STRONG'S
EXHAUSTIVE CONCORDANCE
OF THE BIBLE

UPDATED EDITION

STRONG'S EXHAUSTIVE CONCORDANCE OF THE BIBLE

JAMES STRONG, S.T.D., LL.D.

Strong's Exhaustive Concordance of the Bible:
Updated and Expanded Edition

an imprint of Hendrickson Publishing Group
Hendrickson Publishers, LLC
P. O. Box 3473
Peabody, Massachusetts 01961-3473
www.hendricksonpublishinggroup.com

ISBN 978-1-59856-378-8

Printed in the United States of America

Eleventh Printing — February 2023

Cover Photograph: Avdat, Israel.
Digital Vision Photography/Getty Images. Used with Permission.

Contents

Introduction

Getting the Most Out of Hendrickson Publishers' *Strong's Exhaustive Concordance*

Strong's Exhaustive Concordance deserves a place next to your Bible as one of the most valuable and versatile tools of Bible study ever developed. Students of the Bible have long used concordances to go in search of lost riches within the pages of Scripture. Few, however, make full use of the wealth of resources offered in Strong's—from doing word and thematic studies to probing the deeper meanings embedded in the original languages of the Bible. This guide is designed to help you get the most out of Strong's. Go beyond mere searches for lost verses and hone your skills by utilizing this tool's more advanced features.

Given the vastness of the Bible and the limitations of our own abilities to remember bits of biblical information and put them together in meaningful ways, it is not surprising that often one of the first tools the budding Bible student adds to his or her library is a good concordance. An *exhaustive* concordance—one that lists, alphabetically, every word in the Bible, along with its biblical reference address—is without question one of the most basic and useful tools of Bible study. A concordance makes it far easier for the Bible student to navigate through the great forest of biblical materials in search of that one particular tree—the single Bible verse that meets the need of the moment.

Strong's Exhaustive Concordance was one of the first truly exhaustive concordances to be developed. Compiled painstakingly by James Strong in the late eighteen hundreds (using technology no more elaborate than the index card) the core of this tool is a vast alphabetical listing of every single word that occurs in the entire Bible, along with the chapter and verse citation for every occurrence of that word. The concordance also provides biblical context: every word entry includes an excerpt of the verse where the word appears, making it much easier to recognize the sought-for text. With an exhaustive concordance like Strong's, if you can accurately bring to mind a distinctive word or two from even the most obscure verse, you can, with a bit of patience, track that verse down.

In this edition, Hendrickson Publishers has updated James Strong's monumental effort by re-typesetting the entire work using modern, readable typefaces in larger point sizes; correcting errors that inevitably appear in a work of this size and complexity, and adding visual aids to simplify navigating the pages of this large volume.

In search of that long-lost verse

Nearly everyone interested in the Bible has had the frustrating experience of vaguely remembering a biblical passage but being at a loss when it comes to locating that verse in the pages of Scripture. While not all Bibles are physically large, the Bible itself is huge, in terms of its content. In fact, the Bible is not one book, but a collection of sixty-six books, containing over 790,000 words in a typical English version, making it one of the largest single volumes most people own. In addition, most people remember words and phrases better than Scripture references. For example, you may remember that once familiar verse about how "God so loved the world," but not be able to track it down in the pages of your Bible. However, you may remember bits and pieces of its wording. For example, you may recall that the verse also contains the words "begotten" and "perish."

Hendrickson Publishers' *Strong's Exhaustive Concordance* is structured by listing the words of the KJV Bible in alphabetical order, so it's easy to find key words from your verse. In this case, if you go to the entry for the word "begotten," you'll find this.

BEGOTTEN

Book	Ref.	Context	Number
Gen	5: 4	And the days of Adam after he had **b**	H3205
Lev	18:11	wife's daughter, **b** of thy father, she *is*	H4138
Nu	11:12	all this people? have I **b** them, that thou	H3205
Dt	23: 8	The children that are **b** of them shall	H3205
Jdg	8:30	of his body **b**: for he had many wives.	H3318
Job	38:28	Hath the rain a father? or who hath **b**	H3205
Ps	2: 7	*art* my Son; this day have I **b** thee.	H3205
Isa	49:21	heart, Who hath **b** me these, seeing I	H3205
Hos	5: 7	for they have **b** strange children: now	H3205
Jn	1:14	**b** of the Father,) full of grace and truth.	*G3439*
	18	at any time; the only **b** Son, which is in	*G3439*
	3:16	he gave his only **b** Son, that whosoever	*G3439*
	18	in the name of the only **b** Son of God.	*G3439*
Act	13:33	art my Son, this day have I **b** thee.	*G1080*
1Co	4:15	Jesus I have **b** you through the gospel.	*G1080*
Phlm	10	whom I have **b** in my bonds:	*G1080*
Heb	1: 5	this day have I **b** thee? And again, I will	*G1080*
	5: 5	Thou art my Son, to day have I **b** thee.	*G1080*
	11:17	the promises offered up his only **b** *son*,	*G3439*
1Pt	1: 3	mercy hath **b** us again unto a lively	*G313*
1Jn	4: 9	God sent his only **b** Son into the world,	*G3439*
	5: 1	begat loveth him also that is **b** of him.	*G1080*
	18	not; but he that is **b** of God keepeth	*G1080*
Rev	1: 5	*and* the first **b** of the dead, and the	*G4416*

Under the word "begotten" are twenty-four short excerpts representing all the verses in the King James Bible where the word "begotten" occurs. Scanning through this list, you can quickly locate the verse you want and find its biblical reference in the left column—John 3:16.

It is important to remember that if the word you use to locate the desired text is a very common one, you will need to sort through many more excerpts before finding the verse you're looking for. For this reason, it is very useful to learn a basic rule of concordance usage: *The more uncommon the word, the more helpful it will be in finding the desired biblical context.*

In our example, the word "begotten" is a relatively helpful choice, since it is used only twenty-four times in the entire Bible. The word "believeth" is nearly as useful, with only 45 listings to consider. However, if you were to attempt to locate the same verse using the word "loved," you would find 98 verse contexts to sort through. Using the word "world," you would be confronted with 287 verses.

Following this concept to its logical conclusion, it becomes clear that extremely common words such as "and" and "the" are not very helpful in attempting to locate biblical content using a concordance, since they occur in nearly every verse in the Bible. Because of this, in this edition we have placed many of the most common words in the Bible in the Appendix (pages 1331–1456), where they are listed with all of the verses where they appear. This removes them from the main concordance pages and so saves the reader from having to thumb through these large entries when trying to find other, more useful words.

It is also important to be aware that *Strong's Exhaustive Concordance* was constructed using the King James Version (KJV).* While the King James Version is still one of the most widely used translations in the English-speaking world, other versions of the Bible have somewhat different wording. So if you have become familiar with a passage in a version other than the King James, it may be more difficult to locate the passage using this concordance. The word "begotten," for example, is not found in some recent translations of the Bible. Instead of "only begotten Son," you may find "only Son" or "one and only Son" in your modern version. However, since the various English versions of the Bible share many words in common, you can often overcome the problem of the differences between versions simply by choosing a different word by which to search.

Gaining insight into biblical words

While many people use a concordance merely to search for biblical material, *Strong's Concordance* offers the Bible student far more than a convenient way to find the biblical addresses for vaguely remembered verses. It is also an excellent tool for gaining insight into the meaning and usage of biblical words.

As you reflect on John 3:16, for example, you may become interested in the way a word, such as the word "world," might be used in other biblical contexts. An exhaustive concordance is tailor-made for this kind of word study, since it lists in one place everywhere in the entire Bible where a particular word occurs. The Strong's listing for "world" includes over 280 occurrences, of which 241 are from the New Testament. In a detailed word study, you could examine each of these verses in context, noting the nuances of meaning the words seem to carry in different places, or the varieties of emphasis found in the various contexts.

A more focused and less time-consuming approach might be to scan the list of excerpts under "world" looking for verses that seem to have particular significance or interest. You might want to limit your study further by focusing on a particular biblical book, such as the Gospel of John. You might note, for example, that in John 1:10 the contextual excerpt reads, "and the **w** was made by him." Here, the reference seems to be to the world as God's creation. In the same verse, however, you may note that the word "world" is used a second time, in the phrase "and the **w** knew him not." In this case, the gospel writer seems to have shifted to a meaning of "world" that refers to those who do not know God. John 12:19 contains yet another example of the use of "world," this time quoting the Pharisees as they characterized the impact of Jesus, exclaiming that the population of the entire world had become his followers: "behold, the **w** is gone after him."

* The Hendrickson Publisher's *Strong's Exhaustive Concordance* references the English words in the King James Version, also known as the Authorized Version, originally published in 1611. Specifically, it uses the Oxford edition of 1769, edited by Benjamin Blayney, which is the most common edition in use today. Between 1611 and 1769, numerous printings and editions of the King James Version were published. This 1769 edition carefully updated the original 1611 edition by standardizing the use of italics, updating the spelling, and correcting various minor errors found in different printings.

Even so far in this very limited word study in the Gospel of John, three distinct senses of "world" already seem to have emerged:

1) the world of *God's creation,*
2) the world of unbelievers who do not know God and,
3) the world as *a race of people* occupying this planet.

If we expanded our word study further, we would probably find additional meanings.

Having a good sense of how a particular biblical word is used in a variety of contexts allows you to consider more carefully what that word might mean in a particular verse, such as John 3:16. Which of the above senses best fits the gospel writer's words that "God so loved the world"? Is he speaking of God's love for the *created* world? In the context of John 3, this seems unlikely, since the gospel writer goes on to speak in terms of the need for faith and salvation. Could he be referring to the world as the *human population?* In the light of the universals used in this context ("whosoever believeth"), this meaning cannot be ruled out. However, the meaning that seems to fit best is the third sense: "God so loved *the unbelieving world without God* that he gave his only begotten Son so that those who believe in Him might be saved."

The results of word studies can easily be compiled to create group Bible lessons or sermons. For example, you might take note of the different ways in which biblical passages use the word "love." Then you could gather key examples of passages that use the word in each of these different senses to form a thematic study on the different ways of expressing biblical love.

At its most basic, the development of a theological understanding of the Bible is simply a matter of understanding what the Bible teaches on a host of different topics or themes. Thus the concordance is one of the most useful tools—next to the Bible itself—for constructing a truly biblical theology.

Tracing biblical themes

From basic word studies, more complex thematic studies may be constructed. While there is often a need to limit the scope of a word study, there also may be occasions when you want to *expand* your study beyond the material that results from the analysis of a particular biblical word. One avenue of study may point in other potentially fruitful directions, and study of one word may lead to another, allowing you to focus on themes.

When considering a thematic study, many people turn immediately to theology books, which contain the results of others' Bible study. While there are many excellent theology books available, there are distinct advantages to engaging in a first-hand survey of biblical teaching on a particular topic. The most obvious advantage is the direct knowledge you can gain by thinking through for yourself the bits of biblical data on a particular topic. The person who bakes cookies from a batch of prepared dough may end up with tasty treats, but the person who has whipped up a batch of cookies "from scratch" has a much better sense of the individual ingredients that combine to create the pleasing taste. In the same way, doing your own thematic study from the ground up can give you a much more personal insight into your topic of interest. In addition, because theological books typically cover a wide range of topics, many of the themes treated must be handled in a cursory fashion. By doing your own study, you may uncover thematic nuances others might have skipped over. You can also better adapt and prioritize your selection of biblical material to best address your unique situation and needs.

Strong's Exhaustive Concordance allows you to do first-hand, inductive theological work by expanding word studies into broader thematic investigations. The starting point for such a thematic study is often the word study, as described above. Returning to our example from John 3:16, a concordance study of "world" reveals that one of the ways in which the word is used is to refer to God's creation—the world that God made. Focusing on this theme of creation, you might then review all of the excerpts in the Strong's "world" list, looking in particular for the ones that seem to use "world" in this sense of creation. You could then look up and read in context any verses that seem significant to your study. While reading each passage, it is also helpful to take careful note of the host of other ways creation is referred to. These different modes of expression can lead to additional concordance searches that will further expand your understanding of the creation theme.

Expanding our survey of the "world" entries in Strong's, for instance, we find that Matthew 13:35 speaks of "the foundations of the world" as a reference to God's creative activity. Taking off from this phrase, you may want to perform a parallel word study on the word "foundations" to see what emerges. The Strong's entry for "foundations" reveals several Old Testament contexts that form the background for the New Testament writers' descriptions of creation. Psalm 104, for example, includes a beautiful, poetic depiction of God's creation and sustenance of the world. The Lord is described as the One who "laid the foundations of the earth, that it should not be removed for ever." The language of "foundations" is also found in Isaiah 51:13, in a vivid description of God as "thy Maker," the one who "stretched forth the heavens" and "laid the foundations of the earth." As you examine each new passage, significant terms that emerge (such as "Maker" and "heavens") can become starting points for new concordance word studies that further expand the thematic study. The result is a collection of biblical data that you can organize for personal edification, teaching, or preaching.

Exploring the original languages

Often those interested in Bible study will hear pastors or teachers refer to what a particular passage "really means" in the Hebrew or Greek originals. If you have never studied the biblical languages, you may feel frustrated at your inability to get behind your English translation to the actual words used by the biblical writers. While becoming fluent in the biblical languages requires years of concentrated study, Strong's offers you a simple way to begin penetrating the language barrier without having to do extensive study of ancient Hebrew or Greek. Besides using a comprehensive numbering system to point to the Hebrew and Greek words themselves, Strong's contains vital information related to these original words, and directs you to where they are used in the Bible.

Look again at the Strong's entry for "begotten":

BEGOTTEN

Gen	5: 4	And the days of Adam after he had **b**	H3205
Lev	18:11	wife's daughter, **b** of thy father, she *is*	H4138
Nu	11:12	all this people? have I **b** them, that thou	H3205
Dt	23: 8	The children that are **b** of them shall	H3205
Jdg	8:30	of his body **b**: for he had many wives.	H3318
Job	38:28	Hath the rain a father? or who hath **b**	H3205
Ps	2: 7	*art* my Son; this day have I **b** thee.	H3205
Isa	49:21	heart, Who hath **b** me these, seeing I	H3205
Hos	5: 7	for they have **b** strange children: now	H3205
Jn	1:14	**b** of the Father,) full of grace and truth.	*G3439*
	18	at any time; the only **b** Son, which is in	*G3439*
	3:16	he gave his only **b** Son, that whosoever	*G3439*
	18	in the name of the only **b** Son of God.	*G3439*
Act	13:33	art my Son, this day have I **b** thee.	*G1080*
1Co	4:15	Jesus I have **b** you through the gospel.	*G1080*
Phlm	10	whom I have **b** in my bonds:	*G1080*
Heb	1: 5	this day have I **b** thee? And again, I will	*G1080*
	5: 5	Thou art my Son, to day have I **b** thee.	*G1080*
	11:17	the promises offered up his only **b** *son*,	*G3439*
1Pt	1: 3	mercy hath **b** us again unto a lively	*G313*
1Jn	4: 9	God sent his only **b** Son into the world,	*G3439*
	5: 1	begat loveth him also that is **b** of him.	*G1080*
	18	not; but he that is **b** of God keepeth	*G1080*
Rev	1: 5	*and* the first **b** of the dead, and the	*G4416*

Notice that the biblical reference and the contextual excerpt are followed by the number *G3439*. This number refers to another important feature of *Strong's Concordance*, the Greek Dictionary of the New Testament, one of two original language dictionaries found in the back of the volume. (Italicized numbers, prefaced by the letter "G," refer to the Greek Dictionary (pages 1595–1695), while non-italicized numbers, prefaced by the letter "H," point to the Hebrew/Aramaic Dictionary (pages 1457–1594.) Entry *G3439* in the Greek dictionary contains the following information for the Greek word μονογενής, which is the original word behind the English translation "begotten" in the KJV:

> ***G3439*** **μονογενής** *monogenēs* from *G3441* and *G1096*; *only-born*, i.e. *sole*:— only (begotten, child).

Consider the various elements contained in the Strong's dictionary. Following the Strong's number is the Greek word associated with that number (μονογενής). This is followed by a *transliteration* of the word in italic type (*monogenēs*), which represents the word using a phonetic English alphabet in place of Greek characters. Extra help in working with transliterated forms and pronunciation of Hebrew and Greek words can be found in the "Hebrew Articulation" and "Greek Articulation" sections at the beginning of each dictionary.

Information indicating the word's derivation follows the various representations of the Greek word. In this case, *monogenēs* is derived from two other Greek words (*G3441* and *G1096*). This information is offered because tracking a word's derivation can often yield additional insights into its meaning. Caution should be exercised here, since words sometimes take on completely different meanings when combined with other words. In English, for example, the compound word "understand" derives from the words "under" and "stand," yet means something quite different from the idea of literally "standing under" something. In the case of *monogenēs*, however, the meaning of the compound word is closely related to the meanings of the words from which it is derived: *monos*, "only," and *ginomai*, "to be, become, or come." The *only begotten* Son is the *only* Son who *came* from His Father.

The next bit of information contained in the Strong's Greek Dictionary entry is a brief English definition, representing the normal meaning of the word. The Greek word *monogenēs*, we are told, typically means "*only-born*, i.e. *sole*." The definitions in the Strong's dictionaries should be taken as "rule of thumb" meanings, which apply in most situations, and should not be interpreted rigidly as the precise significance a particular word will have every time it is used. The reason for this is that the meanings of words are strongly influenced by the contexts in which they appear. For more precise and detailed information on the meanings of biblical words in their various contexts, a Hebrew or Greek lexicon should be consulted. (See "Strong's and beyond," p. xi.)

The final piece of information in the Strong's Greek Dictionary entry (following the colon and dash symbols [:—]) is a listing of the several ways in which the term is translated in the KJV. The word *monogenēs* is always rendered "only," yet is translated using the additional words "begotten" or "child." This kind of information is particularly helpful in giving you a grasp of the variety of ways in which a particular Hebrew or Greek word is translated in different contexts, and can provide valuable clues for engaging in original language word studies.

Tracking Hebrew and Greek words

We have already discussed how doing word and thematic studies using *Strong's Concordance* represents an exciting expansion of the function of the exhaustive concordance beyond merely finding lost verses in the Bible. However, you can go further. Not only can you get additional insight into Hebrew and Greek words using the original language dictionaries in Strong's, but you can examine for yourself how these ancient words are used in their various biblical contexts.

Lexicographers track words and take note of the varying nuances of meaning they carry as they are used in various contexts. While becoming an expert in lexicography requires advanced linguistic training, a basic, first-hand knowledge of the way biblical words are used can be gained by using the original language capabilities of *Strong's Concordance*. This knowledge can often lead to a greater insight into nuances of biblical meaning.

Becoming adept at performing even basic Hebrew and Greek word studies using Strong's does require a degree of direction and practice. Doing original language word studies using *Strong's Concordance* requires an integrated and coordinated use of both the concordance and the dictionaries. In particular, it requires paying careful attention to the Strong's numbering system used in both resources.

Returning again to our sample verse, John 3:16, suppose you were particularly interested in finding out more about the original Greek word translated "perish." You consult the "perish" entry in the Strong's Main Concordance, and note that the Strong's number associated with "perish" in John 3:16 is *G622.*

A visit to the Strong's Greek Dictionary to look up the number *G622* will tell you more about the Greek word ἀπόλλυμι (*apollymi*). Then you might also be interested in seeing how the word is used in other biblical contexts. Since a single English word like "perish" could be derived from more than one original Greek word, and since a Greek word like *apollymi* could be translated into English in any number of ways, developing a complete list of verses in which this Greek word appears is more complicated than merely looking at the verses listed under the "perish" listing in *Strong's Concordance.* Remember that the excerpts in Strong's direct you to contexts in which the *English* word "perish" is used, not to all the verses in which *apollymi* is used.

Beginning with the "perish" concordance entry, take note of all the verse excerpts that are followed by the number *G622.* These are all the verses in which *apollymi* is translated "perish" in the KJV. Note that 25 of the 30 New Testament examples of "perish" are derived from *apollymi.* (Since we are studying a Greek word, only New Testament examples need to be considered. Note as well that several other Greek words are also translated "perish" in the KJV.) Since each Greek word will have a slightly different nuanced meaning, you can gain insight into how *this particular Greek word* is employed in its various NT contexts by comparing the verses where *apollymi* is used.

Since *apollymi* is translated in other ways than "perish" in the KJV, you must also consult other concordance entries to create a complete list of verses where *apollymi* appears. Remember that the entry for *apollymi* in the Greek Dictionary lists not only a standard English definition ("to destroy fully," "to perish or lose"), but also the various ways in which the word is translated in the KJV: *destroy, die, lose, mar, perish.* This list of KJV translations is your key to finding out which other concordance entries to consult to develop a full list of verses that use *apollymi.*

If you then turn to the *Strong's Concordance* entry for "destroy," you will find eighteen more examples of verse contexts that are followed by the number *G622.* These are the contexts in which *apollymi* appears. It is important to note at this point, however, that when the Hebrew or Greek dictionary lists the basic form of a word like "destroy," the implication is that *other grammatical forms* of that English word may also represent a translation of the same Greek word. Thus a listing of the verb "destroy" implies that related forms such as "destroyed," "destroyest," "destroyeth," and "destroying" may also represent translations of *apollymi.* You will need to consult the separate concordance entries for each of these forms to get a full list of verses in which *apollymi* appears. A check of the concordance listings for each of the five verbs listed in the Strong's Greek Dictionary (*destroy, die, lose, mar, perish*), along with their related forms, should give a complete view of all the New Testament contexts in which the Greek word *apollymi* is used.

The information gleaned from this kind of original language word study can be quite helpful in shedding light on the nuances of meaning in biblical passages. Very often two verses having the same English word actually derive from the translations of two different Greek words. A careful comparison of the Greek words used can shed light on the different nuances of meaning in these texts. For example, the word "perish" (*apollymi*) used in John 3:16 (*whosoever believeth in him should not* perish *but have everlasting life)* means "to be completely destroyed." Paul uses a different Greek word (*diapherō—"to rot thoroughly" or "to decay utterly"*) in 2 Corinthians 4:16 when he claims that *"though our outward man* perish, *yet the inward man is renewed day by day."* Although believers may indeed "perish" in the second sense, the promise in John 3:16 is that they will never "perish" in the first sense.

Not only can original language word studies enable you to distinguish more clearly between the meanings of the Hebrew and Greek words used in various biblical passages, they can also give you deeper insight into the range of meanings that a particular Greek word may carry as it is used by the biblical writers in different contexts. In English, for example, the word "die" means something quite different in 1 Corinthians 15:31 (*I* die *daily*) from the meaning it carries in Hebrews 9:27 (*it is appointed unto men once to* die). In the same way, the Strong's Greek Dictionary entry for *apollymi* lists both "to destroy fully" and "to perish or lose" as possible meanings. While the first definition fits contexts such as Luke 17:27 (*the flood came and* destroyed *them all*), the second definition is more appropriate for the context of John 3:16.

Strong's and beyond

Once you've become an experienced user of *Strong's Exhaustive Concordance,* you may want to explore a number of other tools that use the Strong's numbering system, and are designed to take you further in the analysis of biblical words and themes. These tools can be used to expand an existing project begun with Strong's, or as standalone resources. The *Englishman's Hebrew Concordance of the Old Testament* and the *Englishman's Greek Concordance of the New Testament,* both edited by George Wigram (Hendrickson, 1996), are similar to Strong's in that they list all the words of the Bible with their biblical references, and with excerpts of each verse context (in English). The key difference between Strong's and the Englishman's resources is that while Strong's is structured around an alphabetical listing of all the *English* words in the King James Version of the Bible, the *Englishman's* resources are organized by the Hebrew and Greek words. However, since the Hebrew and Greek words are listed with Strong's numbers, you needn't learn the Hebrew or Greek alphabets to locate them. The common numbering system also makes it an easy matter to go from the Strong's concordance or dictionary entries to Englishman's entries. Doing original language concordance studies using Englishman's is an even simpler task than with Strong's, because every verse containing a particular Hebrew or Greek word is listed in the same place. The Englishman's concordances also have expanded lexical definitions of Hebrew and Greek words.

Those wanting more depth in original language word studies will also appreciate *The Expository Dictionary of Bible Words*, edited by Stephen D. Renn (Hendrickson, 2005). This recent resource is similar to the older *Vine's Expository Dictionary*, but with updated definitions based on more recent discoveries in biblical studies, and covers both the Old and New Testaments. Articles in this dictionary are listed according to various words from the English Bible, but they discuss the shades of meaning for the various Hebrew and Greek words that lie behind the English. What's more, each Hebrew or Greek word discussed is again keyed to the Strong's number system, making it simple to use this reference to go from a Strong's-based word study to a deeper analysis of words.

If you wish to dig even more deeply into the meanings of particular Hebrew and Greek words, you may want to consult the *Brown-Driver-Briggs Hebrew and English Lexicon* (Hendrickson, 1996) or the *Thayer's Greek-English Lexicon of the New Testament* (Hendrickson, 1996), each of which is also coded using the Strong's numbering system. Both of these classic resources contain detailed breakdowns of the various meanings of each of the biblical words, along with copious biblical examples of how each sense is used. While those untrained in the biblical languages will derive some benefit from the use of these advanced resources, making the most of them requires some knowledge of the Hebrew and Greek languages.

There are many Bible study tools that can help you gain deeper insight into biblical teaching. However, no single resource can offer you a greater variety of ways of mining, polishing, and organizing the gems of biblical teaching than *Strong's Exhaustive Concordance.* In addition to being an essential tool for searching the many corridors of the biblical mine, Strong's enables you to explore the richness and diversity of biblical words and themes, and even equips you in a basic way to penetrate into the often unexplored caverns of the biblical languages. As you become more adept at using this resource to its fullest capacity, you will find it an indispensable and oft-used tool for studying the Scriptures.

Sample Entry

Heading
The heading at the top of each page lists the first and last word found on that page. When the first entry is continued from the previous page, this is indicated by "(cont.)"

Entry
Every word that occurs in the King James Version is listed in boldface.

Chapter & Verse listing. *The entry is followed by every verse in which the word occurs. Chapters and verses are aligned vertically to make entries easy to scan.*

Context
A line of the verse, giving the context of the word, is included.

Bold letters. *Rather than repeating every occurrence of the entry word, just the first letter, in bold, is included.*

See the Appendix
Pronouns, prepositions, and very common words have been moved to the appendix (see page 1331). This makes it simpler to look up key words.

ALPHAEUS (cont.) – ALTAR

Mk 2:14 he saw Levi the *son* of **A** sitting at the *G256*
3:18 James the *son* of **A**, and Thaddaeus, and *G256*
Lk 6:15 the *son* of **A**, and Simon called Zelotes, *G256*
Act 1:13 James *the son* of **A**, and Simon Zelotes, *G256*

ALREADY
Ex 1: 5 seventy souls: for Joseph was in Egypt ***a***.
2Ch 28:13 against the LORD ***a***, ye intend to add
Neh 5: 5 unto bondage ***a***: neither *is it* in our power
Ecc 1:10 **a** of old time, which was before us. H3528
2:12 *even* that which hath been **a** done. H3528
3:15 is to be hath **a** been; and God requireth H3528
4: 2 dead which are **a** dead more than the H3528
6:10 That which hath been is named **a**, and H3528
Mal 2: 2 them **a**, because ye do not lay *it* to heart.
Mt 5:28 adultery with her **a** in his heart. *G2235*
17:12 But I say unto you, That Elias is come **a**, *G2235*
Mk 15:44 And Pilate marvelled if he were **a** dead: *G2235*
Lk 12:49 and what will I, if it be **a** kindled? *G2235*
Jn 3:18 not is condemned **a**, because he hath *G2235*
4:35 fields; for they are white **a** to harvest. *G2235*
9:22 Jews had agreed **a**, that if any man did *G2235*
27 He answered them, I have told you **a**, *G2235*
11:17 he had *lain* in the grave four days **a**. *G2235*
19:33 he was dead **a**, they brake not his legs: *G2235*
Act 11:11 were three men **a** come unto the house *G1824*
27: 9 now **a** past, Paul admonished *them*, *G2235*
1Co 5: 3 spirit, have judged **a**, as though I were *G2235*
2Co 12:21 have sinned **a**, and have not repented *G4258*
Php 3:12 Not as though I had **a** attained, either *G2235*
12 either were **a** perfect: but I follow *G2235*
16 Nevertheless, whereto we have **a** *G5348*
2Th 2: 7 For the mystery of iniquity doth **a** *G2235*
1Ti 5:15 For some are **a** turned aside after *G2235*
2Ti 2:18 past **a**; and overthrow the faith of some. *G2235*
1Jn 4: 3 and even now **a** is it in the world. *G2235*
Rev 2:25 But that which ye have ***a*** hold fast till I

ALSO See the Appendix.

. . . .

ASSAYING
Heb 11:29 **a** to do were drowned. *G3984+G2983*

ASS-COLTS See ASS and COLTS.

ASSEMBLE
Nu 10: 3 the assembly shall **a** themselves to thee H3259
2Sa 20: 4 Then said the king to Amasa, **A** me the H2199
5 So Amasa went to **a** *the men of* Judah: H2199

Strong's number
The KJV word is tied to the original Hebrew or Greek word it translates. This numbering system has become a standard used in a variety of reference tools.

*"H" **numbers** refer to entries in the Hebrew Dictionary, which begins on page 1457.*

*"G" **numbers** refer to entries in the Greek Dictionary. These numbers are also italicized. The Greek Dictionary begins on page 1595.*

Entries with no number
Indicates the English word does not directly translate a Hebrew or Greek word. These words are often auxiliary parts of the English phrase needed to adequately translate a Hebrew or Greek key word in the verse.

Shaded text
Words spoken by Jesus are shaded in gray.

Entries with two or more Strong's numbers
Indicates that two or more Hebrew words or two or more Greek words are translated by one English word.

Cross-Reference
Points to the entry which lists the verses using that word.

Main Concordance

Abbreviations of Biblical Books

Old Testament

Gen	Genesis
Ex	Exodus
Lev	Leviticus
Nu	Numbers
Dt	Deuteronomy
Jos	Joshua
Jdg	Judges
Ru	Ruth
1Sa	1 Samuel
2Sa	2 Samuel
1Ki	1 Kings
2Ki	2 Kings
1Ch	1 Chronicles
2Ch	2 Chronicles
Ezr	Ezra
Neh	Nehemiah
Est	Esther
Job	Job
Ps	Psalms
Prv	Proverbs
Ecc	Ecclesiastes
Song	Song of Solomon
Isa	Isaiah
Jer	Jeremiah
Lam	Lamentations
Ezk	Ezekiel
Dan	Daniel
Hos	Hosea
Joel	Joel
Am	Amos
Oba	Obadiah
Jna	Jonah
Mic	Micah
Nah	Nahum
Hab	Habakkuk
Zep	Zephaniah
Hag	Haggai
Zec	Zechariah
Mal	Malachi

New Testament

Mt	Matthew
Mk	Mark
Lk	Luke
Jn	John
Act	Acts
Ro	Romans
1Co	1 Corinthians
2Co	2 Corinthians
Gal	Galatians
Eph	Ephesians
Php	Philippians
Col	Colossians
1Th	1 Thessalonians
2Th	2 Thessalonians
1Ti	1 Timothy
2Ti	2 Timothy
Tit	Titus
Phlm	Philemon
Heb	Hebrews
Jas	James
1Pt	1 Peter
2Pt	2 Peter
1Jn	1 John
2Jn	2 John
3Jn	3 John
Jude	Jude
Rev	Revelation

A

A See the Appendix.

AARON

Ex 4:14 and he said, *Is* not A the Levite thy H175
27 And the LORD said to A, Go into the H175
28 And Moses told A all the words of the H175
29 And Moses and A went and gathered H175
30 And A spake all the words which the H175
5: 1 And afterward Moses and A went in, H175
4 do ye, Moses and A, let the people from H175
20 And they met Moses and A, who stood in H175
6:13 unto Moses and unto A, and gave them a H175
20 and she bare him A and Moses: and the H175
23 And A took him Elisheba, daughter of H175
26 These *are* that A and Moses, to whom H175
27 from Egypt: these *are* that Moses and A. H175
7: 1 and A thy brother shall be thy prophet. H175
2 thee: and A thy brother shall speak H175
6 And Moses and A did as the LORD H175
7 years old, and A fourscore and three H175
8 spake unto Moses and unto A, saying, H175
9 shalt say unto A, Take thy rod, and cast H175
10 And Moses and A went in unto Pharaoh, H175
10 commanded: and A cast down his rod H175
19 Moses, Say unto A, Take thy rod, and H175
20 And Moses and A did so, as the LORD H175
8: 5 Moses, Say unto A, Stretch forth thine H175
6 And A stretched out his hand over the H175
8 Then Pharaoh called for Moses and A, H175
12 And Moses and A went out from H175
16 Moses, Say unto A, Stretch out thy rod, H175
17 And they did so; for A stretched out his H175
25 And Pharaoh called for Moses and for A, H175
9: 8 Moses and unto A, Take to you handfuls H175
27 for Moses and A, and said unto them, H175
10: 3 And Moses and A came in unto H175
8 And Moses and A were brought again H175
16 Then Pharaoh called for Moses and A in H175
11:10 And Moses and A did all these wonders H175
12: 1 And the LORD spake unto Moses and A H175
28 commanded Moses and A, so did they. H175
31 And he called for Moses and A by night, H175
43 And the LORD said unto Moses and A, H175
50 commanded Moses and A, so did they. H175
15:20 the sister of A, took a timbrel in her H175
16: 2 against Moses and A in the wilderness: H175
6 And Moses and A said unto all the H175
9 And Moses spake unto A, Say unto all the H175
10 And it came to pass, as A spake unto the H175
33 And Moses said unto A, Take a pot, and H175
34 As the LORD commanded Moses, so A H175
17:10 A, and Hur went up to the top of the hill. H175
12 he sat thereon; and A and Hur stayed up H175
18:12 for God: and A came, and all the elders H175
19:24 up, thou, and A with thee: but let not H175
24: 1 LORD, thou, and A, Nadab, and Abihu, H175
9 Then went up Moses, and A, Nadab, and H175
14 you: and, behold, A and Hur *are* with H175
27:21 the testimony, A and his sons shall order H175
28: 1 And take thou unto thee A thy brother, H175
1 priest's office, *even* A, Nadab and Abihu, H175
2 A thy brother for glory and for beauty. H175
4 holy garments for A thy brother, and his H175
12 of Israel: and A shall bear their names H175
29 And A shall bear the names of the H175
30 before the LORD: and A shall bear the H175
35 And it shall be upon A to minister: and H175
38 forehead, that A may bear the iniquity H175
41 And thou shalt put them upon A thy H175
43 And they shall be upon A, and upon his H175
29: 4 And A and his sons thou shalt bring H175
5 and put upon A the coat, and the robe H175
9 And thou shalt gird them with girdles, A H175
9 thou shalt consecrate A and his sons. H175
10 congregation: and A and his sons shall H175
15 Thou shalt also take one ram; and A and H175
19 the other ram; and A and his sons shall H175
20 of the right ear of A, and upon the tip of H175
21 and sprinkle *it* upon A, and upon his H175
24 And thou shalt put all in the hands of A, H175
27 *is* for A, and of *that* which is for his sons: H175
29 And the holy garments of A shall be his H175

Ex 29:32 And A and his sons shall eat the flesh of H175
35 And thus shalt thou do unto A, and to his H175
44 will sanctify also both A and his sons, to H175
30: 7 And A shall burn thereon sweet incense H175
8 And when A lighteth the lamps at even, H175
10 And A shall make an atonement upon H175
19 For A and his sons shall wash their H175
30 And thou shalt anoint A and his sons, H175
31:10 holy garments for A the priest, and the H175
32: 1 together unto A, and said unto him, Up, H175
2 And A said unto them, Break off the H175
3 in their ears, and brought *them* unto A. H175
5 And when A saw *it*, he built an altar H175
5 an altar before it; and A made H175
21 And Moses said unto A, What did this H175
22 And A said, Let not the anger of my lord H175
25 *were* naked; (for A had made them H175
35 they made the calf, which A made. H175
34:30 And when A and all the children of H175
31 And Moses called unto them; and A and H175
35:19 holy garments for A the priest, and the H175
38:21 the hand of Ithamar, son to A the priest. H175
39: 1 for A; as the LORD commanded Moses. H175
27 *of* woven work for A, and for his sons, H175
41 holy garments for A the priest, and his H175
40:12 And thou shalt bring A and his sons H175
13 And thou shalt put upon A the holy H175
31 And Moses and A and his sons washed H175
Lev 1: 7 And the sons of A the priest shall put fire H175
3:13 and the sons of A shall sprinkle the H175
6: 9 Command A and his sons, saying, This H175
14 the sons of A shall offer it before the H175
16 And the remainder thereof shall A and H175
18 All the males among the children of A H175
20 This *is* the offering of A and of his sons, H175
25 Speak unto A and to his sons, saying, H175
7:10 sons of A have, one *as much* as another. H175
33 He among the sons of A, that offereth the H175
34 given them unto A the priest and unto H175
35 This *is the portion* of the anointing of A, H175
8: 2 Take A and his sons with him, and the H175
6 And Moses brought A and his sons, and H175
14 the sin offering: and A and his sons laid H175
18 offering: and A and his sons laid their H175
22 of consecration: and A and his sons laid H175
30 and sprinkled *it* upon A, *and* upon his H175
30 and sanctified A, *and* his garments, and H175
31 And Moses said unto A and to his sons, H175
31 saying, A and his sons shall eat it. H175
36 So A and his sons did all things which H175
9: 1 A and his sons, and the elders of Israel; H175
2 And he said unto A, Take thee a young H175
7 And Moses said unto A, Go unto the H175
8 A therefore went unto the altar, and slew H175
9 And the sons of A brought the blood H175
21 And the breasts and the right shoulder A H175
22 And A lifted up his hand toward the H175
23 And Moses and A went into the H175
10: 1 And Nadab and Abihu, the sons of A, H175
3 Then Moses said unto A, This *is it* that H175
3 I will be glorified. And A held his peace. H175
4 of Uzziel the uncle of A, and said unto H175
6 And Moses said unto A, and unto H175
8 And the LORD spake unto A, saying, H175
12 And Moses spake unto A, and unto H175
16 sons of A *which were* left *alive*, saying, H175
19 And A said unto Moses, Behold, this day H175
11: 1 unto Moses and to A, saying unto them, H175
13: 1 And the LORD spake unto Moses and A, H175
2 be brought unto A the priest, or unto H175
14:33 spake unto Moses and unto A, saying, H175
15: 1 spake unto Moses and to A, saying, H175
16: 1 of the two sons of A, when they offered H175
2 Moses, Speak unto A thy brother, that he H175
3 Thus shall A come into the holy *place*: H175
6 And A shall offer his bullock of the sin H175
8 And A shall cast lots upon the two goats; H175
9 And A shall bring the goat upon which H175
11 And A shall bring the bullock of the sin H175
21 And A shall lay both his hands upon the H175
23 And A shall come into the tabernacle of H175
17: 2 Speak unto A, and unto his sons, and H175

Lev 21: 1 priests the sons of A, and say unto them, H175
17 Speak unto A, saying, Whosoever *he be* H175
21 of the seed of A the priest shall come H175
24 And Moses told *it* unto A, and to his H175
22: 2 Speak unto A and to his sons, that they H175
4 What man soever of the seed of A *is* a H175
18 Speak unto A, and to his sons, and unto H175
24: 3 shall A order it from the evening H175
Nu 1: 3 A shall number them by their armies. H175
17 And Moses and A took these men which H175
44 which Moses and A numbered, and the H175
2: 1 spake unto Moses and unto A, saying, H175
3: 1 These also *are* the generations of A and H175
2 And these *are* the names of the sons of A; H175
3 These *are* the names of the sons of A, the H175
4 office in the sight of A their father. H175
6 them before A the priest, that they H175
9 And thou shalt give the Levites unto A H175
10 And thou shalt appoint A and his sons, H175
32 And Eleazar the son of A the priest *shall* H175
38 *be* Moses, and A and his sons, keeping H175
39 which Moses and A numbered at the H175
48 to be redeemed, unto A and to his sons. H175
51 were redeemed unto A and to his sons, H175
4: 1 spake unto Moses and unto A, saying, H175
5 And when the camp setteth forward, A H175
15 And when A and his sons have made an H175
16 And to the office of Eleazar the son of A H175
17 spake unto Moses and unto A, saying, H175
19 most holy things: A and his sons shall go H175
27 At the appointment of A and his sons H175
28 hand of Ithamar the son of A the priest. H175
33 hand of Ithamar the son of A the priest. H175
34 And Moses and A and the chief of the H175
37 which Moses and A did number H175
41 whom Moses and A did number H175
45 Merari, whom Moses and A numbered H175
46 whom Moses and A and the chief of H175
6:23 Speak unto A and unto his sons, saying, H175
7: 8 hand of Ithamar the son of A the priest. H175
8: 2 Speak unto A, and say unto him, When H175
3 And A did so; he lighted the lamps H175
11 And A shall offer the Levites before the H175
13 And thou shalt set the Levites before A, H175
19 the Levites *as* a gift to A and to his sons H175
20 And Moses, and A, and all the H175
21 their clothes; and A offered them *as* an H175
21 the LORD; and A made an atonement H175
22 before A, and before his sons: H175
9: 6 before Moses and before A on that day: H175
10: 8 And the sons of A, the priests, shall blow H175
12: 1 And Miriam and A spake against Moses H175
4 Moses, and unto A, and unto Miriam, H175
5 and called A and Miriam: and they H175
10 as snow: and A looked upon Miriam, H175
11 And A said unto Moses, Alas, my lord, I H175
13:26 came to Moses, and to A, and to all the H175
14: 2 Moses and against A: and the whole H175
5 Then Moses and A fell on their faces H175
26 spake unto Moses and unto A, saying, H175
15:33 and A, and unto all the congregation. H175
16: 3 Moses and against A, and said unto H175
11 what *is* A, that ye murmur against him? H175
16 LORD, thou, and they, and A, to morrow: H175
17 thou also, and A, each *of you* his censer. H175
18 of the congregation with Moses and A. H175
20 spake unto Moses and unto A, saying, H175
37 Speak unto Eleazar the son of A the H175
40 *is* not of the seed of A, come near to offer H175
41 Moses and against A, saying, Ye have H175
42 Moses and against A, that they looked H175
43 And Moses and A came before the H175
46 And Moses said unto A, Take a censer, H175
47 And A took as Moses commanded, and H175
50 And A returned unto Moses unto the H175
17: 6 and the rod of A *was* among their rods. H175
8 behold, the rod of A for the house of Levi H175
18: 1 And the LORD said unto A, Thou and thy H175
8 And the LORD spake unto A, Behold, I H175
20 And the LORD spake unto A, Thou shalt H175
28 LORD'S heave offering to A the priest. H175
19: 1 spake unto Moses and unto A, saying, H175

Nu 20: 2 together against Moses and against **A**. H175
6 And Moses and **A** went from the H175
8 thou, and **A** thy brother, and speak H175
10 And Moses and **A** gathered the H175
12 And the LORD spake unto Moses and **A**, H175
23 And the LORD spake unto Moses and **A** H175
24 **A** shall be gathered unto his people: for H175
25 Take **A** and Eleazar his son, and bring H175
26 And strip **A** of his garments, and put H175
26 his son: and **A** shall be gathered *unto* H175
28 And Moses stripped **A** of his garments, H175
28 his son; and **A** died there in the top H175
29 saw that **A** was dead, they mourned H175
29 they mourned for **A** thirty days, *even* all H175
25: 7 of Eleazar, the son of **A** the priest, saw *it*, H175
11 of Eleazar, the son of **A** the priest, hath H175
26: 1 Eleazar the son of **A** the priest, saying, H175
9 Moses and against **A** in the company of H175
59 **A** and Moses, and Miriam their sister. H175
60 And unto **A** was born Nadab, and H175
64 them whom Moses and **A** the priest H175
27:13 people, as **A** thy brother was gathered. H175
33: 1 armies under the hand of Moses and **A**. H175
38 And **A** the priest went up into mount H175
39 And **A** *was* an hundred and twenty and H175
Dt 9:20 And the LORD was very angry with **A** to H175
20 and I prayed for **A** also the same time. H175
10: 6 to Mosera: there **A** died, and there he H175
32:50 unto thy people; as **A** thy brother died in H175
Jos 21: 4 and the children of **A** the priest, *which* H175
10 Which the children of **A**, *being* of the H175
13 Thus they gave to the children of **A** the H175
19 All the cities of the children of **A**, the H175
24: 5 I sent Moses also and **A**, and I plagued H175
33 And Eleazar the son of **A** died; and they H175
Jdg 20:28 of Eleazar, the son of **A**, stood before it in H175
1Sa 12: 6 Moses and **A**, and that brought your H175
8 sent Moses and **A**, which brought forth H175
1Ch 6: 3 And the children of Amram; **A**, and H175
3 The sons also of **A**; Nadab, and Abihu, H175
49 But **A** and his sons offered upon the H175
50 And these *are* the sons of **A**; Eleazar his H175
54 of the sons of **A**, of the families of the H175
57 And to the sons of **A** they gave the cities H175
15: 4 And David assembled the children of **A**, H175
23:13 The sons of Amram; **A** and Moses: and H175
13 and Moses: and **A** was separated, that H175
28 to wait on the sons of **A** for the service of H175
32 of the sons of **A** their brethren, in the H175
24: 1 of the sons of **A**. The sons of Aaron; H175
1 Aaron. The sons of **A**; Nadab, and Abihu, H175
19 manner, under **A** their father, as the H175
31 the sons of **A** in the presence of David H175
2Ch 13: 9 the LORD, the sons of **A**, and the Levites, H175
10 *are* the sons of **A**, and the Levites *wait* H175
26:18 the priests the sons of **A**, that are H175
29:21 **A** to offer *them* on the altar of the LORD. H175
31:19 Also of the sons of **A** the priests, *which* H175
35:14 the priests the sons of **A** *were busied* in H175
14 and for the priests the sons of **A**. H175
Ezr 7: 5 of Eleazar, the son of **A** the chief priest: H175
Neh 10:38 And the priest the son of **A** shall be with H175
12:47 sanctified *them* unto the children of **A**. H175
Ps 77:20 like a flock by the hand of Moses and **A**. H175
99: 6 Moses and **A** among his priests, and H175
105:26 He sent Moses his servant; *and* **A** whom H175
106:16 the camp, *and* **A** the saint of the LORD. H175
115:10 O house of **A**, trust in the LORD: he *is* H175
12 of Israel; he will bless the house of **A**. H175
118: 3 Let the house of **A** now say, that his H175
135:19 of Israel: bless the LORD, O house of **A**: H175
Mic 6: 4 I sent before thee Moses, **A**, and Miriam. H175
Lk 1: 5 of **A**, and her name *was* Elisabeth. *G2*
Act 7:40 Saying unto **A**, Make us gods to go before *G2*
Heb 5: 4 but he that is called of God, as *was* **A**. *G2*
7:11 and not be called after the order of **A**? *G2*

AARONITES
1Ch 12:27 And Jehoiada *was* the leader of the **A**, H175
27:17 the son of Kemuel: of the **A**, Zadok: H175

AARON'S
Ex 6:25 And Eleazar **A** son took him *one* of the H175
7:12 but **A** rod swallowed up their rods. H175
28: 1 Abihu, Eleazar and Ithamar, **A** sons. H175
3 that they may make **A** garments to H175
30 and they shall be upon **A** heart, when he H175
38 And it shall be upon **A** forehead, that H175
40 And for **A** sons thou shalt make coats, H175
Ex 29:26 of the ram of **A** consecration, and wave H175
28 And it shall be **A** and his sons' by a H175
Lev 1: 5 and the priests, **A** sons, shall bring the H175
8 And the priests, **A** sons, shall lay the H175
11 and the priests, **A** sons, shall sprinkle H175
2: 2 And he shall bring it to **A** sons the H175
3 offering *shall be* **A** and his sons': *it is* a H175
10 offering *shall be* **A** and his sons': *it is* a H175
3: 2 the congregation: and **A** sons the priests H175
5 And **A** sons shall burn it on the altar H175
8 congregation: and **A** sons shall sprinkle H175
7:31 but the breast shall be **A** and his sons'. H175
8:12 anointing oil upon **A** head, and anointed H175
13 And Moses brought **A** sons, and put H175
23 *it* upon the tip of **A** right ear, and upon H175
24 And he brought **A** sons, and Moses put H175
27 And he put all upon **A** hands, and upon H175
9:12 And he slew the burnt offering; and **A** H175
18 *was* for the people: and **A** sons presented H175
24: 9 And it shall be **A** and his sons'; and they H175
Nu 17: 3 And thou shalt write **A** name upon the H175
10 And the LORD said unto Moses, Bring **A** H175
Ps 133: 2 the beard, *even* **A** beard: that went down H175
Heb 9: 4 had manna, and **A** rod that budded, and *G2*

ABADDON
Rev 9:11 the Hebrew tongue *is* **A**, but in the Greek *G3*

ABAGTHA
Est 1:10 Bigtha, and **A**, Zethar, and Carcas, H5

ABANA
2Ki 5:12 *Are* not **A** and Pharpar, rivers of H71

ABARIM
Nu 27:12 up into this mount **A**, and see the land H5682
33:47 in the mountains of **A**, before Nebo. H5682
48 the mountains of **A**, and pitched in the H5682
Dt 32:49 Get thee up into this mountain **A**, *unto* H5682

ABASE
Job 40:11 every one *that is* proud, and **a** him. H8213
Isa 31: 4 of their voice, nor **a** himself for the H6031
Ezk 21:26 *him that is* low, and **a** *him that is* high. H8213
Dan 4:37 those that walk in pride he is able to **a**. H8214

ABASED
Mt 23:12 himself shall be **a**; and he that shall *G5013*
Lk 14:11 exalteth himself shall be **a**; and he that *G5013*
18:14 exalteth himself shall be **a**; and he that *G5013*
Php 4:12 I know both how to be **a**, and I know *G5013*

ABASING
2Co 11: 7 Have I committed an offence in **a** *G5013*

ABATED
Gen 8: 3 and fifty days the waters were **a**. H2637
8 were **a** from off the face of the ground; H7043
11 the waters were **a** from off the earth. H7043
Lev 27:18 and it shall be **a** from thy estimation. H1639
Dt 34: 7 was not dim, nor his natural force **a**. H5127
Jdg 8: 3 **a** toward him, when he had said that. H7503

ABBA
Mk 14:36 And he said, **A**, Father, all things *are* *G5*
Ro 8:15 of adoption, whereby we cry, **A**, Father. *G5*
Gal 4: 6 Son into your hearts, crying, **A**, Father. *G5*

ABBAS See BARABBAS.

ABDA
1Ki 4: 6 the son of **A** *was* over the tribute. H5653
Neh 11:17 among his brethren, and **A** the son of H5653

ABDEEL
Jer 36:26 the son of **A**, to take Baruch the scribe H5655

ABDI
1Ch 6:44 Kishi, the son of **A**, the son of Malluch, H5660
2Ch 29:12 Kish the son of **A**, and Azariah the son H5660
Ezr 10:26 Jehiel, and **A**, and Jeremoth, and Eliah. H5660

ABDIEL
1Ch 5:15 Ahi the son of **A**, the son of Guni, chief H5661

ABDON
Jos 21:30 with her suburbs, **A** with her suburbs, H5658
Jdg 12:13 And after him **A** the son of Hillel, a H5658
15 And **A** the son of Hillel the Pirathonite H5658
1Ch 6:74 her suburbs, and **A** with her suburbs, H5658
8:23 And **A**, and Zichri, and Hanan, H5658
30 And his firstborn son **A**, and Zur, and H5658
9:36 And his firstborn son **A**, then Zur, and H5658
2Ch 34:20 of Shaphan, and **A** the son of Micah, H5658

ABED-NEGO
Dan 1: 7 of Meshach; and to Azariah, of **A**. H5664
2:49 Meshach, and **A**, over the affairs of the H5665
3:12 Meshach, and **A**; these men, O king, H5665
13 Meshach, and **A**. Then they brought H5665
14 Meshach, and **A**, do not ye serve my H5665
16 Shadrach, Meshach, and **A**, answered H5665
19 Meshach, and **A**: *therefore* he spake, H5665
20 Meshach, and **A**, *and* to cast *them* into H5665
22 took up Shadrach, Meshach, and **A**. H5665
23 Meshach, and **A**, fell down bound into H5665
26 Meshach, and **A**, ye servants of the H5665
26 **A**, came forth of the midst of the fire. H5665
28 Meshach, and **A**, who hath sent his H5665
29 Meshach, and **A**, shall be cut in pieces, H5665
30 and **A**, in the province of Babylon. H5665

ABEL
Gen 4: 2 And she again bare his brother **A**. And H1893
2 brother Abel. And **A** was a keeper of H1893
4 And **A**, he also brought of the firstlings H1893
4 had respect unto **A** and to his offering: H1893
8 And Cain talked with **A** his brother: H1893
8 up against **A** his brother, and slew him. H1893
9 Cain, Where *is* **A** thy brother? And he H1893
25 seed instead of **A**, whom Cain slew. H1893
1Sa 6:18 the great *stone of* **A**, whereon they set H59
2Sa 20:14 of Israel unto **A**, and to Beth-maachah, H59
15 And they came and besieged him in **A** of H59
18 at **A**: and so they ended *the matter.* H59
Mt 23:35 blood of righteous **A** unto the blood of *G6*
Lk 11:51 From the blood of **A** unto the blood of *G6*
Heb 11: 4 By faith **A** offered unto God a more *G6*
12:24 speaketh better things than *that of* **A**. *G6*

ABEL-BETH-MAACHAH
1Ki 15:20 Ijon, and Dan, and **A**, and all Cinneroth, H62
2Ki 15:29 and took Ijon, and **A**, and Janoah, and H62

ABEL-MAIM
2Ch 16: 4 **A**, and all the store cities of Naphtali. H66

ABEL-MEHOLAH
Jdg 7:22 *and* to the border of **A**, unto Tabbath. H65
1Ki 4:12 Beth-shean to **A**, *even* unto *the place* H65
19:16 son of Shaphat of **A** shalt thou anoint *to* H65

ABEL-MIZRAIM
Gen 50:11 it was called **A**, which *is* beyond Jordan. H67

ABEL-SHITTIM
Nu 33:49 *even* unto **A** in the plains of Moab. H63

ABEZ
Jos 19:20 And Rabbith, and Kishion, and **A**, H77

ABHOR
Lev 26:11 you: and my soul shall not **a** you. H1602
15 or if your soul **a** my judgments, so that H1602
30 of your idols, and my soul shall **a** you. H1602
44 neither will I **a** them, to destroy them H1602
Dt 7:26 shalt utterly **a** it; for it *is* a cursed thing. H8581
23: 7 Thou shalt not **a** an Edomite; for he *is* H8581
7 thou shalt not **a** an Egyptian; because H8581
1Sa 27:12 Israel utterly to **a** him; therefore he shall H887
Job 9:31 and mine own clothes shall **a** me. H8581
30:10 They **a** me, they flee far from me, and H8581
42: 6 Wherefore I **a** *myself*, and repent in H3988
Ps 5: 6 will **a** the bloody and deceitful man. H8581
119:163 I hate and **a** lying: *but* thy law do I love. H8581
Prv 24:24 the people curse, nations shall **a** him: H2194
Jer 14:21 Do not **a** *us*, for thy name's sake, do H5006
Am 5:10 they **a** him that speaketh uprightly. H8581
6: 8 the God of hosts, I **a** the excellency of H8374
Mic 3: 9 that **a** judgment, and pervert all equity. H8581
Ro 12: 9 *Let* love be without dissimulation. **A** that *G655*

ABHORRED
Ex 5:21 made our savour to be **a** in the eyes of H887
Lev 20:23 all these things, and therefore I **a** them. H6973
26:43 and because their soul **a** my statutes. H1602
Dt 32:19 And when the LORD saw *it*, he **a** *them*, H5006
1Sa 2:17 for men **a** the offering of the LORD. H5006

2Sa 16:21 hear that thou art **a** of thy father: then H887
1Ki 11:25 and he **a** Israel, and reigned over Syria. H6973
Job 19:19 All my inward friends **a** me: and they H8581
Ps 22:24 For he hath not despised nor **a** the H8262
78:59 *this*, he was wroth, and greatly **a** Israel: H3988
89:38 But thou hast cast off and **a**, thou hast H3988
106:40 that he **a** his own inheritance. H8581
Prv 22:14 that is **a** of the LORD shall fall therein. H2194
Lam 2: 7 his altar, he hath **a** his sanctuary, he H5010
Ezk 16:25 thy beauty to be **a**, and hast opened thy H8581
Zec 11: 8 lothed them, and their soul also **a** me. H973

ABHORREST
Isa 7:16 **a** shall be forsaken of both her kings. H6973
Ro 2:22 that **a** idols, dost thou commit sacrilege? *G948*

ABHORRETH
Job 33:20 So that his life **a** bread, and his soul H2092
Ps 10: 3 the covetous, *whom* the LORD **a**. H5006
36: 4 in a way *that is* not good; he **a** not evil. H3988
107:18 Their soul **a** all manner of meat; and H8581
Isa 49: 7 him whom the nation **a**, to a servant of H8581

ABHORRING
Isa 66:24 and they shall be an **a** unto all flesh. H1860

ABI
2Ki 18: 2 also *was* **A**, the daughter of Zachariah. H21

ABIA
1Ch 3:10 And Solomon's son *was* Rehoboam, **A** H29
Mt 1: 7 Roboam begat **A**; and Abia begat Asa; *G7*
7 Roboam begat Abia; and **A** begat Asa; *G7*
Lk 1: 5 of the course of **A**: and his wife *was* of the *G7*

ABIAH
1Sa 8: 2 **A**: *they were* judges in Beer-sheba. H29
1Ch 2:24 then **A** Hezron's wife bare him H29
6:28 of Samuel; the firstborn Vashni, and **A**. H29
7: 8 and Jerimoth, and **A**, and Anathoth, and H29

ABIALBON
2Sa 23:31 **A** the Arbathite, Azmaveth the H45

ABIASAPH
Ex 6:24 **A**: these *are* the families of the Korhites. H23

ABIATHAR
1Sa 22:20 named **A**, escaped, and fled after David. H54
21 And **A** shewed David that Saul had slain H54
22 And David said unto **A**, I knew *it* that H54
23: 6 And it came to pass, when **A** the son of H54
9 to **A** the priest, Bring hither the ephod. H54
30: 7 And David said to **A** the priest, H54
7 **A** brought thither the ephod to David. H54
2Sa 8:17 the son of **A**, *were* the priests; and H54
15:24 ark of God; and **A** went up, until all the H54
27 thy son, and Jonathan the son of **A**. H54
29 Zadok therefore and **A** carried the ark of H54
35 thee Zadok and **A** the priests? therefore H54
35 shalt tell *it* to Zadok and **A** the priests. H54
17:15 Then said Hushai unto Zadok and to **A** H54
19:11 And king David sent to Zadok and to **A** H54
20:25 And Sheva *was* scribe: and Zadok and **A** H54
1Ki 1: 7 Zeruiah, and with **A** the priest: and they H54
19 of the king, and **A** the priest, and Joab H54
25 of the host, and **A** the priest; and, H54
42 the son of **A** the priest came: and H54
2:22 for him, and for **A** the priest, and for H54
26 And unto **A** the priest said the king, Get H54
27 So Solomon thrust out **A** from being H54
35 priest did the king put in the room of **A**. H54
4: 4 host: and Zadok and **A** *were* the priests: H54
1Ch 15:11 And David called for Zadok and **A** the H54
18:16 the son of **A**, *were* the priests; and H54
24: 6 the son of **A**, and *before* the chief H54
27:34 of Benaiah, and **A**: and the general of the H54
Mk 2:26 God in the days of **A** the high priest, and *G8*

ABIATHAR'S
2Sa 15:36 *son*, and Jonathan **A** *son;* and by them H54

ABIB
Ex 13: 4 This day came ye out in the month **A**. H24
23:15 of the month **A**; for in it thou camest H24
34:18 the time of the month **A**: for in the month H24
18 month **A** thou camest out from Egypt. H24
Dt 16: 1 Observe the month of **A**, and keep the H24
1 for in the month of **A** the LORD thy God H24

ABIDA
Gen 25: 4 and Hanoch, and **A**, and Eldaah. All H28
1Ch 1:33 and Henoch, and **A**, and Eldaah. All H28

ABIDAN
Nu 1:11 Of Benjamin; **A** the son of Gideoni. H27
2:22 Benjamin *shall be* **A** the son of Gideoni. H27
7:60 On the ninth day **A** the son of Gideoni, H27
65 *was* the offering of **A** the son of Gideoni. H27
10:24 of Benjamin *was* **A** the son of Gideoni. H27

ABIDE
Gen 19: 2 but we will **a** in the street all night. H3885
22: 5 his young men, **A** ye here with the ass; H3427
24:55 Let the damsel **a** with us *a few* days, H3427
29:19 give her to another man: **a** with me. H3427
44:33 let thy servant **a** instead of the lad a H3427
Ex 16:29 bread of two days; **a** ye every man in H3427
Lev 8:35 Therefore shall ye **a** *at* the door of the H3427
19:13 **a** with thee all night until the morning. H3885
Nu 22: 5 the earth, and they **a** over against me: H3427
31:19 And do ye **a** without the camp seven H2583
23 Every thing that may **a** the fire, ye shall H935
35:25 fled: and he shall **a** in it unto the death H3427
Dt 3:19 **a** in your cities which I have given you; H3427
Jos 18: 5 parts: Judah shall **a** in their coast on H5975
5 shall **a** in their coasts on the north. H5975
Ru 2: 8 hence, but **a** here fast by my maidens: H1692
1Sa 1:22 before the LORD, and there **a** for ever. H3427
5: 7 God of Israel shall not **a** with us: for his H3427
19: 2 **a** in a secret *place*, and hide thyself: H3427
22: 5 Gad said unto David, **A** not in the hold; H3427
23 **A** thou with me, fear not: for he that H3427
30:21 had made also to **a** at the brook Besor: H3427
2Sa 11:11 Israel, and Judah, **a** in tents; and my H3427
15:19 to thy place, and **a** with the king: for H3427
16:18 his will I be, and with him will I **a**. H3427
1Ki 8:13 a settled place for thee to **a** in for ever. H3427
2Ch 25:19 thee up to boast: **a** now at home; why H3427
32:10 that ye **a** in the siege in Jerusalem? H3427
Job 24:13 thereof, nor **a** in the paths thereof. H3427
38:40 When they couch in *their* dens, *and* **a** H3427
39: 9 willing to serve thee, or **a** by thy crib? H3885
Ps 15: 1 LORD, who shall **a** in thy tabernacle? H1481
61: 4 I will **a** in thy tabernacle for ever: I will H1481
7 He shall **a** before God for ever: O H3427
91: 1 **a** under the shadow of the Almighty. H3885
Prv 7:11 (She *is* loud and stubborn; her feet **a** H7931
19:23 *he that hath it* shall **a** satisfied; he shall H3885
Ecc 8:15 for that shall **a** with him of his labour H3867
Jer 10:10 shall not be able to **a** his indignation. H3557
42:10 If ye will still **a** in this land, then will I H3427
49:18 no man shall **a** there, neither shall H3427
33 **a** there, nor *any* son of man dwell in it. H3427
50:40 *so* shall no man **a** there, neither shall H3427
Hos 3: 3 And I said unto her, Thou shalt **a** for H3427
4 For the children of Israel shall **a** many H3427
11: 6 And the sword shall **a** on his cities, and H2342
Joel 2:11 and very terrible; and who can **a** it? H3557
Mic 5: 4 and they shall **a**: for now shall he be H3427
Nah 1: 6 and who can **a** in the fierceness of H6965
Mal 3: 2 But who may **a** the day of his coming? H3557
Mt 10:11 is worthy; and there **a** till ye go thence. *G3306*
Mk 6:10 there **a** till ye depart from that place. *G3306*
Lk 9: 4 enter into, there **a**, and thence depart. *G3306*
19: 5 down; for to day I must **a** at thy house. *G3306*
24:29 But they constrained him, saying, **A** *G3306*
Jn 12:46 on me should not **a** in darkness. *G3306*
14:16 that he may **a** with you for ever; *G3306*
15: 4 **A** in me, and I in you. As the branch *G3306*
4 of itself, except it **a** in the vine; no more *G3306*
4 no more can ye, except ye **a** in me. *G3306*
6 If a man **a** not in me, he is cast forth as *G3306*
7 If ye **a** in me, and my words abide in *G3306*
7 If ye abide in me, and my words **a** in *G3306*
10 ye shall **a** in my love; even as *G3306*
10 commandments, and **a** in his love. *G3306*
Act 15:34 Notwithstanding it pleased Silas to **a** *G1961*
16:15 and **a** *there*. And she constrained us. *G3306*
20:23 saying that bonds and afflictions **a** me. *G3306*
27:31 these **a** in the ship, ye cannot be saved. *G3306*
Ro 11:23 And they also, if they **a** not still in *G1961*
1Co 3:14 If any man's work **a** which he hath *G3306*
7: 8 It is good for them if they **a** even as I. *G3306*
20 Let every man **a** in the same calling *G3306*
24 he is called, therein **a** with God. *G3306*
40 But she is happier if she so **a**, after my *G3306*
16: 6 And it may be that I will **a**, yea, and *G3887*
Php 1:24 Nevertheless to **a** in the flesh *is* more *G1961*
1:25 I know that I shall **a** and continue with *G3306*
1Ti 1: 3 As I besought thee to **a** still at Ephesus, *G4357*
1Jn 2:24 Let that therefore **a** in you, which ye *G3306*
27 as it hath taught you, ye shall **a** in him. *G3306*
28 And now, little children, **a** in him; that, *G3306*

ABIDETH
Nu 31:23 and all that **a** not the fire ye shall make H935
2Sa 16: 3 king, Behold, he **a** at Jerusalem: for he H3427
Job 39:28 She dwelleth and **a** on the rock, upon H3885
Ps 49:12 Nevertheless man *being* in honour **a** H3885
55:19 them, even he that **a** of old. Selah. H3427
119:90 hast established the earth, and it **a**. H5975
125: 1 cannot be removed, *but* **a** for ever. H3427
Prv 15:31 the reproof of life **a** among the wise. H3885
Ecc 1: 4 cometh: but the earth **a** for ever. H5975
Jer 21: 9 He that **a** in this city shall die by the H3427
Jn 3:36 see life; but the wrath of God **a** on him. *G3306*
8:35 And the servant **a** not in the house for *G3306*
35 the house for ever: *but* the Son **a** ever. *G3306*
12:24 ground and die, it **a** alone: but if it die, *G3306*
34 the law that Christ **a** for ever: and how *G3306*
15: 5 the branches: He that **a** in me, and I in *G3306*
1Co 13:13 And now **a** faith, hope, charity, these *G3306*
2Ti 2:13 If we believe not, *yet* he **a** faithful: he *G3306*
Heb 7: 3 the Son of God; **a** a priest continually. *G3306*
1Pt 1:23 of God, which liveth and **a** for ever. *G3306*
1Jn 2: 6 He that saith he **a** in him ought himself *G3306*
10 He that loveth his brother **a** in the light, *G3306*
14 the word of God **a** in you, and ye have *G3306*
17 he that doeth the will of God **a** for ever. *G3306*
27 received of him **a** in you, and ye need *G3306*
3: 6 Whosoever **a** in him sinneth not: *G3306*
14 that loveth not *his* brother **a** in death. *G3306*
24 we know that he **a** in us, by the Spirit *G3306*
2Jn 9 Whosoever transgresseth, and **a** not in *G3306*
9 not God. He that **a** in the doctrine of *G3306*

ABIDING
Nu 24: 2 eyes, and he saw Israel **a** *in his tents* H7931
Jdg 16: 9 Now *there were* men lying in wait, **a** H3427
12 *were* liers in wait **a** in the chamber. H3427
1Sa 26:19 out this day from **a** in the inheritance H5596
1Ch 29:15 *are* as a shadow, and *there is* none **a**. H4723
Lk 2: 8 country shepherds **a** in the field, keeping *G63*
Jn 5:38 And ye have not his word **a** in you: for *G3306*
Act 16:12 and we were in that city **a** certain days. *G1304*
1Jn 3:15 no murderer hath eternal life **a** in him. *G3306*

ABIEL
1Sa 9: 1 Kish, the son of **A**, the son of Zeror, the H22
14:51 Ner the father of Abner *was* the son of **A**. H22
1Ch 11:32 Hurai of the brooks of Gaash, **A** the H22

ABIEZER
Jos 17: 2 for the children of **A**, and for the children H44
2Sa 23:27 **A** the Anethothite, Mebunnai the H44
1Ch 7:18 bare Ishod, and **A**, and Mahalah. H44
27:12 ninth month *was* **A** the Anetothite, of the H44

ABI-EZER
Jdg 6:34 trumpet; and **A** was gathered after him. H44
8: 2 of Ephraim better than the vintage of **A**? H44
1Ch 11:28 Ira the son of Ikkesh the Tekoite, **A** the H44

ABI-EZRITE
Jdg 6:11 unto Joash the **A**: and his son Gideon H33

ABI-EZRITES
Jdg 6:24 unto this day it *is* yet in Ophrah of the **A**. H33
8:32 of Joash his father, in Ophrah of the **A**. H33

ABIGAIL
1Sa 25: 3 the name of his wife **A**: and *she was* a H26
14 But one of the young men told **A**, Nabal's H26
18 Then **A** made haste, and took two H26
23 And when **A** saw David, she hasted, and H26
32 And David said to **A**, Blessed *be* the H26
36 And **A** came to Nabal; and, behold, he H26
39 with **A**, to take her to him to wife. H26
40 were come to **A** to Carmel, they spake H26
42 And **A** hasted, and arose, and rode upon H26
27: 3 and **A** the Carmelitess, Nabal's wife. H26
30: 5 and **A** the wife of Nabal the Carmelite. H26
2Sa 2: 2 and **A** Nabal's wife the Carmelite. H26
3: 3 And his second, Chileab, of **A** the wife of H26
17:25 that went in to **A** the daughter of H26
1Ch 2:16 Whose sisters *were* Zeruiah, and **A**. And H26
17 And **A** bare Amasa: and the father of H26

1Ch 3: 1 the second Daniel, of **A** the Carmelitess: H26

ABIHAIL
Nu 3:35 Zuriel the son of **A**: *these* shall pitch on H32
1Ch 2:29 **A**, and she bare him Ahban, and Molid. H32
5:14 These *are* the children of **A** the son of H32
2Ch 11:18 **A** the daughter of Eliab the son of Jesse; H32
Est 2:15 the daughter of **A** the uncle of Mordecai, H32
9:29 the daughter of **A**, and Mordecai the Jew, H32

ABIHU
Ex 6:23 Nadab, and **A**, Eleazar, and Ithamar. H30
24: 1 Nadab, and **A**, and seventy of the elders H30
9 and **A**, and seventy of the elders of Israel: H30
28: 1 **A**, Eleazar and Ithamar, Aaron's sons. H30
Lev 10: 1 And Nadab and **A**, the sons of Aaron, H30
Nu 3: 2 firstborn, and **A**, Eleazar, and Ithamar. H30
4 And Nadab and **A** died before the LORD, H30
26:60 And unto Aaron was born Nadab, and **A**, H30
61 And Nadab and **A** died, when they H30
1Ch 6: 3 Nadab, and **A**, Eleazar, and Ithamar. H30
24: 1 Nadab, and **A**, Eleazar, and Ithamar. H30
2 But Nadab and **A** died before their H30

ABIHUD
1Ch 8: 3 of Bela were, Addar, and Gera, and **A**, H31

ABIJAH
1Ki 14: 1 At that time **A** the son of Jeroboam fell H29
1Ch 24:10 The seventh to Hakkoz, the eighth to **A**, H29
2Ch 11:20 **A**, and Attai, and Ziza, and Shelomith. H29
22 And Rehoboam made **A** the son of H29
12:16 and **A** his son reigned in his stead. H29
13: 1 Jeroboam began **A** to reign over Judah. H29
2 there was war between **A** and Jeroboam. H29
3 And **A** set the battle in array with an H29
4 And **A** stood up upon mount Zemaraim, H29
15 and all Israel before **A** and Judah. H29
17 And **A** and his people slew them with a H29
19 And **A** pursued after Jeroboam, and H29
20 in the days of **A**: and the LORD struck H29
21 But **A** waxed mighty, and married H29
22 And the rest of the acts of **A**, and his H29
14: 1 So **A** slept with his fathers, and they H29
29: 1 name *was* **A**, the daughter of Zechariah. H29
Neh 10: 7 Meshullam, **A**, Mijamin, H29
12: 4 Iddo, Ginnetho, **A**, H29
17 Of **A**, Zichri; of Miniamin, of Moadiah, H29

ABIJAM
1Ki 14:31 And **A** his son reigned in his stead. H38
15: 1 the son of Nebat reigned **A** over Judah. H38
7 Now the rest of the acts of **A**, and all that H38
7 there was war between **A** and Jeroboam. H38
8 And **A** slept with his fathers; and they H38

ABILENE
Lk 3: 1 and Lysanias the tetrarch of **A**, *G9*

ABILITY
Lev 27: 8 to his **a** that vowed shall H3027+H5381
Ezr 2:69 They gave after their **a** unto the H3581
Neh 5: 8 And I said unto them, We after our **a** H1767
Dan 1: 4 and such as *had* **a** in them to stand in H3581
Mt 25:15 **a**; and straightway took his journey. *G1411*
Act 11:29 according to his **a**, determined to send *G2141*
1Pt 4:11 *him do it* as of the **a** which God giveth: *G2479*

ABIMAEL
Gen 10:28 And Obal, and **A**, and Sheba, H39
1Ch 1:22 And Ebal, and **A**, and Sheba, H39

ABIMELECH
Gen 20: 2 **A** king of Gerar sent, and took Sarah. H40
3 But God came to **A** in a dream by night, H40
4 But **A** had not come near her: and he H40
8 Therefore **A** rose early in the morning, H40
9 Then **A** called Abraham, and said unto H40
10 And **A** said unto Abraham, What sawest H40
14 And **A** took sheep, and oxen, and H40
15 And **A** said, Behold, my land *is* before H40
17 and God healed **A**, and his wife, and his H40
18 of **A**, because of Sarah Abraham's wife. H40
21:22 And it came to pass at that time, that **A** H40
25 And Abraham reproved **A** because of a H40
26 And **A** said, I wot not who hath done H40
27 **A**; and both of them made a covenant. H40
29 And **A** said unto Abraham, What *mean* H40
32 Beer-sheba: then **A** rose up, and Phichol H40
Gen 26: 1 **A** king of the Philistines unto Gerar. H40
8 a long time, that **A** king of the Philistines H40
9 And **A** called Isaac, and said, Behold, of H40
10 And **A** said, What *is* this thou hast done H40
11 And **A** charged all *his* people, saying, He H40
16 And **A** said unto Isaac, Go from us; for H40
26 Then **A** went to him from Gerar, and H40
Jdg 8:31 bare him a son, whose name he called **A**. H40
9: 1 And **A** the son of Jerubbaal went to H40
3 follow **A**; for they said, He *is* our brother. H40
4 wherewith **A** hired vain and light H40
6 went, and made **A** king, by the plain of H40
16 that ye have made **A** king, and if ye have H40
18 stone, and have made **A**, the son of his H40
19 ye in **A**, and let him also rejoice in you: H40
20 But if not, let fire come out from **A**, and H40
20 from the house of Millo, and devour **A**. H40
21 dwelt there, for fear of **A** his brother. H40
22 When **A** had reigned three years over H40
23 Then God sent an evil spirit between **A** H40
23 of Shechem dealt treacherously with **A**: H40
24 their blood be laid upon **A** their brother, H40
25 that way by them: and it was told **A**. H40
27 and did eat and drink, and cursed **A**. H40
28 And Gaal the son of Ebed said, Who *is* **A**, H40
29 then would I remove **A**. And he said to H40
29 to **A**, Increase thine army, and come out. H40
31 And he sent messengers unto **A** privily, H40
34 And **A** rose up, and all the people that H40
35 of the city: and **A** rose up, and the people H40
38 saidst, Who *is* **A**, that we should serve H40
39 the men of Shechem, and fought with **A**. H40
40 And **A** chased him, and he fled before H40
41 And **A** dwelt at Arumah: and Zebul H40
42 went out into the field; and they told **A**. H40
44 And **A**, and the company that *was* with H40
45 And **A** fought against the city all that H40
47 And it was told **A**, that all the men of the H40
48 And **A** gat him up to mount Zalmon, he H40
48 with him; and **A** took an axe in his hand, H40
49 and followed **A**, and put *them* to the H40
50 Then went **A** to Thebez, and encamped H40
52 And **A** came unto the tower, and fought H40
55 And when the men of Israel saw that **A** H40
56 Thus God rendered the wickedness of **A**, H40
10: 1 And after **A** there arose to defend Israel H40
2Sa 11:21 Who smote **A** the son of Jerubbesheth? H40
1Ch 18:16 And Zadok the son of Ahitub, and **A** the H40
Ps 34: ttl his behaviour before **A**; who drove him H40

ABIMELECH'S
Gen 21:25 **A** servants had violently taken away. H40
Jdg 9:53 upon **A** head, and all to brake his skull. H40

ABINADAB
1Sa 7: 1 it into the house of **A** in the hill, and H41
16: 8 Then Jesse called **A**, and made him pass H41
17:13 unto him **A**, and the third Shammah. H41
31: 2 and **A**, and Malchishua, Saul's sons. H41
2Sa 6: 3 out of the house of **A** that *was* in Gibeah: H41
3 Ahio, the sons of **A**, drave the new cart. H41
4 And they brought it out of the house of **A** H41
1Ki 4:11 The son of **A**, in all the region of Dor; H41
1Ch 2:13 **A** the second, and Shimma the third, H41
8:33 and Malchishua, and **A**, and Eshbaal. H41
9:39 and Malchishua, and **A**, and Eshbaal. H41
10: 2 and **A**, and Malchishua, the sons of Saul. H41
13: 7 of **A**: and Uzza and Ahio drave the cart. H41

ABINOAM
Jdg 4: 6 called Barak the son of **A** out of H42
12 son of **A** was gone up to mount Tabor. H42
5: 1 Barak the son of **A** on that day, saying, H42
12 lead thy captivity captive, thou son of **A**. H42

ABIRAM
Nu 16: 1 and Dathan and **A**, the sons of Eliab, and H48
12 And Moses sent to call Dathan and **A**, the H48
24 the tabernacle of Korah, Dathan, and **A**. H48
25 **A**; and the elders of Israel followed him. H48
27 Korah, Dathan, and **A**, on every side: and H48
27 and Dathan and **A** came out, and stood H48
26: 9 and Dathan, and **A**. This *is that* Dathan H48
9 *is that* Dathan and **A**, *which were* famous H48
Dt 11: 6 And what he did unto Dathan and **A**, the H48
1Ki 16:34 thereof in **A** his firstborn, and set H48
Ps 106:17 Dathan, and covered the company of **A**. H48

ABISHAG
1Ki 1: 3 Israel, and found **A** a Shunammite, and H49
15 was very old; and **A** the Shunammite H49
2:17 he give me **A** the Shunammite to wife. H49
21 And she said, Let **A** the Shunammite be H49
22 why dost thou ask **A** the Shunammite H49

ABISHAI
1Sa 26: 6 the Hittite, and to **A** the son of Zeruiah, H52
6 And **A** said, I will go down with thee. H52
7 So David and **A** came to the people by H52
8 Then said **A** to David, God hath H52
9 And David said to **A**, Destroy him not: H52
2Sa 2:18 there, Joab, and **A**, and Asahel: and H52
24 Joab also and **A** pursued after Abner: H52
3:30 So Joab and **A** his brother slew Abner, H52
10:10 into the hand of **A** his brother, that he H52
14 they also before **A**, and entered into the H52
16: 9 Then said **A** the son of Zeruiah unto the H52
11 And David said to **A**, and to all his H52
18: 2 under the hand of **A** the son of Zeruiah, H52
5 And the king commanded Joab and **A** H52
12 charged thee and **A** and Ittai, saying, H52
19:21 But **A** the son of Zeruiah answered and H52
20: 6 And David said to **A**, Now shall Sheba H52
10 died. So Joab and **A** his brother pursued H52
21:17 But **A** the son of Zeruiah succoured him, H52
23:18 And **A**, the brother of Joab, the son of H52
1Ch 2:16 Zeruiah; **A**, and Joab, and Asahel, three. H52
11:20 And **A** the brother of Joab, he was chief H52
18:12 Moreover **A** the son of Zeruiah slew of H52
19:11 unto the hand of **A** his brother, and they H52
15 fled before **A** his brother, and entered H52

ABISHALOM
1Ki 15: 2 name *was* Maachah, the daughter of **A**. H53
10 name *was* Maachah, the daughter of **A**. H53

ABISHUA
1Ch 6: 4 begat Phinehas, Phinehas begat **A**, H50
5 And **A** begat Bukki, and Bukki begat H50
50 his son, Phinehas his son, **A** his son, H50
8: 4 And **A**, and Naaman, and Ahoah, H50
Ezr 7: 5 The son of **A**, the son of Phinehas, the H50

ABISHUR
1Ch 2:28 the sons of Shammai; Nadab, and **A**. H51
29 And the name of the wife of **A** *was* H51

ABITAL
2Sa 3: 4 and the fifth, Shephatiah the son of **A**; H37
1Ch 3: 3 The fifth, Shephatiah of **A**: the sixth, H37

ABITUB
1Ch 8:11 And of Hushim he begat **A**, and Elpaal. H36

ABIUD
Mt 1:13 And Zorobabel begat **A**; and Abiud begat *G10*
13 And Zorobabel begat Abiud; and **A** *G10*

ABJECTS
Ps 35:15 together: *yea*, the **a** gathered H5222

ABLE
Gen 13: 6 And the land was not **a** to bear them, H5375
15: 5 stars, if thou be **a** to number them: and H3201
33:14 and the children be **a** to endure, until I H7272
Ex 10: 5 one cannot be **a** to see the earth: and H3201
18:18 art not **a** to perform it thyself alone. H3201
21 of all the people **a** men, such as fear H2428
23 then thou shalt be **a** to endure, and all H3201
25 And Moses chose **a** men out of all H2428
40:35 And Moses was not **a** to enter into the H3201
Lev 5: 7 And if he be not **a** to bring a H5060+H1767
11 But if he be not **a** to bring two H5381
12: 8 And if she be not **a** to bring a H4672+H1767
14:22 such as he is **a** to get; and the one shall H5381
31 *Even* such as he is **a** to get, the one *for* H5381
32 whose hand is not **a** to get *that which* H5381
25:26 it, and himself be **a** to redeem it; H1767
28 But if he be not **a** to restore *it* to him, H1767
49 or if he be **a**, he may redeem himself. H5381
Nu 1: 3 all that are **a** to go forth to war in H3318
20 all that were **a** to go forth to war; H3318
22 all that were **a** to go forth to war; H3318
24 all that were **a** to go forth to war; H3318
26 all that were **a** to go forth to war; H3318
28 all that were **a** to go forth to war; H3318
30 all that were **a** to go forth to war; H3318

Nu 1:32 all that were a to go forth to war; H3318
34 all that were a to go forth to war; H3318
36 all that were a to go forth to war; H3318
38 all that were a to go forth to war; H3318
40 all that were a to go forth to war; H3318
42 all that were a to go forth to war; H3318
45 that were a to go forth to war in Israel; H3318
11:14 I am not a to bear all this people alone, H3201
13:30 it; for we are well a to overcome it. H3201
31 said, We be not a to go up against the H3201
14:16 Because the LORD was not a to bring H3201
22:11 I shall be a to overcome them, H3201
37 a indeed to promote thee to honour? H3201
26: 2 all that are a to go to war in Israel. H3318
Dt 1: 9 I am not a to bear you myself alone: H3201
7:24 shall no man be a to stand before thee, H3320
9:28 the LORD was not a to bring them into H3201
11:25 There shall no man be a to stand H3320
14:24 that thou art not a to carry it; *or* if the H3201
16:17 Every man *shall give* as he is a, H4979+H3027
Jos 1: 5 There shall not any man be a to stand H3320
14:12 a to drive them out, as the LORD said.
23: 9 a to stand before you unto this day. H5975
Jdg 8: 3 and what was I a to do in comparison H3201
1Sa 6:20 said, Who is a to stand before this H3201
17: 9 If he be a to fight with me, and to kill H3201
33 And Saul said to David, Thou art not a H3201
1Ki 3: 9 is a to judge this thy so great a people? H3201
9:21 also were not a utterly to destroy, upon H3201
2Ki 3:21 all that were a to put on armour, and H2296
18:23 a on thy part to set riders upon them. H3201
29 not be a to deliver you out of his hand: H3201
1Ch 5:18 valiant men, men a to bear buckler and H5375
9:13 threescore; very a men for the work of H2428
26: 8 their brethren, a men for strength for H2428
29:14 that we should be a to offer so willingly H3581
2Ch 2: 6 But who is a to build him an house, H3581
7: 7 had made was not a to receive the H3201
20: 6 so that none is a to withstand thee?
37 that they were not a to go to Tarshish. H6113
25: 5 choice *men*, *a* to go forth to war, that
9 is a to give thee much more than this.
32:13 lands any ways a to deliver their lands H3201
14 be a to deliver you out of mine hand? H3201
15 or kingdom was a to deliver his people H3201
Ezr 10:13 and we are not a to stand without, H3581
Neh 4:10 so that we are not a to build the wall. H3201
Job 41:10 up: who then is a to stand before me?
Ps 18:38 a to rise: they are fallen under my feet. H3201
21:11 *which* they are not a *to perform*. H3201
36:12 cast down, and shall not be a to rise. H3201
40:12 so that I am not a to look up; they are H3201
Prv 27: 4 but who *is* a to stand before envy?
Ecc 8:17 know *it*, yet shall he not be a to find *it*. H3201
Isa 36: 8 a on thy part to set riders upon them. H3201
14 you: for he shall not be a to deliver you. H3201
47:11 thou shalt not be a to put it off: and H3201
12 a to profit, if so be thou mayest prevail. H3201
Jer 10:10 shall not be a to abide his indignation. H3201
11:11 they shall not be a to escape; and H3201
49:10 he shall not be a to hide himself: his H3201
Lam 1:14 *from whom* I am not a to rise up. H3201
Ezk 7:19 gold shall not be a to deliver them in H3201
33:12 shall the righteous be a to live for his H3201
46: 5 a to give, and an hin of oil to an ephah. H3027
11 a to give, and an hin of oil to an ephah. H3027
Dan 2:26 Art thou a to make known unto H3546
3:17 If it be *so*, our God whom we serve is a H3202
4:18 my kingdom are not a to make known H3202
18 but thou *art* a; for the spirit of the H3546
37 that walk in pride he is a to abase. H3202
6:20 a to deliver thee from the lions? H3202
Am 7:10 the land is not a to bear all his words. H3201
Zep 1:18 their gold shall be a to deliver them in H3201
Mt 3: 9 you, that God is a of these stones to G1410
9:28 ye that I am a to do this? They said G1410
10:28 body, but are not a to kill the soul: but G1410
28 a to destroy both soul and body in hell. G1410
19:12 that is a to receive *it*, let him receive *it*. G1410
20:22 ye ask. Are ye a to drink of the cup that G1410
22 with? They say unto him, We are a. G1410
22:46 And no man was a to answer him a G1410
26:61 And said, This *fellow* said, I am a to G1410
Mk 4:33 unto them, as they were a to hear *it*. G1410
Lk 1:20 be dumb, and not a to speak, until the G1410
3: 8 you, That God is a of these stones to G1410
12:26 If ye then be not a to do that thing G1410
13:24 will seek to enter in, and shall not be a. G2480
14:29 and is not a to finish *it*, all that behold G2480
Lk 14:30 began to build, and was not a to finish. G2480
31 whether he be a with ten thousand to G1415
21:15 shall not be a to gainsay nor resist. G1410
Jn 10:29 all; and no *man* is a to pluck *them* out G1410
21: 6 a to draw it for the multitude of fishes. G2480
Act 6:10 And they were not a to resist the G2480
15:10 our fathers nor we were a to bear? G2480
20:32 of his grace, which is a to build you up, G1410
25: 5 among you are a, go down with *me*, G1415
Ro 4:21 promised, he was a also to perform. G1415
8:39 creature, shall be a to separate us from G1410
11:23 in: for God is a to graff them in again. G1415
14: 4 up: for God is a to make him stand. G1415
15:14 a also to admonish one another. G1410
1Co 3: 2 a *to bear it*, neither yet now are ye able. G1410
2 able *to bear it*, neither yet now are ye a. G1410
6: 5 be a to judge between his brethren? G1410
10:13 above that ye are a; but will with the G1410
13 to escape, that ye may be a to bear *it*. G1410
2Co 1: 4 that we may be a to comfort them G1410
3: 6 Who also hath made us a ministers of G2427
9: 8 And God *is* a to make all grace abound G1415
Eph 3:18 May be a to comprehend with all saints G1840
20 Now unto him that is a to do exceeding G1410
6:11 a to stand against the wiles of the devil. G1410
13 that ye may be a to withstand in the G1410
16 ye shall be a to quench all the fiery G1410
Php 3:21 whereby he is a even to subdue all G1410
2Ti 1:12 that he is a to keep that which I G1415
2: 2 who shall be a to teach others also. G2425
3: 7 Ever learning, and never a to come to G1410
15 which are a to make thee wise unto G1410
Tit 1: 9 that he may be a by sound doctrine G1415
Heb 2:18 is a to succour them that are tempted. G1410
5: 7 unto him that was a to save him from G1410
7:25 Wherefore he is a also to save them to G1410
11:19 Accounting that God *was* a to raise G1415
Jas 1:21 word, which is a to save your souls. G1410
3: 2 *and* a also to bridle the whole body. G1415
4:12 There is one lawgiver, who is a to save G1410
2Pt 1:15 that ye may be a after my decease to G4160
Jude 24 Now unto him that is a to keep you G1410
Rev 5: 3 the earth, was a to open the book, G1410
6:17 is come; and who shall be a to stand? G1410
13: 4 beast? who is a to make war with him? G1410
15: 8 and no man was a to enter into the G1410

ABNER

1Sa 14:50 host *was* A, the son of Ner, Saul's uncle. H74
51 Ner the father of A *was* the son of Abiel. H74
17:55 he said unto A, the captain of the host, H74
55 of the host, A, whose son *is* this youth? H74
55 *is* this youth? And A said, *As* thy soul H74
57 of the Philistine, A took him, and H74
20:25 arose, and A sat by Saul's side, and H74
26: 5 where Saul lay, and A the son of Ner, the H74
7 A and the people lay round about him. H74
14 And David cried to the people, and to A H74
14 thou not, A? Then Abner answered H74
14 not, Abner? Then A answered and said, H74
15 And David said to A, *Art* not thou a H74
2Sa 2: 8 But A the son of Ner, captain of Saul's H74
12 And A the son of Ner, and the servants H74
14 And A said to Joab, Let the young men H74
17 that day; and A was beaten, and the H74
19 And Asahel pursued after A; and in H74
19 hand nor to the left from following A. H74
20 Then A looked behind him, and said, H74
21 And A said to him, Turn thee aside to H74
22 And A said again to Asahel, Turn thee H74
23 aside: wherefore A with the hinder end H74
24 Joab also and Abishai pursued after A: H74
25 together after A, and became one troop, H74
26 Then A called to Joab, and said, Shall H74
29 And A and his men walked all that night H74
30 And Joab returned from following A: and H74
3: 6 of David, that A made himself strong H74
7 said to A, Wherefore hast thou H74
8 Then was A very wroth for the words of H74
9 So do God to A, and more also, except, as H74
11 And he could not answer A a word H74
12 And A sent messengers to David on his H74
16 Then said A unto him, Go, return. H74
17 And A had communication with the H74
19 And A also spake in the ears of H74
19 of Benjamin: and A went also to speak H74
20 So A came to David to Hebron, and H74
20 And David made A and the men that H74
21 And A said unto David, I will arise and H74
2Sa 3:21 sent A away; and he went in peace. H74
22 with them: but A *was* not with David H74
23 told Joab, saying, A the son of Ner came H74
24 thou done? behold, A came unto thee; H74
25 Thou knowest A the son of Ner, that he H74
26 messengers after A, which brought him H74
27 And when A was returned to Hebron, H74
28 ever from the blood of A the son of Ner: H74
30 So Joab and Abishai his brother slew A, H74
31 and mourn before A. And king David H74
32 And they buried A in Hebron: and the H74
32 at the grave of A; and all the people wept. H74
33 And the king lamented over A, and said, H74
33 Abner, and said, Died A as a fool dieth? H74
37 not of the king to slay A the son of Ner. H74
4: 1 And when Saul's son heard that A was H74
12 *it* in the sepulchre of A in Hebron. H74
1Ki 2: 5 of Israel, unto A the son of Ner, and H74
32 *thereof, to wit*, A the son of Ner, captain H74
1Ch 26:28 son of Kish, and A the son of Ner, and H74
27:21 of Benjamin, Jaasiel the son of A: H74

ABNER'S

2Sa 2:31 of Benjamin, and of A men, *so that* three H74

ABOARD

Act 21: 2 unto Phenicia, we went a, and set forth. G1910

ABODE

Gen 29:14 he a with him the space of a month. H3427
49:24 But his bow a in strength, and the arms H3427
Ex 24:16 And the glory of the LORD a upon H7931
40:35 because the cloud a thereon, and the H7931
Nu 9:17 where the cloud a, there the children of H7931
18 long as the cloud a upon the tabernacle H7931
20 of the LORD they a in their tents, and H2583
21 And *so* it was, when the cloud a from H1961
22 children of Israel a in their tents, and H2583
11:35 unto Hazeroth; and a at Hazeroth. H1961
20: 1 and the people a in Kadesh; and H3427
22: 8 the princes of Moab a with Balaam. H3427
25: 1 And Israel a in Shittim, and the people H3427
Dt 1:46 So ye a in Kadesh many days, H3427
46 unto the days that ye a *there*. H3427
3:29 So we a in the valley over against H3427
9: 9 with you, then I a in the mount forty H3427
Jos 2:22 mountain, and a there three days, until H3427
5: 8 people, that they a in their places in the H3427
8: 9 in ambush, and a between Beth-el and H3427
Jdg 5:17 Gilead a beyond Jordan: and why did H7931
17 on the sea shore, and a in his breaches. H7931
11:17 not *consent*: and Israel a in Kadesh. H3427
19: 4 him; and he a with him three days: H3427
20:47 a in the rock Rimmon four months. H3427
21: 2 the house of God, and a there till even H3427
1Sa 1:23 So the woman a, and gave her son suck H3427
7: 2 And it came to pass, while the ark a in H3427
13:16 with them, a in Gibeah of Benjamin: H3427
22: 6 him, (now Saul a in Gibeah under a H3427
23:14 And David a in the wilderness in H3427
18 LORD: and David a in the wood, and H3427
25 into a rock, and a in the wilderness of H3427
25:13 men; and two hundred a by the stuff. H3427
26: 3 the way. But David a in the wilderness, H3427
30:10 for two hundred a behind, which were H5975
2Sa 1: 1 and David had a two days in Ziklag; H3427
11:12 depart. So Uriah a in Jerusalem that H3427
15: 8 For thy servant vowed a vow while I a H3427
1Ki 17:19 he a, and laid him upon his own bed. H3427
2Ki 19:27 But I know thy a, and thy going out, H3427
Ezr 8:15 to Ahava; and there a we in tents three H2583
32 And we came to Jerusalem, and a there H3427
Isa 37:28 But I know thy a, and thy going out, H3427
Jer 38:28 So Jeremiah a in the court of the prison H3427
Mt 17:22 And while they a in Galilee, Jesus said G390
Lk 1:56 And Mary a with her about three G3306
8:27 a in *any* house, but in the tombs. G3306
21:37 he went out, and a in the mount that is G835
Jn 1:32 heaven like a dove, and it a upon him. G3306
39 he dwelt, and a with him that day: for G3306
4:40 with them: and he a there two days. G3306
7: 9 words unto them, he a *still* in Galilee. G3306
8:44 the beginning, and a not in the truth, G2476
10:40 John at first baptized; and there he a. G3306
11: 6 he was sick, he a two days still in the G3306
14:23 unto him, and make our a with him. G3438
Act 1:13 room, where a both Peter, and James, G2258
12:19 from Judaea to Caesarea, and *there* a. G1304
14: 3 Long time therefore a they speaking G1304

Act 14:28 And there they **a** long time with the G1304
17:14 but Silas and Timotheus **a** there still. G5278
18: 3 of the same craft, he **a** with them, and G3306
20: 3 And *there* **a** three months. And when G4160
6 in five days; where we **a** seven days. G1304
21: 7 the brethren, and **a** with them one day. G3306
8 was *one* of the seven; and **a** with him. G3306
Gal 1:18 see Peter, and **a** with him fifteen days. G1961
2Ti 4:20 Erastus **a** at Corinth: but Trophimus G3306

ABODEST
Jdg 5:16 Why **a** thou among the sheepfolds, to H3427

ABOLISH
Isa 2:18 And the idols he shall utterly **a**. H2498

ABOLISHED
Isa 51: 6 and my righteousness shall not be **a**. H2865
Ezk 6: 6 be cut down, and your works may be **a**. H4229
2Co 3:13 look to the end of that which is **a**: G2673
Eph 2:15 Having **a** in his flesh the enmity, *even* G2673
2Ti 1:10 Christ, who hath **a** death, and hath G2673

ABOMINABLE
Lev 7:21 beast, or any **a** unclean *thing,* and H8263
11:43 Ye shall not make yourselves **a** with H8262
18:30 *any one* of these **a** customs, which were H8441
19: 7 day, it *is* **a**; it shall not be accepted. H6292
20:25 make your souls **a** by beast, or by fowl, H8262
Dt 14: 3 Thou shalt not eat any **a** thing. H8441
1Ch 21: 6 for the king's word was **a** to Joab. H8581
2Ch 15: 8 and put away the **a** idols out of all the H8251
Job 15:16 How much more **a** and filthy *is* man, H8581
Ps 14: 1 **a** works, *there is* none that doeth good. H8581
53: 1 and have done **a** iniquity: *there is* none H8581
Isa 14:19 thy grave like an **a** branch, *and as* the H8581
65: 4 and broth of **a** *things is in* their vessels; H6292
Jer 16:18 of their detestable and **a** things. H8441
44: 4 Oh, do not this **a** thing that I hate. H8441
Ezk 4:14 came there **a** flesh into my mouth. H6292
8:10 things, and **a** beasts, and all the idols H8263
16:52 committed more **a** than they: they are H8581
Mic 6:10 wicked, and the scant measure *that is* **a**? H2194
Nah 3: 6 And I will cast **a** filth upon thee, and H8251
Tit 1:16 deny *him*, being **a**, and disobedient, and G947
1Pt 4: 3 revellings, banquetings, and **a** idolatries: G111
Rev 21: 8 and the **a**, and murderers, and G948

ABOMINABLY
1Ki 21:26 And he did very **a** in following idols, H8581

ABOMINATION
Gen 43:32 for that *is* an **a** unto the Egyptians. H8441
46:34 shepherd *is* an **a** unto the Egyptians. H8441
Ex 8:26 shall sacrifice the **a** of the Egyptians to H8441
26 shall we sacrifice the **a** of the Egyptians H8441
Lev 7:18 it: it shall be an **a**, and the soul that H6292
11:10 the waters, they *shall be* an **a** unto you: H8263
11 They shall be even an **a** unto you; ye H8263
11 but ye shall have their carcases in **a**. H8262
12 the waters, that *shall be* an **a** unto you. H8263
13 ye shall have in **a** among the fowls; H8262
13 eaten, they *are* an **a**: the eagle, and the H8263
20 upon *all* four, *shall be* an **a** unto you. H8263
23 have four feet, *shall be* an **a** unto you. H8263
41 earth *shall be* an **a**; it shall not be eaten. H8263
42 them ye shall not eat; for they *are* an **a**. H8263
18:22 mankind, as with womankind: it *is* **a**. H8441
20:13 committed an **a**: they shall surely be H8441
Dt 7:25 for it *is* an **a** to the LORD thy God. H8441
26 Neither shalt thou bring an **a** into thine H8441
12:31 thy God: for every **a** to the LORD, H8441
13:14 *that* such **a** is wrought among you; H8441
17: 1 for that *is* an **a** unto the LORD thy God. H8441
4 *that* such **a** is wrought in Israel: H8441
18:12 For all that do these things *are* an **a** H8441
22: 5 do so *are* **a** unto the LORD thy God. H8441
23:18 these *are* **a** unto the LORD thy God. H8441
24: 4 is defiled; for that *is* **a** before the LORD: H8441
25:16 *are* an **a** unto the LORD thy God. H8441
27:15 molten image, an **a** unto the LORD, the H8441
1Sa 13: 4 also was had in **a** with the Philistines. H887
1Ki 11: 5 after Milcom the **a** of the Ammonites. H8251
7 for Chemosh, the **a** of Moab, in the hill H8251
7 the **a** of the children of Ammon. H8251
2Ki 23:13 for Ashtoreth the **a** of the Zidonians, H8251
13 for Chemosh the **a** of the Moabites, and H8251
13 and for Milcom the **a** of the children of H8441
Ps 88: 8 hast made me an **a** unto them: *I am* H8441
Prv 3:32 For the froward *is* **a** to the LORD: but H8441
6:16 hate: yea, seven *are* an **a** unto him: H8441
8: 7 and wickedness *is* an **a** to my lips. H8441
11: 1 A false balance *is* **a** to the LORD: but a H8441
20 They that are of a froward heart *are* **a** H8441
12:22 Lying lips *are* **a** to the LORD: but they H8441
13:19 but *it is* **a** to fools to depart from evil. H8441
15: 8 The sacrifice of the wicked *is* an **a** to H8441
9 The way of the wicked *is* an **a** unto the H8441
26 The thoughts of the wicked *are* an **a** to H8441
16: 5 Every one *that is* proud in heart *is* an **a** H8441
12 *It is* an **a** to kings to commit H8441
17:15 just, even they both *are* **a** to the LORD. H8441
20:10 both of them *are* alike **a** to the LORD. H8441
23 Divers weights *are* an **a** unto the H8441
21:27 The sacrifice of the wicked *is* **a**: how H8441
24: 9 *is* sin: and the scorner *is* an **a** to men. H8441
28: 9 the law, even his prayer *shall be* **a**. H8441
29:27 An unjust man *is* an **a** to the just: and H8441
27 *is* upright in the way *is* **a** to the wicked. H8441
Isa 1:13 incense is an **a** unto me; the new H8441
41:24 of nought: an **a** *is he that* chooseth you. H8441
44:19 **a**? shall I fall down to the stock of a tree? H8441
66:17 flesh, and the **a**, and the mouse, shall H8263
Jer 2: 7 my land, and made mine heritage an **a**. H8441
6:15 had committed **a**? nay, they were not at H8441
8:12 had committed **a**? nay, they were not at H8441
32:35 should do this **a**, to cause Judah to sin. H8441
Ezk 16:50 and committed **a** before me: therefore H8441
18:12 his eyes to the idols, hath committed **a**, H8441
22:11 And one hath committed **a** with his H8441
33:26 Ye stand upon your sword, ye work **a**, H8441
Dan 11:31 shall place the **a** that maketh desolate. H8251
12:11 away, and the **a** that maketh desolate H8251
Mal 2:11 and an **a** is committed in Israel H8441
Mt 24:15 When ye therefore shall see the **a** of G946
Mk 13:14 But when ye shall see the **a** of desolation, G946
Lk 16:15 among men is **a** in the sight of God. G946
Rev 21:27 worketh **a**, or *maketh* a lie: but G946

ABOMINATIONS
Lev 18:26 *any* of these **a**; *neither* any of your H8441
27 (For all these **a** have the men of the H8441
29 any of these **a**, even the souls that H8441
Dt 18: 9 learn to do after the **a** of those nations. H8441
12 because of these **a** the LORD thy God H8441
20:18 to do after all their **a**, which they have H8441
29:17 And ye have seen their **a**, and their H8251
32:16 with **a** provoked they him to anger. H8441
1Ki 14:24 to all the **a** of the nations which H8441
2Ki 16: 3 fire, according to the **a** of the heathen, H8441
21: 2 the LORD, after the **a** of the heathen, H8441
11 Judah hath done these **a**, *and* hath done H8441
23:24 idols, and all the **a** that were spied in H8251
2Ch 28: 3 in the fire, after the **a** of the heathen H8441
33: 2 like unto the **a** of the heathen, whom H8441
34:33 And Josiah took away all the **a** out of H8441
36: 8 and his **a** which he did, and that H8441
14 much after all the **a** of the heathen; and H8441
Ezr 9: 1 *doing* according to their **a**, *even* of the H8441
11 lands, with their **a**, which have filled it H8441
14 the people of these **a**? wouldest not thou H8441
Prv 26:25 not: for *there are* seven **a** in his heart. H8441
Isa 66: 3 and their soul delighteth in their **a**. H8251
Jer 4: 1 put away thine **a** out of my sight, then H8251
7:10 say, We are delivered to do all these **a**? H8441
30 they have set their **a** in the house which H8251
13:27 *and* thine **a** on the hills in the fields. H8251
32:34 But they set their **a** in the house, which H8251
44:22 *and* because of the **a** which ye have H8441
Ezk 5: 9 more the like, because of all thine **a**. H8441
11 and with all thine **a**, therefore will I also H8441
6: 9 they have committed in all their **a**. H8441
11 for all the evil **a** of the house of Israel! H8441
7: 3 will recompense upon thee all thine **a**. H8441
4 thee, and thine **a** shall be in the midst H8441
8 and will recompense thee for all thine **a**. H8441
9 ways and thine **a** *that* are in the midst H8441
20 the images of their **a** *and* of their H8441
8: 6 do? *even* the great **a** that the house of H8441
6 yet again, *and* thou shalt see greater **a**. H8441
9 behold the wicked **a** that they do here. H8441
13 thou shalt see greater **a** that they do. H8441
15 *and* thou shalt see greater **a** than these. H8441
17 they commit the **a** which they commit H8441
9: 4 the **a** that be done in the midst thereof. H8441
11:18 and all the **a** thereof from thence. H8441
21 things and their **a**, I will recompense H8441
12:16 declare all their **a** among the heathen H8441
Ezk 14: 6 turn away your faces from all your **a**. H8441
16: 2 of man, cause Jerusalem to know her **a**, H8441
22 And in all thine **a** and thy whoredoms H8441
36 all the idols of thy **a**, and by the blood of H8441
43 commit this lewdness above all thine **a**. H8441
47 done after their **a**: but, as *if that were* **a** H8441
51 multiplied thine **a** more than they, and H8441
51 in all thine **a** which thou hast done. H8441
58 lewdness and thine **a**, saith the LORD. H8441
18:13 done all these **a**; he shall surely die; his H8441
24 to all the **a** that the wicked *man* H8441
20: 4 them to know the **a** of their fathers: H8441
7 every man the **a** of his eyes, and defile H8251
8 cast away the **a** of their eyes, neither H8251
30 and commit ye whoredom after their **a**? H8251
22: 2 city? yea, thou shalt shew her all her **a**. H8441
23:36 yea, declare unto them their **a**; H8441
33:29 all their **a** which they have committed. H8441
36:31 sight for your iniquities and for your **a**. H8441
43: 8 holy name by their **a** that they have H8441
44: 6 of Israel, let it suffice you of all your **a**, H8441
7 my covenant because of all your **a**. H8441
13 their **a** which they have committed. H8441
Dan 9:27 the overspreading of **a** he shall make *it* H8251
Hos 9:10 *their* **a** were according as they loved. H8251
Zec 9: 7 his mouth, and his **a** from between his H8251
Rev 17: 4 full of **a** and filthiness of her fornication: G946
5 OF HARLOTS AND **A** OF THE EARTH. G946

ABOUND
Prv 28:20 A faithful man shall **a** with blessings: H7227
Mt 24:12 And because iniquity shall **a**, the love of G4129
Ro 5:20 that the offence might **a**. But where sin G4121
20 sin abounded, grace did much more **a**: G5248
6: 1 we continue in sin, that grace may **a**? G4121
15:13 that ye may **a** in hope, through the G4052
2Co 1: 5 For as the sufferings of Christ **a** in us, G4052
8: 7 Therefore, as ye **a** in every *thing, in* G4052
7 to us, *see* that ye **a** in this grace also. G4052
9: 8 And God *is* able to make all grace **a** G4052
8 in all *things*, may **a** to every good work: G4052
Php 1: 9 And this I pray, that your love may **a** G4052
4:12 I know how to **a**: every where and in G4052
12 be hungry, both to **a** and to suffer need. G4052
17 desire fruit that may **a** to your account. G4121
18 But I have all, and **a**: I am full, having G4052
1Th 3:12 to increase and **a** in love one toward G4052
4: 1 God, *so* ye would **a** more and more. G4052
2Pt 1: 8 For if these things be in you, and **a**, they G4121

ABOUNDED
Ro 3: 7 For if the truth of God hath more **a** G4052
5:15 man, Jesus Christ, hath **a** unto many. G4052
20 sin **a**, grace did much more abound: G4121
2Co 8: 2 **a** unto the riches of their liberality. G4052
Eph 1: 8 Wherein he hath **a** toward us in all G4052

ABOUNDETH
Prv 29:22 and a furious man **a** in transgression. H7227
2Co 1: 5 us, so our consolation also **a** by Christ. G4052
2Th 1: 3 one of you all toward each other **a**; G4121

ABOUNDING
Prv 8:24 *there were* no fountains **a** with water. H3513
1Co 15:58 always **a** in the work of the Lord, G4052
Col 2: 7 taught, **a** therein with thanksgiving. G4052

ABOUT See the Appendix.

ABOVE See the Appendix.

ABRAHAM
Gen 17: 5 thy name shall be **A**; for a father of many H85
9 And God said unto **A**, Thou shalt keep H85
15 And God said unto **A**, As for Sarai thy H85
17 Then **A** fell upon his face, and laughed, H85
18 And **A** said unto God, O that Ishmael H85
22 with him, and God went up from **A**. H85
23 And **A** took Ishmael his son, and all that H85
24 And **A** *was* ninety years old and nine, H85
26 In the selfsame day was **A** circumcised, H85
18: 6 And **A** hastened into the tent unto H85
7 And **A** ran unto the herd, and fetcht a H85
11 Now **A** and Sarah *were* old *and* well H85
13 And the LORD said unto **A**, Wherefore H85
16 Sodom: and **A** went with them to bring H85
17 And the LORD said, Shall I hide from **A** H85
18 Seeing that **A** shall surely become a H85
19 **A** that which he hath spoken of him. H85

Gen 18:22 but A stood yet before the LORD. H85
23 And A drew near, and said, Wilt thou H85
27 And A answered and said, Behold now, I H85
33 A: and Abraham returned unto his place. H85
33 and A returned unto his place. H85
19:27 And A gat up early in the morning to the H85
29 God remembered A, and sent Lot out of H85
20: 1 And A journeyed from thence toward H85
2 And A said of Sarah his wife, She *is* my H85
9 Then Abimelech called A, and said unto H85
10 And Abimelech said unto A, What H85
11 And A said, Because I thought, Surely H85
14 unto A, and restored him Sarah his wife. H85
17 So A prayed unto God: and God healed H85
21: 2 For Sarah conceived, and bare A a son H85
3 And A called the name of his son that H85
4 And A circumcised his son Isaac being H85
5 And A was an hundred years old, when H85
7 have said unto A, that Sarah should have H85
8 was weaned: and A made a great feast H85
9 which she had born unto A, mocking. H85
10 Wherefore she said unto A, Cast out this H85
12 And God said unto A, Let it not be H85
14 And A rose up early in the morning, and H85
22 host spake unto A, saying, God *is* with H85
24 And A said, I will swear. H85
25 And A reproved Abimelech because of a H85
27 And A took sheep and oxen, and gave H85
28 And A set seven ewe lambs of the flock H85
29 And Abimelech said unto A, What *mean* H85
33 And *A* planted a grove in Beer-sheba, H5193
34 And A sojourned in the Philistines' land H85
22: 1 that God did tempt A, and said unto him, H85
1 him, A: and he said, Behold, *here* I *am*. H85
3 And A rose up early in the morning, and H85
4 Then on the third day A lifted up his H85
5 And A said unto his young men, Abide H85
6 And A took the wood of the burnt H85
7 And Isaac spake unto A his father, and H85
8 And A said, My son, God will provide H85
9 told him of; and A built an altar there, H85
10 And A stretched forth his hand, and H85
11 A, Abraham: and he said, Here *am* I. H85
11 Abraham, A: and he said, Here *am* I. H85
13 And A lifted up his eyes, and looked, H85
13 by his horns: and A went and took the H85
14 And A called the name of that place H85
15 And the angel of the LORD called unto A H85
19 So A returned unto his young men, and H85
19 Beer-sheba; and A dwelt at Beer-sheba. H85
20 things, that it was told A, saying, Behold, H85
23: 2 of Canaan: and A came to mourn for H85
3 And A stood up from before his dead, H85
5 And the children of Heth answered A, H85
7 And A stood up, and bowed himself to H85
10 Hittite answered A in the audience of the H85
12 And A bowed down himself before the H85
14 And Ephron answered A, saying unto H85
16 And A hearkened unto Ephron; and H85
16 unto Ephron; and A weighed to Ephron H85
18 Unto A for a possession in the presence H85
19 And after this, A buried Sarah his wife in H85
20 made sure unto A for a possession of a H85
24: 1 And A was old, *and* well stricken in age: H85
1 the LORD had blessed A in all things. H85
2 And A said unto his eldest servant of his H85
6 And A said unto him, Beware thou that H85
9 under the thigh of A his master, and H85
12 God of my master A, I pray thee, send me H85
12 and shew kindness unto my master A. H85
27 God of my master A, who hath not left H85
42 God of my master A, if now thou do H85
48 God of my master A, which had led me in H85
25: 1 Then again A took a wife, and her name H85
5 And A gave all that he had unto Isaac. H85
6 the concubines, which A had, Abraham H85
6 Abraham had, A gave gifts, and sent H85
8 Then A gave up the ghost, and died in a H85
10 The field which A purchased of the sons H85
10 there was A buried, and Sarah his wife. H85
11 And it came to pass after the death of A, H85
12 Sarah's handmaid, bare unto A: H85
19 of Isaac, Abraham's son: A begat Isaac: H85
26: 1 that was in the days of A. And Isaac went H85
3 oath which I sware unto A thy father; H85
5 Because that A obeyed my voice, and H85
15 digged in the days of A his father, the H85
18 digged in the days of A his father; for the H85
18 after the death of A: and he called their H85

Gen 26:24 I *am* the God of A thy father: fear not, H85
28: 4 And give thee the blessing of A, to thee, H85
4 art a stranger, which God gave unto A. H85
13 the LORD God of A thy father, and the H85
31:42 my father, the God of A, and the fear of H85
53 The God of A, and the God of Nahor, the H85
32: 9 And Jacob said, O God of my father A, H85
35:12 And the land which I gave A and Isaac, H85
27 *is* Hebron, where A and Isaac sojourned. H85
48:15 whom my fathers A and Isaac did walk, H85
16 of my fathers A and Isaac; and let them H85
49:30 of Canaan, which A bought with the field H85
31 There they buried A and Sarah his wife; H85
50:13 of Machpelah, which A bought with the H85
24 he sware to A, to Isaac, and to Jacob. H85
Ex 2:24 with A, with Isaac, and with Jacob. H85
3: 6 thy father, the God of A, the God of Isaac, H85
15 fathers, the God of A, the God of Isaac, H85
16 fathers, the God of A, of Isaac, and of H85
4: 5 fathers, the God of A, the God of Isaac, H85
6: 3 And I appeared unto A, unto Isaac, and H85
8 did swear to give it to A, to Isaac, and to H85
32:13 Remember A, Isaac, and Israel, thy H85
33: 1 which I sware unto A, to Isaac, and to H85
Lev 26:42 my covenant with A will I remember; H85
Nu 32:11 which I sware unto A, unto Isaac, and H85
Dt 1: 8 unto your fathers, A, Isaac, and Jacob, to H85
6:10 thy fathers, to A, to Isaac, and to Jacob, H85
9: 5 unto thy fathers, A, Isaac, and Jacob. H85
27 Remember thy servants, A, Isaac, and H85
29:13 thy fathers, to A, to Isaac, and to Jacob. H85
30:20 to A, to Isaac, and to Jacob, to give them. H85
34: 4 which I sware unto A, unto Isaac, and H85
Jos 24: 2 the father of A, and the father of Nachor: H85
3 And I took your father A from the other H85
1Ki 18:36 and said, LORD God of A, Isaac, and of H85
2Ki 13:23 of his covenant with A, Isaac, and Jacob, H85
1Ch 1:27 Abram; the same *is* A. H85
28 The sons of A; Isaac, and Ishmael. H85
34 And A begat Isaac. The sons of Isaac; H85
16:16 made with A, and of his oath unto Isaac; H85
29:18 O LORD God of A, Isaac, and of Israel, H85
2Ch 20: 7 it to the seed of A thy friend for ever? H85
30: 6 the LORD God of A, Isaac, and Israel, H85
Neh 9: 7 Chaldees, and gavest him the name of A; H85
Ps 47: 9 of the God of A: for the shields of the H85
105: 6 O ye seed of A his servant, ye children of H85
9 Which *covenant* he made with A, and his H85
42 his holy promise, *and* A his servant. H85
Isa 29:22 who redeemed A, concerning the house H85
41: 8 I have chosen, the seed of A my friend. H85
51: 2 Look unto A your father, and unto Sarah H85
63:16 Doubtless thou *art* our father, though A H85
Jer 33:26 over the seed of A, Isaac, and Jacob: for H85
Ezk 33:24 Israel speak, saying, A was one, and he H85
Mic 7:20 *and* the mercy to A, which thou hast H85
Mt 1: 1 Christ, the son of David, the son of A. *G11*
2 A begat Isaac; and Isaac begat Jacob; *G11*
17 So all the generations from A to David *G11*
3: 9 We have A to *our* father: for I say *G11*
9 these stones to raise up children unto A. *G11*
8:11 and shall sit down with A, and Isaac, and *G11*
22:32 I am the God of A, and the God of Isaac, *G11*
Mk 12:26 I *am* the God of A, and the God of Isaac, *G11*
Lk 1:55 As he spake to our fathers, to A, and to *G11*
73 The oath which he sware to our father A, *G11*
3: 8 We have A to *our* father: for I say *G11*
8 these stones to raise up children unto A. *G11*
34 was *the son* of A, which was *the son* of *G11*
13:16 being a daughter of A, whom Satan hath *G11*
28 teeth, when ye shall see A, and Isaac, and *G11*
16:23 A afar off, and Lazarus in his bosom. *G11*
24 And he cried and said, Father A, have *G11*
25 But A said, Son, remember that thou in *G11*
29 A saith unto him, They have Moses and *G11*
30 And he said, Nay, father A: but if one *G11*
19: 9 forsomuch as he also is a son of A. *G11*
20:37 Lord the God of A, and the God of Isaac, *G11*
Jn 8:39 They answered and said unto him, A is *G11*
39 children, ye would do the works of A. *G11*
40 I have heard of God: this did not A. *G11*
52 that thou hast a devil. A is dead, and the *G11*
53 Art thou greater than our father A, which *G11*
56 Your father A rejoiced to see my day: *G11*
57 yet fifty years old, and hast thou seen A? *G11*
58 I say unto you, Before A was, I am. *G11*
Act 3:13 The God of A, and of Isaac, and of Jacob, *G11*
25 saying unto A, And in thy seed shall *G11*
7: 2 unto our father A, when he was in *G11*

Act 7: 8 and so *A* begat Isaac, and circumcised
16 the sepulchre that A bought for a sum of *G11*
17 God had sworn to A, the people grew and *G11*
32 thy fathers, the God of A, and the God of *G11*
13:26 of the stock of A, and whosoever among *G11*
Ro 4: 1 What shall we say then that A our *G11*
2 For if A were justified by works, he hath *G11*
3 For what saith the scripture? A believed *G11*
9 was reckoned to A for righteousness. *G11*
12 faith of our father A, which *he had* being *G11*
13 the world, *was* not to A, or to his seed, *G11*
16 the faith of A; who is the father of us all, *G11*
9: 7 Neither, because they are the seed of A, *G11*
11: 1 of the seed of A, *of* the tribe of Benjamin. *G11*
2Co 11:22 so *am* I. Are they the seed of A? so *am* I. *G11*
Gal 3: 6 Even as A believed God, and it was *G11*
7 of faith, the same are the children of A. *G11*
8 the gospel unto A, *saying*, In thee shall *G11*
9 be of faith are blessed with faithful A. *G11*
14 That the blessing of A might come on *G11*
16 Now to A and his seed were the *G11*
18 but God gave *it* to A by promise. *G11*
4:22 For it is written, that A had two sons, the *G11*
Heb 2:16 angels; but he took on *him* the seed of A. *G11*
6:13 For when God made promise to A, *G11*
7: 1 high God, who met A returning from the *G11*
2 To whom also A gave a tenth part of all; *G11*
4 patriarch A gave the tenth of the spoils. *G11*
5 though they come out of the loins of A: *G11*
6 received tithes of A, and blessed him that *G11*
9 who receiveth tithes, payed tithes in A. *G11*
11: 8 By faith A, when he was called to go out *G11*
17 By faith A, when he was tried, offered up *G11*
Jas 2:21 Was not A our father justified by works, *G11*
23 which saith, A believed God, and it *G11*
1Pt 3: 6 Even as Sara obeyed A, calling him lord: *G11*

ABRAHAM'S

Gen 17:23 male among the men of A house; and H85
20:18 of Abimelech, because of Sarah A wife. H85
21:11 And the thing was very grievous in A H85
22:23 Milcah did bear to Nahor, A brother. H85
24:15 the wife of Nahor, A brother, with her H85
34 And he said, I *am* A servant. H85
52 And it came to pass, that, when A H85
59 her nurse, and A servant, and his men. H85
25: 7 And these *are* the days of the years of A H85
12 of Ishmael, A son, whom Hagar the H85
19 of Isaac, A son: Abraham begat Isaac: H85
26:24 multiply thy seed for my servant A sake. H85
28: 9 of Ishmael A son, the sister of Nebajoth, H85
1Ch 1:32 Now the sons of Keturah, A concubine: H85
Lk 16:22 by the angels into A bosom: the rich *G11*
Jn 8:33 They answered him, We be A seed, and *G11*
37 I know that ye are A seed; but ye seek to *G11*
39 them, If ye were A children, ye would do *G11*
Gal 3:29 And if ye *be* Christ's, then are ye A seed, *G11*

ABRAM

Gen 11:26 years, and begat A, Nahor, and Haran. H87
27 Terah begat A, Nahor, and Haran; and H87
29 And A and Nahor took them wives: the H87
31 And Terah took A his son, and Lot the H87
12: 1 Now the LORD had said unto A, Get thee H87
4 So A departed, as the LORD had spoken H87
4 with him: and A *was* seventy and five H87
5 And A took Sarai his wife, and Lot his H87
6 And A passed through the land unto the H87
7 And the LORD appeared unto A, and H87
9 And A journeyed, going on still toward H87
10 in the land: and A went down into Egypt H87
14 And it came to pass, that, when A was H87
16 And he entreated A well for her sake: H87
18 And Pharaoh called A, and said, What *is* H87
13: 1 And A went up out of Egypt, he, and his H87
2 And A *was* very rich in cattle, in silver, H87
4 there A called on the name of the LORD. H87
5 And Lot also, which went with A, had H87
8 And A said unto Lot, Let there be no H87
12 A dwelled in the land of Canaan, and H87
14 And the LORD said unto A, after that Lot H87
18 Then A removed *his* tent, and came and H87
14:13 escaped, and told A the Hebrew; for he H87
13 Aner: and these *were* confederate with A. H87
14 And when A heard that his brother was H87
19 said, Blessed *be* A of the most high God, H87
21 And the king of Sodom said unto A, Give H87
22 And A said to the king of Sodom, I have H87
23 thou shouldest say, I have made A rich: H87

Gen 15: 1 LORD came unto **A** in a vision, saying, H87
1 saying, Fear not, **A**: I *am* thy shield, *and* H87
2 And **A** said, Lord GOD, what wilt thou H87
3 And **A** said, Behold, to me thou hast H87
11 upon the carcases, **A** drove them away. H87
12 sleep fell upon **A**; and, lo, an horror of H87
13 And he said unto **A**, Know of a surety H87
18 a covenant with **A**, saying, Unto thy seed H87
16: 2 And Sarai said unto **A**, Behold now, the H87
2 And **A** hearkened to the voice of Sarai. H87
3 the Egyptian, after **A** had dwelt ten years H87
3 gave her to her husband **A** to be his wife. H87
5 And Sarai said unto **A**, My wrong *be* H87
6 But **A** said unto Sarai, Behold, thy maid H87
15 And Hagar bare **A** a son: and Abram H87
15 And Hagar bare Abram a son: and **A** H87
16 And **A** *was* fourscore and six years old, H87
16 years old, when Hagar bare Ishmael to **A**. H87
17: 1 And when **A** was ninety years old and H87
1 LORD appeared to **A**, and said unto him, H87
3 And **A** fell on his face: and God talked H87
5 any more be called **A**, but thy name shall H87
1Ch 1:27 **A**; the same *is* Abraham. H87
Neh 9: 7 who didst choose **A**, and broughtest him H87

ABRAM'S

Gen 11:29 wives: the name of **A** wife *was* Sarai; and H87
31 in law, his son **A** wife; and they went H87
12:17 great plagues because of Sarai **A** wife. H87
13: 7 between the herdmen of **A** cattle and the H87
14:12 And they took Lot, **A** brother's son, who H87
16: 1 Now Sarai **A** wife bare him no children: H87
3 And Sarai **A** wife took Hagar her maid H87

ABROAD

Gen 10:18 the families of the Canaanites spread **a**. H6327
11: 4 **a** upon the face of the whole earth. H6327
8 So the LORD scattered them **a** from H6527
9 them **a** upon the face of all the earth. H6527
15: 5 And he brought him forth **a**, and said, H2351
19:17 them forth **a**, that he said, Escape H2351
28:14 thou shalt spread **a** to the west, and to H6555
Ex 5:12 So the people were scattered **a** H6327
9:29 city, I will spread **a** my hands unto the H6566
33 and spread **a** his hands unto the LORD: H6566
12:46 ought of the flesh **a** out of the house; H2351
21:19 If he rise again, and walk **a** upon his H2351
40:19 And he spread **a** the tent over the H6566
Lev 13: 7 But if the scab spread much **a** in the H6581
12 And if a leprosy break out **a** in the skin, H6524
22 And if it spread much **a** in the skin, H6581
27 if it be spread much **a** in the skin, then H6581
14: 8 shall tarry **a** out of his tent seven days. H2351
18: 9 born at home, or born **a**, *even* their H2351
Nu 11:32 spread *them* all **a** for themselves round H7849
Dt 23:10 then shall he go **a** out of the camp, he H2351
12 the camp, whither thou shalt go forth **a**: H2351
13 thou wilt ease thyself **a**, thou shalt dig H2351
24:11 Thou shalt stand **a**, and the man to H2351
11 shall bring out the pledge **a** unto thee. H2351
32:11 young, spreadeth **a** her wings, taketh H6566
Jdg 12: 9 *whom* he sent **a**, and took in thirty H2351
9 daughters from **a** for his sons. And he H2351
1Sa 9:26 out both of them, he and Samuel, **a**. H2351
30:16 *they were* spread **a** upon all the earth, H5203
2Sa 22:43 of the street, *and* did spread them **a**. H7554
1Ki 2:42 out, and walkest **a** any whither, that
2Ki 4: 3 Then he said, Go, borrow thee vessels **a** H2351
1Ch 13: 2 God, let us send **a** unto our brethren H6555
14:13 spread themselves **a** in the valley. H6584
2Ch 26: 8 his name spread **a** *even* to the entering
15 his name spread far **a**; for he was H7350
29:16 to carry *it* out **a** into the brook Kidron. H2351
31: 5 came **a**, the children of Israel H6555
Neh 1: 8 I will scatter you **a** among the nations: H6327
Est 1:17 For *this* deed of the queen shall come **a** H3318
3: 8 people scattered **a** and dispersed H6340
Job 4:11 the stout lion's whelps are scattered **a**. H6504
15:23 He wandereth **a** for bread, *saying*, H5074
40:11 Cast **a** the rage of thy wrath: and H6327
Ps 41: 6 to itself; *when* he goeth **a**, he telleth *it*. H2351
77:17 out a sound: thine arrows also went **a**. H1980
Prv 5:16 Let thy fountains be dispersed **a**, *and* H2351
Isa 24: 1 scattereth **a** the inhabitants thereof. H6327
28:25 doth he not cast **a** the fitches, and H6327
44:24 that spreadeth **a** the earth by myself; H7554
Jer 6:11 out upon the children **a**, and upon the H2351
Lam 1:20 rebelled: **a** the sword bereaveth, H2351
Ezk 34:21 horns, till ye have scattered them **a**; H2351
Zec 1:17 shall yet be spread **a**; and the LORD H6327
2: 6 I have spread you **a** as the four winds H6566
Mt 9:26 And the fame hereof went **a** into all *G1831*
31 spread **a** his fame in all that country. *G1310*
36 **a**, as sheep having no shepherd. *G4496*
12:30 that gathereth not with me scattereth **a**. *G4650*
26:31 sheep of the flock shall be scattered **a**. *G1287*
Mk 1:28 And immediately his fame spread **a** *G1831*
45 and to blaze **a** the matter, insomuch *G1310*
4:22 kept secret, but that it should come **a**. *G1519*
6:14 name was spread **a**:) and he said, That *G5318*
Lk 1:65 were noised **a** throughout all the hill *G1255*
2:17 they made known **a** the saying which *G1232*
5:15 went there a fame **a** of him: and great *G1330*
8:17 that shall not be known and come **a**. *G1519*
Jn 11:52 children of God that were scattered **a**. *G1287*
21:23 Then went this saying **a** among the *G1831*
Act 2: 6 Now when this was noised **a**, the *G1096*
8: 1 were all scattered **a** throughout the *G1289*
4 Therefore they that were scattered **a** *G1289*
11:19 Now they which were scattered **a** upon *G1289*
Ro 5: 5 of God is shed **a** in our hearts by the *G1632*
16:19 For your obedience is come **a** unto all *G864*
2Co 9: 9 (As it is written, He hath dispersed **a**; *G4650*
1Th 1: 8 is spread **a**; so that we need not *G1831*
Jas 1: 1 tribes which are scattered **a**, greeting. *G1722*

ABSALOM

2Sa 3: 3 and the third, **A** the son of Maacah the H53
13: 1 And it came to pass after this, that **A** the H53
20 And **A** her brother said unto her, Hath H53
22 And **A** spake unto his brother Amnon H53
22 good nor bad: for **A** hated Amnon, H53
23 two full years, that **A** had sheepshearers H53
23 and **A** invited all the king's sons. H53
24 And **A** came to the king, and said, H53
25 And the king said to **A**, Nay, my son, let H53
26 Then said **A**, If not, I pray thee, let my H53
27 But **A** pressed him, that he let Amnon H53
28 Now **A** had commanded his servants, H53
29 And the servants of **A** did unto Amnon H53
29 did unto Amnon as **A** had commanded. H53
30 to David, saying, **A** hath slain all the H53
32 the appointment of **A** this hath been H53
34 But **A** fled. And the young man that kept H53
37 But **A** fled, and went to Talmai, the son H53
38 So **A** fled, and went to Geshur, and was H53
39 to go forth unto **A**: for he was comforted H53
14: 1 that the king's heart *was* toward **A**. H53
21 therefore, bring the young man **A** again. H53
23 to Geshur, and brought **A** to Jerusalem. H53
24 not see my face. So **A** returned to his H53
25 much praised as **A** for his beauty: from H53
27 And unto **A** there were born three sons, H53
28 So **A** dwelt two full years in Jerusalem, H53
29 Therefore **A** sent for Joab, to have sent H53
31 Then Joab arose, and came to **A** unto *his* H53
32 And **A** answered Joab, Behold, I sent H53
33 he had called for **A**, he came to the king, H53
33 before the king: and the king kissed **A**. H53
15: 1 And it came to pass after this, that **A** H53
2 And **A** rose up early, and stood beside H53
2 for judgment, then **A** called unto him, H53
3 And **A** said unto him, See, thy matters H53
4 **A** said moreover, Oh that I were made H53
6 And on this manner did **A** to all Israel H53
6 so **A** stole the hearts of the men of Israel. H53
7 forty years, that **A** said unto the king, I H53
10 But **A** sent spies throughout all the tribes H53
10 then ye shall say, **A** reigneth in Hebron. H53
11 And with **A** went two hundred men out H53
12 And **A** sent for Ahithophel the Gilonite, H53
12 the people increased continually with **A**. H53
13 hearts of the men of Israel are after **A**. H53
14 not *else* escape from **A**: make speed to H53
31 conspirators with **A**. And David said, O H53
34 city, and say unto **A**, I will be thy servant, H53
37 into the city, and **A** came into Jerusalem. H53
16: 8 into the hand of **A** thy son: and, behold, H53
15 And **A**, and all the people the men of H53
16 was come unto **A**, that Hushai said unto H53
16 **A**, God save the king, God save the king. H53
17 And **A** said to Hushai, *Is* this thy H53
18 And Hushai said unto **A**, Nay; but whom H53
20 Then said **A** to Ahithophel, Give counsel H53
21 And Ahithophel said unto **A**, Go in unto H53
22 So they spread **A** a tent upon the top of H53
22 top of the house; and **A** went in unto his H53
23 Ahithophel both with David and with **A**. H53
2Sa 17: 1 Moreover Ahithophel said unto **A**, Let H53
4 And the saying pleased **A** well, and all H53
5 Then said **A**, Call now Hushai the Archite H53
6 And when Hushai was come to **A**, H53
6 come to Absalom, **A** spake unto him, H53
7 And Hushai said unto **A**, The counsel H53
9 among the people that follow **A**. H53
14 And **A** and all the men of Israel said, H53
14 that the LORD might bring evil upon **A**. H53
15 counsel **A** and the elders of Israel; H53
18 Nevertheless a lad saw them, and told **A**: H53
24 Then David came to Mahanaim. And **A** H53
25 And **A** made Amasa captain of the host H53
26 So Israel and **A** pitched in the land of H53
18: 5 man, *even* with **A**. And all the people H53
5 all the captains charge concerning **A**. H53
9 And **A** met the servants of David. And H53
9 of David. And **A** rode upon a mule, and H53
10 said, Behold, I saw **A** hanged in an oak. H53
12 that none *touch* the young man **A**. H53
14 the heart of **A**, while he *was* yet alive H53
15 about and smote **A**, and slew him. H53
17 And they took **A**, and cast him into a H53
18 Now **A** in his lifetime had taken and H53
29 And the king said, Is the young man **A** H53
32 Is the young man **A** safe? And Cushi H53
33 he said, O my son **A**, my son, my son H53
33 my son, my son **A**! would God I had died H53
33 I had died for thee, O **A**, my son, my son! H53
19: 1 the king weepeth and mourneth for **A**. H53
4 O my son **A**, O Absalom, my son, my son! H53
4 O my son Absalom, O **A**, my son, my son! H53
6 I perceive, that if **A** had lived, and all we H53
9 and now he is fled out of the land for **A**. H53
10 And **A**, whom we anointed over us, is H53
20: 6 harm than *did* **A**: take thou thy lord's H53
1Ki 1: 6 *man;* and *his mother* bare him after **A**. H53
2: 7 me when I fled because of **A** thy brother. H53
28 he turned not after **A**. And Joab fled unto H53
1Ch 3: 2 The third, **A** the son of Maachah the H53
2Ch 11:20 the daughter of **A**; which bare him H53
21 the daughter of **A** above all his wives H53
Ps 3:ttl A Psalm of David, when he fled from **A** H53

ABSALOM'S

2Sa 13: 4 him, I love Tamar, my brother **A** sister. H53
20 desolate in her brother **A** house. H53
14:30 fire. And **A** servants set the field on fire. H53
17:20 And when **A** servants came to the H53
18:18 and it is called unto this day, **A** place. H53

ABSENCE

Lk 22: 6 him unto them in the **a** of the multitude. *G817*
Php 2:12 much more in my **a**, work out your own *G666*

ABSENT

Gen 31:49 thee, when we are **a** one from another. H5641
1Co 5: 3 For I verily, as **a** in body, but present in *G548*
2Co 5: 6 in the body, we are **a** from the Lord: *G1553*
8 rather to be **a** from the body, and *G1553*
9 or **a**, we may be accepted of him. *G1553*
10: 1 you, but being **a** am bold toward you: *G548*
11 by letters when we are **a**, such *will we be* *G548*
13: 2 time; and being **a** now I write to them *G548*
10 Therefore I write these things being **a**, *G548*
Php 1:27 see you, or else be **a**, I may hear of your *G548*
Col 2: 5 For though I be **a** in the flesh, yet am I *G548*

ABSTAIN

Act 15:20 But that we write unto them, that they **a** *G567*
29 That ye **a** from meats offered to idols, *G567*
1Th 4: 3 that ye should **a** from fornication: *G567*
5:22 **A** from all appearance of evil. *G567*
1Ti 4: 3 *commanding* to **a** from meats, which *G567*
1Pt 2:11 and pilgrims, **a** from fleshly lusts, which *G567*

ABSTINENCE

Act 27:21 But after long **a** Paul stood forth in the *G776*

ABUNDANCE

Dt 28:47 gladness of heart, for the **a** of all *things;* H7230
33:19 shall suck *of* the **a** of the seas, and *of* H8228
1Sa 1:16 for out of the **a** of my complaint and H7230
2Sa 12:30 forth the spoil of the city in great **a**. H7235
1Ki 1:19 and sheep in **a**, and hath called all the H7230
25 and sheep in **a**, and hath called all the H7230
10:10 came no more such **a** of spices as these H7230
27 trees that *are* in the vale, for **a**. H7230
18:41 drink; for *there is* a sound of **a** of rain. H1995

1Ch 22: 3 And David prepared iron in **a** for the H7230
3 and brass in **a** without weight; H7230
4 Also cedar trees in **a**: for the H369+H4557
14 weight; for it is in **a**: timber also and H7230
15 with thee in **a**, hewers and workers H7230
29: 2 stones, and marble stones in **a**. H7230
21 and sacrifices in **a** for all Israel: H7230
2Ch 1:15 sycomore trees that *are* in the vale for **a**. H7230
2: 9 Even to prepare me timber in **a**: for the H7230
4:18 vessels in great **a**: for the weight of the H7230
9: 1 bare spices, and gold in **a**, and precious H7230
9 of spices great **a**, and precious stones: H7230
27 trees that *are* in the low plains in **a**. H7230
11:23 in **a**. And he desired many wives. H7230
14:15 camels in **a**, and returned to Jerusalem. H7230
15: 9 out of Israel in **a**, when they saw that H7230
17: 5 and he had riches and honour in **a**. H7230
18: 1 in **a**, and joined affinity with Ahab. H7230
2 oxen for him in **a**, and for the people H7230
20:25 among them in **a** both riches with the H7230
24:11 day by day, and gathered money in **a**. H7230
29:35 And also the burnt offerings *were* in **a**, H7230
31: 5 of Israel brought in **a** the firstfruits of H7235
32: 5 David, and made darts and shields in **a**. H7230
29 and herds in **a**: for God had given him H7230
Neh 9:25 and fruit trees in **a**: so they did eat, and H7230
Est 1: 7 in **a**, according to the state of the king. H7227
Job 22:11 not see; and **a** of waters cover thee. H8229
36:31 he the people; he giveth meat in **a**. H4342
38:34 that **a** of waters may cover thee? H8229
Ps 37:11 delight themselves in the **a** of peace. H7230
52: 7 but trusted in the **a** of his riches, *and* H7230
72: 7 flourish; and **a** of peace so long as H7230
105:30 Their land brought forth frogs in **a**, in H8317
Ecc 5:10 **a** with increase: this *is* also vanity. H1995
12 or much: but the **a** of the rich will not H7647
Isa 7:22 And it shall come to pass, for the **a** of H7230
15: 7 Therefore the **a** they have gotten, and H3502
47: 9 for the great **a** of thine enchantments. H6109
60: 5 because the **a** of the sea shall be H1995
66:11 be delighted with the **a** of her glory. H2123
Jer 33: 6 unto them the **a** of peace and truth. H6283
Ezk 16:49 of bread, and **a** of idleness was in her H7962
26:10 By reason of the **a** of his horses their H8229
Zec 14:14 gold, and silver, and apparel, in great **a**. H7230
Mt 12:34 the **a** of the heart the mouth speaketh. G4051
13:12 shall have more **a**: but whosoever hath G4052
25:29 and he shall have **a**: but from him that G4052
Mk 12:44 For all *they* did cast in of their **a**; but G4052
Lk 6:45 the **a** of the heart his mouth speaketh. G4051
12:15 the **a** of the things which he possesseth. G4052
21: 4 For all these have of their **a** cast in unto G4052
Ro 5:17 they which receive **a** of grace and of the G4050
2Co 8: 2 of affliction the **a** of their joy and their G4050
14 at this time your **a** *may be a supply* for G4051
14 want, that their **a** also may be *a supply* G4051
20 us in this **a** which is administered by us: G100
12: 7 through the **a** of the revelations, there G5236
Rev 18: 3 rich through the **a** of her delicacies. G1411

ABUNDANT
Ex 34: 6 and **a** in goodness and truth, H7227
Isa 56:12 shall be as this day, *and* much more **a**. H3499
Jer 51:13 many waters, **a** in treasures, thine end H7227
1Co 12:23 we bestow more **a** honour; and our G4055
23 *parts* have more **a** comeliness. G4055
24 **a** honour to that *part* which lacked: G4055
2Co 4:15 sakes, that the **a** grace might through G4121
7:15 And his inward affection is more **a** G4056
9:12 of the saints, but is **a** also by many G4052
11:23 in labours more **a**, in stripes above G4056
Php 1:26 That your rejoicing may be more **a** in G4052
1Ti 1:14 was exceeding **a** with faith and love G5250
1Pt 1: 3 according to his **a** mercy hath begotten G4183

ABUNDANTLY
Gen 1:20 the waters bring forth **a** the moving H8317
21 brought forth **a**, after their kind, and H8317
8:17 they may breed **a** in the earth, and be H8317
9: 7 **a** in the earth, and multiply therein. H8317
Ex 1: 7 and increased **a**, and multiplied, and H8317
8: 3 And the river shall bring forth frogs **a**, H8317
Nu 20:11 water came out **a**, and the congregation H7227
1Ch 12:40 and sheep **a**: for *there was* joy in Israel. H7230
22: 5 So David prepared **a** before his death. H7230
8 hast shed blood **a**, and hast made great H7230
2Ch 31: 5 the tithe of all *things* brought they in **a**. H7230
Job 12: 6 secure; into whose hand God bringeth *a*.
36:28 clouds do drop *and* distil upon man **a**. H7227
Ps 36: 8 They shall be **a** satisfied with the H7301
65:10 Thou waterest the ridges thereof **a**: thou H7301
132:15 I will **a** bless her provision: I will satisfy H1288
145: 7 They shall **a** utter the memory of thy H5042
Song 5: 1 friends; drink, yea, drink **a**, O beloved. H7937
Isa 15: 3 streets, every one shall howl, weeping **a**. H3381
35: 2 It shall blossom **a**, and rejoice even with H6524
55: 7 and to our God, for he will **a** pardon. H7235
Jn 10:10 life, and that they might have *it* more **a**. G4053
1Co 15:10 I laboured more **a** than they all: yet not G4054
2Co 1:12 in the world, and more **a** to you-ward. G4056
2: 4 the love which I have more **a** unto you. G4056
10:15 enlarged by you according to our rule **a**, G1519
12:15 more **a** I love you, the less I be loved. G4056
Eph 3:20 to do exceeding **a** above all that we ask G5228
1Th 2:17 **a** to see your face with great desire. G4056
Tit 3: 6 Which he shed on us **a** through Jesus G4146
Heb 6:17 Wherein God, willing more **a** to shew G4054
2Pt 1:11 unto you **a** into the everlasting G4146

ABUSE
1Sa 31: 4 thrust me through, and **a** me. But his H5953
1Ch 10: 4 come and **a** me. But his armourbearer H5953
1Co 9:18 that I **a** not my power in the gospel. G2710

ABUSED
Jdg 19:25 knew her, and **a** her all the night until H5953

ABUSERS
1Co 6: 9 nor **a** of themselves with mankind, G733

ABUSING
1Co 7:31 And they that use this world, as not **a** G2710

ACCAD
Gen 10:10 and **A**, and Calneh, in the land of Shinar. H390

ACCEPT
Gen 32:20 his face; peradventure he will **a** of me. H5375
Ex 22:11 owner of it shall **a** *thereof*, and he shall H3947
Lev 26:41 **a** of the punishment of their iniquity: H7521
43 and they shall **a** of the punishment of H7521
Dt 33:11 Bless, LORD, his substance, and **a** the H7521
1Sa 26:19 me, let him **a** an offering: but if *they* H7306
2Sa 24:23 the king, The LORD thy God **a** thee. H7521
Job 13: 8 Will ye **a** his person? will ye contend for H5375
10 reprove you, if ye do secretly **a** persons. H5375
32:21 Let me not, I pray you, **a** any man's H5375
42: 8 you: for him will I **a**: lest I deal with you H5375
Ps 20: 3 Remember all thy offerings, and **a** thy H1878
82: 2 How long will ye judge unjustly, and **a** H5375
119:108 **A**, I beseech thee, the freewill offerings H7521
Prv 18: 5 *It is* not good to **a** the person of the H5375
Jer 14:10 the LORD doth not **a** them; he will now H7521
12 an oblation, I will not **a** them: but I will H7521
Ezk 20:40 me: there will I **a** them, and there will H7521
41 I will **a** you with your sweet savour, H7521
43:27 and I will **a** you, saith the Lord GOD. H7521
Am 5:22 I will not **a** *them*: neither will I H7521
Mal 1: 8 **a** thy person? saith the LORD of hosts. H5375
10 will I **a** an offering at your hand. H7521
13 I **a** this of your hand? saith the LORD. H7521
Act 24: 3 We **a** *it* always, and in all places, most G588

ACCEPTABLE
Lev 22:20 ye not offer: for it shall not be **a** for you. H7522
Dt 33:24 let him be **a** to his brethren, and H7521
Ps 19:14 of my heart, be **a** in thy sight, O LORD, H7522
69:13 O LORD, *in* an **a** time: O God, in the H7522
Prv 10:32 know what is **a**: but the mouth of the H7522
21: 3 To do justice and judgment *is* more **a** to H977
Ecc 12:10 The preacher sought to find out **a** H2656
Isa 49: 8 Thus saith the LORD, In an **a** time H7522
58: 5 this a fast, and an **a** day to the LORD? H7522
61: 2 To proclaim the **a** year of the LORD, H7522
Jer 6:20 **a**, nor your sacrifices sweet unto me. H7522
Dan 4:27 Wherefore, O king, let my counsel be **a** H8232
Lk 4:19 To preach the **a** year of the Lord. G1184
Ro 12: 1 sacrifice, holy, **a** unto God, *which is* G2101
2 good, and **a**, and perfect, will of God. G2101
14:18 *is* **a** to God, and approved of men. G2101
15:16 **a**, being sanctified by the Holy Ghost. G2144
Eph 5:10 Proving what is **a** unto the Lord. G2101
Php 4:18 smell, a sacrifice **a**, wellpleasing to God. G1184
1Ti 2: 3 For this *is* good and **a** in the sight of God G587
5: 4 for that is good and **a** before God. G587
1Pt 2: 5 sacrifices, **a** to God by Jesus Christ. G2144
20 ye take it patiently, this *is* **a** with God. G5485

ACCEPTABLY
Heb 12:28 God **a** with reverence and godly fear: G2102

ACCEPTANCE
Isa 60: 7 come up with **a** on mine altar, and H7522

A

ACCEPTATION
1Ti 1:15 and worthy of all **a**, that Christ Jesus G594
4: 9 *is* a faithful saying and worthy of all **a**. G594

ACCEPTED
Gen 4: 7 If thou doest well, shalt thou not be **a**? H7613
19:21 And he said unto him, See, I have **a** H5375
Ex 28:38 that they may be **a** before the LORD. H7522
Lev 1: 4 **a** for him to make atonement for him. H7521
7:18 day, it shall not be **a**, neither shall it be H7521
10:19 it have been **a** in the sight of the LORD? H3190
19: 7 day, it *is* abominable; it shall not be **a**. H7521
22:21 be **a**; there shall be no blemish therein. H7522
23 offering; but for a vow it shall not be **a**. H7521
25 *be* in them: they shall not be **a** for you. H7521
27 it shall be **a** for an offering made H7521
23:11 the LORD, to be **a** for you: on the H7522
1Sa 18: 5 war, and he was **a** in the sight of all the H3190
25:35 to thy voice, and have **a** thy person. H5375
Est 10: 3 the Jews, and **a** of the multitude of H7521
Job 42: 9 them: the LORD also **a** Job. H5375
Isa 56: 7 sacrifices *shall be* **a** upon mine altar; H7522
Jer 37:20 I pray thee, be **a** before thee; that thou H5307
42: 2 supplication be **a** before thee, and pray H5307
Lk 4:24 No prophet is **a** in his own country. G1184
Act 10:35 worketh righteousness, is **a** with him. G1184
Ro 15:31 for Jerusalem may be **a** of the saints; G2144
2Co 5: 9 present or absent, we may be **a** of him. G2101
6: 2 heard thee in a time **a**, and in the day of G1184
2 behold, now *is* the **a** time; behold, now G2144
8:12 willing mind, *it is* **a** according to that a G2144
17 For indeed he **a** the exhortation; but G1209
11: 4 have not **a**, ye might well bear with *him*. G1209
Eph 1: 6 he hath made us **a** in the beloved. G5487

ACCEPTEST
Lk 20:21 rightly, neither **a** thou the person *of* G2983

ACCEPTETH
Job 34:19 *How much less to him* that **a** not the H5375
Ecc 9: 7 merry heart; for God now **a** thy works. H7521
Hos 8:13 *it; but* the LORD **a** them not; now will H7521
Gal 2: 6 matter to me: God **a** no man's person:) G2983

ACCEPTING
Heb 11:35 were tortured, not **a** deliverance; that G4327

ACCESS
Ro 5: 2 By whom also we have **a** by faith into G4318
Eph 2:18 For through him we both have **a** by one G4318
3:12 In whom we have boldness and **a** with G4318

ACCHO
Jdg 1:31 out the inhabitants of **A**, nor the H5910

ACCOMPANIED
Act 10:23 certain brethren from Joppa **a** him. G4905
11:12 these six brethren **a** me, and we G2064
20: 4 And there **a** him into Asia Sopater of G4902
38 no more. And they **a** him unto the ship. G4311

ACCOMPANY
Heb 6: 9 that **a** salvation, though we thus speak. G2192

ACCOMPANYING
2Sa 6: 4 *was* at Gibeah, **a** the ark of God: and H5973

ACCOMPLISH
Lev 22:21 unto the LORD to **a** *his* vow, or a H6381
1Ki 5: 9 and thou shalt **a** my desire, in giving H6213
Job 14: 6 till he shall **a**, as an hireling, his day. H7521
Ps 64: 6 They search out iniquities; they **a** a H8552
Isa 55:11 void, but it shall **a** that which I please, H6213
Jer 44:25 her: ye will surely **a** your vows, and H6965
Ezk 6:12 thus will I **a** my fury upon them. H3615
7: 8 fury upon thee, and **a** mine anger upon H3615
13:15 Thus will I **a** my wrath upon the wall, H3615
20: 8 fury upon them, to **a** my anger against H3615
21 fury upon them, to **a** my anger against H3615
Dan 9: 2 that he would **a** seventy years in the H4390
Lk 9:31 which he should **a** at Jerusalem. G4137

ACCOMPLISHED
2Ch 36:22 Jeremiah might be a, the LORD stirred H3615
Est 2:12 their purifications a, *to wit*, six months H4390
Job 15:32 It shall be a before his time, and his H4390
Prv 13:19 The desire a is sweet to the soul: but *it* H1961
Isa 40: 2 that her warfare is a, that her iniquity is H4390
Jer 25:12 seventy years are a, *that* I will punish H4390
34 dispersions are a; and ye shall fall like H4390
29:10 seventy years be a at Babylon I will H4390
39:16 they shall be *a* in that day before thee.
Lam 4:11 The LORD hath a his fury; he hath H3615
22 The punishment of thine iniquity is a, O H8552
Ezk 4: 6 And when thou hast a them, lie again H3615
5:13 Thus shall mine anger be a, and I will H3615
13 zeal, when I have a my fury in them. H3615
Dan 11:36 till the indignation be a: for that that is H3615
12: 7 he shall have a to scatter the power H3615
Lk 1:23 were a, he departed to his own house. G4130
2: 6 were a that she should be delivered. G4130
21 And when eight days were a for the G4130
22 law of Moses were a, they brought him G4130
12:50 and how am I straitened till it be a! G5055
18:31 concerning the Son of man shall be a. G5055
22:37 must yet be a in me, And he was G5055
Jn 19:28 all things were now a, that the scripture G5055
Act 21: 5 And when we had a those days, we G1822
1Pt 5: 9 afflictions are a in your brethren that G2005

ACCOMPLISHING
Heb 9: 6 first tabernacle, a the service *of God*. G2005

ACCOMPLISHMENT
Act 21:26 temple, to signify the a of the days of G1604

ACCORD
Lev 25: 5 That which groweth of its own a of thy H5599
Jos 9: 2 with Joshua and with Israel, with one a. H6310
Act 1:14 These all continued with one a in G3661
2: 1 they were all with one a in one place. G3661
46 And they, continuing daily with one a G3661
4:24 to God with one a, and said, Lord, thou G3661
5:12 were all with one a in Solomon's porch. G3661
7:57 ears, and ran upon him with one a, G3661
8: 6 And the people with one a gave heed G3661
12:10 to them of his own a: and they went out, G844
20 came with one a to him, and, having G3661
15:25 with one a, to send chosen men G3661
18:12 with one a against Paul, and brought G3661
19:29 they rushed with one a into the theatre. G3661
2Co 8:17 forward, of his own a he went unto you. G830
Php 2: 2 same love, *being* of one a, of one mind. G4861

ACCORDING See the Appendix.

ACCORDINGLY See the Appendix.

ACCOUNT
2Ki 12: 4 that passeth *the a*, the money that every
1Ch 27:24 in the a of the chronicles of king David. H4557
2Ch 26:11 number of their a by the hand of Jeiel H6486
Job 33:13 he giveth not a of any of his matters. H6030
Ps 144: 3 son of man, that thou makest a of him! H2803
Ecc 7:27 *counting* one by one, to find out the a: H2808
Mt 12:36 give a thereof in the day of judgment. G3056
18:23 which would take a of his servants. G3056
Lk 16: 2 of thee? give an a of thy stewardship; G3056
Act 19:40 we may give an a of this concourse. G3056
Ro 14:12 So then every one of us shall give a of G3056
1Co 4: 1 Let a man so a of us, as of the G3049
Php 4:17 desire fruit that may abound to your a. G3056
Phlm 18 oweth *thee* ought, put that on mine a; G1677
Heb 13:17 that must give a, that they may do it G3056
1Pt 4: 5 Who shall give a to him that is ready to G3056
2Pt 3:15 And a *that* the longsuffering of our G2233

ACCOUNTED
Dt 2:11 Which also were a giants, as the H2803
20 (That also was a a land of giants: H2803
1Ki 10:21 nothing a of in the days of Solomon. H2803
2Ch 9:20 any thing a of in the days of Solomon. H2803
Ps 22:30 A seed shall serve him; it shall be a to H5608
Isa 2:22 his nostrils: for wherein is he to be a of? H2803
Mk 10:42 that they which are a to rule over the G1380
Lk 20:35 But they which shall be a worthy to G2661
21:36 that ye may be a worthy to escape all G2661
22:24 which of them should be a the greatest. G1380
Ro 8:36 we are a as sheep for the slaughter. G3049
Gal 3: 6 and it was a to him for righteousness. G3049

ACCOUNTING
Heb 11:19 A that God *was* able to raise *him* up, G3049

ACCOUNTS
Dan 6: 2 princes might give a unto them, and H2941

ACCURSED
Dt 21:23 he that is hanged *is* a of God;) that thy H7045
Jos 6:17 And the city shall be a, *even* it, and all H2764
18 from the a thing, lest ye make H2764
18 make *yourselves* a, when ye take of the H2763
18 ye take of the a thing, and make the H2764
7: 1 a trespass in the a thing: for Achan, the H2764
1 of Judah, took of the a thing: and the H2764
11 even taken of the a thing, and have H2764
12 because they were a: neither will I be H2764
12 ye destroy the a from among you. H2764
13 Israel, *There is* an a thing in the midst H2764
13 take away the a thing from among you. H2764
15 is taken with the a thing shall be burnt H2764
22:20 a trespass in the a thing, and wrath fell H2764
1Ch 2: 7 Israel, who transgressed in the thing a. H2764
Isa 65:20 *being* an hundred years old shall be a. H7043
Ro 9: 3 For I could wish that myself were a from G331
1Co 12: 3 God calleth Jesus a: and *that* no man can G331
Gal 1: 8 we have preached unto you, let him be a. G331
9 than that ye have received, let him be a. G331

ACCUSATION
Ezr 4: 6 wrote they *unto him* an a against the H7855
Mt 27:37 And set up over his head his a written, G156
Mk 15:26 And the superscription of his a was G156
Lk 6: 7 that they might find an a against him. G2724
19: 8 man by false a, I restore *him* fourfold. G4811
Jn 18:29 What a bring ye against this man? G2724
Act 25:18 none a of such things as I supposed: G156
1Ti 5:19 Against an elder receive not an a, but G2724
2Pt 2:11 railing a against them before the Lord. G2920
Jude 9 a, but said, The Lord rebuke thee. G2920

ACCUSE
Prv 30:10 A not a servant unto his master, lest he H3960
Mt 12:10 sabbath days? that they might a him. G2723
Mk 3: 2 the sabbath day; that they might a him. G2723
Lk 3:14 no man, neither a *any* falsely; and be G4811
11:54 of his mouth, that they might a him. G2723
23: 2 And they began to a him, saying, We G2723
14 those things whereof ye a him: G2723
Jn 5:45 Do not think that I will a you to the G2723
8: 6 might have to a him. But Jesus stooped G2723
Act 24: 2 forth, Tertullus began to a *him*, saying, G2723
8 of all these things, whereof we a him. G2723
13 the things whereof they now a me. G2723
25: 5 with *me*, and a this man, if there be G2723
11 whereof these a me, no man may G2723
28:19 not that I had ought to a my nation of. G2723
1Pt 3:16 a your good conversation in Christ. G1908

ACCUSED
Dan 3: 8 came near, and a the Jews. H7170+H399
6:24 which had a Daniel, and they H399+H7170
Mt 27:12 And when he was a of the chief priests G2723
Mk 15: 3 And the chief priests a him of many G2723
Lk 16: 1 and the same was a unto him that he G1225
23:10 scribes stood and vehemently a him. G2723
Act 22:30 wherefore he was a of the Jews, he G2723
23:28 wherefore they a him, I brought him G1458
29 Whom I perceived to be a of questions G1458
25:16 that he which is a have the accusers G2723
26: 2 the things whereof I am a of the Jews: G1458
7 sake, king Agrippa, I am a of the Jews. G1458
Tit 1: 6 faithful children not a of riot or unruly. G1722
Rev 12:10 a them before our God day and night. G2723

ACCUSER
Rev 12:10 his Christ: for the a of our brethren is G2725

ACCUSERS
Jn 8:10 thine a? hath no man condemned thee? G2725
Act 23:30 to his a also to say before thee G2725
35 I will hear thee, said he, when thine a G2725
24: 8 Commanding his a to come unto thee: G2725
25:16 is accused have the a face to face, and G2725
18 Against whom when the a stood up, G2725
2Ti 3: 3 false a, incontinent, fierce, G1228
Tit 2: 3 holiness, not false a, not given to much G1228

ACCUSETH
Jn 5:45 a you, *even* Moses, in whom ye trust. G2723

ACCUSING
Ro 2:15 while a or else excusing one another;) G2723

ACCUSTOMED
Jer 13:23 ye also do good, that are a to do evil. H3928

ACELDAMA
Act 1:19 A, that is to say, The field of blood. G184

ACHAIA
Act 18:12 And when Gallio was the deputy of A, the G882
27 to pass into A, the brethren wrote, G882
19:21 Macedonia and A, to go to Jerusalem, G882
Ro 15:26 of Macedonia and A to make a certain G882
16: 5 who is the firstfruits of A unto Christ. G882
1Co 16:15 is the firstfruits of A, and *that* they have G882
2Co 1: 1 with all the saints which are in all A: G882
9: 2 of Macedonia, that A was ready a year G882
11:10 me of this boasting in the regions of A. G882
1Th 1: 7 to all that believe in Macedonia and A. G882
8 in Macedonia and A, but also in every G882

ACHAICUS
1Co 16:17 Fortunatus and A: for that which was G883

ACHAN
Jos 7: 1 thing: for A, the son of Carmi, the H5912
18 man by man; and A, the son of Carmi, H5912
19 And Joshua said unto A, My son, give, I H5912
20 And A answered Joshua, and said, H5912
24 with him, took A the son of Zerah, and H5912
22:20 Did not A the son of Zerah commit a H5912

ACHAR
1Ch 2: 7 And the sons of Carmi; A, the troubler H5917

ACHAZ
Mt 1: 9 begat A; and Achaz begat Ezekias; G881
9 begat Achaz; and A begat Ezekias; G881

ACHBOR
Gen 36:38 the son of A reigned in his stead. H5907
39 And Baal-hanan the son of A died, and H5907
2Ki 22:12 son of Shaphan, and A the son of H5907
14 and Ahikam, and A, and Shaphan, and H5907
1Ch 1:49 the son of A reigned in his stead. H5907
Jer 26:22 the son of A, and *certain* men with H5907
36:12 the son of A, and Gemariah the son H5907

ACHIM
Mt 1:14 Sadoc begat A; and Achim begat Eliud; G885
14 Sadoc begat Achim; and A begat Eliud; G885

ACHISH
1Sa 21:10 of Saul, and went to A the king of Gath. H397
11 And the servants of A said unto him, *Is* H397
12 was sore afraid of A the king of Gath. H397
14 Then said A unto his servants, Lo, ye see H397
27: 2 unto A, the son of Maoch, king of Gath. H397
3 And David dwelt with A at Gath, he and H397
5 And David said unto A, If I have now H397
6 Then A gave him Ziklag that day: H397
9 apparel, and returned, and came to A. H397
10 And A said, Whither have ye made a H397
12 And A believed David, saying, He hath H397
28: 1 fight with Israel. And A said unto David, H397
2 And David said to A, Surely thou shalt H397
2 can do. And A said to David, Therefore H397
29: 2 men passed on in the rearward with A. H397
3 *here?* And A said unto the princes H397
6 Then A called David, and said unto him, H397
8 And David said unto A, But what have I H397
9 And A answered and said to David, I H397
1Ki 2:39 ran away unto A son of Maachah king H397
40 went to Gath to A to seek his servants: H397

ACHMETHA
Ezr 6: 2 And there was found at A, in the palace H307

ACHOR
Jos 7:24 they brought them unto the valley of A. H5911
26 called, The valley of A, unto this day. H5911
15: 7 from the valley of A, and so northward, H5911
Isa 65:10 and the valley of A a place for the herds H5911
Hos 2:15 and the valley of A for a door of hope: H5911

ACHSAH
Jos 15:16 him will I give A my daughter to wife. H5915
17 he gave him A his daughter to wife. H5915

Jdg 1:12 him will I give **A** my daughter to wife. H5915
13 he gave him **A** his daughter to wife. H5915
1Ch 2:49 Gibea: and the daughter of Caleb *was* **A**. H5915

ACHSHAPH
Jos 11: 1 the king of Shimron, and to the king of **A**, H407
12:20 Shimron-meron, one; the king of **A**, one; H407
19:25 was Helkath, and Hali, and Beten, and **A**, H407

ACHZIB
Jos 15:44 And Keilah, and **A**, and Mareshah; nine H392
19:29 thereof are at the sea from the coast to **A**: H392
Jdg 1:31 of Ahlab, nor of **A**, nor of Helbah, nor of H392
Mic 1:14 of **A** *shall be* a lie to the kings of Israel. H392

ACKNOWLEDGE
Dt 21:17 But he shall **a** the son of the hated *for* H5234
33: 9 neither did he **a** his brethren, nor knew H5234
Ps 51: 3 For I **a** my transgressions: and my sin H3045
Prv 3: 6 In all thy ways **a** him, and he shall H3045
Isa 33:13 and, ye *that are* near, **a** my might. H3045
61: 9 see them shall **a** them, that they *are* H5234
63:16 of us, and Israel **a** us not: thou, O H5234
Jer 3:13 Only **a** thine iniquity, that thou hast H3045
14:20 We **a**, O LORD, our wickedness, *and* the H3045
24: 5 good figs, so will I **a** them that are H5234
Dan 11:39 god, whom he shall **a** *and* increase with H5234
Hos 5:15 to my place, till they **a** their offence, and
1Co 14:37 spiritual, let him **a** that the things that *G1921*
16:18 therefore **a** ye them that are such. *G1921*
2Co 1:13 what ye read or **a**; and I trust ye shall *G1921*
13 and I trust ye shall **a** even to the end; *G1921*

ACKNOWLEDGED
Gen 38:26 And Judah **a** *them*, and said, She hath H5234
Ps 32: 5 I **a** my sin unto thee, and mine iniquity H3045
2Co 1:14 As also ye have **a** us in part, that we are *G1921*

ACKNOWLEDGEMENT
Col 2: 2 to the **a** of the mystery of God, *G1922*

ACKNOWLEDGETH
1Jn 2:23 he that **a** the Son hath the Father also.

ACKNOWLEDGING
2Ti 2:25 them repentance to the **a** of the truth; *G1922*
Tit 1: 1 **a** of the truth which is after godliness; *G1922*
Phlm 6 effectual by the **a** of every good thing *G1922*

ACQUAINT
Job 22:21 **A** now thyself with him, and be at H5532

ACQUAINTANCE
2Ki 12: 5 every man of his **a**: and let them repair H4378
7 money of your **a**, but deliver it for the H4378
Job 19:13 mine **a** are verily estranged from me. H3045
42:11 had been of his **a** before, and did eat H3045
Ps 31:11 and a fear to mine **a**: they that did see H3045
55:13 man mine equal, my guide, and mine **a**. H3045
88: 8 Thou hast put away mine **a** far from H3045
18 far from me, *and* mine **a** into darkness. H3045
Lk 2:44 sought him among *their* kinsfolk and **a**. *G1110*
23:49 And all his **a**, and the women that *G1110*
Act 24:23 of his **a** to minister or come unto him. *G2398*

ACQUAINTED
Ps 139: 3 lying down, and art **a** *with* all my ways. H5532
Isa 53: 3 of sorrows, and **a** with grief: and we H3045

ACQUAINTING
Ecc 2: 3 unto wine, yet **a** mine heart with H5090

ACQUIT
Job 10:14 thou wilt not **a** me from mine iniquity. H5352
Nah 1: 3 and will not at all **a** *the wicked*: the H5352

ACRABBIM See MAALEH-ACRABBIM.

ACRE
1Sa 14:14 as it were an half **a** of land, *which* a H4618

ACRES
Isa 5:10 Yea, ten **a** of vineyard shall yield one H6776

ACT
Isa 28:21 and bring to pass his **a**, his strange act. H5656
21 and bring to pass his act, his strange **a**. H5656
59: 6 and the **a** of violence *is* in their hands. H6467
Jn 8: 4 was taken in adultery, in the very **a**. *G1888*

ACTIONS
1Sa 2: 3 knowledge, and by him **a** are weighed. H5949

ACTIVITY
Gen 47: 6 *any* men of **a** among them, then make H2428

ACTS
Dt 11: 3 And his miracles, and his **a**, which he H4639
7 But your eyes have seen all the great **a** H4639
Jdg 5:11 the righteous **a** of the LORD, *even* the H6666
11 LORD, *even* the righteous **a** *toward the* H6666
1Sa 12: 7 all the righteous **a** of the LORD, which H6666
2Sa 23:20 had done many **a**, he slew two lion-like H6467
1Ki 10: 6 own land of thy **a** and of thy wisdom. H1697
11:41 And the rest of the **a** of Solomon, and H1697
41 in the book of the **a** of Solomon? H1697
14:19 And the rest of the **a** of Jeroboam, how H1697
29 Now the rest of the **a** of Rehoboam, H1697
15: 7 Now the rest of the **a** of Abijam, and all H1697
23 The rest of all the **a** of Asa, and all his H1697
31 Now the rest of the **a** of Nadab, and all H1697
16: 5 Now the rest of the **a** of Baasha, and H1697
14 Now the rest of the **a** of Elah, and all H1697
20 Now the rest of the **a** of Zimri, and his H1697
27 Now the rest of the **a** of Omri which he H1697
22:39 Now the rest of the **a** of Ahab, and all H1697
45 Now the rest of the **a** of Jehoshaphat, H1697
2Ki 1:18 Now the rest of the **a** of Ahaziah which H1697
8:23 And the rest of the **a** of Joram, and all H1697
10:34 Now the rest of the **a** of Jehu, and all H1697
12:19 And the rest of the **a** of Joash, and all H1697
13: 8 Now the rest of the **a** of Jehoahaz, and H1697
12 And the rest of the **a** of Joash, and all H1697
14:15 Now the rest of the **a** of Jehoash which H1697
18 And the rest of the **a** of Amaziah, *are* H1697
28 Now the rest of the **a** of Jeroboam, and H1697
15: 6 And the rest of the **a** of Azariah, and all H1697
11 And the rest of the **a** of Zachariah, H1697
15 And the rest of the **a** of Shallum, and H1697
21 And the rest of the **a** of Menahem, and H1697
26 And the rest of the **a** of Pekahiah, and H1697
31 And the rest of the **a** of Pekah, and all H1697
36 Now the rest of the **a** of Jotham, and all H1697
16:19 Now the rest of the **a** of Ahaz which he H1697
20:20 And the rest of the **a** of Hezekiah, and H1697
21:17 Now the rest of the **a** of Manasseh, and H1697
25 Now the rest of the **a** of Amon which he H1697
23:19 to all the **a** that he had done in Beth-el. H4639
28 Now the rest of the **a** of Josiah, and all H1697
24: 5 Now the rest of the **a** of Jehoiakim, and H1697
1Ch 11:22 had done many **a**; he slew two lionlike H6467
29:29 Now the **a** of David the king, first and H1697
2Ch 9: 5 own land of thine **a**, and of thy wisdom: H1697
29 Now the rest of the **a** of Solomon, first H1697
12:15 Now the **a** of Rehoboam, first and last, H1697
13:22 And the rest of the **a** of Abijah, and his H1697
16:11 And, behold, the **a** of Asa, first and H1697
20:34 Now the rest of the **a** of Jehoshaphat, H1697
25:26 Now the rest of the **a** of Amaziah, first H1697
26:22 Now the rest of the **a** of Uzziah, first H1697
27: 7 Now the rest of the **a** of Jotham, and all H1697
28:26 Now the rest of his **a** and of all his H1697
32:32 Now the rest of the **a** of Hezekiah, and H1697
33:18 Now the rest of the **a** of Manasseh, and H1697
35:26 Now the rest of the **a** of Josiah, and his H1697
36: 8 Now the rest of the **a** of Jehoiakim, and H1697
Est 10: 2 And all the **a** of his power and of his H4639
Ps 103: 7 Moses, his **a** unto the children of Israel. H5949
106: 2 Who can utter the mighty **a** of the H1369
145: 4 another, and shall declare thy mighty **a**. H1369
6 **a**: and I will declare thy greatness. H3372
12 of men his mighty **a**, and the glorious H1369
150: 2 Praise him for his mighty **a**: praise him H1369

ADADAH
Jos 15:22 And Kinah, and Dimonah, and **A**, H5735

ADAH
Gen 4:19 *was* **A**, and the name of the other Zillah. H5711
20 And **A** bare Jabal: he was the father of H5711
23 And Lamech said unto his wives, **A** H5711
36: 2 of Canaan; **A** the daughter of Elon H5711
4 And **A** bare to Esau Eliphaz; and H5711
10 Eliphaz the son of **A** the wife of Esau, H5711
12 these *were* the sons of **A** Esau's wife. H5711
16 land of Edom; these *were* the sons of **A**. H5711

ADAIAH
2Ki 22: 1 Jedidah, the daughter of **A** of Boscath. H5718
1Ch 6:41 of Ethni, the son of Zerah, the son of **A**, H5718
8:21 And **A**, and Beraiah, and Shimrath, the H5718
9:12 And **A** the son of Jeroham, the son of H5718
2Ch 23: 1 the son of **A**, and Elishaphat the H5718
Ezr 10:29 and **A**, Jashub, and Sheal, and Ramoth. H5718
39 And Shelemiah, and Nathan, and **A**, H5718
Neh 11: 5 the son of **A**, the son of Joiarib, the H5718
12 and two: and **A** the son of Jeroham, H5718

ADALIA
Est 9: 8 And Poratha, and **A**, and Aridatha, H118

ADAM
Gen 2:19 and brought *them* unto **A** to see what he H120
19 and whatsoever **A** called every living H120
20 And **A** gave names to all cattle, and to H120
20 beast of the field; but for **A** there was not H120
21 sleep to fall upon **A**, and he slept: and he H120
23 And **A** said, This *is* now bone of my H120
3: 8 cool of the day: and **A** and his wife hid H120
9 And the LORD God called unto **A**, and H120
17 And unto **A** he said, Because thou hast H120
20 And **A** called his wife's name Eve; H120
21 Unto **A** also and to his wife did the H120
4: 1 And **A** knew Eve his wife; and she H120
25 And **A** knew his wife again; and she bare H120
5: 1 This *is* the book of the generations of **A**. H120
2 **A**, in the day when they were created. H120
3 And **A** lived an hundred and thirty H120
4 And the days of **A** after he had begotten H120
5 And all the days that **A** lived were nine H120
Dt 32: 8 the sons of **A**, he set the bounds of H120
Jos 3:16 very far from the city **A**, that *is* beside H121
1Ch 1: 1 **A**, Sheth, Enosh, H121
Job 31:33 If I covered my transgressions as **A**, by H120
Lk 3:38 *the son* of **A**, which was *the son* of God. *G76*
Ro 5:14 Nevertheless death reigned from **A** to *G76*
1Co 15:22 For as in **A** all die, even so in Christ shall *G76*
45 And so it is written, The first man **A** was *G76*
45 the last **A** *was made* a quickening spirit. *G76*
1Ti 2:13 For **A** was first formed, then Eve. *G76*
14 And **A** was not deceived, but the woman *G76*
Jude 14 And Enoch also, the seventh from **A**, *G76*

ADAMAH
Jos 19:36 And **A**, and Ramah, and Hazor, H128

ADAMANT
Ezk 3: 9 As an **a** harder than flint have I made H8068
Zec 7:12 Yea, they made their hearts *as* an **a** H8068

ADAMANT-STONE See ADAMANT and STONE.

ADAMI
Jos 19:33 Zaanannim, and **A**, Nekeb, and Jabneel, H129

ADAM'S
Ro 5:14 the similitude of **A** transgression, who is *G76*

ADAR
Jos 15: 3 to **A**, and fetched a compass to Karkaa: H146
Ezr 6:15 day of the month **A**, which was in the H144
Est 3: 7 the twelfth *month*, that *is*, the month **A**. H143
13 is the month **A**, and *to take* the spoil H143
8:12 the twelfth month, which *is* the month **A**. H143
9: 1 that *is*, the month **A**, on the thirteenth H143
15 day also of the month **A**, and slew three H143
17 On the thirteenth day of the month **A**; H143
19 day of the month **A** *a day of* gladness H143
21 day of the month **A**, and the fifteenth day H143

ADBEEL
Gen 25:13 and Kedar, and **A**, and Mibsam, H110
1Ch 1:29 then Kedar, and **A**, and Mibsam, H110

ADD
Gen 30:24 The LORD shall **a** to me another son. H3254
Lev 5:16 thing, and shall **a** the fifth part thereto, H3254
6: 5 and shall **a** the fifth part more thereto, H3254
27:13 it, then he shall **a** a fifth *part* thereof H3254
15 then he shall **a** the fifth *part* of the H3254
19 it, then he shall **a** the fifth *part* of the H3254
27 and shall **a** a fifth *part* of it thereto: H3254
31 he shall **a** thereto the fifth *part* thereof. H3254
Nu 5: 7 thereof, and **a** unto it the fifth *part* H3254
35: 6 to them ye shall **a** forty and two cities. H5414
Dt 4: 2 Ye shall not **a** unto the word which I H3254
12:32 not **a** thereto, nor diminish from it. H3254
19: 9 then shalt thou **a** three cities more for H3254

Dt 29:19 mine heart, to a drunkenness to thirst: H5595
2Sa 24: 3 the LORD thy God **a** unto the people, H3254
1Ki 12:11 a heavy yoke, I will **a** to your yoke: my H3254
14 heavy, and I will **a** to your yoke: my H3254
2Ki 20: 6 And I will **a** unto thy days fifteen years; H3254
1Ch 22:14 I prepared; and thou mayest **a** thereto. H3254
2Ch 10:14 heavy, but I will **a** thereto: my father H3254
28:13 ye intend to **a** *more* to our sins and H3254
Ps 69:27 **A** iniquity unto their iniquity: and let H5414
Prv 3: 2 life, and peace, shall they **a** to thee. H3254
30: 6 **A** thou not unto his words, lest he H3254
Isa 29: 1 David dwelt! **a** ye year to year; let them H5595
30: 1 of my spirit, that they may **a** sin to sin: H5595
38: 5 I will **a** unto thy days fifteen years. H3254
Mt 6:27 Which of you by taking thought can **a** *G4369*
Lk 12:25 thought can **a** to his stature one cubit? *G4369*
Php 1:16 supposing to **a** affliction to my bonds: *G2018*
2Pt 1: 5 And beside this, giving all diligence, **a** *G2023*
Rev 22:18 If any man shall **a** unto these things, *G2007*
18 these things, God shall **a** unto him the *G2007*

ADDAN
Ezr 2:59 Tel-harsa, Cherub, **A**, *and* Immer: but H135

ADDAR
1Ch 8: 3 And the sons of Bela were, **A**, and Gera, H146

ADDED
Dt 5:22 voice: and he **a** no more. And he wrote H3254
1Sa 12:19 not: for we have **a** unto all our sins *this* H3254
Jer 36:32 **a** besides unto them many like words. H3254
45: 3 now! for the LORD hath **a** grief to my H3254
Dan 4:36 and excellent majesty was **a** unto me. H3255
Mt 6:33 and all these things shall be **a** unto you. *G4369*
Lk 3:20 **A** yet this above all, that he shut up *G4369*
12:31 and all these things shall be **a** unto you. *G4369*
19:11 And as they heard these things, he **a** *G4369*
Act 2:41 day there were **a** *unto them* about three *G4369*
47 And the Lord **a** to the church daily *G4369*
5:14 And believers were the more **a** to the *G4369*
11:24 and much people was **a** unto the Lord. *G4369*
Gal 2: 6 in conference **a** nothing to me: *G4323*
3:19 *serveth* the law? It was **a** because of *G4369*

ADDER
Gen 49:17 Dan shall be a serpent by the way, an **a** H8207
Ps 58: 4 like the deaf **a** *that* stoppeth her ear; H6620
91:13 Thou shalt tread upon the lion and **a**: H6620
Prv 23:32 like a serpent, and stingeth like an **a**. H6848

ADDERS'
Ps 140: 3 **a** poison *is* under their lips. Selah. H5919

ADDETH
Job 34:37 For he **a** rebellion unto his sin, he H3254
Prv 10:22 rich, and he **a** no sorrow with it. H3254
16:23 his mouth, and **a** learning to his lips. H3254
Gal 3:15 no man disannulleth, or **a** thereto. *G1928*

ADDI
Lk 3:28 was *the son* of **A**, which was *the son* of *G78*

ADDICTED
1Co 16:15 and *that* they have **a** themselves to the *G5021*

ADDITION
1Ki 7:30 molten, at the side of every **a**. H3914

ADDITIONS
1Ki 7:29 oxen *were* certain **a** made of thin work. H3914
36 of every one, and **a** round about. H3914

ADDON
Neh 7:61 Cherub, **A**, and Immer: but they H114

ADER
1Ch 8:15 And Zebadiah, and Arad, and **A**, H5738

ADIEL
1Ch 4:36 and **A**, and Jesimiel, and Benaiah, H5717
9:12 the son of **A**, the son of Jahzerah, H5717
27:25 the son of **A**: and over the storehouses H5717

ADIN
Ezr 2:15 The children of **A**, four hundred fifty H5720
8: 6 Of the sons also of **A**; Ebed the son of H5720
Neh 7:20 The children of **A**, six hundred fifty and H5720
10:16 Adonijah, Bigvai, **A**, H5720

ADINA
1Ch 11:42 **A** the son of Shiza the Reubenite, a H5721

ADINO
2Sa 23: 8 the same *was* **A** the Eznite: *he lift up* H5722

ADITHAIM
Jos 15:36 And Sharaim, and **A**, and Gederah, and H5723

ADJURE
1Ki 22:16 many times shall I **a** thee that thou tell H7650
2Ch 18:15 many times shall I **a** thee that thou say H7650
Mt 26:63 said unto him, I **a** thee by the living *G1844*
Mk 5: 7 most high God? I **a** thee by God, that *G3726*
Act 19:13 **a** you by Jesus whom Paul preacheth. *G3726*

ADJURED
Jos 6:26 And Joshua **a** *them* at that time, H7650
1Sa 14:24 day: for Saul had **a** the people, saying, H422

ADLAI
1Ch 27:29 in the valleys *was* Shaphat the son of **A**: H5724

ADMAH
Gen 10:19 and **A**, and Zeboim, even unto Lasha. H126
14: 2 Shinab king of **A**, and Shemeber king H126
8 and the king of **A**, and the king of H126
Dt 29:23 and Gomorrah, **A**, and Zeboim, which H126
Hos 11: 8 I make thee as **A**? *how* shall I set thee as H126

ADMATHA
Est 1:14 Shethar, **A**, Tarshish, Meres, Marsena, H133

ADMINISTERED
2Co 8:19 grace, which is **a** by us to the glory of *G1247*
20 us in this abundance which is **a** by us: *G1247*

ADMINISTRATION
2Co 9:12 For the **a** of this service not only *G1248*

ADMINISTRATIONS
1Co 12: 5 And there are differences of **a**, but the *G1248*

ADMIRATION
Jude 16 persons in **a** because of advantage. *G2296*
Rev 17: 6 I saw her, I wondered with great **a**. *G2295*

ADMIRED
2Th 1:10 his saints, and to be **a** in all them that *G2296*

ADMONISH
Ro 15:14 knowledge, able also to **a** one another. *G3560*
1Th 5:12 are over you in the Lord, and **a** you; *G3560*
2Th 3:15 Yet count *him* not as an enemy, but **a** *G3560*

ADMONISHED
Ecc 4:13 and foolish king, who will no more be **a**. H2094
12:12 And further, by these, my son, be **a**: of H2094
Jer 42:19 certainly that I have **a** you this day. H5749
Act 27: 9 was now already past, Paul **a** *them*, *G3867*
Heb 8: 5 as Moses was **a** of God when he was *G5537*

ADMONISHING
Col 3:16 teaching and **a** one another in psalms *G3560*

ADMONITION
1Co 10:11 are written for our **a**, upon whom the *G3559*
Eph 6: 4 up in the nurture and **a** of the Lord. *G3559*
Tit 3:10 after the first and second **a** reject; *G3559*

ADNA
Ezr 10:30 And of the sons of Pahath-moab; **A**, H5733
Neh 12:15 Of Harim, **A**; of Meraioth, Helkai; H5733

ADNAH
1Ch 12:20 him of Manasseh, **A**, and Jozabad, and H5734
2Ch 17:14 of thousands; **A** the chief, and with H5734

ADO
Mk 5:39 Why make ye this **a**, and weep? the *G2350*

ADONI-BEZEK
Jdg 1: 5 And they found **A** in Bezek: and they H137
6 But **A** fled; and they pursued after him, H137
7 And **A** said, Threescore and ten kings, H137

ADONIJAH
2Sa 3: 4 And the fourth, **A** the son of Haggith; H138
1Ki 1: 5 Then **A** the son of Haggith exalted H138
1Ki 1: 7 priest: and they following **A** helped *him*. H138
8 *belonged* to David, were not with **A**. H138
9 And **A** slew sheep and oxen and fat H138
11 not heard that **A** the son of Haggith doth H138
13 upon my throne? why then doth **A** reign? H138
18 And now, behold, **A** reigneth; and now, H138
24 hast thou said, **A** shall reign after me, H138
25 before him, and say, God save king **A**. H138
41 And **A** and all the guests that *were* with H138
42 priest came: and **A** said unto him, Come H138
43 And Jonathan answered and said to **A**, H138
49 And all the guests that *were* with **A** were H138
50 And **A** feared because of Solomon, and H138
51 saying, Behold, **A** feareth king Solomon: H138
2:13 And **A** the son of Haggith came to H138
19 speak unto him for **A**. And the king rose H138
21 be given to **A** thy brother to wife. H138
22 the Shunammite for **A**? ask for him the H138
23 and more also, if **A** have not spoken this H138
24 **A** shall be put to death this day. H138
28 had turned after **A**, though he turned not H138
1Ch 3: 2 Geshur: the fourth, **A** the son of Haggith: H138
2Ch 17: 8 Jehonathan, and **A**, and Tobijah, and H138
Neh 10:16 **A**, Bigvai, Adin, H138

ADONIKAM
Ezr 2:13 The children of **A**, six hundred sixty and H140
8:13 And of the last sons of **A**, whose names H140
Neh 7:18 The children of **A**, six hundred threescore H140

ADONIRAM
1Ki 4: 6 **A** the son of Abda *was* over the tribute. H141
5:14 at home: and **A** *was* over the levy. H141

ADONI-ZEDEK
Jos 10: 1 Now it came to pass, when **A** king of H139
3 Wherefore **A** king of Jerusalem sent unto H139

ADOPTION
Ro 8:15 of **a**, whereby we cry, Abba, Father. *G5206*
23 **a**, *to wit*, the redemption of our body. *G5206*
9: 4 *pertaineth* the **a**, and the glory, and the *G5206*
Gal 4: 5 that we might receive the **a** of sons. *G5206*
Eph 1: 5 Having predestinated us unto the **a** of *G5206*

ADORAIM
2Ch 11: 9 And **A**, and Lachish, and Azekah, H115

ADORAM
2Sa 20:24 And **A** *was* over the tribute: and H151
1Ki 12:18 Then king Rehoboam sent **A**, who *was* H151

ADORN
1Ti 2: 9 In like manner also, that women **a** *G2885*
Tit 2:10 that they may **a** the doctrine of God *G2885*

ADORNED
Jer 31: 4 shalt again be **a** with thy tabrets, and H5710
Lk 21: 5 **a** with goodly stones and gifts, he said, *G2885*
1Pt 3: 5 trusted in God, **a** themselves, being in *G2885*
Rev 21: 2 prepared as a bride **a** for her husband. *G2885*

ADORNETH
Isa 61:10 and as a bride **a** *herself* with her jewels. H5710

ADORNING
1Pt 3: 3 Whose **a** let it not be that outward *G2889*
3 be that outward ***a*** of plaiting the hair,

ADRAMMELECH
2Ki 17:31 children in fire to **A** and Anammelech, H152
19:37 his god, that **A** and Sharezer his sons H152
Isa 37:38 his god, that **A** and Sharezer his sons H152

ADRAMYTTIUM
Act 27: 2 And entering into a ship of **A**, we *G98*

ADRIA
Act 27:27 up and down in **A**, about midnight the *G99*

ADRIEL
1Sa 18:19 given unto **A** the Meholathite to wife. H5741
2Sa 21: 8 **A** the son of Barzillai the Meholathite: H5741

ADULLAM
Jos 12:15 The king of Libnah, one; the king of **A**, H5725
15:35 Jarmuth, and **A**, Socoh, and Azekah, H5725
1Sa 22: 1 to the cave **A**: and when his brethren H5725
2Sa 23:13 unto the cave of **A**: and the troop of the H5725

1Ch 11:15 into the cave of **A**; and the host of the H5725
2Ch 11: 7 And Beth-zur, and Shoco, and **A**, H5725
Neh 11:30 Zanoah, **A**, and *in* their villages, at H5725
Mic 1:15 shall come unto **A** the glory of Israel. H5725

ADULLAMITE
Gen 38: 1 to a certain **A**, whose name *was* Hirah. H5726
12 Timnath, he and his friend Hirah the **A**. H5726
20 of his friend the **A**, to receive *his* pledge H5726

ADULTERER
Lev 20:10 wife, the **a** and the adulteress shall H5003
Job 24:15 The eye also of the **a** waiteth for the H5003
Isa 57: 3 the seed of the **a** and the whore. H5003

ADULTERERS
Ps 50:18 him, and hast been partaker with **a**. H5003
Jer 9: 2 all **a**, an assembly of treacherous men. H5003
23:10 For the land is full of **a**; for because of H5003
Hos 7: 4 They *are* all **a**, as an oven heated by the H5003
Mal 3: 5 and against the **a**, and against false H5003
Lk 18:11 unjust, **a**, or even as this publican. *G3432*
1Co 6: 9 nor idolaters, nor **a**, nor effeminate, nor *G3432*
Heb 13: 4 whoremongers and **a** God will judge. *G3432*
Jas 4: 4 Ye **a** and adulteresses, know ye not *G3432*

ADULTERESS
Lev 20:10 and the **a** shall surely be put to death. H5003
Prv 6:26 **a** will hunt for the precious life. H802+H376
Hos 3: 1 of *her* friend, yet an **a**, according to the H5003
Ro 7: 3 shall be called an **a**: but if her husband *G3428*
3 law; so that she is no **a**, though she be *G3428*

ADULTERESSES
Ezk 23:45 the manner of **a**, and after the manner H5003
45 they *are* **a**, and blood *is* in their hands. H5003
Jas 4: 4 Ye adulterers and **a**, know ye not that *G3428*

ADULTERIES
Jer 13:27 I have seen thine **a**, and thy neighings, H5004
Ezk 23:43 Then said I unto *her that was* old in **a**, H5004
Hos 2: 2 and her **a** from between her breasts; H5005
Mt 15:19 murders, **a**, fornications, thefts, *G3430*
Mk 7:21 evil thoughts, **a**, fornications, murders, *G3430*

ADULTEROUS
Prv 30:20 Such *is* the way of an **a** woman; she H5003
Mt 12:39 them, An evil and **a** generation seeketh *G3428*
16: 4 A wicked and **a** generation seeketh *G3428*
Mk 8:38 of my words in this **a** and sinful *G3428*

ADULTERY
Ex 20:14 Thou shalt not commit **a**. H5003
Lev 20:10 And the man that committeth **a** with H5003
10 that committeth **a** with his neighbour's H5003
Dt 5:18 Neither shalt thou commit **a**. H5003
Prv 6:32 *But* whoso committeth **a** with a woman H5003
Jer 3: 8 Israel committed **a** I had put her away, H5003
9 **a** with stones and with stocks. H5003
5: 7 they then committed **a**, and assembled H5003
7: 9 Will ye steal, murder, and commit **a**, H5003
23:14 they commit **a**, and walk in lies: they H5003
29:23 and have committed **a** with their H5003
Ezk 16:32 *But as* a wife that committeth **a**, *which* H5003
23:37 That they have committed **a**, and blood H5003
37 they committed **a**, and have also caused H5003
Hos 4: 2 and committing **a**, they break out, and H5003
13 and your spouses shall commit **a**. H5003
14 when they commit **a**: for themselves are H5003
Mt 5:27 of old time, Thou shalt not commit **a**: *G3431*
28 **a** with her already in his heart. *G3431*
32 her to commit **a**: and whosoever shall *G3429*
32 her that is divorced committeth **a**. *G3429*
19: 9 committeth **a**: and whoso marrieth *G3429*
9 her which is put away doth commit **a**. *G3429*
18 shalt not commit **a**, Thou shalt not *G3431*
Mk 10:11 another, committeth **a** against her. *G3429*
12 married to another, she committeth **a**. *G3429*
19 Do not commit **a**, Do not kill, Do not *G3431*
Lk 16:18 committeth **a**: and whosoever marrieth *G3431*
18 away from *her* husband committeth **a**. *G3431*
18:20 Do not commit **a**, Do not kill, Do not *G3431*
Jn 8: 3 a woman taken in **a**; and when they had *G3430*
4 woman was taken in **a**, in the very act. *G3431*
Ro 2:22 should not commit **a**, dost thou commit *G3431*
22 adultery, dost thou commit **a**? thou that *G3431*
13: 9 For this, Thou shalt not commit **a**, *G3431*
Gal 5:19 which are *these*; **A**, fornication, *G3430*
Jas 2:11 For he that said, Do not commit **a**, said *G3431*
Jas 2:11 if thou commit no **a**, yet if thou kill, *G3431*
2Pt 2:14 Having eyes full of **a**, and that cannot *G3428*
Rev 2:22 them that commit **a** with her into great *G3431*

ADUMMIM
Jos 15: 7 the going up to **A**, which *is* on the south H131
18:17 the going up of **A**, and descended to the H131

ADVANCED
1Sa 12: 6 *It is* the LORD that **a** Moses and Aaron, H6213
Est 3: 1 the Agagite, and **a** him, and set his seat H5375
5:11 him, and how he had **a** him above the H5375
10: 2 the king **a** him, *are* they not written H1431

ADVANTAGE
Job 35: 3 For thou saidst, What **a** will it be unto H5532
Ro 3: 1 What **a** then hath the Jew? or what *G4053*
2Co 2:11 Lest Satan should get an **a** of us: for we *G4122*
Jude 16 persons in admiration because of **a**. *G5622*

ADVANTAGED
Lk 9:25 For what is a man **a**, if he gain the *G5623*

ADVANTAGETH
1Co 15:32 at Ephesus, what **a** it me, if the dead *G3786*

ADVENTURE
Dt 28:56 which would not **a** to set the sole of her H5254
Act 19:31 he would not **a** himself into the theatre. *G1325*

ADVENTURED
Jdg 9:17 (For my father fought for you, and **a** H7993

ADVERSARIES
Ex 23:22 and an adversary unto thine **a**. H6887
Dt 32:27 the enemy, lest their **a** should behave H6862
43 vengeance to his **a**, and will be merciful H6862
Jos 5:13 unto him, *Art* thou for us, or for our **a**? H6862
1Sa 2:10 The **a** of the LORD shall be broken to H7378
2Sa 19:22 ye should this day be **a** unto me? shall H7854
Ezr 4: 1 Now when the **a** of Judah and H6862
Neh 4:11 And our **a** said, They shall not know, H6862
Ps 38:20 for good are mine **a**; because I follow H7853
69:19 dishonour: mine **a** *are* all before thee. H6887
71:13 that are **a** to my soul; let them H7853
81:14 and turned my hand against their **a**. H6862
89:42 Thou hast set up the right hand of his **a**; H6862
109: 4 For my love they are my **a**: but I *give* H7853
20 *Let* this *be* the reward of mine **a** from H7853
29 Let mine **a** be clothed with shame, and H7853
Isa 1:24 **a**, and avenge me of mine enemies: H6862
9:11 Therefore the LORD shall set up the **a** H6862
11:13 depart, and the **a** of Judah shall be cut H6887
59:18 repay, fury to his **a**, recompence to his H6862
63:18 **a** have trodden down thy sanctuary. H6862
64: 2 known to thine **a**, *that* the nations may H6862
Jer 30:16 and all thine **a**, every one of them, shall H6862
46:10 may avenge him of his **a**: and the sword H6862
50: 7 them: and their **a** said, We offend not, H6862
Lam 1: 5 Her **a** are the chief, her enemies H6862
7 did help her: the **a** saw her, *and* did H6862
17 Jacob, *that* his **a** *should be* round about H6862
2:17 thee, he hath set up the horn of thine **a**. H6862
Mic 5: 9 **a**, and all thine enemies shall be cut off. H6862
Nah 1: 2 vengeance on his **a**, and he reserveth H6862
Lk 13:17 these things, all his **a** were ashamed: *G480*
21:15 **a** shall not be able to gainsay nor resist. *G480*
1Co 16: 9 opened unto me, and *there are* many **a**. *G480*
Php 1:28 And in nothing terrified by your **a**: which *G480*
Heb 10:27 indignation, which shall devour the **a**. *G5227*

ADVERSARY
Ex 23:22 and an **a** unto thine adversaries. H6887
Nu 22:22 in the way for an **a** against him. Now H7854
1Sa 1: 6 And her **a** also provoked her sore, for H6869
29: 4 in the battle he be an **a** to us: for H7854
1Ki 5: 4 *there is* neither **a** nor evil occurrent. H7854
11:14 And the LORD stirred up an **a** unto H7854
23 And God stirred him up *another* **a**, H7854
25 And he was an **a** to Israel all the days H7854
Est 7: 6 And Esther said, The **a** and enemy *is* H6862
Job 31:35 *that* mine **a** had written a book. H376+H7379
Ps 74:10 O God, how long shall the **a** reproach? H6862
Isa 50: 8 **a**? let him come near to me. H1167+H4941
Lam 1:10 The **a** hath spread out his hand upon H6862
2: 4 his right hand as an **a**, and slew all *that* H6862
4:12 have believed that the **a** and the enemy H6862
Am 3:11 the Lord GOD; An **a** *there shall be* even H6862
Mt 5:25 Agree with thine **a** quickly, whiles thou *G476*
Mt 5:25 lest at any time the **a** deliver thee to the *G476*
Lk 12:58 When thou goest with thine **a** to the *G476*
18: 3 unto him, saying, Avenge me of mine **a**. *G476*
1Ti 5:14 occasion to the **a** to speak reproachfully. *G480*
1Pt 5: 8 Be sober, be vigilant; because your **a** the *G476*

ADVERSITIES
1Sa 10:19 saved you out of all your **a** and your H7451
Ps 31: 7 trouble; thou hast known my soul in **a**; H6869

ADVERSITY
2Sa 4: 9 who hath redeemed my soul out of all **a**, H6869
2Ch 15: 6 of city: for God did vex them with all **a**. H6869
Ps 10: 6 not be moved: for *I shall* never *be* in **a**. H7451
35:15 But in mine **a** they rejoiced, and H6761
94:13 **a**, until the pit be digged for the wicked. H7451
Prv 17:17 at all times, and a brother is born for **a**. H6869
24:10 *If* thou faint in the day of **a**, thy strength H6869
Ecc 7:14 but in the day of **a** consider: God also H7451
Isa 30:20 give you the bread of **a**, and the water of H6862
Heb 13: 3 **a**, as being yourselves also in the body. *G2558*

ADVERTISE
Nu 24:14 *and* I will **a** thee what this people H3289
Ru 4: 4 And I thought to **a** thee, saying, H1540+H241

ADVICE
Jdg 19:30 of it, take **a**, and speak *your minds*. H5779
20: 7 of Israel; give here your **a** and counsel. H1697
1Sa 25:33 And blessed *be* thy **a**, and blessed *be* H2940
2Sa 19:43 us, that our **a** should not be first had H1697
2Ch 10: 9 And he said unto them, What **a** give ye H3289
14 And answered them after the **a** of the H6098
25:17 Then Amaziah king of Judah took **a**, H3289
Prv 20:18 by counsel: and with good **a** make war. H8458
2Co 8:10 And herein I give *my* **a**: for this is *G1106*

ADVISE
2Sa 24:13 in thy land? now **a**, and see what H3045
1Ki 12: 6 do ye **a** that I may answer this people? H3289
1Ch 21:12 Now therefore **a** thyself what word I H7200

ADVISED
Prv 13:10 but with the well **a** *is* wisdom. H3289
Act 27:12 in, the more part **a** to depart *G5087+G1012*

ADVISEMENT
1Ch 12:19 the Philistines upon **a** sent him away, H6098

ADVOCATE
1Jn 2: 1 sin, we have an **a** with the Father, Jesus *G3875*

AENEAS
Act 9:33 man named **A**, which had kept his bed *G132*
34 And Peter said unto him, **A**, Jesus Christ *G132*

AENON
Jn 3:23 And John also was baptizing in **A** near *G137*

AFAR
Gen 22: 4 up his eyes, and saw the place **a** off. H7350
37:18 And when they saw him **a** off, even H7350
Ex 2: 4 And his sister stood **a** off, to wit what H7350
20:18 saw *it*, they removed, and stood **a** off. H7350
21 And the people stood **a** off, and Moses H7350
24: 1 elders of Israel; and worship ye **a** off. H7350
33: 7 without the camp, **a** off from the camp, H7368
Nu 9:10 or *be* in a journey **a** off, yet he shall H7350
1Sa 26:13 on the top of an hill **a** off; a great space H7350
2Ki 2: 7 **a** off: and they two stood by Jordan. H7350
4:25 of God saw her **a** off, that he said to H7350
Ezr 3:13 shout, and the noise was heard **a** off. H7350
Neh 12:43 joy of Jerusalem was heard even **a** off. H7350
Job 2:12 And when they lifted up their eyes **a** H7350
36: 3 I will fetch my knowledge from **a**, and H7350
25 may see it; man may behold *it* **a** off. H7350
39:25 smelleth the battle **a** off, the thunder of H7350
29 the prey, *and* her eyes behold **a** off. H7350
Ps 10: 1 Why standest thou **a** off, O LORD? *why* H7350
38:11 my sore; and my kinsmen stand **a** off. H7350
65: 5 and of them that are **a** off *upon* the sea: H7350
138: 6 lowly: but the proud he knoweth **a** off. H4801
139: 2 thou understandest my thought **a** off. H7350
Prv 31:14 ships; she bringeth her food from **a**. H4801
Isa 23: 7 feet shall carry her **a** off to sojourn. H7350
59:14 justice standeth **a** off: for truth is fallen H7350
66:19 Javan, *to* the isles **a** off, that have not H7350
Jer 23:23 saith the LORD, and not a God **a** off? H7350
30:10 save thee from **a**, and thy seed from the H7350

Jer 31:10 *it* in the isles **a** off, and say, He that H4801
46:27 save thee from **a** off, and thy seed from H7350
51:50 the LORD **a** off, and let Jerusalem H7350
Mic 4: 3 strong nations **a** off; and they shall H7350
Mt 26:58 But Peter followed him **a** off unto the *G3113*
27:55 there beholding **a** off, which followed *G3113*
Mk 5: 6 But when he saw Jesus **a** off, he ran *G3113*
11:13 And seeing a fig tree **a** off having *G3113*
14:54 And Peter followed him **a** off, even into *G3113*
15:40 There were also women looking on **a** *G3113*
Lk 16:23 **a** off, and Lazarus in his bosom. *G3113*
17:12 that were lepers, which stood **a** off: *G4207*
18:13 And the publican, standing **a** off, *G3113*
22:54 house. And Peter followed **a** off. *G3113*
23:49 stood **a** off, beholding these things. *G3113*
Act 2:39 and to all that are **a** off, *even* as many *G3112*
Eph 2:17 were **a** off, and to them that were nigh. *G3112*
Heb 11:13 but having seen them **a** off, and were *G4207*
2Pt 1: 9 blind, and cannot see **a** off, and hath *G3467*
Rev 18:10 Standing **a** off for the fear of her *G3113*
15 by her, shall stand **a** off for the fear of *G3113*
17 as many as trade by sea, stood **a** off, *G3113*

AFFAIRS
1Ch 26:32 pertaining to God, and **a** of the king. H1697
Ps 112: 5 he will guide his **a** with discretion. H1697
Dan 2:49 over the **a** of the province of Babylon: H5673
3:12 hast set over the **a** of the province of H5673
Eph 6:21 But that ye also may know my **a**, *and* *G2596*
22 ye might know our **a**, and *that* he might *G4012*
Php 1:27 I may hear of your **a**, that ye stand fast *G4012*
2Ti 2: 4 himself with the **a** of *this* life; that he *G4230*

AFFECT
Gal 4:17 They zealously **a** you, *but* not well; yea, *G2206*
17 exclude you, that ye might **a** them. *G2206*

AFFECTED
Act 14: 2 their minds evil **a** against the brethren. *G2559*
Gal 4:18 But *it is* good to be zealously **a** always *G2206*

AFFECTETH
Lam 3:51 Mine eye **a** mine heart because of all H5953

AFFECTION
1Ch 29: 3 Moreover, because I have set my **a** to H7521
Ro 1:31 natural **a**, implacable, unmerciful: *G794*
2Co 7:15 And his inward **a** is more abundant *G4698*
Col 3: 2 Set your **a** on things above, not on *G5426*
5 inordinate **a**, evil concupiscence, *G3806*
2Ti 3: 3 Without natural **a**, trucebreakers, false *G794*

AFFECTIONATELY
1Th 2: 8 So being **a** desirous of you, we were *G2442*

AFFECTIONED
Ro 12:10 *Be* kindly **a** one to another with *G5387*

AFFECTIONS
Ro 1:26 gave them up unto vile **a**: for even their *G3806*
Gal 5:24 crucified the flesh with the **a** and lusts. *G3804*

AFFINITY
1Ki 3: 1 And Solomon made **a** with Pharaoh H2859
2Ch 18: 1 in abundance, and joined **a** with Ahab. H2859
Ezr 9:14 and join in **a** with the people of these H2859

AFFIRM
Ro 3: 8 and as some **a** that we say,) Let us *G5346*
1Ti 1: 7 what they say, nor whereof they **a**. *G1226*
Tit 3: 8 I will that thou **a** constantly, that they *G1226*

AFFIRMED
Lk 22:59 confidently **a**, saying, Of a truth this *G1340*
Act 12:15 But she constantly **a** that it was even *G1340*
25:19 was dead, whom Paul **a** to be alive. *G5335*

AFFLICT
Gen 15:13 they shall **a** them four hundred years; H6031
31:50 If thou shalt **a** my daughters, or if thou H6031
Ex 1:11 them taskmasters to **a** them with their H6031
22:22 Ye shall not **a** any widow, or fatherless H6031
23 If thou **a** them in any wise, and they H6031
Lev 16:29 month, ye shall **a** your souls, and do no H6031
31 shall **a** your souls, by a statute for ever. H6031
23:27 you; and ye shall **a** your souls, and H6031
32 of rest, and ye shall **a** your souls: in the H6031
Nu 24:24 Chittim, and shall **a** Asshur, and shall H6031
24 Asshur, and shall **a** Eber, and he also H6031
Nu 29: 7 and ye shall **a** your souls: ye shall H6031
30:13 Every vow, and every binding oath to **a** H6031
Jdg 16: 5 we may bind him to **a** him: and we will H6031
6 thou mightest be bound to **a** thee. H6031
19 **a** him, and his strength went from him. H6031
2Sa 7:10 **a** them any more, as beforetime, H6031
1Ki 11:39 And I will for this **a** the seed of David, H6031
2Ch 6:26 from their sin, when thou dost **a** them; H6031
Ezr 8:21 that we might **a** ourselves before our H6031
Job 37:23 and in plenty of justice: he will not **a**. H6031
Ps 44: 2 didst **a** the people, and cast them out. H7489
55:19 God shall hear, and **a** them, even he H6030
89:22 him; nor the son of wickedness **a** him. H6031
94: 5 people, O LORD, and **a** thine heritage. H6031
143:12 that **a** my soul: for I *am* thy servant. H6887
Isa 9: 1 more grievously **a** *her by* the way of the H3513
51:23 hand of them that **a** thee; which have H3013
58: 5 a day for a man to **a** his soul? *is it* to H6031
64:12 hold thy peace, and **a** us very sore? H6031
Jer 31:28 to destroy, and to **a**; so will I watch over H7489
Lam 3:33 For he doth not **a** willingly nor grieve H6031
Am 5:12 mighty sins: they **a** the just, they take a H6887
6:14 and they shall **a** you from the entering H3905
Nah 1:12 afflicted thee, I will **a** thee no more. H6031
Zep 3:19 I will undo all that **a** thee: and I will H6031

AFFLICTED
Ex 1:12 But the more they **a** them, the more H6031
Lev 23:29 that shall not be **a** in that same day, he H6031
Nu 11:11 hast thou **a** thy servant? and wherefore H7489
Dt 26: 6 **a** us, and laid upon us hard bondage: H6031
Ru 1:21 me, and the Almighty hath **a** me? H7489
2Sa 22:28 And the **a** people thou wilt save: but H6041
1Ki 2:26 thou hast been **a** in all wherein my H6031
26 afflicted in all wherein my father was **a**. H6031
2Ki 17:20 the seed of Israel, and **a** them, and H6031
Job 6:14 To him that is **a** pity *should be shewed* H4523
30:11 Because he hath loosed my cord, and **a** H6031
34:28 him, and he heareth the cry of the **a**. H6041
Ps 18:27 For thou wilt save the **a** people; but wilt H6041
22:24 affliction of the **a**; neither hath he hid H6041
25:16 upon me; for I *am* desolate and **a**. H6041
82: 3 do justice to the **a** and needy. H6041
88: 7 hast **a** *me* with all thy waves. Selah. H6031
15 I *am* **a** and ready to die from *my* youth H6041
90:15 *wherein* thou hast **a** us, *and* the years H6031
102:ttl A Prayer of the **a**, when he is H6041
107:17 and because of their iniquities, are **a**. H6031
116:10 therefore have I spoken: I was greatly **a**: H6031
119:67 Before I was **a** I went astray: but now H6031
71 *It is* good for me that I have been **a**; that H6031
75 and *that* thou in faithfulness hast **a** me. H6031
107 I am **a** very much: quicken me, O H6031
129: 1 Many a time have they **a** me from my H6887
2 Many a time have they **a** me from my H6887
140:12 cause of the **a**, *and* the right of the poor. H6041
Prv 15:15 All the days of the **a** *are* evil: but he H6041
22:22 poor: neither oppress the **a** in the gate: H6041
26:28 A lying tongue hateth *those that are* **a** H1790
31: 5 pervert the judgment of any of the **a**. H6040
Isa 9: 1 the first he lightly **a** the land of Zebulun H7043
49:13 people, and will have mercy upon his **a**. H6041
51:21 Therefore hear now this, thou **a**, and H6041
53: 4 him stricken, smitten of God, and **a**. H6031
7 He was oppressed, and he was **a**, yet he H6031
54:11 O thou **a**, tossed with tempest, *and* not H6041
58: 3 have we **a** our soul, and thou takest H6031
10 and satisfy the **a** soul; then shall thy H6031
60:14 The sons also of them that **a** thee shall H6031
63: 9 In all their affliction he was **a**, and the H6862
Lam 1: 4 virgins are **a**, and she *is* in bitterness. H3013
5 for the LORD hath **a** her for the H3013
12 hath **a** *me* in the day of his fierce anger. H3013
Mic 4: 6 that is driven out, and her that I have **a**; H7489
Nah 1:12 I have **a** thee, I will afflict thee no more. H6031
Zep 3:12 the midst of thee an **a** and poor people, H6041
Mt 24: 9 Then shall they deliver you up to be **a**, *G2347*
2Co 1: 6 And whether we be **a**, *it is* for your *G2346*
1Ti 5:10 she have relieved the **a**, if she have *G2346*
Heb 11:37 being destitute, **a**, tormented; *G2346*
Jas 4: 9 Be **a**, and mourn, and weep: let your *G5003*
5:13 Is any among you **a**? let him pray. Is *G2553*

AFFLICTEST
1Ki 8:35 turn from their sin, when thou **a** them: H6031

AFFLICTION
Gen 16:11 because the LORD hath heard thy **a**. H6040
29:32 looked upon my **a**; now therefore my H6040
Gen 31:42 hath seen mine **a** and the labour of my H6040
41:52 me to be fruitful in the land of my **a**. H6040
Ex 3: 7 surely seen the **a** of my people which H6040
17 you up out of the **a** of Egypt unto the H6040
4:31 looked upon their **a**, then they bowed H6040
Dt 16: 3 *even* the bread of **a**; for thou camest H6040
26: 7 **a**, and our labour, and our oppression: H6040
1Sa 1:11 wilt indeed look on the **a** of thine H6040
2Sa 16:12 will look on mine **a**, and that the LORD H6040
1Ki 22:27 him with bread of **a** and with water of H3906
27 with water of **a**, until I come in peace. H3906
2Ki 14:26 For the LORD saw the **a** of Israel, *that* H6040
2Ch 18:26 him with bread of **a** and with water of H3906
26 with water of **a**, until I return in peace. H3906
20: 9 in our **a**, then thou wilt hear and help. H6869
33:12 And when he was in **a**, he besought the H6887
Neh 1: 3 *are* in great **a** and reproach: the wall H7451
9: 9 And didst see the **a** of our fathers in H6040
Job 5: 6 Although **a** cometh not forth of the dust, H205
10:15 of confusion; therefore see thou mine **a**; H6040
30:16 the days of **a** have taken hold upon me. H6040
27 rested not: the days of **a** prevented me. H6040
36: 8 in fetters, *and* be holden in cords of **a**; H6040
15 He delivereth the poor in his **a**, and H6040
21 for this hast thou chosen rather than **a**. H6040
Ps 22:24 nor abhorred the **a** of the afflicted; H6039
25:18 Look upon mine **a** and my pain; and H6040
44:24 forgettest our **a** and our oppression? H6040
66:11 the net; thou laidst **a** upon our loins. H4157
88: 9 Mine eye mourneth by reason of **a**: H6040
106:44 Nevertheless he regarded their **a**, when H6862
107:10 of death, *being* bound in **a** and iron; H6040
39 low through oppression, **a**, and sorrow. H7451
41 Yet setteth he the poor on high from **a**, H6040
119:50 This *is* my comfort in my **a**: for thy H6040
92 I should then have perished in mine **a**. H6040
153 Consider mine **a**, and deliver me: for I H6040
Isa 30:20 and the water of **a**, yet shall not thy H3906
48:10 I have chosen thee in the furnace of **a**. H6040
63: 9 In all their **a** he was afflicted, and the H6869
Jer 4:15 and publisheth **a** from mount Ephraim. H205
15:11 in the time of evil and in the time of **a**. H6869
16:19 in the day of **a**, the Gentiles shall come H6869
30:15 Why criest thou for thine **a**? thy sorrow H7667
48:16 *is* near to come, and his **a** hasteth fast. H7451
Lam 1: 3 because of **a**, and because of great H6040
7 in the days of her **a** and of her miseries H6040
9 LORD, behold my **a**: for the enemy hath H6040
3: 1 I *am* the man *that* hath seen **a** by the H6040
19 Remembering mine **a** and my misery, H6040
Hos 5:15 face: in their **a** they will seek me early. H6862
Am 6: 6 they are not grieved for the **a** of Joseph. H7667
Oba 13 looked on their **a** in the day of their H7451
Jna 2: 2 And said, I cried by reason of mine **a** H6869
Nah 1: 9 **a** shall not rise up the second time. H6869
Hab 3: 7 I saw the tents of Cushan in **a**: *and* the H205
Zec 1:15 and they helped forward the **a**. H7451
8:10 in because of the **a**: for I set all men H6862
10:11 the sea with **a**, and shall smite the H6869
Mk 4:17 time: afterward, when **a** or persecution *G2347*
13:19 For *in* those days shall be **a**, such as was *G2347*
Act 7:11 **a**: and our fathers found no sustenance. *G2347*
34 I have seen, I have seen the **a** of my *G2561*
2Co 2: 4 For out of much **a** and anguish of heart *G2347*
4:17 For our light **a**, which is but for a *G2347*
8: 2 How that in a great trial of **a** the *G2347*
Php 1:16 supposing to add **a** to my bonds: *G2347*
4:14 that ye did communicate with my **a**. *G2347*
1Th 1: 6 in much **a**, with joy of the Holy Ghost: *G2347*
3: 7 in all our **a** and distress by your faith: *G2347*
Heb 11:25 Choosing rather to suffer **a** with the *G4778*
Jas 1:27 widows in their **a**, *and* to keep himself *G2347*
5:10 example of suffering **a**, and of patience. *G2552*

AFFLICTIONS
Ps 34:19 Many *are* the **a** of the righteous: but the H7451
132: 1 LORD, remember David, *and* all his **a**: H6031
Act 7:10 And delivered him out of all his **a**, and *G2347*
20:23 city, saying that bonds and **a** abide me. *G2347*
2Co 6: 4 in **a**, in necessities, in distresses, *G2347*
Col 1:24 is behind of the **a** of Christ in my flesh *G2347*
1Th 3: 3 be moved by these **a**: for yourselves *G2347*
2Ti 1: 8 thou partaker of the **a** of the gospel *G4777*
3:11 Persecutions, **a**, which came unto me at *G3804*
4: 5 But watch thou in all things, endure **a**, *G2553*
Heb 10:32 ye endured a great fight of **a**; *G3804*
33 by reproaches and **a**; and partly, whilst *G2347*
1Pt 5: 9 that the same **a** are accomplished in *G3804*

AFFORDING
Ps 144:13 *That* our garners *may be* full, **a** all H6329

AFFRIGHT
2Ch 32:18 on the wall, to **a** them, and to trouble H3372

AFFRIGHTED
Dt 7:21 Thou shalt not be **a** at them: for the H6206
Job 18:20 as they that went before were **a**. H270+H8178
39:22 He mocketh at fear, and is not **a**; H2865
Isa 21: 4 My heart panted, fearfulness **a** me: the H1204
Jer 51:32 with fire, and the men of war are **a**. H926
Mk 16: 5 a long white garment; and they were **a**. *G1568*
6 And he saith unto them, Be not **a**: Ye *G1568*
Lk 24:37 But they were terrified and **a**, and *G1719*
Rev 11:13 **a**, and gave glory to the God of heaven. *G1719*

A-FISHING See FISHING.

AFOOT
Mk 6:33 him, and ran **a** thither out of all cities, *G3979*
Act 20:13 he appointed, minding himself to go **a**. *G3978*

AFORE
2Ki 20: 4 And it came to pass, **a** Isaiah was gone H3808
Ps 129: 6 which withereth **a** it groweth up: H6927
Isa 18: 5 For **a** the harvest, when the bud is H6440
Ezk 33:22 upon me in the evening, **a** he that was H6440
Ro 1: 2 (Which he had promised **a** by his *G4279*
9:23 which he had **a** prepared unto glory, *G4282*
Eph 3: 3 the mystery; (as I wrote **a** in few words, *G4270*

AFOREHAND
Mk 14: 8 **a** to anoint my body to the burying. *G4301*

AFORETIME
Neh 13: 5 chamber, where **a** they laid the meat H6440
Job 17: 6 of the people; and **a** I was as a tabret. H6440
Isa 52: 4 My people went down **a** into Egypt to H7223
Jer 30:20 Their children also shall be as **a**, and H6924
Dan 6:10 his God, as he did **a**. H4481+H1836+H6928
Jn 9:13 to the Pharisees him that **a** was blind. *G4218*
Ro 15: 4 For whatsoever things were written **a** *G4270*

AFRAID
Gen 3:10 the garden, and I was **a**, because I *was* H3372
18:15 not; for she was **a**. And he said, Nay; H3372
20: 8 in their ears: and the men were sore **a**. H3372
28:17 And he was **a**, and said, How dreadful H3372
31:31 Laban, Because I was **a**: for I said, H3372
32: 7 Then Jacob was greatly **a** and H3372
42:28 and they were **a**, saying one to another, H2729
35 saw the bundles of money, they were **a**. H3372
43:18 And the men were **a**, because they were H3372
Ex 3: 6 his face; for he was **a** to look upon God. H3372
14:10 they were sore **a**: and the children of H3372
15:14 The people shall hear, *and* be **a**: sorrow H7264
34:30 and they were **a** to come nigh him. H3372
Lev 26: 6 shall make *you* **a**: and I will rid evil H2729
Nu 12: 8 **a** to speak against my servant Moses? H3372
22: 3 And Moab was sore **a** of the people, H1481
Dt 1:17 ye shall not be **a** of the face of man; for H1481
29 you, Dread not, neither be **a** of them. H3372
2: 4 and they shall be **a** of you: take ye good H3372
5: 5 LORD: for ye were **a** by reason of the H3372
7:18 Thou shalt not be **a** of them: *but* shalt H3372
19 unto all the people of whom thou art **a**. H3373
9:19 For I was **a** of the anger and hot H3025
18:22 thou shalt not be **a** of him. H1481
20: 1 than thou, be not **a** of them: for the H3372
28:10 the LORD; and they shall be **a** of thee. H3372
60 **a** of; and they shall cleave unto thee. H3025
31: 6 fear not, nor be **a** of them: for the H6206
Jos 1: 9 good courage; be not **a**, neither be thou H6206
9:24 we were sore **a** of our lives because H3372
11: 6 Joshua, Be not **a** because of them: for H3372
Jdg 7: 3 *is* fearful and **a**, let him return and H2730
Ru 3: 8 that the man was **a**, and turned himself: H2729
1Sa 4: 7 And the Philistines were **a**, for they H3372
7: 7 heard *it*, they were **a** of the Philistines. H3372
17:11 they were dismayed, and greatly **a**. H3372
24 man, fled from him, and were sore **a**. H3372
18:12 And Saul was **a** of David, because the H3372
15 himself very wisely, he was **a** of him. H1481
29 And Saul was yet the more **a** of David; H3372
21: 1 and Ahimelech was **a** at the meeting of H2729
12 was sore **a** of Achish the king of Gath. H3372
23: 3 Behold, we be **a** here in Judah: how H3373
28: 5 was **a**, and his heart greatly trembled. H3372
1Sa 28:13 And the king said unto her, Be not **a**: for H3372
20 and was sore **a**, because of the words H3372
31: 4 for he was sore **a**. Therefore Saul took H3372
2Sa 1:14 wast thou not **a** to stretch forth thine H3372
6: 9 And David was **a** of the LORD that day, H3372
14:15 have made me **a**: and thy handmaid H3372
17: 2 will make him **a**: and all the people that H2729
22: 5 the floods of ungodly men made me **a**; H1204
46 they shall be **a** out of their close places. H2296
1Ki 1:49 Adonijah were **a**, and rose up, and went H2729
2Ki 1:15 with him: be not **a** of him. And he H3372
10: 4 But they were exceedingly **a**, and said, H3372
19: 6 the LORD, Be not **a** of the words which H3372
25:26 Egypt: for they were **a** of the Chaldees. H3372
1Ch 10: 4 for he was sore **a**. So Saul took a sword, H3372
13:12 And David was **a** of God that day, H3372
21:30 of God: for he was **a** because of the H1204
2Ch 20:15 unto you, Be not **a** nor dismayed by H3372
32: 7 Be strong and courageous, be not **a** nor H3372
Neh 2: 2 sorrow of heart. Then I was very sore **a**, H3372
4:14 people, Be not ye **a** of them: remember H3372
6: 9 For they all made us **a**, saying, Their H3372
13 that I should be **a**, and do so, and sin, H3372
Est 7: 6 was **a** before the king and the queen. H1204
Job 3:25 that which I was **a** of is come unto me. H3025
5:21 be **a** of destruction when it cometh. H3372
22 thou be **a** of the beasts of the earth. H3372
6:21 ye see *my* casting down, and are **a**. H3372
9:28 I am **a** of all my sorrows, I know that H3025
11:19 **a**; yea, many shall make suit unto thee. H2729
13:11 Shall not his excellency make you **a**? H1204
21 me: and let not thy dread make me **a**. H1204
15:24 Trouble and anguish shall make him **a**; H1204
18:11 Terrors shall make him **a** on every H1204
19:29 Be ye **a** of the sword: for wrath H1481
21: 6 Even when I remember I am **a**, and H926
23:15 when I consider, I am **a** of him. H6342
32: 6 wherefore I was **a**, and durst not shew H2119
33: 7 not make thee **a**, neither shall my hand H1204
39:20 Canst thou make him **a** as a H7493
41:25 himself, the mighty are **a**: by reason of H1481
Ps 3: 6 I will not be **a** of ten thousands of H3372
18: 4 the floods of ungodly men made me **a**. H1204
45 and be **a** out of their close places. H2727
27: 1 strength of my life; of whom shall I be **a**? H6342
49:16 Be not thou **a** when one is made rich, H3372
56: 3 What time I am **a**, I will trust in thee. H3372
11 not be **a** what man can do unto me. H3372
65: 8 parts are **a** at thy tokens: thou H3372
77:16 were **a**: the depths also were troubled. H2342
83:15 and make them **a** with thy storm. H926
91: 5 Thou shalt not be **a** for the terror by H3372
112: 7 He shall not be **a** of evil tidings: his H3372
8 he shall not be **a**, until he see *his desire* H3372
119:120 of thee; and I am **a** of thy judgments. H3372
Prv 3:24 thou shalt not be **a**: yea, thou shalt lie H6342
25 Be not **a** of sudden fear, neither of the H3372
31:21 She is not **a** of the snow for her H3372
Ecc 12: 5 Also *when* they shall be **a** of *that which* H3372
Isa 8:12 neither fear ye their fear, nor be **a**. H6206
10:24 in Zion, be not **a** of the Assyrian: he H3372
29 Ramah is **a**; Gibeah of Saul is fled. H2729
12: 2 will trust, and not be **a**: for the LORD H6342
13: 8 And they shall be **a**: pangs and sorrows H926
17: 2 lie down, and none shall make *them* **a**. H2729
19:16 and it shall be **a** and fear because of H2729
17 thereof shall be **a** in himself, because H6342
20: 5 And they shall be **a** and ashamed of H2865
31: 4 him, *he* will not be **a** of their voice, nor H2865
9 princes shall be **a** of the ensign, saith H2865
33:14 The sinners in Zion are **a**; fearfulness H6342
37: 6 the LORD, Be not **a** of the words that H3372
40: 9 lift *it* up, be not **a**; say unto the cities of H3372
41: 5 the earth were **a**, drew near, and came. H2729
44: 8 Fear ye not, neither be **a**: have not I told H7297
51: 7 men, neither be ye **a** of their revilings. H2865
12 thou shouldest be **a** of a man *that* shall H3372
57:11 And of whom hast thou been **a** or H1672
Jer 1: 8 Be not **a** of their faces: for I *am* with H3372
2:12 **a**, be ye very desolate, saith the LORD. H8175
10: 5 cannot go. Be not **a** of them; for they H3372
26:21 he was **a**, and fled, and went into Egypt; H3372
30:10 be quiet, and none shall make *him* **a**. H2729
36:16 words, they were **a** both one and other, H6342
24 Yet they were not **a**, nor rent their H6342
38:19 Jeremiah, I am **a** of the Jews that are H1672
39:17 hand of the men of whom thou *art* **a**. H3016
41:18 for they were **a** of them, because H3372
42:11 Be not **a** of the king of Babylon, of H3372
Jer 42:11 of whom ye are **a**; be not afraid of him, H3373
11 ye are afraid; be not **a** of him, saith the H3372
16 whereof ye were **a**, shall follow close H1672
46:27 at ease, and none shall make *him* **a**. H2729
Ezk 2: 6 And thou, son of man, be not **a** of H3372
6 of them, neither be not **a** of their words, H3372
6 scorpions: be not **a** of their words, nor H3372
27:35 their kings shall be sore **a**, they shall be H8175
30: 9 Ethiopians **a**, and great pain shall H2729
32:10 shall be horribly **a** for thee, when I H8175
34:28 safely, and none shall make *them* **a**. H2729
39:26 in their land, and none made *them* **a**. H2729
Dan 4: 5 I saw a dream which made me **a**, and H1763
8:17 he came, I was **a**, and fell upon my face: H1204
Joel 2:22 Be not **a**, ye beasts of the field: for the H3372
Am 3: 6 the people not be **a**? shall there be evil in H2729
Jna 1: 5 Then the mariners were **a**, and cried H3372
10 Then were the men exceedingly **a**, and H3372
Mic 4: 4 shall make *them* **a**: for the mouth of the H2729
7:17 they shall be **a** of the LORD our God, H6342
Nah 2:11 lion's whelp, and none made *them* **a**? H2729
Hab 2:17 *which* made them **a**, because of men's H2865
3: 2 speech, *and* was **a**: O LORD, revive thy H3372
Zep 3:13 lie down, and none shall make *them* **a**. H2729
Mal 2: 5 feared me, and was **a** before my name. H2865
Mt 2:22 father Herod, he was **a** to go thither: *G5399*
14:27 saying, Be of good cheer; it is I; be not **a**. *G5399*
30 boisterous, he was **a**; and beginning to *G5399*
17: 6 they fell on their face, and were sore **a**. *G5399*
7 them, and said, Arise, and be not **a**. *G5399*
25:25 And I was **a**, and went and hid thy *G5399*
28:10 Then said Jesus unto them, Be not **a**: go *G5399*
Mk 5:15 and in his right mind: and they were **a**. *G5399*
36 of the synagogue, Be not **a**, only believe. *G5399*
6:50 them, Be of good cheer: it is I; be not **a**. *G5399*
9: 6 not what to say; for they were sore **a**. *G1630*
32 not that saying, and were **a** to ask him. *G5399*
10:32 they were **a**. And he took again the *G5399*
16: 8 any thing to any *man*; for they were **a**. *G5399*
Lk 2: 9 about them: and they were sore **a**. *G5399*
8:25 And they being **a** wondered, saying one *G5399*
35 and in his right mind: and they were **a**. *G5399*
12: 4 my friends, Be not **a** of them that kill *G5399*
24: 5 And as they were **a**, and bowed down *G1719*
Jn 6:19 nigh unto the ship: and they were **a**. *G5399*
20 But he saith unto them, It is I; be not **a**. *G5399*
14:27 heart be troubled, neither let it be **a**. *G1168*
19: 8 heard that saying, he was the more **a**; *G5399*
Act 9:26 but they were all **a** of him, and believed *G5399*
10: 4 And when he looked on him, he was **a**, *G1719*
18: 9 **a**, but speak, and hold not thy peace: *G5399*
22: 9 the light, and were **a**; but they heard not *G1719*
29 captain also was **a**, after he knew that *G5399*
Ro 13: 3 thou then not be **a** of the power? do *G5399*
4 which is evil, be **a**; for he beareth not *G5399*
Gal 4:11 I am **a** of you, lest I have bestowed *G5399*
Heb 11:23 not **a** of the king's commandment. *G5399*
1Pt 3: 6 and are not **a** with any amazement. *G5399*
14 **a** of their terror, neither be troubled; *G5399*
2Pt 2:10 they are not **a** to speak evil of dignities. *G5141*

AFRESH
Heb 6: 6 of God **a**, and put *him* to an open shame. *G388*

AFTER See the Appendix.

AFTERNOON
Jdg 19: 8 tarried until **a**, and they did eat H3117+H5186

AFTERWARD
Gen 10:18 Hamathite: and **a** were the families of H310
15:14 I judge: and **a** shall they come H310+H3651
32:20 before me, and **a** I will see his H310+H3651
38:30 And **a** came out his brother, that had the H310
Ex 5: 1 And **a** Moses and Aaron went in, and H310
34:32 And **a** all the children of Israel H310+H3651
Lev 14:19 and **a** he shall kill the burnt offering: H310
36 unclean: and **a** the priest shall H310+H3651
16:26 and **a** come into the camp. H310+H3651
28 **a** he shall come into the camp. H310+H3651
22: 7 shall be clean, and shall **a** eat of the holy H310
Nu 5:26 *it* upon the altar, and **a** shall cause the H310
12:16 And **a** the people removed from H310
19: 7 flesh in water, and **a** he shall come into H310
31: 2 **a** shalt thou be gathered unto thy people. H310
24 and **a** ye shall come into the camp. H310
32:22 the LORD: then **a** ye shall return, and H310
Dt 17: 7 him to death, and **a** the hands of all the H314
24:21 shalt not glean *it* **a**: it shall be for the H310

Jos 2:16 be returned: and **a** may ye go your way. H310
8:34 And **a** he read all the words of H310+H3651
10:26 And **a** Joshua smote them, and slew H310
24: 5 among them: and **a** I brought you out. H310
Jdg 1: 9 And **a** the children of Judah went down H310
7:11 what they say; and **a** shall thine hands H310
16: 4 And it came to pass **a**, that he H310+H3651
19: 5 a morsel of bread, and **a** go your way. H310
1Sa 24: 5 And it came to pass **a**, that H310+H3651
8 David also arose **a**, and went out H310+H3651
2Sa 3:28 And **a** when David heard *it*, he H310+H3651
1Ch 2:21 And **a** Hezron went in to the daughter of H310
2Ch 35:14 And **a** they made ready for themselves, H310
Ezr 3: 5 And **a** *offered* the continual H310+H3651
Neh 6:10 **A** I came unto the house of Shemaiah
Ps 73:24 thy counsel, and **a** receive me *to* glory. H310
Isa 1:26 at the beginning: **a** thou shalt be H310+H3651
9: 1 of Naphtali, and **a** did more grievously H314
Jer 21: 7 And **a**, saith the LORD, I will H310+H3651
34:11 But **a** they turned, and caused H310+H3651
46:26 his servants: and **a** it shall be H310+H3651
49: 6 And **a** I will bring again the H310+H3651
Ezk 41: 1 **A** he brought me to the temple, and
43: 1 **A** he brought me to the gate, *even* the
47: 1 **A** he brought me again unto the door of
5 **A** he measured a thousand; *and it was* a
Dan 8:27 sick *certain* days; **a** I rose up, and did
Hos 3: 5 **A** shall the children of Israel return, and H310
Joel 2:28 And it shall come to pass **a**, *that* H310+H3651
Mt 4: 2 and forty nights, he was **a** an hungred. *G5305*
21:29 He answered and said, I will not: but **a** *G5305*
32 not **a**, that ye might believe him. *G5305*
25:11 **A** came also the other virgins, saying, *G5305*
Mk 4:17 but for a time: **a**, when affliction or *G1534*
16:14 **A** he appeared unto the eleven as they *G5305*
Lk 4: 2 when they were ended, he **a** hungered. *G5305*
8: 1 And it came to pass **a**, that he went *G2517*
17: 8 **a** thou shalt eat and drink? *G3326+G5023*
18: 4 a while: but **a** he said within *G3326+G5023*
Jn 5:14 **A** Jesus findeth him in the *G3326+G5023*
Act 13:21 And **a** they desired a king: and God *G2547*
1Co 15:23 **a** they that are Christ's at his coming. *G1899*
46 natural; and **a** that which is spiritual. *G1899*
Heb 4: 8 **a** have spoken of another day. *G3326+G5023*
12:11 nevertheless **a** it yieldeth the peaceable *G5305*
17 For ye know how that **a**, when he would *G3347*
Jude 5 **a** destroyed them that believed not. *G1208*

AFTERWARDS
Gen 30:21 And **a** she bare a daughter, and called H310
Ex 11: 1 upon Egypt; **a** he will let you go H310+H3651
Dt 13: 9 death, and **a** the hand of all the people. H314
1Sa 9:13 sacrifice; *and* **a** they eat that be H310+H3651
Job 18: 2 of words? mark, and **a** we will speak. H310
Prv 20:17 Bread of deceit *is* sweet to a man; but **a** H310
24:27 in the field; and **a** build thine house. H310
28:23 He that rebuketh a man **a** shall find H310
29:11 mind: but a wise *man* keepeth it in till **a**. H268
Ezk 11:24 **A** the spirit took me up, and brought me
Jn 13:36 me now; but thou shalt follow me **a**. *G5305*
Gal 1:21 **A** I came into the regions of Syria and *G1899*
3:23 the faith which should **a** be revealed. *G3195*

AGABUS
Act 11:28 of them named **A**, and signified by the *G13*
21:10 from Judaea a certain prophet, named **A**. *G13*

AGAG
Nu 24: 7 **A**, and his kingdom shall be exalted. H90
1Sa 15: 8 And he took **A** the king of the H90
9 But Saul and the people spared **A**, and H90
20 and have brought **A** the king of Amalek, H90
32 Bring ye hither to me **A** the king of the H90
32 the Amalekites. And **A** came unto him H90
32 him delicately. And **A** said, Surely the H90
33 **A** in pieces before the LORD in Gilgal. H90

AGAGITE
Est 3: 1 Hammedatha the **A**, and advanced him, H91
10 of Hammedatha the **A**, the Jews' enemy. H91
8: 3 of Haman the **A**, and his device that he H91
5 of Hammedatha the **A**, which he wrote to H91
9:24 Hammedatha, the **A**, the enemy of all the H91

AGAIN
Gen 4: 2 And she **a** bare his brother Abel. And H3254
25 And Adam knew his wife **a**; and she H5750
8:10 **a** he sent forth the dove out of the ark; H3254
12 returned not **a** unto him any more. H3254
Gen 8:21 heart, I will not **a** curse the ground any H3254
21 neither will I **a** smite any more every H3254
14:16 and also brought **a** his brother Lot, and H7725
15:16 shall come hither **a**: for the iniquity of H7725
18:29 And he spake unto him yet **a**, and said, H3254
19: 9 And they said ***a***, This one *fellow* came
22: 5 and worship, and come **a** to you. H7725
24: 5 bring thy son **a** unto the land from H7725
6 that thou bring not my son thither **a**. H7725
8 oath: only bring not my son thither **a**. H7725
20 trough, and ran **a** unto the well to draw H7725
25: 1 Then **a** Abraham took a wife, and her H3254
26:18 And Isaac digged **a** the wells of water, H7725
28:15 will bring thee **a** into this land; for I H7725
21 So that I come **a** to my father's house in H7725
29: 3 **a** upon the well's mouth in his place. H7725
33 And she conceived **a**, and bare a son; H5750
34 And she conceived **a**, and bare a son; H5750
35 And she conceived **a**, and bare a son; H5750
30: 7 And Bilhah Rachel's maid conceived **a**, H5750
19 And Leah conceived **a**, and bare Jacob H5750
31 for me, I will **a** feed *and* keep thy flock: H7725
35: 9 And God appeared unto Jacob **a**, when H5750
37:14 bring me word **a**. So he sent him out of H7725
22 hands, to deliver him to his father **a**. H7725
38: 4 And she conceived **a**, and bare a son; H5750
5 And she yet **a** conceived, and bare a H5750
26 my son. And he knew her **a** no more. H3254
40:21 his butlership **a**; and he gave the cup H7725
42:24 returned to them **a**, and communed H7725
37 my hand, and I will bring him to thee **a**. H7725
43: 2 unto them, Go **a**, buy us a little food. H7725
12 that was brought **a** in the mouth of H7725
12 your sacks, carry *it* **a** in your hand; H7725
13 Take also your brother, and arise, go **a** H7725
21 and we have brought it **a** in our hand. H7725
44: 8 we brought **a** unto thee out of the H7725
25 And our father said, Go **a**, *and* buy us a H7725
46: 4 bring thee up ***a***: and Joseph shall put
48:21 you **a** unto the land of your fathers. H7725
50: 5 and bury my father, and I will come **a**. H7725
Ex 4: 7 into thy bosom **a**. And he put his hand H7725
7 into his bosom **a**; and plucked it out of H7725
7 it was turned **a** as his *other* flesh. H7725
10: 8 And Moses and Aaron were brought **a** H7725
29 well, I will see thy face **a** no more. H3254
14:13 ye shall see them **a** no more for ever. H3254
26 the waters may come **a** upon the H7725
15:19 the LORD brought **a** the waters of the H7725
21:19 If he rise **a**, and walk abroad upon his
23: 4 thou shalt surely bring it back to him **a**. H7725
24:14 for us, until we come **a** unto you: and, H7725
33:11 And he turned **a** into the camp: but his H7725
34:35 **a**, until he went in to speak with him. H7725
Lev 13: 6 And the priest shall look on him **a** the H8145
7 he shall be seen of the priest **a**: H8145
16 Or if the raw flesh turn **a**, and be H7725
14:39 And the priest shall come **a** the seventh H7725
43 And if the plague come **a**, and break out H7725
20: 2 **A**, thou shalt say to the children of Israel,
24:20 in a man, so shall it be done to him ***a***.
25:48 **a**; one of his brethren may redeem him:
51 them he shall give **a** the price of his H7725
52 give him **a** the price of his redemption. H7725
26:26 *you* your bread **a** by weight: and ye H7725
Nu 11: 4 of Israel also wept **a**, and said, Who H7725
12:14 and after that let her be received in ***a***.
15 not till Miriam was brought in ***a***.
17:10 Moses, Bring Aaron's rod **a** before the H7725
22: 8 bring you word **a**, as the LORD shall H7725
15 And Balak sent yet **a** princes, more, H3254
25 against the wall: and he smote her **a**. H3254
34 if it displease thee, I will get me back **a**. H7725
23:16 said, Go **a** unto Balak, and say thus. H7725
32:15 him, he will yet **a** leave them in the H3254
33: 7 and turned **a** unto Pi-hahiroth, which H7725
35:32 he should come **a** to dwell in the land, H7725
Dt 1:22 and bring us word **a** by what way we H7725
25 and brought us word **a**, and said, *It is* a H7725
5:30 say to them, Get you into your tents **a**. H7725
13:16 an heap for ever; it shall not be built **a**. H5750
15: 3 Of a foreigner thou mayest exact *it* ***a***: but
18:16 Let me not hear **a** the voice of the H3254
22: 1 case bring them **a** unto thy brother. H7725
2 it, and thou shalt restore it to him **a**. H7725
4 shalt surely help him to lift *them* up **a**. H6965
23:11 is down, he shall come into the camp ***a***.
24: 4 may not take her **a** to be his wife, after H7725
13 him the pledge **a** when the sun goeth H7725
Dt 24:19 thou shalt not go **a** to fetch it: it shall be H7725
20 go over the boughs **a**: it shall be for the H310
28:68 thee into Egypt **a** with ships, by the way H7725
68 see it no more **a**: and there ye shall be H7725
30: 9 for the LORD will **a** rejoice over thee H7725
33:11 them that hate him, that they rise not **a**.
Jos 5: 2 **a** the children of Israel the second time. H7725
8:21 they turned **a**, and slew the men of Ai. H7725
14: 7 him word **a** as *it was* in mine heart. H7725
18: 4 of them; and they shall come ***a*** to me.
8 it, and come **a** to me, that I may here H7725
9 came ***a*** to Joshua to the host at Shiloh.
22:28 that we may say ***a***, Behold the pattern of
32 of Israel, and brought them word **a**. H7725
Jdg 3:12 And the children of Israel did evil **a** in H3254
19 But he himself turned **a** from the H7725
4: 1 And the children of Israel **a** did evil in H3254
20 **A** he said unto her, Stand in the door of
6:18 he said, I will tarry until thou come **a**. H7725
8: 9 When I come **a** in peace, I will break H7725
33 of Israel turned **a**, and went a whoring H7725
9:37 And Gaal spake **a** and said, See there H3254
10: 6 And the children of Israel did evil **a** in H3254
11: 8 Therefore we turn **a** to thee now, that H7725
9 ye bring me home **a** to fight against the H7725
13 restore those *lands* **a** peaceably. H7725
14 And Jephthah sent messengers **a** unto H3254
13: 1 And the children of Israel did evil **a** in H3254
8 didst send come **a** unto us, and teach H5750
9 angel of God came **a** unto the woman H5750
15:19 his spirit came **a**, and he revived: H7725
16:22 began to grow **a** after he was shaven.
19: 3 *and* to bring her **a**, having his servant H7725
7 urged him: therefore he lodged there **a**. H7725
20:22 set their battle **a** in array in the place H3254
23 Shall I go up **a** to battle against the H3254
25 children of Israel **a** eighteen thousand H5750
28 saying, Shall I yet **a** go out to battle H3254
41 And when the men of Israel turned **a**, the
48 And the men of Israel turned **a** upon H7725
21:14 And Benjamin came **a** at that time; H7725
Ru 1:11 And Naomi said, Turn **a**, my daughters: H7725
12 Turn **a**, my daughters, go *your way*; for H7725
14 voice, and wept **a**: and Orpah kissed her H5750
21 brought me home **a** empty: why *then* H7725
4: 3 that is come **a** out of the country of H7725
1Sa 3: 5 lie down **a**. And he went and lay down. H7725
6 And the LORD called yet **a**, Samuel. H3254
6 I called not, my son; lie down **a**. H7725
8 And the LORD called Samuel **a** the H3254
21 And the LORD appeared **a** in Shiloh: H3254
4: 5 a great shout, so that the earth rang **a**.
5: 3 took Dagon, and set him in his place **a**. H7725
11 and let it go **a** to his own place, that H7725
6:21 have brought **a** the ark of the LORD; H7725
9: 8 And the servant answered Saul **a**, and H3254
15:25 my sin, and turn **a** with me, that I may H7725
30 Israel, and turn **a** with me, that I may H7725
31 So Samuel turned **a** after Saul; and H7725
16:10 **A**, Jesse made seven of his sons to pass
17:30 him **a** after the former manner. H7725
19: 8 And there was war **a**: and David went H3254
15 And Saul sent the messengers ***a*** to see
21 sent messengers **a** the third time, and H3254
20:17 And Jonathan caused David to swear **a**, H3254
23: 4 Then David inquired of the LORD yet **a**. H3254
23 and come ye **a** to me with the certainty, H7725
25:12 way, and went **a**, and came and told H7725
27: 4 Gath: and he sought no more **a** for him. H3254
29: 4 that he may go **a** to his place which H7725
30:12 his spirit came **a** to him: for he had H7725
2Sa 1: 9 He said unto me **a**, Stand, I pray thee,
2:22 And Abner said **a** to Asahel, H3254+H5750
3:11 word **a**, because he feared him. H3254+H5750
26 brought him **a** from the well of Sirah: H7725
34 And all the people wept **a** over him. H3254
5:22 And the Philistines came up yet **a**, and H3254
6: 1 **A**, David gathered together all *the* H5750
12:23 I bring him back **a**? I shall go to him, H7725
14:13 doth not fetch home **a** his banished. H7725
14 be gathered up **a**; neither doth God
21 bring the young man Absalom **a**. H7725
29 **a** the second time, he would not come. H5750
15: 8 shall bring me **a** indeed to Jerusalem, H7725
25 he will bring me **a**, and shew me *both* it, H7725
29 **a** to Jerusalem: and they tarried there. H7725
16:19 And **a**, whom should I serve? *should I* H8145
18:22 the son of Zadok yet **a** to Joab, But H3254
19:24 until the day he came ***a*** in peace.

2Sa 19:30 is come a in peace unto his own house. H7725
37 Let thy servant, I pray thee, turn back a, H7725
20:10 struck him not a; and he died. So Joab H8138
21:15 Moreover the Philistines had yet war a H5750
18 this, that there was a a battle with the H5750
19 And there was a a battle in Gob with H5750
22:38 not a until I had consumed them. H7725
24: 1 And a the anger of the LORD was H3254
1Ki 1:45 a. This *is* the noise that ye have heard. H1949
2:30 the king word a, saying, Thus said Joab, H7725
41 Jerusalem to Gath, and was come a. H7725
8:33 and shall turn a to thee, and confess H7725
34 and bring them a unto the land which H7725
12: 5 a to me. And the people departed. H7725
12 saying, Come to me a the third day. H7725
20 was come a, that they sent and called H7725
21 a to Rehoboam the son of Solomon. H7725
27 of this people turn a unto their lord, H7725
27 and go a to Rehoboam king of Judah. H7725
13: 4 so that he could not pull it in a to him. H7725
6 be restored me a. And the man of God H7725
6 him a, and became as *it was* before. H7725
9 a by the same way that thou camest. H7725
17 a to go by the way that thou camest. H7725
33 way, but made a of the lowest of the H7725
17:21 let this child's soul come into him a. H7725
22 child came into him a, and he revived. H7725
18:37 *that* thou hast turned their heart back a. H322
43 nothing. And he said, Go a seven times. H7725
19: 6 did eat and drink, and laid him down a. H7725
7 And the angel of the LORD came a the H7725
20 Go back a: for what have I done to thee? H7725
20: 5 And the messengers came a, and said, H7725
9 departed, and brought him word a. H7725
2Ki 1: 6 unto us, Go, turn a unto the king that H7725
11 A also he sent unto him another H7725
13 And he sent a a captain of the third H7725
2:18 And when they came a to him, (for he H7725
4:22 run to the man of God, and come a. H7725
29 answer him not a: and lay my staff upon
31 he went a to meet him, and told H7725
38 And Elisha came a to Gilgal: and *there* H7725
43 men? He said a, Give the people, that
5:10 come a to thee, and thou shalt be clean. H7725
14 and his flesh came a like unto the flesh H7725
26 the man turned a from his chariot to
7: 8 hid *it;* and came a, and entered into H7725
9:18 came to them, but he cometh not a. H7725
20 and cometh not a: and the driving *is* H7725
36 Wherefore they came a, and told him. H7725
13:25 of Jehoahaz took a out of the hand of H7725
19: 9 messengers a unto Hezekiah, saying, H7725
30 house of Judah shall yet a take root H3254
20: 5 Turn a, and tell Hezekiah the captain of H7725
21: 3 For he built up a the high places which H7725
22: 9 the king word a, and said, Thy servants H7725
20 And they brought the king word a. H7725
24: 7 And the king of Egypt came not a any H3254
1Ch 13: 3 And let us bring a the ark of our God to H5437
14:13 And the Philistines yet a spread H3254
14 Therefore David inquired a of God; H5750
20: 5 And there was war a with the H5750
6 And yet a there was war at Gath, where H5750
21:12 I shall bring a to him that sent me. H7725
27 up his sword a into the sheath thereof. H7725
2Ch 6:25 and bring them a unto the land which H7725
10: 5 And he said unto them, Come a unto H7725
12 saying, Come a to me on the third day. H7725
11: 1 bring the kingdom a to Rehoboam. H7725
12:11 them a into the guard chamber. H7725
13:20 recover strength a in the days of H5750
18:18 A he said, Therefore hear the word of the
32 they turned back a from pursuing him. H7725
19: 4 and he went out a through the people H7725
20:27 of them, to go a to Jerusalem with joy; H7725
24:11 it to his place a. Thus they did day by H7725
19 to bring them a unto the LORD; and H7725
25:10 to go home a: wherefore their anger
28:11 the captives a, which ye have taken
17 For a the Edomites had come and
30: 6 of Israel, turn a unto the LORD God H7725
9 For if ye turn a unto the LORD, your H7725
9 they shall come a into this land: for the H7725
32:25 But Hezekiah rendered not a according H7725
33: 3 For he built a the high places which H7725
13 and brought him a to Jerusalem into H7725
34:16 king word back a, saying, All that was H5750
28 same. So they brought the king word a. H7725
Ezr 2: 1 and came a unto Jerusalem and H7725
Ezr 4:13 the walls set up *a, then* will they not pay
16 if this city be builded a, and the walls
6: 5 and brought a unto the temple which H1946
21 which were come a out of captivity, H7725
9:14 Should we a break thy H7725
Neh 7: 6 away, and came a to Jerusalem and to H7725
8:17 that were come a out of the captivity H7725
9:28 But after they had rest, they did evil a H7725
29 bring them a unto thy law: yet they H7725
13: 9 thither brought I a the vessels of the H7725
21 wall? if ye do *so* a, I will lay hands on H8138
Est 4:10 A Esther spake unto Hatach, and gave
6:12 And Mordecai came a to the king's H7725
7: 2 And the king said a unto Esther on the H1571
8: 3 And Esther spake yet a before the king, H3254
Job 2: 1 A there was a day when the sons of God
6:29 yea, return a, my righteousness *is* in it. H5750
10: 9 clay; and wilt thou bring me into dust a? H7725
16 a fierce lion: and a thou shewest thyself H7725
12:14 and it cannot be built a: he shutteth up a
23 the nations, and straiteneth them *a*.
14: 7 that it will sprout a, and that the tender H5750
14 If a man die, shall he live *a*? all the days
20:15 up a: God shall cast them out of his belly.
29:22 After my words they spake not a; and H8138
34:15 and man shall turn a unto dust. H7725
Ps 18:37 did I turn a till they were consumed. H7725
37:21 and payeth not a: but the righteous H7999
60: 1 been displeased; O turn thyself to us a. H7725
68:22 The Lord said, I will bring a from H7725
22 *my people* a from the depths of the sea: H7725
71:20 shalt quicken me a, and shalt bring me H7725
20 me up a from the depths of the earth. H7725
78:39 that passeth away, and cometh not a. H7725
80: 3 Turn us a, O God, and cause thy face to H7725
7 Turn us a, O God of hosts, and cause H7725
19 Turn us a, O LORD God of hosts, cause H7725
85: 6 Wilt thou not revive us a: that thy H7725
8 saints: but let them not turn a to folly. H7725
104: 9 that they turn not a to cover the earth. H7725
107:26 they go down a to the depths: their soul
39 A, they are minished and brought low
126: 1 When the LORD turned a the captivity H7725
4 Turn a our captivity, O LORD, as the H7725
6 shall doubtless come a with rejoicing,
140:10 into deep pits, that they rise not up a.
Prv 2:19 None that go unto her return a, neither H7725
3:28 Go, and come a, and to morrow I will H7725
19:17 which he hath given will he pay him a. H7999
19 thou deliver *him*, yet thou must do it a. H3254
24 not so much as bring it to his mouth a. H7725
23:35 when shall I awake? I will seek it yet a. H5750
24:16 a: but the wicked shall fall into mischief.
26:15 grieveth him to bring it a to his mouth. H7725
Ecc 1: 6 returneth a according to his circuits. H7725
7 the rivers come, thither they return a. H7725
3:20 are of the dust, and all turn to dust a. H7725
4: 4 A, I considered all travail, and every
11 A, if two lie together, then they have H1571
8:14 of the wicked; a, there be wicked *men*,
Isa 7:10 Moreover the LORD spake a unto H3254
8: 5 The LORD spake also unto me a, H3254
10:20 shall no more a stay upon him that H3254
11:11 shall set his hand a the second time to H3254
24:20 upon it; and it shall fall, and not rise a. H3254
37:31 of Judah shall a take root downward, H3254
38: 8 Behold, I will bring a the shadow of the H7725
46: 8 bring *it* a to mind, O ye transgressors. H7725
49: 5 to bring Jacob a to him, Though Israel H7725
20 the other, shall say a in thine ears, The H5750
51:22 my fury; thou shalt no more drink it a: H5750
52: 8 eye, when the LORD shall bring a Zion. H7725
Jer 3: 1 he return unto her a? shall not that land H5750
1 yet return a to me, saith the LORD. H7725
12:15 and will bring them a, every man to his H7725
15:19 will I bring thee a, *and* thou shalt stand H7725
16:15 I will bring them a into their land that H7725
18: 4 so he made it a another vessel, as H7725
19:11 be made whole a: and they shall bury H5750
23: 3 will bring them a to their folds; and H7725
24: 4 A the word of the LORD came unto me,
6 I will bring them a to this land: and I H7725
25: 5 They said, Turn ye a now every one H7725
27:16 shortly be brought a from Babylon: for H7725
28: 3 Within two full years will I bring a into H7725
4 And I will bring a to this place Jeconiah H7725
6 to bring a the vessels of the LORD'S H7725
29:14 I will bring you a into the place whence H7725
30: 3 that I will bring a the captivity of my H7725
Jer 30:18 I will bring a the captivity of Jacob's H7725
31: 4 A I will build thee, and thou shalt be H5750
4 Israel: thou shalt a be adorned with thy H5750
16 come a from the land of the enemy. H7725
17 shall come a to their own border. H7725
21 thou wentest: turn a, O virgin of Israel, H7725
21 of Israel, turn a to these thy cities. H7725
23 when I shall bring a their captivity; The H7725
32:15 shall be possessed a in this land. H5750
37 I will bring them a unto this place, and H7725
33:10 Thus saith the LORD; A there shall be H5750
12 Thus saith the LORD of hosts; A in this H5750
13 the flocks pass a under the hands of H5750
36:28 Take thee a another roll, and write in it H7725
37: 8 And the Chaldeans shall come a, and H7725
41:16 whom he had brought a from Gibeon: H7725
46:16 and let us go a to our own people, H7725
48:47 Yet will I bring a the captivity of Moab H7725
49: 6 And afterward I will bring a the H7725
39 *that* I will bring a the captivity of Elam, H7725
50:19 And I will bring Israel a to his H7725
Lam 3:40 try our ways, and turn a to the LORD. H7725
Ezk 3:20 A, When a righteous *man* doth turn H7725
4: 6 them, lie a on thy right side, and H8145
5: 4 Then take of them a, and cast them into H5750
7: 7 not the sounding a of the mountains. H1906
8: 6 but turn thee yet a, *and* thou shalt see H5750
13 He said also unto me, Turn thee yet a, H5750
15 man? turn thee yet a, *and* thou shalt see H5750
11:14 A the word of the LORD came unto me,
12:26 A the word of the LORD came to me,
14:12 The word of the LORD came a to me,
16: 1 A the word of the LORD came unto me,
53 When I shall bring a their captivity, the H7725
53 then *will I bring a* the captivity of thy
18: 1 The word of the LORD came unto me a,
27 A, when the wicked *man* turneth away
21: 8 A the word of the LORD came unto me,
18 The word of the LORD came unto me a,
23: 1 The word of the LORD came a unto me,
24: 1 A in the ninth year, in the tenth month,
25: 1 The word of the LORD came a unto me,
26:21 never be found a, saith the Lord GOD. H5750
27: 1 The word of the LORD came a unto me,
28: 1 The word of the LORD came a unto me,
20 A the word of the LORD came unto me,
29:14 And I will bring a the captivity of H7725
30: 1 The word of the LORD came a unto me,
33: 1 A the word of the LORD came unto me,
14 A, when I say unto the wicked, Thou
15 *If* the wicked restore the pledge, give a H7999
34: 4 have ye brought a that which was H7725
16 lost, and bring a that which was driven H7725
37: 4 A he said unto me, Prophesy upon these
15 The word of the LORD came a unto me,
39:25 GOD; Now will I bring a the captivity of H7725
27 When I have brought them a from the H7725
47: 1 Afterward he brought me a unto the H7725
4 A he measured a thousand, and brought
4 *were* to the knees. A he measured a
Dan 2: 7 They answered a and said, Let the king H8579
9:25 a, and the wall, even in troublous times. H7725
10:18 Then there came a and touched me *one* H3254
Hos 1: 6 And she conceived a, and bare a H5750
Joel 3: 1 a the captivity of Judah and Jerusalem, H7725
Am 7: 8 I will not a pass by them any more: H3254
13 But prophesy not a any more at H3254
8: 2 I will not a pass by them any more. H3254
14 even they shall fall, and never rise up a. H5750
9:14 And I will bring a the captivity of my H7725
Jna 2: 4 yet I will look a toward thy holy temple. H3254
Mic 7:19 He will turn a, he will have compassion H7725
Zep 3:20 At that time will I bring you a, even in
Hag 2:20 And a the word of the LORD came unto H8145
Zec 2: 1 I lifted up mine eyes a, and looked, and
12 land, and shall choose Jerusalem a. H5750
4: 1 with me came a, and waked me, as a H7725
12 And I answered a, and said unto him, H8145
8: 1 A the word of the LORD of hosts came *to*
15 So a have I thought in these days to do H7725
10: 6 I will bring them a to place them; for I H7725
9 live with their children, and turn a. H7725
10 I will bring them a also out of the land H7725
12: 6 a in her own place, *even* in Jerusalem. H5750
Mal 2:13 And this have ye done a, covering the H8145
Mt 2: 8 bring me word a, that I may come and *G518*
4: 7 Jesus said unto him, It is written a, *G3825*
8 A, the devil taketh him up into an *G3825*
5:33 A, ye have heard that it hath been said *G3825*

Mt 7: 2 ye mete, it shall be measured to you **a**. G488
6 their feet, and turn **a** and rend you. G4762
11: 4 **a** those things which ye do hear and see: G518
13:44 **A**, the kingdom of heaven is like unto G3825
45 **A**, the kingdom of heaven is like unto a G3825
47 **A**, the kingdom of heaven is like unto a G3825
16:21 be killed, and be raised **a** the third day. G1453
17: 9 the Son of man be risen **a** from the dead. G450
23 **a**. And they were exceeding sorry. G1453
18:19 **A** I say unto you, That if two of you G3825
19:24 And **a** I say unto you, It is easier for a G3825
20: 5 **A** he went out about the sixth and G3825
19 *him*: and the third day he shall rise **a**. G450
21:36 **A**, he sent other servants more than the G3825
22: 1 unto them **a** by parables, and said, G3825
4 **A**, he sent forth other servants, saying, G3825
26:32 But after I am risen **a**, I will go before G1453
42 He went away **a** the second time, and G3825
43 And he came and found them asleep **a**: G3825
44 And he left them, and went away **a**, and G3825
52 Then said Jesus unto him, Put up **a** thy G654
72 And **a** he denied with an oath, I do not G3825
27: 3 and brought **a** the thirty pieces of silver G654
50 Jesus, when he had cried **a** with a loud G3825
63 yet alive, After three days I will rise **a**. G1453
Mk 2: 1 And **a** he entered into Capernaum after G3825
13 And he went forth **a** by the sea side; G3825
3: 1 And he entered **a** into the synagogue; G3825
20 And the multitude cometh together **a**, G3825
4: 1 And he began **a** to teach by the sea G3825
5:21 And when Jesus was passed over **a** by G3825
7:31 And **a**, departing from the coasts of G3825
8:13 the ship **a** departed to the other side. G3825
25 After that he put *his* hands **a** upon his G3825
31 and be killed, and after three days rise **a**. G450
10: 1 resort unto him **a**; and, as he was wont, G3825
1 and, as he was wont, he taught them **a**. G3825
10 asked him **a** of the same *matter*. G3825
24 Jesus answereth **a**, and saith unto them, G3825
32 And he took **a** the twelve, and began G3825
34 kill him: and the third day he shall rise **a**. G450
11:27 And they come **a** to Jerusalem: and as G3825
12: 4 And **a** he sent unto them another G3825
5 And **a** he sent another; and him they G3825
13:16 turn back **a** for to take up his garment. G3694
14:39 And **a** he went away, and prayed, and G3825
40 he found them asleep **a**, (for their eyes G3825
61 nothing. **A** the high priest asked G3825
69 And a maid saw him **a**, and began to G3825
70 And he denied it **a**. And a little after, G3825
70 that stood by said **a** to Peter, Surely G3825
15: 4 And Pilate asked him **a**, saying, G3825
12 And Pilate answered and said **a** unto G3825
13 And they cried out **a**, Crucify him. G3825
Lk 2:34 the fall and rising **a** of many in Israel; G386
45 back **a** to Jerusalem, seeking him. G5290
4:20 And he closed the book, and he gave *it* **a** G591
6:30 taketh away thy goods ask *them* not **a**. G523
34 also lend to sinners, to receive as much **a**. G618
35 hoping for nothing **a**; and your reward G560
38 withal it shall be measured to you **a**. G488
8:37 up into the ship, and returned back **a**. G5290
55 And her spirit came **a**, and she arose G1994
9: 8 that one of the old prophets was risen **a**. G450
19 that one of the old prophets is risen **a**. G450
39 that he foameth **a**, and bruising him G3326
42 child, and delivered him **a** to his father. G591
10: 6 rest upon it: if not, it shall turn to you **a**. G344
17 And the seventy returned **a** with joy, G5290
35 more, when I come **a**, I will repay thee. G1880
13:20 And **a** he said, Whereunto shall I liken G3825
14: 6 And they could not answer him **a** to G470
12 thee **a**, and a recompence be made thee. G479
15:24 For this my son was dead, and is alive **a**; G326
32 and is alive **a**; and was lost, and is found. G326
17: 4 in a day turn **a** to thee, saying, I repent; G1994
18:33 death: and the third day he shall rise **a**. G450
20:11 And **a** he sent another servant: and G4369
12 And **a** he sent a third: and they G4369
23:11 gorgeous robe, and sent him **a** to Pilate. G375
20 to release Jesus, spake **a** to them. G3825
24: 7 and be crucified, and the third day rise **a**. G450
Jn 1:35 **A** the next day after John stood, and G3825
3: 3 **a**, he cannot see the kingdom of God. G509
7 that I said unto thee, Ye must be born **a**. G509
4: 3 He left Judaea, and departed **a** into G3825
13 drinketh of this water shall thirst **a**: G3825
46 So Jesus came **a** into Cana of Galilee, G3825
54 This *is* **a** the second miracle *that* Jesus G3825
Jn 6:15 **a** into a mountain himself alone. G3825
39 but should raise it up **a** at the last day. G450
8: 2 And early in the morning he came **a** G3825
8 And **a** he stooped down, and wrote on G3825
12 Then spake Jesus **a** unto them, saying, G3825
21 Then said Jesus **a** unto them, I go my G3825
9:15 Then **a** the Pharisees also asked him G3825
17 They say unto the blind man **a**, What G3825
24 Then **a** called they the man that was G1537
26 Then said they to him **a**, What did he to G3825
27 ye hear *it* **a**? will ye also be his disciples? G3825
10: 7 Then said Jesus unto them **a**, Verily, G3825
17 lay down my life, that I might take it **a**. G3825
18 power to take it **a**. This commandment G3825
19 There was a division therefore **a** G3825
31 Then the Jews took up stones **a** to stone G3825
39 Therefore they sought **a** to take him: G3825
40 And went away **a** beyond Jordan into G3825
11: 7 to *his* disciples, Let us go into Judaea **a**. G3825
8 to stone thee; and goest thou thither **a**? G3825
23 saith unto her, Thy brother shall rise **a**. G450
24 rise **a** in the resurrection at the last day. G450
38 Jesus therefore **a** groaning in himself G3825
12:22 and **a** Andrew and Philip tell Jesus. G3825
28 both glorified *it*, and will glorify *it* **a**. G3825
39 not believe, because that Esaias said **a**, G3825
13:12 and was set down **a**, he said unto them, G3825
14: 3 you, I will come **a**, and receive you unto G3825
28 I go away, and come **a** unto you. If ye
16:16 not see me: and **a**, a little while, and ye G3825
17 not see me: and **a**, a little while, and ye G3825
19 **a**, a little while, and ye shall see me? G3825
22 but I will see you **a**, and your heart shall G3825
28 into the world: **a**, I leave the world, and G3825
18: 7 Then asked he them **a**, Whom seek ye? G3825
27 Peter then denied **a**: and immediately G3825
33 the judgment hall **a**, and called Jesus, G3825
38 this, he went out **a** unto the Jews, and G3825
40 Then cried they all **a**, saying, Not this G3825
19: 4 Pilate therefore went forth **a**, and saith G3825
9 And went **a** into the judgment hall, and G3825
37 And **a** another scripture saith, They G3825
20: 9 that he must rise **a** from the dead. G450
10 Then the disciples went away **a** unto G3825
21 Then said Jesus to them **a**, Peace *be* G3825
26 And after eight days **a** his disciples G3825
21: 1 shewed himself **a** to the disciples at the G3825
16 He saith to him **a** the second time, G3825
Act 1: 6 time restore **a** the kingdom to Israel? G600
7:26 set them at one **a**, saying, Sirs, ye are G1515
39 their hearts turned back **a** into Egypt, G4762
10:15 And the voice *spake* unto him **a** the G3825
16 vessel was received up **a** into heaven. G3825
11: 9 But the voice answered me **a** from G1537
10 and all were drawn up **a** into heaven. G3825
13:33 raised up Jesus **a**; as it is also written in G450
37 But he, whom God raised **a**, saw no G1453
14:21 many, they returned **a** to Lystra, and *to* G5290
15:16 After this I will return, and will build **a** G456
16 **a** the ruins thereof, and I will set it up: G456
36 Let us go **a** and visit our brethren G1994
17: 3 suffered, and risen **a** from the dead; and G450
32 said, We will hear thee **a** of this *matter*. G3825
18:21 but I will return **a** unto you, if God will. G3825
20:11 When he therefore was come up **a**, and G305
21: 6 took ship; and they returned home **a**. G5290
22:17 when I was come **a** to Jerusalem, even G5290
27:28 **a**, and found *it* fifteen fathoms. G3825
Ro 4:25 and was raised **a** for our justification. G1453
8:15 spirit of bondage **a** to fear; but ye have G3825
34 that is risen **a**, who is even at the right G1453
10: 7 is, to bring up Christ **a** from the dead.) G321
11:23 in: for God is able to graff them in **a**. G3825
35 and it shall be recompensed unto him **a**? G467
15:10 And **a** he saith, Rejoice, ye Gentiles, G3825
11 And **a**, Praise the Lord, all ye Gentiles; G3825
12 And **a**, Esaias saith, There shall be a G3825
1Co 3:20 And **a**, The Lord knoweth the thoughts G3825
7: 5 come together **a**, that Satan tempt you G3825
12:21 need of thee: nor **a** the head to the feet, G3825
15: 4 buried, and that he rose **a** the third day G1453
2Co 1:16 and to come **a** out of Macedonia unto G3825
2: 1 I would not come **a** to you in heaviness. G3825
3: 1 Do we begin **a** to commend ourselves? G3825
5:12 For we commend not ourselves **a** unto G3825
15 him which died for them, and rose **a**. G1453
10: 7 of himself think this **a**, that, as he *is* G3825
11:16 I say **a**, Let no man think me a fool; if G3825
12:19 **A**, think ye that we excuse ourselves G3825
2Co 12:21 *And* lest, when I come **a**, my God will G3825
13: 2 other, that, if I come **a**, I will not spare: G3825
Gal 1: 9 As we said before, so say I now **a**, If any G3825
17 and returned **a** unto Damascus. G3825
2: 1 Then fourteen years after I went up **a** G3825
18 For if I build **a** the things which I G3825
4: 9 of God, how turn ye **a** to the weak and G3825
9 whereunto ye desire **a** to be in bondage? G509
19 in birth **a** until Christ be formed in you, G3825
5: 1 entangled **a** with the yoke of bondage. G3825
3 For I testify **a** to every man that is G3825
Php 1:26 Christ for me by my coming to you **a**. G3825
2:28 when ye see him **a**, ye may rejoice, and G3825
4: 4 Rejoice in the Lord alway: *and* **a** I say, G3825
10 of me hath flourished **a**; wherein ye were G330
16 ye sent once and **a** unto my necessity. G1364
1Th 2:18 once and **a**; but Satan hindered us. G1364
3: 9 For what thanks can we render to God **a** G467
4:14 died and rose **a**, even so them also which G450
Tit 2: 9 *them* well in all *things*; not answering **a**; G483
Phlm 12 Whom I have sent **a**: thou therefore G375
Heb 1: 5 thee? And **a**, I will be to him a Father, G3825
6 And **a**, when he bringeth in the G3825
2:13 And **a**, I will put my trust in him. And G3825
13 trust in him. And **a**, Behold I and the G3825
4: 5 And in this *place* **a**, If they shall enter G3825
7 **A**, he limiteth a certain day, saying in G3825
5:12 that one teach you **a** which *be* the first G3825
6: 1 not laying **a** the foundation of G3825
6 If they shall fall away, to renew them **a** G3825
10: 3 remembrance **a** *made* of sins every year. G364
30 And **a**, The Lord shall judge his people. G3825
11:35 dead raised to life **a**: and others were G1537
13:20 Now the God of peace, that brought **a** G321
Jas 5:18 And he prayed **a**, and the heaven gave G3825
1Pt 1: 3 hath begotten us **a** unto a lively hope by G313
23 Being born **a**, not of corruptible seed, but G313
2:23 Who, when he was reviled, reviled not **a**; G486
2Pt 2:20 Christ, they are **a** entangled therein, G3825
22 to his own vomit **a**; and the sow that G1994
1Jn 2: 8 **A**, a new commandment I write unto G3825
Rev 10: 8 spake unto me **a**, and said, Go *and* take G3825
11 must prophesy **a** before many peoples, G3825
19: 3 And **a** they said, Alleluia. And her G1208
20: 5 But the rest of the dead lived not **a** until G326

AGAINST See the Appendix.

AGAR

Gal 4:24 which gendereth to bondage, which is **A**. G28
25 For this **A** is mount Sinai in Arabia, and G28

AGATE

Ex 28:19 And the third row a ligure, an **a**, and an H7618
39:12 And the third row, a ligure, an **a**, and H7618
Ezk 27:16 work, and fine linen, and coral, and **a**. H3539

AGATES

Isa 54:12 And I will make thy windows of **a**, and H3539

AGE

Gen 15:15 thou shalt be buried in a good old **a**. H7872
18:11 well stricken in **a**; *and* it ceased to be H3117
21: 2 a son in his old **a**, at the set time of H2208
7 for I have born *him* a son in his old **a**. H2208
24: 1 well stricken in **a**: and the LORD had H3117
25: 8 died in a good old **a**, an old man, and H7872
37: 3 the son of his old **a**: and he made him a H2208
44:20 a child of his old **a**, a little one; and his H2208
47:28 years: so the whole **a** of Jacob was an H3117
48:10 Now the eyes of Israel were dim for **a**, H2207
Nu 8:25 And from the **a** of fifty years they shall H1121
Jos 23: 1 Joshua waxed old *and* stricken in **a**. H3117
2 unto them, I am old *and* stricken in **a**: H3117
Jdg 8:32 died in a good old **a**, and was buried in H7872
Ru 4:15 of thine old **a**: for thy daughter in H7872
1Sa 2:33 house shall die in the flower of their **a**. H582
1Ki 14: 4 for his eyes were set by reason of his **a**. H7869
15:23 of his old **a** he was diseased in his feet. H2209
1Ch 23: 3 from the **a** of thirty years and upward: H1121
24 the **a** of twenty years and upward. H1121
29:28 And he died in a good old **a**, full of H7872
2Ch 36:17 for **a**: he gave *them* all into his hand. H3486
Job 5:26 Thou shalt come to *thy* grave in a full **a**, H3624
8: 8 For inquire, I pray thee, of the former **a**, H1755
11:17 And *thine* **a** shall be clearer than the H2465
30: 2 *profit* me, in whom old **a** was perished? H3624
Ps 39: 5 and mine **a** *is* as nothing before H2465
71: 9 Cast me not off in the time of old **a**; H2209

Ps 92:14 They shall still bring forth fruit in old a; H7872
Isa 38:12 Mine a is departed, and is removed H1755
46: 4 And even to your old a I am he; and H2209
Zec 8: 4 with his staff in his hand for very a. H3117
Mk 5:42 for she was of the a of twelve years. And
Lk 1:36 a son in her old a: and this is the sixth
2:36 she was of a great a, and had lived with G2250
3:23 about thirty years of a, being (as was
8:42 twelve years of a, and she lay a dying.
Jn 9:21 a; ask him: he shall speak for himself. G2244
23 Therefore said his parents, He is of a; G2244
1Co 7:36 the flower of her a, and need so require, G5230
Heb 5:14 that are of full a, even those who by G5046
11:11 she was past a, because she judged G2244

AGED
2Sa 19:32 Now Barzillai was a very a man, even H2204
Job 12:20 taketh away the understanding of the a. H2205
15:10 a men, much elder than thy father. H3453
29: 8 and the a arose, and stood up. H2205
32: 9 neither do the a understand judgment. H2205
Jer 6:11 the a with him that is full of days. H2205
Tit 2: 2 That the a men be sober, grave, G4246
3 The a women likewise, that they be in G4247
Phlm 9 an one as Paul the a, and now also a G4246

AGEE
2Sa 23:11 the son of A the Hararite. And the H89

AGES
Eph 2: 7 That in the a to come he might shew the G165
3: 5 Which in other a was not made known G1074
21 all a, world without end. Amen. G1074
Col 1:26 which hath been hid from a and from G165

AGO
1Sa 9:20 lost three days a, set not thy mind on H3117
2Ki 19:25 Hast thou not heard long a how I have H7350
Ezr 5:11 these many years a, which a great king H6928
Isa 22:11 unto him that fashioned it long a. H7350
37:26 Hast thou not heard long a, how I have H7350
Mt 11:21 repented long a in sackcloth and ashes. G3819
Mk 9:21 How long is it a since this came unto G5550
Lk 10:13 had a great while a repented, sitting in G3819
Act 10:30 And Cornelius said, Four days a I was G575
15: 7 that a good while a God made choice G575
2Co 8:10 to do, but also to be forward a year a. G575
9: 2 was ready a year a; and your zeal hath G575
12: 2 fourteen years a, (whether in the body, G4253

AGONE
1Sa 30:13 left me, because three days a I fell sick.

AGONY
Lk 22:44 And being in an a he prayed more G74

AGREE
Mt 5:25 A with thine adversary quickly, whiles G2132
18:19 That if two of you shall a on earth as G4856
20:13 didst not thou a with me for a penny? G4856
Mk 14:59 But neither so did their witness a G2470
Act 15:15 And to this a the words of the prophets; G4856
1Jn 5: 8 and the blood: and these three a in one. G1526
Rev 17:17 and to a, and give their G4160+G3391+G1106

AGREED
Am 3: 3 two walk together, except they be a? H3259
Mt 20: 2 And when he had a with the labourers G4856
Mk 14:56 him, but their witness a not together. G2470
Jn 9:22 for the Jews had a already, that if any G4934
Act 5: 9 is it that ye have a together to tempt G4856
40 And to him they a: and when they had G3982
23:20 And he said, The Jews have a to desire G4934
28:25 And when they a not among themselves, G800

AGREEMENT
2Ki 18:31 of Assyria, Make an a with me by a
Isa 28:15 and with hell are we at a; when the H2374
18 and your a with hell shall not stand; H2380
36:16 of Assyria, Make an a with me by a
Dan 11: 6 north to make an a: but she shall not H4339
2Co 6:16 And what a hath the temple of God G4783

AGREETH
Mk 14:70 a Galilaean, and thy speech a thereto. G3662
Lk 5:36 taken out of the new a not with the old. G4856

AGRIPPA
Act 25:13 And after certain days king A and G67
25:22 Then A said unto Festus, I would also G67
23 And on the morrow, when A was come, G67
24 And Festus said, King A, and all men G67
26 specially before thee, O king A, that, after G67
26: 1 Then A said unto Paul, Thou art G67
2 I think myself happy, king A, because I G67
7 sake, king A, I am accused of the Jews. G67
19 Whereupon, O king A, I was not G67
27 King A, believest thou the prophets? I G67
28 Then A said unto Paul, Almost thou G67
32 Then said A unto Festus, This man G67

AGROUND
Act 27:41 they ran the ship a; and the forepart G2027

AGUE
Lev 26:16 and the burning a, that shall consume H6920

AGUR
Prv 30: 1 The words of A the son of Jakeh, even H94

AH
Ps 35:25 Let them not say in their hearts, A, so H1889
Isa 1: 4 A sinful nation, a people laden with H1945
24 One of Israel, A, I will ease me of mine H1945
Jer 1: 6 Then said I, A, Lord GOD! behold, I H162
4:10 Then said I, A, Lord GOD! surely thou H162
14:13 Then said I, A, Lord GOD! behold, the H162
22:18 for him, saying, A my brother! or, Ah H1945
18 my brother! or, A sister! they shall not H1945
18 him, saying, A lord! or, Ah his glory! H1945
18 him, saying, Ah lord! or, A his glory! H1945
32:17 A Lord GOD! behold, thou hast made the H162
34: 5 lament thee, saying, A lord! for I have H1945
Ezk 4:14 Then said I, A Lord GOD! behold, my H162
9: 8 cried, and said, A Lord GOD! wilt thou H162
11:13 voice, and said, A Lord GOD! wilt thou H162
20:49 Then said I, A Lord GOD! they say of me, H162
21:15 be multiplied: a! it is made bright, it is H253
Mk 15:29 and saying, A, thou that destroyest G3758

AHA
Ps 35:21 and said, A, aha, our eye hath seen it. H1889
21 and said, Aha, a, our eye hath seen it. H1889
40:15 of their shame that say unto me, A, aha. H1889
15 of their shame that say unto me, Aha, a. H1889
70: 3 reward of their shame that say, A, aha. H1889
3 reward of their shame that say, Aha, a. H1889
Isa 44:16 A, I am warm, I have seen the fire: H1889
Ezk 25: 3 thou saidst, A, against my sanctuary, H1889
26: 2 Jerusalem, A, she is broken that was H1889
36: 2 said against you, A, even the ancient H1889

AHAB
1Ki 16:28 and A his son reigned in his stead. H256
29 king of Judah began A the son of Omri to H256
29 reign over Israel: and A the son of Omri H256
30 And A the son of Omri did evil in the H256
33 And A made a grove; and Ahab did H256
33 And Ahab made a grove; and A did H256
17: 1 Gilead, said unto A, As the LORD God of H256
18: 1 A; and I will send rain upon the earth. H256
2 And Elijah went to shew himself unto A. H256
3 And A called Obadiah, which was the H256
5 And A said unto Obadiah, Go into the H256
6 to pass throughout it: A went one way by H256
9 servant into the hand of A, to slay me? H256
12 I come and tell A, and he cannot find H256
16 So Obadiah went to meet A, and told H256
16 and told him: and A went to meet Elijah. H256
17 And it came to pass, when A saw Elijah, H256
17 saw Elijah, that A said unto him, Art H256
20 So A sent unto all the children of Israel, H256
41 And Elijah said unto A, Get thee up, eat H256
42 So A went up to eat and to drink. And H256
44 Go up, say unto A, Prepare thy chariot, H256
45 rain. And A rode, and went to Jezreel. H256
46 ran before A to the entrance of Jezreel. H256
19: 1 And A told Jezebel all that Elijah had H256
20: 2 And he sent messengers to A king of H256
13 a prophet unto A king of Israel, saying, H256
14 And A said, By whom? And he said, H256
34 Then said A, I will send thee away
21: 1 hard by the palace of A king of Samaria. H256
2 And A spake unto Naboth, saying, Give H256
3 And Naboth said to A, The LORD forbid H256
4 And A came into his house heavy and H256
15 dead, that Jezebel said to A, Arise, take H256
16 And it came to pass, when A heard that H256
1Ki 21:16 was dead, that A rose up to go down to H256
18 Arise, go down to meet A king of Israel, H256
20 And A said to Elijah, Hast thou found H256
21 and will cut off from A him that pisseth H256
24 Him that dieth of A in the city the dogs H256
25 But there was none like unto A, which H256
27 And it came to pass, when A heard those H256
29 Seest thou how A humbleth himself H256
22:20 shall persuade A, that he may go up and H256
39 Now the rest of the acts of A, and all that H256
40 So A slept with his fathers; and Ahaziah H256
41 in the fourth year of A king of Israel. H256
49 Then said Ahaziah the son of A unto H256
51 Ahaziah the son of A began to reign over H256
2Ki 1: 1 against Israel after the death of A. H256
3: 1 Now Jehoram the son of A began to H256
5 But it came to pass, when A was dead, H256
8:16 year of Joram the son of A king of Israel, H256
18 as did the house of A: for the daughter of H256
18 for the daughter of A was his wife: and H256
25 In the twelfth year of Joram the son of A H256
27 of the house of A, and did evil in the sight H256
27 as did the house of A: for he was the son H256
27 he was the son in law of the house of A. H256
28 And he went with Joram the son of A to H256
29 son of A in Jezreel, because he was sick. H256
9: 7 And thou shalt smite the house of A thy H256
8 For the whole house of A shall perish: H256
8 and I will cut off from A him that pisseth H256
9 And I will make the house of A like the H256
25 thou rode together after A his father, the H256
29 of A began Ahaziah to reign over Judah. H256
10: 1 And A had seventy sons in Samaria. H256
10 the house of A: for the LORD hath done H256
11 of the house of A in Jezreel, and all his H256
17 remained unto A in Samaria, till he had H256
18 said unto them, A served Baal a little; H256
30 unto the house of A according to all that H256
21: 3 a grove, as did A king of Israel; and H256
13 of the house of A: and I will wipe H256
2Ch 18: 1 in abundance, and joined affinity with A. H256
2 he went down to A to Samaria. And H256
2 to Samaria. And A killed sheep and oxen H256
3 And A king of Israel said unto H256
19 And the LORD said, Who shall entice A H256
21: 6 like as did the house of A: for he had the H256
6 had the daughter of A to wife: and he H256
13 of the house of A, and also hast slain thy H256
22: 3 of the house of A: for his mother was his H256
4 like the house of A: for they were his H256
5 Jehoram the son of A king of Israel to H256
6 son of A at Jezreel, because he was sick. H256
7 had anointed to cut off the house of A. H256
8 upon the house of A, and found the H256
Jer 29:21 God of Israel, of A the son of Kolaiah, H256
22 Zedekiah and like A, whom the king of H256
Mic 6:16 of the house of A, and ye walk in their H256

AHAB'S
1Ki 21: 8 So she wrote letters in A name, and H256
2Ki 10: 1 them that brought up A children, saying, H256

AHARAH
1Ch 8: 1 Ashbel the second, and A the third, H315

AHARHEL
1Ch 4: 8 and the families of A the son of Harum. H316

AHASAI
Neh 11:13 of Azareel, the son of A, the son of H273

AHASBAI
2Sa 23:34 Eliphelet the son of A, the son of the H308

AHASUERUS
Ezr 4: 6 And in the reign of A, in the beginning of H325
Est 1: 1 Now it came to pass in the days of A, H325
1 of Ahasuerus, (this is A which reigned, H325
2 That in those days, when the king A sat H325
9 royal house which belonged to king A. H325
10 that served in the presence of A the king, H325
15 of the king A by the chamberlains? H325
16 that are in all the provinces of the king A. H325
17 be reported, The king A commanded H325
19 more before king A; and let the king give H325
2: 1 the wrath of king A was appeased, he H325
12 to go in to king A, after that she had been H325
16 So Esther was taken unto king A into his H325
21 and sought to lay hand on the king A. H325

A

Est 3: 1 After these things did king **A** promote H325
6 of **A**, *even* the people of Mordecai. H325
7 year of king **A**, they cast Pur, that *is*, H325
8 And Haman said unto king **A**, There is a H325
12 in the name of king **A** was it written, and H325
6: 2 who sought to lay hand on the king **A**. H325
7: 5 Then the king **A** answered and said unto H325
8: 1 On that day did the king **A** give the H325
7 Then the king **A** said unto Esther the H325
12 provinces of king **A**, *namely*, upon the H325
9: 2 of the king **A**, to lay hand on such H325
20 of the king **A**, *both* nigh and far, H325
30 of **A**, *with* words of peace and truth, H325
10: 1 And the king **A** laid a tribute upon the H325
3 *was* next unto king **A**, and great among H325
Dan 9: 1 In the first year of Darius the son of **A**, of H325

AHASUERUS'
Est 8:10 And he wrote in the king **A** name, and H325

AHAVA
Ezr 8:15 that runneth to **A**; and there abode we H163
21 at the river of **A**, that we might afflict H163
31 Then we departed from the river of **A** on H163

AHAZ
2Ki 15:38 and **A** his son reigned in his stead. H271
16: 1 the son of Remaliah **A** the son of Jotham H271
2 Twenty years old *was* **A** when he began H271
5 besieged **A**, but could not overcome *him*. H271
7 So **A** sent messengers to Tiglath-pileser H271
8 And **A** took the silver and gold that was H271
10 And king **A** went to Damascus to meet H271
10 and king **A** sent to Urijah the priest H271
11 to all that king **A** had sent from H271
11 *it* against king **A** came from Damascus. H271
15 And king **A** commanded Urijah the H271
16 to all that king **A** commanded. H271
17 And king **A** cut off the borders of the H271
19 Now the rest of the acts of **A** which he H271
20 And **A** slept with his fathers, and was H271
17: 1 In the twelfth year of **A** king of Judah H271
18: 1 son of **A** king of Judah began to reign. H271
20:11 which it had gone down in the dial of **A**. H271
23:12 upper chamber of **A**, which the kings of H271
1Ch 3:13 **A** his son, Hezekiah his son, Manasseh H271
8:35 Pithon, and Melech, and Tarea, and **A**. H271
36 And **A** begat Jehoadah; and Jehoadah H271
9:41 Pithon, and Melech, and Tahrea, *and* **A**.
42 And **A** begat Jarah; and Jarah begat H271
2Ch 27: 9 and **A** his son reigned in his stead. H271
28: 1 **A** *was* twenty years old when he began H271
16 At that time did king **A** send unto the H271
19 low because of **A** king of Israel; for he H271
21 For **A** took away a portion *out* of the H271
22 against the LORD: this *is that* king **A**. H271
24 And **A** gathered together the vessels of H271
27 And **A** slept with his fathers, and they H271
29:19 Moreover all the vessels, which king **A** in H271
Isa 1: 1 Jotham, **A**, *and* Hezekiah, kings of Judah. H271
7: 1 And it came to pass in the days of **A** the H271
3 Go forth now to meet **A**, thou, and H271
10 Moreover the LORD spake again unto **A**, H271
12 But **A** said, I will not ask, neither will I H271
14:28 In the year that king **A** died was this H271
38: 8 down in the sun dial of **A**, ten degrees H271
Hos 1: 1 of Uzziah, Jotham, **A**, *and* Hezekiah, H271
Mic 1: 1 days of Jotham, **A**, *and* Hezekiah, kings H271

AHAZIAH
1Ki 22:40 So Ahab slept with his fathers; and **A** his H274
49 Then said **A** the son of Ahab unto H274
51 **A** the son of Ahab began to reign over H274
2Ki 1: 2 And **A** fell down through a lattice in his H274
18 Now the rest of the acts of **A** which he H274
8:24 and **A** his son reigned in his stead. H274
25 king of Israel did **A** the son of Jehoram H274
26 Two and twenty years old *was* **A** when H274
29 king of Syria. And **A** the son of Jehoram H274
9:16 lay there. And **A** king of Judah was come H274
21 king of Israel and **A** king of Judah went H274
23 said to **A**, *There is* treachery, O Ahaziah. H274
23 said to Ahaziah, *There is* treachery, O **A**. H274
27 But when **A** the king of Judah saw *this*, H274
29 of Ahab began **A** to reign over Judah. H274
10:13 Jehu met with the brethren of **A** king of H274
13 *are* the brethren of **A**; and we go down to H274
11: 1 And when Athaliah the mother of **A** saw H274
2 Joram, sister of **A**, took Joash the son of H274
2Ki 11: 2 Joash the son of **A**, and stole him from H274
12:18 and Jehoram, and **A**, his fathers, kings of H274
13: 1 year of Joash the son of **A** king of Judah H274
14:13 Jehoash the son of **A**, at Beth-she-mesh, H274
1Ch 3:11 Joram his son, **A** his son, Joash his son, H274
2Ch 20:35 **A** king of Israel, who did very wickedly: H274
37 joined thyself with **A**, the LORD hath H274
22: 1 of Jerusalem made **A** his youngest son H274
1 all the eldest. So **A** the son of Jehoram H274
2 Forty and two years old *was* **A** when he H274
7 And the destruction of **A** was of God by H274
8 of the brethren of **A**, that ministered to H274
8 that ministered to **A**, he slew them. H274
9 And he sought **A**: and they caught him, H274
9 So the house of **A** had no power to keep H274
10 But when Athaliah the mother of **A** saw H274
11 Joash the son of **A**, and stole him from H274
11 she was the sister of **A**,) hid him from H274

AHBAN
1Ch 2:29 Abihail, and she bare him **A**, and Molid. H257

AHER
1Ch 7:12 children of Ir, *and* Hushim, the sons of **A**. H313

AHI
1Ch 5:15 **A** the son of Abdiel, the son of Guni, H277
7:34 And the sons of Shamer; **A**, and Rohgah, H277

AHIAH
1Sa 14: 3 And **A**, the son of Ahitub, Ichabod's H281
18 And Saul said unto **A**, Bring hither the H281
1Ki 4: 3 Elihoreph and **A**, the sons of Shisha, H281
1Ch 8: 7 And Naaman, and **A**, and Gera, he H281

AHIAM
2Sa 23:33 Shammah the Hararite, **A** the son of H279
1Ch 11:35 **A** the son of Sacar the Hararite, Eliphal H279

AHIAN
1Ch 7:19 And the sons of Shemida were, **A**, and H291

AHIEZER
Nu 1:12 Of Dan; **A** the son of Ammishaddai. H295
2:25 Dan *shall be* **A** the son of Ammishaddai. H295
7:66 On the tenth day **A** the son of H295
71 offering of **A** the son of Ammishaddai. H295
10:25 his host *was* **A** the son of Ammishaddai. H295
1Ch 12: 3 The chief *was* **A**, then Joash, the sons of H295

AHIHUD
Nu 34:27 children of Asher, **A** the son of Shelomi. H282
1Ch 8: 7 removed them, and begat Uzza, and **A**. H284

AHIJAH
1Ki 11:29 that the prophet **A** the Shilonite found H281
30 And **A** caught the new garment that *was* H281
12:15 the LORD spake by **A** the Shilonite unto H281
14: 2 behold, there *is* **A** the prophet, which H281
4 to the house of **A**. But Ahijah could not H281
4 of Ahijah. But **A** could not see; for his H281
5 And the LORD said unto **A**, Behold, the H281
6 And it was *so*, when **A** heard the sound H281
18 by the hand of his servant **A** the prophet. H281
15:27 And Baasha the son of **A**, of the house of H281
29 he spake by his servant **A** the Shilonite: H281
33 Baasha the son of **A** to reign over all H281
21:22 Baasha the son of **A**, for the provocation H281
2Ki 9: 9 like the house of Baasha the son of **A**: H281
1Ch 2:25 and Bunah, and Oren, and Ozem, *and* **A**. H281
11:36 Hepher the Mecherathite, **A** the Pelonite, H281
26:20 And of the Levites, **A** *was* over the H281
2Ch 9:29 in the prophecy of **A** the Shilonite, and H281
10:15 spake by the hand of **A** the Shilonite to H281
Neh 10:26 And **A**, Hanan, Anan, H281

AHIKAM
2Ki 22:12 the priest, and **A** the son of Shaphan, H296
14 So Hilkiah the priest, and **A**, and Achbor, H296
25:22 the son of **A**, the son of Shaphan, ruler. H296
2Ch 34:20 Hilkiah, and **A** the son of Shaphan, H296
Jer 26:24 Nevertheless the hand of **A** the son of H296
39:14 the son of **A** the son of Shaphan, H296
40: 5 the son of **A** the son of Shaphan, H296
6 the son of **A** to Mizpah; and dwelt H296
7 the son of **A** governor in the land, H296
9 And Gedaliah the son of **A** the son of H296
11 the son of **A** the son of Shaphan; H296
14 Gedaliah the son of **A** believed them not. H296
Jer 40:16 But Gedaliah the son of **A** said unto H296
41: 1 the son of **A** to Mizpah; and there H296
2 the son of **A** the son of Shaphan H296
6 them, Come to Gedaliah the son of **A**. H296
10 the son of **A**: and Ishmael the son H296
16 the son of **A**, *even* mighty men of H296
18 the son of **A**, whom the king of Babylon H296
43: 6 the son of **A** the son of Shaphan, H296

AHILUD
2Sa 8:16 Jehoshaphat the son of **A** *was* recorder; H286
20:24 Jehoshaphat the son of **A** *was* recorder: H286
1Ki 4: 3 Jehoshaphat the son of **A**, the recorder. H286
12 Baana the son of **A**; *to him pertained* H286
1Ch 18:15 and Jehoshaphat the son of **A**, recorder. H286

AHIMAAZ
1Sa 14:50 the daughter of **A**: and the name of the H290
2Sa 15:27 your two sons with you, **A** thy son, and H290
36 them their two sons, **A** Zadok's *son*, and H290
17:17 Now Jonathan and **A** stayed by En-rogel; H290
20 they said, Where *is* **A** and Jonathan? H290
18:19 Then said **A** the son of Zadok, Let me H290
22 Then said **A** the son of Zadok yet again H290
23 him, Run. Then **A** ran by the way of the H290
27 is like the running of **A** the son of Zadok. H290
28 And **A** called, and said unto the king, All H290
29 safe? And **A** answered, When Joab H290
1Ki 4:15 **A** *was* in Naphtali; he also took Basmath H290
1Ch 6: 8 Ahitub begat Zadok, and Zadok begat **A**, H290
9 And **A** begat Azariah, and Azariah begat H290
53 Zadok his son, **A** his son. H290

AHIMAN
Nu 13:22 Hebron; where **A**, Sheshai, and Talmai, H289
Jos 15:14 and **A**, and Talmai, the children of Anak. H289
Jdg 1:10 they slew Sheshai, and **A**, and Talmai. H289
1Ch 9:17 and Talmon, and **A**, and their brethren: H289

AHIMELECH
1Sa 21: 1 Then came David to Nob to **A** the priest: H288
1 the priest: and **A** was afraid at the H288
2 And David said unto **A** the priest, The H288
8 And David said unto **A**, And is there not H288
22: 9 coming to Nob, to **A** the son of Ahitub. H288
11 Then the king sent to call **A** the priest, H288
14 Then **A** answered the king, and said, H288
16 die, **A**, thou, and all thy father's house. H288
20 And one of the sons of **A** the son of H288
23: 6 the son of **A** fled to David to Keilah, H288
26: 6 Then answered David and said to **A** the H288
2Sa 8:17 And Zadok the son of Ahitub, and **A** the H288
1Ch 24: 3 of Eleazar, and **A** of the sons of Ithamar, H288
6 the priest, and **A** the son of Abiathar, H288
31 and Zadok, and **A**, and the chief of the H288
Ps 52:ttl him, David is come to the house of **A**. H288

AHIMELECH'S
1Sa 30: 7 And David said to Abiathar the priest, **A** H288

AHIMOTH
1Ch 6:25 And the sons of Elkanah; Amasai, and **A**. H287

AHINADAB
1Ki 4:14 **A** the son of Iddo *had* Mahanaim: H292

AHINOAM
1Sa 14:50 And the name of Saul's wife *was* **A**, the H293
25:43 David also took **A** of Jezreel; and they H293
27: 3 with his two wives, **A** the Jezreelitess, H293
30: 5 taken captives, **A** the Jezreelitess, and H293
2Sa 2: 2 his two wives also, **A** the Jezreelitess, H293
3: 2 was Amnon, of **A** the Jezreelitess; H293
1Ch 3: 1 Amnon, of **A** the Jezreelitess; the second H293

AHIO
2Sa 6: 3 and Uzzah and **A**, the sons of Abinadab, H283
4 ark of God: and **A** went before the ark. H283
1Ch 8:14 And **A**, Shashak, and Jeremoth, H283
31 And Gedor, and **A**, and Zacher. H283
9:37 And Gedor, and **A**, and Zechariah, and H283
13: 7 and Uzza and **A** drave the cart. H283

AHIRA
Nu 1:15 Of Naphtali; **A** the son of Enan. H299
2:29 of Naphtali *shall be* **A** the son of Enan. H299
7:78 On the twelfth day **A** the son of Enan, H299
83 *was* the offering of **A** the son of Enan. H299
10:27 of Naphtali *was* **A** the son of Enan. H299

AHIRAM
Nu 26:38 of **A**, the family of the Ahiramites: H297

AHIRAMITES
Nu 26:38 of Ahiram, the family of the **A**: H298

AHISAMACH
Ex 31: 6 Aholiab, the son of **A**, of the tribe of Dan: H294
35:34 Aholiab, the son of **A**, of the tribe of Dan. H294
38:23 And with him *was* Aholiab, son of **A**, of H294

AHISHAHAR
1Ch 7:10 and Zethan, and Tharshish, and **A**. H300

AHISHAR
1Ki 4: 6 And **A** *was* over the household: and H301

AHITHOPHEL
2Sa 15:12 And Absalom sent for **A** the Gilonite, H302
31 And *one* told David, saying, **A** *is* among H302
31 turn the counsel of **A** into foolishness. H302
34 thou for me defeat the counsel of **A**. H302
16:15 came to Jerusalem, and **A** with him. H302
20 Then said Absalom to **A**, Give counsel H302
21 And **A** said unto Absalom, Go in unto H302
23 And the counsel of **A**, which he H302
23 of **A** both with David and with Absalom. H302
17: 1 Moreover **A** said unto Absalom, Let me H302
6 unto him, saying, **A** hath spoken after H302
7 **A** hath given *is* not good at this time. H302
14 than the counsel of **A**. For the LORD had H302
14 good counsel of **A**, to the intent that the H302
15 Thus and thus did **A** counsel Absalom H302
21 for thus hath **A** counselled against you. H302
23 And when **A** saw that his counsel was H302
23:34 Eliam the son of **A** the Gilonite, H302
1Ch 27:33 And **A** *was* the king's counsellor: and H302
34 And after **A** *was* Jehoiada the son of H302

AHITUB
1Sa 14: 3 And Ahiah, the son of **A**, Ichabod's H285
22: 9 to Nob, to Ahimelech the son of **A**. H285
11 priest, the son of **A**, and all his father's H285
12 And Saul said, Hear now, thou son of **A**. H285
20 the son of **A**, named Abiathar, escaped, H285
2Sa 8:17 And Zadok the son of **A**, and Ahimelech H285
1Ch 6: 7 begat Amariah, and Amariah begat **A**, H285
8 And **A** begat Zadok, and Zadok begat H285
11 begat Amariah, and Amariah begat **A**, H285
12 And **A** begat Zadok, and Zadok begat H285
52 Meraioth his son, Amariah his son, **A** H285
9:11 son of **A**, the ruler of the house of God; H285
18:16 And Zadok the son of **A**, and Abimelech H285
Ezr 7: 2 Shallum, the son of Zadok, the son of **A**, H285
Neh 11:11 of **A**, *was* the ruler of the house of God. H285

AHLAB
Jdg 1:31 of Zidon, nor of **A**, nor of Achzib, nor of H303

AHLAI
1Ch 2:31 Sheshan. And the children of Sheshan; **A**. H304
11:41 Uriah the Hittite, Zabad the son of **A**, H304

AHOAH
1Ch 8: 4 And Abishua, and Naaman, and **A**, H265

AHOHITE
2Sa 23: 9 the son of Dodo the **A**, *one* of the three H266
28 Zalmon the **A**, Maharai the H266
1Ch 11:12 the **A**, who *was one* of the three mighties. H266
29 Sibbecai the Hushathite, Ilai the **A**, H266
27: 4 *was* Dodai an **A**, and of his course *was* H266

AHOLAH
Ezk 23: 4 And the names of them *were* **A** the elder, H170
4 Samaria *is* **A**, and Jerusalem Aholibah. H170
5 And **A** played the harlot when she was H170
36 wilt thou judge **A** and Aholibah? yea, H170
44 **A** and unto Aholibah, the lewd women. H170

AHOLIAB
Ex 31: 6 And I, behold, I have given with him **A**, H171
35:34 *both* he, and **A**, the son of Ahisamach, H171
36: 1 Then wrought Bezaleel and **A**, and every H171
2 And Moses called Bezaleel and **A**, and H171
38:23 And with him *was* **A**, son of Ahisamach, H171

AHOLIBAH
Ezk 23: 4 the elder, and **A** her sister: and they H172
4 Samaria *is* Aholah, and Jerusalem **A**. H172
11 And when her sister **A** saw *this*, she was H172
22 Therefore, O **A**, thus saith the Lord GOD; H172
36 judge Aholah and **A**? yea, declare unto H172
44 Aholah and unto **A**, the lewd women. H172

AHOLIBAMAH
Gen 36: 2 the Hittite, and **A** the daughter of Anah H173
5 And **A** bare Jeush, and Jaalam, and H173
14 And these were the sons of **A**, the H173
18 And these *are* the sons of **A** Esau's wife; H173
18 of **A** the daughter of Anah, Esau's wife. H173
25 Dishon, and **A** the daughter of Anah. H173
41 Duke **A**, duke Elah, duke Pinon, H173
1Ch 1:52 Duke **A**, duke Elah, duke Pinon, H173

AHUMAI
1Ch 4: 2 and Jahath begat **A**, and Lahad. These H267

AHUZAM
1Ch 4: 6 And Naarah bare him **A**, and Hepher, H275

AHUZZATH
Gen 26:26 from Gerar, and **A** one of his friends, H276

AI
Jos 7: 2 And Joshua sent men from Jericho to **A**, H5857
2 And the men went up and viewed **A**. H5857
3 go up and smite **A**; *and* make not all the H5857
4 men: and they fled before the men of **A**. H5857
5 And the men of **A** smote of them about H5857
8: 1 arise, go up to **A**: see, I have given into H5857
1 hand the king of **A**, and his people, and H5857
2 And thou shalt do to **A** and her king as H5857
3 to go up against **A**: and Joshua chose H5857
9 Beth-el and **A**, on the west side of Ai: H5857
9 on the west side of **A**: but Joshua lodged H5857
10 elders of Israel, before the people to **A**. H5857
11 on the north side of **A**: now *there was* a H5857
11 *there was* a valley between them and **A**. H5857
12 and **A**, on the west side of the city. H5857
14 when the king of **A** saw *it*, that they H5857
16 And all the people that *were* in **A** were H5892
17 And there was not a man left in **A** or H5857
18 thy hand toward **A**; for I will give it into H5857
20 And when the men of **A** looked behind H5857
21 turned again, and slew the men of **A**. H5857
23 And the king of **A** they took alive, and H5857
24 the inhabitants of **A** in the field, in the H5857
24 returned unto **A**, and smote it with the H5857
25 twelve thousand, *even* all the men of **A**. H5857
26 destroyed all the inhabitants of **A**. H5857
28 And Joshua burnt **A**, and made it an H5857
29 And the king of **A** he hanged on a tree H5857
9: 3 Joshua had done unto Jericho and to **A**, H5857
10: 1 Joshua had taken **A**, and had utterly H5857
1 so he had done to **A** and her king; and H5857
2 **A**, and all the men thereof *were* mighty. H5857
12: 9 The king of Jericho, one; the king of **A**, H5857
Ezr 2:28 The men of Beth-el and **A**, two hundred H5857
Neh 7:32 The men of Beth-el and **A**, an hundred H5857
Jer 49: 3 Howl, O Heshbon, for **A** is spoiled: cry, H5857

AIAH
2Sa 3: 7 the daughter of **A**: and *Ish-bosheth* said H345
21: 8 the daughter of **A**, whom she bare unto H345
10 And Rizpah the daughter of **A** took H345
11 of **A**, the concubine of Saul, had done. H345
1Ch 1:40 And the sons of Zibeon; **A**, and Anah. H345

AIATH
Isa 10:28 He is come to **A**, he is passed to Migron; H5857

AIDED
Jdg 9:24 **a** him in the killing of his brethren. H2388

AIJA
Neh 11:31 **A**, and Beth-el, and *in* their villages, H5857

AIJALON
Jos 21:24 **A** with her suburbs, Gath-rimmon with H357
Jdg 1:35 in mount Heres in **A**, and in Shaalbim: H357
12:12 buried in **A** in the country of Zebulun. H357
1Sa 14:31 to **A**: and the people were very faint. H357
1Ch 6:69 And **A** with her suburbs, and H357
8:13 the inhabitants of **A**, who drove away the H357
2Ch 11:10 And Zorah, and **A**, and Hebron, which H357

AIJELETH
Ps 22:ttl To the chief Musician upon **A** Shahar, A H365

AILED
Ps 114: 5 What ***a*** thee, O thou sea, that thou

AILETH
Gen 21:17 unto her, What **a** thee, Hagar? fear not;
Jdg 18:23 said unto Micah, What **a** thee, that thou
24 *is* this *that* ye say unto me, What **a** thee?
1Sa 11: 5 Saul said, What ***a*** the people that they
2Sa 14: 5 And the king said unto her, What **a** thee?
2Ki 6:28 And the king said unto her, What **a** thee?
Isa 22: 1 of vision. What **a** thee now, that thou

AIN
Nu 34:11 on the east side of **A**; and the border H5871
Jos 15:32 And Lebaoth, and Shilhim, and **A**, and H5871
19: 7 **A**, Remmon, and Ether, and Ashan; H5871
21:16 And **A** with her suburbs, and Juttah H5871
1Ch 4:32 And their villages *were*, Etam, and **A**, H5871

AIR
Gen 1:26 the fowl of the **a**, and over the cattle, H8064
28 the fowl of the **a**, and over every living H8064
30 to every fowl of the **a**, and to every thing H8064
2:19 every fowl of the **a**; and brought *them* H8064
20 to the fowl of the **a**, and to every beast H8064
6: 7 the fowls of the **a**; for it repenteth me H8064
7: 3 Of fowls also of the **a** by sevens, the H8064
9: 2 upon every fowl of the **a**, upon all that H8064
Dt 4:17 of any winged fowl that flieth in the **a**, H8064
28:26 all fowls of the **a**, and unto the beasts H8064
1Sa 17:44 of the **a**, and to the beasts of the field. H8064
46 the fowls of the **a**, and to the wild beasts H8064
2Sa 21:10 the birds of the **a** to rest on them by H8064
1Ki 14:11 the **a** eat: for the LORD hath spoken *it*. H8064
16: 4 in the fields shall the fowls of the **a** eat. H8064
21:24 in the field shall the fowls of the **a** eat. H8064
Job 12: 7 fowls of the **a**, and they shall tell thee: H8064
28:21 and kept close from the fowls of the **a**. H8064
41:16 One is so near to another, that no **a** can H7307
Ps 8: 8 The fowl of the **a**, and the fish of the H8064
Prv 30:19 The way of an eagle in the **a**; the way of H8064
Ecc 10:20 for a bird of the **a** shall carry the voice, H8064
Mt 6:26 Behold the fowls of the **a**: for they sow *G3772*
8:20 the birds of the **a** *have* nests; but the *G3772*
13:32 the birds of the **a** come and lodge in the *G3772*
Mk 4: 4 fowls of the **a** came and devoured it up. *G3772*
32 the **a** may lodge under the shadow of it. *G3772*
Lk 8: 5 and the fowls of the **a** devoured it. *G3772*
9:58 and birds of the **a** *have* nests; but the *G3772*
13:19 of the **a** lodged in the branches of it. *G3772*
Act 10:12 and creeping things, and fowls of the **a**. *G3772*
11: 6 and creeping things, and fowls of the **a**. *G3772*
22:23 *their* clothes, and threw dust into the **a**, *G109*
1Co 9:26 so fight I, not as one that beateth the **a**: *G109*
14: 9 is spoken? for ye shall speak into the **a**. *G109*
Eph 2: 2 of the power of the **a**, the spirit that now *G109*
1Th 4:17 **a**: and so shall we ever be with the Lord. *G109*
Rev 9: 2 and the sun and the **a** were darkened by *G109*
16:17 out his vial into the **a**; and there came a *G109*

AJAH
Gen 36:24 of Zibeon; both **A**, and Anah: this *was* H345

AJALON
Jos 10:12 and thou, Moon, in the valley of **A**. H357
19:42 And Shaalabbin, and **A**, and Jethlah, H357
2Ch 28:18 and **A**, and Gederoth, and Shocho H357

AKAN
Gen 36:27 *are* these; Bilhan, and Zaavan, and **A**. H6130

AKKUB
1Ch 3:24 and Pelaiah, and **A**, and Johanan, and H6126
9:17 And the porters *were*, Shallum, and **A**, H6126
Ezr 2:42 the children of **A**, the children of Hatita, H6126
45 children of Hagabah, the children of **A**, H6126
Neh 7:45 the children of **A**, the children of Hatita, H6126
8: 7 and Sherebiah, Jamin, **A**, Shabbethai, H6126
11:19 Moreover the porters, **A**, Talmon, and H6126
12:25 Talmon, **A**, *were* porters keeping H6126

AKRABBIM
Nu 34: 4 to the ascent of **A**, and pass on to Zin: H6137
Jdg 1:36 up to **A**, from the rock, and upward. H6137

ALABASTER
Mt 26: 7 woman having an a box of very precious G211
Mk 14: 3 a woman having an a box of ointment of G211
Lk 7:37 house, brought an a box of ointment, G211

ALABASTER-BOX See ALABASTER and BOX.

ALAMETH
1Ch 7: 8 and A. All these are the sons of Becher. H5964

ALAMMELECH
Jos 19:26 And A, and Amad, and Misheal; and H487

ALAMOTH
1Ch 15:20 and Benaiah, with psalteries on A; H5961
Ps 46:ttl for the sons of Korah, A Song upon A. H5961

ALARM
Nu 10: 5 When ye blow an a, then the camps that H8643
6 When ye blow an a the second time, H8643
6 they shall blow an a for their journeys. H8643
7 shall blow, but ye shall not sound an a. H7321
9 ye shall blow an a with the trumpets; H7321
2Ch 13:12 trumpets to cry a against you. O H7321
Jer 4:19 the sound of the trumpet, the a of war. H8643
49: 2 I will cause an a of war to be heard in H8643
Joel 2: 1 and sound an a in my holy mountain: H7321
Zep 1:16 A day of the trumpet and a against the H8643

ALAS
Nu 12:11 And Aaron said unto Moses, A, my lord, H994
24:23 And he took up his parable, and said, A, H188
Jos 7: 7 And Joshua said, A, O Lord GOD, H162
Jdg 6:22 Gideon said, A, O Lord GOD! for because H162
11:35 clothes, and said, A, my daughter! thou H162
1Ki 13:30 over him, saying, A, my brother! H1945
2Ki 3:10 And the king of Israel said, A! that the H162
6: 5 and said, A, master! for it was borrowed. H162
15 him, A, my master! how shall we do? H162
Jer 30: 7 A! for that day is great, so that none is H1945
Ezk 6:11 with thy foot, and say, A for all the evil H253
Joel 1:15 A for the day! for the day of the LORD is H162
Am 5:16 all the highways, A! alas! and they shall H1930
16 highways, Alas! a! and they shall call H1930
Rev 18:10 torment, saying, A, alas that great city G3759
10 saying, Alas, a that great city Babylon, G3759
16 And saying, A, alas, that great city, that G3759
16 And saying, Alas, a, that great city, that G3759
19 wailing, saying, A, alas, that great city, G3759
19 saying, Alas, a, that great city, wherein G3759

ALBEIT
Ezk 13: 7 The LORD saith it; a I have not spoken?
Phlm 19 I will repay it: a I do not say to thee G2443

ALEMETH
1Ch 6:60 her suburbs, and A with her suburbs, H5964
8:36 Jehoadah begat A, and Azmaveth, and H5964
9:42 and Jarah begat A, and Azmaveth, and H5964

ALEXANDER
Mk 15:21 father of A and Rufus, to bear his cross. G223
Act 4: 6 and John, and A, and as many as were G223
19:33 And they drew A out of the multitude, G223
33 him forward. And A beckoned with the G223
1Ti 1:20 Of whom is Hymenaeus and A; whom I G223
2Ti 4:14 A the coppersmith did me much evil: the G223

ALEXANDRIA
Act 18:24 Apollos, born at A, an eloquent man, and G221
27: 6 found a ship of A sailing into Italy; and G222
28:11 in a ship of A, which had wintered G222

ALEXANDRIANS
Act 6: 9 Cyrenians, and A, and of them of Cilicia G221

ALGUM
2Ch 2: 8 Send me also cedar trees, fir trees, and a H418
9:10 brought a trees and precious stones. H418
11 And the king made of the a trees H418

ALGUM-TREES See ALGUM and TREES.

ALIAH
1Ch 1:51 duke Timnah, duke A, duke Jetheth, H5933

ALIAN
1Ch 1:40 The sons of Shobal; A, and Manahath, H5935

ALIEN
Ex 18: 3 I have been an a in a strange land: H1616
Dt 14:21 sell it unto an a: for thou art an holy H5237
Job 19:15 for a stranger: I am an a in their sight. H5237
Ps 69: 8 and an a unto my mother's children. H5237
Isa 61: 5 the sons of the a shall be your plowmen H5236

ALIENATE
Ezk 48:14 exchange, nor a the firstfruits H5674+H5674

ALIENATED
Ezk 23:17 them, and her mind was a from them. H3363
18 then my mind was a from her, like as H3363
18 like as my mind was a from her sister. H5361
22 whom thy mind is a, and I will bring H5361
28 hand of them from whom thy mind is a: H5361
Eph 4:18 darkened, being a from the life of God G526
Col 1:21 And you, that were sometime a and G526

ALIENS
Lam 5: 2 is turned to strangers, our houses to a. H5237
Eph 2:12 Christ, being a from the commonwealth G526
Heb 11:34 fight, turned to flight the armies of the a. G245

ALIKE
Dt 12:22 and the clean shall eat of them a. H3162
15:22 eat it a, as the roebuck, and as the hart. H3162
1Sa 30:24 tarrieth by the stuff: they shall part a. H3162
Job 21:26 They shall lie down a in the dust, and H3162
Ps 33:15 He fashioneth their hearts a; he H3162
139:12 darkness and the light are both a to thee.
Prv 20:10 them are a abomination to the LORD. H1571
27:15 day and a contentious woman are a. H7737
Ecc 9: 2 All things come a to all: there is one H834
11: 6 or whether they both shall be a good. H259
Ro 14: 5 every day a. Let every man be fully

ALIVE
Gen 6:19 the ark, to keep them a with thee; they H2421
20 shall come unto thee, to keep them a. H2421
7: 3 seed a upon the face of all the earth. H2421
23 a, and they that were with him in the ark.
12:12 will kill me, but they will save thee a. H2421
43: 7 Is your father yet a? have ye another H2416
27 old man of whom ye spake? Is he yet a? H2416
28 health, he is yet a. And they bowed H2416
45:26 And told him, saying, Joseph is yet a, H2416
28 yet a: I will go and see him before I die. H2416
46:30 seen thy face, because thou art yet a. H2416
50:20 as it is this day, to save much people a. H2421
Ex 1:17 them, but saved the men children a. H2421
18 and have saved the men children a? H2421
22 and every daughter ye shall save a. H2421
4:18 they be yet a. And Jethro said to Moses, H2416
22: 4 found in his hand a, whether it be ox, or H2416
Lev 10:16 sons of Aaron which were left a, saying,
14: 4 two birds a and clean, and cedar H2416
16:10 shall be presented a before the LORD, H2416
26:36 And upon them that are left a of you I
Nu 16:33 them, went down a into the pit, and the H2416
21:35 left him a: and they possessed his land. H8300
22:33 also I had slain thee, and saved her a. H2421
31:15 them, Have ye saved all the women a? H2421
18 lying with him, keep a for yourselves. H2421
Dt 4: 4 God are a every one of you this day. H2416
5: 3 us, who are all of us here a this day. H2416
6:24 might preserve us a, as it is at this day. H2421
20:16 shalt save a nothing that breatheth: H2421
31:27 while I am yet a with you this day, ye H2416
32:39 I kill, and I make a; I wound, and I heal: H2421
Jos 2:13 And that ye will save a my father, and H2421
6:25 And Joshua saved Rahab the harlot a, H2421
8:23 And the king of Ai they took a, and H2416
14:10 hath kept me a, as he said, these forty H2421
Jdg 8:19 had saved them a, I would not slay you. H2421
21:14 they had saved a of the women of H2421
1Sa 2: 6 The LORD killeth, and maketh a: he H2421
15: 8 king of the Amalekites a, and utterly H2416
27: 9 man nor woman a, and took away the H2421
11 man nor woman a, to bring tidings to H2421
2Sa 8: 2 full line to keep a. And so the Moabites H2421
12:18 the child was yet a, we spake unto him, H2416
21 child, while it was a; but when the child H2416
22 And he said, While the child was yet a, I H2416
18:14 he was yet a in the midst of the oak. H2416
1Ki 18: 5 mules a, that we lose not all the beasts. H2421
20:18 peace, take them a; or whether they be H2416
18 they be come out for war, take them a. H2416
32 he said, Is he yet a? he is my brother. H2416
1Ki 21:15 money: for Naboth is not a, but dead. H2416
2Ki 5: 7 kill and to make a, that this man doth H2421
7: 4 if they save us a, we shall live; and if H2421
12 shall catch them a, and get into the city. H2416
10:14 And he said, Take them a. And they H2416
14 they took them a, and slew them at the H2416
2Ch 25:12 And other ten thousand left a did the H2416
Ps 22:29 him: and none can keep a his own soul. H2421
30: 3 a, that I should not go down to the pit. H2421
33:19 death, and to keep them a in famine. H2421
41: 2 and keep him a; and he shall be blessed H2421
Prv 1:12 Let us swallow them up a as the grave; H2416
Ecc 4: 2 more than the living which are yet a. H2416
Jer 49:11 them a; and let thy widows trust in me. H2421
Ezk 7:13 they were yet a: for the vision is H2416
13:18 ye save the souls a that come unto you? H2421
19 to save the souls a that should not live, H2421
18:27 and right, he shall save his soul a. H2421
Dan 5:19 he would he kept a; and whom he H2418
Mt 27:63 yet a, After three days I will rise again. G2198
Mk 16:11 heard that he was a, and had been seen G2198
Lk 15:24 For this my son was dead, and is a G326
32 is a again; and was lost, and is found. G326
24:23 of angels, which said that he was a. G2198
Act 1: 3 To whom also he shewed himself a G2198
9:41 the saints and widows, presented her a. G2198
20:12 And they brought the young man a, and G2198
25:19 was dead, whom Paul affirmed to be a. G2198
Ro 6:11 unto sin, but a unto God through Jesus G2198
13 as those that are a from the dead, and G2198
7: 9 For I was a without the law once: but G2198
1Co 15:22 even so in Christ shall all be made a. G2227
1Th 4:15 that we which are a and remain unto G2198
17 Then we which are a and remain shall G2198
Rev 1:18 and, behold, I am a for evermore, G2198
2: 8 and the last, which was dead, and is a; G2198
19:20 both were cast a into a lake of fire G2198

ALL See the Appendix.

ALLEGING
Act 17: 3 Opening and a, that Christ must needs G3908

ALLEGORY
Gal 4:24 Which things are an a: for these are the G238

ALLELUIA
Rev 19: 1 in heaven, saying, A; Salvation, and G239
3 And again they said, A. And her smoke G239
4 that sat on the throne, saying, Amen; A. G239
6 A: for the Lord God omnipotent reigneth. G239

ALLIED
Neh 13: 4 house of our God, was a unto Tobiah: H7138

ALLON
Jos 19:33 from Heleph, from A to Zaanannim, and H438
1Ch 4:37 And Ziza the son of Shiphi, the son of A, H438

ALLON-BACHUTH
Gen 35: 8 an oak: and the name of it was called A. H439

ALLOW
Lk 11:48 Truly ye bear witness that ye a the G4909
Act 24:15 themselves also a, that there shall be a G4327
Ro 7:15 For that which I do I a not: for what I G1097

ALLOWANCE
2Ki 25:30 And his a was a continual allowance H737
30 And his allowance was a continual a H737

ALLOWED
1Th 2: 4 But as we were a of God to be put in G1381

ALLOWETH
Ro 14:22 not himself in that thing which he a. G1381

ALLURE
Hos 2:14 Therefore, behold, I will a her, and H6601
2Pt 2:18 of vanity, they a through the lusts of G1185

ALMIGHTY
Gen 17: 1 him, I am the A God; walk before me, H7706
28: 3 And God A bless thee, and make thee H7706
35:11 And God said unto him, I am God A: be H7706
43:14 And God A give you mercy before the H7706
48: 3 And Jacob said unto Joseph, God A H7706
49:25 thee; and by the A, who shall bless thee H7706
Ex 6: 3 by the name of God A, but by my name H7706

Nu 24: 4 the vision of the A, falling *into a trance,* H7706
16 the vision of the A, falling *into a trance,* H7706
Ru 1:20 the A hath dealt very bitterly with me. H7706
21 me, and the A hath afflicted me? H7706
Job 5:17 not thou the chastening of the A: H7706
6: 4 For the arrows of the A *are* within me, H7706
14 but he forsaketh the fear of the A. H7706
8: 3 or doth the A pervert justice? H7706
5 and make thy supplication to the A; H7706
11: 7 thou find out the A unto perfection? H7706
13: 3 Surely I would speak to the A, and I H7706
15:25 strengtheneth himself against the A. H7706
21:15 What *is* the A, that we should serve H7706
20 and he shall drink of the wrath of the A. H7706
22: 3 *Is it* any pleasure to the A, that thou art H7706
17 us: and what can the A do for them? H7706
23 If thou return to the A, thou shalt be H7706
25 Yea, the A shall be thy defence, and H7706
26 A, and shalt lift up thy face unto God. H7706
23:16 my heart soft, and the A troubleth me: H7706
24: 1 hidden from the A, do they that know H7706
27: 2 and the A, *who* hath vexed my soul; H7706
10 Will he delight himself in the A? will he H7706
11 which *is* with the A will I not conceal. H7706
13 *which* they shall receive of the A. H7706
29: 5 When the A *was* yet with me, *when* my H7706
31: 2 inheritance of the A from on high? H7706
35 desire *is, that* the A would answer me, H7706
32: 8 of the A giveth them understanding. H7706
33: 4 the breath of the A hath given me life. H7706
34:10 the A, *that he should commit* iniquity. H7706
12 neither will the A pervert judgment. H7706
35:13 hear vanity, neither will the A regard it. H7706
37:23 *Touching* the A, we cannot find him H7706
40: 2 Shall he that contendeth with the A H7706
Ps 68:14 When the A scattered kings in it, it was H7706
91: 1 shall abide under the shadow of the A. H7706
Isa 13: 6 shall come as a destruction from the A. H7706
Ezk 1:24 as the voice of the A, the voice of H7706
10: 5 voice of the A God when he speaketh. H7706
Joel 1:15 a destruction from the A shall it come. H7706
2Co 6:18 sons and daughters, saith the Lord A. *G3841*
Rev 1: 8 which was, and which is to come, the A. *G3841*
4: 8 A, which was, and is, and is to come. *G3841*
11:17 O Lord God A, which art, and wast, *G3841*
15: 3 works, Lord God A; just and true *are* *G3841*
16: 7 say, Even so, Lord God A, true and *G3841*
14 to the battle of that great day of God A. *G3841*
19:15 of the fierceness and wrath of A God. *G3841*
21:22 A and the Lamb are the temple of it. *G3841*

ALMODAD
Gen 10:26 And Joktan begat A, and Sheleph, and H486
1Ch 1:20 And Joktan begat A, and Sheleph, and H486

ALMON
Jos 21:18 Anathoth with her suburbs, and A with H5960

ALMOND
Ecc 12: 5 in the way, and the a tree shall flourish, H8247
Jer 1:11 And I said, I see a rod of an a tree. H8247

ALMON-DIBLATHAIM
Nu 33:46 from Dibon-gad, and encamped in A. H5963
47 And they removed from A, and pitched H5963

ALMONDS
Gen 43:11 honey, spices, and myrrh, nuts, and a: H8247
Ex 25:33 Three bowls made like unto a, *with* a H8246
33 bowls made like a in the other branch, H8246
34 a, *with* their knops and their flowers. H8246
37:19 the fashion of a in one branch, a knop H8246
19 bowls made like a in another branch, H8246
20 made like a, his knops, and his flowers: H8246
Nu 17: 8 and bloomed blossoms, and yielded a. H8247

ALMOST
Ex 17: 4 people? they be a ready to stone me. H4592
Ps 73: 2 But as for me, my feet were a gone; my H4592
94:17 help, my soul had a dwelt in silence. H4592
119:87 They had a consumed me upon earth; H4592
Prv 5:14 I was a in all evil in the midst of the H4592
Act 13:44 And the next sabbath day came a the *G4975*
19:26 at Ephesus, but a throughout all Asia, *G4975*
21:27 And when the seven days were a *G3195*
26:28 Then Agrippa said unto Paul, A thou *G1722*
29 day, were both a, and altogether such *G1722*
Heb 9:22 And a all things are by the law purged *G4975*

ALMS
Mt 6: 1 Take heed that ye do not your a before *G1654*
2 Therefore when thou doest *thine* a, do *G1654*
3 But when thou doest a, let not thy left *G1654*
4 That thine a may be in secret: and thy *G1654*
Lk 11:41 But rather give a of such things as ye *G1654*
12:33 Sell that ye have, and give a; provide *G1654*
Act 3: 2 a of them that entered into the temple; *G1654*
3 about to go into the temple asked an a. *G1654*
10 he which sat for a at the Beautiful gate *G1654*
10: 2 which gave much a to the people, and *G1654*
4 prayers and thine a are come up for a *G1654*
31 is heard, and thine a are had in *G1654*
24:17 to bring a to my nation, and offerings. *G1654*

ALMSDEEDS
Act 9:36 full of good works and a which she did. *G1654*

ALMUG
1Ki 10:11 plenty of a trees, and precious stones. H484
12 And the king made of the a trees pillars H484
12 a trees, nor were seen unto this day. H484

ALOES
Nu 24: 6 as the trees of lign a which the LORD H174
Ps 45: 8 All thy garments *smell* of myrrh, and a, H174
Prv 7:17 I have perfumed my bed with myrrh, a, H174
Song 4:14 myrrh and a, with all the chief spices: H174
Jn 19:39 and a, about an hundred pound *weight.* *G250*

ALONE
Gen 2:18 a; I will make him an help meet for him. H905
32:24 And Jacob was left a; and there wrestled H905
42:38 is dead, and he is left a: if mischief befall H905
44:20 is dead, and he a is left of his mother, H905
Ex 14:12 saying, Let us a, that we may serve the H2308
18:14 sittest thou thyself a, and all the people H905
18 thou art not able to perform it thyself a. H905
24: 2 And Moses a shall come near the LORD: H905
32:10 Now therefore let me a, that my wrath
Lev 13:46 he shall dwell a; without the camp *shall* H910
Nu 11:14 I am not able to bear all this people a, H905
17 with thee, that thou bear *it* not thyself a. H905
23: 9 the people shall dwell a, and shall not be H910
Dt 1: 9 I am not able to bear you myself a: H905
12 How can I myself a bear your H905
9:14 Let me a, that I may destroy them, and H7503
32:12 *So* the LORD a did lead him, and *there* H909
33:28 Israel then shall dwell in safety a: the H909
Jos 22:20 that man perished not a in his iniquity. H259
Jdg 3:20 he had for himself a. And Ehud said, I H905
11:37 for me: let me a two months, that I H7503
1Sa 21: 1 Why *art* thou a, and no man with thee? H905
2Sa 16:11 *do it?* let him a, and let him curse; for
18:24 looked, and behold a man running a. H905
25 king said, If he *be* a, *there is* tidings in his H905
26 man running a. And the king said, He H905
1Ki 11:29 and they two *were* a in the field: H905
2Ki 4:27 God said, Let her a; for her soul *is* vexed H7503
19:15 the God, *even* thou a, of all the kingdoms H905
23:18 And he said, Let him a; let no man move
18 they let his bones a, with the bones of H4422
1Ch 29: 1 my son, whom a God hath chosen, *is* H259
Ezr 6: 7 Let the work of this house of God a; let H7662
Neh 9: 6 Thou, *even* thou, *art* LORD a; thou hast H905
Est 3: 6 on Mordecai a; for they had shewed H905
Job 1:15 and I only am escaped a to tell thee. H905
16 and I only am escaped a to tell thee. H905
17 and I only am escaped a to tell thee. H905
19 and I only am escaped a to tell thee. H905
7:16 alway: let me a; for my days *are* vanity. H2308
19 let me a till I swallow down my spittle? H7503
9: 8 Which a spreadeth out the heavens, and H905
10:20 me a, that I may take comfort a little, H7896
13:13 Hold your peace, let me a, that I may
15:19 Unto whom a the earth was given, and H905
31:17 Or have eaten my morsel myself a, and H905
Ps 83:18 thou, whose name a *is* JEHOVAH, *art* H905
86:10 doest wondrous things: thou *art* God a.
102: 7 I watch, and am as a sparrow a upon the H909
136: 4 To him who a doeth great wonders: for H905
148:13 for his name a is excellent; his glory H905
Prv 9:12 but *if* thou scornest, thou a shalt bear *it.* H905
Ecc 4: 8 There is one *a*, and *there is* not a second;
10 woe to him *that is* a when he falleth; for H259
11 have heat: but how can one be warm *a*?
Isa 2:11 the LORD a shall be exalted in that day. H905
17 the LORD a shall be exalted in that day. H905
5: 8 be placed a in the midst of the earth! H905
Isa 14:31 none *shall be* a in his appointed times. H909
37:16 the God, *even* thou a, of all the kingdoms H905
44:24 forth the heavens a; that spreadeth H905
49:21 I was left a; these, where *had* they *been*? H905
51: 2 a, and blessed him, and increased him. H259
63: 3 I have trodden the winepress a; and of H905
Jer 15:17 nor rejoiced; I sat a because of thy hand: H909
49:31 neither gates nor bars, *which* dwell a. H909
Lam 3:28 He sitteth a and keepeth silence, because H905
Dan 10: 7 And I Daniel a saw the vision: for the H905
8 Therefore I was left a, and saw this great H905
Hos 4:17 Ephraim *is* joined to idols: let him a.
8: 9 a by himself: Ephraim hath hired lovers. H909
Mt 4: 4 not live by bread a, but by every word *G3441*
14:23 the evening was come, he was there a. *G3441*
15:14 Let them a: they be blind leaders of the *G863*
18:15 thee and him a: if he shall hear thee, *G3441*
Mk 1:24 Saying, Let *us* a; what have we to do *G1439*
4:10 And when he was a, they that were *G2651*
34 and when they were a, he expounded all *G2596*
6:47 midst of the sea, and he a on the land. *G3441*
14: 6 And Jesus said, Let her a; why trouble ye *G863*
15:36 to drink, saying, Let a; let us see whether *G863*
Lk 4: 4 by bread a, but by every word of God. *G3441*
34 Saying, Let *us* a; what have we to do *G1436*
5:21 Who can forgive sins, but God a? *G3441*
6: 4 is not lawful to eat but for the priests a? *G3441*
9:18 And it came to pass, as he was a *G2651*
36 Jesus was found a. And they kept *it* *G3441*
10:40 a? bid her therefore that she help me. *G3441*
13: 8 him, Lord, let it a this year also, till I *G863*
Jn 6:15 again into a mountain himself a. *G3441*
22 but *that* his disciples were gone away a; *G3441*
8: 9 and Jesus was left a, and the woman *G3441*
16 not a, but I and the Father that sent me. *G3441*
29 hath not left me a; for I do always those *G3441*
11:48 If we let him thus a, all *men* will believe *G863*
12: 7 Then said Jesus, Let her a: against the *G863*
24 and die, it abideth a: but if it die, it *G3441*
16:32 and shall leave me a: and yet I am not *G3441*
32 not a, because the Father is with me. *G3441*
17:20 Neither pray I for these a, but for them *G3440*
Act 5:38 men, and let them a: for if this counsel *G1439*
19:26 Moreover ye see and hear, that not a at *G3440*
Ro 4:23 Now it was not written for his sake a, *G3440*
11: 3 and I am left a, and they seek my life. *G3441*
Gal 6: 4 in himself a, and not in another. *G3441*
1Th 3: 1 thought it good to be left at Athens a; *G3441*
Heb 9: 7 the high priest a once every year, not *G3441*
Jas 2:17 if it hath not works, is dead, being a. *G2596*

ALONG See the Appendix.

ALOOF
Ps 38:11 My lovers and my friends stand a from H5048

ALOTH
1Ki 4:16 son of Hushai *was* in Asher and in A: H1175

ALOUD
Gen 45: 2 And he wept a: and the Egyptians and H6963
1Ki 18:27 and said, Cry a: for he *is* a god; H1419+H6963
28 And they cried a, and cut H1419+H3605
Ezr 3:12 voice; and many shouted a for joy: H7311
Job 19: 7 heard: I cry a, but *there is* no judgment. H7768
Ps 51:14 shall sing a of thy righteousness. H7442
55:17 and cry a: and he shall hear my voice. H1993
59:16 yea, I will sing a of thy mercy in the H7442
81: 1 Sing a unto God our strength: make a H7442
132:16 and her saints shall shout a for joy. H7442
149: 5 glory: let them sing a upon their beds. H7442
Isa 24:14 LORD, they shall cry a from the sea. H6670
54: 1 singing, and cry a, thou *that* didst not H6670
58: 1 Cry a, spare not, lift up thy voice like a H1627
Dan 3: 4 Then an herald cried a, To you it is H2429
4:14 He cried a, and said thus, Hew down H2429
5: 7 The king cried a to bring in the H2429
Hos 5: 8 a *at* Beth-aven, after thee, O Benjamin. H7321
Mic 4: 9 Now why dost thou cry out a? *is there* H7452
Mk 15: 8 And the multitude crying a began to *G310*

ALPHA
Rev 1: 8 I am A and Omega, the beginning and *G1*
11 Saying, I am A and Omega, the first and *G1*
21: 6 And he said unto me, It is done. I am A *G1*
22:13 I am A and Omega, the beginning and *G1*

ALPHAEUS
Mt 10: 3 James *the son* of A, and Lebbaeus, whose *G256*

Mk 2:14 he saw Levi the *son* of A sitting at the *G256*
3:18 James the *son* of A, and Thaddaeus, and *G256*
Lk 6:15 the *son* of A, and Simon called Zelotes, *G256*
Act 1:13 James *the son* of A, and Simon Zelotes, *G256*

ALREADY
Ex 1: 5 seventy souls: for Joseph was in Egypt ***a***.
2Ch 28:13 against the LORD ***a***, ye intend to add
Neh 5: 5 unto bondage ***a***: neither *is it* in our power
Ecc 1:10 **a** of old time, which was before us. H3528
2:12 *even* that which hath been **a** done. H3528
3:15 is to be hath **a** been; and God requireth H3528
4: 2 dead which are **a** dead more than the H3528
6:10 That which hath been is named **a**, and H3528
Mal 2: 2 them **a**, because ye do not lay *it* to heart.
Mt 5:28 adultery with her **a** in his heart. *G2235*
17:12 But I say unto you, That Elias is come **a**, *G2235*
Mk 15:44 And Pilate marvelled if he were **a** dead: *G2235*
Lk 12:49 and what will I, if it be **a** kindled? *G2235*
Jn 3:18 not is condemned **a**, because he hath *G2235*
4:35 fields; for they are white **a** to harvest. *G2235*
9:22 Jews had agreed **a**, that if any man did *G2235*
27 He answered them, I have told you **a**, *G2235*
11:17 he had *lain* in the grave four days **a**. *G2235*
19:33 he was dead **a**, they brake not his legs: *G2235*
Act 11:11 were three men **a** come unto the house *G1824*
27: 9 now **a** past, Paul admonished *them*, *G2235*
1Co 5: 3 spirit, have judged **a**, as though I were *G2235*
2Co 12:21 have sinned **a**, and have not repented *G4258*
Php 3:12 Not as though I had **a** attained, either *G2235*
12 either were **a** perfect: but I follow *G2235*
16 Nevertheless, whereto we have **a** *G5348*
2Th 2: 7 For the mystery of iniquity doth **a** *G2235*
1Ti 5:15 For some are **a** turned aside after *G2235*
2Ti 2:18 past **a**; and overthrow the faith of some. *G2235*
1Jn 4: 3 and even now **a** is it in the world. *G2235*
Rev 2:25 But that which ye have ***a*** hold fast till I

ALSO See the Appendix.

ALTAR
Gen 8:20 And Noah builded an **a** unto the LORD; H4196
20 and offered burnt offerings on the **a**. H4196
12: 7 builded he an **a** unto the LORD, who H4196
8 he builded an **a** unto the LORD, and H4196
13: 4 Unto the place of the **a**, which he had H4196
18 and built there an **a** unto the LORD. H4196
22: 9 Abraham built an **a** there, and laid the H4196
9 and laid him on the **a** upon the wood. H4196
26:25 And he builded an **a** there, and called H4196
33:20 And he erected there an **a**, and called it H4196
35: 1 and make there an **a** unto God, that H4196
3 I will make there an **a** unto God, who H4196
7 And he built there an **a**, and called the H4196
Ex 17:15 And Moses built an **a**, and called the H4196
20:24 An **a** of earth thou shalt make unto me, H4196
25 And if thou wilt make me an **a** of stone, H4196
26 steps unto mine **a**, that thy nakedness H4196
21:14 take him from mine **a**, that he may die. H4196
24: 4 and builded an **a** under the hill, and H4196
6 half of the blood he sprinkled on the **a**. H4196
27: 1 And thou shalt make an **a** *of* shittim H4196
1 cubits broad; the **a** shall be foursquare: H4196
5 compass of the **a** beneath, that the net H4196
5 net may be even to the midst of the **a**. H4196
6 And thou shalt make staves for the **a**, H4196
7 upon the two sides of the **a**, to bear it. H4196
28:43 near unto the **a** to minister in the holy H4196
29:12 the horns of the **a** with thy finger, and H4196
12 all the blood beside the bottom of the **a**. H4196
13 upon them, and burn *them* upon the **a**. H4196
16 and sprinkle *it* round about upon the **a**. H4196
18 ram upon the **a**: it *is* a burnt offering H4196
20 the blood upon the **a** round about. H4196
21 that *is* upon the **a**, and of the anointing H4196
25 *them* upon the **a** for a burnt offering, H4196
36 thou shalt cleanse the **a**, when thou hast H4196
37 an atonement for the **a**, and sanctify it; H4196
37 it; and it shall be an **a** most holy: H4196
37 toucheth the **a** shall be holy. H4196
38 offer upon the **a**; two lambs of the first H4196
44 and the **a**: I will sanctify also both H4196
30: 1 And thou shalt make an **a** to burn H4196
18 the **a**, and thou shalt put water therein. H4196
20 come near to the **a** to minister, to burn H4196
27 and his vessels, and the **a** of incense, H4196
28 And the **a** of burnt offering with all his H4196
31: 8 all his furniture, and the **a** of incense, H4196
9 And the **a** of burnt offering with all his H4196
Ex 32: 5 And when Aaron saw *it*, he built an **a** H4196
35:15 And the incense **a**, and his staves, and H4196
16 The **a** of burnt offering, with his brasen H4196
37:25 And he made the incense **a** *of* shittim H4196
38: 1 And he made the **a** of burnt offering *of* H4196
3 And he made all the vessels of the **a**, the H4196
4 And he made for the **a** a brasen grate H4196
7 on the sides of the **a**, to bear it withal; H4196
7 he made the **a** hollow with boards.
30 and the brasen **a**, and the brasen grate H4196
30 grate for it, and all the vessels of the **a**, H4196
39:38 And the golden **a**, and the anointing oil, H4196
39 The brasen **a**, and his grate of brass, his H4196
40: 5 And thou shalt set the **a** of gold for the H4196
6 And thou shalt set the **a** of the burnt H4196
7 and the **a**, and shalt put water therein. H4196
7 And thou shalt anoint the **a** of the H4196
10 the **a**: and it shall be an altar most holy. H4196
10 altar: and it shall be an **a** most holy. H4196
26 And he put the golden **a** in the tent of H4196
29 And he put the **a** of burnt offering *by* H4196
30 **a**, and put water there, to wash *withal*. H4196
32 near unto the **a**, they washed; as the H4196
33 and the **a**, and set up the hanging H4196
Lev 1: 5 about upon the **a** that *is by* the door of H4196
7 put fire upon the **a**, and lay the wood in H4196
8 that *is* on the fire which *is* upon the **a**: H4196
9 burn all on the **a**, *to be* a burnt sacrifice, H4196
11 And he shall kill it on the side of the **a** H4196
11 his blood round about upon the **a**. H4196
12 that *is* on the fire which *is* upon the **a**: H4196
13 and burn *it* upon the **a**: it *is* a burnt H4196
15 And the priest shall bring it unto the **a**, H4196
15 and burn *it* on the **a**; and the blood H4196
15 shall be wrung out at the side of the **a**: H4196
16 cast it beside the **a** on the east part, by H4196
17 burn it upon the **a**, upon the wood that H4196
2: 2 of it upon the **a**, *to be* an offering made H4196
8 the priest, he shall bring it unto the **a**. H4196
9 shall burn *it* upon the **a**: *it is* an offering H4196
12 be burnt on the **a** for a sweet savour. H4196
3: 2 the blood upon the **a** round about. H4196
5 And Aaron's sons shall burn it on the **a** H4196
8 blood thereof round about upon the **a**. H4196
11 And the priest shall burn it upon the **a**: H4196
13 blood thereof upon the **a** round about. H4196
16 them upon the **a**: *it is* the food of the H4196
4: 7 the horns of the **a** of sweet incense H4196
7 at the bottom of the **a** of the burnt H4196
10 them upon the **a** of the burnt offering. H4196
18 the horns of the **a** which *is* before the H4196
18 at the bottom of the **a** of the burnt H4196
19 fat from him, and burn *it* upon the **a**. H4196
25 the horns of the **a** of burnt offering, H4196
25 at the bottom of the **a** of burnt offering. H4196
26 And he shall burn all his fat upon the **a**, H4196
30 the horns of the **a** of burnt offering, H4196
30 the blood thereof at the bottom of the **a**. H4196
31 burn *it* upon the **a** for a sweet savour H4196
34 the horns of the **a** of burnt offering, H4196
34 the blood thereof at the bottom of the **a**: H4196
35 burn them upon the **a**, according to the H4196
5: 9 the side of the **a**; and the rest of the H4196
9 the bottom of the **a**: it *is* a sin offering. H4196
12 and burn *it* on the **a**, according to the H4196
6: 9 burning upon the **a** all night unto the H4196
9 the fire of the **a** shall be burning in it. H4196
10 offering on the **a**, and he shall put them H4196
10 and he shall put them beside the **a**. H4196
12 And the fire upon the **a** shall be H4196
13 upon the **a**; it shall never go out. H4196
14 offer it before the LORD, before the **a**. H4196
15 burn *it* upon the **a** *for* a sweet savour, H4196
7: 2 he sprinkle round about upon the **a**. H4196
5 them upon the **a** *for* an offering made H4196
31 the fat upon the **a**: but the breast shall H4196
8:11 And he sprinkled thereof upon the **a** H4196
11 and anointed the **a** and all his vessels, H4196
15 the horns of the **a** round about with his H4196
15 and purified the **a**, and poured the H4196
15 the bottom of the **a**, and sanctified it, to H4196
16 fat, and Moses burned *it* upon the **a**. H4196
19 the blood upon the **a** round about. H4196
21 ram upon the **a**: it *was* a burnt sacrifice H4196
24 the blood upon the **a** round about. H4196
28 burnt *them* on the **a** upon the burnt H4196
30 *was* upon the **a**, and sprinkled *it* upon H4196
9: 7 Go unto the **a**, and offer thy sin offering, H4196
8 Aaron therefore went unto the **a**, and H4196
Lev 9: 9 the horns of the **a**, and poured out the H4196
9 out the blood at the bottom of the **a**: H4196
10 the **a**; as the LORD commanded Moses. H4196
12 he sprinkled round about upon the **a**. H4196
13 head: and he burnt *them* upon the **a**. H4196
14 *them* upon the burnt offering on the **a**. H4196
17 burnt *it* upon the **a**, beside the burnt H4196
18 he sprinkled upon the **a** round about, H4196
20 and he burnt the fat upon the **a**: H4196
24 upon the **a** the burnt offering and H4196
10:12 leaven beside the **a**: for it *is* most holy: H4196
14:20 offering upon the **a**: and the priest shall H4196
16:12 of fire from off the **a** before the LORD, H4196
18 And he shall go out unto the **a** that *is* H4196
18 *it* upon the horns of the **a** round about. H4196
20 and the **a**, he shall bring the live goat: H4196
25 sin offering shall he burn upon the **a**. H4196
33 and for the **a**, and he shall make an H4196
17: 6 blood upon the **a** of the LORD *at* the H4196
11 given it to you upon the **a** to make an H4196
21:23 come nigh unto the **a**, because he hath a H4196
22:22 fire of them upon the **a** unto the LORD. H4196
Nu 3:26 and by the **a** round about, and the H4196
4:11 And upon the golden **a** they shall H4196
13 **a**, and spread a purple cloth thereon: H4196
14 all the vessels of the **a**; and they shall H4196
26 and by the **a** round about, and their H4196
5:25 the LORD, and offer it upon the **a**: H4196
26 burn *it* upon the **a**, and afterward shall H4196
7: 1 thereof, both the **a** and all the vessels H4196
10 for dedicating of the **a** in the day that it H4196
10 offered their offering before the **a**. H4196
11 on his day, for the dedicating of the **a**. H4196
84 This *was* the dedication of the **a**, in the H4196
88 of the **a**, after that it was anointed. H4196
16:38 *for* a covering of the **a**: for they offered H4196
39 broad *plates for* a covering of the **a**: H4196
46 from off the **a**, and put on incense, H4196
18: 3 the **a**, that neither they, nor ye also, die. H4196
5 and the charge of the **a**: that there be no H4196
7 every thing of the **a**, and within the vail; H4196
17 blood upon the **a**, and shalt burn their H4196
23: 2 offered on *every* **a** a bullock and a ram. H4196
4 upon *every* **a** a bullock and a ram. H4196
14 offered a bullock and a ram on *every* **a**. H4196
30 offered a bullock and a ram on *every* **a**. H4196
Dt 12:27 blood, upon the **a** of the LORD thy God: H4196
27 out upon the **a** of the LORD thy God, H4196
16:21 near unto the **a** of the LORD thy God, H4196
26: 4 before the **a** of the LORD thy God. H4196
27: 5 And there shalt thou build an **a** unto H4196
5 the LORD thy God, an **a** of stones: thou H4196
6 Thou shalt build the **a** of the LORD thy H4196
33:10 and whole burnt sacrifice upon thine **a**. H4196
Jos 8:30 Then Joshua built an **a** unto the LORD H4196
31 the law of Moses, an **a** of whole stones, H4196
9:27 and for the **a** of the LORD, even unto H4196
22:10 an **a** by Jordan, a great altar to see to. H4196
10 an altar by Jordan, a great **a** to see to. H4196
11 have built an **a** over against the land H4196
16 builded you an **a**, that ye might rebel H4196
19 **a** beside the altar of the LORD our God. H4196
19 altar beside the **a** of the LORD our God. H4196
23 That we have built us an **a** to turn from H4196
26 to build us an **a**, not for burnt offering, H4196
28 the pattern of the **a** of the LORD, which H4196
29 the LORD, to build an **a** for burnt H4196
29 beside the **a** of the LORD our God H4196
34 of Gad called the **a** *Ed*: for it *shall be* a H4196
Jdg 6:24 Then Gideon built an **a** there unto the H4196
25 and throw down the **a** of Baal that thy H4196
26 And build an **a** unto the LORD thy God H4196
28 behold, the **a** of Baal was cast down, H4196
28 was offered upon the **a** *that was* built. H4196
30 cast down the **a** of Baal, and because H4196
31 because *one* hath cast down his **a**. H4196
32 because he hath thrown down his **a**. H4196
13:20 from off the **a**, that the angel of the H4196
20 in the flame of the **a**. And Manoah and H4196
21: 4 and built there an **a**, and offered burnt H4196
1Sa 2:28 offer upon mine **a**, to burn incense, to H4196
33 not cut off from mine **a**, *shall be* to H4196
7:17 and there he built an **a** unto the LORD. H4196
14:35 And Saul built an **a** unto the LORD: the H4196
35 the first **a** that he built unto the LORD. H4196
2Sa 24:18 Go up, rear an **a** unto the LORD in the H4196
21 thee, to build an **a** unto the LORD, that H4196
25 And David built there an **a** unto the H4196
1Ki 1:50 and caught hold on the horns of the **a**. H4196

1Ki 1:51 on the horns of the a, saying, Let king H4196
53 him down from the a. And he came and H4196
2:28 and caught hold on the horns of the a. H4196
29 he is by the a. Then Solomon sent H4196
3: 4 did Solomon offer upon that a. H4196
6:20 so covered the a which was of cedar. H4196
22 also the whole a that was by the oracle H4196
7:48 of the LORD: the a of gold, and the H4196
8:22 And Solomon stood before the a of the H4196
31 oath come before thine a in this house: H4196
54 from before the a of the LORD, from H4196
64 the brasen a that was before the H4196
9:25 offerings upon the a which he built H4196
25 incense upon the a that was before the H4196
12:32 offered upon the a. So did he in Bethel, H4196
33 So he offered upon the a which he had H4196
33 offered upon the a, and burnt incense. H4196
13: 1 stood by the a to burn incense. H4196
2 And he cried against the a in the word H4196
2 and said, O a, altar, thus saith the H4196
2 and said, O altar, a, thus saith the H4196
3 Behold, the a shall be rent, and the H4196
4 cried against the a in Beth-el, that he H4196
4 his hand from the a, saying, Lay hold H4196
5 The a also was rent, and the ashes H4196
5 out from the a, according to the sign H4196
32 the LORD against the a in Beth-el, and H4196
16:32 And he reared up an a for Baal in the H4196
18:26 leaped upon the a which was made. H4196
30 a of the LORD that was broken down. H4196
32 And with the stones he built an a in the H4196
32 a trench about the a, as great as would H4196
35 And the water ran round about the a; H4196
2Ki 11:11 temple, along by the a and the temple. H4196
12: 9 set it beside the a, on the right side as H4196
16:10 and saw an a that was at Damascus: H4196
10 the fashion of the a, and the pattern of H4196
11 And Urijah the priest built an a H4196
12 the king saw the a: and the king H4196
12 to the a, and offered thereon. H4196
13 blood of his peace offerings, upon the a. H4196
14 And he brought also the brasen a, H4196
14 from between the a and the house of H4196
14 and put it on the north side of the a. H4196
15 Upon the great a burn the morning H4196
15 brasen a shall be for me to inquire by. H4196
18:22 worship before this a in Jerusalem? H4196
23: 9 came not up to the a of the LORD in H4196
15 Moreover the a that was at Beth-el, H4196
15 made, both that a and the high place H4196
16 them upon the a, and polluted it, H4196
17 thou hast done against the a of Beth-el. H4196
1Ch 6:49 sons offered upon the a of the burnt H4196
49 and on the a of incense, and were H4196
16:40 LORD upon the a of the burnt offering H4196
21:18 up, and set up an a unto the LORD in H4196
22 that I may build an a therein unto the H4196
26 And David built there an a unto the H4196
26 by fire upon the a of burnt offering. H4196
29 and the a of the burnt offering, H4196
22: 1 is the a of the burnt offering for Israel. H4196
28:18 And for the a of incense refined gold by H4196
2Ch 1: 5 Moreover the brasen a, that Bezaleel H4196
6 to the brasen a before the LORD, which H4196
4: 1 Moreover he made an a of brass, H4196
19 of God, the golden a also, and the H4196
5:12 the east end of the a, and with them an H4196
6:12 And he stood before the a of the LORD H4196
22 oath come before thine a in this house; H4196
7: 7 the brasen a which Solomon had H4196
9 a seven days, and the feast seven days. H4196
8:12 the LORD on the a of the LORD, which H4196
15: 8 and renewed the a of the LORD, that H4196
23:10 along by the a and the temple, by the H4196
26:16 to burn incense upon the a of incense. H4196
19 of the LORD, from beside the incense a. H4196
29:18 the LORD, and the a of burnt offering, H4196
19 they are before the a of the LORD. H4196
21 to offer them on the a of the LORD. H4196
22 sprinkled it on the a: likewise, when H4196
22 blood upon the a: they killed also the H4196
22 they sprinkled the blood upon the a. H4196
24 their blood upon the a, to make an H4196
27 offering upon the a. And when the H4196
32:12 before one a, and burn incense upon it? H4196
33:16 And he repaired the a of the LORD, H4196
35:16 offerings upon the a of the LORD, H4196
Ezr 3: 2 and builded the a of the God of Israel, H4196
3 And they set the a upon his bases; for H4196
Ezr 7:17 them upon the a of the house of your H4056
Neh 10:34 to burn upon the a of the LORD our H4196
Ps 26: 6 so will I compass thine a, O LORD: H4196
43: 4 Then will I go unto the a of God, unto H4196
51:19 shall they offer bullocks upon thine a. H4196
118:27 with cords, even unto the horns of the a. H4196
Isa 6: 6 had taken with the tongs from off the a: H4196
19:19 In that day shall there be an a to the H4196
27: 9 the stones of the a as chalkstones that H4196
36: 7 Ye shall worship before this a? H4196
56: 7 upon mine a; for mine house shall H4196
60: 7 on mine a, and I will glorify the H4196
Lam 2: 7 The Lord hath cast off his a, he hath H4196
Ezk 8: 5 a this image of jealousy in the entry. H4196
16 the porch and the a, were about five H4196
9: 2 went in, and stood beside the brasen a. H4196
40:46 the charge of the a: these are the sons of H4196
47 and the a that was before the house. H4196
41:22 The a of wood was three cubits high, H4196
43:13 And these are the measures of the a H4196
13 this shall be the higher place of the a. H4196
15 So the a shall be four cubits; and H741+H2025
15 the a and upward shall be four horns. H741
16 And the a shall be twelve cubits long, H741
18 the ordinances of the a in the day when H4196
22 shall cleanse the a, as they did cleanse H4196
26 Seven days shall they purge the a and H4196
27 offerings upon the a, and your peace H4196
45:19 of the settle of the a, and upon the posts H4196
47: 1 of the house, at the south side of the a. H4196
Joel 1:13 ye ministers of the a: come, lie all night H4196
2:17 the porch and the a, and let them say, H4196
Am 2: 8 to pledge by every a, and they drink the H4196
3:14 the horns of the a shall be cut off, and H4196
9: 1 I saw the Lord standing upon the a: and H4196
Zec 9:15 like bowls, and as the corners of the a. H4196
14:20 shall be like the bowls before the a. H4196
Mal 1: 7 Ye offer polluted bread upon mine a; H4196
10 fire on mine a for nought. I have no H4196
2:13 covering the a of the LORD with tears, H4196
Mt 5:23 Therefore if thou bring thy gift to the a, G2379
24 Leave there thy gift before the a, and go G2379
23:18 And, Whosoever shall swear by the a, it G2379
19 gift, or the a that sanctifieth the gift? G2379
20 Whoso therefore shall swear by the a, G2379
35 ye slew between the temple and the a. G2379
Lk 1:11 on the right side of the a of incense. G2379
11:51 between the a and the temple: verily G2379
Act 17:23 I found an a with this inscription, G1041
1Co 9:13 at the a are partakers with the altar? G2379
13 at the altar are partakers with the a? G2379
10:18 eat of the sacrifices partakers of the a? G2379
Heb 7:13 which no man gave attendance at the a. G2379
13:10 We have an a, whereof they have no G2379
Jas 2:21 he had offered Isaac his son upon the a? G2379
Rev 6: 9 I saw under the a the souls of them that G2379
8: 3 and stood at the a, having a golden G2379
3 golden a which was before the throne. G2379
5 it with fire of the a, and cast it into the G2379
9:13 of the golden a which is before God, G2379
11: 1 the a, and them that worship therein. G2379
14:18 And another angel came out from the a, G2379
16: 7 And I heard another out of the a say, G2379

ALTARS

Ex 34:13 But ye shall destroy their a, break their H4196
Nu 3:31 and the a, and the vessels of the H4196
23: 1 me here seven a, and prepare me here H4196
4 prepared seven a, and I have offered H4196
14 and built seven a, and offered a bullock H4196
29 me here seven a, and prepare me here H4196
Dt 7: 5 ye shall destroy their a, and break down H4196
12: 3 And ye shall overthrow their a, and H4196
Jdg 2: 2 throw down their a: but ye have not H4196
1Ki 19:10 down thine a, and slain thy prophets H4196
14 down thine a, and slain thy prophets H4196
2Ki 11:18 brake it down; his a and his images H4196
18 of Baal before the a. And the priest H4196
18:22 high places and whose a Hezekiah hath H4196
21: 3 and he reared up a for Baal, and made H4196
4 And he built a in the house of the H4196
5 And he built a for all the host of heaven H4196
23:12 And the a that were on the top of the H4196
12 made, and the a which Manasseh had H4196
20 there upon the a, and burned men's H4196
2Ch 14: 3 For he took away the a of the strange H4196
23:17 and brake his a and his images in H4196
17 Mattan the priest of Baal before the a. H4196
28:24 him a in every corner of Jerusalem. H4196
2Ch 30:14 And they arose and took away the a H4196
14 and all the a for incense took they H4196
31: 1 places and the a out of all Judah and H4196
32:12 high places and his a, and commanded H4196
33: 3 and he reared up a for Baalim, and H4196
4 Also he built a in the house of the H4196
5 And he built a for all the host of heaven H4196
15 LORD, and all the a that he had built in H4196
34: 4 And they brake down the a of Baalim H4196
5 a, and cleansed Judah and Jerusalem. H4196
7 And when he had broken down the a H4196
Ps 84: 3 young, even thine a, O LORD of hosts, H4196
Isa 17: 8 And he shall not look to the a, the work H4196
36: 7 high places and whose a Hezekiah hath H4196
65: 3 and burneth incense upon a of brick;
Jer 11:13 have ye set up a to that shameful thing, H4196
13 even a to burn incense unto Baal. H4196
17: 1 heart, and upon the horns of your a; H4196
2 Whilst their children remember their a H4196
Ezk 6: 4 And your a shall be desolate, and your H4196
5 scatter your bones round about your a. H4196
6 that your a may be laid waste and H4196
13 round about their a, upon every high H4196
Hos 8:11 Because Ephraim hath made many a H4196
11 altars to sin, a shall be unto him to sin. H4196
10: 1 hath increased the a; according to the H4196
2 their a, he shall spoil their images. H4196
8 come up on their a; and they shall say H4196
12:11 Gilgal; yea, their a are as heaps in the H4196
Am 3:14 I will also visit the a of Beth-el: and the H4196
Ro 11: 3 and digged down thine a; and I am left G2379

AL-TASCHITH

Ps 57:ttl To the chief Musician, A, Michtam of H516
58:ttl To the chief Musician, A, Michtam of H516
59:ttl To the chief Musician, A, Michtam of H516
75:ttl To the chief Musician, A, A Psalm or H516

ALTER

Lev 27:10 He shall not a it, nor change it, a good H2498
Ezr 6:11 whosoever shall a this word, let timber H8133
12 to their hand to a and to destroy this H8133
Ps 89:34 My covenant will I not break, nor a the H8138

ALTERED

Est 1:19 that it be not a, That Vashti come no H5674
Lk 9:29 his countenance was a, and his raiment G2087

ALTERETH

Dan 6: 8 the Medes and Persians, which a not. H5709
12 the Medes and Persians, which a not. H5709

ALTHOUGH

Ex 13:17 of the Philistines, a that was near; for H3588
Jos 22:17 until this day, a there was a plague in
2Sa 23: 5 A my house be not so with God; yet he H3588
5 all my desire, a he make it not to grow. H3588
1Ki 20: 5 saying, A I have sent unto thee, H3588
Est 7: 4 held my tongue, a the enemy could not H3588
Job 2: 3 fast his integrity, a thou movedst me
5: 6 A affliction cometh not forth of the H3588
35:14 A thou sayest thou shalt not see him, yet H637
Jer 31:32 they brake, a I was an husband unto
Ezk 7:13 that which is sold, a they were yet alive:
11:16 the Lord GOD; A I have cast them far H3588
16 the heathen, and a I have scattered them H272
Hab 3:17 A the fig tree shall not blossom, neither H272
Mk 14:29 But Peter said unto him, A all shall be G2532
Heb 4: 3 enter into my rest: a the works were G2543

ALTOGETHER

Gen 18:21 they have done a according to the cry H3617
Ex 11: 1 he shall surely thrust you out hence a. H3617
19:18 And mount Sinai was a on a smoke, H3605
Nu 16:13 thou make thyself a a prince over us? H1571
23:11 and, behold, thou hast blessed them a.
24:10 hast a blessed them these three times.
30:14 But if her husband a hold his peace at
Dt 16:20 That which is a just shalt thou follow,
2Ch 12:12 a: and also in Judah things went well. H3617
Est 4:14 For if thou a holdest thy peace at this
Job 13: 5 O that ye would a hold your peace! and
27:12 seen it; why then are ye thus a vain?
Ps 19: 9 of the LORD are true and righteous a. H3162
39: 5 man at his best state is a vanity. Selah. H3605
50:21 that I was a such an one as thyself:
53: 3 back: they are a become filthy; there H3162
62: 9 balance, they are a lighter than vanity. H3162
139: 4 but, lo, O LORD, thou knowest it a. H3605

Song 5:16 His mouth *is* most sweet: yea, he *is* **a**
Isa 10: 8 For he saith, *Are* not my princes **a** H3162
Jer 5: 5 but these have **a** broken the yoke, *and* H3162
10: 8 But they are **a** brutish and foolish: the H259
15:18 wilt thou be **a** unto me as a liar, *and*
30:11 and will not leave thee **a** unpunished.
49:12 thou he *that* shall **a** go unpunished? thou
Jn 9:34 him, Thou wast **a** born in sins, and G3650
Act 26:29 and **a** such as I am, except these bonds. G1722
1Co 5:10 Yet not **a** with the fornicators of this G3843
9:10 Or saith he *it* **a** for our sakes? For our G3843

ALUSH
Nu 33:13 from Dophkah, and encamped in **A**. H442
14 And they removed from **A**, and H442

ALVAH
Gen 36:40 duke Timnah, duke **A**, duke Jetheth, H5933

ALVAN
Gen 36:23 *were* these; **A**, and Manahath, and H5935

ALWAY
Ex 25:30 upon the table shewbread before me **a**. H8548
Nu 9:16 So it was **a**: the cloud covered it *by day,* H8548
Dt 11: 1 and his commandments, **a**. H3605+H3117
28:33 only oppressed and crushed **a**: H3605+H3117
2Sa 9:10 shall eat bread **a** at my table. Now Ziba H8548
1Ki 11:36 have a light **a** before me in H3605+H3117
2Ki 8:19 **a** a light, *and* to his children. H3605+H3117
Job 7:16 I loathe *it*; I would not live **a**: let me H5769
Ps 9:18 For the needy shall not **a** be forgotten: H5331
119:112 thy statutes **a**, *even unto* the end. H5769
Prv 28:14 Happy *is* the man that feareth **a**: but he H8548
Mt 28:20 lo, I am with you **a**, *even* unto the end of G3956
Jn 7: 6 not yet come: but your time is **a** ready. G3842
Act 10: 2 to the people, and prayed to God **a**. G1275
Ro 11:10 not see, and bow down their back **a**. G1275
2Co 4:11 For we which live are **a** delivered unto G104
6:10 As sorrowful, yet **a** rejoicing; as poor, yet G104
Php 4: 4 Rejoice in the Lord **a**: *and* again I say, G3842
Col 4: 6 Let your speech *be* **a** with grace, G3842
1Th 2:16 to fill up their sins **a**: for the wrath is G3842
2Th 2:13 But we are bound to give thanks **a** to G3842
Tit 1:12 *are* **a** liars, evil beasts, slow bellies. G104
Heb 3:10 and said, They do **a** err in *their* heart; G104

ALWAYS
Gen 6: 3 My spirit shall not **a** strive with man, H5769
Ex 27:20 the light, to cause the lamp to burn **a**. H8548
28:38 and it shall be **a** upon his forehead, H8548
Dt 5:29 **a**, that it might be H3605+H3117
6:24 for our good **a**, that he might H3605+H3117
11:12 LORD thy God *are* **a** upon it, from the H8548
14:23 to fear the LORD thy God **a**. H3605+H3117
1Ch 16:15 Be ye mindful **a** of his covenant; the H5769
2Ch 18: 7 unto me, but **a** evil: the same *is* H3605+H3117
Job 27:10 the Almighty? will he **a** call upon God? H6256
32: 9 Great men are not ***a*** wise: neither do the
Ps 10: 5 His ways are **a** grievous; thy judgments H6256
16: 8 I have set the LORD **a** before me: H8548
103: 9 He will not **a** chide: neither will he keep H5331
Prv 5:19 and be thou ravished **a** with her love. H8548
8:30 delight, rejoicing **a** before him; H3605+H6256
Ecc 9: 8 Let thy garments be **a** white; and let thy H6256
Isa 57:16 neither will I be **a** wroth: for the spirit H5331
Jer 20:17 and her womb *to be* **a** great *with me*. H5769
Ezk 38: 8 which have been **a** waste: but it is H8548
Mt 18:10 their angels do **a** behold the face of my G1223
26:11 For ye have the poor **a** with you; but G3842
11 always with you; but me ye have not **a**. G3842
Mk 5: 5 And **a**, night and day, he was in the G1275
14: 7 For ye have the poor with you **a**, and G3842
7 do them good: but me ye have not **a**. G3842
Lk 18: 1 men ought **a** to pray, and not to faint; G3842
21:36 Watch ye therefore, and pray **a**, that ye G1722
Jn 8:29 for I do **a** those things that please him. G3842
11:42 And I knew that thou hearest me **a**: but G3842
12: 8 For the poor **a** ye have with you; but G3842
8 ye have with you; but me ye have not **a**. G3842
18:20 whither the Jews **a** resort; and in secret G3842
Act 2:25 the Lord **a** before my face, G1223+G3956
7:51 and ears, ye do **a** resist the Holy Ghost: G104
24: 3 We accept *it* **a**, and in all places, most G3839
16 myself, to have **a** a conscience void of G1275
Ro 1: 9 make mention of you **a** in my prayers; G3842
1Co 1: 4 I thank my God **a** on your behalf, for G3842
15:58 unmoveable, **a** abounding in the work G3842
2Co 2:14 Now thanks *be* unto God, which **a** G3842
4:10 **A** bearing about in the body the dying G3842
5: 6 Therefore *we are* **a** confident, knowing G3842
9: 8 you; that ye, **a** having all sufficiency G3842
Gal 4:18 But *it is* good to be zealously affected **a** G3842
Eph 5:20 Giving thanks **a** for all things unto God G3842
6:18 Praying **a** with all G1722+G2540+G3956
Php 1: 4 **A** in every prayer of mine for you all G3842
20 all boldness, as **a**, *so* now also Christ G3842
2:12 Wherefore, my beloved, as ye have **a** G3842
Col 1: 3 Lord Jesus Christ, praying **a** for you, G3842
4:12 saluteth you, **a** labouring fervently G3842
1Th 1: 2 We give thanks to God **a** for you all, G3842
3: 6 of us **a**, desiring greatly to see G3842
2Th 1: 3 We are bound to thank God **a** for you, G3842
11 Wherefore also we pray **a** for you, that G3842
3:16 you peace **a** by all means. The G1223+G3956
Phlm 4 mention of thee **a** in my prayers, G3842
Heb 9: 6 the priests went **a** into the first G1275
1Pt 3:15 and *be* ready **a** to *give* an answer to G104
2Pt 1:12 to put you **a** in remembrance of these G104
15 to have these things **a** in remembrance. G1539

AM
See the Appendix.

AMAD
Jos 19:26 And Alammelech, and **A**, and Misheal; H6008

AMAL
1Ch 7:35 Zophah, and Imna, and Shelesh, and **A**. H6000

AMALEK
Gen 36:12 bare to Eliphaz **A**: these *were* the sons H6002
16 Duke Korah, duke Gatam, *and* duke **A**: H6002
Ex 17: 8 Then came **A**, and fought with Israel in H6002
9 go out, fight with **A**: to morrow I will H6002
10 and fought with **A**: and Moses, Aaron, H6002
11 he let down his hand, **A** prevailed. H6002
13 And Joshua discomfited **A** and his H6002
14 remembrance of **A** from under heaven. H6002
16 with **A** from generation to generation. H6002
Nu 24:20 And when he looked on **A**, he took up H6002
20 parable, and said, **A** *was* the first of the H6002
Dt 25:17 Remember what **A** did unto thee by the H6002
19 remembrance of **A** from under heaven; H6002
Jdg 3:13 of Ammon and **A**, and went and smote H6002
5:14 of them against **A**; after thee, Benjamin, H6002
1Sa 15: 2 *that* which **A** did to Israel, how he H6002
3 Now go and smite **A**, and utterly H6002
5 And Saul came to a city of **A**, and laid H6002
20 Agag the king of **A**, and have utterly H6002
28:18 fierce wrath upon **A**, therefore hath the H6002
2Sa 8:12 Philistines, and of **A**, and of the spoil of H6002
1Ch 1:36 and Gatam, Kenaz, and Timna, and **A**. H6002
18:11 and from the Philistines, and from **A**. H6002
Ps 83: 7 Gebal, and Ammon, and **A**; the H6002

AMALEKITE
1Sa 30:13 servant to an **A**; and my master left H6003
2Sa 1: 8 thou? And I answered him, I *am* an **A**. H6003
13 I *am* the son of a stranger, an **A**. H6003

AMALEKITES
Gen 14: 7 all the country of the **A**, and also the H6003
Nu 13:29 The **A** dwell in the land of the south: H6002
14:25 (Now the **A** and the Canaanites dwelt H6003
43 For the **A** and the Canaanites *are* there H6003
45 Then the **A** came down, and the H6003
Jdg 6: 3 came up, and the **A**, and the children of H6002
33 Then all the Midianites and the **A** and H6002
7:12 And the Midianites and the **A** and all H6002
10:12 The Zidonians also, and the **A**, and the H6002
12:15 land of Ephraim, in the mount of the **A**. H6003
1Sa 14:48 and smote the **A**, and delivered Israel H6002
15: 6 from among the **A**, lest I destroy you H6003
6 Kenites departed from among the **A**. H6003
7 And Saul smote the **A** from Havilah H6002
8 And he took Agag the king of the **A** H6002
15 them from the **A**: for the people spared H6003
18 the sinners the **A**, and fight against H6002
20 and have utterly destroyed the **A**. H6002
32 the king of the **A**. And Agag came unto H6002
27: 8 Gezrites, and the **A**: for those *nations* H6003
30: 1 third day, that the **A** had invaded the H6003
18 And David recovered all that the **A** had H6002
2Sa 1: 1 the slaughter of the **A**, and David had H6002
1Ch 4:43 And they smote the rest of the **A** that H6002

AMAM
Jos 15:26 **A**, and Shema, and Moladah, H538

AMANA
Song 4: 8 from the top of **A**, from the top of Shenir H549

AMARIAH
1Ch 6: 7 Meraioth begat **A**, and Amariah begat H568
7 Meraioth begat Amariah, and **A** begat H568
11 And Azariah begat **A**, and Amariah H568
11 And Azariah begat Amariah, and **A** H568
52 Meraioth his son, **A** his son, Ahitub his H568
23:19 Of the sons of Hebron; Jeriah the first, **A** H568
24:23 Jeriah *the first,* **A** the second, Jahaziel H568
2Ch 19:11 And, behold, **A** the chief priest *is* over H568
31:15 and Shemaiah, **A**, and Shecaniah, in the H568
Ezr 7: 3 The son of **A**, the son of Azariah, the son H568
10:42 Shallum, **A**, *and* Joseph. H568
Neh 10: 3 Pashur, **A**, Malchijah, H568
11: 4 the son of **A**, the son of Shephatiah, H568
12: 2 **A**, Malluch, Hattush, H568
13 Of Ezra, Meshullam; of **A**, Jehohanan; H568
Zep 1: 1 the son of **A**, the son of Hizkiah, in H568

AMASA
2Sa 17:25 And Absalom made **A** captain of the H6021
25 of Joab: which **A** *was* a man's son, H6021
19:13 And say ye to **A**, *Art* thou not of my H6021
20: 4 Then said the king to **A**, Assemble me H6021
5 So **A** went to assemble *the men of* H6021
8 *is* in Gibeon, **A** went before them. And H6021
9 And Joab said to **A**, *Art* thou in health, H6021
9 And Joab took **A** by the beard with the H6021
10 But **A** took no heed to the sword that H6021
12 And **A** wallowed in blood in the midst H6021
12 still, he removed **A** out of the highway H6021
1Ki 2: 5 of Ner, and unto **A** the son of Jether, H6021
32 host of Israel, and **A** the son of Jether, H6021
1Ch 2:17 And Abigail bare **A**: and the father of H6021
17 father of **A** *was* Jether the Ishmeelite. H6021
2Ch 28:12 of Shallum, and **A** the son of Hadlai, H6021

AMASAI
1Ch 6:25 And the sons of Elkanah; **A**, and H6022
35 the son of Mahath, the son of **A**, H6022
12:18 Then the spirit came upon **A**, *who was* H6022
15:24 Nethaneel, and **A**, and Zechariah, and H6022
2Ch 29:12 Mahath the son of **A**, and Joel the son of H6022

AMASHAI
Neh 11:13 and two: and **A** the son of Azareel, H6023

AMASIAH
2Ch 17:16 And next him *was* **A** the son of Zichri, H6007

AMAZED
Ex 15:15 Then the dukes of Edom shall be **a**; the H926
Jdg 20:41 of Benjamin were **a**: for they saw that evil H926
Job 32:15 They were **a**, they answered no more: H2865
Isa 13: 8 they shall be **a** one at another; their H8539
Ezk 32:10 Yea, I will make many people **a** at thee, H8074
Mt 12:23 And all the people were **a**, and said, Is G1839
19:25 **a**, saying, Who then can be saved? G1605
Mk 1:27 And they were all **a**, insomuch that they G2284
2:12 that they were all **a**, and glorified God, G1839
6:51 they were sore **a** in themselves beyond G1839
9:15 **a**, and running to *him* saluted him. G1568
10:32 and they were **a**; and as they followed, G2284
14:33 to be sore **a**, and to be very heavy; G1568
16: 8 and were **a**: neither said they any G1611
Lk 2:48 And when they saw him, they were **a**: G1605
4:36 And they were all **a**, and spake among G2285
5:26 And they were all **a**, and they glorified G1611
9:43 And they were all **a** at the mighty G1605
Act 2: 7 And they were all **a** and marvelled, G1839
12 And they were all **a**, and were in doubt, G1839
9:21 But all that heard *him* were **a**, and said; G1839

AMAZEMENT
Act 3:10 with wonder and **a** at that which had G1611
1Pt 3: 6 do well, and are not afraid with any **a**. G4423

AMAZIAH
2Ki 12:21 and **A** his son reigned in his stead. H558
13:12 he fought against **A** king of Judah, *are* H558
14: 1 reigned **A** the son of Joash king of Judah. H558
8 Then **A** sent messengers to Jehoash, the H558
9 And Jehoash the king of Israel sent to **A** H558
11 But **A** would not hear. Therefore Jehoash H558
11 up; and he and **A** king of Judah looked H558
13 And Jehoash king of Israel took **A** king H558
15 he fought with **A** king of Judah, *are* they H558

2Ki 14:17 And **A** the son of Joash king of Judah H558
18 And the rest of the acts of **A**, *are* they not H558
21 made him king instead of his father **A**. H558
23 In the fifteenth year of **A** the son of Joash H558
15: 1 Azariah son of **A** king of Judah to reign. H558
3 to all that his father **A** had done; H558
1Ch 3:12 **A** his son, Azariah his son, Jotham his H558
4:34 and Jamlech, and Joshah the son of **A**, H558
6:45 The son of Hashabiah, the son of **A**, the H558
2Ch 24:27 And **A** his son reigned in his stead. H558
25: 1 **A** *was* twenty and five years old *when* he H558
5 Moreover **A** gathered Judah together, H558
9 And **A** said to the man of God, But what H558
10 Then **A** separated them, *to wit*, the army H558
11 And **A** strengthened himself, and led H558
13 But the soldiers of the army which **A** H558
14 Now it came to pass, after that **A** was H558
15 kindled against **A**, and he sent unto him H558
17 Then **A** king of Judah took advice, and H558
18 And Joash king of Israel sent to **A** king of H558
20 But **A** would not hear; for it *came* of H558
21 the face, *both* he and **A** king of Judah, at H558
23 And Joash the king of Israel took **A** king H558
25 And **A** the son of Joash king of Judah H558
26 Now the rest of the acts of **A**, first and H558
27 Now after the time that **A** did turn away H558
26: 1 him king in the room of his father **A**. H558
4 according to all that his father **A** did. H558
Am 7:10 Then **A** the priest of Beth-el sent to H558
12 Also **A** said unto Amos, O thou seer, go, H558
14 Then answered Amos, and said to **A**, I H558

AMBASSADOR
Prv 13:17 into mischief: but a faithful **a** *is* health. H6735
Jer 49:14 the LORD, and an **a** is sent unto the H6735
Oba 1 the LORD, and an **a** is sent among the H6735
Eph 6:20 For which I am an **a** in bonds: that *G4243*

AMBASSADORS
Jos 9: 4 if they had been **a**, and took old sacks H6737
2Ch 32:31 Howbeit in *the business of* the **a** of the H3887
35:21 But he sent **a** to him, saying, What H4397
Isa 18: 2 That sendeth **a** by the sea, even in H6735
30: 4 For his princes were at Zoan, and his **a** H4397
33: 7 the **a** of peace shall weep bitterly. H4397
Ezk 17:15 him in sending his **a** into Egypt, that H4397
2Co 5:20 Now then we are **a** for Christ, as *G4243*

AMBASSAGE
Lk 14:32 an **a**, and desireth conditions of peace. *G4242*

AMBER
Ezk 1: 4 colour of **a**, out of the midst of the fire. H2830
27 And I saw as the colour of **a**, as the H2830
8: 2 of brightness, as the colour of **a**. H2830

AMBUSH
Jos 8: 2 lay thee an **a** for the city behind it. H693
7 Then ye shall rise up from the **a**, and H693
9 they went to lie in **a**, and abode between H3993
12 set them to lie in **a** between Beth-el and H693
14 liers in **a** against him behind the city. H693
19 And the **a** arose quickly out of their H693
21 Israel saw that the **a** had taken the city, H693

AMBUSHES
Jer 51:12 prepare the **a**: for the LORD hath both H693

AMBUSHMENT
2Ch 13:13 But Jeroboam caused an **a** to come H3993
13 Judah, and the **a** *was* behind them. H3993

AMBUSHMENTS
2Ch 20:22 the LORD set **a** against the children H693

AMEN
Nu 5:22 rot: And the woman shall say, **A**, amen. H543
22 rot: And the woman shall say, Amen, **a**. H543
Dt 27:15 all the people shall answer and say, **A**. H543
16 mother. And all the people shall say, **A**. H543
17 And all the people shall say, **A**. H543
18 the way. And all the people shall say, **A**. H543
19 widow. And all the people shall say, **A**. H543
20 skirt. And all the people shall say, **A**. H543
21 of beast. And all the people shall say, **A**. H543
22 mother. And all the people shall say, **A**. H543
23 in law. And all the people shall say, **A**. H543
24 secretly. And all the people shall say, **A**. H543
25 person. And all the people shall say, **A**. H543
Dt 27:26 do them. And all the people shall say, **A**. H543
1Ki 1:36 the king, and said, **A**: the LORD God of H543
1Ch 16:36 people said, **A**, and praised the LORD. H543
Neh 5:13 the congregation said, **A**, and praised the H543
8: 6 people answered, **A**, Amen, with lifting H543
6 answered, Amen, **A**, with lifting up their H543
Ps 41:13 and to everlasting. **A**, and Amen. H543
13 and to everlasting. Amen, and **A**. H543
72:19 be filled *with* his glory; **A**, and Amen. H543
19 be filled *with* his glory; Amen, and **A**. H543
89:52 Blessed *be* the LORD for evermore. **A**, H543
52 *be* the LORD for evermore. Amen, and **A**. H543
106:48 all the people say, **A**. Praise ye the LORD. H543
Jer 28: 6 Even the prophet Jeremiah said, **A**: the H543
Mt 6:13 and the power, and the glory, for ever. **A**. *G281*
28:20 alway, *even* unto the end of the world. **A**. *G281*
Mk 16:20 the word with signs following. **A**. *G281*
Lk 24:53 the temple, praising and blessing God. **A**. *G281*
Jn 21:25 the books that should be written. **A**. *G281*
Ro 1:25 the Creator, who is blessed for ever. **A**. *G281*
9: 5 who is over all, God blessed for ever. **A**. *G281*
11:36 all things: to whom *be* glory for ever. **A**. *G281*
15:33 Now the God of peace *be* with you all. **A**. *G281*
16:20 of our Lord Jesus Christ *be* with you. **A**. *G281*
24 our Lord Jesus Christ *be* with you all. **A**. *G281*
27 *be* glory through Jesus Christ for ever. **A**. *G281*
1Co 14:16 of the unlearned say **A** at thy giving of *G281*
16:24 My love *be* with you all in Christ Jesus. **A**. *G281*
2Co 1:20 in him **A**, unto the glory of God by us. *G281*
13:14 of the Holy Ghost, *be* with you all. **A**. *G281*
Gal 1: 5 To whom *be* glory for ever and ever. **A**. *G281*
6:18 Lord Jesus Christ *be* with your spirit. **A**. *G281*
Eph 3:21 all ages, world without end. **A**. *G281*
6:24 love our Lord Jesus Christ in sincerity. **A**. *G281*
Php 4:20 our Father *be* glory for ever and ever. **A**. *G281*
23 our Lord Jesus Christ *be* with you all. **A**. *G281*
Col 4:18 my bonds. Grace *be* with you. **A**. *G281*
1Th 5:28 of our Lord Jesus Christ *be* with you. **A**. *G281*
2Th 3:18 our Lord Jesus Christ *be* with you all. **A**. *G281*
1Ti 1:17 *be* honour and glory for ever and ever. **A**. *G281*
6:16 *be* honour and power everlasting. **A**. *G281*
21 the faith. Grace *be* with thee. **A**. *G281*
2Ti 4:18 to whom *be* glory for ever and ever. **A**. *G281*
22 *be* with thy spirit. Grace *be* with you. **A**. *G281*
Tit 3:15 us in the faith. Grace *be* with you all. **A**. *G281*
Phlm 25 Lord Jesus Christ *be* with your spirit. **A**. *G281*
Heb 13:21 to whom *be* glory for ever and ever. **A**. *G281*
25 Grace *be* with you all. **A**. *G281*
1Pt 4:11 and dominion for ever and ever. **A**. *G281*
5:11 glory and dominion for ever and ever. **A**. *G281*
14 *be* with you all that are in Christ Jesus. **A**. *G281*
2Pt 3:18 him *be* glory both now and for ever. **A**. *G281*
1Jn 5:21 children, keep yourselves from idols. **A**. *G281*
2Jn 13 children of thy elect sister greet thee. **A**. *G281*
Jude 25 and power, both now and ever. **A**. *G281*
Rev 1: 6 glory and dominion for ever and ever. **A**. *G281*
7 shall wail because of him. Even so, **A**. *G281*
18 **A**; and have the keys of hell and of death. *G281*
3:14 things saith the **A**, the faithful and true *G281*
5:14 And the four beasts said, **A**. And the four *G281*
7:12 Saying, **A**: Blessing, and glory, and *G281*
12 *be* unto our God for ever and ever. **A**. *G281*
19: 4 sat on the throne, saying, **A**; Alleluia. *G281*
22:20 quickly. **A**. Even so, come, Lord Jesus. *G281*
21 our Lord Jesus Christ *be* with you all. **A**. *G281*

AMEND
2Ch 34:10 of the LORD, to repair and **a** the house: H2388
Jer 7: 3 the God of Israel, **A** your ways and H3190
5 For if ye throughly **a** your ways and H3190
26:13 Therefore now **a** your ways and your H3190
35:15 his evil way, and **a** your doings, and go H3190
Jn 4:52 when he began to **a**. And they said unto *G2192*

AMENDS
Lev 5:16 And he shall make **a** for the harm that H7999

AMERCE
Dt 22:19 And they shall **a** him in an hundred H6064

AMETHYST
Ex 28:19 the third row a ligure, an agate, and an **a**. H306
39:12 third row, a ligure, an agate, and an **a**. H306
Rev 21:20 the eleventh, a jacinth; the twelfth, an **a**. *G271*

AMI
Ezr 2:57 Pochereth of Zebaim, the children of **A**. H532

AMIABLE
Ps 84: 1 How **a** *are* thy tabernacles, O LORD of H3039

AMINADAB
Mt 1: 4 And Aram begat **A**; and Aminadab begat *G284*
4 And Aram begat Aminadab; and **A** *G284*
Lk 3:33 Which was *the son* of **A**, which was *the* *G284*

AMISS
2Ch 6:37 have done **a**, and have dealt wickedly; H5753
Dan 3:29 any thing **a** against the God H7960+H7955
Lk 23:41 deeds: but this man hath done nothing **a**. *G824*
Jas 4: 3 because ye ask **a**, that ye may consume *G2560*

AMITTAI
2Ki 14:25 Jonah, the son of **A**, the prophet, which H573
Jna 1: 1 came unto Jonah the son of **A**, saying, H573

AMMAH
2Sa 2:24 come to the hill of **A**, that *lieth* before H522

AMMI
Hos 2: 1 Say ye unto your brethren, **A**; and to H5971

AMMIEL
Nu 13:12 Of the tribe of Dan, **A** the son of H5988
2Sa 9: 4 of Machir, the son of **A**, in Lo-debar. H5988
5 of Machir, the son of **A**, from Lo-debar. H5988
17:27 Machir the son of **A** of Lo-debar, and H5988
1Ch 3: 5 four, of Bath-shua the daughter of **A**: H5988
26: 5 **A** the sixth, Issachar the seventh, H5988

AMMIHUD
Nu 1:10 the son of **A**: of Manasseh; Gamaliel H5989
2:18 *shall be* Elishama the son of **A**. H5989
7:48 the son of **A**, prince of the children H5989
53 the offering of Elishama the son of **A**. H5989
10:22 his host *was* Elishama the son of **A**. H5989
34:20 of Simeon, Shemuel the son of **A**. H5989
28 of Naphtali, Pedahel the son of **A**. H5989
2Sa 13:37 to Talmai, the son of **A**, king of Geshur. H5989
1Ch 7:26 Laadan his son, **A** his son, Elishama H5989
9: 4 Uthai the son of **A**, the son of Omri, the H5989

AMMINADAB
Ex 6:23 daughter of **A**, sister of Naashon, to H5992
Nu 1: 7 Of Judah; Nahshon the son of **A**. H5992
2: 3 the son of **A** *shall be* captain of the H5992
7:12 the son of **A**, of the tribe of Judah: H5992
17 the offering of Nahshon the son of **A**. H5992
10:14 over his host *was* Nahshon the son of **A**. H5992
Ru 4:19 Hezron begat Ram, and Ram begat **A**, H5992
20 And **A** begat Nahshon, and Nahshon H5992
1Ch 2:10 And Ram begat **A**; and Amminadab H5992
10 And Ram begat Amminadab; and **A** H5992
6:22 The sons of Kohath; **A** his son, Korah H5992
15:10 Of the sons of Uzziel; **A** the chief, and H5992
11 and Joel, Shemaiah, and Eliel, and **A**, H5992

AMMI-NADIB
Song 6:12 *like* the chariots of **A**. H5081+H5971+H5993

AMMISHADDAI
Nu 1:12 Of Dan; Ahiezer the son of **A**. H5996
2:25 of Dan *shall be* Ahiezer the son of **A**. H5996
7:66 On the tenth day Ahiezer the son of **A**, H5996
71 *was* the offering of Ahiezer the son of **A**. H5996
10:25 over his host *was* Ahiezer the son of **A**. H5996

AMMIZABAD
1Ch 27: 6 thirty: and in his course *was* **A** his son. H5990

AMMON
Gen 19:38 of the children of **A** unto this day. H5983
Nu 21:24 the children of **A**: for the border of the H5983
24 border of the children of **A** *was* strong. H5983
Dt 2:19 the children of **A**, distress them not, nor H5983
19 of the children of **A** *any* possession; H5983
37 Only unto the land of the children of **A** H5983
3:11 of the children of **A**? nine cubits *was* the H5983
16 *which is* the border of the children of **A**; H5983
Jos 12: 2 *which is* the border of the children of **A**; H5983
13:10 unto the border of the children of **A**; H5983
25 of **A**, unto Aroer that *is* before Rabbah; H5983
Jdg 3:13 him the children of **A** and Amalek, and H5983
10: 6 of the children of **A**, and the gods of the H5983
7 and into the hands of the children of **A**. H5983
9 Moreover the children of **A** passed over H5983
11 children of **A**, and from the Philistines? H5983

Jdg 10:17 Then the children of A were gathered H5983
18 the children of A? he shall be head over H5983
11: 4 children of A made war against Israel. H5983
5 the children of A made war against H5983
6 we may fight with the children of A. H5983
8 the children of A, and be our head over H5983
9 the children of A, and the LORD deliver H5983
12 of the children of A, saying, What hast H5983
13 And the king of the children of A H5983
14 again unto the king of the children of A: H5983
15 Moab, nor the land of the children of A: H5983
27 children of Israel and the children of A. H5983
28 Howbeit the king of the children of A H5983
29 he passed over *unto* the children of A. H5983
30 the children of A into mine hands, H5983
31 the children of A, shall surely be the H5983
32 the children of A to fight against them; H5983
33 the children of A were subdued before H5983
36 thine enemies, *even* of the children of A. H5983
12: 1 the children of A, and didst not call us H5983
2 the children of A; and when I called H5983
3 against the children of A, and the LORD H5983
1Sa 12:12 of the children of A came against you, H5983
14:47 the children of A, and against Edom, H5983
2Sa 8:12 and of the children of A, and of the H5983
10: 1 of the children of A died, and Hanun H5983
2 came into the land of the children of A. H5983
3 And the princes of the children of A H5983
6 And when the children of A saw that H5983
6 the children of A sent and hired the H5983
8 And the children of A came out, and H5983
10 *them* in array against the children of A. H5983
11 if the children of A be too strong for H5983
14 And when the children of A saw that H5983
14 children of A, and came to Jerusalem. H5983
19 to help the children of A any more. H5983
11: 1 the children of A, and besieged Rabbah. H5983
12: 9 him with the sword of the children of A. H5983
26 children of A, and took the royal city. H5983
31 of the children of A. So David and all H5983
17:27 of the children of A, and Machir the son H5983
1Ki 11: 7 the abomination of the children of A. H5983
33 god of the children of A, and have not H5983
2Ki 23:13 of the children of A, did the king defile. H5983
24: 2 of the children of A, and sent them H5983
1Ch 18:11 from the children of A, and from the H5983
19: 1 of the children of A died, and his son H5983
2 of A to Hanun, to comfort him. H5983
3 But the princes of the children of A H5983
6 And when the children of A saw that H5983
6 and the children of A sent a thousand H5983
7 the children of A gathered themselves H5983
9 And the children of A came out, and H5983
11 in array against the children of A. H5983
12 if the children of A be too strong for H5983
15 And when the children of A saw that H5983
19 help the children of A any more. H5983
20: 1 of the children of A, and came and H5983
3 of the children of A. And David and all H5983
2Ch 20: 1 the children of A, and with them *other* H5983
10 And now, behold, the children of A and H5983
22 the children of A, Moab, and mount H5983
23 For the children of A and Moab stood H5983
27: 5 the children of A gave him the same H5983
5 did the children of A pay unto him, H5983
Neh 13:23 wives of Ashdod, of A, *and* of Moab: H5984
Ps 83: 7 Gebal, and A, and Amalek; the H5983
Isa 11:14 and the children of A shall obey them. H5983
Jer 9:26 the children of A, and Moab, and all H5983
25:21 and Moab, and the children of A, H5983
49: 6 of the children of A, saith the LORD. H5983
Dan 11:41 and the chief of the children of A. H5983
Am 1:13 of the children of A, and for four, I will H5983
Zep 2: 8 of the children of A, whereby they have H5983
9 the children of A as Gomorrah, *even* H5983

AMMONITE
Dt 23: 3 An A or Moabite shall not enter into H5984
1Sa 11: 1 Then Nahash the A came up, and H5984
2 And Nahash the A answered them, On H5984
2Sa 23:37 Zelek the A, Naharai the Beerothite, H5984
1Ch 11:39 Zelek the A, Naharai the Berothite, the H5984
Neh 2:10 the servant, the A, heard *of it*, it grieved H5984
19 the servant, the A, and Geshem the H5984
4: 3 Now Tobiah the A *was* by him, and he H5984
13: 1 written, that the A and the Moabite H5984

AMMONITES
Dt 2:20 and the A call them Zamzummims; H5984
1Sa 11:11 and slew the A until the heat of the H5983
1Ki 11: 1 A, Edomites, Zidonians, *and* Hittites; H5984
5 after Milcom the abomination of the A. H5984
2Ch 20: 1 A, came against Jehoshaphat to battle. H5984
26: 8 And the A gave gifts to Uzziah: and his H5984
27: 5 He fought also with the king of the A, H5984
Ezr 9: 1 the Jebusites, the A, the Moabites, the H5984
Neh 4: 7 the Arabians, and the A, and the H5984
Jer 27: 3 to the king of the A, and to the king of H5984
40:11 and among the A, and in Edom, and H5984
14 the king of the A hath sent Ishmael the H5984
41:10 and departed to go over to the A. H5984
15 with eight men, and went to the A. H5984
49: 1 Concerning the A, thus saith the LORD; H5984
2 in Rabbah of the A; and it shall be a H5984
Ezk 21:20 of the A, and to Judah in H1121+H5984
28 the A, and concerning H1121+H5984
25: 2 A, and prophesy against them; H1121+H5984
3 And say unto the A, Hear the H1121+H5984
5 and the A a couchingplace H1121+H5984
10 east with the A, and will give H1121+H5984
10 that the A may not be H1121+H5984

AMMONITESS
1Ki 14:21 his mother's name *was* Naamah an A. H5984
31 *was* Naamah an A. And Abijam his son H5984
2Ch 12:13 his mother's name *was* Naamah an A. H5984
24:26 of Shimeath an A, and Jehozabad the H5984

AMNON
2Sa 3: 2 was A, of Ahinoam the Jezreelitess; H550
13: 1 and A the son of David loved her. H550
2 And A was so vexed, that he fell sick for H550
2 *was* a virgin; and A thought it hard for H550
3 But A had a friend, whose name *was* H550
4 not tell me? And A said unto him, I love H550
6 So A lay down, and made himself sick: H550
6 come to see him, A said unto the king, I H550
9 refused to eat. And A said, Have out all H550
10 And A said unto Tamar, Bring the meat H550
10 *them* into the chamber to A her brother. H550
15 Then A hated her exceedingly; so that H550
15 her. And A said unto her, Arise, be gone. H550
20 unto her, Hath A thy brother been with H550
22 And Absalom spake unto his brother A H550
22 for Absalom hated A, because he had H550
26 let my brother A go with us. And the H550
27 But Absalom pressed him, that he let A H550
28 unto you, Smite A; then kill him, fear not: H550
29 And the servants of Absalom did unto A H550
32 the king's sons; for A only is dead: for by H550
33 king's sons are dead: for A only is dead. H550
39 concerning A, seeing he was dead. H550
1Ch 3: 1 Hebron; the firstborn A, of Ahinoam the H550
4:20 And the sons of Shimon *were*, A, and H550

AMNON'S
2Sa 13: 7 brother A house, and dress him meat. H550
8 So Tamar went to her brother A house; H550
28 Mark ye now when A heart is merry with H550

AMOK
Neh 12: 7 Sallu, A, Hilkiah, Jedaiah. These *were* H5987
20 Of Sallai, Kallai; of A, Eber; H5987

AMON
1Ki 22:26 him back unto A the governor of the H526
2Ki 21:18 Uzza: and A his son reigned in his stead. H526
19 A *was* twenty and two years old when he H526
23 And the servants of A conspired against H526
24 against king A; and the people of the H526
25 Now the rest of the acts of A which he H526
1Ch 3:14 A his son, Josiah his son. H526
2Ch 18:25 carry him back to A the governor of the H526
33:20 and A his son reigned in his stead. H526
21 A *was* two and twenty years old when he H526
22 his father: for A sacrificed unto all the H526
23 but A trespassed more and more. H526
25 against king A; and the people of the H526
Neh 7:59 Pochereth of Zebaim, the children of A. H526
Jer 1: 2 of Josiah the son of A king of Judah, in H526
25: 3 year of Josiah the son of A king of Judah, H526
Zep 1: 1 of Josiah the son of A, king of Judah. H526
Mt 1:10 begat A; and Amon begat Josias; *G300*
10 begat Amon; and A begat Josias; *G300*

AMONG See the Appendix.

AMONGST See the Appendix.

AMORITE
Gen 10:16 And the Jebusite, and the A, and the H567
14:13 of Mamre the A, brother of Eshcol, and H567
48:22 the A with my sword and with my bow. H567
Ex 33: 2 the Canaanite, the A, and the Hittite, and H567
34:11 out before thee the A, and the Canaanite, H567
Nu 32:39 and dispossessed the A which *was* in it. H567
Dt 2:24 hand Sihon the A, king of Heshbon, and H567
Jos 9: 1 the Hittite, and the A, the Canaanite, the H567
11: 3 west, and *to* the A, and the Hittite, and H567
1Ch 1:14 The Jebusite also, and the A, and the H567
Ezk 16: 3 *was* an A, and thy mother an Hittite. H567
45 *was* an Hittite, and your father an A. H567
Am 2: 9 Yet destroyed I the A before them, H567
10 wilderness, to possess the land of the A. H567

AMORITES
Gen 14: 7 also the A, that dwelt in Hazezon-tamar. H567
15:16 for the iniquity of the A *is* not yet full. H567
21 And the A, and the Canaanites, and the H567
Ex 3: 8 Hittites, and the A, and the Perizzites, H567
17 Hittites, and the A, and the Perizzites, H567
13: 5 Hittites, and the A, and the Hivites, and H567
23:23 thee in unto the A, and the Hittites, and H567
Nu 13:29 the Jebusites, and the A, dwell in the H567
21:13 out of the coasts of the A: for Arnon *is* the H567
13 of Moab, between Moab and the A. H567
21 unto Sihon king of the A, saying, H567
25 all the cities of the A, in Heshbon, and in H567
26 the king of the A, who had fought against H567
29 into captivity unto Sihon king of the A. H567
31 Thus Israel dwelt in the land of the A. H567
32 and drove out the A that *were* there. H567
34 king of the A, which dwelt at Heshbon. H567
22: 2 saw all that Israel had done to the A. H567
32:33 Sihon king of the A, and the kingdom of H567
Dt 1: 4 Sihon the king of the A, which dwelt in H567
7 go to the mount of the A, and unto all *the* H567
19 mountain of the A, as the LORD our God H567
20 mountain of the A, which the LORD our H567
27 us into the hand of the A, to destroy us. H567
44 And the A, which dwelt in that H567
3: 2 king of the A, which dwelt at Heshbon. H567
8 two kings of the A the land that *was* on H567
9 call Sirion; and the A call it Shenir;) H567
4:46 of Sihon king of the A, who dwelt at H567
47 two kings of the A, which *were* on this H567
7: 1 and the A, and the Canaanites, H567
20:17 Hittites, and the A, the Canaanites, and H567
31: 4 to Og, kings of the A, and unto the land H567
Jos 2:10 two kings of the A, that *were* on the other H567
3:10 Girgashites, and the A, and the Jebusites. H567
5: 1 all the kings of the A, which *were* on the H567
7: 7 the hand of the A, to destroy us? would H567
9:10 the two kings of the A, that *were* beyond H567
10: 5 Therefore the five kings of the A, the king H567
6 for all the kings of the A that dwell in the H567
12 delivered up the A before the children of H567
12: 2 Sihon king of the A, who dwelt in H567
8 the Hittites, the A, and the Canaanites, H567
13: 4 unto Aphek, to the borders of the A: H567
10 And all the cities of Sihon king of the A, H567
21 of Sihon king of the A, which reigned in H567
24: 8 And I brought you into the land of the A, H567
11 against you, the A, and the Perizzites, H567
12 the two kings of the A; *but* not with thy H567
15 or the gods of the A, in whose land ye H567
18 the people, even the A which dwelt in the H567
Jdg 1:34 And the A forced the children of Dan H567
35 But the A would dwell in mount Heres in H567
36 And the coast of the A *was* from the H567
3: 5 Hittites, and A, and Perizzites, and H567
6:10 not the gods of the A, in whose land ye H567
10: 8 in the land of the A, which *is* in Gilead. H567
11 and from the A, from the children of H567
11:19 Sihon king of the A, the king of Heshbon; H567
21 of the A, the inhabitants of that country. H567
22 all the coasts of the A, from Arnon even H567
23 hath dispossessed the A from before his H567
1Sa 7:14 was peace between Israel and the A. H567
2Sa 21: 2 the remnant of the A; and the children of H567
1Ki 4:19 of Sihon king of the A, and of Og king of H567
9:20 *And* all the people *that were* left of the A, H567
21:26 *things* as did the A, whom the LORD cast H567
2Ki 21:11 above all that the A did, which *were* H567
2Ch 8: 7 Hittites, and the A, and the Perizzites, H567
Ezr 9: 1 the Moabites, the Egyptians, and the A. H567
Neh 9: 8 the Hittites, the A, and the Perizzites, H567
Ps 135:11 Sihon king of the A, and Og king of H567

Ps 136:19 Sihon king of the A: for his mercy H567

AMOS
Am 1: 1 The words of A, who was among the H5986
7: 8 And the LORD said unto me, A, what H5986
10 king of Israel, saying, A hath conspired H5986
11 For thus A saith, Jeroboam shall die by H5986
12 Also Amaziah said unto A, O thou seer, H5986
14 Then answered A, and said to H5986
8: 2 And he said, A, what seest thou? And I H5986
Lk 3:25 was *the son* of A, which was *the son* of G301

AMOUNTING
2Ch 3: 8 with fine gold, *a* to six hundred talents.

AMOZ
2Ki 19: 2 to Isaiah the prophet the son of A. H531
20 Then Isaiah the son of A sent to H531
20: 1 Isaiah the son of A came to him, and H531
2Ch 26:22 Isaiah the prophet, the son of A, write. H531
32:20 the son of A, prayed and cried to heaven. H531
32 prophet, the son of A, *and* in the book of H531
Isa 1: 1 The vision of Isaiah the son of A, which H531
2: 1 The word that Isaiah the son of A saw H531
13: 1 which Isaiah the son of A did see. H531
20: 2 Isaiah the son of A, saying, Go and loose H531
37: 2 unto Isaiah the prophet the son of A. H531
21 Then Isaiah the son of A sent unto H531
38: 1 the prophet the son of A came unto him, H531

AMPHIPOLIS
Act 17: 1 Now when they had passed through A G295

AMPLIAS
Ro 16: 8 Greet A my beloved in the Lord. G291

AMRAM
Ex 6:18 And the sons of Kohath; A, and Izhar, H6019
20 And A took him Jochebed his father's H6019
20 years of the life of A *were* an hundred H6019
Nu 3:19 A, and Izehar, Hebron, and Uzziel. H6019
26:58 of the Korathites. And Kohath begat A. H6019
59 and she bare unto A Aaron and Moses, H6019
1Ch 1:41 the sons of Dishon; A, and Eshban, and H2566
6: 2 And the sons of Kohath; A, Izhar, and H6019
3 And the children of A; Aaron, and H6019
18 And the sons of Kohath *were*, A, and H6019
23:12 The sons of Kohath; A, Izhar, Hebron, H6019
13 The sons of A; Aaron and Moses: and H6019
24:20 Of the sons of A; Shubael: of the sons H6019
Ezr 10:34 Of the sons of Bani; Maadai, A, and Uel, H6019

AMRAMITES
Nu 3:27 And of Kohath *was* the family of the A, H6020
1Ch 26:23 Of the A, *and* the Izharites, the H6020

AMRAM'S
Nu 26:59 And the name of A wife *was* Jochebed, H6019

AMRAPHEL
Gen 14: 1 And it came to pass in the days of A king H569
9 of nations, and A king of Shinar, and H569

AMZI
1Ch 6:46 The son of A, the son of Bani, the son of H557
Neh 11:12 of Pelaliah, the son of A, the son of H557

AN See the Appendix.

ANAB
Jos 11:21 from Debir, from A, and from all the H6024
15:50 And A, and Eshtemoh, and Anim, H6024

ANAH
Gen 36: 2 of A the daughter of Zibeon the Hivite; H6034
14 the daughter of A the daughter of H6034
18 the daughter of A, Esau's wife. H6034
20 Lotan, and Shobal, and Zibeon, and A, H6034
24 both Ajah, and A: this *was that* Anah H6034
24 this *was that* A that found the mules H6034
25 And the children of A *were* these; H6034
25 and Aholibamah the daughter of A. H6034
29 duke Shobal, duke Zibeon, duke A, H6034
1Ch 1:38 A, and Dishon, and Ezer, and Dishan. H6034
40 And the sons of Zibeon; Aiah, and A. H6034
41 The sons of A; Dishon. And the sons of H6034

ANAHARATH
Jos 19:19 And Hapharaim, and Shion, and A, H588

ANAIAH
Neh 8: 4 and Shema, and A, and Urijah, and H6043
10:22 Pelatiah, Hanan, A, H6043

ANAK
Nu 13:22 the children of A, *were.* (Now Hebron H6061
28 we saw the children of A there. H6061
33 giants, the sons of A, *which come* of the H6061
Dt 9: 2 Who can stand before the children of A! H6061
Jos 15:13 the father of A, which *city is* Hebron. H6061
14 thence the three sons of A, Sheshai, and H6061
14 Ahiman, and Talmai, the children of A. H6061
21:11 of Arba the father of A, which *city is* H6061
Jdg 1:20 he expelled thence the three sons of A. H6061

ANAKIMS
Dt 1:28 we have seen the sons of the A there. H6062
2:10 great, and many, and tall, as the A; H6062
11 A; but the Moabites call them Emims. H6062
21 many, and tall, as the A; but the LORD H6062
9: 2 tall, the children of the A, whom thou H6062
Jos 11:21 and cut off the A from the mountains, H6062
22 There was none of the A left in the land H6062
14:12 in that day how the A *were* there, and H6062
15 the A. And the land had rest from war. H6062

ANAMIM
Gen 10:13 And Mizraim begat Ludim, and A, and H6047
1Ch 1:11 And Mizraim begat Ludim, and A, and H6047

ANAMMELECH
2Ki 17:31 and A, the gods of Sepharvaim. H6048

ANAN
Neh 10:26 And Ahijah, Hanan, A, H6052

ANANI
1Ch 3:24 Johanan, and Dalaiah, and A, seven. H6054

ANANIAH
Neh 3:23 of Maaseiah the son of A by his house. H6055
11:32 *And* at Anathoth, Nob, A, H6055

ANANIAS
Act 5: 1 But a certain man named A, with G367
3 But Peter said, A, why hath Satan filled G367
5 And A hearing these words fell down, G367
9:10 Damascus, named A; and to him said the G367
10 A. And he said, Behold, I *am here*, Lord. G367
12 a man named A coming in, and putting G367
13 Then A answered, Lord, I have heard by G367
17 And A went his way, and entered into G367
22:12 And one A, a devout man according to G367
23: 2 And the high priest A commanded them G367
24: 1 And after five days A the high priest G367

ANATH
Jdg 3:31 Shamgar the son of A, which slew of the H6067
5: 6 In the days of Shamgar the son of A, in H6067

ANATHEMA
1Co 16:22 Jesus Christ, let him be A Maranatha. G331

ANATHOTH
Jos 21:18 A with her suburbs, and Almon with H6068
1Ki 2:26 the king, Get thee to A, unto thine own H6068
1Ch 6:60 her suburbs, and A with her suburbs. H6068
7: 8 and Abiah, and A, and Alameth. All H6068
Ezr 2:23 The men of A, an hundred twenty and H6068
Neh 7:27 The men of A, an hundred twenty and H6068
10:19 Hariph, A, Nebai, H6068
11:32 *And* at A, Nob, Ananiah, H6068
Isa 10:30 it to be heard unto Laish, O poor A. H6068
Jer 1: 1 that *were* in A in the land of Benjamin: H6068
11:21 LORD of the men of A, that seek thy life, H6068
23 of A, *even* the year of their visitation. H6068
29:27 Jeremiah of A, which maketh himself H6069
32: 7 thee my field that *is* in A: for the right of H6068
8 pray thee, that *is* in A, which *is* in the H6068
9 son, that *was* in A, and weighed him the H6068

ANCESTORS
Lev 26:45 the covenant of their a, whom I brought H7223

ANCHOR
Heb 6:19 Which *hope* we have as an a of the soul, G45

ANCHORS
Act 27:29 they cast four a out of the stern, and G45
Act 27:30 would have cast a out of the foreship, G45
40 And when they had taken up the a, they G45

ANCIENT
Dt 33:15 And for the chief things of the a H6924
Jdg 5:21 swept them away, that a river, the river H6917
2Ki 19:25 have done it, *and* of a times that I have H6924
1Ch 4:22 Jashubilehem. And *these are* a things. H6267
Ezr 3:12 fathers, *who were* a men, that had seen H2204
Job 12:12 With the a *is* wisdom; and in length of H3453
Ps 77: 5 the days of old, the years of a times. H5769
Prv 22:28 Remove not the a landmark, which thy H5769
Isa 3: 2 the prophet, and the prudent, and the a, H2205
5 a, and the base against the honourable. H2205
9:15 The a and honourable, he *is* the head; H2205
19:11 the son of the wise, the son of a kings? H6924
23: 7 antiquity *is* of a days? her own feet H6924
37:26 done it; *and* of a times, that I have H6924
44: 7 since I appointed the a people? and the H5769
45:21 declared this from a time? *who* hath H6924
46:10 and from a times *the things* that H6924
47: 6 a hast thou very heavily laid thy yoke. H2205
51: 9 LORD; awake, as in the a days, in the H6924
Jer 5:15 nation, it *is* an a nation, a nation H5769
18:15 their ways *from* the a paths, to walk in H5769
Ezk 9: 6 the a men which *were* before the house. H2205
36: 2 a high places are ours in possession: H5769
Dan 7: 9 down, and the A of days did sit, whose H6268
13 and came to the A of days, and they H6268
22 Until the A of days came, and H6268

ANCIENTS
1Sa 24:13 As saith the proverb of the a, H6931
Ps119:100 I understand more than the a, because I H2205
Isa 3:14 judgment with the a of his people, and H2205
24:23 Jerusalem, and before his a gloriously. H2205
Jer 19: 1 and *take* of the a of the people, and of H2205
1 the people, and of the a of the priests; H2205
Ezk 7:26 from the priest, and counsel from the a. H2205
8:11 men of the a of the house of Israel, H2205
12 seen what the a of the house of Israel H2205
27: 9 The a of Gebal and the wise *men* H2205

AND See the Appendix.

ANDREW
Mt 4:18 called Peter, and A his brother, casting G406
10: 2 is called Peter, and A his brother; James G406
Mk 1:16 he saw Simon and A his brother casting G406
29 of Simon and A, with James and John. G406
3:18 And A, and Philip, and Bartholomew, G406
13: 3 and John and A asked him privately, G406
Lk 6:14 named Peter,) and A his brother, James G406
Jn 1:40 him, was A, Simon Peter's brother. G406
44 was of Bethsaida, the city of A and Peter. G406
6: 8 One of his disciples, A, Simon Peter's G406
12:22 Philip cometh and telleth A: and again G406
22 and again A and Philip tell Jesus. G406
Act 1:13 and John, and A, Philip, and Thomas, G406

ANDRONICUS
Ro 16: 7 Salute A and Junia, my kinsmen, and G408

ANEM
1Ch 6:73 And Ramoth with her suburbs, and A H6046

ANER
Gen 14:13 and brother of A: and these *were* H6063
24 went with me, A, Eshcol, and Mamre; H6063
1Ch 6:70 of Manasseh; A with her suburbs, and H6063

ANETHOTHITE
2Sa 23:27 Abiezer the A, Mebunnai the H6069

ANETOTHITE
1Ch 27:12 *was* Abiezer the A, of the Benjamites: H6069

ANGEL
Gen 16: 7 And the a of the LORD found her by a H4397
9 And the a of the LORD said unto her, H4397
10 And the a of the LORD said unto her, I H4397
11 And the a of the LORD said unto her, H4397
21:17 of the lad; and the a of God called to H4397
22:11 And the a of the LORD called unto him H4397
15 And the a of the LORD called unto H4397
24: 7 he shall send his a before thee, and H4397
40 I walk, will send his a with thee, and H4397
31:11 And the a of God spake unto me in a H4397
48:16 The A which redeemed me from all H4397

Ex 3: 2 And the **a** of the LORD appeared unto H4397
14:19 And the **a** of God, which went before H4397
23:20 Behold, I send an **A** before thee, to keep H4397
23 For mine **A** shall go before thee, and H4397
32:34 behold, mine **A** shall go before thee: H4397
33: 2 And I will send an **a** before thee; and I H4397
Nu 20:16 voice, and sent an **a**, and hath brought H4397
22:22 he went: and the **a** of the LORD stood H4397
23 And the ass saw the **a** of the LORD H4397
24 But the **a** of the LORD stood in a path H4397
25 And when the ass saw the **a** of the H4397
26 And the **a** of the LORD went further, H4397
27 And when the ass saw the **a** of the H4397
31 and he saw the **a** of the LORD standing H4397
32 And the **a** of the LORD said unto him, H4397
34 And Balaam said unto the **a** of the H4397
35 And the **a** of the LORD said unto H4397
Jdg 2: 1 And an **a** of the LORD came up from H4397
4 And it came to pass, when the **a** of the H4397
5:23 Curse ye Meroz, said the **a** of the H4397
6:11 And there came an **a** of the LORD, and H4397
12 And the **a** of the LORD appeared unto H4397
20 And the **a** of God said unto him, Take H4397
21 Then the **a** of the LORD put forth the H4397
21 cakes. Then the **a** of the LORD H4397
22 that he *was* an **a** of the LORD, Gideon H4397
22 seen an **a** of the LORD face to face. H4397
13: 3 And the **a** of the LORD appeared unto H4397
6 the countenance of an **a** of God, very H4397
9 Manoah; and the **a** of God came again H4397
13 And the **a** of the LORD said unto H4397
15 And Manoah said unto the **a** of the H4397
16 And the **a** of the LORD said unto H4397
16 not that he *was* an **a** of the LORD. H4397
17 And Manoah said unto the **a** of the H4397
18 And the **a** of the LORD said unto him, H4397
19 the LORD: and *the* **a** did wondrously;
20 off the altar, that the **a** of the LORD H4397
21 But the **a** of the LORD did no more H4397
21 knew that he *was* an **a** of the LORD. H4397
1Sa 29: 9 good in my sight, as an **a** of God: H4397
2Sa 14:17 for as an **a** of God, so *is* my lord H4397
20 the wisdom of an **a** of God, to know all H4397
19:27 the king *is* as an **a** of God: do therefore H4397
24:16 And when the **a** stretched out his hand H4397
16 and said to the **a** that destroyed the H4397
16 hand. And the **a** of the LORD was by H4397
17 when he saw the **a** that smote the H4397
1Ki 13:18 as thou *art;* and an **a** spake unto me by H4397
19: 5 behold, then an **a** touched him, and H4397
7 And the **a** of the LORD came again the H4397
2Ki 1: 3 But the **a** of the LORD said to Elijah the H4397
15 And the **a** of the LORD said unto H4397
19:35 night, that the **a** of the LORD went out, H4397
1Ch 21:12 in the land, and the **a** of the LORD H4397
15 And God sent an **a** unto Jerusalem to H4397
15 and said to the **a** that destroyed, It is H4397
15 hand. And the **a** of the LORD stood by H4397
16 eyes, and saw the **a** of the LORD stand H4397
18 Then the **a** of the LORD commanded H4397
20 And Ornan turned back, and saw the **a**; H4397
27 And the LORD commanded the **a**; and H4397
30 of the sword of the **a** of the LORD. H4397
2Ch 32:21 And the LORD sent an **a**, which cut off H4397
Ps 34: 7 The **a** of the LORD encampeth round H4397
35: 5 and let the **a** of the LORD chase *them.* H4397
6 let the **a** of the LORD persecute them. H4397
Ecc 5: 6 thou before the **a**, that it *was* an error: H4397
Isa 37:36 Then the **a** of the LORD went forth, and H4397
63: 9 was afflicted, and the **a** of his presence H4397
Dan 3:28 who hath sent his **a**, and delivered his H4398
6:22 My God hath sent his **a**, and hath shut H4398
Hos 12: 4 Yea, he had power over the **a**, and H4397
Zec 1: 9 *are* these? And the **a** that talked with H4397
11 And they answered the **a** of the LORD H4397
12 Then the **a** of the LORD answered and H4397
13 And the LORD answered the **a** that H4397
14 So the **a** that communed with me said H4397
19 And I said unto the **a** that talked with H4397
2: 3 And, behold, the **a** that talked with me H4397
3 and another **a** went out to meet him, H4397
3: 1 before the **a** of the LORD, and Satan H4397
3 filthy garments, and stood before the **a**. H4397
5 And the **a** of the LORD stood by. H4397
6 And the **a** of the LORD protested unto H4397
4: 1 And the **a** that talked with me came H4397
4 So I answered and spake to the **a** that H4397
5 Then the **a** that talked with me H4397
5: 5 Then the **a** that talked with me went H4397
Zec 5:10 Then said I to the **a** that talked with H4397
6: 4 Then I answered and said unto the **a** H4397
5 And the **a** answered and said unto me, H4397
12: 8 God, as the **a** of the LORD before them. H4397
Mt 1:20 these things, behold, the **a** of the Lord *G32*
24 sleep did as the **a** of the Lord had bidden *G32*
2:13 behold, the **a** of the Lord appeareth *G32*
19 But when Herod was dead, behold, an **a** *G32*
28: 2 great earthquake: for the **a** of the Lord *G32*
5 And the **a** answered and said unto the *G32*
Lk 1:11 And there appeared unto him an **a** of the *G32*
13 But the **a** said unto him, Fear not, *G32*
18 And Zacharias said unto the **a**, Whereby *G32*
19 And the **a** answering said unto him, I *G32*
26 And in the sixth month the **a** Gabriel *G32*
28 And the **a** came in unto her, and said, *G32*
30 And the **a** said unto her, Fear not, Mary: *G32*
34 Then said Mary unto the **a**, How shall *G32*
35 And the **a** answered and said unto her, *G32*
38 thy word. And the **a** departed from her. *G32*
2: 9 And, lo, the **a** of the Lord came upon *G32*
10 And the **a** said unto them, Fear not: for, *G32*
13 And suddenly there was with the **a** a *G32*
21 **a** before he was conceived in the womb. *G32*
22:43 And there appeared an **a** unto him from *G32*
Jn 5: 4 For an **a** went down at a certain season *G32*
12:29 others said, An **a** spake to him. *G32*
Act 5:19 But the **a** of the Lord by night opened the *G32*
6:15 his face as it had been the face of an **a**. *G32*
7:30 **a** of the Lord in a flame of fire in a bush. *G32*
35 the **a** which appeared to him in the bush. *G32*
38 with the **a** which spake to him *G32*
8:26 And the **a** of the Lord spake unto Philip, *G32*
10: 3 hour of the day an **a** of God coming in to *G32*
7 And when the **a** which spake unto *G32*
22 God by an holy **a** to send for thee into *G32*
11:13 And he shewed us how he had seen an **a** *G32*
12: 7 And, behold, the **a** of the Lord came *G32*
8 And the **a** said unto him, Gird thyself, *G32*
9 by the **a**; but thought he saw a vision. *G32*
10 and forthwith the **a** departed from him. *G32*
11 Lord hath sent his **a**, and hath delivered *G32*
15 it was even so. Then said they, It is his **a**. *G32*
23 And immediately the **a** of the Lord *G32*
23: 8 neither **a**, nor spirit: but the Pharisees *G32*
9 but if a spirit or an **a** hath spoken to *G32*
27:23 For there stood by me this night the **a** of *G32*
2Co 11:14 himself is transformed into an **a** of light. *G32*
Gal 1: 8 But though we, or an **a** from heaven, *G32*
4:14 me as an **a** of God, *even* as Christ Jesus. *G32*
Rev 1: 1 *it* by his **a** unto his servant John: *G32*
2: 1 Unto the **a** of the church of Ephesus *G32*
8 And unto the **a** of the church in Smyrna *G32*
12 And to the **a** of the church in Pergamos *G32*
18 And unto the **a** of the church in Thyatira *G32*
3: 1 And unto the **a** of the church in Sardis *G32*
7 And to the **a** of the church in *G32*
14 And unto the **a** of the church of the *G32*
5: 2 And I saw a strong **a** proclaiming with a *G32*
7: 2 And I saw another **a** ascending from the *G32*
8: 3 And another **a** came and stood at the *G32*
5 And the **a** took the censer, and filled it *G32*
7 The first **a** sounded, and there followed *G32*
8 And the second **a** sounded, and as it *G32*
10 And the third **a** sounded, and there fell a *G32*
12 And the fourth **a** sounded, and the third *G32*
13 And I beheld, and heard an **a** flying *G32*
9: 1 And the fifth **a** sounded, and I saw a star *G32*
11 them, *which is* the **a** of the bottomless *G32*
13 And the sixth **a** sounded, and I heard a *G32*
14 Saying to the sixth **a** which had the *G32*
10: 1 And I saw another mighty **a** come down *G32*
5 And the **a** which I saw stand upon the *G32*
7 of the seventh **a**, when he shall begin *G32*
8 open in the hand of the **a** which standeth *G32*
9 And I went unto the **a**, and said unto *G32*
11: 1 unto a rod: and the **a** stood, saying, Rise, *G32*
15 And the seventh **a** sounded; and there *G32*
14: 6 And I saw another **a** fly in the midst of *G32*
8 And there followed another **a**, saying, *G32*
9 And the third **a** followed them, saying *G32*
15 And another **a** came out of the temple, *G32*
17 And another **a** came out of the temple *G32*
18 And another **a** came out from the altar, *G32*
19 And the **a** thrust in his sickle into the *G32*
16: 3 And the second **a** poured out his vial *G32*
4 And the third **a** poured out his vial upon *G32*
5 And I heard the **a** of the waters say, *G32*
8 And the fourth **a** poured out his vial *G32*
Rev 16:10 And the fifth **a** poured out his vial upon *G32*
12 And the sixth **a** poured out his vial upon *G32*
17 And the seventh **a** poured out his vial *G32*
17: 7 And the **a** said unto me, Wherefore didst *G32*
18: 1 And after these things I saw another **a** *G32*
21 And a mighty **a** took up a stone like a *G32*
19:17 And I saw an **a** standing in the sun; and *G32*
20: 1 And I saw an **a** come down from heaven, *G32*
21:17 *to* the measure of a man, that is, of the **a**. *G32*
22: 6 holy prophets sent his **a** to shew unto his *G32*
8 of the **a** which shewed me these things. *G32*
16 I Jesus have sent mine **a** to testify unto *G32*

ANGELS
Gen 19: 1 And there came two **a** to Sodom at H4397
15 arose, then the **a** hastened Lot, saying, H4397
28:12 and behold the **a** of God ascending and H4397
32: 1 And Jacob went on his way, and the **a** H4397
Job 4:18 and his **a** he charged with folly: H4397
Ps 8: 5 lower than the **a**, and hast crowned him H430
68:17 *even* thousands of **a**: the Lord *is* among H8136
78:49 trouble, by sending evil **a** *among them.* H4397
91:11 For he shall give his **a** charge over thee, H4397
103:20 Bless the LORD, ye his **a**, that excel in H4397
104: 4 Who maketh his **a** spirits; his ministers H4397
148: 2 Praise ye him, all his **a**: praise ye him, H4397
Mt 4: 6 He shall give his **a** charge concerning *G32*
11 **a** came and ministered unto him. *G32*
13:39 of the world; and the reapers are the **a**. *G32*
41 The Son of man shall send forth his **a**, *G32*
49 of the world: the **a** shall come forth, and *G32*
16:27 of his Father with his **a**; and then he shall *G32*
18:10 in heaven their **a** do always behold the *G32*
22:30 but are as the **a** of God in heaven. *G32*
24:31 And he shall send his **a** with a great *G32*
36 not the **a** of heaven, but my Father only. *G32*
25:31 and all the holy **a** with him, then shall *G32*
41 fire, prepared for the devil and his **a**: *G32*
26:53 give me more than twelve legions of **a**? *G32*
Mk 1:13 beasts; and the **a** ministered unto him. *G32*
8:38 in the glory of his Father with the holy **a**. *G32*
12:25 but are as the **a** which are in heaven. *G32*
13:27 And then shall he send his **a**, and shall *G32*
32 man, no, not the **a** which are in heaven, *G32*
Lk 2:15 And it came to pass, as the **a** were gone *G32*
4:10 For it is written, He shall give his **a** *G32*
9:26 and *in his* Father's, and of the holy **a**. *G32*
12: 8 of man also confess before the **a** of God: *G32*
9 men shall be denied before the **a** of God. *G32*
15:10 **a** of God over one sinner that repenteth. *G32*
16:22 and was carried by the **a** into Abraham's *G32*
20:36 they are equal unto the **a**; and are the *G2465*
24:23 vision of **a**, which said that he was alive. *G32*
Jn 1:51 open, and the **a** of God ascending and *G32*
20:12 And seeth two **a** in white sitting, the one *G32*
Act 7:53 the disposition of **a**, and have not kept *it.* *G32*
Ro 8:38 death, nor life, nor **a**, nor principalities, *G32*
1Co 4: 9 unto the world, and to **a**, and to men. *G32*
6: 3 Know ye not that we shall judge **a**? how *G32*
11:10 have power on *her* head because of the **a**. *G32*
13: 1 of men and of **a**, and have not charity, *G32*
Gal 3:19 ordained by **a** in the hand of a mediator. *G32*
Col 2:18 worshipping of **a**, intruding into those *G32*
2Th 1: 7 revealed from heaven with his mighty **a**, *G32*
1Ti 3:16 in the Spirit, seen of **a**, preached unto the *G32*
5:21 and the elect **a**, that thou observe these *G32*
Heb 1: 4 Being made so much better than the **a**, as *G32*
5 For unto which of the **a** said he at any *G32*
6 And let all the **a** of God worship him. *G32*
7 And of the **a** he saith, Who maketh his *G32*
7 saith, Who maketh his **a** spirits, and his *G32*
13 But to which of the **a** said he at any time, *G32*
2: 2 For if the word spoken by **a** was stedfast, *G32*
5 For unto the **a** hath he not put in *G32*
7 lower than the **a**; thou crownedst him *G32*
9 little lower than the **a** for the suffering of *G32*
16 *him the nature of* **a**; but he took on *him* *G32*
12:22 and to an innumerable company of **a**, *G32*
13: 2 some have entertained **a** unawares. *G32*
1Pt 1:12 which things the **a** desire to look into. *G32*
3:22 right hand of God; **a** and authorities and *G32*
2Pt 2: 4 For if God spared not the **a** that sinned, *G32*
11 Whereas **a**, which are greater in power *G32*
Jude 6 And the **a** which kept not their first *G32*
Rev 1:20 The seven stars are the **a** of the seven *G32*
3: 5 name before my Father, and before his **a**. *G32*
5:11 the voice of many **a** round about the *G32*
7: 1 And after these things I saw four **a** *G32*
2 voice to the four **a**, to whom it was given *G32*

Rev 7:11 And all the **a** stood round about the G32
8: 2 And I saw the seven **a** which stood G32
6 And the seven **a** which had the seven G32
13 of the three **a**, which are yet to sound! G32
9:14 Loose the four **a** which are bound in G32
15 And the four **a** were loosed, which were G32
12: 7 Michael and his **a** fought against the G32
7 dragon; and the dragon fought and his **a**, G32
9 earth, and his **a** were cast out with him. G32
14:10 holy **a**, and in the presence of the Lamb: G32
15: 1 marvellous, seven **a** having the seven G32
6 And the seven **a** came out of the temple, G32
7 unto the seven **a** seven golden vials full G32
8 plagues of the seven **a** were fulfilled. G32
16: 1 saying to the seven **a**, Go your ways, and G32
17: 1 And there came one of the seven **a** which G32
21: 9 one of the seven **a** which had the seven G32
12 at the gates twelve **a**, and names written G32

ANGEL'S

Rev 8: 4 up before God out of the **a** hand. G32
10:10 And I took the little book out of the **a** G32

ANGELS'

Ps 78:25 Man did eat **a** food: he sent them meat H47

ANGER

Gen 27:45 Until thy brother's **a** turn away from H639
30: 2 And Jacob's **a** was kindled against H639
44:18 ears, and let not thine **a** burn against thy H639
49: 6 united: for in their **a** they slew a man, H639
7 Cursed *be* their **a**, for *it was* fierce; and H639
Ex 4:14 And the **a** of the LORD was kindled H639
11: 8 he went out from Pharaoh in a great **a**. H639
32:19 and Moses' **a** waxed hot, and he cast H639
22 And Aaron said, Let not the **a** of my lord H639
Nu 11: 1 heard *it;* and his **a** was kindled; and the H639
10 of his tent: and the **a** of the LORD was H639
12: 9 And the **a** of the LORD was kindled H639
22:22 And God's **a** was kindled because he H639
27 and Balaam's **a** was kindled, and he H639
24:10 And Balak's **a** was kindled against H639
25: 3 Baal-peor: and the **a** of the LORD was H639
4 sun, that the fierce **a** of the LORD may H639
32:10 And the LORD'S **a** was kindled the same H639
13 And the LORD'S **a** was kindled against H639
14 the fierce **a** of the LORD toward Israel. H639
Dt 4:25 the LORD thy God, to provoke him to **a**: H3707
6:15 you) lest the **a** of the LORD thy God H639
7: 4 other gods: so will the **a** of the LORD be H639
9:18 sight of the LORD, to provoke him to **a**. H3707
19 For I was afraid of the **a** and hot H639
13:17 fierceness of his **a**, and shew thee mercy, H639
29:20 him, but then the **a** of the LORD and his H639
23 overthrew in his **a**, and in his wrath: H639
24 what *meaneth* the heat of this great **a**? H639
27 And the **a** of the LORD was kindled H639
28 out of their land in **a**, and in wrath, and H639
31:17 Then my **a** shall be kindled against them H639
29 to **a** through the work of your hands. H3707
32:16 abominations provoked they him to **a**. H3707
21 provoked me to **a** with their vanities: H3707
21 them to **a** with a foolish nation. H3707
22 For a fire is kindled in mine **a**, and shall H639
Jos 7: 1 thing: and the **a** of the LORD was H639
26 fierceness of his **a**. Wherefore the name H639
23:16 then shall the **a** of the LORD be kindled H639
Jdg 2:12 them, and provoked the LORD to **a**. H3707
14 And the **a** of the LORD was hot against H639
20 And the **a** of the LORD was hot against H639
3: 8 Therefore the **a** of the LORD was hot H639
6:39 God, Let not thine **a** be hot against me, H639
8: 3 of you? Then their **a** was abated toward H7307
9:30 Gaal the son of Ebed, his **a** was kindled. H639
10: 7 And the **a** of the LORD was hot against H639
14:19 the riddle. And his **a** was kindled, and he H639
1Sa 11: 6 tidings, and his **a** was kindled greatly. H639
17:28 men; and Eliab's **a** was kindled against H639
20:30 Then Saul's **a** was kindled against H639
34 the table in fierce **a**, and did eat no meat H639
2Sa 6: 7 And the **a** of the LORD was kindled H639
12: 5 And David's **a** was greatly kindled H639
24: 1 And again the **a** of the LORD was H639
1Ki 14: 9 to **a**, and hast cast me behind thy back: H3707
15 their groves, provoking the LORD to **a**. H3707
15:30 provoked the LORD God of Israel to **a**. H3707
16: 2 sin, to provoke me to **a** with their sins; H3707
7 provoking him to **a** with the work of his H3707
13 God of Israel to **a** with their vanities. H3707
1Ki 16:26 God of Israel to **a** with their vanities. H3707
33 God of Israel to **a** than all the kings of H3707
21:22 *me* to **a**, and made Israel to sin. H3707
22:53 and provoked to **a** the LORD God of H3707
2Ki 13: 3 And the **a** of the LORD was kindled H639
17:11 things to provoke the LORD to **a**: H3707
17 sight of the LORD, to provoke him to **a**. H3707
21: 6 sight of the LORD, to provoke *him* to **a**. H3707
15 provoked me to **a**, since the day their H3707
22:17 provoke me to **a** with all the works of H3707
23:19 *the LORD* to **a**, Josiah took away, and H3707
26 wherewith his **a** was kindled against H639
24:20 For through the **a** of the LORD it came to H639
1Ch 13:10 And the **a** of the LORD was kindled H639
2Ch 25:10 wherefore their **a** was greatly kindled H639
10 and they returned home in great **a**. H639
15 Wherefore the **a** of the LORD was H639
28:25 to **a** the LORD God of his fathers. H3707
33: 6 sight of the LORD, to provoke him to **a**. H3707
34:25 provoke me to **a** with all the works of H3707
Neh 4: 5 provoked *thee* to **a** before the builders. H3707
9:17 and merciful, slow to **a**, and of great H639
Est 1:12 very wroth, and his **a** burned in him. H2534
Job 9: 5 not: which overturneth them in his **a**. H639
13 *If* God will not withdraw his **a**, the proud H639
18: 4 He teareth himself in his **a**: shall the H639
21:17 them! *God* distributeth sorrows in his **a**. H639
35:15 he hath visited in his **a**; yet he knoweth *it* H639
Ps 6: 1 O LORD, rebuke me not in thine **a**, H639
7: 6 Arise, O LORD, in thine **a**, lift up thyself H639
21: 9 in the time of thine **a**: the LORD shall H6440
27: 9 thy servant away in **a**: thou hast been my H639
30: 5 For his **a** *endureth but* a moment; in his H639
37: 8 Cease from **a**, and forsake wrath: fret not H639
38: 3 because of thine **a**; neither *is there any* H2195
56: 7 Shall they escape by iniquity? in *thine* **a** H639
69:24 and let thy wrathful **a** take hold of them. H639
74: 1 *why* doth thine **a** smoke against the H639
77: 9 in **a** shut up his tender mercies? Selah. H639
78:21 and **a** also came up against Israel; H639
38 **a** away, and did not stir up all his wrath. H639
49 He cast upon them the fierceness of his **a**, H639
50 He made a way to his **a**; he spared not H639
58 For they provoked him to **a** with their H3707
85: 3 *thyself* from the fierceness of thine **a**. H639
4 and cause thine **a** toward us to cease. H3708
5 thou draw out thine **a** to all generations? H639
90: 7 For we are consumed by thine **a**, and by H639
11 Who knoweth the power of thine **a**? even H639
103: 8 slow to **a**, and plenteous in mercy. H639
9 chide: neither will he keep *his* **a** for ever.
106:29 Thus they provoked *him* to **a** with their H3707
145: 8 slow to **a**, and of great mercy. H639
Prv 15: 1 away wrath: but grievous words stir up **a**. H639
18 but *he that is* slow to **a** appeaseth strife. H639
16:32 *He that is* slow to **a** *is* better than the H639
19:11 The discretion of a man deferreth his **a**; H639
20: 2 him to **a** sinneth *against* his own soul. H5674
21:14 A gift in secret pacifieth **a**: and a reward H639
22: 8 vanity: and the rod of his **a** shall fail. H5678
27: 4 Wrath *is* cruel, and **a** *is* outrageous; but H639
Ecc 7: 9 for **a** resteth in the bosom of fools. H3708
Isa 1: 4 unto **a**, they are gone away backward. H5006
5:25 Therefore is the **a** of the LORD kindled H639
25 For all this his **a** is not turned away, but H639
7: 4 for the fierce **a** of Rezin with Syria, H639
9:12 For all this his **a** is not turned away, but H639
17 For all this his **a** is not turned away, but H639
21 For all this his **a** is not turned away, but H639
10: 4 For all this his **a** is not turned away, but H639
5 O Assyrian, the rod of mine **a**, and the H639
25 cease, and mine **a** in their destruction. H639
12: 1 with me, thine **a** is turned away, and H639
13: 3 **a**, *even* them that rejoice in my highness. H639
9 with wrath and fierce **a**, to lay the land H639
13 of hosts, and in the day of his fierce **a**. H639
14: 6 in **a**, is persecuted, *and* none hindereth. H639
30:27 far, burning *with* his **a**, and the burden H639
30 indignation of *his* **a**, and *with* the flame H639
42:25 him the fury of his **a**, and the strength of H639
48: 9 For my name's sake will I defer mine **a**, H639
63: 3 tread them in mine **a**, and trample them H639
6 the people in mine **a**, and make them H639
65: 3 A people that provoketh me to **a** H3707
66:15 to render his **a** with fury, and his rebuke H639
Jer 2:35 surely his **a** shall turn from me. H639
3: 5 Will he reserve *his* **a** for ever? will he
12 not cause mine **a** to fall upon you: for H6440
12 the LORD, *and* I will not keep *a* for ever.
Jer 4: 8 howl: for the fierce **a** of the LORD is not H639
26 of the LORD, *and* by his fierce **a**. H639
7:18 gods, that they may provoke me to **a**. H3707
19 Do they provoke me to **a**? saith the H3707
20 GOD; Behold, mine **a** and my fury shall H639
8:19 provoked me to **a** with their graven H3707
10:24 in thine **a**, lest thou bring me to nothing. H639
11:17 me to **a** in offering incense unto Baal. H3707
12:13 because of the fierce **a** of the LORD. H639
15:14 in mine **a**, *which* shall burn upon you. H639
17: 4 fire in mine **a**, *which* shall burn for ever. H639
18:23 *thus* with them in the time of thine **a**. H639
21: 5 in **a**, and in fury, and in great wrath. H639
23:20 The **a** of the LORD shall not return, until H639
25: 6 provoke me not to **a** with the works of H3707
7 provoke me to **a** with the works of your H3707
37 because of the fierce **a** of the LORD. H639
38 oppressor, and because of his fierce **a**. H639
30:24 The fierce **a** of the LORD shall not H639
32:29 unto other gods, to provoke me to **a**. H3707
30 only provoked me to **a** with the work of H3707
31 of mine **a** and of my fury from H639
32 to provoke me to **a**, they, their kings, H3707
37 them in mine **a**, and in my fury, and H639
33: 5 have slain in mine **a** and in my fury, and H639
36: 7 for great *is* the **a** and the fury that the H639
42:18 of Israel; As mine **a** and my fury hath H639
44: 3 to provoke me to **a**, in that they went to H3707
6 Wherefore my fury and mine **a** was H639
49:37 *even* my fierce **a**, saith the LORD; and H639
51:45 his soul from the fierce **a** of the LORD. H639
52: 3 For through the **a** of the LORD it came to H639
Lam 1:12 afflicted *me* in the day of his fierce **a**. H639
2: 1 with a cloud in his **a**, *and* cast down from H639
1 not his footstool in the day of his **a**! H639
3 He hath cut off in *his* fierce **a** all the horn H639
6 of his **a** the king and the priest. H639
21 thine **a**; thou hast killed, *and* not pitied. H639
22 day of the LORD'S **a** none escaped nor H639
3:43 Thou hast covered with **a**, and H639
66 Persecute and destroy them in **a** from H639
4:11 out his fierce **a**, and hath kindled a fire H639
16 The **a** of the LORD hath divided them; H6440
Ezk 5:13 Thus shall mine **a** be accomplished, and H639
15 in thee in **a** and in fury and in furious H639
7: 3 I will send mine **a** upon thee, and will H639
8 accomplish mine **a** upon thee: and I will H639
8:17 to provoke me to **a**: and, lo, they put the H3707
13:13 shower in mine **a**, and great hailstones H639
16:26 thy whoredoms, to provoke me to **a**. H3707
20: 8 to accomplish my **a** against them in the H639
21 my **a** against them in the wilderness. H639
22:20 I gather *you* in mine **a** and in my fury, H639
25:14 according to mine **a** and according to H639
35:11 do according to thine **a**, and according to H639
43: 8 I have consumed them in mine **a**. H639
Dan 9:16 thee, let thine **a** and thy fury be turned H639
11:20 be destroyed, neither in **a**, nor in battle. H639
Hos 8: 5 cast *thee* off; mine **a** is kindled against H639
11: 9 fierceness of mine **a**, I will not return to H639
12:14 Ephraim provoked *him* to **a** most H3707
13:11 I gave thee a king in mine **a**, and took H639
14: 4 for mine **a** is turned away from him. H639
Joel 2:13 and merciful, slow to **a**, and of great H639
Am 1:11 cast off all pity, and his **a** did tear H639
Jna 3: 9 from his fierce **a**, that we perish not? H639
4: 2 and merciful, slow to **a**, and of great H639
Mic 5:15 And I will execute vengeance in **a** and H639
7:18 retaineth not his **a** for ever, because he H639
Nah 1: 3 The LORD *is* slow to **a**, and great in H639
6 fierceness of his **a**? his fury is poured out H639
Hab 3: 8 rivers? *was* thine **a** against the rivers? H639
12 thou didst thresh the heathen in **a**. H639
Zep 2: 2 before the fierce **a** of the LORD come H639
2 the day of the LORD'S **a** come upon you. H639
3 shall be hid in the day of the LORD'S **a**. H639
3: 8 *even* all my fierce **a**: for all the earth shall H639
Zec 10: 3 Mine **a** was kindled against the H639
Mk 3: 5 on them with **a**, being grieved for the G3709
Ro 10:19 *and* by a foolish nation I will **a** you. G3949
Eph 4:31 Let all bitterness, and wrath, and **a**, and G3709
Col 3: 8 But now ye also put off all these; **a**, G3709
21 Fathers, provoke not your children *to* **a**,

ANGERED

Ps 106:32 They **a** *him* also at the waters of strife, H7107

ANGLE

Isa 19: 8 all they that cast **a** into the brooks shall H2443

Hab 1:15 They take up all of them with the **a**, they H2443

ANGRY
Gen 18:30 let not the Lord be **a**, and I will speak: H2734
32 And he said, Oh let not the Lord be **a**, H2734
45: 5 Now therefore be not grieved, nor **a** H2734
Lev 10:16 burnt: and he was **a** with Eleazar and H7107
Dt 1:37 Also the LORD was **a** with me for your H599
4:21 Furthermore the LORD was **a** with me H599
9: 8 was **a** with you to have destroyed you. H599
20 And the LORD was very **a** with Aaron to H599
Jdg 18:25 us, lest **a** fellows run upon H4751+H5315
2Sa 19:42 then be ye **a** for this matter? have H2734
1Ki 8:46 not,) and thou be **a** with them, and H599
11: 9 And the LORD was **a** with Solomon, H599
2Ki 17:18 Therefore the LORD was very **a** with H599
2Ch 6:36 not,) and thou be **a** with them, and H599
Ezr 9:14 not thou be **a** with us till thou hadst H599
Neh 5: 6 And I was very **a** when I heard their cry H2734
Ps 2:12 Kiss the Son, lest he be **a**, and ye perish H599
7:11 God is **a** *with the wicked* every day. H2194
76: 7 stand in thy sight when once thou art **a**? H639
79: 5 How long, LORD? wilt thou be **a** for ever? H599
80: 4 be **a** against the prayer of thy people? H6225
85: 5 Wilt thou be **a** with us for ever? wilt thou H599
Prv 14:17 *He that is* soon **a** dealeth foolishly: and a H639
21:19 with a contentious and an **a** woman. H3708
22:24 Make no friendship with an **a** man; and H639
25:23 an **a** countenance a backbiting tongue. H2194
29:22 An **a** man stirreth up strife, and a H639
Ecc 5: 6 should God be **a** at thy voice, and H7107
7: 9 Be not hasty in thy spirit to be **a**: for H3707
Song 1: 6 children were **a** with me; they made H2787
Isa 12: 1 though thou wast **a** with me, thine anger H599
Ezk 16:42 I will be quiet, and will be no more **a**. H3707
Dan 2:12 For this cause the king was **a** and very H1149
Jna 4: 1 Jonah exceedingly, and he was very **a**. H2734
4 said the LORD, Doest thou well to be **a**? H2734
9 thou well to be **a** for the gourd? And H2734
9 said, I do well to be **a**, *even* unto death. H2734
Mt 5:22 But I say unto you, That whosoever is **a** *G3710*
Lk 14:21 of the house being **a** said to his servant, *G3710*
15:28 And he was **a**, and would not go in: *G3710*
Jn 7:23 not be broken; are ye **a** at me, because I *G5520*
Eph 4:26 Be ye **a**, and sin not: let not the sun go *G3710*
Tit 1: 7 not soon **a**, not given to wine, no *G3711*
Rev 11:18 And the nations were **a**, and thy wrath *G3710*

ANGUISH
Gen 42:21 in that we saw the **a** of his soul, when H6869
Ex 6: 9 for **a** of spirit, and for cruel bondage. H7115
Dt 2:25 tremble, and be in **a** because of thee. H2342
2Sa 1: 9 and slay me: for **a** is come upon me, H7661
Job 7:11 I will speak in the **a** of my spirit; I will H6862
15:24 Trouble and **a** shall make him afraid; H4691
Ps119:143 Trouble and **a** have taken hold on me: H4689
Prv 1:27 when distress and **a** cometh upon you. H6695
Isa 8:22 **a**; and *they shall be* driven to darkness. H6695
30: 6 of trouble and **a**, from whence *come* H6695
Jer 4:31 in travail, *and* the **a** as of her that H6869
6:24 hands wax feeble: **a** hath taken hold of H6869
49:24 hath seized on *her*: **a** and sorrows have H6869
50:43 waxed feeble: **a** took hold of him, *and* H6869
Jn 16:21 no more the **a**, for joy that a man is *G2347*
Ro 2: 9 Tribulation and **a**, upon every soul of *G4730*
2Co 2: 4 For out of much affliction and **a** of *G4928*

AN-HUNGERED See HUNGERED.

ANIAM
1Ch 7:19 Ahian, and Shechem, and Likhi, and **A**. H593

ANIM
Jos 15:50 And Anab, and Eshtemoh, and **A**, H6044

ANISE
Mt 23:23 tithe of mint and **a** and cummin, and *G432*

ANKLE
Act 3: 7 his feet and **a** bones received strength. *G4974*

ANKLES
Ezk 47: 3 the waters; the waters *were* to the **a**. H657

ANNA
Lk 2:36 And there was one **A**, a prophetess, the *G451*

ANNAS
Lk 3: 2 **A** and Caiaphas being the high priests, *G452*
Jn 18:13 And led him away to **A** first; for he was *G452*
24 Now **A** had sent him bound unto *G452*
Act 4: 6 And **A** the high priest, and Caiaphas, *G452*

ANNUL See DISANNUL.

ANOINT
Ex 28:41 him; and shalt **a** them, and consecrate H4886
29: 7 and pour *it* upon his head, and **a** him. H4886
36 for it, and thou shalt **a** it, to sanctify it. H4886
30:26 And thou shalt **a** the tabernacle of the H4886
30 And thou shalt **a** Aaron and his sons, H4886
40: 9 the anointing oil, and **a** the tabernacle, H4886
10 And thou shalt **a** the altar of the burnt H4886
11 And thou shalt **a** the laver and his foot, H4886
13 holy garments, and **a** him, and sanctify H4886
15 And thou shalt **a** them, as thou didst H4886
15 as thou didst **a** their father, that they H4886
Lev 16:32 And the priest, whom he shall **a**, and H4886
Dt 28:40 but thou shalt not **a** *thyself* with the oil; H5480
Jdg 9: 8 The trees went forth *on a time* to **a** a H4886
15 trees, If in truth ye **a** me king over you, H4886
Ru 3: 3 Wash thyself therefore, and **a** thee, and H5480
1Sa 9:16 and thou shalt **a** him *to be* captain over H4886
15: 1 LORD sent me to **a** thee *to be* king over H4886
16: 3 shalt do: and thou shalt **a** unto me *him* H4886
12 LORD said, Arise, **a** him: for this *is* he. H4886
2Sa 14: 2 apparel, and **a** not thyself with oil, H5480
1Ki 1:34 the prophet **a** him there king over H4886
19:15 comest, **a** Hazael *to be* king over Syria: H4886
16 of Nimshi shalt thou **a** *to be* king over H4886
16 shalt thou **a** *to be* prophet in thy room. H4886
Isa 21: 5 arise, ye princes, *and* **a** the shield. H4886
Dan 9:24 and prophecy, and to **a** the most Holy. H4886
10: 3 neither did I **a** myself at all, till three H5480
Am 6: 6 That drink wine in bowls, and **a** H4886
Mic 6:15 but thou shalt not **a** thee with oil; and H5480
Mt 6:17 But thou, when thou fastest, **a** thine *G218*
Mk 14: 8 aforehand to **a** my body to the burying. *G3462*
16: 1 spices, that they might come and **a** him. *G218*
Lk 7:46 My head with oil thou didst not **a**: but *G218*
Rev 3:18 do not appear; and **a** thine eyes with *G1472*

ANOINTED
Ex 29: 2 unleavened **a** with oil: *of* wheaten H4886
29 after him, to be **a** therein, and to be H4888
Lev 2: 4 oil, or unleavened wafers **a** with oil. H4886
4: 3 If the priest that is **a** do sin according H4899
5 And the priest that is **a** shall take of the H4899
16 And the priest that is **a** shall bring of H4899
6:20 the day when he is **a**; the tenth part of H4886
22 And the priest of his sons that is **a** in H4899
7:12 wafers **a** with oil, and cakes H4886
36 in the day that he **a** them, *by* a statute H4886
8:10 anointing oil, and **a** the tabernacle and H4886
11 seven times, and **a** the altar and all his H4886
12 head, and **a** him, to sanctify him. H4886
Nu 3: 3 which were **a**, whom he consecrated H4886
6:15 unleavened bread **a** with oil, and their H4886
7: 1 and had **a** it, and sanctified it, H4886
1 and had **a** them, and sanctified them; H4886
10 in the day that it was **a**, even the princes H4886
84 the day when it was **a**, by the princes of H4886
88 of the altar, after that it was **a**. H4886
35:25 priest, which was **a** with the holy oil. H4886
1Sa 2:10 his king, and exalt the horn of his **a**. H4899
35 he shall walk before mine **a** for ever. H4899
10: 1 the LORD hath **a** thee *to be* captain H4886
12: 3 and before his **a**: whose ox have I H4899
5 you, and his **a** *is* witness this day, H4899
15:17 and the LORD **a** thee king over Israel? H4886
16: 6 Surely the LORD'S **a** *is* before him. H4899
13 horn of oil, and **a** him in the midst of H4886
24: 6 the LORD'S **a**, to stretch forth mine H4899
6 him, seeing he *is* the **a** of the LORD. H4899
10 against my lord; for he *is* the LORD'S **a**. H4899
26: 9 against the LORD'S **a**, and be guiltless? H4899
11 the LORD'S **a**: but, I pray thee, take H4899
16 the LORD'S **a**. And now see where H4899
23 forth mine hand against the LORD'S **a**. H4899
2Sa 1:14 thine hand to destroy the LORD'S **a**? H4899
16 thee, saying, I have slain the LORD'S **a**. H4899
21 *as though he had* not *been* **a** with oil. H4899
2: 4 and there they **a** David king over the H4886
7 of Judah have **a** me king over them. H4886
3:39 And I *am* this day weak, though **a** king; H4886
5: 3 and they **a** David king over Israel. H4886
17 that they had **a** David king over Israel, H4886
12: 7 God of Israel, I **a** thee king over Israel, H4886
2Sa 12:20 earth, and washed, and **a** *himself*, and H5480
19:10 And Absalom, whom we **a** over us, is H4886
21 this, because he cursed the LORD'S **a**? H4899
22:51 mercy to his **a**, unto David, and to H4899
23: 1 up on high, the **a** of the God of Jacob, H4899
1Ki 1:39 tabernacle, and **a** Solomon. And they H4886
45 the prophet have **a** him king in Gihon: H4886
5: 1 that they had **a** him king in the room H4886
2Ki 9: 3 saith the LORD, I have **a** thee king over H4886
6 of Israel, I have **a** thee king over the H4886
12 LORD, I have **a** thee king over Israel. H4886
11:12 him king, and **a** him; and they clapped H4886
23:30 the son of Josiah, and **a** him, and made H4886
1Ch 11: 3 the LORD; and they **a** David king over H4886
14: 8 that David was **a** king over all Israel, H4886
16:22 *Saying,* Touch not mine **a**, and do my H4899
29:22 second time, and **a** *him* unto the LORD H4886
2Ch 6:42 away the face of thine **a**: remember the H4899
22: 7 had **a** to cut off the house of Ahab. H4886
23:11 **a** him, and said, God save the king. H4886
28:15 and to drink, and **a** them, and carried H5480
Ps 2: 2 the LORD, and against his **a**, *saying,* H4899
18:50 mercy to his **a**, to David, and to his H4899
20: 6 Now know I that the LORD saveth his **a**; H4899
28: 8 and he *is* the saving strength of his **a**. H4899
45: 7 thy God, hath **a** thee with the oil of H4886
84: 9 and look upon the face of thine **a**. H4899
89:20 servant; with my holy oil have I **a** him: H4886
38 thou hast been wroth with thine **a**. H4899
51 reproached the footsteps of thine **a**. H4899
92:10 an unicorn: I shall be **a** with fresh oil. H1101
105:15 *Saying,* Touch not mine **a**, and do my H4899
132:10 sake turn not away the face of thine **a**. H4899
17 bud: I have ordained a lamp for mine **a**. H4899
Isa 45: 1 Thus saith the LORD to his **a**, to Cyrus, H4899
61: 1 the LORD hath **a** me to preach good H4886
Lam 4:20 The breath of our nostrils, the **a** of the H4899
Ezk 16: 9 blood from thee, and I **a** thee with oil. H5480
28:14 Thou *art* the **a** cherub that covereth; H4473
Hab 3:13 with thine **a**; thou woundedst the H4899
Zec 4:14 Then said he, These *are* the two **a** ones, H3323
Mk 6:13 And they cast out many devils, and **a** *G218*
Lk 4:18 me, because he hath **a** me to preach the *G5548*
7:38 his feet, and **a** *them* with the ointment. *G218*
46 woman hath **a** my feet with ointment. *G218*
Jn 9: 6 of the spittle, and he **a** the eyes of the *G2025*
11 made clay, and **a** mine eyes, and said *G2025*
11: 2 (It was *that* Mary which **a** the Lord with *G218*
12: 3 very costly, and **a** the feet of Jesus, and *G218*
Act 4:27 whom thou hast **a**, both Herod, and *G5548*
10:38 How God **a** Jesus of Nazareth with the *G5548*
2Co 1:21 you in Christ, and hath **a** us, *is* God; *G5548*
Heb 1: 9 thy God, hath **a** thee with the oil of *G5548*

ANOINTEDST
Gen 31:13 I *am* the God of Beth-el, where thou **a** H4886

ANOINTEST
Ps 23: 5 enemies: thou **a** my head with oil; my H1878

ANOINTING
Ex 25: 6 Oil for the light, spices for **a** oil, and for H4888
29: 7 Then shalt thou take the **a** oil, and H4888
21 altar, and of the **a** oil, and sprinkle *it* H4888
30:25 the apothecary: it shall be an holy **a** oil. H4888
31 This shall be an holy **a** oil unto me H4888
31:11 And the **a** oil, and sweet incense for the H4888
35: 8 And oil for the light, and spices for **a** H4888
15 his staves, and the **a** oil, and the sweet H4888
28 for the **a** oil, and for the sweet incense. H4888
37:29 And he made the holy **a** oil, and the H4888
39:38 And the golden altar, and the **a** oil, and H4888
40: 9 And thou shalt take the **a** oil, and H4888
15 office: for their **a** shall surely be an H4888
Lev 7:35 This *is the portion* of the **a** of Aaron, H4888
35 Aaron, and of the **a** of his sons, out of H4888
8: 2 garments, and the **a** oil, and a bullock H4888
10 And Moses took the **a** oil, and anointed H4888
12 And he poured of the **a** oil upon H4888
30 And Moses took of the **a** oil, and of the H4888
10: 7 lest ye die: for the **a** oil of the LORD *is* H4888
21:10 whose head the **a** oil was poured, and H4888
12 for the crown of the **a** oil of his God *is* H4888
Nu 4:16 meat offering, and the **a** oil, *and* the H4888
18: 8 by reason of the **a**, and to thy sons, by H4888
Isa 10:27 shall be destroyed because of the **a**. H8081
Jas 5:14 **a** him with oil in the name of the Lord: *G218*
1Jn 2:27 But the **a** which ye have received of *G5545*
27 but as the same **a** teacheth you of all *G5545*

ANON
Mt 13:20 the word, and a with joy receiveth it; G2117
Mk 1:30 of a fever, and a they tell him of her. G2112

ANOTH See BETH-ANOTH.

ANOTHER
Gen 4:25 a seed instead of Abel, whom Cain slew. H312
11: 3 And they said one to a, Go to, let us H7453
15:10 against a: but the birds divided he not. H7453
26:21 And they digged a well, and strove for H312
22 thence, and digged a well; and for that H312
31 and sware one to a: and Isaac sent them H251
29:19 should give her to a man: abide with me. H312
30:24 said, The LORD shall add to me a son. H312
31:49 thee, when we are absent one from a. H7453
37: 9 And he dreamed yet a dream, and told it H312
19 And they said one to a, Behold, this H251
42: 1 his sons, Why do ye look one upon a?
21 And they said one to a, We *are* verily H251
28 saying one to a, What *is* this *that* God H251
43: 7 yet alive? have ye *a* brother? and we told H251
33 youth: and the men marvelled one at a. H7453
Ex 10:23 They saw not one a, neither rose any H251
16:15 saw *it*, they said one to a, It *is* manna: for H251
18:16 between one and a, and I do make *them* H7453
21:10 If he take him a *wife*; her food, her H312
18 and one smite a with a stone, or with H7453
22: 5 and shall feed in a man's field; of the H312
9 of lost thing, which *a* challengeth to be
25:20 *shall look* one to a; toward the mercy H251
26: 3 together one to a; and *other* five curtains H269
3 five curtains *shall be* coupled one to a. H269
4 *a* curtain, in the coupling of the second.
5 that the loops may take hold one of a. H269
17 in order one against a: thus shalt thou H269
19 under a board for his two tenons. H259
21 board, and two sockets under a board. H259
25 board, and two sockets under a board. H259
36:10 curtains one unto a: and *the other* five H259
10 *other* five curtains he coupled one unto a. H259
11 *a* curtain, in the coupling of the second.
12 second: the loops held one *curtain* to a. H259
13 curtains one unto a with the taches: so it H259
22 distant one from a: thus did he make for H259
24 under a board for his two tenons. H259
26 board, and two sockets under a board. H259
37: 8 on this side, and a cherub on the *other* H259
9 their faces one to a; *even* to the mercy H251
19 like almonds in a branch, a knop and H259
Lev 7:10 sons of Aaron have, one *as much* as a. H251
19:11 neither deal falsely, neither lie one to a. H5997
20:10 adultery with *a* man's wife, *even he* H376
25:14 hand, ye shall not oppress one a: H251
17 Ye shall not therefore oppress one a; H5997
46 ye shall not rule one over a with rigour. H251
26:37 And they shall fall one upon a, as it were H251
27:20 sold the field to a man, it shall not be H312
Nu 5:19 to uncleanness *with a* instead of thy
20 But if thou hast gone aside *to a* instead
29 *a* instead of her husband, and is defiled;
8: 8 with oil, and a young bullock shalt H8145
14: 4 And they said one to a, Let us make a H251
24 But my servant Caleb, because he had a H312
23:13 thee, with me unto a place, from whence H312
27 bring thee unto a place; peradventure H312
36: 9 from *one* tribe to a tribe; but every one H312
Dt 4:34 nation from the midst of *a* nation, by H1471
20: 5 die in the battle, and a man dedicate it. H312
6 he die in the battle, and a man eat of it. H312
7 he die in the battle, and a man take her. H312
21:15 one beloved, and a hated, and they have H259
24: 2 house, she may go and be a man's *wife*. H312
25:11 When men strive together one with a, H251
28:30 Thou shalt betroth a wife, and a man H312
32 *shall be* given unto a people, and thine H312
29:28 cast them into a land, as *it is* this day. H312
Jdg 2:10 and there arose a generation after them, H312
6:29 And they said one to a, Who hath done H7453
9:37 of the land, and a company come along H259
10:18 of Gilead said one to a, What man *is he* H7453
16: 7 then shall I be weak, and be as a man. H259
11 then shall I be weak, and be as a man. H259
Ru 2: 8 Go not to glean in a field, neither go H312
3:14 one could know a. And he said, Let it H7453
1Sa 2:25 If one man sin against a, the judge shall H376
10: 3 three kids, and a carrying three loaves H259
3 of bread, and a carrying a bottle of wine: H259
6 them, and shalt be turned into a man. H312
1Sa 10: 9 God gave him a heart: and all those H312
11 people said one to a, What *is* this *that* is H7453
13:18 And a company turned the way *to* H259
18 *to* Bethhoron: and a company turned *to* H259
14:16 and they went on beating down *one a*.
17:30 And he turned from him toward a, and H312
18: 7 And the women answered *one a* as they
20:41 they kissed one a, and wept one with H7453
41 wept one with a, until David exceeded. H7453
21:11 they not sing one to a of him in dances,
29: 5 they sang one to a in dances, saying,
2Sa 11:25 one as well as a: make thy battle more H2088
18:20 shalt bear tidings a day: but this day H312
26 And the watchman saw a man running: H312
26 and said, Behold *a* man running alone.
1Ki 6:27 one a in the midst of the house. H3671
7: 8 And his house where he dwelt *had* a H312
11:23 And God stirred him up *a* adversary,
13:10 So he went a way, and returned not by H312
14: 5 she shall feign herself *to be* a *woman*. H5234
6 thou thyself *to be* a? for I *am* sent to H5234
18: 6 and Obadiah went a way by himself. H259
20:37 Then he found a man, and said, Smite H312
21: 6 I will give thee *a* vineyard for it: and
22:20 manner, and a said on that manner. H2088
2Ki 1:11 Again also he sent unto him a captain of H312
3:23 a: now therefore, Moab, to the spoil. H7453
7: 3 one to a, Why sit we here until we die? H7453
6 they said one to a, Lo, the king of Israel H251
8 and entered into a a tent, and carried H312
9 Then they said one to a, We do not well: H7453
10:21 house of Baal was full from one end to a.
14: 8 Come, let us look one a in the face.
11 of Judah looked one a in the face at
21:16 from one end to a; beside his sin
1Ch 2:26 Jerahmeel had also a wife, whose name H312
16:20 and from *one* kingdom to a people; H312
17: 5 to tent, and from *one* tabernacle *to a*.
24: 5 lot, one sort with a; for the governors of
26:12 a, to minister in the house of the LORD. H251
2Ch 18:19 and a saying after that manner. H2088
20:23 of Seir, every one helped to destroy a. H7453
25:17 Come, let us see one a in the face.
21 and they saw one a in the face, *both* he
32: 5 to the towers, and a wall without, and H312
Ezr 4:21 not builded, until *a* commandment shall
9:11 one end to a with their uncleanness.
Neh 3:19 ruler of Mizpah, a piece over against H8145
21 the son of Koz a piece, from the door H8145
24 the son of Henadad a piece, from the H8145
27 After them the Tekoites repaired a H8145
30 sixth son of Zalaph, a piece. After him H8145
4:19 separated upon the wall, one far from a. H251
9: 3 part of the day; and *a* fourth part they
Est 1: 7 diverse one from a,) and royal wine in
19 estate unto a that is better than she. H7468
4:14 to the Jews from a place; but thou and H312
9:19 day, and of sending portions one to a. H7453
22 portions one to a, and gifts to the poor. H7453
Job 1:16 there came also a, and said, The fire of H2088
17 there came also a, and said, The H2088
18 there came also a, and said, Thy sons H2088
13: 9 one man mocketh a, do ye *so* mock him?
19:27 behold, and not a; *though* my reins be H2114
21:25 And a dieth in the bitterness of his H2088
31: 8 *Then* let me sow, and let a eat; yea, let H312
10 *Then* let my wife grind unto a, and let H312
41:16 One is so near to a, that no air can come H259
17 They are joined one to a, they stick H251
Ps 16: 4 *that* hasten *after* a *god*: their drink H312
75: 7 he putteth down one, and setteth up a. H2088
105:13 When they went from one nation to a,
13 another, from *one* kingdom to a people; H312
109: 8 Let his days be few; *and* let a take his H312
145: 4 to a, and shall declare thy mighty acts.
Prv 25: 9 *himself*; and discover not a secret to a: H312
27: 2 Let a man praise thee, and not thine H2114
Ecc 1: 4 *One* generation passeth away, and *a*
4:10 for *he hath* not a to help him up. H8145
8: 9 one man ruleth over a to his own hurt.
Song 5: 9 What *is* thy beloved more than *a*
9 *a* beloved, that thou dost so charge us?
Isa 3: 5 every one by a, and every one by his
6: 3 And one cried unto a, and said, Holy, H2088
13: 8 one at a; their faces *shall be as* flames. H7453
28:11 For with stammering lips and a tongue H312
42: 8 to a, neither my praise to graven images. H312
44: 5 One shall say, I *am* the LORD'S; and a H2088
5 of Jacob; and a shall subscribe *with* H2088
Isa 48:11 and I will not give my glory unto a. H312
57: 8 *thyself to a* than me, and art gone
65:15 thee, and call his servants by a name: H312
22 They shall not build, and a inhabit; they H312
22 not plant, and a eat: for as the days of H312
66:23 from one new moon to a, and from one
23 one sabbath to a, shall all flesh come to
Jer 3: 1 from him, and become a man's, shall he H312
13:14 And I will dash them one against a, even H251
18: 4 so he made it again a vessel, as seemed H312
14 that come from a place be forsaken? H2114
22:26 that bare thee, into a country, where ye H312
25:26 far and near, one with a, and all the H251
36:28 Take thee again a roll, and write in it all H312
32 Then took Jeremiah a roll, and gave it to H312
46:16 fall, yea, one fell upon a: and they said, H7453
51:31 One post shall run to meet a, and one
31 messenger to meet a, to shew the king of
46 and after that in *a* year *shall come* a
Ezk 1: 9 Their wings *were* joined one to a; they H269
11 one to a, and two covered their bodies. H376
3:13 that touched one a, and the noise of the H269
4: 8 from one side to a, till thou hast ended
17 a, and consume away for their iniquity. H251
10: 9 by one cherub, and a wheel by another H259
9 and another wheel by a cherub: and the H259
12: 3 from thy place to a place in their sight: it H312
15: 7 out from *one* fire, and *a* fire shall devour
17: 7 There was also a great eagle with great H259
19: 5 lost, then she took a of her whelps, *and* H259
22:11 wife; and a hath lewdly defiled his H376
11 in law; and a in thee hath humbled H376
24:23 your iniquities, and mourn one toward a. H251
33:30 and speak one to a, every one to his H259
37:16 then take a stick, and write upon H259
17 And join them one to a into one stick; H259
40:13 to the roof of a: the breadth *was* five
26 a on that side, upon the posts thereof. H259
49 one on this side, and a on that side. H259
41: 6 three, one over a, and thirty in order; and
11 the north, and a door toward the south: H259
47:14 And ye shall inherit it, one as well as a: H251
Dan 2:39 And after thee shall arise a kingdom H317
39 to thee, and a third kingdom of brass, H317
43 a, even as iron is not mixed with clay. H1836
5: 6 and his knees smote one against a. H1668
17 give thy rewards to a; yet I will read the H321
7: 3 up from the sea, diverse one from a. H1668
5 And behold a beast, a second, like to a H317
6 After this I beheld, and lo a, like a H317
8 up among them a little horn, before H317
24 shall arise: and a shall rise after them; H321
8:13 Then I heard one saint speaking, and a H259
Hos 3: 3 be for *a* man: so *will* I also *be* for thee.
4: 4 Yet let no man strive, nor reprove a: for H376
Joel 1: 3 and their children a generation. H312
2: 8 Neither shall one thrust a; they shall walk H251
Am 4: 7 it not to rain upon a city: one piece was H259
Nah 2: 4 justle one against a in the broad ways: H8264
Zec 2: 3 forth, and a angel went out to meet him, H312
8:21 of one *city* shall go to a, saying, Let us go H259
11: 9 let the rest eat every one the flesh of a. H7468
Mal 3:16 spake often one to a: and the LORD H7453
Mt 2:12 departed into their own country a way. G243
8: 9 he goeth; and to a, Come, and he cometh; G243
21 And a of his disciples said unto him, G2087
10:23 city, flee ye into a: for verily I say unto G243
11: 3 that should come, or do we look for a? G2087
13:24 A parable put he forth unto them, G243
31 A parable put he forth unto them, G243
33 A parable spake he unto them; The G243
19: 9 and shall marry a, committeth adultery: G243
21:33 Hear a parable: There was a certain G243
35 one, and killed a, and stoned another. G3739
35 one, and killed another, and stoned a. G3739
22: 5 one to his farm, a to his merchandise: G3588
24: 2 upon a, that shall not be thrown down. G3037
10 betray one a, and shall hate one another. G240
10 betray one another, and shall hate one a. G240
25:15 And unto one he gave five talents, to a G3739
15 two, and to a one; to every man G3739
32 them one from a, as a shepherd divideth G240
26:71 out into the porch, a *maid* saw him, and G243
27:38 on the right hand, and a on the left. G1520
Mk 4:41 and said one to a, What manner of man G240
9:10 one with a what the rising from G4802
50 in yourselves, and have peace one with a. G240
10:11 a, committeth adultery against her. G243
12 married to a, she committeth adultery. G243

Mk 12: 4 And again he sent unto them a servant; G243
5 And again he sent a; and him they killed, G243
13: 2 upon a, that shall not be thrown down. G3037
14:19 him one by one, Is it I? and a said, Is it I? G243
58 days I will build a made without hands. G243
16:12 After that he appeared in a form unto G2087
Lk 2:15 said one to a, Let us now go even unto G240
6: 6 And it came to pass also on a sabbath, G2087
11 one with a what they might do to Jesus. G4314
7: 8 he goeth; and to a, Come, and he cometh; G243
19 he that should come? or look we for a? G243
20 he that should come? or look we for a? G243
32 and calling one to a, and saying, We G240
8:25 saying one to a, What manner of man G4314
9:56 save them. And they went to a village. G2087
59 And he said unto a, Follow me. But he G2087
61 And a also said, Lord, I will follow G2087
12: 1 trode one upon a, he began to say unto G240
14:19 And a said, I have bought five yoke of G2087
20 And a said, I have married a wife, and G2087
31 to make war against a king, sitteth not G2087
16: 7 Then said he to a, And how much owest G2087
12 in that which is a man's, who shall give G245
18 and marrieth a, committeth adultery: G2087
19:20 And a came, saying, Lord, behold, here G2087
44 thee one stone upon a; because thou G3037
20:11 And again he sent a servant: and they G2087
21: 6 upon a, that shall not be thrown down. G3037
22:58 And after a little while a saw him, and G2087
59 And about the space of one hour after a G243
24:17 have one to a, as ye walk, and are sad? G4314
32 And they said one to a, Did not our G4314
Jn 4:33 Therefore said the disciples one to a, G4314
37 saying true, One soweth, and a reapeth. G243
5: 7 am coming, a steppeth down before me. G243
32 There is a that beareth witness of me; G243
43 ye receive me not: if a shall come in his G243
44 honour one of a, and seek not the G3844
13:22 Then the disciples looked one on a, G1519
34 That ye love one a; as I have loved you, G240
34 I have loved you, that ye also love one a. G240
35 my disciples, if ye have love one to a. G1722
14:16 he shall give you a Comforter, that he G243
15:12 That ye love one a, as I have loved you. G240
17 I command you, that ye love one a. G240
18:15 Jesus, and so did a disciple: that disciple G243
19:37 And again a scripture saith, They shall G2087
21:18 thy hands, and a shall gird thee, and G243
Act 1:20 therein: and his bishoprick let a take. G2087
2: 7 saying one to a, Behold, are not all G4314
12 saying one to a, What meaneth this? G243
7:18 Till a king arose, which knew not G2087
26 are brethren; why do ye wrong one to a? G240
10:28 come unto one of a nation; but God hath G246
12:17 he departed, and went into a place. G2087
13:35 Wherefore he saith also in a psalm, G2087
17: 7 saying that there is a king, one Jesus. G2087
19:32 thing, and some a: for the assembly was G5100
38 are deputies: let them implead one a. G240
21: 6 our leave one of a, we took ship; and they G240
34 And some cried one thing, some a, G5100
Ro 1:27 their lust one toward a; men with men G1519
2: 1 thou judgest a, thou condemnest G2087
15 while accusing or else excusing one a;) G240
21 Thou therefore which teachest a, G2087
7: 3 she be married to a man, she shall be G2087
3 though she be married to a man. G2087
4 be married to a, even to him who is G2087
23 But I see a law in my members, G2087
9:21 unto honour, and a unto dishonour? G3739
12: 5 Christ, and every one members one of a. G240
10 Be kindly affectioned one to a with G1519
10 love; in honour preferring one a; G240
16 Be of the same mind one toward a. G1519
13: 8 Owe no man any thing, but to love one a: G240
8 he that loveth a hath fulfilled the law. G2087
14: 2 all things: a, who is weak, eateth herbs. G3739
4 Who art thou that judgest a man's G245
5 One man esteemeth one day above a: G2250
5 above another: a esteemeth every day G3739
13 Let us not therefore judge one a any G240
19 and things wherewith one may edify a. G240
15: 5 one toward a according to Christ Jesus: G1722
7 Wherefore receive ye one a, as Christ G240
14 knowledge, able also to admonish one a. G240
20 I should build upon a man's foundation: G245
16:16 Salute one a with an holy kiss. The G240
1Co 3: 4 For while one saith, I am of Paul; and a, G2087
10 foundation, and a buildeth thereon. But G243
1Co 4: 6 of you be puffed up for one against a. G2087
7 For who maketh thee to differ from a?
6: 1 a matter against a, go to law before the G2087
7 ye go to law one with a. Why do ye not G3326
7: 7 one after this manner, and a after that. G3739
10:29 my liberty judged of a man's conscience? G243
11:21 and one is hungry, and a is drunken. G3739
33 ye come together to eat, tarry one for a. G240
12: 8 of wisdom; to a the word of knowledge G243
9 To a faith by the same Spirit; to G2087
9 To another faith by the same Spirit; to a G243
10 To a the working of miracles; to another G243
10 To another the working of miracles; to a G243
10 prophecy; to a discerning of spirits; G243
10 of spirits; to a divers kinds of tongues; G2087
10 to a the interpretation of tongues: G243
25 should have the same care one for a. G5228
14:30 If any thing be revealed to a that sitteth G243
15:39 of flesh of men, a flesh of beasts, another G243
39 beasts, a of fishes, and another of birds. G243
39 beasts, another of fishes, and a of birds. G243
40 one, and the glory of the terrestrial is a. G2087
41 There is one glory of the sun, and a glory G243
41 of the moon, and a glory of the stars: for G243
41 one star differeth from a star in glory.
16:20 All the brethren greet you. Greet ye one a G240
2Co 10:16 and not to boast in a man's line of things G245
11: 4 For if he that cometh preacheth a Jesus, G243
4 or if ye receive a spirit, which ye have G2087
4 not received, or a gospel, which ye have G2087
13:12 Greet one a with an holy kiss. G240
Gal 1: 6 into the grace of Christ unto a gospel: G2087
7 Which is not a; but there be some that G243
5:13 to the flesh, but by love serve one a. G240
15 But if ye bite and devour one a, take heed G240
15 heed that ye be not consumed one of a. G240
26 provoking one a, envying one another. G240
26 provoking one another, envying one a. G240
6: 4 rejoicing in himself alone, and not in a. G2087
Eph 4: 2 longsuffering, forbearing one a in love; G240
25 neighbour: for we are members one of a. G240
32 And be ye kind one to a, tenderhearted, G1519
32 forgiving one a, even as God for Christ's G1438
5:21 Submitting yourselves one to a in the G240
Col 3: 9 Lie not one to a, seeing that ye have put G1519
13 Forbearing one a, and forgiving one G240
13 and forgiving one a, if any man have a G1438
16 and admonishing one a in psalms and G1438
1Th 3:12 in love one toward a, and toward all G1519
4: 9 are taught of God to love one a. G240
18 Wherefore comfort one a with these G240
5:11 and edify one a, even as also ye do. G1520
1Ti 5:21 before a, doing nothing by partiality. G4299
Tit 3: 3 and envy, hateful, and hating one a. G240
Heb 3:13 But exhort one a daily, while it is called G1438
4: 8 he not afterward have spoken of a day. G243
5: 6 As he saith also in a place, Thou art a G2087
7:11 was there that a priest should rise after G2087
13 pertaineth to a tribe, of which no man G2087
15 of Melchisedec there ariseth a priest, G2087
10:24 And let us consider one a to provoke G240
25 is; but exhorting one a: and so much the
Jas 2:25 and had sent them out a way? G2087
4:11 Speak not evil one of a, brethren. He that G240
12 to destroy: who art thou that judgest a? G2087
5: 9 Grudge not one against a, brethren, lest G2596
16 Confess your faults one to a, and pray G240
16 and pray one for a, that ye may be G240
1Pt 1:22 ye love one a with a pure heart fervently: G240
3: 8 one of a, love as brethren, be G4835
4: 9 Use hospitality one to a without G1519
10 the same one to a, as good stewards of G1519
5: 5 be subject one to a, and be clothed with G240
14 Greet ye one a with a kiss of charity. G240
1Jn 1: 7 one with a, and the blood of Jesus G3326
3:11 the beginning, that we should love one a. G240
23 love one a, as he gave us commandment. G240
4: 7 Beloved, let us love one a: for love is of G240
11 so loved us, we ought also to love one a. G240
12 If we love one a, God dwelleth in us, and G240
2Jn 5 from the beginning, that we love one a. G240
Rev 6: 4 And there went out a horse that was red: G243
4 should kill one a: and there was given G240
7: 2 And I saw a angel ascending from the G243
8: 3 And a angel came and stood at the altar, G243
10: 1 And I saw a mighty angel come down G243
11:10 send gifts one to a; because these two G240
12: 3 And there appeared a wonder in heaven; G243
13:11 And I beheld a beast coming up out of G243
Rev 14: 6 And I saw a angel fly in the midst of G243
8 And there followed a angel, saying, G243
15 And a angel came out of the temple, G243
17 And a angel came out of the temple G243
18 And a angel came out from the altar, G243
15: 1 And I saw a sign in heaven, great and G243
16: 7 And I heard a out of the altar say, Even G243
18: 1 And after these things I saw a angel G243
4 And I heard a voice from heaven, G243
20:12 were opened: and a book was opened, G243

ANOTHER'S

Gen 11: 7 they may not understand one a speech. H7453
Ex 21:35 And if one man's ox hurt a, that he die; H7453
Jn 13:14 feet; ye also ought to wash one a feet. G240
1Co 10:24 seek his own, but every man a wealth. G2087
Gal 6: 2 Bear ye one a burdens, and so fulfil the G240

ANSWER

Gen 30:33 So shall my righteousness a for me in H6030
41:16 God shall give Pharaoh an a of peace. H6030
45: 3 could not a him; for they were troubled H6030
Dt 20:11 And it shall be, if it make thee a of H6030
21: 7 And they shall a and say, Our hands H6030
25: 9 his face, and shall a and say, So shall it H6030
27:15 all the people shall a and say, Amen. H6030
Jos 4: 7 Then ye shall a them, That the waters of H559
Jdg 5:29 her, yea, she returned a to herself, H561
1Sa 2:16 then he would a him, Nay; but thou shalt H559
20:10 or what if thy father a thee roughly? H6030
2Sa 3:11 And he could not a Abner a word H7725
24:13 a I shall return to him that sent me. H1697
1Ki 9: 9 And they shall a, Because they forsook H559
12: 6 do ye advise that I may a this people? H1697
7 wilt serve them, and a them, and speak H6030
9 ye that we may a this people, who have H1697
18:29 nor any to a, nor any that regarded. H6030
2Ki 4:29 if any salute thee, a him not again: and H6030
18:36 commandment was, saying, A him not. H6030
2Ch 10: 6 give ye me to return a to this people? H1697
9 we may return a to this people, which H1697
10 Thus shalt thou a the people that spake H559
Ezr 4:17 Then sent the king an a unto Rehum H6600
5: 5 a by letter concerning this matter. H8421
11 And thus they returned us a, saying, We H6600
Neh 5: 8 their peace, and found nothing to a. H1696
Est 4:13 Then Mordecai commanded to a H7725
15 Esther bade them return Mordecai this a,
Job 5: 1 Call now, if there be any that will a H6030
9: 3 he cannot a him one of a thousand. H6030
14 How much less shall I a him, and H6030
15 yet would I not a, but I would make H6030
32 as I am, that I should a him, and we H6030
13:22 Then call thou, and I will a: or let me H6030
22 or let me speak, and a thou me. H7725
14:15 Thou shalt call, and I will a thee: thou H6030
19:16 no a; I entreated him with my mouth. H6030
20: 2 me to a, and for this I make haste. H7725
3 of my understanding causeth me to a. H6030
23: 5 which he would a me, and understand H6030
31:14 when he visiteth, what shall I a him? H7725
35 Almighty would a me, and that mine H6030
32: 1 So these three men ceased to a Job, H6030
3 no a, and yet had condemned Job. H4617
5 When Elihu saw that there was no a in H4617
14 neither will I a him with your speeches. H7725
17 I said, I will a also my part, I also will H6030
20 be refreshed: I will open my lips and a. H6030
33: 5 If thou canst a me, set thy words in H7725
12 Behold, in this thou art not just: I will a H6030
32 If thou hast any thing to say, a me: H7725
35: 4 I will a thee, and thy H7725+H4405
12 There they cry, but none giveth a, H6030
38: 3 I will demand of thee, and a thou me. H3045
40: 2 he that reproveth God, let him a it. H6030
4 Behold, I am vile; what shall I a thee? I H7725
5 Once have I spoken; but I will not a: H6030
Ps 27: 7 have mercy also upon me, and a me. H6030
65: 5 wilt thou a us, O God of our salvation; H6030
86: 7 I will call upon thee: for thou wilt a me. H6030
91:15 He shall call upon me, and I will a him: H6030
102: 2 in the day when I call a me speedily. H6030
108: 6 save with thy right hand, and a me. H6030
119:42 So shall I have wherewith to a him that H6030
143: 1 a me, and in thy righteousness. H6030
Prv 1:28 me, but I will not a; they shall seek me H6030
15: 1 A soft a turneth away wrath: but H4617
23 A man hath joy by the a of his mouth: H4617
28 The heart of the righteous studieth to a: H6030

Prv 16: 1 the **a** of the tongue, *is* from the LORD. H4617
22:21 that thou mightest **a** the words of truth H7725
24:26 shall kiss *his* lips that giveth a right **a**. H1697
26: 4 **A** not a fool according to his folly, lest H6030
5 **A** a fool according to his folly, lest he H6030
27:11 **a** him that reproacheth me. H7725+H1697
29:19 for though he understand he will not **a**. H4617
Song 5: 6 him; I called him, but he gave me no **a**. H6030
Isa 14:32 What shall *one* then **a** the messengers H6030
30:19 when he shall hear it, he will **a** thee. H6030
36:21 commandment was, saying, **A** him not. H6030
41:28 when I asked of them, could **a** a word. H7725
46: 7 not **a**, nor save him out of his trouble. H6030
50: 2 called, *was there* none to **a**? Is my hand H6030
58: 9 the LORD shall **a**; thou shalt cry, and H6030
65:12 I called, ye did not **a**; when I spake, ye H6030
24 they call, I will **a**; and while they are yet H6030
66: 4 I called, none did **a**; when I spake, they H6030
Jer 5:19 us? then shalt thou **a** them, Like as ye H559
7:27 call unto them; but they will not **a** thee. H6030
22: 9 Then they shall **a**, Because they have H559
33: 3 Call unto me, and I will **a** thee, and H6030
42: 4 the LORD shall **a** you, I will declare *it* H6030
44:20 had given him *that* **a**, saying, H1697+H6030
Ezk 14: 4 I the LORD will **a** him that cometh H6030
7 me; I the LORD will **a** him by myself: H6030
21: 7 that thou shalt **a**, For the tidings; because H559
Dan 3:16 *are* not careful to **a** thee in this matter. H8421
Joel 2:19 Yea, the LORD will **a** and say unto his H6030
Mic 3: 7 cover their lips; for *there is* no **a** of God. H4617
Hab 2: 1 and what I shall **a** when I am reproved. H7725
11 the beam out of the timber shall **a** it. H6030
Zec 13: 6 Then he shall **a**, *Those* with which I was H559
Mt 22:46 And no man was able to **a** him a word, *G611*
25:37 Then shall the righteous **a** him, saying, *G611*
40 And the King shall **a** and say unto them, *G611*
44 Then shall they also **a** him, saying, Lord, *G611*
45 Then shall he **a** them, saying, Verily I *G611*
Mk 11:29 one question, and **a** me, and I will tell *G611*
30 was *it* from heaven, or of men? **a** me. *G611*
14:40 heavy,) neither wist they what to **a** him. *G611*
Lk 11: 7 And he from within shall **a** and say, *G611*
12:11 thing ye shall **a**, or what ye shall say: *G626*
13:25 us; and he shall **a** and say unto you, I *G611*
14: 6 And they could not **a** him again to these *G470*
20: 3 I will also ask you one thing; and **a** me: *G2036*
26 marvelled at his **a**, and held their peace. *G612*
21:14 not to meditate before what ye shall **a**: *G626*
22:68 And if I also ask *you*, ye will not **a** me, *G611*
Jn 1:22 we may give an **a** to them that sent us. *G612*
19: 9 art thou? But Jesus gave him no **a**. *G612*
Act 24:10 I do the more cheerfully **a** for myself: *G626*
25:16 face, and have licence to **a** for himself *G627*
26: 2 because I shall **a** for myself this day *G636*
Ro 11: 4 But what saith the **a** of God unto him? I *G5538*
1Co 9: 3 Mine **a** to them that do examine me is *G627*
2Co 5:12 have somewhat to *a* them which glory in
Col 4: 6 may know how ye ought to **a** every man. *G611*
2Ti 4:16 At my first **a** no man stood with me, but *G627*
1Pt 3:15 always to *give* an **a** to every man that *G627*
21 of the flesh, but the **a** of a good *G1906*

ANSWERABLE
Ex 38:18 cubits, **a** to the hangings of the court. H5980

ANSWERED
Gen 18:27 And Abraham **a** and said, Behold now, H6030
23: 5 And the children of Heth **a** Abraham, H6030
10 Ephron the Hittite **a** Abraham in the H6030
14 And Ephron **a** Abraham, saying unto H6030
24:50 Then Laban and Bethuel **a** and said, H6030
27:37 And Isaac **a** and said unto Esau, H6030
39 And Isaac his father **a** and said unto H6030
31:14 And Rachel and Leah **a** and said unto H6030
31 And Jacob **a** and said to Laban, H6030
36 Laban: and Jacob **a** and said to Laban, H6030
43 And Laban **a** and said unto Jacob, H6030
34:13 And the sons of Jacob **a** Shechem and H6030
35: 3 unto God, who **a** me in the day of my H6030
40:18 And Joseph **a** and said, This *is* the H6030
41:16 And Joseph **a** Pharaoh, saying, *It is* not H6030
42:22 And Reuben **a** them, saying, Spake I H6030
43:28 And they **a**, Thy servant our father *is* in H559
Ex 4: 1 And Moses **a** and said, But, behold, H6030
15:21 And Miriam **a** them, Sing ye to the H6030
19: 8 And all the people **a** together, and said, H6030
19 spake, and God **a** him by a voice. H6030
24: 3 and all the people **a** with one voice, and H6030
Nu 11:28 of his young men, **a** and said, My lord H6030
22:18 And Balaam **a** and said unto the H6030
23:12 And he **a** and said, Must I not take H6030
26 But Balaam **a** and said unto Balak, H6030
32:31 of Reuben **a**, saying, As the LORD H6030
Dt 1:14 And ye **a** me, and said, The thing H6030
41 Then ye **a** and said unto me, We have H6030
Jos 1:16 And they **a** Joshua, saying, All that H6030
2:14 And the men **a** her, Our life for yours, if H559
7:20 And Achan **a** Joshua, and said, Indeed H6030
9:24 And they **a** Joshua, and said, Because it H6030
15:19 Who **a**, Give me a blessing; for thou hast H559
17:15 And Joshua **a** them, If thou *be* a great H559
22:21 tribe of Manasseh **a**, and said unto the H6030
24:16 And the people **a** and said, God forbid H6030
Jdg 5:29 Her wise ladies **a** her, yea, she returned H6030
7:14 And his fellow **a** and said, This *is* H6030
8: 8 the men of Penuel **a** him as the men of H6030
8 him as the men of Succoth had **a** *him*. H6030
18 at Tabor? And they **a**, As thou *art*, so H559
25 And they **a**, We will willingly give *them*. H559
11:13 of Ammon **a** unto the messengers H559
15: 6 this? And they **a**, Samson, the son in law H559
10 us? And they **a**, To bind Samson are H559
18:14 Then **a** the five men that went to spy H6030
19:28 going. But none **a**. Then the man took H6030
20: 4 that was slain, **a** and said, I came into H6030
Ru 2: 4 And they **a** him, The LORD bless thee. H559
6 set over the reapers **a** and said, It *is* the H6030
11 And Boaz **a** and said unto her, It hath H6030
3: 9 And he said, Who *art* thou? And she **a**, I H559
1Sa 1:15 And Hannah **a** and said, No, my lord, I H6030
17 Then Eli **a** and said, Go in peace: and H6030
3: 4 That the LORD called Samuel: and he **a**, H559
6 he **a**, I called not, my son; lie down again. H559
10 Samuel **a**, Speak; for thy servant heareth. H559
16 Samuel, my son. And he **a**, Here *am* I. H559
4:17 And the messenger **a** and said, Israel is H6030
20 But she **a** not, neither did she regard *it*. H6030
5: 8 of Israel? And they **a**, Let the ark of the H559
6: 4 to him? They **a**, Five golden emerods, H559
9: 8 And the servant **a** Saul again, and said, H6030
12 And they **a** them, and said, He is; H6030
19 And Samuel **a** Saul, and said, I *am* the H6030
21 And Saul **a** and said, *Am* not I a H6030
10:12 And one of the same place **a** and said, H6030
22 And the LORD **a**, Behold, he hath hid H559
11: 2 And Nahash the Ammonite **a** them, On H559
12: 5 in my hand. And they **a**, *He is* witness. H559
14:12 And the men of the garrison **a** H6030
28 Then **a** one of the people, and said, Thy H6030
37 of Israel? But he **a** him not that day. H6030
39 a man among all the people *that* **a** him. H6030
44 And Saul **a**, God do so and more also: for H559
16:18 Then **a** one of the servants, and said, H6030
17:27 And the people **a** him after this manner, H559
30 **a** him again after the former manner. H1697
58 man? And David **a**, I *am* the son of thy H559
18: 7 And the women **a** *one another* as they H6030
19:17 And Michal **a** Saul, He said unto me, H559
20:28 And Jonathan **a** Saul, David earnestly H6030
32 And Jonathan **a** Saul his father, and H6030
21: 4 And the priest **a** David, and said, *There* H6030
5 And David **a** the priest, and said unto H6030
22: 9 Then **a** Doeg the Edomite, which was H6030
12 of Ahitub. And he **a**, Here I *am*, my lord. H559
14 Then Ahimelech **a** the king, and said, H6030
23: 4 And the LORD **a** him and said, Arise, H6030
25:10 And Nabal **a** David's servants, and H6030
26: 6 Then **a** David and said to Ahimelech H6030
14 Then Abner **a** and said, Who *art* thou H6030
22 And David **a** and said, Behold the H6030
28: 6 LORD, the LORD **a** him not, neither by H6030
15 me up? And Saul **a**, I am sore distressed; H559
29: 9 And Achish **a** and said to David, I H6030
30: 8 them? And he **a** him, Pursue: for thou H559
22 Then **a** all the wicked men and *men* of H6030
2Sa 1: 4 tell me. And he **a**, That the people are H559
7 and called unto me. And I **a**, Here *am* I. H559
8 thou? And I **a** him, I *am* an Amalekite. H559
13 *art* thou? And he **a**, I *am* the son of a H559
2:20 said, *Art* thou Asahel? And he **a**, I *am*. H559
4: 9 And David **a** Rechab and Baanah his H6030
9: 6 And he **a**, Behold thy servant! H559
13:12 And she **a** him, Nay, my brother, do not H559
32 David's brother, **a** and said, Let not my H6030
14: 5 thee? And she **a**, I *am* indeed a widow H559
18 Then the king **a** and said unto the H6030
19 And the woman **a** and said, *As* thy soul H6030
32 And Absalom **a** Joab, Behold, I sent unto H559
2Sa 15:21 And Ittai **a** the king, and said, *As* the H6030
18: 3 But the people **a**, Thou shalt not go forth: H559
29 And Ahimaaz **a**, When Joab sent the H559
32 safe? And Cushi **a**, The enemies of my H559
19:21 But Abishai the son of Zeruiah **a** and H6030
26 And he **a**, My lord, O king, my servant H559
38 And the king **a**, Chimham shall go over H559
42 And all the men of Judah **a** the men of H6030
43 And the men of Israel **a** the men of H6030
20:17 thou Joab? And he **a**, I *am he*. Then she H559
17 of thine handmaid. And he **a**, I do hear. H559
20 And Joab **a** and said, Far be it, far be it H6030
21: 1 And the LORD **a**, *It is* for Saul, and for H559
5 And they **a** the king, The man that H559
22:42 unto the LORD, but he **a** them not. H6030
1Ki 1:28 Then king David **a** and said, Call me H6030
36 And Benaiah the son of Jehoiada **a** the H6030
43 And Jonathan **a** and said to Adonijah, H6030
2:22 And king Solomon **a** and said unto his H6030
30 Thus said Joab, and thus he **a** me. H6030
3:27 Then the king **a** and said, Give her the H6030
11:22 country? And he **a**, Nothing: howbeit let H559
12:13 And the king **a** the people roughly, and H6030
16 the people **a** the king, saying, H7725+H1697
13: 6 And the king **a** and said unto the man H6030
18: 8 And he **a** him, I *am*: go, tell thy lord, H559
18 And he **a**, I have not troubled Israel; but H559
21 him. And the people **a** him not a word. H6030
24 the people **a** and said, It is well spoken. H6030
26 nor any that **a**. And they leaped upon H6030
20: 4 And the king of Israel **a** and said, My H6030
11 And the king of Israel **a** and said, Tell H6030
14 shall order the battle? And he **a**, Thou. H559
21: 6 he **a**, I will not give thee my vineyard. H559
20 enemy? And he **a**, I have found *thee*: H559
22:15 shall we forbear? And he **a** him, Go, and H559
2Ki 1: 8 And they **a** him, *He was* an hairy man, H559
10 And Elijah **a** and said to the captain of H6030
11 his fifty. And he **a** and said unto him, H6030
12 And Elijah **a** and said unto them, If I H6030
2: 5 he **a**, Yea, I know *it*; hold ye your peace. H559
3: 8 we go up? And he **a**, The way through the H559
11 of Israel's servants **a** and said, Here *is* H6030
4:13 she **a**, I dwell among mine own people. H559
14 for her? And Gehazi **a**, Verily she hath no H559
26 well with the child? And she **a**, *It is* well. H559
6: 2 where we may dwell. And he **a**, Go ye. H559
3 go with thy servants. And he **a**, I will go. H559
16 And he **a**, Fear not: for they that *be* with H559
22 And he **a**, Thou shalt not smite *them*: H559
28 thee? And she **a**, This woman said unto H559
7: 2 the king leaned **a** the man of God, and H6030
13 And one of his servants **a** and said, Let H6030
19 And that lord **a** the man of God, and H6030
8:12 my lord? And he **a**, Because I know the H559
13 thing? And Elisha **a**, The LORD hath H559
14 to thee? And he **a**, He told me *that* thou H559
9:19 *it* peace? And Jehu **a**, What hast thou to H559
22 Jehu? And he **a**, What peace, so long H559
10:13 *are* ye? And they **a**, We *are* the brethren H559
15 And Jehonadab **a**, It is. If it be, give *me* H559
18:36 But the people held their peace, and **a** H6030
20:10 And Hezekiah **a**, It is a light thing for the H559
15 And Hezekiah **a**, All *the things* that are H559
1Ch 12:17 out to meet them, and **a** and said unto H6030
21: 3 And Joab **a**, The LORD make his people H559
26 the LORD; and he **a** him from heaven H6030
28 that the LORD had **a** him in the H6030
2Ch 2:11 Then Huram the king of Tyre **a** in H559
7:22 And it shall be **a**, Because they forsook H559
10:13 And the king **a** them roughly; and king H6030
14 And **a** them after the advice of the H1696
16 them, the people **a** the king, saying, H7725
18: 3 And he **a** him, I *am* as thou *art*, H559
25: 9 the man of God **a**, The LORD is able to H559
29:31 Then Hezekiah **a** and said, Now ye H6030
31:10 of the house of Zadok **a** him, and said, H559
34:15 And Hilkiah **a** and said to Shaphan the H6030
23 And she **a** them, Thus saith the LORD H559
Ezr 10: 2 the sons of Elam, **a** and said unto Ezra, H6030
12 Then all the congregation **a** and said H6030
Neh 2:20 Then **a** I them, and said unto H7725+H1697
6: 4 and I **a** them after the same manner. H7725
8: 6 And all the people **a**, Amen, Amen, with H6030
Est 1:16 And Memucan **a** before the king and the H559
5: 4 And Esther **a**, If *it seem* good unto the H559
7 Then **a** Esther, and said, My petition H6030
6: 7 And Haman **a** the king, For the man H559
7: 3 Then Esther the queen **a** and said, If I H6030

Est 7: 5 Then the king Ahasuerus **a** and said H559
Job 1: 7 thou? Then Satan **a** the LORD, and H6030
9 Then Satan **a** the LORD, and said, H6030
2: 2 thou? And Satan **a** the LORD, and said, H6030
4 And Satan **a** the LORD, and said, Skin H6030
4: 1 Then Eliphaz the Temanite **a** and said, H6030
6: 1 But Job **a** and said, H6030
8: 1 Then **a** Bildad the Shuhite, and said, H6030
9: 1 Then Job **a** and said, H6030
16 If I had called, and he had **a** me; *yet* H6030
11: 1 Then **a** Zophar the Naamathite, and H6030
2 Should not the multitude of words be **a**? H6030
12: 1 And Job **a** and said, H6030
15: 1 Then **a** Eliphaz the Temanite, and said, H6030
16: 1 Then Job **a** and said, H6030
18: 1 Then **a** Bildad the Shuhite, and said, H6030
19: 1 Then Job **a** and said, H6030
20: 1 Then **a** Zophar the Naamathite, and H6030
21: 1 But Job **a** and said, H6030
22: 1 Then Eliphaz the Temanite **a** and said, H6030
23: 1 Then Job **a** and said, H6030
25: 1 Then **a** Bildad the Shuhite, and said, H6030
26: 1 But Job **a** and said, H6030
32: 6 the Buzite **a** and said, I *am* young, H6030
12 that convinced Job, *or* that **a** his words: H6030
15 They were amazed, they **a** no more: H6030
16 not, but stood still, *and* **a** no more;) H6030
34: 1 Furthermore Elihu **a** and said, H6030
38: 1 Then the LORD **a** Job out of the H6030
40: 1 Moreover the LORD **a** Job, and said, H6030
3 Then Job **a** the LORD, and said, H6030
6 Then **a** the LORD unto Job out of the H6030
42: 1 Then Job **a** the LORD, and said, H6030
Ps 18:41 unto the LORD, but he **a** them not. H6030
81: 7 I delivered thee; I **a** thee in the secret H6030
99: 6 called upon the LORD, and he **a** them. H6030
118: 5 **a** me, *and set me* in a large place. H6030
Isa 6:11 Then said I, Lord, how long? And he **a**, H559
21: 9 horsemen. And he **a** and said, Babylon H6030
36:21 But they held their peace, and **a** him H6030
39: 4 And Hezekiah **a**, All that *is* in mine house H559
Jer 7:13 not; and I called you, but ye **a** not; H6030
11: 5 Then **a** I, and said, So be it, O LORD. H6030
23:35 **a**? and, What hath the LORD spoken? H6030
37 hath the LORD **a** thee? and, What hath H6030
35:17 called unto them, but they have not **a**. H6030
36:18 Then Baruch **a** them, He pronounced all H559
44:15 Egypt, in Pathros, **a** Jeremiah, saying, H6030
Ezk 24:20 Then I **a** them, The word of the LORD H559
37: 3 live? And I **a**, O Lord GOD, thou knowest. H559
Dan 2: 5 The king **a** and said to the Chaldeans, H6032
7 They **a** again and said, Let the king tell H6032
8 The king **a** and said, I know of H6032
10 The Chaldeans **a** before the king, and H6032
14 Then Daniel **a** with counsel and H8421
15 He **a** and said to Arioch the king's H6032
20 Daniel **a** and said, Blessed be the name H6032
26 The king **a** and said to Daniel, whose H6032
27 Daniel **a** in the presence of the king, H6032
47 The king **a** unto Daniel, and said, Of a H6032
3:16 Shadrach, Meshach, and Abed-nego, **a** H6032
24 **a** and said unto the king, True, O king. H6032
25 He **a** and said, Lo, I see four men loose, H6032
4:19 thee. Belteshazzar **a** and said, My lord, H6032
5:17 Then Daniel **a** and said before the king, H6032
6:12 of lions? The king **a** and said, The thing H6032
13 Then **a** they and said before the king, H6032
Am 7:14 Then **a** Amos, and said to Amaziah, I H6030
Mic 6: 5 the son of Beor **a** him from Shittim H6030
Hab 2: 2 And the LORD **a** me, and said, Write H6030
Hag 2:12 be holy? And the priests **a** and said, No. H6030
13 priests **a** and said, It shall be unclean. H6030
14 Then **a** Haggai, and said, So *is* this H6030
Zec 1:10 the myrtle trees **a** and said, These *are* H6030
11 And they **a** the angel of the LORD that H6030
12 Then the angel of the LORD **a** and said, H6030
13 And the LORD **a** the angel that talked H6030
19 *be* these? And he **a** me, These *are* the H559
3: 4 And he **a** and spake unto those that H6030
4: 4 So I **a** and spake to the angel that H6030
5 Then the angel that talked with me **a** H6030
6 Then he **a** and spake unto me, saying, H6030
11 Then **a** I, and said unto him, What *are* H6030
12 And I **a** again, and said unto him, H6030
13 And he **a** me and said, Knowest thou not H559
5: 2 seest thou? And I **a**, I see a flying roll; the H559
6: 4 Then I **a** and said unto the angel that H6030
5 And the angel **a** and said unto me, H6030
Mt 4: 4 But he **a** and said, It is written, Man *G611*
Mt 8: 8 The centurion **a** and said, Lord, I am not *G611*
11: 4 Jesus **a** and said unto them, Go and *G611*
25 At that time Jesus **a** and said, I thank *G611*
12:38 of the Pharisees **a**, saying, Master, we *G611*
39 But he **a** and said unto them, An evil and *G611*
48 But he **a** and said unto him that told *G611*
13:11 He **a** and said unto them, Because it is *G611*
37 He **a** and said unto them, He that soweth *G611*
14:28 And Peter **a** him and said, Lord, if it be *G611*
15: 3 But he **a** and said unto them, Why do ye *G611*
13 But he **a** and said, Every plant, which *G611*
15 Then **a** Peter and said unto him, Declare *G611*
23 But he **a** her not a word. And his *G611*
24 But he **a** and said, I am not sent but unto *G611*
26 But he **a** and said, It is not meet to take *G611*
28 Then Jesus **a** and said unto her, O *G611*
16: 2 He **a** and said unto them, When it is *G611*
16 And Simon Peter **a** and said, Thou art *G611*
17 And Jesus **a** and said unto him, Blessed *G611*
17: 4 Then **a** Peter, and said unto Jesus, Lord, *G611*
11 And Jesus **a** and said unto them, Elias *G611*
17 Then Jesus **a** and said, O faithless and *G611*
19: 4 And he **a** and said unto them, Have ye *G611*
27 Then **a** Peter and said unto him, Behold, *G611*
20:13 But he **a** one of them, and said, Friend, I *G611*
22 But Jesus **a** and said, Ye know not what *G611*
21:21 Jesus **a** and said unto them, Verily I say *G611*
24 And Jesus **a** and said unto them, I also *G611*
27 And they **a** Jesus, and said, We cannot *G611*
29 He **a** and said, I will not: but afterward *G611*
30 he **a** and said, I *go*, sir: and went not. *G611*
22: 1 And Jesus **a** and spake unto them again *G611*
29 Jesus **a** and said unto them, Ye do err, *G611*
24: 4 And Jesus **a** and said unto them, Take *G611*
25: 9 But the wise **a**, saying, *Not so*; lest there *G611*
12 But he **a** and said, Verily I say unto you, *G611*
26 His lord **a** and said unto him, *Thou* *G611*
26:23 And he **a** and said, He that dippeth *his* *G611*
25 Then Judas, which betrayed him, **a** and *G611*
33 Peter **a** and said unto him, Though all *G611*
63 And the high priest **a** and said unto him, *G611*
66 What think ye? They **a** and said, He is *G611*
27:12 chief priests and elders, he **a** nothing. *G611*
14 And he **a** him to never a word; insomuch *G611*
21 The governor **a** and said unto them, *G611*
25 Then **a** all the people, and said, His *G611*
28: 5 And the angel **a** and said unto the *G611*
Mk 3:33 And he **a** them, saying, Who is my *G611*
5: 9 thy name? And he **a**, saying, My name *is* *G611*
6:37 He **a** and said unto them, Give ye them *G611*
7: 6 He **a** and said unto them, Well hath *G611*
28 And she **a** and said unto him, Yes, Lord: *G611*
8: 4 And his disciples **a** him, From whence *G611*
28 And they **a**, John the Baptist: but some *G611*
9: 5 And Peter **a** and said to Jesus, Master, it *G611*
12 And he **a** and told them, Elias verily *G611*
17 And one of the multitude **a** and said, *G611*
38 And John **a** him, saying, Master, we saw *G611*
10: 3 And he **a** and said unto them, What did *G611*
5 And Jesus **a** and said unto them, For the *G611*
20 And he **a** and said unto him, Master, all *G611*
29 And Jesus **a** and said, Verily I say unto *G611*
51 And Jesus **a** and said unto him, What *G611*
11:14 And Jesus **a** and said unto it, No man *G611*
29 And Jesus **a** and said unto them, I will *G611*
33 And they **a** and said unto Jesus, We *G611*
12:28 that he had **a** them well, asked him, *G611*
29 And Jesus **a** him, The first of all the *G611*
34 And when Jesus saw that he **a** discreetly, *G611*
35 And Jesus **a** and said, while he taught in *G611*
14:20 And he **a** and said unto them, *It is* one of *G611*
48 And Jesus **a** and said unto them, Are ye *G611*
61 But he held his peace, and **a** nothing. *G611*
15: 3 him of many things: but he **a** nothing. *G611*
5 But Jesus yet **a** nothing; so that Pilate *G611*
9 But Pilate **a** them, saying, Will ye that I *G611*
12 And Pilate **a** and said again unto them, *G611*
Lk 1:35 And the angel **a** and said unto her, The *G611*
60 And his mother **a** and said, Not *so*; but *G611*
3:16 John **a**, saying unto *them* all, I indeed *G611*
4: 4 And Jesus **a** him, saying, It is written, *G611*
8 And Jesus **a** and said unto him, Get thee *G611*
7:43 Simon **a** and said, I suppose that *he*, to *G611*
8:21 And he **a** and said unto them, My *G611*
50 But when Jesus heard *it*, he **a** him, *G611*
9:49 And John **a** and said, Master, we saw *G611*
10:28 And he said unto him, Thou hast **a** right: *G611*
41 And Jesus **a** and said unto her, Martha, *G611*
11:45 Then **a** one of the lawyers, and said unto *G611*
Lk 13:14 And the ruler of the synagogue **a** with *G611*
15 The Lord then **a** him, and said, *Thou* *G611*
14: 5 And **a** them, saying, Which of you shall *G611*
17:20 should come, he **a** them and said, The *G611*
37 And they **a** and said unto him, Where, *G611*
19:40 And he **a** and said unto them, I tell you *G611*
20: 3 And he **a** and said unto them, I will also *G611*
7 And they **a**, that they could not tell *G611*
24 hath it? They **a** and said, Caesar's. *G611*
22:51 And Jesus **a** and said, Suffer ye thus far. *G611*
23: 3 And he **a** him and said, Thou sayest *it*. *G611*
9 in many words; but he **a** him nothing. *G611*
Jn 1:21 not. Art thou that prophet? And he **a**, No. *G611*
26 John **a** them, saying, I baptize with *G611*
48 thou me? Jesus **a** and said unto him, *G611*
49 Nathanael **a** and saith unto him, Rabbi, *G611*
50 Jesus **a** and said unto him, Because I *G611*
2:18 Then **a** the Jews and said unto him, *G611*
19 Jesus **a** and said unto them, Destroy this *G611*
3: 3 Jesus **a** and said unto him, Verily, verily, *G611*
5 Jesus **a**, Verily, verily, I say unto thee, *G611*
9 Nicodemus **a** and said unto him, How *G611*
10 Jesus **a** and said unto him, Art thou a *G611*
27 John **a** and said, A man can receive *G611*
4:10 Jesus **a** and said unto her, If thou *G611*
13 Jesus **a** and said unto her, Whosoever *G611*
17 The woman **a** and said, I have no *G611*
5: 7 The impotent man **a** him, Sir, I have no *G611*
11 He **a** them, He that made me whole, the *G611*
17 But Jesus **a** them, My Father worketh *G611*
19 Then **a** Jesus and said unto them, Verily, *G611*
6: 7 Philip **a** him, Two hundred pennyworth *G611*
26 Jesus **a** them and said, Verily, verily, I *G611*
29 Jesus **a** and said unto them, This is the *G611*
43 Jesus therefore **a** and said unto them, *G611*
68 Then Simon Peter **a** him, Lord, to whom *G611*
70 Jesus **a** them, Have not I chosen you *G611*
7:16 Jesus **a** them, and said, My doctrine is *G611*
20 The people **a** and said, Thou hast a *G611*
21 Jesus **a** and said unto them, I have done *G611*
46 The officers **a**, Never man spake like this *G611*
47 Then **a** them the Pharisees, Are ye also *G611*
52 They **a** and said unto him, Art thou also *G611*
8:14 Jesus **a** and said unto them, Though I *G611*
19 is thy Father? Jesus **a**, Ye neither know *G611*
33 They **a** him, We be Abraham's seed, and *G611*
34 Jesus **a** them, Verily, verily, I say unto *G611*
39 They **a** and said unto him, Abraham is *G611*
48 Then **a** the Jews, and said unto him, Say *G611*
49 Jesus **a**, I have not a devil; but I honour *G611*
54 Jesus **a**, If I honour myself, my honour is *G611*
9: 3 Jesus **a**, Neither hath this man sinned, *G611*
11 He **a** and said, A man that is called Jesus *G611*
20 His parents **a** them and said, We know *G611*
25 He **a** and said, Whether he be a sinner *or* *G611*
27 He **a** them, I have told you already, and *G611*
30 The man **a** and said unto them, Why *G611*
34 They **a** and said unto him, Thou wast *G611*
36 He **a** and said, Who is he, Lord, that I *G611*
10:25 Jesus **a** them, I told you, and ye believed *G611*
32 Jesus **a** them, Many good works have I *G611*
33 The Jews **a** him, saying, For a good work *G611*
34 Jesus **a** them, Is it not written in your *G611*
11: 9 Jesus **a**, Are there not twelve hours in the *G611*
12:23 And Jesus **a** them, saying, The hour is *G611*
30 Jesus **a** and said, This voice came not *G611*
34 The people **a** him, We have heard out of *G611*
13: 7 Jesus **a** and said unto him, What I do *G611*
8 my feet. Jesus **a** him, If I wash thee not, *G611*
26 Jesus **a**, He it is, to whom I shall give a *G611*
36 goest thou? Jesus **a** him, Whither I go, *G611*
38 Jesus **a** him, Wilt thou lay down thy life *G611*
14:23 Jesus **a** and said unto him, If a man love *G611*
16:31 Jesus **a** them, Do ye now believe? *G611*
18: 5 They **a** him, Jesus of Nazareth. Jesus *G611*
8 Jesus **a**, I have told you that I am *he*: if *G611*
20 Jesus **a** him, I spake openly to the world; *G611*
23 Jesus **a** him, If I have spoken evil, bear *G611*
30 They **a** and said unto him, If he were not *G611*
34 Jesus **a** him, Sayest thou this thing of *G611*
35 Pilate **a**, Am I a Jew? Thine own nation *G611*
36 Jesus **a**, My kingdom is not of this world: *G611*
37 a king then? Jesus **a**, Thou sayest that I *G611*
19: 7 The Jews **a** him, We have a law, and by *G611*
11 Jesus **a**, Thou couldest have no power *at* *G611*
15 priests **a**, We have no king but Caesar. *G611*
22 Pilate **a**, What I have written I have *G611*
20:28 And Thomas **a** and said unto him, My *G611*
21: 5 have ye any meat? They **a** him, No. *G611*

Act 3:12 And when Peter saw *it*, he a unto the G611
4:19 But Peter and John a and said unto G611
5: 8 And Peter a unto her, Tell me whether ye G611
29 Then Peter and the *other* apostles a and G611
8:24 Then a Simon, and said, Pray ye to the G611
34 And the eunuch a Philip, and said, I G611
37 mayest. And he a and said, I believe that G611
9:13 Then Ananias a, Lord, I have heard by G611
10:46 and magnify God. Then a Peter, G611
11: 9 But the voice a me again from heaven, G611
15:13 their peace, James a, saying, Men *and* G611
19:15 And the evil spirit a and said, Jesus I G611
21:13 Then Paul a, What mean ye to weep and G611
22: 8 And I a, Who art thou, Lord? And he said G611
28 And the chief captain a, With a great G611
24:10 unto him to speak, a, Forasmuch as I G611
25 Felix trembled, and a, Go thy way for this G611
25: 4 But Festus a, that Paul should be kept at G611
8 While he a for himself, Neither against G626
9 Jews a pleasure, a Paul, and said, Wilt G611
12 with the council, a, Hast thou appealed G611
16 To whom I a, It is not the manner of the G611
26: 1 forth the hand, and a for himself: G626
Rev 7:13 And one of the elders a, saying unto me, G611

ANSWEREDST
Ps 99: 8 Thou a them, O LORD our God: thou H6030
138: 3 In the day when I cried thou a me, *and* H6030

ANSWEREST
1Sa 26:14 son of Ner, saying, A thou not, Abner? H6030
Job 16: 3 or what emboldeneth thee that thou a? H6030
Mt 26:62 and said unto him, A thou nothing? G611
Mk 14:60 Jesus, saying, A thou nothing? what G611
15: 4 And Pilate asked him again, saying, A G611
Jn 18:22 hand, saying, A thou the high priest so? G611

ANSWERETH
1Sa 28:15 from me, and a me no more, neither H6030
1Ki 18:24 and the God that a by fire, let him be H6030
Job 12: 4 upon God, and he a him: the just H6030
Prv 18:13 He that a a matter before he heareth *it*, H7725
23 useth intreaties; but the rich a roughly. H6030
27:19 As in water face *a* to face, so the heart of
Ecc 5:20 God a *him* in the joy of his heart. H6030
10:19 maketh merry: but money a all *things*. H6030
Mk 8:29 I am? And Peter a and saith unto him, G611
9:19 He a him, and saith, O faithless G611
10:24 words. But Jesus a again, and saith unto G611
Lk 3:11 He a and saith unto them, He that hath G611
Gal 4:25 in Arabia, and a to Jerusalem which G4960

ANSWERING
Mt 3:15 And Jesus a said unto him, Suffer *it to be* G611
Mk 11:22 And Jesus a saith unto them, Have faith G611
33 cannot tell. And Jesus a saith unto them, G611
12:17 And Jesus a said unto them, Render to G611
24 And Jesus a said unto them, Do ye not G611
13: 2 And Jesus a said unto him, Seest thou G611
5 And Jesus a them began to say, Take G611
15: 2 And he a said unto him, Thou sayest *it*. G611
Lk 1:19 And the angel a said unto him, I am G611
4:12 And Jesus a said unto him, It is said, G611
5: 5 And Simon a said unto him, Master, we G611
22 their thoughts, he a said unto them, G611
31 And Jesus a said unto them, They that G611
6: 3 And Jesus a them said, Have ye not read G611
7:22 Then Jesus a said unto them, Go your G611
40 And Jesus a said unto him, Simon, I G611
9:19 They a said, John the Baptist; but some G611
20 I am? Peter a said, The Christ of God. G611
41 And Jesus a said, O faithless and G611
10:27 And he a said, Thou shalt love the Lord G611
30 And Jesus a said, A certain *man* went G5274
13: 2 And Jesus a said unto them, Suppose ye G611
8 And he a said unto him, Lord, let it G611
14: 3 And Jesus a spake unto the lawyers and G611
15:29 And he a said to *his* father, Lo, these G611
17:17 And Jesus a said, Were there not ten G611
20:34 And Jesus a said unto them, The G611
39 Then certain of the scribes a said, G611
23:40 But the other a rebuked him, saying, G611
24:18 name was Cleopas, a said unto him, Art G611
Tit 2: 9 *them* well in all *things*; not a again; G483

ANSWERS
Job 21:34 in your a there remaineth falsehood? H8666
34:36 end because of *his* a for wicked men. H8666
Lk 2:47 astonished at his understanding and a. G612

ANT
Prv 6: 6 Go to the a, thou sluggard; consider her H5244

ANTICHRIST
1Jn 2:18 as ye have heard that a shall come, even G500
22 is a, that denieth the Father and the Son. G500
4: 3 this is that *spirit* of a, whereof ye have G500
2Jn 7 in the flesh. This is a deceiver and an a. G500

ANTICHRISTS
1Jn 2:18 are there many a; whereby we know that G500

ANTIOCH
Act 6: 5 Parmenas, and Nicolas a proselyte of A: G491
11:19 and Cyprus, and A, preaching the word G490
20 they were come to A, spake unto the G490
22 Barnabas, that he should go as far as A. G490
26 brought him unto A. And it came to pass, G490
26 disciples were called Christians first in A. G490
27 came prophets from Jerusalem unto A. G490
13: 1 church that was at A certain prophets G490
14 they came to A in Pisidia, and went G490
14:19 *certain* Jews from A and Iconium, who G490
21 again to Lystra, and *to* Iconium, and A, G490
26 And thence sailed to A, from whence G490
15:22 their own company to A with Paul and G490
23 the Gentiles in A and Syria and Cilicia: G490
30 they came to A: and when they had G490
35 Paul also and Barnabas continued in A, G490
18:22 saluted the church, he went down to A. G490
Gal 2:11 But when Peter was come to A, I G490
2Ti 3:11 which came unto me at A, at Iconium, at G490

ANTIPAS
Rev 2:13 days wherein A *was* my faithful martyr, G493

ANTIPATRIS
Act 23:31 Paul, and brought *him* by night to A. G494

ANTIQUITY
Isa 23: 7 *Is* this your joyous *city*, whose a *is* of H6927

ANTOTHIJAH
1Ch 8:24 And Hananiah, and Elam, and A, H6070

ANTOTHITE
1Ch 11:28 of Ikkesh the Tekoite, Abi-ezer the A, H6069
12: 3 and Berachah, and Jehu the A, H6069

ANTS
Prv 30:25 The a *are* a people not strong, yet they H5244

ANUB
1Ch 4: 8 And Coz begat A, and Zobebah, and the H6036

ANVIL
Isa 41: 7 that smote the a, saying, It *is* ready for H6471

ANY See the Appendix.

APACE
2Sa 18:25 mouth. And he came a, and drew near. H1980
Ps 68:12 Kings of armies did flee a: and she that H5074
Jer 46: 5 and are fled a, and look not back: H4498

APART
Ex 13:12 That thou shalt set a unto the LORD all H5674
Lev 15:19 she shall be put a seven days: and H5079
18:19 as she is put a for her uncleanness. H5079
Ps 4: 3 But know that the LORD hath set a him H6395
Ezk 22:10 her that was set a for pollution. H5079
Zec 12:12 every family a; the family of the house H905
12 of the house of David a, and their wives H905
12 and their wives a; the family of the house H905
12 house of Nathan a, and their wives apart; H905
12 house of Nathan apart, and their wives a; H905
13 The family of the house of Levi a, and H905
13 and their wives a; the family of Shimei H905
13 family of Shimei a, and their wives apart; H905
13 family of Shimei apart, and their wives a; H905
14 every family a, and their wives apart. H905
14 every family apart, and their wives a. H905
Mt 14:13 a desert place a: and when the G2596+G2398
23 into a mountain a to pray: and G2596+G2398
17: 1 up into an high mountain a, G2596+G2398
19 to Jesus a, and said, Why G2596+G2398
20:17 disciples a in the way, and G2596+G2398
Mk 6:31 ye yourselves a into a desert G2596+G2398
9: 2 mountain a by themselves: G2596+G2398

Jas 1:21 Wherefore lay a all filthiness and G659

APELLES
Ro 16:10 Salute A approved in Christ. Salute them G559

APES
1Ki 10:22 and silver, ivory, and a, and peacocks. H6971
2Ch 9:21 and silver, ivory, and a, and peacocks. H6971

APHARSACHITES
Ezr 5: 6 companions the A, which *were* on this H671
6: 6 companions the A, which *are* beyond the H671

APHARSATHCHITES
Ezr 4: 9 the Dinaites, the A, the Tarpelites, the H671

APHARSITES
Ezr 4: 9 the Tarpelites, the A, the Archevites, the H670

APHEK
Jos 12:18 The king of A, one; the king of Lasharon, H663
13: 4 unto A, to the borders of the Amorites: H663
19:30 Ummah also, and A, and Rehob: twenty H663
1Sa 4: 1 and the Philistines pitched in A. H663
29: 1 all their armies to A: and the Israelites H663
1Ki 20:26 and went up to A, to fight against Israel. H663
30 But the rest fled to A, into the city; and H663
2Ki 13:17 in A, till thou have consumed *them*. H663

APHEKAH
Jos 15:53 And Janum, and Beth-tappuah, and A, H664

APHIAH
1Sa 9: 1 A, a Benjamite, a mighty man of power. H647

APHIK
Jdg 1:31 nor of Helbah, nor of A, nor of Rehob: H663

APHRAH
Mic 1:10 the house of A roll thyself in the dust. H1036

APHSES
1Ch 24:15 to Hezir, the eighteenth to A, H6483

APIECE
Nu 3:47 Thou shalt even take five shekels a by
7:86 ten *shekels* a, after the shekel of the
17: 6 gave him a rod a, for each prince one,
1Ki 7:15 cubits high a: and a line of H5982+H259
Ezk 10:21 Every one had four faces a, and every
41:24 And the doors had two leaves a, two
Lk 9: 3 neither money; neither have two coats a. G303
Jn 2: 6 Jews, containing two or three firkins a. G303

APOLLONIA
Act 17: 1 through Amphipolis and A, they came to G624

APOLLOS
Act 18:24 And a certain Jew named A, born at G625
19: 1 And it came to pass, that, while A was at G625
1Co 1:12 I of A; and I of Cephas; and I of Christ. G625
3: 4 another, I *am* of A; are ye not carnal? G625
5 Who then is Paul, and who *is* A, but G625
6 I have planted, A watered; but God gave G625
22 Whether Paul, or A, or Cephas, or the G625
4: 6 to myself and *to* A for your sakes; that G625
16:12 As touching *our* brother A, I greatly G625
Tit 3:13 Bring Zenas the lawyer and A on their G625

APOLLYON
Rev 9:11 but in the Greek tongue hath *his* name A. G623

APOSTLE
Ro 1: 1 an a, separated unto the gospel of God, G652
11:13 a of the Gentiles, I magnify mine office: G652
1Co 1: 1 Paul, called *to be* an a of Jesus Christ G652
9: 1 Am I not an a? am I not free? have I not G652
2 If I be not an a unto others, yet doubtless G652
15: 9 to be called an a, because I persecuted G652
2Co 1: 1 Paul, an a of Jesus Christ by the will of G652
12:12 Truly the signs of an a were wrought G652
Gal 1: 1 Paul, an a, (not of men, neither by man, G652
Eph 1: 1 Paul, an a of Jesus Christ by the will of G652
Col 1: 1 Paul, an a of Jesus Christ by the will of G652
1Ti 1: 1 Paul, an a of Jesus Christ by the G652
2: 7 a preacher, and an a, (I speak the truth G652
2Ti 1: 1 Paul, an a of Jesus Christ by the will of G652
11 and an a, and a teacher of the Gentiles. G652
Tit 1: 1 Paul, a servant of God, and an a of Jesus G652

Heb 3: 1 consider the **A** and High Priest of our G652
1Pt 1: 1 Peter, an **a** of Jesus Christ, to the G652
2Pt 1: 1 Simon Peter, a servant and an **a** of Jesus G652

APOSTLES
Mt 10: 2 Now the names of the twelve **a** are these; G652
Mk 6:30 And the **a** gathered themselves together G652
Lk 6:13 he chose twelve, whom also he named **a**; G652
9:10 And the **a**, when they were returned, told G652
11:49 them prophets and **a**, and *some* of them G652
17: 5 And the **a** said unto the Lord, Increase G652
22:14 he sat down, and the twelve **a** with him. G652
24:10 them, which told these things unto the **a**. G652
Act 1: 2 unto the **a** whom he had chosen: G652
26 and he was numbered with the eleven **a**. G652
2:37 **a**, Men *and* brethren, what shall we do? G652
43 wonders and signs were done by the **a**. G652
4:33 And with great power gave the **a** witness G652
36 And Joses, who by the **a** was surnamed G652
5:12 And by the hands of the **a** were many G652
18 And laid their hands on the **a**, and put G652
29 Then Peter and the *other* **a** answered G652
34 to put the **a** forth a little space; G652
40 they had called the **a**, and beaten *them*, G652
6: 6 Whom they set before the **a**: and when G652
8: 1 of Judaea and Samaria, except the **a**. G652
14 Now when the **a** which were at G652
9:27 brought *him* to the **a**, and declared unto G652
11: 1 And the **a** and brethren that were in G652
14: 4 held with the Jews, and part with the **a**. G652
14 *Which* when the **a**, Barnabas and Paul, G652
15: 2 the **a** and elders about this question. G652
4 church, and *of* the **a** and elders, and they G652
6 And the **a** and elders came together for G652
22 Then pleased it the **a** and elders, with G652
23 after this manner; The **a** and elders and G652
33 go in peace from the brethren unto the **a**. G652
16: 4 **a** and elders which were at Jerusalem. G652
Ro 16: 7 the **a**, who also were in Christ before me. G652
1Co 4: 9 hath set forth us the **a** last, as it were G652
9: 5 as well as other **a**, and *as* the brethren G652
12:28 some in the church, first **a**, secondarily G652
29 *Are* all **a**? *are* all prophets? *are* all G652
15: 7 he was seen of James; then of all the **a**. G652
9 For I am the least of the **a**, that am not G652
2Co 11: 5 was not a whit behind the very chiefest **a**. G652
13 For such *are* false **a**, deceitful workers, G5570
13 themselves into the **a** of Christ. G652
12:11 the very chiefest **a**, though I be nothing. G652
Gal 1:17 them which were **a** before me; but I went G652
19 But other of the **a** saw I none, save G652
Eph 2:20 foundation of the **a** and prophets, Jesus G652
3: 5 his holy **a** and prophets by the Spirit; G652
4:11 And he gave some, **a**; and some, G652
1Th 2: 6 been burdensome, as the **a** of Christ. G652
2Pt 3: 2 of us the **a** of the Lord and Saviour: G652
Jude 17 before of the **a** of our Lord Jesus Christ; G652
Rev 2: 2 which say they are **a**, and are not, and G652
18:20 and *ye* holy **a** and prophets; for God G652
21:14 the names of the twelve **a** of the Lamb. G652

APOSTLES'
Act 2:42 And they continued stedfastly in the **a** G652
4:35 And laid *them* down at the **a** feet: and G652
37 the money, and laid *it* at the **a** feet. G652
5: 2 a certain part, and laid *it* at the **a** feet. G652
8:18 laying on of the **a** hands the Holy Ghost G652

APOSTLESHIP
Act 1:25 this ministry and **a**, from which Judas by G651
Ro 1: 5 By whom we have received grace and **a**, G651
1Co 9: 2 for the seal of mine **a** are ye in the Lord. G651
Gal 2: 8 in Peter to the **a** of the circumcision, G651

APOTHECARIES
Neh 3: 8 son of *one of* the **a**, and they fortified H7546

APOTHECARIES'
2Ch 16:14 prepared by the **a** art: and they made H4842

APOTHECARY
Ex 30:25 the **a**: it shall be an holy anointing oil. H7543
35 **a**, tempered together, pure *and* holy: H7543
37:29 spices, according to the work of the **a**. H7543
Ecc 10: 1 Dead flies cause the ointment of the **a** H7543

APPAIM
1Ch 2:30 And the sons of Nadab; Seled, and **A**: but H649
31 And the sons of **A**; Ishi. And the sons of H649

APPAREL
Jdg 17:10 **a**, and thy victuals. So the Levite went in. H899
1Sa 27: 9 the **a**, and returned, and came to Achish. H899
2Sa 1:24 put on ornaments of gold upon your **a**. H3830
12:20 and changed his **a**, and came into the H8071
14: 2 put on now mourning **a**, and anoint not H899
1Ki 10: 5 and their **a**, and his cupbearers, H4403
2Ch 9: 4 and their **a**; his cupbearers also, H4403
4 also, and their **a**; and his ascent by H4403
Ezr 3:10 set the priests in their **a** with trumpets, H3847
Est 5: 1 put on *her* royal **a**, and stood in the inner
6: 8 Let the royal **a** be brought which the H3830
9 And let this **a** and horse be delivered to H3830
10 *and* take the **a** and the horse, as thou H3830
11 Then took Haman the **a** and the horse, H3830
8:15 of the king in royal **a** of blue and white, H3830
Isa 3:22 The changeable suits of **a**, and the H4254
4: 1 and wear our own **a**: only let us be H8071
63: 1 *that is* glorious in his **a**, travelling in the H3830
2 Wherefore *art thou* red in thine **a**, and H3830
Ezk 27:24 in chests of rich **a**, bound with cords, H1264
Zep 1: 8 all such as are clothed with strange **a**. H4403
Zec 14:14 and silver, and **a**, in great abundance. H899
Act 1:10 two men stood by them in white **a**; G2066
12:21 arrayed in royal **a**, sat upon his throne, G2066
20:33 coveted no man's silver, or gold, or **a**. G2441
1Ti 2: 9 in modest **a**, with shamefacedness G2689
Jas 2: 2 ring, in goodly **a**, and there come in G2066
1Pt 3: 3 of wearing of gold, or of putting on of **a**; G2440

APPARELLED
2Sa 13:18 *that were* virgins **a**. Then his servant H3847
Lk 7:25 are gorgeously **a**, and live delicately, G2441

APPARENTLY
Nu 12: 8 to mouth, even **a**, and not in dark H4758

APPEAL
Act 25:11 deliver me unto them. I **a** unto Caesar. G1941
28:19 constrained to **a** unto Caesar; not that G1941

APPEALED
Act 25:12 Hast thou **a** unto Caesar? unto Caesar G1941
21 But when Paul had **a** to be reserved G1941
25 he himself hath **a** to Augustus, I have G1941
26:32 at liberty, if he had not **a** unto Caesar. G1941

APPEAR
Gen 1: 9 and let the dry *land* **a**: and it was so. H7200
30:37 the white **a** which *was* in the rods. H4286
Ex 23:15 and none shall **a** before me empty:) H7200
17 thy males shall **a** before the Lord GOD. H7200
34:20 And none shall **a** before me empty. H7200
23 all your men children **a** before the Lord H7200
24 shalt go up to **a** before the LORD thy H7200
Lev 9: 4 for to day the LORD will **a** unto you. H7200
6 the glory of the LORD shall **a** unto you. H7200
13:57 And if it **a** still in the garment, either in H7200
16: 2 will **a** in the cloud upon the mercy seat. H7200
Dt 16:16 shall all thy males **a** before the LORD H7200
16 shall not **a** before the LORD empty: H7200
31:11 When all Israel is come to **a** before the H7200
Jdg 13:21 did no more **a** to Manoah and to H7200
1Sa 1:22 him, that he may **a** before the LORD, H7200
2:27 Did I plainly **a** unto the house of thy H1540
2Ch 1: 7 In that night did God **a** unto Solomon, H7200
Ps 42: 2 when shall I come and **a** before God? H7200
90:16 Let thy work **a** unto thy servants, and H7200
102:16 build up Zion, he shall **a** in his glory. H7200
Song 2:12 The flowers **a** on the earth; the time of H7200
4: 1 of goats, that **a** from mount Gilead. H1570
6: 5 *is* as a flock of goats that **a** from Gilead. H1570
7:12 *whether* the tender grape **a**, *and* the H6605
Isa 1:12 When ye come to **a** before me, who H7200
66: 5 but he shall **a** to your joy, and they H7200
Jer 13:26 upon thy face, that thy shame may **a**. H7200
Ezk 21:24 your sins do **a**; because, *I say*, that H7200
Mt 6:16 faces, that they may **a** unto men to fast. G5316
18 That thou **a** not unto men to fast, but G5316
23:27 which indeed **a** beautiful outward, G5316
28 Even so ye also outwardly **a** righteous G5316
24:30 And then shall **a** the sign of the Son of G5316
Lk 11:44 as graves which **a** not, and the men that G82
19:11 kingdom of God should immediately **a**. G398
Act 22:30 all their council to **a**, and brought Paul G2064
26:16 things in the which I will **a** unto thee; G3700
Ro 7:13 sin, that it might **a** sin, working death G5316
2Co 5:10 For we must all **a** before the judgment G5319
7:12 in the sight of God might **a** unto you. G5319
2Co 13: 7 not that we should **a** approved, but G5316
Col 3: 4 When Christ, *who is* our life, shall **a**, G5319
4 then shall ye also **a** with him in glory. G5319
1Ti 4:15 to them; that thy profiting may **a** to all. G5318
Heb 9:24 now to **a** in the presence of God for us: G1718
28 look for him shall he **a** the second time G3700
11: 3 were not made of things which do **a**. G5316
1Pt 4:18 shall the ungodly and the sinner **a**? G5316
5: 4 And when the chief Shepherd shall **a**, ye G5319
1Jn 2:28 that, when he shall **a**, we may have G5319
3: 2 and it doth not yet **a** what we shall be: G5319
2 when he shall **a**, we shall be like him; G5319
Rev 3:18 nakedness do not **a**; and anoint thine G5319

APPEARANCE
Nu 9:15 it were the **a** of fire, until the morning. H4758
16 it *by day*, and the **a** of fire by night. H4758
1Sa 16: 7 **a**, but the LORD looketh on the heart. H5869
Ezk 1: 5 their **a**; they had the likeness of a man. H4758
13 creatures, their **a** *was* like burning H4758
13 fire, *and* like the **a** of lamps: it went up H4758
14 returned as the **a** of a flash of lightning. H4758
16 The **a** of the wheels and their work *was* H4758
16 likeness: and their **a** and their work H4758
26 of a throne, as the **a** of a sapphire H4758
26 as the **a** of a man above upon it. H4758
27 of amber, as the **a** of fire round about H4758
27 within it, from the **a** of his loins even H4758
27 and from the **a** of his loins even H4758
27 I saw as it were the **a** of fire, and it had H4758
28 As the **a** of the bow that is in the cloud H4758
28 of rain, so *was* the **a** of the brightness H4758
28 This *was* the **a** of the likeness of the H4758
8: 2 lo a likeness as the **a** of fire: from the H4758
2 of fire: from the **a** of his loins even H4758
2 **a** of brightness, as the colour of amber. H4758
10: 1 as the **a** of the likeness of a throne. H4758
9 cherub: and the **a** of the wheels *was* as H4758
40: 3 *there was* a man, whose **a** *was* like the H4758
3 *was* like the **a** of brass, with a line H4758
41:21 of the sanctuary; the **a** *of the one* as the H4758
21 *of the one* as the **a** *of the other*. H4758
42:11 And the way before them *was* like the **a** H4758
43: 3 And *it was* according to the **a** of the H4758
Dan 8:15 stood before me as the **a** of a man. H4758
10: 6 and his face as the **a** of lightning, and H4758
18 **a** of a man, and he strengthened me, H4758
Joel 2: 4 The **a** of them *is* as the appearance of H4758
4 The appearance of them *is* as the **a** of H4758
Jn 7:24 Judge not according to the **a**, but judge G3799
2Co 5:12 them which glory in **a**, and not in heart. G4383
10: 7 after the outward **a**? If any man trust to G4383
1Th 5:22 Abstain from all **a** of evil. G1491

APPEARANCES
Ezk 10:10 And *as for* their **a**, they four had one H4758
22 of Chebar, their **a** and themselves: they H4758

APPEARED
Gen 12: 7 And the LORD **a** unto Abram, and H7200
7 altar unto the LORD, who **a** unto him. H7200
17: 1 nine, the LORD **a** to Abram, and said H7200
18: 1 And the LORD **a** unto him in the plains H7200
26: 2 And the LORD **a** unto him, and said, H7200
24 And the LORD **a** unto him the same H7200
35: 1 unto God, that **a** unto thee when thou H7200
7 because there God **a** unto him, when he H1540
9 And God **a** unto Jacob again, when he H7200
48: 3 God Almighty **a** unto me at Luz in the H7200
Ex 3: 2 And the angel of the LORD **a** unto him H7200
16 and of Jacob, **a** unto me, saying, I have H7200
4: 1 say, The LORD hath not **a** unto thee. H7200
5 and the God of Jacob, hath **a** unto thee. H7200
6: 3 And I **a** unto Abraham, unto Isaac, H7200
14:27 when the morning **a**; and the Egyptians H6437
16:10 the glory of the LORD **a** in the cloud. H7200
Lev 9:23 glory of the LORD **a** unto all the people. H7200
Nu 14:10 glory of the LORD **a** in the tabernacle H7200
16:19 the LORD **a** unto all the congregation. H7200
42 covered it, and the glory of the LORD **a**. H7200
20: 6 and the glory of the LORD **a** unto them. H7200
Dt 31:15 And the LORD **a** in the tabernacle in a H7200
Jdg 6:12 And the angel of the LORD **a** unto him, H7200
13: 3 And the angel of the LORD **a** unto the H7200
10 the man hath **a** unto me, that came H7200
1Sa 3:21 And the LORD **a** again in Shiloh: for H7200
2Sa 22:16 And the channels of the sea **a**, the H7200
1Ki 3: 5 In Gibeon the LORD **a** to Solomon in a H7200
9: 2 That the LORD **a** to Solomon the H7200

1Ki 9: 2 time, as he had a unto him at Gibeon. H7200
11: 9 of Israel, which had a unto him twice, H7200
2Ki 2:11 that, behold, *there a* a chariot of fire,
2Ch 3: 1 where *the* LORD a unto David his H7200
7:12 And the LORD a to Solomon by night, H7200
Neh 4:21 the rising of the morning till the stars a. H3318
Jer 31: 3 The LORD hath a of old unto me, H7200
Ezk 10: 1 cherubims there a over them as it were H7200
8 And there a in the cherubims the form H7200
19:11 branches, and she a in her height with H7200
Dan 1:15 countenances a fairer and fatter in H7200
8: 1 a vision a unto me, *even unto* H7200
1 after that which a unto me at the first. H7200
Mt 1:20 the angel of the Lord a unto him in a G5316
2: 7 of them diligently what time the star a. G5316
13:26 forth fruit, then a the tares also. G5316
17: 3 And, behold, there a unto them Moses G3700
27:53 into the holy city, and a unto many. G1718
Mk 9: 4 And there a unto them Elias with G3700
16: 9 *day* of the week, he a first to Mary G5316
12 After that he a in another form unto G5319
14 Afterward he a unto the eleven as they G5319
Lk 1:11 And there a unto him an angel of the G3700
9: 8 And of some, that Elias had a; and of G5316
31 Who a in glory, and spake of his G3700
22:43 And there a an angel unto him from G3700
24:34 is risen indeed, and hath a to Simon. G3700
Act 2: 3 And there a unto them cloven tongues G3700
7: 2 The God of glory a unto our father G3700
30 were expired, there a to him in the G3700
35 of the angel which a to him in the bush. G3700
9:17 *even* Jesus, that a unto thee in the way G3700
16: 9 And a vision a to Paul in the night; G3700
26:16 thy feet: for I have a unto thee for this G3700
27:20 in many days a, and no small tempest G2014
Tit 2:11 bringeth salvation hath a to all men, G2014
3: 4 love of God our Saviour toward man a, G2014
Heb 9:26 the world hath he a to put away sin by G5319
Rev 12: 1 And there a a great wonder in heaven; G3700
3 And there a another wonder in heaven; G3700

APPEARETH
Lev 13:14 But when raw flesh a in him, he shall H7200
43 as the leprosy a in the skin of the flesh; H4758
Dt 2:30 deliver him into thy hand, as *a* this day.
Ps 84: 7 *every one of them* in Zion a before God. H7200
Prv 27:25 The hay a, and the tender grass H1540
Jer 6: 1 for evil a out of the north, and H8259
Mal 3: 2 shall stand when he a? for he *is* like a H7200
Mt 2:13 the angel of the Lord a to Joseph in a G5316
19 Lord a in a dream to Joseph in Egypt, G5316
Jas 4:14 a vapour, that a for a little time, and G5316

APPEARING
1Ti 6:14 until the a of our Lord Jesus Christ: G2015
2Ti 1:10 But is now made manifest by the a of G2015
4: 1 and the dead at his a and his kingdom; G2015
8 but unto all them also that love his a. G2015
Tit 2:13 and the glorious a of the great God and G2015
1Pt 1: 7 honour and glory at the a of Jesus Christ: G602

APPEASE
Gen 32:20 us. For he said, I will a him with the H3722

APPEASED
Est 2: 1 king Ahasuerus was a, he remembered H7918
Act 19:35 And when the townclerk had a the G2687

APPEASETH
Prv 15:18 but *he that is* slow to anger a strife. H8252

APPERTAIN
Nu 16:30 up, with all that *a* unto them, and they
Jer 10: 7 for to thee doth it a: forasmuch as H2969

APPERTAINED
Nu 16:32 that *a* unto Korah, and all *their* goods.
33 They, and all that *a* to them, went down
Neh 2: 8 of the palace which *a* to the house, and

APPERTAINETH
Lev 6: 5 it a, in the day of his trespass offering.
2Ch 26:18 and said unto him, *It a* not unto thee,

APPETITE
Job 38:39 the lion? or fill the a of the young lions, H2416
Prv 23: 2 thy throat, if thou *be* a man given to a. H5315
Ecc 6: 7 his mouth, and yet the a is not filled. H5315
Isa 29: 8 faint, and his soul hath a: so shall the H8264

APPHIA
Phlm 2 And to *our* beloved A, and Archippus our G682

APPII
Act 28:15 meet us as far as A forum, and The three G675

APPII-FORUM See APPII and FORUM.

APPLE
Dt 32:10 him, he kept him as the a of his eye. H380
Ps 17: 8 Keep me as the a of the eye, hide me H380
Prv 7: 2 live; and my law as the a of thine eye. H380
Song 2: 3 As the a tree among the trees of the H8598
8: 5 thee up under the a tree: there thy H8598
Lam 2:18 no rest; let not the a of thine eye cease. H1323
Joel 1:12 tree also, and the a tree, *even* all the H8598
Zec 2: 8 toucheth you toucheth the a of his eye. H892

APPLES
Prv 25:11 A word fitly spoken *is like* a of gold in H8598
Song 2: 5 comfort me with a: for I *am* sick of love. H8598
7: 8 vine, and the smell of thy nose like a; H8598

APPLE-TREE See APPLE and TREE.

APPLIED
Ecc 7:25 I a mine heart to know, and to search, H5437
8: 9 All this have I seen, and a my heart H5414
16 When I a mine heart to know wisdom, H5414

APPLY
Ps 90:12 that we may a *our* hearts unto wisdom. H935
Prv 2: 2 *and* a thine heart to understanding; H5186
22:17 and a thine heart unto my knowledge. H7896
23:12 A thine heart unto instruction, and thine H935

APPOINT
Gen 30:28 And he said, A me thy wages, and I will H5344
41:34 Let Pharaoh do *this*, and let him a H6485
Ex 21:13 will a thee a place whither he shall flee. H7760
30:16 Israel, and shalt a it for the service of H5414
Lev 26:16 I also will do this unto you; I will even a H6485
Nu 1:50 But thou shalt a the Levites over the H6485
3:10 And thou shalt a Aaron and his sons, H6485
4:19 shall go in, and a them every one to his H7760
27 and ye shall a unto them in charge H6485
35: 6 which ye shall a for the manslayer, that H5414
11 Then ye shall a you cities to be cities of H7136
Jos 20: 2 of Israel, saying, A out for you cities of H5414
1Sa 8:11 your sons, and a *them* for himself, for H7760
12 And he will a him captains over H7760
2Sa 6:21 all his house, to a me ruler over the H6680
7:10 Moreover I will a a place for my people H7760
15:15 *do* whatsoever my lord the king shall a. H977
1Ki 5: 6 to all that thou shalt a: for thou knowest H559
9 that thou shalt a me, and will cause H7971
1Ch 15:16 of the Levites to a their brethren *to be* H5975
Neh 7: 3 and bar *them*: and a watches of the H5975
Est 2: 3 And let the king a officers in all the H6485
Job 14:13 a me a set time, and remember me! H7896
Isa 26: 1 will *God* a *for* walls and bulwarks. H7896
61: 3 To a unto them that mourn in Zion, to H7760
Jer 15: 3 And I will a over them four kinds, saith H6485
49:19 *man, that* I may a over her? for who *is* H6485
19 me? and who will a me the time? and
50:44 *man, that* I may a over her? for who *is* H6485
44 me? and who will a me the time? and H3259
51:27 and Ashchenaz; a a captain against H6485
Ezk 21:19 Also, thou son of man, a thee two H7760
20 A a way, that the sword may come to H7760
22 for Jerusalem, to a captains, to open H7760
22 with shouting, to a *battering* rams H7760
45: 6 And ye shall a the possession of the city H5414
Hos 1:11 together, and a themselves one head, H7760
Mt 24:51 And shall cut him asunder, and a *him* G5087
Lk 12:46 a him his portion with the unbelievers. G5087
22:29 And I a unto you a kingdom, as my G1303
Act 6: 3 whom we may a over this business. G2525

APPOINTED
Gen 4:25 God, *said she*, hath a me another seed H7896
18:14 At the time a I will return unto thee, H4150
24:14 *be she that* thou hast a for thy servant H3198
44 LORD hath a out for my master's son. H3198
Ex 9: 5 And the LORD a a set time, saying, To H7760
23:15 thee, in the time a of the month Abib; H4150
Nu 9: 2 also keep the passover at his a season. H4150
3 shall keep it in his a season: according H4150
7 a season among the children of Israel? H4150
9:13 a season, that man shall bear his sin. H4150
Jos 8:14 people, at a time a, before the plain; but H4150
20: 7 And they a Kedesh in Galilee in mount H6942
9 These were the cities a for all the H4152
Jdg 18:11 hundred men a with weapons of war. H2296
16 And the six hundred men a with their H2296
17 men *that were* a with weapons of war. H2296
20:38 Now there was an a sign between the H4150
1Sa 13: 8 that Samuel *had a*: but Samuel came not
11 not within the days a, and *that* the H4150
19:20 standing *as* a over them, the spirit H5324
20:35 a with David, and a little lad with him. H4150
21: 2 thee: and I have a *my* servants to such H3045
25:30 and shall have a thee ruler over Israel; H6680
29: 4 which thou hast a him, and let him not H6485
2Sa 17:14 For the LORD had a to defeat the good H6680
20: 5 than the set time which he had a him. H3259
24:15 even to the time a: and there died of the H4150
1Ki 1:35 stead: and I have a him to be ruler over H6680
11:18 and a him victuals, and gave him land. H559
12:12 as the king had a, saying, Come to me H1696
20:42 a man whom I a to utter destruction, H2764
2Ki 7:17 And the king a the lord on whose hand H6485
8: 6 him. So the king a unto her a certain H5414
10:24 burnt offerings, Jehu a fourscore men H7760
11:18 a officers over the house of the LORD. H7760
18:14 king of Assyria a unto Hezekiah king H7760
1Ch 6:48 Their brethren also the Levites *were* a H5414
49 of incense, *and were* a for all the work of
9:29 *Some* of them also *were* a to oversee H4487
15:17 So the Levites a Heman the son of Joel; H5975
19 *were* a to sound with cymbals of brass;
16: 4 And he a *certain* of the Levites to H5414
2Ch 8:14 And he a, according to the order of H5975
20:21 the people, he a singers unto the LORD, H5975
23:18 Also Jehoiada a the offices of the house H7760
31: 2 And Hezekiah a the courses of the H5975
3 *He* a also the king's portion of his
33: 8 land which I have a for your fathers; so H5975
34:22 that the king *had* a, went to Huldah the
Ezr 3: 8 Jerusalem; and a the Levites, from H5975
8:20 the princes had a for the service of the H5414
10:14 in our cities come at a times, and with H2163
Neh 5:14 Moreover from the time that I was a to H6680
6: 7 And thou hast also a prophets to H5975
7: 1 and the singers and the Levites were a, H6485
9:17 in their rebellion a a captain to return H5414
10:34 fathers, at times a year by year, to burn H2163
12:31 the wall, and a two great *companies* H5975
44 And at that time were some a over the H6485
13:30 all strangers, and a the wards of the H5975
31 And for the wood offering, at times a, H2163
Est 1: 8 so the king had a to all the officers of H3245
2:15 of the women, a. And Esther obtained H559
4: 5 whom he had a to attend upon her, H5975
9:27 and according to their *a* time every year;
31 in their times *a*, according as Mordecai
Job 7: 1 *Is there* not an a time to man upon H6635
3 and wearisome nights are a to me. H4487
14: 5 hast a his bounds that he cannot pass; H6213
14 a time will I wait, till my change come. H6635
20:29 and the heritage a unto him by God. H561
23:14 For he performeth *the thing that is* a H2706
30:23 death, and *to* the house a for all living. H4150
Ps 44:11 Thou hast given us like sheep *a* for meat;
78: 5 in Jacob, and a a law in Israel, which H7760
79:11 preserve thou those that are a to die; H1121
81: 3 in the time a, on our solemn feast day. H3677
102:20 to loose those that are a to death; H1121
104:19 He a the moon for seasons: the sun H6213
Prv 7:20 him, *and* will come home at the day a. H3677
8:29 when he a the foundations of the earth: H2710
31: 8 of all such as are a to destruction. H1121
Isa 1:14 Your new moons and your a feasts my H4150
14:31 and none *shall be* alone in his a times. H4151
28:25 the a barley and the rie in their place? H5567
44: 7 for me, since I a the ancient people? H7760
Jer 5:24 unto us the a weeks of the harvest. H2708
8: 7 knoweth her a times; and the turtle H4150
33:25 a the ordinances of heaven and earth; H7760
46:17 *but* a noise; he hath passed the time a. H4150
47: 7 the sea shore? there hath he a it. H3259
Ezk 4: 6 days: I have a thee each day for a year. H5414
36: 5 which have a my land into their H5414
43:21 shall burn it in the a place of the house, H4662
Dan 1: 5 And the king a them a daily provision H4487
10 king, who hath a your meat and your H4487
8:19 for at the time a the end *shall be*. H4150
10: 1 true, but the time a *was* long: and he H6635

Dan 11:27 for yet the end *shall be* at the time a. H4150
29 At the time a he shall return, and come H4150
35 of the end: because *it is* yet for a time a. H4150
Mic 6: 9 hear ye the rod, and who hath a it. H3259
Hab 2: 3 For the vision *is* yet for an a time, but H4150
Mt 26:19 And the disciples did as Jesus had a G4929
27:10 for the potter's field, as the Lord a me. G4929
28:16 a mountain where Jesus had a them. G5021
Lk 3:13 no more than that which is a you. G1299
10: 1 After these things the Lord a other G322
22:29 as my Father hath a unto me; G1303
Act 1:23 And they a two, Joseph called G2476
7:44 as he had a, speaking unto Moses, G1299
17:26 a, and the bounds of their habitation; G4384
31 Because he hath a a day, in the which G2476
20:13 had he a, minding himself to go afoot. G1299
22:10 of all things which are a for thee to do. G5021
28:23 And when they had a him a day, there G5021
1Co 4: 9 last, as it were a to death: for we are G1935
Gal 4: 2 governors until the time a of the father. G4287
1Th 3: 3 know that we are a thereunto. G2749
5: 9 For God hath not a us to wrath, but to G5087
2Ti 1:11 Whereunto I am a a preacher, and an G5087
Tit 1: 5 elders in every city, as I had a thee: G1299
Heb 1: 2 whom he hath a heir of all things, by G5087
3: 2 Who was faithful to him that a him, as G4160
9:27 And as it is a unto men once to die, but G606
1Pt 2: 8 whereunto also they were a. G5087

APPOINTETH
Dan 5:21 *that* he a over it whomsoever he will. H6966

APPOINTMENT
Nu 4:27 At the a of Aaron and his sons shall be H6310
2Sa 13:32 is dead: for by the a of Absalom this H6310
Ezr 6: 9 according to the a of the priests which H3983
Job 2:11 they had made an a together to come H3259

APPREHEND
2Co 11:32 with a garrison, desirous to a me: G4084
Php 3:12 after, if that I may a that for which also G2638

APPREHENDED
Act 12: 4 And when he had a him, he put *him* in G4084
Php 3:12 for which also I am a of Christ Jesus. G2638
13 Brethren, I count not myself to have a: G2638

APPROACH
Lev 18: 6 None of you shall a to any that is near H7126
14 not a to his wife: she *is* thine aunt. H7126
19 Also thou shalt not a unto a woman to H7126
20:16 And if a woman a unto any beast, and H7126
21:17 him not a to offer the bread of his God. H7126
18 he shall not a: a blind man, or a lame, H7126
Nu 4:19 not die, when they a unto the most holy H5066
Dt 20: 2 shall a and speak unto the people, H5066
3 Hear, O Israel, ye a this day unto battle H7131
31:14 Behold, thy days a that thou must die: H7126
Jos 8: 5 *are* with me, will a unto the city: and it H7126
Job 40:19 him can make his sword to a *unto him*. H5066
Ps 65: 4 and causest to a *unto thee, that* he may H7126
Jer 30:21 near, and he shall a unto me: for who *is* H5066
21 his heart to a unto me? saith the LORD. H5066
Ezk 42:13 the priests that a unto the LORD shall H7138
14 and shall a to *those things* which H7126
43:19 of Zadok, which a unto me, to minister H7138
1Ti 6:16 which no man can a unto; whom no G676

APPROACHED
2Sa 11:20 thee, Wherefore a ye so nigh unto the H5066
2Ki 16:12 king a to the altar, and offered thereon. H7126

APPROACHETH
Lk 12:33 no thief a, neither moth corrupteth. G1448

APPROACHING
Isa 58: 2 justice; they take delight in a to God. H7132
Heb 10:25 so much the more, as ye see the day a. G1448

APPROVE
Ps 49:13 their posterity a their sayings. Selah. H7521
1Co 16: 3 ye shall a by *your* letters, them G1381
Php 1:10 That ye may a things that are excellent; G1381

APPROVED
Act 2:22 Nazareth, a man a of God among you by G584
Ro 14:18 *is* acceptable to God, and a of men. G1384
16:10 Salute Apelles a in Christ. Salute them G1384
1Co 11:19 a may be made manifest among you. G1384
2Co 7:11 a yourselves to be clear in this matter. G4921
10:18 is a, but whom the Lord commendeth. G1384
13: 7 we should appear a, but that ye should G1384
2Ti 2:15 Study to shew thyself a unto God, a G1384

APPROVEST
Ro 2:18 And knowest *his* will, and a the things G1381

APPROVETH
Lam 3:36 a man in his cause, the Lord a not. H7200

APPROVING
2Co 6: 4 But in all *things* a ourselves as the G4921

APPURTENANCE
See PURTENANCE.

APRONS
Gen 3: 7 together, and made themselves a. H2290
Act 19:12 handkerchiefs or a, and the diseases G4612

APT
2Ki 24:16 *were* strong *and* a for war, even them H6213
1Ch 7:40 of them that were a to the war *and* to
1Ti 3: 2 given to hospitality, a to teach; G1317
2Ti 2:24 gentle unto all *men*, a to teach, patient, G1317

AQUILA
Act 18: 2 And found a certain Jew named A, born G207
18 him Priscilla and A; having shorn *his* G207
26 whom when A and Priscilla had heard, G207
Ro 16: 3 Greet Priscilla and A my helpers in G207
1Co 16:19 The churches of Asia salute you. A and G207
2Ti 4:19 Salute Prisca and A, and the household G207

AR
Nu 21:15 A, and lieth upon the border of Moab. H6144
28 it hath consumed A of Moab, *and* the H6144
Dt 2: 9 I have given A unto the children of H6144
18 Thou art to pass over through A, the H6144
29 which dwell in A, did unto me;) until H6144
Isa 15: 1 in the night A of Moab is laid waste, H6144

ARA
1Ch 7:38 of Jether; Jephunneh, and Pispah, and A. H690

ARAB
Jos 15:52 A, and Dumah, and Eshean, H694

ARABAH
Jos 18:18 the side over against A northward, and H6160
18 northward, and went down unto A: H6160

ARABIA
1Ki 10:15 A, and of the governors of the country. H6152
2Ch 9:14 all the kings of A and governors of the H6152
Isa 21:13 The burden upon A. In the forest in H6152
13 In the forest in A shall ye lodge, O ye H6152
Jer 25:24 And all the kings of A, and all the kings H6152
Ezk 27:21 A, and all the princes of Kedar, they H6152
Gal 1:17 A, and returned again unto Damascus. G688
4:25 For this Agar is mount Sinai in A, and G688

ARABIAN
Neh 2:19 and Geshem the A, heard *it*, they H6163
6: 1 and Geshem the A, and the rest of our H6163
Isa 13:20 neither shall the A pitch tent there; H6163
Jer 3: 2 sat for them, as the A in the wilderness; H6163

ARABIANS
2Ch 17:11 silver; and the A brought him flocks, H6163
21:16 of the A, that *were* near the Ethiopians: H6163
22: 1 came with the A to the camp had slain H6163
26: 7 and against the A that dwelt in H6163
Neh 4: 7 Tobiah, and the A, and the Ammonites, H6163
Act 2:11 Cretes and A, we do hear them speak in G690

ARAD
Nu 21: 1 And *when* king A the Canaanite, which H6166
33:40 And king A the Canaanite, which dwelt H6166
Jos 12:14 The king of Hormah, one; the king of A, H6166
Jdg 1:16 in the south of A; and they went and H6166
1Ch 8:15 And Zebadiah, and A, and Ader, H6166

ARAH
1Ch 7:39 And the sons of Ulla; A, and Haniel, and H733
Ezr 2: 5 The children of A, seven hundred seventy H733
Neh 6:18 the son of A; and his son Johanan H733
7:10 The children of A, six hundred fifty and H733

ARAM
Gen 10:22 Asshur, and Arphaxad, and Lud, and A. H758
23 And the children of A; Uz, and Hul, and H758
22:21 his brother, and Kemuel the father of A, H758
Nu 23: 7 brought me from A, out of the mountains H758
1Ch 1:17 and Lud, and A, and Uz, and Hul, and H758
2:23 And he took Geshur, and A, with the H758
7:34 Ahi, and Rohgah, Jehubbah, and A. H758
Mt 1: 3 Phares begat Esrom; and Esrom begat A; G689
4 And A begat Aminadab; and Aminadab G689
Lk 3:33 was *the son* of A, which was *the son* of G689

ARAMITESS
1Ch 7:14 the A bare Machir the father of Gilead: H761

ARAM-NAHARAIM
Ps 60: ttl he strove with A and with Aram-zobah, H763

ARAM-ZOBAH
Ps 60: ttl and with A, when Joab returned, H760

ARAN
Gen 36:28 children of Dishan *are* these; Uz, and A. H765
1Ch 1:42 Jakan. The sons of Dishan; Uz, and A. H765

ARARAT
Gen 8: 4 of the month, upon the mountains of A. H780
Jer 51:27 her the kingdoms of A, Minni, and H780

ARAUNAH
2Sa 24:16 by the threshingplace of A the Jebusite. H728
18 in the threshingfloor of A the Jebusite. H728
20 And A looked, and saw the king and his H728
20 toward him: and A went out, and bowed H728
21 And A said, Wherefore is my lord the H728
22 And A said unto David, Let my lord the H728
23 All these *things* did A, *as* a king, give H728
23 unto the king. And A said unto the king, H728
24 And the king said unto A, Nay; but I will H728

ARBA
Jos 14:15 *which A was* a great man among
15:13 *even* the city of A the father of Anak, H704
21:11 And they gave them the city of A the H704

ARBAH
Gen 35:27 unto the city of A, which *is* Hebron, H7153

ARBATHITE
2Sa 23:31 Abialbon the A, Azmaveth the H6164
1Ch 11:32 of the brooks of Gaash, Abiel the A, H6164

ARBEL
See BETH-ARBEL.

ARBITE
2Sa 23:35 Hezrai the Carmelite, Paarai the A, H701

ARCHANGEL
1Th 4:16 the voice of the a, and with the trump G743
Jude 9 Yet Michael the a, when contending with G743

ARCHELAUS
Mt 2:22 But when he heard that A did reign in G745

ARCHER
Gen 21:20 in the wilderness, and became an a. H7198
Jer 51: 3 Against *him that* bendeth let the a H1869

ARCHERS
Gen 49:23 The a have sorely grieved him, H1167+H2671
Jdg 5:11 from the noise of a in the places of H2686
1Sa 31: 3 Saul, and the a hit him; and he was H3384
3 him; and he was sore wounded of the a. H3384
1Ch 8:40 of valour, a, and had many H1869+H7198
10: 3 Saul, and the a hit him, and he H3384+H7198
3 hit him, and he was wounded of the a. H3384
2Ch 35:23 And the a shot at king Josiah; and the H3384
Job 16:13 His a compass me round about, he H7228
Isa 21:17 And the residue of the number of a, the H7198
22: 3 are bound by the a: all that are found in H7198
Jer 50:29 Call together the a against Babylon: all H7228

ARCHES
Ezk 40:16 and likewise to the a: and windows *were* H361
21 thereof and the a thereof were after the H361
22 And their windows, and their a, and their H361
22 and the a thereof *were* before them. H361
24 a thereof according to these measures. H361
25 in it and in the a thereof round about, H361

Ezk 40:26 go up to it, and the **a** thereof *were* before H361
29 thereof, and the **a** thereof, according to H361
29 in it and in the **a** thereof round about: H361
30 And the **a** round about *were* five and H361
31 And the **a** thereof *were* toward the utter H361
33 posts thereof, and the **a** thereof, *were* H361
33 therein and in the **a** thereof round H361
34 And the **a** thereof *were* toward the H361
36 posts thereof, and the **a** thereof, and the H361

ARCHEVITES
Ezr 4: 9 the Apharsites, the **A**, the Babylonians, H756

ARCHI
Jos 16: 2 along unto the borders of **A** to Ataroth, H757

ARCHIPPUS
Col 4:17 And say to **A**, Take heed to the ministry *G751*
Phlm 2 And to *our* beloved Apphia, and **A** our *G751*

ARCHITE
2Sa 15:32 behold, Hushai the **A** came to meet him H757
16:16 And it came to pass, when Hushai the **A**, H757
17: 5 now Hushai the **A** also, and let us hear H757
14 of Hushai the **A** *is* better than the H757
1Ch 27:33 Hushai the **A** *was* the king's companion: H757

ARCTURUS
Job 9: 9 Which maketh **A**, Orion, and Pleiades, H5906
38:32 or canst thou guide **A** with his sons? H5906

ARD
Gen 46:21 and Rosh, Muppim, and Huppim, and **A**. H714
Nu 26:40 And the sons of Bela were **A** and H714
40 Ard and Naaman: *of A*, the family of the

ARDITES
Nu 26:40 the family of the **A**: *and* of Naaman, the H716

ARDON
1Ch 2:18 *are* these; Jesher, and Shobab, and **A**. H715

ARE See the Appendix.

ARELI
Gen 46:16 Shuni, and Ezbon, Eri, and Arodi, and **A**. H692
Nu 26:17 Of Arod, the family of the Arodites: of **A**, H692

ARELITES
Nu 26:17 the Arodites: of Areli, the family of the **A**. H692

AREOPAGITE
Act 17:34 *was* Dionysius the **A**, and a woman *G698*

AREOPAGUS
Act 17:19 and brought him unto **A**, saying, May we *G697*

ARETAS
2Co 11:32 In Damascus the governor under **A** the *G702*

ARGOB
Dt 3: 4 of **A**, the kingdom of Og in Bashan. H709
13 all the region of **A**, with all Bashan, H709
14 all the country of **A** unto the coasts of H709
1Ki 4:13 the region of **A**, which *is* in Bashan, H709
2Ki 15:25 king's house, with **A** and Arieh, and with H709

ARGUING
Job 6:25 words! but what doth your **a** reprove? H3198

ARGUMENTS
Job 23: 4 before him, and fill my mouth with **a**. H8433

ARIDAI
Est 9: 9 And Parmashta, and Arisai, and **A**, and H742

ARIDATHA
Est 9: 8 And Poratha, and Adalia, and **A**, H743

ARIEH
2Ki 15:25 with Argob and **A**, and with him fifty H745

ARIEL
Ezr 8:16 Then sent I for Eliezer, for **A**, for H740
Isa 29: 1 Woe to **A**, to Ariel, the city *where* David H740
1 Woe to Ariel, to **A**, the city *where* David H740
2 Yet I will distress **A**, and there shall be H740
2 and sorrow: and it shall be unto me as **A**. H740
7 that fight against **A**, even all that fight H740

ARIGHT
Ps 50:23 *a* will I shew the salvation of God.
78: 8 set not their heart **a**, and whose spirit H3559
Prv 15: 2 useth knowledge **a**: but the mouth of H3190
23:31 in the cup, *when* it moveth itself **a**. H4339
Jer 8: 6 *but* they spake not **a**: no man repented H3651

ARIM See KIRJATH-ARIM.

ARIMATHAEA
Mt 27:57 a rich man of **A**, named Joseph, who *G707*
Mk 15:43 Joseph of **A**, an honourable counsellor, *G707*
Lk 23:51 of them;) *he was* of **A**, a city of the Jews: *G707*
Jn 19:38 And after this Joseph of **A**, being a *G707*

ARIOCH
Gen 14: 1 king of Shinar, **A** king of Ellasar, H746
9 **A** king of Ellasar; four kings with five. H746
Dan 2:14 and wisdom to **A** the captain of the H746
15 He answered and said to **A** the king's H746
15 Then **A** made the thing known to Daniel. H746
24 Therefore Daniel went in unto **A**, whom H746
25 Then **A** brought in Daniel before the H746

ARISAI
Est 9: 9 And Parmashta, and **A**, and Aridai, and H747

ARISE
Gen 13:17 **A**, walk through the land in the length H6965
19:15 Lot, saying, **A**, take thy wife, and thy H6965
21:18 **A**, lift up the lad, and hold him in thine H6965
27:19 thou badest me: **a**, I pray thee, sit and H6965
31 Let my father **a**, and eat of his son's H6965
43 my voice; and **a**, flee thou to Laban my H6965
28: 2 **A**, go to Padan-aram, to the house of H6965
31:13 vow unto me: now **a**, get thee out from H6965
35: 1 And God said unto Jacob, **A**, go up to H6965
3 And let us **a**, and go up to Beth-el; and I H6965
41:30 And there shall **a** after them seven H6965
43: 8 me, and we will **a** and go; that we may H6965
13 Take also your brother, and **a**, go again H6965
Dt 9:12 And the LORD said unto me, **A**, get thee H6965
10:11 And the LORD said unto me, **A**, take H6965
13: 1 If there **a** among you a prophet, or a H6965
17: 8 If there **a** a matter too hard for thee in
8 then shalt thou **a**, and get thee up into H6965
Jos 1: 2 now therefore **a**, go over this Jordan, H6965
8: 1 with thee, and **a**, go up to Ai: see, I have H6965
Jdg 5:12 utter a song: **a**, Barak, and lead thy H6965
7: 9 said unto him, **A**, get thee down unto H6965
15 Israel, and said, **A**; for the LORD hath H6965
18: 9 And they said, **A**, that we may go up H6965
20:40 But when the flame began to **a** up out H5927
1Sa 9: 3 with thee, and **a**, go seek the asses. H6965
16:12 LORD said, **A**, anoint him: for this *is* he. H6965
23: 4 him and said, **A**, go down to Keilah; H6965
2Sa 2:14 young men now **a**, and play before us. H6965
14 before us. And Joab said, Let them **a**. H6965
3:21 And Abner said unto David, I will **a** H6965
11:20 And if so be that the king's wrath **a**, and H5927
13:15 And Amnon said unto her, **A**, be gone. H6965
15:14 him at Jerusalem, **A**, and let us flee; for H6965
17: 1 **a** and pursue after David this night: H6965
21 said unto David, **A**, and pass quickly H6965
19: 7 Now therefore **a**, go forth, and speak H6965
22:39 not **a**: yea, they are fallen under my feet. H6965
1Ki 3:12 after thee shall any **a** like unto thee. H6965
14: 2 And Jeroboam said to his wife, **A**, I pray H6965
12 **A** thou therefore, get thee to thine own H6965
17: 9 **A**, get thee to Zarephath, which H6965
19: 5 him, and said unto him, **A** *and* eat. H6965
7 him, and said, **A** *and* eat; because the H6965
21: 7 of Israel? **a**, *and* eat bread, and H6965
15 said to Ahab, **A**, take possession of the H6965
18 **A**, go down to meet Ahab king of Israel, H6965
2Ki 1: 3 Elijah the Tishbite, **A**, go up to meet the H6965
8: 1 to life, saying, **A**, and go thou and thine H6965
9: 2 in, and make him **a** up from among his H6965
1Ch 22:16 *there is* no number. **A** *therefore*, and be H6965
19 LORD your God; **a** therefore, and build H6965
2Ch 6:41 Now therefore **a**, O LORD God, into thy H6965
Ezr 10: 4 **A**; for *this* matter *belongeth* unto thee: H6965
Neh 2:20 we his servants will **a** and build: but ye H6965
Est 1:18 *there a* too much contempt and wrath.
4:14 and deliverance **a** to the Jews from H5975
Job 7: 4 When I lie down, I say, When shall I **a**, H6965
25: 3 and upon whom doth not his light **a**? H6965
Ps 3: 7 **A**, O LORD; save me, O my God: for H6965
7: 6 **A**, O LORD, in thine anger, lift up H6965
9:19 **A**, O LORD; let not man prevail: let the H6965
10:12 **A**, O LORD; O God, lift up thine hand: H6965
12: 5 needy, now will I **a**, saith the LORD; I H6965
17:13 **A**, O LORD, disappoint him, cast him H6965
44:23 Awake, why sleepest thou, O Lord? **a**, H6974
26 **A** for our help, and redeem us for thy H6965
68: 1 Let God **a**, let his enemies be scattered: H6965
74:22 **A**, O God, plead thine own cause: H6965
78: 6 **a** and declare *them* to their children: H6965
82: 8 **A**, O God, judge the earth: for thou shalt H6965
88:10 shall the dead **a** *and* praise thee? Selah. H6965
89: 9 the waves thereof **a**, thou stillest them. H7721
102:13 Thou shalt **a**, *and* have mercy upon H6965
109:28 bless thou: when they **a**, let them be H6965
132: 8 **A**, O LORD, into thy rest; thou, and the H6965
Prv 6: 9 when wilt thou **a** out of thy sleep? H6965
31:28 Her children **a** up, and call her blessed; H6965
Song 2:13 give a *good* smell. **A**, my love, my fair H6965
Isa 21: 5 **a**, ye princes, *and* anoint the shield. H6965
23:12 of Zidon: **a**, pass over to Chittim; H6965
26:19 body shall they **a**. Awake and sing, ye H6965
31: 2 his words: but will **a** against the house H6965
49: 7 Kings shall see and **a**, princes also shall H6965
52: 2 Shake thyself from the dust; **a**, *and* sit H6965
60: 1 **A**, shine; for thy light is come, and the H6965
2 the LORD shall **a** upon thee, and his H2224
Jer 1:17 Thou therefore gird up thy loins, and **a**, H6965
2:27 trouble they will say, **A**, and save us. H6965
28 thee? let them **a**, if they can save thee H6965
6: 4 Prepare ye war against her; **a**, and let us H6965
5 **A**, and let us go by night, and let us H6965
8: 4 **a**? shall he turn away, and not return? H6965
13: 4 thy loins, and **a**, go to Euphrates, and H6965
6 said unto me, **A**, go to Euphrates, and H6965
18: 2 **A**, and go down to the potter's house, H6965
31: 6 shall cry, **A** ye, and let us go up H6965
46:16 and they said, **A**, and let us go again H6965
49:28 saith the LORD; **A** ye, go up to Kedar, H6965
31 **A**, get you up unto the wealthy nation, H6965
Lam 2:19 **A**, cry out in the night: in the beginning H6965
Ezk 3:22 he said unto me, **A**, go forth into the H6965
Dan 2:39 And after thee shall **a** another kingdom H6966
7: 5 said thus unto it, **A**, devour much flesh. H6966
17 kings, *which* shall **a** out of the earth. H6966
24 kings *that* shall **a**: and another shall rise H6966
Hos 10:14 Therefore shall a tumult **a** among thy H6965
Am 7: 2 by whom shall Jacob **a**? for he *is* small. H6965
5 by whom shall Jacob **a**? for he *is* small. H6965
Oba 1 the heathen, **A** ye, and let us rise up H6965
Jna 1: 2 **A**, go to Nineveh, that great city, and H6965
6 thou, O sleeper? **a**, call upon thy God, if H6965
3: 2 **A**, go unto Nineveh, that great city, and H6965
4: 8 when the sun did **a**, that God prepared H2224
Mic 2:10 **A** ye, and depart; for this *is* not *your* H6965
4:13 **A** and thresh, O daughter of Zion: for I H6965
6: 1 Hear ye now what the LORD saith; **A**, H6965
7: 8 when I fall, I shall **a**; when I sit in H6965
Hab 2:19 to the dumb stone, **A**, it shall teach! H5782
Mal 4: 2 of righteousness **a** with healing in his H2224
Mt 2:13 a dream, saying, **A**, and take the young *G1453*
20 Saying, **A**, and take the young child and *G1453*
9: 5 be forgiven thee; or to say, **A**, and walk? *G1453*
6 sick of the palsy,) **A**, take up thy bed, *G1453*
17: 7 them, and said, **A**, and be not afraid. *G1453*
24:24 For there shall **a** false Christs, and false *G1453*
Mk 2: 9 say, **A**, and take up thy bed, and walk? *G1453*
11 I say unto thee, **A**, and take up thy bed, *G1453*
5:41 interpreted, Damsel, I say unto thee, **a**. *G1453*
Lk 5:24 I say unto thee, **A**, and take up thy *G1453*
7:14 he said, Young man, I say unto thee, **A**. *G1453*
8:54 the hand, and called, saying, Maid, **a**. *G1453*
15:18 I will **a** and go to my father, and will say *G450*
17:19 And he said unto him, **A**, go thy way: thy *G450*
24:38 and why do thoughts **a** in your hearts? *G305*
Jn 14:31 even so I do. **A**, let us go hence. *G1453*
Act 8:26 unto Philip, saying, **A**, and go toward the *G450*
9: 6 *said* unto him, **A**, and go into the city, *G450*
11 And the Lord *said* unto him, **A**, and go *G450*
34 thee whole: **a**, and make thy bed. And *G450*
40 said, Tabitha, **a**. And she opened her *G450*
10:20 **A** therefore, and get thee down, and go *G450*
11: 7 And I heard a voice saying unto me, **A**, *G450*
12: 7 him up, saying, **A** up quickly. And his *G450*
20:30 Also of your own selves shall men **a**, *G450*
22:10 the Lord said unto me, **A**, and go into *G450*
16 And now why tarriest thou? **a**, and be *G450*
Eph 5:14 that sleepest, and **a** from the dead, and *G450*
2Pt 1:19 dawn, and the day star **a** in your hearts: *G393*

ARISETH
1Ki 18:44 Behold, there a a little cloud out of H5927
Ps 104:22 The sun a, they gather themselves H2224
112: 4 Unto the upright there a light in the H2224
Ecc 1: 5 The sun also a, and the sun goeth H2224
Isa 2:19 when he a to shake terribly the earth. H6965
21 when he a to shake terribly the earth. H6965
Nah 3:17 *but* when the sun a they flee away, and H2224
Mt 13:21 or persecution a because of the word, *G1096*
Mk 4:17 or persecution a for the word's sake, *G1096*
Jn 7:52 look: for out of Galilee a no prophet. *G1453*
Heb 7:15 of Melchisedec there a another priest, *G450*

ARISING
Est 7: 7 And the king a from the banquet of H6965

ARISTARCHUS
Act 19:29 caught Gaius and A, men of Macedonia, *G708*
20: 4 the Thessalonians, A and Secundus; and *G708*
27: 2 coasts of Asia; *one* A, a Macedonian of *G708*
Col 4:10 A my fellowprisoner saluteth you, and *G708*
Phlm 24 Marcus, A, Demas, Lucas, my *G708*

ARISTOBULUS'
Ro 16:10 Salute them which are of A *household*. *G711*

ARK
Gen 6:14 Make thee an a of gopher wood; rooms H8392
14 thou make in the a, and shalt pitch it H8392
15 *of*: The length of the a *shall be* three H8392
16 A window shalt thou make to the a, and H8392
16 the door of the a shalt thou set in the H8392
18 come into the a, thou, and thy sons, H8392
19 bring into the a, to keep *them* alive with H8392
7: 1 all thy house into the a; for thee have I H8392
7 the a, because of the waters of the flood. H8392
9 unto Noah into the a, the male and the H8392
13 wives of his sons with them, into the a; H8392
15 And they went in unto Noah into the a, H8392
17 the a, and it was lift up above the earth. H8392
18 the a went upon the face of the waters. H8392
23 and they that *were* with him in the a. H8392
8: 1 *was* with him in the a: and God made a H8392
4 And the a rested in the seventh month, H8392
6 window of the a which he had made: H8392
9 unto him into the a, for the waters *were* H8392
9 and pulled her in unto him into the a. H8392
10 he sent forth the dove out of the a; H8392
13 the covering of the a, and looked, and, H8392
16 Go forth of the a, thou, and thy wife, H8392
19 after their kinds, went forth out of the a. H8392
9:10 out of the a, to every beast of the earth. H8392
18 that went forth of the a, were Shem, and H8392
Ex 2: 3 she took for him an a of bulrushes, and H8392
5 when she saw the a among the flags, H8392
25:10 And they shall make an a *of* shittim H727
14 a, that the ark may be borne with them. H727
14 ark, that the a may be borne with them. H727
15 The staves shall be in the rings of the a: H727
16 And thou shalt put into the a the H727
21 above upon the a; and in the ark thou H727
21 the ark; and in the a thou shalt put the H727
22 which *are* upon the a of the testimony, of H727
26:33 within the vail the a of the testimony: H727
34 seat upon the a of the testimony in the H727
30: 6 the vail that *is* by the a of the testimony, H727
26 therewith, and the a of the testimony, H727
31: 7 and the a of the testimony, and H727
35:12 The a, and the staves thereof, *with* the H727
37: 1 And Bezaleel made the a *of* shittim H727
5 by the sides of the a, to bear the ark. H727
5 by the sides of the ark, to bear the a. H727
39:35 The a of the testimony, and the staves H727
40: 3 And thou shalt put therein the a of the H727
3 testimony, and cover the a with the vail. H727
5 incense before the a of the testimony, H727
20 testimony into the a, and set the staves H727
20 set the staves on the a, and put the mercy H727
20 and put the mercy seat above upon the a: H727
21 And he brought the a into the H727
21 and covered the a of the testimony; as H727
Lev 16: 2 which *is* upon the a; that he die not: for I H727
Nu 3:31 And their charge *shall be* the a, and the H727
4: 5 vail, and cover the a of testimony with it: H727
7:89 that *was* upon the a of testimony, from H727
10:33 journey: and the a of the covenant of the H727
35 And it came to pass, when the a set H727
14:44 nevertheless the a of the covenant of the H727
Dt 10: 1 the mount, and make thee an a of wood. H727
Dt 10: 2 brakest, and thou shalt put them in the a. H727
3 And I made an a *of* shittim wood, and H727
5 put the tables in the a which I had made; H727
8 of Levi, to bear the a of the covenant of H727
31: 9 which bare the a of the covenant of the H727
25 a of the covenant of the LORD, saying, H727
26 it in the side of the a of the covenant of H727
Jos 3: 3 When ye see the a of the covenant of the H727
6 Take up the a of the covenant, and H727
6 they took up the a of the covenant, and H727
8 that bare the a of the covenant, saying, H727
11 Behold, the a of the covenant of the Lord H727
13 that bear the a of the LORD, the Lord H727
14 the a of the covenant before the people; H727
15 And as they that bare the a were come H727
15 that bare the a were dipped in the brim H727
17 And the priests that bare the a of the H727
4: 5 over before the a of the LORD your God H727
7 cut off before the a of the covenant of the H727
9 which bare the a of the covenant stood: H727
10 For the priests which bare the a stood in H727
11 over, that the a of the LORD passed H727
16 Command the priests that bear the a of H727
18 that bare the a of the covenant of the H727
6: 4 And seven priests shall bear before the a H727
6 them, Take up the a of the covenant, H727
6 of rams' horns before the a of the LORD. H727
7 armed pass on before the a of the LORD. H727
8 trumpets: and the a of the covenant of H727
9 came after the a, *the priests* going on, H727
11 So the a of the LORD compassed the H727
12 the priests took up the a of the LORD. H727
13 horns before the a of the LORD went on H727
13 came after the a of the LORD, *the priests* H727
7: 6 his face before the a of the LORD until H727
8:33 on this side the a and on that side before H727
33 which bare the a of the covenant of the H727
Jdg 20:27 the LORD, (for the a of the covenant of H727
1Sa 3: 3 the LORD, where the a of God *was*, and H727
4: 3 Let us fetch the a of the covenant of the H727
4 from thence the a of the covenant of the H727
4 there with the a of the covenant of God. H727
5 And when the a of the covenant of the H727
6 a of the LORD was come into the camp. H727
11 And the a of God was taken; and the two H727
13 trembled for the a of God. And when the H727
17 are dead, and the a of God is taken. H727
18 mention of the a of God, that he fell from H727
19 the tidings that the a of God was taken, H727
21 Israel: because the a of God was taken, H727
22 from Israel: for the a of God is taken. H727
5: 1 And the Philistines took the a of God, H727
2 When the Philistines took the a of God, H727
3 earth before the a of the LORD. And they H727
4 ground before the a of the LORD; and H727
7 so, they said, The a of the God of Israel H727
8 we do with the a of the God of Israel? H727
8 answered, Let the a of the God of Israel H727
8 the a of the God of Israel about *thither*. H727
10 Therefore they sent the a of God to H727
10 to pass, as the a of God came to Ekron, H727
10 brought about the a of the God of Israel H727
11 Send away the a of the God of Israel, H727
6: 1 And the a of the LORD was in the H727
2 shall we do to the a of the LORD? tell us H727
3 And they said, If ye send away the a of H727
8 And take the a of the LORD, and lay it H727
11 And they laid the a of the LORD upon H727
13 and saw the a, and rejoiced to see *it*. H727
15 And the Levites took down the a of the H727
18 they set down the a of the LORD: *which* H727
19 looked into the a of the LORD, even he H727
21 brought again the a of the LORD; come H727
7: 1 and fetched up the a of the LORD, and H727
1 his son to keep the a of the LORD. H727
2 And it came to pass, while the a abode H727
14:18 Bring hither the a of God. For the ark of H727
18 ark of God. For the a of God was at that H727
2Sa 6: 2 up from thence the a of God, whose H727
3 And they set the a of God upon a new H727
4 a of God: and Ahio went before the ark. H727
4 ark of God: and Ahio went before the a. H727
6 *his hand* to the a of God, and took hold H727
7 error; and there he died by the a of God. H727
9 shall the a of the LORD come to me? H727
10 So David would not remove the a of the H727
11 And the a of the LORD continued in the H727
12 because of the a of God. So David went H727
12 and brought up the a of God from the H727
2Sa 6:13 they that bare the a of the LORD had H727
15 Israel brought up the a of the LORD with H727
16 And as the a of the LORD came into the H727
17 And they brought in the a of the LORD, H727
7: 2 the a of God dwelleth within curtains. H727
11:11 And Uriah said unto David, The a, and H727
15:24 him, bearing the a of the covenant of H727
24 and they set down the a of God; and H727
25 Carry back the a of God into the city: H727
29 carried the a of God again to Jerusalem: H727
1Ki 2:26 thou barest the a of the Lord GOD before H727
3:15 stood before the a of the covenant of the H727
6:19 there the a of the covenant of the LORD. H727
8: 1 might bring up the a of the covenant of H727
3 came, and the priests took up the a. H727
4 And they brought up the a of the LORD, H727
5 him before the a, sacrificing sheep and H727
6 And the priests brought in the a of the H727
7 the place of the a, and the cherubims H727
7 the a and the staves thereof above. H727
9 *There was* nothing in the a save the two H727
21 And I have set there a place for the a, H727
1Ch 6:31 of the LORD, after that the a had rest. H727
13: 3 And let us bring again the a of our God H727
5 bring the a of God from Kirjath-jearim. H727
6 up thence the a of God the LORD, that H727
7 And they carried the a of God in a new H727
9 to hold the a; for the oxen stumbled. H727
10 to the a: and there he died before God. H727
12 shall I bring the a of God *home* to me? H727
13 So David brought not the a *home* to H727
14 And the a of God remained with the H727
15: 1 for the a of God, and pitched for it a tent. H727
2 None ought to carry the a of God but the H727
2 chosen to carry the a of God, and to H727
3 to bring up the a of the LORD unto his H727
12 may bring up the a of the LORD God of H727
14 bring up the a of the LORD God of Israel. H727
15 the Levites bare the a of God upon their H727
23 and Elkanah *were* doorkeepers for the a. H727
24 before the a of God: and Obed-edom H727
24 and Jehiah *were* doorkeepers for the a. H727
25 to bring up the a of the covenant of the H727
26 that bare the a of the covenant of the H727
27 that bare the a, and the singers, and H727
28 Thus all Israel brought up the a of the H727
29 And it came to pass, *as* the a of the H727
16: 1 So they brought the a of God, and set it H727
4 minister before the a of the LORD, and H727
6 before the a of the covenant of God. H727
37 So he left there before the a of the H727
37 to minister before the a continually, as H727
17: 1 of cedars, but the a of the covenant of H727
22:19 God, to bring the a of the covenant of the H727
28: 2 of rest for the a of the covenant of the H727
18 the a of the covenant of the LORD. H727
2Ch 1: 4 But the a of God had David brought up H727
5: 2 to bring up the a of the covenant of the H727
4 came; and the Levites took up the a. H727
5 And they brought up the a, and the H727
6 him before the a, sacrificed sheep and H727
7 And the priests brought in the a of the H727
8 the place of the a, and the cherubims H727
8 the a and the staves thereof above. H727
9 And they drew out the staves *of the a*,
9 were seen from the a before the oracle; H727
10 *There was* nothing in the a save the two H727
6:11 And in it have I put the a, wherein *is* the H727
41 thou, and the a of thy strength: let thy H727
8:11 whereunto the a of the LORD hath come. H727
35: 3 LORD, Put the holy a in the house which H727
Ps 132: 8 thy rest; thou, and the a of thy strength. H727
Jer 3:16 say no more, The a of the covenant of H727
Mt 24:38 the day that Noe entered into the a, *G2787*
Lk 17:27 entered into the a, and the flood came, *G2787*
Heb 9: 4 Which had the golden censer, and the a *G2787*
11: 7 fear, prepared an a to the saving of his *G2787*
1Pt 3:20 of Noah, while the a was a preparing, *G2787*
Rev 11:19 in his temple the a of his testament: *G2787*

ARKITE
Gen 10:17 And the Hivite, and the A, and the H6208
1Ch 1:15 And the Hivite, and the A, and the H6208

ARM
Ex 6: 6 out a, and with great judgments: H2220
15:16 the greatness of thine a they shall be *as* H2220
Nu 31: 3 people, saying, A some of yourselves H2502
Dt 4:34 and by a stretched out a, and by great H2220

Dt 5:15 and by a stretched out **a**: therefore the H2220
7:19 the stretched out **a**, whereby the LORD H2220
9:29 power and by thy stretched out **a**. H2220
11: 2 mighty hand, and his stretched out **a**, H2220
26: 8 with an outstretched **a**, and with great H2220
33:20 the **a** with the crown of the head. H2220
1Sa 2:31 I will cut off thine **a**, and the arm of thy H2220
31 arm, and the **a** of thy father's house, H2220
2Sa 1:10 that *was* on his **a**, and have brought H2220
1Ki 8:42 thy stretched out **a**;) when he shall come H2220
2Ki 17:36 a stretched out **a**, him shall ye fear, and H2220
2Ch 6:32 **a**; if they come and pray in this house; H2220
32: 8 With him *is* an **a** of flesh; but with us *is* H2220
Job 26: 2 savest thou the **a** *that hath* no strength? H2220
31:22 *Then* let mine **a** fall from my shoulder H3802
22 and mine **a** be broken from the bone. H248
35: 9 out by reason of the **a** of the mighty. H2220
38:15 and the high **a** shall be broken. H2220
40: 9 Hast thou an **a** like God? or canst thou H2220
Ps 10:15 Break thou the **a** of the wicked and the H2220
44: 3 did their own **a** save them: but thy H2220
3 hand, and thine **a**, and the light of thy H2220
77:15 Thou hast with *thine* **a** redeemed thy H2220
89:10 thine enemies with thy strong **a**. H2220
13 Thou hast a mighty **a**: strong is thy H2220
21 mine **a** also shall strengthen him. H2220
98: 1 his holy **a**, hath gotten him the victory. H2220
136:12 out **a**: for his mercy *endureth* for ever. H2220
Song 8: 6 a seal upon thine **a**: for love *is* strong as H2220
Isa 9:20 eat every man the flesh of his own **a**: H2220
17: 5 the ears with his **a**; and it shall be as he H2220
30:30 down of his **a**, with the indignation H2220
33: 2 for thee: be thou their **a** every morning, H2220
40:10 *hand*, and his **a** shall rule for him: H2220
11 the lambs with his **a**, and carry *them* in H2220
48:14 and his **a** *shall be on* the Chaldeans. H2220
51: 5 me, and on mine **a** shall they trust. H2220
9 Awake, awake, put on strength, O **a** of H2220
52:10 The LORD hath made bare his holy **a** H2220
53: 1 to whom is the **a** of the LORD revealed? H2220
59:16 therefore his **a** brought salvation unto H2220
62: 8 hand, and by the **a** of his strength, H2220
63: 5 mine own **a** brought salvation unto H2220
12 with his glorious **a**, dividing the water H2220
Jer 17: 5 maketh flesh his **a**, and whose heart H2220
21: 5 and with a strong **a**, even in anger, and H2220
27: 5 by my outstretched **a**, and have given it H2220
32:17 power and stretched out **a**, *and* there is H2220
21 a stretched out **a**, and with great terror; H248
48:25 The horn of Moab is cut off, and his **a** H2220
Ezk 4: 7 and thine **a** *shall be* uncovered, H2220
20:33 a stretched out **a**, and with fury poured H2220
34 out **a**, and with fury poured out. H2220
30:21 Son of man, I have broken the **a** of H2220
31:17 *they that were* his **a**, *that* dwelt under H2220
Dan 11: 6 the power of the **a**; neither shall he H2220
6 he stand, nor his **a**: but she shall be H2220
Zec 11:17 *shall be* upon his **a**, and upon his right H2220
17 his right eye: his **a** shall be clean dried H2220
Lk 1:51 He hath shewed strength with his **a**; he G1023
Jn 12:38 hath the **a** of the Lord been revealed? G1023
Act 13:17 an high **a** brought he them out of it. G1023
1Pt 4: 1 for us in the flesh, **a** yourselves likewise G3695

ARMAGEDDON

Rev 16:16 a place called in the Hebrew tongue **A**. G717

ARMED

Gen 14:14 was taken captive, he **a** his trained H7324
Nu 31: 5 *every* tribe, twelve thousand **a** for war. H2502
32:17 But we ourselves will go ready **a** before H2502
20 if ye will go **a** before the LORD to war, H2502
21 And will go all of you **a** over Jordan H2502
27 over, every man **a** for war, before the H2502
29 Jordan, every man **a** to battle, before H2502
30 But if they will not pass over with you **a**, H2502
32 We will pass over **a** before the LORD H2502
Dt 3:18 it: ye shall pass over **a** before your H2502
Jos 1:14 your brethren **a**, all the mighty men H2571
4:12 passed over **a** before the children H2571
6: 7 **a** pass on before the ark of the LORD. H2502
9 And the **a** men went before the priests H2502
13 trumpets: and the **a** men went before H2502
Jdg 7:11 of the **a** men that *were* in the host. H2571
1Sa 17: 5 head, and he *was* **a** with a coat of mail; H3847
38 And Saul **a** David with his armour, and H3847
38 head; also he **a** him with a coat of mail. H3847
1Ch 12: 2 *They were* **a** with bows, and could use H5401
23 *that were* ready **a** to the war, *and* came H2502
12:24 and eight hundred, ready **a** to the war. H2502
2Ch 17:17 and with him **a** men with bow and H5401
28:14 So the **a** men left the captives and the H2502
Job 39:21 he goeth on to meet the **a** men. H5402
Ps 78: 9 The children of Ephraim, *being* **a**, *and* H5401
Prv 6:11 travelleth, and thy want as an **a** man. H4043
24:34 travelleth; and thy want as an **a** man. H4043
Isa 15: 4 therefore the **a** soldiers of Moab shall H2502
Lk 11:21 When a strong man **a** keepeth his G2528

ARMENIA

2Ki 19:37 into the land of **A**. And Esarhaddon his H780
Isa 37:38 into the land of **A**: and Esar-haddon his H780

ARMHOLES

Jer 38:12 under thine **a** under the cords. H679+H3027
Ezk 13:18 sew pillows to all **a**, and make H679+H3027

ARMIES

Ex 6:26 the land of Egypt according to their **a**. H6635
7: 4 bring forth mine **a**, *and* my people the H6635
12:17 have I brought your **a** out of the land of H6635
51 out of the land of Egypt by their **a**. H6635
Nu 1: 3 Aaron shall number them by their **a**. H6635
2: 3 throughout their **a**: and Nahshon the H6635
9 their **a**. These shall first set forth. H6635
10 according to their **a**: and the captain of H6635
16 throughout their **a**. And they shall set H6635
18 according to their **a**: and the captain of H6635
24 throughout their **a**. And they shall go H6635
25 north side by their **a**: and the captain of H6635
10:14 according to their **a**: and over his host H6635
18 according to their **a**: and over his host H6635
22 according to their **a**: and over his host H6635
28 to their **a**, when they set forward. H6635
33: 1 **a** under the hand of Moses and Aaron. H6635
Dt 20: 9 captains of the **a** to lead the people. H6635
1Sa 17: 1 together their **a** to battle, and were H4264
8 And he stood and cried unto the **a** of H4634
10 And the Philistine said, I defy the **a** of H4634
23 by name, out of the **a** of the Philistines, H4630
26 he should defy the **a** of the living God? H4634
36 he hath defied the **a** of the living God. H4634
45 the **a** of Israel, whom thou hast defied. H4634
23: 3 Keilah against the **a** of the Philistines? H4634
28: 1 gathered their **a** together for warfare, H4264
29: 1 together all their **a** to Aphek: and the H4264
2Ki 25:23 And when all the captains of the **a**, they H2428
26 the captains of the **a**, arose, and came H2428
1Ch 11:26 Also the valiant men of the **a** *were*, H2428
2Ch 16: 4 the captains of his **a** against the cities H2428
Job 25: 3 Is there any number of his **a**? and upon H1416
Ps 44: 9 shame; and goest not forth with our **a**. H6635
60:10 God, *which* didst not go out with our **a**? H6635
68:12 Kings of **a** did flee apace: and she that H6635
Song 6:13 As it were the company of two **a**. H4264
Isa 34: 2 *his* fury upon all their **a**: he hath utterly H6635
Mt 22: 7 he sent forth his **a**, and destroyed those G4753
Lk 21:20 compassed with **a**, then know that the G4760
Heb 11:34 turned to flight the **a** of the aliens. G3925
Rev 19:14 And the **a** *which were* in heaven G4753
19 earth, and their **a**, gathered together to G4753

ARMONI

2Sa 21: 8 bare unto Saul, **A** and Mephibosheth; H764

ARMOUR

1Sa 14: 1 man that bare his **a**, Come, and let us H3627
6 man that bare his **a**, Come, and let us H3627
17:38 And Saul armed David with his **a**, and H4055
39 And David girded his sword upon his **a**, H4055
54 Jerusalem; but he put his **a** in his tent. H3627
31: 9 stripped off his **a**, and sent into the land H3627
10 And they put his **a** in the house of H3627
2Sa 2:21 and take thee his **a**. But Asahel would H2488
18:15 And ten young men that bare Joab's **a** H3627
1Ki 10:25 garments, and **a**, and spices, horses, H5402
22:38 they washed his **a**; according unto the H2185
2Ki 3:21 **a**, and upward, and stood in the border. H2290
10: 2 and horses, a fenced city also, and **a**; H5402
20:13 *all* the house of his **a**, and all that was H3627
1Ch 10: 9 his head, and his **a**, and sent into the H3627
10 And they put his **a** in the house of their H3627
Isa 22: 8 day to the **a** of the house of the forest. H5402
39: 2 all the house of his **a**, and all that was H3627
Ezk 38: 4 with all sorts *of* **a**, *even* a great company
Lk 11:22 from him all his **a** wherein he trusted, G3833
Ro 13:12 and let us put on the **a** of light. G3696
2Co 6: 7 of God, by the **a** of righteousness on G3696
Eph 6:11 Put on the whole **a** of God, that ye may G3833
13 Wherefore take unto you the whole **a** of G3833

ARMOURBEARER

Jdg 9:54 man his **a**, and said unto him, H5375+H3627
1Sa 14: 7 And his **a** said unto him, Do H5375+H3627
12 and his **a**, and said, Come H5375+H3627
12 said unto his **a**, Come up after H5375+H3627
13 feet, and his **a** after him: and H5375+H3627
13 and his **a** slew after him. H5375+H3627
14 and his **a** made, was about H5375+H3627
17 and his **a** *were* not *there*. H5375+H3627
16:21 greatly; and he became his **a**. H5375+H3627
31: 4 Then said Saul unto his **a**, H5375+H3627
4 me. But his **a** would not; for he H5375+H3627
5 And when his **a** saw that Saul H5375+H3627
6 sons, and his **a**, and all his H5375+H3627
2Sa 23:37 **a** to Joab the son of Zeruiah, H5375+H3627
1Ch 10: 4 Then said Saul to his **a**, Draw H5375+H3627
4 me. But his **a** would not; for he H5375+H3627
5 And when his **a** saw that Saul H5375+H3627
11:39 **a** of Joab the son of Zeruiah, H5375+H3627

ARMOURY

Neh 3:19 up to the **a** at the turning *of the wall*. H5402
Song 4: 4 builded for an **a**, whereon there hang H8530
Jer 50:25 The LORD hath opened his **a**, and hath H214

ARMS

Gen 49:24 in strength, and the **a** of his hands were H2220
Dt 33:27 *are* the everlasting **a**: and he shall H2220
Jdg 15:14 *were* upon his **a** became as flax that H2220
16:12 brake them from off his **a** like a thread. H2220
2Sa 22:35 that a bow of steel is broken by mine **a**. H2220
2Ki 9:24 between his **a**, and the arrow went H2220
Job 22: 9 **a** of the fatherless have been broken. H2220
Ps 18:34 that a bow of steel is broken by mine **a**. H2220
37:17 For the **a** of the wicked shall be broken: H2220
Prv 31:17 with strength, and strengtheneth her **a**. H2220
Isa 44:12 the strength of his **a**: yea, he is hungry, H2220
49:22 thy sons in *their* **a**, and thy daughters H2684
51: 5 gone forth, and mine **a** shall judge the H2220
Ezk 13:20 them from your **a**, and will let the souls H2220
30:22 and will break his **a**, the strong, and H2220
24 And I will strengthen the **a** of the king H2220
24 break Pharaoh's **a**, and he shall groan H2220
25 But I will strengthen the **a** of the king of H2220
25 of Babylon, and the **a** of Pharaoh shall H2220
Dan 2:32 his breast and his **a** of silver, his belly H1872
10: 6 of fire, and his **a** and his feet like in H2220
11:15 cities: and the **a** of the south shall not H2220
22 And with the **a** of a flood shall they be H2220
31 And **a** shall stand on his part, and they H2220
Hos 7:15 *and* strengthened their **a**, yet do they H2220
11: 3 **a**; but they knew not that I healed them. H2220
Mk 9:36 taken him in his **a**, he said unto them, G1723
10:16 And he took them up in his **a**, put *his* G1723
Lk 2:28 Then took he him up in his **a**, and G43

ARMY

Gen 26:26 and Phichol the chief captain of his **a**. H6635
Ex 14: 9 his horsemen, and his **a**, and overtook H2428
Dt 11: 4 And what he did unto the **a** of Egypt, H2428
Jdg 4: 7 captain of Jabin's **a**, with his chariots H6635
8: 6 that we should give bread unto thine **a**? H6635
9:29 Increase thine **a**, and come out. H6635
1Sa 4: 2 **a** in the field about four thousand men. H4634
12 out of the **a**, and came to Shiloh H4634
16 came out of the **a**, and I fled to day out H4634
16 to day out of the **a**. And he said, What H4634
17:21 put the battle in array, **a** against army. H4634
21 put the battle in array, army against **a**. H4634
22 **a**, and came and saluted his brethren. H4634
48 ran toward the **a** to meet the Philistine. H4634
1Ki 20:19 city, and the **a** which followed them. H2428
25 And number thee an **a**, like the army H2428
25 And number thee an army, like the **a** H2428
2Ki 25: 5 And the **a** of the Chaldees pursued H2428
5 and all his **a** were scattered from him. H2428
10 And all the **a** of the Chaldees, that *were* H2428
1Ch 20: 1 forth the power of the **a**, and wasted the H6635
27:34 the general of the king's **a** *was* Joab. H6635
2Ch 13: 3 in array with an **a** of valiant men of H2428
14: 8 And Asa had an **a** *of men* that bare H2428
20:21 out before the **a**, and to say, Praise the H2502
24:24 For the **a** of the Syrians came with a H2428
25: 7 O king, let not the **a** of Israel go with H6635
9 I have given to the **a** of Israel? And the H1416
10 them, *to wit*, the **a** that was come to H1416

2Ch 25:13 But the soldiers of the **a** which H1416
26:13 hand *was* an **a**, three hundred H2428+H6635
Neh 2: 9 of the **a** and horsemen with me. H2428
4: 2 his brethren and the **a** of Samaria, and H2428
Job 29:25 **a**, as one *that* comforteth the mourners. H1416
Song 6: 4 Jerusalem, terrible as *an* **a** with banners.
10 sun, *and* terrible as *an* **a** with banners?
Isa 36: 2 with a great **a**. And he stood by the H2426
43:17 and horse, the **a** and the power; they H2428
Jer 32: 2 For then the king of Babylon's **a** H2428
34: 1 and all his **a**, and all the kingdoms H2428
7 When the king of Babylon's **a** fought H2428
21 **a**, which are gone up from you. H2428
35:11 for fear of the **a** of the Chaldeans, and H2428
11 and for fear of the **a** of the Syrians: so H2428
37: 5 Then Pharaoh's **a** was come forth out H2428
7 me; Behold, Pharaoh's **a**, which is come H2428
10 For though ye had smitten the whole **a** H2428
11 And it came to pass, that when the **a** of H2428
11 from Jerusalem for fear of Pharaoh's **a**, H2428
38: 3 king of Babylon's **a**, which shall take it. H2428
39: 1 and all his **a** against Jerusalem, H2428
5 But the Chaldeans' **a** pursued after H2428
46: 2 Against Egypt, against the **a** of H2428
22 march with an **a**, and come against her H2428
52: 4 he and all his **a**, against Jerusalem, H2428
8 But the **a** of the Chaldeans pursued H2428
8 and all his **a** was scattered from him. H2428
14 And all the **a** of the Chaldeans, that H2428
Ezk 17:17 with *his* mighty **a** and great company H2428
27:10 of Phut were in thine **a**, thy men of war: H2428
11 The men of Arvad with thine **a** *were* H2428
29:18 caused his **a** to serve a great service H2428
18 no wages, nor his **a**, for Tyrus, for the H2428
19 prey; and it shall be the wages for his **a**. H2428
32:31 and all his **a** slain by the sword, H2428
37:10 upon their feet, an exceeding great **a**. H2428
38: 4 and all thine **a**, horses and horsemen, H2428
15 a great company, and a mighty **a**: H2428
Dan 3:20 that *were* in his **a** to bind Shadrach, H2429
4:35 to his will in the **a** of heaven, and H2429
11: 7 come with an **a**, and shall enter into H2428
13 with a great **a** and with much riches. H2428
25 south with a great **a**; and the king of the H2428
25 great and mighty **a**; but he shall not H2428
26 him, and his **a** shall overflow: and H2428
Joel 2:11 voice before his **a**: for his camp *is* very H2428
20 you the northern *a*, and will drive him
25 my great **a** which I sent among you. H2428
Zec 9: 8 because of the **a**, because of him that H4675
Act 23:27 came I with an **a**, and rescued him, *G4753*
Rev 9:16 And the number of the **a** of the *G4753*
19:19 that sat on the horse, and against his **a**. *G4753*

ARNAN
1Ch 3:21 the sons of **A**, the sons of Obadiah, H770

ARNON
Nu 21:13 on the other side of **A**, which *is* in the H769
13 of the Amorites: for **A** *is* the border of H769
14 in the Red sea, and in the brooks of **A**, H769
24 his land from **A** unto Jabbok, even unto H769
26 all his land out of his hand, even unto **A**. H769
28 *and* the lords of the high places of **A**. H769
22:36 border of **A**, which *is* in the utmost coast. H769
Dt 2:24 and pass over the river **A**: behold, I have H769
36 of the river of **A**, and *from* the city that H769
3: 8 from the river of **A** unto mount Hermon; H769
12 *is* by the river **A**, and half mount Gilead, H769
16 even unto the river **A** half the valley, and H769
4:48 the bank of the river **A**, even unto mount H769
Jos 12: 1 the sun, from the river **A** unto mount H769
2 bank of the river **A**, and from the middle H769
13: 9 bank of the river **A**, and the city that *is* in H769
16 bank of the river **A**, and the city that *is* in H769
Jdg 11:13 out of Egypt, from **A** even unto Jabbok, H769
18 the other side of **A**, but came not within H769
18 of Moab: for **A** *was* the border of Moab. H769
22 the Amorites, from **A** even unto Jabbok, H769
26 by the coasts of **A**, three hundred years? H769
2Ki 10:33 by the river **A**, even Gilead and Bashan. H769
Isa 16: 2 of Moab shall be at the fords of **A**. H769
Jer 48:20 cry; tell ye it in **A**, that Moab is spoiled, H769

AROD
Nu 26:17 Of **A**, the family of the Arodites: of Areli, H720

ARODI
Gen 46:16 Shuni, and Ezbon, Eri, and **A**, and Areli. H722

ARODITES
Nu 26:17 Of Arod, the family of the **A**: of Areli, the H722

AROER
Nu 32:34 of Gad built Dibon, and Ataroth, and **A**, H6177
Dt 2:36 From **A**, which *is* by the brink of the H6177
3:12 at that time, from **A**, which *is* by the H6177
4:48 From **A**, which *is* by the bank of the H6177
Jos 12: 2 *and* ruled from **A**, which *is* upon the H6177
13: 9 From **A**, that *is* upon the bank of the H6177
16 And their coast was from **A**, that *is* on H6177
25 Ammon, unto **A** that *is* before Rabbah; H6177
Jdg 11:26 her towns, and in **A** and her towns, and H6177
33 And he smote them from **A**, even till H6177
1Sa 30:28 And to *them* which *were* in **A**, and to H6177
2Sa 24: 5 and pitched in **A**, on the right side of H6177
2Ki 10:33 the Manassites, from **A**, which *is* by the H6177
1Ch 5: 8 in **A**, even unto Nebo and Baalmeon: H6177
Isa 17: 2 The cities of **A** *are* forsaken: they shall H6177
Jer 48:19 O inhabitant of **A**, stand by the way, H6177

AROERITE
1Ch 11:44 and Jehiel the sons of Hothan the **A**, H6200

AROSE
Gen 19:15 And when the morning **a**, then the H5927
33 not when she lay down, nor when she **a**. H6965
35 and the younger **a**, and lay with him; H6965
35 not when she lay down, nor when she **a**. H6965
24:10 in his hand: and he **a**, and went to H6965
61 And Rebekah **a**, and her damsels, and H6965
37: 7 and, lo, my sheaf **a**, and also stood H6965
38:19 And she **a**, and went away, and laid by H6965
Ex 1: 8 Now there **a** up a new king over Egypt, H6965
Dt 34:10 And there **a** not a prophet since in H6965
Jos 8: 3 So Joshua **a**, and all the people of war, H6965
19 And the ambush **a** quickly out of their H6965
18: 8 And the men **a**, and went away: and H6965
24: 9 king of Moab, **a** and warred against H6965
Jdg 2:10 fathers: and there **a** another generation H6965
3:20 God unto thee. And he **a** out of *his* seat. H6965
4: 9 **a**, and went with Barak to Kedesh. H6965
5: 7 **a**, that I arose a mother in Israel. H6965
7 arose, that I **a** a mother in Israel. H6965
6:28 And when the men of the city **a** early in H7925
8:21 And Gideon **a**, and slew Zebah and H6965
10: 1 And after Abimelech there **a** to defend H6965
3 And after him **a** Jair, a Gileadite, and H6965
13:11 And Manoah **a**, and went after his wife, H6965
16: 3 And Samson lay till midnight, and **a** at H6965
19: 3 And her husband **a**, and went after her, H6965
5 day, when they **a** early in the morning, H7925
8 And he **a** early in the morning on the H7925
20: 8 And all the people **a** as one man, H6965
18 And the children of Israel **a**, and went H6965
Ru 1: 6 Then she **a** with her daughters in law, H6965
1Sa 3: 6 And Samuel **a** and went to Eli, and H6965
8 third time. And he **a** and went to Eli, H6965
5: 3 And when they of Ashdod **a** early on H7925
4 And when they **a** early on the morrow H7925
9:26 And they **a** early: and it came to pass H7925
26 away. And Saul **a**, and they went out H6965
13:15 And Samuel **a**, and gat him up from H6965
17:35 and when he **a** against me, I caught H6965
48 the Philistine **a**, and came and drew H6965
52 And the men of Israel and of Judah **a**, H6965
18:27 Wherefore David **a** and went, he and H6965
20:25 wall: and Jonathan **a**, and Abner sat by H6965
34 So Jonathan **a** from the table in fierce H6965
41 lad was gone, David **a** out of *a place* H6965
42 for ever. And he **a** and departed: and H6965
21:10 And David **a**, and fled that day for fear H6965
23:13 six hundred, **a** and departed out of H6965
16 And Jonathan Saul's son **a**, and went to H6965
24 And they **a**, and went to Ziph before H6965
24: 4 thee. Then David **a**, and cut off the skirt H6965
8 David also **a** afterward, and went out H6965
25: 1 And David **a**, and went down to the H6965
41 And she **a**, and bowed herself on *her* H6965
42 And Abigail hasted, and **a**, and rode H6965
26: 2 Then Saul **a**, and went down to the H6965
5 And David **a**, and came to the place H6965
27: 2 And David **a**, and he passed over with H6965
28:23 **a** from the earth, and sat upon the bed. H6965
31:12 All the valiant men **a**, and went all H6965
2Sa 2:15 Then there **a** and went over by number H6965
6: 2 And David **a**, and went with all the H6965
11: 2 that David **a** from off his bed, and H6965
12:17 And the elders of his house **a**, *and went* H6965
2Sa 12:20 Then David **a** from the earth, and H6965
13:29 all the king's sons **a**, and every man gat H6965
31 Then the king **a**, and tare his garments, H6965
14:23 So Joab **a** and went to Geshur, and H6965
31 Then Joab **a**, and came to Absalom H6965
15: 9 in peace. So he **a**, and went to Hebron. H6965
17:22 Then David **a**, and all the people that H6965
23 *his* ass, and **a**, and gat him home to H6965
19: 8 Then the king **a**, and sat in the gate. H6965
23:10 He **a**, and smote the Philistines until his H6965
1Ki 1:50 of Solomon, and **a**, and went, and H6965
2:40 And Shimei **a**, and saddled his ass, and H6965
3:20 And she **a** at midnight, and took my H6965
8:54 unto the LORD, he **a** from before the H6965
11:18 And they **a** out of Midian, and came to H6965
40 And Jeroboam **a**, and fled into Egypt, H6965
14: 4 And Jeroboam's wife did so, and **a**, and H6965
17 And Jeroboam's wife **a**, and departed, H6965
17:10 So he **a** and went to Zarephath. And H6965
19: 3 And when he saw *that*, he **a**, and went H6965
8 And he **a**, and did eat and drink, and H6965
21 they did eat. Then he **a**, and went after H6965
2Ki 1:15 of him. And he **a**, and went down with H6965
4:30 leave thee. And he **a**, and followed her. H6965
7: 7 Wherefore they **a** and fled in the H6965
12 And the king **a** in the night, and said H6965
8: 2 And the woman **a**, and did after the H6965
9: 6 And he **a**, and went into the house; and H6965
10:12 And he **a** and departed, and came to H6965
11: 1 she **a** and destroyed all the seed royal. H6965
12:20 And his servants **a**, and made a H6965
19:35 and when they **a** early in the morning, H7925
23:25 neither after him **a** there *any* like him. H6965
25:26 of the armies, **a**, and came to Egypt: H6965
1Ch 10:12 They **a**, all the valiant men, and took H6965
20: 4 this, that there **a** war at Gezer with the H5975
2Ch 22:10 son was dead, she **a** and destroyed all H6965
29:12 Then the Levites **a**, Mahath the son of H6965
30:14 And they **a** and took away the altars H6965
27 Then the priests the Levites **a** and H6965
36:16 of the LORD **a** against his people, H5927
Ezr 9: 5 And at the evening sacrifice I **a** up H6965
10: 5 Then **a** Ezra, and made the chief H6965
Neh 2:12 And I **a** in the night, I and some few H6965
Est 8: 4 So Esther **a**, and stood before the king, H6965
Job 1:20 Then Job **a**, and rent his mantle, and H6965
19:18 Yea, young children despised me; I **a**, H6965
29: 8 and the aged **a**, *and* stood up. H6965
Ps 76: 9 When God **a** to judgment, to save all H6965
Ecc 1: 5 and hasteth to his place where he **a**. H2224
Isa 37:36 and when they **a** early in the morning, H7925
Jer 41: 2 Then **a** Ishmael the son of Nethaniah, H6965
Ezk 3:23 Then I **a**, and went forth into the plain: H6965
Dan 6:19 Then the king **a** very early in the H6966
Jna 3: 3 So Jonah **a**, and went unto Nineveh, H6965
6 Nineveh, and he **a** from his throne, and H6965
Mt 2:14 When he **a**, he took the young child and *G1453*
21 And he **a**, and took the young child and *G1453*
8:15 and she **a**, and ministered unto them. *G1453*
24 And, behold, there **a** a great tempest in *G1096*
26 faith? Then he **a**, and rebuked the winds *G1453*
9: 7 And he **a**, and departed to his house. *G1453*
9 Follow me. And he **a**, and followed him. *G450*
19 And Jesus **a**, and followed him, and *so* *G1453*
25 took her by the hand, and the maid **a**. *G1453*
25: 7 Then all those virgins **a**, and trimmed *G1453*
26:62 And the high priest **a**, and said unto him, *G450*
27:52 many bodies of the saints which slept **a**, *G1453*
Mk 2:12 And immediately he **a**, took up the bed, *G1453*
14 Follow me. And he **a** and followed him. *G450*
4:37 And there **a** a great storm of wind, and *G1096*
39 And he **a**, and rebuked the wind, and *G1326*
5:42 And straightway the damsel **a**, and *G450*
7:24 And from thence he **a**, and went into the *G450*
9:27 by the hand, and lifted him up; and he **a**. *G450*
10: 1 And he **a** from thence, and cometh into *G450*
14:57 And there **a** certain, and bare false *G450*
Lk 1:39 And Mary **a** in those days, and went into *G450*
4:38 And he **a** out of the synagogue, and *G450*
39 she **a** and ministered unto them. *G450*
6: 8 in the midst. And he **a** and stood forth. *G450*
48 and when the flood **a**, the stream beat *G1096*
8:24 we perish. Then he **a**, and rebuked the *G1453*
55 And her spirit came again, and she **a** *G450*
9:46 Then there **a** a reasoning among them, *G1525*
15:14 And when he had spent all, there **a** a *G1096*
20 And he **a**, and came to his father. But *G450*
23: 1 And the whole multitude of them **a**, and *G450*
24:12 Then **a** Peter, and ran unto the *G450*

Jn 3:25 Then there a a question between *some* G1096
6:18 And the sea a by reason of a great wind G1326
11:29 As soon as she heard *that*, she a G1453
Act 5: 6 And the young men a, wound him up, G450
6: 1 multiplied, there a a murmuring of the G1096
9 Then there a certain of the synagogue, G450
7:18 Till another king a, which knew not G450
8:27 And he a and went: and, behold, a man G450
9: 8 And Saul a from the earth; and when G1453
18 sight forthwith, and a, and was baptized. G450
34 make thy bed. And he a immediately. G450
39 Then Peter a and went with them. When G450
11:19 the persecution that a about Stephen G1096
19:23 And the same time there a no small stir G1096
23: 7 And when he had so said, there a a G1096
9 And there a a great cry: and the scribes G1096
9 the Pharisees' part a, and strove, saying, G450
10 And when there a a great dissension, G1096
27:14 But not long after there a against it a G906
Rev 9: 2 pit; and there a a smoke out of the pit, G305

ARPAD
2Ki 18:34 Where *are* the gods of Hamath, and of A? H774
19:13 and the king of A, and the king of the city H774
Isa 10: 9 as A? *is* not Samaria as Damascus? H774
Jer 49:23 confounded, and A: for they have heard H774

ARPHAD
Isa 36:19 Where *are* the gods of Hamath and A? H774
37:13 and the king of A, and the king of the city H774

ARPHAXAD
Gen 10:22 and Asshur, and A, and Lud, and Aram. H775
24 And A begat Salah; and Salah begat H775
11:10 and begat A two years after the flood: H775
11 And Shem lived after he begat A five H775
12 And A lived five and thirty years, and H775
13 And A lived after he begat Salah four H775
1Ch 1:17 and Asshur, and A, and Lud, and Aram, H775
18 And A begat Shelah, and Shelah begat H775
24 Shem, A, Shelah, H775
Lk 3:36 was *the son* of A, which was *the son* of G742

ARRAY
Jdg 20:20 in a to fight against them at Gibeah. H6186
22 battle again in a in the place where H6186
22 they put themselves in a the first day. H6186
30 in a against Gibeah, as at other times. H6186
33 put themselves in a at Baal-tamar: and H6186
1Sa 4: 2 And the Philistines put themselves in a H6186
17: 2 the battle in a against the Philistines. H6186
8 to set *your* battle in a? *am* not I a H6186
21 put the battle in a, army against army. H6186
2Sa 10: 8 put the battle in a at the entering in of H6186
9 and put *them* in a against the Syrians: H6186
10 in a against the children of Ammon. H6186
17 a against David, and fought with him. H6186
1Ki 20:12 Set *yourselves in* a. And they set
12 they set *themselves in* a against the city.
1Ch 19: 9 put the battle in a before the gate of the H6186
10 and put *them* in a against the Syrians. H6186
11 in a against the children of Ammon. H6186
17 and set *the battle* in a against them. So H6186
17 put the battle in a against the Syrians, H6186
2Ch 13: 3 And Abijah set the battle in a with an H631
3 also set the battle in a against him with H6186
14:10 they set the battle in a in the valley of H6186
Est 6: 9 that they may a the man *withal* whom H3847
Job 6: 4 God do set themselves in a against me. H6186
40:10 and a thyself with glory and beauty. H3847
Isa 22: 7 shall set themselves in a at the gate. H7896
Jer 6:23 horses, set in a as men for war against H6186
43:12 and he shall a himself with the land H5844
50: 9 set themselves in a against her; from H6186
14 Put yourselves in a against Babylon H6186
42 *every one* put in a, like a man to the H6186
Joel 2: 5 as a strong people set in battle a. H6186
1Ti 2: 9 hair, or gold, or pearls, or costly a; G2441

ARRAYED
Gen 41:42 hand, and a him in vestures of fine H3847
2Ch 5:12 brethren, *being* a in white linen, having H3847
28:15 among them, and a them, and shod H3847
Est 6:11 and the horse, and a Mordecai, and H3847
Mt 6:29 all his glory was not a like one of these. G4016
Lk 12:27 all his glory was not a like one of these. G4016
23:11 mocked *him*, and a him in a gorgeous G4016
Act 12:21 And upon a set day Herod, a in royal G1746
Rev 7:13 these which are a in white robes? and G4016
Rev 17: 4 And the woman was a in purple and G4016
19: 8 that she should be a in fine linen, clean G4016

ARRIVED
Lk 8:26 And they a at the country of the G2668
Act 20:15 and the next *day* we a at Samos, and G3846

ARROGANCY
1Sa 2: 3 proudly; let *not* a come out of your H6277
Prv 8:13 evil: pride, and a, and the evil way, and H1347
Isa 13:11 I will cause the a of the proud to cease, H1347
Jer 48:29 loftiness, and his a, and his pride, and H1347

ARROW
1Sa 20:36 the lad ran, he shot an a beyond him. H2678
37 to the place of the a which Jonathan H2678
37 lad, and said, *Is* not the a beyond thee? H2678
2Ki 9:24 his arms, and the a went out at his H2678
13:17 shot. And he said, The a of the LORD'S H2671
17 and the a of deliverance from H2671
19:32 city, nor shoot an a there, nor come H2671
Job 41:28 The a cannot make him flee: H1121+H7198
Ps 11: 2 make ready their a upon the string, H2671
64: 7 But God shall shoot at them *with* an a; H2671
91: 5 night; *nor* for the a *that* flieth by day; H2671
Prv 25:18 *is* a maul, and a sword, and a sharp a. H2671
Isa 37:33 city, nor shoot an a there, nor come H2671
Jer 9: 8 Their tongue *is as* an a shot out; it H2671
Lam 3:12 his bow, and set me as a mark for the a. H2671
Zec 9:14 them, and his a shall go forth as the H2671

ARROWS
Nu 24: 8 and pierce *them* through with his a. H2671
Dt 32:23 them; I will spend mine a upon them. H2671
42 I will make mine a drunk with blood, H2671
1Sa 20:20 And I will shoot three a on the side H2671
21 Go, find out the a. If I expressly say H2671
21 the lad, Behold, the a *are* on this side of H2671
22 man, Behold, the a *are* beyond thee; go H2671
36 find out now the a which I shoot. *And* H2671
38 up the a, and came to his master. H2678
2Sa 22:15 And he sent out a, and scattered them; H2671
2Ki 13:15 Take bow and a. And he took unto him H2671
15 And he took unto him bow and a. H2671
18 And he said, Take the a. And he took H2671
1Ch 12: 2 and *shooting* a out of a bow, *even* of H2671
2Ch 26:15 bulwarks, to shoot a and great stones H2671
Job 6: 4 For the a of the Almighty *are* within H2671
Ps 7:13 his a against the persecutors. H2671
18:14 Yea, he sent out his a, and scattered H2671
21:12 make ready *thine a* upon thy strings
38: 2 For thine a stick fast in me, and thy H2671
45: 5 Thine a *are* sharp in the heart of the H2671
57: 4 and a, and their tongue a sharp sword. H2671
58: 7 *shoot* his a, let them be as cut in pieces. H2671
64: 3 *bows to shoot* their a, *even* bitter words: H2671
76: 3 There brake he the a of the bow, the H7565
77:17 out a sound: thine a also went abroad. H2687
120: 4 Sharp a of the mighty, with coals of H2671
127: 4 As a *are* in the hand of a mighty man; H2671
144: 6 shoot out thine a, and destroy them. H2671
Prv 26:18 who casteth firebrands, a, and death, H2671
Isa 5:28 Whose a *are* sharp, and all their bows H2671
7:24 With a and with bows shall *men* come H2671
Jer 50: 9 be taken: their a *shall be* as of a mighty H2671
14 at her, spare no a: for she hath sinned H2671
51:11 Make bright the a; gather the shields: H2671
Lam 3:13 He hath caused the a of his quiver to H1121
Ezk 5:16 When I shall send upon them the evil a H2671
21:21 he made *his* a bright, he consulted H2671
39: 3 thine a to fall out of thy right hand. H2671
9 the bows and the a, and the handstaves, H2671
Hab 3:11 at the light of thine a they went, *and* at H2671

ART See the Appendix.

ARTAXERXES
Ezr 4: 7 And in the days of A wrote Bishlam, H783
7 companions, unto A king of Persia; and H783
8 Jerusalem to A the king in this sort: H783
11 him, *even* unto A the king; Thy servants H783
6:14 Cyrus, and Darius, and A king of Persia. H783
7: 1 Now after these things, in the reign of A H783
7 in the seventh year of A the king. H783
11 letter that the king A gave unto Ezra the H783
12 A, king of kings, unto Ezra the priest, a H783
21 And I, *even* I A the king, do make a H783
8: 1 from Babylon, in the reign of A the king. H783
Neh 2: 1 twentieth year of A the king, *that* wine H783
Neh 5:14 and thirtieth year of A the king, *that is*, H783
13: 6 thirtieth year of A king of Babylon came H783

ARTAXERXES'
Ezr 4:23 Now when the copy of king A letter *was* H783

ARTEMAS
Tit 3:12 When I shall send A unto thee, or G734

ARTIFICER
Gen 4:22 instructor of every a in brass and iron: H2794
Isa 3: 3 the cunning a, and the eloquent orator. H2796

ARTIFICERS
1Ch 29: 5 by the hands of a. And who *then is* H2796
2Ch 34:11 Even to the a and builders gave they *it*, H2796

ARTILLERY
1Sa 20:40 And Jonathan gave his a unto his lad, H3627

ARTS
Act 19:19 used curious a brought their books G4021

ARUBOTH
1Ki 4:10 The son of Hesed, in A; to him *pertained* H700

ARUMAH
Jdg 9:41 And Abimelech dwelt at A: and Zebul H725

ARVAD
Ezk 27: 8 The inhabitants of Zidon and A were thy H719
11 The men of A with thine army *were* H719

ARVADITE
Gen 10:18 And the A, and the Zemarite, and the H721
1Ch 1:16 And the A, and the Zemarite, and the H721

ARZA
1Ki 16: 9 of A steward of *his* house in Tirzah. H777

AS See the Appendix.

ASA
1Ki 15: 8 and A his son reigned in his stead. H609
9 king of Israel reigned A over Judah. H609
11 And A did *that which was* right in the H609
13 in a grove; and A destroyed her idol, and H609
16 And there was war between A and H609
17 to go out or come in to A king of Judah. H609
18 Then A took all the silver and the gold H609
18 his servants: and king A sent them to H609
20 So Ben-hadad hearkened unto king A, H609
22 Then king A made a proclamation H609
22 had builded; and king A built with them H609
23 The rest of all the acts of A, and all his H609
24 And A slept with his fathers, and was H609
25 the second year of A king of Judah, and H609
28 Even in the third year of A king of Judah H609
32 And there was war between A and H609
33 In the third year of A king of Judah H609
16: 8 In the twenty and sixth year of A king of H609
10 and seventh year of A king of Judah, and H609
15 In the twenty and seventh year of A king H609
23 In the thirty and first year of A king of H609
29 And in the thirty and eighth year of A H609
22:41 And Jehoshaphat the son of A began to H609
43 And he walked in all the ways of A his H609
46 of his father A, he took out of the land. H609
1Ch 3:10 his son, A his son, Jehoshaphat his son, H609
9:16 the son of A, the son of Elkanah, H609
2Ch 14: 1 city of David: and A his son reigned in H609
2 And A did *that which was* good and H609
8 And A had an army *of men* that bare H609
10 Then A went out against him, and they H609
11 And A cried unto the LORD his God, and H609
12 Ethiopians before A, and before Judah; H609
13 And A and the people that *were* with H609
15: 2 And he went out to meet A, and said H609
2 him, Hear ye me, A, and all Judah and H609
8 And when A heard these words, and the H609
10 in the fifteenth year of the reign of A. H609
16 the mother of A the king, he removed H609
16 in a grove: and A cut down her idol, and H609
17 the heart of A was perfect all his days. H609
19 five and thirtieth year of the reign of A. H609
16: 1 year of the reign of A Baasha king of H609
1 go out or come in to A king of Judah. H609
2 Then A brought out silver and gold out H609
4 And Ben-hadad hearkened unto king A, H609

2Ch 16: 6 Then A the king took all Judah; and they H609
7 the seer came to A king of Judah, and H609
10 Then A was wroth with the seer, and put H609
10 of this *thing.* And A oppressed *some* of H609
11 And, behold, the acts of A, first and last, H609
12 And A in the thirty and ninth year of his H609
13 And A slept with his fathers, and died in H609
17: 2 Ephraim, which A his father had taken. H609
20:32 And he walked in the way of A his H609
21:12 nor in the ways of A king of Judah, H609
Jer 41: 9 *was* it which A the king had made for H609
Mt 1: 7 Roboam begat Abia; and Abia begat A; *G760*
8 And A begat Josaphat; and Josaphat *G760*

ASAHEL
2Sa 2:18 and Abishai, and A: and Asahel *was as* H6214
18 and A *was as* light of foot as a wild roe. H6214
19 And A pursued after Abner; and in H6214
20 *Art* thou A? And he answered, I *am.* H6214
21 his armour. But A would not turn aside H6214
22 And Abner said again to A, Turn thee H6214
23 where A fell down and died stood still. H6214
30 David's servants nineteen men and A. H6214
32 And they took up A, and buried him in H6214
3:27 he died, for the blood of A his brother. H6214
30 their brother A at Gibeon in the battle. H6214
23:24 A the brother of Joab *was* one of the H6214
1Ch 2:16 Abishai, and Joab, and A, three. H6214
11:26 the armies *were,* A the brother of Joab, H6214
27: 7 the fourth month *was* A the brother of H6214
2Ch 17: 8 Zebadiah, and A, and Shemiramoth, H6214
31:13 and Nahath, and A, and Jerimoth, and H6214
Ezr 10:15 Only Jonathan the son of A and H6214

ASAHIAH
2Ki 22:12 and A a servant of the king's, saying, H6222
14 Shaphan, and A, went unto Huldah the H6222

ASAIAH
1Ch 4:36 and Jeshohaiah, and A, and Adiel, and H6222
6:30 Shimea his son, Haggiah his son, A his H6222
9: 5 And of the Shilonites; A the firstborn, H6222
15: 6 Of the sons of Merari; A the chief, and H6222
11 the Levites, for Uriel, A, and Joel, H6222
2Ch 34:20 and A a servant of the king's, saying, H6222

ASAPH
2Ki 18:18 and Joah the son of A the recorder. H623
37 and Joah the son of A the recorder, to H623
1Ch 6:39 And his brother A, who stood on his right H623
39 right hand, *even* A the son of Berachiah, H623
9:15 of Micah, the son of Zichri, the son of A; H623
15:17 of his brethren, A the son of Berechiah; H623
19 So the singers, Heman, A, and Ethan, H623
16: 5 A the chief, and next to him Zechariah, H623
5 but A made a sound with cymbals; H623
7 into the hand of A and his brethren. H623
37 of the LORD A and his brethren, to H623
25: 1 of the sons of A, and of Heman, and H623
2 Of the sons of A; Zaccur, and Joseph, and H623
2 the sons of A under the hands of Asaph, H623
2 under the hands of A, which prophesied H623
6 king's order to A, Jeduthun, and Heman. H623
9 Now the first lot came forth for A to H623
26: 1 the son of Kore, of the sons of A. H623
2Ch 5:12 all of them of A, of Heman, of Jeduthun, H623
20:14 of the sons of A, came the spirit of the H623
29:13 the sons of A; Zechariah, and Mattaniah: H623
30 of David, and of A the seer. And they H623
35:15 And the singers the sons of A *were* in H623
15 of David, and A, and Heman, and H623
Ezr 2:41 The singers: the children of A, an H623
3:10 Levites the sons of A with cymbals, to H623
Neh 2: 8 And a letter unto A the keeper of the H623
7:44 The singers: the children of A, an H623
11:17 Zabdi, the son of A, *was* the principal to H623
22 Of the sons of A, the singers *were* over H623
12:35 the son of Zaccur, the son of A: H623
46 For in the days of David and A of old H623
Ps 50:ttl A Psalm of A. H623
73:ttl A Psalm of A. H623
74:ttl Maschil of A. H623
75:ttl Al-taschith, A Psalm *or* Song of A. H623
76:ttl on Neginoth, A Psalm *or* Song of A. H623
77:ttl Musician, to Jeduthun, A Psalm of A. H623
78:ttl Maschil of A. H623
79:ttl A Psalm of A. H623
80:ttl upon Shoshannim-Eduth, A Psalm of A. H623
81:ttl Musician upon Gittith, *A Psalm* of A. H623
Ps 82:ttl A Psalm of A. H623
83:ttl A Song *or* Psalm of A. H623
Isa 36:22 and Joah, the son of A, the recorder, to H623

ASAPH'S
Isa 36: 3 the scribe, and Joah, A son, the recorder. H623

ASAREEL
1Ch 4:16 Ziph, and Ziphah, Tiria, and A. H840

ASARELAH
1Ch 25: 2 and Nethaniah, and A, the sons of Asaph H841

ASA'S
1Ki 15:14 nevertheless A heart was perfect with H609

ASCEND
Jos 6: 5 a up every man straight before him. H5927
Ps 24: 3 Who shall a into the hill of the LORD? H5927
135: 7 He causeth the vapours to a from the H5927
139: 8 If I a up into heaven, thou *art* there: if I H5927
Isa 14:13 thine heart, I will a into heaven, I will H5927
14 I will a above the heights of the clouds; H5927
Jer 10:13 the vapours to a from the ends of the H5927
51:16 the vapours to a from the ends of the H5927
Ezk 38: 9 Thou shalt a and come like a storm, H5927
Jn 6:62 Son of man a up where he was before? *G305*
20:17 say unto them, I a unto my Father, and *G305*
Ro 10: 6 heart, Who shall a into heaven? (that is, *G305*
Rev 17: 8 is not; and shall a out of the bottomless *G305*

ASCENDED
Ex 19:18 the smoke thereof a as the smoke of a H5927
Nu 13:22 And they a by the south, and came H5927
Jos 8:20 smoke of the city a up to heaven, and H5927
21 smoke of the city a, then they turned H5927
10: 7 So Joshua a from Gilgal, he, and all the H5927
15: 3 along to Zin, and a up on the south H5927
Jdg 13:20 angel of the LORD a in the flame of the H5927
20:40 the flame of the city a up to heaven. H5927
Ps 68:18 Thou hast a on high, thou hast led H5927
Prv 30: 4 Who hath a up into heaven, or H5927
Jn 3:13 And no man hath a up to heaven, but he *G305*
20:17 for I am not yet a to my Father: but go *G305*
Act 2:34 For David is not a into the heavens: but *G305*
25: 1 days he a from Caesarea to Jerusalem. *G305*
Eph 4: 8 Wherefore he saith, When he a up on *G305*
9 (Now that he a, what is it but that he also *G305*
10 is the same also that a up far above all *G305*
Rev 8: 4 a up before God out of the angel's hand. *G305*
11:12 up hither. And they a up to heaven in a *G305*

ASCENDETH
Rev 11: 7 the beast that a out of the bottomless *G305*
14:11 And the smoke of their torment a up for *G305*

ASCENDING
Gen 28:12 angels of God a and descending on it. H5927
1Sa 28:13 Saul, I saw gods a out of the earth. H5927
Lk 19:28 he went before, a up to Jerusalem. *G305*
Jn 1:51 a and descending upon the Son of man. *G305*
Rev 7: 2 And I saw another angel a from the east, *G305*

ASCENT
Nu 34: 4 the south to the a of Akrabbim, and H4608
2Sa 15:30 And David went up by the a of *mount* H4608
1Ki 10: 5 and his a by which he went up H5930
2Ch 9: 4 apparel; and his a by which he went up H5944

ASCRIBE
Dt 32: 3 LORD: a ye greatness unto our God. H3051
Job 36: 3 and will a righteousness to my Maker. H5414
Ps 68:34 A ye strength unto God: his excellency H5414

ASCRIBED
1Sa 18: 8 he said, They have a unto David ten H5414
8 to me they have a *but* thousands: and H5414

ASENATH
Gen 41:45 he gave him to wife A the daughter of H621
50 famine came, which A the daughter of H621
46:20 and Ephraim, which A the daughter of H621

ASER
Lk 2:36 of the tribe of A: she was of a great age, *G768*
Rev 7: 6 Of the tribe of A *were* sealed twelve *G768*

ASH
Isa 44:14 an a, and the rain doth nourish *it.* H766

ASHAMED
Gen 2:25 the man and his wife, and were not a. H954
Nu 12:14 should she not be a seven days? let her H3637
Jdg 3:25 And they tarried till they were a: and, H954
2Sa 10: 5 men were greatly a: and the king said, H3637
19: 3 a steal away when they flee in battle. H3637
2Ki 2:17 And when they urged him till he was a, H954
8:11 until he was a: and the man of God wept. H954
1Ch 19: 5 men were greatly a. And the king said, H3637
2Ch 30:15 and the Levites were a, and sanctified H3637
Ezr 8:22 For I was a to require of the king a band H954
9: 6 And said, O my God, I am a and blush to H954
Job 6:20 hoped; they came thither, and were a. H2659
11: 3 mockest, shall no man make thee a? H3637
19: 3 a *that* ye make yourselves strange to me. H954
Ps 6:10 Let all mine enemies be a and sore H954
10 let them return *and* be a suddenly. H954
25: 2 O my God, I trust in thee: let me not be a, H954
3 Yea, let none that wait on thee be a: let H954
3 be a which transgress without cause. H954
20 let me not be a; for I put my trust in thee. H954
31: 1 be a: deliver me in thy righteousness. H954
17 Let me not be a, O LORD; for I have H954
17 be a, *and* let them be silent in the grave. H954
34: 5 lightened: and their faces were not a. H2659
35:26 Let them be a and brought to confusion H954
37:19 They shall not be a in the evil time: and H954
40:14 Let them be a and confounded together H954
69: 6 GOD of hosts, be a for my sake: let not H954
70: 2 Let them be a and confounded that seek H954
74:21 O let not the oppressed return a: let the H3637
86:17 me may see *it,* and be a: because thou, H954
109:28 let them be a; but let thy servant rejoice. H954
119: 6 Then shall I not be a, when I have respect H954
46 also before kings, and will not be a. H954
78 Let the proud be a; for they dealt H954
80 be sound in thy statutes; that I be not a. H954
116 live: and let me not be a of my hope. H954
127: 5 they shall not be a, but they shall speak H954
Prv 12: 4 maketh a *is* as rottenness in his bones. H954
Isa 1:29 For they shall be a of the oaks which ye H954
20: 5 And they shall be afraid and a of H954
23: 4 Be thou a, O Zidon: for the sea hath H954
24:23 and the sun a, when the LORD of hosts H954
26:11 shall see, and be a for *their* envy at the H954
29:22 be a, neither shall his face now wax pale. H954
30: 5 They were all a of a people *that* could H3001
33: 9 Lebanon is a *and* hewn down: Sharon H2659
41:11 thee shall be a and confounded: they H954
42:17 shall be greatly a, that trust in graven H954
44: 9 see not, nor know; that they may be a. H954
11 Behold, all his fellows shall be a: and the H954
11 shall fear, *and* they shall be a together. H954
45:16 They shall be a, and also confounded, all H954
17 be a nor confounded world without end. H954
24 that are incensed against him shall be a. H954
49:23 for they shall not be a that wait for me. H954
50: 7 a flint, and I know that I shall not be a. H954
54: 4 Fear not; for thou shalt not be a: neither H954
65:13 servants shall rejoice, but ye shall be a: H954
66: 5 appear to your joy, and they shall be a. H954
Jer 2:26 As the thief is a when he is found, so is H1322
26 the house of Israel a; they, their kings, H3001
36 thou also shalt be a of Egypt, as thou H954
36 of Egypt, as thou wast a of Assyria. H954
3: 3 forehead, thou refusedst to be a. H3637
6:15 Were they a when they had committed H3001
15 they were not at all a, neither could they H954
8: 9 The wise *men* are a, they are dismayed H3001
12 Were they a when they had committed H3001
12 they were not at all a, neither could they H954
12:13 and they shall be a of your revenues H954
14: 3 empty; they were a and confounded, and H954
4 were a, they covered their heads. H954
15: 9 day: she hath been a and confounded: H954
17:13 thee shall be a, *and* they that depart H954
20:11 they shall be greatly a; for they shall not H954
22:22 then shalt thou be a and confounded for H954
31:19 *my* thigh: I was a, yea, even confounded, H954
48:13 And Moab shall be a of Chemosh, as the H954
13 Israel was a of Beth-el their confidence. H954
50:12 that bare you shall be a: behold, the H2659
Ezk 16:27 which are a of thy lewd way. H3637
61 thy ways, and be a, when thou shalt H3637
32:30 terror they are a of their might; and they H954
36:32 unto you: be a and confounded for H954
43:10 that they may be a of their iniquities: H3637
11 And if they be a of all that they have H3637
Hos 4:19 shall be a because of their sacrifices. H954

Hos 10: 6 and Israel shall be a of his own counsel. H954
Joel 1:11 Be ye a, O ye husbandmen; howl, O ye H3001
2:26 with you: and my people shall never be a. H954
27 else: and my people shall never be a. H954
Mic 3: 7 Then shall the seers be a, and the H954
Zep 3:11 In that day shalt thou not be a for all thy H954
Zec 9: 5 shall be a; and the king shall perish H3001
13: 4 the prophets shall be a every one of his H954
Mk 8:38 Whosoever therefore shall be a of me G1870
38 the Son of man be a, when he cometh in G1870
Lk 9:26 For whosoever shall be a of me and of G1870
26 shall the Son of man be a, when he shall G1870
13:17 adversaries were a: and all the people G2617
16: 3 stewardship: I cannot dig; to beg I am a. G153
Ro 1:16 For I am not a of the gospel of Christ: G1870
5: 5 And hope maketh not a; because the G2617
6:21 a? for the end of those things *is* death. G1870
9:33 believeth on him shall not be a. G2617
10:11 believeth on him shall not be a. G2617
2Co 7:14 of you, I am not a; but as we spake all G2617
9: 4 be a in this same confident boasting. G2617
10: 8 for your destruction, I should not be a: G153
Php 1:20 in nothing I shall be a, but *that* with all G153
2Th 3:14 company with him, that he may be a. G1788
2Ti 1: 8 Be not thou therefore a of the G1870
12 I am not a: for I know whom I have G1870
16 me, and was not a of my chain: G1870
2:15 to be a, rightly dividing the word of truth. G422
Tit 2: 8 be a, having no evil thing to say of you. G1788
Heb 2:11 cause he is not a to call them brethren, G1870
11:16 God is not a to be called their God: G1870
1Pt 3:16 they may be a that falsely accuse your G2617
4:16 a; but let him glorify God on this behalf. G153
1Jn 2:28 and not be a before him at his coming. G153

ASHAN
Jos 15:42 Libnah, and Ether, and A, H6228
19: 7 Ain, Remmon, and Ether, and A; four H6228
1Ch 4:32 and Tochen, and A, five cities: H6228
6:59 And A with her suburbs, and H6228

ASHBEA
1Ch 4:21 that wrought fine linen, of the house of A, H791

ASHBEL
Gen 46:21 and Becher, and A, Gera, and Naaman, H788
Nu 26:38 of the Belaites: of A, the family of the H788
1Ch 8: 1 A the second, and Aharah the third, H788

ASHBELITES
Nu 26:38 the family of the A: of Ahiram, the family H789

ASHCHENAZ
1Ch 1: 6 And the sons of Gomer; A, and Riphath, H813
Jer 51:27 Ararat, Minni, and A; appoint a captain H813

ASHDOD
Jos 11:22 Gaza, in Gath, and in A, there remained. H795
15:46 all that *lay* near A, with their villages: H795
47 A with her towns and her villages, Gaza H795
1Sa 5: 1 and brought it from Eben-ezer unto A. H795
3 And when they of A arose early on the H796
5 threshold of Dagon in A unto this day. H795
6 upon them of A, and he destroyed them, H796
6 emerods, *even* A and the coasts thereof. H795
7 And when the men of A saw that *it was* H795
6:17 unto the LORD; for A one, for Gaza one, H795
2Ch 26: 6 and the wall of A, and built cities about H795
6 about A, and among the Philistines. H795
Neh 13:23 wives of A, of Ammon, *and* of Moab: H796
24 in the speech of A, and could not speak H797
Isa 20: 1 In the year that Tartan came unto A, H795
1 him,) and fought against A, and took it; H795
Jer 25:20 Azzah, and Ekron, and the remnant of A, H795
Am 1: 8 And I will cut off the inhabitant from A, H795
3: 9 Publish in the palaces at A, and in the H795
Zep 2: 4 shall drive out A at the noon day, and H795
Zec 9: 6 And a bastard shall dwell in A, and I will H795

ASHDODITES
Neh 4: 7 and the A, heard that the walls H796

ASHDOTHITES
Jos 13: 3 and the A, the Eshkalonites, the H796

ASHDOTH-PISGAH
Dt 3:17 the salt sea, under A eastward. H798+H6449
Jos 12: 3 and from the south, under A: H798+H6449
13:20 And Beth-peor, and A, and H798+H6449

ASHER
Gen 30:13 me blessed: and she called his name A. H836
35:26 Gad, and A: these *are* the sons of H836
46:17 And the sons of A; Jimnah, and Ishuah, H836
49:20 Out of A his bread *shall be* fat, and he H836
Ex 1: 4 Dan, and Naphtali, Gad, and A. H836
Nu 1:13 Of A; Pagiel the son of Ocran. H836
40 Of the children of A, by their generations, H836
41 *even* of the tribe of A, *were* forty and one H836
2:27 *shall be* the tribe of A: and the captain of H836
27 of A *shall be* Pagiel the son of Ocran. H836
7:72 prince of the children of A, *offered*: H836
10:26 of A *was* Pagiel the son of Ocran. H836
13:13 Of the tribe of A, Sethur the son of H836
26:44 *Of* the children of A after their families: H836
46 And the name of the daughter of A *was* H836
47 These *are* the families of the sons of A H836
34:27 children of A, Ahihud the son of Shelomi. H836
Dt 27:13 and A, and Zebulun, Dan, and Naphtali. H836
33:24 And of A he said, *Let* Asher *be* blessed H836
24 And of Asher he said, *Let* A *be* blessed H836
Jos 17: 7 And the coast of Manasseh was from A H836
10 met together in A on the north, and in H836
11 And Manasseh had in Issachar and in A H836
19:24 children of A according to their families. H836
31 of the children of A according to their H836
34 and reacheth to A on the west side, and H836
21: 6 out of the tribe of A, and out of the tribe H836
30 And out of the tribe of A, Mishal with her H836
Jdg 1:31 Neither did A drive out the inhabitants H836
5:17 remain in ships? A continued on the sea H836
6:35 messengers unto A, and unto Zebulun, H836
7:23 and out of A, and out of all Manasseh, H836
1Ki 4:16 Baanah the son of Hushai *was* in A and H836
1Ch 2: 2 and Benjamin, Naphtali, Gad, and A. H836
6:62 out of the tribe of A, and out of the tribe H836
74 And out of the tribe of A; Mashal with H836
7:30 The sons of A; Imnah, and Isuah, and H836
40 All these *were* the children of A, heads of H836
12:36 And of A, such as went forth to battle, H836
2Ch 30:11 Nevertheless divers of A and Manasseh H836
Ezk 48: 2 side unto the west side, a *portion for* A. H836
3 And by the border of A, from the east H836
34 Gad, one gate of A, one gate of Naphtali. H836

ASHERITES
Jdg 1:32 But the A dwelt among the Canaanites, H843

ASHES
Gen 18:27 unto the Lord, which *am but* dust and a: H665
Ex 9: 8 to you handfuls of a of the furnace, and H6368
10 And they took a of the furnace, and H6368
27: 3 pans to receive his a, and his shovels, H1878
Lev 1:16 on the east part, by the place of the a: H1880
4:12 place, where the a are poured out, and H1880
12 the a are poured out shall he be burnt. H1880
6:10 and take up the a which the fire hath H1880
11 a without the camp unto a clean place. H1880
Nu 4:13 And they shall take away the a from H1878
19: 9 shall gather up the a of the heifer, and H665
10 And he that gathereth the a of the heifer H665
17 shall take of the a of the burnt heifer of H6083
2Sa 13:19 And Tamar put a on her head, and rent H665
1Ki 13: 3 a that *are* upon it shall be poured out. H1880
5 The altar also was rent, and the a H1880
20:38 disguised himself with a upon his face. H666
41 And he hasted, and took the a away H666
2Ki 23: 4 and carried the a of them unto Beth-el. H6083
Est 4: 1 on sackcloth with a, and went out into H665
3 and many lay in sackcloth and a. H665
Job 2: 8 withal; and he sat down among the a. H665
13:12 Your remembrances *are* like unto a, your H665
30:19 mire, and I am become like dust and a. H665
42: 6 I abhor *myself*, and repent in dust and a. H665
Ps 102: 9 For I have eaten a like bread, and H665
147:16 wool: he scattereth the hoarfrost like a. H665
Isa 44:20 He feedeth on a: a deceived heart hath H665
58: 5 sackcloth and a *under him*? wilt thou H665
61: 3 unto them beauty for a, the oil of joy for H665
Jer 6:26 wallow thyself in a: make thee mourning, H665
25:34 yourselves *in the* a, ye principal of the
31:40 bodies, and of the a, and all the fields H1880
Lam 3:16 gravel stones, he hath covered me with a. H665
Ezk 27:30 they shall wallow themselves in the a: H665
28:18 I will bring thee to a upon the earth in H665
Dan 9: 3 with fasting, and sackcloth, and a: H665
Jna 3: 6 covered *him* with sackcloth, and sat in a. H665
Mal 4: 3 for they shall be a under the soles of H665
Mt 11:21 repented long ago in sackcloth and a. G4700
Lk 10:13 ago repented, sitting in sackcloth and a. G4700
Heb 9:13 and of goats, and the a of an heifer G4700
2Pt 2: 6 and Gomorrha into a condemned *them* G5077

ASHIMA
2Ki 17:30 Nergal, and the men of Hamath made A, H807

ASHKELON
Jdg 14:19 he went down to A, and slew thirty men H831
Jer 25:20 the Philistines, and A, and Azzah, and H831
47: 5 Baldness is come upon Gaza; A is cut off H831
7 it a charge against A, and against the sea H831
Am 1: 8 the sceptre from A, and I will turn mine H831
Zep 2: 4 For Gaza shall be forsaken, and A a H831
7 in the houses of A shall they lie down in H831
Zec 9: 5 A shall see *it*, and fear; Gaza also *shall* H831
5 from Gaza, and A shall not be inhabited. H831

ASHKENAZ
Gen 10: 3 And the sons of Gomer; A, and Riphath, H813

ASHNAH
Jos 15:33 in the valley, Eshtaol, and Zoreah, and A, H823
43 And Jiphtah, and A, and Nezib, H823

ASHPENAZ
Dan 1: 3 And the king spake unto A the master of H828

ASHRIEL
1Ch 7:14 The sons of Manasseh; A, whom she H844

ASHTAROTH
Jos 9:10 to Og king of Bashan, which *was* at A. H6252
12: 4 the giants, that dwelt at A and at Edrei, H6252
13:12 which reigned in A and in Edrei, who H6252
31 And half Gilead, and A, and Edrei, H6252
Jdg 2:13 the LORD, and served Baal and A. H6252
10: 6 Baalim, and A, and the gods of Syria, H6252
1Sa 7: 3 strange gods and A from among you, H6252
4 and A, and served the LORD only. H6252
12:10 Baalim and A: but now deliver us out H6252
31:10 in the house of A: and they fastened his H6252
1Ch 6:71 her suburbs, and A with her suburbs: H6252

ASHTERATHITE
1Ch 11:44 Uzzia the A, Shama and Jehiel the sons H6254

ASHTEROTH
Gen 14: 5 the Rephaims in A Karnaim, and the H6255

ASHTORETH
1Ki 11: 5 For Solomon went after A the goddess H6253
33 have worshipped A the goddess of the H6253
2Ki 23:13 had builded for A the abomination of H6253

ASHUR
1Ch 2:24 wife bare him A the father of Tekoa. H806
4: 5 And A the father of Tekoa had two H806

ASHURITES
2Sa 2: 9 and over the A, and over Jezreel, and H805
Ezk 27: 6 company of the A have made thy H839+H838

ASHVATH
1Ch 7:33 A. These *are* the children of Japhlet. H6220

ASIA
Act 2: 9 and Cappadocia, in Pontus, and A, G773
6: 9 Cilicia and of A, disputing with Stephen. G773
16: 6 the Holy Ghost to preach the word in A, G773
19:10 which dwelt in A heard the word of the G773
22 but he himself stayed in A for a season. G773
26 almost throughout all A, this Paul hath G773
27 whom all A and the world worshippeth. G773
31 And certain of the chief of A, which were G775
20: 4 And there accompanied him into A G773
4 and of A, Tychicus and Trophimus. G774
16 spend the time in A: for he hasted, if it G773
18 that I came into A, after what manner I G773
21:27 Jews which were of A, when they saw him G773
24:18 Whereupon certain Jews from A found G773
27: 2 sail by the coasts of A; *one* Aristarchus, a G773
1Co 16:19 The churches of A salute you. Aquila G773
2Co 1: 8 came to us in A, that we were pressed G773
2Ti 1:15 they which are in A be turned away from G773
1Pt 1: 1 Galatia, Cappadocia, A, and Bithynia, G773
Rev 1: 4 which are in A: Grace *be* unto you, and G773
11 which are in A; unto Ephesus, and unto G773

ASIDE
Ex 3: 3 And Moses said, I will now turn a, and H5493
4 that he turned a to see, God called unto H5493
32: 8 They have turned a quickly out of the H5493
Nu 5:12 a, and commit a trespass against him, H7847
19 hast not gone a to uncleanness *with* H7847
20 But if thou hast gone a *to another* H7847
29 when a wife goeth a *to another* instead H7847
22:23 the ass turned a out of the way, and H5186
Dt 5:32 turn a to the right hand or to the left. H5493
9:12 are quickly turned a out of the way H5493
16 ye had turned a quickly out of the way H5493
11:16 and ye turn a, and serve other gods, H5493
28 God, but turn a out of the way which H5493
17:20 and that he turn not a from the H5493
28:14 And thou shalt not go a from any of the H5493
31:29 and turn a from the way which H5493
Jos 23: 6 that ye turn not a therefrom *to* the H5493
Jdg 14: 8 her, and he turned a to see the carcase H5493
19:12 We will not turn a hither into the city H5493
15 And they turned a thither, to go in *and* H5493
Ru 4: 1 such a one! turn a, sit down here. And H5493
1 here. And he turned a, and sat down. H5493
1Sa 6:12 and turned not a *to* the right hand or H5493
8: 3 ways, but turned a after lucre, and took H5186
12:20 yet turn not a from following the H5493
21 And turn ye not a: for *then should ye go* H5493
2Sa 2:21 And Abner said to him, Turn thee a to H5186
21 not turn a from following of him. H5493
22 Asahel, Turn thee a from following me: H5493
23 Howbeit he refused to turn a: wherefore H5493
3:27 Joab took him a in the gate to speak H5186
6:10 but David carried it a into the house of H5186
18:30 And the king said *unto him*, Turn a, H5437
30 here. And he turned a, and stood still. H5437
1Ki 15: 5 and turned not a from any *thing* that H5493
20:39 a man turned a, and brought a man H5493
22:32 And they turned a to fight against him: H5493
43 he turned not a from it, doing *that* H5493
2Ki 4: 4 and thou shalt set a that which is full. H5265
22: 2 not a to the right hand or to the left. H5493
1Ch 13:13 David, but carried it a into the house of H5186
Job 6:18 The paths of their way are turned a; H3943
Ps 14: 3 They are all gone a, they are *all* together H5493
40: 4 the proud, nor such as turn a to lies. H7750
78:57 they were turned a like a deceitful bow. H2015
101: 3 that turn a; *it* shall not cleave to me. H7750
125: 5 As for such as turn a unto their H5186
Song 1: 7 a by the flocks of thy companions? H5844
6: 1 a? that we may seek him with thee. H6437
Isa 10: 2 To turn a the needy from judgment, H5186
29:21 turn a the just for a thing of nought. H5186
30:11 Get you out of the way, turn a out of H5186
44:20 heart hath turned him a, that he cannot H5186
Jer 14: 8 man *that* turneth a to tarry for a night? H5186
15: 5 who shall go a to ask how thou doest? H5493
Lam 3:11 He hath turned a my ways, and pulled H5493
35 To turn a the right of a man before the H5186
Am 2: 7 of the poor, and turn a the way of the H5186
5:12 a the poor in the gate *from their right*. H5186
Mal 3: 5 and that turn a the stranger *from his* H5186
Mt 2:22 he turned a into the parts of Galilee: *G402*
Mk 7: 8 For laying a the commandment of God, *G863*
33 And he took him a from the multitude, *G2596*
Lk 9:10 took them, and went a privately into a *G5298*
Jn 13: 4 He riseth from supper, and laid a his *G5087*
Act 4:15 them to go a out of the council, they *G565*
23:19 and went *with him* a privately, and *G402*
26:31 And when they were gone a, they talked *G402*
1Ti 1: 6 have turned a unto vain jangling; *G1624*
5:15 For some are already turned a after *G1624*
Heb 12: 1 let us lay a every weight, and the *G659*
1Pt 2: 1 Wherefore laying a all malice, and all *G659*

ASIEL
1Ch 4:35 the son of Seraiah, the son of A, H6221

ASK
Gen 32:29 *is it that* thou dost a after my name? H7592
34:12 A me never so much dowry and gift, H7235
Nu 27:21 the priest, who shall a *counsel* for him H7592
Dt 4:32 For a now of the days that are past, H7592
32 the earth, and *a* from the one side of
13:14 make search, and a diligently; and, H7592
32: 7 generations: a thy father, and he will H7592
Jos 4: 6 your children a *their fathers* in time H7592
21 children shall a their fathers in time H7592
15:18 that she moved him to a of her father a H7592
Jdg 1:14 that she moved him to a of her father a H7592
Jdg 18: 5 And they said unto him, A counsel, we H7592
1Sa 12:19 all our sins *this* evil, to a us a king. H7592
25: 8 A thy young men, and they will shew H7592
28:16 then dost thou a of me, seeing the H7592
2Sa 14:18 the thing that I shall a thee. And the H7592
20:18 They shall surely a *counsel* at Abel: H7592
1Ki 2:16 And now I a one petition of thee, deny H7592
20 said unto her, A on, my mother: for H7592
22 And why dost thou a Abishag the H7592
22 for Adonijah? a for him the kingdom H7592
3: 5 and God said, A what I shall give thee. H7592
14: 5 cometh to a a thing of thee for her H1875
2Ki 2: 9 said unto Elisha, A what I shall do for H7592
2Ch 1: 7 said unto him, A what I shall give thee. H7592
20: 4 together, to a *help* of the LORD: even H1245
Job 12: 7 But a now the beasts, and they shall H7592
Ps 2: 8 A of me, and I shall give *thee* the H7592
Isa 7:11 A thee a sign of the LORD thy God; ask H7592
11 Ask thee a sign of the LORD thy God; a H7592
12 But Ahaz said, I will not a, neither will I H7592
45:11 and his Maker, A me of things to come H7592
58: 2 of their God: they a of me the H7592
Jer 6:16 and see, and a for the old paths, where H7592
15: 5 who shall go aside to a how thou doest? H7592
18:13 Therefore thus saith the LORD; A ye H7592
23:33 or a priest, shall a thee, saying, What H7592
30: 6 A ye now, and see whether a man doth H7592
38:14 a thee a thing; hide nothing from me. H7592
48:19 by the way, and espy; a him that fleeth, H7592
50: 5 They shall a the way to Zion with their H7592
Lam 4: 4 young children a bread, *and* no man H7592
Dan 6: 7 whosoever shall a a petition of any God H1156
12 man that shall a *a petition* of any God H1156
Hos 4:12 My people a counsel at their stocks, H7592
Hag 2:11 Thus saith the LORD of hosts; A now H7592
Zec 10: 1 A ye of the LORD rain in the time of the H7592
Mt 6: 8 things ye have need of, before ye a him. *G154*
7: 7 A, and it shall be given you; seek, and ye *G154*
9 his son a bread, will he give him a stone? *G154*
10 Or if he a a fish, will he give him a *G154*
11 give good things to them that a him? *G154*
14: 7 oath to give her whatsoever she would a. *G154*
18:19 that they shall a, it shall be done for them *G154*
20:22 know not what ye a. Are ye able to drink *G154*
21:22 And all things, whatsoever ye shall a in *G154*
24 them, I also will a you one thing, which *G2065*
22:46 day forth a him any more *questions*. *G1905*
27:20 should a Barabbas, and destroy Jesus. *G154*
Mk 6:22 unto the damsel, A of me whatsoever *G154*
23 thou shalt a of me, I will give *it* thee, *G154*
24 What shall I a? And she said, The head *G154*
9:32 that saying, and were afraid to a him. *G1905*
10:38 know not what ye a: can ye drink of the *G154*
11:29 them, I will also a of you one question, *G1905*
12:34 after that durst a him *any question*. *G1905*
Lk 6: 9 Then said Jesus unto them, I will a you *G1905*
30 taketh away thy goods a *them* not again. *G523*
9:45 and they feared to a him of that saying. *G2065*
11: 9 And I say unto you, A, and it shall be *G154*
11 If a son shall a bread of any of you that *G154*
11 a stone? or if *he a* a fish, will he for a fish
12 Or if he shall a an egg, will he offer him a *G154*
13 give the Holy Spirit to them that a him? *G154*
12:48 much, of him they will a the more. *G154*
19:31 And if any man a you, Why do ye loose *G2065*
20: 3 also a you one thing; and answer me: *G2065*
40 And after that they durst not a him any *G1905*
22:68 And if I also a *you*, ye will not answer *G2065*
Jn 1:19 Jerusalem to a him, Who art thou? *G2065*
9:21 age; a him: he shall speak for himself. *G2065*
23 said his parents, He is of age; a him. *G2065*
11:22 thou wilt a of God, God will give *it* thee. *G154*
13:24 a who it should be of whom he spake. *G4441*
14:13 And whatsoever ye shall a in my name, *G154*
14 If ye shall a any thing in my name, I will *G154*
15: 7 in you, ye shall a what ye will, and it *G154*
16 ye shall a of the Father in my name, *G154*
16:19 were desirous to a him, and said unto *G2065*
23 And in that day ye shall a me nothing. *G2065*
23 ye shall a the Father in my name, *G154*
24 in my name: a, and ye shall receive, *G154*
26 At that day ye shall a in my name: and I *G154*
30 that any man should a thee: by this we *G2065*
18:21 Why askest thou me? a them which *G1905*
21:12 of the disciples durst a him, Who art *G1833*
Act 3: 2 called Beautiful, to a alms of them that *G154*
10:29 as I was sent for: I a therefore for what *G4441*
1Co 14:35 any thing, let them a their husbands at *G1905*
Eph 3:20 above all that we a or think, according *G154*
Jas 1: 5 If any of you lack wisdom, let him a of *G154*
6 But let him a in faith, nothing wavering. *G154*
4: 2 war, yet ye have not, because ye a not. *G154*
3 Ye a, and receive not, because ye ask *G154*
3 Ye ask, and receive not, because ye a *G154*
1Jn 3:22 And whatsoever we a, we receive of him, *G154*
5:14 in him, that, if we a any thing according *G154*
15 us, whatsoever we a, we know that we *G154*
16 death, he shall a, and he shall give him *G154*

ASKED
Gen 24:47 And I a her, and said, Whose daughter H7592
26: 7 And the men of the place a *him* of his H7592
32:29 And Jacob a *him*, and said, Tell *me*, I H7592
37:15 man a him, saying, What seekest thou? H7592
38:21 Then he a the men of that place, H7592
40: 7 And he a Pharaoh's officers that *were* H7592
43: 7 And they said, The man a us straitly of H7592
27 And he a them of *their* welfare, and H7592
44:19 My lord a his servants, saying, Have ye H7592
Ex 18: 7 him; and they a each other of *their* H7592
Jos 9:14 their victuals, and a not *counsel* at the H7592
19:50 him the city which he a, *even* H7592
Jdg 1: 1 children of Israel a the LORD, saying, H7592
5:25 He a water, *and* she gave *him* milk; she H7592
6:29 they inquired and a, they said, Gideon H1245
13: 6 very terrible: but I a him not whence he H7592
20:18 house of God, and a counsel of God, H7592
23 until even, and a counsel of the LORD, H7592
1Sa 1:17 thy petition that thou hast a of him. H7592
20 Because I have a him of the LORD. H7592
27 given me my petition which I a of him: H7592
8:10 unto the people that a of him a king. H7592
14:37 And Saul a counsel of God, Shall I go H7592
19:22 in Sechu: and he a and said, Where *are* H7592
20: 6 David earnestly a *leave* of me that he H7592
28 a *leave* of me *to go* to Beth-lehem: H7592
1Ki 3:10 Lord, that Solomon had a this thing. H7592
11 Because thou hast a this thing, and H7592
11 and hast not a for thyself long life; H7592
11 life; neither hast a riches for thyself, H7592
11 for thyself, nor hast a the life of thine H7592
11 thine enemies; but hast a for thyself H7592
13 which thou hast not a, both riches, and H7592
10:13 whatsoever she a, beside *that* which H7592
2Ki 2:10 And he said, Thou hast a a hard thing: H7592
8: 6 And when the king a the woman, she H7592
2Ch 1:11 and thou hast not a riches, wealth, or H7592
11 neither yet hast a long life; but hast H7592
11 asked long life; but hast a wisdom and H7592
9:12 whatsoever she a, beside *that* which she H7592
Ezr 5: 9 Then a we those elders, *and* said unto H7593
10 We a their names also, to certify thee, H7593
Neh 1: 2 of Judah; and I a them concerning the H7592
Job 21:29 Have ye not a them that go by the way? H7592
Ps 21: 4 He a life of thee, *and* thou gavest *it* H7592
105:40 *The people* a, and he brought quails, H7592
Isa 30: 2 Egypt, and have not a at my mouth; to H7592
41:28 when I a of them, could answer a word. H7592
65: 1 I am sought of *them that* a not *for me*; I H7592
Jer 36:17 And they a Baruch, saying, Tell us H7592
37:17 out: and the king a him secretly in his H7592
38:27 Jeremiah, and a him: and he told them H7592
Dan 2:10 nor ruler, *that* a such things at any H7593
7:16 that stood by, and a him the truth of all H1156
Mt 12:10 And they a him, saying, Is it lawful *G1905*
16:13 Philippi, he a his disciples, saying, *G2065*
17:10 And his disciples a him, saying, Why *G1905*
22:23 there is no resurrection, and a him, *G1905*
35 *which was* a lawyer, a *him a question*, *G1905*
41 were gathered together, Jesus a them, *G1905*
27:11 and the governor a him, saying, Art *G1905*
Mk 4:10 with the twelve a of him the parable. *G2065*
5: 9 And he a him, What *is* thy name? And *G1905*
6:25 unto the king, and a, saying, I will that *G154*
7: 5 Then the Pharisees and scribes a him, *G1905*
17 disciples a him concerning the parable. *G1905*
8: 5 And he a them, How many loaves have *G1905*
23 upon him, he a him if he saw ought. *G1905*
27 and by the way he a his disciples, *G1905*
9:11 And they a him, saying, Why say the *G1905*
16 And he a the scribes, What question ye *G1905*
21 And he a his father, How long is it ago *G1905*
28 his disciples a him privately, Why *G1905*
33 in the house he a them, What was it *G1905*
10: 2 And the Pharisees came to him, and a *G1905*
10 And in the house his disciples a him *G1905*
17 to him, and a him, Good Master, *G1905*
12:18 resurrection; and they a him, saying, *G1905*

Mk 12:28 them well, a him, Which is the first G1905
13: 3 and John and Andrew a him privately, G1905
14:60 up in the midst, and a Jesus, saying, G1905
61 the high priest a him, and said unto G1905
15: 2 And Pilate a him, Art thou the King of G1905
4 And Pilate a him again, saying, G1905
44 the centurion, he a him whether he had G1905
Lk 1:63 And he a for a writing table, and wrote, G154
3:10 And the people a him, saying, What G1905
8: 9 And his disciples a him, saying, What G1905
30 And Jesus a him, saying, What is thy G1905
9:18 were with him: and he a them, saying, G1905
15:26 and a what these things meant. G4441
18:18 And a certain ruler a him, saying, G1905
36 multitude pass by, he a what it meant. G4441
40 and when he was come near, he a him, G1905
20:21 And they a him, saying, Master, we G1905
27 is any resurrection; and they a him, G1905
21: 7 And they a him, saying, Master, but G1905
22:64 him on the face, and a him, saying, G1905
23: 3 And Pilate a him, saying, Art thou the G1905
6 When Pilate heard of Galilee, he a G1905
Jn 1:21 And they a him, What then? Art thou G2065
25 And they a him, and said unto him, G2065
4:10 wouldest have a of him, and he would G154
5:12 Then a they him, What man is that G2065
9: 2 And his disciples a him, saying, G2065
15 Then again the Pharisees also a him G2065
19 And they a them, saying, Is this your G2065
16:24 Hitherto have ye a nothing in my name: G154
18: 7 Then a he them again, Whom seek ye? G1905
19 The high priest then a Jesus of his G2065
Act 1: 6 together, they a of him, saying, Lord, G1905
3: 3 about to go into the temple a an alms. G2065
4: 7 in the midst, they a, By what power, or G4441
5:27 the council: and the high priest a them, G1905
10:18 And called, and a whether Simon, G4441
23:19 privately, and a *him*, What is that thou G4441
34 read *the letter*, he a of what province G1905
25:20 of questions, I a *him* whether he would G3004
Ro 10:20 unto them that a not after me. G1905

ASKELON
Jdg 1:18 the coast thereof, and A with the coast H831
1Sa 6:17 for A one, for Gath one, for Ekron one; H831
2Sa 1:20 in the streets of A; lest the daughters of H831

ASKEST
Jdg 13:18 unto him, Why a thou thus after my H7592
Jn 4: 9 thou, being a Jew, a drink of me, which G154
18:21 Why a thou me? ask them which heard G1905

ASKETH
Gen 32:17 meeteth thee, and a thee, saying, H7592
Ex 13:14 And it shall be when thy son a thee in H7592
Dt 6:20 *And* when thy son a thee in time to H7592
Mic 7: 3 the prince a, and the judge *asketh* H7592
3 and the judge *a* for a reward; and the H7592
Mt 5:42 Give to him that a thee, and from him G154
7: 8 For every one that a receiveth; and he G154
Lk 6:30 Give to every man that a of thee; and of G154
11:10 For every one that a receiveth; and he G154
Jn 16: 5 none of you a me, Whither goest thou? G2065
1Pt 3:15 to every man that a you a reason of the G154

ASKING
1Sa 12:17 the sight of the LORD, in a you a king. H7592
1Ch 10:13 not, and also for a *counsel* of *one that* H7592
Ps 78:18 in their heart by a meat for their lust. H7592
Lk 2:46 hearing them, and a them questions. G1905
Jn 8: 7 So when they continued a him, he lifted G2065
1Co 10:25 eat, a no question for conscience sake: G350
27 eat, a no question for conscience sake. G350

ASLEEP
Jdg 4:21 for he was fast a and weary. So he died. H7290
1Sa 26:12 for they *were* all a; because a deep sleep H3463
Song 7: 9 the lips of those that are a to speak. H3463
Jna 1: 5 of the ship; and he lay, and was fast a. H7290
Mt 8:24 covered with the waves: but he was a. G2518
26:40 and findeth them a, and saith unto G2518
43 And he came and found them a again: G2518
Mk 4:38 part of the ship, a on a pillow: and they G2518
14:40 he found them a again, (for their eyes G2518
Lk 8:23 But as they sailed he fell a: and there G879
Act 7:60 And when he had said this, he fell a. G2837
1Co 15: 6 unto this present, but some are fallen a. G2837
18 Then they also which are fallen a in G2837
1Th 4:13 them which are a, that ye sorrow not, G2837
1Th 4:15 shall not prevent them which are a. G2837
2Pt 3: 4 the fathers fell a, all things continue G2837

ASNAH
Ezr 2:50 The children of A, the children of H619

ASNAPPAR
Ezr 4:10 great and noble A brought over, and set H620

ASP
Isa 11: 8 on the hole of the a, and the weaned H6620

ASPATHA
Est 9: 7 And Parshandatha, and Dalphon, and A, H630

ASPS
Dt 32:33 of dragons, and the cruel venom of a. H6620
Job 20:14 is turned, *it is* the gall of a within him. H6620
16 He shall suck the poison of a: the viper's H6620
Ro 3:13 deceit; the poison of a *is* under their lips: G785

ASRIEL
Nu 26:31 And *of* A, the family of the Asrielites: and H844
Jos 17: 2 for the children of A, and for the children H844

ASRIELITES
Nu 26:31 And *of* Asriel, the family of the A: and *of* H845

ASS
Gen 22: 3 and saddled his a, and took two of his H2543
5 ye here with the a; and I and the lad will H2543
42:27 sack to give his a provender in the inn, H2543
44:13 man his a, and returned to the city. H2543
49:14 Issachar *is* a strong a couching down H2543
Ex 4:20 set them upon an a, and he returned to H2543
13:13 And every firstling of an a thou shalt H2543
20:17 a, nor any thing that *is* thy neighbour's. H2543
21:33 cover it, and an ox or an a fall therein; H2543
22: 4 or a, or sheep; he shall restore double. H2543
9 *whether it be* for ox, for a, for sheep, for H2543
10 his neighbour an a, or an ox, or a sheep, H2543
23: 4 If thou meet thine enemy's ox or his a H2543
5 If thou see the a of him that hateth thee H2543
12 thine ox and thine a may rest, and the H2543
34:20 But the firstling of an a thou shalt H2543
Nu 16:15 not taken one a from them, neither H2543
22:21 his a, and went with the princes of Moab. H860
22 a, and his two servants *were* with him. H860
23 And the a saw the angel of the LORD H860
23 his hand: and the a turned aside out of H860
23 smote the a, to turn her into the way. H860
25 And when the a saw the angel of the H860
27 And when the a saw the angel of the H860
27 kindled, and he smote the a with a staff. H860
28 the mouth of the a, and she said unto H860
29 And Balaam said unto the a, Because H860
30 And the a said unto Balaam, *Am* not I H860
30 *Am* not I thine a, upon which thou hast H860
32 thou smitten thine a these three times? H860
33 And the a saw me, and turned from me H860
Dt 5:14 nor thine ox, nor thine a, nor any of thy H2543
21 a, or any *thing* that *is* thy neighbour's. H2543
22: 3 In like manner shalt thou do with his a; H2543
4 Thou shalt not see thy brother's a or H2543
10 not plow with an ox and an a together. H2543
28:31 eat thereof: thine a *shall be* violently H2543
Jos 6:21 and a, with the edge of the sword. H2543
15:18 and she lighted off *her* a; and Caleb said H2543
Jdg 1:14 from off *her* a; and Caleb said unto H2543
6: 4 for Israel, neither sheep, nor ox, nor a. H2543
10: 4 that rode on thirty a colts, and they H5895
12:14 on threescore and ten a colts: and he H5895
15:15 And he found a new jawbone of an a, H2543
16 the jawbone of an a, heaps upon heaps, H2543
16 of an a have I slain a thousand men. H2543
19:28 her *up* upon an a, and the man rose up, H2543
1Sa 12: 3 I taken? or whose a have I taken? or H2543
15: 3 suckling, ox and sheep, camel and a. H2543
16:20 And Jesse took an a *laden* with bread, H2543
25:20 And it was *so, as* she rode on the a, that H2543
23 and lighted off the a, and fell before H2543
42 and rode upon an a, with five damsels H2543
2Sa 17:23 he saddled *his* a, and arose, and gat H2543
19:26 I will saddle me an a, that I may ride H2543
1Ki 2:40 And Shimei arose, and saddled his a, H2543
13:13 Saddle me the a. So they saddled him H2543
13 saddled him the a: and he rode thereon, H2543
23 for him the a, *to wit*, for the prophet H2543
24 the way, and the a stood by it, the lion H2543
1Ki 13:27 Saddle me the a. And they saddled *him*. H2543
28 in the way, and the a and the lion H2543
28 not eaten the carcase, nor torn the a. H2543
29 laid it upon the a, and brought it back: H2543
2Ki 4:24 Then she saddled an a, and said to her H860
Job 6: 5 Doth the wild a bray when he hath H6501
24: 3 They drive away the a of the fatherless, H2543
39: 5 Who hath sent out the wild a free? or H6501
5 hath loosed the bands of the wild a? H6171
Prv 26: 3 A whip for the horse, a bridle for the a, H2543
Isa 1: 3 The ox knoweth his owner, and the a H2543
32:20 forth *thither* the feet of the ox and the a. H2543
Jer 2:24 A wild a used to the wilderness, *that* H6501
22:19 the burial of an a, drawn and cast forth H2543
Hos 8: 9 to Assyria, a wild a alone by himself: H6501
Zec 9: 9 an a, and upon a colt the foal of an ass. H2543
9 an ass, and upon a colt the foal of an a. H860
14:15 the camel, and of the a, and of all the H2543
Mt 21: 2 ye shall find an a tied, and a colt with G3688
5 upon an a, and a colt the foal of an ass. G3688
5 upon an ass, and a colt the foal of an a. G5268
7 And brought the a, and the colt, and G3688
Lk 13:15 loose his ox or *his* a from the stall, and G3688
14: 5 you shall have an a or an ox fallen into G3688
Jn 12:14 a young a, sat thereon; as it is written, G3678
2Pt 2:16 the dumb a speaking with man's G5268

ASSAULT
Est 8:11 that would a them, *both* little ones H6696
Act 14: 5 And when there was an a made both of G3730

ASSAULTED
Act 17: 5 on an uproar, and a the house of Jason, G2186

ASSAY
Job 4: 2 *If* we a to commune with thee, wilt H5254

ASSAYED
Dt 4:34 Or hath God a to go *and* take him a H5254
1Sa 17:39 armour, and he a to go; for he had not H2974
Act 9:26 to Jerusalem, he a to join himself to the G3987
16: 7 After they were come to Mysia, they a G3985

ASSAYING
Heb 11:29 a to do were drowned. G3984+G2983

ASS-COLTS See ASS and COLTS.

ASSEMBLE
Nu 10: 3 the assembly shall a themselves to thee H3259
2Sa 20: 4 Then said the king to Amasa, A me the H2199
5 So Amasa went to a *the men of* Judah: H2199
Isa 11:12 the nations, and shall a the outcasts of H622
45:20 A yourselves and come; draw near H6908
48:14 All ye, a yourselves, and hear; which H6908
Jer 4: 5 together, and say, A yourselves, and let H622
8:14 Why do we sit still? a yourselves, and let H622
12: 9 her; come ye, a all the beasts of the field, H622
21: 4 I will a them into the midst of this city. H622
Ezk 11:17 from the people, and a you out of the H622
39:17 beast of the field, A yourselves, and H6908
Dan 11:10 up, and shall a a multitude of great H622
Hos 7:14 their beds: they a themselves for corn H1481
Joel 2:16 the congregation, a the elders, gather H6908
3:11 A yourselves, and come, all ye heathen, H5789
Am 3: 9 of Egypt, and say, A yourselves upon the H622
Mic 2:12 I will surely a, O Jacob, all of thee; I will H622
4: 6 In that day, saith the LORD, will I a her H622
Zep 3: 8 that I may a the kingdoms, to pour H6908

ASSEMBLED
Ex 38: 8 which a *at* the door of the tabernacle H6633
Nu 1:18 And they a all the congregation H6950
Jos 18: 1 children of Israel a together at Shiloh, H6950
Jdg 10:17 children of Israel a themselves together, H622
1Sa 2:22 the women that a *at* the door of the H6633
14:20 *were* with him a themselves, and they H2199
1Ki 8: 1 Then Solomon a the elders of Israel, H6950
2 And all the men of Israel a themselves H6950
5 Israel, that were a unto him, *were* with H3259
12:21 to Jerusalem, he a all the house of H6950
1Ch 15: 4 And David a the children of Aaron, and H622
28: 1 And David a all the princes of Israel, H6950
2Ch 5: 2 Then Solomon a the elders of Israel, H6950
3 Wherefore all the men of Israel a H6950
6 of Israel that were a unto him before H3259
20:26 And on the fourth day they a H6950
30:13 And there a at Jerusalem much people to H622
Ezr 9: 4 Then were a unto me every one that H622

Ezr 10: 1 of God, there **a** unto him out of Israel H6908
Neh 9: 1 of Israel were **a** with fasting, and with H622
Est 9:18 But the Jews that *were* at Shushan **a** H6950
Ps 48: 4 For, lo, the kings were **a**, they passed by H3259
Isa 43: 9 let the people be **a**: who among them can H622
Jer 5: 7 adultery, and **a** themselves by troops H1413
Ezk 38: 7 company that are **a** unto thee, and be H6950
Dan 6: 6 Then these presidents and princes **a** H7284
11 Then these men **a**, and found Daniel H7284
15 Then these men **a** unto the king, and H7284
Mt 26: 3 Then **a** together the chief priests, and *G4863*
57 where the scribes and the elders were **a**. *G4863*
28:12 And when they were **a** with the elders, *G4863*
Mk 14:53 with him were **a** all the chief priests *G4905*
Jn 20:19 the disciples were **a** for fear of the Jews, *G4863*
Act 1: 4 And, being **a** together with *them*, *G4871*
4:31 where they were **a** together; and they *G4863*
11:26 a whole year they **a** themselves with *G4863*
15:25 It seemed good unto us, being **a** with *G1096*

ASSEMBLIES
Ps 86:14 me, and the **a** of violent *men* have H5712
Ecc 12:11 of **a**, *which* are given from one shepherd. H627
Isa 1:13 the calling of **a**, I cannot away with; H4744
4: 5 and upon her **a**, a cloud and smoke H4744
Ezk 44:24 **a**; and they shall hallow my sabbaths. H4150
Am 5:21 and I will not smell in your solemn **a**. H6116

ASSEMBLING
Ex 38: 8 of *the women* **a**, which assembled *at* H6633
Heb 10:25 Not forsaking the **a** of ourselves *G1997*

ASSEMBLY
Gen 49: 6 secret; unto their **a**, mine honour, be H6951
Ex 12: 6 and the whole **a** of the congregation H6951
16: 3 to kill this whole **a** with hunger. H6951
Lev 4:13 the eyes of the **a**, and they have done H6951
8: 4 him; and the **a** was gathered together H5712
23:36 it *is* a solemn **a**; *and* ye shall do no H6116
Nu 8: 9 **a** of the children of Israel together: H5712
10: 2 **a**, and for the journeying of the camps. H5712
3 with them, all the **a** shall assemble H5712
14: 5 before all the **a** of the congregation H6951
16: 2 and fifty princes of the **a**, famous in the H5712
20: 6 presence of the **a** unto the door of the H6951
8 Take the rod, and gather thou the **a** H5712
29:35 **a**: ye shall do no servile work *therein*: H6116
Dt 5:22 unto all your **a** in the mount out of H6951
9:10 the midst of the fire in the day of the **a**. H6951
10: 4 **a**: and the LORD gave them unto me. H6951
16: 8 *shall be* a solemn **a** to the LORD thy H6116
18:16 in the day of the **a**, saying, Let me not H6951
Jdg 20: 2 themselves in the **a** of the people of H6951
21: 8 the camp from Jabesh-gilead to the **a**. H6951
1Sa 17:47 And all this **a** shall know that the H6951
2Ki 10:20 And Jehu said, Proclaim a solemn **a** for H6116
2Ch 7: 9 they made a solemn **a**: for they kept the H6116
30:23 And the whole **a** took counsel to keep H6951
Neh 5: 7 And I set a great **a** against them. H6952
8:18 a solemn **a**, according unto the manner. H6116
Ps 22:16 For dogs have compassed me: the **a** of H5712
89: 7 God is greatly to be feared in the **a** of H5475
107:32 and praise him in the **a** of the elders. H4186
111: 1 heart, in the **a** of the upright, and H5475
Prv 5:14 in the midst of the congregation and **a**. H5712
Jer 6:11 and upon the **a** of young men together: H5475
9: 2 all adulterers, an **a** of treacherous men. H6116
15:17 I sat not in the **a** of the mockers, nor H5475
26:17 spake to all the **a** of the people, saying, H6951
50: 9 Babylon an **a** of great nations from H6951
Lam 1:15 he hath called an **a** against me to crush H4150
2: 6 his places of the **a**: the LORD hath H4150
Ezk 13: 9 they shall not be in the **a** of my people, H5475
23:24 and with an **a** of people, *which* shall H6951
Joel 1:14 Sanctify ye a fast, call a solemn **a**, H6116
2:15 in Zion, sanctify a fast, call a solemn **a**: H6116
Zep 3:18 for the solemn **a**, *who* are of thee, *to* H4150
Act 19:32 another: for the **a** was confused; and *G1577*
39 it shall be determined in a lawful **a**. *G1577*
41 he had thus spoken, he dismissed the **a**. *G1577*
Heb 12:23 To the general **a** and church of the *G3831*
Jas 2: 2 For if there come unto your **a** a man *G4864*

ASSENT
2Ch 18:12 to the king with one **a**; let thy word H6310

ASSENTED
Act 24: 9 And the Jews also **a**, saying that these *G4934*

ASSES
Gen 12:16 and oxen, and he **a**, and menservants, H2543
16 maidservants, and she **a**, and camels. H860
24:35 and maidservants, and camels, and **a**. H2543
30:43 and menservants, and camels, and **a**. H2543
32: 5 And I have oxen, and **a**, flocks, and H2543
15 and ten bulls, twenty she **a**, and ten foals. H860
34:28 oxen, and their **a**, and that which *was* H2543
36:24 as he fed the **a** of Zibeon his father. H2543
42:26 And they laded their **a** with the corn, H2543
43:18 us, and take us for bondmen, and our **a**. H2543
24 feet; and he gave their **a** provender. H2543
44: 3 men were sent away, they and their **a**. H2543
45:23 this *manner*; ten **a** laden with the good H2543
23 Egypt, and ten she **a** laden with corn and H860
47:17 herds, and for the **a**: and he fed them H2543
Ex 9: 3 horses, upon the **a**, upon the camels, H2543
Nu 31:28 beeves, and of the **a**, and of the sheep: H2543
30 the beeves, of the **a**, and of the flocks, of H2543
34 And threescore and one thousand **a**, H2543
39 And the **a** *were* thirty thousand and H2543
45 And thirty thousand **a** and five H2543
Jos 7:24 his oxen, and his **a**, and his sheep, and H2543
9: 4 sacks upon their **a**, and wine bottles, H2543
Jdg 5:10 Speak, ye that ride on white **a**, ye that sit H860
19: 3 and a couple of **a**: and she brought him H2543
10 *there were* with him two **a** saddled, his H2543
19 provender for our **a**; and there is bread H2543
21 unto the **a**: and they washed their H2543
1Sa 8:16 and your **a**, and put *them* to his work. H2543
9: 3 And the **a** of Kish Saul's father were lost. H860
3 with thee, and arise, go seek the **a**. H860
5 *caring* for the **a**, and take thought for us. H860
20 And as for thine **a** that were lost three H860
10: 2 say unto thee, The **a** which thou wentest H860
2 left the care of the **a**, and sorroweth for H860
14 he said, To seek the **a**: and when we saw H860
16 us plainly that the **a** were found. But of H860
22:19 and oxen, and **a**, and sheep, with the H2543
25:18 cakes of figs, and laid *them* on **a**. H2543
27: 9 the oxen, and the **a**, and the camels, H2543
2Sa 16: 1 with a couple of **a** saddled, and upon H2543
2 And Ziba said, The **a** *be* for the king's H2543
2Ki 4:22 and one of the **a**, that I may run to the H860
7: 7 horses, and their **a**, even the camp as it H2543
10 and **a** tied, and the tents as they *were*. H2543
1Ch 5:21 thousand, and of **a** two thousand, and H2543
12:40 brought bread on **a**, and on camels, and H2543
27:30 the **a** *was* Jehdeiah the Meronothite: H860
2Ch 28:15 of them upon **a**, and brought them to H2543
Ezr 2:67 and five; *their* **a**, six thousand seven H2543
Neh 7:69 thousand seven hundred and twenty **a**. H2543
13:15 and lading **a**; as also wine, grapes, H2543
Job 1: 3 and five hundred she **a**, and a very great H860
14 plowing, and the **a** feeding beside them: H860
24: 5 Behold, *as* wild **a** in the desert, go they H6501
42:12 yoke of oxen, and a thousand she **a**. H860
Ps 104:11 the field: the wild **a** quench their thirst. H6501
Isa 21: 7 a chariot of **a**, *and* a chariot of camels; H2543
30: 6 of young **a**, and their treasures H5895
24 The oxen likewise and the young **a** that H5895
32:14 ever, a joy of wild **a**, a pasture of flocks; H6501
Jer 14: 6 And the wild **a** did stand in the high H6501
Ezk 23:20 *is as* the flesh of **a**, and whose issue *is* H2543
Dan 5:21 *was* with the wild **a**: they fed him with H6167

ASSHUR
Gen 10:11 Out of that land went forth **A**, and H804
22 The children of Shem; Elam, and **A**, and H804
Nu 24:22 until **A** shall carry thee away captive. H804
24 and shall afflict **A**, and shall afflict Eber, H804
1Ch 1:17 The sons of Shem; Elam, and **A**, and H804
Ezk 27:23 **A**, *and* Chilmad, *were* thy merchants. H804
32:22 **A** *is* there and all her company: his H804
Hos 14: 3 **A** shall not save us; we will not ride upon H804

ASSHURIM
Gen 25: 3 were **A**, and Letushim, and Leummim. H805

ASSIGNED
Gen 47:22 had a portion **a** *them* of Pharaoh, and
Jos 20: 8 Jericho eastward, they **a** Bezer in the H5414
2Sa 11:16 the city, that he **a** Uriah unto a place H5414

ASSIR
Ex 6:24 And the sons of Korah; **A**, and Elkanah, H617
1Ch 3:17 And the sons of Jeconiah; **A**, Salathiel his H617
6:22 his son, Korah his son, **A** his son, H617
23 and Ebiasaph his son, and **A** his son, H617
6:37 The son of Tahath, the son of **A**, the son H617

ASSIST
Ro 16: 2 saints, and that ye **a** her in whatsoever *G3936*

ASSOCIATE
Isa 8: 9 **A** yourselves, O ye people, and ye shall H7489

ASSOS
Act 20:13 and sailed unto **A**, there intending to *G789*
14 And when he met with us at **A**, we took *G789*

ASS'S
Gen 49:11 Binding his foal unto the vine, and his **a** H860
2Ki 6:25 besieged it, until an **a** head was *sold* for H2543
Job 11:12 though man be born *like* a wild **a** colt. H6501
Jn 12:15 thy King cometh, sitting on an **a** colt. *G3688*

ASSUAGE See ASSWAGE.

ASSUR
Ezr 4: 2 king of **A**, which brought us up hither. H804
Ps 83: 8 **A** also is joined with them: they have H804

ASSURANCE
Dt 28:66 night, and shalt have none **a** of thy life: H539
Isa 32:17 righteousness quietness and **a** for ever. H983
Act 17:31 he hath given **a** unto all *men*, in that *G4102*
Col 2: 2 riches of the full **a** of understanding, to *G4136*
1Th 1: 5 Ghost, and in much **a**; as ye know what *G4136*
Heb 6:11 to the full **a** of hope unto the end: *G4136*
10:22 a true heart in full **a** of faith, having *G4136*

ASSURE
1Jn 3:19 and shall **a** our hearts before him. *G3982*

ASSURED
Lev 27:19 unto it, and it shall be **a** to him. H6965
Jer 14:13 but I will give you **a** peace in this place. H571
2Ti 3:14 and hast been **a** of, knowing of whom *G4104*

ASSUREDLY
1Sa 28: 1 David, Know thou **a**, that thou shalt go H3045
1Ki 1:13 saying, **A** Solomon thy son shall H3588
17 *saying*, **A** Solomon thy son shall H3588
30 of Israel, saying, **A** Solomon thy son H3588
Jer 32:41 them in this land **a** with my whole heart H571
38:17 of Israel; If thou wilt **a** go forth unto the H3318
49:12 of the cup have **a** drunken; and *art* H8354
Act 2:36 of Israel know **a**, that God hath made *G806*
16:10 into Macedonia, **a** gathering that the *G4822*

ASSWAGE
Job 16: 5 moving of my lips should **a** *your grief*. H2820

ASSWAGED
Gen 8: 1 to pass over the earth, and the waters **a**; H7918
Job 16: 6 Though I speak, my grief is not **a**: and H2820

ASSYRIA
Gen 2:14 of **A**. And the fourth river *is* Euphrates. H804
25:18 thou goest toward **A**: *and* he died in the H804
2Ki 15:19 *And* Pul the king of **A** came against the H804
20 to give to the king of **A**. So the king of H804
20 So the king of **A** turned back, and stayed H804
29 king of **A**, and took Ijon, and H804
29 Naphtali, and carried them captive to **A**. H804
16: 7 king of **A**, saying, I *am* thy servant H804
8 and sent *it for* a present to the king of **A**. H804
9 And the king of **A** hearkened unto him: H804
9 him: for the king of **A** went up against H804
10 king of **A**, and saw an altar that H804
18 the house of the LORD for the king of **A**. H804
17: 3 king of **A**; and Hoshea became H804
4 And the king of **A** found conspiracy in H804
4 to the king of **A**, as *he had done* year H804
4 the king of **A** shut him up, and bound H804
5 Then the king of **A** came up throughout H804
6 In the ninth year of Hoshea the king of **A** H804
6 Israel away into **A**, and placed them in H804
23 out of their own land to **A** unto this day. H804
24 And the king of **A** brought *men* from H804
26 Wherefore they spake to the king of **A**, H804
27 Then the king of **A** commanded, saying, H804
18: 7 the king of **A**, and served him not. H804
9 king of **A** came up against Samaria, H804
11 And the king of **A** did carry away Israel H804
11 away Israel unto **A**, and put them in H804
13 king of **A** come up against all H804

2Ki 18:14 sent to the king of A to Lachish, saying, I H804
14 bear. And the king of A appointed unto H804
16 had overlaid, and gave it to the king of A. H804
17 And the king of A sent Tartan and H804
19 king, the king of A, What confidence *is* H804
23 my lord the king of A, and I will deliver H804
28 the word of the great king, the king of A: H804
30 delivered into the hand of the king of A. H804
31 saith the king of A, Make *an agreement* H804
33 his land out of the hand of the king of A? H804
19: 4 whom the king of A his master hath sent H804
6 of the king of A have blasphemed me. H804
8 and found the king of A warring against H804
10 delivered into the hand of the king of A. H804
11 what the kings of A have done to all H804
17 Of a truth, LORD, the kings of A have H804
20 Sennacherib king of A I have heard. H804
32 the king of A, He shall not come into H804
36 So Sennacherib king of A departed, and H804
20: 6 hand of the king of A; and I will defend H804
23:29 up against the king of A to the river H804
1Ch 5: 6 king of A carried away *captive:* H804
26 spirit of Pul king of A, and the spirit of H804
26 king of A, and he carried them H804
2Ch 28:16 send unto the kings of A to help him. H804
20 And Tilgath-pilneser king of A came H804
21 the king of A: but he helped him not. H804
30: 6 escaped out of the hand of the kings of A. H804
32: 1 king of A came, and entered into H804
4 kings of A come, and find much water? H804
7 for the king of A, nor for all the multitude H804
9 After this did Sennacherib king of A H804
10 Thus saith Sennacherib king of A, H804
11 us out of the hand of the king of A? H804
21 of the king of A. So he returned with H804
22 the king of A, and from the hand of H804
33:11 the host of the king of A, which took H804
Ezr 6:22 the heart of the king of A unto them, to H804
Neh 9:32 the time of the kings of A unto this day. H804
Isa 7:17 departed from Judah; *even* the king of A. H804
18 and for the bee that *is* in the land of A. H804
20 by the king of A, the head, and the hair H804
8: 4 shall be taken away before the king of A. H804
7 *even* the king of A, and all his glory: and H804
10:12 king of A, and the glory of his high looks. H804
11:11 shall be left, from A, and from Egypt, and H804
16 shall be left, from A; like as it was to H804
19:23 out of Egypt to A, and the Assyrian shall H804
23 the Egyptian into A, and the Egyptians H804
24 Egypt and with A, *even* a blessing in the H804
25 my people, and A the work of my hands, H804
20: 1 Sargon the king of A sent him,) and H804
4 So shall the king of A lead away the H804
6 the king of A: and how shall we escape? H804
27:13 in the land of A, and the outcasts in the H804
36: 1 king of A came up against all H804
2 And the king of A sent Rabshakeh from H804
4 king, the king of A, What confidence *is* H804
8 master the king of A, and I will give thee H804
13 the words of the great king, the king of A. H804
15 delivered into the hand of the king of A. H804
16 saith the king of A, Make *an agreement* H804
18 his land out of the hand of the king of A? H804
37: 4 whom the king of A his master hath sent H804
6 of the king of A have blasphemed me. H804
8 and found the king of A warring against H804
10 be given into the hand of the king of A. H804
11 what the kings of A have done to all H804
18 Of a truth, LORD, the kings of A have H804
21 to me against Sennacherib king of A: H804
33 the king of A, He shall not come into H804
37 So Sennacherib king of A departed, and H804
38: 6 the king of A: and I will defend this city. H804
Jer 2:18 way of A, to drink the waters of the river? H804
36 of Egypt, as thou wast ashamed of A. H804
50:17 first the king of A hath devoured him; H804
18 land, as I have punished the king of A. H804
Ezk 23: 7 the chosen men of A, and with all on H804
Hos 7:11 heart: they call to Egypt, they go to A. H804
8: 9 For they are gone up to A, a wild ass H804
9: 3 and they shall eat unclean *things* in A. H804
10: 6 It shall be also carried unto A *for* a H804
11:11 out of the land of A: and I will place them H804
Mic 5: 6 And they shall waste the land of A with H804
7:12 come even to thee from A, and *from* the H804
Nah 3:18 Thy shepherds slumber, O king of A: thy H804
Zep 2:13 the north, and destroy A; and will make H804
Zec 10:10 gather them out of A; and I will bring H804
11 up: and the pride of A shall be brought H804

ASSYRIAN

Isa 10: 5 O A, the rod of mine anger, and the staff H804
24 be not afraid of the A: he shall smite thee H804
14:25 That I will break the A in my land, and H804
19:23 to Assyria, and the A shall come into H804
23:13 was not, *till* the A founded it for them H804
30:31 of the LORD shall the A be beaten down, H804
31: 8 Then shall the A fall with the sword, not H804
52: 4 the A oppressed them without cause. H804
Ezk 31: 3 Behold, the A *was* a cedar in Lebanon H804
Hos 5:13 Ephraim to the A, and sent to king Jareb: H804
11: 5 of Egypt, but the A shall be his king, H804
Mic 5: 5 peace, when the A shall come into our H804
6 he deliver *us* from the A, when he cometh H804

ASSYRIANS

2Ki 19:35 smote in the camp of the A an hundred H804
Isa 19:23 and the Egyptians shall serve with the A. H804
37:36 in the camp of the A a hundred and H804
Lam 5: 6 *and to* the A, to be satisfied with bread. H804
Ezk 16:28 also with the A, because thou H1121+H804
23: 5 on her lovers, on the A *her* neighbours, H804
9 of the A, upon whom she doted. H1121+H804
12 She doted upon the A *her* H1121+H804
23 *and* all the A with them: all of H1121+H804
Hos 12: 1 with the A, and oil is carried into Egypt. H804

ASTAROTH

Dt 1: 4 of Bashan, which dwelt at A in Edrei: H6252

ASTONIED

Ezr 9: 3 head and of my beard, and sat down a. H8074
4 and I sat a until the evening sacrifice. H8074
Job 17: 8 Upright *men* shall be a at this, and the H8074
18:20 They that come after *him* shall be a at H8074
Isa 52:14 As many were a at thee; his visage was H8074
Jer 14: 9 Why shouldest thou be as a man a, as a H1724
Ezk 4:17 and water, and be a one with another, H8074
Dan 3:24 Then Nebuchadnezzar the king was a, H8429
4:19 Belteshazzar, was a for one hour, and H8075
5: 9 changed in him, and his lords were a. H7672

ASTONISHED

Lev 26:32 which dwell therein shall be a at it. H8074
1Ki 9: 8 by it shall be a, and shall hiss; and H8074
Job 21: 5 Mark me, and be a, and lay *your* hand H8074
26:11 The pillars of heaven tremble and are a H8539
Jer 2:12 Be a, O ye heavens, at this, and be H8074
4: 9 be a, and the prophets shall wonder. H8074
18:16 thereby shall be a, and wag his head. H8074
19: 8 thereby shall be a and hiss because of H8074
49:17 by it shall be a, and shall hiss at all H8074
50:13 shall be a, and hiss at all her plagues. H8074
Ezk 3:15 there a among them seven days. H8074
26:16 at *every* moment, and be a at thee. H8074
27:35 of the isles shall be a at thee, and their H8074
28:19 the people shall be a at thee: thou shalt H8074
Dan 8:27 a at the vision, but none understood *it.* H8074
Mt 7:28 the people were a at his doctrine: *G1605*
13:54 that they were a, and said, Whence *G1605*
22:33 heard *this,* they were a at his doctrine. *G1605*
Mk 1:22 And they were a at his doctrine: for he *G1605*
5:42 they were a with a great astonishment. *G1839*
6: 2 many hearing *him* were a, saying, From *G1605*
7:37 And were beyond measure a, saying, *G1605*
10:24 And the disciples were a at his words. *G2284*
26 And they were a out of measure, saying *G1605*
11:18 all the people was a at his doctrine. *G1605*
Lk 2:47 And all that heard him were a at his *G1839*
4:32 And they were a at his doctrine: for his *G1605*
5: 9 For he was a, and all that were with *G4023*
8:56 And her parents were a: but he charged *G1839*
24:22 us a, which were early at the sepulchre; *G1839*
Act 9: 6 And he trembling and a said, Lord, *G2284*
10:45 believed were a, as many as came with *G1839*
12:16 *the door,* and saw him, they were a. *G1839*
13:12 being a at the doctrine of the Lord. *G1605*

ASTONISHMENT

Dt 28:28 and blindness, and a of heart: H8541
37 And thou shalt become an a, a proverb, H8047
2Ch 7:21 is high, shall be an a to every one that H8074
29: 8 to trouble, to a, and to hissing, as ye H8047
Ps 60: 3 hast made us to drink the wine of a. H8653
Jer 8:21 I am black; a hath taken hold on me. H8047
25: 9 make them an a, and an hissing, and H8047
11 *and* an a; and these nations shall H8047
18 a desolation, an a, an hissing, and a H8047
29:18 to be a curse, and an a, and an hissing, H8047
Jer 42:18 and an a, and a curse, and a reproach; H8047
44:12 *and* an a, and a curse, and a reproach. H8047
22 and an a, and a curse, without H8047
51:37 for dragons, an a, and an hissing, H8047
41 become an a among the nations! H8047
Ezk 4:16 drink water by measure, and with a: H8078
5:15 and an a unto the nations that H4923
12:19 their water with a, that her land may be H8078
23:33 with the cup of a and desolation, with H8047
Zec 12: 4 every horse with a, and his rider with H8541
Mk 5:42 they were astonished with a great a. *G1611*

ASTRAY

Ex 23: 4 ox or his ass going a, thou shalt surely H8582
Dt 22: 1 ox or his sheep go a, and hide thyself H5080
Ps 58: 3 the womb: they go a as soon as they be H8582
119:67 Before I was afflicted I went a: but now H7683
176 I have gone a like a lost sheep; seek thy H8582
Prv 5:23 the greatness of his folly he shall go a. H7686
7:25 to her ways, go not a in her paths. H8582
28:10 Whoso causeth the righteous to go a in H7686
Isa 53: 6 All we like sheep have gone a; we have H8582
Jer 50: 6 caused them to go a, they have turned H8582
Ezk 14:11 may go no more a from me, neither be H8582
44:10 when Israel went a, which went astray H8582
10 which went a away from me after H8582
15 of Israel went a from me, they shall H8582
48:11 which went not a when the children of H8582
11 went a, as the Levites went astray. H8582
11 went astray, as the Levites went a. H8582
Mt 18:12 of them be gone a, doth he not leave the *G4105*
12 and seeketh that which is gone a? *G4105*
13 the ninety and nine which went not a. *G4105*
1Pt 2:25 For ye were as sheep going a; but are *G4105*
2Pt 2:15 way, and are gone a, following the way *G4105*

ASTROLOGER

Dan 2:10 at any magician, or a, or Chaldean. H826

ASTROLOGERS

Isa 47:13 Let now the a, the stargazers, H1895+H8064
Dan 1:20 *and* a that *were* in all his realm. H825
2: 2 magicians, and the a, and the sorcerers, H825
27 the wise *men,* the a, the magicians, the H826
4: 7 Then came in the magicians, the a, the H826
5: 7 The king cried aloud to bring in the a, the H826
11 a, Chaldeans, *and* soothsayers; H826
15 And now the wise *men,* the a, have been H826

ASUNDER

Lev 1:17 shall not divide *it* a: and the priest shall
5: 8 from his neck, but shall not divide *it* a:
Nu 16:31 the ground clave a that *was* under them:
2Ki 2:11 parted them both a; and Elijah went up H996
Job 16:12 I was at ease, but he hath broken me a:
13 cleaveth my reins a, and doth not spare;
Ps 2: 3 Let us break their bands a, and cast
129: 4 The LORD *is* righteous: he hath cut a the
Jer 50:23 the whole earth cut a and broken! how is
Ezk 30:16 a, and Noph *shall have* distresses daily.
Hab 3: 6 beheld, and drove a the nations; and the
Zec 11:10 Beauty, and cut it a, that I might break
14 Then I cut a mine other staff, *even*
Mt 19: 6 hath joined together, let not man put a. *G5563*
24:51 And shall cut him a, and appoint *him* *G1371*
Mk 5: 4 had been plucked a by him, and the *G1288*
10: 9 hath joined together, let not man put a. *G5563*
Act 1:18 he burst a in the midst, and all *G2997*
15:39 that they departed a one from the other: *G673*
Heb 4:12 to the dividing a of soul and spirit, and *G3311*
11:37 They were stoned, they were sawn a, *G4249*

ASUPPIM

1Ch 26:15 and to his sons the house of A. H624
17 four a day, and toward A two *and* two. H624

ASYNCRITUS

Ro 16:14 Salute A, Phlegon, Hermas, Patrobas, *G799*

AT See the Appendix.

ATAD

Gen 50:10 And they came to the threshingfloor of A, H329
11 in the floor of A, they said, This *is* a H329

ATARAH

1Ch 2:26 was A; she *was* the mother of Onam. H5851

ATAROTH
Nu 32: 3 **A**, and Dibon, and Jazer, and Nimrah, H5852
34 of Gad built Dibon, and **A**, and Aroer, H5852
Jos 16: 2 along unto the borders of Archi to **A**, H5852
7 And it went down from Janohah to **A**, H5852
1Ch 2:54 the Netophathites, **A**, the house of Joab, H5852

ATAROTH-ADAR
Jos 18:13 descended to **A**, near the hill that *lieth* H5853

ATAROTH-ADDAR
Jos 16: 5 side was **A**, unto Bethhoron the upper; H5853

ATE
Ps 106:28 and **a** the sacrifices of the dead. H398
Dan 10: 3 I **a** no pleasant bread, neither came flesh H398
Rev 10:10 angel's hand, and **a** it up; and it was in *G2719*

ATER
Ezr 2:16 The children of **A** of Hezekiah, ninety H333
42 the children of **A**, the children of Talmon, H333
Neh 7:21 The children of **A** of Hezekiah, ninety H333
45 the children of **A**, the children of Talmon, H333
10:17 **A**, Hizkijah, Azzur, H333

ATHA See MARAN-ATHA.

ATHACH
1Sa 30:30 and to *them* which *were* in **A**, H6269

ATHAIAH
Neh 11: 4 children of Judah; **A** the son of Uzziah, H6265

ATHALIAH
2Ki 8:26 **A**, the daughter of Omri king of Israel. H6271
11: 1 And when **A** the mother of Ahaziah H6271
2 from **A**, so that he was not slain. H6271
3 years. And **A** did reign over the land. H6271
13 And when **A** heard the noise of the H6271
14 trumpets: and **A** rent her clothes, and H6271
20 and they slew **A** with the sword *beside* H6271
1Ch 8:26 Shamsherai, and Sheariah, and **A**, H6271
2Ch 22: 2 name also *was* **A** the daughter of Omri. H6271
10 But when **A** the mother of Ahaziah saw H6271
11 him from **A**, so that she slew him not. H6271
12 six years: and **A** reigned over the land. H6271
23:12 Now when **A** heard the noise of the H6271
13 to sing praise. Then **A** rent her clothes, H6271
21 that they had slain **A** with the sword. H6271
24: 7 For the sons of **A**, that wicked woman, H6271
Ezr 8: 7 son of **A**, and with him seventy males. H6271

ATHENIANS
Act 17:21 (For all the **A** and strangers which were *G117*

ATHENS
Act 17:15 Paul brought him unto **A**: and receiving a *G116*
16 Now while Paul waited for them at **A**, his *G116*
22 said, *Ye* men of **A**, I perceive that in all *G117*
18: 1 After these things Paul departed from **A**, *G116*
1Th 3: 1 we thought it good to be left at **A** alone; *G116*

ATHIRST
Jdg 15:18 And he was sore **a**, and called on the H6770
Ru 2: 9 thee? and when thou art **a**, go unto the H6770
Mt 25:44 thee an hungred, or **a**, or a stranger, or *G1372*
Rev 21: 6 unto him that is **a** of the fountain of the *G1372*
22:17 let him that is **a** come. And whosoever *G1372*

ATHLAI
Ezr 10:28 Jehohanan, Hananiah, Zabbai, *and* **A**. H6270

ATONEMENT
Ex 29:33 things wherewith the **a** was made, to H3722
36 *for* a sin offering for **a**: and thou shalt H3725
36 hast made an **a** for it, and thou shalt H3722
37 Seven days thou shalt make an **a** for H3722
30:10 And Aaron shall make an **a** upon the H3722
10 shall he make **a** upon it throughout H3722
15 the LORD, to make an **a** for your souls. H3722
16 And thou shalt take the **a** money of the H3725
16 the LORD, to make an **a** for your souls. H3722
32:30 I shall make an **a** for your sin. H3722
Lev 1: 4 be accepted for him to make **a** for him. H3722
4:20 shall make an **a** for them, and it shall H3722
26 shall make an **a** for him as concerning H3722
31 **a** for him, and it shall be forgiven him. H3722
35 shall make an **a** for his sin that he hath H3722
5: 6 make an **a** for him concerning his sin. H3722
Lev 5:10 shall make an **a** for him for his sin H3722
13 And the priest shall make an **a** for him H3722
16 shall make an **a** for him with the ram H3722
18 shall make an **a** for him concerning H3722
6: 7 And the priest shall make an **a** for him H3722
7: 7 that maketh **a** therewith shall have *it*. H3722
8:34 to do, to make an **a** for you. H3722
9: 7 and make an **a** for thyself, and for the H3722
7 **a** for them; as the LORD commanded. H3722
10:17 to make **a** for them before the LORD? H3722
12: 7 and make an **a** for her; and she shall H3722
8 an **a** for her, and she shall be clean. H3722
14:18 make an **a** for him before the LORD. H3722
19 and make an **a** for him that is to be H3722
20 an **a** for him, and he shall be clean. H3722
21 to make an **a** for him, and one tenth H3722
29 to make an **a** for him before the LORD. H3722
31 shall make an **a** for him that is to be H3722
53 **a** for the house: and it shall be clean. H3722
15:15 shall make an **a** for him before the H3722
30 shall make an **a** for her before the H3722
16: 6 an **a** for himself, and for his house. H3722
10 LORD, to make an **a** with him, *and* to H3722
11 and shall make an **a** for himself, and H3722
16 And he shall make an **a** for the holy H3722
17 in to make an **a** in the holy *place*, until H3722
17 and have made an **a** for himself, and H3722
18 and make an **a** for it; and shall take H3722
24 an **a** for himself, and for the people. H3722
27 in to make **a** in the holy *place*, shall H3722
30 *the priest* make an **a** for you, to cleanse H3722
32 shall make the **a**, and shall put on the H3722
33 And he shall make an **a** for the holy H3722
33 he shall make an **a** for the tabernacle of H3722
33 he shall make an **a** for the priests, and H3722
34 you, to make an **a** for the children of H3722
17:11 altar to make an **a** for your souls: for it H3722
11 blood *that* maketh an **a** for the soul. H3722
19:22 And the priest shall make an **a** for him H3722
23:27 *shall be* a day of **a**: it shall be an holy H3725
28 day: for it *is* a day of **a**, to make an H3725
28 **a** for you before the LORD your God. H3722
25: 9 in the day of **a** shall ye make the H3725
Nu 5: 8 the ram of the **a**, whereby an atonement H3725
8 whereby an **a** shall be made for him. H3722
6:11 and make an **a** for him, for that he H3722
8:12 the LORD, to make an **a** for the Levites. H3722
19 and to make an **a** for the children of H3722
21 made an **a** for them to cleanse them. H3722
15:25 And the priest shall make an **a** for all H3722
28 And the priest shall make an **a** for the H3722
28 **a** for him; and it shall be forgiven him. H3722
16:46 and make an **a** for them: for there is H3722
47 incense, and made an **a** for the people. H3722
25:13 made an **a** for the children of Israel. H3722
28:22 *for* a sin offering, to make an **a** for you. H3722
30 *And* one kid of the goats, to make an **a** H3722
29: 5 *for* a sin offering, to make an **a** for you: H3722
11 the sin offering of **a**, and the continual H3725
31:50 an **a** for our souls before the LORD. H3722
2Sa 21: 3 shall I make the **a**, that ye may bless the H3722
1Ch 6:49 and to make an **a** for Israel, according H3722
2Ch 29:24 altar, to make an **a** for all Israel: for the H3722
Neh 10:33 to make an **a** for Israel, and *for* all H3722
Ro 5:11 by whom we have now received the **a**. *G2643*

ATONEMENTS
Ex 30:10 of the sin offering of **a**: once in the year H3725

ATROTH
Nu 32:35 And **A**, Shophan, and Jaazer, and H5855

ATTAI
1Ch 2:35 his servant to wife; and she bare him **A**. H6262
36 And **A** begat Nathan, and Nathan H6262
12:11 **A** the sixth, Eliel the seventh, H6262
2Ch 11:20 and **A**, and Ziza, and Shelomith. H6262

ATTAIN
Ps 139: 6 for me; it is high, I cannot ***a*** unto it.
Prv 1: 5 shall **a** unto wise counsels: H7069
Ezk 46: 7 **a** unto, and an hin of oil to an ephah. H5381
Hos 8: 5 long *will it be* ere they **a** to innocency? H3201
Act 27:12 means they might **a** to Phenice, *and* *G2658*
Php 3:11 If by any means I might **a** unto the *G2658*

ATTAINED
Gen 47: 9 and have not **a** unto the days of the H5381
2Sa 23:19 howbeit he **a** not unto the *first* three. H935
2Sa 23:23 the thirty, but he **a** not to the *first* three. H935
1Ch 11:21 howbeit he **a** not to the *first* three. H935
25 the thirty, but **a** not to the *first* three: H935
Ro 9:30 have **a** to righteousness, even *G2638*
31 hath not **a** to the law of righteousness. *G5348*
Php 3:12 Not as though I had already **a**, either *G2983*
16 we have already **a**, let us walk by the *G5348*
1Ti 4: 6 good doctrine, whereunto thou hast **a**. *G3877*

ATTALIA
Act 14:25 word in Perga, they went down into **A**: *G825*

ATTEND
Est 4: 5 had appointed to **a** upon her, and gave H6440
Ps 17: 1 Hear the right, O LORD, **a** unto my cry, H7181
55: 2 **A** unto me, and hear me: I mourn in H7181
61: 1 Hear my cry, O God; **a** unto my prayer. H7181
86: 6 and **a** to the voice of my supplications. H7181
142: 6 **A** unto my cry; for I am brought very H7181
Prv 4: 1 a father, and **a** to know understanding. H7181
20 My son, **a** to my words; incline thine H7181
5: 1 My son, **a** unto my wisdom, *and* bow H7181
7:24 and **a** to the words of my mouth. H7181
1Co 7:35 **a** upon the Lord without distraction. *G2145*

ATTENDANCE
1Ki 10: 5 his servants, and the **a** of his ministers, H4612
2Ch 9: 4 his servants, and the **a** of his ministers, H4612
1Ti 4:13 Till I come, give **a** to reading, to *G4337*
Heb 7:13 of which no man gave **a** at the altar. *G4337*

ATTENDED
Job 32:12 Yea, I **a** unto you, and, behold, *there was* H995
Ps 66:19 *me*; he hath **a** to the voice of my prayer. H7181
Act 16:14 Lord opened, that she **a** unto the things *G4337*

ATTENDING
Ro 13: 6 **a** continually upon this very thing. *G4342*

ATTENT
2Ch 6:40 *let* thine ears *be* **a** unto the prayer *that* H7183
7:15 and mine ears **a** unto the prayer *that* H7183

ATTENTIVE
Neh 1: 6 Let thine ear now be **a**, and thine eyes H7183
11 now thine ear be **a** to the prayer of thy H7183
8: 3 people *were* ***a*** unto the book of the law.
Ps 130: 2 Lord, hear my voice: let thine ears be **a** H7183
Lk 19:48 all the people were very **a** to hear him. *G1582*

ATTENTIVELY
Job 37: 2 Hear **a** the noise of his voice, and the H8085

ATTIRE
Prv 7:10 the **a** of an harlot, and subtil of heart. H7897
Jer 2:32 *or* a bride her **a**? yet my people have H7196
Ezk 23:15 exceeding in dyed **a** upon their heads, H2871

ATTIRED
Lev 16: 4 linen mitre shall he be **a**: these *are* holy H6801

AUDIENCE
Gen 23:10 Abraham in the **a** of the children of H241
13 And he spake unto Ephron in the **a** of H241
16 had named in the **a** of the sons of Heth, H241
Ex 24: 7 and read in the **a** of the people: and they H241
1Sa 25:24 speak in thine **a**, and hear the words H241
1Ch 28: 8 LORD, and in the **a** of our God, keep and H241
Neh 13: 1 book of Moses in the **a** of the people; and H241
Lk 7: 1 all his sayings in the **a** of the people, he *G189*
20:45 Then in the **a** of all the people he said *G191*
Act 13:16 of Israel, and ye that fear God, give **a**. *G191*
15:12 silence, and gave **a** to Barnabas and *G191*
22:22 And they gave him **a** unto this word, and *G191*

AUGHT
Ru 1:17 also, *if* **a** but death part thee and me.

AUGMENT
Nu 32:14 of sinful men, to **a** yet the fierce anger H5595

AUGUSTUS
Lk 2: 1 **A**, that all the world should be taxed. *G828*
Act 25:21 the hearing of **A**, I commanded him *G4575*
25 to **A**, I have determined to send him. *G4575*

AUGUSTUS'
Act 27: 1 named Julius, a centurion of **A** band. *G4575*

A

AUL
Ex 21: 6 an **a**; and he shall serve him for ever. H4836
Dt 15:17 Then thou shalt take an **a**, and thrust *it* H4836

AUNT
Lev 18:14 not approach to his wife: she *is* thine **a**. H1733

AUSTERE
Lk 19:21 For I feared thee, because thou art an **a** *G840*
22 that I was an **a** man, taking up that *G840*

AUTHOR
1Co 14:33 For God is not *the* ***a*** of confusion, but of
Heb 5: 9 he became the **a** of eternal salvation *G159*
12: 2 Looking unto Jesus the **a** and finisher of *G747*

AUTHORITIES
1Pt 3:22 of God; angels and **a** and powers being *G1849*

AUTHORITY
Est 9:29 the Jew, wrote with all **a**, to confirm this H8633
Prv 29: 2 When the righteous are in **a**, the people H7235
Mt 7:29 For he taught them as *one* having **a**, *G1849*
8: 9 For I am a man under **a**, having *G1849*
20:25 that are great exercise **a** upon them. *G1849*
21:23 and said, By what **a** doest thou these *G1849*
23 these things? and who gave thee this **a**? *G1849*
24 will tell you by what **a** I do these things. *G1849*
27 tell I you by what **a** I do these things. *G1849*
Mk 1:22 one that had **a**, and not as the scribes. *G1849*
27 *is* this? for with **a** commandeth he even *G1849*
10:42 their great ones exercise **a** upon them. *G2715*
11:28 And say unto him, By what **a** doest *G1849*
28 who gave thee this **a** to do these things? *G1849*
29 will tell you by what **a** I do these things. *G1849*
33 I tell you by what **a** I do these things. *G1849*
13:34 house, and gave **a** to his servants, and *G1849*
Lk 4:36 word *is* this! for with **a** and power he *G1849*
7: 8 For I also am a man set under **a**, having *G1849*
9: 1 **a** over all devils, and to cure diseases. *G1849*
19:17 a very little, have thou **a** over ten cities. *G1849*
20: 2 Tell us, by what **a** doest thou these *G1849*
2 or who is he that gave thee this **a**? *G1849*
8 tell I you by what **a** I do these things. *G1849*
20 unto the power and **a** of the governor. *G1849*
22:25 **a** upon them are called benefactors. *G1850*
Jn 5:27 And hath given him **a** to execute *G1849*
Act 8:27 an eunuch of great **a** under Candace *G1413*
9:14 And here he hath **a** from the chief *G1849*
26:10 having received **a** from the chief *G1849*
12 to Damascus with **a** and commission *G1849*
1Co 15:24 put down all rule and all **a** and power. *G1849*
2Co 10: 8 more of our **a**, which the Lord hath *G1849*
1Ti 2: 2 For kings, and *for* all that are in **a**; that *G5247*
12 **a** over the man, but to be in silence. *G831*
Tit 2:15 with all **a**. Let no man despise thee. *G2003*
Rev 13: 2 his power, and his seat, and great **a**. *G1849*

AVA
2Ki 17:24 Cuthah, and from **A**, and from Hamath, H5755

AVAILETH
Est 5:13 Yet all this **a** me nothing, so long as I H7737
Gal 5: 6 neither circumcision **a** any thing, nor *G2480*
6:15 neither circumcision **a** any thing, nor *G2480*
Jas 5:16 prayer of a righteous man **a** much. *G2480*

AVEN
Ezk 30:17 The young men of **A** and of Pi-beseth H206
Hos 10: 8 The high places also of **A**, the sin of H206
Am 1: 5 from the plain of **A**, and him that holdeth H206

AVENGE
Lev 19:18 Thou shalt not **a**, nor bear any grudge H5358
26:25 you, that shall **a** the quarrel of *my* H5358
Nu 31: 2 **A** the children of Israel of the H5358+H5360
3 and **a** the LORD of Midian. H5414+H5360
Dt 32:43 his people: for he will **a** the blood of his H5358
1Sa 24:12 and the LORD **a** me of thee: but mine H5358
2Ki 9: 7 master, that I may **a** the blood of my H5358
Est 8:13 day to **a** themselves on their enemies. H5358
Isa 1:24 and **a** me of mine enemies: H5358
Jer 46:10 that he may **a** him of his adversaries: H5358
Hos 1: 4 *while*, and I will **a** the blood of Jezreel H6485
Lk 18: 3 him, saying, **A** me of mine adversary. *G1556*
5 me, I will **a** her, lest by her continual *G1556*
7 And shall not God **a** his own elect, *G1557*
8 I tell you that he will **a** them speedily. *G1557*
Ro 12:19 Dearly beloved, **a** not yourselves, but *G1556*
Rev 6:10 not judge and **a** our blood on them that *G1556*

AVENGED
Gen 4:24 If Cain shall be **a** sevenfold, truly H5358
Jos 10:13 the people had **a** themselves upon their H5358
Jdg 15: 7 I be **a** of you, and after that I will cease. H5358
16:28 **a** of the Philistines for my two eyes. H5358
1Sa 14:24 that I may be **a** on mine enemies. So H5358
18:25 the Philistines, to be **a** of the king's H5358
25:31 that my lord hath **a** himself: but when H3467
2Sa 4: 8 the LORD hath **a** my lord the king this H5360
18:19 the LORD hath **a** him of his enemies. H8199
31 for the LORD hath **a** thee this day of all H8199
Jer 5: 9 my soul be **a** on such a nation as this? H5358
29 my soul be **a** on such a nation as this? H5358
9: 9 my soul be **a** on such a nation as this? H5358
Act 7:24 *him*, and **a** him that was oppressed, *G4160*
Rev 18:20 prophets; for God hath **a** you on her. *G2919*
19: 2 **a** the blood of his servants at her hand. *G1556*

AVENGER
Nu 35:12 refuge from the **a**; that the manslayer H1350
Dt 19: 6 Lest the **a** of the blood pursue the H1350
12 hand of the **a** of blood, that he may die. H1350
Jos 20: 3 be your refuge from the **a** of blood. H1350
5 And if the **a** of blood pursue after him, H1350
9 by the hand of the **a** of blood, until he H1350
Ps 8: 2 thou mightest still the enemy and the **a**. H5358
44:16 by reason of the enemy and **a**. H5358
1Th 4: 6 the Lord *is* the **a** of all such, as we also *G1558*

AVENGETH
2Sa 22:48 It *is* God that **a** me, and that H5414+H5360
Ps 18:47 *It is* God that **a** me, and H5414+H5360

AVENGING
Jdg 5: 2 Praise ye the LORD for the **a** of H6544+H6546
1Sa 25:26 blood, and from **a** thyself with thine H3467
33 from **a** myself with mine own hand. H3467

AVERSE
Mic 2: 8 pass by securely as men **a** from war. H7725

AVIM
Jos 18:23 And **A**, and Parah, and Ophrah, H5761

AVIMS
Dt 2:23 And the **A** which dwelt in Hazerim, H5757

AVITES
Jos 13: 3 Gittites, and the Ekronites; also the **A**: H5757
2Ki 17:31 And the **A** made Nibhaz and Tartak, H5757

AVITH
Gen 36:35 stead: and the name of his city *was* **A**. H5762
1Ch 1:46 stead: and the name of his city *was* **A**. H5762

AVOID
Prv 4:15 **A** it, pass not by it, turn from it, and H6544
Ro 16:17 which ye have learned; and **a** them. *G1578*
1Co 7: 2 Nevertheless, *to* ***a*** fornication, let every *G1223*
2Ti 2:23 But foolish and unlearned questions **a**, *G3868*
Tit 3: 9 But **a** foolish questions, and *G4026*

AVOIDED
1Sa 18:11 And David **a** out of his presence twice. H5437

AVOIDING
2Co 8:20 **A** this, that no man should blame us in *G4724*
1Ti 6:20 to thy trust, **a** profane *and* vain *G1624*

AVOUCHED
Dt 26:17 Thou hast **a** the LORD this day to be thy H559
18 And the LORD hath **a** thee this day to be H559

AWAIT
Act 9:24 But their laying **a** was known of Saul. *G1917*

AWAKE
Jdg 5:12 **A**, awake, Deborah: awake, awake, H5782
12 Awake, **a**, Deborah: awake, awake, H5782
12 Awake, awake, Deborah: **a**, awake, H5782
12 Awake, awake, Deborah: awake, **a**, H5782
Job 8: 6 now he would **a** for thee, and make H5782
14:12 not **a**, nor be raised out of their sleep. H6974
Ps 7: 6 enemies: and **a** for me *to* the judgment H5782
17:15 be satisfied, when I **a**, with thy likeness. H6974
35:23 Stir up thyself, and **a** to my judgment, H6974
44:23 **A**, why sleepest thou, O Lord? arise, cast H5782
57: 8 **A** up, my glory; awake, psaltery and H5782
8 Awake up, my glory; **a**, psaltery and H5782
8 psaltery and harp: I *myself* will **a** early. H5782
59: 4 *my* fault: **a** to help me, and behold. H5782
5 hosts, the God of Israel, **a** to visit all the H6974
108: 2 **A**, psaltery and harp: I *myself* will H5782
2 psaltery and harp: I *myself* will **a** early. H5782
139:18 the sand: when I **a**, I am still with thee. H6974
Prv 23:35 when shall I **a**? I will seek it yet again. H6974
Song 2: 7 stir not up, nor **a** *my* love, till he please. H5782
3: 5 stir not up, nor **a** *my* love, till he please. H5782
4:16 **A**, O north wind; and come, thou south; H5782
8: 4 not up, nor **a** *my* love, until he please. H5782
Isa 26:19 shall they arise. **A** and sing, ye that H6974
51: 9 **A**, awake, put on strength, O arm of the H5782
9 Awake, **a**, put on strength, O arm of the H5782
9 O arm of the LORD; **a**, as in the ancient H5782
17 **A**, awake, stand up, O Jerusalem, which H5782
17 Awake, **a**, stand up, O Jerusalem, which H5782
52: 1 **A**, awake; put on thy strength, O Zion; H5782
1 Awake, **a**; put on thy strength, O Zion; H5782
Dan 12: 2 of the earth shall **a**, some to everlasting H6974
Joel 1: 5 **A**, ye drunkards, and weep; and howl, H6974
Hab 2: 7 bite thee, and **a** that shall vex thee, H3364
19 Woe unto him that saith to the wood, **A**; H6974
Zec 13: 7 **A**, O sword, against my shepherd, and H5782
Mk 4:38 a pillow: and they **a** him, and say unto *G1326*
Lk 9:32 when they were **a**, they saw his glory, *G1235*
Jn 11:11 but I go, that I may **a** him out of sleep. *G1852*
Ro 13:11 *it is* high time to **a** out of sleep: for now *G1453*
1Co 15:34 **A** to righteousness, and sin not; for *G1594*
Eph 5:14 Wherefore he saith, **A** thou that *G1453*

AWAKED
Gen 28:16 And Jacob **a** out of his sleep, and he H3364
Jdg 16:14 Samson. And he **a** out of his sleep, and H3364
1Sa 26:12 nor knew *it*, neither **a**: for they *were* all H6974
1Ki 18:27 he sleepeth, and must be **a**. H3364
2Ki 4:31 and told him, saying, The child is not **a**. H6974
Ps 3: 5 I laid me down and slept; I **a**; for the H6974
78:65 Then the Lord **a** as one out of sleep, H3364
Jer 31:26 Upon this I **a**, and beheld; and my sleep H6974

AWAKEST
Ps 73:20 thou **a**, thou shalt despise their image. H5782
Prv 6:22 and *when* thou **a**, it shall talk with thee. H6974

AWAKETH
Ps 73:20 As a dream when *one* **a**; *so*, O Lord, H6974
Isa 29: 8 he eateth; but he **a**, and his soul is H6974
8 drinketh; but he **a**, and, behold, *he is* H6974

AWAKING
Act 16:27 And the keeper of the prison **a** *G1096+G1853*

AWARE
Song 6:12 Or ever I was **a**, my soul made me *like* H3045
Jer 50:24 and thou wast not **a**: thou art found, H3045
Mt 24:50 *him*, and in an hour that he is not **a** of, *G1097*
Lk 11:44 that walk over *them* are not **a** *of them*. *G1492*
12:46 when he is not **a**, and will cut him in *G1097*

AWAY
Gen 12:20 him **a**, and his wife, and all that he had. H7971
15:11 the carcases, Abram drove them **a**. H5380
18: 3 not **a**, I pray thee, from thy servant: H5674
21:14 child, and sent her **a**: and she departed, H7971
25 servants had violently taken **a**. H1497
24:54 he said, Send me **a** unto my master. H7971
56 send me **a** that I may go to my master. H7971
59 And they sent **a** Rebekah their sister, H7971
25: 6 and sent them **a** from Isaac his son, H7971
26:27 hate me, and have sent me **a** from you? H7971
29 have sent thee **a** in peace: thou *art* now H7971
31 Isaac sent them **a**, and they departed H7971
27:35 subtilty, and hath taken **a** thy blessing. H3947
36 two times: he took **a** my birthright; H3947
36 now he hath taken **a** my blessing. And H3947
44 few days, until thy brother's fury turn **a**; H7725
45 Until thy brother's anger turn **a** from H7725
28: 5 And Isaac sent **a** Jacob: and he went to H7971
6 and sent him **a** to Padan-aram, to take H7971
30:15 thou take **a** my son's mandrakes H3947
23 said, God hath taken **a** my reproach: H622
25 Laban, Send me **a**, that I may go unto H7971
31: 1 Jacob hath taken **a** all that *was* our H3947
9 Thus God hath taken **a** the cattle of H5337
18 And he carried **a** all his cattle, and all H5090
20 And Jacob stole **a** unawares to Laban H1589

Gen 31:26 thou hast stolen **a** unawares to me, and H1589
26 to me, and carried **a** my daughters, as H5090
27 Wherefore didst thou flee **a** secretly, H1272
27 secretly, and steal **a** from me; and didst H1589
27 have sent thee **a** with mirth, and with H7971
42 hadst sent me **a** now empty. God hath H7971
35: 2 with him, Put **a** the strange gods that H5493
38:19 And she arose, and went **a**, and laid by H3212
40:15 For indeed I was stolen **a** out of the H1589
42:36 ***a:*** all these things are against me.
43:14 that he may send **a** your other brother, H7971
44: 3 men were sent **a**, they and their asses. H7971
45:24 So he sent his brethren **a**, and they
Ex 2: 9 Take this child **a**, and nurse it for me, H3212
17 and drove them **a**: but Moses stood up H1644
8: 8 that he may take **a** the frogs from me, H5493
28 ye shall not go very far **a**: intreat for me. H7368
10:17 he may take **a** from me this death only. H5493
19 wind, which took **a** the locusts, and H5375
12:15 day ye shall put **a** leaven out of your H7673
28 And the children of Israel went **a**, and H3212
13:19 carry up my bones **a** hence with you.
22 He took not **a** the pillar of the cloud by H4185
14:11 hast thou taken us **a** to die in the H3947
15:15 the inhabitants of Canaan shall melt **a**. H4127
18:18 Thou wilt surely wear **a**, both thou, and H5034
19:24 And the LORD said unto him, **A**, get thee
22:10 be hurt, or driven **a**, no man seeing *it:* H7617
23:25 take sickness **a** from the midst of thee. H5493
33:23 And I will take **a** mine hand, and thou H5493
Lev 1:16 And he shall pluck **a** his crop with his H5493
3: 4 liver, with the kidneys, it shall he take **a**. H5493
10 liver, with the kidneys, it shall he take **a**. H5493
15 liver, with the kidneys, it shall he take **a**. H5493
4: 9 liver, with the kidneys, it shall he take **a**, H5493
31 And he shall take **a** all the fat thereof, H5493
31 as the fat is taken **a** from off the H5493
35 And he shall take **a** all the fat thereof, H5493
35 the lamb is taken **a** from the sacrifice H5493
6: 2 or in a thing taken **a** by violence, or hath
4 he took violently **a**, or the thing which H1497
7: 4 liver, with the kidneys, it shall he take **a**: H5493
14:40 that they take **a** the stones in which H2502
43 that he hath taken **a** the stones, and H2502
16:21 shall send *him* **a** by the hand of a fit H7971
21: 7 take a woman put **a** from her husband: H1644
25:25 and hath sold **a** *some* of his possession,
26:39 of you shall pine **a** in their iniquity in H4743
39 fathers shall they pine **a** with them. H4743
44 will not cast them **a**, neither will I abhor H3988
Nu 4:13 And they shall take **a** the ashes from the
11: 6 But now our soul *is* dried **a**: *there is* H3002
14:43 ye are turned **a** from the LORD, H7725
17:10 shalt quite take **a** their murmurings H3615
20:21 wherefore Israel turned **a** from him.
21: 7 that he take **a** the serpents from us. H5493
24:22 until Asshur shall carry thee **a** captive.
25: 4 the LORD may be turned **a** from Israel. H7725
11 turned my wrath **a** from the children of H7725
27: 4 of our father be done **a** from among his H1639
32:15 For if ye turn **a** from after him, he will H7725
36: 4 be taken **a** from the inheritance H1639
Dt 7: 4 For they will turn **a** thy son from H5493
15 And the LORD will take **a** from thee all H5493
13: 5 to turn *you* **a** from the LORD your H5627
5 put the evil **a** from the midst of thee. H1197
10 to thrust thee **a** from the LORD thy H5080
15:13 thee, thou shalt not let him go **a** empty: H7971
16 thee, I will not go **a** from thee; because H3318
18 thou sendest him **a** free from thee; for H7971
17: 7 shalt put the evil **a** from among you. H1197
12 thou shalt put **a** the evil from Israel. H1197
17 his heart turn not **a**: neither shall he H5493
19:13 him, but thou shalt put **a** *the guilt of* H1197
19 thou put the evil **a** from among you. H1197
21: 9 So shalt thou put **a** the *guilt of* innocent H1197
21 shalt thou put evil **a** from among you; H1197
22:19 wife; he may not put her **a** all his days. H7971
21 shalt thou put evil **a** from among you. H1197
22 so shalt thou put **a** evil from Israel. H1197
24 thou shalt put **a** evil from among you. H1197
29 her, he may not put her **a** all his days. H7971
23:14 thing in thee, and turn **a** from thee. H7725
24: 4 Her former husband, which sent her **a**, H7971
7 thou shalt put evil **a** from among you. H1197
26:13 I have brought **a** the hallowed things H1197
14 have I taken **a** *ought* thereof for *any* H1197
28:26 earth, and no man shall fray *them* **a**. H2729
31 *be* violently taken **a** from before thy H1497
Dt 29:18 heart turneth **a** this day from the LORD H6437
30:17 But if thine heart turn **a**, so that thou H6437
17 shalt be drawn **a**, and worship other H5080
Jos 2:21 it. And she sent them **a**, and they H7971
5: 9 This day have I rolled **a** the reproach of H1556
7:13 **a** the accursed thing from among you. H5493
8: 3 of valour, and sent them **a** by night. H7971
16 and were drawn **a** from the city. H5423
18: 8 And the men arose, and went **a**: and H3212
22: 6 them **a**: and they went unto their tents. H7971
7 Joshua sent them **a** also unto their H7971
16 God of Israel, to turn **a** this day from H7725
18 But that ye must turn **a** this day from H7725
24:14 in truth: and put **a** the gods which your H5493
23 Now therefore put **a**, *said he,* the H5493
Jdg 3:18 sent **a** the people that bare the present. H7971
4:15 off *his* chariot, and fled **a** on his feet.
17 Howbeit Sisera fled **a** on his feet to the H5127
5:21 The river of Kishon swept them **a**, that H1640
8:21 and took **a** the ornaments that H3947
9:21 And Jotham ran **a**, and fled, and went H5127
10:16 And they put **a** the strange gods from H5493
11:13 Israel took **a** my land, when they
15 Israel took not **a** the land of Moab, nor
38 And he said, Go. And he sent her **a** *for* H7971
15:17 that he cast **a** the jawbone out of his H7993
16: 3 posts, and went **a** with them, bar and H5265
14 sleep, and went **a** with the pin of the H5265
18:24 And he said, Ye have taken **a** my gods H3947
24 and ye are gone **a**: and what have I H3212
19: 2 him, and went **a** from him unto her H3212
20:13 to death, and put **a** evil from Israel. But H1197
31 *and* were drawn **a** from the city; and H5423
1Sa 1:14 be drunken? put **a** thy wine from thee. H5493
5:11 and said, Send **a** the ark of the God of H7971
6: 3 And they said, If ye send **a** the ark of H7971
8 thereof; and send it **a**, that it may go. H7971
7: 3 hearts, *then* put **a** the strange gods and H5493
4 Then the children of Israel did put **a** H5493
9:26 I may send thee **a**. And Saul arose, and H7971
10:25 all the people **a**, every man to his house. H7971
14:16 multitude melted **a**, and they went on H4127
15:27 And as Samuel turned about to go **a**, he H3212
17:26 and taketh **a** the reproach from Israel? H5493
19:10 but he slipped **a** out of Saul's presence, H6362
17 me so, and sent **a** mine enemy, that he H7971
20:13 and send thee **a**, that thou mayest go H7971
22 thy way: for the LORD hath sent thee **a**. H7971
29 eyes, let me get **a**, I pray thee, and see H4422
21: 6 bread in the day when it was taken **a**. H3947
23: 5 and brought **a** their cattle, and smote H5090
26 made haste to get **a** for fear of Saul; for H3212
24:19 will he let him go well **a**? wherefore the H1870
25:10 break **a** every man from his master. H6555
26:12 and they gat them **a**, and no man saw H3212
27: 9 alive, and took **a** the sheep, and the H3947
28: 3 city. And Saul had put **a** those that had H5493
25 they rose up, and went **a** that night. H3212
30: 2 carried *them* **a**, and went on their way. H5090
18 **a**: and David rescued his two wives. H3947
22 that they may lead *them* **a**, and depart. H5090
2Sa 1:21 is vilely cast **a**, the shield of Saul, *as* H1602
3:21 sent Abner **a**; and he went in peace. H7971
22 sent him **a**, and he was gone in peace. H7971
23 sent him **a**, and he is gone in peace. H7971
24 hast sent him **a**, and he is quite gone? H7971
4: 7 gat them **a** through the plain all night.
11 hand, and take you **a** from the earth? H1197
5: 6 Except thou take **a** the blind and the H5493
7:15 But my mercy shall not depart **a** from H5493
15 *it* from Saul, whom I put **a** before thee. H5493
10: 4 *even* to their buttocks, and sent them **a**. H7971
12:13 hath put **a** thy sin; thou shalt not die. H5674
13:16 evil in sending me **a** *is* greater than the H7971
17:18 went both of them **a** quickly, and came
18: 3 forth: for if we flee **a**, they will not care H5127
9 the mule that *was* under him went **a**. H5674
19: 3 steal **a** when they flee in battle. H1589
41 Judah stolen thee **a**, and have brought H1589
22:46 Strangers shall fade **a**, and they shall be H5034
23: 6 as thorns thrust **a**, because they cannot H5074
9 and the men of Israel were gone **a**: H5927
24:10 thee, O LORD, take **a** the iniquity of thy H5674
1Ki 2:31 thou mayest take **a** the innocent blood, H5493
39 of Shimei ran **a** unto Achish son of H1272
8:46 they carry them **a** captives unto the H7617
48 which led them **a** captive, and pray unto
66 On the eighth day he sent the people **a**: H7971
11: 2 they will turn **a** your heart after their H5186
1Ki 11: 3 and his wives turned **a** his heart. H5186
4 his wives turned **a** his heart after other H5186
13 Howbeit I will not rend **a** all the
14: 8 And rent the kingdom **a** from the house
10 and will take **a** the remnant of the H1197
10 a man taketh **a** dung, till it be all gone. H1197
26 And he took **a** the treasures of the H3947
26 he even took **a** all: and he took away H3947
26 all: and he took **a** all the shields of gold H3947
15:12 And he took **a** the sodomites out of the H5674
22 and they took **a** the stones of Ramah, H5375
16: 3 Behold, I will take **a** the posterity of H1197
19: 4 O LORD, take **a** my life; for I *am* not H3947
10 left; and they seek my life, to take it **a**. H3947
14 left; and they seek my life, to take it **a**. H3947
20: 6 shall put *it* in their hand, and take *it* **a**. H3947
24 And do this thing, Take the kings **a**, H5493
34 I will send thee **a** with this covenant. H7971
34 a covenant with him, and sent him **a**. H7971
41 And he hasted, and took the ashes **a** H5493
21: 4 **a** his face, and would eat no bread. H5437
21 thee, and will take **a** thy posterity, and H1197
22:43 were not taken **a**; *for* the people offered H5493
2Ki 2: 3 LORD will take **a** thy master from thy H3947
5 LORD will take **a** thy master from thy H3947
9 before I be taken **a** from thee. And H3947
3: 2 mother: for he put **a** the image of Baal H5493
4:27 near to thrust her **a**. And the man of H1920
5: 2 and had brought **a** captive out of the
11 But Naaman was wroth, and went **a**, H3212
12 So he turned and went **a** in a rage. H3212
6:23 he sent them **a**, and they went to their H7971
32 hath sent to take **a** mine head? look, H5493
7:15 Syrians had cast **a** in their haste. And H7993
12: 3 But the high places were not taken **a**: H5493
18 Syria: and he went **a** from Jerusalem. H5927
14: 4 were not taken **a**: as yet the people did H5493
17: 6 and carried Israel **a** into Assyria, and H1540
11 the LORD carried **a** before them; and H1540
23 So was Israel carried **a** out of their own H1540
28 they had carried **a** from Samaria came H1540
33 whom they carried **a** from thence. H1540
18:11 And the king of Assyria did carry **a** H1540
22 hath taken **a**, and hath said to Judah H5493
24 How then wilt thou turn **a** the face of H7725
32 Until I come and take you **a** to a land H3947
20:18 shall they take **a**; and they shall be H3947
23:11 And he took **a** the horses that the kings H7673
19 to anger, Josiah took **a**, and did to them H5493
24 did Josiah put **a**, that he might perform H1197
34 took Jehoahaz **a**: and he came to Egypt, H3947
24:14 And he carried **a** all Jerusalem, and all H1540
15 And he carried **a** Jehoiachin to H1540
25:11 the fugitives that fell **a** to the king of H5307
11 the captain of the guard carry **a**. H1540
14 wherewith they ministered, took they **a**. H3947
15 silver, the captain of the guard took **a**. H3947
21 Judah was carried **a** out of their land. H1540
1Ch 5: 6 of Assyria carried **a** *captive:* he *was* H1540
21 And they took **a** their cattle; of their H7617
26 he carried them **a**, even the Reubenites, H1540
6:15 when the LORD carried **a** Judah and H1540
7:21 they came down to take **a** their cattle. H3947
8: 8 **a**; Hushim and Baara *were* his wives. H7971
13 who drove **a** the inhabitants of Gath: H1272
9: 1 **a** to Babylon for their transgression. H1540
10:12 men, and took **a** the body of Saul, and H5375
12:19 sent him **a**, saying, He will fall to H7971
14:14 up after them; turn **a** from them, and H5437
17:13 take my mercy **a** from him, as I took H5493
19: 4 hard by their buttocks, and sent them **a**. H7971
21: 8 I beseech thee, do **a** the iniquity of thy H5674
2Ch 6:36 **a** captives unto a land far off or near; H7617
42 O LORD God, turn not **a** the face of H7725
7:10 he sent the people **a** into their tents, H7971
19 But if ye turn **a**, and forsake my statutes H7725
9:12 **a** to her own land, she and her servants.
12: 9 and took **a** the treasures of the house
9 all: he carried **a** also the shields of gold H3947
14: 3 For he took **a** the altars of the strange H5493
5 Also he took **a** out of all the cities of H5493
13 and they carried **a** very much spoil. H5375
15 cattle, and carried **a** sheep and camels H7617
15: 8 courage, and put **a** the abominable H5674
17 But the high places were not taken **a** H5493
16: 6 Judah; and they carried **a** the stones of H5375
17: 6 moreover he took **a** the high places and H5493
19: 3 thou hast taken **a** the groves out of the H1197
20:25 came to take **a** the spoil of them, they H962

2Ch 20:25 they could carry **a**: and they were three H4853
33 were not taken **a**: for as yet the people H5493
21:17 it, and carried **a** all the substance that H7617
25:12 of Judah carry **a** captive, and brought
27 Amaziah did turn **a** from following the H5493
28: 5 him, and carried **a** a great multitude of H7617
8 And the children of Israel carried **a** H7617
8 and took also **a** much spoil from them, H962
17 smitten Judah, and carried **a** captives. H7617
21 For Ahaz took **a** a portion *out* of the
29: 6 and have turned **a** their faces from the H5437
10 his fierce wrath may turn **a** from us. H7725
19 in his reign did cast **a** in his H2186
30: 8 of his wrath may turn **a** from you. H7725
9 and will not turn **a** *his* face from you, if H5493
14 And they arose and took **a** the altars H5493
14 **a**, and cast *them* into the brook Kidron. H5493
32:12 Hath not the same Hezekiah taken **a** H5493
33:15 And he took **a** the strange gods, and H5493
34:33 And Josiah took **a** all the abominations H5493
35:23 Have me **a**; for I am sore wounded. H5674
36:20 sword carried he **a** to Babylon; where H1540
Ezr 2: 1 which had been carried **a**, whom H1473
1 had carried **a** unto Babylon, and came H1540
5:12 and carried the people **a** into Babylon. H1541
8:35 had been carried **a**, which were come out
9: 4 had been carried **a**; and I sat astonied H1473
10: 3 our God to put **a** all the wives, and such H3318
6 of them that had been carried **a**. H1473
8 of those that had been carried **a**. H1473
19 they would put **a** their wives; and *being* H3318
Neh 7: 6 that had been carried **a**, whom H1473
6 had carried **a**, and came again to H1540
Est 2: 6 Who had been carried **a** from H1540
6 had been carried **a** with Jeconiah king H1540
6 the king of Babylon had carried **a**. H1540
4: 4 and to take **a** his sackcloth from him: H5493
8: 3 him with tears to put **a** the mischief of H5674
Job 1:15 and took them **a**; yea, they have slain H3947
17 have carried them **a**, yea, and slain the H3947
21 **a**; blessed be the name of the LORD. H3947
4:21 go **a**? they die, even without wisdom. H5265
6:15 *and* as the stream of brooks they pass **a**; H5674
7: 9 and vanisheth **a**: so he that goeth down
21 and take **a** mine iniquity? for now H5674
8: 4 cast them **a** for their transgression; H7971
20 Behold, God will not cast **a** a perfect H3988
9:12 Behold, he taketh **a**, who can hinder H2862
25 a post: they flee **a**, they see no good. H1272
26 They are passed **a** as the swift ships: as H2498
34 Let him take his rod **a** from me, and let H5493
11:14 If iniquity *be* in thine hand, put it far **a**, H7368
16 *and* remember *it* as waters *that* pass **a**: H5674
12:17 He leadeth counsellors **a** spoiled, and
19 He leadeth princes **a** spoiled, and
20 He removeth **a** the speech of the trusty, H5493
20 taketh **a** the understanding of the aged. H3947
24 He taketh **a** the heart of the chief of the H5493
14:10 But man dieth, and wasteth **a**: yea, man H2522
19 thou washest **a** the things which grow H7857
20 his countenance, and sendest him **a**. H7971
15:12 Why doth thine heart carry thee **a**? and H3947
30 by the breath of his mouth shall he go **a**. H5493
20: 8 He shall fly **a** as a dream, and shall not H5774
8 be chased **a** as a vision of the night. H5074
19 taken **a** an house which he builded not; H1497
28 shall flow **a** in the day of his wrath. H5064
21:18 and as chaff that the storm carrieth **a**. H1589
22: 9 Thou hast sent widows **a** empty, and the
23 put **a** iniquity far from thy tabernacles. H7368
24: 2 take **a** flocks, and feed *thereof*. H1497
3 They drive **a** the ass of the fatherless, H5090
10 they take **a** the sheaf *from* the hungry; H5375
27: 2 *As* God liveth, *who* hath taken **a** my H5493
8 gained, when God taketh **a** his soul? H7953
20 a tempest stealeth him **a** in the night. H1589
21 The east wind carrieth him **a**, and he H5375
28: 4 dried up, they are gone **a** from men. H5128
30:12 youth; they push **a** my feet, and they H7971
15 and my welfare passeth **a** as a cloud. H5674
32:22 *doing* my maker would soon take me **a**. H5375
33:21 His flesh is consumed **a**, that it cannot H3615
34: 5 and God hath taken **a** my judgment. H5493
20 and pass **a**: and the mighty shall H5674
20 mighty shall be taken **a** without hand. H5493
36:18 lest he take thee **a** with *his* stroke: then H5496
Ps 1: 4 like the chaff which the wind driveth **a**. H5086
2: 3 and cast **a** their cords from us. H7993
18:22 I did not put **a** his statutes from me. H5493
Ps 18:45 The strangers shall fade **a**, and be H5034
27: 9 not thy servant **a** in anger: thou hast H5186
28: 3 Draw me not **a** with the wicked, and
31:13 me, they devised to take **a** my life. H3947
34: ttl who drove him **a**, and he departed.
37:20 into smoke shall they consume **a**. H3615
36 Yet he passed **a**, and, lo, he *was* not: H5674
39:10 Remove thy stroke **a** from me: I am H5493
11 to consume **a** like a moth: surely every H4529
48: 5 they were troubled, *and* hasted **a**. H2648
49:17 **a**: his glory shall not descend after him. H3947
51:11 Cast me not **a** from thy presence; and H7993
52: 5 he shall take thee **a**, and pluck thee out H2846
55: 6 *for then* would I fly **a**, and be at rest. H5774
58: 7 Let them melt **a** as waters *which* run
8 *one of them* pass **a**: *like* the untimely H1980
9 thorns, he shall take them **a** as with a
64: 8 all that see them shall flee **a**. H5074
65: 3 thou shalt purge them **a**. H3722
66:20 **a** my prayer, nor his mercy from me. H5493
68: 2 As smoke is driven **a**, *so* drive *them* H5086
2 *so* drive *them* **a**: as wax melteth before H5086
69: 4 then I restored *that* which I took not **a**. H1497
78:38 **a**, and did not stir up all his wrath. H7725
39 that passeth **a**, and cometh not again. H1980
79: 9 purge **a** our sins, for thy name's sake. H3722
85: 3 Thou hast taken **a** all thy wrath: thou H622
88: 8 Thou hast put **a** mine acquaintance far
90: 5 Thou carriest them **a** as with a flood;
9 For all our days are passed **a** in thy H6437
10 for it is soon cut off, and we fly **a**. H5774
102:24 I said, O my God, take me not **a** in the H5927
104: 7 the voice of thy thunder they hasted **a**. H2648
29 thou takest **a** their breath, they die, H622
106:23 the breach, to turn **a** his wrath, lest he H7725
112:10 **a**: the desire of the wicked shall perish. H4549
119:37 Turn **a** mine eyes from beholding H5674
39 Turn **a** my reproach which I fear: for H5674
119 Thou puttest **a** all the wicked of the H7673
132:10 For thy servant David's sake turn not **a** H7725
137: 3 For there they that carried us **a** captive
144: 4 his days *are* as a shadow that passeth **a**. H5674
Prv 1:19 taketh **a** the life of the owners thereof. H3947
32 For the turning **a** of the simple shall H4878
4:15 pass not by it, turn from it, and pass **a**. H5674
16 taken **a**, unless they cause *some* to fall. H1497
24 Put **a** from thee a froward mouth, and H5493
6:33 and his reproach shall not be wiped **a**. H4229
10: 3 casteth **a** the substance of the wicked. H1920
14:32 The wicked is driven **a** in his H1760
15: 1 A soft answer turneth **a** wrath: but
19:26 *and* chaseth **a** *his* mother, *is* a son H1272
20: 8 scattereth **a** all evil with his eyes. H2219
30 The blueness of a wound cleanseth **a**
22:27 he take **a** thy bed from under thee? H3947
23: 5 **a** as an eagle toward heaven. H5774+H5774
24:18 him, and he turn **a** his wrath from him. H7725
25: 4 Take **a** the dross from the silver, and H1898
5 Take **a** the wicked *from* before the H1898
10 to shame, and thine infamy turn not **a**. H7725
20 *As* he that taketh **a** a garment in cold H5710
23 The north wind driveth **a** rain: so *doth* H2342
28: 9 He that turneth **a** his ear from hearing H5493
29: 8 a snare: but wise *men* turn **a** wrath. H7725
30:30 beasts, and turneth not **a** for any; H7725
Ecc 1: 4 *One* generation passeth **a**, and *another* H1980
3: 5 A time to cast **a** stones, and a time to H7993
6 a time to keep, and a time to cast **a**; H7993
5:15 which he may carry **a** in his hand. H3212
11:10 thy heart, and put **a** evil from thy flesh: H5674
Song 2:10 up, my love, my fair one, and come **a**. H3212
13 my love, my fair one, and come **a**. H3212
17 the shadows flee **a**, turn, my beloved, H5127
4: 6 the shadows flee **a**, I will get me to the H5127
5: 7 of the walls took **a** my veil from me. H5375
6: 5 Turn **a** thine eyes from me, for they H5437
Isa 1: 4 unto anger, they are gone **a** backward. H2114
13 I cannot **a** with; *it is* iniquity, even
16 Wash you, make you clean; put **a** the H5493
25 **a** thy dross, and take away all thy tin: H6884
25 away thy dross, and take **a** all thy tin: H5493
3: 1 of hosts, doth take **a** from Jerusalem H5493
18 In that day the Lord will take **a** the H5493
4: 1 by thy name, to take **a** our reproach. H622
4 When the Lord shall have washed **a** the
5: 5 I will take **a** the hedge thereof, and H5493
23 reward, and take **a** the righteousness of H5493
24 they have cast **a** the law of the LORD H3988
25 **a**, but his hand *is* stretched out still. H7725
Isa 5:29 carry *it* **a** safe, and none shall deliver *it*.
6: 7 iniquity is taken **a**, and thy sin purged. H5493
12 And the LORD have removed men far **a**, H7368
8: 4 be taken **a** before the king of Assyria. H5375
9:12 **a**, but his hand *is* stretched out still. H7725
17 **a**, but his hand *is* stretched out still. H7725
21 **a**, but his hand *is* stretched out still. H7725
10: 2 and to take **a** the right from the poor H1497
4 **a**, but his hand *is* stretched out still. H7725
27 shall be taken **a** from off thy shoulder, H5493
12: 1 is turned **a**, and thou comfortedst me. H7725
15: 6 the hay is withered **a**, the grass faileth, H3001
7 they carry **a** to the brook of the willows. H5375
16:10 And gladness is taken **a**, and joy out of H622
17: 1 is taken **a** from *being* a city, and H5493
18: 5 and take **a** *and* cut down the branches. H5493
19: 6 And they shall turn the rivers far **a**; *and* H2186
7 wither, be driven **a**, and be no *more*. H5086
20: 4 So shall the king of Assyria lead **a** the H5090
22: 4 Therefore said I, Look **a** from me; I will H8159
17 Behold, the LORD will carry thee **a** with H2904
24: 4 The earth mourneth *and* fadeth **a**, the H5034
4 *and* fadeth **a**, the haughty people H5034
25: 8 GOD will wipe **a** tears from off all faces; H4229
8 shall he take **a** from off all the earth: H5493
27: 9 *is* all the fruit to take **a** his sin; when he H5493
28:17 the hail shall sweep **a** the refuge of lies, H3261
29: 5 chaff that passeth **a**: yea, it shall be at H5674
30:22 thou shalt cast them **a** as a menstruous H2219
31: 7 For in that day every man shall cast **a** H3988
35:10 and sorrow and sighing shall flee **a**. H5127
36: 7 hath taken **a**, and said to Judah and H5493
9 How then wilt thou turn **a** the face of H7725
17 Until I come and take you **a** to a land
39: 7 shall they take **a**; and they shall be H3947
40:24 whirlwind shall take them **a** as stubble. H5375
41: 9 I have chosen thee, and not cast thee **a**. H3988
16 shall carry them **a**, and the whirlwind H5375
49:19 that swallowed thee up shall be far **a**. H7368
25 shall be taken **a**, and the prey of the H3947
50: 1 whom I have put **a**? or which of my H7971
1 transgressions is your mother put **a**. H7971
5 not rebellious, neither turned **a** back. H5472
51: 6 shall vanish **a** like smoke, and the H4414
11 *and* sorrow and mourning shall flee **a**. H5127
52: 5 people is taken **a** for nought? they that H3947
57: 1 men *are* taken **a**, none considering that H622
1 is taken **a** from the evil *to come*. H622
13 carry them all **a**; vanity shall take *them*: H5375
58: 9 I *am*. If thou take **a** from the midst of H5493
13 If thou turn **a** thy foot from the H7725
59:13 LORD, and departing **a** from our God, H5253
14 And judgment is turned **a** backward, H5253
64: 6 like the wind, have taken us **a**. H5375
Jer 1: 3 Judah, unto the carrying **a** of Jerusalem H1540
2:24 who can turn her **a**? all they that seek H7725
3: 1 They say, If a man put **a** his wife, and H7971
8 I had put her **a**, and given her a bill H7971
19 father; and shalt not turn **a** from me. H7725
4: 1 if thou wilt put **a** thine abominations H5493
4 LORD, and take **a** the foreskins of your H5493
5:10 a full end: take **a** her battlements; for H5493
25 Your iniquities have turned **a** these H5186
6: 4 for the day goeth **a**, for the shadows of H6437
29 vain: for the wicked are not plucked **a**. H5423
7:29 and cast *it* **a**, and take up a lamentation H7993
33 of the earth; and none shall fray *them* **a**. H2729
8: 4 arise? shall he turn **a**, and not return? H7725
13 given them shall pass **a** from them. H5674
13:17 the LORD'S flock is carried **a** captive.
19 shall be carried **a** captive all of it, it shall
19 of it, it shall be wholly carried **a** captive.
24 **a** by the wind of the wilderness. H5674
15:15 take me not **a** in thy longsuffering: H3947
16: 5 for I have taken **a** my peace from this H622
18:20 *and* to turn **a** thy wrath from them. H7725
22:10 for him that goeth **a**: for he shall return H1980
23: 2 and driven them **a**, and have not visited H5080
24: 1 had carried **a** captive Jeconiah the
5 them that are carried **a** captive of Judah,
27:20 when he carried **a** captive Jeconiah the
28: 3 of Babylon took **a** from this place, and H3947
6 **a** captive, from Babylon into this place.
29: 1 which were carried **a** captives, and to
1 **a** captive from Jerusalem to Babylon; H1540
4 all that are carried **a** captives, whom I
4 **a** from Jerusalem unto Babylon; H1540
7 you to be carried **a** captives, and pray
14 and I will turn **a** your captivity, and H7725

Jer 29:14 I caused you to be carried **a** captive.
32:40 that I will not turn **a** from them, to do H7725
33:26 Then will I cast **a** the seed of Jacob, and H3988
37:13 saying, Thou fallest **a** to the Chaldeans. H5307
14 *It is* false; I fall not **a** to the Chaldeans. H5307
38:22 the mire, *and* they are turned **a** back. H5472
39: 9 the guard carried **a** captive into Babylon
9 and those that fell **a**, that fell to him, H5307
40: 1 that were carried **a** captive of Jerusalem
1 were carried **a** captive unto Babylon.
7 were not carried **a** captive to Babylon;
41:10 Then Ishmael carried **a** captive all the
10 carried them **a** captive, and departed
14 had carried **a** captive from Mizpah
43: 3 and carry us **a** captives into Babylon.
12 and carry them **a** captives: and he shall
46: 5 *and* turned **a** back? and their mighty H5472
6 Let not the swift flee **a**, nor the mighty H5127
15 Why are thy valiant *men* swept **a**? they H5502
21 back, *and* are fled **a** together: they did H5127
48: 9 that it may flee and get **a**: for the cities H3318
49:19 make him run **a** from her: and who H7323
29 shall they take **a**: they shall take to H3947
50: 6 have turned them **a** *on* the H7725+H7726
17 lions have driven *him* **a**: first the king of H5080
44 suddenly run **a** from her: and H7323+H7323
51:50 Ye that have escaped the sword, go **a**, H1980
52:15 the guard carried **a** captive *certain* of the
15 and those that fell **a**, that fell to the king H5307
18 wherewith they ministered, took they **a**. H3947
19 silver, took the captain of the guard **a**. H3947
27 carried **a** captive out of his own land.
28 carried **a** captive: in the seventh
29 he carried **a** captive from Jerusalem
30 of the guard carried **a** captive of the Jews
Lam 2: 6 And he hath violently taken **a** his H2554
14 iniquity, to turn **a** thy captivity; but H7725
4: 9 for these pine **a**, stricken through for H2100
15 when they fled **a** and wandered, they H5132
22 no more carry thee **a** into captivity: he
Ezk 3:14 me up, and took me **a**, and I went in H3947
4:17 and consume **a** for their iniquity. H4743
11:18 and they shall take **a** all the detestable H5493
14: 6 idols; and turn **a** your faces from all H7725
16: 9 I throughly washed **a** thy blood from H7857
50 therefore I took them **a** as I saw *good*. H5493
18:24 But when the righteous turneth **a** from H7725
26 When a righteous *man* turneth **a** from H7725
27 Again, when the wicked *man* turneth **a** H7725
28 Because he considereth, and turneth **a** H7725
31 Cast **a** from you all your H7993
20: 7 Then said I unto them, Cast ye **a** every H7993
8 every man cast **a** the abominations of H7993
23:25 they shall take **a** thy nose and thine H5493
26 thy clothes, and take **a** thy fair jewels. H3947
29 and shall take **a** all thy labour, and H3947
24:16 Son of man, behold, I take **a** from thee H3947
23 but ye shall pine **a** for your iniquities, H4743
26:16 thrones, and lay **a** their robes, and put H5493
30: 4 they shall take **a** her multitude, and H3947
33: 4 **a**, his blood shall be upon his own head. H3947
6 them, he is taken **a** in his iniquity; but H3947
10 **a** in them, how should we then live? H4743
34: 4 which was driven **a**, neither have ye H5080
16 which was driven **a**, and will bind up H5080
36:26 and I will take **a** the stony heart out H5493
38:13 a prey? to carry **a** silver and gold, to H5375
13 and gold, to take **a** cattle and goods, to H3947
43: 9 Now let them put **a** their whoredom, H7368
44:10 And the Levites that are gone **a** far from
10 which went astray **a** from me after H8582
22 nor her that is put **a**: but they shall take H1644
45: 9 and justice, take **a** your exactions from H7311
Dan 1:16 Thus Melzar took **a** the portion of their H5375
2:35 wind carried them **a**, that no place was H5376
4:14 let the beasts get **a** from under it, and H5111
7:12 dominion taken **a**: yet their lives were H5709
14 shall not pass **a**, and his kingdom *that* H5709
26 and they shall take **a** his dominion, to H5709
8:11 was taken **a**, and the place of H7311+H7311
9:16 and thy fury be turned **a** from thy city H7725
11:12 *And* when he hath taken **a** the H5375
31 and shall take **a** the daily *sacrifice*, and H5493
44 destroy, and utterly to make **a** many. H2763
12:11 shall be taken **a**, and the abomination H5493
Hos 1: 6 of Israel; but I will utterly take them **a**. H5375
2: 2 her therefore put **a** her whoredoms out H5493
9 Therefore will I return, and take **a** my H3947
17 For I will take **a** the names of Baalim H5493
Hos 4: 3 the fishes of the sea also shall be taken **a**. H622
11 wine and new wine take **a** the heart. H3947
5:14 I, will tear and go **a**; I will take away, H3212
14 I will take **a**, and none shall rescue *him*. H5375
6: 4 cloud, and as the early dew it goeth **a**. H1980
9:11 *As for* Ephraim, their glory shall fly **a** H5774
17 My God will cast them **a**, because they H3988
13: 3 dew that passeth **a**, as the chaff *that* is H1980
11 anger, and took *him* **a** in my wrath. H3947
14: 2 say unto him, Take **a** all iniquity, and H5375
4 for mine anger is turned **a** from him. H7725
Joel 1: 7 **a**; the branches thereof are made white. H7993
12 joy is withered **a** from the sons of men. H3001
Am 1: 3 four, I will not turn **a** *the punishment* H7725
6 four, I will not turn **a** *the punishment* H7725
6 because they carried **a** captive the whole
9 four, I will not turn **a** *the punishment* H7725
11 four, I will not turn **a** *the punishment* H7725
13 four, I will not turn **a** *the punishment* H7725
2: 1 four, I will not turn **a** *the punishment* H7725
4 four, I will not turn **a** *the punishment* H7725
6 four, I will not turn **a** *the punishment* H7725
16 **a** naked in that day, saith the LORD. H5127
4: 2 he will take you **a** with hooks, and your H5375
10 and have taken **a** your horses; and I H7628
5:23 Take thou **a** from me the noise of thy H5493
6: 3 Ye that put far **a** the evil day, and cause H5077
7:11 be led **a** captive out of their own land.
12 seer, go, flee thee **a** into the land of H1272
9: 1 of them shall not flee **a**, and he that H5127
Oba 11 strangers carried **a** captive his forces,
Jna 3: 9 and repent, and turn **a** from his fierce H7725
Mic 1:11 Pass ye **a**, thou inhabitant of Saphir,
2: 2 and take *them* **a**: so they oppress a man H5375
4 turning **a** he hath divided our fields. H7725
9 have ye taken **a** my glory for ever. H3947
Nah 2: 2 For the LORD hath turned **a** the H7725
7 And Huzzab shall be led **a** captive, she
8 yet they shall flee **a**. Stand, stand, *shall* H5127
3:10 Yet *was* she carried **a**, she went into H1473
16 the cankerworm spoileth, and flieth **a**. H5774
17 ariseth they flee **a**, and their place is not H5074
Zep 2: 7 visit them, and turn **a** their captivity. H7725
3:11 for then I will take **a** out of the midst of H5493
15 The LORD hath taken **a** thy judgments, H5493
Zec 3: 4 him, saying, Take **a** the filthy garments H5493
7:11 and pulled **a** the shoulder, and stopped H5637
9: 7 And I will take **a** his blood out of his H5493
10:11 and the sceptre of Egypt shall depart **a**. H5493
14:12 shall consume **a** while they stand upon H4743
12 shall consume **a** in their holes, and H4743
12 tongue shall consume **a** in their mouth. H4743
Mal 2: 3 feasts; and *one* shall take you **a** with it.
6 and did turn many **a** from iniquity. H7725
16 he hateth putting **a**: for *one* covereth H7971
3: 7 ye are gone **a** from mine ordinances, H5493
Mt 1:11 time they were carried **a** to Babylon: G3350
17 until the carrying **a** into Babylon *are* G3350
17 from the carrying **a** into Babylon unto G3350
19 was minded to put her **a** privily. G630
5:31 It hath been said, Whosoever shall put **a** G630
32 shall put **a** his wife, saving for the G630
40 **a** thy coat, let him have *thy* cloke also. G2983
42 would borrow of thee turn not thou **a**. G654
8:31 suffer us to go **a** into the herd of swine. G565
13: 6 they had no root, they withered **a**. G3583
12 him shall be taken **a** even that he hath. G142
19 *one*, and catcheth **a** that which was G726
36 Then Jesus sent the multitude **a**, and G863
48 good into vessels, but cast the bad **a**. G1854
14:15 send the multitude **a**, that they may go G630
22 side, while he sent the multitudes **a**. G630
23 And when he had sent the multitudes **a**, G630
15:23 saying, Send her **a**; for she crieth after us. G630
32 them **a** fasting, lest they faint in the way. G630
39 And he sent **a** the multitude, and took G630
19: 3 a man to put **a** his wife for every cause? G630
7 writing of divorcement, and to put her **a**? G630
8 suffered you to put **a** your wives: but G630
9 shall put **a** his wife, except *it be* G630
9 her which is put **a** doth commit adultery. G630
22 saying, he went **a** sorrowful: for he had G565
21:19 And presently the fig tree withered **a**. G3583
20 How soon is the fig tree withered **a**! G3583
22:13 foot, and take him **a**, and cast *him* into G142
24:35 Heaven and earth shall pass **a**, but my G3928
35 away, but my words shall not pass **a**. G3928
39 and took them all **a**; so shall also the G142
25:29 shall be taken **a** even that which he hath. G142
Mt 25:46 And these shall go **a** into everlasting G565
26:42 He went **a** again the second time, and G565
42 cup may not pass **a** from me, except I G3928
44 And he left them, and went **a** again, and G565
57 on Jesus led *him* **a** to Caiaphas the high G520
27: 2 him, they led *him* **a**, and delivered him to G520
31 on him, and led him **a** to crucify *him*. G520
64 night, and steal him **a**, and say unto the G2813
28:13 by night, and stole him *a* while we slept.
16 Then the eleven disciples went **a** into G4198
Mk 1:43 charged him, and forthwith sent him **a**; G1544
2:20 shall be taken **a** from them, and then G522
21 filled it up taketh **a** from the old, and the G142
4: 6 because it had no root, it withered **a**. G3583
15 **a** the word that was sown in their hearts. G142
36 And when they had sent **a** the multitude, G863
5:10 not send them **a** out of the country.
6:36 Send them **a**, that they may go into the G630
45 Bethsaida, while he sent **a** the people. G630
46 And when he had sent them **a**, he G657
8: 3 And if I send them **a** fasting to their own G630
9 about four thousand: and he sent them **a**. G630
26 And he sent him **a** to his house, saying, G649
9:18 teeth, and pineth **a**: and I spake to thy G3583
10: 2 a man to put **a** *his* wife? tempting him. G630
4 a bill of divorcement, and to put *her* **a**. G630
11 shall put **a** his wife, and marry G630
12 And if a woman shall put **a** her husband, G630
22 **a** grieved: for he had great possessions. G565
50 And he, casting **a** his garment, rose, and G577
11:21 tree which thou cursedst is withered **a**. G3583
12: 3 and beat him, and sent *him* **a** empty. G649
4 and sent *him* **a** shamefully handled. G649
13:31 Heaven and earth shall pass **a**: but my G3928
31 away: but my words shall not pass **a**. G3928
14:36 unto thee; take **a** this cup from me: G3911
39 And again he went **a**, and prayed, and G565
44 is he; take him, and lead *him* **a** safely. G520
53 And they led Jesus **a** to the high priest: G520
15: 1 *him* **a**, and delivered *him* to Pilate. G667
16 And the soldiers led him **a** into the hall, G520
16: 3 Who shall roll us **a** the stone from the G617
4 stone was rolled **a**: for it was very great. G617
Lk 1:25 *me*, to take **a** my reproach among men. G851
53 and the rich he hath sent empty **a**. G1821
2:15 the angels were gone **a** from them into G565
5:35 shall be taken **a** from them, and then G522
6:29 him that taketh **a** thy cloke forbid not G142
30 taketh **a** thy goods ask *them* not again. G142
8: 6 withered **a**, because it lacked moisture. G3583
12 devil, and taketh **a** the word out of their G142
13 believe, and in time of temptation fall **a**. G868
38 be with him: but Jesus sent him **a**, saying, G630
9:12 And when the day began to wear **a**, G2827
12 Send the multitude **a**, that they may go G630
25 world, and lose himself, or be cast **a**? G2210
10:42 which shall not be taken **a** from her. G851
11:52 lawyers! for ye have taken **a** the key of G142
13:15 the stall, and lead *him* **a** to watering? G520
16: 3 do? for my lord taketh **a** from me the G851
18 Whosoever putteth **a** his wife, and G630
18 her that is put **a** from *her* husband G630
17:31 down to take it **a**: and he that is in the G142
19:26 that he hath shall be taken **a** from him. G142
20:10 beat him, and sent *him* **a** empty. G1821
11 *him* shamefully, and sent *him* **a** empty. G1821
21:24 sword, and shall be led **a** captive into all
32 shall not pass **a**, till all be fulfilled. G3928
33 Heaven and earth shall pass **a**: but my G3928
33 away: but my words shall not pass **a**. G3928
23:18 And they cried out all at once, saying, **A**
26 And as they led him **a**, they laid hold G520
24: 2 And they found the stone rolled **a** from G617
Jn 1:29 God, which taketh **a** the sin of the world. G142
4: 8 (For his disciples were gone **a** unto the G565
5:13 **a**, a multitude being in *that* place. G1593
6:22 but *that* his disciples were gone **a** alone; G565
67 Jesus unto the twelve, Will ye also go **a**? G5217
10:40 And went **a** again beyond Jordan into G565
11:39 Jesus said, Take ye **a** the stone. Martha, G142
41 Then they took **a** the stone *from the* G142
48 and take **a** both our place and nation. G142
12:11 the Jews went **a**, and believed on Jesus. G5217
14:28 I said unto you, I go **a**, and come *again* G5217
15: 2 not fruit he taketh **a**: and every *branch* G142
16: 7 for you that I go **a**: for if I go not away, G565
7 for if I go not **a**, the Comforter will not G565
18:13 And led him **a** to Annas first; for he was G520
19:15 But they cried out, **A** with *him*, away

Jn 19:15 But they cried out, Away with *him*, **a**
16 And they took Jesus, and led *him* **a**. *G520*
31 broken, and *that* they might be taken **a**. *G142*
38 that he might take **a** the body of Jesus: *G142*
20: 1 the stone taken **a** from the sepulchre. *G142*
2 They have taken **a** the Lord out of the *G142*
10 Then the disciples went **a** again unto *G565*
13 they have taken **a** my Lord, and I know *G142*
15 thou hast laid him, and I will take him **a**. *G142*
Act 3:26 **a** every one of you from his iniquities. *G654*
5:37 taxing, and drew **a** much people after *G868*
7:27 wrong thrust him **a**, saying, Who made *G683*
43 and I will carry you **a** beyond Babylon. *G3351*
8:33 was taken **a**: and who shall declare *G142*
39 of the Lord caught **a** Philip, that the *G726*
10:23 Peter went **a** with them, and certain *G1831*
13: 3 *their* hands on them, they sent *them* **a**. *G630*
8 to turn **a** the deputy from the faith. *G1294*
17:10 And the brethren immediately sent **a** *G1599*
14 the brethren sent **a** Paul to go as it were *G1821*
19:26 and turned **a** much people, saying *G3179*
20: 6 And we sailed **a** from Philippi after the *G1602*
30 things, to draw **a** disciples after them. *G645*
21:36 followed after, crying, **A** with him. *G142*
22:16 and wash **a** thy sins, calling on the *G628*
22 voices, and said, **A** with such a *fellow*
24: 7 violence took *him* **a** out of our hands, *G520*
27:20 we should be saved was then taken **a**. *G4014*
Ro 11: 1 I say then, Hath God cast **a** his people? *G683*
2 God hath not cast **a** his people which he *G683*
15 For if the casting **a** of them *be* the *G580*
26 and shall turn **a** ungodliness from Jacob: *G654*
27 unto them, when I shall take **a** their sins. *G851*
1Co 5: 2 might be taken **a** from among you. *G1808*
13 judgeth. Therefore put **a** from among *G1808*
7:11 and let not the husband put **a** *his* wife. *G863*
12 to dwell with him, let him not put her **a**. *G863*
31 for the fashion of this world passeth **a**. *G3855*
12: 2 Ye know that ye were Gentiles, carried **a** *G520*
13: 8 *there be* knowledge, it shall vanish **a**. *G2673*
10 that which is in part shall be done **a**. *G2673*
11 became a man, I put **a** childish things. *G2673*
2Co 3: 7 which *glory* was to be done **a**: *G2673*
11 For if that which is done **a** *was* *G2673*
14 same veil untaken **a** in the reading of the *G343*
14 which *veil* is done **a** in Christ. *G2673*
16 to the Lord, the veil shall be taken **a**. *G4014*
5:17 **a**; behold, all things are become new. *G3928*
Gal 2:13 was carried **a** with their dissimulation.
Eph 4:25 Wherefore putting **a** lying, speak every *G659*
31 be put **a** from you, with all malice: *G142*
Col 1:23 and *be* not moved **a** from the hope of *G3334*
2Th 2: 3 come a falling **a** first, and that man of *G646*
1Ti 1:19 some having put **a** concerning faith have *G683*
2Ti 1:15 in Asia be turned **a** from me; of whom *G654*
3: 5 the power thereof: from such turn **a**. *G665*
6 laden with sins, led **a** with divers lusts, *G71*
4: 4 And they shall turn **a** *their* ears from the *G654*
Heb 6: 6 If they shall fall **a**, to renew them again *G3895*
8:13 and waxeth old *is* ready to vanish **a**. *G854*
9:26 to put **a** sin by the sacrifice of himself. *G115*
10: 4 of bulls and of goats should take **a** sins. *G851*
9 O God. He taketh **a** the first, that he may *G337*
11 sacrifices, which can never take **a** sins: *G4014*
35 Cast not **a** therefore your confidence, *G577*
12:25 **a** from him that *speaketh* from heaven:
Jas 1:10 the flower of the grass he shall pass **a**. *G3928*
11 shall the rich man fade **a** in his ways. *G3133*
14 is drawn **a** of his own lust, and enticed. *G1828*
4:14 for a little time, and then vanisheth **a**. *G853*
1Pt 1: 4 fadeth not **a**, reserved in heaven for you, *G263*
24 and the flower thereof falleth **a**: *G1601*
3:21 us (not the putting **a** of the filth of the *G595*
5: 4 a crown of glory that fadeth not **a**. *G262*
2Pt 3:10 heavens shall pass **a** with a great noise, *G3928*
17 ye also, being led **a** with the error of the
1Jn 2:17 And the world passeth **a**, and the lust *G3855*
3: 5 to take **a** our sins; and in him is no sin. *G142*
Rev 7:17 shall wipe **a** all tears from their eyes. *G1813*
12:15 cause her to be carried **a** of the flood.
16:20 And every island fled **a**, and the *G5343*
17: 3 So he carried me **a** in the spirit into the *G667*
20:11 the heaven fled **a**; and there was found *G5343*
21: 1 passed **a**; and there was no more sea. *G3928*
4 And God shall wipe **a** all tears from *G1813*
4 pain: for the former things are passed **a**. *G565*
10 And he carried me **a** in the spirit to a *G667*
22:19 And if any man shall take **a** from the *G851*
19 God shall take **a** his part out of the book *G851*

AWE
Ps 4: 4 Stand in **a**, and sin not: commune with H7264
33: 8 of the world stand in **a** of him.
119:161 but my heart standeth in **a** of thy word. H6342

AWHILE See WHILE.

AWL See AUL.

AWOKE
Gen 9:24 And Noah **a** from his wine, and knew H3364
41: 4 favoured and fat kine. So Pharaoh **a**. H3364
7 Pharaoh **a**, and, behold, *it was* a dream. H3364
21 ill favoured, as at the beginning. So I **a**. H3364
Jdg 16:20 Samson. And he **a** out of his sleep, and H3364
1Ki 3:15 And Solomon **a**; and, behold, *it was* a H3364
Mt 8:25 And his disciples came to *him*, and **a** *G1453*
Lk 8:24 And they came to him, and **a** him, *G1326*

AXE
Dt 19: 5 a stroke with the **a** to cut down the tree, H1631
20:19 by forcing an **a** against them: for thou H1631
Jdg 9:48 took an **a** in his hand, and cut H7134
1Sa 13:20 his coulter, and his **a**, and his mattock. H7134
1Ki 6: 7 hammer nor **a** *nor* any tool of iron H1631
2Ki 6: 5 But as one was felling a beam, the **a**
Isa 10:15 Shall the **a** boast itself against him that H1631
Jer 10: 3 the hands of the workman, with the **a**. H4621
51:20 Thou *art* my battle **a** *and* weapons of H4661
Mt 3:10 And now also the **a** is laid unto the root *G513*
Lk 3: 9 And now also the **a** is laid unto the root *G513*

AXES
1Sa 13:21 and for the **a**, and to sharpen the goads. H7134
2Sa 12:31 of iron, and under **a** of iron, and made H4037
1Ch 20: 3 of iron, and with **a**. Even so dealt David H4050
Ps 74: 5 he had lifted up **a** upon the thick trees. H7134
6 thereof at once with **a** and hammers. H3781
Jer 46:22 against her with **a**, as hewers of wood. H7134
Ezk 26: 9 his **a** he shall break down thy towers. H2719

AX-HEAD See AXE and HEAD.

AXLETREES
1Ki 7:32 wheels; and the **a** of the wheels *were* H3027
33 wheel: their **a**, and their naves, and H3027

AY See NAY.

AZAL
Zec 14: 5 shall reach unto **A**: yea, ye shall flee, like H682

AZALIAH
2Ki 22: 3 the son of **A**, the son of Meshullam, H683
2Ch 34: 8 the son of **A**, and Maaseiah the governor H683

AZANIAH
Neh 10: 9 Jeshua the son of **A**, Binnui of the sons of H245

AZARAEL
Neh 12:36 And his brethren, Shemaiah, and **A**, H5832

AZAREEL
1Ch 12: 6 Elkanah, and Jesiah, and **A**, and Joezer, H5832
25:18 The eleventh to **A**, *he*, his sons, and his H5832
27:22 Of Dan, **A** the son of Jeroham. These H5832
Ezr 10:41 **A**, and Shelemiah, Shemariah, H5832
Neh 11:13 the son of **A**, the son of Ahasai, the H5832

AZARIAH
1Ki 4: 2 he had; **A** the son of Zadok the priest, H5838
5 And **A** the son of Nathan *was* over the H5838
2Ki 14:21 And all the people of Judah took **A**, H5838
15: 1 of Israel began **A** son of Amaziah king H5838
6 And the rest of the acts of **A**, and all H5838
7 So **A** slept with his fathers; and they H5838
8 In the thirty and eighth year of **A** king H5838
17 In the nine and thirtieth year of **A** king H5838
23 In the fiftieth year of **A** king of Judah H5838
27 In the two and fiftieth year of **A** king of H5838
1Ch 2: 8 And the sons of Ethan; **A**. H5838
38 And Obed begat Jehu, and Jehu begat **A**, H5838
39 And **A** begat Helez, and Helez begat H5838
3:12 Amaziah his son, **A** his son, Jotham his H5838
6: 9 And Ahimaaz begat **A**, and Azariah H5838
9 And Ahimaaz begat Azariah, and **A** H5838
10 And Johanan begat **A**, (he *it is* that H5838
11 And **A** begat Amariah, and Amariah H5838
13 begat Hilkiah, and Hilkiah begat **A**, H5838
1Ch 6:14 And **A** begat Seraiah, and Seraiah H5838
36 Joel, the son of **A**, the son of Zephaniah, H5838
9:11 And **A** the son of Hilkiah, the son of H5838
2Ch 15: 1 And the spirit of God came upon **A** the H5838
21: 2 sons of Jehoshaphat, **A**, and Jehiel, and H5838
2 Zechariah, and **A**, and Michael, and H5838
22: 6 Hazael king of Syria. And **A** the son of H5838
23: 1 of hundreds, **A** the son of Jeroham, H5838
1 Jehohanan, and **A** the son of Obed, and H5838
26:17 And **A** the priest went in after him, and H5838
20 And **A** the chief priest, and all the H5838
28:12 of Ephraim, **A** the son of Johanan, H5838
29:12 and Joel the son of **A**, of the sons of the H5838
12 son of Abdi, and **A** the son of Jehalelel: H5838
31:10 And **A** the chief priest of the house of H5838
13 and **A** the ruler of the house of God. H5838
Ezr 7: 1 the son of **A**, the son of Hilkiah, H5838
3 The son of Amariah, the son of **A**, the H5838
Neh 3:23 him repaired **A** the son of Maaseiah H5838
24 from the house of **A** unto the turning *of* H5838
7: 7 Nehemiah, **A**, Raamiah, Nahamani, H5838
8: 7 Maaseiah, Kelita, **A**, Jozabad, Hanan, H5838
10: 2 Seraiah, **A**, Jeremiah, H5838
12:33 And **A**, Ezra, and Meshullam, H5838
Jer 43: 2 Then spake **A** the son of Hoshaiah, and H5838
Dan 1: 6 Daniel, Hananiah, Mishael, and **A**: H5838
7 of Meshach; and to **A**, of Abed-nego. H5838
11 over Daniel, Hananiah, Mishael, and **A**, H5838
19 **A**: therefore stood they before the king. H5838
2:17 Mishael, and **A**, his companions: H5839

AZAZ
1Ch 5: 8 And Bela the son of **A**, the son of H5811

AZAZIAH
1Ch 15:21 **A**, with harps on the Sheminith to excel. H5812
27:20 Hoshea the son of **A**: of the half tribe of H5812
2Ch 31:13 And Jehiel, and **A**, and Nahath, and H5812

AZBUK
Neh 3:16 the son of **A**, the ruler of the half H5802

AZEKAH
Jos 10:10 smote them to **A**, and unto Makkedah. H5825
11 upon them unto **A**, and they died: *they* H5825
15:35 Jarmuth, and Adullam, Socoh, and **A**, H5825
1Sa 17: 1 Shochoh and **A**, in Ephes-dammim. H5825
2Ch 11: 9 And Adoraim, and Lachish, and **A**, H5825
Neh 11:30 fields thereof, at **A**, and *in* the villages H5825
Jer 34: 7 and against **A**: for these defenced cities H5825

AZEL
1Ch 8:37 *was* his son, Eleasah his son, **A** his son: H682
38 And **A** had six sons, whose names *are* H682
38 and Hanan. All these *were* the sons of **A**. H682
9:43 his son, Eleasah his son, **A** his son. H682
44 And **A** had six sons, whose names *are* H682
44 and Hanan: these *were* the sons of **A**. H682

AZEM
Jos 15:29 Baalah, and Iim, and **A**, H6107
19: 3 And Hazar-shual, and Balah, and **A**, H6107

AZGAD
Ezr 2:12 The children of **A**, a thousand two H5803
8:12 And of the sons of **A**; Johanan the son H5803
Neh 7:17 The children of **A**, two thousand three H5803
10:15 Bunni, **A**, Bebai, H5803

AZIEL
1Ch 15:20 And Zechariah, and **A**, and H5815

AZIZA
Ezr 10:27 and Jeremoth, and Zabad, and **A**. H5819

AZMAVETH
2Sa 23:31 Abialbon the Arbathite, **A** the H5820
1Ch 8:36 **A**, and Zimri; and Zimri begat Moza, H5820
9:42 **A**, and Zimri; and Zimri begat Moza; H5820
11:33 **A** the Baharumite, Eliahba the H5820
12: 3 Pelet, the sons of **A**; and Berachah, and H5820
27:25 And over the king's treasures *was* **A** the H5820
Ezr 2:24 The children of **A**, forty and two. H5820
Neh 12:29 fields of Geba and **A**: for the singers had H5820

AZMON
Nu 34: 4 on to Hazar-addar, and pass on to **A**: H6111
5 a compass from **A** unto the river of H6111
Jos 15: 4 *From thence* it passed toward **A**, and H6111

AZNOTHTABOR
Jos 19:34 westward to **A**, and goeth out from H243

AZOR
Mt 1:13 begat Eliakim; and Eliakim begat **A**; *G107*
14 And **A** begat Sadoc; and Sadoc begat *G107*

AZOTUS
Act 8:40 But Philip was found at **A**: and passing *G108*

AZRIEL
1Ch 5:24 and Eliel, and **A**, and Jeremiah, and H5837
27:19 of Naphtali, Jerimoth the son of **A**: H5837
Jer 36:26 Seraiah the son of **A**, and Shelemiah the H5837

AZRIKAM
1Ch 3:23 Elioenai, and Hezekiah, and **A**, three. H5840
8:38 names *are* these, **A**, Bocheru, and H5840
9:14 the son of **A**, the son of Hashabiah, H5840
44 names *are* these, **A**, Bocheru, and H5840
2Ch 28: 7 king's son, and **A** the governor of the H5840
Neh 11:15 the son of **A**, the son of Hashabiah, H5840

AZUBAH
1Ki 22:42 name *was* **A** the daughter of Shilhi. H5806
1Ch 2:18 begat *children* of **A** *his* wife, and of H5806
19 And when **A** was dead, Caleb took unto H5806
2Ch 20:31 name *was* **A** the daughter of Shilhi. H5806

AZUR
Jer 28: 1 the son of **A** the prophet, which H5809
Ezk 11: 1 the son of **A**, and Pelatiah the son H5809

AZZAH
Dt 2:23 *even* unto **A**, the Caphtorims, which H5804
1Ki 4:24 Tiphsah even to **A**, over all the kings on H5804
Jer 25:20 Ashkelon, and **A**, and Ekron, and the H5804

AZZAN
Nu 34:26 of Issachar, Paltiel the son of **A**. H5821

AZZUR
Neh 10:17 Ater, Hizkijah, **A**, H5809

B

BAAL
Nu 22:41 into the high places of **B**, that thence he H1168
Jdg 2:13 LORD, and served **B** and Ashtaroth. H1168
6:25 down the altar of **B** that thy father H1168
28 the altar of **B** was cast down, and H1168
30 down the altar of **B**, and because he H1168
31 Will ye plead for **B**? will ye save him? he H1168
32 saying, Let **B** plead against him, H1168
1Ki 16:31 and served **B**, and worshipped him. H1168
32 And he reared up an altar for **B** in the H1168
32 of **B**, which he had built in Samaria. H1168
18:19 the prophets of **B** four hundred and H1168
21 follow him: but if **B**, *then* follow him. H1168
25 And Elijah said unto the prophets of **B**, H1168
26 on the name of **B** from morning even H1168
26 noon, saying, O **B**, hear us. But *there* H1168
40 the prophets of **B**; let not one of them H1168
19:18 not bowed unto **B**, and every mouth H1168
22:53 For he served **B**, and worshipped him, H1168
2Ki 3: 2 image of **B** that his father had made. H1168
10:18 Ahab served **B** a little; *but* Jehu shall H1168
19 all the prophets of **B**, all his servants, H1168
19 sacrifice *to do* to **B**; whosoever shall be H1168
19 he might destroy the worshippers of **B**. H1168
20 assembly for **B**. And they proclaimed *it*. H1168
21 worshippers of **B** came, so that there H1168
21 into the house of **B**; and the house of H1168
21 of **B** was full from one end to another. H1168
22 worshippers of **B**. And he brought them H1168
23 into the house of **B**, and said unto the H1168
23 worshippers of **B**, Search, and look that H1168
23 LORD, but the worshippers of **B** only. H1168
25 and went to the city of the house of **B**. H1168
26 out of the house of **B**, and burned them. H1168
27 And they brake down the image of **B**, H1168
27 down the house of **B**, and made it a H1168
28 Thus Jehu destroyed **B** out of Israel. H1168
11:18 into the house of **B**, and brake it down; H1168
18 the priest of **B** before the altars. And H1168
17:16 all the host of heaven, and served **B**. H1168
21: 3 up altars for **B**, and made a grove, H1168
23: 4 were made for **B**, and for the grove, and H1168
5 incense unto **B**, to the sun, and to the H1168
1Ch 4:33 same cities, unto **B**. These *were* their H1168
5: 5 Micah his son, Reaia his son, **B** his son, H1168
8:30 and Zur, and Kish, and **B**, and Nadab, H1168
9:36 and Kish, and **B**, and Ner, and Nadab, H1168
2Ch 23:17 to the house of **B**, and brake it down, H1168
17 Mattan the priest of **B** before the altars. H1168
Jer 2: 8 prophesied by **B**, and walked after H1168
7: 9 burn incense unto **B**, and walk after H1168
11:13 *even* altars to burn incense unto **B**. H1168
17 me to anger in offering incense unto **B**. H1168
12:16 to swear by **B**; then shall they be built H1168
19: 5 the high places of **B**, to burn their sons H1168
5 offerings unto **B**, which I commanded H1168
23:13 **B**, and caused my people Israel to err. H1168
27 fathers have forgotten my name for **B**. H1168
32:29 incense unto **B**, and poured out drink H1168
35 And they built the high places of **B**, H1168
Hos 2: 8 and gold, *which* they prepared for **B**. H1168
13: 1 but when he offended in **B**, he died. H1168
Zep 1: 4 off the remnant of **B** from this place, H1168
Ro 11: 4 not bowed the knee to *the image of* **B**. *G896*

BAALAH
Jos 15: 9 drawn to **B**, which *is* Kirjath-jearim: H1173
15:10 And the border compassed from **B** H1173
11 along to mount **B**, and went out unto H1173
29 **B**, and Iim, and Azem, H1173
1Ch 13: 6 And David went up, and all Israel, to **B**, H1173

BAALATH
Jos 19:44 And Eltekeh, and Gibbethon, and **B**, H1191
1Ki 9:18 And **B**, and Tadmor in the wilderness, H1191
2Ch 8: 6 And **B**, and all the store cities that H1191

BAALATH-BEER
Jos 19: 8 these cities to **B**, Ramath of the south. H1192

BAAL-BERITH
Jdg 8:33 after Baalim, and made **B** their god. H1170
9: 4 silver out of the house of **B**, wherewith H1170

BAALE
2Sa 6: 2 with him from **B** of Judah, to bring up H1184

BAAL-GAD
Jos 11:17 up to Seir, even unto **B** in the valley of H1171
12: 7 on the west, from **B** in the valley of H1171
13: 5 the sunrising, from **B** under mount H1171

BAAL-HAMON
Song 8:11 Solomon had a vineyard at **B**; he let out H1174

BAAL-HANAN
Gen 36:38 And Saul died, and **B** the son of Achbor H1177
39 And **B** the son of Achbor died, and H1177
1Ch 1:49 And when Shaul was dead, **B** the son of H1177
50 And when **B** was dead, Hadad reigned H1177
27:28 the low plains *was* **B** the Gederite: and H1177

BAAL-HAZOR
2Sa 13:23 had sheepshearers in **B**, which *is* beside H1178

BAAL-HERMON
Jdg 3: 3 **B** unto the entering in of Hamath. H1179
1Ch 5:23 **B** and Senir, and unto mount Hermon. H1179

BAALI
Hos 2:16 me Ishi; and shalt call me no more **B**. H1180

BAALIM
Jdg 2:11 in the sight of the LORD, and served **B**: H1168
3: 7 their God, and served **B** and the groves. H1168
8:33 **B**, and made Baal-berith their god. H1168
10: 6 LORD, and served **B**, and Ashtaroth, H1168
10 forsaken our God, and also served **B**. H1168
1Sa 7: 4 did put away **B** and Ashtaroth, and H1168
12:10 and have served **B** and Ashtaroth: but H1168
1Ki 18:18 of the LORD, and thou hast followed **B**. H1168
2Ch 17: 3 father David, and sought not unto **B**; H1168
24: 7 of the LORD did they bestow upon **B**. H1168
28: 2 and made also molten images for **B**. H1168
33: 3 up altars for **B**, and made groves, and H1168
34: 4 And they brake down the altars of **B** in H1168
Jer 2:23 have not gone after **B**? see thy way in the H1168
9:14 **B**, which their fathers taught them: H1168
Hos 2:13 And I will visit upon her the days of **B**, H1168
17 For I will take away the names of **B** out H1168
11: 2 sacrificed unto **B**, and burned incense H1168

BAALIS
Jer 40:14 know that **B** the king of the Ammonites H1185

BAALMEON
1Ch 5: 8 dwelt in Aroer, even unto Nebo and **B**: H1186

BAAL-MEON
Nu 32:38 And Nebo, and **B**, (their names being H1186
Ezk 25: 9 Beth-jeshimoth, **B**, and Kiriathaim, H1186

BAAL-PEOR
Nu 25: 3 And Israel joined himself unto **B**: and H1187
5 one his men that were joined unto **B**. H1187
Dt 4: 3 did because of **B**: for all the men that H1187
3 men that followed **B**, the LORD thy God H1187
Ps 106:28 They joined themselves also unto **B**, H1187
Hos 9:10 time: *but* they went to **B**, and separated H1187

BAAL-PERAZIM
2Sa 5:20 And David came to **B**, and David smote H1188
20 he called the name of that place **B**. H1188
1Ch 14:11 So they came up to **B**; and David smote H1188
11 they called the name of that place **B**. H1188

BAAL'S
1Ki 18:22 of the LORD; but **B** prophets *are* four H1168

BAAL-SHALISHA
2Ki 4:42 And there came a man from **B**, and H1190

BAAL-TAMAR
Jdg 20:33 in array at **B**: and the liers in wait H1193

BAALZEBUB
2Ki 1:16 to inquire of **B** the god of Ekron, *is* H1176

BAAL-ZEBUB
2Ki 1: 2 them, Go, inquire of **B** the god of Ekron H1176
3 ye go to inquire of **B** the god of Ekron? H1176
6 to inquire of **B** the god of Ekron? H1176

BAAL-ZEPHON
Ex 14: 2 **B**: before it shall ye encamp by the sea. H1189
9 the sea, beside Pi-hahi-roth, before **B**. H1189
Nu 33: 7 **B**: and they pitched before Migdol. H1189

BAANA
1Ki 4:12 **B** the son of Ahilud; *to him pertained* H1195
Neh 3: 4 unto them repaired Zadok the son of **B**. H1195

BAANAH
2Sa 4: 2 of the one *was* **B**, and the name of the H1196
5 Rechab and **B**, went, and came about H1196
6 and Rechab and **B** his brother escaped. H1196
9 And David answered Rechab and **B** his H1196
23:29 Heleb the son of **B**, a Netophathite, Ittai H1196
1Ki 4:16 **B** the son of Hushai *was* in Asher and H1195
1Ch 11:30 Heled the son of **B** the Netophathite, H1196
Ezr 2: 2 Bigvai, Rehum, **B**. The number of the H1196
Neh 7: 7 Bigvai, Nehum, **B**. The number, *I say*, H1196
10:27 Malluch, Harim, **B**. H1196

BAARA
1Ch 8: 8 away; Hushim and **B** *were* his wives. H1199

BAASEIAH
1Ch 6:40 The son of Michael, the son of **B**, the H1202

BAASHA
1Ki 15:16 And there was war between Asa and **B** H1201
17 And **B** king of Israel went up against H1201

1Ki 15:19 thy league with **B** king of Israel, that he H1201
21 And it came to pass, when **B** heard H1201
22 wherewith **B** had builded; and king H1201
27 And **B** the son of Ahijah, of the house H1201
27 against him; and **B** smote him at H1201
28 **B** slay him, and reigned in his stead. H1201
32 And there was war between Asa and **B** H1201
33 of Judah began **B** the son of Ahijah to H1201
16: 1 the son of Hanani against **B**, saying, H1201
3 the posterity of **B**, and the posterity of H1201
4 Him that dieth of **B** in the city shall the H1201
5 Now the rest of the acts of **B**, and what H1201
6 So **B** slept with his fathers, and was H1201
7 of the LORD against **B**, and against his H1201
8 Elah the son of **B** to reign over Israel H1201
11 all the house of **B**: he left him not one H1201
12 all the house of **B**, according to the H1201
12 he spake against **B** by Jehu the prophet, H1201
13 For all the sins of **B**, and the sins of Elah H1201
21:22 like the house of **B** the son of Ahijah, H1201
2Ki 9: 9 like the house of **B** the son of Ahijah: H1201
2Ch 16: 1 year of the reign of Asa **B** king of Israel H1201
3 thy league with **B** king of Israel, that he H1201
5 And it came to pass, when **B** heard *it*, H1201
6 wherewith **B** was building; and he H1201
Jer 41: 9 made for fear of **B** king of Israel: *and* H1201

BABBLER
Ecc 10:11 and a **b** is no better. H1167+H3956
Act 17:18 What will this **b** say? other some, He *G4691*

BABBLING
Prv 23:29 who hath **b**? who hath wounds without H7879

BABBLINGS
1Ti 6:20 profane *and* vain **b**, and oppositions of *G2757*
2Ti 2:16 But shun profane *and* vain **b**: for they *G2757*

BABE
Ex 2: 6 and, behold, the **b** wept. And she had H5288
Lk 1:41 of Mary, the **b** leaped in her womb; *G1025*
44 ears, the **b** leaped in my womb for joy. *G1025*
2:12 you; Ye shall find the **b** wrapped in *G1025*
16 Joseph, and the **b** lying in a manger. *G1025*
Heb 5:13 the word of righteousness: for he is a **b**. *G3516*

BABEL
Gen 10:10 And the beginning of his kingdom was **B**, H894
11: 9 Therefore is the name of it called **B**; H894

BABES
Ps 8: 2 Out of the mouth of **b** and sucklings H5768
17:14 the rest of their *substance* to their **b**. H5768
Isa 3: 4 princes, and **b** shall rule over them. H8586
Mt 11:25 and hast revealed them unto **b**. *G3516*
21:16 of the mouth of **b** and sucklings thou *G3516*
Lk 10:21 them unto **b**: even so, Father; for *G3516*
Ro 2:20 a teacher of **b**, which hast the form *G3516*
1Co 3: 1 unto carnal, *even* as unto **b** in Christ. *G3516*
1Pt 2: 2 As newborn **b**, desire the sincere milk of *G1025*

BABYLON
2Ki 17:24 brought *men* from **B**, and from Cuthah, H894
30 And the men of **B** made Succoth-benoth, H894
20:12 of Baladan, king of **B**, sent letters and a H894
14 come from a far country, *even* from **B**. H894
17 **B**: nothing shall be left, saith the LORD. H894
18 be eunuchs in the palace of the king of **B**. H894
24: 1 In his days Nebuchadnezzar king of **B** H894
7 for the king of **B** had taken from the H894
10 king of **B** came up against Jerusalem, H894
11 And Nebuchadnezzar king of **B** came H894
12 out to the king of **B**, he, and his mother, H894
12 and the king of **B** took him in the eighth H894
15 And he carried away Jehoiachin to **B**, H894
15 he into captivity from Jerusalem to **B**. H894
16 king of **B** brought captive to Babylon. H894
16 the king of Babylon brought captive to **B**. H894
17 And the king of **B** made Mattaniah his H894
20 Zedekiah rebelled against the king of **B**. H894
25: 1 king of **B** came, he, and all his H894
6 up to the king of **B** to Riblah; and they H894
7 fetters of brass, and carried him to **B**. H894
8 king of **B**, came Nebuzar-adan, H894
8 servant of the king of **B**, unto Jerusalem: H894
11 away to the king of **B**, with the remnant H894
13 and carried the brass of them to **B**. H894
2Ki 25:20 brought them to the king of **B** to Riblah: H894
21 And the king of **B** smote them, and slew H894
22 king of **B** had left, even over them H894
23 that the king of **B** had made Gedaliah H894
24 king of **B**; and it shall be well with you. H894
27 king of **B** in the year that he began H894
28 of the kings that *were* with him in **B**; H894
1Ch 9: 1 away to **B** for their transgression. H894
2Ch 32:31 of the princes of **B**, who sent unto him to H894
33:11 him with fetters, and carried him to **B**. H894
36: 6 king of **B**, and bound him in fetters, H894
6 bound him in fetters, to carry him to **B**. H894
7 of the LORD to **B**, and put them in his H894
7 and put them in his temple at **B**. H894
10 brought him to **B**, with the goodly vessels H894
18 of his princes; all *these* he brought to **B**. H894
20 carried he away to **B**; where they were H894
Ezr 1:11 were brought up from **B** unto Jerusalem. H894
2: 1 the king of **B** had carried away unto H894
1 carried away unto **B**, and came again H894
5:12 the king of **B**, the Chaldean, who H895
12 and carried the people away into **B**. H895
13 Cyrus the king of **B** *the same* king Cyrus H895
14 into the temple of **B**, those did Cyrus the H895
14 out of the temple of **B**, and they were H895
17 which *is* there at **B**, whether it be *so*, that H895
6: 1 where the treasures were laid up in **B**. H895
5 and brought unto **B**, be restored, and H895
7: 6 This Ezra went up from **B**; and he *was* a H894
9 he to go up from **B**, and on the first *day* H894
16 in all the province of **B**, with the freewill H895
8: 1 **B**, in the reign of Artaxerxes the king. H894
Neh 7: 6 the king of **B** had carried away, and H894
13: 6 of Artaxerxes king of **B** came I unto the H894
Est 2: 6 the king of **B** had carried away. H894
Ps 87: 4 I will make mention of Rahab and **B** to H894
137: 1 By the rivers of **B**, there we sat down, yea, H894
8 O daughter of **B**, who art to be destroyed; H894
Isa 13: 1 The burden of **B**, which Isaiah the son of H894
19 And **B**, the glory of kingdoms, the beauty H894
14: 4 against the king of **B**, and say, How hath H894
22 hosts, and cut off from **B** the name, and H894
21: 9 and said, **B** is fallen, is fallen; and H894
39: 1 of Baladan, king of **B**, sent letters and a H894
3 from a far country unto me, *even* from **B**. H894
6 **B**: nothing shall be left, saith the LORD. H894
7 be eunuchs in the palace of the king of **B**. H894
43:14 sake I have sent to **B**, and have brought H894
47: 1 O virgin daughter of **B**, sit on the ground: H894
48:14 **B**, and his arm *shall be on* the Chaldeans. H894
20 Go ye forth of **B**, flee ye from the H894
Jer 20: 4 hand of the king of **B**, and he shall carry H894
4 **B**, and shall slay them with the sword. H894
5 and take them, and carry them to **B**. H894
6 and thou shalt come to **B**, and there thou H894
21: 2 king of **B** maketh war against H894
4 against the king of **B**, and *against* the H894
7 king of **B**, and into the hand of H894
10 king of **B**, and he shall burn it with fire. H894
22:25 of **B**, and into the hand of the Chaldeans. H894
24: 1 king of **B** had carried away captive H894
1 Jerusalem, and had brought them to **B**. H894
25: 1 first year of Nebuchadrezzar king of **B**; H894
9 the king of **B**, my servant, and will H894
11 shall serve the king of **B** seventy years. H894
12 punish the king of **B**, and that nation, H894
27: 6 the king of **B**, my servant; and the H894
8 the king of **B**, and that will not put H894
8 yoke of the king of **B**, that nation will I H894
9 saying, Ye shall not serve the king of **B**: H894
11 the yoke of the king of **B**, and serve him, H894
12 yoke of the king of **B**, and serve him and H894
13 nation that will not serve the king of **B**? H894
14 of **B**: for they prophesy a lie unto you. H894
16 from **B**: for they prophesy a lie unto you. H894
17 serve the king of **B**, and live: wherefore H894
18 of Judah, and at Jerusalem, go not to **B**. H894
20 Which Nebuchadnezzar king of **B** took H894
20 from Jerusalem to **B**, and all the nobles of H894
22 They shall be carried to **B**, and there shall H894
28: 2 I have broken the yoke of the king of **B**. H894
3 king of **B** took away from this H894
3 from this place, and carried them to **B**: H894
4 that went into **B**, saith the LORD: for H894
4 for I will break the yoke of the king of **B**. H894
6 away captive, from **B** into this place. H894
11 king of **B** from the neck of all H894
14 king of **B**; and they shall serve H894
29: 1 away captive from Jerusalem to **B**; H894
Jer 29: 3 of Judah sent unto **B** to Nebuchadnezzar H894
3 to Nebuchadnezzar king of **B**) saying, H894
4 be carried away from Jerusalem unto **B**; H894
10 accomplished at **B** I will visit you, and H894
15 LORD hath raised us up prophets in **B**; H894
20 whom I have sent from Jerusalem to **B**: H894
21 king of **B**; and he shall slay them H894
22 Judah which *are* in **B**, saying, The LORD H894
22 whom the king of **B** roasted in the fire; H894
28 For therefore he sent unto us *in* **B**, H894
32: 3 of the king of **B**, and he shall take it; H894
4 the hand of the king of **B**, and shall speak H894
5 And he shall lead Zedekiah to **B**, and H894
28 king of **B**, and he shall take it: H894
36 hand of the king of **B** by the sword, and H894
34: 1 king of **B**, and all his army, and H894
2 king of **B**, and he shall burn it with fire: H894
3 eyes of the king of **B**, and he shall speak H894
3 mouth to mouth, and thou shalt go to **B**. H894
35:11 king of **B** came up into the land, H894
36:29 saying, The king of **B** shall certainly H894
37: 1 of **B** made king in the land of Judah. H894
17 delivered into the hand of the king of **B**. H894
19 saying, The king of **B** shall not come H894
38:23 the hand of the king of **B**: and thou shalt H894
39: 1 king of **B** and all his army against H894
3 And all the princes of the king of **B** came H894
3 the residue of the princes of the king of **B**. H894
5 king of **B** to Riblah in the land H894
6 Then the king of **B** slew the sons of H894
6 king of **B** slew all the nobles of Judah. H894
7 him with chains, to carry him to **B**. H894
9 away captive into **B** the remnant of the H894
11 Now Nebuchadrezzar king of **B** gave H894
40: 1 which were carried away captive unto **B**. H894
4 to come with me into **B**, come; and I will H894
4 come with me into **B**, forbear: behold, all H894
5 whom the king of **B** hath made governor H894
7 that the king of **B** had made Gedaliah H894
7 that were not carried away captive to **B**; H894
9 king of **B**, and it shall be well with you. H894
11 that the king of **B** had left a remnant of H894
41: 2 of **B** had made governor over the land. H894
18 the king of **B** made governor in the land. H894
42:11 Be not afraid of the king of **B**, of whom ye H894
43: 3 death, and carry us away captives into **B**. H894
10 the king of **B**, my servant, and will H894
44:30 of **B**, his enemy, and that sought his life. H894
46: 2 king of **B** smote in the fourth year H894
13 king of **B** should come *and* smite H894
26 king of **B**, and into the hand of H894
49:28 king of **B** shall smite, thus saith H894
30 king of **B** hath taken counsel against H894
50: 1 The word that the LORD spake against **B** H894
2 *and* conceal not: say, **B** is taken, Bel is H894
8 Remove out of the midst of **B**, and go H894
9 to come up against **B** an assembly of H894
13 one that goeth by **B** shall be astonished, H894
14 Put yourselves in array against **B** round H894
16 Cut off the sower from **B**, and him that H894
17 king of **B** hath broken his bones. H894
18 punish the king of **B** and his land, as I H894
23 asunder and broken! how is **B** become a H894
24 art also taken, O **B**, and thou wast not H894
28 out of the land of **B**, to declare in Zion the H894
29 Call together the archers against **B**: all ye H894
34 land, and disquiet the inhabitants of **B**. H894
35 upon the inhabitants of **B**, and upon her H894
42 the battle, against thee, O daughter of **B**. H894
43 The king of **B** hath heard the report of H894
45 hath taken against **B**; and his purposes, H894
46 At the noise of the taking of **B** the earth H894
51: 1 raise up against **B**, and against them that H894
2 And will send unto **B** fanners, that shall H894
6 Flee out of the midst of **B**, and deliver H894
7 **B** *hath been* a golden cup in the LORD'S H894
8 **B** is suddenly fallen and destroyed: howl H894
9 We would have healed **B**, but she is not H894
11 device *is* against **B**, to destroy it; because H894
12 Set up the standard upon the walls of **B**, H894
12 he spake against the inhabitants of **B**. H894
24 And I will render unto **B** and to all the H894
29 performed against **B**, to make the land of H894
29 of **B** a desolation without an inhabitant. H894
30 The mighty men of **B** have forborn to H894
31 of **B** that his city is taken at *one* end, H894
33 Israel; The daughter of **B** *is* like a H894
34 Nebuchadrezzar the king of **B** hath H894
35 my flesh *be* upon **B**, shall the inhabitant H894

Jer 51:37 And **B** shall become heaps, a H894
41 earth surprised! how is **B** become an H894
42 The sea is come up upon **B**: she is H894
44 And I will punish Bel in **B**, and I will H894
44 unto him: yea, the wall of **B** shall fall. H894
47 graven images of **B**: and her whole land H894
48 shall sing for **B**: for the spoilers shall H894
49 As **B** *hath caused* the slain of Israel to H894
49 so at **B** shall fall the slain of all the earth. H894
53 Though **B** should mount up to heaven, H894
54 A sound of a cry *cometh* from **B**, and H894
55 Because the LORD hath spoiled **B**, and H894
56 her, *even* upon **B**, and her mighty men H894
58 The broad walls of **B** shall be utterly H894
59 king of Judah into **B** in the fourth year of H894
60 that should come upon **B**, *even* all these H894
60 these words that are written against **B**. H894
61 thou comest to **B**, and shalt see, and shalt H894
64 And thou shalt say, Thus shall **B** sink, H894
52: 3 Zedekiah rebelled against the king of **B**. H894
4 king of **B** came, he and all his H894
9 up unto the king of **B** to Riblah in the H894
10 And the king of **B** slew the sons of H894
11 and the king of **B** bound him in chains, H894
11 and carried him to **B**, and put him in H894
12 king of **B**, came Nebuzar-adan, H894
12 served the king of **B**, into Jerusalem, H894
15 king of **B**, and the rest of the multitude. H894
17 and carried all the brass of them to **B**. H894
26 brought them to the king of **B** to Riblah. H894
27 And the king of **B** smote them, and put H894
31 king of **B** in the *first* year of his H894
32 of the kings that *were* with him in **B**, H894
34 him of the king of **B**, every day a portion H894
Ezk 12:13 I will bring him to **B** *to* the land of the H894
17:12 *them*, Behold, the king of **B** is come to H894
12 thereof, and led them with him to **B**; H894
16 with him in the midst of **B** he shall die. H894
20 I will bring him to **B**, and will plead with H894
19: 9 him to the king of **B**: they brought him H894
21:19 of the king of **B** may come: both twain H894
21 For the king of **B** stood at the parting of H894
24: 2 day: the king of **B** set himself against H894
26: 7 king of **B**, a king of kings, from H894
29:18 Son of man, Nebuchadrezzar king of **B** H894
19 king of **B**; and he shall take her H894
30:10 by the hand of Nebuchadrezzar king of **B**. H894
24 arms of the king of **B**, and put my sword H894
25 the arms of the king of **B**, and the arms of H894
25 hand of the king of **B**, and he shall stretch H894
32:11 of the king of **B** shall come upon thee. H894
Dan 1: 1 of **B** unto Jerusalem, and besieged it. H894
2:12 to destroy all the wise *men* of **B**. H895
14 was gone forth to slay the wise *men* of **B**: H895
18 perish with the rest of the wise *men* of **B**. H895
24 the wise *men* of **B**: he went and said thus H895
24 the wise *men* of **B**: bring me in before the H895
48 the whole province of **B**, and chief of the H895
48 the governors over all the wise *men* of **B**. H895
49 **B**: but Daniel *sat* in the gate of the king. H895
3: 1 in the plain of Dura, in the province of **B**. H895
12 of the province of **B**, Shadrach, Meshach, H895
30 and Abed-nego, in the province of **B**. H895
4: 6 in all the wise *men* of **B** before me, that H895
29 walked in the palace of the kingdom of **B**. H895
30 Is not this great **B**, that I have built for H895
5: 7 to the wise *men* of **B**, Whosoever shall H895
7: 1 In the first year of Belshazzar king of **B** H895
Mic 4:10 shalt go *even* to **B**; there shalt thou be H894
Zec 2: 7 that dwellest *with* the daughter of **B**. H894
6:10 are come from **B**, and come thou the H894
Mt 1:11 the time they were carried away to **B**: *G897*
12 And after they were brought to **B**, *G897*
17 the carrying away into **B** *are* fourteen *G897*
17 **B** unto Christ *are* fourteen generations. *G897*
Act 7:43 and I will carry you away beyond **B**. *G897*
1Pt 5:13 The *church that is* at **B**, elected together *G897*
Rev 14: 8 angel, saying, **B** is fallen, is fallen, that *G897*
16:19 fell: and great **B** came in remembrance *G897*
17: 5 written, MYSTERY, **B** THE GREAT, THE *G897*
18: 2 voice, saying, **B** the great is fallen, is *G897*
10 alas that great city **B**, that mighty city! *G897*
21 that great city **B** be thrown down, and *G897*

BABYLONIANS
Ezr 4: 9 the Archevites, the **B**, the Susanchites, H896
Ezk 23:15 manner of the **B** of Chaldea, the H1121+H894
17 And the **B** came to her into the H1121+H894
23 The **B**, and all the Chaldeans, H1121+H894

BABYLONISH
Jos 7:21 the spoils a goodly **B** garment, and two H8152

BABYLON'S
Jer 32: 2 For then the king of **B** army besieged H894
34: 7 When the king of **B** army fought against H894
21 of **B** army, which are gone up from you. H894
38: 3 of the king of **B** army, which shall take it. H894
17 unto the king of **B** princes, then thy soul H894
18 forth to the king of **B** princes, then shall H894
22 forth to the king of **B** princes, and those H894
39:13 Rab-mag, and all the king of **B** princes; H894

BACA
Ps 84: 6 *Who* passing through the valley of **B** H1056

BACHRITES
Nu 26:35 the family of the **B**: of Tahan, the family H1076

BACHUTH See ALLON-BACHUTH.

BACK
Gen 14:16 And he brought **b** all the goods, and H7725
19: 9 And they said, Stand **b**. And they said H1973
26 But his wife looked **b** from behind him, H5027
38:29 And it came to pass, as he drew **b** his H7725
39: 9 hath he kept **b** any thing from me H2820
Ex 14:21 the sea to go ***b*** by a strong east wind
18: 2 Moses' wife, after he had sent her **b**,
23: 4 shalt surely bring it **b** to him again. H7725
33:23 **b** parts: but my face shall not be seen. H268
Nu 9: 7 are we kept **b**, that we may not offer H1639
13:26 and brought **b** word unto them, and H7725
22:34 it displease thee, I will get me **b** again. H7725
24:11 LORD hath kept thee **b** from honour. H4513
Dt 23:13 and shalt turn **b** and cover that which H7725
Jos 8:20 wilderness turned **b** upon the pursuers. H2015
26 For Joshua drew not his hand **b**, H7725
11:10 And Joshua at that time turned **b**, and H7725
23:12 Else if ye do in any wise go **b**, and H7725
Jdg 11:35 unto the LORD, and I cannot go **b**. H7725
18:26 he turned and went **b** unto his house. H7725
Ru 1:15 in law is gone **b** unto her people, and H7725
2: 6 damsel that came **b** with Naomi out of H7725
1Sa 10: 9 he had turned his **b** to go from Samuel, H7926
15:11 for he is turned **b** from following me, H7725
25:34 hath kept me **b** from hurting thee, H4513
2Sa 1:22 turned not **b**, and the sword of Saul H268
12:23 can I bring him **b** again? I shall go to H7725
15:20 thou, and take **b** thy brethren: mercy H7725
25 And the king said unto Zadok, Carry **b** H7725
17: 3 And I will bring **b** all the people unto H7725
18:16 after Israel: for Joab held **b** the people. H2820
19:10 ye not a word of bringing the king **b**? H7725
11 to bring the king **b** to his house? seeing H7725
12 then are ye the last to bring **b** the king? H7725
37 Let thy servant, I pray thee, turn **b** H7725
43 had in bringing **b** our king? And the H7725
1Ki 13:18 saying, Bring him **b** with thee into H7725
19 So he went **b** with him, and did eat H7725
20 unto the prophet that brought him **b**: H7725
22 But camest **b**, and hast eaten bread and H7725
23 the prophet whom he had brought **b**. H7725
26 that brought him **b** from the way heard H7725
29 and brought it **b**: and the old prophet H7725
14: 9 to anger, and hast cast me behind thy **b**: H1458
28 them **b** into the guard chamber. H7725
18:37 thou hast turned their heart **b** again. H322
19:20 **b** again: for what have I done to thee? H7725
21 And he returned **b** from him, and took H7725
22:26 and carry him **b** unto Amon the H7725
33 that they turned **b** from pursuing him. H7725
2Ki 1: 5 And when the messengers turned **b** H7725
5 unto them, Why are ye now turned **b**? H7725
2:13 **b**, and stood by the bank of Jordan; H7725
24 And he turned **b**, and looked on them, H310
8:29 And king Joram went **b** to be healed in H7725
15:20 **b**, and stayed not there in the land. H7725
19:28 **b** by the way by which thou camest. H7725
20: 9 ten degrees, or go **b** ten degrees? H7725
1Ch 21:20 And Ornan turned **b**, and saw the angel; H7725
2Ch 13:14 And when Judah looked **b**, behold, the H6437
18:25 and carry him **b** to Amon the governor H7725
32 turned **b** again from pursuing him. H7725
19: 4 **b** unto the LORD God of their fathers. H7725
25:13 Amaziah sent **b**, that they should not H7725
34:16 the king word **b** again, saying, All that H7725
Neh 2:15 wall, and turned **b**, and entered by the H7725
Job 23:12 Neither have I gone **b** from the H4185
Job 26: 9 He holdeth **b** the face of his throne, *and*
33:18 He keepeth **b** his soul from the pit, and H2820
30 To bring **b** his soul from the pit, to be H7725
34:27 Because they turned **b** from him, and H5493
39:22 neither turneth he **b** from the sword. H7725
Ps 9: 3 When mine enemies are turned **b**, they H268
14: 7 LORD bringeth **b** the captivity of his H7725
19:13 Keep **b** thy servant also from H2820
21:12 them turn their **b**, *when* thou shalt H7926
35: 4 let them be turned **b** and brought to H268
44:10 Thou makest us to turn **b** from the H268
18 Our heart is not turned **b**, neither have H268
53: 3 Every one of them is gone **b**: they are H5472
6 God bringeth **b** the captivity of his H7725
56: 9 turn **b**: this I know; for God *is* for me. H268
70: 3 Let them be turned **b** for a reward of H7725
78: 9 bows, turned **b** in the day of battle. H2015
41 Yea, they turned **b** and tempted God, H7725
57 But turned **b**, and dealt unfaithfully like H5472
80:18 So will not we go **b** from thee: quicken H5472
85: 1 hast brought **b** the captivity of Jacob. H7725
114: 3 sea saw *it*, and fled: Jordan was driven **b**. H268
5 thou Jordan, *that* thou wast driven **b**? H268
129: 3 The plowers plowed upon my **b**: they H1354
5 Let them all be confounded and turned **b** H268
Prv 10:13 **b** of him that is void of understanding. H1460
19:29 scorners, and stripes for the **b** of fools. H1460
26: 3 for the ass, and a rod for the fool's **b**. H1460
Isa 14:27 *is* stretched out, and who shall turn it **b**? H7725
31: 2 and will not call **b** his words: but will H5493
37:29 **b** by the way by which thou camest. H7725
38:17 thou hast cast all my sins behind thy **b**. H1460
42:17 They shall be turned **b**, they shall be H268
43: 6 south, Keep not **b**: bring my sons from H3607
50: 5 not rebellious, neither turned away **b**. H268
6 I gave my **b** to the smiters, and my H1460
Jer 2:27 have turned *their* **b** unto me, and not H6203
4: 8 of the LORD is not turned **b** from us. H7725
28 not repent, neither will I turn **b** from it. H7725
6: 9 Israel as a vine: turn **b** thine hand as a H7725
8: 5 of Jerusalem slidden **b** by a perpetual H7725
11:10 They are turned **b** to the iniquities of H7725
18:17 shew them the **b**, and not the face, in H6203
21: 4 Behold, I will turn **b** the weapons of H5437
32:33 And they have turned unto me the **b**, H6203
38:22 in the mire, *and* they are turned away **b**. H268
40: 5 Now while he was not yet gone **b**, *he* H7725
5 back, *he said*, Go **b** also to Gedaliah the H7725
42: 4 you; I will keep nothing **b** from you. H4513
46: 5 *and* turned away **b**? and their mighty H268
5 and look not **b**: *for* fear *was* round H6437
21 also are turned **b**, *and* are fled away H6437
47: 3 shall not look **b** to *their* children for H6437
48:10 that keepeth **b** his sword from blood. H4513
39 hath Moab turned the **b** with shame! so H6203
49: 8 Flee ye, turn **b**, dwell deep, O H6437
Lam 1:13 he hath turned me **b**: he hath made me H268
2: 3 he hath drawn **b** his right hand from H268
Ezk 23:35 me behind thy **b**, therefore bear thou H1458
24:14 do *it*; I will not go **b**, neither will I spare, H6544
38: 4 And I will turn thee **b**, and put hooks H7725
8 *that is* brought **b** from the sword, *and* H7725
39: 2 And I will turn thee **b**, and leave but the H7725
44: 1 Then he brought me **b** the way of the H7725
Dan 7: 6 had upon the **b** of it four wings of a H1355
Hos 4:16 For Israel slideth **b** as a backsliding H5637
Nah 2: 8 *shall they cry*; but none shall look **b**. H6437
Zep 1: 6 And them that are turned **b** from the H5472
3:20 the earth, when I turn **b** your captivity H7725
Mt 24:18 in the field return **b** to take his clothes. *G3694*
28: 2 came and rolled **b** the stone from the *G617*
Mk 13:16 And let him that is in the field not turn **b** *G617*
Lk 2:45 **b** again to Jerusalem, seeking him. *G5290*
8:37 up into the ship, and returned **b** again. *G5290*
9:62 looking **b**, is fit for the kingdom of God. *G3694*
17:15 **b**, and with a loud voice glorified God, *G5290*
31 the field, let him likewise not return **b**. *G3694*
Jn 6:66 went **b**, and walked no more with him. *G3694*
20:14 she turned herself **b**, and saw Jesus *G3694*
Act 5: 2 And kept **b** *part* of the price, his wife *G3557*
3 to keep **b** *part* of the price of the land? *G3557*
7:39 their hearts turned **b** again into Egypt, *G4762*
20:20 *And* how I kept **b** nothing that was *G5288*
Ro 11:10 not see, and bow down their **b** alway. *G3577*
Heb 10:38 if *any man* draw **b**, my soul shall have *G5288*
39 But we are not of them who draw **b** *G5289*
Jas 5: 4 is of you kept **b** by fraud, crieth: and *G650*

BACKBITERS
Ro 1:30 **B**, haters of God, despiteful, proud, *G2637*

BACKBITETH
Ps 15: 3 *He that* **b** not with his tongue, nor H7270

BACKBITING
Prv 25:23 *doth* an angry countenance a **b** tongue. H5643

BACKBITINGS
2Co 12:20 **b**, whisperings, swellings, tumults: *G2636*

BACKBONE
Lev 3: 9 take off hard by the **b**; and the fat that H6096

BACKS
Ex 23:27 thine enemies turn their **b** unto thee. H6203
Jos 7: 8 turneth their **b** before their enemies! H6203
12 *but* turned *their* **b** before their enemies, H6203
Jdg 20:42 Therefore they turned *their* **b** before the
2Ch 29: 6 of the LORD, and turned *their* **b**. H6203
Neh 9:26 thy law behind their **b**, and slew thy H1458
Ezk 8:16 men, with their **b** toward the temple of H268
10:12 And their whole body, and their **b**, and H1354

BACKSIDE
Ex 3: 1 led the flock to the **b** of the desert, and H310
26:12 shall hang over the **b** of the tabernacle. H268
Rev 5: 1 and on the **b**, sealed with seven seals. *G3693*

BACKSLIDER
Prv 14:14 The **b** in heart shall be filled with his H5472

BACKSLIDING
Jer 3: 6 seen *that* which **b** Israel hath done? she H4878
8 the causes whereby **b** Israel committed H4878
11 And the LORD said unto me, The **b** H4878
12 say, Return, thou **b** Israel, saith the H4878
14 Turn, O **b** children, saith the LORD; for H7726
22 Return, ye **b** children, *and* I will heal H7726
8: 5 by a perpetual **b**? they hold fast deceit, H4878
31:22 How long wilt thou go about, O thou **b** H7728
49: 4 thy flowing valley, O **b** daughter? that H7728
Hos 4:16 For Israel slideth back as a **b** heifer: H5637
11: 7 And my people are bent to **b** from me: H4878
14: 4 I will heal their **b**, I will love them freely: H4878

BACKSLIDINGS
Jer 2:19 thee, and thy **b** shall reprove thee: H4878
3:22 I will heal your **b**. Behold, we come unto H4878
5: 6 are many, *and* their **b** are increased. H4878
14: 7 sake: for our **b** are many; we have H4878

BACKWARD
Gen 9:23 and went **b**, and covered the nakedness H322
23 their faces *were* **b**, and they saw not their H322
49:17 horse heels, so that his rider shall fall **b**. H268
1Sa 4:18 fell from off the seat **b** by the side of the H322
2Ki 20:10 but let the shadow return **b** ten degrees. H322
11 ten degrees **b**, by which it had gone H322
Job 23: 8 *there*; and **b**, but I cannot perceive him: H268
Ps 40:14 **b** and put to shame that wish me evil. H268
70: 2 soul: let them be turned **b**, and put to H268
Isa 1: 4 Israel unto anger, they are gone away **b**. H268
28:13 **b**, and be broken, and snared, and taken. H268
38: 8 Ahaz, ten degrees **b**. So the sun returned H322
44:25 **b**, and maketh their knowledge foolish; H268
59:14 And judgment is turned away **b**, and H268
Jer 7:24 evil heart, and went **b**, and not forward. H268
15: 6 thou art gone **b**: therefore will I stretch H268
Lam 1: 8 yea, she sigheth, and turneth **b**. H268
Jn 18: 6 went **b**, and fell to the ground. *G1519+G3694*

BAD
Gen 24:50 we cannot speak unto thee **b** or good. H7451
31:24 speak not to Jacob either good or **b**. H7451
29 speak not to Jacob either good or **b**. H7451
Lev 27:10 it, a good for a **b**, or a bad for a good: H7451
10 for a bad, or a **b** for a good: and if he H7451
12 it be good or **b**: as thou valuest it, *who* H7451
14 it be good or **b**: as the priest shall H7451
33 it be good or **b**, neither shall he change H7451
Nu 13:19 it *be* good or **b**; and what cities *they* H7451
24:13 do *either* good or **b** of mine own mind; H7451
2Sa 13:22 neither good nor **b**: for Absalom hated H7451
14:17 discern good and **b**: therefore the LORD H7451
1Ki 3: 9 between good and **b**: for who is able to H7451
Ezr 4:12 rebellious and the **b** city, and have set up H873
Jer 24: 2 could not be eaten, they were so **b**. H7455
Mt 13:48 good into vessels, but cast the **b** away. *G4550*
22:10 they found, both **b** and good: and the *G4190*
2Co 5:10 he hath done, whether *it be* good or **b**. *G2556*

BADE
Gen 43:17 And the man did as Joseph **b**; and the H559
Ex 16:24 as Moses **b**: and it did not stink, H6680
Nu 14:10 But all the congregation **b** stone them H559
Jos 11: 9 them as the LORD **b** him: he houghed H559
Ru 3: 6 to all that her mother in law **b** her. H6680
1Sa 24:10 in the cave: and *some* **b** *me* kill thee: but H559
2Sa 1:18 (Also he **b** them teach the children of H559
14:19 servant Joab, he **b** me, and he put all H6680
2Ch 10:12 day, as the king **b**, saying, Come again H1696
Est 4:15 Then Esther **b** *them* return Mordecai H559
Mt 16:12 Then understood they how that he **b** *G2036*
Lk 14: 9 And he that **b** thee and him come and *G2564*
10 that when he that **b** thee cometh, he *G2564*
12 Then said he also to him that **b** him, *G2564*
16 made a great supper, and **b** many: *G2564*
Act 11:12 And the Spirit **b** me go with them, *G2036*
18:21 But **b** them farewell, saying, I must by all *G657*
22:24 into the castle, and **b** that he should be *G2036*

BADEST
Gen 27:19 according as thou **b** me: arise, I pray H1696

BADGERS'
Ex 25: 5 And rams' skins dyed red, and **b** skins, H8476
26:14 red, and a covering above *of* **b** skins. H8476
35: 7 And rams' skins dyed red, and **b** skins, H8476
23 of rams, and **b** skins, brought *them*. H8476
36:19 and a covering *of* **b** skins above *that*. H8476
39:34 of **b** skins, and the vail of the covering, H8476
Nu 4: 6 And shall put thereon the covering of **b** H8476
8 with a covering of **b** skins, and shall H8476
10 of **b** skins, and shall put *it* upon a bar. H8476
11 it with a covering of **b** skins, and shall H8476
12 of **b** skins, and shall put *them* on a bar: H8476
14 of **b** skins, and put to the staves of it. H8476
25 the covering of the **b** skins that *is* above H8476
Ezk 16:10 shod thee with **b** skin, and I girded thee H8476

BADNESS
Gen 41:19 never saw in all the land of Egypt for **b**: H7455

BAG
Dt 25:13 Thou shalt not have in thy **b** divers H3599
1Sa 17:40 in a shepherd's **b** which he had, even H3627
49 And David put his hand in his **b**, and H3627
Job 14:17 My transgression *is* sealed up in a **b**, H6872
Prv 7:20 He hath taken a **b** of money with him, H6872
16:11 all the weights of the **b** *are* his work. H3599
Isa 46: 6 They lavish gold out of the **b**, and weigh H3599
Mic 6:11 and with the **b** of deceitful weights? H3599
Hag 1: 6 wages *to put it* into a **b** with holes. H6872
Jn 12: 6 the **b**, and bare what was put therein. *G1101*
13:29 Judas had the **b**, that Jesus had said *G1101*

BAGS
2Ki 5:23 of silver in two **b**, with two changes of H2754
12:10 up, and they put up in **b**, and told the H6696
Lk 12:33 provide yourselves **b** which wax not old, *G905*

BAH See HEPHZI-BAH.

BAHARUMITE
1Ch 11:33 Azmaveth the **B**, Eliahba the H978

BAHURIM
2Sa 3:16 behind her to **B**. Then said Abner unto H980
16: 5 And when king David came to **B**, behold, H980
17:18 a man's house in **B**, which had a well in H980
19:16 which *was* of **B**, hasted and came down H980
1Ki 2: 8 a Benjamite of **B**, which cursed me with H980

BAJITH
Isa 15: 2 He is gone up to **B**, and to Dibon, the H1006

BAKBAKKAR
1Ch 9:15 And **B**, Heresh, and Galal, and H1230

BAKBUK
Ezr 2:51 The children of **B**, the children of H1227
Neh 7:53 The children of **B**, the children of H1227

BAKBUKIAH
Neh 11:17 in prayer: and **B** the second among his H1229
12: 9 Also **B** and Unni, their brethren, *were* H1229
Neh 12:25 Mattaniah, and **B**, Obadiah, H1229

BAKE
Gen 19: 3 **b** unleavened bread, and they did eat. H644
Ex 16:23 unto the LORD: **b** *that* which ye will H644
23 *that* which ye will **b** *to day*, and seethe H644
Lev 24: 5 And thou shalt take fine flour, and **b** H644
26:26 ten women shall **b** your bread in one H644
1Sa 28:24 *it*, and did **b** unleavened bread thereof: H644
2Sa 13: 8 cakes in his sight, and did **b** the cakes. H1310
Ezk 4:12 and thou shalt **b** it with dung that H5746
46:20 where they shall **b** the meat offering; H644

BAKED
Ex 12:39 And they **b** unleavened cakes of the H644
Nu 11: 8 *it* in a mortar, and **b** *it* in pans, and H1310
1Ch 23:29 for *that which is* **b** *in* the pan, and for
Isa 44:19 yea, also I have **b** bread upon the coals H644

BAKEMEATS
Gen 40:17 all manner of **b** for H3978+H4639+H644

BAKEN
Lev 2: 4 of a meat offering **b** in the oven, *it shall* H644
5 And if thy oblation *be* a meat offering **b**
7 And if thy oblation *be* a meat offering **b**
6:17 It shall not be **b** with leaven. I have given H644
21 oil; *and when it is* **b**, thou shalt bring it H7246
21 bring it in: *and* the **b** pieces of the meat H8601
7: 9 And all the meat offering that is **b** in the H644
23:17 flour; they shall be **b** with leaven; *they* H644
1Ki 19: 6 *there was* a cake **b** on the coals, and a

BAKER
Gen 40: 1 of Egypt and *his* **b** had offended their H644
5 the butler and the **b** of the king of Egypt, H644
16 When the chief **b** saw that the H644
20 and of the chief **b** among his servants. H644
22 But he hanged the chief **b**: as Joseph had H644
41:10 guard's house, *both* me and the chief **b**: H644
Hos 7: 4 oven heated by the **b**, *who* ceaseth from H644
6 lie in wait: their **b** sleepeth all the night; H644

BAKERS
Gen 40: 2 the butlers, and against the chief of the **b**. H644
1Sa 8:13 and *to be* cooks, and *to be* **b**. H644

BAKERS'
Jer 37:21 of bread out of the **b** street, until all the H644

BAKETH
Isa 44:15 yea, he kindleth *it*, and **b** bread; yea, he H644

BALAAM
Nu 22: 5 He sent messengers therefore unto **B** H1109
7 they came unto **B**, and spake unto him H1109
8 and the princes of Moab abode with **B**. H1109
9 And God came unto **B**, and said, What H1109
10 And **B** said unto God, Balak the son of H1109
12 And God said unto **B**, Thou shalt not go H1109
13 And **B** rose up in the morning, and said H1109
14 and said, **B** refuseth to come with us. H1109
16 And they came to **B**, and said to him, H1109
18 And **B** answered and said unto the H1109
20 And God came unto **B** at night, and H1109
21 And **B** rose up in the morning, and H1109
23 into the field: and **B** smote the ass, to H1109
27 fell down under **B**: and Balaam's anger H1109
28 and she said unto **B**, What have I done H1109
29 And **B** said unto the ass, Because thou H1109
30 And the ass said unto **B**, *Am* not I thine H1109
31 Then the LORD opened the eyes of **B**, H1109
34 And **B** said unto the angel of the LORD, H1109
35 And the angel of the LORD said unto **B**, H1109
35 So **B** went with the princes of Balak. H1109
36 And when Balak heard that **B** was H1109
37 And Balak said unto **B**, Did I not H1109
38 And **B** said unto Balak, Lo, I am come H1109
39 And **B** went with Balak, and they came H1109
40 sheep, and sent to **B**, and to the princes H1109
41 that Balak took **B**, and brought him up H1109
23: 1 And **B** said unto Balak, Build me here H1109
2 And Balak did as **B** had spoken; and H1109
2 and Balak and **B** offered on *every* altar H1109
3 And **B** said unto Balak, Stand by thy H1109
4 And God met **B**: and he said unto him, I H1109
11 And Balak said unto **B**, What hast thou H1109
16 And the LORD met **B**, and put a word in H1109
25 And Balak said unto **B**, Neither curse H1109

Nu 23:26 But **B** answered and said unto Balak, H1109
27 And Balak said unto **B**, Come, I pray H1109
28 And Balak brought **B** unto the top of H1109
29 And **B** said unto Balak, Build me here H1109
30 And Balak did as **B** had said, and H1109
24: 1 And when **B** saw that it pleased the H1109
2 And **B** lifted up his eyes, and he saw H1109
3 And he took up his parable, and said, **B** H1109
10 was kindled against **B**, and he smote his H1109
10 Balak said unto **B**, I called thee to curse H1109
12 And **B** said unto Balak, Spake I not H1109
15 And he took up his parable, and said, **B** H1109
25 And **B** rose up, and went and returned H1109
31: 8 kings of Midian: **B** also the son of Beor H1109
16 the counsel of **B**, to commit trespass H1109
Dt 23: 4 hired against thee **B** the son of Beor of H1109
5 not hearken unto **B**; but the LORD thy H1109
Jos 13:22 **B** also the son of Beor, the soothsayer, H1109
24: 9 called **B** the son of Beor to curse you: H1109
10 But I would not hearken unto **B**; H1109
Neh 13: 2 water, but hired **B** against them, that H1109
Mic 6: 5 and what **B** the son of Beor answered H1109
2Pt 2:15 the way of **B** *the son* of Bosor, who *G903*
Jude 11 after the error of **B** for reward, and *G903*
Rev 2:14 the doctrine of **B**, who taught Balac to *G903*

BALAAM'S
Nu 22:25 wall, and crushed **B** foot against the H1109
27 Balaam: and **B** anger was kindled, H1109
23: 5 And the LORD put a word in **B** mouth, H1109

BALAC
Rev 2:14 who taught **B** to cast a stumblingblock *G904*

BALADAN
2Ki 20:12 the son of **B**, king of Babylon, sent H1081
Isa 39: 1 the son of **B**, king of Babylon, sent H1081

BALAH
Jos 19: 3 And Hazar-shual, and **B**, and Azem, H1088

BALAK
Nu 22: 2 And **B** the son of Zippor saw all that H1111
4 of the field. And **B** the son of Zippor H1111
7 and spake unto him the words of **B**. H1111
10 And Balaam said unto God, **B** the son H1111
13 the princes of **B**, Get you into your land: H1111
14 and they went unto **B**, and said, Balaam H1111
15 And **B** sent yet again princes, more, H1111
16 to him, Thus saith **B** the son of Zippor, H1111
18 the servants of **B**, If Balak would give H1111
18 of Balak, If **B** would give me his house H1111
35 So Balaam went with the princes of **B**. H1111
36 And when **B** heard that Balaam was H1111
37 And **B** said unto Balaam, Did I not H1111
38 And Balaam said unto **B**, Lo, I am come H1111
39 And Balaam went with **B**, and they H1111
40 And **B** offered oxen and sheep, and H1111
41 the morrow, that **B** took Balaam, and H1111
23: 1 And Balaam said unto **B**, Build me here H1111
2 And **B** did as Balaam had spoken; and H1111
2 had spoken; and **B** and Balaam offered H1111
3 And Balaam said unto **B**, Stand by thy H1111
5 unto **B**, and thus thou shalt speak. H1111
7 And he took up his parable, and said, **B** H1111
11 And **B** said unto Balaam, What hast H1111
13 And **B** said unto him, Come, I pray H1111
15 And he said unto **B**, Stand here by thy H1111
16 said, Go again unto **B**, and say thus. H1111
17 with him. And **B** said unto him, What H1111
18 and said, Rise up, **B**, and hear; hearken H1111
25 And **B** said unto Balaam, Neither curse H1111
26 But Balaam answered and said unto **B**, H1111
27 And **B** said unto Balaam, Come, I pray H1111
28 And **B** brought Balaam unto the top of H1111
29 And Balaam said unto **B**, Build me here H1111
30 And **B** did as Balaam had said, and H1111
24:10 together: and **B** said unto Balaam, I H1111
12 And Balaam said unto **B**, Spake I not H1111
13 If **B** would give me his house full of H1111
25 to his place: and **B** also went his way. H1111
Jos 24: 9 Then **B** the son of Zippor, king of H1111
Jdg 11:25 thing better than **B** the son of Zippor, H1111
Mic 6: 5 O my people, remember now what **B** H1111

BALAK'S
Nu 24:10 And **B** anger was kindled against H1111

BALANCE
Job 31: 6 Let me be weighed in an even **b**, that H3976
Ps 62: 9 to be laid in the **b**, they *are* altogether H3976
Prv 11: 1 A false **b** *is* abomination to the LORD: H3976
16:11 A just weight and **b** *are* the LORD'S: all H3976
20:23 the LORD; and a false **b** *is* not good. H3976
Isa 40:12 in scales, and the hills in a **b**? H3976
15 small dust of the **b**: behold, he taketh up H3976
46: 6 and weigh silver in the **b**, *and* hire a H7070

BALANCES
Lev 19:36 Just **b**, just weights, a just ephah, and a H3976
Job 6: 2 and my calamity laid in the **b** together! H3976
Jer 32:10 and weighed *him* the money in the **b**. H3976
Ezk 5: 1 thee **b** to weigh, and divide the *hair*. H3976
45:10 Ye shall have just **b**, and a just ephah, H3976
Dan 5:27 TEKEL; Thou art weighed in the **b**, and H3977
Hos 12: 7 *He is* a merchant, the **b** of deceit *are* in H3976
Am 8: 5 great, and falsifying the **b** by deceit? H3976
Mic 6:11 **b**, and with the bag of deceitful weights? H3976
Rev 6: 5 sat on him had a pair of **b** in his hand. *G2218*

BALANCINGS
Job 37:16 Dost thou know the **b** of the clouds, the H4657

BALD
Lev 11:22 after his kind, and the **b** locust after his H5556
13:40 off his head, he *is* **b**; *yet is* he clean. H7142
41 face, he *is* forehead **b**: *yet is* he clean. H1371
42 And if there be in the **b** head, or bald H7146
42 And if there be in the bald head, or **b** H1372
42 up in his **b** head, or his bald forehead. H7146
42 up in his bald head, or his **b** forehead. H1372
43 reddish in his **b** head, or in his bald H7146
43 bald head, or in his **b** forehead, as the H1372
2Ki 2:23 up, thou **b** head; go up, thou bald head. H7142
23 up, thou bald head; go up, thou **b** head. H7142
Jer 16: 6 nor make themselves **b** for them: H7139
48:37 For every head *shall be* **b**, and every H7144
Ezk 27:31 themselves utterly **b** for thee, and gird H7139
29:18 head *was* made **b**, and every shoulder H7139
Mic 1:16 Make thee **b**, and poll thee for thy H7139

BALD-HEAD See BALD and HEAD.

BALD-LOCUST See BALD and LOCUST.

BALDNESS
Lev 21: 5 They shall not make **b** upon their head, H7144
Dt 14: 1 any **b** between your eyes for the dead. H7144
Isa 3:24 of well set hair **b**; and instead of a H7144
15: 2 *shall be* **b**, *and* every beard cut off. H7144
22:12 and to **b**, and to girding with sackcloth: H7144
Jer 47: 5 **B** is come upon Gaza; Ashkelon is cut H7144
Ezk 7:18 all faces, and **b** upon all their heads. H7144
Am 8:10 all loins, and **b** upon every head; and H7144
Mic 1:16 enlarge thy **b** as the eagle; for they H7144

BALL
Isa 22:18 toss thee *like* a **b** into a large country: H1754

BALM
Gen 37:25 spicery and **b** and myrrh, going to H6875
43:11 a present, a little **b**, and a little honey, H6875
Jer 8:22 *Is there* no **b** in Gilead; *is there* no H6875
46:11 Go up into Gilead, and take **b**, O virgin, H6875
51: 8 howl for her; take **b** for her pain, if so H6875
Ezk 27:17 and Pannag, and honey, and oil, and **b**. H6875

BAMAH
Ezk 20:29 name thereof is called **B** unto this day. H1117

BAMOTH
Nu 21:19 to Nahaliel: and from Nahaliel to **B**: H1120
20 And from **B** *in* the valley, that *is* in the H1120

BAMOTH-BAAL
Jos 13:17 Dibon, and **B**, and Beth-baal-meon, H1120

BAND
Ex 39:23 habergeon, *with* a **b** round about the H8193
1Sa 10:26 there went with him a **b** of men, whose H2428
1Ki 11:24 captain over a **b**, when David slew them H1416
2Ki 13:21 they spied a **b** *of men;* and they cast H1416
1Ch 12:18 them, and made them captains of the **b**. H1416
21 And they helped David against the **b** *of* H1416
2Ch 22: 1 in his stead: for the **b** of men that came H1416
Ezr 8:22 require of the king a **b** of soldiers and H2428
Job 39:10 Canst thou bind the unicorn with his **b** H5688
Dan 4:15 earth, even with a **b** of iron and brass, in H613
23 earth, even with a **b** of iron and brass, in H613
Mt 27:27 unto him the whole **b** *of soldiers*. *G4686*
Mk 15:16 and they call together the whole **b**. *G4686*
Jn 18: 3 Judas then, having received a **b** *of men* *G4686*
12 Then the **b** and the captain and officers *G4686*
Act 10: 1 of the **b** called the Italian *band*, *G4686*
1 of the band called the Italian **b**, *G4686*
21:31 **b**, that all Jerusalem was in an uproar. *G4686*
27: 1 Julius, a centurion of Augustus' **b**. *G4686*

BANDED
Act 23:12 of the Jews **b** together, and *H4160+H4963*

BANDS
Gen 32: 7 and herds, and the camels, into two **b**; H4264
10 Jordan; and now I am become two **b**. H4264
Lev 26:13 I have broken the **b** of your yoke, and H4133
Jdg 15:14 fire, and his **b** loosed from off his hands. H612
2Sa 4: 2 *were* captains of **b**: the name of the one H1416
2Ki 6:23 master. So the **b** of Syria came no more H1416
13:20 buried him. And the **b** of the Moabites H1416
23:33 And Pharaoh-nechoh put him in **b** at H631
24: 2 And the LORD sent against him **b** of H1416
2 the Chaldees, and **b** of the Syrians, and H1416
2 the Syrians, and **b** of the Moabites, and H1416
2 the Moabites, and **b** of the children of H1416
1Ch 7: 4 their fathers, *were* **b** of soldiers for war, H1416
12:23 And these *are* the numbers of the **b** H7218
2Ch 26:11 went out to war by **b**, according to the H1416
Job 1:17 made out three **b**, and fell upon the H7218
38:31 of Pleiades, or loose the **b** of Orion? H4189
39: 5 who hath loosed the **b** of the wild ass? H4147
Ps 2: 3 Let us break their **b** asunder, and cast H4147
73: 4 For *there are* no **b** in their death: but H2784
107:14 of death, and brake their **b** in sunder. H4147
119:61 The **b** of the wicked have robbed me: H2256
Prv 30:27 king, yet go they forth all of them by **b**; H2686
Ecc 7:26 *and* her hands *as* **b**: whoso pleaseth God H612
Isa 28:22 mockers, lest your **b** be made strong: H4147
52: 2 loose thyself from the **b** of thy neck, O H4147
58: 6 to loose the **b** of wickedness, to undo H2784
Jer 2:20 *and* burst thy **b**; and thou saidst, I will H4147
Ezk 3:25 they shall put **b** upon thee, and shall H5688
4: 8 And, behold, I will lay **b** upon thee, and H5688
12:14 him, and all his **b**; and I will draw out the H102
17:21 And all his fugitives with all his **b** shall H102
34:27 I have broken the **b** of their yoke, and H4133
38: 6 Gomer, and all his **b**; the house of H102
6 and all his **b**: *and* many people with thee. H102
9 and all thy **b**, and many people with thee. H102
22 him, and upon his **b**, and upon the many H102
39: 4 thou, and all thy **b**, and the people that H102
Hos 11: 4 of a man, with **b** of love: and I was to H5688
Zec 11: 7 the other I called **B**; and I fed the flock. H2256
14 other staff, *even* **B**, that I might break H2256
Lk 8:29 and he brake the **b**, and was driven of *G1199*
Act 16:26 opened, and every one's **b** were loosed. *G1199*
22:30 him from *his* **b**, and commanded the *G1199*
27:40 loosed the rudder **b**, and hoised up the *G2202*
Col 2:19 the body by joints and **b** having *G4886*

BANI
2Sa 23:36 Igal the son of Nathan of Zobah, **B** the H1137
1Ch 6:46 The son of Amzi, the son of **B**, the son of H1137
9: 4 of Imri, the son of **B**, of the children of H1137
Ezr 2:10 The children of **B**, six hundred forty and H1137
10:29 And of the sons of **B**; Meshullam, H1137
34 Of the sons of **B**; Maadai, Amram, and H1137
38 And **B**, and Binnui, Shimei, H1137
Neh 3:17 Rehum the son of **B**. Next unto him H1137
8: 7 Also Jeshua, and **B**, and Sherebiah, H1137
9: 4 Jeshua, and **B**, Kadmiel, Shebaniah, H1137
4 Bunni, Sherebiah, **B**, *and* Chenani, and H1137
5 Jeshua, and Kadmiel, **B**, Hashabniah, H1137
10:13 Hodijah, **B**, Beninu. H1137
14 Parosh, Pahath-moab, Elam, Zatthu, **B**, H1137
11:22 Uzzi the son of **B**, the son of Hashabiah, H1137

BANISHED
2Sa 14:13 king doth not fetch home again his **b**. H5080
14 that his **b** be not expelled from him. H5080

BANISHMENT
Ezr 7:26 unto death, or to **b**, or to confiscation of H8332
Lam 2:14 for thee false burdens and causes of **b**. H4065

BANK
Gen 41:17 behold, I stood upon the **b** of the river: H8193

Dt 4:48 From Aroer, which *is* by the **b** of the H8193
Jos 12: 2 which *is* upon the **b** of the river Arnon, H8193
13: 9 From Aroer, that *is* upon the **b** of the H8193
16 that *is* on the **b** of the river Arnon, and H8193
2Sa 20:15 and they cast up a **b** against the city, H5550
2Ki 2:13 back, and stood by the **b** of Jordan; H8193
19:32 it with shield, nor cast a **b** against it. H5550
Isa 37:33 it with shields, nor cast a **b** against it. H5550
Ezk 47: 7 behold, at the **b** of the river *were* very H8193
12 And by the river upon the **b** thereof, on H8193
Dan 12: 5 on this side of the **b** of the river, and H8193
5 other on that side of the **b** of the river. H8193
Lk 19:23 money into the b, that at my coming I *G5132*

BANKS
Jos 3:15 all his **b** all the time of harvest,) H1415
4:18 flowed over all his **b**, as *they did* before. H1415
1Ch 12:15 had overflown all his **b**; and they put to H1428
Isa 8: 7 all his channels, and go over all his **b**: H1415
Dan 8:16 And I heard a man's voice between *the* **b**

BANNER
Ps 60: 4 Thou hast given a **b** to them that fear H5251
Song 2: 4 house, and his **b** over me *was* love. H1714
Isa 13: 2 Lift ye up a **b** upon the high mountain, H5251

BANNERS
Ps 20: 5 *our* **b**: the LORD fulfil all thy petitions. H1713
Song 6: 4 Jerusalem, terrible as *an army* with **b**. H1713
10 the sun, *and* terrible as *an army* with **b**? H1713

BANQUET
Est 5: 4 the **b** that I have prepared for him. H4960
5 to the **b** that Esther had prepared. H4960
6 And the king said unto Esther at the **b** H4960
8 come to the **b** that I shall prepare H4960
12 with the king unto the **b** that she had H4960
14 with the king unto the **b**. And the thing H4960
6:14 unto the **b** that Esther had prepared. H4960
7: 1 So the king and Haman came to **b** with H8354
2 second day at the **b** of wine, What *is* H4960
7 And the king arising from the **b** of wine H4960
8 the place of the **b** of wine; and Haman H4960
Job 41: 6 Shall the companions make a **b** of him? H3739
Dan 5:10 came into the **b** house: *and* the queen H4961
Am 6: 7 go captive, and the **b** of them that H4797

BANQUETING
Song 2: 4 He brought me to the **b** house, and his H3196

BANQUETINGS
1Pt 4: 3 **b**, and abominable idolatries: *G4224*

BAPTISM
Mt 3: 7 come to his **b**, he said unto them, O *G908*
20:22 baptized with the b that I am baptized *G908*
23 baptized with the b that I am baptized *G908*
21:25 The b of John, whence was it? from *G908*
Mk 1: 4 **b** of repentance for the remission of sins. *G908*
10:38 with the b that I am baptized with? *G908*
39 of; and with the b that I am baptized *G908*
11:30 The b of John, was *it* from heaven, or of *G908*
Lk 3: 3 **b** of repentance for the remission of sins; *G908*
7:29 God, being baptized with the **b** of John. *G908*
12:50 But I have a b to be baptized with; and *G908*
20: 4 The b of John, was it from heaven, or of *G908*
Act 1:22 Beginning from the **b** of John, unto that *G908*
10:37 Galilee, after the **b** which John preached; *G908*
13:24 his coming the **b** of repentance to all the *G908*
18:25 of the Lord, knowing only the **b** of John. *G908*
19: 3 baptized? And they said, Unto John's **b**. *G908*
4 verily baptized with the **b** of repentance, *G908*
Ro 6: 4 Therefore we are buried with him by **b** *G908*
Eph 4: 5 One Lord, one faith, one **b**, *G908*
Col 2:12 Buried with him in **b**, wherein also ye are *G908*
1Pt 3:21 The like figure whereunto *even* **b** doth *G908*

BAPTISMS
Heb 6: 2 Of the doctrine of **b**, and of laying on of *G909*

BAPTIST
Mt 3: 1 In those days came John the **B**, preaching *G910*
11:11 than John the B: notwithstanding he *G910*
12 And from the days of John the B until *G910*
14: 2 This is John the **B**; he is risen from the *G910*
16:14 *that thou art* John the **B**: some, Elias; and *G910*
17:13 that he spake unto them of John the **B**. *G910*
Mk 6:14 said, That John the **B** was risen from the *G907*
24 And she said, The head of John the **B**. *G910*
Mk 6:25 by in a charger the head of John the **B**. *G910*
8:28 And they answered, John the **B**: but some *G910*
Lk 7:20 they said, John **B** hath sent us unto thee, *G910*
28 than John the B: but he that is least in *G910*
33 For John the B came neither eating *G910*
9:19 They answering said, John the **B**; but *G910*

BAPTIST'S
Mt 14: 8 Give me here John **B** head in a charger. *G910*

BAPTIZE
Mt 3:11 I indeed **b** you with water unto *G907*
11 **b** you with the Holy Ghost, and *with* fire: *G907*
Mk 1: 4 John did **b** in the wilderness, and preach *G907*
8 but he shall **b** you with the Holy Ghost. *G907*
Lk 3:16 *them* all, I indeed **b** you with water; but *G907*
16 **b** you with the Holy Ghost and with fire: *G907*
Jn 1:26 John answered them, saying, I **b** with *G907*
33 but he that sent me to **b** with water, the *G907*
1Co 1:17 For Christ sent me not to **b**, but to preach *G907*

BAPTIZED
Mt 3: 6 And were **b** of him in Jordan, confessing *G907*
13 to Jordan unto John, to be **b** of him. *G907*
14 to be **b** of thee, and comest thou to me? *G907*
16 And Jesus, when he was **b**, went up *G907*
20:22 drink of, and to be b with the baptism *G907*
22 **b** with? They say unto him, We are able. *G907*
23 of my cup, and be b with the baptism *G907*
23 baptism that I am b with: but to sit on *G907*
Mk 1: 5 and were all **b** of him in the river of *G907*
8 I indeed have **b** you with water: but he *G907*
9 of Galilee, and was **b** of John in Jordan. *G907*
10:38 I drink of? and be b with the baptism *G907*
38 with the baptism that I am b with? *G907*
39 that I am b withal shall ye be baptized: *G907*
39 that I am baptized withal shall ye be b: *G907*
16:16 He that believeth and is b shall be saved; *G907*
Lk 3: 7 came forth to be **b** of him, O generation *G907*
12 Then came also publicans to be **b**, and *G907*
21 Now when all the people were **b**, it came *G907*
21 **b**, and praying, the heaven was opened, *G907*
7:29 God, being **b** with the baptism of John. *G907*
30 against themselves, being not **b** of him. *G907*
12:50 But I have a baptism to be b with; and *G907*
Jn 3:22 and there he tarried with them, and **b**. *G907*
23 water there: and they came, and were **b**. *G907*
4: 1 made and **b** more disciples than John, *G907*
2 (Though Jesus himself **b** not, but his *G907*
10:40 where John at first **b**; and there he abode. *G907*
Act 1: 5 For John truly b with water; but ye shall *G907*
5 but ye shall be b with the Holy Ghost *G907*
2:38 Repent, and be **b** every one of you in the *G907*
41 his word were **b**: and the same day there *G907*
8:12 they were **b**, both men and women. *G907*
13 and when he was **b**, he continued with *G907*
16 were **b** in the name of the Lord Jesus.) *G907*
36 *is* water; what doth hinder me to be **b**? *G907*
38 Philip and the eunuch; and he **b** him. *G907*
9:18 sight forthwith, and arose, and was **b**. *G907*
10:47 should not be **b**, which have received *G907*
48 And he commanded them to be **b** in the *G907*
11:16 he said, John indeed b with water; but ye *G907*
16 but ye shall be b with the Holy Ghost. *G907*
16:15 And when she was **b**, and her household, *G907*
33 and was **b**, he and all his, straightway. *G907*
18: 8 hearing believed, and were **b**. *G907*
19: 3 ye **b**? And they said, Unto John's baptism. *G907*
4 Then said Paul, John verily **b** with the *G907*
5 When they heard *this*, they were **b** in the *G907*
22:16 thou? arise, and be **b**, and wash away thy *G907*
Ro 6: 3 so many of us as were **b** into Jesus Christ *G907*
3 into Jesus Christ were **b** into his death? *G907*
1Co 1:13 you? or were ye **b** in the name of Paul? *G907*
14 I thank God that I **b** none of you, but *G907*
15 Lest any should say that I had **b** in mine *G907*
16 And I **b** also the household of Stephanas: *G907*
16 I know not whether I **b** any other. *G907*
10: 2 And were all **b** unto Moses in the cloud *G907*
12:13 For by one Spirit are we all **b** into one *G907*
15:29 Else what shall they do which are **b** for *G907*
29 at all? why are they then **b** for the dead? *G907*
Gal 3:27 For as many of you as have been **b** into *G907*

BAPTIZEST
Jn 1:25 unto him, Why **b** thou then, if thou be *G907*

BAPTIZETH
Jn 1:33 same is he which **b** with the Holy Ghost. *G907*
Jn 3:26 the same **b**, and all *men* come to him. *G907*

BAPTIZING
Mt 28:19 Go ye therefore, and teach all nations, b *G907*
Jn 1:28 beyond Jordan, where John was **b**. *G907*
31 Israel, therefore am I come **b** with water. *G907*
3:23 And John also was **b** in Aenon near to *G907*

BAR
Ex 26:28 And the middle **b** in the midst of the H1280
36:33 And he made the middle **b** to shoot H1280
Nu 4:10 skins, and shall put *it* upon a **b**. H4132
12 skins, and shall put *them* on a **b**: H4132
Jdg 16: 3 away with them, **b** and all, and put H1280
Neh 7: 3 shut the doors, and **b** *them*: and appoint H270
Am 1: 5 I will break also the **b** of Damascus, H1280

BARABBAS
Mt 27:16 had then a notable prisoner, called **B**. *G912*
17 you? **B**, or Jesus which is called Christ? *G912*
20 they should ask **B**, and destroy Jesus. *G912*
21 ye that I release unto you? They said, **B**. *G912*
26 Then released he **B** unto them: and when *G912*
Mk 15: 7 And there was *one* named **B**, *which lay* *G912*
11 he should rather release **B** unto them. *G912*
15 the people, released **B** unto them, and *G912*
Lk 23:18 with this *man*, and release unto us **B**: *G912*
Jn 18:40 man, but **B**. Now Barabbas was a robber. *G912*
40 but Barabbas. Now **B** was a robber. *G912*

BARACHEL
Job 32: 2 of Elihu the son of **B** the Buzite, of the H1292
6 And Elihu the son of **B** the Buzite H1292

BARACHIAS
Mt 23:35 of Zacharias son of B, whom ye slew *G914*

BARAH See BETH-BARAH.

BARAK
Jdg 4: 6 And she sent and called **B** the son of H1301
8 And **B** said unto her, If thou wilt go H1301
9 arose, and went with **B** to Kedesh. H1301
10 And **B** called Zebulun and Naphtali to H1301
12 And they shewed Sisera that **B** the son H1301
14 And Deborah said unto **B**, Up; for this H1301
14 out before thee? So **B** went down from H1301
15 of the sword before **B**; so that Sisera H1301
16 But **B** pursued after the chariots, and H1301
22 And, behold, as **B** pursued Sisera, Jael H1301
5: 1 Then sang Deborah and **B** the son of H1301
12 a song: arise, **B**, and lead thy captivity H1301
15 Issachar, and also **B**: he was sent on H1301
Heb 11:32 of Gedeon, and *of* **B**, and *of* Samson, and *G913*

BARBARIAN
1Co 14:11 that speaketh a **b**, and he that speaketh *G915*
11 he that speaketh *shall be* a **b** unto me. *G915*
Col 3:11 uncircumcision, **B**, Scythian, bond *nor* *G915*

BARBARIANS
Act 28: 4 And when the **b** saw the *venomous* beast *G915*
Ro 1:14 **B**; both to the wise, and to the unwise. *G915*

BARBAROUS
Act 28: 2 And the **b** people shewed us no little *G915*

BARBED
Job 41: 7 Canst thou fill his skin with **b** irons? or H7905

BARBER'S
Ezk 5: 1 knife, take thee a **b** razor, and cause *it* H1532

BARE
Gen 4: 1 conceived, and **b** Cain, and said, I have H3205
2 And she again **b** his brother Abel. And H3205
17 she conceived, and **b** Enoch: and he H3205
20 And Adah **b** Jabal: he was the father of H3205
22 And Zillah, she also **b** Tubal-cain, an H3205
25 again; and she **b** a son, and called his H3205
6: 4 of men, and they **b** *children* to them, H3205
7:17 increased, and **b** up the ark, and it was H5375
16: 1 Now Sarai Abram's wife **b** him no H3205
15 And Hagar **b** Abram a son: and Abram H3205
15 son's name, which Hagar **b**, Ishmael. H3205
16 old, when Hagar **b** Ishmael to Abram. H3205
19:37 And the firstborn **b** a son, and called H3205
38 And the younger, she also **b** a son, and H3205
20:17 his maidservants; and they **b** *children*. H3205

Gen 21: 2 For Sarah conceived, and **b** Abraham a H3205
3 unto him, whom Sarah **b** to him, Isaac. H3205
22:24 *was* Reumah, she **b** also Tebah, and H3205
24:24 son of Milcah, which she **b** unto Nahor. H3205
36 And Sarah my master's wife **b** a son to H3205
47 son, whom Milcah **b** unto him: and I H3205
25: 2 And she **b** him Zimran, and Jokshan, H3205
12 Sarah's handmaid, **b** unto Abraham: H3205
26 threescore years old when she **b** them. H3205
29:32 And Leah conceived, and **b** a son, and H3205
33 And she conceived again, and **b** a son; H3205
34 And she conceived again, and **b** a son; H3205
35 And she conceived again, and **b** a son: H3205
30: 1 And when Rachel saw that she **b** Jacob H3205
5 And Bilhah conceived, and **b** Jacob a H3205
7 again, and **b** Jacob a second son. H3205
10 And Zilpah Leah's maid **b** Jacob a son. H3205
12 And Zilpah Leah's maid **b** Jacob a H3205
17 conceived, and **b** Jacob the fifth son. H3205
19 And Leah conceived again, and **b** H3205
21 And afterwards she **b** a daughter, and H3205
23 And she conceived, and **b** a son; and H3205
31: 8 then all the cattle **b** speckled: and if he H3205
8 hire; then **b** all the cattle ringstraked. H3205
39 not unto thee; I **b** the loss of it; of my H2398
34: 1 of Leah, which she **b** unto Jacob, went H3205
36: 4 And Adah **b** to Esau Eliphaz; and H3205
4 Esau Eliphaz; and Bashemath **b** Reuel; H3205
5 And Aholibamah **b** Jeush, and Jaalam, H3205
12 son; and she **b** to Eliphaz Amalek: H3205
14 wife: and she **b** to Esau Jeush, and H3205
38: 3 And she conceived, and **b** a son; and he H3205
4 And she conceived again, and **b** a son; H3205
5 And she yet again conceived, and **b** a H3205
5 and he was at Chezib, when she **b** him. H3205
41:50 of Potipherah priest of On **b** unto him. H3205
44:27 Ye know that my wife **b** me two *sons:* H3205
46:15 These *be* the sons of Leah, which she **b** H3205
18 she **b** unto Jacob, *even* sixteen souls. H3205
20 of Potipherah priest of On **b** unto him. H3205
25 daughter, and she **b** these unto Jacob: H3205
Ex 2: 2 And the woman conceived, and **b** a H3205
22 And she **b** *him* a son, and he called his H3205
6:20 sister to wife; and she **b** him Aaron and H3205
23 to wife; and she **b** him Nadab, and H3205
25 to wife; and she **b** him Phinehas: these H3205
19: 4 and *how* I **b** you on eagles' wings, H5375
Lev 13:45 rent, and his head **b**, and he shall put a H6544
55 *whether* it *be* **b** within or without. H7146
Nu 13:23 grapes, and they **b** it between two upon H5375
26:59 whom *her mother* **b** to Levi in Egypt: H3205
59 Levi in Egypt: and she **b** unto Amram H3205
Dt 1:31 the LORD thy God **b** thee, as a man H5375
31: 9 of Levi, which **b** the ark of the covenant H5375
25 the Levites, which **b** the ark of the H5375
Jos 3:15 And as they that **b** the ark were come H5375
15 feet of the priests that **b** the ark were H5375
17 And the priests that **b** the ark of the H5375
4: 9 of the priests which **b** the ark of the H5375
10 For the priests which **b** the ark stood in H5375
18 when the priests that **b** the ark of the H5375
8:33 the Levites, which **b** the ark of the H5375
Jdg 3:18 away the people that **b** the present. H5375
8:31 Shechem, she also **b** him a son, whose H3205
11: 2 And Gilead's wife **b** him sons; and his H3205
13: 2 and his wife *was* barren, and **b** not. H3205
24 And the woman **b** a son, and called his H3205
Ru 4:12 whom Tamar **b** unto Judah, of the seed H3205
13 gave her conception, and she **b** a son. H3205
1Sa 1:20 that she **b** a son, and called his H3205
2:21 conceived, and **b** three sons and two H3205
14: 1 young man that **b** his armour, Come, H5375
6 young man that **b** his armour, Come, H5375
17:41 man that **b** the shield *went* before him. H5375
2Sa 6:13 And it was *so*, that when they that **b** H5375
11:27 his wife, and **b** him a son. But the thing H3205
12:15 wife **b** unto David, and it was very sick. H3205
24 with her: and she **b** a son, and he called H3205
18:15 And ten young men that **b** Joab's H5375
21: 8 Aiah, whom she **b** unto Saul, Armoni H3205
1Ki 1: 6 and *his mother* **b** him after Absalom. H3205
5:15 and ten thousand that **b** burdens, and H5375
9:23 and fifty, which **b** rule over the people H7287
10: 2 with camels that **b** spices, and very H5375
11:20 And the sister of Tahpenes **b** him H3205
14:28 that the guard **b** them, and brought H5375
2Ki 4:17 And the woman conceived, and **b** a son H3205
5:23 servants; and they **b** *them* before him. H5375
1Ch 1:32 concubine: she **b** Zimran, and Jokshan, H3205
1Ch 2: 4 And Tamar his daughter in law **b** him H3205
17 And Abigail **b** Amasa: and the father of H3205
19 unto him Ephrath, which **b** him Hur. H3205
21 years old; and she **b** him Segub. H3205
24 wife **b** him Ashur the father of Tekoa. H3205
29 and she **b** him Ahban, and Molid. H3205
35 servant to wife; and she **b** him Attai. H3205
46 And Ephah, Caleb's concubine, **b** H3205
48 Maachah, Caleb's concubine, **b** Sheber, H3205
49 She **b** also Shaaph the father of H3205
4: 6 And Naarah **b** him Ahuzam, and H3205
9 saying, Because I **b** him with sorrow. H3205
17 and Jalon: and she **b** Miriam, and H2029
18 And his wife Jehudijah **b** Jered the H3205
7:14 Ashriel, whom she **b**: (*but* his H3205
14 **b** Machir the father of Gilead: H3205
16 And Maachah the wife of Machir **b** a H3205
18 And his sister Hammoleketh **b** Ishod, H3205
23 conceived, and **b** a son, and he called H3205
12:24 The children of Judah that **b** shield and H5375
15:15 And the children of the Levites **b** the H5375
26 helped the Levites that **b** the ark of the H5375
27 all the Levites that **b** the ark, and the H5375
2Ch 8:10 and fifty, that **b** rule over the people. H7287
9: 1 and camels that **b** spices, and gold in H5375
11:19 Which **b** him children; Jeush, and H3205
20 of Absalom; which **b** him Abijah, and H3205
14: 8 And Asa had an army *of men* that **b** H5375
8 of Benjamin, that **b** shields and drew H5375
Neh 4:17 and they that **b** burdens, with those H5375
5:15 their servants **b** rule over the people: H7980
Prv 17:25 and bitterness to her that **b** him. H3205
23:25 glad, and she that **b** thee shall rejoice. H3205
Song 6: 9 *one* of her that **b** her. The daughters H3205
8: 5 she brought thee forth *that* **b** thee. H3205
Isa 8: 3 conceived, and **b** a son. Then said the H3205
22: 6 And Elam **b** the quiver with chariots of H5375
32:11 **b**, and gird *sackcloth* upon *your* loins. H6209
47: 2 thy locks, make **b** the leg, uncover the H2834
51: 2 unto Sarah *that* **b** you: for I called him H2342
52:10 The LORD hath made **b** his holy arm in H2834
53:12 and he **b** the sin of many, and H5375
63: 9 them; and he **b** them, and carried them H5190
Jer 13:22 skirts discovered, *and* thy heels made **b**. H2554
16: 3 their mothers that **b** them, and H3205
20:14 wherein my mother **b** me be blessed. H3205
22:26 thy mother that **b** thee, into another H3205
49:10 But I have made Esau **b**, I have H2834
50:12 she that **b** you shall be ashamed: H3205
Ezk 12: 7 I **b** *it* upon *my* shoulder in their sight. H5375
16: 7 grown, whereas thou *wast* naked and **b**. H6181
22 and **b**, *and* wast polluted in thy blood. H6181
39 fair jewels, and leave thee naked and **b**. H6181
19:11 of them that **b** rule, and her stature H4910
23: 4 mine, and they **b** sons and daughters. H3205
29 thee naked and **b**: and the nakedness H6181
37 sons, whom they **b** unto me, to pass for H3205
Hos 1: 3 which conceived, and **b** him a son. H3205
6 And she conceived again, and **b** a H3205
8 she conceived, and **b** a son. H3205
Joel 1: 7 made it clean **b**, and cast *it* away; the H2834
Mt 8:17 our infirmities, and **b** *our* sicknesses. *G941*
Mk 14:56 For many **b** false witness against him, *G5576*
57 And there arose certain, and **b** false *G5576*
Lk 4:22 And all **b** him witness, and wondered *G3140*
7:14 bier: and they that **b** *him* stood still. And *G941*
8: 8 sprang up, and **b** fruit an hundredfold. *G4160*
11:27 *is* the womb that **b** thee, and the paps *G941*
23:29 **b**, and the paps which never gave suck. *G1080*
Jn 1:15 John **b** witness of him, and cried, *G3140*
32 And John **b** record, saying, I saw the *G3140*
34 And I saw, and **b** record that this is the *G3140*
2: 8 the governor of the feast. And they **b** *it*. *G5342*
5:33 Ye sent unto John, and he **b** witness *G3140*
12: 6 had the bag, and **b** what was put therein. *G941*
17 raised him from the dead, **b** record. *G3140*
19:35 And he that saw *it* **b** record, and his *G3140*
Act 15: 8 And God, which knoweth the hearts, **b** *G3140*
1Co 15:37 body that shall be, but **b** grain, it may *G1131*
1Pt 2:24 Who his own self **b** our sins in his own *G399*
Rev 1: 2 Who **b** record of the word of God, and *G3140*
22: 2 tree of life, which **b** twelve *manner of* *G4160*

BAREFOOT
2Sa 15:30 and he went **b**: and all the people that H3182
Isa 20: 2 And he did so, walking naked and **b**. H3182
3 walked naked and **b** three years *for* a H3182
4 and old, naked and **b**, even with *their* H3182

BAREST
1Ki 2:26 because thou **b** the ark of the Lord H5375
Isa 63:19 We are *thine*: thou never **b** rule over H4910
Jn 3:26 to whom thou **b** witness, behold, the *G3140*

BARHUMITE
2Sa 23:31 the Arbathite, Azmaveth the **B**, H1273

BARIAH
1Ch 3:22 and **B**, and Neariah, and Shaphat, six. H1282

BARJESUS
Act 13: 6 false prophet, a Jew, whose name *was* **B**: *G919*

BARJONA
Mt 16:17 art thou, Simon **B**: for flesh and blood *G920*

BARK
Isa 56:10 dogs, they cannot **b**; sleeping, lying H5024

BARKED
Joel 1: 7 He hath laid my vine waste, and **b** my H7111

BARKOS
Ezr 2:53 The children of **B**, the children of Sisera, H1302
Neh 7:55 The children of **B**, the children of Sisera, H1302

BARLEY
Ex 9:31 And the flax and the **b** was smitten: for H8184
31 smitten: for the **b** *was* in the ear, and H8184
Lev 27:16 an homer of **b** seed *shall be valued* H8184
Nu 5:15 of an ephah of **b** meal; he shall pour H8184
Dt 8: 8 A land of wheat, and **b**, and vines, and H8184
Jdg 7:13 and, lo, a cake of **b** bread tumbled into H8184
Ru 1:22 in the beginning of **b** harvest. H8184
2:17 and it was about an ephah of **b**. H8184
23 unto the end of **b** harvest and of wheat H8184
3: 2 **b** to night in the threshingfloor. H8184
15 six *measures* of **b**, and laid *it* on her: H8184
17 And she said, These six *measures* of **b** H8184
2Sa 14:30 mine, and he hath **b** there; go and set it H8184
17:28 and wheat, and **b**, and flour, and H8184
21: 9 *days*, in the beginning of **b** harvest. H8184
1Ki 4:28 **B** also and straw for the horses and H8184
2Ki 4:42 twenty loaves of **b**, and full ears of corn H8184
7: 1 **b** for a shekel, in the gate of Samaria. H8184
16 and two measures of **b** for a shekel, H8184
18 Two measures of **b** for a shekel, and a H8184
1Ch 11:13 of ground full of **b**; and the people fled H8184
2Ch 2:10 measures of **b**, and twenty thousand H8184
15 Now therefore the wheat, and the **b**, the H8184
27: 5 and ten thousand of **b**. So much did the H8184
Job 31:40 of **b**. The words of Job are ended. H8184
Isa 28:25 appointed **b** and the rie in their place? H8184
Jer 41: 8 of wheat, and of **b**, and of oil, and of H8184
Ezk 4: 9 Take thou also unto thee wheat, and **b**, H8184
12 And thou shalt eat it *as* **b** cakes, and H8184
13:19 for handfuls of **b** and for pieces of H8184
45:13 sixth part of an ephah of an homer of **b**: H8184
Hos 3: 2 of **b**, and an half homer of barley: H8184
2 of barley, and an half homer of **b**: H8184
Joel 1:11 the wheat and for the **b**; because the H8184
Jn 6: 9 There is a lad here, which hath five **b** *G2916*
13 of the five **b** loaves, which remained *G2916*
Rev 6: 6 three measures of **b** for a penny; and *G2915*

BARN
Job 39:12 home thy seed, and gather *it into* thy **b**? H1637
Hag 2:19 Is the seed yet in the **b**? yea, as yet the H4035
Mt 13:30 them: but gather the wheat into my **b**. *G596*
Lk 12:24 storehouse nor **b**; and God feedeth them: *G596*

BARNABAS
Act 4:36 was surnamed **B**, (which is, being *G921*
9:27 But **B** took him, and brought *him* to the *G921*
11:22 **B**, that he should go as far as Antioch. *G921*
25 Then departed **B** to Tarsus, for to seek *G921*
30 to the elders by the hands of **B** and Saul. *G921*
12:25 And **B** and Saul returned from *G921*
13: 1 and teachers; as **B**, and Simeon that was *G921*
2 said, Separate me **B** and Saul for the *G921*
7 who called for **B** and Saul, and desired *G921*
43 followed Paul and **B**: who, speaking to *G921*
46 Then Paul and **B** waxed bold, and said, *G921*
50 **B**, and expelled them out of their coasts. *G921*
14:12 And they called **B**, Jupiter; and Paul, *G921*
14 *Which* when the apostles, **B** and Paul, *G921*
20 next day he departed with **B** to Derbe. *G921*
15: 2 When therefore Paul and **B** had no small *G921*

1Ch 19: 9 out, and put the **b** in array before the H4421
10 Now when Joab saw that the **b** was set H4421
14 unto the **b**; and they fled before him. H4421
17 them, and set *the* **b** in array against
17 David had put the **b** in array against H4421
20: 1 that kings go out *to* **b**, Joab led forth the
2Ch 13: 3 And Abijah set the **b** in array with an H4421
3 also set the **b** in array against him H4421
14 back, behold, the **b** *was* before and H4421
14:10 and they set the **b** in array in the valley H4421
18: 5 Ramoth-gilead to **b**, or shall I forbear? H4421
14 Ramoth-gilead to **b**, or shall I forbear? H4421
29 and will go to the **b**; but put thou on thy H4421
29 himself; and they went to the **b**. H4421
34 And the **b** increased that day: howbeit H4421
20: 1 came against Jehoshaphat to **b**. H4421
15 for the **b** *is* not yours, but God's. H4421
17 Ye shall not *need* to fight in this **b**: set
25: 8 be strong for the **b**: God shall make thee H4421
13 not go with him to **b**, fell upon the cities H4421
Job 15:24 against him, as a king ready to the **b**. H3593
38:23 trouble, against the day of **b** and war? H7128
39:25 he smelleth the **b** afar off, the thunder H4421
41: 8 him, remember the **b**, do no more. H4421
Ps 18:39 strength unto the **b**: thou hast subdued H4421
24: 8 and mighty, the LORD mighty in **b**. H4421
55:18 in peace from the **b** *that was* against H7128
76: 3 shield, and the sword, and the **b**. Selah. H4421
78: 9 bows, turned back in the day of **b**. H7128
89:43 hast not made him to stand in the **b**. H4421
140: 7 hast covered my head in the day of **b**. H5402
Prv 21:31 the day of **b**: but safety *is* of the LORD. H4421
Ecc 9:11 to the swift, nor the **b** to the strong, H4421
Isa 9: 5 For every **b** of the warrior *is* with H5430
13: 4 of hosts mustereth the host of the **b**. H4421
22: 2 not slain with the sword, nor dead in **b**. H4421
27: 4 against me in **b**? I would go through H4421
28: 6 to them that turn the **b** to the gate. H4421
42:25 the strength of **b**: and it hath set him H4421
Jer 8: 6 course, as the horse rusheth into the **b**. H4421
18:21 young men *be* slain by the sword in **b**. H4421
46: 3 buckler and shield, and draw near to **b**. H4421
49:14 come against her, and rise up to the **b**. H4421
50:22 A sound of **b** *is* in the land, and of great H4421
42 **b**, against thee, O daughter of Babylon. H4421
51:20 Thou *art* my **b** axe *and* weapons of H4661
Ezk 7:14 but none goeth to the **b**: for my wrath *is* H4421
13: 5 stand in the **b** in the day of the LORD. H4421
Dan 11:20 be destroyed, neither in anger, nor in **b**. H4421
25 be stirred up to **b** with a very great and H4421
Hos 1: 7 nor by **b**, by horses, nor by horsemen. H4421
2:18 the sword and the **b** out of the earth, H4421
10: 9 they stood: the **b** in Gibeah against the H4421
14 in the day of **b**: the mother was dashed H4421
Joel 2: 5 as a strong people set in **b** array. H4421
Am 1:14 in the day of **b**, with a tempest in the H4421
Oba 1 ye, and let us rise up against her in **b**. H4421
Zec 9:10 and the **b** bow shall be cut off: H4421
10: 3 made them as his goodly horse in the **b**. H4421
4 out of him the **b** bow, out of him every H4421
5 the streets in the **b**: and they shall fight, H4421
14: 2 Jerusalem to **b**; and the city shall be H4421
3 as when he fought in the day of **b**. H7128
1Co 14: 8 who shall prepare himself to the **b**? G4171
Rev 9: 7 prepared unto **b**; and on their heads G4171
9 chariots of many horses running to **b**. G4171
16:14 **b** of that great day of God Almighty. G4171
20: 8 them together to **b**: the number of G4171

BATTLE-AXE See BATTLE and AXE.

BATTLE-BOW See BATTLE and BOW.

BATTLEMENT
Dt 22: 8 thou shalt make a **b** for thy roof, that H4624

BATTLEMENTS
Jer 5:10 her **b**; for they *are* not the LORD'S. H5189

BATTLES
1Sa 8:20 and go out before us, and fight our **b**. H4421
18:17 fight the LORD'S **b**. For Saul said, Let H4421
25:28 lord fighteth the **b** of the LORD, and H4421
1Ch 26:27 Out of the spoils won in **b** did they H4421
2Ch 32: 8 us, and to fight our **b**. And the people H4421
Isa 30:32 and in **b** of shaking will he fight with it. H4421

BAVAI
Neh 3:18 After him repaired their brethren, **B** the H942

BAY
Jos 15: 2 sea, from the **b** that looketh southward: H3956
5 quarter *was* from the **b** of the sea at the H3956
18:19 were at the north **b** of the salt sea at the H3956
Ps 37:35 spreading himself like a green **b** tree. H249
Zec 6: 3 the fourth chariot grisled and **b** horses. H554
7 And the **b** went forth, and sought to go H554

BAY-TREE See BAY and TREE.

BAZ See MAHER-SHALAL-HASH-BAZ.

BAZLITH
Neh 7:54 The children of **B**, the children of H1213

BAZLUTH
Ezr 2:52 The children of **B**, the children of H1213

BDELLIUM
Gen 2:12 *is* good: there *is* **b** and the onyx stone. H916
Nu 11: 7 and the colour thereof as the colour of **b**. H916

BE See the Appendix.

BEACON
Isa 30:17 till ye be left as a **b** upon the top of a H8650

BEALIAH
1Ch 12: 5 Eluzai, and Jerimoth, and **B**, and H1183

BEALOTH
Jos 15:24 Ziph, and Telem, and **B**, H1175

BEAM
Jdg 16:14 with the pin of the **b**, and with the web. H708
1Sa 17: 7 like a weaver's **b**; and his spear's head H4500
2Sa 21:19 of whose spear *was* like a weaver's **b**. H4500
1Ki 7: 6 and the thick **b** *were* before them. H5646
2Ki 6: 2 every man a **b**, and let us make us H6982
5 But as one was felling a **b**, the axe head H6982
1Ch 11:23 like a weaver's **b**; and he went down to H4500
20: 5 whose spear staff *was* like a weaver's **b**. H4500
Hab 2:11 the **b** out of the timber shall answer it. H3714
Mt 7: 3 not the **b** that is in thine own eye? G1385
4 and, behold, a **b** *is* in thine own eye? G1385
5 Thou hypocrite, first cast out the **b** out G1385
Lk 6:41 not the **b** that is in thine own eye? G1385
42 beholdest not the **b** that is in thine own G1385
42 cast out first the **b** out of thine own eye, G1385

BEAMS
1Ki 6: 6 about, that *the* **b** should not be fastened
9 the house with **b** and boards of cedar. H1356
36 of hewed stone, and a row of cedar **b**. H3773
7: 2 pillars, with cedar **b** upon the pillars. H3773
3 above upon the **b**, that *lay* on forty five H6763
12 and a row of cedar **b**, both for the inner H3773
2Ch 3: 7 He overlaid also the house, the **b**, the H6982
Neh 2: 8 timber to make **b** for the gates of the H7136
3: 3 who *also* laid the **b** thereof, and set up H7136
6 they laid the **b** thereof, and set up H7136
Ps 104: 3 Who layeth the **b** of his chambers in H7136
Song 1:17 The **b** of our house *are* cedar, *and* our H6982

BEANS
2Sa 17:28 and **b**, and lentiles, and parched *pulse*, H6321
Ezk 4: 9 and barley, and **b**, and lentiles, and H6321

BEAR
Gen 4:13 My punishment *is* greater than I can **b**. H5375
13: 6 And the land was not able to **b** them, H5375
16:11 child, and shalt **b** a son, and shalt call H3205
17:17 shall Sarah, that is ninety years old, **b**? H3205
19 And God said, Sarah thy wife shall **b** H3205
21 which Sarah shall **b** unto thee at this H3205
18:13 I of a surety **b** a child, which am old? H3205
22:23 did **b** to Nahor, Abraham's brother. H3205
30: 3 her; and she shall **b** upon my knees, H3205
36: 7 not **b** them because of their cattle. H5375
43: 9 thee, then let me **b** the blame for ever: H2398
44:32 shall **b** the blame to my father for ever. H2398
49:15 **b**, and became a servant unto tribute. H5445
Ex 18:22 and they shall **b** *the burden* with thee. H5375
20:16 Thou shalt not **b** false witness against H6030
25:27 for places of the staves to **b** the table. H5375
27: 7 upon the two sides of the altar, to **b** it. H5375
28:12 and Aaron shall **b** their names before H5375
29 And Aaron shall **b** the names of the H5375
30 and Aaron shall **b** the judgment of the H5375
Ex 28:38 that Aaron may **b** the iniquity of the H5375
43 *place;* that they **b** not iniquity, and die: H5375
30: 4 for places for the staves to **b** it withal. H5375
37: 5 by the sides of the ark, to **b** the ark. H5375
14 the places for the staves to **b** the table. H5375
15 overlaid them with gold, to **b** the table. H5375
27 to be places for the staves to **b** it withal. H5375
38: 7 of the altar, to **b** it withal; he made the H5375
Lev 5: 1 not utter *it,* then he shall **b** his iniquity. H5375
17 yet is he guilty, and shall **b** his iniquity. H5375
7:18 that eateth of it shall **b** his iniquity. H5375
10:17 hath given it you to **b** the iniquity of the H5375
12: 5 But if she **b** a maid child, then she shall H3205
16:22 And the goat shall **b** upon him all their H5375
17:16 his flesh; then he shall **b** his iniquity. H5375
19: 8 *one* that eateth it shall **b** his iniquity, H5375
18 Thou shalt not avenge, nor **b** any H5201
20:17 nakedness; he shall **b** his iniquity. H5375
19 his near kin: they shall **b** their iniquity. H5375
20 **b** their sin; they shall die childless. H5375
22: 9 lest they **b** sin for it, and die therefore, H5375
16 Or suffer them to **b** the iniquity of H5375
24:15 curseth his God shall **b** his sin. H5375
Nu 1:50 to it: they shall **b** the tabernacle, and H5375
4:15 shall come to **b** *it*: but they shall not H5375
25 And they shall **b** the curtains of the H5375
5:31 and this woman shall **b** her iniquity. H5375
7: 9 they should **b** upon their shoulders. H5375
9:13 season, that man shall **b** his sin. H5375
11:14 I am not able to **b** all this people alone, H5375
17 and they shall **b** the burden of the H5375
17 thee, that thou **b** *it* not thyself alone. H5375
14:27 How long *shall I* **b** *with* this evil
33 forty years, and **b** your whoredoms, H5375
34 for a year, shall ye **b** your iniquities, H5375
18: 1 with thee shall **b** the iniquity of the H5375
1 shall **b** the iniquity of your priesthood. H5375
22 congregation, lest they **b** sin, and die. H5375
23 and they shall **b** their iniquity: *it shall* H5375
32 And ye shall **b** no sin by reason of it, H5375
30:15 *them;* then he shall **b** her iniquity. H5375
Dt 1: 9 I am not able to **b** you myself alone: H5375
12 How can I myself alone **b** your H5375
31 as a man doth **b** his son, in all the way H5375
5:20 Neither shalt thou **b** false witness H6030
10: 8 the tribe of Levi, to **b** the ark of the H5375
28:57 which she shall **b**: for she shall eat them H3205
Jos 3: 8 the priests that **b** the ark of the H5375
13 feet of the priests that **b** the ark of the H5375
4:16 Command the priests that **b** the ark of H5375
6: 4 And seven priests shall **b** before the ark H5375
6 let seven priests **b** seven trumpets of H5375
Jdg 13: 3 but thou shalt conceive, and **b** a son. H3205
5 For, lo, thou shalt conceive, and **b** a H3205
7 conceive, and **b** a son; and now drink H3205
Ru 1:12 also to night, and should also **b** sons; H3205
1Sa 17:34 a **b**, and took a lamb out of the flock: H1677
36 both the lion and the **b**: and this H1677
37 of the paw of the **b**, he will deliver me H1677
2Sa 17: 8 in their minds, as a **b** robbed of her H1677
18:19 Let me now run, and **b** the king tidings, H1319
20 Thou shalt not **b** tidings this day, but H1319
20 but thou shalt **b** tidings another day: H1319
20 day thou shalt **b** no tidings, because H1319
1Ki 3:21 it was not my son, which I did **b**. H3205
21:10 before him, to **b** witness against him, H5749
2Ki 18:14 on me will I **b**. And the king of Assyria H5375
19:30 root downward, and **b** fruit upward. H6213
1Ch 5:18 men, men able to **b** buckler and sword, H5375
2Ch 2: 2 ten thousand men to **b** burdens, and H5445
Est 1:22 every man should **b** rule in his own H8323
Ps 75: 3 dissolved: I **b** up the pillars of it. Selah. H8505
89:50 servants; *how* I do **b** in my bosom *the* H5375
91:12 They shall **b** thee up in *their* hands, lest H5375
Prv 9:12 *if* thou scornest, thou alone shalt **b** *it*. H5375
12:24 The hand of the diligent shall **b** rule: H4910
17:12 Let a **b** robbed of her whelps meet a H1677
18:14 but a wounded spirit who can **b**? H5375
28:15 *As* a roaring lion, and a ranging **b**; *so is* H1677
30:21 and for four *which* it cannot **b**: H5375
Song 4: 2 whereof every one **b** twins, and none *is* H8382
Isa 1:14 trouble unto me; I am weary to **b** *them*. H5375
7:14 conceive, and **b** a son, and shall call H3205
11: 7 And the cow and the **b** shall feed; their H1677
37:31 root downward, and **b** fruit upward: H6213
46: 4 **b**; even I will carry, and will deliver *you*. H5375
7 They **b** him upon the shoulder, they H5375
52:11 clean, that **b** the vessels of the LORD. H5375
53:11 many; for he shall **b** their iniquities. H5445

Isa 54: 1 Sing, O barren, thou *that* didst not **b**; H3205
Jer 5:31 and the priests **b** rule by their means; H7287
10:19 Truly this *is* a grief, and I must **b** it. H5375
17:21 to yourselves, and **b** no burden on the H5375
27 day, and not to **b** a burden, even H5375
29: 6 that they may **b** sons and daughters; H3205
31:19 I did **b** the reproach of my youth. H5375
44:22 So that the LORD could no longer **b**, H5375
Lam 3:10 He *was* unto me *as* a **b** lying in wait, H1677
27 *It is* good for a man that he **b** the yoke H5375
Ezk 4: 4 lie upon it thou shalt **b** their iniquity. H5375
5 **b** the iniquity of the house of Israel. H5375
6 and thou shalt **b** the iniquity of the H5375
12: 6 In their sight shalt thou **b** *it* upon *thy* H5375
12 among them shall **b** upon *his* shoulder H5375
14:10 And they shall **b** the punishment of H5375
16:52 judged thy sisters, **b** thine own shame H5375
52 also, and **b** thy shame, in that thou H5375
54 That thou mayest **b** thine own shame, H5375
17: 8 **b** fruit, that it might be a goodly vine. H5375
23 forth boughs, and **b** fruit, and be a H6213
18:19 Yet say ye, Why? doth not the son **b** the H5375
20 The son shalt not **b** the iniquity of the H5375
20 shall the father **b** the iniquity of the H5375
23:35 thy back, therefore **b** thou also thy H5375
49 you, and ye shall **b** the sins of your H5375
32:30 by the sword, and **b** their shame with H5375
34:29 **b** the shame of the heathen any more. H5375
36: 7 about you, they shall **b** their shame. H5375
15 neither shalt thou **b** the reproach of the H5375
44:10 idols; they shall even **b** their iniquity. H5375
12 GOD, and they shall **b** their iniquity. H5375
13 but they shall **b** their shame, and their H5375
46:20 offering; that they **b** *them* not out into H3318
Dan 2:39 which shall **b** rule over all the earth. H7981
7: 5 a second, like to a **b**, and it raised up H1678
Hos 9:16 up, they shall **b** no fruit: yea, though H6213
13: 8 I will meet them as a **b** *that is* bereaved H1677
Am 5:19 from a lion, and a **b** met him; or went H1677
7:10 the land is not able to **b** all his words. H3557
Mic 6:16 ye shall **b** the reproach of my people. H5375
7: 9 I will **b** the indignation of the LORD, H5375
Zep 1:11 down; all they that **b** silver are cut off. H5187
Hag 2:12 If one **b** holy flesh in the skirt of his H5375
Zec 5:10 me, Whither do these **b** the ephah? H3212
6:13 and he shall **b** the glory, and shall H5375
Mt 3:11 I am not worthy to **b**: he shall baptize you *G941*
4: 6 hands they shall **b** thee up, lest at any *G142*
19:18 steal, Thou shalt not **b** false witness, *G5576*
27:32 name: him they compelled to **b** his cross. *G142*
Mk 10:19 Do not steal, Do not **b** false witness, *G5576*
15:21 of Alexander and Rufus, to **b** his cross. *G142*
Lk 1:13 Elisabeth shall **b** thee a son, and thou *G1080*
4:11 And in *their* hands they shall **b** thee up, *G142*
11:48 Truly ye **b** witness that ye allow the *G3140*
13: 9 And if it **b** fruit, *well*: and if not, *then* *G4160*
14:27 And whosoever doth not **b** his cross, and *G941*
18: 7 unto him, though he **b** long with them? *G3114*
20 Do not steal, Do not **b** false witness, *G5576*
23:26 the cross, that he might **b** *it* after Jesus. *G5342*
Jn 1: 7 The same came for a witness, to **b** *G3140*
8 but *was sent* to **b** witness of that Light. *G3140*
2: 8 out now, and **b** unto the governor of *G5342*
3:28 Ye yourselves **b** me witness, that I said, *G3140*
5:31 If I **b** witness of myself, my witness is *G3140*
36 works that I do, **b** witness of me, that *G3140*
8:14 them, Though I **b** record of myself, *yet* *G3140*
18 I am one that **b** witness of myself, and *G3140*
10:25 Father's name, they **b** witness of me. *G3140*
15: 4 As the branch cannot **b** fruit of itself, *G5342*
8 Herein is my Father glorified, that ye **b** *G5342*
27 And ye also shall **b** witness, because ye *G3140*
16:12 say unto you, but ye cannot **b** them now. *G941*
18:23 I have spoken evil, **b** witness of the evil: *G3140*
37 that I should **b** witness unto the truth. *G3140*
Act 9:15 vessel unto me, to **b** my name before the *G941*
15:10 neither our fathers nor we were able to **b**? *G941*
18:14 reason would that I should **b** with you: *G430*
22: 5 As also the high priest doth **b** me *G3140*
23:11 so must thou **b** witness also at Rome. *G3140*
27:15 not **b** up into the wind, we let *her* drive. *G503*
Ro 10: 2 For I **b** them record that they have a *G3140*
13: 9 Thou shalt not **b** false witness, Thou *G5576*
15: 1 We then that are strong ought to **b** the *G941*
1Co 3: 2 able *to* **b** *it*, neither yet now are ye able.
10:13 to escape, that ye may be able to **b** *it*. *G5297*
15:49 shall also **b** the image of the heavenly. *G5409*
2Co 8: 3 For to *their* power, I **b** record, yea, and *G3140*
11: 1 Would to God ye could **b** with me a little *G430*
2Co 11: 1 a little in *my* folly: and indeed **b** with me. *G430*
4 not accepted, ye might well **b** with *him*. *G430*
Gal 4:15 ye spake of? for I **b** you record, that, if *G3140*
5:10 shall **b** his judgment, whosoever he be. *G941*
6: 2 **B** ye one another's burdens, and so fulfil *G941*
5 For every man shall **b** his own burden. *G941*
17 trouble me: for I **b** in my body the marks *G941*
Col 4:13 For I **b** him record, that he hath a great *G3140*
1Ti 5:14 women marry, **b** children, guide the *G5041*
Heb 9:28 So Christ was once offered to **b** the sins *G399*
Jas 3:12 Can the fig tree, my brethren, **b** olive *G4160*
1Jn 1: 2 have seen *it*, and **b** witness, and shew *G3140*
5: 7 For there are three that **b** record in *G3140*
8 And there are three that **b** witness in *G3140*
3Jn 12 yea, and we *also* **b** record; and ye know *G3140*
Rev 2: 2 how thou canst not **b** them which are *G941*
13: 2 as *the feet* of a **b**, and his mouth as the *G715*

BEARD

Lev 13:29 have a plague upon the head or the **b**; H2206
30 scall, *even* a leprosy upon the head or **b**. H2206
14: 9 his head and his **b** and his eyebrows, H2206
19:27 shalt thou mar the corners of thy **b**. H2206
21: 5 **b**, nor make any cuttings in their flesh. H2206
1Sa 17:35 by his **b**, and smote him, and slew him. H2206
21:13 and let his spittle fall down upon his **b**. H2206
2Sa 19:24 feet, nor trimmed his **b**, nor washed his H8222
20: 9 the **b** with the right hand to kiss him. H2206
Ezr 9: 3 and of my **b**, and sat down astonied. H2206
Ps 133: 2 down upon the **b**, *even* Aaron's beard: H2206
2 *even* Aaron's **b**: that went down to the H2206
Isa 7:20 the feet: and it shall also consume the **b**. H2206
15: 2 *shall be* baldness, *and* every **b** cut off. H2206
Jer 48:37 *be* bald, and every **b** clipped: upon all H2206
Ezk 5: 1 and upon thy **b**: then take thee balances H2206

BEARDS

2Sa 10: 4 the one half of their **b**, and cut off their H2206
5 until your **b** be grown, and *then* return. H2206
1Ch 19: 5 until your **b** be grown, and *then* return. H2206
Jer 41: 5 men, having their **b** shaven, and their H2206

BEARERS

2Ch 2:18 of them *to be* **b** of burdens, and H5449
34:13 Also *they were* over the **b** of burdens, H5449
Neh 4:10 And Judah said, The strength of the **b** H5449

BEAREST

Jdg 13: 3 *art* barren, and **b** not: but thou shalt H3205
Ps 106: 4 the favour *that thou* **b** *unto* thy people: O
Jn 8:13 unto him, Thou **b** record of thyself; thy *G3140*
Ro 11:18 thou **b** not the root, but the root thee. *G941*
Gal 4:27 *thou* barren that **b** not; break forth and *G5088*

BEARETH

Lev 11:25 And whosoever **b** *ought* of the carcase H5375
28 And he that **b** the carcase of them shall H5375
40 the even: he also that **b** the carcase of it H5375
15:10 even: and he that **b** *any of* those things H5375
Nu 11:12 as a nursing father **b** the sucking child, H5375
Dt 25: 6 which she **b** shall succeed in the H3205
29:18 you a root that **b** gall and wormwood; H6509
23 *that* it is not sown, nor **b**, nor any grass H6779
32:11 taketh them, **b** them on her wings: H5375
Job 16: 8 rising up in me **b** witness to my face. H6030
24:21 He evil entreateth the barren *that* **b** H3205
Prv 25:18 A man that **b** false witness against his H6030
29: 2 the wicked **b** rule, the people mourn. H4910
Song 6: 6 whereof every one **b** twins, and *there is* H8382
Joel 2:22 spring, for the tree **b** her fruit, the fig H5375
Mt 13:23 *it*; which also **b** fruit, and bringeth *G2592*
Jn 5:32 There is another that **b** witness of me; *G3140*
8:18 Father that sent me **b** witness of me. *G3140*
15: 2 Every branch in me that **b** not fruit he *G5342*
2 every *branch* that **b** fruit, he purgeth it, *G5342*
Ro 8:16 The Spirit itself **b** witness with our *G4828*
13: 4 evil, be afraid; for he **b** not the sword in *G5409*
1Co 13: 7 **B** all things, believeth all things, hopeth *G4722*
Heb 6: 8 But that which **b** thorns and briers *is* *G1627*
1Jn 5: 6 **b** witness, because the Spirit is truth. *G3140*

BEARING

Gen 1:29 you every herb **b** seed, which *is* upon H2232
16: 2 me from **b**: I pray thee, go in unto H3205
29:35 she called his name Judah; and left **b**. H3205
30: 9 When Leah saw that she had left **b**, she H3205
37:25 with their camels **b** spicery and balm H5375
Nu 10:17 of Merari set forward, **b** the tabernacle. H5375
21 And the Kohathites set forward, **b** the H5375
Jos 3: 3 the priests the Levites **b** it, then ye shall H5375
14 Jordan, and the priests **b** the ark of the H5375
6: 8 the seven priests **b** the seven trumpets H5375
13 And seven priests **b** seven trumpets of H5375
1Sa 17: 7 and one **b** a shield went before him. H5375
2Sa 15:24 Levites *were* with him, **b** the ark of the H5375
Ps 126: 6 He that goeth forth and weepeth, **b** H5375
Mk 14:13 a man **b** a pitcher of water: follow him. *G941*
Lk 22:10 a man meet you, **b** a pitcher of water; *G941*
Jn 19:17 And he **b** his cross went forth into a *G941*
Ro 2:15 conscience also **b** witness, and *their* *G4828*
9: 1 also **b** me witness in the Holy Ghost, *G4828*
2Co 4:10 Always **b** about in the body the dying *G4064*
Heb 2: 4 God also **b** *them* witness, both with *G4901*
13:13 him without the camp, **b** his reproach. *G5342*

BEARS

2Ki 2:24 forth two she **b** out of the wood, and H1677
Isa 59:11 We roar all like **b**, and mourn sore like H1677

BEAST

Gen 1:24 thing, and **b** of the earth after his H2416
25 And God made the **b** of the earth after H2416
30 And to every **b** of the earth, and to H2416
2:19 God formed every **b** of the field, and H2416
20 air, and to every **b** of the field; but for H2416
3: 1 subtil than any **b** of the field which the H2416
14 and above every **b** of the field; upon thy H2416
6: 7 both man, and **b**, and the creeping thing, H929
7: 2 Of every clean **b** thou shalt take to thee H929
14 They, and every **b** after his kind, and H2416
21 of cattle, and of **b**, and of every creeping H2416
8:19 Every **b**, every creeping thing, and every H2416
20 took of every clean **b**, and of every clean H929
9: 2 be upon every **b** of the earth, and upon H2416
5 the hand of every **b** will I require it, and H2416
10 and of every **b** of the earth with you; H2416
10 out of the ark, to every **b** of the earth. H2416
34:23 and every **b** of theirs *be* ours? only H929
37:20 we will say, Some evil **b** hath devoured H2416
33 my son's coat; an evil **b** hath devoured H2416
Ex 8:17 lice in man, and in **b**; all the dust of the H929
18 so there were lice upon man, and upon **b**. H929
9: 9 upon **b**, throughout all the land of Egypt. H929
10 forth *with* blains upon man, and upon **b**. H929
19 every man and **b** which shall be found H929
22 man, and upon **b**, and upon every herb H929
25 field, both man and **b**; and the hail smote H929
11: 7 against man or **b**: that ye may know how H929
12:12 both man and **b**; and against all the gods H929
13: 2 of Israel, *both* of man and of **b**: it *is* mine. H929
12 that cometh of a **b** which thou hast; the H929
15 the firstborn of **b**: therefore I sacrifice H929
19:13 whether *it be* **b** or man, it shall not live: H929
21:34 of them; and the dead *b* shall be his.
22: 5 and shall put in his **b**, and shall feed in H1165
10 or a sheep, or any **b**, to keep; and it die, H929
19 Whosoever lieth with a **b** shall surely be H929
23:29 the **b** of the field multiply against thee. H2416
Lev 5: 2 of an unclean **b**, or a carcase of unclean H2416
7:21 or *any* unclean **b**, or any abominable H929
24 And the fat of the **b** that dieth of itself, H5038
25 For whosoever eateth the fat of the **b**, of H929
26 of fowl or of **b**, in any of your dwellings. H929
11:26 *The carcases* of every **b** which divideth H929
39 And if any **b**, of which ye may eat, die; he H929
47 and between the **b** that may be eaten H2416
47 eaten and the **b** that may not be eaten. H2416
17:13 and catcheth any **b** or fowl that may be H2416
18:23 Neither shalt thou lie with any **b** to defile H929
23 a **b** to lie down thereto: it *is* confusion. H929
20:15 And if a man lie with a **b**, he shall surely H929
15 be put to death: and ye shall slay the **b**. H929
16 And if a woman approach unto any **b**, H929
16 woman, and the **b**: they shall surely be H929
25 abominable by **b**, or by fowl, or by any H929
24:18 And he that killeth a **b** shall make it H929
18 a beast shall make it good; **b** for beast. H5315
18 a beast shall make it good; beast for **b**. H5315
21 And he that killeth a **b**, he shall restore it: H929
25: 7 And for thy cattle, and for the **b** that H2416
27: 9 And if *it be* a **b**, whereof men bring an H929
10 he shall at all change **b** for beast, then it H929
10 all change beast for **b**, then it and the H929
11 And if *it be* any unclean **b**, of which they H929
11 he shall present the **b** before the priest: H929
27 And if *it be* of an unclean **b**, then he shall H929
28 *both* of man and **b**, and of the field of his H929
Nu 3:13 **b**: mine shall they be: I *am* the LORD. H929

Nu 8:17 *both* man and **b**: on the day that I smote H929
31:26 *both* of man and of **b**, thou, and Eleazar H929
47 *both* of man and of **b**, and gave them H929
Dt 4:17 The likeness of any **b** that *is* on the H929
14: 6 And every **b** that parteth the hoof, and H929
27:21 of **b**. And all the people shall say, Amen. H929
Jdg 20:48 of *every* city, as the **b**, and all that came H929
2Ki 14: 9 there passed by a wild **b** that *was* in H2416
2Ch 25:18 there passed by a wild **b** that *was* in H2416
Neh 2:12 *was there any* **b** with me, save the beast H929
12 with me, save the **b** that I rode upon. H929
14 for the **b** *that was* under me to pass. H929
Job 39:15 or that the wild **b** may break them. H2416
Ps 36: 6 O LORD, thou preservest man and **b**. H929
50:10 For every **b** of the forest *is* mine, *and* H2416
73:22 I, and ignorant: I was *as* a **b** before thee. H929
80:13 the wild **b** of the field doth devour it. H2123
104:11 They give drink to every **b** of the field: H2416
135: 8 firstborn of Egypt, both of man and **b**. H929
147: 9 He giveth to the **b** his food, *and* to the H929
Prv 12:10 the life of his **b**: but the tender mercies H929
Ecc 3:19 preeminence above a **b**: for all *is* vanity. H929
21 the **b** that goeth downward to the earth? H929
Isa 35: 9 there, nor *any* ravenous **b** shall go up H2416
43:20 The **b** of the field shall honour me, the H2416
46: 1 loaden; *they are* a burden to the weary ***b***.
63:14 As a **b** goeth down into the valley, the H929
Jer 7:20 man, and upon **b**, and upon the trees of H929
9:10 and the **b** are fled; they are gone. H929
21: 6 and **b**: they shall die of a great pestilence. H929
27: 5 the man and the **b** that *are* upon the H929
31:27 the seed of man, and with the seed of **b**. H929
32:43 without man or **b**; it is given into the H929
33:10 man and without **b**, *even* in the cities of H929
10 and without inhabitant, and without **b**, H929
12 man and without **b**, and in all the cities H929
36:29 cause to cease from thence man and **b**? H929
50: 3 they shall depart, both man and **b**. H929
51:62 **b**, but that it shall be desolate for ever. H929
Ezk 14:13 it, and will cut off man and **b** from it: H929
17 land; so that I cut off man and **b** from it: H929
19 it in blood, to cut off from it man and **b**: H929
21 and the noisome **b**, and the pestilence, H2416
21 pestilence, to cut off from it man and **b**? H929
25:13 will cut off man and **b** from it; and I will H929
29: 8 thee, and cut off man and **b** out of thee. H929
11 it, nor foot of **b** shall pass through it, H929
34: 8 meat to every **b** of the field, because H2416
28 neither shall the **b** of the land devour H2416
36:11 And I will multiply upon you man and **b**; H929
39:17 fowl, and to every **b** of the field, H2416
44:31 of itself, or torn, whether it be fowl or **b**. H929
Dan 7: 5 And behold another **b**, a second, like to H2423
6 of a fowl; the **b** had also four heads; H2423
7 behold a fourth **b**, dreadful and terrible, H2423
11 *even* till the **b** was slain, and his body H2423
19 truth of the fourth **b**, which was diverse H2423
23 Thus he said, The fourth **b** shall be the H2423
Hos 13: 8 like a lion: the wild **b** shall tear them. H2416
Jna 3: 7 neither man nor **b**, herd nor flock, taste H929
8 But let man and **b** be covered with H929
Mic 1:13 to the swift **b**: she *is* the beginning H7409
Zep 1: 3 I will consume man and **b**; I will H929
Zec 8:10 nor any hire for **b**; neither *was there any* H929
Lk 10:34 him on his own **b**, and brought him to G2934
Act 28: 4 saw the *venomous* **b** hang on his hand, G2342
5 And he shook off the **b** into the fire, G2342
Heb 12:20 if so much as a **b** touch the mountain, G2342
Rev 4: 7 And the first **b** *was* like a lion, and the G2226
7 and the second **b** like a calf, and the G2226
7 a calf, and the third **b** had a face as a G2226
7 and the fourth **b** *was* like a flying eagle. G2226
6: 3 heard the second **b** say, Come and see. G2226
5 I heard the third **b** say, Come and see. G2226
7 of the fourth **b** say, Come and see. G2226
11: 7 testimony, the **b** that ascendeth out G2342
13: 1 the sea, and saw a **b** rise up out of the G2342
2 And the **b** which I saw was like unto a G2342
3 and all the world wondered after the **b**. G2342
4 power unto the **b**: and they worshipped G2342
4 worshipped the **b**, saying, Who *is* like G2342
4 **b**? who is able to make war with him? G2342
11 And I beheld another **b** coming up out G2342
12 the power of the first **b** before him, and G2342
12 **b**, whose deadly wound was healed. G2342
14 in the sight of the **b**; saying to them that G2342
14 an image to the **b**, which had the wound G2342
15 the image of the **b**, that the image of the G2342
15 the image of the **b** should both speak, G2342
Rev 13:15 the image of the **b** should be killed. G2342
17 of the **b**, or the number of his name. G2342
18 the number of the **b**: for it is the number G2342
14: 9 man worship the **b** and his image, and G2342
11 who worship the **b** and his image, and G2342
15: 2 victory over the **b**, and over his image, G2342
16: 2 had the mark of the **b**, and *upon* them G2342
10 the seat of the **b**; and his kingdom was G2342
13 of the mouth of the **b**, and out of the G2342
17: 3 a scarlet coloured **b**, full of names of G2342
7 and of the **b** that carrieth her, which G2342
8 The **b** that thou sawest was, and is not; G2342
8 the **b** that was, and is not, and yet is. G2342
11 And the **b** that was, and is not, even he G2342
12 power as kings one hour with the **b**. G2342
13 their power and strength unto the **b**. G2342
16 sawest upon the **b**, these shall hate the G2342
17 kingdom unto the **b**, until the words of G2342
19:19 And I saw the **b**, and the kings of the G2342
20 And the **b** was taken, and with him the G2342
20 the mark of the **b**, and them that G2342
20: 4 worshipped the **b**, neither his image, G2342
10 where the **b** and the false prophet G2342

BEASTS

Gen 7: 2 his female: and of **b** that *are* not clean by H929
8 Of clean **b**, and of beasts that *are* not H929
8 Of clean beasts, and of **b** that *are* not H929
31:39 That which was torn *of* **b** I brought not H2966
36: 6 his cattle, and all his **b**, and all his H929
45:17 do ye; lade your **b**, and go, get you unto H1165
Ex 11: 5 behind the mill; and all the firstborn of **b**. H929
22:31 *that is* torn of **b** in the field; ye shall H2966
23:11 they leave the **b** of the field shall eat. H2416
Lev 7:24 which is torn with **b**, may be used in H2966
11: 2 These *are* the **b** which ye shall eat H2416
2 eat among all the **b** that *are* on the earth. H929
3 the cud, among the **b**, that shall ye eat. H929
27 all manner of **b** that go on *all* four, H2416
46 This *is* the law of the **b**, and of the fowl, H929
17:15 was torn *with* **b**, *whether it be* one of H2966
20:25 between clean **b** and unclean, and H929
22: 8 or is torn *with* **b**, he shall not eat to H2966
26: 6 and I will rid evil **b** out of the land, H2416
22 I will also send wild **b** among you, H2416
27:26 Only the firstling of the **b**, which should H929
Nu 18:15 *whether it be* of men or **b**, shall be thine: H929
15 firstling of unclean **b** shalt thou redeem. H929
20: 8 the congregation and their **b** drink. H1165
11 congregation drank, and their **b** *also*. H1165
31:11 and all the prey, *both* of men and of **b**. H929
30 of all manner of **b**, and give them unto H929
35: 3 and for their goods, and for all their **b**. H2416
Dt 7:22 the **b** of the field increase upon thee. H2416
14: 4 These *are* the **b** which ye shall eat: the H929
6 the cud among the **b**, that ye shall eat. H929
28:26 air, and unto the **b** of the earth, and no H929
32:24 send the teeth of **b** upon them, with the H929
1Sa 17:44 fowls of the air, and to the **b** of the field. H929
46 and to the wild **b** of the earth; that all H2416
2Sa 21:10 by day, nor the **b** of the field by night. H2416
1Ki 4:33 he spake also of **b**, and of fowl, and of H929
18: 5 mules alive, that we lose not all the **b**. H929
2Ki 3:17 both ye, and your cattle, and your **b**. H929
2Ch 32:28 for all manner of **b**, and cotes for flocks. H929
Ezr 1: 4 goods, and with **b**, beside the freewill H929
6 goods, and with **b**, and with precious H929
Job 5:22 thou be afraid of the **b** of the earth. H2416
23 the field: and the **b** of the field shall be H2416
12: 7 But ask now the **b**, and they shall teach H929
18: 3 Wherefore are we counted as **b**, *and* H929
35:11 Who teacheth us more than the **b** of the H929
37: 8 Then the **b** go into dens, and remain in H2416
40:20 food, where all the **b** of the field play. H2416
Ps 8: 7 All sheep and oxen, yea, and the **b** of the H929
49:12 abideth not: he is like the **b** *that* perish. H929
20 not, is like the **b** *that* perish. H929
50:11 and the wild **b** of the field *are* mine. H2123
79: 2 of thy saints unto the **b** of the earth. H2416
104:20 all the **b** of the forest do creep *forth*. H2416
25 innumerable, both small and great **b**. H2416
148:10 **B**, and all cattle; creeping things, and H2416
Prv 9: 2 She hath killed her **b**; she hath mingled H2874
30:30 A lion *which is* strongest among **b**, and H929
Ecc 3:18 might see that they themselves are **b**. H929
19 sons of men befalleth **b**; even one thing H929
Isa 1:11 and the fat of fed **b**; and I delight not in H4806
13:21 But wild **b** of the desert shall lie there; H6728
22 And the wild **b** of the islands shall cry in H338
Isa 18: 6 and to the **b** of the earth: and the H929
6 **b** of the earth shall winter upon them. H929
30: 6 The burden of the **b** of the south: into the H929
34:14 The wild **b** of the desert shall also meet H6728
14 meet with the wild **b** of the island, and H338
40:16 **b** thereof sufficient for a burnt offering. H2416
46: 1 were upon the **b**, and upon the cattle: H2416
56: 9 All ye **b** of the field, come to devour, H2416
9 to devour, *yea*, all ye **b** in the forest. H2416
66:20 and upon swift **b**, to my holy mountain H3753
Jer 7:33 and for the **b** of the earth; and none H929
12: 4 dwell therein? the **b** are consumed, and H929
9 all the **b** of the field, come to devour. H2416
15: 3 the **b** of the earth, to devour and destroy. H929
16: 4 of heaven, and for the **b** of the earth. H929
19: 7 of the heaven, and for the **b** of the earth. H929
27: 6 servant; and the **b** of the field have I H2416
28:14 I have given him the **b** of the field also. H2416
34:20 of the heaven, and to the **b** of the earth. H929
50:39 Therefore the wild **b** of the desert with H6728
39 with the wild **b** of the islands shall dwell H338
Ezk 5:17 you famine and evil **b**, and they shall H2416
8:10 and abominable **b**, and all the idols of H929
14:15 If I cause noisome **b** to pass through H2416
15 may pass through because of the **b**: H2416
29: 5 for meat to the **b** of the field and to the H2416
31: 6 did all the **b** of the field bring forth H2416
13 and all the **b** of the field shall be H2416
32: 4 fill the **b** of the whole earth with thee. H2416
13 I will destroy also all the **b** thereof from H929
13 more, nor the hoofs of **b** trouble them. H929
33:27 will I give to the **b** to be devoured, and H2416
34: 5 **b** of the field, when they were scattered. H2416
25 will cause the evil **b** to cease out of the H2416
38:20 heaven, and the **b** of the field, and all H2416
39: 4 and *to* the **b** of the field to be devoured. H2416
Dan 2:38 of men dwell, the **b** of the field and the H2423
4:12 *was* meat for all: the **b** of the field had H2423
14 his fruit: let the **b** get away from under H2423
15 *be* with the **b** in the grass of the earth: H2423
21 all; under which the **b** of the field dwelt, H2423
23 *be* with the **b** of the field, till seven H2423
25 shall be with the **b** of the field, and they H2423
32 *shall be* with the **b** of the field: they H2423
5:21 was made like the **b**, and his dwelling H2423
7: 3 And four great **b** came up from the sea, H2423
7 from all the **b** that *were* before it; H2423
12 As concerning the rest of the **b**, they H2423
17 These great **b**, which are four, *are* four H2423
8: 4 so that no **b** might stand before H2416
Hos 2:12 and the **b** of the field shall eat them. H2416
18 for them with the **b** of the field, and H2416
4: 3 languish, with the **b** of the field, and H2416
Joel 1:18 How do the **b** groan! the herds of cattle H929
20 The **b** of the field cry also unto thee: for H929
2:22 Be not afraid, ye **b** of the field: for the H929
Am 5:22 regard the peace offerings of your fat **b**. H4806
Mic 5: 8 as a lion among the **b** of the forest, as a H929
Hab 2:17 and the spoil of **b**, *which* made them H929
Zep 2:14 of her, all the **b** of the nations: both H2416
15 a place for **b** to lie down in! every H2416
Zec 14:15 ass, and of all the **b** that shall be in these H929
Mk 1:13 **b**; and the angels ministered unto him. G2342
Act 7:42 to me slain **b** and sacrifices *by the* G4968
10:12 of fourfooted **b** of the earth, and wild G5074
12 earth, and wild **b**, and creeping things, G2342
11: 6 saw fourfooted **b** of the earth, and wild G5074
6 earth, and wild **b**, and creeping things, G2342
23:24 And provide *them* **b**, that they may set G2934
Ro 1:23 and fourfooted **b**, and creeping things. G5074
1Co 15:32 I have fought with **b** at Ephesus, what G2341
39 another flesh of **b**, another of fishes, G2934
Tit 1:12 *are* alway liars, evil **b**, slow bellies. G2342
Heb 13:11 For the bodies of those **b**, whose blood G2226
Jas 3: 7 For every kind of **b**, and of birds, and of G2342
2Pt 2:12 But these, as natural brute **b**, made to G2226
Jude 10 naturally, as brute **b**, in those things G2226
Rev 4: 6 four **b** full of eyes before and behind. G2226
8 And the four **b** had each of them six G2226
9 And when those **b** give glory and G2226
5: 6 and of the four **b**, and in the midst of G2226
8 taken the book, the four **b** and four *and* G2226
11 the throne and the **b** and the elders: G2226
14 And the four **b** said, Amen. And the G2226
6: 1 one of the four **b** saying, Come and see. G2226
6 midst of the four **b** say, A measure of G2226
8 with death, and with the **b** of the earth. G2342
7:11 elders and the four **b**, and fell before the G2226
14: 3 before the four **b**, and the elders: and G2226

Rev 15: 7 And one of the four **b** gave unto the *G2226*
18:13 flour, and wheat, and **b**, and sheep, and *G2934*
19: 4 elders and the four **b** fell down and *G2226*

BEAST'S
Dan 4:16 man's, and let a **b** heart be given unto H2423

BEAT
Ex 30:36 And thou shalt **b** *some* of it very small, H7833
39: 3 And they did **b** the gold into thin H7554
Nu 11: 8 *it* in mills, or **b** *it* in a mortar, and H1743
Dt 25: 3 exceed, and **b** him above these with H5221
Jdg 8:17 And he **b** down the tower of Penuel, H5422
9:45 **b** down the city, and sowed it with salt. H5422
19:22 round about, *and* **b** at the door, and H1849
Ru 2:17 field until even, and **b** out that she had H2251
2Sa 22:43 Then did I **b** them as small as the dust H7833
2Ki 3:25 And they **b** down the cities, and on H2040
13:25 times did Joash **b** him, and recovered H5221
23:12 did the king **b** down, and brake *them* H5422
Ps 18:42 Then did I **b** them small as the dust H7833
89:23 And I will **b** down his foes before his H3807
Prv 23:14 Thou shalt **b** him with the rod, and H5221
Isa 2: 4 and they shall **b** their swords into H3807
3:15 What mean ye *that* ye **b** my people to H1792
27:12 the LORD shall **b** off from the channel H2251
41:15 the mountains, and **b** *them* small, and H1854
Joel 3:10 **B** your plowshares into swords, and H3807
Jna 4: 8 wind; and the sun **b** upon the head of H5221
Mic 4: 3 off; and they shall **b** their swords into H3807
13 brass: and thou shalt **b** in pieces many H1854
Mt 7:25 the winds blew, and **b** upon that house; *G4363*
27 the winds blew, and **b** upon that house; *G4350*
21:35 took his servants, and **b** one, and killed *G1194*
Mk 4:37 **b** into the ship, so that it was now full. *G1911*
12: 3 And they caught *him*, and **b** him, and *G1194*
Lk 6:48 arose, the stream **b** vehemently upon *G4366*
49 the stream did **b** vehemently, and *G4366*
12:45 and shall begin to **b** the menservants *G5180*
20:10 **b** him, and sent *him* away empty. *G1194*
11 servant: and they **b** him also, and *G1194*
Act 16:22 clothes, and commanded to **b** *them*. *G4463*
18:17 the synagogue, and **b** *him* before the *G5180*
22:19 I imprisoned and **b** in every synagogue *G1194*

BEATEN
Ex 5:14 set over them, were **b**, *and* demanded, H5221
16 **b**; but the fault *is* in thine own people. H5221
25:18 *of* gold, *of* **b** work shalt thou make H4749
31 *of* pure gold: *of* **b** work shall the H4749
36 all it *shall be* one **b** work *of* pure gold. H4749
27:20 thee pure oil olive **b** for the light, to H3795
29:40 part of an hin of **b** oil; and the fourth H3795
37: 7 And he made two cherubims *of* gold, **b** H4749
17 *of* pure gold: *of* **b** work made he the H4749
22 all of it *was* one **b** work *of* pure gold. H4749
Lev 2:14 by the fire, *even* corn **b** out of full ears. H1643
16 of it, *part* of the **b** corn thereof, and H1643
16:12 **b** small, and bring *it* within the vail: H1851
24: 2 thee pure oil olive **b** for the light, to H3795
Nu 8: 4 the candlestick *was of* **b** gold, unto the H4749
4 thereof, *was* **b** work: according unto H4749
28: 5 with the fourth *part* of an hin of **b** oil. H3795
Dt 25: 2 *be* worthy to be **b**, that the judge shall H5221
2 lie down, and to be **b** before his face, H5221
Jos 8:15 as if they were **b** before them, and fled H5060
2Sa 2:17 and Abner was **b**, and the men of Israel, H5062
1Ki 10:16 targets *of* **b** gold: six hundred *shekels* H7820
17 shields *of* **b** gold; three pound of H7820
2Ch 2:10 measures of **b** wheat, and twenty H4347
9:15 targets *of* **b** gold: six hundred *shekels* H7820
15 *shekels* of **b** gold went to one target. H7820
16 *made he of* **b** gold: three hundred H7820
34: 7 groves, and had **b** the graven images H3807
Prv 23:35 sick; they have **b** me, *and* I felt *it* not: H1986
Isa 27: 9 that are **b** in sunder, the groves H5310
28:27 but the fitches are **b** out with a staff, H2251
30:31 be **b** down, *which* smote with a rod. H2865
Jer 46: 5 mighty ones are **b** down, and are fled H3807
Mic 1: 7 thereof shall be **b** to pieces, and all the H3807
Mk 13: 9 ye shall be **b**: and ye shall be brought *G1194*
Lk 12:47 to his will, shall be **b** with many *stripes*. *G1194*
48 of stripes, shall be **b** with few *stripes*. *G1194*
Act 5:40 called the apostles, and **b** *them*, they *G1194*
16:37 But Paul said unto them, They have **b** *G1194*
2Co 11:25 Thrice was I **b** with rods, once was I *G4463*

BEATEST
Dt 24:20 When thou **b** thine olive tree, thou H2251

Prv 23:13 **b** him with the rod, he shall not die. H5221

BEATETH
1Co 9:26 so fight I, not as one that **b** the air: *G1194*

BEATING
1Sa 14:16 and they went on **b** down *one another*. H1986
Mk 12: 5 many others; **b** some, and killing some. *G1194*
Act 21:32 and the soldiers, they left **b** of Paul. *G5180*

BEAUTIES
Ps 110: 3 thy power, in the **b** of holiness from the H1926

BEAUTIFUL
Gen 29:17 was **b** and well favoured. H3303+H8389
Dt 21:11 the captives a **b** woman, and H3303+H8389
1Sa 16:12 *and* withal of a **b** countenance, and H3303
25: 3 and of a **b** countenance: but the H3303
2Sa 11: 2 the woman *was* very **b** to look upon. H2896
Est 2: 7 maid *was* fair and **b**; whom H2896+H4758
Ps 48: 2 **B** for situation, the joy of the whole H3303
Ecc 3:11 He hath made every *thing* **b** in his time: H3303
Song 6: 4 Thou *art* **b**, O my love, as Tirzah, H3303
7: 1 How **b** are thy feet with shoes, O H3302
Isa 4: 2 of the LORD be **b** and glorious, and the H6643
52: 1 O Zion; put on thy **b** garments, O H8597
7 How **b** upon the mountains are the feet H4998
64:11 Our holy and our **b** house, where our H8597
Jer 13:20 flock *that* was given thee, thy **b** flock? H8597
48:17 the strong staff broken, *and* the **b** rod! H8597
Ezk 16:12 ears, and a **b** crown upon thine head. H8597
13 thou wast exceeding **b**, and thou didst H3302
23:42 hands, and **b** crowns upon their heads. H8597
Mt 23:27 indeed appear **b** outward, but are *G5611*
Act 3: 2 which is called **B**, to ask alms of them *G5611*
10 sat for alms at the **B** gate of the temple: *G5611*
Ro 10:15 it is written, How **b** are the feet of them *G5611*

BEAUTIFY
Ezr 7:27 the king's heart, to **b** the house of the H6286
Ps 149: 4 he will **b** the meek with salvation. H6286
Isa 60:13 the box together, to **b** the place of my H6286

BEAUTY
Ex 28: 2 Aaron thy brother for glory and for **b**. H8597
40 thou make for them, for glory and for **b**. H8597
2Sa 1:19 The **b** of Israel is slain upon thy high H6643
14:25 Absalom for his **b**: from the sole of his H3303
1Ch 16:29 worship the LORD in the **b** of holiness. H1927
2Ch 3: 6 for **b**: and the gold *was* gold of Parvaim. H8597
20:21 should praise the **b** of holiness, as they H1927
Est 1:11 her **b**: for she *was* fair to look on. H3308
Job 40:10 and array thyself with glory and **b**. H1926
Ps 27: 4 life, to behold the **b** of the LORD, and H5278
29: 2 worship the LORD in the **b** of holiness. H1927
39:11 thou makest his **b** to consume away H2530
45:11 So shall the king greatly desire thy **b**: for H3308
49:14 and their **b** shall consume in the H6736
50: 2 Out of Zion, the perfection of **b**, God H3308
90:17 And let the **b** of the LORD our God be H5278
96: 6 strength and **b** *are* in his sanctuary. H8597
9 O worship the LORD in the **b** of H1927
Prv 6:25 Lust not after her **b** in thine heart; H3308
20:29 and the **b** of old men *is* the gray head. H1926
31:30 Favour *is* deceitful, and **b** *is* vain: *but* a H3308
Isa 3:24 of sackcloth; *and* burning instead of **b**. H3308
13:19 of kingdoms, the **b** of the Chaldees' H8597
28: 1 whose glorious **b** *is* a fading flower, H8597
4 And the glorious **b**, which *is* on the H8597
5 of **b**, unto the residue of his people, H8597
33:17 Thine eyes shall see the king in his **b**: H3308
44:13 according to the **b** of a man; that it H8597
53: 2 *there is* no **b** that we should desire him. H4758
61: 3 to give unto them **b** for ashes, the oil of H6287
Lam 1: 6 And from the daughter of Zion all her **b** H1926
2: 1 unto the earth the **b** of Israel, and H8597
15 of **b**, The joy of the whole earth? H3308
Ezk 7:20 As for the **b** of his ornament, he set it in H6643
16:14 the heathen for thy **b**: for it *was* perfect H3308
15 But thou didst trust in thine own **b**, and H3308
25 hast made thy **b** to be abhorred, and H3308
27: 3 Tyrus, thou hast said, I *am* of perfect **b**. H3308
4 seas, thy builders have perfected thy **b**. H3308
11 about; they have made thy **b** perfect. H3308
28: 7 against the **b** of thy wisdom, and H3308
12 sum, full of wisdom, and perfect in **b**. H3308
17 lifted up because of thy **b**, thou hast H3308
31: 8 of God was like unto him in his **b**. H3308
32:19 Whom dost thou pass in **b**? go down, H5276

Hos 14: 6 His branches shall spread, and his **b** H1935
Zec 9:17 how great *is* his **b**! corn shall make the H3308
11: 7 the one I called **B**, and the other I called H5278
10 And I took my staff, *even* **B**, and cut it H5278

BEBAI
Ezr 2:11 The children of **B**, six hundred twenty H893
8:11 And of the sons of **B**; Zechariah the son H893
11 **B**, and with him twenty and eight males. H893
10:28 Of the sons also of **B**; Jehohanan, H893
Neh 7:16 The children of **B**, six hundred twenty H893
10:15 Bunni, Azgad, **B**, H893

BECAME See the Appendix.

BECAMEST See the Appendix.

BECAUSE See the Appendix.

BECHER
Gen 46:21 *were* Belah, and **B**, and Ashbel, Gera, H1071
Nu 26:35 the Shuthalhites: of **B**, the family of the H1071
1Ch 7: 6 *The sons* of Benjamin; Bela, and **B**, and H1071
8 And the sons of **B**; Zemira, and Joash, H1071
8 Alameth. All these *are* the sons of **B**. H1071

BECHORATH
1Sa 9: 1 Zeror, the son of **B**, the son of Aphiah, a H1064

BECKONED
Lk 1:22 **b** unto them, and remained speechless. *G2258*
5: 7 And they **b** unto *their* partners, which *G2656*
Jn 13:24 Simon Peter therefore **b** to him, that he *G3506*
Act 19:33 And Alexander **b** with the hand, and *G2678*
21:40 on the stairs, and **b** with the hand unto *G2678*
24:10 the governor had **b** unto him to speak, *G3506*

BECKONING
Act 12:17 But he, **b** unto them with the hand to *G2678*
13:16 Then Paul stood up, and **b** with *his* *G2678*

BECOME See the Appendix.

BECOMETH See the Appendix.

BED
Gen 48: 2 himself, and sat upon the **b**. H4296
49: 4 up to thy father's **b**; then defiledst thou H4904
33 up his feet into the **b**, and yielded up the H4296
Ex 8: 3 and upon thy **b**, and into the house H4296
21:18 fist, and he die not, but keepeth *his* **b**: H4904
Lev 15: 4 Every **b**, whereon he lieth that hath the H4904
5 And whosoever toucheth his **b** shall H4904
21 And whosoever toucheth her **b** shall H4904
23 And if it *be* on *her* **b**, or on any thing H4904
24 the **b** whereon he lieth shall be unclean. H4904
26 Every **b** whereon she lieth all the days H4904
26 be unto her as the **b** of her separation: H4904
1Sa 19:13 and laid *it* in the **b**, and put a pillow of H4296
15 up to me in the **b**, that I may slay him. H4296
16 *was* an image in the **b**, with a pillow of H4296
28:23 from the earth, and sat upon the **b**. H4296
2Sa 4: 5 of Ish-bosheth, who lay on a **b** at noon. H4904
7 he lay on his **b** in his bedchamber, H4296
11 house upon his **b**? shall I not therefore H4904
11: 2 arose from off his **b**, and walked upon H4904
13 out to lie on his **b** with the servants of H4904
13: 5 thee down on thy **b**, and make thyself H4904
1Ki 1:47 And the king bowed himself upon the **b**. H4904
17:19 he abode, and laid him upon his own **b**. H4296
21: 4 down upon his **b**, and turned away his H4296
2Ki 1: 4 down from that **b** on which thou art H4296
6 down from that **b** on which thou art H4296
16 down off that **b** on which thou art gone H4296
4:10 set for him there a **b**, and a table, and a H4296
21 And she went up, and laid him on the **b** H4296
32 the child was dead, *and* laid upon his **b**. H4296
1Ch 5: 1 his father's **b**, his birthright was given H3326
2Ch 16:14 laid him in the **b** which was filled with H4904
24:25 and slew him on his **b**, and he died: and H4296
Est 7: 8 fallen upon the **b** whereon Esther *was*. H4296
Job 7:13 When I say, My **b** shall comfort me, my H6210
17:13 I have made my **b** in the darkness. H3326
33:15 upon men, in slumberings upon the **b**; H4904
19 pain upon his **b**, and the multitude of H4904
Ps 4: 4 heart upon your **b**, and be still. Selah. H4904
6: 6 night make I my **b** to swim; I water my H4296
36: 4 He deviseth mischief upon his **b**; he H4904
41: 3 him upon the **b** of languishing: thou H6210

Ps 41: 3 thou wilt make all his **b** in his sickness. H4904
63: 6 When I remember thee upon my **b**, *and* H3326
132: 3 my house, nor go up into my **b**; H6210+H3326
139: 8 my **b** in hell, behold, thou *art there.* H3331
Prv 7:16 I have decked my **b** with coverings of H6210
17 I have perfumed my **b** with myrrh, H4904
22:27 he take away thy **b** from under thee? H4904
26:14 hinges, so *doth* the slothful upon his **b**. H4296
Song 1:16 yea, pleasant: also our **b** *is* green. H6210
3: 1 By night on my **b** I sought him whom H4904
7 Behold his **b**, which *is* Solomon's; H4296
5:13 His cheeks *are* as a **b** of spices, *as* sweet H6170
Isa 28:20 For the **b** is shorter than that *a man* H4702
57: 7 hast thou set thy **b**: even thither wentest H4904
8 hast enlarged thy **b**, and made thee *a* H4904
8 lovedst their **b** where thou sawest *it*. H4904
Ezk 23:17 came to her into the **b** of love, and they H4904
41 And satest upon a stately **b**, and a table H4296
32:25 They have set her a **b** in the midst of H4904
Dan 2:28 of thy head upon thy **b**, are these; H4903
29 *mind* upon thy **b**, what should come to H4903
4: 5 thoughts upon my **b** and the visions of H4903
10 mine head in my **b**; I saw, and behold a H4903
13 of my head upon my **b**, and, behold, a H4903
7: 1 his head upon his **b**: then he wrote the H4903
Am 3:12 of a **b**, and in Damascus *in* a couch. H4296
Mt 9: 2 the palsy, lying on a **b**: and Jesus seeing G2825
6 take up thy **b**, and go unto thine house. G2825
Mk 2: 4 the **b** wherein the sick of the palsy lay. G2895
9 say, Arise, and take up thy **b**, and walk? G2895
11 thy **b**, and go thy way into thine house. G2895
12 he arose, took up the **b**, and went forth G2895
4:21 a **b**? and not to be set on a candlestick? G2825
7:30 out, and her daughter laid upon the **b**. G2825
Lk 5:18 And, behold, men brought in a **b** a man G2825
8:16 putteth *it* under a **b**; but setteth *it* on a G2825
11: 7 me in **b**; I cannot rise and give thee. G2845
17:34 be two *men* in one **b**; the one shall be G2825
Jn 5: 8 unto him, Rise, take up thy **b**, and walk. G2895
9 and took up his **b**, and walked: and on G2895
10 it is not lawful for thee to carry *thy* **b**. G2895
11 said unto me, Take up thy **b**, and walk. G2895
12 unto thee, Take up thy **b**, and walk? G2895
Act 9:33 **b** eight years, and was sick of the palsy. G2895
34 make thy **b**. And he arose immediately. G4766
Heb 13: 4 in all, and the **b** undefiled: but G2845
Rev 2:22 Behold, I will cast her into a **b**, and G2825

BEDAD
Gen 36:35 Hadad the son of **B**, who smote Midian H911
1Ch 1:46 Hadad the son of **B**, which smote Midian H911

BEDAN
1Sa 12:11 And the LORD sent Jerubbaal, and **B**, H917
1Ch 7:17 And the sons of Ulam; **B**. These *were* the H917

BEDCHAMBER
Ex 8: 3 and into thy **b**, and upon thy bed, and H4904
2Sa 4: 7 on his bed in his **b**, and they smote him, H4904
2Ki 6:12 the words that thou speakest in thy **b**. H4904
11: 2 his nurse, in the **b** from Athaliah, so H4296
2Ch 22:11 and his nurse in a **b**. So Jehoshabeath, H4296
Ecc 10:20 not the rich in thy **b**: for a bird of the air H4296

BEDEIAH
Ezr 10:35 Benaiah, **B**, Chelluh, H912

BEDS
2Sa 17:28 Brought **b**, and basons, and earthen H4904
Est 1: 6 of marble: the **b** *were of* gold and H4296
Ps 149: 5 glory: let them sing aloud upon their **b**. H4904
Song 6: 2 his garden, to the **b** of spices, to feed in H6170
Isa 57: 2 **b**, *each one* walking *in* his uprightness. H4904
Hos 7:14 howled upon their **b**: they assemble H4904
Am 6: 4 That lie upon **b** of ivory, and stretch H4296
Mic 2: 1 evil upon their **b**! when the morning is H4904
Mk 6:55 to carry about in **b** those that were sick, G2895
Act 5:15 and laid *them* on **b** and couches, that G2825

BED'S
Gen 47:31 Israel bowed himself upon the **b** head. H4296

BEDSTEAD
Dt 3:11 giants; behold, his **b** *was* a bedstead of H6210
11 his bedstead *was* a **b** of iron; *is* it not in H6210

BEE
Isa 7:18 for the **b** that *is* in the land of Assyria. H1682

BEELIADA
1Ch 14: 7 And Elishama, and **B**, and Eliphalet. H1182

BEELZEBUB
Mt 10:25 of the house **B**, how much more *shall* G954
12:24 devils, but by **B** the prince of the devils. G954
27 And if I by **B** cast out devils, by whom do G954
Mk 3:22 said, He hath **B**, and by the prince of G954
Lk 11:15 devils through **B** the chief of the devils. G954
18 ye say that I cast out devils through **B**. G954
19 And if I by **B** cast out devils, by whom do G954

BEEN See the Appendix.

BEER
Nu 21:16 And from thence *they went* to **B**: that *is* H876
Jdg 9:21 fled, and went to **B**, and dwelt there, for H876

BEERA
1Ch 7:37 and Shilshah, and Ithran, and **B**. H878

BEERAH
1Ch 5: 6 **B** his son, whom Tilgath-pilneser king of H880

BEER-ELIM
Isa 15: 8 Eglaim, and the howling thereof unto **B**. H879

BEERI
Gen 26:34 Judith the daughter of **B** the Hittite, and H882
Hos 1: 1 unto Hosea, the son of **B**, in the days of H882

BEER-LAHAI-ROI
Gen 16:14 Wherefore the well was called **B**; behold, H883

BEEROTH
Dt 10: 6 their journey from **B** of the children of H881
Jos 9:17 Chephirah, and **B**, and Kirjath-jearim. H881
18:25 Gibeon, and Ramah, and **B**, H881
2Sa 4: 2 (for **B** also was reckoned to Benjamin: H881
Ezr 2:25 **B**, seven hundred and forty and three. H881
Neh 7:29 and **B**, seven hundred forty and three. H881

BEEROTHITE
2Sa 4: 2 sons of Rimmon a **B**, of the children of H886
5 And the sons of Rimmon the **B**, Rechab H886
9 of Rimmon the **B**, and said unto them, H886
23:37 Zelek the Ammonite, Naharai the **B**, H886

BEEROTHITES
2Sa 4: 3 And the **B** fled to Gittaim, and were H886

BEERSHEBA
1Ki 4:25 Dan even to **B**, all the days of Solomon. H884

BEER-SHEBA
Gen 21:14 and wandered in the wilderness of **B**. H884
31 Wherefore he called that place **B**; H884
32 Thus they made a covenant at **B**: then H884
33 And *Abraham* planted a grove in **B**, and H884
22:19 to **B**; and Abraham dwelt at Beer-sheba. H884
19 to Beer-sheba; and Abraham dwelt at **B**. H884
26:23 And he went up from thence to **B**. H884
33 the name of the city *is* **B** unto this day. H884
28:10 And Jacob went out from **B**, and went H884
46: 1 he had, and came to **B**, and offered H884
5 And Jacob rose up from **B**: and the sons H884
Jos 15:28 And Hazar-shual, and **B**, and Bizjothjah, H884
19: 2 And they had in their inheritance **B**, or H884
Jdg 20: 1 from Dan even to **B**, with the land of H884
1Sa 3:20 And all Israel from Dan even to **B** knew H884
8: 2 his second, Abiah: *they were* judges in **B**. H884
2Sa 3:10 and over Judah, from Dan even to **B**. H884
17:11 from Dan even to **B**, as the sand that *is* H884
24: 2 from Dan even to **B**, and number ye the H884
7 went out to the south of Judah, *even* to **B**. H884
15 Dan even to **B** seventy thousand men. H884
1Ki 19: 3 life, and came to **B**, which *belongeth* to H884
2Ki 12: 1 And his mother's name *was* Zibiah of **B**. H884
23: 8 from Geba to **B**, and brake down the H884
1Ch 4:28 And they dwelt at **B**, and Moladah, and H884
21: 2 Israel from **B** even to Dan; and bring H884
2Ch 19: 4 the people from **B** to mount Ephraim, H884
24: 1 His mother's name also *was* Zibiah of **B**. H884
30: 5 all Israel, from **B** even to Dan, that they H884
Neh 11:27 And at Hazar-shual, and at **B**, and *in* the H884
30 dwelt from **B** unto the valley of Hinnom. H884
Am 5: 5 and pass not to **B**: for Gilgal shall surely H884
8:14 The manner of **B** liveth; even they shall H884

BEES
Dt 1:44 chased you, as **b** do, and destroyed you H1682
Jdg 14: 8 **b** and honey in the carcase of the lion. H1682
Ps 118:12 They compassed me about like **b**; they H1682

BEESH-TERAH
Jos 21:27 and **B** with her suburbs; two cities. H1203

BEETLE
Lev 11:22 his kind, and the **b** after his kind, and H2728

BEEVES
Lev 22:19 of the **b**, of the sheep, or of the goats. H1241
21 a freewill offering in **b** or sheep, it shall H1241
Nu 31:28 **b**, and of the asses, and of the sheep: H1241
30 the persons, of the **b**, of the asses, and H1241
33 And threescore and twelve thousand **b**, H1241
38 And the **b** *were* thirty and six H1241
44 And thirty and six thousand **b**, H1241

BEFALL
Gen 42: 4 Lest peradventure mischief **b** him. H7122
38 alone: if mischief **b** him by the way in H7122
44:29 me, and mischief **b** him, ye shall bring H7136
49: 1 *that* which shall **b** you in the last days. H7122
Dt 31:17 and troubles shall **b** them; so that they H4672
29 you; and evil will **b** you in the latter H7122
Ps 91:10 There shall no evil **b** thee, neither shall H579
Dan 10:14 what shall **b** thy people in the latter H7136
Act 20:22 the things that shall **b** me there: G4876

BEFALLEN
Lev 10:19 and such things have **b** me: and *if* I had H7122
Nu 20:14 knowest all the travail that hath **b** us: H4672
Dt 31:21 and troubles are **b** them, that this song H4672
Jdg 6:13 then is all this **b** us? and where *be* all H4672
1Sa 20:26 Something hath **b** him, he *is* not clean; H4745
Est 6:13 *thing* that had **b** him. Then said his H7136
Mt 8:33 was **b** to the possessed of the devils. G4876

BEFALLETH
Ecc 3:19 For that which **b** the sons of men H4745
19 the sons of men **b** beasts; even one H4745
19 even one thing **b** them: as the one H4745

BEFELL
Gen 42:29 told him all that **b** unto them; saying, H7136
Jos 2:23 and told him all *things* that **b** them: H4672
2Sa 19: 7 that **b** thee from thy youth until now. H935
Mk 5:16 And they that saw *it* told them how it **b** G1096
Act 20:19 **b** me by the lying in wait of the Jews: G4819

BEFORE See the Appendix.

BEFOREHAND
Mk 13:11 take no thought **b** what ye shall speak, G4305
2Co 9: 5 unto you, and make up **b** your bounty, G4294
1Ti 5:24 Some men's sins are open **b**, going G4271
25 *some* are manifest **b**; and they that are G4271
1Pt 1:11 when it testified **b** the sufferings of G4303

BEFORETIME
Dt 2:12 The Horims also dwelt in Seir **b**; but the H6440
Jos 11:10 **b** was the head of all those kingdoms. H6440
20: 5 and hated him not **b**. H8543+H8032
1Sa 9: 9 (**B** in Israel, when a man went to inquire H6440
9 *called* a Prophet was **b** called a Seer.) H6440
10:11 all that knew him **b** saw that, H865+H8032
2Sa 7:10 wickedness afflict them any more, as **b**, H7223
2Ki 13: 5 Israel dwelt in their tents, as **b**. H8032+H8543
Neh 2: 1 I had not been *b* sad in his presence.
Isa 41:26 may know? and **b**, that we may say, *He* H6440
Act 8: 9 Simon, which **b** in the same city used G4391

BEG
Ps 109:10 vagabonds, and **b**: let them seek *their* H7592
Prv 20: 4 shall he **b** in harvest, and H7592+H7592
Lk 16: 3 I cannot dig; to **b** I am ashamed. G1871

BEGAN
Gen 4:26 name Enos; then **b** men to call upon H2490
6: 1 And it came to pass, when men **b** to H2490
9:20 And Noah **b** *to be* an husbandman, H2490
10: 8 And Cush begat Nimrod: he **b** to be a H2490
41:54 And the seven years of dearth **b** to H2490
44:12 And he searched, *and* **b** at the eldest, H2490
Nu 25: 1 and the people **b** to commit whoredom H2490
Dt 1: 5 **b** Moses to declare this law, saying, H2974
Jdg 13:25 And the spirit of the LORD **b** to move H2490

Jdg 16:19 his head; and she **b** to afflict him, and H2490
22 Howbeit the hair of his head **b** to grow H2490
19:25 when the day **b** to spring, they let her go.
20:31 from the city; and they **b** to smite of the H2490
39 battle, Benjamin **b** to smite *and* kill of H2490
40 But when the flame **b** to arise up out of H2490
1Sa 3: 2 **b** to wax dim, *that* he could not see; H2490
2Sa 2:10 years old when he **b** to reign over Israel,
5: 4 David *was* thirty years old when he **b** to
1Ki 6: 1 that he **b** to build the house of the LORD.
14:21 one years old when he **b** to reign, and he
15:25 And Nadab the son of Jeroboam **b** to
33 In the third year of Asa king of Judah **b**
16: 8 of Asa king of Judah **b** Elah the son of
11 And it came to pass, when he **b** to reign,
23 Asa king of Judah **b** Omri to reign over
29 of Asa king of Judah **b** Ahab the son of
22:41 And Jehoshaphat the son of Asa **b** to
42 five years old when he **b** to reign; and he
51 Ahaziah the son of Ahab **b** to reign over
2Ki 3: 1 Now Jehoram the son of Ahab **b** to reign
8:16 of Jehoshaphat king of Judah **b** to reign.
17 old was he when he **b** to reign; and he
26 *was* Ahaziah when he **b** to reign; and he
9:29 of Ahab **b** Ahaziah to reign over Judah.
10:32 In those days the LORD **b** to cut Israel H2490
11:21 Seven years old *was* Jehoash when he **b**
12: 1 In the seventh year of Jehu Jehoash **b** to
13: 1 the son of Jehu **b** to reign over Israel in
10 Joash king of Judah **b** Jehoash the son of
14: 2 five years old when he **b** to reign, and
23 king of Israel **b** to reign in Samaria,
15: 1 king of Israel **b** Azariah son of Amaziah
2 Sixteen years old was he when he **b** to
13 Shallum the son of Jabesh **b** to reign in
17 king of Judah **b** Menahem the son of
23 son of Menahem **b** to reign over Israel in
27 son of Remaliah **b** to reign over Israel in
32 king of Israel **b** Jotham the son of Uzziah
33 old was he when he **b** to reign, and he
37 In those days the LORD **b** to send H2490
16: 1 son of Jotham king of Judah **b** to reign.
2 Twenty years old *was* Ahaz when he **b** to
17: 1 Ahaz king of Judah **b** Ho-shea the son of
18: 1 the son of Ahaz king of Judah **b** to reign.
2 old was he when he **b** to reign; and he
21: 1 twelve years old when he **b** to reign, and
19 two years old when he **b** to reign, and he
22: 1 Josiah *was* eight years old when he **b** to
23:31 years old when he **b** to reign; and he
36 five years old when he **b** to reign; and he
24: 8 years old when he **b** to reign, and he
18 one years old when he **b** to reign, and he
25:27 in the year that he **b** to reign did lift up
1Ch 1:10 And Cush begat Nimrod: he **b** to be H2490
27:24 Joab the son of Zeruiah **b** to number, H2490
2Ch 3: 1 Then Solomon **b** to build the house of H2490
2 And he **b** to build in the second *day* of H2490
12:13 years old when he **b** to reign, and he
13: 1 Jeroboam **b** Abijah to reign over Judah.
20:22 And when they **b** to sing and to praise, H2490
31 five years old when he **b** to reign, and he
21: 5 two years old when he **b** to reign, and he
20 old was he when he **b** to reign, and he
22: 2 *was* Ahaziah when he **b** to reign, and he
24: 1 Joash *was* seven years old when he **b** to
25: 1 five years old *when* he **b** to reign, and he
26: 3 Sixteen years old *was* Uzziah when he **b**
27: 1 five years old when he **b** to reign, and he
8 twenty years old when he **b** to reign, and
28: 1 Ahaz *was* twenty years old when he **b** to
29: 1 Hezekiah **b** to reign *when he was* five
17 Now they **b** on the first *day* of the first H2490
27 the burnt offering **b**, the song of the H2490
27 the song of the LORD **b** *also* with the H2490
31: 7 In the third month they **b** to lay the H2490
10 said, Since *the people* **b** to bring the H2490
21 And in every work that he **b** in the H2490
33: 1 years old when he **b** to reign, and he
21 twenty years old when he **b** to reign, and
34: 1 Josiah *was* eight years old when he **b** to
3 he was yet young, he **b** to seek after the H2490
3 in the twelfth year he **b** to purge Judah H2490
36: 2 years old when he **b** to reign, and he
5 five years old when he **b** to reign, and he
9 years old when he **b** to reign, and he
11 twenty years old when he **b** to reign, and
Ezr 3: 6 the seventh month **b** they to offer burnt H2490
8 in the second month, **b** Zerubbabel the H2490
Ezr 5: 2 of Jozadak, and **b** to build the house of H8271
7: 9 of the first month **b** he to go up from H3246
Neh 4: 7 that the breaches **b** to be stopped, then H2490
13:19 gates of Jerusalem **b** to be dark before
Jer 52: 1 years old when he **b** to reign, and he
Ezk 9: 6 Then they **b** at the ancient men H2490
Jna 3: 4 And Jonah **b** to enter into the city a H2490
Mt 4:17 From that time Jesus **b** to preach, and to *G756*
11: 7 And as they departed, Jesus **b** to say *G756*
20 Then **b** he to upbraid the cities wherein *G756*
12: 1 **b** to pluck the ears of corn, and to eat. *G756*
16:21 From that time forth **b** Jesus to shew *G756*
22 Then Peter took him, and **b** to rebuke *G756*
26:22 sorrowful, and **b** every one of them to *G756*
37 and **b** to be sorrowful and very heavy. *G756*
74 Then **b** he to curse and to swear, *saying*, *G756*
28: 1 In the end of the sabbath, as it **b** to *G2020*
Mk 1:45 But he went out, and **b** to publish *it* *G756*
2:23 **b**, as they went, to pluck the ears of corn. *G756*
4: 1 And he **b** again to teach by the sea side: *G756*
5:17 And they **b** to pray him to depart out of *G756*
20 And he departed, and **b** to publish in *G756*
6: 2 day was come, he **b** to teach in the *G756*
7 And he called *unto him* the twelve, and **b** *G756*
34 and he **b** to teach them many things. *G756*
55 round about, and **b** to carry about in *G756*
8:11 And the Pharisees came forth, and **b** to *G756*
31 And he **b** to teach them, that the Son of *G756*
32 Peter took him, and **b** to rebuke him. *G756*
10:28 Then Peter **b** to say unto him, Lo, we *G756*
32 again the twelve, and **b** to tell them what *G756*
41 And when the ten heard *it*, they **b** to be *G756*
47 of Nazareth, he **b** to cry out, and say, *G756*
11:15 the temple, and **b** to cast out them that *G756*
12: 1 And he **b** to speak unto them by *G756*
13: 5 And Jesus answering them **b** to say, *G756*
14:19 And they **b** to be sorrowful, and to say *G756*
33 and John, and **b** to be sore amazed, and *G756*
65 And some **b** to spit on him, and to cover *G756*
69 And a maid saw him again, and **b** to say *G756*
71 But he **b** to curse and to swear, *saying*, I *G756*
15: 8 And the multitude crying aloud **b** to *G756*
18 And **b** to salute him, Hail, King of the *G756*
Lk 1:70 which have been since the world **b**:
3:23 And Jesus himself **b** to be about thirty *G756*
4:21 And he **b** to say unto them, This day is *G756*
5: 7 both the ships, so that they **b** to sink.
21 And the scribes and the Pharisees **b** to *G756*
7:15 And he that was dead sat up, and **b** to *G756*
24 were departed, he **b** to speak unto the *G756*
38 *him* weeping, and **b** to wash his feet with *G756*
49 And they that sat at meat with him **b** to *G756*
9:12 And when the day **b** to wear away, then *G756*
11:29 thick together, he **b** to say, This is an evil *G756*
53 scribes and the Pharisees **b** to urge *him* *G756*
12: 1 one upon another, he **b** to say unto his *G756*
14:18 And they all with one *consent* **b** to make *G756*
30 Saying, This man **b** to build, and was *G756*
15:14 in that land; and he **b** to be in want. *G756*
24 and is found. And they **b** to be merry. *G756*
19:37 of the disciples **b** to rejoice and praise *G756*
45 And he went into the temple, and **b** to *G756*
20: 9 Then **b** he to speak to the people this *G756*
22:23 And they **b** to enquire among *G756*
23: 2 And they **b** to accuse him, saying, We *G756*
Jn 4:52 the hour when he **b** to amend. And they *G2192*
9:32 Since the world **b** was it not heard that
13: 5 water into a bason, and **b** to wash the *G756*
Act 1: 1 of all that Jesus **b** both to do and teach, *G756*
2: 4 Holy Ghost, and **b** to speak with other *G756*
3:21 of all his holy prophets since the world **b**.
8:35 Then Philip opened his mouth, and **b** at *G756*
10:37 all Judaea, and **b** from Galilee, after the *G756*
11:15 And as I **b** to speak, the Holy Ghost fell *G756*
18:26 And he **b** to speak boldly in the *G756*
24: 2 forth, Tertullus **b** to accuse *him*, saying, *G756*
27:35 and when he had broken *it*, he **b** to eat. *G756*
Ro 16:25 which was kept secret since the world **b**,
2Ti 1: 9 us in Christ Jesus before the world **b**,
Tit 1: 2 cannot lie, promised before the world **b**;
Heb 2: 3 which at the first **b** to be spoken by the *G2983*

BEGAT

Gen 4:18 born Irad: and Irad **b** Mehujael: and H3205
18 and Mehujael **b** Methusael: and H3205
18 Methusael: and Methusael **b** Lamech. H3205
5: 3 thirty years, and **b** *a son* in his own H3205
4 years: and he **b** sons and daughters: H3205
6 an hundred and five years, and **b** Enos: H3205
Gen 5: 7 And Seth lived after he **b** Enos eight H3205
7 seven years, and **b** sons and daughters: H3205
9 And Enos lived ninety years, and **b** H3205
10 And Enos lived after he **b** Cainan eight H3205
10 years, and **b** sons and daughters: H3205
12 And Cainan lived seventy years, and **b** H3205
13 And Cainan lived after he **b** Mahalaleel H3205
13 forty years, and **b** sons and daughters: H3205
15 lived sixty and five years, and **b** Jared: H3205
16 And Mahalaleel lived after he **b** Jared H3205
16 thirty years, and **b** sons and daughters: H3205
18 sixty and two years, and he **b** Enoch: H3205
19 And Jared lived after he **b** Enoch eight H3205
19 years, and **b** sons and daughters: H3205
21 sixty and five years, and **b** Methuselah: H3205
22 And Enoch walked with God after he **b** H3205
22 years, and **b** sons and daughters: H3205
25 eighty and seven years, and **b** Lamech: H3205
26 And Methuselah lived after he **b** H3205
26 two years, and **b** sons and daughters: H3205
28 eighty and two years, and **b** a son: H3205
30 And Lamech lived after he **b** Noah five H3205
30 five years, and **b** sons and daughters: H3205
32 and Noah **b** Shem, Ham, and Japheth. H3205
6:10 And Noah **b** three sons, Shem, Ham, H3205
10: 8 And Cush **b** Nimrod: he began to be a H3205
13 And Mizraim **b** Ludim, and Anamim, H3205
15 And Canaan **b** Sidon his firstborn, and H3205
24 And Arphaxad **b** Salah; and Salah H3205
24 begat Salah; and Salah **b** Eber. H3205
26 And Joktan **b** Almodad, and Sheleph, H3205
11:10 **b** Arphaxad two years after the flood: H3205
11 And Shem lived after he **b** Arphaxad H3205
11 years, and **b** sons and daughters. H3205
12 lived five and thirty years, and **b** Salah: H3205
13 And Arphaxad lived after he **b** Salah H3205
13 three years, and **b** sons and daughters. H3205
14 And Salah lived thirty years, and **b** H3205
15 And Salah lived after he **b** Eber four H3205
15 three years, and **b** sons and daughters. H3205
16 lived four and thirty years, and **b** Peleg: H3205
17 And Eber lived after he **b** Peleg four H3205
17 thirty years, and **b** sons and daughters. H3205
18 And Peleg lived thirty years, and **b** Reu: H3205
19 And Peleg lived after he **b** Reu two H3205
19 nine years, and **b** sons and daughters. H3205
20 lived two and thirty years, and **b** Serug: H3205
21 And Reu lived after he **b** Serug two H3205
21 seven years, and **b** sons and daughters. H3205
22 And Serug lived thirty years, and **b** H3205
23 And Serug lived after he **b** Nahor two H3205
23 years, and **b** sons and daughters. H3205
24 nine and twenty years, and **b** Terah: H3205
25 And Nahor lived after he **b** Terah an H3205
25 years, and **b** sons and daughters. H3205
26 And Terah lived seventy years, and **b** H3205
27 of Terah: Terah **b** Abram, Nahor, and H3205
27 Nahor, and Haran; and Haran **b** Lot. H3205
22:23 And Bethuel **b** Rebekah: these eight H3205
25: 3 And Jokshan **b** Sheba, and Dedan. And H3205
19 Abraham's son: Abraham **b** Isaac: H3205
Lev 25:45 you, which they **b** in your land: and H3205
Nu 26:29 and Machir **b** Gilead: of Gilead *come* H3205
58 the Korathites. And Kohath **b** Amram. H3205
Dt 32:18 Of the Rock *that* **b** thee thou art H3205
Jdg 11: 1 of an harlot: and Gilead **b** Jephthah. H3205
Ru 4:18 of Pharez: Pharez **b** Hezron, H3205
19 And Hezron **b** Ram, and Ram begat H3205
19 And Hezron begat Ram, and Ram **b** H3205
20 And Amminadab **b** Nahshon, and H3205
20 Nahshon, and Nahshon **b** Salmon, H3205
21 And Salmon **b** Boaz, and Boaz begat H3205
21 And Salmon begat Boaz, and Boaz **b** H3205
22 And Obed **b** Jesse, and Jesse begat H3205
22 And Obed begat Jesse, and Jesse **b** H3205
1Ch 1:10 And Cush **b** Nimrod: he began to be H3205
11 And Mizraim **b** Ludim, and Anamim, H3205
13 And Canaan **b** Zidon his firstborn, and H3205
18 And Arphaxad **b** Shelah, and Shelah H3205
18 begat Shelah, and Shelah **b** Eber. H3205
20 And Joktan **b** Almodad, and Sheleph, H3205
34 And Abraham **b** Isaac. The sons of H3205
2:10 And Ram **b** Amminadab; and H3205
10 and Amminadab **b** Nahshon, prince of H3205
11 And Nahshon **b** Salma, and Salma H3205
11 begat Salma, and Salma **b** Boaz, H3205
12 And Boaz **b** Obed, and Obed begat H3205
12 And Boaz begat Obed, and Obed **b** H3205
13 And Jesse **b** his firstborn Eliab, and H3205

1Ch 2:18 And Caleb the son of Hezron **b** *children* H3205
20 And Hur **b** Uri, and Uri begat Bezaleel. H3205
20 And Hur begat Uri, and Uri **b** Bezaleel. H3205
22 And Segub **b** Jair, who had three and H3205
36 And Attai **b** Nathan, and Nathan begat H3205
36 And Attai begat Nathan, and Nathan **b** H3205
37 And Zabad **b** Ephlal, and Ephlal begat H3205
37 And Zabad begat Ephlal, and Ephlal **b** H3205
38 And Obed **b** Jehu, and Jehu begat H3205
38 And Obed begat Jehu, and Jehu **b** H3205
39 And Azariah **b** Helez, and Helez begat H3205
39 And Azariah begat Helez, and Helez **b** H3205
40 And Eleasah **b** Sisamai, and Sisamai H3205
40 begat Sisamai, and Sisamai **b** Shallum, H3205
41 And Shallum **b** Jekamiah, and H3205
41 Jekamiah, and Jekamiah **b** Elishama. H3205
44 And Shema **b** Raham, the father of H3205
44 of Jorkoam: and Rekem **b** Shammai. H3205
46 Moza, and Gazez: and Haran **b** Gazez. H3205
4: 2 And Reaiah the son of Shobal **b** Jahath; H3205
2 and Jahath **b** Ahumai, and Lahad. H3205
8 And Coz **b** Anub, and Zobebah, and H3205
11 And Chelub the brother of Shuah **b** H3205
12 And Eshton **b** Beth-rapha, and Paseah, H3205
14 And Meonothai **b** Ophrah: and Seraiah H3205
14 and Seraiah **b** Joab, the father of the H3205
6: 4 Eleazar **b** Phinehas, Phinehas begat H3205
4 Eleazar begat Phinehas, Phinehas **b** H3205
5 And Abishua **b** Bukki, and Bukki begat H3205
5 And Abishua begat Bukki, and Bukki **b** H3205
6 And Uzzi **b** Zerahiah, and Zerahiah H3205
6 Zerahiah, and Zerahiah **b** Meraioth, H3205
7 Meraioth **b** Amariah, and Amariah H3205
7 Amariah, and Amariah **b** Ahitub, H3205
8 And Ahitub **b** Zadok, and Zadok begat H3205
8 And Ahitub begat Zadok, and Zadok **b** H3205
9 And Ahimaaz **b** Azariah, and Azariah H3205
9 begat Azariah, and Azariah **b** Johanan, H3205
10 And Johanan **b** Azariah, (he *it is* that H3205
11 And Azariah **b** Amariah, and Amariah H3205
11 Amariah, and Amariah **b** Ahitub, H3205
12 And Ahitub **b** Zadok, and Zadok begat H3205
12 And Ahitub begat Zadok, and Zadok **b** H3205
13 And Shallum **b** Hilkiah, and Hilkiah H3205
13 begat Hilkiah, and Hilkiah **b** Azariah, H3205
14 And Azariah **b** Seraiah, and Seraiah H3205
14 Seraiah, and Seraiah **b** Jehozadak, H3205
7:32 And Heber **b** Japhlet, and Shomer, and H3205
8: 1 Now Benjamin **b** Bela his firstborn, H3205
7 them, and **b** Uzza, and Ahihud. H3205
8 And Shaharaim **b** *children* in the H3205
9 And he **b** of Hodesh his wife, Jobab, H3205
11 And of Hushim he **b** Abitub, and H3205
32 And Mikloth **b** Shimeah. And these H3205
33 And Ner **b** Kish, and Kish begat Saul, H3205
33 And Ner begat Kish, and Kish **b** Saul, H3205
33 begat Saul, and Saul **b** Jonathan, and H3205
34 Merib-baal; and Merib-baal **b** Micah. H3205
36 And Ahaz **b** Jehoadah; and Jehoadah H3205
36 and Jehoadah **b** Alemeth, and H3205
36 and Zimri; and Zimri **b** Moza, H3205
37 And Moza **b** Binea: Rapha *was* his son, H3205
9:38 And Mikloth **b** Shimeam. And they H3205
39 And Ner **b** Kish; and Kish begat Saul; H3205
39 And Ner begat Kish; and Kish **b** Saul; H3205
39 begat Saul; and Saul **b** Jonathan, and H3205
40 Merib-baal: and Meribbaal **b** Micah. H3205
42 And Ahaz **b** Jarah; and Jarah begat H3205
42 And Ahaz begat Jarah; and Jarah **b** H3205
42 and Zimri; and Zimri **b** Moza; H3205
43 And Moza **b** Binea; and Rephaiah his H3205
14: 3 and David **b** more sons and daughters. H3205
2Ch 11:21 concubines; and **b** twenty and eight H3205
13:21 wives, and **b** twenty and two sons, H3205
24: 3 wives; and he **b** sons and daughters. H3205
Neh 12:10 And Jeshua **b** Joiakim, Joiakim also H3205
10 **b** Eliashib, and Eliashib begat Joiada, H3205
10 begat Eliashib, and Eliashib **b** Joiada, H3205
11 And Joiada **b** Jonathan, and Jonathan H3205
11 Jonathan, and Jonathan **b** Jaddua. H3205
Prv 23:22 Hearken unto thy father that **b** thee, H3205
Jer 16: 3 their fathers that **b** them in this land; H3205
Dan 11: 6 her, and he that **b** her, and he that H3205
Zec 13: 3 his mother that **b** him shall say unto H3205
3 his mother that **b** him shall thrust him H3205
Mt 1: 2 Abraham **b** Isaac; and Isaac begat *G1080*
2 Abraham begat Isaac; and Isaac **b** *G1080*
2 and Jacob **b** Judas and his brethren; *G1080*
3 And Judas **b** Phares and Zara of *G1080*

Mt 1: 3 **b** Esrom; and Esrom begat Aram; *G1080*
3 begat Esrom; and Esrom **b** Aram; *G1080*
4 And Aram **b** Aminadab; and *G1080*
4 and Aminadab **b** Naasson; and *G1080*
4 Naasson; and Naasson **b** Salmon; *G1080*
5 And Salmon **b** Booz of Rachab; and *G1080*
5 **b** Obed of Ruth; and Obed begat Jesse; *G1080*
5 begat Obed of Ruth; and Obed **b** Jesse; *G1080*
6 And Jesse **b** David the king; and David *G1080*
6 David the king **b** Solomon of her *that* *G1080*
7 And Solomon **b** Roboam; and Roboam *G1080*
7 Roboam **b** Abia; and Abia begat Asa; *G1080*
7 Roboam begat Abia; and Abia **b** Asa; *G1080*
8 And Asa **b** Josaphat; and Josaphat *G1080*
8 **b** Joram; and Joram begat Ozias; *G1080*
8 begat Joram; and Joram **b** Ozias; *G1080*
9 And Ozias **b** Joatham; and Joatham *G1080*
9 **b** Achaz; and Achaz begat Ezekias; *G1080*
9 begat Achaz; and Achaz **b** Ezekias; *G1080*
10 And Ezekias **b** Manasses; and *G1080*
10 **b** Amon; and Amon begat Josias; *G1080*
10 begat Amon; and Amon **b** Josias; *G1080*
11 And Josias **b** Jechonias and his *G1080*
12 Jechonias **b** Salathiel; and Salathiel *G1080*
12 Salathiel; and Salathiel **b** Zorobabel; *G1080*
13 And Zorobabel **b** Abiud; and Abiud *G1080*
13 **b** Eliakim; and Eliakim begat Azor; *G1080*
13 begat Eliakim; and Eliakim **b** Azor; *G1080*
14 And Azor **b** Sadoc; and Sadoc begat *G1080*
14 And Azor begat Sadoc; and Sadoc **b** *G1080*
14 begat Achim; and Achim **b** Eliud; *G1080*
15 And Eliud **b** Eleazar; and Eleazar begat *G1080*
15 And Eliud begat Eleazar; and Eleazar **b** *G1080*
15 begat Matthan; and Matthan **b** Jacob; *G1080*
16 And Jacob **b** Joseph the husband of *G1080*
Act 7: 8 and so *Abraham* **b** Isaac, and *G1080*
8 day; and Isaac ***b*** Jacob; and Jacob *begat*
8 Jacob; and Jacob ***b*** the twelve patriarchs.
29 land of Madian, where he **b** two sons. *G1080*
Jas 1:18 Of his own will **b** he us with the word of *G616*
1Jn 5: 1 loveth him that **b** loveth him also that *G1080*

BEGET
Gen 17:20 **b**, and I will make him a great nation. H3205
Dt 4:25 When thou shalt **b** children, and H3205
28:41 Thou shalt **b** sons and daughters, but H3205
2Ki 20:18 thee, which thou shalt **b**, shall they take H3205
Ecc 6: 3 If a man **b** an hundred *children*, and H3205
Isa 39: 7 thee, which thou shalt **b**, shall they take H3205
Jer 29: 6 Take ye wives, and **b** sons and H3205
Ezk 18:10 If he **b** a son *that is* a robber, a shedder H3205
14 Now, lo, *if* he **b** a son, that seeth all his H3205
47:22 you, which shall **b** children among you: H3205

BEGETTEST
Gen 48: 6 And thy issue, which thou **b** after them, H3205
Isa 45:10 unto *his* father, What **b** thou? or to the H3205

BEGETTETH
Prv 17:21 He that **b** a fool *doeth it* to his sorrow: H3205
23:24 **b** a wise *child* shall have joy of him. H3205
Ecc 5:14 evil travail: and he **b** a son, and *there is* H3205

BEGGAR
1Sa 2: 8 *and* lifteth up the **b** from the dunghill, to H34
Lk 16:20 And there was a certain **b** named *G4434*
22 And it came to pass, that the **b** died, *G4434*

BEGGARLY
Gal 4: 9 to the weak and **b** elements, whereunto *G4434*

BEGGED
Mt 27:58 He went to Pilate, and **b** the body of *G154*
Lk 23:52 This *man* went unto Pilate, and **b** the *G154*
Jn 9: 8 blind, said, Is not this he that sat and **b**? *G4319*

BEGGING
Ps 37:25 forsaken, nor his seed **b** bread. H1245
Mk 10:46 of Timaeus, sat by the highway side **b**. *G4319*
Lk 18:35 certain blind man sat by the way side **b**: *G4319*

BEGIN
Gen 11: 6 and this they **b** to do: and now nothing H2490
Dt 2:24 and his land: **b** to possess *it*, and H2490
25 This day will I **b** to put the dread of H2490
31 his land before thee: **b** to possess, that H2490
16: 9 unto thee: **b** to number the seven H2490
Jos 3: 7 This day will I **b** to magnify thee in the H2490
Jdg 10:18 man *is he* that will **b** to fight against H2490

Jdg 13: 5 and he shall **b** to deliver Israel out H2490
1Sa 3:12 when I **b**, I will also make an end. H2490
22:15 Did I then **b** to inquire of God for him? H2490
2Ki 8:25 son of Jehoram king of Judah **b** to reign.
Neh 11:17 the principal to **b** the thanksgiving in H8462
Jer 25:29 For, lo, I **b** to bring evil on the city H2490
Ezk 9: 6 *is* the mark; and **b** at my sanctuary. H2490
Mt 24:49 And shall **b** to smite *his* fellowservants, *G756*
Lk 3: 8 of repentance, and **b** not to say within *G756*
12:45 his coming; and shall **b** to beat the *G756*
13:25 to the door, and ye **b** to stand without, *G756*
26 Then shall ye **b** to say, We have eaten *G756*
14: 9 **b** with shame to take the lowest room. *G756*
29 *it*, all that behold *it* **b** to mock him, *G756*
21:28 And when these things **b** to come to *G756*
23:30 Then shall they **b** to say to the *G756*
2Co 3: 1 Do we **b** again to commend ourselves? or *G756*
1Pt 4:17 judgment must **b** at the house of God: *G756*
17 God: and if *it* first ***b*** at us, what shall the
Rev 10: 7 when he shall **b** to sound, the mystery *G3195*

BEGINNEST
Dt 16: 9 *as* thou **b** *to put* the sickle to the corn. H2490

BEGINNING
Gen 1: 1 In the **b** God created the heaven and H7225
10:10 And the **b** of his kingdom was Babel, H7225
13: 3 been at the **b**, between Beth-el and Hai; H8462
41:21 still ill favoured, as at the **b**. So I awoke. H8462
49: 3 my might, and the **b** of my strength, H7225
Ex 12: 2 This month *shall be* unto you the **b** of H7218
Dt 11:12 upon it, from the **b** of the year even H7225
21:17 hath: for he *is* the **b** of his strength; the H7225
32:42 the **b** of revenges upon the enemy. H7218
Jdg 7:19 of the camp in the **b** of the middle H7218
Ru 1:22 Beth-lehem in the **b** of barley harvest. H8462
3:10 end than at the **b**, inasmuch as thou H7223
2Sa 21: 9 first *days*, in the **b** of barley harvest. H8462
10 the rock, from the **b** of harvest until H8462
2Ki 17:25 And *so* it was at the **b** of their dwelling H8462
1Ch 17: 9 waste them any more, as at the **b**, H7223
Ezr 4: 6 And in the reign of Ahasuerus, in the **b** H8462
Job 8: 7 Though thy **b** was small, yet thy latter H7225
42:12 Job more than his **b**: for he had fourteen H7225
Ps 111:10 The fear of the LORD *is* the **b** of H7225
119:160 Thy word *is* true *from* the **b**: and every H7218
Prv 1: 7 The fear of the LORD *is* the **b** of H7225
8:22 The LORD possessed me in the **b** of his H7225
23 from the **b**, or ever the earth was. H7218
9:10 The fear of the LORD *is* the **b** of H8462
17:14 The **b** of strife *is as* when one letteth H7225
20:21 hastily at the **b**; but the end thereof H7223
Ecc 3:11 that God maketh from the **b** to the end. H7218
7: 8 Better *is* the end of a thing than the **b** H7225
10:13 The **b** of the words of his mouth *is* H8462
Isa 1:26 as at the **b**: afterward thou shalt H8462
18: 2 terrible from their **b** hitherto; a nation H1931
7 terrible from their **b** hitherto; a nation H1931
40:21 been told you from the **b**? have ye not H7218
41: 4 from the **b**? I the LORD, the first, H7218
26 Who hath declared from the **b**, that we H7218
46:10 Declaring the end from the **b**, and from H7225
48: 3 things from the **b**; and they went forth H227
5 I have even from the **b** declared *it* to H227
7 and not from the **b**; even before the day H227
16 in secret from the **b**; from the time that H7218
64: 4 For since the **b** of the world *men* have H5769
Jer 17:12 A glorious high throne from the **b** *is* the H7223
26: 1 In the **b** of the reign of Jehoiakim the H7225
27: 1 In the **b** of the reign of Jehoiakim the H7225
28: 1 the same year, in the **b** of the reign of H7225
49:34 Elam in the **b** of the reign of Zedekiah H7225
Lam 2:19 Arise, cry out in the night: in the **b** of H7218
Ezk 40: 1 our captivity, in the **b** of the year, in the H7218
Dan 9:21 in the vision at the **b**, being caused to H8462
23 At the **b** of thy supplications the H8462
Hos 1: 2 The **b** of the word of the LORD by H8462
Am 7: 1 in the **b** of the shooting up of H8462
Mic 1:13 swift beast: she *is* the **b** of the sin to the H7225
Mt 14:30 he was afraid; and **b** to sink, he cried, *G756*
19: 4 at the **b** made them male and female, *G746*
8 your wives: but from the **b** it was not so. *G746*
20: 8 *their* hire, **b** from the last unto the first. *G756*
24: 8 All these *are* the **b** of sorrows. *G746*
21 was not since the **b** of the world to this *G746*
Mk 1: 1 The **b** of the gospel of Jesus Christ, the *G746*
10: 6 But from the **b** of the creation God made *G746*
13:19 was not from the **b** of the creation which *G746*
Lk 1: 2 us, which from the **b** were eyewitnesses, *G746*

Lk 23: 5 all Jewry, **b** from Galilee to this place. *G756*
24:27 And **b** at Moses and all the prophets, he *G756*
47 name among all nations, **b** at Jerusalem. *G756*
Jn 1: 1 In the **b** was the Word, and the Word *G746*
2 The same was in the **b** with God. *G746*
2:10 Every man at the **b** doth set forth good *G4412*
11 This **b** of miracles did Jesus in Cana of *G746*
6:64 knew from the **b** who they were that *G746*
8: 9 out one by one, **b** at the eldest, *even* unto *G756*
25 *the same* that I said unto you from the **b**. *G746*
44 a murderer from the **b**, and abode not in *G746*
15:27 ye have been with me from the **b**. *G746*
16: 4 you at the **b**, because I was with you. *G746*
Act 1:22 **B** from the baptism of John, unto that *G756*
11: 4 *matter* from the **b**, and expounded *it* by *G756*
15 Ghost fell on them, as on us at the **b**. *G746*
15:18 are all his works from the **b** of the world. *G165*
26: 5 Which knew me from the **b**, if they would *G509*
Eph 3: 9 which from the **b** of the world hath been *G165*
Php 4:15 also, that in the **b** of the gospel, when I *G746*
Col 1:18 church: who is the **b**, the firstborn from *G746*
2Th 2:13 God hath from the **b** chosen you to *G746*
Heb 1:10 And, Thou, Lord, in the **b** hast laid the *G746*
3:14 Christ, if we hold the **b** of our confidence *G746*
7: 3 having neither **b** of days, nor end of life; *G746*
2Pt 2:20 end is worse with them than the **b**. *G4413*
3: 4 as *they were* from the **b** of the creation. *G746*
1Jn 1: 1 That which was from the **b**, which we *G746*
2: 7 which ye had from the **b**. The old *G746*
7 the word which ye have heard from the **b**. *G746*
13 him *that is* from the **b**. I write unto you, *G746*
14 *that is* from the **b**. I have written unto *G746*
24 heard from the **b**. If that which ye have *G746*
24 heard from the **b** shall remain in you, *G746*
3: 8 sinneth from the **b**. For this purpose the *G746*
11 the **b**, that we should love one another. *G746*
2Jn 5 had from the **b**, that we love one another. *G746*
6 heard from the **b**, ye should walk in it. *G746*
Rev 1: 8 I am Alpha and Omega, the **b** and the *G746*
3:14 witness, the **b** of the creation of God; *G746*
21: 6 and Omega, the **b** and the end. I will give *G746*
22:13 I am Alpha and Omega, the **b** and the *G746*

BEGINNINGS
Nu 10:10 days, and in the **b** of your months, ye *H7218*
28:11 And in the **b** of your months ye shall *H7218*
Ezk 36:11 *you* than at your **b**: and ye shall know *H7221*
Mk 13: 8 and troubles: these *are* the **b** of sorrows. *G746*

BEGOTTEN
Gen 5: 4 And the days of Adam after he had **b** H3205
Lev 18:11 wife's daughter, **b** of thy father, she *is* H4138
Nu 11:12 all this people? have I **b** them, that thou H3205
Dt 23: 8 The children that are **b** of them shall H3205
Jdg 8:30 of his body **b**: for he had many wives. H3318
Job 38:28 Hath the rain a father? or who hath **b** H3205
Ps 2: 7 *art* my Son; this day have I **b** thee. H3205
Isa 49:21 heart, Who hath **b** me these, seeing I H3205
Hos 5: 7 for they have **b** strange children: now H3205
Jn 1:14 **b** of the Father,) full of grace and truth. *G3439*
18 at any time; the only **b** Son, which is in *G3439*
3:16 he gave his only **b** Son, that whosoever *G3439*
18 in the name of the only **b** Son of God. *G3439*
Act 13:33 art my Son, this day have I **b** thee. *G1080*
1Co 4:15 Jesus I have **b** you through the gospel. *G1080*
Phlm 10 whom I have **b** in my bonds: *G1080*
Heb 1: 5 this day have I **b** thee? And again, I will *G1080*
5: 5 Thou art my Son, to day have I **b** thee. *G1080*
11:17 the promises offered up his only **b** *son*, *G3439*
1Pt 1: 3 mercy hath **b** us again unto a lively *G313*
1Jn 4: 9 God sent his only **b** Son into the world, *G3439*
5: 1 begat loveth him also that is **b** of him. *G1080*
18 not; but he that is **b** of God keepeth *G1080*
Rev 1: 5 *and* the first **b** of the dead, and the *G4416*

BEGUILE
Col 2: 4 And this I say, lest any man should **b** *G3884*
18 Let no man **b** you of your reward in a *G2603*

BEGUILED
Gen 3:13 said, The serpent **b** me, and I did eat. H5377
29:25 wherefore then hast thou **b** me? H7411
Nu 25:18 they have **b** you in the matter of H5230
Jos 9:22 have ye **b** us, saying, We *are* very H7411
2Co 11: 3 as the serpent **b** Eve through his *G1818*

BEGUILING
2Pt 2:14 cease from sin; **b** unstable souls: an *G1185*

BEGUN
Nu 16:46 out from the LORD; the plague is **b**. H2490
47 the plague was **b** among the people: H2490
Dt 2:31 me, Behold, I have **b** to give Sihon and H2490
3:24 O Lord GOD, thou hast **b** to shew thy H2490
Est 6:13 whom thou hast **b** to fall, thou shalt H2490
9:23 to do as they had **b**, and as Mordecai H2490
Mt 18:24 And when he had **b** to reckon, one was *G756*
2Co 8: 6 that as he had **b**, so he would also finish *G4278*
10 for you, who have **b** before, not only to *G4278*
Gal 3: 3 Are ye so foolish? having **b** in the Spirit, *G1728*
Php 1: 6 he which hath **b** a good work in you *G1728*
1Ti 5:11 for when they have **b** to wax wanton *G2691*

BEHALF
Ex 27:21 on the **b** of the children of Israel. H854
2Sa 3:12 to David on his **b**, saying, Whose *is* the H8478
2Ch 16: 9 strong in the **b** of *them* whose heart H5973
Job 36: 2 thee that *I have* yet to speak on God's **b**.
Dan 11:18 a prince for his own **b** shall cause the
Ro 16:19 therefore on your **b**: but yet I would *G1909*
1Co 1: 4 I thank my God always on your **b**, for *G4012*
2Co 1:11 thanks may be given by many on our **b**. *G5228*
5:12 to glory on our **b**, that ye may have *G5228*
8:24 love, and of our boasting on your **b**. *G5228*
9: 3 this **b**; that, as I said, ye may be ready: *G3313*
Php 1:29 For unto you it is given in the **b** of *G5228*
1Pt 4:16 but let him glorify God on this **b**. *G3313*

BEHAVE
Dt 32:27 should **b** themselves strangely, H5234
1Ch 19:13 Be of good courage, and let us **b** H2388
Ps 101: 2 I will **b** myself wisely in a perfect way. H7919
Isa 3: 5 the child shall **b** himself proudly H7292
1Co 13: 5 Doth not **b** itself unseemly, seeketh not *G807*
1Ti 3:15 thou oughtest to **b** thyself in the house *G390*

BEHAVED
1Sa 18: 5 sent him, *and* **b** himself wisely: and H7919
14 And David **b** himself wisely in all his H7919
15 Wherefore when Saul saw that he **b** H7919
30 forth, *that* David **b** himself more wisely H7919
Ps 35:14 I **b** myself as though *he had been* my H1980
131: 2 Surely I have **b** and quieted myself, as H7737
Mic 3: 4 have **b** themselves ill in their doings. H7489
1Th 2:10 we **b** ourselves among you that believe: *G1096*
2Th 3: 7 **b** not ourselves disorderly among you; *G812*

BEHAVETH
1Co 7:36 But if any man think that he **b** himself *G807*

BEHAVIOUR
1Sa 21:13 And he changed his **b** before them, and H2940
Ps 34:ttl he changed his **b** before Abimelech; H2940
1Ti 3: 2 **b**, given to hospitality, apt to teach; *G2887*
Tit 2: 3 that *they be* in **b** as becometh holiness, *G2688*

BEHEADED
Dt 21: 6 over the heifer that is **b** in the valley: H6202
2Sa 4: 7 slew him, and **b** him, and took H5493+H7218
Mt 14:10 And he sent, and **b** John in the prison. *G607*
Mk 6:16 whom I **b**: he is risen from the dead. *G607*
27 and he went and **b** him in the prison, *G607*
Lk 9: 9 And Herod said, John have I **b**: but who *G607*
Rev 20: 4 of them that were **b** for the witness of *G3990*

BEHELD
Gen 12:14 **b** the woman that she *was* very fair. H7200
13:10 And Lot lifted up his eyes, and **b** all the H7200
19:28 of the plain, and **b**, and, lo, the smoke H7200
31: 2 And Jacob **b** the countenance of Laban, H7200
48: 8 And Israel **b** Joseph's sons, and said, H7200
Nu 21: 9 he **b** the serpent of brass, he lived. H5027
23:21 He hath not **b** iniquity in Jacob, neither H5027
Jdg 16:27 that **b** while Samson made sport. H7200
1Sa 26: 5 and David **b** the place where Saul H7200
1Ch 21:15 the LORD **b**, and he repented him H7200
Job 31:26 If I **b** the sun when it shined, or the H7200
Ps119:158 I **b** the transgressors, and was grieved; H7200
142: 4 I looked on *my* right hand, and **b**, but H7200
Prv 7: 7 And **b** among the simple ones, I H7200
Ecc 8:17 Then I **b** all the work of God, that a H7200
Isa 41:28 For I **b**, and *there was* no man; even H7200
Jer 4:23 I **b** the earth, and, lo, *it was* without H7200
24 I **b** the mountains, and, lo, they H7200
25 I **b**, and, lo, *there was* no man, and all H7200
26 I **b**, and, lo, the fruitful place *was* a H7200
31:26 Upon this I awaked, and **b**; and my H7200
Ezk 1:15 Now as I **b** the living creatures, behold H7200
8: 2 Then I **b**, and lo a likeness as the H7200
37: 8 And when I **b**, lo, the sinews and the H7200
Dan 7: 4 wings: I **b** till the wings thereof H1934+H2370
6 After this I **b**, and lo another, H1934+H2370
9 I **b** till the thrones were cast H1934+H2370
11 I **b** then because of the voice of H1934+H2370
11 the horn spake: I **b** *even* till the H1934+H2370
21 I **b**, and the same horn made H1934+H2370
Hab 3: 6 He stood, and measured the earth: he **b**, H7200
Mt 19:26 But Jesus **b** *them*, and said unto them, *G1689*
Mk 9:15 people, when they **b** him, were greatly *G1492*
12:41 the treasury, and **b** how the people cast *G2334*
15:47 *mother* of Joses **b** where he was laid. *G2334*
Lk 10:18 And he said unto them, I **b** Satan as *G2334*
19:41 And when he was come near, he **b** the *G1492*
20:17 And he **b** them, and said, What is this *G1689*
22:56 But a certain maid **b** him as he sat by *G1492*
23:55 after, and **b** the sepulchre, and how *G2300*
24:12 stooping down, he **b** the linen clothes *G991*
Jn 1:14 us, (and we **b** his glory, the glory as *G2300*
42 And when Jesus **b** him, he said, Thou *G1689*
Act 1: 9 things, while they **b**, he was taken up; *G991*
17:23 For as I passed by, and **b** your *G333*
Rev 5: 6 And I **b**, and, lo, in the midst of the *G1492*
11 And I **b**, and I heard the voice of many *G1492*
6: 5 and see. And I **b**, and lo a black horse; *G1492*
12 And I **b** when he had opened the sixth *G1492*
7: 9 After this I **b**, and, lo, a great multitude, *G1492*
8:13 And I **b**, and heard an angel flying *G1492*
11:12 in a cloud; and their enemies **b** them. *G2334*
13:11 And I **b** another beast coming up out of *G1492*

BEHEMOTH
Job 40:15 Behold now **b**, which I made with thee; H930

BEHIND
Gen 18:10 *it* in the tent door, which *was* **b** him. H310
19:17 for thy life; look not **b** thee, neither stay H310
26 But his wife looked back from **b** him, H310
22:13 looked, and behold **b** *him* a ram caught H310
32:18 lord Esau: and, behold, also he *is* **b** us. H310
20 servant Jacob *is* **b** us. For he said, I will H310
Ex 10:26 not an hoof be left **b**; for thereof must we
11: 5 **b** the mill; and all the firstborn of beasts. H310
14:19 removed and went **b** them; and the pillar H310
19 before their face, and stood **b** them: H310
Lev 25:51 If *there be* yet many years *b*, according
Nu 3:23 shall pitch **b** the tabernacle westward. H310
Dt 25:18 all *that were* feeble **b** thee, when thou H310
Jos 8: 2 lay thee an ambush for the city **b** it. H310
4 the city, *even* **b** the city: go not very H310
14 liers in ambush against him **b** the city. H310
20 And when the men of Ai looked **b** them, H310
Jdg 18:12 this day: behold, *it is* **b** Kirjath-jearim. H310
20:40 Benjamites looked **b** them, and, behold, H310
1Sa 21: 9 wrapped in a cloth **b** the ephod: if thou H310
24: 8 when Saul looked **b** him, David stooped H310
30: 9 where those that were left **b** stayed. H3498
10 hundred abode **b**, which were so faint H5975
2Sa 1: 7 And when he looked **b** him, he saw me, H310
2:20 Then Abner looked **b** him, and said, *Art* H310
23 the spear came out **b** him; and he fell H310
3:16 her along weeping **b** her to Bahurim. H310
5:23 fetch a compass **b** them, and come upon H310
10: 9 him before and **b**, he chose of all the H268
13:34 people by the way of the hill side **b** him. H310
1Ki 10:19 throne *was* round **b**: and *there were* stays H310
14: 9 to anger, and hast cast me **b** thy back: H310
2Ki 6:32 not the sound of his master's feet **b** him? H310
9:18 with peace? turn thee **b** me. And the H310
19 thou to do with peace? turn thee **b** me. H310
11: 6 part at the gate **b** the guard: so shall ye H310
1Ch 19:10 him before and **b**, he chose out of all the H268
2Ch 13:13 to come about **b** them: so they were H310
13 and the ambushment *was* **b** them. H310
14 *was* before and **b**: and they cried unto H268
Neh 4:13 Therefore set I in the lower places **b** the H310
16 the rulers *were* **b** all the house of Judah. H310
9:26 and cast thy law **b** their backs, and slew H310
Ps 50:17 and castest my words **b** thee. H310
139: 5 Thou hast beset me **b** and before, and H268
Song 2: 9 he standeth **b** our wall, he looketh H310
Isa 9:12 The Syrians before, and the Philistines **b**; H268
30:21 And thine ears shall hear a word **b** thee, H310
38:17 for thou hast cast all my sins **b** thy back. H310
57: 8 **B** the doors also and the posts hast thou H310
66:17 in the gardens **b** one *tree* in the midst, H310
Ezk 3:12 me up, and I heard **b** me a voice of a H310
23:35 me, and cast me **b** thy back, therefore H310

Ezk 41:15 place which *was* **b** it, and the galleries H310
Joel 2: 3 A fire devoureth before them; and **b** H310
3 before them, and **b** them a desolate H310
14 and leave a blessing **b** him; *even* a meat H310
Zec 1: 8 in the bottom; and **b** him *were there* red H310
Mt 9:20 years, came **b** *him*, and touched the G3693
16:23 Peter, Get thee **b** me, Satan: thou art G3694
Mk 5:27 the press **b**, and touched his garment. G3693
8:33 saying, Get thee **b** me, Satan: for thou G3694
12:19 and leave *his* wife **b** *him*, and leave no G2641
Lk 2:43 child Jesus tarried **b** in Jerusalem; and G5278
4: 8 unto him, Get thee **b** me, Satan: for it is G3694
7:38 And stood at his feet **b** *him* weeping, G3694
8:44 Came **b** *him*, and touched the border of G3693
1Co 1: 7 So that ye come **b** in no gift; waiting for G5302
2Co 11: 5 For I suppose I was not a whit **b** the G5302
12:11 for in nothing am I **b** the very chiefest G5302
Php 3:13 things which are **b**, and reaching forth G3694
Col 1:24 up that which is **b** of the afflictions of G5303
Rev 1:10 **b** me a great voice, as of a trumpet, G3694
4: 6 four beasts full of eyes before and **b**. G3693

BEHOLD

Gen 1:29 And God said, **B**, I have given you every H2009
31 he had made, and, **b**, *it was* very good. H2009
3:22 And the LORD God said, **B**, the man is H2005
4:14 **B**, thou hast driven me out this day H2005
6:12 And God looked upon the earth, and, **b**, H2009
13 **b**, I will destroy them with the earth. H2005
17 And, **b**, I, even I, do bring a flood of H2009
8:13 and, **b**, the face of the ground was dry. H2009
9: 9 And I, **b**, I establish my covenant with H2005
11: 6 And the LORD said, **B**, the people *is* H2005
12:11 Sarai his wife, **B** now, I know that thou H2009
19 **b** thy wife, take *her*, and go thy way. H2009
15: 3 And Abram said, **B**, to me thou hast H2005
4 And, **b**, the word of the LORD *came* H2009
17 and it was dark, **b** a smoking furnace, H2009
16: 2 And Sarai said unto Abram, **B** now, the H2009
6 But Abram said unto Sarai, **B**, thy maid H2009
11 said unto her, **B**, thou *art* with child, H2009
14 **b**, *it is* between Kadesh and Bered. H2009
17: 4 As for me, **b**, my covenant *is* with thee, H2009
20 I have heard thee: **B**, I have blessed H2009
18: 9 thy wife? And he said, **B**, in the tent. H2009
27 And Abraham answered and said, **B** H2009
31 And he said, **B** now, I have taken upon H2009
19: 2 And he said, **B** now, my lords, turn in, I H2009
8 **B** now, I have two daughters which H2009
19 **B** now, thy servant hath found grace in H2009
20 **B** now, this city *is* near to flee unto, and H2009
34 unto the younger, **B**, I lay yesternight H2005
20: 3 and said to him, **B**, thou *art but* a dead H2009
15 And Abimelech said, **B**, my land *is* H2009
16 And unto Sarah he said, **B**, I have given H2009
16 *pieces* of silver: **b**, he *is* to thee a H2009
22: 1 Abraham: and he said, **B**, *here* I *am*. H2009
7 my son. And he said, **B** the fire and the H2009
13 and looked, and **b** behind *him* a ram H2009
20 Abraham, saying, **B**, Milcah, she hath H2009
24:13 **B**, I stand *here* by the well of water; and H2009
15 speaking, that, **b**, Rebekah came out, H2009
30 **b**, he stood by the camels at the well. H2009
43 **B**, I stand by the well of water; and it H2009
45 in mine heart, **b**, Rebekah came forth H2009
51 **B**, Rebekah *is* before thee, take *her*, and H2009
63 saw, and, **b**, the camels *were* coming. H2009
25:24 **b**, *there were* twins in her womb. H2009
32 And Esau said, **B**, I *am* at the point to H2009
26: 8 and saw, and, **b**, Isaac *was* sporting H2009
9 Isaac, and said, **B**, of a surety she *is* thy H2009
27: 1 son: and he said unto him, **B**, *here am* I. H2009
2 And he said, **B** now, I am old, I know H2009
6 her son, saying, **B**, I heard thy father H2009
11 his mother, **B**, Esau my brother *is* H2005
36 birthright; and, **b**, now he hath taken H2009
37 said unto Esau, **B**, I have made him thy H2005
39 said unto him, **B**, thy dwelling shall be H2009
42 said unto him, **B**, thy brother Esau, as H2009
28:12 And he dreamed, and **b** a ladder set up H2009
12 to heaven: and **b** the angels of God H2009
13 And, **b**, the LORD stood above it, and H2009
15 And, **b**, I *am* with thee, and will keep H2009
29: 2 And he looked, and **b** a well in the field, H2009
6 *He is* well: and, **b**, Rachel his daughter H2009
25 in the morning, **b**, it *was* Leah: and he H2009
30: 3 And she said, **B** my maid Bilhah, go in H2009
34 And Laban said, **B**, I would it might be H2005
31: 2 and, **b**, it *was* not toward him as before. H2009

Gen 31:10 saw in a dream, and, **b**, the rams which H2009
51 And Laban said to Jacob, **B** this heap, H2009
51 this heap, and **b** *this* pillar, which I H2009
32:18 lord Esau: and, **b**, also he *is* behind us. H2009
20 And say ye moreover, **B**, thy servant H2009
33: 1 and looked, and, **b**, Esau came, and H2009
34:21 for the land, **b**, *it is* large enough for H2009
37: 7 For, **b**, we *were* binding sheaves in the H2009
7 upright; and, **b**, your sheaves stood H2009
9 and said, **B**, I have dreamed a dream H2009
9 a dream more; and, **b**, the sun and the H2009
15 And a certain man found him, and, **b**, H2009
19 And they said one to another, **B**, this H2009
25 eyes and looked, and, **b**, a company of H2009
29 unto the pit; and, **b**, Joseph *was* not in H2009
38:13 And it was told Tamar, saying, **B** thy H2009
23 we be shamed: **b**, I sent this kid, and H2009
24 harlot; and also, **b**, she *is* with child by H2009
27 of travail, that, **b**, twins *were* in her womb. H2009
29 his hand, that, **b**, his brother came out: H2009
39: 8 his master's wife, **B**, my master wotteth H2005
40: 6 upon them, and, **b**, they *were* sad. H2009
9 In my dream, **b**, a vine *was* before me; H2009
16 in my dream, and, **b**, *I had* three white H2009
41: 1 dreamed: and, **b**, he stood by the river. H2009
2 And, **b**, there came up out of the river H2009
3 And, **b**, seven other kine came up after H2009
5 second time: and, **b**, seven ears of corn H2009
6 And, **b**, seven thin ears and blasted with H2009
7 Pharaoh awoke, and, **b**, *it was* a dream. H2009
17 **B**, I stood upon the bank of the river: H2005
18 And, **b**, there came up out of the river H2009
19 And, **b**, seven other kine came up after H2009
22 And I saw in my dream, and, **b**, seven H2009
23 And, **b**, seven ears, withered, thin, *and* H2009
29 **B**, there come seven years of great H2009
42: 2 And he said, **B**, I have heard that there H2009
13 of Canaan; and, **b**, the youngest *is* this H2009
22 therefore, **b**, also his blood is required. H2009
27 for, **b**, it *was* in his sack's mouth. H2009
35 their sacks, that, **b**, every man's bundle H2009
43:21 our sacks, and, **b**, *every* man's money H2009
44: 8 **B**, the money, which we found in our H2005
16 of thy servants: **b**, we *are* my lord's H2009
45:12 And, **b**, your eyes see, and the eyes of H2009
47: 1 and, **b**, they *are* in the land of Goshen. H2009
23 Then Joseph said unto the people, **B**, I H2009
48: 1 *one* told Joseph, **B**, thy father *is* sick: H2009
2 And *one* told Jacob, and said, **B**, thy son H2009
4 And said unto me, **B**, I will make thee H2005
21 And Israel said unto Joseph, **B**, I die: H2009
50:18 and they said, **B**, we *be* thy servants. H2009
Ex 1: 9 And he said unto his people, **B**, the H2009
2: 6 the child: and, **b**, the babe wept. And H2009
13 out the second day, **b**, two men of the H2009
3: 2 he looked, and, **b**, the bush burned with H2009
9 Now therefore, **b**, the cry of the children H2009
13 And Moses said unto God, **B**, *when* I H2009
4: 1 And Moses answered and said, But, **b**, H2005
6 it out, **b**, his hand *was* leprous as snow. H2009
7 **b**, it was turned again as his *other* flesh. H2009
14 well. And also, **b**, he cometh forth to H2009
23 **b**, I will slay thy son, *even* thy firstborn. H2009
5: 5 And Pharaoh said, **B**, the people of the H2005
16 us, Make brick: and, **b**, thy servants *are* H2009
6:12 the LORD, saying, **B**, the children of H2005
30 And Moses said before the LORD, **B**, I H2005
7:16 and, **b**, hitherto thou wouldest not hear. H2009
17 I *am* the LORD: **b**, I will smite with the H2009
8: 2 And if thou refuse to let *them* go, **b**, I H2009
21 Else, if thou wilt not let my people go, **b**, H2005
29 And Moses said, **B**, I go out from thee, H2009
9: 3 **B**, the hand of the LORD is upon thy H2009
7 And Pharaoh sent, and, **b**, there was H2009
18 **B**, to morrow about this time I will H2005
10: 4 to let my people go, **b**, to morrow will I H2009
14:10 up their eyes, and, **b**, the Egyptians H2009
17 And I, **b**, I will harden the hearts of the H2005
16: 4 Then said the LORD unto Moses, **B**, I H2005
10 the wilderness, and, **b**, the glory of the H2009
14 lay was gone up, **b**, upon the face of the H2009
17: 6 **B**, I will stand before thee there upon H2005
23:20 **B**, I send an Angel before thee, to keep H2009
24: 8 the people, and said, **B** the blood of the H2009
14 unto you: and, **b**, Aaron and Hur *are* H2009
31: 6 And I, **b**, I have given with him Aholiab, H2009
32: 9 people, and, **b**, it *is* a stiffnecked people: H2009
34 spoken unto thee: **b**, mine Angel shall H2009
33:21 And the LORD said, **B**, *there is* a place H2009

Ex 34:10 And he said, **B**, I make a covenant: H2009
11 thee this day: **b**, I drive out before thee H2005
30 Israel saw Moses, **b**, the skin of his face H2009
39:43 all the work, and, **b**, they had done it as H2009
Lev 10:16 sin offering, and, **b**, it was burnt: and he H2009
18 **B**, the blood of it was not brought in H2005
19 And Aaron said unto Moses, **B**, this day H2005
13: 5 seventh day: and, **b**, *if* the plague in his H2009
6 the seventh day: and, **b**, *if* the plague *be* H2009
8 And *if* the priest see that, **b**, the scab H2009
10 And the priest shall see *him*: and, **b**, *if* H2009
13 Then the priest shall consider: and, **b**, *if* H2009
17 And the priest shall see him: and, **b**, *if* H2009
20 And if, when the priest seeth it, **b**, it *be* H2009
21 But if the priest look on it, and, **b**, *there* H2009
25 look upon it: and, **b**, *if* the hair in the H2009
26 But if the priest look on it, and, **b**, *there* H2009
30 see the plague: and, **b**, if it *be* in sight H2009
31 of the scall, and, **b**, it *be* not in sight H2009
32 on the plague: and, **b**, *if* the scall spread H2009
34 on the scall: and, **b**, *if* the scall be not H2009
36 shall look on him: and, **b**, if the scall be H2009
39 Then the priest shall look: and, **b**, *if* the H2009
43 look upon it: and, **b**, *if* the rising of the H2009
53 And if the priest shall look, and, **b**, the H2009
55 it is washed: and, **b**, *if* the plague have H2009
56 And if the priest look, and, **b**, the plague H2009
14: 3 priest shall look, and, **b**, *if* the plague of H2009
37 And he shall look on the plague, and, **b**, H2009
39 and shall look: and, **b**, *if* the plague be H2009
44 and look, and, **b**, *if* the plague be spread H2009
48 look *upon it*, and, **b**, the plague hath H2009
25:20 the seventh year? **b**, we shall not sow, H2005
Nu 3:12 And I, **b**, I have taken the Levites from H2009
12: 8 of the LORD shall he **b**: wherefore then H5027
10 the tabernacle; and, **b**, Miriam *became* H2009
10 upon Miriam, and, **b**, *she was* leprous. H2009
16:42 and, **b**, the cloud covered it, H2009
47 and, **b**, the plague was begun H2009
17: 8 of witness; and, **b**, the rod of Aaron for H2009
12 **B**, we die, we perish, we all perish. H2005
18: 6 And I, **b**, I have taken your brethren the H2009
8 And the LORD spake unto Aaron, **B**, I H2009
21 And, **b**, I have given the children of Levi H2009
20:16 out of Egypt: and, **b**, we *are* in Kadesh, H2009
22: 5 to call him, saying, **B**, there is a people H2009
5 out from Egypt: **b**, they cover the face of H2009
11 **B**, *there is* a people come out of Egypt, H2009
32 ass these three times? **b**, I went out to H2009
23: 9 from the hills I **b** him: lo, the people H7789
11 **b**, thou hast blessed *them* altogether. H2009
17 And when he came to him, **b**, he stood H2009
20 **B**, I have received *commandment* to H2009
24 **B**, the people shall rise up as a great H2005
24:10 enemies, and, **b**, thou hast altogether H2005
14 And now, **b**, I go unto my people: come H2005
17 I shall see him, but not now: I shall **b** H7789
25: 6 And, **b**, one of the children of Israel H2009
12 Wherefore say, **B**, I give unto him my H2005
31:16 **B**, these caused the children of Israel, H2005
32: 1 that, **b**, the place *was* a place for cattle; H2009
14 And, **b**, ye are risen up in your fathers' H2009
23 But if ye will not do so, **b**, ye have H2009
Dt 1: 8 **B**, I have set the land before you: go in H7200
10 you, and, **b**, ye *are* this day as the H2009
21 **B**, the LORD thy God hath set the land H7200
2:24 the river Arnon: **b**, I have given into H7200
31 And the LORD said unto me, **B**, I have H7200
3:11 remnant of giants; **b**, his bedstead *was* H2009
27 eastward, and **b** *it* with thine eyes: for H7200
4: 5 **B**, I have taught you statutes and H7200
5:24 And ye said, **B**, the LORD our God hath H2005
9:13 people, and, **b**, it *is* a stiffnecked people: H2009
16 And I looked, and, **b**, ye had sinned H2009
10:14 **B**, the heaven and the heaven of H2005
11:26 **B**, I set before you this day a blessing H7200
13:14 diligently; and, **b**, *if it be* truth, *and* the H2009
17: 4 diligently, and, **b**, *it be* true, *and* the H2009
19:18 inquisition: and, **b**, *if* the witness *be* a H2009
26:10 And now, **b**, I have brought the H2009
31:14 And the LORD said unto Moses, **B**, thy H2005
16 And the LORD said unto Moses, **B**, thou H2009
27 and thy stiff neck: **b**, while I am yet H2005
32:49 Jericho; and **b** the land of Canaan, H7200
Jos 2: 2 of Jericho, saying, **B**, there came men in H2009
18 **B**, *when* we come into the land, thou H2009
3:11 **B**, the ark of the covenant of the Lord of H2009
5:13 and looked, and, **b**, there stood a man H2009
7:21 took them; and, **b**, they *are* hid in the H2009

Jos 7:22 unto the tent; and, **b**, *it was* hid in his H2009
8: 4 And he commanded them, saying, **B**, ye H7200
20 they saw, and, **b**, the smoke of the city H2009
9:12 but now, **b**, it is dry, and it is mouldy: H2009
13 *were* new; and, **b**, they be rent: and H2009
25 And now, **b**, we *are* in thine hand: as it H2005
14:10 And now, **b**, the LORD hath kept me H2009
22:11 And the children of Israel heard say, **B**, H2009
28 we may say *again*, **B** the pattern of the H7200
23: 4 **B**, I have divided unto you by lot these H7200
14 And, **b**, this day I *am* going the way of H2009
24:27 And Joshua said unto all the people, **B**, H2009
Jdg 1: 2 Judah shall go up: **b**, I have delivered H2009
3:24 when they saw that, **b**, the doors of the H2009
25 ashamed: and, **b**, he opened not the H2009
25 *them*: and, **b**, their lord *was* fallen H2009
4:22 And, **b**, as Barak pursued Sisera, Jael H2009
22 into her *tent*, **b**, Sisera lay dead, and H2009
6:15 shall I save Israel? **b**, my family *is* poor H2009
28 in the morning, **b**, the altar of Baal was H2009
37 **B**, I will put a fleece of wool in the floor; H2009
7:13 And when Gideon was come, **b**, *there* H2009
13 fellow, and said, **B**, I dreamed a dream, H2009
17 do likewise; and, **b**, when I come to the H2009
8:15 of Succoth, and said, **B** Zebah and H2009
9:31 privily, saying, **B**, Gaal the son of Ebed H2009
31 and, **b**, they fortify the city against thee. H2009
33 the city: and, **b**, *when* he and the people H2009
36 he said to Zebul, **B**, there come people H2009
43 and looked, and, **b**, the people *were* H2009
11:34 his house, and, **b**, his daughter came H2009
13: 3 and said unto her, **B** now, thou *art* H2009
7 But he said unto me, **B**, thou shalt H2009
10 and said unto him, **B**, the man hath H2009
14: 5 **b**, a young lion roared against him. H2009
8 of the lion: and, **b**, *there was* a swarm H2009
16 he said unto her, **B**, I have not told *it* my H2009
16:10 And Delilah said unto Samson, **B**, thou H2009
17: 2 of also in mine ears, **b**, the silver *is* with H2009
18: 9 the land, and, **b**, it *is* very good: and H2009
12 this day: **b**, *it is* behind Kirjath-jearim. H2009
19: 9 said unto him, **B**, now the day draweth H2009
9 tarry all night: **b**, the day groweth to H2009
16 And, **b**, there came an old man from his H2009
22 hearts merry, **b**, the men of the city, H2009
24 **B**, *here is* my daughter a maiden, and H2009
27 to go his way: and, **b**, the woman his H2009
20: 7 **B**, ye *are* all children of Israel; give here H2009
40 behind them, and, **b**, the flame of the H2009
21: 8 the LORD? And, **b**, there came none to H2009
9 For the people were numbered, and, **b**, H2009
19 Then they said, **B**, *there is* a feast of the H2009
21 And see, and, **b**, if the daughters of H2009
Ru 1:15 And she said, **B**, thy sister in law is gone H2009
2: 4 And, **b**, Boaz came from Beth-lehem, H2009
3: 2 thou wast? **B**, he winnoweth barley H2009
8 himself: and, **b**, a woman lay at his feet. H2009
4: 1 him down there: and, **b**, the kinsman of H2009
1Sa 2:31 **B**, the days come, that I will cut off H2009
3:11 And the LORD said to Samuel, **B**, I will H2009
5: 3 on the morrow, **b**, Dagon *was* fallen H2009
4 morrow morning, **b**, Dagon *was* fallen H2009
8: 5 And said unto him, **B**, thou art old, and H2009
9: 6 And he said unto him, **B** now, *there is* H2009
7 Then said Saul to his servant, But, **b**, *if* H2009
8 again, and said, **B**, I have here at hand H2009
12 and said, He is; **b**, *he is* before you: H2009
14 come into the city, **b**, Samuel came out H2009
17 said unto him, **B** the man whom I H2009
24 And *Samuel* said, **B** that which is left! H2009
10: 8 me to Gilgal; and, **b**, I will come down H2009
10 came thither to the hill, **b**, a company of H2009
11 saw that, **b**, he prophesied among H2009
22 **B**, he hath hid himself among the stuff. H2009
11: 5 And, **b**, Saul came after the herd out of H2009
12: 1 And Samuel said unto all Israel, **B**, I H2009
2 And now, **b**, the king walketh before H2009
2 grayheaded; and, **b**, my sons *are* with H2009
3 **B**, here I *am*: witness against me before H2009
13 Now therefore **b** the king whom ye H2009
13 **b**, the LORD hath set a king over you. H2009
13:10 the burnt offering, **b**, Samuel came; and H2009
14: 7 **b**, I *am* with thee according to thy heart. H2005
8 Then said Jonathan, **B**, we will pass H2009
11 Philistines said, **B**, the Hebrews come H2009
16 looked; and, **b**, the multitude melted H2009
17 had numbered, **b**, Jonathan and his H2009
20 to the battle: and, **b**, every man's sword H2009
26 into the wood, **b**, the honey dropped; H2009
1Sa 14:33 Then they told Saul, saying, **B**, the H2009
15:12 came to Carmel, and, **b**, he set him up a H2009
22 of the LORD? **B**, to obey *is* better than H2009
16:11 yet the youngest, and, **b**, he keepeth the H2009
15 And Saul's servants said unto him, **B** H2009
18 and said, **B**, I have seen a son of H2009
17:23 And as he talked with them, **b**, there H2009
18:17 And Saul said to David, **B** my elder H2009
22 secretly, and say, **B**, the king hath H2009
19:16 were come in, **b**, *there was* an image H2009
19 And it was told Saul, saying, **B**, David *is* H2009
22 said, **B**, *they be* at Naioth in Ramah. H2009
20: 2 thou shalt not die: **b**, my father will do H2009
5 And David said unto Jonathan, **B**, to H2009
12 *or* the third *day*, and, **b**, *if there be* good H2009
21 And, **b**, I will send a lad, *saying*, Go, H2009
21 say unto the lad, **B**, the arrows *are* on H2009
22 But if I say thus unto the young man, **B**, H2009
23 and I have spoken of, **b**, the LORD *be* H2009
21: 9 the valley of Elah, **b**, it *is here* wrapped H2009
23: 1 Then they told David, saying, **B**, the H2009
3 And David's men said unto him, **B**, we H2009
24: 1 **B**, David *is* in the wilderness of En-gedi. H2009
4 And the men of David said unto him, **B** H2009
4 said unto thee, **B**, I will deliver thine H2009
9 saying, **B**, David seeketh thy hurt? H2009
10 **B**, this day thine eyes have seen how H2009
20 And now, **b**, I know well that thou shalt H2009
25:14 wife, saying, **B**, David sent messengers H2009
19 Go on before me; **b**, I come after you. H2005
20 of the hill, and, **b**, David and his men H2009
36 And Abigail came to Nabal; and, **b**, he H2009
41 earth, and said, **B**, *let* thine handmaid H2009
26: 7 by night: and, **b**, Saul lay sleeping H2009
21 eyes this day: **b**, I have played the fool, H2009
22 And David answered and said, **B** the H2009
24 And, **b**, as thy life was much set by this H2009
28: 7 said to him, **B**, *there is* a woman that H2009
9 And the woman said unto him, **B**, thou H2009
21 said unto him, **B**, thine handmaid hath H2009
30: 3 to the city, and, **b**, *it was* burned with H2009
16 And when he had brought him down, **b**, H2009
26 friends, saying, **B** a present for you of H2009
2Sa 1: 2 third day, that, **b**, a man came out of H2009
6 mount Gilboa, **b**, Saul leaned upon his H2009
18 **b**, *it is* written in the book of Jasher.) H2009
3:12 with me, and, **b**, my hand *shall be* with H2009
22 And, **b**, the servants of David and Joab H2009
24 hast thou done? **b**, Abner came unto H2009
4: 8 and said to the king, **B** the head of H2009
10 When one told me, saying, **B**, Saul is H2009
5: 1 saying, **B**, we *are* thy bone and thy flesh. H2005
9: 4 unto the king, **B**, he *is* in the house of H2009
6 And he answered, **B** thy servant! H2009
12:11 Thus saith the LORD, **B**, I will raise up H2005
18 for they said, **B**, while the child was H2009
13:24 king, and said, **B** now, thy servant hath H2009
34 and looked, and, **b**, there came much H2009
35 And Jonadab said unto the king, **B**, the H2009
36 end of speaking, that, **b**, the king's sons H2009
14: 7 And, **b**, the whole family is risen H2009
21 And the king said unto Joab, **B** now, I H2009
32 And Absalom answered Joab, **B**, I sent H2009
15:15 unto the king, **B**, thy servants *are ready* H2009
26 no delight in thee; **b**, *here am* I, let him H2005
32 worshipped God, **b**, Hushai the Archite H2009
36 **B**, *they have* there with them their two H2009
16: 1 the top *of the hill*, **b**, Ziba the servant of H2009
3 said unto the king, **B**, he abideth at H2009
4 Then said the king to Ziba, **B**, thine *are* H2009
5 came to Bahurim, **b**, thence came out a H2009
8 thy son: and, **b**, thou *art taken* in thy H2009
11 to all his servants, **B**, my son, which H2009
17: 9 **B**, he is hid now in some pit, or in some H2009
18:10 **B**, I saw Absalom hanged in an oak. H2009
11 told him, And, **b**, thou sawest *him*, and H2009
24 looked, and **b** a man running alone. H2009
26 the porter, and said, **B** *another* man H2009
31 And, **b**, Cushi came; and Cushi said, H2009
19: 1 And it was told Joab, **B**, the king H2009
8 people, saying, **B**, the king doth sit in H2009
20 sinned: therefore, **b**, I am come the first H2009
37 and of my mother. But **b** thy servant H2009
41 And, **b**, all the men of Israel came to the H2009
20:21 said unto Joab, **B**, his head shall be H2009
24:22 good unto him: **b**, *here be* oxen for H7200
1Ki 1:14 **B**, while thou yet talkest there with the H2009
18 And now, **b**, Adonijah reigneth; and H2009
23 And they told the king, saying, **B** H2009
1Ki 1:25 the priest; and, **b**, they eat and drink H2009
42 And while he yet spake, **b**, Jonathan the H2009
51 And it was told Solomon, saying, **B**, H2009
2: 8 And, **b**, *thou hast* with thee Shimei the H2009
29 of the LORD; and, **b**, *he is* by the altar. H2009
39 saying, **B**, thy servants *be* in Gath. H2009
3:12 **B**, I have done according to thy words: H2009
15 And Solomon awoke; and, **b**, *it was* a H2009
21 my child suck, **b**, it was dead: but when H2009
21 **b**, it was not my son, which I did bear. H2009
5: 5 And, **b**, I purpose to build an house H2005
8:27 on the earth? **b**, the heaven and heaven H2009
10: 7 had seen *it*: and, **b**, the half was not told H2009
11:22 with me, that, **b**, thou seekest to go to H2009
31 the God of Israel, **B**, I will rend the H2005
12:28 up to Jerusalem: **b** thy gods, O Israel, H2009
13: 1 And, **b**, there came a man of God out of H2009
2 saith the LORD; **B**, a child shall be born H2009
3 hath spoken; **B**, the altar shall be rent, H2009
25 And, **b**, men passed by, and saw the H2009
14: 2 get thee to Shiloh: **b**, there *is* Ahijah the H2009
5 And the LORD said unto Ahijah, **B**, the H2009
10 Therefore, **b**, I will bring evil upon the H2005
19 how he reigned, **b**, they *are* written in H2009
15:19 and thy father: **b**, I have sent unto thee H2009
16: 3 **B**, I will take away the posterity of H2005
17: 9 and dwell there: **b**, I have commanded H2009
10 gate of the city, **b**, the widow woman H2009
12 oil in a cruse: and, **b**, I *am* gathering H2005
18: 7 And as Obadiah was in the way, **b**, H2009
8 I *am*: go, tell thy lord, **B**, Elijah *is here*. H2009
11 sayest, Go, tell thy lord, **B**, Elijah *is here*. H2009
14 **B**, Elijah *is here*: and he shall slay me. H2009
44 time, that he said, **B**, there ariseth a H2009
19: 5 a juniper tree, **b**, then an angel touched H2009
6 And he looked, and, **b**, *there was* a cake H2009
9 lodged there; and, **b**, the word of the H2009
11 the LORD. And, **b**, the LORD passed by, H2009
13 of the cave. And, **b**, *there came* a voice H2009
20:13 And, **b**, there came a prophet unto H2009
13 great multitude? **b**, I will deliver it into H2005
31 And his servants said unto him, **B** now, H2009
36 of the LORD, **b**, as soon as thou art H2009
39 of the battle; and, **b**, a man turned H2009
21:18 *is* in Samaria: **b**, *he is* in the vineyard H2009
21 **B**, I will bring evil upon thee, and will H2005
22:13 unto him, saying, **B** now, the words of H2009
23 Now therefore, **b**, the LORD hath put a H2009
25 And Micaiah said, **B**, thou shalt see in H2009
2Ki 1: 9 up to him: and, **b**, he sat on the top of H2009
14 **B**, there came fire down from heaven, H2009
2:11 and talked, that, **b**, *there appeared* a H2009
16 And they said unto him, **B** now, there H2009
19 city said unto Elisha, **B**, I pray thee, the H2009
3:20 was offered, that, **b**, there came water H2009
4: 9 And she said unto her husband, **B** now, H2009
13 Say now unto her, **B**, thou hast been H2009
25 servant, **B**, *yonder is* that Shunammite: H2009
32 into the house, **b**, the child was dead, H2009
5: 6 is come unto thee, **b**, I have *therewith* H2009
11 away, and said, **B**, I thought, He will H2009
15 him: and he said, **B**, now I know that H2009
20 man of God, said, **B**, my master hath H2009
22 sent me, saying, **B**, even now there be H2009
6: 1 said unto Elisha, **B** now, the place H2009
13 told him, saying, **B**, *he is* in Dothan. H2009
15 and gone forth, **b**, an host compassed H2009
17 and he saw: and, **b**, the mountain *was* H2009
20 **b**, *they were* in the midst of Samaria. H2009
25 in Samaria: and, **b**, they besieged it, H2009
30 looked, and, **b**, *he had* sackcloth within H2009
33 And while he yet talked with them, **b**, H2009
33 him: and he said, **B**, this evil *is* of the H2009
7: 2 of God, and said, **B**, *if* the LORD would H2009
2 be? And he said, **B**, thou shalt see *it* with H2009
5 of Syria, **b**, *there was* no man there. H2009
10 the Syrians, and, **b**, *there was* no man H2009
13 are left in the city, (**b**, they *are* as all the H2009
13 that are left in it: **b**, *I say*, they *are* even H2009
19 and said, Now, **b**, *if* the LORD should H2009
19 be? And he said, **B**, thou shalt see it with H2009
8: 5 body to life, that, **b**, the woman, whose H2009
9: 5 And when he came, **b**, the captains of H2009
10: 4 afraid, and said, **B**, two kings stood not H2009
9 Ye *be* righteous: **b**, I conspired against H2009
11:14 And when she looked, **b**, the king stood H2009
13:21 a man, that, **b**, they spied a band *of* H2009
15:11 And the rest of the acts of Zachariah, **b**, H2009
15 which he made, **b**, they *are* written in H2009

2Ki 15:26 all that he did, **b**, they *are* written in the H2009
31 all that he did, **b**, they *are* written in the H2009
17:26 among them, and, **b**, they slay them, H2009
18:21 Now, **b**, thou trustest upon the staff of H2009
19: 7 **B**, I will send a blast upon him, and he H2005
9 king of Ethiopia, **B**, he is come out to H2009
11 **B**, thou hast heard what the kings of H2009
35 morning, **b**, they *were* all dead corpses. H2009
20: 5 seen thy tears: **b**, I will heal thee: on the H2005
17 **B**, the days come, that all that *is* in H2009
21:12 God of Israel, **B**, I *am* bringing *such* H2009
22:16 Thus saith the LORD, **B**, I will bring evil H2005
20 **B** therefore, I will gather thee unto thy H2005
1Ch 9: 1 genealogies; and, **b**, they *were* written H2009
11: 1 saying, **B**, we *are* thy bone and thy flesh. H2009
25 **B**, he was honourable among the thirty, H2009
22: 9 **B**, a son shall be born to thee, who shall H2009
14 Now, **b**, in my trouble I have prepared H2009
28:21 And, **b**, the courses of the priests and H2009
29:29 first and last, **b**, they *are* written in the H2009
2Ch 2: 4 **B**, I build an house to the name of the H2009
8 in Lebanon; and, **b**, my servants *shall* H2009
10 And, **b**, I will give to thy servants, the H2009
6:18 men on the earth? **b**, heaven and the H2009
9: 6 had seen *it*: and, **b**, the one half of the H2009
13:12 And, **b**, God himself *is* with us for *our* H2009
14 And when Judah looked back, **b**, the H2009
16: 3 and thy father: **b**, I have sent thee silver H2009
11 And, **b**, the acts of Asa, first and last, lo, H2009
18:12 to him, saying, **B**, the words of the H2009
22 Now therefore, **b**, the LORD hath put a H2009
24 And Micaiah said, **B**, thou shalt see on H2009
19:11 And, **b**, Amariah the chief priest *is* over H2009
20: 2 this side Syria; and, **b**, they *be* in H2009
10 And now, **b**, the children of Ammon H2009
11 **B**, *I say, how* they reward us, to come to H2009
16 To morrow go ye down against them: **b**, H2009
24 the multitude, and, **b**, they *were* dead H2009
34 first and last, **b**, they *are* written in the H2009
21:14 **B**, with a great plague will the LORD H2009
23: 3 said unto them, **B**, the king's son shall H2009
13 And she looked, and, **b**, the king stood H2009
24:27 the house of God, **b**, they *are* written in H2009
25:26 first and last, **b**, *are* they not written H2009
26:20 upon him, and, **b**, he *was* leprous in his H2009
28: 9 said unto them, **B**, because the LORD H2009
26 first and last, **b**, they *are* written in the H2009
29:19 **b**, they *are* before the altar of the LORD. H2009
32:32 and his goodness, **b**, they *are* written in H2009
33:18 God of Israel, **b**, they *are written* in the H2009
19 he was humbled: **b**, they *are* written H2009
34:24 Thus saith the LORD, **B**, I will bring evil H2005
28 **B**, I will gather thee to thy fathers, and H2005
35:25 **b**, they *are* written in the lamentations. H2009
27 And his deeds, first and last, **b**, they *are* H2009
36: 8 was found in him, **b**, they *are* written in H2009
Ezr 9:15 as *it is* this day: **b**, we *are* before thee in H2005
Neh 9:36 **B**, we *are* servants this day, and *for* the H2009
36 good thereof, **b**, we *are* servants in it: H2009
Est 6: 5 said unto him, **B**, Haman standeth in H2009
7: 9 before the king, **B** also, the gallows fifty H2009
8: 7 to Mordecai the Jew, **B**, I have given H2009
Job 1:12 And the LORD said unto Satan, **B**, all H2009
19 And, **b**, there came a great wind from H2009
2: 6 And the LORD said unto Satan, **B**, he *is* H2009
4: 3 **B**, thou hast instructed many, and thou H2009
18 **B**, he put no trust in his servants; and H2005
5:17 **B**, happy *is* the man whom God H2009
8:19 **B**, this *is* the joy of his way, and out of H2005
20 **B**, God will not cast away a perfect H2005
9:12 **B**, he taketh away, who can hinder him? H2005
12:14 **B**, he breaketh down, and it cannot be H2005
15 **B**, he withholdeth the waters, and they H2005
13:18 **B** now, I have ordered *my* cause; I H2009
15:15 **B**, he putteth no trust in his saints; yea, H2005
16:19 Also now, **b**, my witness *is* in heaven, H2009
19: 7 **B**, I cry out of wrong, but I am not H2005
27 and mine eyes shall **b**, and not another; H7200
20: 9 neither shall his place any more **b** him. H7789
21:27 **B**, I know your thoughts, and the H2005
22:12 of heaven? and **b** the height of the H7200
23: 8 **B**, I go forward, but he *is* not *there*; and H2005
9 work, but I cannot **b** *him*: he hideth H2372
24: 5 **B**, *as* wild asses in the desert, go they H2005
25: 5 **B** even to the moon, and it shineth not; H2005
27:12 **B**, all ye yourselves have seen *it*; why H2005
28:28 And unto man he said, **B**, the fear of the H2005
31:35 Oh that one would hear me! **b**, my H2005
32:11 **B**, I waited for your words; I gave ear to H2005
Job 32:12 Yea, I attended unto you, and, **b**, *there* H2009
19 **B**, my belly *is* as wine *which* hath no H2009
33: 2 **B**, now I have opened my mouth, my H2009
6 **B**, I *am* according to thy wish in God's H2005
7 **B**, my terror shall not make thee afraid, H2009
10 **B**, he findeth occasions against me, he H2005
12 **B**, *in* this thou art not just: I will answer H2005
34:29 face, who then can **b** him? whether *it be* H7789
35: 5 Look unto the heavens, and see; and **b** H7789
36: 5 **B**, God *is* mighty, and despiseth not H2005
22 **B**, God exalteth by his power: who H2005
24 thou magnify his work, which men **b**. H7891
25 Every man may see it; man may **b** *it* H5027
26 **B**, God *is* great, and we know *him* not, H2005
30 **B**, he spreadeth his light upon it, and H2005
39:29 the prey, *and* her eyes **b** afar off. H5027
40: 4 **B**, I am vile; what shall I answer thee? I H2005
11 of thy wrath: and **b** every one *that is* H7200
15 **B** now behemoth, which I made with H2009
23 **B**, he drinketh up a river, *and* hasteth H2005
41: 9 **B**, the hope of him is in vain: shall not H2005
Ps 7:14 **B**, he travaileth with iniquity, and hath H2009
11: 4 **b**, his eyelids try, the children of men. H2372
7 his countenance doth **b** the upright. H2372
17: 2 thine eyes **b** the things that are equal. H2372
15 As for me, I will **b** thy face in H2372
27: 4 days of my life, to **b** the beauty of the H2372
33:18 **B**, the eye of the LORD *is* upon them H2009
37:37 Mark the perfect *man*, and **b** the H7200
39: 5 **B**, thou hast made my days *as* an H2009
46: 8 Come, **b** the works of the LORD, what H2372
51: 5 **B**, I was shapen in iniquity; and in sin H2005
6 **B**, thou desirest truth in the inward H2005
54: 4 **B**, God *is* mine helper: the Lord *is* with H2009
59: 4 *my* fault: awake to help me, and **b**. H7200
7 **B**, they belch out with their mouth: H2009
66: 7 for ever; his eyes **b** the nations: let not H6822
73:12 **B**, these *are* the ungodly, who prosper H2009
15 If I say, I will speak thus; **b**, I should H2009
78:20 **B**, he smote the rock, that the waters H2005
80:14 from heaven, and **b**, and visit this vine; H7200
84: 9 **B**, O God our shield, and look upon the H7200
87: 4 that know me: **b** Philistia, and Tyre, H2009
91: 8 Only with thine eyes shalt thou **b** and H5027
102:19 from heaven did the LORD **b** the earth; H5027
113: 6 Who humbleth *himself* to **b** *the things* H7200
119:18 Open thou mine eyes, that I may **b** H5027
40 **B**, I have longed after thy precepts: H2009
121: 4 **B**, he that keepeth Israel shall neither H2009
123: 2 **B**, as the eyes of servants *look* unto the H2009
128: 4 **B**, that thus shall the man be blessed H2009
133: 1 **B**, how good and how pleasant *it is* for H2009
134: 1 **B**, bless ye the LORD, all *ye* servants of H2009
139: 8 I make my bed in hell, **b**, thou *art there*. H2009
Prv 1:23 Turn you at my reproof: **b**, I will pour H2009
7:10 And, **b**, there met him a woman *with* H2009
11:31 **B**, the righteous shall be recompensed H2005
23:33 Thine eyes shall **b** strange women, and H7200
24:12 If thou sayest, **B**, we knew it not; doth H2005
Ecc 1:14 **b**, all *is* vanity and vexation of spirit. H2009
2: 1 pleasure: and, **b**, this also *is* vanity. H2009
11 to do: and, **b**, all *was* vanity and H2009
12 And I turned myself to **b** wisdom, and H7200
4: 1 the sun: and **b** the tears of *such as* H2009
5:18 **B** *that* which I have seen: *it is* good and H2009
7:27 **B**, this have I found, saith the preacher, H7200
11: 7 *thing it is* for the eyes to **b** the sun: H7200
Song 1:15 **B**, thou *art* fair, my love; behold, thou H2009
15 Behold, thou *art* fair, my love; **b**, thou H2009
16 **B**, thou *art* fair, my beloved, yea, H2009
2: 8 The voice of my beloved! **b**, he cometh H2009
9 or a young hart: **b**, he standeth behind H2009
3: 7 **B** his bed, which *is* Solomon's; H2009
11 Go forth, O ye daughters of Zion, and **b** H7200
4: 1 **B**, thou *art* fair, my love; behold, thou H2009
1 Behold, thou *art* fair, my love; **b**, thou H2009
Isa 3: 1 For, **b**, the Lord, the LORD of hosts, H2009
5: 7 for judgment, but **b** oppression; for H2009
7 for righteousness, but **b** a cry. H2009
26 **b**, they shall come with speed swiftly: H2009
30 unto the land, **b** darkness *and* sorrow, H2009
7:14 shall give you a sign; **B**, a virgin shall H2009
8: 7 Now therefore, **b**, the Lord bringeth up H2009
18 **B**, I and the children whom the LORD H2009
22 the earth; and **b** trouble and darkness, H2009
10:33 **B**, the Lord, the LORD of hosts, shall lop H2009
12: 2 **B**, God *is* my salvation; I will trust, and H2009
13: 9 **B**, the day of the LORD cometh, cruel H2009
17 **B**, I will stir up the Medes against them, H2005
Isa 17: 1 The burden of Damascus. **B**, Damascus H2009
14 And **b** at eveningtide trouble; *and* H2009
19: 1 The burden of Egypt. **B**, the LORD H2009
20: 6 shall say in that day, **B**, such *is* our H2009
21: 9 And, **b**, here cometh a chariot of men, H2009
22:13 And **b** joy and gladness, slaying oxen, H2009
17 **B**, the LORD will carry thee away with a H2009
23:13 **B** the land of the Chaldeans; this H2005
24: 1 **B**, the LORD maketh the earth empty, H2009
26:10 and will not **b** the majesty of the LORD. H7200
21 For, **b**, the LORD cometh out of his H2009
28: 2 **B**, the Lord hath a mighty and strong H2009
16 Therefore thus saith the Lord GOD, **B**, I H2005
29: 8 *man* dreameth, and, **b**, he eateth; but he H2009
8 dreameth, and, **b**, he drinketh; but he H2009
8 he awaketh, and, **b**, *he is* faint, and his H2009
14 Therefore, **b**, I will proceed to do a H2005
30:27 **B**, the name of the LORD cometh from H2009
32: 1 **B**, a king shall reign in righteousness, H2005
33: 7 **B**, their valiant ones shall cry without: H2005
17 they shall **b** the land that is very far off. H7200
34: 5 bathed in heaven: **b**, it shall come down H2009
35: 4 strong, fear not: **b**, your God will come H2009
37: 7 **B**, I will send a blast upon him, and he H2005
11 **B**, thou hast heard what the kings of H2009
36 morning, **b**, they *were* all dead corpses. H2009
38: 5 **b**, I will add unto thy days fifteen years. H2005
8 **B**, I will bring again the shadow of the H2005
11 the living: I shall **b** man no more with H7200
17 **B**, for peace I had great bitterness: but H2009
39: 6 **B**, the days come, that all that *is* in H2009
40: 9 unto the cities of Judah, **B** your God! H2009
10 **B**, the Lord GOD will come with strong H2009
10 shall rule for him: **b**, his reward *is* with H2009
15 **B**, the nations *are* as a drop of a bucket, H2005
15 of the balance: **b**, he taketh up the isles H2005
26 Lift up your eyes on high, and **b** who H7200
41:11 **B**, all they that were incensed against H2005
15 **B**, I will make thee a new sharp H2009
23 we may be dismayed, and **b** *it* together. H7200
24 **B**, ye *are* of nothing, and your work of H2005
27 The first *shall say* to Zion, **B**, behold H2009
27 The first *shall say* to Zion, Behold, **b** H2009
29 **B**, they *are* all vanity; their works *are* H2005
42: 1 **B** my servant, whom I uphold; mine H2005
9 **B**, the former things are come to pass, H2009
43:19 **B**, I will do a new thing; now it shall H2005
44:11 **B**, all his fellows shall be ashamed: and H2005
47:14 **B**, they shall be as stubble; the fire shall H2009
48: 7 lest thou shouldest say, **B**, I knew them. H2009
10 **B**, I have refined thee, but not with H2009
49:12 **B**, these shall come from far: and, lo, H2009
16 **B**, I have graven thee upon the palms of H2005
18 Lift up thine eyes round about, and **b**: H7200
21 brought up these? **B**, I was left alone; H2005
22 Thus saith the Lord GOD, **B**, I will lift H2009
50: 1 I have sold you? **B**, for your iniquities H2005
2 power to deliver? **b**, at my rebuke I dry H2005
9 **B**, the Lord GOD will help me; who *is* he H2005
11 **B**, all ye that kindle a fire, that compass H2005
51:22 of his people, **B**, I have taken out of H2009
52: 6 that I *am* he that doth speak: **b**, *it is* I. H2009
13 **B**, my servant shall deal prudently, he H2009
54:11 not comforted, **b**, I will lay thy stones H2009
15 **B**, they shall surely gather together, *but* H2005
16 **B**, I have created the smith that bloweth H2005
55: 4 **B**, I have given him *for* a witness to the H2005
5 **B**, thou shalt call a nation *that* thou H2005
56: 3 let the eunuch say, **B**, I *am* a dry tree. H2005
58: 3 no knowledge? **B**, in the day of your fast H2005
4 **B**, ye fast for strife and debate, and to H2005
59: 1 **B**, the LORD'S hand is not shortened, H2005
9 we wait for light, but **b** obscurity; for H2009
60: 2 For, **b**, the darkness shall cover the H2009
62:11 **B**, the LORD hath proclaimed unto the H2009
11 the daughter of Zion, **B**, thy salvation H2009
11 salvation cometh; **b**, his reward *is* with H2009
63:15 Look down from heaven, and **b** from H7200
64: 5 thee in thy ways: **b**, thou art wroth; for H2005
9 iniquity for ever: **b**, see, we beseech H2005
65: 1 me not: I said, **B** me, behold me, unto H2009
1 I said, Behold me, **b** me, unto a nation H2009
6 **B**, *it is* written before me: I will not keep H2009
13 Therefore thus saith the Lord GOD, **B**, H2009
13 ye shall be hungry: **b**, my servants shall H2005
13 ye shall be thirsty: **b**, my servants shall H2005
14 **B**, my servants shall sing for joy of H2005
17 For, **b**, I create new heavens and a new H2005
18 I create: for, **b**, I create Jerusalem a H2005

Isa 66:12 For thus saith the LORD, **B**, I will H2005
15 For, **b**, the LORD will come with fire, H2009
Jer 1: 6 Then said I, Ah, Lord GOD! **b**, I cannot H2009
9 **B**, I have put my words in thy mouth. H2009
18 For, **b**, I have made thee this day a H2009
2:35 turn from me. **B**, I will plead with thee, H2005
3: 5 keep *it* to the end? **B**, thou hast spoken H2009
22 your backslidings. **B**, we come unto H2005
4:13 **B**, he shall come up as clouds, and his H2009
16 Make ye mention to the nations; **b**, H2009
5:14 ye speak this word, **b**, I will make my H2005
6:10 that they may hear? **b**, their ear *is* H2009
10 they cannot hearken: **b**, the word of the H2009
19 Hear, O earth: **b**, I will bring evil upon H2009
21 Therefore thus saith the LORD, **B**, I will H2005
22 Thus saith the LORD, **B**, a people H2009
7: 8 **B**, ye trust in lying words, that cannot H2009
11 **B**, even I have seen *it*, saith the LORD. H2009
20 Therefore thus saith the Lord GOD; **B**, H2009
32 Therefore, **b**, the days come, saith the H2009
8:15 *and* for a time of health, and **b** trouble! H2009
17 For, **b**, I will send serpents, cockatrices, H2005
19 **B** the voice of the cry of the daughter of H2009
9: 7 LORD of hosts, **B**, I will melt them, and H2005
15 the God of Israel; **B**, I will feed them, H2009
25 **B**, the days come, saith the LORD, that I H2009
10:18 For thus saith the LORD, **B**, I will sling H2005
22 **B**, the noise of the bruit is come, and a H2009
11:11 Therefore thus saith the LORD, **B**, I will H2005
22 LORD of hosts, **B**, I will punish them: H2005
12:14 Israel to inherit; **B**, I will pluck them out H2005
13: 7 I had hid it: and, **b**, the girdle was H2009
13 Thus saith the LORD, **B**, I will fill all the H2005
20 Lift up your eyes, and **b** them that H7200
14:13 Then said I, Ah, Lord GOD! **b**, the H2009
18 If I go forth into the field, then **b** the H2009
18 into the city, then **b** them that are sick H2009
19 for the time of healing, and **b** trouble! H2009
16: 9 the God of Israel; **B**, I will cause to cease H2005
12 your fathers; for, **b**, ye walk every one H2009
14 Therefore, **b**, the days come, saith the H2009
16 **B**, I will send for many fishers, saith the H2005
21 Therefore, **b**, I will this once cause them H2005
17:15 **B**, they say unto me, Where *is* the word H2009
18: 3 **b**, he wrought a work on the wheels. H2009
6 saith the LORD. **B**, as the clay *is* in the H2009
11 saith the LORD; **B**, I frame evil against H2009
19: 3 the God of Israel; **B**, I will bring evil H2005
6 Therefore, **b**, the days come, saith the H2009
15 the God of Israel; **B**, I will bring upon H2005
20: 4 For thus saith the LORD, **B**, I will make H2005
4 thine eyes shall **b** *it*: and I will give all H7200
21: 4 Thus saith the LORD God of Israel; **B**, I H2005
8 saith the LORD; **B**, I set before you the H2005
13 **B**, I *am* against thee, O inhabitant of the H2005
23: 2 not visited them: **b**, I will visit upon you H2005
5 **B**, the days come, saith the LORD, that I H2009
7 Therefore, **b**, the days come, saith the H2009
15 the prophets; **B**, I will feed them with H2005
19 **B**, a whirlwind of the LORD is gone H2009
30 Therefore, **b**, I *am* against the prophets, H2005
31 **B**, I *am* against the prophets, saith the H2005
32 **B**, I *am* against them that prophesy H2005
39 Therefore, **b**, I, even I, will utterly forget H2005
24: 1 The LORD shewed me, and, **b**, two H2009
25: 9 **B**, I will send and take all the families of H2005
32 Thus saith the LORD of hosts, **B**, evil H2009
26:14 As for me, **b**, I *am* in your hand: do with H2005
27:16 unto you, saying, **B**, the vessels of the H2009
28:16 Therefore thus saith the LORD; **B**, I will H2005
29:17 Thus saith the LORD of hosts; **B**, I will H2005
21 you in my name; **B**, I will deliver them H2005
32 Therefore thus saith the LORD; **B**, I will H2005
32 neither shall he **b** the good that I will H7200
30:18 Thus saith the LORD;; **B**, I will bring H2005
23 **B**, the whirlwind of the LORD goeth H2009
31: 8 **B**, I will bring them from the north H2005
27 **B**, the days come, saith the LORD, that I H2009
31 **B**, the days come, saith the LORD, that I H2009
38 **B**, the days come, saith the LORD, that H2009
32: 3 saith the LORD, **B**, I will give this city H2005
4 to mouth, and his eyes shall **b** his eyes; H7200
7 **B**, Hanameel the son of Shallum thine H2009
17 Ah Lord GOD! **b**, thou hast made the H2009
24 **B** the mounts, they are come unto the H2009
24 is come to pass; and, **b**, thou seest *it*. H2009
27 **B**, I *am* the LORD, the God of all flesh: is H2009
28 Therefore thus saith the LORD; **B**, I will H2005
37 **B**, I will gather them out of all H2005

Jer 33: 6 **B**, I will bring it health and cure, and I H2005
14 **B**, the days come, saith the LORD, that I H2009
34: 2 saith the LORD; **B**, I will give this city H2005
3 thine eyes shall **b** the eyes of the king H7200
17 to his neighbour: **b**, I proclaim a liberty H2005
22 **B**, I will command, saith the LORD, and H2005
35:17 the God of Israel; **B**, I will bring upon H2005
37: 7 me to inquire of me; **B**, Pharaoh's army, H2005
38: 5 Then Zedekiah the king said, **B**, he *is* in H2009
22 And, **b**, all the women that are left in H2009
39:16 the God of Israel; **B**, I will bring my H2005
40: 4 And now, **b**, I loose thee this day from H2009
4 into Babylon, forbear: **b**, all the land *is* H7200
10 As for me, **b**, I will dwell at Mizpah to H2005
42: 2 a few of many, as thine eyes do **b** us:) H7200
4 I have heard *you*; **b**, I will pray unto the H2005
43:10 the God of Israel; **B**, I will send and take H2005
44: 2 of Judah; and, **b**, this day they *are* a H2009
11 the God of Israel; **B**, I will set my face H2005
26 in the land of Egypt; **B**, I have sworn by H2005
27 **B**, I will watch over them for evil, and H2005
30 Thus saith the LORD; **B**, I will give H2005
45: 4 LORD saith thus; **B**, *that* which I have H2009
5 *them* not: for, **b**, I will bring evil upon H2005
46:25 God of Israel, saith; **B**, I will punish the H2005
27 O Israel: for, **b**, I will save thee from H2005
47: 2 Thus saith the LORD; **B**, waters rise up H2009
48:12 Therefore, **b**, the days come, saith the H2009
40 For thus saith the LORD; **B**, he shall fly H2009
49: 2 Therefore, **b**, the days come, saith the H2009
5 **B**, I will bring a fear upon thee, saith the H2005
12 For thus saith the LORD; **B**, they whose H2009
19 **B**, he shall come up like a lion from the H2009
22 **B**, he shall come up and fly as the eagle, H2009
35 Thus saith the LORD of hosts; **B**, I will H2005
50:12 shall be ashamed: **b**, the hindermost of H2009
18 the God of Israel; **B**, I will punish the H2005
31 **B**, I *am* against thee, *O thou* most H2005
41 **B**, a people shall come from the north, H2009
44 **B**, he shall come up like a lion from the H2009
51: 1 Thus saith the LORD; **B**, I will raise up H2005
25 **B**, I *am* against thee, O destroying H2005
36 Therefore thus saith the LORD; **B**, I will H2005
47 Therefore, **b**, the days come, that I will H2009
52 Wherefore, **b**, the days come, saith the H2009
Lam 1: 9 O LORD, **b** my affliction: for the H7200
12 all ye that pass by? **b**, and see if there be H5027
18 you, all people, and **b** my sorrow: my H7200
20 **B**, O LORD; for I *am* in distress: my H7200
2:20 **B**, O LORD, and consider to whom thou H7200
3:50 Till the LORD look down, and **b** from H7200
63 **B** their sitting down, and their rising H5027
5: 1 upon us: consider, and **b** our reproach. H7200
Ezk 1: 4 And I looked, and, **b**, a whirlwind came H2009
15 Now as I beheld the living creatures, **b** H2009
2: 9 And when I looked, **b**, an hand *was* sent H2009
3: 8 **B**, I have made thy face strong against H2009
23 the plain: and, **b**, the glory of the LORD H2009
25 But thou, O son of man, **b**, they shall H2009
4: 8 And, **b**, I will lay bands upon thee, and H2009
14 Then said I, Ah Lord GOD! **b**, my soul H2009
16 me, Son of man, **b**, I will break the staff H2005
5: 8 Therefore thus saith the Lord GOD; **B**, I, H2005
6: 3 and to the valleys; **B**, I, *even* I, will bring H2005
7: 5 GOD; An evil, an only evil, **b**, is come. H2009
6 come: it watcheth for thee; **b**, it is come. H2009
10 **B** the day, behold, it is come: the H2009
10 Behold the day, **b**, it is come: the H2009
8: 4 And, **b**, the glory of the God of Israel H2009
5 the north, and **b** northward at the gate H2009
7 and when I looked, **b** a hole in the wall. H2009
8 when I had digged in the wall, **b** a door. H2009
9 And he said unto me, Go in, and **b** the H7200
10 So I went in and saw; and **b** every form H2009
14 the north; and, **b**, there sat women H2009
16 house, and, **b**, at the door of the temple H2009
9: 2 And, **b**, six men came from the way of H2009
11 And, **b**, the man clothed with linen, H2009
10: 1 Then I looked, and, **b**, in the firmament H2009
9 And when I looked, **b** the four wheels H2009
11: 1 eastward: and **b** at the door of the gate H2009
12:27 Son of man, **b**, *they of* the house of H2009
13: 8 seen lies, therefore, **b**, I *am* against you, H2005
20 Wherefore thus saith the Lord GOD; **B**, I H2005
14:22 Yet, **b**, therein shall be left a remnant H2009
22 and daughters: **b**, they shall come forth H2009
15: 4 **B**, it is cast into the fire for fuel; the fire H2009
5 **B**, when it was whole, it was meet for no H2009
16: 8 looked upon thee, **b**, thy time *was* the H2009

Ezk 16:27 **B**, therefore I have stretched out my H2009
37 **B**, therefore I will gather all thy lovers, H2005
43 me in all these *things*; **b**, therefore I also H1887
44 **B**, every one that useth proverbs shall H2009
49 **B**, this was the iniquity of thy sister H2009
17: 7 feathers: and, **b**, this vine did bend her H2009
10 Yea, **b**, *being* planted, shall it prosper? H2009
12 *mean*? tell *them*, **B**, the king of Babylon H2009
18: 4 **B**, all souls are mine; as the soul of the H2005
20:47 the Lord GOD; **B**, I will kindle a fire in H2005
21: 3 saith the LORD; **B**, I *am* against thee, H2005
7 be weak *as* water: **b**, it cometh, and H2009
22: 6 **B**, the princes of Israel, every one were H2009
13 **B**, therefore I have smitten mine hand H2009
19 are all become dross, **b**, therefore I will H2005
23:22 the Lord GOD; **B**, I will raise up thy H2005
28 For thus saith the Lord GOD; **B**, I will H2005
24:16 Son of man, **b**, I take away from thee H2005
21 the Lord GOD; **B**, I will profane my H2005
25: 4 **B**, therefore I will deliver thee to the H2005
7 **B**, therefore I will stretch out mine hand H2005
8 and Seir do say, **B**, the house of Judah H2009
9 Therefore, **b**, I will open the side of H2005
16 Therefore thus saith the Lord GOD; **B**, I H2005
26: 3 Therefore thus saith the Lord GOD; **B**, I H2005
7 For thus saith the Lord GOD; **B**, I will H2005
28: 3 **B**, thou *art* wiser than Daniel; there is H2009
7 **B**, therefore I will bring strangers upon H2005
17 thee before kings, that they may **b** thee. H7200
18 in the sight of all them that **b** thee. H7200
22 And say, Thus saith the Lord GOD; **B**, I H2005
29: 3 the Lord GOD; **B**, I *am* against thee, H2005
8 Therefore thus saith the Lord GOD; **B**, I H2005
10 **B**, therefore I *am* against thee, and H2005
19 Therefore thus saith the Lord GOD; **B**, I H2005
30:22 Therefore thus saith the Lord GOD; **B**, I H2005
31: 3 **B**, the Assyrian *was* a cedar in Lebanon H2009
34:10 Thus saith the Lord GOD; **B**, I *am* H2005
11 For thus saith the Lord GOD; **B**, I, *even* H2005
17 the Lord GOD; **B**, I judge between cattle H2005
20 GOD unto them; **B**, I, *even* I, will judge H2005
35: 3 the Lord GOD; **B**, O mount Seir, I *am* H2005
36: 6 the Lord GOD; **B**, I have spoken in my H2005
9 For, **b**, I *am* for you, and I will turn unto H2005
37: 2 round about: and, **b**, *there were* very H2009
5 unto these bones; **B**, I will cause breath H2009
7 was a noise, and **b** a shaking, and the H2009
11 house of Israel: **b**, they say, Our bones H2009
12 the Lord GOD; **B**, O my people, I will H2009
19 the Lord GOD; **B**, I will take the stick H2009
21 the Lord GOD; **B**, I will take the children H2009
38: 3 And say, Thus saith the Lord GOD; **B**, I H2005
39: 1 the Lord GOD; **B**, I *am* against thee, O H2005
8 **B**, it is come, and it is done, saith the H2009
40: 3 And he brought me thither, and, **b**, H2009
4 me, Son of man, **b** with thine eyes, and H7200
5 And **b** a wall on the outside of the H2009
24 the south, and **b** a gate toward the H2009
43: 2 And, **b**, the glory of the God of Israel H2009
5 the inner court; and, **b**, the glory of the H2009
12 holy. **B**, this *is* the law of the house. H2009
44: 4 and I looked, and, **b**, the glory of the H2009
5 mark well, and **b** with thine eyes, and H7200
46:19 the north: and, **b**, there *was* a place on H2009
21 of the court; and, **b**, in every corner of H2009
47: 1 of the house; and, **b**, waters issued out H2009
2 **b**, there ran out waters on the right side. H2009
7 Now when I had returned, **b**, at the H2009
Dan 2:31 Thou, O king, sawest, and **b** a great H431
4:10 my bed; I saw, and **b** a tree in the midst H431
13 upon my bed, and, **b**, a watcher and an H431
7: 2 by night, and, **b**, the four winds of the H718
5 And **b** another beast, a second, like to a H718
7 the night visions, and **b** a fourth beast, H718
8 I considered the horns, and, **b**, there H431
8 up by the roots: and, **b**, in this horn *were* H431
13 I saw in the night visions, and, **b**, *one* like H718
8: 3 and saw, and, **b**, there stood before the H2009
5 And as I was considering, **b**, an he goat H2009
15 meaning, then, **b**, there stood before me H2009
19 And he said, **B**, I will make thee know H2005
9:18 thine eyes, and **b** our desolations, and H7200
10: 5 eyes, and looked, and **b** a certain man H2009
10 And, **b**, an hand touched me, which set H2009
16 And, **b**, *one* like the similitude of the H2009
11: 2 And now will I shew thee the truth. **B**, H2009
12: 5 Then I Daniel looked, and, **b**, there H2009
Hos 2: 6 Therefore, **b**, I will hedge up thy way H2005
14 Therefore, **b**, I will allure her, and bring H2009

Joel 2:19 unto his people, **B**, I will send you corn, H2005
3: 1 For, **b**, in those days, and in that time, H2005
7 **B**, I will raise them out of the place H2005
Am 2:13 **B**, I am pressed under you, as a cart is H2009
3: 9 of Samaria, and **b** the great tumults in H7200
6:11 For, **b**, the LORD commandeth, and he H2005
14 But, **b**, I will raise up against you a H2009
7: 1 shewed unto me; and, **b**, he formed H2009
4 unto me: and, **b**, the Lord GOD called H2009
7 Thus he shewed me: and, **b**, the Lord H2009
8 said the Lord, **B**, I will set a plumbline H2005
8: 1 me: and **b** a basket of summer fruit. H2009
11 **B**, the days come, saith the Lord GOD, H2009
9: 8 **B**, the eyes of the Lord GOD *are* upon H2009
13 **B**, the days come, saith the LORD, that H2009
Oba 2 **B**, I have made thee small among the H2009
Mic 1: 3 For, **b**, the LORD cometh forth out of H2009
2: 3 Therefore thus saith the LORD; **B**, H2005
7: 9 light, *and* I shall **b** his righteousness. H7200
10 mine eyes shall **b** her: now shall she be H7200
Nah 1:15 **B** upon the mountains the feet of him H2009
2:13 **B**, I *am* against thee, saith the LORD of H2005
3: 5 **B**, I *am* against thee, saith the LORD of H2005
13 **B**, thy people in the midst of thee *are* H2009
Hab 1: 3 and cause *me* to **b** grievance? for H5027
5 **B** ye among the heathen, and regard, H7200
13 *Thou art* of purer eyes than to **b** evil, H7200
2: 4 **B**, his soul *which* is lifted up is not H2009
13 **B**, *is it* not of the LORD of hosts that the H2009
19 it shall teach! **B**, it *is* laid over with gold H2009
Zep 3:19 **B**, at that time I will undo all that afflict H2005
Zec 1: 8 I saw by night, and **b** a man riding H2009
11 the earth, and, **b**, all the earth sitteth H2009
18 mine eyes, and saw, and **b** four horns. H2009
2: 1 again, and looked, and **b** a man with a H2009
3 And, **b**, the angel that talked with me H2009
9 For, **b**, I will shake mine hand upon H2005
3: 4 unto him he said, **B**, I have caused thine H7200
8 wondered at: for, **b**, I will bring forth H2005
9 For **b** the stone that I have laid before H2009
9 *shall be* seven eyes: **b**, I will engrave the H2005
4: 2 I have looked, and **b** a candlestick all *of* H2005
5: 1 eyes, and looked, and **b** a flying roll. H2009
7 And, **b**, there was lifted up a talent of H2009
9 and looked, and, **b**, there came out two H2009
6: 1 and looked, and, **b**, there came four H2009
8 spake unto me, saying, **B**, these that go H7200
12 of hosts, saying, **B** the man whose H2009
8: 7 Thus saith the LORD of hosts; **B**, I will H2005
9: 4 **B**, the Lord will cast her out, and he will H2009
9 of Jerusalem: **b**, thy King cometh unto H2009
12: 2 **B**, I will make Jerusalem a cup of H2009
14: 1 **B**, the day of the LORD cometh, and thy H2009
Mal 1:13 Ye said also, **B**, what a weariness *is it*! H2009
2: 3 **B**, I will corrupt your seed, and spread H2005
3: 1 **B**, I will send my messenger, and he H2005
1 ye delight in: **b**, he shall come, saith H2009
4: 1 For, **b**, the day cometh, that shall burn H2009
5 **B**, I will send you Elijah the prophet H2009
Mt 1:20 But while he thought on these things, **b**, G2400
23 **B**, a virgin shall be with child, and shall G2400
2: 1 of Herod the king, **b**, there came wise G2400
13 And when they were departed, **b**, the G2400
19 But when Herod was dead, **b**, an angel G2400
4:11 Then the devil leaveth him, and, **b**, G2400
6:26 **B** the fowls of the air: for they sow not, G1689
7: 4 eye; and, **b**, a beam *is* in thine own eye? G2400
8: 2 And, **b**, there came a leper and G2400
24 And, **b**, there arose a great tempest in G2400
29 And, **b**, they cried out, saying, What G2400
32 herd of swine: and, **b**, the whole herd of G2400
34 And, **b**, the whole city came out to meet G2400
9: 2 And, **b**, they brought to him a man sick G2400
3 And, **b**, certain of the scribes said G2400
10 at meat in the house, **b**, many publicans G2400
18 these things unto them, **b**, there came a G2400
20 And, **b**, a woman, which was diseased G2400
32 As they went out, **b**, they brought to G2400
10:16 **B**, I send you forth as sheep in the midst G2400
11: 8 in soft raiment? **b**, they that wear soft G2400
10 For this is *he*, of whom it is written, **B**, I G2400
19 and they say, **B** a man gluttonous, and G2400
12: 2 said unto him, **B**, thy disciples do that G2400
10 And, **b**, there was a man which had *his* G2400
18 **B** my servant, whom I have chosen; my G2400
41 and, **b**, a greater than Jonas *is* here. G2400
42 and, **b**, a greater than Solomon *is* here. G2400
46 While he yet talked to the people, **b**, *his* G2400
47 Then one said unto him, **B**, thy mother G2400
Mt 12:49 said, **B** my mother and my brethren! G2400
13: 3 saying, **B**, a sower went forth to sow; G2400
15:22 And, **b**, a woman of Canaan came out G2400
17: 3 And, **b**, there appeared unto them G2400
5 While he yet spake, **b**, a bright cloud G2400
5 them: and **b** a voice out of the cloud, G2400
18:10 angels do always **b** the face of my Father G991
19:16 And, **b**, one came and said unto him, G2400
27 said unto him, **B**, we have forsaken all, G2400
20:18 **B**, we go up to Jerusalem; and the Son G2400
30 And, **b**, two blind men sitting by the G2400
21: 5 Tell ye the daughter of Sion, **B**, thy King G2400
22: 4 which are bidden, **B**, I have prepared G2400
23:34 Wherefore, **b**, I send unto you prophets, G2400
38 **B**, your house is left unto you desolate. G2400
24:25 **B**, I have told you before. G2400
26 Wherefore if they shall say unto you, **B**, G2400
26 desert; go not forth: **b**, *he is* in the secret G2400
25: 6 was a cry made, **B**, the bridegroom G2400
20 me five talents: **b**, I have gained beside G2396
22 me two talents: **b**, I have gained two G2396
26:45 take *your* rest: **b**, the hour is at hand, G2400
46 Rise, let us be going: **b**, he is at hand G2400
51 And, **b**, one of them which were with G2400
65 **b**, now ye have heard his blasphemy. G2396
27:51 And, **b**, the veil of the temple was rent G2400
28: 2 And, **b**, there was a great earthquake: G2400
7 the dead; and, **b**, he goeth before you G2400
9 And as they went to tell his disciples, **b**, G2400
11 Now when they were going, **b**, some of G2400
Mk 1: 2 As it is written in the prophets, **B**, I send G2400
2:24 And the Pharisees said unto him, **B**, G2396
3:32 said unto him, **B**, thy mother and thy G2400
34 said, **B** my mother and my brethren! G2396
4: 3 Hearken; **B**, there went out a sower to G2400
5:22 And, **b**, there cometh one of the rulers G2400
10:33 *Saying*, **B**, we go up to Jerusalem; and G2400
11:21 unto him, Master, **b**, the fig tree which G2396
13:23 But take ye heed: **b**, I have foretold you G2400
14:41 the hour is come; **b**, the Son of man is G2400
15: 4 thou nothing? **b** how many things they G2396
35 they heard *it*, said, **B**, he calleth Elias. G2400
16: 6 here: **b** the place where they laid him. G2396
Lk 1:20 And, **b**, thou shalt be dumb, and not G2400
31 And, **b**, thou shalt conceive in thy G2400
36 And, **b**, thy cousin Elisabeth, she hath G2400
38 And Mary said, **B** the handmaid of the G2400
48 handmaiden: for, **b**, from henceforth all G2400
2:10 Fear not: for, **b**, I bring you good tidings G2400
25 And, **b**, there was a man in Jerusalem, G2400
34 Mary his mother, **B**, this *child* is set for G2400
48 dealt with us? **b**, thy father and I have G2400
5:12 was in a certain city, **b** a man full of G2400
18 And, **b**, men brought in a bed a man G2400
6:23 leap for joy: for, **b**, your reward *is* great G2400
7:12 the gate of the city, **b**, there was a dead G2400
25 in soft raiment? **B**, they which are G2400
27 This is *he*, of whom it is written, **B**, I G2400
34 and ye say, **B** a gluttonous man, and G2400
37 And, **b**, a woman in the city, which was G2400
8:41 And, **b**, there came a man named G2400
9:30 And, **b**, there talked with him two men, G2400
38 And, **b**, a man of the company cried G2400
10: 3 Go your ways: **b**, I send you forth as G2400
19 **B**, I give unto you power to tread on G2400
25 And, **b**, a certain lawyer stood up, and G2400
11:31 and, **b**, a greater than Solomon *is* here. G2400
32 and, **b**, a greater than Jonas *is* here. G2400
41 and, **b**, all things are clean unto you. G2400
13: 7 of his vineyard, **B**, these three years I G2400
11 And, **b**, there was a woman which had a G2400
30 And, **b**, there are last which shall be G2400
32 ye, and tell that fox, **B**, I cast out devils, G2400
35 **B**, your house is left unto you desolate: G2400
14: 2 And, **b**, there was a certain man before G2400
29 *it*, all that **b** *it* begin to mock him, G2334
17:21 **b**, the kingdom of God is within you. G2400
18:31 and said unto them, **B**, we go up to G2400
19: 2 And, **b**, *there was* a man named G2400
8 unto the Lord; **B**, Lord, the half of my G2400
20 And another came, saying, Lord, **b**, G2400
21: 6 *As for* these things which ye **b**, the days G2334
29 And he spake to them a parable; **B** the G1492
22:10 And he said unto them, **B**, when ye are G2400
21 But, **b**, the hand of him that betrayeth G2400
31 And the Lord said, Simon, Simon, **b**, G2400
38 And they said, Lord, **b**, here *are* two G2400
47 And while he yet spake, **b** a multitude, G2400
23:14 the people: and, **b**, I, having examined G2400
Lk 23:29 For, **b**, the days are coming, in the G2400
50 And, **b**, *there was* a man named Joseph, G2400
24: 4 thereabout, **b**, two men stood by them G2400
13 And, **b**, two of them went that same day G2400
39 **B** my hands and my feet, that it is I G1492
49 And, **b**, I send the promise of my Father G2400
Jn 1:29 him, and saith, **B** the Lamb of God, G2396
36 walked, he saith, **B** the Lamb of God! G2396
47 and saith of him, **B** an Israelite indeed, G2396
3:26 barest witness, **b**, the same baptizeth, G2396
4:35 cometh harvest? **b**, I say unto you, Lift G2400
5:14 said unto him, **B**, thou art made whole: G2396
11: 3 Lord, **b**, he whom thou lovest is sick. G2396
36 Then said the Jews, **B** how he loved G2396
12:15 Fear not, daughter of Sion: **b**, thy King G2400
19 nothing? **b**, the world is gone after him. G2396
16:32 **B**, the hour cometh, yea, is now come, G2400
17:24 I am; that they may **b** my glory, which G2334
18:21 unto them: **b**, they know what I said. G2396
19: 4 saith unto them, **B**, I bring him forth to G2396
5 And *Pilate* saith unto them, **B** the man! G2396
14 he saith unto the Jews, **B** your King! G2396
26 unto his mother, Woman, **b** thy son! G2400
27 Then saith he to the disciple, **B** thy G2400
20:27 thy finger, and **b** my hands; and reach G1492
Act 1:10 as he went up, **b**, two men stood by G2400
2: 7 one to another, **B**, are not all these G2400
4:29 And now, Lord, **b** their threatenings: G1896
5: 9 Spirit of the Lord? **b**, the feet of them G2400
25 told them, saying, **B**, the men whom ye G2400
28 in this name? and, **b**, ye have filled G2400
7:31 as he drew near to **b** *it*, the voice of the G2657
32 Then Moses trembled, and durst not **b**. G2657
56 And said, **B**, I see the heavens opened, G2400
8:27 And he arose and went: and, **b**, a man G2400
9:10 And he said, **B**, I *am here*, Lord. G2400
11 Saul, of Tarsus: for, **b**, he prayeth, G2400
10:17 should mean, **b**, the men which were G2400
19 said unto him, **B**, three men seek thee. G2400
21 and said, **B**, I am he whom ye seek: G2400
30 in my house, and, **b**, a man stood G2400
11:11 And, **b**, immediately there were three G2400
12: 7 And, **b**, the angel of the Lord came G2400
13:11 And now, **b**, the hand of the Lord *is* G2400
25 I am not *he*. But, **b**, there cometh one G2400
41 **B**, ye despisers, and wonder, and G1492
16: 1 and Lystra: and, **b**, a certain disciple G2400
20:22 And now, **b**, I go bound in the spirit G2400
25 And now, **b**, I know that ye all, among G2400
Ro 2:17 **B**, thou art called a Jew, and restest in G2396
9:33 As it is written, **B**, I lay in Sion a G2400
11:22 **B** therefore the goodness and severity G1492
1Co 10:18 **B** Israel after the flesh: are not they G991
15:51 **B**, I shew you a mystery; We shall not G2400
2Co 3: 7 not stedfastly **b** the face of Moses for G816
5:17 away; **b**, all things are become new. G2400
6: 2 I succoured thee: **b**, now *is* the accepted G2400
2 time; **b**, now *is* the day of salvation.) G2400
9 **b**, we live; as chastened, and not killed; G2400
7:11 For **b** this selfsame thing, that ye G2400
12:14 **B**, the third time I am ready to come to G2400
Gal 1:20 I write unto you, **b**, before God, I lie not. G2400
5: 2 **B**, I Paul say unto you, that if ye be G2396
Heb 2:13 in him. And again, **B** I and the children G2400
8: 8 For finding fault with them, he saith, **B**, G2400
Jas 3: 3 **B**, we put bits in the horses' mouths, G2400
4 **B** also the ships, which though *they be* G2400
5 great things. **B**, how great a matter G2400
5: 4 **B**, the hire of the labourers who have G2400
7 of the Lord. **B**, the husbandman waiteth G2400
9 **b**, the judge standeth before the door. G2400
11 **B**, we count them happy which endure. G2400
1Pt 2: 6 in the scripture, **B**, I lay in Sion a chief G2400
12 **b**, glorify God in the day of visitation. G2029
3: 2 While they **b** your chaste conversation G2029
1Jn 3: 1 **B**, what manner of love the Father hath G1492
Jude 14 of these, saying, **B**, the Lord cometh G2400
Rev 1: 7 **B**, he cometh with clouds; and every eye G2400
18 and was dead; and, **b**, I am alive for G2400
2:10 thou shalt suffer: **b**, the devil shall cast G2400
22 **B**, I will cast her into a bed, and them G2400
3: 8 I know thy works: **b**, I have set before G2400
9 **B**, I will make them of the synagogue of G2400
9 are not, but do lie; **b**, I will make them G2400
11 **B**, I come quickly: hold that fast which G2400
20 **B**, I stand at the door, and knock: if any G2400
4: 1 After this I looked, and, **b**, a door *was* G2400
2 in the spirit: and, **b**, a throne was set in G2400
5: 5 me, Weep not: **b**, the Lion of the tribe G2400

Rev 6: 2 And I saw, and **b** a white horse: and he G2400
8 And I looked, and **b** a pale horse: and G2400
9:12 One woe is past; *and*, **b**, there come two G2400
11:14 The second woe is past; *and*, **b**, the G2400
12: 3 in heaven; and **b** a great red dragon, G2400
14:14 And I looked, and **b** a white cloud, and G2400
15: 5 And after that I looked, and, **b**, the G2400
16:15 **B**, I come as a thief. Blessed *is* he that G2400
17: 8 world, when they **b** the beast that was, G991
19:11 And I saw heaven opened, and **b** a G2400
21: 3 of heaven saying, **B**, the tabernacle of G2400
5 And he that sat upon the throne said, **B**, G2400
22: 7 **B**, I come quickly: blessed *is* he that G2400
12 And, **b**, I come quickly; and my reward G2400

BEHOLDEST
Ps 10:14 Thou hast seen *it*; for thou **b** mischief H5027
Mt 7: 3 And why **b** thou the mote that is in thy G991
Lk 6:41 And why **b** thou the mote that is in thy G991
42 when thou thyself **b** not the beam that is G991

BEHOLDETH
Job 24:18 he **b** not the way of the vineyards. H6437
41:34 He **b** all high *things*: he *is* a king over H7200
Ps 33:13 The LORD looketh from heaven; he **b** H7200
Jas 1:24 For he **b** himself, and goeth his way, G2657

BEHOLDING
Ps 119:37 Turn away mine eyes from **b** vanity; H7200
Prv 15: 3 in every place, **b** the evil and the good. H6822
Ecc 5:11 saving the **b** *of them* with their eyes? H7200
Mt 27:55 And many women were there **b** afar G2334
Mk 10:21 Then Jesus **b** him loved him, and said G1689
Lk 23:35 And the people stood **b**. And the rulers G2334
48 to that sight, **b** the things which were G2334
49 Galilee, stood afar off, **b** these things. G3708
Act 4:14 And **b** the man which was healed G991
8:13 and wondered, **b** the miracles and G2334
14: 9 who stedfastly **b** him, and perceiving G816
23: 1 And Paul, earnestly **b** the council, said, G816
2Co 3:18 But we all, with open face **b** as in a G2734
Col 2: 5 spirit, joying and **b** your order, and the G991
Jas 1:23 a man **b** his natural face in a glass: G2657

BEHOVED
Lk 24:46 and thus it **b** Christ to suffer, and G1163
Heb 2:17 Wherefore in all things it **b** him to be G3784

BEING See the Appendix.

BEKAH
Ex 38:26 A **b** for every man, *that is*, half a H1235

BEL
Isa 46: 1 **B** boweth down, Nebo stoopeth, their H1078
Jer 50: 2 say, Babylon is taken, **B** is confounded, H1078
51:44 And I will punish **B** in Babylon, and I H1078

BELA
Gen 14: 2 and the king of **B**, which is Zoar. H1106
8 and the king of **B** (the same *is* Zoar;) H1106
36:32 And **B** the son of Beor reigned in H1106
33 And **B** died, and Jobab the son of Zerah H1106
Nu 26:38 their families: of **B**, the family of the H1106
40 And the sons of **B** were Ard and H1106
1Ch 1:43 the children of Israel; **B** the son of Beor: H1106
44 And when **B** was dead, Jobab the son of H1106
5: 8 And **B** the son of Azaz, the son of H1106
7: 6 *The sons* of Benjamin; **B**, and Becher, H1106
7 And the sons of **B**; Ezbon, and Uzzi, and H1106
8: 1 Now Benjamin begat **B** his firstborn, H1106
3 And the sons of **B** were, Addar, and H1106

BELAH
Gen 46:21 And the sons of Benjamin *were* **B**, and H1106

BELAITES
Nu 26:38 the family of the **B**: of Ashbel, the family H1108

BELCH
Ps 59: 7 Behold, they **b** out with their mouth: H5042

BELIAL
Dt 13:13 *Certain* men, the children of **B**, are gone H1100
Jdg 19:22 certain sons of **B**, beset the house round H1100
20:13 the children of **B**, which *are* in Gibeah, H1100
1Sa 1:16 for a daughter of **B**: for out of the H1100
2:12 Now the sons of Eli *were* sons of **B**; they H1100
10:27 But the children of **B** said, How shall H1100
1Sa 25:17 of **B**, that *a man* cannot speak to him. H1100
25 this man of **B**, *even* Nabal: for as his H1100
30:22 men and *men* of **B**, of those that went H1100
2Sa 16: 7 thou bloody man, and thou man of **B**: H1100
20: 1 to be there a man of **B**, whose name *was* H1100
23: 6 But *the sons* of **B** *shall be* all of them as H1100
1Ki 21:10 And set two men, sons of **B**, before him, H1100
13 men, children of **B**, and sat before him: H1100
13 and the men of **B** witnessed against H1100
2Ch 13: 7 men, the children of **B**, and have H1100
2Co 6:15 And what concord hath Christ with **B**? or G955

BELIED
Jer 5:12 They have **b** the LORD, and said, *It is* H3584

BELIEF
2Th 2:13 of the Spirit and **b** of the truth: G4102

BELIEVE
Ex 4: 1 they will not **b** me, nor hearken unto H539
5 That they may **b** that the LORD God of H539
8 if they will not **b** thee, neither hearken H539
8 they will **b** the voice of the latter sign. H539
9 if they will not **b** also these two signs, H539
19: 9 speak with thee, and **b** thee for ever. And H539
Nu 14:11 will it be ere they **b** me, for all the signs H539
Dt 1:32 Yet in this thing ye did not **b** the LORD H539
2Ki 17:14 that did not **b** in the LORD their God. H539
2Ch 20:20 of Jerusalem; **B** in the LORD your God, H539
20 **b** his prophets, so shall ye prosper. H539
32:15 neither yet **b** him: for no god of any H539
Job 9:16 **b** that he had hearkened unto my voice. H539
39:12 Wilt thou **b** him, that he will bring home H539
Prv 26:25 When he speaketh fair, **b** him not: for H539
Isa 7: 9 not **b**, surely ye shall not be established. H539
43:10 ye may know and **b** me, and understand H539
Jer 12: 6 after thee: **b** them not, though they H539
Hab 1: 5 *which* ye will not **b**, though it be told *you*. H539
Mt 9:28 saith unto them, **B** ye that I am able to G4100
18: 6 little ones which **b** in me, it were better G4100
21:25 unto us, Why did ye not then **b** him? G4100
32 not afterward, that ye might **b** him. G4100
24:23 Lo, here *is* Christ, or there; **b** *it* not. G4100
26 *he is* in the secret chambers; **b** *it* not. G4100
27:42 from the cross, and we will **b** him. G4100
Mk 1:15 repent ye, and **b** the gospel. G4100+G1722
5:36 of the synagogue, Be not afraid, only **b**. G4100
9:23 Jesus said unto him, If thou canst **b**, all G4100
24 Lord, I **b**; help thou mine unbelief. G4100
42 little ones that **b** in me, it is better for G4100
11:23 his heart, but shall **b** that those things G4100
24 when ye pray, **b** that ye receive *them*, G4100
31 he will say, Why then did ye not **b** him? G4100
13:21 *is* Christ; or, lo, *he is* there; **b** *him* not: G4100
15:32 we may see and **b**. And they that were G4100
16:17 follow them that **b**; In my name shall G4100
Lk 8:12 hearts, lest they should **b** and be saved. G4100
13 **b**, and in time of temptation fall away. G4100
50 **b** only, and she shall be made whole. G4100
22:67 unto them, If I tell you, ye will not **b**: G4100
24:25 slow of heart to **b** all that the G4100+G1909
Jn 1: 7 that all *men* through him might **b**. G4100
12 God, *even* to them that **b** on his name: G4100
3:12 things, and ye **b** not, how shall ye G4100
12 ye **b**, if I tell you *of* heavenly things? G4100
4:21 Jesus saith unto her, Woman, **b** me, the G4100
42 And said unto the woman, Now we **b**, G4100
48 ye see signs and wonders, ye will not **b**. G4100
5:38 for whom he hath sent, him ye **b** not. G4100
44 How can ye **b**, which receive honour G4100
47 But if ye **b** not his writings, how shall G4100
47 his writings, how shall ye **b** my words? G4100
6:29 that ye **b** on him whom he hath sent. G4100
30 see, and **b** thee? what dost thou work? G4100
36 That ye also have seen me, and **b** not. G4100
64 But there are some of you that **b** not. G4100
69 And we **b** and are sure that thou art G4100
7: 5 For neither did his brethren **b** in him. G4100
39 Spirit, which they that **b** on him should G4100
8:24 in your sins: for if ye **b** not that I am *he*, G4100
45 And because I tell *you* the truth, ye **b** G4100
46 if I say the truth, why do ye not **b** me? G4100
9:18 But the Jews did not **b** concerning him, G4100
35 him, Dost thou **b** on the Son of God? G4100
36 Who is he, Lord, that I might **b** on him? G4100
38 And he said, Lord, I **b**. And he G4100
10:26 But ye **b** not, because ye are not of my G4100
37 If I do not the works of my Father, **b** G4100
38 But if I do, though ye **b** not me, believe G4100
Jn 10:38 But if I do, though ye believe not me, **b** G4100
38 **b**, that the Father *is* in me, and I in him. G4100
11:15 may **b**; nevertheless let us go unto him. G4100
27 She saith unto him, Yea, Lord: I **b** that G4100
40 **b**, thou shouldest see the glory of God? G4100
42 that they may **b** that thou hast sent me. G4100
48 If we let him thus alone, all *men* will **b** G4100
12:36 While ye have light, **b** in the light, that G4100
39 Therefore they could not **b**, because G4100
47 And if any man hear my words, and **b** G4100
13:19 is come to pass, ye may **b** that I am *he*. G4100
14: 1 Let not your heart be troubled: ye **b** in G4100
1 ye believe in God, **b** also in me. G4100
11 **B** me that I *am* in the Father, and the G4100
11 or else **b** me for the very works' sake. G4100
29 when it is come to pass, ye might **b**. G4100
16: 9 Of sin, because they **b** not on me; G4100
30 we **b** that thou camest forth from God. G4100
31 Jesus answered them, Do ye now **b**? G4100
17:20 shall **b** on me through their word; G4100
21 world may **b** that thou hast sent me. G4100
19:35 that he saith true, that ye might **b**. G4100
20:25 my hand into his side, I will not **b**. G4100
31 But these are written, that ye might **b** G4100
Act 8:37 I **b** that Jesus Christ is the Son of God. G4100
13:39 And by him all that **b** are justified from G4100
41 **b**, though a man declare it unto you. G4100
15: 7 hear the word of the gospel, and **b**. G4100
11 But we **b** that through the grace of the G4100
16:31 And they said, **B** on the Lord Jesus G4100
19: 4 that they should **b** on him which G4100
21:20 **b**; and they are all zealous of the law: G4100
25 As touching the Gentiles which **b**, we G4100
27:25 good cheer: for I **b** God, that it shall be G4100
Ro 3: 3 For what if some did not **b**? shall their G569
22 them that **b**: for there is no difference: G4100
4:11 of all them that **b**, though they be not G4100
24 be imputed, if we **b** on him that raised G4100
6: 8 Now if we be dead with Christ, we **b** G4100
10: 9 Jesus, and shalt **b** in thine heart that G4100
14 how shall they **b** in him of whom they G4100
15:31 them that do not **b** in Judaea; and that G544
1Co 1:21 of preaching to save them that **b**. G4100
10:27 If any of them that **b** not bid you *to a* G571
11:18 divisions among you; and I partly **b** it. G4100
14:22 not to them that **b**, but to them that G4100
22 but to them that **b** not: but prophesying G571
22 that **b** not, but for them which believe. G571
22 that believe not, but for them which **b**. G4100
2Co 4: 4 of them which **b** not, lest the light of the G571
13 spoken; we also **b**, and therefore speak; G4100
Gal 3:22 Christ might be given to them that **b**. G4100
Eph 1:19 to us-ward who **b**, according to the G4100
Php 1:29 Christ, not only to **b** on him, but also to G4100
1Th 1: 7 So that ye were ensamples to all that **b** G4100
2:10 behaved ourselves among you that **b**: G4100
13 effectually worketh also in you that **b**. G4100
4:14 For if we **b** that Jesus died and rose G4100
2Th 1:10 in all them that **b** (because our G4100
2:11 delusion, that they should **b** a lie: G4100
1Ti 1:16 hereafter **b** on him to life everlasting. G4100
4: 3 of them which **b** and know the truth. G4103
10 of all men, specially of those that **b**. G4103
2Ti 2:13 If we **b** not, *yet* he abideth faithful: he G569
Heb 10:39 of them that **b** to the saving of the soul. G4102
11: 6 to God must **b** that he is, and *that* G4100
Jas 2:19 well: the devils also **b**, and tremble. G4100
1Pt 1:21 Who by him do **b** in God, that raised G4100
2: 7 Unto you therefore which **b** *he is* G4100
1Jn 3:23 That we should **b** on the name of his G4100
4: 1 Beloved, **b** not every spirit, but try the G4100
5:13 unto you that **b** on the name of the G4100
13 may **b** on the name of the Son of God. G4100

BELIEVED
Gen 15: 6 And he **b** in the LORD; and he counted it H539
45:26 Jacob's heart fainted, for he **b** them not. H539
Ex 4:31 And the people **b**: and when they heard H539
14:31 and **b** the LORD, and his servant Moses. H539
Nu 20:12 Aaron, Because ye **b** me not, to sanctify H539
Dt 9:23 ye **b** him not, nor hearkened to his voice. H539
1Sa 27:12 And Achish **b** David, saying, He hath H539
1Ki 10: 7 Howbeit I **b** not the words, until I came, H539
2Ch 9: 6 Howbeit I **b** not their words, until I H539
Job 29:24 *If* I laughed on them, they **b** *it* not; and H539
Ps 27:13 *I had fainted*, unless I had **b** to see the H539
78:22 Because they **b** not in God, and trusted H539
32 For all this they sinned still, and **b** not H539
106:12 Then **b** they his words; they sang his H539

Ps 106:24 the pleasant land, they **b** not his word: H539
116:10 I **b**, therefore have I spoken: I was greatly H539
119:66 for I have **b** thy commandments. H539
Isa 53: 1 Who hath **b** our report? and to whom is H539
Jer 40:14 Gedaliah the son of Ahikam **b** them not. H539
Lam 4:12 would not have **b** that the adversary and H539
Dan 6:23 upon him, because he **b** in his God. H540
Jna 3: 5 So the people of Nineveh **b** God, and H539
Mt 8:13 and as thou hast **b**, *so* be it done unto G4100
21:32 and ye **b** him not: but the publicans G4100
32 and the harlots **b** him: and ye, when ye G4100
Mk 16:11 alive, and had been seen of her, **b** not. G569
13 unto the residue: neither **b** they them. G4100
14 because they **b** not them which had G4100
Lk 1: 1 which are most surely **b** among us, G4135
45 And blessed *is* she that **b**: for there shall G4100
20: 5 he will say, Why then **b** ye him not? G4100
24:11 them as idle tales, and they **b** them not. G569
41 And while they yet **b** not for joy, and G569
Jn 2:11 his glory; and his disciples **b** on him. G4100
22 them; and they **b** the scripture, and the G4100
23 feast *day*, many **b** in his name, when G4100
3:18 he hath not **b** in the name of the only G4100
4:39 of that city **b** on him for the saying G4100
41 And many more **b** because of his own G4100
50 And the man **b** the word that Jesus G4100
53 and himself **b**, and his whole house. G4100
5:46 For had ye **b** Moses, ye would have G4100
46 would have **b** me: for he wrote of me. G4100
6:64 that **b** not, and who should betray him. G4100
7:31 And many of the people **b** on him, and G4100
48 the rulers or of the Pharisees **b** on him? G4100
8:30 As he spake these words, many **b** on G4100
31 Then said Jesus to those Jews which **b** G4100
10:25 I told you, and ye **b** not: the works that G4100
42 And many **b** on him there. G4100
11:45 the things which Jesus did, **b** on him. G4100
12:11 of the Jews went away, and **b** on Jesus. G4100
37 before them, yet they **b** not on him: G4100
38 Lord, who hath **b** our report? and to G4100
42 rulers also many **b** on him; but because G4100
16:27 and have **b** that I came out from God. G4100
17: 8 they have **b** that thou didst send me. G4100
20: 8 to the sepulchre, and he saw, and **b**. G4100
29 me, thou hast **b**: blessed *are* they that G4100
29 they that have not seen, and *yet* have **b**. G4100
Act 2:44 And all that **b** were together, and had G4100
4: 4 heard the word **b**; and the number of G4100
32 And the multitude of them that **b** were G4100
8:12 But when they **b** Philip preaching the G4100
13 Then Simon himself **b** also: and when G4100
9:26 him, and **b** not that he was a disciple. G4100
42 all Joppa; and many **b** in the Lord. G4100
10:45 And they of the circumcision which **b** G4103
11:17 *he did* unto us, who **b** on the Lord Jesus G4100
21 number **b**, and turned unto the Lord. G4100
13:12 what was done, **b**, being astonished at G4100
48 many as were ordained to eternal life **b**. G4100
14: 1 of the Jews and also of the Greeks **b**. G4100
23 them to the Lord, on whom they **b**. G4100
15: 5 Pharisees which **b**, saying, That it was G4100
16: 1 and **b**; but his father *was* a Greek: G4103
17: 4 And some of them **b**, and consorted G3982
5 But the Jews which **b** not, moved with G544
12 Therefore many of them **b**; also of G4100
34 unto him, and **b**: among the which *was* G4100
18: 8 of the synagogue, **b** on the Lord with all G4100
8 hearing **b**, and were baptized. G4100
27 them much which had **b** through grace: G4100
19: 2 Ghost since ye **b**? And they said unto G4100
9 But when divers were hardened, and **b** G544
18 And many that **b** came, and confessed, G4100
22:19 every synagogue them that **b** on thee: G4100
27:11 Nevertheless the centurion **b** the G3982
28:24 And some **b** the things which were G3982
24 which were spoken, and some **b** not.
Ro 4: 3 Abraham **b** God, and it was counted G4100
17 before him whom he **b**, *even* God, who G4100
18 Who against hope **b** in hope, that he G4100
10:14 they have not **b**? and how shall they G4100
16 saith, Lord, who hath **b** our report? G4100
11:30 For as ye in times past have not **b** God, G544
31 Even so have these also now not **b**, that G544
13:11 *is* our salvation nearer than when we **b**. G4100
1Co 3: 5 **b**, even as the Lord gave to every man? G4100
15: 2 unto you, unless ye have **b** in vain. G4100
11 I or they, so we preach, and so ye **b**. G4100
2Co 4:13 as it is written, I **b**, and therefore have G4100
Gal 2:16 even we have **b** in Jesus Christ, that G4100
Gal 3: 6 Even as Abraham **b** God, and it was G4100
Eph 1:13 also after that ye **b**, ye were sealed with G4100
2Th 1:10 among you was **b**) in that day. G4100
2:12 That they all might be damned who **b** G4100
1Ti 3:16 unto the Gentiles, **b** on in the world, G4100
2Ti 1:12 whom I have **b**, and am persuaded G4100
Tit 3: 8 that they which have **b** in God might be G4100
Heb 3:18 into his rest, but to them that **b** not? G544
4: 3 For we which have **b** do enter into rest, G4100
11:31 not with them that **b** not, when she had G544
Jas 2:23 saith, Abraham **b** God, and it was G4100
1Jn 4:16 And we have known and **b** the love that G4100
Jude 5 afterward destroyed them that **b** not. G4100

BELIEVERS
Act 5:14 And **b** were the more added to the G4100
1Ti 4:12 thou an example of the **b**, in word, in G4103

BELIEVEST
Lk 1:20 because thou **b** not my words, which G4100
Jn 1:50 under the fig tree, **b** thou? thou shalt G4100
11:26 in me shall never die. **B** thou this? G4100
14:10 **B** thou not that I am in the Father, and G4100
Act 8:37 And Philip said, If thou **b** with all thine G4100
26:27 King Agrippa, **b** thou the prophets? I G4100
27 thou the prophets? I know that thou **b**. G4100
Jas 2:19 Thou **b** that there is one God; thou G4100

BELIEVETH
Job 15:22 He **b** not that he shall return out of H539
39:24 he **b** that *it is* the sound of the trumpet. H539
Prv 14:15 The simple **b** every word: but the H539
Isa 28:16 he that **b** shall not make haste. H539
Mk 9:23 all things *are* possible to him that **b**. G4100
16:16 He that **b** and is baptized shall be G4100
16 but he that **b** not shall be damned. G4100
Jn 3:15 That whosoever **b** in him should not G4100
16 that whosoever **b** in him should not G4100
18 He that **b** on him is not condemned: G4100
18 but he that **b** not is condemned G4100
36 He that **b** on the Son hath everlasting G4100
36 life: and he that **b** not the Son shall not G544
5:24 my word, and **b** on him that sent me, G4100
6:35 and he that **b** on me shall never thirst. G4100
40 seeth the Son, and **b** on him, may have G4100
47 Verily, verily, I say unto you, He that **b** G4100
7:38 He that **b** on me, as the scripture hath G4100
11:25 the life: he that **b** in me, though he were G4100
26 And whosoever liveth and **b** in me shall G4100
12:44 Jesus cried and said, He that **b** on me, G4100
44 **b** not on me, but on him that sent me. G4100
46 **b** on me should not abide in darkness. G4100
14:12 Verily, verily, I say unto you, He that **b** G4100
Act 10:43 **b** in him shall receive remission of sins. G4100
Ro 1:16 **b**; to the Jew first, and also to the Greek. G4100
3:26 of him which **b** in Jesus. G1537+G4102
4: 5 But to him that worketh not, but **b** on G4100
9:33 **b** on him shall not be ashamed. G4100
10: 4 for righteousness to every one that **b**. G4100
10 For with the heart man **b** unto G4100
11 For the scripture saith, Whosoever **b** G4100
14: 2 For one **b** that he may eat all things: G4100
1Co 7:12 hath a wife that **b** not, and she be G571
13 hath an husband that **b** not, and if he be G571
13: 7 Beareth all things, **b** all things, hopeth G4100
14:24 there come in one that **b** not, or *one* G571
2Co 6:15 part hath he that **b** with an infidel? G4103
1Ti 5:16 If any man or woman that **b** have G4103
1Pt 2: 6 that **b** on him shall not be confounded. G4100
1Jn 5: 1 Whosoever **b** that Jesus is the Christ is G4100
5 he that **b** that Jesus is the Son of God? G4100
10 He that **b** on the Son of God hath the G4100
10 in himself: he that **b** not God hath G4100
10 a liar; because he **b** not the record that G4100

BELIEVING
Mt 21:22 shall ask in prayer, **b**, ye shall receive. G4100
Jn 20:27 into my side: and be not faithless, but **b**. G4103
31 **b** ye might have life through his name. G4100
Act 16:34 rejoiced, **b** in God with all his house. G4100
24:14 God of my fathers, **b** all things which G4100
Ro 15:13 joy and peace in **b**, that ye may abound G4100
1Ti 6: 2 And they that have **b** masters, let them G4103
1Pt 1: 8 ye see *him* not, yet **b**, ye rejoice with joy G4100

BELL
Ex 28:34 A golden **b** and a pomegranate, a H6472
34 a golden **b** and a pomegranate, H6472
39:26 A **b** and a pomegranate, a bell and a H6472
Ex 39:26 A bell and a pomegranate, a **b** and a H6472

BELLIES
Tit 1:12 *are* alway liars, evil beasts, slow **b**. G1064

BELLOW
Jer 50:11 fat as the heifer at grass, and **b** as bulls; H6670

BELLOWS
Jer 6:29 The **b** are burned, the lead is consumed H4647

BELLS
Ex 28:33 **b** of gold between them round about: H6472
39:25 And they made **b** *of* pure gold, and put H6472
25 pure gold, and put the **b** between the H6472
Zec 14:20 In that day shall there be upon the **b** of H4698

BELLY
Gen 3:14 the field; upon thy **b** shalt thou go, and H1512
Lev 11:42 Whatsoever goeth upon the **b**, and H1512
Nu 5:21 make thy thigh to rot, and thy **b** to swell; H990
22 to make *thy* **b** to swell, and *thy* thigh H990
27 bitter, and her **b** shall swell, and her H990
25: 8 through her **b**. So the plague was stayed H6897
Jdg 3:21 his right thigh, and thrust it into his **b**: H990
22 out of his **b**; and the dirt came out. H990
1Ki 7:20 over against the **b** which *was* by the H990
Job 3:11 up the ghost when I came out of the **b**? H990
15: 2 and fill his **b** with the east wind? H990
35 vanity, and their **b** prepareth deceit. H990
20:15 again: God shall cast them out of his **b**. H990
20 Surely he shall not feel quietness in his **b**, H990
23 *When* he is about to fill his **b**, *God* shall H990
32:19 Behold, my **b** *is* as wine *which* hath no H990
40:16 and his force *is* in the navel of his **b**. H990
Ps 17:14 in *this* life, and whose **b** thou fillest with H990
22:10 thou *art* my God from my mother's **b**. H990
31: 9 with grief, *yea*, my soul and my **b**. H990
44:25 the dust: our **b** cleaveth unto the earth. H990
Prv 13:25 soul: but the **b** of the wicked shall want. H990
18: 8 down into the innermost parts of the **b**. H990
20 A man's **b** shall be satisfied with the fruit H990
20:27 searching all the inward parts of the **b**. H990
30 so *do* stripes the inward parts of the **b**. H990
26:22 down into the innermost parts of the **b**. H990
Song 5:14 with the beryl: his **b** *is as* bright ivory H4578
7: 2 not liquor: thy **b** *is like* an heap of wheat H990
Isa 46: 3 the **b**, which are carried from the womb: H990
Jer 1: 5 Before I formed thee in the **b** I knew H990
51:34 he hath filled his **b** with my delicates, H3770
Ezk 3: 3 of man, cause thy **b** to eat, and fill thy H990
Dan 2:32 of silver, his **b** and his thighs of brass, H4577
Jna 1:17 And Jonah was in the **b** of the fish three H4578
2: 1 the LORD his God out of the fish's **b**, H4578
2 me; out of the **b** of hell cried I, *and* thou H990
Hab 3:16 When I heard, my **b** trembled; my lips H990
Mt 12:40 in the whale's **b**; so shall the Son of man G2836
15:17 the **b**, and is cast out into the draught? G2836
Mk 7:19 heart, but into the **b**, and goeth out into G2836
Lk 15:16 And he would fain have filled his **b** G2836
Jn 7:38 of his **b** shall flow rivers of living water. G2836
Ro 16:18 but their own **b**; and by good words G2836
1Co 6:13 Meats for the **b**, and the belly for meats: G2836
13 Meats for the belly, and the **b** for G2836
Php 3:19 whose God *is their* **b**, and *whose* glory *is* G2836
Rev 10: 9 it shall make thy **b** bitter, but it shall be G2836
10 soon as I had eaten it, my **b** was bitter. G2836

BELONG
Gen 40: 8 ***b*** to God? tell me *them*, I pray you.
Lev 27:24 to whom the possession of the land *did* ***b***.
Nu 1:50 and over all things that ***b*** to it: they shall
Dt 29:29 The secret *things* ***b*** unto the LORD our
29 *which are* revealed ***b*** unto us and to our
Ps 47: 9 earth ***b*** unto God: he is greatly exalted.
68:20 GOD the Lord ***b*** the issues from death.
Prv 24:23 These *things* also ***b*** to the wise. *It is* not
Dan 9: 9 To the Lord our God ***b*** mercies and
Mk 9:41 name, because ye **b** to Christ, verily I G1510
Lk 19:42 the things *which* **b** unto thy peace! but
1Co 7:32 for the things that **b** to the Lord, how he

BELONGED
Jos 17: 8 Manasseh ***b*** to the children of Ephraim;
1Sa 21: 7 chiefest of the herdmen that ***b*** to Saul.
1Ki 1: 8 ***b*** to David, were not with Adonijah.
15:27 Gibbethon, which ***b*** to the Philistines; for
16:15 Gibbethon, which ***b*** to the Philistines.
2Ki 14:28 Hamath, *which* ***b*** to Judah, for Israel,

1Ch 2:23 cities. All these ***b*** *to* the sons of Machir
13: 6 which ***b*** to Judah, to bring up
2Ch 26:23 of the burial which ***b*** to the kings; for
Est 1: 9 royal house which ***b*** to king Ahasuerus.
2: 9 with such things as ***b*** to her, and seven H4490
Lk 23: 7 And as soon as he knew that he **b** unto *G1510*

BELONGEST
1Sa 30:13 And David said unto him, To whom ***b***

BELONGETH
Nu 8:24 This *is it* that ***b*** unto the Levites: from
Dt 32:35 To me ***b*** vengeance, and recompence;
Jdg 19:14 *were* by Gibeah, which ***b*** to Benjamin.
20: 4 into Gibeah that ***b*** to Benjamin, I and
1Sa 17: 1 at Shochoh, which ***b*** to Judah, and
30:14 *the coast* which ***b*** to Judah, and upon
1Ki 17: 9 Arise, get thee to Zarephath, which ***b*** to
19: 3 ***b*** to Judah, and left his servant there.
2Ki 14:11 face at Beth-shemesh, which ***b*** to Judah.
2Ch 25:21 at Beth-shemesh, which ***b*** to Judah.
Ezr 10: 4 Arise; for *this* matter ***b*** unto thee: we
Ps 3: 8 Salvation ***b*** unto the LORD: thy blessing
62:11 I heard this; that power ***b*** unto God.
12 Also unto thee, O Lord, ***b*** mercy: for
94: 1 O LORD God, to whom vengeance **b**; O
1 God, to whom vengeance **b**, shew thyself.
Dan 9: 7 O Lord, righteousness ***b*** unto thee, but
8 O Lord, to us ***b*** confusion of face, to our
Heb 5:14 But strong meat ***b*** to them that are of *G1510*
10:30 hath said, Vengeance ***b*** unto me, I will

BELONGING
Nu 7: 9 of the sanctuary **b** unto them *was that*
Ru 2: 3 a part of the field ***b*** unto Boaz, who *was*
1Sa 6:18 of the Philistines ***b*** to the five lords, *both*
Prv 26:17 with strife ***b*** not to him, *is like* one
Lk 9:10 place **b** to the city called Bethsaida.

BELOVED
Dt 21:15 If a man have two wives, one **b**, and H157
15 children, *both* the **b** and the hated; and H157
16 the son of the **b** firstborn before the H157
33:12 *And* of Benjamin he said, The **b** of the H3039
Neh 13:26 like him, who was **b** of his God, and God H157
Ps 60: 5 That thy **b** may be delivered; save *with* H3039
108: 6 That thy **b** may be delivered: save *with* H3039
127: 2 of sorrows: *for* so he giveth his **b** sleep. H3039
Prv 4: 3 and only ***b*** in the sight of my mother.
Song 1:14 My **b** *is* unto me *as* a cluster of H1730
16 Behold, thou *art* fair, my **b**, yea, H1730
2: 3 the wood, so *is* my **b** among the sons. I H1730
8 The voice of my **b**! behold, he cometh H1730
9 My **b** is like a roe or a young hart: H1730
10 My **b** spake, and said unto me, Rise up, H1730
16 My **b** *is* mine, and I *am* his: he feedeth H1730
17 away, turn, my **b**, and be thou like a roe H1730
4:16 may flow out. Let my **b** come into his H1730
5: 1 drink, yea, drink abundantly, O **b**. H1730
2 *it is* the voice of my **b** that knocketh, H1730
4 My **b** put in his hand by the hole *of the* H1730
5 I rose up to open to my **b**; and my H1730
6 I opened to my **b**; but my beloved had H1730
6 I opened to my beloved; but my **b** had H1730
8 **b**, that ye tell him, that I *am* sick of love. H1730
9 What *is* thy **b** more than *another* H1730
9 than *another* **b**, O thou fairest among H1730
9 what *is* thy **b** more than *another* H1730
9 *another* **b**, that thou dost so charge us? H1730
10 My **b** *is* white and ruddy, the chiefest H1730
16 lovely. This *is* my **b**, and this *is* my H1730
6: 1 Whither is thy **b** gone, O thou fairest H1730
1 whither is thy **b** turned aside? that we H1730
2 My **b** is gone down into his garden, to H1730
3 I *am* my beloved's, and my **b** *is* mine: H1730
7: 9 the best wine for my **b**, that goeth *down* H1730
11 Come, my **b**, let us go forth into the H1730
13 *which* I have laid up for thee, O my **b**. H1730
8: 5 leaning upon her **b**? I raised thee up H1730
14 Make haste, my **b**, and be thou like to a H1730
Isa 5: 1 a song of my **b** touching his vineyard. H1730
Jer 11:15 What hath my **b** to do in mine house, H3039
12: 7 given the dearly **b** of my soul into the H3033
Dan 9:23 thou *art* greatly **b**: therefore understand H2532
10:11 a man greatly **b**, understand the words H2532
19 And said, O man greatly **b**, fear not: H2532
Hos 3: 1 yet, love a woman **b** of *her* friend, yet an H157
9:16 I slay *even* the **b** *fruit* of their womb. H4261
Mt 3:17 is my **b** Son, in whom I am well pleased. *G27*
Mt 12:18 I have chosen; my **b**, in whom my soul is *G27*
17: 5 said, This is my **b** Son, in whom I am *G27*
Mk 1:11 my **b** Son, in whom I am well pleased. *G27*
9: 7 saying, This is my **b** Son: hear him. *G27*
Lk 3:22 art my **b** Son; in thee I am well pleased. *G27*
9:35 saying, This is my **b** Son: hear him. *G27*
20:13 I do? I will send my **b** son: it may be they *G27*
Act 15:25 unto you with our **b** Barnabas and Paul, *G27*
Ro 1: 7 To all that be in Rome, **b** of God, called *G27*
9:25 and her **b**, which was not beloved. *G25*
25 and her beloved, which was not **b**. *G25*
11:28 election, *they are* **b** for the fathers' sakes. *G27*
12:19 Dearly **b**, avenge not yourselves, but *G27*
16: 5 Salute my well **b** Epaenetus, who is the *G27*
8 Greet Amplias my **b** in the Lord. *G27*
9 our helper in Christ, and Stachys my **b**. *G27*
12 the Lord. Salute the **b** Persis, which *G27*
1Co 4:14 shame you, but as my **b** sons I warn *you*. *G27*
17 who is my **b** son, and faithful in the *G27*
10:14 Wherefore, my dearly **b**, flee from *G27*
15:58 Therefore, my **b** brethren, be ye stedfast, *G27*
2Co 7: 1 these promises, dearly **b**, let us cleanse *G27*
12:19 *do* all things, dearly **b**, for your edifying. *G27*
Eph 1: 6 he hath made us accepted in the **b**. *G25*
6:21 I do, Tychicus, a **b** brother and faithful *G27*
Php 2:12 Wherefore, my **b**, as ye have always *G27*
4: 1 Therefore, my brethren dearly **b** and *G27*
1 so stand fast in the Lord, *my* dearly **b**. *G27*
Col 3:12 of God, holy and **b**, bowels of mercies, *G25*
4: 7 unto you, *who is a* **b** brother, and a *G27*
9 With Onesimus, a faithful and **b** brother, *G27*
14 Luke, the **b** physician, and Demas, greet *G27*
1Th 1: 4 Knowing, brethren **b**, your election of *G25*
2Th 2:13 for you, brethren **b** of the Lord, because *G25*
1Ti 6: 2 they are faithful and **b**, partakers of the *G27*
2Ti 1: 2 To Timothy, *my* dearly **b** son: Grace, *G27*
Phlm 1 our dearly **b**, and fellowlabourer, *G27*
2 And to *our* **b** Apphia, and Archippus our *G27*
16 servant, a brother **b**, specially to me, but *G27*
Heb 6: 9 But, **b**, we are persuaded better things of *G27*
Jas 1:16 Do not err, my **b** brethren. *G27*
19 Wherefore, my **b** brethren, let every man *G27*
2: 5 Hearken, my **b** brethren, Hath not God *G27*
1Pt 2:11 Dearly **b**, I beseech *you* as strangers and *G27*
4:12 **B**, think it not strange concerning the *G27*
2Pt 1:17 is my **b** Son, in whom I am well pleased. *G27*
3: 1 This second epistle, **b**, I now write unto *G27*
8 But, **b**, be not ignorant of this one thing, *G27*
14 Wherefore, **b**, seeing that ye look for such *G27*
15 even as our **b** brother Paul also *G27*
17 Ye therefore, **b**, seeing ye know *these* *G27*
1Jn 3: 2 **B**, now are we the sons of God, and it *G27*
21 **B**, if our heart condemn us not, *then* have *G27*
4: 1 **B**, believe not every spirit, but try the *G27*
7 **B**, let us love one another: for love is of *G27*
11 **B**, if God so loved us, we ought also to *G27*
3Jn 2 **B**, I wish above all things that thou *G27*
5 **B**, thou dost faithfully whatsoever thou *G27*
11 **B**, follow not that which is evil, but that *G27*
Jude 3 **B**, when I gave all diligence to write unto *G27*
17 But, **b**, remember ye the words which *G27*
20 But ye, **b**, building up yourselves on your *G27*
Rev 20: 9 about, and the **b** city: and fire came *G25*

BELOVED'S
Song 6: 3 I *am* my **b**, and my beloved *is* mine: he H1730
7:10 I *am* my **b**, and his desire *is* toward me. H1730

BELOW See the Appendix.

BELSHAZZAR
Dan 5: 1 **B** the king made a great feast to a H1113
2 **B**, whiles he tasted the wine, H1113
9 Then was king **B** greatly troubled, and H1113
22 And thou his son, O **B**, hast not H1113
29 Then commanded **B**, and they clothed H1113
30 In that night was **B** the king of the H1113
7: 1 In the first year of **B** king of Babylon H1113
8: 1 In the third year of the reign of king **B** a H1113

BELTESHAZZAR
Dan 1: 7 *the name* of **B**; and to Hananiah, of H1095
2:26 whose name *was* **B**, Art thou able to H1096
4: 8 whose name *was* **B**, according to the H1096
9 O **B**, master of the magicians, because I H1096
18 have seen. Now thou, O **B**, declare the H1096
19 Then Daniel, whose name *was* **B**, was H1096
19 spake, and said, **B**, let not the dream, or H1096
19 trouble thee. **B** answered and said, H1096
Dan 5:12 the king named **B**: now let Daniel be H1096
10: 1 name was called **B**; and the thing *was* H1095

BEMOAN
Jer 15: 5 or who shall **b** thee? or who shall go H5110
16: 5 go to lament nor **b** them: for I have H5110
22:10 Weep ye not for the dead, neither **b** H5110
48:17 All ye that are about him, **b** him; and H5110
Nah 3: 7 waste: who will **b** her? whence shall I H5110

BEMOANED
Job 42:11 house: and they **b** him, and comforted H5110

BEMOANING
Jer 31:18 I have surely heard Ephraim **b** himself H5110

BEN
1Ch 15:18 *degree,* Zechariah, **B**, and Jaaziel, and H1122

BENAIAH
2Sa 8:18 And **B** the son of Jehoiada *was over* H1141
20:23 the host of Israel: and **B** the son of H1141
23:20 And **B** the son of Jehoiada, the son of a H1141
22 These *things* did **B** the son of Jehoiada, H1141
30 **B** the Pirathonite, Hiddai of the brooks H1141
1Ki 1: 8 But Zadok the priest, and **B** the son of H1141
10 But Nathan the prophet, and **B**, and the H1141
26 the priest, and **B** the son of Jehoiada, H1141
32 the prophet, and **B** the son of Jehoiada. H1141
36 And **B** the son of Jehoiada answered H1141
38 the prophet, and **B** the son of Jehoiada, H1141
44 the prophet, and **B** the son of Jehoiada, H1141
2:25 by the hand of **B** the son of Jehoiada; H1141
29 Solomon sent **B** the son of Jehoiada, H1141
30 And **B** came to the tabernacle of the H1141
30 I will die here. And **B** brought the king H1141
34 So **B** the son of Jehoiada went up, and H1141
35 And the king put **B** the son of Jehoiada H1141
46 So the king commanded **B** the son of H1141
4: 4 And **B** the son of Jehoiada *was* over the H1141
1Ch 4:36 Asaiah, and Adiel, and Jesimiel, and **B**, H1141
11:22 **B** the son of Jehoiada, the son of a H1141
24 These *things* did **B** the son of Jehoiada, H1141
31 of Benjamin, **B** the Pirathonite, H1141
15:18 Unni, Eliab, and **B**, and Maaseiah, and H1141
20 and **B**, with psalteries on Alamoth; H1141
24 and Zechariah, and **B**, and Eliezer, the H1141
16: 5 and Eliab, and **B**, and Obed-edom: and H1141
6 **B** also and Jahaziel the priests with H1141
18:17 And **B** the son of Jehoiada *was* over the H1141
27: 5 third month *was* **B** the son of Jehoiada, H1141
6 This *is that* **B**, *who was* mighty *among* H1141
14 month *was* **B** the Pirathonite, of the H1141
34 the son of **B**, and Abiathar: and H1141
2Ch 20:14 the son of **B**, the son of Jeiel, the H1141
31:13 and Mahath, and **B**, *were* overseers H1141
Ezr 10:25 and Eleazar, and Malchijah, and **B**. H1141
30 Adna, and Chelal, **B**, Maaseiah, H1141
35 **B**, Bedeiah, Chelluh, H1141
43 Zabad, Zebina, Jadau, and Joel, **B**. H1141
Ezk 11: 1 the son of **B**, princes of the people. H1141
13 the son of **B** died. Then fell I down H1141

BEN-AMMI
Gen 19:38 and called his name **B**: the same *is* the H1151

BENCHES
Ezk 27: 6 have made thy **b** *of* ivory, *brought* out H7175

BEND
Ps 11: 2 For, lo, the wicked **b** *their* bow, they H1869
64: 3 like a sword, *and* **b** *their bows to shoot* H1869
Jer 9: 3 And they **b** their tongues *like* their bow H1869
46: 9 Lydians, that handle *and* **b** the bow. H1869
50:14 about: all ye that **b** the bow, shoot at H1869
29 all ye that **b** the bow, camp against H1869
51: 3 let the archer **b** his bow, and against H1869
Ezk 17: 7 this vine did **b** her roots toward him, H3719

BENDETH
Ps 58: 7 *when* he **b** *his bow to shoot* his H1869
Jer 51: 3 Against *him that* **b** let the archer bend H1869

BENDING
Isa 60:14 thee shall come **b** unto thee; and all H7817

BENEATH
Gen 35: 8 she was buried **b** Beth-el under an oak: H8478
Ex 20: 4 or that *is* in the earth **b**, or that *is* in the H8478

Ex 26:24 And they shall be coupled together **b**, H4295
27: 5 of the altar **b**, that the net may be H4295
28:33 And ***b*** upon the hem of it thou shalt
32:19 hands, and brake them **b** the mount. H8478
36:29 And they were coupled **b**, and coupled H4295
38: 4 compass thereof **b** unto the midst of it. H4295
Dt 4:18 fish that *is* in the waters **b** the earth: H8478
39 and upon the earth **b**: *there is* none else. H8478
5: 8 or that *is* in the earth **b**, or that *is* in the H8478
8 or that *is* in the waters **b** the earth: H8478
28:13 thou shalt not be **b**; if that thou hearken H4295
33:13 dew, and for the deep that coucheth **b**, H8478
Jos 2:11 *is* God in heaven above, and in earth **b**. H8478
Jdg 7: 8 host of Midian was **b** him in the valley. H8478
1Ki 4:12 which *is* by Zartanah **b** Jezreel, from H8478
7:29 a base above: and **b** the lions and oxen H8478
8:23 above, or on earth **b**, who keepest H8478
Job 18:16 His roots shall be dried up **b**, and above H8478
Prv 15:24 wise, that he may depart from hell **b**. H4295
Isa 14: 9 Hell from **b** is moved for thee to meet H8478
51: 6 upon the earth **b**: for the heavens shall H8478
Jer 31:37 searched out **b**, I will also cast off all H4295
Am 2: 9 fruit from above, and his roots from **b**. H8478
Mk 14:66 And as Peter was **b** in the palace, there *G2736*
Jn 8:23 And he said unto them, Ye are from **b**; I *G2736*
Act 2:19 signs in the earth **b**; blood, and fire, and *G2736*

BENE-BERAK
Jos 19:45 And Jehud, and **B**, and Gath-rimmon, H1139

BENEFACTORS
Lk 22:25 authority upon them are called **b**. *G2110*

BENEFIT
2Ch 32:25 according to the **b** *done* unto him; for H1576
Jer 18:10 good, wherewith I said I would **b** them. H3190
2Co 1:15 before, that ye might have a second **b**; *G5485*
1Ti 6: 2 of the **b**. These things teach and exhort. *G2108*
Phlm 14 do nothing; that thy **b** should not be as it *G18*

BENEFITS
Ps 68:19 ***b***, *even* the God of our salvation. Selah.
103: 2 O my soul, and forget not all his **b**: H1576
116:12 unto the LORD *for* all his **b** toward me? H8408

BENE-JAAKAN
Nu 33:31 from Moseroth, and pitched in **B**. H1142
32 And they removed from **B**, and H1142

BENEVOLENCE
1Co 7: 3 unto the wife due **b**: and likewise also *G2133*

BEN-HADAD
1Ki 15:18 king Asa sent them to **B**, the son of H1130
20 So **B** hearkened unto king Asa, and H1130
20: 1 And **B** the king of Syria gathered all his H1130
2 city, and said unto him, Thus saith **B**, H1130
5 Thus speaketh **B**, saying, Although I H1130
9 the messengers of **B**, Tell my lord the H1130
10 And **B** sent unto him, and said, The H1130
12 And it came to pass, when ***B*** heard this
16 And they went out at noon. But **B** *was* H1130
17 went out first; and **B** sent out, and they H1130
20 them: and **B** the king of Syria escaped H1130
26 return of the year, that **B** numbered the H1130
30 *were* left. And **B** fled, and came into H1130
32 said, Thy servant **B** saith, I pray thee, H1130
33 said, Thy brother **B**. Then he said, Go H1130
33 bring him. Then **B** came forth to him; H1130
34 And ***B*** said unto him, The cities, which
2Ki 6:24 And it came to pass after this, that **B** H1130
8: 7 And Elisha came to Damascus; and **B** H1130
9 and said, Thy son **B** king of Syria hath H1130
13: 3 of **B** the son of Hazael, all *their* days. H1130
24 So Hazael king of Syria died; and **B** his H1130
25 out of the hand of **B** the son of Hazael H1130
2Ch 16: 2 house, and sent to **B** king of Syria, that H1130
4 And **B** hearkened unto king Asa, and H1130
Jer 49:27 and it shall consume the palaces of **B**. H1130
Am 1: 4 which shall devour the palaces of **B**. H1130

BEN-HAIL
2Ch 17: 7 princes, *even* to **B**, and to Obadiah, and H1134

BEN-HANAN
1Ch 4:20 and Rinnah, **B**, and Tilon. And the H1135

BENINU
Neh 10:13 Hodijah, Bani, **B**. H1148

BENJAMIN
Gen 35:18 Ben-oni: but his father called him **B**. H1144
24 The sons of Rachel; Joseph, and **B**: H1144
42: 4 But **B**, Joseph's brother, Jacob sent not H1144
36 **B** *away:* all these things are against me. H1144
43:14 other brother, and **B**. If I be bereaved *of* H1144
15 in their hand, and **B**; and rose up, and H1144
16 And when Joseph saw **B** with them, he H1144
29 saw his brother **B**, his mother's son, H1144
45:12 of my brother **B**, that *it is* my mouth H1144
14 and wept; and **B** wept upon his neck. H1144
22 of raiment; but to **B** he gave three H1144
46:19 of Rachel Jacob's wife; Joseph, and **B**. H1144
21 And the sons of **B** *were* Belah, and H1144
49:27 **B** shall ravin *as* a wolf: in the morning H1144
Ex 1: 3 Issachar, Zebulun, and **B**, H1144
Nu 1:11 Of **B**; Abidan the son of Gideoni. H1144
36 Of the children of **B**, by their H1144
37 of the tribe of **B**, *were* thirty and five H1144
2:22 Then the tribe of **B**: and the captain of H1144
22 of **B** *shall be* Abidan the son of Gideoni. H1144
7:60 prince of the children of **B**, *offered*: H1144
10:24 of **B** *was* Abidan the son of Gideoni. H1144
13: 9 Of the tribe of **B**, Palti the son of Raphu. H1144
26:38 The sons of **B** after their families: of H1144
41 These *are* the sons of **B** after their H1144
34:21 Of the tribe of **B**, Elidad the son of H1144
Dt 27:12 and Issachar, and Joseph, and **B**: H1144
33:12 *And* of **B** he said, The beloved of the H1144
Jos 18:11 of the children of **B** came up according H1144
20 of the children of **B**, by the coasts H1144
21 of the children of **B** according to their H1144
28 of **B** according to their families. H1144
21: 4 and out of the tribe of **B**, thirteen cities. H1144
17 And out of the tribe of **B**, Gibeon with H1144
Jdg 1:21 And the children of **B** did not drive out H1144
21 of **B** in Jerusalem unto this day. H1144
5:14 after thee, **B**, among thy people; H1144
10: 9 and against **B**, and against the house H1144
19:14 *were* by Gibeah, which *belongeth* to **B**. H1144
20: 3 (Now the children of **B** heard that the H1144
4 to **B**, I and my concubine, to lodge. H1144
10 come to Gibeah of **B**, according to all H1144
12 through all the tribe of **B**, saying, What H1144
13 the children of **B** would not hearken H1144
14 But the children of **B** gathered H1144
15 And the children of **B** were numbered H1144
17 And the men of Israel, beside **B**, were H1144
18 the children of **B**? And the LORD said, H1144
20 out to battle against **B**; and the men of H1144
21 And the children of **B** came forth out of H1144
23 the children of **B** my brother? And the H1144
24 the children of **B** the second day. H1144
25 And **B** went forth against them out of H1144
28 the children of **B** my brother, or shall H1144
30 the children of **B** on the third day, and H1144
31 And the children of **B** went out against H1144
32 And the children of **B** said, They *are* H1144
35 And the LORD smote **B** before Israel: H1144
36 So the children of **B** saw that they were H1144
39 in the battle, **B** began to smite *and* H1144
41 again, the men of **B** were amazed: for H1144
44 And there fell of **B** eighteen thousand H1144
46 So that all which fell that day of **B** were H1144
48 the children of **B**, and smote them with H1144
21: 1 of us give his daughter unto **B** to wife. H1144
6 repented them for **B** their brother, and H1144
13 to the children of **B** that *were* in the H1144
14 And **B** came again at that time; and H1144
15 And the people repented them for **B**, H1144
16 the women are destroyed out of **B**? H1144
17 that be escaped of **B**, that a tribe be not H1144
18 Cursed *be* he that giveth a wife to **B**. H1144
20 the children of **B**, saying, Go and lie in H1144
21 of Shiloh, and go to the land of **B**. H1144
23 And the children of **B** did so, and took H1144
1Sa 4:12 And there ran a man of **B** out of the H1144
9: 1 Now there was a man of **B**, whose name H1144
16 man out of the land of **B**, and thou shalt H1144
21 of the tribe of **B**? wherefore then H1144
10: 2 in the border of **B** at Zelzah; and they H1144
20 to come near, the tribe of **B** was taken. H1144
21 When he had caused the tribe of **B** to H1144
13: 2 in Gibeah of **B**: and the rest of the H1144
15 unto Gibeah of **B**. And Saul numbered H1144
16 abode in Gibeah of **B**: but the Philistines H1144
14:16 of Saul in Gibeah of **B** looked; and, H1144
2Sa 2: 9 and over **B**, and over all Israel. H1144
15 number twelve of **B**, which *pertained* to H1144
2Sa 2:25 And the children of **B** gathered H1144
31 had smitten of **B**, and of Abner's men, H1144
3:19 And Abner also spake in the ears of **B**: H1144
19 seemed good to the whole house of **B**. H1144
4: 2 of the children of **B**: (for Beeroth also H1144
2 (for Beeroth also was reckoned to **B**: H1144
19:17 And *there were* a thousand men of **B** H1144
21:14 they in the country of **B** in Zelah, in the H1144
23:29 Ribai out of Gibeah of the children of **B**, H1144
1Ki 4:18 Shimei the son of Elah, in **B**: H1144
12:21 with the tribe of **B**, an hundred and H1144
23 of Judah and **B**, and to the remnant H1144
15:22 built with them Geba of **B**, and Mizpah. H1144
1Ch 2: 2 Dan, Joseph, and **B**, Naphtali, Gad, and H1144
6:60 And out of the tribe of **B**; Geba with her H1144
65 of the children of **B**, these cities, which H1144
7: 6 *The sons* of **B**; Bela, and Becher, and H1144
10 of Bilhan; Jeush, and **B**, and Ehud, and H1144
8: 1 Now **B** begat Bela his firstborn, Ashbel H1144
40 and fifty. All these *are* of the sons of **B**. H1144
9: 3 of the children of **B**, and of the children H1144
7 And of the sons of **B**; Sallu the son of H1144
11:31 children of **B**, Benaiah the Pirathonite, H1144
12: 2 of a bow, *even* of Saul's brethren of **B**. H1144
16 And there came of the children of **B** H1144
29 And of the children of **B**, the kindred of H1144
21: 6 But Levi and **B** counted he not among H1144
27:21 of **B**, Jaasiel the son of Abner: H1144
2Ch 11: 1 house of Judah and **B** an hundred and H1144
3 and to all Israel in Judah and **B**, saying, H1144
10 *are* in Judah and in **B** fenced cities. H1144
12 strong, having Judah and **B** on his side. H1144
23 of Judah and **B**, unto every fenced city: H1144
14: 8 and out of **B**, that bare shields and H1144
15: 2 and all Judah and **B**; The LORD *is* with H1144
8 the land of Judah and **B**, and out of the H1144
9 And he gathered all Judah and **B**, and H1144
17:17 And of **B**; Eliada a mighty man of H1144
25: 5 all Judah and **B**: and he numbered them H1144
31: 1 of all Judah and **B**, in Ephraim also and H1144
34: 9 and **B**; and they returned to Jerusalem. H1144
32 in Jerusalem and **B** to stand *to it*. And H1144
Ezr 1: 5 of Judah and **B**, and the priests, and H1144
4: 1 of Judah and **B** heard that the children H1144
10: 9 Then all the men of Judah and **B** H1144
32 **B**, Malluch, *and* Shemariah. H1144
Neh 3:23 After him repaired **B** and Hashub over H1144
11: 4 of the children of **B**. Of the children of H1144
7 And these *are* the sons of **B**; Sallu the H1144
31 The children also of **B** from Geba *dwelt* H1144
36 *were* divisions *in* Judah, *and* in **B**. H1144
12:34 Judah, and **B**, and Shemaiah, and H1144
Ps 68:27 There *is* little **B** *with* their ruler, the H1144
80: 2 Before Ephraim and **B** and Manasseh H1144
Jer 1: 1 that *were* in Anathoth in the land of **B**: H1144
6: 1 O ye children of **B**, gather yourselves to H1144
17:26 from the land of **B**, and from the plain, H1144
20: 2 **B**, which *was* by the house of the LORD. H1144
32: 8 *is* in the country of **B**: for the right of H1144
44 in the land of **B**, and in the places about H1144
33:13 and in the land of **B**, and in the places H1144
37:12 to go into the land of **B**, to separate H1144
13 And when he was in the gate of **B**, a H1144
38: 7 the king then sitting in the gate of **B**; H1144
Ezk 48:22 the border of **B**, shall be for the prince. H1144
23 the west side, **B** *shall have a portion*. H1144
24 And by the border of **B**, from the east H1144
32 Joseph, one gate of **B**, one gate of Dan. H1144
Hos 5: 8 cry aloud *at* Beth-aven, after thee, O **B**. H1144
Oba 19 of Samaria: and **B** *shall possess* Gilead. H1144
Act 13:21 the tribe of **B**, by the space of forty years. *G958*
Ro 11: 1 of the seed of Abraham, *of* the tribe of **B**. *G958*
Php 3: 5 Israel, *of* the tribe of **B**, an Hebrew of the *G958*
Rev 7: 8 tribe of **B** *were* sealed twelve thousand. *G958*

BENJAMIN'S
Gen 43:34 before him: but **B** mess was five times H1144
44:12 and the cup was found in **B** sack. H1144
45:14 And he fell upon his brother **B** neck, H1144
Zec 14:10 in her place, from **B** gate unto the place H1144

BENJAMITE
Jdg 3:15 the son of Gera, a **B**, a man lefthanded: H1145
1Sa 9: 1 of Aphiah, a **B**, a mighty man of power. H1145
21 said, *Am* not I a **B**, of the smallest of the H1145
2Sa 16:11 now *may this* **B** *do it?* let him alone, H1145
19:16 And Shimei the son of Gera, a **B**, which H1145
20: 1 the son of Bichri, a **B**: and he blew a H1145
1Ki 2: 8 the son of Gera, a **B** of Bahurim, which H1145

Est 2: 5 the son of Shimei, the son of Kish, a **B**; H1145
Ps 7:ttl concerning the words of Cush the **B**. H1145

BENJAMITES
Jdg 19:16 but the men of the place *were* **B**. H1145
20:35 destroyed of the **B** that day twenty and H1145
36 Israel gave place to the **B**, because they H1145
40 of smoke, the **B** looked behind them, H1145
43 *Thus* they inclosed the **B** round about, H1145
1Sa 9: 4 land of the **B**, but they found *them* not. H1145
22: 7 him, Hear now, ye **B**; will the son of H1145
1Ch 27:12 Anetothite, of the **B**: and in his course H1145

BENO
1Ch 24:26 and Mushi: the sons of Jaaziah; **B**. H1121
27 The sons of Merari by Jaaziah; **B**, and H1121

BENOB See ISBI-BENOB.

BEN-ONI
Gen 35:18 **B**: but his father called him Benjamin. H1126

BENOTH See ISBI-BENOTH.

BENT
Ps 7:12 he hath **b** his bow, and made it ready. H1869
37:14 sword, and have **b** their bow, to cast H1869
Isa 5:28 and all their bows **b**, their horses' hoofs H1869
21:15 and from the **b** bow, and from the H1869
Lam 2: 4 He hath **b** his bow like an enemy: he H1869
3:12 He hath **b** his bow, and set me as a H1869
Hos 11: 7 And my people are **b** to backsliding H8511
Zec 9:13 When I have **b** Judah for me, filled the H1869

BEN-ZOHETH
1Ch 4:20 the sons of Ishi *were*, Zoheth, and **B**. H1132

BEON
Nu 32: 3 Elealeh, and Shebam, and Nebo, and **B**, H1194

BEOR
Gen 36:32 And Bela the son of **B** reigned in Edom: H1160
Nu 22: 5 Balaam the son of **B** to Pethor, which *is* H1160
24: 3 Balaam the son of **B** hath said, and the H1160
15 Balaam the son of **B** hath said, and the H1160
31: 8 the son of **B** they slew with the sword. H1160
Dt 23: 4 thee Balaam the son of **B** of Pethor of H1160
Jos 13:22 Balaam also the son of **B**, the H1160
24: 9 Balaam the son of **B** to curse you: H1160
1Ch 1:43 Bela the son of **B**: and the name of his H1160
Mic 6: 5 Balaam the son of **B** answered him H1160

BERA
Gen 14: 2 *That these* made war with **B** king of H1298

BERACHAH
1Ch 12: 3 and **B**, and Jehu the Antothite, H1294
2Ch 20:26 in the valley of **B**; for there they blessed H1294
26 called, The valley of **B**, unto this day. H1294

BERACHIAH
1Ch 6:39 Asaph the son of **B**, the son of Shimea, H1296

BERAIAH
1Ch 8:21 And Adaiah, and **B**, and Shimrath, the H1256

BEREA
Act 17:10 Silas by night unto **B**: who coming *thither* *G960*
13 of Paul at **B**, they came thither also, *G960*
20: 4 into Asia Sopater of **B**; and of the *G960*

BEREAVE
Ecc 4: 8 do I labour, and **b** my soul of good? H2637
Jer 15: 7 of the land; I will **b** *them* of children, I H7921
Ezk 5:17 and they shall **b** thee; and pestilence H7921
36:12 no more henceforth **b** them *of men*. H7921
14 no more, neither **b** thy nations H7921+H3782
Hos 9:12 children, yet will I **b** them, *that there* H7921

BEREAVED
Gen 42:36 them, Me have ye **b** *of my children*: H7921
43:14 If I be **b** *of my children*, I am bereaved. H7921
14 If I be bereaved *of my children*, I am **b**. H7921
Jer 18:21 let their wives be **b** of their children, H7909
Ezk 36:13 up men, and hast **b** thy nations; H7921
Hos 13: 8 I will meet them as a bear *that is* **b** *of* H7909

BEREAVETH
Lam 1:20 the sword **b**, at home *there is* as death. H7921

BERECHIAH
1Ch 3:20 And Hashubah, and Ohel, and **B**, and H1296
9:16 of Jeduthun, and **B** the son of Asa, the H1296
15:17 Asaph the son of **B**; and of the sons of H1296
23 And **B** and Elkanah *were* doorkeepers H1296
2Ch 28:12 the son of Johanan, **B** the son of H1296
Neh 3: 4 the son of **B**, the son of Meshezabeel. H1296
30 the son of **B** over against his chamber. H1296
6:18 the daughter of Meshullam the son of **B**. H1296
Zec 1: 1 **B**, the son of Iddo the prophet, saying, H1296
7 **B**, the son of Iddo the prophet, saying, H1296

BERED
Gen 16:14 behold, *it is* between Kadesh and **B**. H1260
1Ch 7:20 Shuthelah, and **B** his son, and Tahath H1260

BERI
1Ch 7:36 and Shual, and **B**, and Imrah, H1275

BERIAH
Gen 46:17 and Isui, and **B**, and Serah their sister: H1283
17 and the sons of **B**; Heber, and Malchiel. H1283
Nu 26:44 Jesuites: of **B**, the family of the Beriites. H1283
45 Of the sons of **B**: of Heber, the family of H1283
1Ch 7:23 **B**, because it went evil with his house. H1283
30 Ishuai, and **B**, and Serah their sister. H1283
31 And the sons of **B**; Heber, and Malchiel, H1283
8:13 **B** also, and Shema, who *were* heads of H1283
16 and Ispah, and Joha, the sons of **B**; H1283
23:10 **B**. These four *were* the sons of Shimei. H1283
11 but Jeush and **B** had not many sons; H1283

BERIITES
Nu 26:44 Jesuites: of Beriah, the family of the **B**. H1284

BERITES
2Sa 20:14 and all the **B**: and they were gathered H1276

BERITH
Jdg 9:46 into an hold of the house of the god **B**. H1286

BERNICE
Act 25:13 **B** came unto Caesarea to salute Festus. *G959*
23 was come, and **B**, with great pomp, and *G959*
26:30 and **B**, and they that sat with them: *G959*

BERODACH-BALADAN
2Ki 20:12 At that time **B**, the son of Baladan, king H1255

BEROEA See BEREA.

BEROTHAH
Ezk 47:16 Hamath, **B**, Sibraim, which *is* between H1268

BEROTHAI
2Sa 8: 8 And from Betah, and from **B**, cities of H1268

BEROTHITE
1Ch 11:39 Zelek the Ammonite, Naharai the **B**, the H1307

BERRIES
Isa 17: 6 tree, two *or* three **b** in the top of the H1620
Jas 3:12 bear olive **b**? either a vine, figs? so *G1636*

BERYL
Ex 28:20 And the fourth row a **b**, and an onyx, H8658
39:13 And the fourth row, a **b**, an onyx, and a H8658
Song 5:14 rings set with the **b**: his belly *is as* bright H8658
Ezk 1:16 the colour of a **b**: and they four had one H8658
10: 9 wheels *was* as the colour of a **b** stone. H8658
28:13 the diamond, the **b**, the onyx, and the H8658
Dan 10: 6 His body also *was* like the **b**, and his H8658
Rev 21:20 the eighth, **b**; the ninth, a topaz; the *G969*

BESAI
Ezr 2:49 children of Paseah, the children of **B**, H1153
Neh 7:52 The children of **B**, the children of H1153

BESEECH
Ex 3:18 now let us go, we **b** thee, three days' H4994
33:18 And he said, I **b** thee, shew me thy H4994
Nu 12:11 Alas, my lord, I **b** thee, lay not the sin H4994
13 saying, Heal her now, O God, I **b** thee. H4994
14:17 And now, I **b** thee, let the power of my H4994
19 Pardon, I **b** thee, the iniquity of this H4994
1Sa 23:11 God of Israel, I **b** thee, tell thy servant. H4994
2Sa 13:24 let the king, I **b** thee, and his servants H4994
16: 4 said, I humbly **b** thee *that* I may find
24:10 done: and now, I **b** thee, O LORD, take H4994
2Ki 19:19 Now therefore, O LORD our God, I **b** H4994
20: 3 I **b** thee, O LORD, remember now how I H577
1Ch 21: 8 thing: but now, I **b** thee, do away the H4994
2Ch 6:40 Now, my God, let, I **b** thee, thine eyes H4994
Neh 1: 5 And said, I **b** thee, O LORD God of H577
8 Remember, I **b** thee, the word that thou H4994
11 O Lord, I **b** thee, let now thine ear be H577
Job 10: 9 Remember, I **b** thee, that thou hast H4994
42: 4 Hear, I **b** thee, and I will speak: I will H4994
Ps 80:14 Return, we **b** thee, O God of hosts: look H4994
116: 4 O LORD, I **b** thee, deliver my soul. H577
118:25 Save now, I **b** thee, O LORD: O LORD, I H577
25 O LORD, I **b** thee, send now prosperity. H577
119:108 Accept, I **b** thee, the freewill offerings H4994
Isa 38: 3 And said, Remember now, O LORD, I **b** H577
64: 9 see, we **b** thee, we *are* all thy people. H4994
Jer 38: 4 unto the king, We **b** thee, let this man H4994
20 *thee*. Obey, I **b** thee, the voice of the H4994
42: 2 the prophet, Let, we **b** thee, our H4994
Dan 1:12 Prove thy servants, I **b** thee, ten days; H4994
9:16 righteousness, I **b** thee, let thine anger H4994
Am 7: 2 GOD, forgive, I **b** thee: by whom shall H4994
5 Then said I, O Lord GOD, cease, I **b** H4994
Jna 1:14 LORD, and said, We **b** thee, O LORD, we H577
14 thee, O LORD, we **b** thee, let us not H577
4: 3 Therefore now, O LORD, take, I **b** thee, H4994
Mal 1: 9 And now, I pray you, **b** God H2470+H6440
Mk 7:32 they **b** him to put his hand upon him. *G3870*
Lk 8:28 most high? I **b** thee, torment me not. *G1189*
9:38 saying, Master, I **b** thee, look upon my *G1189*
Act 21:39 mean city: and, I **b** thee, suffer me to *G1189*
26: 3 wherefore I **b** thee to hear me patiently. *G1189*
Ro 12: 1 I **b** you therefore, brethren, by the *G3870*
15:30 Now I **b** you, brethren, for the Lord *G3870*
16:17 Now I **b** you, brethren, mark them *G3870*
1Co 1:10 Now I **b** you, brethren, by the name of *G3870*
4:16 Wherefore I **b** you, be ye followers of *G3870*
16:15 I **b** you, brethren, (ye know the house *G3870*
2Co 2: 8 Wherefore I **b** you that ye would *G3870*
5:20 as though God did **b** *you* by us: we pray *G3870*
6: 1 together *with him*, **b** *you* also that ye *G3870*
10: 1 Now I Paul myself **b** you by the *G3870*
2 But I **b** *you*, that I may not be bold *G1189*
Gal 4:12 Brethren, I **b** you, be as I *am*; for I *am* *G1189*
Eph 4: 1 I therefore, the prisoner of the Lord, **b** *G2065*
Php 4: 2 I **b** Euodias, and beseech Syntyche, *G3870*
2 I beseech Euodias, and **b** Syntyche, *G3870*
1Th 4: 1 Furthermore then we **b** you, brethren, *G2065*
10 but we **b** you, brethren, that *G3870*
5:12 And we **b** you, brethren, to know them *G2065*
2Th 2: 1 Now we **b** you, brethren, by the coming *G2065*
Phlm 9 Yet for love's sake I rather **b** *thee*, being *G3870*
10 I **b** thee for my son Onesimus, whom I *G3870*
Heb 13:19 But I **b** *you* the rather to do this, that I *G3870*
22 And I **b** you, brethren, suffer the word *G3870*
1Pt 2:11 Dearly beloved, I **b** *you* as strangers *G3870*
2Jn 5 And now I **b** thee, lady, not as though I *G2065*

BESEECHING
Mt 8: 5 came unto him a centurion, **b** him, *G3870*
Mk 1:40 And there came a leper to him, **b** him, *G3870*
Lk 7: 3 elders of the Jews, **b** him that he would *G2065*

BESET
Jdg 19:22 sons of Belial, **b** the house round H5437
20: 5 against me, and **b** the house round H5437
Ps 22:12 *bulls* of Bashan have **b** me round. H3803
139: 5 Thou hast **b** me behind and before, H6696
Hos 7: 2 **b** them about; they are before my face. H5437
Heb 12: 1 doth so easily **b** *us*, and let us run with *G2139*

BESETH See PI-BESETH.

BESIDE
Gen 26: 1 And there was a famine in the land, **b** H905
31:50 take *other* wives **b** my daughters, no H5921
Ex 12:37 on foot *that were* men, **b** children. H905
14: 9 **b** Pi-hahi-roth, before Baal-zephon. H5921
29:12 all the blood **b** the bottom of the altar. H413
Lev 1:16 and cast it **b** the altar on the east H681
6:10 altar, and he shall put them **b** the altar. H681
9:17 **b** the burnt sacrifice of the morning. H905
10:12 leaven **b** the altar: for it *is* most holy: H681
18:18 nakedness, **b** the other in her life *time*. H5921
23:38 **B** the sabbaths of the LORD, and beside H905
38 Beside the sabbaths of the LORD, and **b** H905
38 your gifts, and **b** all your vows, and H905
38 all your vows, and **b** all your freewill H905
Nu 5: 8 *even* to the priest; **b** the ram of the H905

Nu 5:20 have lain with thee **b** thine husband: H1107
6:21 for his separation, **b** *that* that his hand H905
11: 6 at all, **b** this manna, *before* our eyes. H1115
16:49 seven hundred, **b** them that died about H905
24: 6 *and* as cedar trees **b** the waters. H5921
28:10 of every sabbath, **b** the continual burnt H5921
15 shall be offered, **b** the continual burnt H5921
23 Ye shall offer these **b** the burnt offering H905
24 it shall be offered **b** the continual burnt H5921
31 Ye shall offer *them* **b** the continual burnt H905
29: 6 **B** the burnt offering of the month, and H905
11 One kid of the goats *for* a sin offering; **b** H905
16 *for* a sin offering; **b** the continual burnt H905
19 *for* a sin offering; **b** the continual burnt H905
22 And one goat *for* a sin offering; **b** the H905
25 *for* a sin offering; **b** the continual burnt H905
28 And one goat *for* a sin offering; **b** the H905
31 And one goat *for* a sin offering; **b** the H905
34 And one goat *for* a sin offering; **b** the H905
38 And one goat *for* a sin offering; **b** the H905
39 in your set feasts, **b** your vows, and your H905
31: 8 And they slew the kings of Midian, **b** H5921
Dt 3: 5 bars; **b** unwalled towns a great many. H905
4:35 he *is* God; *there is* none else **b** him. H905
11:30 against Gilgal, **b** the plains of Moreh? H681
18: 8 They shall have like portions to eat, **b** H905
19: 9 three cities more for thee, **b** these three: H5921
29: 1 the land of Moab, **b** the covenant which H905
Jos 3:16 city Adam, that *is* **b** Zaretan: and those H6654
7: 2 to Ai, which *is* **b** Beth-aven, on the east H5973
12: 9 the king of Ai, which *is* **b** Beth-el, one; H6654
13: 4 and Mearah that *is* **b** the Sidonians,
17: 5 to Manasseh, **b** the land of Gilead and H905
22:19 altar **b** the altar of the LORD our God. H1107
29 or for sacrifices, **b** the altar of the LORD H905
Jdg 6:37 upon all the earth ***b***, then shall I know
7: 1 early, and pitched **b** the well of Harod: H5921
8:26 *shekels* of gold; **b** ornaments, and H905
26 of Midian, and **b** the chains that *were* H905
11:34 **b** her he had neither son nor daughter.
20:15 that drew sword, **b** the inhabitants of H905
17 And the men of Israel, **b** Benjamin, were H905
36 in wait which they had set **b** Gibeah. H413
Ru 2:14 And she sat **b** the reapers: and he H6654
4: 4 *is* none to redeem *it* **b** thee; and I *am* H2108
1Sa 2: 2 for *there is* none **b** thee: neither *is there* H1115
4: 1 and pitched **b** Eben-ezer: and the H5921
19: 3 And I will go out and stand **b** my father H3027
2Sa 7:22 *is there any* God **b** thee, according to H2108
13:23 which *is* **b** Ephraim: and Absalom H5973
15: 2 early, and stood **b** the way of the gate: H3027
18 And all his servants passed on **b** him; H3027
1Ki 3:20 and took my son from **b** me, while thine H681
4:23 and an hundred sheep, **b** harts, and H905
5:16 **B** the chief of Solomon's officers which H905
9:26 which *is* **b** Eloth, on the shore of H854
10:13 she asked, **b** *that* which Solomon H905
15 **B** *that he had* of the merchantmen, and H905
19 the seat, and two lions stood **b** the stays. H681
11:25 the days of Solomon, **b** the mischief that H854
13:31 God *is* buried; lay my bones **b** his bones: H681
2Ki 11:20 with the sword ***b*** the king's house.
12: 9 the lid of it, and set it **b** the altar, on the H681
21:16 end to another; **b** his sin wherewith he H905
1Ch 3: 9 *These were* all the sons of David, **b** the H905
17:20 *is there any* God **b** thee, according to H2108
2Ch 9:12 she asked, **b** *that* which she had brought H905
14 **B** *that which* chapmen and merchants H905
17:19 These waited on the king, **b** *those* whom H905
20: 1 with them *other* **b** the Ammonites, came
26:19 of the LORD, from **b** the incense altar. H5921
31:16 **B** their genealogy of males, from three H905
Ezr 1: 4 and with beasts, **b** the freewill offering H5973
6 **b** all *that* was willingly offered. H905+H5921
2:65 **B** their servants and their maids, of H905
Neh 5:15 bread and wine, **b** forty shekels of silver; H310
17 Jews and rulers, **b** those that came unto
7:67 **B** their manservants and their H905
8: 4 for the purpose; and **b** him stood H681
Job 1:14 and the asses feeding **b** them: H5921+H3027
Ps 23: 2 he leadeth me **b** the still waters. H5921
73:25 *is* none upon earth *that* I desire **b** thee. H5973
Song 1: 8 feed thy kids **b** the shepherds' tents. H5921
Isa 26:13 O LORD our God, *other* lords **b** thee H2108
32:20 Blessed *are* ye that sow **b** all waters, H5921
43:11 I, *even* I, *am* the LORD; and **b** me *there* H1107
44: 6 I *am* the last; and **b** me *there is* no God. H1107
8 Is there a God **b** me? yea, *there is* no H1107
45: 5 *there is* no God **b** me: I girded thee, H2108
Isa 45: 6 west, that *there is* none **b** me. I *am* the H1107
21 *is* no God else **b** me; a just God and H1107
21 God and a Saviour; *there is* none **b** me. H2108
47: 8 *am*, and none else **b** me; I shall not sit *as* H657
10 in thine heart, I *am*, and none else **b** me. H657
56: 8 him, **b** those that are gathered unto him.
64: 4 eye seen, O God, **b** thee, *what* he hath H2108
Jer 36:21 all the princes which stood **b** the king. H5921
Ezk 9: 2 went in, and stood **b** the brasen altar. H681
10: 6 then he went in, and stood **b** the wheels. H681
16 wheels also turned not from **b** them. H681
19 wheels also *were* **b** them, and *every one* H5980
11:22 and the wheels **b** them; and the glory H5980
32:13 thereof from **b** the great waters; neither H5921
Dan 11: 4 be plucked up, even for others **b** those. H905
Hos 13: 4 but me: for *there is* no saviour **b** me. H1115
Zep 2:15 *am*, and *there is* none **b** me: how is she H657
Mt 14:21 thousand men, **b** women and children. G5565
15:38 thousand men, **b** women and children. G5565
25:20 I have gained **b** them five talents more. G1909
22 I have gained two other talents **b** them. G1909
Mk 3:21 on him: for they said, He is **b** himself. G1839
Lk 16:26 And **b** all this, between us and you G1909
24:21 Israel: and **b** all this, to day is the G4862
Act 26:24 Paul, thou art **b** thyself; much learning G3105
2Co 5:13 For whether we be **b** ourselves, *it is* to G1839
11:28 **B** those things that are without, that G5565
2Pt 1: 5 And **b** this, giving all diligence, add to G846

BESIDES
Gen 19:12 thou here any **b**? son in law, and thy H5750
46:26 out of his loins, **b** Jacob's sons' wives, H905
Lev 7:13 **B** the cakes, he shall offer *for* his H5921
1Ki 22: 7 LORD **b**, that we might inquire of him? H5750
2Ch 18: 6 LORD **b**, that we might inquire of him? H5750
Jer 36:32 added **b** unto them many like words. H5750
1Co 1:16 of Stephanas: **b**, I know not whether G3063
Phlm 19 owest unto me even thine own self **b**. G4359

BESIEGE
Dt 20:12 war against thee, then thou shalt **b** it: H6696
19 When thou shalt **b** a city a long time, in H6696
28:52 And he shall **b** thee in all thy gates, H6887
52 land: and he shall **b** thee in all thy gates H6887
1Sa 23: 8 to Keilah, to **b** David and his men. H6696
1Ki 8:37 if their enemy **b** them in the land of H6887
2Ki 24:11 the city, and his servants did **b** it. H6696
2Ch 6:28 if their enemies **b** them in the cities of H6696
Isa 21: 2 Go up, O Elam: **b**, O Media; all the H6696
Jer 21: 4 the Chaldeans, which **b** you without the H6696
9 Chaldeans that **b** you, he shall live, and H6696

BESIEGED
2Sa 11: 1 of Ammon, and **b** Rabbah. But David H6696
20:15 And they came and **b** him in Abel of H6696
1Ki 16:17 all Israel with him, and they **b** Tirzah. H6696
20: 1 and **b** Samaria, and warred against it. H6696
2Ki 6:24 his host, and went up, and **b** Samaria. H6696
25 and, behold, they **b** it, until an ass's H6696
16: 5 **b** Ahaz, but could not overcome *him*. H6696
17: 5 up to Samaria, and **b** it three years. H6696
18: 9 came up against Samaria, and **b** it. H6696
19:24 I dried up all the rivers of **b** places. H4693
24:10 Jerusalem, and the city was **b**. H935+H4692
25: 2 And the city was **b** unto the H935+H4692
1Ch 20: 1 and came and **b** Rabbah. But David H6696
Ecc 9:14 king against it, and **b** it, and built great H5437
Isa 1: 8 in a garden of cucumbers, as a **b** city. H5341
37:25 I dried up all the rivers of the **b** places. H4693
Jer 32: 2 For then the king of Babylon's army **b** H6696
37: 5 the Chaldeans that **b** Jerusalem heard H6696
39: 1 army against Jerusalem, and they **b** it. H6696
52: 5 So the city was **b** unto the eleventh year H4692
Ezk 4: 3 it, and it shall be **b**, and thou shalt lay H4692
6:12 that remaineth and is **b** shall die by the H5341
Dan 1: 1 of Babylon unto Jerusalem, and **b** it. H6696

BESODEIAH
Neh 3: 6 the son of **B**; they laid the beams H1152

BESOM
Isa 14:23 sweep it with the **b** of destruction, saith H4292

BESOR
1Sa 30: 9 came to the brook **B**, where those that H1308
10 that they could not go over the brook **B**. H1308
21 to abide at the brook **B**: and they went H1308

BESOUGHT
Gen 42:21 of his soul, when he **b** us, and we would H2603
Ex 32:11 And Moses **b** the LORD his God, and H2470
Dt 3:23 And I **b** the LORD at that time, saying, H2603
2Sa 12:16 David therefore **b** God for the child; H1245
1Ki 13: 6 the man of God **b** the LORD, and the H2470
2Ki 1:13 before Elijah, and **b** him, and said unto H2603
13: 4 And Jehoahaz **b** the LORD, and the H2470
2Ch 33:12 And when he was in affliction, he **b** the H2470
Ezr 8:23 So we fasted and **b** our God for this: H1245
Est 8: 3 at his feet, and **b** him with tears to put H2603
Jer 26:19 the LORD, and **b** the LORD, and the H2470
Mt 8:31 So the devils **b** him, saying, If thou cast G3870
34 they saw him, they **b** *him* that he would G3870
14:36 And **b** him that they might only touch G3870
15:23 came and **b** him, saying, Send her G2065
18:29 at his feet, and **b** him, saying, Have G3870
Mk 5:10 And he **b** him much that he would not G3870
12 And all the devils **b** him, saying, Send G3870
23 And **b** him greatly, saying, My little G3870
6:56 sick in the streets, and **b** him that they G3870
7:26 by nation; and she **b** him that he would G2065
8:22 unto him, and **b** him to touch him. G3870
Lk 4:38 a great fever; and they **b** him for her. G2065
5:12 on *his* face, and **b** him, saying, Lord, if G1189
7: 4 And when they came to Jesus, they **b** G3870
8:31 And they **b** him that he would not G3870
32 and they **b** him that he would suffer G3870
37 round about **b** him to depart from G2065
38 were departed **b** him that he might be G1189
41 at Jesus' feet, and **b** him that he would G3870
9:40 And I **b** thy disciples to cast him out; G1189
11:37 And as he spake, a certain Pharisee **b** G2065
Jn 4:40 unto him, they **b** him that he would G2065
47 unto him, and **b** him that he would G2065
19:31 was an high day,) **b** Pilate that their G2065
38 fear of the Jews, **b** Pilate that he might G2065
Act 13:42 the Gentiles **b** that these words might G3870
16:15 household, she **b** *us*, saying, If ye have G3870
39 And they came and **b** them, and G3870
21:12 place, **b** him not to go up to Jerusalem. G3870
25: 2 informed him against Paul, and **b** him, G3870
27:33 was coming on, Paul **b** *them* all to take G3870
2Co 12: 8 For this thing I **b** the Lord thrice, that it G3870
1Ti 1: 3 As I **b** thee to abide still at Ephesus, G3870

BEST
Gen 43:11 do this; take of the **b** fruits in the land H2173
47: 6 *is* before thee; in the **b** of the land make H4315
11 of Egypt, in the **b** of the land, in the H4315
Ex 22: 5 man's field; of the **b** of his own field, H4315
5 field, and of the **b** of his own vineyard, H4315
Nu 18:12 All the **b** of the oil, and all the best of H2459
12 All the best of the oil, and all the **b** of H2459
29 the LORD, of all the **b** thereof, *even* the H2459
30 have heaved the **b** thereof from it, then H2459
32 heaved from it the **b** of it: neither shall H2459
36: 6 whom they think **b**; only to the family of H2896
Dt 23:16 him **b**: thou shalt not oppress him. H2896
1Sa 8:14 *even* the **b** *of them*, and give *them* H2896
15: 9 Agag, and the **b** of the sheep, and of H4315
15 people spared the **b** of the sheep and of H4315
2Sa 18: 4 seemeth you **b** I will do. And the king H3190
1Ki 10:18 of ivory, and overlaid it with the **b** gold. H6338
2Ki 10: 3 Look even out the **b** and meetest of H2896
Est 2: 9 the **b** *place* of the house of the women. H2896
Ps 39: 5 his **b** state *is* altogether vanity. Selah. H5324
Song 7: 9 And the roof of thy mouth like the **b** H2896
Ezk 31:16 the choice and **b** of Lebanon, all that H2896
Mic 7: 4 The **b** of them *is* as a brier: the most H2896
Lk 15:22 Bring forth the **b** robe, and put *it* on G4413
1Co 12:31 But covet earnestly the **b** gifts: and yet G2909

BESTEAD
Isa 8:21 through it, hardly **b** and hungry: and it H7185

BESTIR
2Sa 5:24 then thou shalt **b** thyself: for then shall H2782

BESTOW
Ex 32:29 he may **b** upon you a blessing this day. H5414
Dt 14:26 And thou shalt **b** that money for H5414
2Ch 24: 7 of the LORD did they **b** upon Baalim. H6213
Ezr 7:20 have occasion to **b**, bestow *it* out of the H5415
20 **b** *it* out of the king's treasure house. H5415
Lk 12:17 I have no room where to **b** my fruits? G4863
18 will I **b** all my fruits and my goods. G4863
1Co 12:23 upon these we **b** more abundant G4060
13: 3 And though I **b** all my goods to feed *the* G5595

BESTOWED
1Ki 10:26 whom he **b** in the cities for chariots, H5148
2Ki 5:24 their hand, and **b** *them* in the house: H6485
12:15 **b** on workmen: for they dealt faithfully. H5414
1Ch 29:25 of all Israel, and **b** upon him *such* royal H5414
2Ch 9:25 whom he **b** in the chariot cities, H3240
Isa 63: 7 the LORD hath **b** on us, and the great H1580
7 which he hath **b** on them according H1580
Jn 4:38 I sent you to reap that whereon ye **b** no *G2872*
Ro 16: 6 Greet Mary, who **b** much labour on us. *G2872*
1Co 15:10 grace which *was* **b** upon me was not in
2Co 1:11 for us, that for the gift ***b*** upon us by the
8: 1 God **b** on the churches of Macedonia; *G1325*
Gal 4:11 I am afraid of you, lest I have **b** upon *G2872*
1Jn 3: 1 love the Father hath **b** upon us, that we *G1325*

BETAH
2Sa 8: 8 And from **B**, and from Berothai, cities of H984

BETEN
Jos 19:25 Helkath, and Hali, and **B**, and Achshaph, H991

BETHABARA
Jn 1:28 These things were done in **B** beyond *G962*

BETH-ANATH
Jos 19:38 Horem, and **B**, and Beth-shemesh; H1043
Jdg 1:33 nor the inhabitants of **B**; but he dwelt H1043
33 and of **B** became tributaries unto them. H1043

BETH-ANOTH
Jos 15:59 And Maarath, and **B**, and Eltekon; six H1042

BETHANY
Mt 21:17 of the city into **B**; and he lodged there. *G963*
26: 6 Now when Jesus was in **B**, in the house of *G963*
Mk 11: 1 Bethphage and **B**, at the mount of Olives, *G963*
11 he went out unto **B** with the twelve. *G963*
12 they were come from **B**, he was hungry: *G963*
14: 3 And being in **B** in the house of Simon the *G963*
Lk 19:29 to Bethphage and **B**, at the mount called *G963*
24:50 And he led them out as far as to **B**, and *G963*
Jn 11: 1 *named* Lazarus, of **B**, the town of Mary *G963*
18 Now **B** was nigh unto Jerusalem, about *G963*
12: 1 passover came to **B**, where Lazarus was *G963*

BETH-ARABAH
Jos 15: 6 by the north of **B**; and the border went H1026
61 In the wilderness, **B**, Middin, and H1026
18:22 And **B**, and Zemaraim, and Beth-el, H1026

BETH-ARAM
Jos 13:27 And in the valley, **B**, and Beth-nimrah, H1027

BETH-ARBEL
Hos 10:14 Shalman spoiled **B** in the day of battle: H1009

BETH-AVEN
Jos 7: 2 Ai, which *is* beside **B**, on the east side of H1007
18:12 out thereof were at the wilderness of **B**. H1007
1Sa 13: 5 pitched in Michmash, eastward from **B**. H1007
14:23 day: and the battle passed over unto **B**. H1007
Hos 4:15 ye up to **B**, nor swear, The LORD liveth. H1007
5: 8 cry aloud *at* **B**, after thee, O Benjamin. H1007
10: 5 of the calves of **B**: for the people thereof H1007

BETH-AZMAVETH
Neh 7:28 The men of **B**, forty and two. H1041

BETH-BAAL-MEON
Jos 13:17 plain; Dibon, and Bamoth-baal, and **B**, H1010

BETH-BARAH
Jdg 7:24 the waters unto **B** and Jordan. Then all H1012
24 and took the waters unto **B** and Jordan. H1012

BETH-BIREI
1Ch 4:31 and at **B**, and at Shaaraim. These H1011

BETH-CAR
1Sa 7:11 smote them, until *they came* under **B**. H1033

BETH-DAGON
Jos 15:41 And Gederoth, **B**, and Naamah, and H1016
19:27 And turneth toward the sunrising to **B**, H1016

BETHDIBLATHAIM
Jer 48:22 Dibon, and upon Nebo, and upon **B**, H1015

BETH-EL
Gen 12: 8 on the east of **B**, and pitched his tent, H1008
8 his tent, *having* **B** on the west, and Hai H1008
13: 3 from the south even to **B**, unto the place H1008
3 at the beginning, between **B** and Hai; H1008
28:19 And he called the name of that place **B**: H1008
31:13 I *am* the God of **B**, where thou H1008
35: 1 Arise, go up to **B**, and dwell there: and H1008
3 And let us arise, and go up to **B**; and I H1008
6 land of Canaan, that *is*, **B**, he and all the H1008
8 buried beneath **B** under an oak: and H1008
15 the place where God spake with him, **B**. H1008
16 And they journeyed from **B**; and there H1008
Jos 7: 2 on the east side of **B**, and spake unto H1008
8: 9 abode between **B** and Ai, on the west H1008
12 **B** and Ai, on the west side of the city. H1008
17 And there was not a man left in Ai or **B**, H1008
12: 9 the king of Ai, which *is* beside **B**, one; H1008
16 of Makkedah, one; the king of **B**, one; H1008
16: 1 up from Jericho throughout mount **B**, H1008
2 And goeth out from **B** to Luz, and H1008
18:13 of Luz, which *is* **B**, southward; and the H1008
22 Beth-arabah, and Zemaraim, and **B**, H1008
Jdg 1:22 **B**: and the LORD *was* with them. H1008
23 sent to descry **B**. (Now the name of the H1008
4: 5 Ramah and **B** in mount Ephraim: H1008
21:19 the north side of **B**, on the east side of H1008
19 goeth up from **B** to Shechem, and on H1008
1Sa 7:16 to year in circuit to **B**, and Gilgal, and H1008
10: 3 going up to God to **B**, one carrying three H1008
13: 2 and in mount **B**, and a thousand were H1008
30:27 To *them* which *were* in **B**, and to *them* H1008
1Ki 12:29 And he set the one in **B**, and the other H1008
32 altar. So did he in **B**, sacrificing unto H1008
32 and he placed in **B** the priests of the H1008
33 he had made in **B** the fifteenth day of H1008
13: 1 of the LORD unto **B**: and Jeroboam H1008
4 the altar in **B**, that he put forth his H1008
10 not by the way that he came to **B**. H1008
11 Now there dwelt an old prophet in **B**; H1008
11 done that day in **B**: the words which he H1008
32 the altar in **B**, and against all the H1008
2Ki 2: 2 hath sent me to **B**. And Elisha said *unto* H1008
2 not leave thee. So they went down to **B**. H1008
3 that *were* at **B** came forth to Elisha, H1008
23 And he went up from thence unto **B**: H1008
10:29 that *were* in **B**, and that *were* in Dan. H1008
17:28 came and dwelt in **B**, and taught them H1008
23: 4 and carried the ashes of them unto **B**. H1008
15 Moreover the altar that *was* at **B**, *and* H1008
17 thou hast done against the altar of **B**. H1008
19 to all the acts that he had done in **B**. H1008
1Ch 7:28 and habitations *were*, **B** and the towns H1008
2Ch 13:19 took cities from him, **B** with the towns H1008
Ezr 2:28 The men of **B** and Ai, two hundred H1008
Neh 7:32 The men of **B** and Ai, an hundred H1008
11:31 and Aija, and **B**, and *in* their villages, H1008
Jer 48:13 was ashamed of **B** their confidence. H1008
Hos 10:15 So shall **B** do unto you because of your H1008
12: 4 him *in* **B**, and there he spake with us; H1008
Am 3:14 visit the altars of **B**: and the horns of the H1008
4: 4 Come to **B**, and transgress; at Gilgal H1008
5: 5 But seek not **B**, nor enter into Gilgal, H1008
5 captivity, and **B** shall come to nought. H1008
6 *it*, and *there be* none to quench *it* in **B**. H1008
7:10 Then Amaziah the priest of **B** sent to H1008
13 But prophesy not again any more at **B**: H1008

BETH-ELITE
1Ki 16:34 In his days did Hiel the **B** build Jericho: H1017

BETH-EMEK
Jos 19:27 the north side of **B**, and Neiel, and H1025

BETHER
Song 2:17 a young hart upon the mountains of **B**. H1336

BETHESDA
Jn 5: 2 Hebrew tongue **B**, having five porches. *G964*

BETH-EZEL
Mic 1:11 **B**; he shall receive of you his standing. H1018

BETH-GADER
1Ch 2:51 of Beth-lehem, Hareph the father of **B**. H1013

BETH-GAMUL
Jer 48:23 And upon Kiriathaim, and upon **B**, and H1014

BETH-HACCEREM
Neh 3:14 the ruler of part of **B**; he built it, and set H1021
Jer 6: 1 up a sign of fire in **B**: for evil appeareth H1021

BETH-HANAN See ELON-BETH-HANAN.

BETH-HARAN
Nu 32:36 And Beth-nimrah, and **B**, fenced cities: H1028

BETH-HOGLA
Jos 15: 6 And the border went up to **B**, and H1031

BETH-HOGLAH
Jos 18:19 to the side of **B** northward: and the H1031
21 Jericho, and **B**, and the valley of Keziz, H1031

BETH-HORON
Jos 10:10 that goeth up to **B**, and smote them to H1032
11 the going down to **B**, that the LORD cast H1032
16: 3 unto the coast of **B** the nether, and to H1032
5 was Ataroth-addar, unto **B** the upper; H1032
18:13 *lieth* on the south side of the nether **B**. H1032
14 that *lieth* before **B** southward; and the H1032
21:22 And Kibzaim with her suburbs, and **B** H1032
1Sa 13:18 turned the way *to* **B**: and another H1032
1Ki 9:17 And Solomon built Gezer, and **B** the H1032
1Ch 6:68 And Jokmeam with her suburbs, and **B** H1032
7:24 Sherah, who built **B** the nether, and the H1032
2Ch 8: 5 Also he built **B** the upper, and H1032
5 the upper, and **B** the nether, fenced H1032
25:13 even unto **B**, and smote three thousand H1032

BETHINK
1Ki 8:47 *Yet* if they shall **b** themselves H7725+H3820
2Ch 6:37 Yet *if* they **b** themselves in the H7725+H3820

BETH-JESHIMOTH
Jos 12: 3 east, the way to **B**; and from the south, H1020
13:20 Beth-peor, and Ashdoth-pisgah, and **B**, H1020
Ezk 25: 9 country, **B**, Baal-meon, and Kiriathaim, H1020

BETH-JESIMOTH
Nu 33:49 And they pitched by Jordan, from **B** H1020

BETH-LEBAOTH
Jos 19: 6 And **B**, and Sharuhen; thirteen cities H1034

BETH-LEHEM
Gen 35:19 in the way to Ephrath, which *is* **B**. H1035
48: 7 in the way of Ephrath; the same *is* **B**. H1035
Jos 19:15 and **B**: twelve cities with their villages. H1035
Jdg 12: 8 And after him Ibzan of **B** judged Israel. H1035
10 Then died Ibzan, and was buried at **B**. H1035
Ru 1:19 So they two went until they came to **B**. H1035
19 they were come to **B**, that all the city H1035
22 to **B** in the beginning of barley harvest. H1035
2: 4 And, behold, Boaz came from **B**, and H1035
4:11 in Ephratah, and be famous in **B**: H1035
1Sa 16: 4 and came to **B**. And the elders of the H1035
17:15 from Saul to feed his father's sheep at **B**. H1035
20: 6 he might run to **B** his city: for *there is* H1035
28 earnestly asked *leave* of me *to go* to **B**: H1035
2Sa 2:32 which *was in* **B**. And Joab and his men H1035
23:14 of the Philistines *was* then *in* **B**. H1035
15 of the well of **B**, which *is* by the gate! H1035
16 out of the well of **B**, that *was* by the H1035
24 thirty; Elhanan the son of Dodo of **B**, H1035
1Ch 2:51 Salma the father of **B**, Hareph the father H1035
54 The sons of Salma; **B**, and the H1035
4: 4 firstborn of Ephratah, the father of **B**. H1035
11:16 the Philistines' garrison *was* then at **B**. H1035
17 water of the well of **B**, that *is* at the gate! H1035
18 out of the well of **B**, that *was* by the H1035
26 of Joab, Elhanan the son of Dodo of **B**, H1035
2Ch 11: 6 He built even **B**, and Etam, and Tekoa, H1035
Ezr 2:21 The children of **B**, an hundred twenty H1035
Neh 7:26 The men of **B** and Netophah, an H1035
Jer 41:17 which is by **B**, to go to enter into Egypt, H1035
Mic 5: 2 But thou, **B** Ephratah, *though* thou be H1035
Mt 2: 1 Now when Jesus was born in **B** of Judaea *G965*
5 And they said unto him, In **B** of Judaea: *G965*
6 And thou **B**, *in* the land of Juda, art not *G965*
8 And he sent them to **B**, and said, Go and *G965*
16 that were in **B**, and in all the coasts *G965*
Lk 2: 4 which is called **B**; (because he was of the *G965*
15 us now go even unto **B**, and see this thing *G965*
Jn 7:42 out of the town of **B**, where David was? *G965*

BETH-LEHEMITE
1Sa 16: 1 thee to Jesse the **B**: for I have provided H1022
18 a son of Jesse the **B**, *that is* cunning in H1022
17:58 I *am* the son of thy servant Jesse the **B**. H1022
2Sa 21:19 of Jaare-oregim, a **B**, slew *the brother of* H1022

BETH-LEHEM-JUDAH
Jdg 17: 7 And there was a young man out of **B** of H1035
8 of the city from **B** to sojourn where he H1035
9 I *am* a Levite of **B**, and I go to sojourn H1035
19: 1 who took to him a concubine out of **B**. H1035
2 to **B**, and was there four whole months. H1035
18 *are* passing from **B** toward the side of H1035
18 I: and I went to **B**, but I *am now* going H1035
Ru 1: 1 a certain man of **B** went to sojourn in H1035
2 Ephrathites of **B**. And they came into H1035
1Sa 17:12 that Ephrathite of **B**, whose name *was* H1035

BETH-MAACHAH
2Sa 20:14 unto Abel, and to **B**, and all the Berites: H1038
15 him in Abel of **B**, and they cast up a H1038

BETH-MARCABOTH
Jos 19: 5 And Ziklag, and **B**, and Hazar-susah, H1024
1Ch 4:31 And at **B**, and Hazar-susim, and at H1024

BETH-MEON
Jer 48:23 and upon Beth-gamul, and upon **B**, H1010

BETH-NIMRAH
Nu 32:36 And **B**, and Beth-haran, fenced cities: H1039
Jos 13:27 And in the valley, Beth-aram, and **B**, H1039

BETH-PALET
Jos 15:27 Hazar-gaddah, and Heshmon, and **B**, H1046

BETH-PAZZEZ
Jos 19:21 En-gannim, and En-haddah, and **B**; H1048

BETH-PEOR
Dt 3:29 we abode in the valley over against **B**. H1047
4:46 over against **B**, in the land of Sihon H1047
34: 6 over against **B**: but no man knoweth H1047
Jos 13:20 And **B**, and Ashdoth-pisgah, and H1047

BETHPHAGE
Mt 21: 1 and were come to **B**, unto the mount of *G967*
Mk 11: 1 to Jerusalem, unto **B** and Bethany, at the *G967*
Lk 19:29 was come nigh to **B** and Bethany, at the *G967*

BETH-PHELET
Neh 11:26 at Jeshua, and at Moladah, and at **B**, H1046

BETH-RAPHA
1Ch 4:12 And Eshton begat **B**, and Paseah, and H1051

BETH-REHOB
Jdg 18:28 valley that *lieth* by **B**. And they built a H1050
2Sa 10: 6 the Syrians of **B**, and the Syrians of H1050

BETHSAIDA
Mt 11:21 woe unto thee, **B**! for if the mighty works, *G966*
Mk 6:45 unto **B**, while he sent away the people. *G966*
8:22 And he cometh to **B**; and they bring a *G966*
Lk 9:10 place belonging to the city called **B**. *G966*
10:13 woe unto thee, **B**! for if the mighty works *G966*
Jn 1:44 Now Philip was of **B**, the city of Andrew *G966*
12:21 which was of **B** of Galilee, and desired *G966*

BETH-SHAN
1Sa 31:10 they fastened his body to the wall of **B**. H1052
12 from the wall of **B**, and came to Jabesh, H1052
2Sa 21:12 them from the street of **B**, where the H1052

BETH-SHEAN
Jos 17:11 and in Asher **B** and her towns, and H1052
16 *they* who *are* of **B** and her towns, and H1052
Jdg 1:27 *the inhabitants of* **B** and her towns, nor H1052
1Ki 4:12 and Megiddo, and all **B**, which *is* by H1052
12 Jezreel, from **B** to Abel-meholah, *even* H1052
1Ch 7:29 of Manasseh, **B** and her towns, H1052

BETH-SHEMESH
Jos 15:10 down to **B**, and passed on to Timnah: H1053
19:22 Shahazimah, and **B**; and the outgoings H1053
38 **B**; nineteen cities with their villages. H1053
21:16 her suburbs, *and* **B** with her suburbs; H1053
Jdg 1:33 out the inhabitants of **B**, nor the H1053
33 the inhabitants of **B** and of Beth-anath H1053
1Sa 6: 9 of his own coast to **B**, *then* he hath done H1053
12 way to the way of **B**, *and* went along the H1053
12 went after them unto the border of **B**. H1053
13 And *they of* **B** *were* reaping their wheat H1053
15 stone: and the men of **B** offered burnt H1053
19 And he smote the men of **B**, because H1053
20 And the men of **B** said, Who is able to H1053
1Ki 4: 9 and **B**, and Elon-beth-hanan: H1053
2Ki 14:11 the face at **B**, which *belongeth* to Judah. H1053
13 the son of Ahaziah, at **B**, and came to H1053
1Ch 6:59 And Ashan with her suburbs, and **B** H1053
2Ch 25:21 Judah, at **B**, which *belongeth* to Judah. H1053
23 of Jehoahaz, at **B**, and brought him to H1053
28:18 and had taken **B**, and Ajalon, and H1053
Jer 43:13 He shall break also the images of **B**, H1053

BETHSHEMITE
1Sa 6:14 the field of Joshua, a **B**, and stood there, H1030

BETH-SHEMITE
1Sa 6:18 this day in the field of Joshua, the **B**. H1030

BETH-SHITTAH
Jdg 7:22 the host fled to **B** in Zererath, *and* to H1029

BETH-TAPPUAH
Jos 15:53 And Janum, and **B**, and Aphekah, H1054

BETHUEL
Gen 22:22 Hazo, and Pildash, and Jidlaph, and **B**. H1328
23 And **B** begat Rebekah: these eight H1328
24:15 who was born to **B**, son of Milcah, the H1328
24 the daughter of **B** the son of Milcah, H1328
47 The daughter of **B**, Nahor's son, whom H1328
50 Then Laban and **B** answered and said, H1328
25:20 wife, the daughter of **B** the Syrian of H1328
28: 2 to the house of **B** thy mother's father; H1328
5 Laban, son of **B** the Syrian, the brother H1328
1Ch 4:30 And at **B**, and at Hormah, and at H1328

BETHUL
Jos 19: 4 And Eltolad, and **B**, and Hormah, H1329

BETH-ZUR
Jos 15:58 Halhul, **B**, and Gedor, H1049
1Ch 2:45 Maon: and Maon *was* the father of **B**. H1049
2Ch 11: 7 And **B**, and Shoco, and Adullam, H1049
Neh 3:16 of the half part of **B**, unto *the place* over H1049

BETIMES
Gen 26:31 And they rose up **b** in the morning, and H7925
2Ch 36:15 rising up **b**, and sending; because H7925
Job 8: 5 If thou wouldest seek unto God **b**, and H7836
24: 5 to their work; rising **b** for a prey: the H7836
Prv 13:24 he that loveth him chasteneth him **b**. H7836

BETONIM
Jos 13:26 and **B**; and from Mahanaim H993

BETRAY
1Ch 12:17 if *ye be come* to **b** me to mine enemies, H7411
Mt 24:10 and shall **b** one another, and shall *G3860*
26:16 time he sought opportunity to **b** him. *G3860*
21 unto you, that one of you shall **b** me. *G3860*
23 me in the dish, the same shall **b** me. *G3860*
46 behold, he is at hand that doth **b** me. *G3860*
Mk 13:12 Now the brother shall **b** the brother to *G3860*
14:10 the chief priests, to **b** him unto them. *G3860*
11 how he might conveniently **b** him. *G3860*
18 you which eateth with me shall **b** me. *G3860*
Lk 22: 4 how he might **b** him unto them. *G3860*
6 opportunity to **b** him unto them in the *G3860*
Jn 6:64 believed not, and who should **b** him. *G3860*
71 should **b** him, being one of the twelve. *G3860*
12: 4 Simon's *son*, which should **b** him, *G3860*
13: 2 Judas Iscariot, Simon's *son*, to **b** him; *G3860*
11 For he knew who should **b** him; *G3860*
21 unto you, that one of you shall **b** me. *G3860*

BETRAYED
Mt 10: 4 and Judas Iscariot, who also **b** him. *G3860*
17:22 man shall be **b** into the hands of men: *G3860*
20:18 of man shall be **b** unto the chief priests *G3860*
26: 2 and the Son of man is **b** to be crucified. *G3860*
24 the Son of man is **b**! it had been good *G3860*
25 Then Judas, which **b** him, answered *G3860*
45 of man is **b** into the hands of sinners. *G3860*
48 Now he that **b** him gave them a sign, *G3860*
27: 3 Then Judas, which had **b** him, when he *G3860*
Mt 27: 4 Saying, I have sinned in that I have **b** *G3860*
Mk 3:19 And Judas Iscariot, which also **b** him: *G3860*
14:21 the Son of man is **b**! good were it for *G3860*
41 of man is **b** into the hands of sinners. *G3860*
44 And he that **b** him had given them a *G3860*
Lk 21:16 And ye shall be **b** both by parents, and *G3860*
22:22 woe unto that man by whom he is **b**! *G3860*
Jn 18: 2 And Judas also, which **b** him, knew the *G3860*
5 also, which **b** him, stood with them. *G3860*
1Co 11:23 night in which he was **b** took bread: *G3860*

BETRAYERS
Act 7:52 ye have been now the **b** and murderers: *G4273*

BETRAYEST
Lk 22:48 But Jesus said unto him, Judas, **b** thou *G3860*

BETRAYETH
Mk 14:42 Rise up, let us go; lo, he that **b** me is at *G3860*
Lk 22:21 But, behold, the hand of him that **b** me *G3860*
Jn 21:20 and said, Lord, which is he that **b** thee? *G3860*

BETROTH
Dt 28:30 Thou shalt **b** a wife, and another man H781
Hos 2:19 And I will **b** thee unto me for ever; yea, I H781
19 me for ever; yea, I will **b** thee unto me in H781
20 I will even **b** thee unto me in H781

BETROTHED
Ex 21: 8 master, who hath **b** her to himself, then H3259
9 And if he have **b** her unto his son, he H3259
22:16 And if a man entice a maid that is not **b**, H781
Lev 19:20 *is* a bondmaid, **b** to an husband, and H2778
Dt 20: 7 And what man *is there* that hath **b** a H781
22:23 If a damsel *that is* a virgin be **b** unto an H781
25 But if a man find a **b** damsel in the field, H781
27 For he found her in the field, *and* the **b** H781
28 a virgin, which is not **b**, and lay hold on H781

BETTER
Gen 29:19 And Laban said, *It is* **b** that I give her H2896
Ex 14:12 For *it had been* **b** for us to serve the H2896
Nu 14: 3 it not **b** for us to return into Egypt? H2896
Jdg 8: 2 **b** than the vintage of Abi-ezer? H2896
9: 2 Whether *is* **b** for you, either that H2896
11:25 And now *art* thou any thing **b** than H2896
18:19 and a priest: *is it* **b** for thee to be a H2896
Ru 4:15 thee, which is **b** to thee than seven H2896
1Sa 1: 8 *am* not I **b** to thee than ten sons? H2896
15:22 Behold, to obey *is* **b** than sacrifice, *and* H2896
28 neighbour of thine, *that is* **b** than thou. H2896
27: 1 *there is* nothing **b** for me than that I H2896
2Sa 17:14 the Archite *is* **b** than the counsel of H2896
18: 3 *is* **b** that thou succour us out of the city. H2896
1Ki 1:47 the name of Solomon **b** than thy name, H3190
2:32 righteous and **b** than he, and slew H2896
19: 4 my life; for I *am* not **b** than my fathers. H2896
21: 2 give thee for it a **b** vineyard than it; *or*, H2896
2Ki 5:12 of Damascus, **b** than all the waters of H2896
2Ch 21:13 house, *which were* **b** than thyself: H2896
Est 1:19 estate unto another that is **b** than she. H2896
Ps 37:16 A little that a righteous man hath *is* **b** H2896
63: 3 Because thy lovingkindness *is* **b** than H2896
69:31 *This* also shall please the LORD **b** than H3190
84:10 For a day in thy courts *is* **b** than a H2896
118: 8 *It is* **b** to trust in the LORD than to put H2896
9 *It is* **b** to trust in the LORD than to put H2896
119:72 The law of thy mouth *is* **b** unto me than H2896
Prv 3:14 For the merchandise of it *is* **b** than the H2896
8:11 For wisdom *is* **b** than rubies; and all H2896
19 My fruit *is* **b** than gold, yea, than fine H2896
12: 9 and hath a servant, *is* **b** than he that H2896
15:16 **B** *is* little with the fear of the LORD H2896
17 **B** *is* a dinner of herbs where love is, H2896
16: 8 **B** *is* a little with righteousness than H2896
16 How much **b** *is it* to get wisdom than H2896
19 **B** *it is to be* of an humble spirit with the H2896
32 *He that is* slow to anger *is* **b** than the H2896
17: 1 **B** *is* a dry morsel, and quietness H2896
19: 1 **B** *is* the poor that walketh in his H2896
22 and a poor man *is* **b** than a liar. H2896
21: 9 *It is* **b** to dwell in a corner of the H2896
19 *It is* **b** to dwell in the wilderness, than H2896
25: 7 For **b** *it is* that it be said unto thee, H2896
24 *It is* **b** to dwell in the corner of the H2896
27: 5 Open rebuke *is* **b** than secret love. H2896
10 thy calamity: *for* **b** *is* a neighbour *that* H2896
28: 6 **B** *is* the poor that walketh in his H2896
Ecc 2:24 *There is* nothing **b** for a man, *than* that H2896

Ecc 3:22 that *there is* nothing **b**, than that a man H2896
4: 3 Yea, **b** *is he* than both they, which hath H2896
6 **B** *is* an handful *with* quietness, than H2896
9 Two *are* **b** than one; because they have H2896
13 **B** *is* a poor and a wise child than an old H2896
5: 5 **B** *is it* that thou shouldest not vow, H2896
6: 3 say, *that* an untimely birth *is* **b** than he. H2896
9 **B** *is* the sight of the eyes than the H2896
11 that increase vanity, what *is* man the **b**? H3148
7: 1 A good name *is* **b** than precious H2896
2 *It is* **b** to go to the house of mourning, H2896
3 Sorrow *is* **b** than laughter: for by the H2896
3 of the countenance the heart is made **b**. H3190
5 *It is* **b** to hear the rebuke of the wise, H2896
8 **B** *is* the end of a thing than the H2896
8 in spirit *is* **b** than the proud in spirit. H2896
10 the former days were **b** than these? for H2896
8:15 a man hath no **b** thing under the sun, H2896
9: 4 for a living dog is **b** than a dead lion. H2896
16 Then said I, Wisdom *is* **b** than H2896
18 Wisdom *is* **b** than weapons of war: but H2896
10:11 enchantment; and a babbler is no **b**. H3504
Song 1: 2 his mouth: for thy love *is* **b** than wine. H2896
4:10 how much **b** is thy love than wine! H2895
Isa 56: 5 place and a name **b** than of sons and of H2896
Lam 4: 9 *They that be* slain with the sword are **b** H2896
Ezk 36:11 and will do **b** *unto you* than at your H2895
Dan 1:20 found them ten times **b** than all the H3027
Hos 2: 7 for then *was it* **b** with me than now. H2896
Am 6: 2 *be they* **b** than these kingdoms? H2896
Jna 4: 3 me; for *it is* **b** for me to die than to live. H2896
8 said, *It is* **b** for me to die than to live. H2896
Nah 3: 8 Art thou **b** than populous No, that was H3190
Mt 6:26 them. Are ye not much **b** than they? *G1308*
12:12 How much then is a man **b** than a *G1308*
18: 6 believe in me, it were **b** for him that a *G4851*
8 from thee: it is **b** for thee to enter into *G2570*
9 *it* from thee: it is **b** for thee to enter into *G2570*
Mk 9:42 that believe in me, it is **b** for him that a *G2570*
43 thee, cut it off: it is **b** for thee to enter *G2570*
45 thee, cut it off: it is **b** for thee to enter *G2570*
47 pluck it out: it is **b** for thee to enter into *G2570*
Lk 5:39 desireth new: for he saith, The old is **b**. *G5543*
12:24 much more are ye **b** than the fowls? *G1308*
17: 2 It were **b** for him that a millstone were *G3081*
Ro 3: 9 What then? are we **b** *than they*? No, in *G4284*
1Co 7: 9 marry: for it is **b** to marry than to burn. *G2909*
38 that giveth *her* not in marriage doeth **b**. *G2908*
8: 8 if we eat, are we the **b**; neither, if we eat *G4052*
9:15 me: for *it were* **b** for me to die, than *G2570*
11:17 together not for the **b**, but for the worse. *G2909*
Php 1:23 and to be with Christ; which is far **b**: *G2909*
2: 3 each esteem other **b** than themselves. *G5242*
Heb 1: 4 Being made so much **b** than the angels, *G2909*
6: 9 But, beloved, we are persuaded **b** *G2909*
7: 7 the less is blessed of the **b**. *G2909*
19 the bringing in of a **b** hope *did*; by the *G2909*
22 Jesus made a surety of a **b** testament. *G2909*
8: 6 is the mediator of a **b** covenant, which *G2909*
6 was established upon **b** promises. *G2909*
9:23 themselves with **b** sacrifices than these. *G2909*
10:34 heaven a **b** and an enduring substance. *G2909*
11:16 But now they desire a **b** *country*, that *G2909*
35 they might obtain a **b** resurrection: *G2909*
40 God having provided some **b** thing for *G2909*
12:24 speaketh **b** things than *that of* Abel. *G2909*
1Pt 3:17 For *it is* **b**, if the will of God be so, that *G2909*
2Pt 2:21 For it had been **b** for them not to have *G2909*

BETTERED
Mk 5:26 was nothing **b**, but rather grew worse, *G5623*

BETWEEN See the Appendix.

BETWIXT
Gen 17:11 a token of the covenant **b** me and you. H996
23:15 **b** me and thee? bury therefore thy dead. H996
26:28 be now an oath **b** us, *even* betwixt us H996
28 betwixt us, *even* **b** us and thee, and let H996
30:36 And he set three days' journey **b** himself H996
31:37 brethren, that they may judge **b** us both. H996
50 us; see, God *is* witness **b** me and thee. H996
51 pillar, which I have cast **b** me and thee; H996
53 their father, judge **b** us. And Jacob sware H996
32:16 me, and put a space **b** drove and drove. H996
Job 9:33 Neither is there any daysman **b** us, *that* H996
36:32 *not to shine* by *the cloud* that cometh **b**. H6293
Song 1:13 me; he shall lie all night **b** my breasts. H996
Isa 5: 3 I pray you, **b** me and my vineyard. H996
Jer 39: 4 garden, by the gate **b** the two walls: and H996
Php 1:23 For I am in a strait **b** two, having a *G1537*

BEULAH
Isa 62: 4 and thy land **B**: for the LORD delighteth H1166

BEWAIL
Lev 10: 6 house of Israel, **b** the burning which H1058
Dt 21:13 thine house, and **b** her father and her H1058
Jdg 11:37 and **b** my virginity, I and my fellows. H1058
Isa 16: 9 Therefore I will **b** with the weeping of H1058
2Co 12:21 and *that* I shall **b** many which have *G3996*
Rev 18: 9 with her, shall **b** her, and lament for *G2799*

BEWAILED
Jdg 11:38 **b** her virginity upon the mountains. H1058
Lk 8:52 And all wept, and **b** her: but he said, *G2875*
23:27 which also **b** and lamented him. *G2875*

BEWAILETH
Jer 4:31 of Zion, *that* **b** herself, *that* spreadeth H3306

BEWARE
Gen 24: 6 And Abraham said unto him, **B** thou H8104
Ex 23:21 **B** of him, and obey his voice, provoke H8104
Dt 6:12 *Then* **b** lest thou forget the LORD, H8104
8:11 **B** that thou forget not the LORD thy H8104
15: 9 **B** that there be not a thought in thy H8104
Jdg 13: 4 Now therefore **b**, I pray thee, and drink H8104
13 all that I said unto the woman let her **b**. H8104
2Sa 18:12 and Ittai, saying, **B** that none *touch* the H8104
2Ki 6: 9 of Israel, saying, **B** that thou pass not H8104
Job 36:18 Because *there is* wrath, **b** lest he take
Prv 19:25 Smite a scorner, and the simple will **b**: H6191
Isa 36:18 **B** lest Hezekiah persuade you, saying,
Mt 7:15 **B** of false prophets, which come to you *G4337*
10:17 But **b** of men: for they will deliver you *G4337*
16: 6 Take heed and **b** of the leaven of the *G4337*
11 that ye should **b** of the leaven of the *G4337*
12 he bade *them* not **b** of the leaven of *G4337*
Mk 8:15 saying, Take heed, **b** of the leaven of the *G991*
12:38 And he said unto them in his doctrine, **B** *G991*
Lk 12: 1 first of all, **B** ye of the leaven of the *G4337*
15 Take heed, and **b** of covetousness: for *G5442*
20:46 **B** of the scribes, which desire to walk in *G4337*
Act 13:40 **B** therefore, lest that come upon you, *G991*
Php 3: 2 **B** of dogs, beware of evil workers, *G991*
2 Beware of dogs, **b** of evil workers, *G991*
2 of evil workers, **b** of the concision. *G991*
Col 2: 8 **B** lest any man spoil you through *G991*
2Pt 3:17 *things* before, **b** lest ye also, being led *G5442*

BEWITCHED
Act 8: 9 city used sorcery, and **b** the people of *G1839*
11 long time he had **b** them with sorceries. *G1839*
Gal 3: 1 O foolish Galatians, who hath **b** you, *G940*

BEWRAY
Isa 16: 3 the outcasts; **b** not him that wandereth. H1540

BEWRAYETH
Prv 27:16 of his right hand, *which* **b** *itself*. H7121
29:24 soul: he heareth cursing, and **b** *it* not. H5046
Mt 26:73 art *one* of them; for thy speech **b** thee. *G1212*

BEYOND
Gen 35:21 spread his tent **b** the tower of Edar. H1973
50:10 of Atad, which *is* **b** Jordan, and there H5676
11 Abel-mizraim, which *is* **b** Jordan. H5676
Lev 15:25 or if it run **b** the time of her separation; H5921
Nu 22:18 and gold, I cannot go **b** the word of the H5674
24:13 gold, I cannot go **b** the commandment H5674
Dt 3:20 hath given them **b** Jordan: and *then* H5676
25 good land that *is* **b** Jordan, that goodly H5676
30:13 Neither *is* it **b** the sea, that thou H5676
Jos 9:10 that *were* **b** Jordan, to Sihon king H5676
13: 8 Moses gave them, **b** Jordan eastward, H5676
18: 7 their inheritance **b** Jordan on the east, H5676
Jdg 3:26 and passed **b** the quarries, and escaped H5674
5:17 Gilead abode **b** Jordan: and why did H5676
1Sa 20:22 the arrows *are* **b** thee; go thy way: for H1973
36 as the lad ran, he shot an arrow **b** him. H5674
37 lad, and said, *Is* not the arrow **b** thee? H1973
2Sa 10:16 Syrians that *were* **b** the river: and they H5676
1Ki 4:12 *even* unto *the place that is* **b** Jokneam: H5676
14:15 shall scatter them **b** the river, because H5676
1Ch 19:16 the Syrians that *were* **b** the river: and H5676
2Ch 20: 2 against thee from **b** the sea on this side H5676
Ezr 4:17 **b** the river, Peace, and at such a time. H5675
4:20 over all *countries* **b** the river; and toll, H5675
6: 6 Now *therefore*, Tatnai, governor **b** the H5675
6 *are* **b** the river, be ye far from thence: H5675
8 goods, *even* of the tribute **b** the river, H5675
7:21 which *are* **b** the river, that whatsoever H5675
25 people that *are* **b** the river, all such as H5675
Neh 2: 7 to the governors **b** the river, that they H5676
9 Then I came to the governors **b** the H5676
12:38 upon the wall, from **b** the tower of the H5921
Isa 7:20 *namely*, by them **b** the river, by the H5676
9: 1 sea, **b** Jordan, in Galilee of the nations. H5676
18: 1 wings, which *is* **b** the rivers of Ethiopia: H5676
Jer 22:19 and cast forth **b** the gates of Jerusalem. H1973
25:22 kings of the isles which *are* **b** the sea, H5676
Am 5:27 go into captivity **b** Damascus, saith the H1973
Zep 3:10 From **b** the rivers of Ethiopia my H5676
Mt 4:15 sea, **b** Jordan, Galilee of the Gentiles; *G4008*
25 and *from* Judaea, and *from* **b** Jordan. *G4008*
19: 1 into the coasts of Judaea **b** Jordan; *G4008*
Mk 3: 8 and *from* **b** Jordan; and they about *G4008*
6:51 themselves **b** measure, and wondered. *G1537*
7:37 And were **b** measure astonished, *G5249*
Jn 1:28 These things were done in Bethabara **b** *G4008*
3:26 that was with thee **b** Jordan, to whom *G4008*
10:40 And went away again **b** Jordan into the *G4008*
Act 7:43 and I will carry you away **b** Babylon. *G1900*
2Co 8: 3 record, yea, and **b** *their* power *they* *G5228*
10:14 For we stretch not ourselves **b** *our* *G5239*
16 To preach the gospel in the *regions* **b** *G5238*
Gal 1:13 religion, how that **b** measure I *G2596+G5236*
1Th 4: 6 That no *man* go **b** and defraud his *G5233*

BEZAI
Ezr 2:17 The children of **B**, three hundred twenty H1209
Neh 7:23 The children of **B**, three hundred twenty H1209
10:18 Hodijah, Hashum, **B**, H1209

BEZALEEL
Ex 31: 2 See, I have called by name **B** the son of H1212
35:30 called by name **B** the son of Uri, the H1212
36: 1 Then wrought **B** and Aholiab, and H1212
2 And Moses called **B** and Aholiab, and H1212
37: 1 And **B** made the ark *of* shittim wood: H1212
38:22 And **B** the son of Uri, the son of Hur, of H1212
1Ch 2:20 And Hur begat Uri, and Uri begat **B**. H1212
2Ch 1: 5 Moreover the brasen altar, that **B** the H1212
Ezr 10:30 **B**, and Binnui, and Manasseh. H1212

BEZEK
Jdg 1: 4 slew of them in **B** ten thousand men. H966
5 And they found Adoni-bezek in **B**: and H966
1Sa 11: 8 And when he numbered them in **B**, the H966

BEZER
Dt 4:43 *Namely*, **B** in the wilderness, in the H1221
Jos 20: 8 they assigned **B** in the wilderness upon H1221
21:36 And out of the tribe of Reuben, **B** with H1221
1Ch 6:78 the tribe of Reuben, **B** in the wilderness H1221
7:37 **B**, and Hod, and Shamma, and H1221

BICHRI
2Sa 20: 1 Sheba, the son of **B**, a Benjamite: and H1075
2 Sheba the son of **B**: but the men of H1075
6 Sheba the son of **B** do us more harm H1075
7 to pursue after Sheba the son of **B**. H1075
10 pursued after Sheba the son of **B**. H1075
13 Joab, to pursue after Sheba the son of **B**. H1075
21 Sheba the son of **B** by name, hath lifted H1075
22 of Sheba the son of **B**, and cast *it* out to H1075

BID
Nu 15:38 Speak unto the children of Israel, and **b** H559
Jos 6:10 day I **b** you shout; then shall ye shout. H559
1Sa 9:27 said to Saul, **B** the servant pass on H559
2Sa 2:26 it be then, ere thou **b** the people return H559
2Ki 4:24 not *thy* riding for me, except I **b** thee. H559
5:13 *if* the prophet had **b** thee *do some* great H1696
10: 5 all that thou shalt **b** us; we will not make H559
Jna 3: 2 unto it the preaching that I **b** thee. H1696
Zep 1: 7 a sacrifice, he hath **b** his guests. H6942
Mt 14:28 **b** me come unto thee on the water. *G2753*
22: 9 as ye shall find, **b** to the marriage. *G2564*
23: 3 All therefore whatsoever they **b** you *G2036*
Lk 9:61 but let me first go **b** them farewell, which *G657*
10:40 alone? **b** her therefore that she help me. *G2036*
14:12 lest they also **b** thee again, and a *G479*
1Co 10:27 If any of them that believe not **b** you *to* *G2564*
2Jn 10 *your* house, neither **b** him God speed: *G3004*

BIDDEN
1Sa 9:13 they eat that be **b**. Now therefore get H7121
22 **b**, which *were* about thirty persons. H7121
2Sa 16:11 let him curse; for the LORD hath **b** him. H559
Mt 1:24 had **b** him, and took unto him his wife: *G4367*
22: 3 them that were **b** to the wedding: and *G2564*
4 Tell them which are **b**, Behold, I have *G2564*
8 but they which were **b** were not worthy. *G2564*
Lk 7:39 Now when the Pharisee which had **b** *G2564*
14: 7 to those which were **b**, when he marked *G2564*
8 When thou art **b** of any *man* to a *G2564*
8 man than thou be **b** of him; *G2564*
10 But when thou art **b**, go and sit down in *G2564*
17 **b**, Come; for all things are now ready. *G2564*
24 which were **b** shall taste of my supper. *G2564*
Lk 16: 6 **b**, and sit down quickly, and write fifty. *G1121*
7 him, Take thy **b**, and write fourscore. *G1121*

BIDDETH
2Jn 11 For he that **b** him God speed is *G3004*

BIDDING
1Sa 22:14 thy **b**, and is honourable in thine house? H4928

BIDKAR
2Ki 9:25 Then said *Jehu* to **B** his captain, Take H920

BIER
2Sa 3:31 And king David *himself* followed the **b**. H4296
Lk 7:14 And he came and touched the **b**: and *G4673*

BIGTHA
Est 1:10 Biztha, Harbona, **B**, and Abagtha, H903

BIGTHAN
Est 2:21 chamberlains, **B** and Teresh, of those H904

BIGTHANA
Est 6: 2 had told of **B** and Teresh, two of the H904

BIGVAI
Ezr 2: 2 Bilshan, Mispar, **B**, Rehum, Baanah. The H902
14 The children of **B**, two thousand fifty and H902
8:14 Of the sons also of **B**; Uthai, and Zabbud, H902
Neh 7: 7 Mispereth, **B**, Nehum, Baanah. The H902
19 The children of **B**, two thousand H902
10:16 Adonijah, **B**, Adin, H902

BILDAD
Job 2:11 the Temanite, and **B** the Shuhite, and H1085
8: 1 Then answered **B** the Shuhite, and H1085
18: 1 Then answered **B** the Shuhite, and H1085
25: 1 Then answered **B** the Shuhite, and H1085
42: 9 So Eliphaz the Temanite and **B** the H1085

BILEAM
1Ch 6:70 her suburbs, and **B** with her suburbs, H1109

BILGAH
1Ch 24:14 The fifteenth to **B**, the sixteenth to H1083
Neh 12: 5 Miamin, Maadiah, **B**, H1083
18 Of **B**, Shammua; of Shemaiah, H1083

BILGAI
Neh 10: 8 Maaziah, **B**, Shemaiah: these *were* the H1084

BILHAH
Gen 29:29 **B** his handmaid to be her maid. H1090
30: 3 And she said, Behold my maid **B**, go in H1090
4 And she gave him **B** her handmaid to H1090
5 And **B** conceived, and bare Jacob a H1090
7 And **B** Rachel's maid conceived again, H1090
35:22 went and lay with **B** his father's H1090
25 And the sons of **B**, Rachel's handmaid; H1090
37: 2 with the sons of **B**, and with the sons of H1090
46:25 These *are* the sons of **B**, which Laban H1090
1Ch 4:29 And at **B**, and at Ezem, and at Tolad, H1090
7:13 and Jezer, and Shallum, the sons of **B**. H1090

BILHAN
Gen 36:27 The children of Ezer *are* these; **B**, and H1092
1Ch 1:42 The sons of Ezer; **B**, and Zavan, *and* H1092
7:10 The sons also of Jediael; **B**: and the sons H1092
10 and the sons of **B**; Jeush, and Benjamin, H1092

BILL
Dt 24: 1 let him write her a **b** of divorcement, H5612
3 and write her a **b** of divorcement, and H5612
Isa 50: 1 Thus saith the LORD, Where *is* the **b** of H5612
Jer 3: 8 and given her a **b** of divorce; yet her H5612
Mk 10: 4 a **b** of divorcement, and to put *her* away. *G975*

BILLOWS
Ps 42: 7 thy waves and thy **b** are gone over me. H1530
Jna 2: 3 thy **b** and thy waves passed over me. H4867

BILSHAN
Ezr 2: 2 Mordecai, **B**, Mispar, Bigvai, Rehum, H1114
Neh 7: 7 Mordecai, **B**, Mispereth, Bigvai, H1114

BIMHAL
1Ch 7:33 And the sons of Japhlet; Pasach, and **B**, H1118

BIND
Ex 28:28 And they shall **b** the breastplate by the H7405
39:21 And they did **b** the breastplate by his H7405
Nu 30: 2 swear an oath to **b** his soul with a bond; H631
3 unto the LORD, and **b** herself by a bond, H631
Dt 6: 8 And thou shalt **b** them for a sign upon H7194
11:18 and in your soul, and **b** them for a sign H7194
14:25 *it* into money, and **b** up the money in H6696
Jos 2:18 the land, thou shalt **b** this line of scarlet H7194
Jdg 15:10 And they answered, To **b** Samson are we H631
12 are come down to **b** thee, that we may H631
13 No; but we will **b** thee fast, and deliver H631
16: 5 him, that we may **b** him to afflict him: H631
7 And Samson said unto her, If they **b** me H631
11 And he said unto her, If they **b** me fast H631
Job 31:36 my shoulder, *and* **b** it *as* a crown to me. H6029
38:31 Canst thou **b** the sweet influences of H7194
39:10 Canst thou **b** the unicorn with his band H7194
40:13 Hide them in the dust together; *and* **b** H2280
41: 5 or wilt thou **b** him for thy maidens? H7194
Ps 105:22 To **b** his princes at his pleasure; and H631
118:27 hath shewed us light: **b** the sacrifice with H631
149: 8 To **b** their kings with chains, and their H631
Prv 3: 3 Let not mercy and truth forsake thee: **b** H7194
6:21 **B** them continually upon thine heart, H7194
7: 3 **B** them upon thy fingers, write them H7194
Isa 8:16 **B** up the testimony, seal the law among H6887
49:18 and **b** them *on thee*, as a bride *doeth*. H7194
61: 1 meek; he hath sent me to **b** up the H2280
Jer 51:63 *that* thou shalt **b** a stone to it, and cast H7194
Ezk 3:25 thee, and shall **b** thee with them, and H631
5: 3 in number, and **b** them in thy skirts. H6696
24:17 for the dead, **b** the tire of thine head H2280
30:21 to put a roller to **b** it, to make it strong H2280
34:16 away, and will **b** up *that which was* H2280
Dan 3:20 in his army to **b** Shadrach, Meshach, H3729
Hos 6: 1 he hath smitten, and he will **b** us up. H2280
10:10 shall **b** themselves in their two furrows. H631
Mic 1:13 O thou inhabitant of Lachish, **b** the H7573
Mt 12:29 except he first **b** the strong man? and *G1210*
13:30 first the tares, and **b** them in bundles to *G1210*
16:19 thou shalt **b** on earth shall be bound *G1210*
18:18 ye shall **b** on earth shall be bound *G1210*
22:13 Then said the king to the servants, **B** *G1210*
23: 4 For they **b** heavy burdens and grievous *G1195*
Mk 3:27 except he will first **b** the strong man; *G1210*
5: 3 man could **b** him, no, not with chains: *G1210*
Act 9:14 priests to **b** all that call on thy name. *G1210*
12: 8 Gird thyself, and **b** on thy sandals. And *G5265*
21:11 the Jews at Jerusalem **b** the man that *G1210*

BINDETH
Job 5:18 For he maketh sore, and **b** up: he H2280
26: 8 He **b** up the waters in his thick clouds; H6887
28:11 He **b** the floods from overflowing; and H2280
30:18 it **b** me about as the collar of my coat. H247
36:13 up wrath: they cry not when he **b** them. H631
Ps 129: 7 hand; nor he that **b** sheaves his bosom. H6014
147: 3 He healeth the broken in heart, and **b** H2280
Prv 26: 8 As he that **b** a stone in a sling, so *is* he H6887
Isa 30:26 that the LORD **b** up the breach of his H2280

BINDING
Gen 37: 7 For, behold, we *were* **b** sheaves in the H481
49:11 **B** his foal unto the vine, and his ass's H631
Ex 28:32 it shall have a **b** of woven work round H8193
Nu 30:13 Every vow, and every **b** oath to afflict the H632
Act 22: 4 unto the death, **b** and delivering into *G1195*

BINEA
1Ch 8:37 And Moza begat **B**: Rapha *was* his son, H1150
9:43 And Moza begat **B**; and Rephaiah his H1150

BINNUI
Ezr 8:33 and Noadiah the son of **B**, Levites; H1131
Ezr 10:30 Bezaleel, and **B**, and Manasseh. H1131
38 And Bani, and **B**, Shimei, H1131
Neh 3:24 After him repaired **B** the son of H1131
7:15 The children of **B**, six hundred forty and H1131
10: 9 **B** of the sons of Henadad, Kadmiel; H1131
12: 8 Moreover the Levites: Jeshua, **B**, H1131

BIRD
Gen 7:14 after his kind, every **b** of every sort. H6833
Lev 14: 6 As for the living **b**, he shall take it, and H6833
6 and the living **b** in the blood of the bird H6833
6 in the blood of the **b** *that was* killed H6833
7 let the living **b** loose into the open field. H6833
51 and the living **b**, and dip them in the H6833
51 blood of the slain **b**, and in the running H6833
52 the blood of the **b**, and with the running H6833
52 with the living **b**, and with the cedar H6833
53 But he shall let go the living **b** out of the H6833
Job 41: 5 Wilt thou play with him as *with* a **b**? or H6833
Ps 11: 1 my soul, Flee *as* a **b** to your mountain? H6833
124: 7 Our soul is escaped as a **b** out of the H6833
Prv 1:17 the net is spread in the sight of any **b**. H6833
6: 5 and as a **b** from the hand of the fowler. H6833
7:23 his liver; as a **b** hasteth to the snare, H6833
26: 2 As the **b** by wandering, as the swallow H6833
27: 8 As a **b** that wandereth from her nest, so H6833
Ecc 10:20 thy bedchamber: for a **b** of the air shall H5775
12: 4 up at the voice of the **b**, and all the H6833
Isa 16: 2 For it shall be, *that*, as a wandering **b** H5775
46:11 Calling a ravenous **b** from the east, the H5861
Jer 12: 9 me *as* a speckled **b**, the birds round H5861
Lam 3:52 Mine enemies chased me sore, like a **b**, H6833
Hos 9:11 fly away like a **b**, from the birth, and H5775
11:11 They shall tremble as a **b** out of Egypt, H6833
Am 3: 5 Can a **b** fall in a snare upon the earth, H6833
Rev 18: 2 a cage of every unclean and hateful **b**. *G3732*

BIRDS
Gen 15:10 another: but the **b** divided he not. H6833
40:17 Pharaoh; and the **b** did eat them out of H5775
19 the **b** shall eat thy flesh from off thee. H5775
Lev 14: 4 is to be cleansed two **b** alive *and* clean, H6833
5 that one of the **b** be killed in an earthen H6833
49 the house two **b**, and cedar wood, and H6833
50 And he shall kill the one of the **b** in an H6833
Dt 14:11 *Of* all clean **b** ye shall eat. H6833
2Sa 21:10 neither the **b** of the air to rest on H5775
Ps 104:17 Where the **b** make their nests: *as for* H6833
Ecc 9:12 net, and as the **b** that are caught in the H6833
Song 2:12 of the singing *of* **b** is come, and the voice
Isa 31: 5 As **b** flying, so will the LORD of hosts H6833
Jer 4:25 and all the **b** of the heavens were fled. H5775
5:27 As a cage is full of **b**, so *are* their houses H5775
12: 4 and the **b**; because they said, He H5775
9 a speckled bird, the **b** round about *are* H5861
Ezk 39: 4 unto the ravenous **b** of every sort, and H6833
Mt 8:20 holes, and the **b** of the air *have* nests; *G4071*
13:32 a tree, so that the **b** of the air come and *G4071*
Lk 9:58 have holes, and **b** of the air *have* nests; *G4071*
Ro 1:23 man, and to **b**, and fourfooted beasts, *G4071*
1Co 15:39 another of fishes, *and* another of **b**. *G4421*
Jas 3: 7 For every kind of beasts, and of **b**, and *G4071*

BIRD'S
Dt 22: 6 If a **b** nest chance to be before thee in H6833

BIRDS'
Dan 4:33 *feathers*, and his nails like **b** *claws*. H6853

BIREI See BETH-BIREI.

BIRSHA
Gen 14: 2 Sodom, and with **B** king of Gomorrah, H1306

BIRTH
Ex 28:10 on the other stone, according to their **b**. H8435
2Ki 19: 3 are come to the **b**, and *there is* not H4866
Job 3:16 Or as an hidden untimely **b** I had not H5309
Ps 58: 8 *like* the untimely **b** of a woman, *that* H5309
Ecc 6: 3 *that* an untimely **b** *is* better than he. H5309
7: 1 the day of death than the day of one's **b**. H3205
Isa 37: 3 are come to the **b**, and *there is* not H4866
66: 9 Shall I bring to the **b**, and not cause to H7665
Ezk 16: 3 Jerusalem; Thy **b** and thy nativity *is* of H4351
Hos 9:11 a bird, from the **b**, and from the womb, H3205
Mt 1:18 Now the **b** of Jesus Christ was on this *G1083*
Lk 1:14 and many shall rejoice at his **b**. *G1083*
Jn 9: 1 saw a man which was blind from *his* **b**. *G1079*
Gal 4:19 **b** again until Christ be formed in you, *G5605*

Rev 12: 2 in **b**, and pained to be delivered. *G5605*

BIRTHDAY
Gen 40:20 Pharaoh's **b**, that he made a H3205+H3117
Mt 14: 6 But when Herod's **b** was kept, the *G1077*
Mk 6:21 that Herod on his **b** made a supper to *G1077*

BIRTHRIGHT
Gen 25:31 And Jacob said, Sell me this day thy **b**. H1062
32 and what profit shall this **b** do to me? H1062
33 unto him: and he sold his **b** unto Jacob. H1062
34 went his way: thus Esau despised *his* **b**. H1062
27:36 he took away my **b**; and, behold, now H1062
43:33 according to his **b**, and the youngest H1062
1Ch 5: 1 father's bed, his **b** was given unto the H1062
1 is not to be reckoned after the **b**. H1062
2 the chief ruler; but the **b** *was* Joseph's:) H1062
Heb 12:16 who for one morsel of meat sold his **b**. *G4415*

BIRZAVITH
1Ch 7:31 and Malchiel, who *is* the father of **B**. H1269

BISHLAM
Ezr 4: 7 And in the days of Artaxerxes wrote **B**, H1312

BISHOP
1Ti 3: 1 office of a **b**, he desireth a good work. *G1984*
2 A **b** then must be blameless, the *G1985*
Tit 1: 7 For a **b** must be blameless, as the *G1985*
1Pt 2:25 unto the Shepherd and **B** of your souls. *G1985*

BISHOPRICK
Act 1:20 therein: and his **b** let another take. *G1984*

BISHOPS
Php 1: 1 are at Philippi, with the **b** and deacons: *G1985*

BIT
Nu 21: 6 the people, and they **b** the people; and H5391
Ps 32: 9 be held in with **b** and bridle, lest they H4964
Am 5:19 hand on the wall, and a serpent **b** him. H5391

BITE
Ecc 10: 8 an hedge, a serpent shall **b** him. H5391
11 Surely the serpent will **b** without H5391
Jer 8:17 and they shall **b** you, saith the LORD. H5391
Am 9: 3 the serpent, and he shall **b** them: H5391
Mic 3: 5 people err, that **b** with their teeth, and H5391
Hab 2: 7 that shall **b** thee, and awake that H5391
Gal 5:15 But if ye **b** and devour one another, *G1143*

BITETH
Gen 49:17 in the path, that **b** the horse heels, so H5391
Prv 23:32 At the last it **b** like a serpent, and H5391

BITHIAH
1Ch 4:18 these *are* the sons of **B** the daughter of H1332

BITHRON
2Sa 2:29 all **B**, and they came to Mahanaim. H1338

BITHYNIA
Act 16: 7 into **B**: but the Spirit suffered them not. *G978*
1Pt 1: 1 Galatia, Cappadocia, Asia, and **B**, *G978*

BITS
Jas 3: 3 Behold, we put **b** in the horses' mouths, *G5469*

BITTEN
Nu 21: 8 is **b**, when he looketh upon it, shall live. H5391
9 if a serpent had **b** any man, when he H5391

BITTER
Gen 27:34 and exceeding **b** cry, and said unto his H4751
Ex 1:14 And they made their lives **b** with hard H4843
12: 8 *and* with **b** *herbs* they shall eat it. H4844
15:23 for they *were* **b**: therefore the name H4751
Nu 5:18 the **b** water that causeth the curse: H4751
19 this **b** water that causeth the curse: H4751
23 he shall blot *them* out with the **b** water: H4751
24 to drink the **b** water that causeth H4751
24 shall enter into her, *and become* **b**. H4751
27 her, *and become* **b**, and her belly shall H4751
9:11 it with unleavened bread and **b** *herbs*. H4844
Dt 32:24 heat, and with **b** destruction: I will also H4815
32 *are* grapes of gall, their clusters *are* **b**: H4846
2Ki 14:26 *that it was* very **b**: for *there was* not any H4784
Est 4: 1 city, and cried with a loud and a **b** cry; H4751
Job 3:20 is in misery, and life unto the **b** *in* soul; H4751
Job 13:26 For thou writest **b** things against me, H4846
23: 2 Even to day *is* my complaint **b**: my H4805
Ps 64: 3 *to shoot* their arrows, *even* **b** words: H4751
Prv 5: 4 But her end is **b** as wormwood, sharp H4751
27: 7 the hungry soul every **b** thing is sweet. H4751
Ecc 7:26 And I find more **b** than death the H4751
Isa 5:20 put **b** for sweet, and sweet for bitter! H4751
20 put bitter for sweet, and sweet for **b**! H4751
24: 9 drink shall be **b** to them that drink it. H4843
Jer 2:19 *is* an evil *thing* and **b**, that thou hast H4751
4:18 **b**, because it reacheth unto thine heart. H4751
6:26 an only son, most **b** lamentation: for H8563
31:15 lamentation, *and* **b** weeping; Rahel H8563
Ezk 27:31 with bitterness of heart *and* **b** wailing. H4751
Am 8:10 *son*, and the end thereof as a **b** day. H4751
Hab 1: 6 For, lo, I raise up the Chaldeans, *that* **b** H4751
Col 3:19 *your* wives, and be not **b** against them. *G4087*
Jas 3:11 at the same place sweet *water* and **b**? *G4089*
14 But if ye have **b** envying and strife in *G4089*
Rev 8:11 the waters, because they were made **b**. *G4087*
10: 9 make thy belly **b**, but it shall be in thy *G4087*
10 soon as I had eaten it, my belly was **b**. *G4087*

BITTERLY
Jdg 5:23 of the LORD, curse ye **b** the inhabitants H779
Ru 1:20 Almighty hath dealt very **b** with me. H4843
Isa 22: 4 me; I will weep **b**, labour not to comfort H4843
33: 7 the ambassadors of peace shall weep **b**. H4751
Ezk 27:30 thee, and shall cry **b**, and shall cast up H4751
Hos 12:14 *him* to anger most **b**: therefore shall he H8563
Zep 1:14 the mighty man shall cry there **b**. H4751
Mt 26:75 me thrice. And he went out, and wept **b**. *G4090*
Lk 22:62 And Peter went out, and wept **b**. *G4090*

BITTERN
Isa 14:23 possession for the **b**, and pools of water: H7090
34:11 But the cormorant and the **b** shall H7090
Zep 2:14 and the **b** shall lodge in the upper H7090

BITTERNESS
1Sa 1:10 And she *was* in **b** of soul, and prayed H4751
15:32 Agag said, Surely the **b** of death is past. H4751
2Sa 2:26 not that it will be **b** in the latter end? H4751
Job 7:11 I will complain in the **b** of my soul. H4751
9:18 to take my breath, but filleth me with **b**. H4472
10: 1 myself; I will speak in the **b** of my soul. H4751
21:25 And another dieth in the **b** of his soul, H4751
Prv 14:10 The heart knoweth his own **b**; and a H4787
17:25 his father, and **b** to her that bare him. H4470
Isa 38:15 softly all my years in the **b** of my soul. H4751
17 Behold, for peace I had great **b**: but H4751
Lam 1: 4 her virgins are afflicted, and she *is* in **b**. H4843
3:15 He hath filled me with **b**, he hath made H4844
Ezk 3:14 and I went in **b**, in the heat of my spirit; H4751
21: 6 loins; and with **b** sigh before their eyes. H4814
27:31 thee with **b** of heart *and* bitter wailing. H4751
Zec 12:10 and shall be in **b** for him, as one that H4843
10 as one that is in **b** for *his* firstborn. H4843
Act 8:23 gall of **b**, and *in* the bond of iniquity. *G4088*
Ro 3:14 Whose mouth *is* full of cursing and **b**: *G4088*
Eph 4:31 Let all **b**, and wrath, and anger, and *G4088*
Heb 12:15 lest any root of **b** springing up trouble *G4088*

BIZJOTHJAH
Jos 15:28 Hazar-shual, and Beer-sheba, and **B**, H964

BIZTHA
Est 1:10 Mehuman, **B**, Harbona, Bigtha, and H968

BLACK
Lev 13:31 *that there is* no **b** hair in it; then the H7838
37 stay, and *that* there is **b** hair grown up H7838
1Ki 18:45 that the heaven was **b** with clouds and H6937
Est 1: 6 and blue, and white, and **b**, marble. H5508
Job 30:30 My skin is **b** upon me, and my bones H7835
Prv 7: 9 In the twilight, in the evening, in the **b** H380
Song 1: 5 I *am* **b**, but comely, O ye daughters of H7838
6 Look not upon me, because I *am* **b**, H7840
5:11 his locks *are* bushy, *and* **b** as a raven. H7838
Jer 4:28 the heavens above be **b**: because I have H6937
8:21 **b**; astonishment hath taken hold on me. H6937
14: 2 languish; they are **b** unto the ground; H6937
Lam 5:10 Our skin was **b** like an oven because of H3648
Zec 6: 2 and in the second chariot **b** horses; H7838
6 The **b** horses which *are* therein go forth H7838
Mt 5:36 canst not make one hair white or **b**. *G3189*
Rev 6: 5 I beheld, and lo a **b** horse; and he that *G3189*
12 the sun became **b** as sackcloth of hair, *G3189*

BLACKER
Lam 4: 8 Their visage is **b** than a coal; they are H2821

BLACKISH
Job 6:16 Which are **b** by reason of the ice, *and* H6937

BLACKNESS
Job 3: 5 upon it; let the **b** of the day terrify it. H3650
Isa 50: 3 I clothe the heavens with **b**, and I make H6940
Joel 2: 6 be much pained: all faces shall gather **b**. H6289
Nah 2:10 loins, and the faces of them all gather **b**. H6289
Heb 12:18 nor unto **b**, and darkness, and tempest, *G1105*
Jude 13 is reserved the **b** of darkness for ever. *G2217*

BLADE
Jdg 3:22 And the haft also went in after the **b**; H3851
22 closed upon the **b**, so that he could not H3851
Job 31:22 from my shoulder **b**, and mine arm be H7929
Mt 13:26 But when the **b** was sprung up, and *G5528*
Mk 4:28 of herself; first the **b**, then the ear, after *G5528*

BLAINS
Ex 9: 9 forth *with* **b** upon man, and upon H76
10 forth *with* **b** upon man, and upon beast. H76

BLAME
Gen 43: 9 thee, then let me bear the **b** for ever: H2398
44:32 I shall bear the **b** to my father for ever. H2398
2Co 8:20 Avoiding this, that no man should **b** us *G3469*
Eph 1: 4 holy and without **b** before him in love: *G299*

BLAMED
2Co 6: 3 in any thing, that the ministry be not **b**: *G3469*
Gal 2:11 him to the face, because he was to be **b**. *G2607*

BLAMELESS
Gen 44:10 shall be my servant; and ye shall be **b**. H5355
Jos 2:17 unto her, We *will be* **b** of this thine oath H5355
Jdg 15: 3 shall I be more **b** than the Philistines, H5352
Mt 12: 5 temple profane the sabbath, and are **b**? *G338*
Lk 1: 6 and ordinances of the Lord **b**. *G273*
1Co 1: 8 *be* **b** in the day of our Lord Jesus Christ. *G410*
Php 2:15 That ye may be **b** and harmless, the sons *G273*
3: 6 the righteousness which is in the law, **b**. *G273*
1Th 5:23 body be preserved **b** unto the coming of *G274*
1Ti 3: 2 A bishop then must be **b**, the husband of *G423*
10 use the office of a deacon, being *found* **b**. *G410*
5: 7 things give in charge, that they may be **b**. *G423*
Tit 1: 6 If any be **b**, the husband of one wife, *G410*
7 For a bishop must be **b**, as the steward of *G410*
2Pt 3:14 of him in peace, without spot, and **b**. *G298*

BLASPHEME
2Sa 12:14 of the LORD to **b**, the child also *that is* H5006
1Ki 21:10 Thou didst **b** God and the king. And H1288
13 Naboth did **b** God and the king. Then H1288
Ps 74:10 shall the enemy **b** thy name for ever? H5006
Mk 3:28 wherewith soever they shall **b**: *G987*
29 But he that shall **b** against the Holy *G987*
Act 26:11 and compelled *them* to **b**; and being *G987*
1Ti 1:20 unto Satan, that they may learn not to **b**. *G987*
Jas 2: 7 Do not they **b** that worthy name by the *G987*
Rev 13: 6 against God, to **b** his name, and his *G987*

BLASPHEMED
Lev 24:11 And the Israelitish woman's son **b** the H5344
2Ki 19: 6 of the king of Assyria have **b** me. H1442
22 Whom hast thou reproached and **b**? H1442
Ps 74:18 the foolish people have **b** thy name. H5006
Isa 37: 6 of the king of Assyria have **b** me. H1442
23 Whom hast thou reproached and **b**? H1442
52: 5 my name continually every day *is* **b**. H5006
65: 7 mountains, and **b** me upon the hills: H2778
Ezk 20:27 your fathers have **b** me, in that they H1442
Act 18: 6 themselves, and **b**, he shook *his* raiment, *G987*
Ro 2:24 For the name of God is **b** among the *G987*
1Ti 6: 1 name of God and *his* doctrine be not **b**. *G987*
Tit 2: 5 husbands, that the word of God be not **b**. *G987*
Rev 16: 9 with great heat, and **b** the name of God, *G987*
11 And **b** the God of heaven because of *G987*
21 a talent: and men **b** God because of the *G987*

BLASPHEMER
1Ti 1:13 Who was before a **b**, and a persecutor, *G989*

BLASPHEMERS
Act 19:37 of churches, nor yet **b** of your goddess. *G987*
2Ti 3: 2 boasters, proud, **b**, disobedient to *G989*

BLASPHEMEST
Jn 10:36 **b**; because I said, I am the Son of God? G987

BLASPHEMETH
Lev 24:16 And he that **b** the name of the LORD, H5344
16 in the land, when he **b** the name *of the* H5344
Ps 44:16 **b**; by reason of the enemy and avenger. H1442
Mt 9: 3 said within themselves, This *man* **b**. G987
Lk 12:10 but unto him that **b** against the Holy G987

BLASPHEMIES
Ezk 35:12 I have heard all thy **b** which thou hast H5007
Mt 15:19 fornications, thefts, false witness, **b**: G988
Mk 2: 7 Why doth this *man* thus speak **b**? who G988
3:28 the sons of men, and **b** wherewith soever G988
Lk 5:21 **b**? Who can forgive sins, but God alone? G988
Rev 13: 5 great things and **b**; and power was given G988

BLASPHEMING
Act 13:45 spoken by Paul, contradicting and **b**. G987

BLASPHEMOUS
Act 6:11 heard him speak **b** words against Moses, G989
13 not to speak **b** words against this holy G989

BLASPHEMOUSLY
Lk 22:65 And many other things **b** spake they G987

BLASPHEMY
2Ki 19: 3 of rebuke, and **b**: for the children are H5007
Isa 37: 3 of rebuke, and of **b**: for the children are H5007
Mt 12:31 All manner of sin and **b** shall be forgiven G988
31 unto men: but the **b** *against* the *Holy* G988
26:65 He hath spoken **b**; what further need G987
65 behold, now ye have heard his **b**. G988
Mk 7:22 an evil eye, **b**, pride, foolishness: G988
14:64 Ye have heard the **b**: what think ye? And G988
Jn 10:33 thee not; but for **b**; and because that G988
Col 3: 8 wrath, malice, **b**, filthy communication G988
Rev 2: 9 and *I know* the **b** of them which say they G988
13: 1 and upon his heads the name of **b**. G988
6 And he opened his mouth in **b** against G988
17: 3 of **b**, having seven heads and ten horns. G988

BLAST
Ex 15: 8 And with the **b** of thy nostrils the H7307
Jos 6: 5 they make a long *b* with the ram's horn,
2Sa 22:16 at the **b** of the breath of his nostrils. H5397
2Ki 19: 7 Behold, I will send a **b** upon him, and H7307
Job 4: 9 By the **b** of God they perish, and by the H5397
Ps 18:15 at the **b** of the breath of thy nostrils. H5397
Isa 25: 4 the heat, when the **b** of the terrible ones H7307
37: 7 Behold, I will send a **b** upon him, and H7307

BLASTED
Gen 41: 6 And, behold, seven thin ears and **b** H7710
23 thin, *and* **b** with the east wind, H7710
27 seven empty ears **b** with the east wind H7710
2Ki 19:26 and *as corn* **b** before it be grown up. H7711
Isa 37:27 and *as corn* **b** before it be grown up. H7709

BLASTING
Dt 28:22 sword, and with **b**, and with mildew; H7711
1Ki 8:37 be pestilence, **b**, mildew, locust, *or* if H7711
2Ch 6:28 if there be **b**, or mildew, locusts, H7711
Am 4: 9 I have smitten you with **b** and mildew: H7711
Hag 2:17 I smote you with **b** and with mildew H7711

BLASTUS
Act 12:20 him, and, having made **B** the king's G986

BLAZE
Mk 1:45 *it* much, and to **b** abroad the matter, G1310

BLEATING
1Sa 15:14 *meaneth* then this **b** of the sheep in H6963

BLEATINGS
Jdg 5:16 to hear the **b** of the flocks? For the H8292

BLEMISH
Ex 12: 5 Your lamb shall be without **b**, a male of H8549
29: 1 young bullock, and two rams without **b**, H8549
Lev 1: 3 a male without **b**: he shall offer it of his H8549
10 he shall bring it a male without **b**. H8549
3: 1 offer it without **b** before the LORD. H8549
6 or female, he shall offer it without **b**. H8549
4: 3 **b** unto the LORD for a sin offering. H8549
23 a kid of the goats, a male without **b**: H8549
Lev 4:28 **b**, for his sin which he hath sinned. H8549
32 he shall bring it a female without **b**. H8549
5:15 a ram without **b** out of the flocks, with H8549
18 And he shall bring a ram without **b** out H8549
6: 6 a ram without **b** out of the flock, with H8549
9: 2 **b**, and offer *them* before the LORD. H8549
3 year, without **b**, for a burnt offering; H8549
14:10 he lambs without **b**, and one ewe lamb H8549
10 the first year without **b**, and three tenth H8549
21:17 that hath *any* **b**, let him not approach H3971
18 man *he be* that hath a **b**, he shall not H3971
20 or that hath a **b** in his eye, or be scurvy, H8400
21 No man that hath a **b** of the seed of H3971
21 by fire: he hath a **b**; he shall not come H3971
23 because he hath a **b**; that he profane not H3971
22:19 a male without **b**, of the beeves, of the H8549
20 *But* whatsoever hath a **b**, *that* shall ye H3971
21 accepted; there shall be no **b** therein. H3971
23:12 he lamb without **b** of the first year for H8549
18 lambs without **b** of the first year, and H8549
24:19 And if a man cause a **b** in his H3971
20 he hath caused a **b** in a man, so shall it H3971
Nu 6:14 the first year without **b** for a burnt H8549
14 first year without **b** for a sin offering, H8549
14 one ram without **b** for peace offerings, H8549
19: 2 no **b**, *and* upon which never came yoke: H3971
28:19 year: they shall be unto you without **b**: H8549
31 without **b**) and their drink offerings. H8549
29: 2 seven lambs of the first year without **b**: H8549
8 year; they shall be unto you without **b**: H8549
13 of the first year; they shall be without **b**: H8549
20 lambs of the first year without **b**; H8549
23 lambs of the first year without **b**: H8549
29 lambs of the first year without **b**: H8549
32 lambs of the first year without **b**: H8549
36 seven lambs of the first year without **b**: H8549
Dt 15:21 And if there be *any* **b** therein, *as if it be* H3971
21 *or have* any ill **b**, thou shalt not sacrifice H3971
17: 1 or sheep, wherein is **b**, *or* any H3971
2Sa 14:25 of his head there was no **b** in him. H3971
Ezk 43:22 of the goats without **b** for a sin offering; H8549
23 bullock without **b**, and a ram out of the H8549
23 and a ram out of the flock without **b**. H8549
25 and a ram out of the flock, without **b**. H8549
45:18 without **b**, and cleanse the sanctuary: H8549
23 rams without **b** daily the seven days; H8549
46: 4 without **b**, and a ram without blemish. H8549
4 without blemish, and a ram without **b**. H8549
6 bullock without **b**, and six lambs, and H8549
6 and a ram: they shall be without **b**. H8549
13 **b**: thou shalt prepare it every morning. H8549
Dan 1: 4 Children in whom *was* no **b**, but well H3971
Eph 5:27 but that it should be holy and without **b**. G299
1Pt 1:19 as of a lamb without **b** and without spot: G299

BLEMISHES
Lev 22:25 *is* in them, *and* **b** *be* in them: they shall H3971
2Pt 2:13 time. Spots *they are* and **b**, sporting G3470

BLESS
Gen 12: 2 nation, and I will **b** thee, and make thy H1288
3 And I will **b** them that bless thee, and H1288
3 And I will bless them that **b** thee, and H1288
17:16 And I will **b** her, and give thee a son H1288
16 of her: yea, I will **b** her, and she shall be H1288
22:17 That in blessing I will **b** thee, and in H1288
26: 3 be with thee, and will **b** thee; for unto H1288
24 with thee, and will **b** thee, and multiply H1288
27: 4 that my soul may **b** thee before I die. H1288
7 I may eat, and **b** thee before the LORD H1288
10 that he may **b** thee before his death. H1288
19 of my venison, that thy soul may **b** me. H1288
25 that my soul may **b** thee. And he H1288
31 son's venison, that thy soul may **b** me. H1288
34 **B** me, *even* me also, O my father. H1288
38 my father? **b** me, *even* me also, O H1288
28: 3 And God Almighty **b** thee, and make H1288
32:26 I will not let thee go, except thou **b** me. H1288
48: 9 I pray thee, unto me, and I will **b** them. H1288
16 me from all evil, **b** the lads; and let my H1288
20 In thee shall Israel **b**, saying, God make H1288
49:25 who shall **b** thee with blessings H1288
Ex 12:32 have said, and be gone; and **b** me also. H1288
20:24 I will come unto thee, and I will **b** thee. H1288
23:25 God, and he shall **b** thy bread, and thy H1288
Nu 6:23 On this wise ye shall **b** the children of H1288
24 The LORD **b** thee, and keep thee: H1288
27 the children of Israel; and I will **b** them. H1288
23:20 *commandment* to **b**: and he hath H1288
Nu 23:25 curse them at all, nor **b** them at all. H1288
24: 1 the LORD to **b** Israel, he went not, H1288
Dt 1:11 and **b** you, as he hath promised you!) H1288
7:13 And he will love thee, and **b** thee, and H1288
13 thee: he will also **b** the fruit of thy H1288
8:10 then thou shalt **b** the LORD thy God for H1288
10: 8 and to **b** in his name, unto this day. H1288
14:29 thy God may **b** thee in all the work H1288
15: 4 shall greatly **b** thee in the land which H1288
10 thy God shall **b** thee in all thy works, H1288
18 God shall **b** thee in all that thou doest. H1288
16:15 LORD thy God shall **b** thee in all thine H1288
21: 5 unto him, and to **b** in the name of the H1288
23:20 thy God may **b** thee in all that thou H1288
24:13 own raiment, and **b** thee: and it shall H1288
19 **b** thee in all the work of thine hands. H1288
26:15 from heaven, and **b** thy people Israel, H1288
27:12 mount Gerizim to **b** the people, when H1288
28: 8 unto; and he shall **b** thee in the land H1288
12 in his season, and to **b** all the work of H1288
29:19 of this curse, that he **b** himself in his H1288
30:16 thy God shall **b** thee in the land whither H1288
33:11 **B**, LORD, his substance, and accept the H1288
Jos 8:33 that they should **b** the people of Israel. H1288
Jdg 5: 9 among the people. **B** ye the LORD. H1288
Ru 2: 4 they answered him, The LORD **b** thee. H1288
1Sa 9:13 because he doth **b** the sacrifice; *and* H1288
2Sa 6:20 Then David returned to **b** his H1288
7:29 Therefore now let it please thee to **b** the H1288
8:10 to salute him, and to **b** him, because he H1288
21: 3 ye may **b** the inheritance of the LORD? H1288
1Ki 1:47 king's servants came to **b** our lord king H1288
1Ch 4:10 that thou wouldest **b** me indeed, and H1288
16:43 and David returned to **b** his house. H1288
17:27 Now therefore let it please thee to **b** the H1288
23:13 him, and to **b** in his name for ever. H1288
29:20 Now **b** the LORD your God. H1288
Neh 9: 5 Stand up *and* **b** the LORD your God H1288
Ps 5:12 For thou, LORD, wilt **b** the righteous; H1288
16: 7 I will **b** the LORD, who hath given me H1288
26:12 in the congregations will I **b** the LORD. H1288
28: 9 Save thy people, and **b** thine H1288
29:11 the LORD will **b** his people with peace. H1288
34: 1 I will **b** the LORD at all times: his H1288
62: 4 in lies: they **b** with their mouth, but H1288
63: 4 Thus will I **b** thee while I live: I will lift H1288
66: 8 O **b** our God, ye people, and make the H1288
67: 1 God be merciful unto us, and **b** us; *and* H1288
6 *and* God, *even* our own God, shall **b** us. H1288
7 God shall **b** us; and all the ends of the H1288
68:26 **B** ye God in the congregations, *even* the H1288
96: 2 Sing unto the LORD, **b** his name; shew H1288
100: 4 be thankful unto him, *and* **b** his name. H1288
103: 1 **B** the LORD, O my soul: and all that is H1288
1 all that is within me, *b* his holy name.
2 **B** the LORD, O my soul, and forget not H1288
20 **B** the LORD, ye his angels, that excel in H1288
21 **B** ye the LORD, all *ye* his hosts; *ye* H1288
22 **B** the LORD, all his works in all places H1288
22 his dominion: **b** the LORD, O my soul. H1288
104: 1 **B** the LORD, O my soul. O LORD my H1288
35 be no more. **B** thou the LORD, O my H1288
109:28 Let them curse, but **b** thou: when they H1288
115:12 of us: he will **b** *us*; he will bless the H1288
12 bless *us*; he will **b** the house of Israel; H1288
12 of Israel; he will **b** the house of Aaron. H1288
13 He will **b** them that fear the LORD, H1288
18 But we will **b** the LORD from this time H1288
128: 5 The LORD shall **b** thee out of Zion: and H1288
129: 8 we **b** you in the name of the LORD. H1288
132:15 I will abundantly **b** her provision: I will H1288
134: 1 Behold, **b** ye the LORD, all *ye* servants H1288
2 *in* the sanctuary, and **b** the LORD. H1288
3 heaven and earth **b** thee out of Zion. H1288
135:19 **B** the LORD, O house of Israel: bless the H1288
19 Bless the LORD, O house of Israel: **b** the H1288
20 **B** the LORD, O house of Levi: ye that H1288
20 ye that fear the LORD, **b** the LORD. H1288
145: 1 and I will **b** thy name for ever and ever. H1288
2 Every day will I **b** thee; and I will praise H1288
10 O LORD; and thy saints shall **b** thee. H1288
21 flesh **b** his holy name for ever and ever. H1288
Prv 30:11 father, and doth not **b** their mother. H1288
Isa 19:25 Whom the LORD of hosts shall **b**, H1288
65:16 in the earth shall **b** himself in the God H1288
Jer 4: 2 the nations shall **b** themselves in him, H1288
31:23 The LORD **b** thee, O habitation of H1288
Hag 2:19 forth: from this day will I **b** *you*. H1288
Mt 5:44 your enemies, **b** them that curse you, G2127

Lk 6:28 **B** them that curse you, and pray for G2127
Act 3:26 Son Jesus, sent him to **b** you, in turning G2127
Ro 12:14 **B** them which persecute you: bless, and G2127
14 Bless them which persecute you: **b**, and G2127
1Co 4:12 we **b**; being persecuted, we suffer it: G2127
10:16 The cup of blessing which we **b**, is it not G2127
14:16 Else when thou shalt **b** with the spirit, G2127
Heb 6:14 Saying, Surely blessing I will **b** thee, G2127
Jas 3: 9 Therewith **b** we God, even the Father; G2127

BLESSED

Gen 1:22 And God **b** them, saying, Be fruitful, H1288
28 And God **b** them, and God said unto H1288
2: 3 And God **b** the seventh day, and H1288
5: 2 he them; and **b** them, and called their H1288
9: 1 And God **b** Noah and his sons, and H1288
26 And he said, **B** *be* the LORD God of H1288
12: 3 thee shall all families of the earth be **b**. H1288
14:19 And he **b** him, and said, Blessed *be* H1288
19 And he blessed him, and said, **B** *be* H1288
20 And **b** be the most high God, which H1288
17:20 Behold, I have **b** him, and will make H1288
18:18 nations of the earth shall be **b** in him? H1288
22:18 **b**; because thou hast obeyed my voice. H1288
24: 1 the LORD had **b** Abraham in all things. H1288
27 And he said, **B** *be* the LORD God of my H1288
31 And he said, Come in, thou **b** of the H1288
35 And the LORD hath **b** my master H1288
48 the LORD, and **b** the LORD God of my H1288
60 And they **b** Rebekah, and said unto H1288
25:11 that God **b** his son Isaac; and Isaac H1288
26: 4 shall all the nations of the earth be **b**; H1288
12 an hundredfold: and the LORD **b** him. H1288
29 peace: thou *art* now the **b** of the LORD. H1288
27:23 his brother Esau's hands: so he **b** him. H1288
27 his raiment, and **b** him, and said, See, H1288
27 smell of a field which the LORD hath **b**: H1288
29 thee, and **b** *be* he that blesseth thee. H1288
33 **b** him? yea, *and* he shall be blessed. H1288
33 blessed him? yea, *and* he shall be **b**. H1288
41 his father **b** him: and Esau said H1288
28: 1 And Isaac called Jacob, and **b** him, and H1288
6 When Esau saw that Isaac had **b** Jacob, H1288
6 and that as he **b** him he gave him a H1288
14 shall all the families of the earth be **b**. H1288
30:13 call me **b**: and she called his name Asher. H833
27 that the LORD hath **b** me for thy sake. H1288
30 and the LORD hath **b** thee since my H1288
31:55 his daughters, and **b** them: and Laban H1288
32:29 after my name? And he **b** him there. H1288
35: 9 came out of Padan-aram, and **b** him. H1288
39: 5 that the LORD **b** the Egyptian's house H1288
47: 7 before Pharaoh: and Jacob **b** Pharaoh. H1288
10 And Jacob **b** Pharaoh, and went out H1288
48: 3 Luz in the land of Canaan, and **b** me, H1288
15 And he **b** Joseph, and said, God, before H1288
20 And he **b** them that day, saying, In thee H1288
49:28 unto them, and **b** them; every one H1288
28 according to his blessing he **b** them. H1288
Ex 18:10 And Jethro said, **B** *be* the LORD, who H1288
20:11 **b** the sabbath day, and hallowed it. H1288
39:43 so had they done it: and Moses **b** them. H1288
Lev 9:22 the people, and **b** them, and came H1288
23 came out, and **b** the people: and the H1288
Nu 22: 6 **b**, and he whom thou cursest is cursed. H1288
12 not curse the people: for they *are* **b**. H1288
23:11 behold, thou hast **b** *them* altogether. H1288
20 and he hath **b**; and I cannot reverse it. H1288
24: 9 shall stir him up? **B** *is* he that blesseth H1288
10 altogether **b** *them* these three times. H1288
Dt 2: 7 For the LORD thy God hath **b** thee in all H1288
7:14 Thou shalt be **b** above all people: there H1288
12: 7 wherein the LORD thy God hath **b** thee. H1288
14:24 when the LORD thy God hath **b** thee: H1288
15:14 hath **b** thee thou shalt give unto him. H1288
16:10 as the LORD thy God hath **b** thee: H1288
28: 3 **B** *shalt* thou *be* in the city, and blessed H1288
3 Blessed *shalt* thou *be* in the city, and **b** H1288
4 **B** *shall be* the fruit of thy body, and the H1288
5 **B** *shall be* thy basket and thy store. H1288
6 **B** *shalt* thou *be* when thou comest in, H1288
6 **b** *shalt* thou *be* when thou goest out. H1288
33: 1 the man of God **b** the children of Israel H1288
13 And of Joseph he said, **B** of the LORD H1288
20 And of Gad he said, **B** *be* he that H1288
24 And of Asher he said, *Let* Asher *be* **b** H1288
Jos 14:13 And Joshua **b** him, and gave unto H1288
17:14 as the LORD hath **b** me hitherto? H1288
22: 6 So Joshua **b** them, and sent them away: H1288
Jos 22: 7 also unto their tents, then he **b** them, H1288
33 children of Israel **b** God, and did not H1288
24:10 therefore he **b** you still: so I delivered H1288
Jdg 5:24 **B** above women shall Jael the wife of H1288
24 **b** shall she be above women in the tent. H1288
13:24 the child grew, and the LORD **b** him. H1288
17: 2 said, **B** *be thou* of the LORD, my son. H1288
Ru 2:19 wroughtest thou? **b** be he that did take H1288
20 daughter in law, **B** *be* he of the LORD, H1288
3:10 And he said, **B** *be* thou of the LORD, H1288
4:14 And the women said unto Naomi, **B** *be* H1288
1Sa 2:20 And Eli **b** Elkanah and his wife, and H1288
15:13 said unto him, **B** *be* thou of the LORD: H1288
23:21 And Saul said, **B** *be* ye of the LORD; for H1288
25:32 And David said to Abigail, **B** *be* the H1288
33 And **b** *be* thy advice, and blessed *be* H1288
33 And blessed *be* thy advice, and **b** *be* H1288
39 was dead, he said, **B** *be* the LORD, that H1288
26:25 Then Saul said to David, **B** *be* thou, my H1288
2Sa 2: 5 said unto them, **B** *be* ye of the LORD, H1288
6:11 **b** Obed-edom, and all his household. H1288
12 saying, The LORD hath **b** the house of H1288
18 offerings, he **b** the people in the name H1288
7:29 the house of thy servant be **b** for ever. H1288
13:25 howbeit he would not go, but **b** him. H1288
18:28 king, and said, **B** *be* the LORD thy God, H1288
19:39 Barzillai, and **b** him; and he returned H1288
22:47 The LORD liveth; and **b** *be* my rock; H1288
1Ki 1:48 And also thus said the king, **B** *be* the H1288
2:45 And king Solomon *shall be* **b**, and the H1288
5: 7 greatly, and said, **B** *be* the LORD this H1288
8:14 face about, and **b** all the congregation H1288
15 And he said, **B** *be* the LORD God of H1288
55 And he stood, and **b** all the H1288
56 **B** *be* the LORD, that hath given rest H1288
66 away: and they **b** the king, and went H1288
10: 9 **B** be the LORD thy God, which H1288
1Ch 13:14 months. And the LORD **b** the house of H1288
16: 2 **b** the people in the name of the LORD. H1288
36 **B** *be* the LORD God of Israel for ever H1288
17:27 O LORD, and *it shall be* **b** for ever. H1288
26: 5 Peulthai the eighth: for God **b** him. H1288
29:10 Wherefore David **b** the LORD before all H1288
10 and David said, **B** *be* thou, LORD God H1288
20 all the congregation **b** the LORD God of H1288
2Ch 2:12 Huram said moreover, **B** *be* the LORD H1288
6: 3 And the king turned his face, and **b** the H1288
4 And he said, **B** *be* the LORD God of H1288
9: 8 **B** be the LORD thy God, which H1288
20:26 for there they **b** the LORD: therefore H1288
30:27 the Levites arose and **b** the people: and H1288
31: 8 they **b** the LORD, and his people Israel. H1288
10 for the LORD hath **b** his people; and H1288
Ezr 7:27 **B** *be* the LORD God of our fathers, H1288
Neh 8: 6 And Ezra **b** the LORD, the great God. H1288
9: 5 for ever and ever: and **b** be thy glorious H1288
11: 2 And the people **b** all the men, that H1288
Job 1:10 side? thou hast **b** the work of his hands, H1288
21 away; **b** be the name of the LORD. H1288
29:11 When the ear heard *me*, then it **b** me; H833
31:20 If his loins have not **b** me, and *if* he H1288
42:12 So the LORD **b** the latter end of Job H1288
Ps 1: 1 **B** *is* the man that walketh not in the H835
2:12 **B** *are* all they that put their trust in him. H835
18:46 The LORD liveth; and **b** *be* my rock; H1288
21: 6 For thou hast made him most **b** for H1293
28: 6 **B** *be* the LORD, because he hath heard H1288
31:21 **B** *be* the LORD: for he hath shewed me H1288
32: 1 **B** *is he whose* transgression *is* forgiven, H835
2 **B** *is* the man unto whom the LORD H835
33:12 **B** *is* the nation whose God *is* the LORD; H835
34: 8 O taste and see that the LORD *is* good: **b** H835
37:22 For *such as be* **b** of him shall inherit the H1288
26 merciful, and lendeth; and his seed *is* **b**. H1293
40: 4 **B** *is* that man that maketh the LORD his H835
41: 1 **B** *is* he that considereth the poor: the H835
2 *and* he shall be **b** upon the earth: and H833
13 **B** *be* the LORD God of Israel from H1288
45: 2 lips: therefore God hath **b** thee for ever. H1288
49:18 Though while he lived he **b** his soul: H1288
65: 4 **B** *is the man whom* thou choosest, and H835
66:20 **B** *be* God, which hath not turned away H1288
68:19 **B** *be* the Lord, *who* daily loadeth us H1288
35 and power unto *his* people. **B** *be* God. H1288
72:17 and *men* shall be **b** in him: all nations H1288
17 in him: all nations shall call him **b**. H833
18 **B** *be* the LORD God, the God of Israel, H1288
19 And **b** *be* his glorious name for ever: H1288
84: 4 **B** *are* they that dwell in thy house: they H835
Ps 84: 5 **B** *is* the man whose strength *is* in thee; in H835
12 O LORD of hosts, **b** *is* the man that H835
89:15 **B** *is* the people that know the joyful H835
52 **B** *be* the LORD for evermore. Amen, H1288
94:12 **B** *is* the man whom thou chastenest, O H835
106: 3 **B** *are* they that keep judgment, *and* he H835
48 **B** *be* the LORD God of Israel from H1288
112: 1 Praise ye the LORD. **B** *is* the man *that* H835
2 the generation of the upright shall be **b**. H1288
113: 2 **B** be the name of the LORD from this H1288
115:15 Ye *are* **b** of the LORD which made H1288
118:26 **B** *be* he that cometh in the name of the H1288
26 **b** you out of the house of the LORD. H1288
119: 1 **B** *are* the undefiled in the way, who walk H835
2 **B** *are* they that keep his testimonies, *and* H835
12 **B** *art* thou, O LORD: teach me thy H1288
124: 6 **B** *be* the LORD, who hath not given us H1288
128: 1 **B** *is* every one that feareth the LORD; H835
4 Behold, that thus shall the man be **b** H1288
135:21 **B** be the LORD out of Zion, which H1288
144: 1 **B** *be* the LORD my strength, which H1288
147:13 he hath **b** thy children within thee. H1288
Prv 5:18 Let thy fountain be **b**: and rejoice with H1288
8:32 for **b** *are they that* keep my ways. H835
34 **B** *is* the man that heareth me, watching H835
10: 7 The memory of the just *is* **b**: but the H1293
20: 7 integrity: his children *are* **b** after him. H835
21 but the end thereof shall not be **b**. H1288
22: 9 He that hath a bountiful eye shall be **b**; H1288
31:28 Her children arise up, and call her **b**; her H833
Ecc 10:17 **B** *art* thou, O land, when thy king *is* the H835
Song 6: 9 saw her, and **b** her; *yea*, the queens H833
Isa 19:25 bless, saying, **B** *be* Egypt my people, H1288
30:18 **b** *are* all they that wait for him. H835
32:20 **B** *are* ye that sow beside all waters, that H835
51: 2 alone, and **b** him, and increased him. H1288
56: 2 **B** *is* the man *that* doeth this, and the son H835
61: 9 *are* the seed *which* the LORD hath **b**. H1288
65:23 *are* the seed of the **b** of the LORD, and H1288
66: 3 incense, *as if* he **b** an idol. Yea, they H1288
Jer 17: 7 **B** *is* the man that trusteth in the LORD, H1288
20:14 day wherein my mother bare me be **b**. H1288
Ezk 3:12 rushing, *saying*, **B** *be* the glory of the H1288
Dan 2:19 Then Daniel **b** the God of heaven. H1289
20 Daniel answered and said, **B** be the H1289
3:28 spake, and said, **B** *be* the God of H1289
4:34 unto me, and I **b** the most High, and H1289
12:12 **B** *is* he that waiteth, and cometh to the H835
Zec 11: 5 that sell them say, **B** *be* the LORD; for I H1288
Mal 3:12 And all nations shall call you **b**: for ye H833
Mt 5: 3 **B** *are* the poor in spirit: for theirs is the G3107
4 **B** *are* they that mourn: for they shall be G3107
5 **B** *are* the meek: for they shall inherit G3107
6 **B** *are* they which do hunger and thirst G3107
7 **B** *are* the merciful: for they shall obtain G3107
8 **B** *are* the pure in heart: for they shall G3107
9 **B** *are* the peacemakers: for they shall G3107
10 **B** *are* they which are persecuted for G3107
11 **B** are ye, when *men* shall revile you, G3107
11: 6 And **b** is *he*, whosoever shall not be G3107
13:16 But **b** *are* your eyes, for they see: and G3107
14:19 up to heaven, he **b**, and brake, and gave G2127
16:17 and said unto him, **B** art thou, Simon G3107
21: 9 the son of David: **B** is he that cometh in G2127
23:39 till ye shall say, **B** *is* he that cometh in G2127
24:46 **B** is that servant, whom his lord when G3107
25:34 hand, Come, ye **b** of my Father, inherit G2127
26:26 took bread, and **b** *it*, and brake *it*, and G2127
Mk 6:41 up to heaven, and **b**, and brake the G2127
8: 7 fishes: and he **b**, and commanded to G2127
10:16 put *his* hands upon them, and **b** them. G2127
11: 9 saying, Hosanna; **B** *is* he that cometh G2127
10 **B** *be* the kingdom of our father David, G2127
14:22 took bread, and **b**, and brake *it*, and G2127
61 Art thou the Christ, the Son of the **B**? G2128
Lk 1:28 *is* with thee: **b** *art* thou among women. G2127
42 loud voice, and said, **B** *art* thou among G2127
42 women, and **b** *is* the fruit of thy womb. G2127
45 And **b** *is* she that believed: for there G3107
48 all generations shall call me **b**. G3106
68 **B** *be* the Lord God of Israel; for he hath G2128
2:28 Then took he him up in his arms, and **b** G2127
34 And Simeon **b** them, and said unto G2127
6:20 and said, **B** *be ye* poor: for yours G3107
21 **B** *are ye* that hunger now: for ye shall G3107
21 for ye shall be filled. **B** *are ye* that weep G3107
22 **B** are ye, when men shall hate you, and G3107
7:23 And **b** is *he*, whosoever shall not be G3107
9:16 up to heaven, he **b** them, and brake, G2127

Lk 10:23 said privately, **B** *are* the eyes which see G3107
11:27 said unto him, **B** *is* the womb that bare G3107
28 But he said, Yea rather, **b** *are* they that G3107
12:37 **B** *are* those servants, whom the lord G3107
38 and find *them* so, **b** are those servants. G3107
43 **B** *is* that servant, whom his lord when G3107
13:35 when ye shall say, **B** *is* he that cometh G2127
14:14 And thou shalt be **b**; for they cannot G3107
15 he said unto him, **B** *is* he that shall eat G3107
19:38 Saying, **B** *be* the King that cometh in G2127
23:29 they shall say, **B** *are* the barren, and G3107
24:30 and **b** *it*, and brake, and gave to them. G2127
50 and he lifted up his hands, and **b** them. G2127
51 And it came to pass, while he **b** them, G2127
Jn 12:13 cried, Hosanna: **B** *is* the King of Israel G2127
20:29 hast believed: **b** *are* they that have not G3107
Act 3:25 shall all the kindreds of the earth be **b**. G1757
20:35 It is more **b** to give than to receive. G3107
Ro 1:25 the Creator, who is **b** for ever. Amen. G2128
4: 7 *Saying*, **B** *are* they whose iniquities are G3107
8 **B** *is* the man to whom the Lord will not G3107
9: 5 who is over all, God **b** for ever. Amen. G2128
2Co 1: 3 **B** *be* God, even the Father of our Lord G2128
11:31 **b** for evermore, knoweth that I lie not. G2128
Gal 3: 8 *saying*, In thee shall all nations be **b**. G1757
9 So then they which be of faith are **b** G2127
Eph 1: 3 **B** *be* the God and Father of our Lord G2128
3 Christ, who hath **b** us with all spiritual G2127
1Ti 1:11 glorious gospel of the **b** God, which was G3107
6:15 shew, *who is* the **b** and only Potentate, G3107
Tit 2:13 Looking for that **b** hope, and the G3107
Heb 7: 1 the slaughter of the kings, and **b** him; G2127
6 and **b** him that had the promises. G2127
7 contradiction the less is **b** of the better. G2127
11:20 By faith Isaac **b** Jacob and Esau G2127
21 By faith Jacob, when he was a dying, **b** G2127
Jas 1:12 **B** *is* the man that endureth temptation: G3107
25 work, this man shall be **b** in his deed. G3107
1Pt 1: 3 **B** *be* the God and Father of our Lord G2128
Rev 1: 3 **B** *is* he that readeth, and they that hear G3107
14:13 unto me, Write, **B** *are* the dead which G3107
16:15 Behold, I come as a thief. **B** *is* he that G3107
19: 9 And he saith unto me, Write, **B** *are* G3107
20: 6 **B** and holy *is* he that hath part in the G3107
22: 7 Behold, I come quickly: **b** *is* he that G3107
14 **B** *are* they that do his commandments, G3107

BLESSEDNESS
Ro 4: 6 Even as David also describeth the **b** of G3108
9 *Cometh* this **b** then upon the G3108
Gal 4:15 Where is then the **b** ye spake of? for I G3108

BLESSEST
Nu 22: 6 that he whom thou **b** *is* blessed, and he H1288
1Ch 17:27 thee for ever: for thou **b**, O LORD, and *it* H1288
Ps 65:10 showers: thou **b** the springing thereof. H1288

BLESSETH
Gen 27:29 thee, and blessed *be* he that **b** thee. H1288
Nu 24: 9 Blessed *is* he that **b** thee, and cursed *is* H1288
Dt 15: 6 For the LORD thy God **b** thee, as he H1288
Ps 10: 3 his heart's desire, and **b** the covetous, H1288
107:38 He **b** them also, so that they are H1288
Prv 3:33 but he **b** the habitation of the just. H1288
27:14 He that **b** his friend with a loud voice, H1288
Isa 65:16 That he who **b** himself in the earth H1288

BLESSING
Gen 12: 2 thy name great; and thou shalt be a **b**: H1293
22:17 That in **b** I will bless thee, and in H1288
27:12 bring a curse upon me, and not a **b**. H1293
30 made an end of **b** Jacob, and Jacob was H1288
35 subtilty, and hath taken away thy **b**. H1293
36 taken away my **b**. And he said, Hast H1293
36 Hast thou not reserved a **b** for me? H1293
38 Hast thou but one **b**, my father? bless H1293
41 And Esau hated Jacob because of the **b** H1293
28: 4 And give thee the **b** of Abraham, to H1293
33:11 Take, I pray thee, my **b** that is brought H1293
39: 5 sake; and the **b** of the LORD was upon H1293
49:28 one according to his **b** he blessed them. H1293
Ex 32:29 he may bestow upon you a **b** this day. H1293
Lev 25:21 Then I will command my **b** upon you H1293
Dt 11:26 Behold, I set before you this day a **b** H1293
27 A **b**, if ye obey the commandments of H1293
29 that thou shalt put the **b** upon mount H1293
12:15 according to the **b** of the LORD thy God H1293
16:17 according to the **b** of the LORD thy God H1293
23: 5 the curse into a **b** unto thee, because H1293
Dt 28: 8 The LORD shall command the **b** upon H1293
30: 1 upon thee, the **b** and the curse, which H1293
19 life and death, **b** and cursing: therefore H1293
33: 1 And this *is* the **b**, wherewith Moses the H1293
7 And this *is the* **b** of Judah: and he said,
16 in the bush: let *the* **b** come upon the
23 favour, and full with the **b** of the LORD: H1293
Jos 15:19 Who answered, Give me a **b**; for thou H1293
Jdg 1:15 And she said unto him, Give me a **b**: for H1293
1Sa 25:27 And now this **b** which thine handmaid H1293
2Sa 7:29 *it*: and with thy **b** let the house of thy H1293
2Ki 5:15 I pray thee, take a **b** of thy servant. H1293
Neh 9: 5 which is exalted above all **b** and praise. H1293
13: 2 our God turned the curse into a **b**. H1293
Job 29:13 The **b** of him that was ready to perish H1293
Ps 3: 8 LORD: thy **b** *is* upon thy people. Selah. H1293
24: 5 He shall receive the **b** from the LORD, H1293
109:17 not in **b**, so let it be far from him. H1293
129: 8 Neither do they which go by say, The **b** H1293
133: 3 the **b**, *even* life for evermore. H1293
Prv 10:22 The **b** of the LORD, it maketh rich, and H1293
11:11 By the **b** of the upright the city is H1293
26 curse him: but **b** *shall be* upon the head H1293
24:25 and a good **b** shall come upon them. H1293
Isa 19:24 *even* a **b** in the midst of the land: H1293
44: 3 seed, and my **b** upon thine offspring: H1293
65: 8 it not; for a **b** *is* in it: so will I do for H1293
Ezk 34:26 about my hill a **b**; and I will cause the H1293
26 his season; there shall be showers of **b**. H1293
44:30 may cause the **b** to rest in thine house. H1293
Joel 2:14 and leave a **b** behind him; *even* a H1293
Zec 8:13 and ye shall be a **b**: fear not, *but* let your H1293
Mal 3:10 pour you out a **b**, that *there shall* not H1293
Lk 24:53 the temple, praising and **b** God. Amen. G2127
Ro 15:29 fulness of the **b** of the gospel of Christ. G2129
1Co 10:16 The cup of **b** which we bless, is it not G2129
Gal 3:14 That the **b** of Abraham might come on G2129
Heb 6: 7 it is dressed, receiveth **b** from God: G2129
14 Saying, Surely **b** I will bless thee, and G2127
12:17 have inherited the **b**, he was rejected: G2129
Jas 3:10 Out of the same mouth proceedeth **b** G2129
1Pt 3: 9 but contrariwise **b**; knowing that ye are G2127
9 called, that ye should inherit a **b**. G2129
Rev 5:12 strength, and honour, and glory, and **b**. G2129
13 heard I saying, **B**, and honour, and G2129
7:12 Saying, Amen: **B**, and glory, and G2129

BLESSINGS
Gen 49:25 shall bless thee with **b** of heaven above, H1293
25 of heaven above, **b** of the deep that H1293
25 **b** of the breasts, and of the womb: H1293
26 The **b** of thy father have prevailed H1293
26 above the **b** of my progenitors unto H1293
Dt 28: 2 And all these **b** shall come on thee, and H1293
Jos 8:34 words of the law, the **b** and cursings, H1293
Ps 21: 3 For thou preventest him with the **b** of H1293
Prv 10: 6 **B** *are* upon the head of the just: but H1293
28:20 A faithful man shall abound with **b**: but H1293
Mal 2: 2 I will curse your **b**: yea, I have cursed H1293
Eph 1: 3 spiritual **b** in heavenly *places* in Christ: G2129

BLEW
Jos 6: 8 the LORD, and **b** with the trumpets: H8628
9 the priests that **b** with the trumpets, H8628
13 continually, and **b** with the trumpets: H8628
16 when the priests **b** with the trumpets, H8628
20 when *the priests* **b** with the trumpets: H8628
Jdg 3:27 he was come, that he **b** a trumpet in the H8628
6:34 upon Gideon, and he **b** a trumpet; and H8628
7:19 watch: and they **b** the trumpets, and H8628
20 And the three companies **b** the H8628
22 And the three hundred **b** the trumpets, H8628
1Sa 13: 3 heard *of it*. And Saul **b** the trumpet H8628
2Sa 2:28 So Joab **b** a trumpet, and all the people H8628
18:16 And Joab **b** the trumpet, and the H8628
20: 1 a Benjamite: and he **b** a trumpet, and H8628
22 to Joab. And he **b** a trumpet, and they H8628
1Ki 1:39 And they **b** the trumpet; and all H8628
2Ki 9:13 **b** with trumpets, saying, Jehu is king. H8628
11:14 the land rejoiced, and **b** with trumpets: H8628
Mt 7:25 and the winds **b**, and beat upon that G4154
27 and the winds **b**, and beat upon that G4154
Jn 6:18 arose by reason of a great wind that **b**. G4154
Act 27:13 And when the south wind **b** softly, G5285
28:13 **b**, and we came the next day to Puteoli: G1920

BLIND
Ex 4:11 seeing, or the **b**? have not I the LORD? H5787
Lev 19:14 before the **b**, but shalt fear thy God: H5787
Lev 21:18 not approach: a **b** man, or a lame, or H5787
22:22 **B**, or broken, or maimed, or having a H5788
Dt 15:21 *as if it be* lame, or **b**, *or have* any ill H5787
16:19 a gift: for a gift doth **b** the eyes of the H5786
27:18 Cursed *be* he that maketh the **b** to H5787
28:29 grope at noonday, as the **b** gropeth in H5787
1Sa 12: 3 *any* bribe to **b** mine eyes therewith? H5956
2Sa 5: 6 take away the **b** and the lame, thou H5787
8 the lame and the **b**, *that are* hated of H5787
8 they said, The **b** and the lame shall not H5787
Job 29:15 I was eyes to the **b**, and feet *was* I to the H5787
Ps 146: 8 The LORD openeth *the eyes of* the **b**: the H5787
Isa 29:18 and the eyes of the **b** shall see out of H5787
35: 5 Then the eyes of the **b** shall be opened, H5787
42: 7 To open the **b** eyes, to bring out the H5787
16 And I will bring the **b** by a way *that* H5787
18 Hear, ye deaf; and look, ye **b**, that ye H5787
19 Who *is* **b**, but my servant? or deaf, as H5787
19 *that* I sent? who *is* **b** as *he that is* H5787
19 perfect, and **b** as the LORD'S servant? H5787
43: 8 Bring forth the **b** people that have eyes, H5787
56:10 His watchmen *are* **b**: they are all H5787
59:10 We grope for the wall like the **b**, and we H5787
Jer 31: 8 *and* with them the **b** and the lame, the H5787
Lam 4:14 They have wandered *as* **b** *men* in the H5787
Zep 1:17 shall walk like **b** men, because they H5787
Mal 1: 8 And if ye offer the **b** for sacrifice, *is it* H5787
Mt 9:27 And when Jesus departed thence, two **b** G5185
28 into the house, the **b** men came to him: G5185
11: 5 The **b** receive their sight, and the lame G5185
12:22 with a devil, **b**, and dumb: and he G5185
22 the **b** and dumb both spake and saw. G5185
15:14 Let them alone: they be **b** leaders of the G5185
14 leaders of the **b**. And if the blind lead G5185
14 blind. And if the **b** lead the blind, both G5185
14 lead the **b**, both shall fall into the ditch. G5185
30 *that were* lame, **b**, dumb, maimed, and G5185
31 lame to walk, and the **b** to see: and they G5185
20:30 And, behold, two **b** men sitting by the G5185
21:14 And the **b** and the lame came to him in G5185
23:16 Woe unto you, *ye* **b** guides, which say, G5185
17 *Ye* fools and **b**: for whether is greater, G5185
19 *Ye* fools and **b**: for whether *is* greater, G5185
24 *Ye* **b** guides, which strain at a gnat, and G5185
26 *Thou* **b** Pharisee, cleanse first that G5185
Mk 8:22 and they bring a **b** man unto him, and G5185
23 And he took the **b** man by the hand, G5185
10:46 number of people, **b** Bartimaeus, the G5185
49 And they call the **b** man, saying unto G5185
51 do unto thee? The **b** man said unto G5185
Lk 4:18 of sight to the **b**, to set at liberty them G5185
6:39 them, Can the **b** lead the blind? shall G5185
39 **b**? shall they not both fall into the ditch? G5185
7:21 unto many *that were* **b** he gave sight. G5185
22 how that the **b** see, the lame walk, G5185
14:13 the poor, the maimed, the lame, the **b**: G5185
21 the maimed, and the halt, and the **b**. G5185
18:35 **b** man sat by the way side begging: G5185
Jn 5: 3 of impotent folk, of **b**, halt, withered, G5185
9: 1 saw a man which was **b** from *his* birth. G5185
2 man, or his parents, that he was born **b**? G5185
6 the eyes of the **b** man with the clay, G5185
8 him that he was **b**, said, Is not this he G5185
13 the Pharisees him that aforetime was **b**. G5185
17 They say unto the **b** man again, What G5185
18 that he had been **b**, and received his G5185
19 was born **b**? how then doth he now see? G5185
20 this is our son, and that he was born **b**: G5185
24 the man that was **b**, and said unto him, G5185
25 know, that, whereas I was **b**, now I see. G5185
32 opened the eyes of one that was born **b**. G5185
39 that they which see might be made **b**. G5185
40 and said unto him, Are we **b** also? G5185
41 Jesus said unto them, If ye were **b**, ye G5185
10:21 devil. Can a devil open the eyes of the **b**? G5185
11:37 the eyes of the **b**, have caused that even G5185
Act 13:11 and thou shalt be **b**, not seeing the sun G5185
Ro 2:19 art a guide of the **b**, a light of them G5185
2Pt 1: 9 But he that lacketh these things is **b**, G5185
Rev 3:17 miserable, and poor, and **b**, and naked: G5185

BLINDED
Jn 12:40 He hath **b** their eyes, and hardened G5186
Ro 11: 7 hath obtained it, and the rest were **b** G4456
2Co 3:14 But their minds were **b**: for until this G4456
4: 4 In whom the god of this world hath **b** G5186
1Jn 2:11 because that darkness hath **b** his eyes. G5186

BLINDETH
Ex 23: 8 take no gift: for the gift **b** the wise, and H5786

BLINDFOLDED
Lk 22:64 And when they had **b** him, they struck *G4028*

BLINDNESS
Gen 19:11 of the house with **b**, both small and H5575
Dt 28:28 and **b**, and astonishment of heart: H5788
2Ki 6:18 I pray thee, with **b**. And he smote them H5575
18 with **b** according to the word of Elisha. H5575
Zec 12: 4 smite every horse of the people with **b**. H5788
Ro 11:25 your own conceits; that **b** in part is *G4457*
Eph 4:18 in them, because of the **b** of their heart: *G4457*

BLOOD
Gen 4:10 **b** crieth unto me from the ground. H1818
11 receive thy brother's **b** from thy hand; H1818
9: 4 *which is* the **b** thereof, shall ye not eat. H1818
5 And surely your **b** of your lives will I H1818
6 Whoso sheddeth man's **b**, by man shall H1818
6 by man shall his **b** be shed: for in the H1818
37:22 And Reuben said unto them, Shed no **b**, H1818
26 we slay our brother, and conceal his **b**? H1818
31 the goats, and dipped the coat in the **b**; H1818
42:22 behold, also his **b** is required. H1818
49:11 wine, and his clothes in the **b** of grapes: H1818
Ex 4: 9 river shall become **b** upon the dry *land*. H1818
7:17 the river, and they shall be turned to **b**. H1818
19 they may become **b**; and *that* there may H1818
19 *that* there may be **b** throughout all the H1818
20 that *were* in the river were turned to **b**. H1818
21 was **b** throughout all the land of Egypt. H1818
12: 7 And they shall take of the **b**, and strike H1818
13 And the **b** shall be to you for a token H1818
13 and when I see the **b**, I will pass over H1818
22 and dip *it* in the **b** that *is* in the bason, H1818
22 two side posts with the **b** that *is* in the H1818
23 when he seeth the **b** upon the lintel, H1818
22: 2 he die, *there shall* no **b** *be shed* for him. H1818
3 him, *there shall be* **b** *shed* for him; *for* H1818
23:18 Thou shalt not offer the **b** of my H1818
24: 6 And Moses took half of the **b**, and put *it* H1818
6 half of the **b** he sprinkled on the altar. H1818
8 And Moses took the **b**, and sprinkled *it* H1818
8 and said, Behold the **b** of the covenant, H1818
29:12 And thou shalt take of the **b** of the H1818
12 all the **b** beside the bottom of the altar. H1818
16 thou shalt take his **b**, and sprinkle *it* H1818
20 and take of his **b**, and put *it* upon the H1818
20 the **b** upon the altar round about. H1818
21 And thou shalt take of the **b** that *is* H1818
30:10 in a year with the **b** of the sin offering H1818
34:25 Thou shalt not offer the **b** of my H1818
Lev 1: 5 shall bring the **b**, and sprinkle the blood H1818
5 and sprinkle the **b** round about upon H1818
11 his **b** round about upon the altar. H1818
15 on the altar; and the **b** thereof shall be H1818
3: 2 the **b** upon the altar round about. H1818
8 **b** thereof round about upon the altar. H1818
13 **b** thereof upon the altar round about. H1818
17 dwellings, that ye eat neither fat nor **b**. H1818
4: 5 of the bullock's **b**, and bring it to the H1818
6 his finger in the **b**, and sprinkle of the H1818
6 sprinkle of the **b** seven times before H1818
7 And the priest shall put *some* of the **b** H1818
7 shall pour all the **b** of the bullock at the H1818
16 **b** to the tabernacle of the congregation: H1818
17 *in some* of the **b**, and sprinkle *it* seven H1818
18 And he shall put *some* of the **b** upon H1818
18 pour out all the **b** at the bottom of the H1818
25 And the priest shall take of the **b** of the H1818
25 shall pour out his **b** at the bottom of H1818
30 And the priest shall take of the **b** H1818
30 the **b** thereof at the bottom of the altar. H1818
34 And the priest shall take of the **b** of the H1818
34 the **b** thereof at the bottom of the altar: H1818
5: 9 And he shall sprinkle of the **b** of the sin H1818
9 and the rest of the **b** shall be wrung out H1818
6:27 is sprinkled of the **b** thereof upon any H1818
30 whereof *any* of the **b** is brought into the H1818
7: 2 offering: and the **b** thereof shall he H1818
14 sprinkleth the **b** of the peace offerings. H1818
26 Moreover ye shall eat no manner of **b**, H1818
27 any manner of **b**, even that soul shall H1818
33 Aaron, that offereth the **b** of the peace H1818
8:15 And he slew *it;* and Moses took the **b**, H1818
15 and poured the **b** at the bottom of the H1818
19 the **b** upon the altar round about. H1818
Lev 8:23 And he slew *it;* and Moses took of the **b** H1818
24 Moses put of the **b** upon the tip of their H1818
24 the **b** upon the altar round about. H1818
30 oil, and of the **b** which *was* upon the H1818
9: 9 And the sons of Aaron brought the **b** H1818
9 his finger in the **b**, and put *it* upon the H1818
9 out the **b** at the bottom of the altar: H1818
12 unto him the **b**, which he sprinkled H1818
18 unto him the **b**, which he sprinkled H1818
10:18 Behold, the **b** of it was not brought in H1818
12: 4 And she shall then continue in the **b** of H1818
5 shall continue in the **b** of her purifying H1818
7 the issue of her **b**. This *is* the law for her H1818
14: 6 living bird in the **b** of the bird *that was* H1818
14 And the priest shall take *some* of the **b** H1818
17 upon the **b** of the trespass offering: H1818
25 shall take *some* of the **b** of the trespass H1818
28 place of the **b** of the trespass offering: H1818
51 dip them in the **b** of the slain bird, and H1818
52 the house with the **b** of the bird, and H1818
15:19 in her flesh be **b**, she shall be put apart H1818
25 And if a woman have an issue of her **b** H1818
16:14 And he shall take of the **b** of the H1818
14 of the **b** with his finger seven times. H1818
15 and bring his **b** within the vail, and H1818
15 and do with that **b** as he did with the H1818
15 as he did with the **b** of the bullock, and H1818
18 shall take of the **b** of the bullock, and H1818
18 and of the **b** of the goat, and put H1818
19 And he shall sprinkle of the **b** upon it H1818
27 sin offering, whose **b** was brought in to H1818
17: 4 of the LORD; **b** shall be imputed unto H1818
4 that man; he hath shed **b**; and that man H1818
6 And the priest shall sprinkle the **b** H1818
10 any manner of **b**; I will even set my face H1818
10 soul that eateth **b**, and will cut him off H1818
11 For the life of the flesh *is* in the **b**: and I H1818
11 souls: for it *is* the **b** *that* maketh an H1818
12 soul of you shall eat **b**, neither shall any H1818
12 that sojourneth among you eat **b**. H1818
13 the **b** thereof, and cover it with dust. H1818
14 For *it is* the life of all flesh; the **b** of it *is* H1818
14 Ye shall eat the **b** of no manner of flesh: H1818
14 of all flesh *is* the **b** thereof: whosoever H1818
19:16 the **b** of thy neighbour: I *am* the LORD. H1818
26 Ye shall not eat *any thing* with the **b**: H1818
20: 9 or his mother; his **b** *shall be* upon him. H1818
11 to death; their **b** *shall be* upon them. H1818
12 confusion; their **b** *shall be* upon them. H1818
13 to death; their **b** *shall be* upon them. H1818
16 to death; their **b** *shall be* upon them. H1818
18 the fountain of her **b**: and both of them H1818
27 with stones: their **b** *shall be* upon them. H1818
Nu 18:17 sprinkle their **b** upon the altar, and H1818
19: 4 shall take of her **b** with his finger, and H1818
4 and sprinkle of her **b** directly before the H1818
5 and her **b**, with her dung, shall he burn: H1818
23:24 *of* the prey, and drink the **b** of the slain. H1818
35:19 The revenger of **b** himself shall slay the H1818
21 the revenger of **b** shall slay the H1818
24 of **b** according to these judgments: H1818
25 hand of the revenger of **b**, and the H1818
27 And the revenger of **b** find him without H1818
27 the revenger of **b** kill the slayer; he shall H1818
27 the slayer; he shall not be guilty of **b**: H1818
33 *ye are*: for **b** it defileth the land: H1818
33 cannot be cleansed of the **b** that is shed H1818
33 but by the **b** of him that shed it. H1818
Dt 12:16 Only ye shall not eat the **b**; ye shall pour H1818
23 Only be sure that thou eat not the **b**: for H1818
23 the blood: for the **b** *is* the life; and thou H1818
27 the flesh and the **b**, upon the altar of the H1818
27 thy God: and the **b** of thy sacrifices H1818
15:23 Only thou shalt not eat the **b** thereof; H1818
17: 8 between **b** and blood, between H1818
8 blood and **b**, between plea and plea, H1818
19: 6 Lest the avenger of the **b** pursue the H1818
10 That innocent **b** be not shed in thy H1818
10 an inheritance, and *so* **b** be upon thee. H1818
12 of the avenger of **b**, that he may die. H1818
13 *guilt of* innocent **b** from Israel, that it H1818
21: 7 this **b**, neither have our eyes seen *it*. H1818
8 lay not innocent **b** unto thy people of H1818
8 And the **b** shall be forgiven them. H1818
9 *guilt of* innocent **b** from among you, H1818
22: 8 thou bring not **b** upon thine house, if H1818
32:14 didst drink the pure **b** of the grape. H1818
42 I will make mine arrows drunk with **b**, H1818
42 *and that* with the **b** of the slain and of H1818
Dt 32:43 for he will avenge the **b** of his servants, H1818
Jos 2:19 into the street, his **b** *shall be* upon his H1818
19 thee in the house, his **b** *shall be* on our H1818
20: 3 be your refuge from the avenger of **b**. H1818
5 And if the avenger of **b** pursue after H1818
9 hand of the avenger of **b**, until he stood H1818
Jdg 9:24 might come, and their **b** be laid upon H1818
1Sa 14:32 and the people did eat *them* with the **b**. H1818
33 that they eat with the **b**. And he said, Ye H1818
34 in eating with the **b**. And all the people H1818
19: 5 **b**, to slay David without a cause? H1818
25:26 coming to *shed* **b**, and from avenging H1818
31 thou hast shed **b** causeless, or that my H1818
33 coming to *shed* **b**, and from avenging H1818
26:20 Now therefore, let not my **b** fall to the H1818
2Sa 1:16 And David said unto him, Thy **b** *be* H1818
22 From the **b** of the slain, from the fat of H1818
3:27 he died, for the **b** of Asahel his brother. H1818
28 from the **b** of Abner the son of Ner: H1818
4:11 now require his **b** of your hand, and H1818
14:11 the revengers of **b** to destroy any more, H1818
16: 8 upon thee all the **b** of the house of Saul, H1818
20:12 And Amasa wallowed in **b** in the midst H1818
23:17 do this: *is not this* the **b** of the men that H1818
1Ki 2: 5 he slew, and shed the **b** of war in peace, H1818
5 in peace, and put the **b** of war upon his H1818
9 bring thou down to the grave with **b**. H1818
31 away the innocent **b**, which Joab shed, H1818
32 And the LORD shall return his **b** upon H1818
33 Their **b** shall therefore return upon the H1818
37 thy **b** shall be upon thine own head. H1818
18:28 till the **b** gushed out upon them. H1818
21:19 dogs licked the **b** of Naboth shall dogs H1818
19 Naboth shall dogs lick thy **b**, even thine. H1818
22:35 at even: and the **b** ran out of the wound H1818
38 dogs licked up his **b**; and they washed H1818
2Ki 3:22 the water on the other side *as* red as **b**: H1818
23 And they said, This *is* **b**: the kings are H1818
9: 7 I may avenge the **b** of my servants the H1818
7 prophets, and the **b** of all the servants H1818
26 Surely I have seen yesterday the **b** of H1818
26 Naboth, and the **b** of his sons, saith the H1818
33 and *some* of her **b** was sprinkled on the H1818
16:13 **b** of his peace offerings, upon the altar. H1818
15 upon it all the **b** of the burnt offering, H1818
15 and all the **b** of the sacrifice: and H1818
21:16 Moreover Manasseh shed innocent **b** H1818
24: 4 And also for the innocent **b** that he H1818
4 **b**; which the LORD would not pardon. H1818
1Ch 11:19 shall I drink the **b** of these men that H1818
22: 8 Thou hast shed **b** abundantly, and hast H1818
8 much **b** upon the earth in my sight. H1818
28: 3 *been* a man of war, and hast shed **b**. H1818
2Ch 19:10 cities, between **b** and blood, between H1818
10 between blood and **b**, between law and H1818
24:25 him for the **b** of the sons of Jehoiada H1818
29:22 received the **b**, and sprinkled *it* on H1818
22 they sprinkled the **b** upon the altar: H1818
22 they sprinkled the **b** upon the altar. H1818
24 with their **b** upon the altar, to make H1818
30:16 sprinkled the **b**, *which they received* H1818
35:11 sprinkled *the* **b** from their hands, and
Job 16:18 O earth, cover not thou my **b**, and let H1818
39:30 Her young ones also suck up **b**: and H1818
Ps 9:12 When he maketh inquisition for **b**, he H1818
16: 4 drink offerings of **b** will I not offer, nor H1818
30: 9 What profit *is there* in my **b**, when I go H1818
50:13 flesh of bulls, or drink the **b** of goats? H1818
58:10 wash his feet in the **b** of the wicked. H1818
68:23 That thy foot may be dipped in the **b** of H1818
72:14 precious shall their **b** be in his sight. H1818
78:44 And had turned their rivers into **b**; and H1818
79: 3 Their **b** have they shed like water H1818
10 of the **b** of thy servants *which is* shed. H1818
94:21 righteous, and condemn the innocent **b**. H1818
105:29 He turned their waters into **b**, and slew H1818
106:38 And shed innocent **b**, *even* the blood of H1818
38 And shed innocent blood, *even* the **b** of H1818
38 and the land was polluted with **b**. H1818
Prv 1:11 let us lay wait for **b**, let us lurk privily H1818
16 run to evil, and make haste to shed **b**. H1818
18 And they lay wait for their *own* **b**; they H1818
6:17 and hands that shed innocent **b**, H1818
12: 6 to lie in wait for **b**: but the mouth of the H1818
28:17 A man that doeth violence to the **b** of H1818
30:33 bringeth forth **b**: so the forcing of wrath H1818
Isa 1:11 I delight not in the **b** of bullocks, or of H1818
15 I will not hear: your hands are full of **b**. H1818
4: 4 have purged the **b** of Jerusalem from H1818

Isa 9: 5 garments rolled in **b**; but *this* shall be H1818
15: 9 shall be full of **b**: for I will bring more H1818
26:21 **b**, and shall no more cover her slain. H1818
33:15 from hearing of **b**, and shutteth his eyes H1818
34: 3 mountains shall be melted with their **b**. H1818
6 The sword of the LORD is filled with **b**, H1818
6 *and* with the **b** of lambs and goats, H1818
7 **b**, and their dust made fat with fatness. H1818
49:26 with their own **b**, as with sweet wine: H1818
59: 3 For your hands are defiled with **b**, and H1818
7 to shed innocent **b**: their thoughts *are* H1818
63: 3 my fury; and their **b** shall be sprinkled H5332
66: 3 *if he offered* swine's **b**; he that burneth H1818
Jer 2:34 Also in thy skirts is found the **b** of the H1818
7: 6 and shed not innocent **b** in this place, H1818
18:21 and pour out their ***b*** by the force of the
19: 4 filled this place with the **b** of innocents; H1818
22: 3 neither shed innocent **b** in this place. H1818
17 to shed innocent **b**, and for oppression, H1818
26:15 bring innocent **b** upon yourselves, and H1818
46:10 drunk with their **b**: for the Lord GOD of H1818
48:10 he that keepeth back his sword from **b**. H1818
51:35 of Zion say; and my **b** upon the H1818
Lam 4:13 the **b** of the just in the midst of her, H1818
14 themselves with **b**, so that men could H1818
Ezk 3:18 but his **b** will I require at thine hand. H1818
20 but his **b** will I require at thine hand. H1818
5:17 pestilence and **b** shall pass through H1818
9: 9 the land is full of **b**, and the city full of H1818
14:19 it in **b**, to cut off from it man and beast: H1818
16: 6 in thine own **b**, I said unto thee *when* H1818
6 *thou wast* in thy **b**, Live; yea, I said unto H1818
6 unto thee *when thou wast* in thy **b**, Live. H1818
9 washed away thy **b** from thee, and I H1818
22 and bare, *and* wast polluted in thy **b**. H1818
36 and by the **b** of thy children, which H1818
38 wedlock and shed **b** are judged; and I H1818
38 I will give thee **b** in fury and jealousy. H1818
18:10 a shedder of **b**, and *that* doeth the like H1818
13 surely die; his **b** shall be upon him. H1818
19:10 Thy mother *is* like a vine in thy **b**, H1818
21:32 Thou shalt be for fuel to the fire; thy **b** H1818
22: 3 The city sheddeth **b** in the midst of it, H1818
4 Thou art become guilty in thy **b** that H1818
6 were in thee to their power to shed **b**. H1818
9 carry tales to shed **b**: and in thee they H1818
12 In thee have they taken gifts to shed **b**; H1818
13 **b** which hath been in the midst of thee. H1818
27 the prey, to shed **b**, *and* to destroy H1818
23:37 adultery, and **b** *is* in their hands, and H1818
45 of women that shed **b**; because they *are* H1818
45 adulteresses, and **b** *is* in their hands. H1818
24: 7 For her **b** is in the midst of her; she set H1818
8 I have set her **b** upon the top of a rock, H1818
28:23 pestilence, and **b** into her streets; and H1818
32: 6 I will also water with thy **b** the land H1818
33: 4 his **b** shall be upon his own head. H1818
5 not warning; his **b** shall be upon him. H1818
6 iniquity; but his **b** will I require at the H1818
8 but his **b** will I require at thine hand. H1818
25 Ye eat with the **b**, and lift up your eyes H1818
25 shed **b**: and shall ye possess the land? H1818
35: 5 and hast shed *the* ***b*** *of* the children of
6 prepare thee unto **b**, and blood shall H1818
6 unto blood, and **b** shall pursue thee: H1818
6 hated **b**, even blood shall pursue thee. H1818
6 hated blood, even **b** shall pursue thee. H1818
36:18 upon them for the **b** that they had shed H1818
38:22 and with **b**; and I will rain upon H1818
39:17 that ye may eat flesh, and drink **b**. H1818
18 and drink the **b** of the princes of the H1818
19 be full, and drink **b** till ye be drunken, H1818
43:18 thereon, and to sprinkle **b** thereon. H1818
20 And thou shalt take of the **b** thereof, H1818
44: 7 the fat and the **b**, and they have broken H1818
15 the fat and the **b**, saith the Lord GOD: H1818
45:19 And the priest shall take of the **b** of the H1818
Hos 1: 4 I will avenge the **b** of Jezreel upon the H1818
4: 2 they break out, and **b** toucheth blood. H1818
2 they break out, and blood toucheth **b**. H1818
6: 8 work iniquity, *and is* polluted with **b**. H1818
12:14 shall he leave his **b** upon him, and his H1818
Joel 2:30 earth, **b**, and fire, and pillars of smoke. H1818
31 and the moon into **b**, before the great H1818
3:19 have shed innocent **b** in their land. H1818
21 For I will cleanse their **b** *that* I have not H1818
Jna 1:14 upon us innocent **b**: for thou, O LORD, H1818
Mic 3:10 They build up Zion with **b**, and H1818
7: 2 all lie in wait for **b**; they hunt every man H1818

Hab 2: 8 because of men's **b**, and *for* the violence H1818
12 Woe to him that buildeth a town with **b**, H1818
17 because of men's **b**, and for the violence H1818
Zep 1:17 LORD: and their **b** shall be poured out H1818
Zec 9: 7 And I will take away his **b** out of his H1818
11 As for thee also, by the **b** of thy H1818
Mt 9:20 with an issue of **b** twelve years, came *G131*
16:17 for flesh and **b** hath not revealed *it* *G129*
23:30 with them in the **b** of the prophets. *G129*
35 all the righteous **b** shed upon the earth, *G129*
35 the earth, from the **b** of righteous Abel *G129*
35 Abel unto the **b** of Zacharias son of *G129*
26:28 For this is my **b** of the new testament, *G129*
27: 4 the innocent **b**. And they said, What *G129*
6 the treasury, because it is the price of **b**. *G129*
8 was called, The field of **b**, unto this day. *G129*
24 of the **b** of this just person: see ye *to it*. *G129*
25 His **b** *be* on us, and on our children. *G129*
Mk 5:25 which had an issue of **b** twelve years, *G129*
29 And straightway the fountain of her **b** *G129*
14:24 And he said unto them, This is my **b** of *G129*
Lk 8:43 And a woman having an issue of **b** *G129*
44 immediately her issue of **b** stanched. *G129*
11:50 That the **b** of all the prophets, which was *G129*
51 From the **b** of Abel unto the blood of *G129*
51 From the blood of Abel unto the **b** of *G129*
13: 1 Galilaeans, whose **b** Pilate had mingled *G129*
22:20 testament in my **b**, which is shed for you. *G129*
44 drops of **b** falling down to the ground. *G129*
Jn 1:13 Which were born, not of **b**, nor of the will *G129*
6:53 and drink his **b**, ye have no life in you. *G129*
54 and drinketh my **b**, hath eternal life; and *G129*
55 For my flesh is meat indeed, and my **b** is *G129*
56 my **b**, dwelleth in me, and I in him. *G129*
19:34 forthwith came there out **b** and water. *G129*
Act 1:19 Aceldama, that is to say, The field of **b**. *G129*
2:19 **b**, and fire, and vapour of smoke: *G129*
20 and the moon into **b**, before that great *G129*
5:28 intend to bring this man's **b** upon us. *G129*
15:20 and *from* things strangled, and *from* **b**. *G129*
29 to idols, and from **b**, and from things *G129*
17:26 And hath made of one **b** all nations of *G129*
18: 6 unto them, Your **b** *be* upon your own *G129*
20:26 that I *am* pure from the **b** of all *men*. *G129*
28 which he hath purchased with his own **b**. *G129*
21:25 to idols, and from **b**, and from strangled, *G129*
22:20 And when the **b** of thy martyr Stephen *G129*
Ro 3:15 Their feet *are* swift to shed **b**: *G129*
25 faith in his **b**, to declare his righteousness *G129*
5: 9 justified by his **b**, we shall be saved from *G129*
1Co 10:16 the communion of the **b** of Christ? The *G129*
11:25 testament in my **b**: this do ye, as oft as ye *G129*
27 be guilty of the body and **b** of the Lord. *G129*
15:50 Now this I say, brethren, that flesh and **b** *G129*
Gal 1:16 I conferred not with flesh and **b**: *G129*
Eph 1: 7 through his **b**, the forgiveness of sins, *G129*
2:13 far off are made nigh by the **b** of Christ. *G129*
6:12 For we wrestle not against flesh and **b**, *G129*
Col 1:14 his **b**, *even* the forgiveness of sins: *G129*
20 And, having made peace through the **b** *G129*
Heb 2:14 of flesh and **b**, he also himself likewise *G129*
9: 7 year, not without **b**, which he offered for *G129*
12 Neither by the **b** of goats and calves, but *G129*
12 but by his own **b** he entered in once into *G129*
13 For if the **b** of bulls and of goats, and the *G129*
14 How much more shall the **b** of Christ, *G129*
18 first *testament* was dedicated without **b**. *G129*
19 law, he took the **b** of calves and of goats, *G129*
20 Saying, This *is* the **b** of the testament *G129*
21 Moreover he sprinkled with **b** both the *G129*
22 law purged with **b**; and without shedding *G129*
22 without shedding of **b** is no remission. *G130*
25 holy place every year with **b** of others; *G129*
10: 4 For *it is* not possible that the **b** of bulls *G129*
19 to enter into the holiest by the **b** of Jesus, *G129*
29 and hath counted the **b** of the covenant, *G129*
11:28 the sprinkling of **b**, lest he that destroyed *G129*
12: 4 Ye have not yet resisted unto **b**, striving *G129*
24 and to the **b** of sprinkling, that speaketh *G129*
13:11 For the bodies of those beasts, whose **b** *G129*
12 with his own **b**, suffered without the gate. *G129*
20 the **b** of the everlasting covenant, *G129*
1Pt 1: 2 sprinkling of the **b** of Jesus Christ: Grace *G129*
19 But with the precious **b** of Christ, as of a *G129*
1Jn 1: 7 another, and the **b** of Jesus Christ his *G129*
5: 6 This is he that came by water and **b**, *even* *G129*
6 but by water and **b**. And it is the Spirit *G129*
8 and the **b**: and these three agree in one. *G129*
Rev 1: 5 washed us from our sins in his own **b**, *G129*

Rev 5: 9 us to God by thy **b** out of every kindred, *G129*
6:10 our **b** on them that dwell on the earth? *G129*
12 of hair, and the moon became as **b**; *G129*
7:14 made them white in the **b** of the Lamb. *G129*
8: 7 fire mingled with **b**, and they were cast *G129*
8 and the third part of the sea became **b**; *G129*
11: 6 to turn them to **b**, and to smite the earth *G129*
12:11 And they overcame him by the **b** of the *G129*
14:20 without the city, and **b** came out of the *G129*
16: 3 it became as the **b** of a dead *man*: and *G129*
4 fountains of waters; and they became **b**. *G129*
6 For they have shed the **b** of saints and *G129*
6 them **b** to drink; for they are worthy. *G129*
17: 6 drunken with the **b** of the saints, and *G129*
6 and with the **b** of the martyrs of Jesus: *G129*
18:24 And in her was found the **b** of prophets, *G129*
19: 2 the **b** of his servants at her hand. *G129*
13 a vesture dipped in **b**: and his name is *G129*

BLOODGUILTINESS
Ps 51:14 Deliver me from **b**, O God, thou God of H1818

BLOODTHIRSTY
Prv 29:10 The **b** hate the upright: but the H582+H1818

BLOODY
Ex 4:25 Surely a **b** husband *art* thou to me. H1818
26 So he let him go: then she said, A **b** H1818
2Sa 16: 7 thou **b** man, and thou man of Belial: H1818
8 thy mischief, because thou *art* a **b** man. H1818
21: 1 Saul, and for *his* **b** house, because he H1818
Ps 5: 6 will abhor the **b** and deceitful man. H1818
26: 9 with sinners, nor my life with **b** men: H1818
55:23 pit of destruction: **b** and deceitful men H1818
59: 2 of iniquity, and save me from **b** men. H1818
139:19 depart from me therefore, ye **b** men. H1818
Ezk 7:23 Make a chain: for the land is full of **b** H1818
22: 2 thou judge the **b** city? yea, thou shalt H1818
24: 6 Lord GOD; Woe to the **b** city, to the pot H1818
9 Lord GOD; Woe to the **b** city! I will even H1818
Nah 3: 1 Woe to the **b** city! it *is* all full of lies *and* H1818
Act 28: 8 of a fever and of a **b** flux: to whom Paul *G1420*

BLOOMED
Nu 17: 8 and **b** blossoms, and yielded almonds. H6692

BLOSSOM
Nu 17: 5 shall choose, shall **b**: and I will make to H6524
Isa 5:24 and their **b** shall go up as dust: H6525
27: 6 root: Israel shall **b** and bud, and fill the H6692
35: 1 desert shall rejoice, and **b** as the rose. H6524
2 It shall **b** abundantly, and rejoice even H6524
Hab 3:17 Although the fig tree shall not **b**, neither H6524

BLOSSOMED
Ezk 7:10 the rod hath **b**, pride hath budded. H6692

BLOSSOMS
Gen 40:10 it budded, *and* her **b** shot forth; and the H5322
Nu 17: 8 and bloomed **b**, and yielded almonds. H6731

BLOT
Ex 32:32 sin—; and if not, **b** me, I pray thee, out H4229
33 me, him will I **b** out of my book. H4229
Nu 5:23 shall **b** *them* out with the bitter water: H4229
Dt 9:14 destroy them, and **b** out their name H4229
25:19 possess it, *that* thou shalt **b** out the H4229
29:20 **b** out his name from under heaven. H4229
2Ki 14:27 And the LORD said not that he would **b** H4229
Job 31: 7 if any **b** hath cleaved to mine hands; H3971
Ps 51: 1 mercies **b** out my transgressions. H4229
9 Hide thy face from my sins, and **b** out H4229
Prv 9: 7 a wicked *man getteth* himself a **b**. H3971
Jer 18:23 iniquity, neither **b** out their sin from H4229
Rev 3: 5 and I will not **b** out his name out of *G1813*

BLOTTED
Neh 4: 5 let not their sin be **b** out from before H4229
Ps 69:28 Let them be **b** out of the book of the H4229
109:13 following let their name be **b** out. H4229
14 let not the sin of his mother be **b** out. H4229
Isa 44:22 I have **b** out, as a thick cloud, thy H4229
Act 3:19 your sins may be **b** out, when the times *G1813*

BLOTTETH
Isa 43:25 I, *even* I, *am* he that **b** out thy H4229

BLOTTING
Col 2:14 **B** out the handwriting of ordinances *G1813*

B

BLOW
Ex 15:10 Thou didst **b** with thy wind, the sea H5398
Nu 10: 3 And when they shall **b** with them, all H8628
4 And if they **b** *but* with one *trumpet,* H8628
5 When ye **b** an alarm, then the camps H8628
6 When ye **b** an alarm the second time, H8628
6 shall **b** an alarm for their journeys. H8628
7 **b**, but ye shall not sound an alarm. H8628
8 the priests, shall **b** with the trumpets; H8628
9 you, then ye shall **b** an alarm with the H7321
10 months, ye shall **b** with the trumpets H8628
31: 6 and the trumpets to **b** in his hand. H8643
Jos 6: 4 the priests shall **b** with the trumpets. H8628
Jdg 7:18 When I **b** with a trumpet, I and all that H8628
18 *are* with me, then **b** ye the trumpets H8628
20 right hands to **b** *withal*: and they cried, H8628
1Ki 1:34 over Israel: and **b** ye with the trumpet, H8628
1Ch 15:24 the priests, did **b** with the trumpets H2690
Ps 39:10 I am consumed by the **b** of thine hand. H8409
78:26 He caused an east wind to **b** in the H5265
81: 3 **B** up the trumpet in the new moon, in H8628
147:18 his wind to **b**, *and* the waters flow. H5380
Song 4:16 come, thou south; **b** upon my garden, H6315
Isa 40:24 and he shall also **b** upon them, and H5398
Jer 4: 5 and say, **B** ye the trumpet in the H8628
6: 1 of Jerusalem, and **b** the trumpet in H8628
14:17 a great breach, with a very grievous **b**. H4347
51:27 Set ye up a standard in the land, **b** the H8628
Ezk 21:31 upon thee, I will **b** against thee in the H6315
22:20 of the furnace, to **b** the fire upon it, to H5301
21 Yea, I will gather you, and **b** upon you H5301
33: 3 he **b** the trumpet, and warn the people; H8628
6 sword come, and **b** not the trumpet, H8628
Hos 5: 8 **B** ye the cornet in Gibeah, *and* the H8628
Joel 2: 1 **B** ye the trumpet in Zion, and sound an H8628
15 **B** the trumpet in Zion, sanctify a fast, H8628
Hag 1: 9 *it* home, I did **b** upon it. Why? saith H5301
Zec 9:14 the Lord GOD shall **b** the trumpet, and H8628
Lk 12:55 And when *ye see* the south wind **b**, ye *G4154*
Rev 7: 1 wind should not **b** on the earth, nor on *G4154*

BLOWETH
Isa 18: 3 and when he **b** a trumpet, hear ye. H8628
40: 7 **b** upon it: surely the people *is* grass. H5380
54:16 Behold, I have created the smith that **b** H5301
Jn 3: 8 The wind **b** where it listeth, and thou *G4154*

BLOWING
Lev 23:24 of **b** of trumpets, an holy convocation. H8643
Nu 29: 1 it is a day of **b** the trumpets unto you. H8643
Jos 6: 9 going on, and **b** with the trumpets. H8628
13 going on, and **b** with the trumpets. H8628

BLOWN
Job 20:26 places: a fire not **b** shall consume him; H5301
Isa 27:13 trumpet shall be **b**, and they shall come H8628
Ezk 7:14 They have **b** the trumpet, even to make H8628
Am 3: 6 Shall a trumpet be **b** in the city, and the H8628

BLUE
Ex 25: 4 And **b**, and purple, and scarlet, and fine H8504
26: 1 twined linen, and **b**, and purple, and H8504
4 And thou shalt make loops of **b** upon H8504
31 And thou shalt make a vail *of* **b**, and H8504
36 door of the tent, *of* **b**, and purple, and H8504
27:16 of twenty cubits, *of* **b**, and purple, and H8504
28: 5 And they shall take gold, and **b**, and H8504
6 the ephod *of* gold, *of* **b**, and *of* purple, *of* H8504
8 *even of* gold, *of* **b**, and purple, and H8504
15 it; *of* gold, *of* **b**, and *of* purple, and *of* H8504
28 with a lace of **b**, that *it* may be above H8504
31 make the robe of the ephod all *of* **b**. H8504
33 pomegranates *of* **b**, and *of* purple, and H8504
37 And thou shalt put it on a **b** lace, that it H8504
35: 6 And **b**, and purple, and scarlet, and fine H8504
23 whom was found **b**, and purple, and H8504
25 had spun, *both* of **b**, and *of* purple, *and* H8504
35 the embroiderer, in **b**, and in purple, in H8504
36: 8 twined linen, and **b**, and purple, and H8504
11 And he made loops of **b** on the edge of H8504
35 And he made a vail *of* **b**, and purple, H8504
37 tabernacle door *of* **b**, and purple, and H8504
38:18 *was* needlework, *of* **b**, and purple, and H8504
23 an embroiderer in **b**, and in purple, and H8504
39: 1 And of the **b**, and purple, and scarlet, H8504
2 And he made the ephod *of* gold, **b**, and H8504
3 to work *it* in the **b**, and in the purple, H8504
5 thereof; *of* gold, **b**, and purple, and H8504
8 of the ephod; *of* gold, **b**, and purple, and H8504
Ex 39:21 with a lace of **b**, that it might be above H8504
22 of the ephod *of* woven work, all *of* **b**. H8504
24 pomegranates *of* **b**, and purple, and H8504
29 And a girdle *of* fine twined linen, and **b**, H8504
31 And they tied unto it a lace of **b**, to H8504
Nu 4: 6 of **b**, and shall put in the staves thereof. H8504
7 spread a cloth of **b**, and put thereon the H8504
9 And they shall take a cloth of **b**, and H8504
11 spread a cloth of **b**, and cover it with a H8504
12 put *them* in a cloth of **b**, and cover them H8504
15:38 the fringe of the borders a ribband of **b**: H8504
2Ch 2: 7 and crimson, and **b**, and that can skill H8504
14 in purple, in **b**, and in fine linen, and H8504
3:14 And he made the vail *of* **b**, and purple, H8504
Est 1: 6 *Where were* white, green, and **b**, H8504
6 and **b**, and white, and black, marble. H8336
8:15 in royal apparel of **b** and white, and H8504
Jer 10: 9 of the founder: **b** and purple *is* their H8504
Ezk 23: 6 *Which were* clothed with **b**, captains H8504
27: 7 to be thy sail; **b** and purple from the H8504
24 all sorts *of things*, in **b** clothes, and H8504

BLUENESS
Prv 20:30 The **b** of a wound cleanseth away evil: H2250

BLUNT
Ecc 10:10 If the iron be **b**, and he do not whet the H6949

BLUSH
Ezr 9: 6 am ashamed and **b** to lift up my face to H3637
Jer 6:15 neither could they **b**: therefore they H3637
8:12 neither could they **b**: therefore shall H3637

BOANERGES
Mk 3:17 them **B**, which is, The sons of thunder: *G993*

BOAR
Ps 80:13 The **b** out of the wood doth waste it, H2386

BOARD
Ex 26:16 Ten cubits *shall be* the length of a **b**, H7175
16 and a half *shall be* the breadth of one **b**. H7175
17 Two tenons *shall there be* in one **b**, set H7175
19 sockets under one **b** for his two tenons, H7175
19 under another **b** for his two tenons. H7175
21 sockets under one **b**, and two sockets H7175
21 and two sockets under another **b**. H7175
25 sockets under one **b**, and two sockets H7175
25 and two sockets under another **b**. H7175
36:21 The length of a **b** *was* ten cubits, and H7175
21 the breadth of a **b** one cubit and a half. H7175
22 One **b** had two tenons, equally distant H7175
24 sockets under one **b** for his two tenons, H7175
24 under another **b** for his two tenons. H7175
26 sockets under one **b**, and two sockets H7175
26 and two sockets under another **b**. H7175
30 of silver, under every **b** two sockets. H7175

BOARDS
Ex 26:15 And thou shalt make **b** for the H7175
17 make for all the **b** of the tabernacle. H7175
18 And thou shalt make the **b** for the H7175
18 twenty **b** on the south side southward. H7175
19 under the twenty **b**; two sockets under H7175
20 the north side *there shall be* twenty **b**: H7175
22 westward thou shalt make six **b**. H7175
23 And two **b** shalt thou make for the H7175
25 And they shall be eight **b**, and their H7175
26 the **b** of the one side of the tabernacle, H7175
27 And five bars for the **b** of the other side H7175
27 and five bars for the **b** of the side of the H7175
28 of the **b** shall reach from end to end. H7175
29 And thou shalt overlay the **b** with gold, H7175
27: 8 Hollow with **b** shalt thou make it: as it H3871
35:11 **b**, his bars, his pillars, and his sockets, H7175
36:20 And he made **b** for the tabernacle *of* H7175
22 he make for all the **b** of the tabernacle. H7175
23 And he made **b** for the tabernacle; H7175
23 twenty **b** for the south side southward: H7175
24 under the twenty **b**; two sockets under H7175
25 the north corner, he made twenty **b**, H7175
27 the tabernacle westward he made six **b**. H7175
28 And two **b** made he for the corners of H7175
30 And there were eight **b**; and their H7175
31 the **b** of the one side of the tabernacle, H7175
32 And five bars for the **b** of the other side H7175
32 five bars for the **b** of the tabernacle for H7175
33 the **b** from the one end to the other. H7175
34 And he overlaid the **b** with gold, and H7175
Ex 38: 7 withal; he made the altar hollow with **b**. H3871
39:33 his taches, his **b**, his bars, and his H7175
40:18 and set up the **b** thereof, and put in H7175
Nu 3:36 *shall be* the **b** of the tabernacle, and H7175
4:31 congregation; the **b** of the tabernacle, H7175
1Ki 6: 9 the house with beams and **b** of cedar. H7713
15 house within with **b** of cedar, both the H6763
16 and the walls with **b** of cedar: he even H6763
Song 8: 9 we will inclose her with **b** of cedar. H3871
Ezk 27: 5 They have made all thy *ship* **b** of fir H3871
Act 27:44 And the rest, some on **b**, and some on *G4548*

BOAST
1Ki 20:11 **b** himself as he that putteth it off. H1984
2Ch 25:19 lifteth thee up to **b**: abide now at home; H3513
Ps 34: 2 My soul shall make her **b** in the LORD: H1984
44: 8 In God we **b** all the day long, and H1984
49: 6 They that trust in their wealth, and **b** H1984
94: 4 all the workers of iniquity **b** themselves? H559
97: 7 images, that **b** themselves of idols: H1984
Prv 27: 1 **B** not thyself of to morrow; for thou H1984
Isa 10:15 Shall the axe **b** itself against him that H6286
61: 6 and in their glory shall ye **b** yourselves. H3235
Ro 2:17 in the law, and makest thy **b** of God, *G2744*
23 Thou that makest thy **b** of the law, *G2744*
11:18 **B** not against the branches. But if thou *G2620*
18 But if thou **b**, thou bearest not the *G2620*
2Co 9: 2 mind, for which I **b** of you to them of *G2744*
10: 8 For though I should **b** somewhat more *G2744*
13 But we will not **b** of things without *our* *G2744*
16 you, *and* not to **b** in another man's line *G2744*
11:16 receive me, that I may **b** myself a little. *G2744*
Eph 2: 9 Not of works, lest any man should **b**. *G2744*

BOASTED
Ezk 35:13 Thus with your mouth ye have **b** H1431
2Co 7:14 For if I have **b** any thing to him of you, *G2744*

BOASTERS
Ro 1:30 despiteful, proud, **b**, inventors of evil *G213*
2Ti 3: 2 selves, covetous, **b**, proud, blasphemers, *G213*

BOASTEST
Ps 52: 1 Why **b** thou thyself in mischief, O H1984

BOASTETH
Ps 10: 3 For the wicked **b** of his heart's desire, H1984
Prv 20:14 but when he is gone his way, then he **b**. H1984
25:14 Whoso **b** himself of a false gift *is like* H1984
Jas 3: 5 a little member, and **b** great things. *G3166*

BOASTING
Act 5:36 days rose up Theudas, **b** himself to be *G3004*
Ro 3:27 Where *is* **b** then? It is excluded. By *G2746*
2Co 7:14 in truth, even so our **b**, which *I made* *G2746*
8:24 your love, and of our **b** on your behalf. *G2746*
9: 3 Yet have I sent the brethren, lest our **b** *G2745*
4 be ashamed in this same confident **b**. *G2746*
10:15 Not **b** of things without *our* measure, *G2744*
11:10 me of this **b** in the regions of Achaia. *G2746*
17 it were foolishly, in this confidence of **b**. *G2746*

BOASTINGS
Jas 4:16 But now ye rejoice in your **b**: all such *G212*

BOAT
2Sa 19:18 And there went over a ferry **b** to carry H5679
Jn 6:22 was none other **b** there, save that one *G4142*
22 his disciples into the **b**, but *that* his *G4142*
Act 27:16 we had much work to come by the **b**: *G4627*
30 had let down the **b** into the sea, under *G4627*
32 off the ropes of the **b**, and let her fall off. *G4627*

BOATS
Jn 6:23 (Howbeit there came other **b** from *G4142*

BOAZ
Ru 2: 1 of Elimelech; and his name *was* **B**. H1162
3 **B**, who *was* of the kindred of Elimelech. H1162
4 And, behold, **B** came from Beth-lehem, H1162
5 Then said **B** unto his servant that was H1162
8 Then said **B** unto Ruth, Hearest thou H1162
11 And **B** answered and said unto her, It H1162
14 And **B** said unto her, At mealtime H1162
15 And when she was risen up to glean, **B** H1162
19 name with whom I wrought to day *is* **B**. H1162
23 So she kept fast by the maidens of **B** to H1162
3: 2 And now *is* not **B** of our kindred, with H1162
7 And when **B** had eaten and drunk, and H1162

Ru 4: 1 Then went **B** up to the gate, and sat H1162
1 kinsman of whom **B** spake came by; H1162
5 Then said **B**, What day thou buyest the H1162
8 Therefore the kinsman said unto **B**, Buy H1162
9 And **B** said unto the elders, and *unto* H1162
13 So **B** took Ruth, and she was his wife: H1162
21 And Salmon begat **B**, and Boaz begat H1162
21 And Salmon begat Boaz, and **B** begat H1162
1Ki 7:21 pillar, and called the name thereof **B**. H1162
1Ch 2:11 begat Salma, and Salma begat **B**, H1162
12 And **B** begat Obed, and Obed begat H1162
2Ch 3:17 and the name of that on the left **B**. H1162

BOCHERU
1Ch 8:38 these, Azrikam, **B**, and Ishmael, and H1074
9:44 these, Azrikam, **B**, and Ishmael, and H1074

BOCHIM
Jdg 2: 1 up from Gilgal to **B**, and said, I made H1066
5 of that place **B**: and they sacrificed H1066

BODIES
Gen 47:18 of my lord, but our **b**, and our lands: H1472
1Sa 31:12 of Saul and the **b** of his sons from the H1472
1Ch 10:12 body of Saul, and the **b** of his sons, and H1480
2Ch 20:24 **b** fallen to the earth, and none escaped. H6297
25 with the dead **b**, and precious jewels, H6297
Neh 9:37 over our **b**, and over our cattle, H1472
Job 13:12 unto ashes, your **b** to bodies of clay. H1354
12 unto ashes, your bodies to **b** of clay. H1354
Ps 79: 2 The dead **b** of thy servants have they H5038
110: 6 with the dead **b**; he shall wound the H1472
Jer 31:40 And the whole valley of the dead **b**, and H6297
33: 5 with the dead **b** of men, whom I have H6297
34:20 and their dead **b** shall be for meat unto H5038
41: 9 cast all the dead **b** of the men, whom H6297
Ezk 1:11 one to another, and two covered their **b**. H1472
23 two, which covered on that side, their **b**. H1472
Dan 3:27 men, upon whose **b** the fire had no H1655
28 and yielded their **b**, that they might not H1655
Am 8: 3 *be* many dead **b** in every place; they H6297
Mt 27:52 many **b** of the saints which slept arose, G4983
Jn 19:31 that the **b** should not remain upon G4983
Ro 1:24 their own **b** between themselves: G4983
8:11 **b** by his Spirit that dwelleth in you. G4983
12: 1 that ye present your **b** a living sacrifice, G4983
1Co 6:15 Know ye not that your **b** are the G4983
15:40 *There are* also celestial **b**, and bodies G4983
40 *There are* also celestial bodies, and **b** G4983
Eph 5:28 **b**. He that loveth his wife loveth himself. G4983
Heb 10:22 and our **b** washed with pure water. G4983
13:11 For the **b** of those beasts, whose blood G4983
Rev 11: 8 And their dead **b** *shall lie* in the street G4430
9 see their dead **b** three days and an half, G4430
9 suffer their dead **b** to be put in graves. G4430

BODILY
Lk 3:22 And the Holy Ghost descended in a **b** G4984
2Co 10:10 powerful; but *his* **b** presence *is* weak, G4983
Col 2: 9 all the fulness of the Godhead **b**. G4985
1Ti 4: 8 For **b** exercise profiteth little: but G4984

BODY
Ex 24:10 it were the **b** of heaven in *his* clearness. H6106
Lev 21:11 Neither shall he go in to any dead **b**, nor H5315
Nu 6: 6 the LORD he shall come at no dead **b**. H5315
9: 6 by the dead **b** of a man, that they H5315
7 by the dead **b** of a man: wherefore H5315
10 by reason of a dead **b**, or *be* in a journey H5315
19:11 He that toucheth the dead **b** of any H5315
13 Whosoever toucheth the dead **b** of any H5315
16 fields, or a dead **b**, or a bone of a man, H5315
Dt 21:23 His **b** shall not remain all night upon H5038
28: 4 Blessed *shall be* the fruit of thy **b**, and the H990
11 in the fruit of thy **b**, and in the fruit of thy H990
18 Cursed *shall be* the fruit of thy **b**, and the H990
53 fruit of thine own **b**, the flesh of thy sons H990
30: 9 in the fruit of thy **b**, and in the fruit of thy H990
Jdg 8:30 his **b** begotten: for he had many wives. H3409
1Sa 31:10 fastened his **b** to the wall of Beth-shan. H1472
12 and took the **b** of Saul and the bodies H1472
2Ki 8: 5 restored a dead **b** to life, that, behold,
1Ch 10:12 and took away the **b** of Saul, and the H1480
Job 19:17 for the children's *sake* of mine own **b**. H990
26 this *b*, yet in my flesh shall I see God:
20:25 It is drawn, and cometh out of the **b**; H1465
Ps 132:11 fruit of thy **b** will I set upon thy throne. H990
Prv 5:11 thy flesh and thy **b** are consumed, H7607
Isa 10:18 both soul and **b**: and they shall be as H1320
Isa 26:19 *with* my dead **b** shall they arise. Awake H5038
51:23 thou hast laid thy **b** as the ground, and H1460
Jer 26:23 and cast his dead **b** into the graves of H5038
36:30 and his dead **b** shall be cast out in H5038
Lam 4: 7 were more ruddy in **b** than rubies, their H6106
Ezk 10:12 And their whole **b**, and their backs, and H1320
Dan 4:33 as oxen, and his **b** was wet with the H1655
5:21 like oxen, and his **b** was wet with the H1655
7:11 was slain, and his **b** destroyed, and H1655
15 in the midst of *my* **b**, and the visions of H5085
10: 6 His **b** also *was* like the beryl, and his H1472
Mic 6: 7 the fruit of my **b** *for* the sin of my soul? H990
Hag 2:13 unclean by a dead **b** touch any of these, H5315
Mt 5:29 thy whole **b** should be cast into hell. G4983
30 thy whole **b** should be cast into hell. G4983
6:22 The light of the **b** is the eye: if therefore G4983
22 single, thy whole **b** shall be full of light. G4983
23 But if thine eye be evil, thy whole **b** G4983
25 nor yet for your **b**, what ye shall put on. G4983
25 than meat, and the **b** than raiment? G4983
10:28 And fear not them which kill the **b**, but G4983
28 able to destroy both soul and **b** in hell. G4983
14:12 and took up the **b**, and buried it, and G4983
26:12 on my **b**, she did *it* for my burial. G4983
26 and said, Take, eat; this is my **b**. G4983
27:58 He went to Pilate, and begged the **b** of G4983
58 commanded the **b** to be delivered. G4983
59 And when Joseph had taken the **b**, he G4983
Mk 5:29 **b** that she was healed of that plague. G4983
14: 8 to anoint my **b** to the burying. G4983
22 them, and said, Take, eat: this is my **b**. G4983
51 *b*; and the young men laid hold on him: G4983
15:43 unto Pilate, and craved the **b** of Jesus. G4983
45 the centurion, he gave the **b** to Joseph. G4983
Lk 11:34 The light of the **b** is the eye: therefore G4983
34 single, thy whole **b** also is full of light; G4983
34 *eye* is evil, thy **b** also *is* full of darkness. G4983
36 If thy whole **b** therefore *be* full of light, G4983
12: 4 them that kill the **b**, and after that have G4983
22 neither for the **b**, what ye shall put on. G4983
23 The life is more than meat, and the **b** *is* G4983
17:37 Wheresoever the **b** *is*, thither will the G4983
22:19 saying, This is my **b** which is given for G4983
23:52 unto Pilate, and begged the **b** of Jesus. G4983
55 the sepulchre, and how his **b** was laid. G4983
24: 3 and found not the **b** of the Lord Jesus. G4983
23 And when they found not his **b**, they G4983
Jn 2:21 But he spake of the temple of his **b**. G4983
19:38 take away the **b** of Jesus: and Pilate G4983
38 came therefore, and took the **b** of Jesus. G4983
40 Then took they the **b** of Jesus, and G4983
20:12 the feet, where the **b** of Jesus had lain. G4983
Act 9:40 and turning *him* to the **b** said, Tabitha, G4983
19:12 So that from his **b** were brought unto G5559
Ro 4:19 not his own **b** now dead, when he G4983
6: 6 with *him*, that the **b** of sin might be G4983
12 in your mortal **b**, that ye should obey G4983
7: 4 to the law by the **b** of Christ; that ye G4983
24 deliver me from the **b** of this death? G4983
8:10 And if Christ *be* in you, the **b** *is* dead G4983
13 mortify the deeds of the **b**, ye shall live. G4983
23 *to wit*, the redemption of our **b**. G4983
12: 4 members in one **b**, and all members G4983
5 So we, *being* many, are one **b** in Christ, G4983
1Co 5: 3 For I verily, as absent in **b**, but present G4983
6:13 them. Now the **b** *is* not for fornication, G4983
13 but for the Lord; and the Lord for the **b**. G4983
16 **b**? for two, saith he, shall be one flesh. G4983
18 is without the **b**; but he that committeth G4983
18 fornication sinneth against his own **b**. G4983
19 What? know ye not that your **b** is the G4983
20 **b**, and in your spirit, which are God's. G4983
7: 4 The wife hath not power of her own **b**, G4983
4 not power of his own **b**, but the wife. G4983
34 be holy both in **b** and in spirit: but she G4983
9:27 But I keep under my **b**, and bring *it* into G4983
10:16 not the communion of the **b** of Christ? G4983
17 one bread, *and* one **b**: for we are all G4983
11:24 eat: this is my **b**, which is broken for G4983
27 be guilty of the **b** and blood of the Lord. G4983
29 to himself, not discerning the Lord's **b**. G4983
12:12 For as the **b** is one, and hath many G4983
12 of that one **b**, being many, are one G4983
12 being many, are one **b**: so also *is* Christ. G4983
13 baptized into one **b**, whether *we be* Jews G4983
14 For the **b** is not one member, but G4983
15 of the **b**; is it therefore not of the body? G4983
15 of the body; is it therefore not of the **b**? G4983
16 of the **b**; is it therefore not of the body? G4983
1Co 12:16 of the body; is it therefore not of the **b**? G4983
17 If the whole **b** *were* an eye, where *were* G4983
18 of them in the **b**, as it hath pleased him. G4983
19 were all one member, where *were* the **b**? G4983
20 *are they* many members, yet but one **b**. G4983
22 members of the **b**, which seem to be G4983
23 And those *members* of the **b**, which we G4983
24 hath tempered the **b** together, having G4983
25 That there should be no schism in the **b**; G4983
27 Now ye are the **b** of Christ, and G4983
13: 3 though I give my **b** to be burned, and G4983
15:35 up? and with what **b** do they come? G4983
37 sowest not that **b** that shall be, but bare G4983
38 But God giveth it a **b** as it hath pleased G4983
38 him, and to every seed his own **b**. G4983
44 It is sown a natural **b**; it is raised a G4983
44 is raised a spiritual **b**. There is a natural G4983
44 natural **b**, and there is a spiritual body. G4983
44 natural body, and there is a spiritual **b**. G4983
2Co 4:10 Always bearing about in the **b** the G4983
10 Jesus might be made manifest in our **b**. G4983
5: 6 in the **b**, we are absent from the Lord: G4983
8 the **b**, and to be present with the Lord. G4983
10 things *done* in *his* **b**, according to that G4983
12: 2 ago, (whether in the **b**, I cannot tell; or G4983
2 whether out of the **b**, I cannot tell: God G4983
3 (whether in the **b**, or out of the body, I G4983
3 of the **b**, I cannot tell: God knoweth;) G4983
Gal 6:17 in my **b** the marks of the Lord Jesus. G4983
Eph 1:23 Which is his **b**, the fulness of him that G4983
2:16 unto God in one **b** by the cross, having G4983
3: 6 and of the same **b**, and partakers of his G4954
4: 4 *There is* one **b**, and one Spirit, even as G4983
12 for the edifying of the **b** of Christ: G4983
16 From whom the whole **b** fitly joined G4983
16 the **b** unto the edifying of itself in love. G4983
5:23 church: and he is the saviour of the **b**. G4983
30 For we are members of his **b**, of his G4983
Php 1:20 my **b**, whether *it be* by life, or by death. G4983
3:21 Who shall change our vile **b**, that it may G4983
21 unto his glorious **b**, according to the G4983
Col 1:18 And he is the head of the **b**, the church: G4983
22 In the **b** of his flesh through death, to G4983
2:11 in putting off the **b** of the sins of the G4983
17 of things to come; but the **b** *is* of Christ. G4983
19 from which all the **b** by joints and G4983
23 neglecting of the **b**; not in any honour to G4983
3:15 are called in one **b**; and be ye thankful. G4983
1Th 5:23 and soul and **b** be preserved blameless G4983
Heb 10: 5 not, but a **b** hast thou prepared me: G4983
10 of the **b** of Jesus Christ once *for all*. G4983
13: 3 as being yourselves also in the **b**. G4983
Jas 2:16 are needful to the **b**; what *doth it* profit? G4983
26 For as the **b** without the spirit is dead, G4983
3: 2 *and* able also to bridle the whole **b**. G4983
3 us; and we turn about their whole **b**. G4983
6 defileth the whole **b**, and setteth on fire G4983
1Pt 2:24 sins in his own **b** on the tree, that we, G4983
Jude 9 about the **b** of Moses, durst not G4983

BODY'S
Col 1:24 for his **b** sake, which is the church: G4983

BOHAN
Jos 15: 6 up to the stone of **B** the son of Reuben: H932
18:17 to the stone of **B** the son of Reuben, H932

BOIL
Ex 9: 9 and shall be a **b** breaking forth *with* H7822
10 and it became a **b** breaking forth *with* H7822
11 of the boils; for the **b** was upon the H7822
Lev 8:31 and to his sons, **B** the flesh *at* the door H1310
13:18 the skin thereof, was a **b**, and is healed, H7822
19 And in the place of the **b** there be a H7822
20 a plague of leprosy broken out of the **b**. H7822
23 not, it *is* a burning **b**; and the priest H7822
2Ki 20: 7 and laid *it* on the **b**, and he recovered. H7822
Job 41:31 He maketh the deep to **b** like a pot: he H7570
Isa 38:21 upon the **b**, and he shall recover. H7822
64: 2 the waters to **b**, to make thy name H1158
Ezk 24: 5 it, *and* make it **b** well, and let them H7570
46:20 the priests shall **b** the trespass offering H1310
24 of them that **b**, where the ministers H1310
24 shall **b** the sacrifice of the people. H1310

BOILED
1Ki 19:21 slew them, and **b** their flesh with the H1310
2Ki 6:29 So we **b** my son, and did eat him: and I H1310
Job 30:27 My bowels **b**, and rested not: the days H7570

BOILING
Ezk 46:23 **b** places under the rows round about. H4018

BOILING-PLACES See BOILING and PLACES.

BOILS
Ex 9:11 because of the **b**; for the boil was upon H7822
Job 2: 7 Job with sore **b** from the sole of his H7822

BOISTEROUS
Mt 14:30 But when he saw the wind **b**, he was *G2478*

BOLD
Prv 28: 1 but the righteous are **b** as a lion. H982
Act 13:46 Then Paul and Barnabas waxed **b**, and *G3955*
Ro 10:20 But Esaias is very **b**, and saith, I was *G662*
2Co 10: 1 but being absent am **b** toward you: *G2292*
2 But I beseech *you*, that I may not be **b** *G2292*
2 I think to be **b** against some, which *G5111*
11:21 is **b**, (I speak foolishly,) I am bold also. *G5111*
21 is bold, (I speak foolishly,) I am **b** also. *G5111*
Php 1:14 more **b** to speak the word without fear. *G5111*
1Th 2: 2 Philippi, we were **b** in our God to speak *G3955*
Phlm 8 Wherefore, though I might be much **b** *G3954*

BOLDLY
Gen 34:25 upon the city **b**, and slew all the males. H983
Mk 15:43 came, and went in **b** unto Pilate, and *G5111*
Jn 7:26 But, lo, he speaketh **b**, and they say *G3954*
Act 9:27 **b** at Damascus in the name of Jesus. *G3955*
29 And he spake **b** in the name of the Lord *G3955*
14: 3 they speaking **b** in the Lord, which *G3955*
18:26 And he began to speak **b** in the *G3955*
19: 8 and spake **b** for the space of three *G3955*
Ro 15:15 written the more **b** unto you in some *G5112*
Eph 6:19 open my mouth **b**, to make known the *G1722*
20 I may speak **b**, as I ought to speak. *G3955*
Heb 4:16 Let us therefore come **b** unto the *G3326*
13: 6 So that we may **b** say, The Lord *is* my *G2292*

BOLDNESS
Ecc 8: 1 and the **b** of his face shall be changed. H5797
Act 4:13 Now when they saw the **b** of Peter and *G3954*
29 with all **b** they may speak thy word, *G3954*
31 and they spake the word of God with **b**. *G3954*
2Co 7: 4 Great *is* my **b** of speech toward you, *G3954*
Eph 3:12 In whom we have **b** and access with *G3954*
Php 1:20 but *that* with all **b**, as always, *so* now *G3954*
1Ti 3:13 **b** in the faith which is in Christ Jesus. *G3954*
Heb 10:19 Having therefore, brethren, **b** to enter *G3954*
1Jn 4:17 that we may have **b** in the day of *G3954*

BOLLED
Ex 9:31 *was* in the ear, and the flax *was* **b**. H1392

BOLSTER
1Sa 19:13 for his **b**, and covered *it* with a cloth. H4763
16 with a pillow of goats' *hair* for his **b**. H4763
26: 7 the ground at his **b**: but Abner and the H4763
11 **b**, and the cruse of water, and let us go. H4763
12 water from Saul's **b**; and they gat them H7226
16 and the cruse of water that *was* at his **b**. H4763

BOLT
2Sa 13:17 out from me, and **b** the door after her. H5274

BOLTED
2Sa 13:18 her out, and **b** the door after her. H5274

BOND
Nu 30: 2 his soul with a **b**; he shall not break his H632
3 bind herself by a **b**, *being* in her father's H632
4 And her father hear her vow, and her **b** H632
4 stand, and every **b** wherewith she hath H632
10 or bound her soul by a **b** with an oath; H632
11 stand, and every **b** wherewith she bound H632
12 or concerning the **b** of her soul, shall not H632
Job 12:18 He looseth the **b** of kings, and girdeth H4148
Ezk 20:37 bring you into the **b** of the covenant: H4562
Lk 13:16 loosed from this **b** on the sabbath day? *G1199*
Act 8:23 of bitterness, and *in* the **b** of iniquity. *G4886*
1Co 12:13 whether *we be* **b** or free; and have been *G1401*
Gal 3:28 there is neither **b** nor free, there is *G1401*
Eph 4: 3 the unity of the Spirit in the **b** of peace. *G4886*
6: 8 of the Lord, whether *he be* **b** or free. *G1401*
Col 3:11 **b** *nor* free: but Christ *is* all, and in all. *G1401*
14 charity, which is the **b** of perfectness. *G4886*
Rev 13:16 and poor, free and **b**, to receive a mark *G1401*
19:18 *both* free and **b**, both small and great. *G1401*

BONDAGE
Ex 1:14 bitter with hard **b**, in morter, and in H5656
2:23 by reason of the **b**, and they cried, and H5656
23 came up unto God by reason of the **b**. H5656
6: 5 the Egyptians keep in **b**; and I have H5647
6 you out of their **b**, and I will redeem you H5656
9 for anguish of spirit, and for cruel **b**. H5656
13: 3 out of the house of **b**; for by strength of H5650
14 us out from Egypt, from the house of **b**: H5650
20: 2 the land of Egypt, out of the house of **b**. H5650
Dt 5: 6 the land of Egypt, from the house of **b**. H5650
6:12 the land of Egypt, from the house of **b**. H5650
8:14 the land of Egypt, from the house of **b**; H5650
13: 5 out of the house of **b**, to thrust thee out H5650
10 the land of Egypt, from the house of **b**. H5650
26: 6 afflicted us, and laid upon us hard **b**: H5656
Jos 24:17 from the house of **b**, and which did H5650
Jdg 6: 8 brought you forth out of the house of **b**; H5650
Ezr 9: 8 and give us a little reviving in our **b**. H5659
9 forsaken us in our **b**, but hath extended H5659
Neh 5: 5 lo, we bring into **b** our sons and our H3533
5 are brought unto **b** *already*: neither *is it* H3533
18 the **b** was heavy upon this people. H5656
9:17 to return to their **b**: but thou *art* a God H5659
Isa 14: 3 **b** wherein thou wast made to serve, H5656
Jn 8:33 and were never in **b** to any man: how *G1398*
Act 7: 6 bring them into **b**, and entreat *them* evil *G1402*
7 they shall be in **b** will I judge, said God: *G1398*
Ro 8:15 For ye have not received the spirit of **b** *G1397*
21 delivered from the **b** of corruption into *G1397*
1Co 7:15 sister is not under **b** in such *cases*: but *G1402*
2Co 11:20 For ye suffer, if a man bring you into **b**, *G2615*
Gal 2: 4 Jesus, that they might bring us into **b**: *G2615*
4: 3 in **b** under the elements of the world: *G1402*
9 whereunto ye desire again to be in **b**? *G1398*
24 which gendereth to **b**, which is Agar. *G1397*
25 now is, and is in **b** with her children. *G1398*
5: 1 not entangled again with the yoke of **b**. *G1397*
Heb 2:15 were all their lifetime subject to **b**. *G1397*
2Pt 2:19 of the same is he brought in **b**. *G1402*

BONDMAID
Lev 19:20 a woman, that *is* a **b**, betrothed to an H8198
Gal 4:22 one by a **b**, the other by a freewoman. *G3814*

BONDMAIDS
Lev 25:44 Both thy bondmen, and thy **b**, which H519
44 of them shall ye buy bondmen and **b**. H519

BONDMAN
Gen 44:33 of the lad a **b** to my lord; and let the H5650
Dt 15:15 that thou wast a **b** in the land of Egypt, H5650
16:12 that thou wast a **b** in Egypt: and thou H5650
24:18 that thou wast a **b** in Egypt, and the H5650
22 that thou wast a **b** in the land of Egypt: H5650
Rev 6:15 men, and every **b**, and every free man, *G1401*

BONDMEN
Gen 43:18 us, and take us for **b**, and our asses. H5650
44: 9 him die, and we also will be my lord's **b**. H5650
Lev 25:42 of Egypt: they shall not be sold as **b**. H5650
44 Both thy **b**, and thy bondmaids, which H5650
44 of them shall ye buy **b** and bondmaids. H5650
46 they shall be your **b** for ever: but over H5647
26:13 not be their **b**; and I have broken the H5650
Dt 6:21 We were Pharaoh's **b** in Egypt; and the H5650
7: 8 out of the house of **b**, from the hand of H5650
28:68 your enemies for **b** and bondwomen, H5650
Jos 9:23 freed from being **b**, and hewers of wood H5650
1Ki 9:22 Solomon make no **b**: but they *were* men H5650
2Ki 4: 1 to take unto him my two sons to be **b**. H5650
2Ch 28:10 and Jerusalem for **b** and bondwomen H5650
Ezr 9: 9 For we *were* **b**; yet our God hath not H5650
Est 7: 4 had been sold for **b** and bondwomen, I H5650
Jer 34:13 of Egypt, out of the house of **b**, saying, H5650

BONDS
Nu 30: 5 her vows, or of her **b** wherewith she hath H632
7 stand, and her **b** wherewith she bound H632
14 all her vows, or all her **b**, which *are* upon H632
Ps 116:16 thine handmaid: thou hast loosed my **b**. H4147
Jer 5: 5 broken the yoke, *and* burst the **b**. H4147
27: 2 to me; Make thee **b** and yokes, and put H4147
30: 8 and will burst thy **b**, and strangers shall H4147
Nah 1:13 off thee, and will burst thy **b** in sunder. H4147
Act 20:23 saying that **b** and afflictions abide me. *G1199*
23:29 to his charge worthy of death or of **b**. *G1199*
25:14 is a certain man left in **b** by Felix: *G1198*
26:29 altogether such as I am, except these **b**. *G1199*
Act 26:31 doeth nothing worthy of death or of **b**. *G1199*
Eph 6:20 For which I am an ambassador in **b**: that *G254*
Php 1: 7 as both in my **b**, and in the defence and *G1199*
13 So that my **b** in Christ are manifest in *G1199*
14 confident by my **b**, are much more bold *G1199*
16 supposing to add affliction to my **b**: *G1199*
Col 4: 3 of Christ, for which I am also in **b**: *G1210*
18 my **b**. Grace *be* with you. Amen. *G1199*
2Ti 2: 9 **b**; but the word of God is not bound. *G1199*
Phlm 10 whom I have begotten in my **b**: *G1199*
13 unto me in the **b** of the gospel: *G1199*
Heb 10:34 For ye had compassion of me in my **b**, *G1199*
11:36 yea, moreover of **b** and imprisonment: *G1199*
13: 3 Remember them that are in **b**, as bound *G1198*

BONDSERVANT
Lev 25:39 shalt not compel him to serve as a **b**: H5650

BONDSERVICE
1Ki 9:21 levy a tribute of **b** unto this day. H5647

BONDWOMAN
Gen 21:10 Cast out this **b** and her son: for the H519
10 for the son of this **b** shall not be heir with H519
12 and because of thy **b**; in all that Sarah H519
13 And also of the son of the **b** will I make a H519
Gal 4:23 But he *who was* of the **b** was born after *G3814*
30 Cast out the **b** and her son: for the *G3814*
30 for the son of the **b** shall not be heir *G3814*
31 are not children of the **b**, but of the free. *G3814*

BONDWOMEN
Dt 28:68 and **b**, and no man shall buy *you*. H8198
2Ch 28:10 for bondmen and **b** unto you: *but are* H8198
Est 7: 4 sold for bondmen and **b**, I had held my H8198

BONE
Gen 2:23 And Adam said, This *is* now **b** of my H6106
29:14 thou *art* my **b** and my flesh. And he H6106
Ex 12:46 neither shall ye break a **b** thereof. H6106
Nu 9:12 nor break any **b** of it: according to all H6106
19:16 or a dead body, or a **b** of a man, or a H6106
18 **b**, or one slain, or one dead, or a grave: H6106
Jdg 9: 2 also that I *am* your **b** and your flesh. H6106
2Sa 5: 1 Behold, we *are* thy **b** and thy flesh. H6106
19:13 *Art* thou not of my **b**, and of my flesh? H6106
1Ch 11: 1 Behold, we *are* thy **b** and thy flesh. H6106
Job 2: 5 and touch his **b** and his flesh, and he H6106
19:20 My **b** cleaveth to my skin and to my H6106
31:22 and mine arm be broken from the **b**. H7070
Ps 3: 7 *upon* the cheek **b**; thou hast broken the H3895
Prv 25:15 and a soft tongue breaketh the **b**. H1634
Ezk 37: 7 the bones came together, **b** to his bone. H6106
7 the bones came together, bone to his **b**. H6106
39:15 *any* seeth a man's **b**, then shall he set up H6106
Jn 19:36 A **b** of him shall not be broken. *G3747*

BONES
Gen 2:23 *is* now bone of my **b**, and flesh of my H6106
50:25 and ye shall carry up my **b** from hence. H6106
Ex 13:19 And Moses took the **b** of Joseph with H6106
19 carry up my **b** away hence with you. H6106
Nu 24: 8 and shall break their **b**, and pierce *them* H6106
Jos 24:32 And the **b** of Joseph, which the children H6106
Jdg 19:29 *together* with her **b**, into twelve pieces, H6106
1Sa 31:13 And they took their **b**, and buried *them* H6106
2Sa 19:12 Ye *are* my brethren, ye *are* my **b** and H6106
21:12 And David went and took the **b** of Saul H6106
12 of Saul and the **b** of Jonathan his son H6106
13 And he brought up from thence the **b** H6106
13 of Saul and the **b** of Jonathan his son; H6106
13 the **b** of them that were hanged. H6106
14 And the **b** of Saul and Jonathan his son H6106
1Ki 13: 2 and men's **b** shall be burnt upon thee. H6106
31 *is* buried; lay my **b** beside his bones: H6106
31 *is* buried; lay my bones beside his **b**: H6106
2Ki 13:21 and touched the **b** of Elisha, he revived, H6106
23:14 filled their places with the **b** of men. H6106
16 and sent, and took the **b** out of the H6106
18 let no man move his **b**. So they let his H6106
18 So they let his **b** alone, with the bones H6106
18 alone, with the **b** of the prophet that H6106
20 and burned men's **b** upon them, and H6106
1Ch 10:12 and buried their **b** under the oak in H6106
2Ch 34: 5 And he burnt the **b** of the priests upon H6106
Job 4:14 which made all my **b** to shake. H6106
10:11 and hast fenced me with **b** and sinews. H6106
20:11 His **b** are full *of the sin* of his youth, H6106
21:24 His breasts are full of milk, and his **b** H6106

Job 30:17 My **b** are pierced in me in the night H6106
30 My skin is black upon me, and my **b** H6106
33:19 the multitude of his **b** with strong *pain*: H6106
21 and his **b** *that* were not seen stick out. H6106
40:18 His **b** *are as* strong pieces of brass; his H6106
18 of brass; his **b** *are* like bars of iron. H1634
Ps 6: 2 heal me; for my **b** are vexed. H6106
22:14 water, and all my **b** are out of joint: my H6106
17 I may tell all my **b**: they look *and* stare H6106
31:10 mine iniquity, and my **b** are consumed. H6106
32: 3 When I kept silence, my **b** waxed old H6106
34:20 He keepeth all his **b**: not one of them is H6106
35:10 All my **b** shall say, LORD, who *is* like H6106
38: 3 *any* rest in my **b** because of my sin. H6106
42:10 *As* with a sword in my **b**, mine enemies H6106
51: 8 **b** *which* thou hast broken may rejoice. H6106
53: 5 God hath scattered the **b** of him that H6106
102: 3 and my **b** are burned as an hearth. H6106
5 of my groaning my **b** cleave to my skin. H6106
109:18 bowels like water, and like oil into his **b**. H6106
141: 7 Our **b** are scattered at the grave's H6106
Prv 3: 8 to thy navel, and marrow to thy **b**. H6106
12: 4 ashamed *is* as rottenness in his **b**. H6106
14:30 flesh: but envy the rottenness of the **b**. H6106
15:30 *and* a good report maketh the **b** fat. H6106
16:24 sweet to the soul, and health to the **b**. H6106
17:22 but a broken spirit drieth the **b**. H1634
Ecc 11: 5 the spirit, *nor* how the **b** *do grow* in the H6106
Isa 38:13 will he break all my **b**: from day *even* to H6106
58:11 and make fat thy **b**: and thou shalt be H6106
66:14 rejoice, and your **b** shall flourish like H6106
Jer 8: 1 shall bring out the **b** of the kings of H6106
1 of Judah, and the **b** of his princes, and H6106
1 princes, and the **b** of the priests, and H6106
1 priests, and the **b** of the prophets, and H6106
1 prophets, and the **b** of the inhabitants H6106
20: 9 fire shut up in my **b**, and I was weary H6106
23: 9 prophets; all my **b** shake; I am like a H6106
50:17 king of Babylon hath broken his **b**. H6105
Lam 1:13 From above hath he sent fire into my **b**, H6106
3: 4 hath he made old; he hath broken my **b**. H6106
4: 8 cleaveth to their **b**; it is withered, it is H6106
Ezk 6: 5 scatter your **b** round about your altars. H6106
24: 4 the shoulder; fill *it* with the choice **b**. H6106
5 and burn also the **b** under it, *and* make H6106
5 and let them seethe the **b** of it therein. H6106
10 spice it well, and let the **b** be burned. H6106
32:27 be upon their **b**, though *they were* the H6106
37: 1 midst of the valley which *was* full of **b**, H6106
3 Son of man, can these **b** live? And I H6106
4 upon these **b**, and say unto them, H6106
4 O ye dry **b**, hear the word of the LORD. H6106
5 Thus saith the Lord GOD unto these **b**; H6106
7 the **b** came together, bone to his bone. H6106
11 me, Son of man, these **b** are the whole H6106
11 they say, Our **b** are dried, and our hope H6106
Dan 6:24 and brake all their **b** in pieces or ever H1635
Am 2: 1 the **b** of the king of Edom into lime: H6106
6:10 to bring out the **b** out of the house, and H6106
Mic 3: 2 them, and their flesh from off their **b**; H6106
3 they break their **b**, and chop them in H6106
Hab 3:16 entered into my **b**, and I trembled in H6106
Zep 3: 3 they gnaw not the **b** till the morrow. H1633
Mt 23:27 of dead *men's* **b**, and of all uncleanness. *G3747*
Lk 24:39 hath not flesh and **b**, as ye see me have. *G3747*
Act 3: 7 his feet and ankle **b** received strength. *G4974*
Eph 5:30 of his body, of his flesh, and of his **b**. *G3747*
Heb 11:22 gave commandment concerning his **b**. *G3747*

BONNETS
Ex 28:40 them girdles, and **b** shalt thou make H4021
29: 9 sons, and put the **b** on them: and the H4021
39:28 And a mitre *of* fine linen, and goodly **b** H4021
Lev 8:13 girdles, and put **b** upon them; as the H4021
Isa 3:20 The **b**, and the ornaments of the legs, H6287
Ezk 44:18 They shall have linen **b** upon their H6287

BOOK
Gen 5: 1 This *is* the **b** of the generations of H5612
Ex 17:14 *for* a memorial in a **b**, and rehearse *it* in H5612
24: 7 And he took the **b** of the covenant, and H5612
32:32 out of thy **b** which thou hast written. H5612
33 against me, him will I blot out of my **b**. H5612
Nu 5:23 these curses in a **b**, and he shall blot H5612
21:14 Wherefore it is said in the **b** of the wars H5612
Dt 17:18 of this law in a **b** out of *that which is* H5612
28:58 are written in this **b**, that thou mayest H5612
61 *is* not written in the **b** of this law, them H5612
29:20 are written in this **b** shall lie upon him, H5612
29:21 that are written in this **b** of the law: H5612
27 all the curses that are written in this **b**: H5612
30:10 are written in this **b** of the law, *and* if H5612
31:24 this law in a **b**, until they were finished, H5612
26 Take this **b** of the law, and put it in the H5612
Jos 1: 8 This **b** of the law shall not depart out of H5612
8:31 as it is written in the **b** of the law of H5612
34 to all that is written in the **b** of the law. H5612
10:13 this written in the **b** of Jasher? So the H5612
18: 9 seven parts in a **b**, and came *again* to H5612
23: 6 is written in the **b** of the law of Moses, H5612
24:26 And Joshua wrote these words in the **b** H5612
1Sa 10:25 and wrote *it* in a **b**, and laid *it* up before H5612
2Sa 1:18 behold, *it is* written in the **b** of Jasher.) H5612
1Ki 11:41 written in the **b** of the acts of Solomon? H5612
14:19 *are* written in the **b** of the chronicles of H5612
29 not written in the **b** of the chronicles of H5612
15: 7 not written in the **b** of the chronicles of H5612
23 not written in the **b** of the chronicles of H5612
31 not written in the **b** of the chronicles of H5612
16: 5 not written in the **b** of the chronicles of H5612
14 not written in the **b** of the chronicles of H5612
20 not written in the **b** of the chronicles of H5612
27 not written in the **b** of the chronicles of H5612
22:39 not written in the **b** of the chronicles of H5612
45 not written in the **b** of the chronicles of H5612
2Ki 1:18 not written in the **b** of the chronicles of H5612
8:23 not written in the **b** of the chronicles of H5612
10:34 not written in the **b** of the chronicles of H5612
12:19 not written in the **b** of the chronicles of H5612
13: 8 not written in the **b** of the chronicles of H5612
12 not written in the **b** of the chronicles of H5612
14: 6 is written in the **b** of the law of Moses, H5612
15 not written in the **b** of the chronicles of H5612
18 not written in the **b** of the chronicles of H5612
28 not written in the **b** of the chronicles of H5612
15: 6 not written in the **b** of the chronicles of H5612
11 *are* written in the **b** of the chronicles of H5612
15 *are* written in the **b** of the chronicles of H5612
21 not written in the **b** of the chronicles of H5612
26 *are* written in the **b** of the chronicles of H5612
31 *are* written in the **b** of the chronicles of H5612
36 not written in the **b** of the chronicles of H5612
16:19 not written in the **b** of the chronicles of H5612
20:20 not written in the **b** of the chronicles of H5612
21:17 not written in the **b** of the chronicles of H5612
25 not written in the **b** of the chronicles of H5612
22: 8 I have found the **b** of the law in the H5612
8 gave the **b** to Shaphan, and he read it. H5612
10 **b**. And Shaphan read it before the king. H5612
11 **b** of the law, that he rent his clothes. H5612
13 the words of this **b** that is found: for H5612
13 the words of this **b**, to do according H5612
16 **b** which the king of Judah hath read: H5612
23: 2 all the words of the **b** of the covenant H5612
3 written in this **b**. And all the people H5612
21 as *it is* written in the **b** of this covenant. H5612
24 written in the **b** that Hilkiah the priest H5612
28 not written in the **b** of the chronicles of H5612
24: 5 not written in the **b** of the chronicles of H5612
1Ch 9: 1 written in the **b** of the kings of Israel H5612
29:29 *are* written in the **b** of Samuel the seer, H1697
29 the seer, and in the **b** of Nathan the H1697
29 prophet, and in the **b** of Gad the seer, H1697
2Ch 9:29 they not written in the **b** of Nathan the H1697
12:15 not written in the **b** of Shemaiah the H1697
16:11 the **b** of the kings of Judah and Israel. H5612
17: 9 and *had* the **b** of the law of the LORD H5612
20:34 *are* written in the **b** of Jehu the son of H1697
34 in the **b** of the kings of Israel. H5612
24:27 in the story of the **b** of the kings. And H5612
25: 4 in the law in the **b** of Moses, where the H5612
26 the **b** of the kings of Judah and Israel? H5612
27: 7 the **b** of the kings of Israel and Judah. H5612
28:26 the **b** of the kings of Judah and Israel. H5612
32:32 the **b** of the kings of Judah and Israel. H5612
33:18 *written* in the **b** of the kings of Israel. H1697
34:14 the priest found a **b** of the law of the H5612
15 I have found the **b** of the law in the H5612
15 Hilkiah delivered the **b** to Shaphan. H5612
16 And Shaphan carried the **b** to the king, H5612
18 **b**. And Shaphan read it before the king. H5612
21 the words of the **b** that is found: for H5612
21 to do after all that is written in this **b**. H5612
24 are written in the **b** which they have H5612
30 the words of the **b** of the covenant that H5612
31 covenant which are written in this **b**. H5612
35:12 *it is* written in the **b** of Moses. And so H5612
27 the **b** of the kings of Israel and Judah. H5612
2Ch 36: 8 they *are* written in the **b** of the kings of H5612
Ezr 4:15 That search may be made in the **b** of H5609
15 thou find in the **b** of the records, and H5609
6:18 as it is written in the **b** of Moses. H5609
Neh 8: 1 the scribe to bring the **b** of the law of H5612
3 *were attentive* unto the **b** of the law. H5612
5 And Ezra opened the **b** in the sight of H5612
8 So they read in the **b** in the law of God H5612
18 day, he read in the **b** of the law of God. H5612
9: 3 and read in the **b** of the law of the H5612
12:23 written in the **b** of the chronicles, even H5612
13: 1 On that day they read in the **b** of Moses H5612
Est 2:23 the **b** of the chronicles before the king. H5612
6: 1 to bring the **b** of records of the H5612
9:32 of Purim; and it was written in the **b**. H5612
10: 2 not written in the **b** of the chronicles of H5612
Job 19:23 oh that they were printed in a **b**! H5612
31:35 *that* mine adversary had written a **b**. H5612
Ps 40: 7 the volume of the **b** *it is* written of me, H5612
56: 8 into thy bottle: *are they* not in thy **b**? H5612
69:28 Let them be blotted out of the **b** of the H5612
139:16 and in thy **b** all *my members* were H5612
Isa 29:11 you as the words of a **b** that is sealed, H5612
12 And the **b** is delivered to him that is H5612
18 the words of the **b**, and the eyes of the H5612
30: 8 and note it in a **b**, that it may be for the H5612
34:16 Seek ye out of the **b** of the LORD, and H5612
Jer 25:13 that is written in this **b**, which Jeremiah H5612
30: 2 that I have spoken unto thee in a **b**. H5612
32:12 that subscribed the **b** of the purchase, H5612
36: 2 Take thee a roll of a **b**, and write therein H5612
4 spoken unto him, upon a roll of a **b**. H5612
8 reading in the **b** the words of the LORD H5612
10 Then read Baruch in the **b** the words of H5612
11 out of the **b** all the words of the LORD, H5612
13 read the **b** in the ears of the people. H5612
18 and I wrote *them* with ink in the **b**. H5612
32 all the words of the **b** which Jehoiakim H5612
45: 1 these words in a **b** at the mouth of H5612
51:60 So Jeremiah wrote in a **b** all the evil H5612
63 of reading this **b**, *that* thou shalt bind H5612
Ezk 2: 9 me; and, lo, a roll of a **b** *was* therein; H5612
Dan 12: 1 one that shall be found written in the **b**. H5612
4 and seal the **b**, *even* to the time of the H5612
Nah 1: 1 The burden of Nineveh. The **b** of the H5612
Mal 3:16 heard *it*, and a **b** of remembrance was H5612
Mt 1: 1 The **b** of the generation of Jesus Christ, *G976*
Mk 12:26 ye not read in the **b** of Moses, how in the *G976*
Lk 3: 4 As it is written in the **b** of the words of *G976*
4:17 And there was delivered unto him the **b** *G975*
17 he had opened the **b**, he found the place *G975*
20 And he closed the **b**, and he gave *it* again *G975*
20:42 And David himself saith in the **b** of *G976*
Jn 20:30 disciples, which are not written in this **b**: *G975*
Act 1:20 For it is written in the **b** of Psalms, Let *G976*
7:42 it is written in the **b** of the prophets, O ye *G976*
Gal 3:10 written in the **b** of the law to do them. *G975*
Php 4: 3 whose names *are* in the **b** of life. *G976*
Heb 9:19 sprinkled both the **b**, and all the people, *G975*
10: 7 the volume of the **b** it is written of me,) *G975*
Rev 1:11 seest, write in a **b**, and send *it* unto the *G975*
3: 5 his name out of the **b** of life, but I will *G976*
5: 1 sat on the throne a **b** written within and *G975*
2 open the **b**, and to loose the seals thereof? *G975*
3 to open the **b**, neither to look thereon. *G975*
4 to read the **b**, neither to look thereon. *G975*
5 **b**, and to loose the seven seals thereof. *G975*
7 And he came and took the **b** out of the *G975*
8 And when he had taken the **b**, the four *G975*
9 art worthy to take the **b**, and to open the *G975*
10: 2 And he had in his hand a little **b** open: *G974*
8 *and* take the little **b** which is open in the *G974*
9 Give me the little **b**. And he said unto me, *G974*
10 And I took the little **b** out of the angel's *G974*
13: 8 not written in the **b** of life of the Lamb *G976*
17: 8 were not written in the **b** of life from the *G975*
20:12 and another **b** was opened, which is *G975*
12 which is *the* **b** of life: and the dead *G976*
15 the **b** of life was cast into the lake of fire. *G976*
21:27 which are written in the Lamb's **b** of life. *G975*
22: 7 the sayings of the prophecy of this **b**. *G975*
9 keep the sayings of this **b**: worship God. *G975*
10 of this **b**: for the time is at hand. *G975*
18 prophecy of this **b**, If any man shall add *G975*
18 him the plagues that are written in this **b**: *G975*
19 the words of the **b** of this prophecy, God *G976*
19 his part out of the **b** of life, and out of the *G976*
19 the things which are written in this **b**. *G975*

BOOKS
Ecc 12:12 of making many **b** *there is* no end; and H5612
Dan 7:10 was set, and the **b** were opened. H5609
9: 2 understood by **b** the number of the H5612
Jn 21:25 the **b** that should be written. Amen. *G975*
Act 19:19 arts brought their **b** together, and *G976*
2Ti 4:13 and the **b**, *but* especially the parchments. *G975*
Rev 20:12 before God; and the **b** were opened: and *G975*
12 in the **b**, according to their works. *G975*

BOOTH
Job 27:18 and as a **b** *that* the keeper maketh. H5521
Jna 4: 5 there made him a **b**, and sat under it in H5521

BOOTHS
Gen 33:17 an house, and made **b** for his cattle: H5521
Lev 23:42 Ye shall dwell in **b** seven days; all that H5521
42 that are Israelites born shall dwell in **b**: H5521
43 of Israel to dwell in **b**, when I brought H5521
Neh 8:14 in **b** in the feast of the seventh month: H5521
15 of thick trees, to make **b**, as *it is* written. H5521
16 made themselves **b**, every one upon the H5521
17 the captivity made **b**, and sat under the H5521
17 and sat under the **b**: for since the days H5521

BOOTIES
Hab 2: 7 and thou shalt be for **b** unto them? H4933

BOOTY
Nu 31:32 And the **b**, *being* the rest of the prey H4455
Jer 49:32 And their camels shall be a **b**, and the H957
Zep 1:13 Therefore their goods shall become a **b**, H4933

BOOZ
Mt 1: 5 And Salmon begat **B** of Rachab; and *G1003*
5 of Rachab; and **B** begat Obed of Ruth; *G1003*
Lk 3:32 was *the son* of **B**, which was *the son* of *G1003*

BORDER
Gen 10:19 And the **b** of the Canaanites was from H1366
49:13 of ships; and his **b** *shall be* unto Zidon. H3411
Ex 19:12 mount, or touch the **b** of it: whosoever H7097
25:25 And thou shalt make unto it a **b** of an H4526
25 crown to the **b** thereof round about. H4526
27 Over against the **b** shall the rings be for H4526
28:26 breastplate in the **b** thereof, which *is* in H8193
37:12 Also he made thereunto a **b** of an H4526
12 of gold for the **b** thereof round about. H4526
14 Over against the **b** were the rings, the H4526
39:19 upon the **b** of it, which *was* on H8193
Nu 20:16 Kadesh, a city in the uttermost of thy **b**: H1366
21 through his **b**: wherefore Israel turned H1366
21:13 for Arnon *is* the **b** of Moab, between H1366
15 of Ar, and lieth upon the **b** of Moab. H1366
23 pass through his **b**: but Sihon gathered H1366
24 of Ammon: for the **b** of the children of H1366
22:36 which *is* in the **b** of Arnon, which *is* in H1366
33:44 pitched in Ijeabarim, in the **b** of Moab. H1366
34: 3 and your south **b** shall be the outmost H1366
4 And your **b** shall turn from the south to H1366
5 And the **b** shall fetch a compass from H1366
6 And *as for* the western **b**, ye shall even H1366
6 for a **b**: this shall be your west border. H1366
6 for a border: this shall be your west **b**. H1366
7 And this shall be your north **b**: from the H1366
8 point out *your* **b** unto the entrance of
8 goings forth of the **b** shall be to Zedad: H1366
9 And the **b** shall go on to Ziphron, and H1366
9 Hazar-enan: this shall be your north **b**. H1366
10 And ye shall point out your east **b** from H1366
11 of Ain; and the **b** shall descend, and H1366
12 And the **b** shall go down to Jordan, and H1366
35:26 come without the **b** of the city of his H1366
Dt 3:16 the valley, and the **b** even unto the river H1366
16 *is* the **b** of the children of Ammon; H1366
12:20 shall enlarge thy **b**, as he hath promised H1366
Jos 4:19 in Gilgal, in the east **b** of Jericho. H7097
12: 2 *is* the **b** of the children of Ammon; H1366
5 all Bashan, unto the **b** of the Geshurites H1366
5 Gilead, the **b** of Sihon king of Heshbon. H1366
13:10 unto the **b** of the children of Ammon; H1366
11 And Gilead, and the **b** of the Geshurites H1366
23 And the **b** of the children of Reuben H1366
23 Jordan, and the **b** *thereof*. This *was* the H1366
26 from Mahanaim unto the **b** of Debir; H1366
27 Jordan and *his* **b**, *even* unto the edge H1366
15: 1 *even* to the **b** of Edom the wilderness H1366
2 And their south **b** was from the shore H1366
5 And the east **b** *was* the salt sea, *even* H1366
Jos 15: 5 of Jordan. And *their* **b** in the north H1366
6 And the **b** went up to Beth-hogla, and H1366
6 and the **b** went up to the stone H1366
7 And the **b** went up toward Debir from H1366
7 the river: and the **b** passed toward the H1366
8 And the **b** went up by the valley of the H1366
8 and the **b** went up to the top of H1366
9 And the **b** was drawn from the top of H1366
9 mount Ephron; and the **b** was drawn to H1366
10 And the **b** compassed from Baalah H1366
11 And the **b** went out unto the side of H1366
11 and the **b** was drawn to Shicron, H1366
11 the goings out of the **b** were at the sea. H1366
12 And the west **b** *was* to the great sea, H1366
47 and the great sea, and the **b** *thereof*: H1366
16: 5 And the **b** of the children of Ephraim H1366
5 families was *thus*: even the **b** of their H1366
6 And the **b** went out toward the sea to H1366
6 side; and the **b** went about eastward H1366
8 The **b** went out from Tappuah H1366
17: 7 Shechem; and the **b** went along on the H1366
8 but Tappuah on the **b** of Manasseh H1366
10 and the sea is his **b**; and they met H1366
18:12 And their **b** on the north side was from H1366
12 Jordan; and the **b** went up to the side H1366
13 And the **b** went over from thence H1366
13 and the **b** descended to Ataroth-adar, H1366
14 And the **b** was drawn *thence*, and H1366
15 and the **b** went out on the west, H1366
16 And the **b** came down to the end of the H1366
19 And the **b** passed along to the side of H1366
19 the outgoings of the **b** were at the north H1366
20 And Jordan was the **b** of it on the east H1379
19:10 **b** of their inheritance was unto Sarid: H1366
11 And their **b** went up toward the sea, H1366
12 unto the **b** of Chisloth-tabor, and H1366
14 And the **b** compasseth it on the north H1366
18 And their **b** was toward Jezreel, and H1366
22 the outgoings of their **b** were at Jordan: H1366
25 And their **b** was Helkath, and Hali, and H1366
46 and Rakkon, with the **b** before Japho. H1366
22:25 For the LORD hath made Jordan a **b** H1366
24:30 And they buried him in the **b** of his H1366
Jdg 2: 9 And they buried him in the **b** of his H1366
7:22 the **b** of Abel-meholah, unto Tabbath. H8193
11:18 not within the **b** of Moab: for Arnon H1366
18 of Moab: for Arnon *was* the **b** of Moab. H1366
1Sa 6:12 after them unto the **b** of Beth-shemesh. H1366
10: 2 sepulchre in the **b** of Benjamin at H1366
13:18 *to* the way of the **b** that looketh to the H1366
2Sa 8: 3 to recover his **b** at the river Euphrates. H3027
1Ki 4:21 and unto the **b** of Egypt: they brought H1366
2Ki 3:21 and upward, and stood in the **b**. H1366
2Ch 9:26 of the Philistines, and to the **b** of Egypt. H1366
Ps 78:54 And he brought them to the **b** of his H1366
Prv 15:25 but he will establish the **b** of the widow. H1366
Isa 19:19 a pillar at the **b** thereof to the LORD. H1366
37:24 of his **b**, *and* the forest of his Carmel. H7093
Jer 31:17 shall come again to their own **b**. H1366
50:26 Come against her from the utmost **b**, H7093
Ezk 11:10 will judge you in the **b** of Israel; and ye H1366
11 *but* I will judge you in the **b** of Israel: H1366
29:10 of Syene even unto the **b** of Ethiopia. H1366
43:13 a cubit, and the **b** thereof by the edge H1366
17 thereof; and the **b** about it *shall be* half H1366
20 and upon the **b** round about: thus shalt H1366
45: 7 from the west **b** unto the east border. H1366
7 from the west border unto the east **b**. H1366
47:13 This *shall be* the **b**, whereby ye shall H1366
15 And this *shall be* the **b** of the land H1366
16 *is* between the **b** of Damascus and the H1366
16 and the **b** of Hamath; Hazar-hatticon, H1366
17 And the **b** from the sea shall be H1366
17 Hazar-enan, the **b** of Damascus, and H1366
17 and the **b** of Hamath. And *this* H1366
18 *by* Jordan, from the **b** unto the east sea. H1366
20 great sea from the **b**, till a man come H1366
48: 1 Hazar-enan, the **b** of Damascus H1366
2 And by the **b** of Dan, from the east side H1366
3 And by the **b** of Asher, from the east H1366
4 And by the **b** of Naphtali, from the east H1366
5 And by the **b** of Manasseh, from the H1366
6 And by the **b** of Ephraim, from the east H1366
7 And by the **b** of Reuben, from the east H1366
8 And by the **b** of Judah, from the east H1366
12 thing most holy by the **b** of the Levites. H1366
13 And over against the **b** of the priests H1366
21 toward the east **b**, and westward over H1366
21 toward the west **b**, over against the H1366
Ezk 48:22 between the **b** of Judah and the border H1366
22 **b** of Benjamin, shall be for the prince. H1366
24 And by the **b** of Benjamin, from the H1366
25 And by the **b** of Simeon, from the east H1366
26 And by the **b** of Issachar, from the east H1366
27 And by the **b** of Zebulun, from the east H1366
28 And by the **b** of Gad, at the south side H1366
28 southward, the **b** shall be even from H1366
Joel 3: 6 ye might remove them far from their **b**. H1366
Am 1:13 Gilead, that they might enlarge their **b**: H1366
6: 2 or their **b** greater than your border? H1366
2 or their border greater than your **b**? H1366
Oba 7 thee *even* to the **b**: the men that were at H1366
Zep 2: 8 magnified *themselves* against their **b**. H1366
Zec 9: 2 And Hamath also shall **b** thereby; H1379
Mal 1: 4 call them, The **b** of wickedness, and, H1366
5 will be magnified from the **b** of Israel. H1366
Mk 6:56 if it were but the **b** of his garment: and *G2899*
Lk 8:44 Came behind *him*, and touched the **b** *G2899*

BORDERS
Gen 23:17 all the **b** round about, were made sure H1366
47:21 *one* end of the **b** of Egypt even to the H1366
Ex 8: 2 behold, I will smite all thy **b** with frogs: H1366
16:35 came unto the **b** of the land of Canaan. H7097
34:24 and enlarge thy **b**: neither shall any H1366
Nu 15:38 them fringes in the **b** of their garments H3671
38 the fringe of the **b** a ribband of blue: H3671
20:17 to the left, until we have passed thy **b**. H1366
21:22 king's *high* way, until we be past thy **b**. H1366
35:27 find him without the **b** of the city of his H1366
Jos 11: 2 valley, and in the **b** of Dor on the west, H5299
13: 2 the **b** of the Philistines, and all Geshuri, H1552
3 even unto the **b** of Ekron northward, H1366
4 unto Aphek, to the **b** of the Amorites: H1366
16: 2 along unto the **b** of Archi to Ataroth, H1366
22:10 And when they came unto the **b** of H1552
11 of Canaan, in the **b** of Jordan, at the H1552
1Ki 7:28 *manner*: they had **b**, and the borders H4526
28 and the **b** *were* between the ledges: H4526
29 And on the **b** that *were* between the H4526
31 with their **b**, foursquare, not round. H4526
32 And under the **b** *were* four wheels; and H4526
35 and the **b** thereof *were* of the same. H4526
36 thereof, and on the **b** thereof, he graved H4526
2Ki 16:17 And king Ahaz cut off the **b** of the H4526
18: 8 Gaza, and the **b** thereof, from the tower H1366
19:23 his **b**, *and into* the forest of his Carmel. H7093
1Ch 5:16 all the suburbs of Sharon, upon their **b**. H8444
7:29 And by the **b** of the children of H3027
Ps 74:17 Thou hast set all the **b** of the earth: H1367
147:14 He maketh peace *in* thy **b**, *and* filleth H1366
Song 1:11 We will make thee **b** of gold with studs H8447
Isa 15: 8 For the cry is gone round about the **b** of H1366
54:12 and all thy **b** of pleasant stones. H1366
60:18 within thy **b**; but thou shalt call thy H1366
Jer 15:13 *that* for all thy sins, even in all thy **b**. H1366
17: 3 high places for sin, throughout all thy **b**. H1366
Ezk 27: 4 Thy **b** *are* in the midst of the seas, thy H1366
45: 1 holy in all the **b** thereof round about. H1366
Mic 5: 6 and when he treadeth within our **b**. H1366
Mt 4:13 in the **b** of Zabulon and Nephthalim: *G3725*
23: 5 and enlarge the **b** of their garments, *G2899*
Mk 7:24 and went into the **b** of Tyre and Sidon, *G3181*

BORE
Ex 21: 6 his master shall **b** his ear through with H7527
Job 41: 2 or **b** his jaw through with a thorn? H5344

BORED
2Ki 12: 9 took a chest, and **b** a hole in the lid of H5344

BORN
Gen 4:18 And unto Enoch was **b** Irad: and Irad H3205
26 And to Seth, to him also there was **b** a H3205
6: 1 and daughters were **b** unto them, H3205
10: 1 unto them were sons **b** after the flood. H3205
21 the elder, even to him were *children* **b**. H3205
25 And unto Eber were **b** two sons: the H3205
14:14 trained *servants*, **b** in his own house, H3211
15: 3 and, lo, one **b** in my house is mine heir. H1121
17:12 he that is **b** in the house, or bought H3211
13 He that is **b** in thy house, and he that is H3211
17 Shall *a child* be **b** unto him that is an H3205
23 and all that were **b** in his house, and all H3211
27 And all the men of his house, **b** in the H3211
21: 3 of his son that was **b** unto him, whom H3205
5 when his son Isaac was **b** unto him. H3205
7 for I have **b** *him* a son in his old age. H3205

Gen 21: 9 she had **b** unto Abraham, mocking. H3205
22:20 also **b** children unto thy brother Nahor; H3205
24:15 came out, who was **b** to Bethuel, son of H3205
29:34 me, because I have **b** him three sons: H3205
30:20 because I have **b** him six sons: and she H3205
25 when Rachel had **b** Joseph, that Jacob H3205
31:43 unto their children which they have **b**? H3205
35:26 which were **b** to him in Padan-aram. H3205
36: 5 were **b** unto him in the land of Canaan. H3205
41:50 And unto Joseph were **b** two sons H3205
46:20 land of Egypt were **b** Manasseh and H3205
22 **b** to Jacob: all the souls *were* fourteen. H3205
27 And the sons of Joseph, which were **b** H3205
48: 5 which were **b** unto thee in the land H3205
Ex 1:22 Every son that is **b** ye shall cast into the H3209
12:19 he be a stranger, or **b** in the land. H249
48 be as one that is **b** in the land: for no H249
21: 4 a wife, and she have **b** him sons or H3205
Lev 12: 2 seed, and **b** a man child: then she H3205
7 for her that hath **b** a male or a female. H3205
18: 9 *whether she be* **b** at home, or born H4138
9 born at home, or **b** abroad, *even* their H4138
19:34 be unto you as one **b** among you, and H249
22:11 of it, and he that is **b** in his house: they H3211
23:42 are Israelites **b** shall dwell in booths: H249
24:16 as he that is **b** in the land, when he H249
Nu 9:14 and for him that was **b** in the land. H249
15:13 All that are **b** of the country shall do H249
29 *for* him that is **b** among the children H249
30 *whether he be* **b** in the land, or a H249
26:60 And unto Aaron was **b** Nadab, and H3205
Dt 21:15 and they have **b** him children, *both* H3205
Jos 5: 5 people *that were* **b** in the wilderness by H3209
8:33 as he that was **b** among them; half of H249
Jdg 13: 8 shall do unto the child that shall be **b**. H3205
18:29 father, who was **b** unto Israel: howbeit H3205
Ru 4:15 to thee than seven sons, hath **b** him. H3205
17 There is a son **b** to Naomi; and they H3205
1Sa 2: 5 the barren hath **b** seven; and she that H3205
4:20 Fear not; for thou hast **b** a son. But she H3205
2Sa 3: 2 And unto David were sons **b** in H3205
5 wife. These were **b** to David in Hebron. H3205
5:13 yet sons and daughters **b** to David. H3205
14 names of those that were **b** unto him in H3209
12:14 also *that is* **b** unto thee shall surely die. H3209
14:27 And unto Absalom there were **b** three H3205
21:20 number; and he also was **b** to the giant. H3205
22 These four were **b** to the giant in Gath, H3205
1Ki 13: 2 a child shall be **b** unto the house of H3205
1Ch 1:19 And unto Eber were **b** two sons: the H3205
2: 3 *which* three were **b** unto him of the H3205
9 The sons also of Hezron, that were **b** H3205
3: 1 of David, which were **b** unto him in H3205
4 *These* six were **b** unto him in Hebron; H3205
5 And these were **b** unto him in H3205
7:21 of Gath *that were* **b** in *that* land slew, H3205
20: 8 These were **b** unto the giant in Gath; H3205
22: 9 Behold, a son shall be **b** to thee, who H3205
26: 6 his son were sons **b**, that ruled H3205
Ezr 10: 3 and such as are **b** of them, according H3205
Job 1: 2 And there were **b** unto him seven sons H3205
3: 3 Let the day perish wherein I was **b**, and H3205
5: 7 Yet man is **b** unto trouble, as the H3205
11:12 though man be **b** *like* a wild ass's colt. H3205
14: 1 Man *that is* **b** of a woman *is* of few H3205
15: 7 *Art* thou the first man *that* was **b**? or H3205
14 and *he which is* **b** of a woman, that he H3205
25: 4 can he be clean *that is* **b** of a woman? H3205
38:21 thou wast then **b**? or *because* the H3205
Ps 22:31 that shall be **b**, that he hath done *this*. H3205
58: 3 astray as soon as they be **b**, speaking lies. H990
78: 6 *which* should be **b**; *who* should arise H3205
87: 4 with Ethiopia; this *man* was **b** there. H3205
5 and that man was **b** in her: and the H3205
6 *that* this *man* was **b** there. Selah. H3205
Prv 17:17 times, and a brother is **b** for adversity. H3205
Ecc 2: 7 and had servants **b** in my house; also I H1121
3: 2 A time to be **b**, and a time to die; a time H3205
4:14 *is* **b** in his kingdom becometh poor. H3205
Isa 9: 6 For unto us a child is **b**, unto us a son is H3205
66: 8 shall a nation be **b** at once? for as soon H3205
Jer 16: 3 daughters that are **b** in this place, and H3209
20:14 Cursed *be* the day wherein I was **b**: let H3205
15 is **b** unto thee; making him very glad. H3205
22:26 ye were not **b**; and there shall ye die. H3205
Ezk 16: 4 the day thou wast **b** thy navel was not H3205
5 thy person, in the day that thou wast **b**. H3205
47:22 be unto you as **b** in the country among H249
Hos 2: 3 day that she was **b**, and make her as a H3205
Mt 1:16 was **b** Jesus, who is called Christ. *G1080*
2: 1 Now when Jesus was **b** in Bethlehem of *G1080*
2 Saying, Where is he that is **b** King of *G5088*
4 of them where Christ should be **b**. *G1080*
11:11 them that are **b** of women there hath *G1084*
19:12 which were so **b** from *their* mother's *G1080*
26:24 good for that man if he had not been **b**. *G1080*
Mk 14:21 it for that man if he had never been **b**. *G1080*
Lk 1:35 **b** of thee shall be called the Son of God. *G1080*
2:11 For unto you is **b** this day in the city of *G5088*
7:28 those that are **b** of women there is not *G1084*
Jn 1:13 Which were **b**, not of blood, nor of the *G1080*
3: 3 Except a man be **b** again, he cannot see *G1080*
4 can a man be **b** when he is old? can *G1080*
4 time into his mother's womb, and be **b**? *G1080*
5 Except a man be **b** of water and *of* the *G1080*
6 That which is **b** of the flesh is flesh; and *G1080*
6 that which is **b** of the Spirit is spirit. *G1080*
7 I said unto thee, Ye must be **b** again. *G1080*
8 so is every one that is **b** of the Spirit. *G1080*
8:41 to him, We be not **b** of fornication; we *G1080*
9: 2 or his parents, that he was **b** blind? *G1080*
19 **b** blind? how then doth he now see? *G1080*
20 this is our son, and that he was **b** blind: *G1080*
32 the eyes of one that was **b** blind. *G1080*
34 wast altogether **b** in sins, and dost thou *G1080*
16:21 for joy that a man is **b** into the world. *G1080*
18:37 To this end was I **b**, and for this cause *G1080*
Act 2: 8 in our own tongue, wherein we were **b**? *G1080*
7:20 In which time Moses was **b**, and was *G1080*
18: 2 named Aquila, **b** in Pontus, lately come *G1085*
24 And a certain Jew named Apollos, **b** at *G1085*
22: 3 I am verily a man *which am* a Jew, **b** in *G1080*
28 And Paul said, But I was *free* **b**. *G1080*
Ro 9:11 (For *the children* being not yet **b**, *G1080*
1Co 15: 8 of me also, as of one **b** out of due time. *G1626*
Gal 4:23 bondwoman was **b** after the flesh; but *G1080*
29 But as then he that was **b** after the flesh *G1080*
29 *was* **b** after the Spirit, even so *it is* now. *G1080*
Heb 11:23 By faith Moses, when he was **b**, was hid *G1080*
1Pt 1:23 Being **b** again, not of corruptible seed, *G313*
1Jn 2:29 that doeth righteousness is **b** of him. *G1080*
3: 9 Whosoever is **b** of God doth not *G1080*
9 he cannot sin, because he is **b** of God. *G1080*
4: 7 loveth is **b** of God, and knoweth God. *G1080*
5: 1 is the Christ is **b** of God: and every one *G1080*
4 For whatsoever is **b** of God overcometh *G1080*
18 We know that whosoever is **b** of God *G1080*
Rev 12: 4 to devour her child as soon as it was **b**. *G5088*

BORNE
Ex 25:14 ark, that the ark may be **b** with them. H5375
28 that the table may be **b** with them. H5375
Jdg 16:29 on which it was **b** up, of the one with H5564
Job 34:31 unto God, I have **b** *chastisement*, I will H5375
Ps 55:12 then I could have **b** *it*: neither *was it* he H5375
69: 7 Because for thy sake I have **b** reproach; H5375
Isa 46: 3 of Israel, which are **b** *by me* from the H6006
53: 4 Surely he hath **b** our griefs, and carried H5375
66:12 suck, ye shall be **b** upon *her* sides, and H5375
Jer 10: 5 must needs be **b**, because they cannot H5375
15: 9 She that hath **b** seven languisheth: she H3205
10 that thou hast **b** me a man of strife and H3205
Lam 3:28 silence, because he hath **b** *it* upon him. H5190
5: 7 *are* not; and we have **b** their iniquities. H5445
Ezk 16:20 whom thou hast **b** unto me, and these H3205
58 Thou hast **b** thy lewdness and thine H5375
32:24 yet have they **b** their shame with them H5375
25 yet have they **b** their shame with them H5375
36: 6 ye have **b** the shame of the heathen: H5375
39:26 After that they have **b** their shame, and H5375
Am 5:26 But ye have **b** the tabernacle of your H5375
Mt 20:12 have **b** the burden and heat of the day. *G941*
23: 4 and grievous to be **b**, and lay *them* on *G1419*
Mk 2: 3 sick of the palsy, which was **b** of four. *G142*
Lk 11:46 grievous to be **b**, and ye yourselves *G1419*
Jn 5:37 hath sent me, hath **b** witness of me. Ye
20:15 Sir, if thou have **b** him hence, tell me *G941*
Act 21:35 it was, that he was **b** of the soldiers for *G941*
1Co 15:49 And as we have **b** the image of the *G5409*
3Jn 6 Which have **b** witness of thy charity
Rev 2: 3 And hast **b**, and hast patience, and for *G941*

BORROW
Ex 3:22 But every woman shall **b** of her H7592
11: 2 and let every man **b** of his neighbour, H7592
22:14 And if a man **b** *ought* of his neighbour, H7592
Dt 15: 6 but thou shalt not **b**; and thou shalt H5670
28:12 many nations, and thou shalt not **b**. H3867
2Ki 4: 3 Then he said, Go, **b** thee vessels abroad H7592
3 *even* empty vessels; **b** not a few.
Mt 5:42 would **b** of thee turn not thou away. *G1155*

BORROWED
Ex 12:35 of Moses; and they **b** of the Egyptians H7592
2Ki 6: 5 and said, Alas, master! for it was **b**. H7592
Neh 5: 4 There were also that said, We have **b** H3867

BORROWER
Prv 22: 7 The rich ruleth over the poor, and the **b** H3867
Isa 24: 2 lender, so with the **b**; as with the taker H3867

BORROWETH
Ps 37:21 The wicked **b**, and payeth not again: H3867

BOSCATH
2Ki 22: 1 Jedidah, the daughter of Adaiah of **B**. H1218

BOSKETH See ISH-BOSKETH.

BOSOM
Gen 16: 5 my maid into thy **b**; and when she saw H2436
Ex 4: 6 hand into thy **b**. And he put his hand H2436
6 his hand into his **b**: and when he took it H2436
7 And he said, Put thine hand into thy **b** H2436
7 his hand into his **b** again; and plucked H2436
7 it out of his **b**, and, behold, it was H2436
Nu 11:12 Carry them in thy **b**, as a nursing father H2436
Dt 13: 6 or the wife of thy **b**, or thy friend, which H2436
28:54 toward the wife of his **b**, and toward the H2436
56 husband of her **b**, and toward her son, H2436
Ru 4:16 it in her **b**, and became nurse unto it. H2436
2Sa 12: 3 his **b**, and was unto him as a daughter. H2436
8 wives into thy **b**, and gave thee the H2436
1Ki 1: 2 **b**, that my lord the king may get heat. H2436
3:20 **b**, and laid her dead child in my bosom. H2436
20 bosom, and laid her dead child in my **b**. H2436
17:19 him out of her **b**, and carried him up H2436
Job 31:33 Adam, by hiding mine iniquity in my **b**: H2243
Ps 35:13 my prayer returned into mine own **b**. H2436
74:11 thy right hand? pluck *it* out of thy **b**. H2436
79:12 into their **b** their reproach, wherewith H2436
89:50 **b** *the reproach of* all the mighty people; H2436
129: 7 hand; nor he that bindeth sheaves his **b**. H2683
Prv 5:20 and embrace the **b** of a stranger? H2436
6:27 Can a man take fire in his **b**, and his H2436
17:23 A wicked *man* taketh a gift out of the **b** H2436
19:24 A slothful *man* hideth his hand in *his* **b**, H6747
21:14 and a reward in the **b** strong wrath. H2436
26:15 The slothful hideth his hand in *his* **b**; it H6747
Ecc 7: 9 for anger resteth in the **b** of fools. H2436
Isa 40:11 carry *them* in his **b**, *and* shall gently H2436
65: 6 even recompense into their **b**, H2436
7 measure their former work into their **b**. H2436
Jer 32:18 fathers into the **b** of their children after H2436
Lam 2:12 was poured out into their mothers' **b**. H2436
Mic 7: 5 thy mouth from her that lieth in thy **b**. H2436
Lk 6:38 men give into your **b**. For with the same *G2859*
16:22 into Abraham's **b**: the rich man also *G2859*
23 Abraham afar off, and Lazarus in his **b**. *G2859*
Jn 1:18 **b** of the Father, he hath declared *him*. *G2859*
13:23 Now there was leaning on Jesus' **b** one *G2859*

BOSOR
2Pt 2:15 of Balaam *the son* of **B**, who loved the *G1007*

BOSSES
Job 15:26 neck, upon the thick **b** of his bucklers: H1354

BOTCH
Dt 28:27 The LORD will smite thee with the **b** of H7822
35 the legs, with a sore **b** that cannot be H7822

BOTH
Gen 2:25 And they were **b** naked, the man and H8147
3: 7 And the eyes of them **b** were opened, H8147
6: 7 face of the earth; **b** man, and beast, and
7:21 upon the earth, **b** of fowl, and of cattle,
23 face of the ground, **b** man, and cattle,
8:17 thee, of all flesh, ***b*** of fowl, and of cattle,
9:23 and laid *it* upon **b** their shoulders, and H8147
19: 4 the house round, **b** old and young, all
11 with blindness, **b** small and great: so
36 Thus were **b** the daughters of Lot with H8147
21:27 and **b** of them made a covenant. H8147
31 because there they sware **b** of them. H8147
22: 6 and they went **b** of them together. H8147
8 so they went **b** of them together. H8147

Gen 24:25 him, We have **b** straw and provender H1571
44 And she say to me, **B** drink thou, and I
27:45 I be deprived also of you **b** in one day? H8147
31:37 that they may judge betwixt us **b**. H8147
36:24 And these *are* the children of Zibeon; **b**
40: 5 And they dreamed a dream **b** of them, H8147
41:10 guard's house, **b** me and the chief baker:
42:35 in his sack: and when **b** they and their
43: 8 **b** we, and thou, *and* also our little ones.
44: 9 it be found, **b** let him die, and we also
16 lord's servants, **b** we, and *he* also with H1571
46:34 youth even until now, **b** we, *and* also our
47: 3 shepherds, **b** we, *and* also our fathers.
19 die before thine eyes, **b** we and our land?
48:13 And Joseph took them **b**, Ephraim in H8147
50: 9 And there went up with him **b** chariots
Ex 5:14 **b** yesterday and to day, as heretofore?
7:19 the land of Egypt, **b** in *vessels of* wood,
8: 4 And the frogs shall come up **b** on thee,
9:25 *was* in the field, **b** man and beast; and
12:12 the land of Egypt, **b** man and beast; and
31 among my people, **b** ye and the children
13: 2 Israel, **b** of man and of beast: it *is* mine.
15 the land of Egypt, **b** the firstborn of man,
18:18 Thou wilt surely wear away, **b** thou, and
22: 9 be his, the cause of **b** parties shall come
11 be between them **b**, that he hath not put H8147
26:24 **b**; they shall be for the two corners. H8147
29:44 I will sanctify also **b** Aaron and his sons,
32:15 *were* written on **b** their sides; on the H8147
35:22 And they came, **b** men and women, as H5921
25 they had spun, **b** of blue, and of purple,
34 that he may teach, **b** he, and Aholiab,
36:29 he did to **b** of them in both the corners. H8147
29 he did to both of them in **b** the corners. H8147
37:26 And he overlaid it with pure gold, **b** the
Lev 6:28 shall be **b** scoured, and rinsed in water.
8:11 and all his vessels, **b** the laver and his
9: 3 and a calf and a lamb, **b** of the first year,
15:18 they shall **b** bathe *themselves* in
16:21 And Aaron shall lay **b** his hands upon H8147
17:15 a stranger, he shall **b** wash his clothes,
20:11 nakedness: **b** of them shall surely H8147
12 daughter in law, **b** of them shall surely H8147
13 lieth with a woman, **b** of them have H8147
14 be burnt with fire, **b** he and they; that
18 of her blood: and **b** of them shall be cut H8147
21:22 He shall eat the bread of his God, **b** of
22:28 not kill it and her young **b** in one day.
25:41 And *then* shall he depart from thee, **b** he
44 **B** thy bondmen, and thy bondmaids,
54 jubile, **b** he, and his children with him.
27:28 of all that he hath, **b** of man and beast,
33 it at all, then **b** it and the change thereof
Nu 3:13 the firstborn in Israel, **b** man and beast:
5: 3 **B** male and female shall ye put out,
7: 1 thereof, **b** the altar and all the
13 of the sanctuary; **b** of them *were* full of H8147
19 of the sanctuary; **b** of them full of fine H8147
25 of the sanctuary; **b** of them full of fine H8147
31 of the sanctuary; **b** of them full of fine H8147
37 of the sanctuary; **b** of them full of fine H8147
43 of the sanctuary; **b** of them full of fine H8147
49 of the sanctuary; **b** of them full of fine H8147
55 of the sanctuary; **b** of them full of fine H8147
61 of the sanctuary; **b** of them full of fine H8147
67 of the sanctuary; **b** of them full of fine H8147
73 of the sanctuary; **b** of them full of fine H8147
79 of the sanctuary; **b** of them full of fine H8147
8:17 of Israel *are* mine, **b** man and beast: on
9:14 one ordinance, **b** for the stranger, and
12: 5 and Miriam: and they **b** came forth. H8147
15:15 One ordinance *shall be* **b** for you of the
29 through ignorance, **b** *for* him that is
16:11 For which cause **b** thou and all thy
25: 8 tent, and thrust **b** of them through, the H8147
27:21 word they shall come in, **b** he, and all the
31:11 and all the prey, **b** of men and of beasts.
19 any slain, purify **b** yourselves and your
26 that was taken, **b** of man and of beast,
28 of five hundred, **b** of the persons, and of
47 portion of fifty, **b** of man and of beast,
35:15 These six cities shall be a refuge, **b** for
Dt 19:17 Then **b** the men, between whom the H8147
21:15 born him children, **b** the beloved and the
22:22 then they shall **b** of them die, *both* the H8147
22 both of them die, **b** the man that lay with
24 Then ye shall bring them **b** out unto the H8147
23:18 for any vow: for even **b** these *are* H8147

Dt 30:19 life, that **b** thou and thy seed may live:
32:25 shall destroy **b** the young man and
Jos 6:21 that *was* in the city, **b** man and woman,
8:25 that fell that day, **b** of men and women,
14:11 for war, **b** to go out, and to come in.
17:16 have chariots of iron, **b** *they* who *are* of
Jdg 5:30 of needlework on **b** sides, *meet* for the
6: 5 for multitude; *for* **b** they and their
8:22 Rule thou over us, **b** thou, and thy son,
10:10 sinned against thee, **b** because we have
15: 5 and burnt up **b** the shocks, and also
19: 6 did eat and drink **b** of them together: H8147
8 afternoon, and they did eat **b** of them. H8147
19 Yet there is **b** straw and provender for
Ru 1: 5 And Mahlon and Chilion died also **b** of H8147
1Sa 2:26 **b** with the LORD, and also with men.
34 in one day they shall die **b** of them. H8147
3:11 in Israel, at which **b** the ears of every H8147
5: 4 of Dagon and **b** the palms of his hands H8147
9 the men of the city, **b** small and great,
6:18 to the five lords, **b** of fenced cities, and
9:26 out **b** of them, he and Samuel, abroad. H8147
12:14 LORD, then shall **b** ye and also the king
25 shall be consumed, **b** ye and your king.
14:11 And **b** of them discovered themselves H8147
15: 3 them not; but slay **b** man and woman,
17:36 Thy servant slew **b** the lion and the bear:
20:11 they went out **b** of them into the field. H8147
42 as we have sworn **b** of us in the name H8147
22:19 edge of the sword, **b** men and women,
25: 6 Peace *be* **b** to thee, and peace *be*
16 They were a wall unto us **b** by night and
43 and they were also **b** of them his wives. H8147
26:25 David: thou shalt **b** do great *things*, and
2Sa 8:18 Jehoiada *was over* **b** the Cherethites and
9:13 table; and was lame on **b** his feet. H8147
15:25 and shew me **b** it, and his habitation:
16:23 **b** with David and with Absalom.
17:18 but they went **b** of them away quickly, H8147
1Ki 3:13 hast not asked, **b** riches, and honour:
6: 5 round about, **b** of the temple and of
15 boards of cedar, **b** the floor of the house,
16 the sides of the house, **b** the floor and the
25 And the other cherub *was* ten cubits: **b** H8147
7:12 of cedar beams, **b** for the inner court of
50 the hinges *of* gold, **b** for the doors of the
2Ki 2:11 and parted them **b** asunder; and Elijah H8147
3:17 **b** ye, and your cattle, and your beasts.
6:15 compassed the city **b** with horses and
17:41 graven images, **b** their children, and
21:12 heareth of it, **b** his ears shall tingle. H8147
23: 2 and all the people, **b** small and great:
15 to sin, had made, **b** that altar and the
25:26 And all the people, **b** small and great,
1Ch 12: 2 and could use **b** the right hand and the
15 **b** toward the east, and toward the west.
15:12 yourselves, **b** ye and your brethren,
16: 3 And he dealt to every one of Israel, **b**
23:29 **B** for the shewbread, and for the fine
24: 3 And David distributed them, **b** Zadok of
28:15 of silver by weight, **b** for the candlestick,
29:12 **B** riches and honour *come* of thee, and
2Ch 20:25 in abundance **b** riches with the dead
24:16 **b** toward God, and toward his house.
25:21 in the face, **b** he and Amaziah king
26:10 he had much cattle, **b** in the low country,
27: 5 him, **b** the second year, and the third.
31:17 **B** to the genealogy of the priests by the
32:26 the pride of his heart, **b** he and the
Ezr 3: 5 burnt offering, **b** of the new moons, and
6: 9 And that which they have need of, **b**
Neh 1: 6 **b** I and my father's house have sinned.
4:16 other half of them held **b** the spears, the
8: 2 the congregation **b** of men and women,
10: 9 And the Levites: **b** Jeshua the son of
12:27 with gladness, **b** with thanksgivings,
28 together, **b** out of the plain country
45 And **b** the singers and the porters kept
Est 1: 5 the palace, **b** unto great and small,
20 husbands honour, **b** to great and small.
2:23 they were **b** hanged on a tree: and H8147
3:13 to perish, all Jews, **b** young and old, little
8:11 assault them, **b** little ones and women,
9:20 of the king Ahasuerus, **b** nigh and far,
Job 9:33 us, *that* might lay his hand upon us **b**. H8147
15:10 With us *are* **b** the grayheaded and very
Ps 4: 8 I will **b** lay me down in peace, and H3162
49: 2 **B** low and high, rich and poor, together.
58: 9 a whirlwind, **b** living, and in *his* wrath.

Ps 64: 6 a diligent search: **b** the inward *thought*
76: 6 At thy rebuke, O God of Jacob, **b** the
104:25 innumerable, **b** small and great beasts.
115:13 He will bless them that fear the LORD, **b**
135: 8 Who smote the firstborn of Egypt, **b** of
139:12 and the light *are* **b** alike *to thee*.
148:12 **B** young men, and maidens; old men,
Prv 17:15 they **b** *are* abomination to the LORD. H8147
20:10 Divers weights, *and* divers measures, **b** H8147
12 the LORD hath made even **b** of them. H8147
24:22 and who knoweth the ruin of them **b**? H8147
26:10 The great *God* that formed all *things* **b**
27: 3 a fool's wrath *is* heavier than them **b**. H8147
29:13 the LORD lighteneth **b** their eyes. H8147
Ecc 4: 3 Yea, better *is he* than **b** they, which H8147
6 quietness, than **b** the hands full *with*
8: 5 heart discerneth **b** time and judgment.
11: 6 or whether they **b** *shall be* alike good. H8147
Isa 1:31 and they shall **b** burn together, and H8147
7:16 shall be forsaken of **b** her kings. H8147
8:14 a rock of offence to **b** the houses of H8147
10:18 of his fruitful field, **b** soul and body: and
13: 9 cometh, cruel **b** with wrath and fierce
18: 5 in the flower, he shall **b** cut off the sprigs
31: 3 out his hand, **b** he that helpeth shall
38:15 What shall I say? he hath **b** spoken unto
44:12 The smith with the tongs **b** worketh in
Jer 5:24 that giveth rain, **b** the former and the
9:10 the voice of the cattle; **b** the fowl of the
14:18 with famine! yea, **b** the prophet and the
16: 6 **B** the great and the small shall die in this
21: 6 of this city, **b** man and beast: they
23:11 For **b** prophet and priest are profane;
26: 5 I sent unto you, **b** rising up early, and
28: 8 thee of old prophesied **b** against many
31:13 in the dance, **b** young men and old
32:11 So I took the evidence of the purchase, **b**
14 of the purchase, **b** which is sealed, and
36:16 they were afraid **b** one and other, and H413
44:25 and your wives have **b** spoken with your
46:12 mighty, *and* they are fallen **b** together. H8147
50: 3 they shall depart, **b** man and beast.
51:12 for the LORD hath **b** devised and done
46 a rumour shall **b** come *one* year, and
Lam 3:26 *It is* good that *a man* should **b** hope and
Ezk 9: 6 Slay utterly old *and* young, **b** maids, and
14:22 be brought forth, **b** sons and daughters:
15: 4 the fire devoureth **b** the ends of it, and H8147
21:19 may come: **b** twain shall come forth
23:13 was defiled, *that* they *took* **b** one way, H8147
29 **b** thy lewdness and thy whoredoms.
34:11 **b** search my sheep, and seek them out.
39: 9 burn the weapons, **b** the shields and the
42:11 goings out *were* **b** according to their
Dan 8:13 desolation, to give **b** the sanctuary and
11:27 And **b** these kings' hearts *shall be* to do H8147
Mic 5: 8 if he go through, **b** treadeth down, and
7: 3 That they may do evil with **b** hands
Nah 3: 3 The horseman lifteth up **b** the bright
Zep 2:14 of the nations: **b** the cormorant and the
Zec 6:13 of peace shall be between them **b**. H8147
12: 2 **b** against Judah *and* against Jerusalem.
Mt 9:17 into new bottles, and **b** are preserved. *G297*
10:28 able to destroy **b** soul and body in hell. *G2532*
12:22 the blind and dumb **b** spake and saw. *G2532*
13:30 Let **b** grow together until the harvest: *G297*
15:14 lead the blind, **b** shall fall into the ditch. *G297*
22:10 as they found, **b** bad and good: and *G5037*
Mk 6:30 him all things, **b** what they had done, *G2532*
7:37 well: he maketh **b** the deaf to hear, and *G2532*
Lk 1: 6 And they were **b** righteous before God, *G297*
7 they **b** were *now* well stricken in years. *G297*
2:46 of the doctors, **b** hearing them, and *G2532*
5: 7 **b** the ships, so that they began to sink. *G297*
36 if otherwise, then **b** the new maketh a *G2532*
38 into new bottles; and **b** are preserved. *G297*
6:39 blind? shall they not **b** fall into the ditch? *G297*
7:42 forgave them **b**. Tell me therefore, which *G297*
21:16 And ye shall be betrayed **b** by parents, *G2532*
22:33 with thee, **b** into prison, and to death. *G2532*
Jn 2: 2 And **b** Jesus was called, and his *G2532*
4:36 life eternal: that **b** he that soweth and *G2532*
7:28 he taught, saying, Ye **b** know me, and ye
9:37 And Jesus said unto him, Thou hast **b** *G2532*
11:48 and take away **b** our place and nation. *G2532*
57 Now **b** the chief priests and the *G2532*
12:28 **b** glorified *it*, and will glorify *it* again. *G2532*
15:24 but now have they **b** seen and hated *G2532*
24 seen and hated **b** me and my Father. *G2532*

Jn 20: 4 So they ran **b** together: and the other G1417
Act 1: 1 all that Jesus began **b** to do and teach, G5037
8 witnesses unto me **b** in Jerusalem, and G5037
13 where abode **b** Peter, and James, and G5037
2:29 David, that he is **b** dead and buried, G2532
36 ye have crucified, **b** Lord and Christ. G2532
4:27 hast anointed, **b** Herod, and Pontius G5037
5:14 multitudes **b** of men and women.) G5037
8:12 they were baptized, **b** men and women. G5037
38 they went down **b** into the water, both G297
38 both into the water, **b** Philip and the G5037
10:39 which he did **b** in the land of the Jews, G5037
14: 1 that they went **b** together into the
1 a great multitude **b** of the Jews and G5037
5 And when there was an assault made **b** G5037
19:10 of the Lord Jesus, **b** Jews and Greeks. G5037
20:21 Testifying **b** to the Jews, and also to the G5037
21:12 And when we heard these things, **b** we, G5037
22: 4 into prisons **b** men and women. G5037
23: 8 nor spirit: but the Pharisees confess **b**. G297
24:15 of the dead, **b** of the just and unjust. G5037
25:24 dealt with me, **b** at Jerusalem, and *also* G5037
26:16 and a witness **b** of these things which G5037
22 day, witnessing **b** to small and great, G5037
29 hear me this day, were **b** almost, and G2532
28:23 concerning Jesus, **b** out of the law of G5037
Ro 1:12 by the mutual faith **b** of you and me. G5037
14 I am debtor **b** to the Greeks, and to the G5037
14 **b** to the wise, and to the unwise. G5037
3: 9 before proved **b** Jews and Gentiles, that G5037
11:33 O the depth of the riches **b** of the G2532
14: 9 For to this end Christ **b** died, and rose, G2532
9 might be Lord **b** of the dead and living. G2532
1Co 1: 2 Christ our Lord, **b** theirs and ours: G5037
24 But unto them which are called, **b** Jews G5037
4: 5 Lord come, who **b** will bring to light the G2532
11 Even unto this present hour we **b** G2532
6:13 God shall destroy **b** it and them. Now G2532
14 And God hath **b** raised up the Lord, G2532
7:29 it remaineth, that **b** they that have G2532
34 she may be holy **b** in body and in spirit: G2532
2Co 9:10 seed to the sower **b** minister bread for G2532
Eph 1:10 things in Christ, **b** which are in heaven, G5037
2:14 For he is our peace, who hath made **b** G297
16 And that he might reconcile **b** unto God G297
18 For through him we **b** have access by G297
Php 1: 7 inasmuch as **b** in my bonds, and in G5037
2:13 For it is God which worketh in you **b** to G2532
4: 9 Those things, which ye have **b** learned, G2532
12 I know **b** how to be abased, and I know
12 I am instructed **b** to be full and to be G2532
12 **b** to abound and to suffer need. G2532
1Th 2:15 Who **b** killed the Lord Jesus, and their G2532
5:15 **b** among yourselves, and to all *men*. G2532
2Th 3: 4 you, that ye **b** do and will do the things G2532
1Ti 4:10 For therefore we **b** labour and suffer G2532
16 **b** save thyself, and them that hear thee. G2532
Tit 1: 9 by sound doctrine **b** to exhort and to G2532
Phlm 16 thee, **b** in the flesh, and in the Lord? G2532
Heb 2: 4 God also bearing *them* witness, **b** with G5037
11 For **b** he that sanctifieth and they who G5037
5: 1 may offer **b** gifts and sacrifices for sins: G5037
14 exercised to discern **b** good and evil. G5037
6:19 of the soul, **b** sure and stedfast, and G5037
9: 9 were offered **b** gifts and sacrifices, G5037
19 **b** the book, and all the people, G5037
21 Moreover he sprinkled with blood **b** the G2532
10:33 a gazingstock **b** by reproaches and G5037
11:21 a dying, blessed **b** the sons of Joseph; G1538
Jas 3:12 no fountain **b** yield salt water and fresh.
2Pt 3: 1 write unto you; in **b** which I stir up your
18 *be* glory **b** now and for ever. Amen. G2532
2Jn 9 he hath **b** the Father and the Son. G2532
Jude 25 and power, **b** now and ever. Amen. G2532
Rev 13:15 of the beast should **b** speak, and cause G2532
16 And he causeth all, **b** small and great,
19: 5 ye that fear him, **b** small and great. G2532
18 ***b*** free and bond, both small and great.
18 *both* free and bond, **b** small and great. G2532
20 his image. These **b** were cast alive into G1417

BOTTLE

Gen 21:14 took bread, and a **b** of water, and gave H2573
15 And the water was spent in the **b**, and H2573
19 **b** with water, and gave the lad drink. H2573
Jdg 4:19 And she opened a **b** of milk, and gave H4997
1Sa 1:24 of flour, and a **b** of wine, and brought H5035
10: 3 and another carrying a **b** of wine: H5035
16:20 with bread, and a **b** of wine, and a kid, H4997
2Sa 16: 1 of summer fruits, and a **b** of wine. H5035
Ps 56: 8 into thy **b**: *are they* not in thy book? H4997
119:83 For I am become like a **b** in the smoke; H4997
Jer 13:12 of Israel, Every **b** shall be filled with H5035
12 that every **b** shall be filled with wine? H5035
19: 1 get a potter's earthen **b**, and *take* of the H1228
10 Then shalt thou break the **b** in the sight H1228
Hab 2:15 that puttest thy **b** to *him*, and makest H2573

BOTTLES

Jos 9: 4 wine **b**, old, and rent, and bound up; H4997
13 And these **b** of wine, which we filled, H4997
1Sa 25:18 loaves, and two **b** of wine, and five H5035
Job 32:19 no vent; it is ready to burst like new **b**. H178
38:37 or who can stay the **b** of heaven, H5035
Jer 48:12 empty his vessels, and break their **b**. H5035
Hos 7: 5 *him* sick with **b** of wine; he stretched H2534
Mt 9:17 Neither do men put new wine into old **b**: G779
17 into old bottles: else the **b** break, and the G779
17 out, and the **b** perish: but they put G779
17 wine into new **b**, and both are preserved. G779
Mk 2:22 And no man putteth new wine into old **b**: G779
22 doth burst the **b**, and the wine is spilled, G779
22 is spilled, and the **b** will be marred: but G779
22 but new wine must be put into new **b**. G779
Lk 5:37 And no man putteth new wine into old **b**; G779
37 wine will burst the **b**, and be spilled, and G779
37 and be spilled, and the **b** shall perish. G779
38 But new wine must be put into new **b**; G779

BOTTOM

Ex 15: 5 them: they sank into the **b** as a stone. H4688
29:12 all the blood beside the **b** of the altar. H3247
Lev 4: 7 of the bullock at the **b** of the altar of the H3247
18 all the blood at the **b** of the altar of the H3247
25 at the **b** of the altar of burnt offering. H3247
30 the blood thereof at the **b** of the altar. H3247
34 the blood thereof at the **b** of the altar: H3247
5: 9 at the **b** of the altar: it *is* a sin offering. H3247
8:15 the blood at the **b** of the altar, and H3247
9: 9 out the blood at the **b** of the altar: H3247
Job 36:30 upon it, and covereth the **b** of the sea. H8328
Song 3:10 *of* silver, the **b** thereof *of* gold, the H7507
Ezk 43:13 breadth; even the **b** *shall be* a cubit, H2436
14 And from the **b** *upon* the ground *even* H2436
17 half a cubit; and the **b** thereof *shall be* a H2436
Dan 6:24 or ever they came at the **b** of the den. H773
Am 9: 3 my sight in the **b** of the sea, thence will H7172
Zec 1: 8 that *were* in the **b**; and behind him *were* H4699
Mt 27:51 from the top to the **b**; and the earth did G2736
Mk 15:38 was rent in twain from the top to the **b**. G2736

BOTTOMLESS

Rev 9: 1 to him was given the key of the **b** pit. G12
2 And he opened the **b** pit; and there arose G12
11 *is* the angel of the **b** pit, whose name in G12
11: 7 out of the **b** pit shall make war against G12
17: 8 shall ascend out of the **b** pit, and go into G12
20: 1 the **b** pit and a great chain in his hand. G12
3 And cast him into the **b** pit, and shut G12

BOTTOMS

Jna 2: 6 I went down to the **b** of the mountains; H7095

BOUGH

Gen 49:22 Joseph *is* a fruitful **b**, *even* a fruitful H1121
22 *even* a fruitful **b** by a well; *whose* H1121
Jdg 9:48 and cut down a **b** from the trees, and H7754
49 down every man his **b**, and followed H7754
Isa 10:33 shall lop the **b** with terror: and the H6288
17: 6 top of the uppermost **b**, four *or* five in the H534
9 be as a forsaken **b**, and an uppermost H2793

BOUGHS

Lev 23:40 on the first day the **b** of goodly trees, H6529
40 trees, and the **b** of thick trees, and H6057
Dt 24:20 not go over the **b** again: it shall be for H6286
2Sa 18: 9 under the thick **b** of a great oak, and H7730
Job 14: 9 will bud, and bring forth **b** like a plant. H7105
Ps 80:10 **b** thereof *were like* the goodly cedars. H6057
11 She sent out her **b** unto the sea, and her H7105
Song 7: 8 take hold of the **b** thereof: now also thy H5577
Isa 27:11 When the **b** thereof are withered, they H7105
Ezk 17:23 it shall bring forth **b**, and bear fruit, H6057
31: 3 and his top was among the thick **b**. H5688
5 of the field, and his **b** were multiplied, H5634
6 made their nests in his **b**, and under his H5589
8 were not like his **b**, and the chesnut H5589
10 top among the thick **b**, and his heart is H5688
Ezk 31:12 are fallen, and his **b** are broken by all H6288
14 among the thick **b**, neither their trees H5688
Dan 4:12 the **b** thereof, and all flesh was fed of it. H6056

BOUGHT

Gen 17:12 in the house, or **b** with money of any H4736
13 and he that is **b** with thy money, must H4736
23 and all that were **b** with his money, H4736
27 in the house, and **b** with money of the H4736
33:19 And he **b** a parcel of a field, where he H7069
39: 1 an Egyptian, **b** him of the hands of H7069
47:14 corn which they **b**: and Joseph brought H7666
20 And Joseph **b** all the land of Egypt for H7069
22 Only the land of the priests **b** he not; H7069
23 Behold, I have **b** you this day and your H7069
49:30 which Abraham **b** with the field of H7069
50:13 which Abraham **b** with the field for a H7069
Ex 12:44 But every man's servant that is **b** for H4736
Lev 25:28 of him that hath **b** it until the year of H7069
30 for ever to him that **b** it throughout his H7069
50 And he shall reckon with him that **b** H7069
51 out of the money that he was **b** for. H4736
27:22 which he hath **b**, which *is* not of the H4736
24 of whom it was **b**, *even* to him to whom H7069
Dt 32: 6 thy father *that* hath **b** thee? hath he not H7069
Jos 24:32 which Jacob **b** of the sons of Hamor H7069
Ru 4: 9 this day, that I have **b** all that *was* H7069
2Sa 12: 3 which he had **b** and nourished up: and H7069
24:24 nothing. So David **b** the threshingfloor H7069
1Ki 16:24 And he **b** the hill Samaria of Shemer H7069
Neh 5:16 this wall, neither **b** we any land: and all H7069
Isa 43:24 Thou hast **b** me no sweet cane with H7069
Jer 32: 9 And I **b** the field of Hanameel my H7069
43 And fields shall be **b** in this land, H7069
Hos 3: 2 So I **b** her to me for fifteen *pieces* of H3739
Mt 13:46 went and sold all that he had, and **b** it. G59
21:12 them that sold and **b** in the temple, and G59
27: 7 And they took counsel, and **b** with them G59
Mk 11:15 them that sold and **b** in the temple, and G59
15:46 And he **b** fine linen, and took him down, G59
16: 1 and Salome, had **b** sweet spices, that G59
Lk 14:18 unto him, I have **b** a piece of ground, G59
19 And another said, I have **b** five yoke of G59
17:28 **b**, they sold, they planted, they builded; G59
19:45 them that sold therein, and them that **b**; G59
Act 7:16 that Abraham **b** for a sum of money G5608
1Co 6:20 For ye are **b** with a price: therefore G59
7:23 Ye are **b** with a price; be not ye the G59
2Pt 2: 1 the Lord that **b** them, and bring upon G59

BOUND

Gen 22: 9 in order, and **b** Isaac his son, and laid H6123
38:28 midwife took and **b** upon his hand a H7194
39:20 *were* **b**: and he was there in the prison. H631
40: 3 the prison, the place where Joseph *was* **b**. H631
5 of Egypt, which *were* **b** in the prison. H631
42:19 one of your brethren be **b** in the house of H631
24 Simeon, and **b** him before their eyes. H631
44:30 that his life is **b** up in the lad's life; H7194
49:26 unto the utmost **b** of the everlasting H8379
Ex 12:34 being **b** up in their clothes upon H6887
Lev 8: 7 the ephod, and **b** *it* unto him therewith. H640
Nu 19:15 hath no covering **b** upon it, *is* unclean. H6616
30: 4 she hath **b** her soul, and her father H631
4 she hath **b** her soul shall stand. H631
5 she hath **b** her soul, shall stand: H631
6 out of her lips, wherewith she **b** her soul; H631
7 wherewith she **b** her soul shall stand. H631
8 lips, wherewith she **b** her soul, of none H631
9 **b** their souls, shall stand against her. H631
10 or **b** her soul by a bond with an oath; H631
11 wherewith she **b** her soul shall stand. H631
Jos 2:21 she **b** the scarlet line in the window. H7194
9: 4 wine bottles, old, and rent, and **b** up; H6887
Jdg 15:13 kill thee. And they **b** him with two new H631
16: 6 thou mightest be **b** to afflict thee. H631
8 been dried, and she **b** him with them. H631
10 pray thee, wherewith thou mightest be **b**. H631
12 Delilah therefore took new ropes, and **b** H631
13 thou mightest be **b**. And he said unto her, H631
21 down to Gaza, and **b** him with fetters of H631
1Sa 25:29 of my lord shall be **b** in the bundle of H6887
2Sa 3:34 Thy hands *were* not **b**, nor thy feet put H631
2Ki 5:23 And he urged him, and **b** two talents of H6696
17: 4 shut him up, and **b** him in prison. H631
25: 7 of Zedekiah, and **b** him with fetters of H631
2Ch 33:11 the thorns, and **b** him with fetters, and H631
36: 6 **b** him in fetters, to carry him to Babylon. H631
Job 36: 8 And if *they be* **b** in fetters, *and* be holden H631

Job 38:20 That thou shouldest take it to the **b** H1366
Ps 68: 6 those which are **b** with chains: but the H615
104: 9 Thou hast set a **b** that they may not H1366
107:10 of death, *being* **b** in affliction and iron; H615
Prv 22:15 Foolishness *is* **b** in the heart of a child; H7194
30: 4 in his fists? who hath **b** the waters in a H6887
Isa 1: 6 **b** up, neither mollified with ointment. H2280
22: 3 together, they are **b** by the archers: all H631
3 are **b** together, *which* have fled from far. H631
61: 1 opening of the prison to *them that are* **b**; H631
Jer 5:22 placed the sand *for* the **b** of the sea by a H1366
30:13 **b** up: thou hast no healing medicines. H4205
39: 7 eyes, and **b** him with chains, to H631
40: 1 taken him being **b** in chains among all H631
52:11 the king of Babylon **b** him in chains, and H631
Lam 1:14 The yoke of my transgressions is **b** by H8244
Ezk 27:24 of rich apparel, **b** with cords, and made H2280
30:21 lo, it shall not be **b** up to be healed, to H2280
34: 4 neither have ye **b** up *that which was* H2280
Dan 3:21 Then these men were **b** in their coats, H3729
23 fell down **b** into the midst of the H3729
24 we cast three men **b** into the midst of H3729
Hos 4:19 The wind hath **b** her up in her wings, H6887
5:10 that remove the **b**: *therefore* I will pour H1366
7:15 Though I have **b** *and* strengthened H3256
13:12 The iniquity of Ephraim *is* **b** up; his sin H6887
Nah 3:10 and all her great men were **b** in chains. H7576
Mt 14: 3 For Herod had laid hold on John, and **b** *G1210*
16:19 bind on earth shall be **b** in heaven: and *G1210*
18:18 bind on earth shall be **b** in heaven: and *G1210*
27: 2 And when they had **b** him, they led *him* *G1210*
Mk 5: 4 Because that he had been often **b** with *G1210*
6:17 upon John, and **b** him in prison for *G1210*
15: 1 council, and **b** Jesus, and carried *him* *G1210*
7 *which lay* **b** with them that had *G1210*
Lk 8:29 and he was kept **b** with chains and in *G1196*
10:34 And went to *him*, and **b** up his wounds, *G2611*
13:16 whom Satan hath **b**, lo, these eighteen *G1210*
Jn 11:44 And he that was dead came forth, **b** *G1210*
44 and his face was **b** about with a *G4019*
18:12 of the Jews took Jesus, and **b** him, *G1210*
24 Now Annas had sent him **b** unto *G1210*
Act 9: 2 he might bring them **b** unto Jerusalem. *G1210*
21 bring them **b** unto the chief priests? *G1210*
12: 6 two soldiers, **b** with two chains: and *G1210*
20:22 And now, behold, I go **b** in the spirit *G1210*
21:11 Paul's girdle, and **b** his own hands and *G1210*
13 ready not to be **b** only, but also to die *G1210*
33 *him* to be **b** with two chains; and *G1210*
22: 5 **b** unto Jerusalem, for to be punished. *G1210*
25 And as they **b** him with thongs, Paul *G4385*
29 a Roman, and because he had **b** him. *G1210*
23:12 together, and **b** themselves under a *G332*
14 and said, We have **b** ourselves under a *G332*
21 men, which have **b** themselves with an *G332*
24:27 to shew the Jews a pleasure, left Paul **b**. *G1210*
28:20 hope of Israel I am **b** with this chain. *G4029*
Ro 7: 2 hath an husband is **b** by the law to *her* *G1210*
1Co 7:27 Art thou **b** unto a wife? seek not to be *G1210*
39 The wife is **b** by the law as long as her *G1210*
2Th 1: 3 We are **b** to thank God always for you, *G3784*
2:13 But we are **b** to give thanks alway to *G3784*
2Ti 2: 9 bonds; but the word of God is not **b**. *G1210*
Heb 13: 3 are in bonds, as **b** with them; *and* them *G4887*
Rev 9:14 are **b** in the great river Euphrates. *G1210*
20: 2 Satan, and **b** him a thousand years, *G1210*

BOUNDS
Ex 19:12 And thou shalt set **b** unto the people H1379
23 Set **b** about the mount, and sanctify it. H1379
23:31 And I will set thy **b** from the Red sea H1366
Dt 32: 8 of Adam, he set the **b** of the people H1367
Job 14: 5 appointed his **b** that he cannot pass; H2706
26:10 He hath compassed the waters with **b**, H2706
Isa 10:13 I have removed the **b** of the people, and H1367
Act 17:26 and the **b** of their habitation; *G3734*

BOUNTIFUL
Prv 22: 9 He that hath a **b** eye shall be blessed; H2896
Isa 32: 5 called liberal, nor the churl said *to be* **b**. H7771

BOUNTIFULLY
Ps 13: 6 because he hath dealt **b** with me. H1580
116: 7 for the LORD hath dealt **b** with thee. H1580
119:17 Deal **b** with thy servant, *that* I may live, H1580
142: 7 for thou shalt deal **b** with me. H1580
2Co 9: 6 soweth **b** shall reap also bountifully. *G1909*
6 soweth bountifully shall reap also **b**. *G1909*

BOUNTIFULNESS
2Co 9:11 Being enriched in every thing to all **b**, *G572*

BOUNTY
1Ki 10:13 her of his royal **b**. So she turned and H3027
2Co 9: 5 up beforehand your **b**, whereof ye had *G2129*
5 *matter of* **b**, and not as *of* covetousness. *G2129*

BOW
Gen 9:13 I do set my **b** in the cloud, and it shall H7198
14 that the **b** shall be seen in the cloud: H7198
16 And the **b** shall be in the cloud; and I H7198
27: 3 thy quiver and thy **b**, and go out to the H7198
29 Let people serve thee, and nations **b** H7812
29 let thy mother's sons **b** down to thee: H7812
37:10 **b** down ourselves to thee to the earth? H7812
41:43 they cried before him, **B** the knee: and he H86
48:22 Amorite with my sword and with my **b**. H7198
49: 8 children shall **b** down before thee. H7812
24 But his **b** abode in strength, and the H7198
Ex 11: 8 unto me, and **b** down themselves unto H7812
20: 5 Thou shalt not **b** down thyself to them, H7812
23:24 Thou shalt not **b** down to their gods, H7812
Lev 26: 1 in your land, to **b** down unto it: for I H7812
Dt 5: 9 Thou shalt not **b** down thyself unto H7812
Jos 23: 7 them, nor **b** yourselves unto them: H7812
24:12 *but* not with thy sword, nor with thy **b**. H7198
Jdg 2:19 serve them, and to **b** down unto them; H7812
1Sa 18: 4 sword, and to his **b**, and to his girdle. H7198
2Sa 1:18 *the use of* the **b**: behold, *it is* written H7198
22 of the mighty, the **b** of Jonathan turned H7198
22:35 a **b** of steel is broken by mine arms. H7198
1Ki 22:34 And a *certain* man drew a **b** at a H7198
2Ki 5:18 on my hand, and I **b** myself in the H7812
18 Rimmon: when I **b** down myself in the H7812
6:22 and with thy **b**? set bread and water H7198
9:24 And Jehu drew a **b** with his full H7198
13:15 And Elisha said unto him, Take **b** and H7198
15 And he took unto him **b** and arrows. H7198
16 hand upon the **b**. And he put his hand H7198
17:35 other gods, nor **b** yourselves to them, H7812
19:16 LORD, **b** down thine ear, and hear: H5186
1Ch 5:18 and to shoot with **b**, and skilful in war, H7198
12: 2 **b**, *even* of Saul's brethren of Benjamin. H7198
2Ch 17:17 **b** and shield two hundred thousand. H7198
18:33 And a *certain* man drew a **b** at a H7198
Job 20:24 the **b** of steel shall strike him through. H7198
29:20 My glory *was* fresh in me, and my **b** H7198
31:10 and let others **b** down upon her. H3766
39: 3 They **b** themselves, they bring forth H3766
Ps 7:12 he hath bent his **b**, and made it ready. H7198
11: 2 For, lo, the wicked bend *their* **b**, they H7198
18:34 a **b** of steel is broken by mine arms. H7198
22:29 to the dust shall **b** before him: and H3766
31: 2 **B** down thine ear to me; deliver me H5186
37:14 have bent their **b**, to cast down the poor H7198
44: 6 For I will not trust in my **b**, neither shall H7198
46: 9 he breaketh the **b**, and cutteth the spear H7198
58: 7 he bendeth *his* **b** *to shoot* his arrows,
72: 9 wilderness shall **b** before him; and his H3766
76: 3 There brake he the arrows of the **b**, the H7198
78:57 were turned aside like a deceitful **b**. H7198
86: 1 **B** down thine ear, O LORD, hear me: H5186
95: 6 O come, let us worship and **b** down: let H3766
144: 5 **B** thy heavens, O LORD, and come H5186
Prv 5: 1 My son, attend unto my wisdom, *and* **b** H5186
14:19 The evil **b** before the good; and the H7817
22:17 **B** down thine ear, and hear the words H5186
Ecc 12: 3 strong men shall **b** themselves, and the H5791
Isa 10: 4 Without me they shall **b** down under H3766
21:15 **b**, and from the grievousness of war. H7198
41: 2 sword, *and* as driven stubble to his **b**. H7198
45:23 knee shall **b**, every tongue shall swear. H3766
46: 2 They stoop, they **b** down together; they H3766
49:23 they shall **b** down to thee with *their* H7812
51:23 said to thy soul, **B** down, that we may H7812
58: 5 his soul? *is it* to **b** down his head as a H3721
60:14 thee shall **b** themselves down at H7812
65:12 sword, and ye shall all **b** down to the H3766
66:19 that draw the **b**, *to* Tubal, and Javan, H7198
Jer 6:23 They shall lay hold on **b** and spear; H7198
9: 3 tongues *like* their **b** *for* lies: but they H7198
46: 9 Lydians, that handle *and* bend the **b**. H7198
49:35 the **b** of Elam, the chief of their might. H7198
50:14 ye that bend the **b**, shoot at her, spare H7198
29 all ye that bend the **b**, camp against it H7198
42 They shall hold the **b** and the lance: H7198
51: 3 archer bend his **b**, and against *him that* H7198
Lam 2: 4 He hath bent his **b** like an enemy: he H7198
3:12 He hath bent his **b**, and set me as a H7198
Ezk 1:28 As the appearance of the **b** that is in H7198
39: 3 And I will smite thy **b** out of thy left H7198
Hos 1: 5 the **b** of Israel in the valley of Jezreel. H7198
7 not save them by **b**, nor by sword, nor H7198
2:18 I will break the **b** and the sword and H7198
7:16 are like a deceitful **b**: their princes shall H7198
Am 2:15 that handleth the **b**; and *he that is* swift H7198
Mic 6: 6 the LORD, *and* **b** myself before the high H3721
Hab 3: 6 hills did **b**: his ways *are* everlasting. H7817
9 Thy **b** was made quite naked, H7198
Zec 9:10 and the battle **b** shall be cut off: and H7198
13 for me, filled the **b** with Ephraim, and H7198
10: 4 **b**, out of him every oppressor together. H7198
Ro 11:10 not see, and **b** down their back alway. *G4781*
14:11 every knee shall **b** to me, and every *G2578*
Eph 3:14 For this cause I **b** my knees unto the *G2578*
Php 2:10 Jesus every knee should **b**, of *things* in *G2578*
Rev 6: 2 sat on him had a **b**; and a crown was *G5115*

BOWED
Gen 18: 2 door, and **b** himself toward the ground, H7812
19: 1 them; and he **b** himself with his face H7812
23: 7 And Abraham stood up, and **b** himself H7812
12 And Abraham **b** down himself before H7812
24:26 And the man **b** down his head, and H6915
48 And I **b** down my head, and H6915
33: 3 And he passed over before them, and **b** H7812
6 their children, and they **b** themselves. H7812
7 came near, and **b** themselves: and after H7812
7 and Rachel, and they **b** themselves. H7812
42: 6 came, and **b** down themselves before H7812
43:26 and **b** themselves to him to the earth. H7812
28 yet alive. And they **b** down their heads, H7812
47:31 Israel **b** himself upon the bed's head. H7812
48:12 he **b** himself with his face to the earth. H7812
49:15 *it was* pleasant; and **b** his shoulder to H5186
Ex 4:31 they **b** their heads and worshipped. H6915
12:27 the people **b** the head and worshipped. H6915
34: 8 And Moses made haste, and **b** his head H6915
Nu 22:31 his hand: and he **b** down his head, and H6915
25: 2 did eat, and **b** down to their gods. H7812
Jos 23:16 other gods, and **b** yourselves to them; H7812
Jdg 2:12 about them, and **b** themselves unto H7812
17 other gods, and **b** themselves unto H7812
5:27 At her feet he **b**, he fell, he lay down: at H3766
27 at her feet he **b**, he fell: where he bowed, H3766
27 fell: where he **b**, there he fell down dead. H3766
7: 6 rest of the people **b** down upon their H3766
16:30 And he **b** himself with *all his* H5186
Ru 2:10 Then she fell on her face, and **b** herself H7812
1Sa 4:19 were dead, she **b** herself and travailed; H3766
20:41 the ground, and **b** himself three times: H7812
24: 8 his face to the earth, and **b** himself. H7812
25:23 her face, and **b** herself to the ground, H7812
41 And she arose, and **b** herself on *her* H7812
28:14 *his* face to the ground, and **b** himself. H7812
2Sa 9: 8 And he **b** himself, and said, What *is* thy H7812
14:22 on his face, and **b** himself, and thanked H7812
33 to the king, and **b** himself on his face H7812
18:21 Cushi **b** himself unto Joab, and ran. H7812
19:14 And he **b** the heart of all the men of H5186
22:10 He **b** the heavens also, and came down; H5186
24:20 went out, and **b** himself before the king H7812
1Ki 1:16 And Bath-sheba **b**, and did obeisance H6915
23 before the king, he **b** himself before the H7812
31 Then Bath-sheba **b** with *her* face to the H6915
47 And the king **b** himself upon the bed. H7812
53 And he came and **b** himself to king H7812
2:19 up to meet her, and **b** himself unto her, H7812
19:18 which have not **b** unto Baal, and every H3766
2Ki 2:15 **b** themselves to the ground before him. H7812
4:37 and fell at his feet, and **b** herself to the H7812
1Ch 21:21 and **b** himself to David with H7812
29:20 their fathers, and **b** down their heads, H6915
2Ch 7: 3 the house, they **b** themselves with their H3766
20:18 And Jehoshaphat **b** his head with *his* H6915
25:14 *be* his gods, and **b** down himself before H7812
29:29 him **b** themselves, and worshipped. H3766
30 they **b** their heads and worshipped. H6915
Neh 8: 6 hands: and they **b** their heads, and H6915
Est 3: 2 in the king's gate, **b**, and reverenced H3766
2 Mordecai **b** not, nor did *him* reverence. H3766
5 And when Haman saw that Mordecai **b** H3766
Ps 18: 9 He **b** the heavens also, and came down: H5186
35:14 *or* brother: I **b** down heavily, as one H7817
38: 6 I am troubled; I am **b** down greatly; I H7743
44:25 For our soul is **b** down to the dust: our H3721
57: 6 my steps; my soul is **b** down: they have H3721

Ps 145:14 raiseth up all *those that be* b down. H3721
146: 8 b down: the LORD loveth the righteous: H3721
Isa 2:11 of men shall be b down, and the LORD H7817
17 And the loftiness of man shall be b H7817
21: 3 travaileth: I was b down at the hearing H5791
Mt 27:29 hand: and they b the knee before him, *G1120*
Lk 13:11 years, and was b together, and could *G4794*
24: 5 And as they were afraid, and b down *G2827*
Jn 19:30 he b his head, and gave up the ghost. *G2827*
Ro 11: 4 not b the knee to *the image of* Baal. *G2578*

BOWELS
Gen 15: 4 out of thine own b shall be thine heir. H4578
25:23 from thy b; and *the one* people H4578
43:30 And Joseph made haste; for his b did H7356
Nu 5:22 shall go into thy b, to make *thy* belly to H4578
2Sa 7:12 thy b, and I will establish his kingdom. H4578
16:11 came forth of my b, seeketh my life: H4578
20:10 and shed out his b to the ground, and H4578
1Ki 3:26 the king, for her b yearned upon her H7356
2Ch 21:15 by disease of thy b, until thy bowels fall H4578
15 bowels, until thy b fall out by reason of H4578
18 him in his b with an incurable disease. H4578
19 of two years, his b fell out by reason of H4578
32:21 own b slew him there with the sword. H4578
Job 20:14 *Yet* his meat in his b is turned, *it is* the H4578
30:27 My b boiled, and rested not: the days of H4578
Ps 22:14 wax; it is melted in the midst of my b. H4578
71: 6 out of my mother's b: my praise *shall be* H4578
109:18 b like water, and like oil into his bones. H7130
Song 5: 4 *door,* and my b were moved for him. H4578
Isa 16:11 Wherefore my b shall sound like an H4578
48:19 the offspring of thy b like the gravel H4578
49: 1 womb; from the b of my mother hath H4578
63:15 the sounding of thy b and of thy mercies H4578
Jer 4:19 My b, my bowels! I am pained at my H4578
19 My bowels, my b! I am pained at my H4578
31:20 still: therefore my b are troubled for H4578
Lam 1:20 *am* in distress: my b are troubled; mine H4578
2:11 Mine eyes do fail with tears, my b are H4578
Ezk 3: 3 to eat, and fill thy b with this roll that I H4578
7:19 neither fill their b: because it is the H4578
Act 1:18 in the midst, and all his b gushed out. *G4698*
2Co 6:12 us, but ye are straitened in your own b. *G4698*
Php 1: 8 after you all in the b of Jesus Christ. *G4698*
2: 1 of the Spirit, if any b and mercies, *G4698*
Col 3:12 God, holy and beloved, b of mercies, *G4698*
Phlm 7 thy love, because the b of the saints are *G4698*
12 receive him, that is, mine own b: *G4698*
20 in the Lord: refresh my b in the Lord. *G4698*
1Jn 3:17 shutteth up his b *of compassion* from *G4698*

BOWETH
Jdg 7: 5 that b down upon his knees to drink. H3766
Isa 2: 9 And the mean man b down, and the H7817
46: 1 Bel b down, Nebo stoopeth, their idols H3766

BOWING
Gen 24:52 the LORD, *b himself* to the earth.
Ps 17:11 have set their eyes b down to the earth; H5186
62: 3 all of you: as a b wall *shall ye be, and* H5186
Mk 15:19 and b *their* knees worshipped him. *G5087*

BOWL
Nu 7:13 *shekels,* one silver b of seventy shekels, H4219
19 *shekels,* one silver b of seventy shekels, H4219
25 *shekels,* one silver b of seventy shekels, H4219
31 *shekels,* one silver b of seventy shekels, H4219
37 *shekels,* one silver b of seventy shekels, H4219
43 *shekels,* a silver b of seventy shekels, H4219
49 *shekels,* one silver b of seventy shekels, H4219
55 *shekels,* one silver b of seventy shekels, H4219
61 *shekels,* one silver b of seventy shekels, H4219
67 *shekels,* one silver b of seventy shekels, H4219
73 *shekels,* one silver b of seventy shekels, H4219
79 *shekels,* one silver b of seventy shekels, H4219
85 *shekels,* each b seventy: all the silver H4219
Jdg 6:38 dew out of the fleece, a b full of water. H5602
Ecc 12: 6 or the golden b be broken, or the H1543
Zec 4: 2 all *of* gold, with a b upon the top of it, H1531
3 right *side* of the b, and the other upon H1543

BOWLS
Ex 25:29 thereof, and b thereof, to cover withal: H4518
31 his branches, his b, his knops, and his H1375
33 Three b made like unto almonds, *with* H1375
33 branch; and three b made like almonds H1375
34 And in the candlestick *shall be* four b H1375
37:16 his spoons, and his b, and his covers to H4518
Ex 37:17 his branch, his b, his knops, and his H1375
19 Three b made after the fashion of H1375
19 flower; and three b made like almonds H1375
20 And in the candlestick *were* four b H1375
Nu 4: 7 spoons, and the b, and covers to cover H4518
7:84 twelve silver b, twelve spoons of gold: H4219
1Ki 7:41 The two pillars, and the *two* b of the H1543
41 to cover the two b of the chapiters H1543
42 to cover the two b of the chapiters that H1543
50 And the b, and the snuffers, and the H5592
2Ki 12:13 house of the LORD b of silver, snuffers, H5592
25:15 And the firepans, and the b, *and* such H4219
1Ch 28:17 and the b, and the cups: and for H4219
Jer 52:18 snuffers, and the b, and the spoons, and H4219
19 firepans, and the b, and the caldrons, H4219
Am 6: 6 That drink wine in b, and anoint H4219
Zec 9:15 like b, *and* as the corners of the altar. H4219
14:20 shall be like the b before the altar. H4219

BOWMEN
Jer 4:29 and b; they shall go into H7198+H7411

BOWS
1Sa 2: 4 The b of the mighty men *are* broken, H7198
1Ch 12: 2 *They were* armed with b, and could use H7198
2Ch 14: 8 shields and drew b, two hundred and H7198
26:14 and b, and slings *to cast* stones. H7198
Neh 4:13 their swords, their spears, and their b. H7198
16 shields, and the b, and the habergeons; H7198
Ps 37:15 own heart, and their b shall be broken. H7198
64: 3 *and* bend *their b to shoot* their arrows,
78: 9 b, turned back in the day of battle. H7198
Isa 5:28 and all their b bent, their horses' hoofs H7198
7:24 With arrows and with b shall *men* H7198
13:18 *Their* b also shall dash the young men H7198
Jer 51:56 every one of their b is broken: for the H7198
Ezk 39: 9 the bucklers, the b and the arrows, and H7198

BOWSHOT
Gen 21:16 as it were a b: for she said, Let H2909+H7198

BOX
2Ki 9: 1 and take this b of oil in thine hand, H6378
3 Then take the b of oil, and pour *it* on H6378
Isa 41:19 *and* the pine, and the b tree together: H8391
60:13 the pine tree, and the b together, to H8391
Mt 26: 7 having an alabaster b of very precious *G211*
Mk 14: 3 an alabaster b of ointment of spikenard *G211*
3 brake the b, and poured *it* on his head. *G211*
Lk 7:37 brought an alabaster b of ointment, *G211*

BOX-TREE See BOX and TREE.

BOY
Joel 3: 3 and have given a b for an harlot, and H3206

BOYS
Gen 25:27 And the b grew: and Esau was a H5288
Zec 8: 5 city shall be full of b and girls playing H3206

BOZEZ
1Sa 14: 4 *was* B, and the name of the other Seneh. H949

BOZKATH
Jos 15:39 Lachish, and B, and Eglon, H1218

BOZNAI See SHETHAR-BOZNAI.

BOZRAH
Gen 36:33 son of Zerah of B reigned in his stead. H1224
1Ch 1:44 son of Zerah of B reigned in his stead. H1224
Isa 34: 6 LORD hath a sacrifice in B, and a great H1224
63: 1 garments from B? this *that is* glorious H1224
Jer 48:24 And upon Kerioth, and upon B, and H1224
49:13 saith the LORD, that B shall become a H1224
22 his wings over B: and at that day shall H1224
Am 1:12 which shall devour the palaces of B. H1224
Mic 2:12 as the sheep of B, as the flock in the H1224

BRACELET
2Sa 1:10 his head, and the b that *was* on his arm, H685

BRACELETS
Gen 24:22 weight, and two b for her hands of ten H6781
30 saw the earring and b upon his sister's H6781
47 her face, and the b upon her hands. H6781
38:18 signet, and thy b, and thy staff that *is* H6616
25 *are* these, the signet, and b, and staff. H6616
Ex 35:22 *and* brought b, and earrings, and rings, H2397
Nu 31:50 gold, chains, and b, rings, earrings, and H6781
Isa 3:19 The chains, and the b, and the mufflers, H8285
Ezk 16:11 and I put b upon thy hands, and H6781
23:42 which put b upon their hands, and H6781

BRAIDED See BROIDED.

BRAKE
Ex 9:25 of the field, and b every tree of the field. H7665
32: 3 And all the people b off the golden H6561
19 hands, and b them beneath the mount. H7665
Dt 9:17 hands, and b them before your eyes. H7665
Jdg 7:19 b the pitchers that *were* in their hands. H5310
20 the trumpets, and b the pitchers, and H7665
9:53 head, and all to b his skull. H7533
16: 9 thee, Samson. And he b the withs, as a H5423
12 b them from off his arms like a thread. H5423
1Sa 4:18 gate, and his neck b, and he died: for he H7665
2Sa 23:16 And the three mighty men b through H1234
1Ki 19:11 mountains, and b in pieces the rocks H7665
2Ki 10:27 And they b down the image of Baal, H5422
27 of Baal, and b down the house of Baal, H5422
11:18 house of Baal, and b it down; his altars H5422
18 altars and his images b they in pieces H7665
14:13 to Jerusalem, and b down the wall of H6555
18: 4 He removed the high places, and b the H7665
4 the groves, and b in pieces the brasen H3807
23: 7 And he b down the houses of the H5422
8 to Beer-sheba, and b down the high H5422
12 beat down, and b *them* down from H7323
14 And he b in pieces the images, and cut H7665
15 the high place he b down, and burned H5422
25:10 of the guard, b down the walls of H5422
1Ch 11:18 And the three b through the host of the H1234
2Ch 14: 3 high places, and b down the images, H7665
21:17 And they came up into Judah, and b H1234
23:17 the house of Baal, and b it down, and H5422
17 brake it down, and b his altars and his H7665
25:23 to Jerusalem, and b down the wall of H6555
26: 6 the Philistines, and b down the wall of H6555
31: 1 of Judah, and b the images in pieces, H7665
34: 4 And they b down the altars of Baalim H5422
4 the molten images, he b in pieces, and H7665
36:19 And they burnt the house of God, and b H5422
Job 29:17 And I b the jaws of the wicked, and H7665
38: 8 with doors, when it b forth, *as if* it had H1518
10 And b up for it my decreed *place,* and H7665
Ps 76: 3 There b he the arrows of the bow, the H7665
105:16 the land: he b the whole staff of bread. H7665
33 fig trees; and b the trees of their coasts. H7665
106:29 and the plague b in upon them. H6555
107:14 of death, and b their bands in sunder. H5423
Jer 28:10 the prophet Jeremiah's neck, and b it. H7665
31:32 my covenant they b, although I was an H6565
39: 8 and b down the walls of Jerusalem. H5422
52:14 of the guard, b down all the walls of H5422
17 the Chaldeans b, and carried all the H7665
Ezk 17:16 covenant he b, *even* with him in the H6565
Dan 2: 1 troubled, and his sleep b from him. H1961
34 of iron and clay, and b them to pieces. H1855
45 hands, and that it b in pieces the iron, H1855
6:24 of them, and b all their bones in pieces H1855
7: 7 teeth: it devoured and b in pieces, and H1855
19 brass; *which* devoured, b in pieces, and H1855
8: 7 the ram, and b his two horns: and H7665
Mt 14:19 he blessed, and b, and gave the loaves *G2806*
15:36 gave thanks, and b *them,* and gave to *G2806*
26:26 blessed *it,* and b *it,* and gave *it* to the *G2806*
Mk 6:41 and blessed, and b the loaves, and gave *G2622*
8: 6 and gave thanks, and b, and gave to his *G2806*
19 When I b the five loaves among five *G2806*
14: 3 b the box, and poured *it* on his head. *G4937*
22 and blessed, and b *it,* and gave to *G2806*
Lk 5: 6 multitude of fishes: and their net b. *G1284*
8:29 in fetters; and he b the bands, and was *G1284*
9:16 he blessed them, and b, and gave to the *G2622*
22:19 gave thanks, and b *it,* and gave unto *G2806*
24:30 and blessed *it,* and b, and gave to them. *G2806*
Jn 19:32 Then came the soldiers, and b the legs *G2608*
33 was dead already, they b not his legs: *G2608*
1Co 11:24 And when he had given thanks, he b *it,* *G2806*

BRAKEST
Ex 34: 1 were in the first tables, which thou b. H7665
Dt 10: 2 b, and thou shalt put them in the ark. H7665
Ps 74:13 by thy strength: thou b the heads of the H7665
14 Thou b the heads of leviathan in H7533
Ezk 29: 7 upon thee, thou b, and madest all their H7665

BRAMBLE
Jdg 9:14 Then said all the trees unto the **b**, Come H329
15 And the **b** said unto the trees, If in truth H329
15 the **b**, and devour the cedars of Lebanon. H329
Lk 6:44 figs, nor of a **b** bush gather they grapes. *G942*

BRAMBLES
Isa 34:13 nettles and **b** in the fortresses thereof: H2336

BRANCH
Ex 25:33 a flower in one **b**; and three bowls made H7070
33 in the other **b**, *with* a knop and a flower: H7070
37:17 his shaft, and his **b**, his bowls, his H7070
19 of almonds in one **b**, a knop and a H7070
19 in another **b**, a knop and a flower: H7070
Nu 13:23 from thence a **b** with one cluster of H2156
Job 8:16 He *is* green before the sun, and his **b** H3127
14: 7 that the tender **b** thereof will not cease. H3127
15:32 his time, and his **b** shall not be green. H3712
18:16 and above shall his **b** be cut off. H7105
29:19 and the dew lay all night upon my **b**. H7105
Ps 80:15 **b** *that* thou madest strong for thyself. H1121
Prv 11:28 but the righteous shall flourish as a **b**. H5929
Isa 4: 2 In that day shall the **b** of the LORD be H6780
9:14 head and tail, **b** and rush, in one day. H3712
11: 1 and a **B** shall grow out of his roots: H5342
14:19 an abominable **b**, *and as* the raiment H5342
17: 9 and an uppermost **b**, which they left H534
19:15 the head or tail, **b** or rush, may do. H3712
25: 5 of a cloud: the **b** of the terrible ones H2159
60:21 land for ever, the **b** of my planting, the H5342
Jer 23: 5 David a righteous **B**, and a King shall H6780
33:15 will I cause the **B** of righteousness to H6780
Ezk 8:17 and, lo, they put the **b** to their nose. H2156
15: 2 any tree, *or than* a **b** which is among H2156
17: 3 and took the highest **b** of the cedar: H6788
22 take of the highest **b** of the high cedar, H6788
Dan 11: 7 But out of a **b** of her roots shall *one* H5342
Zec 3: 8 I will bring forth my servant the **B**. H6780
6:12 name *is* The **B**; and he shall grow up H6780
Mal 4: 1 it shall leave them neither root nor **b**. H6057
Mt 24:32 fig tree; When his **b** is yet tender, and *G2798*
Mk 13:28 fig tree; When her **b** is yet tender, and *G2798*
Jn 15: 2 Every **b** in me that beareth not fruit he *G2814*
2 away: and every *b* that beareth fruit, he
4 Abide in me, and I in you. As the **b** *G2814*
6 is cast forth as a **b**, and is withered; and *G2814*

BRANCHES
Gen 40:10 And in the vine *were* three **b**: and it *was* H8299
12 of it: The three **b** *are* three days: H8299
49:22 by a well; *whose* **b** run over the wall: H1323
Ex 25:31 his shaft, and his **b**, his bowls, his H7070
32 And six **b** shall come out of the sides of H7070
32 the sides of it; three **b** of the candlestick H7070
32 side, and three **b** of the candlestick out H7070
33 six **b** that come out of the candlestick. H7070
35 And *there shall be* a knop under two **b** H7070
35 a knop under two **b** of the same, and a H7070
35 and a knop under two **b** of the same, H7070
35 **b** that proceed out of the candlestick. H7070
36 Their knops and their **b** shall be of the H7070
37:18 And six **b** going out of the sides thereof; H7070
18 thereof; three **b** of the candlestick out H7070
18 thereof, and three **b** of the candlestick H7070
19 the six **b** going out of the candlestick. H7070
21 And a knop under two **b** of the same, H7070
21 a knop under two **b** of the same, and a H7070
21 and a knop under two **b** of the same, H7070
21 according to the six **b** going out of it. H7070
22 Their knops and their **b** were of the H7070
Lev 23:40 of goodly trees, **b** of palm trees, and the H3709
Neh 8:15 and fetch olive **b**, and pine branches, H5929
15 and pine **b**, and myrtle branches, H5929
15 and myrtle **b**, and palm branches, H5929
15 and palm **b**, and branches of thick H5929
15 branches, and **b** of thick trees, to make H5929
Job 15:30 shall dry up his **b**, and by the breath of H3127
Ps 80:11 unto the sea, and her **b** unto the river. H3127
104:12 habitation, *which* sing among the **b**. H6073
Isa 16: 8 the wilderness: her **b** are stretched out, H7976
17: 6 **b** thereof, saith the LORD God of Israel. H5585
18: 5 and take away *and* cut down the **b**. H5189
27:10 lie down, and consume the **b** thereof. H5585
Jer 11:16 fire upon it, and the **b** of it are broken. H1808
Ezk 17: 6 stature, whose **b** turned toward him, H1808
6 brought forth **b**, and shot forth sprigs. H905
7 and shot forth her **b** toward him, that H1808
8 it might bring forth **b**, and that it might H6057
Ezk 17:23 of the **b** thereof shall they dwell. H1808
19:10 and full of **b** by reason of many waters. H6058
11 among the thick **b**, and she appeared in H5688
11 her height with the multitude of her **b**. H1808
14 And fire is gone out of a rod of her **b**, H905
31: 3 in Lebanon with fair **b**, and with a H6057
5 and his **b** became long because H6288
6 and under his **b** did all the beasts of H6288
7 his **b**: for his root was by great waters. H1808
8 were not like his **b**; nor any tree in the H6288
9 multitude of his **b**: so that all the trees H1808
12 all the valleys his **b** are fallen, and his H1808
13 beasts of the field shall be upon his **b**: H6288
36: 8 shoot forth your **b**, and yield your fruit H6057
Dan 4:14 and cut off his **b**, shake off his leaves, H6056
14 from under it, and the fowls from his **b**: H6056
21 and upon whose **b** the fowls of the H6056
Hos 11: 6 shall consume his **b**, and devour *them*, H905
14: 6 His **b** shall spread, and his beauty shall H3127
Joel 1: 7 *it* away; the **b** thereof are made white. H8299
Nah 2: 2 them out, and marred their vine **b**. H2156
Zec 4:12 *be these* two olive **b** which through the H7641
Mt 13:32 the air come and lodge in the **b** thereof. *G2798*
21: 8 others cut down **b** from the trees, and *G2798*
Mk 4:32 shooteth out great **b**; so that the fowls of *G2798*
11: 8 others cut down **b** off the trees, and *G4746*
Lk 13:19 the fowls of the air lodged in the **b** of it. *G2798*
Jn 12:13 Took **b** of palm trees, and went forth to *G902*
15: 5 I am the vine, ye *are* the **b**: He that *G2814*
Ro 11:16 and if the root *be* holy, so *are* the **b**. *G2798*
17 And if some of the **b** be broken off, and *G2798*
18 Boast not against the **b**. But if thou *G2798*
19 Thou wilt say then, The **b** were broken *G2798*
21 For if God spared not the natural **b**, *G2798*
24 *b*, be graffed into their own olive tree?

BRAND
Zec 3: 2 *is* not this a **b** plucked out of the fire? H181

BRANDISH
Ezk 32:10 thee, when I shall **b** my sword before H5774

BRANDS
Jdg 15: 5 And when he had set the **b** on fire, he H3940

BRASEN
Ex 27: 4 four **b** rings in the four corners thereof. H5178
35:16 The altar of burnt offering, with his **b** H5178
38: 4 And he made for the altar a **b** grate of H5178
10 Their pillars *were* twenty, and their **b** H5178
30 and the **b** altar, and the brasen H5178
30 altar, and the **b** grate for it, and all H5178
39:39 The **b** altar, and his grate of brass, his H5178
Lev 6:28 and if it be sodden in a **b** pot, it shall be H5178
Nu 16:39 And Eleazar the priest took the **b** H5178
1Ki 4:13 great cities with walls and **b** bars: H5178
7:30 And every base had four **b** wheels, and H5178
8:64 because the **b** altar that *was* before H5178
14:27 in their stead **b** shields, and committed H5178
2Ki 16:14 And he brought also the **b** altar, which H5178
15 **b** altar shall be for me to inquire *by*. H5178
17 sea from off the **b** oxen that *were* under H5178
18: 4 in pieces the **b** serpent that Moses H5178
25:13 the bases, and the **b** sea that *was* in the H5178
1Ch 18: 8 made the **b** sea, and the pillars, H5178
2Ch 1: 5 Moreover the **b** altar, that Bezaleel the H5178
6 And Solomon went up thither to the **b** H5178
6:13 For Solomon had made a **b** scaffold, of H5178
7: 7 because the **b** altar which Solomon H5178
Jer 1:18 an iron pillar, and **b** walls against the H5178
15:20 people a fenced **b** wall: and they shall H5178
52:17 the bases, and the **b** sea that *was* in the H5178
20 The two pillars, one sea, and twelve **b** H5178
Ezk 9: 2 went in, and stood beside the **b** altar. H5178
Mk 7: 4 cups, and pots, **b** vessels, and of tables. *G5473*

BRASS
Gen 4:22 of every artificer in **b** and iron: and the H5178
Ex 25: 3 take of them; gold, and silver, and **b**, H5178
26:11 And thou shalt make fifty taches of **b**, H5178
37 shalt cast five sockets of **b** for them. H5178
27: 2 same: and thou shalt overlay it with **b**. H5178
3 the vessels thereof thou shalt make *of* **b**. H5178
4 of network *of* **b**; and upon the net shalt H5178
6 shittim wood, and overlay them with **b**. H5178
10 sockets *shall be of* **b**; the hooks of the H5178
11 twenty sockets *of* **b**; the hooks of the H5178
17 *shall be of* silver, and their sockets *of* **b**. H5178
18 fine twined linen, and their sockets *of* **b**. H5178
Ex 27:19 all the pins of the court, *shall be of* **b**. H5178
30:18 Thou shalt also make a laver *of* **b**, and H5178
18 his foot *also of* **b**, to wash *withal:* and H5178
31: 4 to work in gold, and in silver, and in **b**, H5178
35: 5 of the LORD; gold, and silver, and **b**, H5178
24 of silver and **b** brought the LORD'S H5178
32 to work in gold, and in silver, and in **b**, H5178
36:18 And he made fifty taches *of* **b** to couple H5178
38 gold: but their five sockets *were of* **b**. H5178
38: 2 of the same: and he overlaid it with **b**. H5178
3 all the vessels thereof made he *of* **b**. H5178
5 grate of **b**, *to be* places for the staves. H5178
6 wood, and overlaid them with **b**. H5178
8 And he made the laver *of* **b**, and the H5178
8 the foot of it *of* **b**, of the looking-glasses H5178
11 their sockets of **b** twenty; the hooks of H5178
17 And the sockets for the pillars *were of* **b**; H5178
19 their sockets *of* **b** four; their hooks *of* H5178
20 and of the court round about, *were of* **b**. H5178
29 And the **b** of the offering *was* seventy H5178
39:39 The brasen altar, and his grate of **b**, his H5178
Lev 26:19 heaven as iron, and your earth as **b**: H5154
Nu 21: 9 And Moses made a serpent of **b**, and H5178
9 he beheld the serpent of **b**, he lived. H5178
31:22 Only the gold, and the silver, the **b**, the H5178
Dt 8: 9 out of whose hills thou mayest dig **b**. H5178
28:23 thy head shall be **b**, and the earth that is H5178
33:25 Thy shoes *shall be* iron and **b**; and as H5178
Jos 6:19 gold, and vessels of **b** and iron, *are* H5178
24 and the vessels of **b** and of iron, they H5178
22: 8 gold, and with **b**, and with iron, and H5178
Jdg 16:21 **b**; and he did grind in the prison house. H5178
1Sa 17: 5 And *he had* an helmet of **b** upon his H5178
5 the coat *was* five thousand shekels of **b**. H5178
6 And *he had* greaves of **b** upon his legs, H5178
6 a target of **b** between his shoulders. H5178
38 put an helmet of **b** upon his head; also H5178
2Sa 8: 8 king David took exceeding much **b**. H5178
10 and vessels of gold, and vessels of **b**: H5178
21:16 *shekels* of **b** in weight, he being H5178
1Ki 7:14 of Tyre, a worker in **b**: and he was filled H5178
14 to work all works in **b**. And he came to H5178
15 For he cast two pillars of **b**, of eighteen H5178
16 And he made two chapiters *of* molten **b**, H5178
27 And he made ten bases of **b**; four cubits H5178
30 and plates of **b**: and the four corners H5178
38 Then made he ten lavers of **b**: one laver H5178
45 the house of the LORD, *were of* bright **b**. H5178
47 was the weight of the **b** found out. H5178
2Ki 25: 7 fetters of **b**, and carried him to Babylon. H5178
13 And the pillars of **b** that *were* in the H5178
13 and carried the **b** of them to Babylon. H5178
14 and all the vessels of **b** wherewith they H5178
16 of the LORD; the **b** of all these vessels H5178
17 upon it *was* **b**: and the height of the H5178
17 about, all of **b**: and like unto these H5178
1Ch 15:19 *appointed* to sound with cymbals of **b**; H5178
18: 8 brought David very much **b**, wherewith H5178
8 sea, and the pillars, and the vessels of **b**. H5178
10 of vessels of gold and silver and **b**. H5178
22: 3 and **b** in abundance without weight; H5178
14 of silver; and of **b** and iron without H5178
16 Of the gold, the silver, and the **b**, and H5178
29: 2 of silver, and the **b** for *things* of brass, H5178
2 brass for *things* of **b**, the iron for *things* H5178
7 talents, and of **b** eighteen thousand H5178
2Ch 2: 7 in silver, and in **b**, and in iron, and in H5178
14 and in silver, in **b**, in iron, in stone, and H5178
4: 1 Moreover he made an altar of **b**, twenty H5178
9 and overlaid the doors of them with **b**. H5178
16 for the house of the LORD of bright **b**. H5178
18 weight of the **b** could not be found out. H5178
12:10 made shields of **b**, and committed *them* H5178
24:12 and **b** to mend the house of the LORD. H5178
Job 6:12 strength of stones? or *is* my flesh of **b**? H5153
28: 2 Iron is taken out of the earth, and **b** *is* H5154
40:18 His bones *are as* strong pieces of **b**; his H5154
41:27 He esteemeth iron as straw, *and* **b** as H5154
Ps 107:16 For he hath broken the gates of **b**, and H5178
Isa 45: 2 of **b**, and cut in sunder the bars of iron: H5154
48: 4 neck *is* an iron sinew, and thy brow **b**; H5154
60:17 For **b** I will bring gold, and for iron I H5178
17 and for wood **b**, and for stones iron: H5178
Jer 6:28 *are* **b** and iron; they *are* all corrupters. H5178
52:17 Also the pillars of **b** that *were* in the H5178
17 carried all the **b** of them to Babylon. H5178
18 and all the vessels of **b** wherewith they H5178
20 of the LORD: the **b** of all these vessels H5178
22 And a chapiter of **b** *was* upon it; and H5178

Jer 52:22 about, all *of* **b**. The second pillar also H5178
Ezk 1: 7 sparkled like the colour of burnished **b**. H5178
22:18 dross: all they *are* **b**, and tin, and iron, H5178
20 *As* they gather silver, and **b**, and iron, H5178
24:11 thereof, that the **b** of it may be hot, and H5178
27:13 of men and vessels of **b** in thy market. H5178
40: 3 the appearance of **b**, with a line of flax H5178
Dan 2:32 of silver, his belly and his thighs of **b**, H5174
35 Then was the iron, the clay, the **b**, the H5174
39 third kingdom of **b**, which shall bear H5174
45 the iron, the **b**, the clay, the silver, H5174
4:15 band of iron and **b**, in the tender grass H5174
23 band of iron and **b**, in the tender grass H5174
5: 4 of **b**, of iron, of wood, and of stone. H5174
23 of silver, and gold, of **b**, iron, wood, and H5174
7:19 and his nails *of* **b**; *which* devoured, H5174
10: 6 in colour to polished **b**, and the voice of H5178
Mic 4:13 make thy hoofs **b**: and thou shalt beat H5154
Zec 6: 1 the mountains *were* mountains of **b**. H5178
Mt 10: 9 Provide neither gold, nor silver, nor **b** *G5475*
1Co 13: 1 *as* sounding **b**, or a tinkling cymbal. *G5475*
Rev 1:15 And his feet like unto fine **b**, as if they *G5474*
2:18 flame of fire, and his feet *are* like fine **b**; *G5474*
9:20 and silver, and **b**, and stone, and of *G5470*
18:12 wood, and of **b**, and iron, and marble, *G5475*

BRAVERY
Isa 3:18 will take away the **b** of *their* tinkling H8597

BRAWLER
1Ti 3: 3 lucre; but patient, not a **b**, not covetous; *G269*

BRAWLERS
Tit 3: 2 To speak evil of no man, to be no **b**, *but* *G269*

BRAWLING
Prv 21: 9 than with a **b** woman in a wide house. H4090
25:24 with a **b** woman and in a wide house. H4090

BRAY
Job 6: 5 Doth the wild ass **b** when he hath H5101
Prv 27:22 Though thou shouldest **b** a fool in a H3806

BRAYED
Job 30: 7 Among the bushes they **b**; under the H5101

BRAZEN See BRASEN.

BREACH
Gen 38:29 thou broken forth? *this* **b** *be* upon thee: H6556
Lev 24:20 **B** for breach, eye for eye, tooth for H7667
20 Breach for **b**, eye for eye, tooth for H7667
Nu 14:34 and ye shall know my **b** of promise. H8569
Jdg 21:15 had made a **b** in the tribes of Israel. H6556
2Sa 5:20 enemies before me, as the **b** of waters. H6556
6: 8 LORD had made a **b** upon Uzzah: and H6556
2Ki 12: 5 wheresoever any **b** shall be found. H919
1Ch 13:11 the LORD had made a **b** upon Uzza: H6556
15:13 our God made a **b** upon us, for that we H6555
Neh 6: 1 and *that* there was no **b** left therein; H6556
Job 16:14 He breaketh me with **b** upon breach, he H6556
14 He breaketh me with breach upon **b**, he H6556
Ps 106:23 before him in the **b**, to turn away his H6556
Prv 15: 4 perverseness therein *is* a **b** in the spirit. H7667
Isa 7: 6 and let us make a **b** therein for us, and H1234
30:13 be to you as a **b** ready to fall, swelling H6556
26 bindeth up the **b** of his people, and H7667
58:12 the **b**, The restorer of paths to dwell in. H6556
Jer 14:17 a great **b**, with a very grievous blow. H7667
Lam 2:13 of Zion? for thy **b** *is* great like the sea: H7667
Ezk 26:10 enter into a city wherein is made a **b**. H1234

BREACHES
Jdg 5:17 on the sea shore, and abode in his **b**. H4664
1Ki 11:27 the **b** of the city of David his father. H6556
2Ki 12: 5 and let them repair the **b** of the house, H919
6 had not repaired the **b** of the house. H919
7 repair ye not the **b** of the house? now H919
7 but deliver it for the **b** of the house. H919
8 neither to repair the **b** of the house. H919
12 stone to repair the **b** of the house of the H919
22: 5 the LORD, to repair the **b** of the house, H919
Neh 4: 7 up, *and* that the **b** began to be stopped, H6555
Ps 60: 2 it: heal the **b** thereof; for it shaketh. H7667
Isa 22: 9 Ye have seen also the **b** of the city of H1233
Am 4: 3 And ye shall go out at the **b**, every *cow* H6556
6:11 with **b**, and the little house with clefts. H7447
9:11 and close up the **b** thereof; and I will H6556

BREAD
Gen 3:19 In the sweat of thy face shalt thou eat **b**, H3899
14:18 brought forth **b** and wine: and he *was* H3899
18: 5 And I will fetch a morsel of **b**, and H3899
19: 3 bake unleavened **b**, and they did eat. H4682
21:14 and took **b**, and a bottle of water, H3899
25:34 Then Jacob gave Esau **b** and pottage of H3899
27:17 savoury meat and the **b**, which she had H3899
28:20 me **b** to eat, and raiment to put on, H3899
31:54 his brethren to eat **b**: and they did eat H3899
54 **b**, and tarried all night in the mount. H3899
37:25 And they sat down to eat **b**: and they H3899
39: 6 he had, save the **b** which he did eat. H3899
41:54 but in all the land of Egypt there was **b**. H3899
55 to Pharaoh for **b**: and Pharaoh said H3899
43:25 they heard that they should eat **b** there. H3899
31 refrained himself, and said, Set on **b**. H3899
32 might not eat **b** with the Hebrews; for H3899
45:23 **b** and meat for his father by the way. H3899
47:12 with **b**, according to *their* families. H3899
13 And *there was* no **b** in all the land; for H3899
15 and said, Give us **b**: for why should we H3899
17 Joseph gave them **b** *in exchange* for H3899
17 with **b** for all their cattle for that year. H3899
19 and our land for **b**, and we and our land H3899
49:20 Out of Asher his **b** *shall be* fat, and he H3899
Ex 2:20 the man? call him, that he may eat **b**. H3899
12: 8 **b**; *and* with bitter *herbs* they shall eat it. H4682
15 Seven days shall ye eat unleavened **b**; H4682
15 eateth leavened **b** from the first day H2557
17 *of* unleavened **b**; for in this selfsame H4682
18 eat unleavened **b**, until the one and H4682
20 habitations shall ye eat unleavened **b**. H4682
13: 3 there shall no leavened **b** be eaten. H2557
6 Seven days thou shalt eat unleavened **b**, H4682
7 Unleavened **b** shall be eaten seven H4682
7 shall no leavened **b** be seen with thee, H2557
16: 3 *and* when we did eat **b** to the full; for ye H3899
4 Behold, I will rain **b** from heaven for H3899
8 in the morning **b** to the full; for that the H3899
12 shall be filled with **b**; and ye shall know H3899
15 them, This *is* the **b** which the LORD H3899
22 twice as much **b**, two omers for one H3899
29 the sixth day the **b** of two days; abide H3899
32 they may see the **b** wherewith I have H3899
18:12 **b** with Moses' father in law before God. H3899
23:15 feast of unleavened **b**: (thou shalt eat H4682
15 shalt eat unleavened **b** seven days, as I H4682
18 with leavened **b**; neither shall the fat H2557
25 he shall bless thy **b**, and thy water; and H3899
29: 2 And unleavened **b**, and cakes H3899
23 And one loaf of **b**, and one cake of oiled H3899
23 one cake of oiled **b**, and one wafer out H3899
23 unleavened **b** that *is* before the LORD: H4682
32 the ram, and the **b** that *is* in the basket, H3899
34 or of the **b**, remain unto the morning, H3899
34:18 The feast of unleavened **b** shalt thou H4682
18 eat unleavened **b**, as I commanded H4682
28 he did neither eat **b**, nor drink water. H3899
40:23 And he set the **b** in order upon it before H3899
Lev 6:16 with unleavened **b** shall it be eaten in H4682
7:13 offering leavened **b** with the sacrifice of H3899
8: 2 rams, and a basket of unleavened **b**; H4682
26 And out of the basket of unleavened **b**, H3899
26 and a cake of oiled **b**, and one wafer, and
31 eat it with the **b** that *is* in the basket H3899
32 and of the **b** shall ye burn with fire. H3899
21: 6 by fire, *and* the **b** of their God, they do H3899
8 for he offereth the **b** of thy God: he shall H3899
17 not approach to offer the **b** of his God. H3899
21 not come nigh to offer the **b** of his God. H3899
22 He shall eat the **b** of his God, *both* of H3899
22:25 shall ye offer the **b** of your God of any H3899
23: 6 of unleavened **b** unto the LORD: seven H4682
6 seven days ye must eat unleavened **b**. H4682
14 And ye shall eat neither **b**, nor parched H3899
18 And ye shall offer with the **b** seven H3899
20 them with the **b** of the firstfruits *for* H3899
24: 7 it may be on the **b** for a memorial, *even* H3899
26: 5 ye shall eat your **b** to the full, and dwell H3899
26 the staff of your **b**, ten women shall H3899
26 shall bake your **b** in one oven, and they H3899
26 deliver *you* your **b** again by weight: and H3899
Nu 4: 7 and the continual **b** shall be thereon: H3899
6:15 And a basket of unleavened **b**, cakes of H4682
15 of unleavened **b** anointed with oil, and H4682
17 of unleavened **b**: the priest shall offer H4682
9:11 it with unleavened **b** and bitter *herbs*. H4682
14: 9 land; for they *are* **b** for us: their defence H3899
Nu 15:19 when ye eat of the **b** of the land, ye H3899
21: 5 for *there is* no **b**, neither *is there any* H3899
5 water; and our soul loatheth this light **b**. H3899
28: 2 My offering, *and* my **b** for my sacrifices H3899
17 days shall unleavened **b** be eaten. H4682
Dt 8: 3 doth not live by **b** only, but by every H3899
9 A land wherein thou shalt eat **b** H3899
9: 9 I neither did eat **b** nor drink water: H3899
18 I did neither eat **b**, nor drink water, H3899
16: 3 Thou shalt eat no leavened **b** with it; H2557
3 eat unleavened **b** therewith, *even* the H4682
3 *even* the **b** of affliction; for thou H3899
4 And there shall be no leavened **b** seen
8 Six days thou shalt eat unleavened **b**: H4682
16 of unleavened **b**, and in the feast of H4682
23: 4 Because they met you not with **b** and H3899
29: 6 Ye have not eaten **b**, neither have ye H3899
Jos 9: 5 them; and all the **b** of their provision H3899
12 This our **b** we took hot *for* our H3899
Jdg 7:13 lo, a cake of barley **b** tumbled into the H3899
8: 5 you, loaves of **b** unto the people that H3899
6 that we should give **b** unto thine army? H3899
15 give **b** unto thy men *that are* weary? H3899
13:16 I will not eat of thy **b**: and if thou wilt H3899
19: 5 morsel of **b**, and afterward go your way. H3899
19 asses; and there is **b** and wine also for H3899
Ru 1: 6 had visited his people in giving them **b**. H3899
2:14 and eat of the **b**, and dip thy morsel H3899
1Sa 2: 5 out themselves for **b**; and *they that were* H3899
36 and a morsel of **b**, and shall say, Put H3899
36 offices, that I may eat a piece of **b**. H3899
9: 7 bring the man? for the **b** is spent in our H3899
10: 3 three loaves of **b**, and another carrying H3899
4 thee two *loaves* of **b**; which thou shalt H3899
16:20 And Jesse took an ass *laden* with **b**, and H3899
21: 3 *me* five *loaves of* **b** in mine hand, or H3899
4 *is* no common **b** under mine hand, but H3899
4 there is hallowed **b**; if the young men H3899
5 men are holy, and *the* **b** *is* in a manner
6 So the priest gave him hallowed *b:* for
6 *bread:* for there was no **b** there but the H3899
6 **b** in the day when it was taken away. H3899
22:13 hast given him **b**, and a sword, and hast H3899
25:11 Shall I then take my **b**, and my water, H3899
28:20 eaten no **b** all the day, nor all the night. H3899
22 me set a morsel of **b** before thee; and H3899
24 *it*, and did bake unleavened **b** thereof: H4682
30:11 and gave him **b**, and he did eat; and H3899
12 for he had eaten no **b**, nor drunk *any* H3899
2Sa 3:29 falleth on the sword, or that lacketh **b**. H3899
35 **b**, or ought else, till the sun be down. H3899
6:19 one a cake of **b**, and a good piece *of* H3899
9: 7 shalt eat **b** at my table continually. H3899
10 son shall eat **b** alway at my table. Now H3899
12:17 not, neither did he eat **b** with them. H3899
20 they set **b** before him, and he did eat. H3899
21 was dead, thou didst rise and eat **b**. H3899
16: 1 hundred *loaves* of **b**, and an hundred H3899
2 to ride on; and the **b** and summer fruit H3899
1Ki 13: 8 I eat **b** nor drink water in this place: H3899
9 saying, Eat no **b**, nor drink water, nor H3899
15 him, Come home with me, and eat **b**. H3899
16 neither will I eat **b** nor drink water with H3899
17 Thou shalt eat no **b** nor drink water H3899
18 that he may eat **b** and drink water. *But* H3899
19 eat **b** in his house, and drank water. H3899
22 But camest back, and hast eaten **b** and H3899
22 did say to thee, Eat no **b**, and drink no H3899
23 after he had eaten **b**, and after he had H3899
17: 6 And the ravens brought him **b** and H3899
6 in the morning, and **b** and flesh in the H3899
11 I pray thee, a morsel of **b** in thine hand. H3899
18: 4 cave, and fed them with **b** and water.) H3899
13 a cave, and fed them with **b** and water? H3899
21: 4 away his face, and would eat no **b**. H3899
5 thy spirit so sad, that thou eatest no **b**? H3899
7 arise, *and* eat **b**, and let thine heart be H3899
22:27 and feed him with **b** of affliction and H3899
2Ki 4: 8 him to eat **b**. And *so* it was, *that* H3899
8 passed by, he turned in thither to eat **b**. H3899
42 the man of God **b** of the firstfruits, H3899
6:22 with thy bow? set **b** and water before H3899
18:32 wine, a land of **b** and vineyards, a land H3899
23: 9 unleavened **b** among their brethren. H4682
25: 3 was no **b** for the people of the land. H3899
29 and he did eat **b** continually before him H3899
1Ch 12:40 Naphtali, brought **b** on asses, and on H3899
16: 3 every one a loaf of **b**, and a good piece H3899
2Ch 8:13 of unleavened **b**, and in the feast of H4682

B

2Ch 18:26 and feed him with **b** of affliction and H3899
30:13 of unleavened **b** in the second month, H4682
21 of unleavened **b** seven days with great H4682
35:17 the feast of unleavened **b** seven days. H4682
Ezr 6:22 And kept the feast of unleavened **b** H4682
10: 6 he did eat no **b**, nor drink water: for H3899
Neh 5:14 have not eaten the **b** of the governor. H3899
15 had taken of them **b** and wine, beside H3899
18 required not I the **b** of the governor, H3899
9:15 And gavest them **b** from heaven for H3899
13: 2 of Israel with **b** and with water, but H3899
Job 15:23 He wandereth abroad for **b**, *saying*, H3899
22: 7 hast withholden **b** from the hungry. H3899
27:14 offspring shall not be satisfied with **b**. H3899
28: 5 *As for* the earth, out of it cometh **b**: and H3899
33:20 So that his life abhorreth **b**, and his soul H3899
42:11 and did eat **b** with him in his house: H3899
Ps 14: 4 they eat **b**, and call not upon the LORD. H3899
37:25 forsaken, nor his seed begging **b**. H3899
41: 9 my **b**, hath lifted up *his* heel against me. H3899
53: 4 eat **b**: they have not called upon God. H3899
78:20 can he give **b** also? can he provide H3899
80: 5 Thou feedest them with the **b** of tears; H3899
102: 4 like grass; so that I forget to eat my **b**. H3899
9 For I have eaten ashes like **b**, and H3899
104:15 **b** *which* strengtheneth man's heart. H3899
105:16 the land: he brake the whole staff of **b**. H3899
40 satisfied them with the **b** of heaven. H3899
109:10 *their* ***b*** also out of their desolate places.
127: 2 up late, to eat the **b** of sorrows: *for* so H3899
132:15 provision: I will satisfy her poor with **b**. H3899
Prv 4:17 For they eat the **b** of wickedness, and H3899
6:26 to a piece of **b**: and the adulteress will H3899
9: 5 Come, eat of my **b**, and drink of the H3899
17 Stolen waters are sweet, and **b** *eaten* in H3899
12: 9 that honoureth himself, and lacketh **b**. H3899
11 be satisfied with **b**: but he that followeth H3899
20:13 eyes, *and* thou shalt be satisfied with **b**. H3899
17 **B** of deceit *is* sweet to a man; but H3899
22: 9 for he giveth of his **b** to the poor. H3899
23: 6 Eat thou not the **b** of *him that hath* an H3899
25:21 If thine enemy be hungry, give him **b** to H3899
28:19 have plenty of **b**: but he that followeth H3899
21 a piece of **b** *that* man will transgress. H3899
31:27 and eateth not the **b** of idleness. H3899
Ecc 9: 7 Go thy way, eat thy **b** with joy, and H3899
11 strong, neither yet **b** to the wise, nor yet H3899
11: 1 Cast thy **b** upon the waters: for thou H3899
Isa 3: 1 stay of **b**, and the whole stay of water, H3899
7 house *is* neither **b** nor clothing: make H3899
4: 1 will eat our own **b**, and wear our own H3899
21:14 prevented with their **b** him that fled. H3899
28:28 **B** *corn* is bruised; because he will not H3899
30:20 And *though* the Lord give you the **b** of H3899
23 withal; and **b** of the increase of the H3899
33:16 of rocks: **b** shall be given him; H3899
36:17 and wine, a land of **b** and vineyards. H3899
44:15 *it*, and baketh **b**; yea, he maketh a god, H3899
19 yea, also I have baked **b** upon the coals H3899
51:14 die in the pit, nor that his **b** should fail. H3899
55: 2 *that which is* not **b**? and your labour for H3899
10 seed to the sower, and **b** to the eater: H3899
58: 7 *Is it* not to deal thy **b** to the hungry, H3899
Jer 5:17 harvest, and thy **b**, *which* thy sons and H3899
37:21 him daily a piece of **b** out of the bakers' H3899
21 street, until all the **b** in the city were H3899
38: 9 he is: for *there is* no more **b** in the city. H3899
41: 1 there they did eat **b** together in Mizpah. H3899
42:14 hunger of **b**; and there will we dwell: H3899
52: 6 was no **b** for the people of the land. H3899
33 eat **b** before him all the days of his life. H3899
Lam 1:11 All her people sigh, they seek **b**; they H3899
4: 4 **b**, *and* no man breaketh *it* unto them. H3899
5: 6 *to* the Assyrians, to be satisfied with **b**. H3899
9 We gat our **b** with *the peril of* our lives H3899
Ezk 4: 9 and make thee **b** thereof, *according* to H3899
13 eat their defiled **b** among the Gentiles, H3899
15 and thou shalt prepare thy **b** therewith. H3899
16 break the staff of **b** in Jerusalem: and H3899
16 and they shall eat **b** by weight, and H3899
17 That they may want **b** and water, and H3899
5:16 upon you, and will break your staff of **b**: H3899
12:18 Son of man, eat thy **b** with quaking, H3899
19 shall eat their **b** with carefulness, and H3899
13:19 and for pieces of **b**, to slay the souls that H3899
14:13 the staff of the **b** thereof, and will send H3899
16:49 pride, fulness of **b**, and abundance of H3899
18: 7 hath given his **b** to the hungry, and H3899
16 *but* hath given his **b** to the hungry, and H3899
Ezk 24:17 not *thy* lips, and eat not the **b** of men. H3899
22 cover *your* lips, nor eat the **b** of men. H3899
44: 3 shall sit in it to eat **b** before the LORD; H3899
7 when ye offer my **b**, the fat and the H3899
45:21 days; unleavened **b** shall be eaten. H4682
Dan 10: 3 I ate no pleasant **b**, neither came flesh H3899
Hos 2: 5 that give *me* my **b** and my water, my H3899
9: 4 *be* unto them as the **b** of mourners; all H3899
4 polluted: for their **b** for their soul shall H3899
Am 4: 6 cities, and want of **b** in all your places: H3899
7:12 and there eat **b**, and prophesy there: H3899
8:11 not a famine of **b**, nor a thirst for water, H3899
Oba 7 *they that eat* thy **b** have laid a wound H3899
Hag 2:12 his skirt do touch **b**, or pottage, or wine, H3899
Mal 1: 7 Ye offer polluted **b** upon mine altar; H3899
Mt 4: 3 command that these stones be made **b**. *G740*
4 shall not live by **b** alone, but by every *G740*
6:11 Give us this day our daily **b**. *G740*
7: 9 if his son ask **b**, will he give him a stone? *G740*
15: 2 wash not their hands when they eat **b**. *G740*
26 the children's **b**, and to cast *it* to dogs. *G740*
33 we have so much **b** in the wilderness, as *G740*
16: 5 other side, they had forgotten to take **b**. *G740*
7 saying, *It is* because we have taken no **b**. *G740*
8 because ye have brought no **b**? *G740*
11 not to you concerning **b**, that ye should *G740*
12 of the leaven of **b**, but of the doctrine of *G740*
26:17 *of* unleavened **b** the disciples came to *G106*
26 And as they were eating, Jesus took **b**, *G740*
Mk 3:20 so that they could not so much as eat **b**. *G740*
6: 8 no scrip, no **b**, no money in *their* purse: *G740*
36 **b**: for they have nothing to eat. *G740*
37 pennyworth of **b**, and give them to eat? *G740*
7: 2 of his disciples eat **b** with defiled, that is *G740*
5 elders, but eat **b** with unwashen hands? *G740*
27 children's **b**, and to cast *it* unto the dogs. *G740*
8: 4 these *men* with **b** here in the wilderness? *G740*
14 forgotten to take **b**, neither had they in *G740*
16 saying, *It is* because we have no **b**. *G740*
17 because ye have no **b**? perceive ye not yet, *G740*
14: 1 and of unleavened **b**: and the chief *G106*
12 And the first day of unleavened **b**, when *G106*
22 And as they did eat, Jesus took **b**, and *G740*
Lk 4: 3 command this stone that it be made **b**. *G740*
4 by **b** alone, but by every word of God. *G740*
7:33 neither eating **b** nor drinking wine; and *G740*
9: 3 nor scrip, neither **b**, neither money; *G740*
11: 3 Give us day by day our daily **b**. *G740*
11 If a son shall ask **b** of any of you that is a *G740*
14: 1 Pharisees to eat **b** on the sabbath day, *G740*
15 that shall eat **b** in the kingdom of God. *G740*
15:17 of my father's have **b** enough and to *G740*
22: 1 Now the feast of unleavened **b** drew *G106*
7 Then came the day of unleavened **b**, *G106*
19 And he took **b**, and gave thanks, and *G740*
24:30 with them, he took **b**, and blessed *it*, and *G740*
35 he was known of them in breaking of **b**. *G740*
Jn 6: 5 shall we buy **b**, that these may eat? *G740*
7 pennyworth of **b** is not sufficient for *G740*
23 **b**, after that the Lord had given thanks:) *G740*
31 He gave them **b** from heaven to eat. *G740*
32 gave you not that **b** from heaven; but my *G740*
32 giveth you the true **b** from heaven. *G740*
33 For the **b** of God is he which cometh *G740*
34 unto him, Lord, evermore give us this **b**. *G740*
35 And Jesus said unto them, I am the **b** of *G740*
41 the **b** which came down from heaven. *G740*
48 I am that **b** of life. *G740*
50 This is the **b** which cometh down from *G740*
51 I am the living **b** which came down from *G740*
51 if any man eat of this **b**, he shall live for *G740*
51 for ever: and the **b** that I will give is my *G740*
58 This is that **b** which came down from *G740*
58 he that eateth of this **b** shall live for ever. *G740*
13:18 He that eateth **b** with me hath lifted up *G740*
21: 9 coals there, and fish laid thereon, and **b**. *G740*
13 Jesus then cometh, and taketh **b**, and *G740*
Act 2:42 and in breaking of **b**, and in prayers. *G740*
46 and breaking **b** from house to house, *G740*
12: 3 (Then were the days of unleavened **b**.) *G106*
20: 6 of unleavened **b**, and came unto them *G106*
7 together to break **b**, Paul preached unto *G740*
11 and had broken **b**, and eaten, and talked *G740*
27:35 And when he had thus spoken, he took **b**, *G740*
1Co 5: 8 the unleavened ***b*** of sincerity and truth.
10:16 of Christ? The **b** which we break, is it *G740*
17 For we *being* many are one **b**, *and* one *G740*
17 for we are all partakers of that one **b**. *G740*
11:23 night in which he was betrayed took **b**: *G740*
1Co 11:26 For as often as ye eat this **b**, and drink *G740*
27 Wherefore whosoever shall eat this **b**, *G740*
28 him eat of *that* **b**, and drink of *that* cup. *G740*
2Co 9:10 sower both minister **b** for *your* food, and *G740*
2Th 3: 8 Neither did we eat any man's **b** for *G740*
12 quietness they work, and eat their own **b**. *G740*

BREADTH

Gen 6:15 cubits, the **b** of it fifty cubits, and H7341
13:17 in the **b** of it; for I will give it unto thee. H7341
Ex 25:10 and a half the **b** thereof, and a cubit H7341
17 and a cubit and a half the **b** thereof. H7341
23 and a cubit the **b** thereof, and a cubit H7341
25 border of an hand **b** round about, and H2948
26: 2 cubits, and the **b** of one curtain four H7341
8 cubits, and the **b** of one curtain four H7341
16 and a half *shall be* the **b** of one board. H7341
27:12 And *for* the **b** of the court on the west H7341
13 And the **b** of the court on the east side H7341
18 cubits, and the **b** fifty every where, and H7341
28:16 and a span *shall be* the **b** thereof. H7341
30: 2 and a cubit the **b** thereof; foursquare H7341
36: 9 cubits, and the **b** of one curtain four H7341
15 cubits *was* the **b** of one curtain: the H7341
21 the **b** of a board one cubit and a half. H7341
37: 1 and a half the **b** of it, and a cubit and H7341
6 and one cubit and a half the **b** thereof. H7341
10 and a cubit the **b** thereof, and a cubit H7341
25 a cubit, and the **b** of it a cubit; *it was* H7341
38: 1 and five cubits the **b** thereof; *it was* H7341
18 and the height in the **b** *was* five cubits, H7341
39: 9 a span the **b** thereof, *being* doubled. H7341
Dt 2: 5 not so much as a foot **b**; because I have H4096
3:11 the **b** of it, after the cubit of a man. H7341
Jdg 20:16 sling stones at an hair ***b***, and not miss.
1Ki 6: 2 cubits, and the **b** thereof twenty *cubits*, H7341
3 according to the **b** of the house; *and* ten H7341
3 *was* the **b** thereof before the house. H7341
20 twenty cubits in **b**, and twenty cubits in H7341
7: 2 cubits, and the **b** thereof fifty cubits, H7341
6 cubits, and the **b** thereof thirty cubits: H7341
26 And it *was* an hand **b** thick, and the H2947
27 and four cubits the **b** thereof, and three H7341
2Ch 3: 3 cubits, and the **b** twenty cubits. H7341
4 according to the **b** of the house, twenty H7341
8 according to the **b** of the house, twenty H7341
8 cubits, and the **b** thereof twenty cubits: H7341
4: 1 twenty cubits the **b** thereof, and ten H7341
Ezr 6: 3 *and* the **b** thereof threescore cubits; H6613
Job 37:10 and the **b** of the waters is straitened. H7341
38:18 Hast thou perceived the **b** of the earth? H7338
Isa 8: 8 shall fill the **b** of thy land, O Immanuel. H7341
Ezk 40: 5 cubit and an hand **b**: so he measured H2948
5 he measured the **b** of the building, one H7341
11 And he measured the **b** of the entry of H7341
13 of another: the **b** *was* five and twenty H7341
19 Then he measured the **b** from the H7341
20 the length thereof, and the **b** thereof. H7341
21 and the **b** five and twenty cubits. H7341
25 and the **b** five and twenty cubits. H7341
36 and the **b** five and twenty cubits. H7341
48 on that side: and the **b** of the gate *was* H7341
49 cubits, and the **b** eleven cubits; and *he* H7341
41: 1 side, *which was* the **b** of the tabernacle. H7341
2 And the **b** of the door *was* ten cubits; H7341
2 forty cubits: and the **b**, twenty cubits. H7341
3 and the **b** of the door, seven cubits. H7341
4 cubits; and the **b**, twenty cubits, before H7341
5 six cubits; and the **b** of *every* side H7341
7 therefore the **b** of the house *was still* H7341
11 the south: and the **b** of the place that H7341
14 Also the **b** of the face of the house, and H7341
42: 2 north door, and the **b** *was* fifty cubits. H7341
4 a walk of ten cubits **b** inward, a way of H7341
43:13 a cubit and an hand **b**; even the bottom H2948
13 *be* a cubit, and the **b** a cubit, and the H7341
14 cubits, and the **b** one cubit; and from H7341
14 *be* four cubits, and the **b** *one* cubit. H7341
45: 1 *reeds*, and the **b** *shall be* ten thousand. H7341
2 five hundred *in* **b**, square round about; H7341
3 thousand, and the **b** of ten thousand: H7341
5 ten thousand of **b**, shall also the Levites, H7341
48: 8 thousand *reeds in* **b**, and *in* length as H7341
9 in length, and of ten thousand in **b**. H7341
10 ten thousand in **b**, and toward the east H7341
10 east ten thousand in **b**, and toward the H7341
13 ten thousand in **b**: all the length *shall be* H7341
13 thousand, and the **b** ten thousand. H7341
15 that are left in the **b** over against the H7341

Dan 3: 1 cubits, *and* the **b** thereof six cubits: he H6613
Hab 1: 6 through the **b** of the land, to possess H4800
Zec 2: 2 to see what *is* the **b** thereof, and what *is* H7341
5: 2 cubits, and the **b** thereof ten cubits. H7341
Eph 3:18 **b**, and length, and depth, and height; *G4114*
Rev 20: 9 And they went up on the **b** of the earth, *G4114*
21:16 is as large as the **b**: and he measured *G4114*
16 and the **b** and the height of it are equal. *G4114*

BREAK
Gen 19: 9 *even* Lot, and came near to **b** the door. H7665
27:40 thou shalt **b** his yoke from off thy neck. H6561
Ex 12:46 neither shall ye **b** a bone thereof. H7665
13:13 it, then thou shalt **b** his neck: and all H6202
19:21 the people, lest they **b** through unto the H2040
22 lest the LORD **b** forth upon them. H6555
24 and the people **b** through to come up H2040
24 the LORD, lest he **b** forth upon them. H6555
22: 6 If fire **b** out, and catch in thorns, so H3318
23:24 them, and quite **b** down their images. H7665
32: 2 And Aaron said unto them, **B** off the H6561
24 any gold, let them **b** *it* off. So they gave H6561
34:13 But ye shall destroy their altars, **b** their H7665
20 not, then shalt thou **b** his neck. All the H6202
Lev 11:33 in it shall be unclean; and ye shall **b** it. H7665
13:12 And if a leprosy **b** out abroad in the H6524
14:43 And if the plague come again, and **b** H6524
45 And he shall **b** down the house, the H5422
26:15 *but* that ye **b** my covenant: H6565
19 And I will **b** the pride of your power; H7665
44 utterly, and to **b** my covenant with H6565
Nu 9:12 unto the morning, nor **b** any bone of it: H7665
24: 8 and shall **b** their bones, and pierce H1633
30: 2 bond; he shall not **b** his word, he shall H2490
Dt 7: 5 their altars, and **b** down their images, H7665
12: 3 their altars, and **b** their pillars, and H7665
31:16 forsake me, and **b** my covenant which H6565
20 and provoke me, and **b** my covenant. H6565
Jdg 2: 1 I will never **b** my covenant with you. H6565
8: 9 in peace, I will **b** down this tower. H5422
1Sa 25:10 **b** away every man from his master. H6555
2Sa 2:32 and they came to Hebron at **b** of day. H215
1Ki 15:19 and gold; come and **b** thy league with H6565
2Ki 3:26 drew swords, to **b** through *even* unto H1234
25:13 did the Chaldees **b** in pieces, and H7665
2Ch 16: 3 and gold; go, **b** thy league with Baasha H6565
Ezr 9:14 Should we again **b** thy H6565
Neh 4: 3 he shall even **b** down their stone wall. H6565
Job 13:25 Wilt thou **b** a leaf driven to and fro? H6206
19: 2 How long will ye vex my soul, and **b** me H1792
34:24 He shall **b** in pieces mighty men H7489
39:15 or that the wild beast may **b** them. H1758
Ps 2: 3 Let us **b** their bands asunder, and cast H5423
9 Thou shalt **b** them with a rod of iron; H7489
10:15 **B** thou the arm of the wicked and the H7665
58: 6 **B** their teeth, O God, in their mouth: H2040
6 in their mouth: **b** out the great teeth of H5422
72: 4 and shall **b** in pieces the oppressor. H1792
74: 6 But now they **b** down the carved work H1986
89:31 If they **b** my statutes, and keep not my H2490
34 My covenant will I not **b**, nor alter the H2490
94: 5 They **b** in pieces thy people, O LORD, H1792
141: 5 *which* shall not **b** my head: for yet my H5106
Ecc 3: 3 time to **b** down, and a time to build up; H6555
Song 2:17 Until the day **b**, and the shadows flee H6315
4: 6 Until the day **b**, and the shadows flee H6315
Isa 5: 5 shall be eaten up; *and* **b** down the wall H6555
14: 7 *and* is quiet: they **b** forth into singing. H6476
25 That I will **b** the Assyrian in my land, H7665
28:24 he open and **b** the clods of his ground? H7702
28 threshing it, nor **b** *it with* the wheel of H2000
30:14 And he shall **b** it as the breaking of the H7665
35: 6 waters **b** out, and streams in the desert. H1234
38:13 a lion, so will he **b** all my bones: from H7665
42: 3 A bruised reed shall he not **b**, and the H7665
44:23 parts of the earth: **b** forth into singing, H6476
45: 2 straight: I will **b** in pieces the gates of H7665
49:13 O earth; and **b** forth into singing, O H6476
52: 9 **B** forth into joy, sing together, ye waste H6476
54: 1 didst not bear; **b** forth into singing, and H6476
3 For thou shalt **b** forth on the right hand H6555
55:12 and the hills shall **b** forth before you H6476
58: 6 go free, and that ye **b** every yoke? H5423
8 Then shall thy light **b** forth as the H1234
Jer 1:14 north an evil shall **b** forth upon all the H6605
4: 3 Judah and Jerusalem, **B** up your fallow H5214
14:21 remember, **b** not thy covenant with us. H6565
15:12 Shall iron **b** the northern iron and the H7489
19:10 Then shalt thou **b** the bottle in the sight H7665
Jer 19:11 Even so will I **b** this people and this H7665
28: 4 I will **b** the yoke of the king of Babylon. H7665
11 LORD; Even so will I **b** the yoke of H7665
30: 8 of hosts, *that* I will **b** his yoke from off H7665
31:28 pluck up, and to **b** down, and to throw H5422
33:20 Thus saith the LORD; If ye can **b** my H6565
43:13 He shall **b** also the images of H7665
45: 4 I have built will I **b** down, and that H2040
48:12 empty his vessels, and **b** their bottles. H5310
49:35 Behold, I will **b** the bow of Elam, the H7665
51:20 war: for with thee will I **b** in pieces the H5310
21 And with thee will I **b** in pieces the H5310
21 I **b** in pieces the chariot and his rider; H5310
22 With thee also will I **b** in pieces man H5310
22 and with thee will I **b** in pieces old and H5310
22 with thee will I **b** in pieces the young H5310
23 I will also **b** in pieces with thee the H5310
23 and with thee will I **b** in pieces the H5310
23 will I **b** in pieces captains and rulers. H5310
Ezk 4:16 behold, I will **b** the staff of bread in H7665
5:16 you, and will **b** your staff of bread: H7665
13:14 So will I **b** down the wall that ye have H2040
14:13 upon it, and will **b** the staff of the bread H7665
16:38 And I will judge thee, as women that **b** H5003
39 place, and shall **b** down thy high H5422
17:15 he **b** the covenant, and be delivered? H6565
23:34 and thou shalt **b** the sherds thereof, H1633
26: 4 of Tyrus, and **b** down her towers: I H2040
9 his axes he shall **b** down thy towers. H5422
12 and they shall **b** down thy walls, and H2040
29: 7 hand, thou didst **b**, and rend all their H7533
30:18 when I shall **b** there the yokes of Egypt: H7665
22 king of Egypt, and will **b** his arms, the H7665
24 hand: but I will **b** Pharaoh's arms, and H7665
Dan 2:40 all these, shall it **b** in pieces and bruise. H1854
44 people, *but* it shall **b** in pieces and H1854
4:27 unto thee, and **b** off thy sins by H6562
7:23 shall tread it down, and **b** it in pieces. H1854
Hos 1: 5 day, that I will **b** the bow of Israel in H7665
2:18 ground: and I will **b** the bow and the H7665
4: 2 they **b** out, and blood toucheth blood. H6555
10: 2 faulty: he shall **b** down their altars, he H6202
11 shall plow, *and* Jacob shall **b** his clods. H7702
12 reap in mercy; **b** up your fallow H5214
Joel 2: 7 ways, and they shall not **b** their ranks: H5670
Am 1: 5 I will **b** also the bar of Damascus, and H7665
5: 6 ye shall live; lest he **b** out like fire in the H6743
Mic 3: 3 off them; and they **b** their bones, and H6476
Nah 1:13 For now will I **b** his yoke from off thee, H7665
Zec 11:10 that I might **b** my covenant which H6565
14 that I might **b** the brotherhood between H6565
Mt 5:19 Whosoever therefore shall **b** one of *G3089*
6:19 and where thieves **b** through and steal: *G1358*
20 thieves do not **b** through nor steal: *G1358*
9:17 else the bottles **b**, and the wine runneth *G4486*
12:20 A bruised reed shall he not **b**, and *G2608*
Act 20: 7 came together to **b** bread, Paul *G2806*
11 while, even till **b** of day, so he departed. *G827*
21:13 ye to weep and to **b** mine heart? for I *G4919*
1Co 10:16 The bread which we **b**, is it not the *G2806*
Gal 4:27 that bearest not; **b** forth and cry, thou *G4486*

BREAKER
Mic 2:13 The **b** is come up before them: they H6555
Ro 2:25 law: but if thou be a **b** of the law, thy *G3848*

BREAKEST
Ps 48: 7 Thou **b** the ships of Tarshish with an H7665

BREAKETH
Gen 32:26 And he said, Let me go, for the day **b**. H5927
Job 9:17 For he **b** me with a tempest, and H7779
12:14 Behold, he **b** down, and it cannot be H2040
16:14 He **b** me with breach upon breach, he H6555
28: 4 The flood **b** out from the inhabitant; H6555
Ps 29: 5 The voice of the LORD **b** the cedars; H7665
5 the LORD **b** the cedars of Lebanon. H7665
46: 9 of the earth; he **b** the bow, and cutteth H7665
119:20 My soul **b** for the longing *that it hath* H1638
Prv 25:15 and a soft tongue **b** the bone. H7665
Ecc 10: 8 **b** an hedge, a serpent shall bite him. H6555
Isa 59: 5 which is crushed **b** out into a viper. H1234
Jer 19:11 this city, as *one* **b** a potter's vessel, that H7665
23:29 a hammer *that* **b** the rock in pieces? H6327
Lam 4: 4 ask bread, *and* no man **b** *it* unto them. H6566
Dan 2:40 iron: forasmuch as iron **b** in pieces and H1855
40 and as iron that **b** all these, shall it H7490

BREAKING
Gen 32:24 a man with him until the **b** of the day. H5927
Ex 9: 9 and shall be a boil **b** forth *with* blains H6524
10 and it became a boil **b** forth *with* blains H6524
22: 2 If a thief be found **b** up, and be smitten H4290
1Ch 14:11 mine hand like the **b** forth of waters: H6556
Job 30:14 They came *upon me* as a wide **b** in *of* H6556
Ps 144:14 *that there be* no **b** in, nor going out; H6556
Isa 22: 5 valley of vision, **b** down the walls, and H6979
30:13 **b** cometh suddenly at an instant. H7667
14 And he shall break it as the **b** of the H7667
Ezk 16:59 despised the oath in **b** the covenant. H6565
17:18 Seeing he despised the oath by **b** the H6565
21: 6 son of man, with the **b** of *thy* loins; and H7670
Hos 13:13 in *the place of* the **b** forth of children. H4866
Lk 24:35 he was known of them in **b** of bread. *G2800*
Act 2:42 and in **b** of bread, and in prayers. *G2800*
46 in the temple, and **b** bread from house *G2806*
Ro 2:23 **b** the law dishonourest thou God? *G3847*

BREAKINGS
Job 41:25 by reason of **b** they purify themselves. H7667

BREAST
Ex 29:26 And thou shalt take the **b** of the ram of H2373
27 And thou shalt sanctify the **b** of the H2373
Lev 7:30 the fat with the **b**, it shall he bring, that H2373
30 he bring, that the **b** may be waved *for* a H2373
31 the **b** shall be Aaron's and his sons'. H2373
34 For the wave **b** and the heave shoulder H2373
8:29 And Moses took the **b**, and waved it *for* H2373
10:14 And the wave **b** and heave shoulder H2373
15 The heave shoulder and the wave **b** H2373
Nu 6:20 with the wave **b** and heave shoulder: H2373
18:18 **b** and as the right shoulder are thine. H2373
Job 24: 9 They pluck the fatherless from the **b**, H7699
Isa 60:16 and shalt suck the **b** of kings: and thou H7699
Lam 4: 3 Even the sea monsters draw out the **b**, H7699
Dan 2:32 *was* of fine gold, his **b** and his arms of H2306
Lk 18:13 but smote upon his **b**, saying, God be *G4738*
Jn 13:25 He then lying on Jesus' **b** saith unto *G4738*
21:20 also leaned on his **b** at supper, and *G4738*

BREASTPLATE
Ex 25: 7 to be set in the ephod, and in the **b**. H2833
28: 4 they shall make; a **b**, and an ephod, and H2833
15 And thou shalt make the **b** of judgment H2833
22 And thou shalt make upon the **b** chains H2833
23 And thou shalt make upon the **b** two H2833
23 the two rings on the two ends of the **b**. H2833
24 rings *which are* on the ends of the **b**. H2833
26 two ends of the **b** in the border thereof, H2833
28 And they shall bind the **b** by the rings H2833
28 the **b** be not loosed from the ephod. H2833
29 of Israel in the **b** of judgment upon his H2833
30 And thou shalt put in the **b** of H2833
29: 5 ephod, and the **b**, and gird him with the H2833
35: 9 to be set for the ephod, and for the **b**. H2833
27 to be set, for the ephod, and for the **b**; H2833
39: 8 And he made the **b** *of* cunning work, H2833
9 It was foursquare; they made the **b** H2833
15 And they made upon the **b** chains at H2833
16 the two rings in the two ends of the **b**. H2833
17 in the two rings on the ends of the **b**. H2833
19 two ends of the **b**, upon the border of H2833
21 And they did bind the **b** by his rings H2833
21 and that the **b** might not be loosed H2833
Lev 8: 8 And he put the **b** upon him: also he put H2833
8 in the **b** the Urim and the Thummim. H2833
Isa 59:17 For he put on righteousness as a **b**, and H8302
Eph 6:14 and having on the **b** of righteousness; *G2382*
1Th 5: 8 putting on the **b** of faith and love; and *G2382*

BREASTPLATES
Rev 9: 9 And they had **b**, as it were breastplates *G2382*
9 And they had breastplates, as it were **b** *G2382*
17 sat on them, having **b** of fire, and of *G2382*

BREASTS
Gen 49:25 blessings of the **b**, and of the womb: H7699
Lev 9:20 And they put the fat upon the **b**, and he H2373
21 And the **b** and the right shoulder Aaron H2373
Job 3:12 me? or why the **b** that I should suck? H7699
21:24 His **b** are full of milk, and his bones are H5845
Ps 22: 9 hope *when I was* upon my mother's **b**. H7699
Prv 5:19 roe; let her **b** satisfy thee at all times; H1717
Song 1:13 me; he shall lie all night betwixt my **b**. H7699
4: 5 Thy two **b** *are* like two young roes that H7699
7: 3 Thy two **b** *are* like two young roes *that* H7699

Song 7: 7 tree, and thy **b** to clusters *of grapes*. H7699
8 now also thy **b** shall be as clusters H7699
8: 1 that sucked the **b** of my mother! *when* H7699
8 and she hath no **b**: what shall we do for H7699
10 I *am* a wall, and my **b** like towers: then H7699
Isa 28: 9 from the milk, *and* drawn from the **b**. H7699
66:11 satisfied with the **b** of her consolations; H7699
Ezk 16: 7 ornaments: *thy* **b** are fashioned, and H7699
23: 3 there were their **b** pressed, and there H7699
8 they bruised the **b** of her virginity, and H1717
34 off thine own **b**: for I have spoken *it*, H7699
Hos 2: 2 and her adulteries from between her **b**; H7699
9:14 them a miscarrying womb and dry **b**. H7699
Joel 2:16 that suck the **b**: let the bridegroom H7699
Nah 2: 7 voice of doves, tabering upon their **b**. H3824
Lk 23:48 were done, smote their **b**, and returned. *G4738*
Rev 15: 6 their **b** girded with golden girdles. *G4738*

BREATH
Gen 2: 7 **b** of life; and man became a living soul. H5397
6:17 wherein *is* the **b** of life, from under H7307
7:15 two of all flesh, wherein *is* the **b** of life. H7307
22 All in whose nostrils *was* the **b** of life, H5397
2Sa 22:16 at the blast of the **b** of his nostrils. H7307
1Ki 17:17 so sore, that there was no **b** left in him. H5397
Job 4: 9 the **b** of his nostrils are they consumed. H7307
9:18 He will not suffer me to take my **b**, but H7307
12:10 living thing, and the **b** of all mankind. H7307
15:30 by the **b** of his mouth shall he go away. H7307
17: 1 My **b** is corrupt, my days are extinct, H7307
19:17 My **b** is strange to my wife, though I H7307
27: 3 All the while my **b** *is* in me, and the H5397
33: 4 **b** of the Almighty hath given me life. H5397
34:14 gather unto himself his spirit and his **b**; H5397
37:10 By the **b** of God frost is given: and the H5397
41:21 His **b** kindleth coals, and a flame goeth H5315
Ps 18:15 at the blast of the **b** of thy nostrils. H7307
33: 6 the host of them by the **b** of his mouth. H7307
104:29 **b**, they die, and return to their dust. H7307
135:17 neither is there *any* **b** in their mouths. H7307
146: 4 His **b** goeth forth, he returneth to his H7307
150: 6 Let every thing that hath **b** praise the H5397
Ecc 3:19 they have all one **b**; so that a man hath H7307
Isa 2:22 Cease ye from man, whose **b** *is* in his H5397
11: 4 **b** of his lips shall he slay the wicked. H7307
30:28 And his **b**, as an overflowing stream, H7307
33 much wood; the **b** of the LORD, like a H5397
33:11 your **b**, *as* fire, shall devour you. H7307
42: 5 of it; he that giveth **b** unto the people H5397
Jer 10:14 *is* falsehood, and *there is* no **b** in them. H7307
51:17 *is* falsehood, and *there is* no **b** in them. H7307
Lam 4:20 The **b** of our nostrils, the anointed of H7307
Ezk 37: 5 **b** to enter into you, and ye shall live: H7307
6 you with skin, and put **b** in you, and ye H7307
8 above: but *there was* no **b** in them. H7307
9 the four winds, O **b**, and breathe upon H7307
10 me, and the **b** came into them, and H7307
Dan 5:23 in whose hand thy **b** *is*, and whose *are* H5396
10:17 in me, neither is there **b** left in me. H5397
Hab 2:19 *there is* no **b** at all in the midst of it. H7307
Act 17:25 giveth to all life, and **b**, and all things; *G4157*

BREATHE
Jos 11:11 left to **b**: and he burnt Hazor with fire. H5397
14 them, neither left they any to **b**. H5397
Ps 27:12 against me, and such as **b** out cruelty. H3307
Ezk 37: 9 **b** upon these slain, that they may live. H5301

BREATHED
Gen 2: 7 of the ground, and **b** into his nostrils H5301
Jos 10:40 destroyed all that **b**, as the LORD God H5397
1Ki 15:29 any that **b**, until he had destroyed H5397
Jn 20:22 And when he had said this, he **b** on *G1720*

BREATHETH
Dt 20:16 thou shalt save alive nothing that **b**: H5397

BREATHING
Lam 3:56 hide not thine ear at my **b**, at my cry. H7309
Act 9: 1 And Saul, yet **b** out threatenings and *G1709*

BRED
Ex 16:20 morning, and it **b** worms, and stank: H7311

BREECHES
Ex 28:42 And thou shalt make them linen **b** to H4370
39:28 linen, and linen **b** *of* fine twined linen, H4370
Lev 6:10 and his linen **b** shall he put upon his H4370
16: 4 have the linen **b** upon his flesh, and H4370
Ezk 44:18 shall have linen **b** upon their loins; they H4370

BREED
Gen 8:17 that they may **b** abundantly in the H8317
Dt 32:14 and rams of the **b** of Bashan, and H1121

BREEDING
Zep 2: 9 *even* the **b** of nettles, and saltpits, H4476

BRETHREN
Gen 9:22 of his father, and told his two **b** without. H251
25 servant of servants shall he be unto his **b**. H251
13: 8 herdmen and thy herdmen; for we *be* **b**. H251
16:12 he shall dwell in the presence of all his **b**. H251
19: 7 And said, I pray you, **b**, do not so H251
24:27 led me to the house of my master's **b**. H251
25:18 *and* he died in the presence of all his **b**. H251
27:29 be lord over thy **b**, and let thy mother's H251
37 lord, and all his **b** have I given to him for H251
29: 4 And Jacob said unto them, My **b**, whence H251
31:23 And he took his **b** with him, and H251
25 his **b** pitched in the mount of Gilead. H251
32 not live: before our **b** discern thou what H251
37 set *it* here before my **b** and thy brethren, H251
37 **b**, that they may judge betwixt us both. H251
46 And Jacob said unto his **b**, Gather stones; H251
54 and called his **b** to eat bread: and they H251
34:11 and unto her **b**, Let me find grace in H251
25 and Levi, Dinah's **b**, took each man his H251
37: 2 the flock with his **b**; and the lad *was* with H251
4 And when his **b** saw that their father H251
4 more than all his **b**, they hated him, and H251
5 *it* his **b**: and they hated him yet the more. H251
8 And his **b** said to him, Shalt thou indeed H251
9 and told it his **b**, and said, Behold, I have H251
10 And he told *it* to his father, and to his **b**: H251
10 mother and thy **b** indeed come to bow H251
11 And his **b** envied him; but his father H251
12 And his **b** went to feed their father's H251
13 Joseph, Do not thy **b** feed *the flock* in H251
14 it be well with thy **b**, and well with the H251
16 And he said, I seek my **b**: tell me, I pray H251
17 after his **b**, and found them in Dothan. H251
23 was come unto his **b**, that they stript H251
26 And Judah said unto his **b**, What profit *is* H251
27 *and* our flesh. And his **b** were content. H251
30 And he returned unto his **b**, and said, H251
38: 1 went down from his **b**, and turned in to a H251
11 he die also, as his **b** *did*. And Tamar H251
42: 3 And Joseph's ten **b** went down to buy H251
4 sent not with his **b**; for he said, Lest H251
6 land: and Joseph's **b** came, and bowed H251
7 And Joseph saw his **b**, and he knew them, H251
8 And Joseph knew his **b**, but they knew H251
13 And they said, Thy servants *are* twelve **b**, H251
19 If ye *be* true *men*, let one of your **b** be H251
28 And he said unto his **b**, My money is H251
32 We *be* twelve **b**, sons of our father; one *is* H251
33 leave one of your **b** *here* with me, and H251
44:14 And Judah and his **b** came to Joseph's H251
33 my lord; and let the lad go up with his **b**. H251
45: 1 Joseph made himself known unto his **b**. H251
3 And Joseph said unto his **b**, I *am* Joseph; H251
3 yet live? And his **b** could not answer H251
4 And Joseph said unto his **b**, Come near to H251
15 Moreover he kissed all his **b**, and wept H251
15 and after that his **b** talked with him. H251
16 saying, Joseph's **b** are come: and it H251
17 Say unto thy **b**, This do ye; lade your H251
24 So he sent his **b** away, and they H251
46:31 And Joseph said unto his **b**, and unto his H251
31 and say unto him, My **b**, and my father's H251
47: 1 My father and my **b**, and their flocks, H251
2 And he took some of his **b**, *even* five men, H251
3 And Pharaoh said unto his **b**, What *is* H251
5 Thy father and thy **b** are come unto thee: H251
6 thy father and **b** to dwell; in the land H251
11 And Joseph placed his father and his **b**, H251
12 his father, and his **b**, and all his father's H251
48: 6 the name of their **b** in their inheritance. H251
22 portion above thy **b**, which I took out of H251
49: 5 Simeon and Levi *are* **b**; instruments of H251
8 Judah, thou *art he* whom thy **b** shall H251
26 of him that was separate from his **b**. H251
50: 8 And all the house of Joseph, and his **b**, H251
14 Egypt, he, and his **b**, and all that went up H251
15 And when Joseph's **b** saw that their H251
17 the trespass of thy **b**, and their sin; for H251
18 And his **b** also went and fell down before H251
Gen 50:24 And Joseph said unto his **b**, I die: and H251
Ex 1: 6 And Joseph died, and all his **b**, and all H251
2:11 went out unto his **b**, and looked on their H251
11 smiting an Hebrew, one of his **b**. H251
4:18 return unto my **b** which *are* in Egypt, H251
Lev 10: 4 Come near, carry your **b** from before the H251
6 but let your **b**, the whole house of Israel, H251
21:10 priest among his **b**, upon whose head the H251
25:46 for ever: but over your **b** the children of H251
48 again; one of his **b** may redeem him: H251
Nu 8:26 But shall minister with their **b** in the H251
16:10 *to him*, and all thy **b** the sons of Levi H251
18: 2 And thy **b** also of the tribe of Levi, the H251
6 And I, behold, I have taken your **b** the H251
20: 3 died when our **b** died before the LORD! H251
25: 6 brought unto his **b** a Midianitish woman H251
27: 4 a possession among the **b** of our father. H251
7 their father's **b**; and thou shalt cause H251
9 ye shall give his inheritance unto his **b**. H251
10 And if he have no **b**, then ye shall give his H251
10 give his inheritance unto his father's **b**. H251
11 And if his father have no **b**, then ye shall H251
32: 6 your **b** go to war, and shall ye sit here? H251
Dt 1:16 between your **b**, and judge righteously H251
28 Whither shall we go up? our **b** have H251
2: 4 the coast of your **b** the children of Esau, H251
8 And when we passed by from our **b** the H251
3:18 over armed before your **b** the children of H251
20 rest unto your **b**, as well as unto you, H251
10: 9 with his **b**; the LORD *is* his inheritance, H251
15: 7 man of one of thy **b** within any of thy H251
17:15 from among thy **b** shalt thou set king H251
20 lifted up above his **b**, and that he turn H251
18: 2 among their **b**: the LORD *is* their H251
7 his God, as all his **b** the Levites *do*, which H251
15 of thee, of thy **b**, like unto me; unto him H251
18 from among their **b**, like unto thee, and H251
24: 7 If a man be found stealing any of his **b** of H251
14 *he be* of thy **b**, or of thy strangers that H251
25: 5 If **b** dwell together, and one of them die, H251
33: 9 he acknowledge his **b**, nor knew his own H251
16 of him *that was* separated from his **b**. H251
24 to his **b**, and let him dip his foot in oil. H251
Jos 1:14 pass before your **b** armed, all the mighty H251
15 Until the LORD have given your **b** rest, H251
2:13 mother, and my **b**, and my sisters, and H251
18 mother, and thy **b**, and all thy father's H251
6:23 mother, and her **b**, and all that she had; H251
14: 8 Nevertheless my **b** that went up with me H251
17: 4 among our **b**. Therefore according H251
4 inheritance among the **b** of their father. H251
22: 3 Ye have not left your **b** these many days H251
4 rest unto your **b**, as he promised them: H251
7 among their **b** on this side Jordan H251
8 the spoil of your enemies with your **b**. H251
Jdg 8:19 And he said, They *were* my **b**, *even* the H251
9: 1 unto his mother's **b**, and communed with H251
3 And his mother's **b** spake of him in the H251
5 and slew his **b** the sons of Jerubbaal, H251
24 which aided him in the killing of his **b**. H251
26 Ebed came with his **b**, and went over to H251
31 of Ebed and his **b** be come to Shechem; H251
41 **b**, that they should not dwell in Shechem. H251
56 unto his father, in slaying his seventy **b**: H251
11: 3 Then Jephthah fled from his **b**, and dwelt H251
14: 3 the daughters of thy **b**, or among all my H251
16:31 Then his **b** and all the house of his father H251
18: 8 And they came unto their **b** to Zorah H251
8 their **b** said unto them, What *say* ye? H251
14 and said unto their **b**, Do ye know that H251
19:23 them, Nay, my **b**, *nay*, I pray you, do not H251
20:13 the voice of their **b** the children of Israel: H251
21:22 their fathers or their **b** come unto us to H251
Ru 4:10 off from among his **b**, and from the gate H251
1Sa 16:13 in the midst of his **b**: and the spirit of the H251
17:17 son, Take now for thy **b** an ephah of this H251
17 ten loaves, and run to the camp to thy **b**; H251
18 how thy **b** fare, and take their pledge. H251
22 the army, and came and saluted his **b**. H251
20:29 thee, and see my **b**. Therefore he cometh H251
22: 1 and when his **b** and all his father's house H251
30:23 shall not do so, my **b**, with that which the H251
2Sa 2:26 the people return from following their **b**? H251
3: 8 thy father, to his **b**, and to his friends, H251
15:20 back thy **b**: mercy and truth *be* with thee. H251
19:12 Ye *are* my **b**, ye *are* my bones and my H251
41 Why have our **b** the men of Judah stolen H251
1Ki 1: 9 and called all his **b** the king's sons, and H251
12:24 nor fight against your **b** the children of H251

2Ki 9: 2 **b**, and carry him to an inner chamber; H251
10:13 Jehu met with the **b** of Ahaziah king of H251
13 We *are* the **b** of Ahaziah; and we go H251
23: 9 of the unleavened bread among their **b**. H251
1Ch 4: 9 than his **b**: and his mother called H251
27 six daughters; but his **b** had not many H251
5: 2 For Judah prevailed above his **b**, and of H251
7 And his **b** by their families, when the H251
13 And their **b** of the house of their fathers H251
6:44 And their **b** the sons of Merari *stood* on H251
48 Their **b** also the Levites *were* appointed H251
7: 5 And their **b** among all the families of H251
22 days, and his **b** came to comfort him. H251
8:32 their **b** in Jerusalem, over against them. H251
9: 6 and their **b**, six hundred and ninety. H251
9 And their **b**, according to their H251
13 And their **b**, heads of the house of their H251
17 and their **b**: Shallum *was* the chief; H251
19 of Korah, and his **b**, of the house of his H251
25 And their **b**, *which were* in their villages, H251
32 And *other* of their **b**, of the sons of the H251
38 dwelt with their **b** at Jerusalem, over H251
38 at Jerusalem, over against their **b**. H251
12: 2 of a bow, *even* of Saul's **b** of Benjamin. H251
32 all their **b** *were* at their commandment. H251
39 for their **b** had prepared for them. H251
13: 2 abroad unto our **b** every where, *that are* H251
15: 5 chief, and his **b** an hundred and twenty: H251
6 and his **b** two hundred and twenty: H251
7 chief, and his **b** an hundred and thirty: H251
8 the chief, and his **b** two hundred: H251
9 Eliel the chief, and his **b** fourscore: H251
10 chief, and his **b** an hundred and twelve. H251
12 *both* ye and your **b**, that ye may bring up H251
16 to appoint their **b** *to be* the singers with H251
17 son of Joel; and of his **b**, Asaph the son of H251
17 their **b**, Ethan the son of Kushaiah; H251
18 And with them their **b** of the second H251
16: 7 LORD into the hand of Asaph and his **b**. H251
37 Asaph and his **b**, to minister before the H251
38 And Obed-edom with their **b**, threescore H251
39 And Zadok the priest, and his **b** the H251
23:22 and their **b** the sons of Kish took them. H251
32 sons of Aaron their **b**, in the service of H251
24:31 over against their **b** the sons of Aaron in H251
31 fathers over against their younger **b**. H251
25: 7 So the number of them, with their **b** that H251
9 who with his **b** and sons *were* twelve: H251
10 *he*, his sons, and his **b**, *were* twelve: H251
11 The fourth to Izri, *he*, his sons, and his **b**, H251
12 *he*, his sons, and his **b**, *were* twelve: H251
13 *he*, his sons, and his **b**, *were* twelve: H251
14 *he*, his sons, and his **b**, *were* twelve: H251
15 *he*, his sons, and his **b**, *were* twelve: H251
16 *he*, his sons, and his **b**, *were* twelve: H251
17 *he*, his sons, and his **b**, *were* twelve: H251
18 *he*, his sons, and his **b**, *were* twelve: H251
19 *he*, his sons, and his **b**, *were* twelve: H251
20 *he*, his sons, and his **b**, *were* twelve: H251
21 *he*, his sons, and his **b**, *were* twelve: H251
22 *he*, his sons, and his **b**, *were* twelve: H251
23 *he*, his sons, and his **b**, *were* twelve: H251
24 *he*, his sons, and his **b**, *were* twelve: H251
25 *he*, his sons, and his **b**, *were* twelve: H251
26 *he*, his sons, and his **b**, *were* twelve: H251
27 *he*, his sons, and his **b**, *were* twelve: H251
28 *he*, his sons, and his **b**, *were* twelve: H251
29 *he*, his sons, and his **b**, *were* twelve: H251
30 *he*, his sons, and his **b**, *were* twelve: H251
31 *he*, his sons, and his **b**, *were* twelve. H251
26: 7 Elzabad, whose **b** *were* strong men, H251
8 sons and their **b**, able men for strength H251
9 And Meshelemiah had sons and **b**, H251
11 the sons and **b** of Hosah *were* thirteen. H251
25 And his **b** by Eliezer; Rehabiah his son, H251
26 Which Shelomith and his **b** *were* over all H251
28 the hand of Shelomith, and of his **b**. H251
30 Hashabiah and his **b**, men of valour, a H251
32 And his **b**, men of valour, *were* two H251
27:18 Of Judah, Elihu, *one* of the **b** of David: of H251
28: 2 said, Hear me, my **b**, and my people: *As* H251
2Ch 5:12 sons and their **b**, *being* arrayed in white H251
11: 4 fight against your **b**: return every man to H251
22 his **b**: for *he thought* to make him king. H251
19:10 to you of your **b** that dwell in their cities, H251
10 your **b**: this do, and ye shall not trespass. H251
21: 2 And he had **b** the sons of Jehoshaphat, H251
4 and slew all his **b** with the sword, and H251
13 and also hast slain thy **b** of thy father's H251

2Ch 22: 8 and the sons of the **b** of Ahaziah, that H251
28: 8 away captive of their **b** two hundred H251
11 captive of your **b**: for the fierce wrath of H251
15 to their **b**: then they returned to Samaria. H251
29:15 And they gathered their **b**, and sanctified H251
34 wherefore their **b** the Levites did help H251
30: 7 and like your **b**, which trespassed against H251
9 the LORD, your **b** and your children H251
31:15 to give to their **b** by courses, as well to H251
35: 5 of the fathers of your **b** the people, and H251
6 and prepare your **b**, that *they* may do H251
9 and Nethaneel, his **b**, and Hashabiah H251
15 for their **b** the Levites prepared for them. H251
Ezr 3: 2 of Jozadak, and his **b** the priests, and H251
2 Shealtiel, and his **b**, and builded the altar H251
8 remnant of their **b** the priests and the H251
9 his sons and his **b**, Kadmiel and his sons, H251
9 *with* their sons and their **b** the Levites. H251
6:20 their **b** the priests, and for themselves. H251
7:18 to thee, and to thy **b**, to do with the rest H252
8:17 Iddo, *and* to his **b** the Nethinims, at the H251
18 with his sons and his **b**, eighteen; H251
19 of Merari, his **b** and their sons, twenty; H251
24 Hashabiah, and ten of their **b** with them, H251
10:18 son of Jozadak, and his **b**; Maaseiah, and H251
Neh 1: 2 That Hanani, one of my **b**, came, he and H251
3: 1 rose up with his **b** the priests, and they H251
18 After him repaired their **b**, Bavai the son H251
4: 2 And he spake before his **b** and the army H251
14 and fight for your **b**, your sons, and your H251
23 So neither I, nor my **b**, nor my servants, H251
5: 1 of their wives against their **b** the Jews. H251
5 Yet now our flesh *is* as the flesh of our **b**, H251
8 have redeemed our **b** the Jews, which H251
8 ye even sell your **b**? or shall they be sold H251
10 I likewise, *and* my **b**, and my servants, H251
14 years, I and my **b** have not eaten the H251
10:10 And their **b**, Shebaniah, Hodijah, Kelita, H251
29 They clave to their **b**, their nobles, and H251
11:12 And their **b** that did the work of the H251
13 And his **b**, chief of the fathers, two H251
14 And their **b**, mighty men of valour, an H251
17 second among his **b**, and Abda the son of H251
19 Talmon, and their **b** that kept the gates, H251
12: 7 and of their **b** in the days of Jeshua. H251
8 *was* over the thanksgiving, he and his **b**. H251
9 Also Bakbukiah and Unni, their **b**, *were* H251
24 with their **b** over against them, to H251
36 And his **b**, Shemaiah, and Azarael, H251
13:13 their office *was* to distribute unto their **b**. H251
Est 10: 3 multitude of his **b**, seeking the wealth of H251
Job 6:15 My **b** have dealt deceitfully as a brook, H251
19:13 He hath put my **b** far from me, and mine H251
42:11 Then came there unto him all his **b**, and H251
15 gave them inheritance among their **b**. H251
Ps 22:22 I will declare thy name unto my **b**: in the H251
69: 8 I am become a stranger unto my **b**, and H251
122: 8 For my **b** and companions' sakes, I will H251
133: 1 *it is* for **b** to dwell together in unity! H251
Prv 6:19 and he that soweth discord among **b**. H251
17: 2 have part of the inheritance among the **b**. H251
19: 7 All the **b** of the poor do hate him: how H251
Isa 66: 5 at his word; Your **b** that hated you, that H251
20 And they shall bring all your **b** *for* an H251
Jer 7:15 your **b**, *even* the whole seed of Ephraim. H251
12: 6 For even thy **b**, and the house of thy H251
29:16 this city, *and* of your **b** that are not gone H251
35: 3 and his **b**, and all his sons, and H251
41: 8 and slew them not among their **b**. H251
49:10 his **b**, and his neighbours, and he *is* not. H251
Ezk 11:15 Son of man, thy **b**, *even* thy brethren, the H251
15 Son of man, thy brethren, *even* thy **b**, the H251
Hos 2: 1 Say ye unto your **b**, Ammi; and to your H251
13:15 Though he be fruitful among *his* **b**, an H251
Mic 5: 3 **b** shall return unto the children of Israel. H251
Mt 1: 2 Jacob; and Jacob begat Judas and his **b**; *G80*
11 And Josias begat Jechonias and his **b**, *G80*
4:18 of Galilee, saw two **b**, Simon called Peter, *G80*
21 he saw other two **b**, James *the son* of *G80*
5:47 And if ye salute your **b** only, what do ye *G80*
12:46 *his* mother and his **b** stood without, *G80*
47 thy mother and thy **b** stand without, *G80*
48 Who is my mother? and who are my **b**? *G80*
49 and said, Behold my mother and my **b**! *G80*
13:55 Mary? and his **b**, James, and Joses, and *G80*
19:29 houses, or **b**, or sisters, or father, *G80*
20:24 with indignation against the two **b**. *G80*
22:25 Now there were with us seven **b**: and the *G80*
23: 8 Master, *even* Christ; and all ye are **b**. *G80*

Mt 25:40 of these my **b**, ye have done *it* unto me. *G80*
28:10 not afraid: go tell my **b** that they go into *G80*
Mk 3:31 There came then his **b** and his mother, *G80*
32 mother and thy **b** without seek for thee. *G80*
33 saying, Who is my mother, or my **b**? *G80*
34 and said, Behold my mother and my **b**! *G80*
10:29 hath left house, or **b**, or sisters, or father, *G80*
30 this time, houses, and **b**, and sisters, and *G80*
12:20 Now there were seven **b**: and the first *G80*
Lk 8:19 Then came to him *his* mother and his **b**, *G80*
20 thy **b** stand without, desiring to see thee. *G80*
21 mother and my **b** are these which hear *G80*
14:12 not thy friends, nor thy **b**, neither thy *G80*
26 and children, and **b**, and sisters, yea, and *G80*
16:28 For I have five **b**; that he may testify unto *G80*
18:29 or parents, or **b**, or wife, or children, *G80*
20:29 There were therefore seven **b**: and the *G80*
21:16 by parents, and **b**, and kinsfolks, and *G80*
22:32 thou art converted, strengthen thy **b**. *G80*
Jn 2:12 mother, and his **b**, and his disciples: and *G80*
7: 3 His **b** therefore said unto him, Depart *G80*
5 For neither did his **b** believe in him. *G80*
10 But when his **b** were gone up, then went *G80*
20:17 but go to my **b**, and say unto them, *G80*
21:23 abroad among the **b**, that that disciple *G80*
Act 1:14 Mary the mother of Jesus, and with his **b**. *G80*
16 Men *and* **b**, this scripture must needs *G80*
2:29 Men *and* **b**, let me freely speak unto you *G80*
37 apostles, Men *and* **b**, what shall we do? *G80*
3:17 And now, **b**, I wot that through ignorance *G80*
22 up unto you of your **b**, like unto me; him *G80*
6: 3 Wherefore, **b**, look ye out among you *G80*
7: 2 And he said, Men, **b**, and fathers, *G80*
13 was made known to his **b**; and Joseph's *G80*
23 heart to visit his **b** the children of Israel. *G80*
25 For he supposed his **b** would have *G80*
26 are **b**; why do ye wrong one to another? *G80*
37 of your **b**, like unto me; him shall ye hear. *G80*
9:30 *Which* when the **b** knew, they brought *G80*
10:23 certain **b** from Joppa accompanied him. *G80*
11: 1 And the apostles and **b** that were in *G80*
12 Moreover these six **b** accompanied me, *G80*
29 relief unto the **b** which dwelt in Judaea: *G80*
12:17 James, and to the **b**. And he departed, *G80*
13:15 *Ye* men *and* **b**, if ye have any word *G80*
26 Men *and* **b**, children of the stock of *G80*
38 therefore, men *and* **b**, that through this *G80*
14: 2 their minds evil affected against the **b**. *G80*
15: 1 Judaea taught the **b**, *and said*, Except ye *G80*
3 and they caused great joy unto all the **b**. *G80*
7 them, Men *and* **b**, ye know how that a *G80*
13 saying, Men *and* **b**, hearken unto me: *G80*
22 and Silas, chief men among the **b**: *G80*
23 and elders and **b** *send* greeting unto the *G80*
23 *send* greeting unto the **b** which are of the *G80*
32 exhorted the **b** with many words, and *G80*
33 go in peace from the **b** unto the apostles. *G80*
36 again and visit our **b** in every city where *G80*
40 by the **b** unto the grace of God. *G80*
16: 2 Which was well reported of by the **b** that *G80*
40 **b**, they comforted them, and departed. *G80*
17: 6 Jason and certain **b** unto the rulers of *G80*
10 And the **b** immediately sent away Paul *G80*
14 And then immediately the **b** sent away *G80*
18:18 his leave of the **b**, and sailed thence into *G80*
27 into Achaia, the **b** wrote, exhorting the *G80*
20:32 And now, **b**, I commend you to God, and *G80*
21: 7 the **b**, and abode with them one day. *G80*
17 to Jerusalem, the **b** received us gladly. *G80*
22: 1 Men, **b**, and fathers, hear ye my defence *G80*
5 received letters unto the **b**, and went to *G80*
23: 1 said, Men *and* **b**, I have lived in all good *G80*
5 Then said Paul, I wist not, **b**, that he was *G80*
6 council, Men *and* **b**, I am a Pharisee, the *G80*
28:14 Where we found **b**, and were desired to *G80*
15 And from thence, when the **b** heard of *G80*
17 unto them, Men *and* **b**, though I have *G80*
21 neither any of the **b** that came shewed or *G80*
Ro 1:13 Now I would not have you ignorant, **b**, *G80*
7: 1 Know ye not, **b**, (for I speak to them that *G80*
4 Wherefore, my **b**, ye also are become *G80*
8:12 Therefore, **b**, we are debtors, not to the *G80*
29 he might be the firstborn among many **b**. *G80*
9: 3 my **b**, my kinsmen according to the flesh: *G80*
10: 1 **B**, my heart's desire and prayer to God *G80*
11:25 For I would not, **b**, that ye should be *G80*
12: 1 I beseech you therefore, **b**, by the mercies *G80*
15:14 of you, my **b**, that ye also are full of *G80*
15 Nevertheless, **b**, I have written the more *G80*

Ro 15:30 Now I beseech you, **b**, for the Lord Jesus G80
16:14 Hermes, and the **b** which are with them. G80
17 Now I beseech you, **b**, mark them which G80
1Co 1:10 Now I beseech you, **b**, by the name of our G80
11 me of you, my **b**, by them *which are of* G80
26 For ye see your calling, **b**, how that not G80
2: 1 And I, **b**, when I came to you, came not G80
3: 1 And I, **b**, could not speak unto you as G80
4: 6 And these things, **b**, I have in a figure G80
6: 5 that shall be able to judge between his **b**? G80
8 do wrong, and defraud, and that *your* **b**. G80
7:24 **B**, let every man, wherein he is called, G80
29 But this I say, **b**, the time *is* short: it G80
8:12 But when ye sin so against the **b**, and G80
9: 5 and *as* the **b** of the Lord, and Cephas? G80
10: 1 Moreover, **b**, I would not that ye should G80
11: 2 Now I praise you, **b**, that ye remember G80
33 Wherefore, my **b**, when ye come together G80
12: 1 Now concerning spiritual *gifts*, **b**, I would G80
14: 6 Now, **b**, if I come unto you speaking with G80
20 **B**, be not children in understanding: G80
26 How is it then, **b**? when ye come together, G80
39 Wherefore, **b**, covet to prophesy, and G80
15: 1 Moreover, **b**, I declare unto you the G80
6 five hundred **b** at once; of whom the G80
50 Now this I say, **b**, that flesh and blood G80
58 Therefore, my beloved **b**, be ye stedfast, G80
16:11 unto me: for I look for him with the **b**. G80
12 unto you with the **b**: but his will was not G80
15 I beseech you, **b**, (ye know the house of G80
20 All the **b** greet you. Greet ye one another G80
2Co 1: 8 For we would not, **b**, have you ignorant G80
8: 1 Moreover, **b**, we do you to wit of the G80
23 you: or our **b** *be inquired of, they* G80
9: 3 Yet have I sent the **b**, lest our boasting of G80
5 to exhort the **b**, that they would go before G80
11: 9 lacking to me the **b** which came from G80
26 in the sea, *in* perils among false **b**; G5569
13:11 Finally, **b**, farewell. Be perfect, be of good G80
Gal 1: 2 And all the **b** which are with me, unto G80
11 But I certify you, **b**, that the gospel which G80
2: 4 And that because of false **b** unawares G5569
3:15 **B**, I speak after the manner of men; G80
4:12 **B**, I beseech you, be as I *am*; for I *am* as G80
28 Now we, **b**, as Isaac was, are the children G80
31 So then, **b**, we are not children of the G80
5:11 And I, **b**, if I yet preach circumcision, G80
13 For, **b**, ye have been called unto liberty; G80
6: 1 **B**, if a man be overtaken in a fault, ye G80
18 **B**, the grace of our Lord Jesus Christ *be* G80
Eph 6:10 Finally, my **b**, be strong in the Lord, and G80
23 Peace *be* to the **b**, and love with faith, G80
Php 1:12 But I would ye should understand, **b**, G80
14 And many of the **b** in the Lord, waxing G80
3: 1 Finally, my **b**, rejoice in the Lord. To G80
13 **B**, I count not myself to have G80
17 **B**, be followers together of me, and mark G80
4: 1 Therefore, my **b** dearly beloved and G80
8 Finally, **b**, whatsoever things are true, G80
21 Salute every saint in Christ Jesus. The **b** G80
Col 1: 2 To the saints and faithful **b** in Christ G80
4:15 Salute the **b** which are in Laodicea, and G80
1Th 1: 4 Knowing, **b** beloved, your election of G80
2: 1 For yourselves, **b**, know our entrance in G80
9 For ye remember, **b**, our labour and G80
14 For ye, **b**, became followers of the G80
17 But we, **b**, being taken from you for a G80
3: 7 Therefore, **b**, we were comforted over G80
4: 1 Furthermore then we beseech you, **b**, and G80
10 And indeed ye do it toward all the **b** G80
10 you, **b**, that ye increase more and more; G80
13 you to be ignorant, **b**, concerning them G80
5: 1 But of the times and the seasons, **b**, ye G80
4 But ye, **b**, are not in darkness, that that G80
12 And we beseech you, **b**, to know them G80
14 Now we exhort you, **b**, warn them that G80
25 **B**, pray for us. G80
26 Greet all the **b** with an holy kiss. G80
27 this epistle be read unto all the holy **b**. G80
2Th 1: 3 always for you, **b**, as it is meet, because G80
2: 1 Now we beseech you, **b**, by the coming of G80
13 to God for you, **b** beloved of the Lord, G80
15 Therefore, **b**, stand fast, and hold the G80
3: 1 Finally, **b**, pray for us, that the word of G80
6 Now we command you, **b**, in the name of G80
13 But ye, **b**, be not weary in well doing. G80
1Ti 4: 6 If thou put the **b** in remembrance of G80
5: 1 as a father; *and* the younger men as **b**; G80
6: 2 because they are **b**; but rather do *them* G80
2Ti 4:21 and Linus, and Claudia, and all the **b**. G80
Heb 2:11 cause he is not ashamed to call them **b**, G80
12 thy name unto my **b**, in the midst of the G80
17 made like unto *his* **b**, that he might be a G80
3: 1 Wherefore, holy **b**, partakers of the G80
12 Take heed, **b**, lest there be in any of you G80
7: 5 that is, of their **b**, though they come out G80
10:19 Having therefore, **b**, boldness to enter G80
13:22 And I beseech you, **b**, suffer the word of G80
Jas 1: 2 My **b**, count it all joy when ye fall into G80
16 Do not err, my beloved **b**. G80
19 Wherefore, my beloved **b**, let every man G80
2: 1 My **b**, have not the faith of our Lord Jesus G80
5 Hearken, my beloved **b**, Hath not God G80
14 What *doth it* profit, my **b**, though a man G80
3: 1 My **b**, be not many masters, knowing G80
10 My **b**, these things ought not so to be. G80
12 Can the fig tree, my **b**, bear olive berries? G80
4:11 Speak not evil one of another, **b**. He that G80
5: 7 Be patient therefore, **b**, unto the coming G80
9 Grudge not one against another, **b**, lest G80
10 Take, my **b**, the prophets, who have G80
12 But above all things, my **b**, swear not, G80
19 **B**, if any of you do err from the truth, and G80
1Pt 1:22 love of the **b**, *see that ye* love one G5360
3: 8 love as **b**, *be* pitiful, *be* courteous: G5361
5: 9 in your **b** that are in the world. G81
2Pt 1:10 Wherefore the rather, **b**, give diligence to G80
1Jn 2: 7 **B**, I write no new commandment unto G80
3:13 Marvel not, my **b**, if the world hate you. G80
14 we love the **b**. He that loveth not *his* G80
16 we ought to lay down *our* lives for the **b**. G80
3Jn 3 For I rejoiced greatly, when the **b** came G80
5 thou doest to the **b**, and to strangers; G80
10 he himself receive the **b**, and forbiddeth G80
Rev 6:11 also and their **b**, that should be killed G80
12:10 the accuser of our **b** is cast down, which G80
19:10 and of thy **b** that have the testimony G80
22: 9 and of thy **b** the prophets, and of G80

BRETHREN'S
Dt 20: 8 lest his **b** heart faint as well as his heart. H251

BRIBE
1Sa 12: 3 I received *any* **b** to blind mine eyes H3724
Am 5:12 just, they take a **b**, and they turn aside H3724

BRIBERY
Job 15:34 fire shall consume the tabernacles of **b**. H7810

BRIBES
1Sa 8: 3 and took **b**, and perverted judgment. H7810
Ps 26:10 and their right hand is full of **b**. H7810
Isa 33:15 from holding of **b**, that stoppeth his H7810

BRICK
Gen 11: 3 Go to, let us make **b**, and burn them H3843
3 And they had **b** for stone, and slime H3843
Ex 1:14 in morter, and in **b**, and in all manner H3843
5: 7 straw to make **b**, as heretofore: let them H3843
14 task in making **b** both yesterday and H3835
16 they say to us, Make **b**: and, behold, thy H3843
Isa 65: 3 and burneth incense upon altars of **b**; H3843

BRICKKILN
2Sa 12:31 pass through the **b**: and thus did he H4404
Jer 43: 9 in the clay in the **b**, which *is* at the entry H4404
Nah 3:14 tread the morter, make strong the **b**. H4404

BRICKS
Ex 5: 8 And the tale of the **b**, which they did H3843
18 you, yet shall ye deliver the tale of **b**. H3843
19 *ought* from your **b** of your daily task. H3843
Isa 9:10 The **b** are fallen down, but we will build H3843

BRIDE
Isa 49:18 and bind them *on thee*, as a **b** *doeth*. H3618
61:10 as a **b** adorneth *herself* with her jewels. H3618
62: 5 the **b**, *so* shall thy God rejoice over thee. H3618
Jer 2:32 ornaments, *or* a **b** her attire? yet my H3618
7:34 of the **b**: for the land shall be desolate. H3618
16: 9 the bridegroom, and the voice of the **b**. H3618
25:10 and the voice of the **b**, the sound of the H3618
33:11 the voice of the **b**, the voice of them that H3618
Joel 2:16 chamber, and the **b** out of her closet. H3618
Jn 3:29 He that hath the **b** is the bridegroom: G3565
Rev 18:23 and of the **b** shall be heard no more G3565
21: 2 as a **b** adorned for her husband. G3565
9 I will shew thee the **b**, the Lamb's wife. G3565
22:17 And the Spirit and the **b** say, Come. G3565

BRIDECHAMBER
Mt 9:15 the children of the **b** mourn, as long as G3567
Mk 2:19 Can the children of the **b** fast, while the G3567
Lk 5:34 the children of the **b** fast, while the G3567

BRIDEGROOM
Ps 19: 5 Which *is* as a **b** coming out of his H2860
Isa 61:10 as a **b** decketh *himself* with H2860
62: 5 thee: and *as* the **b** rejoiceth over the H2860
Jer 7:34 the voice of the **b**, and the voice of the H2860
16: 9 of the **b**, and the voice of the bride. H2860
25:10 the voice of the **b**, and the voice of the H2860
33:11 the voice of the **b**, and the voice of the H2860
Joel 2:16 the breasts: let the **b** go forth of his H2860
Mt 9:15 as long as the **b** is with them? but the G3566
15 come, when the **b** shall be taken from G3566
25: 1 lamps, and went forth to meet the **b**. G3566
5 While the **b** tarried, they all slumbered G3566
6 the **b** cometh; go ye out to meet him. G3566
10 And while they went to buy, the **b** G3566
Mk 2:19 fast, while the **b** is with them? as long G3566
19 have the **b** with them, they cannot fast. G3566
20 But the days will come, when the **b** G3566
Lk 5:34 fast, while the **b** is with them? G3566
35 But the days will come, when the **b** G3566
Jn 2: 9 the governor of the feast called the **b**, G3566
3:29 He that hath the bride is the **b**: but the G3566
29 the friend of the **b**, which standeth and G3566
Rev 18:23 the voice of the **b** and of the bride shall G3566

BRIDEGROOM'S
Jn 3:29 because of the **b** voice: this my joy G3566

BRIDLE
2Ki 19:28 in thy nose, and my **b** in thy lips, and I H4964
Job 30:11 have also let loose the **b** before me. H7448
41:13 who can come *to him* with his double **b**? H7448
Ps 32: 9 bit and **b**, lest they come near unto thee. H7448
39: 1 with a **b**, while the wicked is before me. H4269
Prv 26: 3 A whip for the horse, a **b** for the ass, H4964
Isa 30:28 and *there shall be* a **b** in the jaws of the H7448
37:29 in thy nose, and my **b** in thy lips, and I H4964
Jas 3: 2 *and* able also to **b** the whole body. G5468

BRIDLES
Rev 14:20 even unto the horse **b**, by the space of a G5469

BRIDLETH
Jas 1:26 be religious, and **b** not his tongue, but G5468

BRIEFLY
Ro 13: 9 it is **b** comprehended in this G346
1Pt 5:12 I have written **b**, exhorting, and G1223+G3641

BRIER
Isa 55:13 and instead of the **b** shall come up the H5636
Ezk 28:24 no more a pricking **b** unto the house of H5544
Mic 7: 4 The best of them *is* as a **b**: the most H2312

BRIERS
Jdg 8: 7 the thorns of the wilderness and with **b**. H1303
16 the wilderness and **b**, and with them he H1303
Isa 5: 6 shall come up **b** and thorns: I will also H8068
7:23 it shall *even* be for **b** and thorns. H8068
24 all the land shall become **b** and thorns. H8068
25 thither the fear of **b** and thorns: but it H8068
9:18 it shall devour the **b** and thorns, and H8068
10:17 devour his thorns and his **b** in one day; H8068
27: 4 Fury *is* not in me: who would set the **b** H8068
32:13 come up thorns *and* **b**; yea, upon all the H8068
Ezk 2: 6 words, though **b** and thorns *be* with H5621
Heb 6: 8 But that which beareth thorns and **b** *is* G5146

BRIGANDINE
Jer 51: 3 himself up in his **b**: and spare ye not her H5630

BRIGANDINES
Jer 46: 4 furbish the spears, *and* put on the **b**. H5630

BRIGHT
Lev 13: 2 a rising, a scab, or **b** spot, and it be in H934
4 If the **b** spot *be* white in the skin of his H934
19 be a white rising, or a **b** spot, white, and H934
23 But if the **b** spot stay in his place, *and* H934
24 **b** spot, somewhat reddish, or white; H934
25 *if* the hair in the **b** spot be turned white, H934
26 no white hair in the **b** spot, and it *be* no H934

Lev 13:28 And if the **b** spot stay in his place, *and* H934
38 flesh **b** spots, *even* white bright spots; H934
38 flesh bright spots, *even* white **b** spots; H934
39 and, behold, *if* the **b** spots in the skin of H934
14:56 a rising, and for a scab, and for a **b** spot: H934
1Ki 7:45 the house of the LORD, *were of* **b** brass. H4803
2Ch 4:16 for the house of the LORD of **b** brass. H4838
Job 37:11 the thick cloud: he scattereth his **b** cloud: H216
21 And now *men* see not the **b** light which H925
Song 5:14 *is as* **b** ivory overlaid *with* sapphires. H6247
Jer 51:11 Make **b** the arrows; gather the shields: H1305
Ezk 1:13 and the fire was **b**, and out of the fire H5051
21:15 **b**, *it is* wrapped up for the slaughter. H1300
21 made *his* arrows **b**, he consulted with H7043
27:19 in thy fairs: **b** iron, cassia, and H6219
32: 8 All the **b** lights of heaven will I make H3974
Nah 3: 3 The horseman lifteth up both the **b** H3851
Zec 10: 1 LORD shall make **b** clouds, and give H2385
Mt 17: 5 While he yet spake, behold, a **b** cloud *G5460*
Lk 11:36 light, as when the **b** shining of a candle *G796*
Act 10:30 a man stood before me in **b** clothing, *G2986*
Rev 22:16 of David, *and* the **b** and morning star. *G2986*

BRIGHTNESS
2Sa 22:13 Through the **b** before him were coals of H5051
Job 31:26 it shined, or the moon walking *in* **b**; H3368
Ps 18:12 At the **b** *that was* before him his thick H5051
Isa 59: 9 for **b**, *but* we walk in darkness. H5054
60: 3 light, and kings to the **b** of thy rising. H5051
19 by day; neither for **b** shall the moon H5051
62: 1 thereof go forth as **b**, and the salvation H5051
Ezk 1: 4 itself, and a **b** *was* about it, and out H5051
27 of fire, and it had **b** round about. H5051
28 appearance of the **b** round about. This H5051
8: 2 of **b**, as the colour of amber. H2096
10: 4 was full of the **b** of the LORD'S glory. H5051
28: 7 thy wisdom, and they shall defile thy **b**. H3314
17 by reason of thy **b**: I will cast thee to the H3314
Dan 2:31 image, whose **b** *was* excellent, stood H2122
4:36 mine honour and **b** returned unto me; H2122
12: 3 shall shine as the **b** of the firmament; H2096
Am 5:20 light? even very dark, and no **b** in it? H5051
Hab 3: 4 And *his* **b** was as the light; he had H5051
Act 26:13 heaven, above the **b** of the sun, shining *G2987*
2Th 2: 8 shall destroy with the **b** of his coming: *G2015*
Heb 1: 3 Who being the **b** of *his* glory, and the *G541*

BRIM
Jos 3:15 were dipped in the **b** of the water, (for H7097
1Ki 7:23 from the one **b** to the other: *it was* H8193
24 And under the **b** of it round about H8193
26 thick, and the **b** thereof was wrought H8193
26 was wrought like the **b** of a cup, with H8193
2Ch 4: 2 of ten cubits from **b** to brim, round in H8193
2 from brim to **b**, round in compass, H8193
5 and the **b** of it like the work of H8193
5 the work of the **b** of a cup, with flowers H8193
Jn 2: 7 water. And they filled them up to the **b**. *G507*

BRIMSTONE
Gen 19:24 upon Gomorrah **b** and fire from the H1614
Dt 29:23 *And that* the whole land thereof *is* **b**, H1614
Job 18:15 *it is* none of his: **b** shall be scattered H1614
Ps 11: 6 rain snares, fire and **b**, and an horrible H1614
Isa 30:33 LORD, like a stream of **b**, doth kindle it. H1614
34: 9 dust thereof into **b**, and the land thereof H1614
Ezk 38:22 rain, and great hailstones, fire, and **b**. H1614
Lk 17:29 **b** from heaven, and destroyed *them* all. *G2303*
Rev 9:17 of jacinth, and **b**: and the heads of the *G2306*
17 mouths issued fire and smoke and **b**. *G2303*
18 the **b**, which issued out of their mouths. *G2303*
14:10 with fire and **b** in the presence of the *G2303*
19:20 alive into a lake of fire burning with **b**. *G2303*
20:10 lake of fire and **b**, where the beast and *G2303*
21: 8 fire and **b**: which is the second death. *G2303*

BRING
Gen 1:11 And God said, Let the earth **b** forth H1876
20 And God said, Let the waters **b** forth H8317
24 And God said, Let the earth **b** forth the H3318
3:16 sorrow thou shalt **b** forth children; and H3205
18 Thorns also and thistles shall it **b** forth H6779
6:17 And, behold, I, even I, do **b** a flood of H935
19 *sort* shalt thou **b** into the ark, to keep H935
8:17 **B** forth with thee every living thing that H3318
9: 7 And you, be ye fruitful, and multiply; **b** H8317
14 And it shall come to pass, when I **b** a H6049
18:16 went with them to **b** them on the way. H7971
19 the LORD may **b** upon Abraham that H935
Gen 19: 5 to thee this night? **b** them out unto us, H3318
8 let me, I pray you, **b** them out unto H3318
12 in the city, **b** *them* out of this place: H3318
24: 5 this land: must I needs **b** thy son again H7725
6 that thou **b** not my son thither again. H7725
8 oath: only **b** not my son thither again. H7725
27: 4 such as I love, and **b** *it* to me, that I may H935
5 the field to hunt *for* venison, *and* to **b** *it*. H935
7 **B** me venison, and make me savoury H935
10 And thou shalt **b** *it* to thy father, that he H935
12 **b** a curse upon me, and not a blessing. H935
25 And he said, **B** *it* near to me, and I will H5066
28:15 goest, and will **b** thee again into this H7725
37:14 the flocks; and **b** me word again. So H7725
38:24 said, **B** her forth, and let her be burnt. H3318
40:14 Pharaoh, and **b** me out of this house: H3318
41:32 God, and God will shortly **b** it to pass. H6213
42:20 But **b** your youngest brother unto me; so H935
34 And **b** your youngest brother unto me: H935
37 Slay my two sons, if I **b** him not to thee: H935
37 my hand, and I will **b** him to thee again. H935
38 go, then shall ye **b** down my gray hairs H3381
43: 7 he would say, **B** your brother down? H3381
9 require him: if I **b** him not unto thee, H935
16 ruler of his house, **B** *these* men home, H935
44:21 And thou saidst unto thy servants, **B**
29 him, ye shall **b** down my gray hairs H3381
31 and thy servants shall **b** down the gray H3381
32 father, saying, If I **b** him not unto thee, H935
45:13 haste and **b** down my father hither. H3381
19 wives, and **b** your father, and come. H5375
46: 4 I will also surely **b** thee up *again*: and H5927
48: 9 And he said, **B** them, I pray thee, unto H3947
21 be with you, and **b** you again unto the H7725
50:20 it unto good, to **b** to pass, as *it is* this H6213
24 visit you, and **b** you out of this land H5927
Ex 3: 8 Egyptians, and to **b** them up out of that H5927
10 that thou mayest **b** forth my people the H3318
11 and that I should **b** forth the children H3318
17 And I have said, I will **b** you up out of H5297
6: 6 LORD, and I will **b** you out from under H3318
8 And I will **b** you in unto the land, H935
13 king of Egypt, to **b** the children of Israel H3318
26 the LORD said, **B** out the children of H3318
27 king of Egypt, to **b** out the children of H3318
7: 4 upon Egypt, and **b** forth mine armies, H3318
5 upon Egypt, and **b** out the children of H3318
8: 3 And the river shall **b** forth frogs H8317
18 enchantments to **b** forth lice, but they H3318
10: 4 will I **b** the locusts into thy coast: H935
11: 1 unto Moses, Yet will I **b** one plague *more* H935
12:51 *that* the LORD did **b** the children of H3318
13: 5 And it shall be when the LORD shall **b** H935
11 And it shall be when the LORD shall **b** H935
15:17 Thou shalt **b** them in, and plant them in H935
16: 5 *that* which they **b** in; and it shall be twice H935
18:19 that thou mayest **b** the causes unto God: H935
22 matter they shall **b** unto thee, but every H935
21: 6 Then his master shall **b** him unto the H5066
6 he shall also **b** him to the door, or H5066
22:13 If it be torn in pieces, *then* let him **b** it H935
23: 4 shalt surely **b** it back to him again. H7725
19 of thy land thou shalt **b** into the house of H935
20 in the way, and to **b** thee into the place H935
23 go before thee, and **b** thee in unto the H935
25: 2 of Israel, that they **b** me an offering: of H3947
26:33 that thou mayest **b** in thither within the H935
27:20 of Israel, that they **b** thee pure oil olive H3947
29: 3 one basket, and **b** them in the basket, H7126
4 And Aaron and his sons thou shalt **b** H7126
8 And thou shalt **b** his sons, and put H7126
32: 2 of your daughters, and **b** *them* unto me. H935
12 For mischief did he **b** them out, to slay H3318
33:12 sayest unto me, **B** up this people: and H5927
34:26 thy land thou shalt **b** unto the house of H935
35: 5 heart, let him **b** it, an offering of the H935
29 them willing to **b** for all manner of work, H935
36: 5 saying, The people **b** much more than H935
40: 4 And thou shalt **b** in the table, and set in H935
4 it; and thou shalt **b** in the candlestick, H935
12 And thou shalt **b** Aaron and his sons H7126
14 And thou shalt **b** his sons, and clothe H7126
Lev 1: 2 If any man of you **b** an offering unto H7126
2 the LORD, ye shall **b** your offering of H7126
5 sons, shall **b** the blood, and sprinkle H7126
10 he shall **b** it a male without blemish. H7126
13 and the priest shall **b** *it* all, and burn *it* H7126
14 fowls, then he shall **b** his offering of H7126
15 And the priest shall **b** it unto the altar, H7126
Lev 2: 2 And he shall **b** it to Aaron's sons the H935
4 And if thou **b** an oblation of a meat H7126
8 And thou shalt **b** the meat offering that H935
8 the priest, he shall **b** it unto the altar. H5066
11 No meat offering, which ye shall **b** unto H7126
4: 3 then let him **b** for his sin, which he H7126
4 And he shall **b** the bullock unto the door H935
5 blood, and **b** it to the tabernacle of H935
14 bullock for the sin, and **b** him before the H935
16 And the priest that is anointed shall **b** of H935
23 he shall **b** his offering, a kid of H935
28 then he shall **b** his offering, a kid of H935
32 And if he **b** a lamb for a sin offering, he H935
32 he shall **b** it a female without blemish. H935
5: 6 And he shall **b** his trespass offering unto H935
7 And if he be not able to **b** a lamb, then H5060
7 a lamb, then he shall **b** for his trespass, H935
8 And he shall **b** them unto the priest, who H935
11 But if he be not able to **b** two H5381
11 he that sinned shall **b** for his offering the H935
12 Then shall he **b** it to the priest, and the H935
15 then he shall **b** for his trespass unto H935
18 And he shall **b** a ram without blemish H935
6: 6 And he shall **b** his trespass offering unto H935
21 baken, thou shalt **b** it in: *and* the baken H935
7:29 the LORD shall **b** his oblation unto the H935
30 His own hands shall **b** the offerings of H935
30 breast, it shall he **b**, that the breast may H935
10:15 breast shall they **b** with the offerings H935
12: 6 a daughter, she shall **b** a lamb of the first H935
8 And if she be not able to **b** a lamb, then H4672
8 then she shall **b** two turtles, or two H3947
14:23 And he shall **b** them on the eighth day H935
15:29 pigeons, and **b** them unto the priest, H935
16: 9 And Aaron shall **b** the goat upon which H7126
11 And Aaron shall **b** the bullock of the H7126
12 beaten small, and **b** *it* within the vail: H935
15 *is* for the people, and **b** his blood within H935
20 and the altar, he shall **b** the live goat: H7126
17: 5 of Israel may **b** their sacrifices, which H935
5 even that they may **b** them unto the H935
18: 3 Canaan, whither I **b** you, shall ye not do: H935
19:21 And he shall **b** his trespass offering unto H935
20:22 **b** you to dwell therein, spue you not out. H935
23:10 then ye shall **b** a sheaf of the firstfruits H935
17 Ye shall **b** out of your habitations two H935
24: 2 of Israel, that they **b** unto thee pure oil H3947
14 **B** forth him that hath cursed without H3318
23 that they should **b** forth him that had H3318
25:21 and it shall **b** forth fruit for three years. H6213
26:10 And ye shall eat old store, and **b** forth H3318
21 unto me; I will **b** seven times more H3254
25 And I will **b** a sword upon you, that shall H935
31 cities waste, and **b** your sanctuaries H8074
32 And I will **b** the land into desolation: H8074
27: 9 And if *it be* a beast, whereof men **b** an H7126
Nu 3: 6 **B** the tribe of Levi near, and present H7126
5: 9 they **b** unto the priest, shall be his. H7126
15 Then shall the man **b** his wife unto the H935
15 the priest, and he shall **b** her offering for H935
16 And the priest shall **b** her near, and set H7126
6:10 And on the eighth day he shall **b** two H935
12 and shall **b** a lamb of the first year H935
16 And the priest shall **b** *them* before the H7126
8: 9 And thou shalt **b** the Levites before the H7126
10 And thou shalt **b** the Levites before the H7126
11:16 over them; and **b** them unto the H3947
13:20 good courage, and **b** of the fruit of the H3947
14: 8 If the LORD delight in us, then he will **b** H935
16 Because the LORD was not able to **b** this H935
24 me fully, him will I **b** into the land H935
31 be a prey, them will I **b** in, and they shall H935
37 Even those men that did **b** up the evil H3318
15: 4 unto the LORD **b** a meat offering of a H7126
9 Then shall he **b** with a bullock a meat H7126
10 And thou shalt **b** for a drink offering H7126
18 ye come into the land whither I **b** you, H935
25 and they shall **b** their offering, a sacrifice H935
27 then he shall **b** a she goat of the first H7126
16: 9 of Israel, to **b** you near to himself H7126
17 and **b** ye before the LORD H7126
17:10 And the LORD said unto Moses, **B** H7725
18: 2 the tribe of thy father, **b** thou with thee, H7126
13 which they shall **b** unto the LORD, shall H935
15 all flesh, which they **b** unto the LORD, H7126
19: 2 of Israel, that they **b** thee a red heifer H3947
3 that he may **b** her forth without the H3318
20: 5 up out of Egypt, to **b** us in unto this evil H935
8 and thou shalt **b** forth to them water H3318

B

Nu 20:12 ye shall not **b** this congregation into H935
25 Take Aaron and Eleazar his son, and **b** H5927
22: 8 night, and I will **b** you word again, as H7725
23:27 I pray thee, I will **b** thee unto another H3947
27:17 out, and which may **b** them in; that the H935
28:26 when ye **b** a new meat offering H7126
32: 5 a possession, *and* **b** us not over Jordan. H5674
Dt 1:17 for you, **b** *it* unto me, and I will hear it. H7126
22 us out the land, and **b** us word again by H7725
4:38 than thou *art,* to **b** thee in, to give thee H935
6:23 that he might **b** us in, to give us the land H935
7: 1 When the LORD thy God shall **b** thee H935
26 Neither shalt thou **b** an abomination H935
9: 3 them, and he shall **b** them down before H3665
28 was not able to **b** them into the land H935
12: 6 And thither ye shall **b** your burnt H935
11 thither shall ye **b** all that I command H935
14:28 At the end of three years thou shalt **b** H3318
17: 5 Then shalt thou **b** forth that man or H3318
21: 4 And the elders of that city shall **b** down H3381
12 Then thou shalt **b** her home to thine H935
19 hold on him, and **b** him out unto the H3318
22: 1 case **b** them again unto thy brother. H7725
2 not, then thou shalt **b** it unto thine own H622
8 for thy roof, that thou **b** not blood upon H7760
14 against her, and **b** up an evil name H3318
15 mother, take and **b** forth *the tokens of* H3318
21 Then they shall **b** out the damsel to the H3318
24 Then ye shall **b** them both out unto the H3318
23:18 Thou shalt not **b** the hire of a whore, or H935
24:11 **b** out the pledge abroad unto thee. H3318
26: 2 which thou shalt **b** of thy land that the H935
28:36 The LORD shall **b** thee, and thy king H3212
49 The LORD shall **b** a nation against thee H5375
60 Moreover he will **b** upon thee all the H7725
61 **b** upon thee, until thou be destroyed. H5927
63 you, and to **b** you to nought; and H8045
68 And the LORD shall **b** thee into Egypt H7725
29:27 this land, to **b** upon it all the curses H935
30: 5 And the LORD thy God will **b** thee into H935
12 us to heaven, and **b** it unto us, that we H3947
13 the sea for us, and **b** it unto us, that we H3947
31:23 for thou shalt **b** the children of Israel H935
33: 7 of Judah, and **b** him unto his people: H935
Jos 2: 3 Rahab, saying, **B** forth the men that are H3318
18 by: and thou shalt **b** thy father, and thy H622
6:22 house, and **b** out thence the woman, H3318
10:22 of the cave, and **b** out those five kings H3318
18: 6 seven parts, and **b** *the description* hither H935
23:15 so shall the LORD **b** upon you all evil H935
Jdg 6:13 Did not the LORD **b** us up from Egypt? H5927
18 unto thee, and **b** forth my present, and H3318
30 said unto Joash, **B** out thy son, that he H3318
7: 4 *are* yet *too* many; **b** them down unto the H338
11: 9 of Gilead, If ye **b** me home again to H7725
19: 3 unto her, *and* to **b** her again, having his H7725
22 old man, saying, **B** forth the man that H3318
24 them I will **b** out now, and humble H3318
Ru 3:15 Also he said, **B** the vail that *thou hast* H3051
1Sa 1:22 and *then* I will **b** him, that he may H935
4: 4 that they might **b** from thence the ark H5375
6: 7 and **b** their calves home from them: H7725
9: 7 we go, what shall we **b** the man? for the H935
7 to **b** to the man of God: what have we? H935
23 And Samuel said unto the cook, **B** the H5414
11:12 reign over us? **b** the men, that we may H5414
13: 9 And Saul said, **B** hither a burnt offering H5066
14:18 And Saul said unto Ahiah, **B** hither the H5066
34 say unto them, **B** me hither every man H5066
15:32 Then said Samuel, **B** ye hither to me H5066
16:17 that can play well, and **b** *him* to me. H935
19:15 to see David, saying, **B** him up to me in H5927
20: 8 why shouldest thou **b** me to thy father? H935
23: 9 Abiathar the priest, **B** hither the ephod. H5066
27:11 nor woman alive, to **b** *tidings* to Gath, H935
28: 8 spirit, and **b** me *him* up, whom I H5927
11 Then said the woman, Whom shall I **b** H5927
11 thee? And he said, **B** me up Samuel. H5927
15 disquieted me, to **b** me up? And Saul H5927
30: 7 son, I pray thee, **b** me hither the ephod. H5066
15 And David said to him, Canst thou **b** H3381
15 and I will **b** thee down to this company. H3381
2Sa 2: 3 him did David **b** up, every man with H5927
3:12 thee, to **b** about all Israel unto thee. H5437
13 face, except thou first **b** Michal Saul's H935
6: 2 Baale of Judah, to **b** up from thence the H5927
9:10 and thou shalt **b** in *the fruits,* that thy H935
12:23 I fast? can I **b** him back again? I shall H7725
13:10 And Amnon said unto Tamar, **B** the H935

2Sa 14:10 *ought* unto thee, **b** him to me, and he H935
21 **b** the young man Absalom again. H7725
15: 8 If the LORD shall **b** me again indeed to H7725
14 us suddenly, and **b** evil upon us, and H5080
25 of the LORD, he will **b** me again, and H7725
17: 3 And I will **b** back all the people unto H7725
13 shall all Israel **b** ropes to that city, and H5375
14 the LORD might **b** evil upon Absalom. H935
19:11 are ye the last to **b** the king back to his H7725
12 then are ye the last to **b** back the king? H7725
22:28 *that* thou mayest **b** *them* down. H8213
1Ki 1:33 own mule, and **b** him down to Gihon: H3381
2: 9 **b** thou down to the grave with blood. H3381
3:24 And the king said, **B** me a sword. And H3947
5: 9 My servants shall **b** *them* down from H3381
8: 1 that they might **b** up the ark of the H5927
4 did the priests and the Levites **b** up. H5927
32 the wicked, to **b** his way upon his head; H5414
34 people Israel, and **b** them again unto H7725
10:29 did they **b** *them* out by their means. H3318
12:21 house of Israel, to **b** the kingdom again H7725
13:18 of the LORD, saying, **B** him back with H7725
14:10 Therefore, behold, I will **b** evil upon the H935
17:11 to her, and said, **B** me, I pray thee, a H3947
13 cake first, and **b** *it* unto me, and after H3318
20:33 he said, Go ye, **b** him. Then Ben-hadad H3947
21:21 Behold, I will **b** evil upon thee, and will H935
29 me, I will not **b** the evil in his days: *but* H935
29 days will I **b** the evil upon his house. H935
2Ki 2:20 And he said, **B** me a new cruse, and put H3947
3:15 But now **b** me a minstrel. And it came H3947
4: 6 said unto her son, **B** me yet a vessel. H5066
41 But he said, Then **b** meal. And he cast H3947
6:19 me, and I will **b** you to the man whom H3212
10:22 over the vestry, **B** forth vestments for H3318
12: 4 heart to **b** into the house of the LORD, H935
19: 3 and *there is* not strength to **b** forth. H3205
22:16 Thus saith the LORD, Behold, I will **b** H935
20 evil which I will **b** upon this place. And H935
23: 4 of the door, to **b** forth out of the temple H3318
1Ch 9:28 **b** them in and out by tale. H935+H3318
13: 3 And let us **b** again the ark of our God to H5497
5 to **b** the ark of God from Kirjath-jearim. H935
6 to Judah, to **b** up thence the ark of H5927
12 shall I **b** the ark of God *home* to me? H935
15: 3 to Jerusalem, to **b** up the ark of the H5927
12 that ye may **b** up the ark of the LORD H5927
14 **b** up the ark of the LORD God of Israel. H5927
25 went to **b** up the ark of the covenant H5927
16:29 unto his name: **b** an offering, and come H5375
21: 2 even to Dan; and **b** the number of them H935
12 I shall **b** again to him that sent me. H7725
22:19 of the LORD God, to **b** the ark of the H935
2Ch 2:16 need: and we will **b** it to thee in floats by H935
5: 2 unto Jerusalem, to **b** up the ark of the H5927
5 did the priests *and* the Levites **b** up. H5927
6:25 people Israel, and **b** them again unto H7725
11: 1 **b** the kingdom again to Rehoboam. H7725
24: 6 of the Levites to **b** in out of Judah and H935
9 and Jerusalem, to **b** in to the LORD the H935
19 Yet he sent prophets to them, to **b** them H935
28:13 And said unto them, Ye shall not **b** in the H935
29:31 come near and **b** sacrifices and thank H935
31:10 *people* began to **b** the offerings into the H935
34:24 Thus saith the LORD, Behold, I will **b** H935
28 the evil that I will **b** upon this place, and H935
Ezr 1: 8 Even those did Cyrus king of Persia **b** H3318
11 did Sheshbazzar **b** up with *them of* the H5927
3: 7 to them of Tyre, to **b** cedar trees from H935
8:17 that they should **b** unto us ministers for H935
30 and the vessels, to **b** *them* to Jerusalem H935
Neh 1: 9 thence, and will **b** them unto the place H935
5: 5 and, lo, we **b** into bondage our sons H3533
8: 1 Ezra the scribe to **b** the book of the law H935
9:29 that thou mightest **b** them again unto H7725
10:31 And *if* the people of the land **b** ware or H935
34 wood offering, to **b** *it* into the house of H935
35 And to **b** the firstfruits of our ground, H935
36 of our flocks, to **b** to the house of our H935
37 And *that* we should **b** the firstfruits of H935
38 the Levites shall **b** up the tithe of the H5927
39 of Levi shall **b** the offering of the corn, H935
11: 1 also cast lots, to **b** one of ten to dwell in H935
12:27 all their places, to **b** them to Jerusalem, H935
13:18 did not our God **b** all this evil upon us, H935
18 upon this city? yet ye **b** more wrath upon H935
Est 1:11 To **b** Vashti the queen before the king H935
3: 9 to **b** *it* into the king's treasuries. H935
6: 1 he commanded to **b** the book of records H935

Est 6: 9 to honour, and **b** him on horseback H7392
14 and hasted to **b** Haman unto the H935
Job 6:22 Did I say, **B** unto me? or, Give a reward H3051
10: 9 and wilt thou **b** me into dust again? H7725
14: 4 Who can **b** a clean *thing* out of an H5414
9 bud, and **b** forth boughs like a plant. H6213
15:35 They conceive mischief, and **b** forth H3205
18:14 and it shall **b** him to the king of terrors. H6805
30:23 For I know *that* thou wilt **b** me *to* H7725
33:30 To **b** back his soul from the pit, to be H7725
38:32 Canst thou **b** forth Mazzaroth in his H3318
39: 1 goats of the rock **b** forth? *or* canst thou H3205
2 thou the time when they **b** forth? H3205
3 They bow themselves, they **b** forth their H6398
12 Wilt thou believe him, that he will **b** H7725
40:12 Look on every one *that is* proud, *and* **b** H3665
20 Surely the mountains **b** him forth food, H5375
Ps 18:27 people; but wilt **b** down high looks. H8213
25:17 *O* **b** thou me out of my distresses. H3318
37: 5 also in him; and he shall **b** *it* to pass. H6213
6 And he shall **b** forth thy righteousness H3318
38:ttl A Psalm of David, to **b** to H2142
43: 3 lead me; let them **b** me unto thy holy hill, H935
55:23 But thou, O God, shalt **b** them down H3381
59:11 and **b** them down, O Lord our shield. H3381
60: 9 Who will **b** me *into* the strong city? who H2986
68:22 The Lord said, I will **b** again from H7725
22 Bashan, I will **b** *my people* again from H7725
29 shall kings **b** presents unto thee. H2986
70:ttl *Psalm* of David, to **b** to remembrance. H2142
71:20 again, and shalt **b** me up again from H5927
72: 3 The mountains shall **b** peace to the H5375
10 of the isles shall **b** presents: the kings H7725
76:11 round about him **b** presents unto him H2986
81: 2 Take a psalm, and **b** hither the timbrel, H5414
92:14 They shall still **b** forth fruit in old age; H5107
94:23 And he shall **b** upon them their own H7725
96: 8 **b** an offering, and come into his courts. H5375
104:14 he may **b** forth food out of the earth; H3318
108:10 Who will **b** me into the strong city? who H2986
142: 7 **B** my soul out of prison, that I may H3318
143:11 sake **b** my soul out of trouble. H3318
144:13 our sheep may **b** forth thousands and H503
Prv 4: 8 thee: she shall **b** thee to honour, when H3513
19:24 not so much as **b** it to his mouth again. H7725
26:15 grieveth him to **b** it again to his mouth. H7725
27: 1 knowest not what a day may **b** forth. H3205
29: 8 Scornful men **b** a city into a snare: but H6315
23 A man's pride shall **b** him low: but H8213
Ecc 3:22 **b** him to see what shall be after him? H935
11: 9 *things* God will **b** thee into judgment. H935
12:14 For God shall **b** every work into H935
Song 8: 2 I would lead thee, *and* **b** thee into my H935
11 was to **b** a thousand *pieces* of silver. H935
Isa 1:13 **B** no more vain oblations; incense is an H935
5: 2 that it should **b** forth grapes, and it H6213
4 that it should **b** forth grapes, brought H6213
7:17 The LORD shall **b** upon thee, and upon H935
14: 2 And the people shall take them, and **b** H935
15: 9 of blood: for I will **b** more upon Dimon, H7896
23: 4 I travail not, nor **b** forth children, H3205
4 up young men, *nor* **b** up virgins. H7311
9 of all glory, *and* to **b** into contempt all H7034
25: 5 Thou shalt **b** down the noise of H3665
11 swim: and he shall **b** down their pride H8213
12 thy walls shall he **b** down, lay low, *and* H7817
12 *and* **b** to the ground, *even* to the dust. H5060
28:21 and **b** to pass his act, his strange act. H5647
31: 2 Yet he also *is* wise, and will **b** evil, and H935
33:11 Ye shall conceive chaff, ye shall **b** forth H3205
37: 3 and *there is* not strength to **b** forth. H3205
38: 8 Behold, I will **b** again the shadow of the H7725
41:21 Produce your cause, saith the LORD; **b** H5066
22 Let them **b** *them* forth, and shew us H5066
42: 1 shall **b** forth judgment to the Gentiles. H3318
3 he shall **b** forth judgment unto truth. H3318
7 To open the blind eyes, to **b** out the H3318
16 And I will **b** the blind by a way *that* H3212
43: 5 Fear not: for I *am* with thee: I will **b** thy H935
6 Keep not back: **b** my sons from far, and H935
8 **B** forth the blind people that have eyes, H3318
9 things? let them **b** forth their witnesses, H5414
45: 8 and let them **b** forth salvation, and H6509
21 Tell ye, and **b** *them* near; yea, let them H5066
46: 8 **b** *it* again to mind, O ye transgressors. H7725
11 *it,* I will also **b** it to pass; I have purposed H935
13 I **b** near my righteousness; it shall not H7126
49: 5 *be* his servant, to **b** Jacob again to him, H7725
22 and they shall **b** thy sons in *their* arms, H935

Isa 52: 8 eye, when the LORD shall **b** again Zion. H7725
55:10 and maketh it **b** forth and bud, that H3205
56: 7 Even them will I **b** to my holy mountain, H935
58: 7 and that thou **b** the poor that are cast H935
59: 4 conceive mischief, and **b** forth iniquity. H3205
60: 6 come: they shall **b** gold and incense; H5375
9 of Tarshish first, to **b** thy sons from far, H935
11 that *men* may **b** unto thee the forces H935
17 For brass I will **b** gold, and for iron I will H935
17 and for iron I will **b** silver, and for wood H935
63: 6 will **b** down their strength to the earth. H3381
65: 9 And I will **b** forth a seed out of Jacob, H3318
23 They shall not labour in vain, nor **b** H3205
66: 4 delusions, and will **b** their fears upon H935
8 earth be made to **b** forth in one day? *or* H2342
9 Shall I **b** to the birth, and not cause to H7665
9 and not cause to **b** forth? saith the H3205
9 shall I cause to **b** forth, and shut *the* H3205
20 And they shall **b** all your brethren *for* an H935
20 children of Israel **b** an offering in a clean H935
Jer 3:14 two of a family, and I will **b** you to Zion: H935
4: 6 stay not: for I will **b** evil from the north, H935
5:15 Lo, I will **b** a nation upon you from far, H935
6:19 Hear, O earth: behold, I will **b** evil upon H935
8: 1 LORD, they shall **b** out the bones of the H3318
10:24 in thine anger, lest thou **b** me to nothing.
11: 8 therefore I will **b** upon them all the H935
11 Behold, I will **b** evil upon them, which H935
23 of them: for I will **b** evil upon the men of H935
12: 2 grow, yea, they **b** forth fruit: thou *art* H6213
15 on them, and will **b** them again, every H7725
15:19 return, then will I **b** thee again, *and* H7725
16:15 them: and I will **b** them again into their H7725
17:18 me be dismayed: **b** upon them the day of H935
21 day, nor **b** *it* in by the gates of Jerusalem; H935
24 me, saith the LORD, to **b** in no burden H935
18:22 when thou shalt **b** a troop suddenly H935
19: 3 Behold, I will **b** evil upon this place, H935
15 Behold, I will **b** upon this city and upon H935
23: 3 them, and will **b** them again to their H7725
12 therein: for I will **b** evil upon them, *even* H935
40 And I will **b** an everlasting reproach H5414
24: 6 for good, and I will **b** them again to this H7725
25: 9 my servant, and will **b** them against this H935
13 And I will **b** upon that land all my words H935
29 For, lo, I begin to **b** evil on the city which H935
26:15 ye shall surely **b** innocent blood upon H5414
27:11 But the nations that **b** their neck under H935
12 words, saying, **B** your necks under the H935
22 the LORD; then will I **b** them up, and H5927
28: 3 Within two full years will I **b** again into H7725
4 And I will **b** again to this place H7725
6 prophesied, to **b** again the vessels of H7725
29:14 LORD; and I will **b** you again into the H7725
30: 3 LORD, that I will **b** again the captivity H7725
18 Thus saith the LORD;; Behold, I will **b** H7725
31: 8 Behold, I will **b** them from the north H935
23 when I shall **b** again their captivity; H7725
32 by the hand to **b** them out of the land H3318
32:37 wrath; and I will **b** them again unto H7725
42 this people, so will I **b** upon them all the H935
33: 6 Behold, I will **b** it health and cure, and H5927
11 *and* of them that shall **b** the sacrifice of H935
35: 2 unto them, and **b** them into the house H935
17 Behold, I will **b** upon Judah and upon H935
36:31 iniquity; and I will **b** upon them, and H935
38:23 So they shall **b** out all thy wives and thy H4672
39:16 Behold, I will **b** my words upon this H935
41: 5 to **b** *them* to the house of the LORD. H935
42:17 from the evil that I will **b** upon them. H935
45: 5 for, behold, I will **b** evil upon all flesh, H935
48:44 the snare: for I will **b** upon it, *even* upon H935
47 Yet will I **b** again the captivity of Moab H7725
49: 5 Behold, I will **b** a fear upon thee, saith H935
6 And afterward I will **b** again the H7725
8 of Dedan; for I will **b** the calamity of H935
16 as the eagle, I will **b** thee down from H3381
32 corners; and I will **b** their calamity from H935
36 And upon Elam will I **b** the four winds H935
37 their life: and I will **b** evil upon them, H935
39 days, *that* I will **b** again the captivity H7725
50:19 And I will **b** Israel again to his H7725
51:40 I will **b** them down like lambs to the H3381
44 and I will **b** forth out of his mouth H3318
64 the evil that I will **b** upon her: and they H935
Lam 1:21 done *it*: thou wilt **b** the day *that* thou H935
Ezk 5:17 thee; and I will **b** the sword upon thee. H935
6: 3 I, *even* I, will **b** a sword upon you, and H935
7:24 Wherefore I will **b** the worst of the H935

Ezk 11: 7 I will **b** you forth out of the midst of it. H3318
8 Ye have feared the sword; and I will **b** a H935
9 And I will **b** you out of the midst H3318
12: 4 Then shalt thou **b** forth thy stuff by day H3318
13 snare: and I will **b** him to Babylon *to* the H935
13:14 *morter*, and **b** it down to the ground, H5060
14:17 Or *if* I **b** a sword upon that land, and H935
16:40 They shall also **b** up a company against H5927
53 When I shall **b** again their captivity, H7725
53 then *will I b again* the captivity of
17: 8 that it might **b** forth branches, and H6213
20 snare, and I will **b** him to Babylon, and H935
23 it: and it shall **b** forth boughs, and bear H5375
20: 6 unto them, to **b** them forth of the land H3318
15 that I would not **b** them into the land H935
34 And I will **b** you out from the people, H3318
35 And I will **b** you into the wilderness of H935
37 will **b** you into the bond of the covenant: H935
38 against me: I will **b** them forth out of H3318
41 savour, when I **b** you out from the H3318
42 when I shall **b** you into the land of H935
21:29 a lie unto thee, to **b** thee upon the necks H5414
23:22 I will **b** them against thee on every side; H935
46 For thus saith the Lord GOD; I will **b** up H5927
24: 6 is not gone out of it! **b** it out piece by H3318
26: 7 Lord GOD; Behold, I will **b** upon Tyrus H935
19 when I shall **b** up the deep upon thee, H5927
20 When I shall **b** thee down with them H3381
28: 7 Behold, therefore I will **b** strangers upon H935
8 They shall **b** thee down to the pit, and H3381
18 therefore will I **b** forth a fire from the H3318
18 thee, and I will **b** thee to ashes upon H5414
29: 4 scales, and I will **b** thee up out of the H5927
8 GOD; Behold, I will **b** a sword upon thee, H935
14 And I will **b** again the captivity of H7725
31: 6 beasts of the field **b** forth their young, H3205
32: 3 and they shall **b** thee up in my net. H5927
9 when I shall **b** thy destruction among H935
33: 2 unto them, When I **b** the sword upon a H935
34:13 And I will **b** them out from the people, H3318
13 countries, and will **b** them to their own H935
16 I will seek that which was lost, and **b** H7725
36:11 shall increase and **b** fruit: and I will H6509
24 and will **b** you into your own land. H935
37: 6 you, and will **b** up flesh upon you, and H5927
12 graves, and **b** you into the land of Israel. H935
21 side, and **b** them into their own land: H935
38: 4 thy jaws, and I will **b** thee forth, and all H3318
16 days, and I will **b** thee against my land, H935
17 years that I would **b** thee against them? H935
39: 2 will **b** thee upon the mountains of Israel: H935
25 GOD; Now will I **b** again the captivity H7725
47:12 be consumed: it shall **b** forth new fruit H1069
Dan 1: 3 that he should **b** *certain* of the children H935
18 had said he should **b** them in, then the H935
2:24 *men* of Babylon: **b** me in before the H5924
3:13 commanded to **b** Shadrach, Meshach, H858
4: 6 Therefore made I a decree to **b** in all H5924
5: 2 commanded to **b** the golden and silver H858
7 The king cried aloud to **b** in the H5924
9:24 for iniquity, and to **b** in everlasting H935
Hos 2:14 will allure her, and **b** her into the H1980
7:12 upon them; I will **b** them down as the H3318
9:12 Though they **b** up their children, yet H1431
13 **b** forth his children to the murderer. H3318
16 yea, though they **b** forth, yet will I slay H3205
Joel 3: 1 time, when I shall **b** again the captivity H7725
2 I will also gather all nations, and will **b** H3381
Am 3:11 land; and he shall **b** down thy strength H3381
4: 1 say to their masters, **B**, and let us drink. H935
4 transgression; and **b** your sacrifices H935
6:10 burneth him, to **b** out the bones out of H3318
8:10 and I will **b** up sackcloth upon all H5927
9: 2 to heaven, thence will I **b** them down: H3381
14 And I will **b** again the captivity of my H7725
Oba 3 Who shall **b** me down to the ground? H3381
4 will I **b** thee down, saith the LORD. H3381
Jna 1:13 Nevertheless the men rowed hard to **b** H7725
Mic 1:15 Yet will I **b** an heir unto thee, O H935
4:10 Be in pain, and labour to **b** forth, O H1518
7: 9 for me: he will **b** me forth to the light, H3318
Zep 1:17 And I will **b** distress upon men, that they
2: 2 Before the decree **b** forth, *before* the H3205
3: 5 morning doth he **b** his judgment to H5414
10 of my dispersed, shall **b** mine offering. H2986
20 At that time will I **b** you *again*, even in H935
Hag 1: 6 Ye have sown much, and **b** in little; ye H935
8 Go up to the mountain, and **b** wood, and H935
Zec 3: 8 I will **b** forth my servant the BRANCH. H935

Zec 4: 7 a plain: and he shall **b** forth the H3318
5: 4 I will **b** it forth, saith the LORD of H3318
8: 8 And I will **b** them, and they shall dwell H935
10: 6 Joseph, and I will **b** them again to place H7725
10 I will **b** them again also out of the land H7725
10 Assyria; and I will **b** them into the land H935
13: 9 And I will **b** the third part through the H935
Mal 3:10 **B** ye all the tithes into the storehouse, H935
Mt 1:21 And she shall **b** forth a son, and thou *G5088*
23 child, and shall **b** forth a son, and they *G5088*
2: 8 ye have found *him*, **b** me word again, *G518*
13 be thou there until I **b** thee word: for *G2036*
3: 8 **B** forth therefore fruits meet for *G4160*
5:23 Therefore if thou **b** thy gift to the altar, *G4374*
7:18 A good tree cannot **b** forth evil fruit, *G4160*
18 *can* a corrupt tree **b** forth good fruit. *G4160*
14:18 He said, **B** them hither to me. *G5342*
17:17 shall I suffer you? **b** him hither to me. *G5342*
21: 2 her: loose *them*, and **b** *them* unto me. *G71*
28: 8 joy; and did run to **b** his disciples word. *G518*
Mk 4:20 and receive *it*, and **b** forth fruit, some *G2592*
7:32 And they **b** unto him one that was deaf, *G5342*
8:22 and they **b** a blind man unto him, *G5342*
9:19 long shall I suffer you? **b** him unto me. *G5342*
11: 2 never man sat; loose him, and **b** *him*. *G71*
12:15 ye me? **b** me a penny, that I may see *it*. *G5342*
15:22 And they **b** him unto the place *G5342*
Lk 1:31 in thy womb, and **b** forth a son, and *G5088*
2:10 not: for, behold, I **b** you good tidings of *G2097*
3: 8 **B** forth therefore fruits worthy of *G4160*
5:18 to **b** him in, and to lay *him* before him. *G1533*
19 *way* they might **b** him in because of the *G1533*
6:43 doth a corrupt tree **b** forth good fruit. *G4160*
8:14 of *this* life, and **b** no fruit to perfection. *G5052*
15 keep *it*, and **b** forth fruit with patience. *G2592*
9:41 you, and suffer you? **B** thy son hither. *G4317*
12:11 And when they **b** you unto the *G4374*
14:21 of the city, and **b** in hither the poor, *G1521*
15:22 But the father said to his servants, **B** *G1627*
23 And **b** hither the fatted calf, and kill *it*; *G5342*
19:27 them, **b** hither, and slay *them* before me. *G71*
30 man sat: loose him, and **b** *him hither*. *G71*
Jn 10:16 them also I must **b**, and they shall hear *G71*
14:26 you all things, and **b** all things to your *G5179*
15: 2 it, that it may **b** forth more fruit. *G5342*
16 ye should go and **b** forth fruit, and *that* *G5342*
18:29 accusation **b** ye against this man? *G5342*
19: 4 them, Behold, I **b** him forth to you, that *G71*
21:10 Jesus saith unto them, **B** of the fish *G5342*
Act 5:28 intend to **b** this man's blood upon us. *G1863*
7: 6 that they should **b** them into bondage, *G1402*
9: 2 he might **b** them bound unto Jerusalem. *G71*
21 **b** them bound unto the chief priests? *G71*
12: 4 after Easter to **b** him forth to the people. *G321*
17: 5 and sought to **b** them out to the people. *G71*
22: 5 to Damascus, to **b** them which were *G71*
23:10 them, and to **b** *him* into the castle. *G71*
15 captain that he **b** him down unto you *G2609*
17 *him*, and said, **B** this young man unto *G520*
18 and prayed me to **b** this young man unto *G71*
20 thou wouldest **b** down Paul to morrow *G2609*
24 and **b** *him* safe unto Felix the governor. *G1295*
24:17 Now after many years I came to **b** alms *G4160*
Ro 7: 4 that we should **b** forth fruit unto God. *H2592*
5 members to **b** forth fruit unto death. *G1519*
10: 6 (that is, to **b** Christ down *from above*:) *G2609*
7 is, to **b** up Christ again from the dead.) *G321*
15 and **b** glad tidings of good things! *G2097*
1Co 1:19 of the wise, and will **b** to nothing the *G114*
28 are not, to **b** to nought things that are: *G2673*
4: 5 who both will **b** to light the hidden *G5461*
17 in the Lord, who shall **b** you into *G363*
9:27 But I keep under my body, and **b** *it* into *G1396*
16: 3 send to **b** your liberality unto Jerusalem. *G667*
6 you, that ye may **b** me on my journey *G4311*
2Co 11:20 For ye suffer, if a man **b** you into *G2615*
Gal 2: 4 that they might **b** us into bondage: *G2615*
3:24 schoolmaster *to b us* unto Christ, that
Eph 6: 4 to wrath: but **b** them up in the nurture *G1625*
1Th 4:14 which sleep in Jesus will God **b** with him. *G71*
2Ti 4:11 Only Luke is with me. Take Mark, and **b** *G71*
13 when thou comest, **b** *with thee*, and the *G5342*
Tit 3:13 **B** Zenas the lawyer and Apollos on *G4311*
1Pt 3:18 that he might **b** us to God, being put *G4317*
2Pt 2: 1 you, who privily shall **b** in damnable *G3918*
1 **b** upon themselves swift destruction. *G3918*
11 in power and might, **b** not railing *G5342*
2Jn 10 If there come any unto you, and **b** not *G5342*
3Jn 6 whom if thou **b** forward on their *G4311*

B

Jude 9 of Moses, durst not **b** against him a *G2018*
Rev 21:24 do **b** their glory and honour into it. *G5342*
26 And they shall **b** the glory and honour *G5342*

BRINGERS
2Ki 10: 5 also, and the **b** up *of the children,* sent H539

BRINGEST
1Ki 1:42 *art* a valiant man, and **b** good tidings. H1319
Job 14: 3 one, and **b** me into judgment with thee? H935
Isa 40: 9 O Zion, that **b** good tidings, get thee up H1319
9 O Jerusalem, that **b** good tidings, lift up H1319
Act 17:20 For thou **b** certain strange things to our *G1533*

BRINGETH
Ex 6: 7 your God, which **b** you out from under H3318
Lev 11:45 For I *am* the LORD that **b** you up out of H5927
17: 4 And **b** it not unto the door of the H935
9 And **b** it not unto the door of the H935
Dt 8: 7 For the LORD thy God **b** thee into a good H935
14:22 seed, that the field **b** forth year by year. H3318
1Sa 2: 6 **b** down to the grave, and bringeth up. H3381
6 bringeth down to the grave, and **b** up. H5927
7 maketh rich: he **b** low, and lifteth up. H8213
2Sa 18:26 And the king said, He also **b** tidings. H1319
22:48 It *is* God that avengeth me, and that **b** H3381
49 And that **b** me forth from mine H3318
Job 12: 6 into whose hand God **b** *abundantly.* H935
22 and **b** out to light the shadow of death. H3318
19:29 Be ye afraid of the sword: for wrath ***b*** the
28:11 *the thing that is* hid **b** he forth to light. H3318
Ps 1: 3 of water, that **b** forth his fruit in his H5414
14: 7 when the LORD **b** back the captivity of H7725
33:10 The LORD **b** the counsel of the heathen H6331
37: 7 the man who **b** wicked devices to pass. H6213
53: 6 Zion! When God **b** back the captivity of H7725
68: 6 in families: he **b** out those which are H3318
107:28 and he **b** them out of their distresses. H3318
30 so he **b** them unto their desired haven. H5148
135: 7 he **b** the wind out of his treasures. H3318
Prv 10:31 The mouth of the just **b** forth wisdom: H5107
16:30 moving his lips he **b** evil to pass. H3615
18:16 for him, and **b** him before great men. H5148
19:26 that causeth shame, and **b** reproach. H2659
20:26 the wicked, and **b** the wheel over them. H7725
21:27 more, *when* he **b** it with a wicked mind? H935
29:15 left *to himself* **b** his mother to shame.
21 He that delicately **b** up his servant H6445
25 The fear of man **b** a snare: but whoso H5414
30:33 Surely the churning of milk **b** forth H3318
33 of the nose **b** forth blood: so the forcing H3318
33 so the forcing of wrath **b** forth strife. H3318
31:14 She is like the merchants' ships; she **b** H935
Ecc 2: 6 therewith the wood that **b** forth trees: H6779
Isa 8: 7 Now therefore, behold, the Lord **b** up H5927
26: 5 For he **b** down them that dwell on high; H7817
5 to the ground; he **b** it *even* to the dust. H5060
40:23 That **b** the princes to nothing; he H5414
26 these *things,* that **b** out their host by H3318
41:27 to Jerusalem one that **b** good tidings. H1319
43:17 Which **b** forth the chariot and horse, H3318
52: 7 the feet of him that **b** good tidings, that H1319
7 peace; that **b** good tidings of good, H1319
54:16 the fire, and that **b** forth an instrument H3318
61:11 For as the earth **b** forth her bud, and as H3318
Jer 4:31 as of her that **b** forth her first child, H1069
10:13 **b** forth the wind out of his treasures. H3318
51:16 **b** forth the wind out of his treasures. H3318
Ezk 29:16 of Israel, which **b** *their* iniquity to H2142
Hos 10: 1 Israel *is* an empty vine, he **b** forth fruit H7737
Nah 1:15 the feet of him that **b** good tidings, that H1319
Hag 1:11 which the ground **b** forth, and upon H3318
Mt 3:10 every tree which **b** not forth good fruit *G4160*
7:17 Even so every good tree **b** forth good *G4160*
17 but a corrupt tree **b** forth evil fruit. *G4160*
19 Every tree that **b** not forth good fruit is *G4160*
12:35 of the heart **b** forth good things: and *G1544*
35 of the evil treasure **b** forth evil things. *G4160*
13:23 also beareth fruit, and **b** forth, some an *G1544*
52 which **b** forth out of his treasure *G399*
17: 1 **b** them up into an high mountain apart, *G399*
Mk 4:28 For the earth **b** forth fruit of herself; *G2592*
Lk 3: 9 therefore which **b** not forth good fruit *G4160*
6:43 For a good tree **b** not forth corrupt *G4160*
45 of his heart **b** forth that which is good; *G4393*
45 of his heart **b** forth that which is evil: *G4393*
Jn 12:24 alone: but if it die, it **b** forth much fruit. *G5342*
15: 5 I in him, the same **b** forth much fruit: *G5342*
Col 1: 6 in all the world; and **b** forth fruit, as *it* *G2592*
Tit 2:11 For the grace of God that **b** salvation *G4992*
Heb 1: 6 And again, when he **b** in the *G1521*
6: 7 oft upon it, and **b** forth herbs meet for *G5088*
Jas 1:15 Then when lust hath conceived, it **b** *G616*
15 sin, when it is finished, **b** forth death. *G5088*

BRINGING
Ex 12:42 unto the LORD for **b** them out from the H3318
36: 6 So the people were restrained from **b**. H935
Nu 5:15 memorial, **b** iniquity to remembrance. H2142
14:36 him, by **b** up a slander upon the land, H3318
2Sa 19:10 speak ye not a word of **b** the king back? H7725
43 not be first had in **b** back our king? H7725
1Ki 10:22 of Tharshish, **b** gold, and silver, ivory, H5375
2Ki 21:12 Behold, I *am* **b** *such* evil upon Jerusalem H935
2Ch 9:21 the ships of Tarshish **b** gold, and silver, H5375
Neh 13:15 on the sabbath, and **b** in sheaves, and H935
Ps 126: 6 with rejoicing, **b** his sheaves *with him.* H5375
Jer 17:26 from the south, **b** burnt offerings, and H935
26 and incense, and **b** sacrifices of praise, H935
Ezk 20: 9 **b** them forth out of the land of Egypt. H3318
Dan 9:12 that judged us, by **b** upon us a great evil: H935
Mt 21:43 to a nation **b** forth the fruits thereof. *G4160*
Mk 2: 3 And they come unto him, **b** one sick of *G5342*
Lk 24: 1 the sepulchre, **b** the spices which they *G5342*
Act 5:16 unto Jerusalem, **b** sick folks, and them *G5342*
Ro 7:23 of my mind, and **b** me into captivity to *G163*
2Co 10: 5 of God, and **b** into captivity every *G163*
Heb 2:10 *are* all things, in **b** many sons unto glory, *G71*
7:19 perfect, but the **b** in of a better hope *G1898*
2Pt 2: 5 of righteousness, **b** in the flood upon *G1863*

BRINK
Gen 41: 3 the *other* kine upon the **b** of the river. H8193
Ex 2: 3 she laid *it* in the flags by the river's **b**. H8193
7:15 by the river's **b** against he come; and H8193
Dt 2:36 From Aroer, which *is* by the **b** of the H8193
Jos 3: 8 ye are come to the **b** of the water of H7097
Ezk 47: 6 me to return to the **b** of the river. H8193

BROAD
Ex 27: 1 long, and five cubits **b**; the altar shall be H7341
Nu 16:38 let them make them **b** plates *for* a H7555
39 **b** *plates for* a covering of the altar: H7554
1Ki 6: 6 *was* five cubits **b**, and the middle *was* H7341
6 *was* six cubits **b**, and the third *was* H7341
6 *was* seven cubits **b**: for without *in the* H7341
2Ch 6:13 and five cubits **b**, and three cubits high, H7341
Neh 3: 8 fortified Jerusalem unto the **b** wall. H7342
12:38 of the furnaces even unto the **b** wall; H7342
Job 36:16 of the strait *into* a **b** place, where *there* H7338
Ps 119:96 *but* thy commandment *is* exceeding **b**. H7342
Song 3: 2 the streets, and in the **b** ways I will seek H7339
Isa 33:21 unto us a place of **b** rivers *and* H7338+H3027
Jer 5: 1 and seek in the **b** places thereof, if ye H7339
51:58 Thus saith the LORD of hosts; The **b** H7342
Ezk 40: 6 *was* one reed **b**; and the other threshold H7341
6 *of the gate, which was* one reed **b**. H7341
7 long, and one reed **b**; and between the H7341
29 long, and five and twenty cubits **b**. H7341
30 twenty cubits long, and five cubits **b**. H7341
33 long, and five and twenty cubits **b**. H7341
42 cubit and an half **b**, and one cubit high: H7341
43 And within *were* hooks, an hand **b**,
47 an hundred cubits **b**, foursquare; and H7341
41: 1 posts, six cubits **b** on the one side, and H7341
1 side, and six cubits **b** on the other side, H7341
12 *was* seventy cubits **b**; and the wall of the H7341
42:11 as they, *and* as **b** as they: and all their H7342
20 long, and five hundred **b**, to make a H7341
43:16 **b**, square in the four squares thereof. H7341
17 long and fourteen **b** in the four squares H7341
45: 6 the city five thousand **b**, and five and H7341
46:22 long and thirty **b**: these four corners H7341
Nah 2: 4 another in the **b** ways: they shall seem H7339
Mt 7:13 wide *is* the gate, and **b** *is* the way, that *G2149*
23: 5 of men: they make **b** their phylacteries, *G4115*

BROADER
Job 11: 9 than the earth, and **b** than the sea. H7342

BROIDED
1Ti 2: 9 sobriety; not with **b** hair, or gold, or *G4117*

BROIDERED
Ex 28: 4 and a robe, and a **b** coat, a mitre, and a H8665
Ezk 16:10 I clothed thee also with **b** work, and H7553
13 and silk, and **b** work; thou didst eat H7553
18 And tookest thy **b** garments, and H7553
26:16 and put off their **b** garments: they shall H7553
27: 7 Fine linen with **b** work from Egypt was H7553
16 purple, and **b** work, and fine linen, H7553
24 blue clothes, and **b** work, and in chests H7553

BROILED
Lk 24:42 And they gave him a piece of a **b** fish, *G3702*

BROKE See BRAKE.

BROKEN
Gen 7:11 of the great deep **b** up, and the H1234
17:14 his people; he hath **b** my covenant. H6565
38:29 How hast thou **b** forth? *this* breach *be* H6555
Lev 6:28 is sodden shall be **b**: and if it be sodden H7665
11:35 pots, they shall be **b** down: *for* they *are* H5422
13:20 *is* a plague of leprosy **b** out of the boil. H6524
25 it *is* a leprosy **b** out of the burning: H6524
15:12 the issue, shall be **b**: and every vessel of H7665
21:20 scurvy, or scabbed, or hath his stones **b**; H4790
22:22 Blind, or **b**, or maimed, or having a H7665
24 or crushed, or **b**, or cut; neither shall H5423
26:13 and I have **b** the bands of your yoke, H7665
26 *And* when I have **b** the staff of your H7665
Nu 15:31 LORD, and hath **b** his commandment, H6565
Jdg 5:22 Then were the horsehoofs **b** by the H1986
16: 9 as a thread of tow is **b** when it toucheth H5423
1Sa 2: 4 The bows of the mighty men *are* **b**, and H2844
10 The adversaries of the LORD shall be **b** H2865
2Sa 5:20 The LORD hath **b** forth upon mine H6555
22:35 that a bow of steel is **b** by mine arms. H5181
1Ki 18:30 the altar of the LORD *that was* **b** down. H2040
22:48 for the ships were **b** at Ezion-geber. H7665
2Ki 11: 6 of the house, that it be not **b** down. H4535
25: 4 And the city was **b** up, and all the men H1234
1Ch 14:11 said, God hath **b** in upon mine enemies H6555
2Ch 20:37 the LORD hath **b** thy works. And the H6555
37 the ships were **b**, that they were not able H7665
24: 7 woman, had **b** up the house of God; H6555
25:12 the rock, that they all were **b** in pieces. H1234
32: 5 the wall that was **b**, and raised *it* up to H6555
33: 3 his father had **b** down, and he reared H5422
34: 7 And when he had **b** down the altars H5422
Neh 1: 3 Jerusalem also *is* **b** down, and the gates H6555
2:13 which were **b** down, and the gates H6555
Job 4:10 and the teeth of the young lions, are **b**. H5421
7: 5 my skin is **b**, and become loathsome. H7280
16:12 I was at ease, but he hath **b** me H6565
17:11 My days are past, my purposes are **b** H5423
22: 9 the arms of the fatherless have been **b**. H1792
24:20 and wickedness shall be **b** as a tree. H7665
31:22 and mine arm be **b** from the bone. H7665
38:15 and the high arm shall be **b**. H7665
Ps 3: 7 thou hast **b** the teeth of the ungodly. H7665
18:34 that a bow of steel is **b** by mine arms. H5181
31:12 man out of mind: I am like a **b** vessel. H6
34:18 them that are of a **b** heart; and saveth H7665
20 all his bones: not one of them is **b**. H7665
37:15 own heart, and their bows shall be **b**. H7665
17 For the arms of the wicked shall be **b**: H7665
38: 8 I am feeble and sore **b**: I have roared by H1794
44:19 Though thou hast sore **b** us in the place H1794
51: 8 bones *which* thou hast **b** may rejoice. H1794
17 The sacrifices of God *are* a **b** spirit: a H7665
17 *are* a broken spirit: a **b** and a contrite H7665
55:20 with him: he hath **b** his covenant. H2490
60: 2 to tremble; thou hast **b** it: heal the H6480
69:20 Reproach hath **b** my heart; and I am H7665
80:12 Why hast thou *then* **b** down her H6555
89:10 Thou hast **b** Rahab in pieces, as one H1792
40 Thou hast **b** down all his hedges; thou H6555
107:16 For he hath **b** the gates of brass, and H7665
109:16 that he might even slay the **b** in heart. H5218
124: 7 the snare is **b**, and we are escaped. H7665
147: 3 He healeth the **b** in heart, and bindeth H7665
Prv 3:20 By his knowledge the depths are **b** up, H1234
6:15 suddenly shall he be **b** without remedy. H7665
15:13 but by sorrow of the heart the spirit is **b**. H5218
17:22 but a **b** spirit drieth the bones. H5218
24:31 and the stone wall thereof was **b** down. H2040
25:19 *is like* a **b** tooth, and a foot out of joint. H7465
28 city *that is* **b** down, *and* without walls. H6555
Ecc 4:12 and a threefold cord is not quickly **b**. H5423
12: 6 the golden bowl be **b**, or the pitcher be H7533
6 or the pitcher be **b** at the fountain, or H7665
6 fountain, or the wheel **b** at the cistern. H7533
Isa 5:27 nor the latchet of their shoes be **b**: H5423
7: 8 Ephraim be **b**, that it be not a people. H2844
8: 9 and ye shall be **b** in pieces; and give H2844

Isa 8: 9 and ye shall be **b** in pieces; gird H2844
9 yourselves, and ye shall be **b** in pieces. H2844
15 and be **b**, and be snared, and be taken. H7665
9: 4 For thou hast **b** the yoke of his burden, H2865
14: 5 The LORD hath **b** the staff of the H7665
29 him that smote thee is **b**: for out of the H7665
16: 8 the heathen have **b** down the principal H1986
19:10 And they shall be **b** in the purposes H1792
21: 9 of her gods he hath **b** unto the ground. H7665
22:10 have ye **b** down to fortify the wall. H5422
24: 5 ordinance, **b** the everlasting covenant. H6565
10 The city of confusion is **b** down: every H7665
19 The earth is utterly **b** down, the earth is H7489
27:11 they shall be **b** off: the women come, H7665
28:13 and be **b**, and snared, and taken. H7665
30:14 vessel that is **b** in pieces; he shall not H3807
33: 8 ceaseth: he hath **b** the covenant, he H6565
20 shall any of the cords thereof be **b**. H5423
36: 6 Lo, thou trustest in the staff of this **b** H7533
Jer 2:13 **b** cisterns, that can hold no water. H7665
16 have **b** the crown of thy head. H7462
20 For of old time I have **b** thy yoke, *and* H7665
4:26 the cities thereof were **b** down at the H5422
5: 5 **b** the yoke, *and* burst the bonds. H7665
10:20 and all my cords are **b**: my children are H5423
11:10 of Judah have **b** my covenant which H6565
16 upon it, and the branches of it are **b**. H7489
14:17 of my people is **b** with a great breach, H7665
22:28 *Is* this man Coniah a despised **b** idol? *is* H5310
23: 9 Mine heart within me is **b** because of H7665
28: 2 have **b** the yoke of the king of Babylon. H7665
12 the prophet had **b** the yoke from off the H7665
13 LORD; Thou hast **b** the yokes of wood; H7665
33:21 *Then* may also my covenant be **b** with H6565
37:11 Chaldeans was **b** up from Jerusalem H5927
39: 2 *day* of the month, the city was **b** up. H1234
48:17 the strong staff **b**, *and* the beautiful rod! H7665
20 Moab is confounded; for it is **b** down: H2865
25 off, and his arm is **b**, saith the LORD. H7665
38 thereof: for I have **b** Moab like a vessel H7665
39 They shall howl, *saying*, How is it **b** H2865
50: 2 Merodach is **b** in pieces; her idols are H2844
2 her images are **b** in pieces. H2865
17 king of Babylon hath **b** his bones. H6105
23 cut asunder and **b**! how is Babylon H7665
51:30 her dwellingplaces; her bars are **b**. H7665
56 of their bows is **b**: for the LORD God of H2865
58 shall be utterly **b**, and her high gates H6209
52: 7 Then the city was **b** up, and all the men H1234
Lam 2: 9 destroyed and **b** her bars: her king and H7665
3: 4 hath he made old; he hath **b** my bones. H7665
16 He hath also **b** my teeth with gravel H1638
Ezk 6: 4 images shall be **b**: and I will cast down H7665
6 your idols may be **b** and cease, and H7665
9 because I am **b** with their whorish H7665
17:19 that he hath **b**, even it will I recompense H6331
19:12 strong rods were **b** and withered; the H6561
26: 2 Aha, she is **b** *that was* the gates of H7665
27:26 hath **b** thee in the midst of the seas. H7665
34 In the time *when* thou shalt be **b** by the H7665
30: 4 and her foundations shall be **b** down. H2040
21 Son of man, I have **b** the arm of H7665
22 that which was **b**; and I will cause the H7665
31:12 his boughs are **b** by all the rivers of the H7665
32:28 Yea, thou shalt be **b** in the midst of the H7665
34: 4 up *that which was* **b**, neither have ye H7665
16 bind up *that which was* **b**, and will H7665
27 when I have **b** the bands of their yoke, H7665
44: 7 and they have **b** my covenant because H6565
Dan 2:35 and the gold, **b** to pieces together, and H1854
42 shall be partly strong, and partly **b**. H8406
8: 8 the great horn was **b**; and for it came up H7665
22 Now that being **b**, whereas four stood H7665
25 princes; but he shall be **b** without hand. H7665
11: 4 his kingdom shall be **b**, and shall be H7665
22 **b**; yea, also the prince of the covenant. H7665
Hos 5:11 Ephraim *is* oppressed *and* **b** in H7533
8: 6 the calf of Samaria shall be **b** in pieces. H7616
Joel 1:17 are **b** down; for the corn is withered. H2040
Jna 1: 4 the sea, so that the ship was like to be **b**. H7665
Mic 2:13 them: they have **b** up, and have passed H6555
Zec 11:11 And it was **b** in that day: and so the H6565
16 heal that that is **b**, nor feed that that H7665
Mt 15:37 **b** *meat* that was left seven baskets full. *G2801*
21:44 on this stone shall be **b**: but on *G4917*
24:43 not have suffered his house to be **b** up. *G1358*
Mk 2: 4 when they had **b** *it* up, they let down *G1846*
5: 4 him, and the fetters **b** in pieces: neither *G4937*
8: 8 the **b** *meat* that was left seven baskets. *G2801*
Lk 12:39 suffered his house to be **b** through. *G1358*
20:18 upon that stone shall be **b**; but on *G4917*
Jn 5:18 he not only had **b** the sabbath, but said *G3089*
7:23 should not be **b**; are ye angry at me, *G3089*
10:35 came, and the scripture cannot be **b**; *G3089*
19:31 **b**, and *that* they might be taken away. *G2608*
36 fulfilled, A bone of him shall not be **b**. *G4937*
21:11 were so many, yet was not the net **b**. *G4977*
Act 13:43 Now when the congregation was **b** up, *G3089*
20:11 up again, and had **b** bread, and eaten, *G2806*
27:35 and when he had **b** *it*, he began to eat. *G2806*
41 was **b** with the violence of the waves. *G3089*
44 and some on **b** *pieces* of the ship. And
Ro 11:17 And if some of the branches be **b** off, *G1575*
19 were **b** off, that I might be graffed in. *G1575*
20 Well; because of unbelief they were **b** *G1575*
1Co 11:24 my body, which is **b** for you: this do in *G2806*
Eph 2:14 one, and hath **b** down the middle wall *G3089*
Rev 2:27 shall they be **b** to shivers: even as I *G4937*

BROKENFOOTED
Lev 21:19 Or a man that is **b**, or H7667+H7272

BROKENHANDED
Lev 21:19 man that is brokenfooted, or **b**, H7667+H3027

BROKENHEARTED
Isa 61: 1 to bind up the **b**, to proclaim H7665+H3820
Lk 4:18 sent me to heal the **b**, to preach *G4937+G2588*

BROOD
Lk 13:34 **b** under *her* wings, and ye would not! *G3555*

BROOK
Gen 32:23 over the **b**, and sent over that he had. H5158
Lev 23:40 trees, and willows of the **b**; and ye shall H5158
Nu 13:23 And they came unto the **b** of Eshcol, H5158
24 The place was called the **b** Eshcol, H5158
Dt 2:13 get you over the **b** Zered. And we went H5158
13 Zered. And we went over the **b** Zered. H5158
14 come over the **b** Zered, *was* thirty and H5158
9:21 the **b** that descended out of the mount. H5158
1Sa 17:40 stones out of the **b**, and put them in a H5158
30: 9 and came to the **b** Besor, where those H5158
10 that they could not go over the **b** Besor. H5158
21 to abide at the **b** Besor: and they went H5158
2Sa 15:23 passed over the **b** Kidron, and all the H5158
17:20 be gone over the **b** of water. And when H4323
1Ki 2:37 passest over the **b** Kidron, thou shalt H5158
15:13 her idol, and burnt *it* by the **b** Kidron. H5158
17: 3 by the **b** Cherith, that *is* before Jordan. H5158
4 thou shalt drink of the **b**; and I have H5158
5 by the **b** Cherith, that *is* before Jordan. H5158
6 in the evening; and he drank of the **b**. H5158
7 a while, that the **b** dried up, because H5158
18:40 to the **b** Kishon, and slew them there. H5158
2Ki 23: 6 unto the **b** Kidron, and burned H5158
6 burned it at the **b** Kidron, and stamped H5158
12 cast the dust of them into the **b** Kidron. H5158
2Ch 15:16 *it*, and burnt *it* at the **b** Kidron. H5158
20:16 of the **b**, before the wilderness of Jeruel. H5158
29:16 carry *it* out abroad into the **b** Kidron. H5158
30:14 away, and cast *them* into the **b** Kidron. H5158
32: 4 fountains, and the **b** that ran through H5158
Neh 2:15 Then went I up in the night by the **b**, H5158
Job 6:15 deceitfully as a **b**, *and* as the stream of H5158
40:22 willows of the **b** compass him about. H5158
Ps 83: 9 *to* Sisera, as *to* Jabin, at the **b** of Kison: H5158
110: 7 He shall drink of the **b** in the way: H5158
Prv 18: 4 the wellspring of wisdom *as* a flowing **b**. H5158
Isa 15: 7 they carry away to the **b** of the willows. H5158
Jer 31:40 the fields unto the **b** of Kidron, unto the H5158
Jn 18: 1 disciples over the **b** Cedron, where was *G5493*

BROOKS
Nu 21:14 in the Red sea, and in the **b** of Arnon, H5158
15 And at the stream of the **b** that goeth H5158
Dt 8: 7 land, a land of **b** of water, of fountains H5158
2Sa 23:30 Pirathonite, Hiddai of the **b** of Gaash, H5158
1Ki 18: 5 and unto all **b**: peradventure we may H5158
1Ch 11:32 Hurai of the **b** of Gaash, Abiel the H5158
Job 6:15 *and* as the stream of **b** they pass away; H5158
20:17 the floods, the **b** of honey and butter. H5158
22:24 the *gold* of Ophir as the stones of the **b**. H5158
Ps 42: 1 As the hart panteth after the water **b**, so H650
Isa 19: 6 far away; *and* the **b** of defence shall be H2975
7 The paper reeds by the **b**, by the mouth H2975
7 by the mouth of the **b**, and every thing H2975
7 thing sown by the **b**, shall wither, be H2975
Isa 19: 8 cast angle into the **b** shall lament, and H2975

BROTH
Jdg 6:19 and he put the **b** in a pot, and brought H4839
20 rock, and pour out the **b**. And he did so. H4839
Isa 65: 4 eat swine's flesh, and **b** of abominable H6564

BROTHER
Gen 4: 2 And she again bare his **b** Abel. And Abel H251
8 And Cain talked with Abel his **b**: and it H251
8 rose up against Abel his **b**, and slew him. H251
9 Where *is* Abel thy **b**? And he said, I know H251
9: 5 man's **b** will I require the life of man. H251
10:21 of Eber, the **b** of Japheth the elder, H251
14:13 the Amorite, **b** of Eshcol, and brother H251
13 of Eshcol, and **b** of Aner: and these *were* H251
14 And when Abram heard that his **b** was H251
16 brought again his **b** Lot, and his goods, H251
20: 5 said, He *is* my **b**: in the integrity of my H251
13 we shall come, say of me, He *is* my **b**. H251
16 I have given thy **b** a thousand *pieces* of H251
22:20 also born children unto thy **b** Nahor; H251
21 Huz his firstborn, and Buz his **b**, and H251
23 Milcah did bear to Nahor, Abraham's **b**. H251
24:15 **b**, with her pitcher upon her shoulder. H251
29 And Rebekah had a **b**, and his name *was* H251
53 her **b** and to her mother precious things. H251
55 And her **b** and her mother said, Let the H251
25:26 And after that came his **b** out, and his H251
27: 6 thy father speak unto Esau thy **b**, saying, H251
11 Behold, Esau my **b** *is* a hairy man, and H251
23 as his **b** Esau's hands: so he blessed him. H251
30 Esau his **b** came in from his hunting. H251
35 And he said, Thy **b** came with subtilty, H251
40 and shalt serve thy **b**; and it shall come to H251
41 are at hand; then will I slay my **b** Jacob. H251
42 him, Behold, thy **b** Esau, as touching H251
43 arise, flee thou to Laban my **b** to Haran; H251
28: 2 of the daughters of Laban thy mother's **b**. H251
5 the Syrian, the **b** of Rebekah, Jacob's H251
29:10 his mother's **b**, and the sheep of Laban H251
10 his mother's **b**, that Jacob went near, H251
10 the flock of Laban his mother's **b**. H251
12 he *was* her father's **b**, and that he *was* H251
15 thou *art* my **b**, shouldest thou therefore H251
32: 3 him to Esau his **b** unto the land of Seir, H251
6 We came to thy **b** Esau, and also he H251
11 the hand of my **b**, from the hand of Esau: H251
13 to his hand a present for Esau his **b**; H251
17 When Esau my **b** meeteth thee, and H251
33: 3 seven times, until he came near to his **b**. H251
9 And Esau said, I have enough, my **b**; H251
35: 1 thou fleddest from the face of Esau thy **b**. H251
7 him, when he fled from the face of his **b**. H251
36: 6 the country from the face of his **b** Jacob. H251
37:26 *it* if we slay our **b**, and conceal his blood? H251
27 him; for he *is* our **b** *and* our flesh. And H251
38: 8 marry her, and raise up seed to thy **b**. H251
9 lest that he should give seed to his **b**. H251
29 that, behold, his **b** came out: and she H251
30 And afterward came out his **b**, that had H251
42: 4 But Benjamin, Joseph's **b**, Jacob sent not H251
15 except your youngest **b** come hither. H251
16 let him fetch your **b**, and ye shall be kept H251
20 But bring your youngest **b** unto me; so H251
21 concerning our **b**, in that we saw the H251
34 And bring your youngest **b** unto me: H251
34 your **b**, and ye shall traffick in the land. H251
38 with you; for his **b** is dead, and he is left H251
43: 3 see my face, except your **b** *be* with you. H251
4 If thou wilt send our **b** with us, we will H251
5 see my face, except your **b** *be* with you. H251
6 *as* to tell the man whether ye had yet a **b**? H251
7 alive? have ye *another* **b**? and we told him H251
7 that he would say, Bring your **b** down? H251
13 Take also your **b**, and arise, go again H251
14 away your other **b**, and Benjamin. If I be H251
29 And he lifted up his eyes, and saw his **b** H251
29 *Is* this your younger **b**, of whom ye spake H251
30 did yearn upon his **b**: and he sought H251
44:19 servants, saying, Have ye a father, or a **b**? H251
20 a little one; and his **b** is dead, and he H251
23 your youngest **b** come down with you, H251
26 if our youngest **b** be with us, then will H251
26 face, except our youngest **b** *be* with us. H251
45: 4 Joseph your **b**, whom ye sold into Egypt. H251
12 and the eyes of my **b** Benjamin, that *it is* H251
14 And he fell upon his **b** Benjamin's neck, H251
48:19 truly his younger **b** shall be greater than H251

Ex 4:14 the Levite thy **b**? I know that he can speak H251
7: 1 and Aaron thy **b** shall be thy prophet. H251
2 thee: and Aaron thy **b** shall speak unto H251
28: 1 And take thou unto thee Aaron thy **b**, H251
2 for Aaron thy **b** for glory and for beauty. H251
4 for Aaron thy **b**, and his sons, that he H251
41 upon Aaron thy **b**, and his sons with him; H251
32:27 slay every man his **b**, and every man his H251
29 son, and upon his **b**; that he may bestow H251
Lev 16: 2 unto Aaron thy **b**, that he come not at H251
18:14 of thy father's **b**, thou shalt not approach H251
19:17 Thou shalt not hate thy **b** in thine heart: H251
21: 2 son, and for his daughter, and for his **b**, H251
25:25 If thy **b** be waxen poor, and hath sold H251
25 shall he redeem that which his **b** sold. H251
35 And if thy **b** be waxen poor, and fallen in H251
36 thy God; that thy **b** may live with thee. H251
39 And if thy **b** *that dwelleth* by thee be H251
47 by thee, and thy **b** *that dwelleth* by him H251
Nu 6: 7 for his mother, for his **b**, or for his sister, H251
20: 8 and Aaron thy **b**, and speak ye unto the H251
14 Thus saith thy **b** Israel, Thou knowest H251
27:13 thy people, as Aaron thy **b** was gathered. H251
36: 2 of Zelophehad our **b** unto his daughters. H251
Dt 1:16 his **b**, and the stranger *that is* with him. H251
13: 6 If thy **b**, the son of thy mother, or thy son, H251
15: 2 **b**; because it is called the LORD'S release. H251
3 thine with thy **b** thine hand shall release; H251
7 nor shut thine hand from thy poor **b**: H251
9 against thy poor **b**, and thou givest him H251
11 wide unto thy **b**, to thy poor, and to thy H251
12 *And* if thy **b**, an Hebrew man, or an H251
17:15 a stranger over thee, which *is* not thy **b**. H251
19:18 *and* hath testified falsely against his **b**; H251
19 to have done unto his **b**: so shalt thou put H251
22: 1 in any case bring them again unto thy **b**. H251
2 And if thy **b** *be* not nigh unto thee, or if H251
2 be with thee until thy **b** seek after it, and H251
23: 7 for he *is* thy **b**: thou shalt not abhor H251
19 Thou shalt not lend upon usury to thy **b**; H251
20 usury; but unto thy **b** thou shalt not lend H251
24:10 When thou dost lend thy **b** any thing, H7453
25: 3 then thy **b** should seem vile unto thee. H251
5 her husband's **b** shall go in unto her, H2993
5 the duty of an husband's **b** unto her. H2992
6 in the name of his **b** *which is* dead, that H251
7 My husband's **b** refuseth to raise up H2993
7 raise up unto his **b** a name in Israel, he H251
7 perform the duty of my husband's **b**. H2992
28:54 be evil toward his **b**, and toward the wife H251
32:50 as Aaron thy **b** died in mount Hor, and H251
Jos 15:17 And Othniel the son of Kenaz, the **b** of H251
Jdg 1: 3 And Judah said unto Simeon his **b**, Come H251
13 Caleb's younger **b**, took it: and he gave H251
17 And Judah went with Simeon his **b**, and H251
3: 9 the son of Kenaz, Caleb's younger **b**. H251
9: 3 Abimelech; for they said, He *is* our **b**. H251
18 men of Shechem, because he *is* your **b**;) H251
21 dwelt there, for fear of Abimelech his **b**. H251
24 Abimelech their **b**, which slew them; and H251
20:23 of Benjamin my **b**? And the LORD said, H251
28 of Benjamin my **b**, or shall I cease? And H251
21: 6 for Benjamin their **b**, and said, There is H251
Ru 4: 3 of land, which *was* our **b** Elimelech's: H251
1Sa 14: 3 Ahitub, Ichabod's **b**, the son of Phinehas, H251
17:28 And Eliab his eldest **b** heard when he H251
20:29 sacrifice in the city; and my **b**, he hath H251
26: 6 the son of Zeruiah, **b** to Joab, saying, H251
2Sa 1:26 I am distressed for thee, my **b** Jonathan: H251
2:22 should I hold up my face to Joab thy **b**? H251
27 gone up every one from following his **b**. H251
3:27 he died, for the blood of Asahel his **b**. H251
30 So Joab and Abishai his **b** slew Abner, H251
30 their **b** Asahel at Gibeon in the battle. H251
4: 6 and Rechab and Baanah his **b** escaped. H251
9 and Baanah his **b**, the sons of Rimmon H251
10:10 of Abishai his **b**, that he might put *them* H251
13: 3 **b**: and Jonadab *was* a very subtil man. H251
4 I love Tamar, my **b** Absalom's sister. H251
7 **b** Amnon's house, and dress him meat. H251
8 So Tamar went to her **b** Amnon's house; H251
10 *them* into the chamber to Amnon her **b**. H251
12 And she answered him, Nay, my **b**, do H251
20 And Absalom her **b** said unto her, Hath H251
20 Hath Amnon thy **b** been with thee? but H251
20 my sister: he *is* thy **b**; regard not this H251
20 desolate in her **b** Absalom's house. H251
22 And Absalom spake unto his **b** Amnon
26 I pray thee, let my **b** Amnon go with us. H251

2Sa 13:32 Shimeah David's **b**, answered and said, H251
14: 7 him that smote his **b**, that we may kill H251
7 for the life of his **b** whom he slew; and H251
18: 2 son of Zeruiah, Joab's **b**, and a third part H251
20: 9 *Art* thou in health, my **b**? And Joab took H251
10 **b** pursued after Sheba the son of Bichri. H251
21:19 slew *the* **b** *of* Goliath the Gittite,
21 son of Shimea the **b** of David slew him. H251
23:18 And Abishai, the **b** of Joab, the son of H251
24 Asahel the **b** of Joab *was* one of the H251
1Ki 1:10 men, and Solomon his **b**, he called not. H251
2: 7 me when I fled because of Absalom thy **b**. H251
21 be given to Adonijah thy **b** to wife. H251
22 for he *is* mine elder **b**; even for him, and H251
9:13 hast given me, my **b**? And he called them H251
13:30 mourned over him, *saying*, Alas, my **b**! H251
20:32 And he said, *Is* he yet alive? he *is* my **b**. H251
33 and they said, Thy **b** Ben-hadad. Then H251
2Ki 24:17 his father's **b** king in his stead, and H251
1Ch 2:32 And the sons of Jada the **b** of Shammai; H251
42 Now the sons of Caleb the **b** of Jerahmeel H251
4:11 And Chelub the **b** of Shuah begat Mehir, H251
6:39 And his **b** Asaph, who stood on his right H251
7:16 the name of his **b** *was* Sheresh; and his H251
35 And the sons of his **b** Helem; Zophah, H251
8:39 And the sons of Eshek his **b** *were*, Ulam H251
11:20 And Abishai the **b** of Joab, he was chief H251
26 *were*, Asahel the **b** of Joab, Elhanan the H251
38 Joel the **b** of Nathan, Mibhar the son of H251
45 Jediael the son of Shimri, and Joha his **b**, H251
19:11 of Abishai his **b**, and they set *themselves* H251
15 before Abishai his **b**, and entered into the H251
20: 5 slew Lahmi the **b** of Goliath the Gittite, H251
7 the son of Shimea David's **b** slew him. H251
24:25 The **b** of Michah *was* Isshiah: of the H1730
26:22 and Joel his **b**, *which were* over the H251
27: 7 *was* Asahel the **b** of Joab, and Zebadiah H251
2Ch 31:12 *was* ruler, and Shimei his **b** *was* the next. H251
13 and Shimei his **b**, at the commandment H251
36: 4 made Eliakim his **b** king over Judah and H251
4 Jehoahaz his **b**, and carried him to Egypt. H251
10 his **b** king over Judah and Jerusalem. H251
Neh 5: 7 every one of his **b**. And I set a great H251
7: 2 That I gave my **b** Hanani, and Hananiah H251
Job 22: 6 For thou hast taken a pledge from thy **b** H251
30:29 I am a **b** to dragons, and a companion to H251
Ps 35:14 *had been* my friend *or* **b**: I bowed down H251
49: 7 his **b**, nor give to God a ransom for him: H251
50:20 Thou sittest *and* speakest against thy **b**; H251
Prv 17:17 A friend loveth at all times, and a **b** is H251
18: 9 He also that is slothful in his work is **b** to H251
19 A **b** offended *is harder to be won* than a H251
24 is a friend *that* sticketh closer than a **b**. H251
27:10 a neighbour *that is* near than a **b** far off. H251
Ecc 4: 8 neither child nor **b**: yet *is there* no end of H251
Song 8: 1 O that thou *wert* as my **b**, that sucked the H251
Isa 3: 6 When a man shall take hold of his **b** of H251
9:19 fuel of the fire: no man shall spare his **b**. H251
19: 2 one against his **b**, and every one against H251
41: 6 *one* said to his **b**, Be of good courage. H251
Jer 9: 4 trust ye not in any **b**: for every brother H251
4 brother: for every **b** will utterly supplant, H251
22:18 *saying*, Ah my **b**! or, Ah sister! they shall H251
23:35 every one to his **b**, What hath the LORD H251
31:34 and every man his **b**, saying, Know the H251
34: 9 himself of them, *to wit*, of a Jew his **b**. H251
14 ye go every man his **b** an Hebrew, which H251
17 every one to his **b**, and every man to his H251
Ezk 18:18 spoiled his **b** by violence, and did H251
33:30 every one to his **b**, saying, Come, I pray H251
38:21 every man's sword shall be against his **b**. H251
44:25 for daughter, for **b**, or for sister that hath H251
Hos 12: 3 He took his **b** by the heel in the womb, H251
Am 1:11 he did pursue his **b** with the sword, and H251
Oba 10 For *thy* violence against thy **b** Jacob H251
12 on the day of thy **b** in the day that he H251
Mic 7: 2 they hunt every man his **b** with a net. H251
Hag 2:22 down, every one by the sword of his **b**. H251
Zec 7: 9 and compassions every man to his **b**: H251
10 imagine evil against his **b** in your heart. H251
Mal 1: 2 **b**? saith the LORD: yet I loved Jacob, H251
2:10 man against his **b**, by profaning the H251
Mt 4:18 and Andrew his **b**, casting a net into the *G80*
21 and John his **b**, in a ship with Zebedee *G80*
5:22 is angry with his **b** without a cause shall *G80*
22 shall say to his **b**, Raca, shall be in *G80*
23 that thy **b** hath ought against thee; *G80*
24 to thy **b**, and then come and offer thy gift. *G80*
7: 4 Or how wilt thou say to thy **b**, Let me pull *G80*

Mt 10: 2 and Andrew his **b**; James *the son* of *G80*
2 James *the son* of Zebedee, and John his **b**; *G80*
21 And the **b** shall deliver up the brother to *G80*
21 And the brother shall deliver up the **b** to *G80*
12:50 the same is my **b**, and sister, and mother. *G80*
14: 3 for Herodias' sake, his **b** Philip's wife. *G80*
17: 1 and John his **b**, and bringeth them up *G80*
18:15 Moreover if thy **b** shall trespass against *G80*
15 shall hear thee, thou hast gained thy **b**. *G80*
21 how oft shall my **b** sin against me, and *G80*
35 not every one his **b** their trespasses. *G80*
22:24 no children, his **b** shall marry his wife, *G80*
24 his wife, and raise up seed unto his **b**. *G80*
25 having no issue, left his wife unto his **b**: *G80*
Mk 1:16 and Andrew his **b** casting a net into the *G80*
19 and John his **b**, who also were in the *G80*
3:17 and John the **b** of James; and he *G80*
35 same is my **b**, and my sister, and mother. *G80*
5:37 and James, and John the **b** of James. *G80*
6: 3 son of Mary, the **b** of James, and Joses, *G80*
17 **b** Philip's wife: for he had married her. *G80*
12:19 unto us, If a man's **b** die, and leave *his* *G80*
19 children, that his **b** should take his wife, *G80*
19 his wife, and raise up seed unto his **b**. *G80*
13:12 Now the **b** shall betray the brother to *G80*
12 Now the brother shall betray the **b** to *G80*
Lk 3: 1 of Galilee, and his **b** Philip tetrarch of *G80*
19 for Herodias his **b** Philip's wife, and for *G80*
6:14 and Andrew his **b**, James and John, *G80*
16 And Judas *the* **b** of James, and Judas
42 Either how canst thou say to thy **b**, *G80*
42 say to thy brother, **B**, let me pull out the *G80*
12:13 **b**, that he divide the inheritance with me. *G80*
15:27 And he said unto him, Thy **b** is come; *G80*
32 glad: for this thy **b** was dead, and is alive *G80*
17: 3 Take heed to yourselves: If thy **b** *G80*
20:28 us, If any man's **b** die, having a wife, and *G80*
28 children, that his **b** should take his wife, *G80*
28 his wife, and raise up seed unto his **b**. *G80*
Jn 1:40 him, was Andrew, Simon Peter's **b**. *G80*
41 He first findeth his own **b** Simon, and *G80*
6: 8 Andrew, Simon Peter's **b**, saith unto him, *G80*
11: 2 her hair, whose **b** Lazarus was sick.) *G80*
19 to comfort them concerning their **b**. *G80*
21 hadst been here, my **b** had not died. *G80*
23 Jesus saith unto her, Thy **b** shall rise *G80*
32 hadst been here, my **b** had not died. *G80*
Act 1:13 Simon Zelotes, and Judas *the* **b** of James.
9:17 on him said, **B** Saul, the Lord, *even* *G80*
12: 2 And he killed James the **b** of John with *G80*
21:20 him, Thou seest, **b**, how many thousands *G80*
22:13 and said unto me, **B** Saul, receive thy *G80*
Ro 14:10 But why dost thou judge thy **b**? or why *G80*
10 set at nought thy **b**? for we shall all stand *G80*
15 But if thy **b** be grieved with *thy* meat, *G80*
21 *any thing* whereby thy **b** stumbleth, or is *G80*
16:23 of the city saluteth you, and Quartus a **b**. *G80*
1Co 1: 1 the will of God, and Sosthenes *our* **b**, *G80*
5:11 man that is called a **b** be a fornicator, or *G80*
6: 6 But **b** goeth to law with brother, and that *G80*
6 But brother goeth to law with **b**, and that *G80*
7:12 not the Lord: If any **b** hath a wife that *G80*
15 let him depart. A **b** or a sister is not *G80*
8:11 the weak **b** perish, for whom Christ died? *G80*
13 Wherefore, if meat make my **b** to offend, *G80*
13 standeth, lest I make my **b** to offend. *G80*
16:12 As touching *our* **b** Apollos, I greatly *G80*
2Co 1: 1 and Timothy *our* **b**, unto the church of *G80*
2:13 not Titus my **b**: but taking my leave *G80*
8:18 And we have sent with him the **b**, whose *G80*
22 And we have sent with them our **b**, *G80*
12:18 I desired Titus, and with *him* I sent a **b**. *G80*
Gal 1:19 saw I none, save James the Lord's **b**. *G80*
Eph 6:21 a beloved **b** and faithful minister *G80*
Php 2:25 Epaphroditus, my **b**, and companion in *G80*
Col 1: 1 by the will of God, and Timotheus *our* **b**, *G80*
4: 7 you, *who is* a beloved **b**, and a faithful *G80*
9 With Onesimus, a faithful and beloved **b**, *G80*
1Th 3: 2 And sent Timotheus, our **b**, and minister *G80*
4: 6 beyond and defraud his **b** in *any* matter: *G80*
2Th 3: 6 from every **b** that walketh disorderly, *G80*
15 as an enemy, but admonish *him* as a **b**. *G80*
Phlm 1 and Timothy *our* **b**, unto Philemon our *G80*
7 of the saints are refreshed by thee, **b**. *G80*
16 above a servant, a **b** beloved, specially to *G80*
20 Yea, **b**, let me have joy of thee in the *G80*
Heb 8:11 and every man his **b**, saying, Know the *G80*
13:23 Know ye that *our* **b** Timothy is set at *G80*
Jas 1: 9 Let the **b** of low degree rejoice in that he *G80*

Jas 2:15 If a **b** or sister be naked, and destitute of G80
4:11 speaketh evil of *his* **b**, and judgeth his G80
11 and judgeth his **b**, speaketh evil of the G80
1Pt 5:12 By Silvanus, a faithful **b** unto you, as I G80
2Pt 3:15 as our beloved **b** Paul also according G80
1Jn 2: 9 his **b**, is in darkness even until now. G80
10 He that loveth his **b** abideth in the light, G80
11 But he that hateth his **b** is in darkness, G80
3:10 of God, neither he that loveth not his **b**. G80
12 one, and slew his **b**. And wherefore slew G80
14 that loveth not *his* **b** abideth in death. G80
15 Whosoever hateth his **b** is a murderer: G80
17 good, and seeth his **b** have need, and G80
4:20 and hateth his **b**, he is a liar: for he that G80
20 that loveth not his **b** whom he hath seen, G80
21 That he who loveth God love his **b** also. G80
5:16 If any man see his **b** sin a sin *which is* G80
Jude 1 Jude, the servant of Jesus Christ, and **b** G80
Rev 1: 9 I John, who also am your **b**, and G80

BROTHERHOOD
Zec 11:14 break the **b** between Judah and Israel. H264
1Pt 2:17 Honour all *men*. Love the **b**. Fear God. G81

BROTHERLY
Am 1: 9 and remembered not the **b** covenant: H251
Ro 12:10 one to another with **b** love; in honour G5360
1Th 4: 9 But as touching **b** love ye need not that G5360
Heb 13: 1 Let **b** love continue. G5360
2Pt 1: 7 And to godliness **b** kindness; and to G5360
7 kindness; and to **b** kindness charity. G5360

BROTHER'S
Gen 4: 9 he said, I know not: *Am* I my **b** keeper? H251
10 **b** blood crieth unto me from the ground. H251
11 to receive thy **b** blood from thy hand; H251
21 And his **b** name *was* Jubal: he was the H251
10:25 divided; and his **b** name *was* Joktan. H251
12: 5 his wife, and Lot his **b** son, and all their H251
14:12 And they took Lot, Abram's **b** son, who H251
24:48 my master's **b** daughter unto his son. H251
27:44 a few days, until thy **b** fury turn away; H251
45 Until thy **b** anger turn away from thee, H251
38: 8 Go in unto thy **b** wife, and marry her, H251
9 he went in unto his **b** wife, that he spilled H251
Lev 18:16 thy **b** wife: it *is* thy brother's nakedness. H251
16 thy brother's wife: it *is* thy **b** nakedness. H251
20:21 And if a man shall take his **b** wife, it *is* H251
21 his **b** nakedness; they shall be childless. H251
Dt 22: 1 Thou shalt not see thy **b** ox or his sheep H251
3 all lost thing of thy **b**, which he hath lost, H251
4 Thou shalt not see thy **b** ass or his ox fall H251
25: 7 And if the man like not to take his **b** H2994
7 wife, then let his **b** wife go up to the H2994
9 Then shall his **b** wife come unto him in H2994
9 man that will not build up his **b** house. H251
1Ki 2:15 my **b**: for it was his from the LORD. H251
1Ch 1:19 was divided: and his **b** name *was* Joktan. H251
Job 1:13 drinking wine in their eldest **b** house: H251
18 drinking wine in their eldest **b** house: H251
Prv 27:10 neither go into thy **b** house in the day of H251
Mt 7: 3 mote that is in thy **b** eye, but considerest G80
5 to cast out the mote out of thy **b** eye. G80
Mk 6:18 is not lawful for thee to have thy **b** wife. G80
Lk 6:41 mote that is in thy **b** eye, but perceivest G80
42 to pull out the mote that is in thy **b** eye. G80
Ro 14:13 or an occasion to fall in *his* **b** way. G80
1Jn 3:12 works were evil, and his **b** righteous. G80

BROTHERS'
Nu 36:11 married unto their father's **b** sons: H1730

BROUGHT
Gen 1:12 And the earth **b** forth grass, *and* herb H3318
21 which the waters **b** forth abundantly, H8317
2:19 fowl of the air; and **b** *them* unto Adam to H935
22 he a woman, and **b** her unto the man. H935
4: 3 to pass, that Cain **b** of the fruit of the H935
4 And Abel, he also **b** of the firstlings of H935
14:16 And he **b** back all the goods, and also H7725
16 the goods, and also **b** again his brother H7725
18 And Melchizedek king of Salem **b** forth H3318
15: 5 And he **b** him forth abroad, and said, H3318
7 I *am* the LORD that **b** thee out of Ur of H3318
19:16 him: and they **b** him forth, and set him H3318
17 And it came to pass, when they had **b** H3318
20: 9 thee, that thou hast **b** on me and on my H935
24:53 And the servant **b** forth jewels of silver, H3318
67 And Isaac **b** her into his mother Sarah's H935
Gen 26:10 shouldest have **b** guiltiness upon us. H935
27:14 And he went, and fetched, and **b** *them* to H935
20 Because the LORD thy God **b** *it* to me. H7136
25 bless thee. And he **b** *it* near to him, and H5066
25 eat: and he **b** him wine, and he drank. H935
31 savoury meat, and **b** it unto his father, H935
33 taken venison, and **b** *it* me, and I have H935
29:13 kissed him, and **b** him to his house. And H935
23 **b** her to him; and he went in unto her. H935
30:14 in the field, and **b** them unto his mother H935
39 the rods, and **b** forth cattle ringstraked, H3205
31:39 That which was torn *of beasts* I **b** not H935
33:11 Take, I pray thee, my blessing that is **b** H935
37: 2 Joseph **b** unto his father their evil report. H935
28 of silver: and they **b** Joseph into Egypt. H935
32 colours, and they **b** *it* to their father; and H935
38:25 When she *was* **b** forth, she sent to her H3318
39: 1 And Joseph was **b** down to Egypt; and H3381
1 which had **b** him down thither. H3381
14 See, he hath **b** in an Hebrew unto us H935
17 **b** unto us, came in unto me to mock me: H935
40:10 the clusters thereof **b** forth ripe grapes: H1310
41:14 Joseph, and they **b** him hastily out of H7323
47 years the earth **b** forth by handfuls. H6213
43: 2 corn which they had **b** out of Egypt, their H935
12 money that was **b** again in the mouth H7725
17 the man **b** the men into Joseph's house. H935
18 because they were **b** into Joseph's house; H935
18 first time are we **b** in; that he may seek H935
21 and we have **b** it again in our hand. H7725
22 And other money have we **b** down in H3381
23 And he **b** Simeon out unto them. H3318
24 And the man **b** the men into Joseph's H935
26 And when Joseph came home, they **b** H935
44: 8 sacks' mouths, we **b** again unto thee H7725
46: 7 all his seed **b** he with him into Egypt. H935
32 and they have **b** their flocks, and their H935
47: 7 And Joseph **b** in Jacob his father, and set H935
14 **b** the money into Pharaoh's house. H935
17 And they **b** their cattle unto Joseph: and H935
48:10 not see. And he **b** them near unto him; H5066
12 And Joseph **b** them out from between H3318
13 right hand, and **b** *them* near unto him. H5066
50:23 were **b** up upon Joseph's knees. H3205
Ex 2:10 And the child grew, and she **b** him unto H935
3:12 When thou hast **b** forth the people out H3318
8: 7 and **b** up frogs upon the land of Egypt. H5927
12 frogs which he had **b** against Pharaoh. H7760
9:19 and shall not be **b** home, the hail shall H622
10: 8 And Moses and Aaron were **b** again H7725
13 and the LORD **b** an east wind upon the H5090
13 morning, the east wind **b** the locusts. H5375
12:17 day have I **b** your armies out of the H3318
39 dough which they **b** forth out of Egypt, H3318
13: 3 of hand the LORD **b** you out from this H3318
9 hath the LORD **b** thee out of Egypt. H3318
14 of hand the LORD **b** us out from Egypt, H3318
16 hand the LORD **b** us forth out of Egypt. H3318
15:19 and the LORD **b** again the waters of H7725
22 So Moses **b** Israel from the Red sea, H5265
26 upon thee, which I have **b** upon the H7760
16: 3 the full; for ye have **b** us forth into this H3318
6 hath **b** you out from the land of Egypt: H3318
32 I **b** you forth from the land of Egypt. H3318
17: 3 this *that* thou hast **b** us up out of Egypt, H5927
18: 1 the LORD had **b** Israel out of Egypt; H3318
26 the hard causes they **b** unto Moses, but H935
19: 4 on eagles' wings, and **b** you unto myself. H935
17 And Moses **b** forth the people out of the H3318
20: 2 I *am* the LORD thy God, which have **b** H3318
22: 8 the house shall be **b** unto the judges, *to* H7126
29:10 And thou shalt cause a bullock to be **b** H7126
46 their God, that **b** them forth out of the H3318
32: 1 the man that **b** us up out of the land H5927
3 in their ears, and **b** *them* unto Aaron. H935
4 **b** thee up out of the land of Egypt. H5927
6 offerings, and **b** peace offerings; and H5066
8 have **b** thee up out of the land of Egypt. H5927
11 which thou hast **b** forth out of the land H3318
21 thou hast **b** so great a sin upon them? H935
23 the man that **b** us up out of the land H5927
33: 1 which thou hast **b** up out of the land of H5927
35:21 willing, *and* they **b** the LORD'S offering H935
22 hearted, *and* **b** bracelets, and earrings, H935
23 of rams, and badgers' skins, **b** *them*. H935
24 offering of silver and brass **b** the LORD'S H935
24 wood for any work of the service, **b** *it*. H935
25 their hands, and **b** that which they had H935
27 And the rulers **b** onyx stones, and stones H935
Ex 35:29 The children of Israel **b** a willing offering H935
36: 3 of Israel had **b** for the work of the service H935
3 it *withal*. And they **b** yet unto him free H935
39:33 And they **b** the tabernacle unto Moses, H935
40:21 And he **b** the ark into the tabernacle, H935
Lev 6:30 *any* of the blood is **b** into the tabernacle H935
8: 6 And Moses **b** Aaron and his sons, and H7126
13 And Moses **b** Aaron's sons, and put H7126
14 And he **b** the bullock for the sin H5066
18 And he **b** the ram for the burnt H7126
22 And he **b** the other ram, the ram of H7126
24 And he **b** Aaron's sons, and Moses put H7126
9: 5 And they **b** *that* which Moses H3947
9 And the sons of Aaron **b** the blood unto H7126
15 And he **b** the people's offering, and H7126
16 And he **b** the burnt offering, and H7126
17 And he **b** the meat offering, and took H7126
10:18 Behold, the blood of it was not **b** in H935
13: 2 then he shall be **b** unto Aaron the priest, H935
9 a man, then he shall be **b** unto the priest; H935
14: 2 cleansing: He shall be **b** unto the priest: H935
16:27 offering, whose blood was **b** in to make H935
19:36 which **b** you out of the land of Egypt. H3318
22:27 sheep, or a goat, is **b** forth, then it shall H3205
33 That **b** you out of the land of Egypt, to H3318
23:14 day that ye have **b** an offering unto your H935
15 the day that ye **b** the sheaf of the wave H935
43 in booths, when I **b** them out of the H3318
24:11 and cursed. And they **b** him unto Moses: H935
25:38 I *am* the LORD your God, which **b** you H3318
42 For they *are* my servants, which I **b** H3318
55 servants whom I **b** forth out of the land H3318
26:13 I *am* the LORD your God, which **b** you H3318
41 them, and have **b** them into the land of H935
45 ancestors, whom I **b** forth out of the H3318
Nu 6:13 he shall be **b** unto the door of the H935
7: 3 And they **b** their offering before the H935
3 and they **b** them before the tabernacle. H7126
9:13 because he **b** not the offering of the H7126
11:31 the LORD, and **b** quails from the sea, H1468
12:15 not till Miriam was **b** in *again*. H622
13:23 ***b*** of the pomegranates, and of the figs.
26 to Kadesh; and **b** back word unto H7725
32 And they **b** up an evil report of the land H3318
14: 3 And wherefore hath the LORD **b** us unto H935
15:33 gathering sticks **b** him unto Moses and H7126
36 And all the congregation **b** him without H3318
41 I *am* the LORD your God, which **b** you H3318
16:10 And he hath **b** thee near *to him*, and all H7126
13 *Is it* a small thing that thou hast **b** us H5927
14 Moreover thou hast not **b** us into a land H935
17: 8 was budded, and **b** forth buds, and H3318
9 And Moses **b** out all the rods from H3318
20: 4 And why have ye **b** up the congregation H935
16 angel, and hath **b** us forth out of Egypt: H3318
21: 5 have ye **b** us up out of Egypt to H5927
22:41 took Balaam, and **b** him up into the H5927
23: 7 king of Moab hath **b** me from Aram, H5148
14 And he **b** him into the field of Zophim, H3947
22 God **b** them out of Egypt; he hath as it H3318
28 And Balak **b** Balaam unto the top of H3947
24: 8 God **b** him forth out of Egypt; he hath H3318
25: 6 of Israel came and **b** unto his brethren H7126
27: 5 And Moses **b** their cause before the H7126
31:12 And they **b** the captives, and the prey, H935
50 We have therefore **b** an oblation for the H7126
54 of hundreds, and **b** it into the tabernacle H935
32:17 until we have **b** them unto their place: H935
Dt 1:25 in their hands, and **b** *it* down unto us, H3381
25 unto us, and **b** us word again, and H7725
27 hated us, he hath **b** us forth out of the H3318
4:20 But the LORD hath taken you, and **b** H3318
37 after them, and **b** thee out in his sight H3318
5: 6 I *am* the LORD thy God, which **b** thee H3318
15 the LORD thy God **b** thee out thence H3318
6:10 thy God shall have **b** thee into the land H935
12 the LORD, which **b** thee forth out of the H3318
21 **b** us out of Egypt with a mighty hand: H3318
23 And he **b** us out from thence, that he H3318
7: 8 hath the LORD **b** you out with a mighty H3318
19 the LORD thy God **b** thee out: so shall H3318
8:14 thy God, which **b** thee forth out of the H3318
15 no water; who **b** thee forth water out H3318
9: 4 the LORD hath **b** me in to possess this H935
12 which thou hast **b** forth out of Egypt H3318
26 which thou hast **b** forth out of Egypt H3318
28 them, he hath **b** them out to slay them H3318
11:29 thy God hath **b** thee in unto the land H935
13: 5 your God, which **b** you out of the land H3318

Dt 13:10 thy God, which **b** thee out of the land H3318
16: 1 God **b** thee forth out of Egypt by night. H3318
20: 1 **b** thee up out of the land of Egypt. H5927
22:19 because he hath **b** up an evil name H3318
26: 8 And the LORD **b** us forth out of Egypt H3318
9 And he hath **b** us into this place, and H935
10 And now, behold, I have **b** the firstfruits H935
13 thy God, I have **b** away the hallowed H1197
29:25 **b** them forth out of the land of Egypt: H3318
31:20 For when I shall have **b** them into the H935
21 have **b** them into the land which I sware. H935
33:14 And for the precious fruits ***b** forth* by the
Jos 2: 6 But she had **b** them up to the roof of H5927
6:23 spies went in, and **b** out Rahab, and H3318
23 she had; and they **b** out all her kindred, H3318
7: 7 hast thou at all **b** this people over H5674
14 In the morning therefore ye shall be **b** H7126
16 in the morning, and **b** Israel by their H7126
17 And he **b** the family of Judah; and he H7126
17 the Zarhites: and he **b** the family of the H7126
18 And he **b** his household man by man; H7126
23 of the tent, and **b** them unto Joshua, and H935
24 they **b** them unto the valley of Achor. H5927
8:23 Ai they took alive, and **b** him to Joshua. H7126
10:23 And they did so, and **b** forth those five H3318
24 And it came to pass, when they **b** out H3318
14: 7 out the land; and I **b** him word again H7725
22:32 of Israel, and **b** them word again. H7725
24: 5 them: and afterward I **b** you out. H3318
6 And I **b** your fathers out of Egypt: and H3318
7 the Egyptians, and **b** the sea upon them, H935
8 And I **b** you into the land of the H935
17 For the LORD our God, he *it is* that **b** us H5927
32 the children of Israel **b** up out of Egypt, H5927
Jdg 1: 7 **b** him to Jerusalem, and there he died. H935
2: 1 of Egypt, and have **b** you unto the land H935
12 fathers, which **b** them out of the land H3318
3:17 And he **b** the present unto Eglon king H7126
5:25 milk; she **b** forth butter in a lordly dish. H7126
6: 8 God of Israel, I **b** you up from Egypt, H5927
8 from Egypt, and **b** you forth out of the H3318
19 in a pot, and **b** *it* out unto him under H3318
7: 5 So he **b** down the people unto the H3381
25 Midian, and **b** the heads of Oreb and H935
11:35 thou hast **b** me very low, and thou H3766
14:11 **b** thirty companions to be with him. H3947
15:13 cords, and **b** him up from the rock. H5927
16: 8 Then the lords of the Philistines **b** up to H5927
18 unto her, and **b** money in their hand. H5927
21 out his eyes, and **b** him down to Gaza, H3381
31 and took him, and **b** *him* up, and H5927
18: 3 unto him, Who **b** thee hither? and what H935
19: 3 of asses: and she **b** him into her father's H935
21 So he **b** him into his house, and gave H935
25 concubine, and **b** her forth unto them; H3318
21:12 with any male: and they **b** them unto the H935
Ru 1:21 I went out full, and the LORD hath **b** H7725
2:18 gleaned: and she **b** forth, and gave to H3318
1Sa 1:24 bottle of wine, and **b** him unto the house H935
25 And they slew a bullock, and **b** the child H935
2:14 that the fleshhook **b** up the priest took H5927
19 a little coat, and **b** *it* to him from year H5927
5: 1 and **b** it from Eben-ezer unto Ashdod. H935
2 the ark of God, they **b** it into the house of H935
10 saying, They have **b** about the ark of H5437
6:21 Philistines have **b** again the ark of the H7725
7: 1 of the LORD, and **b** it into the house of H935
8: 8 the day that I **b** them up out of Egypt H5927
9:22 his servant, and **b** them into the parlour, H935
10:18 God of Israel, I **b** up Israel out of Egypt, H5927
27 **b** him no presents. But he held his peace. H935
12: 6 Aaron, and that **b** your fathers up out H5927
8 and Aaron, which **b** forth your fathers H3318
14:34 And all the people **b** every man his ox H5066
15:15 And Saul said, They have **b** them from H935
20 sent me, and have **b** Agag the king of H935
16:12 And he sent, and **b** him in. Now he *was* H935
17:54 the Philistine, and **b** it to Jerusalem; but H935
57 took him, and **b** him before Saul with H935
18:27 men; and David **b** their foreskins, and H935
19: 7 And Jonathan **b** David to Saul, and he H935
20: 8 for thou hast **b** thy servant into a H935
21: 8 for I have neither **b** my sword nor my H3947
14 wherefore *then* have ye **b** him to me? H935
15 Have I need of mad men, that ye have **b** H935
22: 4 And he **b** them before the king of H5148
23: 5 the Philistines, and **b** away their cattle, H5090
25:27 handmaid hath **b** unto my lord, let it H935
35 *that* which she had **b** him, and said unto H935
1Sa 28:25 And she **b** *it* before Saul, and before his H5066
30: 7 Abiathar **b** thither the ephod to David. H5066
11 in the field, and **b** him to David, and H3947
16 And when he had **b** him down, behold, H3381
2Sa 1:10 and have **b** them hither unto my lord. H935
2: 8 of Saul, and **b** him over to Mahanaim; H5674
3:22 a troop, and **b** in a great spoil with H935
26 Abner, which **b** him again from the H7725
4: 8 And they **b** the head of Ish-bosheth unto H935
10 thinking to have **b** good tidings, I took H1319
6: 3 a new cart, and **b** it out of the house of H5375
4 And they **b** it out of the house of H5375
12 So David went and **b** up the ark of God H5927
15 So David and all the house of Israel **b** H5927
17 And they **b** in the ark of the LORD, and H935
7: 6 the time that I **b** up the children of H5927
18 my house, that thou hast **b** me hitherto? H935
8: 2 became David's servants, *and* **b** gifts. H5375
6 to David, *and* **b** gifts. And the LORD H5375
7 of Hadadezer, and **b** them to Jerusalem. H935
10 Toi. And *Joram* **b** with him vessels of H1961
10:16 And Hadarezer sent, and **b** out the H3318
12:30 head. And he **b** forth the spoil of the H3318
31 And he **b** forth the people that *were* H3318
13:10 she had made, and **b** *them* into the H935
11 And when she had **b** *them* unto him to H5066
18 Then his servant **b** her out, and bolted H3318
14:23 So Joab arose and went to Geshur, and **b** H935
17:28 **B** beds, and basons, and earthen H5066
19:41 thee away, and have **b** the king, and his H5674
21: 8 of Saul, whom she **b** up for Adriel the H3205
13 And he **b** up from thence the bones of H5927
22:20 He **b** me forth also into a large place: H3318
23:16 gate, and took *it,* and **b** *it* to David: H935
1Ki 1: 3 a Shunammite, and **b** her to the king. H935
38 king David's mule, and **b** him to Gihon. H3212
53 So king Solomon sent, and they **b** him H3381
2:30 And Benaiah **b** the king word again, H7725
40 went, and **b** his servants from Gath. H935
3: 1 daughter, and **b** her into the city of H935
24 And they **b** a sword before the king. H935
4:21 of Egypt: they **b** presents, and served H5066
28 and dromedaries **b** they unto the place H935
5:17 And the king commanded, and they **b** H5265
6: 7 before it was **b** thither: so that there H4551
7:51 And Solomon **b** in the things which H935
8: 4 And they **b** up the ark of the LORD, H5927
6 And the priests **b** in the ark of the H935
16 Since the day that I **b** forth my people H3318
21 he **b** them out of the land of Egypt. H3318
9: 9 their God, who **b** forth their fathers out H3318
9 hath the LORD **b** upon them all this evil. H935
28 twenty talents, and **b** *it* to king Solomon. H935
10:11 And the navy also of Hiram, that **b** H5375
11 gold from Ophir, **b** in from Ophir great H935
25 And they **b** every man his present, H935
28 And Solomon had horses **b** out of H4161
12:28 **b** thee up out of the land of Egypt. H5927
13:20 unto the prophet that **b** him back: H7725
23 for the prophet whom he had **b** back. H7725
26 And when the prophet that **b** him back H7725
29 upon the ass, and **b** it back: and the old H7725
14:28 **b** them back into the guard chamber. H7725
15:15 And he **b** in the things which his father H935
17: 6 And the ravens **b** him bread and flesh in H935
20 hast thou also **b** evil upon the widow
23 And Elijah took the child, and **b** him H3381
18:40 them: and Elijah **b** them down to the H3381
20: 9 departed, and **b** him word again. H7725
39 turned aside, and **b** a man unto me, and H935
22:37 So the king died, and was **b** to Samaria; H935
2Ki 2:20 put salt therein. And they **b** *it* to him. H3947
4: 5 her sons, who **b** *the vessels* to her; and H5066
20 And when he had taken him, and **b** him H935
42 Baal-shalisha, and **b** the man of God H935
5: 2 and had **b** away captive out of H7617
6 And he **b** the letter to the king of Israel, H935
20 that which he **b**: but, *as* the LORD liveth, H935
10: 1 them that **b** up Ahab's *children,* saying, H539
6 great men of the city, which **b** them up. H1431
8 saying, They have **b** the heads of the H935
22 Baal. And he **b** them forth vestments. H3318
24 the men whom I have **b** into your hands H935
26 And they **b** forth the images out of the H3318
11: 4 and the guard, and **b** them to him into H935
12 And he **b** forth the king's son, and put H3318
19 of the land; and they **b** down the king H3381
12: 4 things that is **b** into the house of the H935
9 *that was* **b** into the house of the LORD. H935
2Ki 12:13 *that was* **b** into the house of the LORD: H935
16 sin money was not **b** into the house of H935
14:20 And they **b** him on horses: and he was H5375
16:14 And he **b** also the brasen altar, which H7126
17: 4 king of Egypt, and **b** no present to the H5927
7 God, which had **b** them up out of the H5927
24 And the king of Assyria **b** *men* from H935
27 priests whom ye **b** from thence; and let H1540
36 But the LORD, who **b** you up out of the H5927
19:25 it? now have I **b** it to pass, that thou H935
20:11 the LORD: and he **b** the shadow ten H7725
20 and a conduit, and **b** water into the city, H935
22: 4 the silver which is **b** into the house of the H935
9 to the king, and **b** the king word again, H7725
20 place. And they **b** the king word again. H7725
23: 6 And he **b** out the grove from the house H3318
8 And he **b** all the priests out of the cities H935
30 Megiddo, and **b** him to Jerusalem, and H935
24:16 king of Babylon **b** captive to Babylon. H935
25: 6 So they took the king, and **b** him up to H5927
20 took these, and **b** them to the king of H3212
1Ch 5:26 of Manasseh, and **b** them unto Halah, H935
10:12 of his sons, and **b** them to Jabesh, and H935
11:18 and took *it,* and **b** *it* to David: but David H935
19 *of* their lives they **b** it. Therefore he H935
12:40 and Naphtali, **b** bread on asses, and H935
13:13 So David **b** not the ark *home* to himself H5493
14:17 **b** the fear of him upon all nations. H5414
15:28 Thus all Israel **b** up the ark of the H5927
16: 1 So they **b** the ark of God, and set it in the H935
17: 5 the day that I **b** up Israel unto this day; H5927
16 house, that thou hast **b** me hitherto? H935
18: 2 became David's servants, *and* **b** gifts. H5375
6 servants, *and* **b** gifts. Thus the LORD H5375
7 of Hadarezer, and **b** them to Jerusalem. H935
8 cities of Hadarezer, **b** David very much H3947
11 and the gold that he **b** from all *these* H5375
20: 2 head: and he **b** also exceeding much H3318
3 And he **b** out the people that *were* in it, H3318
22: 4 of Tyre **b** much cedar wood to David. H935
2Ch 1: 4 But the ark of God had David **b** up H5927
16 And Solomon had horses **b** out of H4161
17 And they fetched up, and **b** forth out of H3318
17 and fifty: and so **b** they out *horses* for H3318
5: 1 and Solomon **b** in *all* the things that H935
5 And they **b** up the ark, and the H5927
7 And the priests **b** in the ark of the H935
6: 5 Since the day that I **b** forth my people H3318
7:22 fathers, which **b** them forth out of the H3318
22 hath he **b** all this evil upon them. H935
8:11 And Solomon **b** up the daughter of H5927
18 of gold, and **b** *them* to king Solomon. H935
9:10 of Solomon, which **b** gold from Ophir, H935
10 **b** algum trees and precious stones. H935
12 *that* which she had **b** unto the king. So H935
14 and merchants **b**. And all the kings of H935
14 country **b** gold and silver to Solomon. H935
24 And they **b** every man his present, H935
28 And they **b** unto Solomon horses out of H3318
10: 8 **b** up with him, that stood before him. H1431
10 And the young men that were **b** up H1431
12:11 **b** them again into the guard chamber. H7725
13:18 Thus the children of Israel were **b** H3665
15:11 *which* they had **b**, seven hundred oxen H935
18 And he **b** into the house of God the H935
16: 2 Then Asa **b** out silver and gold out of H3318
17: 5 hand; and all Judah **b** to Jehoshaphat H5414
11 Also *some* of the Philistines **b** H935
11 and the Arabians **b** him flocks, seven H935
19: 4 Ephraim, and **b** them back unto the H7725
22: 9 hid in Samaria,) and **b** him to Jehu: and H935
23:11 Then they **b** out the king's son, and put H3318
14 Then Jehoiada the priest **b** out the H3318
20 of the land, and **b** down the king from H3381
24:10 rejoiced, and **b** in, and cast into the H935
11 time the chest was **b** unto the king's H935
14 And when they had finished *it,* they **b** H935
25:12 away captive, and **b** them unto the top H935
14 the Edomites, that he **b** the gods of the H935
23 and **b** him to Jerusalem, and H935
28 And they **b** him upon horses, and H5375
28: 5 them captives, and **b** *them* to Damascus. H935
8 from them, and **b** the spoil to Samaria. H935
15 upon asses, and **b** them to Jericho, the H935
19 For the LORD **b** Judah low because of H3665
27 but they **b** him not into the sepulchres H935
29: 4 And he **b** in the priests and the Levites, H935
16 LORD, to cleanse *it,* and **b** out all the H3318
21 And they **b** seven bullocks, and seven H935

2Ch 29:23 And they **b** forth the he goats *for* the H5066
31 And the congregation **b** in sacrifices and H935
32 the congregation **b**, was threescore and H935
30:15 themselves, and **b** in the burnt offerings H935
31: 5 the children of Israel **b** in abundance the H935
5 tithe of all *things* **b** they in abundantly. H935
6 of Judah, they also **b** in the tithe of oxen H935
12 And **b** in the offerings and the tithes and H935
32:23 And many **b** gifts unto the LORD to H935
30 of Gihon, and **b** it straight down to the H3474
33:11 Wherefore the LORD **b** upon them the H935
13 his supplication, and **b** him again to H7725
34: 9 money that was **b** into the house of God, H935
14 And when they **b** out the money that H3318
14 money that was **b** into the house of the H935
16 to the king, and **b** the king word back H7725
28 same. So they **b** the king word again. H7725
35:24 he had; and they **b** him to Jerusalem, H3212
36:10 sent, and **b** him to Babylon, with H935
17 Therefore he **b** upon them the king of H5927
18 of his princes; all *these* he **b** to Babylon. H935
Ezr 1: 7 Also Cyrus the king **b** forth the vessels H3318
7 had **b** forth out of Jerusalem, H3318
11 **b** up from Babylon unto Jerusalem. H5927
4: 2 king of Assur, which **b** us up hither. H5927
10 noble Asnappar **b** over, and set in the H1541
5:14 *was* in Jerusalem, and **b** them into the H2987
6: 5 *is* at Jerusalem, and **b** unto Babylon, be H2987
5 be restored, and **b** again unto the H1946
8:18 our God upon us they **b** us a man of H935
Neh 4:15 unto us, and God had **b** their counsel to H6565
5: 5 of our daughters are **b** unto bondage H3533
8: 2 And Ezra the priest **b** the law before the H935
16 So the people went forth, and **b** *them*, H935
9:18 *is* thy God that **b** thee up out of Egypt, H5927
33 Howbeit thou *art* just in all that is **b** H935
12:31 Then I **b** up the princes of Judah upon H5927
13: 9 and thither **b** I again the vessels of H7725
12 Then **b** all Judah the tithe of the corn H935
15 which they **b** into Jerusalem on the H935
16 Tyre also therein, which **b** fish, and all H935
19 no burden be **b** in on the sabbath day. H935
Est 1:17 to be **b** in before him, but she came not. H935
2: 7 And he **b** up Hadassah, that *is*, Esther, H539
8 that Esther was **b** also unto the king's H3947
20 like as when she was **b** up with him. H539
6: 8 Let the royal apparel be **b** which the king H935
11 Mordecai, and **b** him on horseback H7392
9:11 the palace was **b** before the king. H935
Job 4:12 Now a thing was secretly **b** to me, and H1589
10:18 Wherefore then hast thou **b** me forth H3318
14:21 **b** low, but he perceiveth *it* not of them. H6819
21:30 shall be **b** forth to the day of wrath. H2986
32 Yet shall he be **b** to the grave, and shall H2986
24:24 but are gone and **b** low; they are taken H4355
31:18 (For from my youth he was **b** up with H1431
42:11 that the LORD had **b** upon him: every H935
Ps 7:14 mischief, and **b** forth falsehood. H3205
18:19 He **b** me forth also into a large place; H3318
20: 8 They are **b** down and fallen: but we are H3766
22:15 thou hast **b** me into the dust of death. H8239
30: 3 O LORD, thou hast **b** up my soul from H5927
35: 4 and **b** to confusion that devise my hurt. H2659
26 Let them be ashamed and **b** to H2659
40: 2 He **b** me up also out of an horrible pit, H5927
45:14 She shall be **b** unto the king in raiment H2986
14 that follow her shall be **b** unto thee. H935
15 shall they be **b**: they shall enter into H2986
71:24 are **b** unto shame, that seek my hurt. H2659
73:19 How are they *b* into desolation, as in a
78:16 He **b** streams also out of the rock, and H3318
26 by his power he **b** in the south wind. H5090
54 And he **b** them to the border of his H935
71 with young he **b** him to feed Jacob his H935
79: 8 prevent us: for we are **b** very low. H1809
80: 8 Thou hast **b** a vine out of Egypt: thou H5265
81:10 I *am* the LORD thy God, which **b** thee H5927
85: 1 thou hast **b** back the captivity of Jacob. H7725
89:40 thou hast **b** his strong holds to ruin. H7760
90: 2 Before the mountains were **b** forth, or H3205
105:30 Their land **b** forth frogs in abundance, H8317
37 He **b** them forth also with silver and H3318
40 *The people* asked, and he **b** quails, and H935
43 And he **b** forth his people with joy, *and* H3318
106:42 **b** into subjection under their hand. H3665
43 and were **b** low for their iniquity. H4355
107:12 Therefore he **b** down their heart with H3665
14 He **b** them out of darkness and the H3318
39 Again, they are minished and **b** low H7817

Ps 116: 6 simple: I was **b** low, and he helped me. H1809
136:11 And **b** out Israel from among them: for H3318
142: 6 Attend unto my cry; for I am **b** very H1809
Prv 6:26 woman *a man is b* to a piece of bread:
8:24 When *there were* no depths, I was **b** H2342
25 settled, before the hills was I **b** forth: H2342
30 Then I was by him, *as* one **b** up *with* H539
Ecc 12: 4 the daughters of musick shall be **b** low; H7817
Song 1: 4 after thee: the king hath **b** me into his H935
2: 4 He **b** me to the banqueting house, and H935
3: 4 let him go, until I had **b** him into my H935
8: 5 there thy mother **b** thee forth: there she H2254
5 there she **b** thee forth *that* bare thee. H2254
Isa 1: 2 nourished and **b** up children, and they H7311
2:12 *that is* lifted up; and he shall be **b** low: H8213
5: 2 forth grapes, and it **b** forth wild grapes. H6213
4 forth grapes, **b** it forth wild grapes? H6213
15 And the mean man shall be **b** down, H7817
14:11 Thy pomp is **b** down to the grave, *and* H3381
15 Yet thou shalt be **b** down to hell, to the H3381
15: 1 is laid waste, *and* **b** to silence; because H1820
1 of Moab is laid waste, *and* **b** to silence; H1820
18: 7 In that time shall the present be **b** unto H2986
21:14 The inhabitants of the land of Tema **b** H857
23:13 the palaces thereof; *and* he **b** it to ruin. H7760
25: 5 of the terrible ones shall be **b** low. H6030
26:18 we have as it were **b** forth wind; we H3205
29: 4 And thou shalt be **b** down, *and* shalt H8213
20 For the terrible one is **b** to nought, and H656
37:26 it? now have I **b** it to pass, that thou H935
43:14 and have **b** down all their nobles, H3381
23 Thou hast not **b** me the small cattle of H935
45:10 to the woman, What hast thou **b** forth? H2342
48:15 called him: I have **b** him, and he shall H935
49:21 fro? and who hath **b** up these? Behold, I H1431
51:18 *whom* she hath **b** forth; neither *is there* H3205
18 hand of all the sons *that* she hath **b** up. H1431
53: 7 not his mouth: he is **b** as a lamb to the H2986
59:16 therefore his arm **b** salvation unto him; H3467
60:11 Gentiles, and *that* their kings *may be* **b**. H5090
62: 9 they that have **b** it together shall drink H6908
63: 5 mine own arm **b** salvation unto me; H3467
11 Where *is* he that **b** them up out of the H5927
66: 7 Before she travailed, she **b** forth; before H3205
8 Zion travailed, she **b** forth her children. H3205
Jer 2: 6 *is* the LORD that **b** us up out of the H5927
7 And I **b** you into a plentiful country, to H935
27 a stone, Thou hast **b** me forth: for they H3205
7:22 in the day that I **b** them out of the land H3318
10: 9 Silver spread into plates is **b** from H935
11: 4 in the day *that* I **b** them forth out of the H3318
7 in the day *that* I **b** them up out of the H5927
19 But I *was* like a lamb *or* an ox *that* is **b** H2986
15: 8 of the seas: I have **b** upon them against H935
16:14 LORD liveth, that **b** up the children of H5927
15 But, The LORD liveth, that **b** up the H5927
20: 3 that Pashur **b** forth Jeremiah out of H3318
15 Cursed *be* the man who **b** tidings to my H1319
23: 7 liveth, which **b** up the children of Israel H5927
8 But, The LORD liveth, which **b** up and H5927
24: 1 Jerusalem, and had **b** them to Babylon. H935
26:23 out of Egypt, and **b** him unto Jehoiakim H935
27:16 now shortly be **b** again from Babylon: H7725
32:21 And hast **b** forth thy people Israel out H3318
42 Like as I have **b** all this great evil upon H935
34:11 to return, and **b** them into subjection H3533
13 in the day that I **b** them forth out of the H3318
16 to return, and **b** them into subjection, H3533
35: 4 And I **b** them into the house of the H935
37:14 took Jeremiah, and **b** him to the princes. H935
38:22 house *shall be* **b** forth to the king of H3318
39: 5 had taken him, they **b** him up to H5927
40: 3 Now the LORD hath **b** *it*, and done H935
41:16 whom he had **b** again from Gibeon: H7725
44: 2 all the evil that I have **b** upon Jerusalem, H935
50:25 and hath **b** forth the weapons of H3318
51:10 The LORD hath **b** forth our H3318
52:26 took them, and **b** them to the king of H3212
31 of Judah, and **b** him forth out of prison, H3218
Lam 2: 2 of Judah; he hath **b** *them* down to the H5060
22 and **b** up hath mine enemy consumed. H7235
3: 2 He hath led me, and **b** *me into* H3212
4: 5 were **b** up in scarlet embrace dunghills. H539
Ezk 8: 3 the heaven, and **b** me in the visions of H935
7 And he **b** me to the door of the court; H935
14 Then he **b** me to the door of the gate of H935
16 And he **b** me into the inner court of the H935
11: 1 Moreover the spirit lifted me up, and **b** H935
24 Afterwards the spirit took me up, and **b** H935

Ezk 12: 7 And I did so as I was commanded: I **b** H3318
7 wall with mine hand; I **b** *it* forth in the H3318
14:22 that shall be **b** forth, *both* sons and H3318
22 the evil that I have **b** upon Jerusalem, H935
22 *even* concerning all that I have **b** upon it. H935
17: 6 **b** forth branches, and shot forth sprigs. H5375
24 I the LORD have **b** down the high tree, H8213
19: 3 And she **b** up one of her whelps: it H5927
4 in their pit, and they **b** him with chains H935
9 ward in chains, and **b** him to the king of H935
9 of Babylon: they **b** him into holds, that H935
20:10 Egypt, and **b** them into the wilderness. H935
14 heathen, in whose sight I **b** them out. H3318
22 heathen, in whose sight I **b** them forth. H3318
28 *For* when I had **b** them into the land, *for* H935
21: 7 shall be **b** to pass, saith the Lord GOD. H1961
23: 8 Neither left she her whoredoms *b* from
27 and thy whoredom *b* from the land of
42 common sort *were* **b** Sabeans from the H935
27: 6 *of* ivory, *b* out of the isles of Chittim.
15 of thine hand: they **b** thee *for* a present H7725
26 Thy rowers have **b** thee into great H935
29: 5 fields; thou shalt not be **b** together, nor H622
30:11 nations, shall be **b** to destroy the land: H935
31:18 yet shalt thou be **b** down with the trees H3381
34: 4 neither have ye **b** again that which was H7725
37:13 and **b** you up out of your graves, H5927
38: 8 the land *that is* **b** back from the sword, H7725
8 always waste: but it is **b** forth out of the H3318
39:27 When I have **b** them again from the H7725
40: 1 LORD was upon me, and **b** me thither. H935
2 In the visions of God **b** he me into the H935
3 And he **b** me thither, and, behold, *there* H935
4 unto thee *art* thou **b** hither: declare all H935
17 Then **b** he me into the outward court, H935
24 After that he **b** me toward the south, H3212
28 And he **b** me to the inner court by the H935
32 And he **b** me into the inner court toward H935
35 And he **b** me to the north gate, and H935
48 And he **b** me to the porch of the house, H935
49 cubits; and *he b me* by the steps whereby
41: 1 Afterward he **b** me to the temple, and H935
42: 1 Then he **b** me forth into the utter court, H3318
1 the north: and he **b** me into the chamber H935
15 inner house, he **b** me forth toward the H3318
43: 1 Afterward he **b** me to the gate, *even* the H3212
5 So the spirit took me up, and **b** me into H935
44: 1 Then he **b** me back the way of the gate H7725
4 Then **b** he me the way of the north gate H935
7 In that ye have **b** *into my sanctuary* H935
46:19 After he **b** me through the entry, which H935
21 Then he **b** me forth into the utter court, H3318
47: 1 Afterward he **b** me again unto the door H7725
2 Then **b** he me out of the way of the gate H3318
3 cubits, and he **b** me through the H5674
4 Again he measured a thousand, and **b** H5674
4 a thousand, and **b** me through; the H5674
6 seen *this*? Then he **b** me, and caused H3212
8 sea: *which being* **b** forth into the sea, H3318
Dan 1: 2 of his god; and he **b** the vessels into the H935
9 Now God had **b** Daniel into favour and H5414
18 **b** them in before Nebuchadnezzar. H935
2:25 Then Arioch **b** in Daniel before the H5954
3:13 Then they **b** these men before the king. H858
5: 3 Then they **b** the golden vessels that were H858
13 Then was Daniel **b** in before the king. H5954
13 whom the king my father **b** out of Jewry? H858
15 have been **b** in before me, that they H5954
23 and they have **b** the vessels of his house H858
6:16 Then the king commanded, and they **b** H858
17 And a stone was **b**, and laid upon the H858
18 of musick **b** before him: and his H5954
24 And the king commanded, and they **b** H858
7:13 days, and they **b** him near before him. H7127
9:14 upon the evil, and **b** it upon us: for the H935
15 And now, O Lord our God, that hast **b** H3318
11: 6 up, and they that **b** her, and he that H935
Hos 12:13 And by a prophet the LORD **b** Israel H5927
Am 2:10 Also I **b** you up from the land of Egypt, H5927
3: 1 I **b** up from the land of Egypt, saying, H5927
9: 7 LORD. Have not I **b** up Israel out of the H5927
Oba 7 All the men of thy confederacy have **b** H7971
Jna 2: 6 ever: yet hast thou **b** up my life from H5927
Mic 5: 3 which travaileth hath **b** forth: then the H3205
6: 4 For I **b** thee up out of the land of Egypt, H5927
Nah 2: 7 she shall be **b** up, and her maids shall H5927
Hag 1: 9 little; and when ye **b** *it* home, I did blow H935
2:19 **b** forth: from this day will I bless *you*. H5375
Zec 10:11 of Assyria shall be **b** down, and the H3381

Mal 1:13 of hosts; and ye **b** *that which was* torn, H935
13 the sick; thus ye **b** an offering: should I H935
Mt 1:12 And after they were **b** to Babylon, *G3350*
25 And knew her not till she had **b** forth *G5088*
4:24 all Syria: and they **b** unto him all sick *G4374*
8:16 When the even was come, they **b** unto *G4374*
9: 2 And, behold, they **b** to him a man sick *G4374*
32 As they went out, behold, they **b** to him *G4374*
10:18 And ye shall be **b** before governors and *G71*
11:23 heaven, shalt be **b** down to hell: for if *G2601*
12:22 Then was **b** unto him one possessed *G4374*
25 against itself is **b** to desolation; and *G2049*
13: 8 But other fell into good ground, and **b** *G1325*
26 was sprung up, and **b** forth fruit, then *G4160*
14:11 And his head was **b** in a charger, and *G5342*
11 the damsel: and she **b** *it* to her mother. *G5342*
35 and **b** unto him all that were diseased; *G4374*
16: 8 because ye have **b** no bread? *G2983*
17:16 And I **b** him to thy disciples, and they *G4374*
18:24 to reckon, one was **b** unto him, which *G4374*
19:13 Then were there **b** unto him little *G4374*
21: 7 And **b** the ass, and the colt, and put on *G71*
22:19 Shew me the tribute money. And they **b** *G4374*
25:20 talents came and **b** other five talents, *G4374*
27: 3 himself, and **b** again the thirty pieces *G654*
Mk 1:32 the sun did set, they **b** unto him all that *G5342*
4: 8 increased; and **b** forth, some thirty, *G5342*
21 And he said unto them, Is a candle **b** to *G2064*
29 But when the fruit is **b** forth, *G3860*
6:27 his head to be **b**: and he went and *G5342*
28 And **b** his head in a charger, and gave *G5342*
9:17 Master, I have **b** unto thee my son, *G5342*
20 And they **b** him unto him: and when he *G5342*
10:13 And they **b** young children to him, that *G4374*
13 disciples rebuked those that **b** *them*. *G4374*
11: 7 And they **b** the colt to Jesus, and cast *G71*
12:16 And they **b** *it*. And he saith unto them, *G5342*
13: 9 and ye shall be **b** before rulers and *G2476*
Lk 1:57 be delivered; and she **b** forth a son. *G1080*
2: 7 And she **b** forth her firstborn son, and *G5088*
22 they **b** him to Jerusalem, to *G321*
27 when the parents **b** in the child Jesus, *G1521*
3: 5 and hill shall be **b** low; and the crooked *G5013*
4: 9 And he **b** him to Jerusalem, and set him *G71*
16 he had been **b** up: and, as his custom *G5142*
40 divers diseases **b** them unto him; and *G71*
5:11 And when they had **b** their ships to *G2609*
18 And, behold, men **b** in a bed a man *G5342*
7:37 house, **b** an alabaster box of ointment, *G2865*
10:34 **b** him to an inn, and took care of him. *G71*
11:17 against itself is **b** to desolation; and a *G2049*
12:16 a certain rich man **b** forth plentifully: *G2164*
18:15 And they **b** unto him also infants, that *G4374*
40 him to be **b** unto him: and when *G71*
19:35 And they **b** him to Jesus: and they cast *G71*
21:12 into prisons, being **b** before kings and *G71*
22:54 and led *him*, and **b** him into the high *G1521*
23:14 Said unto them, Ye have **b** this man *G4374*
Jn 1:42 And he **b** him to Jesus. And when Jesus *G71*
4:33 Hath any man **b** him *ought* to eat? *G5342*
7:45 said unto them, Why have ye not **b** him? *G71*
8: 3 And the scribes and Pharisees **b** unto *G71*
9:13 They **b** to the Pharisees him that *G71*
18:16 her that kept the door, and **b** in Peter. *G1521*
19:13 that saying, he **b** Jesus forth, and sat *G71*
39 by night, and **b** a mixture of myrrh *G5342*
Act 4:34 sold them, and **b** the prices of the *G5342*
37 Having land, sold *it*, and **b** the money, *G5342*
5: 2 privy *to it*, and **b** a certain part, and *G5342*
15 Insomuch that they **b** forth the sick *G1627*
19 doors, and **b** them forth, and said, *G1806*
21 and sent to the prison to have them **b**. *G71*
26 with the officers, and **b** them without *G71*
27 And when they had **b** them, they set *G71*
36 him, were scattered, and **b** to nought. *G1096*
6:12 caught him, and **b** *him* to the council, *G71*
7:36 He **b** them out, after that he had *G1806*
40 this Moses, which **b** us out of the land *G1806*
45 that came after **b** in with Jesus into the *G1521*
9: 8 the hand, and **b** *him* into Damascus. *G1521*
27 But Barnabas took him, and **b** *him* to *G71*
30 *Which* when the brethren knew, they **b** *G2609*
39 he was come, they **b** him into the upper *G321*
11:26 And when he had found him, he **b** him *G71*
12: 6 And when Herod would have **b** him *G4254*
17 how the Lord had **b** him out of the *G1806*
13: 1 **b** up with Herod the tetrarch, and Saul. *G4939*
17 with an high arm **b** he them out of it. *G1806*
14:13 before their city, **b** oxen and garlands *G5342*
Act 15: 3 And being **b** on their way by the *G4311*
16:16 met us, which **b** her masters much gain *G3930*
20 And **b** them to the magistrates, saying, *G4317*
30 And **b** them out, and said, Sirs, what *G4254*
34 And when he had **b** them into his house, *G321*
39 them, and **b** *them* out, and desired *G1806*
17:15 And they that conducted Paul **b** him *G71*
19 And they took him, and **b** him unto *G71*
18:12 Paul, and **b** him to the judgment seat, *G71*
19:12 So that from his body were **b** unto the *G2018*
19 which used curious arts **b** their books *G4851*
24 **b** no small gain unto the craftsmen; *G3930*
37 For ye have **b** hither these men, which *G71*
20:12 And they **b** the young man alive, and *G71*
21: 5 way; and they all **b** us on our way, with *G4311*
16 of Caesarea, and **b** with them one *G71*
28 place: and further **b** Greeks also into *G1521*
29 that Paul had **b** into the temple.) *G1521*
22: 3 *a city* in Cilicia, yet **b** up in this city at *G397*
24 him to be **b** into the castle, and bade *G71*
30 **b** Paul down, and set him before them. *G2609*
23:18 So he took him, and **b** *him* to the chief *G71*
28 him, I **b** him forth into their council: *G2609*
31 Paul, and **b** *him* by night to Antipatris. *G71*
25: 6 judgment seat commanded Paul to be **b**. *G71*
17 and commanded the man to be **b** forth. *G71*
18 stood up, they **b** none accusation of *G2018*
23 Festus' commandment Paul was **b** forth. *G71*
26 Wherefore I have **b** him forth before *G4254*
27:24 Saying, Fear not, Paul; thou must be **b** *G3936*
Ro 15:24 my journey, and to be **b** on my way *G4311*
1Co 6:12 I will not be **b** under the power of any. *G1850*
15:54 then shall be **b** to pass the saying that *G1096*
2Co 1:16 you to be **b** on my way toward Judaea. *G4311*
Gal 2: 4 unawares **b** in, who came in privily *G3920*
1Th 3: 6 you unto us, and **b** us good tidings of *G2097*
1Ti 5:10 works; if she have **b** up children, if she *G5044*
6: 7 For we **b** nothing into *this* world, *and it* *G1533*
2Ti 1:10 death, and hath **b** life and immortality *G5461*
Heb 13:11 whose blood is **b** into the sanctuary by *G1533*
20 Now the God of peace, that **b** again from *G321*
Jas 5:18 gave rain, and the earth **b** forth her fruit. *G985*
1Pt 1:13 the grace that is to be **b** unto you at the *G5342*
2Pt 2:19 of the same is he **b** in bondage. *G1402*
Rev 12: 5 And she **b** forth a man child, who was *G5088*
13 woman which **b** forth the man *child*. *G5088*

BROUGHTEST
Ex 32: 7 which thou **b** out of the land of Egypt, H5927
Nu 14:13 hear *it*, (for thou **b** up this people in thy H5927
Dt 9:28 Lest the land whence thou **b** us out say, H3318
29 which thou **b** out by thy mighty power H3318
2Sa 5: 2 that leddest out and **b** in Israel: and the H935
1Ki 8:51 which thou **b** forth out of Egypt, from H3318
53 when thou **b** our fathers out of Egypt, H3318
1Ch 11: 2 that leddest out and **b** in Israel: and the H935
Neh 9: 7 Abram, and **b** him forth out of Ur H3318
15 for their hunger, and **b** forth water for H3318
23 of heaven, and **b** them into the land, H935
Ps 66:11 Thou **b** us into the net; thou laidst H935
12 but thou **b** us out into a wealthy *place*. H3318

BROW
Isa 48: 4 neck *is* an iron sinew, and thy **b** brass; H4696
Lk 4:29 led him unto the **b** of the hill whereon *G3790*

BROWN
Gen 30:32 cattle, and all the **b** cattle among the H2345
33 the goats, and **b** among the sheep, that H2345
35 in it, and all the **b** among the sheep, H2345
40 and all the **b** in the flock of Laban; H2345

BRUISE
Gen 3:15 her seed; it shall **b** thy head, and thou H7779
15 thy head, and thou shalt **b** his heel. H7779
Isa 28:28 of his cart, nor **b** it *with* his horsemen. H1854
53:10 Yet it pleased the LORD to **b** him; he H1792
Jer 30:12 For thus saith the LORD, Thy **b** *is* H7667
Dan 2:40 all these, shall it break in pieces and **b**. H7490
Nah 3:19 *There is* no healing of thy **b**; thy wound H7667
Ro 16:20 And the God of peace shall **b** Satan *G4937*

BRUISED
Lev 22:24 that which is **b**, or crushed, or broken, H4600
2Ki 18:21 upon the staff of this **b** reed, *even* upon H7533
Isa 28:28 Bread *corn* is **b**; because he will not ever H1854
42: 3 A **b** reed shall he not break, and the H7533
53: 5 *he was* **b** for our iniquities: the H1792
Ezk 23: 3 there they **b** the teats of their virginity. H6213
Ezk 23: 8 with her, and they **b** the breasts of her H6213
Mt 12:20 A **b** reed shall he not break, and *G4937*
Lk 4:18 blind, to set at liberty them that are **b**, *G2352*

BRUISES
Isa 1: 6 it; *but* wounds, and **b**, and putrifying H2250

BRUISING
Ezk 23:21 of thy youth, in **b** thy teats by the H6213
Lk 9:39 and **b** him hardly departeth from him. *G4937*

BRUIT
Jer 10:22 Behold, the noise of the **b** is come, and H8052
Nah 3:19 all that hear the **b** of thee shall clap the H8088

BRUTE
2Pt 2:12 But these, as natural **b** beasts, made to *G249*
Jude 10 know naturally, as **b** beasts, in those *G249*

BRUTISH
Ps 49:10 the fool and the **b** person perish, and H1197
92: 6 A **b** man knoweth not; neither doth a H1197
94: 8 Understand, ye **b** among the people: H1197
Prv 12: 1 but he that hateth reproof *is* **b**. H1197
30: 2 Surely I *am* more **b** than *any* man, and H1197
Isa 19:11 is become **b**: how say ye unto Pharaoh, H1197
Jer 10: 8 But they are altogether **b** and foolish: H1197
14 Every man is **b** in *his* knowledge: every H1197
21 For the pastors are become **b**, and have H1197
51:17 Every man is **b** by *his* knowledge; every H1197
Ezk 21:31 hand of **b** men, *and* skilful to destroy. H1197

BUCK See ROEBUCK.

BUCKET
Isa 40:15 Behold, the nations *are* as a drop of a **b**, H1805

BUCKETS
Nu 24: 7 He shall pour the water out of his **b**, and H1805

BUCKLER
2Sa 22:31 he *is* a **b** to all them that trust in him. H4043
1Ch 5:18 men able to bear **b** and sword, and to H4043
12: 8 handle shield and **b**, whose faces *were* H7420
Ps 18: 2 I will trust; my **b**, and the horn of my H4043
30 he *is* a **b** to all those that trust in him. H4043
35: 2 Take hold of shield and **b**, and stand up H6793
91: 4 trust: his truth *shall be thy* shield and **b**. H5507
Prv 2: 7 *he is* a **b** to them that walk uprightly. H4043
Jer 46: 3 Order ye the **b** and shield, and draw H4043
Ezk 23:24 shall set against thee **b** and shield and H6793
26: 8 thee, and lift up the **b** against thee. H6793

BUCKLERS
2Ch 23: 9 spears, and **b**, and shields, that *had* H4043
Job 15:26 *his* neck, upon the thick bosses of his **b**: H4043
Song 4: 4 a thousand **b**, all shields of mighty men. H4043
Ezk 38: 4 company *with* **b** and shields, all of H6793
39: 9 the shields and the **b**, the bows and the H6793

BUD
Job 14: 9 *Yet* through the scent of water it will **b**, H6524
38:27 the **b** of the tender herb to spring forth? H4161
Ps 132:17 horn of David to **b**: I have ordained a H6779
Song 7:12 **b** forth: there will I give thee my loves. H5132
Isa 18: 5 For afore the harvest, when the **b** is H6525
27: 6 shall blossom and **b**, and fill the face of H6524
55:10 it bring forth and **b**, that it may give H6779
61:11 For as the earth bringeth forth her **b**, H6779
Ezk 16: 7 I have caused thee to multiply as the **b** H6779
29:21 the house of Israel to **b** forth, and I will H6779
Hos 8: 7 hath no stalk: the **b** shall yield no meal: H6779

BUDDED
Gen 40:10 it *was* as though it **b**, *and* her blossoms H6524
Nu 17: 8 house of Levi was **b**, and brought forth H6524
Song 6:11 flourished, *and* the pomegranates **b**. H5132
Ezk 7:10 the rod hath blossomed, pride hath **b**. H6524
Heb 9: 4 that **b**, and the tables of the covenant; *G985*

BUDS
Nu 17: 8 and brought forth **b**, and bloomed H6525

BUFFET
Mk 14:65 his face, and to **b** him, and to say unto *G2852*
2Co 12: 7 of Satan to **b** me, lest I should be *G2852*

BUFFETED
Mt 26:67 Then did they spit in his face, and **b** *G2852*

1Co 4:11 **b**, and have no certain dwellingplace; G2852
1Pt 2:20 For what glory *is it*, if, when ye be **b** for G2852

BUILD

Gen 11: 4 And they said, Go to, let us **b** us a city H1129
8 the earth: and they left off to **b** the city. H1129
Ex 20:25 thou shalt not **b** it of hewn stone: for H1129
Nu 23: 1 And Balaam said unto Balak, **B** me H1129
29 And Balaam said unto Balak, **B** me H1129
32:16 and said, We will **b** sheepfolds here for H1129
24 **B** you cities for your little ones, and H1129
Dt 20:20 and thou shalt **b** bulwarks against the H1129
25: 9 that will not **b** up his brother's house. H1129
27: 5 And there shalt thou **b** an altar unto H1129
6 Thou shalt **b** the altar of the LORD thy H1129
28:30 her: thou shalt **b** an house, and thou H1129
Jos 22:26 us now prepare to **b** us an altar, not for H1129
29 the LORD, to **b** an altar for burnt H1129
Jdg 6:26 And **b** an altar unto the LORD thy God H1129
Ru 4:11 which two did **b** the house of Israel: H1129
1Sa 2:35 mind: and I will **b** him a sure house; H1129
2Sa 7: 5 thou **b** me an house for me to dwell in? H1129
7 Why **b** ye not me an house of cedar? H1129
13 He shall **b** an house for my name, and I H1129
27 saying, I will **b** thee an house: therefore H1129
24:21 of thee, to **b** an altar unto the LORD, H1129
1Ki 2:36 and said unto him, **B** thee an house in H1129
5: 3 father could not **b** an house unto the H1129
5 And, behold, I purpose to **b** an house H1129
5 he shall **b** an house unto my name. H1129
18 timber and stones to **b** the house. H1129
6: 1 he began to **b** the house of the LORD. H1129
8:16 tribes of Israel to **b** an house, that my H1129
17 my father to **b** an house for the name H1129
18 in thine heart to **b** an house unto my H1129
19 Nevertheless thou shalt not **b** the H1129
19 he shall **b** the house unto my name. H1129
9:15 raised; for to **b** the house of the LORD, H1129
19 desired to **b** in Jerusalem, and in H1129
24 had built for her: then did he **b** Millo. H1129
11: 7 Then did Solomon **b** an high place for H1129
38 be with thee, and **b** thee a sure house, H1129
16:34 In his days did Hiel the Beth-elite **b** H1129
1Ch 14: 1 and carpenters, to **b** him an house. H1129
17: 4 shalt not **b** me an house to dwell in: H1129
10 that the LORD will **b** thee an house. H1129
12 He shall **b** me an house, and I will H1129
25 servant that thou wilt **b** him an house: H1129
21:22 that I may **b** an altar therein unto H1129
22: 2 wrought stones to **b** the house of God. H1129
6 **b** an house for the LORD God of Israel. H1129
7 was in my mind to **b** an house unto the H1129
8 thou shalt not **b** an house unto my H1129
10 He shall **b** an house for my name; and H1129
11 prosper thou, and **b** the house of the H1129
19 therefore, and **b** ye the sanctuary of H1129
28: 2 in mine heart to **b** an house of rest for H1129
3 But God said unto me, Thou shalt not **b** H1129
6 thy son, he shall **b** my house and my H1129
10 hath chosen thee to **b** an house for the H1129
29:16 have prepared to **b** thee an house for H1129
19 *things*, and to **b** the palace, *for* the H1129
2Ch 2: 1 And Solomon determined to **b** an H1129
3 him cedars to **b** him an house to dwell H1129
4 Behold, I **b** an house to the name of the H1129
5 And the house which I **b** *is* great: for H1129
6 But who is able to **b** him an house, H1129
6 I then, that I should **b** him an house, H1129
9 am about to **b** *shall be* wonderful great. H1129
12 that might **b** an house for the LORD, H1129
3: 1 Then Solomon began to **b** the house of H1129
2 And he began to **b** in the second *day* of H1129
6: 5 tribes of Israel to **b** an house in, that H1129
7 my father to **b** an house for the name H1129
8 was in thine heart to **b** an house for my H1129
9 Notwithstanding thou shalt not **b** the H1129
9 he shall **b** the house for my name. H1129
8: 6 desired to **b** in Jerusalem, and in H1129
14: 7 Therefore he said unto Judah, Let us **b** H1129
35: 3 king of Israel did **b**; *it shall* not *be* a H1129
36:23 hath charged me to **b** him an house in H1129
Ezr 1: 2 hath charged me to **b** him an house at H1129
3 *is* in Judah, and **b** the house of the H1129
5 raised, to go up to **b** the house of the H1129
4: 2 unto them, Let us **b** with you: for we H1129
3 to do with us to **b** an house unto our H1129
3 together will **b** unto the LORD God H1129
5: 2 and began to **b** the house of God which H1124
3 **b** this house, and to make up this wall? H1124
Ezr 5: 9 you to **b** this house, and to make H1124
11 and earth, and **b** the house that was H1124
13 made a decree to **b** this house of God. H1124
17 Cyrus the king to **b** this house of God at H1124
6: 7 Jews **b** this house of God in his place. H1124
Neh 2: 5 my fathers' sepulchres, that I may **b** it. H1129
17 fire: come, and let us **b** up the wall of H1129
18 said, Let us rise up and **b**. So they H1129
20 will arise and **b**: but ye have no portion, H1129
3: 3 sons of Hassenaah **b**, who *also* laid the H1129
4: 3 that which they **b**, if a fox go up, he H1129
10 so that we are not able to **b** the wall. H1129
Ps 28: 5 shall destroy them, and not **b** them up. H1129
51:18 Zion: **b** thou the walls of Jerusalem. H1129
69:35 For God will save Zion, and will **b** the H1129
89: 4 Thy seed will I establish for ever, and **b** H1129
102:16 When the LORD shall **b** up Zion, he H1129
127: 1 Except the LORD **b** the house, they H1129
1 in vain that **b** it: except the LORD H1129
147: 2 The LORD doth **b** up Jerusalem: he H1129
Prv 24:27 the field; and afterwards **b** thine house. H1129
Ecc 3: 3 to break down, and a time to **b** up; H1129
Song 8: 9 If she *be* a wall, we will **b** upon her a H1129
Isa 9:10 down, but we will **b** with hewn stones: H1129
45:13 all his ways: he shall **b** my city, and he H1129
58:12 And *they that shall be* of thee shall **b** H1129
60:10 And the sons of strangers shall **b** up H1129
61: 4 And they shall **b** the old wastes, they H1129
65:21 And they shall **b** houses, and inhabit H1129
22 They shall not **b**, and another inhabit; H1129
66: 1 *is* the house that ye **b** unto me? and H1129
Jer 1:10 and to throw down, to **b**, and to plant. H1129
18: 9 a kingdom, to **b** and to plant *it*; H1129
22:14 That saith, I will **b** me a wide house H1129
24: 6 land: and I will **b** them, and not pull H1129
29: 5 **B** ye houses, and dwell *in them*; and H1129
28 *captivity is* long: **b** ye houses, and dwell H1129
31: 4 Again I will **b** thee, and thou shalt be H1129
28 to **b**, and to plant, saith the LORD. H1129
33: 7 return, and will **b** them, as at the first. H1129
35: 7 Neither shall ye **b** house, nor sow seed, H1129
9 Nor to **b** houses for us to dwell in: H1129
42:10 land, then will I **b** you, and not pull *you* H1129
Ezk 4: 2 And lay siege against it, and **b** a fort H1129
11: 3 Which say, *It is* not near; let us **b** H1129
21:22 gates, to cast a mount, *and* to **b** a fort. H1129
28:26 therein, and shall **b** houses, and plant H1129
36:36 that I the LORD **b** the ruined *places*, H1129
Dan 9:25 to restore and to **b** Jerusalem unto the H1129
Am 9:11 and I will **b** it as in the days of old: H1129
14 and they shall **b** the waste cities, and H1129
Mic 3:10 They **b** up Zion with blood, and H1129
Zep 1:13 they shall also **b** houses, but not H1129
Hag 1: 8 bring wood, and **b** the house; and I will H1129
Zec 5:11 And he said unto me, To **b** it an house H1129
6:12 and he shall **b** the temple of the LORD: H1129
13 Even he shall **b** the temple of the H1129
15 off shall come and **b** in the temple of H1129
9: 3 And Tyrus did **b** herself a strong hold, H1129
Mal 1: 4 but we will return and **b** the desolate H1129
4 of hosts, They shall **b**, but I will throw H1129
Mt 16:18 this rock I will **b** my church; and the G3618
23:29 because ye **b** the tombs of the prophets, G3618
26:61 temple of God, and to **b** it in three days. G3618
Mk 14:58 I will **b** another made without hands. G3618
Lk 11:47 Woe unto you! for ye **b** the sepulchres G3618
48 killed them, and ye **b** their sepulchres. G3618
12:18 my barns, and **b** greater; and there will G3618
14:28 For which of you, intending to **b** a G3618
30 Saying, This man began to **b**, and was G3618
Act 7:49 what house will ye **b** me? saith the G3618
15:16 After this I will return, and will **b** again G456
16 fallen down; and I will **b** again the ruins G456
20:32 which is able to **b** you up, and to give G456
Ro 15:20 **b** upon another man's foundation: G3618
1Co 3:12 Now if any man **b** upon this G2026
Gal 2:18 For if I **b** again the things which I G3618

BUILDED

Gen 4:17 Enoch: and he **b** a city, and called the H1129
8:20 And Noah **b** an altar unto the LORD; H1129
10:11 forth Asshur, and **b** Nineveh, and the H1129
11: 5 the tower, which the children of men **b**. H1129
12: 7 land: and there **b** he an altar unto the H1129
8 east: and there he **b** an altar unto the H1129
26:25 And he **b** an altar there, and called H1129
Ex 24: 4 the morning, and **b** an altar under the H1129
Nu 32:38 names unto the cities which they **b**. H1129
Jos 22:16 in that ye have **b** you an altar, that ye H1129
1Ki 8:27 how much less this house that I have **b**? H1129
43 which I have **b**, is called by thy name. H1129
15:22 Baasha had **b**; and king Asa built with H1129
2Ki 23:13 king of Israel had **b** for Ashtoreth the H1129
1Ch 22: 5 house *that is* to be **b** for the LORD *must* H1129
Ezr 3: 2 his brethren, and **b** the altar of the God H1129
4: 1 of the captivity **b** the temple unto the H1129
13 that, if this city be **b**, and the walls set H1124
16 We certify the king that, if this city be **b** H1124
21 that this city be not **b**, until *another* H1124
5: 8 God, which is **b** with great stones, and H1124
11 the house that was **b** these many years H1124
11 a great king of Israel **b** and set up. H1124
15 let the house of God be **b** in his place. H1124
6: 3 Let the house be **b**, the place where they H1124
14 And the elders of the Jews **b**, and they H1124
14 son of Iddo. And they **b**, and finished *it*, H1124
Neh 3: 1 priests, and they **b** the sheep gate; they H1129
2 And next unto him **b** the men of H1129
2 next to them **b** Zaccur the son of Imri. H1129
4: 1 heard that we **b** the wall, he was wroth, H1129
17 They which **b** on the wall, and they that H1129
18 girded by his side, and *so* **b**. And he that H1129
6: 1 heard that I had **b** the wall, and *that* H1129
7: 4 few therein, and the houses *were* not **b**. H1129
12:29 **b** them villages round about Jerusalem. H1129
Job 20:19 taken away an house which he **b** not; H1129
Ps 122: 3 Jerusalem is **b** as a city that is compact H1129
Prv 9: 1 Wisdom hath **b** her house, she hath H1129
24: 3 Through wisdom is an house **b**; and by H1129
Ecc 2: 4 I made me great works; I **b** me houses; H1129
Song 4: 4 Thy neck *is* like the tower of David **b** H1129
Jer 30:18 the city shall be **b** upon her own heap, H1129
Lam 3: 5 He hath **b** against me, and compassed H1129
Ezk 36:10 be inhabited, and the wastes shall be **b**: H1129
33 in the cities, and the wastes shall be **b**. H1129
Lk 17:28 bought, they sold, they planted, they **b**; G3618
Eph 2:22 In whom ye also are **b** together for an G4925
Heb 3: 3 as he who hath **b** the house hath more G2680
4 For every house is **b** by some *man*; but G2680

BUILDEDST

Dt 6:10 and goodly cities, which thou **b** not, H1129

BUILDER

Heb 11:10 whose **b** and maker *is* God. G5079

BUILDERS

1Ki 5:18 And Solomon's **b** and Hiram's builders H1129
18 And Solomon's builders and Hiram's **b** H1129
2Ki 12:11 carpenters and **b**, that wrought upon H1129
22: 6 Unto carpenters, and **b**, and masons, H1129
2Ch 34:11 Even to the artificers and **b** gave they H1129
Ezr 3:10 And when the **b** laid the foundation of H1129
Neh 4: 5 provoked *thee* to anger before the **b**. H1129
18 For the **b**, every one had his sword H1129
Ps 118:22 The stone *which* the **b** refused is H1129
Ezk 27: 4 seas, thy **b** have perfected thy beauty. H1129
Mt 21:42 stone which the **b** rejected, the same is G3618
Mk 12:10 stone which the **b** rejected is become G3618
Lk 20:17 stone which the **b** rejected, the same is G3618
Act 4:11 at nought of you **b**, which is become the G3618
1Pt 2: 7 stone which the **b** disallowed, the same G3618

BUILDEST

Dt 22: 8 When thou **b** a new house, then thou H1129
Neh 6: 6 which cause thou **b** the wall, that thou H1129
Ezk 16:31 In that thou **b** thine eminent place in H1129
Mt 27:40 the temple, and **b** *it* in three days, save G3618
Mk 15:29 the temple, and **b** *it* in three days, G3618

BUILDETH

Jos 6:26 that riseth up and **b** this city Jericho: he H1129
Job 27:18 He **b** his house as a moth, and as a H1129
Prv 14: 1 Every wise woman **b** her house: but the H1129
Jer 22:13 Woe unto him that **b** his house by H1129
Hos 8:14 his Maker, and **b** temples; and Judah H1129
Am 9: 6 *It is* he that **b** his stories in the heaven, H1129
Hab 2:12 Woe to him that **b** a town with blood, H1129
1Co 3:10 and another **b** thereon. But let every G4925
10 man take heed how he **b** thereupon. G4925

BUILDING

Jos 22:19 against us, in **b** you an altar beside H1129
1Ki 3: 1 made an end of **b** his own house, and H1129
6: 7 And the house, when it was in **b**, was H1129
7 heard in the house, while it was in **b**. H1129
12 which thou art in **b**, if thou wilt walk in H1129
38 of it. So was he seven years in **b** it. H1129

1Ki 7: 1 But Solomon was **b** his own house H1129
9: 1 had finished the **b** of the house of the H1129
15:21 off **b** of Ramah, and dwelt in Tirzah. H1129
1Ch 28: 2 our God, and had made ready for the **b**: H1129
2Ch 3: 3 was instructed for the **b** of the house of H1129
16: 5 off **b** of Ramah, and let his work cease. H1129
6 Baasha was **b**; and he built therewith H1129
Ezr 4: 4 of Judah, and troubled them in **b**, H1129
12 unto Jerusalem, **b** the rebellious and H1124
5: 4 the names of the men that make this **b**? H1147
16 it been in **b**, and *yet* it is not finished. H1124
6: 8 of these Jews for the **b** of this house of H1124
Ecc 10:18 By much slothfulness the **b** decayeth; H4746
Ezk 17:17 and **b** forts, to cut off many persons: H1129
40: 5 **b**, one reed; and the height, one reed. H1146
41:12 Now the **b** that *was* before the separate H1146
12 and the wall of the **b** *was* five cubits H1146
13 place, and the **b**, with the walls thereof, H1140
15 And he measured the length of the **b** H1146
42: 1 *was* before the **b** toward the north. H1146
5 and than the middlemost of the **b**. H1146
6 therefore *the* **b** was straitened more
10 separate place, and over against the **b**. H1146
46:23 And *there was* a row *of* **b** round about in
Jn 2:20 **b**, and wilt thou rear it up in three days? *G3618*
1Co 3: 9 ye are God's husbandry, *ye are* God's **b**. *G3619*
2Co 5: 1 we have a **b** of God, an house not *G3619*
Eph 2:21 In whom all the **b** fitly framed together *G3619*
Heb 9:11 with hands, that is to say, not of this **b**; *G2937*
Jude 20 But ye, beloved, **b** up yourselves on *G2026*
Rev 21:18 And the **b** of the wall of it was *of* jasper: *G1739*

BUILDINGS
Mt 24: 1 for to shew him the **b** of the temple. *G3619*
Mk 13: 1 manner of stones and what **b** *are here*! *G3619*
2 thou these great **b**? there shall not be left *G3619*

BUILT
Gen 13:18 and **b** there an altar unto the LORD. H1129
22: 9 of; and Abraham **b** an altar there, and H1129
33:17 And Jacob journeyed to Succoth, and **b** H1129
35: 7 And he **b** there an altar, and called the H1129
Ex 1:11 their burdens. And they **b** for Pharaoh H1129
17:15 And Moses **b** an altar, and called the H1129
32: 5 And when Aaron saw *it*, he **b** an altar H1129
Nu 13:22 **b** seven years before Zoan in Egypt.) H1129
21:27 let the city of Sihon be **b** and prepared: H1129
23:14 top of Pisgah, and **b** seven altars, and H1129
32:34 And the children of Gad **b** Dibon, and H1129
37 And the children of Reuben **b** Heshbon, H1129
Dt 8:12 **b** goodly houses, and dwelt *therein*; H1129
13:16 heap for ever; it shall not be **b** again. H1129
20: 5 *is there* that hath **b** a new house, and H1129
Jos 8:30 Then Joshua **b** an altar unto the LORD H1129
19:50 and he **b** the city, and dwelt therein. H1129
22:10 tribe of Manasseh **b** there an altar by H1129
11 tribe of Manasseh have **b** an altar over H1129
23 That we have **b** us an altar to turn from H1129
24:13 cities which ye **b** not, and ye dwell in H1129
Jdg 1:26 the Hittites, and **b** a city, and called the H1129
6:24 Then Gideon **b** an altar there unto the H1129
28 was offered upon the altar *that was* **b**. H1129
18:28 And they **b** a city, and dwelt therein. H1129
21: 4 rose early, and **b** there an altar, and H1129
1Sa 7:17 and there he **b** an altar unto the LORD. H1129
14:35 And Saul **b** an altar unto the LORD: the H1129
35 the first altar that he **b** unto the LORD. H1129
2Sa 5: 9 **b** round about from Millo and inward. H1129
11 masons: and they **b** David an house. H1129
24:25 And David **b** there an altar unto the H1129
1Ki 3: 2 was no house **b** unto the name of the H1129
6: 2 And the house which king Solomon **b** H1129
5 And against the wall of the house he **b** H1129
7 in building, was **b** of stone made ready H1129
9 So he **b** the house, and finished it; and H1129
10 And *then* he **b** chambers against all the H1129
14 So Solomon **b** the house, and finished H1129
15 And he **b** the walls of the house within H1129
16 And he **b** twenty cubits on the sides of H1129
16 of cedar: he even **b** *them* for it within, H1129
36 And he **b** the inner court with three H1129
7: 2 He **b** also the house of the forest of H1129
8:13 I have surely **b** thee an house to dwell H1129
20 and have **b** an house for the name H1129
44 the house that I have **b** for thy name: H1129
48 the house which I have **b** for thy name: H1129
9: 3 which thou hast **b**, to put my name H1129
10 Solomon had **b** the two houses, the H1129
17 And Solomon **b** Gezer, and Beth-horon H1129
1Ki 9:24 had **b** for her: then did he build Millo. H1129
25 the altar which he **b** unto the LORD, H1129
10: 4 wisdom, and the house that he had **b**, H1129
11:27 against the king: Solomon **b** Millo, *and* H1129
38 a sure house, as I **b** for David, and will H1129
12:25 Then Jeroboam **b** Shechem in mount H1129
25 went out from thence, and **b** Penuel. H1129
14:23 For they also **b** them high places, and H1129
15:17 Judah, and **b** Ramah, that he might H1129
22 and king Asa **b** with them Geba of H1129
23 and the cities which he **b**, *are* they not H1129
16:24 of silver, and **b** on the hill, and called H1129
24 of the city which he **b**, after the name of H1129
32 of Baal, which he had **b** in Samaria. H1129
18:32 And with the stones he **b** an altar in the H1129
22:39 the cities that he **b**, *are* they not written H1129
2Ki 14:22 He **b** Elath, and restored it to Judah, H1129
15:35 high places. He **b** the higher gate of the H1129
16:11 And Urijah the priest **b** an altar H1129
18 that they had **b** in the house, and the H1129
17: 9 God, and they **b** them high places in H1129
21: 3 For he **b** up again the high places H1129
4 And he **b** altars in the house of the H1129
5 And he **b** altars for all the host of H1129
25: 1 and they **b** forts against it round about. H1129
1Ch 6:10 temple that Solomon **b** in Jerusalem:) H1129
32 Solomon had **b** the house of the LORD H1129
7:24 (And his daughter *was* Sherah, who **b** H1129
8:12 and Shamed, who **b** Ono, and Lod, H1129
11: 8 And he **b** the city round about, even H1129
17: 6 have ye not **b** me an house of cedars? H1129
21:26 And David **b** there an altar unto the H1129
22:19 that is to be **b** to the name of the LORD. H1129
2Ch 6: 2 But I have **b** an house of habitation for H1129
10 and have **b** the house for the name H1129
18 much less this house which I have **b**! H1129
33 which I have **b** is called by thy name. H1129
34 the house which I have **b** for thy name; H1129
38 the house which I have **b** for thy name: H1129
8: 1 Solomon had **b** the house of the LORD, H1129
2 Solomon **b** them, and caused the H1129
4 And he **b** Tadmor in the wilderness, H1129
4 the store cities, which he **b** in Hamath. H1129
5 Also he **b** Beth-horon the upper, and H1129
11 house that he had **b** for her: for he said, H1129
12 which he had **b** before the porch, H1129
9: 3 Solomon, and the house that he had **b**, H1129
11: 5 and **b** cities for defence in Judah. H1129
6 He **b** even Beth-lehem, and Etam, and H1129
14: 6 And he **b** fenced cities in Judah: for the H1129
7 on every side. So they **b** and prospered. H1129
16: 1 Judah, and **b** Ramah, to the intent H1129
6 and he **b** therewith Geba and Mizpah. H1129
17:12 **b** in Judah castles, and cities of store. H1129
20: 8 And they dwelt therein, and have **b** H1129
26: 2 He **b** Eloth, and restored it to Judah, H1129
6 of Ashdod, and **b** cities about Ashdod, H1129
9 Moreover Uzziah **b** towers in H1129
10 Also he **b** towers in the desert, and H1129
27: 3 He **b** the high gate of the house of the H1129
3 and on the wall of Ophel he **b** much. H1129
4 Moreover he **b** cities in the mountains H1129
4 in the forests he **b** castles and towers. H1129
32: 5 Also he strengthened himself, and **b** up H1129
33: 3 For he **b** again the high places which H1129
4 Also he **b** altars in the house of the H1129
5 And he **b** altars for all the host of H1129
14 Now after this he **b** a wall without the H1129
15 altars that he had **b** in the mount of the H1129
19 places wherein he **b** high places, and H1129
Neh 3:13 of Zanoah; they **b** it, and set up the H1129
14 he **b** it, and set up the doors H1129
15 part of Mizpah; he **b** it, and covered it, H1129
4: 6 So **b** we the wall; and all the wall was H1129
7: 1 when the wall was **b**, and I had set up H1129
Job 3:14 which **b** desolate places for themselves; H1129
12:14 and it cannot be **b** again: he shutteth H1129
22:23 thou shalt be **b** up, thou shalt put away H1129
Ps 78:69 And he **b** his sanctuary like high H1129
89: 2 For I have said, Mercy shall be **b** up for H1129
Ecc 9:14 it, and **b** great bulwarks against it: H1129
Isa 5: 2 the choicest vine, and **b** a tower in the H1129
25: 2 to be no city; it shall never be **b**. H1129
44:26 Judah, Ye shall be **b**, and I will raise up H1129
28 Thou shalt be **b**; and to the temple, Thy H1129
Jer 7:31 And they have **b** the high places of H1129
12:16 they be **b** in the midst of my people. H1129
19: 5 They have **b** also the high places of H1129
31: 4 and thou shalt be **b**, O virgin of Israel: H1129
Jer 31:38 the city shall be **b** to the LORD from the H1129
32:31 the day that they **b** it even unto this H1129
35 And they **b** the high places of Baal, H1129
45: 4 *that* which I have **b** will I break down, H1129
52: 4 it, and **b** forts against it round about. H1129
Ezk 13:10 no peace; and one **b** up a wall, and, lo, H1129
16:24 *That* thou hast also **b** unto thee an H1129
25 Thou hast **b** thy high place at every H1129
26:14 thou shalt be **b** no more: for I the LORD H1129
Dan 4:30 that I have **b** for the house of the H1124
9:25 the street shall be **b** again, and the H1129
Am 5:11 of wheat: ye have **b** houses of hewn H1129
Mic 7:11 *In* the day that thy walls are to be **b**, *in* H1129
Hag 1: 2 that the LORD'S house should be **b**. H1129
Zec 1:16 my house shall be **b** in it, saith the H1129
8: 9 was laid, that the temple might be **b**. H1129
Mt 7:24 man, which **b** his house upon a rock: *G3618*
26 man, which **b** his house upon the sand: *G3618*
21:33 in it, and **b** a tower, and let it out *G3618*
Mk 12: 1 the winefat, and **b** a tower, and let it *G3618*
Lk 4:29 their city was **b**, that they might cast *G3618*
6:48 He is like a man which **b** an house, and *G3618*
49 a foundation **b** an house upon the *G3618*
7: 5 For he loveth our nation, and he hath **b** *G3618*
Act 7:47 But Solomon **b** him an house. *G3618*
1Co 3:14 **b** thereupon, he shall receive a reward. *G2026*
Eph 2:20 And are **b** upon the foundation of the *G2026*
Col 2: 7 Rooted and **b** up in him, and *G2026*
Heb 3: 4 *man*; but he that **b** all things *is* God. *G2680*
1Pt 2: 5 Ye also, as lively stones, are **b** up a *G3618*

BUKKI
Nu 34:22 the children of Dan, **B** the son of Jogli. H1231
1Ch 6: 5 And Abishua begat **B**, and Bukki begat H1231
5 And Abishua begat Bukki, and **B** begat H1231
51 **B** his son, Uzzi his son, Zerahiah his H1231
Ezr 7: 4 Zerahiah, the son of Uzzi, the son of **B**, H1231

BUKKIAH
1Ch 25: 4 Of Heman: the sons of Heman; **B**, H1232
13 The sixth to **B**, *he*, his sons, and his H1232

BUL
1Ki 6:38 And in the eleventh year, in the month **B**, H945

BULL
Job 21:10 Their **b** gendereth, and faileth not; H7794
Isa 51:20 streets, as a wild **b** in a net: they are full H8377

BULLOCK
Ex 29: 1 **b**, and two rams without blemish, H6499
3 basket, with the **b** and the two rams. H6499
10 And thou shalt cause a **b** to be brought H6499
10 put their hands upon the head of the **b**. H6499
11 And thou shalt kill the **b** before the H6499
12 of the blood of the **b**, and put *it* upon H6499
14 But the flesh of the **b**, and his skin, and H6499
36 And thou shalt offer every day a **b** *for* a H6499
Lev 1: 5 And he shall kill the **b** before H1121+H1241
4: 3 sinned, a young **b** without blemish H6499
4 And he shall bring the **b** unto the door H6499
4 head, and kill the **b** before the LORD. H6499
7 the blood of the **b** at the bottom of the H6499
8 it all the fat of the **b** for the sin offering; H6499
10 As it was taken off from the **b** of the H7794
11 And the skin of the **b**, and all his flesh, H6499
12 Even the whole **b** shall he carry forth H6499
14 shall offer a young **b** for the sin, and H6499
15 the head of the **b** before the LORD: and H6499
15 the **b** shall be killed before the LORD. H6499
20 And he shall do with the **b** as he did H6499
20 as he did with the **b** for a sin offering, H6499
21 And he shall carry forth the **b** without H6499
21 he burned the first **b**: it *is* a sin offering H6499
8: 2 oil, and a **b** for the sin offering, H6499
14 And he brought the **b** for the sin H6499
14 the head of the **b** for the sin offering. H6499
17 But the **b**, and his hide, his flesh, and H6499
9: 4 Also a **b** and a ram for peace offerings, H7794
18 He slew also the **b** and the ram *for* a H7794
19 And the fat of the **b** and of the ram, the H7794
16: 3 with a young **b** for a sin offering, and H6499
6 And Aaron shall offer his **b** of the sin H6499
11 And Aaron shall bring the **b** of the sin H6499
11 and shall kill the **b** of the sin offering H6499
14 And he shall take of the blood of the **b**, H6499
15 the blood of the **b**, and sprinkle it upon H6499
18 of the blood of the **b**, and of the blood of H6499
27 And the **b** *for* the sin offering, and the H6499

Lev 22:23 Either a **b** or a lamb that hath any H7794
27 When a **b**, or a sheep, or a goat, is H7794
23:18 and one young **b**, and two rams: they H6499
Nu 7:15 One young **b**, one ram, one lamb of the H6499
21 One young **b**, one ram, one lamb of the H6499
27 One young **b**, one ram, one lamb of the H6499
33 One young **b**, one ram, one lamb of the H6499
39 One young **b**, one ram, one lamb of the H6499
45 One young **b**, one ram, one lamb of the H6499
51 One young **b**, one ram, one lamb of the H6499
57 One young **b**, one ram, one lamb of the H6499
63 One young **b**, one ram, one lamb of the H6499
69 One young **b**, one ram, one lamb of the H6499
75 One young **b**, one ram, one lamb of the H6499
81 One young **b**, one ram, one lamb of the H6499
8: 8 Then let them take a young **b** with his H6499
8 **b** shalt thou take for a sin offering. H6499
15: 8 And when thou preparest a **b** H1121+H1241
9 Then shall he bring with a **b** a H1121+H1241
11 Thus shall it be done for one **b**, or for H7794
24 offer one young **b** for a burnt offering, H6499
23: 2 offered on *every* altar a **b** and a ram. H6499
4 offered upon *every* altar a **b** and a ram. H6499
14 offered a **b** and a ram on *every* altar. H6499
30 offered a **b** and a ram on *every* altar. H6499
28:12 with oil, for one **b**; and two tenth deals H6499
14 hin of wine unto a **b**, and the third *part* H6499
20 for a **b**, and two tenth deals for a ram; H6499
28 one **b**, two tenth deals unto one ram, H6499
29: 2 the LORD; one young **b**, one ram, *and* H6499
3 for a **b**, *and* two tenth deals for a ram, H6499
8 savour; one young **b**, one ram, *and* H6499
9 to a **b**, *and* two tenth deals to one ram, H6499
14 tenth deals unto every **b** of the thirteen H6499
36 the LORD: one **b**, one ram, seven lambs H6499
37 offerings for the **b**, for the ram, and for H6499
Dt 15:19 **b**, nor shear the firstling of thy sheep. H7794
17: 1 thy God *any* **b**, or sheep, wherein is H7794
33:17 His glory *is like* the firstling of his **b**, H7794
Jdg 6:25 thy father's young **b**, even the second H7794
25 even the second **b** of seven years old, H6499
26 and take the second **b**, and offer a burnt H6499
28 it, and the second **b** was offered upon H6499
1Sa 1:25 And they slew a **b**, and brought the H6499
1Ki 18:23 them choose one **b** for themselves, and H6499
23 dress the other **b**, and lay *it* on wood, H6499
25 Choose you one **b** for yourselves, and H6499
26 And they took the **b** which was given H6499
33 order, and cut the **b** in pieces, and laid H6499
2Ch 13: 9 with a young **b** and seven rams, *the* H6499
Ps 50: 9 I will take no **b** out of thy house, *nor* he H6499
69:31 an ox *or* **b** that hath horns and hoofs. H6499
Isa 65:25 eat straw like the **b**: and dust *shall be* H1241
Jer 31:18 chastised, as a **b** unaccustomed *to the* H5695
Ezk 43:19 Lord GOD, a young **b** for a sin offering. H6499
21 Thou shalt take the **b** also of the sin H6499
22 altar, as they did cleanse *it* with the **b**. H6499
23 offer a young **b** without blemish, and H6499
25 prepare a young **b**, and a ram out of the H6499
45:18 shalt take a young **b** without blemish, H6499
22 people of the land a **b** *for* a sin offering. H6499
24 of an ephah for a **b**, and an ephah for a H6499
46: 6 *it shall be* a young **b** without blemish, H6499
7 an ephah for a **b**, and an ephah for a H6499
11 be an ephah to a **b**, and an ephah to a H6499

BULLOCKS
Nu 7:87 *were* twelve **b**, the rams twelve, the H6499
88 twenty and four **b**, the rams sixty, the H6499
8:12 the heads of the **b**: and thou shalt offer H6499
23:29 me here seven **b** and seven rams. H6499
28:11 the LORD; two young **b**, and one ram, H6499
19 LORD; two young **b**, and one ram, and H6499
27 the LORD; two young **b**, one ram, seven H6499
29:13 LORD; thirteen young **b**, two rams, *and* H6499
14 of the thirteen **b**, two tenth deals to each H6499
17 *shall offer* twelve young **b**, two rams, H6499
18 offerings for the **b**, for the rams, and for H6499
20 And on the third day eleven **b**, two H6499
21 offerings for the **b**, for the rams, and for H6499
23 And on the fourth day ten **b**, two rams, H6499
24 offerings for the **b**, for the rams, and for H6499
26 And on the fifth day nine **b**, two rams, H6499
27 offerings for the **b**, for the rams, and for H6499
29 And on the sixth day eight **b**, two rams, H6499
30 offerings for the **b**, for the rams, and for H6499
32 And on the seventh day seven **b**, two H6499
33 offerings for the **b**, for the rams, and for H6499
1Sa 1:24 with her, with three **b**, and one ephah of H6499
1Ki 18:23 Let them therefore give us two **b**; and let H6499
1Ch 15:26 they offered seven **b** and seven rams. H6499
29:21 *even* a thousand **b**, a thousand rams, H6499
2Ch 29:21 And they brought seven **b**, and seven H6499
22 So they killed the **b**, and the priests H1241
32 and ten **b**, an hundred rams, *and* H1241
30:24 a thousand **b** and seven thousand H6499
24 a thousand **b** and ten thousand sheep: H6499
35: 7 **b**: these *were* of the king's substance. H1241
Ezr 6: 9 of, both young **b**, and rams, and lambs, H8450
17 God an hundred **b**, two hundred rams, H8450
7:17 with this money **b**, rams, lambs, with H8450
8:35 of Israel, twelve **b** for all Israel, ninety H6499
Job 42: 8 Therefore take unto you now seven **b** H6499
Ps 51:19 then shall they offer **b** upon thine altar. H6499
66:15 of rams; I will offer **b** with goats. Selah. H1241
Isa 1:11 blood of **b**, or of lambs, or of he goats. H6499
34: 7 them, and the **b** with the bulls; and H6499
Jer 46:21 of her like fatted **b**; for they also are H5695
50:27 Slay all her **b**; let them go down to the H6499
Ezk 39:18 of **b**, all of them fatlings of Bashan. H6499
45:23 to the LORD, seven **b** and seven rams H6499
Hos 12:11 they sacrifice **b** in Gilgal; yea, their H7794

BULLOCK'S
Lev 4: 4 his hand upon the **b** head, and kill the H6499
5 shall take of the **b** blood, and bring it H6499
16 shall bring of the **b** blood to the H6499

BULLS
Gen 32:15 ten **b**, twenty she asses, and ten foals. H6499
Ps 22:12 Many **b** have compassed me: strong H6499
12 strong *b* of Bashan have beset me round.
50:13 Will I eat the flesh of **b**, or drink the H47
68:30 multitude of the **b**, with the calves of the H47
Isa 34: 7 bullocks with the **b**, and their land shall H47
Jer 50:11 fat as the heifer at grass, and bellow as **b**; H47
52:20 and twelve brasen **b** that *were* under H1241
Heb 9:13 For if the blood of **b** and of goats, and *G5022*
10: 4 For *it is* not possible that the blood of **b** *G5022*

BULRUSH
Isa 58: 5 bow down his head as a **b**, and to spread H100

BULRUSHES
Ex 2: 3 for him an ark of **b**, and daubed it with H1573
Isa 18: 2 even in vessels of **b** upon the waters, H1573

BULWARKS
Dt 20:20 thou shalt build **b** against the city that H4692
2Ch 26:15 and upon the **b**, to shoot arrows and H6438
Ps 48:13 Mark ye well her **b**, consider her H2430
Ecc 9:14 besieged it, and built great **b** against it: H4685
Isa 26: 1 will *God* appoint *for* walls and **b**. H2426

BUNAH
1Ch 2:25 and **B**, and Oren, and Ozem, *and* Ahijah. H946

BUNCH
Ex 12:22 And ye shall take a **b** of hyssop, and dip H92

BUNCHES
2Sa 16: 1 and an hundred **b** of raisins, and an H6778
1Ch 12:40 cakes of figs, and **b** of raisins, and H6778
Isa 30: 6 upon the **b** of camels, to a people H1707

BUNDLE
Gen 42:35 every man's **b** of money *was* in his H6872
1Sa 25:29 be bound in the **b** of life with the LORD H6872
Song 1:13 A **b** of myrrh *is* my well-beloved unto H6872
Act 28: 3 And when Paul had gathered a **b** of *G4128*

BUNDLES
Gen 42:35 saw the **b** of money, they were afraid. H6872
Mt 13:30 and bind them in **b** to burn them: but *G1197*

BUNNI
Neh 9: 4 Shebaniah, **B**, Sherebiah, Bani, *and* H1138
10:15 **B**, Azgad, Bebai, H1138
11:15 the son of Hashabiah, the son of **B**; H1138

BURDEN
Ex 18:22 and they shall bear *the* **b** with thee.
23: 5 lying under his **b**, and wouldest forbear H4853
Nu 4:15 *things are* the **b** of the sons of Kohath H4853
19 every one to his service and to his **b**: H4853
31 And this *is* the charge of their **b**, H4853
32 the instruments of the charge of their **b**. H4853
47 **b** in the tabernacle of the congregation, H4853
Nu 4:49 and according to his **b**: thus were they H4853
11:11 layest the **b** of all this people upon me? H4853
17 they shall bear the **b** of the people with H4853
Dt 1:12 and your **b**, and your strife? H4853
2Sa 15:33 me, then thou shalt be a **b** unto me: H4853
19:35 be yet a **b** unto my lord the king? H4853
2Ki 5:17 two mules' **b** of earth? for thy servant H4853
8: 9 forty camels' **b**, and came and stood H4853
9:25 father, the LORD laid this **b** upon him; H4853
2Ch 35: 3 *it shall* not *be* a **b** upon *your* shoulders: H4853
Neh 13:19 no **b** be brought in on the sabbath day. H4853
Job 7:20 against thee, so that I am a **b** to myself? H4853
Ps 38: 4 an heavy **b** they are too heavy for me. H4853
55:22 Cast thy **b** upon the LORD, and he shall H3053
81: 6 I removed his shoulder from the **b**: his H5447
Ecc 12: 5 shall be a **b**, and desire shall fail: H5445
Isa 9: 4 For thou hast broken the yoke of his **b**, H5448
10:27 that day, *that* his **b** shall be taken away H5448
13: 1 The **b** of Babylon, which Isaiah the son H4853
14:25 his **b** depart from off their shoulders. H5448
28 the year that king Ahaz died was this **b**. H4853
15: 1 The **b** of Moab. Because in the night Ar H4853
17: 1 The **b** of Damascus. Behold, Damascus H4853
19: 1 The **b** of Egypt. Behold, the LORD H4853
21: 1 The **b** of the desert of the sea. As H4853
11 The **b** of Dumah. He calleth to me out H4853
13 The **b** upon Arabia. In the forest in H4853
22: 1 The **b** of the valley of vision. What H4853
25 and fall; and the **b** that *was* upon it H4853
23: 1 The **b** of Tyre. Howl, ye ships of H4853
30: 6 The **b** of the beasts of the south: into H4853
27 his anger, and the **b** *thereof is* heavy: H4858
46: 1 loaden; *they are* a **b** to the weary *beast*. H4853
2 not deliver the **b**, but themselves are H4853
Jer 17:21 and bear no **b** on the sabbath day, H4853
22 Neither carry forth a **b** out of your H4853
24 to bring in no **b** through the gates of H4853
27 and not to bear a **b**, even entering in at H4853
23:33 What *is* the **b** of the LORD? thou shalt H4853
33 unto them, What **b**? I will even forsake H4853
34 that shall say, The **b** of the LORD, I will H4853
36 And the **b** of the LORD shall ye H4853
36 man's word shall be his **b**; for ye have H4853
38 But since ye say, The **b** of the LORD; H4853
38 say this word, The **b** of the LORD, and I H4853
38 Ye shall not say, The **b** of the LORD; H4853
Ezk 12:10 the Lord GOD; This **b** *concerneth* the H4853
Hos 8:10 a little for the **b** of the king of princes. H4853
Nah 1: 1 The **b** of Nineveh. The book of the H4853
Hab 1: 1 The **b** which Habakkuk the prophet did H4853
Zep 3:18 *to whom* the reproach of it *was* a **b**. H4864
Zec 9: 1 The **b** of the word of the LORD in the H4853
12: 1 The **b** of the word of the LORD for H4853
3 all people: all that **b** themselves with it H6006
Mal 1: 1 The **b** of the word of the LORD to Israel H4853
Mt 11:30 For my yoke *is* easy, and my **b** is light. *G5413*
20:12 have borne the **b** and heat of the day. *G922*
Act 15:28 no greater **b** than these necessary things; *G922*
21: 3 for there the ship was to unlade her **b**. *G1117*
2Co 12:16 But be it so, I did not **b** you: *G2599*
Gal 6: 5 For every man shall bear his own **b**. *G5413*
Rev 2:24 speak; I will put upon you none other **b**. *G922*

BURDENED
2Co 5: 4 do groan, being **b**: not for that we would *G916*
8:13 not that other men be eased, and ye **b**: *G2347*

BURDENS
Gen 49:14 ass couching down between two **b**: H4942
Ex 1:11 them with their **b**. And they built for H5450
2:11 and looked on their **b**: and he spied an H5450
5: 4 from their works? get you unto your **b**. H5450
5 and ye make them rest from their **b**. H5450
6: 6 from under the **b** of the Egyptians, and H5450
7 out from under the **b** of the Egyptians. H5450
Nu 4:24 of the Gershonites, to serve, and for **b**: H4853
27 in all their **b**, and in all their service: H4853
27 appoint unto them in charge all their **b**. H4853
1Ki 5:15 that bare **b**, and fourscore thousand H5449
2Ch 2: 2 men to bear **b**, and fourscore thousand H5449
18 them *to be* bearers of **b**, and fourscore H5449
24:27 greatness of the **b** *laid* upon him, and H4853
34:13 Also *they were* over the bearers of **b**, H5449
Neh 4:10 of the bearers of **b** is decayed, and H5449
17 and they that bare **b**, with those that H5447
13:15 figs, and all *manner of* **b**, which they H4853
Isa 58: 6 to undo the heavy **b**, and to let the H92
Lam 2:14 thee false **b** and causes of banishment. H4864
Am 5:11 ye take from him **b** of wheat: ye have H4864

Mt 23: 4 For they bind heavy **b** and grievous to *G5413*
Lk 11:46 for ye lade men with **b** grievous to be *G5413*
46 not the **b** with one of your fingers. *G5413*
Gal 6: 2 Bear ye one another's **b**, and so fulfil the *G922*

BURDENSOME
Zec 12: 3 I make Jerusalem a **b** stone for all H4614
2Co 11: 9 **b** unto you, and *so* will I keep *myself*. *G4*
12:13 not **b** to you? forgive me this wrong. *G2655*
14 and I will not be **b** to you: for I seek not *G2655*
1Th 2: 6 been **b**, as the apostles of Christ. *G1722+G922*

BURIAL
2Ch 26:23 in the field of the **b** which *belonged* to H6900
Ecc 6: 3 also *that* he have no **b**; I say, *that* an H6900
Isa 14:20 Thou shalt not be joined with them in **b**, H6900
Jer 22:19 He shall be buried with the **b** of an ass, H6900
Mt 26:12 on my body, she did *it* for my **b**. *G1779*
Act 8: 2 And devout men carried Stephen *to his* **b**,

BURIED
Gen 15:15 thou shalt be **b** in a good old age. H6912
23:19 And after this, Abraham **b** Sarah his H6912
25: 9 And his sons Isaac and Ishmael **b** him H6912
10 was Abraham **b**, and Sarah his wife. H6912
35: 8 died, and she was **b** beneath Beth-el H6912
19 And Rachel died, and was **b** in the way H6912
29 and his sons Esau and Jacob **b** him. H6912
48: 7 Ephrath: and I **b** her there in the way H6912
49:31 There they **b** Abraham and Sarah his H6912
31 wife; there they **b** Isaac and Rebekah H6912
31 Rebekah his wife; and there I **b** Leah. H6912
50:13 of Canaan, and **b** him in the cave of the H6912
14 his father, after he had **b** his father. H6912
Nu 11:34 there they **b** the people that lusted. H6912
20: 1 Miriam died there, and was **b** there. H6912
33: 4 For the Egyptians **b** all *their* firstborn, H6912
Dt 10: 6 and there he was **b**; and Eleazar his son H6912
34: 6 And he **b** him in a valley in the land of H6912
Jos 24:30 And they **b** him in the border of his H6912
32 up out of Egypt, **b** they in Shechem, in H6912
33 died; and they **b** him in a hill *that* H6912
Jdg 2: 9 And they **b** him in the border of his H6912
8:32 old age, and was **b** in the sepulchre of H6912
10: 2 years, and died, and was **b** in Shamir. H6912
5 And Jair died, and was **b** in Camon. H6912
12: 7 and was **b** in *one of* the cities of Gilead. H6912
10 Then died Ibzan, and was **b** at H6912
12 **b** in Aijalon in the country of Zebulun. H6912
15 died, and was **b** in Pirathon in the land H6912
16:31 *him* up, and **b** him between Zorah H6912
Ru 1:17 and there will I be **b**: the LORD do so to H6912
1Sa 25: 1 him, and **b** him in his house at H6912
28: 3 him, and **b** him in Ramah, even H6912
31:13 And they took their bones, and **b** *them* H6912
2Sa 2: 4 of Jabesh-gilead *were they* that **b** Saul. H6912
5 lord, *even* unto Saul, and have **b** him. H6912
32 And they took up Asahel, and **b** him in H6912
3:32 And they **b** Abner in Hebron: and the H6912
4:12 Ish-bosheth, and **b** *it* in the sepulchre H6912
17:23 was **b** in the sepulchre of his father. H6912
19:37 own city, *and be* **b** by the grave of my
21:14 Jonathan his son **b** they in the country H6912
1Ki 2:10 fathers, and was **b** in the city of David. H6912
34 **b** in his own house in the wilderness. H6912
11:43 fathers, and was **b** in the city of David H6912
13:31 And it came to pass, after he had **b** H6912
31 God *is* **b**; lay my bones beside his bones: H6912
14:18 And they **b** him; and all Israel H6912
31 fathers, and was **b** with his fathers in H6912
15: 8 fathers; and they **b** him in the city of H6912
24 fathers, and was **b** with his fathers in H6912
16: 6 fathers, and was **b** in Tirzah: and Elah H6912
28 his fathers, and was **b** in Samaria: and H6912
22:37 and they **b** the king in Samaria. H6912
50 fathers, and was **b** with his fathers in H6912
2Ki 8:24 fathers, and was **b** with his fathers in H6912
9:28 chariot to Jerusalem, and **b** him in his H6912
10:35 his fathers: and they **b** him in Samaria. H6912
12:21 and he died; and they **b** him with his H6912
13: 9 his fathers; and they **b** him in Samaria: H6912
13 **b** in Samaria with the kings of Israel. H6912
20 And Elisha died, and they **b** him. And H6912
14:16 fathers, and was **b** in Samaria with the H6912
20 and he was **b** at Jerusalem with his H6912
15: 7 fathers; and they **b** him with his fathers H6912
38 fathers, and was **b** with his fathers in H6912
16:20 fathers, and was **b** with his fathers in H6912
21:18 fathers, and was **b** in the garden of his H6912
2Ki 21:26 And he was **b** in his sepulchre in the H6912
23:30 to Jerusalem, and **b** him in his own H6912
1Ch 10:12 to Jabesh, and **b** their bones under the H6912
2Ch 9:31 and he was **b** in the city of David H6912
12:16 fathers, and was **b** in the city of David: H6912
14: 1 fathers, and they **b** him in the city of H6912
16:14 And they **b** him in his own sepulchres, H6912
21: 1 fathers, and was **b** with his fathers in H6912
20 Howbeit they **b** him in the city of H6912
22: 9 slain him, they **b** him: Because, said H6912
24:16 And they **b** him in the city of David H6912
25 he died: and they **b** him in the city of H6912
25 city of David, but they **b** him not in the H6912
25:28 him upon horses, and **b** him with his H6912
26:23 fathers, and they **b** him with his fathers H6912
27: 9 fathers, and they **b** him in the city of H6912
28:27 fathers, and they **b** him in the city, *even* H6912
32:33 fathers, and they **b** him in the chiefest H6912
33:20 his fathers, and they **b** him in his own H6912
35:24 and he died, and was **b** in *one of* the H6912
Job 27:15 Those that remain of him shall be **b** in H6912
Ecc 8:10 And so I saw the wicked **b**, who had H6912
Jer 8: 2 be gathered, nor be **b**; they shall be for H6912
16: 4 shall they be **b**; *but* they shall be as H6912
6 they shall not be **b**, neither shall *men* H6912
20: 6 die, and shalt be **b** there, thou, and all H6912
22:19 He shall be **b** with the burial of an ass, H6912
25:33 **b**; they shall be dung upon the ground. H6912
Ezk 39:15 have **b** it in the valley of Hamongog. H6912
Mt 14:12 and **b** it, and went and told Jesus. *G2290*
Lk 16:22 the rich man also died, and was **b**; *G2290*
Act 2:29 is both dead and **b**, and his sepulchre is *G2290*
5: 6 up, and carried *him* out, and **b** *him*. *G2290*
9 them which have **b** thy husband *are* at *G2290*
10 *her* forth, **b** *her* by her husband. *G2290*
Ro 6: 4 Therefore we are **b** with him by *G4916*
1Co 15: 4 And that he was **b**, and that he rose *G2290*
Col 2:12 **B** with him in baptism, wherein also ye *G4916*

BURIERS
Ezk 39:15 a sign by it, till the **b** have buried it in H6912

BURN
Gen 11: 3 us make brick, and **b** them throughly. H8313
44:18 and let not thine anger **b** against thy H2734
Ex 12:10 it until the morning ye shall **b** with fire. H8313
27:20 the light, to cause the lamp to **b** always. H5927
29:13 upon them, and **b** *them* upon the altar. H6999
14 dung, shalt thou **b** with fire without the H8313
18 And thou shalt **b** the whole ram upon H6999
25 their hands, and **b** *them* upon the altar H6999
34 then thou shalt **b** the remainder with H8313
30: 1 And thou shalt make an altar to **b** H4729
7 And Aaron shall **b** thereon sweet H6999
7 the lamps, he shall **b** incense upon it. H6999
8 at even, he shall **b** incense upon it, a H6999
20 **b** offering made by fire unto the LORD: H6999
Lev 1: 9 the priest shall **b** all on the altar, *to be* H6999
13 bring *it* all, and **b** *it* upon the altar: it H6999
15 off his head, and **b** *it* on the altar; and H6999
17 and the priest shall **b** it upon the altar, H6999
2: 2 the priest shall **b** the memorial of it H6999
9 thereof, and shall **b** *it* upon the altar: *it* H6999
11 for ye shall **b** no leaven, nor any honey, H6999
16 And the priest shall **b** the memorial of H6999
3: 5 And Aaron's sons shall **b** it on the altar H6999
11 And the priest shall **b** it upon the altar: H6999
16 And the priest shall **b** them upon the H6999
4:10 the priest shall **b** them upon the altar H6999
12 are poured out, and **b** him on the wood H8313
19 fat from him, and **b** *it* upon the altar. H6999
21 the camp, and **b** him as he burned the H8313
26 And he shall **b** all his fat upon the altar, H6999
31 the priest shall **b** *it* upon the altar for H6999
35 the priest shall **b** them upon the altar, H6999
5:12 thereof, and **b** *it* on the altar, according H6999
6:12 and the priest shall **b** wood on it every H1197
12 **b** thereon the fat of the peace offerings. H6999
15 offering, and shall **b** *it* upon the altar H6999
7: 5 And the priest shall **b** them upon the H6999
31 And the priest shall **b** the fat upon the H6999
8:32 and of the bread shall ye **b** with fire. H8313
13:52 He shall therefore **b** that garment, H8313
55 thou shalt **b** it in the fire; it *is* fret H8313
57 **b** that wherein the plague *is* with fire. H8313
16:25 And the fat of the sin offering shall he **b** H6999
27 and they shall **b** in the fire their skins, H8313
17: 6 congregation, and **b** the fat for a sweet H6999
24: 2 to cause the lamps to **b** continually. H5927
Nu 5:26 thereof, and **b** *it* upon the altar, and H6999
18:17 the altar, and shalt **b** their fat *for* an H6999
19: 5 And *one* shall **b** the heifer in his sight; H8313
5 her blood, with her dung, shall he **b**: H8313
Dt 5:23 the mountain did **b** with fire,) that ye H1197
7: 5 and **b** their graven images with fire. H8313
25 of their gods shall ye **b** with fire: thou H8313
12: 3 their pillars, and **b** their groves with H8313
13:16 thereof, and shalt **b** with fire the city, H8313
32:22 anger, and shall **b** unto the lowest hell, H3344
Jos 11: 6 horses, and **b** their chariots with fire. H8313
13 save Hazor only; *that* did Joshua **b**. H8313
Jdg 9:52 the door of the tower to **b** it with fire. H8313
12: 1 will **b** thine house upon thee with fire. H8313
14:15 us the riddle, lest we **b** thee and thy H8313
1Sa 2:16 them not fail to **b** the fat presently, and H6999
28 mine altar, to **b** incense, to wear an H6999
1Ki 13: 1 stood by the altar to **b** incense. H6999
2 high places that **b** incense upon thee, H6999
2Ki 16:15 the great altar **b** the morning burnt H6999
18: 4 of Israel did **b** incense to it: and he H6999
23: 5 had ordained to **b** incense in the high H6999
1Ch 23:13 sons for ever, to **b** incense before the H6999
2Ch 2: 4 *it* to him, *and* to **b** before him sweet H6999
6 save only to **b** sacrifice before him? H6999
4:20 that they should **b** after the manner H1197
13:11 And they **b** unto the LORD every H6999
11 lamps thereof, to **b** every evening: for H1197
26:16 to **b** incense upon the altar of incense. H6999
18 thee, Uzziah, to **b** incense unto the H6999
18 are consecrated to **b** incense: go out of H6999
19 in his hand to **b** incense: and while he H6999
28:25 high places to **b** incense unto other H6999
29:11 minister unto him, and **b** incense. H6999
32:12 before one altar, and **b** incense upon it? H6999
Neh 10:34 year by year, to **b** upon the altar of the H1197
Ps 79: 5 for ever? shall thy jealousy **b** like fire? H1197
89:46 for ever? shall thy wrath **b** like fire? H1197
Isa 1:31 they shall both **b** together, and none H1197
10:17 a flame: and it shall **b** and devour his H1197
27: 4 through them, I would **b** them together. H6702
40:16 And Lebanon *is* not sufficient to **b**, nor H1197
44:15 Then shall it be for a man to **b**: for he H1197
47:14 the fire shall **b** them; they shall not H8313
Jer 4: 4 forth like fire, and **b** that none can H1197
7: 9 swear falsely, and **b** incense unto Baal, H6999
20 it shall **b**, and shall not be quenched. H1197
31 the son of Hinnom, to **b** their sons and H8313
11:13 *even* altars to **b** incense unto Baal. H6999
15:14 in mine anger, *which* shall **b** upon you. H3344
17: 4 in mine anger, *which* shall **b** for ever. H3344
19: 5 places of Baal, to **b** their sons with fire H8313
21:10 of Babylon, and he shall **b** it with fire. H8313
12 go out like fire, and **b** that none can H1197
32:29 on this city, and **b** it with the houses, H8313
34: 2 of Babylon, and he shall **b** it with fire: H8313
5 thee, so shall they **b** *odours* for thee; H8313
22 it, and take it, and **b** it with fire: and I H8313
36:25 **b** the roll: but he would not hear them. H8313
37: 8 this city, and take it, and **b** it with fire. H8313
10 in his tent, and **b** this city with fire. H8313
38:18 and they shall **b** it with fire, and thou H8313
43:12 and he shall **b** them, and carry them H8313
13 of the Egyptians shall he **b** with fire. H8313
44: 3 in that they went to **b** incense, *and* to H6999
5 to **b** no incense unto other gods. H6999
17 our own mouth, to **b** incense unto the H6999
18 But since we left off to **b** incense to the H6999
25 that we have vowed, to **b** incense to the H6999
Ezk 5: 2 Thou shalt **b** with fire a third part in H1197
4 of the fire, and **b** them in the fire; *for* H8313
16:41 And they shall **b** thine houses with fire, H8313
23:47 and **b** up their houses with fire. H8313
24: 5 Take the choice of the flock, and **b** also H1754
11 may be hot, and may **b**, and *that* the H2787
39: 9 set on fire and **b** the weapons, both the H5400
9 they shall **b** them with fire seven years: H1197
10 for they shall **b** the weapons with fire: H1197
43:21 and he shall **b** it in the appointed place H8313
Hos 4:13 the mountains, and **b** incense upon the H6999
Nah 2:13 of hosts, and I will **b** her chariots in the H1197
Hab 1:16 unto their net, and **b** incense unto their H6999
Mal 4: 1 cometh, that shall **b** as an oven; and all H1197
1 that cometh shall **b** them up, saith the H3857
Mt 3:12 **b** up the chaff with unquenchable fire. *G2618*
13:30 in bundles to **b** them: but gather the *G2618*
Lk 1: 9 his lot was to **b** incense when he went *G2370*
3:17 chaff he will **b** with fire unquenchable. *G2618*
24:32 Did not our heart **b** within us, while he *G2545*

1Co 7: 9 for it is better to marry than to **b**. *G4448*
2Co 11:29 not weak? who is offended, and I **b** not? *G4448*
Rev 17:16 shall eat her flesh, and **b** her with fire. *G2618*

BURNED
Ex 3: 2 behold, the bush **b** with fire, and the H1197
Lev 4:21 burn him as he **b** the first bullock: it *is* H8313
8:16 their fat, and Moses **b** *it* upon the altar. H6999
Dt 4:11 and the mountain **b** with fire unto the H1197
9:15 and the mount **b** with fire: and the two H1197
Jos 7:25 with stones, and **b** them with fire, after H8313
11:13 strength, Israel **b** none of them, save H8313
1Sa 30: 1 and smitten Ziklag, and **b** it with fire; H8313
3 behold, *it was* **b** with fire; and their H8313
14 of Caleb; and we **b** Ziklag with fire. H8313
2Sa 5:21 and David and his men **b** them. H5375
23: 7 be utterly **b** with fire in the *same* place. H8313
2Ki 10:26 out of the house of Baal, and **b** them. H8313
15:35 sacrificed and **b** incense still in the H6999
22:17 me, and have **b** incense unto other H6999
23: 4 host of heaven: and he **b** them without H8313
5 them also that **b** incense unto Baal, to H6999
6 Kidron, and **b** it at the brook Kidron, H8313
8 the priests had **b** incense, from Geba H6999
11 and **b** the chariots of the sun with fire. H8313
15 brake down, and **b** the high place, *and* H8313
15 *it* small to powder, and **b** the grove. H8313
16 sepulchres, and **b** *them* upon the altar, H8313
20 the altars, and **b** men's bones upon H8313
1Ch 14:12 and they were **b** with fire. H8313
2Ch 25:14 before them, and **b** incense unto them. H6999
29: 7 and have not **b** incense nor offered H6999
34:25 me, and have **b** incense unto other H6999
Neh 1: 3 and the gates thereof are **b** with fire. H3341
2:17 gates thereof are **b** with fire: come, and H3341
4: 2 of the heaps of the rubbish which are **b**? H8313
Est 1:12 very wroth, and his anger **b** in him. H1197
Job 1:16 heaven, and hath **b** up the sheep, and H1197
30:30 me, and my bones are **b** with heat. H2787
Ps 39: 3 the fire **b**: *then* spake I with my tongue, H1197
74: 8 they have **b** up all the synagogues H8313
80:16 *It is* **b** with fire, *it is* cut down: they H8313
102: 3 and my bones are **b** as an hearth. H2787
106:18 company; the flame **b** up the wicked. H3857
Prv 6:27 in his bosom, and his clothes not be **b**? H8313
28 go upon hot coals, and his feet not be **b**? H3554
Isa 1: 7 your cities *are* **b** with fire: your land, H8313
24: 6 of the earth are **b**, and few men left. H2787
33:12 thorns cut up shall they be **b** in the fire. H3341
42:25 and it **b** him, yet he laid *it* not to heart. H1197
43: 2 thou shalt not be **b**; neither shall the H3554
44:19 to say, I have **b** part of it in the fire; H8313
64:11 praised thee, is **b** up with fire: and all H8316
65: 7 LORD, which have **b** incense upon the H6999
Jer 1:16 me, and have **b** incense unto other H6999
2:15 his cities are **b** without inhabitant. H3341
6:29 The bellows are **b**, the lead is consumed H2787
9:10 because they are **b** up, so that none can H3341
12 perisheth *and* is **b** up like a wilderness, H3341
18:15 me, they have **b** incense to vanity, and H6999
19: 4 place, and have **b** incense in it unto H6999
13 roofs they have **b** incense unto all the H6999
36:27 that the king had **b** the roll, and the H8313
28 Jehoiakim the king of Judah hath **b**. H8313
29 the LORD; Thou hast **b** this roll, saying, H8313
32 king of Judah had **b** in the fire: and H8313
38:17 city shall not be **b** with fire; and thou H8313
23 shalt cause this city to be **b** with fire. H8313
39: 8 And the Chaldeans **b** the king's house, H8313
44:15 their wives had **b** incense unto other H6999
19 And when we **b** incense to the queen of H6999
21 The incense that ye **b** in the cities of H6999
23 Because ye have **b** incense, and H6999
49: 2 her daughters shall be **b** with fire: then H3341
51:30 as women: they have **b** her H3341
32 the reeds they have **b** with fire, and the H8313
58 high gates shall be **b** with fire; and the H3341
52:13 And **b** the house of the LORD, and the H8313
13 houses of the great *men*, **b** he with fire: H8313
Lam 2: 3 the enemy, and he **b** against Jacob like H1197
Ezk 15: 4 midst of it is **b**. Is it meet for *any* work? H2787
5 the fire hath devoured it, and it is **b**? H2787
20:47 south to the north shall be **b** therein. H6866
24:10 and spice it well, and let the bones be **b**. H2787
Hos 2:13 wherein she **b** incense to them, and H6999
11: 2 and **b** incense to graven images. H6999
Joel 1:19 flame hath **b** all the trees of the field. H3857
Am 2: 1 because he **b** the bones of the king H8313
Mic 1: 7 thereof shall be **b** with the fire, and all H8313
Nah 1: 5 and the earth is **b** at his presence, yea, H5375
Mt 13:40 are gathered and **b** in the fire; so shall *G2618*
22: 7 those murderers, and **b** up their city. *G1714*
Jn 15: 6 cast *them* into the fire, and they are **b**. *G2545*
Act 19:19 together, and **b** them before all *men*: *G2618*
Ro 1:27 use of the woman, **b** in their lust one *G1572*
1Co 3:15 If any man's work shall be **b**, he shall *G2618*
13: 3 my body to be **b**, and have not charity, *G2545*
Heb 6: 8 nigh unto cursing; whose end *is* to be **b**. *G1519*
12:18 touched, and that **b** with fire, nor unto *G2545*
13:11 priest for sin, are **b** without the camp. *G2618*
2Pt 3:10 works that are therein shall be **b** up. *G2618*
Rev 1:15 brass, as if they **b** in a furnace; and his *G4448*
18: 8 shall be utterly **b** with fire: for strong *G2618*

BURNETH
Lev 13:24 quick *flesh* that **b** have a white bright H4348
16:28 And he that **b** them shall wash his H8313
Nu 19: 8 And he that **b** her shall wash his H8313
Ps 46: 9 in sunder; he **b** the chariot in the fire. H8313
83:14 As the fire **b** a wood, and as the flame H1197
97: 3 A fire goeth before him, and **b** up his H3857
Isa 9:18 For wickedness **b** as the fire: it shall H1197
44:16 He **b** part thereof in the fire; with part H8313
62: 1 the salvation thereof as a lamp *that* **b**. H1197
64: 2 As *when* the melting fire **b**, the fire H6919
65: 3 and **b** incense upon altars of brick; H6999
5 in my nose, a fire that **b** all the day. H3344
66: 3 blood; he that **b** incense, *as if* he H2142
Jer 48:35 and him that **b** incense to his gods. H6999
Hos 7: 6 in the morning it **b** as a flaming fire. H1197
Joel 2: 3 them a flame **b**: the land *is* as the H3857
Am 6:10 up, and he that **b** him, to bring out the H5635
Rev 21: 8 part in the lake which **b** with fire and *G2545*

BURNING
Gen 15:17 furnace, and a **b** lamp that passed H784
Ex 21:25 **B** for burning, wound for wound, stripe H3555
25 Burning for **b**, wound for wound, stripe H3555
Lev 6: 9 because of the **b** upon the altar all H4169
9 and the fire of the altar shall be **b** in it. H3344
12 And the fire upon the altar shall be **b** in H3344
13 The fire shall ever be **b** upon the altar; H3344
10: 6 the **b** which the LORD hath kindled. H8316
13:23 spread not, it *is* a **b** boil; and the priest H6867
24 *there is* a hot **b**, and the quick *flesh* H4348
25 broken out of the **b**: wherefore the H4348
28 it *is* a rising of the **b**, and the priest shall H4348
28 clean: for it *is* an inflammation of the **b**. H4348
16:12 And he shall take a censer full of **b** coals H784
26:16 and the **b** ague, that shall consume H6920
Nu 16:37 censers out of the **b**, and scatter thou H8316
19: 6 *it* into the midst of the **b** of the heifer. H8316
Dt 28:22 with an extreme **b**, and with the sword, H2746
29:23 and salt, *and* **b**, *that* it is not sown, nor H8316
32:24 and devoured with **b** heat, and with
2Ch 16:14 and they made a very great **b** for him. H8316
21:19 his people made no **b** for him, like the H8316
19 for him, like the **b** of his fathers. H8316
Job 41:19 Out of his mouth go **b** lamps, *and* H3940
Ps 140:10 Let **b** coals fall upon them: let them be H784
Prv 16:27 evil: and in his lips *there is* as a **b** fire. H6867
26:21 *As* coals *are* to **b** coals, and wood to H1513
23 **B** lips and a wicked heart *are like* a H1814
Isa 3:24 of sackcloth; *and* **b** instead of beauty. H3587
4: 4 of judgment, and by the spirit of **b**. H1197
9: 5 but *this* shall be with **b** *and* fuel of fire. H8316
10:16 kindle a **b** like the burning of a fire. H3350
16 kindle a burning like the **b** of a fire. H1197
30:27 cometh from far, **b** *with* his anger, and H1197
34: 9 the land thereof shall become **b** pitch. H1197
Jer 20: 9 in mine heart as a **b** fire shut up in my H1197
36:22 *was a fire* on the hearth **b** before him. H1197
44: 8 of your hands, **b** incense unto other H6999
Ezk 1:13 *was* like **b** coals of fire, *and* like H1197
Dan 3: 6 cast into the midst of a **b** fiery furnace. H3345
11 cast into the midst of a **b** fiery furnace. H3345
15 into the midst of a **b** fiery furnace; and H3345
17 us from the **b** fiery furnace, and he H3345
20 to cast *them* into the **b** fiery furnace. H3345
21 into the midst of the **b** fiery furnace. H3345
23 into the midst of the **b** fiery furnace. H3345
26 to the mouth of the **b** fiery furnace, *and* H3345
7: 9 the fiery flame, *and* his wheels *as* **b** fire. H1815
11 destroyed, and given to the **b** flame. H3346
Am 4:11 plucked out of the **b**: yet have ye not H8316
Hab 3: 5 Before him went the pestilence, and **b** H7565
Lk 12:35 loins be girded about, and *your* lights **b**; *G2545*
Jn 5:35 He was a **b** and a shining light: and ye *G2545*
Jas 1:11 For the sun is no sooner risen with a **b** *G2742*
Rev 4: 5 lamps of fire **b** before the throne, which *G2545*
8: 8 a great mountain **b** with fire was cast *G2545*
10 star from heaven, **b** as it were a lamp, *G2545*
18: 9 when they shall see the smoke of her **b**, *G4451*
18 the smoke of her **b**, saying, What *city is* *G4451*
19:20 into a lake of fire **b** with brimstone. *G2545*

B

BURNINGS
Isa 33:12 And the people shall be *as* the **b** of H4955
14 among us shall dwell with everlasting **b**? H4168
Jer 34: 5 peace: and with the **b** of thy fathers, the H4955

BURNISHED
Ezk 1: 7 they sparkled like the colour of **b** brass. H7044

BURNT
Gen 8:20 and offered **b** offerings on the altar. H5930
22: 2 him there for a **b** offering upon one of H5930
3 the wood for the **b** offering, and rose H5930
6 And Abraham took the wood of the **b** H5930
7 but where *is* the lamb for a **b** offering? H5930
8 a lamb for a **b** offering: so they went H5930
13 for a **b** offering in the stead of his son. H5930
38:24 said, Bring her forth, and let her be **b**. H8313
Ex 3: 3 this great sight, why the bush is not **b**. H1197
10:25 also sacrifices and **b** offerings, that we H5930
18:12 in law, took a **b** offering and sacrifices H5930
20:24 thereon thy **b** offerings, and thy peace H5930
24: 5 Israel, which offered **b** offerings, and H5930
29:18 the altar: it *is* a **b** offering unto the H5930
25 the altar for a **b** offering, for a sweet H5930
42 *This shall be* a continual **b** offering H5930
30: 9 thereon, nor **b** sacrifice, nor meat H5930
28 And the altar of **b** offering with all his H5930
31: 9 And the altar of **b** offering with all his H5930
32: 6 and offered **b** offerings, and brought H5930
20 they had made, and **b** *it* in the fire, and H8313
35:16 The altar of **b** offering, with his brasen H5930
38: 1 And he made the altar of **b** offering *of* H5930
40: 6 And thou shalt set the altar of the **b** H5930
10 And thou shalt anoint the altar of the **b** H5930
27 And he **b** sweet incense thereon; as the H6999
29 And he put the altar of **b** offering *by* the H5930
29 offered upon it the **b** offering and the H5930
Lev 1: 3 If his offering *be* a **b** sacrifice of the H5930
4 the head of the **b** offering; and it shall H5930
6 And he shall flay the **b** offering, and cut H5930
9 the altar, *to be* a **b** sacrifice, an offering H5930
10 of the goats, for a **b** sacrifice; he shall H5930
13 the altar: it *is* a **b** sacrifice, an offering H5930
14 And if the **b** sacrifice for his offering to H5930
17 the fire: it *is* a **b** sacrifice, an offering H5930
2:12 be **b** on the altar for a sweet savour. H5927
3: 5 the altar upon the **b** sacrifice, which *is* H5930
4: 7 of the altar of the **b** offering, which *is at* H5930
10 them upon the altar of the **b** offering. H5930
12 the ashes are poured out shall he be **b**. H8313
18 of the altar of the **b** offering, which *is at* H5930
24 where they kill the **b** offering before the H5930
25 of the altar of **b** offering, and shall pour H5930
25 at the bottom of the altar of **b** offering. H5930
29 offering in the place of the **b** offering. H5930
30 of the altar of **b** offering, and shall pour H5930
33 the place where they kill the **b** offering. H5930
34 of the altar of **b** offering, and shall pour H5930
5: 7 offering, and the other for a **b** offering. H5930
10 And he shall offer the second *for* a **b** H5930
6: 9 This *is* the law of the **b** offering: It *is* the H5930
9 offering: It *is* the **b** offering, because of H5930
10 with the **b** offering on the altar, H5930
12 and lay the **b** offering in order upon H5930
22 unto the LORD; it shall be wholly **b**. H6999
23 shall be wholly **b**: it shall not be eaten.
25 place where the **b** offering is killed shall H5930
30 shall be eaten: it shall be **b** in the fire. H8313
7: 2 In the place where they kill the **b** H5930
8 any man's **b** offering, *even* the priest H5930
8 of the **b** offering which he hath offered. H5930
17 on the third day shall be **b** with fire. H8313
19 eaten; it shall be **b** with fire: and as for H8313
37 This *is* the law of the **b** offering, of the H5930
8:17 and his dung, he **b** with fire without the H8313
18 And he brought the ram for the **b** H5930
20 **b** the head, and the pieces, and the fat. H6999
21 in water; and Moses **b** the whole ram H6999
21 the altar: it *was* a **b** sacrifice for a sweet H5930
28 off their hands, and **b** *them* on the altar H6999
28 the altar upon the **b** offering: they *were* H5930

Lev 9: 2 and a ram for a **b** offering, without H5930
3 year, without blemish, for a **b** offering; H5930
7 offering, and thy **b** offering, and make H5930
10 sin offering, he **b** upon the altar; as the H6999
11 And the flesh and the hide he **b** with H8313
12 And he slew the **b** offering; and Aaron's H5930
13 And they presented the **b** offering unto H5930
13 the head: and he **b** *them* upon the altar. H6999
14 and the legs, and **b** *them* upon the H6999
14 *them* upon the **b** offering on the altar. H5930
16 And he brought the **b** offering, and H5930
17 thereof, and **b** *it* upon the altar, beside H6999
17 beside the **b** sacrifice of the morning. H5930
20 breasts, and he **b** the fat upon the altar: H6999
22 and the **b** offering, and peace offerings. H5930
24 upon the altar the **b** offering and the H5930
10:16 behold, it was **b**: and he was angry with H8313
19 offering and their **b** offering before the H5930
12: 6 of the first year for a **b** offering, and a H5930
8 the one for the **b** offering, and the other H5930
13:52 fretting leprosy; it shall be **b** in the fire. H8313
14:13 offering and the **b** offering, in the holy H5930
19 afterward he shall kill the **b** offering: H5930
20 And the priest shall offer the **b** offering H5930
22 sin offering, and the other a **b** offering. H5930
31 the other *for* a **b** offering, with the meat H5930
15:15 the other *for* a **b** offering; and the priest H5930
30 the other *for* a **b** offering; and the priest H5930
16: 3 sin offering, and a ram for a **b** offering. H5930
5 offering, and one ram for a **b** offering. H5930
24 and offer his **b** offering, and the burnt H5930
24 burnt offering, and the **b** offering of the H5930
17: 8 that offereth a **b** offering or sacrifice, H5930
19: 6 the third day, it shall be **b** in the fire. H8313
20:14 they shall be **b** with fire, both he and H8313
21: 9 her father: she shall be **b** with fire. H8313
22:18 offer unto the LORD for a **b** offering; H5930
23:12 year for a **b** offering unto the LORD. H5930
18 they shall be *for* a **b** offering unto the H5930
37 fire unto the LORD, a **b** offering, and a H5930
Nu 6:11 the other for a **b** offering, and make H5930
14 blemish for a **b** offering, and one ewe H5930
16 his sin offering, and his **b** offering: H5930
7:15 lamb of the first year, for a **b** offering: H5930
21 lamb of the first year, for a **b** offering: H5930
27 lamb of the first year, for a **b** offering: H5930
33 lamb of the first year, for a **b** offering: H5930
39 lamb of the first year, for a **b** offering: H5930
45 lamb of the first year, for a **b** offering: H5930
51 lamb of the first year, for a **b** offering: H5930
57 lamb of the first year, for a **b** offering: H5930
63 lamb of the first year, for a **b** offering: H5930
69 lamb of the first year, for a **b** offering: H5930
75 lamb of the first year, for a **b** offering: H5930
81 lamb of the first year, for a **b** offering: H5930
87 All the oxen for the **b** offering *were* H5930
8:12 and the other *for* a **b** offering, unto the H5930
10:10 over your **b** offerings, and over H5930
11: 1 fire of the LORD **b** among them, and H1197
3 the fire of the LORD **b** among them. H1197
15: 3 fire unto the LORD, a **b** offering, or a H5930
5 **b** offering or sacrifice, for one lamb. H5930
8 a bullock *for* a **b** offering, or *for* a H5930
24 bullock for a **b** offering, for a sweet H5930
16:39 they that were **b** had offered; and they H8313
19:17 take of the ashes of the **b** heifer of H8316
23: 3 Stand by thy **b** offering, and I will go: H5930
6 lo, he stood by his **b** sacrifice, he, and H5930
15 Stand here by thy **b** offering, while I H5930
17 he stood by his **b** offering, and the H5930
28: 3 day by day, *for* a continual **b** offering. H5930
6 *It is* a continual **b** offering, which was H5930
10 *This is* the **b** offering of every sabbath, H5930
10 **b** offering, and his drink offering. H5930
11 ye shall offer a **b** offering unto the H5930
13 one lamb; *for* a **b** offering of a sweet H5930
14 a lamb: this *is* the **b** offering of every H5930
15 **b** offering, and his drink offering. H5930
19 made by fire *for* a **b** offering unto the H5930
23 Ye shall offer these beside the **b** H5930
23 which *is* for a continual **b** offering. H5930
24 **b** offering, and his drink offering. H5930
27 But ye shall offer the **b** offering for a H5930
31 the continual **b** offering, and his meat H5930
29: 2 And ye shall offer a **b** offering for a H5930
6 Beside the **b** offering of the month, and H5930
6 and the daily **b** offering, and his meat H5930
8 But ye shall offer a **b** offering unto the H5930
11 and the continual **b** offering, and the H5930

Nu 29:13 And ye shall offer a **b** offering, a H5930
16 the continual **b** offering, his meat H5930
19 the continual **b** offering, and the meat H5930
22 the continual **b** offering, and his meat H5930
25 the continual **b** offering, his meat H5930
28 the continual **b** offering, and his meat H5930
31 the continual **b** offering, his meat H5930
34 the continual **b** offering, his meat H5930
36 But ye shall offer a **b** offering, a H5930
38 the continual **b** offering, and his meat H5930
39 offerings, for your **b** offerings, and for H5930
31:10 And they **b** all their cities wherein they H8313
Dt 9:21 ye had made, and **b** it with fire, and H8313
12: 6 And thither ye shall bring your **b** H5930
11 you; your **b** offerings, and your H5930
13 thou offer not thy **b** offerings in every H5930
14 shalt offer thy **b** offerings, and there H5930
27 And thou shalt offer thy **b** offerings, the H5930
31 they have **b** in the fire to their gods. H8313
27: 6 and thou shalt offer **b** offerings thereon H5930
32:24 *They shall be* **b** with hunger, and H4198
33:10 and whole **b** sacrifice upon thine altar. H3632
Jos 6:24 And they **b** the city with fire, and all H8313
7:15 thing shall be **b** with fire, he and all H8313
8:28 And Joshua **b** Ai, and made it an heap H8313
31 offered thereon **b** offerings unto the H5930
11: 9 horses, and **b** their chariots with fire. H8313
11 to breathe: and he **b** Hazor with fire. H8313
22:23 or if to offer thereon **b** offering or meat H5930
26 not for **b** offering, nor for sacrifice: H5930
27 him with our **b** offerings, and with H5930
28 made, not for **b** offerings, nor for H5930
29 build an altar for **b** offerings, for meat H5930
Jdg 6:26 and offer a **b** sacrifice with the wood H5930
11:31 and I will offer it up for a **b** offering. H5930
13:16 and if thou wilt offer a **b** offering, thou H5930
23 have received a **b** offering and a meat H5930
15: 5 Philistines, and **b** up both the shocks, H1197
6 up, and **b** her and her father with fire. H8313
14 as flax that was **b** with fire, and his H1197
18:27 of the sword, and **b** the city with fire. H8313
20:26 even, and offered **b** offerings and peace H5930
21: 4 offered **b** offerings and peace offerings. H5930
1Sa 2:15 Also before they **b** the fat, the priest's H6999
6:14 the kine a **b** offering unto the LORD. H5930
15 offered **b** offerings and sacrificed H5930
7: 9 offered *it for* a **b** offering wholly unto H5930
10 And as Samuel was offering up the **b** H5930
10: 8 unto thee, to offer **b** offerings, *and* to H5930
13: 9 And Saul said, Bring hither a **b** offering H5930
9 offerings. And he offered the **b** offering. H5930
10 end of offering the **b** offering, behold, H5930
12 therefore, and offered a **b** offering. H5930
15:22 *as great* delight in **b** offerings and H5930
31:12 and came to Jabesh, and **b** them there. H8313
2Sa 6:17 it: and David offered **b** offerings and H5930
18 an end of offering **b** offerings and H5930
24:22 *here be* oxen for **b** sacrifice, and H5930
24 neither will I offer **b** offerings unto the H5930
25 and offered **b** offerings and peace H5930
1Ki 3: 3 sacrificed and **b** incense in high places. H6999
4 high place: a thousand **b** offerings did H5930
15 and offered up **b** offerings, and offered H5930
8:64 there he offered **b** offerings, and meat H5930
64 too little to receive the **b** offerings, and H5930
9:16 and taken Gezer, and **b** it with fire, and H8313
25 year did Solomon offer **b** offerings and H5930
25 the LORD, and he **b** incense upon the H6999
11: 8 wives, which **b** incense and sacrificed H6999
12:33 offered upon the altar, and **b** incense. H6999
13: 2 and men's bones shall be **b** upon thee. H8313
15:13 her idol, and **b** *it* by the brook Kidron. H8313
16:18 king's house, and **b** the king's house H8313
18:33 *it* on the **b** sacrifice, and on the wood. H5930
38 and consumed the **b** sacrifice, and the H5930
22:43 and **b** incense yet in the high places. H6999
2Ki 1:14 from heaven, and **b** up the two captains H398
3:27 offered him *for* a **b** offering upon the H5930
5:17 offer neither **b** offering nor sacrifice H5930
10:24 offer sacrifices and **b** offerings, Jehu H5930
25 end of offering the **b** offering, that Jehu H5930
12: 3 and **b** incense in the high places. H6999
14: 4 and **b** incense on the high places. H6999
15: 4 and **b** incense still on the high places. H6999
16: 4 And he sacrificed and **b** incense in the H6999
13 And he **b** his burnt offering and his H5930
13 And he burnt his **b** offering and his H5930
15 burn the morning **b** offering, and the H5930
15 and the king's **b** sacrifice, and his meat H5930

2Ki 16:15 offering, with the **b** offering of all the H5930
15 the blood of the **b** offering, and all the H5930
17:11 And there they **b** incense in all the high H6999
31 the Sepharvites **b** their children in fire H8313
25: 9 And he **b** the house of the LORD, and H8313
9 every great *man's* house **b** he with fire. H8313
1Ch 6:49 the altar of the **b** offering, and on the H5930
16: 1 and they offered **b** sacrifices and peace H5930
2 end of offering the **b** offerings and the H5930
40 To offer **b** offerings unto the LORD H5930
40 the altar of the **b** offering continually H5930
21:23 the oxen *also* for **b** offerings, and the H5930
24 nor offer **b** offerings without cost. H5930
26 and offered **b** offerings and peace H5930
26 by fire upon the altar of **b** offering. H5930
29 the altar of the **b** offering, *were* at that H5930
22: 1 *is* the altar of the **b** offering for Israel. H5930
23:31 And to offer all **b** sacrifices unto the H5930
29:21 and offered **b** offerings unto the LORD, H5930
2Ch 1: 6 offered a thousand **b** offerings upon it. H5930
2: 4 and for the **b** offerings morning and H5930
4: 6 offered for the **b** offering they washed H5930
7: 1 and consumed the **b** offering and the H5930
7 there he offered **b** offerings, and the fat H5930
7 able to receive the **b** offerings, and the H5930
8:12 Then Solomon offered **b** offerings unto H5930
13:11 and every evening **b** sacrifices and H5930
15:16 *it*, and **b** *it* at the brook Kidron. H8313
23:18 the LORD, to offer the **b** offerings of the H5930
24:14 And they offered **b** offerings in the H5930
28: 3 Moreover he **b** incense in the valley of H6999
3 of Hinnom, and **b** his children in the H1197
4 He sacrificed also and **b** incense in the H6999
29: 7 nor offered **b** offerings in the holy H5930
18 and the altar of **b** offering, with all the H5930
24 *that* the **b** offering and the sin H5930
27 to offer the **b** offering upon the altar. H5930
27 And when the **b** offering began, the H5930
28 until the **b** offering was finished. H5930
31 as were of a free heart **b** offerings. H5930
32 And the number of the **b** offerings, H5930
32 these *were* for a **b** offering to the LORD. H5930
34 not flay all the **b** offerings: wherefore H5930
35 And also the **b** offerings *were* in H5930
35 offerings for *every* **b** offering. So the H5930
30:15 **b** offerings into the house of the LORD. H5930
31: 2 and Levites for **b** offerings and for H5930
3 substance for the **b** offerings, *to wit*, for H5930
3 and evening **b** offerings, and the burnt H5930
3 offerings, and the **b** offerings for the H5930
34: 5 And he **b** the bones of the priests upon H8313
35:12 And they removed the **b** offerings, that H5930
14 in offering of **b** offerings and the fat H5930
16 and to offer **b** offerings upon the altar H5930
36:19 And they **b** the house of God, and H8313
19 wall of Jerusalem, and **b** all the palaces H8313
Ezr 3: 2 of Israel, to offer **b** offerings thereon, as H5930
3 and they offered **b** offerings thereon H5930
3 *even* **b** offerings morning and evening. H5930
4 and *offered* the daily **b** offerings by H5930
5 And afterward *offered* the continual **b** H5930
6 they to offer **b** offerings unto the LORD. H5930
6: 9 and lambs, for the **b** offerings of the H5928
8:35 captivity, offered **b** offerings unto the H5930
35 all *this was* a **b** offering unto the LORD. H5930
Neh 10:33 and for the continual **b** offering, of the H5930
Job 1: 5 and offered **b** offerings *according* H5930
42: 8 up for yourselves a **b** offering; and my H5930
Ps 20: 3 and accept thy **b** sacrifice; Selah. H5930
40: 6 hast thou opened: **b** offering and sin H5930
50: 8 thy sacrifices or thy **b** offerings, *to have* H5930
51:16 give *it*: thou delightest not in **b** offering. H5930
19 with **b** offering and whole H5930
19 and whole **b** offering: then shall H5930
66:13 I will go into thy house with **b** H5930
15 I will offer unto thee **b** sacrifices of H5930
Isa 1:11 I am full of the **b** offerings of rams, and H5930
40:16 thereof sufficient for a **b** offering. H5930
43:23 small cattle of thy **b** offerings; neither H5930
56: 7 of prayer: their **b** offerings and their H5930
61: 8 I hate robbery for **b** offering; and I will H5930
Jer 6:20 a far country? your **b** offerings *are* not H5930
7:21 God of Israel; Put your **b** offerings unto H5930
22 concerning **b** offerings or sacrifices: H5930
14:12 and when they offer **b** offering and an H5930
17:26 the south, bringing **b** offerings, and H5930
19: 5 sons with fire *for* **b** offerings unto Baal, H5930
33:18 before me to offer **b** offerings, and to H5930
51:25 and will make thee a **b** mountain. H8316

Ezk 40:38 where they washed the **b** offering. H5930
39 to slay thereon the **b** offering and the H5930
42 hewn stone for the **b** offering, of a cubit H5930
42 slew the **b** offering and the sacrifice. H5930
43:18 make it, to offer **b** offerings thereon, H5930
24 up *for* a **b** offering unto the LORD. H5930
27 shall make your **b** offerings upon the H5930
44:11 they shall slay the **b** offering and the H5930
45:15 offering, and for a **b** offering, and for H5930
17 part *to give* **b** offerings, and meat H5930
17 offering, and the **b** offering, and the H5930
23 he shall prepare a **b** offering to the H5930
25 according to the **b** offering, and H5930
46: 2 shall prepare his **b** offering and his H5930
4 And the **b** offering that the prince shall H5930
12 prepare a voluntary **b** offering or peace H5930
12 he shall prepare his **b** offering and his H5930
13 Thou shalt daily prepare a **b** offering H5930
15 morning *for* a continual **b** offering. H5930
Hos 6: 6 of God more than **b** offerings. H5930
Am 5:22 Though ye offer me **b** offerings and H5930
Mic 6: 6 **b** offerings, with calves of a year old? H5930
Mk 12:33 all whole **b** offerings and sacrifices. G3646
Heb 10: 6 In **b** offerings and *sacrifices* for sin G3646
8 and offering and **b** offerings and G3646
Rev 8: 7 **b** up, and all green grass was burnt up. G2618
7 burnt up, and all green grass was **b** up. G2618

BURNT-OFFERING See BURNT and OFFERING.

BURNT-SACRIFICE See BURNT and SACRIFICE.

BURST
Job 32:19 no vent; it is ready to **b** like new bottles. H1234
Prv 3:10 thy presses shall **b** out with new wine. H6555
Jer 2:20 thy yoke, *and* **b** thy bands; and thou H5423
5: 5 broken the yoke, *and* **b** the bonds. H5423
30: 8 off thy neck, and will **b** thy bonds, and H5423
Nah 1:13 thee, and will **b** thy bonds in sunder. H5423
Mk 2:22 the new wine doth **b** the bottles, and G4486
Lk 5:37 the new wine will **b** the bottles, and be G4486
Act 1:18 headlong, he **b** asunder in the midst, G2997

BURSTING
Isa 30:14 be found in the **b** of it a sherd to take H4386

BURY
Gen 23: 4 that I may **b** my dead out of my sight. H6912
6 of our sepulchres **b** thy dead; none of H6912
6 but that thou mayest **b** thy dead. H6912
8 that I should **b** my dead out of my H6912
11 of my people give I it thee: **b** thy dead. H6912
13 *it* of me, and I will **b** my dead there. H6912
15 me and thee? **b** therefore thy dead. H6912
47:29 me; **b** me not, I pray thee, in Egypt: H6912
30 me out of Egypt, and **b** me in their H6912
49:29 unto my people: **b** me with my fathers H6912
50: 5 there shalt thou **b** me. Now therefore H6912
5 and **b** my father, and I will come again. H6912
6 And Pharaoh said, Go up, and **b** thy H6912
7 And Joseph went up to **b** his father: H6912
14 up with him to **b** his father, after he H6912
Dt 21:23 shalt in any wise **b** him that day; (for H6912
1Ki 2:31 fall upon him, and **b** him; that thou H6912
11:15 was gone up to **b** the slain, after he had H6912
13:29 to the city, to mourn and to **b** him. H6912
31 I am dead, then **b** me in the sepulchre H6912
14:13 for him, and **b** him: for he only of H6912
2Ki 9:10 *shall be* none to **b** *her.* And he opened H6912
34 and **b** her: for she *is* a king's daughter. H6912
35 And they went to **b** her: but they found H6912
Ps 79: 3 and *there was* none to **b** *them.* H6912
Jer 7:32 shall **b** in Tophet, till there be no place. H6912
14:16 shall have none to **b** them, them, their H6912
19:11 and they shall **b** *them* in Tophet, till H6912
11 in Tophet, till *there be* no place to **b**. H6912
Ezk 39:11 and there shall they **b** Gog and all his H6912
13 Yea, all the people of the land shall **b** H6912
14 the land to **b** with the passengers H6912
Hos 9: 6 Memphis shall **b** them: the pleasant H6912
Mt 8:21 suffer me first to go and **b** my father. G2290
22 me; and let the dead **b** their dead. G2290
27: 7 the potter's field, to **b** strangers in. G5027
Lk 9:59 suffer me first to go and **b** my father. G2290
60 Jesus said unto him, Let the dead **b** G2290
Jn 19:40 spices, as the manner of the Jews is to **b**. G1779

BURYING
2Ki 13:21 And it came to pass, as they were **b** a H6912
Ezk 39:12 house of Israel be **b** of them, that they H6912
Mk 14: 8 aforehand to anoint my body to the **b**. G1780
Jn 12: 7 the day of my **b** hath she kept this. G1780

BURYINGPLACE
Gen 23: 4 a possession of a **b** with you, that I may H6913
9 for a possession of a **b** amongst you. H6913
47:30 bury me in their **b**. And he said, I will H6900
49:30 the Hittite for a possession of a **b**. H6913
50:13 **b** of Ephron the Hittite, before Mamre. H6913

BURYING-PLACE
Gen 23:20 a possession of a **b** by the sons of Heth. H6913
Jdg 16:31 and Eshtaol in the **b** of Manoah his H6913

BUSH
Ex 3: 2 of the midst of a **b**: and he looked, and, H5572
2 and, behold, the **b** burned with fire, H5572
2 with fire, and the **b** *was* not consumed. H5572
3 this great sight, why the **b** is not burnt. H5572
4 of the midst of the **b**, and said, Moses, H5572
Dt 33:16 that dwelt in the **b**: let *the blessing* come H5572
Mk 12:26 of Moses, how in the **b** God spake unto G942
Lk 6:44 nor of a bramble **b** gather they grapes. G942
20:37 shewed at the **b**, when he calleth the Lord G942
Act 7:30 angel of the Lord in a flame of fire in a **b**. G942
35 the angel which appeared to him in the **b**. G942

BUSHEL
Mt 5:15 candle, and put it under a **b**, but on a G3426
Mk 4:21 to be put under a **b**, or under a bed? and G3426
Lk 11:33 neither under a **b**, but on a candlestick, G3426

BUSHES
Job 30: 4 Who cut up mallows by the **b**, and H7880
7 Among the **b** they brayed; under the H7880
Isa 7:19 and upon all thorns, and upon all **b**. H5097

BUSHY
Song 5:11 his locks *are* **b**, *and* black as a raven. H8534

BUSIED
2Ch 35:14 sons of Aaron *were* **b** in offering of burnt

BUSINESS
Gen 39:11 house to do his **b**; and *there was* none H4399
Dt 24: 5 charged with any **b**: *but* he shall be free H1697
Jos 2:14 ye utter not this our **b**. And it shall be, H1697
20 And if thou utter this our **b**, then we will H1697
Jdg 18: 7 and had no **b** with *any* man. H1697
28 and they had no **b** with *any* man; and H1697
1Sa 20:19 thyself when the **b** was *in hand,* and H4639
21: 2 commanded me a **b**, and hath said unto H1697
2 any thing of the **b** whereabout I send H1697
8 because the king's **b** required haste. H1697
1Ch 26:29 **b** over Israel, for officers and judges. H4399
30 in all the **b** of the LORD, and in H4399
2Ch 13:10 and the Levites *wait* upon *their* **b**: H4399
17:13 And he had much **b** in the cities of H4399
32:31 Howbeit in *the* **b** *of* the ambassadors of
Neh 11:16 of the outward **b** of the house of God. H4399
22 *were* over the **b** of the house of God. H4399
13:30 and the Levites, every one in his **b**; H4399
Est 3: 9 **b**, to bring *it* into the king's treasuries. H4399
Ps 107:23 sea in ships, that do **b** in great waters; H4399
Prv 22:29 Seest thou a man diligent in his **b**? he H4399
Ecc 5: 3 the multitude of **b**; and a fool's voice *is* H6045
8:16 and to see the **b** that is done upon the H6045
Dan 8:27 up, and did the king's **b**; and I was H4399
Lk 2:49 not that I must be about my Father's **b**? G3588
Act 6: 3 whom we may appoint over this **b**. G5532
Ro 12:11 Not slothful in **b**; fervent in spirit; G4710
16: 2 her in whatsoever **b** she hath need of G4229
1Th 4:11 and to do your own **b**, and to work with G4238

BUSY
1Ki 20:40 And as thy servant was **b** here and H6213

BUSYBODIES
2Th 3:11 disorderly, working not at all, but are **b**. G4020
1Ti 5:13 but tattlers also and **b**, speaking things G4021

BUSYBODY
1Pt 4:15 or as a **b** in other men's matters. G244

BUT See the Appendix.

BUTLER
Gen 40: 1 things, *that* the **b** of the king of Egypt H4945
5 of his dream, the **b** and the baker of the H4945
9 And the chief **b** told his dream to H4945
13 former manner when thou wast his **b**. H4945
20 the head of the chief **b** and of the chief H4945
21 And he restored the chief **b** unto his H4945
23 Yet did not the chief **b** remember H4945
41: 9 Then spake the chief **b** unto Pharaoh, H4945

B

BUTLERS
Gen 40: 2 **b**, and against the chief of the bakers. H4945

BUTLERSHIP
Gen 40:21 butler unto his **b** again; and he gave H4945

BUTTER
Gen 18: 8 And he took **b**, and milk, and the calf H2529
Dt 32:14 **B** of kine, and milk of sheep, with fat of H2529
Jdg 5:25 she brought forth **b** in a lordly dish. H2529
2Sa 17:29 And honey, and **b**, and sheep, and H2529
Job 20:17 the floods, the brooks of honey and **b**. H2529
29: 6 When I washed my steps with **b**, and H2529
Ps 55:21 smoother than **b**, but war *was* in his H4260
Prv 30:33 bringeth forth **b**, and the wringing of H2529
Isa 7:15 **B** and honey shall he eat, that he may H2529
22 give he shall eat **b**: for butter and honey H2529
22 eat butter: for **b** and honey shall every H2529

BUTTOCKS
2Sa 10: 4 *even* to their **b**, and sent them away. H8357
1Ch 19: 4 hard by their **b**, and sent them away. H4667
Isa 20: 4 **b** uncovered, to the shame of Egypt. H8357

BUY
Gen 41:57 to Joseph for to **b** *corn;* because that H7666
42: 2 down thither, and **b** for us from thence; H7666
3 brethren went down to **b** corn in Egypt. H7666
5 And the sons of Israel came to **b** *corn* H7666
7 From the land of Canaan to **b** food. H7666
10 but to **b** food are thy servants come. H7666
43: 2 unto them, Go again, **b** us a little food. H7666
4 us, we will go down and **b** thee food: H7666
20 indeed down at the first time to **b** food: H7666
22 in our hands to **b** food: we cannot tell H7666
44:25 And our father said, Go again, *and* **b** us H7666
47:19 we and our land? **b** us and our land for H7069
Ex 21: 2 If thou **b** an Hebrew servant, six years H7069
Lev 22:11 But if the priest **b** *any* soul with his H7069
25:15 the jubile thou shalt **b** of thy neighbour, H7069
44 shall ye **b** bondmen and bondmaids. H7069
45 of them shall ye **b**, and of their families H7069
Dt 2: 6 Ye shall **b** meat of them for money, H7666
6 and ye shall also **b** water of them for H3739
28:68 bondwomen, and no man shall **b** *you.* H7069
Ru 4: 4 advertise thee, saying, **B** *it* before the H7069
5 Naomi, thou must **b** *it* also of Ruth the H7069
8 **B** *it* for thee. So he drew off his shoe. H7069
2Sa 24:21 David said, To **b** the threshingfloor of H7069
24 but I will surely **b** *it* of thee at a price: H7069
2Ki 12:12 of stone, and to **b** timber and hewed H7069
22: 6 and masons, and to **b** timber and hewn H7069
1Ch 21:24 but I will verily **b** it for the full price: for H7069
2Ch 34:11 gave they *it,* to **b** hewn stone, and H7069
Ezr 7:17 That thou mayest **b** speedily with this H7066
Neh 5: 3 we might **b** corn, because of the dearth. H3947
10:31 *that* we would not **b** it of them on the H3947
Prv 23:23 **B** the truth, and sell *it* not; *also* H7069
Isa 55: 1 money; come ye, **b**, and eat; yea, come, H7666
1 and eat; yea, come, **b** wine and milk H7666
Jer 32: 7 unto thee, saying, **B** thee my field that H7069
7 the right of redemption *is* thine to **b** *it.* H7069
8 and said unto me, **B** my field, I pray H7069
8 *is* thine; **b** *it* for thyself. Then I H7069
25 me, O Lord GOD, **B** thee the field for H7069
44 Men shall **b** fields for money, and H7069
Am 8: 6 That we may **b** the poor for silver, and H7069
Mt 14:15 the villages, and **b** themselves victuals. G59
25: 9 to them that sell, and **b** for yourselves. G59
10 And while they went to **b**, the bridegroom G59
Mk 6:36 the villages, and **b** themselves bread: for G59
37 him, Shall we go and **b** two hundred G59
Lk 9:13 should go and **b** meat for all this people. G59
22:36 let him sell his garment, and **b** one. G59
Jn 4: 8 were gone away unto the city to **b** meat.) G59
6: 5 shall we **b** bread, that these may eat? G59
13:29 had said unto him, **B** *those things* that G59
1Co 7:30 that **b**, as though they possessed not; G59
Jas 4:13 a year, and **b** and sell, and get gain: G1710
Rev 3:18 I counsel thee to **b** of me gold tried in the G59
13:17 And that no man might **b** or sell, save he G59

BUYER
Prv 20:14 *It is* naught, *it is* naught, saith the **b**: but H7069
Isa 24: 2 as with the **b**, so with the seller; as H7069
Ezk 7:12 near: let not the **b** rejoice, nor the seller H7069

BUYEST
Lev 25:14 unto thy neighbour, or **b** *ought* of thy H7069
Ru 4: 5 Then said Boaz, What day thou **b** the H7069

BUYETH
Prv 31:16 She considereth a field, and **b** it: with H3947
Mt 13:44 selleth all that he hath, and **b** that field. *G59*
Rev 18:11 no man **b** their merchandise any more: *G59*

BUZ
Gen 22:21 Huz his firstborn, and **B** his brother, and H938
1Ch 5:14 Jeshishai, the son of Jahdo, the son of **B**; H938
Jer 25:23 Dedan, and Tema, and **B**, and all *that are* H938

BUZI
Ezk 1: 3 the priest, the son of **B**, in the land of the H941

BUZITE
Job 32: 2 son of Barachel the **B**, of the kindred of H940
6 And Elihu the son of Barachel the **B** H940

BY See the Appendix.

BYWAYS
Jdg 5: 6 the travellers walked through **b**. H734+H6128

BYWORD
Dt 28:37 a proverb, and a **b**, among all nations H8148
1Ki 9: 7 be a proverb and a **b** among all people: H8148
2Ch 7:20 a proverb and a **b** among all nations. H8148
Job 17: 6 He hath made me also a **b** of the H4914
30: 9 now am I their song, yea, I am their **b**. H4405
Ps 44:14 Thou makest us a **b** among the H4912

C

CAB
2Ki 6:25 **c** of dove's dung for five *pieces* of silver. H6894

CABBON
Jos 15:40 And **C**, and Lahmam, and Kithlish, H3522

CABINS
Jer 37:16 and into the **c**, and Jeremiah had H2588

CABUL
Jos 19:27 and goeth out to **C** on the left hand, H3521
1Ki 9:13 called them the land of **C** unto this day. H3521

CAESAR
Mt 22:17 it lawful to give tribute unto **C**, or not? *G2541*
21 therefore unto **C** the things which are *G2541*
Mk 12:14 Is it lawful to give tribute to **C**, or not? *G2541*
17 them, Render to **C** the things that are *G2541*
Lk 2: 1 out a decree from **C** Augustus, that all *G2541*
3: 1 reign of Tiberius **C**, Pontius Pilate being *G2541*
20:22 Is it lawful for us to give tribute unto **C**, *G2541*
25 therefore unto **C** the things which be *G2541*
23: 2 to give tribute to **C**, saying that he *G2541*
Jn 19:12 himself a king speaketh against **C**. *G2541*
15 answered, We have no king but **C**. *G2541*
Act 11:28 came to pass in the days of Claudius **C**. *G2541*
17: 7 to the decrees of **C**, saying that there is *G2541*
25: 8 **C**, have I offended any thing at all. *G2541*
11 deliver me unto them. I appeal unto **C**. *G2541*
12 unto **C**? unto Caesar shalt thou go. *G2541*
12 unto Caesar? unto **C** shalt thou go. *G2541*
21 to be kept till I might send him to **C**. *G2541*
26:32 liberty, if he had not appealed unto **C**. *G2541*
27:24 be brought before **C**: and, lo, God hath *G2541*
28:19 to appeal unto **C**; not that I had ought *G2541*

CAESAR AUGUSTUS See CAESAR and AUGUSTUS.

CAESAREA
Mt 16:13 When Jesus came into the coasts of **C** *G2542*
Mk 8:27 into the towns of **C** Philippi: and by the *G2542*
Act 8:40 in all the cities, till he came to **C**. *G2542*
9:30 to **C**, and sent him forth to Tarsus. *G2542*
10: 1 There was a certain man in **C** called *G2542*
24 after they entered into **C**. And Cornelius *G2542*
11:11 where I was, sent from **C** unto me. *G2542*
12:19 from Judaea to **C**, and *there* abode. *G2542*
18:22 And when he had landed at **C**, and gone *G2542*
21: 8 and came unto **C**: and we entered into *G2542*
16 of the disciples of **C**, and brought with *G2542*
23:23 soldiers to go to **C**, and horsemen *G2542*
33 Who, when they came to **C**, and *G2542*
25: 1 days he ascended from **C** to Jerusalem. *G2542*
4 should be kept at **C**, and that he himself *G2542*
6 he went down unto **C**; and the next day *G2542*
13 Bernice came unto **C** to salute Festus. *G2542*

CAESAREA-PHILIPPI See CAESAREA and PHILIPPI.

CAESAR'S
Mt 22:21 They say unto him, **C**. Then saith he *G2541*
21 things which are **C**; and unto God the *G2541*
Mk 12:16 And they said unto him, **C**. *G2541*
17 the things that are **C**, and to God the *G2541*
Lk 20:24 hath it? They answered and said, **C**. *G2541*
25 the things which be **C**, and unto God the *G2541*
Jn 19:12 go, thou art not **C** friend: whosoever *G2541*
Act 25:10 Then said Paul, I stand at **C** judgment *G2541*
Php 4:22 chiefly they that are of **C** household. *G2541*

CAGE
Jer 5:27 As a **c** is full of birds, so *are* their H3619
Rev 18: 2 a **c** of every unclean and hateful bird. *G5438*

CAIAPHAS
Mt 26: 3 of the high priest, who was called **C**, *G2533*
57 Jesus led *him* away to **C** the high priest, *G2533*
Lk 3: 2 Annas and **C** being the high priests, the *G2533*
Jn 11:49 And one of them, *named* **C**, being the *G2533*
18:13 father in law to **C**, which was the high *G2533*
14 Now **C** was he, which gave counsel to *G2533*
24 sent him bound unto **C** the high priest. *G2533*
28 Then led they Jesus from **C** unto the *G2533*
Act 4: 6 And Annas the high priest, and **C**, and *G2533*

CAIN
Gen 4: 1 and bare **C**, and said, I have gotten H7014
2 sheep, but **C** was a tiller of the ground. H7014
3 it came to pass, that **C** brought of the H7014
5 But unto **C** and to his offering he had H7014
5 not respect. And **C** was very wroth, and H7014
6 And the LORD said unto **C**, Why art H7014
8 And **C** talked with Abel his brother: H7014
8 in the field, that **C** rose up against Abel H7014
9 And the LORD said unto **C**, Where *is* H7014
13 And **C** said unto the LORD, My H7014
15 whosoever slayeth **C**, vengeance shall H7014
15 **C**, lest any finding him should kill him. H7014
16 And **C** went out from the presence of H7014
17 And **C** knew his wife; and she H7014
24 If **C** shall be avenged sevenfold, truly H7014
25 seed instead of Abel, whom **C** slew. H7014
Jos 15:57 **C**, Gibeah, and Timnah; ten cities with H7014
Heb 11: 4 sacrifice than **C**, by which he obtained *G2535*
1Jn 3:12 Not as **C**, *who* was of that wicked one, *G2535*
Jude 11 gone in the way of **C**, and ran greedily *G2535*

CAINAN
Gen 5: 9 Enos lived ninety years, and begat **C**: H7018
10 And Enos lived after he begat **C** eight H7018
12 And **C** lived seventy years, and begat H7018
13 And **C** lived after he begat Mahalaleel H7018
14 And all the days of **C** were nine H7018
Lk 3:36 Which was *the son* of **C**, which was *the* *G2536*
37 *son* of Maleleel, which was *the son* of **C**, *G2536*

CAKE
Ex 29:23 And one loaf of bread, and one **c** of H2471
Lev 8:26 one unleavened **c**, and a cake of oiled H2471
26 cake, and a **c** of oiled bread, and H2471
24: 5 two tenth deals shall be in one **c**. H2471
Nu 6:19 one unleavened **c** out of the basket, H2471
15:20 Ye shall offer up a **c** of the first of your H2471
Jdg 7:13 a dream, and, lo, a **c** of barley bread H6742
1Sa 30:12 And they gave him a piece of a **c** of figs, H1690
2Sa 6:19 to every one a **c** of bread, and a good H2471
1Ki 17:12 liveth, I have not a **c**, but an handful of H4580
13 me thereof a little **c** first, and bring *it* H5692
19: 6 *there was* a **c** baken on the coals, H5692
Hos 7: 8 the people; Ephraim is a **c** not turned. H5692

CAKES
Gen 18: 6 knead *it*, and make **c** upon the hearth. H5692
Ex 12:39 And they baked unleavened **c** of the H5692
29: 2 And unleavened bread, and **c** H2471
Lev 2: 4 *be* unleavened **c** of fine flour mingled H2471
7:12 unleavened **c** mingled with oil, and H2471
Lev 7:12 **c** mingled with oil, of fine flour, fried. H2471
13 Besides the **c**, he shall offer *for* his H2471
24: 5 and bake twelve **c** thereof: two tenth H2471
Nu 6:15 And a basket of unleavened bread, **c** of H2471
11: 8 in pans, and made **c** of it: and the taste H5692
Jos 5:11 unleavened **c**, and parched *corn* in H4682
Jdg 6:19 and unleavened **c** of an ephah of flour: H4682
20 the unleavened **c**, and lay *them* upon H4682
21 the unleavened **c**; and there rose up fire H4682
21 the unleavened **c**. Then the angel of the H4682
1Sa 25:18 **c** of figs, and laid *them* on asses. H1690
2Sa 13: 6 me a couple of **c** in my sight, that I may H3834
8 **c** in his sight, and did bake the cakes. H3823
8 cakes in his sight, and did bake the **c**. H3834
10 Tamar took the **c** which she had made, H3834
1Ch 12:40 *and* meat, meal, **c** of figs, and bunches H1690
23:29 the unleavened **c**, and for *that which is* H7550
Jer 7:18 *their* dough, to make **c** to the queen of H3561
44:19 did we make her **c** to worship her, and H3561
Ezk 4:12 And thou shalt eat it *as* barley **c**, and H5692

CALAH
Gen 10:11 Nineveh, and the city Rehoboth, and **C**, H3625
12 And Resen between Nineveh and **C**: the H3625

CALAMITIES
Ps 57: 1 my refuge, until *these* **c** be overpast. H1942
141: 5 yet my prayer also *shall be* in their **c**. H7451
Prv 17: 5 that is glad at **c** shall not be unpunished. H343

CALAMITY
Dt 32:35 for the day of their **c** *is* at hand, and the H343
2Sa 22:19 They prevented me in the day of my **c**: H343
Job 6: 2 and my **c** laid in the balances together! H1942
30:13 set forward my **c**, they have no helper. H1942
Ps 18:18 They prevented me in the day of my **c**: H343
Prv 1:26 I also will laugh at your **c**; I will mock H343
6:15 Therefore shall his **c** come suddenly; H343
19:13 A foolish son *is* the **c** of his father: and H1942
24:22 For their **c** shall rise suddenly; and who H343
27:10 house in the day of thy **c**: *for* better *is* a H343
Jer 18:17 and not the face, in the day of their **c**. H343
46:21 the day of their **c** was come upon them, H343
48:16 The **c** of Moab *is* near to come, and his H343
49: 8 for I will bring the **c** of Esau upon him, H343
32 **c** from all sides thereof, saith the LORD. H343
Ezk 35: 5 in the time of their **c**, in the time *that* H343
Oba 13 in the day of their **c**; yea, thou shouldest H343
13 in the day of their **c**, nor have laid *hands* H343
13 on their substance in the day of their **c**; H343

CALAMUS
Ex 30:23 sweet **c** two hundred and fifty *shekels*, H7070
Song 4:14 Spikenard and saffron; **c** and H7070
Ezk 27:19 iron, cassia, and **c**, were in thy market. H7070

CALCOL
1Ch 2: 6 and **C**, and Dara: five of them in all. H3633

CALDRON
1Sa 2:14 pan, or kettle, or **c**, or pot; all that the H7037
Job 41:20 smoke, as *out* of a seething pot or **c**. H100
Ezk 11: 3 this *city is* the **c**, and we *be* the flesh. H5518
7 and this *city is* the **c**: but I will bring you H5518
11 This *city* shall not be your **c**, neither H5518
Mic 3: 3 as for the pot, and as flesh within the **c**. H7037

CALDRONS
2Ch 35:13 they in pots, and in **c**, and in pans, and H1731

Jer 52:18 The **c** also, and the shovels, and the H5518
19 and the bowls, and the **c**, and the H5518

CALEB

Nu 13: 6 Of the tribe of Judah, **C** the son of H3612
30 And **C** stilled the people before Moses, H3612
14: 6 And Joshua the son of Nun, and **C** the H3612
24 But my servant **C**, because he had H3612
30 therein, save **C** the son of Jephunneh, H3612
38 But Joshua the son of Nun, and **C** the H3612
26:65 a man of them, save **C** the son of H3612
32:12 Save **C** the son of Jephunneh the H3612
34:19 tribe of Judah, **C** the son of Jephunneh. H3612
Dt 1:36 Save **C** the son of Jephunneh; he shall H3612
Jos 14: 6 in Gilgal: and **C** the son of Jephunneh H3612
13 and gave unto **C** the son of Jephunneh H3612
14 became the inheritance of **C** the son of H3612
15:13 And unto **C** the son of Jephunneh he H3612
14 And **C** drove thence the three sons of H3612
16 And **C** said, He that smiteth H3612
17 the brother of **C**, took it: and he gave H3612
18 **C** said unto her, What wouldest thou? H3612
21:12 gave they to **C** the son of Jephunneh H3612
Jdg 1:12 And **C** said, He that smiteth H3612
14 and **C** said unto her, What wilt thou? H3612
15 of water. And **C** gave her the upper H3612
20 And they gave Hebron unto **C**, as Moses H3612
1Sa 25: 3 doings; and he *was* of the house of **C**. H3614
30:14 of **C**; and we burned Ziklag with fire. H3612
1Ch 2:18 And **C** the son of Hezron begat *children* H3612
19 And when Azubah was dead, **C** took H3612
42 Now the sons of **C** the brother of H3612
49 and the daughter of **C** *was* Achsah. H3612
50 These were the sons of **C** the son of H3612
4:15 And the sons of **C** the son of H3612
6:56 they gave to **C** the son of Jephunneh. H3612

CALEB-EPHRATAH

1Ch 2:24 And after that Hezron was dead in **C**, H3613

CALEB'S

Jdg 1:13 And Othniel the son of Kenaz, **C** H3612
3: 9 the son of Kenaz, **C** younger brother. H3612
1Ch 2:46 And Ephah, **C** concubine, bare Haran, H3612
48 Maachah, **C** concubine, bare Sheber, H3612

CALF

Gen 18: 7 and fetcht a **c** tender and good, H1121+H1241
8 milk, and the **c** which he had H1121+H1241
Ex 32: 4 had made it a molten **c**: and they said, H5695
8 them a molten **c**, and have worshipped H5695
19 that he saw the **c**, and the dancing: and H5695
20 And he took the **c** which they had H5695
24 into the fire, and there came out this **c**. H5695
35 they made the **c**, which Aaron made. H5695
Lev 9: 2 Take thee a young **c** for a sin offering, H5695
3 a sin offering; and a **c** and a lamb, *both* H5695
8 altar, and slew the **c** of the sin offering, H5695
Dt 9:16 you a molten **c**: ye had turned aside H5695
21 And I took your sin, the **c** which ye had H5695
1Sa 28:24 And the woman had a fat **c** in the H5695
Neh 9:18 them a molten **c**, and said, This *is* thy H5695
Job 21:10 cow calveth, and casteth not her **c**. H7921
Ps 29: 6 He maketh them also to skip like a **c**; H5695
106:19 They made a **c** in Horeb, and H5695
Isa 11: 6 the kid; and the **c** and the young lion H5695
27:10 there shall the **c** feed, and there shall H5695
Jer 34:18 me, when they cut the **c** in twain, and H5695
19 passed between the parts of the **c**; H5695
Hos 8: 5 Thy **c**, O Samaria, hath cast *thee* off; H5695
6 **c** of Samaria shall be broken in pieces. H5695
Lk 15:23 And bring hither the fatted **c**, and kill *it*; *G3448*
27 hath killed the fatted **c**, because he hath *G3448*
30 thou hast killed for him the fatted **c**. *G3448*
Act 7:41 And they made a **c** in those days, and *G3447*
Rev 4: 7 beast like a **c**, and the third beast *G3448*

CALF'S

Ezk 1: 7 *was* like the sole of a **c** foot: and they H5695

CALKERS

Ezk 27: 9 in thee thy **c**: all the ships of the H919+H2388
27 and thy pilots, thy **c**, and the H919+H2388

CALL

Gen 2:19 to see what he would **c** them: and H7121
4:26 men to **c** upon the name of the LORD. H7121
16:11 a son, and shalt **c** his name Ishmael; H7121
17:15 thou shalt not **c** her name Sarai, but H7121
Gen 17:19 and thou shalt **c** his name Isaac: and H7121
24:57 And they said, We will **c** the damsel, H7121
30:13 the daughters will **c** me blessed: and she H833
46:33 Pharaoh shall **c** you, and shall say, H7121
Ex 2: 7 Shall I go and **c** to thee a nurse of the H7121
20 the man? **c** him, that he may eat bread. H7121
34:15 *one* **c** thee, and thou eat of his sacrifice; H7121
Nu 16:12 And Moses sent to **c** Dathan and H7121
22: 5 of his people, to **c** him, saying, Behold, H7121
20 the men come to **c** thee, rise up, *and* go H7121
37 send unto thee to **c** thee? wherefore H7121
Dt 2:11 but the Moabites **c** them Emims. H7121
20 the Ammonites **c** them Zamzummims; H7121
3: 9 (*Which* Hermon the Sidonians **c** H7121
9 Sirion; and the Amorites **c** it Shenir;) H7121
4: 7 *is* in all *things that* we **c** upon him *for*? H7121
26 I **c** heaven and earth to witness against H5749
25: 8 Then the elders of his city shall **c** him, H7121
30: 1 and thou shalt **c** *them* to mind among H7725
19 I **c** heaven and earth to record this day H5749
31:14 thou must die: **c** Joshua, and present H7121
28 in their ears, and **c** heaven and earth to H5749
33:19 They shall **c** the people unto the H7121
Jdg 12: 1 and didst not **c** us to go with thee? we H7121
16:25 that they said, **C** for Samson, that he H7121
21:13 and to **c** peaceably unto them. H7121
Ru 1:20 And she said unto them, **C** me not H7121
20 Call me not Naomi, **c** me Mara: for the H7121
21 again empty: why *then* **c** ye me Naomi, H7121
1Sa 3: 6 *am* I; for thou didst **c** me. And he H7121
8 *am* I; for thou didst **c** me. And Eli H7121
9 it shall be, if he **c** thee, that thou shalt H7121
12:17 *Is it* not wheat harvest to day? I will **c** H7121
16: 3 And **c** Jesse to the sacrifice, and I will H7121
22:11 Then the king sent to **c** Ahimelech the H7121
2Sa 17: 5 Then said Absalom, **C** now Hushai the H7121
22: 4 I will **c** on the LORD, *who is* worthy to H7121
1Ki 1:28 Then king David answered and said, **C** H7121
32 And king David said, **C** me Zadok the H7121
8:52 them in all that they **c** for unto thee. H7121
17:18 thou come unto me to **c** my sin to H2142
18:24 And **c** ye on the name of your gods, H7121
24 gods, and I will **c** on the name of the H7121
25 for ye *are* many; and **c** on the name of H7121
22:13 And the messenger that was gone to **c** H7121
2Ki 4:12 And he said to Gehazi his servant, **C** H7121
15 And he said, **C** her. And when he had H7121
36 And he called Gehazi, and said, **C** this H7121
5:11 and stand, and **c** on the name of the H7121
10:19 Now therefore **c** unto me all the H7121
1Ch 16: 8 Give thanks unto the LORD, **c** upon his H7121
2Ch 18:12 And the messenger that went to **c** H7121
Job 5: 1 **C** now, if there be any that will answer H7121
13:22 Then **c** thou, and I will answer: or let H7121
14:15 Thou shalt **c**, and I will answer thee: H7121
27:10 Almighty? will he always **c** upon God? H7121
Ps 4: 1 Hear me when I **c**, O God of my H7121
3 the LORD will hear when I **c** unto him. H7121
14: 4 eat bread, and **c** not upon the LORD. H7121
18: 3 I will **c** upon the LORD, *who is worthy* H7121
20: 9 LORD: let the king hear us when we **c**. H7121
49:11 **c** *their* lands after their own names. H7121
50: 4 He shall **c** to the heavens from above, H7121
15 And **c** upon me in the day of trouble: I H7121
55:16 As for me, I will **c** upon God; and the H7121
72:17 in him: all nations shall **c** him blessed. H833
77: 6 I **c** to remembrance my song in the H2142
80:18 us, and we will **c** upon thy name. H7121
86: 5 mercy unto all them that **c** upon thee. H7121
7 In the day of my trouble I will **c** upon H7121
91:15 He shall **c** upon me, and I will answer H7121
99: 6 among them that **c** upon his name; H7121
102: 2 the day *when* I **c** answer me speedily. H7121
105: 1 O give thanks unto the LORD; **c** upon H7121
116: 2 will I **c** upon *him* as long as I live. H7121
13 I will take the cup of salvation, and **c** H7121
17 and will **c** upon the name of the LORD. H7121
145:18 The LORD *is* nigh unto all them that **c** H7121
18 him, to all that **c** upon him in truth. H7121
Prv 1:28 Then shall they **c** upon me, but I will H7121
7: 4 and **c** understanding *thy* kinswoman: H7121
8: 4 Unto you, O men, I **c**; and my voice *is* to H7121
9:15 To **c** passengers who go right on their H7121
31:28 Her children arise up, and **c** her blessed; H833
Isa 5:20 Woe unto them that **c** evil good, and H559
7:14 a son, and shall **c** his name Immanuel. H7121
8: 3 **C** his name Maher-shalal-hash-baz. H7121
12: 4 say, Praise the LORD, **c** upon his name, H7121
22:12 Lord GOD of hosts **c** to weeping, and to H7121
Isa 22:20 day, that I will **c** my servant Eliakim H7121
31: 2 evil, and will not **c** back his words: but H5493
34:12 They shall **c** the nobles thereof to the H7121
41:25 of the sun shall he **c** upon my name: H7121
44: 5 and another shall **c** *himself* by the H7121
7 And who, as I, shall **c**, and shall declare H7121
45: 3 I, the LORD, which **c** *thee* by thy name, H7121
48: 2 For they **c** themselves of the holy city, H7121
13 I **c** unto them, they stand up together. H7121
55: 5 Behold, thou shalt **c** a nation *that* thou H7121
6 found, **c** ye upon him while he is near: H7121
58: 5 *him*? wilt thou **c** this a fast, and an H7121
9 Then shalt thou **c**, and the LORD shall H7121
13 on my holy day; and **c** the sabbath a H7121
60:14 and they shall **c** thee, The city of the H7121
18 but thou shalt **c** thy walls Salvation, H7121
61: 6 LORD: *men* shall **c** you the Ministers of H559
62:12 And they shall **c** them, The holy people, H7121
65:15 and **c** his servants by another name: H7121
24 that before they **c**, I will answer; and H7121
Jer 1:15 For, lo, I will **c** all the families of the H7121
3:17 At that time they shall **c** Jerusalem the H7121
19 I said, Thou shalt **c** me, My father; and H7121
6:30 Reprobate silver shall *men* **c** them, H7121
7:27 thou shalt also **c** unto them; but they H7121
9:17 Consider ye, and **c** for the mourning H7121
10:25 the families that **c** not on thy name: for H7121
25:29 for I will **c** for a sword upon all H7121
29:12 Then shall ye **c** upon me, and ye shall H7121
33: 3 **C** unto me, and I will answer thee, and H7121
50:29 **C** together the archers against Babylon: H8085
51:27 against her, **c** together against her H8085
Lam 2:15 this the city that *men* **c** The perfection of H559
Ezk 21:23 oaths: but he will **c** to remembrance H2142
36:29 and I will **c** for the corn, and will H7121
38:21 And I will **c** for a sword against him H7121
39:11 shall **c** *it* The valley of Hamon-gog. H7121
Dan 2: 2 Then the king commanded to **c** the H7121
Hos 1: 4 And the LORD said unto him, **C** his H7121
6 *God* said unto him, **C** her name H7121
9 Then said *God*, **C** his name Lo-ammi: H7121
2:16 *that* thou shalt **c** me Ishi; and shalt call H7121
16 me Ishi; and shalt **c** me no more Baali. H7121
7:11 they **c** to Egypt, they go to Assyria. H7121
Joel 1:14 Sanctify ye a fast, **c** a solemn assembly, H7121
2:15 sanctify a fast, **c** a solemn assembly: H7121
32 whosoever shall **c** on the name of the H7121
32 in the remnant whom the LORD shall **c**. H7121
Am 5:16 and they shall **c** the husbandman to H7121
Jna 1: 6 O sleeper? arise, **c** upon thy God, if so H7121
Zep 3: 9 that they may all **c** upon the name of H7121
Zec 3:10 LORD of hosts, shall ye **c** every man his H7121
13: 9 is tried: they shall **c** on my name, and I H7121
Mal 1: 4 and they shall **c** them, The border of H7121
3:12 And all nations shall **c** you blessed: for H833
15 And now we **c** the proud happy; yea, H833
Mt 1:21 and thou shalt **c** his name JESUS: for *G2564*
23 and they shall **c** his name Emmanuel, *G2564*
9:13 I am not come to **c** the righteous, but *G2564*
10:25 *shall they* **c** them of his household? *G2564*
20: 8 unto his steward, **C** the labourers, and *G2564*
22: 3 And sent forth his servants to **c** them *G2564*
43 doth David in spirit **c** him Lord, saying, *G2564*
45 If David then **c** him Lord, how is he his *G2564*
23: 9 And **c** no *man* your father upon the *G2564*
Mk 2:17 sick: I came not to **c** the righteous, but *G2564*
10:49 be called. And they **c** the blind man, *G5455*
15:12 *him* whom ye **c** the King of the Jews? *G3004*
16 and they **c** together the whole band. *G4779*
Lk 1:13 a son, and thou shalt **c** his name John. *G2564*
31 a son, and shalt **c** his name JESUS. *G2564*
48 all generations shall **c** me blessed. *G3106*
5:32 I came not to **c** the righteous, but *G2564*
6:46 And why **c** ye me, Lord, Lord, and do *G2564*
14:12 or a supper, **c** not thy friends, nor *G5455*
13 But when thou makest a feast, **c** the *G2564*
Jn 4:16 Jesus saith unto her, Go, **c** thy *G5455*
13:13 Ye **c** me Master and Lord: and ye say *G5455*
15:15 Henceforth I **c** you not servants; for the *G3004*
Act 2:21 whosoever shall **c** on the name of the *G1941*
39 as many as the Lord our God shall **c**. *G4341*
9:14 priests to bind all that **c** on thy name. *G1941*
10: 5 And now send men to Joppa, and **c** for *G3343*
15 cleansed, *that* **c** not thou common. *G2840*
28 not **c** any man common or unclean. *G3004*
32 Send therefore to Joppa, and **c** hither *G3333*
11: 9 cleansed, *that* **c** not thou common. *G2840*
13 **c** for Simon, whose surname is Peter; *G3343*
19:13 took upon them to **c** over them which *G3687*

Act 24:14 way which they c heresy, so worship I *G3004*
25 a convenient season, I will c for thee. *G3333*
Ro 9:25 As he saith also in Osee, I will c them *G2564*
10:12 over all is rich unto all that c upon him. *G1941*
13 For whosoever shall c upon the name *G1941*
14 How then shall they c on him in whom *G1941*
1Co 1: 2 that in every place c upon the name of *G1941*
2Co 1:23 Moreover I c God for a record upon my *G1941*
2Ti 1: 5 When I c to remembrance the *G2983*
2:22 that c on the Lord out of a pure heart. *G1941*
Heb 2:11 he is not ashamed to c them brethren, *G2564*
10:32 But c to remembrance the former days, *G363*
Jas 5:14 Is any sick among you? let him c for the *G4341*
1Pt 1:17 And if ye c on the Father, who without *G4341*

CALLED
Gen 1: 5 And God c the light Day, and the H7121
5 and the darkness he c Night. And the H7121
8 And God c the firmament Heaven. And H7121
10 And God c the dry *land* Earth; and the H7121
10 of the waters c he Seas: and God saw H7121
2:19 and whatsoever Adam c every living H7121
23 flesh: she shall be c Woman, because H7121
3: 9 And the LORD God c unto Adam, and H7121
20 And Adam c his wife's name Eve; H7121
4:17 he builded a city, and c the name of the H7121
25 bare a son, and c his name Seth: For H7121
26 born a son; and he c his name Enos; H7121
5: 2 blessed them, and c their name Adam, H7121
3 after his image; and c his name Seth: H7121
29 And he c his name Noah, saying, This H7121
11: 9 Therefore is the name of it c Babel; H7121
12: 8 and c upon the name of the LORD. H7121
18 And Pharaoh c Abram, and said, What H7121
13: 4 Abram c on the name of the LORD. H7121
16:13 And she c the name of the LORD that H7121
14 Wherefore the well was c H7121
15 a son: and Abram c his son's name, H7121
17: 5 Neither shall thy name any more be c H7121
19: 5 And they c unto Lot, and said unto H7121
22 the name of the city was c Zoar. H7121
37 And the firstborn bare a son, and c his H7121
38 bare a son, and c his name Ben-ammi: H7121
20: 8 in the morning, and c all his servants, H7121
9 Then Abimelech c Abraham, and said H7121
21: 3 And Abraham c the name of his son H7121
12 voice; for in Isaac shall thy seed be c. H7121
17 and the angel of God c to Hagar out of H7121
31 Wherefore he c that place Beer-sheba; H7121
33 Beer-sheba, and c there on the name of H7121
22:11 And the angel of the LORD c unto him H7121
14 And Abraham c the name of that place H7121
15 And the angel of the LORD c unto H7121
24:58 And they c Rebekah, and said unto her, H7121
25:25 garment; and they c his name Esau. H7121
26 and his name was c Jacob: and Isaac H7121
30 faint: therefore was his name c Edom. H7121
26: 9 And Abimelech c Isaac, and said, H7121
18 of Abraham: and he c their names after H7121
18 names by which his father had c them. H7121
20 *is* ours: and he c the name of the well H7121
21 also: and he c the name of it Sitnah. H7121
22 they strove not: and he c the name of it H7121
25 And he builded an altar there, and c H7121
33 And he c it Shebah: therefore the name H7121
27: 1 could not see, he c Esau his eldest son, H7121
42 and she sent and c Jacob her younger H7121
28: 1 And Isaac c Jacob, and blessed him, H7121
19 And he c the name of that place H7121
19 name of that city *was* c Luz at the first.
29:32 a son, and she c his name Reuben: for H7121
33 *son* also: and she c his name Simeon. H7121
34 sons: therefore was his name c Levi. H7121
35 she c his name Judah; and left bearing. H7121
30: 6 a son: therefore c she his name Dan. H7121
8 and she c his name Naphtali. H7121
11 troop cometh: and she c his name Gad. H7121
13 me blessed: and she c his name Asher. H7121
18 husband: and she c his name Issachar. H7121
20 six sons: and she c his name Zebulun. H7121
21 a daughter, and c her name Dinah. H7121
24 And she c his name Joseph; and said, H7121
31: 4 And Jacob sent and c Rachel and Leah H7121
47 And Laban c it Jegar-sahadutha: but H7121
47 Jegar-sahadutha: but Jacob c it Galeed. H7121
48 Therefore was the name of it c Galeed; H7121
54 the mount, and c his brethren to eat H7121
32: 2 he c the name of that place Mahanaim. H7121
28 And he said, Thy name shall be c no H559

Gen 32:30 And Jacob c the name of the place H7121
33:17 the name of the place is c Succoth. H7121
20 And he erected there an altar, and c it H7121
35: 7 And he built there an altar, and c the H7121
8 the name of it was c Allon-bachuth. H7121
10 name shall not be c any more Jacob, H7121
10 be thy name: and he c his name Israel. H7121
15 And Jacob c the name of the place H7121
18 she died) that she c his name Ben-oni: H7121
18 but his father c him Benjamin. H7121
38: 3 and bare a son; and he c his name Er. H7121
4 bare a son; and she c his name Onan. H7121
5 bare a son; and c his name Shelah: and H7121
29 thee: therefore his name was c Pharez. H7121
30 his hand: and his name was c Zarah. H7121
39:14 That she c unto the men of her house, H7121
41: 8 and he sent and c for all the magicians H7121
14 Then Pharaoh sent and c Joseph, and H7121
45 And Pharaoh c Joseph's name H7121
51 And Joseph c the name of the firstborn H7121
52 And the name of the second c he H7121
47:29 must die: and he c his son Joseph, and H7121
48: 6 thine, *and* shall be c after the name of H7121
49: 1 And Jacob c unto his sons, and said, H7121
50:11 the name of it was c Abel-mizraim, H7121
Ex 1:18 And the king of Egypt c for the H7121
2: 8 maid went and c the child's mother. H7121
10 her son. And she c his name Moses: H7121
22 And she bare *him* a son, and he c his H7121
3: 4 aside to see, God c unto him out of the H7121
7:11 Then Pharaoh also c the wise men and H7121
8: 8 Then Pharaoh c for Moses and Aaron, H7121
25 And Pharaoh c for Moses and for H7121
9:27 And Pharaoh sent, and c for Moses H7121
10:16 Then Pharaoh c for Moses and Aaron H7121
24 And Pharaoh c unto Moses, and said, H7121
12:21 Then Moses c for all the elders of H7121
31 And he c for Moses and Aaron by H7121
15:23 therefore the name of it was c Marah. H7121
16:31 And the house of Israel c the name H7121
17: 7 And he c the name of the place H7121
15 And Moses built an altar, and c the H7121
19: 3 and the LORD c unto him out of the H7121
7 And Moses came and c for the elders of H7121
20 and the LORD c Moses *up* to the top H7121
24:16 the seventh day he c unto Moses out of H7121
31: 2 See, I have c by name Bezaleel the son H7121
33: 7 the camp, and c it the Tabernacle of H7121
34:31 And Moses c unto them; and Aaron H7121
35:30 the LORD hath c by name Bezaleel the H7121
36: 2 And Moses c Bezaleel and Aholiab, and H7121
Lev 1: 1 And the LORD c unto Moses, and H7121
9: 1 day, *that* Moses c Aaron and his sons, H7121
10: 4 And Moses c Mishael and Elzaphan, H7121
Nu 11: 3 And he c the name of the place H7121
34 And he c the name of that place H7121
12: 5 tabernacle, and c Aaron and Miriam: H7121
13:16 c Oshea the son of Nun Jehoshua. H7121
24 The place was c the brook Eshcol, H7121
21: 3 he c the name of the place Hormah. H7121
24:10 unto Balaam, I c thee to curse mine H7121
25: 2 And they c the people unto the H7121
32:41 towns thereof, and c them Havoth-jair. H7121
42 and c it Nobah, after his own name. H7121
Dt 3:13 Bashan, which was c the land of giants. H7121
14 Maachathi; and c them after his own H7121
5: 1 And Moses c all Israel, and said unto H7121
15: 2 because it is c the LORD'S release. H7121
25:10 And his name shall be c in Israel, The H7121
28:10 see that thou art c by the name of the H7121
29: 2 And Moses c unto all Israel, and said H7121
31: 7 And Moses c unto Joshua, and said H7121
Jos 4: 4 Then Joshua c the twelve men, whom H7121
5: 9 of the place is c Gilgal unto this day. H7121
6: 6 And Joshua the son of Nun c the H7121
7:26 c, The valley of Achor, unto this day. H7121
8:16 *were* in Ai were c together to pursue H2199
9:22 And Joshua c for them, and he spake H7121
10:24 that Joshua c for all the men of Israel, H7121
19:47 dwelt therein, and c Leshem, Dan, after H7121
22: 1 Then Joshua c the Reubenites, and the H7121
34 the children of Gad c the altar *Ed*: for it H7121
23: 2 And Joshua c for all Israel, *and* for H7121
24: 1 to Shechem, and c for the elders of H7121
9 c Balaam the son of Beor to curse you: H7121
Jdg 1:17 the name of the city was c Hormah. H7121
26 and built a city, and c the name thereof H7121
2: 5 And they c the name of that place H7121
4: 6 And she sent and c Barak the son of H7121

Jdg 4:10 And Barak c Zebulun and Naphtali to H2199
6:24 the LORD, and c it Jehovah-shalom: H7121
32 Therefore on that day he c him H7121
8:31 a son, whose name he c Abimelech. H7760
9:54 Then he c hastily unto the young man H7121
10: 4 cities, which are c Havoth-jair unto H7121
12: 2 and when I c you, ye delivered me H2199
13:24 And the woman bare a son, and c his H7121
14:15 c us to take that we have? *is it* not *so*? H7121
15:17 hand, and c that place Ramath-lehi. H7121
18 And he was sore athirst, and c on the H7121
19 wherefore he c the name thereof H7121
16:18 heart, she sent and c for the lords of the H7121
19 her knees; and she c for a man, and she H7121
25 us sport. And they c for Samson out of H7121
28 And Samson c unto the LORD, and H7121
18:12 Judah: wherefore they c that place H7121
29 And they c the name of the city Dan, H7121
Ru 4:17 Naomi; and they c his name Obed: he H7121
1Sa 1:20 she bare a son, and c his name Samuel, H7121
3: 4 That the LORD c Samuel: and he H7121
5 me. And he said, I c not; lie down H7121
6 And the LORD c yet again, Samuel. H7121
6 I c not, my son; lie down again. H7121
8 And the LORD c Samuel again the H7121
8 that the LORD had c the child. H7121
10 And the LORD came, and stood, and c H7121
16 Then Eli c Samuel, and said, Samuel, H7121
6: 2 And the Philistines c for the priests and H7121
7:12 Mizpeh and Shen, and c the name of it H7121
9: 9 seer: for *he that is* now c a Prophet was
9 a Prophet was beforetime c a Seer.) H7121
26 day, that Samuel c Saul to the top of H7121
10:17 And Samuel c the people together unto H6817
12:18 So Samuel c unto the LORD; and the H7121
13: 4 were c together after Saul to Gilgal. H6817
16: 5 his sons, and c them to the sacrifice. H7121
8 Then Jesse c Abinadab, and made him H7121
19: 7 And Jonathan c David, and Jonathan H7121
23: 8 And Saul c all the people together to H8085
28 they c that place Sela-hammahlekoth. H7121
28:15 therefore I have c thee, that thou H7121
29: 6 Then Achish c David, and said unto H7121
2Sa 1: 7 c unto me. And I answered, Here *am* I. H7121
15 And David c one of the young men, H7121
2:16 that place was c Helkath-hazzurim, H7121
26 Then Abner c to Joab, and said, Shall H7121
5: 9 So David dwelt in the fort, and c it the H7121
20 c the name of that place Baal-perazim. H7121
6: 2 whose name is c by the name of the H7121
8 Uzzah: and he c the name of the place H7121
9: 2 when they had c him unto David, the H7121
9 Then the king c to Ziba, Saul's servant, H7121
11:13 And when David had c him, he did eat H7121
12:24 she bare a son, and he c his name H7121
25 prophet; and he c his name Jedidiah, H7121
28 take the city, and it be c after my name. H7121
13:17 Then he c his servant that ministered H7121
14:33 and when he had c for Absalom, he H7121
15: 2 then Absalom c unto him, and said, H7121
11 *that were* c; and they went in their H7121
18:18 and he c the pillar after his own H7121
18 it is c unto this day, Absalom's place. H7121
26 the watchman c unto the porter, and H7121
28 And Ahimaaz c, and said unto the king, H7121
21: 2 And the king c the Gibeonites, and said H7121
22: 7 In my distress I c upon the LORD, and H7121
1Ki 1: 9 by En-rogel, and c all his brethren the H7121
10 and Solomon his brother, he c not. H7121
19 and hath c all the sons of the king, H7121
19 but Solomon thy servant hath he not c. H7121
25 and hath c all the king's sons, and H7121
26 and thy servant Solomon, hath he not c. H7121
2:36 And the king sent and c for Shimei, H7121
42 And the king sent and c for Shimei, H7121
7:21 the right pillar, and c the name thereof H7121
21 left pillar, and c the name thereof Boaz. H7121
8:43 which I have builded, is c by thy name. H7121
9:13 c them the land of Cabul unto this day. H7121
12: 3 That they sent and c him. And H7121
20 that they sent and c him unto the H7121
16:24 on the hill, and c the name of the city H7121
17:10 of sticks: and he c to her, and said, H7121
11 And as she was going to fetch *it*, he c to H7121
18: 3 And Ahab c Obadiah, which *was* the H7121
26 dressed *it*, and c on the name of Baal H7121
20: 7 Then the king of Israel c all the elders H7121
22: 9 Then the king of Israel c an officer, and H7121
2Ki 3:10 that the LORD hath c these three kings H7121

2Ki 3:13 for the LORD hath c these three kings H7121
4:12 he had c her, she stood before him. H7121
15 he had c her, she stood in the door. H7121
22 And she c unto her husband, and said, H7121
36 And he c Gehazi, and said, Call this H7121
36 So he c her. And when she was H7121
6:11 this thing; and he c his servants, and H7121
7:10 So they came and c unto the porter of H7121
11 And he c the porters; and they told *it* to H7121
8: 1 for the LORD hath c for a famine; and H7121
9: 1 And Elisha the prophet c one of the H7121
12: 7 Then king Jehoash c for Jehoiada the H7121
14: 7 c the name of it Joktheel unto this day. H7121
18: 4 incense to it: and he c it Nehushtan. H7121
18 And when they had c to the king, there H7121
1Ch 4: 9 and his mother c his name Jabez, H7121
10 And Jabez c on the God of Israel, H7121
6:65 cities, which are c by *their* names. H7121
7:16 a son, and she c his name Peresh; and H7121
23 bare a son, and he c his name Beriah, H7121
11: 7 therefore they c it the city of David. H7121
13: 6 the cherubims, whose name is c *on it*. H7121
11 that place is c Perez-uzza to this day. H7121
14:11 therefore they c the name of that place H7121
15:11 And David c for Zadok and Abiathar H7121
21:26 offerings, and c upon the LORD; and H7121
22: 6 Then he c for Solomon his son, and H7121
2Ch 3:17 on the left; and c the name of that on H7121
6:33 which I have built is c by thy name. H7121
7:14 If my people, which are c by my name, H7121
10: 3 And they sent and c him. So Jeroboam H7121
18: 8 And the king of Israel c for one *of his* H7121
20:26 c, The valley of Berachah, unto this day. H7121
24: 6 And the king c for Jehoiada the chief, H7121
Ezr 2:61 Gileadite, and was c after their name: H7121
Neh 5:12 sayest. Then I c the priests, and took H7121
7:63 to wife, and was c after their name. H7121
Est 2:14 in her, and that she were c by name. H7121
3:12 Then were the king's scribes c on the H7121
4: 5 Then c Esther for Hatach, *one* of the H7121
11 court, who is not c, *there is* one law of H7121
11 I have not been c to come in unto the H7121
5:10 c for his friends, and Zeresh his wife. H935
8: 9 Then were the king's scribes c at that H7121
9:26 Wherefore they c these days Purim H7121
Job 1: 4 his day; and sent and c for their three H7121
9:16 If I had c, and he had answered me; *yet* H7121
19:16 I c my servant, and he gave *me* no H7121
42:14 And he c the name of the first, Jemima; H7121
Ps 17: 6 I have c upon thee, for thou wilt hear H7121
18: 6 In my distress I c upon the LORD, and H7121
31:17 O LORD; for I have c upon thee: let the H7121
50: 1 hath spoken, and c the earth from the H7121
53: 4 eat bread: they have not c upon God. H7121
79: 6 that have not c upon thy name. H7121
88: 9 LORD, I have c daily upon thee, I have H7121
99: 6 his name; they c upon the LORD, and H7121
105:16 Moreover he c for a famine upon the H7121
116: 4 Then c I upon the name of the LORD; O H7121
118: 5 I c upon the LORD in distress: the H7121
Prv 1:24 Because I have c, and ye refused; I have H7121
16:21 The wise in heart shall be c prudent: H7121
24: 8 He that deviseth to do evil shall be c a H7121
Song 5: 6 I c him, but he gave me no answer. H7121
Isa 1:26 afterward thou shalt be c, The city of H7121
4: 1 only let us be c by thy name, to take H7121
3 in Jerusalem, shall be c holy, *even* every H559
9: 6 and his name shall be c Wonderful, H7121
13: 3 ones, I have also c my mighty ones for H7121
19:18 one shall be c, The city of destruction. H559
31: 4 of shepherds is c forth against him, *he* H7121
32: 5 The vile person shall be no more c H7121
35: 8 and it shall be c The way of holiness; H7121
41: 2 from the east, c him to his foot, gave H7121
9 of the earth, and c thee from the chief H7121
42: 6 I the LORD have c thee in H7121
43: 1 c *thee* by thy name; thou *art* mine. H7121
7 *Even* every one that is c by my name: H7121
22 But thou hast not c upon me, O Jacob; H7121
45: 4 elect, I have even c thee by thy name: I H7121
47: 1 shalt no more be c tender and delicate. H7121
5 no more be c, The lady of kingdoms. H7121
48: 1 of Jacob, which are c by the name of H7121
8 wast c a transgressor from the womb. H7121
12 and Israel, my c; I *am* he; I *am* the first, H7121
15 I, *even* I, have spoken; yea, I have c H7121
49: 1 The LORD hath c me from the womb; H7121
50: 2 no man? when I c, *was there* none to H7121
51: 2 bare you: for I c him alone, and blessed H7121

Isa 54: 5 God of the whole earth shall he be c. H7121
6 For the LORD hath c thee as a woman H7121
56: 7 be c an house of prayer for all people. H7121
58:12 and thou shalt be c, The repairer of the H7121
61: 3 heaviness; that they might be c trees of H7121
62: 2 and thou shalt be c by a new name, H7121
4 but thou shalt be c Hephzi-bah, and H7121
12 be c, Sought out, A city not forsaken. H7121
63:19 them; they were not c by thy name. H7121
65: 1 a nation *that* was not c by my name. H7121
12 because when I c, ye did not answer; H7121
66: 4 because when I c, none did answer; H7121
Jer 7:10 house, which is c by my name, and say, H7121
11 Is this house, which is c by my name, H7121
13 not; and I c you, but ye answered not; H7121
14 house, which is c by my name, wherein H7121
30 which is c by my name, to pollute it. H7121
32 that it shall no more be c Tophet, nor the H559
11:16 The LORD c thy name, A green olive H7121
12: 6 yea, they have c a multitude after thee: H7121
14: 9 and we are c by thy name; leave us not. H7121
15:16 c by thy name, O LORD God of hosts. H7121
19: 6 shall no more be c Tophet, nor The H7121
20: 3 LORD hath not c thy name Pashur, but H7121
23: 6 c, THE LORD OUR RIGHTEOUSNESS. H7121
25:29 on the city which is c by my name, and H7121
30:17 because they c thee an Outcast, *saying*, H7121
32:34 which is c by my name, to defile it. H7121
33:16 shall be c, The LORD our righteousness. H7121
34:15 in the house which is c by my name: H7121
35:17 heard; and I have c unto them, but they H7121
36: 4 Then Jeremiah c Baruch the son of H7121
42: 8 Then c he Johanan the son of Kareah, H7121
Lam 1:15 of me: he hath c an assembly against H7121
19 I c for my lovers, *but* they deceived me: H7121
21 hast c, and they shall be like unto me. H7121
2:22 Thou hast c as in a solemn day my H7121
3:55 I c upon thy name, O LORD, out of the H7121
57 Thou drewest near in the day *that* I c H7121
Ezk 9: 3 the house. And he c to the man clothed H7121
20:29 name thereof is c Bamah unto this day. H7121
Dan 5:12 c, and he will shew the interpretation. H7123
8:16 *of* Ulai, which c, and said, Gabriel, H7121
9:18 the city which is c by thy name: for we H7121
19 city and thy people are c by thy name. H7121
10: 1 whose name was c Belteshazzar; and H7121
Hos 11: 1 I loved him, and c my son out of Egypt. H7121
2 *As* they c them, so they went from H7121
7 me: though they c them to the most H7121
Am 7: 4 the Lord GOD c to contend by fire, and H7121
9:12 which are c by my name, saith the H7121
Hag 1:11 And I c for a drought upon the land, H7121
Zec 8: 3 Jerusalem shall be c a city of truth; and H7121
11: 7 two staves; the one I c Beauty, and the H7121
7 the other I c Bands; and I fed the flock. H7121
Mt 1:16 whom was born Jesus, who is c Christ. G3004
25 son: and he c his name JESUS. G2564
2: 7 Then Herod, when he had privily c the G2564
15 saying, Out of Egypt have I c my son. G2564
23 And he came and dwelt in a city c G3004
23 the prophets, He shall be c a Nazarene. G2564
4:18 brethren, Simon c Peter, and Andrew G3004
21 mending their nets; and he c them. G2564
5: 9 for they shall be c the children of God. G2564
19 men so, he shall be c the least in the G2564
19 be c great in the kingdom of heaven. G2564
10: 1 And when he had c unto *him* his twelve G4341
2 Simon, who is c Peter, and Andrew G3004
25 his lord. If they have c the master of the G2564
13:55 son? is not his mother c Mary? and his G3004
15:10 And he c the multitude, and said unto G4341
32 Then Jesus c his disciples *unto him*, G4341
18: 2 And Jesus c a little child unto him, and G4341
32 Then his lord, after that he had c him, G4341
20:16 first last: for many be c, but few chosen. G2822
25 But Jesus c them *unto him*, and said, G4341
32 And Jesus stood still, and c them, and G5455
21:13 My house shall be c the house of G2564
22:14 For many are c, but few *are* chosen. G2822
23: 7 and to be c of men, Rabbi, Rabbi. G2564
8 But be not ye c Rabbi: for one is your G2564
10 Neither be ye c masters: for one is your G2564
25:14 a far country, *who* c his own servants, G2564
26: 3 of the high priest, who was c Caiaphas, G3004
14 Then one of the twelve, c Judas G3004
36 them unto a place c Gethsemane, and G3004
27: 8 Wherefore that field was c, The field of G2564
16 then a notable prisoner, c Barabbas. G3004
17 Barabbas, or Jesus which is c Christ? G3004

Mt 27:22 Jesus which is c Christ? *They* all say G3004
33 come unto a place c Golgotha, that is to G3004
Mk 1:20 And straightway he c them: and they G2564
3:23 And he c them *unto him*, and said unto G4341
6: 7 And he c *unto him* the twelve, and G4341
7:14 And when he had c all the people *unto* G4341
8: 1 to eat, Jesus c his disciples *unto him*, G4341
34 And when he had c the people *unto* G4341
9:35 And he sat down, and c the twelve, and G5455
10:42 But Jesus c them *to him*, and saith unto G4341
49 him to be c. And they call the blind G5455
11:17 My house shall be c of all nations the G2564
12:43 And he c *unto him* his disciples, and G4341
14:72 crew. And Peter c to mind the word that G363
15:16 away into the hall, c Praetorium; and G2076
Lk 1:32 He shall be great, and shall be c the G2564
35 born of thee shall be c the Son of God. G2564
36 month with her, who was c barren. G2564
59 the child; and they c him Zacharias, G2564
60 and said, Not *so*; but he shall be c John. G2564
61 of thy kindred that is c by this name. G2564
62 to his father, how he would have him c. G2564
76 And thou, child, shalt be c the prophet G2564
2: 4 city of David, which is c Bethlehem; G2564
21 his name was c JESUS, which was so G2564
23 the womb shall be c holy to the Lord;) G2564
6:13 And when it was day, he c *unto him* his G4377
15 *son* of Alphaeus, and Simon c Zelotes, G2564
7:11 he went into a city c Nain; and many of G2564
8: 2 infirmities, Mary c Magdalene, out of G2564
54 by the hand, and c, saying, Maid, arise. G5455
9: 1 Then he c his twelve disciples together, G4779
10 place belonging to the city c Bethsaida. G2564
10:39 And she had a sister c Mary, which G2564
13:12 And when Jesus saw her, he c *her to* G4377
15:19 And am no more worthy to be c thy G2564
21 am no more worthy to be c thy son. G2564
26 And he c one of the servants, and G4341
16: 2 And he c him, and said unto him, How G5455
5 So he c every one of his lord's debtors G4341
18:16 But Jesus c them *unto him*, and said, G4341
19:13 And he c his ten servants, and G2564
15 servants to be c unto him, to whom G5455
29 at the mount c *the mount* of Olives, G2564
21:37 the mount that is c *the mount* of Olives. G2564
22: 1 drew nigh, which is c the Passover. G3004
25 authority upon them are c benefactors. G2564
47 and he that was c Judas, one of the G3004
23:13 And Pilate, when he had c together the G4779
33 the place, which is c Calvary, there they G2564
24:13 day to a village c Emmaus, which was G3686
Jn 1:42 thou shalt be c Cephas, which is by G2564
48 Before that Philip c thee, when thou G5455
2: 2 And both Jesus was c, and his disciples, G2564
9 governor of the feast c the bridegroom, G5455
4: 5 Samaria, which is c Sychar, near to the G3004
25 cometh, which is c Christ: when he is G3004
5: 2 a pool, which is c in the Hebrew tongue G1951
9:11 He answered and said, A man that is c G3004
18 sight, until they c the parents of him G5455
24 Then again c they the man that was G5455
10:35 If he c them gods, unto whom the word G2036
11:16 Then said Thomas, which is c G3004
28 went her way, and c Mary her sister G5455
54 into a city c Ephraim, and there G3004
12:17 with him when he c Lazarus out of his G5455
15:15 doeth: but I have c you friends; for all G2046
18:33 hall again, and c Jesus, and said unto G5455
19:13 in a place that is c the Pavement, but in G3004
17 forth into a place c *the place* of a skull, G3004
17 which is c in the Hebrew Golgotha: G3004
20:24 But Thomas, one of the twelve, c G3004
21: 2 Peter, and Thomas c Didymus, and G3004
Act 1:12 from the mount c Olivet, which is from G2564
19 as that field is c in their proper tongue, G2564
23 And they appointed two, Joseph c G2564
3: 2 the temple which is c Beautiful, to ask G3004
11 that is c Solomon's, greatly wondering. G2564
4:18 And they c them, and commanded G2564
5:21 with him, and c the council together, G4779
40 and when they had c the apostles, and G4341
6: 2 Then the twelve c the multitude of the G4341
9 which is c *the synagogue* of the G3004
7:14 Then sent Joseph, and c his father G3333
8: 9 But there was a certain man, c Simon, G3686
9:11 into the street which is c Straight, and G2564
11 of Judas for *one* c Saul, of Tarsus: for, G3686
21 them which c on this name in G1941
36 interpretation is c Dorcas: this woman G3004

C

Act 9:41 up, and when he had c the saints and G5455
10: 1 There was a certain man in Caesarea c G3686
1 of the band c the Italian *band*, G2564
7 Cornelius was departed, he c two of his G5455
18 And c, and asked whether Simon, G5455
23 Then c he them in, and lodged *them*. G1528
24 waited for them, and had c together his G4779
11:26 were c Christians first in Antioch. G5537
13: 1 Simeon that was c Niger, and Lucius of G2564
2 for the work whereunto I have c them. G4341
7 prudent man; who c for Barnabas and G4341
9 Then Saul, (who also *is* c Paul,) filled
14:12 And they c Barnabas, Jupiter; and G2564
15:17 whom my name is c, saith the Lord, G1941
16:10 c us for to preach the gospel unto them. G4341
29 Then he c for a light, and sprang in, and G154
19:25 Whom he c together with the workmen G4867
40 For we are in danger to be c in question G1458
20: 1 uproar was ceased, Paul c unto *him* the G4341
17 and c the elders of the church. G3333
23: 6 of the dead I am c in question. G2919
17 Then Paul c one of the centurions unto G4341
18 Paul the prisoner c me unto *him*, and G4341
23 And he c unto *him* two centurions, G4341
24: 2 And when he was c forth, Tertullus G2564
21 I am c in question by you this day. G2919
27: 8 a place which is c The fair havens; nigh G2564
14 it a tempestuous wind, c Euroclydon. G2564
16 island which is c Clauda, we had much G2564
28: 1 they knew that the island was c Melita. G2564
17 three days Paul c the chief of the Jews G4779
20 For this cause therefore have I c for G3870
Ro 1: 1 Paul, a servant of Jesus Christ, c *to be* G2822
6 Among whom are ye also the c of Jesus G2822
7 beloved of God, c *to be* saints: Grace to G2822
2:17 Behold, thou art c a Jew, and restest in G2028
7: 3 man, she shall be c an adulteress: but if G5537
8:28 who are the c according to *his* purpose. G2822
30 them he also c: and whom he called, G2564
30 and whom he c, them he also justified: G2564
9: 7 but, In Isaac shall thy seed be c. G2564
24 Even us, whom he hath c, not of the G2564
26 they be c the children of the living God. G2564
1Co 1: 1 Paul, c *to be* an apostle of Jesus Christ G2822
2 in Christ Jesus, c *to be* saints, with all G2822
9 God *is* faithful, by whom ye were c unto G2564
24 But unto them which are c, both Jews G2822
26 not many mighty, not many noble, *are c*:
5:11 if any man that is c a brother be a G3687
7:15 such *cases*: but God hath c us to peace. G2564
17 as the Lord hath c every one, so let him G2564
18 Is any man c being circumcised? let G2564
18 Is any c in uncircumcision? G2564
20 in the same calling wherein he was c. G2564
21 Art thou c *being* a servant? care not for G2564
22 For he that is c in the Lord, *being* a G2564
22 that is c, *being* free, is Christ's servant. G2564
24 Brethren, let every man, wherein he is c, G2564
8: 5 For though there be that are c gods, G3004
15: 9 that am not meet to be c an apostle, G2564
Gal 1: 6 from him that c you into the grace of G2564
15 mother's womb, and c *me* by his grace, G2564
5:13 For, brethren, ye have been c unto G2564
Eph 2:11 the flesh, who are c Uncircumcision by G3004
11 by that which is c the Circumcision in G3004
4: 1 of the vocation wherewith ye are c, G2564
4 as ye are c in one hope of your calling; G2564
Col 3:15 are c in one body; and be ye thankful. G2564
4:11 And Jesus, which is c Justus, who are of G3004
1Th 2:12 hath c you unto his kingdom and glory. G2564
4: 7 For God hath not c us unto G2564
2Th 2: 4 above all that is c God, or that is G3004
14 Whereunto he c you by our gospel, to G2564
1Ti 6:12 thou art also c, and hast professed G2564
20 and oppositions of science falsely so c: G5581
2Ti 1: 9 Who hath saved us, and c *us* with an G2564
Heb 3:13 daily, while it is c To day; lest any of G2564
5: 4 but he that is c of God, as *was* Aaron. G2564
10 C of God an high priest after the order G4316
7:11 and not be c after the order of Aaron? G3004
9: 2 shewbread; which is c the sanctuary. G3004
3 tabernacle which is c the Holiest of all; G3004
15 they which are c might receive the G2564
11: 8 By faith Abraham, when he was c to go G2564
16 is not ashamed to be c their God: for he G1941
18 said, That in Isaac shall thy seed be c: G2564
24 to be c the son of Pharaoh's daughter; G3004
Jas 2: 7 that worthy name by the which ye are c? G1941
23 and he was c the Friend of God. G2564
1Pt 1:15 But as he which hath c you is holy, so G2564
2: 9 of him who hath c you out of darkness G2564
21 For even hereunto were ye c: because G2564
3: 9 c, that ye should inherit a blessing. G2564
5:10 But the God of all grace, who hath c us G2564
2Pt 1: 3 him that hath c us to glory and virtue: G2564
1Jn 3: 1 us, that we should be c the sons of God: G2564
Jude 1 and preserved in Jesus Christ, *and c*: G2822
Rev 1: 9 was in the isle that is c Patmos, for the G2564
8:11 And the name of the star is c G3004
11: 8 spiritually is c Sodom and Egypt, G2564
12: 9 that old serpent, c the Devil, and Satan, G2564
16:16 c in the Hebrew tongue Armageddon. G2564
17:14 him *are* c, and chosen, and faithful. G2822
19: 9 *are* they which are c unto the marriage G2564
11 sat upon him *was* c Faithful and True, G2564
13 and his name is c The Word of God. G2564

CALLEDST
Jdg 8: 1 us thus, that thou c us not, when thou H7121
1Sa 3: 5 Here *am* I; for thou c me. And he said, I H7121
Ps 81: 7 Thou c in trouble, and I delivered thee; H7121
Ezk 23:21 Thus thou c to remembrance the H6485

CALLEST
Mt 19:17 And he said unto him, Why c thou me G3004
Mk 10:18 And Jesus said unto him, Why c thou G3004
Lk 18:19 And Jesus said unto him, Why c thou G3004

CALLETH
1Ki 8:43 that the stranger c to thee for: that all H7121
2Ch 6:33 that the stranger c to thee for; that all H7121
Job 12: 4 his neighbour, who c upon God, and he H7121
Ps 42: 7 Deep c unto deep at the noise of thy H7121
147: 4 He telleth the number of the stars; he c H7121
Prv 18: 6 and his mouth c for strokes. H7121
Isa 21:11 The burden of Dumah. He c to me out H7121
40:26 by number: he c them all by names by H7121
59: 4 None c for justice, nor *any* pleadeth for H7121
64: 7 And *there is* none that c upon thy H7121
Hos 7: 7 *is* none among them that c unto me. H7121
Am 5: 8 with night: that c for the waters of the H7121
9: 6 the earth; he that c for the waters of the H7121
Mt 27:47 heard *that*, said, This *man* c for Elias. G5455
Mk 3:13 a mountain, and c *unto him* whom he G4341
10:49 him, Be of good comfort, rise; he c thee. G5455
12:37 David therefore himself c him Lord; G3004
15:35 they heard *it*, said, Behold, he c Elias. G5455
Lk 15: 6 And when he cometh home, he c G4779
9 And when she hath found *it*, she c *her* G4779
20:37 the bush, when he c the Lord the God G3004
44 David therefore c him Lord, how is he G2564
Jn 10: 3 his voice: and he c his own sheep by G2564
11:28 The Master is come, and c for thee. G5455
Ro 4:17 the dead, and c those things which G2564
9:11 stand, not of works, but of him that c;) G2564
1Co 12: 3 the Spirit of God c Jesus accursed: and G3004
Gal 5: 8 *cometh* not of him that c you. G2564
1Th 5:24 Faithful *is* he that c you, who also will G2564
Rev 2:20 Jezebel, which c herself a prophetess, G3004

CALLING
Nu 10: 2 use them for the c of the assembly, and H4744
Isa 1:13 and sabbaths, the c of assemblies, I H7121
41: 4 Who hath wrought and done *it*, c the H7121
46:11 C a ravenous bird from the east, the H7121
Ezk 23:19 Yet she multiplied her whoredoms, in c H2142
Mt 11:16 the markets, and c unto their fellows, G4377
Mk 3:31 without, sent unto him, c him. G5455
11:21 And Peter c to remembrance saith unto G363
15:44 were already dead: and c *unto him* the G4341
Lk 7:19 And John c *unto him* two of his G4341
32 marketplace, and c one to another, and G4377
Act 7:59 And they stoned Stephen, c upon *God*, G1941
22:16 thy sins, c on the name of the Lord. G1941
Ro 11:29 For the gifts and c of God *are* without G2821
1Co 1:26 For ye see your c, brethren, how that G2821
7:20 Let every man abide in the same c G2821
Eph 1:18 is the hope of his c, and what the riches G2821
4: 4 as ye are called in one hope of your c; G2821
Php 3:14 of the high c of God in Christ Jesus. G2821
2Th 1:11 you worthy of *this* c, and fulfil all the G2821
2Ti 1: 9 *us* with an holy c, not according to our G2821
Heb 3: 1 of the heavenly c, consider the Apostle G2821
1Pt 3: 6 Even as Sara obeyed Abraham, c him G2564
2Pt 1:10 to make your c and election sure: for G2821

CALM
Ps 107:29 He maketh the storm a c, so that the H1827
Jna 1:11 the sea may be c unto us? for the sea H8367
12 sea; so shall the sea be c unto you: for I H8367
Mt 8:26 and the sea; and there was a great c. G1055
Mk 4:39 wind ceased, and there was a great c. G1055
Lk 8:24 and they ceased, and there was a c. G1055

CALNEH
Gen 10:10 and Accad, and C, in the land of Shinar. H3641
Am 6: 2 Pass ye unto C, and see; and from H3641

CALNO
Isa 10: 9 *Is* not C as Carchemish? *is* not Hamath H3641

CALVARY
Lk 23:33 which is called C, there they crucified G2898

CALVE
Job 39: 1 canst thou mark when the hinds do c? H2342
Ps 29: 9 the hinds to c, and discovereth the H2342

CALVED
Jer 14: 5 Yea, the hind also c in the field, and H3205

CALVES
1Sa 6: 7 and bring their c home from them: H1121
10 the cart, and shut up their c at home: H1121
14:32 and oxen, and c, and slew *them* H1121+H1241
1Ki 12:28 and made two c *of* gold, and said unto H5695
32 unto the c that he had made: and H5695
2Ki 10:29 them, *to wit*, the golden c that *were* in H5695
17:16 images, *even* two c, and made a grove, H5695
2Ch 11:15 and for the c which he had made. H5695
13: 8 c, which Jeroboam made you for gods. H5695
Ps 68:30 of the bulls, with the c of the people, *till* H5695
Hos 10: 5 because of the c of Beth-aven: for the H5697
13: 2 Let the men that sacrifice kiss the c. H5695
14: 2 so will we render the c of our lips. H6499
Am 6: 4 and the c out of the midst of the stall; H5695
Mic 6: 6 burnt offerings, with c of a year old? H5695
Mal 4: 2 go forth, and grow up as c of the stall. H5695
Heb 9:12 Neither by the blood of goats and c, but G3448
19 took the blood of c and of goats, with G3448

CALVETH
Job 21:10 their cow c, and casteth not her calf. H6403

CAME
Gen 4: 3 And in process of time it c to pass, that H1961
8 his brother: and it c to pass, when they H1961
6: 1 And it c to pass, when men began to H1961
4 the sons of God c in unto the daughters H935
7:10 And it c to pass after seven days, that H1961
8: 6 And it c to pass at the end of forty H1961
11 And the dove c in to him in the evening; H935
13 And it c to pass in the six hundredth H1961
10:14 of whom c Philistim,) and Caphtorim. H3318
11: 2 And it c to pass, as they journeyed H1961
5 And the LORD c down to see the city H3381
31 and they c unto Haran, and dwelt there. H935
12: 5 and into the land of Canaan they c. H935
11 And it c to pass, when he was come H1961
14 And it c to pass, that, when Abram was H1961
13:18 Then Abram removed *his* tent, and c H935
14: 1 And it c to pass in the days of H1961
5 And in the fourteenth year c H935
7 And they returned, and c to En-mishpat, H935
13 And there c one that had escaped, and H935
15: 1 word of the LORD c unto Abram in a H1961
4 And, behold, the word of the LORD c
11 And when the fowls c down upon the H3381
17 And it c to pass, that, when the sun H1961
19: 1 And there c two angels to Sodom at H935
5 *are* the men which c in to thee this night? H935
8 c they under the shadow of my roof. H935
9 This one *fellow* c in to sojourn, and he H935
9 *even* Lot, and c near to break the door. H5066
17 And it c to pass, when they had H1961
29 And it c to pass, when God destroyed H1961
34 And it c to pass on the morrow, that H1961
20: 3 But God c to Abimelech in a dream by H935
13 And it c to pass, when God caused me H1961
21:22 And it c to pass at that time, that H1961
22: 1 And it c to pass after these things, that H1961
9 And they c to the place which God had H935
20 And it c to pass after these things, that H1961
23: 2 and Abraham c to mourn for Sarah, H935
24:15 And it c to pass, before he had done H1961
15 behold, Rebekah c out, who was born H3318
16 well, and filled her pitcher, and c up. H5927

Gen 24:22 And it c to pass, as the camels had H1961
30 And it c to pass, when he saw the H1961
30 unto me; that he c unto the man; and, H935
32 And the man c into the house: and he H935
42 And I c this day unto the well, and said, H935
45 heart, behold, Rebekah c forth with her H3318
52 And it c to pass, that, when Abraham's H1961
62 And Isaac c from the way of the well H935
25:11 And it c to pass after the death of H1961
25 And the first c out red, all over like an H3318
26 And after that c his brother out, and H3318
29 And Jacob sod pottage: and Esau c from H935
26: 8 And it c to pass, when he had been H1961
32 And it c to pass the same day, that H1961
32 that Isaac's servants c, and told him H935
27: 1 And it c to pass, that when Isaac was H1961
18 And he c unto his father, and said, My H935
27 And he c near, and kissed him: and he H5066
30 And it c to pass, as soon as Isaac had H1961
30 Esau his brother c in from his hunting. H935
35 And he said, Thy brother c with subtilty, H935
29: 1 Then Jacob went on his journey, and c H3212
9 with them, Rachel c with her father's H935
10 And it c to pass, when Jacob saw H1961
13 And it c to pass, when Laban heard the H1961
23 And it c to pass in the evening, that he H1961
25 And it c to pass, that in the morning, H1961
30:16 And Jacob c out of the field in the H935
25 And it c to pass, when Rachel had born H1961
30 which thou hadst before I *c*, and it is *now*
38 when the flocks c to drink, that they H935
38 should conceive when they c to drink. H935
41 And it c to pass, whensoever the H1961
31:10 And it c to pass at the time that the H1961
24 And God c to Laban the Syrian in a H935
32: 6 Jacob, saying, We c to thy brother Esau, H935
13 and took of that which c to his hand a H935
33: 1 and, behold, Esau c, and with him four H935
3 times, until he c near to his brother. H5066
6 Then the handmaidens c near, they H5066
7 And Leah also with her children c near, H5066
7 and after c Joseph near and Rachel, H5066
18 And Jacob c to Shalem, a city of H935
18 of Canaan, when he c from Padan-aram; H935
34: 7 And the sons of Jacob c out of the field H935
20 And Hamor and Shechem his son c unto H935
25 And it c to pass on the third day, when H1961
25 his sword, and c upon the city boldly, H935
27 The sons of Jacob c upon the slain, and H935
35: 6 So Jacob c to Luz, which *is* in the land of H935
9 c out of Padan-aram, and blessed him. H935
17 And it c to pass, when she was in hard H1961
18 And it c to pass, as her soul was in H1961
22 And it c to pass, when Israel dwelt in H1961
27 And Jacob c unto Isaac his father unto H935
36:16 *are* the dukes *that* c of Eliphaz in the
17 *are* the dukes *that* c of Reuel in the land
18 *were* the dukes *that* c of Aholibamah the
29 These *are* the dukes *that* c of the Horites;
30 *are* the dukes *that* c of Hori, among their
40 of the dukes *that* c of Esau, according to
37:14 the vale of Hebron, and he c to Shechem. H935
18 off, even before he c near unto them, H7126
23 And it c to pass, when Joseph was H1961
25 of Ishmeelites c from Gilead with their H935
38: 1 And it c to pass at that time, that Judah H1961
9 not be his; and it c to pass, when he H1961
18 c in unto her, and she conceived by him. H935
24 And it c to pass about three months H1961
27 And it c to pass in the time of her H1961
28 And it c to pass, when she travailed, H1961
28 scarlet thread, saying, This c out first. H3318
29 And it c to pass, as he drew back his H1961
29 his brother c out: and she said, How H3318
30 And afterward c out his brother, that H3318
39: 5 And it c to pass from the time *that* he H1961
7 And it c to pass after these things, that H1961
10 And it c to pass, as she spake to Joseph H1961
11 And it c to pass about this time, that H1961
13 And it c to pass, when she saw that he H1961
14 us to mock us; he c in unto me to lie with H935
15 And it c to pass, when he heard that I H1961
16 garment by her, until his lord c home. H935
17 unto us, c in unto me to mock me: H935
18 And it c to pass, as I lifted up my voice H1961
19 And it c to pass, when his master heard H1961
40: 1 And it c to pass after these things, *that* H1961
6 And Joseph c in unto them in the H935
20 And it c to pass the third day, *which* H1961

Gen 41: 1 And it c to pass at the end of two full H1961
2 And, behold, there c up out of the river H5927
3 And, behold, seven other kine c up H5927
5 c up upon one stalk, rank and good. H5927
8 And it c to pass in the morning that his H1961
13 And it c to pass, as he interpreted to us, H1961
14 his raiment, and c in unto Pharaoh. H935
18 And, behold, there c up out of the river H5927
19 And, behold, seven other kine c up H5927
22 ears c up in one stalk, full and good: H5927
27 favoured kine that c up after them *are* H5927
50 the years of famine c, which Asenath the H935
57 And all countries c into Egypt to Joseph H935
42: 5 And the sons of Israel c to buy *corn* H935
5 among those that c: for the famine was in H935
6 Joseph's brethren c, and bowed down H935
29 And they c unto Jacob their father unto H935
35 And it c to pass as they emptied their H1961
43: 2 And it c to pass, when they had eaten H1961
19 And they c near to the steward of H5066
20 And said, O sir, we c indeed down at H3381
21 And it c to pass, when we came to the H1961
21 And it came to pass, when we c to the H935
25 against Joseph c at noon: for they heard H935
26 And when Joseph c home, they brought H935
44:14 And Judah and his brethren c to Joseph's H935
18 Then Judah c near unto him, and said, H5066
24 And it c to pass when we came up unto H1961
24 And it came to pass when we c up unto H5927
45: 4 you. And they c near. And he said, I H5066
25 And they went up out of Egypt, and c H935
46: 1 all that he had, and c to Beer-sheba, and H935
6 of Canaan, and c into Egypt, Jacob, and H935
8 of Israel, which c into Egypt, Jacob and H935
26 All the souls that c with Jacob into H935
26 into Egypt, which c out of his loins, H3318
27 c into Egypt, *were* threescore and ten. H935
28 and they c into the land of Goshen. H935
47: 1 Then Joseph c and told Pharaoh, and H935
15 all the Egyptians c unto Joseph, and H935
18 When that year was ended, they c unto H935
48: 1 And it c to pass after these things, that H1961
5 of Egypt before I c unto thee into Egypt, H935
7 And as for me, when I c from Padan, H935
50:10 And they c to the threshingfloor of Atad, H935
Ex 1: 1 of Israel, which c into Egypt; every man H935
1 man and his household c with Jacob. H935
5 And all the souls that c out of the loins H3318
21 And it c to pass, because the midwives H1961
2: 5 And the daughter of Pharaoh c down H3381
11 And it c to pass in those days, when H1961
16 and they c and drew *water*, and H935
17 And the shepherds c and drove them H935
18 And when they c to Reuel their father, he H935
23 And it c to pass in process of time, that H1961
23 and their cry c up unto God by reason H5927
3: 1 c to the mountain of God, *even* to Horeb. H935
4:24 And it c to pass by the way in the inn, H1961
5:15 the children of Israel c and cried unto H935
20 the way, as they c forth from Pharaoh: H3318
23 For since I c to Pharaoh to speak in thy H935
6:28 And it c to pass on the day *when* the H1961
8: 6 c up, and covered the land of Egypt. H5927
24 And the LORD did so; and there c a H935
10: 3 And Moses and Aaron c in unto H935
12:29 And it c to pass, that at midnight the H1961
41 And it c to pass at the end of the four H1961
41 the selfsame day it c to pass, that all H1961
51 And it c to pass the selfsame day, *that* H1961
13: 3 day, in which ye c out from Egypt, out H3318
4 This day c ye out in the month Abib. H3318
8 unto me when I c forth out of Egypt. H3318
15 And it c to pass, when Pharaoh would H1961
17 And it c to pass, when Pharaoh had let H1961
14:20 And it c between the camp of the H935
20 one c not near the other all the night. H7126
24 And it c to pass, that in the morning H1961
28 host of Pharaoh that c into the sea after H935
15:23 And when they c to Marah, they could H935
27 And they c to Elim, where *were* twelve H935
16: 1 children of Israel c unto the wilderness H935
10 And it c to pass, as Aaron spake unto H1961
13 And it c to pass, that at even the quails H1961
13 at even the quails c up, and covered the H5927
22 And it c to pass, *that* on the sixth day H1961
22 of the congregation c and told Moses. H935
27 And it c to pass, *that* there went out H1961
35 years, until they c to a land inhabited; H935
35 manna, until they c unto the borders of H935

Ex 17: 8 Then c Amalek, and fought with Israel H935
11 And it c to pass, when Moses held up H1961
18: 5 And Jethro, Moses' father in law, c with H935
7 of *their* welfare; and they c into the tent. H935
12 God: and Aaron c, and all the elders of H935
13 And it c to pass on the morrow, that H1961
19: 1 day c they *into* the wilderness of Sinai. H935
7 And Moses c and called for the elders of H935
16 And it c to pass on the third day in the H1961
20 And the LORD c down upon mount H3381
21: 3 If he c in by himself, he shall go out by H935
22:15 if it *be* an hired *thing*, it c for his hire. H935
24: 3 And Moses c and told the people all the H935
32:19 And it c to pass, as soon as he came H7126
19 And it came to pass, as soon as he c H7126
24 it into the fire, and there c out this calf. H3318
30 And it c to pass on the morrow, that H1961
33: 7 And it c to pass, *that* every one H1961
8 And it c to pass, when Moses went out H1961
9 And it c to pass, as Moses entered into H1961
34:29 And it c to pass, when Moses came H1961
29 And it came to pass, when Moses c H3381
29 hand, when he c down from the mount, H3381
32 children of Israel c nigh: and he gave H5066
34 the vail off, until he c out. And he came H3318
34 he came out. And he c out, and spake H3318
35:21 And they c, every one whose heart stirred H935
22 And they c, both men and women, as H935
36: 4 of the sanctuary, c every man from his H935
40:17 And it c to pass in the first month in H1961
32 and when they c near unto the altar, H7126
Lev 9: 1 And it c to pass on the eighth day, *that* H3381
22 and blessed them, and c down from H1961
23 congregation, and c out, and blessed H3318
24 And there c a fire out from before the H3318
Nu 4:47 old, every one that c to do the service of H935
7: 1 And it c to pass on the day that Moses H1961
9: 6 that day: and they c before Moses and H7126
10:11 And it c to pass on the twentieth *day* of H1961
21 did set up the tabernacle against they c. H935
35 And it c to pass, when the ark set H1961
11:20 saying, Why c we forth out of Egypt? H3318
25 And the LORD c down in a cloud, and H3381
25 elders: and it c to pass, *that*, when H1961
12: 4 the congregation. And they three c out. H3318
5 And the LORD c down in the pillar of H3381
5 and Miriam: and they both c forth. H3381
13:22 And they ascended by the south, and c H935
23 And they c unto the brook of Eshcol, and H935
26 And they went and c to Moses, and to H935
27 And they told him, and said, We c unto H935
14:45 Then the Amalekites c down, and the H3381
16:27 and Abiram c out, and stood in the H3318
31 And it c to pass, as he had made an H1961
35 And there c out a fire from the LORD, H3318
42 And it c to pass, when the congregation H1961
43 And Moses and Aaron c before the H935
17: 8 And it c to pass, that on the morrow H1961
19: 2 blemish, *and* upon which never c yoke: H5927
20: 1 Then c the children of Israel, *even* the H935
11 and the water c out abundantly, and H3318
20 And Edom c out against him with H3318
22 from Kadesh, and c unto mount Hor. H935
28 and Eleazar c down from the mount. H3381
21: 1 tell that Israel c by the way of the spies; H935
7 Therefore the people c to Moses, and H935
9 a pole, and it c to pass, that if a serpent H1961
23 he c to Jahaz, and fought against Israel. H935
22: 7 their hand; and they c unto Balaam, and H935
9 And God c unto Balaam, and said, What H935
16 And they c to Balaam, and said to him, H935
20 And God c unto Balaam at night, and H935
39 And Balaam went with Balak, and they c H935
41 And it c to pass on the morrow, that H1961
23:17 And when he c to him, behold, he stood H935
24: 2 and the spirit of God c upon him. H1961
25: 6 children of Israel c and brought unto his H935
26: 1 And it c to pass after the plague, that H1961
27: 1 Then c the daughters of Zelophehad, H7126
31:14 over hundreds, which c from the battle. H935
48 of hundreds, c near unto Moses: H7126
32: 2 the children of Reuben c and spake unto H935
11 Surely none of the men that c up out of H5927
16 And they c near unto him, and said, H5066
33: 9 And they removed from Marah, and c H935
36: 1 of the sons of Joseph, c near, and spake H7126
Dt 1: 3 And it c to pass in the fortieth year, in H1961
19 us; and we c to Kadeshbarnea. H935
22 And ye c near unto me every one of H7126

Dt 1:24 the mountain, and **c** unto the valley of H935
31 that ye went, until ye **c** into this place. H935
44 in that mountain, **c** out against you, H3318
2:14 And the space in which we **c** from H1980
16 So it **c** to pass, when all the men of war H1961
23 which **c** forth out of Caphtor, H3318
32 Then Sihon **c** out against us, he and all H3318
3: 1 king of Bashan **c** out against us, he and H3318
4:11 And ye **c** near and stood under the H7126
45 of Israel, after they **c** forth out of Egypt, H3318
5:23 And it **c** to pass, when ye heard the H1961
23 with fire,) that ye **c** near unto me, *even* H7126
9: 7 of Egypt, until ye **c** unto this place, ye H935
11 And it **c** to pass at the end of forty days H1961
15 So I turned and **c** down from the H3381
10: 5 And I turned myself and **c** down from H3381
11: 5 the wilderness, until ye **c** into this place; H935
10 from whence ye **c** out, where thou H3318
22:14 when I **c** to her, I found her not a maid: H7126
23: 4 the way, when ye **c** forth out of Egypt; H3318
29: 7 And when ye **c** unto this place, Sihon the H935
7 king of Bashan, **c** out against us unto H3318
16 and how we **c** through the nations H5674
31:24 And it **c** to pass, when Moses had made H1961
32:17 to new *gods that* **c** newly up, whom your H935
44 And Moses **c** and spake all the words of H935
33: 2 And he said, The LORD **c** from Sinai, H935
2 Paran, and he **c** with ten thousands of H857
21 *he* seated; and he **c** with the heads of the H857
Jos 1: 1 of the LORD it **c** to pass, that the LORD H1961
2: 1 they went, and **c** into an harlot's house, H935
2 Behold, there **c** men in hither to night H935
4 said thus, There **c** men unto me, but I H935
5 And it **c** to pass *about the time* of H1961
8 And before they were laid down, she **c** H5927
10 for you, when ye **c** out of Egypt; and H3318
22 And they went, and **c** unto the H935
23 passed over, and **c** to Joshua the son of H935
3: 1 from Shittim, and **c** to Jordan, he and all H935
2 And it **c** to pass after three days, that H1961
14 And it **c** to pass, when the people H1961
16 That the waters which **c** down from H3381
16 and those that **c** down toward the sea H3381
4: 1 And it **c** to pass, when all the people H1961
11 And it **c** to pass, when all the people H1961
18 And it **c** to pass, when the priests that H1961
19 And the people **c** up out of Jordan on H5927
22 Israel **c** over this Jordan on dry land. H5674
5: 1 And it **c** to pass, when all the kings of H1961
4 All the people that **c** out of Egypt, *that* H3318
4 by the way, after they **c** out of Egypt. H3318
5 Now all the people that **c** out were H3318
5 by the way as they **c** forth out of Egypt, H3318
6 men of war, which **c** out of Egypt, were H3318
8 And it **c** to pass, when they had done H1961
13 And it **c** to pass, when Joshua was by H1961
6: 1 of Israel: none went out, and none **c** in. H935
8 And it **c** to pass, when Joshua had H1961
9 and the rearward **c** after the ark, *the* H1980
11 **c** into the camp, and lodged in the camp. H935
13 but the rearward **c** after the ark of the H1980
15 And it **c** to pass on the seventh day, H1961
16 And it **c** to pass at the seventh time, H1961
20 the trumpets: and it **c** to pass, when the H1961
8:11 and drew nigh, and **c** before the city, and H935
14 And it **c** to pass, when the king of Ai H1961
24 And it **c** to pass, when Israel had made H1961
9: 1 And it **c** to pass, when all the kings H1961
12 on the day we **c** forth to go unto you; H3318
16 And it **c** to pass at the end of three days H1961
17 journeyed, and **c** unto their cities on the H935
10: 1 Now it **c** to pass, when Adoni-zedek H1961
9 Joshua therefore **c** unto them suddenly, H935
11 And it **c** to pass, as they fled from H1961
20 And it **c** to pass, when Joshua and the H1961
24 And it **c** to pass, when they brought out H1961
24 kings. And they **c** near, and put their H7126
27 And it **c** to pass at the time of the going H1961
33 Then Horam king of Gezer **c** up to help H5927
11: 1 And it **c** to pass, when Jabin king of H1961
5 were met together, they **c** and pitched H935
7 So Joshua **c**, and all the people of war H935
21 And at that time **c** Joshua, and cut off H935
14: 6 Then the children of Judah **c** unto H5066
15:18 And it **c** to pass, as she came *unto him,* H1961
18 And it came to pass, as she **c** *unto him,* H935
16: 7 **c** to Jericho, and went out at Jordan. H6293
17: 4 And they **c** near before Eleazar the H7126
13 Yet it **c** to pass, when the children of H1961

Jos 18: 9 **c** *again* to Joshua to the host at Shiloh. H935
11 of Benjamin **c** up according to their H5927
11 coast of their lot **c** forth between the H3318
16 And the border **c** down to the end of H3381
19: 1 And the second lot **c** forth to Simeon, H3318
10 And the third lot **c** up for the children H5927
17 *And* the fourth lot **c** out to Issachar, for H3318
24 And the fifth lot **c** out for the tribe of H3318
32 The sixth lot **c** out to the children of H3318
40 *And* the seventh lot **c** out for the tribe H3318
21: 1 Then **c** near the heads of the fathers of H5066
4 And the lot **c** out for the families of the H3318
45 unto the house of Israel; all **c** to pass. H935
22:10 And when they **c** unto the borders of H935
15 And they **c** unto the children of Reuben, H935
23: 1 And it **c** to pass a long time after that H1961
24: 6 of Egypt: and ye **c** unto the sea; and the H935
11 And ye went over Jordan, and **c** unto H935
29 And it **c** to pass after these things, that H1961
Jdg 1: 1 Now after the death of Joshua it **c** to H1961
14 And it **c** to pass, when she came *to* H1961
14 And it came to pass, when she **c** *to him,* H935
28 And it **c** to pass, when Israel was H1961
2: 1 And an angel of the LORD **c** up from H5927
4 And it **c** to pass, when the angel of the H1961
19 And it **c** to pass, when the judge was H1961
3:10 And the spirit of the LORD **c** upon him, H1961
20 And Ehud **c** unto him; and he was sitting H935
22 out of his belly; and the dirt **c** out. H3318
24 When he was gone out, his servants **c**; H935
27 And it **c** to pass, when he was come, H1961
4: 5 of Israel **c** up to her for judgment. H5927
22 Sisera, Jael **c** out to meet him, and H3318
22 And when he **c** into her *tent,* behold, H935
5:14 out of Machir **c** down governors, and H3381
19 The kings **c** *and* fought, then fought the H935
23 because they **c** not to the help of the H935
6: 3 that the Midianites **c** up, and the H5927
3 the east, even they **c** up against them; H5927
5 For they **c** up with their cattle and their H5927
5 tents, and they **c** as grasshoppers for H935
7 And it **c** to pass, when the children of H1961
11 And there **c** an angel of the LORD, and H935
25 And it **c** to pass the same night, that H1961
34 But the spirit of the LORD **c** upon H3847
35 Naphtali; and they **c** up to meet them. H5927
7: 9 And it **c** to pass the same night, that H1961
13 of Midian, and **c** unto a tent, and smote H935
19 *were* with him, **c** unto the outside of the H935
8: 4 And Gideon **c** to Jordan, *and* passed H935
15 And he **c** unto the men of Succoth, and H935
33 And it **c** to pass, as soon as Gideon was H1961
9:25 they robbed all that **c** along that way by H5674
26 And Gaal the son of Ebed **c** with his H935
42 And it **c** to pass on the morrow, that H1961
52 And Abimelech **c** unto the tower, and H935
57 and upon them **c** the curse of Jotham H935
11: 4 And it **c** to pass in process of time, that H1961
13 land, when they **c** up out of Egypt, from H5927
16 But when Israel **c** up from Egypt, and H5927
16 unto the Red sea, and **c** to Kadesh; H935
18 land of Moab, and **c** by the east side of H935
18 other side of Arnon, but **c** not within the H935
29 Then the spirit of the LORD **c** upon H1961
34 And Jephthah **c** to Mizpeh unto his H935
34 his daughter **c** out to meet him with H3318
35 And it **c** to pass, when he saw her, that H1961
39 And it **c** to pass at the end of two H1961
13: 6 Then the woman **c** and told her H935
6 saying, A man of God **c** unto me, and his H935
9 and the angel of God **c** again unto the H935
10 unto me, that **c** unto me the *other* day. H935
11 after his wife, and **c** to the man, and said H935
20 For it **c** to pass, when the flame went H1961
14: 2 And he **c** up, and told his father and his H5927
5 to Timnath, and **c** to the vineyards of H935
6 And the spirit of the LORD **c** mightily H6743
9 went on eating, and **c** to his father and H1980
11 And it **c** to pass, when they saw him, H1961
14 Out of the eater **c** forth meat, and out H3318
14 out of the strong **c** forth sweetness. And H3318
15 And it **c** to pass on the seventh day, H1961
17 feast lasted: and it **c** to pass on the H1961
19 And the spirit of the LORD **c** upon him, H6743
15: 1 But it **c** to pass within a while after, in H1961
6 the Philistines **c** up, and burnt her and H5927
14 *And* when he **c** unto Lehi, the Philistines H935
14 spirit of the LORD **c** mightily upon him, H935
17 And it **c** to pass, when he had made an H1961

Jdg 15:19 in the jaw, and there **c** water thereout; H3318
19 had drunk, his spirit **c** again, and he H7725
16: 4 And it **c** to pass afterward, that he H1961
5 And the lords of the Philistines **c** up H5927
16 And it **c** to pass, when she pressed him H1961
18 of the Philistines **c** up unto her, and H5927
25 And it **c** to pass, when their hearts were H1961
31 house of his father **c** down, and took H3381
17: 8 *a place*: and he **c** to mount Ephraim to H935
18: 2 who when they **c** to mount Ephraim, to H935
7 Then the five men departed, and **c** to H935
8 And they **c** unto their brethren to Zorah H935
13 and **c** unto the house of Micah. H935
15 And they turned thitherward, and **c** to H935
17 land went up, *and* **c** in thither, *and* took H935
27 which he had, and **c** unto Laish, unto a H935
19: 1 And it **c** to pass in those days, when H1961
5 And it **c** to pass on the fourth day, H1961
10 and departed, and **c** over against Jebus, H935
16 And, behold, there **c** an old man from H935
22 forth the man that **c** into thine house, H935
26 Then **c** the woman in the dawning of the H935
30 children of Israel **c** up out of the land of H5927
20: 4 and said, I **c** into Gibeah that *belongeth* H935
21 And the children of Benjamin **c** forth H3318
24 And the children of Israel **c** near H7126
26 went up, and **c** unto the house of God, H935
33 liers in wait of Israel **c** forth out of their H1518
34 And there **c** against Gibeah ten H935
42 and them which **c** out of the cities they
48 beast, and all that **c** to hand: also they H4672
48 set on fire all the cities that they **c** to. H4672
21: 2 And the people **c** to the house of God, H935
4 And it **c** to pass on the morrow, that H1961
5 tribes of Israel that **c** not up with the H5927
5 him that **c** not up to the LORD H5927
8 of Israel that **c** not up to Mizpeh to H5927
8 And, behold, there **c** none to the camp H935
14 And Benjamin **c** again at that time; H7725
Ru 1: 1 Now it **c** to pass in the days when the H1961
2 And they **c** into the country of Moab, H935
19 So they two went until they **c** to H935
19 And it **c** to pass, when they were H1961
22 of Moab: and they **c** to Beth-lehem in the H935
2: 3 And she went, and **c**, and gleaned in the H935
4 And, behold, Boaz **c** from Beth-lehem, H935
6 damsel that **c** back with Naomi out H77252
7 the sheaves: so she **c**, and hath continued H935
3: 7 of corn: and she **c** softly, and uncovered H935
8 And it **c** to pass at midnight, that the H1961
14 be known that a woman **c** into the floor. H935
16 And when she **c** to her mother in law, H935
4: 1 whom Boaz spake **c** by; unto whom he H5674
1Sa 1:12 And it **c** to pass, as she continued H1961
19 and returned, and **c** to their house to H935
20 Wherefore it **c** to pass, when the time H1961
2:13 the priest's servant **c**, while the flesh was H935
14 unto all the Israelites that **c** thither. H935
15 fat, the priest's servant **c**, and said to the H935
19 year to year, when she **c** up with her H5927
27 And there **c** a man of God unto Eli, and H935
3: 2 And it **c** to pass at that time, when Eli H1961
10 And the LORD **c**, and stood, and called H935
4: 1 And the word of Samuel **c** to all Israel. H1961
5 of the LORD **c** into the camp, all Israel H935
12 of the army, and **c** to Shiloh the same H935
13 And when he **c**, lo, Eli sat upon a seat by H935
13 And when the man **c** into the city, and H935
14 And the man **c** in hastily, and told Eli. H935
16 Eli, I *am* he that **c** out of the army, and H935
18 And it **c** to pass, when he made H1961
19 and travailed; for her pains **c** upon her. H2015
5:10 to Ekron. And it **c** to pass, as the ark of H1961
10 as the ark of God **c** to Ekron, that the H935
6:14 And the cart **c** into the field of Joshua, a H935
7: 1 And the men of Kirjath-jearim **c**, and H935
2 And it **c** to pass, while the ark abode in H1961
11 smote them, until *they* **c** under Beth-car.
13 subdued, and they **c** no more into the H935
8: 1 And it **c** to pass, when Samuel was old, H1961
4 together, and **c** to Samuel unto Ramah, H935
9:12 haste now, for he **c** to day to the city; for H935
14 behold, Samuel **c** out against them, for H3318
15 in his ear a day before Saul **c**, saying, H935
26 And they arose early: and it **c** to pass H1961
10: 9 and all those signs **c** to pass that day. H935
10 And when they **c** thither to the hill, H935
10 the spirit of God **c** upon him, and he H6743
11 And it **c** to pass, when all that knew H1961

1Sa 10:13 of prophesying, he c to the high place. H935
14 that *they were* no where, we c to Samuel. H935
11: 1 Then Nahash the Ammonite c up, and H5927
4 Then c the messengers to Gibeah of Saul, H935
5 And, behold, Saul c after the herd out of H935
6 And the spirit of God c upon Saul when H6743
7 and they c out with one consent. H3318
9 messengers that c, Thus shall ye say unto H935
9 the messengers c and shewed *it* to the H935
11 and they c into the midst of the H935
11 of the day: and it c to pass, that they H1961
12:12 of Ammon c against you, ye said H935
13: 5 and they c up, and pitched in H5927
8 but Samuel c not to Gilgal; and the H935
10 And it c to pass, that as soon as he had H1961
10 behold, Samuel c; and Saul went out to H935
17 And the spoilers c out of the camp of H3318
22 So it c to pass in the day of battle, that H1961
14: 1 Now it c to pass upon a day, that H1961
19 And it c to pass, while Saul talked unto H1961
20 and they c to the battle: and, behold, H935
25 And all *they of* the land c to a wood; and H935
15: 2 in the way, when he c up from Egypt. H5927
5 And Saul c to a city of Amalek, and laid H935
6 Israel, when they c up out of Egypt. So H5927
10 Then c the word of the LORD unto H1961
12 saying, Saul c to Carmel, and, behold, H935
13 And Samuel c to Saul: and Saul said H935
32 And Agag c unto him delicately. H1980
35 And Samuel c no more to see Saul until
16: 4 LORD spake, and c to Beth-lehem. And H935
6 And it c to pass, when they were come, H1961
13 spirit of the LORD c upon David from H6743
21 And David c to Saul, and stood before H935
23 And it c to pass, when the *evil* spirit H1961
17:20 him; and he c to the trench, as the H935
22 army, and c and saluted his brethren. H935
23 behold, there c up the champion, the H5927
34 sheep, and there c a lion, and a bear, H935
41 And the Philistine c on and drew near H3212
48 And it c to pass, when the Philistine H1961
48 arose, and c and drew nigh to meet H3212
18: 1 And it c to pass, when he had made an H1961
6 And it c to pass as they came, when H1961
6 And it came to pass as they c, when H935
6 that the women c out of all cities of H3318
10 And it c to pass on the morrow, that H1961
10 spirit from God c upon Saul, and he H6743
13 he went out and c in before the people. H935
16 he went out and c in before them. H935
19 But it c to pass at the time when Merab H1961
30 went forth: and it c to pass, after they H1961
19:18 So David fled, and escaped, and c to H935
22 Then went he also to Ramah, and c to a H935
23 until he c to Naioth in Ramah. H935
20: 1 Naioth in Ramah, and c and said before H935
27 And it c to pass on the morrow, *which* H1961
35 And it c to pass in the morning, that H1961
38 up the arrows, and c to his master. H935
21: 1 Then c David to Nob to Ahimelech the H935
5 these three days, since I c out, and the H3318
22: 5 departed, and c into the forest of Hareth. H935
11 Nob: and they c all of them to the king. H935
23: 6 And it c to pass, when Abiathar the son H1961
6 he c down *with* an ephod in his hand. H3381
19 Then c up the Ziphites to Saul to H5927
25 wherefore he c down into a rock, and H3381
27 But there c a messenger unto Saul, H935
24: 1 And it c to pass, when Saul was H1961
3 And he c to the sheepcotes by the way, H935
5 And it c to pass afterward, that David's H1961
16 And it c to pass, when David had made H1961
25: 9 And when David's young men c, they H935
12 and c and told him all those sayings. H935
20 the ass, that she c down by the covert H3381
20 c down against her; and she met them. H3381
36 And Abigail c to Nabal; and, behold, he H935
37 But it c to pass in the morning, when H1916
38 And it c to pass about ten days *after,* H1916
26: 1 And the Ziphites c unto Saul to Gibeah, H935
3 that Saul c after him into the wilderness. H935
5 And David arose, and c to the place H935
7 So David and Abishai c to the people by H935
15 the king? for there c one of the people in H935
27: 9 apparel, and returned, and c to Achish. H935
28: 1 And it c to pass in those days, that the H1961
4 together, and c and pitched in Shunem: H935
8 with him, and they c to the woman by H935
21 And the woman c unto Saul, and saw H935

1Sa 30: 1 And it c to pass, when David and his H1961
3 So David and his men c to the city, and, H935
9 *were* with him, and c to the brook Besor, H935
12 eaten, his spirit c again to him: for he H7725
21 And David c to the two hundred men, H935
21 c near to the people, he saluted them. H5066
23 that c against us into our hand. H935
26 And when David c to Ziklag, he sent of H935
31: 7 and the Philistines c and dwelt in them. H935
8 And it c to pass on the morrow, when H1691
8 the Philistines c to strip the slain, that H935
12 and c to Jabesh, and burnt them there. H935
2Sa 1: 1 Now it c to pass after the death of Saul, H1961
2 It c even to pass on the third day, that, H1961
2 behold, a man c out of the camp from H935
2 *so* it was, when he c to David, that he fell H935
2: 1 And it c to pass after this, that David H1961
4 And the men of Judah c, and there they H935
23 *rib,* that the spear c out behind him; H3318
23 the same place: and it c to pass, *that* as H935
23 *that* as many as c to the place where H935
29 all Bithron, and they c to Mahanaim. H935
32 and they c to Hebron at break of day. H935
3: 6 And it c to pass, while there was war H1961
20 So Abner c to David to Hebron, and H935
22 of David and Joab c from *pursuing* a H935
23 the son of Ner c to the king, and he hath H935
24 Then Joab c to the king, and said, What H935
24 behold, Abner c unto thee; why *is it that* H935
25 son of Ner, that he c to deceive thee, and H935
35 And when all the people c to cause H935
4: 4 when the tidings c of Saul and Jonathan H935
4 and fled: and it c to pass, as she made H1961
5 Baanah, went, and c about the heat of H935
6 And they c thither into the midst of the H935
7 For when they c into the house, he lay on H935
5: 1 Then c all the tribes of Israel to David H935
3 So all the elders of Israel c to the king to H935
17 all the Philistines c up to seek David; H5927
18 The Philistines also c and spread H935
20 And David c to Baal-perazim, and David H935
22 And the Philistines c up yet again, and H5927
6: 6 And when they c to Nachon's H935
16 And as the ark of the LORD c into the H935
20 daughter of Saul c out to meet David, H3318
7: 1 And it c to pass, when the king sat in H1961
4 And it c to pass that night, that the H1961
4 of the LORD c unto Nathan, saying, H1961
8: 1 And after this it c to pass, that David H1961
5 And when the Syrians of Damascus c to H935
10: 1 And it c to pass after this, that the king H1961
2 David's servants c into the land of the H935
8 And the children of Ammon c out, and H3318
14 children of Ammon, and c to Jerusalem. H935
16 the river: and they c to Helam; and H935
17 over Jordan, and c to Helam. And the H935
11: 1 And it c to pass, after the year was H1961
2 And it c to pass in an eveningtide, that H1961
4 took her; and she c in unto him, and he H935
14 And it c to pass in the morning, that H1961
16 And it c to pass, when Joab observed H1961
22 So the messenger went, and c and H935
23 against us, and c out unto us into the H3318
12: 1 David. And he c unto him, and said unto H935
4 And there c a traveller unto the rich H935
18 And it c to pass on the seventh day, H1961
20 his apparel, and c into the house of the H935
20 then he c to his own house; and H935
13: 1 And it c to pass after this, that H1961
23 And it c to pass after two full years, H1961
24 And Absalom c to the king, and said, H935
30 And it c to pass, while they were in the H1961
30 the way, that tidings c to David, saying, H935
34 and, behold, there c much people by H1980
36 And it c to pass, as soon as he had H1961
36 the king's sons c, and lifted up their voice H935
14:31 Then Joab arose, and c to Absalom unto H935
33 So Joab c to the king, and told him: and H935
33 called for Absalom, he c to the king, and H935
15: 1 And it c to pass after this, that H1961
2 that had a controversy c to the king for H935
5 And it was *so,* that when any man c H7126
6 to all Israel that c to the king for H935
7 And it c to pass after forty years, that H1961
13 And there c a messenger to David, H935
18 men which c after him from Gath, H935
32 And it c to pass, that *when* David was H1961
32 Hushai the Archite c to meet him with
37 So Hushai David's friend c into the city, H935

2Sa 15:37 the city, and Absalom c into Jerusalem. H935
16: 5 And when king David c to Bahurim, H935
5 behold, thence c out a man of the H3318
5 he c forth, and cursed still as he came. H3318
5 he came forth, and cursed still as he c. H3318
11 my son, which c forth of my bowels, H3318
14 c weary, and refreshed themselves there. H935
15 the men of Israel, c to Jerusalem, and H935
16 And it c to pass, when Hushai the H1961
17:18 away quickly, and c to a man's house in H935
20 And when Absalom's servants c to the H935
21 And it c to pass, after they were H1961
21 that they c up out of the well, and H5927
24 Then David c to Mahanaim. And H935
27 And it c to pass, when David was come H1961
18: 4 c out by hundreds and by thousands. H3318
25 mouth. And he c apace, and drew near. H3212
31 And, behold, Cushi c; and Cushi said, H935
19: 5 And Joab c into the house to the king, H935
8 And all the people c before the king: for H935
15 So the king returned, and c to Jordan. H935
15 to Jordan. And Judah c to Gilgal, to go to H935
16 hasted and c down with the men H3381
24 And Mephibosheth the son of Saul c H3381
24 until the day he c *again* in peace. H935
25 And it c to pass, when he was come to H1961
31 And Barzillai the Gileadite c down H3381
41 And, behold, all the men of Israel c to H935
20: 3 And David c to his house at Jerusalem; H935
12 that every one that c by him stood still. H935
15 And they c and besieged him in Abel of H935
21:18 And it c to pass after this, that there H1961
22:10 He bowed the heavens also, and c H3381
23:13 chief went down, and c to David in the H935
24: 6 Then they c to Gilead, and to the land of H935
6 they c to Dan-jaan, and about to Zidon, H935
7 And c to the strong hold of Tyre, and to H935
8 all the land, they c to Jerusalem at the H935
11 word of the LORD c unto the prophet H1961
13 So Gad c to David, and told him, and H935
18 And Gad c that day to David, and said H935
1Ki 1:22 the king, Nathan the prophet also c in. H935
28 And she c into the king's presence, H935
32 of Jehoiada. And they c before the king. H935
40 And all the people c up after him, and H5927
42 Abiathar the priest c: and Adonijah said H935
47 And moreover the king's servants c to H935
53 the altar. And he c and bowed himself to H935
2: 7 table: for so they c to me when I fled H7126
8 Mahanaim: but he c down to meet me H3381
13 And Adonijah the son of Haggith c to H935
28 Then tidings c to Joab: for Joab had H935
30 And Benaiah c to the tabernacle of the H935
39 And it c to pass at the end of three H1961
3:15 a dream. And he c to Jerusalem, and H935
16 Then c there two women, *that were* H935
18 And it c to pass the third day after that H1961
4:27 and for all that c unto king Solomon's H7131
34 And there c of all people to hear the H935
5: 7 And it c to pass, when Hiram heard the H1961
6: 1 And it c to pass in the four hundred H1961
11 And the word of the LORD c to H1961
7:14 in brass. And he c to king Solomon, and H935
8: 3 And all the elders of Israel c, and the H935
9 when they c out of the land of Egypt. H3318
10 And it c to pass, when the priests were H1961
9: 1 And it c to pass, when Solomon had H1961
10 And it c to pass at the end of twenty H1961
12 And Hiram c out from Tyre to see the H3318
24 But Pharaoh's daughter c up out of the H5927
28 And they c to Ophir, and fetched from H935
10: 1 she c to prove him with hard questions. H935
2 And she c to Jerusalem with a very great H935
7 the words, until I c, and mine eyes had H935
10 stones: there c no more such abundance H935
12 for singers: there c no such almug trees, H935
14 Now the weight of gold that c to H935
22 Hiram: once in three years c the navy of H935
29 And a chariot c up and went out of H5927
11: 4 For it c to pass, when Solomon was old, H1961
15 For it c to pass, when David was in H1961
18 And they arose out of Midian, and c to H935
18 out of Paran, and they c to Egypt, unto H935
29 And it c to pass at that time when H1961
12: 2 And it c to pass, when Jeroboam the H1961
3 c, and spake unto Rehoboam, saying, H935
12 So Jeroboam and all the people c to H935
20 And it c to pass, when all Israel heard H1961
22 But the word of God c unto Shemaiah H1961

1Ki 13: 1 And, behold, there c a man of God out of H935
4 And it c to pass, when king Jeroboam H1961
10 not by the way that he c to Beth-el. H935
11 and his sons c and told him all the H935
12 man of God went, which c from Judah. H935
20 And it c to pass, as they sat at the table, H1961
20 word of the LORD c unto the prophet H1961
21 And he cried unto the man of God that c H935
23 And it c to pass, after he had eaten H1961
25 carcase: and they c and told *it* in the city H935
29 c to the city, to mourn and to bury him. H935
31 And it c to pass, after he had buried H1961
14: 4 and went to Shiloh, and c to the house of H935
6 of her feet, as she c in at the door, that H935
17 and departed, and c to Tirzah: *and* when H935
17 *and* when she c to the threshold of the H935
25 And it c to pass in the fifth year of king H1961
25 king of Egypt c up against Jerusalem: H5927
15:21 And it c to pass, when Baasha heard H1961
29 And it c to pass, when he reigned, *that* H1961
16: 1 Then the word of the LORD c to Jehu H1961
7 the son of Hanani c the word of the H1961
11 And it c to pass, when he began to H1961
18 And it c to pass, when Zimri saw that H1961
31 And it c to pass, as if it had been a light H1961
17: 2 And the word of the LORD c unto him, H1961
7 And it c to pass after a while, that the H1961
8 And the word of the LORD c unto him, H1961
10 And when he c to the gate of the city, H935
17 And it c to pass after these things, *that* H1961
22 child c into him again, and he revived. H7725
18: 1 And it c to pass *after* many days, that H1961
1 the word of the LORD c to Elijah in the H1961
17 And it c to pass, when Ahab saw Elijah, H1961
21 And Elijah c unto all the people, and H5066
27 And it c to pass at noon, that Elijah H1961
29 And it c to pass, when midday was H1961
30 me. And all the people c near unto him. H5066
31 c, saying, Israel shall be thy name: H1961
36 And it c to pass at *the time of* the H1961
36 Elijah the prophet c near, and said, H5066
44 And it c to pass at the seventh time, H1961
45 And it c to pass in the mean while, that H1961
19: 3 for his life, and c to Beer-sheba, which H935
4 wilderness, and c and sat down under H935
7 And the angel of the LORD c again the H7725
9 And he c thither unto a cave, and lodged H935
9 word of the LORD c to him, and he said
13 And, behold, *there c* a voice unto him, H7725
20: 5 And the messengers c again, and said, H7725
12 And it c to pass, when *Ben-hadad* H1961
13 And, behold, there c a prophet unto H5066
19 of the provinces c out of the city, and H3318
22 And the prophet c to the king of Israel, H5066
26 And it c to pass at the return of the H1961
28 And there c a man of God, and spake H5066
30 c into the city, into an inner chamber. H935
32 ropes on their heads, and c to the king of H935
33 Then Ben-hadad c forth to him; and he H3318
43 heavy and displeased, and c to Samaria. H935
21: 1 And it c to pass after these things, *that* H1961
4 And Ahab c into his house heavy and H935
5 But Jezebel his wife c to him, and said H935
13 And there c in two men, children of H935
15 And it c to pass, when Jezebel heard H1961
16 And it c to pass, when Ahab heard that H1961
17 And the word of the LORD c to Elijah H1961
27 And it c to pass, when Ahab heard H1961
28 And the word of the LORD c to Elijah H1961
22: 2 And it c to pass in the third year, that H1961
2 of Judah c down to the king of Israel. H3381
15 So he c to the king. And the king said H935
21 And there c forth a spirit, and stood H3318
32 And it c to pass, when the captains of H1961
33 And it c to pass, when the captains of H1961
2Ki 1: 6 And they said unto him, There c a man H5927
7 of man *was he* which c up to meet you, H5927
10 thy fifty. And there c down fire from H3381
12 the fire of God c down from heaven, H3381
13 fifty went up, and c and fell on his knees H935
14 Behold, there c fire down from heaven, H3381
2: 1 And it c to pass, when the LORD would H1961
3 *were* at Beth-el c forth to Elisha, and H3318
4 I will not leave thee. So they c to Jericho. H935
5 *were* at Jericho c to Elisha, and said H5066
9 And it c to pass, when they were gone H1961
11 And it c to pass, as they still went on, H1961
15 on Elisha. And they c to meet him, and H935
18 And when they c again to him, (for he H7725

2Ki 2:23 by the way, there c forth little children H3318
24 LORD. And there c forth two she bears H3318
3: 5 But it c to pass, when Ahab was dead, H1961
15 But now bring me a minstrel. And it c H1961
15 that the hand of the LORD c upon him. H1961
20 And it c to pass in the morning, when H1961
20 that, behold, there c water by the way of H935
24 And when they c to the camp of Israel, H935
4: 6 And it c to pass, when the vessels were H1961
7 Then she c and told the man of God. H935
11 And it fell on a day, that he c thither, H935
25 So she went and c unto the man of God H935
25 Carmel. And it c to pass, when the man H1961
27 And when she c to the man of God to the H935
27 the feet: but Gehazi c near to thrust her H5066
38 And Elisha c again to Gilgal: and *there* H7725
39 his lap full, and c and shred *them* into H935
40 the men to eat. And it c to pass, as they H1961
42 And there c a man from Baal-shalisha, H935
5: 7 And it c to pass, when the king of Israel H1961
9 So Naaman c with his horses and with H935
13 And his servants c near, and spake H5066
14 God: and his flesh c again like unto the H7725
15 all his company, and c, and stood before H935
24 And when he c to the tower, he took H935
6: 4 So he went with them. And when they c H935
14 great host: and they c by night, and H935
18 And when they c down to him, Elisha H3381
20 And it c to pass, when they were come H1961
23 of Syria c no more into the land of Israel. H935
24 And it c to pass after this, that H1961
30 And it c to pass, when the king heard H1961
32 ere the messenger c to him, he said to H935
33 the messenger c down unto him: and H3381
7: 8 And when these lepers c to the uttermost H935
8 and hid *it;* and c again, and entered H7725
10 So they c and called unto the porter of H935
10 them, saying, We c to the camp of the H935
17 spake when the king c down to him. H3381
18 And it c to pass as the man of God had H1961
8: 3 And it c to pass at the seven years' end, H1961
5 And it c to pass, as he was telling the H1961
7 And Elisha c to Damascus; and H935
9 burden, and c and stood before him, H935
14 So he departed from Elisha, and c to his H935
15 And it c to pass on the morrow, that he H1961
9: 5 And when he c, behold, the captains of H935
11 Then Jehu c forth to the servants of his H3318
11 *Is* all well? wherefore c this mad *fellow* to H935
17 company of Jehu as he c, and said, I see a H935
18 c to them, but he cometh not again. H935
19 horseback, which c to them, and said, H935
20 And the watchman told, saying, He c H935
22 And it c to pass, when Joram saw Jehu, H1961
36 Wherefore they c again, and told him. H7725
10: 7 And it c to pass, when the letter came H1961
7 And it came to pass, when the letter c to H935
8 And there c a messenger, and told him, H935
9 And it c to pass in the morning, that he H1961
12 And he arose and departed, and c to H1980
17 And when he c to Samaria, he slew all H935
21 of Baal c, so that there was not H935
21 not a man left that c not. And they came H935
21 not. And they c into the house of Baal; H935
25 And it c to pass, as soon as he had H1961
11: 9 sabbath, and c to Jehoiada the priest. H935
13 of the people, she c to the people into the H935
16 the which the horses c into the king's H3996
19 of the LORD, and c by the way of the H935
12:10 the high priest c up, and they put up H5927
13:14 the king of Israel c down unto him, and H3381
21 And it c to pass, as they were burying a H1961
14: 5 And it c to pass, as soon as the H1961
13 and c to Jerusalem, and brake H935
15:12 fourth *generation.* And so it c to pass. H1961
14 up from Tirzah, and c to Samaria, and H935
19 *And* Pul the king of Assyria c against the H935
29 In the days of Pekah king of Israel c H935
16: 5 king of Israel c up to Jerusalem to war: H5927
6 c to Elath, and dwelt there unto this day. H935
11 *it* against king Ahaz c from Damascus. H935
17: 3 Against him c up Shalmaneser king of H5927
5 Then the king of Assyria c up H5927
28 from Samaria c and dwelt in Beth-el, H935
18: 1 Now it c to pass in the third year of H1961
9 And it c to pass in the fourth year of H1961
9 c up against Samaria, and besieged it. H5927
17 they went up and c to Jerusalem. And H935
17 were come up, they c and stood by the H935

2Ki 18:18 to the king, there c out to them Eliakim H3318
37 Then c Eliakim the son of Hilkiah, which H935
19: 1 And it c to pass, when king Hezekiah H1961
5 So the servants of king Hezekiah c to H935
33 By the way that he c, by the same shall he H935
35 And it c to pass that night, that the H1961
37 And it c to pass, as he was worshipping H1961
20: 1 the son of Amoz c to him, and said unto H935
4 And it c to pass, afore Isaiah was gone H1961
4 the word of the LORD c to him, saying, H1961
14 Then c Isaiah the prophet unto king H935
14 and from whence c they unto thee? And H935
21:15 c forth out of Egypt, even unto this day. H3315
22: 3 And it c to pass in the eighteenth year H1961
9 And Shaphan the scribe c to the king, H935
11 And it c to pass, when the king had H1961
23: 9 of the high places c not up to the altar H5927
17 man of God, which c from Judah, and H935
18 of the prophet that c out of Samaria. H935
34 away: and he c to Egypt, and died there. H935
24: 1 king of Babylon c up, and Jehoiakim H5927
3 of the LORD c *this* upon Judah, to H1961
7 And the king of Egypt c not again any H3318
10 king of Babylon c up against H5927
11 And Nebuchadnezzar king of Babylon c H935
20 For through the anger of the LORD it c H1961
25: 1 And it c to pass in the ninth year of his H1961
1 king of Babylon c, he, and all his host, H935
8 king of Babylon, c Nebuzar-adan, H935
23 governor, there c to Gedaliah to Mizpah, H935
25 But it c to pass in the seventh month, H1961
25 of the seed royal, c, and ten men with H935
26 armies, arose, and c to Egypt: for they H935
27 And it c to pass in the seven and H1961
1Ch 1:12 c the Philistines,) and Caphthorim. H3318
2:53 c the Zareathites, and the Eshtaulites. H3318
55 the Kenites that c of Hemath, the father H935
4:41 And these written by name c in the days H935
5: 2 and of him *c* the chief ruler; but the
7:21 they c down to take away their cattle. H3381
22 days, and his brethren c to comfort him. H935
10: 7 and the Philistines c and dwelt in them. H935
8 And it c to pass on the morrow, when H1961
8 the Philistines c to strip the slain, that H935
11: 3 Therefore c all the elders of Israel to the H935
12: 1 Now these *are* they that c to David to H935
16 And there c of the children of Benjamin H935
18 Then the spirit c upon Amasai, *who* H3847
19 to David, when he c with the Philistines H935
22 For at *that* time day by day there c to H935
23 to the war, *and* c to David to Hebron, H935
38 could keep rank, c with a perfect heart H935
13: 9 And when they c unto the threshingfloor H935
14: 9 And the Philistines c and spread H935
11 So they c up to Baal-perazim; and H5927
15:26 And it c to pass, when God helped the H1961
29 And it c to pass, *as* the ark of the H1961
29 of the LORD c to the city of David, H935
17: 1 Now it c to pass, as David sat in his H1961
3 And it c to pass the same night, that H1961
3 the word of God c to Nathan, saying, H1961
16 And David the king c and sat before the H935
18: 1 Now after this it c to pass, that David H1961
5 And when the Syrians of Damascus c to H935
19: 1 Now it c to pass after this, that Nahash H1961
2 servants of David c into the land of the H935
7 and his people; who c and pitched before H935
7 from their cities, and c to battle. H935
9 And the children of Ammon c out, and H3318
15 into the city. Then Joab c to Jerusalem. H935
17 over Jordan, and c upon them, and set H935
20: 1 And it c to pass, that after the year was H1961
1 of Ammon, and c and besieged Rabbah. H935
4 And it c to pass after this, that there H1961
21: 4 all Israel, and c to Jerusalem. H935
11 So Gad c to David, and said unto him, H935
21 And as David c to Ornan, Ornan looked H935
22: 8 But the word of the LORD c to me, H1961
24: 7 Now the first lot c forth to Jehoiarib, H3318
28 Of Mahli c Eleazar, who had no sons.
25: 9 Now the first lot c forth for Asaph to H3318
26:14 cast lots; and his lot c out northward. H3318
16 To Shuppim and Hosah *the lot c forth*
27: 1 of the courses, which c in and went out H935
2Ch 1:13 Then Solomon c *from his journey* to the H935
5: 4 And all the elders of Israel c; and the H935
10 of Israel, when they c out of Egypt. H3318
11 And it c to pass, when the priests were H1961
13 It c even to pass, as the trumpeters and H1961

2Ch 7: 1 end of praying, the fire c down from H3381
3 saw how the fire c down, and the glory H3381
11 house: and all that c into Solomon's H935
8: 1 And it c to pass at the end of twenty H1961
9: 1 of Solomon, she c to prove Solomon with H935
6 their words, until I c, and mine eyes had H935
13 Now the weight of gold that c to H935
21 three years once c the ships of Tarshish H935
10: 2 And it c to pass, when Jeroboam the H1961
3 Israel c and spake to Rehoboam, saying, H935
12 So Jeroboam and all the people c to H935
11: 2 But the word of the LORD c to H1961
14 their possession, and c to Judah and H3212
16 God of Israel c to Jerusalem, to sacrifice H935
12: 1 And it c to pass, when Rehoboam had H1961
2 And it c to pass, *that* in the fifth year of H1961
2 king of Egypt c up against Jerusalem, H5927
3 number that c with him out of Egypt; H935
4 *pertained* to Judah, and c to Jerusalem. H935
5 Then c Shemaiah the prophet to H935
7 the word of the LORD c to Shemaiah, H1961
9 So Shishak king of Egypt c up against H5927
11 the LORD, the guard c and fetched them, H935
13:15 of Judah shouted, it c to pass, that God H1961
14: 9 And there c out against them Zerah the H3318
9 hundred chariots; and c unto Mareshah. H935
14 the fear of the LORD c upon them: and H1961
15: 1 And the spirit of God c upon Azariah H1961
5 nor to him that c in, but great vexations H935
16: 1 king of Israel c up against Judah, and H5927
5 And it c to pass, when Baasha heard *it*, H1961
7 And at that time Hanani the seer c to H935
18:20 Then there c out a spirit, and stood H3318
23 Then Zedekiah the son of Chenaanah c H5066
31 And it c to pass, when the captains of H1961
32 For it c to pass, that, when the captains H1961
20: 1 It c to pass after this also, *that* the H1961
1 c against Jehoshaphat to battle. H935
2 Then there c some that told H935
4 cities of Judah they c to seek the LORD. H935
10 invade, when they c out of the land of H935
14 of the sons of Asaph, c the spirit of the H1961
24 And when Judah c toward the watch H935
25 And when Jehoshaphat and his people c H935
28 And they c to Jerusalem with psalteries H935
21:12 And there c a writing to him from Elijah H935
17 And they c up into Judah, and brake H5927
19 And it c to pass, that in process of time, H1961
22: 1 band of men that c with the Arabians to H935
8 And it c to pass, that, when Jehu was H1961
23: 2 of Israel, and they c to Jerusalem. H935
12 the king, she c to the people into the H935
20 LORD: and they c through the high gate H935
24: 4 And it c to pass after this, *that* Joash H1961
11 Now it c to pass, that at what time the H1961
11 high priest's officer c and emptied the H935
17 Now after the death of Jehoiada c the H935
18 and idols: and wrath c upon Judah and H1961
20 And the spirit of God c upon Zechariah H3847
23 And it c to pass at the end of the year, H1961
23 the host of Syria c up against him: and H5927
23 him: and they c to Judah and Jerusalem, H935
24 For the army of the Syrians c with a H935
25: 3 Now it c to pass, when the kingdom H1961
7 But there c a man of God to him, saying, H935
14 Now it c to pass, after that Amaziah H1961
16 And it c to pass, as he talked with him, H1961
20 But Amaziah would not hear; for it c of
28: 9 the host that c to Samaria, and said H935
12 up against them that c from the war, H935
20 And Tilgath-pilneser king of Assyria c H935
29:15 themselves, and c, according to the H935
17 day of the month c they to the porch of H935
30:11 themselves, and c to Jerusalem. H935
25 congregation that c out of Israel, and the H935
25 the strangers that c out of the land of H935
27 heard, and their prayer c *up* to his holy H935
31: 5 And as soon as the commandment c H6555
8 And when Hezekiah and the princes c H935
32: 1 king of Assyria c, and entered into Judah, H935
21 of his god, they that c forth of his own H3329
26 wrath of the LORD c not upon them in H935
34: 9 And when they c to Hilkiah the high H935
19 And it c to pass, when the king had H1961
35:20 king of Egypt c up to fight against H5927
22 and c to fight in the valley of Megiddo. H935
36: 6 Against him c up Nebuchadnezzar H5927
Ezr 2: 1 away unto Babylon, and c again unto H7725
2 Which c with Zerubbabel: Jeshua, H935

Ezr 2:68 fathers, when they c to the house of the H935
4: 2 Then they c to Zerubbabel, and to the H5066
12 the Jews which c up from thee to us are H5559
5: 3 At the same time c to them Tatnai, H858
5 till the matter c to Darius: and then H1946
16 Then c the same Sheshbazzar, *and* laid H858
7: 8 And he c to Jerusalem in the fifth month, H935
9 *day* of the fifth month c he to Jerusalem, H935
8:32 And we c to Jerusalem, and abode there H935
9: 1 done, the princes c to me, saying, The H5066
10: 6 and *when* he c thither, he did eat no H3212
Neh 1: 1 of Hachaliah. And it c to pass in the H1961
2 That Hanani, one of my brethren, c, he H935
4 And it c to pass, when I heard these H1961
2: 1 And it c to pass in the month Nisan, in H1961
9 Then I c to the governors beyond the H935
11 So I c to Jerusalem, and was there three H935
4: 1 But it c to pass, that when Sanballat H1961
7 But it c to pass, *that* when Sanballat, H1961
12 And it c to pass, that when the Jews H1961
12 dwelt by them c, they said unto us ten H935
15 And it c to pass, when our enemies H1961
16 And it c to pass from that time forth, H1961
5:17 beside those that c unto us from among H935
6: 1 Now it c to pass, when Sanballat, and H1961
10 Afterward I c unto the house of H935
16 And it c to pass, that when all our H1961
17 and *the letters* of Tobiah c unto them. H935
7: 1 Now it c to pass, when the wall was H1961
5 of them which c up at the first, and H5927
6 carried away, and c again to Jerusalem H7725
7 Who c with Zerubbabel, Jeshua, H935
73 the seventh month c, the children of H5060
13: 3 Now it c to pass, when they had heard H1961
6 king of Babylon c I unto the king, and H935
7 And I c to Jerusalem, and understood of H935
19 And it c to pass, that when the gates of H1961
21 forth c they no *more* on the sabbath. H935
Est 1: 1 Now it c to pass in the days of H1961
17 be brought in before him, but she c not. H935
2: 8 So it c to pass, when the king's H1961
13 Then thus c *every* maiden unto the king; H935
14 the concubines: she c in unto the king no H935
3: 4 Now it c to pass, when they spake daily H1961
4: 2 And c even before the king's gate: for H935
3 and his decree c, *there was* great H5060
4 her chamberlains c and told *it* her. Then H935
9 And Hatach c and told Esther the words H935
5: 1 Now it c to pass on the third day, that H1961
5 king and Haman c to the banquet that H935
10 and when he c home, he sent and called H935
6: 6 So Haman c in. And the king said unto H935
12 And Mordecai c again to the king's H7725
14 yet talking with him, c the king's H5060
7: 1 So the king and Haman c to banquet H935
8: 1 And Mordecai c before the king; for H935
17 and his decree c, the Jews had joy and H5060
9:25 But when *Esther* c before the king, he H935
Job 1: 6 the sons of God c to present themselves H935
6 LORD, and Satan c also among them. H935
14 And there c a messenger unto Job, and H935
16 While he *was* yet speaking, there c also H935
17 While he *was* yet speaking, there c also H935
18 While he *was* yet speaking, there c also H935
19 And, behold, there c a great wind from H935
21 And said, Naked c I out of my mother's H3318
2: 1 the sons of God c to present themselves H935
1 LORD, and Satan c also among them to H935
11 upon him, they c every one from his own H935
3:11 up the ghost when I c out of the belly? H3318
26 I rest, neither was I quiet; yet trouble c. H935
4:14 Fear c upon me, and trembling, which H7122
6:20 they c thither, and were ashamed. H935
26: 4 words? and whose spirit c from thee? H3318
29:13 ready to perish c upon me: and I caused H935
30:14 They c *upon me* as a wide breaking in *of* H857
26 When I looked for good, then evil c *unto* H935
26 when I waited for light, there c darkness. H935
38:29 Out of whose womb c the ice? and the H3318
42:11 Then c there unto him all his brethren, H935
Ps 18: 6 my cry c before him, *even* into his ears. H935
9 He bowed the heavens also, and c H3381
27: 2 and my foes, c upon me to eat up my H7126
51:ttl the prophet c unto him, after he had H935
52:ttl Doeg the Edomite c and told Saul, and H935
54:ttl when the Ziphims c and said to Saul, H935
78:21 and anger also c up against Israel; H5927
31 The wrath of God c upon them, and H5927
88:17 They c round about me daily like H5437

Ps 105:19 Until the time that his word c: the word H935
23 Israel also c into Egypt; and Jacob H935
31 He spake, and there c divers sorts of H935
34 He spake, and the locusts c, and H935
Prv 7:15 Therefore c I forth to meet thee, H3318
Ecc 5:15 As he c forth of his mother's womb, H3318
15 he return to go as he c, and shall take H935
16 in all points as he c, so shall he go: and H935
9:14 men within it; and there c a great king H935
Song 4: 2 *are even* shorn, which c up from the H5927
Isa 7: 1 And it c to pass in the days of Ahaz the H1961
11:16 that he c up out of the land of Egypt. H5927
20: 1 In the year that Tartan c unto Ashdod, H935
30: 4 Zoan, and his ambassadors c to Hanes. H5060
36: 1 Now it c to pass in the fourteenth year H1961
1 king of Assyria c up against all the H5927
3 Then c forth unto him Eliakim, H3318
22 Then c Eliakim, the son of Hilkiah, that H935
37: 1 And it c to pass, when king Hezekiah H1961
5 So the servants of king Hezekiah c to H935
34 By the way that he c, by the same shall he H935
38 And it c to pass, as he was worshipping H1961
38: 1 the son of Amoz c unto him, and said H935
4 Then c the word of the LORD to Isaiah, H1961
39: 3 Then c Isaiah the prophet unto king H935
3 and from whence c they unto thee? And H935
41: 5 the earth were afraid, drew near, and c. H857
48: 3 I did *them* suddenly, and they c to pass. H935
5 *it* to thee; before it c to pass I shewed *it* H935
50: 2 Wherefore, when I c, *was there* no man? H935
66: 7 pain c, she was delivered of a man child. H935
Jer 1: 2 To whom the word of the LORD c in H1961
3 It c also in the days of Jehoiakim the H1961
4 Then the word of the LORD c unto me, H1961
11 Moreover the word of the LORD c unto H1961
13 And the word of the LORD c unto me H1961
2: 1 Moreover the word of the LORD c to H1961
3: 9 And it c to pass through the lightness H1961
7: 1 The word that c to Jeremiah from the H1961
25 Since the day that your fathers c forth H3318
31 *them* not, neither c it into my heart. H5927
8:15 We looked for peace, but no good *c; and*
11: 1 The word that c to Jeremiah from the H1961
13: 3 And the word of the LORD c unto me H1961
6 And it c to pass after many days, that H1961
8 Then the word of the LORD c unto me, H1961
14: 1 The word of the LORD that c to H1961
3 ones to the waters: they c to the pits, *and* H935
16: 1 The word of the LORD c also unto me, H1961
17:16 c out of my lips was *right* before thee. H4161
18: 1 The word which c to Jeremiah from the H1961
5 Then the word of the LORD c to me, H1961
19: 5 nor spake *it*, neither c *it* into my mind: H5927
14 Then c Jeremiah from Tophet, whither H935
20: 3 And it c to pass on the morrow, that H1961
18 Wherefore c I forth out of the womb to H3318
21: 1 The word which c unto Jeremiah from H1961
24: 4 Again the word of the LORD c unto me, H1961
25: 1 The word that c to Jeremiah H1961
26: 1 c this word from the LORD, saying, H1961
8 Now it c to pass, when Jeremiah had H1961
10 things, then they c up from the king's H5927
27: 1 Josiah king of Judah c this word unto H1961
28: 1 And it c to pass the same year, in the H1961
12 Then the word of the LORD c unto H1961
29:30 Then c the word of the LORD unto H1961
30: 1 The word that c to Jeremiah from the H1961
32: 1 The word that c to Jeremiah from the H1961
6 word of the LORD c unto me, saying, H1961
8 So Hanameel mine uncle's son c to me in H935
23 And they c in, and possessed it; but they H935
26 Then c the word of the LORD unto H1961
35 them not, neither c it into my mind, H5927
33: 1 Moreover the word of the LORD c unto H1961
19 And the word of the LORD c unto H1961
23 Moreover the word of the LORD c to H1961
34: 1 The word which c unto Jeremiah from H1961
8 *This is* the word that c unto Jeremiah H1961
12 Therefore the word of the LORD c to H1961
35: 1 The word which c unto Jeremiah from H1961
11 But it c to pass, when Nebuchadrezzar H1961
11 king of Babylon c up into the land, that H5927
12 Then c the word of the LORD unto H1961
36: 1 And it c to pass in the fourth year of H1961
1 *that* this word c unto Jeremiah from H1961
9 And it c to pass in the fifth year of H1961
9 to all the people that c from the cities of H935
14 the roll in his hand, and c unto them. H935
16 Now it c to pass, when they had heard H1961

Jer 36:23 And it c to pass, that when Jehudi had H1961
27 Then the word of the LORD c to H1961
37: 4 Now Jeremiah c in and went out among H935
6 Then c the word of the LORD unto the H1961
11 And it c to pass, that when the army of H1961
38:27 Then c all the princes unto Jeremiah, H935
39: 1 in the tenth month, c Nebuchadrezzar H935
3 the king of Babylon c in, and sat in the H935
4 And it c to pass, that when Zedekiah H1961
15 Now the word of the LORD c unto H1961
40: 1 The word that c to Jeremiah from the H1961
8 Then they c to Gedaliah to Mizpah, even H935
12 were driven, and c to the land of Judah, H935
13 in the fields, c to Gedaliah to Mizpah, H935
41: 1 Now it c to pass in the seventh month, H1961
1 ten men with him, c unto Gedaliah the H935
4 And it c to pass the second day after he H1961
5 That there c certain from Shechem, from H935
6 as he went: and it c to pass, as he met H1961
7 And it was so, when they c into the H935
13 Now it c to pass, that when all the H1961
42: 1 the least even unto the greatest, c near, H5066
7 And it c to pass after ten days, that the H1961
7 the word of the LORD c unto Jeremiah. H1961
43: 1 And it c to pass, that when Jeremiah H1961
7 So they c into the land of Egypt: for they H935
7 LORD: thus c they even to Tahpanhes. H935
8 Then c the word of the LORD unto H1961
44: 1 The word that c to Jeremiah H1961
21 them, and c it not into his mind? H5927
46: 1 The word of the LORD which c to H1961
47: 1 The word of the LORD that c to H1961
49:34 The word of the LORD that c to H1961
52: 3 For through the anger of the LORD it c H1961
4 And it c to pass in the ninth year of his H1961
4 king of Babylon c, he and all his army, H935
12 king of Babylon, c Nebuzar-adan, H935
31 And it c to pass in the seven and H1961
Lam 1: 9 end; therefore she c down wonderfully: H3381
Ezk 1: 1 Now it c to pass in the thirtieth year, in H1961
3 The word of the LORD c expressly unto H1961
4 And I looked, and, behold, a whirlwind c H935
5 Also out of the midst thereof c the
3:15 Then I c to them of the captivity at H935
16 And it c to pass at the end of seven H1961
16 word of the LORD c unto me, saying, H1961
4:14 c there abominable flesh into my mouth. H935
6: 1 And the word of the LORD c unto me, H1961
7: 1 Moreover the word of the LORD c unto H1961
8: 1 And it c to pass in the sixth year, in the H1961
9: 2 And, behold, six men c from the way of H935
8 And it c to pass, while they were H1961
10: 6 And it c to pass, that when he had H1961
11:13 And it c to pass, when I prophesied, H1961
14 Again the word of the LORD c unto me, H1961
12: 1 The word of the LORD also c unto me, H1961
8 And in the morning c the word of the H1961
17 Moreover the word of the LORD c to H1961
21 And the word of the LORD c unto me, H1961
26 Again the word of the LORD c to me, H1961
13: 1 And the word of the LORD c unto me, H1961
14: 1 Then c certain of the elders of Israel H935
2 And the word of the LORD c unto me, H1961
12 The word of the LORD c again to me, H1961
15: 1 And the word of the LORD c unto me, H1961
16: 1 Again the word of the LORD c unto me, H1961
23 And it c to pass after all thy H1961
17: 1 And the word of the LORD c unto me, H1961
3 had divers colours, c unto Lebanon, and H935
11 Moreover the word of the LORD c unto H1961
18: 1 The word of the LORD c unto me H1961
20: 1 And it c to pass in the seventh year, in H1961
1 of the elders of Israel c to inquire of the H935
2 Then c the word of the LORD unto me, H1961
45 Moreover the word of the LORD c unto H1961
21: 1 And the word of the LORD c unto me, H1961
8 Again the word of the LORD c unto me, H1961
18 The word of the LORD c unto me H1961
22: 1 Moreover the word of the LORD c unto H1961
17 And the word of the LORD c unto me, H1961
23 And the word of the LORD c unto me, H1961
23: 1 The word of the LORD c again unto H1961
17 And the Babylonians c to her into the H935
39 idols, then they c the same day into my H935
40 sent; and, lo, they c: for whom thou didst H935
24: 1 word of the LORD c unto me, saying, H1961
15 Also the word of the LORD c unto me, H1961
20 word of the LORD c unto me, saying, H1961
25: 1 The word of the LORD c again unto H1961

Ezk 26: 1 And it c to pass in the eleventh year, in H1961
1 word of the LORD c unto me, saying, H1961
27: 1 The word of the LORD c again unto H1961
28: 1 The word of the LORD c again unto H1961
11 Moreover the word of the LORD c unto H1961
20 Again the word of the LORD c unto me, H1961
29: 1 word of the LORD c unto me, saying, H1961
17 And it c to pass in the seven and H1961
17 word of the LORD c unto me, saying, H1961
30: 1 The word of the LORD c again unto H1961
20 And it c to pass in the eleventh year, in H1961
20 word of the LORD c unto me, saying, H1961
31: 1 And it c to pass in the eleventh year, in H1961
1 word of the LORD c unto me, saying, H1961
32: 1 And it c to pass in the twelfth year, in H1961
1 word of the LORD c unto me, saying, H1961
17 It c to pass also in the twelfth year, in H1961
17 word of the LORD c unto me, saying, H1961
33: 1 Again the word of the LORD c unto me, H1961
21 And it c to pass in the twelfth year of H1961
21 c unto me, saying, The city is smitten. H935
22 that was escaped c; and had opened my H935
22 my mouth, until he c to me in the H935
23 Then the word of the LORD c unto me, H1961
34: 1 And the word of the LORD c unto me, H1961
35: 1 Moreover the word of the LORD c unto H1961
36:16 Moreover the word of the LORD c unto H1961
37: 7 the bones c together, bone to his bone. H7126
8 and the flesh c up upon them, and H5927
10 me, and the breath c into them, and they H935
15 The word of the LORD c again unto H1961
38: 1 And the word of the LORD c unto me, H1961
40: 6 Then c he unto the gate which looketh H935
43: 2 of the God of Israel c from the way of the H935
3 that I saw when I c to destroy the city: H935
4 And the glory of the LORD c into the H935
46: 9 he c in, but shall go forth over against it. H935
47: 1 and the waters c down from under H3381
Dan 1: 1 king of Judah c Nebuchadnezzar king H935
2: 2 So they c and stood before the king. H935
29 As for thee, O king, thy thoughts c into H5559
3: 8 c near, and accused the Jews. H7127
26 Then Nebuchadnezzar c near to the H7127
26 c forth of the midst of the fire. H5312
4: 7 Then c in the magicians, the H5954
8 But at the last Daniel c in before me, H5954
13 and an holy one c down from heaven; H5182
28 All this c upon the king H4291
5: 5 In the same hour c forth fingers of a H5312
8 Then c in all the king's wise men: but H5954
10 king and his lords, c into the banquet H5954
6:12 Then they c near, and spake before the H7127
20 And when he c to the den, he cried with H7127
24 or ever they c at the bottom of the den. H4291
7: 3 And four great beasts c up from the H5559
8 and, behold, there c up among them H5559
10 A fiery stream issued and c forth from H5312
13 the Son of man c with the clouds H1934+H858
13 of heaven, and c to the Ancient of days, H4291
16 I c near unto one of them that stood by, H7127
20 and of the other which c up, and before H5559
22 Until the Ancient of days c, and H858
22 High; and the time c that the saints H4291
8: 2 And I saw in a vision; and it c to pass, H1961
3 than the other, and the higher c up last. H5927
5 behold, an he goat c from the west on H935
6 And he c to the ram that had two horns, H935
8 broken; and for it c up four notable H5927
9 And out of one of them c forth a little H3318
15 And it c to pass, when I, even I Daniel, H1961
17 So he c near where I stood: and when he H935
17 and when he c, I was afraid, and fell H935
9: 2 the word of the LORD c to Jeremiah the H1961
23 commandment c forth, and I am come H3318
10: 3 I ate no pleasant bread, neither c flesh H935
13 of the chief princes, c to help me; and I H935
18 Then there c again and touched me one
Hos 1: 1 The word of the LORD that c unto H1961
2:15 when she c up out of the land of Egypt. H5927
Joel 1: 1 The word of the LORD that c to Joel the H1961
Am 6: 1 nations, to whom the house of Israel c! H935
7: 2 And it c to pass, that when they had H1961
Oba 5 If thieves c to thee, if robbers by night, H935
5 the grape-gatherers c to thee, would they H935
Jna 1: 1 Now the word of the LORD c unto H1961
6 So the shipmaster c to him, and said H7126
2: 7 c in unto thee, into thine holy temple. H935
3: 1 And the word of the LORD c unto H1961
6 For word c unto the king of Nineveh, H5060

Jna 4: 8 And it c to pass, when the sun did H1961
10 c up in a night, and perished in a night: H1961
Mic 1: 1 The word of the LORD that c to Micah H1961
11 of Zaanan c not forth in the mourning H3318
12 for good: but evil c down from the H3381
Hab 3: 3 God c from Teman, and the Holy One H935
14 of his villages: they c out as a whirlwind
Zep 1: 1 The word of the LORD which c unto H1961
Hag 1: 1 day of the month, c the word of the H1961
3 Then c the word of the LORD by H1961
9 Ye looked for much, and, lo, it c to little;
14 people; and they c and did work in the H935
2: 1 day of the month, c the word of the H1961
5 with you when ye c out of Egypt, so my H3318
10 year of Darius, c the word of the LORD H1961
16 Since those days were, when one c to an H935
16 but ten: when one c to the pressfat for to H935
20 And again the word of the LORD c unto H1961
Zec 1: 1 year of Darius, c the word of the LORD H1961
7 year of Darius, c the word of the LORD H1961
4: 1 And the angel that talked with me c H7725
8 Moreover the word of the LORD c unto H1961
5: 9 and, behold, there c out two women, H3318
6: 1 and, behold, there c four chariots out H3318
9 And the word of the LORD c unto me, H1961
7: 1 And it c to pass in the fourth year of H1961
1 word of the LORD c unto Zechariah in H1961
4 Then c the word of the LORD of hosts H1961
8 And the word of the LORD c unto H1961
12 therefore c a great wrath from H1961
8: 1 Again the word of the LORD of hosts c H1961
10 him that went out or c in because of the H935
18 And the word of the LORD of hosts c H1961
10: 4 Out of him c forth the corner, out of H3318
14:16 the nations which c against Jerusalem H935
Mt 1:18 before they c together, she was found G4905
2: 1 c wise men from the east to Jerusalem, G3854
9 before them, till it c and stood over G2064
21 mother, and c into the land of Israel. G2064
23 And he c and dwelt in a city called G2064
3: 1 In those days c John the Baptist, G3854
4: 3 And when the tempter c to him, he G4334
11 angels c and ministered unto him. G4334
13 And leaving Nazareth, he c and dwelt G2064
5: 1 he was set, his disciples c unto him: G4334
7:25 and the floods c, and the winds blew, G2064
27 and the floods c, and the winds blew, G2064
28 And it c to pass, when Jesus had ended G1096
8: 2 And, behold, there c a leper and G2064
5 into Capernaum, there c unto him a G4334
19 And a certain scribe c, and said unto G4334
25 And his disciples c to him, and awoke G4334
34 And, behold, the whole city c out to G1831
9: 1 passed over, and c into his own city. G2064
10 And it c to pass, as Jesus sat at meat in G1096
10 and sinners c and sat down with him G2064
14 Then c to him the disciples of John, G4334
18 behold, there c a certain ruler, and G2064
20 blood twelve years, c behind him, and G4334
23 And when Jesus c into the ruler's G2064
28 the blind men c to him: and Jesus saith G4334
10:34 I c not to send peace, but a sword. G2064
11: 1 And it c to pass, when Jesus had made G1096
18 For John c neither eating nor drinking, G2064
19 The Son of man c eating and drinking, G2064
12:42 it: for she c from the uttermost G2064
44 from whence I c out; and when he is G1831
13: 4 and the fowls c and devoured them up: G2064
10 And the disciples c, and said unto him, G4334
25 But while men slept, his enemy c and G2064
27 So the servants of the householder c G4334
36 and his disciples c unto him, saying, G4334
53 And it c to pass, that when Jesus had G1096
14:12 And his disciples c, and took up the G4334
15 his disciples c to him, saying, This G4334
33 Then they that were in the ship c and G2064
34 And when they were gone over, they c G2064
15: 1 Then c to Jesus scribes and Pharisees, G4334
12 Then c his disciples, and said unto G4334
22 And, behold, a woman of Canaan c out G1831
23 And his disciples c and besought him, G4334
25 Then c she and worshipped him, G2064
29 And Jesus departed from thence, and c G2064
30 And great multitudes c unto him, G4334
39 ship, and c into the coasts of Magdala. G2064
16: 1 the Sadducees c, and tempting desired G4334
13 When Jesus c into the coasts of G2064
17: 7 And Jesus c and touched them, and G4334
9 And as they c down from the G2597

Mt 17:14 the multitude, there **c** to him a *certain* G4334
19 Then **c** the disciples to Jesus apart, and G4334
24 tribute *money* **c** to Peter, and said, G4334
18: 1 At the same time **c** the disciples unto G4334
21 Then **c** Peter to him, and said, Lord, G4334
31 very sorry, and **c** and told unto their G2064
19: 1 And it **c** to pass, *that* when Jesus had G1096
1 from Galilee, and **c** into the coasts of G2064
3 The Pharisees also **c** unto him, G4334
16 And, behold, one **c** and said unto him, G4334
20: 9 And when they **c** that *were hired* about G2064
10 But when the first **c**, they supposed that G2064
20 Then **c** to him the mother of Zebedee's G4334
28 Even as the Son of man **c** not to be G2064
21:14 And the blind and the lame **c** to him in G4334
19 fig tree in the way, he **c** to it, and found G2064
23 of the people **c** unto him as he was G4334
28 had two sons; and he **c** to the first, and G4334
30 And he **c** to the second, and said G4334
32 For John **c** unto you in the way of G2064
22:11 And when the king **c** in to see the G1525
23 The same day **c** to him the Sadducees, G4334
24: 1 and his disciples **c** to *him* for to shew G4334
3 the disciples **c** unto him privately, G4334
39 And knew not until the flood **c**, and G2064
25:10 the bridegroom **c**; and they that were G2064
11 Afterward **c** also the other virgins, G2064
20 five talents **c** and brought other five G4334
22 He also that had received two talents **c** G4334
24 the one talent **c** and said, Lord, I knew G4334
36 me: I was in prison, and ye **c** unto me. G2064
39 thee sick, or in prison, and **c** unto thee? G2064
26: 1 And it **c** to pass, when Jesus had G1096
7 There **c** unto him a woman having an G4334
17 the disciples **c** to Jesus, saying unto G4334
43 And he **c** and found them asleep again: G2064
47 one of the twelve, **c**, and with him a G2064
49 And forthwith he **c** to Jesus, and said, G4334
50 art thou come? Then **c** they, and laid G4334
60 false witnesses **c**, *yet* found they none. G4334
60 none. At the last **c** two false witnesses, G4334
69 and a damsel **c** unto him, saying, Thou G4334
73 And after a while **c** unto *him* they that G4334
27:32 And as they **c** out, they found a man of G1831
53 And **c** out of the graves after his G1831
57 When the even was come, there **c** a rich G2064
62 and Pharisees **c** together unto Pilate, G4863
28: 1 *day* of the week, **c** Mary Magdalene G2064
2 from heaven, and **c** and rolled back the G4334
9 All hail. And they **c** and held him by G4334
11 some of the watch **c** into the city, and G2064
13 Saying, Say ye, His disciples **c** by night, G2064
18 And Jesus **c** and spake unto them, G4334
Mk 1: 9 And it **c** to pass in those days, that G1096
9 days, that Jesus **c** from Nazareth of G2064
11 And there **c** a voice from heaven, G1096
14 put in prison, Jesus **c** into Galilee, G2064
26 cried with a loud voice, he **c** out of him. G1831
31 And he **c** and took her by the hand, and G4334
38 there also: for therefore **c** I forth. G1831
40 And there **c** a leper to him, beseeching G2064
45 and they **c** to him from every quarter. G2064
2:15 And it **c** to pass, that, as Jesus sat at G1096
17 they that are sick: I **c** not to call the G2064
23 And it **c** to pass, that he went through G1096
3: 8 what great things he did, **c** unto him. G2064
13 whom he would: and they **c** unto him. G565
22 And the scribes which **c** down from G2597
31 There **c** then his brethren and his G2064
4: 4 And it **c** to pass, as he sowed, some fell G1096
4 fowls of the air **c** and devoured it up. G2064
5: 1 And they **c** over unto the other side of G2064
27 When she had heard of Jesus, **c** in the G2064
33 was done in her, **c** and fell down before G2064
35 While he yet spake, there **c** from the G2064
6: 1 And he went out from thence, and **c** G2064
22 of the said Herodias **c** in, and danced, G1525
25 And she **c** in straightway with haste G1525
29 heard *of it*, they **c** and took up his G2064
33 them, and **c** together unto him. G4905
34 And Jesus, when he **c** out, saw much G1831
35 his disciples **c** unto him, and said, G4334
53 And when they had passed over, they **c** G2064
7: 1 Then **c** together unto him the G4863
1 of the scribes, which **c** from Jerusalem. G2064
25 heard of him, and **c** and fell at his feet: G2064
31 and Sidon, he **c** unto the sea of Galilee, G2064
8: 3 the way: for divers of them **c** from far. G2240
10 and **c** into the parts of Dalmanutha. G2064

Mk 8:11 And the Pharisees **c** forth, and began to G1831
9: 7 them: and a voice **c** out of the cloud, G2064
9 And as they **c** down from the G2597
14 And when he **c** to *his* disciples, he saw G2064
21 **c** unto him? And he said, Of a child. G1096
25 When Jesus saw that the people **c** G1998
26 rent him sore, and **c** out of him: and he G1831
33 And he **c** to Capernaum: and being in G2064
10: 2 And the Pharisees **c** to him, and asked G4334
17 into the way, there **c** one running, and G4370
45 For even the Son of man **c** not to be G2064
46 And they **c** to Jericho: and as he went G2064
50 away his garment, rose, and **c** to Jesus. G2064
11: 1 And when they **c** nigh to Jerusalem, G1448
13 off having leaves, he **c**, if haply he might G2064
13 and when he **c** to it, he found nothing G2064
12:28 And one of the scribes **c**, and having G4334
42 And there **c** a certain poor widow, and G2064
14: 3 sat at meat, there **c** a woman having an G2064
16 And his disciples went forth, and **c** into G2064
32 And they **c** to a place which was named G2064
15:41 which **c** up with him unto Jerusalem. G4872
43 kingdom of God, **c**, and went in boldly G2064
16: 2 of the week, they **c** unto the sepulchre G2064
Lk 1: 8 And it **c** to pass, that while he executed G1096
22 And when he **c** out, he could not speak G1881
23 And it **c** to pass, that, as soon as the G1096
28 And the angel **c** in unto her, and said, G1525
41 And it **c** to pass, that, when Elisabeth G1096
57 Now Elisabeth's full time **c** that she G4130
59 And it **c** to pass, that on the eighth day G1096
59 the eighth day they **c** to circumcise the G2064
65 And fear **c** on all that dwelt round G1096
2: 1 And it **c** to pass in those days, that G1096
9 And, lo, the angel of the Lord **c** upon G2186
15 And it **c** to pass, as the angels were G1096
16 And they **c** with haste, and found G2064
27 And he **c** by the Spirit into the temple: G2064
46 And it **c** to pass, that after three days G1096
51 And he went down with them, and **c** to G2064
3: 2 the word of God **c** unto John the son of G1096
3 And he **c** into all the country about G2064
7 Then said he to the multitude that **c** G1607
12 Then **c** also publicans to be baptized, G2064
21 were baptized, it **c** to pass, that Jesus G1096
22 him, and a voice **c** from heaven, which G1096
4:16 And he **c** to Nazareth, where he had G2064
31 And **c** down to Capernaum, a city of G2718
35 he **c** out of him, and hurt him not. G1831
41 And devils also **c** out of many, crying G1831
42 sought him, and **c** unto him, and G2064
5: 1 And it **c** to pass, that, as the people G1096
7 them. And they **c**, and filled both the G2064
12 And it **c** to pass, when he was in a G1096
15 great multitudes **c** together to hear, G4905
17 And it **c** to pass on a certain day, as he G1096
32 I **c** not to call the righteous, but sinners G2064
6: 1 And it **c** to pass on the second sabbath G1096
6 And it **c** to pass also on another G1096
12 And it **c** to pass in those days, that he G1096
17 And he **c** down with them, and stood in G2597
17 and Sidon, which **c** to hear him, and to G2064
7: 4 And when they **c** to Jesus, they G3854
11 And it **c** to pass the day after, that he G1096
12 Now when he **c** nigh to the gate of the G1448
14 And he **c** and touched the bier: and G4334
16 And there **c** a fear on all: and they G2983
33 For John the Baptist **c** neither eating G2064
45 I **c** in hath not ceased to kiss my feet. G1525
8: 1 And it **c** to pass afterward, that he went G1096
19 Then **c** to him *his* mother and his G3854
22 Now it **c** to pass on a certain day, that G1096
23 fell asleep: and there **c** down a storm of G2597
24 And they **c** to him, and awoke him, G4334
35 was done; and **c** to Jesus, and found G2064
40 And it **c** to pass, that, when Jesus was G1096
41 And, behold, there **c** a man named G2064
44 **C** behind *him*, and touched the border G4334
47 she was not hid, she **c** trembling, and G2064
51 And when he **c** into the house, he G1525
55 And her spirit **c** again, and she arose G1994
9:12 wear away, then **c** the twelve, and said G4334
18 And it **c** to pass, as he was alone G1096
28 And it **c** to pass about an eight days G1096
33 And it **c** to pass, as they departed from G1096
34 While he thus spake, there **c** a cloud, G1096
35 And there **c** a voice out of the cloud, G1096
37 And it **c** to pass, that on the next day, G1096
51 And it **c** to pass, when the time was G1096

Lk 9:57 And it **c** to pass, that, as they went in G1096
10:31 And by chance there **c** down a certain G2597
32 was at the place, **c** and looked *on him*, G2064
33 as he journeyed, **c** where he was: and G2064
38 Now it **c** to pass, as they went, that he G1096
40 much serving, and **c** to him, and said, G2186
11: 1 And it **c** to pass, that, as he was G1096
14 it was dumb. And it **c** to pass, when the G1096
24 return unto my house whence I **c** out. G1831
27 And it **c** to pass, as he spake these G1096
31 them: for she **c** from the utmost parts G2064
13: 6 his vineyard; and he **c** and sought fruit G2064
31 The same day there **c** certain of the G4334
14: 1 And it **c** to pass, as he went into the G1096
21 So that servant **c**, and shewed his lord G3854
15:17 And when he **c** to himself, he said, How G2064
20 And he arose, and **c** to his father. But G2064
25 field: and as he **c** and drew nigh to the G2064
28 **c** his father out, and intreated him. G1831
16:21 the dogs **c** and licked his sores. G2064
22 And it **c** to pass, that the beggar died, G1096
17:11 And it **c** to pass, as he went to G1096
14 the priests. And it **c** to pass, that, as G1096
27 and the flood **c**, and destroyed them all. G2064
18: 3 in that city; and she **c** unto him, saying, G2064
35 And it **c** to pass, that as he was come G1096
19: 5 And when Jesus **c** to the place, he G2064
6 And he made haste, and **c** down, and G2597
15 And it **c** to pass, that when he was G1096
16 Then **c** the first, saying, Lord, thy G3854
18 And the second **c**, saying, Lord, thy G2064
20 And another **c**, saying, Lord, behold, G2064
29 And it **c** to pass, when he was come G1096
20: 1 And it **c** to pass, *that* on one of those G1096
1 the scribes **c** upon *him* with the elders, G2186
27 Then **c** to *him* certain of the Sadducees, G4334
21:38 And all the people **c** early in the G3719
22: 7 Then **c** the day of unleavened bread, G2064
39 And he **c** out, and went, as he was G1831
66 and the scribes **c** together, and led him G4863
23:48 And all the people that **c** together to G4836
55 And the women also, which **c** with him G4905
24: 1 the morning, they **c** unto the sepulchre, G2064
4 And it **c** to pass, as they were much G1096
15 And it **c** to pass, that, while they G1096
23 not his body, they **c**, saying, that they G2064
30 And it **c** to pass, as he sat at meat with G2064
51 And it **c** to pass, while he blessed them, G1096
Jn 1: 7 The same **c** for a witness, to bear G2064
11 He **c** unto his own, and his own G2064
17 *but* grace and truth **c** by Jesus Christ. G1096
39 and see. They **c** and saw where he G2064
3: 2 The same **c** to Jesus by night, and said G2064
13 but he that **c** down from heaven, G2597
22 After these things **c** Jesus and his G2064
23 there: and they **c**, and were baptized. G3854
26 And they **c** unto John, and said unto G2064
4:27 And upon this **c** his disciples, and G2064
30 Then they went out of the city, and **c** G2064
46 So Jesus **c** again into Cana of Galilee, G2064
6:23 (Howbeit there **c** other boats from G2064
24 and **c** to Capernaum, seeking for Jesus. G2064
38 For I **c** down from heaven, not to do G2597
41 the bread which **c** down from heaven. G2597
42 that he saith, I **c** down from heaven? G2597
51 I am the living bread which **c** down G2597
58 This is that bread which **c** down from G2597
7:45 Then **c** the officers to the chief priests G2064
50 Nicodemus saith unto them, (he that **c** G2064
8: 2 And early in the morning he **c** again G3854
2 and all the people **c** unto him; and he G2064
14 I know whence I **c**, and whither I go; but G2064
42 forth and **c** from God; neither came G2240
42 neither **c** I of myself, but he sent me. G2064
9: 7 therefore, and washed, and **c** seeing. G2064
10: 8 All that ever **c** before me are thieves G2064
24 Then **c** the Jews round about him, and G2944
35 **c**, and the scripture cannot be broken; G1096
11:17 Then when Jesus **c**, he found that he G2064
19 And many of the Jews **c** to Martha and G2064
29 *that*, she arose quickly, and **c** unto him. G2064
33 weeping which **c** with her, he groaned G4905
44 And he that was dead **c** forth, bound G1831
45 Then many of the Jews which **c** to G2064
12: 1 the passover **c** to Bethany, where G2064
9 there: and they **c** not for Jesus' sake G2064
20 them that **c** up to worship at the feast: G305
21 The same **c** therefore to Philip, which G4334
27 but for this cause **c** I unto this hour. G2064

Jn 12:28 Father, glorify thy name. Then **c** there G2064
30 Jesus answered and said, This voice **c** G1096
47 him not: for I **c** not to judge the world, G2064
16:27 have believed that I **c** out from God. G1831
28 I **c** forth from the Father, and am come G1831
17: 8 surely that I **c** out from thee, and they G1831
18:37 and for this cause **c** I into the world, G2064
19: 5 Then **c** Jesus forth, wearing the crown G1831
32 Then **c** the soldiers, and brake the legs G2064
33 But when they **c** to Jesus, and saw that G2064
34 forthwith **c** there out blood and water. G1831
38 **c** therefore, and took the body of Jesus. G2064
39 And there **c** also Nicodemus, which at G2064
39 which at the first **c** to Jesus by night, G2064
20: 3 other disciple, and **c** to the sepulchre. G2064
4 Peter, and **c** first to the sepulchre. G2064
8 disciple, which **c** first to the sepulchre, G2064
18 Mary Magdalene **c** and told the G2064
19 fear of the Jews, **c** Jesus and stood in G2064
24 was not with them when Jesus **c**. G2064
26 with them: *then* **c** Jesus, the doors G2064
21: 8 And the other disciples **c** in a little ship; G2064
Act 2: 2 And suddenly there **c** a sound from G1096
6 the multitude **c** together, and were G4905
43 And fear **c** upon every soul: and many G1096
4: 1 and the Sadducees, **c** upon them, G2186
5 And it **c** to pass on the morrow, that G1096
5: 5 **c** on all them that heard these things. G1096
7 wife, not knowing what was done, **c** in. G1525
10 and the young men **c** in, and found her G1525
11 And great fear **c** upon all the church, G1096
16 There **c** also a multitude *out* of the G4905
21 But the high priest **c**, and they that were G3854
22 But when the officers **c**, and found them G3854
25 Then **c** one and told them, saying, G3854
6:12 and the scribes, and **c** upon *him*, and G2186
7: 4 Then **c** he out of the land of the G1881
11 Now there **c** a dearth over all the land G2064
23 And when he was full forty years old, it **c** G305
31 *it*, the voice of the Lord **c** unto him, G1096
45 Which also our fathers that **c** after G1237
8: 7 with loud voice, **c** out of many that G1831
36 And as they went on *their* way, they **c** G2064
40 in all the cities, till he **c** to Caesarea. G2064
9: 3 And as he journeyed, he **c** near G1096
21 in Jerusalem, and **c** hither for that G2064
32 And it **c** to pass, as Peter passed G1096
32 all *quarters*, he **c** down also to the G2718
37 And it **c** to pass in those days, that she G1096
43 And it **c** to pass, that he tarried many G1096
10:13 And there **c** a voice to him, Rise, Peter; G1096
29 Therefore **c** I *unto you* without G2064
45 as many as **c** with Peter, because G4905
11: 5 by four corners; and it **c** even to me: G2064
22 Then tidings of these things **c** unto the G191
23 Who, when he **c**, and had seen the grace G3854
26 Antioch. And it **c** to pass, that a whole G1096
27 And in these days **c** prophets from G2718
28 the world: which **c** to pass in the days G1096
12: 7 And, behold, the angel of the Lord **c** G2186
10 second ward, they **c** unto the iron gate G2064
12 *the thing*, he **c** to the house of Mary G2064
13 a damsel **c** to hearken, named Rhoda. G4334
20 Sidon: but they **c** with one accord to G3918
13:13 loosed from Paphos, they **c** to Perga in G2064
14 from Perga, they **c** to Antioch in G3854
31 days of them which **c** up with him from G4872
44 And the next sabbath day **c** almost the G4863
51 feet against them, and **c** unto Iconium. G2064
14: 1 And it **c** to pass in Iconium, that they G1096
19 And there **c** thither *certain* Jews from G1904
20 he rose up, and **c** into the city: and the G1525
24 Pisidia, they **c** to Pamphylia. G2064
15: 1 And certain men which **c** down from G2718
6 And the apostles and elders **c** together G4863
30 So when they were dismissed, they **c** to G2064
16: 1 Then **c** he to Derbe and Lystra: and, G2658
8 And they passing by Mysia **c** down to G2597
11 Therefore loosing from Troas, we **c** G2113
16 And it **c** to pass, as we went to prayer, G1096
18 out of her. And he **c** out the same hour. G1831
29 sprang in, and **c** trembling, and fell G1096
39 And they **c** and besought them, and G2064
17: 1 and Apollonia, they **c** to Thessalonica, G2064
13 Paul at Berea, they **c** thither also, and G2064
18: 1 from Athens, and **c** to Corinth; G2064
2 depart from Rome:) and **c** unto them. G4334
19 And he **c** to Ephesus, and left them G2658
24 mighty in the scriptures, **c** to Ephesus. G2658
Act 19: 1 And it **c** to pass, that, while Apollos G1096
1 the upper coasts **c** to Ephesus: and G2064
6 the Holy Ghost **c** on them; and they G2064
18 And many that believed **c**, and G2064
20: 2 much exhortation, he **c** into Greece, G2064
6 bread, and **c** unto them to Troas G2064
7 when the disciples **c** together to break G4863
14 we took him in, and **c** to Mitylene. G2064
15 And we sailed thence, and **c** the next G2658
15 and the next *day* we **c** to Miletus. G2064
18 the first day that I **c** into Asia, after G1910
21: 1 And it **c** to pass, that after we were G1096
1 and had launched, we **c** with a straight G2064
7 from Tyre, we **c** to Ptolemais, and G2658
8 departed, and **c** unto Caesarea: and G2064
10 many days, there **c** down from Judaea G2718
31 about to kill him, tidings **c** unto the chief G305
33 Then the chief captain **c** near, and took G1448
35 And when he **c** upon the stairs, so it G1096
22: 6 And it **c** to pass, that, as I made my G1096
11 that were with me, I **c** into Damascus. G2064
13 **C** unto me, and stood, and said unto G2064
17 And it **c** to pass, that, when I was come G1096
27 Then the chief captain **c**, and said unto G4334
23:14 And they **c** to the chief priests and G4334
27 of them: then **c** I with an army, and G2186
33 Who, when they **c** to Caesarea, and G1525
24: 7 But the chief captain Lysias **c** *upon us*, G3928
17 Now after many years I **c** to bring alms G3854
24 And after certain days, when Felix **c** G3854
27 Festus **c** into Felix' room: G2983+G1240
25: 7 the Jews which **c** down from Jerusalem G2597
13 **c** unto Caesarea to salute Festus. G2658
27: 5 we **c** to Myra, *a city* of Lycia. G2718
8 And, hardly passing it, **c** unto a place G2064
44 the ship. And so it **c** to pass, that they G1096
28: 3 on the fire, there **c** a viper out of the G1831
8 And it **c** to pass, that the father of G1096
9 in the island, **c**, and were healed: G4334
13 a compass, and **c** to Rhegium: and G2658
13 blew, and we **c** the next day to Puteoli: G2064
15 heard of us, they **c** to meet us as far as G1831
16 And when we **c** to Rome, the centurion G2064
17 And it **c** to pass, that after three days G1096
21 **c** shewed or spake any harm of thee. G3854
23 him a day, there **c** many to him into *his* G2240
30 and received all that **c** in unto him, G1531
Ro 5:18 of one *judgment* **c** upon all men to
18 *c* upon all men unto justification of life.
7: 9 **c**, sin revived, and I died. G2064
9: 5 the flesh Christ *c*, who is over all, God
1Co 2: 1 And I, brethren, when I **c** to you, came G2064
1 And I, brethren, when I came to you, **c** G2064
14:36 What? **c** the word of God out from you? G1831
36 out from you? or **c** it unto you only? G2658
15:21 For since by man *c* death, by man *came*
21 For since by man *came* death, by man *c*
2Co 1: 8 our trouble which **c** to us in Asia, that G1096
23 to spare you I **c** not as yet unto Corinth. G2064
2: 3 you, lest, when I **c**, I should have sorrow G2064
12 Furthermore, when I **c** to Troas to G2064
11: 9 the brethren which **c** from Macedonia G2064
Gal 1:21 Afterwards I **c** into the regions of Syria G2064
2: 4 brought in, who **c** in privily to spy out G3922
12 For before that certain **c** from James, G2064
3:23 But before faith **c**, we were kept under G2064
Eph 2:17 And **c** and preached peace to you G2064
1Th 1: 5 For our gospel **c** not unto you in word G1096
3: 4 even as it **c** to pass, and ye know. G1096
6 But now when Timotheus **c** from you G2064
1Ti 1:15 that Christ Jesus **c** into the world to G2064
2Ti 3:11 Persecutions, afflictions, which **c** unto G1096
Heb 3:16 not all that **c** out of Egypt by Moses. G1831
11:15 from whence they **c** out, they might G1831
2Pt 1:17 glory, when there **c** such a voice to him G5342
18 And this voice which **c** from heaven we G5342
21 For the prophecy **c** not in old time by G5342
1Jn 5: 6 This is he that **c** by water and blood, G2064
3Jn 3 when the brethren **c** and testified of the G2064
Rev 5: 7 And he **c** and took the book out of the G2064
7:13 in white robes? and whence **c** they? G2064
14 These are they which **c** out of great G2064
8: 3 And another angel **c** and stood at the G2064
4 And the smoke of the incense, *which c*
9: 3 And there **c** out of the smoke locusts G1831
14:15 And another angel **c** out of the temple, G1831
17 And another angel **c** out of the temple G1831
18 And another angel **c** out from the altar, G1831
20 without the city, and blood **c** out of the G1831
Rev 15: 6 And the seven angels **c** out of the G1831
16:17 the air; and there **c** a great voice out of G1831
19 and great Babylon **c** in remembrance G8415
17: 1 And there **c** one of the seven angels G2064
19: 5 And a voice **c** out of the throne, saying, G1831
20: 9 city: and fire **c** down from God out G2597
21: 9 And there **c** unto me one of the seven G2064

CAMEL

Gen 24:64 she saw Isaac, she lighted off the **c**. H1581
Lev 11: 4 the hoof: *as* the **c**, because he cheweth H1581
Dt 14: 7 cloven hoof; *as* the **c**, and the hare, and H1581
1Sa 15: 3 and suckling, ox and sheep, **c** and ass. H1581
Zec 14:15 of the mule, of the **c**, and of the ass, and H1581
Mt 19:24 It is easier for a **c** to go through the eye G2574
23:24 which strain at a gnat, and swallow a **c**. G2574
Mk 10:25 It is easier for a **c** to go through the eye G2574
Lk 18:25 For it is easier for a **c** to go through a G2574

CAMELS

Gen 12:16 maidservants, and she asses, and **c**. H1581
24:10 And the servant took ten **c** of the H1581
10 ten camels of the **c** of his master, and H1581
11 And he made his **c** to kneel down H1581
14 and I will give thy **c** drink also: *let the* H1581
19 **c** also, until they have done drinking. H1581
20 to draw *water*, and drew for all his **c**. H1581
22 And it came to pass, as the **c** had done H1581
30 behold, he stood by the **c** at the well. H1581
31 prepared the house, and room for the **c**. H1581
32 he ungirded his **c**, and gave straw and H1581
32 provender for the **c**, and water to wash H1581
35 and maidservants, and **c**, and asses. H1581
44 also draw for thy **c**: *let the same be* the H1581
46 and I will give thy **c** drink also: so I H1581
46 I drank, and she made the **c** drink also. H1581
61 rode upon the **c**, and followed the man: H1581
63 saw, and, behold, the **c** *were* coming. H1581
30:43 and menservants, and **c**, and asses. H1581
31:17 and set his sons and his wives upon **c**; H1581
32: 7 and herds, and the **c**, into two bands; H1581
15 Thirty milch **c** with their colts, forty H1581
37:25 Gilead with their **c** bearing spicery and H1581
Ex 9: 3 asses, upon the **c**, upon the oxen, and H1581
Jdg 6: 5 they and their **c** were without number: H1581
7:12 and their **c** *were* without number, H1581
1Sa 27: 9 the asses, and the **c**, and the apparel, H1581
30:17 men, which rode upon **c**, and fled. H1581
1Ki 10: 2 great train, with **c** that bare spices, and H1581
1Ch 5:21 cattle; of their **c** fifty thousand, and H1581
12:40 on asses, and on **c**, and on mules, and H1581
27:30 Over the **c** also *was* Obil the Ishmaelite: H1581
2Ch 9: 1 company, and **c** that bare spices, and H1581
14:15 away sheep and **c** in abundance, and H1581
Ezr 2:67 Their **c**, four hundred thirty and five; H1581
Neh 7:69 *Their* **c**, four hundred thirty and five: H1581
Est 8:10 on mules, **c**, *and* young dromedaries: H327
14 *So* the posts that rode upon mules *and* **c** H327
Job 1: 3 and three thousand **c**, and five hundred H1581
17 and fell upon the **c**, and have carried H1581
42:12 and six thousand **c**, and a thousand H1581
Isa 21: 7 *and* a chariot of **c**; and he hearkened H1581
30: 6 **c**, to a people *that* shall not profit *them*. H1581
60: 6 The multitude of **c** shall cover thee, the H1581
Jer 49:29 vessels, and their **c**; and they shall cry H1581
32 And their **c** shall be a booty, and the H1581
Ezk 25: 5 And I will make Rabbah a stable for **c**, H1581

CAMEL'S

Gen 31:34 put them in the **c** furniture, and sat H1581
Mt 3: 4 John had his raiment of **c** hair, and a G2574
Mk 1: 6 And John was clothed with **c** hair, and G2574

CAMELS'

Jdg 8:21 ornaments that *were* on their **c** necks. H1581
26 chains that *were* about their **c** necks. H1581
2Ki 8: 9 of Damascus, forty **c** burden, and came H1581

CAMEST

Gen 16: 8 maid, whence **c** thou? and whither wilt H935
24: 5 unto the land from whence thou **c**? H3318
27:33 of all before thou **c**, and have blessed H935
Ex 23:15 Abib; for in it thou **c** out from Egypt: H3318
34:18 the month Abib thou **c** out from Egypt. H3318
Nu 22:37 thee? wherefore **c** thou not unto me? H1980
Dt 2:37 of Ammon thou **c** not, *nor* unto any H7126
16: 3 of affliction; for thou **c** forth out of the H3318
3 the day when thou **c** forth out of the H3318
6 season that thou **c** forth out of Egypt. H3318

1Sa 13:11 me, and *that* thou **c** not within the days H935
17:28 and he said, Why **c** thou down hither? H3381
2Sa 11:10 said unto Uriah, **C** thou not from *thy* H935
15:20 Whereas thou **c** *but* yesterday, should I H935
1Ki 13: 9 turn again by the same way that thou **c**. H1980
14 that **c** from Judah? And he said, I *am*. H935
17 turn again to go by the way that thou **c**. H1980
22 But **c** back, and hast eaten bread and H7725
2Ki 19:28 thee back by the way by which thou **c**. H935
Neh 9:13 Thou **c** down also upon mount Sinai, H3381
Isa 37:29 thee back by the way by which thou **c**. H935
64: 3 not for, thou **c** down, the mountains H3381
Jer 1: 5 thee; and before thou **c** forth out of the H3318
Ezk 32: 2 in the seas: and thou **c** forth with thy H1518
Mt 22:12 And he saith unto him, Friend, how **c** G1525
Jn 6:25 unto him, Rabbi, when **c** thou hither? G1096
16:30 we believe that thou **c** forth from God. G1831
Act 9:17 in the way as thou **c**, hath sent me, that G2064

CAMON
Jdg 10: 5 And Jair died, and was buried in **C**. H7056

CAMP
Ex 14:19 went before the **c** of Israel, removed H4264
20 And it came between the **c** of the H4264
20 the Egyptians and the **c** of Israel; and it H4264
16:13 and covered the **c**: and in the morning H4264
19:16 the people that *was* in the **c** trembled. H4264
17 people out of the **c** to meet with God; H4264
29:14 fire without the **c**: it *is* a sin offering. H4264
32:17 Moses, *There is* a noise of war in the **c**. H4264
19 nigh unto the **c**, that he saw the calf, H4264
26 Then Moses stood in the gate of the **c**, H4264
27 throughout the **c**, and slay every man H4264
33: 7 it without the **c**, afar off from the camp, H4264
7 afar off from the **c**, and called it the H4264
7 congregation, which *was* without the **c**. H4264
11 again into the **c**: but his servant Joshua, H4264
36: 6 throughout the **c**, saying, Let neither H4264
Lev 4:12 forth without the **c** unto a clean place, H4264
21 without the **c**, and burn him as he H4264
6:11 ashes without the **c** unto a clean place. H4264
8:17 the **c**; as the LORD commanded Moses. H4264
9:11 hide he burnt with fire without the **c**. H4264
10: 4 from before the sanctuary out of the **c**. H4264
5 coats out of the **c**; as Moses had said. H4264
13:46 without the **c** *shall* his habitation *be*. H4264
14: 3 go forth out of the **c**; and the priest shall H4264
8 come into the **c**, and shall tarry abroad H4264
16:26 water, and afterward come into the **c**. H4264
27 forth without the **c**; and they shall burn H4264
28 and afterward he shall come into the **c**. H4264
17: 3 the **c**, or that killeth *it* out of the camp, H4264
3 the camp, or that killeth *it* out of the **c**, H4264
24:10 a man of Israel strove together in the **c**; H4264
14 cursed without the **c**; and let all that H4264
23 cursed out of the **c**, and stone him with H4264
Nu 1:52 man by his own **c**, and every man by his H4264
2: 3 the standard of the **c** of Judah pitch H4264
9 All that were numbered in the **c** of H4264
10 standard of the **c** of Reuben according H4264
16 All that were numbered in the **c** of H4264
17 forward with the **c** of the Levites in the H4264
17 in the midst of the **c**: as they encamp, so H4264
18 standard of the **c** of Ephraim according H4264
24 All that were numbered of the **c** of H4264
25 The standard of the **c** of Dan *shall be* H4264
31 All they that were numbered in the **c** of H4264
4: 5 And when the **c** setteth forward, Aaron H4264
15 sanctuary, as the **c** is to set forward; H4264
5: 2 they put out of the **c** every leper, and H4264
3 out, without the **c** shall ye put them; H4264
4 out without the **c**: as the LORD spake H4264
10:14 the standard of the **c** of the children of H4264
18 And the standard of the **c** of Reuben set H4264
22 And the standard of the **c** of the H4264
25 And the standard of the **c** of the H4264
34 by day, when they went out of the **c**. H4264
11: 1 *were* in the uttermost parts of the **c**. H4264
9 And when the dew fell upon the **c** in the H4264
26 *of the* men in the **c**, the name of the one H4264
26 and they prophesied in the **c**. H4264
27 Eldad and Medad do prophesy in the **c**. H4264
30 And Moses gat him into the **c**, he and H4264
31 let *them* fall by the **c**, as it were a day's H4264
31 round about the **c**, and as it were two H4264
32 for themselves round about the **c**. H4264
12:14 be shut out from the **c** seven days, and H4264
15 And Miriam was shut out from the **c** H4264
Nu 14:44 and Moses, departed not out of the **c**. H4264
15:35 stone him with stones without the **c**. H4264
36 him without the **c**, and stoned him with H4264
19: 3 **c**, and *one* shall slay her before his face: H4264
7 come into the **c**, and the priest shall H4264
9 up without the **c** in a clean place, and H4264
31:12 of Israel, unto the **c** at the plains of H4264
13 went forth to meet them without the **c**. H4264
19 And do ye abide without the **c** seven H4264
24 and afterward ye shall come into the **c**. H4264
Dt 23:10 **c**, he shall not come within the camp: H4264
10 camp, he shall not come within the **c**: H4264
11 is down, he shall come into the **c** *again*. H4264
12 **c**, whither thou shalt go forth abroad: H4264
14 in the midst of thy **c**, to deliver thee, H4264
14 therefore shall thy **c** be holy: that he see H4264
29:11 that *is* in thy **c**, from the hewer of thy H4264
Jos 5: 8 places in the **c**, till they were whole. H4264
6:11 into the **c**, and lodged in the camp. H4264
11 into the camp, and lodged in the **c**. H4264
14 returned into the **c**: so they did six days. H4264
18 the **c** of Israel a curse, and trouble it. H4264
23 and left them without the **c** of Israel. H4264
9: 6 And they went to Joshua unto the **c** at H4264
10: 6 unto Joshua to the **c** to Gilgal, saying, H4264
15 all Israel with him, unto the **c** to Gilgal. H4264
21 And all the people returned to the **c** to H4264
43 all Israel with him, unto the **c** to Gilgal. H4264
Jdg 7:17 **c**, it shall be *that*, as I do, so shall ye do. H4264
18 side of all the **c**, and say, *The sword* H4264
19 the outside of the **c** in the beginning of H4264
21 round about the **c**: and all the host ran, H4264
13:25 **c** of Dan between Zorah and Eshtaol. H4264
21: 8 **c** from Jabesh-gilead to the assembly. H4264
12 them unto the **c** to Shiloh, which *is* in H4264
1Sa 4: 3 were come into the **c**, the elders of Israel H4264
5 came into the **c**, all Israel shouted with H4264
6 great shout in the **c** of the Hebrews? H4264
6 ark of the LORD was come into the **c**. H4264
7 is come into the **c**. And they said, Woe H4264
13:17 And the spoilers came out of the **c** of H4264
14:21 with them into the **c** *from the country* H4264
17: 4 out of the **c** of the Philistines, named H4264
17 loaves, and run to the **c** to thy brethren; H4264
26: 6 me to Saul to the **c**? And Abishai said, I H4264
2Sa 1: 2 came out of the **c** from Saul with his H4264
3 Out of the **c** of Israel am I escaped. H4264
1Ki 16:16 host, king over Israel that day in the **c**. H4264
2Ki 3:24 And when they came to the **c** of Israel, H4264
6: 8 In such and such a place *shall be* my **c**. H8466
7: 5 to go unto the **c** of the Syrians: and H4264
5 part of the **c** of Syria, behold, *there* H4264
7 the **c** as it *was*, and fled for their life. H4264
8 part of the **c**, they went into one tent, H4264
10 We came to the **c** of the Syrians, and, H4264
12 gone out of the **c** to hide themselves in H4264
19:35 and smote in the **c** of the Assyrians an H4264
2Ch 22: 1 the Arabians to the **c** had slain all the H4264
32:21 captains in the **c** of the king of Assyria. H4264
Ps 78:28 And he let *it* fall in the midst of their **c**, H4264
106:16 They envied Moses also in the **c**, *and* H4264
Isa 29: 3 And I will **c** against thee round about, H2583
37:36 and smote in the **c** of the Assyrians a H4264
Jer 50:29 that bend the bow, **c** against it round H2583
Ezk 4: 2 against it; set the **c** also against it, and H4264
Joel 2:11 his army: for his **c** *is* very great: for *he* H4264
Nah 3:17 which **c** in the hedges in the H2583
Heb 13:11 priest for sin, are burned without the **c**. G3925
13 without the **c**, bearing his reproach. G3925
Rev 20: 9 compassed the **c** of the saints about, G3925

CAMPED
Ex 19: 2 and there Israel **c** before the mount. H2583

CAMPHIRE
Song 1:14 My beloved *is* unto me *as* a cluster of **c** H3724
4:13 with pleasant fruits; **c**, with spikenard, H3724

CAMPS
Nu 2:32 numbered of the **c** throughout their H4264
5: 3 not their **c**, in the midst whereof I dwell. H4264
10: 2 and for the journeying of the **c**. H4264
5 When ye blow an alarm, then the **c** that H4264
6 time, then the **c** that lie on the south H4264
25 rearward of all the **c** throughout their H4264
Am 4:10 the stink of your **c** to come up unto H4264

CAN
Gen 4:13 My punishment *is* greater than I **c** bear.
Gen 13:16 so that if a man **c** number the dust of H3201
31:43 *is* mine: and what **c** I do this day unto
39: 9 *art* his wife: how then **c** I do this great
41:15 *there is* none that **c** interpret it: and I H6622
38 And Pharaoh said unto his servants, **C**
44: 1 as much as they **c** carry, and put every H3201
15 that such a man as I **c** certainly divine? H5172
Ex 4:14 I know that he **c** speak well. And also,
5:11 Go ye, get you straw where ye **c** find it:
Lev 14:30 or of the young pigeons, such as he **c** get;
Nu 23:10 Who **c** count the dust of Jacob, and the H4487
Dt 1:12 How **c** I myself alone bear your
3:24 or in earth, that **c** do according to thy H6213
7:17 more than I; how **c** I dispossess them? H3201
9: 2 **c** stand before the children of Anak! H3320
31: 2 old this day; I **c** no more go out and H3201
32:39 *there any* that **c** deliver out of my hand. H5337
Jdg 14:12 unto you: if ye **c** certainly declare it me
1Sa 9: 6 he **c** shew us our way that we should go.
16: 2 And Samuel said, How **c** I go? if Saul
17 that **c** play well, and bring *him* to me.
18: 8 *what* **c** he have more but the kingdom?
26: 9 him not: for who **c** stretch forth his hand
28: 2 what thy servant **c** do. And Achish said
2Sa 7:20 And what **c** David say more unto thee? H3254
12:22 for I said, Who **c** tell *whether* GOD will
23 should I fast? **c** I bring him back again? H3201
14:19 my lord the king, none **c** turn to the right
15:36 send unto me every thing that ye **c** hear.
19:35 I *am* this day fourscore years old: *and* **c** I
35 good and evil? **c** thy servant taste what
35 or what I drink? **c** I hear any more the
1Ki 5: 6 among us any that **c** skill to hew timber
1Ch 17:18 What **c** David *speak* more to thee for H3254
2Ch 1:10 **c** judge this thy people, *that is so* great?
2: 7 and blue, and that **c** skill to grave with
8 that thy servants **c** skill to cut timber in
Est 8: 6 For how **c** I endure to see the evil that
6 my people? or how **c** I endure to see the
Job 3:22 *and* are glad, when they **c** find the grave?
4: 2 who **c** withhold himself from speaking? H3201
6: 6 **C** that which is unsavoury be eaten
8:11 **C** the rush grow up without mire? can
11 Can the rush grow up without mire? **c** H7685
9:12 Behold, he taketh away, who **c** hinder
10: 7 *is* none that **c** deliver out of thine hand.
11:10 gather together, then who **c** hinder him?
12:14 up a man, and there **c** be no opening.
14: 4 Who **c** bring a clean *thing* out of an
15: 3 speeches wherewith he **c** do no good?
22: 2 **C** a man be profitable unto God, as he
13 And thou sayest, How doth God know? **c**
17 and what **c** the Almighty do for them?
23:13 But he *is* in one *mind*, and who **c** turn
25: 4 How then **c** man be justified with God?
4 **c** he be clean *that is* born of a woman?
26:14 thunder of his power who **c** understand?
34:29 When he giveth quietness, who then **c**
29 hideth *his* face, who then **c** behold him?
36:23 who **c** say, Thou hast wrought iniquity?
26 *him* not, neither **c** the number of his
29 Also **c** *any* understand the spreadings of
38:37 Who **c** number the clouds in wisdom? or
37 or who **c** stay the bottles of heaven,
40:14 that thine own right hand **c** save thee.
19 **c** make his sword to approach *unto him*.
23 that he **c** draw up Jordan into his mouth.
41:13 Who **c** discover the face of his garment?
13 **c** come *to him* with his double bridle?
14 Who **c** open the doors of his face? his
16 One is so near to another, that no air **c**
42: 2 no thought **c** be withholden from thee.
Ps 11: 3 If the foundations be destroyed, what **c**
19:12 Who **c** understand *his* errors? cleanse
22:29 him: and none **c** keep alive his own soul.
40: 5 they are more than **c** be numbered.
49: 7 None *of them* **c** by any means redeem H376
56: 4 I will not fear what flesh **c** do unto me.
11 not be afraid what man **c** do unto me.
58: 9 Before your pots **c** feel the thorns, he
78:19 God; they said, **C** God furnish a table H3201
20 overflowed; **c** he give bread also? H3201
20 also? **c** he provide flesh for his people?
89: 6 For who in the heaven **c** be compared
6 the mighty **c** be likened unto the LORD?
106: 2 Who **c** utter the mighty acts of the
2 LORD? *who* **c** shew forth all his praise?
118: 6 I will not fear: what **c** man do unto me?
147:17 morsels: who **c** stand before his cold?

Prv 6:27 C a man take fire in his bosom, and his
28 C one go upon hot coals, and his feet not
18:14 but a wounded spirit who c bear?
20: 6 goodness: but a faithful man who c find?
9 Who c say, I have made my heart clean,
24 Man's goings *are* of the LORD; how c a
26:16 than seven men that c render a reason.
31:10 Who c find a virtuous woman? for her
Ecc 2:12 and folly: for what c the man *do* that
25 For who c eat, or who else can hasten
25 For who can eat, or who else c hasten
3:11 so that no man c find out the work that
14 for ever: nothing c be put to it, nor any
4:11 heat: but how c one be warm *alone*?
6:12 as a shadow? for who c tell a man what
7:13 Consider the work of God: for who c H3201
24 and exceeding deep, who c find it out?
8: 7 be: for who c tell him when it shall be?
10:14 what shall be after him, who c tell him?
Song 8: 7 love, neither c the floods drown it:
Isa 28:20 For the bed is shorter than that *a man* c
20 than that he c wrap himself *in it*.
38:18 For the grave cannot praise thee, death c
43: 9 who among them c declare this, and
13 *there is* none that c deliver out of my
46: 7 cry unto him, yet c he not answer, nor
49:15 C a woman forget her sucking child, that
56:11 Yea, *they are* greedy dogs *which* c never
Jer 2:13 broken cisterns, that c hold no water.
24 in her occasion who c turn her away? all
28 them arise, if they c save thee in the time
32 C a maid forget her ornaments, *or* a
4: 4 burn that none c quench *it*, because of
5: 1 places thereof, if ye c find a man, if there
22 toss themselves, yet c they not prevail;
22 they roar, yet c they not pass over it?
9:10 up, so that none c pass through *them*;
10 *them*; neither c *men* hear the voice of
13:23 C the Ethiopian change his skin, or the
14:22 of the Gentiles that c cause rain? or can
22 can cause rain? or c the heavens give
17: 9 and desperately wicked: who c know it?
21:12 burn that none c quench *it*, because of
23:24 C any hide himself in secret places that I
31:37 Thus saith the LORD; If heaven above c
33:20 Thus saith the LORD; If ye c break my
38: 5 not *he that* c do *any* thing against you. H3201
47: 7 How c it be quiet, seeing the LORD hath
Lam 2:13 *is* great like the sea: who c heal thee?
Ezk 22:14 C thine heart endure, or can thine hands
14 Can thine heart endure, or c thine hands
28: 3 is no secret that they c hide from thee:
33:32 a pleasant voice, and c play well on an
37: 3 And he said unto me, Son of man, c
Dan 2: 9 ye c shew me the interpretation thereof.
10 the earth that c shew the king's matter: H3202
11 is none other that c shew it before the
3:29 other God that c deliver after this sort. H3202
4:35 earth: and none c stay his hand, or say H383
10:17 For how c the servant of this my lord H3201
Joel 2:11 and very terrible; and who c abide it?
Am 3: 3 C two walk together, except they be
5 C a bird fall in a snare upon the earth,
8 GOD hath spoken, who c but prophesy?
Jna 3: 9 Who c tell *if* God will turn and repent,
Mic 3:11 among us? none evil c come upon us.
5: 8 teareth in pieces, and none c deliver.
Nah 1: 6 Who c stand before his indignation? and
6 and who c abide in the fierceness
Mt 6:24 No man c serve two masters: for either *G1410*
27 Which of you by taking thought c add *G1410*
7:18 *c* a corrupt tree bring forth good fruit.
9:15 And Jesus said unto them, C the *G3361*
12:29 Or else how c one enter into a strong *G1410*
34 O generation of vipers, how c ye, being
16: 3 O *ye* hypocrites, ye c discern the face of *G1097*
3 c ye not *discern* the signs of the times?
19:25 amazed, saying, Who then c be saved? *G1410*
23:33 how c ye escape the damnation of hell?
27:65 go your way, make *it* as sure as ye c. *G1492*
Mk 2: 7 who c forgive sins but God only? *G1410*
19 And Jesus said unto them, C the *G1410*
3:23 parables, How c Satan cast out Satan? *G1410*
27 No man c enter into a strong man's *G1410*
7:15 entering into him c defile him: but the *G1410*
8: 4 From whence c a man satisfy these *G1410*
9: 3 so as no fuller on earth c white them. *G1410*
29 And he said unto them, This kind c *G1410*
39 name, that c lightly speak evil of me. *G1410*
Mk 10:26 themselves, Who then c be saved? *G1410*
38 not what ye ask: c ye drink of the cup
39 And they said unto him, We c. And *G1410*
Lk 5:21 Who c forgive sins, but God alone? *G1410*
34 And he said unto them, C ye make the *G1410*
6:39 And he spake a parable unto them, C *G1410*
12: 4 after that have no more that they c do.
25 thought c add to his stature one cubit? *G1410*
56 *Ye* hypocrites, ye c discern the face of *G1492*
16:13 No servant c serve two masters: for *G1410*
26 cannot; neither c they pass to us, that
18:26 And they that heard *it* said, Who then c *G1410*
20:36 Neither c they die any more: for they *G1410*
Jn 1:46 And Nathanael said unto him, C there *G1410*
3: 2 God: for no man c do these miracles *G1410*
4 Nicodemus saith unto him, How c a *G1410*
4 when he is old? c he enter the second *G1410*
9 said unto him, How c these things be? *G1410*
27 John answered and said, A man c *G1410*
5:19 say unto you, The Son c do nothing of *G1410*
30 I c of mine own self do nothing: as I *G1410*
44 How c ye believe, which receive honour *G1410*
6:44 No man c come to me, except the *G1410*
52 How c this man give us *his* flesh to eat? *G1410*
60 This is an hard saying; who c hear it? *G1410*
65 unto you, that no man c come unto me, *G1410*
9: 4 night cometh, when no man c work. *G1410*
16 day. Others said, How c a man that is a *G1410*
10:21 C a devil open the eyes of the blind? *G1410*
14: 5 thou goest; and how c we know the way?
15: 4 no more c ye, except ye abide in me.
5 fruit: for without me ye c do nothing. *G1410*
Act 8:31 And he said, How c I, except some man
10:47 C any man forbid water, that these *G1410*
24:13 Neither c they prove the things whereof *G1410*
Ro 8: 7 to the law of God, neither indeed c be. *G1410*
31 If God *be* for us, who c *be* against us?
1Co 2:14 unto him: neither c he know *them*, *G1410*
3:11 For other foundation c no man lay *G1410*
12: 3 and *that* no man c say that Jesus is the *G1410*
2Co 13: 8 For we c do nothing against the truth,
Php 4:13 I c do all things through Christ which
1Th 3: 9 For what thanks c we render to God
1Ti 6: 7 *and it is* certain we c carry nothing out. *G1410*
16 the light which no man c approach unto;
16 man hath seen, nor c see: to whom *be* *G1410*
Heb 5: 2 Who c have compassion on the *G1410*
10: 1 image of the things, c never with those *G1410*
11 which c never take away sins: *G1410*
Jas 2:14 and have not works? c faith save him? *G1410*
3: 8 But the tongue c no man tame; *it is* an *G1410*
12 C the fig tree, my brethren, bear olive *G1410*
12 a vine, figs? so c no fountain both yield
1Jn 4:20 c he love God whom he hath not seen? *G1410*
Rev 3: 8 door, and no man c shut it: for thou *G1410*
9:20 which neither c see, nor hear, nor walk: *G1410*

CANA

Jn 2: 1 was a marriage in C of Galilee; and the *G2580*
11 miracles did Jesus in C of Galilee, and *G2580*
4:46 So Jesus came again into C of Galilee, *G2580*
21: 2 and Nathanael of C in Galilee, and the *G2580*

CANAAN

Gen 9:18 Japheth: and Ham *is* the father of C. H3667
22 And Ham, the father of C, saw the H3667
25 And he said, Cursed *be* C; a servant of H3667
26 of Shem; and C shall be his servant. H3667
27 of Shem; and C shall be his servant. H3667
10: 6 Cush, and Mizraim, and Phut, and C. H3667
15 And C begat Sidon his firstborn, and H3667
11:31 to go into the land of C; and they came H3667
12: 5 go into the land of C; and into the land H3667
5 and into the land of C they came. H3667
13:12 Abram dwelled in the land of C, and Lot H3667
16: 3 in the land of C, and gave her to her H3667
17: 8 all the land of C, for an everlasting H3667
23: 2 in the land of C: and Abraham came H3667
19 the same *is* Hebron in the land of C. H3667
28: 1 not take a wife of the daughters of C. H3667
6 not take a wife of the daughters of C; H3667
8 of C pleased not Isaac his father; H3667
31:18 to go to Isaac his father in the land of C. H3667
33:18 *is* in the land of C, when he came from H3667
35: 6 *is* in the land of C, that *is*, Beth-el, he H3667
36: 2 the daughters of C; Adah the daughter H3667
5 were born unto him in the land of C. H3667
6 got in the land of C; and went into the H3667
37: 1 father was a stranger, in the land of C. H3667
Gen 42: 5 for the famine was in the land of C. H3667
7 said, From the land of C to buy food. H3667
13 man in the land of C; and, behold, the H3667
29 unto the land of C, and told him all that H3667
32 this day with our father in the land of C. H3667
44: 8 out of the land of C: how then should we H3667
45:17 and go, get you unto the land of C; H3667
25 the land of C unto Jacob their father, H3667
46: 6 in the land of C, and came into Egypt, H3667
12 died in the land of C. And the sons of H3667
31 in the land of C, are come unto me; H3667
47: 1 out of the land of C; and, behold, they H3667
4 sore in the land of C: now therefore, we H3667
13 of C fainted by reason of the famine. H3667
14 and in the land of C, for the corn which H3667
15 and in the land of C, all the Egyptians H3667
48: 3 at Luz in the land of C, and blessed me, H3667
7 by me in the land of C in the way, when H3667
49:30 in the land of C, which Abraham H3667
50: 5 for me in the land of C, there shalt thou H3667
13 into the land of C, and buried him in H3667
Ex 6: 4 them the land of C, the land of their H3667
15:15 the inhabitants of C shall melt away. H3667
16:35 came unto the borders of the land of C. H3667
Lev 14:34 When ye be come into the land of C, H3667
18: 3 of the land of C, whither I bring you, H3667
25:38 you the land of C, *and* to be your God. H3667
Nu 13: 2 search the land of C, which I give unto H3667
17 out the land of C, and said unto them, H3667
26:19 and Er and Onan died in the land of C. H3667
32:30 possessions among you in the land of C. H3667
32 into the land of C, that the possession H3667
33:40 in the land of C, heard of the coming H3667
51 passed over Jordan into the land of C; H3667
34: 2 into the land of C; (this *is* the land that H3667
2 the land of C with the coasts thereof:) H3667
29 the children of Israel in the land of C. H3667
35:10 be come over Jordan into the land of C; H3667
14 land of C, *which* shall be cities of refuge. H3667
Dt 32:49 behold the land of C, which I give unto H3667
Jos 5:12 of the fruit of the land of C that year. H3667
14: 1 in the land of C, which Eleazar the H3667
21: 2 in the land of C, saying, The LORD H3667
22: 9 which *is* in the land of C, to go unto the H3667
10 that *are* in the land of C, the children of H3667
11 the land of C, in the borders of Jordan, H3667
32 unto the land of C, to the children of H3667
24: 3 all the land of C, and multiplied his H3667
Jdg 3: 1 as had not known all the wars of C; H3667
4: 2 hand of Jabin king of C, that reigned in H3667
23 king of C before the children of Israel. H3667
24 Jabin the king of C, until they had H3667
24 they had destroyed Jabin king of C. H3667
5:19 the kings of C in Taanach by the waters H3667
21:12 to Shiloh, which *is* in the land of C. H3667
1Ch 1: 8 Ham; Cush, and Mizraim, Put, and C. H3667
13 And C begat Zidon his firstborn, and H3667
16:18 land of C, the lot of your inheritance; H3667
Ps 105:11 land of C, the lot of your inheritance: H3667
106:38 unto the idols of C: and the land was H3667
135:11 of Bashan, and all the kingdoms of C: H3667
Isa 19:18 the language of C, and swear to the H3667
Ezk 16: 3 *is* of the land of C; thy father *was* an H3669
29 in the land of C unto Chaldea; and yet H3667
Zep 2: 5 *is* against you; O C, the land of the H3667
Mt 15:22 And, behold, a woman of C came out of *G5478*

CANAANITE

Gen 12: 6 Moreh. And the C *was* then in the land. H3669
13: 7 Lot's cattle: and the C and the Perizzite H3669
38: 2 of a certain C, whose name *was* Shuah; H3669
Ex 23:28 the C, and the Hittite, from before thee. H3669
33: 2 I will drive out the C, the Amorite, and H3669
34:11 Amorite, and the C, and the Hittite, and H3669
Nu 21: 1 And *when* king Arad the C, which dwelt H3669
33:40 And king Arad the C, which dwelt in the H3669
Jos 9: 1 the Amorite, the C, the Perizzite, the H3669
11: 3 *And to* the C on the east and on the H3669
13: 3 is counted to the C: five lords of the H3669
Zec 14:21 C in the house of the LORD of hosts. H3669
Mt 10: 4 Simon the C, and Judas Iscariot, who *G2581*
Mk 3:18 and Thaddaeus, and Simon the C, *G2581*

CANAANITES

Gen 10:18 the families of the C spread abroad. H3669
19 And the border of the C was from H3669
15:21 And the Amorites, and the C, and the H3669
24: 3 of the C, among whom I dwell: H3669
37 of the C, in whose land I dwell: H3669

Gen 34:30 land, among the C and the Perizzites: H3669
50:11 of the land, the C, saw the mourning in H3669
Ex 3: 8 the place of the C, and the Hittites, and H3669
17 the land of the C, and the Hittites, and H3669
13: 5 the land of the C, and the Hittites, and H3669
11 the land of the C, as he sware unto thee H3669
23:23 Perizzites, and the C, the Hivites, and H3669
Nu 13:29 and the C dwell by the sea, and H3669
14:25 (Now the Amalekites and the C dwelt H3669
43 For the Amalekites and the C *are* there H3669
45 down, and the C which dwelt in that H3669
21: 3 and delivered up the C; and they utterly H3669
Dt 1: 7 to the land of the C, and unto Lebanon, H3669
7: 1 Amorites, and the C, and the Perizzites, H3669
11:30 in the land of the C, which dwell in the H3669
20:17 the Amorites, the C, and the Perizzites, H3669
Jos 3:10 before you the C, and the Hittites, and H3669
5: 1 all the kings of the C, which *were* by the H3669
7: 9 For the C and all the inhabitants of the H3669
12: 8 Amorites, and the C, the Perizzites, the H3669
13: 4 From the south, all the land of the C, H3669
16:10 And they drave not out the C that dwelt H3669
10 in Gezer: but the C dwell among the H3669
17:12 but the C would dwell in that land. H3669
13 that they put the C to tribute; but did H3669
16 for us: and all the C that dwell in the H3669
18 shalt drive out the C, though they have H3669
24:11 Perizzites, and the C, and the Hittites, H3669
Jdg 1: 1 the C first, to fight against them? H3669
3 fight against the C; and I likewise will H3669
4 delivered the C and the Perizzites into H3669
5 and they slew the C and the Perizzites. H3669
9 to fight against the C, that dwelt in the H3669
10 And Judah went against the C that H3669
17 and they slew the C that inhabited H3669
27 but the C would dwell in that land. H3669
28 that they put the C to tribute, and did H3669
29 Neither did Ephraim drive out the C H3669
29 but the C dwelt in Gezer among them. H3669
30 Nahalol; but the C dwelt among them, H3669
32 But the Asherites dwelt among the C, H3669
33 dwelt among the C, the inhabitants of H3669
3: 3 and all the C, and the Sidonians, H3669
5 Israel dwelt among the C, Hittites, and H3669
2Sa 24: 7 Hivites, and of the C: and they went out H3669
1Ki 9:16 fire, and slain the C that dwelt in the H3669
Ezr 9: 1 *even* of the C, the Hittites, the H3669
Neh 9: 8 give the land of the C, the Hittites, the H3669
24 of the land, the C, and gavest them into H3669
Oba 20 *shall possess* that of the C, *even* unto H3669

CANAANITESS
1Ch 2: 3 of Shua the C. And Er, the firstborn H3669

CANAANITISH
Gen 46:10 and Shaul the son of a C woman. H3669
Ex 6:15 Shaul the son of a C woman: these *are* H3669

CANDACE
Act 8:27 great authority under C queen of the *G2582*

CANDLE
Job 18: 6 and his c shall be put out with him. H5216
21:17 How oft is the c of the wicked put out! H5216
29: 3 When his c shined upon my head, *and* H5216
Ps 18:28 For thou wilt light my c: the LORD my H5216
Prv 20:27 The spirit of man *is* the c of the LORD, H5216
24:20 the c of the wicked shall be put out. H5216
31:18 *is* good: her c goeth not out by night. H5216
Jer 25:10 of the millstones, and the light of the c. H5216
Mt 5:15 Neither do men light a c, and put it *G3088*
Mk 4:21 And he said unto them, Is a c brought *G3088*
Lk 8:16 No man, when he hath lighted a c, *G3088*
11:33 No man, when he hath lighted a c, *G3088*
36 shining of a c doth give thee light. *G3088*
15: 8 doth not light a c, and sweep the house, *G3088*
Rev 18:23 And the light of a c shall shine no more *G3088*
22: 5 and they need no c, neither light of the *G3088*

CANDLES
Zep 1:12 Jerusalem with c, and punish the men H5216

CANDLESTICK
Ex 25:31 And thou shalt make a c *of* pure gold: H4501
31 work shall the c be made: his shaft, H4501
32 branches of the c out of the one side, H4501
32 branches of the c out of the other side: H4501
33 the six branches that come out of the c. H4501
34 And in the c *shall be* four bowls made H4501
Ex 25:35 six branches that proceed out of the c. H4501
26:35 the vail, and the c over against the H4501
30:27 vessels, and the c and his vessels, and H4501
31: 8 and the pure c with all his furniture, H4501
35:14 The c also for the light, and his H4501
37:17 And he made the c *of* pure gold: *of* H4501
17 work made he the c; his shaft, and his H4501
18 branches of the c out of the one side H4501
18 of the c out of the other side thereof: H4501
19 the six branches going out of the c. H4501
20 And in the c *were* four bowls made like H4501
39:37 The pure c, *with* the lamps thereof, *even* H4501
40: 4 in the c, and light the lamps thereof. H4501
24 And he put the c in the tent of the H4501
Lev 24: 4 pure c before the LORD continually. H4501
Nu 3:31 the table, and the c, and the altars, and H4501
4: 9 and cover the c of the light, and his H4501
8: 2 lamps shall give light over against the c. H4501
3 the c, as the LORD commanded Moses. H4501
4 And this work of the c *was of* beaten H4501
4 had shewed Moses, so he made the c. H4501
2Ki 4:10 and a stool, and a c: and it shall be, H4501
1Ch 28:15 by weight for every c, and for the lamps H4501
15 *both* for the c, and *also* for the lamps H4501
15 thereof, according to the use of every c. H4501
2Ch 13:11 table; and the c of gold with the lamps H4501
Dan 5: 5 over against the c upon the plaister of H5043
Zec 4: 2 and behold a c all *of* gold, with a bowl H4501
11 of the c and upon the left *side* thereof? H4501
Mt 5:15 a bushel, but on a c; and it giveth light *G3087*
Mk 4:21 or under a bed? and not to be set on a c? *G3087*
Lk 8:16 but setteth *it* on a c, that they which *G3087*
11:33 a bushel, but on a c, that they which *G3087*
Heb 9: 2 wherein *was* the c, and the table, and *G3087*
Rev 2: 5 c out of his place, except thou repent. *G3087*

CANDLESTICKS
1Ki 7:49 And the c of pure gold, five on the right H4501
1Ch 28:15 Even the weight for the c of gold, and H4501
15 and for the c of silver by weight, H4501
2Ch 4: 7 And he made ten c of gold according to H4501
20 Moreover the c with their lamps, that H4501
Jer 52:19 the caldrons, and the c, and the spoons, H4501
Rev 1:12 And being turned, I saw seven golden c; *G3087*
13 And in the midst of the seven c *one* like *G3087*
20 the seven golden c. The seven stars are *G3087*
20 and the seven c which thou sawest are *G3087*
2: 1 in the midst of the seven golden c; *G3087*
11: 4 c standing before the God of the earth. *G3087*

CANE
Isa 43:24 Thou hast bought me no sweet c with H7070
Jer 6:20 and the sweet c from a far country? H7070

CANKER
2Ti 2:17 And their word will eat as doth a c: of *G1044*

CANKERED
Jas 5: 3 Your gold and silver is c; and the rust of *G2728*

CANKERWORM
Joel 1: 4 hath left hath the c eaten; and that H3218
4 c hath left hath the caterpiller eaten. H3218
2:25 hath eaten, the c, and the caterpiller, H3218
Nah 3:15 thee up like the c: make thyself many H3218
15 the c, make thyself many as the locusts. H3218
16 heaven: the c spoileth, and flieth away. H3218

CANNEH
Ezk 27:23 Haran, and C, and Eden, the merchants H3656

CANNOT
Gen 19:19 my life; and I c escape to the H3808+H3201
22 thither; for I c do any thing till H3808+H3201
24:50 c speak unto thee bad or good. H3808+H3201
29: 8 And they said, We c, until all H3808+H3201
31:35 my lord that I c rise up before H3808+H3201
32:12 which c be numbered for multitude. H3808
34:14 And they said unto them, We c H3808+H3201
38:22 And he returned to Judah, and said, I c H3808
43:22 c tell who put our money in our sacks. H3045
44:22 lord, The lad c leave his father: H3808+H3201
26 And we said, We c go down: if H3808+H3201
Ex 10: 5 the earth, that one c be able to see the H3808
19:23 The people c come up to H3808+H3201
Lev 14:21 And if he *be* poor, and c get so H369+H3027
Nu 22:18 and gold, I c go beyond the H3808+H3201
23:20 and he hath blessed; and I c reverse it. H3808
24:13 and gold, I c go beyond the H3808+H3201
Nu 35:33 land: and the land c be cleansed of the H3308
Dt 28:35 botch that c be healed, from H3808+H3201
Jos 24:19 unto the people, Ye c serve the H3808+H3201
Jdg 11:35 the LORD, and I c go back. H3808+H3201
14:13 But if ye c declare *it* me, then H3808+H3201
Ru 4: 6 And the kinsman said, I c H3808+H3201
6 to thyself; for I c redeem *it*. H3808+H3201
1Sa 12:21 c profit nor deliver; for they *are* vain. H3308
17:39 said unto Saul, I c go with these; for I H3308
55 said, *As* thy soul liveth, O king, I c tell. H518
25:17 son of Belial, that *a man* c speak to him.
2Sa 5: 6 thinking, David c come in hither. H3808
14:14 on the ground, which c be gathered up H3808
23: 6 because they c be taken with hands: H3808
1Ki 3: 8 a great people, that c be numbered nor H3808
8:27 heaven of heavens c contain thee; how H3808
18:12 tell Ahab, and he c find thee, he shall H3808
2Ch 2: 6 heaven of heavens c contain him? who H3808
6:18 heaven of heavens c contain thee; how H3808
24:20 the LORD, that ye c prosper? because H3808
Ezr 9:15 we c stand before thee because of this. H3808
Neh 6: 3 work, so that I c come down: why should H369
Job 5:12 c perform *their* enterprise. H3808+H3201
6:30 Is there iniquity in my tongue? c my H3808
9: 3 If he will contend with him, he c H3808
12:14 Behold, he breaketh down, and it c be H3808
14: 5 appointed his bounds that he c pass; H3808
17:10 for I c find *one* wise *man* among you. H3808
19: 8 He hath fenced up my way that I c H3808
23: 8 and backward, but I c perceive him: H3808
9 he doth work, but I c behold *him*: he H3808
9 on the right hand, that I c see *him*: H3808
28:15 It c be gotten for gold, neither shall H3808
16 It c be valued with the gold of Ophir, H3808
17 The gold and the crystal c equal it: and H3808
31:31 we had of his flesh! we c be satisfied. H3808
33:21 His flesh is consumed away, that it c be H3808
36:18 then a great ransom c deliver thee. H3808
37: 5 doeth he, which we c comprehend. H408
19 unto him; *for* we c order *our speech* by H3808
23 *Touching* the Almighty, we c find him H3808
41:17 stick together, that they c be sundered. H3808
23 firm in themselves; they c be moved. H1077
26 The sword of him that layeth at him c H1097
28 The arrow c make him flee: slingstones H3808
Ps 40: 5 *are* to us-ward: they c be reckoned up in H408
77: 4 I am so troubled that I c speak. H3808
88: 8 them: *I am* shut up, and I c come forth. H3808
93: 1 also is stablished, that it c be moved. H1077
125: 1 c be removed, *but* abideth for ever. H3808
139: 6 me; it is high, I c *attain* unto it. H3808+H3201
Prv 30:21 and for four *which* it c bear: H3808+H3201
Ecc 1: 8 labour; man c utter *it*: the eye H3808+H3201
15 *That which is* crooked c be H3808+H3201
15 is wanting c be numbered. H3808+H3201
8:17 that a man c find out the work H3808+H3201
10:14 A fool also is full of words: a man c tell H3045
Song 8: 7 Many waters c quench love, H3808+H3201
Isa 1:13 assemblies, I c away with; *it is* H3808+H3201
29:11 and he saith, I c; for it *is* sealed: H3808+H3201
38:18 For the grave c praise thee, death can H3808
18 down into the pit c hope for thy truth. H3808
44:18 eyes, that they c see; *and* their hearts,
18 *and* their hearts, that they c understand.
20 him aside, that he c deliver his soul, H3808
45:20 image, and pray unto a god *that* c save. H3808
50: 2 at all, that it c redeem? or have I no
56:10 dogs, they c bark; sleeping, H3808+H3201
11 *that* c understand: they H3808+H3045
57:20 sea, when it c rest, whose H3808+H3201
59: 1 shortened, that it c save; neither his ear H3808
1 neither his ear heavy, that it c hear: H3808
14 the street, and equity c enter. H3808+H3201
Jer 1: 6 Then said I, Ah, Lord GOD! behold, I c H3808
4:19 a noise in me; I c hold my peace, H3808
5:22 decree, that it c pass it: and though H3808
6:10 and they c hearken: behold, H3808+H3201
7: 8 Behold, ye trust in lying words, that c H1115
10: 5 because they c go. Be not afraid of H3808
5 of them; for they c do evil, neither also H3808
14: 9 man *that* c save? yet thou, H3808+H3201
18: 6 O house of Israel, c I do with H3808+H3201
19:11 vessel, that c be made whole H3808+H3201
24: 3 evil, that c be eaten, they are so evil. H3808
8 And as the evil figs, which c be eaten, H3808
29:17 figs, that c be eaten, they are so evil. H3808
33:22 As the host of heaven c be numbered, H3808
36: 5 I *am* shut up; I c go into the H3808+H3201
46:23 the LORD, though it c be searched; H3808

Jer 49:23 sorrow on the sea; it c be quiet. H3808+H3201
Lam 3: 7 He hath hedged me about, that I c get H3808
4:18 They hunt our steps, that we c go in H3808
Dan 2:27 demanded c the wise *men*, the H3809+H3202
Hos 1:10 of the sea, which c be measured nor H3808
Jna 4:11 persons that c discern between their H3808
Hab 2: 5 and *is* as death, and c be satisfied, but H3808
Mt 5:14 that is set on an hill c be hid. G3756+G1410
6:24 Ye c serve God and mammon. G3756+G1410
7:18 A good tree c bring forth evil G3756+G1410
19:11 But he said unto them, All *men* c G3756
21:27 and said, We c tell. And he G3756+G1492
26:53 Thinkest thou that I c now G3756+G1410
27:42 He saved others; himself he c G3756+G1410
Mk 2:19 with them, they c fast. G3756+G1410
3:24 itself, that kingdom c stand. G3756+G1410
25 itself, that house c stand. G3756+G1410
26 he c stand, but hath an end. G3756+G1410
7:18 into the man, *it* c defile him; G3756+G1410
11:33 Jesus, We c tell. And Jesus G3756+G1492
15:31 others; himself he c save. G3756+G1410
Lk 11: 7 in bed; I c rise and give thee. G3756+G1410
13:33 for it c be that a prophet G3756+G1735
14:14 for they c recompense thee: G3756+G2192
20 a wife, and therefore I c come. G3756+G1410
26 life also, he c be my disciple. G3756+G1410
27 after me, c be my disciple. G3756+G1410
33 he hath, he c be my disciple. G3756+G1410
16: 3 I c dig; to beg I am ashamed. G3756+G2480
13 Ye c serve God and mammon. G3756+G1410
26 hence to you c; neither can they G3361+G1410
Jn 3: 3 he c see the kingdom of God. G3756+G1410
5 *of* the Spirit, he c enter into the G3756+G1410
7: 7 The world c hate you; but me it G3756+G1410
34 where I am, *thither* ye c come. G3756+G1410
36 where I am, *thither* ye c come? G3756+G1410
8:14 I go; but ye c tell whence I G3756+G1492
21 sins: whither I go, ye c come. G3756+G1410
22 saith, Whither I go, ye c come. G3756+G1410
43 because ye c hear my word. G3756+G1410
10:35 and the scripture c be broken; G3756+G1410
13:33 ye c come; so now I say to you. G3756+G1410
37 Lord, why c I follow thee now? G3756+G1410
14:17 the world c receive, because G3756+G1410
15: 4 As the branch c bear fruit of G3756+G1410
16:12 you, but ye c bear them now. G3756+G1410
18 while? we c tell what he saith. G3756+G1492
Act 4:16 in Jerusalem; and we c deny *it*. G3756+G1410
20 For we c but speak the things G3756+G1410
5:39 But if it be of God, ye c G3756+G1410
15: 1 of Moses, ye c be saved. G3756+G1410
19:36 Seeing then that these things c be spoken G868
27:31 in the ship, ye c be saved. G3756+G1410
Ro 8: 8 are in the flesh c please God. G3756+G1410
26 for us with groanings which c be uttered. G215
1Co 7: 9 But if they c contain, let them marry: G3756
10:21 Ye c drink the cup of the Lord, G3756+G1410
21 of devils: ye c be partakers of G3756+G1410
12:21 And the eye c say unto the G3756+G1410
15:50 flesh and blood c inherit the G3756+G1410
2Co 12: 2 in the body, I c tell; or whether G3756+G1492
2 out of the body, I c tell: God G3756+G1492
3 body, I c tell: God knoweth;) G3756+G1492
Gal 3:17 thirty years after, c disannul, that it G3756
5:17 so that ye c do the things that ye would. G3361
1Ti 5:25 that are otherwise c be hid. G3756+G1410
2Ti 2:13 faithful: he c deny himself. G3756+G1410
Tit 1: 2 In hope of eternal life, which God, that c G893
2: 8 Sound speech, that c be condemned; G176
Heb 4:15 priest which c be touched with G3361+G1410
9: 5 of which we c now speak particularly. G3756
12:27 things which c be shaken may remain. G3361
28 a kingdom which c be moved, let us G761
Jas 1:13 of God: for God c be tempted with evil, G551
4: 2 to have, and c obtain: ye fight G3756+G1410
2Pt 1: 9 is blind, and c see afar off, and hath G3467
2:14 Having eyes full of adultery, and that c G180
1Jn 3: 9 him: and he c sin, because he G3756+G1410

CANST
Gen 41:15 c understand a dream to interpret it.
Ex 33:20 And he said, Thou c not see my face: H3201
Dt 28:27 the itch, whereof thou c not be healed. H3201
Jos 7:13 O Israel: thou c not stand before thine H3201
Jdg 16:15 And she said unto him, How c thou say,
1Sa 30:15 And David said to him, C thou bring me
2Ki 8: 1 wheresoever thou c sojourn: for the
Ezr 7:16 And all the silver and gold that thou c
Job 11: 7 C thou by searching find out God? canst
Job 11: 7 Canst thou by searching find out God? c
8 *It is* as high as heaven; what c thou do?
8 do? deeper than hell; what c thou know?
22:11 Or darkness, *that* thou c not see; and
33: 5 If thou c answer me, set *thy words* in H3201
38:31 C thou bind the sweet influences of
32 C thou bring forth Mazzaroth in his
32 or c thou guide Arcturus with his sons?
33 of heaven? c thou set the dominion
34 C thou lift up thy voice to the clouds,
35 C thou send lightnings, that they may
39: 1 *or* c thou mark when the hinds do calve?
2 C thou number the months *that* they
10 C thou bind the unicorn with his band in
20 C thou make him afraid as a
40: 9 Hast thou an arm like God? or c thou
41: 1 C thou draw out leviathan with an hook?
2 C thou put an hook into his nose? or
7 C thou fill his skin with barbed irons? or
42: 2 I know that thou c do every *thing*, and H3201
Prv 3:15 all the things thou c desire are not to be
5: 6 moveable, *that* thou c not know *them*.
30: 4 and what *is* his son's name, if thou c tell?
Isa 33:19 deeper speech than thou c perceive; of a
19 tongue, *that thou* c not understand.
Jer 2:23 How c thou say, I am not polluted, I
12: 5 thee, then how c thou contend with
Ezk 3: 6 whose words thou c not understand.
Dan 5:16 And I have heard of thee, that thou c H3202
16 now if thou c read the writing, and H3202
Hab 1:13 than to behold evil, and c not look on H3201
Mt 5:36 c not make one hair white or black. G1410
8: 2 if thou wilt, thou c make me clean. G1410
Mk 1:40 If thou wilt, thou c make me clean. G1410
9:22 him: but if thou c do any thing, have G1410
23 Jesus said unto him, If thou c believe, G1410
Lk 5:12 if thou wilt, thou c make me clean. G1410
6:42 Either how c thou say to thy brother, G1410
Jn 3: 8 sound thereof, but c not tell whence it G1492
13:36 him, Whither I go, thou c not follow me G1410
Act 21:37 thee? Who said, C thou speak Greek? G1097
Rev 2: 2 and how thou c not bear them which G1410

CAPERNAUM
Mt 4:13 came and dwelt in C, which is upon the G2584
8: 5 And when Jesus was entered into C, G2584
11:23 And thou, C, which art exalted unto G2584
17:24 And when they were come to C, they G2584
Mk 1:21 And they went into C; and straightway G2584
2: 1 And again he entered into C after *some* G2584
9:33 And he came to C: and being in the G2584
Lk 4:23 done in C, do also here in thy country. G2584
31 And came down to C, a city of Galilee, G2584
7: 1 of the people, he entered into C. G2584
10:15 And thou, C, which art exalted to G2584
Jn 2:12 After this he went down to C, he, and G2584
4:46 nobleman, whose son was sick at C. G2584
6:17 the sea toward C. And it was now dark, G2584
24 and came to C, seeking for Jesus. G2584
59 he in the synagogue, as he taught in C. G2584

CAPHTHORIM
1Ch 1:12 (of whom came the Philistines,) and C. H3732

CAPHTOR
Dt 2:23 came forth out of C, destroyed them, H3731
Jer 47: 4 the remnant of the country of C. H3731
Am 9: 7 from C, and the Syrians from Kir? H3731

CAPHTORIM
Gen 10:14 (out of whom came Philistim,) and C. H3732

CAPHTORIMS
Dt 2:23 unto Azzah, the C, which came forth H3732

CAPITAL
See CHAPITER.

CAPPADOCIA
Act 2: 9 in Judaea, and C, in Pontus, and Asia, G2587
1Pt 1: 1 Pontus, Galatia, C, Asia, and Bithynia, G2587

CAPTAIN
Gen 21:22 Phichol the chief c of his host spake H8269
32 Phichol the chief c of his host, and they H8269
26:26 and Phichol the chief c of his army. H8269
37:36 of Pharaoh's, *and* c of the guard. H8269
39: 1 officer of Pharaoh, c of the guard, an H8269
40: 3 in the house of the c of the guard, into H8269
4 And the c of the guard charged Joseph H8269
Gen 41:10 put me in ward in the c of the guard's H8269
12 servant to the c of the guard; and we H8269
Nu 2: 3 *shall be* c of the children of Judah. H5387
5 *shall be* c of the children of Issachar. H5387
7 *shall be* c of the children of Zebulun. H5387
10 armies: and the c of the children of H5387
12 of Simeon: and the c of the children of H5387
14 Then the tribe of Gad: and the c of the H5387
18 their armies: and the c of the sons of H5387
20 and the c of the children of Manasseh H5387
22 Then the tribe of Benjamin: and the c H5387
25 armies: and the c of the children of H5387
27 of Asher: and the c of the children of H5387
29 Then the tribe of Naphtali: and the c of H5387
14: 4 make a c, and let us return into Egypt. H7218
Jos 5:14 And he said, Nay; but *as* c of the host of H8269
15 And the c of the LORD'S host said unto H8269
Jdg 4: 2 in Hazor; the c of whose host *was* H8269
7 Kishon Sisera, the c of Jabin's army, H8269
11: 6 Come, and be our c, that we may fight H7101
11 made him head and c over them: and H7101
1Sa 9:16 shalt anoint him *to be* c over my people H5057
10: 1 thee *to be* c over his inheritance? H5057
12: 9 into the hand of Sisera, c of the host of H8269
13:14 him *to be* c over his people, because H5057
14:50 and the name of the c of his host *was* H8269
17:18 And carry these ten cheeses unto the c H8269
55 unto Abner, the c of the host, Abner, H8269
18:13 and made him his c over a thousand; H8269
22: 2 him; and he became a c over them: and H8269
26: 5 the son of Ner, the c of his host: and H8269
2Sa 2: 8 But Abner the son of Ner, c of Saul's H8269
5: 2 Israel, and thou shalt be a c over Israel. H5057
8 *shall be chief and c.* Wherefore they said,
10:16 and Shobach the c of the host of H8269
18 the c of their host, who died there. H8269
17:25 And Absalom made Amasa c of the H5921
19:13 also, if thou be not c of the host before H8269
23:19 he was their c: howbeit he attained H8269
24: 2 For the king said to Joab the c of the H8269
1Ki 1:19 and Joab the c of the host: but Solomon H8269
2:32 the son of Ner, c of the host of Israel, H8269
32 the son of Jether, c of the host of Judah. H8269
11:15 and Joab the c of the host was gone H8269
21 and that Joab the c of the host was H8269
24 him, and became c over a band, when H8269
16: 9 And his servant Zimri, c of half *his* H8269
16 made Omri, the c of the host, king over H8269
2Ki 1: 9 Then the king sent unto him a c of fifty H8269
10 And Elijah answered and said to the c H8269
11 Again also he sent unto him another c H8269
13 And he sent again a c of the third fifty H8269
13 fifty. And the third c of fifty went up, H8269
4:13 to the king, or to the c of the host? And H8269
5: 1 Now Naaman, c of the host of the king H8269
9: 5 errand to thee, O c. And Jehu said, Unto H8269
5 of all us? And he said, To thee, O c. H8269
25 Then said *Jehu* to Bidkar his c, Take up, H7991
15:25 But Pekah the son of Remaliah, a c of H7991
18:24 away the face of one c of the least of my H6346
20: 5 Turn again, and tell Hezekiah the c of H5057
25: 8 came Nebuzar-adan, c of the guard, a H7227
10 that *were with* the c of the guard, brake H7227
11 the c of the guard carry away. H7227
12 But the c of the guard left of the poor of H7227
15 *in* silver, the c of the guard took away. H7227
18 And the c of the guard took Seraiah the H7227
20 And Nebuzar-adan c of the guard took H7227
1Ch 11: 6 shall be chief and c. So Joab the son of H8269
21 for he was their c: howbeit he attained H8269
42 the Reubenite, a c of the Reubenites, H7218
19:16 river: and Shophach the c of the host of H8269
18 and killed Shophach the c of the host. H8269
27: 5 The third c of the host for the third H8269
7 The fourth c for the fourth month *was*
8 The fifth c for the fifth month *was* H8269
9 The sixth c for the sixth month *was* Ira
10 The seventh c for the seventh month *was*
11 The eighth c for the eighth month *was*
12 The ninth c for the ninth month *was*
13 The tenth c for the tenth month *was*
14 The eleventh c for the eleventh month
15 The twelfth c for the twelfth month *was*
2Ch 13:12 *is* with us for *our* c, and his priests with H7218
17:15 And next to him *was* Jehohanan the c, H8269
Neh 9:17 appointed a c to return to their H7218
Isa 3: 3 The c of fifty, and the honourable man, H8269
36: 9 away the face of one c of the least of my H6346
Jer 37:13 of Benjamin, a c of the ward *was* there, H1167

Jer 39: 9 Then Nebuzar-adan the **c** of the guard H7227
10 But Nebuzar-adan the **c** of the guard H7227
11 the **c** of the guard, saying, H7227
13 So Nebuzar-adan the **c** of the guard H7227
40: 1 Nebuzar-adan the **c** of the guard had H7227
2 And the **c** of the guard took Jeremiah, H7227
5 thee to go. So the **c** of the guard gave H7227
41:10 the **c** of the guard had committed H7227
43: 6 Nebuzar-adan the **c** of the guard had H7227
51:27 appoint a **c** against her; cause the H2951
52:12 Nebuzar-adan, **c** of the guard, *which* H7227
14 that *were* with the **c** of the guard, brake H7227
15 Then Nebuzar-adan the **c** of the guard H7227
16 But Nebuzar-adan the **c** of the guard H7227
19 *in* silver, took the **c** of the guard away. H7227
24 And the **c** of the guard took Seraiah the H7227
26 So Nebuzar-adan the **c** of the guard H7227
30 Nebuzar-adan the **c** of the guard H7227
Dan 2:14 to Arioch the **c** of the king's guard, H7229
15 Arioch the king's **c**, Why *is* the decree *so* H7990
Jn 18:12 Then the band and the **c** and officers of G5506
Act 4: 1 priests, and the **c** of the temple, and the G4755
5:24 Now when the high priest and the **c** of G4755
26 Then went the **c** with the officers, and G4755
21:31 unto the chief **c** of the band, that all G5506
32 they saw the chief **c** and the soldiers, G5506
33 Then the chief **c** came near, and took G5506
37 said unto the chief **c**, May I speak unto G5506
22:24 The chief **c** commanded him to be G5506
26 and told the chief **c**, saying, Take heed G5506
27 Then the chief **c** came, and said unto G5506
28 And the chief **c** answered, With a great G5506
29 him: and the chief **c** also was afraid, G5506
23:10 the chief **c**, fearing lest Paul should G5506
15 signify to the chief **c** that he bring him G5506
17 **c**: for he hath a certain thing to tell him. G5506
18 *him* to the chief **c**, and said, Paul the G5506
19 Then the chief **c** took him by the hand, G5506
22 So the chief **c** *then* let the young man G5506
24: 7 But the chief **c** Lysias came *upon us*, G5506
22 Lysias the chief **c** shall come down, I G5506
28:16 the prisoners to the **c** of the guard: but G4759
Heb 2:10 glory, to make the **c** of their salvation G747

CAPTAINS
Ex 14: 7 of Egypt, and **c** over every one of them. H7991
15: 4 **c** also are drowned in the Red sea. H7991
Nu 31:14 of the host, *with* the **c** over thousands, H8269
14 thousands, and **c** over hundreds, which H8269
48 of the host, the **c** of thousands, and H8269
48 **c** of hundreds, came near unto Moses: H8269
52 the LORD, of the **c** of thousands, and of H8269
52 and of the **c** of hundreds, was sixteen H8269
54 the gold of the **c** of thousands and of H8269
Dt 1:15 heads over you, **c** over thousands, and H8269
15 thousands, and **c** over hundreds, and H8269
15 over hundreds, and **c** over fifties, and H8269
15 over fifties, and **c** over tens, and H8269
20: 9 **c** of the armies to lead the people. H8269
29:10 your God; your **c** of your tribes, your H7218
Jos 10:24 and said unto the **c** of the men of war H7101
1Sa 8:12 And he will appoint him **c** over H8269
12 thousands, and **c** over fifties; and *will* H8269
22: 7 *and* make you all **c** of thousands, and H8269
7 of thousands, and **c** of hundreds; H8269
2Sa 4: 2 had two men *that were* **c** of bands: the H8269
18: 1 with him, and set **c** of thousands and H8269
1 and **c** of hundreds over them. H8269
5 all the **c** charge concerning Absalom. H8269
23: 8 chief among the **c**; the same *was* Adino H7991
24: 4 and against the **c** of the host. And Joab H8269
4 And Joab and the **c** of the host went out H8269
1Ki 1:25 king's sons, and the **c** of the host, and H8269
2: 5 what he did to the two **c** of the hosts of H8269
9:22 his princes, and his **c**, and rulers of his H7991
15:20 Asa, and sent the **c** of the hosts which H8269
20:24 of his place, and put **c** in their rooms: H6346
22:31 his thirty and two **c** that had rule over H8269
32 And it came to pass, when the **c** of the H8269
33 And it came to pass, when the **c** of the H8269
2Ki 1:14 burnt up the two **c** of the former fifties H8269
8:21 about, and the **c** of the chariots: and H8269
9: 5 And when he came, behold, the **c** of the H8269
10:25 the guard and to the **c**, Go in, *and* slay H7991
25 the guard and the **c** cast *them* out, and H7991
11: 4 with the **c** and the guard, and H3746
9 And the **c** over the hundreds did H8269
10 And to the **c** over hundreds did the H8269
15 commanded the **c** of the hundreds, the H8269
2Ki 11:19 hundreds, and the **c**, and the guard, H3746
25:23 And when all the **c** of the armies, they H8269
26 and great, and the **c** of the armies, H8269
1Ch 4:42 Seir, having for their **c** Pelatiah, and H7218
11:11 the chief of the **c**: he lifted up his spear H7991
15 Now three of the thirty **c** went down to H7218
12:14 These *were* of the sons of Gad, **c** of the H7218
18 *was* chief of the **c**, *and he said*, Thine H7991
18 them, and made them **c** of the band. H7218
20 Elihu, and Zilthai, **c** of the thousands H7218
21 men of valour, and were **c** in the host. H8269
28 of his father's house twenty and two **c**. H8269
34 And of Naphtali a thousand **c**, and with H8269
13: 1 And David consulted with the **c** of H8269
15:25 of Israel, and the **c** over thousands, H8269
25: 1 Moreover David and the **c** of the host H8269
26:26 chief fathers, the **c** over thousands and H8269
26 and the **c** of the host, had dedicated. H8269
27: 1 chief fathers and **c** of thousands and H8269
3 all the **c** of the host for the first month. H8269
28: 1 the tribes, and the **c** of the companies H8269
1 king by course, and the **c** over the H8269
1 thousands, and **c** over the hundreds, H8269
29: 6 of Israel, and the **c** of thousands and of H8269
2Ch 1: 2 all Israel, to the **c** of thousands and of H8269
8: 9 and chief of his **c**, and captains of his H7991
9 and **c** of his chariots and horsemen. H8269
11:11 holds, and put **c** in them, and store of H5057
16: 4 king Asa, and sent the **c** of his armies H8269
17:14 Of Judah, the **c** of thousands; Adnah H8269
18:30 commanded the **c** of the chariots that H8269
31 And it came to pass, when the **c** of the H8269
32 For it came to pass, that, when the **c** of H8269
21: 9 him in, and the **c** of the chariots. H8269
23: 1 and took the **c** of hundreds, Azariah H8269
9 delivered to the **c** of hundreds spears, H8269
14 brought out the **c** of hundreds that H8269
20 And he took the **c** of hundreds, and the H8269
25: 5 and made them **c** over thousands, and H8269
5 over thousands, and **c** over hundreds, H8269
26:11 hand of Hananiah, *one* of the king's **c**. H8269
32: 6 And he set **c** of war over the people, H8269
21 the leaders and **c** in the camp of the H8269
33:11 upon them the **c** of the host of the king H8269
14 great height, and put **c** of war in all the H8269
Neh 2: 9 **c** of the army and horsemen with me. H8269
Job 39:25 the thunder of the **c**, and the shouting. H8269
Jer 13:21 taught them *to be* **c**, *and* as chief over H441
40: 7 Now when all the **c** of the forces which H8269
13 and all the **c** of the forces that *were* H8269
41:11 and all the **c** of the forces that *were* H8269
13 and all the **c** of the forces that *were* H8269
16 and all the **c** of the forces that *were* H8269
42: 1 Then all the **c** of the forces, and H8269
8 and all the **c** of the forces which H8269
43: 4 and all the **c** of the forces, and all H8269
5 and all the **c** of the forces, took all H8269
51:23 thee will I break in pieces **c** and rulers. H6346
28 of the Medes, the **c** thereof, and all the H6346
57 her wise *men*, her **c**, and her rulers, and H6346
Ezk 21:22 to appoint **c**, to open the mouth in H3733
23: 6 *Which were* clothed with blue, **c** and H6346
12 *her* neighbours, **c** and rulers clothed H6346
23 young men, **c** and rulers, great lords H6346
Dan 3: 2 and the **c**, the judges, the treasurers, H6347
3 Then the princes, the governors, and **c**, H6347
27 And the princes, governors, and **c**, and H6347
6: 7 and the **c**, have consulted together H6347
Nah 3:17 the locusts, and thy **c** as the great H2951
Mk 6:21 high **c**, and chief *estates* of Galilee; G5506
Lk 22: 4 **c**, how he might betray him unto them. G4755
52 chief priests, and **c** of the temple, and G4755
Act 25:23 with the chief **c**, and principal men of G5506
Rev 6:15 men, and the chief **c**, and the mighty G5506
19:18 kings, and the flesh of **c**, and the flesh of G5506

CAPTIVE
Gen 14:14 his brother was taken **c**, he armed his H7617
34:29 wives took they **c**, and spoiled even all H7617
Ex 12:29 the firstborn of the **c** that *was* in the H7628
Nu 24:22 until Asshur shall carry thee away **c**. H7617
Dt 21:10 hands, and thou hast taken them **c**, H7628
Jdg 5:12 thy captivity **c**, thou son of Abinoam. H7617
1Ki 8:48 led them away **c**, and pray unto thee H7617
50 who carried them **c**, that they may have H7617
2Ki 5: 2 had brought away **c** out of the land of H7617
6:22 thou hast taken **c** with thy sword and H7617
15:29 and carried them **c** to Assyria. H1540
16: 9 *the people of* it **c** to Kir, and slew Rezin. H1540
2Ki 24:16 king of Babylon brought **c** to Babylon. H1473
1Ch 5: 6 **c**: he *was* prince of the Reubenites. H1540
2Ch 6:37 they are carried **c**, and turn and pray H7617
25:12 Judah carry away **c**, and brought them H7617
28: 8 carried away **c** of their brethren two H7617
11 ye have taken **c** of your brethren: for H7617
30: 9 them that lead them **c**, so that they shall H7617
Ps 68:18 hast led captivity **c**: thou hast received H7617
137: 3 For there they that carried us away **c** H7617
Isa 49:21 am desolate, a **c**, and removing to and H1540
24 the mighty, or the lawful **c** delivered? H7628
51:14 The **c** exile hasteneth that he may be H6808
52: 2 of thy neck, O **c** daughter of Zion. H7628
Jer 1: 3 away of Jerusalem **c** in the fifth month. H1540
13:17 the LORD'S flock is carried away **c**. H7617
19 be carried away **c** all of it, it shall be H1540
19 of it, it shall be wholly carried away **c**. H1540
20: 4 he shall carry them **c** into Babylon, and H1540
22:12 him **c**, and shall see this land no more. H1540
24: 1 had carried away **c** Jeconiah the son of H1540
5 are carried away **c** of Judah, whom I H1546
27:20 he carried away **c** Jeconiah the son of H1540
28: 6 away **c**, from Babylon into this place. H1473
29: 1 away **c** from Jerusalem to Babylon; H1473
14 I caused you to be carried away **c**. H1540
39: 9 guard carried away **c** into Babylon the H1540
40: 1 were carried away **c** of Jerusalem and H1546
1 were carried away **c** unto Babylon. H1540
7 were not carried away **c** to Babylon; H1540
41:10 Then Ishmael carried away **c** all the H7617
10 them away **c**, and departed to go H7617
14 had carried away **c** from Mizpah cast H7617
52:15 carried away **c** *certain* of the poor of H1540
27 was carried away **c** out of his own land. H1540
28 carried away **c**: in the seventh year H1540
29 he carried away **c** from Jerusalem eight H1540
30 guard carried away **c** of the Jews seven H1540
Am 1: 6 because they carried away **c** the whole H1540
6: 7 Therefore now shall they go **c** with the H1540
7 the first that go **c**, and the banquet of H1540
7:11 be led away **c** out of their own land. H1540
Oba 11 carried away **c** his forces, and H7617
Nah 2: 7 And Huzzab shall be led away **c**, she H1540
Lk 21:24 shall be led away **c** into all nations: and G163
Eph 4: 8 led captivity **c**, and gave gifts unto men. G162
2Ti 2:26 who are taken **c** by him at his will. G2221
3: 6 houses, and lead **c** silly women laden G162

CAPTIVES
Gen 31:26 daughters, as **c** *taken* with the sword? H7617
Nu 31: 9 the women of Midian **c**, and their little H7617
12 And they brought the **c**, and the prey, H7628
19 and your **c** on the third day, and H7628
Dt 21:11 And seest among the **c** a beautiful H7633
32:42 slain and of the **c**, from the beginning H7633
1Sa 30: 2 And had taken the women **c**, that *were* H7617
3 sons, and their daughters, were taken **c**. H7617
5 And David's two wives were taken **c**, H7617
1Ki 8:46 carry them away **c** unto the land of the H7617
47 they were carried **c**, and repent, and H7617
47 that carried them **c**, saying, We have H7617
2Ki 24:14 valour, *even* ten thousand **c**, and all the H1540
2Ch 6:36 away **c** unto a land far off or near; H7617
38 have carried them **c**, and pray toward H7617
28: 5 multitude of them **c**, and brought *them* H7633
11 and deliver the **c** again, which ye have H7633
13 not bring in the **c** hither: for whereas H7633
14 So the armed men left the **c** and the H7633
15 up, and took the **c**, and with the spoil H7633
17 and smitten Judah, and carried away **c**. H7628
Ps 106:46 pitied of all those that carried them **c**. H7617
Isa 14: 2 shall take them **c**, whose captives they H7617
2 captives, whose **c** they were; and they H7617
20: 4 the Ethiopians **c**, young and old, naked H1546
45:13 he shall let go my **c**, not for price nor H1546
49:25 But thus saith the LORD, Even the **c** of H7628
61: 1 liberty to the **c**, and the opening of H7617
Jer 28: 4 of Judah, with all the **c** of Judah, that H1546
29: 1 were carried away **c**, and to the priests, H1473
4 are carried away **c**, whom I have caused H1473
7 to be carried away **c**, and pray unto the H1540
43: 3 and carry us away **c** into Babylon. H1540
12 carry them away **c**: and he shall array H7617
48:46 are taken **c**, and thy daughters captives. H7628
46 are taken captives, and thy daughters **c**. H7633
50:33 and all that took them **c** held them fast; H7617
Ezk 1: 1 as I *was* among the **c** by the river of H1473
6: 9 shall be carried **c**, because I am broken H7617
16:53 captivity of thy **c** in the midst of them: H7628

Dan 2:25 a man of the c of Judah, that H1123+H1547
11: 8 And shall also carry c into Egypt their H7628
Lk 4:18 deliverance to the c, and recovering of G164

CAPTIVITY
Nu 21:29 into c unto Sihon king of the Amorites. H7622
Dt 21:13 And she shall put the raiment of her c H7628
28:41 not enjoy them; for they shall go into c. H7628
30: 3 thy God will turn thy c, and have H7622
Jdg 5:12 thy c captive, thou son of Abinoam. H7628
18:30 Dan until the day of the c of the land. H1540
2Ki 24:15 he into c from Jerusalem to Babylon. H1473
25:27 year of the c of Jehoiachin king of H1546
1Ch 5:22 they dwelt in their steads until the c. H1473
6:15 And Jehozadak went *into c*, when the
2Ch 6:37 in the land of their c, saying, We have H7628
38 in the land of their c, whither they have H7628
29: 9 and our wives *are* in c for this. H7628
Ezr 1:11 with *them of* the c that were brought H1473
2: 1 went up out of the c, of those which had H7628
3: 8 come out of the c unto Jerusalem; and H7628
4: 1 the children of the c builded the temple H1473
6:16 of the children of the c, kept the H1547
19 And the children of the c kept the H1473
20 all the children of the c, and for their H1473
21 come again out of c, and all such as had H1473
8:35 were come out of the c, offered burnt H7628
9: 7 to the sword, to c, and to a spoil, and to H7628
10: 7 the children of the c, that they should H1473
16 And the children of the c did so. And H1473
Neh 1: 2 left of the c, and concerning Jerusalem. H7628
3 that are left of the c there in the H7628
4: 4 give them for a prey in the land of c: H7633
7: 6 went up out of the c, of those that had H7628
8:17 again out of the c made booths, and sat H7628
Est 2: 6 with the c which had been carried H1473
Job 42:10 And the LORD turned the c of Job, H7622
Ps 14: 7 bringeth back the c of his people, Jacob H7622
53: 6 bringeth back the c of his people, Jacob H7622
68:18 high, thou hast led c captive: thou hast H7628
78:61 And delivered his strength into c, and H7628
85: 1 thou hast brought back the c of Jacob. H7622
126: 1 When the LORD turned again the c of H7622
4 Turn again our c, O LORD, as the H7622
Isa 5:13 Therefore my people are gone into c, H1540
22:17 a mighty c, and will surely cover thee. H2925
46: 2 burden, but themselves are gone into c. H7628
Jer 15: 2 such as *are* for the c, to the captivity. H7628
2 such as *are* for the captivity, to the c. H7628
20: 6 shall go into c: and thou shalt come H7628
22:22 shall go into c: surely then shalt thou H7628
29:14 turn away your c, and I will gather you H7622
16 that are not gone forth with you into c; H1473
20 LORD, all ye of the c, whom I have sent H1473
22 a curse by all the c of Judah which *are* H1546
28 saying, This *c is* long: build ye houses,
31 Send to all them of the c, saying, Thus H1473
30: 3 bring again the c of my people Israel H7622
10 from the land of their c; and Jacob shall H7628
16 them, shall go into c; and they that spoil H7628
18 bring again the c of Jacob's tents, and H7622
31:23 bring again their c; The LORD bless H7622
32:44 cause their c to return, saith the LORD. H7622
33: 7 And I will cause the c of Judah and the H7622
7 of Judah and the c of Israel to return, H7622
11 to return the c of the land, as at the H7622
26 c to return, and have mercy on them. H7622
43:11 such *as are* for c to captivity; and such H7628
11 *as are* for captivity to c; and such *as are* H7628
46:19 thyself to go into c: for Noph shall be H1473
27 from the land of their c; and Jacob shall H7628
48: 7 shall go forth into c *with* his priests H1473
11 hath he gone into c: therefore his taste H1473
47 Yet will I bring again the c of Moab in H7622
49: 3 king shall go into c, *and* his priests and H1473
6 And afterward I will bring again the c H7622
39 again the c of Elam, saith the LORD. H7622
52:31 year of the c of Jehoiachin king of H1546
Lam 1: 3 Judah is gone into c because of H1540
5 are gone into c before the enemy. H7628
18 and my young men are gone into c. H7628
2:14 to turn away thy c; but have seen for H7622
4:22 thee away into c: he will visit thine H1540
Ezk 1: 2 *was* the fifth year of king Jehoiachin's c, H1546
3:11 And go, get thee to them of the c, unto H1473
15 Then I came to them of the c at H1473
11:24 to them of the c. So the vision that I H1473
25 Then I spake unto them of the c all the H1473
12: 4 their sight, as they that go forth into c. H1473
Ezk 12: 7 by day, as stuff for c, and in the even I H1473
11 them: they shall remove *and* go into c. H7628
16:53 When I shall bring again their c, the H7622
53 their captivity, the c of Sodom and her H7622
53 and the c of Samaria and her H7622
53 c of thy captives in the midst of them: H7622
25: 3 house of Judah, when they went into c; H1473
29:14 And I will bring again the c of Egypt, H7622
30:17 sword: and these *cities* shall go into c. H7628
18 her, and her daughters shall go into c. H7628
33:21 the twelfth year of our c, in the tenth H1546
39:23 of Israel went into c for their iniquity: H1540
25 I bring again the c of Jacob, and have H7622
28 to be led into c among the heathen: H1540
40: 1 In the five and twentieth year of our c, H1546
Dan 5:13 of the children of the c of Judah, whom H1547
6:13 of the children of the c of Judah, H1547
11:33 by flame, by c, and by spoil, *many* days. H7628
Hos 6:11 when I returned the c of my people. H7622
Joel 3: 1 again the c of Judah and Jerusalem, H7622
Am 1: 5 go into c unto Kir, saith the LORD. H1540
6 whole c, to deliver *them* up to Edom: H1546
9 delivered up the whole c to Edom, and H1546
15 And their king shall go into c, he and H1473
5: 5 c, and Beth-el shall come to nought. H1540
27 Therefore will I cause you to go into c H1540
7:17 shall surely go into c forth of his land. H1540
9: 4 And though they go into c before their H7628
14 And I will bring again the c of my H7622
Oba 20 And the c of this host of the children of H1546
20 and the c of Jerusalem, which H1546
Mic 1:16 for they are gone into c from thee. H1540
Nah 3:10 she went into c: her young children H7628
Hab 1: 9 and they shall gather the c as the sand. H7628
Zep 2: 7 shall visit them, and turn away their c. H7622
3:20 c before your eyes, saith the LORD. H7622
Zec 6:10 Take of *them of* the c, *even* of Heldai, of H1473
14: 2 shall go forth into c, and the residue of H1473
Ro 7:23 and bringing me into c to the law of sin G163
2Co 10: 5 and bringing into c every thought to the G163
Eph 4: 8 led c captive, and gave gifts unto men. G161
Rev 13:10 He that leadeth into c shall go into G161
10 shall go into c: he that killeth with the G161

CAR See BETH-CAR.

CARBUNCLE
Ex 28:17 and a c: *this shall be* the first row. H1304
39:10 a topaz, and a c: this *was* the first row. H1304
Ezk 28:13 the emerald, and the c, and gold: the H1304

CARBUNCLES
Isa 54:12 and thy gates of c, and all thy H68+H688

CARCAS
Est 1:10 Zethar, and C, the seven chamberlains H3752

CARCASE
Lev 5: 2 whether *it be* a c of an unclean beast, H5038
2 beast, or a c of unclean cattle, or H5038
2 cattle, or the c of unclean creeping H5038
11: 8 not eat, and their c shall ye not touch; H5038
24 toucheth the c of them shall be unclean H5038
25 And whosoever beareth *ought* of the c H5038
27 their c shall be unclean until the even. H5038
28 And he that beareth the c of them shall H5038
35 *any part* of their c falleth shall be H5038
36 toucheth their c shall be unclean. H5038
37 And if *any part* of their c fall upon any H5038
38 *any part* of their c fall thereon, it *shall* H5038
39 he that toucheth the c thereof shall be H5038
40 And he that eateth of the c of it shall H5038
40 that beareth the c of it shall wash his H5038
Dt 14: 8 eat of their flesh, nor touch their dead c. H5038
28:26 And thy c shall be meat unto all fowls H5038
Jos 8:29 should take his c down from the tree, H5038
Jdg 14: 8 aside to see the c of the lion: and, H4658
8 of bees and honey in the c of the lion. H1472
9 taken the honey out of the c of the lion. H1472
1Ki 13:22 no water; thy c shall not come unto H5038
24 and slew him: and his c was cast in the H5038
24 stood by it, the lion also stood by the c. H5038
25 by, and saw the c cast in the way, and H5038
25 standing by the c: and they came and H5038
28 And he went and found his c cast in the H5038
28 standing by the c: the lion had not eaten H5038
28 had not eaten the c, nor torn the ass. H5038
29 And the prophet took up the c of the H5038
30 And he laid his c in his own grave; and H5038
2Ki 9:37 And the c of Jezebel shall be as dung H5038
Isa 14:19 of the pit; as a c trodden under feet. H6297
Mt 24:28 For wheresoever the c is, there will the G4430

CARCASES
Gen 15:11 upon the c, Abram drove them away. H6297
Lev 11:11 ye shall have their c in abomination. H5038
26 *The* c of every beast which divideth the
26:30 and cast your c upon the carcases of H6297
30 carcases upon the c of your idols, and H6297
Nu 14:29 Your c shall fall in this wilderness; and H6297
32 But *as for* you, your c, they shall fall in H6297
33 your c be wasted in the wilderness. H6297
1Sa 17:46 and I will give the c of the host of the H6297
Isa 5:25 tremble, and their c *were* torn in the H5038
34: 3 up out of their c, and the mountains H6297
66:24 and look upon the c of the men that H6297
Jer 7:33 And the c of this people shall be meat H5038
9:22 LORD, Even the c of men shall fall as H5038
16: 4 by famine; and their c shall be meat for H5038
18 with the c of their detestable and H5038
19: 7 lives: and their c will I give to be meat H5038
Ezk 6: 5 And I will lay the dead c of the children H6297
43: 7 the c of their kings in their high places. H6297
9 and the c of their kings, far from H6297
Nah 3: 3 a great number of c; and *there is* none H6297
Heb 3:17 sinned, whose c fell in the wilderness? G2966

CARCASS See CARCASE.

CARCHEMISH
2Ch 35:20 up to fight against C by Euphrates: and H3751
Isa 10: 9 *Is* not Calno as C? *is* not Hamath as H3751
Jer 46: 2 the river Euphrates in C, which H3751

CARE
1Sa 10: 2 father hath left the c of the asses, and H1697
2Sa 18: 3 they will not c for us; neither if H7760+H3820
3 die, will they c for us: but now H7760+H3820
2Ki 4:13 for us with all this c; what *is* to be done H2731
Jer 49:31 that dwelleth without c, saith the LORD, H983
Ezk 4:16 weight, and with c; and they shall drink H1674
Mt 13:22 the word; and the c of this world, and G3308
Lk 10:34 him to an inn, and took c of him. G1959
35 said unto him, Take c of him; and G1959
40 dost thou not c that my sister hath G3199
1Co 7:21 Art thou called *being* a servant? c not G3199
9: 9 out the corn. Doth God take c for oxen? G3199
12:25 have the same c one for another. G3309
2Co 7:12 but that our c for you in the sight G4710
8:16 c into the heart of Titus for you. G4710
11:28 me daily, the c of all the churches. G3308
Php 2:20 who will naturally c for your state. G3309
4:10 at the last your c of me hath flourished G5426
1Ti 3: 5 shall he take c of the church of God?) G1959
1Pt 5: 7 Casting all your c upon him; for he G3308

CAREAH
2Ki 25:23 the son of C, and Seraiah the son H7143

CARED
Ps 142: 4 refuge failed me; no man c for my soul. H1875
Jn 12: 6 This he said, not that he c for the poor; G3199
Act 18:17 And Gallio c for none of those things. G3199

CAREFUL
2Ki 4:13 thou hast been c for us with all this H2729
Jer 17: 8 green; and shall not be c in the year of H1672
Dan 3:16 *are* not c to answer thee in this matter. H2818
Lk 10:41 art c and troubled about many things: G3309
Php 4: 6 Be c for nothing; but in every thing by G3309
10 were also c, but ye lacked opportunity. G5426
Tit 3: 8 in God might be c to maintain good G5431

CAREFULLY
Dt 15: 5 Only if thou c hearken unto the voice of H8085
Mic 1:12 For the inhabitant of Maroth waited c H2342
Php 2:28 I sent him therefore the more c, that, G4708
Heb 12:17 though he sought it c with tears. G1567

CAREFULNESS
Ezk 12:18 thy water with trembling and with c; H1674
19 eat their bread with c, and drink their H1674
1Co 7:32 But I would have you without c. He that G275
2Co 7:11 a godly sort, what c it wrought in you, G4710

CARELESS
Jdg 18: 7 how they dwelt c, after the manner of H983
Isa 32: 9 ye c daughters; give ear unto my speech. H982

Isa 32:10 shall ye be troubled, ye **c** women: for the H982
11 be troubled, ye **c** ones: strip you, and H982
Ezk 30: 9 in ships to make the **c** Ethiopians afraid, H983

CARELESSLY
Isa 47: 8 that dwellest **c**, that sayest in thine heart, H983
Ezk 39: 6 them that dwell **c** in the isles: and they H983
Zep 2:15 This *is* the rejoicing city that dwelt **c**, that H983

CARES
Mk 4:19 And the **c** of this world, and the G3308
Lk 8:14 and are choked with **c** and riches and G3308
21:34 drunkenness, and **c** of this life, and *so* G3308

CAREST
Mt 22:16 in truth, neither **c** thou for any *man*: G3199
Mk 4:38 him, Master, **c** thou not that we perish? G3199
12:14 thou art true, and **c** for no man: for G3199

CARETH
Dt 11:12 A land which the LORD thy God **c** for: H1875
Jn 10:13 is an hireling, and **c** not for the sheep. G3199
1Co 7:32 that is unmarried **c** for the things that G3309
33 But he that is married **c** for the things G3309
34 woman **c** for the things of the G3309
34 that is married **c** for the things of the G3309
1Pt 5: 7 Casting all your care upon him; for he **c** G3199

CARING
1Sa 9: 5 *c* for the asses, and take thought for us.

CARMEL
Jos 12:22 one; the king of Jokneam of **C**, one; H3760
15:55 Maon, **C**, and Ziph, and Juttah, H3760
19:26 to **C** westward, and to Shihor-libnath; H3760
1Sa 15:12 Saul came to **C**, and, behold, he set H3760
25: 2 *were* in **C**; and the man *was* very H3760
2 and he was shearing his sheep in **C**. H3760
5 Get you up to **C**, and go to Nabal, and H3760
7 unto them, all the while they were in **C**. H3760
40 come to Abigail to **C**, they spake unto H3760
1Ki 18:19 Israel unto mount **C**, and the prophets H3760
20 the prophets together unto mount **C**. H3760
42 up to the top of **C**; and he cast himself H3760
2Ki 2:25 And he went from thence to mount **C**, H3760
4:25 of God to mount **C**. And it came to pass, H3760
19:23 his borders, *and into* the forest of his **C**. H3760
2Ch 26:10 and in **C**: for he loved husbandry. H3760
Song 7: 5 Thine head upon thee *is* like **C**, and the H3760
Isa 33: 9 Bashan and **C** shake off *their fruits*. H3760
35: 2 it, the excellency of **C** and Sharon, they H3760
37:24 of his border, *and* the forest of his **C**. H3760
Jer 46:18 and as **C** by the sea, *so* shall he come. H3760
50:19 he shall feed on **C** and Bashan, and his H3760
Am 1: 2 mourn, and the top of **C** shall wither. H3760
9: 3 in the top of **C**, I will search and take H3760
Mic 7:14 wood, in the midst of **C**: let them feed *in* H3760
Nah 1: 4 languisheth, and **C**, and the flower of H3760

CARMELITE
1Sa 30: 5 and Abigail the wife of Nabal the **C**. H3761
2Sa 2: 2 and Abigail Nabal's wife the **C**. H3761
3: 3 the wife of Nabal the **C**; and the third, H3761
23:35 Hezrai the **C**, Paarai the Arbite, H3761
1Ch 11:37 Hezro the **C**, Naarai the son of Ezbai, H3761

CARMELITESS
1Sa 27: 3 and Abigail the **C**, Nabal's wife. H3762
1Ch 3: 1 the second Daniel, of Abigail the **C**: H3762

CARMI
Gen 46: 9 and Phallu, and Hezron, and **C**. H3756
Ex 6:14 and **C**: these *be* the families of Reuben. H3756
Nu 26: 6 of **C**, the family of the Carmites. H3756
Jos 7: 1 Achan, the son of **C**, the son of Zabdi, H3756
18 Achan, the son of **C**, the son of Zabdi, H3756
1Ch 2: 7 And the sons of **C**; Achar, the troubler H3756
4: 1 Hezron, and **C**, and Hur, and Shobal. H3756
5: 3 Hanoch, and Pallu, Hezron, and **C**. H3756

CARMITES
Nu 26: 6 of Carmi, the family of the **C**. H3757

CARNAL
Ro 7:14 is spiritual: but I am **c**, sold under sin. G4559
8: 7 Because the **c** mind *is* enmity against G4561
15:27 also to minister unto them in **c** things. G4559
1Co 3: 1 as unto **c**, *even* as unto babes in Christ. G4559
3 For ye are yet **c**: for whereas *there is* G4559
1Co 3: 3 are ye not **c**, and walk as men? G4559
4 another, I *am* of Apollos; are ye not **c**? G4559
9:11 thing if we shall reap your **c** things? G4559
2Co 10: 4 warfare *are* not **c**, but mighty through G4559
Heb 7:16 Who is made, not after the law of a **c** G4559
9:10 washings, and **c** ordinances, imposed G4561

CARNALLY
Lev 18:20 Moreover thou shalt not lie **c** H7903+H2233
19:20 And whosoever lieth **c** with a H7902+H2233
Nu 5:13 And a man lie with her **c**, and it H7902+H2233
Ro 8: 6 For to be **c** minded *is* death; but to be G4561

CARPENTER
Isa 41: 7 So the **c** encouraged the goldsmith, *and* H2796
44:13 The **c** stretcheth out *his* rule; H2796+H6086
Mk 6: 3 Is not this the **c**, the son of Mary, the G5045

CARPENTERS
2Sa 5:11 trees, and **c**, and masons: and H2796+H6086
2Ki 12:11 it out to the **c** and builders, H2796+H6086
22: 6 Unto **c**, and builders, and masons, and H2796
1Ch 14: 1 and **c**, to build him an house. H2796+H6086
2Ch 24:12 hired masons and **c** to repair the house H2796
Ezr 3: 7 and to the **c**; and meat, and drink, H2796
Jer 24: 1 of Judah, with the **c** and smiths, from H2796
29: 2 and the **c**, and the smiths, were H2796
Zec 1:20 And the LORD shewed me four **c**. H2796

CARPENTER'S
Mt 13:55 Is not this the **c** son? is not his mother G5045

CARPUS
2Ti 4:13 The cloak that I left at Troas with **C**, G2591

CARRIAGE
Jdg 18:21 and the cattle and the **c** before them. H3520
1Sa 17:22 And David left his **c** in the hand of the H3627
22 of the keeper of the **c**, and ran into the H3627

CARRIAGES
Isa 10:28 at Michmash he hath laid up his **c**: H3627
46: 1 the cattle: your **c** *were* heavy loaden; H5385
Act 21:15 And after those days we took up our **c**, G643

CARRIED
Gen 31:18 And he **c** away all his cattle, and all his H5090
26 to me, and **c** away my daughters, H5090
46: 5 the sons of Israel **c** Jacob their father, H5375
50:13 For his sons **c** him into the land of H5375
Lev 10: 5 So they went near, and **c** them in their H5375
Jos 4: 8 of Israel, and **c** them over with them H5674
Jdg 16: 3 his shoulders, and **c** them up to the top H5927
1Sa 5: 8 the God of Israel be **c** about unto Gath. H5437
8 Gath. And they **c** the ark of the God of H5437
9 And it was *so*, that, after they had **c** it H5437
30: 2 **c** *them* away, and went on their way. H5090
18 the Amalekites had **c** away: and David H3947
2Sa 6:10 of David: but David **c** it aside into the H5186
15:29 Zadok therefore and Abiathar **c** the ark H7725
1Ki 8:47 land whither they were **c** captives, and
47 the land of them that **c** them captives,
50 before them who **c** them captive, that
17:19 of her bosom, and **c** him up into a loft, H5927
21:13 king. Then they **c** him forth out of the H3318
2Ki 7: 8 eat and drink, and **c** thence silver, and H5375
8 and **c** thence *also*, and went and hid *it*. H5375
9:28 And his servants **c** him in a chariot to H7392
15:29 Naphtali, and **c** them captive to Assyria.
16: 9 and took it, and **c** *the people of* it captive
17: 6 took Samaria, and **c** Israel away into H1540
11 whom the LORD **c** away before them; H1540
23 So was Israel **c** away out of their own H1540
28 whom they had **c** away from Samaria H1540
33 whom they **c** away from thence. H1540
20:17 unto this day, shall be **c** into Babylon: H5375
23: 4 and **c** the ashes of them unto Beth-el. H5375
30 And his servants **c** him in a chariot H7392
24:13 And he **c** out thence all the treasures of H3318
14 And he **c** away all Jerusalem, and all H1540
15 And he **c** away Jehoiachin to Babylon, H1540
15 of the land, *those* **c** he into captivity H1980
25: 7 fetters of brass, and **c** him to Babylon. H935
13 and **c** the brass of them to Babylon. H5375
21 So Judah was **c** away out of their land. H1540
1Ch 5: 6 king of Assyria **c** away *captive*: he *was* H1540
26 of Assyria, and he **c** them away, even H1540
6:15 when the LORD **c** away Judah and H1540
9: 1 Judah, *who* were **c** away to Babylon for H1540
1Ch 13: 7 And they **c** the ark of God in a new cart H7392
13 the city of David, but **c** it aside into the H5186
2Ch 6:37 whither they are **c** captive, and turn and
38 whither they have **c** them captives, and
12: 9 he took all: he **c** away also the shields H3947
14:13 host; and they **c** away very much spoil. H5375
15 tents of cattle, and **c** away sheep and H7617
16: 6 all Judah; and they **c** away the stones of H5375
21:17 and brake into it, and **c** away all the H7617
24:11 and took it, and **c** it to his place again. H7725
28: 5 they smote him, and **c** away a great H7616
8 And the children of Israel **c** away H7616
15 them, and **c** all the feeble of them H5095
17 and smitten Judah, and **c** away captives.
33:11 him with fetters, and **c** him to Babylon. H3212
34:16 And Shaphan **c** the book to the king, and H935
36: 4 his brother, and **c** him to Egypt. H935
7 Nebuchadnezzar also **c** of the vessels of H935
20 from the sword **c** he away to Babylon; H1473
Ezr 2: 1 those which had been **c** away, whom H1540
1 of Babylon had **c** away unto Babylon, H1540
5:12 and **c** the people away into Babylon. H1541
8:35 that had been **c** away, which were H1473
9: 4 those that had been **c** away; and I sat H1473
10: 6 of them that had been **c** away. H1473
8 of those that had been **c** away. H1473
Neh 7: 6 those that had been **c** away, whom H1473
6 king of Babylon had **c** away, and came H1540
Est 2: 6 Who had been **c** away from Jerusalem H1540
6 which had been **c** away with Jeconiah H1540
6 the king of Babylon had **c** away. H1540
Job 1:17 the camels, and have **c** them away, yea, H3947
5:13 counsel of the froward is **c** headlong. H4116
10:19 been **c** from the womb to the grave. H2986
Ps 46: 2 be **c** into the midst of the sea; H4131
106:46 pitied of all those that **c** them captives.
137: 3 For there they that **c** us away captive
Isa 39: 6 this day, shall be **c** to Babylon: nothing H5375
46: 3 the belly, which are **c** from the womb: H5375
49:22 shall be **c** upon *their* shoulders. H5375
53: 4 Surely he hath borne our griefs, and **c** H5445
63: 9 them, and **c** them all the days of old. H5375
Jer 13:17 the LORD'S flock is **c** away captive.
19 Judah shall be **c** away captive all of it,
19 all of it, it shall be wholly **c** away captive.
24: 1 of Babylon had **c** away captive Jeconiah
5 them that are **c** away captive of Judah,
27:20 took not, when he **c** away captive
22 They shall be **c** to Babylon, and there H935
28: 3 from this place, and **c** them to Babylon: H935
6 and all that is **c** away captive, from
29: 1 elders which were **c** away captives, and
1 had **c** away captive from Jerusalem
4 unto all that are **c** away captives, whom
4 **c** away from Jerusalem unto Babylon; H1540
7 caused you to be **c** away captives, and
14 I caused you to be **c** away captive.
39: 9 of the guard **c** away captive into Babylon
40: 1 all that were **c** away captive of Jerusalem
1 were **c** away captive unto Babylon.
7 that were not **c** away captive to Babylon;
41:10 Then Ishmael **c** away captive all the
10 son of Nethaniah **c** them away captive,
14 So all the people that Ishmael had **c**
52: 9 Then they took the king, and **c** him up H5927
11 him in chains, and **c** him to Babylon, H935
15 of the guard **c** away captive *certain*
17 and **c** all the brass of them to Babylon. H5375
27 was **c** away captive out of his own land.
28 Nebuchadrezzar **c** away captive: in the
29 he **c** away captive from Jerusalem
30 of the guard **c** away captive of the Jews
Ezk 6: 9 they shall be **c** captives, because I am
17: 4 his young twigs, and **c** it into a land of H935
37: 1 was upon me, and **c** me out in the H3318
Dan 1: 2 house of God: which he **c** into the land of H935
2:35 and the wind **c** them away, that no H5376
Hos 10: 6 It shall be also **c** unto Assyria *for* a H2986
12: 1 the Assyrians, and oil is **c** into Egypt. H2986
Joel 3: 5 my gold, and have **c** into your temples H935
Am 1: 6 because they **c** away captive the whole
Oba 11 day that the strangers **c** away captive his
Nah 3:10 Yet *was* she **c** away, she went into H1473
Mt 1:11 the time they were **c** away to Babylon: G3350
Mk 15: 1 **c** *him* away, and delivered *him* to Pilate. G667
Lk 7:12 was a dead man **c** out, the only son of G1580
16:22 died, and was **c** by the angels into G667
24:51 parted from them, and **c** up into heaven. G399
Act 3: 2 womb was **c**, whom they laid daily G941

Act 5: 6 up, and c *him* out, and buried *him*. G1627
7:16 And were c over into Sychem, and laid G3346
8: 2 And devout men c Stephen *to his* G4792
21:34 commanded him to be c into the castle. G71
1Co 12: 2 Ye know that ye were Gentiles, c away G520
Gal 2:13 was c away with their dissimulation. G4879
Eph 4:14 to and fro, and c about with every wind G4064
Heb 13: 9 Be not c about with divers and strange G4064
2Pt 2:17 clouds that are c with a tempest; to G1643
Jude 12 *are* without water, c about of winds; G4064
Rev 12:15 cause her to be c away of the flood. G4216
17: 3 So he c me away in the spirit into the G667
21:10 And he c me away in the spirit to a great G667

CARRIEST
Ps 90: 5 Thou c them away as with a flood; they H2229

CARRIETH
Job 21:18 and as chaff that the storm c away. H1589
27:21 The east wind c him away, and he H5375
Rev 17: 7 of the beast that c her, which hath the G941

CARRY
Gen 37:25 and myrrh, going to c *it* down to Egypt. H3381
42:19 ye, c corn for the famine of your houses: H935
43:11 in your vessels, and c down the man a H3381
12 of your sacks, c *it* again in your hand; H7725
44: 1 as much as they can c, and put every H5375
45:27 Joseph had sent to c him, the spirit of H5375
46: 5 which Pharaoh had sent to c him. H5375
47:30 and thou shalt c me out of Egypt, and H5375
50:25 and ye shall c up my bones from hence. H5927
Ex 12:46 thou shalt not c forth ought of the flesh H3318
13:19 c up my bones away hence with you. H5927
14:11 thus with us, to c us forth out of Egypt? H3318
33:15 go not *with me*, c us not up hence. H5927
Lev 4:12 Even the whole bullock shall he c forth H3318
21 And he shall c forth the bullock without H3318
6:11 other garments, and c forth the ashes H3318
10: 4 them, Come near, c your brethren from H5375
14:45 and he shall c *them* forth out of the H3318
16:27 holy *place*, shall *one* c forth without the H3318
Nu 11:12 say unto me, C them in thy bosom, H5375
24:22 until Asshur shall c thee away captive.
Dt 14:24 art not able to c it; *or* if the place be H5375
28:38 Thou shalt c much seed out into the H3318
Jos 4: 3 and ye shall c them over with you, H5674
1Sa 17:18 And c these ten cheeses unto the captain H935
20:40 said unto him, Go, c *them* to the city. H935
2Sa 15:25 And the king said unto Zadok, C back H7725
19:18 And there went over a ferry boat to c H5674
1Ki 8:46 so that they c them away captives
18:12 of the LORD shall c thee whither I H5375
21:10 and the king. And *then* c him out, and H3318
22:26 Micaiah, and c him back unto Amon H7725
34 c me out of the host; for I am wounded. H3318
2Ki 4:19 he said to a lad, C him to his mother. H5375
9: 2 and c him to an inner chamber; H935
17:27 saying, C thither one of the priests H1980
18:11 And the king of Assyria did c away H1540
25:11 the captain of the guard c away. H1540
1Ch 10: 9 round about, to c tidings unto their H1319
15: 2 Then David said, None ought to c the H5375
2 LORD chosen to c the ark of God, and H5375
23:26 they shall no *more* c the tabernacle, H5375
2Ch 2:16 and thou shalt c it up to Jerusalem. H5927
6:36 enemies, and they c them away captives
18:25 ye Micaiah, and c him back to Amon H7725
33 c me out of the host; for I am wounded. H3318
20:25 than they could c away: and they were H4853
25:12 children of Judah c away captive, and
29: 5 your fathers, and c forth the filthiness H3318
16 c *it* out abroad into the brook Kidron. H3318
36: 6 him in fetters, to c him to Babylon. H3212
Ezr 5:15 Take these vessels, go, c them into the H5182
7:15 And to c the silver and gold, which the H2987
Job 15:12 Why doth thine heart c thee away? and H3947
Ps 49:17 For when he dieth he shall c nothing H3947
Ecc 5:15 which he may c away in his hand. H3212
10:20 of the air shall c the voice, and that H3212
Isa 5:29 c *it* away safe, and none shall deliver *it*. H6403
15: 7 they c away to the brook of the willows. H5375
22:17 Behold, the LORD will c thee away with H2904
23: 7 own feet shall c her afar off to sojourn. H2986
30: 6 serpent, they will c their riches upon H5375
40:11 with his arm, and c *them* in his bosom, H5375
41:16 and the wind shall c them away, and H5375
46: 4 to hoar hairs will I c *you*: I have made, H5445
4 bear; even I will c, and will deliver *you*. H5445
Isa 46: 7 the shoulder, they c him, and set him H5445
57:13 but the wind shall c them all away; H5375
Jer 17:22 Neither c forth a burden out of your H3318
20: 4 and he shall c them captive into
5 and take them, and c them to Babylon. H935
39: 7 him with chains, to c him to Babylon. H935
14 that he should c him home: so he dwelt H3318
43: 3 and c us away captives into Babylon.
12 burn them, and c them away captives:
Lam 4:22 Zion; he will no more c thee away into
Ezk 12: 5 wall in their sight, and c out thereby. H3318
6 *thy* shoulders, *and* c *it* forth in the H3318
12 the wall to c out thereby: he shall H3318
22: 9 In thee are men that c tales to shed H7400
38:13 to take a prey? to c away silver and H5375
Dan 11: 8 And shall also c captives into Egypt their H935
Mk 6:55 and began to c about in beds those G4064
11:16 should c *any* vessel through the temple. G1308
Lk 10: 4 C neither purse, nor scrip, nor shoes: G941
Jn 5:10 day: it is not lawful for thee to c *thy* bed. G142
21:18 and c *thee* whither thou wouldest not. G5342
Act 5: 9 *are* at the door, and shall c thee out. G1627
7:43 and I will c you away beyond Babylon. G3351
1Ti 6: 7 *and it is* certain we can c nothing out. G1627

CARRYING
1Sa 10: 3 God to Beth-el, one c three kids, and H5375
3 kids, and another c three loaves of H5375
3 bread, and another c a bottle of wine: H5375
Ps 78: 9 *being* armed, *and* c bows, turned back H7411
Jer 1: 3 of Judah, unto the c away of Jerusalem H1540
Mt 1:17 David until the c away into Babylon G3350
17 and from the c away into Babylon G3350
Act 5:10 c *her* forth, buried *her* by her husband. G1627

CARSHENA
Est 1:14 And the next unto him *was* C, Shethar, H3771

CART
1Sa 6: 7 Now therefore make a new c, and take H5699
7 and tie the kine to the c, and bring their H5699
8 lay it upon the c; and put the jewels of H5699
10 the c, and shut up their calves at home: H5699
11 LORD upon the c, and the coffer with H5699
14 And the c came into the field of Joshua, H5699
14 the wood of the c, and offered the kine H5699
2Sa 6: 3 God upon a new c, and brought it out of H5699
3 the sons of Abinadab, drave the new c. H5699
1Ch 13: 7 of God in a new c out of the house of H5699
7 and Uzza and Ahio drave the c. H5699
Isa 5:18 vanity, and sin as it were with a c rope: H5699
28:27 neither is a c wheel turned about H5699
28 his c, nor bruise it *with* his horsemen. H5699
Am 2:13 Behold, I am pressed under you, as a c H5699

CARVED
Jdg 18:18 and fetched the c image, the ephod, H6459
1Ki 6:18 the house within *was* c with knops and H4734
29 And he c all the walls of the house H7049
29 house round about with c figures of H6603
32 olive tree; and he c upon them carvings H7049
35 And he c *thereon* cherubims and palm H7049
35 *them* with gold fitted upon the c work. H2707
2Ch 33: 7 And he set a c image, the idol which he H6459
22 unto all the c images which Manasseh H6456
34: 3 the c images, and the molten images. H6456
4 the groves, and the c images, and the H6456
Ps 74: 6 But now they break down the c work H6603
Prv 7:16 with c *works*, with fine linen of Egypt. H2405

CARVING
Ex 31: 5 to set *them*, and in c of timber, to work H2799
35:33 to set *them*, and in c of wood, to make H2799

CARVINGS
1Ki 6:32 carved upon them c of cherubims and H4734

CASE
Ex 5:19 they *were* in evil c, after it was said, Ye
Dt 19: 4 And this *is* the c of the slayer, which H1697
22: 1 c bring them again unto thy brother. H7725
24:13 In any c thou shalt deliver him the H7725
Ps 144:15 Happy *is that* people, that is in such a c: H3602
Mt 5:20 no c enter into the kingdom of heaven. G3364
19:10 His disciples say unto him, If the c of the G156
Jn 5: 6 a long time *in that* c, he saith unto him,

CASEMENT
Prv 7: 6 of my house I looked through my c, H822

CASES
1Co 7:15 such *c*: but God hath called us to peace.

CASIPHIA
Ezr 8:17 the chief at the place C, and I told them H3703
17 at the place C, that they should bring H3703

CASLUHIM
Gen 10:14 And Pathrusim, and C, (out of whom H3695
1Ch 1:12 And Pathrusim, and C, (of whom came H3695

CASSIA
Ex 30:24 And of c five hundred *shekels*, after the H6916
Ps 45: 8 myrrh, and aloes, *and* c, out of the ivory H7102
Ezk 27:19 c, and calamus, were in thy market. H6916

CAST
Gen 21:10 Wherefore she said unto Abraham, C H1644
15 she c the child under one of the shrubs. H7993
31:38 she goats have not c their young, and H7921
51 which I have c betwixt me and thee; H3384
37:20 us slay him, and c him into some pit, H7993
22 no blood, *but* c him into this pit that H7993
24 And they took him, and c him into a H7993
39: 7 that his master's wife c her eyes upon H5375
Ex 1:22 is born ye shall c into the river, and H7993
4: 3 And he said, C it on the ground. And he H7993
3 ground. And he c it on the ground, and H7993
25 of her son, and c *it* at his feet, and said, H5060
7: 9 Take thy rod, and c *it* before Pharaoh, H7993
10 and Aaron c down his rod before H7993
12 For they c down every man his rod, H7993
10:19 the locusts, and c them into the Red H8628
15: 4 and his host hath he c into the sea: his H3384
25 when he had c into the waters, the H7993
22:31 in the field; ye shall c it to the dogs. H7993
23:26 There shall nothing c their young, nor H7921
25:12 And thou shalt c four rings of gold for H3332
26:37 shalt c five sockets of brass for them. H3332
32:19 waxed hot, and he c the tables out of H7993
24 gave *it* me: then I c it into the fire, and H7993
34:24 For I will c out the nations before thee, H3423
36:36 and he c for them four sockets of silver. H3332
37: 3 And he c for it four rings of gold, *to be* H3332
13 And he c for it four rings of gold, and H3332
38: 5 And he c four rings for the four ends of H3332
27 of silver were c the sockets of the H3332
Lev 1:16 his feathers, and c it beside the altar on H7993
14:40 plague *is*, and they shall c them into an H7993
16: 8 And Aaron shall c lots upon the two H5414
18:24 are defiled which I c out before you: H7971
20:23 the nation, which I c out before you: for H7971
26:30 your images, and c your carcases upon H5414
44 their enemies, I will not c them away, H3988
Nu 19: 6 and scarlet, and c *it* into the midst of H7993
35:22 enmity, or have c upon him any thing H7993
23 *him* not, and c *it* upon him, that he H5307
Dt 6:19 To c out all thine enemies from before H1920
7: 1 it, and hath c out many nations before H5394
9: 4 thy God hath c them out from before H1920
17 And I took the two tables, and c them H7993
21 as dust: and I c the dust thereof into H7993
28:40 the oil; for thine olive shall c *his fruit*. H5394
29:28 indignation, and c them into another H7993
Jos 8:29 from the tree, and c it at the entering of H7993
10:11 that the LORD c down great stones H7993
27 off the trees, and c them into the cave H7993
13:12 these did Moses smite, and c them out. H3423
18: 6 to me, that I may c lots for you here H3384
8 that I may here c lots for you before the H7993
10 And Joshua c lots for them in Shiloh H7993
Jdg 6:28 altar of Baal was c down, and the grove H5422
30 because he hath c down the altar of H5422
31 because *one* hath c down his altar. H5422
8:25 garment, and did c therein every man H7993
9:53 And a certain woman c a piece of a H7993
15:17 speaking, that he c away the jawbone H7993
1Sa 14:42 And Saul said, C *lots* between me and H5307
18:11 And Saul c the javelin; for he said, I H2904
20:33 And Saul c a javelin at him to smite H2904
2Sa 1:21 mighty is vilely c away, the shield of H1602
11:21 did not a woman c a piece of a H7993
16: 6 And he c stones at David, and at all the H5619
13 and threw stones at him, and c dust. H6080
18:17 And they took Absalom, and c him into H7993
20:12 into the field, and c a cloth upon him, H7993
15 and they c up a bank against the H8210
22 son of Bichri, and c *it* out to Joab. And H7993
1Ki 7:15 For he c two pillars of brass, of H6696

1Ki 7:24 *were* c in two rows, when it was cast. H3332
24 *were* cast in two rows, when it was c. H3333
46 In the plain of Jordan did the king c H3332
9: 7 my name, will I c out of my sight; and H7971
13:24 his carcase was c in the way, and the H7993
25 saw the carcase c in the way, and the H7993
28 And he went and found his carcase c in H7993
14: 9 anger, and hast c me behind thy back: H7993
24 c out before the children of Israel. H3423
18:42 of Carmel; and he c himself down upon H1457
19:19 by him, and c his mantle upon him. H7993
21:26 c out before the children of Israel. H3423
2Ki 2:16 taken him up, and c him upon some H7993
21 of the waters, and c the salt in there, H7993
3:25 good piece of land c every man his H7993
4:41 But he said, Then bring meal. And he c H7993
6: 6 c *it* in thither; and the iron did swim. H7993
7:15 the Syrians had c away in their haste. H7993
9:25 Take up, *and* c him in the portion of H7993
26 therefore take *and* c him into the plat H7993
10:25 and the captains c *them* out, and went H7993
13:21 *of men;* and they c the man into the H7993
23 c he them from his presence as yet. H7993
16: 3 c out from before the children of Israel. H3423
17: 8 whom the LORD c out from before the H3423
20 until he had c them out of his sight. H7993
19:18 And have c their gods into the fire: for H5414
32 it with shield, nor c a bank against it. H8210
21: 2 c out before the children of Israel. H3423
23: 6 to powder, and c the powder thereof H7993
12 from thence, and c the dust of them H7993
27 Israel, and will c off this city Jerusalem H3988
24:20 Judah, until he had c them out from his H7993
1Ch 24:31 These likewise c lots over against their H5307
25: 8 And they c lots, ward against *ward*, as H5307
26:13 And they c lots, as well the small as the H5307
14 c lots; and his lot came out northward. H5307
28: 9 forsake him, he will c thee off for ever. H2186
2Ch 4: 3 rows of oxen *were* c, when it was cast. H3332
3 rows of oxen *were* cast, when it was c. H4166
17 In the plain of Jordan did the king c H3332
7:20 my name, will I c out of my sight, and H7993
11:14 and his sons had c them off from H2186
13: 9 Have ye not c out the priests of the H5080
20:11 reward us, to come to c us out of thy H1644
24:10 brought in, and c into the chest, until H7993
25: 8 God hath power to help, and to c down. H3782
12 of the rock, and c them down from the H7993
26:14 and bows, and slings *to* c stones.
28: 3 had c out before the children of Israel. H3423
29:19 Ahaz in his reign did c away in his H2186
30:14 and c *them* into the brook Kidron. H7993
33: 2 had c out before the children of Israel. H3423
15 Jerusalem, and c *them* out of the city. H7993
Neh 1: 9 though there were of you c out unto the H5080
6:16 they were much c down in their own H5307
9:26 against thee, and c thy law behind their H7993
10:34 And we c the lots among the priests, H5307
11: 1 of the people also c lots, to bring one of H5307
13: 8 And it grieved me sore: therefore I c H7993
Est 3: 7 Ahasuerus, they c Pur, that *is*, the lot, H5307
9:24 them, and had c Pur, that *is*, the lot, H5307
Job 8: 4 c them away for their transgression; H7971
20 Behold, God will not c away a perfect H3988
15:33 and shall c off his flower as the olive. H7993
18: 7 and his own counsel shall c him down. H7993
8 For he is c into a net by his own feet, H7971
20:15 again: God shall c them out of his belly. H3423
23 belly, *God* shall c the fury of his wrath H7971
22:29 When *men* are c down, then thou shalt H8213
27:22 For *God* shall c upon him, and not H7993
29:24 of my countenance they c not down. H5307
30:19 He hath c me into the mire, and I am H3384
39: 3 young ones, they c out their sorrows. H7971
40:11 C abroad the rage of thy wrath: and H6327
41: 9 *one* be c down even at the sight of him? H2904
Ps 2: 3 and c away their cords from us. H7993
5:10 their own counsels; c them out in the H5080
17:13 Arise, O LORD, disappoint him, c him H3766
18:42 did c them out as the dirt in the streets. H7324
22:10 I was c upon thee from the womb: thou H7993
18 them, and c lots upon my vesture. H5307
36:12 c down, and shall not be able to rise. H1760
37:14 bent their bow, to c down the poor and H5307
24 Though he fall, he shall not be utterly c H2904
42: 5 Why art thou c down, O my soul? and H7817
6 O my God, my soul is c down within H7817
11 Why art thou c down, O my soul? and H7817
43: 2 why dost thou c me off? why go I H2186

Ps 43: 5 Why art thou c down, O my soul? and H7817
44: 2 didst afflict the people, and c them out. H7971
9 But thou hast c off, and put us to H2186
23 O Lord? arise, c *us* not off for ever. H2186
51:11 C me not away from thy presence; and H7993
55: 3 wicked: for they c iniquity upon me, H4131
22 C thy burden upon the LORD, and he H7993
56: 7 *thine* anger c down the people, O God. H3381
60: 1 O God, thou hast c us off, thou hast H2186
8 over Edom will I c out my shoe: H7993
10 *Wilt* not thou, O God, *which* hadst c us H2186
62: 4 They only consult to c *him* down from H5080
71: 9 C me not off in the time of old age; H7993
74: 1 O God, why hast thou c *us* off for ever? H2186
7 They have c fire into thy sanctuary, H7971
76: 6 and horse are c into a dead sleep. H7290
77: 7 Will the Lord c off for ever? and will he H2186
78:49 He c upon them the fierceness of his H7971
55 He c out the heathen also before them, H1644
80: 8 hast c out the heathen, and planted it. H1644
89:38 But thou hast c off and abhorred, thou H2186
44 and c his throne down to the ground. H4048
94:14 For the LORD will not c off his people, H5203
102:10 thou hast lifted me up, and c me down. H7993
108: 9 over Edom will I c out my shoe; over H7993
11 *Wilt* not *thou*, O God, *who* hast c us off? H2186
140:10 them: let them be c into the fire; into H5307
144: 6 C forth lightning, and scatter them: H1299
Prv 1:14 C in thy lot among us; let us all have H5307
7:26 For she hath c down many wounded: H5307
16:33 The lot is c into the lap; but the whole H2904
22:10 C out the scorner, and contention shall H1644
Ecc 3: 5 A time to c away stones, and a time to H7993
6 a time to keep, and a time to c away; H7993
11: 1 C thy bread upon the waters: for thou H7971
Isa 2:20 In that day a man shall c his idols of H7993
5:24 because they have c away the law of H3988
6:13 them, when they c *their leaves: so* the H7995
14:19 But thou art c out of thy grave like an H7993
16: 2 a wandering bird c out of the nest, *so* H7971
19: 8 and all they that c angle into the H7993
25: 7 of the covering c over all people, and H3874
26:19 and the earth shall c out the dead. H5307
28: 2 c down to the earth with the hand. H3240
25 doth he not c abroad the fitches, and H6327
25 the cummin, and c in the principal H7760
30:22 of gold: thou shalt c them away as a H2219
31: 7 For in that day every man shall c away H3988
34: 3 Their slain also shall be c out, and their H7993
17 And he hath c the lot for them, and his H5307
37:19 And have c their gods into the fire: for H5414
33 it with shields, nor c a bank against it. H8210
38:17 hast c all my sins behind thy back. H7993
41: 9 have chosen thee, and not c thee away. H3988
57:14 And shall say, C ye up, cast ye up, H5549
14 And shall say, Cast ye up, c ye up, H1644
20 rest, whose waters c up mire and dirt. H4788
58: 7 the poor that are c out to thy house? H5549
62:10 the way of the people; c up, cast up the H5077
10 the people; cast up, c up the highway; H8210
66: 5 that hated you, that c you out for my H3782
Jer 6: 6 ye down trees, and c a mount against H8210
15 they shall be c down, saith the LORD. H3782
7:15 And I will c you out of my sight, as I H7993
15 of my sight, as I have c out all your H7993
29 Cut off thine hair, *O Jerusalem*, and c *it* H7993
8:12 they shall be c down, saith the LORD. H3782
9:19 because our dwellings have c *us* out. H7933
14:16 prophesy shall be c out in the streets of H7933
15: 1 this people: c *them* out of my sight, H7971
16:13 Therefore will I c you out of this land H2904
18:15 to walk in paths, *in* a way not c up; H5549
22: 7 choice cedars, and c *them* into the fire. H5307
19 c forth beyond the gates of Jerusalem. H7993
26 And I will c thee out, and thy mother H2904
28 wherefore are they c out, he and his H7993
28 are c into a land which they know not? H7993
23:39 fathers, *and* c *you* out of my presence: H7993
26:23 the sword, and c his dead body into the H7993
28:16 Behold, I will c thee from off the face H7971
31:37 I will also c off all the seed of Israel H3988
33:24 he hath even c them off? thus they H3988
26 Then will I c away the seed of Jacob, H3988
36:23 the penknife, and c *it* into the fire that H7993
30 dead body shall be c out in the day to H7993
38: 6 Then took they Jeremiah, and c him H7993
9 whom they have c into the dungeon; H7993
11 took thence old c clouts and old rotten H5499
12 Put now *these* old c clouts and rotten H5499

Jer 41: 7 slew them, *and* c *them* into the midst
9 Now the pit wherein Ishmael had c all H7993
14 from Mizpah c about and returned, H5437
50:26 her storehouses: c her up as heaps, and H5549
51:34 with my delicates, he hath c me out. H1740
63 it, and c it into the midst of Euphrates: H7993
52: 3 Judah, till he had c them out from his H7993
Lam 2: 1 in his anger, *and* c down from heaven H7993
7 The Lord hath c off his altar, he hath H2186
10 silence: they have c up dust upon their H5927
3:31 For the Lord will not c off for ever: H2186
53 in the dungeon, and c a stone upon me. H3034
Ezk 4: 2 a fort against it, and c a mount against H8210
5: 4 Then take of them again, and c them H7993
6: 4 be broken: and I will c down your slain H5307
7:19 They shall c their silver in the streets, H7993
11:16 Although I have c them far off among H7368
15: 4 Behold, it is c into the fire for fuel; the H5414
16: 5 but thou wast c out in the open field, H7993
18:31 C away from you all your H7993
19:12 in fury, she was c down to the ground, H7993
20: 7 Then said I unto them, C ye away every H7993
8 they did not every man c away the H7993
21:22 gates, to c a mount, *and* to build a fort. H8210
23:35 hast forgotten me, and c me behind thy H7993
26: 8 against thee, and c a mount against H8210
27:30 bitterly, and shall c up dust upon their H5927
28:16 therefore I will c thee as profane out H2490
17 brightness: I will c thee to the ground, H7993
31:16 of his fall, when I c him down to hell H3381
32: 4 the land, I will c thee forth upon the H2904
18 of Egypt, and c them down, *even* her, H3381
36: 5 despiteful minds, to c it out for a prey. H4054
43:24 the priests shall c salt upon them, and H7993
Dan 3: 6 the same hour be c into the midst of a H7412
11 *that* he should be c into the midst of a H7412
15 not, ye shall be c the same hour into H7412
20 c *them* into the burning fiery furnace. H7412
21 and were c into the midst of the H7412
24 Did not we c three men bound into H7412
6: 7 king, he shall be c into the den of lions. H7412
12 O king, shall be c into the den of lions? H7412
16 Daniel, and c *him* into the den of H7412
24 Daniel, and they c *them* into the den of H7412
7: 9 I beheld till the thrones were c down, H7412
8: 7 before him, but he c him down to the H7993
10 of heaven; and it c down *some* of the H5307
11 the place of his sanctuary was c down. H7993
12 and it c down the truth to the H7993
11:12 lifted up; and he shall c down *many* ten H5307
15 shall come, and c up a mount, and take H8210
Hos 8: 3 Israel hath c off *the thing that is* good: H2186
5 Thy calf, O Samaria, hath c *thee* off; H2186
9:17 My God will c them away, because they H3988
14: 5 lily, and c forth his roots as Lebanon. H5221
Joel 1: 7 made it clean bare, and c *it* away; the H7993
3: 3 And they have c lots for my people; and H3032
Am 1:11 sword, and did c off all pity, and his H7843
4: 3 c *them* into the palace, saith the LORD. H7993
8: 3 they shall c *them* forth with silence. H7993
8 and it shall be c out and drowned, as H16444
Oba 11 entered into his gates, and c lots upon H3032
Jna 1: 5 unto his god, and c forth the wares that H2904
7 Come, and let us c lots, that we may H5307
7 they c lots, and the lot fell upon Jonah. H5307
12 Take me up, and c me forth into the H2904
15 So they took up Jonah, and c him forth H2904
2: 3 For thou hadst c me into the deep, in H7993
4 Then I said, I am c out of thy sight; yet H1644
Mic 2: 5 none that shall c a cord by lot in the H7993
9 The women of my people have ye c out H1644
4: 7 and her that was c far off a strong H1972
7:19 and thou wilt c all their sins into the H7993
Nah 3: 6 And I will c abominable filth upon H7993
10 the streets: and they c lots for her H3032
Zep 3:15 he hath c out thine enemy: the H6437
Zec 1:21 to fray them, to c out the horns of the H3034
5: 8 And he c it into the midst of the H7993
8 the ephah; and he c the weight of lead H7993
9: 4 Behold, the Lord will c her out, and he H3423
10: 6 as though I had not c them off: for I *am* H2186
11:13 And the LORD said unto me, C it unto H7993
13 of silver, and c them to the potter in H7993
Mal 3:11 shall your vine c her fruit before the H7921
Mt 3:10 fruit is hewn down, and c into the fire. *G906*
4: 6 be the Son of God, c thyself down: for it *G906*
12 c into prison, he departed into Galilee; *G3860*
5:13 for nothing, but to be c out, and to be *G906*
25 to the officer, and thou be c into prison. *G906*

Mt 5:29 pluck it out, and c *it* from thee: for it is G906
29 thy whole body should be c into hell. G906
30 thee, cut it off, and c *it* from thee: for it is G906
30 thy whole body should be c into hell. G906
6:30 and to morrow is c into the oven, *shall* G906
7: 5 Thou hypocrite, first c out the beam G1544
5 c out the mote out of thy brother's eye. G1544
6 the dogs, neither c ye your pearls before G906
19 fruit is hewn down, and c into the fire. G906
22 in thy name have c out devils? and in G1544
8:12 the kingdom shall be c out into outer G1544
16 devils: and he c out the spirits with G1544
31 saying, If thou c us out, suffer us to go G1544
9:33 And when the devil was c out, the G1544
10: 1 unclean spirits, to c them out, and to G1544
8 raise the dead, c out devils: freely ye G1544
12:24 This *fellow* doth not c out devils, but by G1544
26 And if Satan c out Satan, he is divided G1544
27 And if I by Beelzebub c out devils, by G1544
27 do your children c *them* out? therefore G1544
28 But if I c out devils by the Spirit of God, G1544
13:42 And shall c them into a furnace of fire: G906
47 unto a net, that was c into the sea, and G906
48 good into vessels, but c the bad away. G906
50 And shall c them into the furnace of fire: G906
15:17 the belly, and is c out into the draught? G1544
26 the children's bread, and to c *it* to dogs. G906
30 and many others, and c them down at G4496
17:19 and said, Why could not we c him out? G1544
27 to the sea, and c an hook, and take up G906
18: 8 cut them off, and c *them* from thee: it is G906
8 or two feet to be c into everlasting fire. G906
9 thee, pluck it out, and c *it* from thee: it is G906
9 having two eyes to be c into hell fire. G906
30 And he would not: but went and c him G906
21:12 of God, and c out all them that sold G1544
21 be thou c into the sea; it shall be done. G906
39 And they caught him, and c *him* out of G1544
22:13 take him away, and c *him* into outer G1544
25:30 And c ye the unprofitable servant into G1544
27: 5 And he c down the pieces of silver in G4496
35 and upon my vesture did they c lots. G906
44 with him, c the same in his teeth. G3679
Mk 1:34 diseases, and c out many devils; and G1544
39 throughout all Galilee, and c out devils. G1544
3:15 to heal sicknesses, and to c out devils: G1544
23 parables, How can Satan c out Satan? G1544
4:26 if a man should c seed into the ground; G906
6:13 And they c out many devils, and G1544
7:26 c forth the devil out of her daughter. G1544
27 bread, and to c *it* unto the dogs. G906
9:18 should c him out; and they could not. G1544
22 And ofttimes it hath c him into the fire, G906
28 privately, Why could not we c him out? G1544
42 his neck, and he were c into the sea. G906
45 two feet to be c into hell, into the fire G906
47 having two eyes to be c into hell fire: G906
11: 7 colt to Jesus, and c their garments on G1911
15 and began to c out them that sold and G1544
23 and be thou c into the sea; and shall G906
12: 4 and at him they c stones, and wounded G3086
8 *him*, and c *him* out of the vineyard. G1544
41 beheld how the people c money into the G906
41 and many that were rich c in much. G906
43 poor widow hath c more in, than all they G906
43 all they which have c into the treasury: G906
44 For all *they* did c in of their abundance; G906
44 c in all that she had, *even* all her living. G906
14:51 a linen cloth c about *his* naked *body*; G4016
16: 9 out of whom he had c seven devils. G1544
17 name shall they c out devils; they shall G1544
Lk 1:29 at his saying, and c in her mind what G1260
3: 9 fruit is hewn down, and c into the fire. G906
4: 9 Son of God, c thyself down from hence: G906
29 that they might c him down headlong. G2630
6:22 reproach *you*, and c out your name as G1544
42 Thou hypocrite, c out first the beam G1544
9:25 world, and lose himself, or be c away? G2210
40 And I besought thy disciples to c him G1544
11:18 that I c out devils through Beelzebub. G1544
19 And if I by Beelzebub c out devils, by G1544
19 do your sons c *them* out? therefore G1544
20 But if I with the finger of God c out G1544
12: 5 hath power to c into hell; yea, I say G1685
28 and to morrow is c into the oven; how G906
58 officer, and the officer c thee into prison. G906
13:19 a man took, and c into his garden; and G906
32 that fox, Behold, I c out devils, and I do G1544
14:35 dunghill; *but* men c it out. He that hath G906

Lk 17: 2 his neck, and he c into the sea, than G4496
19:35 him to Jesus: and they c their garments G1977
43 enemies shall c a trench about thee, G4016
45 and began to c out them that sold G1544
20:12 they wounded him also, and c *him* out. G1544
15 So they c him out of the vineyard, and G1544
21: 3 poor widow hath c in more than they all: G906
4 For all these have of their abundance c G906
4 hath c in all the living that she had. G906
22:41 c, and kneeled down, and prayed, G1000
23:19 city, and for murder, was c into prison.) G906
25 and murder was c into prison, whom G906
34 And they parted his raiment, and c lots. G906
Jn 3:24 For John was not yet c into prison. G906
6:37 cometh to me I will in no wise c out. G1544
8: 7 among you, let him first c a stone at her. G906
59 Then took they up stones to c at him: but G906
9:34 dost thou teach us? And they c him out. G1544
35 Jesus heard that they had c him out; G1544
12:31 shall the prince of this world be c out. G1544
15: 6 If a man abide not in me, he is c forth as G906
6 gather them, and c *them* into the fire, G906
19:24 us not rend it, but c lots for it, whose it G2975
24 my vesture they did c lots. These things G906
21: 6 And he said unto them, C the net on the G906
6 ye shall find. They c therefore, and now G906
7 naked,) and did c himself into the sea. G906
Act 7:19 so that they c out their young G4160+G1570
21 And when he was c out, Pharaoh's G1620
58 And c *him* out of the city, and stoned G1544
12: 8 he saith unto him, C thy garment about G4016
16:23 upon them, they c *them* into prison, G906
37 Romans, and have c *us* into prison; and G906
22:23 And as they cried out, and c off *their* G4496
27:19 And the third *day* we c out with our G4496
26 Howbeit we must be c upon a certain G1601
29 upon rocks, they c four anchors out of G4496
30 have c anchors out of the foreship, G1614
38 ship, and c out the wheat into the sea. G1544
43 could swim should c *themselves* first G641
Ro 11: 1 I say then, Hath God c away his people? G683
2 God hath not c away his people which he G683
13:12 hand: let us therefore c off the works of G656
1Co 7:35 not that I may c a snare upon you, but G1911
2Co 4: 9 Persecuted, but not forsaken; c down, G2598
7: 6 those that are c down, comforted us G5011
Gal 4:30 the scripture? C out the bondwoman G1544
1Ti 5:12 Having damnation, because they have c G114
Heb 10:35 C not away therefore your confidence, G577
2Pt 2: 4 that sinned, but c *them* down to hell, G5020
Rev 2:10 the devil shall c *some* of you into prison, G906
14 who taught Balac to c a stumblingblock G906
22 Behold, I will c her into a bed, and them G906
4:10 c their crowns before the throne, saying, G906
8: 5 of the altar, and c *it* into the earth: and G906
7 and they were c upon the earth: and G906
8 with fire was c into the sea: and the G906
12: 4 of heaven, and did c them to the earth: G906
9 And the great dragon was c out, that old G906
9 world: he was c out into the earth, and G906
9 and his angels were c out with him. G906
10 of our brethren is c down, which G2598
13 And when the dragon saw that he was c G906
15 And the serpent c out of his mouth water G906
16 which the dragon c out of his mouth. G906
14:19 vine of the earth, and c *it* into the great G906
18:19 And they c dust on their heads, and G906
21 millstone, and c *it* into the sea, saying, G906
19:20 These both were c alive into a lake of fire G906
20: 3 And c him into the bottomless pit, and G906
10 And the devil that deceived them was c G906
14 And death and hell were c into the lake G906
15 the book of life was c into the lake of fire. G906

CASTAWAY

1Co 9:27 to others, I myself should be a c. G96

CASTEDST

Ps 73:18 thou c them down into destruction. H5307

CASTEST

Job 15: 4 Yea, thou c off fear, and restrainest H6565
Ps 50:17 Seeing thou hatest instruction, and c H7993
88:14 LORD, why c thou off my soul? *why* H2186

CASTETH

Job 21:10 their cow calveth, and c not her calf. H7921
Ps 147: 6 The LORD lifteth up the meek: he c the H8213
17 He c forth his ice like morsels: who can H7993

Prv 10: 3 he c away the substance of the wicked. H1920
19:15 Slothfulness c into a deep sleep; and an H5307
21:22 of the mighty, and c down the strength H3381
26:18 As a mad *man* who c firebrands, H3384
Isa 40:19 it over with gold, and c silver chains. H6884
Jer 6: 7 As a fountain c out her waters, so she H6979
7 out her waters, so she c out her H6979
Mt 9:34 But the Pharisees said, He c out devils G1544
Mk 3:22 the prince of the devils c he out devils. G1544
Lk 11:15 But some of them said, He c out devils G1544
1Jn 4:18 but perfect love c out fear: because fear G906
3Jn 10 would, and c *them* out of the church. G1544
Rev 6:13 even as a fig tree c her untimely figs, G906

CASTING

2Sa 8: 2 them with a line, c them down to the H7901
1Ki 7:37 had one c, one measure, *and* one size. H4165
Ezr 10: 1 weeping and c himself down before H5307
Job 6:21 For now ye are nothing; ye see *my* c H2866
Ps 74: 7 they have defiled *by c down* the dwelling
89:39 profaned his crown *by c it* to the ground.
Ezk 17:17 him in the war, by c up mounts, and H8210
Mic 6:14 satisfied; and thy c down *shall be* in the H3445
Mt 4:18 c a net into the sea: for they were fishers. G906
27:35 his garments, c lots: that it might be G906
Mk 1:16 c a net into the sea: for they were fishers. G906
9:38 we saw one c out devils in thy name, G1544
10:50 And he, c away his garment, rose, and G577
15:24 his garments, c lots upon them, what G906
Lk 9:49 we saw one c out devils in thy name; G1544
11:14 And he was c out a devil, and it was G1544
21: 1 rich men c their gifts into the treasury. G906
2 And he saw also a certain poor widow c G906
Ro 11:15 For if the c away of them *be* the G580
2Co 10: 5 C down imaginations, and every high G2507
1Pt 5: 7 C all your care upon him; for he careth G1977

CASTLE

1Ch 11: 5 the c of Zion, which *is* the city of David. H4686
7 And David dwelt in the c; therefore they H4679
Prv 18:19 *their* contentions *are* like the bars of a c. H759
Act 21:34 him to be carried into the c. G3925
37 And as Paul was to be led into the c, he G3925
22:24 be brought into the c, and bade that he G3925
23:10 them, and to bring *him* into the c. G3925
16 and entered into the c, and told Paul. G3925
32 to go with him, and returned to the c: G3925

CASTLES

Gen 25:16 and by their c; twelve princes according H2918
Nu 31:10 dwelt, and all their goodly c, with fire. H2918
1Ch 6:54 throughout their c in their coasts, of H2918
27:25 c, *was* Jehonathan the son of Uzziah: H4026
2Ch 17:12 he built in Judah c, and cities of store. H1003
27: 4 and in the forests he built c and towers. H1003

CASTOR

Act 28:11 the isle, whose sign was C and Pollux. G1359

CATCH

Ex 22: 6 If fire break out, and c in thorns, so H4672
Jdg 21:21 the vineyards, and c you every man his H2414
1Ki 20:33 and did hastily c *it*: and they said, Thy H2480
2Ki 7:12 shall c them alive, and get into the city. H8610
Ps 10: 9 he lieth in wait to c the poor: he doth H2414
9 the poor: he doth c the poor, when he H2414
35: 8 net that he hath hid c himself: into that H3920
109:11 Let the extortioner c all that he hath; H5367
Jer 5:26 snares; they set a trap, they c men. H3920
Ezk 19: 3 learned to c the prey; it devoured men. H2963
6 to c the prey, *and* devoured men. H2963
Hab 1:15 the angle, they c them in their net, and H1641
Mk 12:13 of the Herodians, to c him in *his* words. G64
Lk 5:10 not; from henceforth thou shalt c men. G2221
11:54 Laying wait for him, and seeking to c G2340

CATCHETH

Lev 17:13 hunteth and c any beast or fowl that H6718
Mt 13:19 wicked *one*, and c away that which was G726
Jn 10:12 wolf c them, and scattereth the sheep. G726

CATERPILLER

1Ki 8:37 *or* if there be c; if their enemy besiege H2625
Ps 78:46 He gave also their increase unto the c, H2625
Isa 33: 4 gathering of the c: as the running to and H2625
Joel 1: 4 cankerworm hath left hath the c eaten. H2625
2:25 and the c, and the palmerworm, H2625

CATERPILLERS
2Ch 6:28 locusts, or **c**; if their enemies besiege H2625
Ps 105:34 He spake, and the locusts came, and **c**, H3218
Jer 51:14 with men, as with **c**; and they shall lift H3218
27 the horses to come up as the rough **c**. H3218

CATTLE
Gen 1:24 after his kind, **c**, and creeping thing, H929
25 after his kind, and **c** after their kind, and H929
26 air, and over the **c**, and over all the earth, H929
2:20 And Adam gave names to all **c**, and to H929
3:14 cursed above all **c**, and above every beast H929
4:20 as dwell in tents, and *of such as have* **c**. H4735
6:20 Of fowls after their kind, and of **c** after H929
7:14 kind, and all the **c** after their kind, and H929
21 of fowl, and of **c**, and of beast, and of H929
23 both man, and **c**, and the creeping H929
8: 1 thing, and all the **c** that *was* with him in H929
17 of fowl, and of **c**, and of every creeping H929
9:10 of the fowl, of the **c**, and of every beast of H929
13: 2 And Abram *was* very rich in **c**, in silver, H4735
7 of Abram's **c** and the herdmen of H4735
7 herdmen of Lot's **c**: and the Canaanite H4735
29: 7 *is it* time that the **c** should be gathered H4735
30:29 thee, and how thy **c** was with me. H4735
32 and spotted **c**, and all the brown cattle H7716
32 and all the brown **c** among the sheep, H7716
39 **c** ringstraked, speckled, and spotted. H6629
40 and put them not unto Laban's **c**. H6629
41 the stronger **c** did conceive, that Jacob H6629
41 the eyes of the **c** in the gutters, that H6629
42 But when the **c** were feeble, he put H6629
43 and had much **c**, and maidservants, H6629
31: 8 wages; then all the **c** bare speckled: and H6629
8 hire; then bare all the **c** ringstraked. H6629
9 Thus God hath taken away the **c** of H4735
10 at the time that the **c** conceived, that I H6629
10 leaped upon the **c** *were* ringstraked, H6629
12 which leap upon the **c** *are* ringstraked, H6629
18 And he carried away all his **c**, and all H4735
18 he had gotten, the **c** of his getting, H4735
41 and six years for thy **c**: and thou hast H6629
43 and *these* **c** *are* my cattle, and all H6629
43 cattle *are* my **c**, and all that thou seest H6629
33:14 according as the **c** that goeth before me H4399
17 booths for his **c**: therefore the name H4735
34: 5 sons were with his **c** in the field: and H4735
23 *Shall* not their **c** and their substance H4735
36: 6 his house, and his **c**, and all his beasts, H4735
7 could not bear them because of their **c**. H4735
46: 6 And they took their **c**, and their goods, H4735
32 trade hath been to feed **c**; and they have H4735
34 hath been about **c** from our youth even H4735
47: 6 them, then make them rulers over my **c**. H4735
16 And Joseph said, Give your **c**; and I will H4735
16 I will give you for your **c**, if money fail. H4735
17 And they brought their **c** unto Joseph: H4735
17 flocks, and for the **c** of the herds, and H4735
17 with bread for all their **c** for that year. H4735
18 hath our herds of **c**; there is not ought left H929
Ex 9: 3 the LORD is upon thy **c** which *is* in the H4735
4 sever between the **c** of Israel and the H4735
4 of Israel and the **c** of Egypt: and there H4735
6 and all the **c** of Egypt died: but of H4735
6 **c** of the children of Israel died not one. H4735
7 was not one of the **c** of the Israelites H4735
19 Send therefore now, *and* gather thy **c**, H4735
20 servants and his **c** flee into the houses: H4735
21 left his servants and his **c** in the field. H4735
10:26 Our **c** also shall go with us; there shall H4735
12:29 in the dungeon; and all the firstborn of **c**. H929
38 flocks, and herds, *even* very much **c**. H4735
17: 3 and our children and our **c** with thirst? H4735
20:10 nor thy **c**, nor thy stranger that H929
34:19 thy **c**, *whether* ox or sheep, *that is male*. H4735
Lev 1: 2 the **c**, *even* of the herd, and of the flock. H929
5: 2 a carcase of unclean **c**, or the carcase of H929
19:19 shalt not let thy **c** gender with a diverse H929
25: 7 And for thy **c**, and for the beast that *are* H929
26:22 and destroy your **c**, and make you few in H929
Nu 3:41 of Israel; and the **c** of the Levites instead H929
41 among the **c** of the children of Israel. H929
45 of Israel, and the **c** of the Levites instead H929
45 instead of their **c**; and the Levites shall H929
20: 4 that we and our **c** should die there? H1165
19 and if I and my **c** drink of thy water, H4735
31: 9 **c**, and all their flocks, and all their goods. H929
32: 1 great multitude of **c**: and when they saw H4735
1 that, behold, the place *was* a place for **c**; H4735
Nu 32: 4 land for **c**, and thy servants have cattle: H4735
4 land for cattle, and thy servants have **c**: H4735
16 for our **c**, and cities for our little ones: H4735
26 **c**, shall be there in the cities of Gilead: H929
35: 3 shall be for their **c**, and for their goods, H929
Dt 2:35 Only the **c** we took for a prey unto H929
3: 7 But all the **c**, and the spoil of the cities, H929
19 ones, and your **c**, (*for* I know that ye H4735
19 that ye have much **c**,) shall abide in your H4735
5:14 ass, nor any of thy **c**, nor thy stranger H929
7:14 barren among you, or among your **c**. H929
11:15 thy **c**, that thou mayest eat and be full. H929
13:15 the **c** thereof, with the edge of the sword. H929
20:14 little ones, and the **c**, and all that is in the H929
28: 4 and the fruit of thy **c**, the increase of thy H929
11 in the fruit of thy **c**, and in the fruit of thy H929
51 And he shall eat the fruit of thy **c**, and the H929
30: 9 in the fruit of thy **c**, and in the fruit of thy H929
Jos 1:14 Your wives, your little ones, and your **c**, H4735
8: 2 thereof, and the **c** thereof, shall ye take H929
27 Only the **c** and the spoil of that city H929
11:14 And all the spoil of these cities, and the **c**, H929
14: 4 for their **c** and for their substance. H4735
21: 2 in, with the suburbs thereof for our **c**. H929
22: 8 with very much **c**, with silver, and with H4735
Jdg 6: 5 For they came up with their **c** and their H4735
18:21 and the **c** and the carriage before them. H4735
1Sa 23: 5 away their **c**, and smote them with H4735
30:20 *other* **c**, and said, This *is* David's spoil. H4735
1Ki 1: 9 and oxen and fat **c** by the stone of H4806
19 And he hath slain oxen and fat **c** and H4806
25 hath slain oxen and fat **c** and sheep in H4806
2Ki 3: 9 host, and for the **c** that followed them. H929
17 both ye, and your **c**, and your beasts. H4735
1Ch 5: 9 **c** were multiplied in the land of Gilead. H4735
21 And they took away their **c**; of their H4735
7:21 they came down to take away their **c**. H4735
2Ch 14:15 They smote also the tents of **c**, and H4735
26:10 for he had much **c**, both in the low H4735
35: 8 *small* **c**, and three hundred oxen.
9 *small* **c**, and five hundred oxen.
Neh 9:37 and over our **c**, at their pleasure, and H929
10:36 sons, and of our **c**, as *it is* written in the H929
Job 36:33 it, the **c** also concerning the vapour. H4735
Ps 50:10 *is* mine, *and* the **c** upon a thousand hills. H929
78:48 He gave up their **c** also to the hail, and H1165
104:14 He causeth the grass to grow for the **c**, H929
107:38 and suffereth not their **c** to decrease. H929
148:10 Beasts, and all **c**; creeping things, and H929
Ecc 2: 7 of great and small **c** above all that were H6629
Isa 7:25 of oxen, and for the treading of lesser **c**. H7716
30:23 day shall thy **c** feed in large pastures. H4735
43:23 Thou hast not brought me the small **c** H7716
46: 1 and upon the **c**: your carriages *were* H929
Jer 9:10 the voice of the **c**; both the fowl of the H4735
49:32 multitude of their **c** a spoil: and I will H4735
Ezk 34:17 I judge between **c** and cattle, between H7716
17 **c**, between the rams and the he goats. H7716
20 the fat **c** and between the lean cattle. H7716
20 the fat cattle and between the lean **c**. H7716
22 and I will judge between **c** and cattle. H7716
22 and I will judge between cattle and **c**. H7716
38:12 which have gotten **c** and goods, that H4735
13 away **c** and goods, to take a great spoil? H4735
Joel 1:18 How do the beasts groan! the herds of **c** H1241
Jna 4:11 and their left hand; and *also* much **c**? H929
Hag 1:11 **c**, and upon all the labour of the hands. H929
Zec 2: 4 for the multitude of men and **c** therein: H929
13: 5 taught me to keep **c** from my youth. H7069
Lk 17: 7 plowing or feeding **c**, will say unto him G4165
Jn 4:12 himself, and his children, and his **c**? G2353

CAUGHT
Gen 22:13 behind *him* a ram **c** in a thicket by his H270
39:12 And she **c** him by his garment, saying, H8610
Ex 4: 4 **c** it, and it became a rod in his hand: H2388
Nu 31:32 the men of war had **c**, was six hundred H962
Jdg 1: 6 after him, and **c** him, and cut off his H270
8:14 And **c** a young man of the men of H3920
15: 4 And Samson went and **c** three hundred H3920
21:23 whom they **c**: and they went and H1497
1Sa 17:35 against me, I **c** *him* by his beard, and H2388
2Sa 2:16 And they **c** every one his fellow by the H2388
18: 9 oak, and his head **c** hold of the oak, H2388
1Ki 1:50 and **c** hold on the horns of the altar. H2388
51 for, lo, he hath **c** hold on the horns of H270
2:28 and **c** hold on the horns of the altar. H2388
11:30 And Ahijah **c** the new garment that H8610
2Ki 4:27 of God to the hill, she **c** him by the feet: H2388
2Ch 22: 9 And he sought Ahaziah: and they **c** H3920
Prv 7:13 So she **c** him, and kissed him, *and* with H2388
Ecc 9:12 the birds that are **c** in the snare; so *are* H270
Jer 50:24 art found, and also **c**, because thou hast H8610
Mt 14:31 *his* hand, and **c** him, and said unto G1949
21:39 And they **c** him, and cast *him* out of the G2983
Mk 12: 3 And they **c** *him*, and beat him, and sent G2983
Lk 8:29 oftentimes it had **c** him: and he was G4884
Jn 21: 3 and that night they **c** nothing. G4084
10 Bring of the fish which ye have now **c**. G4084
Act 6:12 **c** him, and brought *him* to the council, G4884
8:39 Spirit of the Lord **c** away Philip, that the G726
16:19 was gone, they **c** Paul and Silas, and G1949
19:29 and having **c** Gaius and Aristarchus, G4884
26:21 For these causes the Jews **c** me in the G4815
27:15 And when the ship was **c**, and could not G4884
2Co 12: 2 such an one **c** up to the third heaven. G726
4 How that he was **c** up into paradise, and G726
16 being crafty, I **c** you with guile. G2983
1Th 4:17 remain shall be **c** up together with them G726
Rev 12: 5 was **c** up unto God, and *to* his throne. G726

CAUL
Ex 29:13 the inwards, and the **c** *that is* above the H3508
22 inwards, and the **c** *above* the liver, and H3508
Lev 3: 4 by the flanks, and the **c** above the liver, H3508
10 by the flanks, and the **c** above the liver, H3508
15 by the flanks, and the **c** above the liver, H3508
4: 9 by the flanks, and the **c** above the liver, H3508
7: 4 the flanks, and the **c** *that is* above the H3508
8:16 inwards, and the **c** *above* the liver, and H3508
25 inwards, and the **c** *above* the liver, and H3508
9:10 But the fat, and the kidneys, and the **c** H3508
19 the kidneys, and the **c** *above* the liver: H3508
Hos 13: 8 and will rend the **c** of their heart, and H5458

CAULS
Isa 3:18 **c**, and *their* round tires like the moon, H7636

CAUSE
Gen 7: 4 For yet seven days, and I will **c** it to rain
45: 1 him; and he cried, **C** every man to go out
Ex 8: 5 the ponds, and **c** frogs to come up upon
9:16 And in very deed for this **c** have I H5668
18 this time I will **c** it to rain a very grievous
21:19 and shall **c** *him* to be thoroughly healed.
22: 5 If a man shall **c** a field or vineyard to be
9 to be his, the **c** of both parties shall H1697
23: 2 thou speak in a **c** to decline after many H7379
3 thou countenance a poor man in his **c**. H7379
6 wrest the judgment of thy poor in his **c**. H7379
27:20 the light, to **c** the lamp to burn always.
29:10 And thou shalt **c** a bullock to be brought
Lev 14:41 And he shall **c** the house to be scraped
19:29 Do not prostitute thy daughter, to **c** her
24: 2 light, to **c** the lamps to burn continually.
19 And if a man **c** a blemish in his H5414
25: 9 Then shalt thou **c** the trumpet of the
26:16 the eyes, and **c** sorrow of heart: and
Nu 5:24 And he shall **c** the woman to drink the
26 shall **c** the woman to drink the water.
16: 5 *is* holy; and will **c** *him* to come near unto
5 chosen will he **c** to come near unto him.
11 For which **c** *both* thou and all thy H3651
27: 5 And Moses brought their **c** before the H4941
7 and thou shalt **c** the inheritance of their
8 no son, then ye shall **c** his inheritance to
28: 7 *place* shalt thou **c** the strong wine to be
35:30 against any person *to* **c** *him* to die.
Dt 1:17 *is* God's: and the **c** that is too hard for H1697
38 him: for he shall **c** Israel to inherit it.
3:28 and he shall **c** them to inherit the land
12:11 shall choose to **c** his name to dwell there;
17:16 to himself, nor **c** the people to return
24: 4 and thou shalt not **c** the land to sin,
25: 2 that the judge shall **c** him to lie down,
28: 7 The LORD shall **c** thine enemies that H5414
25 The LORD shall **c** thee to be smitten H5414
31: 7 them; and thou shalt **c** them to inherit it.
Jos 5: 4 And this *is* the **c** why Joshua did H1697
20: 4 and shall declare his **c** in the ears of the H1697
23: 7 of their gods, nor **c** to swear *by them*,
1Sa 17:29 What have I now done? *Is there* not a **c**? H1697
19: 5 blood, to slay David without a **c**? H2600
24:15 my **c**, and deliver me out of thine hand. H7379
25:39 that hath pleaded the **c** of my reproach H7379
28: 9 thou a snare for my life, to **c** me to die?
2Sa 3:35 And when all the people came to **c** David
13:13 And I, whither shall I **c** my shame to go?

2Sa 13:16 And she said unto him, *There is* no c: this
15: 4 hath any suit or c might come unto me, H4941
1Ki 1:33 of your lord, and c Solomon my son to
5: 9 me, and will c them to be discharged
8:31 laid upon him to c him to swear, and the
45 supplication, and maintain their c. H4941
49 dwelling place, and maintain their c, H4941
59 he maintain the c of his servant, and H4941
59 servant, and the c of his people Israel H4941
11:27 And this *was* the c that he lifted up *his* H1697
12:15 unto the people; for the c was from the H5438
2Ki 19: 7 land; and I will c him to fall by the sword
1Ch 21: 3 why will he be a c of trespass to Israel?
2Ch 6:35 supplication, and maintain their c. H4941
39 maintain their c, and forgive thy people H4941
10:15 the people: for the c was of God, that H5252
19:10 And what c soever shall come to you of H7379
32:20 And for this c Hezekiah the king, and the
Ezr 4:15 time: for which c was this city destroyed.
21 Give ye now commandment to c these
5: 5 that they could not c them to cease, till
Neh 4:11 and slay them, and c the work to cease.
6: 6 to rebel: for which c thou buildest the
13:26 even him did outlandish women c to sin.
Est 3:13 to kill, and to c to perish, all Jews, both
5: 5 Then the king said, C Haman to make
8:11 to slay, and to c to perish, all the power
Job 2: 3 against him, to destroy him without c. H2600
5: 8 and unto God would I commit my c: H1700
6:24 hold my tongue: and c me to understand
9:17 and multiplieth my wounds without c. H2600
13:18 Behold now, I have ordered *my* c; I H4941
20: 2 Therefore do my thoughts c me to
23: 4 I would order *my* c before him, and fill H4941
24: 7 They c the naked to lodge without
10 They c *him* to go naked without
29:16 I *was* a father to the poor: and the c H7379
31:13 If I did despise the c of my manservant H4941
34:11 unto him, and c every man to find
28 So that they c the cry of the poor to come
38:26 To c it to rain on the earth, *where* no
27 *ground*; and to c the bud of the tender
Ps 7: 4 him that without c is mine enemy:) H7387
9: 4 my right and my c; thou satest in the H1779
10:17 their heart, thou wilt c thine ear to hear:
25: 3 ashamed which transgress without c. H7387
35: 1 Plead *my c*, O LORD, with them that
7 For without c have they hid for me H2600
7 without c they have digged for my soul. H2600
19 with the eye that hate me without a c. H2600
23 *even* unto my c, my God and my Lord. H7379
27 favour my righteous c: yea, let them say
43: 1 Judge me, O God, and plead my c H7379
67: 1 *and* c his face to shine upon us; Selah.
69: 4 They that hate me without a c are more H2600
71: 2 Deliver me in thy righteousness, and c
74:22 Arise, O God, plead thine own c: H7379
76: 8 Thou didst c judgment to be heard from
80: 3 Turn us again, O God, and c thy face to
7 Turn us again, O God of hosts, and c thy
9 before it, and didst c it to take deep root,
19 Turn us again, O LORD God of hosts, c
85: 4 Turn us, O God of our salvation, and c
109: 3 and fought against me without a c. H2600
119:78 a c: *but* I will meditate in thy precepts. H8267
154 Plead my c, and deliver me: quicken me H7379
161 Princes have persecuted me without a c: H2600
140:12 will maintain the c of the afflicted, *and* H1779
143: 8 C me to hear thy lovingkindness in the
8 in thee do I trust: c me to know the way
Prv 1:11 lurk privily for the innocent without c: H2600
3:30 Strive not with a man without c, if he H2600
4:16 is taken away, unless they c *some* to fall.
8:21 That I may c those that love me to
18:17 *He that is* first in his own c *seemeth* H7379
22:23 For the LORD will plead their c, and H7379
23:11 mighty; he shall plead their c with thee. H7379
29 without c? who hath redness of eyes? H2600
24:28 without c; and deceive *not* with thy lips. H2600
25: 9 Debate thy c with thy neighbour H7379
29: 7 The righteous considereth the c of the H1779
31: 8 Open thy mouth for the dumb in the c H1779
9 and plead the c of the poor and needy.
Ecc 2:20 Therefore I went about to c my heart to
5: 6 Suffer not thy mouth to c thy flesh to sin;
7:10 Say not thou, What is *the* c that the H1961
10: 1 Dead flies c the ointment of the
Song 8: 2 me: I would c thee to drink of spiced
13 hearken to thy voice: c me to hear *it*.

Isa 1:23 the c of the widow come unto them. H7379
3:12 they which lead thee c *thee* to err, and
9:16 For the leaders of this people c *them* to
10:30 Lift up thy voice, O daughter of Gallim: c
13:10 the moon shall not c her light to shine.
11 iniquity; and I will c the arrogancy of the
27: 6 He shall c them that come of Jacob to
28:12 *wherewith* ye may c the weary to rest;
30:11 out of the path, c the Holy One of Israel
30 And the LORD shall c his glorious voice
32: 6 he will c the drink of the thirsty to fail.
37: 7 land; and I will c him to fall by the sword
41:21 Produce your c, saith the LORD; bring H7379
42: 2 He shall not cry, nor lift up, nor c his
49: 8 to c to inherit the desolate heritages;
51:22 *that* pleadeth the c of his people, Behold,
52: 4 the Assyrian oppressed them without c. H657
58:14 LORD; and I will c thee to ride upon the
61:11 the Lord GOD will c righteousness and
66: 9 Shall I bring to the birth, and not c to
9 the LORD: shall I c to bring forth, and
Jer 3:12 *and* I will not c mine anger to fall upon
5:28 they judge not the c, the cause of the H1779
28 not the cause, the c of the fatherless, H1779
7: 3 and I will c you to dwell in this place.
7 Then will I c you to dwell in this place, in
34 Then will I c to cease from the cities of
11:20 for unto thee have I revealed my c. H7379
13:16 God, before he c darkness, and before
14:22 the Gentiles that can c rain? or can the
15: 4 And I will c them to be removed into all H5414
11 verily I will c the enemy to entreat
16: 9 Behold, I will c to cease out of this place
21 Therefore, behold, I will this once c them
21 to know, I will c them to know mine
17: 4 gave thee; and I will c thee to serve thine
18: 2 and there I will c thee to hear my words.
19: 7 this place; and I will c them to fall by the
9 And I will c them to eat the flesh of their
20:12 them: for unto thee have I opened my c. H7379
22:16 He judged the c of the poor and needy; H1779
23:27 Which think to c my people to forget my
32 do tell them, and c my people to err by
25:15 fury at my hand, and c all the nations, to
29: 8 your dreams which ye c to be dreamed.
30: 3 LORD: and I will c them to return to the
13 *There is* none to plead thy c, that thou H1779
21 of them; and I will c him to draw near,
31: 2 *even* Israel, when I went to c him to rest.
9 I lead them: I will c them to walk by the
32:35 the son of Hinnom, to c their sons and H4616
35 do this abomination, to c Judah to sin.
37 place, and I will c them to dwell safely:
44 of the south: for I will c their captivity to
33: 7 And I will c the captivity of Judah and
11 LORD. For I will c to return the captivity
15 In those days, and at that time, will I c
26 and Jacob: for I will c their captivity to
34:22 the LORD, and c them to return to this
36:29 c to cease from thence man and beast?
37:20 thee; that thou c me not to return to the
38:23 shalt c this city to be burned with fire.
26 king, that he would not c me to return to
42:12 and c you to return to your own land.
48:12 that shall c him to wander, and
35 Moreover I will c to cease in Moab, saith
49: 2 LORD, that I will c an alarm of war to be
37 For I will c Elam to be dismayed before
50: 9 For, lo, I will raise and c to come up
34 plead their c, that he may give rest H7379
51:27 against her; c the horses to come up
36 I will plead thy c, and take vengeance H7379
Lam 3:32 But though he c grief, yet will he have
36 To subvert a man in his c, the Lord H7379
52 chased me sore, like a bird, without c. H2600
59 hast seen my wrong: judge thou my c. H4941
Ezk 3: 3 And he said unto me, Son of man, c thy
5: 1 a barber's razor, and c *it* to pass upon
13 and I will c my fury to rest upon
9: 1 a loud voice, saying, C them that have
14:15 If I c noisome beasts to pass through the
23 not done without c all that I have done H2600
16: 2 Son of man, c Jerusalem to know her
21 c them to pass through *the fire* for them?
41 women: and I will c thee to cease from
20: 4 thou judge *them*? c them to know the
37 And I will c you to pass under the rod,
21:17 together, and I will c my fury to rest: I
30 Shall I c *it* to return into his sheath? I

Ezk 23:48 Thus will I c lewdness to cease out of the
24: 8 That it might c fury to come up to take
26 thee, to c *thee* to hear *it* with *thine* ears?
25: 7 people, and I will c thee to perish out of
26: 3 O Tyrus, and will c many nations to
13 And I will c the noise of thy songs to
17 c their terror *to be* on all that haunt it! H5414
27:30 And shall c their voice to be heard
29: 4 thy jaws, and I will c the fish of thy rivers
14 of Egypt, and will c them to return *into*
21 In that day will I c the horn of the house
30:13 the idols, and I will c *their* images to
22 I will c the sword to fall out of his hand.
32: 4 open field, and will c all the fowls of the
12 By the swords of the mighty will I c thy
14 waters deep, and c their rivers to run
34:10 at their hand, and c them to cease from
15 I will feed my flock, and I will c them to
25 of peace, and will c the evil beasts to
26 blessing; and I will c the shower to come
36:12 Yea, I will c men to walk upon you, *even*
15 Neither will I c *men* to hear in thee the
15 neither shalt thou c thy nations to fall
27 within you, and c you to walk in my
33 I will also c *you* to dwell in the cities,
37: 5 Behold, I will c breath to enter into
12 your graves, and c you to come up out of
39: 2 of thee, and will c thee to come up from
3 left hand, and will c thine arrows to fall
44:23 holy and profane, and c them to discern
30 may c the blessing to rest in thine house.
Dan 2:12 For this c the king was H3606+H6903+H1836
8:25 And through his policy also he shall c
9:17 his supplications, and c thy face to shine
27 the week he shall c the sacrifice and the
11:18 own behalf shall c the reproach offered
18 reproach he shall c *it* to turn upon him.
39 glory: and he shall c them to rule over
Hos 1: 4 of Jehu, and will c to cease the kingdom
2:11 I will also c all her mirth to cease, her
Joel 2:23 and he will c to come down for you
3:11 about: thither c thy mighty ones to come
Am 5:27 Therefore will I c you to go into captivity
6: 3 Ye that put far away the evil day, and c
8: 9 GOD, that I will c the sun to go down at
Jna 1: 7 know for whose c this evil *is* upon us. H7945
8 thee, for whose c this evil *is* upon us; H3834
Mic 7: 9 him, until he plead my c, and execute H7379
Hab 1: 3 Why dost thou shew me iniquity, and c
Zec 8:12 dew; and I will c the remnant of this
13: 2 and also I will c the prophets and the
Mt 5:22 brother without a c shall be in danger *G1500*
32 saving for the c of fornication, causeth *G3056*
10:21 parents, and c them to be put to death. *G2289*
19: 3 a man to put away his wife for every c? *G156*
5 And said, For this c shall a man leave *G1752*
Mk 10: 7 For this c shall a man leave his father *G1752*
13:12 and shall c them to be put to death. *G2289*
Lk 8:47 all the people for what c she had touched *G156*
21:16 of you shall they c to be put to death. *G2289*
23:22 I have found no c of death in him: I will *G158*
Jn 12:18 For this c the people also met him, for *G1223*
27 but for this c came I unto this hour. *G1223*
15:25 in their law, They hated me without a c. *G1432*
18:37 I born, and for this c came I into the *G5124*
Act 10:21 what *is* the c wherefore ye are come? *G156*
13:28 And though they found no c of death *in* *G156*
19:40 there being no c whereby we may give *G158*
23:28 And when I would have known the c *G156*
25:14 declared Paul's c unto the king, saying, *G2596*
28:18 because there was no c of death in me. *G156*
20 For this c therefore have I called for you, *G156*
Ro 1:26 For this c God gave them up unto vile *G1223*
13: 6 For for this c pay ye tribute also: for *G1223*
15: 9 it is written, For this c I will confess to *G1223*
22 For which c also I have been much *G1352*
16:17 mark them which c divisions and *G4160*
1Co 4:17 For this c have I sent unto you *G1223*
11:10 For this c ought the woman to have *G1223*
30 For this c many *are* weak and sickly *G1223*
2Co 4:16 For which c we faint not; but though *G1352*
5:13 or whether we be sober, *it is* for your c. *G5213*
7:12 *I did it* not for his c that had done the *G1752*
12 the wrong, nor for his c that suffered *G1752*
Eph 3: 1 For this c I Paul, the prisoner of Jesus *G5127*
14 For this c I bow my knees unto the *G5127*
5:31 For this c shall a man leave his father *G5127*
Php 2:18 For the same c also do ye joy, and rejoice *G846*
Col 1: 9 For this c we also, since the day we *G5124*

Col 4:16 read among you, c that it be read also G4160
1Th 2:13 For this c also thank we God without G1223
3: 5 For this c, when I could no longer G1223
2Th 2:11 And for this c God shall send them G1223
1Ti 1:16 Howbeit for this c I obtained mercy, G1223
2Ti 1:12 For the which c I also suffer these things: G156
Tit 1: 5 For this c left I thee in Crete, that thou G5127
Heb 2:11 of one: for which c he is not ashamed to G156
9:15 And for this c he is the mediator of the G1223
1Pt 4: 6 For for this c was the gospel preached G5124
Rev 12:15 c her to be carried away of the flood. G4160
13:15 both speak, and c that as many as G4160

CAUSED
Gen 2: 5 LORD God had not c it to rain upon the
21 And the LORD God c a deep sleep to fall
20:13 And it came to pass, when God c me to
41:52 For God hath c me to be fruitful in the
Ex 14:21 sea; and the LORD c the sea to go *back*
36: 6 and they c it to be proclaimed
Lev 24:20 tooth: as he hath c a blemish in a man, H5414
Nu 31:16 Behold, these c the children of Israel, H1961
Dt 34: 4 thy seed: I have c thee to see *it* with thine
Jdg 16:19 for a man, and she c him to shave off the
1Sa 10:20 And when Samuel had c all the tribes of
21 When he had c the tribe of Benjamin to
20:17 And Jonathan c David to swear again,
2Sa 7:11 Israel, and have c thee to rest from all
1Ki 1:38 went down, and c Solomon to ride upon
44 have c him to ride upon the king's mule:
2:19 on his throne, and c a seat to be set for
20:33 he c him to come up into the chariot.
2Ki 17:17 And they c their sons and their
2Ch 8: 2 c the children of Israel to dwell there.
13:13 But Jeroboam c an ambushment to
21:11 of Judah, and c the inhabitants of
33: 6 And he c his children to pass through
34:32 And he c all that were present in
Ezr 6:12 And the God that hath c his name to
Neh 8: 7 Pelaiah, and the Levites, c the people to
8 and c *them* to understand the reading.
Est 5:14 and he c the gallows to be made.
Job 29:13 and I c the widow's heart to sing for joy.
31:16 or have c the eyes of the widow to fail;
39 c the owners thereof to lose their life:
37:15 and c the light of his cloud to shine?
38:12 *and* c the dayspring to know his place;
Ps 66:12 Thou hast c men to ride over our heads;
78:13 He divided the sea, and c them to pass
16 and c waters to run down like rivers.
26 He c an east wind to blow in the heaven:
119:49 upon which thou hast c me to hope.
Prv 7:21 With her much fair speech she c him to
Isa 19:14 and they have c Egypt to err in every
43:23 I have not c thee to serve with an
48:21 the deserts: he c the waters to flow out
63:14 Spirit of the LORD c him to rest: so didst
Jer 12:14 which I have c my people Israel to
13:11 of a man, so have I c to cleave unto me
15: 8 at noonday: I have c *him* to fall upon it
18:15 and they have c them to stumble in their
23:13 in Baal, and c my people Israel to err.
22 counsel, and had c my people to hear my
29: 4 whom I have c to be carried away from
7 city whither I have c you to be carried
14 I c you to be carried away captive.
31 him not, and he c you to trust in a lie:
32:23 hast c all this evil to come upon them:
34:11 But afterward they turned, and c the
16 my name, and c every man his servant,
48: 4 Moab is destroyed; her little ones have c
33 Moab; and I have c wine to fail from the
50: 6 shepherds have c them to go astray, they
51:49 As Babylon *hath* c the slain of Israel to
Lam 2: 6 the LORD hath c the solemn feasts and
17 not pitied: and he hath c *thine* enemy to
3:13 He hath c the arrows of his quiver to
Ezk 3: 2 So I opened my mouth, and he c me to
16: 7 I have c thee to multiply as the bud of H5414
20:10 Wherefore I c them to go forth out of the
26 gifts, in that they c to pass through *the*
22: 4 and thou hast c thy days to draw near,
23:37 and have also c their sons, whom they
24:13 till I have c my fury to rest upon thee.
29:18 king of Babylon c his army to serve a
31:15 went down to the grave I c a mourning: I
15 were stayed: and I c Lebanon to mourn
32:23 which c terror in the land of the living. H5414
24 of the earth, which c their terror in the H5414
Ezk 32:25 their terror was c in the land of the H5414
26 c their terror in the land of the living. H5414
32 For I have c my terror in the land of the H5414
37: 2 And c me to pass by them round about:
39:28 their God, which c them to be led into
44:12 their idols, and c the house of Israel to
46:21 utter court, and c me to pass by the four
47: 6 c me to return to the brink of the river.
Dan 9:21 beginning, being c to fly swiftly, touched
Hos 4:12 whoredoms hath c *them* to err, and they
Am 2: 4 and their lies c them to err, after the
4: 7 to the harvest: and I c it to rain upon one
7 upon one city, and c it not to rain upon
Jna 3: 7 And he c *it* to be proclaimed and
Zec 3: 4 Behold, I have c thine iniquity to pass
Mal 2: 8 of the way; ye have c many to stumble at
Jn 11:37 of the blind, have c that even this man G4160
Act 15: 3 they c great joy unto all the brethren. G4160
2Co 2: 5 But if any have c grief, he hath not G3076

CAUSELESS
1Sa 25:31 hast shed blood c, or that my lord hath H2600
Prv 26: 2 by flying, so the curse c shall not come. H2600

CAUSES
Ex 18:19 that thou mayest bring the c unto God: H1697
26 seasons: the hard c they brought unto H1697
Dt 1:16 time, saying, Hear *the* c between your
Jer 3: 8 And I saw, when for all the c whereby H182
Lam 2:14 thee false burdens and c of banishment.
3:58 O Lord, thou hast pleaded the c of my H7379
Act 26:21 For these c the Jews caught me in the G1752

CAUSEST
Job 30:22 Thou liftest me up to the wind; thou c
Ps 65: 4 thou choosest, and c to approach *unto*

CAUSETH
Nu 5:18 hand the bitter water that c the curse:
19 from this bitter water that c the curse:
22 And this water that c the curse shall go
24 the bitter water that c the curse: and the
24 and the water that c the curse shall enter
27 that the water that c the curse shall enter
Job 12:24 of the earth, and c them to wander in a
20: 3 of my understanding c me to answer.
37:13 He c it to come, whether for correction,
Ps 104:14 He c the grass to grow for the cattle, and
107:40 upon princes, and c them to wander in
135: 7 He c the vapours to ascend from the
147:18 c his wind to blow, *and* the waters flow.
Prv 10: 5 sleepeth in harvest *is* a son that c shame.
10 He that winketh with the eye c sorrow: H5414
14:35 his wrath is *against* him that c shame.
17: 2 rule over a son that c shame, and shall
18:18 The lot c contentions to cease, and
19:26 that c shame, and bringeth reproach.
27 c to err from the words of knowledge.
28:10 Whoso c the righteous to go astray in an
Isa 61:11 and as the garden c the things that are
64: 2 burneth, the fire c the waters to boil, to
Jer 10:13 heavens, and he c the vapours to ascend
51:16 heavens; and he c the vapours to ascend
Ezk 26: 3 thee, as the sea c his waves to come up.
44:18 *themselves* with any thing that c sweat.
Mt 5:32 cause of fornication, c her to commit G4160
2Co 2:14 which always c us to triumph in Christ, G2358
9:11 c through us thanksgiving to God. G2716
Rev 13:12 before him, and c the earth and them G4160
16 And he c all, both small and great, rich G4160

CAUSEWAY
1Ch 26:16 c of the going up, ward against ward. H4546
18 At Parbar westward, four at the c, *and* H4546

CAUSING
Song 7: 9 *down* sweetly, c the lips of those that
Isa 30:28 in the jaws of the people, c *them* to err.
Jer 29:10 you, in c you to return to this place.
33:12 of shepherds c *their* flocks to lie down.

CAVE
Gen 19:30 dwelt in a c, he and his two daughters. H4631
23: 9 That he may give me the c of H4631
11 I thee, and the c that *is* therein, I give H4631
17 the field, and the c which *was* therein, H4631
19 Sarah his wife in the c of the field of H4631
20 And the field, and the c that *is* therein, H4631
25: 9 buried him in the c of Machpelah, in H4631
Gen 49:29 my fathers in the c that *is* in the field of H4631
30 In the c that *is* in the field of H4631
32 The purchase of the field and of the c H4631
50:13 and buried him in the c of the field of H4631
Jos 10:16 hid themselves in a c at Makkedah. H4631
17 are found hid in a c at Makkedah. H4631
18 c, and set men by it for to keep them: H4631
22 the mouth of the c, and bring out those H4631
22 those five kings unto me out of the c. H4631
23 him out of the c, the king of Jerusalem, H4631
27 cast them into the c wherein they had H4631
1Sa 22: 1 escaped to the c Adullam: and when H4631
24: 3 way, where *was* a c; and Saul went in to H4631
3 his men remained in the sides of the c. H4631
7 up out of the c, and went on *his* way. H4631
8 went out of the c, and cried after Saul, H4631
10 mine hand in the c: and *some* bade *me* H4631
2Sa 23:13 time unto the c of Adullam: and the H4631
1Ki 18: 4 c, and fed them with bread and water.) H4631
13 a c, and fed them with bread and water? H4631
19: 9 And he came thither unto a c, and H4631
13 entering in of the c. And, behold, *there* H4631
1Ch 11:15 to David, into the c of Adullam; and H4631
Ps 57:ttl David, when he fled from Saul in the c. H4631
142:ttl David; A Prayer when he was in the c. H4631
Jn 11:38 It was a c, and a stone lay upon it. G4693

CAVES
Jdg 6: 2 the mountains, and c, and strong holds. H4631
1Sa 13: 6 hide themselves in c, and in thickets, H4631
Job 30: 6 To dwell in the clifts of the valleys, *in* c H2356
Isa 2:19 and into the c of the earth, for fear H4247
Ezk 33:27 and in the c shall die of the pestilence. H4631
Heb 11:38 and *in* dens and c of the earth. G3692

CAVE'S
Jos 10:27 laid great stones in the c mouth, *which* H4631

CEASE
Gen 8:22 winter, and day and night shall not c. H7673
Ex 9:29 the thunder shall c, neither shall there H2308
Nu 8:25 fifty years they shall c waiting upon the H7725
11:25 them, they prophesied, and did not c. H3254
17: 5 and I will make to c from me the H7918
Dt 15:11 For the poor shall never c out of the H2308
32:26 of them to c from among men: H7673
Jos 22:25 our children c from fearing the LORD: H7673
Jdg 15: 7 avenged of you, and after that I will c. H2308
20:28 my brother, or shall I c? And the LORD H2308
1Sa 7: 8 said to Samuel, C not to cry unto the H2790
2Ch 16: 5 building of Ramah, and let his work c. H7673
Ezr 4:21 cause these men to c, and that this city be H989
23 and made them to c by force and power. H989
5: 5 not cause them to c, till the matter came H989
Neh 4:11 and slay them, and cause the work to c. H7673
6: 3 should the work c, whilst I leave it, and H7673
Job 3:17 There the wicked c *from* troubling; and H2308
10:20 *Are* not my days few? c *then, and* let H2308
14: 7 the tender branch thereof will not c. H2308
Ps 37: 8 C from anger, and forsake wrath: fret H7503
46: 9 He maketh wars to c unto the end of H7673
85: 4 and cause thine anger toward us to c. H6565
89:44 Thou hast made his glory to c, and cast H7673
Prv 18:18 The lot causeth contentions to c, and H7673
19:27 C, my son, to hear the instruction *that* H2308
20: 3 *It is* an honour for a man to c from H7674
22:10 go out; yea, strife and reproach shall c. H7673
23: 4 Labour not to be rich: c from thine own H2308
Ecc 12: 3 and the grinders c because they are few, H988
Isa 1:16 from before mine eyes; c to do evil; H2308
2:22 C ye from man, whose breath *is* in his H2308
10:25 c, and mine anger in their destruction. H3615
13:11 of the proud to c, and will lay low the H7673
16:10 I have made *their vintage* shouting to c. H7673
17: 3 The fortress also shall c from Ephraim, H7673
21: 2 all the sighing thereof have I made to c. H7673
30:11 Holy One of Israel to c from before us. H7673
33: 1 when thou shalt c to spoil, thou shalt H8552
Jer 7:34 Then will I cause to c from the cities of H7673
14:17 day, and let them not c: for the virgin H1820
16: 9 I will cause to c out of this place in your H7673
17: 8 neither shall c from yielding fruit. H4185
31:36 seed of Israel also shall c from being a H7673
36:29 cause to c from thence man and beast? H7673
48:35 Moreover I will cause to c in Moab, H7673
Lam 2:18 no rest; let not the apple of thine eye c. H1826
Ezk 6: 6 be broken and c, and your images may H7673
7:24 c; and their holy places shall be defiled. H7673
12:23 this proverb to c, and they shall no H7673

Ezk 16:41 I will cause thee to c from playing the H7673
23:27 Thus will I make thy lewdness to c H7673
48 Thus will I cause lewdness to c out of H7673
26:13 of thy songs to c; and the sound of thy H7673
30:10 multitude of Egypt to c by the hand of H7673
13 *their* images to c out of Noph; and H7673
18 her strength shall c in her: as for her, a H7673
33:28 her strength shall c; and the mountains H7673
34:10 and cause them to c from feeding the H7673
25 the evil beasts to c out of the land: and H7673
Dan 9:27 and the oblation to c, and for the H7673
11:18 offered by him to c; without his own H7673
Hos 1: 4 to c the kingdom of the house of Israel. H7673
2:11 I will also cause all her mirth to c, her H7673
Am 7: 5 Then said I, O Lord GOD, c, I beseech H2308
Act 13:10 c to pervert the right ways of the Lord? *G3973*
1Co 13: 8 tongues, they shall c; whether *there be* *G3973*
Eph 1:16 C not to give thanks for you, making *G3973*
Col 1: 9 heard *it*, do not c to pray for you, and *G3973*
2Pt 2:14 and that cannot c from sin; beguiling *G180*

CEASED
Gen 18:11 in age; *and* it c to be with Sarah after H2308
Ex 9:33 thunders and hail c, and the rain was H2308
34 and the thunders were c, he sinned yet H2308
Jos 5:12 And the manna c on the morrow after H7673
Jdg 2:19 unto them; they c not from their own H5307
5: 7 *The inhabitants of* the villages c, they H2308
7 ceased, they c in Israel, until that H2308
1Sa 2: 5 *that were* hungry c: so that the barren H2308
25: 9 words in the name of David, and c. H5117
Ezr 4:24 Then c the work of the house of God H989
24 So it c unto the second H1934+H989
Job 32: 1 So these three men c to answer Job, H7673
Ps 35:15 *it* not; they did tear *me*, and c not: H1826
77: 2 c not: my soul refused to be comforted. H6313
Isa 14: 4 the oppressor c! the golden city ceased! H7673
4 the oppressor ceased! the golden city c! H7673
Lam 5:14 The elders have c from the gate, the H7673
15 The joy of our heart is c; our dance is H7673
Jna 1:15 the sea: and the sea c from her raging. H5975
Mt 14:32 were come into the ship, the wind c. *G2869*
Mk 4:39 the wind c, and there was a great calm. *G2869*
6:51 ship; and the wind c: and they were sore *G2869*
Lk 7:45 I came in hath not c to kiss my feet. *G1257*
8:24 and they c, and there was a calm. *G3973*
11: 1 place, when he c, one of his disciples *G3973*
Act 5:42 c not to teach and preach Jesus Christ. *G3973*
20: 1 And after the uproar was c, Paul called *G3973*
31 of three years I c not to warn every one *G3973*
21:14 c, saying, The will of the Lord be done. *G2270*
Gal 5:11 then is the offence of the cross c. *G2673*
Heb 4:10 his rest, he also hath c from his own *G2664*
10: 2 For then would they not have c to be *G3973*
1Pt 4: 1 suffered in the flesh hath c from sin; *G3973*

CEASETH
Ps 12: 1 Help, LORD; for the godly man c; for H1584
49: 8 their soul *is* precious, and it c for ever:) H2308
Prv 26:20 where *there is* no talebearer, the strife c. H8367
Isa 16: 4 an end, the spoiler c, the oppressors are H3615
24: 8 The mirth of tabrets c, the noise of H7673
8 rejoice endeth, the joy of the harp c. H7673
33: 8 wayfaring man c: he hath broken the H7673
Lam 3:49 Mine eye trickleth down, and c not, H1820
Hos 7: 4 by the baker, *who* c from raising after H7673
Act 6:13 which said, This man c not to speak *G3973*

CEASING
1Sa 12:23 the LORD in c to pray for you: but H2308
Act 12: 5 c of the church unto God for him. *G1618*
Ro 1: 9 Son, that without c I make mention of *G89*
1Th 1: 3 Remembering without c your work of *G89*
2:13 we God without c, because, when ye *G89*
5:17 Pray without c. *G89*
2Ti 1: 3 that without c I have remembrance *G88*

CEDAR
Lev 14: 4 and c wood, and scarlet, and hyssop: H730
6 take it, and the c wood, and the scarlet, H730
49 and c wood, and scarlet, and hyssop: H730
51 And he shall take the c wood, and the H730
52 bird, and with the c wood, and with the H730
Nu 19: 6 And the priest shall take c wood, and H730
24: 6 planted, *and* as c trees beside the waters. H730
2Sa 5:11 to David, and c trees, and carpenters, H730
7: 2 dwell in an house of c, but the ark of God H730
7 Why build ye not me an house of c? H730
1Ki 4:33 And he spake of trees, from the c tree H730
5: 6 that they hew me c trees out of Lebanon; H730
8 timber of c, and concerning timber of fir. H730
10 So Hiram gave Solomon c trees and fir H730
6: 9 the house with beams and boards of c. H730
10 they rested on the house *with* timber of c. H730
15 with boards of c, both the floor of the H730
16 with boards of c: he even built *them* for H730
18 And the c of the house within *was* H730
18 all *was* c; there was no stone seen. H730
20 and *so* covered the altar *which was of* c. H730
36 of hewed stone, and a row of c beams. H730
7: 2 upon four rows of c pillars, with cedar H730
2 pillars, with c beams upon the pillars. H730
3 And *it was* covered with c above upon H730
7 c from one side of the floor to the other. H730
12 and a row of c beams, both for the H730
9:11 Solomon with c trees and fir trees, and H730
2Ki 14: 9 sent to the c that *was* in Lebanon, H730
19:23 cut down the tall c trees thereof, *and* the H730
1Ch 22: 4 Also c trees in abundance: for the H730
4 of Tyre brought much c wood to David. H730
2Ch 1:15 as stones, and c trees made he as the H730
2: 8 Send me also c trees, fir trees, and H730
9:27 as stones, and c trees made he as the H730
25:18 sent to the c that *was* in Lebanon, H730
Ezr 3: 7 of Tyre, to bring c trees from Lebanon H730
Job 40:17 He moveth his tail like a c: the sinews of H730
Ps 92:12 tree: he shall grow like a c in Lebanon. H730
Song 1:17 The beams of our house *are* c, *and* our H730
8: 9 door, we will inclose her with boards of c. H730
Isa 41:19 I will plant in the wilderness the c, the H730
Jer 22:14 with c, and painted with vermilion. H730
15 closest *thyself* in c? did not thy father eat H730
Ezk 17: 3 and took the highest branch of the c: H730
22 branch of the high c, and will set *it*; I will H730
23 and be a goodly c: and under it shall H730
27:24 and made of c, among thy merchandise. H729
31: 3 Behold, the Assyrian *was* a c in Lebanon H730
Zep 2:14 for he shall uncover the c work. H731
Zec 11: 2 Howl, fir tree; for the c is fallen; because H730

CEDARS
Jdg 9:15 bramble, and devour the c of Lebanon. H730
1Ki 7:11 the measures of hewed stones, and c. H730
10:27 as stones, and c made he *to be* as the H730
1Ch 14: 1 David, and timber of c, with masons and H730
17: 1 dwell in an house of c, but the ark of the H730
6 Why have ye not built me an house of c? H730
2Ch 2: 3 and didst send him c to build him an H730
Ps 29: 5 The voice of the LORD breaketh the c; H730
5 the LORD breaketh the c of Lebanon. H730
80:10 the boughs thereof *were like* the goodly c. H730
104:16 the c of Lebanon, which he hath planted; H730
148: 9 and all hills; fruitful trees, and all c: H730
Song 5:15 *is* as Lebanon, excellent as the c. H730
Isa 2:13 And upon all the c of Lebanon, *that are* H730
9:10 cut down, but we will change *them into* c. H730
14: 8 at thee, *and* the c of Lebanon, *saying*, H730
37:24 will cut down the tall c thereof, *and* the H730
44:14 He heweth him down c, and taketh the H730
Jer 22: 7 thy choice c, and cast *them* into the fire. H730
23 thy nest in the c, how gracious shalt thou H730
Ezk 27: 5 c from Lebanon to make masts for thee. H730
31: 8 The c in the garden of God could not H730
Am 2: 9 the height of the c, and he *was* strong as H730
Zec 11: 1 Lebanon, that the fire may devour thy c. H730

CEDAR-TREE See CEDAR and TREE.

CEDAR-WOOD See CEDAR and WOOD.

CEDRON
Jn 18: 1 over the brook C, where was a garden, *G2748*

CEILED See CIELED.

CEILING See CIELING.

CELEBRATE
Lev 23:32 unto even, shall ye c your sabbath. H7673
41 ye shall c it in the seventh month. H2287
Isa 38:18 death can *not* c thee: they that go down H1984

CELESTIAL
1Co 15:40 *There are* also c bodies, and bodies *G2032*
40 the glory of the c *is* one, and the *glory* *G2032*

CELLARS
1Ch 27:27 for the wine c *was* Zabdi the Shiphmite: H214
27:28 Gederite: and over the c of oil *was* Joash: H214

CENCHREA
Act 18:18 shorn *his* head in C: for he had a vow. *G2747*
Ro 16: 1 is a servant of the church which is at C: *G2747*

CENSER
Lev 10: 1 took either of them his c, and put fire H4289
16:12 And he shall take a c full of burning H4289
Nu 16:17 And take every man his c, and put H4289
17 every man his c, two hundred and fifty H4289
17 thou also, and Aaron, each *of you* his c. H4289
18 And they took every man his c, and put H4289
46 And Moses said unto Aaron, Take a c, H4289
2Ch 26:19 Then Uzziah was wroth, and *had* a c in H4730
Ezk 8:11 with every man his c in his hand; and a H4730
Heb 9: 4 Which had the golden c, and the ark of *G2369*
Rev 8: 3 having a golden c; and there was given *G3031*
5 And the angel took the c, and filled it *G3031*

CENSERS
Nu 4:14 about it, *even* the c, the fleshhooks, and H4289
16: 6 This do; Take you c, Korah, and all his H4289
17 two hundred and fifty c; thou also, and H4289
37 priest, that he take up the c out of the H4289
38 The c of these sinners against their H4289
39 took the brasen c, wherewith they that H4289
1Ki 7:50 spoons, and the c *of* pure gold; and the H4289
2Ch 4:22 spoons, and the c, *of* pure gold: and the H4289

CENTURION
Mt 8: 5 came unto him a c, beseeching him, *G1543*
8 The c answered and said, Lord, I am *G1543*
13 And Jesus said unto the c, Go thy way; *G1543*
27:54 Now when the c, and they that were *G1543*
Mk 15:39 And when the c, which stood over *G2760*
44 *unto him* the c, he asked him whether *G2760*
45 And when he knew *it* of the c, he gave *G2760*
Lk 7: 6 the house, the c sent friends to him, *G1543*
23:47 Now when the c saw what was done, he *G1543*
Act 10: 1 a c of the band called the Italian *band*, *G1543*
22 And they said, Cornelius the c, a just *G1543*
22:25 Paul said unto the c that stood by, Is it *G1543*
26 When the c heard *that*, he went and *G1543*
24:23 And he commanded a c to keep Paul, *G1543*
27: 1 named Julius, a c of Augustus' band. *G1543*
6 And there the c found a ship of *G1543*
11 Nevertheless the c believed the master *G1543*
31 Paul said to the c and to the soldiers, *G1543*
43 But the c, willing to save Paul, kept *G1543*
28:16 And when we came to Rome, the c *G1543*

CENTURIONS
Act 21:32 Who immediately took soldiers and c, *G1543*
23:17 Then Paul called one of the c unto *him*, *G1543*
23 And he called unto *him* two c, saying, *G1543*

CENTURION'S
Lk 7: 2 And a certain c servant, who was dear *G1543*

CEPHAS
Jn 1:42 C, which is by interpretation, A stone. *G2786*
1Co 1:12 I of Apollos; and I of C; and I of Christ. *G2786*
3:22 Whether Paul, or Apollos, or C, or the *G2786*
9: 5 and *as* the brethren of the Lord, and C? *G2786*
15: 5 And that he was seen of C, then of the *G2786*
Gal 2: 9 And when James, C, and John, who *G2786*

CEREMONIES
Nu 9: 3 to all the c thereof, shall ye keep it. H4941

CERTAIN
Gen 28:11 And he lighted upon a c place, and
37:15 And a c man found him, and, behold, *he*
38: 1 a c Adullamite, whose name *was* Hirah. H376
2 And Judah saw there a daughter of a c H376
Ex 16: 4 out and gather a c rate every day, that H1697
Nu 9: 6 And there were c men, who were defiled
16: 2 And they rose up before Moses, with c of H582
Dt 13:13 C men, the children of Belial, are gone
14 *and* the thing c, *that* such abomination H3559
17: 4 *be* true, *and* the thing c, *that* such H3559
25: 2 according to his fault, by a c number.
Jdg 9:53 And a c woman cast a piece of a H259
13: 2 And there was a c man of Zorah, of the H259
19: 1 that there was a c Levite sojourning on H376
22 the men of the city, c sons of Belial, beset H582
Ru 1: 1 famine in the land. And a c man of
1Sa 1: 1 Now there was a c man of H259

1Sa 21: 7 Now a **c** man of the servants of Saul *was*
2Sa 18:10 And a **c** man saw *it*, and told Joab, and H259
1Ki 2:37 shalt know for **c** that thou shalt surely H3045
42 Know for a **c**, on the day thou goest H3045
7:29 *were* **c** additions made of thin work.
11:17 That Hadad fled, he and **c** Edomites of H582
20:35 And a **c** man of the sons of the prophets H259
22:34 And a **c** man drew a bow at a venture,
2Ki 4: 1 Now there cried a **c** woman of the wives H259
8: 6 unto her a **c** officer, saying, Restore H259
1Ch 9:28 And **c** of them had the charge of the
16: 4 And he appointed **c** of the Levites to
19: 5 Then there went **c**, and told David how
2Ch 8:13 Even after a **c** rate every day, offering H1697
18: 2 And after **c** years he went down to Ahab
33 And a **c** man drew a bow at a venture,
28:12 Then **c** of the heads of the children of H582
Ezr 10:16 the priest, *with* **c** chief of the fathers, H582
Neh 1: 2 came, he and **c** men of Judah; and I
4 and mourned **c** days, and fasted, and
11: 4 And at Jerusalem dwelt **c** of the children
23 them, that a **c** portion should be for
12:35 And **c** of the priests' sons with trumpets;
13: 6 after **c** days obtained I leave of the king:
25 them, and smote **c** of them, and plucked H582
Est 2: 5 *Now* in Shushan the palace there was a **c** H376
3: 8 There is a **c** people scattered abroad H259
Jer 26:15 But know ye for **c**, that if ye put me to H3045
17 Then rose up **c** of the elders of the land, H582
22 Achbor, and **c** men with him into Egypt.
41: 5 That there came **c** from Shechem, from H582
52:15 away captive **c** of the poor of the people,
16 of the guard left **c** of the poor of the land
Ezk 14: 1 Then came **c** of the elders of Israel unto H582
20: 1 *day* of the month, *that* **c** of the elders of H582
Dan 1: 3 that he should bring **c** of the children of
2:45 *is* **c**, and the interpretation thereof sure. H3330
3: 8 Wherefore at that time **c** Chaldeans H1400
12 There are **c** Jews whom thou hast set H1400
8:13 said unto that **c** *saint* which spake, H6422
27 And I Daniel fainted, and was sick **c**
10: 5 and behold a **c** man clothed in linen, H259
11:13 come after **c** years with a great army H6256
Mt 8:19 And a **c** scribe came, and said unto G1520
9: 3 And, behold, **c** of the scribes said G5100
18 there came a **c** ruler, and worshipped
12:38 Then **c** of the scribes and of the G5100
17:14 came to him a **c** man, kneeling down
18:23 likened unto a **c** king, which would take G444
20:20 *him*, and desiring a **c** thing of him. G5100
21:28 But what think ye? A **c** man had two
33 There was a **c** householder, G444+G5100
22: 2 The kingdom of heaven is like unto a **c** G444
Mk 2: 6 But there were **c** of the scribes sitting G5100
5:25 And a **c** woman, which had an issue of G5100
35 the synagogue's *house* **c** which said, Thy
7: 1 him the Pharisees, and **c** of the scribes, G5100
25 For a **c** woman, whose young daughter
11: 5 And **c** of them that stood there said G5100
12: 1 them by parables. A **c** man planted a
13 And they send unto him **c** of the G5100
42 And there came a **c** poor widow, and G1520
14:51 And there followed him a **c** young man, G5100
57 And there arose **c**, and bare false G5100
Lk 1: 5 the king of Judaea, a **c** priest named G5100
5:12 when he was in a **c** city, behold a man G1520
17 And it came to pass on a **c** day, as he G1520
6: 2 And **c** of the Pharisees said unto them, G5100
7: 2 And a **c** centurion's servant, who was G5100
41 There was a **c** creditor which had two G5100
8: 2 And **c** women, which had been healed G5100
20 And it was told him *by* **c** which said, Thy
22 Now it came to pass on a **c** day, that he G1520
27 him out of the city a **c** man, which had G5100
9:57 went in the way, a **c** *man* said unto G5100
10:25 And, behold, a **c** lawyer stood up, and G5100
30 And Jesus answering said, A **c** *man* G5100
31 And by chance there came down a **c** G5100
33 But a **c** Samaritan, as he journeyed, G5100
38 that he entered into a **c** village: and a G5100
38 village: and a **c** woman named Martha G5100
11: 1 he was praying in a **c** place, when he G5100
27 spake these things, a **c** woman of the G5100
37 And as he spake, a **c** Pharisee besought G5100
12:16 a **c** rich man brought forth plentifully: G5100
13: 6 He spake also this parable; A **c** *man* G5100
31 The same day there came **c** of the G5100
14: 2 And, behold, there was a **c** man before G5100
16 Then said he unto him, A **c** man made G5100
Lk 15:11 And he said, A **c** man had two sons: G5100
16: 1 There was a **c** rich man, which had G5100
19 There was a **c** rich man, which was G5100
20 And there was a **c** beggar named G5100
17:12 And as he entered into a **c** village, there G5100
18: 9 And he spake this parable unto **c** which G5100
18 And a **c** ruler asked him, saying, Good G5100
35 unto Jericho, a **c** blind man sat by the G5100
19:12 He said therefore, A **c** nobleman went G5100
20: 9 people this parable; A **c** man planted a G5100
27 Then came to *him* **c** of the Sadducees, G5100
39 Then **c** of the scribes answering said, G5100
21: 2 And he saw also a **c** poor widow G5100
22:56 But a **c** maid beheld him as he sat by G5100
23:19 (Who for a **c** sedition made in the city, G5100
24: 1 had prepared, and **c** *others* with them.
22 Yea, and **c** women also of our company G5100
24 And **c** of them which were with us went G5100
Jn 4:46 And there was a **c** nobleman, whose G5100
5: 4 For an angel went down at a **c** season
5 And a **c** man was there, which had an G5100
11: 1 Now a **c** *man* was sick, *named* Lazarus, G5100
12:20 And there were **c** Greeks among them G5100
Act 3: 2 And a **c** man lame from his mother's G5100
5: 1 But a **c** man named Ananias, with G5100
2 a **c** part, and laid *it* at the apostles' feet. G5100
6: 9 Then there arose **c** of the synagogue, G5100
8: 9 But there was a **c** man, called Simon, G5100
36 way, they came unto a **c** water: and the G5100
9:10 And there was a **c** disciple at G5100
19 Then was Saul **c** days with the disciples G5100
33 And there he found a **c** man named G5100
36 Now there was at Joppa a **c** disciple G5100
10: 1 There was a **c** man in Caesarea called G5100
11 And saw heaven opened, and a **c** vessel G5100
23 with them, and **c** brethren from Joppa G5100
48 Then prayed they him to tarry **c** days. G5100
11: 5 I saw a vision, A **c** vessel descend, as it G5100
12: 1 forth *his* hands to vex **c** of the church. G5100
13: 1 that was at Antioch **c** prophets and G5100
6 Paphos, they found a **c** sorcerer, a false G5100
14: 8 And there sat a **c** man at Lystra, G5100
19 And there came thither **c** Jews from
15: 1 And **c** men which came down from G5100
2 Barnabas, and **c** other of them, should G5100
5 But there rose up **c** of the sect of the G5100
24 Forasmuch as we have heard, that **c** G5100
16: 1 and, behold, a **c** disciple was there, G5100
1 the son of a **c** woman, which was G5100
12 and we were in that city abiding **c** days. G5100
14 And a **c** woman named Lydia, a seller G5100
16 went to prayer, a **c** damsel possessed G5100
17: 5 took unto them **c** lewd fellows of the G5100
6 drew Jason and **c** brethren unto the G5100
18 Then **c** philosophers of the Epicureans, G5100
20 For thou bringest **c** strange things to G5100
28 have our being; as **c** also of your own G5100
34 Howbeit **c** men clave unto him, and G5100
18: 2 And found a **c** Jew named Aquila, born G5100
7 and entered into a **c** *man's* house, G5100
24 And a **c** Jew named Apollos, born at G5100
19: 1 to Ephesus: and finding **c** disciples, G5100
13 Then **c** of the vagabond Jews, exorcists, G5100
24 For a **c** *man* named Demetrius, a G5100
31 And **c** of the chief of Asia, which were G5100
20: 9 And there sat in a window a **c** young G5100
21:10 Judaea a **c** prophet, named Agabus. G5100
16 There went with us also **c** of the disciples
23:12 And when it was day, **c** of the Jews G5100
17 for he hath a **c** thing to tell him. G5100
24: 1 the elders, and *with* a **c** orator *named* G5100
18 Whereupon **c** Jews from Asia found me G5100
24 And after **c** days, when Felix came with G5100
25:13 And after **c** days king Agrippa and G5100
14 There is a **c** man left in bonds by Felix: G5100
19 But had **c** questions against him of G5100
26 Of whom I have no **c** thing to write unto G804
27: 1 Paul and **c** other prisoners unto G5100
16 And running under a **c** island which is G5100
26 Howbeit we must be cast upon a **c** G5100
39 they discovered a **c** creek with a shore, G5100
Ro 15:26 Achaia to make a **c** contribution for the G5100
1Co 4:11 buffeted, and have no **c** dwellingplace; G790
Gal 2:12 For before that **c** came from James, he G5100
1Ti 6: 7 *and it is* **c** we can carry nothing out. G1212
Heb 2: 6 But one in a **c** place testified, saying, G4225
4: 4 For he spake in a **c** place of the seventh G4225
7 Again, he limiteth a **c** day, saying in G5100
10:27 But a **c** fearful looking for of judgment G5100
Jude 4 For there are **c** men crept in unawares, G5100

CERTAINLY
Gen 18:10 And he said, I will **c** return unto thee
26:28 And they said, We saw **c** that the LORD
43: 7 words: could we **c** know that he would
44:15 ye not that such a man as I can **c** divine?
50:15 hate us, and will **c** requite us all the evil
Ex 3:12 And he said, **C** I will be with thee; and H3588
22: 4 If the theft be **c** found in his hand alive,
Lev 5:19 It *is* a trespass offering: he hath **c**
24:16 congregation shall **c** stone him: as well
Jos 9:24 Because it was **c** told thy servants, how
Jdg 14:12 unto you: if ye can **c** declare it me within
1Sa 20: 3 said, Thy father **c** knoweth that I have
9 from thee: for if I knew **c** that evil were
23:10 Israel, thy servant hath **c** heard that Saul
25:28 for the LORD will **c** make my lord a sure
1Ki 1:30 in my stead; even so will I **c** do this day.
2Ki 8:10 him, Thou mayest **c** recover: howbeit the
2Ch 18:27 And Micaiah said, If thou **c** return in
Prv 23: 5 is not? for *riches* **c** make themselves
Jer 8: 8 *is* with us? Lo, **c** in vain made he *it*; the H403
13:12 thee, Do we not **c** know that every bottle
25:28 saith the LORD of hosts; Ye shall **c** drink.
36:29 of Babylon shall **c** come and destroy this
40:14 And said unto him, Dost thou **c** know
42:19 **c** that I have admonished you this day.
22 Now therefore know **c** that ye shall die
44:17 But we will **c** do whatsoever thing goeth
Lam 2:16 swallowed *her* up: **c** this *is* the day that H389
Dan 11:10 and *one* shall **c** come, and overflow,
13 former, and shall **c** come after certain
Lk 23:47 saying, **C** this was a righteous man. G3689

CERTAINTY
Jos 23:13 Know for a **c** that the LORD your God
1Sa 23:23 to me with the **c**, and I will go with you: H3559
Prv 22:21 That I might make thee know the **c** of H7189
Dan 2: 8 said, I know of **c** that ye would gain the H3330
Lk 1: 4 That thou mightest know the **c** of those G803
Act 21:34 could not know the **c** for the tumult, he G804
22:30 have known the **c** wherefore he was G804

CERTIFIED
Ezr 4:14 therefore have we sent and **c** the king; H3046
Est 2:22 **c** the king *thereof* in Mordecai's name. H559

CERTIFY
2Sa 15:28 there come word from you to **c** me. H5046
Ezr 4:16 We **c** the king that, if this city be H3046
5:10 We asked their names also, to **c** thee, H3046
7:24 Also we **c** you, that touching any of the H3046
Gal 1:11 But I **c** you, brethren, that the gospel G1107

CESAR See CAESAR.

CESAREA See CAESAREA.

CHABOD See I-CHABOD.

CHAFED
2Sa 17: 8 men, and they *be* **c** in their minds, as a H4751

CHAFF
Job 21:18 and as **c** that the storm carrieth away. H4671
Ps 1: 4 like the **c** which the wind driveth away. H4671
35: 5 Let them be as **c** before the wind: and H4671
Isa 5:24 consumeth the **c**, *so* their root shall be H2842
17:13 be chased as the **c** of the mountains H4671
29: 5 ones *shall be* as **c** that passeth away: H4671
33:11 Ye shall conceive **c**, ye shall bring forth H2842
41:15 small, and shalt make the hills as **c**. H4671
Jer 23:28 *is* the **c** to the wheat? saith the LORD. H8401
Dan 2:35 and became like the **c** of the summer H5784
Hos 13: 3 away, as the **c** *that* is driven with the H4671
Zep 2: 2 the day pass as the **c**, before the fierce H4671
Mt 3:12 burn up the **c** with unquenchable fire. G892
Lk 3:17 **c** he will burn with fire unquenchable. G892

CHAIN
Gen 41:42 linen, and put a gold **c** about his neck; H7242
1Ki 7:17 work, and wreaths of **c** work, for the H8333
Ps 73: 6 **c**; violence covereth them *as* a garment. H6059
Song 4: 9 of thine eyes, with one **c** of thy neck. H6060
Lam 3: 7 get out: he hath made my **c** heavy. H5178
Ezk 7:23 Make a **c**: for the land is full of bloody H7569
16:11 upon thy hands, and a **c** on thy neck. H7242
Dan 5: 7 and *have* a **c** of gold about his neck, H2002

Dan 5:16 and *have* a c of gold about thy neck, H2002
29 scarlet, and *put* a c of gold about his H2002
Act 28:20 the hope of Israel I am bound with this c. *G254*
2Ti 1:16 me, and was not ashamed of my c: *G254*
Rev 20: 1 bottomless pit and a great c in his hand. *G254*

CHAINS
Ex 28:14 And two c *of* pure gold at the ends; *of* H8333
14 fasten the wreathen c to the ouches. H8333
22 upon the breastplate c at the ends *of* H8331
24 And thou shalt put the two wreathen *c* H5688
25 the two wreathen c thou shalt fasten in
39:15 And they made upon the breastplate c H8333
17 And they put the two wreathen c of H5688
18 And the two ends of the two wreathen c H5688
Nu 31:50 of jewels of gold, c, and bracelets, rings, H685
Jdg 8:26 c that *were* about their camels' necks. H6060
1Ki 6:21 a partition by the c of gold before the H7569
2Ch 3: 5 gold, and set thereon palm trees and c. H8333
16 And he made c, *as* in the oracle, and H8333
16 pomegranates, and put *them* on the c. H8333
Ps 68: 6 c: but the rebellious dwell in a dry *land.* H3574
149: 8 To bind their kings with c, and their H2131
Prv 1: 9 unto thy head, and c about thy neck. H6060
Song 1:10 rows *of jewels,* thy neck with c *of gold.* H2737
Isa 3:19 The c, and the bracelets, and the H5188
40:19 it over with gold, and casteth silver c. H7577
45:14 come after thee; in c they shall come H2131
Jer 39: 7 him with c, to carry him to Babylon. H5178
40: 1 being bound in c among all that were H246
4 this day from the c which *were* upon H246
52:11 bound him in c, and carried him to H5178
Ezk 19: 4 him with c unto the land of Egypt. H2397
9 And they put him in ward in c, and H2397
Nah 3:10 and all her great men were bound in c. H2131
Mk 5: 3 no man could bind him, no, not with c: *G254*
4 with fetters and c, and the chains had *G254*
4 and chains, and the c had been plucked *G254*
Lk 8:29 kept bound with c and in fetters; and he *G254*
Act 12: 6 bound with two c: and the keepers before *G254*
7 And his c fell off from *his* hands. *G254*
21:33 be bound with two c; and demanded who *G254*
2Pt 2: 4 *them* into c of darkness, to be reserved *G4577*
Jude 6 in everlasting c under darkness unto *G1199*

CHAIN-WORK See CHAIN and WORK.

CHALCEDONY
Rev 21:19 the third, a c; the fourth, an emerald; *G5472*

CHALCOL
1Ki 4:31 and Heman, and C, and Darda, the H3633

CHALDAEANS
Act 7: 4 Then came he out of the land of the C, *G5466*

CHALDEA
Jer 50:10 And C shall be a spoil: all that spoil her H3778
51:24 the inhabitants of C all their evil that H3778
35 inhabitants of C, shall Jerusalem say. H3778
Ezk 11:24 the Spirit of God into C, to them of the H3778
16:29 of Canaan unto C; and yet thou wast H3778
23:15 of C, the land of their nativity: H3778
16 and sent messengers unto them into C. H3778

CHALDEAN
Ezr 5:12 of Babylon, the C, who destroyed this H3777
Dan 2:10 at any magician, or astrologer, or C. H3777

CHALDEANS
Job 1:17 and said, The C made out three bands, H3778
Isa 23:13 Behold the land of the C; this people H3778
43:14 and the C, whose cry *is* in the ships. H3778
47: 1 O daughter of the C: for thou shalt no H3778
5 O daughter of the C: for thou shalt no H3778
48:14 Babylon, and his arm *shall be on* the C. H3778
20 flee ye from the C, with a voice of H3778
Jer 21: 4 and *against* the C, which besiege you H3778
9 and falleth to the C that besiege you, he H3778
22:25 of Babylon, and into the hand of the C. H3778
24: 5 into the land of the C for *their* good. H3778
25:12 and the land of the C, and will make it H3778
32: 4 of the hand of the C, but shall surely be H3778
5 ye fight with the C, ye shall not prosper. H3778
24 the hand of the C, that fight against it, H3778
25 the city is given into the hand of the C. H3778
28 the hand of the C, and into the hand of H3778
29 And the C, that fight against this city, H3778
43 beast; it is given into the hand of the C. H3778
Jer 33: 5 They come to fight with the C, but *it is* H3778
35:11 of the army of the C, and for fear of the H3778
37: 5 Egypt: and when the C that besieged H3778
8 And the C shall come again, and fight H3778
9 saying, The C shall surely depart H3778
10 whole army of the C that fight against H3778
11 the army of the C was broken up from H3778
13 saying, Thou fallest away to the C. H3778
14 not away to the C. But he hearkened not H3778
38: 2 goeth forth to the C shall live; for he H3778
18 the hand of the C, and they shall burn H3778
19 are fallen to the C, lest they deliver me H3778
23 thy children to the C: and thou shalt not H3778
39: 8 And the C burned the king's house, and H3778
40: 9 not to serve the C: dwell in the land, and H3778
10 to serve the C, which will come unto H3778
41: 3 at Mizpah, and the C that were found H3778
18 Because of the C: for they were afraid of H3778
43: 3 the hand of the C, that they might put H3778
50: 1 land of the C by Jeremiah the prophet. H3778
8 out of the land of the C, and be as the he H3778
25 Lord GOD of hosts in the land of the C. H3778
35 A sword *is* upon the C, saith the LORD, H3778
45 the land of the C: Surely the least of the H3778
51: 4 in the land of the C, and *they that are* H3778
54 destruction from the land of the C: H3778
52: 7 garden; (now the C *were* by the city H3778
8 But the army of the C pursued after the H3778
14 And all the army of the C, that *were* H3778
17 of the LORD, the C brake, and carried H3778
Ezk 1: 3 in the land of the C by the river Chebar; H3778
12:13 *to* the land of the C; yet shall he not see H3778
23:14 of the C pourtrayed with vermilion, H3778
23 The Babylonians, and all the C, Pekod, H3778
Dan 1: 4 the learning and the tongue of the C. H3778
2: 2 the sorcerers, and the C, for to shew the H3778
4 Then spake the C to the king in H3778
5 The king answered and said to the C, H3779
10 The C answered before the king, and H3779
3: 8 Wherefore at that time certain C came H3779
4: 7 astrologers, the C, and the soothsayers: H3779
5: 7 astrologers, the C, and the soothsayers. H3779
11 astrologers, C, *and* soothsayers; H3779
30 was Belshazzar the king of the C slain. H3779
9: 1 was made king over the realm of the C; H3778
Hab 1: 6 For, lo, I raise up the C, *that* bitter and H3778

CHALDEANS'
Jer 39: 5 But the C army pursued after them, H3778

CHALDEES
Gen 11:28 the land of his nativity, in Ur of the C. H3778
31 from Ur of the C, to go into the land of H3778
15: 7 the C, to give thee this land to inherit it. H3778
2Ki 24: 2 him bands of the C, and bands of the H3778
25: 4 garden: (now the C *were* against the H3778
5 And the army of the C pursued after H3778
10 And all the army of the C, that *were* H3778
13 of the LORD, did the C break in pieces, H3778
24 the servants of the C: dwell in the land, H3778
25 the C that were with him at Mizpah. H3778
26 to Egypt: for they were afraid of the C. H3778
2Ch 36:17 the king of the C, who slew their young H3778
Neh 9: 7 out of Ur of the C, and gavest him the H3778

CHALDEES'
Isa 13:19 the beauty of the C excellency, shall be H3778

CHALKSTONES
Isa 27: 9 of the altar as c that are beaten in H68+H1615

CHALLENGETH
Ex 22: 9 which *another* c to be his, the cause of H559

CHAMBER
Gen 43:30 he entered into *his* c, and wept there. H2315
Jdg 3:24 he covereth his feet in his summer c. H2315
15: 1 in to my wife into the c. But her father H2315
16: 9 with her in the c. And she said unto H2315
12 abiding in the c. And he brake them H2315
2Sa 13:10 the meat into the c, that I may eat of H2315
10 *them* into the c to Amnon her brother. H2315
18:33 and went up to the c over the gate, and H5944
1Ki 1:15 the king into the c: and the king was H2315
6: 6 The nethermost c *was* five cubits H3326
8 The door for the middle c *was* in the H6763
8 *c*, and out of the middle into the third.
14:28 brought them back into the guard c. H8372
17:23 down out of the c into the house, and H5944
1Ki 20:30 and came into the city, into an inner c. H2315
22:25 shalt go into an inner c to hide thyself. H2315
2Ki 1: 2 in his upper c that *was* in Samaria, H5944
4:10 Let us make a little c, I pray thee, on the H5944
11 and he turned into the c, and lay there. H5944
9: 2 brethren, and carry him to an inner c; H2315
23:11 the LORD, by the c of Nathan-melech H3957
12 top of the upper c of Ahaz, which the H5944
2Ch 12:11 brought them again into the guard c. H8372
18:24 shalt go into an inner c to hide thyself. H2315
Ezr 10: 6 and went into the c of Johanan the son H3957
Neh 3:30 the son of Berechiah over against his c. H5393
13: 4 oversight of the c of the house of our H3957
5 And he had prepared for him a great c, H3957
7 a c in the courts of the house of God. H5393
8 household stuff of Tobiah out of the c. H3957
Ps 19: 5 coming out of his c, *and* rejoiceth as a H2646
Song 3: 4 and into the c of her that conceived me. H2315
Jer 35: 4 of the LORD, into the c of the sons of H3957
4 God, which *was* by the c of the princes, H3957
4 *was* above the c of Maaseiah the son H3957
36:10 the LORD, in the c of Gemariah the son H3957
12 house, into the scribe's c: and, lo, all the H3957
20 laid up the roll in the c of Elishama the H3957
21 the scribe's c. And Jehudi read it in H3957
Ezk 40: 7 And *every* little c *was* one reed long, H8372
13 the roof of *one* little c to the roof of H8372
45 And he said unto me, This c, whose H3957
46 And the c whose prospect *is* toward the H3957
41: 5 of *every* side c, four cubits, round about H6763
7 the lowest *c* to the highest by the midst.
9 *was* for the side c without, *was* five H6763
42: 1 me into the c that *was* over against H3957
Dan 6:10 being open in his c toward Jerusalem, H5952
Joel 2:16 of his c, and the bride out of her closet. H2315
Act 9:37 had washed, they laid *her* in an upper c. *G5253*
39 into the upper c: and all the widows *G5253*
20: 8 c, where they were gathered together. *G5253*

CHAMBERING
Ro 13:13 not in c and wantonness, not *G2845*

CHAMBERLAIN
2Ki 23:11 the c, which *was* in the suburbs, H5631
Est 2: 3 of Hege the king's c, keeper of the H5631
14 the king's c, which kept the concubines: H5631
15 Hegai the king's c, the keeper of the H5631
Act 12:20 made Blastus the king's c their friend, *G1909*
Ro 16:23 you. Erastus the c of the city saluteth *G3623*

CHAMBERLAINS
Est 1:10 Carcas, the seven c that served in the H5631
12 by *his* c: therefore was the king H5631
15 of the king Ahasuerus by the c? H5631
2:21 two of the king's c, Bigthan and Teresh, H5631
4: 4 So Esther's maids and her c came and H5631
5 *one* of the king's c, whom he had H5631
6: 2 two of the king's c, the keepers of the H5631
14 came the king's c, and hasted to bring H5631
7: 9 And Harbonah, one of the c, said before H5631

CHAMBERS
1Ki 6: 5 of the house he built c round about, H3326
5 the oracle: and he made c round about: H6763
10 And *then* he built c against all the H3326
1Ch 9:26 c and treasuries of the house of God. H3957
33 *remaining* in the c *were* free: for they H3957
23:28 the courts, and in the c, and in the H3957
28:11 and of the upper c thereof, and of the H5944
12 and of all the c round about, of the H3957
2Ch 3: 9 And he overlaid the upper c with gold. H5944
31:11 to prepare c in the house of the LORD; H3957
Ezr 8:29 in the c of the house of the LORD. H3957
Neh 10:37 the priests, to the c of the house of our H3957
38 God, to the c, into the treasure house. H3957
39 the oil, unto the c, where *are* the vessels H3957
12:44 over the c for the treasures, for H5393
13: 9 they cleansed the c: and thither brought H3957
Job 9: 9 and Pleiades, and the c of the south. H2315
Ps 104: 3 Who layeth the beams of his c in the H5944
13 He watereth the hills from his c: the H5944
105:30 in abundance, in the c of their kings. H2315
Prv 7:27 to hell, going down to the c of death. H2315
24: 4 And by knowledge shall the c be filled H2315
Song 1: 4 me into his c: we will be glad and H2315
Isa 26:20 Come, my people, enter thou into thy c, H2315
Jer 22:13 and his c by wrong; *that* useth H5944
14 house and large c, and cutteth him out H5944
35: 2 of the c, and give them wine to drink. H3957

Ezk 8:12 every man in the **c** of his imagery? for H2315
21:14 slain, which entereth into their privy **c**. H2314
40: 7 between the little **c** *were* five cubits; H8372
10 And the little **c** of the gate eastward H8372
12 The space also before the little **c** *was* H8372
12 side: and the little **c** *were* six cubits on H8372
16 to the little **c**, and to their posts within H8372
17 and, lo, *there were* **c**, and a pavement H3957
17 thirty **c** *were* upon the pavement. H3957
21 And the little **c** thereof *were* three on H8372
29 And the little **c** thereof, and the posts H8372
33 And the little **c** thereof, and the posts H8372
36 The little **c** thereof, the posts thereof, H8372
38 And the **c** and the entries thereof *were* H3957
44 And without the inner gate *were* the **c** H3957
41: 6 And the side **c** *were* three, one over H6763
6 house for the side **c** round about, that H6763
7 upward to the side **c**: for the winding H6763
8 **c** *were* a full reed of six great cubits. H6763
9 the place of the side **c** that *were* within. H6763
10 And between the **c** *was* the wideness of H3957
11 And the doors of the side **c** *were* H6763
26 side **c** of the house, and thick planks. H6763
42: 4 And before the **c** *was* a walk of ten H3957
5 Now the upper **c** *were* shorter: for the H3957
7 over against the **c**, toward the utter H3957
7 the **c**, the length thereof *was* fifty cubits. H3957
8 For the length of the **c** that *were* in the H3957
9 And from under these **c** *was* the entry H3957
10 The **c** *were* in the thickness of the wall H3957
11 appearance of the **c** which *were* toward H3957
12 And according to the doors of the **c** H3957
13 Then said he unto me, The north **c** *and* H3957
13 *and* the south **c**, which *are* before the H3957
13 place, they *be* holy **c**, where the priests H3957
44:19 them in the holy **c**, and they shall put on H3957
45: 5 for a possession for twenty **c**. H3957
46:19 the gate, into the holy **c** of the priests, H3957
Mt 24:26 he *is* in the secret **c**; believe *it* not. G5009

CHAMELEON
Lev 11:30 And the ferret, and the **c**, and the lizard, H3581

CHAMOIS
Dt 14: 5 the pygarg, and the wild ox, and the **c**. H2169

CHAMPAIGN
Dt 11:30 which dwell in the **c** over against H6160

CHAMPION
1Sa 17: 4 And there went out a **c** out of H376+H1143
23 came up the **c**, the Philistine of H376+H1143
51 saw their **c** was dead, they fled. H1368

CHANAAN
Act 7:11 the land of Egypt and **C**, and great G5477
13:19 **C**, he divided their land to them by lot. G5477

CHANCE
Dt 22: 6 If a bird's nest **c** to be before thee in the H7122
1Sa 6: 9 us: it *was* a **c** *that* happened to us. H4745
2Sa 1: 6 said, As I happened by **c** upon mount H7122
Ecc 9:11 but time and **c** happeneth to them all. H6294
Lk 10:31 And by **c** there came down a certain G4795
1Co 15:37 may **c** of wheat, or of some other *grain*: G1487

CHANCELLOR
Ezr 4: 8 Rehum the **c** and Shimshai the H1169+H2942
9 Then *wrote* Rehum the **c**, and H1169+H2942
17 Rehum the **c**, and *to* Shimshai H1169+H2942

CHANCETH
Dt 23:10 uncleanness that **c** him by night, then H7137

CHANGE
Gen 35: 2 and be clean, and **c** your garments: H2498
Lev 27:10 He shall not alter it, nor **c** it, a good for H4171
10 if he shall at all **c** beast for beast, then H4171
33 neither shall he **c** it: and if he change H4171
33 it: and if he **c** it at all, then both it H4171
33 both it and the **c** thereof shall be holy; H8545
Jdg 14:12 thirty sheets and thirty **c** of garments: H2487
13 sheets and thirty **c** of garments. And H2487
19 spoil, and gave **c** of garments unto H2487
Job 14:14 time will I wait, till my **c** come. H2487
17:12 They **c** the night into day: the light *is* H7760
Ps 102:26 **c** them, and they shall be changed: H2498
Prv 24:21 not with them that are given to **c**: H8138
Isa 9:10 down, but we will **c** *them into* cedars. H2498
Jer 2:36 Why gaddest thou about so much to **c** H8138
13:23 Can the Ethiopian **c** his skin, or the H2015
Dan 7:25 High, and think to **c** times and laws: H8133
Hos 4: 7 will I **c** their glory into shame. H4171
Hab 1:11 Then shall *his* mind **c**, and he shall pass H2498
Zec 3: 4 and I will clothe thee with **c** of raiment. H4254
Mal 3: 6 For I *am* the LORD, I **c** not; therefore ye H8138
Act 6:14 **c** the customs which Moses delivered us. G236
Ro 1:26 their women did **c** the natural use into G3337
Gal 4:20 **c** my voice; for I stand in doubt of you. G236
Php 3:21 Who shall **c** our vile body, that it may G3345
Heb 7:12 is made of necessity a **c** also of the law. G3331

CHANGEABLE
Isa 3:22 The **c** suits of apparel, and the mantles, H4254

CHANGED
Gen 31: 7 hath deceived me, and **c** my wages ten H2498
41 and thou hast **c** my wages ten times. H2498
41:14 *himself*, and **c** his raiment, and came H2498
Lev 13:16 Or if the raw flesh turn again, and be **c** H2015
55 plague have not **c** his colour, and the H2015
Nu 32:38 names being **c**,) and Shibmah: and gave H4142
1Sa 21:13 And he **c** his behaviour before them, H8138
2Sa 12:20 *himself*, and **c** his apparel, and came H2498
2Ki 24:17 his stead, and **c** his name to Zedekiah. H5437
25:29 And **c** his prison garments: and he did H8132
Job 30:18 is my garment **c**: it bindeth me about H2664
Ps 34:ttl *A Psalm* of David, when he **c** his H8138
102:26 thou change them, and they shall be **c**: H2498
106:20 Thus they **c** their glory into the H4171
Ecc 8: 1 and the boldness of his face shall be **c**. H8132
Isa 24: 5 the laws, **c** the ordinance, broken H2498
Jer 2:11 Hath a nation **c** *their* gods, which *are* H4171
11 my people have **c** their glory for *that* H4171
48:11 remained in him, and his scent is not **c**. H4171
52:33 And **c** his prison garments: and he did H8138
Lam 4: 1 is the most fine gold **c**! the stones of the H8132
Ezk 5: 6 And she hath **c** my judgments into H4171
Dan 2: 9 me, till the time be **c**: therefore tell me H8133
3:19 of his visage was **c** against Shadrach, H8133
27 were their coats **c**, nor the smell of fire H8133
28 in him, and have **c** the king's word, and H8133
4:16 Let his heart be **c** from man's, and let a H8133
5: 6 Then the king's countenance was **c**, and H8133
9 **c** in him, and his lords were astonied. H8133
10 thee, nor let thy countenance be **c**: H8133
6: 8 that it be not **c**, according to the law H8133
15 which the king establisheth may be **c**. H8133
17 might not be **c** concerning Daniel. H8133
7:28 my countenance **c** in me: but I kept the H8133
Mic 2: 4 spoiled: he hath **c** the portion of my H4171
Act 28: 6 come to him, they **c** their minds, and G3328
Ro 1:23 And **c** the glory of the uncorruptible God G236
25 Who **c** the truth of God into a lie, and G3337
1Co 15:51 shall not all sleep, but we shall all be **c**, G236
52 raised incorruptible, and we shall be **c**. G236
2Co 3:18 of the Lord, are **c** into the same image G3339
Heb 1:12 up, and they shall be **c**: but thou art the G236
7:12 For the priesthood being **c**, there is G3346

CHANGERS
Jn 2:14 and doves, and the **c** of money sitting: G2773

CHANGERS'
Jn 2:15 the **c** money, and overthrew the tables; G2855

CHANGES
Gen 45:22 To all of them he gave each man **c** of H2487
22 *pieces* of silver, and five **c** of raiment. H2487
2Ki 5: 5 *pieces* of gold, and ten **c** of raiment. H2487
22 talent of silver, and two **c** of garments. H2487
23 bags, with two **c** of garments, and laid H2487
Job 10:17 upon me; **c** and war *are* against me. H2487
Ps 55:19 have no **c**, therefore they fear not God. H2487

CHANGEST
Job 14:20 he passeth: thou **c** his countenance, H8138

CHANGETH
Ps 15: 4 sweareth to *his own* hurt, and **c** not. H4171
Dan 2:21 And he **c** the times and the seasons: he H8133

CHANGING
Ru 4: 7 and concerning **c**, for to confirm all H8545

CHANNEL
Isa 27:12 beat off from the **c** of the river unto the H7641

CHANNELS
2Sa 22:16 And the **c** of the sea appeared, the H650
Ps 18:15 Then the **c** of waters were seen, and the H650
Isa 8: 7 over all his **c**, and go over all his banks: H650

CHANT
Am 6: 5 That **c** to the sound of the viol, *and* H6527

CHAPEL
Am 7:13 *is* the king's **c**, and it *is* the king's court. H4720

C

CHAPITER
1Ki 7:16 height of the one **c** *was* five cubits, and H3805
16 the height of the other **c** *was* five cubits: H3805
17 one **c**, and seven for the other chapiter. H3805
17 one chapiter, and seven for the other **c**. H3805
18 and so did he for the other **c**. H3805
20 in rows round about upon the other **c**. H3805
31 And the mouth of it within the **c** and H3805
2Ki 25:17 cubits, and the **c** upon it *was* brass: H3805
17 the height of the **c** three cubits; and the H3805
17 upon the **c** round about, all of brass: H3805
2Ch 3:15 high, and the **c** that *was* on the top H6858
Jer 52:22 And a **c** of brass *was* upon it; and the H3805
22 the height of one **c** *was* five cubits, with H3805

CHAPITERS
Ex 36:38 he overlaid their **c** and their fillets with H7218
38:17 overlaying of their **c** *of* silver; and all H7218
19 of their **c** and their fillets *of* silver. H7218
28 and overlaid their **c**, and filleted them. H7218
1Ki 7:16 And he made two **c** *of* molten brass, to H3805
17 work, for the **c** which *were* upon the H3805
18 to cover the **c** that *were* upon the H3805
19 And the **c** that *were* upon the top of the H3805
20 And the **c** upon the two pillars *had* H3805
41 *two* bowls of the **c** that *were* on the top H3805
41 two bowls of the **c** which *were* upon the H3805
42 of the **c** that *were* upon the pillars; H3805
2Ch 4:12 pommels, and the **c** *which were* on the H3805
12 **c** which *were* on the top of the pillars; H3805
13 of the **c** which *were* upon the pillars. H3805
Jer 52:22 upon the **c** round about, all *of* brass. H3805

CHAPMEN
2Ch 9:14 Beside *that which* **c** and H582+H8446

CHAPT
Jer 14: 4 Because the ground is **c**, for there was H2865

CHARASHIM
1Ch 4:14 the valley of **C**; for they were craftsmen. H3751

CHARGE
Gen 26: 5 and kept my **c**, my commandments, H4931
28: 6 him he gave him a **c**, saying, Thou shalt H6680
Ex 6:13 and gave them a **c** unto the children of H6680
19:21 Moses, Go down, **c** the people, lest they H5749
Lev 8:35 days, and keep the **c** of the LORD, that H4931
Nu 1:53 the **c** of the tabernacle of testimony. H4931
3: 7 And they shall keep his **c**, and the H4931
7 his charge, and the **c** of the whole H4931
8 and the **c** of the children of Israel, H4931
25 And the **c** of the sons of Gershon in the H4931
28 keeping the **c** of the sanctuary. H4931
31 And their **c** *shall be* the ark, and the H4931
32 them that keep the **c** of the sanctuary. H4931
36 And *under* the custody and **c** of the H4931
38 sons, keeping the **c** of the sanctuary for H4931
38 sanctuary for the **c** of the children of H4931
4:27 unto them in **c** all their burdens. H4931
28 and their **c** *shall be* under the hand H4931
31 And this *is* the **c** of their burden, H4931
32 instruments of the **c** of their burden. H4931
5:19 And the priest shall **c** her by an oath, H7650
21 Then the priest shall **c** the woman with H7650
8:26 to keep the **c**, and shall do no service. H4931
26 do unto the Levites touching their **c**. H4931
9:19 the **c** of the LORD, and journeyed not. H4931
23 they kept the **c** of the LORD, at the H4931
18: 3 And they shall keep thy **c**, and the H4931
3 charge, and the **c** of all the tabernacle: H4931
4 thee, and keep the **c** of the tabernacle H4931
5 And ye shall keep the **c** of the H4931
5 and the **c** of the altar: that there H4931
8 given thee the **c** of mine heave offerings H4931
27:19 and give him a **c** in their sight. H6680
23 him, and gave him a **c**, as the LORD H6680
31:30 the **c** of the tabernacle of the LORD. H4931

Nu 31:47 which kept the c of the tabernacle of H4931
49 c, and there lacketh not one man of us. H3027
Dt 3:28 But c Joshua, and encourage him, and H6680
11: 1 God, and keep his c, and his statutes, H4931
21: 8 c. And the blood shall be forgiven them. H7130
31:14 that I may give him a c. And Moses and H6680
23 And he gave Joshua the son of Nun a c, H6680
Jos 22: 3 day, but have kept the c of the H4931
2Sa 14: 8 and I will give c concerning thee. H6680
18: 5 all the captains c concerning Absalom. H6680
1Ki 2: 3 And keep the c of the LORD thy God, to H4931
4:28 were, every man according to his c. H4941
11:28 over all the c of the house of Joseph. H5447
2Ki 7:17 leaned to have the c of the gate: and the H5921
1Ch 9:27 of God, because the c *was* upon them, H4931
28 And *certain* of them had the c of the H5921
22:12 and give thee c concerning Israel, that H6680
23:32 And that they should keep the c of the H4931
32 and the c of the holy *place*, and H4931
32 *place*, and the c of the sons of Aaron H4931
2Ch 13:11 for we keep the c of the LORD our God; H4931
30:17 Levites had the c of the killing of the H5921
Neh 7: 2 of the palace, c over Jerusalem: for H6680
10:32 Also we made ordinances for us, to c H5414
Est 3: 9 that have the c of the business, to bring H6213
4: 8 *it* unto her, and to c her that she should H6680
Job 34:13 Who hath given him a c over the earth? H6485
Ps 35:11 laid to my c *things* that I knew not. H7592
91:11 For he shall give his angels c over thee, H6680
Song 2: 7 I c you, O ye daughters of Jerusalem, by H7650
3: 5 I c you, O ye daughters of Jerusalem, by H7650
5: 8 I c you, O daughters of Jerusalem, if ye H7650
9 *another* beloved, that thou dost so c us? H7650
8: 4 I c you, O daughters of Jerusalem, that H7650
Isa 10: 6 will I give him a c, to take the spoil, and H6680
Jer 39:11 of Babylon gave c concerning Jeremiah H6680
47: 7 hath given it a c against Ashkelon, and H6680
52:25 which had the c of the men of war; and H6496
Ezk 9: 1 them that have c over the city to draw H6486
40:45 the keepers of the c of the house. H4931
46 the keepers of the c of the altar: these H4931
44: 8 And ye have not kept the c of mine holy H4931
8 of my c in my sanctuary for yourselves. H4931
11 sanctuary, *having* c at the gates of the H6486
14 But I will make them keepers of the c of H4931
15 that kept the c of my sanctuary when H4931
16 unto me, and they shall keep my c. H4931
48:11 have kept my c, which went not astray H4931
Zec 3: 7 if thou wilt keep my c, then thou shalt H4931
Mt 4: 6 give his angels c concerning thee: and G1781
Mk 9:25 and deaf spirit, I c thee, come out of G2004
Lk 4:10 his angels c over thee, to keep thee: G1781
Act 7:60 this sin to their c. And when he had said G2476
8:27 who had the c of all her treasure, and G1909
16:24 Who, having received such a c, thrust G3852
23:29 to his c worthy of death or of bonds. G1462
Ro 8:33 Who shall lay any thing to the c of G2596
1Co 9:18 of Christ without c, that I abuse not my G77
1Th 5:27 I c you by the Lord that this epistle be G3726
1Ti 1: 3 that thou mightest c some that they G3853
18 This c I commit unto thee, son G3852
5: 7 And these things give in c, that they G3853
21 I c *thee* before God, and the Lord Jesus G1263
6:13 I give thee c in the sight of God, who G3853
17 C them that are rich in this world, that G3853
2Ti 4: 1 I c *thee* therefore before God, and the G1263
16 *God* that it may not be laid to their c. G3049

CHARGEABLE

2Sa 13:25 now go, lest we be c unto thee. And he H3513
Neh 5:15 before me were c unto the people, and H3513
2Co 11: 9 and wanted, I was c to no man: for that G2655
1Th 2: 9 we would not be c unto any of you, we G1912
2Th 3: 8 that we might not be c to any of you: G1912

CHARGED

Gen 26:11 And Abimelech c all *his* people, saying, H6680
28: 1 blessed him, and c him, and said unto H6680
40: 4 And the captain of the guard c Joseph H6485
49:29 And he c them, and said unto them, I H6680
Ex 1:22 And Pharaoh c all his people, saying, H6680
Dt 1:16 And I c your judges at that time, H6680
24: 5 neither shall he be c with any business: H5674
27:11 And Moses c the people the same day, H6680
Jos 18: 8 away: and Joshua c them that went to H6680
22: 5 of the LORD c you, to love the LORD H6680
Ru 2: 9 them: have I not c the young men that H6680
1Sa 14:27 when his father c the people with the H7650
28 Thy father straitly c the people with an H7650
2Sa 11:19 And c the messenger, saying, When H6680
18:12 our hearing the king c thee and Abishai H6680
1Ki 2: 1 die; and he c Solomon his son, saying, H6680
43 commandment that I have c thee with? H6680
13: 9 For so was it c me by the word of the H6680
2Ki 17:15 the LORD had c them, that they should H6680
35 a covenant, and c them, saying, Ye H6680
1Ch 22: 6 his son, and c him to build an house H6680
13 which the LORD c Moses with H6680
2Ch 19: 9 And he c them, saying, Thus shall ye H6680
36:23 me; and he hath c me to build him an H6485
Ezr 1: 2 earth; and he hath c me to build him H6485
Neh 13:19 be shut, and c that they should not H559
Est 2:10 had c her that she should not shew *it*. H6680
20 as Mordecai had c her: for Esther did H6680
Job 1:22 In all this Job sinned not, nor c God H5414
4:18 servants; and his angels he c with folly: H7760
Jer 32:13 And I c Baruch before them, saying, H6680
35: 8 in all that he hath c us, to drink no H6680
Mt 9:30 and Jesus straitly c them, saying, See G1690
12:16 And c them that they should not make G2008
16:20 Then c he his disciples that they should G1291
17: 9 mountain, Jesus c them, saying, Tell G1781
Mk 1:43 And he straitly c him, and forthwith G1690
3:12 And he straitly c them that they should G2008
5:43 And he c them straitly that no man G1291
7:36 And he c them that they should tell no G1291
36 but the more he c them, so much the G1291
8:15 And he c them, saying, Take heed, G1291
30 And he c them that they should tell no G2008
9: 9 from the mountain, he c them that they G1291
10:48 And many c him that he should hold G2008
Lk 5:14 And he c him to tell no man: but go, G3853
8:56 astonished: but he c them that they G3853
9:21 And he straitly c them, and G2008
Act 23:22 man depart, and c *him, See thou* tell no G3853
1Th 2:11 comforted and c every one of you, as G3140
1Ti 5:16 let not the church be c; that it may relieve G916

CHARGEDST

Ex 19:23 Sinai: for thou c us, saying, Set bounds H5749

CHARGER

Nu 7:13 And his offering *was* one silver c, the H7086
19 He offered *for* his offering one silver c, H7086
25 His offering *was* one silver c, the weight H7086
31 His offering *was* one silver c of the H7086
37 His offering *was* one silver c, the weight H7086
43 His offering *was* one silver c of the H7086
49 His offering *was* one silver c, the weight H7086
55 His offering *was* one silver c of the H7086
61 His offering *was* one silver c, the weight H7086
67 His offering *was* one silver c, the weight H7086
73 His offering *was* one silver c, the weight H7086
79 His offering *was* one silver c, the weight H7086
85 Each c of silver *weighing* an hundred H7086
Mt 14: 8 Give me here John Baptist's head in a c. G4094
11 And his head was brought in a c, and G4094
Mk 6:25 by in a c the head of John the Baptist. G4094
28 And brought his head in a c, and gave it G4094

CHARGERS

Nu 7:84 of Israel: twelve c of silver, twelve silver H7086
Ezr 1: 9 And this *is* the number of them: thirty c H105
9 c of silver, nine and twenty knives, H105

CHARGES

2Ch 8:14 and the Levites to their c, to praise and H4931
31:16 in their c according to their courses; H4931
17 and upward, in their c by their courses; H4931
35: 2 And he set the priests in their c, and H4931
Act 21:24 them, and be at c with them, that they G1159
1Co 9: 7 any time at his own c? who planteth a G3800

CHARGEST

2Sa 3: 8 of David, that thou c me to day with a H6485

CHARGING

Act 16:23 prison, c the jailor to keep them safely: G3853
2Ti 2:14 in remembrance, c *them* before the G1263

CHARIOT

Gen 41:43 ride in the second c which he had; and H4818
46:29 And Joseph made ready his c, and went H4818
Ex 14: 6 And he made ready his c, and took his H7393
25 And took off their c wheels, that they H4818
Jdg 4:15 off *his* c, and fled away on his feet. H4818
5:28 lattice, Why is his c *so* long in coming? H7393
2Sa 8: 4 houghed all the c *horses*, but reserved H7393
1Ki 7:33 *was* like the work of a c wheel: their H4818
10:29 And a c came up and went out of Egypt H4818
12:18 get him up to his c, to flee to Jerusalem. H4818
18:44 Ahab, Prepare *thy c*, and get thee down,
20:25 for horse, and c for chariot: and we H7393
25 and chariot for c: and we will fight H7393
33 he caused him to come up into the c. H4818
22:34 the driver of his c, Turn thine hand, and H7395
35 stayed up in his c against the Syrians, H4818
35 out of the wound into the midst of the c. H7393
38 And *one* washed the c in the pool of H7393
2Ki 2:11 *there appeared* a c of fire, and horses H7393
12 my father, the c of Israel, and the H7393
5: 9 and with his c, and stood at the door H7393
21 the c to meet him, and said, *Is* all well? H4818
26 again from his c to meet thee? *Is it* a H4818
7:14 They took therefore two c horses; and H7393
9:16 So Jehu rode in a c, and went to Jezreel;
21 And Joram said, Make ready. And his c H7393
21 out, each in his c, and they went out H7393
24 at his heart, and he sunk down in his c. H7393
27 him also in the c. *And they did so* at the H4818
28 And his servants carried him in a c to
10:15 and he took him up to him into the c. H4818
16 LORD. So they made him ride in his c. H7393
13:14 c of Israel, and the horsemen thereof. H7393
23:30 And his servants carried him in a c dead
1Ch 18: 4 houghed all the c *horses*, but reserved H7393
28:18 the pattern of the c of the cherubims, H4818
2Ch 1:14 c cities, and with the king at Jerusalem. H7393
17 out of Egypt a c for six hundred *shekels* H4818
8: 6 had, and all the c cities, and the cities H7393
9:25 c cities, and with the king at Jerusalem. H7393
10:18 get him up to *his* c, to flee to Jerusalem. H4818
18:33 he said to his c man, Turn thine hand, H7395
34 *himself* up in *his* c against the Syrians H4818
35:24 him out of that c, and put him in the H4818
24 him in the second c that he had; and H7393
Ps 46: 9 in sunder; he burneth the c in the fire. H5699
76: 6 c and horse are cast into a dead sleep. H7393
104: 3 the clouds his c: who walketh upon the H7398
Song 3: 9 King Solomon made himself a c of the H668
Isa 21: 7 And he saw a c *with* a couple of H7393
7 of horsemen, a c of asses, *and* a chariot H7393
7 of asses, *and* a c of camels; and he H7393
9 And, behold, here cometh a c of men, H7393
43:17 Which bringeth forth the c and horse, H7393
Jer 51:21 I break in pieces the c and his rider; H7393
Mic 1:13 Lachish, bind the c to the swift beast: H4818
Zec 6: 2 In the first c *were* red horses; and in H4818
2 and in the second c black horses; H4818
3 And in the third c white horses; and in H4818
3 in the fourth c grisled and bay horses. H4818
9:10 And I will cut off the c from Ephraim, H7393
Act 8:28 Was returning, and sitting in his c read G716
29 Philip, Go near, and join thyself to this c. G716
38 And he commanded the c to stand still: G716

CHARIOT-CITIES See CHARIOT and CITIES.

CHARIOT-HORSES See CHARIOT and HORSES.

CHARIOT-MAN See CHARIOT and MAN.

CHARIOTS

Gen 50: 9 And there went up with him both c and H7393
Ex 14: 7 And he took six hundred chosen c, and H7393
7 and all the c of Egypt, and captains H7393
9 all the horses *and* c of Pharaoh, and his H7393
17 upon his c, and upon his horsemen. H7393
18 upon his c, and upon his horsemen. H7393
23 horses, his c, and his horsemen. H7393
26 upon their c, and upon their horsemen. H7393
28 and covered the c, and the horsemen, H7393
15: 4 Pharaoh's c and his host hath he cast H4818
19 went in with his c and with his H7393
Dt 11: 4 and to their c; how he made the water H7393
20: 1 seest horses, and c, *and* a people more H7393
Jos 11: 4 with horses and c very many. H7393
6 their horses, and burn their c with fire. H4818
9 their horses, and burnt their c with fire. H4818
17:16 of the valley have c of iron, *both they* H7393
18 have iron c, *and* though they *be* strong. H7393
24: 6 with c and horsemen unto the Red sea. H7393
Jdg 1:19 the valley, because they had c of iron. H7393
4: 3 had nine hundred c of iron; and twenty H7393
7 army, with his c and his multitude; and H7393
13 And Sisera gathered together all his c, H7393
13 *even* nine hundred c of iron, and all the H7393

Jdg 4:15 Sisera, and all *his* c, and all *his* host, H7393
16 But Barak pursued after the c, and after H7393
5:28 coming? why tarry the wheels of his c? H4818
1Sa 8:11 *them* for himself, for his c, and *to be* his H4818
11 and *some* shall run before his c. H4818
12 of war, and instruments of his c. H7393
13: 5 thirty thousand c, and six thousand H7393
2Sa 1: 6 his spear; and, lo, the c and horsemen H7393
8: 4 And David took from him a thousand c,
4 but reserved of them *for* an hundred c. H7393
10:18 *of* seven hundred c of the Syrians, and H7393
15: 1 prepared him c and horses, and fifty H4818
1Ki 1: 5 he prepared him c and horsemen, and H7393
4:26 his c, and twelve thousand horsemen. H4817
9:19 and cities for his c, and cities for his H7393
22 and rulers of his c, and his horsemen. H7393
10:26 And Solomon gathered together c and H7393
26 and four hundred c, and twelve H7393
26 for c, and with the king at Jerusalem. H7393
16: 9 captain of half *his* c, conspired against H7393
20: 1 and horses, and c: and he went up and H7393
21 the horses and c, and slew the Syrians H7393
22:31 that had rule over his c, saying, Fight H7393
32 the captains of the c saw Jehoshaphat, H7393
33 the captains of the c perceived that it H7393
2Ki 6:14 Therefore sent he thither horses, and c, H7393
15 with horses and c. And his servant said H7393
17 horses and c of fire round about Elisha. H7393
7: 6 to hear a noise of c, and a noise of H7393
8:21 to Zair, and all the c with him: and he H7393
21 c: and the people fled into their tents. H7393
10: 2 and *there are* with you c and horses, a H7393
13: 7 and ten c, and ten thousand footmen; H7393
18:24 trust on Egypt for c and for horsemen? H7393
19:23 multitude of my c I am come up to the H7393
23:11 and burned the c of the sun with fire. H4818
1Ch 18: 4 And David took from him a thousand c, H7393
4 but reserved of them an hundred c. H7393
19: 6 silver to hire them c and horsemen out H7393
7 and two thousand c, and the king of H7393
18 *which fought in* c, and forty thousand H7393
2Ch 1:14 And Solomon gathered c and H7393
14 and four hundred c, and twelve H7393
8: 9 and captains of his c and horsemen. H7393
9:25 for horses and c, and twelve thousand H4818
12: 3 With twelve hundred c, and threescore H7393
14: 9 hundred c; and came unto Mareshah. H4818
16: 8 with very many c and horsemen? yet, H7393
18:30 the captains of the c that *were* with H7393
31 the captains of the c saw Jehoshaphat, H7393
32 the captains of the c perceived that it H7393
21: 9 and all his c with him: and he rose H7393
9 him in, and the captains of the c. H7393
Ps 20: 7 Some *trust* in c, and some in horses: but H7393
68:17 The c of God *are* twenty thousand, H7393
Song 1: 9 to a company of horses in Pharaoh's c. H7393
6:12 made me *like* the c of Ammi-nadib. H4818
Isa 2: 7 neither *is there any* end of their c: H4818
22: 6 And Elam bare the quiver with c of H7393
7 shall be full of c, and the horsemen H7393
18 die, and there the c of thy glory *shall be* H4818
31: 1 and trust in c, because *they are* many; H7393
36: 9 trust on Egypt for c and for horsemen? H7393
37:24 multitude of my c am I come up to the H7393
66:15 fire, and with his c like a whirlwind, to H4818
20 horses, and in c, and in litters, and H7393
Jer 4:13 up as clouds, and his c *shall be* as a H4818
17:25 of David, riding in c and on horses, H7393
22: 4 of David, riding in c and on horses, he, H7393
46: 9 Come up, ye horses; and rage, ye c; and H7393
47: 3 at the rushing of his c, *and at* the H7393
50:37 and upon their c, and upon all the H7393
Ezk 23:24 come against thee with c, wagons, and H2021
26: 7 horses, and with c, and with horsemen, H7393
10 wheels, and of the c, when he shall enter H7393
27:20 thy merchant in precious clothes for c. H7396
39:20 with horses and c, with mighty men, H7393
Dan 11:40 like a whirlwind, with c, and with H7393
Joel 2: 5 Like the noise of c on the tops of H4818
Mic 5:10 midst of thee, and I will destroy thy c: H4818
Nah 2: 3 men *are* in scarlet: the c *shall be* with H7393
4 The c shall rage in the streets, they H7393
13 and I will burn her c in the smoke, and H7393
3: 2 pransing horses, and of the jumping c. H4818
Hab 3: 8 thine horses *and* thy c of salvation? H4818
Hag 2:22 will overthrow the c, and those that ride H4818
Zec 6: 1 there came four c out from between H4818
Rev 9: 9 of c of many horses running to battle. G716
18:13 and c, and slaves, and souls of men. G4480

CHARITABLY
Ro 14:15 thou not c. Destroy not him G2596+G26

CHARITY
1Co 8: 1 Knowledge puffeth up, but c edifieth. G26
13: 1 and have not c, I am become *as* sounding G26
2 and have not c, I am nothing. G26
3 and have not c, it profiteth me nothing. G26
4 C suffereth long, *and* is kind; charity G26
4 Charity suffereth long, *and* is kind; c G26
4 c vaunteth not itself, is not puffed up, G26
8 C never faileth: but whether *there be* G26
13 And now abideth faith, hope, c, these G26
13 these three; but the greatest of these *is* c. G26
14: 1 Follow after c, and desire spiritual *gifts*, G26
16:14 Let all your things be done with c. G26
Col 3:14 And above all these things *put on* c, G26
1Th 3: 6 of your faith and c, and that ye have G26
2Th 1: 3 and the c of every one of you all G26
1Ti 1: 5 Now the end of the commandment is c G26
2:15 in faith and c and holiness with sobriety. G26
4:12 in c, in spirit, in faith, in purity. G26
2Ti 2:22 faith, c, peace, with them that G26
3:10 purpose, faith, longsuffering, c, patience, G26
Tit 2: 2 sound in faith, in c, in patience. G26
1Pt 4: 8 And above all things have fervent c G26
8 for c shall cover the multitude of sins. G26
5:14 Greet ye one another with a kiss of c. G26
2Pt 1: 7 kindness; and to brotherly kindness c. G26
3Jn 6 Which have borne witness of thy c G26
Jude 12 These are spots in your feasts of c, when G26
Rev 2:19 I know thy works, and c, and service, and G26

CHARMED
Jer 8:17 which *will* not *be* c, and they shall bite H3908

CHARMER
Dt 18:11 Or a c, or a consulter with H2266+H2267

CHARMERS
Ps 58: 5 Which will not hearken to the voice of c, H3907
Isa 19: 3 idols, and to the c, and to them that have H328

CHARMING
Ps 58: 5 of charmers, c never so wisely. H2266+H2267

CHARRAN
Act 7: 2 in Mesopotamia, before he dwelt in C, G5488
4 and dwelt in C: and from thence, when G5488

CHASE
Lev 26: 7 And ye shall c your enemies, and they H7291
8 And five of you shall c an hundred, and H7291
36 of a shaken leaf shall c them; and they H7291
Dt 32:30 How should one c a thousand, and two H7291
Jos 23:10 One man of you shall c a thousand: for H7291
Ps 35: 5 and let the angel of the LORD c *them*. H1760

CHASED
Dt 1:44 against you, and c you, as bees do, and H7291
Jos 7: 5 six men: for they c them *from* before H7291
8:24 wherein they c them, and when they H7291
10:10 at Gibeon, and c them along the way H7291
11: 8 smote them, and c them unto great H7291
Jdg 9:40 And Abimelech c him, and he fled H7291
20:43 round about, *and* c them, *and* trode H7291
Neh 13:28 Horonite: therefore I c him from me. H1272
Job 18:18 into darkness, and c out of the world. H5074
20: 8 shall be c away as a vision of the night. H5074
Isa 13:14 And it shall be as the c roe, and as a H5080
17:13 far off, and shall be c as the chaff of the H7291
Lam 3:52 Mine enemies c me sore, like a bird, H6679

CHASETH
Prv 19:26 He that wasteth *his* father, *and* c away H1272

CHASING
1Sa 17:53 returned from c after the Philistines, H1814

CHASTE
2Co 11: 2 I may present *you as* a c virgin to Christ. G53
Tit 2: 5 *To be* discreet, c, keepers at home, good, G53
1Pt 3: 2 While they behold your c conversation G53

CHASTEN
2Sa 7:14 iniquity, I will c him with the rod of H3198
Ps 6: 1 neither c me in thy hot displeasure. H3256
38: 1 neither c me in thy hot displeasure. H3256
Prv 19:18 C thy son while there is hope, and let H3256
Dan 10:12 and to c thyself before thy God, H6031
Rev 3:19 As many as I love, I rebuke and c: be G3811

CHASTENED
Dt 21:18 c him, will not hearken unto them: H3256
Job 33:19 He is c also with pain upon his bed, H3198
Ps 69:10 When I wept, *and* c my soul with fasting,
73:14 I been plagued, and c every morning. H8433
118:18 The LORD hath c me sore: but he hath H3256
1Co 11:32 But when we are judged, we are c of the G3811
2Co 6: 9 behold, we live; as c, and not killed; G3811
Heb 12:10 For they verily for a few days c *us* after G3811

CHASTENEST
Ps 94:12 Blessed *is* the man whom thou c, O H3256

CHASTENETH
Dt 8: 5 that, as a man c his son, *so* the LORD H3256
5 his son, *so* the LORD thy God c thee. H3256
Prv 13:24 but he that loveth him c him betimes. H4148
Heb 12: 6 For whom the Lord loveth he c, and G3811
7 what son is he whom the father c not? G3811

CHASTENING
Job 5:17 despise not thou the c of the Almighty: H4148
Prv 3:11 My son, despise not the c of the LORD; H4148
Isa 26:16 a prayer *when* thy c *was* upon them. H4148
Heb 12: 5 not thou the c of the Lord, nor faint G3809
7 If ye endure c, God dealeth with you as G3809
11 Now no c for the present seemeth to be G3809

CHASTISE
Lev 26:28 I, will c you seven times for your sins. H3256
Dt 22:18 that city shall take that man and c him; H3256
1Ki 12:11 whips, but I will c you with scorpions. H3256
14 whips, but I will c you with scorpions. H3256
2Ch 10:11 whips, but I *will c you* with scorpions.
14 whips, but I *will c you* with scorpions.
Hos 7:12 of the heaven; I will c them, as their H3256
10:10 *It is* in my desire that I should c them; H3256
Lk 23:16 I will therefore c him, and release *him*. G3811
22 I will therefore c him, and let *him* go. G3811

CHASTISED
1Ki 12:11 my father hath c you with whips, but H3256
14 my father *also* c you with whips, but H3256
2Ch 10:11 yoke: my father c you with whips, but H3256
14 thereto: my father c you with whips, H3256
Jer 31:18 *thus*; Thou hast c me, and I was H3256
18 chastised me, and I was c, as a bullock H3256

CHASTISEMENT
Dt 11: 2 have not seen the c of the LORD your H4148
Job 34:31 have borne c, I will not offend *any more*:
Isa 53: 5 our iniquities: the c of our peace *was* H4148
Jer 30:14 enemy, with the c of a cruel one, for the H4148
Heb 12: 8 But if ye be without c, whereof all are G3809

CHASTISETH
Ps 94:10 He that c the heathen, shall not he H3256

CHATTER
Isa 38:14 Like a crane *or* a swallow, so did I c: I H6850

CHEBAR
Ezk 1: 1 by the river of C, *that* the heavens were H3529
3 by the river C; and the hand of the H3529
3:15 by the river of C, and I sat where they H3529
23 by the river of C: and I fell on my face. H3529
10:15 creature that I saw by the river of C. H3529
20 by the river of C; and I knew that they H3529
22 saw by the river of C, their appearances H3529
43: 3 by the river C; and I fell upon my face. H3529

CHECK
Job 20: 3 I have heard the c of my reproach, and H4148

CHECKER
1Ki 7:17 *And* nets of c work, and wreaths of H7639

CHECKER-WORK See CHECKER and WORK.

CHEDORLAOMER
Gen 14: 1 king of Ellasar, C king of Elam, and H3540
4 Twelve years they served C, and in the H3540
5 And in the fourteenth year came C, and H3540
9 With C the king of Elam, and with H3540
17 the slaughter of C, and of the kings that H3540

CHEEK
1Ki 22:24 Micaiah on the c, and said, Which way H3895
2Ch 18:23 Micaiah upon the c, and said, Which H3895
Job 16:10 me upon the c reproachfully; they H3895
Ps 3: 7 enemies upon the c bone; thou hast H3895
Lam 3:30 He giveth his c to him that smiteth H3895
Joel 1: 6 and he hath the c teeth of a great lion. H4973
Mic 5: 1 judge of Israel with a rod upon the c. H3895
Mt 5:39 thy right c, turn to him the other also. G4600
Lk 6:29 thee on the one c offer also the other; G4600

CHEEK-BONE See CHEEK and BONE.

CHEEKS
Dt 18: 3 shoulder, and the two c, and the maw. H3895
Song 1:10 Thy c are comely with rows of jewels, H3895
5:13 His c are as a bed of spices, as sweet H3895
Isa 50: 6 smiters, and my c to them that plucked H3895
Lam 1: 2 tears are on her c: among all her lovers H3895

CHEER
Dt 24: 5 shall c up his wife which he hath taken. H8055
Ecc 11: 9 and let thy heart c thee in the days of H2895
Mt 9: 2 be of good c; thy sins be forgiven thee. G2293
14:27 Be of good c; it is I; be not afraid. G2293
Mk 6:50 them, Be of good c: it is I; be not afraid. G2293
Jn 16:33 of good c; I have overcome the world. G2293
Act 23:11 said, Be of good c, Paul: for as thou hast G2293
27:22 And now I exhort you to be of good c: G2114
25 Wherefore, sirs, be of good c: for I G2114
36 Then were they all of good c, and they G2115

CHEERETH
Jdg 9:13 my wine, which c God and man, and H8055

CHEERFUL
Prv 15:13 A merry heart maketh a c H3190
Zec 8:19 and gladness, and c feasts; therefore H2896
9:17 young men c, and new wine the maids. H5107
2Co 9: 7 or of necessity: for God loveth a c giver. G2431

CHEERFULLY
Act 24:10 I do the more c answer for myself: G2115

CHEERFULNESS
Ro 12: 8 he that sheweth mercy, with c. G2432

CHEESE
2Sa 17:29 and sheep, and c of kine, for David, H8194
Job 10:10 me out as milk, and curdled me like c? H1385

CHEESES
1Sa 17:18 And carry these ten c unto the H2461+H2757

CHELAL
Ezr 10:30 Adna, and C, Benaiah, Maaseiah, H3636

CHELLUH
Ezr 10:35 Benaiah, Bedeiah, C, H3622

CHELUB
1Ch 4:11 And C the brother of Shuah begat H3620
27:26 of the ground was Ezri the son of C: H3620

CHELUBAI
1Ch 2: 9 unto him; Jerahmeel, and Ram, and C. H3621

CHEMARIMS
Zep 1: 4 and the name of the C with the priests; H3649

CHEMOSH
Nu 21:29 O people of C: he hath given his sons H3645
Jdg 11:24 Wilt not thou possess that which C thy H3645
1Ki 11: 7 an high place for C, the abomination of H3645
33 of the Zidonians, C the god of the H3645
2Ki 23:13 and for C the abomination of H3645
Jer 48: 7 also be taken: and C shall go forth into H3645
13 And Moab shall be ashamed of C, as the H3645
46 the people of C perisheth: for thy sons H3645

CHENAANAH
1Ki 22:11 And Zedekiah the son of C made him H3668
24 But Zedekiah the son of C went near, H3668
1Ch 7:10 and Ehud, and C, and Zethan, and H3668
2Ch 18:10 And Zedekiah the son of C had made H3668
23 Then Zedekiah the son of C came near, H3668

CHENANI
Neh 9: 4 Bani, and C, and cried with a loud H3662

CHENANIAH
1Ch 15:22 And C, chief of the Levites, was for H3663
27 the singers, and C the master of the H3663
26:29 Of the Izharites, C and his sons were H3663

CHEPHAR-HAAMMONAI
Jos 18:24 And C, and Ophni, and Gaba; twelve H3726

CHEPHIRAH
Jos 9:17 C, and Beeroth, and Kirjath-jearim. H3716
18:26 And Mizpeh, and C, and Mozah, H3716
Ezr 2:25 The children of Kirjath-arim, C, and H3716
Neh 7:29 The men of Kirjath-jearim, C, and H3716

CHERAN
Gen 36:26 and Eshban, and Ithran, and C. H3763
1Ch 1:41 and Eshban, and Ithran, and C. H3763

CHERETHIMS
Ezk 25:16 and I will cut off the C, and destroy the H3774

CHERETHITES
1Sa 30:14 the south of the C, and upon the coast H3774
2Sa 8:18 was over both the C and the Pelethites; H3774
15:18 beside him; and all the C, and all the H3774
20: 7 men, and the C, and the Pelethites, and H3774
23 was over the C and over the Pelethites: H3774
1Ki 1:38 Jehoiada, and the C, and the Pelethites, H3746
44 Jehoiada, and the C, and the Pelethites, H3774
1Ch 18:17 was over the C and the Pelethites; and H3774
Zep 2: 5 the nation of the C! the word of the H3774

CHERISH
1Ki 1: 2 king, and let her c him, and let her lie H5532

CHERISHED
1Ki 1: 4 And the damsel was very fair, and c the H5532

CHERISHETH
Eph 5:29 and c it, even as the Lord the church: G2282
1Th 2: 7 you, even as a nurse c her children: G2282

CHERITH
1Ki 17: 3 by the brook C, that is before Jordan. H3747
5 by the brook C, that is before Jordan. H3747

CHERUB
Ex 25:19 And make one c on the one end, and H3742
19 end, and the other c on the other end: H3742
37: 8 One c on the end on this side, and H3742
8 side, and another c on the other end on H3742
2Sa 22:11 And he rode upon a c, and did fly: and H3742
1Ki 6:24 the one wing of the c, and five cubits the H3742
24 other wing of the c: from the uttermost H3742
25 And the other c was ten cubits: both H3742
26 The height of the one c was ten cubits, H3742
26 ten cubits, and so was it of the other c. H3742
27 wing of the other c touched the other H3742
2Ch 3:11 one wing of the one c was five cubits,
11 reaching to the wing of the other c. H3742
12 And one wing of the other c was five H3742
12 also, joining to the wing of the other c. H3742
Ezr 2:59 Tel-harsa, C, Addan, and Immer: H3743
Neh 7:61 Tel-haresha, C, Addon, and Immer: H3743
Ps 18:10 And he rode upon a c, and did fly: yea, H3742
Ezk 9: 3 gone up from the c, whereupon he was, H3742
10: 2 even under the c, and fill thine hand H3742
4 went up from the c, and stood over the H3742
7 And one c stretched forth his hand H3742
9 one wheel by one c, and another wheel H3742
9 wheel by another c: and the appearance H3742
14 was the face of a c, and the second face H3742
28:14 Thou art the anointed c that covereth; H3742
16 c, from the midst of the stones of fire. H3742
41:18 tree was between a c and a cherub; and H3742
18 a c; and every cherub had two faces; H3742
18 a cherub; and every c had two faces; H3742

CHERUBIMS
Gen 3:24 garden of Eden C, and a flaming sword H3742
Ex 25:18 And thou shalt make two c of gold, of H3742
19 ye make the c on the two ends thereof. H3742
20 And the c shall stretch forth their wings H3742
20 mercy seat shall the faces of the c be. H3742
22 between the two c which are upon the H3742
26: 1 and scarlet: with c of cunning work H3742
31 cunning work: with c shall it be made: H3742
36: 8 with c of cunning work made he them. H3742
35 with c made he it of cunning work. H3742
Ex 37: 7 And he made two c of gold, beaten out H3742
8 made he the c on the two ends thereof. H3742
9 And the c spread out their wings on H3742
9 mercy seatward were the faces of the c. H3742
Nu 7:89 the two c: and he spake unto him. H3742
1Sa 4: 4 between the c: and the two sons of H3742
2Sa 6: 2 of hosts that dwelleth between the c. H3742
1Ki 6:23 And within the oracle he made two c of H3742
25 the c were of one measure and one size. H3742
27 And he set the c within the inner house: H3742
27 the wings of the c, so that the wing of H3742
28 And he overlaid the c with gold. H3742
29 carved figures of c and palm trees and H3742
32 them carvings of c and palm trees and H3742
32 upon the c, and upon the palm trees. H3742
35 And he carved thereon c and palm H3742
7:29 lions, oxen, and c: and upon the ledges H3742
36 thereof, he graved c, lions, and palm H3742
8: 6 place, even under the wings of the c. H3742
7 For the c spread forth their two wings H3742
7 of the ark, and the c covered the ark H3742
2Ki 19:15 between the c, thou art the God, even H3742
1Ch 13: 6 the c, whose name is called on it. H3742
28:18 of the chariot of the c, that spread out H3742
2Ch 3: 7 with gold; and graved c on the walls. H3742
10 he made two c of image work, and H3742
11 And the wings of the c were twenty H3742
13 The wings of these c spread themselves H3742
14 and fine linen, and wrought c thereon. H3742
5: 7 place, even under the wings of the c: H3742
8 For the c spread forth their wings over H3742
8 of the ark, and the c covered the ark H3742
Ps 80: 1 that dwellest between the c, shine forth. H3742
99: 1 between the c; let the earth be moved. H3742
Isa 37:16 between the c, thou art the God, even H3742
Ezk 10: 1 the head of the c there appeared over H3742
2 from between the c, and scatter them H3742
3 Now the c stood on the right side of the H3742
6 from between the c; then he went in, H3742
7 from between the c unto the fire that H3742
7 was between the c, and took thereof, H3742
8 And there appeared in the c the form of H3742
9 four wheels by the c, one wheel by one H3742
15 And the c were lifted up. This is the H3742
16 And when the c went, the wheels went H3742
16 and when the c lifted up their wings H3742
18 of the house, and stood over the c. H3742
19 And the c lifted up their wings, and H3742
20 and I knew that they were the c. H3742
11:22 Then did the c lift up their wings, and H3742
41:18 And it was made with c and palm H3742
20 the door were c and palm trees made, H3742
25 of the temple, c and palm trees, like H3742
Heb 9: 5 And over it the c of glory shadowing G5502

CHERUBIMS'
Ezk 10: 5 And the sound of the c wings was H3742

CHESALON
Jos 15:10 Jearim, which is C, on the north side, H3693

CHESED
Gen 22:22 And C, and Hazo, and Pildash, and H3777

CHESIL
Jos 15:30 And Eltolad, and C, and Hormah, H3686

CHESNUT
Gen 30:37 of the hazel and c tree; and pilled white H6196
Ezk 31: 8 boughs, and the c trees were not like H6196

CHEST
2Ki 12: 9 But Jehoiada the priest took a c, and H727
10 was much money in the c, that the king's H727
2Ch 24: 8 they made a c, and set it without at H727
10 into the c, until they had made an end. H727
11 at what time the c was brought unto the H727
11 came and emptied the c, and took it, and H727

CHESTNUT See CHESNUT

CHESTNUT-TREE See CHESNUT and TREE.

CHESTS
Ezk 27:24 work, and in c of rich apparel, bound H1595

CHESULLOTH
Jos 19:18 toward Jezreel, and C, and Shunem, H3694

CHEW

Lev 11: 4 eat of them that **c** the cud, or of them H5927
Dt 14: 7 eat of them that **c** the cud, or of them H5927
7 the coney: for they **c** the cud, but divide H5927

CHEWED

Nu 11:33 their teeth, ere it was **c**, the wrath of the H3772

CHEWETH

Lev 11: 3 clovenfooted, *and* **c** the cud, among the H5927
4 the camel, because he **c** the cud, but H5927
5 And the coney, because he **c** the cud, H5927
6 And the hare, because he **c** the cud, but H5927
7 he **c** not the cud; he *is* unclean to you. H1641
26 not clovenfooted, nor **c** the cud, *are* H5927
Dt 14: 6 two claws, *and* **c** the cud among the H5927
8 the hoof, yet **c** not the cud, it *is* unclean

CHEZIB

Gen 38: 5 and he was at **C**, when she bare him. H3580

CHICKENS

Mt 23:37 **c** under *her* wings, and ye would not! *G3556*

CHIDE

Ex 17: 2 Wherefore the people did **c** with Moses, H7378
2 said unto them, Why **c** ye with me? H7378
Jdg 8: 1 And they did **c** with him sharply. H7378
Ps 103: 9 He will not always **c**: neither will he H7378

CHIDED See CHODE.

CHIDING

Ex 17: 7 because of the **c** of the children of H7379

CHIDON

1Ch 13: 9 threshingfloor of **C**, Uzza put forth his H3592

CHIEF

Gen 21:22 and Phichol the **c** captain of his host H8269
32 and Phichol the **c** captain of his host, H8269
26:26 and Phichol the **c** captain of his army. H8269
40: 2 against the **c** of the butlers, and against H8269
2 butlers, and against the **c** of the bakers. H8269
9 And the **c** butler told his dream to H8269
16 When the **c** baker saw that the H8269
20 up the head of the **c** butler and of the H8269
20 and of the **c** baker among his servants. H8269
21 And he restored the **c** butler unto his H8269
22 But he hanged the **c** baker: as Joseph H8269
23 Yet did not the **c** butler remember H8269
41: 9 Then spake the **c** butler unto Pharaoh, H8269
10 house, *both* me and the **c** baker: H8269
Lev 21: 4 himself, *being* a **c** man among his H1167
Nu 3:24 And the **c** of the house of the father of H5387
30 And the **c** of the house of the father of H5387
32 the priest *shall be* **c** over the chief of the H5387
32 *be* chief over the **c** of the Levites, *and* H5387
35 And the **c** of the house of the father of H5387
4:34 And Moses and Aaron and the **c** of the H5387
46 Aaron and the **c** of Israel numbered, H5387
25:14 of a **c** house among the Simeonites. H1
15 a people, *and* of a **c** house in Midian. H1
31:26 and the **c** fathers of the congregation: H7218
32:28 of Nun, and the **c** fathers of the tribes H7218
36: 1 And the **c** fathers of the families of the H7218
1 the **c** fathers of the children of Israel: H7218
Dt 1:15 So I took the **c** of your tribes, wise men, H7218
33:15 And for the **c** things of the ancient H7218
Jos 22:14 And with him ten princes, of each **c** H1
Jdg 20: 2 And the **c** of all the people, *even* of all H6438
1Sa 14:38 near hither, all the **c** of the people: and H6438
15:21 and oxen, the **c** of the things which H7225
2Sa 5: 8 David's soul, *he shall be* **c** *and captain.*
8:18 and David's sons were **c** rulers. H3548
20:26 And Ira also the Jairite was a **c** ruler H3548
23: 8 that satin the seat, **c** among the H7218
13 And three of the thirty **c** went down, H7218
18 of Zeruiah, was **c** among three. And he H7218
1Ki 5:16 Beside the **c** of Solomon's officers H8269
8: 1 of the tribes, the **c** of the fathers of the H5387
9:23 These *were* the **c** of the officers that H8269
14:27 the hands of the **c** of the guard, which H8269
2Ki 25:18 guard took Seraiah the **c** priest, and H7218
1Ch 5: 2 and of him *came* the **c** ruler; but the H5057
7 *were* the **c**, Jeiel, and Zechariah, H7218
12 Joel the **c**, and Shapham the next, and H7218
15 of Guni, **c** of the house of their fathers. H7218
7: 3 Joel, Ishiah, five: all of them **c** men. H7218
1Ch 7:40 men of valour, **c** of the princes. And H7218
8:28 **c** *men.* These dwelt in Jerusalem. H7218
9: 9 these men *were* **c** of the fathers in the H7218
17 and their brethren: Shallum *was* the **c**; H7218
26 For these Levites, the four **c** porters, H1368
33 And these *are* the singers, **c** of the H7218
34 These **c** fathers of the Levites *were* H7218
34 of the Levites *were* **c** throughout their H7218
11: 6 first shall be **c** and captain. So Joab H7218
6 son of Zeruiah went first up, and was **c**. H7218
10 These also *are* the **c** of the mighty men H7218
11 Hachmonite, the **c** of the captains: he H7218
20 of Joab, he was **c** of the three: for lifting H7218
12: 3 The **c** *was* Ahiezer, then Joash, the sons H7218
18 Amasai, *who was* **c** of the captains, H7218
15: 5 Of the sons of Kohath; Uriel the **c**, and H8269
6 Of the sons of Merari; Asaiah the **c**, and H8269
7 Of the sons of Gershom; Joel the **c**, and H8269
8 the **c**, and his brethren two hundred: H8269
9 Of the sons of Hebron; Eliel the **c**, and H8269
10 Of the sons of Uzziel; Amminadab the **c**, H8269
12 And said unto them, Ye *are* the **c** of the H7218
16 And David spake to the **c** of the Levites H8269
22 And Chenaniah, **c** of the Levites, *was* H8269
16: 5 Asaph the **c**, and next to him Zechariah, H7218
18:17 sons of David *were* **c** about the king. H7223
23: 8 The sons of Laadan; the **c** *was* Jehiel, H7218
9 *were* the **c** of the fathers of Laadan. H7218
11 And Jahath was the **c**, and Zizah the H7218
16 the sons of Gershom, Shebuel *was* the **c**. H7218
17 Rehabiah the **c**. And Eliezer had none H7218
18 Of the sons of Izhar; Shelomith the **c**. H7218
24 fathers; *even* the **c** of the fathers, as H7218
24: 4 And there were more **c** men found of H7218
4 *there were* sixteen **c** men of the house H7218
6 and *before* the **c** of the fathers of the H7218
31 and the **c** of the fathers of the H7218
26:10 sons; Simri the **c**, (for *though* he was H7218
10 firstborn, yet his father made him the **c**;) H7218
12 *even* among the **c** men, *having* wards H7218
21 Laadan, **c** fathers, *even* of Laadan H7218
26 the king, and the **c** fathers, the captains H7218
31 *was* Jerijah the **c**, *even* among the H7218
32 seven hundred **c** fathers, whom king H7218
27: 1 *to wit,* the **c** fathers and captains H7218
3 Of the children of Perez *was* the **c** of all H7218
5 son of Jehoiada, a **c** priest: and in his H7218
29: 6 Then the **c** of the fathers and princes of H8269
22 the **c** governor, and Zadok *to be* priest. H8269
2Ch 1: 2 in all Israel, the **c** of the fathers. H7218
5: 2 of the tribes, the **c** of the fathers of the H5387
8: 9 men of war, and **c** of his captains, and H8269
10 And these *were* the **c** of king Solomon's H8269
11:22 of Maachah the **c**, *to be* ruler among his H7218
12:10 to the hands of the **c** of the guard, that H8269
17:14 Adnah the **c**, and with him mighty H8269
19: 8 the priests, and of the **c** of the fathers of H7218
11 And, behold, Amariah the **c** priest *is* H7218
23: 2 of Judah, and the **c** of the fathers of H7218
24: 6 And the king called for Jehoiada the **c**, H7218
26:12 The whole number of the **c** of the H7218
20 And Azariah the **c** priest, and all the H7218
31:10 And Azariah the **c** priest of the house H7218
35: 9 Jeiel and Jozabad, **c** of the Levites, gave H8269
36:14 Moreover all the **c** of the priests, and H8269
Ezr 1: 5 Then rose up the **c** of the fathers of H7218
2:68 And *some* of the **c** of the fathers, when H7218
3:12 and Levites and **c** of the fathers, *who* H7218
4: 2 and to the **c** of the fathers, and said H7218
3 and the rest of the **c** of the fathers of H7218
5:10 of the men that *were* the **c** of them. H7217
7: 5 Eleazar, the son of Aaron the **c** priest: H7218
28 out of Israel **c** men to go up with me. H7218
8: 1 These *are* now the **c** of their fathers, H7218
16 for Meshullam, **c** men; also for Joiarib, H7218
17 unto Iddo the **c** at the place Casiphia, H7218
24 Then I separated twelve of the **c** of the H8269
29 *them* before the **c** of the priests and the H8269
29 and the Levites, and **c** of the fathers of H8269
9: 2 and rulers hath been **c** in this trespass. H7223
10: 5 Then arose Ezra, and made the **c** H8269
16 *with* certain **c** of the fathers, after H7218
Neh 7:70 And some of the **c** of the fathers gave H7218
71 And *some* of the **c** of the fathers gave to H7218
8:13 together the **c** of the fathers of all H7218
10:14 The **c** of the people; Parosh, H7218
11: 3 Now these *are* the **c** of the province H7218
13 And his brethren, **c** of the fathers, two H7218
16 And Shabbethai and Jozabad, of the **c** H7218
Neh 12: 7 These *were* the **c** of the priests and of H7218
12 were priests, the **c** of the fathers: of H7218
22 *were* recorded **c** of the fathers: also the H7218
23 The sons of Levi, the **c** of the fathers, H7218
24 And the **c** of the Levites: Hashabiah, H7218
46 of old *there were* **c** of the singers, and H7218
Job 12:24 He taketh away the heart of the **c** of the H7218
29:25 I chose out their way, and sat **c**, and H7218
40:19 He *is* the **c** of the ways of God: he that H7225
Ps 4:ttl To the **c** Musician on Neginoth, A H5329
5:ttl To the **c** Musician upon Nehiloth, A H5329
6:ttl To the **c** Musician on Neginoth upon H5329
8:ttl To the **c** Musician upon Gittith, A Psalm
9:ttl To the **c** Musician upon Muth-labben, H5329
11:ttl To the **c** Musician, *A Psalm* of David. H5329
12:ttl To the **c** Musician upon Sheminith, A H5329
13:ttl To the **c** Musician, A Psalm of David. H5329
14:ttl To the **c** Musician, *A Psalm* of David. H5329
18:ttl To the **c** Musician, *A Psalm* of David, H5329
19:ttl To the **c** Musician, A Psalm of David. H5329
20:ttl To the **c** Musician, A Psalm of David. H5329
21:ttl To the **c** Musician, A Psalm of David. H5329
22:ttl To the **c** Musician upon Aijeleth H5329
31:ttl To the **c** Musician, A Psalm of David. H5329
36:ttl To the **c** Musician, *A Psalm* of David H5329
39:ttl To the **c** Musician, *even* to Jeduthun, A H5329
40:ttl To the **c** Musician, A Psalm of David. H5329
41:ttl To the **c** Musician, A Psalm of David. H5329
42:ttl To the **c** Musician, Maschil, for the H5329
44:ttl To the **c** Musician for the sons of H5329
45:ttl To the **c** Musician upon Shoshannim, H5329
46:ttl To the **c** Musician for the sons of H5329
47:ttl To the **c** Musician, A Psalm for the H5329
49:ttl To the **c** Musician, A Psalm for the H5329
51:ttl To the **c** Musician, A Psalm of David, H5329
52:ttl To the **c** Musician, Maschil, *A Psalm* of H5329
53:ttl To the **c** Musician upon Mahalath, H5329
54:ttl To the **c** Musician on Neginoth, H5329
55:ttl To the **c** Musician on Neginoth, H5329
56:ttl To the **c** Musician upon H5329
57:ttl To the **c** Musician, Al-taschith, H5329
58:ttl To the **c** Musician, Al-taschith, H5329
59:ttl To the **c** Musician, Al-taschith, H5329
60:ttl To the **c** Musician upon H5329
61:ttl To the **c** Musician upon Neginah, *A* H5329
62:ttl To the **c** Musician, to Jeduthun, A H5329
64:ttl To the **c** Musician, A Psalm of David. H5329
65:ttl To the **c** Musician, A Psalm *and* Song H5329
66:ttl To the **c** Musician, A Song *or* Psalm. H5329
67:ttl To the **c** Musician on Neginoth, A H5329
68:ttl To the **c** Musician, A Psalm *or* Song of H5329
69:ttl To the **c** Musician upon Shoshannim, H5329
70:ttl To the **c** Musician, *A Psalm* of David, H5329
75:ttl To the **c** Musician, Al-taschith, A Psalm H5329
76:ttl To the **c** Musician on Neginoth, A H5329
77:ttl To the **c** Musician, to Jeduthun, A H5329
78:51 in Egypt; the **c** of *their* strength in the H7225
80:ttl To the **c** Musician upon H5329
81:ttl To the **c** Musician upon Gittith, *A* H5329
84:ttl To the **c** Musician upon Gittith, A H5329
85:ttl To the **c** Musician, A Psalm for the H5329
88:ttl sons of Korah, to the **c** Musician upon H5329
105:36 in their land, the **c** of all their strength. H7225
109:ttl To the **c** Musician, A Psalm of David. H5329
137: 6 I prefer not Jerusalem above my **c** joy. H7218
139:ttl To the **c** Musician, A Psalm of David. H5329
140:ttl To the **c** Musician, A Psalm of David. H5329
Prv 1:21 She crieth in the **c** place of concourse, H7218
16:28 and a whisperer separateth **c** friends. H441
Song 4:14 myrrh and aloes, with all the **c** spices: H7218
Isa 14: 9 thee, *even* all the **c** ones of the earth; it H6260
41: 9 thee from the **c** men thereof, and said H678
Jer 13:21 captains, *and* as **c** over thee: shall not H7218
20: 1 who *was* also **c** governor in the house H5057
31: 7 and shout among the **c** of the nations: H7218
49:35 the bow of Elam, the **c** of their might. H7225
52:24 guard took Seraiah the **c** priest, and H7218
Lam 1: 5 Her adversaries are the **c**, her enemies H7218
Ezk 27:22 in thy fairs with **c** of all spices, and H7218
38: 2 of Magog, the **c** prince of Meshech and H7218
3 the **c** prince of Meshech and Tubal: H7218
39: 1 the **c** prince of Meshech and Tubal: H7218
Dan 2:48 of Babylon, and **c** of the governors over H7229
10:13 one of the **c** princes, came to help H7223
11:41 and the **c** of the children of Ammon. H7225
Am 6: 1 *which are* named **c** of the nations, to H7225
6 with the **c** ointments: but they H7225
Hab 3:19 **c** singer on my stringed instruments. H5329
Mt 2: 4 And when he had gathered all the **c** *G749*

Mt 16:21 of the elders and c priests and scribes, G749
20:18 betrayed unto the c priests and unto the G749
27 And whosoever will be c among you, G4413
21:15 And when the c priests and scribes saw G749
23 the temple, the c priests and the elders G749
45 And when the c priests and Pharisees G749
23: 6 and the c seats in the synagogues, G4410
26: 3 Then assembled together the c priests, G749
14 Judas Iscariot, went unto the c priests, G749
47 the c priests and elders of the people. G749
59 Now the c priests, and elders, and all the G749
27: 1 When the morning was come, all the c G749
3 of silver to the c priests and elders, G749
6 And the c priests took the silver pieces, G749
12 And when he was accused of the c G749
20 But the c priests and elders persuaded G749
41 Likewise also the c priests mocking *him*, G749
62 preparation, the c priests and Pharisees G749
28:11 c priests all the things that were done. G749
Mk 6:21 high captains, and c *estates* of Galilee; G4413
8:31 elders, and *of* the c priests, and scribes, G749
10:33 be delivered unto the c priests, and unto G749
11:18 And the scribes and c priests heard *it*, G749
27 c priests, and the scribes, and the elders, G749
12:39 And the c seats in the synagogues, and G749
14: 1 bread: and the c priests and the scribes G749
10 the c priests, to betray him unto them. G749
43 c priests and the scribes and the elders. G749
53 c priests and the elders and the scribes. G749
55 And the c priests and all the council G749
15: 1 And straightway in the morning the c G749
3 And the c priests accused him of many G749
10 For he knew that the c priests had G749
11 But the c priests moved the people, that G749
31 Likewise also the c priests mocking said G749
Lk 9:22 of the elders and c priests and scribes, G749
11:15 through Beelzebub the c of the devils. G758
14: 1 the house of one of the c Pharisees to eat G758
7 out the c rooms; saying unto them, G4411
19: 2 c among the publicans, and he was rich. G754
47 in the temple. But the c priests and the G749
47 c of the people sought to destroy him, G4413
20: 1 the gospel, the c priests and the scribes G749
19 And the c priests and the scribes the G749
46 synagogues, and the c rooms at feasts; G4411
22: 2 And the c priests and scribes sought how G749
4 with the c priests and captains, G749
26 and he that is c, as he that doth serve. G2233
52 Then Jesus said unto the c priests, and G749
66 of the people and the c priests and the G749
23: 4 Then said Pilate to the c priests and *to* G749
10 And the c priests and scribes stood and G749
13 c priests and the rulers and the people, G749
23 of them and of the c priests prevailed. G749
24:20 And how the c priests and our rulers G749
Jn 7:32 the c priests sent officers to take him. G749
45 Then came the officers to the c priests G749
11:47 Then gathered the c priests and the G749
57 Now both the c priests and the Pharisees G749
12:10 But the c priests consulted that they G749
42 Nevertheless among the c rulers also G758
18: 3 officers from the c priests and Pharisees, G749
35 nation and the c priests have delivered G749
19: 6 When the c priests therefore and officers G749
15 your King? The c priests answered, We G749
21 Then said the c priests of the Jews to G749
Act 4:23 c priests and elders had said unto them. G749
5:24 the temple and the c priests heard these G749
9:14 And here he hath authority from the c G749
21 bring them bound unto the c priests? G749
13:50 women, and the c men of the city, and G4413
14:12 because he was the c speaker. G2233
15:22 and Silas, c men among the brethren: G2233
16:12 which is the c city of that part of G4413
17: 4 and of the c women not a few. G4413
18: 8 And Crispus, the c ruler of the G752
17 Then all the Greeks took Sosthenes, the c G752
19:14 a Jew, *and* c of the priests, which did so. G749
31 And certain of the c of Asia, which were G775
21:31 came unto the c captain of the band, G5506
32 when they saw the c captain and the G5506
33 Then the c captain came near, and G5506
37 he said unto the c captain, May I speak G5506
22:24 The c captain commanded him to be G5506
26 he went and told the c captain, saying, G5506
27 Then the c captain came, and said G5506
28 And the c captain answered, With a G5506
29 him: and the c captain also was afraid, G5506
30 commanded the c priests and all their G749
Act 23:10 dissension, the c captain, fearing lest G5506
14 And they came to the c priests and G749
15 signify to the c captain that he bring G5506
17 man unto the c captain: for he hath G5506
18 *him* to the c captain, and said, Paul G5506
19 Then the c captain took him by the G5506
22 So the c captain *then* let the young man G5506
24: 7 But the c captain Lysias came *upon us*, G5506
22 When Lysias the c captain shall come G5506
25: 2 Then the high priest and the c of the G4413
15 at Jerusalem, the c priests and the elders G749
23 of hearing, with the c captains, and G5506
26:10 authority from the c priests; and when G749
12 and commission from the c priests, G749
28: 7 possessions of the c man of the island, G4413
17 Paul called the c of the Jews together: G4413
Eph 2:20 Christ himself being the c corner *stone*; G204
1Ti 1:15 world to save sinners; of whom I am c. G4413
1Pt 2: 6 I lay in Sion a c corner stone, elect, G204
5: 4 And when the c Shepherd shall appear, G750
Rev 6:15 rich men, and the c captains, and the G5506

CHIEFEST

1Sa 2:29 fat with the c of all the offerings of H7225
9:22 them sit in the c place among them H7218
21: 7 c of the herdmen that *belonged* to Saul. H47
2Ch 32:33 buried him in the c of the sepulchres of H4608
Song 5:10 My beloved *is* white and ruddy, the c H1713
Mk 10:44 And whosoever of you will be the c, G4413
2Co 11: 5 behind the very c apostles. G5228+G3029
12:11 the very c apostles, though G5228+G3029

CHIEFLY

Ro 3: 2 Much every way: c, because that unto G4412
Php 4:22 All the saints salute you, c they that are G3122
2Pt 2:10 But c them that walk after the flesh in G3122

CHIEF-PRIEST See CHIEF and PRIEST.

CHILD

Gen 11:30 But Sarai was barren; she *had* no c. H2056
16:11 thou *art* with c, and shalt bear a son, H2030
17:10 c among you shall be circumcised. H2145
12 you, every man c in your generations, H2145
14 And the uncircumcised man c whose H2145
17 in his heart, Shall *a* c be born unto him
18:13 Shall I of a surety bear a c, which am old?
19:36 daughters of Lot with c by their father. H2029
21: 8 And the c grew, and was weaned: and H3206
14 shoulder, and the c, and sent her away: H3206
15 she cast the c under one of the shrubs. H3206
16 see the death of the c. And she sat over H3206
37:30 The c *is* not; and I, whither shall I go? H3206
38:24 behold, she *is* with c by whoredom. H2030
25 *are, am* I with c: and she said, Discern, H2030
42:22 not sin against the c; and ye would not H3206
44:20 an old man, and a c of his old age, a H3206
Ex 2: 2 *a* goodly *c*, she hid him three months.
3 pitch, and put the c therein; and she H3206
6 *it*, she saw the c: and, behold, the babe H3206
7 that she may nurse the c for thee? H3206
9 her, Take this c away, and nurse it for H3206
9 the woman took the c, and nursed it. H3206
10 And the c grew, and she brought him H3206
21:22 If men strive, and hurt a woman with c, H2030
22:22 not afflict any widow, or fatherless c. H3490
Lev 12: 2 and born a man c: then she shall be H2145
5 But if she bear a maid c, then she shall H5347
22:13 and have no c, and is returned unto H2233
Nu 11:12 the sucking c, unto the land which H3243
Dt 25: 5 die, and have no c, the wife of the dead H1121
Jdg 11:34 she *was his* only c; beside her he had H3173
13: 5 his head: for the c shall be a Nazarite H5288
7 *thing*: for the c shall be a Nazarite to H5288
8 shall do unto the c that shall be born. H5288
12 the c, and *how* shall we do unto him? H5288
24 the c grew, and the LORD blessed him. H5288
Ru 4:16 And Naomi took the c, and laid it in her H3206
1Sa 1:11 handmaid a man c, then I will give him H2233
22 *not go up* until the c be weaned, and H5288
24 LORD in Shiloh: and the c *was* young. H5288
25 slew a bullock, and brought the c to Eli. H5288
27 For this c I prayed; and the LORD hath H5288
2:11 his house. And the c did minister unto H5288
18 *being* a c, girded with a linen ephod. H5288
21 the c Samuel grew before the LORD. H5288
26 And the c Samuel grew on, and was in H5288
3: 1 And the c Samuel ministered unto the H5288
8 that the LORD had called the c. H5288
1Sa 4:19 wife, was with c, *near* to be delivered: H2030
21 And she named the c Ichabod, saying, H5288
2Sa 6:23 had no c unto the day of her death. H3206
11: 5 and told David, and said, I *am* with c. H2030
12:14 to blaspheme, the c also *that is* born H1121
15 the LORD struck the c that Uriah's wife H3206
16 David therefore besought God for the c; H5288
18 day, that the c died. And the servants H3206
18 to tell him that the c was dead: for they H3206
18 Behold, while the c was yet alive, we H3206
18 if we tell him that the c is dead? H3206
19 David perceived that the c was dead: H3206
19 the c dead? And they said, He is dead. H3206
21 and weep for the c, *while it was* alive; H3206
21 but when the c was dead, thou didst H3206
22 And he said, While the c was yet alive, H3206
22 be gracious to me, that the c may live? H3206
1Ki 3: 7 c: I know not *how* to go out or come in. H5288
17 delivered of a c with her in the house. H3205
19 And this woman's c died in the night; H1121
20 and laid her dead c in my bosom. H1121
21 to give my c suck, behold, it was H1121
25 And the king said, Divide the living c in H3206
26 whose the living c *was* unto the king, H1121
26 give her the living c, and in no wise slay H3205
27 Give her the living c, and in no wise slay H3205
11:17 go into Egypt; Hadad *being* yet a little c. H5288
13: 2 LORD; Behold, a c shall be born unto H1121
14: 3 tell thee what shall become of the c. H5288
12 feet enter into the city, the c shall die. H3206
17 to the threshold of the door, the c died; H5288
17:21 And he stretched himself upon the c H3206
22 c came into him again, and he revived. H3206
23 And Elijah took the c, and brought him H3206
2Ki 4:14 she hath no c, and her husband is old. H1121
18 And when the c was grown, it fell on a H3206
26 with the c? And she answered, *It is* well. H3206
29 and lay my staff upon the face of the c. H5288
30 And the mother of the c said, *As* the H5288
31 the face of the c; but *there was* neither H5288
31 told him, saying, The c is not awaked. H5288
32 the c was dead, *and* laid upon his bed. H5288
34 And he went up, and lay upon the c, H3206
34 c; and the flesh of the child waxed warm.
34 and the flesh of the c waxed warm. H3206
35 upon him: and the c sneezed seven H5288
35 seven times, and the c opened his eyes. H5288
5:14 the flesh of a little c, and he was clean. H5288
8:12 and rip up their women with c. H2030
15:16 therein that were with c he ripped up. H2030
Job 3: 3 it was said, There is a man c conceived.
Ps 131: 2 myself, as a c that is weaned of his
2 mother: my soul *is* even as a weaned c.
Prv 20:11 Even a c is known by his doings, H5288
22: 6 Train up a c in the way he should go: H5288
15 Foolishness *is* bound in the heart of a c; H5288
23:13 Withhold not correction from the c: for H5288
24 begetteth a wise c shall have joy of him.
29:15 wisdom: but a c left *to himself* bringeth H5288
21 up his servant from a c shall have him H5290
Ecc 4: 8 he hath neither c nor brother: yet *is* H1121
13 Better *is* a poor and a wise c than an H3206
15 c that shall stand up in his stead. H3206
10:16 a c, and thy princes eat in the morning! H5288
11: 5 womb of her that is with c: even so thou H4392
Isa 3: 5 by his neighbour: the c shall behave H5288
7:16 For before the c shall know to refuse H5288
8: 4 For before the c shall have knowledge H5288
9: 6 For unto us a c is born, unto us a son is H3206
10:19 shall be few, that a c may write them. H5288
11: 6 together; and a little c shall lead them. H5288
8 And the sucking c shall play on the hole
8 and the weaned c shall put his hand on
26:17 Like as a woman with c, *that* draweth H2030
18 We have been with c, we have been in H2029
49:15 Can a woman forget her sucking c, that
54: 1 didst not travail with c: for more *are* the
65:20 his days: for the c shall die an hundred H5288
66: 7 pain came, she was delivered of a man c.
Jer 1: 6 behold, I cannot speak: for I *am* a c. H5288
7 Say not, I *am* a c: for thou shalt go to H5288
4:31 forth her first c, the voice of the daughter
20:15 saying, A man c is born unto thee; H1121
30: 6 doth travail with c? wherefore do I see H3205
31: 8 lame, the woman with c and her that H2030
8 that travaileth with c together: a great H3205
20 son? *is he* a pleasant c? for since I spake H3206
44: 7 man and woman, c and suckling, out H5768
Lam 4: 4 The tongue of the sucking c cleaveth to

Hos 11: 1 When Israel was a c, then I loved him, H5288
13:16 their women with c shall be ripped up. H2030
Am 1:13 the women with c of Gilead, that they H2030
Mt 1:18 c of the Holy Ghost. G1722+G1064+G2192
23 be with c, and shall G1722+G1064+G2192
2: 8 for the young c; and when ye have G3813
9 and stood over where the young c was. G3813
11 saw the young c with Mary his mother, G3813
13 take the young c and his mother, and G3813
13 will seek the young c to destroy him. G3813
14 When he arose, he took the young c G3813
20 Saying, Arise, and take the young c and G3813
21 And he arose, and took the young c G3813
10:21 and the father the c: and the children G5043
17:18 the c was cured from that very hour. G3816
18: 2 And Jesus called a little c unto him, G3813
4 as this little c, the same is greatest G3813
5 such little c in my name receiveth me. G3813
23:15 more the c of hell than yourselves. G5207
24:19 are with c, and to them G1722+G1064+G2192
Mk 9:21 came unto him? And he said, Of a c. G3812
24 And straightway the father of the c G3813
36 And he took a c, and set him in the G3813
10:15 as a little c, he shall not enter therein. G3813
13:17 are with c, and to them G1722+G1064+G2192
Lk 1: 7 And they had no c, because that G5043
59 to circumcise the c; and they called him G3813
66 What manner of c shall this be! And G3813
76 And thou, c, shalt be called the prophet G3813
80 And the c grew, and waxed strong in G3813
2: 5 his espoused wife, being great with c. G1471
17 which was told them concerning this c. G3813
21 of the c, his name was called G3813
27 brought in the c Jesus, to do for him G3813
34 Behold, this c is set for the fall and
40 And the c grew, and waxed strong in G3813
43 as they returned, the c Jesus tarried G3816
9:38 look upon my son: for he is mine only c. G3439
42 c, and delivered him again to his father. G3816
47 heart, took a c, and set him by him, G3813
48 shall receive this c in my name G3813
18:17 a little c shall in no wise enter therein. G3813
21:23 are with c, and to them G1722+G1064+G2192
Jn 4:49 unto him, Sir, come down ere my c die. G3813
16:21 is delivered of the c, she remembereth G3813
Act 4:27 For of a truth against thy holy c Jesus, G3816
30 done by the name of thy holy c Jesus. G3816
7: 5 seed after him, when as yet he had no c. G5043
13:10 all mischief, thou c of the devil, thou G5207
1Co 13:11 When I was a c, I spake as a child, I G3516
11 When I was a child, I spake as a c, I G3516
11 I understood as a c, I thought as a child: G3516
11 I thought as a c: but when I became G3516
Gal 4: 1 as long as he is a c, differeth nothing G3516
1Th 5: 3 with c; and they shall G1722+G1064+G2192
2Ti 3:15 And that from a c thou hast known the G1025
Heb 11:11 was delivered of a c when she was past G5088
23 he was a proper c; and they were not G3813
Rev 12: 2 And she being with c cried, travailing G1064
4 to devour her c as soon as it was born. G5043
5 And she brought forth a man c, who G5207
5 of iron: and her c was caught up unto G5043
13 woman which brought forth the man c.

CHILDBEARING
1Ti 2:15 shall be saved in c, if they continue in G5042

CHILDHOOD
1Sa 12: 2 before you from my c unto this day. H5271
Ecc 11:10 thy flesh: for c and youth are vanity. H3208

CHILDISH
1Co 13:11 I became a man, I put away c things. G3516

CHILDLESS
Gen 15: 2 me, seeing I go c, and the steward of my H6185
Lev 20:20 they shall bear their sin; they shall die c. H6185
21 his brother's nakedness; they shall be c. H6185
1Sa 15:33 made women c, so shall thy mother H7921
33 thy mother be c among women. And H7921
Jer 22:30 Write ye this man c, a man that shall H6185
Lk 20:30 second took her to wife, and he died c. G815

CHILDREN
Gen 3:16 shalt bring forth c; and thy desire shall H1121
6: 4 men, and they bare c to them, the same
10:21 Unto Shem also, the father of all the c H1121
21 the elder, even to him were c born. H1121
22 The c of Shem; Elam, and Asshur, and H1121
Gen 10:23 And the c of Aram; Uz, and Hul, and H1121
11: 5 the tower, which the c of men builded. H1121
16: 1 Now Sarai Abram's wife bare him no c:
2 that I may obtain c by her. And Abram H1129
18:19 will command his c and his household H1121
19:38 father of the c of Ammon unto this day. H1121
20:17 and his maidservants; and they bare c.
21: 7 should have given c suck? for I have H1121
22:20 also born c unto thy brother Nahor; H1121
23: 5 And the c of Heth answered Abraham, H1121
7 of the land, even to the c of Heth. H1121
10 And Ephron dwelt among the c of H1121
10 audience of the c of Heth, even of all H1121
18 the presence of the c of Heth, before all H1121
25: 4 Eldaah. All these were the c of Keturah. H1121
22 And the c struggled together within H1121
30: 1 she bare Jacob no c, Rachel envied her
1 said unto Jacob, Give me c, or else I die. H1121
3 knees, that I may also have c by her. H1129
26 Give me my wives and my c, for whom I H3206
31:43 and these c are my children, and H1121
43 children are my c, and these cattle are H1121
43 or unto their c which they have born? H1121
32:11 smite me, and the mother with the c. H1121
32 Therefore the c of Israel eat not of the H1121
33: 1 he divided the c unto Leah, and unto H3206
2 And he put the handmaids and their c H3206
2 and Leah and her c after, and Rachel H3206
5 women and the c; and said, Who are H3206
5 And he said, The c which God hath H3206
6 and their c, and they bowed themselves. H3206
7 And Leah also with her c came near, H3206
13 knoweth that the c are tender, and the H3206
14 before me and the c be able to endure, H3206
19 tent, at the hand of the c of Hamor, H1121
36:21 the c of Seir in the land of Edom. H1121
22 And the c of Lotan were Hori and H1121
23 And the c of Shobal were these; Alvan, H1121
24 And these are the c of Zibeon; both H1121
25 And the c of Anah were these; Dishon, H1121
26 And these are the c of Dishon; H1121
27 The c of Ezer are these; Bilhan, and H1121
28 The c of Dishan are these; Uz, and H1121
31 reigned any king over the c of Israel. H1121
37: 3 more than all his c, because he was the H1121
42:36 ye bereaved of my c: Joseph is not, and
43:14 If I be bereaved of my c, I am bereaved.
45:10 me, thou, and thy c, and thy children's H1121
10 and thy children's c, and thy flocks, and H1121
21 And the c of Israel did so: and Joseph H1121
46: 8 And these are the names of the c of H1121
49: 8 father's c shall bow down before thee. H1121
32 that is therein was from the c of Heth. H1121
50:23 And Joseph saw Ephraim's c of the H1121
23 generation: the c also of Machir the son H1121
25 And Joseph took an oath of the c of H1121
Ex 1: 1 Now these are the names of the c of H1121
7 And the c of Israel were fruitful, and H1121
9 the people of the c of Israel are more H1121
12 were grieved because of the c of Israel. H1121
13 And the Egyptians made the c of Israel H1121
17 them, but saved the men c alive. H3206
18 thing, and have saved the men c alive? H3206
2: 6 and said, This is one of the Hebrews' c. H3206
23 died: and the c of Israel sighed by H1121
25 And God looked upon the c of Israel, H1121
3: 9 Now therefore, behold, the cry of the c H1121
10 my people the c of Israel out of Egypt. H1121
11 bring forth the c of Israel out of Egypt? H1121
13 I come unto the c of Israel, and shall H1121
14 thou say unto the c of Israel, I AM hath H1121
15 thou say unto the c of Israel, The LORD H1121
4:29 together all the elders of the c of Israel: H1121
31 had visited the c of Israel, and that he H1121
5:14 And the officers of the c of Israel, H1121
15 Then the officers of the c of Israel came H1121
19 And the officers of the c of Israel did H1121
6: 5 groaning of the c of Israel, whom the H1121
6 Wherefore say unto the c of Israel, I H1121
9 And Moses spake so unto the c of H1121
11 he let the c of Israel go out of his land. H1121
12 saying, Behold, the c of Israel have not H1121
13 a charge unto the c of Israel, and unto H1121
13 the c of Israel out of the land of Egypt. H1121
26 said, Bring out the c of Israel from the H1121
27 to bring out the c of Israel from Egypt: H1121
7: 2 he send the c of Israel out of his land. H1121
4 and my people the c of Israel, out of the H1121
5 out the c of Israel from among them. H1121
Ex 9: 6 the cattle of the c of Israel died not one. H1121
26 Only in the land of Goshen, where the c H1121
35 would he let the c of Israel go; as the H1121
10:20 that he would not let the c of Israel go. H1121
23 c of Israel had light in their dwellings. H1121
11: 7 But against any of the c of Israel shall H1121
10 not let the c of Israel go out of his land. H1121
12:26 And it shall come to pass, when your c H1121
27 the houses of the c of Israel in Egypt, H1121
28 And the c of Israel went away, and did H1121
31 both ye and the c of Israel; and go, H1121
35 And the c of Israel did according to the H1121
37 And the c of Israel journeyed from H1121
37 on foot that were men, beside c. H2945
40 Now the sojourning of the c of Israel, H1121
42 all the c of Israel in their generations. H1121
50 Thus did all the c of Israel; as the H1121
51 did bring the c of Israel out of the land H1121
13: 2 womb among the c of Israel, both of H1121
13 of man among thy c shalt thou redeem. H1121
15 but all the firstborn of my c I redeem. H1121
18 the Red sea: and the c of Israel went up H1121
19 straitly sworn the c of Israel, saying, H1121
14: 2 Speak unto the c of Israel, that they H1121
3 For Pharaoh will say of the c of Israel, H1121
8 he pursued after the c of Israel: and the H1121
8 c of Israel went out with an high hand. H1121
10 And when Pharaoh drew nigh, the c of H1121
10 the c of Israel cried out unto the LORD. H1121
15 the c of Israel, that they go forward: H1121
16 divide it: and the c of Israel shall go on H1121
22 And the c of Israel went into the midst H1121
29 But the c of Israel walked upon dry H1121
15: 1 Then sang Moses and the c of Israel H1121
19 them; but the c of Israel went on dry H1121
16: 1 of the c of Israel came unto H1121
2 And the whole congregation of the c of H1121
3 And the c of Israel said unto them, H1121
6 said unto all the c of Israel, At even, H1121
9 of the c of Israel, Come near H1121
10 of the c of Israel, that they looked H1121
12 I have heard the murmurings of the c H1121
15 And when the c of Israel saw it, they H1121
17 And the c of Israel did so, and H1121
35 And the c of Israel did eat manna forty H1121
17: 1 And all the congregation of the c of H1121
3 us and our c and our cattle with thirst? H1121
7 of the chiding of the c of Israel, and H1121
19: 1 In the third month, when the c of Israel H1121
3 house of Jacob, and tell the c of Israel; H1121
6 thou shalt speak unto the c of Israel. H1121
20: 5 fathers upon the c unto the third and H1121
22 shalt say unto the c of Israel, Ye have H1121
21: 4 the wife and her c shall be her master's, H3206
5 my wife, and my c; I will not go out free: H1121
22:24 shall be widows, and your c fatherless. H1121
24: 5 And he sent young men of the c of H1121
11 And upon the nobles of the c of Israel H1121
17 the mount in the eyes of the c of Israel. H1121
25: 2 Speak unto the c of Israel, that they H1121
22 in commandment unto the c of Israel. H1121
27:20 And thou shalt command the c of H1121
21 on the behalf of the c of Israel. H1121
28: 1 from among the c of Israel, that he H1121
9 on them the names of the c of Israel: H1121
11 the names of the c of Israel: thou shalt H1121
12 unto the c of Israel: and Aaron H1121
21 the names of the c of Israel, twelve, H1121
29 bear the names of the c of Israel in the H1121
30 the judgment of the c of Israel upon his H1121
38 holy things, which the c of Israel shall H1121
29:28 for ever from the c of Israel: for it is an H1121
28 offering from the c of Israel of the H1121
43 And there I will meet with the c of H1121
45 And I will dwell among the c of Israel, H1121
30:12 When thou takest the sum of the c of H1121
16 money of the c of Israel, and shalt H1121
16 unto the c of Israel before the H1121
31 And thou shalt speak unto the c of H1121
31:13 Speak thou also unto the c of Israel, H1121
16 Wherefore the c of Israel shall keep the H1121
17 It is a sign between me and the c of H1121
32:20 and made the c of Israel drink of it. H1121
28 And the c of Levi did according to the H1121
33: 5 Say unto the c of Israel, Ye are a H1121
6 And the c of Israel stripped themselves H1121
34: 7 the fathers upon the c, and upon the H1121
7 upon the children's c, unto the third and
23 Thrice in the year shall all your men c

Ex 34:30 And when Aaron and all the c of Israel H1121
32 And afterward all the c of Israel came H1121
34 spake unto the c of Israel *that* which H1121
35 And the c of Israel saw the face of H1121
35: 1 of the c of Israel together, and H1121
4 of the c of Israel, saying, This H1121
20 And all the congregation of the c of H1121
29 The c of Israel brought a willing H1121
30 And Moses said unto the c of Israel, H1121
36: 3 which the c of Israel had brought H1121
39: 6 with the names of the c of Israel. H1121
7 for a memorial to the c of Israel; as the H1121
14 to the names of the c of Israel, twelve, H1121
32 finished: and the c of Israel did H1121
42 so the c of Israel made all the work. H1121
40:36 over the tabernacle, the c of Israel went H1121
Lev 1: 2 Speak unto the c of Israel, and say unto H1121
4: 2 Speak unto the c of Israel, saying, If a H1121
6:18 All the males among the c of Aaron H1121
7:23 Speak unto the c of Israel, saying, Ye H1121
29 Speak unto the c of Israel, saying, He H1121
34 have I taken of the c of Israel from off H1121
34 for ever from among the c of Israel. H1121
36 given them of the c of Israel, in the day H1121
38 he commanded the c of Israel to offer H1121
9: 3 And unto the c of Israel thou shalt H1121
10:11 And that ye may teach the c of Israel H1121
14 of peace offerings of the c of Israel. H1121
11: 2 Speak unto the c of Israel, saying, H1121
12: 2 Speak unto the c of Israel, saying, If a H1121
15: 2 Speak unto the c of Israel, and say unto H1121
31 Thus shall ye separate the c of Israel H1121
16: 5 of the c of Israel two kids of H1121
16 the uncleanness of the c of Israel, and H1121
19 from the uncleanness of the c of Israel. H1121
21 iniquities of the c of Israel, and all their H1121
34 an atonement for the c of Israel for all H1121
17: 2 and unto all the c of Israel, and say H1121
5 To the end that the c of Israel may H1121
12 Therefore I said unto the c of Israel, No H1121
13 And whatsoever man *there be* of the c H1121
14 I said unto the c of Israel, Ye shall eat H1121
18: 2 Speak unto the c of Israel, and say unto H1121
19: 2 Speak unto all the congregation of the c H1121
18 grudge against the c of thy people, but H1121
20: 2 Again, thou shalt say to the c of Israel, H1121
2 *he be* of the c of Israel, or of the H1121
21:24 to his sons, and unto all the c of Israel. H1121
22: 2 holy things of the c of Israel, and that H1121
3 things, which the c of Israel hallow H1121
15 the holy things of the c of Israel, which H1121
18 and unto all the c of Israel, and say H1121
32 among the c of Israel: I *am* the LORD H1121
23: 2 Speak unto the c of Israel, and say unto H1121
10 Speak unto the c of Israel, and say unto H1121
24 Speak unto the c of Israel, saying, In H1121
34 Speak unto the c of Israel, saying, The H1121
43 that I made the c of Israel to dwell in H1121
44 And Moses declared unto the c of H1121
24: 2 Command the c of Israel, that they H1121
8 c of Israel by an everlasting covenant. H1121
10 out among the c of Israel: and this son H1121
15 And thou shalt speak unto the c of H1121
23 And Moses spake to the c of Israel, that H1121
23 stones. And the c of Israel did as the H1121
25: 2 Speak unto the c of Israel, and say unto H1121
33 their possession among the c of Israel. H1121
41 *both* he and his c with him, and shall H1121
45 Moreover of the c of the strangers that H1121
46 for your c after you, to inherit H1121
46 your brethren the c of Israel, ye shall H1121
54 of jubile, *both* he, and his c with him. H1121
55 For unto me the c of Israel *are* H1121
26:22 shall rob you of your c, and destroy your
46 him and the c of Israel in mount Sinai H1121
27: 2 Speak unto the c of Israel, and say unto H1121
34 for the c of Israel in mount Sinai. H1121
Nu 1: 2 of the c of Israel, after their H1121
10 Of the c of Joseph: of Ephraim; H1121
20 And the c of Reuben, Israel's eldest H1121
22 Of the c of Simeon, by their H1121
24 Of the c of Gad, by their generations, H1121
26 Of the c of Judah, by their generations, H1121
28 Of the c of Issachar, by their H1121
30 Of the c of Zebulun, by their H1121
32 Of the c of Joseph, *namely,* of the H1121
32 *namely,* of the c of Ephraim, by their H1121
34 Of the c of Manasseh, by their H1121
36 Of the c of Benjamin, by their H1121

Nu 1:38 Of the c of Dan, by their generations, H1121
40 Of the c of Asher, by their generations, H1121
42 Of the c of Naphtali, throughout their H1121
45 were numbered of the c of Israel, by the H1121
49 the sum of them among the c of Israel: H1121
52 And the c of Israel shall pitch their H1121
53 of the c of Israel: and the Levites H1121
54 And the c of Israel did according to all H1121
2: 2 Every man of the c of Israel shall pitch H1121
3 *shall be* captain of the c of Judah. H1121
5 *shall be* captain of the c of Issachar. H1121
7 *shall be* captain of the c of Zebulun. H1121
10 the captain of the c of Reuben *shall be* H1121
12 the captain of the c of Simeon *shall be* H1121
20 the captain of the c of Manasseh *shall* H1121
25 and the captain of the c of Dan *shall be* H1121
27 the captain of the c of Asher *shall be* H1121
29 the captain of the c of Naphtali *shall be* H1121
32 were numbered of the c of Israel by the H1121
33 among the c of Israel; as the LORD H1121
34 And the c of Israel did according to all H1121
3: 4 and they had no c: and Eleazar and H1121
8 the charge of the c of Israel, to do the H1121
9 given unto him out of the c of Israel. H1121
12 from among the c of Israel instead of H1121
12 matrix among the c of Israel: therefore H1121
15 Number the c of Levi after the house of H1121
38 for the charge of the c of Israel; and the H1121
40 of the males of the c of Israel from a H1121
41 among the c of Israel; and the cattle H1121
41 among the cattle of the c of Israel. H1121
42 all the firstborn among the c of Israel. H1121
45 among the c of Israel, and the cattle H1121
46 firstborn of the c of Israel, which are H1121
50 Of the firstborn of the c of Israel took H1121
5: 2 Command the c of Israel, that they put H1121
4 And the c of Israel did so, and put H1121
4 unto Moses, so did the c of Israel. H1121
6 Speak unto the c of Israel, When a man H1121
9 the holy things of the c of Israel, which H1121
12 Speak unto the c of Israel, and say unto H1121
6: 2 Speak unto the c of Israel, and say unto H1121
23 bless the c of Israel, saying unto them, H1121
27 And they shall put my name upon the c H1121
7:24 prince of the c of Zebulun, *did offer*: H1121
30 prince of the c of Reuben, *did offer*: H1121
36 prince of the c of Simeon, *did offer*: H1121
42 Deuel, prince of the c of Gad, *offered*: H1121
48 prince of the c of Ephraim, *offered*: H1121
54 Pedahzur, prince of the c of Manasseh: H1121
60 prince of the c of Benjamin, *offered*: H1121
66 prince of the c of Dan, *offered*: H1121
72 Ocran, prince of the c of Asher, *offered*: H1121
78 prince of the c of Naphtali, *offered*: H1121
8: 6 Take the Levites from among the c of H1121
9 assembly of the c of Israel together: H1121
10 the LORD: and the c of Israel shall put H1121
11 an offering of the c of Israel, that they H1121
14 from among the c of Israel: and the H1121
16 from among the c of Israel; instead of H1121
16 c of Israel, have I taken them unto me. H1121
17 For all the firstborn of the c of Israel H1121
18 for all the firstborn of the c of Israel. H1121
19 from among the c of Israel, to do the H1121
19 do the service of the c of Israel in the H1121
19 atonement for the c of Israel: that there H1121
19 plague among the c of Israel, when the H1121
19 of Israel, when the c of Israel come H1121
20 of the c of Israel, did to the H1121
20 so did the c of Israel unto them. H1121
9: 2 Let the c of Israel also keep the H1121
4 And Moses spake unto the c of Israel, H1121
5 Moses, so did the c of Israel. H1121
7 season among the c of Israel? H1121
10 Speak unto the c of Israel, saying, If H1121
17 then after that the c of Israel H1121
17 there the c of Israel pitched their tents. H1121
18 of the LORD the c of Israel journeyed, H1121
19 many days, then the c of Israel kept the H1121
22 thereon, the c of Israel abode in their H1121
10:12 And the c of Israel took their journeys H1121
14 of the camp of the c of Judah according H1121
15 And over the host of the tribe of the c of H1121
16 And over the host of the tribe of the c of H1121
19 And over the host of the tribe of the c of H1121
20 And over the host of the tribe of the c of H1121
22 And the standard of the camp of the c H1121
23 And over the host of the tribe of the c of H1121
24 And over the host of the tribe of the c of H1121

Nu 10:25 And the standard of the camp of the c H1121
26 And over the host of the tribe of the c of H1121
27 And over the host of the tribe of the c of H1121
28 Thus *were* the journeyings of the c of H1121
11: 4 a lusting: and the c of Israel also wept H1121
13: 2 I give unto the c of Israel: of every tribe H1121
3 those men *were* heads of the c of Israel. H1121
22 and Talmai, the c of Anak, *were.* (Now H3211
24 the c of Israel cut down from thence. H1121
26 of the c of Israel, unto the wilderness H1121
28 moreover we saw the c of Anak there. H3211
32 searched unto the c of Israel, saying, H1121
14: 2 And all the c of Israel murmured H1121
3 our wives and our c should be a prey? H2945
5 of the congregation of the c of Israel. H1121
7 company of the c of Israel, saying, The H1121
10 congregation before all the c of Israel. H1121
18 c unto the third and fourth *generation*. H1121
27 of the c of Israel, which they H1121
33 And your c shall wander in the H1121
39 unto all the c of Israel: and the people H1121
15: 2 Speak unto the c of Israel, and say unto H1121
18 Speak unto the c of Israel, and say unto H1121
25 of the c of Israel, and it shall H1121
26 of the c of Israel, and the stranger H1121
29 is born among the c of Israel, and for H1121
32 And while the c of Israel were in the H1121
38 Speak unto the c of Israel, and bid H1121
16: 2 with certain of the c of Israel, two H1121
27 wives, and their sons, and their little c. H2945
38 they shall be a sign unto the c of Israel. H1121
40 *To be* a memorial unto the c of Israel, H1121
41 of the c of Israel murmured H1121
17: 2 Speak unto the c of Israel, and take of H1121
5 of the c of Israel, whereby they H1121
6 And Moses spake unto the c of Israel, H1121
9 LORD unto all the c of Israel: and they H1121
12 And the c of Israel spake unto Moses, H1121
18: 5 no wrath any more upon the c of Israel. H1121
6 from among the c of Israel: to you *they* H1121
8 things of the c of Israel; unto thee H1121
11 offerings of the c of Israel: I have given H1121
19 things, which the c of Israel offer unto H1121
20 thine inheritance among the c of Israel. H1121
21 And, behold, I have given the c of Levi H1121
22 Neither must the c of Israel henceforth H1121
23 the c of Israel they have no inheritance. H1121
24 But the tithes of the c of Israel, which H1121
24 them, Among the c of Israel they shall H1121
26 ye take of the c of Israel the tithes H1121
28 ye receive of the c of Israel; and ye shall H1121
32 holy things of the c of Israel, lest ye die. H1121
19: 2 Speak unto the c of Israel, that they H1121
9 of the c of Israel for a water H1121
10 it shall be unto the c of Israel, and unto H1121
20: 1 Then came the c of Israel, *even* the H1121
12 in the eyes of the c of Israel, therefore H1121
13 because the c of Israel strove with H1121
19 And the c of Israel said unto him, We H1121
22 And the c of Israel, *even* the whole H1121
24 given unto the c of Israel, because ye H1121
21:10 And the c of Israel set forward, and H1121
24 even unto the c of Ammon: for the H1121
24 border of the c of Ammon *was* strong. H1121
22: 1 And the c of Israel set forward, and H1121
3 distressed because of the c of Israel. H1121
5 of the land of the c of his people, to call H1121
24:17 of Moab, and destroy all the c of Sheth. H1121
25: 6 And, behold, one of the c of Israel came H1121
6 of the c of Israel, who *were* H1121
8 plague was stayed from the c of Israel. H1121
11 away from the c of Israel, while he was H1121
11 not the c of Israel in my jealousy. H1121
13 made an atonement for the c of Israel. H1121
26: 2 of the c of Israel, from twenty H1121
4 Moses and the c of Israel, which went H1121
5 Reuben, the eldest son of Israel: the c H1121
11 Notwithstanding the c of Korah died H1121
15 The c of Gad after their families: of H1121
18 These *are* the families of the c of Gad H1121
44 *Of* the c of Asher after their families: of H1121
51 These *were* the numbered of the c of H1121
62 among the c of Israel, because there H1121
62 given them among the c of Israel. H1121
63 numbered the c of Israel in the plains H1121
64 c of Israel in the wilderness of Sinai. H1121
27: 8 And thou shalt speak unto the c of H1121
11 it shall be unto the c of Israel a statute H1121
12 which I have given unto the c of Israel. H1121

Nu 27:20 of the **c** of Israel may be obedient. H1121
21 he, and all the **c** of Israel with him, H1121
28: 2 Command the **c** of Israel, and say unto H1121
29:40 And Moses told the **c** of Israel H1121
30: 1 concerning the **c** of Israel, saying, This H1121
31: 2 Avenge the **c** of Israel of the H1121
9 And the **c** of Israel took *all* the women H1121
12 of the **c** of Israel, unto the camp H1121
16 Behold, these caused the **c** of Israel, H1121
18 But all the women **c**, that have not H2945
30 And of the **c** of Israel's half, thou shalt H1121
42 And of the **c** of Israel's half, which H1121
47 Even of the **c** of Israel's half, Moses H1121
54 for the **c** of Israel before the LORD. H1121
32: 1 Now the **c** of Reuben and the children H1121
1 Now the children of Reuben and the **c** H1121
2 The **c** of Gad and the children of H1121
2 The children of Gad and the **c** of H1121
6 And Moses said unto the **c** of Gad and H1121
6 of Gad and to the **c** of Reuben, Shall H1121
7 ye the heart of the **c** of Israel from H1121
9 the heart of the **c** of Israel, that they H1121
17 armed before the **c** of Israel, until we H1121
18 our houses, until the **c** of Israel have H1121
25 And the **c** of Gad and the children of H1121
25 And the children of Gad and the **c** of H1121
28 fathers of the tribes of the **c** of Israel: H1121
29 And Moses said unto them, If the **c** of H1121
29 of Gad and the **c** of Reuben will pass H1121
31 And the **c** of Gad and the children of H1121
31 And the children of Gad and the **c** of H1121
33 them, *even* to the **c** of Gad, and to the H1121
33 of Gad, and to the **c** of Reuben, and H1121
34 And the **c** of Gad built Dibon, and H1121
37 And the **c** of Reuben built Heshbon, H1121
39 And the **c** of Machir the son of H1121
33: 1 These *are* the journeys of the **c** of H1121
3 the passover the **c** of Israel went out H1121
5 And the **c** of Israel removed from H1121
38 year after the **c** of Israel were come H1121
40 heard of the coming of the **c** of Israel. H1121
51 Speak unto the **c** of Israel, and say unto H1121
34: 2 Command the **c** of Israel, and say unto H1121
13 And Moses commanded the **c** of Israel, H1121
14 For the tribe of the **c** of Reuben H1121
14 the tribe of the **c** of Gad according to H1121
20 And of the tribe of the **c** of Simeon, H1121
22 And the prince of the tribe of the **c** of H1121
23 The prince of the **c** of Joseph, for the H1121
23 for the tribe of the **c** of Manasseh, H1121
24 And the prince of the tribe of the **c** of H1121
25 And the prince of the tribe of the **c** of H1121
26 And the prince of the tribe of the **c** of H1121
27 And the prince of the tribe of the **c** of H1121
28 And the prince of the tribe of the **c** of H1121
29 the **c** of Israel in the land of Canaan. H1121
35: 2 Command the **c** of Israel, that they give H1121
8 possession of the **c** of Israel: from *them* H1121
10 Speak unto the **c** of Israel, and say unto H1121
15 *both* for the **c** of Israel, and for the H1121
34 I the LORD dwell among the **c** of Israel. H1121
36: 1 the families of the **c** of Gilead, the son H1121
1 the chief fathers of the **c** of Israel: H1121
2 by lot to the **c** of Israel: and my lord H1121
3 *other* tribes of the **c** of Israel, then shall H1121
4 And when the jubile of the **c** of Israel H1121
5 And Moses commanded the **c** of Israel H1121
7 So shall not the inheritance of the **c** of H1121
7 every one of the **c** of Israel shall keep H1121
8 in any tribe of the **c** of Israel, shall be H1121
8 father, that the **c** of Israel may enjoy H1121
9 of the tribes of the **c** of Israel shall keep H1121
13 of Moses unto the **c** of Israel in the H1121
Dt 1: 3 spake unto the **c** of Israel, according H1121
36 upon, and to his **c**, because he hath H1121
39 be a prey, and your **c**, which in that day H1121
2: 4 of your brethren the **c** of Esau, which H1121
8 our brethren the **c** of Esau, which dwelt H1121
9 Ar unto the **c** of Lot *for* a possession. H1121
12 but the **c** of Esau succeeded them, H1121
19 over against the **c** of Ammon, distress H1121
19 thee of the land of the **c** of Ammon *any* H1121
19 it unto the **c** of Lot *for* a possession. H1121
22 As he did to the **c** of Esau, which dwelt H1121
29 (As the **c** of Esau which dwell in Seir, H1121
37 Only unto the land of the **c** of Ammon H1121
3: 6 the men, women, and **c**, of every city. H2945
11 in Rabbath of the **c** of Ammon? nine H1121
16 *which is* the border of the **c** of Ammon; H1121

Dt 3:18 **c** of Israel, all *that are* meet for the war. H1121
4:10 earth, and *that* they may teach their **c**. H1121
25 When thou shalt beget **c**, and children's H1121
25 and children's **c**, and ye shall have H1121
40 thee, and with thy **c** after thee, and that H1121
44 which Moses set before the **c** of Israel: H1121
45 spake unto the **c** of Israel, after they H1121
46 Moses and the **c** of Israel smote, after H1121
5: 9 fathers upon the **c** unto the third and H1121
29 with them, and with their **c** for ever! H1121
6: 7 diligently unto thy **c**, and shalt talk of H1121
9: 2 A people great and tall, the **c** of the H1121
2 Who can stand before the **c** of Anak! H1121
10: 6 And the **c** of Israel took their journey H1121
6 Beeroth of the **c** of Jaakan to Mosera: H1121
11: 2 not with your **c** which have not known, H1121
19 And ye shall teach them your **c**, H1121
21 the days of your **c**, in the land which the H1121
12:25 thee, and with thy **c** after thee, when H1121
28 thee, and with thy **c** after thee for ever, H1121
13:13 *Certain* men, the **c** of Belial, are gone H1121
14: 1 Ye *are* the **c** of the LORD your God: ye H1121
17:20 he, and his **c**, in the midst of Israel. H1121
21:15 have born him **c**, *both* the beloved and H1121
23: 8 The **c** that are begotten of them shall H1121
24: 7 of his brethren of the **c** of Israel, and H1121
16 put to death for the **c**, neither shall the H1121
16 neither shall the **c** be put to death for H1121
28:54 remnant of his **c** which he shall leave: H1121
55 of the flesh of his **c** whom he shall eat: H1121
57 and toward her **c** which she shall bear: H1121
29: 1 to make with the **c** of Israel in the land H1121
22 to come of your **c** that shall rise up H1121
29 unto us and to our **c** for ever, that *we* H1121
30: 2 day, thou and thy **c**, with all thine heart, H1121
31:12 and women, and **c**, and thy stranger H2945
13 And *that* their **c**, which have not known H1121
19 and teach it the **c** of Israel: put it in H1121
19 a witness for me against the **c** of Israel. H1121
22 same day, and taught it the **c** of Israel. H1121
23 shalt bring the **c** of Israel into the land H1121
32: 5 not *the spot* of his **c**: *they are* a perverse H1121
8 to the number of the **c** of Israel. H1121
20 generation, **c** in whom *is* no faith. H1121
46 command your **c** to observe to do, all H1121
49 unto the **c** of Israel for a possession: H1121
51 me among the **c** of Israel at the waters H1121
51 me not in the midst of the **c** of Israel. H1121
52 the land which I give the **c** of Israel. H1121
33: 1 blessed the **c** of Israel before his death. H1121
9 nor knew his own **c**: for they have H1121
24 *be* blessed with **c**; let him be acceptable H1121
34: 8 And the **c** of Israel wept for Moses in H1121
9 hands upon him: and the **c** of Israel H1121
Jos 1: 2 do give to them, *even* to the **c** of Israel. H1121
2: 2 **c** of Israel to search out the country. H1121
3: 1 he and all the **c** of Israel, and lodged H1121
9 And Joshua said unto the **c** of Israel, H1121
4: 4 the **c** of Israel, out of every tribe a man: H1121
5 number of the tribes of the **c** of Israel: H1121
6 *that* when your **c** ask *their fathers* in H1121
7 memorial unto the **c** of Israel for ever. H1121
8 And the **c** of Israel did so as Joshua H1121
8 of the tribes of the **c** of Israel, and H1121
12 And the **c** of Reuben, and the children H1121
12 And the children of Reuben, and the **c** H1121
12 **c** of Israel, as Moses spake unto them: H1121
21 And he spake unto the **c** of Israel, H1121
21 When your **c** shall ask their fathers H1121
22 Then ye shall let your **c** know, saying, H1121
5: 1 from before the **c** of Israel, until we H1121
1 any more, because of the **c** of Israel. H1121
2 again the **c** of Israel the second time. H1121
3 **c** of Israel at the hill of the foreskins. H1121
6 For the **c** of Israel walked forty years in H1121
7 And their **c**, *whom* he raised up in their H1121
10 And the **c** of Israel encamped in Gilgal, H1121
12 neither had the **c** of Israel manna any H1121
6: 1 up because of the **c** of Israel: none went H1121
7: 1 But the **c** of Israel committed a H1121
1 was kindled against the **c** of Israel. H1121
12 Therefore the **c** of Israel could not H1121
23 and unto all the **c** of Israel, and laid H1121
8:31 commanded the **c** of Israel, as it is H1121
32 wrote in the presence of the **c** of Israel. H1121
9:17 And the **c** of Israel journeyed, and H1121
18 And the **c** of Israel smote them not, H1121
26 the **c** of Israel, that they slew them not. H1121
10: 4 with Joshua and with the **c** of Israel. H1121

Jos 10:11 the **c** of Israel slew with the sword. H1121
12 before the **c** of Israel, and he said H1121
20 Joshua and the **c** of Israel had made H1121
21 tongue against any of the **c** of Israel. H1121
11:14 and the cattle, the **c** of Israel took for a H1121
19 peace with the **c** of Israel, save the H1121
22 left in the land of the **c** of Israel: only in H1121
12: 1 land, which the **c** of Israel smote, and H1121
2 *which is* the border of the **c** of Ammon; H1121
6 the LORD and the **c** of Israel smite: and H1121
7 Joshua and the **c** of Israel smote on this H1121
13: 6 from before the **c** of Israel: only divide H1121
10 unto the border of the **c** of Ammon; H1121
13 Nevertheless the **c** of Israel expelled not H1121
15 And Moses gave unto the tribe of the **c** H1121
22 did the **c** of Israel slay with the H1121
23 And the border of the **c** of Reuben was H1121
23 the inheritance of the **c** of Reuben after H1121
24 the **c** of Gad according to their families. H1121
25 the land of the **c** of Ammon, unto Aroer H1121
28 This *is* the inheritance of the **c** of Gad H1121
29 of the **c** of Manasseh by their families. H1121
31 unto the **c** of Machir the son of H1121
31 half of the **c** of Machir by their families. H1121
14: 1 And these *are the countries* which the **c** H1121
1 fathers of the tribes of the **c** of Israel, H1121
4 For the **c** of Joseph were two tribes, H1121
5 Moses, so the **c** of Israel did, and they H1121
6 Then the **c** of Judah came unto Joshua H1121
10 Moses, while *the c of* Israel wandered in
15: 1 lot of the tribe of the **c** of Judah by their H1121
12 *is* the coast of the **c** of Judah round H1121
13 a part among the **c** of Judah, according H1121
14 Ahiman, and Talmai, the **c** of Anak. H3211
20 **c** of Judah according to their families. H1121
21 of the tribe of the **c** of Judah toward the H1121
63 of Jerusalem, the **c** of Judah could not H1121
63 **c** of Judah at Jerusalem unto this day. H1121
16: 1 And the lot of the **c** of Joseph fell from H1121
4 So the **c** of Joseph, Manasseh and H1121
5 And the border of the **c** of Ephraim H1121
8 of the **c** of Ephraim by their families. H1121
9 And the separate cities for the **c** of H1121
9 inheritance of the **c** of Manasseh, all H1121
17: 2 There was also *a lot* for the rest of the **c** H1121
2 families; for the **c** of Abiezer, and for H1121
2 and for the **c** of Helek, and for the H1121
2 of Helek, and for the **c** of Asriel, and for H1121
2 of Asriel, and for the **c** of Shechem, and H1121
2 and for the **c** of Hepher, and for the H1121
2 and for the **c** of Shemida: these *were* H1121
2 *were* the male **c** of Manasseh the son H1121
8 *belonged* to the **c** of Ephraim; H1121
12 Yet the **c** of Manasseh could not drive H1121
13 Yet it came to pass, when the **c** of Israel H1121
14 And the **c** of Joseph spake unto Joshua, H1121
16 And the **c** of Joseph said, The hill is not H1121
18: 1 And the whole congregation of the **c** of H1121
2 And there remained among the **c** of H1121
3 And Joshua said unto the **c** of Israel, H1121
10 **c** of Israel according to their divisions. H1121
11 And the lot of the tribe of the **c** of H1121
11 **c** of Judah and the children of Joseph. H1121
11 children of Judah and the **c** of Joseph. H1121
14 **c** of Judah: this *was* the west quarter. H1121
20 inheritance of the **c** of Benjamin, by the H1121
21 Now the cities of the tribe of the **c** of H1121
28 the inheritance of the **c** of Benjamin H1121
19: 1 *even* for the tribe of the **c** of Simeon H1121
1 the inheritance of the **c** of Judah. H1121
8 **c** of Simeon according to their families. H1121
9 Out of the portion of the **c** of Judah *was* H1121
9 inheritance of the **c** of Simeon: for the H1121
9 for the part of the **c** of Judah was too H1121
9 therefore the **c** of Simeon had their H1121
10 And the third lot came up for the **c** of H1121
16 This *is* the inheritance of the **c** of H1121
17 to Issachar, for the **c** of Issachar H1121
23 of the tribe of the **c** of Issachar H1121
24 **c** of Asher according to their families. H1121
31 of the tribe of the **c** of Asher according H1121
32 The sixth lot came out to the **c** of H1121
32 *even* for the **c** of Naphtali according H1121
39 of the tribe of the **c** of Naphtali H1121
40 **c** of Dan according to their families. H1121
47 And the coast of the **c** of Dan went out H1121
47 therefore the **c** of Dan went up to fight H1121
48 of the tribe of the **c** of Dan according to H1121
49 by their coasts, the **c** of Israel gave an H1121

C

Jos 19:51 of the tribes of the **c** of Israel, divided H1121
20: 2 Speak to the **c** of Israel, saying, H1121
9 for all the **c** of Israel, and for the H1121
21: 1 fathers of the tribes of the **c** of Israel; H1121
3 And the **c** of Israel gave unto the H1121
4 and the **c** of Aaron the priest, H1121
5 And the rest of the **c** of Kohath *had* by H1121
6 And the **c** of Gershon *had* by lot out of H1121
7 The **c** of Merari by their families *had* H1121
8 And the **c** of Israel gave by lot unto the H1121
9 And they gave out of the tribe of the **c** H1121
9 out of the tribe of the **c** of Simeon, these H1121
10 Which the **c** of Aaron, *being* of the H1121
10 *who were* of the **c** of Levi, had: for H1121
13 Thus they gave to the **c** of Aaron the H1121
19 All the cities of the **c** of Aaron, the H1121
20 And the families of the **c** of Kohath, the H1121
20 remained of the **c** of Kohath, even they H1121
26 of the **c** of Kohath that remained. H1121
27 And unto the **c** of Gershon, of the H1121
34 And unto the families of the **c** of H1121
40 So all the cities for the **c** of Merari by H1121
41 possession of the **c** of Israel *were* forty H1121
22: 9 And the **c** of Reuben and the children H1121
9 And the children of Reuben and the **c** H1121
9 and departed from the **c** of Israel out of H1121
10 of Canaan, the **c** of Reuben and the H1121
10 of Reuben and the **c** of Gad and the H1121
11 And the **c** of Israel heard say, Behold, H1121
11 say, Behold, the **c** of Reuben and the H1121
11 of Reuben and the **c** of Gad and the H1121
11 Jordan, at the passage of the **c** of Israel. H1121
12 And when the **c** of Israel heard *of it*, the H1121
12 of the **c** of Israel gathered themselves H1121
13 And the **c** of Israel sent unto the H1121
13 sent unto the **c** of Reuben, and to the H1121
13 and to the **c** of Gad, and to the half H1121
15 And they came unto the **c** of Reuben, H1121
15 and to the **c** of Gad, and to the half H1121
21 Then the **c** of Reuben and the children H1121
21 Then the children of Reuben and the **c** H1121
24 time to come your **c** might speak unto H1121
24 speak unto our **c**, saying, What have ye H1121
25 us and you, ye **c** of Reuben and H1121
25 of Reuben and **c** of Gad; ye have no H1121
25 so shall your **c** make our children cease H1121
25 our **c** cease from fearing the LORD: H1121
27 that your **c** may not say to our H1121
27 not say to our **c** in time to come, Ye H1121
30 the words that the **c** of Reuben and the H1121
30 of Reuben and the **c** of Gad and the H1121
30 **c** of Manasseh spake, it pleased them. H1121
31 said unto the **c** of Reuben, and to the H1121
31 and to the **c** of Gad, and to the children H1121
31 of Gad, and to the **c** of Manasseh, This H1121
31 **c** of Israel out of the hand of the LORD. H1121
32 returned from the **c** of Reuben, and H1121
32 and from the **c** of Gad, out of the land H1121
32 land of Canaan, to the **c** of Israel, and H1121
33 And the thing pleased the **c** of Israel; H1121
33 of Israel; and the **c** of Israel blessed H1121
33 the **c** of Reuben and Gad dwelt. H1121
34 And the **c** of Reuben and the children H1121
34 And the children of Reuben and the **c** H1121
24: 4 Jacob and his **c** went down into Egypt. H1121
32 And the bones of Joseph, which the **c** of H1121
32 the inheritance of the **c** of Joseph. H1121
Jdg 1: 1 to pass, that the **c** of Israel asked the H1121
8 Now the **c** of Judah had fought against H1121
9 And afterward the **c** of Judah went H1121
16 And the **c** of the Kenite, Moses' father H1121
16 palm trees with the **c** of Judah into the H1121
21 And the **c** of Benjamin did not drive H1121
21 dwell with the **c** of Benjamin in H1121
34 And the Amorites forced the **c** of Dan H1121
2: 4 words unto all the **c** of Israel, that the H1121
6 the people go, the **c** of Israel went every H1121
11 And the **c** of Israel did evil in the sight H1121
3: 2 Only that the generations of the **c** of H1121
5 And the **c** of Israel dwelt among the H1121
7 And the **c** of Israel did evil in the sight H1121
8 and the **c** of Israel served H1121
9 And when the **c** of Israel cried unto the H1121
9 up a deliverer to the **c** of Israel, who H1121
12 And the **c** of Israel did evil again in the H1121
13 And he gathered unto him the **c** of H1121
14 So the **c** of Israel served Eglon the king H1121
15 But when the **c** of Israel cried unto the H1121
15 and by him the **c** of Israel sent a H1121

Jdg 3:27 Ephraim, and the **c** of Israel went down H1121
4: 1 And the **c** of Israel again did evil in the H1121
3 And the **c** of Israel cried unto the H1121
3 he mightily oppressed the **c** of Israel. H1121
5 **c** of Israel came up to her for judgment. H1121
6 men of the **c** of Naphtali and of the H1121
6 of Naphtali and of the **c** of Zebulun? H1121
11 *which was* of the **c** of Hobab the father H1121
23 king of Canaan before the **c** of Israel. H1121
24 And the hand of the **c** of Israel H1121
6: 1 And the **c** of Israel did evil in the sight H1121
2 of the Midianites the **c** of Israel made H1121
3 and the **c** of the east, even they H1121
6 the **c** of Israel cried unto the LORD. H1121
7 And it came to pass, when the **c** of H1121
8 a prophet unto the **c** of Israel, which H1121
33 and the **c** of the east were gathered H1121
7:12 and all the **c** of the east lay along H1121
8:10 of all the hosts of the **c** of the east: for H1121
18 each one resembled the **c** of a king. H1121
28 Thus was Midian subdued before the **c** H1121
33 was dead, that the **c** of Israel turned H1121
34 And the **c** of Israel remembered not the H1121
10: 6 And the **c** of Israel did evil again in the H1121
6 the gods of the **c** of Ammon, and the H1121
7 and into the hands of the **c** of Ammon. H1121
8 and oppressed the **c** of Israel: eighteen H1121
8 years, all the **c** of Israel that *were* on H1121
9 Moreover the **c** of Ammon passed over H1121
10 And the **c** of Israel cried unto the H1121
11 And the LORD said unto the **c** of Israel, H1121
11 **c** of Ammon, and from the Philistines? H1121
15 And the **c** of Israel said unto the LORD, H1121
17 Then the **c** of Ammon were gathered H1121
17 encamped in Gilead. And the **c** of Israel H1121
18 fight against the **c** of Ammon? he shall H1121
11: 4 **c** of Ammon made war against Israel. H1121
5 And it was so, that when the **c** of H1121
6 we may fight with the **c** of Ammon. H1121
8 fight against the **c** of Ammon, and be H1121
9 fight against the **c** of Ammon, and the H1121
12 the king of the **c** of Ammon, saying, H1121
13 And the king of the **c** of Ammon H1121
14 again unto the king of the **c** of Ammon: H1121
15 Moab, nor the land of the **c** of Ammon: H1121
27 **c** of Israel and the children of Ammon. H1121
27 children of Israel and the **c** of Ammon. H1121
28 Howbeit the king of the **c** of Ammon H1121
29 he passed over *unto* the **c** of Ammon. H1121
30 the **c** of Ammon into mine hands, H1121
31 in peace from the **c** of Ammon, shall H1121
32 So Jephthah passed over unto the **c** of H1121
33 Thus the **c** of Ammon were subdued H1121
33 were subdued before the **c** of Israel. H1121
36 thine enemies, *even* of the **c** of Ammon. H1121
12: 1 to fight against the **c** of Ammon, and H1121
2 strife with the **c** of Ammon; and when H1121
3 over against the **c** of Ammon, and the H1121
13: 1 And the **c** of Israel did evil again in the H1121
14:16 a riddle unto the **c** of my people, and H1121
17 told the riddle to the **c** of her people. H1121
18: 2 And the **c** of Dan sent of their family H1121
16 which *were* of the **c** of Dan, stood by H1121
22 together, and overtook the **c** of Dan. H1121
23 And they cried unto the **c** of Dan. And H1121
25 And the **c** of Dan said unto him, Let H1121
26 And the **c** of Dan went their way: and H1121
30 And the **c** of Dan set up the graven H1121
19:12 **c** of Israel; we will pass over to Gibeah. H1121
30 the day that the **c** of Israel came up out H1121
20: 1 Then all the **c** of Israel went out, and H1121
3 (Now the **c** of Benjamin heard that the H1121
3 heard that the **c** of Israel were gone H1121
3 Then said the **c** of Israel, Tell *us*, how H1121
7 Behold, ye *are* all **c** of Israel; give here H1121
13 Now therefore deliver *us* the men, the **c** H1121
13 Israel. But the **c** of Benjamin would H1121
13 voice of their brethren the **c** of Israel: H1121
14 But the **c** of Benjamin gathered H1121
14 go out to battle against the **c** of Israel. H1121
15 And the **c** of Benjamin were numbered H1121
18 And the **c** of Israel arose, and went up H1121
18 battle against the **c** of Benjamin? And H1121
19 And the **c** of Israel rose up in the H1121
21 And the **c** of Benjamin came forth out H1121
23 (And the **c** of Israel went up and wept H1121
23 to battle against the **c** of Benjamin my H1121
24 And the **c** of Israel came near against H1121
24 the **c** of Benjamin the second day. H1121

Jdg 20:25 to the ground of the **c** of Israel again H1121
26 Then all the **c** of Israel, and all the H1121
27 And the **c** of Israel inquired of the H1121
28 to battle against the **c** of Benjamin my H1121
30 And the **c** of Israel went up against the H1121
30 up against the **c** of Benjamin on the H1121
31 And the **c** of Benjamin went out H1121
32 And the **c** of Benjamin said, They *are* H1121
32 at the first. But the **c** of Israel said, Let H1121
35 Israel: and the **c** of Israel destroyed of H1121
36 So the **c** of Benjamin saw that they H1121
48 again upon the **c** of Benjamin, and H1121
21: 5 And the **c** of Israel said, Who *is there* H1121
6 And the **c** of Israel repented them for H1121
10 of the sword, with the women and the **c**. H2945
13 to speak to the **c** of Benjamin that *were* H1121
18 our daughters: for the **c** of Israel have H1121
20 Therefore they commanded the **c** of H1121
23 And the **c** of Benjamin did so, and took H1121
24 And the **c** of Israel departed thence at H1121
1Sa 1: 2 had **c**, but Hannah had no children. H3206
2 had children, but Hannah had no **c**. H3206
2: 5 she that hath many **c** is waxed feeble. H1121
28 offerings made by fire of the **c** of Israel? H1121
7: 4 Then the **c** of Israel did put away H1121
6 judged the **c** of Israel in Mizpeh. H1121
7 heard that the **c** of Israel were gathered H1121
7 And when the **c** of Israel heard *it*, they H1121
8 And the **c** of Israel said to Samuel, H1121
9: 2 not among the **c** of Israel a goodlier H1121
10:18 And said unto the **c** of Israel, Thus H1121
27 But the **c** of Belial said, How shall this H1121
11: 8 them in Bezek, the **c** of Israel were H1121
12:12 the king of the **c** of Ammon came H1121
14:18 was at that time with the **c** of Israel. H1121
47 and against the **c** of Ammon, and H1121
15: 6 kindness to all the **c** of Israel, when H1121
16:11 Are here all *thy* **c**? And he said, There H5288
17:53 And the **c** of Israel returned from H1121
22:19 men and women, **c** and sucklings, and H5768
26:19 but if *they be* the **c** of men, cursed *be* H1121
30:22 his wife and his **c**, that they may lead H1121
2Sa 1:18 (Also he bade them teach the **c** of H1121
2:25 And the **c** of Benjamin gathered H1121
4: 2 a Beerothite, of the **c** of Benjamin: (for H1121
7: 6 that I brought up the **c** of Israel out of H1121
7 with all the **c** of Israel spake I a word H1121
10 neither shall the **c** of wickedness afflict H1121
14 and with the stripes of the **c** of men: H1121
8:12 Of Syria, and of Moab, and of the **c** of H1121
10: 1 the king of the **c** of Ammon died, and H1121
2 came into the land of the **c** of Ammon. H1121
3 And the princes of the **c** of Ammon H1121
6 And when the **c** of Ammon saw that H1121
6 before David, the **c** of Ammon sent and H1121
8 And the **c** of Ammon came out, and H1121
10 *them* in array against the **c** of Ammon. H1121
11 help me: but if the **c** of Ammon be too H1121
14 And when the **c** of Ammon saw that H1121
14 **c** of Ammon, and came to Jerusalem. H1121
19 to help the **c** of Ammon any more. H1121
11: 1 they destroyed the **c** of Ammon, and H1121
12: 3 him, and with his **c**; it did eat of his own H1121
9 him with the sword of the **c** of Ammon. H1121
26 **c** of Ammon, and took the royal city. H1121
31 all the cities of the **c** of Ammon. So H1121
17:27 of Rabbah of the **c** of Ammon, and H1121
21: 2 *were* not of the **c** of Israel, but of the H1121
2 Amorites; and the **c** of Israel had sworn H1121
2 in his zeal to the **c** of Israel and Judah.) H1121
23:29 out of Gibeah of the **c** of Benjamin, H1121
1Ki 2: 4 me, saying, If thy **c** take heed to their H1121
4:30 wisdom of all the **c** of the east country, H1121
6: 1 year after the **c** of Israel were come H1121
13 And I will dwell among the **c** of Israel, H1121
8: 1 the fathers of the **c** of Israel, unto king H1121
9 *a covenant* with the **c** of Israel, when H1121
25 of Israel; so that thy **c** take heed to their H1121
39 knowest the hearts of all the **c** of men;) H1121
63 king and all the **c** of Israel dedicated H1121
9: 6 me, ye or your **c**, and will not keep my H1121
20 which *were* not of the **c** of Israel, H1121
21 Their **c** that were left after them in the H1121
21 land, whom the **c** of Israel also were H1121
22 But of the **c** of Israel did Solomon make H1121
11: 2 said unto the **c** of Israel, Ye shall not H1121
7 the abomination of the **c** of Ammon. H1121
33 the god of the **c** of Ammon, and have H1121
12:17 But *as for* the **c** of Israel which dwelt in H1121

1Ki 12:24 your brethren the c of Israel: return H1121
33 a feast unto the c of Israel: and he H1121
14:24 LORD cast out before the c of Israel. H1121
18:20 So Ahab sent unto all the c of Israel, H1121
19:10 God of hosts: for the c of Israel have H1121
14 of hosts: because the c of Israel have H1121
20: 3 and thy c, *even* the goodliest, *are* mine. H1121
5 and thy gold, and thy wives, and thy c; H1121
7 wives, and for my c, and for my silver, H1121
15 the c of Israel, *being* seven thousand. H1121
27 And the c of Israel were numbered, H1121
27 them: and the c of Israel pitched before H1121
29 joined: and the c of Israel slew of the H1121
21:13 And there came in two men, c of Belial, H1121
26 LORD cast out before the c of Israel. H1121
2Ki 2:23 came forth little c out of the city, and H5288
24 wood, and tare forty and two c of them. H3206
4: 7 and live thou and thy c of the rest. H1121
8:12 wilt do unto the c of Israel: their strong H1121
12 c, and rip up their women with child. H5768
19 to give him alway a light, *and* to his c. H1121
9: 1 called one of the c of the prophets, and H1121
10: 1 to them that brought up Ahab's c, saying,
5 bringers up *of the* c, sent to Jehu, saying,
13 down to salute the c of the king and the H1121
13 of the king and the c of the queen. H1121
30 *was* in mine heart, thy c of the fourth H1121
13: 5 the Syrians: and the c of Israel dwelt in H1121
14: 6 But the c of the murderers he slew not: H1121
6 to death for the c, nor the children be H1121
6 children, nor the c be put to death for H1121
16: 3 cast out from before the c of Israel. H1121
17: 7 For *so* it was, that the c of Israel had H1121
8 from before the c of Israel, and of the H1121
9 And the c of Israel did secretly *those* H1121
22 For the c of Israel walked in all the sins H1121
24 instead of the c of Israel: and they H1121
31 burnt their c in fire to Adrammelech H1121
34 the c of Jacob, whom he named Israel; H1121
41 graven images, both their c, and their H1121
41 their children's c: as did their fathers, H1121
18: 4 unto those days the c of Israel did burn H1121
19: 3 for the c are come to the birth, H1121
12 the c of Eden which *were* in Thelasar? H1121
21: 2 LORD cast out before the c of Israel. H1121
9 LORD destroyed before the c of Israel. H1121
23: 6 upon the graves of the c of the people. H1121
10 *is* in the valley of the c of Hinnom, that H1121
13 of the c of Ammon, did the king defile. H1121
24: 2 and bands of the c of Ammon, and sent H1121
1Ch 1:43 reigned over the c of Israel; Bela the H1121
2:10 Nahshon, prince of the c of Judah; H1121
18 And Caleb the son of Hezron begat *c* of
30 and Appaim: but Seled died without c. H1121
31 Sheshan. And the c of Sheshan; Ahlai. H1121
32 Jonathan: and Jether died without c. H1121
4:27 had not many c, neither did all their H1121
27 family multiply, like to the c of Judah. H1121
5:11 And the c of Gad dwelt over against H1121
14 These *are* the c of Abihail the son of H1121
23 And the c of the half tribe of Manasseh H1121
6: 3 And the c of Amram; Aaron, and H1121
33 waited with their c. Of the sons of the H1121
64 And the c of Israel gave to the Levites H1121
65 of the tribe of the c of Judah, and out of H1121
65 of the tribe of the c of Simeon, and out H1121
65 of the tribe of the c of Benjamin, these H1121
77 Unto the rest of the c of Merari *were* H1121
7:12 Shuppim also, and Huppim, the c of Ir, H1121
29 And by the borders of the c of H1121
29 dwelt the c of Joseph the son of Israel. H1121
33 Ashvath. These *are* the c of Japhlet. H1121
40 All these *were* the c of Asher, heads of H1121
8: 8 And Shaharaim begat *c* in the country of
9: 3 And in Jerusalem dwelt of the c of H1121
3 Judah, and of the c of Benjamin, and of H1121
3 of the c of Ephraim, and Manasseh; H1121
4 of the c of Pharez the son of Judah. H1121
18 in the companies of the c of Levi. H1121
23 So they and their c *had* the oversight of H1121
11:31 *that pertained* to the c of Benjamin, H1121
12:16 And there came of the c of Benjamin H1121
24 The c of Judah that bare shield and H1121
25 Of the c of Simeon, mighty men of H1121
26 Of the c of Levi four thousand and six H1121
29 And of the c of Benjamin, the kindred H1121
30 And of the c of Ephraim twenty H1121
32 And of the c of Issachar, *which were* H1121
14: 4 Now these *are* the names of *his* c which H3205

1Ch 15: 4 And David assembled the c of Aaron, H1121
15 And the c of the Levites bare the ark of H1121
16:13 O ye seed of Israel his servant, ye c of H1121
17: 9 neither shall the c of wickedness waste H1121
18:11 and from the c of Ammon, and from H1121
19: 1 the king of the c of Ammon died, and H1121
2 c of Ammon to Hanun, to comfort him. H1121
3 But the princes of the c of Ammon said H1121
6 And when the c of Ammon saw that H1121
6 Hanun and the c of Ammon sent a H1121
7 Medeba. And the c of Ammon gathered H1121
9 And the c of Ammon came out, and H1121
11 in array against the c of Ammon. H1121
12 help me: but if the c of Ammon be too H1121
15 And when the c of Ammon saw that H1121
19 help the c of Ammon any more. H1121
20: 1 the country of the c of Ammon, and H1121
3 all the cities of the c of Ammon. And H1121
4 c of the giant: and they were subdued. H3211
24: 2 father, and had no c: therefore Eleazar H1121
26:10 Also Hosah, of the c of Merari, had H1121
27: 1 Now the c of Israel after their number, H1121
3 Of the c of Perez *was* the chief of all the H1121
10 the Pelonite, of the c of Ephraim: and H1121
14 Pirathonite, of the c of Ephraim: and in H1121
20 Of the c of Ephraim, Hoshea the son of H1121
28: 8 for your c after you for ever. H1121
2Ch 5: 2 of the fathers of the c of Israel, unto H1121
10 *a covenant* with the c of Israel, when H1121
6:11 that he made with the c of Israel. H1121
16 yet so that thy c take heed to their way H1121
30 knowest the hearts of the c of men:) H1121
7: 3 And when all the c of Israel saw how H1121
8: 2 caused the c of Israel to dwell there. H1121
8 *But* of their c, who were left after them H1121
8 land, whom the c of Israel consumed H1121
9 But of the c of Israel did Solomon make H1121
10:17 But *as for* the c of Israel that dwelt in H1121
18 tribute; and the c of Israel stoned him H1121
11:19 Which bare him c; Jeush, and H1121
23 of all his c throughout all the countries H1121
13: 7 him vain men, the c of Belial, and have H1121
12 against you. O c of Israel, fight ye not H1121
16 And the c of Israel fled before Judah: H1121
18 Thus the c of Israel were brought under H1121
18 that time, and the c of Judah prevailed, H1121
20: 1 this also, *that* the c of Moab, and the H1121
1 of Moab, and the c of Ammon, and H1121
10 And now, behold, the c of Ammon and H1121
13 their little ones, their wives, and their c. H1121
19 And the Levites, of the c of the H1121
19 and of the c of the Korhites, stood H1121
22 against the c of Ammon, Moab, and H1121
23 For the c of Ammon and Moab stood H1121
21:14 thy c, and thy wives, and all thy goods: H1121
25: 4 But he slew not their c, but *did* as *it is* H1121
4 shall not die for the c, neither shall the H1121
4 neither shall the c die for the fathers, H1121
7 Israel, *to wit, with* all the c of Ephraim. H1121
11 smote of the c of Seir ten thousand. H1121
12 *left* alive did the c of Judah carry away H1121
14 the gods of the c of Seir, and set them H1121
27: 5 them. And the c of Ammon gave him H1121
5 So much did the c of Ammon pay unto H1121
28: 3 and burnt his c in the fire, after the H1121
3 had cast out before the c of Israel. H1121
8 And the c of Israel carried away H1121
10 to keep under the c of Judah and H1121
12 Then certain of the heads of the c of H1121
30: 6 king, saying, Ye c of Israel, turn again H1121
9 your brethren and your c *shall find* H1121
21 And the c of Israel that were present at H1121
31: 1 all. Then all the c of Israel returned, H1121
5 came abroad, the c of Israel brought in H1121
6 And *concerning* the c of Israel and H1121
33: 2 had cast out before the c of Israel. H1121
6 And he caused his c to pass through H1121
9 had destroyed before the c of Israel. H1121
34:33 *pertained* to the c of Israel, and made H1121
35:17 And the c of Israel that were present H1121
Ezr 2: 1 Now these *are* the c of the province H1121
3 The c of Parosh, two thousand an H1121
4 The c of Shephatiah, three hundred H1121
5 The c of Arah, seven hundred seventy H1121
6 The c of Pahath-moab, of the children H1121
6 The children of Pahath-moab, of the c H1121
7 The c of Elam, a thousand two H1121
8 The c of Zattu, nine hundred forty and H1121
9 The c of Zaccai, seven hundred and H1121

Ezr 2:10 The c of Bani, six hundred forty and H1121
11 The c of Bebai, six hundred twenty and H1121
12 The c of Azgad, a thousand two H1121
13 The c of Adonikam, six hundred sixty H1121
14 The c of Bigvai, two thousand fifty and H1121
15 The c of Adin, four hundred fifty and H1121
16 The c of Ater of Hezekiah, ninety and H1121
17 The c of Bezai, three hundred twenty H1121
18 The c of Jorah, an hundred and twelve. H1121
19 The c of Hashum, two hundred twenty H1121
20 The c of Gibbar, ninety and five. H1121
21 The c of Beth-lehem, an hundred H1121
24 The c of Azmaveth, forty and two. H1121
25 The c of Kirjath-arim, Chephirah, and H1121
26 The c of Ramah and Gaba, six hundred H1121
29 The c of Nebo, fifty and two. H1121
30 The c of Magbish, an hundred fifty and H1121
31 The c of the other Elam, a thousand H1121
32 The c of Harim, three hundred and H1121
33 The c of Lod, Hadid, and Ono, seven H1121
34 The c of Jericho, three hundred forty H1121
35 The c of Senaah, three thousand and H1121
36 The priests: the c of Jedaiah, of the H1121
37 The c of Immer, a thousand fifty and H1121
38 The c of Pashur, a thousand two H1121
39 The c of Harim, a thousand and H1121
40 The Levites: the c of Jeshua and H1121
40 of the c of Hodaviah, seventy and four. H1121
41 The singers: the c of Asaph, an H1121
42 The c of the porters: the children of H1121
42 The children of the porters: the c of H1121
42 of Shallum, the c of Ater, the children H1121
42 of Ater, the c of Talmon, the children H1121
42 of Talmon, the c of Akkub, the children H1121
42 of Akkub, the c of Hatita, the children H1121
42 of Hatita, the c of Shobai, *in* all an H1121
43 The Nethinims: the c of Ziha, the H1121
43 of Ziha, the c of Hasupha, the children H1121
43 of Hasupha, the c of Tabbaoth, H1121
44 The c of Keros, the children of Siaha, H1121
44 The children of Keros, the c of Siaha, H1121
44 the children of Siaha, the c of Padon, H1121
45 The c of Lebanah, the children of H1121
45 The children of Lebanah, the c of H1121
45 children of Hagabah, the c of Akkub, H1121
46 The c of Hagab, the children of H1121
46 The children of Hagab, the c of H1121
46 children of Shalmai, the c of Hanan, H1121
47 The c of Giddel, the children of Gahar, H1121
47 The children of Giddel, the c of Gahar, H1121
47 the children of Gahar, the c of Reaiah, H1121
48 The c of Rezin, the children of Nekoda, H1121
48 The children of Rezin, the c of Nekoda, H1121
48 children of Nekoda, the c of Gazzam, H1121
49 The c of Uzza, the children of Paseah, H1121
49 The children of Uzza, the c of Paseah, H1121
49 the children of Paseah, the c of Besai, H1121
50 The c of Asnah, the children of H1121
50 The children of Asnah, the c of H1121
50 of Mehunim, the c of Nephusim, H1121
51 The c of Bakbuk, the children of H1121
51 The children of Bakbuk, the c of H1121
51 children of Hakupha, the c of Harhur, H1121
52 The c of Bazluth, the children of H1121
52 The children of Bazluth, the c of H1121
52 children of Mehida, the c of Harsha, H1121
53 The c of Barkos, the children of Sisera, H1121
53 The children of Barkos, the c of Sisera, H1121
53 the children of Sisera, the c of Thamah, H1121
54 The c of Neziah, the children of H1121
54 The children of Neziah, the c of H1121
55 The c of Solomon's servants: the H1121
55 servants: the c of Sotai, the children H1121
55 c of Sophereth, the children of Peruda, H1121
55 children of Sophereth, the c of Peruda, H1121
56 The c of Jaalah, the children of Darkon, H1121
56 The children of Jaalah, the c of Darkon, H1121
56 the children of Darkon, the c of Giddel, H1121
57 The c of Shephatiah, the children of H1121
57 The children of Shephatiah, the c of H1121
57 of Hattil, the c of Pochereth of Zebaim, H1121
57 of Pochereth of Zebaim, the c of Ami. H1121
58 All the Nethinims, and the c of H1121
60 The c of Delaiah, the children of H1121
60 The children of Delaiah, the c of H1121
60 c of Nekoda, six hundred fifty and two. H1121
61 And of the c of the priests: the children H1121
61 And of the children of the priests: the c H1121
61 of Habaiah, the c of Koz, the children H1121

Ezr 2:61 of Koz, the c of Barzillai; which took H1121
3: 1 was come, and the c of Israel *were* in H1121
4: 1 heard that the c of the captivity builded H1121
6:16 And the c of Israel, the priests, and the H1123
16 and the rest of the c of the captivity, H1123
19 And the c of the captivity kept the H1121
20 for all the c of the captivity, and H1121
21 And the c of Israel, which were come H1121
7: 7 And there went up *some* of the c of H1121
8:35 *Also* the c of those that had been H1121
9:12 *it* for an inheritance to your c for ever. H1121
10: 1 and c: for the people wept very sore. H3206
7 unto all the c of the captivity, that H1121
16 And the c of the captivity did so. And H1121
44 of them had wives by whom they had c. H1121
Neh 1: 6 day and night, for the c of Israel thy H1121
6 the sins of the c of Israel, which we H1121
2:10 to seek the welfare of the c of Israel. H1121
5: 5 of our brethren, our c as their children: H1121
5 our children as their c: and, lo, we bring H1121
7: 6 These *are* the c of the province, that H1121
8 The c of Parosh, two thousand an H1121
9 The c of Shephatiah, three hundred H1121
10 The c of Arah, six hundred fifty and H1121
11 The c of Pahath-moab, of the children H1121
11 The children of Pahath-moab, of the c H1121
12 The c of Elam, a thousand two H1121
13 The c of Zattu, eight hundred forty and H1121
14 The c of Zaccai, seven hundred and H1121
15 The c of Binnui, six hundred forty and H1121
16 The c of Bebai, six hundred twenty and H1121
17 The c of Azgad, two thousand three H1121
18 The c of Adonikam, six hundred H1121
19 The c of Bigvai, two thousand H1121
20 The c of Adin, six hundred fifty and H1121
21 The c of Ater of Hezekiah, ninety and H1121
22 The c of Hashum, three hundred H1121
23 The c of Bezai, three hundred twenty H1121
24 The c of Hariph, an hundred and H1121
25 The c of Gibeon, ninety and five. H1121
34 The c of the other Elam, a thousand H1121
35 The c of Harim, three hundred and H1121
36 The c of Jericho, three hundred forty H1121
37 The c of Lod, Hadid, and Ono, seven H1121
38 The c of Senaah, three thousand nine H1121
39 The priests: the c of Jedaiah, of the H1121
40 The c of Immer, a thousand fifty and H1121
41 The c of Pashur, a thousand two H1121
42 The c of Harim, a thousand and H1121
43 The Levites: the c of Jeshua, of H1121
43 of the c of Hodevah, seventy and four. H1121
44 The singers: the c of Asaph, an H1121
45 The porters: the c of Shallum, the H1121
45 of Shallum, the c of Ater, the children H1121
45 of Ater, the c of Talmon, the children H1121
45 of Talmon, the c of Akkub, the children H1121
45 of Akkub, the c of Hatita, the children H1121
45 of Hatita, the c of Shobai, an hundred H1121
46 The Nethinims: the c of Ziha, the H1121
46 of Ziha, the c of Hashupha, the H1121
46 of Hashupha, the c of Tabbaoth, H1121
47 The c of Keros, the children of Sia, the H1121
47 The children of Keros, the c of Sia, the H1121
47 the children of Sia, the c of Padon, H1121
48 The c of Lebana, the children of H1121
48 The children of Lebana, the c of H1121
48 children of Hagaba, the c of Shalmai, H1121
49 The c of Hanan, the children of Giddel, H1121
49 The children of Hanan, the c of Giddel, H1121
49 the children of Giddel, the c of Gahar, H1121
50 The c of Reaiah, the children of Rezin, H1121
50 The children of Reaiah, the c of Rezin, H1121
50 the children of Rezin, the c of Nekoda, H1121
51 The c of Gazzam, the children of Uzza, H1121
51 The children of Gazzam, the c of Uzza, H1121
51 the children of Uzza, the c of Phaseah, H1121
52 The c of Besai, the children of Meunim, H1121
52 The children of Besai, the c of Meunim, H1121
52 of Meunim, the c of Nephishesim, H1121
53 The c of Bakbuk, the children of H1121
53 The children of Bakbuk, the c of H1121
53 children of Hakupha, the c of Harhur, H1121
54 The c of Bazlith, the children of H1121
54 The children of Bazlith, the c of H1121
54 children of Mehida, the c of Harsha, H1121
55 The c of Barkos, the children of Sisera, H1121
55 The children of Barkos, the c of Sisera, H1121
55 the children of Sisera, the c of Tamah, H1121
56 The c of Neziah, the children of H1121
Neh 7:56 The children of Neziah, the c of H1121
57 The c of Solomon's servants: the H1121
57 servants: the c of Sotai, the children H1121
57 c of Sophereth, the children of Perida, H1121
57 children of Sophereth, the c of Perida, H1121
58 The c of Jaala, the children of Darkon, H1121
58 The children of Jaala, the c of Darkon, H1121
58 the children of Darkon, the c of Giddel, H1121
59 The c of Shephatiah, the children of H1121
59 The children of Shephatiah, the c of H1121
59 of Hattil, the c of Pochereth of Zebaim, H1121
59 of Pochereth of Zebaim, the c of Amon. H1121
60 All the Nethinims, and the c of H1121
62 The c of Delaiah, the children of H1121
62 The children of Delaiah, the c of H1121
62 children of Tobiah, the c of Nekoda, six H1121
63 And of the priests: the c of Habaiah, H1121
63 of Habaiah, the c of Koz, the children H1121
63 of Koz, the c of Barzillai, which took H1121
73 the c of Israel *were* in their cities. H1121
8:14 by Moses, that the c of Israel should H1121
17 that day had not the c of Israel done so. H1121
9: 1 day of this month the c of Israel were H1121
23 Their c also multipliedst thou as the H1121
24 So the c went in and possessed the H1121
10:39 For the c of Israel and the children of H1121
39 For the children of Israel and the c of H1121
11: 3 and the c of Solomon's servants. H1121
4 And at Jerusalem dwelt *certain* of the c H1121
4 Judah, and of the c of Benjamin. Of the H1121
4 of Benjamin. Of the c of Judah; Athaiah H1121
4 the son of Mahalaleel, of the c of Perez; H1121
24 of the c of Zerah the son of Judah, H1121
25 fields, *some* of the c of Judah dwelt at H1121
31 The c also of Benjamin from Geba H1121
12:43 wives also and the c rejoiced: so that H3206
47 sanctified *them* unto the c of Aaron. H1121
13: 2 Because they met not the c of Israel H1121
16 unto the c of Judah, and in Jerusalem. H1121
24 And their c spake half in the speech of H1121
Est 3:13 and old, little c and women, in one H2945
5:11 the multitude of his c, and all *the things* H1121
Job 5: 4 His c are far from safety, and they are H1121
8: 4 If thy c have sinned against him, and H1121
17: 5 friends, even the eyes of his c shall fail. H1121
19:18 Yea, young c despised me; I arose, and H5759
20:10 His c shall seek to please the poor, and H1121
21:11 ones like a flock, and their c dance. H3206
19 God layeth up his iniquity for his c: he H1121
24: 5 *yieldeth* food for them *and* for *their* c. H5288
27:14 If his c be multiplied, *it is* for the H1121
29: 5 yet with me, *when* my c *were* about me; H5288
30: 8 *They were* c of fools, yea, children of H1121
8 *They were* children of fools, yea, c of H1121
41:34 he *is* a king over all the c of pride. H1121
Ps 11: 4 behold, his eyelids try, the c of men. H1121
12: 1 faithful fail from among the c of men. H1121
14: 2 heaven upon the c of men, to see if H1121
17:14 they are full of c, and leave the rest of H1121
21:10 their seed from among the c of men. H1121
34:11 Come, ye c, hearken unto me: I will H1121
36: 7 O God! therefore the c of men put their H1121
45: 2 Thou art fairer than the c of men: grace H1121
16 Instead of thy fathers shall be thy c, H1121
53: 2 heaven upon the c of men, to see if H1121
66: 5 *in his* doing toward the c of men. H1121
69: 8 and an alien unto my mother's c. H1121
72: 4 he shall save the c of the needy, and H1121
73:15 offend *against* the generation of thy c. H1121
78: 4 We will not hide *them* from their c, H1121
5 should make them known to their c: H1121
6 *them, even* the c *which* should be born; H1121
6 arise and declare *them* to their c: H1121
9 The c of Ephraim, *being* armed, *and* H1121
82: 6 and all of you *are* c of the most High. H1121
83: 8 they have holpen the c of Lot. Selah. H1121
89:30 If his c forsake my law, and walk not in H1121
90: 3 and sayest, Return, ye c of men. H1121
16 thy servants, and thy glory unto their c. H1121
102:28 The c of thy servants shall continue, H1121
103: 7 Moses, his acts unto the c of Israel. H1121
13 Like as a father pitieth *his* c, *so* the H1121
17 and his righteousness unto children's c; H1121
105: 6 O ye seed of Abraham his servant, ye c H1121
107: 8 his wonderful works to the c of men! H1121
15 his wonderful works to the c of men! H1121
21 his wonderful works to the c of men! H1121
31 his wonderful works to the c of men! H1121
109: 9 Let his c be fatherless, and his wife a H1121
Ps 109:10 Let his c be continually vagabonds, H1121
12 there be any to favour his fatherless c. H3490
113: 9 joyful mother of c. Praise ye the LORD. H1121
115:14 you more and more, you and your c. H1121
16 the earth hath he given to the c of men. H1121
127: 3 Lo, c *are* an heritage of the LORD: *and* H1121
4 of a mighty man; so *are* c of the youth. H1121
128: 3 of thine house: thy c like olive plants H1121
6 Yea, thou shalt see thy children's c, *and* H1121
132:12 If thy c will keep my covenant and my H1121
12 teach them, their c shall also sit upon H1121
137: 7 Remember, O LORD, the c of Edom in H1121
144: 7 waters, from the hand of strange c; H1121
11 the hand of strange c, whose mouth H1121
147:13 gates; he hath blessed thy c within thee. H1121
148:12 men, and maidens; old men, and c: H5288
14 saints; *even* of the c of Israel, a people H1121
149: 2 let the c of Zion be joyful in their King. H1121
Prv 4: 1 Hear, ye c, the instruction of a father, H1121
5: 7 Hear me now therefore, O ye c, and H1121
7:24 Hearken unto me now therefore, O ye c, H1121
8:32 Now therefore hearken unto me, O ye c: H1121
13:22 to his children's c: and the wealth of the H1121
14:26 and his c shall have a place of refuge. H1121
15:11 more then the hearts of the c of men? H1121
17: 6 Children's c *are* the crown of old men; H1121
6 and the glory of c *are* their fathers. H1121
20: 7 integrity: his c *are* blessed after him. H1121
31:28 Her c arise up, and call her blessed; her H1121
Ecc 6: 3 If a man beget an hundred c, and live
Song 1: 6 me: my mother's c were angry with me; H1121
Isa 1: 2 c, and they have rebelled against me. H1121
4 seed of evildoers, c that are corrupters: H1121
2: 6 please themselves in the c of strangers. H3206
3: 4 And I will give c *to be* their princes, H5288
12 *As for* my people, c *are* their H5768
8:18 Behold, I and the c whom the LORD H3206
11:14 and the c of Ammon shall obey them. H1121
13:16 Their c also shall be dashed to pieces H5768
18 of the womb; their eye shall not spare c. H1121
14:21 Prepare slaughter for his c for the H1121
17: 3 the c of Israel, saith the LORD of hosts. H1121
9 left because of the c of Israel: and there H1121
21:17 mighty men of the c of Kedar, shall be H1121
23: 4 nor bring forth c, neither do I nourish H3205
27:12 be gathered one by one, O ye c of Israel. H1121
29:23 But when he seeth his c, the work of H3206
30: 1 Woe to the rebellious c, saith the LORD, H1121
9 That this *is* a rebellious people, lying c, H1121
9 lying children, c *that* will not hear the H1121
31: 6 Turn ye unto *him from* whom the c of H1121
37: 3 for the c are come to the birth, H1121
12 the c of Eden which *were* in Telassar? H1121
38:19 to the c shall make known thy truth. H1121
47: 8 neither shall I know the loss of c: H7908
9 day, the loss of c, and widowhood: they H7908
49:17 Thy c shall make haste; thy destroyers H1121
20 The c which thou shalt have, after thou H1121
21 I have lost my c, and am desolate, a H7921
25 with thee, and I will save thy c. H1121
54: 1 for more *are* the c of the desolate than H1121
1 c of the married wife, saith the LORD. H1121
13 And all thy c *shall be* taught of the H1121
13 and great *shall be* the peace of thy c. H1121
57: 4 c of transgression, a seed of falsehood, H3206
5 tree, slaying the c in the valleys under H3206
63: 8 *are* my people, c *that* will not lie: so he H1121
66: 8 Zion travailed, she brought forth her c. H1121
20 the LORD, as the c of Israel bring an H1121
Jer 2: 9 and with your children's c will I plead. H1121
16 Also the c of Noph and Tahapanes H1121
30 In vain have I smitten your c; they H1121
3:14 Turn, O backsliding c, saith the LORD; H1121
19 put thee among the c, and give thee a H1121
21 of the c of Israel: for they have H1121
22 Return, ye backsliding c, *and* I will heal H1121
4:22 they *are* sottish c, and they have none H1121
5: 7 How shall I pardon thee for this? thy c H1121
6: 1 O ye c of Benjamin, gather yourselves H1121
11 it out upon the c abroad, and upon the H5768
7:18 The c gather wood, and the fathers H1121
30 For the c of Judah have done evil in my H1121
9:21 to cut off the c from without, *and* the H5768
26 Egypt, and Judah, and Edom, and the c H1121
10:20 are broken: my c are gone forth of me, H1121
15: 7 will bereave *them* of c, I will destroy my H7921
16:14 the c of Israel out of the land of Egypt; H1121
15 brought up the c of Israel from the land H1121
17: 2 Whilst their c remember their altars H1121

Jer 17:19 stand in the gate of the c of the people, H1121
18:21 Therefore deliver up their c to the H1121
21 bereaved of their c, and *be* widows; and
23: 7 the c of Israel out of the land of Egypt; H1121
25:21 Edom, and Moab, and the c of H1121
30:20 Their c also shall be as aforetime, and H1121
31:15 Rahel weeping for her c refused to be H1121
15 for her c, because they *were* not. H1121
17 c shall come again to their own border. H1121
32:18 the bosom of their c after them: the H1121
30 For the c of Israel and the children of H1121
30 For the children of Israel and the c of H1121
30 their youth: for the c of Israel have only H1121
32 Because of all the evil of the c of Israel H1121
32 Israel and of the c of Judah, which they H1121
39 good of them, and of their c after them: H1121
38:23 thy wives and thy c to the Chaldeans: H1121
40: 7 and women, and c, and of the poor of H2945
41:16 the women, and the c, and the eunuchs, H2945
43: 6 *Even* men, and women, and c, and the H2945
47: 3 back to *their* c for feebleness of hands; H1121
49: 6 of the c of Ammon, saith the LORD. H1121
11 Leave thy fatherless c, I will preserve H3490
50: 4 the LORD, the c of Israel shall come, H1121
4 they and the c of Judah together, going H1121
33 Thus saith the LORD of hosts; The c of H1121
33 of Israel and the c of Judah *were* H1121
Lam 1: 5 her c are gone into captivity H5768
16 soul is far from me: my c are desolate, H1121
2:11 because the c and the sucklings swoon H5768
19 life of thy young c, that faint for hunger H5768
20 eat their fruit, *and* c of a span long? H5768
3:33 afflict willingly nor grieve the c of men. H1121
4: 4 thirst: the young c ask bread, *and* no H5768
10 sodden their own c: they were their H3206
5:13 to grind, and the c fell under the wood. H5288
Ezk 2: 3 man, I send thee to the c of Israel, to a H1121
4 For *they are* impudent c and H1121
3:11 captivity, unto the c of thy people, and H1121
4:13 Even thus shall the c of Israel eat their H1121
6: 5 And I will lay the dead carcases of the c H1121
9: 6 maids, and little c, and women: but H2945
16:21 That thou hast slain my c, and H1121
36 thy c, which thou didst give unto them; H1121
45 her husband and her c; and thou *art* the H1121
45 and their c: your mother *was* an H1121
20:18 But I said unto their c in the H1121
21 Notwithstanding the c rebelled against H1121
23:39 For when they had slain their c to their H1121
31:14 in the midst of the c of men, with them H1121
33: 2 Son of man, speak to the c of thy H1121
12 man, say unto the c of thy people, The H1121
17 Yet the c of thy people say, The way of H1121
30 Also, thou son of man, the c of thy H1121
35: 5 *the blood of* the c of Israel by the force H1121
37:16 For Judah, and for the c of Israel his H1121
18 And when the c of thy people shall H1121
21 I will take the c of Israel from among H1121
25 they, and their c, and their children's H1121
25 and their children's c for ever: and my H1121
43: 7 in the midst of the c of Israel for ever, H1121
44: 9 stranger that *is* among the c of Israel. H1121
15 when the c of Israel went astray H1121
47:22 which shall beget c among you: and H1121
22 among the c of Israel; they shall H1121
48:11 astray when the c of Israel went astray, H1121
Dan 1: 3 *certain* of the c of Israel, and of the H1121
4 C in whom *was* no blemish, but well H3206
6 Now among these were of the c of H1121
10 liking than the c which *are* of your sort? H3206
13 of the c that eat of the portion H3206
15 in flesh than all the c which did eat the H3206
17 As for these four c, God gave them H3206
2:38 And wheresoever the c of men dwell, H1123
5:13 which *art* of the c of the captivity of H1123
6:13 which *is* of the c of the captivity of H1123
24 of lions, them, their c, and their wives; H1123
11:41 and the chief of the c of Ammon. H1121
12: 1 standeth for the c of thy people: and H1121
Hos 1: 2 of whoredoms and c of whoredoms: for H3206
10 Yet the number of the c of Israel shall H1121
11 Then shall the c of Judah and the H1121
11 of Judah and the c of Israel be gathered H1121
2: 4 And I will not have mercy upon her c; H1121
4 for they *be* the c of whoredoms. H1121
3: 1 LORD toward the c of Israel, who look H1121
4 For the c of Israel shall abide many H1121
5 Afterward shall the c of Israel return, H1121
4: 1 Hear the word of the LORD, ye c of H1121

Hos 4: 6 law of thy God, I will also forget thy c. H1121
5: 7 begotten strange c: now shall a month H1121
9:12 Though they bring up their c, yet will I H1121
13 shall bring forth his c to the murderer. H1121
10: 9 the c of iniquity did not overtake them. H1121
14 was dashed in pieces upon *her* c. H1121
11:10 then the c shall tremble from the west. H1121
13:13 in *the place of* the breaking forth of c. H1121
Joel 1: 3 Tell ye your c of it, and *let* your H1121
3 of it, and *let* your c *tell* their children, H1121
3 children *tell* their c, and their children H1121
3 and their c another generation. H1121
2:16 elders, gather the c, and those that suck H5768
23 Be glad then, ye c of Zion, and rejoice H1121
3: 6 The c also of Judah and the children of H1121
6 The children also of Judah and the c of H1121
8 the hand of the c of Judah, and they H1121
16 and the strength of the c of Israel. H1121
19 *against* the c of Judah, because they H1121
Am 1:13 of the c of Ammon, and for H1121
2:11 thus, O ye c of Israel? saith the LORD. H1121
3: 1 against you, O c of Israel, against the H1121
12 ear; so shall the c of Israel be taken out H1121
4: 5 O ye c of Israel, saith the Lord GOD. H1121
9: 7 *Are* ye not as c of the Ethiopians unto H1121
7 unto me, O c of Israel? saith the LORD. H1121
Oba 12 rejoiced over the c of Judah in the day H1121
20 And the captivity of this host of the c of H1121
Mic 1:16 for thy delicate c; enlarge thy baldness H1121
2: 9 c have ye taken away my glory for ever. H5768
5: 3 shall return unto the c of Israel. H1121
Nah 3:10 her young c also were dashed in H5768
Zep 1: 8 and the king's c, and all such as are H1121
2: 8 and the revilings of the c of Ammon, H1121
9 be as Sodom, and the c of Ammon as H1121
Zec 10: 7 wine: yea, their c shall see *it*, and be H1121
9 shall live with their c, and turn again. H1121
Mal 4: 6 the fathers to the c, and the heart of the H1121
6 the heart of the c to their fathers, lest H1121
Mt 2:16 forth, and slew all the c that were in G3816
18 weeping *for* her c, and would not be G5043
3: 9 stones to raise up c unto Abraham. G5043
5: 9 for they shall be called the c of God. G5207
45 That ye may be the c of your Father G5207
7:11 gifts unto your c, how much more shall G5043
8:12 But the c of the kingdom shall be cast G5207
9:15 And Jesus said unto them, Can the c of G5207
10:21 father the child: and the c shall rise up G5043
11:16 It is like unto c sitting in the markets, G3808
19 sinners. But wisdom is justified of her c. G5043
12:27 by whom do your c cast *them* out? G5207
13:38 good seed are the c of the kingdom; but G5207
38 the tares are the c of the wicked *one*; G5207
14:21 thousand men, beside women and c. G3813
15:38 thousand men, beside women and c. G3813
17:25 tribute? of their own c, or of strangers? G5207
26 saith unto him, Then are the c free. G5207
18: 3 become as little c, ye shall not enter into G3813
25 and his wife, and c, and all that he had, G5043
19:13 unto him little c, that he should put *his* G3813
14 But Jesus said, Suffer little c, and forbid G3813
29 or mother, or wife, or c, or lands, for my G5043
20:20 mother of Zebedee's c with her sons, G5207
21:15 he did, and the c crying in the temple, G3816
22:24 man die, having no c, his brother shall G5043
23:31 the c of them which killed the prophets. G5207
37 have gathered thy c together, even as a G5043
27: 9 whom they of the c of Israel did value; G5207
25 said, His blood *be* on us, and on our c. G5043
56 Joses, and the mother of Zebedee's c. G5207
Mk 2:19 And Jesus said unto them, Can the c of G5207
7:27 But Jesus said unto her, Let the c first G5043
9:37 Whosoever shall receive one of such c G3813
10:13 And they brought young c to him, that G3813
14 Suffer the little c to come unto me, and G3813
24 saith unto them, C, how hard is it for G5043
29 or mother, or wife, or c, or lands, for my G5043
30 and mothers, and c, and lands, with G5043
12:19 *him*, and leave no c, that his brother G5043
13:12 the son; and c shall rise up against G5043
Lk 1:16 And many of the c of Israel shall he G5207
17 the fathers to the c, and the disobedient G5043
3: 8 stones to raise up c unto Abraham. G5043
5:34 Can ye make the c of the bridechamber G5207
6:35 and ye shall be the c of the Highest: for G5207
7:32 They are like unto c sitting in the G3813
35 But wisdom is justified of all her c. G5043
11: 7 now shut, and my c are with me in bed; G3813
13 gifts unto your c: how much more shall G5043

Lk 13:34 I have gathered thy c together, as a hen G5043
14:26 and wife, and c, and brethren, and G5043
16: 8 wisely: for the c of this world are in G5207
8 generation wiser than the c of light. G5207
18:16 said, Suffer little c to come unto me, G3813
29 or c, for the kingdom of God's sake, G5043
19:44 ground, and thy c within thee; and they G5043
20:28 and he die without c, that his brother G815
29 the first took a wife, and died without c. G815
31 seven also: and they left no c, and died. G5043
34 unto them, The c of this world marry, G5207
36 and are the c of God, being the children G5207
36 of God, being the c of the resurrection. G5207
23:28 but weep for yourselves, and for your c. G5043
Jn 4:12 himself, and his c, and his cattle? G5207
8:39 c, ye would do the works of Abraham. G5043
11:52 c of God that were scattered abroad. G5043
12:36 that ye may be the c of light. These G5207
13:33 Little c, yet a little while I am with you. G5040
21: 5 Then Jesus saith unto them, C, have ye G3813
Act 2:39 you, and to your c, and to all that are G5043
3:25 Ye are the c of the prophets, and of the G5207
5:21 the senate of the c of Israel, and sent to G5207
7:19 young c, to the end they might not live. G1025
23 to visit his brethren the c of Israel. G5207
37 said unto the c of Israel, A prophet G5207
9:15 Gentiles, and kings, and the c of Israel: G5207
10:36 The word which *God* sent unto the c of G5207
13:26 Men *and* brethren, c of the stock of G5207
33 the same unto us their c, in that he hath G5043
21: 5 with wives and c, till *we were* out of the G5043
21 c, neither to walk after the customs. G5043
Ro 8:16 our spirit, that we are the c of God: G5043
17 And if c, then heirs; heirs of God, and G5043
21 into the glorious liberty of the c of God. G5043
9: 7 c: but, In Isaac shall thy seed be called. G5043
8 That is, They which are the c of the G5043
8 flesh, these *are* not the c of God: but the G5043
8 of God: but the c of the promise are G5043
11 (For *the* c being not yet born, neither
26 they be called the c of the living God. G5207
27 the number of the c of Israel be as the G5207
1Co 7:14 your c unclean; but now are they holy. G5043
14:20 Brethren, be not c in understanding: G3813
20 be ye c, but in understanding be men. G3515
2Co 3: 7 so that the c of Israel could not G5207
13 his face, that the c of Israel could not G5207
6:13 speak as unto *my* c,) be ye also enlarged. G5043
12:14 but you: for the c ought not to lay up G5043
14 the parents, but the parents for the c. G5043
Gal 3: 7 faith, the same are the c of Abraham. G5207
26 For ye are all the c of God by faith in G5207
4: 3 Even so we, when we were c, were in G3516
19 My little c, of whom I travail in birth G5040
25 now is, and is in bondage with her c. G5043
27 c than she which hath an husband. G5043
28 as Isaac was, are the c of promise. G5043
31 So then, brethren, we are not c of the G5043
Eph 1: 5 the adoption of c by Jesus Christ to G5206
2: 2 now worketh in the c of disobedience: G5207
3 nature the c of wrath, even as others. G5043
4:14 That we *henceforth* be no more c, G3516
5: 1 ye therefore followers of God, as dear c; G5043
6 of God upon the c of disobedience. G5207
8 *ye* light in the Lord: walk as c of light: G5043
6: 1 C, obey your parents in the Lord: for G5043
4 And, ye fathers, provoke not your c to G5043
Col 3: 6 God cometh on the c of disobedience: G5207
20 C, obey *your* parents in all things: for G5043
21 Fathers, provoke not your c *to anger*, G5043
1Th 2: 7 you, even as a nurse cherisheth her c: G5043
11 every one of you, as a father *doth* his c, G5043
5: 5 Ye are all the c of light, and the G5207
5 of light, and the c of the day: we are not G5207
1Ti 3: 4 his c in subjection with all gravity; G5043
12 their c and their own houses well. G5043
5: 4 But if any widow have c or nephews, let G5043
10 have brought up c, if she have lodged G5044
14 marry, bear c, guide the house, give G5041
Tit 1: 6 faithful c not accused of riot or unruly. G5043
2: 4 to love their husbands, to love their c, G5388
Heb 2:13 I and the c which God hath given me. G3813
14 Forasmuch then as the c are partakers G3813
11:22 departing of the c of Israel; and gave G5207
12: 5 unto you as unto c, My son, despise not G5207
1Pt 1:14 As obedient c, not fashioning G5043
2Pt 2:14 with covetous practices; cursed c: G5043
1Jn 2: 1 My little c, these things write I unto G5040
12 I write unto you, little c, because your G5040

C

1Jn 2:13 c, because ye have known the Father. G3813
18 Little c, it is the last time: and as ye G3813
28 And now, little c, abide in him; that, G5040
3: 7 Little c, let no man deceive you: he that G5040
10 In this the c of God are manifest, and G5043
10 are manifest, and the c of the devil: G5043
18 My little c, let us not love in word, G5040
4: 4 Ye are of God, little c, and have G5040
5: 2 By this we know that we love the c of G5043
21 Little c, keep yourselves from idols. G5040
2Jn 1 The elder unto the elect lady and her c, G5043
4 I rejoiced greatly that I found of thy c G5043
13 The c of thy elect sister greet thee. G5043
3Jn 4 than to hear that my c walk in truth. G5043
Rev 2:14 before the c of Israel, to eat things G5207
23 And I will kill her c with death; and all G5043
7: 4 of all the tribes of the c of Israel. G5207
21:12 of the twelve tribes of the c of Israel: G5207

CHILDREN'S
Gen 31:16 that *is* ours, and our c: now then, H1121
45:10 children, and thy c children, and thy H1121
Ex 9: 4 nothing die of all *that is* the c of Israel. H1121
34: 7 and upon the c children, unto the third H1121
Dt 4:25 When thou shalt beget children, and c H1121
Jos 14: 9 and thy c for ever, because thou H1121
2Ki 17:41 children, and their c children: as did H1121
Job 19:17 for the c *sake* of mine own body. H1121
Ps 103:17 and his righteousness unto c children; H1121
128: 6 Yea, thou shalt see thy c children, *and* H1121
Prv 13:22 inheritance to his c children: and the H1121
17: 6 C children *are* the crown of old men; H1121
Jer 2: 9 and with your c children will I plead. H1121
31:29 grape, and the c teeth are set on edge. H1121
Ezk 18: 2 grapes, and the c teeth are set on edge? H1121
37:25 children, and their c children for ever: H1121
Mt 15:26 take the c bread, and to cast *it* to dogs. G5043
Mk 7:27 c bread, and to cast *it* unto the dogs. G5043
28 under the table eat of the c crumbs. G3813

CHILD'S
Ex 2: 8 the maid went and called the c mother. H3206
1Ki 17:21 let this c soul come into him again. H3206
Job 33:25 His flesh shall be fresher than a c: he H5290
Mt 2:20 are dead which sought the young c life. G3813

CHILEAB
2Sa 3: 3 And his second, C, of Abigail the wife of H3609

CHILION
Ru 1: 2 two sons Mahlon and C, Ephrathites of H3630
5 And Mahlon and C died also both of H3630

CHILION'S
Ru 4: 9 C and Mahlon's, of the hand of Naomi. H3630

CHILMAD
Ezk 27:23 Asshur, *and* C, *were* thy merchants. H3638

CHIMHAM
2Sa 19:37 thy servant C; let him go over with H3643
38 And the king answered, C shall go over H3643
40 Then the king went on to Gilgal, and C H3643
Jer 41:17 in the habitation of C, which is by H3643

CHIMNEY
Hos 13: 3 the floor, and as the smoke out of the c. H699

CHINNERETH
Nu 34:11 unto the side of the sea of C eastward: H3672
Dt 3:17 *thereof,* from C even unto the sea of H3672
Jos 13:27 of C on the other side Jordan eastward. H3672
19:35 Zer, and Ham-math, Rakkath, and C, H3672

CHINNEROTH
Jos 11: 2 plains south of C, and in the valley, and H3672
12: 3 And from the plain to the sea of C on H3672

CHIOS
Act 20:15 *day* over against C; and the next *day* we G5508

CHISLEU
Neh 1: 1 to pass in the month C, in the twentieth H3691
Zec 7: 1 *day* of the ninth month, *even* in C; H3691

CHISLON
Nu 34:21 tribe of Benjamin, Elidad the son of C. H3692

CHISLOTH-TABOR
Jos 19:12 unto the border of C, and then goeth H3696

CHITTIM
Nu 24:24 from the coast of C, and shall afflict H3794
Isa 23: 1 the land of C it is revealed to them. H3794
12 to C; there also shalt thou have no rest. H3794
Jer 2:10 For pass over the isles of C, and see; H3794
Ezk 27: 6 *of* ivory, *brought* out of the isles of C. H3794
Dan 11:30 For the ships of C shall come against H3794

CHIUN
Am 5:26 of your Moloch and C your images, the H3594

CHLOE
1Co 1:11 *are of the house* of C, that there are G5514

CHODE
Gen 31:36 And Jacob was wroth, and c with H7378
Nu 20: 3 And the people c with Moses, and H7378

CHOICE
Gen 23: 6 among us: in the c of our sepulchres H4005
49:11 ass's colt unto the c vine; he washed his H8321
Dt 12:11 c vows which ye vow unto the LORD: H4005
1Sa 9: 2 name *was* Saul, a c young man, and a H970
2Sa 10: 9 he chose of all the c *men* of Israel, and H977
2Ki 3:19 city, and every c city, and shall fell H4004
19:23 thereof, *and* the c fir trees thereof: and H4004
1Ch 7:40 father's house, c *and* mighty men of H1305
19:10 he chose out of all the c of Israel, and put H977
2Ch 25: 5 hundred thousand c *men, able* to go H977
Neh 5:18 one ox *and* six c sheep; also fowls were H1305
Prv 8:10 silver; and knowledge rather than c gold. H977
19 fine gold; and my revenue than c silver. H977
10:20 The tongue of the just *is as* c silver: the H977
Song 6: 9 her mother, she *is* the c *one* of her that H1249
Isa 37:24 thereof, *and* the c fir trees thereof: and H4005
Jer 22: 7 c cedars, and cast *them* into the fire. H4005
Ezk 24: 4 the shoulder; fill *it* with the c bones. H4005
5 Take the c of the flock, and burn also H4005
31:16 the trees of Eden, the c and best of H4005
Act 15: 7 ago God made c among us, that the G1586

CHOICEST
Isa 5: 2 planted it with the c vine, and built a H8321
22: 7 And it shall come to pass, *that* thy c H4005

CHOKE
Mt 13:22 of riches, c the word, and he becometh G4846
Mk 4:19 c the word, and it becometh unfruitful. G4846

CHOKED
Mt 13: 7 and the thorns sprung up, and c them: G638
Mk 4: 7 up, and c it, and it yielded no fruit. G4846
5:13 two thousand;) and were c in the sea. G4155
Lk 8: 7 the thorns sprang up with it, and c it. G638
14 go forth, and are c with cares and G4846
33 a steep place into the lake, and were c. G638

CHOLER
Dan 8: 7 he was moved with c against him, and H4843
11:11 be moved with c, and shall come forth H4843

CHOOSE
Ex 17: 9 And Moses said unto Joshua, C us out H977
Nu 16: 7 the LORD doth c, he *shall be* holy: *ye take* H977
17: 5 rod, whom I shall c, shall blossom: and I H977
Dt 7: 7 his love upon you, nor c you, because ye H977
12: 5 your God shall c out of all your tribes H977
11 your God shall c to cause his name to H977
14 But in the place which the LORD shall c H977
18 thy God shall c, thou, and thy son, and H977
26 unto the place which the LORD shall c: H977
14:23 which he shall c to place his name there, H977
24 thy God shall c to set his name there, H977
25 place which the LORD thy God shall c: H977
15:20 LORD shall c, thou and thy household. H977
16: 2 LORD shall c to place his name there. H977
6 thy God shall c to place his name in, H977
7 thy God shall c: and thou shalt turn H977
15 the LORD shall c: because the LORD thy H977
16 place which he shall c; in the feast of H977
17: 8 place which the LORD thy God shall c; H977
10 the LORD shall c shall shew thee; and H977
15 thy God shall c: *one* from among thy H977
18: 6 unto the place which the LORD shall c; H977
23:16 which he shall c in one of thy gates, H977
26: 2 thy God shall c to place his name there. H977
Dt 30:19 cursing: therefore c life, that both thou H977
31:11 which he shall c, thou shalt read this H977
Jos 9:27 this day, in the place which he should c. H977
24:15 to serve the LORD, c you this day whom H977
1Sa 2:28 And did I c him out of all the tribes of H977
17: 8 servants to Saul? c you a man for you, H1262
2Sa 16:18 c, his will I be, and with him will I abide. H977
17: 1 Let me now c out twelve thousand H977
21: 6 did c. And the king said, I will give *them.* H972
24:12 thee three *things;* c thee one of them, H977
1Ki 14:21 the LORD did c out of all the tribes of H977
18:23 bullocks; and let them c one bullock for H977
25 prophets of Baal, C you one bullock for H977
1Ch 21:10 thee three *things:* c thee one of them, H977
11 unto him, Thus saith the LORD, C thee H6901
Neh 9: 7 Thou *art* the LORD the God, who didst c H977
Job 9:14 How much less shall I answer him, *and* c H977
34: 4 Let us c to us judgment: let us know H977
33 or whether thou c; and not I: therefore H977
Ps 25:12 shall he teach in the way *that* he shall c. H977
47: 4 He shall c our inheritance for us, the H977
Prv 1:29 and did not c the fear of the LORD: H977
3:31 Envy thou not the oppressor, and c none H977
Isa 7:15 know to refuse the evil, and c the good. H977
16 refuse the evil, and c the good, the land H977
14: 1 Jacob, and will yet c Israel, and set them H977
49: 7 Holy One of Israel, and he shall c thee. H977
56: 4 keep my sabbaths, and c *the things* that H977
65:12 and did c *that* wherein I delighted not. H977
66: 4 I also will c their delusions, and will H977
Ezk 21:19 of one land: and c thou a place, choose H1254
19 c *it* at the head of the way to the city. H1254
Zec 1:17 comfort Zion, and shall yet c Jerusalem. H977
2:12 holy land, and shall c Jerusalem again. H977
Php 1:22 of my labour: yet what I shall c I wot not. G138

CHOOSEST
Job 15: 5 and thou c the tongue of the crafty. H977
Ps 65: 4 Blessed *is the man whom* thou c, and H977

CHOOSETH
Job 7:15 So that my soul c strangling, *and* death H977
Isa 40:20 he hath no oblation c a tree *that* will not H977
41:24 nought: an abomination *is he that* c you. H977

CHOOSING
Heb 11:25 C rather to suffer affliction with the G138

CHOP
Mic 3: 3 their bones, and c them in pieces, as H6566

CHOR-ASHAN
1Sa 30:30 C, and to *them* which *were* in Athach, H3565

CHORAZIN
Mt 11:21 Woe unto thee, C! woe unto thee, G5523
Lk 10:13 Woe unto thee, C! woe unto thee, G5523

CHOSE
Gen 6: 2 they took them wives of all which they c. H977
13:11 Then Lot c him all the plain of Jordan; H977
Ex 18:25 And Moses c able men out of all Israel, H977
Dt 4:37 therefore he c their seed after them, H977
10:15 to love them, and he c their seed after H977
Jos 8: 3 Ai: and Joshua c out thirty thousand H977
Jdg 5: 8 They c new gods; then *was* war in the H977
1Sa 13: 2 Saul c him three thousand *men* of Israel; H977
17:40 And he took his staff in his hand, and c H977
2Sa 6:21 the LORD, which c me before thy father, H977
10: 9 and behind, he c of all the choice *men* H977
1Ki 8:16 out of Egypt, I c no city out of all the H977
16 I c David to be over my people Israel. H977
11:34 sake, whom I c, because he kept my H977
1Ch 19:10 and behind, he c out of all the choice H977
28: 4 Howbeit the LORD God of Israel c me H977
2Ch 6: 5 of the land of Egypt I c no city among all H977
5 be there; neither c I any man to be a H977
Job 29:25 I c out their way, and sat chief, and H977
Ps 78:67 Joseph, and c not the tribe of Ephraim: H977
68 But c the tribe of Judah, the mount Zion H977
70 He c David also his servant, and took H977
Isa 66: 4 eyes, and c *that* in which I delighted not. H977
Ezk 20: 5 In the day when I c Israel, and lifted up H977
Lk 6:13 and of them he c twelve, whom also he G1586
14: 7 he marked how they c out the chief G1586
Act 6: 5 and they c Stephen, a man full G1586
13:17 The God of this people of Israel c our G1586
15:40 And Paul c Silas, and departed, being G1951

CHOSEN

Ex 14: 7 And he took six hundred c chariots, and H977
15: 4 cast into the sea: his c captains also are H4005
Nu 16: 5 c will he cause to come near unto him. H977
Dt 7: 6 LORD thy God hath c thee to be a special H977
12:21 thy God hath c to put his name there H977
14: 2 the LORD hath c thee to be a peculiar H977
16:11 thy God hath c to place his name there. H977
18: 5 For the LORD thy God hath c him out of H977
21: 5 thy God hath c to minister unto him, H977
Jos 24:22 that ye have c you the LORD, to serve H977
Jdg 10:14 the gods which ye have c; let them deliver H977
20:15 were numbered seven hundred c men. H977
16 seven hundred c men lefthanded; every H977
34 ten thousand c men out of all Israel, H977
1Sa 8:18 ye shall have c you; and the LORD will H977
10:24 the LORD hath c, that *there is* none like H977
12:13 king whom ye have c, *and* whom ye have H977
16: 8 he said, Neither hath the LORD c this. H977
9 he said, Neither hath the LORD c this. H977
10 unto Jesse, The LORD hath not c these. H977
20:30 that thou hast c the son of Jesse to thine H977
24: 2 Then Saul took three thousand c men H977
26: 2 three thousand c men of Israel with him, H977
2Sa 6: 1 Again, David gathered together all *the* c H977
1Ki 3: 8 which thou hast c, a great people, that H977
8:44 which thou hast c, and *toward* the house H977
48 which thou hast c, and the house which H977
11:13 and for Jerusalem's sake which I have c. H977
32 I have c out of all the tribes of Israel:) H977
36 which I have c me to put my name there. H977
12:21 thousand c men, which were warriors, H970
2Ki 21: 7 which I have c out of all tribes of Israel, H977
23:27 which I have c, and the house of which H977
1Ch 9:22 All these *which were* c to be porters in H1305
15: 2 hath the LORD c to carry the ark of God, H977
16:13 servant, ye children of Jacob, his c ones. H972
41 the rest that were c, who were expressed H1305
28: 4 ever: for he hath c Judah *to be* the ruler; H977
5 sons,) he hath c Solomon my son to sit H977
6 my courts: for I have c him *to be* my son, H977
10 Take heed now; for the LORD hath c H977
29: 1 whom alone God hath c, *is yet* young and H977
2Ch 6: 6 But I have c Jerusalem, that my name H977
6 c David to be over my people Israel. H977
34 which thou hast c, and the house which H977
38 which thou hast c, and toward the house H977
7:12 prayer, and have c this place to myself H977
16 For now have I c and sanctified this H977
11: 1 thousand c *men,* which were warriors, H977
12:13 the LORD had c out of all the tribes of H977
13: 3 hundred thousand c men: Jeroboam H977
3 c men, *being* mighty men of valour. H977
17 of Israel five hundred thousand c men. H977
29:11 for the LORD hath c you to stand before H977
33: 7 which I have c before all the tribes of H977
Neh 1: 9 place that I have c to set my name there. H977
Job 36:21 this hast thou c rather than affliction. H977
Ps 33:12 *whom* he hath c for his own inheritance. H977
78:31 and smote down the c *men* of Israel. H970
89: 3 I have made a covenant with my c, I have H972
19 I have exalted *one* c out of the people. H977
105: 6 his servant, ye children of Jacob his c. H972
26 his servant; *and* Aaron whom he had c. H977
43 people with joy, *and* his c with gladness: H972
106: 5 That I may see the good of thy c, that I H972
23 had not Moses his c stood before him in H972
119:30 I have c the way of truth: thy judgments H977
173 Let thine hand help me; for I have c thy H977
132:13 For the LORD hath c Zion; he hath H977
135: 4 For the LORD hath c Jacob unto himself, H977
Prv 16:16 understanding rather to be c than silver! H977
22: 1 A *good* name *is* rather to be c than great H977
Isa 1:29 for the gardens that ye have c. H977
41: 8 I have c, the seed of Abraham my friend. H977
9 I have c thee, and not cast thee away. H977
43:10 whom I have c: that ye may know and H977
20 desert, to give drink to my people, my c. H972
44: 1 my servant; and Israel, whom I have c: H977
2 and thou, Jesurun, whom I have c. H977
48:10 I have c thee in the furnace of affliction. H977
58: 5 Is it such a fast that I have c? a day for a H977
6 *Is* not this the fast that I have c? to loose H977
65:15 a curse unto my c: for the Lord GOD shall H972
66: 3 Yea, they have c their own ways, and H977
Jer 8: 3 And death shall be c rather than life by H977
33:24 the LORD hath c, he hath even cast them H977
48:15 *of* her cities, and his c young men are H4005
49:19 from her: and who *is* a c *man, that* I may H977
Jer 50:44 from her: and who *is* a c *man, that* I may H977
Ezk 23: 7 *that were* the c men of Assyria, and H4005
Dan 11:15 neither his c people, neither *shall* H4005
Hag 2:23 I have c thee, saith the LORD of hosts. H977
Zec 3: 2 the LORD that hath c Jerusalem rebuke H977
Mt 12:18 Behold my servant, whom I have c; my G140
20:16 first last: for many be called, but few c. G1588
22:14 For many are called, but few *are* c. G1588
Mk 13:20 he hath c, he hath shortened the days. G1586
Lk 10:42 and Mary hath c that good part, which G1586
23:35 himself, if he be Christ, the c of God. G1588
Jn 6:70 Jesus answered them, Have not I c you G1586
13:18 whom I have c: but that the scripture G1586
15:16 Ye have not c me, but I have chosen G1586
16 Ye have not chosen me, but I have c G1586
19 the world, but I have c you out of the G1586
Act 1: 2 unto the apostles whom he had c: G1586
24 shew whether of these two thou hast c, G1586
9:15 thy way: for he is a c vessel unto me, to G1589
10:41 unto witnesses c before of God, *even* G4401
15:22 church, to send c men of their own G1586
25 accord, to send c men unto you with G1586
22:14 of our fathers hath c thee, that thou G4400
Ro 16:13 Salute Rufus c in the Lord, and his G1588
1Co 1:27 But God hath c the foolish things of the G1586
27 and God hath c the weak things of the G1586
28 hath God c, *yea,* and things which G1586
2Co 8:19 And not *that* only, but who was also c G5500
Eph 1: 4 According as he hath c us in him G1586
2Th 2:13 from the beginning c you to salvation G138
2Ti 2: 4 him who hath c him to be a soldier. G4758
Jas 2: 5 Hath not God c the poor of this world G1586
1Pt 2: 4 of men, but c of God, *and* precious, G1588
9 But ye *are* a c generation, a royal G1588
Rev 17:14 with him *are* called, and c, and faithful. G1588

CHOZEBA

1Ch 4:22 And Jokim, and the men of C, and H3578

CHRIST

Mt 1: 1 The book of the generation of Jesus C, G5547
16 whom was born Jesus, who is called C. G5547
17 unto C *are* fourteen generations. G5547
18 Now the birth of Jesus C was on this G5547
2: 4 of them where C should be born. G5547
11: 2 works of C, he sent two of his disciples, G5547
16:16 art the C, the Son of the living God. G5547
20 tell no man that he was Jesus the C. G5547
22:42 Saying, What think ye of C? whose son G5547
23: 8 Master, *even* C; and all ye are brethren. G5547
10 masters: for one is your Master, *even* C. G5547
24: 5 saying, I am C; and shall deceive many. G5547
23 Lo, here *is* C, or there; believe *it* not. G5547
26:63 whether thou be the C, the Son of God. G5547
68 Saying, Prophesy unto us, thou C, Who G5547
27:17 Barabbas, or Jesus which is called C? G5547
22 which is called C? *They* all say unto him, G5547
Mk 1: 1 The beginning of the gospel of Jesus C, G5547
8:29 and saith unto him, Thou art the C. G5547
9:41 ye belong to C, verily I say unto you, G5547
12:35 the scribes that C is the son of David? G5547
13: 6 saying, I am C; and shall deceive many.
21 *is* C; or, lo, *he is* there; believe *him* not: G5547
14:61 Art thou the C, the Son of the Blessed? G5547
15:32 Let C the King of Israel descend now G5547
Lk 2:11 David a Saviour, which is C the Lord. G5547
26 death, before he had seen the Lord's C. G5547
3:15 of John, whether he were the C, or not; G5547
4:41 saying, Thou art C the Son of God. And G5547
41 to speak: for they knew that he was C. G5547
9:20 Peter answering said, The C of God. G5547
20:41 How say they that C is David's son? G5547
21: 8 my name, saying, I am C; and the time
22:67 Art thou the C? tell us. And he said unto G5547
23: 2 saying that he himself is C a King. G5547
35 himself, if he be C, the chosen of God. G5547
39 saying, If thou be C, save thyself and us. G5547
24:26 Ought not C to have suffered these G5547
46 thus it behoved C to suffer, and to rise G5547
Jn 1:17 *but* grace and truth came by Jesus C. G5547
20 not; but confessed, I am not the C. G5547
25 that C, nor Elias, neither that prophet? G5547
41 which is, being interpreted, the C. G5547
3:28 not the C, but that I am sent before him. G5547
4:25 which is called C: when he is come, he G5547
29 things that ever I did: is not this the C? G5547
42 indeed the C, the Saviour of the world. G5547
6:69 art that C, the Son of the living God. G5547
7:26 know indeed that this is the very C? G5547
Jn 7:27 he is: but when C cometh, no man G5547
31 and said, When C cometh, will he do G5547
41 Others said, This is the C. But some G5547
41 some said, Shall C come out of Galilee? G5547
42 Hath not the scripture said, That C G5547
9:22 that he was C, he should be put out G5547
10:24 doubt? If thou be the C, tell us plainly. G5547
11:27 that thou art the C, the Son of God, G5547
12:34 out of the law that C abideth for ever: G5547
17: 3 God, and Jesus C, whom thou hast sent. G5547
20:31 that Jesus is the C, the Son of God; and G5547
Act 2:30 would raise up C to sit on his throne; G5547
31 resurrection of C, that his soul was not G5547
36 ye have crucified, both Lord and C. G5547
38 the name of Jesus C for the remission G5547
3: 6 Jesus C of Nazareth rise up and walk. G5547
18 C should suffer, he hath so fulfilled. G5547
20 And he shall send Jesus C, which before G5547
4:10 the name of Jesus C of Nazareth, whom G5547
26 against the Lord, and against his C. G5547
5:42 ceased not to teach and preach Jesus C. G5547
8: 5 of Samaria, and preached C unto them. G5547
12 and the name of Jesus C, they were G5547
37 I believe that Jesus C is the Son of God. G5547
9:20 And straightway he preached C in the G5547
22 Damascus, proving that this is very C. G5547
34 Aeneas, Jesus C maketh thee whole: G5547
10:36 peace by Jesus C: (he is Lord of all:) G5547
11:17 on the Lord Jesus C; what was I, that I G5547
15:11 Jesus C we shall be saved, even as they. G5547
26 lives for the name of our Lord Jesus C. G5547
16:18 the name of Jesus C to come out of her. G5547
31 on the Lord Jesus C, and thou shalt be G5547
17: 3 Opening and alleging, that C must G5547
3 Jesus, whom I preach unto you, is C. G5547
18: 5 testified to the Jews *that* Jesus *was* C. G5547
28 by the scriptures that Jesus was C. G5547
19: 4 come after him, that is, on C Jesus. G5547
20:21 God, and faith toward our Lord Jesus C. G5547
24:24 heard him concerning the faith in C. G5547
26:23 That C should suffer, *and* that he G5547
28:31 the Lord Jesus C, with all confidence, G5547
Ro 1: 1 Paul, a servant of Jesus C, called *to be* G5547
3 Concerning his Son Jesus C our Lord, G5547
6 whom are ye also the called of Jesus C: G5547
7 God our Father, and the Lord Jesus C. G5547
8 First, I thank my God through Jesus C G5547
16 of the gospel of C: for it is the power of G5547
2:16 men by Jesus C according to my gospel. G5547
3:22 *is* by faith of Jesus C unto all and upon G5547
24 the redemption that is in C Jesus: G5547
5: 1 with God through our Lord Jesus C: G5547
6 in due time C died for the ungodly. G5547
8 we were yet sinners, C died for us. G5547
11 our Lord Jesus C, by whom we have G5547
15 Jesus C, hath abounded unto many. G5547
17 shall reign in life by one, Jesus C.) G5547
21 unto eternal life by Jesus C our Lord. G5547
6: 3 Jesus C were baptized into his death? G5547
4 into death: that like as C was raised up G5547
8 Now if we be dead with C, we believe G5547
9 Knowing that C being raised from the G5547
11 unto God through Jesus C our Lord. G5547
23 *is* eternal life through Jesus C our Lord. G5547
7: 4 law by the body of C; that ye should be G5547
25 I thank God through Jesus C our Lord. G5547
8: 1 to them which are in C Jesus, who walk G5547
2 For the law of the Spirit of life in C G5547
9 not the Spirit of C, he is none of his. G5547
10 And if C *be* in you, the body *is* dead G5547
11 he that raised up C from the dead shall G5547
17 joint-heirs with C; if so be that we suffer G5547
34 Who *is* he that condemneth? *It is* C that G5547
35 from the love of C? *shall* tribulation, or G5547
39 of God, which is in C Jesus our Lord. G5547
9: 1 I say the truth in C, I lie not, my G5547
3 accursed from C for my brethren, my G5547
5 the flesh C *came,* who is over all, G5547
10: 4 For C *is* the end of the law for G5547
6 (that is, to bring C down *from above:*) G5547
7 is, to bring up C again from the dead.) G5547
12: 5 So we, *being* many, are one body in C, G5547
13:14 But put ye on the Lord Jesus C, and G5547
14: 9 For to this end C both died, and rose, G5547
10 all stand before the judgment seat of C. G5547
15 him with thy meat, for whom C died. G5547
18 For he that in these things serveth C *is* G5547
15: 3 For even C pleased not himself; but, as G5547
5 toward another according to C Jesus: G5547

Ro 15: 6 even the Father of our Lord Jesus C. G5547
7 Wherefore receive ye one another, as C G5547
8 Now I say that Jesus C was a minister G5547
16 That I should be the minister of Jesus C G5547
17 C in those things which pertain to God. G5547
18 things which C hath not wrought by G5547
19 I have fully preached the gospel of C. G5547
20 gospel, not where C was named, lest I G5547
29 fulness of the blessing of the gospel of C. G5547
16: 3 and Aquila my helpers in C Jesus: G5547
5 who is the firstfruits of Achaia unto C. G5547
7 apostles, who also were in C before me. G5547
9 Salute Urbane, our helper in C, and G5547
10 Salute Apelles approved in C. Salute G5547
16 holy kiss. The churches of C salute you. G5547
18 not our Lord Jesus C, but their own G5547
20 of our Lord Jesus C *be* with you. Amen. G5547
24 The grace of our Lord Jesus C *be* with G5547
25 preaching of Jesus C, according to the G5547
27 glory through Jesus C for ever. Amen. G5547
1Co 1: 1 Paul, called *to be* an apostle of Jesus C G5547
2 are sanctified in C Jesus, called *to be* G5547
2 Jesus C our Lord, both theirs and ours: G5547
3 our Father, and *from* the Lord Jesus C. G5547
4 of God which is given you by Jesus C; G5547
6 Even as the testimony of C was G5547
7 for the coming of our Lord Jesus C: G5547
8 in the day of our Lord Jesus C. G5547
9 fellowship of his Son Jesus C our Lord. G5547
10 of our Lord Jesus C, that ye all speak the G5547
12 I of Apollos; and I of Cephas; and I of C. G5547
13 Is C divided? was Paul crucified for G5547
17 For C sent me not to baptize, but to G5547
17 of C should be made of none effect. G5547
23 But we preach C crucified, unto the G5547
24 Jews and Greeks, C the power of God, G5547
30 But of him are ye in C Jesus, who of G5547
2: 2 you, save Jesus C, and him crucified. G5547
16 him? But we have the mind of C. G5547
3: 1 as unto carnal, *even* as unto babes in C. G5547
11 lay than that is laid, which is Jesus C. G5547
23 And ye are Christ's; and C *is* God's. G5547
4: 1 as of the ministers of C, and stewards of G5547
10 but ye *are* wise in C; we *are* weak, but ye G5547
15 instructors in C, yet *have ye* not many G5547
15 fathers: for in C Jesus I have begotten G5547
17 my ways which be in C, as I teach every G5547
5: 4 In the name of our Lord Jesus C, when G5547
4 with the power of our Lord Jesus C, G5547
7 even C our passover is sacrificed for us: G5547
6:15 the members of C? shall I then take the G5547
15 the members of C, and make *them* the G5547
8: 6 and one Lord Jesus C, by whom *are* all G5547
11 weak brother perish, for whom C died? G5547
12 their weak conscience, ye sin against C. G5547
9: 1 I not seen Jesus C our Lord? are not ye G5547
12 lest we should hinder the gospel of C. G5547
18 the gospel of C without charge, that G5547
21 under the law to C,) that I might gain G5547
10: 4 followed them: and that Rock was C. G5547
9 Neither let us tempt C, as some of them G5547
16 of the blood of C? The bread which we G5547
16 it not the communion of the body of C? G5547
11: 1 followers of me, even as I also *am* of C. G5547
3 of every man is C; and the head of the G5547
3 *is* the man; and the head of C *is* God. G5547
12:12 being many, are one body: so also *is* C. G5547
27 Now ye are the body of C, and members G5547
15: 3 received, how that C died for our sins G5547
12 Now if C be preached that he rose from G5547
13 of the dead, then is C not risen: G5547
14 And if C be not risen, then *is* our G5547
15 that he raised up C: whom he raised not G5547
16 For if the dead rise not, then is not C G5547
17 And if C be not raised, your faith *is* G5547
18 are fallen asleep in C are perished. G5547
19 If in this life only we have hope in C, we G5547
20 But now is C risen from the dead, *and* G5547
22 For as in Adam all die, even so in C G5547
23 But every man in his own order: C the G5547
31 I have in C Jesus our Lord, I die daily. G5547
57 us the victory through our Lord Jesus C. G5547
16:22 If any man love not the Lord Jesus C, let G5547
23 The grace of our Lord Jesus C *be* with G5547
24 My love *be* with you all in C Jesus. G5547
2Co 1: 1 Paul, an apostle of Jesus C by the will G5547
2 our Father, and *from* the Lord Jesus C. G5547
3 Father of our Lord Jesus C, the Father of G5547
5 For as the sufferings of C abound in us, G5547
2Co 1: 5 our consolation also aboundeth by C. G5547
19 For the Son of God, Jesus C, who was G5547
21 you in C, and hath anointed us, *is* God; G5547
2:10 sakes *forgave I it* in the person of C; G5547
14 causeth us to triumph in C, and maketh G5547
15 a sweet savour of C, in them that are G5547
17 God, in the sight of God speak we in C. G5547
3: 3 to be the epistle of C ministered by us, G5547
4 And such trust have we through C to G5547
14 testament; which *veil* is done away in C. G5547
4: 4 glorious gospel of C, who is the image of G5547
5 For we preach not ourselves, but C G5547
6 of the glory of God in the face of Jesus C. G5547
5:10 judgment seat of C; that every one may G5547
14 For the love of C constraineth us; G5547
16 we have known C after the flesh, yet G5547
17 Therefore if any man *be* in C, *he is* a G5547
18 himself by Jesus C, and hath given to us G5547
19 To wit, that God was in C, reconciling G5547
20 Now then we are ambassadors for C, as G5547
6:15 And what concord hath C with Belial? G5547
8: 9 of our Lord Jesus C, that, though he was G5547
23 of the churches, *and* the glory of C. G5547
9:13 unto the gospel of C, and for *your* G5547
10: 1 and gentleness of C, who in presence G5547
5 every thought to the obedience of C; G5547
14 to you also in *preaching* the gospel of C: G5547
11: 2 may present *you as* a chaste virgin to C. G5547
3 from the simplicity that is in C. G5547
10 As the truth of C is in me, no man shall G5547
13 themselves into the apostles of C. G5547
23 Are they ministers of C? (I speak as a G5547
31 of our Lord Jesus C, which is blessed for G5547
12: 2 I knew a man in C above fourteen G5547
9 that the power of C may rest upon me. G5547
19 before God in C: but *we do* all things, G5547
13: 3 Since ye seek a proof of C speaking in G5547
5 C is in you, except ye be reprobates? G5547
14 The grace of the Lord Jesus C, and the G5547
Gal 1: 1 by man, but by Jesus C, and God the G5547
3 the Father, and *from* our Lord Jesus C, G5547
6 into the grace of C unto another gospel: G5547
7 you, and would pervert the gospel of C. G5547
10 men, I should not be the servant of C. G5547
12 *it*, but by the revelation of Jesus C. G5547
22 the churches of Judaea which were in C: G5547
2: 4 which we have in C Jesus, that they G5547
16 by the faith of Jesus C, even we have G5547
16 believed in Jesus C, that we might be G5547
16 by the faith of C, and not by the works G5547
17 But if, while we seek to be justified by C, G5547
17 C the minister of sin? God forbid. G5547
20 I am crucified with C: nevertheless I G5547
20 I live; yet not I, but C liveth in me: and G5547
21 by the law, then C is dead in vain. G5547
3: 1 whose eyes Jesus C hath been evidently G5547
13 C hath redeemed us from the curse of G5547
14 through Jesus C; that we might receive G5547
16 as of one, And to thy seed, which is C. G5547
17 before of God in C, the law, which was G5547
22 C might be given to them that believe. G5547
24 C, that we might be justified by faith. G5547
26 the children of God by faith in C Jesus. G5547
27 baptized into C have put on Christ. G5547
27 baptized into Christ have put on C. G5547
28 nor female: for ye are all one in C Jesus. G5547
4: 7 if a son, then an heir of God through C. G5547
14 me as an angel of God, *even* as C Jesus. G5547
19 in birth again until C be formed in you, G5547
5: 1 liberty wherewith C hath made us free, G5547
2 C shall profit you nothing. G5547
4 C is become of no effect unto you, G5547
6 For in Jesus C neither circumcision G5547
6: 2 burdens, and so fulfil the law of C. G5547
12 suffer persecution for the cross of C. G5547
14 of our Lord Jesus C, by whom the world G5547
15 For in C Jesus neither circumcision G5547
18 Brethren, the grace of our Lord Jesus C G5547
Eph 1: 1 Paul, an apostle of Jesus C by the will G5547
1 Ephesus, and to the faithful in C Jesus: G5547
2 our Father, and *from* the Lord Jesus C. G5547
3 of our Lord Jesus C, who hath blessed G5547
3 blessings in heavenly *places* in C: G5547
5 of children by Jesus C to himself, G5547
10 in one all things in C, both which are in G5547
12 of his glory, who first trusted in C. G5547
17 That the God of our Lord Jesus C, the G5547
20 Which he wrought in C, when he raised G5547
2: 5 with C, (by grace ye are saved;) G5547
Eph 2: 6 together in heavenly *places* in C Jesus: G5547
7 kindness toward us through C Jesus. G5547
10 created in C Jesus unto good works, G5547
12 That at that time ye were without C, G5547
13 But now in C Jesus ye who sometimes G5547
13 far off are made nigh by the blood of C. G5547
20 C himself being the chief corner *stone*; G5547
3: 1 the prisoner of Jesus C for you Gentiles, G5547
4 my knowledge in the mystery of C) G5547
6 of his promise in C by the gospel: G5547
8 Gentiles the unsearchable riches of C; G5547
9 God, who created all things by Jesus C: G5547
11 which he purposed in C Jesus our Lord: G5547
14 unto the Father of our Lord Jesus C, G5547
17 That C may dwell in your hearts by G5547
19 And to know the love of C, which G5547
21 Unto him *be* glory in the church by C G5547
4: 7 to the measure of the gift of C. G5547
12 for the edifying of the body of C: G5547
13 of the stature of the fulness of C: G5547
15 in all things, which is the head, *even* C: G5547
20 But ye have not so learned C; G5547
5: 2 And walk in love, as C also hath loved G5547
5 in the kingdom of C and of God. G5547
14 the dead, and C shall give thee light. G5547
20 Father in the name of our Lord Jesus C; G5547
23 of the wife, even as C is the head of the G5547
24 is subject unto C, so *let* the wives *be* to G5547
25 Husbands, love your wives, even as C G5547
32 I speak concerning C and the church. G5547
6: 5 in singleness of your heart, as unto C; G5547
6 C, doing the will of God from the heart; G5547
23 God the Father and the Lord Jesus C. G5547
24 our Lord Jesus C in sincerity. Amen. G5547
Php 1: 1 servants of Jesus C, to all the saints in G5547
1 to all the saints in C Jesus which are at G5547
2 our Father, and *from* the Lord Jesus C. G5547
6 will perform *it* until the day of Jesus C: G5547
8 after you all in the bowels of Jesus C. G5547
10 and without offence till the day of C; G5547
11 C, unto the glory and praise of God. G5547
13 So that my bonds in C are manifest in G5547
15 Some indeed preach C even of envy G5547
16 The one preach C of contention, not G5547
18 or in truth, C is preached; and I therein G5547
19 and the supply of the Spirit of Jesus C, G5547
20 *so* now also C shall be magnified in G5547
21 For to me to live *is* C, and to die *is* gain. G5547
23 and to be with C; which is far better: G5547
26 C for me by my coming to you again. G5547
27 the gospel of C: that whether I come G5547
29 in the behalf of C, not only to believe on G5547
2: 1 consolation in C, if any comfort of love, G5547
5 be in you, which was also in C Jesus: G5547
11 confess that Jesus C *is* Lord, to the G5547
16 in the day of C, that I have not run G5547
30 Because for the work of C he was nigh G5547
3: 3 and rejoice in C Jesus, and have no G5547
7 gain to me, those I counted loss for C. G5547
8 the knowledge of C Jesus my Lord: for G5547
8 count them *but* dung, that I may win C, G5547
9 the faith of C, the righteousness which G5547
12 also I am apprehended of C Jesus. G5547
14 of the high calling of God in C Jesus. G5547
18 *they are* the enemies of the cross of C: G5547
20 look for the Saviour, the Lord Jesus C: G5547
4: 7 hearts and minds through C Jesus. G5547
13 I can do all things through C which G5547
19 to his riches in glory by C Jesus. G5547
21 Salute every saint in C Jesus. The G5547
23 The grace of our Lord Jesus C *be* with G5547
Col 1: 1 Paul, an apostle of Jesus C by the will G5547
2 To the saints and faithful brethren in C G5547
2 God our Father and the Lord Jesus C. G5547
3 Lord Jesus C, praying always for you, G5547
4 Since we heard of your faith in C Jesus, G5547
7 who is for you a faithful minister of C; G5547
24 of the afflictions of C in my flesh for his G5547
27 which is C in you, the hope of glory: G5547
28 present every man perfect in C Jesus: G5547
2: 2 of God, and of the Father, and of C; G5547
5 and the stedfastness of your faith in C. G5547
6 As ye have therefore received C Jesus G5547
8 rudiments of the world, and not after C. G5547
11 of the flesh by the circumcision of C: G5547
17 of things to come; but the body *is* of C. G5547
20 Wherefore if ye be dead with C from G5547
3: 1 If ye then be risen with C, seek those G5547
1 C sitteth on the right hand of God. G5547

Col 3: 3 and your life is hid with C in God. *G5547*
4 When C, *who is* our life, shall appear, *G5547*
11 bond *nor* free: but C *is* all, and in all. *G5547*
13 even as C forgave you, so also *do* ye. *G5547*
16 Let the word of C dwell in you richly in *G5547*
24 the inheritance: for ye serve the Lord C. *G5547*
4: 3 of C, for which I am also in bonds: *G5547*
12 you, a servant of C, saluteth you, always *G5547*
1Th 1: 1 *in* the Lord Jesus C: Grace *be* unto you, *G5547*
1 God our Father, and the Lord Jesus C. *G5547*
3 C, in the sight of God and our Father; *G5547*
2: 6 been burdensome, as the apostles of C. *G5547*
14 in Judaea are in C Jesus: for ye also *G5547*
19 of our Lord Jesus C at his coming? *G5547*
3: 2 in the gospel of C, to establish you, and *G5547*
11 Lord Jesus C, direct our way unto you. *G5547*
13 of our Lord Jesus C with all his saints. *G5547*
4:16 God: and the dead in C shall rise first: *G5547*
5: 9 to obtain salvation by our Lord Jesus C, *G5547*
18 will of God in C Jesus concerning you. *G5547*
23 unto the coming of our Lord Jesus C. *G5547*
28 The grace of our Lord Jesus C *be* with *G5547*
2Th 1: 1 in God our Father and the Lord Jesus C: *G5547*
2 God our Father and the Lord Jesus C. *G5547*
8 obey not the gospel of our Lord Jesus C: *G5547*
12 That the name of our Lord Jesus C may *G5547*
12 grace of our God and the Lord Jesus C. *G5547*
2: 1 coming of our Lord Jesus C, and *by* our *G5547*
2 from us, as that the day of C is at hand. *G5547*
14 of the glory of our Lord Jesus C. *G5547*
16 Now our Lord Jesus C himself, and *G5547*
3: 5 God, and into the patient waiting for C. *G5547*
6 of our Lord Jesus C, that ye withdraw *G5547*
12 by our Lord Jesus C, that with quietness *G5547*
18 The grace of our Lord Jesus C *be* with *G5547*
1Ti 1: 1 Paul, an apostle of Jesus C by the *G5547*
1 and Lord Jesus C, *which is* our hope; *G5547*
2 God our Father and Jesus C our Lord. *G5547*
12 And I thank C Jesus our Lord, who *G5547*
14 with faith and love which is in C Jesus. *G5547*
15 acceptation, that C Jesus came into the *G5547*
16 in me first Jesus C might shew forth all *G5547*
2: 5 God and men, the man C Jesus; *G5547*
7 (I speak the truth in C, *and* lie not;) a *G5547*
3:13 in the faith which is in C Jesus. *G5547*
4: 6 minister of Jesus C, nourished up in the *G5547*
5:11 wax wanton against C, they will marry; *G5547*
21 the Lord Jesus C, and the elect angels, *G5547*
6: 3 of our Lord Jesus C, and to the doctrine *G5547*
13 things, and *before* C Jesus, who before *G5547*
14 until the appearing of our Lord Jesus C: *G5547*
2Ti 1: 1 Paul, an apostle of Jesus C by the will *G5547*
1 the promise of life which is in C Jesus, *G5547*
2 God the Father and C Jesus our Lord. *G5547*
9 us in C Jesus before the world began, *G5547*
10 of our Saviour Jesus C, who hath *G5547*
13 in faith and love which is in C Jesus. *G5547*
2: 1 be strong in the grace that is in C Jesus. *G5547*
3 hardness, as a good soldier of Jesus C. *G5547*
8 Remember that Jesus C of the seed of *G5547*
10 which is in C Jesus with eternal glory. *G5547*
19 the name of C depart from iniquity. *G5547*
3:12 Yea, and all that will live godly in C *G5547*
15 through faith which is in C Jesus. *G5547*
4: 1 the Lord Jesus C, who shall judge the *G5547*
22 The Lord Jesus C *be* with thy spirit. *G5547*
Tit 1: 1 apostle of Jesus C, according to the faith *G5547*
4 and the Lord Jesus C our Saviour. *G5547*
2:13 the great God and our Saviour Jesus C; *G5547*
3: 6 through Jesus C our Saviour; *G5547*
Phlm 1 Paul, a prisoner of Jesus C, and *G5547*
3 God our Father and the Lord Jesus C. *G5547*
6 good thing which is in you in C Jesus. *G5547*
8 be much bold in C to enjoin thee that *G5547*
9 and now also a prisoner of Jesus C. *G5547*
23 my fellowprisoner in C Jesus; *G5547*
25 The grace of our Lord Jesus C *be* with *G5547*
Heb 3: 1 High Priest of our profession, C Jesus; *G5547*
6 But C as a son over his own house; *G5547*
14 For we are made partakers of C, if we *G5547*
5: 5 So also C glorified not himself to be *G5547*
6: 1 of the doctrine of C, let us go on unto *G5547*
9:11 But C being come an high priest of *G5547*
14 How much more shall the blood of C, *G5547*
24 For C is not entered into the holy *G5547*
28 So C was once offered to bear the sins *G5547*
10:10 of the body of Jesus C once *for all*. *G5547*
11:26 Esteeming the reproach of C greater *G5547*
13: 8 Jesus C the same yesterday, and to day, *G5547*
Heb 13:21 through Jesus C; to whom *be* glory for *G5547*
Jas 1: 1 of the Lord Jesus C, to the twelve tribes *G5547*
2: 1 of our Lord Jesus C, *the Lord* of glory, *G5547*
1Pt 1: 1 Peter, an apostle of Jesus C, to the *G5547*
2 of the blood of Jesus C: Grace unto you, *G5547*
3 of our Lord Jesus C, which according to *G5547*
3 resurrection of Jesus C from the dead, *G5547*
7 and glory at the appearing of Jesus C: *G5547*
11 time the Spirit of C which was in them *G5547*
11 of C, and the glory that should follow. *G5547*
13 unto you at the revelation of Jesus C; *G5547*
19 But with the precious blood of C, as of a *G5547*
2: 5 sacrifices, acceptable to God by Jesus C. *G5547*
21 ye called: because C also suffered for *G5547*
3:16 accuse your good conversation in C. *G5547*
18 For C also hath once suffered for sins, *G5547*
21 God,) by the resurrection of Jesus C: *G5547*
4: 1 Forasmuch then as C hath suffered for *G5547*
11 through Jesus C, to whom be praise and *G5547*
14 If ye be reproached for the name of C, *G5547*
5: 1 the sufferings of C, and also a partaker *G5547*
10 eternal glory by C Jesus, after that ye *G5547*
14 with you all that are in C Jesus. Amen. *G5547*
2Pt 1: 1 an apostle of Jesus C, to them that have *G5547*
1 of God and our Saviour Jesus C: *G5547*
8 in the knowledge of our Lord Jesus C. *G5547*
11 of our Lord and Saviour Jesus C. *G5547*
14 as our Lord Jesus C hath shewed me. *G5547*
16 C, but were eyewitnesses of his majesty. *G5547*
2:20 and Saviour Jesus C, they are again *G5547*
3:18 and Saviour Jesus C. To him *be* glory *G5547*
1Jn 1: 3 the Father, and with his Son Jesus C. *G5547*
7 C his Son cleanseth us from all sin. *G5547*
2: 1 with the Father, Jesus C the righteous: *G5547*
22 that Jesus is the C? He is antichrist, that *G5547*
3:23 name of his Son Jesus C, and love one *G5547*
4: 2 Jesus C is come in the flesh is of God: *G5547*
3 not that Jesus C is come in the flesh *G5547*
5: 1 Whosoever believeth that Jesus is the C *G5547*
6 blood, *even* Jesus C; not by water only, *G5547*
20 C. This is the true God, and eternal life. *G5547*
2Jn 3 the Lord Jesus C, the Son of the Father, *G5547*
7 not that Jesus C is come in the flesh. *G5547*
9 in the doctrine of C, hath not God. He *G5547*
9 C, he hath both the Father and the Son. *G5547*
Jude 1 Jude, the servant of Jesus C, and *G5547*
1 and preserved in Jesus C, *and* called: *G5547*
4 only Lord God, and our Lord Jesus C. *G5547*
17 of the apostles of our Lord Jesus C; *G5547*
21 of our Lord Jesus C unto eternal life. *G5547*
Rev 1: 1 The Revelation of Jesus C, which God *G5547*
2 of Jesus C, and of all things that he saw. *G5547*
5 And from Jesus C, *who is* the faithful *G5547*
9 patience of Jesus C, was in the isle that *G5547*
9 God, and for the testimony of Jesus C. *G5547*
11:15 C; and he shall reign for ever and ever. *G5547*
12:10 the power of his C: for the accuser of *G5547*
17 God, and have the testimony of Jesus C. *G5547*
20: 4 and reigned with C a thousand years. *G5547*
6 of God and of C, and shall reign with *G5547*
22:21 The grace of our Lord Jesus C *be* with *G5547*

CHRIST JESUS See CHRIST and JESUS.

CHRISTIAN
Act 26:28 Almost thou persuadest me to be a C. *G5546*
1Pt 4:16 Yet if *any man suffer* as a C, let him not *G5546*

CHRISTIANS
Act 11:26 disciples were called C first in Antioch. *G5546*

CHRISTS
Mt 24:24 For there shall arise false C, and false *G5580*
Mk 13:22 For false C and false prophets shall *G5580*

CHRIST'S
Ro 15:30 for the Lord Jesus C sake, and for the *G5547*
1Co 3:23 And ye are C; and Christ *is* God's. *G5547*
4:10 We *are* fools for C sake, but ye *are* wise *G5547*
7:22 that is called, *being* free, is C servant. *G5547*
15:23 they that are C at his coming. *G5547*
2Co 2:12 to Troas to *preach* C gospel, and a door *G5547*
5:20 *you* in C stead, be ye reconciled to God. *G5547*
10: 7 himself that he is C, let him of himself *G5547*
7 that, as he *is* C, even so *are* we Christ's. *G5547*
7 that, as he *is* Christ's, even so *are* we C. *G5547*
12:10 in distresses for C sake: for when I am *G5547*
Gal 3:29 And if ye *be* C, then are ye Abraham's *G5547*
5:24 And they that are C have crucified the *G5547*
Eph 4:32 as God for C sake hath forgiven you. *G5547*
Php 2:21 own, not the things which are Jesus C. *G5547*
1Pt 4:13 ye are partakers of C sufferings; that, *G5547*

CHRONICLES
1Ki 14:19 of the c of the kings of Israel. H1697+H3117
29 of the c of the kings of Judah? H1697+H3117
15: 7 the book of the c of the kings of H1697+H3117
23 the book of the c of the kings of H1697+H3117
31 of the c of the kings of Israel? H1697+H3117
16: 5 of the c of the kings of Israel? H1697+H3117
14 of the c of the kings of Israel? H1697+H3117
20 of the c of the kings of Israel? H1697+H3117
27 of the c of the kings of Israel? H1697+H3117
22:39 of the c of the kings of Israel? H1697+H3117
45 of the c of the kings of Judah? H1697+H3117
2Ki 1:18 of the c of the kings of Israel? H1697+H3117
8:23 of the c of the kings of Judah? H1697+H3117
10:34 of the c of the kings of Israel? H1697+H3117
12:19 of the c of the kings of Judah? H1697+H3117
13: 8 of the c of the kings of Israel? H1697+H3117
12 of the c of the kings of Israel? H1697+H3117
14:15 of the c of the kings of Israel? H1697+H3117
18 of the c of the kings of Judah? H1697+H3117
28 of the c of the kings of Israel? H1697+H3117
15: 6 of the c of the kings of Judah? H1697+H3117
11 of the c of the kings of Israel. H1697+H3117
15 of the c of the kings of Israel. H1697+H3117
21 of the c of the kings of Israel? H1697+H3117
26 of the c of the kings of Israel. H1697+H3117
31 of the c of the kings of Israel. H1697+H3117
36 of the c of the kings of Judah? H1697+H3117
16:19 of the c of the kings of Judah? H1697+H3117
20:20 of the c of the kings of Judah? H1697+H3117
21:17 of the c of the kings of Judah? H1697+H3117
25 of the c of the kings of Judah? H1697+H3117
23:28 of the c of the kings of Judah? H1697+H3117
24: 5 of the c of the kings of Judah? H1697+H3117
1Ch 27:24 account of the c of king David. H1697+H3117
Neh 12:23 the book of the c, even until the H1697+H3117
Est 2:23 book of the c before the king. H1697+H3117
6: 1 records of the c; and they were H1697+H3117
10: 2 the book of the c of the kings of H1697+H3117

CHRYSOLYTE
Rev 21:20 the seventh, c; the eighth, beryl; the *G5555*

CHRYSOPRASUS
Rev 21:20 a topaz; the tenth, a c; the eleventh, a *G5556*

CHUB
Ezk 30: 5 people, and C, and the men of the H3552

CHUN
1Ch 18: 8 Likewise from Tibhath, and from C, H3560

CHURCH
Mt 16:18 I will build my c; and the gates of hell *G1577*
18:17 tell *it* unto the c: but if he neglect to *G1577*
17 he neglect to hear the c, let him be unto *G1577*
Act 2:47 to the c daily such as should be saved. *G1577*
5:11 And great fear came upon all the c, and *G1577*
7:38 This is he, that was in the c in the *G1577*
8: 1 against the c which was at Jerusalem; *G1577*
3 As for Saul, he made havock of the c, *G1577*
11:22 unto the ears of the c which was in *G1577*
26 with the c, and taught much people. *G1577*
12: 1 forth *his* hands to vex certain of the c. *G1577*
5 ceasing of the c unto God for him. *G1577*
13: 1 Now there were in the c that was at *G1577*
14:23 elders in every c, and had prayed with *G1577*
27 and had gathered the c together, they *G1577*
15: 3 their way by the c, they passed through *G1577*
4 received of the c, and *of* the apostles *G1577*
22 with the whole c, to send chosen men *G1577*
18:22 saluted the c, he went down to Antioch. *G1577*
20:17 Ephesus, and called the elders of the c. *G1577*
28 to feed the c of God, which he hath *G1577*
Ro 16: 1 a servant of the c which is at Cenchrea: *G1577*
5 Likewise *greet* the c that is in their *G1577*
23 Gaius mine host, and of the whole c, *G1577*
1Co 1: 2 Unto the c of God which is at Corinth, *G1577*
4:17 Christ, as I teach every where in every c. *G1577*
6: 4 judge who are least esteemed in the c. *G1577*
10:32 nor to the Gentiles, nor to the c of God: *G1577*
11:18 together in the c, I hear that there be *G1577*
22 or despise ye the c of God, and shame *G1577*
12:28 And God hath set some in the c, first *G1577*
14: 4 but he that prophesieth edifieth the c. *G1577*

1Co 14: 5 that the c may receive edifying. G1577
12 ye may excel to the edifying of the c. G1577
19 Yet in the c I had rather speak five G1577
23 If therefore the whole c be come G1577
28 keep silence in the c; and let him speak G1577
35 is a shame for women to speak in the c. G1577
15: 9 because I persecuted the c of God. G1577
16:19 Lord, with the c that is in their house. G1577
2Co 1: 1 brother, unto the c of God which is at G1577
Gal 1:13 persecuted the c of God, and wasted it: G1577
Eph 1:22 *to be* the head over all *things* to the c, G1577
3:10 by the c the manifold wisdom of God, G1577
21 Unto him *be* glory in the c by Christ G1577
5:23 the c: and he is the saviour of the body. G1577
24 Therefore as the c is subject unto G1577
25 also loved the c, and gave himself for it; G1577
27 himself a glorious c, not having spot, or G1577
29 cherisheth it, even as the Lord the c: G1577
32 but I speak concerning Christ and the c. G1577
Php 3: 6 Concerning zeal, persecuting the c; G1577
4:15 Macedonia, no c communicated with G1577
Col 1:18 And he is the head of the body, the c: G1577
24 flesh for his body's sake, which is the c: G1577
4:15 and the c which is in his house. G1577
16 be read also in the c of the Laodiceans; G1577
1Th 1: 1 unto the c of the Thessalonians G1577
2Th 1: 1 unto the c of the Thessalonians G1577
1Ti 3: 5 how shall he take care of the c of God?) G1577
15 of God, which is the c of the living God, G1577
5:16 and let not the c be charged; that it G1577
Phlm 2 fellowsoldier, and to the c in thy house: G1577
Heb 2:12 of the c will I sing praise unto thee. G1577
12:23 To the general assembly and c of the G1577
Jas 5:14 for the elders of the c; and let them pray G1577
1Pt 5:13 The *c that is* at Babylon, elected G1577
3Jn 6 charity before the c: whom if thou bring G1577
9 I wrote unto the c: but Diotrephes, who G1577
10 would, and casteth *them* out of the c. G1577
Rev 2: 1 Unto the angel of the c of Ephesus G1577
8 And unto the angel of the c in Smyrna G1577
12 And to the angel of the c in Pergamos G1577
18 And unto the angel of the c in Thyatira G1577
3: 1 And unto the angel of the c in Sardis G1577
7 And to the angel of the c in G1577
14 And unto the angel of the c of the G1577

CHURCHES
Act 9:31 Then had the c rest throughout all G1577
15:41 Syria and Cilicia, confirming the c. G1577
16: 5 And so were the c established in the G1577
19:37 c, nor yet blasphemers of your goddess. G1577
Ro 16: 4 but also all the c of the Gentiles. G1577
16 an holy kiss. The c of Christ salute you. G1577
1Co 7:17 so let him walk. And so ordain I in all c. G1577
11:16 no such custom, neither the c of God. G1577
14:33 but of peace, as in all c of the saints. G1577
34 Let your women keep silence in the c: G1577
16: 1 order to the c of Galatia, even so do ye. G1577
19 The c of Asia salute you. Aquila and G1577
2Co 8: 1 God bestowed on the c of Macedonia; G1577
18 *is* in the gospel throughout all the c; G1577
19 also chosen of the c to travel with us G1577
23 of the c, *and* the glory of Christ. G1577
24 and before the c, the proof of your love, G1577
11: 8 I robbed other c, taking wages *of them*, G1577
28 upon me daily, the care of all the c. G1577
12:13 inferior to other c, except *it be* that I G1577
Gal 1: 2 are with me, unto the c of Galatia: G1577
22 And was unknown by face unto the c of G1577
1Th 2:14 followers of the c of God which in G1577
2Th 1: 4 glory in you in the c of God for your G1577
Rev 1: 4 John to the seven c which are in Asia: G1577
11 *it* unto the seven c which are in Asia; G1577
20 angels of the seven c: and the seven G1577
20 which thou sawest are the seven c. G1577
2: 7 Spirit saith unto the c; To him that G1577
11 saith unto the c; He that overcometh G1577
17 Spirit saith unto the c; To him that G1577
23 death; and all the c shall know that I G1577
29 hear what the Spirit saith unto the c. G1577
3: 6 hear what the Spirit saith unto the c. G1577
13 hear what the Spirit saith unto the c. G1577
22 hear what the Spirit saith unto the c. G1577
22:16 these things in the c. I am the root and G1577

CHURL
Isa 32: 5 liberal, nor the c said *to be* bountiful. H3596
7 The instruments also of the c *are* evil: H3596

CHURLISH
1Sa 25: 3 but the man *was* c and evil in his H7186

CHURNING
Prv 30:33 Surely the c of milk bringeth forth H4330

CHUSHAN-RISHATHAIM
Jdg 3: 8 them into the hand of C king of H3573
8 children of Israel served C eight years. H3573
10 the LORD delivered C king of H3573
10 hand; and his hand prevailed against C. H3573

CHUZA
Lk 8: 3 And Joanna the wife of C Herod's G5529

CIELED
2Ch 3: 5 And the greater house he c with fir tree, H2645
Jer 22:14 windows; and *it is* c with cedar, and H5603
Ezk 41:16 against the door, c with wood round H7824
Hag 1: 4 your c houses, and this house *lie* waste? H5603

CIELING
1Ki 6:15 the walls of the c: *and* he covered *them* H5604

CILICIA
Act 6: 9 C and of Asia, disputing with Stephen. G2791
15:23 the Gentiles in Antioch and Syria and C: G2791
41 And he went through Syria and C, G2791
21:39 Jew of Tarsus, *a city* in C, a citizen of no G2791
22: 3 in Tarsus, *a city* in C, yet brought up in G2791
23:34 when he understood that *he was* of C; G2791
27: 5 over the sea of C and Pamphylia, we G2791
Gal 1:21 I came into the regions of Syria and C; G2791

CINNAMON
Ex 30:23 and of sweet c half so much, *even* H7076
Prv 7:17 my bed with myrrh, aloes, and c. H7076
Song 4:14 Spikenard and saffron; calamus and c, H7076
Rev 18:13 And c, and odours, and ointments, and G2792

CINNEROTH
1Ki 15:20 and all C, with all the land of Naphtali. H3672

CIRCLE
Isa 40:22 *It is* he that sitteth upon the c of the H2329

CIRCUIT
1Sa 7:16 And he went from year to year in c to H5437
Job 22:14 not; and he walketh in the c of heaven. H2329
Ps 19: 6 heaven, and his c unto the ends of it: H8622

CIRCUITS
Ecc 1: 6 wind returneth again according to his c. H5439

CIRCUMCISE
Gen 17:11 And ye shall c the flesh of your H5243
Dt 10:16 C therefore the foreskin of your heart, H4135
30: 6 And the LORD thy God will c thine H4135
Jos 5: 2 sharp knives, and c again the children H4135
4 And this *is* the cause why Joshua did c: H4135
Jer 4: 4 C yourselves to the LORD, and take H4135
Lk 1:59 day they came to c the child; and they G4059
Jn 7:22 and ye on the sabbath day c a man. G4059
Act 15: 5 That it was needful to c them, and to G4059
21:21 that they ought not to c *their* children, G4059

CIRCUMCISED
Gen 17:10 Every man child among you shall be c. H4135
12 And he that is eight days old shall be c H4135
13 must needs be c: and my covenant shall H4135
14 of his foreskin is not c, that soul shall be H4135
23 house; and c the flesh of their foreskin H4135
24 he was c in the flesh of his foreskin. H4135
25 he was c in the flesh of his foreskin. H4135
26 In the selfsame day was Abraham c, H4135
27 of the stranger, were c with him. H4135
21: 4 And Abraham c his son Isaac being H4135
34:15 be as we *be*, that every male of you be c; H4135
17 unto us, to be c; then will we take our H4135
22 among us be c, as they *are* circumcised. H4135
22 among us be circumcised, as they *are* c. H4135
24 every male was c, all that went out of H4135
Ex 12:44 hast c him, then shall he eat thereof. H4135
48 let all his males be c, and then let him H4135
Lev 12: 3 day the flesh of his foreskin shall be c. H4135
Jos 5: 3 him sharp knives, and c the children of H4135
5 came out were c: but all the people *that* H4135
5 forth out of Egypt, *them* they had not c. H4135
7 stead, them Joshua c: for they were H4135
5: 7 they had not c them by the way. H4135
Jer 9:25 *which are* c with the uncircumcised; H4135
Act 7: 8 begat Isaac, and c him the eighth day; G4059
15: 1 *said*, Except ye be c after the manner of G4059
24 *Ye must* be c, and keep the law: to G4059
16: 3 him; and took and c him because of the G4059
Ro 4:11 they be not c; that righteousness might G1223
1Co 7:18 Is any man called being c? let him not G4059
18 in uncircumcision? let him not be c. G4059
Gal 2: 3 being a Greek, was compelled to be c: G4059
5: 2 ye be c, Christ shall profit you nothing. G4059
3 every man that is c, that he is a debtor G4059
6:12 you to be c; only lest they should G4059
13 For neither they themselves who are c G4059
13 you c, that they may glory in your flesh. G4059
Php 3: 5 C the eighth day, of the stock of Israel, G4061
Col 2:11 In whom also ye are c with the G4059

CIRCUMCISING
Jos 5: 8 they had done c all the people, that H4135
Lk 2:21 for the c of the child, his name G4059

CIRCUMCISION
Ex 4:26 husband *thou art*, because of the c. H4139
Jn 7:22 Moses therefore gave unto you c; (not G4061
23 If a man on the sabbath day receive c, G4061
Act 7: 8 And he gave him the covenant of c: and G4061
10:45 And they of the c which believed were G4061
11: 2 that were of the c contended with him, G4061
Ro 2:25 For c verily profiteth, if thou keep the G4061
25 the law, thy c is made uncircumcision. G4061
26 his uncircumcision be counted for c? G4061
27 the letter and c dost transgress the law? G4061
28 *is that* c, which is outward in the flesh: G4061
29 one inwardly; and c *is that* of the heart, G4061
3: 1 the Jew? or what profit *is there* of c? G4061
30 which shall justify the c by faith, and G4061
4: 9 then upon the c *only*, or upon the G4061
10 when he was in c, or in uncircumcision? G4061
10 Not in c, but in uncircumcision. G4061
11 And he received the sign of c, a seal of G4061
12 And the father of c to them who are not G4061
12 who are not of the c only, but who also G4061
15: 8 a minister of the c for the truth of God, G4061
1Co 7:19 C is nothing, and uncircumcision is G4061
Gal 2: 7 as *the gospel* of the c *was* unto Peter; G4061
8 the apostleship of the c, the same was G4061
9 unto the heathen, and they unto the c. G4061
12 fearing them which were of the c. G4061
5: 6 For in Jesus Christ neither c availeth G4061
11 And I, brethren, if I yet preach c, why G4061
6:15 For in Christ Jesus neither c availeth G4061
Eph 2:11 the C in the flesh made by hands; G4061
Php 3: 3 For we are the c, which worship God in G4061
Col 2:11 with the c made without hands, G4061
11 the sins of the flesh by the c of Christ: G4061
3:11 Where there is neither Greek nor Jew, c G4061
4:11 who are of the c. These only *are my* G4061
Tit 1:10 and deceivers, specially they of the c: G4061

CIRCUMSPECT
Ex 23:13 have said unto you be c: and make no H8104

CIRCUMSPECTLY
Eph 5:15 See then that ye walk c, not as fools, but G199

CIS
Act 13:21 Saul the son of C, a man of the tribe of G2797

CISTERN
2Ki 18:31 drink ye every one the waters of his c: H953
Prv 5:15 Drink waters out of thine own c, and H953
Ecc 12: 6 fountain, or the wheel broken at the c. H953
Isa 36:16 ye every one the waters of his own c; H953

CISTERNS
Jer 2:13 hewed them out c, broken cisterns, that H877
13 broken c, that can hold no water. H877

CITIES
Gen 13:12 Lot dwelled in the c of the plain, and H5892
19:25 And he overthrew those c, and all the H5892
25 the inhabitants of the c, and that which H5892
29 God destroyed the c of the plain, that H5892
29 overthrew the c in the which Lot dwelt. H5892
35: 5 of God was upon the c that *were* round H5892
41:35 and let them keep food in the c. H5892
48 laid up the food in the c: the food of the H5892
47:21 removed them to c from *one* end of the H5892

Ex 1:11 treasure c, Pithom and Raamses. H5892
Lev 25:32 Notwithstanding the c of the Levites, H5892
32 the houses of the c of their possession, H5892
33 for the houses of the c of the Levites *are* H5892
34 But the field of the suburbs of their c H5892
26:25 within your c, I will send the pestilence H5892
31 And I will make your c waste, and H5892
33 shall be desolate, and your c waste. H5892
Nu 13:19 or bad; and what c *they be* that they H5892
28 the land, and the c *are* walled, *and* very H5892
21: 2 hand, then I will utterly destroy their c. H5892
3 them and their c: and he called the H5892
25 And Israel took all these c: and Israel H5892
25 dwelt in all the c of the Amorites, in H5892
31:10 And they burnt all their c wherein they H5892
32:16 for our cattle, and c for our little ones: H5892
17 dwell in the fenced c because of the H5892
24 Build you c for your little ones, and H5892
26 cattle, shall be there in the c of Gilead: H5892
33 the land, with the c thereof in the H5892
33 *even* the c of the country round about. H5892
36 fenced c: and folds for sheep. H5892
38 names unto the c which they builded. H5892
35: 2 of their possession c to dwell in; and ye H5892
2 suburbs for the c round about them. H5892
3 And the c shall they have to dwell in; H5892
4 And the suburbs of the c, which ye shall H5892
5 shall be to them the suburbs of the c. H5892
6 And among the c which ye shall give H5892
6 *there shall be* six c for refuge, which ye H5892
6 to them ye shall add forty and two c. H5892
7 *So* all the c which ye shall give to the H5892
7 c: them *shall ye give* with their suburbs. H5892
8 And the c which ye shall give *shall be* of H5892
8 one shall give of his c unto the Levites H5892
11 Then ye shall appoint you c to be cities H5892
11 Then ye shall appoint you cities to be c H5892
12 And they shall be unto you c for refuge H5892
13 And of these c which ye shall give six H5892
13 shall give six c shall ye have for refuge. H5892
14 Ye shall give three c on this side H5892
14 Jordan, and three c shall ye give in the H5892
14 of Canaan, *which* shall be c of refuge. H5892
15 These six c shall be a refuge, *both* for H5892
Dt 1:22 go up, and into what c we shall come. H5892
28 and taller than we; the c *are* great and H5892
2:34 And we took all his c at that time, and H5892
35 and the spoil of the c which we took. H5892
37 nor unto the c in the mountains, nor H5892
3: 4 And we took all his c at that time, there H5892
4 them, threescore c, all the region of H5892
5 All these c *were* fenced with high walls, H5892
7 But all the cattle, and the spoil of the c, H5892
10 All the c of the plain, and all Gilead, H5892
10 c of the kingdom of Og in Bashan. H5892
12 Gilead, and the c thereof, gave I unto H5892
19 abide in your c which I have given you; H5892
4:41 Then Moses severed three c on this side H5892
42 unto one of these c he might live: H5892
6:10 and goodly c, which thou buildedst not, H5892
9: 1 c great and fenced up to heaven, H5892
13:12 If thou shalt hear *say* in one of thy c, H5892
19: 1 dwellest in their c, and in their houses; H5892
2 Thou shalt separate three c for thee in H5892
5 shall flee unto one of those c, and live: H5892
7 Thou shalt separate three c for thee. H5892
9 c more for thee, beside these three: H5892
11 he die, and fleeth into one of these c: H5892
20:15 Thus shalt thou do unto all the c *which* H5892
15 which *are* not of the c of these nations. H5892
16 But of the c of these people, which the H5892
21: 2 measure unto the c which *are* round H5892
Jos 9:17 and came unto their c on the third day. H5892
17 day. Now their c *were* Gibeon, and H5892
10: 2 as one of the royal c, and because it *was* H5892
19 to enter into their c: for the LORD your H5892
20 remained of them entered into fenced c. H5892
37 and all the c thereof, and all the H5892
39 and all the c thereof; and they smote H5892
11:12 And all the c of those kings, and all the H5892
13 But *as for* the c that stood still in their H5892
14 And all the spoil of these c, and the H5892
21 destroyed them utterly with their c. H5892
13:10 And all the c of Sihon king of the H5892
17 Heshbon, and all her c that *are* in the H5892
21 And all the c of the plain, and all the H5892
23 families, the c and the villages thereof. H5892
25 And their coast was Jazer, and all the c H5892
28 their families, the c, and their villages. H5892
Jos 13:30 Jair, which *are* in Bashan, threescore c: H5892
31 and Edrei, c of the kingdom of Og H5892
14: 4 in the land, save c to dwell *in*, with H5892
12 there, and *that* the c *were* great *and* H5892
15: 9 went out to the c of mount Ephron; and H5892
21 And the uttermost c of the tribe of the H5892
32 Rimmon: all the c *are* twenty and nine, H5892
36 fourteen c with their villages: H5892
41 sixteen c with their villages: H5892
44 Mareshah; nine c with their villages: H5892
51 and Giloh; eleven c with their villages: H5892
54 and Zior; nine c with their villages: H5892
57 Cain, Gibeah, and Timnah; ten c with H5892
59 and Eltekon; six c with their villages: H5892
60 and Rabbah; two c with their villages: H5892
62 and En-gedi; six c with their villages. H5892
16: 9 And the separate c for the children of H5892
9 Manasseh, all the c with their villages. H5892
17: 9 of the river: these c of Ephraim *are* H5892
9 *are* among the c of Manasseh: the coast H5892
12 *of* those c; but the Canaanites H5892
18: 9 described it by c into seven parts in a H5892
21 Now the c of the tribe of the children of H5892
24 and Gaba; twelve c with their villages: H5892
28 Kirjath; fourteen c with their villages. H5892
19: 6 Sharuhen; thirteen c and their villages: H5892
7 and Ashan; four c and their villages: H5892
8 round about these c to Baalath-beer, H5892
15 twelve c with their villages. H5892
16 families, these c with their villages. H5892
22 at Jordan: sixteen c with their villages. H5892
23 their families, the c and their villages. H5892
30 twenty and two c with their villages. H5892
31 families, these c with their villages. H5892
35 And the fenced c *are* Ziddim, Zer, and H5892
38 nineteen c with their villages. H5892
39 their families, the c and their villages. H5892
48 families, these c with their villages. H5892
20: 2 out for you c of refuge, whereof I H5892
4 unto one of those c shall stand at the H5892
9 These were the c appointed for all the H5892
21: 2 Moses to give us c to dwell in, with the H5892
3 of the LORD, these c and their suburbs. H5892
4 out of the tribe of Benjamin, thirteen c. H5892
5 out of the half tribe of Manasseh, ten c. H5892
6 tribe of Manasseh in Bashan, thirteen c. H5892
7 out of the tribe of Zebulun, twelve c. H5892
8 the Levites these c with their suburbs, H5892
9 c which are *here* mentioned by name, H5892
16 suburbs; nine c out of those two tribes. H5892
18 and Almon with her suburbs; four c. H5892
19 All the c of the children of Aaron, the H5892
19 *were* thirteen c with their suburbs. H5892
20 even they had the c of their lot out of H5892
22 Beth-horon with her suburbs; four c. H5892
24 Gath-rimmon with her suburbs; four c. H5892
25 Gath-rimmon with her suburbs; two c. H5892
26 All the c *were* ten with their suburbs for H5892
27 Beesh-terah with her suburbs; two c. H5892
29 En-gannim with her suburbs; four c. H5892
31 and Rehob with her suburbs; four c. H5892
32 and Kartan with her suburbs; three c. H5892
33 All the c of the Gershonites according H5892
33 *were* thirteen c with their suburbs. H5892
35 Nahalal with her suburbs; four c. H5892
37 and Mephaath with her suburbs; four c. H5892
39 Jazer with her suburbs; four c in all. H5892
40 So all the c for the children of Merari H5892
40 of the Levites, were *by* their lot twelve c. H5892
41 All the c of the Levites within the H5892
41 forty and eight c with their suburbs. H5892
42 These c were every one with their H5892
42 round about them: thus *were* all these c. H5892
24:13 not labour, and c which ye built not, H5892
Jdg 10: 4 and they had thirty c, which are called H5892
11:26 and in all the c that *be* along by the H5892
33 *even* twenty c, and unto the plain of H5892
12: 7 was buried in *one of* the c of Gilead. H5892
20:14 together out of the c unto Gibeah, to go H5892
15 that time out of the c twenty and six H5892
42 c they destroyed in the midst of them. H5892
48 set on fire all the c that they came to. H5892
21:23 and repaired the c, and dwelt in them. H5892
1Sa 6:18 number of all the c of the Philistines H5892
18 lords, *both* of fenced c, and of country H5892
7:14 And the c which the Philistines had H5892
18: 6 came out of all c of Israel, singing and H5892
30:29 *them* which *were* in the c of the H5892
29 which *were* in the c of the Kenites, H5892
1Sa 31: 7 they forsook the c, and fled; and the H5892
2Sa 2: 1 up into any of the c of Judah? And the H5892
3 and they dwelt in the c of Hebron. H5892
8: 8 And from Betah, and from Berothai, c H5892
10:12 and for the c of our God: and the H5892
12:31 did he unto all the c of the children of H5892
20: 6 lest he get him fenced c, and escape us. H5892
24: 7 and to all the c of the Hivites, and of H5892
1Ki 4:13 great c with walls and brasen bars: H5892
8:37 them in the land of their c; whatsoever H8179
9:11 Hiram twenty c in the land of Galilee. H5892
12 Tyre to see the c which Solomon had H5892
13 And he said, What c *are* these which H5892
19 And all the c of store that Solomon H5892
19 Solomon had, and c for his chariots, H5892
19 his chariots, and c for his horsemen, H5892
10:26 he bestowed in the c for chariots, and H5892
12:17 Israel which dwelt in the c of Judah, H5892
13:32 c of Samaria, shall surely come to pass. H5892
15:20 he had against the c of Israel, and H5892
23 he did, and the c which he built, *are* H5892
20:34 And *Ben-hadad* said unto him, The c, H5892
22:39 he made, and all the c that he built, *are* H5892
2Ki 3:25 And they beat down the c, and on every H5892
13:25 son of Hazael the c, which he had taken H5892
25 beat him, and recovered the c of Israel. H5892
17: 6 of Gozan, and in the c of the Medes. H5892
9 places in all their c, from the tower of H5892
24 and placed *them* in the c of Samaria H5892
24 Samaria, and dwelt in the c thereof. H5892
26 and placed in the c of Samaria, know H5892
29 nation in their c wherein they dwelt. H5892
18:11 of Gozan, and in the c of the Medes: H5892
13 the fenced c of Judah, and took them. H5892
19:25 lay waste fenced c *into* ruinous heaps. H5892
23: 5 high places in the c of Judah, and in the H5892
8 the priests out of the c of Judah, and H5892
19 that *were* in the c of Samaria, which H5892
1Ch 2:22 and twenty c in the land of Gilead. H5892
23 *even* threescore c. All these *belonged to* H5892
4:31 *were* their c unto the reign of David. H5892
32 and Tochen, and Ashan, five c: H5892
33 about the same c, unto Baal. These H5892
6:57 they gave the c of Judah, *namely,* H5892
60 suburbs. All their c throughout their H5892
60 their families *were* thirteen c. H5892
61 of that tribe, *were* c *given* out of the half
61 the half *tribe* of Manasseh, by lot, ten c. H5892
62 tribe of Manasseh in Bashan, thirteen c. H5892
63 out of the tribe of Zebulun, twelve c. H5892
64 the Levites *these* c with their suburbs. H5892
65 c, which are called by *their* names. H5892
66 of Kohath had c of their coasts out of H5892
67 And they gave unto them, *of* the c of H5892
9: 2 in their c *were*, the Israelites, H5892
10: 7 they forsook their c, and fled: and the H5892
13: 2 *which are* in their c *and* suburbs, that H5892
18: 8 and from Chun, c of Hadarezer, H5892
19: 7 from their c, and came to battle. H5892
13 and for the c of our God: and let the H5892
20: 3 David with all the c of the children of H5892
27:25 in the fields, in the c, and in the villages, H5892
2Ch 1:14 c, and with the king at Jerusalem. H5892
6:28 them in the c of their land; whatsoever H8179
8: 2 That the c which Huram had restored H5892
4 the store c, which he built in Hamath. H5892
5 fenced c, with walls, gates, and bars; H5892
6 And Baalath, and all the store c that H5892
6 and all the chariot c, and the cities of H5892
6 cities, and the c of the horsemen, and H5892
9:25 c, and with the king at Jerusalem. H5892
10:17 that dwelt in the c of Judah, Rehoboam H5892
11: 5 and built c for defence in Judah. H5892
10 *are* in Judah and in Benjamin fenced c. H5892
12: 4 And he took the fenced c which H5892
13:19 and took c from him, Beth-el with H5892
14: 5 Also he took away out of all the c of H5892
6 And he built fenced c in Judah: for the H5892
7 Let us build these c, and make about H5892
14 And they smote all the c round about H5892
14 they spoiled all the c; for there was H5892
15: 8 and out of the c which he had taken H5892
16: 4 armies against the c of Israel; and they H5892
4 and all the store c of Naphtali. H5892
17: 2 And he placed forces in all the fenced c H5892
2 Judah, and in the c of Ephraim, which H5892
7 to Michaiah, to teach in the c of Judah. H5892
9 the c of Judah, and taught the people. H5892
12 he built in Judah castles, and c of store. H5892

2Ch 17:13 And he had much business in the c of H5892
19 in the fenced c throughout all Judah. H5892
19: 5 all the fenced c of Judah, city by city, H5892
10 that dwell in their c, between blood and H5892
20: 4 c of Judah they came to seek the LORD. H5892
21: 3 things, with fenced c in Judah: but the H5892
23: 2 out of all the c of Judah, and the chief H5892
24: 5 Go out unto the c of Judah, and gather H5892
25:13 fell upon the c of Judah, from Samaria H5892
26: 6 Ashdod, and built c about Ashdod, and H5892
27: 4 Moreover he built c in the mountains H5892
28:18 The Philistines also had invaded the c H5892
31: 1 went out to the c of Judah, and brake H5892
1 man to his possession, into their own c. H5892
6 that dwelt in the c of Judah, they also H5892
15 Shecaniah, in the c of the priests, in H5892
19 suburbs of their c, in every several city, H5892
32: 1 c, and thought to win them for himself. H5892
29 Moreover he provided him c, and H5892
33:14 of war in all the fenced c of Judah. H5892
34: 6 And *so did he* in the c of Manasseh, H5892
Ezr 2:70 in their c, and all Israel in their cities. H5892
70 in their cities, and all Israel in their c. H5892
3: 1 Israel *were* in the c, the people gathered H5892
4:10 and set in the c of Samaria, and the H7149
10:14 wives in our c come at appointed H5892
Neh 7:73 dwelt in their c; and when the seventh H5892
73 the children of Israel *were* in their c. H5892
8:15 in all their c, and in Jerusalem, saying, H5892
9:25 And they took strong c, and a fat land, H5892
10:37 have the tithes in all the c of our tillage. H5892
11: 1 city, and nine parts *to dwell* in *other* c. H5892
3 but in the c of Judah dwelt every H5892
3 in their c, *to wit*, Israel, the priests, H5892
20 *were* in all the c of Judah, every one H5892
12:44 of the fields of the c the portions of the H5892
Est 9: 2 together in their c throughout all the H5892
Job 15:28 And he dwelleth in desolate c, *and* in H5892
Ps 9: 6 c; their memorial is perished with them. H5892
69:35 and will build the c of Judah: that they H5892
Isa 1: 7 Your country *is* desolate, your c *are* H5892
6:11 Until the c be wasted without H5892
14:17 and destroyed the c thereof; *that* H5892
21 nor fill the face of the world with c. H5892
17: 2 The c of Aroer *are* forsaken: they shall H5892
9 In that day shall his strong c be as a H5892
19:18 In that day shall five c in the land of H5892
33: 8 despised the c, he regardeth no man. H5892
36: 1 defenced c of Judah, and took them. H5892
37:26 waste defenced c *into* ruinous heaps. H5892
40: 9 unto the c of Judah, Behold your God! H5892
42:11 Let the wilderness and the c thereof lift H5892
44:26 and to the c of Judah, Ye shall be H5892
54: 3 make the desolate c to be inhabited. H5892
61: 4 c, the desolations of many generations. H5892
64:10 Thy holy c are a wilderness, Zion is a H5892
Jer 1:15 about, and against all the c of Judah. H5892
2:15 his c are burned without inhabitant. H5892
28 number of thy c are thy gods, O Judah. H5892
4: 5 and let us go into the defenced c. H5892
7 desolate; *and* thy c shall be laid waste, H5892
16 out their voice against the c of Judah. H5892
26 and all the c thereof were broken H5892
5: 6 watch over their c: every one that goeth H5892
17 thy fenced c, wherein thou trustedst, H5892
7:17 Seest thou not what they do in the c of H5892
34 Then will I cause to cease from the c of H5892
8:14 into the defenced c, and let us be silent H5892
9:11 and I will make the c of Judah desolate, H5892
10:22 to make the c of Judah desolate, *and* H5892
11: 6 all these words in the c of Judah, and in H5892
12 Then shall the c of Judah and H5892
13 For *according to* the number of thy c H5892
13:19 The c of the south shall be shut up, and H5892
17:26 And they shall come from the c of H5892
20:16 And let that man be as the c which the H5892
22: 6 *and* c *which* are not inhabited. H5892
25:18 *To wit*, Jerusalem, and the c of Judah, H5892
26: 2 speak unto all the c of Judah, which H5892
31:21 of Israel, turn again to these thy c. H5892
23 Judah and in the c thereof, when I shall H5892
24 itself, and in all the c thereof together, H5892
32:44 and in the c of Judah, and in the H5892
44 Judah, and in the c of the mountains, H5892
44 and in the c of the valley, and in H5892
44 valley, and in the c of the south: for I H5892
33:10 beast, *even* in the c of Judah, and in the H5892
12 and in all the c thereof, shall be an H5892
13 In the c of the mountains, in the cities H5892
Jer 33:13 In the cities of the mountains, in the c H5892
13 vale, and in the c of the south, and in H5892
13 and in the c of Judah, shall the flocks H5892
34: 1 and against all the c thereof, saying, H5892
7 and against all the c of Judah that were H5892
7 c remained of the cities of Judah. H5892
7 cities remained of the c of Judah. H5892
22 I will make the c of Judah a desolation H5892
36: 6 of all Judah that come out of their c. H5892
9 from the c of Judah unto Jerusalem. H5892
40: 5 governor over the c of Judah, and dwell H5892
10 and dwell in your c that ye have taken. H5892
44: 2 and upon all the c of Judah; and, H5892
6 was kindled in the c of Judah and in H5892
17 our princes, in the c of Judah, and in H5892
21 The incense that ye burned in the c of H5892
48: 9 and get away: for the c thereof shall be H5892
15 gone up *out of* her c, and his chosen H5892
24 the c of the land of Moab, far or near. H5892
28 O ye that dwell in Moab, leave the c, H5892
49: 1 Gad, and his people dwell in his c? H5892
13 the c thereof shall be perpetual wastes. H5892
18 and the neighbour *c* thereof, saith the
50:32 kindle a fire in his c, and it shall devour H5892
40 and the neighbour *c* thereof, saith the
51:43 Her c are a desolation, a dry land, and H5892
Lam 5:11 Zion, *and* the maids in the c of Judah. H5892
Ezk 6: 6 In all your dwellingplaces the c shall be H5892
12:20 And the c that are inhabited shall be H5892
19: 7 he laid waste their c; and the land was H5892
25: 9 side of Moab from the c, from his cities H5892
9 the cities, from his c *which are* on his H5892
26:19 city, like the c that are not inhabited; H5892
29:12 desolate, and her c among the cities H5892
12 cities among the c *that are* laid waste H5892
30: 7 *are* desolate, and her c shall be in the H5892
7 be in the midst of the c *that are* wasted. H5892
17 and these c shall go into captivity.
35: 4 I will lay thy c waste, and thou shalt be H5892
9 and thy c shall not return: and H5892
36: 4 wastes, and to the c that are forsaken, H5892
10 all of it: and the c shall be inhabited, H5892
33 the c, and the wastes shall be builded. H5892
35 and ruined c *are become* fenced, H5892
38 so shall the waste c be filled with flocks H5892
39: 9 And they that dwell in the c of Israel H5892
Dan 11:15 the most fenced c: and the arms of the H5892
Hos 8:14 multiplied fenced c: but I will send a H5892
14 a fire upon his c, and it shall devour H5892
11: 6 And the sword shall abide on his c, and H5892
13:10 save thee in all thy c? and thy judges of H5892
Am 4: 6 of teeth in all your c, and want of bread H5892
8 So two *or* three c wandered unto one H5892
9:14 build the waste c, and inhabit *them*; H5892
Oba 20 shall possess the c of the south. H5892
Mic 5:11 And I will cut off the c of thy land, and H5892
14 the midst of thee: so will I destroy thy c. H5892
7:12 and *from* the fortified c, and from the H5892
Zep 1:16 fenced c, and against the high towers. H5892
3: 6 passeth by: their c are destroyed, so H5892
Zec 1:12 and on the c of Judah, against which H5892
17 of hosts; My c through prosperity H5892
7: 7 and the c thereof round about H5892
8:20 people, and the inhabitants of many c: H5892
Mt 9:35 And Jesus went about all the c and *G4172*
10:23 c of Israel, till the Son of man be come. *G4172*
11: 1 thence to teach and to preach in their c. *G4172*
20 Then began he to upbraid the c *G4172*
14:13 they followed him on foot out of the c. *G4172*
Mk 6:33 thither out of all c, and outwent them, *G4172*
56 into villages, or c, or country, they laid *G4172*
Lk 4:43 to other c also: for therefore am I sent. *G4172*
13:22 And he went through the c and *G4172*
19:17 little, have thou authority over ten c. *G4172*
19 likewise to him, Be thou also over five c. *G4172*
Act 5:16 *out of* the c round about unto *G4172*
8:40 in all the c, till he came to Caesarea. *G4172*
14: 6 Lystra and Derbe, c of Lycaonia, and *G4172*
16: 4 And as they went through the c, they *G4172*
26:11 I persecuted *them* even unto strange c. *G4172*
2Pt 2: 6 And turning the c of Sodom and *G4172*
Jude 7 and the c about them in like manner, *G4172*
Rev 16:19 parts, and the c of the nations fell: and *G4172*

CITIZEN

Lk 15:15 And he went and joined himself to a c *G4177*
Act 21:39 *a city* in Cilicia, a c of no mean city: *G4177*

CITIZENS

Lk 19:14 But his c hated him, and sent a *G4177*

CITY

Gen 4:17 and he builded a c, and called the name H5892
17 the c, after the name of his son, Enoch. H5892
10:11 and the c Rehoboth, and Calah, H5892
12 and Calah: the same *is* a great c. H5892
11: 4 And they said, Go to, let us build us a c H5892
5 And the LORD came down to see the c H5892
8 the earth: and they left off to build the c. H5892
18:24 within the c: wilt thou also destroy H5892
26 within the c, then I will spare all H5892
28 destroy all the c for *lack of* five? And H5892
19: 4 down, the men of the c, *even* the men of H5892
12 in the c, bring *them* out of this place: H5892
14 will destroy this c. But he seemed as one H5892
15 be consumed in the iniquity of the c. H5892
16 him forth, and set him without the c. H5892
20 Behold now, this c *is* near to flee unto, H5892
21 this c, for the which thou hast spoken. H5892
22 the name of the c was called Zoar. H5892
23:10 that went in at the gate of his c, saying, H5892
18 all that went in at the gate of his c. H5892
24:10 to Mesopotamia, unto the c of Nahor. H5892
11 down without the c by a well of water H5892
13 men of the c come out to draw water: H5892
26:33 of the c *is* Beer-sheba unto this day. H5892
28:19 of that c *was called* Luz at the first. H5892
33:18 And Jacob came to Shalem, a c of H5892
18 and pitched his tent before the c. H5892
34:20 the gate of their c, and communed with H5892
20 with the men of their c, saying, H5892
24 of the gate of his c; and every male was H5892
24 all that went out of the gate of his c. H5892
25 the c boldly, and slew all the males. H5892
27 c, because they had defiled their sister. H5892
28 in the c, and that which *was* in the field, H5892
35:27 Mamre, unto the c of Arbah, which *is* H7151
36:32 and the name of his c *was* Dinhabah. H5892
35 stead: and the name of his c *was* Avith. H5892
39 and the name of his c *was* Pau; and his H5892
41:48 about every c, laid he up in the same. H5892
44: 4 *And* when they were gone out of the c, H5892
13 man his ass, and returned to the c. H5892
Ex 9:29 I am gone out of the c, I will spread H5892
33 And Moses went out of the c from H5892
Lev 14:40 into an unclean place without the c: H5892
41 off without the c into an unclean place: H5892
45 forth out of the c into an unclean place. H5892
53 bird out of the c into the open fields, H5892
25:29 house in a walled c, then he may H5892
30 *is* in the walled c shall be established H5892
33 was sold, and the c of his possession, H5892
Nu 20:16 a c in the uttermost of thy border: H5892
21:26 For Heshbon *was* the c of Sihon the H5892
27 let the c of Sihon be built and prepared: H5892
28 a flame from the c of Sihon: it hath H7151
22:36 meet him unto a c of Moab, which *is* in H5892
24:19 destroy him that remaineth of the c. H5892
35: 4 from the wall of the c and outward a H5892
5 from without the c on the east side two H5892
5 cubits; and the c *shall be* in the midst: H5892
25 shall restore him to the c of his refuge, H5892
26 the c of his refuge, whither he was fled; H5892
27 the borders of the c of his refuge, and H5892
28 remained in the c of his refuge until the H5892
32 that is fled to the c of his refuge, that he H5892
Dt 2:34 ones, of every c, we left none to remain: H5892
36 and *from* the c that *is* by the river, H5892
36 there was not one c too strong for us: H7151
3: 4 there was not a c which we took not H7151
6 men, women, and children, of every c. H5892
13:13 of their c, saying, Let us go and H5892
15 of that c with the edge of the H5892
16 burn with fire the c, and all the spoil H5892
19:12 Then the elders of his c shall send and H5892
20:10 When thou comest nigh unto a c to H5892
14 and all that is in the c, *even* all the spoil H5892
19 When thou shalt besiege a c a long H5892
20 against the c that maketh war with H5892
21: 3 And it shall be, *that* the c *which is* next H5892
3 the elders of that c shall take an heifer, H5892
4 And the elders of that c shall bring H5892
6 And all the elders of that c, *that are* next H5892
19 of his c, and unto the gate of his place; H5892
20 unto the elders of his c, This our son *is* H5892
21 And all the men of his c shall stone him H5892
22:15 unto the elders of the c in the gate: H5892

Dt 22:17 the cloth before the elders of the c. H5892
18 And the elders of that c shall take that H5892
21 the men of her c shall stone her with H5892
23 a man find her in the c, and lie with her; H5892
24 the gate of that c, and ye shall stone H5892
24 cried not, *being* in the c; and the man, H5892
25: 8 Then the elders of his c shall call him, H5892
28: 3 Blessed *shalt* thou *be* in the c, and H5892
16 Cursed *shalt* thou *be* in the c, and H5892
34: 3 Jericho, the c of palm trees, unto Zoar. H5892
Jos 3:16 heap very far from the c Adam, that *is* H5892
6: 3 And ye shall compass the c, all *ye* men H5892
3 the c once. Thus shalt thou do six days. H5892
4 ye shall compass the c seven times, and H5892
5 and the wall of the c shall fall down H5892
7 and compass the c, and let him that is H5892
11 compassed the c, going about *it* once: H5892
14 compassed the c once, and returned H5892
15 and compassed the c after the same H5892
15 day they compassed the c seven times. H5892
16 for the LORD hath given you the c. H5892
17 And the c shall be accursed, *even* it, H5892
20 went up into the c, every man straight H5892
20 straight before him, and they took the c. H5892
21 all that *was* in the c, both man and H5892
24 And they burnt the c with fire, and all H5892
26 and buildeth this c Jericho: he shall lay H5892
8: 1 and his people, and his c, and his land: H5892
2 lay thee an ambush for the c behind it. H5892
4 lie in wait against the c, *even* behind the H5892
4 *even* behind the c: go not very far from H5892
4 very far from the c, but be ye all ready: H5892
5 approach unto the c: and it shall come H5892
6 them from the c; for they will say, They H5892
7 seize upon the c: for the LORD your God H5892
8 ye have taken the c, *that* ye shall set the H5892
8 ye shall set the c on fire: according to H5892
11 came before the c, and pitched on the H5892
12 Beth-el and Ai, on the west side of the c. H5892
13 on the north of the c, and their liers in H5892
13 on the west of the c, Joshua went that H5892
14 the men of the c went out against Israel H5892
14 in ambush against him behind the c. H5892
16 and were drawn away from the c. H5892
17 the c open, and pursued after Israel. H5892
18 that *he had* in his hand toward the c. H5892
19 they entered into the c, and took it, and H5892
19 took it, and hasted and set the c on fire. H5892
20 the smoke of the c ascended up to H5892
21 had taken the c, and that the smoke H5892
21 the smoke of the c ascended, then they H5892
22 And the other issued out of the c H5892
27 Only the cattle and the spoil of that c H5892
29 of the gate of the c, and raise thereon a H5892
10: 2 *was* a great c, as one of the royal cities, H5892
11:19 There was not a c that made peace H5892
13: 9 Arnon, and the c that *is* in the midst H5892
16 Arnon, and the c that *is* in the midst H5892
15:13 Joshua, *even* the c of Arba the father of H7151
13 the father of Anak, which *c is* Hebron.
62 And Nibshan, and the c of Salt, and H5892
18:14 *is* Kirjath-jearim, a c of the children of H5892
19:29 and to the strong c Tyre; and the coast H5892
50 they gave him the c which he asked, H5892
50 and he built the c, and dwelt therein. H5892
20: 4 of the gate of the c, and shall declare his H5892
4 the elders of that c, they shall take him H5892
4 take him into the c unto them, and give H5892
6 And he shall dwell in that c, until he H5892
6 come unto his own c, and unto his own H5892
6 house, unto the c from whence he fled. H5892
21:11 And they gave them the c of Arba the H7151
11 of Anak, which *c is* Hebron, in the hill
12 But the fields of the c, and the villages H5892
13 her suburbs, *to be* a c of refuge for the H5892
21 Ephraim, *to be* a c of refuge for the H5892
27 her suburbs, *to be* a c of refuge for the H5892
32 her suburbs, *to be* a c of refuge for the H5892
38 her suburbs, *to be* a c of refuge for the H5892
Jdg 1: 8 edge of the sword, and set the c on fire. H5892
16 went up out of the c of palm trees with H5892
17 the name of the c was called Hormah. H5892
23 the name of the c before *was* Luz.) H5892
24 forth out of the c, and they said unto H5892
24 into the c, and we will shew thee mercy. H5892
25 entrance into the c, they smote the city H5892
25 they smote the c with the edge of the H5892
26 and built a c, and called the name H5892
3:13 and possessed the c of palm trees. H5892
Jdg 6:27 the men of the c, that he could not do H5892
28 And when the men of the c arose early H5892
30 Then the men of the c said unto Joash, H5892
8:16 And he took the elders of the c, and H5892
17 of Penuel, and slew the men of the c. H5892
27 and put it in his c, *even* in Ophrah: and H5892
9:30 And when Zebul the ruler of the c H5892
31 behold, they fortify the c against thee. H5892
33 and set upon the c: and, behold, *when* H5892
35 of the gate of the c: and Abimelech rose H5892
43 come forth out of the c; and he rose up H5892
44 of the gate of the c: and the two *other* H5892
45 And Abimelech fought against the c all H5892
45 and he took the c, and slew the people H5892
45 beat down the c, and sowed it with salt. H5892
51 tower within the c, and thither fled all H5892
51 and all they of the c, and shut *it* to H5892
14:18 And the men of the c said unto him on H5892
16: 2 in the gate of the c, and were quiet all H5892
3 of the gate of the c, and the two posts, H5892
17: 8 And the man departed out of the c H5892
18:27 of the sword, and burnt the c with fire. H5892
28 And they built a c, and dwelt therein. H5892
29 And they called the name of the c Dan, H5892
29 the name of the c *was* Laish at the first. H5892
19:11 this c of the Jebusites, and lodge in it. H5892
12 hither into the c of a stranger, that *is* H5892
15 in a street of the c: for *there was* no man H5892
17 in the street of the c: and the old man H5892
22 the men of the c, certain sons of Belial, H5892
20:11 against the c, knit together as one man. H5892
31 away from the c; and they began to H5892
32 them from the c unto the highways. H5892
37 all the c with the edge of the sword. H5892
38 flame with smoke rise up out of the c. H5892
40 to arise up out of the c with a pillar of H5892
40 flame of the c ascended up to heaven. H5892
48 the men of *every* c, as the beast, and all H5892
Ru 1:19 that all the c was moved about them, H5892
2:18 And she took *it* up, and went into the c: H5892
3:11 for all the c of my people doth know H8179
15 laid *it* on her: and she went into the c. H5892
4: 2 of the elders of the c, and said, Sit ye H5892
1Sa 1: 3 And this man went up out of his c H5892
4:13 the c, and told *it*, all the city cried out. H5892
13 the city, and told *it*, all the c cried out. H5892
5: 9 was against the c with a very great H5892
9 the men of the c, both small and great, H5892
11 throughout all the c; the hand of God H5892
12 and the cry of the c went up to heaven. H5892
8:22 of Israel, Go ye every man unto his c. H5892
9: 6 *there is* in this c a man of God, and *he* H5892
10 unto the c where the man of God *was*. H5892
11 *And* as they went up the hill to the c, H5892
12 he came to day to the c; for *there is* a H5892
13 As soon as ye be come into the c, ye H5892
14 And they went up into the c: *and* when H5892
14 come into the c, behold, Samuel came H5892
25 the high place into the c, *Samuel* H5892
27 to the end of the c, Samuel said to Saul, H5892
10: 5 thither to the c, that thou shalt meet H5892
15: 5 And Saul came to a c of Amalek, and H5892
20: 6 to Beth-lehem his c: for *there is* a yearly H5892
29 a sacrifice in the c; and my brother, he H5892
40 said unto him, Go, carry *them* to the c. H5892
42 departed: and Jonathan went into the c. H5892
22:19 And Nob, the c of the priests, smote he H5892
23:10 to Keilah, to destroy the c for my sake. H5892
27: 5 servant dwell in the royal c with thee? H5892
28: 3 even in his own c. And Saul had put H5892
30: 3 So David and his men came to the c, H5892
2Sa 5: 7 hold of Zion: the same *is* the c of David. H5892
9 and called it the c of David. And David H5892
6:10 unto him into the c of David: but David H5892
12 into the c of David with gladness. H5892
16 came into the c of David, Michal Saul's H5892
10: 3 c, and to spy it out, and to overthrow it? H5892
14 and entered into the c. So Joab returned H5892
11:16 Joab observed the c, that he assigned H5892
17 And the men of the c went out, and H5892
20 ye so nigh unto the c when ye did fight? H5892
25 strong against the c, and overthrow it: H5892
12: 1 one c; the one rich, and the other poor. H5892
26 of Ammon, and took the royal c. H5892
27 and have taken the c of waters. H5892
28 against the c, and take it: lest I take H5892
28 the c, and it be called after my name. H5892
30 the spoil of the c in great abundance. H5892
15: 2 and said, Of what c *art* thou? And he H5892
2Sa 15:12 from his c, *even* from Giloh, while H5892
14 smite the c with the edge of the sword. H5892
24 people had done passing out of the c. H5892
25 of God into the c: if I shall find favour H5892
27 return into the c in peace, and your two H5892
34 But if thou return to the c, and say unto H5892
37 c, and Absalom came into Jerusalem. H5892
17:13 Moreover, if he be gotten into a c, then H5892
13 bring ropes to that c, and we will draw H5892
17 to come into the c: and a wench went H5892
23 home to his house, to his c, and put his H5892
18: 3 better that thou succour us out of the c. H5892
19: 3 that day into the c, as people being H5892
37 die in mine own c, *and be buried* by the H5892
20:15 a bank against the c, and it stood in the H5892
16 Then cried a wise woman out of the c, H5892
19 to destroy a c and a mother in Israel: H5892
21 depart from the c. And the woman said H5892
22 they retired from the c, every man to his H5892
24: 5 right side of the c that *lieth* in the midst H5892
1Ki 1:41 *this* noise of the c being in an uproar? H7151
45 so that the c rang again. This *is* the H7151
2:10 and was buried in the c of David. H5892
3: 1 her into the c of David, until he had H5892
8: 1 out of the c of David, which *is* Zion. H5892
16 Egypt, I chose no c out of all the tribes H5892
44 the LORD toward the c which thou hast H5892
48 their fathers, the c which thou hast H5892
9:16 that dwelt in the c, and given it *for* a H5892
24 came up out of the c of David unto her H5892
11:27 breaches of the c of David his father. H5892
32 sake, the c which I have chosen H5892
36 in Jerusalem, the c which I have chosen H5892
43 was buried in the c of David his father: H5892
13:25 *it* in the c where the old prophet dwelt. H5892
29 to the c, to mourn and to bury him. H5892
14:11 Him that dieth of Jeroboam in the c H5892
12 feet enter into the c, the child shall die. H5892
21 in Jerusalem, the c which the LORD did H5892
31 his fathers in the c of David. And his H5892
15: 8 buried him in the c of David: and Asa H5892
24 his fathers in the c of David his father: H5892
16: 4 Him that dieth of Baasha in the c shall H5892
18 Zimri saw that the c was taken, that he H5892
24 the name of the c which he built, after H5892
17:10 to the gate of the c, behold, the widow H5892
20: 2 of Israel into the c, and said unto him, H5892
12 set *themselves in array* against the c. H5892
19 c, and the army which followed them. H5892
30 But the rest fled to Aphek, into the c; H5892
30 came into the c, into an inner chamber. H5892
21: 8 *were* in his c, dwelling with Naboth. H5892
11 And the men of his c, *even* the elders H5892
11 inhabitants in his c, did as Jezebel had H5892
13 forth out of the c, and stoned him with H5892
24 Him that dieth of Ahab in the c the H5892
22:26 of the c, and to Joash the king's son; H5892
36 c, and every man to his own country. H5892
50 his fathers in the c of David his father: H5892
2Ki 2:19 And the men of the c said unto Elisha, H5892
19 the situation of this c *is* pleasant, as my H5892
23 children out of the c, and mocked him, H5892
3:19 And ye shall smite every fenced c, and H5892
19 and every choice c, and shall fell every H5892
6:14 by night, and compassed the c about. H5892
15 compassed the c both with horses and H5892
19 neither *is* this the c: follow me, and I H5892
7: 4 If we say, We will enter into the c, then H5892
4 the famine *is* in the c, and we shall die H5892
10 the porter of the c: and they told them, H5892
12 come out of the c, we shall catch them H5892
12 catch them alive, and get into the c. H5892
13 are left in the c, (behold, they *are* as
8:24 with his fathers in the c of David: and H5892
9:15 out of the c to go to tell *it* in Jezreel. H5892
28 with his fathers in the c of David. H5892
10: 2 horses, a fenced c also, and armour; H5892
5 that *was* over the c, the elders also, and H5892
6 men of the c, which brought them up. H5892
25 and went to the c of the house of Baal. H5892
11:20 rejoiced, and the c was in quiet: and H5892
12:21 with his fathers in the c of David: and H5892
14:20 with his fathers in the c of David. H5892
15: 7 with his fathers in the c of David: and H5892
38 his fathers in the c of David his father: H5892
16:20 with his fathers in the c of David: and H5892
17: 9 tower of the watchmen to the fenced c. H5892
18: 8 tower of the watchmen to the fenced c. H5892
30 us, and this c shall not be delivered H5892

2Ki 19:13 c of Sepharvaim, of Hena, and Ivah? H5892
32 shall not come into this c, nor shoot an H5892
33 not come into this c, saith the LORD. H5892
34 For I will defend this c, to save it, for H5892
20: 6 thee and this c out of the hand of the H5892
6 I will defend this c for mine own sake, H5892
20 water into the c, are they not written H5892
23: 8 the governor of the c, which were on a H5892
8 on a man's left hand at the gate of the c. H5892
17 And the men of the c told him, It is the H5892
27 will cast off this c Jerusalem which I H5892
24:10 Jerusalem, and the c was besieged. H5892
11 the c, and his servants did besiege it. H5892
25: 2 And the c was besieged unto the H5892
3 prevailed in the c, and there was no H5892
4 And the c was broken up, and all the H5892
4 were against the c round about:) and H5892
11 were left in the c, and the fugitives that H5892
19 And out of the c he took an officer that H5892
19 were found in the c, and the principal H5892
19 of the land that were found in the c: H5892
1Ch 1:43 and the name of his c was Dinhabah. H5892
46 stead: and the name of his c was Avith. H5892
50 and the name of his c was Pai; and his H5892
6:56 But the fields of the c, and the villages H5892
57 Hebron, the c of refuge, and Libnah
11: 5 castle of Zion, which is the c of David. H5892
7 therefore they called it the c of David. H5892
8 And he built the c round about, even H5892
8 and Joab repaired the rest of the c. H5892
13:13 to himself to the c of David, but carried H5892
15: 1 And David made him houses in the c of H5892
29 the LORD came to the c of David, that H5892
19: 9 the gate of the c: and the kings that H5892
15 the c. Then Joab came to Jerusalem. H5892
20: 2 also exceeding much spoil out of the c. H5892
2Ch 5: 2 out of the c of David, which is Zion. H5892
6: 5 Egypt I chose no c among all the tribes H5892
34 thee toward this c which thou hast H5892
38 and toward the c which thou hast H5892
8:11 Pharaoh out of the c of David unto the H5892
9:31 was buried in the c of David his father: H5892
11:12 And in every several c he put shields H5892
23 unto every fenced c: and he gave them H5892
12:13 in Jerusalem, the c which the LORD H5892
16 and was buried in the c of David: and H5892
14: 1 buried him in the c of David: and Asa H5892
15: 6 of nation, and c of city: for God did vex H5892
6 of nation, and city of c: for God did vex H5892
16:14 for himself in the c of David, and laid H5892
18:25 of the c, and to Joash the king's son; H5892
19: 5 all the fenced cities of Judah, c by city, H5892
5 all the fenced cities of Judah, city by c, H5892
21: 1 with his fathers in the c of David. And H5892
20 buried him in the c of David, but not in H5892
23:21 rejoiced: and the c was quiet, after that H5892
24:16 And they buried him in the c of David H5892
25 buried him in the c of David, but they H5892
25:28 him with his fathers in the c of Judah. H5892
27: 9 buried him in the c of David: and Ahaz H5892
28:15 to Jericho, the c of palm trees, to their H5892
25 And in every several c of Judah he H5892
27 buried him in the c, even in Jerusalem: H5892
29:20 the rulers of the c, and went up to the H5892
30:10 So the posts passed from c to city H5892
10 So the posts passed from city to c H5892
31:19 in every several c, the men that were H5892
32: 3 without the c: and they did help him. H5892
5 Millo in the c of David, and made H5892
6 street of the gate of the c, and spake H5892
18 them; that they might take the c. H5892
30 the west side of the c of David. And H5892
33:14 a wall without the c of David, on the H5892
15 Jerusalem, and cast them out of the c. H5892
34: 8 governor of the c, and Joah the son of H5892
Ezr 2: 1 and Judah, every one unto his c; H5892
4:12 and the bad c, and have set up the H7149
13 king, that, if this c be builded, and the H7149
15 know that this c is a rebellious city, H7149
15 city is a rebellious c, and hurtful unto H7149
15 for which cause was this c destroyed. H7149
16 We certify the king that, if this c be H7149
19 it is found that this c of old time hath H7149
21 and that this c be not builded, until H7149
10:14 the elders of every c, and the judges H5892
Neh 2: 3 be sad, when the c, the place of my H5892
5 unto Judah, unto the c of my fathers' H5892
8 for the wall of the c, and for the house H5892
3:15 that go down from the c of David. H5892

Neh 7: 4 Now the c was large and great: but the H5892
6 and to Judah, every one unto his c; H5892
11: 1 c, and nine parts to dwell in other cities. H5892
9 son of Senuah was second over the c. H5892
18 All the Levites in the holy c were two H5892
12:37 up by the stairs of the c of David, at the H5892
13:18 us, and upon this c? yet ye bring more H5892
Est 3:15 but the c Shushan was perplexed. H5892
4: 1 c, and cried with a loud and a bitter cry; H5892
6 the c, which was before the king's gate. H5892
6: 9 the street of the c, and proclaim before H5892
11 the street of the c, and proclaimed H5892
8:11 were in every c to gather themselves H5892
15 the c of Shushan rejoiced and was glad. H5892
17 And in every province, and in every c, H5892
9:28 and every c; and that these days H5892
Job 24:12 Men groan from out of the c, and the H5892
29: 7 c, when I prepared my seat in the street! H7176
39: 7 He scorneth the multitude of the c, H7151
Ps 31:21 his marvellous kindness in a strong c. H5892
46: 4 make glad the c of God, the holy place H5892
48: 1 to be praised in the c of our God, in the H5892
2 of the north, the c of the great King. H7151
8 we seen in the c of the LORD of hosts, H5892
8 of hosts, in the c of our God: God will H5892
55: 9 I have seen violence and strife in the c. H5892
59: 6 like a dog, and go round about the c. H5892
14 like a dog, and go round about the c. H5892
60: 9 Who will bring me into the strong c? H5892
72:16 c shall flourish like grass of the earth. H5892
87: 3 Glorious things are spoken of thee, O c H5892
101: 8 wicked doers from the c of the LORD. H5892
107: 4 way; they found no c to dwell in. H5892
7 that they might go to a c of habitation. H5892
36 they may prepare a c for habitation; H5892
108:10 Who will bring me into the strong c? H5892
122: 3 Jerusalem is builded as a c that is H5892
127: 1 c, the watchman waketh but in vain. H5892
Prv 1:21 in the c she uttereth her words, saying, H5892
8: 3 of the c, at the coming in at the doors. H7176
9: 3 crieth upon the highest places of the c, H7176
14 on a seat in the high places of the c, H7176
10:15 The rich man's wealth is his strong c: H7151
11:10 the righteous, the c rejoiceth: and when H7151
11 By the blessing of the upright the c is H7176
16:32 ruleth his spirit than he that taketh a c. H5892
18:11 The rich man's wealth is his strong c, H7151
19 be won than a strong c: and their H7151
21:22 A wise man scaleth the c of the mighty, H5892
25:28 his own spirit is like a c that is broken H5892
29: 8 Scornful men bring a c into a snare: H7151
Ecc 7:19 than ten mighty men which are in the c. H5892
8:10 forgotten in the c where they had so H5892
9:14 There was a little c, and few men within H5892
15 wisdom delivered the c; yet no man H5892
10:15 he knoweth not how to go to the c. H5892
Song 3: 2 I will rise now, and go about the c in H5892
3 The watchmen that go about the c H5892
5: 7 The watchmen that went about the c H5892
Isa 1: 8 a garden of cucumbers, as a besieged c. H5892
21 How is the faithful c become an harlot! H7151
26 The c of righteousness, the faithful city. H5892
26 The city of righteousness, the faithful c. H7151
14: 4 oppressor ceased! the golden c ceased! H4062
31 Howl, O gate; cry, O c; thou, whole H5892
17: 1 a c, and it shall be a ruinous heap. H5892
19: 2 his neighbour; c against city, and H5892
2 c, and kingdom against kingdom. H5892
18 shall be called, The c of destruction. H5892
22: 2 a tumultuous c, a joyous city: thy slain H5892
2 city, a joyous c: thy slain men are not H7151
9 Ye have seen also the breaches of the c H5892
23: 7 Is this your joyous c, whose antiquity is
8 Tyre, the crowning c, whose merchants
11 c, to destroy the strong holds thereof.
16 Take an harp, go about the c, thou H5892
24:10 The c of confusion is broken down: H7151
12 In the c is left desolation, and the gate H5892
25: 2 For thou hast made of a c an heap; of a H5892
2 heap; of a defenced c a ruin: a palace of H7151
2 to be no c; it shall never be built. H5892
3 c of the terrible nations shall fear thee. H7151
26: 1 We have a strong c; salvation will God H5892
5 on high; the lofty c, he layeth it low; he H7151
27:10 Yet the defenced c shall be desolate, H5892
29: 1 Woe to Ariel, to Ariel, the c where H7151
32:13 all the houses of joy in the joyous c: H7151
14 multitude of the c shall be left; the forts H5892
19 and the c shall be low in a low place. H5892

Isa 33:20 Look upon Zion, the c of our H7151
36:15 deliver us: this c shall not be delivered H5892
37:13 the c of Sepharvaim, Hena, and Ivah? H5892
33 shall not come into this c, nor shoot an H5892
34 not come into this c, saith the LORD. H5892
35 For I will defend this c to save it for H5892
38: 6 And I will deliver thee and this c out of H5892
6 king of Assyria: and I will defend this c. H5892
45:13 he shall build my c, and he shall let go H5892
48: 2 For they call themselves of the holy c, H5892
52: 1 the holy c: for henceforth there H5892
60:14 shall call thee, The c of the LORD, The H5892
62:12 be called, Sought out, A c not forsaken. H5892
66: 6 A voice of noise from the c, a voice from H5892
Jer 1:18 day a defenced c, and an iron pillar, H5892
3:14 take you one of a c, and two of a family, H5892
4:29 The whole c shall flee for the noise of H5892
29 the rocks: every c shall be forsaken, H5892
6: 6 this is the c to be visited; she is H5892
8:16 in it; the c, and those that dwell therein. H5892
14:18 if I enter into the c, then behold them H5892
15: 8 it suddenly, and terrors upon the c. H5892
17:24 the gates of this c on the sabbath day, H5892
25 the gates of this c kings and princes H5892
25 and this c shall remain for ever. H5892
19: 8 And I will make this c desolate, and an H5892
11 this people and this c, as one breaketh a H5892
12 and even make this c as Tophet: H5892
15 will bring upon this c and upon all her H5892
20: 5 strength of this c, and all the labours H5892
21: 4 assemble them into the midst of this c. H5892
6 the inhabitants of this c, both man and H5892
7 as are left in this c from the pestilence, H5892
9 He that abideth in this c shall die by H5892
10 For I have set my face against this c for H5892
22: 8 And many nations shall pass by this c, H5892
8 the LORD done thus unto this great c? H5892
23:39 you, and the c that I gave you and H5892
25:29 For, lo, I begin to bring evil on the c H5892
26: 6 c a curse to all the nations of the earth. H5892
9 like Shiloh, and this c shall be desolate H5892
11 this c, as ye have heard with your ears. H5892
12 this c all the words that ye have heard. H5892
15 and upon this c, and upon the H5892
20 against this c and against this land H5892
27:17 wherefore should this c be laid waste? H5892
19 of the vessels that remain in this c, H5892
29: 7 And seek the peace of the c whither I H5892
16 dwelleth in this c, and of your brethren H5892
30:18 and the c shall be builded upon H5892
31:38 LORD, that the c shall be built to the H5892
32: 3 I will give this c into the hand of the H5892
24 are come unto the c to take it; and the H5892
24 to take it; and the c is given into the H5892
25 witnesses; for the c is given into the H5892
28 I will give this c into the hand of the H5892
29 fight against this c, shall come and set H5892
29 and set fire on this c, and burn it with H5892
31 For this c hath been to me as a H5892
36 concerning this c, whereof ye say, It H5892
33: 4 the houses of this c, and concerning the H5892
5 I have hid my face from this c. H5892
34: 2 I will give this c into the hand of the H5892
22 to return to this c; and they shall fight H5892
37: 8 this c, and take it, and burn it with fire. H5892
10 in his tent, and burn this c with fire. H5892
21 all the bread in the c were spent. Thus H5892
38: 2 that remaineth in this c shall die by the H5892
3 Thus saith the LORD, This c shall H5892
4 remain in this c, and the hands of all H5892
9 is: for there is no more bread in the c. H5892
17 soul shall live, and this c shall not be H5892
18 then shall this c be given into the hand H5892
23 cause this c to be burned with fire. H5892
39: 2 day of the month, the c was broken up. H5892
4 forth out of the c by night, by the way H5892
9 remained in the c, and those that fell H5892
16 words upon this c for evil, and not for H5892
41: 7 the midst of the c, that Ishmael the son H5892
46: 8 the c and the inhabitants thereof. H5892
47: 2 all that is therein; the c, and them that H5892
48: 8 come upon every c, and no city shall H5892
8 every city, and no c shall escape: the H5892
49:25 How is the c of praise not left, the city H5892
25 How is the city of praise not left, the c H7151
51:31 Babylon that his c is taken at one end, H5892
52: 5 So the c was besieged unto the eleventh H5892
6 was sore in the c, so that there was no H5892
7 Then the c was broken up, and all the H5892

Jer 52: 7 forth out of the c by night by the way H5892
7 were by the c round about:) and they H5892
15 remained in the c, and those that fell H5892
25 He took also out of the c an eunuch, H5892
25 were found in the c; and the principal H5892
25 that were found in the midst of the c. H5892
Lam 1: 1 How doth the c sit solitary, that was H5892
19 up the ghost in the c, while they sought H5892
2:11 sucklings swoon in the streets of the c. H7151
12 the streets of the c, when their soul was H5892
15 saying, Is this the c that men call The H5892
3:51 because of all the daughters of my c. H5892
Ezk 4: 1 pourtray upon it the c, even Jerusalem: H5892
3 thee and the c: and set thy face against H5892
5: 2 in the midst of the c, when the days of H5892
7:15 and he that is in the c, famine and H5892
23 crimes, and the c is full of violence. H5892
9: 1 charge over the c to draw near, even H5892
4 the midst of the c, through the midst of H5892
5 him through the c, and smite: let not H5892
7 And they went forth, and slew in the c. H5892
9 of blood, and the c full of perverseness: H5892
10: 2 over the c. And he went in in my sight. H5892
11: 2 and give wicked counsel in this c: H5892
3 this c is the caldron, and we be the flesh.
6 Ye have multiplied your slain in this c, H5892
7 the flesh, and this c is the caldron: but I
11 This c shall not be your caldron, neither
23 the midst of the c, and stood upon the H5892
23 which is on the east side of the c. H5892
17: 4 of traffick; he set it in a c of merchants. H5892
21:19 choose it at the head of the way to the c. H5892
22: 2 judge the bloody c? yea, thou shalt shew H5892
3 Lord GOD, The c sheddeth blood in the H5892
24: 6 Woe to the bloody c, to the pot whose H5892
9 c! I will even make the pile for fire great. H5892
26:10 into a c wherein is made a breach. H5892
17 the renowned c, which wast strong in H5892
19 thee a desolate c, like the cities that are H5892
27:32 thee, saying, What c is like Tyrus, like
33:21 unto me, saying, The c is smitten. H5892
39:16 And also the name of the c shall be H5892
40: 1 year after that the c was smitten, in the H5892
2 was as the frame of a c on the south. H5892
43: 3 to destroy the c: and the visions were H5892
45: 6 the possession of the c five thousand H5892
7 possession of the c, before the oblation H5892
7 possession of the c, from the west side H5892
48:15 place for the c, for dwelling, and for H5892
15 and the c shall be in the midst thereof. H5892
17 And the suburbs of the c shall be H5892
18 be for food unto them that serve the c. H5892
19 And they that serve the c shall serve it H5892
20 foursquare, with the possession of the c. H5892
21 possession of the c, over against the five H5892
22 possession of the c, being in the midst H5892
30 And these are the goings out of the c on H5892
31 And the gates of the c shall be after the H5892
35 the name of the c from that day shall H5892
Dan 9:16 away from thy c Jerusalem, thy holy H5892
18 and the c which is called by thy H5892
19 O my God: for thy c and thy people are H5892
24 people and upon thy holy c, to finish the H5892
26 shall destroy the c and the sanctuary; H5892
Hos 6: 8 Gilead is a c of them that work H7151
11: 9 of thee: and I will not enter into the c. H5892
Joel 2: 9 They shall run to and fro in the c; they H5892
Am 3: 6 Shall a trumpet be blown in the c, and H5892
6 in a c, and the LORD hath not done it? H5892
4: 7 it to rain upon one c, and caused it not H5892
7 to rain upon another c: one piece was H5892
8 unto one c, to drink water; but H5892
5: 3 For thus saith the Lord GOD; The c that H5892
6: 8 deliver up the c with all that is therein. H5892
7:17 be an harlot in the c, and thy sons and H5892
Jna 1: 2 Arise, go to Nineveh, that great c, and H5892
3: 2 Arise, go unto Nineveh, that great c, H5892
3 great c of three days' journey. H5892
4 And Jonah began to enter into the c a H5892
4: 5 So Jonah went out of the c, and sat on H5892
5 the east side of the c, and there made H5892
5 might see what would become of the c. H5892
11 that great c, wherein are more than H5892
Mic 4:10 go forth out of the c, and thou shalt H7151
6: 9 The LORD'S voice crieth unto the c, and H5892
Nah 3: 1 Woe to the bloody c! it is all full of lies H5892
Hab 2: 8 of the c, and of all that dwell therein. H7151
12 blood, and stablisheth a c by iniquity! H7151
17 of the c, and of all that dwell therein. H7151
Zep 2:15 This is the rejoicing c that dwelt H5892
3: 1 filthy and polluted, to the oppressing c! H5892
Zec 8: 3 shall be called a c of truth; and the H5892
5 And the streets of the c shall be full of H5892
21 And the inhabitants of one c shall go to
14: 2 to battle; and the c shall be taken, and H5892
2 and half of the c shall go forth into H5892
2 people shall not be cut off from the c. H5892
Mt 2:23 And he came and dwelt in a c called G4172
4: 5 up into the holy c, and setteth him on G4172
5:14 Ye are the light of the world. A c that is G4172
35 for it is the c of the great King. G4172
8:33 their ways into the c, and told every G4172
34 And, behold, the whole c came out to G4172
9: 1 passed over, and came into his own c. G4172
10: 5 any c of the Samaritans enter ye not: G4172
11 And into whatsoever c or town ye shall G4172
14 or c, shake off the dust of your feet. G4172
15 in the day of judgment, than for that c. G4172
23 But when they persecute you in this c, G4172
12:25 and every c or house divided against G4172
21:10 the c was moved, saying, Who is this? G4172
17 And he left them, and went out of the c G4172
18 as he returned into the c, he hungered. G4172
22: 7 those murderers, and burned up their c. G4172
23:34 and persecute them from c to city: G4172
34 and persecute them from city to c: G4172
26:18 And he said, Go into the c to such a G4172
27:53 the holy c, and appeared unto many. G4172
28:11 came into the c, and shewed unto the G4172
Mk 1:33 And all the c was gathered together at G4172
45 enter into the c, but was without in G4172
5:14 and told it in the c, and in the country. G4172
6:11 in the day of judgment, than for that c. G4172
11:19 even was come, he went out of the c. G4172
14:13 Go ye into the c, and there shall meet G4172
16 and came into the c, and found as he G4172
Lk 1:26 unto a c of Galilee, named Nazareth, G4172
39 hill country with haste, into a c of Juda; G4172
2: 3 to be taxed, every one into his own c. G4172
4 Galilee, out of the c of Nazareth, into G4172
4 Judaea, unto the c of David, which is G4172
11 For unto you is born this day in the c of G4172
39 into Galilee, to their own c Nazareth. G4172
4:26 save unto Sarepta, a c of Sidon, unto a G4172
29 him out of the c, and led him unto the G4172
29 hill whereon their c was built, that they G4172
31 And came down to Capernaum, a c of G4172
5:12 was in a certain c, behold a man full of G4172
7:11 he went into a c called Nain; and many G4172
12 to the gate of the c, behold, there was a G4172
12 and much people of the c was with her. G4172
37 And, behold, a woman in the c, which G4172
8: 1 went throughout every c and village, G4172
4 out of every c, he spake by a parable: G4172
27 met him out of the c a certain man, G4172
34 and told it in the c and in the country. G4172
39 the whole c how great things Jesus G4172
9: 5 ye go out of that c, shake off the very G4172
10 belonging to the c called Bethsaida. G4172
10: 1 his face into every c and place, whither G4172
8 And into whatsoever c ye enter, and G4172
10 But into whatsoever c ye enter, and G4172
11 Even the very dust of your c, which G4172
12 in that day for Sodom, than for that c. G4172
14:21 and lanes of the c, and bring in hither G4172
18: 2 Saying, There was in a c a judge, which G4172
3 And there was a widow in that c; and G4172
19:41 near, he beheld the c, and wept over it, G4172
22:10 are entered into the c, there shall a man G4172
23:19 made in the c, and for murder, was G4172
51 of Arimathaea, a c of the Jews: who G4172
24:49 but tarry ye in the c of Jerusalem, until G4172
Jn 1:44 Now Philip was of Bethsaida, the c of G4172
4: 5 Then cometh he to a c of Samaria, G4172
8 gone away unto the c to buy meat.) G4172
28 her way into the c, and saith to the men, G4172
30 Then they went out of the c, and came G4172
39 And many of the Samaritans of that c G4172
11:54 the wilderness, into a c called Ephraim, G4172
19:20 was nigh to the c: and it was written in G4172
Act 7:58 And cast him out of the c, and stoned G4172
8: 5 Then Philip went down to the c of G4172
8 And there was great joy in that c. G4172
9 in the same c used sorcery, and G4172
9: 6 and go into the c, and it shall be told G4172
10: 9 nigh unto the c, Peter went up upon G4172
11: 5 I was in the c of Joppa praying: and in G4172
12:10 that leadeth unto the c; which opened to G4172
Act 13:44 c together to hear the word of God. G4172
50 the chief men of the c, and raised G4172
14: 4 But the multitude of the c was divided: G4172
13 was before their c, brought oxen and G4172
19 of the c, supposing he had been dead. G4172
20 and came into the c: and the next day G4172
21 the gospel to that c, and had taught G4172
15:21 For Moses of old time hath in every c G2596
36 our brethren in every c where we have G4172
16:12 which is the chief c of that part of G4172
12 we were in that c abiding certain days. G4172
13 we went out of the c by a river side, G4172
14 of purple, of the c of Thyatira, which G4172
20 Jews, do exceedingly trouble our c, G4172
39 and desired them to depart out of the c. G4172
17: 5 and set all the c on an uproar, and G4172
6 the rulers of the c, crying, These that G4173
8 of the c, when they heard these things. G4173
16 he saw the c wholly given to idolatry. G4172
18:10 thee: for I have much people in this c. G4172
19:29 And the whole c was filled with G4172
35 not how that the c of the Ephesians is G4172
20:23 in every c, saying that bonds and G2596
21: 5 till we were out of the c: and we kneeled G4172
29 before with him in the c Trophimus an G4172
30 And all the c was moved, and the G4172
39 a Jew of Tarsus, a c in Cilicia, a citizen of
39 a citizen of no mean c: and, I beseech G4172
22: 3 born in Tarsus, a c in Cilicia, yet brought
3 yet brought up in this c at the feet of G4172
24:12 neither in the synagogues, nor in the c: G4172
25:23 men of the c, at Festus' commandment G4172
27: 5 we came to Myra, a c of Lycia.
8 nigh whereunto was the c of Lasea. G4172
Ro 16:23 c saluteth you, and Quartus a brother. G4172
2Co 11:26 in perils in the c, in perils in the G4172
32 the king kept the c of the Damascenes G4172
Tit 1: 5 in every c, as I had appointed thee: G4172
Heb 11:10 For he looked for a c which hath G4172
16 God: for he hath prepared for them a c. G4172
12:22 Sion, and unto the c of the living God, G4172
13:14 For here have we no continuing c, but G4172
Jas 4:13 will go into such a c, and continue there G4172
Rev 3:12 the name of the c of my God, which is G4172
11: 2 and the holy c shall they tread under G4172
8 street of the great c, which spiritually is G4172
13 the tenth part of the c fell, and in the G4172
14: 8 is fallen, that great c, because she made G4172
20 without the c, and blood came out G4172
16:19 And the great c was divided into three G4172
17:18 is that great c, which reigneth over G4172
18:10 alas that great c Babylon, that mighty G4172
10 c! for in one hour is thy judgment come. G4172
16 And saying, Alas, alas, that great c, that G4172
18 What c is like unto this great city! G4172
18 What city is like unto this great c! G4172
19 alas, that great c, wherein were made G4172
21 shall that great c Babylon be thrown G4172
20: 9 and the beloved c: and fire came down G4172
21: 2 And I John saw the holy c, new G4172
10 me that great c, the holy Jerusalem, G4172
14 And the wall of the c had twelve G4172
15 to measure the c, and the gates thereof, G4172
16 And the c lieth foursquare, and the G4172
16 he measured the c with the reed, twelve G4172
18 c was pure gold, like unto clear glass. G4172
19 And the foundations of the wall of the c G4172
21 the street of the c was pure gold, as it G4172
23 And the c had no need of the sun, G4172
22:14 enter in through the gates into the c. G4172
19 out of the holy c, and from the things G4172

CLAD

1Ki 11:29 way; and he had c himself with a new H3680
Isa 59:17 and was c with zeal as a cloak. H5844

CLAMOROUS

Prv 9:13 A foolish woman is c: she is simple, and H1993

CLAMOUR

Eph 4:31 and anger, and c, and evil speaking, be G2906

CLAP

Job 27:23 Men shall c their hands at him, and H5606
Ps 47: 1 O c your hands, all ye people; shout H8628
98: 8 Let the floods c their hands: let the hills H4222
Isa 55:12 the trees of the field shall c their hands. H4222
Lam 2:15 All that pass by c their hands at thee; H5606
Nah 3:19 the bruit of thee shall c the hands over H8628

CLAPPED
2Ki 11:12 him; and they c their hands, and said, H5221
Ezk 25: 6 Because thou hast c *thine* hands, and H4222

CLAPPETH
Job 34:37 unto his sin, he c *his hands* among us, H5606

CLAUDA
Act 27:16 which is called C, we had much work *G2802*

CLAUDIA
2Ti 4:21 and Linus, and C, and all the brethren. *G2803*

CLAUDIUS
Act 11:28 came to pass in the days of C Caesar. *G2804*
18: 2 (because that C had commanded all *G2804*
23:26 C Lysias unto the most excellent *G2804*

CLAVE
Gen 22: 3 Isaac his son, and c the wood for the H1234
34: 3 And his soul c unto Dinah the daughter H1692
Nu 16:31 c asunder that *was* under them: H1234
Jdg 15:19 But God c an hollow place that *was* in H1234
Ru 1:14 her mother in law; but Ruth c unto her. H1692
1Sa 6:14 stone: and they c the wood of the cart, H1234
2Sa 20: 2 but the men of Judah c unto their king, H1692
23:10 and his hand c unto the sword: and H1692
1Ki 11: 2 gods: Solomon c unto these in love. H1692
2Ki 18: 6 For he c to the LORD, *and* departed not H1692
Neh 10:29 They c to their brethren, their nobles, H2388
Ps 78:15 He c the rocks in the wilderness, and H1234
Isa 48:21 rock for them: he c the rock also, and H1234
Act 17:34 Howbeit certain men c unto him, and *G2853*

CLAWS
Dt 14: 6 the cleft into two c, *and* cheweth the cud H6541
Dan 4:33 *feathers,* and his nails like birds' *c.*
Zec 11:16 of the fat, and tear their c in pieces. H6541

CLAY
1Ki 7:46 cast them, in the c ground between H4568
2Ch 4:17 cast them, in the c ground between H4568
Job 4:19 dwell in houses of c, whose foundation H2563
10: 9 made me as the c; and wilt thou bring H2563
13:12 unto ashes, your bodies to bodies of c. H2563
27:16 the dust, and prepare raiment as the c; H2563
33: 6 stead: I also am formed out of the c. H2563
38:14 It is turned as c *to* the seal; and they H2563
Ps 40: 2 out of the miry c, and set my feet upon H2916
Isa 29:16 as the potter's c: for shall the work say H2563
41:25 morter, and as the potter treadeth c. H2916
45: 9 the earth. Shall the c say to him that H2563
64: 8 our father; we *are* the c, and thou our H2563
Jer 18: 4 And the vessel that he made of c was H2563
6 Behold, as the c *is* in the potter's hand, H2563
43: 9 and hide them in the c in the brickkiln, H4423
Dan 2:33 iron, his feet part of iron and part of c. H2635
34 of iron and c, and brake them to pieces. H2635
35 Then was the iron, the c, the brass, the H2635
41 part of potters' c, and part of iron, the H2635
41 thou sawest the iron mixed with miry c. H2635
42 iron, and part of c, *so* the kingdom shall H2635
43 mixed with miry c, they shall mingle H2635
43 even as iron is not mixed with c. H2635
45 the brass, the c, the silver, and the gold; H2635
Nah 3:14 holds: go into c, and tread the morter, H2916
Hab 2: 6 to him that ladeth himself with thick c! H5671
Jn 9: 6 ground, and made c of the spittle, and *G4081*
6 the eyes of the blind man with the c, *G4081*
11 called Jesus made c, and anointed mine *G4081*
14 Jesus made the c, and opened his eyes. *G4081*
15 unto them, He put c upon mine eyes, *G4081*
Ro 9:21 Hath not the potter power over the c, of *G4081*

CLEAN
Gen 7: 2 Of every c beast thou shalt take to thee H2889
2 not c by two, the male and his female. H2889
8 Of c beasts, and of beasts that *are* not H2889
8 beasts that *are* not c, and of fowls, and H2889
8:20 and took of every c beast, and of every H2889
20 and of every c fowl, and offered burnt H2889
35: 2 and be c, and change your garments: H2891
Lev 4:12 the camp unto a c place, where the H2889
6:11 ashes without the camp unto a c place. H2889
7:19 the flesh, all that be c shall eat thereof. H2889
10:10 unholy, and between unclean and c; H2889
14 shall ye eat in a c place; thou, and thy H2889
11:36 of water, shall be c: but that which H2889
37 seed which is to be sown, it *shall be* c. H2889
Lev 11:47 the unclean and the c, and between the H2889
12: 8 atonement for her, and she shall be c. H2891
13: 6 pronounce him c: it *is but* a scab: and H2891
6 and he shall wash his clothes, and be c. H2891
13 pronounce *him* c *that hath* the plague: H2891
13 the plague: it is all turned white: he *is* c. H2889
17 *him* c *that hath* the plague: he *is* clean. H2891
17 *him* clean *that hath* the plague: he *is* c. H2889
23 and the priest shall pronounce him c. H2891
28 shall pronounce him c: for it *is* an H2891
34 pronounce him c: and he shall wash his H2891
34 and he shall wash his clothes, and be c. H2891
37 is healed, he *is* c: and the priest shall H2889
37 and the priest shall pronounce him c. H2891
39 spot *that* groweth in the skin; he *is* c. H2889
40 fallen off his head, he *is* bald; *yet is* he c. H2889
41 his face, he *is* forehead bald: *yet is* he c. H2889
58 washed the second time, and shall be c. H2891
59 it c, or to pronounce it unclean. H2891
14: 4 birds alive *and* c, and cedar wood, and H2889
7 shall pronounce him c, and shall let the H2891
8 that he may be c: and after that he shall H2891
9 his flesh in water, and he shall be c. H2891
11 And the priest that maketh *him* c shall H2891
11 that is to be made c, and those things, H2891
20 atonement for him, and he shall be c. H2891
48 house c, because the plague is healed. H2891
53 for the house: and it shall be c. H2891
57 when *it is* c: this *is* the law of leprosy. H2889
15: 8 upon him that is c; then he shall wash H2889
13 flesh in running water, and shall be c. H2891
28 seven days, and after that she shall be c. H2891
16:30 c from all your sins before the LORD. H2891
17:15 until the even: then shall he be c. H2891
20:25 between c beasts and unclean, H2889
25 unclean fowls and c: and ye shall not H2889
22: 4 holy things, until he be c. And whoso H2891
7 down, he shall be c, and shall afterward H2891
23:22 shalt not make c riddance of the corners
Nu 5:28 not defiled, but be c; then she shall be H2889
8: 7 their clothes, and *so* make themselves c. H2891
9:13 But the man that *is* c, and is not in a H2889
18:11 one that is c in thy house shall eat of it. H2889
13 that is c in thine house shall eat *of* it. H2889
19: 9 And a man *that is* c shall gather up the H2889
9 the camp in a c place, and it shall be H2889
12 day he shall be c: but if he purify not H2891
12 then the seventh day he shall not be c. H2891
18 And a c person shall take hyssop, and H2889
19 And the c *person* shall sprinkle upon H2889
19 himself in water, and shall be c at even. H2891
31:23 the fire, and it shall be c: nevertheless it H2891
24 and ye shall be c, and afterward ye shall H2891
Dt 12:15 unclean and the c may eat thereof, as H2889
22 and the c shall eat *of* them alike. H2889
14:11 *Of* all c birds ye shall eat. H2889
20 *But of* all c fowls ye may eat. H2889
15:22 unclean and the c *person shall eat it* H2889
23:10 any man, that is not c by reason of H2889
Jos 3:17 the people were passed c over Jordan. H8552
4: 1 when all the people were c passed over H8552
11 all the people were c passed over, that H8552
1Sa 20:26 him, he *is* not c; surely he *is* not clean. H2889
26 him, he *is* not clean; surely he *is* not c. H2889
2Ki 5:10 come again to thee, and thou shalt be c. H2891
12 in them, and be c? So he turned and H2891
13 when he saith to thee, Wash, and be c? H2891
14 the flesh of a little child, and he was c. H2891
2Ch 30:17 not c, to sanctify *them* unto the LORD. H2889
Job 9:30 water, and make my hands never so c; H2141
11: 4 *is* pure, and I am c in thine eyes. H1249
14: 4 Who can bring a c *thing* out of an H2889
15:14 What *is* man, that he should be c? and H2135
15 yea, the heavens are not c in his sight. H2141
17: 9 c hands shall be stronger and stronger. H2890
25: 4 can he be c *that is* born of a woman? H2135
33: 9 I am c without transgression, I *am* H2134
Ps 19: 9 The fear of the LORD *is* c, enduring for H2889
24: 4 He that hath c hands, and a pure heart; H5355
51: 7 Purge me with hyssop, and I shall be c: H2891
10 Create in me a c heart, O God; and H2889
73: 1 Israel, *even* to such as are of a c heart. H1249
77: 8 Is his mercy c gone for ever? doth *his* H6565
Prv 14: 4 Where no oxen *are,* the crib *is* c: but H1249
16: 2 All the ways of a man *are* c in his own H2134
20: 9 Who can say, I have made my heart c, I H2135
Ecc 9: 2 good and to the c, and to the unclean; H2889
Isa 1:16 Wash you, make you c; put away the H2135
24:19 down, the earth is c dissolved, the H6565
Isa 28: 8 *and* filthiness, *so that there is* no place c.
30:24 ground shall eat c provender, which H2548
52:11 ye c, that bear the vessels of the LORD. H1305
66:20 a c vessel into the house of the LORD. H2889
Jer 13:27 not be made c? when *shall it* once *be*? H2891
Ezk 22:26 unclean and the c, and have hid their H2889
36:25 Then will I sprinkle c water upon you, H2889
25 you, and ye shall be c: from all your H2891
44:23 discern between the unclean and the c. H2889
Joel 1: 7 he hath made it c bare, and cast *it* away;
Zec 11:17 his arm shall be c dried up, and his right
Mt 8: 2 if thou wilt, thou canst make me c. *G2511*
3 I will; be thou c. And immediately his *G2511*
23:25 for ye make c the outside of the cup *G2511*
26 that the outside of them may be c also. *G2513*
27:59 body, he wrapped it in a c linen cloth, *G2513*
Mk 1:40 him, If thou wilt, thou canst make me c. *G2511*
41 and saith unto him, I will; be thou c. *G2511*
Lk 5:12 if thou wilt, thou canst make me c. *G2511*
13 I will: be thou c. And immediately the *G2511*
11:39 ye Pharisees make c the outside of the *G2511*
41 and, behold, all things are c unto you. *G2513*
Jn 13:10 *his* feet, but is c every whit: and ye are *G2513*
10 every whit: and ye are c, but not all. *G2513*
11 him; therefore said he, Ye are not all c. *G2513*
15: 3 Now ye are c through the word which I *G2513*
Act 18: 6 own heads; I *am* c: from henceforth I *G2513*
2Pt 2:18 c escaped from them who live in error. *G3689*
Rev 19: 8 in fine linen, c and white: for the fine *G2513*
14 clothed in fine linen, white and c. *G2513*

CLEANNESS
2Sa 22:21 according to the c of my hands hath he H1252
25 according to my c in his eye sight. H1252
Ps 18:20 according to the c of my hands hath he H1252
24 to the c of my hands in his eyesight. H1252
Am 4: 6 And I also have given you c of teeth in H5356

CLEANSE
Ex 29:36 and thou shalt c the altar, when thou H2398
Lev 14:49 And he shall take to c the house two H2398
52 And he shall c the house with the blood H2398
16:19 seven times, and c it, and hallow it H2891
30 for you, to c you, *that* ye may be H2891
Nu 8: 6 the children of Israel, and c them. H2891
7 And thus shalt thou do unto them, to c H2891
15 c them, and offer them *for* an offering. H2891
21 an atonement for them to c them. H2891
2Ch 29:15 the LORD, to c the house of the LORD. H2891
16 of the LORD, to c *it,* and brought out H2891
Neh 13:22 that they should c themselves, and *that* H2891
Ps 19:12 Who can understand *his* errors? c thou H5352
51: 2 mine iniquity, and c me from my sin. H2891
119: 9 Wherewithal shall a young man c his H2135
Jer 4:11 of my people, not to fan, nor to c, H1305
33: 8 And I will c them from all their H2891
Ezk 36:25 and from all your idols, will I c you. H2891
37:23 sinned, and will c them: so shall they H2891
39:12 of them, that they may c the land. H2891
14 face of the earth, to c it: after the end of H2891
16 Hamonah. Thus shall they c the land. H2891
43:20 about: thus shalt thou c and purge it. H2398
22 and they shall c the altar, as they did H2398
22 altar, as they did c *it* with the bullock. H2398
45:18 without blemish, and c the sanctuary: H2398
Joel 3:21 For I will c their blood *that* I have not H5352
Mt 10: 8 Heal the sick, c the lepers, raise the *G2511*
23:26 *Thou* blind Pharisee, c first that *which* *G2511*
2Co 7: 1 beloved, let us c ourselves from all *G2511*
Eph 5:26 That he might sanctify and c it with the *G2511*
Jas 4: 8 will draw nigh to you. C *your* hands, *ye* *G2511*
1Jn 1: 9 and to c us from all unrighteousness. *G2511*

CLEANSED
Lev 11:32 unclean until the even; so it shall be c. H2891
12: 7 and she shall be c from the issue of her H2891
14: 4 him that is to be c two birds alive *and* H2891
7 him that is to be c from the leprosy H2891
8 And he that is to be c shall wash his H2891
14 him that is to be c, and upon the thumb H2891
17 him that is to be c, and upon the thumb H2891
18 him that is to be c: and the priest shall H2891
19 for him that is to be c from his H2891
25 him that is to be c, and upon the thumb H2891
28 him that is to be c, and upon the thumb H2891
29 of him that is to be c, to make an H2891
31 for him that is to be c before the LORD. H2891
15:13 And when he that hath an issue is c of H2891
28 But if she be c of her issue, then she H2891

Nu 35:33 the land cannot be c of the blood that is H3722
Jos 22:17 from which we are not c until this day, H2891
2Ch 29:18 and said, We have c all the house of the H2891
30:18 Zebulun, had not c themselves, yet did H2891
19 though *he be* not c according to the
34: 5 altars, and c Judah and Jerusalem. H2891
Neh 13: 9 Then I commanded, and they c the H2891
30 Thus c I them from all strangers, and H2891
Job 35: 3 profit shall I have, *if I be* c from my sin?
Ps 73:13 Verily I have c my heart *in* vain, and H2135
Ezk 22:24 land that is not c, nor rained upon in H2891
36:33 that I shall have c you from all your H2891
44:26 And after he is c, they shall reckon unto H2893
Dan 8:14 days; then shall the sanctuary be c. H6663
Joel 3:21 not c: for the LORD dwelleth in Zion. H5352
Mt 8: 3 And immediately his leprosy was c. *G2511*
11: 5 the lepers are c, and the deaf hear, the *G2511*
Mk 1:42 departed from him, and he was c. *G2511*
Lk 4:27 them was c, saving Naaman the Syrian. *G2511*
7:22 the lepers are c, the deaf hear, the dead *G2511*
17:14 to pass, that, as they went, they were c. *G2511*
17 there not ten c? but where *are* the nine? *G2511*
Act 10:15 God hath c, *that* call not thou common. *G2511*
11: 9 God hath c, *that* call not thou common. *G2511*

CLEANSETH
Job 37:21 but the wind passeth, and c them. H2891
Prv 20:30 The blueness of a wound c away evil: H8562
1Jn 1: 7 of Jesus Christ his Son c us from all sin. *G2511*

CLEANSING
Lev 13: 7 c, he shall be seen of the priest again: H2893
35 spread much in the skin after his c; H2893
14: 2 c: He shall be brought unto the priest: H2893
23 the eighth day for his c unto the priest, H2893
32 to get *that which pertaineth* to his c. H2893
15:13 seven days for his c, and wash his H2893
Nu 6: 9 c, on the seventh day shall he shave it. H2893
Ezk 43:23 When thou hast made an end of c *it*, H2398
Mk 1:44 and offer for thy c those things which *G2512*
Lk 5:14 and offer for thy c, according as Moses *G2512*

CLEAR
Gen 24: 8 then thou shalt be c from this my oath: H5352
41 Then shalt thou be c from *this* my oath, H5352
41 thee *one*, thou shalt be c from my oath. H5355
44:16 or how shall we c ourselves? God hath H6663
Ex 34: 7 will by no means c *the guilty;* visiting H5352
2Sa 23: 4 out of the earth by c shining after rain.
Ps 51: 4 speakest, *and* be c when thou judgest. H2135
Song 6:10 fair as the moon, c as the sun, *and* H1249
Isa 18: 4 place like a c heat upon herbs, *and* H6703
Am 8: 9 and I will darken the earth in the c day: H216
Zec 14: 6 *that* the light shall not be c, *nor* dark: H3368
2Co 7:11 yourselves to be c in this matter. *G53*
Rev 21:11 even like a jasper stone, c as crystal; *G2929*
18 the city *was* pure gold, like unto c glass. *G2513*
22: 1 of water of life, c as crystal, proceeding *G2986*

CLEARER
Job 11:17 And *thine* age shall be c than the H6965

CLEARING
Nu 14:18 and by no means c *the guilty,* visiting H5352
2Co 7:11 in you, yea, *what* c of yourselves, yea, *G627*

CLEARLY
Job 33: 3 and my lips shall utter knowledge c. H1305
Mt 7: 5 shalt thou see c to cast out the mote *G1227*
Mk 8:25 he was restored, and saw every man c. *G5081*
Lk 6:42 shalt thou see c to pull out the mote *G1227*
Ro 1:20 creation of the world are c seen, being *G2529*

CLEARNESS
Ex 24:10 as it were the body of heaven in *his* c. H2892

CLEAVE
Gen 2:24 mother, and shall c unto his wife: and H1692
Lev 1:17 And he shall c it with the wings thereof, H8156
Dt 4: 4 But ye that did c unto the LORD your H1695
10:20 shalt thou c, and swear by his name. H1692
11:22 walk in all his ways, and to c unto him; H1692
13: 4 and ye shall serve him, and c unto him. H1692
17 And there shall c nought of the cursed H1692
28:21 The LORD shall make the pestilence c H1692
60 afraid of; and they shall c unto thee. H1692
30:20 that thou mayest c unto him: for he *is* H1692
Jos 22: 5 and to c unto him, and to serve H1692
23: 8 But c unto the LORD your God, as ye H1692
Jos 23:12 Else if ye do in any wise go back, and c H1692
2Ki 5:27 of Naaman shall c unto thee, and unto H1692
Job 38:38 hardness, and the clods c fast together? H1692
Ps 74:15 Thou didst c the fountain and the H1234
101: 3 that turn aside; *it* shall not c to me. H1692
102: 5 of my groaning my bones c to my skin. H1692
137: 6 thee, let my tongue c to the roof of my H1692
Isa 14: 1 and they shall c to the house of Jacob. H5596
Jer 13:11 have I caused to c unto me the whole H1692
Ezk 3:26 And I will make thy tongue c to the H1692
Dan 2:43 but they shall not c one to another, H1693
11:34 many shall c to them with flatteries. H3867
Hab 3: 9 Thou didst c the earth with rivers. H1234
Zec 14: 4 of Olives shall c in the midst thereof H1234
Mt 19: 5 mother, and shall c to his wife: and *G4347*
Mk 10: 7 father and mother, and c to his wife; *G4347*
Act 11:23 of heart they would c unto the Lord. *G4347*
Ro 12: 9 which is evil; c to that which is good. *G2853*

CLEAVED
2Ki 3: 3 Nevertheless he c unto the sins of H1692
Job 29:10 tongue c to the roof of their mouth. H1692
31: 7 and if any blot hath c to mine hands; H1692

CLEAVETH
Dt 14: 6 the hoof, and c the cleft into two claws, H8157
Job 16:13 round about, he c my reins asunder, H6398
19:20 My bone c to my skin and to my flesh, H1692
Ps 22:15 and my tongue c to my jaws; and thou H1692
41: 8 An evil disease, *say they,* c fast unto H3332
44:25 to the dust: our belly c unto the earth. H1692
119:25 My soul c unto the dust: quicken thou H1692
141: 7 one cutteth and c *wood* upon the earth. H1234
Ecc 10: 9 c wood shall be endangered thereby. H1234
Jer 13:11 For as the girdle c to the loins of a man, H1692
Lam 4: 4 The tongue of the sucking child c to the H1692
8 streets: their skin c to their bones; it is H6821
Lk 10:11 Even the very dust of your city, which c *G2853*

CLEFT
Dt 14: 6 and cleaveth the c into two claws, *and* H8157
Mic 1: 4 valleys shall be c, as wax before the fire, H1234

CLEFTS
Song 2:14 O my dove, *that art* in the c of the rock, H2288
Isa 2:21 To go into the c of the rocks, and into H5366
Jer 49:16 that dwellest in the c of the rock, that H2288
Am 6:11 breaches, and the little house with c. H1233
Oba 3 that dwellest in the c of the rock, whose H2288

CLEMENCY
Act 24: 4 wouldest hear us of thy c a few words. *G1932*

CLEMENT
Php 4: 3 me in the gospel, with C also, and *with* *G2815*

CLEOPAS
Lk 24:18 whose name was C, answering said *G2810*

CLEOPHAS
Jn 19:25 the *wife* of C, and Mary Magdalene. *G2832*

CLERK See TOWNCLERK.

CLIFF
2Ch 20:16 come up by the c of Ziz; and ye shall H4608

CLIFT
Ex 33:22 I will put thee in a c of the rock, and H5366

CLIFTS
Job 30: 6 To dwell in the c of the valleys, *in* caves H6178
Isa 57: 5 in the valleys under the c of the rocks? H5585

CLIMB
Jer 4:29 into thickets, and c up upon the rocks: H5927
Joel 2: 7 men; they shall c the wall like men of H5927
9 upon the wall, they shall c up upon the H5927
Am 9: 2 take them; though they c up to heaven, H5927

CLIMBED
1Sa 14:13 And Jonathan c up upon his hands and H5927
Lk 19: 4 And he ran before, and c up into a *G305*

CLIMBETH
Jn 10: 1 the sheepfold, but c up some other way, *G305*

CLIPPED
Jer 48:37 and every beard c: upon all the hands H1639

CLOAK
Isa 59:17 clothing, and was clad with zeal as a c. H4598
Mt 5:40 away thy coat, let him have *thy* c also. *G2440*
Lk 6:29 thy c forbid not *to take thy* coat also. *G2440*
Jn 15:22 but now they have no c for their sin. *G4392*
1Th 2: 5 nor a c of covetousness; God *is* witness: *G4392*
2Ti 4:13 The c that I left at Troas with Carpus, *G5341*
1Pt 2:16 *your* liberty for a c of maliciousness, *G1942*

CLODS
Job 7: 5 My flesh is clothed with worms and c H1487
21:33 The c of the valley shall be sweet unto H7263
38:38 and the c cleave fast together? H7263
Isa 28:24 he open and break the c of his ground? H7702
Hos 10:11 shall plow, *and* Jacob shall break his c. H7702
Joel 1:17 The seed is rotten under their c, the H4053

CLOKE See CLOAK.

CLOSE
Nu 5:13 and be kept c, and she be defiled, and H5641
2Sa 22:46 shall be afraid out of their c places. H4526
1Ch 12: 1 yet kept himself c because of Saul the H6113
Job 28:21 and kept c from the fowls of the air. H5641
41:15 pride, shut up together *as with* a c seal. H6862
Ps 18:45 and be afraid out of their c places. H4526
Jer 42:16 shall follow c after you there in Egypt; H1692
Dan 8: 7 And I saw him come c unto the ram, and H681
Am 9:11 that is fallen, and c up the breaches H1443
Lk 9:36 And they kept *it* c, and told no man in *G4601*
Act 27:13 loosing *thence*, they sailed c by Crete. *G788*

CLOSED
Gen 2:21 ribs, and c up the flesh instead thereof; H5462
20:18 For the LORD had fast c up all the H6113
Nu 16:33 the pit, and the earth c upon them: and H3680
Jdg 3:22 blade; and the fat c upon the blade, so H5462
Isa 1: 6 they have not been c, neither bound up, H2115
29:10 deep sleep, and hath c your eyes: the H6105
Dan 12: 9 c up and sealed till the time of the end. H5640
Jna 2: 5 the soul: the depth c me round about, H5437
Mt 13:15 eyes they have c; lest at any time they *G2576*
Lk 4:20 And he c the book, and he gave *it* again *G4428*
Act 28:27 eyes have they c; lest they should see *G2576*

CLOSER
Prv 18:24 is a friend *that* sticketh c than a brother.

CLOSEST
Jer 22:15 Shalt thou reign, because thou c *thyself* H8474

CLOSET
Joel 2:16 his chamber, and the bride out of her c. H2646
Mt 6: 6 enter into thy c, and when thou hast *G5009*

CLOSETS
Lk 12: 3 in the ear in c shall be proclaimed *G5009*

CLOTH
Nu 4: 6 spread over *it* a c wholly of blue, and H899
7 they shall spread a c of blue, and put H899
8 And they shall spread upon them a c of H899
9 And they shall take a c of blue, and H899
11 they shall spread a c of blue, and cover it H899
12 and put *them* in a c of blue, and cover H899
13 the altar, and spread a purple c thereon: H899
Dt 22:17 the c before the elders of the city. H8071
1Sa 19:13 for his bolster, and covered *it* with a c. H899
21: 9 *here* wrapped in a c behind the ephod: H8071
2Sa 20:12 the field, and cast a c upon him, when he H899
2Ki 8:15 that he took a thick c, and dipped *it* in H4346
Isa 30:22 c; thou shalt say unto it, Get thee hence.
Mt 9:16 No man putteth a piece of new c unto *G4470*
27:59 body, he wrapped it in a clean linen c, *G4616*
Mk 2:21 No man also seweth a piece of new c on *G4470*
14:51 having a linen c cast about *his* naked *G4616*
52 And he left the linen c, and fled from *G4616*

CLOTHE
Ex 40:14 And thou shalt bring his sons, and c H3847
Est 4: 4 sent raiment to c Mordecai, and to take H3847
Ps 132:16 I will also c her priests with salvation: H3847
18 His enemies will I c with shame: but H3847
Prv 23:21 drowsiness shall c *a man* with rags. H3847
Isa 22:21 And I will c him with thy robe, and H3847
49:18 thou shalt surely c thee with them all, H3847
50: 3 I c the heavens with blackness, and I H3847
Ezk 26:16 they shall c themselves with trembling; H3847
34: 3 Ye eat the fat, and ye c you with the H3847

Hag 1: 6 with drink; ye c you, but there is none H3847
Zec 3: 4 I will c thee with change of raiment. H3847
Mt 6:30 Wherefore, if God so c the grass of the G294
30 not much more c you, O ye of little faith?
Lk 12:28 If then God so c the grass, which is to G294
28 more will he c you, O ye of little faith?

CLOTHED

Gen 3:21 God make coats of skins, and c them. H3847
Lev 8: 7 the girdle, and c him with the robe, and H3847
2Sa 1:24 over Saul, who c you in scarlet, with H3847
1Ch 15:27 And David was c with a robe of fine H3736
21:16 c in sackcloth, fell upon their faces. H3680
2Ch 6:41 O LORD God, be c with salvation, and H3847
18: 9 on his throne, c in their robes, and they H3847
28:15 and with the spoil c all that were naked H3847
Est 4: 2 into the king's gate c with sackcloth. H3830
Job 7: 5 My flesh is c with worms and clods of H3847
8:22 They that hate thee shall be c with H3847
10:11 Thou hast c me with skin and flesh, H3847
29:14 I put on righteousness, and it c me: my H3847
39:19 hast thou c his neck with thunder? H3847
Ps 35:26 hurt: let them be c with shame and H3847
65:13 The pastures are c with flocks; the H3847
93: 1 The LORD reigneth, he is c with H3847
1 the LORD is c with strength, wherewith H3847
104: 1 thou art c with honour and majesty. H3847
109:18 As he c himself with cursing like as H3847
29 Let mine adversaries be c with shame, H3847
132: 9 Let thy priests be c with righteousness; H3847
Prv 31:21 for all her household are c with scarlet. H3847
Isa 61:10 my God; for he hath c me with the H3847
Ezk 7:27 the prince shall be c with desolation, H3847
9: 2 among them was c with linen, with a H3847
3 called to the man c with linen, which H3847
11 And, behold, the man c with linen, H3847
10: 2 And he spake unto the man c with H3847
6 the man c with linen, saying, Take H3847
7 c with linen: who took it, and went out. H3847
16:10 I c thee also with broidered work, and H3847
23: 6 Which were c with blue, captains and H3847
12 captains and rulers c most gorgeously, H3847
38: 4 all of them c with all sorts of armour, H3847
44:17 they shall be c with linen garments; H3847
Dan 5: 7 thereof, shall be c with scarlet, and H3848
16 thou shalt be c with scarlet, and have H3848
29 and they c Daniel with scarlet, H3848
10: 5 a certain man c in linen, whose loins H3847
12: 6 And one said to the man c in linen, H3847
7 And I heard the man c in linen, which H3847
Zep 1: 8 all such as are c with strange apparel. H3847
Zec 3: 3 Now Joshua was c with filthy H3847
5 his head, and c him with garments. H3847
Mt 6:31 drink? or, Wherewithal shall we be c? G4016
11: 8 But what went ye out for to see? A man c G294
25:36 Naked, and ye c me: I was sick, and ye G4016
38 and took thee in? or naked, and c thee? G4016
43 in: naked, and ye c me not: sick, and in G4016
Mk 1: 6 And John was c with camel's hair, and G1746
5:15 sitting, and c, and in his right mind: G2439
15:17 And they c him with purple, and G1746
16: 5 on the right side, c in a long white G4016
Lk 7:25 But what went ye out for to see? A man c G294
8:35 at the feet of Jesus, c, and in his right G2439
16:19 man, which was c in purple and fine G1737
2Co 5: 2 desiring to be c upon with our house G1902
3 If so be that being c we shall not be G1746
4 would be unclothed, but c upon, that G1902
1Pt 5: 5 to another, and be c with humility: for G1463
Rev 1:13 the Son of man, c with a garment down G1746
3: 5 the same shall be c in white raiment; G4016
18 thou mayest be c, and that the shame G4016
4: 4 elders sitting, c in white raiment; and G4016
7: 9 before the Lamb, c with white robes, G4016
10: 1 from heaven, c with a cloud: and a G4016
11: 3 and threescore days, c in sackcloth. G4016
12: 1 heaven; a woman c with the sun, and G4016
15: 6 the seven plagues, c in pure and white G1746
18:16 great city, that was c in fine linen, and G4016
19:13 And he was c with a vesture dipped in G4016
14 horses, c in fine linen, white and clean. G1746

CLOTHES

Gen 37:29 was not in the pit; and he rent his c. H899
34 And Jacob rent his c, and put sackcloth H8071
44:13 Then they rent their c, and laded every H8071
49:11 wine, and his c in the blood of grapes: H5497
Ex 12:34 up in their c upon their shoulders. H8071
19:10 to morrow, and let them wash their c, H8071
Ex 19:14 the people; and they washed their c. H8071
Lev 10: 6 neither rend your c; lest ye die, and lest H899
11:25 his c, and be unclean until the even. H899
28 shall wash his c, and be unclean until H899
40 of it shall wash his c, and be unclean H899
40 his c, and be unclean until the even. H899
13: 6 and he shall wash his c, and be clean. H899
34 and he shall wash his c, and be clean. H899
45 the plague is, his c shall be rent, and his H899
14: 8 shall wash his c, and shave off all his H899
9 he shall wash his c, also he shall wash his H899
47 shall wash his c; and he that eateth in H899
47 that eateth in the house shall wash his c. H899
15: 5 bed shall wash his c, and bathe himself H899
6 shall wash his c, and bathe himself in H899
7 shall wash his c, and bathe himself in H899
8 he shall wash his c, and bathe himself in H899
10 shall wash his c, and bathe himself in H899
11 he shall wash his c, and bathe himself in H899
13 and wash his c, and bathe his flesh in H899
21 bed shall wash his c, and bathe himself H899
22 shall wash his c, and bathe himself in H899
27 and shall wash his c, and bathe himself H899
16:26 shall wash his c, and bathe his flesh in H899
28 shall wash his c, and bathe his flesh in H899
32 on the linen c, even the holy garments: H899
17:15 shall both wash his c, and bathe himself H899
21:10 not uncover his head, nor rend his c; H899
Nu 8: 7 their c, and so make themselves clean. H899
21 they washed their c; and Aaron offered H899
14: 6 them that searched the land, rent their c: H899
19: 7 Then the priest shall wash his c, and he H899
8 And he that burneth her shall wash his c H899
10 shall wash his c, and be unclean until H899
19 and wash his c, and bathe himself in H899
21 shall wash his c; and he that toucheth H899
31:24 And ye shall wash your c on the seventh H899
Dt 29: 5 wilderness: your c are not waxen old H8008
Jos 7: 6 And Joshua rent his c, and fell to the H8071
Jdg 11:35 her, that he rent his c, and said, Alas, my H899
1Sa 4:12 c rent, and with earth upon his head. H4055
19:24 And he stripped off his c also, and H899
2Sa 1: 2 from Saul with his c rent, and earth H899
11 Then David took hold on his c, and rent H899
3:31 with him, Rend your c, and gird you with H899
13:31 his servants stood by with their c rent. H899
19:24 nor washed his c, from the day the king H899
1Ki 1: 1 covered him with c, but he gat no heat. H899
21:27 that he rent his c, and put sackcloth upon H899
2Ki 2:12 of his own c, and rent them in two pieces. H899
5: 7 that he rent his c, and said, Am I God, H899
8 of Israel had rent his c, that he sent to the H899
8 hast thou rent thy c? let him come now to H899
6:30 that he rent his c; and he passed by upon H899
11:14 rent her c, and cried, Treason, Treason. H899
18:37 with their c rent, and told him the H899
19: 1 it, that he rent his c, and covered himself H899
22:11 of the book of the law, that he rent his c. H899
19 and hast rent thy c, and wept before me; H899
2Ch 23:13 rent her c, and said, Treason, Treason. H899
34:19 the words of the law, that he rent his c. H899
27 and didst rend thy c, and weep before H899
Neh 4:23 of us put off our c, saving that every one H899
9:21 nothing; their c waxed not old, and H8008
Est 4: 1 Mordecai rent his c, and put on sackcloth H899
Job 9:31 ditch, and mine own c shall abhor me. H8008
Prv 6:27 in his bosom, and his c not be burned? H899
Isa 36:22 with their c rent, and told him the H899
37: 1 it, that he rent his c, and covered himself H899
Jer 41: 5 shaven, and their c rent, and having cut H899
Ezk 16:39 thee also of thy c, and shall take thy fair H899
23:26 They shall also strip thee out of thy c, H899
27:20 Dedan was thy merchant in precious c H899
24 of things, in blue c, and broidered work, H1545
Am 2: 8 And they lay themselves down upon c H899
Mt 21: 7 them their c, and they set him thereon. G2440
24:18 is in the field return back to take his c. G2440
26:65 Then the high priest rent his c, saying, G2440
Mk 5:28 For she said, If I may touch but his c, I G2440
30 the press, and said, Who touched my c? G2440
14:63 Then the high priest rent his c, and G5509
15:20 and put his own c on him, and led him G2440
Lk 2: 7 him in swaddling c, and laid him in a G4683
12 in swaddling c, lying in a manger. G4683
8:27 time, and ware no c, neither abode in G2440
19:36 And as he went, they spread their c in G2440
24:12 beheld the linen c laid by themselves, G3608
Jn 19:40 wound it in linen c with the spices, as G3608
20: 5 the linen c lying; yet went he not in. G3608
Jn 20: 6 the sepulchre, and seeth the linen c lie, G3608
7 with the linen c, but wrapped together G3608
Act 7:58 laid down their c at a young man's feet, G2440
14:14 of, they rent their c, and ran in among G2440
16:22 their c, and commanded to beat them. G2440
22:23 off their c, and threw dust into the air, G2440

CLOTHEST

Jer 4:30 thou do? Though thou c thyself with H3847

CLOTHING

Job 22: 6 and stripped the naked of their c. H899
24: 7 to lodge without c, that they have no H3830
10 They cause him to go naked without c, H3830
31:19 If I have seen any perish for want of c, H3830
Ps 35:13 they were sick, my c was sackcloth: I H3830
45:13 within: her c is of wrought gold. H3830
Prv 27:26 The lambs are for thy c, and the goats H3830
31:22 of tapestry; her c is silk and purple. H3830
25 Strength and honour are her c; and she H3830
Isa 3: 6 saying, Thou hast c, be thou our ruler, H8071
7 c: make me not a ruler of the people. H8071
23:18 to eat sufficiently, and for durable c. H4374
59:17 for c, and was clad with zeal as a cloak. H8516
Jer 10: 9 c: they are all the work of cunning men. H3830
Mt 7:15 to you in sheep's c, but inwardly they G1742
11: 8 that wear soft c are in kings' houses.
Mk 12:38 love to go in long c, and love salutations G4749
Act 10:30 a man stood before me in bright c, G2066
Jas 2: 3 weareth the gay c, and say unto him, Sit G2066

CLOTHS

Ex 31:10 And the c of service, and the holy H899
35:19 The c of service, to do service in the holy H899
39: 1 and scarlet, they made c of service, to do H899
41 The c of service to do service in the holy H899

CLOUD

Gen 9:13 I do set my bow in the c, and it shall be H6051
14 when I bring a c over the earth, that H6051
14 that the bow shall be seen in the c: H6051
16 And the bow shall be in the c; and I will H6051
Ex 13:21 by day in a pillar of a c, to lead them the H6051
22 He took not away the pillar of the c by H6051
14:19 and the pillar of the c went from before H6051
20 and it was a c and darkness to them, H6051
24 of fire and of the c, and troubled the H6051
16:10 the glory of the LORD appeared in the c. H6051
19: 9 thee in a thick c, that the people may H6051
16 and a thick c upon the mount, and H6051
24:15 the mount, and a c covered the mount. H6051
16 Sinai, and the c covered it six days: H6051
16 unto Moses out of the midst of the c. H6051
18 And Moses went into the midst of the c, H6051
34: 5 And the LORD descended in the c, and H6051
40:34 Then a c covered the tent of the H6051
35 because the c abode thereon, and H6051
36 And when the c was taken up from H6051
37 But if the c were not taken up, then H6051
38 For the c of the LORD was upon the H6051
Lev 16: 2 appear in the c upon the mercy seat. H6051
13 LORD, that the c of the incense may H6051
Nu 9:15 was reared up the c covered the H6051
16 So it was alway: the c covered it by day, H6051
17 And when the c was taken up from the H6051
17 the place where the c abode, there the H6051
18 as long as the c abode upon the H6051
19 And when the c tarried long upon the H6051
20 And so it was, when the c was a few H6051
21 And so it was, when the c abode from H6051
21 and that the c was taken up in the H6051
21 the c was taken up, they journeyed. H6051
22 or a year, that the c tarried upon the H6051
10:11 year, that the c was taken up from H6051
12 the c rested in the wilderness of Paran. H6051
34 And the c of the LORD was upon them H6051
11:25 And the LORD came down in a c, and H6051
12: 5 in the pillar of the c, and stood in the H6051
10 And the c departed from off the H6051
14:14 to face, and that thy c standeth over H6051
14 of a c, and in a pillar of fire by night. H6051
16:42 and, behold, the c covered it, and the H6051
Dt 1:33 way ye should go, and in a c by day. H6051
5:22 of the fire, of the c, and of the thick H6051
31:15 in a pillar of a c: and the pillar of the H6051
15 c stood over the door of the tabernacle. H6051
1Ki 8:10 that the c filled the house of the LORD, H6051
11 because of the c: for the glory of the H6051
18:44 ariseth a little c out of the sea, like a H5645

2Ch 5:13 with a c, *even* the house of the LORD; H6051
14 by reason of the c: for the glory of the H6051
Neh 9:19 the pillar of the c departed not from H6051
Job 3: 5 death stain it; let a c dwell upon it; let H6053
7: 9 *As* the c is consumed and vanisheth H6051
22:13 know? can he judge through the dark c? H6205
26: 8 and the c is not rent under them. H6051
9 his throne, *and* spreadeth his c upon it. H6051
30:15 and my welfare passeth away as a c. H5645
36:32 *to shine* by *the* c that cometh betwixt.
37:11 thick c: he scattereth his bright cloud: H5645
11 thick cloud: he scattereth his bright c: H6051
15 and caused the light of his c to shine? H6051
38: 9 When I made the c the garment H6051
Ps 78:14 a c, and all the night with a light of fire. H6051
105:39 He spread a c for a covering; and fire to H6051
Prv 16:15 his favour *is* as a c of the latter rain. H5645
Isa 4: 5 her assemblies, a c and smoke by day, H6051
18: 4 like a c of dew in the heat of harvest. H5645
19: 1 upon a swift c, and shall come into H5645
25: 5 the shadow of a c: the branch of the H5645
44:22 I have blotted out, as a thick c, thy H5645
22 and, as a c, thy sins: return unto H6051
60: 8 Who *are* these *that* fly as a c, and as the H5645
Lam 2: 1 of Zion with a c in his anger, *and* cast H5743
3:44 Thou hast covered thyself with a c, that H6051
Ezk 1: 4 the north, a great c, and a fire infolding H6051
28 bow that is in the c in the day of rain, H6051
8:11 hand; and a thick c of incense went up. H6051
10: 3 went in; and the c filled the inner court. H6051
4 was filled with the c, and the court was H6051
30:18 her: as for her, a c shall cover her, and H6051
32: 7 c, and the moon shall not give her light. H6051
38: 9 shalt be like a c to cover the land, thou, H6051
16 of Israel, as a c to cover the land; it H6051
Hos 6: 4 c, and as the early dew it goeth away. H6051
13: 3 be as the morning c, and as the early H6051
Mt 17: 5 While he yet spake, behold, a bright c G3507
5 a voice out of the c, which said, This is G3507
Mk 9: 7 And there was a c that overshadowed G3507
7 came out of the c, saying, This is my G3507
Lk 9:34 While he thus spake, there came a c, G3507
34 they feared as they entered into the c. G3507
35 And there came a voice out of the c, G3507
12:54 When ye see a c rise out of the west, G3507
21:27 in a c with power and great glory. G3507
Act 1: 9 and a c received him out of their sight. G3507
1Co 10: 1 the c, and all passed through the sea; G3507
2 unto Moses in the c and in the sea; G3507
Heb 12: 1 with so great a c of witnesses, let us lay G3509
Rev 10: 1 clothed with a c: and a rainbow *was* G3507
11:12 in a c; and their enemies beheld them. G3507
14:14 And I looked, and behold a white c, and G3507
14 and upon the c *one* sat like unto the G3507
15 that sat on the c, Thrust in thy sickle, G3507
16 And he that sat on the c thrust in his G3507

CLOUDS
Dt 4:11 with darkness, c, and thick darkness. H6051
Jdg 5: 4 dropped, the c also dropped water. H5645
2Sa 22:12 dark waters, *and* thick c of the skies. H5645
23: 4 morning without c; *as* the tender grass H5645
1Ki 18:45 was black with c and wind, and there H5645
Job 20: 6 heavens, and his head reach unto the c; H5645
22:14 Thick c *are* a covering to him, that he H5645
26: 8 He bindeth up the waters in his thick c; H5645
35: 5 the c *which* are higher than thou. H7834
36:28 Which the c do drop *and* distil upon H7834
29 of the c, *or* the noise of his tabernacle? H5645
32 With c he covereth the light; and H3709
37:16 Dost thou know the balancings of the c, H5645
21 which *is* in the c: but the wind passeth, H7834
38:34 Canst thou lift up thy voice to the c, that H5645
37 Who can number the c in wisdom? or H7834
Ps 18:11 dark waters *and* thick c of the skies. H5645
12 c passed, hail *stones* and coals of fire. H5645
36: 5 thy faithfulness *reacheth* unto the c. H7834
57:10 the heavens, and thy truth unto the c. H7834
68:34 over Israel, and his strength *is* in the c. H7834
77:17 The c poured out water: the skies sent H5645
78:23 Though he had commanded the c from H7834
97: 2 C and darkness *are* round about him: H6051
104: 3 who maketh the c his chariot: who H5645
108: 4 and thy truth *reacheth* unto the c. H7834
147: 8 Who covereth the heaven with c, who H5645
Prv 3:20 up, and the c drop down the dew. H7834
8:28 When he established the c above: when H7834
25:14 gift *is like* c and wind without rain. H5387
Ecc 11: 3 If the c be full of rain, they empty H5645
Ecc 11: 4 he that regardeth the c shall not reap. H5645
12: 2 nor the c return after the rain: H5645
Isa 5: 6 the c that they rain no rain upon it. H5645
14:14 I will ascend above the heights of the c; H5645
Jer 4:13 Behold, he shall come up as c, and his H6051
Dan 7:13 came with the c of heaven, and came H6050
Joel 2: 2 a day of c and of thick darkness, H6051
Nah 1: 3 storm, and the c *are* the dust of his feet. H6051
Zep 1:15 a day of c and thick darkness, H6051
Zec 10: 1 shall make bright c, and give them H2385
Mt 24:30 c of heaven with power and great glory. G3507
26:64 power, and coming in the c of heaven. G3507
Mk 13:26 in the c with great power and glory. G3507
14:62 power, and coming in the c of heaven. G3507
1Th 4:17 with them in the c, to meet the Lord in G3507
2Pt 2:17 These are wells without water, c that G3507
Jude 12 without fear: c *they are* without water, G3507
Rev 1: 7 Behold, he cometh with c; and every eye G3507

CLOUDY
Ex 33: 9 the tabernacle, the c pillar descended, H6051
10 And all the people saw the c pillar H6051
Neh 9:12 in the day by a c pillar; and in the night H6051
Ps 99: 7 He spake unto them in the c pillar: they H6051
Ezk 30: 3 LORD *is* near, a c day; it shall be the H6051
34:12 been scattered in the c and dark day. H6051

CLOUTED
Jos 9: 5 And old shoes and c upon their feet, H2921

CLOUTS
Jer 38:11 thence old cast c and old rotten rags, H5499
12 now *these* old cast c and rotten rags H5499

CLOVE See CLAVE.

CLOVEN
Dt 14: 7 that divide the c hoof; *as* the camel, H8156
Act 2: 3 And there appeared unto them c G1266

CLOVENFOOTED
Lev 11: 3 Whatsoever parteth the hoof, and is c, H8156
7 the hoof, and be c, yet he cheweth not H8156
26 hoof, and *is* not c, nor cheweth the cud, H8156

CLUSTER
Nu 13:23 a branch with one c of grapes, and they H811
24 because of the c of grapes which the H811
Song 1:14 My beloved *is* unto me *as* a c of H811
Isa 65: 8 is found in the c, and *one* saith, Destroy H811
Mic 7: 1 the vintage: *there is* no c to eat: my soul H811

CLUSTERS
Gen 40:10 the c thereof brought forth ripe grapes: H811
Dt 32:32 *are* grapes of gall, their c *are* bitter: H811
1Sa 25:18 and an hundred c of raisins, and two H6778
30:12 of figs, and two c of raisins: and when H6778
Song 7: 7 palm tree, and thy breasts to c *of grapes*. H811
8 breasts shall be as c of the vine, and the H811
Rev 14:18 and gather the c of the vine of the G1009

CNIDUS
Act 27: 7 were come over against C, the wind not G2834

COAL
2Sa 14: 7 shall quench my c which is left, and H1513
Isa 6: 6 me, having a live c in his hand, *which* H7531
47:14 a c to warm at, *nor* fire to sit before it. H1513
Lam 4: 8 Their visage is blacker than a c; they H7815

COALS
Lev 16:12 full of burning c of fire from off the H1513
2Sa 22: 9 mouth devoured: c were kindled by it. H1513
13 before him were c of fire kindled. H1513
1Ki 19: 6 a cake baken on the c, and a cruse of H7529
Job 41:21 His breath kindleth c, and a flame H1513
Ps 18: 8 mouth devoured: c were kindled by it. H1513
12 clouds passed, hail *stones* and c of fire. H1513
13 gave his voice; hail *stones* and c of fire. H1513
120: 4 Sharp arrows of the mighty, with c of H1513
140:10 Let burning c fall upon them: let them H1513
Prv 6:28 Can one go upon hot c, and his feet not H1513
25:22 For thou shalt heap c of fire upon his H1513
26:21 *As* c *are* to burning coals, and wood to H6352
21 *As* coals *are* to burning c, and wood to H1513
Song 8: 6 as the grave: the c thereof *are* coals of H7565
6 coals thereof *are* c of fire, *which hath a* H7565
Isa 44:12 worketh in the c, and fashioneth it with H6352
19 baked bread upon the c thereof; I have H1513
Isa 54:16 that bloweth the c in the fire, and that H6352
Ezk 1:13 *was* like burning c of fire, *and* like the H1513
10: 2 thine hand with c of fire from between H1513
24:11 Then set it empty upon the c thereof, H1513
Hab 3: 5 and burning c went forth at his feet. H7565
Jn 18:18 had made a fire of c; for it was cold: and *G439*
21: 9 c there, and fish laid thereon, and bread. *G439*
Ro 12:20 thou shalt heap c of fire on his head. *G440*

COAST
Ex 10: 4 will I bring the locusts into thy c: H1366
Nu 13:29 by the sea, and by the c of Jordan. H3027
20:23 by the c of the land of Edom, saying, H1366
22:36 of Arnon, which *is* in the utmost c. H1366
24:24 And ships *shall come* from the c of H3027
34: 3 of Zin along by the c of Edom, and your H3027
3 the outmost c of the salt sea eastward: H7097
11 And the c shall go down from Shepham H1366
Dt 2: 4 pass through the c of your brethren the H1366
18 Thou art to pass over through Ar, the c H1366
3:17 The plain also, and Jordan, and the c H1366
11:24 unto the uttermost sea shall your c be. H1366
16: 4 seen with thee in all thy c seven days; H1366
19: 8 And if the LORD thy God enlarge thy c, H1366
Jos 1: 4 going down of the sun, shall be your c. H1366
12: 4 And the c of Og king of Bashan, *which* H1366
23 The king of Dor in the c of Dor, one; the H5299
13:16 And their c was from Aroer, that *is* on H1366
25 And their c was Jazer, and all the cities H1366
30 And their c was from Mahanaim, all H1366
15: 1 *was* the uttermost part of the south c. H1366
4 goings out of that c were at the sea: this H1366
4 at the sea: this shall be your south c. H1366
12 great sea, and the c *thereof*. This *is* the H1366
12 *thereof*. This *is* the c of the children of H1366
21 Judah toward the c of Edom southward H1366
16: 3 And goeth down westward to the c of H1366
3 Japhleti, unto the c of Beth-horon the H1366
17: 7 And the c of Manasseh was from Asher H1366
9 And the c descended unto the river H1366
9 of Manasseh: the c of Manasseh also H1366
18: 5 abide in their c on the south, and the H1366
11 families: and the c of their lot came H1366
19 end of Jordan: this *was* the south c. H1366
19:22 And the c reacheth to Tabor, and H1366
29 And *then* the c turneth to Ramah, and H1366
29 city Tyre; and the c turneth to Hosah; H1366
29 are at the sea from the c to Achzib: H2256
33 And their c was from Heleph, from H1366
34 And *then* the c turneth westward to H1366
41 And the c of their inheritance was H1366
47 And the c of the children of Dan went H1366
Jdg 1:18 Also Judah took Gaza with the c H1366
18 Askelon with the c thereof, and Ekron H1366
18 thereof, and Ekron with the c thereof. H1366
36 And the c of the Amorites *was* from the H1366
11:20 pass through his c: but Sihon gathered H1366
1Sa 6: 9 the way of his own c to Beth-shemesh, H1366
7:13 no more into the c of Israel: and the H1366
27: 1 any more in any c of Israel: so shall I H1366
30:14 and upon *the c* which *belongeth* to
2Ki 14:25 He restored the c of Israel from the H1366
1Ch 4:10 and enlarge my c, and that thine hand H1366
Ezk 25:16 and destroy the remnant of the sea c. H2348
47:16 which *is* by the c of Hauran. H1366
48: 1 the north end to the c of the way of H3027
1 northward, to the c of Hamath; for H3027
Zep 2: 5 Woe unto the inhabitants of the sea c, H2256
6 And the sea c shall be dwellings *and* H2256
7 And the c shall be for the remnant of H2256
Mt 4:13 is upon the sea c, in the borders of *G3864*
Lk 6:17 and from the sea c of Tyre and Sidon, *G3882*

COASTS
Ex 10:14 and rested in all the c of Egypt: very H1366
19 not one locust in all the c of Egypt. H1366
Nu 21:13 cometh out of the c of the Amorites: for H1366
32:33 thereof in the c, *even* the cities of the H1367
34: 2 the land of Canaan with the c thereof:) H1367
12 land with the c thereof round about. H1367
Dt 3:14 of Argob unto the c of Geshuri and H1366
19: 3 and divide the c of thy land, which the H1366
28:40 throughout all thy c, but thou shalt not H1366
Jos 9: 1 and in all the c of the great sea over H2348
18: 5 shall abide in their c on the north. H1366
20 of Benjamin, by the c thereof round H1367
19:49 by their c, the children of Israel H1367
Jdg 11:22 And they possessed all the c of the H1366
26 that *be* along by the c of Arnon, three H3027

C

Jdg 18: 2 men from their c, men of valour, from H7098
19:29 and sent her into all the c of Israel. H1366
1Sa 5: 6 *even* Ashdod and the c thereof. H1366
7:14 unto Gath; and the c thereof did Israel H1366
11: 3 unto all the c of Israel: and then, H1366
7 throughout all the c of Israel by the H1366
2Sa 21: 5 remaining in any of the c of Israel, H1366
1Ki 1: 3 throughout all the c of Israel, and H1366
2Ki 10:32 Hazael smote them in all the c of Israel; H1366
15:16 therein, and the c thereof from Tirzah: H1366
1Ch 6:54 castles in their c, of the sons of Aaron, H1366
66 of their c out of the tribe of Ephraim. H1366
21:12 throughout all the c of Israel. Now H1366
2Ch 11:13 Israel resorted to him out of all their c. H1366
Ps 105:31 sorts of flies, *and* lice in all their c. H1366
33 fig trees; and brake the trees of their c. H1366
Jer 25:32 be raised up from the c of the earth. H3411
31: 8 them from the c of the earth, *and* with H3411
50:41 be raised up from the c of the earth. H3411
Ezk 33: 2 their c, and set him for their watchman: H7097
Joel 3: 4 Zidon, and all the c of Palestine? will ye H1552
Mt 2:16 and in all the c thereof, from two years *G3725*
8:34 *him* that he would depart out of their c. *G3725*
15:21 departed into the c of Tyre and Sidon. *G3313*
22 out of the same c, and cried unto him, *G3725*
39 ship, and came into the c of Magdala. *G3725*
16:13 When Jesus came into the c of *G3313*
19: 1 into the c of Judaea beyond Jordan; *G3725*
Mk 5:17 to pray him to depart out of their c. *G3725*
7:31 And again, departing from the c of *G3725*
31 through the midst of the c of Decapolis. *G3725*
10: 1 and cometh into the c of Judaea by the *G3725*
Act 13:50 and expelled them out of their c. *G3725*
19: 1 through the upper c came to Ephesus: *G3313*
26:20 and throughout all the c of Judaea, and *G5561*
27: 2 meaning to sail by the c of Asia; *one* *G5117*

COAT
Gen 37: 3 and he made him a c of *many* colours. H3801
23 Joseph out of his c, *his* coat of *many* H3801
23 *his* c of *many* colours that *was* on him; H3801
31 And they took Joseph's c, and killed a H3801
31 goats, and dipped the c in the blood; H3801
32 And they sent the c of *many* colours, H3801
32 now whether it *be* thy son's c or no. H3801
33 said, *It is* my son's c; an evil beast hath H3801
Ex 28: 4 and a broidered c, a mitre, and a girdle: H3801
39 And thou shalt embroider the c of fine H3801
29: 5 upon Aaron the c, and the robe of the H3801
Lev 8: 7 And he put upon him the c, and girded H3801
16: 4 He shall put on the holy linen c, and he H3801
1Sa 2:19 made him a little c, and brought *it* to H4598
17: 5 he *was* armed with a c of mail; and the H8302
5 c *was* five thousand shekels of brass. H8302
38 also he armed him with a c of mail. H8302
2Sa 15:32 his c rent, and earth upon his head: H3801
Job 30:18 bindeth me about as the collar of my c. H3801
Song 5: 3 I have put off my c; how shall I put it H3801
Mt 5:40 away thy c, let him have *thy* cloak also. *G5509*
Lk 6:29 thy cloak forbid not *to take thy* c also. *G5509*
Jn 19:23 a part; and also *his* c: now the coat was *G5509*
23 *his* coat: now the c was without seam, *G5509*
21: 7 he girt *his* fisher's c *unto him*, (for he *G1903*

COATS
Gen 3:21 God make c of skins, and clothed them. H3801
Ex 28:40 And for Aaron's sons thou shalt make c, H3801
29: 8 bring his sons, and put c upon them. H3801
39:27 And they made c *of* fine linen *of* woven H3801
40:14 bring his sons, and clothe them with c: H3801
Lev 8:13 sons, and put c upon them, and girded H3801
10: 5 c out of the camp; as Moses had said. H3801
Dan 3:21 Then these men were bound in their c, H5622
27 neither were their c changed, nor the H5622
Mt 10:10 neither two c, neither shoes, nor yet *G5509*
Mk 6: 9 with sandals; and not put on two c. *G5509*
Lk 3:11 He that hath two c, let him impart to *G5509*
9: 3 money; neither have two c apiece. *G5509*
Act 9:39 and shewing the c and garments which *G5509*

COCK
Mt 26:34 the c crow, thou shalt deny me thrice. *G220*
74 the man. And immediately the c crew. *G220*
75 him, Before the c crow, thou shalt deny *G220*
Mk 14:30 c crow twice, thou shalt deny me thrice. *G220*
68 went out into the porch; and the c crew. *G220*
72 And the second time the c crew. And *G220*
72 him, Before the c crow twice, thou shalt *G220*
Lk 22:34 And he said, I tell thee, Peter, the c shall *G220*
22:60 while he yet spake, the c crew. *G220*
61 the c crow, thou shalt deny me thrice. *G220*
Jn 13:38 I say unto thee, The c shall not crow, till *G220*
18:27 again: and immediately the c crew. *G220*

COCKATRICE
Isa 14:29 shall come forth a c, and his fruit *shall* H6848

COCKATRICE'
Isa 11: 8 child shall put his hand on the c den. H6848
59: 5 They hatch c eggs, and weave the H6848

COCKATRICES
Jer 8:17 For, behold, I will send serpents, c, H6848

COCKCROWING
Mk 13:35 midnight, or at the c, or in the morning: *G219*

COCKLE
Job 31:40 Let thistles grow instead of wheat, and c H890

COFFER
1Sa 6: 8 offering, in a c by the side thereof; and H712
11 the cart, and the c with the mice of gold H712
15 of the LORD, and the c that *was* with it, H712

COFFIN
Gen 50:26 him, and he was put in a c in Egypt. H727

COGITATIONS
Dan 7:28 for me Daniel, my c much troubled me, H7476

COL See COL-HOZEH.

COLD
Gen 8:22 and harvest, and c and heat, and H7120
Job 24: 7 that *they have* no covering in the c. H7135
37: 9 the whirlwind: and c out of the north. H7135
Ps 147:17 morsels: who can stand before his c? H7135
Prv 20: 4 by reason of the c; *therefore* shall he beg H2779
25:13 As the c of snow in the time of harvest, H6793
20 *As* he that taketh away a garment in c H7135
25 *As* c waters to a thirsty soul, so *is* good H7119
Jer 18:14 field? *or* shall the c flowing waters that H7119
Nah 3:17 in the hedges in the c day, *but* when the H7135
Mt 10:42 little ones a cup of c *water* only in the *G5593*
24:12 abound, the love of many shall wax c. *G5594*
Jn 18:18 of coals; for it was c: and they warmed *G5592*
Act 28: 2 the present rain, and because of the c. *G5592*
2Co 11:27 in fastings often, in c and nakedness. *G5592*
Rev 3:15 thou art neither c nor hot: I would thou *G5593*
15 nor hot: I would thou wert c or hot. *G5593*
16 and neither c nor hot, I will spue *G5593*

COL-HOZEH
Neh 3:15 Shallun the son of C, the ruler of part of H3626
11: 5 of Baruch, the son of C, the son of H3626

COLLAR
Job 30:18 it bindeth me about as the c of my coat. H6310

COLLARS
Jdg 8:26 ornaments, and c, and purple raiment H5188

COLLECTION
2Ch 24: 6 out of Jerusalem the c, *according to the* H4864
9 in to the LORD the c *that* Moses the H4864
1Co 16: 1 Now concerning the c for the saints, as *G3048*

COLLEGE
2Ki 22:14 in the c;) and they communed with her. H4932
2Ch 34:22 c:) and they spake to her to that *effect*. H4932

COLLOPS
Job 15:27 and maketh c of fat on *his* flanks. H6371

COLONY
Act 16:12 of Macedonia, *and* a c: and we were in *G2862*

COLOR See COLOUR.

COLOSSAE See COLOSSE.

COLOSSE
Col 1: 2 which are at C: Grace *be* unto you, *G2857*

COLOUR
Lev 13:55 not changed his c, and the plague be H5869
Nu 11: 7 the c thereof as the colour of bdellium. H5869
Nu 11: 7 the colour thereof as the c of bdellium. H5869
Prv 23:31 when it giveth his c in the cup, *when* it H5869
Ezk 1: 4 c of amber, out of the midst of the fire. H5869
7 sparkled like the c of burnished brass. H5869
16 *was* like unto the c of a beryl: and they H5869
22 *was* as the c of the terrible crystal, H5869
27 And I saw as the c of amber, as the H5869
8: 2 of brightness, as the c of amber. H5869
10: 9 the wheels *was* as the c of a beryl stone. H5869
Dan 10: 6 and his feet like in c to polished brass, H5869
Act 27:30 into the sea, under c as though they *G4392*
Rev 17: 4 in purple and scarlet c, and decked with *G2847*

COLOURED
Rev 17: 3 sit upon a scarlet c beast, full of names *G2847*

COLOURS
Gen 37: 3 age: and he made him a coat of *many* c. H6446
23 *his* coat of *many* c that *was* on him; H6446
32 And they sent the coat of *many* c, and H6446
Jdg 5:30 a prey of divers c, a prey of divers H6648
30 a prey of divers c of needlework, of H6648
30 of divers c of needlework on both H6648
2Sa 13:18 And *she had* a garment of divers c H6446
19 garment of divers c that *was* on her, H6446
1Ch 29: 2 and of divers c, and all manner of H7553
Isa 54:11 thy stones with fair c, and lay thy H6320
Ezk 16:16 places with divers c, and playedst the H2921
17: 3 feathers, which had divers c, came unto H7553

COLT
Gen 49:11 the vine, and his ass's c unto the choice H1121
Job 11:12 though man be born *like* a wild ass's c. H5895
Zec 9: 9 an ass, and upon a c the foal of an ass. H5895
Mt 21: 2 find an ass tied, and a c with her: loose *G4454*
5 upon an ass, and a c the foal of an ass. *G4454*
7 And brought the ass, and the c, and put *G4454*
Mk 11: 2 it, ye shall find a c tied, whereon never *G4454*
4 way, and found the c tied by the door *G4454*
5 unto them, What do ye, loosing the c? *G4454*
7 And they brought the c to Jesus, and *G4454*
Lk 19:30 ye shall find a c tied, whereon yet never *G4454*
33 And as they were loosing the c, the *G4454*
33 said unto them, Why loose ye the c? *G4454*
35 upon the c, and they set Jesus thereon. *G4454*
Jn 12:15 thy King cometh, sitting on an ass's c. *G4454*

COLTS
Gen 32:15 Thirty milch camels with their c, forty H1121
Jdg 10: 4 rode on thirty ass c, and they had thirty H5895
12:14 ass c: and he judged Israel eight years. H5895

COMBS See HONEYCOMBS.

COME
Gen 4:14 earth; and it shall c to pass, *that* every H1961
6:13 The end of all flesh is c before me; for the H935
18 and thou shalt c into the ark, thou, and H935
20 *sort* shall c unto thee, to keep *them* alive. H935
7: 1 And the LORD said unto Noah, C thou H935
9:14 And it shall c to pass, when I bring a H1961
12:11 And it came to pass, when he was c H7126
12 Therefore it shall c to pass, when the
14 that, when Abram was c into Egypt, the H935
15: 4 but he that shall c forth out of thine H3318
14 shall they c out with great substance. H3318
16 they shall c hither again: for the H7725
17: 6 of thee, and kings shall c out of thee. H3318
18: 5 therefore are ye c to your servant. And H5674
21 is c unto me; and if not, I will know. H935
19:22 thing till thou be c thither. Therefore the H935
31 man in the earth to c in unto us after the H935
32 C, let us make our father drink wine, H3212
20: 4 But Abimelech had not c near her: and H7126
13 we shall c, say of me, He *is* my brother. H935
22: 5 and worship, and c again to you. H7725
24:13 the men of the city c out to draw water: H3318
14 And let it c to pass, that the damsel to H1961
31 And he said, C in, thou blessed of the H935
43 water; and it shall c to pass, that when H1961
26:27 And Isaac said unto them, Wherefore c H935
27:21 And Isaac said unto Jacob, C near, I H5066
26 And his father Isaac said unto him, C H5066
40 and it shall c to pass when thou shalt H1961
28:21 So that I c again to my father's house H7725
30:16 said, Thou must c in unto me; for surely H935
33 for me in time to c, when it shall come H4279
33 come, when it shall c for my hire before H935
31:44 Now therefore c thou, let us make a H3212

Gen 32: 8 And said, If Esau c to the one company, H935
11 him, lest he will c and smite me, *and* the H935
33:14 endure, until I c unto my lord unto Seir. H935
34: 5 Jacob held his peace until they were c. H935
35:11 thee, and kings shall c out of thy loins; H3318
16 was but a little way to c to Ephrath: and H935
37:10 thy brethren indeed c to bow down H935
13 *flock* in Shechem? c, and I will send thee H3212
20 C now therefore, and let us slay him, H3212
23 And it came to pass, when Joseph was c H935
27 C, and let us sell him to the Ishmeelites, H3212
38:16 I pray thee, let me c in unto thee; (for he H935
16 give me, that thou mayest c in unto me? H935
41:29 Behold, there c seven years of great H935
35 good years that c, and lay up corn under H935
54 And the seven years of dearth began to c, H935
42: 7 them, Whence c ye? And they said, From H935
9 to see the nakedness of the land ye are c. H935
10 lord, but to buy food are thy servants c. H935
12 to see the nakedness of the land ye are c. H935
15 except your youngest brother c hither. H935
21 hear; therefore is this distress c upon us. H935
44:23 youngest brother c down with you, ye H3381
30 Now therefore when I c to thy servant H935
31 It shall c to pass, when he seeth that H1961
34 I see the evil that shall c on my father. H4672
45: 4 And Joseph said unto his brethren, C H5066
9 of all Egypt: c down unto me, tarry not: H3381
11 and all that thou hast, c to poverty.
16 brethren are c: and it pleased Pharaoh H935
18 households, and c unto me: and I will H935
19 your wives, and bring your father, and c. H935
46:31 in the land of Canaan, are c unto me; H935
33 And it shall c to pass, when Pharaoh
47: 1 all that they have, are c out of the land of H935
4 in the land are we c; for thy servants H935
5 father and thy brethren are c unto thee: H935
24 And it shall c to pass in the increase, H1961
48: 7 but a little way to c unto Ephrath: and I H935
49: 6 O my soul, c not thou into their secret; H935
10 feet, until Shiloh c; and unto him *shall* H935
50: 5 and bury my father, and I will c again. H7725
Ex 1:10 C on, let us deal wisely with them; lest H3051
10 multiply, and it c to pass, that, when H1961
19 ere the midwives c in unto them. H935
2:18 How *is it that* ye are c so soon to day? H935
3: 8 And I am c down to deliver them out of H3381
9 the children of Israel is c unto me: and I H935
10 C now therefore, and I will send thee H3212
13 Behold, *when* I c unto the children of H935
18 and thou shalt c, thou and the elders of H935
21 and it shall c to pass, that, when H1961
4: 8 And it shall c to pass, if they will not H1961
9 And it shall c to pass, if they will not H1961
7:15 brink against he c; and the rod which H7125
8: 3 shall go up and c into thine house, and H935
4 And the frogs shall c up both on thee, H5927
5 frogs to c up upon the land of Egypt. H5927
9:19 c down upon them, and they shall die. H3381
10:12 that they may c up upon the land of H5927
26 must serve the LORD, until we c thither. H935
11: 8 And all these thy servants shall c down H3381
12:23 to c in unto your houses to smite *you*. H935
25 And it shall c to pass, when ye be come H1961
25 And it shall come to pass, when ye be c H935
26 And it shall c to pass, when your H1961
48 and then let him c near and keep it; H7126
13:14 thee in time to c, saying, What *is* this? H4279
14:26 that the waters may c again upon the H7725
16: 5 And it shall c to pass, that on the sixth H1961
9 the children of Israel, C near before the H7126
17: 6 and there shall c water out of it, that H3318
18: 6 in law Jethro am c unto thee, and thy H935
8 the travail that had c upon them by the H4672
15 the people c unto me to inquire of God: H935
16 When they have a matter, they c unto H935
19: 2 and were c *to* the desert of Sinai, H935
9 And the LORD said unto Moses, Lo, I c H935
11 day the LORD will c down in the sight H3381
13 long, they shall c up to the mount. H5927
15 the third day: c not at *your* wives. H5066
22 And let the priests also, which c near to H5066
23 The people cannot c up to mount Sinai: H5927
24 and thou shalt c up, thou, and Aaron H5927
24 break through to c up unto the LORD, H5927
20:20 Fear not: for God is c to prove you, and H935
24 I will c unto thee, and I will bless thee. H935
21:14 But if a man c presumptuously upon his
22: 9 of both parties shall c before the judges; H935

Ex 22:27 he sleep? and it shall c to pass, when he H1961
23:27 to whom thou shalt c, and I will make all H935
24: 1 And he said unto Moses, C up unto the H5927
2 And Moses alone shall c near the H5066
2 but they shall not c nigh; neither shall H5066
12 And the LORD said unto Moses, C up H5927
14 for us, until we c again unto you: and, H7725
14 any matters to do, let him c unto them. H5066
25:32 And six branches shall c out of the H3318
33 branches that c out of the candlestick. H3318
28:43 sons, when they c in unto the tabernacle H935
43 or when they c near unto the altar H5066
30:20 not; or when they c near to the altar to H5066
32: 1 Moses delayed to c down out of the H3381
26 side? *let him* c unto me. And all the
33: 5 people: I will c up into the midst of H5927
22 And it shall c to pass, while my glory H1961
34: 2 And be ready in the morning, and c up H5927
3 And no man shall c up with thee, H5927
30 and they were afraid to c nigh him. H5066
35:10 among you shall c, and make all that the H935
36: 2 him up to c unto the work to do it: H7126
Lev 4:23 Or if his sin, wherein he hath sinned, c H3045
28 Or if his sin, which he hath sinned, c to H3045
10: 3 in them that c nigh me, and before H7138
4 and said unto them, C near, carry your H7126
6 die, and lest wrath c upon all the people:
12: 4 thing, nor c into the sanctuary, until H935
13:16 unto white, he shall c unto the priest; H935
14: 8 after that he shall c into the camp, and H935
34 When ye be c into the land of Canaan, H935
35 And he that owneth the house shall c H935
39 And the priest shall c again the seventh H7725
43 And if the plague c again, and break H7725
44 Then the priest shall c and look, and, H935
48 And if the priest shall c in, and look H935
15:14 pigeons, and c before the LORD unto H935
16: 2 brother, that he c not at all times into H935
3 Thus shall Aaron c into the holy *place*: H935
17 *place*, until he c out, and have made H3318
23 And Aaron shall c into the tabernacle of H935
24 his garments, and c forth, and offer his H3318
26 in water, and afterward c into the camp. H935
28 and afterward he shall c into the camp. H935
19:19 of linen and woollen c upon thee. H5927
23 And when ye shall c into the land, and H935
21:21 the priest shall c nigh to offer the H5066
21 not c nigh to offer the bread of his God. H5066
23 unto the vail, nor c nigh unto the altar, H5066
23:10 them, When ye be c into the land which I H935
25: 2 them, When ye c into the land which I H935
22 fruits c in ye shall eat *of* the old *store*. H935
25 if any of his kin c to redeem it, then shall H935
Nu 1: 1 were c out of the land of Egypt, saying, H3318
4: 5 Aaron shall c, and his sons, and they H935
15 sons of Kohath shall c to bear *it*: but they H935
5:14 And the spirit of jealousy c upon him, H5674
14 spirit of jealousy c upon him, and he be H5674
27 water, then it shall c to pass, *that*, if she H1961
6: 5 shall no razor c upon his head: until H5674
6 the LORD he shall c at no dead body. H935
8:19 of Israel c nigh unto the sanctuary. H5066
9: 1 were c out of the land of Egypt, saying, H3318
10:29 I will give it you: c thou with us, and we H3212
11:17 And I will c down and talk with thee H3381
20 *But* even a whole month, until it c out H3318
23 word shall c to pass unto thee or not. H7136
12: 4 and unto Miriam, C out ye three unto H3318
13:21 of Zin unto Rehob, as men c to Hamath. H935
33 of Anak, *which* c of the giants: and we
14:30 Doubtless ye shall not c into the land, H935
15: 2 them, When ye be c into the land of your H935
18 ye c into the land whither I bring you, H935
16: 5 will cause *him* to c near unto him: even H7126
5 will he cause to c near unto him. H7126
12 of Eliab: which said, We will not c up: H5927
14 the eyes of these men? we will not c up. H5927
40 of the seed of Aaron, c near to offer H7126
17: 5 And it shall c to pass, *that* the man's H1961
18: 3 only they shall not c nigh the vessels of H7126
4 a stranger shall not c nigh unto you. H7126
22 Israel henceforth c nigh the tabernacle H7126
19: 7 afterward he shall c into the camp, and H935
14 in a tent: all that c into the tent, and all H935
20: 5 And wherefore have ye made us to c up H5927
18 lest I c out against thee with the sword. H3318
21: 8 a pole: and it shall c to pass, that every H1961
27 in proverbs say, C into Heshbon, let the H935
22: 5 there is a people c out from Egypt: H3318

Nu 22: 6 C now therefore, I pray thee, curse me H3212
11 Behold, *there is* a people c out of Egypt, H3318
11 the face of the earth: c now, curse me H3212
14 and said, Balaam refuseth to c with us. H1980
17 sayest unto me: c therefore, I pray thee, H3212
20 him, If the men c to call thee, rise up, H935
36 that Balaam was c, he went out to meet H935
38 And Balaam said unto Balak, Lo, I am c H935
23: 3 the LORD will c to meet me: and H7136
7 the east, *saying*, C, curse me Jacob, and H3212
7 curse me Jacob, and c, defy Israel. H3212
13 And Balak said unto him, C, I pray H3212
27 And Balak said unto Balaam, C, I pray H3212
24:14 unto my people: c *therefore, and* I will H3212
17 nigh: there shall c a Star out of Jacob, H1869
19 Out of Jacob shall c he that shall have H3381
24 And ships *shall* c from the coast of
26:29 of Gilead c the family of the Gileadites.
27:21 his word they shall c in, *both* he, and all H935
31:24 and afterward ye shall c into the camp. H935
33:38 of Israel were c out of the land of H3318
55 you; then it shall c to pass, that those H1961
56 Moreover it shall c to pass, *that* I shall H1961
34: 2 unto them, When ye c into the land of H935
35:10 c over Jordan into the land of Canaan; H5674
26 But if the slayer shall at any time c H3318
32 that he should c again to dwell in the H7725
Dt 1:20 And I said unto you, Ye are c unto the H935
22 go up, and into what cities we shall c. H935
2:14 until we were c over the brook Zered, H5674
4:30 all these things are c upon thee, *even* in H4672
46 after they were c forth out of Egypt: H3318
6:20 thee in time to c, saying, What *mean* H4279
7:12 Wherefore it shall c to pass, if ye H1961
10: 1 unto the first, and c up unto me into H5927
11:13 And it shall c to pass, if ye shall H1961
29 And it shall c to pass, when the LORD H1961
12: 5 shall ye seek, and thither thou shalt c: H935
9 For ye are not as yet c to the rest and to H935
13: 2 And the sign or the wonder c to pass, H935
14:29 thy gates, shall c, and shall eat and be H935
15:19 All the firstling males that c of thy herd H3205
17: 9 And thou shalt c unto the priests the H935
14 When thou art c unto the land which the H935
18: 6 And if a Levite c from any of thy gates H935
6 he sojourned, and c with all the desire of H935
9 When thou art c into the land which the H935
19 And it shall c to pass, *that* whosoever H1961
22 follow not, nor c to pass, that *is* the thing H935
20: 2 And it shall be, when ye are c nigh unto H7126
21: 2 Then thy elders and thy judges shall c H3318
5 And the priests the sons of Levi shall c H5066
23:10 camp, he shall not c within the camp: H935
11 is down, he shall c into the camp *again*. H935
24: 1 her, and it c to pass that she find H1961
9 after that ye were c forth out of Egypt. H3318
25: 1 men, and they c unto judgment, that H5066
9 Then shall his brother's wife c unto H5066
17 way, when ye were c forth out of Egypt; H3318
26: 1 And it shall be, when thou *art* c in unto H935
3 thy God, that I am c unto the country H935
27:12 when ye are c over Jordan; Simeon, H5674
28: 1 And it shall c to pass, if thou shalt H1961
2 And all these blessings shall c on thee, H935
7 thy face: they shall c out against thee H3318
15 But it shall c to pass, if thou wilt not H1961
15 shall c upon thee, and overtake thee: H935
24 heaven shall it c down upon thee, until H3381
43 high; and thou shalt c down very low. H3381
45 Moreover all these curses shall c upon H935
52 and fenced walls c down, wherein thou H3381
63 And it shall c to pass, *that* as the LORD H1961
29:19 And it c to pass, when he heareth the H1961
22 So that the generation to c of your H314
22 the stranger that shall c from a far land, H935
30: 1 And it shall c to pass, when all these H1961
1 all these things are c upon thee, the H935
31: 2 no more go out and c in: also the LORD H935
11 When all Israel is c to appear before the H935
17 Are not these evils c upon us, because H4672
21 And it shall c to pass, when many evils H1961
32:35 that shall c upon them make haste. H6264
33:16 bush: let *the blessing* c upon the head of H935
Jos 2: 3 the men that are c to thee, which are H935
3 they be c to search out all the country. H935
18 Behold, *when* we c into the land, thou H935
3: 4 by measure: c not near unto it, that H7126
8 When ye are c to the brink of the water H935
9 children of Israel, C hither, and hear H5066

Jos 3:13 And it shall c to pass, as soon as the H1961
13 the waters that c down from above; H3381
15 And as they that bare the ark were c H935
4: 6 *fathers* in time to c, saying, What *mean* H4279
16 testimony, that they c up out of Jordan. H5927
17 priests, saying, C ye up out of Jordan. H5927
18 of the LORD were c up out of the midst H5927
21 to c, saying, What *mean* these stones? H4279
5:14 LORD am I now c. And Joshua fell on his H935
6: 5 And it shall c to pass, that when they H1961
19 shall c into the treasury of the LORD. H935
7:14 LORD taketh shall c according to the H7126
14 shall take shall c by households; and H7126
14 LORD shall take shall c man by man. H7126
8: 5 city: and it shall c to pass, when they H1961
5 to pass, when they c out against us, as H3318
6 (For they will c out after us) till we H3318
9: 6 of Israel, We be c from a far country: H935
8 Who *are* ye? and from whence c ye? H935
9 thy servants are c because of the name H935
10: 4 C up unto me, and help me, that we H5927
6 from thy servants; c up to us quickly, H5927
24 went with him, C near, put your feet H7126
11:20 that they should c against Israel in H7122
14:11 now, for war, both to go out, and to c in. H935
18: 4 of them; and they shall c *again* to me. H935
8 describe it, and c again to me, that I H7725
20: 6 slayer return, and c unto his own city, H935
22:24 saying, In time to c your children H4279
27 time to c, Ye have no part in the LORD. H4279
28 in time to c, that we may say *again*, H4279
23: 7 That ye c not among these nations, these H935
14 you; all are c to pass unto you, *and* H935
15 Therefore it shall c to pass, *that* as all H1961
15 as all good things are c upon you, which H935
Jdg 1: 3 his brother, C up with me into my H5927
24 And the spies saw a man c forth out of H3318
34 not suffer them to c down to the valley: H3381
3:27 And it came to pass, when he was c, that H935
4:20 any man doth c and inquire of thee, H935
22 said unto him, C, and I will shew thee H3212
6: 4 the earth, till thou c unto Gaza, and left H935
18 Depart not hence, I pray thee, until I c H935
18 he said, I will tarry until thou c again. H7725
7:13 And when Gideon was c, behold, *there* H935
17 behold, when I c to the outside of the H935
24 Ephraim, saying, C down against the H3381
8: 9 saying, When I c again in peace, I will H7725
9:10 And the trees said to the fig tree, C H3212
12 Then said the trees unto the vine, C H3212
14 the bramble, C thou, *and* reign over us. H3212
15 king over you, *then* c *and* put your trust H935
15 and if not, let fire c out of the bramble, H3318
20 But if not, let fire c out from H3318
20 Millo; and let fire c out from the men of H3318
24 of Jerubbaal might c, and their blood be H935
29 Increase thine army, and c out. H3318
31 and his brethren be c to Shechem; and, H935
33 that *is* with him c out against thee, H3318
36 Behold, there c people down from the H3381
37 said, See there c people down by the H3381
37 c along by the plain of Meonenim. H935
43 the people *were* c forth out of the city; H3318
11: 6 And they said unto Jephthah, C, and be H3212
7 c unto me now when ye are in distress? H935
12 art c against me to fight in my land? H935
33 even till thou c to Minnith, *even* twenty H935
12: 3 then are ye c up unto me this day, H5927
13: 5 and no razor shall c on his head: for H5927
8 thou didst send c again unto us, and H935
12 And Manoah said, Now let thy words c H935
17 c to pass we may do thee honour? H935
15:10 said, Why are ye c up against us? And H5927
10 Samson are we c up, to do to him as H5927
12 And they said unto him, We are c H3381
16: 2 saying, Samson is c hither. And they H935
17 There hath not c a razor upon mine H5927
18 saying, C up this once, for he H5927
18:10 When ye go, ye shall c unto a people H935
19:11 unto his master, C, I pray thee, and let H3212
13 And he said unto his servant, C, and let H3212
23 is c into mine house, do not this folly. H935
29 And when he was c into his house, he H935
20:10 they may do, when they c to Gibeah of H935
41 for they saw that evil was c upon them. H5060
21: 3 of Israel, why is this c to pass in Israel, H1961
21 of Shiloh c out to dance in dances, H3318
21 dance in dances, then c ye out of the H3318
22 or their brethren c unto us to complain, H935
Ru 1:19 when they were c to Beth-lehem, that all H935
2:11 nativity, and art c unto a people which H3212
12 under whose wings thou art c to trust. H935
14 And Boaz said unto her, At mealtime c H5066
4: 3 Naomi, that is c again out of the H7725
11 the woman that is c into thine house like H935
1Sa 1:11 there shall no razor c upon his head. H5927
20 pass, when the time was c about after H8622
2: 3 let *not* arrogancy c out of your mouth: H3318
31 Behold, the days c, that I will cut off thine H935
34 thee, that shall c upon thy two sons, on H935
36 And it shall c to pass, *that* every one H1961
36 in thine house shall c *and* crouch to him H935
4: 3 And when the people were c into the H935
6 ark of the LORD was c into the camp. H935
7 they said, God is c into the camp. And H935
5: 5 nor any that c into Dagon's house, H935
6: 7 which there hath c no yoke, and tie the H5927
21 c ye down, *and* fetch it up to you. H3381
9: 5 *And* when they were c to the land of H935
5 *was* with him, C, and let us return; lest H3212
9 thus he spake, C, and let us go to the H3212
10 servant, Well said; c, let us go. So they H3212
13 As soon as ye be c into the city, ye shall H935
13 will not eat until he c, because he doth H935
14 when they were c into the city, behold, H935
16 people, because their cry is c unto me. H935
25 And when they were c down from the H3381
10: 3 and thou shalt c to the plain of Tabor, H935
5 After that thou shalt c to the hill of God, H935
5 and it shall c to pass, when thou H1961
5 when thou art c thither to the city, that H935
6 And the spirit of the LORD will c upon H6743
7 And let it be, when these signs are c unto H935
8 and, behold, I will c down unto thee, to H3381
8 thou tarry, till I c to thee, and shew thee H935
11 *is* this *that* is c unto the son of Kish? H1961
20 the tribes of Israel to c near, the tribe of H7126
21 of Benjamin to c near by their families, H7126
22 if the man should yet c thither. And the H935
11: 3 no man to save us, we will c out to thee. H3318
10 morrow we will c out unto you, and ye H3318
14 Then said Samuel to the people, C, and H3212
12: 8 When Jacob was c into Egypt, and your H935
13:12 Therefore said I, The Philistines will c H3381
14: 1 bare his armour, C, and let us go over to H3212
6 bare his armour, C, and let us go over H3212
9 us, Tarry until we c to you; then we will H5060
10 But if they say thus, C up unto us; then H5927
11 the Hebrews c forth out of the holes H3318
12 and said, C up to us, and we will H5927
12 his armourbearer, C up after me: for H5927
26 And when the people were c into the H935
16: 2 and say, I am c to sacrifice to the LORD. H935
5 And he said, Peaceably: I am c to H935
5 sanctify yourselves, and c with me to the H935
6 And it came to pass, when they were c, H935
11 for we will not sit down till he c hither. H935
16 harp: and it shall c to pass, when the H1961
17: 8 unto them, Why are ye c out to set *your* H3318
8 man for you, and let him c down to me. H3381
25 this man that is c up? surely to defy H5927
25 to defy Israel is he c up: and it shall be, H5927
28 heart; for thou art c down that thou H3381
44 And the Philistine said to David, C to H3212
45 with a shield: but I c to thee in the name H935
52 until thou c to the valley, and to H935
19:16 And when the messengers were c in, H935
20: 9 c upon thee, then would not I tell it thee? H935
11 And Jonathan said unto David, C, and H3212
19 down quickly, and c to the place where H935
21 take them; then c thou: for *there is* peace H935
24 c, the king sat him down to eat meat. H1961
37 And when the lad was c to the place of H935
21:15 shall this *fellow* c into my house? H935
22: 3 I pray thee, c forth, *and be* with you, H3318
23: 3 more then if we c to Keilah against the H3212
7 And it was told Saul that David was c to H935
10 Saul seeketh to c to Keilah, to destroy H935
11 into his hand? will Saul c down, as thy H3381
11 And the LORD said, He will c down. H3381
15 And David saw that Saul was c out to H3318
20 Now therefore, O king, c down H3381
20 of thy soul to c down; and our part H3381
23 himself, and c ye again to me with H7725
23 you: and it shall c to pass, if he be in H1961
27 Haste thee, and c; for the Philistines H3212
24:14 After whom is the king of Israel c out? H3318
25: 8 thine eyes: for we c in a good day: give, I H935
1Sa 25:19 me; behold, I c after you. But she told H935
30 And it shall c to pass, when the LORD H1961
34 hadst hasted and c to meet me, surely H935
40 And when the servants of David were c H935
26: 4 understood that Saul was c in very deed. H935
10 him; or his day shall c to die; or he shall H935
20 king of Israel is c out to seek a flea, as H3318
22 of the young men c over and fetch it. H5674
29:10 servants that are c with thee: and as H935
30: 1 and his men were c to Ziklag on the H935
31: 4 uncircumcised c and thrust me through, H935
2Sa 1: 9 me: for anguish is c upon me, because H270
2:24 when they were c to the hill of Ammah, H935
3:23 that *was* with him were c, they told Joab, H935
26 And when Joab was c out from David, H3318
5: 6 thou shalt not c in hither: thinking, H935
6 thinking, David cannot c in hither. H935
8 and the lame shall not c into the house. H935
13 after he was c from Hebron: and there H935
23 behind them, and c upon them over H935
25 from Geba until thou c to Gazer. H935
6: 9 How shall the ark of the LORD c to me? H935
7:19 for a great while to c. And *is* this the H7350
9: 6 son of Saul, was c unto David, he fell on H935
10:11 for thee, then I will c and help thee. H1980
11: 7 And when Uriah was c unto him, David H935
12: 4 man that was c unto him; but took the H935
4 dressed it for the man that was c to him. H935
13: 5 let my sister Tamar c, and give me meat, H935
6 when the king was c to see him, Amnon H935
6 let Tamar my sister c, and make me a H935
11 said unto her, C lie with me, my sister. H935
35 king's sons c: as thy servant said, so it is. H935
14: 3 And c to the king, and speak on this H935
15 Now therefore that I am c to speak of H935
29 but he would not c to him: and when he H935
29 again the second time, he would not c. H935
32 unto thee, saying, C hither, that I may H935
32 Wherefore am I c from Geshur? *it had* H935
15: 4 c unto me, and I would do him justice! H935
28 there c word from you to certify me. H935
32 that *when* David was c to the top *of the* H935
16: 7 when he cursed, C out, come out, thou H3318
7 cursed, Come out, c out, thou bloody H3318
16 David's friend, was c unto Absalom, that H935
17: 2 And I will c upon him while he *is* weary H935
6 And when Hushai was c to Absalom, H935
9 place: and it will c to pass, when some H1961
12 So shall we c upon him in some place H935
17 not be seen to c into the city: and a H935
27 And it came to pass, when David was c H935
19:11 Israel is c to the king, *even* to his house. H935
18 the king, as he was c over Jordan; H5674
20 behold, I am c the first this day of all H935
25 And it came to pass, when he was c to H935
30 is c again in peace unto his own house. H935
33 And the king said unto Barzillai, C H5674
39 And when the king was c over, the king H5674
20:16 you, unto Joab, C near hither, that I H7126
17 And when he was c near unto her, the H7126
24:13 years of famine c unto thee in thy land? H935
21 is my lord the king c to his servant? And H935
1Ki 1:12 Now therefore c, let me, I pray thee, H3212
14 c in after thee, and confirm thy words. H935
21 Otherwise it shall c to pass, when my H1961
23 And when he was c in before the king, he H935
35 Then ye shall c up after him, that he H5927
35 after him, that he may c and sit upon my H935
42 said unto him, C in; for thou *art* a H935
45 Gihon: and they are c up from thence H5927
2:30 saith the king, C forth. And he said, H3318
41 Jerusalem to Gath, and was c again. H7725
3: 7 child: I know not *how* to go out or c in. H935
6: 1 of Israel were c out of the land of H3318
8:10 the priests were c out of the holy *place*, H3318
19 but thy son that shall c forth out of thy H3318
31 oath c before thine altar in this house: H935
42 he shall c and pray toward this house; H935
10: 2 and when she was c to Solomon, she H935
11: 2 neither shall they c in unto you: *for* H935
12: 1 were c to Shechem to make him king. H935
5 three days, then c again to me. And the H7725
12 saying, C to me again the third day. H7725
20 Jeroboam was c again, that they sent H7725
21 And when Rehoboam was c to H935
13: 7 the man of God, C home with me, and H935
15 Then he said unto him, C home with H3212
22 not c unto the sepulchre of thy fathers. H935
32 cities of Samaria, shall surely c to pass. H1961

1Ki 14: 6 the door, that he said, **C** in, thou wife of H935
13 of Jeroboam shall **c** to the grave, because H935
15:17 to go out or **c** in to Asa king of Judah. H935
19 of silver and gold; **c** and break thy H3212
17:18 of God? art thou **c** unto me to call my sin H935
21 let this child's soul **c** into him again. H7725
18:12 And it shall **c** to pass, *as soon as* I am H1961
12 not; and *so* when I **c** and tell Ahab, and H935
30 And Elijah said unto all the people, **C** H5066
19:17 And it shall **c** to pass, *that* him that H1961
20:17 There are men **c** out of Samaria. H3318
18 And he said, Whether they be **c** out for H3318
18 they be **c** out for war, take them alive. H3318
22 the king of Syria will **c** up against thee. H5927
33 *any thing would* **c** from him, and did
33 he caused him to **c** up into the chariot. H5927
22:27 water of affliction, until I **c** in peace. H935
2Ki 1: 4 Thou shalt not **c** down from that bed H3381
6 thou shalt not **c** down from that bed H3381
9 of God, the king hath said, **C** down. H3381
10 God, then let fire **c** down from heaven, H3381
11 hath the king said, **C** down quickly. H3381
12 of God, let fire **c** down from heaven, H3381
16 thou shalt not **c** down off that bed on H3381
3:21 that the kings were **c** up to fight against H5927
4: 1 and the creditor is **c** to take unto him my H935
4 And when thou art **c** in, thou shalt shut H935
22 run to the man of God, and **c** again. H7725
32 And when Elisha was **c** into the house, H935
36 **c** in unto him, he said, Take up thy son. H935
5: 6 when this letter is **c** unto thee, behold, I H935
8 thy clothes? let him **c** now to me, and he H935
10 and thy flesh shall **c** again to thee, and H7725
11 He will surely **c** out to me, and stand, H3318
22 even now there be **c** to me from mount H935
6: 9 for thither the Syrians are **c** down. H5185
20 And it came to pass, when they were **c** H935
7: 4 Now therefore **c**, and let us fall unto the H3212
5 when they were **c** to the uttermost part H935
6 the kings of the Egyptians, to **c** upon us. H935
9 some mischief will **c** upon us: now H4672
9 us: now therefore **c**, that we may go and H3212
12 saying, When they **c** out of the city, we H3318
8: 1 it shall also **c** upon the land seven years. H935
7 him, saying, The man of God is **c** hither. H935
9:16 king of Judah was **c** down to see Joram. H3381
30 And when Jehu was **c** to Jezreel, Jezebel H935
34 And when he was **c** in, he did eat and H935
10: 6 master's sons, and **c** to me to Jezreel by H935
16 And he said, **C** with me, and see my H3212
25 them; let none **c** forth. And they smote H3381
11: 9 his men that were to **c** in on the sabbath, H935
14: 8 **C**, let us look one another in the face. H3212
16: 7 and thy son: **c** up, and save me out H5927
12 And when the king was **c** from H935
18:13 king of Assyria **c** up against all the H5927
17 when they were **c** up, they came and H5927
25 Am I now **c** up without the LORD H5927
31 by a present, and **c** out to me, and *then* H3318
32 Until I **c** and take you away to a land H935
19: 3 for the children are **c** to the birth, and H935
9 Behold, he is **c** out to fight against H3318
23 my chariots I am **c** up to the height of H5927
28 and thy tumult is **c** up into mine ears, H5927
32 He shall not **c** into this city, nor shoot H935
32 arrow there, nor **c** before it with shield, H6923
33 shall not **c** into this city, saith the LORD. H935
20:14 **c** from a far country, *even* from Babylon. H935
17 Behold, the days **c**, that all that *is* in thine H935
1Ch 9:25 villages, *were* to **c** after seven days from H935
10: 4 uncircumcised **c** and abuse me. But his H935
11: 5 Thou shalt not **c** hither. Nevertheless H935
12:17 unto them, If ye be **c** peaceably unto me H935
17 you: but if *ye be* **c** to betray me to mine H935
31 by name, to **c** and make David king. H935
14:14 away from them, and **c** upon them over H935
16:29 an offering, and **c** before him: worship H935
17:11 And it shall **c** to pass, when thy days be H1961
17 for a great while to **c**, and hast regarded
19: 3 are not his servants **c** unto thee for to H935
9 were **c** *were* by themselves in the field. H935
24:19 in their service to **c** into the house of the H935
29:12 Both riches and honour *c* of thee, and
14 sort? for all things *c* of thee, and of thine
2Ch 1:10 I may go out and **c** in before this people: H935
5:11 the priests were **c** out of the holy *place:* H3318
6: 9 son which shall **c** forth out of thy loins, H3318
22 oath **c** before thine altar in this house; H935
32 Israel, but is **c** from a far country for H935

2Ch 6:32 out arm; if they **c** and pray in this house; H935
8:11 whereunto the ark of the LORD hath **c**. H935
9: 1 and when she was **c** to Solomon, she H935
10: 1 were all Israel **c** to make him king. H935
5 And he said unto them, **C** again unto H7725
12 saying, **C** again to me on the third day. H7725
11: 1 And when Rehoboam was **c** to H935
13:13 an ambushment to **c** about behind H935
16: 1 none go out or **c** in to Asa king of Judah. H935
18:14 And when he was **c** to the king, the king H935
19:10 And what cause soever shall **c** to you of H935
10 and *so* wrath **c** upon you, and upon H1961
20:11 Behold, *I say, how* they reward us, to **c** H935
16 them: behold, they **c** up by the cliff of H5927
22 **c** against Judah; and they were smitten. H935
22: 7 for when he was **c**, he went out with H935
23: 6 But let none **c** into the house of the H935
8 his men that were to **c** in on the sabbath, H935
15 and when she was **c** to the entering of H935
25:10 *wit*, the army that was **c** to him out of H935
14 that Amaziah was **c** from the slaughter H935
17 **C**, let us see one another in the face. H3212
28:17 For again the Edomites had **c** and H935
29:31 unto the LORD, **c** near and bring H5066
30: 1 that they should **c** to the house of the H935
5 that they should **c** to keep the passover H935
9 so that they shall **c** again into this land: H7725
32: 2 that Sennacherib was **c**, and that he was H935
4 kings of Assyria **c**, and find much water? H935
21 And when he was **c** into the house of his H935
35:21 king of Judah? *I c* not against thee this
Ezr 3: 1 And when the seventh month was **c**, H5060
8 all they that were **c** out of the captivity H935
4:12 up from thee to us are **c** unto Jerusalem, H858
6:21 of Israel, which were **c** again out of H7725
8:35 away, which were **c** out of the captivity, H935
9:13 And after all that is **c** upon us for our H935
10: 8 And that whosoever would not **c** within H935
14 wives in our cities **c** at appointed times, H935
Neh 2: 7 may convey me over till I **c** into Judah; H935
10 that there was **c** a man to seek the H935
17 burned with fire: **c**, and let us build up H3212
4: 8 And conspired all of them together to **c** H935
11 neither see, till we **c** in the midst among H935
6: 2 unto me, saying, **C**, let us meet together H3212
3 so that I cannot **c** down: why should H3381
3 whilst I leave it, and **c** down to you? H3381
7 to these words. **C** now therefore, and H3212
10 for they will **c** to slay thee; yea, in the H935
10 yea, in the night will they **c** to slay thee. H935
8:17 of them that were **c** again out of the H7725
9:32 thee, that hath **c** upon us, on our kings, H4672
13: 1 **c** into the congregation of God for ever; H935
22 *that* they should **c** *and* keep the gates, to H935
Est 1:12 But the queen Vashti refused to **c** at the H935
17 For *this* deed of the queen shall **c** H3318
19 That Vashti **c** no more before king H935
2:12 Now when every maid's turn was **c** to H5060
15 his daughter, was **c** to go in unto the H5060
4:11 or woman, shall **c** unto the king into the H935
11 to **c** in unto the king these thirty days. H935
14 whether thou art **c** to the kingdom for H5060
5: 4 the king and Haman **c** this day unto the H935
8 king and Haman **c** to the banquet that I H935
12 did let no man **c** in with the king unto H935
6: 4 Now Haman was **c** into the outward H935
5 court. And the king said, Let him **c** in. H935
8: 6 the evil that shall **c** unto my people? or H4672
9:26 matter, and which had **c** unto them, H5060
Job 2:11 this evil that was **c** upon him, they came H935
11 together to **c** to mourn with him and H935
3: 6 it not **c** into the number of the months. H935
7 be solitary, let no joyful voice **c** therein. H935
25 For the thing which I greatly feared is **c** H857
25 that which I was afraid of is **c** unto me. H935
4: 5 But now it is **c** upon thee, and thou H935
5:26 Thou shalt **c** to *thy* grave in a full age, H935
7: 9 down to the grave shall **c** up no *more*. H5927
8:22 place of the wicked shall **c** to nought.
9:32 *and* we should **c** together in judgment. H935
13:13 I may speak, and let **c** on me what *will*. H5674
16 for an hypocrite shall not **c** before him. H935
14:14 time will I wait, till my change **c**. H935
21 His sons **c** to honour, and he knoweth *it*
15:21 the destroyer shall **c** upon him. H935
16:22 When a few years are **c**, then I shall go H857
17:10 But as for you all, do ye return, and **c** H935
18:20 They that **c** after *him* shall be astonied
19:12 His troops **c** together, and raise up their H935

Job 20:22 hand of the wicked shall **c** upon him. H935
22:21 at peace: thereby good shall **c** unto thee. H935
23: 3 find him! *that* I might **c** *even* to his seat! H935
10 he hath tried me, I shall **c** forth as gold. H3318
26:10 until the day and night **c** to an end.
34:28 the cry of the poor to **c** unto him, and he H935
37:13 He causeth it to **c**, whether for H4672
38:11 And said, Hitherto shalt thou **c**, but no H935
41:13 who can **c** *to him* with his double bridle? H935
16 another, that no air can **c** between them. H935
Ps 5: 7 But as for me, I will **c** *into* thy house in H935
7: 9 Oh let the wickedness of the wicked **c** to
16 shall **c** down upon his own pate. H3381
9: 6 O thou enemy, destructions are **c** to a
14: 7 Oh that the salvation of Israel *were* **c** out
17: 2 Let my sentence **c** forth from thy H3318
22:31 They shall **c**, and shall declare his H935
24: 7 doors; and the King of glory shall **c** in. H935
9 doors; and the King of glory shall **c** in. H935
32: 6 waters they shall not **c** nigh unto him. H5060
9 and bridle, lest they **c** near unto thee. H7126
34:11 **C**, ye children, hearken unto me: I will H3212
35: 8 Let destruction **c** upon him at unawares; H935
36:11 Let not the foot of pride **c** against me, H935
40: 7 Then said I, Lo, I **c**: in the volume of the H935
41: 6 And if he **c** to see *me*, he speaketh H935
42: 2 when shall I **c** and appear before God? H935
44:17 All this is **c** upon us; yet have we not H935
46: 8 **C**, behold the works of the LORD, what H3212
50: 3 Our God shall **c**, and shall not keep H935
52:ttl David is **c** to the house of Ahimelech. H935
53: 6 Oh that the salvation of Israel *were* **c** out
55: 5 Fearfulness and trembling are **c** upon H935
65: 2 hearest prayer, unto thee shall all flesh **c**. H935
66: 5 **C** and see the works of God: *he is* H3212
16 **C** *and* hear, all ye that fear God, and I H3212
68:31 Princes shall **c** out of Egypt; Ethiopia H857
69: 1 Save me, O God; for the waters are **c** in H935
2 *is* no standing: I am **c** into deep waters, H935
27 let them not **c** into thy righteousness. H935
71:18 *and* thy power to every one *that* is to **c**. H935
72: 6 He shall **c** down like rain upon the H3381
78: 4 to the generation to **c** the praises of the H314
6 That the generation to **c** might know H314
79: 1 O God, the heathen are **c** into thine H935
11 Let the sighing of the prisoner **c** before H935
80: 2 stir up thy strength, and **c** *and* save us. H3212
83: 4 They have said, **C**, and let us cut them H3212
86: 9 All nations whom thou hast made shall **c** H935
88: 2 Let my prayer **c** before thee: incline H935
8 *I am* shut up, and I cannot **c** forth. H3318
91: 7 right hand; *but* it shall not **c** nigh thee. H5066
10 shall any plague **c** nigh thy dwelling. H7126
95: 1 O **c**, let us sing unto the LORD: let us H3212
2 Let us **c** before his presence with H6923
6 O **c**, let us worship and bow down: let us H935
96: 8 bring an offering, and **c** into his courts. H935
100: 2 Serve the LORD with gladness: **c** before H935
101: 2 O when wilt thou **c** unto me? I will walk H935
102: 1 O LORD, and let my cry **c** unto thee. H935
13 time to favour her, yea, the set time, is **c**. H935
18 the generation to **c**: and the people which H314
109:17 As he loved cursing, so let it **c** unto him: H935
18 garment, so let it **c** into his bowels like H935
119:41 Let thy mercies **c** also unto me, O LORD, H935
77 Let thy tender mercies **c** unto me, that I H935
169 Let my cry **c** near before thee, O LORD: H7126
170 Let my supplication **c** before thee: H935
126: 6 shall doubtless **c** again with rejoicing, H935
132: 3 Surely I will not **c** into the tabernacle of H935
144: 5 Bow thy heavens, O LORD, and **c** H3381
Prv 1:11 If they say, **C** with us, let us lay wait for H3212
3:28 Say not unto thy neighbour, Go, and **c** H7725
5: 8 Remove thy way far from her, and **c** H7126
6: 3 when thou art **c** into the hand of thy H935
11 So shall thy poverty **c** as one that H935
15 Therefore shall his calamity **c** suddenly; H935
7:18 **C**, let us take our fill of love until the H3212
20 *and* will **c** home at the day appointed. H935
9: 5 **C**, eat of my bread, and drink of the H3212
10:24 The fear of the wicked, it shall **c** upon H935
11:27 seeketh mischief, it shall **c** unto him. H935
12:13 lips: but the just shall **c** out of trouble. H3318
20:13 Love not sleep, lest thou **c** to poverty;
22:16 giveth to the rich, *shall* surely **c** to want.
23:21 For the drunkard and the glutton shall **c**
24:25 and a good blessing shall **c** upon them. H935
34 So shall thy poverty **c** *as* one that H935
25: 4 there shall **c** forth a vessel for the finer. H3318

Prv 25: 7 it be said unto thee, C up hither; than H5927
26: 2 flying, so the curse causeless shall not c. H935
28:22 not that poverty shall c upon him. H935
31:25 and she shall rejoice in time to c. H314
Ecc 1: 7 the rivers c, thither they return again. H1980
11 are to c with *those* that shall come after. H314
11 to come with *those* that shall c after. H1961
16 saying, Lo, I am c to great estate, and
2:16 *is* in the days to c shall all be forgotten. H935
4:16 they also that c after shall not rejoice H314
7:18 feareth God shall c forth of them all. H3318
8:10 buried, who had c and gone from the H935
9: 2 All *things* c alike to all: *there is* one event
12: 1 while the evil days c not, nor the years H935
Song 2:10 up, my love, my fair one, and c away. H3212
12 singing *of birds* is c, and the voice of the H5060
13 my love, my fair one, and c away. H3212
4: 8 C with me from Lebanon, *my* spouse, H935
16 Awake, O north wind; and c, thou south; H935
16 Let my beloved c into his garden, and H935
5: 1 I am c into my garden, my sister, *my* H935
7:11 C, my beloved, let us go forth into the H3212
Isa 1:12 When ye c to appear before me, who H935
18 C now, and let us reason together, saith H3212
23 the cause of the widow c unto them. H935
2: 2 And it shall c to pass in the last days, H1961
3 And many people shall go and say, C H3212
5 O house of Jacob, c ye, and let us walk H3212
3:24 And it shall c to pass, *that* instead of H1961
4: 3 And it shall c to pass, *that he that is* left H1961
5: 6 but there shall c up briers and thorns: H5927
19 draw nigh and c, that we may know *it*! H935
26 behold, they shall c with speed swiftly: H935
7: 7 not stand, neither shall it c to pass. H1961
17 days that have not c, from the day that H935
18 And it shall c to pass in that day, *that* H1961
19 And they shall c, and shall rest all of H935
21 And it shall c to pass in that day, *that* a H1961
22 And it shall c to pass, for the H1961
23 And it shall c to pass in that day, *that* H1961
24 With arrows and with bows shall *men* c H935
25 there shall not c thither the fear of briers H935
8: 7 his glory: and he shall c up over all his H5927
10 Take counsel together, and it shall c to
21 and it shall c to pass, that when they H1961
10: 3 *which* shall c from far? to whom will H935
12 Wherefore it shall c to pass, *that* when H1961
20 And it shall c to pass in that day, *that* H1961
27 And it shall c to pass in that day, *that* H1961
28 He is c to Aiath, he is passed to Migron; H935
11: 1 And there shall c forth a rod out of the H3318
11 And it shall c to pass in that day, *that* H1961
13: 5 They c from a far country, from the end H935
6 c as a destruction from the Almighty. H935
22 to c, and her days shall not be prolonged. H935
14: 3 And it shall c to pass in the day that the H1961
8 laid down, no feller is c up against us. H5927
24 thought, so shall it c to pass; and as I H1961
29 root shall c forth a cockatrice, and H3318
31 for there shall c from the north a smoke, H935
16: 8 thereof, they are c *even* unto Jazer, they H5060
12 And it shall c to pass, when it is seen H1961
12 place, that he shall c to his sanctuary to H935
17: 4 And in that day it shall c to pass, *that* H1961
19: 1 cloud, and shall c into Egypt: and the H935
23 the Assyrian shall c into Egypt, and the H935
21:12 if ye will inquire, inquire ye: return, c. H857
22: 7 And it shall c to pass, *that* thy choicest H1961
20 And it shall c to pass in that day, that I H1961
23:15 And it shall c to pass in that day, that H1961
17 And it shall c to pass after the end of H1961
24:10 house is shut up, that no man may c in. H935
18 And it shall c to pass, *that* he who H1961
21 And it shall c to pass in that day, *that* H1961
26:20 C, my people, enter thou into thy H3212
27: 6 He shall cause them that c of Jacob to H935
11 off: the women c, *and* set them on fire: H935
12 And it shall c to pass in that day, *that* H1961
13 And it shall c to pass in that day, *that* H1961
13 and they shall c which were ready to H935
28:15 it shall not c unto us: for we have H935
29:24 They also that erred in spirit shall c to H3045
30: 6 from whence c the young and old lion, H935
8 be for the time to c for ever and ever: H314
29 with a pipe to c into the mountain of H935
31: 4 the LORD of hosts c down to fight for H3381
32:10 shall fail, the gathering shall not c. H935
13 Upon the land of my people shall c up H5927
34: 1 C near, ye nations, to hear; and H7126

Isa 34: 1 world, and all things that c forth of it. H6631
3 and their stink shall c up out of their H5927
5 behold, it shall c down upon Idumea, H3381
7 And the unicorns shall c down with H3381
13 And thorns shall c up in her palaces, H5927
35: 4 your God will c *with* vengeance, *even* H935
4 a recompence; he will c and save you. H935
10 shall return, and c to Zion with songs H935
36:10 And am I now c up without the LORD H5927
16 *by* a present, and c out to me: and eat H3318
17 Until I c and take you away to a land H935
37: 3 for the children are c to the birth, and H935
9 of Ethiopia, He is c forth to make war H3318
24 my chariots am I c up to the height of H5927
29 and thy tumult, is c up into mine ears, H5927
33 He shall not c into this city, nor shoot H935
33 an arrow there, nor c before it with H6923
34 shall not c into this city, saith the LORD. H935
39: 3 said, They are c from a far country unto H935
6 Behold, the days c, that all that *is* in thine H935
40:10 Behold, the Lord GOD will c with strong H935
41: 1 strength: let them c near; then let them H5066
1 let us c near together to judgment. H7126
22 end of them; or declare us things for to c. H935
23 Shew the things that are to c hereafter, H857
25 north, and he shall c: from the rising of H857
25 my name: and he shall c upon princes as H935
42: 9 Behold, the former things are c to pass, H935
23 will hearken and hear for the time to c?
44: 7 and shall c, let them shew unto them. H935
45:11 Ask me of things to c concerning my H857
14 of stature, shall c over unto thee, and H5674
14 thine: they shall c after thee; in chains H3212
14 chains they shall c over, and they shall H5674
20 Assemble yourselves and c; draw near H935
24 *even* to him shall *men* c; and all that are H935
47: 1 C down, and sit in the dust, O virgin H3381
9 But these two *things* shall c to thee in a H935
9 they shall c upon thee in their perfection H935
11 Therefore shall evil c upon thee; thou H935
11 desolation shall c upon thee suddenly, H935
13 from *these things* that shall c upon thee. H935
48: 1 of Israel, and are c forth out of the H3318
16 C ye near unto me, hear ye this; I have H7126
49:12 Behold, these shall c from far: and, lo, H935
18 together, *and* c to thee. *As* I live, saith H935
50: 8 mine adversary? let him c near to me. H5066
51:11 shall return, and c with singing unto H935
19 These two *things* are c unto thee; who H7122
52: 1 there shall no more c into thee the H935
54:14 from terror; for it shall not c near thee. H7126
55: 1 Ho, every one that thirsteth, c ye to the H3212
1 hath no money; c ye, buy, and eat; yea, H3212
1 buy, and eat; yea, c, buy wine and milk H3212
3 Incline your ear, and c unto me: hear, H3212
13 Instead of the thorn shall c up the fir H5927
13 of the brier shall c up the myrtle tree: H5927
56: 1 c, and my righteousness to be revealed. H935
9 All ye beasts of the field, c to devour, H857
12 C ye, *say they*, I will fetch wine, and we H857
57: 1 is taken away from the evil *to c*.
59:19 the enemy shall c in like a flood, the H935
20 And the Redeemer shall c to Zion, and H935
60: 1 Arise, shine; for thy light is c, and the H935
3 And the Gentiles shall c to thy light, H1980
4 together, they c to thee: thy sons shall H935
4 to thee: thy sons shall c from far, and thy H935
5 forces of the Gentiles shall c unto thee. H935
6 from Sheba shall c: they shall bring gold H935
7 thee: they shall c up with acceptance H5927
13 The glory of Lebanon shall c unto thee, H935
14 afflicted thee shall c bending unto thee; H1980
63: 4 heart, and the year of my redeemed is c. H935
64: 1 that thou wouldest c down, that the H3381
65: 5 Which say, Stand by thyself, c not near H5066
17 not be remembered, nor c into mind. H5927
24 And it shall c to pass, that before they H1961
66:15 For, behold, the LORD will c with fire, H935
18 thoughts: it shall c, that I will gather all H935
18 and they shall c, and see my glory. H935
23 And it shall c to pass, *that* from one H1961
23 c to worship before me, saith the LORD. H935
Jer 1:15 and they shall c, and they shall set every H935
2: 3 evil shall c upon them, saith the LORD. H935
31 are lords; we will c no more unto thee? H935
3:16 And it shall c to pass, when ye be H1961
16 neither shall it c to mind: neither shall H5927
18 and they shall c together out of the land H935
22 Behold, we c unto thee; for thou *art* H857

Jer 4: 4 lest my fury c forth like fire, and burn H3318
7 The lion is c up from his thicket, and H5927
9 And it shall c to pass at that day, saith H1961
12 those *places* shall c unto me: now also H935
13 Behold, he shall c up as clouds, and his H5927
16 *that* watchers c from a far country, and H935
5:12 neither shall evil c upon us; neither shall H935
19 And it shall c to pass, when ye shall H1961
6: 3 The shepherds with their flocks shall c H935
26 for the spoiler shall suddenly c upon us. H935
7:10 And c and stand before me in this house, H935
32 Therefore, behold, the days c, saith the H935
8:16 ones; for they are c, and have devoured H935
9:17 that they may c; and send for cunning H935
17 for cunning *women*, that they may c: H935
21 For death is c up into our windows, H5927
25 Behold, the days c, saith the LORD, that I H935
10:22 Behold, the noise of the bruit is c, and a H935
12: 9 *are* against her; c ye, assemble all the H3212
9 all the beasts of the field, c to devour. H857
12 The spoilers are c upon all high places H935
15 And it shall c to pass, after that I have H1961
16 And it shall c to pass, if they will H1961
13:18 c down, *even* the crown of your glory. H3381
20 and behold them that c from the north: H935
22 heart, Wherefore c these things upon H7122
15: 2 And it shall c to pass, if they say unto H1961
16:10 And it shall c to pass, when thou shalt H1961
14 Therefore, behold, the days c, saith the H935
19 the Gentiles shall c unto thee from the H935
17:15 *is* the word of the LORD? let it c now. H935
19 the kings of Judah c in, and by the which H935
24 And it shall c to pass, if ye diligently H1961
26 And they shall c from the cities of Judah, H935
18:14 that c from another place be forsaken?
18 Then said they, C, and let us devise H3212
18 from the prophet. C, and let us smite H3212
19: 6 Therefore, behold, the days c, saith the H935
20: 6 and thou shalt c to Babylon, and there H935
21:13 say, Who shall c down against us? or H5181
22:23 be when pangs c upon thee, the pain as H935
23: 5 Behold, the days c, saith the LORD, that I H935
7 Therefore, behold, the days c, saith the H935
17 his own heart, No evil shall c upon you. H935
25: 3 of the LORD hath c unto me, and I H1961
12 And it shall c to pass, when seventy H1961
31 A noise shall c *even* to the ends of the H935
26: 2 cities of Judah, which c to worship in the H935
27: 3 messengers which c to Jerusalem unto H935
7 very time of his land c: and then many H935
8 And it shall c to pass, *that* the nation H1961
28: 9 the prophet shall c to pass, *then* shall the H935
30: 3 For, lo, the days c, saith the LORD, that I H935
8 For it shall c to pass in that day, saith H1961
31: 9 They shall c with weeping, and with H935
12 Therefore they shall c and sing in the H935
16 c again from the land of the enemy. H7725
17 shall c again to their own border. H7725
27 Behold, the days c, saith the LORD, that I H935
28 And it shall c to pass, *that* like as I have H1961
31 Behold, the days c, saith the LORD, that I H935
38 Behold, the days c, saith the LORD, that H935
32: 7 thine uncle shall c unto thee, saying, Buy H935
23 hast caused all this evil to c upon them: H7122
24 Behold the mounts, they are c unto the H935
24 is c to pass; and, behold, thou seest *it*. H935
29 this city, shall c and set fire on this city, H935
33: 5 They c to fight with the Chaldeans, but *it* H935
14 Behold, the days c, saith the LORD, that I H935
35:11 the land, that we said, C, and let us go to H935
36: 6 ears of all Judah that c out of their cities. H935
14 of the people, and c. So Baruch the son H3212
29 shall certainly c and destroy this land, H935
37: 5 Then Pharaoh's army was c forth out H3318
7 army, which is c forth to help you, shall H3318
8 And the Chaldeans shall c again, and H7725
19 not c against you, nor against this land? H935
38:25 with thee, and they c unto thee, and say H935
40: 3 therefore this thing is c upon you. H1961
4 seem good unto thee to c with me into H935
4 me into Babylon, c; and I will look well H935
4 ill unto thee to c with me into Babylon, H935
10 which will c unto us: but ye, gather H935
41: 6 them, C to Gedaliah the son of Ahikam. H935
42: 4 your words; and it shall c to pass, *that* H1961
16 Then it shall c to pass, *that* the sword, H1961
46: 9 C up, ye horses; and rage, ye chariots; H5927
9 the mighty men c forth; the Ethiopians H3318
13 should c *and* smite the land of Egypt. H935

Jer 46:18 and as Carmel by the sea, *so* shall he c. H935
21 their calamity was c upon them, *and* the H935
22 with an army, and c against her with H935
47: 5 Baldness is c upon Gaza; Ashkelon is cut H935
48: 2 evil against it; c, and let us cut it off H3212
8 And the spoiler shall c upon every city, H935
12 Therefore, behold, the days c, saith the H935
16 The calamity of Moab *is* near to c, and H935
18 inhabit Dibon, c down from *thy* glory, H3381
18 of Moab shall c upon thee, *and* he shall H5927
21 And judgment is c upon the plain H935
45 but a fire shall c forth out of Heshbon, H3318
49: 2 Therefore, behold, the days c, saith the H935
4 treasures, *saying*, Who shall c unto me? H935
9 If grapegatherers c to thee, would they H935
14 c against her, and rise up to the battle. H935
19 Behold, he shall c up like a lion from H5927
22 Behold, he shall c up and fly as the H5927
36 whither the outcasts of Elam shall not c. H935
39 But it shall c to pass in the latter days, H1961
50: 4 of Israel shall c, they and the children H935
5 *saying*, C, and let us join ourselves H935
9 For, lo, I will raise and cause to c up H5927
26 C against her from the utmost border, H935
27 their day is c, the time of their visitation. H935
31 thy day is c, the time *that* I will visit thee. H935
41 Behold, a people shall c from the north, H935
44 Behold, he shall c up like a lion from H5927
51:10 our righteousness: c, and let us declare in H935
13 c, *and* the measure of thy covetousness. H935
27 horses to c up as the rough caterpillers. H5927
33 while, and the time of her harvest shall c. H935
42 The sea is c up upon Babylon: she is H5927
46 rumour shall both c *one* year, and after H935
46 in *another* year *shall* c a rumour, and
47 Therefore, behold, the days c, that I will H935
48 for the spoilers shall c unto her from the H935
50 off, and let Jerusalem c into your mind. H5927
51 for strangers are c into the sanctuaries H935
52 Wherefore, behold, the days c, saith the H935
53 shall spoilers c unto her, saith the LORD. H935
56 Because the spoiler is c upon her, *even* H935
60 all the evil that should c upon Babylon, H935
Lam 1: 4 because none c to the solemn feasts: H935
14 are wreathed, *and* c up upon my neck: H5927
22 Let all their wickedness c before thee; H935
3:47 Fear and a snare is c upon us, H1961
4:18 our days are fulfilled; for our end is c. H935
5: 1 Remember, O LORD, what is c upon H1961
Ezk 5: 4 a fire c forth into all the house of Israel. H3318
7: 2 is c upon the four corners of the land. H935
3 Now *is* the end c upon thee, and I will
5 GOD; An evil, an only evil, behold, is c. H935
6 An end is c, the end is come: it watcheth H935
6 An end is come, the end is c: it watcheth H935
6 come: it watcheth for thee; behold, it is c. H935
7 The morning is c unto thee, O thou that H935
7 land: the time is c, the day of trouble *is* H935
10 Behold the day, behold, it is c: the H935
12 The time is c, the day draweth near: let H935
26 Mischief shall c upon mischief, and H935
9: 6 and women: but c not near any man H5066
11: 5 c into your mind, *every one of* them. H4609
16 in the countries where they shall c. H935
18 And they shall c thither, and they shall H935
12:16 whither they c; and they shall know H935
25 I shall speak shall c to pass; it shall be H6213
27 *is* for many days *to* c, and he prophesieth
13:18 ye save the souls alive *that* c unto you?
14:22 behold, they shall c forth unto you, and H3318
16: 7 waxen great, and thou art c to excellent H935
16 *things* shall not c, neither shall it be *so*. H935
33 that they may c unto thee on every side H935
17:12 king of Babylon is c to Jerusalem, and H935
18: 6 hath c near to a menstruous woman, H7126
20: 3 Lord GOD; Are ye c to inquire of me? *As* H935
21:19 of Babylon may c: both twain shall come H935
19 both twain shall c forth out of one land: H935
20 Appoint a way, that the sword may c to H935
24 *I say*, that ye are c to remembrance, ye
25 day is c, when iniquity *shall have* an end, H935
27 c whose right it is; and I will give it *him*. H935
29 c, when their iniquity *shall have* an end. H935
22: 3 it, that her time may c, and maketh idols H935
4 to draw near, and art c *even* unto thy H935
23:24 And they shall c against thee with H935
40 sent for men to c from far, unto whom H935
24: 8 That it might cause fury to c up to take H5927
14 I the LORD have spoken *it*: it shall c to H935

Ezk 24:26 *That* he that escapeth in that day shall c H935
26: 3 many nations to c up against thee, as H5927
3 as the sea causeth his waves to c up. H5927
16 Then all the princes of the sea shall c H3381
27:29 of the sea, shall c down from their H3381
30: 4 And the sword shall c upon Egypt, and H935
6 of her power shall c down: from the H3381
9 great pain shall c upon them, as in the H1961
32:11 of the king of Babylon shall c upon thee. H935
33: 3 If when he seeth the sword c upon the H935
4 if the sword c, and take him away, H935
6 But if the watchman see the sword c, and H935
6 if the sword c, and take *any* person H935
30 brother, saying, C, I pray you, and hear H935
31 And they c unto thee as the people H935
33 to pass, (lo, it will c,) then shall they know H935
34:26 the shower to c down in his season; H3381
36: 8 people of Israel; for they are at hand to c. H935
37: 9 the Lord GOD; C from the four winds, H935
12 and cause you to c up out of your H5927
38: 8 years thou shalt c into the land *that is* H935
9 Thou shalt ascend and c like a storm, H935
10 Thus saith the Lord GOD; It shall also c H1961
10 time shall things c into thy mind, and H5927
13 unto thee, Art thou c to take a spoil? hast H935
15 And thou shalt c from thy place out of H935
16 And thou shalt c up against my people H5927
18 And it shall c to pass at the same time H1961
18 when Gog shall c against the land of H935
18 *that* my fury shall c up in my face. H5927
39: 2 will cause thee to c up from the north H5927
8 Behold, it is c, and it is done, saith the H935
11 And it shall c to pass in that day, *that* I H1961
17 yourselves, and c; gather yourselves on H935
40:46 of Levi, which c near to the LORD to H7131
44:13 And they shall not c near unto me, to H5066
13 unto me, nor to c near to any of my H5066
15 me, they shall c near to me to minister H7126
16 and they shall c near to my table, to H7126
17 And it shall c to pass, *that* when they H1961
17 and no wool shall c upon them, whiles H5927
25 And they shall c at no dead person to H935
45: 4 which shall c near to minister unto H7131
46: 9 But when the people of the land shall c H935
47: 9 And it shall c to pass, *that* every thing H1961
9 the rivers shall c, shall live: and there H935
9 these waters shall c thither: for they shall H935
10 And it shall c to pass, *that* the fishers H1961
20 the border, till a man c over against H935
22 And it shall c to pass, *that* ye shall H1961
23 And it shall c to pass, *that* in what tribe H1961
Dan 2:29 bed, what should c to pass hereafter: H1934
29 known to thee what shall c to pass. H1934
45 king what shall c to pass hereafter: and H1934
3: 2 of the provinces, to c to the dedication of H858
26 the most high God, c forth, and come H5312
26 God, come forth, and c *hither*. Then H858
4:24 High, which is c upon my lord the king: H4291
8: 7 And I saw him c close unto the ram, H5060
23 transgressors are c to the full, a king of
9:13 all this evil is c upon us: yet made we H935
22 O Daniel, I am now c forth to give thee H3318
23 forth, and I am c to shew *thee*; for thou H935
26 prince that shall c shall destroy the city H935
10:12 were heard, and I am c for thy words. H935
14 Now I am c to make thee understand H935
20 thou wherefore I c unto thee? and now H935
20 forth, lo, the prince of Grecia shall c. H935
11: 6 of the south shall c to the king of the H935
7 estate, which shall c with an army, and H935
9 So the king of the south shall c into *his* H935
10 *one* shall certainly c, and overflow, and H935
11 choler, and shall c forth and fight with H3318
13 and shall certainly c after certain years H935
15 So the king of the north shall c, and cast H935
21 but he shall c in peaceably, and obtain H935
23 for he shall c up, and shall become H5927
29 shall return, and c toward the south; but H935
30 For the ships of Chittim shall c against H935
40 of the north shall c against him like a H8175
45 c to his end, and none shall help him. H935
Hos 1: 5 And it shall c to pass at that day, that I H1961
10 and it shall c to pass, *that* in the place H1961
11 and they shall c up out of the land: for H5927
2:21 And it shall c to pass in that day, I will H1961
4:15 Judah offend; and c not ye unto Gilgal, H935
6: 1 C, and let us return unto the LORD: for H3212
3 and he shall c unto us as the rain, as H935
8: 1 *Set* the trumpet to thy mouth. *He shall* c

Hos 9: 4 shall not c into the house of the LORD. H935
7 The days of visitation are c, the days of H935
7 of recompence are c; Israel shall know *it*: H935
10: 8 the thistle shall c up on their altars; H5927
12 he c and rain righteousness upon you. H935
13:13 woman shall c upon him: he *is* an H935
15 an east wind shall c, the wind of the H935
15 wind of the LORD shall c up from the H5927
Joel 1: 6 For a nation is c up upon my land, H5927
13 of the altar: c, lie all night in sackcloth, H935
15 destruction from the Almighty shall it c. H935
2:20 sea, and his stink shall c up, and his ill H5927
20 and his ill savour shall c up, because he H5927
23 and he will cause to c down for you the H3381
28 And it shall c to pass afterward, *that* I H1961
31 great and the terrible day of the LORD c. H935
32 And it shall c to pass, *that* whosoever H1961
3: 9 men of war draw near; let them c up: H5927
11 Assemble yourselves, and c, all ye H935
11 thy mighty ones to c down, O LORD. H5181
12 Let the heathen be wakened, and c up H5927
13 the harvest is ripe: c, get you down; for H935
18 And it shall c to pass in that day, *that* H1961
18 a fountain shall c forth of the house of H3318
Am 4: 2 lo, the days shall c upon you, that he will H935
4 C to Beth-el, and transgress; at Gilgal H935
10 stink of your camps to c up unto your H5927
5: 5 captivity, and Beth-el shall c to nought. H1961
9 the spoiled shall c against the fortress. H935
6: 3 and cause the seat of violence to c near; H5066
9 And it shall c to pass, if there remain H1961
8: 2 unto me, The end is c upon my people of H935
9 And it shall c to pass in that day, saith H1961
11 Behold, the days c, saith the Lord GOD, H935
9:13 Behold, the days c, saith the LORD, that H935
Oba 21 And saviours shall c up on mount Zion H5927
Jna 1: 2 for their wickedness is c up before me. H5927
7 And they said every one to his fellow, C, H3212
4: 6 and made *it* to c up over Jonah, that H5927
Mic 1: 3 of his place, and will c down, and tread H3381
9 For her wound *is* incurable; for it is c H935
9 unto Judah; he is c unto the gate of my H5060
15 shall c unto Adullam the glory of Israel. H935
2:13 The breaker is c up before them: they H5927
3:11 among us? none evil can c upon us. H935
4: 1 But in the last days it shall c to pass, H1961
2 And many nations shall c, and say, H1980
2 come, and say, C, and let us go up to the H3212
8 Zion, unto thee shall it c, even the first H857
8 shall c to the daughter of Jerusalem. H935
5: 2 of thee shall he c forth unto me *that is* H3318
5 the Assyrian shall c into our land: and H935
10 And it shall c to pass in that day, saith H1961
6: 6 Wherewith shall I c before the LORD, H6923
6 the high God? shall I c before him with H6923
7:12 *In* that day *also* he shall c even to thee H935
Nah 1:11 There is *one* c out of thee, that H3318
2: 1 He that dasheth in pieces is c up before H5927
3: 7 And it shall c to pass, *that* all they that H1961
Hab 1: 8 horsemen shall c from far; they shall fly H935
9 They shall c all for violence: their faces H935
2: 3 because it will surely c, it will not tarry. H935
Zep 1: 8 And it shall c to pass in the day of the H1961
10 And it shall c to pass in that day, saith H1961
12 And it shall c to pass at that time, *that* H1961
2: 2 anger of the LORD c upon you, before H935
2 the day of the LORD'S anger c upon you. H935
Hag 1: 2 say, The time is not c, the time that the H935
2: 7 of all nations shall c: and I will fill this H935
22 their riders shall c down, every one by H935
Zec 1:21 Then said I, What c these to do? And he H935
21 his head: but these are c to fray them, to H935
2: 6 Ho, ho, *c forth*, and flee from the land of
10 of Zion: for, lo, I c, and I will dwell in the H935
6:10 Jedaiah, which are c from Babylon, and H935
10 from Babylon, and c thou the same day, H935
15 And they *that are* far off shall c and H935
15 you. And *this* shall c to pass, if ye will H1961
7:13 Therefore it is c to pass, *that* as he H1961
8:13 And it shall c to pass, *that* as ye were a H1961
20 of hosts; *It shall* yet c *to pass*, that there
20 *pass*, that there shall c people, and the H935
22 nations shall c to seek the LORD of H935
23 In those days *it shall c to pass*, that ten
11: 2 for the forest of the vintage is c down. H3381
12: 9 And it shall c to pass in that day, *that* I H1961
9 all the nations that c against Jerusalem. H935
13: 2 And it shall c to pass in that day, saith H1961
3 And it shall c to pass, *that* when any H1961

Zec 13: 4 And it shall c to pass in that day, *that* H1961
8 And it shall c to pass, *that* in all the H1961
14: 5 God shall c, *and* all the saints with thee. H935
6 And it shall c to pass in that day, *that* H1961
7 nor night: but it shall c to pass, *that* at H1961
13 And it shall c to pass in that day, *that* a H1961
16 And it shall c to pass, *that* every one H1961
17 And it shall be, *that* whoso will not c up H5927
18 go not up, and c not, that *have* no *rain*; H935
18 the heathen that c not up to keep the H5927
19 of all nations that c not up to keep the H5927
21 that sacrifice shall c and take of them, H935
Mal 3: 1 shall suddenly c to his temple, even the H935
1 he shall c, saith the LORD of hosts. H935
5 And I will c near to you to judgment; H7126
4: 6 lest I c and smite the earth with a curse. H935
Mt 2: 2 in the east, and are c to worship him. G2064
6 for out of thee shall c a Governor, that G1831
8 that I may c and worship him also. G2064
11 And when they were c into the house, G2064
3: 7 and Sadducees c to his baptism, he G2064
7 warned you to flee from the wrath to c? G3195
5:17 Think not that I am c to destroy the G2064
17 I am not c to destroy, but to fulfil. G2064
24 brother, and then c and offer thy gift. G2064
26 shalt by no means c out thence, till G1831
6:10 Thy kingdom c. Thy will be done in G2064
7:15 Beware of false prophets, which c to G2064
8: 1 When he was c down from the G2597
7 And Jesus saith unto him, I will c and G2064
8 thou shouldest c under my roof: but G1525
9 and to another, C, and he cometh; and G2064
11 And I say unto you, That many shall c G2240
14 And when Jesus was c into Peter's G2064
16 When the even was c, they brought unto G1096
28 And when he was c to the other side G2064
29 c hither to torment us before the time? G2064
32 when they were c out, they went into G1831
9:13 for I am not c to call the righteous, G2064
15 them? but the days will c, when the G2064
18 now dead: but c and lay thy hand upon G2064
28 And when he was c into the house, the G2064
10:12 And when ye c into an house, salute it. G1525
13 let your peace c upon it: but if it be not G2064
23 cities of Israel, till the Son of man be c. G2064
34 Think not that I am c to send peace on G2064
35 For I am c to set a man at variance G2064
11: 3 should c, or do we look for another? G2064
14 *it*, this is Elias, which was for to c. G2064
28 C unto me, all *ye* that labour and are G1205
12:28 then the kingdom of God is c unto you. G5348
32 in this world, neither in the *world* to c. G3195
44 and when he is c, he findeth *it* empty, G2064
13:32 air c and lodge in the branches thereof. G2064
49 the angels shall c forth, and sever the G1831
54 And when he was c into his own G2064
14:23 the evening was c, he was there alone. G1096
28 thou, bid me c unto thee on the water. G2064
29 And he said, C. And when Peter was G2064
29 when Peter was c down out of the ship, G2064
32 And when they were c into the ship, the G1684
15:18 out of the mouth c forth from the heart; G1831
16: 5 And when his disciples were c to the G2064
24 If any *man* will c after me, let him deny G2064
27 For the Son of man shall c in the glory G2064
17:10 say the scribes that Elias must first c? G2064
11 truly shall first c, and restore all things. G2064
12 But I say unto you, That Elias is c G2064
14 And when they were c to the multitude, G2064
24 And when they were c to Capernaum, G2064
25 He saith, Yes. And when he was c into G1525
18: 7 be that offences c; but woe to that man G2064
11 For the Son of man is c to save that G2064
19:14 them not, to c unto me: for of such G2064
21 in heaven: and c *and* follow me. G1204
20: 8 So when even was c, the lord of the G1096
21: 1 and were c to Bethphage, unto G2064
10 And when he was c into Jerusalem, all G1525
23 And when he was c into the temple, the G2064
38 This is the heir; c, let us kill him, and let G1205
22: 3 to the wedding: and they would not c. G2064
4 things *are* ready: c unto the marriage. G1205
23:35 That upon you may c all the righteous G2064
36 things shall c upon this generation. G2240
24: 5 For many shall c in my name, saying, I G2064
6 must c to pass, but the end is not yet. G1096
14 all nations; and then shall the end c. G2240
17 Let him which is on the housetop not c G2597
42 know not what hour your Lord doth c. G2064
Mt 24:43 watch the thief would c, he would have G2064
50 The lord of that servant shall c in a day G2240
25:31 When the Son of man shall c in his G2064
34 on his right hand, C, ye blessed of my G1205
26:20 Now when the even was c, he sat down G1096
50 art thou c? Then came they, and G3918
55 multitudes, Are ye c out as against a G1831
27: 1 When the morning was c, all the chief G1096
33 And when they were c unto a place G2064
40 the Son of God, c down from the cross. G2597
42 of Israel, let him now c down from the G2597
49 us see whether Elias will c to save him. G2064
57 When the even was c, there came a rich G1096
64 lest his disciples c by night, and steal G2064
28: 6 C, see the place where the Lord lay. G1205
14 And if this c to the governor's ears, we G191
Mk 1:17 And Jesus said unto them, C ye after G1205
24 art thou c to destroy us? I know G2064
25 Hold thy peace, and c out of him. G1831
29 And forthwith, when they were c out of G1831
2: 3 And they c unto him, bringing one sick G2064
4 And when they could not c nigh unto G4331
18 to fast: and they c and say unto him, G2064
20 But the days will c, when the G2064
4:22 kept secret, but that it should c abroad. G2064
29 in the sickle, because the harvest is c. G3936
35 And the same day, when the even was c, G1096
5: 2 And when he was c out of the ship, G1831
8 For he said unto him, C out of the man, G1831
15 And they c to Jesus, and see him that G2064
18 And when he was c into the ship, he G1684
23 death: *I pray thee*, c and lay thy hands G2064
39 And when he was c in, he saith unto G1525
6: 2 And when the sabbath day was c, he G1096
21 And when a convenient day was c, that G1096
31 And he said unto them, C ye yourselves G1205
47 And when even was c, the ship was in G1096
54 And when they were c out of the ship, G1831
7: 4 And *when they* c from the market,
15 the things which c out of him, those are G1607
23 All these evil things c from within, and G1607
30 And when she was c to her house, she G565
8:34 Whosoever will c after me, let him G2064
9: 1 seen the kingdom of God c with power. G2064
11 say the scribes that Elias must first c? G2064
13 Elias is indeed c, and they have done G2064
25 I charge thee, c out of him, and enter G1831
28 And when he was c into the house, his G1525
29 And he said unto them, This kind can c G1831
10:14 little children to c unto me, and forbid G2064
21 and c, take up the cross, and follow me. G1204
30 and in the world to c eternal life. G2064
35 sons of Zebedee, c unto him, saying, G4365
11:11 the eventide was c, he went out unto G5607
12 And on the morrow, when they were c G1831
15 And they c to Jerusalem: and Jesus G2064
19 And when even was c, he went out of G1096
23 he saith shall c to pass; he shall have G1096
27 And they c again to Jerusalem: and as G2064
27 in the temple, there c to him the chief G2064
12: 7 This is the heir; c, let us kill him, and G1205
9 vineyard do? he will c and destroy the G2064
14 And when they were c, they say unto G2064
18 Then c unto him the Sadducees, which G2064
13: 6 For many shall c in my name, saying, I G2064
29 see these things c to pass, know that it G1096
14: 8 She hath done what she could: she is c G4301
41 the hour is c; behold, the Son of man G2064
45 And as soon as he was c, he goeth G2064
48 unto them, Are ye c out, as against a G4301
15:30 Save thyself, and c down from the G2064
33 And when the sixth hour was c, there G1096
36 whether Elias will c to take him down. G2064
42 And now when the even was c, because G1096
16: 1 that they might c and anoint him. G2064
Lk 1:35 Holy Ghost shall c upon thee, and the G1904
43 the mother of my Lord should c to me? G2064
2:15 this thing which is c to pass, which the G1096
3: 7 warned you to flee from the wrath to c? G3195
4:34 art thou c to destroy us? I know G2064
35 thy peace, and c out of him. And when G1831
36 the unclean spirits, and they c out. G1831
5: 7 that they should c and help them. And G2064
17 by, which were c out of every town of G2064
35 But the days will c, when the G2064
7: 3 that he would c and heal his servant. G2064
7 I myself worthy to c unto thee: but say G2064
8 and to another, C, and he cometh; and G2064
19 he that should c? or look we for another? G2064
Lk 7:20 When the men were c unto him, they G3854
20 he that should c? or look we for another? G2064
34 The Son of man is c eating and G2064
8: 4 together, and were c to him out of G1975
17 that shall not be known and c abroad. G2064
19 and could not c at him for the press. G4940
29 unclean spirit to c out of the man. For G1831
41 him that he would c into his house: G1525
9:23 If any *man* will c after me, let him deny G2064
26 when he shall c in his own glory, and G2064
37 when they were c down from the hill, G2718
51 when the time was c that he should be G4845
54 command fire to c down from heaven, G2597
56 For the Son of man is not c to destroy G2064
10: 1 and place, whither he himself would c. G2064
9 The kingdom of God is c nigh unto you. G1448
11 the kingdom of God is c nigh unto you. G1448
35 more, when I c again, I will repay thee. G1880
11: 2 Thy kingdom c. Thy will be done, as G2064
6 For a friend of mine in his journey is c G3854
20 the kingdom of God is c upon you. G5348
22 But when a stronger than he shall c G1904
33 that they which c in may see the light. G1531
12:37 meat, and will c forth and serve them. G3928
38 And if he shall c in the second watch, G2064
38 second watch, or c in the third watch, G2064
39 hour the thief would c, he would have G2064
46 The lord of that servant will c in a day G2240
49 I am c to send fire on the earth; and G2064
51 Suppose ye that I am c to give peace on G3854
13: 7 these three years I c seeking fruit on G2064
14 in them therefore c and be healed, and G2064
29 And they shall c from the east, and G2240
35 me, until *the time* c when ye shall say, G2240
14: 9 And he that bade thee and him c and G2064
17 bidden, C; for all things are now ready. G2064
20 a wife, and therefore I cannot c. G2064
23 to c in, that my house may be filled. G1525
26 If any *man* c to me, and hate not his G2064
27 and c after me, cannot be my disciple. G2064
15:27 And he said unto him, Thy brother is c; G2240
30 But as soon as this thy son was c, which G2064
16:26 pass to us, that *would* c from thence.
28 they also c into this place of torment. G2064
17: 1 that offences will c: but woe *unto him*, G2064
1 woe *unto him*, through whom they c! G2064
7 and by, when he is c from the field, Go G1525
20 of God should c, he answered them and G2064
22 The days will c, when ye shall desire G2064
31 the house, let him not c down to take it G2597
18:16 little children to c unto me, and forbid G2064
22 treasure in heaven: and c, follow me. G1204
30 and in the world to c life everlasting. G2064
35 And it came to pass, that as he was c G1448
40 and when he was c near, he asked him, G1448
19: 5 make haste, and c down; for to day I G2597
9 This day is salvation c to this house, G1096
10 For the Son of man is c to seek and to G2064
13 and said unto them, Occupy till I c. G2064
29 And it came to pass, when he was c G1448
37 And when he was c nigh, even now at G1448
41 And when he was c near, he beheld the G1448
43 For the days shall c upon thee, that G2240
20:14 This is the heir: c, let us kill him, that G1205
16 He shall c and destroy these G2064
21: 6 the days will c, in the which there shall G2064
7 *be* when these things shall c to pass? G1096
8 for many shall c in my name, saying, G2064
9 c to pass; but the end *is* not by and by. G1096
28 And when these things begin to c to G1096
31 ye see these things c to pass, know ye G1096
34 and *so* that day c upon you unawares. G2186
35 For as a snare shall it c on all them that G1904
36 things that shall c to pass, and to stand G1096
22:14 And when the hour was c, he sat down, G1096
18 vine, until the kingdom of God shall c. G2064
45 prayer, and was c to his disciples, he G2064
52 the elders, which were c to him, Be ye G3854
52 to him, Be ye c out, as against a thief, G1831
23:33 And when they were c to the place, G565
24:12 in himself at that which was c to pass. G1096
18 which are c to pass there in these days? G1096
Jn 1:31 therefore am I c baptizing with water. G2064
39 He saith unto them, C and see. They G2064
46 there any good thing c out of Nazareth? G1511
46 Philip saith unto him, C and see. G2064
2: 4 I to do with thee? mine hour is not yet c. G2240
3: 2 thou art a teacher c from God: for no G2064
19 that light is c into the world, and G2064

Jn 3:26 same baptizeth, and all *men* **c** to him. G2064
4:15 I thirst not, neither **c** hither to draw. G2064
16 her, Go, call thy husband, and **c** hither. G2064
25 when he is **c**, he will tell us all things. G2064
29 **C**, see a man, which told me all things G1205
40 So when the Samaritans were **c** unto G2064
45 Then when he was **c** into Galilee, the G2064
47 When he heard that Jesus was **c** out of G2240
47 him that he would **c** down, and heal his G2597
49 The nobleman saith unto him, Sir, **c** G2597
54 he was **c** out of Judaea into Galilee. G2064
5:14 no more, lest a worse thing **c** unto thee. G1096
24 life, and shall not **c** into condemnation; G2064
29 And shall **c** forth; they that have done G1607
40 And ye will not **c** to me, that ye might G2064
43 I am **c** in my Father's name, and ye G2064
43 **c** in his own name, him ye will receive. G2064
6: 5 a great company **c** unto him, he saith G2064
14 prophet that should **c** into the world. G2064
15 that they would **c** and take him by G2064
16 And when even was *now* **c**, his disciples G1096
17 now dark, and Jesus was not **c** to them. G2064
37 All that the Father giveth me shall **c** to G2240
44 No man can **c** to me, except the Father G2064
65 that no man can **c** unto me, except it G2064
7: 6 not yet **c**: but your time is alway ready. G3918
8 this feast; for my time is not yet full **c**. G4137
28 I am: and I am not **c** of myself, but he G2064
30 on him, because his hour was not yet **c**. G2064
34 and where I am, *thither* ye cannot **c**. G2064
36 and where I am, *thither* ye cannot **c**? G2064
37 thirst, let him **c** unto me, and drink. G2064
41 some said, Shall Christ **c** out of Galilee? G2064
8:14 cannot tell whence I **c**, and whither I go. G2064
20 on him; for his hour was not yet **c**. G2064
21 in your sins: whither I go, ye cannot **c**. G2064
22 he saith, Whither I go, ye cannot **c**. G2064
9:39 And Jesus said, For judgment I am **c** G2064
10:10 to destroy: I am **c** that they might have G2064
11:27 of God, which should **c** into the world. G2064
28 The Master is **c**, and calleth for thee. G3918
30 Now Jesus was not yet **c** into the town, G2064
32 Then when Mary was **c** where Jesus G2064
34 They said unto him, Lord, **c** and see. G2064
43 with a loud voice, Lazarus, **c** forth. G1204
48 the Romans shall **c** and take away both G2064
56 think ye, that he will not **c** to the feast? G2064
12:12 people that were **c** to the feast, when G2064
23 The hour is **c**, that the Son of man G2064
35 lest darkness **c** upon you: for he that G2638
46 I am **c** a light into the world, that G2064
13: 1 that his hour was **c** that he should G2064
3 he was **c** from God, and went to God; G1831
19 Now I tell you before it **c**, that, when it G1096
19 **c** to pass, ye may believe that I am *he*. G1096
33 I go, ye cannot **c**; so now I say to you. G2064
14: 3 for you, I will **c** again, and receive you G2064
18 I will not leave you comfortless: I will **c** G2064
23 him, and we will **c** unto him, and make G2064
28 I go away, and **c** *again* unto you. If ye G2064
29 And now I have told you before it **c** to G1096
29 when it is **c** to pass, ye might believe. G1096
15:22 If I had not **c** and spoken unto them, G2064
26 But when the Comforter is **c**, whom I G2064
16: 4 the time shall **c**, ye may remember that G2064
7 Comforter will not **c** unto you; but if I G2064
8 And when he is **c**, he will reprove the G2064
13 the Spirit of truth, is **c**, he will guide you G2064
13 speak: and he will shew you things to **c**. G2064
21 her hour is **c**: but as soon as she is G2064
28 I came forth from the Father, and am **c** G2064
32 Behold, the hour cometh, yea, is now **c**, G2064
17: 1 Father, the hour is **c**; glorify thy Son, G2064
11 are in the world, and I **c** to thee. Holy G2064
13 And now **c** I to thee; and these things I G2064
18: 4 all things that should **c** upon him, went G2064
21: 4 But when the morning was now **c**, Jesus G1096
9 As soon then as they were **c** to land, they G576
12 Jesus saith unto them, **C** *and* dine. And G1205
22 I **c**, what *is that* to thee? follow thou me. G2064
23 that he tarry till I **c**, what *is that* to thee? G2064
Act 1: 6 When they therefore were **c** together, G4905
8 the Holy Ghost is **c** upon you: and ye G1904
11 heaven, shall so **c** in like manner as ye G2064
13 And when they were **c** in, they went up G1525
2: 1 was fully **c**, they were all with one G4845
17 And it shall **c** to pass in the last days, G1511
20 great and notable day of the Lord **c**: G2064
21 And it shall **c** to pass, *that* whosoever G1511
Act 3:19 shall **c** from the presence of the Lord; G2064
23 And it shall **c** to pass, *that* every soul, G1511
5:38 this work be of men, it will **c** to nought: G2647
7: 3 **c** into the land which I shall shew thee. G1204
7 they **c** forth, and serve me in this place. G1834
34 groaning, and am **c** down to deliver G2597
34 And now **c**, I will send thee into Egypt. G1204
8:15 Who, when they were **c** down, prayed G2597
24 which ye have spoken **c** upon me. G1904
27 and had **c** to Jerusalem for to worship, G2064
31 that he would **c** up and sit with him. G5927
39 And when they were **c** up out of the G5927
9:26 And when Saul was **c** to Jerusalem, he G3854
38 that he would not delay to **c** to them. G1330
39 When he was **c**, they brought him into G3854
10: 4 are **c** up for a memorial before God. G5927
21 what *is* the cause wherefore ye are **c**? G3918
27 and found many that were **c** together. G4905
28 to keep company, or **c** unto one of G4334
33 done that thou art **c**. Now therefore are G3854
11: 2 And when Peter was **c** up to Jerusalem, G5927
11 three men already **c** unto the house G2186
20 when they were **c** to Antioch, spake G1525
12:11 And when Peter was **c** to himself, he G1096
13:40 Beware therefore, lest that **c** upon you, G1904
14:11 are **c** down to us in the likeness of men. G2597
27 And when they were **c**, and had G3854
15: 4 And when they were **c** to Jerusalem, G3854
16: 7 After they were **c** to Mysia, they G2064
9 **C** over into Macedonia, and help us. G1224
15 to the Lord, **c** into my house, and G1525
18 of Jesus Christ to **c** out of her. And he G1831
37 let them **c** themselves and fetch us out. G2064
17: 6 world upside down are **c** hither also; G3918
15 **c** to him with all speed, they departed. G2064
18: 2 in Pontus, lately **c** from Italy, with his G2064
5 And when Silas and Timotheus were **c** G2718
27 who, when he was **c**, helped them much G3854
19: 4 **c** after him, that is, on Christ Jesus. G2064
32 not wherefore they were **c** together. G4905
20:11 When he therefore was **c** up again, and G5927
18 And when they were **c** to him, he said G3854
21:11 And when he was **c** unto us, he took G2064
17 And when we were **c** to Jerusalem, the G1096
22 must needs **c** together: for they will G4905
22 for they will hear that thou art **c**. G2064
22: 6 my journey, and was **c** nigh unto G1448
17 And it came to pass, that, when I was **c** G5290
23:15 or ever he **c** near, are ready to kill him. G1448
35 thine accusers are also **c**. And he G3854
24: 8 Commanding his accusers to **c** unto G2064
22 chief captain shall **c** down, I will know G2597
23 to minister or **c** unto him. G4334
25 judgment to **c**, Felix trembled, G3195+G1510
25: 1 Now when Festus was **c** into the G1910
7 And when he was **c**, the Jews which G3854
17 Therefore, when they were **c** hither, G4905
23 when Agrippa was **c**, and Bernice, with G2064
26: 7 and night, hope to **c**. For which hope's G2658
22 prophets and Moses did say should **c**: G1096
27: 7 and scarce were **c** over against Cnidus, G1096
16 much work to **c** by the boat: G4031+G1096
27 But when the fourteenth night was **c**, as G1096
28: 6 while, and saw no harm **c** to him, they G1096
17 when they were **c** together, he said unto G4905
Ro 1:10 by the will of God to **c** unto you. G2064
13 I purposed to **c** unto you, (but was G2064
3: 8 good may **c**? whose damnation is just. G2064
23 For all have sinned, and **c** short of the G5302
5:14 who is the figure of him that was to **c**. G3195
8:38 nor things present, nor things to **c**, G3195
9: 9 will I **c**, and Sarah shall have a son. G2064
26 And it shall **c** to pass, *that* in the place G1511
11:11 fall salvation *is* **c** unto the Gentiles, for
25 until the fulness of the Gentiles be **c** in. G1525
26 There shall **c** out of Sion the Deliverer, G2240
15:23 desire these many years to **c** unto you; G2064
24 into Spain, I will **c** to you: for I trust to G2064
28 them this fruit, I will **c** by you into Spain. G565
29 And I am sure that, when I **c** unto you, G2064
29 unto you, I shall **c** in the fulness of the G2064
32 That I may **c** unto you with joy by the G2064
16:19 For your obedience is **c** abroad unto all G864
1Co 1: 7 So that ye **c** behind in no gift; waiting G5302
2: 6 princes of this world, that **c** to nought: G2673
3:22 present, or things to **c**; all are yours; G3195
4: 5 until the Lord **c**, who both will bring G2064
18 up, as though I would not **c** to you. G2064
19 But I will **c** to you shortly, if the Lord G2064
1Co 4:21 What will ye? shall I **c** unto you with a G2064
7: 5 and prayer; and **c** together again, that G4905
10:11 upon whom the ends of the world are **c**. G2658
11:17 *you* not, that ye **c** together not for the G4905
18 For first of all, when ye **c** together in G4905
20 When ye **c** together therefore into one G4905
26 ye do shew the Lord's death till he **c**. G2064
33 Wherefore, my brethren, when ye **c** G4905
34 eat at home; that ye **c** not together unto G4905
34 And the rest will I set in order when I **c**. G2064
13:10 But when that which is perfect is **c**, then G2064
14: 6 Now, brethren, if I **c** unto you speaking G2064
23 If therefore the whole church be **c** G4905
23 tongues, and there **c** in *those that are* G1525
24 But if all prophesy, and there **c** in one G1525
26 How is it then, brethren? when ye **c** G4905
15:35 up? and with what body do they **c**? G2064
16: 2 that there be no gatherings when I **c**. G2064
3 And when I **c**, whomsoever ye shall G3854
5 Now I will **c** unto you, when I shall pass G2064
10 Now if Timotheus **c**, see that he may be G2064
11 that he may **c** unto me: for I look for G2064
12 desired him to **c** unto you with the G2064
12 was not at all to **c** at this time; but he G2064
12 **c** when he shall have convenient time. G2064
2Co 1:15 I was minded to **c** unto you before, that G2064
16 and to **c** again out of Macedonia G2064
2: 1 would not **c** again to you in heaviness. G2064
6:17 Wherefore **c** out from among them, G1831
7: 5 For, when we were **c** into Macedonia, G2064
9: 4 Lest haply if they of Macedonia **c** with G2064
10:14 you: for we are **c** as far as to you also G5348
12: 1 **c** to visions and revelations of the Lord. G2064
14 Behold, the third time I am ready to **c** G2064
20 For I fear, lest, when I **c**, I shall not find G2064
21 *And* lest, when I **c** again, my God will G2064
13: 2 other, that, if I **c** again, I will not spare: G2064
Gal 2:11 But when Peter was **c** to Antioch, I G2064
12 but when they were **c**, he withdrew and G2064
21 **c** by the law, then Christ is dead in vain.
3:14 That the blessing of Abraham might **c** G1096
19 till the seed should **c** to whom the G2064
25 But after that faith is **c**, we are no G2064
4: 4 But when the fulness of the time was **c**, G2064
Eph 1:21 this world, but also in that which is to **c**: G3195
2: 7 That in the ages to **c** he might shew the G1904
4:13 Till we all **c** in the unity of the faith, G2658
Php 1:27 that whether I **c** and see you, or else G2064
2:24 Lord that I also myself shall **c** shortly. G2064
Col 1: 6 Which is **c** unto you, as *it is* in all the G3918
2:17 Which are a shadow of things to **c**; but G3195
4:10 if he **c** unto you, receive him;) G2064
1Th 1:10 which delivered us from the wrath to **c**. G2064
2:16 wrath is **c** upon them to the uttermost. G5348
18 Wherefore we would have **c** unto you, G2064
2Th 1:10 When he shall **c** to be glorified in his G2064
2: 3 *that day shall not* **c**, except there come a G2064
3 except there **c** a falling away first, G2064
1Ti 2: 4 to **c** unto the knowledge of the truth. G2064
3:14 thee, hoping to **c** unto thee shortly: G2064
4: 8 that now is, and of that which is to **c**. G3195
13 Till I **c**, give attendance to reading, to G2064
6:19 **c**, that they may lay hold on eternal life. G3195
2Ti 3: 1 in the last days perilous times shall **c**. G1764
7 Ever learning, and never able to **c** to G2064
4: 3 For the time will **c** when they will not G2071
9 Do thy diligence to **c** shortly unto me: G2064
21 Do thy diligence to **c** before winter. G2064
Tit 3:12 be diligent to **c** unto me to Nicopolis: G2064
Heb 2: 5 the world to **c**, whereof we speak. G3195
4: 1 any of you should seem to **c** short of it. G5302
16 Let us therefore **c** boldly unto the G4334
6: 5 God, and the powers of the world to **c**, G3195
7: 5 they **c** out of the loins of Abraham: G1831
25 the uttermost that **c** unto God by him, G4334
8: 8 Behold, the days **c**, saith the Lord, when G2064
9:11 But Christ being **c** an high priest of G3854
11 of good things to **c**, by a greater and G3195
10: 1 of good things to **c**, *and* not the very G3195
7 Then said I, Lo, I **c** (in the volume of G2240
9 Then said he, Lo, I **c** to do thy will, O G2240
37 For yet a little while, and he that shall **c** G2064
37 shall come will **c**, and will not tarry. G2240
11:20 Jacob and Esau concerning things to **c**. G3195
24 By faith Moses, when he was **c** to years, G1096
12:18 For ye are not **c** unto the mount that G4334
22 But ye are **c** unto mount Sion, and unto G4334
13:14 no continuing city, but we seek one to **c**. G3195
23 whom, if he **c** shortly, I will see you. G2064

Jas 2: 2 For if there c unto your assembly a G1525
2 c in also a poor man in vile raiment; G1525
4: 1 From whence c wars and fightings
1 among you? c they not hence, even
5: 1 for your miseries that shall c upon you. G1904
1Pt 1:10 of the grace that should c unto you:
4:17 For the time is c that judgment must
2Pt 3: 3 Knowing this first, that there shall c in G2064
9 but that all should c to repentance. G5562
10 But the day of the Lord will c as a thief G2240
1Jn 2:18 antichrist shall c, even now are there G2064
4: 2 Jesus Christ is c in the flesh is of God: G2064
3 that Jesus Christ is c in the flesh is not G2064
3 that it should c; and even now already G2064
5:20 And we know that the Son of God is c, G2240
2Jn 7 that Jesus Christ is c in the flesh. This is G2064
10 If there c any unto you, and bring not G2064
12 ink: but I trust to c unto you, and speak G2064
3Jn 10 Wherefore, if I c, I will remember his G2064
Rev 1: 1 must shortly c to pass; and he sent G1096
4 and which is to c; and from the seven G2064
8 was, and which is to c, the Almighty. G2064
2: 5 or else I will c unto thee quickly, and G2064
16 Repent; or else I will c unto thee G2064
25 which ye have already hold fast till I c. G2240
3: 3 not watch, I will c on thee as a thief, G2240
3 not know what hour I will c upon thee. G2240
9 I will make them to c and worship G2240
10 which shall c upon all the world, G3195
11 Behold, I c quickly: hold that fast G2064
20 the door, I will c in to him, and will sup G1525
4: 1 me; which said, C up hither, and I will G305
8 which was, and is, and is to c. G2064
6: 1 of the four beasts saying, C and see. G2064
3 heard the second beast say, C and see. G2064
5 the third beast say, C and see. And I G2064
7 voice of the fourth beast say, C and see. G2064
17 For the great day of his wrath is c; and G2064
9:12 One woe is past; and, behold, there c G2064
10: 1 And I saw another mighty angel c G2597
11:12 saying unto them, C up hither. And they G305
17 wast, and art to c; because thou hast G2064
18 and thy wrath is c, and the time of the G2064
12:10 in heaven, Now is c salvation, and G1096
12 sea! for the devil is c down unto you, G2597
13:13 he maketh fire c down from heaven G2597
14: 7 of his judgment is c: and worship him G2064
15 for the time is c for thee to reap; for G2064
15: 4 all nations shall c and worship before G2240
16:13 spirits like frogs c out of the mouth of
15 Behold, I c as a thief. Blessed is he that G2064
17: 1 saying unto me, C hither; I will shew G1204
10 and the other is not yet c; and when he G2064
18: 1 I saw another angel c down from G2597
4 from heaven, saying, C out of her, my G1831
8 Therefore shall her plagues c in one G2240
10 city! for in one hour is thy judgment c. G2064
17 For in one hour so great riches is c to G2049
19: 7 c, and his wife hath made herself ready. G2064
17 the midst of heaven, C and gather G1205
20: 1 And I saw an angel c down from G2597
21: 9 with me, saying, C hither, I will shew G1204
22: 7 Behold, I c quickly: blessed is he that G2064
12 And, behold, I c quickly; and my G2064
17 And the Spirit and the bride say, C. And G2064
17 that heareth say, C. And let him that is G2064
17 let him that is athirst c. And whosoever G2064
20 saith, Surely I c quickly. Amen. Even G2064
20 quickly. Amen. Even so, c, Lord Jesus. G2064

COMELINESS

Isa 53: 2 hath no form nor c; and when we shall H1926
Ezk 16:14 through my c, which I had put upon H1926
27:10 and helmet in thee; they set forth thy c. H1926
Dan 10: 8 in me: for my c was turned in me into H1935
1Co 12:23 uncomely parts have more abundant c. G2157

COMELY

1Sa 16:18 a c person, and the LORD is with him. H8389
Job 41:12 nor his power, nor his c proportion. H2433
Ps 33: 1 for praise is c for the upright. H5000
147: 1 God; for it is pleasant; and praise is c. H5000
Prv 30:29 which go well, yea, four are c in going: H3190
Ecc 5:18 it is good and c for one to eat and to H3303
Song 1: 5 I am black, but c, O ye daughters of H5000
10 Thy cheeks are c with rows of jewels, H4998
2:14 is thy voice, and thy countenance is c. H5000
4: 3 and thy speech is c: thy temples are like H5000
6: 4 love, as Tirzah, c as Jerusalem, terrible H5000

Isa 4: 2 c for them that are escaped of Israel. H8597
Jer 6: 2 of Zion to a c and delicate woman. H5116
1Co 7:35 but for that which is c, and that ye may G2158
11:13 Judge in yourselves: is it c that a G4241
12:24 For our c parts have no need: but God G2158

COMERS

Heb 10: 1 make the c thereunto perfect. G4334

COMEST

Gen 10:19 Sidon, as thou c to Gerar, unto Gaza; H935
13:10 the land of Egypt, as thou c unto Zoar. H935
24:41 oath, when thou c to my kindred; and if H935
Dt 2:19 And when thou c nigh over against the H7126
20:10 When thou c nigh unto a city to fight H7126
23:24 When thou c into thy neighbour's H935
25 When thou c into the standing corn of H935
28: 6 Blessed shalt thou be when thou c in, H935
19 Cursed shalt thou be when thou c in, and H935
Jdg 17: 9 And Micah said unto him, Whence c H935
18:23 thee, that thou c with such a company? H2199
19:17 Whither goest thou? and whence c thou? H935
1Sa 15: 7 c to Shur, that is over against Egypt. H935
16: 4 his coming, and said, C thou peaceably? H935
17:43 I a dog, that thou c to me with staves? H935
45 Then said David to the Philistine, Thou c H935
2Sa 1: 3 him, From whence c thou? And he said H935
3:13 daughter, when thou c to see my face. H935
1Ki 2:13 And she said, C thou peaceably? And H935
19:15 c, anoint Hazael to be king over Syria: H935
2Ki 5:25 unto him, Whence c thou, Gehazi? And
9: 2 And when thou c thither, look out there H935
Job 1: 7 unto Satan, Whence c thou? Then Satan H935
2: 2 Satan, From whence c thou? And Satan H935
Jer 51:61 When thou c to Babylon, and shalt H935
Jna 1: 8 and whence c thou? what is thy country? H935
Mt 3:14 be baptized of thee, and c thou to me? G2064
Lk 23:42 me when thou c into thy kingdom. G2064
2Ti 4:13 when thou c, bring with thee, and G2064

COMETH

Gen 24:43 when the virgin c forth to draw water, H3318
29: 6 Rachel his daughter c with the sheep. H935
30:11 And Leah said, A troop c: and she called H935
32: 6 Esau, and also he c to meet thee, and H1980
37:19 one to another, Behold, this dreamer c. H935
48: 2 thy son Joseph c unto thee: and Israel H935
Ex 4:14 also, behold, he c forth to meet thee: H3318
8:20 Pharaoh; lo, he c forth to the water; H3318
13:12 every firstling that c of a beast which H7698
28:35 and when he c out, that he die not. H3318
29:30 days, when he c into the tabernacle of H935
Lev 11:34 which such water c shall be unclean: and H935
Nu 1:51 that c nigh shall be put to death. H7131
3:10 that c nigh shall be put to death. H7131
38 that c nigh shall be put to death. H7131
5:30 Or when the spirit of jealousy c upon H5674
12:12 when he c out of his mother's womb. H3318
17:13 Whosoever c any thing near unto the H7131
18: 7 that c nigh shall be put to death. H7131
21:13 wilderness that c out of the coasts of H3318
26: 5 Hanoch, of whom c the family of the
Dt 18: 8 that which c of the sale of his patrimony.
23:11 But it shall be, when evening c on, he H6437
13 back and cover that which c from thee: H6627
28:57 And toward her young one that c out H3318
Jdg 11:31 Then it shall be, that whatsoever c H3318
13:14 She may not eat of any thing that c of H3318
1Sa 4: 3 us, that, when it c among us, it may save H935
9: 6 all that he saith c surely to pass: now let H935
11: 7 Whosoever c not forth after Saul H3318
20:27 his son, Wherefore c not the son of Jesse H935
29 Therefore he c not unto the king's table. H935
25: 8 thee, whatsoever c to thine hand unto H4672
28:14 she said, An old man c up; and he is H5927
2Sa 13: 5 when thy father c to see thee, say unto H935
18:27 is a good man, and c with good tidings. H935
1Ki 8:41 people Israel, but c out of a far country H935
14: 5 wife of Jeroboam c to ask a thing of thee H935
5 it shall be, when she c in, that she shall H935
2Ki 4:10 he c to us, that he shall turn in thither. H935
6:32 the messenger c, shut the door, and hold H935
9:18 came to them, but he c not again. H7725
20 unto them, and c not again: and the H7725
10: 2 Now as soon as this letter c to you, H935
11: 8 hand: and he that c within the ranges, H935
8 the king as he goeth out and as he c in. H935
12: 4 all the money that c into any man's H5927
9 right side as one c into the house of the H935
1Ch 16:33 LORD, because he c to judge the earth. H935
29:16 c of thine hand, and is all thine own.
2Ch 13: 9 lands? so that whosoever c to consecrate H935
20: 2 saying, There c a great multitude H935
9 If, when evil c upon us, as the sword, H935
12 company that c against us; neither know H935
23: 7 whosoever else c into the house, he shall H935
7 when he c in, and when he goeth out. H935
Job 3:21 Which long for death, but it c not; and
24 For my sighing c before I eat, and my H935
5: 6 Although affliction c not forth of the H3318
21 thou be afraid of destruction when it c. H935
26 as a shock of corn c in in his season. H5927
14: 2 He c forth like a flower, and is cut H3318
18 And surely the mountain falling c to H5034
20:25 It is drawn, and c out of the body; yea, H3318
25 c out of his gall: terrors are upon him. H1980
21:17 put out! and how oft c their destruction H935
27: 9 Will God hear his cry when trouble c H935
28: 5 As for the earth, out of it c bread: and H3318
20 Whence then c wisdom? and where is H935
36:32 not to shine by the cloud that c betwixt. H6293
37: 9 Out of the south c the whirlwind: and H935
22 Fair weather c out of the north: with God H857
Ps 30: 5 for a night, but joy c in the morning.
62: 1 upon God: from him c my salvation.
75: 6 For promotion c neither from the east,
78:39 that passeth away, and c not again. H7725
96:13 Before the LORD: for he c, for he cometh H935
13 Before the LORD: for he cometh, for he c H935
98: 9 Before the LORD; for he c to judge the H935
118:26 Blessed be he that c in the name of the H935
121: 1 unto the hills, from whence c my help. H935
2 My help c from the LORD, which made
Prv 1:26 calamity; I will mock when your fear c; H935
27 When your fear c as desolation, and H935
27 your destruction c as a whirlwind; when H857
27 when distress and anguish c upon you. H935
2: 6 mouth c knowledge and understanding.
3:25 of the desolation of the wicked, when it c. H935
11: 2 When pride c, then cometh shame: but H935
2 When pride cometh, then c shame: but H935
8 of trouble, and the wicked c in his stead. H935
13: 5 man is loathsome, and c to shame.
10 Only by pride c contention: but with H5414
12 but when the desire c, it is a tree of life. H935
18: 3 When the wicked c, then cometh also H935
3 When the wicked cometh, then c also H935
17 but his neighbour c and searcheth him. H935
29:26 every man's judgment c from the LORD.
Ecc 1: 4 c: but the earth abideth for ever. H935
2:12 the man do that c after the king? even H935
4:14 For out of prison he c to reign; whereas H3318
5: 3 For a dream c through the multitude of H935
6: 4 For he c in with vanity, and departeth in H935
11: 8 they shall be many. All that c is vanity. H935
Song 2: 8 The voice of my beloved! behold, he c H935
3: 6 Who is this that c out of the wilderness H5927
8: 5 Who is this that c up from the H5927
Isa 13: 9 Behold, the day of the LORD c, cruel both H935
21: 1 it c from the desert, from a terrible land. H935
9 And, behold, here c a chariot of men, H935
12 The watchman said, The morning c, and H857
24:18 pit; and he that c up out of the midst H5927
26:21 For, behold, the LORD c out of his H3318
28:29 This also c forth from the LORD of H3318
30:13 breaking c suddenly at an instant. H935
27 Behold, the name of the LORD c from H935
42: 5 and that which c out of it; he that H6631
55:10 For as the rain c down, and the snow H3381
62:11 thy salvation c; behold, his reward is H935
63: 1 Who is this that c from Edom, with dyed H935
Jer 6:20 To what purpose c there to me incense H935
22 Thus saith the LORD, Behold, a people c H935
17: 6 not see when good c; but shall inhabit the H935
8 not see when heat c, but her leaf shall be H935
18:14 of Lebanon which c from the rock of the
43:11 And when he c, he shall smite the land of H935
46: 7 Who is this that c up as a flood, whose H5927
20 destruction c; it cometh out of the north. H935
20 destruction cometh; it c out of the north. H935
47: 4 Because of the day that c to spoil all the H935
50: 3 For out of the north there c up a nation H5927
51:54 A sound of a cry c from Babylon, and H1961
Lam 3:37 Who is he that saith, and it c to pass, H1961
Ezk 4:12 dung that c out of man, in their sight. H6627
7:25 Destruction c; and they shall seek peace, H935
14: 4 his face, and c to the prophet; I the H935
4 c according to the multitude of his idols; H935

Ezk 14: 7 his face, and c to a prophet to inquire H935
20:32 And that which c into your mind shall H5927
21: 7 the tidings; because it c: and every heart H935
7 weak *as* water: behold, it c, and shall be H935
24:24 c, ye shall know that I *am* the Lord GOD. H935
30: 9 them, as in the day of Egypt: for, lo, it c. H935
33:30 is the word that c forth from the LORD. H3318
31 And they come unto thee as the people c, H935
33 And when this c to pass, (lo, it will H935
47: 9 every thing shall live whither the river c. H935
Dan 11:16 But he that c against him shall do H935
12:12 Blessed *is* he that waiteth, and c to the H5060
Hos 7: 1 and the thief c in, *and* the troop of H935
Joel 2: 1 day of the LORD c, for *it is* nigh at hand; H935
Mic 1: 3 For, behold, the LORD c forth out of his H3318
5: 6 Assyrian, when he c into our land, and H935
7: 4 visitation c; now shall be their perplexity. H935
Hab 3:16 trouble: when he c up unto the people, H5927
Zec 9: 9 behold, thy King c unto thee: he *is* just, H935
14: 1 Behold, the day of the LORD c, and thy H935
Mal 4: 1 For, behold, the day c, that shall burn as H935
1 and the day that c shall burn them up, H935
Mt 3:11 but he that c after me is mightier G2064
13 Then c Jesus from Galilee to Jordan G3854
5:37 whatsoever is more than these c of evil. G2076
8: 9 Come, and he c; and to my servant, G2064
13:19 *it* not, then c the wicked *one*, and G2064
15:11 c out of the mouth, this defileth a man. G1607
17:27 up the fish that first c up; and when thou G305
18: 7 woe to that man by whom the offence c! G2064
21: 5 Behold, thy King c unto thee, meek, G2064
9 Blessed *is* he that c in the name of the G2064
40 of the vineyard c, what will he do unto G2064
23:39 *is* he that c in the name of the Lord. G2064
24:27 For as the lightning c out of the east, G1831
44 hour as ye think not the Son of man c. G2064
46 his lord when he c shall find so doing. G2064
25: 6 bridegroom c; go ye out to meet him. G2064
13 nor the hour wherein the Son of man c. G2064
19 servants c, and reckoneth with them. G2064
26:36 Then c Jesus with them unto a place G2064
40 And he c unto the disciples, and G2064
45 Then c he to his disciples, and saith G2064
Mk 1: 7 And preached, saying, There c one G2064
3:20 And the multitude c together again, so G4905
4:15 have heard, Satan c immediately, and G2064
5:22 And, behold, there c one of the rulers of G2064
38 And he c to the house of the ruler of the G2064
6:48 of the night he c unto them, walking G2064
7:20 And he said, That which c out of the G1607
8:22 And he c to Bethsaida; and they bring a G2064
38 when he c in the glory of his Father G2064
9:12 them, Elias verily c first, and restoreth G2064
10: 1 And he arose from thence, and c into G2064
11: 9 *is* he that c in the name of the Lord: G2064
10 father David, that c in the name of the G2064
13:35 of the house c, at even, or at midnight, G2064
14:17 And in the evening he c with the G2064
37 And he c, and findeth them sleeping, G2064
41 And he c the third time, and saith unto G2064
43 And immediately, while he yet spake, c G3854
66 c one of the maids of the high priest: G2064
Lk 3:16 mightier than I c, the latchet of whose G2064
6:47 Whosoever c to me, and heareth my G2064
7: 8 Come, and he c; and to my servant, G2064
8:12 that hear; then c the devil, and taketh G2064
49 While he yet spake, there c one from G2064
11:25 And when he c, he findeth *it* swept and G2064
12:36 that when he c and knocketh, they G2064
37 the lord when he c shall find watching: G2064
40 of man c at an hour when ye think not. G2064
43 his lord when he c shall find so doing. G2064
54 ye say, There c a shower; and so it is. G2064
55 say, There will be heat; and it c to pass. G1096
13:35 *is* he that c in the name of the Lord. G2064
14:10 he that bade thee c, he may say unto G2064
31 c against him with twenty thousand? G2064
15: 6 And when he c home, he calleth G2064
17:20 of God c not with observation: G2064
18: 8 man c, shall he find faith on the earth? G2064
19:38 Saying, Blessed *be* the King that c in G2064
Jn 1: 9 every man that c into the world. G2064
15 I spake, He that c after me is preferred G2064
30 This is he of whom I said, After me c a G2064
3: 8 canst not tell whence it c, and whither it G2064
20 the light, neither c to the light, lest his G2064
21 But he that doeth truth c to the light, G2064
31 He that c from above is above all: he G2064
31 he that c from heaven is above all. G2064
Jn 4: 5 Then c he to a city of Samaria, which is G2064
7 There c a woman of Samaria to draw G2064
21 me, the hour c, when ye shall neither G2064
23 But the hour c, and now is, when the G2064
25 that Messias c, which is called Christ: G2064
35 months, and *then* c harvest? behold, I G2064
5:44 not the honour that *c* from God only?
6:33 For the bread of God is he which c G2597
35 bread of life: he that c to me shall never G2064
37 that c to me I will in no wise cast out. G2064
45 hath learned of the Father, c unto me. G2064
50 This is the bread which c down from G2597
7:27 Christ c, no man knoweth whence he is. G2064
31 said, When Christ c, will he do more G2064
42 said, That Christ c of the seed of David, G2064
9: 4 the night c, when no man can work. G2064
10:10 The thief c not, but for to steal, and to G2064
11:38 in himself c to the grave. It was G2064
12:13 of Israel that c in the name of the Lord. G2064
15 thy King c, sitting on an ass's colt. G2064
22 Philip c and telleth Andrew: and again G2064
13: 6 Then c he to Simon Peter: and Peter G2064
14: 6 no man c unto the Father, but by me. G2064
30 of this world c, and hath nothing in me. G2064
15:25 But *this c to pass*, that the word might
16: 2 yea, the time c, that whosoever killeth G2064
25 but the time c, when I shall no more G2064
32 Behold, the hour c, yea, is now come, G2064
18: 3 and Pharisees, c thither with lanterns G2064
20: 1 The first *day* of the week c Mary G2064
2 Then she runneth, and c to Simon G2064
6 Then c Simon Peter following him, and G2064
21:13 Jesus then c, and taketh bread, and G2064
Act 10:32 who, when he c, shall speak unto thee. G3854
13:25 *he*. But, behold, there c one after me, G2064
18:21 this feast that c in Jerusalem: but I will G2064
Ro 4: 9 *C* this blessedness then upon the
10:17 So then faith c by hearing, and hearing
1Co 15:24 Then c the end, when he shall have
2Co 11: 4 For if he that c preacheth another G2064
28 that which c upon me daily, the care G1999
Gal 5: 8 This persuasion *c* not of him that calleth
Eph 5: 6 of these things c the wrath of God upon G2064
Col 3: 6 God c on the children of disobedience: G2064
1Th 5: 2 of the Lord so c as a thief in the night. G2064
3 destruction c upon them, as travail G2186
1Ti 6: 4 c envy, strife, railings, evil surmisings, G1096
Heb 6: 7 in the rain that c oft upon it, and G2064
10: 5 Wherefore when he c into the world, he G1525
11: 6 *him*: for he that c to God must believe G4334
Jas 1:17 is from above, and c down from the G2591
Jude 14 Lord c with ten thousands of his saints, G2064
Rev 1: 7 Behold, he c with clouds; and every eye G2064
3:12 Jerusalem, which c down out of heaven G2597
11:14 *and*, behold, the third woe c quickly. G2064
17:10 he c, he must continue a short space. G2064

COMFORT
Gen 5:29 This *same* shall c us concerning our H5162
18: 5 of bread, and c ye your hearts; after H5582
27:42 doth c himself, *purposing* to kill thee. H5162
37:35 rose up to c him; but he refused H5162
Jdg 19: 5 his son in law, C thine heart with a H5582
8 father said, C thine heart, I pray thee. H5582
2Sa 10: 2 And David sent to c him by the hand of H5162
1Ch 7:22 days, and his brethren came to c him. H5162
19: 2 messengers to c him concerning his H5162
2 of Ammon to Hanun, to c him. H5162
Job 2:11 come to mourn with him and to c him. H5162
6:10 Then should I yet have c; yea, I would H5165
7:13 When I say, My bed shall c me, my H5162
9:27 leave off my heaviness, and c *myself*: H1082
10:20 let me alone, that I may take c a little, H1082
21:34 How then c ye me in vain, seeing in H5162
Ps 23: 4 me; thy rod and thy staff they c me. H5162
71:21 my greatness, and c me on every side. H5162
119:50 This *is* my c in my affliction: for thy H5165
76 be for my c, according to thy word H5162
82 thy word, saying, When wilt thou c me? H5162
Song 2: 5 Stay me with flagons, c me with apples: H7502
Isa 22: 4 labour not to c me, because of the H5162
40: 1 C ye, comfort ye my people, saith your H5162
1 Comfort ye, c ye my people, saith your H5162
51: 3 For the LORD shall c Zion: he will H5162
3 Zion: he will c all her waste places; H5162
19 and the sword: by whom shall I c thee? H5162
57: 6 offering. Should I receive c in these? H5162
61: 2 of our God; to c all that mourn; H5162
66:13 so will I c you; and ye shall be H5162
Jer 8:18 *When* I would c myself against sorrow, H4010
16: 7 in mourning, to c them for the dead; H5162
31:13 into joy, and will c them, and make H5162
Lam 1: 2 she hath none to c *her*: all her friends H5162
17 *there is* none to c her: the LORD hath H5162
21 *there is* none to c me: all mine enemies H5162
2:13 to thee, that I may c thee, O virgin H5162
Ezk 14:23 And they shall c you, when ye see their H5162
16:54 done, in that thou art a c unto them. H5162
Zec 1:17 c Zion, and shall yet choose Jerusalem. H5162
10: 2 false dreams; they c in vain: therefore H5162
Mt 9:22 be of good c; thy faith hath made G2293
Mk 10:49 him, Be of good c, rise; he calleth thee. G2293
Lk 8:48 be of good c: thy faith hath made G2293
Jn 11:19 to c them concerning their brother. G3888
Act 9:31 c of the Holy Ghost, were multiplied. G3874
Ro 15: 4 c of the scriptures might have hope. G3874
1Co 14: 3 *to* edification, and exhortation, and c. G3889
2Co 1: 3 Father of mercies, and the God of all c; G3874
4 we may be able to c them which are in G3870
4 any trouble, by the c wherewith we G3874
2: 7 to forgive *him*, and c *him*, lest perhaps G3870
7: 4 I am filled with c, I am exceeding joyful G3874
13 Therefore we were comforted in your c: G3874
13:11 Be perfect, be of good c, be of one mind, G3870
Eph 6:22 and *that* he might c your hearts. G3870
Php 2: 1 in Christ, if any c of love, if any G3890
19 be of good c, when I know your state. G2174
Col 4: 8 know your estate, and c your hearts; G3870
11 of God, which have been a c unto me. G3931
1Th 3: 2 and to c you concerning your faith: G3870
4:18 Wherefore c one another with these G3870
5:11 Wherefore c yourselves together, and G3870
14 that are unruly, c the feebleminded, G3888
2Th 2:17 C your hearts, and stablish you in G3870

COMFORTABLE
2Sa 14:17 king shall now be c: for as an angel of H4496
Zec 1:13 with me *with* good words *and* c words. H5150

COMFORTABLY
2Sa 19: 7 forth, and speak c unto thy servants: H3820
2Ch 30:22 And Hezekiah spake c unto all the H3820
32: 6 of the city, and spake c to them, saying, H3824
Isa 40: 2 Speak ye c to Jerusalem, and cry unto H3820
Hos 2:14 the wilderness, and speak c unto her. H3820

COMFORTED
Gen 24:67 Isaac was c after his mother's *death*. H5162
37:35 but he refused to be c; and he said, For I H5162
38:12 and Judah was c, and went up unto his H5162
50:21 c them, and spake kindly unto them. H5162
Ru 2:13 for that thou hast c me, and for that H5162
2Sa 12:24 And David c Bath-sheba his wife, and H5162
13:39 for he was c concerning Amnon, H5162
Job 42:11 him, and c him over all the evil H5162
Ps 77: 2 and ceased not: my soul refused to be c. H5162
86:17 thou, LORD, hast holpen me, and c me. H5162
119:52 of old, O LORD; and have c myself. H5162
Isa 49:13 for the LORD hath c his people, and H5162
52: 9 for the LORD hath c his people, he hath H5162
54:11 tempest, *and* not c, behold, I will lay thy H5162
66:13 you; and ye shall be c in Jerusalem. H5162
Jer 31:15 refused to be c for her children, H5162
Ezk 5:13 them, and I will be c: and they shall H5162
14:22 and ye shall be c concerning the evil H5162
31:16 be c in the nether parts of the earth. H5162
32:31 Pharaoh shall see them, and shall be c H5162
Mt 2:18 would not be c, because they are not. G3870
5: 4 *are* they that mourn: for they shall be c. G3870
Lk 16:25 now he is c, and thou art tormented. G3870
Jn 11:31 in the house, and c her, when they saw G3888
Act 16:40 brethren, they c them, and departed. G3870
20:12 young man alive, and were not a little c. G3870
Ro 1:12 That is, that I may be c together with G4837
1Co 14:31 that all may learn, and all may be c. G3870
2Co 1: 4 wherewith we ourselves are c of God. G3870
6 suffer: or whether we be c, *it is* for your G3870
7: 6 cast down, c us by the coming of Titus; G3870
7 wherewith he was c in you, when he G3870
13 Therefore we were c in your comfort: G3870
Col 2: 2 That their hearts might be c, being knit G3870
1Th 2:11 As ye know how we exhorted and c and G3888
3: 7 Therefore, brethren, we were c over G3870

COMFORTEDST
Isa 12: 1 anger is turned away, and thou c me. H5162

COMFORTER
Ecc 4: 1 and they had no c; and on the side of H5162
1 *there was* power; but they had no c. H5162
Lam 1: 9 she had no c. O LORD, behold my H5162
16 water, because the c that should relieve H5162
Jn 14:16 C, that he may abide with you for ever; G3875
26 But the C, *which is* the Holy Ghost, G3875
15:26 But when the C is come, whom I will G3875
16: 7 I go not away, the C will not come unto G3875

COMFORTERS
2Sa 10: 3 that he hath sent c unto thee? hath not H5162
1Ch 19: 3 that he hath sent c unto thee? are not H5162
Job 16: 2 such things: miserable c *are* ye all. H5162
Ps 69:20 *was* none; and for c, but I found none. H5162
Nah 3: 7 her? whence shall I seek c for thee? H5162

COMFORTETH
Job 29:25 the army, as one *that* c the mourners. H5162
Isa 51:12 I, *even* I, *am* he that c you: who *art* H5162
66:13 As one whom his mother c, so will I H5162
2Co 1: 4 Who c us in all our tribulation, that we G3870
7: 6 Nevertheless God, that c those that are G3870

COMFORTLESS
Jn 14:18 I will not leave you c: I will come to you. G3737

COMFORTS
Ps 94:19 within me thy c delight my soul. H8575
Isa 57:18 c unto him and to his mourners. H5150

COMING
Gen 24:63 and saw, and, behold, the camels *were* c. H935
30:30 thee since my c: and now when shall H7272
Nu 22:16 pray thee, hinder thee from c unto me: H1980
33:40 heard of the c of the children of Israel. H935
Jdg 5:28 in c? why tarry the wheels of his chariots? H935
1Sa 10: 5 of prophets c down from the high H3381
16: 4 his c, and said, Comest thou peaceably? H7122
22: 9 the son of Jesse c to Nob, to Ahimelech H935
25:26 thee from c to *shed* blood, and from H935
33 me this day from c to *shed* blood, and H935
29: 6 thy going out and thy c in with me in the H935
6 since the day of thy c unto me unto this H935
2Sa 3:25 c in, and to know all that thou doest. H4126
24:20 and his servants c on toward him: and H5674
2Ki 10:15 the son of Rechab *c* to meet him: and he
13:20 invaded the land at the c in of the year. H935
19:27 and thy c in, and thy rage against me. H935
2Ch 22: 7 was of God by c to Joram: for when he H935
Ezr 3: 8 Now in the second year of their c unto H935
Ps 19: 5 Which *is* as a bridegroom c out of his H3318
37:13 at him: for he seeth that his day is c. H935
121: 8 thy going out and thy c in from this time H935
Prv 8: 3 of the city, at the c in at the doors. H3996
Isa 14: 9 to meet *thee* at thy c: it stirreth up the H935
32:19 When it shall hail, c down on the H3381
37:28 and thy c in, and thy rage against me. H935
44: 7 the things that are c, and shall come, let H857
Jer 8: 7 the time of their c; but my people know H935
Dan 4:23 and an holy one c down from heaven, H5182
Mic 7:15 According to the days of thy c out of H3318
Hab 3: 4 the light; he had horns *c* out of his hand:
Mal 3: 2 But who may abide the day of his c? and H935
4: 5 the prophet before the c of the great and H935
Mt 8:28 with devils, c out of the tombs, G1831
16:28 see the Son of man c in his kingdom. G2064
24: 3 of thy c, and of the end of the world? G3952
27 so shall also the c of the Son of man be. G3952
30 see the Son of man c in the clouds of G2064
37 so shall also the c of the Son of man be. G3952
39 so shall also the c of the Son of man be. G3952
48 say in his heart, My lord delayeth his c; G2064
25:27 and *then* at my c I should have G2064
26:64 power, and c in the clouds of heaven. G2064
Mk 1:10 And straightway c up out of the water, G305
6:31 there were many c and going, and they G2064
13:26 see the Son of man c in the clouds with G2064
36 Lest c suddenly he find you sleeping. G2064
14:62 power, and c in the clouds of heaven. G2064
15:21 who passed by, c out of the country, G2064
Lk 2:38 And she c in that instant gave thanks G2186
9:42 And as he was yet a c, the devil threw G4334
12:45 lord delayeth his c; and shall begin to G2064
18: 5 lest by her continual c she weary me. G2064
19:23 the bank, that at my c I might have G2064
21:26 things which are c on the earth: for the G1904
27 the Son of man c in a cloud with power G2064
23:26 a Cyrenian, c out of the country, and G2064
Lk 23:29 For, behold, the days are c, in the which G2064
36 And the soldiers also mocked him, c to G4334
Jn 1:27 He it is, who c after me is preferred G2064
29 The next day John seeth Jesus c unto G2064
47 Jesus saw Nathanael c to him, and G2064
5: 7 c, another steppeth down before me. G2064
25 you, The hour is c, and now is, when the G2064
28 Marvel not at this: for the hour is c, in G2064
10:12 are not, seeth the wolf c, and leaveth the G2064
11:20 that Jesus was c, went and met him: G2064
12:12 heard that Jesus was c to Jerusalem, G2064
Act 7:52 before of the c of the Just One; of whom G1660
9:12 named Ananias c in, and putting *his* G1525
28 And he was with them c in and going G1531
10: 3 an angel of God c in to him, and saying G1525
25 And as Peter was c in, Cornelius met G1525
13:24 before his c the baptism of repentance G1529
17:10 unto Berea: who c *thither* went into the G3854
27:33 And while the day was c on, G3195+G1096
Ro 15:22 been much hindered from c to you. G2064
1Co 1: 7 for the c of our Lord Jesus Christ: G602
15:23 afterward they that are Christ's at his c. G3952
16:17 I am glad of the c of Stephanas and G3952
2Co 7: 6 down, comforted us by the c of Titus; G3952
7 And not by his c only, but by the G3952
13: 1 This *is* the third *time* I am c to you. In G2064
Php 1:26 Christ for me by my c to you again. G3952
1Th 2:19 of our Lord Jesus Christ at his c? G3952
3:13 our Father, at the c of our Lord Jesus G3952
4:15 remain unto the c of the Lord shall not G3952
5:23 unto the c of our Lord Jesus Christ. G3952
2Th 2: 1 Now we beseech you, brethren, by the c G3952
8 destroy with the brightness of his c: G3952
9 *Even him*, whose c is after the working G3952
Jas 5: 7 brethren, unto the c of the Lord. G3952
8 for the c of the Lord draweth nigh. G3952
1Pt 2: 4 To whom c, *as unto* a living stone, G4334
2Pt 1:16 you the power and c of our Lord Jesus G3952
3: 4 is the promise of his c? for since the G3952
12 Looking for and hasting unto the c of G3952
1Jn 2:28 and not be ashamed before him at his c. G3952
Rev 13:11 And I beheld another beast c up out of G305
21: 2 new Jerusalem, c down from God out G2597

COMINGS
Ezk 43:11 thereof, and the c in thereof, and all the H4126

COMMAND
Gen 18:19 For I know him, that he will c his H6680
27: 8 voice according to that which I c thee. H6680
50:16 Thy father did c before he died, saying, H6680
Ex 7: 2 Thou shalt speak all that I c thee: and H6680
8:27 to the LORD our God, as he shall c us. H559
18:23 If thou shalt do this thing, and God c H6680
27:20 And thou shalt c the children of Israel, H6680
34:11 Observe thou that which I c thee this H6680
Lev 6: 9 C Aaron and his sons, saying, This *is* H6680
13:54 Then the priest shall c that they wash H6680
14: 4 Then shall the priest c to take for him H6680
5 And the priest shall c that one of the H6680
36 Then the priest shall c that they empty H6680
40 Then the priest shall c that they take H6680
24: 2 C the children of Israel, that they bring H6680
25:21 Then I will c my blessing upon you in H6680
Nu 5: 2 C the children of Israel, that they put H6680
9: 8 what the LORD will c concerning you. H6680
28: 2 C the children of Israel, and say unto H6680
34: 2 C the children of Israel, and say unto H6680
35: 2 C the children of Israel, that they give H6680
36: 6 which the LORD doth c concerning the H6680
Dt 2: 4 And c thou the people, saying, Ye *are* H6680
4: 2 the word which I c you, neither shall ye H6680
2 of the LORD your God which I c you. H6680
40 which I c thee this day, that it H6680
6: 2 which I c thee, thou, and thy H6680
6 And these words, which I c thee this H6680
7:11 which I c thee this day, to do them. H6680
8: 1 All the commandments which I c thee H6680
11 his statutes, which I c thee this day: H6680
10:13 which I c thee this day for thy good? H6680
11: 8 which I c you this day, that ye H6680
13 which I c you this day, to love H6680
22 which I c you, to do them, to H6680
27 LORD your God, which I c you this day: H6680
28 of the way which I c you this day, to go H6680
12:11 ye bring all that I c you; your burnt H6680
14 and there thou shalt do all that I c thee. H6680
28 words which I c thee, that it may go H6680
32 What thing soever I c you, observe to H6680
Dt 13:18 which I c thee this day, to do H6680
15: 5 which I c thee this day. H6680
11 land: therefore I c thee, saying, Thou H6680
15 therefore I c thee this thing to day. H6680
18:18 speak unto them all that I shall c him. H6680
19: 7 Wherefore I c thee, saying, Thou shalt H6680
9 do them, which I c thee this day, to love H6680
24:18 therefore I c thee to do this thing. H6680
22 therefore I c thee to do this thing. H6680
27: 1 commandments which I c you this day. H6680
4 these stones, which I c you this day, in H6680
10 his statutes, which I c thee this day. H6680
28: 1 which I c thee this day, that the H6680
8 The LORD shall c the blessing upon H6680
13 thy God, which I c thee this day, to H6680
14 the words which I c thee this day, *to* the H6680
15 statutes which I c thee this day; that all H6680
30: 2 to all that I c thee this day, thou and H6680
8 which I c thee this day. H6680
11 For this commandment which I c thee H6680
16 In that I c thee this day to love the H6680
32:46 day, which ye shall c your children to H6680
Jos 1:11 Pass through the host, and c the H6680
3: 8 And thou shalt c the priests that bear H6680
4: 3 And c ye them, saying, Take you hence H6680
16 C the priests that bear the ark of the H6680
11:15 so did Moses c Joshua, and so did H6680
1Sa 16:16 Let our lord now c thy servants, *which* H559
1Ki 5: 6 Now therefore c thou that they hew me H6680
11:38 unto all that I c thee, and wilt walk H6680
2Ch 7:13 there be no rain, or if I c the locusts to H6680
Job 39:27 Doth the eagle mount up at thy c, and H6310
Ps 42: 8 *Yet* the LORD will c his lovingkindness H6680
44: 4 Thou art my King, O God: c H6680
Isa 5: 6 thorns: I will also c the clouds that they H6680
45:11 the work of my hands c ye me. H6680
Jer 1: 7 whatsoever I c thee thou shalt speak. H6680
17 them all that I c thee: be not dismayed H6680
11: 4 to all which I c you: so shall ye be my H6680
26: 2 all the words that I c thee to speak unto H6680
27: 4 And c them to say unto their masters, H6680
34:22 Behold, I will c, saith the LORD, and H6680
Lam 1:10 whom thou didst c *that* they should not H6680
Am 9: 3 I c the serpent, and he shall bite them: H6680
4 thence will I c the sword, and it shall H6680
9 For, lo, I will c, and I will sift the house H6680
Mt 4: 3 c that these stones be made bread. G2036
19: 7 did Moses then c to give a writing of G1781
27:64 C therefore that the sepulchre be made G2753
Mk 10: 3 said unto them, What did Moses c you? G1781
Lk 4: 3 God, c this stone that it be made bread. G2036
8:31 not c them to go out into the deep. G2004
9:54 wilt thou that we c fire to come down G2036
Jn 15:14 my friends, if ye do whatsoever I c you. G1781
17 These things I c you, that ye love one G1781
Act 5:28 Saying, Did not we straitly c you that G3853
15: 5 and to c *them* to keep the law of Moses. G3853
16:18 said to the spirit, I c thee in the name G3853
1Co 7:10 And unto the married I c, *yet* not I, but G3853
2Th 3: 4 and will do the things which we c you. G3853
6 Now we c you, brethren, in the name of G3853
12 Now them that are such we c and G3853
1Ti 4:11 These things c and teach. G3853

COMMANDED
Gen 2:16 And the LORD God c the man, saying, H6680
3:11 I c thee that thou shouldest not eat? H6680
17 the tree, of which I c thee, saying, Thou H6680
6:22 to all that God c him, so did he. H6680
7: 5 unto all that the LORD c him. H6680
9 and the female, as God had c Noah. H6680
16 had c him: and the LORD shut him in. H6680
12:20 And Pharaoh c *his* men concerning H6680
21: 4 being eight days old, as God had c him. H6680
32: 4 And he c them, saying, Thus shall ye H6680
17 And he c the foremost, saying, When H6680
19 And so c he the second, and the third, H6680
42:25 Then Joseph c to fill their sacks with H6680
44: 1 And he c the steward of his house, H6680
45:19 Now thou art c, this do ye; take you H6680
47:11 the land of Rameses, as Pharaoh had c. H6680
50: 2 And Joseph c his servants the H6680
12 did unto him according as he c them: H6680
Ex 1:17 the king of Egypt c them, but saved the H1696
4:28 and all the signs which he had c him. H6680
5: 6 And Pharaoh c the same day the H6680
7: 6 did as the LORD c them, so did they. H6680
10 so as the LORD had c: and Aaron cast H6680
20 so, as the LORD c; and he lifted up the H6680

Ex 12:28 had c Moses and Aaron, so did they. H6680
50 LORD c Moses and Aaron, so did they. H6680
16:16 the LORD hath c, Gather of it every H6680
34 As the LORD c Moses, so Aaron laid it H6680
19: 7 all these words which the LORD c him. H6680
23:15 seven days, as I c thee, in the time H6680
29:35 which I have c thee: seven days shalt H6680
31: 6 they may make all that I have c thee; H6680
11 to all that I have c thee shall they do. H6680
32: 8 of the way which I c them: they have H6680
34: 4 as the LORD had c him, and took in his H6680
18 bread, as I c thee, in the time of the H6680
34 children of Israel *that* which he was c. H6680
35: 1 LORD hath c, that *ye* should do them. H6680
4 *is* the thing which the LORD c, saying, H6680
10 and make all that the LORD hath c; H6680
29 had c to be made by the hand of Moses. H6680
36: 1 according to all that the LORD had c. H6680
5 the work, which the LORD c to make. H6680
38:22 made all that the LORD c Moses. H6680
39: 1 for Aaron; as the LORD c Moses. H6680
5 twined linen; as the LORD c Moses. H6680
7 of Israel; as the LORD c Moses. H6680
21 from the ephod; as the LORD c Moses. H6680
26 to minister *in;* as the LORD c Moses. H6680
29 *of* needlework; as the LORD c Moses. H6680
31 upon the mitre; as the LORD c Moses. H6680
32 all that the LORD c Moses, so did they. H6680
42 According to all that the LORD c H6680
43 it as the LORD had c, even so had they H6680
40:16 to all that the LORD c him, so did he. H6680
19 above upon it; as the LORD c Moses. H6680
21 of the testimony; as the LORD c Moses. H6680
23 the LORD; as the LORD had c Moses. H6680
25 the LORD; as the LORD c Moses. H6680
27 incense thereon; as the LORD c Moses. H6680
29 meat offering; as the LORD c Moses. H6680
32 they washed; as the LORD c Moses. H6680
Lev 7:36 Which the LORD c to be given them of H6680
38 Which the LORD c Moses in mount H6680
38 in the day that he c the children of H6680
8: 4 And Moses did as the LORD c him; and H6680
5 the thing which the LORD c to be done. H6680
9 the holy crown; as the LORD c Moses. H6680
13 upon them; as the LORD c Moses. H6680
17 the camp; as the LORD c Moses. H6680
21 unto the LORD; as the LORD c Moses. H6680
29 was Moses' part; as the LORD c Moses. H6680
31 consecrations, as I c, saying, Aaron and H6680
34 c to do, to make an atonement for you. H6680
35 the LORD, that ye die not: for so I am c. H6680
36 the LORD c by the hand of Moses. H6680
9: 5 And they brought *that* which Moses c H6680
6 which the LORD c that ye should do: H6680
7 an atonement for them; as the LORD c. H6680
10 upon the altar; as the LORD c Moses. H6680
21 offering before the LORD; as Moses c. H6680
10: 1 before the LORD, which he c them not. H6680
13 of the LORD made by fire: for so I am c. H6680
15 a statute for ever; as the LORD hath c. H6680
18 have eaten it in the holy *place,* as I c. H6680
16:34 year. And he did as the LORD c Moses. H6680
17: 2 thing which the LORD hath c, saying, H6680
24:23 of Israel did as the LORD c Moses. H6680
27:34 which the LORD c Moses for the H6680
Nu 1:19 As the LORD c Moses, so he numbered H6680
54 all that the LORD c Moses, so did they. H6680
2:33 of Israel; as the LORD c Moses. H6680
34 to all that the LORD c Moses: so they H6680
3:16 to the word of the LORD, as he was c. H6680
42 And Moses numbered, as the LORD c H6680
51 of the LORD, as the LORD c Moses. H6680
4:49 of him, as the LORD c Moses. H6680
8: 3 the candlestick, as the LORD c Moses. H6680
20 all that the LORD c Moses concerning H6680
22 as the LORD had c Moses concerning H6680
9: 5 c Moses, so did the children of Israel. H6680
15:23 *Even* all that the LORD hath c you by H6680
23 the day that the LORD c *Moses,* and H6680
36 and he died; as the LORD c Moses. H6680
16:47 And Aaron took as Moses c, and ran H1696
17:11 And Moses did *so:* as the LORD c him, H6680
19: 2 the LORD hath c, saying, Speak unto H6680
20: 9 rod from before the LORD, as he c him. H6680
27 And Moses did as the LORD c: and they H6680
26: 4 as the LORD c Moses and the children H6680
27:11 of judgment, as the LORD c Moses. H6680
22 And Moses did as the LORD c him: and H6680
23 as the LORD c by the hand of Moses. H1696

Nu 29:40 to all that the LORD c Moses. H6680
30: 1 *is* the thing which the LORD hath c. H6680
16 which the LORD c Moses, between a H6680
31: 7 c Moses; and they slew all the males. H6680
21 of the law which the LORD c Moses; H6680
31 the priest did as the LORD c Moses. H6680
41 the priest, as the LORD c Moses. H6680
47 of the LORD; as the LORD c Moses. H6680
32:28 So concerning them Moses c Eleazar H6680
34:13 And Moses c the children of Israel, H6680
13 which the LORD c to give unto the nine H6680
29 These *are they* whom the LORD c to H6680
36: 2 And they said, The LORD c my lord to H6680
2 and my lord was c by the LORD to give H6680
5 And Moses c the children of Israel H6680
10 Even as the LORD c Moses, so did the H6680
13 which the LORD c by the hand of H6680
Dt 1:18 And I c you at that time all the things H6680
19 c us; and we came to Kadeshbarnea. H6680
41 the LORD our God c us. And when ye H6680
3:18 And I c you at that time, saying, The H6680
21 And I c Joshua at that time, saying, H6680
4: 5 the LORD my God c me, that ye should H6680
13 which he c you to perform, *even* H6680
14 And the LORD c me at that time to H6680
5:12 it, as the LORD thy God hath c thee. H6680
15 thy God c thee to keep the sabbath day. H6680
16 thy God hath c thee; that thy days may H6680
32 your God hath c you: ye shall not turn H6680
33 your God hath c you, that ye may live, H6680
6: 1 LORD your God c to teach you, that ye H6680
17 and his statutes, which he hath c thee. H6680
20 which the LORD our God hath c you? H6680
24 And the LORD c us to do all these H6680
25 the LORD our God, as he hath c us. H6680
9:12 of the way which I c them; they have H6680
16 of the way which the LORD had c you. H6680
10: 5 and there they be, as the LORD c me. H6680
12:21 thee, as I have c thee, and thou shalt H6680
13: 5 the LORD thy God c thee to walk in. So H6680
17: 3 the host of heaven, which I have not c; H6680
18:20 which I have not c him to speak, or H6680
20:17 as the LORD thy God hath c thee: H6680
24: 8 as I c them, *so* ye shall observe to do. H6680
26:13 which thou hast c me: I have not H6680
14 according to all that thou hast c me. H6680
16 This day the LORD thy God hath c thee H6680
27: 1 And Moses with the elders of Israel c H6680
28:45 and his statutes which he c thee: H6680
29: 1 which the LORD c Moses to make with H6680
31: 5 commandments which I have c you. H6680
10 And Moses c them, saying, At the end H6680
25 That Moses c the Levites, which bare H6680
29 way which I have c you; and evil will H6680
33: 4 Moses c us a law, *even* the inheritance H6680
34: 9 him, and did as the LORD c Moses. H6680
Jos 1: 7 Moses my servant c thee: turn not from H6680
9 Have not I c thee? Be strong and of a H6680
10 Then Joshua c the officers of the H6680
13 of the LORD c you, saying, The LORD H6680
3: 3 And they c the people, saying, When ye H6680
4: 8 did so as Joshua c, and took up twelve H6680
10 that the LORD c Joshua to speak unto H6680
10 to all that Moses c Joshua: and the H6680
17 Joshua therefore c the priests, saying, H6680
6:10 And Joshua had c the people, saying, H6680
7:11 covenant which I c them: for they have H6680
8: 4 And he c them, saying, Behold, ye shall H6680
8 the LORD shall ye do. See, I have c you. H6680
27 word of the LORD which he c Joshua. H6680
29 was down, Joshua c that they should H6680
31 As Moses the servant of the LORD c the H6680
33 of the LORD had c before, that they H6680
35 of all that Moses c, which Joshua read H6680
9:24 the LORD thy God c his servant Moses H6680
10:27 sun, *that* Joshua c, and they took them H6680
40 breathed, as the LORD God of Israel c. H6680
11:12 as Moses the servant of the LORD c. H6680
15 As the LORD c Moses his servant, so H6680
15 undone of all that the LORD c Moses. H6680
20 destroy them, as the LORD c Moses. H6680
13: 6 for an inheritance, as I have c thee. H6680
14: 2 as the LORD c by the hand of Moses, H6680
5 As the LORD c Moses, so the children H6680
17: 4 saying, The LORD c Moses to give us H6680
21: 2 saying, The LORD c by the hand of H6680
8 as the LORD c by the hand of Moses. H6680
22: 2 of the LORD c you, and have obeyed H6680
2 obeyed my voice in all that I c you: H6680

Jos 23:16 God, which he c you, and have gone H6680
Jdg 2:20 covenant which I c their fathers, and H6680
3: 4 he c their fathers by the hand of Moses. H6680
4: 6 God of Israel c, *saying,* Go and draw H6680
13:14 *thing:* all that I c her let her observe. H6680
21:10 the valiantest, and c them, saying, Go H6680
20 Therefore they c the children of H6680
Ru 2:15 up to glean, Boaz c his young men, H6680
1Sa 2:29 which I have c *in my* habitation; and H6680
13:13 thy God, which he c thee: for now H6680
14 and the LORD hath c him *to be* captain H6680
14 not kept *that* which the LORD c thee. H6680
17:20 went, as Jesse had c him; and he came H6680
18:22 And Saul c his servants, *saying,* H6680
20:29 brother, he hath c me *to be there:* and H6680
21: 2 The king hath c me a business, and H6680
2 and what I have c thee: and I have H6680
2Sa 4:12 And David c his young men, and they H6680
5:25 And David did so, as the LORD had c H6680
7: 7 of Israel, whom I c to feed my people H6680
11 And as since the time that I c judges *to* H6680
9:11 my lord the king hath c his servant, so H6680
13:28 Now Absalom had c his servants, H6680
28 I c you? be courageous, and be valiant. H6680
29 as Absalom had c. Then all the king's H6680
18: 5 And the king c Joab and Abishai and H6680
21:14 all that the king c. And after that God H6680
24:19 saying of Gad, went up as the LORD c. H6680
1Ki 2:46 So the king c Benaiah the son of H6680
5:17 And the king c, and they brought great H6680
8:58 his judgments, which he c our fathers. H6680
9: 4 to all that I have c thee, *and* wilt keep H6680
11:10 And had c him concerning this thing, H6680
10 but he kept not that which the LORD c. H6680
11 which I have c thee, I will surely rend H6680
13:21 which the LORD thy God c thee, H6680
15: 5 any *thing* that he c him all the days of H6680
17: 4 I have c the ravens to feed thee there. H6680
9 behold, I have c a widow woman there H6680
22:31 But the king of Syria c his thirty and H6680
2Ki 11: 5 And he c them, saying, This *is* the thing H6680
9 the priest c: and they took every H6680
15 But Jehoiada the priest c the captains H6680
14: 6 wherein the LORD c, saying, The H6680
16:15 And king Ahaz c Urijah the priest, H6680
16 priest, according to all that king Ahaz c. H6680
17:13 all the law which I c your fathers, and H6680
27 Then the king of Assyria c, saying, H6680
34 which the LORD c the children of H6680
18: 6 which the LORD c Moses. H6680
12 of the LORD c, and would not hear H6680
21: 8 to all that I have c them, and according H6680
8 the law that my servant Moses c them. H6680
22:12 And the king c Hilkiah the priest, and H6680
23: 4 And the king c Hilkiah the high priest, H6680
21 And the king c all the people, saying, H6680
1Ch 6:49 all that Moses the servant of God had c. H6680
14:16 David therefore did as God c him: and H6680
15:15 c according to the word of the LORD. H6680
16:15 *which* he c to a thousand generations; H6680
40 the law of the LORD, which he c Israel; H6680
17: 6 of Israel, whom I c to feed my people, H6680
10 And since the time that I c judges *to be* H6680
21:17 God, *Is it* not I *that* c the people to be H559
18 Then the angel of the LORD c Gad to say H559
27 And the LORD c the angel; and he put up H559
22: 2 And David c to gather together the H559
17 David also c all the princes of Israel to H6680
23:31 to the order c unto them, continually
24:19 as the LORD God of Israel had c him. H6680
2Ch 7:17 to all that I have c thee, and shalt H6680
8:14 for so had David the man of God c. H4687
14: 4 And c Judah to seek the LORD God of H559
18:30 Now the king of Syria had c the H6680
23: 8 the priest had c, and took every man H6680
25: 4 where the LORD c, saying, The fathers H6680
29:21 for Judah. And he c the priests the sons H559
24 all Israel: for the king c *that* the burnt H559
27 And Hezekiah c to offer the burnt H559
30 king and the princes c the Levites to sing H559
31: 4 Moreover he c the people that dwelt in H559
11 Then Hezekiah c to prepare chambers in H559
32:12 places and his altars, and c Judah and H559
33: 8 do all that I have c them, according to H6680
16 c Judah to serve the LORD God of Israel. H559
34:20 And the king c Hilkiah, and Ahikam H6680
35:21 I have war: for God c me to make haste: H559
Ezr 4: 3 king Cyrus the king of Persia hath c us. H6680
19 And I c, and search hath been H7761+H2942

Ezr 5: 3 Who hath c you to build this H7761+H2942
9 thus, Who c you to build this H7761+H2942
7:23 Whatsoever is c by the God of H4480+H2941
9:11 Which thou hast c by thy servants the H6680
Neh 8: 1 Moses, which the LORD had c to Israel. H6680
14 the LORD had c by Moses, that the H6680
13: 5 the oil, which was c *to be given* to the H4687
9 Then I c, and they cleansed the H559
19 the sabbath, I c that the gates should H559
22 And I c the Levites that they should H559
Est 1:10 merry with wine, he c Mehuman, Biztha, H559
17 king Ahasuerus c Vashti the queen to H559
3: 2 for the king had so c concerning him. H6680
12 all that Haman had c unto the king's H6680
4:13 Then Mordecai c to answer Esther, H559
17 according to all that Esther had c him. H6680
6: 1 king sleep, and he c to bring the book of H559
8: 9 all that Mordecai c unto the Jews, and H6680
9:14 And the king c it so to be done: and the H559
25 before the king, he c by letters that his H559
Job 38:12 Hast thou c the morning since thy H6680
42: 9 c them: the LORD also accepted Job. H1696
Ps 7: 6 for me *to* the judgment *that* thou hast c. H6680
33: 9 For he spake, and it was *done*; he c, and H6680
68:28 Thy God hath c thy strength: H6680
78: 5 in Israel, which he c our fathers, that H6680
23 Though he had c the clouds from H6680
105: 8 *which* he c to a thousand generations. H6680
106:34 concerning whom the LORD c them: H559
111: 9 people: he hath c his covenant for ever: H6680
119: 4 Thou hast c *us* to keep thy precepts H6680
138 Thy testimonies *that* thou hast c *are* H6680
133: 3 c the blessing, *even* life for evermore. H6680
148: 5 LORD: for he c, and they were created. H6680
Isa 13: 3 I have c my sanctified ones, I have also H6680
34:16 c, and his spirit it hath gathered them. H6680
45:12 the heavens, and all their host have I c. H6680
48: 5 and my molten image, hath c them. H6680
Jer 7:22 For I spake not unto your fathers, nor c H6680
23 But this thing c I them, saying, Obey H6680
23 c you, that it may be well unto you. H6680
31 in the fire; which I c *them* not, neither H6680
11: 4 Which I c your fathers in the day *that* I H6680
8 I c *them* to do; but they did *them* not. H6680
13: 5 hid it by Euphrates, as the LORD c me. H6680
6 thence, which I c thee to hide there. H6680
14:14 not, neither have I c them, neither H6680
17:22 ye the sabbath day, as I c your fathers. H6680
19: 5 unto Baal, which I c not, nor spake *it*, H6680
23:32 I sent them not, nor c them: therefore H6680
26: 8 the LORD had c *him* to speak unto all H6680
29:23 which I have not c them; even I know, H6680
32:35 Molech; which I c them not, neither H6680
35: 6 Rechab our father c us, saying, Ye shall H6680
10 to all that Jonadab our father c us. H6680
14 son of Rechab, that he c his sons not to H6680
16 father, which he c them; but this people H6680
18 according unto all that he hath c you: H6680
36: 5 And Jeremiah c Baruch, saying, I *am* H6680
8 the prophet c him, reading in the H6680
26 But the king c Jerahmeel the son of H6680
37:21 Then Zedekiah the king c that they H6680
38:10 Then the king c Ebed-melech the H6680
27 that the king had c. So they left off H6680
50:21 do according to all that I have c thee. H6680
51:59 the prophet c Seraiah the son of H6680
Lam 1:17 the LORD hath c concerning Jacob, H6680
2:17 word that he had c in the days of old: H6680
Ezk 9:11 saying, I have done as thou hast c me. H6680
10: 6 *that* when he had c the man clothed H6680
12: 7 And I did so as I was c: I brought forth H6680
24:18 and I did in the morning as I was c. H6680
37: 7 So I prophesied as I was c: and as I H6680
10 So I prophesied as he c me, and the H6680
Dan 2: 2 Then the king c to call the magicians, H559
12 c to destroy all the wise *men* of Babylon. H560
46 Daniel, and c that they should offer H560
3: 4 it is c, O people, nations, and languages, H560
13 in *his* rage and fury c to bring Shadrach, H560
19 he spake, and c that they should heat H560
20 And he c the most mighty men that *were* H560
4:26 And whereas they c to leave the stump of H560
5: 2 Belshazzar, whiles he tasted the wine, c H560
29 Then c Belshazzar, and they clothed H560
6:16 Then the king c, and they brought H560
23 glad for him, and c that they should take H560
24 And the king c, and they brought those H560
Am 2:12 c the prophets, saying, Prophesy not. H6680
Zec 1: 6 my statutes, which I c my servants the H6680
Mal 4: 4 servant, which I c unto him in Horeb H6680
Mt 8: 4 Moses c, for a testimony unto them. G4367
10: 5 These twelve Jesus sent forth, and c G3853
14: 9 him at meat, he c *it* to be given *her*. G2753
19 And he c the multitude to sit down on G2753
15: 4 For God c, saying, Honour thy father G1781
35 And he c the multitude to sit down on G2753
18:25 to pay, his lord c him to be sold, and G2753
21: 6 disciples went, and did as Jesus c them, G4367
27:58 Then Pilate c the body to be delivered. G2753
28:20 whatsoever I have c you: and, lo, I am G1781
Mk 1:44 Moses c, for a testimony unto them. G4367
5:43 know it; and c that something should G2036
6: 8 And c them that they should take G3853
27 an executioner, and c his head to be G2004
39 And he c them to make all sit down by G2004
8: 6 And he c the people to sit down on the G3853
7 and c to set them also before *them*. G2036
10:49 And Jesus stood still, and c him to be G2036
11: 6 as Jesus had c: and they let them go. G1781
13:34 his work, and c the porter to watch. G1781
Lk 5:14 as Moses c, for a testimony unto them. G4367
8:29 (For he had c the unclean spirit to G3853
55 straightway: and he c to give her meat. G1299
9:21 And he straitly charged them, and c G3853
14:22 as thou hast c, and yet there is room. G2004
17: 9 the things that were c him? I trow not. G1299
10 things which are c you, say, We are G1299
18:40 And Jesus stood, and c him to be G2753
19:15 kingdom, then he c these servants to be G2036
Jn 8: 5 Now Moses in the law c us, that such G1781
Act 1: 4 with *them*, c them that they should G3853
4:15 But when they had c them to go aside G2753
18 And they called them, and c them not G3853
5:34 c to put the apostles forth a little space; G2753
40 beaten *them*, they c that they should G3853
8:38 And he c the chariot to stand still: and G2753
10:33 to hear all things that are c thee of God. G4367
42 And he c us to preach unto the people, G3853
48 And he c them to be baptized in the G4367
12:19 the keepers, and c that *they* should be G2753
13:47 For so hath the Lord c us, *saying*, I G1781
16:22 off their clothes, and c to beat *them*. G2753
18: 2 that Claudius had c all Jews to depart G1299
21:33 and took him, and c *him* to be bound G2753
34 he c him to be carried into the castle. G2753
22:24 The chief captain c him to be brought G2753
30 *his* bands, and c the chief priests and G2753
23: 2 And the high priest Ananias c them G2004
10 in pieces of them, c the soldiers to go G2753
31 Then the soldiers, as it was c them, G1299
35 also come. And he c him to be kept in G2753
24:23 And he c a centurion to keep Paul, and G1299
25: 6 the judgment seat c Paul to be brought. G2753
17 and c the man to be brought forth. G2753
21 of Augustus, I c him to be kept till I G2753
27:43 *their* purpose; and c that they which G2753
1Co 14:34 to speak; but *they are* c to be under
2Co 4: 6 For God, who c the light to shine out of G2036
1Th 4:11 with your own hands, as we c you; G3853
2Th 3:10 were with you, this we c you, that if any G3853
Heb 12:20 that which was c, And if so much as a G1291
Rev 9: 4 And it was c them that they should not G4483

COMMANDEDST

Neh 1: 7 which thou c thy servant Moses. H6680
8 thee, the word that thou c thy servant H6680
9:14 thy holy sabbath, and c them precepts, H6680
Jer 32:23 of all that thou c them to do: therefore H6680

COMMANDER

Isa 55: 4 the people, a leader and c to the people. H6680

COMMANDEST

Jos 1:16 All that thou c us we will do, and H6680
18 in all that thou c him, he shall be put H6680
Act 23: 3 c me to be smitten contrary to the law? G2753

COMMANDETH

Ex 16:32 which the LORD c, Fill an omer of it to H6680
Nu 32:25 Thy servants will do as my lord c. H6680
Job 9: 7 Which c the sun, and it riseth not; and H559
36:10 and c that they return from iniquity. H559
32 the light; and c it *not to shine* by *the* H6680
37:12 do whatsoever he c them upon the face H6680
Ps 107:25 For he c, and raiseth the stormy wind, H559
Lam 3:37 cometh to pass, *when* the Lord c *it* not? H6680
Am 6:11 For, behold, the LORD c, and he will H6680
Mk 1:27 this? for with authority c he even the G2004
Lk 4:36 and power he c the unclean spirits, G2004
8:25 of man is this! for he c even the winds G2004
Act 17:30 now c all men every where to repent: G3853

COMMANDING

Gen 49:33 And when Jacob had made an end of c H6680
Mt 11: 1 made an end of c his twelve disciples, G1299
Act 24: 8 C his accusers to come unto thee: by G2753
1Ti 4: 3 Forbidding to marry, *and* c to abstain

COMMANDMENT

Gen 45:21 according to the c of Pharaoh, and H6310
Ex 17: 1 according to the c of the LORD, and H6310
25:22 thee in c unto the children of Israel. H6680
34:32 he gave them in c all that the LORD H6680
36: 6 And Moses gave c, and they caused it to H6680
38:21 according to the c of Moses, *for* the H6310
Nu 3:39 Aaron numbered at the c of the LORD, H6310
4:37 c of the LORD by the hand of Moses. H6310
41 according to the c of the LORD. H6310
49 According to the c of the LORD they H6310
9:18 At the c of the LORD the children of H6310
18 and at the c of the LORD they pitched: H6310
20 according to the c of the LORD they H6310
20 to the c of the LORD they journeyed. H6310
23 At the c of the LORD they rested in the H6310
23 the tents, and at the c of the LORD they H6310
23 c of the LORD by the hand of Moses. H6310
10:13 c of the LORD by the hand of Moses. H6310
13: 3 And Moses by the c of the LORD sent H6310
14:41 c of the LORD? but it shall not prosper. H6310
15:31 hath broken his c, that soul shall utterly H4687
23:20 Behold, I have received *c* to bless: and he
24:13 go beyond the c of the LORD, to do H6310
27:14 For ye rebelled against my c in the H6310
33: 2 journeys by the c of the LORD: and H6310
38 mount Hor at the c of the LORD, and H6310
Dt 1: 3 LORD had given him in c unto them; H6680
26 against the c of the LORD your God: H6310
43 against the c of the LORD, and went H6310
9:23 against the c of the LORD your God, H6310
17:20 not aside from the c, *to* the right hand, H4687
30:11 For this c which I command thee this H4687
Jos 1:18 rebel against thy c, and will not hearken H6310
8: 8 according to the c of the LORD shall ye H1697
15:13 according to the c of the LORD to H6310
17: 4 according to the c of the LORD he gave H6310
21: 3 inheritance, at the c of the LORD, these H6310
22: 3 charge of the c of the LORD your God. H4687
5 But take diligent heed to do the c and H4687
1Sa 12:14 rebel against the c of the LORD, then H6310
15 rebel against the c of the LORD, then H6310
13:13 hast not kept the c of the LORD thy H4687
15:13 I have performed the c of the LORD. H1697
24 transgressed the c of the LORD, and H6310
2Sa 12: 9 Wherefore hast thou despised the c of H1697
1Ki 2:43 the c that I have charged thee with? H4687
13:21 hast not kept the c which the LORD thy H4687
2Ki 17:34 or after the law and c which the LORD H4687
37 the law, and the c, which he wrote for H4687
18:36 king's c was, saying, Answer him not. H4687
23:35 according to the c of Pharaoh: he H6310
24: 3 Surely at the c of the LORD came *this* H6310
1Ch 12:32 and all their brethren *were* at their c. H6310
14:12 gave a c, and they were burned with fire. H559
28:21 all the people *will be* wholly at thy c. H1697
2Ch 8:13 according to the c of Moses, on the H4687
15 And they departed not from the c of the H4687
14: 4 fathers, and to do the law and the c. H4687
19:10 blood, between law and c, statutes and H4687
24: 6 *according to the* c of Moses the servant
8 And at the king's c they made a chest, H559
21 with stones at the c of the king in the H4687
29:15 according to the c of the king, by the H4687
25 according to the c of David, and of Gad H4687
25 *was* the c of the LORD by his prophets. H4687
30: 6 according to the c of the king, saying, H4687
12 heart to do the c of the king and of the H4687
31: 5 And as soon as the c came abroad, the H1697
13 his brother, at the c of Hezekiah the H4662
35:10 their courses, according to the king's c. H4687
15 place, according to the c of David, and H4687
16 according to the c of king Josiah. H4687
Ezr 4:21 Give ye now c to cause these men to H2942
21 until *another* c shall be given from me. H2941
6:14 according to the c of the God of Israel, H2941
14 and according to the c of Cyrus, and H2942
8:17 And I sent them with c unto Iddo the H3318
10: 3 that tremble at the c of our God; and let H4687

Neh 11:23 For *it was* the king's **c** concerning H4687
12:24 according to the **c** of David the man of H4687
45 the **c** of David, *and* of Solomon his son. H4687
Est 1:12 to come at the king's **c** by *his* H1697
15 hath not performed the **c** of the king H3982
19 let there go a royal **c** from him, and let H1697
2: 8 So it came to pass, when the king's **c** H1697
20 for Esther did the **c** of Mordecai, like as H3982
3: 3 Why transgressest thou the king's **c**? H4687
14 The copy of the writing for a **c** to be H1881
15 by the king's **c**, and the decree was H1697
4: 3 the king's **c** and his decree came, H1697
5 and gave him a **c** to Mordecai, to know H6680
10 and gave him **c** unto Mordecai; H6680
8:13 The copy of the writing for a **c** to be H1881
14 on by the king's **c**. And the decree was H1697
17 the king's **c** and his decree came, H1697
9: 1 when the king's **c** and his decree drew H1697
Job 23:12 Neither have I gone back from the **c** of H4687
Ps 19: 8 the heart: the **c** of the LORD *is* pure, H4687
71: 3 thou hast given **c** to save me; for thou H6680
119:96 *but* thy **c** *is* exceeding broad. H4687
147:15 He sendeth forth his **c** *upon* earth: his H565
Prv 6:20 My son, keep thy father's **c**, and forsake H4687
23 For the **c** *is* a lamp; and the law *is* light; H4687
8:29 not pass his **c**: when he appointed H6310
13:13 he that feareth the **c** shall be rewarded. H4687
19:16 He that keepeth the **c** keepeth his own H4687
Ecc 8: 2 I *counsel thee* to keep the king's **c**, and H6310
5 Whoso keepeth the **c** shall feel no evil H4687
Isa 23:11 hath given a **c** against the merchant H6680
36:21 king's **c** was, saying, Answer him not. H4687
Jer 35:14 obey their father's **c**: notwithstanding I H4687
16 performed the **c** of their father, which H4687
18 ye have obeyed the **c** of Jonadab your H4687
Lam 1:18 against his **c**: hear, I pray you, all H6310
Dan 3:22 Therefore because the king's **c** was H4406
9:23 supplications the **c** came forth, and I H1697
25 going forth of the **c** to restore and to H1697
Hos 5:11 because he willingly walked after the **c**. H6673
Nah 1:14 And the LORD hath given a **c** H6680
Mal 2: 1 And now, O ye priests, this **c** *is* for you. H4687
4 I have sent this **c** unto you, that my H4687
Mt 8:18 he gave **c** to depart unto the other side. G2753
15: 3 the **c** of God by your tradition? G1785
6 have ye made the **c** of God of none G1785
22:36 Master, which *is* the great **c** in the law? G1785
38 This is the first and great **c**. G1785
Mk 7: 8 For laying aside the **c** of God, ye hold G1785
9 well ye reject the **c** of God, that ye may G1785
12:28 asked him, Which is the first **c** of all? G1785
30 with all thy strength: this *is* the first **c**. G1785
31 is none other **c** greater than these. G1785
Lk 15:29 I at any time thy **c**: and yet thou never G1785
23:56 the sabbath day according to the **c**. G1785
Jn 10:18 This **c** have I received of my Father. G1785
11:57 had given a **c**, that, if any man knew G1785
12:49 me, he gave me a **c**, what I should say, G1785
50 And I know that his **c** is life everlasting: G1785
13:34 A new **c** I give unto you, That ye love G1785
14:31 **c**, even so I do. Arise, let us go hence. G1781
15:12 This is my **c**, That ye love one another, G1785
Act 15:24 the law: to whom we gave no *such* **c**: G1291
17:15 and receiving a **c** unto Silas and G1785
23:30 to thee, and gave **c** to his accusers also G3853
25:23 at Festus' **c** Paul was brought forth. G2753
Ro 7: 8 But sin, taking occasion by the **c**, G1785
9 the **c** came, sin revived, and I died. G1785
10 And the **c**, which *was ordained* to life, I G1785
11 For sin, taking occasion by the **c**, G1785
12 Wherefore the law *is* holy, and the **c** G1785
13 the **c** might become exceeding sinful. G1785
13: 9 if *there be* any other **c**, it is briefly G1785
16:26 according to the **c** of the everlasting G2003
1Co 7: 6 I speak this by permission, *and* not of **c**. G2003
25 Now concerning virgins I have no **c** of G2003
2Co 8: 8 I speak not by **c**, but by occasion of the G2003
Eph 6: 2 which is the first **c** with promise; G1785
1Ti 1: 1 Paul, an apostle of Jesus Christ by the **c** G2003
5 Now the end of the **c** is charity out of a G3852
6:14 That thou keep *this* **c** without spot, G1785
Tit 1: 3 according to the **c** of God our Saviour; G2003
Heb 7: 5 priesthood, have a **c** to take tithes of G1785
16 **c**, but after the power of an endless life. G1785
18 of the **c** going before for the G1785
11:22 and gave **c** concerning his bones. G1781
23 and they were not afraid of the king's **c**. G1297
2Pt 2:21 from the holy **c** delivered unto them. G1785
3: 2 and of the **c** of us the apostles of G1785
1Jn 2: 7 Brethren, I write no new **c** unto you, G1785
7 you, but an old **c** which ye had from the G1785
7 The old **c** is the word which ye G1785
8 Again, a new **c** I write unto you, which G1785
3:23 And this is his **c**, That we should believe G1785
23 and love one another, as he gave us **c**. G1785
4:21 And this **c** have we from him, That he G1785
2Jn 4 we have received a **c** from the Father. G1785
5 I wrote a new **c** unto thee, but that G1785
6 This is the **c**, That, as ye have heard G1785

COMMANDMENTS

Gen 26: 5 charge, my **c**, my statutes, and my laws. H4687
Ex 15:26 wilt give ear to his **c**, and keep all his H4687
16:28 refuse ye to keep my **c** and my laws? H4687
20: 6 of them that love me, and keep my **c**. H4687
24:12 and a law, and **c** which I have written; H4687
34:28 the words of the covenant, the ten **c**. H1697
Lev 4: 2 against any of the **c** of the LORD H4687
13 *against* any of the **c** of the LORD H4687
22 *against* any of the **c** of the LORD his H4687
27 *against* any of the **c** of the LORD H4687
5:17 to be done by the **c** of the LORD; H4687
22:31 Therefore shall ye keep my **c**, and do H4687
26: 3 statutes, and keep my **c**, and do them; H4687
14 unto me, and will not do all these **c**; H4687
15 all my **c**, *but* that ye break my covenant: H4687
27:34 These *are* the **c**, which the LORD H4687
Nu 15:22 observed all these **c**, which the LORD H4687
39 remember all the **c** of the LORD, and H4687
40 do all my **c**, and be holy unto your God. H4687
36:13 These *are* the **c** and the judgments, H4687
Dt 4: 2 ye may keep the **c** of the LORD your H4687
13 perform, *even* ten **c**; and he wrote them H1697
40 statutes, and his **c**, which I command H4687
5:10 of them that love me and keep my **c**. H4687
29 and keep all my **c** always, that it might H4687
31 unto thee all the **c**, and the statutes, and H4687
6: 1 Now these *are* the **c**, the statutes, and H4687
2 statutes and his **c**, which I command H4687
17 Ye shall diligently keep the **c** of the H4687
25 to do all these **c** before the LORD our H4687
7: 9 keep his **c** to a thousand generations; H4687
11 Thou shalt therefore keep the **c**, and the H4687
8: 1 All the **c** which I command thee this H4687
2 thou wouldest keep his **c**, or no. H4687
6 Therefore thou shalt keep the **c** of the H4687
11 in not keeping his **c**, and his judgments, H4687
10: 4 first writing, the ten **c**, which the LORD H1697
13 To keep the **c** of the LORD, and his H4687
11: 1 and his judgments, and his **c**, alway. H4687
8 Therefore shall ye keep all the **c** which I H4687
13 diligently unto my **c** which I command H4687
22 For if ye shall diligently keep all these **c** H4687
27 A blessing, if ye obey the **c** of the LORD H4687
28 And a curse, if ye will not obey the **c** of H4687
13: 4 him, and keep his **c**, and obey his voice, H4687
18 to keep all his **c** which I command thee H4687
15: 5 these **c** which I command thee this day. H4687
19: 9 If thou shalt keep all these **c** to do H4687
26:13 according to all thy **c** which thou hast H4687
13 thy **c**, neither have I forgotten *them*: H4687
17 statutes, and his **c**, and his judgments, H4687
18 and that *thou* shouldest keep all his **c**; H4687
27: 1 the **c** which I command you this day. H4687
10 thy God, and do his **c** and his statutes, H4687
28: 1 *and* to do all his **c** which I command H4687
9 shalt keep the **c** of the LORD thy God, H4687
13 hearken unto the **c** of the LORD thy H4687
15 to do all his **c** and his statutes which H4687
45 thy God, to keep his **c** and his statutes H4687
30: 8 his **c** which I command thee this day. H4687
10 thy God, to keep his **c** and his statutes H4687
16 and to keep his **c** and his statutes and H4687
31: 5 all the **c** which I have commanded you. H4687
Jos 22: 5 and to keep his **c**, and to cleave unto H4687
Jdg 2:17 the **c** of the LORD; *but* they did not so. H4687
3: 4 hearken unto the **c** of the LORD, which H4687
1Sa 15:11 not performed my **c**. And it grieved H1697
1Ki 2: 3 statutes, and his **c**, and his judgments, H4687
3:14 statutes and my **c**, as thy father David H4687
6:12 and keep all my **c** to walk in them; then H4687
8:58 and to keep his **c**, and his statutes, and H4687
61 and to keep his **c**, as at this day. H4687
9: 6 and will not keep my **c** *and* my statutes H4687
11:34 because he kept my **c** and my statutes: H4687
38 statutes and my **c**, as David my servant H4687
14: 8 who kept my **c**, and who followed me H4687
18:18 have forsaken the **c** of the LORD, and H4687
2Ki 17:13 ways, and keep my **c** *and* my statutes, H4687
16 And they left all the **c** of the LORD their H4687
19 Also Judah kept not the **c** of the LORD H4687
18: 6 **c**, which the LORD commanded Moses. H4687
23: 3 and to keep his **c** and his testimonies H4687
1Ch 28: 7 my **c** and my judgments, as at this day. H4687
8 seek for all the **c** of the LORD your God: H4687
29:19 heart, to keep thy **c**, thy testimonies, H4687
2Ch 7:19 my statutes and my **c**, which I have set H4687
17: 4 his **c**, and not after the doings of Israel. H4687
24:20 transgress ye the **c** of the LORD, that ye H4687
31:21 the law, and in the **c**, to seek his God, he H4687
34:31 and to keep his **c**, and his testimonies, H4687
Ezr 7:11 of the words of the **c** of the LORD, and H4687
9:10 after this? for we have forsaken thy **c**, H4687
14 Should we again break thy **c**, and join H4687
Neh 1: 5 them that love him and observe his **c**: H4687
7 have not kept the **c**, nor the statutes, H4687
9 But *if* ye turn unto me, and keep my **c**, H4687
9:13 and true laws, good statutes and **c**: H4687
16 their necks, and hearkened not to thy **c**, H4687
29 not unto thy **c**, but sinned against thy H4687
34 unto thy **c** and thy testimonies, H4687
10:29 and do all the **c** of the LORD our Lord, H4687
Ps 78: 7 forget the works of God, but keep his **c**: H4687
89:31 break my statutes, and keep not my **c**; H4687
103:18 those that remember his **c** to do them. H6490
20 that do his **c**, hearkening unto the H1697
111: 7 verity and judgment; all his **c** *are* sure. H6490
10 do *his* **c**: his praise endureth for ever.
112: 1 LORD, *that* delighteth greatly in his **c**. H4687
119: 6 when I have respect unto all thy **c**. H4687
10 thee: O let me not wander from thy **c**. H4687
19 in the earth: hide not thy **c** from me. H4687
21 *are* cursed, which do err from thy **c**. H4687
32 I will run the way of thy **c**, when thou H4687
35 Make me to go in the path of thy **c**; for H4687
47 And I will delight myself in thy **c**, which H4687
48 My hands also will I lift up unto thy **c**, H4687
60 haste, and delayed not to keep thy **c**. H4687
66 knowledge: for I have believed thy **c**. H4687
73 understanding, that I may learn thy **c**. H4687
86 All thy **c** *are* faithful: they persecute me H4687
98 Thou through thy **c** hast made me H4687
115 for I will keep the **c** of my God. H4687
127 Therefore I love thy **c** above gold; yea, H4687
131 and panted: for I longed for thy **c**. H4687
143 hold on me: *yet* thy **c** *are* my delights. H4687
151 Thou *art* near, O LORD; and all thy **c** H4687
166 hoped for thy salvation, and done thy **c**. H4687
172 word: for all thy **c** *are* righteousness. H4687
176 thy servant; for I do not forget thy **c**. H4687
Prv 2: 1 my words, and hide my **c** with thee; H4687
3: 1 my law; but let thine heart keep my **c**: H4687
4: 4 retain my words: keep my **c**, and live. H4687
7: 1 my words, and lay up my **c** with thee. H4687
2 Keep my **c**, and live; and my law as the H4687
10: 8 The wise in heart will receive **c**: but a H4687
Ecc 12:13 his **c**: for this *is* the whole *duty* of man. H4687
Isa 48:18 O that thou hadst hearkened to my **c**! H4687
Dan 9: 4 love him, and to them that keep his **c**; H4687
Am 2: 4 and have not kept his **c**, and their lies H2706
Mt 5:19 one of these least **c**, and shall teach men G1785
15: 9 teaching *for* doctrines the **c** of men. G1778
19:17 if thou wilt enter into life, keep the **c**. G1785
22:40 On these two **c** hang all the law and the G1785
Mk 7: 7 teaching *for* doctrines the **c** of men. G1778
10:19 Thou knowest the **c**, Do not commit G1785
12:29 The first of all the **c** *is*, Hear, O Israel; G1785
Lk 1: 6 walking in all the **c** and ordinances of G1785
18:20 Thou knowest the **c**, Do not commit G1785
Jn 14:15 If ye love me, keep my **c**. G1785
21 He that hath my **c**, and keepeth them, G1785
15:10 If ye keep my **c**, ye shall abide in my G1785
10 my Father's **c**, and abide in his love. G1785
Act 1: 2 Ghost had given **c** unto the apostles G1781
1Co 7:19 but the keeping of the **c** of God. G1785
14:37 I write unto you are the **c** of the Lord. G1785
Eph 2:15 enmity, *even* the law of **c** *contained* in G1785
Col 2:22 after the **c** and doctrines of men? G1778
4:10 **c**: if he come unto you, receive him;) G1785
1Th 4: 2 For ye know what **c** we gave you by the G3852
Tit 1:14 Not giving heed to Jewish fables, and **c** G1785
1Jn 2: 3 that we know him, if we keep his **c**. G1785
4 **c**, is a liar, and the truth is not in him. G1785
3:22 we keep his **c**, and do those things G1785
24 And he that keepeth his **c** dwelleth in G1785
5: 2 God, when we love God, and keep his **c**. G1785
3 God, that we keep his **c**: and his G1785

1Jn 5: 3 and his **c** are not grievous. *G1785*
2Jn 6 that we walk after his **c**. This is the *G1785*
Rev 12:17 which keep the **c** of God, and have the *G1785*
14:12 the **c** of God, and the faith of Jesus. *G1785*
22:14 Blessed *are* they that do his **c**, that they *G1785*

COMMEND

Lk 23:46 into thy hands I **c** my spirit: and *G3908*
Act 20:32 And now, brethren, I **c** you to God, and *G3908*
Ro 3: 5 But if our unrighteousness **c** the *G4921*
16: 1 I **c** unto you Phebe our sister, which is *G4921*
2Co 3: 1 Do we begin again to **c** ourselves? or *G4921*
5:12 For we **c** not ourselves again unto you, *G4921*
10:12 with some that **c** themselves: but they *G4921*

COMMENDATION

2Co 3: 1 *others*, epistles of **c** to you, or *letters* of *G4956*
1 to you, or *letters* of **c** from you? *G4956*

COMMENDED

Gen 12:15 saw her, and **c** her before Pharaoh: H1984
Prv 12: 8 A man shall be **c** according to his H1984
Ecc 8:15 Then I **c** mirth, because a man hath no H7623
Lk 16: 8 And the lord **c** the unjust steward, *G1867*
Act 14:23 with fasting, they **c** them to the Lord, *G3908*
2Co 12:11 to have been **c** of you: for in nothing *G4921*

COMMENDETH

Ro 5: 8 But God **c** his love toward us, in that, *G4921*
1Co 8: 8 But meat **c** us not to God: for neither, if *G3936*
2Co 10:18 For not he that **c** himself is approved, *G4921*
18 is approved, but whom the Lord **c**. *G4921*

COMMENDING

2Co 4: 2 of the truth **c** ourselves to every man's *G4921*

COMMISSION

Act 26:12 authority and **c** from the chief priests, *G2011*

COMMISSIONS

Ezr 8:36 And they delivered the king's **c** unto the H1881

COMMIT

Ex 20:14 Thou shalt not **c** adultery. H5003
Lev 5:15 If a soul **c** a trespass, and sin through H4603
17 And if a soul sin, and **c** any of these H6213
6: 2 If a soul sin, and **c** a trespass against H4603
18:26 judgments, and shall not **c** *any* of these H6213
29 For whosoever shall **c** any of these H6213
29 even the souls that **c** *them* shall be cut H6213
30 ordinance, that *ye* **c** not *any one* of H6213
20: 5 after him, to **c** whoredom with Molech, H2181
Nu 5: 6 or woman shall **c** any sin that men H6213
6 any sin that men **c**, to do a trespass
12 go aside, and **c** a trespass against him, H4603
25: 1 people began to **c** whoredom with the H2181
31:16 of Balaam, to **c** trespass against the H4560
Dt 5:18 Neither shalt thou **c** adultery. H5003
19:20 **c** no more any such evil among you. H6213
Jos 22:20 Did not Achan the son of Zerah **c** a H4603
2Sa 7:14 shall be my son. If he **c** iniquity, I will H5753
2Ch 21:11 of Jerusalem to **c** fornication, and H2181
Job 5: 8 God, and unto God would I **c** my cause: H7760
34:10 the Almighty, *that he should* **c** iniquity.
Ps 31: 5 Into thine hand I **c** my spirit: thou hast H6485
37: 5 **C** thy way unto the LORD; trust also in H1556
Prv 16: 3 **C** thy works unto the LORD, and thy H1556
12 *It is* an abomination to kings to **c** H6213
Isa 22:21 girdle, and I will **c** thy government into H5414
23:17 to her hire, and shall **c** fornication with H2181
Jer 7: 9 Will ye steal, murder, and **c** adultery, H5003
9: 5 *and* weary themselves to **c** iniquity. H5753
23:14 thing: they **c** adultery, and walk H5003
37:21 that they should **c** Jeremiah into the H6485
44: 7 of Israel; Wherefore **c** ye *this* great evil H6213
Ezk 3:20 and **c** iniquity, and I lay a H6213
8:17 of Judah that they **c** the abominations H6213
17 which they **c** here? for they have H6213
16:17 men, and didst **c** whoredom with them, H2181
34 followeth thee to **c** whoredoms: and in H2181
43 and thou shalt not **c** this lewdness H6213
20:30 your fathers? and **c** ye whoredom after H2181
22: 9 in the midst of thee they **c** lewdness. H6213
23:43 Will they now **c** whoredoms with her, H2181
33:13 and **c** iniquity, all his righteousnesses H6213
Hos 4:10 enough: they shall **c** whoredom, and H2181
13 daughters shall **c** whoredom, and your H2181
13 and your spouses shall **c** adultery. H5003
14 when they **c** whoredom, nor your H2181
Hos 4:14 when they **c** adultery: for themselves H5003
6: 9 way by consent: for they **c** lewdness. H6213
7: 1 Samaria: for they **c** falsehood; and the H6466
Mt 5:27 of old time, Thou shalt not **c** adultery: *G3431*
32 causeth her to **c** adultery: and *G3429*
19: 9 her which is put away doth **c** adultery. *G3429*
18 Thou shalt not **c** adultery, Thou shalt *G3431*
Mk 10:19 Do not **c** adultery, Do not kill, *G3431*
Lk 12:48 But he that knew not, and did **c** things *G4160*
16:11 who will **c** to your trust the true *riches*? *G4100*
18:20 Do not **c** adultery, Do not kill, *G3431*
Jn 2:24 But Jesus did not **c** himself unto them, *G4100*
Ro 1:32 God, that they which **c** such things are *G4238*
2: 2 against them which **c** such things. *G4238*
22 Thou that sayest a man should not **c** *G3431*
22 dost thou **c** adultery? thou that *G3431*
22 abhorrest idols, dost thou **c** sacrilege? *G2416*
13: 9 For this, Thou shalt not **c** adultery, *G3431*
1Co 10: 8 Neither let us **c** fornication, as some of *G4203*
1Ti 1:18 This charge I **c** unto thee, son Timothy, *G3908*
2Ti 2: 2 the same **c** thou to faithful men, *G3908*
Jas 2: 9 But if ye have respect to persons, ye **c** *G2038*
11 For he that said, Do not **c** adultery, *G3431*
11 kill. Now if thou **c** no adultery, yet if *G3431*
1Pt 4:19 to the will of God **c** the keeping of their *G3908*
1Jn 3: 9 Whosoever is born of God doth not **c** *G4160*
Rev 2:14 unto idols, and to **c** fornication. *G4203*
20 my servants to **c** fornication, and to *G4203*
22 and them that **c** adultery with her into *G3431*

COMMITTED

Gen 39: 8 he hath **c** all that he hath to my hand; H5414
22 And the keeper of the prison **c** to H5414
Lev 4:35 he hath **c**, and it shall be forgiven him. H2398
5: 7 which he hath **c**, two turtledoves, or H2398
18:30 which were **c** before you, and that H6213
20:13 both of them have **c** an abomination: H6213
23 you: for they **c** all these things, and H6213
Nu 15:24 Then it shall be, if *ought* be **c** by H6213
Dt 17: 5 which have **c** that wicked thing, unto H6213
21:22 And if a man have **c** a sin worthy of H1961
Jos 7: 1 But the children of Israel **c** a trespass H4600
22:16 *is* this that ye have **c** against the God of H4600
31 ye have not **c** this trespass against H4600
Jdg 20: 6 have **c** lewdness and folly in Israel. H6213
1Ki 8:47 done perversely, we have **c** wickedness; H7561
14:22 **c**, above all that their fathers had done. H2398
27 shields, and **c** *them* unto the hands H6485
1Ch 10:13 which he **c** against the LORD, *even* H4603
2Ch 12:10 of brass, and **c** *them* to the hands of H6485
34:16 that was **c** to thy servants, they do *it*. H5414
Ps 106: 6 **c** iniquity, we have done wickedly. H5753
Jer 2:13 For my people have **c** two evils; they H6213
3: 8 backsliding Israel **c** adultery I had put H5003
9 **c** adultery with stones and with stocks. H5003
5: 7 to the full, they then **c** adultery, and H5003
30 A wonderful and horrible thing is **c** in H1961
6:15 Were they ashamed when they had **c** H6213
8:12 Were they ashamed when they had **c** H6213
16:10 we have **c** against the LORD our God? H2398
29:23 Because they have **c** villany in Israel, H6213
23 in Israel, and have **c** adultery with their H6213
39:14 of the prison, and **c** him unto Gedaliah H5414
40: 7 the land, and had **c** unto him men, and H6485
41:10 of the guard had **c** to Gedaliah the son H6485
44: 3 which they have **c** to provoke me to H6213
9 which they have **c** in the land of Judah, H6213
22 which ye have **c**; therefore is your land H6213
Ezk 6: 9 they have **c** in all their abominations. H6213
15: 8 have **c** a trespass, saith the Lord GOD. H4603
16:26 Thou hast also **c** fornication with the H2181
50 And they were haughty, and **c** H6213
51 Neither hath Samaria **c** half of thy sins; H2398
52 sins that thou hast **c** more abominable H8581
18:12 eyes to the idols, hath **c** abomination, H6213
21 his sins that he hath **c**, and keep all my H6213
22 All his transgressions that he hath **c**, H6213
27 that he hath **c**, and doeth that which H6213
28 **c**, he shall surely live, he shall not die. H6213
20:27 that they have **c** a trespass against me. H4603
43 sight for all your evils that ye have **c**. H6213
22:11 And one hath **c** abomination with his H6213
23: 3 And they **c** whoredoms in Egypt; they H2181
3 in Egypt; they **c** whoredoms in their H2181
7 Thus she **c** her whoredoms with them, H5414
37 That they have **c** adultery, and blood *is* H5003
37 idols have they **c** adultery, and have H5003
33:13 that he hath **c**, he shall die for it. H6213
16 None of his sins that he hath **c** shall be H2398
Ezk 33:29 their abominations which they have **c**. H6213
43: 8 that they have **c**: wherefore I have H6213
44:13 their abominations which they have **c**. H6213
Dan 9: 5 We have sinned, and have **c** iniquity, H5753
Hos 1: 2 for the land hath **c** great whoredom, H2181
4:18 Their drink is sour: they have **c** H2181
Mal 2:11 an abomination is **c** in Israel and in H6213
Mt 5:28 **c** adultery with her already in his heart. *G3431*
Mk 15: 7 who had **c** murder in the insurrection. *G4160*
Lk 12:48 **c** much, of him they will ask the more. *G3908*
Jn 5:22 but hath **c** all judgment unto the Son: *G1325*
Act 8: 3 men and women **c** *them* to prison. *G3860*
25:11 For if I be an offender, or have **c** any *G4238*
25 But when I found that he had **c** nothing *G4238*
27:40 the anchors, they **c** *themselves* unto the *G1439*
28:17 though I have **c** nothing against the *G4160*
Ro 3: 2 unto them were **c** the oracles of God. *G4100*
1Co 9:17 dispensation *of the gospel* is **c** unto me. *G4100*
10: 8 as some of them **c**, and fell in one day *G4203*
2Co 5:19 **c** unto us the word of reconciliation. *G5087*
11: 7 Have I **c** an offence in abasing myself *G4160*
12:21 and lasciviousness which they have **c**. *G4238*
Gal 2: 7 was **c** unto me, as *the gospel* *G4100*
1Ti 1:11 blessed God, which was **c** to my trust. *G4100*
6:20 O Timothy, keep that which is **c** to thy *G3872*
2Ti 1:12 I have **c** unto him against that day. *G3866*
14 That good thing which was **c** unto thee *G3872*
Tit 1: 3 which is **c** unto me according *G4100*
Jas 5:15 have **c** sins, they shall be forgiven him. *G4160*
1Pt 2:23 not; but **c** *himself* to him that *G3860*
Jude 15 they have ungodly **c**, and of all their hard *G764*
Rev 17: 2 of the earth have **c** fornication, and the *G4203*
18: 3 of the earth have **c** fornication with *G4203*
9 And the kings of the earth, who have **c** *G4203*

COMMITTEST

Hos 5: 3 thou **c** whoredom, *and* Israel is defiled. H2181

COMMITTETH

Lev 20:10 And the man that **c** adultery with H5003
10 wife, *even he* that **c** adultery with his H5003
Ps 10:14 thy hand: the poor **c** himself unto thee; H5800
Prv 6:32 *But* whoso **c** adultery with a woman H5003
Ezk 8: 6 the house of Israel **c** here, that I should H6213
16:32 *But as* a wife that **c** adultery, *which* H5003
18:24 and **c** iniquity, *and* doeth H6213
26 and **c** iniquity, and dieth in H6213
33:18 **c** iniquity, he shall even die thereby. H6213
Mt 5:32 marry her that is divorced **c** adultery. *G3429*
19: 9 marry another, **c** adultery: and whoso *G3429*
Mk 10:11 marry another, **c** adultery against her. *G3429*
12 be married to another, she **c** adultery. *G3429*
Lk 16:18 and marrieth another, **c** adultery: and *G3431*
18 put away from *her* husband **c** adultery. *G3431*
Jn 8:34 Whosoever **c** sin is the servant of sin. *G4160*
1Co 6:18 body; but he that **c** fornication sinneth *G4203*
1Jn 3: 4 Whosoever **c** sin transgresseth also the *G4160*
8 He that **c** sin is of the devil; for the devil *G4160*

COMMITTING

Ezk 33:15 of life, without **c** iniquity; he shall H6213
Hos 4: 2 and stealing, and **c** adultery, they H5003

COMMODIOUS

Act 27:12 And because the haven was not **c** to *G428*

COMMON

Lev 4:27 And if any one of the **c** people sin H776
Nu 16:29 If these men die the **c** death of all men,
1Sa 21: 4 said, *There is* no **c** bread under mine H2455
5 *is* in a manner **c**, yea, though it were H2455
Ecc 6: 1 under the sun, and it *is* **c** among men: H7227
Jer 26:23 body into the graves of the **c** people. H1121
31: 5 plant, and shall eat *them* as **c** things. H2490
Ezk 23:42 with the men of the **c** sort *were* brought H7230
Mt 27:27 took Jesus into the **c** hall, and gathered *G4232*
Mk 12:37 And the **c** people heard him gladly. *G4183*
Act 2:44 were together, and had all things **c**; *G2839*
4:32 was his own; but they had all things **c**. *G2839*
5:18 apostles, and put them in the **c** prison. *G1219*
10:14 eaten any thing that is **c** or unclean. *G2839*
15 God hath cleansed, *that* call not thou **c**. *G2840*
28 I should not call any man **c** or unclean. *G2839*
11: 8 But I said, Not so, Lord: for nothing **c** *G2839*
9 God hath cleansed, *that* call not thou **c**. *G2840*
1Co 10:13 you but such as is **c** to man: but God *is* *G442*
Tit 1: 4 To Titus, *mine* own son after the **c** *G2839*
Jude 3 write unto you of the **c** salvation, it was *G2839*

COMMONLY
Mt 28:15 and this saying is c reported among the G1310
1Co 5: 1 It is reported c *that there is* fornication G3654

COMMONWEALTH
Eph 2:12 being aliens from the c of Israel, and G4174

COMMOTION
Jer 10:22 is come, and a great c out of the north H7494

COMMOTIONS
Lk 21: 9 But when ye shall hear of wars and c, be G181

COMMUNE
Gen 34: 6 went out unto Jacob to c with him. H1696
Ex 25:22 thee, and I will c with thee from above H1696
1Sa 18:22 servants, *saying,* C with David secretly, H1696
19: 3 thou *art,* and I will c with my father of H1696
Job 4: 2 *If* we assay to c with thee, wilt thou be H1697
Ps 4: 4 Stand in awe, and sin not: c with your H559
64: 5 an evil matter: they c of laying snares H5608
77: 6 in the night: I c with mine own heart: H7878

COMMUNED
Gen 23: 8 And he c with them, saying, If it be H1696
34: 8 And Hamor c with them, saying, The H1696
20 and c with the men of their city, saying, H1696
42:24 them again, and c with them, and took H1696
43:19 c with him at the door of the house, H1696
Jdg 9: 1 brethren, and c with them, and with H1696
1Sa 9:25 c with Saul upon the top of the house. H1696
25:39 David sent and c with Abigail, to take H1696
1Ki 10: 2 c with him of all that was in her heart. H1696
2Ki 22:14 in the college;) and they c with her. H1696
2Ch 9: 1 c with him of all that was in her heart. H1696
Ecc 1:16 I c with mine own heart, saying, Lo, I H1696
Dan 1:19 And the king c with them; and among H1696
Zec 1:14 So the angel that c with me said unto H1696
Lk 6:11 madness; and c one with another what G1255
22: 4 And he went his way, and c with the G4814
24:15 And it came to pass, that, while they c G3656
Act 24:26 for him the oftener, and c with him. G3656

COMMUNICATE
Gal 6: 6 Let him that is taught in the word c G2841
Php 4:14 done, that ye did c with my affliction. G394
1Ti 6:18 works, ready to distribute, willing to c; G2843
Heb 13:16 But to do good and to c forget not: for G2842

COMMUNICATED
Gal 2: 2 And I went up by revelation, and c unto G394
Php 4:15 no church c with me as concerning G2841

COMMUNICATION
2Sa 3:17 And Abner had c with the elders of H1697
2Ki 9:11 unto them, Ye know the man, and his c. H7879
Mt 5:37 But let your c be, Yea, yea; Nay, nay: G3056
Eph 4:29 Let no corrupt c proceed out of your G3956
Col 3: 8 blasphemy, filthy c out of your mouth. G148
Phlm 6 That the c of thy faith may become G2842

COMMUNICATIONS
Lk 24:17 What manner of c *are* these that ye G3056
1Co 15:33 Be not deceived: evil c corrupt good G3657

COMMUNING
Gen 18:33 as soon as he had left c with Abraham: H1696
Ex 31:18 had made an end of c with him upon H1696

COMMUNION
1Co 10:16 we bless, is it not the c of the blood of G2842
16 is it not the c of the body of Christ? G2842
2Co 6:14 and what c hath light with darkness? G2842
13:14 of God, and the c of the Holy Ghost, *be* G2842

COMPACT
Ps 122: 3 Jerusalem is builded as a city that is c H2266

COMPACTED
Eph 4:16 together and c by that which every G4822

COMPANIED
Act 1:21 Wherefore of these men which have c G4905

COMPANIES
Jdg 7:16 men *into* three c, and he put a trumpet H7218
20 And the three c blew the trumpets, and H7218
9:34 laid wait against Shechem in four c. H7218
43 them into three c, and laid wait in the H7218
Jdg 9:44 and the two *other* c ran upon all *the* H7218
1Sa 11:11 put the people in three c; and they came H7218
13:17 in three c: one company turned H7218
2Ki 5: 2 And the Syrians had gone out by c, and H1416
1Ch 9:18 porters in the c of the children of Levi. H4264
28: 1 the captains of the c that ministered to H4256
Neh 12:31 two great c *of them that gave* thanks,
40 So stood the two c *of them that gave*
Job 6:19 The troops of Tema looked, the c of H1979
Isa 21:13 ye lodge, O ye travelling c of Dedanim. H736
57:13 When thou criest, let thy c deliver thee; H6899
Ezk 26: 7 horsemen, and c, and much people. H6951
Mk 6:39 all sit down by c upon the green grass. G4849

COMPANION
Ex 32:27 his c, and every man his neighbour. H7453
Jdg 14:20 But Samson's wife was *given* to his c, H4828
15: 2 I gave her to thy c: *is* not her younger H4828
6 given her to his c. And the Philistines H4828
1Ch 27:33 and Hushai the Archite *was* the king's c: H7453
Job 30:29 I am a brother to dragons, and a c to H7453
Ps 119:63 I *am* a c of all *them* that fear thee, and H2270
Prv 13:20 wise: but a c of fools shall be destroyed. H7462
28: 7 a c of riotous *men* shameth his father. H7462
24 the same *is* the c of a destroyer. H2270
Mal 2:14 she thy c, and the wife of thy covenant. H2278
Php 2:25 my brother, and c in labour, and G4904
Rev 1: 9 your brother, and c in tribulation, and G4791

COMPANIONS
Jdg 11:38 she went with her c, and bewailed her H7464
14:11 they brought thirty c to be with him. H4828
Ezr 4: 7 the rest of their c, unto Artaxerxes king H3674
9 and the rest of their c; the Dinaites, the H3675
17 and *to* the rest of their c that dwell in H3675
23 the scribe, and their c, they went up in H3675
5: 3 and their c, and said thus unto H3675
6 and his c the Apharsachites, H3675
6: 6 and your c the Apharsachites, H3675
13 and their c, according to that which H3675
Job 35: 4 I will answer thee, and thy c with thee. H7453
41: 6 Shall the c make a banquet of him? H2271
Ps 45:14 the virgins her c that follow her shall H7464
Song 1: 7 that turneth aside by the flocks of thy c? H2270
8:13 Thou that dwellest in the gardens, the c H2270
Isa 1:23 Thy princes *are* rebellious, and c of H2270
Ezk 37:16 of Israel his c: then take another stick, H2270
16 and *for* all the house of Israel his c: H2270
Dan 2:17 Hananiah, Mishael, and Azariah, his c: H2269
Act 19:29 of Macedonia, Paul's c in travel, they G4898
Heb 10:33 ye became c of them that were so used. G2844

COMPANIONS'
Ps 122: 8 For my brethren and c sakes, I will now H7453

COMPANY
Gen 32: 8 And said, If Esau come to the one c, H4264
8 the other c which is left shall escape. H4264
21 and himself lodged that night in the c. H4264
35:11 a nation and a c of nations shall be of H6951
37:25 and, behold, a c of Ishmeelites came H736
50: 9 horsemen: and it was a very great c. H4264
Nu 14: 7 And they spake unto all the c of the H5712
16: 5 and unto all his c, saying, Even to H5712
6 Take you censers, Korah, and all his c; H5712
11 For which cause *both* thou and all thy c H5712
16 Be thou and all thy c before the LORD, H5712
40 Korah, and as his c: as the LORD said H5712
22: 4 Now shall this c lick up all *that are* H6951
26: 9 Aaron in the c of Korah, when they H5712
10 Korah, when that c died, what time the H5712
27: 3 and he was not in the c of them that H5712
3 the LORD in the c of Korah; but died in H5712
Jdg 9:37 land, and another c come along by the H7218
44 And Abimelech, and the c that *was* H7218
18:23 thee, that thou comest with such a c? H2199
1Sa 10: 5 thou shalt meet a c of prophets coming H2256
10 to the hill, behold, a c of prophets met H2256
13:17 companies: one c turned unto the way H7218
18 And another c turned the way *to* H7218
18 and another c turned *to* the way of H7218
19:20 when they saw the c of the prophets H3862
30:15 me down to this c? And he said, Swear H1416
15 and I will bring thee down to this c. H1416
23 c that came against us into our hand. H1416
2Ki 5:15 of God, he and all his c, and came, and H4264
9:17 and he spied the c of Jehu as he came, H8229
17 and said, I see a c. And Joram said, H8229
2Ch 9: 1 with a very great c, and camels that H2428
2Ch 20:12 might against this great c that cometh H1995
24:24 came with a small c of men, and the
Neh 12:38 And the other c *of them that gave* thanks
Job 16: 7 thou hast made desolate all my c. H5712
34: 8 Which goeth in c with the workers of H2274
Ps 55:14 *and* walked unto the house of God in c. H7285
68:11 *was* the c of those that published *it.* H6635
30 Rebuke the c of spearmen, the H2416
106:17 Dathan, and covered the c of Abiram. H5712
18 And a fire was kindled in their c; the H5712
Prv 29: 3 c with harlots spendeth *his* substance. H7462
Song 1: 9 I have compared thee, O my love, to a c
6:13 As it were the c of two armies. H4246
Jer 31: 8 together: a great c shall return thither. H6951
Ezk 16:40 They shall also bring up a c against H6951
17:17 army and great c make for him in the H6951
23:46 I will bring up a c upon them, and will H6951
47 And the c shall stone them with stones, H6951
27: 6 thine oars; the c of the Ashurites have H1323
27 in thee, and in all thy c which *is* in the H6951
34 all thy c in the midst of thee shall fall. H6951
32: 3 over thee with a c of many people; and H6951
22 Asshur *is* there and all her c: his graves H6951
23 of the pit, and her c is round about her H6951
38: 4 *even* a great c *with* bucklers and H6951
7 thou, and all thy c that are assembled H6951
13 thou gathered thy c to take a prey? to H6951
15 horses, a great c, and a mighty army: H6951
Hos 6: 9 for a man, *so* the c of priests murder in H2267
Lk 2:44 to have been in the c, went a day's G4923
5:29 there was a great c of publicans and of G3793
6:17 the plain, and the c of his disciples, and G3793
22 you *from their c,* and shall reproach *you,*
9:14 Make them sit down by fifties in a c. G2828
38 And, behold, a man of the c cried out, G3793
11:27 woman of the c lifted up her voice, and G3793
12:13 And one of the c said unto him, G3793
23:27 And there followed him a great c of G4128
24:22 Yea, and certain women also of our c G2257
Jn 6: 5 and saw a great c come unto him, he G3793
Act 4:23 went to their own c, and reported all G2398
6: 7 and a great c of the priests were G3793
10:28 is a Jew to keep c, or come unto one of G2853
13:13 Now when Paul and his c loosed from G4012
15:22 men of their own c to Antioch with Paul G846
17: 5 and gathered a c, and set all the city on G3792
21: 8 we that were of Paul's c departed, and G4012
Ro 15:24 if first I be somewhat filled with your *c.*
1Co 5: 9 I wrote unto you in an epistle not to c G4874
11 you not to keep c, if any man that is G4874
2Th 3:14 no c with him, that he may be ashamed.
Heb 12:22 and to an innumerable c of angels, G3461
Rev 18:17 and all the c in ships, and sailors, G3658

COMPARABLE
Lam 4: 2 The precious sons of Zion, c to fine H5537

COMPARE
Isa 40:18 or what likeness will ye c unto him? H6186
46: 5 equal, and c me, that we may be like? H4911
Mk 4:30 or with what comparison shall we c it? G3846
2Co 10:12 of the number, or c ourselves with G4793

COMPARED
Ps 89: 6 For who in the heaven can be c unto H6186
Prv 3:15 canst desire are not to be c unto her. H7737
8:11 may be desired are not to be c to it. H7737
Song 1: 9 I have c thee, O my love, to a company H1819
Ro 8:18 not worthy *to be* c with the glory which

COMPARING
1Co 2:13 c spiritual things with spiritual. G4793
2Co 10:12 themselves, and c themselves among G4793

COMPARISON
Jdg 8: 2 have I done now in c of you? *Is* not the
3 was I able to do in c of you? Then their
Hag 2: 3 *it* not in your eyes in c of it as nothing? H3644
Mk 4:30 or with what c shall we compare it? G3850

COMPASS
Ex 27: 5 And thou shalt put it under the c of the H3749
38: 4 c thereof beneath unto the midst of it. H3749
Nu 21: 4 of the Red sea, to c the land of Edom: H5437
34: 5 And the border shall fetch a c from H5437
Jos 6: 3 And ye shall c the city, all *ye* men of H5437
4 day ye shall c the city seven times, H5437
7 Pass on, and c the city, and let him H5437
15: 3 up to Adar, and fetched a c to Karkaa: H5437

C

2Sa 5:23 go up; *but* fetch a c behind them, and H5437
1Ki 7:15 cubits did c either of them about. H5437
23 of thirty cubits did c it round about. H5437
35 base *was there* a round c of half a cubit H5439
2Ki 3: 9 and they fetched a c of seven days' H5437
11: 8 And ye shall c the king round about, H5362
2Ch 4: 2 to brim, round in c, and five cubits the H5439
2 of thirty cubits did c it round about. H5437
3 of oxen, which did c it round about: ten H5437
23: 7 And the Levites shall c the king round H5362
Job 16:13 His archers c me round about, he H5437
40:22 the willows of the brook c him about. H5437
Ps 5:12 favour wilt thou c him as *with* a shield. H5849
7: 7 of the people c thee about: for their H5437
17: 9 my deadly enemies, *who* c me about. H5362
26: 6 so will I c thine altar, O LORD: H5437
32: 7 trouble; thou shalt c me about with H5437
10 in the LORD, mercy shall c him about. H5437
49: 5 iniquity of my heels shall c me about? H5437
140: 9 *As for* the head of those that c me H4524
142: 7 the righteous shall c me about; for thou H3803
Prv 8:27 he set a c upon the face of the depth: H2329
Isa 44:13 it out with the c, and maketh it after H4230
50:11 Behold, all ye that kindle a fire, that c H247
Jer 31:22 in the earth, A woman shall c a man. H5437
39 hill Gareb, and shall c about to Goath. H5437
52:21 twelve cubits did c it; and the thickness H5437
Hab 1: 4 the wicked doth c about the righteous; H3803
Mt 23:15 hypocrites! for ye c sea and land to G4013
Lk 19:43 about thee, and c thee round, and keep G4033
Act 28:13 And from thence we fetched a c, and G4022

COMPASSED
Gen 19: 4 men of Sodom, c the house round, both H5437
Dt 2: 1 me: and we c mount Seir many days. H5437
3 Ye have c this mountain long enough: H5437
Jos 6:11 So the ark of the LORD c the city, going H5437
14 And the second day they c the city H5437
15 of the day, and c the city after the same H5437
15 on that day they c the city seven times. H5437
15:10 And the border c from Baalah H5437
18:14 *thence,* and c the corner of the sea H5437
Jdg 11:18 the wilderness, and c the land of Edom, H5437
16: 2 hither. And they c *him* in, and laid wait H5437
1Sa 23:26 Saul and his men c David and his men H5849
2Sa 18:15 bare Joab's armour c about and smote H5437
22: 5 When the waves of death c me, the H661
6 The sorrows of hell c me about; the H5437
2Ki 6:14 came by night, and c the city about. H5362
15 behold, an host c the city both with H5437
8:21 Edomites which c him about, and the H5437
2Ch 18:31 Therefore they c about him to fight: H5437
21: 9 the Edomites which c him in, and the H5437
33:14 at the fish gate, and c about Ophel, and H5437
Job 19: 6 me, and hath c me with his net. H5362
26:10 He hath c the waters with bounds, until H2328
Ps 17:11 They have now c us in our steps: they H5437
18: 4 The sorrows of death c me, and the H661
5 The sorrows of hell c me about: the H5437
22:12 Many bulls have c me: strong *bulls* of H5437
16 For dogs have c me: the assembly of H5437
40:12 For innumerable evils have c me about: H661
88:17 like water; they c me about together. H5362
109: 3 They c me about also with words of H5437
116: 3 The sorrows of death c me, and the H661
118:10 All nations c me about: but in the H5437
11 They c me about; yea, they compassed H5437
11 They compassed me about; yea, they c H5437
12 They c me about like bees; they are H5437
Lam 3: 5 He hath builded against me, and c *me* H5362
Jna 2: 3 seas; and the floods c me about: all thy H5437
5 The waters c me about, *even* to the soul: H661
Lk 21:20 And when ye shall see Jerusalem c with G2944
Heb 5: 2 that he himself also is c with infirmity. G4029
11:30 after they were c about seven days. G2944
12: 1 Wherefore seeing we also are c about G4029
Rev 20: 9 of the earth, and c the camp of the G2944

COMPASSEST
Ps 139: 3 Thou c my path and my lying down, H2219

COMPASSETH
Gen 2:11 that *is* it which c the whole land of H5437
13 *is* it that c the whole land of Ethiopia. H5437
Jos 19:14 And the border c it on the north side to H5437
Ps 73: 6 Therefore pride c them about as a H6059
Hos 11:12 Ephraim c me about with lies, and the H5437

COMPASSING
1Ki 7:24 *there were* knops c it, ten in a cubit, H5437
24 it, ten in a cubit, c the sea round about: H5362
2Ch 4: 3 ten in a cubit, c the sea round about. H5362

COMPASSION
Ex 2: 6 wept. And she had c on him, and said, H2550
Dt 13:17 thee mercy, and have c upon thee, and H7355
30: 3 and have c upon thee, and will H7355
1Sa 23:21 *be* ye of the LORD; for ye have c on me. H2550
1Ki 8:50 thee, and give them c before them who H7356
50 captive, that they may have c on them: H7355
2Ki 13:23 them, and had c on them, and had H7355
2Ch 30: 9 children *shall find* c before them that H7356
36:15 because he had c on his people, and on H2550
17 and had no c upon young man or H2550
Ps 78:38 But he, *being* full of c, forgave *their* H7349
86:15 But thou, O Lord, *art* a God full of c, H7349
111: 4 the LORD *is* gracious and full of c. H7349
112: 4 *is* gracious, and full of c, and righteous. H7349
145: 8 The LORD *is* gracious, and full of c; H7349
Isa 49:15 she should not have c on the son of her H7355
Jer 12:15 return, and have c on them, and will H7355
Lam 3:32 grief, yet will he have c according to the H7355
Ezk 16: 5 unto thee, to have c upon thee; but H2550
Mic 7:19 He will turn again, he will have c upon H7355
Mt 9:36 he was moved with c on them, because G4697
14:14 was moved with c toward them, and he G4697
15:32 and said, I have c on the multitude, G4697
18:27 was moved with c, and loosed him, and G4697
33 Shouldest not thou also have had c on G1653
20:34 So Jesus had c *on them,* and touched G4697
Mk 1:41 And Jesus, moved with c, put forth *his* G4697
5:19 done for thee, and hath had c on thee. G1653
6:34 and was moved with c toward them, G4697
8: 2 I have c on the multitude, because they G4697
9:22 do any thing, have c on us, and help us. G4697
Lk 7:13 And when the Lord saw her, he had c G4697
10:33 when he saw him, he had c *on him,* G4697
15:20 saw him, and had c, and ran, and fell G4697
Ro 9:15 c on whom I will have compassion. G3627
15 compassion on whom I will have c. G3627
Heb 5: 2 Who can have c on the ignorant, and G3356
10:34 For ye had c of me in my bonds, and G4834
1Pt 3: 8 Finally, *be ye* all of one mind, having c G4885
1Jn 3:17 up his bowels *of* c from him, how
Jude 22 And of some have c, making a G1653

COMPASSIONS
Lam 3:22 not consumed, because his c fail not. H7356
Zec 7: 9 mercy and c every man to his brother: H7356

COMPEL
Lev 25:39 not c him to serve as a bondservant: H5647
Est 1: 8 to the law; none did c: for so the king had H597
Mt 5:41 And whosoever shall c thee to go a mile, G29
Mk 15:21 And they c one Simon a Cyrenian, who G29
Lk 14:23 and hedges, and c *them* to come in, that G315

COMPELLED
1Sa 28:23 with the woman, c him; and he H6555
2Ch 21:11 fornication, and c Judah *thereto.* H5080
Mt 27:32 by name: him they c to bear his cross. G29
Act 26:11 synagogue, and c *them* to blaspheme; G315
2Co 12:11 I am become a fool in glorying; ye have c G315
Gal 2: 3 being a Greek, was c to be circumcised: G315

COMPELLEST
Gal 2:14 c thou the Gentiles to live as do the Jews? G315

COMPLAIN
Jdg 21:22 come unto us to c, that we will say unto H7378
Job 7:11 I will c in the bitterness of my soul. H7878
31:38 or that the furrows likewise thereof c; H1058
Lam 3:39 Wherefore doth a living man c, a man for H596

COMPLAINED
Nu 11: 1 And *when* the people c, it displeased the H596
Ps 77: 3 and was troubled: I c, and my spirit was H7878

COMPLAINERS
Jude 16 These are murmurers, c, walking after G3202

COMPLAINING
Ps 144:14 out; that *there be* no c in our streets. H6682

COMPLAINT
1Sa 1:16 my c and grief have I spoken hitherto. H7879
Job 7:13 comfort me, my couch shall ease my c; H7879
9:27 If I say, I will forget my c, I will leave off H7879
10: 1 life; I will leave my c upon myself; I will H7879
21: 4 As for me, *is* my c to man? and if *it* H7879
23: 2 Even to day *is* my c bitter: my stroke is H7879
Ps 55: 2 me: I mourn in my c, and make a noise; H7879
102: ttl and poureth out his c before the LORD. H7879
142: 2 I poured out my c before him; I shewed H7879

COMPLAINTS
Act 25: 7 laid many and grievous c against Paul, G157

COMPLETE
Lev 23:15 offering; seven sabbaths shall be c: H8549
Col 2:10 And ye are c in him, which is the head G4137
4:12 perfect and c in all the will of God. G4137

COMPOSITION
Ex 30:32 like it, after the c of it: it *is* holy, *and* it H4971
37 according to the c thereof: it shall be H4971

COMPOUND
Ex 30:25 an ointment c after the art of the H4842

COMPOUNDETH
Ex 30:33 Whosoever c *any* like it, or whosoever H7543

COMPREHEND
Job 37: 5 things doeth he, which we cannot c. H3045
Eph 3:18 May be able to c with all saints what *is* G2638

COMPREHENDED
Isa 40:12 with the span, and c the dust of the H3557
Jn 1: 5 in darkness; and the darkness c it not. G2638
Ro 13: 9 it is briefly c in this saying, namely, G346

CONANIAH
2Ch 35: 9 C also, and Shemaiah and Nethaneel, H3562

CONCEAL
Gen 37:26 if we slay our brother, and c his blood? H3680
Dt 13: 8 thou spare, neither shalt thou c him: H3680
Job 27:11 which *is* with the Almighty will I not c. H3582
41:12 I will not c his parts, nor his power, nor H2790
Prv 25: 2 *It is* the glory of God to c a thing: but H5641
Jer 50: 2 publish, *and* c not: say, Babylon is H3582

CONCEALED
Job 6:10 I have not c the words of the Holy One. H3582
Ps 40:10 I have not c thy lovingkindness H3582

CONCEALETH
Prv 11:13 that is of a faithful spirit c the matter. H3680
12:23 A prudent man c knowledge: but the H3680

CONCEIT
Prv 18:11 city, and as an high wall in his own c. H4906
26: 5 to his folly, lest he be wise in his own c. H5869
12 Seest thou a man wise in his own c? H5869
16 The sluggard *is* wiser in his own c than H5869
28:11 The rich man *is* wise in his own c; but H5869

CONCEITS
Ro 11:25 be wise in your own c; that blindness in G1438
12:16 of low estate. Be not wise in your own c. G1438

CONCEIVE
Gen 30:38 they should c when they came to drink. H3179
41 stronger cattle did c, that Jacob laid the H3179
41 that they might c among the rods. H3179
Nu 5:28 then she shall be free, and shall c seed. H2232
Jdg 13: 3 not: but thou shalt c, and bear a son. H2029
5 For, lo, thou shalt c, and bear a son; H2030
7 Behold, thou shalt c, and bear a son; H2030
Job 15:35 They c mischief, and bring forth H2029
Ps 51: 5 and in sin did my mother c me. H3179
Isa 7:14 a virgin shall c, and bear a son, and H2030
33:11 Ye shall c chaff, ye shall bring forth H2029
59: 4 c mischief, and bring forth iniquity. H2029
Lk 1:31 And, behold, thou shalt c in thy womb, G4815
Heb 11:11 strength to c seed, and was delivered G2602

CONCEIVED
Gen 4: 1 his wife; and she c, and bare Cain, and H2029
17 And Cain knew his wife; and she c, and H2029
16: 4 And he went in unto Hagar, and she c: H2029
4 c, her mistress was despised in her eyes. H2029
5 saw that she had c, I was despised in H2029
21: 2 For Sarah c, and bare Abraham a son H2029
25:21 of him, and Rebekah his wife c. H2029

Gen 29:32 And Leah c, and bare a son, and she H2029
33 And she c again, and bare a son; and H2029
34 And she c again, and bare a son; and H2029
35 And she c again, and bare a son: and H2029
30: 5 And Bilhah c, and bare Jacob a son. H2029
7 And Bilhah Rachel's maid c again, and H2029
17 and she c, and bare Jacob the fifth son. H2029
19 And Leah c again, and bare Jacob the H2029
23 And she c, and bare a son; and said, H2029
39 And the flocks c before the rods, and H3179
31:10 that the cattle c, that I lifted up mine H3179
38: 3 And she c, and bare a son; and he H2029
4 And she c again, and bare a son; and H2029
5 And she yet again c, and bare a son; H3254
18 came in unto her, and she c by him. H2029
Ex 2: 2 And the woman c, and bare a son: and H2029
Lev 12: 2 If a woman have c seed, and born a H2232
Nu 11:12 Have I c all this people? have I begotten H2029
1Sa 1:20 after Hannah had c, that she bare a H2029
2:21 so that she c, and bare three sons H2029
2Sa 11: 5 And the woman c, and sent and told H2029
2Ki 4:17 And the woman c, and bare a son at H2029
1Ch 7:23 And when he went in to his wife, she c, H2029
Job 3: 3 it was said, There is a man child c. H2029
Ps 7:14 with iniquity, and hath c mischief, and H2029
Song 3: 4 and into the chamber of her that c me. H2029
Isa 8: 3 and she c, and bare a son. Then H2029
Jer 49:30 you, and hath c a purpose against you. H2803
Hos 1: 3 Diblaim; which c, and bare him a son. H2029
6 And she c again, and bare a daughter. H2029
8 Lo-ruhamah, she c, and bare a son. H2029
2: 5 the harlot: she that c them hath done H2029
Mt 1:20 which is c in her is of the Holy Ghost. G1080
Lk 1:24 c, and hid herself five months, saying, G4815
36 she hath also c a son in her old age: G4815
2:21 the angel before he was c in the womb. G4815
Act 5: 4 why hast thou c this thing in thine G5087
Ro 9:10 had c by one, *even* by our father Isaac; G2845
Jas 1:15 Then when lust hath c, it bringeth forth G4815

CONCEIVING
Isa 59:13 and revolt, c and uttering from the H2029

CONCEPTION
Gen 3:16 sorrow and thy c; in sorrow thou shalt H2032
Ru 4:13 LORD gave her c, and she bare a son. H2032
Hos 9:11 and from the womb, and from the c. H2032

CONCERN
Act 28:31 things which c the Lord Jesus Christ, G4012
2Co 11:30 of the things which c mine infirmities. G769

CONCERNETH
Ps 138: 8 The LORD will perfect *that which* c me: H1157
Ezk 12:10 Lord GOD; This burden c the prince in

CONCERNING
Gen 5:29 shall comfort us c our work and toil of
12:20 And Pharaoh commanded *his* men c
19:21 have accepted thee c this thing also, that
24: 9 and sware to him c that matter. H5921
26:32 and told him c the well which H5921+H182
42:21 *are* verily guilty c our brother, in that H5921
Ex 6: 8 And I will bring you in unto the land, c
24: 8 hath made with you c all these words. H5921
Lev 4: 2 of the LORD c *things* which ought not
13 of the LORD c *things* which should
22 the LORD his God c *things* which should
26 as c his sin, and it shall be forgiven him.
27 of the LORD c *things* which ought not
5: 6 make an atonement for him c his sin.
18 for him c his ignorance wherein H5921
6: 3 was lost, and lieth c it, and sweareth
18 in your generations c the offerings of the
23: 2 say unto them, C the feasts of the LORD,
27:32 And c the tithe of the herd, or of the
Nu 8:20 Moses c the Levites, so did the
22 c the Levites, so did they unto them. H5921
9: 8 what the LORD will command c you.
10:29 the LORD hath spoken good c Israel. H5921
14:30 come into the land, c which I sware to
30: 1 the heads of the tribes c the children of
12 out of her lips c her vows, or concerning
12 her vows, or c the bond of her soul,
32:28 So c them Moses commanded Eleazar
36: 6 LORD doth command c the daughters of
Jos 14: 6 c me and thee in Kadeshbarnea. H5921+H182
23:14 your God spake c you; all are come to H5921
Jdg 15: 3 And Samson said c them, Now shall I be
21: 5 made a great oath c him that came not
Ru 4: 7 former time in Israel c redeeming and H5921
7 redeeming and c changing, for to H5921
1Sa 3:12 I have spoken c his house: when I begin, H413
25:30 he hath spoken c thee, and shall have H5921
2Sa 3: 8 me to day with a fault c this woman?
7:25 thou hast spoken c thy servant, and H5921
25 thy servant, and c his house, establish H5921
11:18 and told David all the things c the war;
13:39 c Amnon, seeing he was dead. H5921
14: 8 house, and I will give charge c thee. H5921
18: 5 captains charge c Absalom. H5921+H1697
1Ki 2: 4 which he spake c me, saying, If thy H5921
27 he spake c the house of Eli in Shiloh. H5921
5: 8 do all thy desire c timber of cedar, and
8 timber of cedar, and c timber of fir.
6:12 C this house which thou art in building,
8:41 Moreover c a stranger, that *is* not of thy H413
10: 1 the fame of Solomon c the name of the
11: 2 Of the nations c which the LORD said
10 And had commanded him c this thing, H5921
22: 8 not prophesy good c me, but evil. And H5921
18 would prophesy no good c me, but evil? H5921
23 and the LORD hath spoken evil c thee. H5921
2Ki 10:10 the LORD spake c the house of Ahab: H5921
17:15 about them, c whom the LORD had H5921
19:21 hath spoken c him; The virgin the H5921
32 Therefore thus saith the LORD c the king H413
22:13 and for all Judah, c the words of this H5921
13 unto all that which is written c us. H5921
1Ch 11:10 to the word of the LORD c Israel. H5921
17:23 thou hast spoken c thy servant and H5921
23 thy servant and c his house be H5921
19: 2 to comfort him c his father. So the H5921
22:12 and give thee charge c Israel, that thou
13 Moses with c Israel: be strong, and
23:14 Now c Moses the man of God, his sons
24:21 C Rehabiah: of the sons of Rehabiah, the
29 C Kish: the son of Kish *was* Jerahmeel.
26: 1 C the divisions of the porters: Of the
21 *As* c the sons of Laadan; the sons of the H413
2Ch 6:32 Moreover c the stranger, which is not of
8:15 the priests and Levites c any matter, or
15 any matter, or c the treasures.
12:15 of Iddo the seer c genealogies? And *there*
15:16 And also c Maachah the mother of Asa
24:27 Now c his sons, and the greatness of the
31: 6 And c the children of Israel and Judah,
9 the priests and the Levites c the heaps. H5921
34:21 and in Judah, c the words of the book H5921
26 c the words which thou hast heard;
Ezr 5: 5 returned answer by letter c this *matter.* H5922
17 send his pleasure to us c this matter. H5922
6: 3 king made a decree c the house of God at
7:14 to inquire c Judah and Jerusalem, H5922
10: 2 now there is hope in Israel c this thing. H5921
Neh 1: 2 and I asked them c the Jews that had H5921
2 left of the captivity, and c Jerusalem. H5921
9:23 them into the land, c which thou hadst
11:23 For *it was* the king's commandment c H5921
24 king's hand in all matters c the people.
13:14 Remember me, O my God, c this, and H5921
22 me, O my God, c this also, and spare
Est 3: 2 had so commanded c him. But Mordecai
9:26 they had seen c this matter, and which H5921
Job 36:33 The noise thereof sheweth c it, the H5921
33 it, the cattle also c the vapour. H5921
Ps 7:ttl c the words of Cush the Benjamite. H5921
17: 4 C the works of men, by the word of thy
73: 8 They are corrupt, and speak wickedly c
90:13 and let it repent thee c thy servants. H5921
106:34 They did not destroy the nations, c
119:128 Therefore I esteem all *thy* precepts c all
152 C thy testimonies, I have known of old
135:14 he will repent himself c his servants. H5921
Ecc 1:13 out by wisdom c all *things* that are H5921
3:18 I said in mine heart c the estate of the H5921
7:10 for thou dost not inquire wisely c this. H5921
Isa 1: 1 which he saw c Judah and Jerusalem H5921
2: 1 of Amoz saw c Judah and Jerusalem. H5921
8: 1 a man's pen c Maher-shalal-hash-baz.
16:13 hath spoken c Moab since that time. H413
23: 5 As at the report c Egypt, *so* shall they be
29:22 Abraham, c the house of Jacob, Jacob H413
30: 7 I cried c this, Their strength *is* to sit still.
37: 9 And he heard say c Tirhakah king of H5921
22 hath spoken c him; The virgin, the H5921
33 Therefore thus saith the LORD c the king H413
45:11 me of things to come c my sons, and H5921
Isa 45:11 my sons, and c the work of my hands H5921
Jer 7:22 c burnt offerings or sacrifices: H5921+H1697
14: 1 came to Jeremiah c the dearth. H5921+H1697
15 Therefore thus saith the LORD c the H5921
16: 3 For thus saith the LORD c the sons and H5921
3 the sons and c the daughters that are H5921
3 in this place, and c their mothers that H5921
3 that bare them, and c their fathers that H5921
18: 7 *At what* instant I shall speak c a H5921
7 a nation, and c a kingdom, to pluck H5921
9 And *at what* instant I shall speak c a H5921
9 c a kingdom, to build and to plant *it;* H5921
22:18 Therefore thus saith the LORD c H413
23:15 saith the LORD of hosts c the prophets; H5921
25: 1 The word that came to Jeremiah c all H5921
27:19 For thus saith the LORD of hosts c the H5921
19 the pillars, and c the sea, and H5921
19 the sea, and c the bases, and H5921
19 the bases, and c the residue of the H5921
21 the God of Israel, c the vessels that H5921
29:31 Thus saith the LORD c Shemaiah the H413
30: 4 spake c Israel and concerning Judah. H413
4 spake concerning Israel and c Judah. H413
32:36 the God of Israel, c this city, whereof ye H413
33: 4 the God of Israel, c the houses of this H5921
4 of this city, and c the houses of the H5921
39:11 Babylon gave charge c Jeremiah to H5921
42:19 The LORD hath said c you, O ye H5921
44: 1 The word that came to Jeremiah c all the H413
49: 1 C the Ammonites, thus saith the LORD;
7 C Edom, thus saith the LORD of hosts; *Is*
23 C Damascus. Hamath is confounded,
28 C Kedar, and concerning the kingdoms
28 Concerning Kedar, and c the kingdoms
52:21 And c the pillars, the height of one pillar
Lam 1:17 hath commanded c Jacob, *that* his
Ezk 13:16 which prophesy c Jerusalem, and which H413
14: 7 to inquire of him c me; I the LORD will
22 shall be comforted c the evil that I have H5921
22 *even* c all that I have brought upon it. H854
18: 2 ye use this proverb c the land of Israel, H5921
21:28 saith the Lord GOD c the Ammonites, H413
28 Ammonites, and c their reproach; even H413
36: 6 Prophesy therefore c the land of Israel, H5921
44: 5 that I say unto thee c all the ordinances
45:14 C the ordinance of oil, the bath of oil, *ye*
47:14 as well as another: c the which I lifted up
Dan 2:18 of the God of heaven c this secret; that H5922
5:29 a proclamation c him, that he should H5922
6: 4 against Daniel c the kingdom; but they H6655
5 find *it* against him c the law of his God.
12 before the king c the king's decree; H5922
17 purpose might not be changed c Daniel.
7:12 As c the rest of the beasts, they had their
8:13 *shall be* the vision c the daily *sacrifice,*
Am 1: 1 which he saw c Israel in the days of H5921
Oba 1 saith the Lord GOD c Edom; We have
Mic 1: 1 he saw c Samaria and Jerusalem. H5921
3: 5 Thus saith the LORD c the prophets H5921
Nah 1:14 a commandment c thee, *that* no more H5921
Hag 2:11 Ask now the priests c the law, saying,
Mt 4: 6 his angels charge c thee: and in *their* G4012
11: 7 the multitudes c John, What went ye G4012
16:11 I spake *it* not to you c bread, that ye G4012
Mk 5:16 with the devil, and *also* c the swine. G4012
7:17 his disciples asked him c the parable. G4012
Lk 2:17 which was told them c this child. G4012
7:24 unto the people c John, What went ye G4012
18:31 c the Son of man shall be accomplished.
22:37 for the things c me have an end. G4012
24:19 said unto him, C Jesus of Nazareth, G4012
27 all the scriptures the things c himself. G4012
44 the prophets, and *in* the psalms, c me. G4012
Jn 7:12 among the people c him: for some said, G4012
32 such things c him; and the Pharisees G4012
9:18 But the Jews did not believe c him, that G4012
11:19 Mary, to comfort them c their brother. G4012
Act 1:16 spake before c Judas, which was guide G4012
2:25 For David speaketh c him, I foresaw G1519
8:12 the things c the kingdom of God, G4012
13:34 And as c that he raised him up from G3754
19: 8 the things c the kingdom of God. G4012
39 But if ye inquire any thing c other G4012
21:24 were informed c thee, are nothing; but G4012
22:18 will not receive thy testimony c me. G4012
23:15 more perfectly c him: and we, or ever G4012
24:24 and heard him c the faith in Christ. G4012
25:16 himself c the crime laid against him. G4012
28:21 out of Judaea c thee, neither any of G4012

Act 28:22 thinkest: for as c this sect, we know G4012
23 persuading them c Jesus, both out of G4012
Ro 1: 3 C his Son Jesus Christ our Lord, which G4012
9: 5 and of whom as c the flesh Christ G2596
27 Esaias also crieth c Israel, Though the G5228
11:28 As c the gospel, *they are* enemies for G2596
16:19 that which is good, and simple c evil. G1519
1Co 5: 3 c him that hath so done this deed,
7: 1 Now c the things whereof ye wrote unto G4012
25 Now c virgins I have no G4012
8: 4 As c therefore the eating of those things G4012
12: 1 Now c spiritual *gifts*, brethren, I would G4012
16: 1 Now c the collection for the saints, as I G4012
2Co 8:23 and fellowhelper c you: or our brethren G1519
11:21 I speak as c reproach, as though we G2596
Eph 4:22 That ye put off c the former G2596
5:32 This is a great mystery: but I speak c G1519
Php 3: 6 C zeal, persecuting the church; G2596
4:15 as c giving and receiving, but ye only. G1519
1Th 3: 2 you, and to comfort you c your faith: G4012
4:13 brethren, c them which are asleep, G4012
5:18 is the will of God in Christ Jesus c you. G1519
1Ti 1:19 put away c faith have made shipwreck: G4012
6:21 Which some professing have erred c G4012
2Ti 2:18 Who c the truth have erred, saying that G4012
3: 8 of corrupt minds, reprobate c the faith. G4012
Heb 7:14 Moses spake nothing c priesthood. G4012
11:20 By faith Isaac blessed Jacob and Esau c G4012
22 and gave commandment c his bones. G4012
1Pt 4:12 Beloved, think it not strange c the fiery G4012
2Pt 3: 9 The Lord is not slack c his promise, as G4314
1Jn 2:26 These *things* have I written unto you c G4012

CONCISION
Php 3: 2 beware of evil workers, beware of the c. G2699

CONCLUDE
Ro 3:28 Therefore we c that a man is justified G3049

CONCLUDED
Act 21:25 have written *and* c that they observe no G2919
Ro 11:32 For God hath c them all in unbelief, G4788
Gal 3:22 But the scripture hath c all under sin, G4788

CONCLUSION
Ecc 12:13 Let us hear the c of the whole matter: H5490

CONCORD
2Co 6:15 And what c hath Christ with Belial? or G4857

CONCOURSE
Prv 1:21 She crieth in the chief place of c, in the H1993
Act 19:40 we may give an account of this c. G4963

CONCUBINE
Gen 22:24 And his c, whose name *was* Reumah, H6370
35:22 Bilhah his father's c: and Israel heard *it*. H6370
36:12 And Timna was c to Eliphaz Esau's H6370
Jdg 8:31 And his c that *was* in Shechem, she H6370
19: 1 to him a c out of Beth-lehem-judah. H6370
2 And his c played the whore against H6370
9 he, and his c, and his servant, his H6370
10 asses saddled, his c also *was* with him. H6370
24 a maiden, and his c; them I will bring H6370
25 so the man took his c, and brought her H6370
27 the woman his c was fallen down *at* H6370
29 and laid hold on his c, and divided her, H6370
20: 4 to Benjamin, I and my c, to lodge. H6370
5 my c have they forced, that she is dead. H6370
6 And I took my c, and cut her in pieces, H6370
2Sa 3: 7 And Saul had a c, whose name *was* H6370
7 hast thou gone in unto my father's c? H6370
21:11 of Aiah, the c of Saul, had done. H6370
1Ch 1:32 Now the sons of Keturah, Abraham's c: H6370
2:46 And Ephah, Caleb's c, bare Haran, and H6370
48 Maachah, Caleb's c, bare Sheber, and H6370
7:14 she bare: (*but* his c the Aramitess bare H6370

CONCUBINES
Gen 25: 6 But unto the sons of the c, which H6370
2Sa 5:13 And David took *him* more c and wives H6370
15:16 *which were* c, to keep the house. H6370
16:21 unto thy father's c, which he hath left to H6370
22 his father's c in the sight of all Israel. H6370
19: 5 lives of thy wives, and the lives of thy c; H6370
20: 3 the ten women *his* c, whom he had left H6370
1Ki 11: 3 c: and his wives turned away his heart. H6370
1Ch 3: 9 sons of the c, and Tamar their sister. H6370
2Ch 11:21 all his wives and his c: (for he took H6370
2Ch 11:21 and threescore c; and begat twenty and H6370
Est 2:14 which kept the c: she came in unto the H6370
Song 6: 8 c, and virgins without number. H6370
9 queens and the c, and they praised her. H6370
Dan 5: 2 wives, and his c, might drink therein. H3904
3 his wives, and his c, drank in them. H3904
23 thy wives, and thy c, have drunk wine H3904

CONCUPISCENCE
Ro 7: 8 of c. For without the law sin *was* dead. G1939
Col 3: 5 c, and covetousness, which is idolatry: G1939
1Th 4: 5 Not in the lust of c, even as the Gentiles G1939

CONDEMN
Ex 22: 9 the judges shall c, he shall pay double H7561
Dt 25: 1 justify the righteous, and c the wicked. H7561
Job 9:20 own mouth shall c me: *if I say*, I *am* H7561
10: 2 I will say unto God, Do not c me; shew H7561
34:17 and wilt thou c him that is most just? H7561
40: 8 c me, that thou mayest be righteous? H7561
Ps 37:33 his hand, nor c him when he is judged. H7561
94:21 righteous, and c the innocent blood. H7561
109:31 to save *him* from those that c his soul. H8199
Prv 12: 2 but a man of wicked devices will he c. H7561
Isa 50: 9 *is* he *that* shall c me? lo, they all shall H7561
54:17 thou shalt c. This *is* the heritage H7561
Mt 12:41 and shall c it: because they repented G2632
42 and shall c it: for she came from G2632
20:18 scribes, and they shall c him to death, G2632
Mk 10:33 and they shall c him to death, and shall G2632
Lk 6:37 Judge not, and ye shall not be judged: c G2613
11:31 generation, and c them: for she came G2632
32 and shall c it: for they repented G2632
Jn 3:17 into the world to c the world; but that G2919
8:11 do I c thee: go, and sin no more. G2632
2Co 7: 3 I speak not *this* to c *you*: for I have said G2633
1Jn 3:20 For if our heart c us, God is greater G2607
21 Beloved, if our heart c us not, *then* G2607

CONDEMNATION
Lk 23:40 fear God, seeing thou art in the same c? G2917
Jn 3:19 And this is the c, that light is come into G2920
5:24 c; but is passed from death unto life. G2920
Ro 5:16 *was* by one to c, but the free gift *is* of G2631
18 *came* upon all men to c; even so by the G2631
8: 1 *There is* therefore now no c to them G2631
1Co 11:34 not together unto c. And the rest will I G2917
2Co 3: 9 For if the ministration of c *be* glory, G2633
1Ti 3: 6 with pride he fall into the c of the devil. G2917
Jas 3: 1 that we shall receive the greater c. G2917
5:12 and *your* nay, nay; lest ye fall into c. G5272
Jude 4 old ordained to this c, ungodly men, G2917

CONDEMNED
2Ch 36: 3 at Jerusalem, and c the land in an H6064
Job 32: 3 found no answer, and *yet* had c Job. H7561
Ps 109: 7 When he shall be judged, let him be c: H7563
Am 2: 8 wine of the c *in* the house of their god. H6064
Mt 12: 7 ye would not have c the guiltless. G2613
37 and by thy words thou shalt be c. G2613
27: 3 he saw that he was c, repented himself, G2632
Mk 14:64 And they all c him to be guilty of death. G2632
Lk 6:37 be c: forgive, and ye shall be forgiven: G2613
24:20 be c to death, and have crucified him. G2917
Jn 3:18 He that believeth on him is not c: but he G2919
18 believeth not is c already, because he G2919
8:10 thine accusers? hath no man c thee? G2632
Ro 8: 3 flesh, and for sin, c sin in the flesh: G2632
1Co 11:32 that we should not be c with the world. G2632
Tit 2: 8 Sound speech, that cannot be c; that he G176
3:11 and sinneth, being c of himself. G843
Heb 11: 7 house; by the which he c the world, and G2632
Jas 5: 6 Ye have c *and* killed the just; *and* he G2613
9 lest ye be c: behold, the judge standeth G2632
2Pt 2: 6 into ashes c *them* with an overthrow, G2632

CONDEMNEST
Ro 2: 1 another, thou c thyself; for thou that G2632

CONDEMNETH
Job 15: 6 Thine own mouth c thee, and not I: H7561
Prv 17:15 and he that c the just, even they both H7561
Ro 8:34 Who *is* he that c? *It is* Christ that died, G2632
14:22 Happy *is* he that c not himself in that G2919

CONDEMNING
1Ki 8:32 thy servants, c the wicked, to bring H7561
Act 13:27 day, they have fulfilled *them* in c *him*. G2919

CONDESCEND
Ro 12:16 high things, but c to men of low estate. G4879

CONDITION
1Sa 11: 2 them, On this c will I make *a covenant*

CONDITIONS
Lk 14:32 an ambassage, and desireth c of peace. G3588

CONDUCT
2Sa 19:15 the king, to c the king over Jordan. H5674
31 with the king, to c him over Jordan. H7971
1Co 16:11 despise him: but c him forth in peace, G4311

CONDUCTED
2Sa 19:40 the people of Judah c the king, and also H5674
Act 17:15 And they that c Paul brought him unto G2525

CONDUIT
2Ki 18:17 and stood by the c of the upper pool, H8585
20:20 a pool, and a c, and brought water into H8585
Isa 7: 3 at the end of the c of the upper pool in H8585
36: 2 he stood by the c of the upper pool in H8585

CONEY
Lev 11: 5 And the c, because he cheweth the cud, H8227
Dt 14: 7 the hare, and the c: for they chew the H8227

CONFECTION
Ex 30:35 And thou shalt make it a perfume, a c H7545

CONFECTIONARIES
1Sa 8:13 And he will take your daughters *to be* c, H7548

CONFEDERACY
Isa 8:12 Say ye not, A c, to all *them to* whom this H7195
12 this people shall say, A c; neither fear ye H7195
Oba 7 All the men of thy c have brought thee H1285

CONFEDERATE
Gen 14:13 and these *were* c with Abram. H1167+H1285
Ps 83: 5 one consent: they are c against thee: H1285
Isa 7: 2 saying, Syria is c with Ephraim. And H5117

CONFERENCE
Gal 2: 6 *be somewhat* in c added nothing to me: G4323

CONFERRED
1Ki 1: 7 And he c with Joab the son of Zeruiah, H1697
Act 4:15 the council, they c among themselves, G4820
25:12 Then Festus, when he had c with the G4814
Gal 1:16 I c not with flesh and blood: G4323

CONFESS
Lev 5: 5 c that he hath sinned in that *thing*: H3034
16:21 of the live goat, and c over him all the H3034
26:40 If they shall c their iniquity, and the H3034
Nu 5: 7 Then they shall c their sin which they H3034
1Ki 8:33 turn again to thee, and c thy name, and H3034
35 this place, and c thy name, and turn H3034
2Ch 6:24 shall return and c thy name, and pray H3034
26 this place, and c thy name, and turn H3034
Neh 1: 6 Israel thy servants, and c the sins of the H3034
Job 40:14 Then will I also c unto thee that thine H3034
Ps 32: 5 hid. I said, I will c my transgressions H3034
Mt 10:32 Whosoever therefore shall c me before G3670
32 men, him will I c also before my Father G3670
Lk 12: 8 Also I say unto you, Whosoever shall c G3670
8 of man also c before the angels of God: G3670
Jn 9:22 if any man did c that he was Christ, he G3670
12:42 they did not c *him*, lest they should G3670
Act 23: 8 nor spirit: but the Pharisees c both. G3670
24:14 But this I c unto thee, that after the way G3670
Ro 10: 9 That if thou shalt c with thy mouth the G3670
14:11 to me, and every tongue shall c to God. G1843
15: 9 this cause I will c to thee among the G1843
Php 2:11 And *that* every tongue should c that G1843
Jas 5:16 C *your* faults one to another, and pray G1843
1Jn 1: 9 If we c our sins, he is faithful and just G3670
4:15 Whosoever shall c that Jesus is the Son G3670
2Jn 7 the world, who c not that Jesus Christ G3670
Rev 3: 5 of life, but I will c his name before my G1843

CONFESSED
Ezr 10: 1 and when he had c, weeping and H3034
Neh 9: 2 and stood and c their sins, and the H3034
3 c, and worshipped the LORD their God. H3034
Jn 1:20 And he c, and denied not; but G3670
20 denied not; but c, I am not the Christ. G3670

Act 19:18 And many that believed came, and **c**, G1843
Heb 11:13 *them*, and **c** that they were strangers G3670

CONFESSETH
Prv 28:13 **c** and forsaketh *them* shall have mercy. H3034
1Jn 4: 2 Every spirit that **c** that Jesus Christ is G3670
3 And every spirit that **c** not that Jesus G3670

CONFESSING
Dan 9:20 and praying, and **c** my sin and the sin H3034
Mt 3: 6 And were baptized of him in Jordan, **c** G1843
Mk 1: 5 him in the river of Jordan, **c** their sins. G1843

CONFESSION
Jos 7:19 of Israel, and make **c** unto him; and tell H8426
2Ch 30:22 **c** to the LORD God of their fathers. H3034
Ezr 10:11 Now therefore make **c** unto the LORD H8426
Dan 9: 4 and made my **c**, and said, O Lord, the H3034
Ro 10:10 the mouth **c** is made unto salvation. G3670
1Ti 6:13 Pontius Pilate witnessed a good **c**; G3671

CONFIDENCE
Jdg 9:26 the men of Shechem put their **c** in him. H982
2Ki 18:19 What **c** *is* this wherein thou trustest? H986
Job 4: 6 *Is* not *this* thy fear, thy **c**, thy hope, and H3690
18:14 His **c** shall be rooted out of his H4009
31:24 said to the fine gold, *Thou art* my **c**; H4009
Ps 65: 5 *who art* the **c** of all the ends of the H4009
118: 8 trust in the LORD than to put **c** in man. H982
9 in the LORD than to put **c** in princes. H982
Prv 3:26 For the LORD shall be thy **c**, and shall H3689
14:26 In the fear of the LORD *is* strong **c**: and H4009
21:22 down the strength of the **c** thereof. H4009
25:19 **C** in an unfaithful man in time of H4009
Isa 30:15 in quietness and in **c** shall be your H985
36: 4 What **c** *is* this wherein thou trustest? H986
Jer 48:13 of Israel was ashamed of Beth-el their **c**. H4009
Ezk 28:26 shall dwell with **c**, when I have executed H983
29:16 And it shall be no more the **c** of the H4009
Mic 7: 5 Trust ye not in a friend, put ye not **c** in a H982
Act 28:31 with all **c**, no man forbidding him. G3954
2Co 1:15 And in this **c** I was minded to come G4006
2: 3 to rejoice; having **c** in you all, that my G3982
7:16 I rejoice therefore that I have **c** in you G2292
8:22 upon the great **c** which *I have* in you. G4006
10: 2 present with that **c**, wherewith I think G4006
11:17 it were foolishly, in this **c** of boasting. G5287
Gal 5:10 I have **c** in you through the Lord, that G3982
Eph 3:12 and access with **c** by the faith of him. G4006
Php 1:25 And having this **c**, I know that I shall G3982
3: 3 Christ Jesus, and have no **c** in the flesh. G3982
4 Though I might also have **c** in the flesh. G4006
2Th 3: 4 And we have **c** in the Lord touching G3982
Phlm 21 Having **c** in thy obedience I wrote unto G3982
Heb 3: 6 if we hold fast the **c** and the rejoicing of G3954
14 of our **c** stedfast unto the end; G5287
10:35 Cast not away therefore your **c**, which G3954
1Jn 2:28 we may have **c**, and not be ashamed G3954
3:21 us not, *then* have we **c** toward God. G3954
5:14 And this is the **c** that we have in him, G3954

CONFIDENCES
Jer 2:37 **c**, and thou shalt not prosper in them. H4009

CONFIDENT
Ps 27: 3 should rise against me, in this *will* I *be* **c**. H982
Prv 14:16 from evil: but the fool rageth, and is **c**. H982
Ro 2:19 And art **c** that thou thyself art a guide G3982
2Co 5: 6 Therefore *we are* always **c**, knowing G2292
8 We are **c**, *I say*, and willing rather to be G2292
9: 4 be ashamed in this same **c** boasting. G5287
Php 1: 6 Being **c** of this very thing, that he which G3982
14 in the Lord, waxing **c** by my bonds, are G3982

CONFIDENTLY
Lk 22:59 hour after another **c** affirmed, saying, G1340

CONFIRM
Ru 4: 7 changing, for to **c** all things; a man H6965
1Ki 1:14 come in after thee, and **c** thy words. H4390
2Ki 15:19 with him to **c** the kingdom in his hand. H2388
Est 9:29 to **c** this second letter of Purim. H6965
31 To **c** these days of Purim in their times H6965
Ps 68: 9 **c** thine inheritance, when it was weary. H3559
Isa 35: 3 Strengthen ye the weak hands, and **c** the H553
Ezk 13: 6 to hope that they would **c** the word. H6965
Dan 9:27 And he shall **c** the covenant with many H1396
11: 1 I, stood to **c** and to strengthen him. H2388
Ro 15: 8 to **c** the promises *made* unto the fathers: G950
1Co 1: 8 Who shall also **c** you unto the end, *that* G950
2Co 2: 8 that ye would **c** *your* love toward him. G2964

CONFIRMATION
Php 1: 7 in the defence and **c** of the gospel, ye all G951
Heb 6:16 oath for **c** *is* to them an end of all strife. G951

CONFIRMED
2Sa 7:24 For thou hast **c** to thyself thy people H3559
2Ki 14: 5 the kingdom was **c** in his hand, that he H2388
1Ch 14: 2 the LORD had **c** him king over Israel, H3559
16:17 And hath **c** the same to Jacob for a law, H5975
Est 9:32 And the decree of Esther **c** these H6965
Ps 105:10 And **c** the same unto Jacob for a law, H5975
Dan 9:12 And he hath **c** his words, which he H6965
Act 15:32 with many words, and **c** *them*. G1991
1Co 1: 6 Even as the testimony of Christ was **c** in G950
Gal 3:15 yet *if it be* **c**, no man disannulleth, G2964
17 that was **c** before of God in Christ, G4300
Heb 2: 3 was **c** unto us by them that heard *him*; G950
6:17 of his counsel, **c** *it* by an oath: G3315

CONFIRMETH
Nu 30:14 *are* upon her: he **c** them, because he H6965
Dt 27:26 Cursed *be* he that **c** not *all* the words of H6965
Isa 44:26 That **c** the word of his servant, and H6965

CONFIRMING
Mk 16:20 **c** the word with signs following. Amen. G950
Act 14:22 **C** the souls of the disciples, *and* G1991
15:41 Syria and Cilicia, **c** the churches. G1991

CONFISCATION
Ezr 7:26 or to **c** of goods, or to imprisonment. H6065

CONFLICT
Php 1:30 Having the same **c** which ye saw in me, G73
Col 2: 1 For I would that ye knew what great **c** I G73

CONFORMABLE
Php 3:10 being made **c** unto his death; G4833

CONFORMED
Ro 8:29 predestinate *to be* **c** to the image of his G4832
12: 2 And be not **c** to this world: but be ye G4964

CONFOUND
Gen 11: 7 Go to, let us go down, and there **c** their H1101
9 LORD did there **c** the language of all H1101
Jer 1:17 at their faces, lest I **c** thee before them. H2865
1Co 1:27 of the world to **c** the wise; and God G2617
27 world to **c** the things which are mighty; G2617

CONFOUNDED
2Ki 19:26 dismayed and **c**; they were *as* the grass H954
Job 6:20 They were **c** because they had hoped; H954
Ps 22: 5 they trusted in thee, and were not **c**. H954
35: 4 Let them be **c** and put to shame that H954
40:14 Let them be ashamed and **c** together H2659
69: 6 thee be **c** for my sake, O God of Israel. H3637
70: 2 Let them be ashamed and **c** that seek H2659
71:13 Let them be **c** *and* consumed that are H954
24 long: for they are **c**, for they are brought H954
83:17 Let them be **c** and troubled for ever; yea, H954
97: 7 **C** be all they that serve graven images, H954
129: 5 Let them all be **c** and turned back that H954
Isa 1:29 **c** for the gardens that ye have chosen. H2659
19: 9 and they that weave networks, shall be **c**. H954
24:23 Then the moon shall be **c**, and the sun H2659
37:27 dismayed and **c**: they were *as* the grass H954
41:11 shall be ashamed and **c**: they shall be as H3637
45:16 They shall be ashamed, and also **c**, all H3637
17 be ashamed nor **c** world without end. H3637
50: 7 shall I not be **c**: therefore have I set H3637
54: 4 neither be thou **c**; for thou shalt not be H3637
Jer 9:19 we are greatly **c**, because we have H954
10:14 every founder is **c** by the graven image: H3001
14: 3 and **c**, and covered their heads. H3637
15: 9 ashamed and **c**: and the residue of them H2659
17:18 Let them be **c** that persecute me, but let H954
18 me, but let not me be **c**: let them be H954
22:22 ashamed and **c** for all thy wickedness. H3637
31:19 yea, even **c**, because I did bear the H3637
46:24 The daughter of Egypt shall be **c**; she H3001
48: 1 Kiriathaim is **c** *and* taken: Misgab H3001
1 *and* taken: Misgab is **c** and dismayed. H3001
20 Moab is **c**; for it is broken down: howl H3001
49:23 Concerning Damascus. Hamath is **c**, and H954
50: 2 is taken, Bel is **c**, Merodach is broken H3001
Jer 50: 2 are **c**, her images are broken in pieces. H3001
12 Your mother shall be sore **c**; she that H954
51:17 every founder is **c** by the graven image: H3001
47 whole land shall be **c**, and all her slain H954
51 We are **c**, because we have heard H954
Ezk 16:52 thou: yea, be thou **c** also, and bear thy H954
54 and mayest be **c** in all that thou hast H3637
63 That thou mayest remember, and be **c**, H954
36:32 **c** for your own ways, O house of Israel. H3637
Mic 3: 7 and the diviners **c**: yea, they shall all H2659
7:16 The nations shall see and be **c** at all their H954
Zec 10: 5 and the riders on horses shall be **c**. H3001
Act 2: 6 together, and were **c**, because that every G4797
9:22 in strength, and **c** the Jews which dwelt G4797
1Pt 2: 6 he that believeth on him shall not be **c**. G2617

CONFUSED
Isa 9: 5 For every battle of the warrior *is* with **c** H7494
Act 19:32 the assembly was **c**; and the more part G4797

CONFUSION
Lev 18:23 a beast to lie down thereto: it *is* **c**. H8397
20:12 **c**; their blood *shall be* upon them. H8397
1Sa 20:30 of Jesse to thine own **c**, and unto the H1322
30 unto the **c** of thy mother's nakedness? H1322
Ezr 9: 7 spoil, and to **c** of face, as *it is* this day. H1322
Job 10:15 of **c**; therefore see thou mine affliction; H7036
Ps 35: 4 and brought to **c** that devise my hurt. H2659
26 Let them be ashamed and brought to **c** H2659
44:15 My **c** *is* continually before me, and the H3639
70: 2 and put to **c**, that desire my hurt. H3637
71: 1 I put my trust: let me never be put to **c**. H954
109:29 with their own **c**, as with a mantle. H1322
Isa 24:10 The city of **c** is broken down: every H8414
30: 3 the trust in the shadow of Egypt *your* **c**. H3639
34:11 line of **c**, and the stones of emptiness. H8414
41:29 their molten images *are* wind and **c**. H8414
45:16 to **c** together *that are* makers of idols. H3639
61: 7 double; and *for* **c** they shall rejoice in H3639
Jer 3:25 We lie down in our shame, and our **c** H3639
7:19 themselves to the **c** of their own faces? H1322
20:11 everlasting **c** shall never be forgotten. H3639
Dan 9: 7 thee, but unto us **c** of faces, as at this H1322
8 O Lord, to us *belongeth* **c** of face, to our H1322
Act 19:29 And the whole city was filled with **c**: G4799
1Co 14:33 For God is not *the author* of **c**, but of G181
Jas 3:16 strife *is*, there *is* **c** and every evil work. G181

CONGEALED
Ex 15: 8 depths were **c** in the heart of the sea. H7087

CONGRATULATE
1Ch 18:10 of his welfare, and to **c** him, because he H1288

CONGREGATION
Ex 12: 3 Speak ye unto all the **c** of Israel, saying, H5712
6 **c** of Israel shall kill it in the evening. H5712
19 be cut off from the **c** of Israel, whether H5712
47 All the **c** of Israel shall keep it. H5712
16: 1 Elim, and all the **c** of the children of H5712
2 And the whole **c** of the children of H5712
9 Say unto all the **c** of the children of H5712
10 unto the whole **c** of the children of H5712
22 rulers of the **c** came and told Moses. H5712
17: 1 And all the **c** of the children of Israel H5712
27:21 In the tabernacle of the **c** without the H4150
28:43 tabernacle of the **c**, or when they come H4150
29: 4 the **c**, and shalt wash them with water. H4150
10 tabernacle of the **c**: and Aaron and his H4150
11 *by* the door of the tabernacle of the **c**. H4150
30 of the **c** to minister in the holy *place*. H4150
32 *by* the door of the tabernacle of the **c**. H4150
42 tabernacle of the **c** before the LORD: H4150
44 tabernacle of the **c**, and the altar: I will H4150
30:16 the tabernacle of the **c**; that it may be a H4150
18 tabernacle of the **c** and the altar, and H4150
20 tabernacle of the **c**, they shall wash with H4150
26 tabernacle of the **c** therewith, and the H4150
36 tabernacle of the **c**, where I will meet H4150
31: 7 The tabernacle of the **c**, and the ark of H4150
33: 7 the Tabernacle of the **c**. And it came to H4150
7 of the **c**, which *was* without the camp. H4150
34:31 the rulers of the **c** returned unto him: H5712
35: 1 And Moses gathered all the **c** of the H5712
4 And Moses spake unto all the **c** of the H5712
20 And all the **c** of the children of Israel H5712
21 the tabernacle of the **c**, and for all his H4150
38: 8 *at* the door of the tabernacle of the **c**. H4150
25 numbered of the **c** *was* an hundred H5712

Ex 38:30 the tabernacle of the **c**, and the brasen H4150
39:32 of the tent of the **c** finished: and the H4150
40 of the tabernacle, for the tent of the **c**, H4150
40: 2 set up the tabernacle of the tent of the **c**. H4150
6 of the tabernacle of the tent of the **c**. H4150
7 the tent of the **c** and the altar, and shalt H4150
12 of the **c**, and wash them with water. H4150
22 And he put the table in the tent of the **c**, H4150
24 in the tent of the **c**, over against the H4150
26 altar in the tent of the **c** before the vail: H4150
29 of the tent of the **c**, and offered upon it H4150
30 the tent of the **c** and the altar, and put H4150
32 When they went into the tent of the **c**, H4150
34 Then a cloud covered the tent of the **c**, H4150
35 into the tent of the **c**, because the cloud H4150
Lev 1: 1 out of the tabernacle of the **c**, saying, H4150
3 tabernacle of the **c** before the LORD. H4150
5 *is by* the door of the tabernacle of the **c**. H4150
3: 2 tabernacle of the **c**: and Aaron's sons H4150
8 tabernacle of the **c**: and Aaron's sons H4150
13 the tabernacle of the **c**: and the sons of H4150
4: 4 tabernacle of the **c** before the LORD; H4150
5 and bring it to the tabernacle of the **c**: H4150
7 tabernacle of the **c**; and shall pour all H4150
7 *is at* the door of the tabernacle of the **c**. H4150
13 And if the whole **c** of Israel sin through H5712
14 is known, then the **c** shall offer a young H6951
14 bring him before the tabernacle of the **c**. H4150
15 And the elders of the **c** shall lay their H5712
16 blood to the tabernacle of the **c**: H4150
18 tabernacle of the **c**, and shall pour out H4150
18 *is at* the door of the tabernacle of the **c**. H4150
21 first bullock: it *is* a sin offering for the **c**. H6951
6:16 the tabernacle of the **c** they shall eat it. H4150
26 in the court of the tabernacle of the **c**. H4150
30 tabernacle of the **c** to reconcile *withal* H4150
8: 3 And gather thou all the **c** together unto H5712
3 unto the door of the tabernacle of the **c**. H4150
4 unto the door of the tabernacle of the **c**. H4150
5 And Moses said unto the **c**, This *is* the H5712
31 tabernacle of the **c**: and there eat it with H4150
33 tabernacle of the **c** *in* seven days, until H4150
35 tabernacle of the **c** day and night seven H4150
9: 5 the tabernacle of the **c**: and all the H4150
5 and all the **c** drew near and stood H5712
23 tabernacle of the **c**, and came out, and H4150
10: 7 tabernacle of the **c**, lest ye die: for the H4150
9 tabernacle of the **c**, lest ye die: *it shall be* H4150
17 the iniquity of the **c**, to make atonement H5712
12: 6 the tabernacle of the **c**, unto the priest: H4150
14:11 *at* the door of the tabernacle of the **c**: H4150
23 tabernacle of the **c**, before the LORD. H4150
15:14 of the **c**, and give them unto the priest: H4150
29 to the door of the tabernacle of the **c**. H4150
16: 5 And he shall take of the **c** of the H5712
7 *at* the door of the tabernacle of the **c**. H4150
16 the tabernacle of the **c**, that remaineth H4150
17 tabernacle of the **c** when he goeth in to H4150
17 household, and for all the **c** of Israel. H6951
20 the tabernacle of the **c**, and the altar, he H4150
23 tabernacle of the **c**, and shall put off the H4150
33 tabernacle of the **c**, and for the altar, H4150
33 priests, and for all the people of the **c**. H6951
17: 4 tabernacle of the **c**, to offer an offering H4150
5 tabernacle of the **c**, unto the priest, and H4150
6 tabernacle of the **c**, and burn the fat for H4150
9 tabernacle of the **c**, to offer it unto the H4150
19: 2 Speak unto all the **c** of the children of H5712
21 the **c**, *even* a ram for a trespass offering. H4150
24: 3 tabernacle of the **c**, shall Aaron order it H4150
14 his head, and let all the **c** stone him. H5712
16 to death, *and* all the **c** shall certainly H5712
Nu 1: 1 tabernacle of the **c**, on the first *day* of H4150
2 Take ye the sum of all the **c** of the H5712
16 These *were* the renowned of the **c**, H5712
18 And they assembled all the **c** together H5712
53 no wrath upon the **c** of the children of H5712
2: 2 the tabernacle of the **c** shall they pitch. H4150
17 Then the tabernacle of the **c** shall set H4150
3: 7 of the whole **c** before the tabernacle H5712
7 the **c**, to do the service of the tabernacle. H4150
8 tabernacle of the **c**, and the charge of H4150
25 the tabernacle of the **c** *shall be* the H4150
25 for the door of the tabernacle of the **c**, H4150
38 tabernacle of the **c** eastward, *shall be* H4150
4: 3 do the work in the tabernacle of the **c**. H4150
4 of the **c**, *about* the most holy things: H4150
15 of Kohath in the tabernacle of the **c**. H4150
23 do the work in the tabernacle of the **c**. H4150

Nu 4:25 tabernacle of the **c**, his covering, and H4150
25 for the door of the tabernacle of the **c**, H4150
28 the tabernacle of the **c**: and their charge H4150
30 to do the work of the tabernacle of the **c**. H4150
31 the tabernacle of the **c**; the boards of the H4150
33 tabernacle of the **c**, under the hand of H4150
34 the chief of the **c** numbered the sons H5712
35 for the work in the tabernacle of the **c**: H4150
37 tabernacle of the **c**, which Moses and H4150
39 for the work in the tabernacle of the **c**, H4150
41 tabernacle of the **c**, whom Moses and H4150
43 for the work in the tabernacle of the **c**, H4150
47 of the burden in the tabernacle of the **c**, H4150
6:10 to the door of the tabernacle of the **c**: H4150
13 unto the door of the tabernacle of the **c**: H4150
18 tabernacle of the **c**, and shall take the H4150
7: 5 tabernacle of the **c**; and thou shalt give H4150
89 tabernacle of the **c** to speak with him, H4150
8: 9 the tabernacle of the **c**: and thou shalt H4150
15 the tabernacle of the **c**: and thou shalt H4150
19 the tabernacle of the **c**, and to make an H4150
20 And Moses, and Aaron, and all the **c** of H5712
22 tabernacle of the **c** before Aaron, and H4150
24 the service of the tabernacle of the **c**: H4150
26 tabernacle of the **c**, to keep the charge, H4150
10: 3 at the door of the tabernacle of the **c**. H4150
7 But when the **c** is to be gathered H6951
11:16 **c**, that they may stand there with thee. H4150
12: 4 of the **c**. And they three came out. H4150
13:26 and to all the **c** of the children of Israel, H5712
26 and unto all the **c**, and shewed them the H5712
14: 1 And all the **c** lifted up their voice, and H5712
2 and the whole **c** said unto them, Would H5712
5 of the **c** of the children of Israel. H5712
10 But all the **c** bade stone them with H5712
10 of the **c** before all the children of Israel. H4150
27 How long *shall I bear with* this evil **c**, H5712
35 it unto all this evil **c**, that are gathered H5712
36 and made all the **c** to murmur against H5712
15:15 *be both* for you of the **c**, and also for the H6951
24 the knowledge of the **c**, that all the H5712
24 that all the **c** shall offer one young H5712
25 for all the **c** of the children of Israel, H5712
26 And it shall be forgiven all the **c** of the H5712
33 Moses and Aaron, and unto all the **c**. H5712
35 to death: all the **c** shall stone him with H5712
36 And all the **c** brought him without the H5712
16: 2 famous in the **c**, men of renown: H4150
3 you, seeing all the **c** *are* holy, every one H5712
3 up yourselves above the **c** of the LORD? H6951
9 you from the **c** of Israel, to bring you H5712
9 before the **c** to minister unto them? H5712
18 of the **c** with Moses and Aaron. H4150
19 And Korah gathered all the **c** against H5712
19 tabernacle of the **c**: and the glory of the H4150
19 of the LORD appeared unto all the **c**. H5712
21 Separate yourselves from among this **c**, H5712
22 and wilt thou be wroth with all the **c**? H5712
24 Speak unto the **c**, saying, Get you up H5712
26 And he spake unto the **c**, saying, H5712
33 and they perished from among the **c**. H6951
41 But on the morrow all the **c** of the H5712
42 And it came to pass, when the **c** was H5712
42 the tabernacle of the **c**: and, behold, the H4150
43 came before the tabernacle of the **c**. H4150
45 Get you up from among this **c**, that I H5712
46 go quickly unto the **c**, and make an H5712
47 into the midst of the **c**; and, behold, the H6951
50 of the **c**: and the plague was stayed. H4150
17: 4 the tabernacle of the **c** before the H4150
18: 4 tabernacle of the **c**, for all the service of H4150
6 do the service of the tabernacle of the **c**. H4150
21 the service of the tabernacle of the **c**. H4150
22 of the **c**, lest they bear sin, and die. H4150
23 tabernacle of the **c**, and they shall bear H4150
31 your service in the tabernacle of the **c**. H4150
19: 4 the tabernacle of the **c** seven times: H4150
9 shall be kept for the **c** of the children of H5712
20 off from among the **c**, because he hath H6951
20: 1 *even* the whole **c**, into the desert of Zin H5712
2 And there was no water for the **c**: and H5712
4 And why have ye brought up the **c** of H6951
6 tabernacle of the **c**, and they fell upon H4150
8 shalt give the **c** and their beasts drink. H5712
10 And Moses and Aaron gathered the **c** H6951
11 and the **c** drank, and their beasts *also*. H5712
12 not bring this **c** into the land which H6951
22 Israel, *even* the whole **c**, journeyed from H5712
27 into mount Hor in the sight of all the **c**. H5712

Nu 20:29 And when all the **c** saw that Aaron was H5712
25: 6 in the sight of all the **c** of the children of H5712
6 the door of the tabernacle of the **c**. H4150
7 the **c**, and took a javelin in his hand; H5712
26: 2 Take the sum of all the **c** of the children H5712
9 famous in the **c**, who strove against H5712
27: 2 princes and all the **c**, *by* the door of the H5712
2 door of the tabernacle of the **c**, saying, H4150
14 in the strife of the **c**, to sanctify me at H5712
16 spirits of all flesh, set a man over the **c**, H5712
17 them in; that the **c** of the LORD be not H5712
19 **c**; and give him a charge in their sight. H5712
20 him, that all the **c** of the children of H5712
21 of Israel with him, even all the **c**. H5712
22 Eleazar the priest, and before all the **c**: H5712
31:12 and unto the **c** of the children of Israel, H5712
13 the princes of the **c**, went forth to meet H5712
16 was a plague among the **c** of the LORD. H5712
26 the priest, and the chief fathers of the **c**: H5712
27 out to battle, and between all the **c**: H5712
43 (Now the half *that pertained unto* the **c** H5712
54 tabernacle of the **c**, *for* a memorial for H4150
32: 2 and unto the princes of the **c**, saying, H5712
4 smote before the **c** of Israel, *is* a land H5712
35:12 until he stand before the **c** in judgment. H5712
24 Then the **c** shall judge between the H5712
25 And the **c** shall deliver the slayer out of H5712
25 of blood, and the **c** shall restore him to H5712
Dt 23: 1 shall not enter into the **c** of the LORD. H6951
2 A bastard shall not enter into the **c** of H6951
2 he not enter into the **c** of the LORD. H6951
3 not enter into the **c** of the LORD; even H6951
3 enter into the **c** of the LORD for ever: H6951
8 **c** of the LORD in their third generation. H6951
31:14 tabernacle of the **c**, that I may give him H4150
14 themselves in the tabernacle of the **c**. H4150
30 And Moses spake in the ears of all the **c** H6951
33: 4 *even* the inheritance of the **c** of Jacob. H6952
Jos 8:35 not before all the **c** of Israel, with the H6951
9:15 the princes of the **c** sware unto them. H5712
18 the princes of the **c** had sworn unto H5712
18 all the **c** murmured against the princes. H5712
19 But all the princes said unto all the **c**, H5712
21 **c**; as the princes had promised them. H5712
27 of water for the **c**, and for the altar of H5712
18: 1 And the whole **c** of the children of H5712
1 tabernacle of the **c** there. And the land H4150
19:51 the tabernacle of the **c**. So they made an H4150
20: 6 he stand before the **c** for judgment, *and* H5712
9 of blood, until he stood before the **c**. H5712
22:12 *of it*, the whole **c** of the children of H5712
16 Thus saith the whole **c** of the LORD, H5712
17 was a plague in the **c** of the LORD, H5712
18 will be wroth with the whole **c** of Israel. H5712
20 fell on all the **c** of Israel? and that man H5712
30 the princes of the **c** and heads of the H5712
Jdg 20: 1 Israel went out, and the **c** was gathered H5712
21: 5 not up with the **c** unto the LORD? For H6951
10 And the **c** sent thither twelve thousand H5712
13 And the whole **c** sent *some* to speak to H5712
16 Then the elders of the **c** said, How shall H5712
1Sa 2:22 *at* the door of the tabernacle of the **c**. H4150
1Ki 8: 4 the tabernacle of the **c**, and all the holy H4150
5 And king Solomon, and all the **c** of H5712
14 and blessed all the **c** of Israel: (and all H6951
14 of Israel: (and all the **c** of Israel stood;) H6951
22 the presence of all the **c** of Israel, and H6951
55 And he stood, and blessed all the **c** of H6951
65 with him, a great **c**, from the entering in H6951
12: 3 and all the **c** of Israel came, and H6951
20 him unto the **c**, and made him king H5712
1Ch 6:32 tabernacle of the **c** with singing, until H4150
9:21 of the door of the tabernacle of the **c**. H4150
13: 2 And David said unto all the **c** of Israel, H6951
4 And all the **c** said that they would do H6951
23:32 tabernacle of the **c**, and the charge of H4150
28: 8 of all Israel the **c** of the LORD, and in H6951
29: 1 said unto all the **c**, Solomon my son, H6951
10 before all the **c**: and David said, Blessed H6951
20 And David said to all the **c**, Now bless H6951
20 God. And all the **c** blessed the LORD H6951
2Ch 1: 3 So Solomon, and all the **c** with him, H6951
3 the tabernacle of the **c** of God, which H4150
5 and Solomon and the **c** sought unto it. H6951
6 the tabernacle of the **c**, and offered a H4150
13 of the **c**, and reigned over Israel. H4150
5: 5 the tabernacle of the **c**, and all the holy H4150
6 Also king Solomon, and all the **c** of H5712
6: 3 blessed the whole **c** of Israel: and all H6951

2Ch 6: 3 of Israel: and all the c of Israel stood. H6951
12 c of Israel, and spread forth his hands: H6951
13 before all the c of Israel, and spread H6951
7: 8 him, a very great c, from the entering in H6951
20: 5 And Jehoshaphat stood in the c of H6951
14 spirit of the LORD in the midst of the c; H6951
23: 3 And all the c made a covenant with the H6951
24: 6 the LORD, and of the c of Israel, for the H6951
28:14 spoil before the princes and all the c. H6951
29:23 c; and they laid their hands upon them: H6951
28 And all the c worshipped, and the H6951
31 LORD. And the c brought in sacrifices H6951
32 which the c brought, was threescore H6951
30: 2 and all the c in Jerusalem, to keep H6951
4 the thing pleased the king and all the c. H6951
13 in the second month, a very great c. H6951
17 For *there were* many in the c that were H6951
24 did give to the c a thousand bullocks H6951
24 gave to the c a thousand bullocks H6951
25 And all the c of Judah, with the priests H6951
25 and all the c that came out of Israel, H6951
31:18 through all the c: for in their set office H6951
Ezr 2:64 The whole c together *was* forty and two H6951
10: 1 Israel a very great c of men and women H6951
8 c of those that had been carried away. H6951
12 Then all the c answered and said with H6951
14 Let now our rulers of all the c stand, H6951
Neh 5:13 And all the c said, Amen, and praised H6951
7:66 The whole c together *was* forty and two H6951
8: 2 the law before the c both of men and H6951
17 And all the c of them that were come H6951
13: 1 not come into the c of God for ever; H6951
Job 15:34 For the c of hypocrites *shall be* H5712
30:28 the sun: I stood up, *and* I cried in the c. H6951
Ps 1: 5 nor sinners in the c of the righteous. H5712
7: 7 So shall the c of the people compass H5712
22:22 in the midst of the c will I praise thee. H6951
25 My praise *shall be* of thee in the great c: H6951
26: 5 I have hated the c of evil doers; and will H6951
35:18 I will give thee thanks in the great c: I H6951
40: 9 in the great c: lo, I have not refrained H6951
10 and thy truth from the great c. H6951
58: 1 Do ye indeed speak righteousness, O c? H482
68:10 Thy c hath dwelt therein: thou, O God, H2416
74: 2 Remember thy c, *which* thou hast H5712
19 forget not the c of thy poor for ever. H2416
75: 2 When I shall receive the c I will judge H4150
82: 1 God standeth in the c of the mighty; he H5712
89: 5 faithfulness also in the c of the saints. H6951
107:32 Let them exalt him also in the c of the H6951
111: 1 assembly of the upright, and *in* the c. H5712
149: 1 song, *and* his praise in the c of saints. H6951
Prv 5:14 evil in the midst of the c and assembly. H6951
21:16 shall remain in the c of the dead. H6951
26:26 shall be shewed before the *whole* c. H6951
Isa 14:13 mount of the c, in the sides of the north: H4150
Jer 6:18 and know, O c, what *is* among them. H5712
30:20 and their c shall be established H5712
Lam 1:10 *that* they should not enter into thy c. H6951
Hos 7:12 chastise them, as their c hath heard. H5712
Joel 2:16 Gather the people, sanctify the c, H6951
Mic 2: 5 cast a cord by lot in the c of the LORD. H6951
Act 13:43 Now when the c was broken up, many G4864

CONGREGATIONS
Ps 26:12 place: in the c will I bless the LORD. H4721
68:26 Bless ye God in the c, *even* the Lord, H4721
74: 4 thy c; they set up their ensigns *for* signs. H4150

CONIAH
Jer 22:24 *As* I live, saith the LORD, though C the H3659
28 *Is* this man C a despised broken idol? *is* H3659
37: 1 Josiah reigned instead of C the son of H3659

CONIES
Ps 104:18 the wild goats; *and* the rocks for the c. H8226
Prv 30:26 The c *are but* a feeble folk, yet make H8226

CONONIAH
2Ch 31:12 over which C the Levite *was* ruler, H3562
13 under the hand of C and Shimei his H3562

CONQUER
Rev 6: 2 and he went forth conquering, and to c. G3528

CONQUERING
Rev 6: 2 and he went forth c, and to conquer. G3528

CONQUERORS
Ro 8:37 more than c through him that loved us. G5245

CONSCIENCE
Jn 8: 9 by *their own* c, went out one by one, G4893
Act 23: 1 in all good c before God until this day. G4893
24:16 to have always a c void of offence G4893
Ro 2:15 in their hearts, their c also bearing G4893
9: 1 I say the truth in Christ, I lie not, my c G4893
13: 5 not only for wrath, but also for c sake. G4893
1Co 8: 7 for some with c of the idol unto this G4893
7 idol; and their c being weak is defiled. G4893
10 shall not the c of him which is weak G4893
12 their weak c, ye sin against Christ. G4893
10:25 *that* eat, asking no question for c sake: G4893
27 you, eat, asking no question for c sake. G4893
28 shewed it, and for c sake: for the earth G4893
29 C, I say, not thine own, but of the other: G4893
29 is my liberty judged of another *man's* c? G4893
2Co 1:12 the testimony of our c, that in simplicity G4893
4: 2 to every man's c in the sight of God. G4893
1Ti 1: 5 and *of* a good c, and *of* faith unfeigned: G4893
19 Holding faith, and a good c; which G4893
3: 9 the mystery of the faith in a pure c. G4893
4: 2 having their c seared with a hot iron; G4893
2Ti 1: 3 with pure c, that without ceasing G4893
Tit 1:15 but even their mind and c is defiled. G4893
Heb 9: 9 service perfect, as pertaining to the c; G4893
14 God, purge your c from dead works to G4893
10: 2 should have had no more c of sins. G4893
22 from an evil c, and our bodies washed G4893
13:18 c, in all things willing to live honestly. G4893
1Pt 2:19 For this *is* thankworthy, if a man for c G4893
3:16 Having a good c; that, whereas they G4893
21 answer of a good c toward God,) by the G4893

CONSCIENCES
2Co 5:11 I trust also are made manifest in your c. G4893

CONSECRATE
Ex 28: 3 garments to c him, that he may H6942
41 them, and c them, and sanctify H4390+H3027
29: 9 shalt c Aaron and his sons. H4390+H3027
33 was made, to c *and* to sanctify H4390+H3027
35 seven days shalt thou c them. H4390+H3027
30:30 and his sons, and c them, that *they* H6942
32:29 For Moses had said, C yourselves to H4390
Lev 8:33 for seven days shall he c you. H4390+H3027
16:32 he shall c to minister in the H4390+H3027
Nu 6:12 And he shall c unto the LORD the days H5144
1Ch 29: 5 is willing to c his service this H4390+H3027
2Ch 13: 9 cometh to c himself with a H4390+H3027
Ezk 43:26 it; and they shall c themselves. H4390+H3027
Mic 4:13 people: and I will c their gain unto the H2763

CONSECRATED
Ex 29:29 therein, and to be c in them. H4390+H3027
Lev 21:10 and that is c to put on the H4390+H3027
Nu 3: 3 whom he c to minister in the H4390+H3027
Jos 6:19 and iron, *are* c unto the LORD: they H6944
Jdg 17: 5 and teraphim, and c one of his H4390+H3027
12 And Micah c the Levite; and H4390+H3027
1Ki 13:33 would, he c him, and he became H4390
2Ch 26:18 of Aaron, that are c to burn incense: go H6942
29:31 Now ye have c yourselves unto H4390+H3027
33 And the c things *were* six hundred H6942
31: 6 things which were c unto the LORD H6942
Ezr 3: 5 LORD that were c, and of every one that H6942
Heb 7:28 *maketh* the Son, who is c for evermore. G5048
10:20 which he hath c for us, through the G1457

CONSECRATION
Ex 29:22 the right shoulder; for it *is* a ram of c: H4394
26 the ram of Aaron's c, and wave it *for* a H4394
27 of the ram of the c, *even* of *that* which *is* H4394
31 And thou shalt take the ram of the c, H4394
Lev 8:22 ram, the ram of c: and Aaron and his H4394
29 *for* of the ram of c it was Moses' part; H4394
33 the days of your c be at an end: for H4394
Nu 6: 7 the c of his God *is* upon his head. H5145
9 the head of his c; then he shall shave H5145

CONSECRATIONS
Ex 29:34 And if ought of the flesh of the c, or of H4394
Lev 7:37 and of the c, and of the sacrifice H4394
8:28 burnt offering: they *were* c for a sweet H4394
31 *is* in the basket of c, as I commanded, H4394

CONSENT
Gen 34:15 But in this will we c unto you: If ye will H225
22 Only herein will the men c unto us for to H225
23 c unto them, and they will dwell with us. H225
Dt 13: 8 Thou shalt not c unto him, nor hearken H14
Jdg 11:17 would not c: and Israel abode in Kadesh. H14
1Sa 11: 7 the people, and they came out with one c. H376
1Ki 20: 8 unto him, Hearken not *unto him*, nor c. H14
Ps 83: 5 c: they are confederate against thee: H3820
Prv 1:10 My son, if sinners entice thee, c thou H14
Hos 6: 9 the way by c: for they commit lewdness. H7926
Zep 3: 9 of the LORD, to serve him with one c. H7926
Lk 14:18 And they all with one c began to make
Ro 7:16 If then I do that which I would not, I c G4852
1Co 7: 5 except *it be* with c for a time, that ye G4859
1Ti 6: 3 If any man teach otherwise, and c not G4334

CONSENTED
2Ki 12: 8 And the priests c to receive no *more* H225
Dan 1:14 So he c to them in this matter, and H8085
Lk 23:51 (The same had not c to the counsel and G4784
Act 18:20 tarry longer time with them, he c not; G1962

CONSENTEDST
Ps 50:18 When thou sawest a thief, then thou c H7521

CONSENTING
Act 8: 1 And Saul was c unto his death. And at G4909
22:20 standing by, and c unto his death, and G4909

CONSIDER
Ex 33:13 and c that this nation *is* thy people. H7200
Lev 13:13 Then the priest shall c: and, behold, *if* H7200
Dt 4:39 Know therefore this day, and c *it* in H7725
8: 5 Thou shalt also c in thine heart, that, H3045
32: 7 Remember the days of old, c the years of H995
29 this, *that* they would c their latter end! H995
Jdg 18:14 now therefore c what ye have to do. H3045
19:30 unto this day: c of it, take advice, and H7760
1Sa 12:24 all your heart: for c how great *things* he H7200
25:17 Now therefore know and c what thou H7200
2Ki 5: 7 wherefore c, I pray you, and see H3045
Job 11:11 wickedness also; will he not then c *it*? H995
23:15 presence: when I c, I am afraid of him. H995
34:27 him, and would not c any of his ways: H7919
37:14 still, and c the wondrous works of God. H995
Ps 5: 1 Give ear to my words, O LORD, c my H995
8: 3 When I c thy heavens, the work of thy H7200
9:13 Have mercy upon me, O LORD; c my H7200
13: 3 C *and* hear me, O LORD my God: H5027
25:19 C mine enemies; for they are many; H7200
37:10 diligently c his place, and it *shall* not *be*. H995
45:10 Hearken, O daughter, and c, and incline H7200
48:13 Mark ye well her bulwarks, c her H6448
50:22 Now c this, ye that forget God, lest I tear H995
64: 9 for they shall wisely c of his doing. H7919
119:95 destroy me: *but* I will c thy testimonies. H995
153 C mine affliction, and deliver me: for I H7200
159 C how I love thy precepts: quicken me, H7200
Prv 6: 6 Go to the ant, thou sluggard; c her H7200
23: 1 When thou sittest to eat with a ruler, c H995
24:12 the heart c *it*? and he that keepeth H995
Ecc 5: 1 of fools: for they c not that they do evil. H3045
7:13 C the work of God: for who can make H7200
14 day of adversity c: God also hath set the H7200
Isa 1: 3 doth not know, my people doth not c. H995
5:12 neither c the operation of his hands. H7200
14:16 upon thee, *and* c thee, *saying, Is* this the H995
18: 4 my rest, and I will c in my dwelling H5027
41:20 That they may see, and know, and c, H7760
22 that we may c them, and know H7760+H3820
43:18 things, neither c the things of old. H995
52:15 which they had not heard shall they c. H995
Jer 2:10 unto Kedar, and c diligently, and see if H995
9:17 Thus saith the LORD of hosts, C ye, and H995
23:20 in the latter days ye shall c it perfectly. H995
30:24 his heart: in the latter days ye shall c it. H995
Lam 1:11 O LORD, and c; for I am become vile. H5027
2:20 Behold, O LORD, and c to whom thou H5027
5: 1 upon us: c, and behold our reproach. H5027
Ezk 12: 3 c, though they *be* a rebellious house. H7200
Dan 9:23 understand the matter, and c the vision. H995
Hos 7: 2 And they c not in their hearts *that* I H559
Hag 1: 5 LORD of hosts; C your ways. H7760+H3824
7 LORD of hosts; C your ways. H7760+H3824
2:15 And now, I pray you, c from H7760+H3824
18 C now from this day and H7760+H3824
18 LORD'S temple was laid, c *it*. H7760+H3824
Mt 6:28 for raiment? C the lilies of the field, G2648

Lk 12:24 C the ravens: for they neither sow nor G2657
27 C the lilies how they grow: they toil not, G2657
Jn 11:50 Nor c that it is expedient for us, that G1260
Act 15: 6 came together for to c of this matter. G1492
2Ti 2: 7 C what I say; and the Lord give thee G3539
Heb 3: 1 the heavenly calling, c the Apostle and G2657
7: 4 Now c how great this man was, unto G2334
10:24 And let us c one another to provoke G2657
12: 3 For c him that endured such G357

CONSIDERED
1Ki 3:21 dead: but when I had c it in the morning, H995
5: 8 saying, I have c the things which thou H8085
Job 1: 8 Hast thou c my servant Job, H7760+H3820
2: 3 Hast thou c my servant Job, H7760+H3820
Ps 31: 7 for thou hast c my trouble; thou hast H7200
77: 5 I have c the days of old, the years of H2803
Prv 24:32 Then I saw, and c it well: I H7896+H3820
Ecc 4: 1 So I returned, and c all the oppressions H7200
4 Again, I c all travail, and every right H7200
15 I c all the living which walk under the H7200
9: 1 For all this I c in my heart even to H5414
Dan 7: 8 I c the horns, and, behold, there came H7920
Mk 6:52 For they c not the miracle of the loaves: G4920
Act 11: 6 mine eyes, I c, and saw fourfooted G2657
12:12 And when he had c the thing, he came G4894
Ro 4:19 And being not weak in faith, he c not G2657

CONSIDEREST
Jer 33:24 C thou not what this people have H7200
Mt 7: 3 c not the beam that is in thine own eye? G2657

CONSIDERETH
Ps 33:15 He fashioneth their hearts alike; he c all H995
41: 1 Blessed is he that c the poor: the LORD H7919
Prv 21:12 The righteous man wisely c the house H7919
28:22 an evil eye, and c not that poverty shall H3045
29: 7 The righteous c the cause of the poor: H3045
31:16 She c a field, and buyeth it: with the H2161
Isa 44:19 And none c in his heart, neither is there H7725
Ezk 18:14 done, and c, and doeth not such like, H7200
28 Because he c, and turneth away from all H7200

CONSIDERING
Isa 57: 1 taken away, none c that the righteous is H995
Dan 8: 5 And as I was c, behold, an he goat came H995
Gal 6: 1 c thyself, lest thou also be tempted. G4648
Heb 13: 7 follow, c the end of their conversation. G333

CONSIST
Col 1:17 all things, and by him all things c. G4921

CONSISTETH
Lk 12:15 for a man's life c not in the abundance G2076

CONSOLATION
Jer 16: 7 give them the cup of c to drink for their H8575
Lk 2:25 waiting for the c of Israel: and the Holy G3874
6:24 are rich! for ye have received your c. G3874
Act 4:36 The son of c,) a Levite, and of the G3874
15:31 they had read, they rejoiced for the c. G3874
Ro 15: 5 Now the God of patience and c grant G3874
2Co 1: 5 us, so our c also aboundeth by Christ. G3874
6 it is for your c and salvation, which G3874
6 it is for your c and salvation. G3874
7 sufferings, so shall ye be also of the c. G3874
7: 7 only, but by the c wherewith he was G3874
Php 2: 1 If there be therefore any c in Christ, if G3874
2Th 2:16 c and good hope through grace, G3874
Phlm 7 For we have great joy and c in thy love, G3874
Heb 6:18 might have a strong c, who have fled for G3874

CONSOLATIONS
Job 15:11 Are the c of God small with thee? is H8575
21: 2 my speech, and let this be your c. H8575
Isa 66:11 the breasts of her c; that ye may milk H8575

CONSORTED
Act 17: 4 And some of them believed, and c with G4345

CONSPIRACY
2Sa 15:12 sacrifices. And the c was strong; for the H7195
2Ki 12:20 And his servants arose, and made a c, H7195
14:19 Now they made a c against him in H7195
15:15 of Shallum, and his c which he made, H7195
30 And Hoshea the son of Elah made a c H7195
17: 4 And the king of Assyria found c in H7195
2Ch 25:27 LORD they made a c against him in H7195
Jer 11: 9 And the LORD said unto me, A c is H7195
Ezk 22:25 There is a c of her prophets in the H7195
Act 23:13 more than forty which had made this c. G4945

CONSPIRATORS
2Sa 15:31 is among the c with Absalom. And H7194

CONSPIRED
Gen 37:18 them, they c against him to slay him. H5230
1Sa 22: 8 That all of you have c against me, and H7194
13 And Saul said unto him, Why have ye c H7194
1Ki 15:27 house of Issachar, c against him; and H7194
16: 9 half his chariots, c against him, as he H7194
16 say, Zimri hath c, and hath also slain H7194
2Ki 9:14 the son of Nimshi c against Joram. H7194
10: 9 behold, I c against my master, H7194
15:10 And Shallum the son of Jabesh c H7194
25 a captain of his, c against him, and H7194
21:23 And the servants of Amon c against H7194
24 all them that had c against king Amon; H7194
2Ch 24:21 And they c against him, and stoned H7194
25 his own servants c against him for the H7194
26 And these are they that c against him; H7194
33:24 And his servants c against him, and H7194
25 all them that had c against king Amon; H7194
Neh 4: 8 And c all of them together to come and H7194
Am 7:10 Amos hath c against thee in the midst H7194

CONSTANT
1Ch 28: 7 kingdom for ever, if he be c to do my H2388

CONSTANTLY
Prv 21:28 but the man that heareth speaketh c. H5331
Act 12:15 art mad. But she c affirmed that it was G1340
Tit 3: 8 that thou affirm c, that they which have G1226

CONSTELLATIONS
Isa 13:10 For the stars of heaven and the c H3685

CONSTRAIN
Gal 6:12 shew in the flesh, they c you to be G315

CONSTRAINED
2Ki 4: 8 woman; and she c him to eat bread. H2388
Mt 14:22 And straightway Jesus c his disciples to G315
Mk 6:45 And straightway he c his disciples to get G315
Lk 24:29 But they c him, saying, Abide with us: G3849
Act 16:15 house, and abide there. And she c us. G3849
28:19 against it, I was c to appeal unto Caesar; G315

CONSTRAINETH
Job 32:18 of matter, the spirit within me c me. H6693
2Co 5:14 For the love of Christ c us; because we G4912

CONSTRAINT
1Pt 5: 2 thereof, not by c, but willingly; not for G317

CONSULT
Ps 62: 4 They only c to cast him down from his H3289

CONSULTATION
Mk 15: 1 priests held a c with the elders and G4824

CONSULTED
1Ki 12: 6 And king Rehoboam c with the old H3289
8 given him, and c with the young men H3289
1Ch 13: 1 And David c with the captains of H3289
2Ch 20:21 And when he had c with the people, he H3289
Neh 5: 7 Then I c with myself, and I rebuked the H4427
Ps 83: 3 people, and c against thy hidden ones. H3289
5 For they have c together with one H3289
Ezk 21:21 he c with images, he looked in the liver. H7592
Dan 6: 7 and the captains, have c together to H3272
Mic 6: 5 king of Moab c, and what Balaam the H3289
Hab 2:10 Thou hast c shame to thy house by H3289
Mt 26: 4 And c that they might take Jesus by G4823
Jn 12:10 But the chief priests c that they might G1011

CONSULTER
Dt 18:11 Or a charmer, or a c with familiar H7592

CONSULTETH
Lk 14:31 down first, and c whether he be able G1011

CONSUME
Gen 41:30 Egypt; and the famine shall c the land; H3615
Ex 32:10 and that I may c them: and I will make H3615
12 the mountains, and to c them from the H3615
33: 3 people: lest I c thee in the way. H3615
5 in a moment, and c thee: therefore now H3615
Lev 26:16 ague, that shall c the eyes, and cause H3615
Nu 16:21 that I may c them in a moment. H3615
45 that I may c them as in a moment. H3615
Dt 5:25 for this great fire will c us: if we hear the H398
7:16 And thou shalt c all the people which the H398
22 thou mayest not c them at once, lest H3615
28:38 but little in; for the locust shall c it. H2628
42 and fruit of thy land shall the locust c. H3423
32:22 lowest hell, and shall c the earth with her H398
Jos 24:20 do you hurt, and c you, after that he H3615
1Sa 2:33 altar, shall be to c thine eyes, and to H3615
2Ki 1:10 from heaven, and c thee and thy fifty. H398
12 from heaven, and c thee and thy fifty. H398
Neh 9:31 didst not utterly c them, nor forsake H3617
Est 9:24 the lot, to c them, and to destroy them; H2000
Job 15:34 fire shall c the tabernacles of bribery. H398
20:26 a fire not blown shall c him; it shall go ill H398
24:19 Drought and heat c the snow waters: so H1497
Ps 37:20 c; into smoke shall they consume away. H3615
20 into smoke shall they c away. H3615
39:11 his beauty to c away like a moth: surely H4529
49:14 shall c in the grave from their dwelling. H1086
59:13 C them in wrath, consume them, that H3615
13 Consume them in wrath, c them, that H3615
78:33 Therefore their days did he c in vanity, H3615
Isa 7:20 of the feet: and it shall also c the beard. H5595
10:18 And shall c the glory of his forest, and H3615
27:10 lie down, and c the branches thereof. H3615
Jer 8:13 I will surely c them, saith the LORD: H5486
14:12 them: but I will c them by the sword, H3615
49:27 and it shall c the palaces of Ben-hadad. H398
Ezk 4:17 another, and c away for their iniquity. H4743
13:13 and great hailstones in my fury to c it. H3617
20:13 upon them in the wilderness, to c them. H3615
21:28 furbished, to c because of the glittering: H398
22:15 and will c thy filthiness out of thee. H8552
24:10 Heap on wood, kindle the fire, c the H8552
35:12 are laid desolate, they are given us to c. H402
Dan 2:44 in pieces and c all these kingdoms, H5487
7:26 to c and to destroy it unto the end. H8046
Hos 11: 6 his cities, and shall c his branches, and H3615
Zep 1: 2 I will utterly c all things from off the H5486
3 I will c man and beast; I will consume H5486
3 I will consume man and beast; I will c H5486
Zec 5: 4 his house, and shall c it with the timber H3615
14:12 Their flesh shall c away while they H4743
12 their eyes shall c away in their holes, H4743
12 tongue shall c away in their mouth. H4743
Lk 9:54 heaven, and c them, even as Elias did? G355
2Th 2: 8 the Lord shall c with the spirit of his G355
Jas 4: 3 amiss, that ye may c it upon your lusts. G1159

CONSUMED
Gen 19:15 lest thou be c in the iniquity of the city. H5595
17 escape to the mountain, lest thou be c. H5595
31:40 Thus I was; in the day the drought c me, H398
Ex 3: 2 burned with fire, and the bush was not c. H398
15: 7 thy wrath, which c them as stubble. H398
22: 6 corn, or the field, be c therewith; he that H398
Lev 6:10 which the fire hath c with the burnt H398
9:24 the LORD, and c upon the altar the H398
Nu 11: 1 among them, and c them that were in H398
12:12 the flesh is half c when he cometh out H398
14:35 they shall be c, and there they shall die. H8552
16:26 of theirs, lest ye be c in all their sins. H5595
35 the LORD, and c the two hundred and H398
17:13 shall die: shall we be c with dying? H8552
21:28 of Sihon: it hath c Ar of Moab, and the H398
25:11 them, that I c not the children of Israel H3615
32:13 evil in the sight of the LORD, was c. H8552
Dt 2:15 from among the host, until they were c. H8552
16 c and dead from among the people, H8552
28:21 thee, until he have c thee from off the H3615
Jos 5: 6 came out of Egypt, were c, because they H8552
8:24 until they were c, that all the Israelites H8552
10:20 till they were c, that the rest which H8552
Jdg 6:21 out of the rock, and c the flesh and the H398
1Sa 12:25 ye shall be c, both ye and your king. H5595
15:18 and fight against them until they be c. H3615
2Sa 21: 5 The man that c us, and that devised H3615
22:38 turned not again until I had c them. H3615
39 And I have c them, and wounded them, H3615
1Ki 18:38 Then the fire of the LORD fell, and c the H398
22:11 the Syrians, until thou have c them. H3615
2Ki 1:10 from heaven, and c him and his fifty. H398
12 from heaven, and c him and his fifty. H398
7:13 that are c:) and let us send and see. H8552
13:17 Syrians in Aphek, till thou have c them. H3615
19 till thou hadst c it: whereas now thou H3615

2Ch 7: 1 from heaven, and c the burnt offering H398
8: 8 the children of Israel c not, them did H3615
18:10 thou shalt push Syria until they be c. H3615
Ezr 9:14 us till thou hadst c *us*, so that *there* H3615
Neh 2: 3 and the gates thereof are c with fire? H398
13 and the gates thereof were c with fire. H398
Job 1:16 the servants, and c them; and I only am H398
4: 9 by the breath of his nostrils are they c. H3615
6:17 it is hot, they are c out of their place. H1846
7: 9 *As* the cloud is c and vanisheth away: H3615
19:27 *though* my reins be c within me. H3615
33:21 His flesh is c away, that it cannot be H3615
Ps 6: 7 Mine eye is c because of grief; it waxeth H6244
18:37 neither did I turn again till they were c. H3615
31: 9 c with grief, *yea*, my soul and my belly. H6244
10 of mine iniquity, and my bones are c. H6244
39:10 me: I am c by the blow of thine hand. H3615
71:13 Let them be confounded *and* c that are H3615
73:19 moment! they are utterly c with terrors. H8552
78:63 The fire c their young men; and their H398
90: 7 For we are c by thine anger, and by thy H3615
102: 3 For my days are c like smoke, and my H3615
104:35 Let the sinners be c out of the earth, H8552
119:87 They had almost c me upon earth; but H3615
139 My zeal hath c me, because mine H6789
Prv 5:11 last, when thy flesh and thy body are c, H3615
Isa 1:28 they that forsake the LORD shall be c. H3615
16: 4 the oppressors are c out of the land. H8552
29:20 and the scorner is c, and all that watch H3615
64: 7 and hast c us, because of our iniquities. H4127
66:17 shall be c together, saith the LORD. H5486
Jer 5: 3 not grieved; thou hast c them, *but* they H3615
6:29 The bellows are burned, the lead is c of H8552
9:16 a sword after them, till I have c them. H3615
10:25 him, and c him, and have made H3615
12: 4 the beasts are c, and the birds; because H5595
14:15 and famine shall those prophets be c. H8552
16: 4 and they shall be c by the sword, and H3615
20:18 that my days should be c with shame? H3615
24:10 them, till they be c from off the land H8552
27: 8 until I have c them by his hand. H8552
36:23 was c in the fire that *was* on the hearth. H8552
44:12 they shall all be c, *and* fall in the land H8552
12 they shall *even* be c by the sword *and* H8552
18 been c by the sword and by the famine. H8552
27 of Egypt shall be c by the sword and by H8552
49:37 the sword after them, till I have c them: H3615
Lam 2:22 and brought up hath mine enemy c. H3615
3:22 not c, because his compassions fail not. H8552
Ezk 5:12 shall they be c in the midst of thee: H3615
13:14 and ye shall be c in the midst thereof: H3615
19:12 broken and withered; the fire c them. H398
22:31 upon them; I have c them with the fire H3615
24:11 in it, *that* the scum of it may be c. H8552
34:29 shall be no more c with hunger in the H622
43: 8 wherefore I have c them in mine anger. H3615
47:12 the fruit thereof be c: it shall bring forth H8552
Dan 11:16 land, which by his hand shall be c. H3617
Mal 3: 6 not; therefore ye sons of Jacob are not c. H3615
Gal 5:15 heed that ye be not c one of another. G355

CONSUMETH
Job 13:28 And he, as a rotten thing, c, as a H1086
22:20 down, but the remnant of them the fire c. H398
31:12 For it *is* a fire *that* c to destruction, and H398
Isa 5:24 and the flame c the chaff, *so* their root H7503

CONSUMING
Dt 4:24 For the LORD thy God *is* a c fire, *even* a H398
9: 3 before thee; *as* a c fire he shall destroy H398
Heb 12:29 For our God *is* a c fire. G2654

CONSUMMATION
Dan 9:27 even until the c, and that determined H3617

CONSUMPTION
Lev 26:16 over you terror, c, and the burning H7829
Dt 28:22 The LORD shall smite thee with a c, and H7829
Isa 10:22 them shall return: the c decreed shall H3631
23 hosts shall make a c, even determined, H3617
28:22 Lord GOD of hosts a c, even determined H3617

CONTAIN
1Ki 8:27 of heavens cannot c thee; how much H3557
18:32 great as would c two measures of seed. H1004
2Ch 2: 6 of heavens cannot c him? who *am* I H3557
6:18 of heavens cannot c thee; how much H3557
Ezk 45:11 that the bath may c the tenth part of an H5375
Jn 21:25 itself could not c the books that should G5562
1Co 7: 9 But if they cannot c, let them marry: for G1467

CONTAINED
1Ki 7:26 of lilies: it c two thousand baths. H3557
38 of brass: one laver c forty baths: *and* H3557
Ro 2:14 by nature the things c in the law, these,
Eph 2:15 of commandments c in ordinances; for
1Pt 2: 6 Wherefore also it is c in the scripture, G4023

CONTAINETH
Ezk 23:32 to scorn and had in derision; it c much. H3557

CONTAINING
Jn 2: 6 the Jews, c two or three firkins apiece. G5562

CONTEMN
Ps 10:13 Wherefore doth the wicked c God? he H5006
Ezk 21:13 and what if *the sword* c even the rod? it H3988

CONTEMNED
Ps 15: 4 In whose eyes a vile person is c; but he H959
107:11 and c the counsel of the most High: H5006
Song 8: 7 his house for love, it would utterly be c. H936
Isa 16:14 of Moab shall be c, with all that great H7034

CONTEMNETH
Ezk 21:10 it c the rod of my son, *as* every tree. H3988

CONTEMPT
Est 1:18 *shall there arise* too much c and wrath. H963
Job 12:21 He poureth c upon princes, and H937
31:34 Did I fear a great multitude, or did the c H937
Ps 107:40 He poureth c upon princes, and causeth H937
119:22 Remove from me reproach and c; for I H937
123: 3 us: for we are exceedingly filled with c. H937
4 are at ease, *and* with the c of the proud. H937
Prv 18: 3 also c, and with ignominy reproach. H937
Isa 23: 9 into c all the honourable of the earth. H7043
Dan 12: 2 and some to shame *and* everlasting c. H1860

CONTEMPTIBLE
Mal 1: 7 In that ye say, The table of the LORD *is* c. H959
12 and the fruit thereof, *even* his meat, *is* c. H959
2: 9 Therefore have I also made you c and H959
2Co 10:10 presence *is* weak, and *his* speech c. G1848

CONTEMPTUOUSLY
Ps 31:18 proudly and c against the righteous. H937

CONTEND
Dt 2: 9 Moabites, neither c with them in battle: H1624
24 to possess *it*, and c with him in battle. H1624
Job 9: 3 If he will c with him, he cannot answer H7378
13: 8 Will ye accept his person? will ye c for H7378
Prv 28: 4 but such as keep the law c with them. H1624
Ecc 6:10 he c with him that is mightier than he. H1777
Isa 49:25 for I will c with him that contendeth H7378
50: 8 *He is* near that justifieth me; who will c H7378
57:16 For I will not c for ever, neither will I be H7378
Jer 12: 5 how canst thou c with horses? and *if* H8474
18:19 to the voice of them that c with me. H3401
Am 7: 4 GOD called to c by fire, and it devoured H7378
Mic 6: 1 LORD saith; Arise, c thou before the H7378
Jude 3 should earnestly c for the faith which G1864

CONTENDED
Neh 13:11 Then c I with the rulers, and said, Why H7378
17 Then I c with the nobles of Judah, and H7378
25 And I c with them, and cursed them, H7378
Job 31:13 my maidservant, when they c with me; H7379
Isa 41:12 *even* them that c with thee: they that H4695
Act 11: 2 were of the circumcision c with him, G1252

CONTENDEST
Job 10: 2 shew me wherefore thou c with me. H7378

CONTENDETH
Job 40: 2 Shall he that c with the Almighty H7378
Prv 29: 9 *If* a wise man c with a foolish man, H8199
Isa 49:25 with him that c with thee, and I will H3401

CONTENDING
Jude 9 Yet Michael the archangel, when c with G1252

CONTENT
Gen 37:27 *and* our flesh. And his brethren were c. H8085
Ex 2:21 And Moses was c to dwell with the H2974
Lev 10:20 And when Moses heard *that*, he was c. H3190
Jos 7: 7 c, and dwelt on the other side Jordan! H2974
Jdg 17:11 And the Levite was c to dwell with the H2974
19: 6 unto the man, Be c, I pray thee, and H2974
2Ki 5:23 And Naaman said, Be c, take two H2974
6: 3 And one said, Be c, I pray thee, and go H2974
Job 6:28 Now therefore be c, look upon me; for *it* H2974
Prv 6:35 he rest c, though thou givest many gifts. H14
Mk 15:15 And *so* Pilate, willing to c the people, G2425
Lk 3:14 *any* falsely; and be c with your wages. G714
Php 4:11 whatsoever state I am, *therewith* to be c. G842
1Ti 6: 8 food and raiment let us be therewith c. G714
Heb 13: 5 *and be* c with such things as ye G714
3Jn 10 words: and not c therewith, neither doth G714

CONTENTION
Prv 13:10 Only by pride cometh c: but with the H4683
17:14 leave off c, before it be meddled with. H7379
18: 6 A fool's lips enter into c, and his mouth H7379
22:10 Cast out the scorner, and c shall go out; H4066
Jer 15:10 and a man of c to the whole earth! I H4066
Hab 1: 3 and there are *that* raise up strife and c. H4066
Act 15:39 And the c was so sharp between them, G3948
Php 1:16 The one preach Christ of c, not G2052
1Th 2: 2 unto you the gospel of God with much c. G73

CONTENTIONS
Prv 18:18 The lot causeth c to cease, and parteth H4079
19 and *their* c *are* like the bars of a castle. H4079
19:13 c of a wife *are* a continual dropping. H4079
23:29 hath sorrow? who hath c? who hath H4079
1Co 1:11 of Chloe, that there are c among you. G2054
Tit 3: 9 genealogies, and c, and strivings about G2054

CONTENTIOUS
Prv 21:19 than with a c and an angry woman. H4066
26:21 to fire; so *is* a c man to kindle strife. H4066
27:15 rainy day and a c woman are alike. H4066
Ro 2: 8 But unto them that are c, and G1537+G2052
1Co 11:16 But if any man seem to be c, we have no G5380

CONTENTMENT
1Ti 6: 6 But godliness with c is great gain. G841

CONTINENCE See INCONTINENCY.

CONTINUAL
Ex 29:42 *This shall be* a c burnt offering H8548
Nu 4: 7 and the c bread shall be thereon: H8548
28: 3 spot day by day, *for* a c burnt offering. H8548
6 *It is* a c burnt offering, which was H8548
10 c burnt offering, and his drink offering. H8548
15 c burnt offering, and his drink offering. H8548
23 which *is* for a c burnt offering. H8548
24 c burnt offering, and his drink offering. H8548
31 Ye shall offer *them* beside the c burnt H8548
29:11 and the c burnt offering, and H8548
16 beside the c burnt offering, his meat H8548
19 beside the c burnt offering, and H8548
22 beside the c burnt offering, and H8548
25 beside the c burnt offering, his meat H8548
28 beside the c burnt offering, and H8548
31 beside the c burnt offering, his meat H8548
34 beside the c burnt offering, his meat H8548
38 beside the c burnt offering, and H8548
2Ki 25:30 And his allowance *was* a c allowance H8548
2Ch 2: 4 and for the c shewbread, and for H8548
Ezr 3: 5 And afterward *offered* the c burnt H8548
Neh 10:33 For the shewbread, and for the c meat H8548
33 and for the c burnt offering, of the H8548
Prv 15:15 that is of a merry heart *hath* a c feast. H8548
19:13 contentions of a wife *are* a c dropping. H2956
27:15 A c dropping in a very rainy day and a H2956
Isa 14: 6 wrath with a c stroke, he that H1115+H5627
Jer 48: 5 For in the going up of Luhith c weeping
52:34 And *for* his diet, there was a c diet H8548
Ezk 39:14 And they shall sever out men of c
46:15 every morning *for* a c burnt offering. H8548
Lk 18: 5 by her c coming she weary me. G1519+G5056
Ro 9: 2 That I have great heaviness and c G88

CONTINUALLY
Gen 6: 5 of his heart *was* only evil c. H3605+H3117
8: 3 off the earth c: and after the H1980+H7725
5 And the waters decreased c until the H1980
Ex 28:29 for a memorial before the LORD c. H8548
30 upon his heart before the LORD c. H8548
29:38 two lambs of the first year day by day c. H8548
Lev 24: 2 the light, to cause the lamps to burn c. H8548
3 before the LORD c: *it shall be* a statute H8548
4 the pure candlestick before the LORD c. H8548

Lev 24: 8 before the LORD c, *being taken* from H8548
Jos 6:13 the LORD went on c, and blew with the H1980
1Sa 18:29 Saul became David's enemy c. H3605+H3117
2Sa 9: 7 and thou shalt eat bread at my table c. H8548
13 for he did eat c at the king's table; and H8548
15:12 the people increased c with Absalom. H1980
19:13 me c in the room of Joab. H3605+H3117
1Ki 10: 8 which stand c before thee, *and* that H8548
2Ki 4: 9 holy man of God, which passeth by us c. H8548
25:29 c before him all the days of his life. H8548
1Ch 16: 6 c before the ark of the covenant of God. H8548
11 LORD and his strength, seek his face c. H8548
37 the ark c, as every day's work required: H8548
40 of the burnt offering c morning and H8548
23:31 unto them, c before the LORD: H8548
2Ch 9: 7 c before thee, and hear thy wisdom. H8548
12:15 Rehoboam and Jeroboam c. H3605+H3117
24:14 of the LORD c all the days of Jehoiada. H8548
Job 1: 5 in their hearts. Thus did Job c. H3605+H3117
Ps 34: 1 his praise *shall* c *be* in my mouth. H8548
35:27 yea, let them say c, Let the LORD be H8548
38:17 to halt, and my sorrow *is* c before me. H8548
40:11 and thy truth c preserve me. H8548
16 say c, The LORD be magnified. H8548
42: 3 while they c say unto me, H3605+H3117
44:15 My confusion *is* c before me, H3605+H3117
50: 8 offerings, *to have been* c before me. H8548
52: 1 goodness of God *endureth* c. H3605+H3117
58: 7 waters *which* run c: *when* he bendeth *his*
69:23 not; and make their loins c to shake. H8548
70: 4 salvation say c, Let God be magnified. H8548
71: 3 whereunto I may c resort: thou hast H8548
6 bowels: my praise *shall be* c of thee. H8548
14 But I will hope c, and will yet praise H8548
72:15 for him c; *and* daily shall he be praised. H8548
73:23 Nevertheless I *am* c with thee: thou H8548
74:23 that rise up against thee increaseth c. H8548
109:10 Let his children be c vagabonds, and H5128
15 Let them be before the LORD c, that he H8548
19 for a girdle wherewith he is girded c. H8548
119:44 So shall I keep thy law c for ever and H8548
109 My soul *is* c in my hand: yet do I not H8548
117 I will have respect unto thy statutes c. H8548
140: 2 in *their* heart; c are they H3605+H3117
Prv 6:14 deviseth mischief c; he soweth discord. H6256
21 Bind them c upon thine heart, *and* tie H8548
Ecc 1: 6 north; it whirleth about c, and the wind
Isa 21: 8 And he cried, A lion: My lord, I stand c H8548
49:16 of *my* hands; thy walls *are* c before me. H8548
51:13 and hast feared c every day because of H8548
52: 5 my name c every day *is* blasphemed. H8548
58:11 And the LORD shall guide thee c, and H8548
60:11 Therefore thy gates shall be open c; they H8548
65: 3 A people that provoketh me to anger c H8548
Jer 6: 7 in her; before me c *is* grief and wounds. H8548
33:18 offerings, and to do sacrifice c. H3605+H3117
52:33 and he did c eat bread before him H8548
Ezk 46:14 flour; a meat offering c by a perpetual H8548
Dan 6:16 thou servest c, he will deliver thee. H8411
20 c, able to deliver thee from the lions? H8411
Hos 4:18 whoredom c: her rulers *with* shame H2181
12: 6 and judgment, and wait on thy God c. H8548
Oba 16 all the heathen drink c, yea, they shall H8548
Nah 3:19 hath not thy wickedness passed c? H8548
Hab 1:17 net, and not spare c to slay the nations? H8548
Lk 24:53 And were c in the temple, praising and *G1275*
Act 6: 4 But we will give ourselves c to prayer, *G4342*
10: 7 soldier of them that waited on him c; *G4342*
Ro 13: 6 attending c upon this very thing. *G4342*
Heb 7: 3 Son of God; abideth a priest c. *G1519+G1336*
10: 1 year by year c make the *G1519+G1336*
13:15 of praise to God c, that is, the fruit of *G1275*

CONTINUANCE

Dt 28:59 and of long c, and sore sicknesses, H539
59 and sore sicknesses, and of long c. H539
Ps 139:16 written, *which* in c were fashioned, H3117
Isa 64: 5 in those is c, and we shall be saved. H5769
Ro 2: 7 To them who by patient c in well doing *G5281*

CONTINUE

Ex 21:21 Notwithstanding, if he c a day or two, H5975
Lev 12: 4 And she shall then c in the blood of her H3427
5 and she shall c in the blood of her H3427
1Sa 12:14 you c following the LORD your God: H1961
13:14 But now thy kingdom shall not c: the H6965
2Sa 7:29 that it may c for ever before thee: H1961
1Ki 2: 4 That the LORD may c his word which H6965
Job 15:29 his substance c, neither shall he prolong H6965
Job 17: 2 not mine eye c in their provocation? H3885
Ps 36:10 O c thy lovingkindness unto them that H4900
49:11 their houses *shall* c for ever, *and* their
102:28 The children of thy servants shall c, and H7931
119:91 They c this day according to thine H5975
Isa 5:11 that c until night, *till* wine inflame them! H309
Jer 32:14 vessel, that they may c many days. H5975
Dan 11: 8 of gold; and he shall c *more* years than H5975
Mt 15:32 because they c with me now three days, *G4357*
Jn 8:31 on him, If ye c in my word, *then* are *G3306*
15: 9 so have I loved you: c ye in my love. *G3306*
Act 13:43 them to c in the grace of God. *G1961*
14:22 exhorting them to c in the faith, and *G1696*
26:22 obtained help of God, I c unto this day, *G2476*
Ro 6: 1 What shall we say then? Shall we c in *G1961*
11:22 goodness, if thou c in *his* goodness: *G1961*
Gal 2: 5 truth of the gospel might c with you. *G1265*
Php 1:25 I shall abide and c with you all for your *G4839*
Col 1:23 If ye c in the faith grounded and *G1961*
4: 2 C in prayer, and watch in the same *G4342*
1Ti 2:15 if they c in faith and charity *G3306*
4:16 and unto the doctrine; c in them: for in *G1961*
2Ti 3:14 But c thou in the things which thou *G3306*
Heb 7:23 not suffered to c by reason of death: *G3887*
13: 1 Let brotherly love c. *G3306*
Jas 4:13 such a city, and c there a year, and buy *G4160*
2Pt 3: 4 asleep, all things c as *they were* from *G1265*
1Jn 2:24 shall c in the Son, and in the Father. *G3306*
Rev 13: 5 unto him to c forty *and* two months. *G4160*
17:10 he cometh, he must c a short space. *G3306*

CONTINUED

Gen 40: 4 them: and they c a season in ward. H1961
Jdg 5:17 in ships? Asher c on the sea shore, and H3427
Ru 1: 2 into the country of Moab, and c there. H1961
2: 7 she came, and hath c even from the H5975
1Sa 1:12 And it came to pass, as she c praying H7235
2Sa 6:11 And the ark of the LORD c in the house H3427
1Ki 22: 1 And they c three years without war H3427
2Ch 29:28 c until the burnt offering was finished.
Neh 5:16 Yea, also I c in the work of this wall, H2388
Job 27: 1 Moreover Job c his parable, and said, H3254
29: 1 Moreover Job c his parable, and said, H3254
Ps 72:17 his name shall be c as long as the sun: H5125
Dan 1:21 And Daniel c *even* unto the first year of H1961
Lk 6:12 pray, and c all night in prayer to God. *G1273*
22:28 Ye are they which have c with me in my *G1265*
Jn 2:12 and they c there not many days. *G3306*
8: 7 So when they c asking him, he lifted up *G1961*
11:54 and there c with his disciples. *G1304*
Act 1:14 These all c with one accord in prayer *G4342*
2:42 And they c stedfastly in the apostles' *G4342*
8:13 he was baptized, he c with Philip, and *G4342*
12:16 But Peter c knocking: and when they *G1961*
15:35 Paul also and Barnabas c in Antioch, *G1304*
18:11 And he c *there* a year and six months, *G2523*
19:10 And this c by the space of two years; so *G1096*
20: 7 and c his speech until midnight. *G3905*
27:33 and c fasting, having taken nothing. *G1300*
Heb 8: 9 because they c not in my covenant, *G1696*
1Jn 2:19 *no doubt* have c with us: but *they went* *G3306*

CONTINUETH

Job 14: 2 he fleeth also as a shadow, and c not. H5975
Gal 3:10 *is* every one that c not in all things *G1696*
1Ti 5: 5 in God, and c in supplications and *G4357*
Heb 7:24 But this *man*, because he c ever, hath *G3306*
Jas 1:25 law of liberty, and c *therein*, he being *G3887*

CONTINUING

Jer 30:23 forth with fury, a c whirlwind: it shall H1641
Act 2:46 And they, c daily with one accord in *G4342*
Ro 12:12 in tribulation; c instant in prayer; *G4342*
Heb 13:14 For here have we no c city, but we seek *G3306*

CONTRADICTING

Act 13:45 spoken by Paul, c and blaspheming. *G483*

CONTRADICTION

Heb 7: 7 And without all c the less is blessed of *G485*
12: 3 For consider him that endured such c of *G485*

CONTRARIWISE

2Co 2: 7 So that c ye *ought* rather to forgive *G5121*
Gal 2: 7 But c, when they saw that the gospel of *G5121*
1Pt 3: 9 for railing: but c blessing; knowing that *G5121*

CONTRARY

Lev 26:21 And if ye walk c unto me, and will not H7147
Lev 26:23 these things, but will walk c unto me; H7147
24 Then will I also walk c unto you, and H7147
27 hearken unto me, but walk c unto me; H7147
28 Then I will walk c unto you also in fury; H7147
40 that also they have walked c unto me; H7147
41 And *that* I also have walked c unto H7147
Est 9: 1 it was turned to the c, that the Jews had
Ezk 16:34 And the c is in thee from *other* women H2016
34 is given unto thee, therefore thou art c. H2016
Mt 14:24 tossed with waves: for the wind was c. *G1727*
Mk 6:48 for the wind was c unto them: and *G1727*
Act 17: 7 and these all do c to the decrees of *G561*
18:13 men to worship God c to the law. *G3844*
23: 3 me to be smitten c to the law? *G3891*
26: 9 c to the name of Jesus of Nazareth. *G1727*
27: 4 Cyprus, because the winds were c. *G1727*
Ro 11:24 and wert graffed c to nature into a *G3844*
16:17 and offences c to the doctrine which *G3844*
Gal 5:17 the flesh: and these are c the one to the *G480*
Col 2:14 us, which was c to us, and took it out *G5227*
1Th 2:15 please not God, and are c to all men: *G1727*
1Ti 1:10 other thing that is c to sound doctrine; *G480*
Tit 2: 8 that he that is of the c part may be *G1727*

CONTRIBUTION

Ro 15:26 to make a certain c for the poor saints *G2842*

CONTRITE

Ps 34:18 and saveth such as be of a c spirit. H1793
51:17 a c heart, O God, thou wilt not despise. H1794
Isa 57:15 also *that is* of a c and humble spirit, to H1793
15 and to revive the heart of the c ones. H1792
66: 2 of a c spirit, and trembleth at my word. H5223

CONTROVERSIES

2Ch 19: 8 for c, when they returned to Jerusalem. H7379

CONTROVERSY

Dt 17: 8 *being* matters of c within thy gates: H7379
19:17 whom the c *is*, shall stand before H7379
21: 5 shall every c and every stroke be *tried*: H7379
25: 1 If there be a c between men, and they H7379
2Sa 15: 2 man that had a c came to the king for H7379
Isa 34: 8 year of recompences for the c of Zion. H7379
Jer 25:31 the LORD hath a c with the nations, he H7379
Ezk 44:24 And in c they shall stand in judgment; H7379
Hos 4: 1 the LORD hath a c with the inhabitants H7379
12: 2 The LORD hath also a c with Judah, H7379
Mic 6: 2 Hear ye, O mountains, the LORD'S c, H7379
2 the LORD hath a c with his people, and H7379
1Ti 3:16 And without c great is the mystery of *G3672*

CONVENIENT

Prv 30: 8 nor riches; feed me with food c for me: H2706
Jer 40: 4 good and c for thee to go, thither go. H3477
5 it seemeth c unto thee to go. So the H3477
Mk 6:21 And when a c day was come, that *G2121*
Act 24:25 I have a c season, I will call for thee. *G2540*
Ro 1:28 to do those things which are not c; *G2520*
1Co 16:12 he will come when he shall have c time. *G2119*
Eph 5: 4 are not c: but rather giving of thanks. *G433*
Phlm 8 in Christ to enjoin thee that which is c, *G433*

CONVENIENTLY

Mk 14:11 he sought how he might c betray him. *G2122*

CONVERSANT

Jos 8:35 the strangers that were c among them. H1980
1Sa 25:15 as long as we were c with them, when H1980

CONVERSATION

Ps 37:14 *and* to slay such as be of upright c. H1870
50:23 that ordereth *his* c *aright* will I shew H1870
2Co 1:12 we have had our c in the world, and *G390*
Gal 1:13 For ye have heard of my c in time past in *G391*
Eph 2: 3 Among whom also we all had our c in *G390*
4:22 That ye put off concerning the former c *G391*
Php 1:27 Only let your c be as it becometh the *G4176*
3:20 For our c is in heaven; from whence *G4175*
1Ti 4:12 c, in charity, in spirit, in faith, in purity. *G391*
Heb 13: 5 *Let your* c *be* without covetousness; *G5158*
7 follow, considering the end of *their* c. *G391*
Jas 3:13 c his works with meekness of wisdom. *G391*
1Pt 1:15 is holy, so be ye holy in all manner of c; *G391*
18 from your vain c *received* by tradition *G391*
2:12 Having your c honest among the *G391*
3: 1 the word be won by the c of the wives; *G391*
2 While they behold your chaste c *coupled* *G391*
16 that falsely accuse your good c in Christ. *G391*

2Pt 2: 7 Lot, vexed with the filthy **c** of the wicked: *G391*
3:11 ye to be in *all* holy **c** and godliness, *G391*

CONVERSION
Act 15: 3 declaring the **c** of the Gentiles: and *G1995*

CONVERT
Isa 6:10 with their heart, and **c**, and be healed. H7725
Jas 5:19 do err from the truth, and one **c** him; *G1994*

CONVERTED
Ps 51:13 ways; and sinners shall be **c** unto thee. H7725
Isa 60: 5 of the sea shall be **c** unto thee, the H2015
Mt 13:15 should be **c**, and I should heal them. *G1994*
18: 3 you, Except ye be **c**, and become as little *G4762*
Mk 4:12 they should be **c**, and *their* sins should *G1994*
Lk 22:32 thou art **c**, strengthen thy brethren. *G1994*
Jn 12:40 heart, and be **c**, and I should heal them. *G1994*
Act 3:19 Repent ye therefore, and be **c**, that your *G1994*
28:27 should be **c**, and I should heal them. *G1994*

CONVERTETH
Jas 5:20 Let him know, that he which **c** the *G1994*

CONVERTING
Ps 19: 7 The law of the LORD *is* perfect, **c** the H7725

CONVERTS
Isa 1:27 and her **c** with righteousness. H7725

CONVEY
1Ki 5: 9 unto the sea: and I will **c** them by sea in H7760
Neh 2: 7 may **c** me over till I come into Judah; H5674

CONVEYED
Jn 5:13 it was: for Jesus had **c** himself away, a *G1593*

CONVICTED
Jn 8: 9 And they which heard *it*, being **c** by *G1651*

CONVINCE
Tit 1: 9 both to exhort and to **c** the gainsayers. *G1651*
Jude 15 To execute judgment upon all, and to **c** *G1827*

CONVINCED
Job 32:12 that **c** Job, *or* that answered his words: H3198
Act 18:28 For he mightily **c** the Jews, *and that* *G1246*
1Co 14:24 he is **c** of all, he is judged of all: *G1651*
Jas 2: 9 and are **c** of the law as transgressors. *G1651*

CONVINCETH
Jn 8:46 Which of you **c** me of sin? And if I say *G1651*

CONVOCATION
Ex 12:16 *shall be* an holy **c**, and in the seventh H4744
16 shall be an holy **c** to you; no manner of H4744
Lev 23: 3 of rest, an holy **c**; ye shall do no work H4744
7 In the first day ye shall have an holy **c**: H4744
8 **c**: ye shall do no servile work *therein*. H4744
21 it may be an holy **c** unto you: ye shall H4744
24 of blowing of trumpets, an holy **c**. H4744
27 it shall be an holy **c** unto you; and ye H4744
35 On the first day *shall be* an holy **c**: ye H4744
36 day shall be an holy **c** unto you; and ye H4744
Nu 28:18 In the first day *shall be* an holy **c**; ye H4744
25 an holy **c**; ye shall do no servile work. H4744
26 an holy **c**; ye shall do no servile work: H4744
29: 1 ye shall have an holy **c**; ye shall do no H4744
7 month an holy **c**; and ye shall afflict H4744
12 ye shall have an holy **c**; ye shall do no H4744

CONVOCATIONS
Lev 23: 2 *to be* holy **c**, *even* these *are* my feasts. H4744
4 the LORD, *even* holy **c**, which ye shall H4744
37 *to be* holy **c**, to offer an offering H4744

COOK
1Sa 9:23 And Samuel said unto the **c**, Bring the H2876
24 And the **c** took up the shoulder, and H2876

COOKS
1Sa 8:13 and *to be* **c**, and *to be* bakers. H2879

COOL
Gen 3: 8 in the garden in the **c** of the day: and H7307
Lk 16:24 in water, and **c** my tongue; for I am *G2711*

COOS
Act 21: 1 course unto **C**, and the *day* following *G2972*

COPIED
Prv 25: 1 men of Hezekiah king of Judah **c** out. H6275

COPING
1Ki 7: 9 unto the **c**, and *so* on the outside H2947

COPPER
Ezr 8:27 two vessels of fine **c**, precious as gold. H5178

COPPERSMITH
2Ti 4:14 Alexander the **c** did me much evil: the *G5471*

COPULATION
Lev 15:16 And if any man's seed of **c** go out from H7902
17 is the seed of **c**, shall be washed with H7902
18 lie *with* seed of **c**, they shall *both* bathe H7902

COPY
Dt 17:18 shall write him a **c** of this law in a book H4932
Jos 8:32 And he wrote there upon the stones a **c** H4932
Ezr 4:11 This *is* the **c** of the letter that they sent H6573
23 Now when the **c** of king Artaxerxes' H6573
5: 6 The **c** of the letter that Tatnai, governor H6573
7:11 Now this *is* the **c** of the letter that the H6572
Est 3:14 The **c** of the writing for a H6572
4: 8 Also he gave him the **c** of the writing of H6572
8:13 The **c** of the writing for a H6572

COR
Ezk 45:14 a bath out of the **c**, *which is* an homer of H3734

CORAL
Job 28:18 No mention shall be made of **c**, or of H7215
Ezk 27:16 work, and fine linen, and **c**, and agate. H7215

CORBAN
Mk 7:11 or mother, *It is* **C**, that is to say, a gift, *G2878*

CORD
Jos 2:15 Then she let them down by a **c** through H2256
Job 30:11 Because he hath loosed my **c**, and H3499
41: 1 with a **c** *which* thou lettest down? H2256
Ecc 4:12 and a threefold **c** is not quickly broken. H2339
12: 6 Or ever the silver **c** be loosed, or the H2256
Mic 2: 5 none that shall cast a **c** by lot in the H2256

CORDS
Ex 35:18 and the pins of the court, and their **c**, H4340
39:40 the court gate, his **c**, and his pins, and H4340
Nu 3:26 the **c** of it for all the service thereof. H4340
37 sockets, and their pins, and their **c**. H4340
4:26 round about, and their **c**, and all the H4340
32 their pins, and their **c**, with all their H4340
Jdg 15:13 **c**, and brought him up from the rock. H5688
14 upon him, and the **c** that *were* upon his H5688
Est 1: 6 fastened with **c** of fine linen and purple H2256
Job 36: 8 fetters, *and* be holden in **c** of affliction; H2256
Ps 2: 3 asunder, and cast away their **c** from us. H5688
118:27 with **c**, *even* unto the horns of the altar. H5688
129: 4 hath cut asunder the **c** of the wicked. H5688
140: 5 snare for me, and **c**; they have spread a H2256
Prv 5:22 he shall be holden with the **c** of his sins. H2256
Isa 5:18 draw iniquity with **c** of vanity, and sin H2256
33:20 shall any of the **c** thereof be broken. H2256
54: 2 thy **c**, and strengthen thy stakes; H4340
Jer 10:20 My tabernacle is spoiled, and all my **c** H4340
38: 6 Jeremiah with **c**. And in the dungeon H2256
11 by **c** into the dungeon to Jeremiah. H2256
12 under the **c**. And Jeremiah did so. H2256
13 So they drew up Jeremiah with **c**, and H2256
Ezk 27:24 bound with **c**, and made of cedar, H2256
Hos 11: 4 I drew them with **c** of a man, with H2256
Jn 2:15 a scourge of small **c**, he drove them all *G4979*

CORE
Jude 11 and perished in the gainsaying of **C**. *G2879*

CORIANDER
Ex 16:31 and it *was* like **c** seed, white; and the H1407
Nu 11: 7 And the manna *was* as **c** seed, and the H1407

CORINTH
Act 18: 1 departed from Athens, and came to **C**; *G2882*
19: 1 Apollos was at **C**, Paul having passed *G2882*
1Co 1: 2 Unto the church of God which is at **C**, to *G2882*
2Co 1: 1 of God which is at **C**, with all the saints *G2882*
23 to spare you I came not as yet unto **C**. *G2882*
2Ti 4:20 Erastus abode at **C**: but Trophimus *G2882*

CORINTHIANS
Act 18: 8 **C** hearing believed, and were baptized. *G2881*
2Co 6:11 O *ye* **C**, our mouth is open unto you, our *G2881*

CORMORANT
Lev 11:17 And the little owl, and the **c**, and the H7994
Dt 14:17 pelican, and the gier eagle, and the **c**, H7994
Isa 34:11 But the **c** and the bittern shall possess H6893
Zep 2:14 nations: both the **c** and the bittern shall H6893

CORN
Gen 27:28 of the earth, and plenty of **c** and wine: H1715
37 servants; and with **c** and wine have I H1715
41: 5 seven ears of **c** came up upon one H7641
35 come, and lay up **c** under the hand of H1250
49 And Joseph gathered **c** as the sand of H1250
57 to Joseph for to buy **c**; because that the
42: 1 Now when Jacob saw that there was **c** H7668
2 heard that there is **c** in Egypt: get you H7668
3 brethren went down to buy **c** in Egypt. H1250
5 And the sons of Israel came to buy **c**
19 carry **c** for the famine of your houses: H7668
25 their sacks with **c**, and to restore every H1250
26 And they laded their asses with the **c**, H7668
43: 2 they had eaten up the **c** which they had H7668
44: 2 youngest, and his **c** money. And he did H7668
45:23 asses laden with **c** and bread and meat H1250
47:14 of Canaan, for the **c** which they bought: H7668
Ex 22: 6 so that the stacks of **c**, or the standing H1430
6 corn, or the standing **c**, or the field, be H7054
Lev 2:14 green ears of **c** dried by the fire, *even* H24
14 the fire, *even* **c** beaten out of full ears. H1643
16 *part* of the beaten **c** thereof, and *part* of H1643
23:14 bread, nor parched **c**, nor green ears,
Nu 18:27 as though *it were* the **c** of the H1715
Dt 7:13 of thy land, thy **c**, and thy wine, and H1715
11:14 in thy **c**, and thy wine, and thine oil. H1715
12:17 the tithe of thy **c**, or of thy wine, or of H1715
14:23 the tithe of thy **c**, of thy wine, and of H1715
16: 9 thou beginnest *to put* the sickle to the **c**. H7054
13 hast gathered in thy **c** and thy wine: H1637
18: 4 The firstfruit *also* of thy **c**, of thy wine, H1715
23:25 When thou comest into the standing **c** H7054
25 sickle unto thy neighbour's standing **c**. H7054
25: 4 muzzle the ox when he treadeth out *the* **c**.
28:51 leave thee *either* **c**, wine, or oil, *or* the H1715
33:28 *be* upon a land of **c** and wine; also his H1715
Jos 5:11 And they did eat of the old **c** of the land H5669
11 and parched **c** in the selfsame day.
12 eaten of the old **c** of the land; neither H5669
Jdg 15: 5 go into the standing **c** of the Philistines, H7054
5 **c**, with the vineyards *and* olives. H7054
Ru 2: 2 and glean ears of **c** after *him* in whose
14 her parched **c**, and she did eat, and
3: 7 the end of the heap of **c**: and she came H6194
1Sa 17:17 of this parched **c**, and these ten loaves,
25:18 of parched **c**, and an hundred clusters
2Sa 17:19 spread ground **c** thereon; and the thing H7383
28 and flour, and parched **c**, and beans, and
2Ki 4:42 and full ears of **c** in the husk thereof. H3759
18:32 land, a land of **c** and wine, a land of H1715
19:26 and *as* **c** blasted before it be grown up. H1715
2Ch 31: 5 the firstfruits of **c**, wine, and oil, and H1715
32:28 Storehouses also for the increase of **c**, H1715
Neh 5: 2 **c** *for them*, that we may eat, and live. H1715
3 we might buy **c**, because of the dearth. H1715
10 **c**: I pray you, let us leave off this usury. H1715
11 money, and of the **c**, the wine, and the H1715
10:39 the offering of the **c**, of the new wine, H1715
13: 5 the tithes of the **c**, the new wine, and the H1715
12 the tithe of the **c** and the new wine and H1715
Job 5:26 as a shock of **c** cometh in in his season.
24: 6 They reap *every one* his **c** in the field: H1098
24 and cut off as the tops of the ears of **c**.
39: 4 they grow up with **c**; they go forth, and H1250
Ps 4: 7 *that* their **c** and their wine increased. H1715
65: 9 **c**, when thou hast so provided for it. H1715
13 with **c**; they shout for joy, they also sing. H1250
72:16 There shall be an handful of **c** in the H1250
78:24 and had given them of the **c** of heaven. H1715
Prv 11:26 He that withholdeth **c**, the people shall H1250
Isa 17: 5 gathereth the **c**, and reapeth the ears H7054
21:10 O my threshing, and the **c** of my floor: H1121
28:28 Bread **c** is bruised; because he will not
36:17 land, a land of **c** and wine, a land of H1715
37:27 and *as* **c** blasted before it be grown up.
62: 8 no more give thy **c** *to be* meat for thine H1715
Lam 2:12 They say to their mothers, Where *is* **c** H1715
Ezk 36:29 I will call for the **c**, and will increase it, H1715

Hos 2: 8 For she did not know that I gave her **c**, H1715
9 and take away my **c** in the time thereof, H1715
22 And the earth shall hear the **c**, and the H1715
7:14 **c** and wine, *and* they rebel against me. H1715
10:11 to tread out *the c*; but I passed over upon
14: 7 shall revive *as* the **c**, and grow as the H1715
Joel 1:10 mourneth; for the **c** is wasted: the new H1715
17 are broken down; for the **c** is withered. H1715
2:19 I will send you **c**, and wine, and oil, and H1715
Am 8: 5 that we may sell **c**? and the sabbath, H7668
9: 9 all nations, like as *c* is sifted in a sieve,
Hag 1:11 and upon the **c**, and upon the new wine, H1715
Zec 9:17 *is* his beauty! **c** shall make the young H1715
Mt 12: 1 day through the **c**; and his disciples G4702
1 began to pluck the ears of **c**, and to eat. G4719
Mk 2:23 he went through the **c** fields on the G4702
23 as they went, to pluck the ears of **c**. G4719
4:28 the ear, after that the full **c** in the ear. G4621
Lk 6: 1 he went through the **c** fields; and his G4702
1 the ears of **c**, and did eat, rubbing G4719
Jn 12:24 Verily, verily, I say unto you, Except a **c** G2848
Act 7:12 But when Jacob heard that there was **c** G4621
1Co 9: 9 out the **c**. Doth God take care for oxen? G248
1Ti 5:18 treadeth out the **c**. And, The labourer *is* G248

CORNELIUS
Act 10: 1 in Caesarea called **C**, a centurion of the G2883
3 in to him, and saying unto him, **C**. G2883
7 which spake unto **C** was departed, he G2883
17 were sent from **C** had made inquiry for G2883
21 unto him from **C**; and said, Behold, I G2883
22 And they said, **C** the centurion, a just G2883
24 Caesarea. And **C** waited for them, and G2883
25 And as Peter was coming in, **C** met G2883
30 And **C** said, Four days ago I was G2883
31 And said, **C**, thy prayer is heard, and G2883

CORNER
Ex 36:25 the north **c**, he made twenty boards, H6285
Lev 21: 5 they shave off the **c** of their beard, nor H6285
Jos 18:14 compassed the **c** of the sea southward, H6285
2Ki 11:11 from the right **c** of the temple to the H3802
11 temple to the left **c** of the temple, *along* H3802
14:13 unto the **c** gate, four hundred cubits. H6438
2Ch 25:23 to the **c** gate, four hundred cubits. H6437
26: 9 in Jerusalem at the **c** gate, and at the H6438
28:24 him altars in every **c** of Jerusalem. H6438
Neh 3:24 the turning *of the wall*, even unto the **c**. H6438
31 Miphkad, and to the going up of the **c**. H6438
32 And between the going up of the **c** unto H6438
Job 38: 6 or who laid the **c** stone thereof; H6438
Ps 118:22 is become the head *stone* of the **c**. H6438
144:12 *may be* as **c** stones, polished *after* H2106
Prv 7: 8 Passing through the street near her **c**; H6438
12 the streets, and lieth in wait at every **c**.) H6438
21: 9 *It is* better to dwell in a **c** of the H6438
25:24 *It is* better to dwell in the **c** of the H6438
Isa 28:16 tried stone, a precious **c** *stone*, a sure H6438
30:20 be removed into a **c** any more, but H3670
Jer 31:38 of Hananeel unto the gate of the **c**. H6438
40 of Kidron, unto the **c** of the horse gate H6438
48:45 shall devour the **c** of Moab, and the H6285
51:26 of thee a stone for a **c**, nor a stone for H6438
Ezk 46:21 every **c** of the court *there was* a court. H4742
Am 3:12 in Samaria in the **c** of a bed, and in H6285
Zec 10: 4 Out of him came forth the **c**, out of him H6438
14:10 first gate, unto the **c** gate, and *from* the H6434
Mt 21:42 the head of the **c**: this is the Lord's G1137
Mk 12:10 rejected is become the head of the **c**: G1137
Lk 20:17 the same is become the head of the **c**? G1137
Act 4:11 which is become the head of the **c**. G1137
26:26 him; for this thing was not done in a **c**. G1137
Eph 2:20 Christ himself being the chief **c** *stone*; G204
1Pt 2: 6 I lay in Sion a chief **c** stone, elect, G204
7 the same is made the head of the **c**, G1137

CORNER-GATE See CORNER and GATE.

CORNERS
Ex 25:12 put *them* in the four **c** thereof; and two H6471
26 four **c** that *are* on the four feet thereof. H6285
26:23 the **c** of the tabernacle in the two sides. H4742
24 them both; they shall be for the two **c**. H4740
27: 2 of it upon the four **c** thereof: his horns H6438
4 four brasen rings in the four **c** thereof. H7098
30: 4 of it, by the two **c** thereof, upon the two H6763
36:28 And two boards made he for the **c** of H4742
29 he did to both of them in both the **c**. H4740
37: 3 *be set* by the four **c** of it; even two rings H6471
Ex 37:13 four **c** that *were* in the four feet thereof. H6285
27 thereof, by the two **c** of it, upon the two H6763
38: 2 thereof on the four **c** of it; the horns H6438
Lev 19: 9 wholly reap the **c** of thy field, neither H6285
27 Ye shall not round the **c** of your heads, H6285
27 shalt thou mar the **c** of thy beard. H6285
23:22 riddance of the **c** of thy field when thou H6285
Nu 24:17 shall smite the **c** of Moab, and destroy H6285
Dt 32:26 I said, I would scatter them into **c**, I H6284
1Ki 7:30 brass: and the four **c** thereof had H6471
34 to the four **c** of one base: *and* the H6438
Neh 9:22 divide them into **c**: so they possessed H6285
Job 1:19 smote the four **c** of the house, and it H6438
Isa 11:12 of Judah from the four **c** of the earth. H3671
Jer 9:26 *are* in the utmost **c**, that dwell in the H6285
25:23 Buz, and all *that are* in the utmost **c**, H6285
49:32 *that are* in the utmost **c**; and I will bring H6285
Ezk 7: 2 end is come upon the four **c** of the land. H3671
41:22 two cubits; and the **c** thereof, and the H4740
43:20 of it, and on the four **c** of the settle, and H6438
45:19 and upon the four **c** of the settle of the H6438
46:21 to pass by the four **c** of the court; and, H4740
22 In the four **c** of the court *there were* H4740
22 these four **c** *were* of one measure. H7106
Zec 9:15 like bowls, *and* as the **c** of the altar. H2106
Mt 6: 5 and in the **c** of the streets, that they G1137
Act 10:11 at the four **c**, and let down to the earth: G746
11: 5 heaven by four **c**; and it came even to me: G746
Rev 7: 1 on the four **c** of the earth, holding G1137

CORNER-STONE See CORNER and STONE.

CORNET
1Ch 15:28 with sound of the **c**, and with trumpets, H7782
Ps 98: 6 With trumpets and sound of **c** make a H7782
Dan 3: 5 the sound of the **c**, flute, harp, sackbut, H7162
7 the sound of the **c**, flute, harp, sackbut, H7162
10 the sound of the **c**, flute, harp, sackbut, H7162
15 the sound of the **c**, flute, harp, sackbut, H7162
Hos 5: 8 Blow ye the **c** in Gibeah, *and* the H7782

CORNETS
2Sa 6: 5 on timbrels, and on **c**, and on cymbals. H4517
2Ch 15:14 and with trumpets, and with **c**. H7782

CORNFLOOR
Hos 9: 1 loved a reward upon every **c**. H1637+H1715

CORPSE
Mk 6:29 and took up his **c**, and laid it in a tomb. G4430

CORPSES
2Ki 19:35 morning, behold, they *were* all dead **c**. H6297
Isa 37:36 morning, behold, they *were* all dead **c**. H6297
Nah 3: 3 **c**; they stumble upon their corpses: H1472
3 corpses; they stumble upon their **c**: H1472

CORRECT
Ps 39:11 When thou with rebukes dost **c** man H3256
94:10 shall not he **c**? he that teacheth man H3198
Prv 29:17 **C** thy son, and he shall give thee rest; H3256
Jer 2:19 Thine own wickedness shall **c** thee, and H3256
10:24 O LORD, **c** me, but with judgment; not H3256
30:11 of thee: but I will **c** thee in measure, H3256
46:28 end of thee, but **c** thee in measure; yet H3256

CORRECTED
Prv 29:19 A servant will not be **c** by words: for H3256
Heb 12: 9 of our flesh which **c** *us*, and we gave G3810

CORRECTETH
Job 5:17 Behold, happy *is* the man whom God **c**: H3198
Prv 3:12 For whom the LORD loveth he **c**; even H3198

CORRECTION
Job 37:13 He causeth it to come, whether for **c**, or H7626
Prv 3:11 of the LORD; neither be weary of his **c**: H8433
7:22 or as a fool to the **c** of the stocks; H4148
15:10 **C** *is* grievous unto him that forsaketh H4148
22:15 the rod of **c** shall drive it far from him. H4148
23:13 Withhold not **c** from the child: for *if* H4148
Jer 2:30 they received no **c**: your own sword H4148
5: 3 refused to receive **c**: they have made H4148
7:28 God, nor receiveth **c**: truth is perished, H4148
Hab 1:12 God, thou hast established them for **c**. H3198
Zep 3: 2 she received not **c**; she trusted not in the H4148
2Ti 3:16 for **c**, for instruction in righteousness: G1882

CORRUPT
Gen 6:11 The earth also was **c** before God, and H7843
12 and, behold, it was **c**; for all flesh had H7843
Dt 4:16 Lest ye **c** *yourselves*, and make you a H7843
25 in the land, and shall **c** *yourselves*, and H7843
31:29 ye will utterly **c** *yourselves*, and turn H7843
Job 17: 1 My breath is **c**, my days are extinct, the H2254
Ps 14: 1 *is* no God. They are **c**, they have done H7843
38: 5 My wounds stink *and* are **c** because of H4743
53: 1 *There is* no God. **C** are they, and have H7843
73: 8 They are **c**, and speak wickedly H4167
Prv 25:26 *as* a troubled fountain, and a **c** spring. H7843
Ezk 20:44 according to your **c** doings, O ye house H7843
23:11 *this*, she was more **c** in her inordinate H7843
Dan 2: 9 lying and **c** words to speak before H7844
11:32 covenant shall he **c** by flatteries: but H2610
Mal 1:14 unto the Lord a **c** thing: for I *am* a H7843
2: 3 Behold, I will **c** your seed, and spread H1605
Mt 6:19 and rust doth **c**, and where thieves break G853
20 moth nor rust doth **c**, and where thieves G853
7:17 but a **c** tree bringeth forth evil fruit. G4550
18 *can* a **c** tree bring forth good fruit. G4550
12:33 or else make the tree **c**, and his fruit G4550
33 fruit **c**: for the tree is known by *his* fruit. G4550
Lk 6:43 For a good tree bringeth not forth **c** G4550
43 doth a **c** tree bring forth good fruit. G4550
1Co 15:33 evil communications **c** good manners. G5351
2Co 2:17 For we are not as many, which **c** the G2585
Eph 4:22 is **c** according to the deceitful lusts; G5351
29 Let no **c** communication proceed out of G4550
1Ti 6: 5 Perverse disputings of men of **c** minds, G1311
2Ti 3: 8 the truth: men of **c** minds, reprobate G2704
Jude 10 in those things they **c** themselves. G5351
Rev 19: 2 whore, which did **c** the earth with her G5351

CORRUPTED
Gen 6:12 all flesh had **c** his way upon the earth. H7843
Ex 8:24 was **c** by reason of the swarm *of flies*. H7843
32: 7 of the land of Egypt, have **c** *themselves*: H7843
Dt 9:12 out of Egypt have **c** *themselves*; they H7843
32: 5 They have **c** themselves, their spot *is* H7843
Jdg 2:19 they returned, and **c** *themselves* more H7843
Ezk 16:47 wast **c** more than they in all thy ways. H7843
28:17 thy beauty, thou hast **c** thy wisdom by H7843
Hos 9: 9 They have deeply **c** *themselves*, as in H7843
Zep 3: 7 they rose early, *and* **c** all their doings. H7843
Mal 2: 8 at the law; ye have **c** the covenant of H7843
2Co 7: 2 **c** no man, we have defrauded no man. G5351
11: 3 **c** from the simplicity that is in Christ. G5351
Jas 5: 2 Your riches are **c**, and your garments G4595

CORRUPTERS
Isa 1: 4 children that are **c**: they have forsaken H7843
Jer 6:28 *they are* brass and iron; they *are* all **c**. H7843

CORRUPTETH
Lk 12:33 no thief approacheth, neither moth **c**. G1311

CORRUPTIBLE
Ro 1:23 made like to **c** man, and to birds, and G5349
1Co 9:25 a **c** crown; but we an incorruptible. G5349
15:53 For this **c** must put on incorruption, G5349
54 So when this **c** shall have put on G5349
1Pt 1:18 redeemed with **c** things, *as* silver and G5349
23 Being born again, not of **c** seed, but of G5349
3: 4 in that which is not **c**, *even the ornament* G862

CORRUPTING
Dan 11:17 of women, **c** her: but she shall not H7843

CORRUPTION
Lev 22:25 these; because their **c** *is* in them, *and* H4893
2Ki 23:13 of the mount of **c**, which Solomon the H4889
Job 17:14 I have said to **c**, Thou *art* my father: to H7845
Ps 16:10 wilt thou suffer thine Holy One to see **c**. H7845
49: 9 should still live for ever, *and* not see **c**. H7845
Isa 38:17 *it* from the pit of **c**: for thou hast cast all H1097
Dan 10: 8 in me into **c**, and I retained no strength. H4889
Jna 2: 6 up my life from **c**, O LORD my God. H7845
Act 2:27 wilt thou suffer thine Holy One to see **c**. G1312
31 left in hell, neither his flesh did see **c**. G1312
13:34 more to return to **c**, he said on this wise, G1312
35 shalt not suffer thine Holy One to see **c**. G1312
36 was laid unto his fathers, and saw **c**: G1312
37 he, whom God raised again, saw no **c**. G1312
Ro 8:21 from the bondage of **c** into the glorious G5356
1Co 15:42 is sown in **c**; it is raised in incorruption: G5356
50 neither doth **c** inherit incorruption. G5356
Gal 6: 8 of the flesh reap **c**; but he that soweth to G5356

2Pt 1: 4 the c that is in the world through lust. G5356
2:12 and shall utterly perish in their own c; G5356
19 are the servants of c: for of whom a G5356

CORRUPTLY
2Ch 27: 2 of the LORD. And the people did yet c. H7843
Neh 1: 7 We have dealt very c against thee, and H2254

COSAM
Lk 3:28 was *the son* of C, which was *the son* of G2973

COST
2Sa 19:42 the king's *c?* or hath he given us any gift?
24:24 of that which doth c me nothing. So H2600
1Ch 21:24 nor offer burnt offerings without c. H2600
Lk 14:28 c, whether he have *sufficient* to finish *it?* G1160

COSTLINESS
Rev 18:19 c! for in one hour is she made desolate. G5094

COSTLY
1Ki 5:17 great stones, c stones, *and* hewed H3368
7: 9 All these *were of* c stones, according to H3368
10 And the foundation *was of* c stones, H3368
11 And above *were* c stones, after the H3368
Jn 12: 3 of spikenard, very c, and anointed the G4186
1Ti 2: 9 hair, or gold, or pearls, or c array; G4185

COTES
2Ch 32:28 for all manner of beasts, and c for flocks. H220

COTTAGE
Isa 1: 8 And the daughter of Zion is left as a c H5521
24:20 shall be removed like a c; and the H4412

COTTAGES
Zep 2: 6 c for shepherds, and folds for flocks. H3741

COUCH
Gen 49: 4 defiledst thou *it*: he went up to my c. H3326
Job 7:13 me, my c shall ease my complaint; H4904
38:40 When they c in *their* dens, *and* abide in H7817
Ps 6: 6 to swim; I water my c with my tears. H6210
Am 3:12 of a bed, and in Damascus *in* a c. H6210
Lk 5:19 with *his* c into the midst before Jesus. G2826
24 take up thy c, and go into thine house. G2826

COUCHED
Gen 49: 9 stooped down, he c as a lion, and as an H7257
Nu 24: 9 He c, he lay down as a lion, and as a H3766

COUCHES
Am 6: 4 upon their c, and eat the lambs out H6210
Act 5:15 *them* on beds and c, that at the least the G2895

COUCHETH
Dt 33:13 dew, and for the deep that c beneath, H7257

COUCHING
Gen 49:14 Issachar *is* a strong ass c down H7257

COUCHINGPLACE
Ezk 25: 5 the Ammonites a c for flocks: and ye H4769

COULD
Gen 13: 6 great, so that they c not dwell together. H3201
27: 1 dim, so that he c not see, he called Esau
36: 7 c not bear them because of their cattle. H3201
37: 4 and c not speak peaceably unto him. H3201
41: 8 that c interpret them unto Pharaoh. H6622
21 And when they had eaten them up, it c
24 *there was* none that c declare *it* to me.
43: 7 of these words: c we certainly know that
45: 1 Then Joseph c not refrain himself H3201
3 And his brethren c not answer him; for H3201
48:10 for age, *so that* he c not see. And he H3201
Ex 2: 3 And when she c not longer hide him, H3201
7:21 and the Egyptians c not drink of the H3201
24 c not drink of the water of the river. H3201
8:18 forth lice, but they c not: so there were H3201
9:11 And the magicians c not stand before H3201
12:39 out of Egypt, and c not tarry, neither H3201
15:23 And when they came to Marah, they c H3201
Nu 9: 6 of a man, that they c not keep the H3201
Jos 7:12 Therefore the children of Israel c not H3201
15:63 children of Judah c not drive them out: H3201
17:12 Yet the children of Manasseh c not H3201
Jdg 1:19 *of* the mountain; but c not drive out the
2:14 about, so that they c not any longer H3201
3:22 blade, so that he c not draw the dagger
6:27 c not do *it* by day, that he did *it* by night.
12: 6 said Sibboleth: for he c not frame to
14:14 c not in three days expound the riddle. H3201
17: 8 sojourn where he c find *a place*: and he
20:16 every one c sling stones at an hair
Ru 3:14 rose up before one c know another. And
1Sa 3: 2 began to wax dim, *that* he c not see; H3201
4:15 his eyes were dim, that he c not see. H3201
10:21 they sought him, he c not be found.
23:13 whithersoever they c go. And it was told
30:10 that they c not go over the brook Besor.
21 so faint that they c not follow David,
2Sa 1:10 I was sure that he c not live after that he
3:11 And he c not answer Abner a word H3201
17:20 had sought and c not find *them*, they
22:39 them, that they c not arise: yea, they are
1Ki 5: 3 David my father c not build an house H3201
8: 5 sheep and oxen, that c not be told nor
11 So that the priests c not stand to H3201
13: 4 so that he c not pull it in again to him. H3201
14: 4 But Ahijah c not see; for his eyes H3201
2Ki 3:26 unto the king of Edom: but they c not. H3201
4:40 in the pot. And they c not eat *thereof*. H3201
16: 5 Ahaz, but c not overcome *him*. H3201
1Ch 12: 2 *They were* armed with bows, and c use
8 *fit* for the battle, that c handle shield and
33 thousand, which c keep rank: *they were*
38 All these men of war, that c keep rank,
21:30 But David c not go before it to inquire H3201
2Ch 4:18 weight of the brass c not be found out.
5: 6 sheep and oxen, which c not be told nor
14 So that the priests c not stand to H3201
7: 2 And the priests c not enter into the H3201
13: 7 and c not withstand them.
14:13 that they c not recover themselves;
20:25 more than they c carry away: and they
25: 5 to war, that c handle spear and shield.
15 the people, which c not deliver their own
29:34 few, so that they c not flay all the burnt H3201
30: 3 For they c not keep it at that time, H3201
32:14 destroyed, that c deliver his people out H3201
34:12 all that c skill of instruments of musick.
Ezr 2:59 *and* Immer: but they c not shew their H3201
3:13 So that the people c not discern the noise
5: 5 of the Jews, that they c not cause them to
Neh 7:61 and Immer: but they c not shew their H3201
8: 2 and all that c hear with understanding,
3 and those that c understand; and the
13:24 of Ashdod, and c not speak in the Jews' H5234
Est 6: 1 On that night c not the king sleep, and H5074
7: 4 c not countervail the king's damage.
9: 2 hurt: and no man c withstand them; for
Job 4:16 It stood still, but I c not discern the form
16: 4 I also c speak as ye *do*: if your soul were
4 in my soul's stead, I c heap up words
31:23 reason of his highness I c not endure. H3201
Ps 37:36 yea, I sought him, but he c not be found.
55:12 me; then I c have borne *it*: neither
73: 7 they have more than heart c wish.
78:44 and their floods, that they c not drink.
Song 5: 6 I sought him, but I c not find him; I
Isa 5: 4 What c have been done more to my
7: 1 against it, but c not prevail against it. H3201
30: 5 They were all ashamed of a people *that* c
33:23 Thy tacklings are loosed; they c not well
23 their mast, they c not spread the sail:
41:28 when I asked of them, c answer a word.
46: 2 together; they c not deliver the burden, H3201
Jer 6:15 all ashamed, neither c they blush: H3045
8:12 all ashamed, neither c they blush: H3045
15: 1 me, *yet* my mind c not *be* toward this
20: 9 weary with forbearing, and I c not *stay*. H3201
24: 2 which c not be eaten, they were so bad.
44:22 So that the LORD c no longer bear, H3201
Lam 4:14 so that men c not touch their garments. H3201
17 watched for a nation *that* c not save *us*.
Ezk 31: 8 The cedars in the garden of God c not
47: 5 *it was* a river that I c not pass over: for H3201
5 in, a river that c not be passed over.
Dan 5: 8 *men*: but they c not read the writing, H3546
15 thereof: but they c not shew the H3546
6: 4 kingdom; but they c find none occasion H3202
8: 4 *was there any* that c deliver out of his
7 that c deliver the ram out of his hand.
Hos 5:13 to king Jareb; yet c he not heal you, nor H3201
Jna 1:13 to the land; but they c not: for the sea H3201
Mt 17:16 thy disciples, and they c not cure him. G1410
19 and said, Why c not we cast him out? G1410
26:40 c ye not watch with me one hour? G2480
27:24 When Pilate saw that he c prevail
Mk 1:45 that Jesus c no more openly enter G1410
2: 4 And when they c not come nigh unto G1410
3:20 so that they c not so much as eat bread. G1410
5: 3 man c bind him, no, not with chains: G1410
4 in pieces: neither c any *man* tame him. G2480
6: 5 And he c there do no mighty work, G1410
19 would have killed him; but she c not: G1410
7:24 no man know *it*: but he c not be hid. G1410
9:18 should cast him out; and they c not. G2480
28 privately, Why c not we cast him out? G1410
14: 8 She hath done what she c: she is come G2192
Lk 1:22 And when he came out, he c not speak G1410
5:19 And when they c not find by what *way*
6:48 that house, and c not shake it: for it G2480
8:19 and c not come at him for the press. G1410
43 physicians, neither c be healed of any, G2480
9:40 to cast him out; and they c not. G1410
13:11 and c in no wise lift up *herself*. G1410
14: 6 And they c not answer him again to G2480
19: 3 who he was; and c not for the press, G1410
48 And c not find what they might do: for G2147
20: 7 And they answered, that they c not tell G5342
26 And they c not take hold of his words G2480
Jn 9:33 If this man were not of God, he c do G1410
11:37 And some of them said, C not this G1410
12:39 Therefore they c not believe, because G1410
21:25 the world itself c not contain the books
Act 4:14 them, they c say nothing against it. G2192
11:17 what was I, that I c withstand God? G1415
13:39 c not be justified by the law of Moses. G1410
21:34 and when he c not know the certainty G1410
22:11 And when I c not see for the glory of that
25: 7 against Paul, which they c not prove. G2480
27:15 And when the ship was caught, and c G1410
43 that they which c swim should cast G1410
Ro 8: 3 For what the law c not do, in that it was G102
9: 3 For I c wish that myself were accursed
1Co 3: 1 And I, brethren, c not speak unto you G1410
13: 2 all faith, so that I c remove mountains,
2Co 3: 7 the children of Israel c not stedfastly G1410
13 children of Israel c not stedfastly look to
11: 1 Would to God ye c bear with me a little
Gal 3:21 a law given which c have given life, G1410
1Th 3: 1 Wherefore when we c no longer forbear,
5 For this cause, when I c no longer
Heb 3:19 So we see that they c not enter in G1410
6:13 because he c swear by no greater, G2192
9: 9 sacrifices, that c not make him that did G1410
12:20 (For they c not endure that which was
Rev 7: 9 which no man c number, of all nations, G1410
14: 3 and no man c learn that song but G1410

COULDEST
Jer 3: 5 spoken and done evil things as thou c. H3201
Ezk 16:28 with them, and yet c not be satisfied.
Dan 2:47 secrets, seeing thou c reveal this secret. H3202
Mk 14:37 thou? c not thou watch one hour? G2480
Jn 19:11 Jesus answered, Thou c have no power

COULTER
1Sa 13:20 and his c, and his axe, and his mattock. H855

COULTERS
1Sa 13:21 and for the c, and for the forks, and H855

COUNCIL
Ps 68:27 of Judah *and* their c, the princes of H7277
Mt 5:22 be in danger of the c: but whosoever G4892
12:14 out, and held a c against him, how they G4824
26:59 and elders, and all the c, sought false G4892
Mk 14:55 And the chief priests and all the c G4892
15: 1 and the whole c, and bound Jesus, and G4892
Lk 22:66 and led him into their c, saying, G4892
Jn 11:47 the Pharisees a c, and said, What do G4892
Act 4:15 c, they conferred among themselves, G4892
5:21 and called the c together, and all the G4892
27 the c: and the high priest asked them, G4892
34 Then stood there up one in the c, a G4892
41 the presence of the c, rejoicing that they G4892
6:12 caught him, and brought *him* to the c, G4892
15 And all that sat in the c, looking G4892
22:30 and all their c to appear, and brought G4892
23: 1 And Paul, earnestly beholding the c, G4892
6 he cried out in the c, Men *and* brethren, G4892
15 Now therefore ye with the c signify to G4892
20 to morrow into the c, as though they G4892
28 him, I brought him forth into their c: G4892

Act 24:20 doing in me, while I stood before the c, G4892
25:12 conferred with the c, answered, Hast G4824

COUNCILS
Mt 10:17 you up to the c, and they will scourge G4892
Mk 13: 9 shall deliver you up to c; and in the G4892

COUNSEL
Ex 18:19 I will give thee c, and God shall be with H3289
Nu 27:21 priest, who shall ask c for him after the
31:16 of Israel, through the c of Balaam, to H1697
Dt 32:28 For they *are* a nation void of c, neither H6098
Jos 9:14 asked not c at the mouth of the LORD.
Jdg 18: 5 And they said unto him, Ask c, we pray
20: 7 of Israel; give here your advice and c. H6098
18 of God, and asked c of God, and said,
23 even, and asked c of the LORD, saying,
1Sa 14:37 And Saul asked c of God, Shall I go down
2Sa 15:31 the c of Ahithophel into foolishness. H6098
34 thou for me defeat the c of Ahithophel. H6098
16:20 Give c among you what we shall do. H6098
23 And the c of Ahithophel, which he H6098
23 of God: so *was* all the c of Ahithophel H6098
17: 7 And Hushai said unto Absalom, The c H6098
11 Therefore I c that all Israel be generally H3289
14 men of Israel said, The c of Hushai the H6098
14 *is* better than the c of Ahithophel. For H6098
14 to defeat the good c of Ahithophel, to H6098
15 thus did Ahithophel c Absalom and the H3289
23 And when Ahithophel saw that his c H6098
20:18 c at Abel: and so they ended *the matter.*
1Ki 1:12 thee, give thee c, that thou mayest save H6098
12: 8 But he forsook the c of the old men, H6098
9 And he said unto them, What c give ye H3289
13 the old men's c that they gave him; H6098
14 And spake to them after the c of the H6098
28 Whereupon the king took c, and made H3289
2Ki 6: 8 Israel, and took c with his servants, H3289
18:20 words,) *I have* c and strength for the H6098
1Ch 10:13 and also for asking c of *one that had* a
2Ch 10: 6 And king Rehoboam took c with the H3289
6 saying, What c give ye *me* to return H3289
8 But he forsook the c which the old men H6098
8 him, and took c with the young men H3289
13 forsook the c of the old men, H6098
22: 5 He walked also after their c, and went H6098
25:16 thou made of the king's c? forbear; why H3289
16 this, and hast not hearkened unto my c. H6098
30: 2 For the king had taken c, and his H3289
23 And the whole assembly took c to keep H3289
32: 3 He took c with his princes and his H3289
Ezr 10: 3 according to the c of my lord, and of H6098
8 according to the c of the princes and H6098
Neh 4:15 had brought their c to nought, that we H6098
6: 7 therefore, and let us take c together. H3289
Job 5:13 c of the froward is carried headlong. H6098
10: 3 and shine upon the c of the wicked? H6098
12:13 strength, he hath c and understanding. H6098
18: 7 and his own c shall cast him down. H6098
21:16 the c of the wicked is far from me. H6098
22:18 but the c of the wicked is far from me. H6098
29:21 and waited, and kept silence at my c. H6098
38: 2 Who *is* this that darkeneth c by words H6098
42: 3 Who *is* he that hideth c without H6098
Ps 1: 1 walketh not in the c of the ungodly, nor H6098
2: 2 the rulers take c together, against the H3245
13: 2 How long shall I take c in my soul, H6098
14: 6 Ye have shamed the c of the poor, H6098
16: 7 hath given me c: my reins also instruct H3289
20: 4 and fulfil all thy c. H6098
31:13 while they took c together against me, H3245
33:10 The LORD bringeth the c of the H6098
11 The c of the LORD standeth for ever, H6098
55:14 We took sweet c together, *and* walked H5475
64: 2 Hide me from the secret c of the H5475
71:10 lay wait for my soul take c together, H3289
73:24 Thou shalt guide me with thy c, and H6098
83: 3 They have taken crafty c against thy H5475
106:13 his works; they waited not for his c: H6098
43 *him* with their c, and were brought low H6098
107:11 and contemned the c of the most High: H6098
Prv 1:25 But ye have set at nought all my c, and H6098
30 They would none of my c: they despised H6098
8:14 C *is* mine, and sound wisdom: I *am* H6098
11:14 Where no c *is*, the people fall: but in the H8458
12:15 but he that hearkeneth unto c *is* wise. H6098
15:22 Without c purposes are disappointed: H5475
19:20 Hear c, and receive instruction, that H6098
21 the c of the LORD, that shall stand. H6098
Prv 20: 5 C in the heart of man *is like* deep H6098
18 *Every* purpose is established by c: and H6098
21:30 understanding nor c against the LORD. H6098
24: 6 For by wise c thou shalt make thy war: H8458
27: 9 sweetness of a man's friend by hearty c. H6098
Ecc 8: 2 I *c thee* to keep the king's
Isa 5:19 see *it*: and let the c of the Holy One of H6098
7: 5 have taken evil c against thee, saying, H3289
8:10 Take c together, and it shall come to H6098
11: 2 the spirit of c and might, the spirit H6098
16: 3 Take c, execute judgment; make thy H6098
19: 3 I will destroy the c thereof: and they H6098
11 of Zoan *are* fools, the c of the wise H6098
17 because of the c of the LORD of hosts, H6098
23: 8 Who hath taken this c against Tyre, the H3289
28:29 in c, *and* excellent in working. H6098
29:15 deep to hide their c from the LORD, H6098
30: 1 LORD, that take c, but not of me; and H6098
36: 5 words) *I have* c and strength for war: H6098
40:14 With whom took he c, and *who* H3289
44:26 performeth the c of his messengers; H6098
45:21 yea, let them take c together: who hath H3289
46:10 done, saying, My c shall stand, and I H6098
11 that executeth my c from a far country: H6098
Jer 18:18 the priest, nor c from the wise, nor the H6098
23 Yet, LORD, thou knowest all their c H6098
19: 7 And I will make void the c of Judah H6098
23:18 For who hath stood in the c of the H5475
22 But if they had stood in my c, and had H5475
32:19 Great in c, and mighty in work: for H6098
38:15 thee c, wilt thou not hearken unto me? H3289
49: 7 more in Teman? is c perished from the H6098
20 Therefore hear the c of the LORD, that H6098
30 hath taken c against you, and hath H6098
50:45 Therefore hear ye the c of the LORD, H6098
Ezk 7:26 the priest, and c from the ancients. H6098
11: 2 mischief, and give wicked c in this city: H6098
Dan 2:14 Then Daniel answered with c and H5843
4:27 Wherefore, O king, let my c be H4431
Hos 4:12 My people ask c at their stocks, and
10: 6 Israel shall be ashamed of his own c. H6098
Mic 4:12 they his c: for he shall gather them H6098
Zec 6:13 c of peace shall be between them both. H6098
Mt 22:15 Then went the Pharisees, and took c G4824
27: 1 c against Jesus to put him to death: G4824
7 And they took c, and bought with them G4824
28:12 and had taken c, they gave large money G4824
Mk 3: 6 straightway took c with the Herodians G4824
Lk 7:30 lawyers rejected the c of God against G1012
23:51 (The same had not consented to the c G1012
Jn 11:53 Then from that day forth they took c G4823
18:14 Now Caiaphas was he, which gave c to G4823
Act 2:23 the determinate c and foreknowledge G1012
4:28 thy c determined before to be done. G1012
5:33 *to the heart*, and took c to slay them. G1011
38 alone: for if this c or this work be of G1012
9:23 fulfilled, the Jews took c to kill him: G4823
20:27 to declare unto you all the c of God. G1012
27:42 And the soldiers' c was to kill the G1012
Eph 1:11 all things after the c of his own will: G1012
Heb 6:17 of his c, confirmed *it* by an oath: G1012
Rev 3:18 I c thee to buy of me gold tried in the G4823

COUNSELLED
2Sa 16:23 which he c in those days, *was* as H3289
17:15 of Israel; and thus and thus have I c. H3289
21 for thus hath Ahithophel c against you. H3289
Job 26: 3 How hast thou c *him that hath* no H3289

COUNSELLOR
2Sa 15:12 Gilonite, David's c, from his city, *even* H3289
1Ch 26:14 his son, a wise c, they cast lots; and his H3289
27:32 Also Jonathan David's uncle was a c, a H3289
33 And Ahithophel *was* the king's c: and H3289
2Ch 22: 3 for his mother was his c to do wickedly. H3289
Isa 3: 3 man, and the c, and the cunning H3289
9: 6 called Wonderful, C, The mighty God, H3289
40:13 LORD, or *being* his c hath taught him? H6098
41:28 and *there was* no c, that, when I asked H3289
Mic 4: 9 no king in thee? is thy c perished? for H3289
Nah 1:11 evil against the LORD, a wicked c. H3289
Mk 15:43 Joseph of Arimathaea, an honourable c, G1010
Lk 23:50 a c; *and he was* a good man, and a just: G1010
Ro 11:34 of the Lord? or who hath been his c? G4825

COUNSELLORS
2Ch 22: 4 for they were his c after the death of his H3289
Ezr 4: 5 And hired c against them, to frustrate H3289
7:14 king, and of his seven c, to inquire H3272
Ezr 7:15 the king and his c have freely offered H3272
28 the king, and his c, and before all the H3289
8:25 the king, and his c, and his lords, and H3289
Job 3:14 With kings and c of the earth, which H3289
12:17 He leadeth c away spoiled, and maketh H3289
Ps 119:24 also *are* my delight *and* my c. H6098
Prv 11:14 but in the multitude of c *there is* safety. H3289
12:20 evil: but to the c of peace *is* joy. H3289
15:22 the multitude of c they are established. H3289
24: 6 and in multitude of c *there is* safety. H3289
Isa 1:26 the first, and thy c as at the beginning: H3289
19:11 of the wise c of Pharaoh is become H3289
Dan 3: 2 the treasurers, the c, the sheriffs, and all H1884
3 the treasurers, the c, the sheriffs, and all H1884
24 and said unto his c, Did not we cast H1907
27 and the king's c, being gathered H1907
4:36 unto me; and my c and my lords H1907
6: 7 and the princes, the c, and the captains, H1907

COUNSELS
Job 37:12 And it is turned round about by his c: H8458
Ps 5:10 fall by their own c; cast them out in the H4156
81:12 lust: *and* they walked in their own c. H4156
Prv 1: 5 understanding shall attain unto wise c: H8458
12: 5 right: *but* the c of the wicked *are* deceit. H8458
22:20 excellent things in c and knowledge, H4156
Isa 25: 1 *thy* c of old *are* faithfulness *and* truth. H6098
47:13 the multitude of thy c. Let now the H6098
Jer 7:24 ear, but walked in the c *and* in the H4156
Hos 11: 6 devour *them*, because of their own c. H4156
Mic 6:16 ye walk in their c; that I should make H4156
1Co 4: 5 make manifest the c of the hearts: and G1012

COUNT
Ex 12: 4 eating shall make your c for the lamb. H3699
Lev 19:23 food, then ye shall c the fruit thereof as
23:15 And ye shall c unto you from the H5608
25:27 Then let him c the years of the sale H2803
52 then he shall c with him, *and* according H2803
Nu 23:10 Who can c the dust of Jacob, and the H4487
1Sa 1:16 C not thine handmaid for a daughter of H5414
Job 19:15 and my maids, c me for a stranger: I H2803
31: 4 Doth not he see my ways, and c all my H5608
Ps 87: 6 The LORD shall c, when he writeth up H5608
139:18 *If* I should c them, they are more in H5608
22 I hate them with perfect hatred: I c H1961
Mic 6:11 Shall I c *them* pure with the wicked
Act 20:24 move me, neither c I my life dear unto G2192
Php 3: 8 Yea doubtless, and I c all things *but* G2233
8 c them *but* dung, that I may win Christ, G2233
13 Brethren, I c not myself to have G3049
2Th 1:11 that our God would c you worthy of *this* G515
3:15 Yet c *him* not as an enemy, but G2233
1Ti 6: 1 are under the yoke c their own masters G2233
Phlm 17 If thou c me therefore a partner, G2192
Jas 1: 2 My brethren, c it all joy when ye fall G2233
5:11 Behold, we c them happy which G3106
2Pt 2:13 *as* they that c it pleasure to riot in G2233
3: 9 as some men c slackness; but is G2233
Rev 13:18 understanding c the number of the G5585

COUNTED
Gen 15: 6 And he believed in the LORD; and he c H2803
30:33 the sheep, that shall be c stolen with me.
31:15 Are we not c of him strangers? for he H2803
Ex 38:21 testimony, as it was c, according to the H6485
Lev 25:31 them shall be c as the fields of the H2803
Nu 18:30 it, then it shall be c unto the Levites as H2803
Jos 13: 3 *which* is c to the Canaanite: five H2803
1Ki 1:21 my son Solomon shall be c offenders.
3: 8 be numbered nor c for multitude. H5608
1Ch 21: 6 But Levi and Benjamin c he not among H6485
23:24 as they were c by number of names H6485
Neh 13:13 for they were c faithful, and their office H2803
Job 18: 3 Wherefore are we c as beasts, *and* H2803
41:29 Darts are c as stubble: he laugheth at H2803
Ps 44:22 we are c as sheep for the slaughter. H2803
88: 4 I am c with them that go down into the H2803
106:31 And that was c unto him for H2803
Prv 17:28 holdeth his peace, is c wise: *and* he that H2803
27:14 morning, it shall be c a curse to him. H2803
Isa 5:28 hoofs shall be c like flint, and their H2803
32:15 and the fruitful field be c for a forest. H2803
33:18 receiver? where *is* he that c the towers? H5608
40:15 a bucket, and are c as the small dust of H2803
17 c to him less than nothing, and vanity. H2803
Hos 8:12 law, *but* they were c as a strange thing. H2803
Mt 14: 5 because they c him as a prophet. G2192
Mk 11:32 c John, that he was a prophet indeed. G2192

Act 5:41 c worthy to suffer shame for his name. G2661
19:19 all *men*: and they c the price of them, G4860
Ro 2:26 uncircumcision be c for circumcision? G3049
4: 3 it was c unto him for righteousness. G3049
5 his faith is c for righteousness. G3049
9: 8 of the promise are c for the seed. G3049
Php 3: 7 gain to me, those I c loss for Christ. G2233
2Th 1: 5 God, that ye may be c worthy of the G2661
1Ti 1:12 me, for that he c me faithful, putting G2233
5:17 Let the elders that rule well be c worthy G515
Heb 3: 3 For this *man* was c worthy of more glory G515
7: 6 But he whose descent is not c from G1075
10:29 Son of God, and hath c the blood of the G2233

COUNTENANCE
Gen 4: 5 Cain was very wroth, and his c fell. H6440
6 art thou wroth? and why is thy c fallen? H6440
31: 2 And Jacob beheld the c of Laban, and, H6440
5 them, I see your father's c, that it *is* not H6440
Ex 23: 3 Neither shalt thou c a poor man in his H1921
Nu 6:26 The LORD lift up his c upon thee, and H6440
Dt 28:50 A nation of fierce c, which shall not H6440
Jdg 13: 6 came unto me, and his c *was* like the H4758
6 *was* like the c of an angel of God, H4758
1Sa 1:18 did eat, and her c was no more *sad*. H6440
16: 7 Look not on his c, or on the height of his H4758
12 of a beautiful c, and goodly to look to. H5869
17:42 *but* a youth, and ruddy, and of a fair c. H4758
25: 3 and of a beautiful c: but the man *was* H8389
2Sa 14:27 Tamar: she was a woman of a fair c. H4758
2Ki 8:11 And he settled his c stedfastly, until he H6440
Neh 2: 2 me, Why *is* thy c sad, seeing thou *art* H6440
3 should not my c be sad, when the city, H6440
Job 14:20 changest his c, and sendest him away. H6440
29:24 the light of my c they cast not down. H6440
Ps 4: 6 lift thou up the light of thy c upon us. H6440
10: 4 The wicked, through the pride of his c, H639
11: 7 his c doth behold the upright. H6440
21: 6 made him exceeding glad with thy c. H6440
42: 5 shall yet praise him *for* the help of his c. H6440
11 *who is* the health of my c, and my God. H6440
43: 5 *who is* the health of my c, and my God. H6440
44: 3 the light of thy c, because thou hadst H6440
80:16 down: they perish at the rebuke of thy c. H6440
89:15 shall walk, O LORD, in the light of thy c. H6440
90: 8 thee, our secret *sins* in the light of thy c. H6440
Prv 15:13 A merry heart maketh a cheerful c: but H6440
16:15 In the light of the king's c *is* life; and H6440
25:23 *doth* an angry c a backbiting tongue. H6440
27:17 a man sharpeneth the c of his friend. H6440
Ecc 7: 3 of the c the heart is made better. H6440
Song 2:14 let me see thy c, let me hear thy voice; H4758
14 sweet *is* thy voice, and thy c *is* comely. H4758
5:15 of fine gold: his c *is* as Lebanon, H4758
Isa 3: 9 The shew of their c doth witness H6440
Ezk 27:35 afraid, they shall be troubled in *their* c. H6440
Dan 1:13 thee, and the c of the children that H4758
5: 6 Then the king's c was changed, and his H2122
9 troubled, and his c was changed in H2122
10 trouble thee, nor let thy c be changed: H2122
7:28 me, and my c changed in me: but H2122
8:23 a king of fierce c, and understanding H6440
Mt 6:16 of a sad c: for they disfigure their G4659
28: 3 His c was like lightning, and his G2397
Lk 9:29 And as he prayed, the fashion of his c G4383
Act 2:28 shalt make me full of joy with thy c. G4383
2Co 3: 7 his c; which *glory* was to be done away: G4383
Rev 1:16 sword: and his c *was* as the sun shineth G3799

COUNTENANCES
Dan 1:13 Then let our c be looked upon before H4758
15 And at the end of ten days their c H4758

COUNTERVAIL
Est 7: 4 enemy could not c the king's damage. H7737

COUNTETH
Job 19:11 c me unto him as *one of* his enemies. H2803
33:10 against me, he c me for his enemy, H2803
Lk 14:28 down first, and c the cost, whether he G5585

COUNTING
Ecc 7:27 c one by one, to find out the account:

COUNTRIES
Gen 10:20 tongues, in their c, *and* in their nations. H776
26: 3 I will give all these c, and I will perform H776
4 thy seed all these c; and in thy seed shall H776
41:57 And all c came into Egypt to Joseph for H776
Jos 13:32 These *are the* c which Moses did
14: 1 And these *are the* c which the children of
17:11 of Megiddo and her towns, *even* three c. H5316
2Ki 18:35 Who *are* they among all the gods of the c, H776
1Ch 22: 5 throughout all c: I will *therefore* now H776
29:30 Israel, and over all the kingdoms of the c. H776
2Ch 11:23 throughout all the c of Judah and H776
12: 8 and the service of the kingdoms of the c. H776
15: 5 *were* upon all the inhabitants of the c. H776
20:29 the kingdoms of *those* c, when they had H776
34:33 out of all the c that *pertained* to the H776
Ezr 3: 3 of the people of those c: and they offered H776
4:20 have ruled over all c beyond the river;
Ps 110: 6 he shall wound the heads over many c. H776
Isa 8: 9 ear, all ye of far c: gird yourselves, and H776
37:18 laid waste all the nations, and their c, H776
Jer 23: 3 of my flock out of all c whither I have H776
8 and from all c whither I had driven H776
28: 8 both against many c, and against great H776
32:37 Behold, I will gather them out of all c, H776
40:11 that *were* in all the c, heard that the king H776
Ezk 5: 5 nations and c *that are* round about her. H776
6 more than the c that *are* round about H776
6: 8 when ye shall be scattered through the c. H776
11:16 them among the c, yet will I be to them H776
16 in the c where they shall come. H776
17 you out of the c where ye have been H776
12:15 the nations, and disperse them in the c. H776
20:23 and disperse them through the c; H776
32 of the c, to serve wood and stone. H776
34 you out of the c wherein ye are scattered, H776
41 you out of the c wherein ye have been H776
22: 4 unto the heathen, and a mocking to all c. H776
15 disperse thee in the c, and will consume H776
25: 7 to perish out of the c: I will destroy thee; H776
29:12 in the midst of the c *that are* desolate, H776
12 and will disperse them through the c. H776
30: 7 in the midst of the c *that are* desolate, H776
23 and will disperse them through the c. H776
26 them among the c; and they shall know H776
32: 9 into the c which thou hast not known. H776
34:13 them from the c, and will bring them H776
35:10 and these two c shall be mine, and we H776
36:19 through the c: according to their way H776
24 c, and will bring you into your own land. H776
Dan 9: 7 off, through all the c whither thou hast H776
11:40 the c, and shall overflow and pass over. H776
41 land, and many c shall be overthrown: H776
42 c: and the land of Egypt shall not escape. H776
Zec 10: 9 me in far c; and they shall live with H4801
Lk 21:21 them that are in the c enter thereinto. G5561

COUNTRY
Gen 12: 1 Get thee out of thy c, and from thy H776
14: 7 and smote all the c of the Amalekites, H7704
19:28 the c went up as the smoke of a furnace. H776
20: 1 toward the south c, and dwelled between H776
24: 4 But thou shalt go unto my c, and to my H776
62 Lahai-roi; for he dwelt in the south c. H776
25: 6 he yet lived, eastward, unto the east c. H776
29:26 be so done in our c, to give the younger H4725
30:25 go unto mine own place, and to my c. H776
32: 3 unto the land of Seir, the c of Edom. H7704
9 Return unto thy c, and to thy kindred, H776
34: 2 prince of the c, saw her, he took her, H776
36: 6 the c from the face of his brother Jacob. H776
42:30 to us, and took us for spies of the c. H776
33 And the man, the lord of the c, said unto H776
47:27 of Egypt, in the c of Goshen; and they H776
Lev 16:29 *it be* one of your own c, or a stranger that H249
17:15 *it be* one of your own c, or a stranger, he H249
24:22 your own c: for I *am* the LORD your God. H249
25:31 as the fields of the c: they may be H776
Nu 15:13 All that are born of the c shall do these H249
20:17 Let us pass, I pray thee, through thy c: we H776
21:20 that *is* in the c of Moab, to the top H7704
32: 4 *Even* the c which the LORD smote before H776
33 *even* the cities of the c round about. H776
Dt 3:14 Jair the son of Manasseh took all the c H2256
4:43 in the plain c, of the Reubenites; and H776
26: 3 I am come unto the c which the LORD H776
Jos 2: 2 the children of Israel to search out the c. H776
3 for they be come to search out all the c. H776
24 of the c do faint because of us. H776
6:22 had spied out the c, Go into the harlot's H776
27 his fame was *noised* throughout all the c. H776
7: 2 c. And the men went up and viewed Ai. H776
9: 6 We be come from a far c: now therefore H776
9 From a very far c thy servants are come H776
Jos 9:11 inhabitants of our c spake to us, saying, H776
10:40 So Joshua smote all the c of the hills, and H776
41 all the c of Goshen, even unto Gibeon. H776
11:16 and all the south c, and all the land of H5045
12: 7 And these *are* the kings of the c which H776
8 and in the south c; the Hittites, the H5045
13: 6 All the inhabitants of the hill c from H2022
21 *were* dukes of Sihon, dwelling in the c. H776
17:15 thee up to the wood c, and cut down for
19:51 So they made an end of dividing the c. H776
21:11 *is* Hebron, in the hill c of Judah, with the
22: 9 to go unto the c of Gilead, to the land H776
Jdg 8:28 no more. And the c was in quietness H776
11:21 of the Amorites, the inhabitants of that c. H776
12:12 buried in Aijalon in the c of Zebulun. H776
16:24 of our c, which slew many of us. H776
18:14 went to spy out the c of Laish, and said H776
20: 6 throughout all the c of the inheritance H7704
Ru 1: 1 to sojourn in the c of Moab, he, and his H7704
2 the c of Moab, and continued there. H7704
6 return from the c of Moab: for she had H7704
6 had heard in the c of Moab how that H7704
22 out of the c of Moab: and they came H7704
2: 6 back with Naomi out of the c of Moab: H7704
4: 3 again out of the c of Moab, selleth a H7704
1Sa 6: 1 And the ark of the LORD was in the c of H7704
18 cities, and of c villages, even unto the H6521
14:21 the camp *from the* c round about, even
27: 5 in some town in the c, that I may dwell H7704
7 And the time that David dwelt in the c H7704
11 he dwelleth in the c of the Philistines. H7704
2Sa 15:23 And all the c wept with a loud voice, and H776
18: 8 over the face of all the c: and the wood H776
21:14 son buried they in the c of Benjamin in H776
1Ki 4:19 Geber the son of Uri *was* in the c of H776
19 of Gilead, *in* the c of Sihon king of the H776
30 of the east c, and all the wisdom of Egypt.
8:41 out of a far c for thy name's sake; H776
10:13 went to her own c, she and her servants. H776
15 of Arabia, and of the governors of the c. H776
11:21 me depart, that I may go to mine own c. H776
22 to go to thine own c? And he answered, H776
20:27 flocks of kids; but the Syrians filled the c. H776
22:36 to his city, and every man to his own c. H776
2Ki 3:20 of Edom, and the c was filled with water. H776
24 smiting the Moabites, even in *their* c.
18:35 delivered their c out of mine hand, that H776
20:14 come from a far c, *even* from Babylon. H776
1Ch 8: 8 And Shaharaim begat *children* in the c H7704
20: 1 army, and wasted the c of the children of H776
2Ch 6:32 is come from a far c for thy great name's H776
9:14 c brought gold and silver to Solomon. H776
26:10 both in the low c, and in the plains: H8219
28:18 cities of the low c, and of the south of H8219
30:10 city to city through the c of Ephraim and H776
Neh 12:28 both out of the plain c round about
Prv 25:25 thirsty soul, so *is* good news from a far c. H776
Isa 1: 7 Your c *is* desolate, your cities *are* burned H776
13: 5 They come from a far c, from the end of H776
22:18 a ball into a large c: there shalt thou die, H776
39: 3 a far c unto me, *even* from Babylon. H776
46:11 counsel from a far c: yea, I have spoken H776
Jer 2: 7 And I brought you into a plentiful c, to H776
4:16 come from a far c, and give out their H776
6:20 cane from a far c? your burnt offerings H776
22 from the north c, and a great nation shall H776
8:19 that dwell in a far c: *Is* not the LORD in H776
10:22 out of the north c, to make the cities of H776
22:10 shall return no more, nor see his native c. H776
26 thee, into another c, where ye were not H776
23: 8 out of the north c, and from all countries H776
31: 8 from the north c, and gather them from H776
32: 8 which *is* in the c of Benjamin: for the H776
44: 1 at Noph, and in the c of Pathros, saying, H776
46:10 in the north c by the river Euphrates. H776
47: 4 the remnant of the c of Caphtor. H339
48:21 And judgment is come upon the plain c; H776
50: 9 from the north c: and they shall set H776
51: 9 one into his own c: for her judgment H776
Ezk 20:38 forth out of the c where they sojourn, H776
42 of Israel, into the c *for* the which I lifted H776
25: 9 the glory of the c, Beth-jeshimoth, H776
32:15 desolate, and the c shall be destitute of H776
34:13 and in all the inhabited places of the c. H776
47: 8 toward the east c, and go down into the H1552
22 you as born in the c among the children H249
Hos 12:12 And Jacob fled into the c of Syria, and H7704
Jna 1: 8 *is* thy c? and of what people *art* thou? H776
4: 2 I was yet in my c? Therefore I fled before H127

Zec 6: 6 forth into the north **c**; and the white go H776
6 the grisled go forth toward the south **c**. H776
8 go toward the north **c** have quieted my H776
8 have quieted my spirit in the north **c**. H776
8: 7 the east **c**, and from the west country; H776
7 the east country, and from the west **c**; H776
Mt 2:12 departed into their own **c** another way. *G5561*
8:28 other side into the **c** of the Gergesenes, *G5561*
9:31 spread abroad his fame in all that **c**. *G1093*
13:54 And when he was come into his own **c**, *G3968*
57 save in his own **c**, and in his own house. *G3968*
14:35 out into all that **c** round about, and *G4066*
21:33 to husbandmen, and went into a far **c**: *G589*
25:14 travelling into a far **c**, *who* called his own *G589*
Mk 5: 1 of the sea, into the **c** of the Gadarenes. *G5561*
10 would not send them away out of the **c**. *G5561*
14 the city, and in the **c**. And they went out *G68*
6: 1 his own **c**; and his disciples follow him. *G3968*
4 but in his own **c**, and among his own *G3968*
36 may go into the **c** round about, and into *G68*
56 or cities, or **c**, they laid the sick in *G68*
12: 1 to husbandmen, and went into a far **c**. *G589*
15:21 by, coming out of the **c**, the father of *G68*
16:12 as they walked, and went into the **c**. *G68*
Lk 1:39 the hill **c** with haste, into a city of Juda; *G3714*
65 throughout all the hill **c** of Judaea. *G3714*
2: 8 And there were in the same **c** *G5561*
3: 3 And he came into all the **c** about *G4066*
4:23 in Capernaum, do also here in thy **c**. *G3968*
24 No prophet is accepted in his own **c**. *G3968*
37 into every place of the **c** round about. *G4066*
8:26 And they arrived at the **c** of the *G5561*
34 went and told *it* in the city and in the **c**. *G68*
37 Then the whole multitude of the **c** of *G4066*
9:12 into the towns and **c** round about, and *G68*
15:13 journey into a far **c**, and there wasted *G5561*
15 to a citizen of that **c**; and he sent him *G5561*
19:12 went into a far **c** to receive for himself *G5561*
20: 9 and went into a far **c** for a long time. *G589*
23:26 coming out of the **c**, and on him they laid *G68*
Jn 4:44 a prophet hath no honour in his own **c**. *G3968*
11:54 thence unto a **c** near to the wilderness, *G5561*
55 many went out of the **c** up to Jerusalem *G5561*
Act 4:36 a Levite, *and* of the **c** of Cyprus, *G1085*
7: 3 him, Get thee out of thy **c**, and from thy *G1093*
12:20 **c** was nourished by the king's *country*. *G5561*
20 country was nourished by the king's **c**. *G5561*
13: 7 Which was with the deputy of the **c**, *G446*
18:23 and went over *all* the **c** of Galatia and *G5561*
27:27 deemed that they drew near to some **c**; *G5561*
Heb 11: 9 as *in* a strange **c**, dwelling in tabernacles *G245*
14 things declare plainly that they seek a **c**. *G3968*
15 been mindful of that *c* from whence they
16 But now they desire a better *c*, that is, an

COUNTRYMEN
2Co 11:26 by *mine own* **c**, *in* perils by the heathen, *G1085*
1Th 2:14 own **c**, even as they *have* of the Jews: *G4853*

COUPLE
Ex 26: 6 of gold, and **c** the curtains together H2266
9 And thou shalt **c** five curtains by H2266
11 **c** the tent together, that it may be one. H2266
36:18 And he made fifty taches *of* brass to **c** H2266
39: 4 They made shoulderpieces for it, to **c** *it* H2266
Jdg 19: 3 with him, and a **c** of asses: and she H6776
2Sa 13: 6 and make me a **c** of cakes in my sight, H8147
16: 1 met him, with a **c** of asses saddled, and H6776
Isa 21: 7 And he saw a chariot *with* a **c** of H6776
9 of men, *with* a **c** of horsemen. And he H6776

COUPLED
Ex 26: 3 The five curtains shall be **c** together H2266
3 five curtains *shall be* **c** one to another. H2266
24 And they shall be **c** together beneath, H8382
24 and they shall be **c** together above the H8382
36:10 And he **c** the five curtains one unto H2266
10 five curtains he **c** one unto another. H2266
13 And he made fifty taches of gold, and **c** H2266
16 And he **c** five curtains by themselves, H2266
29 And they were **c** beneath, and coupled H8382
29 And they were coupled beneath, and **c** H8382
39: 4 by the two edges was it **c** together. H2266
1Pt 3: 2 your chaste conversation *c* with fear.

COUPLETH
Ex 26:10 edge of the curtain which **c** the second. H2279
36:17 edge of the curtain which **c** the second. H2279

COUPLING
Ex 26: 4 the selvedge in the **c**; and likewise shalt H2279
4 *another* curtain, in the **c** of the second. H4225
5 that *is* in the **c** of the second; that the H4225
10 *is* outmost in the **c**, and fifty loops in H2279
28:27 against the *other* **c** thereof, above the H4225
36:11 the selvedge in the **c**: likewise he made H4225
11 *another* curtain, in the **c** of the second. H4225
12 which *was* in the **c** of the second: the H4225
17 of the curtain in the **c**, and fifty loops H4225
39:20 against the *other* **c** thereof, above the H4225

COUPLINGS
2Ch 34:11 stone, and timber for **c**, and to floor the H4226

COURAGE
Nu 13:20 And be ye of good **c**, and bring of the H2388
Dt 31: 6 Be strong and of a good **c**, fear not, nor H553
7 and of a good **c**: for thou must go with H553
23 and of a good **c**: for thou shalt bring H553
Jos 1: 6 Be strong and of a good **c**: for unto this H553
9 and of a good **c**; be not afraid, neither H553
18 to death: only be strong and of a good **c**. H553
2:11 there remain any more **c** in any man, H7307
10:25 be strong and of good **c**: for thus shall the H553
2Sa 10:12 Be of good **c**, and let us play the men for H2388
1Ch 19:13 Be of good **c**, and let us behave H2388
22:13 of good **c**; dread not, nor be dismayed. H553
28:20 strong and of good **c**, and do *it:* fear not, H553
2Ch 15: 8 prophet, he took **c**, and put away the H2388
Ezr 10: 4 *will be* with thee: be of good **c**, and do *it*. H2388
Ps 27:14 Wait on the LORD: be of good **c**, and he H2388
31:24 Be of good **c**, and he shall strengthen H2388
Isa 41: 6 *one* said to his brother, Be of good **c**. H2388
Dan 11:25 And he shall stir up his power and his **c** H3824
Act 28:15 Paul saw, he thanked God, and took **c**. *G2294*

COURAGEOUS
Jos 1: 7 Only be thou strong and very **c**, that thou H553
23: 6 Be ye therefore very **c** to keep and to do H2388
2Sa 13:28 I commanded you? be **c**, and be valiant. H2388
2Ch 32: 7 Be strong and **c**, be not afraid nor H553
Am 2:16 And *he that is* **c** among the mighty H3820

COURAGEOUSLY
2Ch 19:11 **c**, and the LORD shall be with the good. H2388

COURSE
1Ch 27: 1 every **c** *were* twenty and four thousand. H4256
2 Over the first **c** for the first month *was* H4256
2 his **c** *were* twenty and four thousand. H4256
4 And over the **c** of the second month H4256
4 and of his **c** *was* Mikloth also the H4256
4 the ruler: in his **c** likewise *were* twenty H4256
5 his **c** *were* twenty and four thousand. H4256
6 and in his **c** *was* Ammizabad his son. H4256
7 his **c** *were* twenty and four thousand. H4256
8 his **c** *were* twenty and four thousand. H4256
9 his **c** *were* twenty and four thousand. H4256
10 his **c** *were* twenty and four thousand. H4256
11 his **c** *were* twenty and four thousand. H4256
12 his **c** *were* twenty and four thousand. H4256
13 his **c** *were* twenty and four thousand. H4256
14 his **c** *were* twenty and four thousand. H4256
15 his **c** *were* twenty and four thousand. H4256
28: 1 to the king by **c**, and the captains over H4256
2Ch 5:11 sanctified, *and* did not *then* wait by **c**: H4256
Ezr 3:11 And they sang together by **c** in praising
Ps 82: 5 foundations of the earth are out of **c**. H4131
Jer 8: 6 **c**, as the horse rusheth into the battle. H4794
23:10 **c** is evil, and their force *is* not right. H4794
Lk 1: 5 Zacharias, of the **c** of Abia: and his wife *G2183*
8 office before God in the order of his **c**, *G2183*
Act 13:25 And as John fulfilled his **c**, he said, *G1408*
16:11 with a straight **c** to Samothracia, and *G2113*
20:24 I might finish my **c** with joy, and the *G1408*
21: 1 with a straight **c** unto Coos, and the *G2113*
7 And when we had finished *our* **c** from *G4144*
1Co 14:27 and *that* by **c**; and let one interpret. *G3313*
Eph 2: 2 walked according to the **c** of this world, *G165*
2Th 3: 1 may have *free* **c**, and be glorified, even *G5143*
2Ti 4: 7 finished *my* **c**, I have kept the faith: *G1408*
Jas 3: 6 **c** of nature; and it is set on fire of hell. *G5164*

COURSES
Jdg 5:20 stars in their **c** fought against Sisera. H4546
1Ki 5:14 a month by **c**: a month they were in H2487
1Ch 23: 6 And David divided them into **c** among H4256
27: 1 any matter of the **c**, which came in and H4256
28:13 Also for the **c** of the priests and the H4256
21 And, behold, the **c** of the priests and H4256
2Ch 8:14 his father, the **c** of the priests to their H4256
14 also by their **c** at every gate: for so H4256
23: 8 Jehoiada the priest dismissed not the **c**. H4256
31: 2 And Hezekiah appointed the **c** of the H4256
2 the Levites after their **c**, every man H4256
15 by **c**, as well to the great as to the small: H4256
16 in their charges according to their **c**; H4256
17 and upward, in their charges by their **c**; H4256
35: 4 fathers, after your **c**, according to the H4256
10 the Levites in their **c**, according to the H4256
Ezr 6:18 the Levites in their **c**, for the service of H4255
Isa 44: 4 the grass, as willows by the water **c**. H2988

COURT
Ex 27: 9 And thou shalt make the **c** of the H2691
9 hangings for the **c** *of* fine twined linen H2691
12 And *for* the breadth of the **c** on the west H2691
13 And the breadth of the **c** on the east H2691
16 And for the gate of the **c** *shall be* an H2691
17 All the pillars round about the **c** *shall* H2691
18 The length of the **c** *shall be* an hundred H2691
19 all the pins of the **c**, *shall be of* brass. H2691
35:17 The hangings of the **c**, his pillars, and H2691
17 and the hanging for the door of the **c**, H2691
18 and the pins of the **c**, and their cords, H2691
38: 9 And he made the **c**: on the south side H2691
9 hangings of the **c** *were of* fine twined H2691
15 And for the other side of the **c** gate, on H2691
16 All the hangings of the **c** round about H2691
17 pillars of the **c** *were* filleted with silver. H2691
18 And the hanging for the gate of the **c** H2691
18 answerable to the hangings of the **c**. H2691
20 of the **c** round about, *were of* brass. H2691
31 And the sockets of the **c** round about, H2691
31 the sockets of the **c** gate, and all the H2691
31 and all the pins of the **c** round about. H2691
39:40 The hangings of the **c**, his pillars, and H2691
40 hanging for the **c** gate, his cords, and H2691
40: 8 And thou shalt set up the **c** round H2691
8 and hang up the hanging at the **c** gate. H2691
33 And he reared up the **c** round about the H2691
33 the **c** gate. So Moses finished the work. H2691
Lev 6:16 holy place; in the **c** of the tabernacle of H2691
26 **c** of the tabernacle of the congregation. H2691
Nu 3:26 And the hangings of the **c**, and the H2691
26 for the door of the **c**, which *is* by the H2691
37 And the pillars of the **c** round about, H2691
4:26 And the hangings of the **c**, and the H2691
26 door of the gate of the **c**, which *is* by the H2691
32 And the pillars of the **c** round about, H2691
2Sa 17:18 a well in his **c**; whither they went down. H2691
1Ki 6:36 And he built the inner **c** with three H2691
7: 8 dwelt *had* another **c** within the porch, H2691
9 *so* on the outside toward the great **c**. H2691
12 And the great **c** round about *was* with H2691
12 both for the inner **c** of the house of the H2691
8:64 the middle of the **c** that *was* before the H2691
2Ki 20: 4 into the middle **c**, that the word of the H5892
2Ch 4: 9 Furthermore he made the **c** of the H2691
9 and the great **c**, and doors for the court, H5835
9 and doors for the **c**, and overlaid the H5835
6:13 it in the midst of the **c**: and upon it he H5835
7: 7 the middle of the **c** that *was* before the H2691
20: 5 house of the LORD, before the new **c**, H2691
24:21 king in the **c** of the house of the LORD. H2691
29:16 the LORD into the **c** of the house of the H2691
Neh 3:25 that *was* by the **c** of the prison. After H2691
Est 1: 5 the **c** of the garden of the king's palace; H2691
2:11 day before the **c** of the women's house, H2691
4:11 king into the inner **c**, who is not called, H2691
5: 1 stood in the inner **c** of the king's house, H2691
2 standing in the **c**, *that* she obtained H2691
6: 4 And the king said, Who *is* in the **c**? Now H2691
4 into the outward **c** of the king's house, H2691
5 **c**. And the king said, Let him come in. H2691
Isa 34:13 habitation of dragons, *and* a **c** for owls. H2681
Jer 19:14 he stood in the **c** of the LORD's house; H2691
26: 2 Thus saith the LORD; Stand in the **c** of H2691
32: 2 was shut up in the **c** of the prison, H2691
8 son came to me in the **c** of the prison H2691
12 the Jews that sat in the **c** of the prison. H2691
33: 1 shut up in the **c** of the prison, saying, H2691
36:10 in the higher **c**, at the entry of the new H2691
20 And they went in to the king into the **c**, H2691
37:21 Jeremiah into the **c** of the prison, and H2691
21 remained in the **c** of the prison. H2691
38: 6 that *was* in the **c** of the prison: and they H2691

Jer 38:13 remained in the **c** of the prison. H2691
28 So Jeremiah abode in the **c** of the H2691
39:14 Jeremiah out of the **c** of the prison, and H2691
15 shut up in the **c** of the prison, saying, H2691
Ezk 8: 7 And he brought me to the door of the **c**; H2691
16 And he brought me into the inner **c** of H2691
10: 3 went in; and the cloud filled the inner **c**. H2691
4 with the cloud, and the **c** was full of the H2691
5 *even* to the outer **c**, as the voice of the H2691
40:14 the post of the **c** round about the gate. H2691
17 Then brought he me into the outward **c**, H2691
17 made for the **c** round about: thirty H2691
19 of the inner **c** without, an hundred H2691
20 And the gate of the outward **c** that H2691
23 And the gate of the inner **c** *was* over H2691
27 And *there was* a gate in the inner **c** H2691
28 And he brought me to the inner **c** by H2691
31 toward the utter **c**; and palm trees *were* H2691
32 And he brought me into the inner **c** H2691
34 the outward **c**; and palm trees *were* H2691
37 toward the utter **c**; and palm trees *were* H2691
44 in the inner **c**, which *was* at the side H2691
47 So he measured the **c**, an hundred H2691
41:15 inner temple, and the porches of the **c**; H2691
42: 1 forth into the utter **c**, the way toward H2691
3 *were* for the inner **c**, and over against H2691
3 *was* for the utter **c**, *was* gallery against H2691
7 toward the utter **c** on the forepart of H2691
8 *were* in the utter **c** *was* fifty cubits: and, H2691
9 as one goeth into them from the utter **c**. H2691
10 of the wall of the **c** toward the east, H2691
14 into the utter **c**, but there they shall H2691
43: 5 me into the inner **c**; and, behold, the H2691
44:17 the gates of the inner **c**, they shall be H2691
17 in the gates of the inner **c**, and within. H2691
19 And when they go forth into the utter **c**, H2691
19 *even* into the utter **c** to the people, they H2691
21 wine, when they enter into the inner **c**. H2691
27 unto the inner **c**, to minister in the H2691
45:19 upon the posts of the gate of the inner **c**. H2691
46: 1 gate of the inner **c** that looketh toward H2691
20 into the utter **c**, to sanctify the people. H2691
21 forth into the utter **c**, and caused me to H2691
21 the four corners of the **c**; and, behold, in H2691
21 every corner of the **c** *there was* a court. H2691
21 every corner of the court *there was* a **c**. H2691
22 In the four corners of the **c** *there were* H2691
Am 7:13 the king's chapel, and it *is* the king's **c**. H1004
Rev 11: 2 But the **c** which is without the temple *G833*

COURTEOUS
1Pt 3: 8 love as brethren, *be* pitiful, *be* **c**: *G5391*

COURTEOUSLY
Act 27: 3 Sidon. And Julius **c** entreated Paul, and *G5364*
28: 7 received us, and lodged us three days **c**. *G5390*

COURTS
2Ki 21: 5 in the two **c** of the house of the LORD. H2691
23:12 made in the two **c** of the house of the H2691
1Ch 23:28 of the LORD, in the **c**, and in the H2691
28: 6 my house and my **c**: for I have chosen H2691
12 by the spirit, of the **c** of the house of the H2691
2Ch 23: 5 *be* in the **c** of the house of the LORD. H2691
33: 5 in the two **c** of the house of the LORD. H2691
Neh 8:16 and in their **c**, and in the courts of H2691
16 courts, and in the **c** of the house of H2691
13: 7 a chamber in the **c** of the house of God. H2691
Ps 65: 4 may dwell in thy **c**: we shall be satisfied H2691
84: 2 even fainteth for the **c** of the LORD: my H2691
10 For a day in thy **c** *is* better than a H2691
92:13 LORD shall flourish in the **c** of our God. H2691
96: 8 bring an offering, and come into his **c**. H2691
100: 4 *and* into his **c** with praise: be thankful H2691
116:19 In the **c** of the LORD'S house, in the H2691
135: 2 LORD, in the **c** of the house of our God, H2691
Isa 1:12 this at your hand, to tread my **c**? H2691
62: 9 shall drink it in the **c** of my holiness. H2691
Ezk 9: 7 house, and fill the **c** with the slain: go H2691
42: 6 as the pillars of the **c**: therefore *the* H2691
46:22 court *there were* **c** joined of forty *cubits* H2691
Zec 3: 7 shalt also keep my **c**, and I will give thee H2691
Lk 7:25 and live delicately, are in kings' **c**.

COUSIN
Lk 1:36 And, behold, thy **c** Elisabeth, she hath *G4773*

COUSINS
Lk 1:58 And her neighbours and her **c** heard *G4773*

COVENANT
Gen 6:18 But with thee will I establish my **c**; and H1285
9: 9 And I, behold, I establish my **c** with H1285
11 And I will establish my **c** with you; H1285
12 And God said, This *is* the token of the **c** H1285
13 token of a **c** between me and the earth. H1285
15 And I will remember my **c**, which *is* H1285
16 the everlasting **c** between God and H1285
17 This *is* the token of the **c**, which I have H1285
15:18 In the same day the LORD made a **c** H1285
17: 2 And I will make my **c** between me and H1285
4 As for me, behold, my **c** *is* with thee, H1285
7 And I will establish my **c** between me H1285
7 for an everlasting **c**, to be a God unto H1285
9 shalt keep my **c** therefore, thou, and H1285
10 This *is* my **c**, which ye shall keep, H1285
11 be a token of the **c** betwixt me and you. H1285
13 and my **c** shall be in your flesh H1285
13 be in your flesh for an everlasting **c**. H1285
14 from his people; he hath broken my **c**. H1285
19 I will establish my **c** with him for an H1285
19 **c**, *and* with his seed after him. H1285
21 But my **c** will I establish with Isaac, H1285
21:27 Abimelech; and both of them made a **c**. H1285
32 Thus they made a **c** at Beer-sheba: then H1285
26:28 and thee, and let us make a **c** with thee; H1285
31:44 let us make a **c**, I and thou; and let it H1285
Ex 2:24 remembered his **c** with Abraham, with H1285
6: 4 And I have also established my **c** with H1285
5 bondage; and I have remembered my **c**. H1285
19: 5 and keep my **c**, then ye shall be a H1285
23:32 Thou shalt make no **c** with them, nor H1285
24: 7 And he took the book of the **c**, and read H1285
8 the blood of the **c**, which the LORD hath H1285
31:16 their generations, *for* a perpetual **c**. H1285
34:10 And he said, Behold, I make a **c**: before H1285
12 Take heed to thyself, lest thou make a **c** H1285
15 Lest thou make a **c** with the H1285
27 made a **c** with thee and with Israel. H1285
28 words of the **c**, the ten commandments. H1285
Lev 2:13 the salt of the **c** of thy God to be lacking H1285
24: 8 children of Israel by an everlasting **c**. H1285
26: 9 you, and establish my **c** with you. H1285
15 *but* that ye break my **c**: H1285
25 the quarrel of *my* **c**: and when ye are H1285
42 Then will I remember my **c** with Jacob, H1285
42 and also my **c** with Isaac, and also H1285
42 and also my **c** with Abraham will H1285
44 and to break my **c** with them: for I *am* H1285
45 remember the **c** of their ancestors, H1285
Nu 10:33 and the ark of the **c** of the LORD went H1285
14:44 the ark of the **c** of the LORD, and H1285
18:19 for ever: it *is* a **c** of salt for ever before H1285
25:12 Behold, I give unto him my **c** of peace: H1285
13 after him, *even* the **c** of an everlasting H1285
Dt 4:13 And he declared unto you his **c**, which H1285
23 lest ye forget the **c** of the LORD your H1285
31 nor forget the **c** of thy fathers which H1285
5: 2 The LORD our God made a **c** with us in H1285
3 The LORD made not this **c** with our H1285
7: 2 shalt make no **c** with them, nor shew H1285
9 which keepeth **c** and mercy with them H1285
12 keep unto thee the **c** and the mercy H1285
8:18 he may establish his **c** which he sware H1285
9: 9 the tables of the **c** which the LORD H1285
11 tables of stone, *even* the tables of the **c**. H1285
15 tables of the **c** *were* in my two hands. H1285
10: 8 to bear the ark of the **c** of the LORD, to H1285
17: 2 LORD thy God, in transgressing his **c**, H1285
29: 1 These *are* the words of the **c**, which the H1285
1 **c** which he made with them in Horeb. H1285
9 Keep therefore the words of this **c**, and H1285
12 That thou shouldest enter into **c** with H1285
14 Neither with you only do I make this **c** H1285
21 the curses of the **c** that are written in H1285
25 have forsaken the **c** of the LORD God of H1285
31: 9 bare the ark of the **c** of the LORD, and H1285
16 my **c** which I have made with them. H1285
20 them, and provoke me, and break my **c**. H1285
25 the ark of the **c** of the LORD, saying, H1285
26 of the ark of the **c** of the LORD your H1285
33: 9 have observed thy word, and kept thy **c**. H1285
Jos 3: 3 ye see the ark of the **c** of the LORD your H1285
6 up the ark of the **c**, and pass over before H1285
6 ark of the **c**, and went before the people. H1285
8 bear the ark of the **c**, saying, When ye H1285
11 Behold, the ark of the **c** of the Lord of H1285
14 the ark of the **c** before the people; H1285
17 bare the ark of the **c** of the LORD stood H1285
Jos 4: 7 the ark of the **c** of the LORD; when H1285
9 bare the ark of the **c** stood: and they H1285
18 bare the ark of the **c** of the LORD were H1285
6: 6 up the ark of the **c**, and let seven priests H1285
8 ark of the **c** of the LORD followed them. H1285
7:11 transgressed my **c** which I commanded H1285
15 transgressed the **c** of the LORD, and H1285
8:33 bare the ark of the **c** of the LORD, as H1285
23:16 When ye have transgressed the **c** of the H1285
24:25 So Joshua made a **c** with the people H1285
Jdg 2: 1 I said, I will never break my **c** with you. H1285
20 transgressed my **c** which I commanded H1285
20:27 of the **c** of God *was* there in those days, H1285
1Sa 4: 3 the ark of the **c** of the LORD out of H1285
4 the ark of the **c** of the LORD of hosts, H1285
4 *were* there with the ark of the **c** of God. H1285
5 And when the ark of the **c** of the LORD H1285
11: 1 a **c** with us, and we will serve thee. H1285
2 will I make *a c* with you, that I may
18: 3 Then Jonathan and David made a **c**, H1285
20: 8 thy servant into a **c** of the LORD with H1285
16 So Jonathan made *a c* with the house of
23:18 And they two made a **c** before the H1285
2Sa 15:24 the ark of the **c** of God: and they set H1285
23: 5 with me an everlasting **c**, ordered in all H1285
1Ki 3:15 the ark of the **c** of the LORD, and H1285
6:19 set there the ark of the **c** of the LORD. H1285
8: 1 up the ark of the **c** of the LORD out of H1285
6 in the ark of the **c** of the LORD unto his H1285
9 the LORD made *a c* with the children of
21 the ark, wherein *is* the **c** of the LORD, H1285
23 who keepest **c** and mercy with thy H1285
11:11 hast not kept my **c** and my statutes, H1285
19:10 have forsaken thy **c**, thrown down thine H1285
14 have forsaken thy **c**, thrown down thine H1285
20:34 thee away with this **c**. So he made a H1285
34 made a **c** with him, and sent him away. H1285
2Ki 11: 4 and made a **c** with them, and took H1285
17 And Jehoiada made a **c** between the H1285
13:23 because of his **c** with Abraham, Isaac, H1285
17:15 statutes, and his **c** that he made with H1285
35 With whom the LORD had made a **c**, H1285
38 And the **c** that I have made with you ye H1285
18:12 transgressed his **c**, *and* all that Moses H1285
23: 2 of the book of the **c** which was found in H1285
3 pillar, and made a **c** before the LORD, H1285
3 the words of this **c** that were written in H1285
3 book. And all the people stood to the **c**. H1285
21 as *it is* written in the book of this **c**. H1285
1Ch 11: 3 and David made a **c** with them in H1285
15:25 up the ark of the **c** of the LORD out of H1285
26 bare the ark of the **c** of the LORD, that H1285
28 up the ark of the **c** of the LORD with H1285
29 And it came to pass, *as* the ark of the **c** H1285
16: 6 before the ark of the **c** of God. H1285
15 Be ye mindful always of his **c**; the word H1285
16 *Even of the* **c** which he made with H1285
17 a law, *and* to Israel *for* an everlasting **c**, H1285
37 So he left there before the ark of the **c** of H1285
17: 1 cedars, but the ark of the **c** of the LORD H1285
22:19 the ark of the **c** of the LORD, and the H1285
28: 2 for the ark of the **c** of the LORD, and H1285
18 covered the ark of the **c** of the LORD. H1285
2Ch 5: 2 up the ark of the **c** of the LORD out of H1285
7 in the ark of the **c** of the LORD unto his H1285
10 the LORD made *a c* with the children of
6:11 ark, wherein *is* the **c** of the LORD, that H1285
14 which keepest **c**, and *shewest* mercy H1285
13: 5 to him and to his sons by a **c** of salt? H1285
15:12 And they entered into a **c** to seek the H1285
21: 7 because of the **c** that he had made with H1285
23: 1 the son of Zichri, into **c** with him. H1285
3 And all the congregation made a **c** with H1285
16 And Jehoiada made a **c** between him, H1285
29:10 Now *it is* in mine heart to make a **c** H1285
34:30 of the book of the **c** that was found in H1285
31 place, and made a **c** before the LORD, H1285
31 of the **c** which are written in this book. H1285
32 to the **c** of God, the God of their fathers. H1285
Ezr 10: 3 Now therefore let us make a **c** with our H1285
Neh 1: 5 God, that keepeth **c** and mercy for H1285
9: 8 and madest a **c** with him to give the H1285
32 God, who keepest **c** and mercy, let not H1285
38 And because of all this we make a sure **c**,
13:29 **c** of the priesthood, and of the Levites. H1285
Job 31: 1 I made a **c** with mine eyes; why then H1285
41: 4 Will he make a **c** with thee? wilt thou H1285
Ps 25:10 such as keep his **c** and his testimonies. H1285
14 fear him; and he will shew them his **c**. H1285

Ps 44:17 neither have we dealt falsely in thy c. H1285
50: 5 have made a c with me by sacrifice. H1285
16 thou shouldest take my c in thy mouth? H1285
55:20 at peace with him: he hath broken his c. H1285
74:20 Have respect unto the c: for the dark H1285
78:10 They kept not the c of God, and refused H1285
37 him, neither were they stedfast in his c. H1285
89: 3 I have made a c with my chosen, I have H1285
28 and my c shall stand fast with him. H1285
34 My c will I not break, nor alter the H1285
39 Thou hast made void the c of thy H1285
103:18 To such as keep his c, and to those that H1285
105: 8 He hath remembered his c for ever, the H1285
9 Which c he made with Abraham, and
10 a law, *and* to Israel *for* an everlasting c: H1285
106:45 And he remembered for them his c, and H1285
111: 5 him: he will ever be mindful of his c. H1285
9 commanded his c for ever: holy and H1285
132:12 If thy children will keep my c and my H1285
Prv 2:17 youth, and forgetteth the c of her God. H1285
Isa 24: 5 the ordinance, broken the everlasting c. H1285
28:15 We have made a c with death, and with H1285
18 And your c with death shall be H1285
33: 8 hath broken the c, he hath despised the H1285
42: 6 and give thee for a c of the people, for a H1285
49: 8 and give thee for a c of the people, to H1285
54:10 thee, neither shall the c of my peace be H1285
55: 3 an everlasting c with you, *even* the sure H1285
56: 4 that please me, and take hold of my c; H1285
6 polluting it, and taketh hold of my c; H1285
57: 8 bed, and made thee *a* c with them; thou
59:21 As for me, this *is* my c with them, saith H1285
61: 8 I will make an everlasting c with them. H1285
Jer 3:16 The ark of the c of the LORD: neither H1285
11: 2 Hear ye the words of this c, and speak H1285
3 that obeyeth not the words of this c, H1285
6 ye the words of this c, and do them. H1285
8 the words of this c, which I commanded H1285
10 my c which I made with their fathers. H1285
14:21 remember, break not thy c with us. H1285
22: 9 have forsaken the c of the LORD their H1285
31:31 I will make a new c with the house of H1285
32 Not according to the c that I made with H1285
32 Egypt; which my c they brake, although H1285
33 But this *shall be* the c that I will make H1285
32:40 And I will make an everlasting c with H1285
33:20 If ye can break my c of the day, and my H1285
20 of the day, and my c of the night, and H1285
21 *Then* may also my c be broken with H1285
25 Thus saith the LORD; If my c *be* not H1285
34: 8 had made a c with all the people which H1285
10 entered into the c, heard that every one H1285
13 of Israel; I made a c with your fathers H1285
15 ye had made a c before me in the house H1285
18 have transgressed my c, which have not H1285
18 the words of the c which they had H1285
50: 5 perpetual c *that* shall not be forgotten. H1285
Ezk 16: 8 and entered into a c with thee, saith the H1285
59 despised the oath in breaking the c. H1285
60 Nevertheless I will remember my c H1285
60 will establish unto thee an everlasting c. H1285
61 thee for daughters, but not by thy c. H1285
62 And I will establish my c with thee; and H1285
17:13 seed, and made a c with him, and hath H1285
14 that by keeping of his c it might stand. H1285
15 shall he break the c, and be delivered? H1285
16 and whose c he brake, *even* with H1285
18 oath by breaking the c, when, lo, he had H1285
19 hath despised, and my c that he hath H1285
20:37 I will bring you into the bond of the c: H1285
34:25 And I will make with them a c of peace, H1285
37:26 Moreover I will make a c of peace with H1285
26 be an everlasting c with them: and I H1285
44: 7 my c because of all your abominations. H1285
Dan 9: 4 God, keeping the c and mercy to them H1285
27 And he shall confirm the c with many H1285
11:22 be broken; yea, also the prince of the c. H1285
28 *be* against the holy c; and he shall do H1285
30 against the holy c: so shall he do; he H1285
30 with them that forsake the holy c. H1285
32 And such as do wickedly against the c H1285
Hos 2:18 And in that day will I make a c for H1285
6: 7 transgressed the c: there have they dealt H1285
8: 1 my c, and trespassed against my law. H1285
10: 4 in making a c: thus judgment springeth H1285
12: 1 they do make a c with the Assyrians, H1285
Am 1: 9 and remembered not the brotherly c: H1285
Zec 9:11 As for thee also, by the blood of thy c I H1285
11:10 c which I had made with all the people. H1285

Mal 2: 4 unto you, that my c might be with Levi, H1285
5 My c was with him of life and peace; H1285
8 the c of Levi, saith the LORD of hosts. H1285
10 by profaning the c of our fathers? H1285
14 thy companion, and the wife of thy c. H1285
3: 1 messenger of the c, whom ye delight in: H1285
Lk 1:72 fathers, and to remember his holy c; G1242
Act 3:25 and of the c which God made with G1242
7: 8 And he gave him the c of circumcision: G1242
Ro 11:27 For this *is* my c unto them, when I shall G1242
Gal 3:15 Though *it be* but a man's c, yet *if it be* G1242
17 And this I say, *that* the c, that was G1242
Heb 8: 6 of a better c, which was established G1242
7 For if that first c had been faultless, then
8 I will make a new c with the house of G1242
9 Not according to the c that I made with G1242
9 not in my c, and I regarded them G1242
10 For this *is* the c that I will make with G1242
13 In that he saith, A new *c*, he hath made
9: 1 Then verily the first *c* had also
4 and the ark of the c overlaid round G1242
4 rod that budded, and the tables of the c; G1242
10:16 This *is* the c that I will make with them G1242
29 the blood of the c, wherewith he was G1242
12:24 And to Jesus the mediator of the new c, G1242
13:20 through the blood of the everlasting c, G1242

COVENANTBREAKERS
Ro 1:31 Without understanding, c, without G802

COVENANTED
2Ch 7:18 as I have c with David thy father, H3772
Hag 2: 5 *According to* the word that I c with you H3772
Mt 26:15 c with him for thirty pieces of silver. G2476
Lk 22: 5 And they were glad, and c to give him G4934

COVENANTS
Ro 9: 4 the glory, and the c, and the giving of G1242
Gal 4:24 for these are the two c; the one from the G1242
Eph 2:12 strangers from the c of promise, having G1242

COVER
Ex 10: 5 And they shall c the face of the earth, H3680
21:33 c it, and an ox or an ass fall therein; H3680
25:29 bowls thereof, to c withal: *of* pure gold H5258
26:13 on this side and on that side, to c it. H3680
28:42 linen breeches to c their nakedness; H3680
33:22 c thee with my hand while I pass by: H5526
37:16 and his covers to c withal, *of* pure gold. H5258
40: 3 testimony, and c the ark with the vail. H5526
Lev 13:12 and the leprosy c all the skin of *him* H3680
16:13 of the incense may c the mercy seat H3680
17:13 the blood thereof, and c it with dust. H3680
Nu 4: 5 vail, and c the ark of testimony with it: H3680
7 bowls, and covers to c withal: and the H5258
8 cloth of scarlet, and c the same with a H3680
9 a cloth of blue, and c the candlestick of H3680
11 cloth of blue, and c it with a covering of H3680
12 a cloth of blue, and c them with a H3680
22: 5 behold, they c the face of the earth, H3680
Dt 23:13 and c that which cometh from thee: H3680
33:12 *the LORD* shall c him all the day long, H2653
1Sa 24: 3 Saul went in to c his feet: and David H5526
1Ki 7:18 the one network, to c the chapiters that H3680
41 two networks, to c the two bowls of the H3680
42 one network, to c the two bowls of the H3680
2Ch 4:12 the two wreaths to c the two pommels H3680
13 on each wreath, to c the two pommels H3680
Neh 4: 5 And c not their iniquity, and let not H3680
Job 16:18 O earth, c not thou my blood, and let H3680
21:26 the dust, and the worms shall c them. H3680
22:11 see; and abundance of waters c thee. H3680
38:34 that abundance of waters may c thee? H3680
40:22 The shady trees c him *with* their H5526
Ps 91: 4 He shall c thee with his feathers, and H5526
104: 9 that they turn not again to c the earth. H3680
109:29 and let them c themselves with their H5844
139:11 If I say, Surely the darkness shall c me; H7779
140: 9 the mischief of their own lips c them. H3680
Isa 11: 9 of the LORD, as the waters c the sea. H3680
14:11 under thee, and the worms c thee. H4374
22:17 mighty captivity, and will surely c thee. H5844
26:21 blood, and shall no more c her slain. H3680
30: 1 of me; and that c with a covering, but H5258
58: 7 naked, that thou c him; and that thou H3680
59: 6 neither shall they c themselves with H3680
60: 2 For, behold, the darkness shall c the H3680
6 The multitude of camels shall c thee, H3680
Jer 46: 8 will go up, *and* will c the earth; I will H3680

Ezk 7:18 and horror shall c them; and shame H3680
12: 6 thou shalt c thy face, that thou see H3680
12 thereby: he shall c his face, that he see H3680
24: 7 not upon the ground, to c it with dust; H3680
17 upon thy feet, and c not *thy* lips, and H5844
22 c *your* lips, nor eat the bread of men. H5844
26:10 their dust shall c thee: thy walls shall H3680
19 thee, and great waters shall c thee; H3680
30:18 for her, a cloud shall c her, and her H3680
32: 7 And when I shall put thee out, I will c H3680
7 thereof dark; I will c the sun with a H3680
37: 6 upon you, and c you with skin, and put H7159
38: 9 be like a cloud to c the land, thou, and H3680
16 as a cloud to c the land; it shall be H3680
Hos 2: 9 and my flax *given* to c her nakedness. H3680
10: 8 C us; and to the hills, Fall on us. H3680
Oba 10 Jacob shame shall c thee, and thou H3680
Mic 3: 7 yea, they shall all c their lips; for *there* H5844
7:10 and shame shall c her which said unto H3680
Hab 2:14 of the LORD, as the waters c the sea. H3680
17 For the violence of Lebanon shall c H3680
Mk 14:65 on him, and to c his face, and to buffet G4028
Lk 23:30 Fall on us; and to the hills, C us. G2572
1Co 11: 7 For a man indeed ought not to c *his* G2619
1Pt 4: 8 for charity shall c the multitude of sins. G2572

COVERED
Gen 7:19 *were* under the whole heaven, were c. H3680
20 prevail; and the mountains were c. H3680
9:23 backward, and c the nakedness of their H3680
24:65 therefore she took a vail, and c herself. H3680
38:14 off from her, and c her with a vail, and H3680
15 an harlot; because she had c her face. H3680
Ex 8: 6 frogs came up, and c the land of Egypt. H3680
10:15 For they c the face of the whole earth, H3680
14:28 And the waters returned, and c the H3680
15: 5 The depths have c them: they sank into H3680
10 thy wind, the sea c them: they sank as H3680
16:13 came up, and c the camp: and in the H3680
24:15 the mount, and a cloud c the mount. H3680
16 and the cloud c it six days: and the H3680
37: 9 on high, *and* c with their wings over H5526
40:21 of the covering, and c the ark of the H5526
34 Then a cloud c the tent of the H3680
Lev 13:13 *if* the leprosy have c all his flesh, he H3680
Nu 4:20 when the holy things are c, lest they die. H1104
7: 3 the LORD, six c wagons, and twelve H6632
9:15 up the cloud c the tabernacle, *namely,* H3680
16 So it was alway: the cloud c it *by day,* H3680
16:42 behold, the cloud c it, and the glory of H3680
Dt 32:15 thick, thou art c *with fatness*; then he H3780
Jos 24: 7 upon them, and c them; and your eyes H3680
Jdg 4:18 into the tent, she c him with a mantle. H3680
19 milk, and gave him drink, and c him. H3680
1Sa 19:13 for his bolster, and c *it* with a cloth. H3680
28:14 up; and he *is* c with a mantle. And H5844
2Sa 15:30 up, and had his head c, and he went H2645
30 that *was* with him c every man his H2645
19: 4 But the king c his face, and the king H3813
1Ki 1: 1 c him with clothes, but he gat no heat. H3680
6: 9 finished it; and c the house with beams H5603
15 the cieling: *and* he c *them* on the inside H6823
15 with wood, and c the floor of the house H6823
20 and *so* c the altar *which was of* cedar. H6823
35 and open flowers: and c *them* with gold H6823
7: 3 And *it was* c with cedar above upon the H5603
7 and *it was* c with cedar from one H5603
8: 7 c the ark and the staves thereof above. H5526
2Ki 19: 1 rent his clothes, and c himself with H3680
2 of the priests, c with sackcloth, to H3680
1Ch 28:18 c the ark of the covenant of the LORD. H5526
2Ch 5: 8 c the ark and the staves thereof above. H3680
Neh 3:15 he built it, and c it, and set up the H2926
Est 6:12 mourning, and having his head c. H2645
7: 8 the king's mouth, they c Haman's face. H2645
Job 23:17 hath he c the darkness from my face. H3680
31:33 If I c my transgressions as Adam, by H3680
Ps 32: 1 transgression *is* forgiven, *whose* sin *is* c. H3680
44:15 and the shame of my face hath c me, H3680
19 and c us with the shadow of death. H3680
65:13 valleys also are c over with corn; they H5848
68:13 wings of a dove c with silver, and her H2645
69: 7 borne reproach; shame hath c my face. H3680
71:13 soul; let them be c *with* reproach and H5844
80:10 The hills were c with the shadow of it, H3680
85: 2 people, thou hast c all their sin. Selah. H3680
89:45 thou hast c him with shame. Selah. H5844
106:11 And the waters c their enemies: there H3680
17 Dathan, and c the company of Abiram. H3680

Ps 139:13 thou hast **c** me in my mother's womb. H5526
140: 7 hast **c** my head in the day of battle. H5526
Prv 24:31 *and* nettles had **c** the face thereof, and H3680
26:23 *are like* a potsherd **c** with silver dross. H6823
26 *Whose* hatred is **c** by deceit, his H3680
Ecc 6: 4 and his name shall be **c** with darkness. H3680
Isa 6: 2 with twain he **c** his face, and with H3680
2 he **c** his feet, and with twain he did fly. H3680
29:10 and your rulers, the seers hath he **c**. H3680
37: 1 rent his clothes, and **c** himself with H3680
2 of the priests **c** with sackcloth, unto H3680
51:16 mouth, and I have **c** thee in the shadow H3680
61:10 salvation, he hath **c** me with the robe of H3271
Jer 14: 3 and confounded, and **c** their heads. H2645
4 were ashamed, they **c** their heads. H2645
51:42 Babylon: she is **c** with the multitude of H3680
51 shame hath **c** our faces: for strangers H3680
Lam 2: 1 How hath the Lord **c** the daughter of H5743
3:16 gravel stones, he hath **c** me with ashes. H3728
43 Thou hast **c** with anger, and persecuted H5526
44 Thou hast **c** thyself with a cloud, that H5526
Ezk 1:11 one to another, and two **c** their bodies. H3680
23 one had two, which **c** on this side, and H3680
23 two, which **c** on that side, their bodies. H3680
16: 8 over thee, and **c** thy nakedness: yea, H3680
10 with fine linen, and I **c** thee with silk. H3680
18: 7 and hath **c** the naked with a garment; H3680
16 and hath **c** the naked with a garment, H3680
24: 8 the top of a rock, that it should not be **c**. H3680
27: 7 isles of Elishah was that which **c** thee. H4374
31:15 a mourning: I **c** the deep for him, and H3680
37: 8 and the skin **c** them above: but *there* H7159
41:16 the windows, and the windows *were* **c**; H3680
Jna 3: 6 **c** *him* with sackcloth, and sat in ashes. H3680
8 But let man and beast be **c** with H3680
Hab 3: 3 Selah. His glory **c** the heavens, and the H3680
Mt 8:24 **c** with the waves: but he was asleep. *G2572*
10:26 for there is nothing **c**, that shall not be *G2572*
Lk 12: 2 For there is nothing **c**, that shall not be *G4780*
Ro 4: 7 are forgiven, and whose sins are **c**. *G1943*
1Co 11: 4 *his* head **c**, dishonoureth his head. *G2596*
6 For if the woman be not **c**, let her also *G2619*
6 to be shorn or shaven, let her be **c**. *G2619*

COVEREDST
Ps 104: 6 Thou **c** it with the deep as *with* a H3680
Ezk 16:18 garments, and **c** them: and thou hast H3680

COVEREST
Dt 22:12 thy vesture, wherewith thou **c** *thyself.* H3680
Ps 104: 2 Who **c** *thyself* with light as *with* a H5844

COVERETH
Ex 29:13 And thou shalt take all the fat that **c** H3680
22 and the fat that **c** the inwards, and the H3680
Lev 3: 3 LORD; the fat that **c** the inwards, and H3680
9 and the fat that **c** the inwards, and all H3680
14 LORD; the fat that **c** the inwards, and H3680
4: 8 the fat that **c** the inwards, and all H3680
7: 3 rump, and the fat that **c** the inwards, H3680
9:19 and that which **c** *the inwards,* and the H4374
Nu 22:11 of Egypt, which **c** the face of the earth: H3680
Jdg 3:24 he **c** his feet in his summer chamber. H5526
Job 9:24 of the wicked: he **c** the faces of the H3680
15:27 Because he **c** his face with his fatness, H3680
36:30 upon it, and **c** the bottom of the sea. H3680
32 With clouds he **c** the light; and H3680
Ps 73: 6 a chain; violence **c** them *as* a garment. H5848
109:19 garment *which* **c** him, and for a girdle H5844
147: 8 Who **c** the heaven with clouds, who H3680
Prv 10: 6 but violence **c** the mouth of the wicked. H3680
11 but violence **c** the mouth of the wicked. H3680
12 Hatred stirreth up strifes: but love **c** all H3680
12:16 known: but a prudent *man* **c** shame. H3680
17: 9 He that **c** a transgression seeketh love; H3680
28:13 He that **c** his sins shall not prosper: but H3680
Jer 3:25 and our confusion **c** us: for we have H3680
Ezk 28:14 Thou *art* the anointed cherub that **c**; H5526
Mal 2:16 away: for *one* **c** violence with his H3680
Lk 8:16 lighted a candle, **c** it with a vessel, or *G2572*

COVERING
Gen 8:13 Noah removed the **c** of the ark, and H4372
20:16 he *is* to thee a **c** of the eyes, unto all H3682
Ex 22:27 For that *is* his **c** only, it *is* his raiment H3682
25:20 wings on high, **c** the mercy seat with H5526
26: 7 goats' *hair* to be a **c** upon the tabernacle: H168
14 And thou shalt make a **c** for the tent *of* H4372
14 red, and a **c** above *of* badgers' skins. H4372
Ex 35:11 The tabernacle, his tent, and his **c**, his H4372
12 the mercy seat, and the vail of the **c**, H4539
36:19 And he made a **c** for the tent *of* rams' H4372
19 and a **c** *of* badgers' skins above *that.* H4372
39:34 And the **c** of rams' skins dyed red, and H4372
34 dyed red, and the **c** of badgers' skins, H4372
34 of badgers' skins, and the vail of the **c**, H4539
40:19 and put the **c** of the tent above upon H4372
21 up the vail of the **c**, and covered the ark H4539
Lev 13:45 and he shall put a **c** upon his upper lip, H5844
Nu 3:25 and the tent, the **c** thereof, and the H4372
4: 5 take down the **c** vail, and cover the ark H4539
6 And shall put thereon the **c** of badgers' H3681
8 the same with a **c** of badgers' skins, H4372
10 thereof within a **c** of badgers' skins, H4372
11 and cover it with a **c** of badgers' skins, H4372
12 cover them with a **c** of badgers' skins, H4372
14 spread upon it a **c** of badgers' skins, H3681
15 made an end of **c** the sanctuary, and H3680
25 congregation, his **c**, and the covering of H4372
25 his covering, and the **c** of the badgers' H4372
16:38 broad plates *for* a **c** of the altar: for H6826
39 made broad *plates for* a **c** of the altar: H6826
19:15 And every open vessel, which hath no **c** H6781
2Sa 17:19 And the woman took and spread a **c** H4539
Job 22:14 Thick clouds *are* a **c** to him, that he H5643
24: 7 that *they have* no **c** in the cold. H3682
26: 6 before him, and destruction hath no **c**. H3682
31:19 want of clothing, or any poor without **c**; H3682
Ps 105:39 He spread a cloud for a **c**; and fire to H4539
Song 3:10 *of* gold, the **c** of it *of* purple, the midst H4817
Isa 22: 8 And he discovered the **c** of Judah, and H4539
25: 7 the face of the **c** cast over all people, H3875
28:20 *on it*: and the **c** narrower than that H4541
30: 1 that cover with a **c**, but not of my spirit, H4541
22 Ye shall defile also the **c** of thy graven H6826
50: 3 blackness, and I make sackcloth their **c**. H3682
Ezk 28:13 stone *was* thy **c**, the sardius, topaz, and H4540
16 will destroy thee, O **c** cherub, from the H5526
Mal 2:13 And this have ye done again, **c** the altar H3680
1Co 11:15 to her: for *her* hair is given her for a **c**. *G4018*

COVERINGS
Prv 7:16 I have decked my bed with **c** of H4765
31:22 She maketh herself **c** of tapestry; her H4765

COVERS
Ex 25:29 thereof, and **c** thereof, and bowls H7184
37:16 and his **c** to cover withal, *of* pure gold. H7184
Nu 4: 7 the bowls, and **c** to cover withal: and H7184

COVERT
1Sa 25:20 she came down by the **c** of the hill, and, H5643
2Ki 16:18 And the **c** for the sabbath that they had H4329
Job 38:40 dens, *and* abide in the **c** to lie in wait? H5521
40:21 He lieth under the shady trees, in the **c** H5643
Ps 61: 4 I will trust in the **c** of thy wings. Selah. H5643
Isa 4: 6 and for a **c** from storm and from rain. H4563
16: 4 Moab; be thou a **c** to them from the H5643
32: 2 the wind, and a **c** from the tempest; as H5643
Jer 25:38 He hath forsaken his **c**, as the lion: for H5520

COVET
Ex 20:17 Thou shalt not **c** thy neighbour's house, H2530
17 thou shalt not **c** thy neighbour's wife, H2530
Dt 5:21 wife, neither shalt thou **c** thy neighbour's H183
Mic 2: 2 And they **c** fields, and take *them* by H2530
Ro 7: 7 the law had said, Thou shalt not **c**. *G1937*
13: 9 Thou shalt not **c**; and if *there be* any *G1937*
1Co 12:31 But **c** earnestly the best gifts: and yet *G2206*
14:39 Wherefore, brethren, **c** to prophesy, *G2206*

COVETED
Jos 7:21 weight, then I **c** them, and took them; H2530
Act 20:33 I have **c** no man's silver, or gold, or *G1937*
1Ti 6:10 which while some **c** after, they have *G3713*

COVETETH
Prv 21:26 He **c** greedily all the day long: but the H183
Hab 2: 9 Woe to him that **c** an evil covetousness H1214

COVETOUS
Ps 10: 3 the **c**, *whom* the LORD abhorreth. H1214
Lk 16:14 And the Pharisees also, who were **c**, *G5366*
1Co 5:10 world, or with the **c**, or extortioners, or *G4123*
11 be a fornicator, or **c**, or an idolater, or a *G4123*
6:10 Nor thieves, nor **c**, nor drunkards, nor *G4123*
Eph 5: 5 person, nor **c** man, who is an idolater, *G4123*
1Ti 3: 3 lucre; but patient, not a brawler, not **c**; *G866*
2Ti 3: 2 of their own selves, **c**, boasters, proud, *G5366*
2Pt 2:14 with **c** practices; cursed children: *G4124*

COVETOUSNESS
Ex 18:21 of truth, hating **c**; and place *such* over H1215
Ps 119:36 heart unto thy testimonies, and not to **c**. H1215
Prv 28:16 he that hateth **c** shall prolong *his* days. H1215
Isa 57:17 For the iniquity of his **c** was I wroth, H1215
Jer 6:13 one *is* given to **c**; and from the prophet H1215
8:10 greatest is given to **c**, from the prophet H1215
22:17 *are* not but for thy **c**, and for to shed H1215
51:13 end is come, *and* the measure of thy **c**. H1215
Ezk 33:31 love, *but* their heart goeth after their **c**. H1215
Hab 2: 9 Woe to him that coveteth an evil **c** to H1215
Mk 7:22 Thefts, **c**, wickedness, deceit, *G4124*
Lk 12:15 heed, and beware of **c**: for a man's life *G4124*
Ro 1:29 wickedness, **c**, maliciousness; full *G4124*
2Co 9: 5 as *a matter of* bounty, and not as *of* **c**. *G4124*
Eph 5: 3 all uncleanness, or **c**, let it not be once *G4124*
Col 3: 5 concupiscence, and **c**, which is idolatry: *G4124*
1Th 2: 5 know, nor a cloak of **c**; God *is* witness: *G4124*
Heb 13: 5 *Let your* conversation *be* without **c**; *and* *G866*
2Pt 2: 3 And through **c** shall they with feigned *G4124*

COW
Lev 22:28 And *whether it be* **c** or ewe, ye shall not H7794
Nu 18:17 But the firstling of a **c**, or the firstling of H7794
Job 21:10 **c** calveth, and casteth not her calf. H6510
Isa 7:21 shall nourish a young **c**, and two sheep; H5697
11: 7 And the **c** and the bear shall feed; their H6510
Am 4: 3 at the breaches, every **c** *at that which is*

COW'S
Ezk 4:15 Lo, I have given thee **c** dung for man's H1241

COZ
1Ch 4: 8 And **C** begat Anub, and Zobebah, and H6976

COZBI
Nu 25:15 that was slain *was* **C**, the daughter of H3579
18 in the matter of **C**, the daughter of a H3579

CRACKLING
Ecc 7: 6 For as the **c** of thorns under a pot, so *is* H6963

CRACKNELS
1Ki 14: 3 And take with thee ten loaves, and **c**, H5350

CRAFT
Dan 8:25 also he shall cause **c** to prosper in his H4820
Mk 14: 1 take him by **c**, and put *him* to death. *G1388*
Act 18: 3 And because he was of the same **c**, he *G3673*
19:25 know that by this **c** we have our wealth. *G2039*
27 So that not only this our **c** is in danger *G3313*
Rev 18:22 of whatsoever **c** *he be*, shall be found *G5078*

CRAFTINESS
Job 5:13 He taketh the wise in their own **c**: and H6193
Lk 20:23 But he perceived their **c**, and said unto *G3834*
1Co 3:19 He taketh the wise in their own **c**. *G3834*
2Co 4: 2 not walking in **c**, nor handling the word *G3834*
Eph 4:14 **c**, whereby they lie in wait to deceive; *G3834*

CRAFTSMAN
Dt 27:15 of the hands of the **c**, and putteth *it* in *a* H2796
Rev 18:22 all in thee; and no **c**, of whatsoever craft *G5079*

CRAFTSMEN
2Ki 24:14 captives, and all the **c** and smiths: none H2796
16 seven thousand, and **c** and smiths a H2796
1Ch 4:14 the valley of Charashim; for they were **c**. H2796
Neh 11:35 Lod, and Ono, the valley of **c**. H2796
Hos 13: 2 of it the work of the **c**: they say of them, H2796
Act 19:24 brought no small gain unto the **c**; *G5079*
38 Wherefore if Demetrius, and the **c** *G5079*

CRAFTY
Job 5:12 He disappointeth the devices of the **c**, so H6175
15: 5 and thou choosest the tongue of the **c**. H6175
Ps 83: 3 They have taken **c** counsel against thy H6191
2Co 12:16 being **c**, I caught you with guile. *G3835*

CRAG
Job 39:28 the **c** of the rock, and the strong place. H8127

CRANE
Isa 38:14 Like a **c** *or* a swallow, so did I chatter: I H5483
Jer 8: 7 the turtle and the **c** and the swallow H5483

CRASHING
Zep 1:10 the second, and a great **c** from the hills. H7667

CRAVED
Mk 15:43 unto Pilate, and **c** the body of Jesus. *G154*

CRAVETH
Prv 16:26 for himself; for his mouth **c** it of him. H404

CREATE
Ps 51:10 **C** in me a clean heart, O God; and H1254
Isa 4: 5 And the LORD will **c** upon every H1254
45: 7 I form the light, and **c** darkness: I make H1254
7 **c** evil: I the LORD do all these *things*. H1254
57:19 I **c** the fruit of the lips; Peace, peace to H1254
65:17 For, behold, I **c** new heavens and a new H1254
18 *in that* which I **c**: for, behold, I create H1254
18 for, behold, I **c** Jerusalem a rejoicing, H1254

CREATED
Gen 1: 1 In the beginning God **c** the heaven and H1254
21 And God **c** great whales, and every H1254
27 So God **c** man in his *own* image, in the H1254
27 in the image of God **c** he him; male and H1254
27 he him; male and female **c** he them. H1254
2: 3 all his work which God **c** and made. H1254
4 when they were **c**, in the day that the H1254
5: 1 the day that God **c** man, in the likeness H1254
2 Male and female **c** he them; and H1254
2 Adam, in the day when they were **c**. H1254
6: 7 man whom I have **c** from the face of H1254
Dt 4:32 the day that God **c** man upon the earth, H1254
Ps 89:12 The north and the south thou hast **c** H1254
102:18 which shall be **c** shall praise the LORD. H1254
104:30 Thou sendest forth thy spirit, they are **c**: H1254
148: 5 for he commanded, and they were **c**. H1254
Isa 40:26 behold who hath **c** these *things*, that H1254
41:20 and the Holy One of Israel hath **c** it. H1254
42: 5 Thus saith God the LORD, he that **c** the H1254
43: 1 But now thus saith the LORD that **c** H1254
7 name: for I have **c** him for my glory, I H1254
45: 8 up together; I the LORD have **c** it. H1254
12 I have made the earth, and **c** man upon H1254
18 For thus saith the LORD that **c** the H1254
18 established it, he **c** it not in vain, he H1254
48: 7 They are **c** now, and not from the H1254
54:16 Behold, I have **c** the smith that bloweth H1254
16 and I have **c** the waster to destroy. H1254
Jer 31:22 for the LORD hath **c** a new thing in the H1254
Ezk 21:30 thou wast **c**, in the land of thy nativity. H1254
28:13 in thee in the day that thou wast **c**. H1254
15 wast **c**, till iniquity was found in thee. H1254
Mal 2:10 hath not one God **c** us? why do we deal H1254
Mk 13:19 God **c** unto this time, neither shall be. *G2936*
1Co 11: 9 Neither was the man **c** for the woman; *G2936*
Eph 2:10 For we are his workmanship, **c** in *G2936*
3: 9 in God, who **c** all things by Jesus Christ: *G2936*
4:24 is **c** in righteousness and true holiness. *G2936*
Col 1:16 For by him were all things **c**, that are in *G2936*
16 all things were **c** by him, and for him: *G2936*
3:10 after the image of him that **c** him: *G2936*
1Ti 4: 3 which God hath **c** to be received with *G2936*
Rev 4:11 for thou hast **c** all things, and for thy *G2936*
11 for thy pleasure they are and were **c**. *G2936*
10: 6 and ever, who **c** heaven, and the things *G2936*

CREATETH
Am 4:13 the mountains, and **c** the wind, and H1254

CREATION
Mk 10: 6 But from the beginning of the **c** God *G2937*
13:19 beginning of the **c** which God created *G2937*
Ro 1:20 of him from the **c** of the world are *G2937*
8:22 For we know that the whole **c** groaneth *G2937*
2Pt 3: 4 *they were* from the beginning of the **c**. *G2937*
Rev 3:14 witness, the beginning of the **c** of God; *G2937*

CREATOR
Ecc 12: 1 Remember now thy **C** in the days of thy H1254
Isa 40:28 God, the LORD, the **C** of the ends of the H1254
43:15 I *am* the LORD, your Holy One, the **c** of H1254
Ro 1:25 the **C**, who is blessed for ever. Amen. *G2936*
1Pt 4:19 *him* in well doing, as unto a faithful **C**. *G2939*

CREATURE
Gen 1:20 the moving **c** that hath life, and fowl H8318
21 and every living **c** that moveth, which H5315
24 forth the living **c** after his kind, cattle, H5315
2:19 living **c**, that *was* the name thereof. H5315
9:10 And with every living **c** that *is* with H5315
12 and every living **c** that *is* with you, for H5315
15 and every living **c** of all flesh; and the H5315
16 **c** of all flesh that *is* upon the earth. H5315
Lev 11:46 and of every living **c** that moveth in the H5315
46 of every **c** that creepeth upon the earth: H5315
Ezk 1:20 spirit of the living **c** *was* in the wheels. H2416
21 spirit of the living **c** *was* in the wheels. H2416
22 heads of the living **c** *was* as the colour H2416
10:15 **c** that I saw by the river of Chebar. H2416
17 the spirit of the living **c** *was* in them. H2416
20 This *is* the living **c** that I saw under the H2416
Mk 16:15 world, and preach the gospel to every **c**. *G2937*
Ro 1:25 and served the **c** more than the *G2937*
8:19 For the earnest expectation of the **c** *G2937*
20 For the **c** was made subject to vanity, *G2937*
21 Because the **c** itself also shall be *G2937*
39 Nor height, nor depth, nor any other **c**, *G2937*
2Co 5:17 in Christ, *he is* a new **c**: old things are *G2937*
Gal 6:15 thing, nor uncircumcision, but a new **c**. *G2937*
Col 1:15 invisible God, the firstborn of every **c**: *G2937*
23 was preached to every **c** which is under *G2937*
1Ti 4: 4 For every **c** of God *is* good, and nothing *G2938*
Heb 4:13 Neither is there any **c** that is not *G2937*
Rev 5:13 And every **c** which is in heaven, and on *G2938*

CREATURES
Isa 13:21 be full of doleful **c**; and owls shall dwell H255
Ezk 1: 5 of four living **c**. And this *was* their H2416
13 As for the likeness of the living **c**, their H2416
13 among the living **c**; and the fire was H2416
14 And the living **c** ran and returned as H2416
15 Now as I beheld the living **c**, behold one H2416
15 earth by the living **c**, with his four faces. H2416
19 And when the living **c** went, the wheels H2416
19 when the living **c** were lifted up from H2416
3:13 wings of the living **c** that touched one H2416
Jas 1:18 should be a kind of firstfruits of his **c**. *G2938*
Rev 8: 9 And the third part of the **c** which were *G2938*

CREDIBLE See INCREDIBLE.

CREDITOR
Dt 15: 2 Every **c** that lendeth H1167+H4874+H3027
2Ki 4: 1 the LORD: and the **c** is come to take H5383
Lk 7:41 There was a certain **c** which had two *G1157*

CREDITORS
Isa 50: 1 or which of my **c** *is it* to whom I have H5383

CREEK
Act 27:39 a certain **c** with a shore, into the *G2859*

CREEP
Lev 11:20 All fowls that **c**, going upon *all* four, H8318
29 things that **c** upon the earth; the H8317
31 among all that **c**: whosoever doth touch H8318
42 things that **c** upon the earth, them H8317
Ps 104:20 all the beasts of the forest do **c** *forth*. H7430
Ezk 38:20 things that **c** upon the earth, and H7430
2Ti 3: 6 For of this sort are they which **c** into *G1744*

CREEPETH
Gen 1:25 every thing that **c** upon the earth after H7431
26 creeping thing that **c** upon the earth. H7430
30 to every thing that **c** upon the earth, H7430
7: 8 of every thing that **c** upon the earth, H7430
14 thing that **c** upon the earth after H7430
21 that **c** upon the earth, and every man: H8317
8:17 thing that **c** upon the earth; that H7430
19 *and* whatsoever **c** upon the earth, after H7430
Lev 11:41 And every creeping thing that **c** upon H8317
43 thing that **c**, neither shall ye make H8317
44 of creeping thing that **c** upon the earth. H7430
46 of every creature that **c** upon the earth: H8317
20:25 of living thing that **c** on the ground, H7430
Dt 4:18 The likeness of any thing that **c** on the H7430

CREEPING
Gen 1:24 kind, cattle, and **c** thing, and beast of H7431
26 **c** thing that creepeth upon the earth. H7431
6: 7 and beast, and the **c** thing, and the H7431
20 kind, of every **c** thing of the earth after H7431
7:14 kind, and every **c** thing that creepeth H7431
21 and of every **c** thing that creepeth H8318
23 and cattle, and the **c** things, and the H7431
8:17 and of every **c** thing that creepeth H7431
19 Every beast, every **c** thing, and every H7431
Lev 5: 2 carcase of unclean **c** things, and *if* it be H8313
11:21 Yet these may ye eat of every flying **c** H8313
23 But all *other* flying **c** things, which have H8313
29 unto you among the **c** things that creep H8313
41 And every **c** thing that creepeth upon H8313
42 feet among all **c** things that creep upon H8313
43 with any **c** thing that creepeth, H8313
44 of **c** thing that creepeth upon the earth. H8313
22: 5 Or whosoever toucheth any **c** thing, H8313
Dt 14:19 And every **c** thing that flieth *is* unclean H8313
1Ki 4:33 of fowl, and of **c** things, and of fishes. H7431
Ps 104:25 wherein *are* things **c** innumerable, both H7431
148:10 Beasts, and all cattle; **c** things, and H7431
Ezk 8:10 every form of **c** things, and abominable H7431
38:20 of the field, and all **c** things that creep H7431
Hos 2:18 and *with* the **c** things of the ground: H7431
Hab 1:14 **c** things, *that have* no ruler over them? H7431
Act 10:12 and **c** things, and fowls of the air. *G2062*
11: 6 and **c** things, and fowls of the air. *G2062*
Ro 1:23 and fourfooted beasts, and **c** things. *G2062*

CREPT
Jude 4 For there are certain men **c** in *G3921*

CRESCENS
2Ti 4:10 **C** to Galatia, Titus unto Dalmatia. *G2913*

CRETANS See CRETES and CRETIANS.

CRETE
Act 27: 7 sailed under **C**, over against Salmone; *G2914*
12 *is* an haven of **C**, and lieth toward the *G2914*
13 loosing *thence*, they sailed close by **C**. *G2914*
21 have loosed from **C**, and to have gained *G2914*
Tit 1: 5 For this cause left I thee in **C**, that thou *G2914*

CRETES
Act 2:11 **C** and Arabians, we do hear them *G2912*

CRETIANS
Tit 1:12 own, said, The **C** *are* alway liars, evil *G2912*

CREW
Mt 26:74 the man. And immediately the cock **c**. *G5455*
Mk 14:68 went out into the porch; and the cock **c**. *G5455*
72 And the second time the cock **c**. And *G5455*
Lk 22:60 while he yet spake, the cock **c**. *G5455*
Jn 18:27 again: and immediately the cock **c**. *G5455*

CRIB
Job 39: 9 be willing to serve thee, or abide by thy **c**? H18
Prv 14: 4 Where no oxen *are*, the **c** *is* clean: but H18
Isa 1: 3 the ass his master's **c**: *but* Israel doth not H18

CRIED
Gen 27:34 of his father, he **c** with a great and H6817
39:14 lie with me, and I **c** with a loud voice: H7121
15 lifted up my voice and **c**, that he left his H7121
18 lifted up my voice and **c**, that he left his H7121
41:43 he had; and they **c** before him, Bow the H7121
55 the people **c** to Pharaoh for bread: H6817
45: 1 by him; and he **c**, Cause every man to H7121
Ex 2:23 bondage, and they **c**, and their cry came H2199
5:15 of Israel came and **c** unto Pharaoh, H6817
8:12 and Moses **c** unto the LORD because H6817
14:10 children of Israel **c** out unto the LORD. H6817
15:25 And he **c** unto the LORD; and the H6817
17: 4 And Moses **c** unto the LORD, saying, H6817
Nu 11: 2 And the people **c** unto Moses; and H6817
12:13 And Moses **c** unto the LORD, saying, H6817
14: 1 and **c**; and the people wept that night. H5414
20:16 And when we **c** unto the LORD, he H6817
Dt 22:24 because she **c** not, *being* in the city; H6817
27 **c**, and *there was* none to save her. H6817
26: 7 And when we **c** unto the LORD God of H6817
Jos 24: 7 And when they **c** unto the LORD, he H6817
Jdg 3: 9 And when the children of Israel **c** unto H2199
15 But when the children of Israel **c** unto H2199
4: 3 And the children of Israel **c** unto the H6817
5:28 at a window, and **c** through the lattice, H2980
6: 6 the children of Israel **c** unto the LORD. H2199
7 the children of Israel **c** unto the LORD H2199
7:20 *withal*: and they **c**, The sword of the H7121
21 and all the host ran, and **c**, and fled. H7321
9: 7 up his voice, and **c**, and said unto them, H7121
10:10 And the children of Israel **c** unto the H2199
12 you; and ye **c** to me, and I delivered H6817
18:23 And they **c** unto the children of Dan. H7121
1Sa 4:13 the city, and told *it*, all the city **c** out. H2199
5:10 that the Ekronites **c** out, saying, They H2199

1Sa 7: 9 and Samuel **c** unto the LORD for Israel; H2199
12: 8 and your fathers **c** unto the LORD, then H2199
10 And they **c** unto the LORD, and said, H2199
15:11 and he **c** unto the LORD all night. H2199
17: 8 And he stood and **c** unto the armies of H7121
20:37 shot, Jonathan **c** after the lad, and said, H7121
38 And Jonathan **c** after the lad, Make H7121
24: 8 of the cave, and **c** after Saul, saying, H7121
26:14 And David **c** to the people, and to H7121
28:12 saw Samuel, she **c** with a loud voice: H2199
2Sa 18:25 And the watchman **c**, and told the king. H7121
19: 4 face, and the king **c** with a loud voice, H2199
20:16 Then **c** a wise woman out of the city, H7121
22: 7 the LORD, and **c** to my God: and he did H7121
1Ki 13: 2 And he **c** against the altar in the word H7121
4 of God, which had **c** against the altar in H7121
21 And he **c** unto the man of God that H7121
32 For the saying which he **c** by the word H7121
17:20 And he **c** unto the LORD, and said, O H7121
21 three times, and **c** unto the LORD, and H7121
18:28 And they **c** aloud, and cut themselves H7121
20:39 And as the king passed by, he **c** unto H6817
22:32 against him: and Jehoshaphat **c** out. H2199
2Ki 2:12 And Elisha saw *it*, and he **c**, My father, H6817
4: 1 Now there **c** a certain woman of the H6817
40 the pottage, that they **c** out, and said, O H6817
6: 5 into the water: and he **c**, and said, Alas, H6817
26 the wall, there **c** a woman unto him, H6817
8: 5 restored to life, **c** to the king for her H6817
11:14 her clothes, and **c**, Treason, Treason. H7121
18:28 Then Rab-shakeh stood and **c** with a H7121
20:11 And Isaiah the prophet **c** unto the H7121
1Ch 5:20 them: for they **c** to God in the battle, H2199
2Ch 13:14 behind: and they **c** unto the LORD, and H6817
14:11 And Asa **c** unto the LORD his God, and H7121
18:31 but Jehoshaphat **c** out, and the LORD H2199
32:18 Then they **c** with a loud voice in the H7121
20 son of Amoz, prayed and **c** to heaven. H2199
Neh 9: 4 *and* Chenani, and **c** with a loud voice H2199
27 trouble, when they **c** unto thee, thou H6817
28 they returned, and **c** unto thee, thou H2199
Est 4: 1 city, and **c** with a loud and a bitter cry; H2199
Job 29:12 Because I delivered the poor that **c**, and H7768
30: 5 (they **c** after them as *after* a thief;) H7321
28 I stood up, *and* I **c** in the congregation. H7768
Ps 3: 4 I **c** unto the LORD with my voice, and H7121
18: 6 upon the LORD, and **c** unto my God: he H7768
41 They **c**, but *there was* none to save H7768
22: 5 They **c** unto thee, and were delivered: H2199
24 him; but when he **c** unto him, he heard. H7768
30: 2 O LORD my God, I **c** unto thee, and H7768
8 I **c** to thee, O LORD; and unto the H7121
31:22 of my supplications when I **c** unto thee. H7768
34: 6 This poor man **c**, and the LORD heard H7121
66:17 I **c** unto him with my mouth, and he H7121
77: 1 I **c** unto God with my voice, *even* unto H6817
88: 1 O LORD God of my salvation, I have **c** H6817
13 But unto thee have I **c**, O LORD; and in H7768
107: 6 Then they **c** unto the LORD in their H6817
13 Then they **c** unto the LORD in their H2199
119:145 I **c** with *my* whole heart; hear me, O H7121
146 I **c** unto thee; save me, and I shall keep H7121
147 morning, and **c**: I hoped in thy word. H7768
120: 1 In my distress I **c** unto the LORD, and H7121
130: 1 Out of the depths have I **c** unto thee, O H7121
138: 3 In the day when I **c** thou answeredst H7121
142: 1 I **c** unto the LORD with my voice; with H2199
5 I **c** unto thee, O LORD: I said, Thou *art* H2199
Isa 6: 3 And one **c** unto another, and said, H7121
4 **c**, and the house was filled with smoke. H7121
21: 8 And he **c**, A lion: My lord, I stand H7121
30: 7 therefore have I **c** concerning this, H7121
36:13 Then Rabshakeh stood, and **c** with a H7121
Jer 4:20 Destruction upon destruction is **c**; for H7121
20: 8 For since I spake, I **c** out, I cried H2199
8 For since I spake, I cried out, I **c** H7121
Lam 2:18 Their heart **c** unto the Lord, O wall of H6817
4:15 They **c** unto them, Depart ye; *it is* H7121
Ezk 9: 1 He **c** also in mine ears with a loud H7121
8 upon my face, and **c**, and said, Ah Lord H2199
10:13 As for the wheels, it was **c** unto them in H7121
11:13 upon my face, and **c** with a loud voice, H2199
Dan 3: 4 Then an herald **c** aloud, To you it is H7123
4:14 He **c** aloud, and said thus, Hew down H7123
5: 7 The king **c** aloud to bring in the H7123
6:20 And when he came to the den, he **c** H2200
Hos 7:14 And they have not **c** unto me with their H2199
Jna 1: 5 Then the mariners were afraid, and **c** H2199
14 Wherefore they **c** unto the LORD, and H7121
Jna 2: 2 And said, I **c** by reason of mine H7121
2 of hell **c** I, *and* thou heardest my voice. H7768
3: 4 journey, and he **c**, and said, Yet forty H7121
Zec 1: 4 prophets have **c**, saying, Thus saith the H7121
6: 8 Then **c** he upon me, and spake unto H2199
7: 7 which the LORD hath **c** by the former H7121
13 to pass, *that* as he **c**, and they would not H7121
13 not hear; so they **c**, and I would not H7121
Mt 8:29 And, behold, they **c** out, saying, What *G2896*
14:26 It is a spirit; and they **c** out for fear. *G2896*
30 to sink, he **c**, saying, Lord, save me. *G2896*
15:22 same coasts, and **c** unto him, saying, *G2905*
20:30 Jesus passed by, **c** out, saying, Have *G2896*
31 peace: but they **c** the more, saying, *G2896*
21: 9 and that followed, **c**, saying, Hosanna *G2896*
27:23 hath he done? But they **c** out the more, *G2896*
46 And about the ninth hour Jesus **c** with a *G310*
50 Jesus, when he had **c** again with a loud *G2896*
Mk 1:23 with an unclean spirit; and he **c** out, *G349*
26 had torn him, and **c** with a loud voice, *G2896*
3:11 and **c**, saying, Thou art the Son of God. *G2896*
5: 7 And **c** with a loud voice, and said, *G2896*
6:49 supposed it had been a spirit, and **c** out: *G349*
9:24 father of the child **c** out, and said with *G2896*
26 And *the spirit* **c**, and rent him sore, and *G2896*
10:48 his peace: but he **c** the more a great *G2896*
11: 9 they that followed, **c**, saying, Hosanna; *G2896*
15:13 And they **c** out again, Crucify him. *G2896*
14 hath he done? And they **c** out the more *G2896*
34 And at the ninth hour Jesus **c** with a loud *G994*
37 And Jesus **c** with a loud voice, and gave *G863*
39 saw that he so **c** out, and gave up the *G2896*
Lk 4:33 devil, and **c** out with a loud voice, *G349*
8: 8 these things, he **c**, He that hath ears to *G5455*
28 When he saw Jesus, he **c** out, and fell *G349*
9:38 And, behold, a man of the company **c** *G310*
16:24 And he **c** and said, Father Abraham, *G5455*
18:38 And he **c**, saying, Jesus, *thou* son of *G994*
39 his peace: but he **c** so much the more, *G2896*
23:18 And they **c** out all at once, saying, Away *G349*
21 But they **c**, saying, Crucify *him*, crucify *G2019*
46 And when Jesus had **c** with a loud *G5455*
Jn 1:15 John bare witness of him, and **c**, saying, *G2896*
7:28 Then **c** Jesus in the temple as he *G2896*
37 Jesus stood and **c**, saying, If any man *G2896*
11:43 And when he thus had spoken, he **c** *G2905*
12:13 to meet him, and **c**, Hosanna: Blessed *is* *G2896*
44 Jesus **c** and said, He that believeth on *G2896*
18:40 Then **c** they all again, saying, Not this *G2905*
19: 6 saw him, they **c** out, saying, Crucify *G2905*
12 him: but the Jews **c** out, saying, If thou *G2896*
15 But they **c** out, Away with *him*, away *G2905*
Act 7:57 Then they **c** out with a loud voice, and *G2896*
60 And he kneeled down, and **c** with a *G2896*
16:17 The same followed Paul and us, and **c**, *G2896*
28 But Paul **c** with a loud voice, saying, Do *G5455*
19:28 full of wrath, and **c** out, saying, Great *is* *G2896*
32 Some therefore **c** one thing, and some *G2896*
34 **c** out, Great *is* Diana of the Ephesians. *G2896*
21:34 And some **c** one thing, some another, *G994*
22:23 And as they **c** out, and cast off *their* *G2905*
24 know wherefore they **c** so against him. *G2019*
23: 6 Pharisees, he **c** out in the council, Men *G2896*
24:21 Except it be for this one voice, that I **c** *G2896*
Rev 6:10 And they **c** with a loud voice, saying, *G2896*
7: 2 living God: and he **c** with a loud voice *G2896*
10 And **c** with a loud voice, saying, *G2896*
10: 3 And **c** with a loud voice, as *when* a lion *G2896*
3 **c**, seven thunders uttered their voices. *G2896*
12: 2 And she being with child **c**, travailing in *G2896*
14:18 over fire; and **c** with a loud cry to him *G5455*
18: 2 And he **c** mightily with a strong voice, *G2896*
18 And **c** when they saw the smoke of her *G2896*
19 on their heads, and **c**, weeping and *G2896*
19:17 in the sun; and he **c** with a loud voice, *G2896*

CRIES
Jas 5: 4 crieth: and the **c** of them which have *G995*

CRIEST
Ex 14:15 Moses, Wherefore **c** thou unto me? H6817
1Sa 26:14 said, Who *art* thou *that* **c** to the king? H7121
Prv 2: 3 Yea, if thou **c** after knowledge, *and* H7121
Isa 57:13 When thou **c**, let thy companies deliver H2199
Jer 30:15 Why **c** thou for thine affliction? thy H2199

CRIETH
Gen 4:10 blood **c** unto me from the ground. H6817
Ex 22:27 to pass, when he **c** unto me, that I will H6817
Job 24:12 **c** out: yet God layeth not folly *to them*. H7768
Ps 72:12 the needy when he **c**; the poor also, and H7768
84: 2 and my flesh **c** out for the living God. H7442
Prv 1:20 Wisdom **c** without; she uttereth her H7442
21 She **c** in the chief place of concourse, in H7121
8: 3 She **c** at the gates, at the entry of the H7442
9: 3 She hath sent forth her maidens: she **c** H7121
Isa 26:17 is in pain, *and* **c** out in her pangs; so H2199
40: 3 The voice of him that **c** in the H7121
Jer 12: 8 lion in the forest; it **c** out against me: H5414
Mic 6: 9 The LORD'S voice **c** unto the city, and H7121
Mt 15:23 Send her away; for she **c** after us. *G2896*
Lk 9:39 and he suddenly **c** out; and it teareth *G2896*
Ro 9:27 Esaias also **c** concerning Israel, *G2896*
Jas 5: 4 back by fraud, **c**: and the cries of them *G2896*

CRIME
Job 31:11 For this *is* an heinous **c**; yea, it *is* an H2154
Act 25:16 concerning the **c** laid against him. *G1462*

CRIMES
Ezk 7:23 bloody **c**, and the city is full of violence. H4941
Act 25:27 withal to signify the **c** *laid* against him. *G156*

CRIMSON
2Ch 2: 7 and in purple, and **c**, and blue, and that H3758
14 in fine linen, and in **c**; also to grave any H3758
3:14 and purple, and **c**, and fine linen, and H3758
Isa 1:18 they be red like **c**, they shall be as wool. H8438
Jer 4:30 thyself with **c**, though thou deckest H8144

CRIPPLE
Act 14: 8 in his feet, being a **c** from his mother's *G5560*

CRISPING
Isa 3:22 and the wimples, and the **c** pins, H2754

CRISPING-PINS See CRISPING and PINS.

CRISPUS
Act 18: 8 And **C**, the chief ruler of the synagogue, *G2921*
1Co 1:14 baptized none of you, but **C** and Gaius; *G2921*

CROOKBACKT
Lev 21:20 Or **c**, or a dwarf, or that hath a blemish H1384

CROOKED
Dt 32: 5 *they are* a perverse and **c** generation. H6618
Job 26:13 his hand hath formed the **c** serpent. H1281
Ps 125: 5 As for such as turn aside unto their **c** H6128
Prv 2:15 Whose ways *are* **c**, and *they* froward in H6141
Ecc 1:15 *That which is* **c** cannot be made H5791
7:13 *that* straight, which he hath made **c**? H5791
Isa 27: 1 leviathan that **c** serpent; and he shall H6129
40: 4 be made low: and the **c** shall be made H6121
42:16 before them, and **c** things straight. H4625
45: 2 I will go before thee, and make the **c** H1921
59: 8 have made them **c** paths: whosoever H6140
Lam 3: 9 hewn stone, he hath made my paths **c**. H5753
Lk 3: 5 low; and the **c** shall be made straight, *G4646*
Php 2:15 in the midst of a **c** and perverse nation, *G4646*

CROP
Lev 1:16 And he shall pluck away his **c** with his H4760
Ezk 17:22 will set *it*; I will **c** off from the top of his H6998

CROPPED
Ezk 17: 4 He **c** off the top of his young twigs, and H6998

CROSS
Mt 10:38 And he that taketh not his **c**, and *G4716*
16:24 and take up his **c**, and follow me. *G4716*
27:32 name: him they compelled to bear his **c**. *G4716*
40 the Son of God, come down from the **c**. *G4716*
42 from the **c**, and we will believe him. *G4716*
Mk 8:34 and take up his **c**, and follow me. *G4716*
10:21 and come, take up the **c**, and follow me. *G4716*
15:21 of Alexander and Rufus, to bear his **c**. *G4716*
30 thyself, and come down from the **c**. *G4716*
32 now from the **c**, that we may see and *G4716*
Lk 9:23 and take up his **c** daily, and follow me. *G4716*
14:27 And whosoever doth not bear his **c**, and *G4716*
23:26 the **c**, that he might bear *it* after Jesus. *G4716*
Jn 19:17 And he bearing his **c** went forth into a *G4716*
19 and put *it* on the **c**. And the writing was, *G4716*
25 Now there stood by the **c** of Jesus his *G4716*
31 remain upon the **c** on the sabbath day, *G4716*
1Co 1:17 of words, lest the **c** of Christ should be *G4716*
18 For the preaching of the **c** is to them *G4716*

Gal 5:11 then is the offence of the c ceased. G4716
6:12 suffer persecution for the c of Christ. G4716
14 glory, save in the c of our Lord Jesus G4716
Eph 2:16 the c, having slain the enmity thereby: G4716
Php 2: 8 unto death, even the death of the c. G4716
3:18 *they are* the enemies of the c of Christ: G4716
Col 1:20 the blood of his c, by him to reconcile G4716
2:14 took it out of the way, nailing it to his c; G4716
Heb 12: 2 before him endured the c, despising the G4716

CROSSWAY
Oba 14 have stood in the c, to cut off those of H6563

CROUCH
1Sa 2:36 shall come *and* c to him for a piece of H7812

CROUCHETH
Ps 10:10 He c, *and* humbleth himself, that the H1794

CROW
Mt 26:34 the cock c, thou shalt deny me thrice. G5455
75 Before the cock c, thou shalt deny me G5455
Mk 14:30 cock c twice, thou shalt deny me thrice. G5455
72 Before the cock c twice, thou shalt deny G5455
Lk 22:34 the cock shall not c this day, before G5455
61 the cock c, thou shalt deny me thrice. G5455
Jn 13:38 not c, till thou hast denied me thrice. G5455

CROWN
Gen 49:26 Joseph, and on the c of the head of him H6936
Ex 25:11 make upon it a c of gold round about. H2213
24 make thereto a c of gold round about. H2213
25 c to the border thereof round about. H2213
29: 6 and put the holy c upon the mitre. H5145
30: 3 make unto it a c of gold round about. H2213
4 make to it under the c of it, by the two H2213
37: 2 and made a c of gold to it round about. H2213
11 thereunto a c of gold round about. H2213
12 and made a c of gold for the border H2213
26 made unto it a c of gold round about. H2213
27 for it under the c thereof, by the two H2213
39:30 And they made the plate of the holy c H5145
Lev 8: 9 c; as the LORD commanded Moses. H5145
21:12 of his God; for the c of the anointing oil H5145
Dt 33:20 teareth the arm with the c of the head. H6936
2Sa 1:10 and I took the c that *was* upon his H5145
12:30 And he took their king's c from off his H5850
14:25 foot even to the c of his head there was H6936
2Ki 11:12 son, and put the c upon him, and *gave* H5145
1Ch 20: 2 And David took the c of their king from H5850
2Ch 23:11 put upon him the c, and *gave him* the H5145
Est 1:11 the king with the c royal, to shew the H3804
2:17 he set the royal c upon her head, and H3804
6: 8 the c royal which is set upon his head: H3804
8:15 and with a great c of gold, and with a H5850
Job 2: 7 boils from the sole of his foot unto his c. H6936
19: 9 glory, and taken the c *from* my head. H5850
31:36 my shoulder, *and* bind it *as* a c to me. H5850
Ps 21: 3 settest a c of pure gold on his head. H5850
89:39 his c *by casting it* to the ground. H5145
132:18 but upon himself shall his c flourish. H5145
Prv 4: 9 a c of glory shall she deliver to thee. H5850
12: 4 A virtuous woman *is* a c to her H5850
14:24 The c of the wise *is* their riches: *but* the H5850
16:31 The hoary head *is* a c of glory, *if* it be H5850
17: 6 Children's children *are* the c of old H5850
27:24 doth the c *endure* to every generation? H5145
Song 3:11 king Solomon with the c wherewith his H5850
Isa 3:17 with a scab the c of the head of the H6936
28: 1 Woe to the c of pride, to the drunkards H5850
3 The c of pride, the drunkards of H5850
5 of hosts be for a c of glory, and for a H5850
62: 3 Thou shalt also be a c of glory in the H5850
Jer 2:16 have broken the c of thy head. H6936
13:18 come down, *even* the c of your glory. H5850
48:45 c of the head of the tumultuous ones. H6936
Lam 5:16 The c is fallen *from* our head: woe unto H5850
Ezk 16:12 and a beautiful c upon thine head. H5850
21:26 and take off the c: this *shall* not *be* the H5850
Zec 9:16 c, lifted up as an ensign upon his land. H5145
Mt 27:29 And when they had platted a c of G4735
Mk 15:17 a c of thorns, and put it about his *head*, G4735
Jn 19: 2 And the soldiers platted a c of thorns, G4735
5 Then came Jesus forth, wearing the c of G4735
1Co 9:25 a corruptible c; but we an incorruptible. G4735
Php 4: 1 for, my joy and c, so stand fast in the G4735
1Th 2:19 For what *is* our hope, or joy, or c of G4735
2Ti 4: 8 Henceforth there is laid up for me a c G4735
Jas 1:12 he shall receive the c of life, which the G4735
1Pt 5: 4 a c of glory that fadeth not away. G4735
Rev 2:10 death, and I will give thee a c of life. G4735
3:11 thou hast, that no man take thy c. G4735
6: 2 him had a bow; and a c was given unto G4735
12: 1 and upon her head a c of twelve stars: G4735
14:14 golden c, and in his hand a sharp sickle. G4735

CROWNED
Ps 8: 5 and hast c him with glory and honour. H5849
Prv 14:18 but the prudent are c with knowledge. H3803
Song 3:11 his mother c him in the day of his H5849
Nah 3:17 Thy c *are* as the locusts, and thy H4502
2Ti 2: 5 *yet* is he not c, except he strive lawfully. G4737
Heb 2: 9 the suffering of death, c with glory and G4737

CROWNEDST
Heb 2: 7 the angels; thou c him with glory and G4737

CROWNEST
Ps 65:11 Thou c the year with thy goodness; and H5849

CROWNETH
Ps 103: 4 from destruction; who c thee with H5849

CROWNING
Isa 23: 8 counsel against Tyre, the c *city*, whose H5849

CROWNS
Ezk 23:42 and beautiful c upon their heads. H5850
Zec 6:11 Then take silver and gold, and make c, H5850
14 And the c shall be to Helem, and to H5850
Rev 4: 4 and they had on their heads c of gold. G4735
10 cast their c before the throne, saying, G4735
9: 7 *were* as it were c like gold, and their G4735
12: 3 ten horns, and seven c upon his heads. G1238
13: 1 his horns ten c, and upon his heads G1238
19:12 head *were* many c; and he had a name G1238

CRUCIFIED
Mt 26: 2 and the Son of man is betrayed to be c. G4717
27:22 *They* all say unto him, Let him be c. G4717
23 cried out the more, saying, Let him be c. G4717
26 Jesus, he delivered *him* to be c. G4717
35 And they c him, and parted his G4717
38 Then were there two thieves c with G4717
44 The thieves also, which were c with G4957
28: 5 I know that ye seek Jesus, which was c. G4717
Mk 15:15 when he had scourged *him*, to be c. G4717
24 And when they had c him, they parted G4717
25 And it was the third hour, and they c G4717
32 they that were c with him reviled him. G4957
16: 6 which was c: he is risen; he is not G4717
Lk 23:23 that he might be c. And the voices of G4717
33 there they c him, and the malefactors, G4717
24: 7 and be c, and the third day rise again. G4717
20 condemned to death, and have c him. G4717
Jn 19:16 unto them to be c. And they took Jesus, G4717
18 Where they c him, and two other with G4717
20 where Jesus was c was nigh to the city: G4717
23 Then the soldiers, when they had c G4717
32 and of the other which was c with him. G4957
41 Now in the place where he was c there G4717
Act 2:23 and by wicked hands have c and slain: G4362
36 whom ye have c, both Lord and Christ. G4717
4:10 whom ye c, whom God raised from G4717
Ro 6: 6 Knowing this, that our old man is c G4957
1Co 1:13 Is Christ divided? was Paul c for you? G4717
23 But we preach Christ c, unto the Jews a G4717
2: 2 you, save Jesus Christ, and him c. G4717
8 would not have c the Lord of glory. G4717
2Co 13: 4 For though he was c through weakness, G4717
Gal 2:20 I am c with Christ: nevertheless I live; G4957
3: 1 been evidently set forth, c among you? G4717
5:24 And they that are Christ's have c the G4717
6:14 is c unto me, and I unto the world. G4717
Rev 11: 8 and Egypt, where also our Lord was c. G4717

CRUCIFY
Mt 20:19 to scourge, and to c *him*: and the third G4717
23:34 ye shall kill and c; and *some* of them G4717
27:31 on him, and led him away to c *him*. G4717
Mk 15:13 And they cried out again, C him. G4717
14 cried out the more exceedingly, C him. G4717
20 on him, and led him out to c him. G4717
27 And with him they c two thieves; the G4717
Lk 23:21 But they cried, saying, C *him*, crucify G4717
21 But they cried, saying, Crucify *him*, c G4717
Jn 19: 6 cried out, saying, C *him*, crucify *him*. G4717
6 Crucify *him*, c *him*. Pilate saith unto G4717
Jn 19: 6 and c *him*: for I find no fault in him. G4717
10 c thee, and have power to release thee? G4717
15 away with *him*, c him. Pilate saith unto G4717
15 unto them, Shall I c your King? The G4717
Heb 6: 6 seeing they c to themselves the Son G388

CRUEL
Gen 49: 7 wrath, for it was c: I will divide them in H7185
Ex 6: 9 anguish of spirit, and for c bondage. H7186
Dt 32:33 of dragons, and the c venom of asps. H393
Job 30:21 Thou art become c to me: with thy H393
Ps 25:19 many; and they hate me with c hatred. H2555
71: 4 hand of the unrighteous and c man. H2556
Prv 5: 9 unto others, and thy years unto the c: H394
11:17 but *he that is* c troubleth his own flesh. H394
12:10 the tender mercies of the wicked *are* c. H394
17:11 a c messenger shall be sent against him. H394
27: 4 Wrath *is* c, and anger *is* outrageous; but H395
Song 8: 6 as death; jealousy *is* c as the grave: the H7186
Isa 13: 9 Behold, the day of the LORD cometh, c H394
19: 4 into the hand of a c lord; and a fierce H7186
Jer 6:23 bow and spear; they *are* c, and have no H394
30:14 the chastisement of a c one, for the H394
50:42 the lance: they *are* c, and will not shew H394
Lam 4: 3 c, like the ostriches in the wilderness. H393
Heb 11:36 And others had trial of c mockings and

CRUELLY
Ezk 18:18 *As for* his father, because he c H6233

CRUELTY
Gen 49: 5 of c *are in* their habitations. H2555
Jdg 9:24 That the c *done* to the threescore and H2555
Ps 27:12 against me, and such as breathe out c. H2555
74:20 the earth are full of the habitations of c. H2555
Ezk 34: 4 force and with c have ye ruled them. H6531

CRUMBS
Mt 15:27 c which fall from their masters' table. G5589
Mk 7:28 under the table eat of the children's c. G5589
Lk 16:21 And desiring to be fed with the c which G5589

CRUSE
1Sa 26:11 and the c of water, and let us go. H6835
12 So David took the spear and the c of H6835
16 the c of water that *was* at his bolster. H6835
1Ki 14: 3 cracknels, and a c of honey, and go to H1228
17:12 and a little oil in a c: and, behold, I *am* H6835
14 neither shall the c of oil fail, until the H6835
16 neither did the c of oil fail, according H6835
19: 6 the coals, and a c of water at his head. H6835
2Ki 2:20 And he said, Bring me a new c, and put H6746

CRUSH
Job 39:15 And forgetteth that the foot may c H2115
Lam 1:15 against me to c my young men: the H7665
3:34 To c under his feet all the prisoners of H1792
Am 4: 1 the poor, which c the needy, which say H7533

CRUSHED
Lev 22:24 which is bruised, or c, or broken, or cut; H3807
Nu 22:25 unto the wall, and c Balaam's foot H3905
Dt 28:33 shalt be only oppressed and c alway: H7533
Job 4:19 the dust, *which* are c before the moth? H1792
5: 4 and they are c in the gate, neither H1792
Isa 59: 5 which is c breaketh out into a viper. H2116
Jer 51:34 me, he hath c me, he hath made me H2000

CRY
Gen 18:20 And the LORD said, Because the c of H2201
21 according to the c of it, which is come H6818
19:13 place, because the c of them is waxen H6818
27:34 exceeding bitter c, and said unto his H6818
Ex 2:23 cried, and their c came up unto God by H7775
3: 7 have heard their c by reason of their H6818
9 Now therefore, behold, the c of the H6818
5: 8 therefore they c, saying, Let us go *and* H6817
11: 6 And there shall be a great c throughout H6818
12:30 there was a great c in Egypt; for *there* H6818
22:23 in any wise, and they c at all unto me, I H6817
23 at all unto me, I will surely hear their c; H6818
32:18 the voice of *them that* c for being H6030
Lev 13:45 lip, and shall c, Unclean, unclean. H7121
Nu 16:34 them fled at the c of them: for they H6963
Dt 15: 9 him nought; and he c unto the LORD H7121
24:15 upon it: lest he c against thee unto the H7121
Jdg 10:14 Go and c unto the gods which ye have H2199
1Sa 5:12 and the c of the city went up to heaven. H7775
7: 8 Cease not to c unto the LORD our H2199

1Sa 8:18 And ye shall c out in that day because H2199
9:16 because their c is come unto me. H6818
2Sa 19:28 have I yet to c any more unto the king? H2199
22: 7 and my c *did enter* into his ears. H7775
1Ki 8:28 hearken unto the c and to the prayer, H7440
18:27 them, and said, C aloud: for he *is* a H7121
2Ki 8: 3 she went forth to c unto the king for H6817
2Ch 6:19 to hearken unto the c and the prayer H7440
13:12 trumpets to c alarm against you. H7321
20: 9 in this house,) and c unto thee in our H2199
Neh 5: 1 And there was a great c of the people H6818
6 when I heard their c and these words. H2201
9: 9 and heardest their c by the Red sea; H2201
Est 4: 1 and cried with a loud and a bitter c; H2201
9:31 the matters of the fastings and their c. H2201
Job 16:18 my blood, and let my c have no place. H2201
19: 7 Behold, I c out of wrong, but I am not H6817
7 I c aloud, but *there is* no judgment. H7768
27: 9 Will God hear his c when trouble H6818
30:20 I c unto thee, and thou dost not hear H7768
24 grave, though they c in his destruction. H7769
31:38 If my land c against me, or that the H2199
34:28 So that they cause the c of the poor to H6818
28 and he heareth the c of the afflicted. H6818
35: 9 make *the oppressed* to c: they cry out by H2199
9 to cry: they c out by reason of the H7768
12 There they c, but none giveth answer, H6817
36:13 they c not when he bindeth them. H7768
38:41 when his young ones c unto God, they H7768
Ps 5: 2 Hearken unto the voice of my c, my H7773
9:12 he forgetteth not the c of the humble. H6818
17: 1 attend unto my c, give ear unto my H7440
18: 6 c came before him, *even* into his ears. H7775
22: 2 O my God, I c in the daytime, but thou H7121
27: 7 Hear, O LORD, *when* I c with my voice: H7121
28: 1 Unto thee will I c, O LORD my rock; be H7121
2 when I c unto thee, when I lift H7768
34:15 and his ears *are open* unto their c. H7775
17 *The righteous* c, and the LORD heareth, H6817
39:12 give ear unto my c; hold not thy peace H7775
40: 1 he inclined unto me, and heard my c. H7775
55:17 c aloud: and he shall hear my voice. H1993
56: 9 When I c *unto thee*, then shall mine H7121
57: 2 I will c unto God most high; unto God H7121
61: 1 Hear my c, O God; attend unto my H7440
2 From the end of the earth will I c unto H7121
86: 3 Be merciful unto me, O Lord: for I c H7121
88: 2 before thee: incline thine ear unto my c; H7440
89:26 He shall c unto me, Thou *art* my father, H7121
102: 1 Hear my prayer, O LORD, and let my c H7775
106:44 their affliction, when he heard their c: H7440
107:19 Then they c unto the LORD in their H2199
28 Then they c unto the LORD in their H6817
119:169 Let my c come near before thee, O H7440
141: 1 LORD, I c unto thee: make haste unto H7121
1 ear unto my voice, when I c unto thee. H7121
142: 6 Attend unto my c; for I am brought very H7440
145:19 will hear their c, and will save them. H7775
147: 9 food, *and* to the young ravens which c. H7121
Prv 8: 1 Doth not wisdom c? and understanding H7121
21:13 Whoso stoppeth his ears at the c of the H2201
13 shall c himself, but shall not be heard. H7121
Ecc 9:17 the c of him that ruleth among fools. H2201
Isa 5: 7 for righteousness, but behold a c. H6818
8: 4 have knowledge to c, My father, and my H7121
12: 6 C out and shout, thou inhabitant of H6670
13:22 of the islands shall c in their desolate H6030
14:31 Howl, O gate; c, O city; thou, whole H2199
15: 4 And Heshbon shall c, and Elealeh: their H2199
4 of Moab shall c out; his life shall be H7321
5 My heart shall c out for Moab; his H2199
5 they shall raise up a c of destruction. H2201
8 For the c is gone round about the H2201
19:20 for they shall c unto the LORD because H6817
24:14 LORD, they shall c aloud from the sea. H6670
29: 9 Stay yourselves, and wonder; c ye out, H8173
9 cry ye out, and c: they are drunken, but H8173
30:19 at the voice of thy c; when he shall hear H2199
33: 7 Behold, their valiant ones shall c H6817
34:14 and the satyr shall c to his fellow; the H7121
40: 2 to Jerusalem, and c unto her, that her H7121
6 The voice said, C. And he said, What H7121
6 he said, What shall I c? All flesh *is* grass, H7121
42: 2 He shall not c, nor lift up, nor cause his H6817
13 of war: he shall c, yea, roar; he shall H7321
14 myself: *now* will I c like a travailing H6463
43:14 the Chaldeans, whose c *is* in the ships. H7440
46: 7 yea, *one* shall c unto him, yet can he H6817
54: 1 into singing, and c aloud, thou *that* H6670
Isa 58: 1 C aloud, spare not, lift up thy voice like H7121
9 answer; thou shalt c, and he shall say, H7768
65:14 heart, but ye shall c for sorrow of heart, H6817
Jer 2: 2 Go and c in the ears of Jerusalem, H7121
3: 4 Wilt thou not from this time c unto me, H7121
4: 5 in the land: c, gather together, and H7121
7:16 neither lift up c nor prayer for them, H7440
8:19 Behold the voice of the c of the H7775
11:11 though they shall c unto me, I will not H2199
12 Jerusalem go, and c unto the gods unto H2199
14 neither lift up a c or prayer for them: H7440
14 that they c unto me for their trouble. H7121
14: 2 and the c of Jerusalem is gone up. H6682
12 When they fast, I will not hear their c; H7440
18:22 Let a c be heard from their houses, H2201
20:16 let him hear the c in the morning, and H2201
22:20 Go up to Lebanon, and c; and lift up thy H6817
20 in Bashan, and c from the passages: H6817
25:34 Howl, ye shepherds, and c; and wallow H2199
36 A voice of the c of the shepherds, and H6818
31: 6 Ephraim shall c, Arise ye, and let us H7121
46:12 shame, and thy c hath filled the land: H6682
17 They did c there, Pharaoh king of H7121
47: 2 then the men shall c, and all the H2199
48: 4 little ones have caused a c to be heard. H2201
5 enemies have heard a c of destruction. H6818
20 down: howl and c; tell ye it in Arnon, H2199
31 for Moab, and I will c out for all Moab; H2199
34 From the c of Heshbon *even* unto H2201
49: 3 Howl, O Heshbon, for Ai is spoiled: c, ye H6817
21 of their fall, at the c the noise thereof H6818
29 shall c unto them, Fear *is* on every side. H7121
50:46 and the c is heard among the nations. H2201
51:54 A sound of a c *cometh* from Babylon, H2201
Lam 2:19 Arise, c out in the night: in the H7442
3: 8 Also when I c and shout, he shutteth H2199
56 not thine ear at my breathing, at my c. H7775
Ezk 8:18 and though they c in mine ears with a H7121
9: 4 men that sigh and that c for all the H602
21:12 C and howl, son of man: for it shall be H2199
24:17 Forbear to c, make no mourning for the H602
26:15 when the wounded c, when the slaughter H602
27:28 at the sound of the c of thy pilots. H2201
30 thee, and shall c bitterly, and shall cast H2199
Hos 5: 8 in Ramah: c aloud *at* Beth-aven, H7321
8: 2 Israel shall c unto me, My God, we H2199
Joel 1:14 LORD your God, and c unto the LORD, H2199
19 O LORD, to thee will I c: for the fire hath H7121
20 The beasts of the field c also unto thee: H6165
Am 3: 4 will a young lion c out of his den, if he H6963
Jna 1: 2 great city, and c against it; for their H7121
3: 8 sackcloth, and c mightily unto God: H7121
Mic 3: 4 Then shall they c unto the LORD, but H2199
5 their teeth, and c, Peace; and he that H7121
4: 9 Now why dost thou c out aloud? *is* H7321
Nah 2: 8 *shall they* c; but none shall look back.
Hab 1: 2 O LORD, how long shall I c, and thou H7768
2 wilt not hear! *even* c out unto thee *of* H2199
2:11 For the stone shall c out of the wall, H2199
Zep 1:10 *be* the noise of a c from the fish gate, H6818
14 the mighty man shall c there bitterly. H6873
Zec 1:14 me said unto me, C thou, saying, Thus H7121
17 C yet, saying, Thus saith the LORD of H7121
Mt 12:19 He shall not strive, nor c; neither shall *G2905*
25: 6 And at midnight there was a c made, *G2906*
Mk 10:47 he began to c out, and say, Jesus, *G2896*
Lk 18: 7 own elect, which c day and night unto *G994*
19:40 the stones would immediately c out. *G2896*
Act 23: 9 And there arose a great c: and the *G2906*
Ro 8:15 adoption, whereby we c, Abba, Father. *G2896*
Gal 4:27 break forth and c, thou that travailest *G994*
Rev 14:18 cried with a loud c to him that had the *G2906*

CRYING
1Sa 4:14 And when Eli heard the noise of the c, H6818
2Sa 13:19 her hand on her head, and went on c. H2199
Job 39: 7 neither regardeth he the c of the driver. H8663
Ps 69: 3 I am weary of my c: my throat is dried: H7121
Prv 19:18 and let not thy soul spare for his c. H4191
30:15 The horseleach hath two daughters, c,
Isa 22: 5 the walls, and of c to the mountains. H7771
24:11 *There is* a c for wine in the streets; all H6682
65:19 no more heard in her, nor the voice of c. H2201
Jer 48: 3 A voice of c *shall be* from Horonaim, H6818
Zec 4: 7 *with* shoutings, c, Grace, grace unto it.
Mal 2:13 weeping, and with c out, insomuch H6030
Mt 3: 3 The voice of one c in the wilderness, *G994*
9:27 followed him, c, and saying, *Thou* son *G2896*
21:15 and the children c in the temple, and *G2896*
Mk 1: 3 The voice of one c in the wilderness, *G994*
5: 5 c, and cutting himself with stones. *G2896*
15: 8 And the multitude c aloud began to *G310*
Lk 3: 4 The voice of one c in the wilderness, *G994*
4:41 And devils also came out of many, c *G2896*
Jn 1:23 He said, I *am* the voice of one c in the *G994*
Act 8: 7 For unclean spirits, c with loud voice, *G994*
14:14 and ran in among the people, c out, *G2896*
17: 6 the rulers of the city, c, These that have *G994*
21:28 C out, Men of Israel, help: This is the *G2896*
36 followed after, c, Away with him. *G2896*
25:24 c that he ought not to live any longer. *G1916*
Gal 4: 6 Son into your hearts, c, Abba, Father. *G2896*
Heb 5: 7 with strong c and tears unto him *G2906*
Rev 14:15 out of the temple, c with a loud voice to *G2896*
21: 4 sorrow, nor c, neither shall there be *G2906*

CRYSTAL
Job 28:17 The gold and the c cannot equal it: and H2137
Ezk 1:22 of the terrible c, stretched forth over H7140
Rev 4: 6 of glass like unto c: and in the midst of *G2930*
21:11 even like a jasper stone, clear as c; *G2929*
22: 1 of life, clear as c, proceeding out of the *G2930*

CUBIT
Gen 6:16 to the ark, and in a c shalt thou finish it H520
Ex 25:10 thereof, and a c and a half the breadth H520
10 and a c and a half the height thereof. H520
17 and a c and a half the breadth thereof. H520
23 thereof, and a c the breadth thereof, H520
23 and a c and a half the height thereof. H520
26:13 And a c on the one side, and a cubit on H520
13 And a cubit on the one side, and a c on H520
16 of a board, and a c and a half *shall be* H520
30: 2 A c *shall be* the length thereof, and a H520
2 thereof, and a c the breadth thereof; H520
36:21 the breadth of a board one c and a half. H520
37: 1 the length of it, and a c and a half the H520
1 of it, and a c and a half the height of it: H520
6 and one c and a half the breadth thereof. H520
10 thereof, and a c the breadth thereof, H520
10 and a c and a half the height thereof: H520
25 length of it *was* a c, and the breadth of it H520
25 the breadth of it a c; *it was* foursquare; H520
Dt 3:11 the breadth of it, after the c of a man. H520
Jdg 3:16 had two edges, of a c length; and he did H1574
1Ki 7:24 it, ten in a c, compassing the sea H520
31 and above *was* a c: but the mouth thereof H520
31 work of the base, a c and an half: and H520
32 of a wheel *was* a c and half a cubit. H520
32 of a wheel *was* a cubit and half a c. H520
35 compass of half a c high: and on the top H520
2Ch 4: 3 about: ten in a c, compassing the sea H520
Ezk 40: 5 six cubits *long* by the c and an hand H520
12 chambers *was* one c *on this side*, and the H520
12 the space *was* one c on that side: and the H520
42 burnt offering, of a c and an half long, H520
42 an half long, and a c and an half broad, H520
42 broad, and one c high: whereupon also H520
42: 4 one c; and their doors toward the north. H520
43:13 the cubits: The c *is* a cubit and an hand H520
13 The cubit *is* a c and an hand breadth; H520
13 the bottom *shall be* a c, and the breadth a H520
13 and the breadth a c, and the border H520
14 the breadth one c; and from the lesser H520
14 *be* four cubits, and the breadth *one* c. H520
17 about it *shall be* half a c; and the bottom H520
17 thereof *shall be* a c about; and his stairs H520
Mt 6:27 thought can add one c unto his stature? *G4083*
Lk 12:25 thought can add to his stature one c? *G4083*

CUBITS
Gen 6:15 *be* three hundred c, the breadth of it fifty H520
15 it fifty c, and the height of it thirty cubits. H520
15 it fifty cubits, and the height of it thirty c. H520
7:20 Fifteen c upward did the waters prevail; H520
Ex 25:10 shittim wood: two c and a half *shall be* H520
17 *of* pure gold: two c and a half *shall be* H520
23 *of* shittim wood: two c *shall be* the length H520
26: 2 *be* eight and twenty c, and the breadth of H520
2 of one curtain four c: and every one of H520
8 *shall be* thirty c, and the breadth of one H520
8 of one curtain four c: and the eleven H520
16 Ten c *shall be* the length of a board, and H520
27: 1 shittim wood, five c long, and five cubits H520
1 long, and five c broad; the altar shall H520
1 and the height thereof *shall be* three c. H520
9 linen of an hundred c long for one side: H520
11 of an hundred c long, and his twenty

Ex 27:12 c: their pillars ten, and their sockets ten. H520
13 on the east side eastward *shall be* fifty c. H520
14 *gate shall be* fifteen c: their pillars three, H520
15 *be* hangings fifteen c: their pillars three,
16 hanging of twenty c, *of* blue, and purple, H520
18 *be* an hundred c, and the breadth fifty H520
18 and the height five c *of* fine twined linen, H520
30: 2 shall it be: and two c *shall be* the height H520
36: 9 twenty and eight c, and the breadth of H520
9 four c: the curtains *were* all of one size. H520
15 The length of one curtain *was* thirty c, H520
15 cubits, and four c *was* the breadth of one H520
21 The length of a board *was* ten c, and the H520
37: 1 shittim wood: two c and a half *was* the H520
6 *of* pure gold: two c and a half *was* the H520
10 *of* shittim wood: two c *was* the length H520
25 and two c *was* the height of it; H520
38: 1 *of* shittim wood: five c *was* the length H520
1 thereof, and five c the breadth thereof; H520
1 and three c the height thereof. H520
9 *were of* fine twined linen, an hundred c: H520
11 *were* an hundred c, their pillars *were* H520
12 hangings of fifty c, their pillars ten, and H520
13 And for the east side eastward fifty c. H520
14 *the gate were* fifteen c; their pillars three, H520
15 hangings of fifteen c; their pillars three, H520
18 linen: and twenty c *was* the length, and H520
18 the breadth *was* five c, answerable to the H520
Nu 11:31 two c *high* upon the face of the earth. H520
35: 4 and outward a thousand c round about. H520
5 side two thousand c, and on the south H520
5 side two thousand c, and on the west side H520
5 side two thousand c, and on the north H520
5 side two thousand c; and the city *shall be* H520
Dt 3:11 of Ammon? nine c *was* the length H520
11 thereof, and four c the breadth of it, H520
Jos 3: 4 two thousand c by measure: come not H520
1Sa 17: 4 Gath, whose height *was* six c and a span. H520
1Ki 6: 2 *was* threescore c, and the breadth thereof H520
2 c, and the height thereof thirty cubits.
2 *cubits*, and the height thereof thirty c. H520
3 of the house, twenty c *was* the length H520
3 of the house; *and* ten c *was* the breadth H520
6 The nethermost chamber *was* five c H520
6 and the middle *was* six c broad, and the H520
6 the third *was* seven c broad: for without H520
10 all the house, five c high: and they rested H520
16 And he built twenty c on the sides of the H520
17 *is*, the temple before it, was forty c *long*. H520
20 *was* twenty c in length, and twenty H520
20 in length, and twenty c in breadth, and H520
20 and twenty c in the height thereof: H520
23 cherubims *of* olive tree, *each* ten c high. H520
24 And five c *was* the one wing of the H520
24 cherub, and five c the other wing of the H520
24 uttermost part of the other *were* ten c. H520
25 And the other cherub *was* ten c: both the H520
26 The height of the one cherub *was* ten c, H520
7: 2 *was* an hundred c, and the breadth H520
2 thereof fifty c, and the height thereof H520
2 thereof thirty c, upon four rows of cedar H520
6 thereof *was* fifty c, and the breadth H520
6 thereof thirty c: and the porch *was* before H520
10 stones of ten c, and stones of eight cubits. H520
10 stones of ten cubits, and stones of eight c. H520
15 of brass, of eighteen c high apiece: and a H520
15 c did compass either of them about. H520
16 chapiter *was* five c, and the height of the H520
16 height of the other chapiter *was* five c: H520
19 *were* of lily work in the porch, four c. H520
23 And he made a molten sea, ten c from H520
23 his height *was* five c: and a line of thirty H520
23 of thirty c did compass it round about. H520
27 And he made ten bases of brass; four c H520
27 one base, and four c the breadth thereof, H520
27 thereof, and three c the height of it. H520
38 laver was four c: *and* upon every one H520
2Ki 14:13 unto the corner gate, four hundred c. H520
25:17 pillar *was* eighteen c, and the chapiter H520
17 of the chapiter three c; and the wreathen H520
1Ch 11:23 of *great* stature, five c high; and in the H520
2Ch 3: 3 of God. The length by c after the first H520
3 c, and the breadth twenty cubits. H520
3 cubits, and the breadth twenty c. H520
4 the house, twenty c, and the height *was* H520
8 of the house, twenty c, and the breadth H520
8 thereof twenty c: and he overlaid it with H520
11 *were* twenty c long: one wing *of the* H520
11 *cherub was* five c, reaching to the wall H520
2Ch 3:11 *was likewise* five c, reaching to the wing H520
12 cherub *was* five c, reaching to the wall H520
12 other wing *was* five c *also*, joining to the H520
13 forth twenty c: and they stood on their H520
15 of thirty and five c high, and the chapiter H520
15 *was* on the top of each of them *was* five c. H520
4: 1 of brass, twenty c the length thereof, and H520
1 and twenty c the breadth thereof, H520
1 thereof, and ten c the height thereof. H520
2 Also he made a molten sea of ten c from H520
2 compass, and five c the height thereof; H520
2 of thirty c did compass it round about. H520
6:13 scaffold, of five c long, and five cubits H520
13 long, and five c broad, and three cubits H520
13 broad, and three c high, and had set it in H520
25:23 to the corner gate, four hundred c. H520
Ezr 6: 3 thereof threescore c, *and* the breadth H521
3 *and* the breadth thereof threescore c; H521
Neh 3:13 c on the wall unto the dung gate. H520
Est 5:14 be made of fifty c high, and to morrow H520
7: 9 the gallows fifty c high, which Haman H520
Jer 52:21 one pillar *was* eighteen c; and a fillet of H520
21 a fillet of twelve c did compass it; and H520
22 chapiter *was* five c, with network and H520
Ezk 40: 5 reed of six c *long* by the cubit and H520
7 chambers *were* five c; and the threshold H520
9 of the gate, eight c; and the posts thereof, H520
9 c; and the porch of the gate *was* inward. H520
11 of the gate, ten c; *and* the length of the H520
11 *and* the length of the gate, thirteen c. H520
12 chambers *were* six c on this side, and six H520
12 on this side, and six c on that side. H520
13 *was* five and twenty c, door against door. H520
14 He made also posts of threescore c, even H520
15 of the porch of the inner gate *were* fifty c. H520
19 an hundred c eastward and northward. H520
21 c, and the breadth five and twenty cubits. H520
21 cubits, and the breadth five and twenty c. H520
23 from gate to gate an hundred c. H520
25 c, and the breadth five and twenty cubits. H520
25 cubits, and the breadth five and twenty c. H520
27 to gate toward the south an hundred c. H520
29 c long, and five and twenty cubits broad. H520
29 cubits long, and five and twenty c broad. H520
30 and twenty c long, and five cubits broad. H520
30 and twenty cubits long, and five c broad. H520
33 c long, and five and twenty cubits broad. H520
33 cubits long, and five and twenty c broad. H520
36 c, and the breadth five and twenty cubits. H520
36 cubits, and the breadth five and twenty c. H520
47 So he measured the court, an hundred c H520
47 and an hundred c broad, foursquare; H520
48 of the porch, five c on this side, and five H520
48 this side, and five c on that side: and the H520
48 of the gate *was* three c on this side, and H520
48 on this side, and three c on that side. H520
49 The length of the porch *was* twenty c, H520
49 the breadth eleven c; and *he brought me* H520
41: 1 the posts, six c broad on the one side, H520
1 one side, and six c broad on the other H520
2 And the breadth of the door *was* ten c; H520
2 the door *were* five c on the one side, and H520
2 the one side, and five c on the other side: H520
2 forty c: and the breadth, twenty cubits. H520
2 forty cubits: and the breadth, twenty c. H520
3 post of the door, two c; and the door, six H520
3 and the door, six c; and the breadth of H520
3 and the breadth of the door, seven c. H520
4 length thereof, twenty c; and the breadth, H520
4 breadth, twenty c, before the temple: and H520
5 of the house, six c; and the breadth of H520
5 c, round about the house on every side. H520
8 chambers *were* a full reed of six great c. H520
9 without, *was* five c: and *that* which *was* H520
10 c round about the house on every side. H520
11 that was left *was* five c round about. H520
12 west *was* seventy c broad; and the wall H520
12 building *was* five c thick round about, H520
12 about, and the length thereof ninety c. H520
13 So he measured the house, an hundred c H520
13 the walls thereof, an hundred c long; H520
14 place toward the east, an hundred c. H520
15 other side, an hundred c, with the inner H520
22 The altar of wood *was* three c high, and H520
22 the length thereof two c; and the corners H520
42: 2 Before the length of an hundred c *was* H520
2 north door, and the breadth *was* fifty c. H520
3 Over against the twenty *c* which *were* for
4 *was* a walk of ten c breadth inward, a H520
Ezk 42: 7 chambers, the length thereof *was* fifty c. H520
8 utter court *was* fifty c: and, lo, before the H520
8 lo, before the temple *were* an hundred c. H520
43:13 the altar after the c: The cubit *is* a cubit H520
14 settle *shall be* two c, and the breadth one H520
14 *be* four c, and the breadth *one* cubit. H520
15 So the altar *shall be* four c; and from the H520
16 And the altar *shall be* twelve c long,
17 And the settle *shall be* fourteen c long
45: 2 c round about for the suburbs thereof. H520
46:22 joined of forty c long and thirty broad:
47: 3 a thousand c, and he brought me H520
Dan 3: 1 *was* threescore c, *and* the breadth thereof H521
1 breadth thereof six c: he set it up in the H521
Zec 5: 2 c, and the breadth thereof ten cubits. H520
2 cubits, and the breadth thereof ten c. H520
Jn 21: 8 hundred c,) dragging the net with fishes. *G4083*
Rev 21:17 *and* forty *and* four c, *according to* the *G4083*

CUCKOW

Lev 11:16 and the c, and the hawk after his kind, H7828
Dt 14:15 and the c, and the hawk after his kind, H7828

CUCUMBERS

Nu 11: 5 Egypt freely; the c, and the melons, and H7180
Isa 1: 8 in a garden of c, as a besieged city. H4750

CUD

Lev 11: 3 c, among the beasts, that shall ye eat. H1625
4 that chew the c, or of them that divide H1625
4 he cheweth the c, but divideth not the H1625
5 he cheweth the c, but divideth not the H1625
6 And the hare, because he cheweth the c, H1625
7 cheweth not the c; he *is* unclean to you. H1625
26 nor cheweth the c, *are* unclean unto H1625
Dt 14: 6 c among the beasts, that ye shall eat. H1625
7 that chew the c, or of them that divide H1625
7 for they chew the c, but divide not the H1625
8 yet cheweth not the c, it *is* unclean unto H1625

CUMBERED

Lk 10:40 But Martha was c about much serving, *G4049*

CUMBERETH

Lk 13: 7 none: cut it down; why c it the ground? *G2673*

CUMBRANCE

Dt 1:12 How can I myself alone bear your c, H2960

CUMI

Mk 5:41 said unto her, Talitha c; which is, being *G2891*

CUMMIN

Isa 28:25 fitches, and scatter the c, and cast in the H3646
27 about upon the c; but the fitches are H3646
27 out with a staff, and the c with a rod. H3646
Mt 23:23 and anise and c, and have omitted the *G2951*

CUNNING

Gen 25:27 And the boys grew: and Esau was a c H3045
Ex 26: 1 of c work shalt thou make them. H2803
31 twined linen of c work: with cherubims H2803
28: 6 and fine twined linen, with c work. H2803
15 of judgment with c work; after the H2803
31: 4 To devise c works, to work in gold, and H4284
35:33 wood, to make any manner of c work. H4284
35 and of the c workman, and of the H2803
35 work, and of those that devise c work. H4284
36: 8 cherubims of c work made he them. H2803
35 *with* cherubims made he it of c work. H2803
38:23 an engraver, and a c workman, and an H2803
39: 3 and in the fine linen, *with* c work. H2803
8 And he made the breastplate *of* c work, H2803
1Sa 16:16 a man, *who is* a c player on an harp: H3045
18 *that is* c in playing, and a mighty H3045
1Ki 7:14 and c to work all works in H1847
1Ch 22:15 of c men for every manner of work. H2450
25: 7 c, was two hundred fourscore and eight. H995
2Ch 2: 7 Send me now therefore a man c to H2450
7 to grave with the c men that *are* with H2450
13 And now I have sent a c man, endued H2450
14 to him, with thy c men, and with the H2450
14 the c men of my lord David thy father. H2450
26:15 invented by c men, to be on the towers H2803
Ps 137: 5 Jerusalem, let my right hand forget *her* c.
Song 7: 1 the work of the hands of a c workman. H542
Isa 3: 3 the c artificer, and the eloquent orator. H2450
40:20 unto him a c workman to prepare H2450
Jer 9:17 send for c *women*, that they may come: H2450

Jer 10: 9 clothing: they *are* all the work of c *men*. H2450
Dan 1: 4 in all wisdom, and c in knowledge, and H3045
Eph 4:14 sleight of men, *and* c craftiness, whereby

CUNNINGLY
2Pt 1:16 For we have not followed c devised

CUP
Gen 40:11 And Pharaoh's c *was* in my hand: and I H3563
11 into Pharaoh's c, and I gave the cup H3563
11 and I gave the c into Pharaoh's hand. H3563
13 deliver Pharaoh's c into his hand, after H3563
21 and he gave the c into Pharaoh's hand: H3563
44: 2 And put my c, the silver cup, in the H1375
2 And put my cup, the silver c, in the H1375
12 the c was found in Benjamin's sack. H1375
16 and *he* also with whom the c is found. H1375
17 in whose hand the c is found, he shall H1375
2Sa 12: 3 and drank of his own c, and lay in his H3563
1Ki 7:26 like the brim of a c, with flowers of H3563
2Ch 4: 5 of the brim of a c, with flowers of lilies; H3563
Ps 11: 6 *this shall be* the portion of their c. H3563
16: 5 and of my c: thou maintainest my lot. H3563
23: 5 my head with oil; my c runneth over. H3563
73:10 waters of a full *c* are wrung out to them.
75: 8 LORD *there is* a c, and the wine is red; H3563
116:13 I will take the c of salvation, and call H3563
Prv 23:31 in the c, *when* it moveth itself aright. H3599
Isa 51:17 of the LORD the c of his fury; thou hast H3563
17 c of trembling, *and* wrung *them* out. H3563
22 of thine hand the c of trembling, *even* H3563
22 the dregs of the c of my fury; thou shalt H3563
Jer 16: 7 *men* give them the c of consolation to H3563
25:15 me; Take the wine c of this fury at my H3563
17 Then took I the c at the LORD'S hand, H3563
28 refuse to take the c at thine hand to H3563
49:12 not to drink of the c have assuredly H3563
51: 7 Babylon *hath been* a golden c in the H3563
Lam 4:21 in the land of Uz; the c also shall pass H3563
Ezk 23:31 will I give her c into thine hand. H3563
32 of thy sister's c deep and large: thou H3563
33 sorrow, with the c of astonishment and H3563
33 with the c of thy sister Samaria. H3563
Hab 2:16 be uncovered: the c of the LORD'S right H3563
Zec 12: 2 Behold, I will make Jerusalem a c of H5592
Mt 10:42 these little ones a c of cold *water* only G4221
20:22 to drink of the c that I shall drink of, G4221
23 indeed of my c, and be baptized with G4221
23:25 the outside of the c and of the platter, G4221
26 *is* within the c and platter, that the G4221
26:27 And he took the c, and gave thanks, G4221
39 be possible, let this c pass from me: G4221
42 my Father, if this c may not pass away G4221
Mk 9:41 For whosoever shall give you a c of G4221
10:38 can ye drink of the c that I drink of? G4221
39 drink of the c that I drink of; and G4221
14:23 And he took the c, and when he had G4221
36 take away this c from me: nevertheless G4221
Lk 11:39 the outside of the c and the platter; but G4221
22:17 And he took the c, and gave thanks, G4221
20 Likewise also the c after supper, G4221
20 saying, This c *is* the new testament G4221
42 remove this c from me: nevertheless G4221
Jn 18:11 the sheath: the c which my Father hath G4221
1Co 10:16 The c of blessing which we bless, is it G4221
21 Ye cannot drink the c of the Lord, and G4221
21 the Lord, and the c of devils: ye cannot G4221
11:25 also *he took* the c, when he had supped, G4221
25 saying, This c is the new testament G4221
26 and drink this c, ye do shew the Lord's G4221
27 bread, and drink *this* c of the Lord, G4221
28 eat of *that* bread, and drink of *that* c. G4221
Rev 14:10 mixture into the c of his indignation; G4221
16:19 to give unto her the c of the wine of the G4221
17: 4 having a golden c in her hand full of G4221
18: 6 to her works: in the c which she hath G4221

CUPBEARER
Neh 1:11 sight of this man. For I was the king's c. H4945

CUPBEARERS
1Ki 10: 5 apparel, and his c, and his ascent by H4945
2Ch 9: 4 and their apparel; his c also, and their H4945

CUPS
1Ch 28:17 the bowls, and the c: and for the golden H7184
Isa 22:24 of c, even to all the vessels of flagons. H101
Jer 35: 5 c, and I said unto them, Drink ye wine. H3563
52:19 the spoons, and the c; *that* which *was* of H4518

Mk 7: 4 *as* the washing of c, and pots, brasen G4221
8 of pots and c: and many other such G4221

CURDLED
Job 10:10 me out as milk, and c me like cheese? H7087

CURE
Jer 33: 6 Behold, I will bring it health and c, and H4832
6 cure, and I will c them, and will reveal H7495
Hos 5:13 not heal you, nor c you of your wound. H1455
Mt 17:16 thy disciples, and they could not c him. G2323
Lk 9: 1 over all devils, and to c diseases. G2323

CURED
Jer 46:11 medicines; *for* thou shalt not be c. H8585
Mt 17:18 the child was c from that very hour. G2323
Lk 7:21 And in that same hour he c many of G2323
Jn 5:10 unto him that was c, It is the sabbath G2323

CURES
Lk 13:32 out devils, and I do c to day and to G2392

CURIOUS
Ex 28: 8 And the c girdle of the ephod, which *is*
27 thereof, above the c girdle of the ephod.
28 may be above the c girdle of the ephod,
29: 5 gird him with the c girdle of the ephod:
35:32 And to devise c works, to work in gold, H4284
39: 5 And the c girdle of his ephod, that *was*
20 thereof, above the c girdle of the ephod.
21 might be above the c girdle of the ephod,
Lev 8: 7 him with the c girdle of the ephod, and
Act 19:19 Many of them also which used c arts G4021

CURIOUSLY
Ps 139:15 in secret, *and* c wrought in the lowest H7551

CURRENT
Gen 23:16 of silver, c *money* with the merchant. H5674

CURSE
Gen 8:21 I will not again c the ground any more H7043
12: 3 that bless thee, and c him that curseth H779
27:12 bring a c upon me, and not a blessing. H7045
13 Upon me *be* thy c, my son: only obey H7045
Ex 22:28 Thou shalt not revile the gods, nor c the H779
Lev 19:14 Thou shalt not c the deaf, nor put a H7043
Nu 5:18 hand the bitter water that causeth the c: H779
19 from this bitter water that causeth the c: H779
21 LORD make thee a c and an oath among H423
22 And this water that causeth the c shall H779
24 that causeth the c: and the water that H779
24 c shall enter into her, *and become* bitter. H779
27 that causeth the c shall enter into her, H779
27 woman shall be a c among her people. H423
22: 6 Come now therefore, I pray thee, c me H779
11 the earth: come now, c me them; H6895
12 not c the people: for they *are* blessed. H779
17 therefore, I pray thee, c me this people. H6895
23: 7 c me Jacob, and come, defy Israel. H779
8 How shall I c, whom God hath not H5344
11 me? I took thee to c mine enemies, and, H6895
13 them all: and c me them from thence. H6895
25 And Balak said unto Balaam, Neither c H5344
27 thou mayest c me them from thence. H6895
24:10 I called thee to c mine enemies, and, H6895
Dt 11:26 before you this day a blessing and a c; H7045
28 And a c, if ye will not obey the H7045
29 Gerizim, and the c upon mount Ebal. H7045
23: 4 of Pethor of Mesopotamia, to c thee. H7043
5 God turned the c into a blessing unto H7045
27:13 mount Ebal to c; Reuben, Gad, and H7045
29:19 the words of this c, that he bless himself H423
30: 1 the blessing and the c, which I have set H7045
Jos 6:18 the camp of Israel a c, and trouble it. H2764
24: 9 called Balaam the son of Beor to c you: H7043
Jdg 5:23 C ye Meroz, said the angel of the LORD, H779
23 the angel of the LORD, c ye bitterly the H779
9:57 the c of Jotham the son of Jerubbaal. H7045
2Sa 16: 9 this dead dog c my lord the king? let H7043
10 so let him c, because the LORD hath H7043
10 said unto him, C David. Who shall then H7043
11 him c; for the LORD hath bidden him. H7043
1Ki 2: 8 me with a grievous c in the day when I H7045
2Ki 22:19 a desolation and a c, and hast rent thy H7045
Neh 10:29 and entered into a c, and into an oath, to H423
13: 2 that he should c them: howbeit our H7043
2 our God turned the c into a blessing. H7045
Job 1:11 he hath, and he will c thee to thy face. H1288
2: 5 his flesh, and he will c thee to thy face. H1288
9 retain thine integrity? c God, and die. H1288
3: 8 Let them c it that curse the day, who H5344
8 Let them curse it that c the day, who are H779
31:30 mouth to sin by wishing a c to his soul. H423
Ps 62: 4 mouth, but they c inwardly. Selah. H7043
109:28 Let them c, but bless thou: when they H7043
Prv 3:33 The c of the LORD *is* in the house of the H3994
11:26 the people shall c him: but blessing H5344
24:24 the people c, nations shall abhor him: H5344
26: 2 so the c causeless shall not come. H7045
27:14 morning, it shall be counted a c to him. H7045
28:27 hideth his eyes shall have many a c. H3994
30:10 lest he c thee, and thou be found guilty. H7043
Ecc 7:21 lest thou hear thy servant c thee: H7043
10:20 C not the king, no not in thy thought; H7043
20 in thy thought; and c not the rich in thy H7043
Isa 8:21 themselves, and c their king and their H7043
24: 6 Therefore hath the c devoured the earth, H423
34: 5 upon the people of my c, to judgment. H2764
43:28 Jacob to the c, and Israel to reproaches. H2764
65:15 And ye shall leave your name for a c H7621
Jer 15:10 usury; *yet* every one of them doth c me. H7043
24: 9 a taunt and a c, in all places whither H7045
25:18 an hissing, and a c; as *it is* this day; H7045
26: 6 city a c to all the nations of the earth. H7045
29:18 kingdoms of the earth, to be a c, and an H423
22 And of them shall be taken up a c by all H7045
42:18 and a c, and a reproach; and H7045
44: 8 that ye might be a c and a reproach H7045
12 astonishment, and a c, and a reproach. H7045
22 c, without an inhabitant, as at this day. H7045
49:13 a waste, and a c; and all the cities H7045
Lam 3:65 Give them sorrow of heart, thy c unto H8381
Dan 9:11 voice; therefore the c is poured upon us, H423
Zec 5: 3 Then said he unto me, This *is* the c that H423
8:13 *that* as ye were a c among the heathen, H7045
Mal 2: 2 I will even send a c upon you, and I will H3994
2 you, and I will c your blessings: yea, H779
3: 9 Ye *are* cursed with a c: for ye have H3994
4: 6 lest I come and smite the earth with a c. H2764
Mt 5:44 bless them that c you, do good to them G2672
26:74 Then began he to c and to swear, G2653
Mk 14:71 But he began to c and to swear, *saying*, I G332
Lk 6:28 Bless them that c you, and pray for G2672
Act 23:12 themselves under a c, saying that they G332
14 under a great c, that we will eat nothing G331
Ro 12:14 which persecute you: bless, and c not. G2672
Gal 3:10 the law are under the c: for it is written, G2671
13 Christ hath redeemed us from the c of G2671
13 the law, being made a c for us: for it is G2671
Jas 3: 9 and therewith c we men, which are G2672
Rev 22: 3 And there shall be no more c: but the G2652

CURSED
Gen 3:14 done this, thou *art* c above all cattle, and H779
17 shalt not eat of it: c *is* the ground for thy H779
4:11 And now *art* thou c from the earth, H779
5:29 of the ground which the LORD hath c. H779
9:25 And he said, C *be* Canaan; a servant of H779
27:29 bow down to thee: c *be* every one that H779
49: 7 C *be* their anger, for *it was* fierce; and H779
Lev 20: 9 put to death: he hath c his father or his H7043
24:11 *of the LORD*, and c. And they brought H7043
14 Bring forth him that hath c without the H7043
23 forth him that had c out of the camp, H7043
Nu 22: 6 blessed, and he whom thou cursest is c. H779
23: 8 God hath not c? or how shall I defy, H6895
24: 9 thee, and c *is* he that curseth thee. H779
Dt 7:26 lest thou be a c thing like it: *but* thou H2764
26 shalt utterly abhor it; for it *is* a c thing. H2764
13:17 And there shall cleave nought of the c H2764
27:15 C *be* the man that maketh *any* graven or H779
16 C *be* he that setteth light by his father or H779
17 C *be* he that removeth his neighbour's H779
18 C *be* he that maketh the blind to wander H779
19 C *be* he that perverteth the judgment of H779
20 C *be* he that lieth with his father's wife; H779
21 C *be* he that lieth with any manner of H779
22 C *be* he that lieth with his sister, the H779
23 C *be* he that lieth with his mother in law. H779
24 C *be* he that smiteth his neighbour H779
25 C *be* he that taketh reward to slay an H779
26 C *be* he that confirmeth not *all* the words H779
28:16 C *shalt* thou *be* in the city, and cursed H779
16 Cursed *shalt* thou *be* in the city, and c H779
17 C *shall be* thy basket and thy store. H779
18 C *shall be* the fruit of thy body, and the H779
19 C *shalt* thou *be* when thou comest in, H779

Dt 28:19 and c *shalt* thou *be* when thou goest out. H779
Jos 6:26 at that time, saying, C *be* the man before H779
9:23 Now therefore ye *are* c, and there shall H779
Jdg 9:27 did eat and drink, and c Abimelech. H7043
21:18 C *be* he that giveth a wife to Benjamin. H779
1Sa 14:24 the people, saying, C *be* the man that H779
28 with an oath, saying, C *be* the man that H779
17:43 And the Philistine c David by his gods. H7043
26:19 the children of men, c *be* they before the H779
2Sa 16: 5 he came forth, and c still as he came. H7043
7 And thus said Shimei when he c, Come H7043
13 against him, and c as he went, and H7043
19:21 because he c the LORD'S anointed? H7043
1Ki 2: 8 of Bahurim, which c me with a H7043
2Ki 2:24 on them, and c them in the name of H7043
9:34 Go, see now this c *woman,* and bury her: H779
Neh 13:25 And I contended with them, and c H7043
Job 1: 5 have sinned, and c God in their hearts. H1288
3: 1 After this opened Job his mouth, and c H7043
5: 3 root: but suddenly I c his habitation. H5344
24:18 their portion is c in the earth: he H7043
Ps 37:22 *they that be* c of him shall be cut off. H7043
119:21 Thou hast rebuked the proud *that are* c, H779
Ecc 7:22 that thou thyself likewise hast c others. H7043
Jer 11: 3 God of Israel; C *be* the man that obeyeth H779
17: 5 Thus saith the LORD; C *be* the man that H779
20:14 C *be* the day wherein I was born: let not H779
15 C *be* the man who brought tidings to my H779
48:10 C *be* he that doeth the work of the LORD H779
10 deceitfully, and c *be* he that keepeth H779
Mal 1:14 But c *be* the deceiver, which hath in his H779
2: 2 yea, I have c them already, because H779
3: 9 Ye *are* c with a curse: for ye have robbed H779
Mt 25:41 from me, ye c, into everlasting fire, *G2672*
Jn 7:49 people who knoweth not the law are c. *G1944*
Gal 3:10 for it is written, C *is* every one that *G1944*
13 C *is* every one that hangeth on a tree: *G1944*
2Pt 2:14 with covetous practices; c children: *G2671*

CURSEDST
Jdg 17: 2 about which thou c, and spakest of also H422
Mk 11:21 fig tree which thou c is withered away. *G2672*

CURSES
Nu 5:23 And the priest shall write these c in a H423
Dt 28:15 day; that all these c shall come upon H7045
45 Moreover all these c shall come upon H7045
29:20 man, and all the c that are written in H423
21 according to all the c of the covenant H423
27 it all the c that are written in this book: H7045
30: 7 will put all these c upon thine enemies, H423
2Ch 34:24 *even* all the c that are written in the H423

CURSEST
Nu 22: 6 blessed, and he whom thou c is cursed. H779

CURSETH
Gen 12: 3 curse him that c thee: and in thee shall H7043
27:29 *be* every one that c thee, and blessed *be* H779
Ex 21:17 And he that c his father, or his mother, H7043
Lev 20: 9 For every one that c his father or his H7043
24:15 Whosoever c his God shall bear his sin. H7043
Nu 24: 9 thee, and cursed *is* he that c thee. H779
Prv 20:20 Whoso c his father or his mother, his H7043
30:11 *There is* a generation *that* c their H7043
Mt 15: 4 and, He that c father or mother, let *G2551*
Mk 7:10 and, Whoso c father or mother, let *G2551*

CURSING
Nu 5:21 with an oath of c, and the priest shall say H423
Dt 28:20 The LORD shall send upon thee c, H3994
30:19 blessing and c: therefore choose life, H7045
2Sa 16:12 will requite me good for his c this day. H7045
Ps 10: 7 His mouth is full of c and deceit and H423
59:12 and for c and lying *which* they speak. H423
109:17 As he loved c, so let it come unto him: H7045
18 As he clothed himself with c like as H7045
Prv 29:24 soul: he heareth c, and bewrayeth *it* not. H423
Ro 3:14 Whose mouth *is* full of c and bitterness: *G685*
Heb 6: 8 nigh unto c; whose end *is* to be burned. *G2671*
Jas 3:10 blessing and c. My brethren, these *G2671*

CURSINGS
Jos 8:34 the blessings and c, according to all H7045

CURTAIN
Ex 26: 2 The length of one c *shall be* eight and H3407
2 the breadth of one c four cubits: and H3407
4 the edge of the one c from the selvedge H3407
Ex 26: 4 *another* c, in the coupling of the second. H3407
5 Fifty loops shalt thou make in the one c, H3407
5 make in the edge of the c that *is* in the H3407
8 The length of one c *shall be* thirty H3407
8 the breadth of one c four cubits: and H3407
9 c in the forefront of the tabernacle. H3407
10 the edge of the one c *that is* outmost in H3407
10 of the c which coupleth the second. H3407
12 the tent, the half c that remaineth, shall H3407
36: 9 The length of one c *was* twenty and H3407
9 the breadth of one c four cubits: the H3407
11 on the edge of one c from the selvedge H3407
11 *another* c, in the coupling of the second. H3407
12 Fifty loops made he in one c, and fifty H3407
12 he in the edge of the c which *was* in the H3407
12 second: the loops held one c to another.
15 The length of one c *was* thirty cubits, H3407
15 c: the eleven curtains *were* of one size. H3407
17 edge of the c in the coupling, and H3407
17 of the c which coupleth the second. H3407
Nu 3:26 the court, and the c for the door of the H4539
Ps 104: 2 who stretchest out the heavens like a c: H3407
Isa 40:22 the heavens as a c, and spreadeth them H1852

CURTAINS
Ex 26: 1 *with* ten c *of* fine twined linen, H3407
2 one of the c shall have one measure. H3407
3 The five c shall be coupled together one H3407
3 five c *shall be* coupled one to another. H3407
6 gold, and couple the c together with the H3407
7 And thou shalt make c *of* goats' *hair* to H3407
7 tabernacle: eleven c shalt thou make. H3407
8 the eleven c *shall be all* of one measure. H3407
9 And thou shalt couple five c by H3407
9 and six c by themselves, and H3407
12 remaineth of the c of the tent, the half H3407
13 in the length of the c of the tent, it shall H3407
36: 8 made ten c *of* fine twined linen, H3407
9 four cubits: the c *were* all of one size. H3407
10 And he coupled the five c one unto H3407
10 five c he coupled one unto another. H3407
13 and coupled the c one unto another H3407
14 And he made c *of* goats' *hair* for the H3407
14 the tabernacle: eleven c he made them. H3407
15 curtain: the eleven c *were* of one size. H3407
16 And he coupled five c by themselves, H3407
16 by themselves, and six c by themselves. H3407
Nu 4:25 And they shall bear the c of the H3407
2Sa 7: 2 but the ark of God dwelleth within c. H3407
1Ch 17: 1 of the LORD *remaineth* under c. H3407
Song 1: 5 the tents of Kedar, as the c of Solomon. H3407
Isa 54: 2 stretch forth the c of thine habitations: H3407
Jer 4:20 tents spoiled, *and* my c in a moment. H3407
10:20 my tent any more, and to set up my c. H3407
49:29 themselves their c, and all their vessels, H3407
Hab 3: 7 the c of the land of Midian did tremble. H3407

CUSH
Gen 10: 6 And the sons of Ham; C, and Mizraim, H3568
7 And the sons of C; Seba, and Havilah, H3568
8 And C begat Nimrod: he began to be a H3568
1Ch 1: 8 The sons of Ham; C, and Mizraim, Put, H3568
9 And the sons of C; Seba, and Havilah, H3568
10 And C begat Nimrod: he began to be H3568
Ps 7:ttl the words of C the Benjamite. H3568
Isa 11:11 Pathros, and from C, and from Elam, H3568

CUSHAN
Hab 3: 7 I saw the tents of C in affliction: *and* H3572

CUSHI
2Sa 18:21 Then said Joab to C, Go tell the king H3569
21 C bowed himself unto Joab, and ran. H3569
22 thee, also run after C. And Joab said, H3569
23 by the way of the plain, and overran C. H3569
31 And, behold, C came; and Cushi said, H3569
31 And, behold, Cushi came; and C said, H3569
32 And the king said unto C, Is the young H3569
32 safe? And C answered, The enemies H3569
Jer 36:14 the son of C, unto Baruch, saying, H3569
Zep 1: 1 the son of C, the son of Gedaliah, H3569

CUSTODY
Nu 3:36 And *under* the c and charge of the sons H6486
Est 2: 3 women, unto the c of Hege the king's H3027
8 the palace, to the c of Hegai, that H3027
8 to the c of Hegai, keeper of the women. H3027
14 the women, to the c of Shaashgaz, the H3027

CUSTOM
Gen 31:35 thee; for the c of women *is* upon me. H1870
Jdg 11:39 knew no man. And it was a c in Israel, H2706
1Sa 2:13 And the priests' c with the people *was,* H4941
Ezr 3: 4 the c, as the duty of every day required; H4941
4:13 toll, tribute, and c, and *so* thou shalt H1983
20 toll, tribute, and c, was paid unto them. H1983
7:24 to impose toll, tribute, or c, upon them. H1983
Jer 32:11 the law and c, and that which was open: H2706
Mt 9: 9 at the receipt of c: and he saith unto *G5058*
17:25 of the earth take c or tribute? of their *G5056*
Mk 2:14 at the receipt of c, and said unto him, *G5058*
Lk 1: 9 According to the c of the priest's office, *G1485*
2:27 to do for him after the c of the law, *G1480*
42 up to Jerusalem after the c of the feast. *G1485*
4:16 up: and, as his c was, he went into the *G1486*
5:27 of c: and he said unto him, Follow me. *G5058*
Jn 18:39 But ye have a c, that I should release *G4914*
Ro 13: 7 tribute *is due;* c to whom custom; fear *G5056*
7 custom to whom c; fear to whom fear; *G5056*
1Co 11:16 no such c, neither the churches of God. *G4914*

CUSTOMS
Lev 18:30 of these abominable c, which were H2708
Jer 10: 3 For the c of the people *are* vain: for *one* H2708
Act 6:14 change the c which Moses delivered us. *G1485*
16:21 And teach c, which are not lawful for us *G1485*
21:21 children, neither to walk after the c. *G1485*
26: 3 thee to be expert in all c and questions *G1485*
28:17 the people, or c of our fathers, yet was *G1485*

CUT
Gen 9:11 shall all flesh be c off any more by the H3772
17:14 that soul shall be c off from his people; H3772
Ex 4:25 a sharp stone, and c off the foreskin of H3772
9:15 and thou shalt be c off from the earth. H3582
12:15 day, that soul shall be c off from Israel. H3772
19 even that soul shall be c off from the H3772
23:23 and the Jebusites: and I will c them off. H3582
29:17 And thou shalt c the ram in pieces, and H5408
30:33 shall even be c off from his people. H3772
38 shall even be c off from his people. H3772
31:14 shall be c off from among his people. H3772
34:13 their images, and c down their groves: H3772
39: 3 thin plates, and c *it into* wires, to work H7112
Lev 1: 6 burnt offering, and c it into his pieces. H5408
12 And he shall c it into his pieces, with H5408
7:20 that soul shall be c off from his people. H3772
21 that soul shall be c off from his people. H3772
25 eateth *it* shall be c off from his people. H3772
27 that soul shall be c off from his people. H3772
8:20 And he c the ram into pieces; and H5408
17: 4 shall be c off from among his people: H3772
9 shall be c off from among his people. H3772
10 will c him off from among his people. H3772
14 whosoever eateth it shall be c off. H3772
18:29 shall be c off from among their people. H3772
19: 8 shall be c off from among his people. H3772
20: 3 that man, and will c him off from H3772
5 family, and will c him off, and all that H3772
6 will c him off from among his people. H3772
17 and they shall be c off in the sight of H3772
18 shall be c off from among their people. H3772
22: 3 him, that soul shall be c off from my H3772
24 or broken, or c; neither shall ye make H3772
23:29 shall be c off from among his people. H3772
26:30 high places, and c down your images, H3772
Nu 4:18 C ye not off the tribe of the families of H3772
9:13 same soul shall be c off from among H3772
13:23 of Eshcol, and c down from thence a H3772
24 children of Israel c down from thence. H3772
15:30 shall be c off from among his people. H3772
31 be c off; his iniquity *shall be* upon him. H3772
19:13 and that soul shall be c off from Israel: H3772
20 that soul shall be c off from among the H3772
Dt 7: 5 their images, and c down their groves, H3772
12:29 When the LORD thy God shall c off the H3772
14: 1 your God: ye shall not c yourselves, nor H1413
19: 1 When the LORD thy God hath c off the H3772
5 with the axe to c down the tree, and H3772
20:19 and thou shalt not c them down (for H3772
20 shalt destroy and c them down; and H3772
23: 1 his privy member c off, shall not enter H3772
25:12 Then thou shalt c off her hand, thine H7112
Jos 3:13 of Jordan shall be c off *from* the waters H3772
16 failed, *and* were c off: and the people H3772
4: 7 of Jordan were c off before the ark of H3772
7 of Jordan were c off: and these stones H3772
7: 9 us round, and c off our name from the H3772

Jos 11:21 And at that time came Joshua, and c H3772
17:15 *country,* and c down for thyself there H1254
18 and thou shalt c it down: and the H1254
23: 4 c off, even unto the great sea westward. H3772
Jdg 1: 6 and c off his thumbs and his great toes. H7112
7 their great toes c off, gathered *their* H7112
6:25 hath, and c down the grove that *is* by it: H3772
26 of the grove which thou shalt c down. H3772
28 and the grove was c down that *was* by H3772
30 hath c down the grove that *was* by it. H3772
9:48 in his hand, and c down a bough from H3772
49 And all the people likewise c down H3772
20: 6 And I took my concubine, and c her in H5408
21: 6 is one tribe c off from Israel this day. H1438
Ru 4:10 of the dead be not c off from among his H3772
1Sa 2:31 Behold, the days come, that I will c off H1438
33 *whom* I shall not c off from mine altar, H3772
5: 4 palms of his hands *were* c off upon the H3772
17:51 and slew him, and c off his head H3772
20:15 But *also* thou shalt not c off thy H3772
15 the LORD hath c off the enemies of H3772
24: 4 and c off the skirt of Saul's robe privily. H3772
5 him, because he had c off Saul's skirt. H3772
11 hand: for in that I c off the skirt of thy H3772
21 that thou wilt not c off my seed after H3772
28: 9 done, how he hath c off those that have H3772
31: 9 And they c off his head, and stripped H3772
2Sa 4:12 slew them, and c off their hands and H7112
7: 9 thou wentest, and have c off all thine H3772
10: 4 their beards, and c off their garments H3772
20:22 her wisdom. And they c off the head of H3772
1Ki 9: 7 Then will I c off Israel out of the land H3772
11:16 until he had c off every male in Edom:) H3772
13:34 of Jeroboam, even to c *it* off, and to H3582
14:10 and will c off from Jeroboam him H3772
14 over Israel, who shall c off the house of H3772
18: 4 For it was *so,* when Jezebel c off the H3772
23 themselves, and c it in pieces, and lay H5408
28 And they cried aloud, and c themselves H1413
33 And he put the wood in order, and c H5408
21:21 posterity, and will c off from Ahab him H3772
2Ki 6: 4 came to Jordan, they c down wood. H1504
6 the place. And he c down a stick, and H7094
9: 8 perish: and I will c off from Ahab him H3772
10:32 In those days the LORD began to c H7096
16:17 And king Ahaz c off the borders of the H7112
18: 4 the images, and c down the groves, and H3772
16 At that time did Hezekiah c off *the gold* H7112
19:23 Lebanon, and will c down the tall cedar H3772
23:14 the images, and c down the groves, and H3772
24:13 the king's house, and c in pieces all the H7112
1Ch 17: 8 hast walked, and have c off all thine H3772
19: 4 shaved them, and c off their garments H3772
20: 3 *were* in it, and c *them* with saws, and H7787
2Ch 2: 8 can skill to c timber in Lebanon; H3772
10 the hewers that c timber, twenty H3772
16 And we will c wood out of Lebanon, as H3772
14: 3 the images, and c down the groves: H1438
15:16 a grove: and Asa c down her idol, and H3772
22: 7 anointed to c off the house of Ahab. H3772
26:21 a leper; for he was c off from the house H1504
28:24 the house of God, and c in pieces the H7112
31: 1 in pieces, and c down the groves, and H1438
32:21 And the LORD sent an angel, which c H3582
34: 4 above them, he c down; and the groves, H1438
7 into powder, and c down all the idols H1438
Job 4: 7 or where were the righteous c off? H3582
6: 9 would let loose his hand, and c me off! H1214
8:12 *and* not c down, it withereth before H6998
14 Whose hope shall be c off, and whose H6990
11:10 If he c off, and shut up, or gather H2498
14: 2 He cometh forth like a flower, and is c H5243
7 For there is hope of a tree, if it be c H3772
18:16 and above shall his branch be c off. H5243
21:21 of his months is c off in the midst? H2686
22:16 Which were c down out of time, whose H7059
20 Whereas our substance is not c down, H3582
23:17 Because I was not c off before the H6789
24:24 and c off as the tops of the ears of corn. H5243
30: 4 Who c up mallows by the bushes, and H6998
36:20 Desire not the night, when people are c H5927
Ps 12: 3 The LORD shall c off all flattering lips, H3772
31:22 For I said in my haste, I am c off from H1629
34:16 that do evil, to c off the remembrance H3772
37: 2 For they shall soon be c down like the H5243
9 For evildoers shall be c off: but those H3772
22 *that be* cursed of him shall be c off. H3772
28 but the seed of the wicked shall be c off. H3772
34 the wicked are c off, thou shalt see *it.* H3772
Ps 37:38 the end of the wicked shall be c off. H3772
54: 5 mine enemies: c them off in thy truth. H6789
58: 7 his arrows, let them be as c in pieces. H4135
75:10 All the horns of the wicked also will I c H1438
76:12 He shall c off the spirit of princes: *he is* H1219
80:16 *It is* burned with fire, *it is* c down: they H3683
83: 4 They have said, Come, and let us c H3582
88: 5 more: and they are c off from thy hand. H1504
16 over me; thy terrors have c me off. H6789
90: 6 the evening it is c down, and withereth. H4135
10 for it is soon c off, and we fly away. H1504
94:23 iniquity, and shall c them off in their H6789
23 the LORD our God shall c them off. H6789
101: 5 him will I c off: him that hath an H6789
8 land; that I may c off all wicked doers H3772
107:16 brass, and c the bars of iron in sunder. H1438
109:13 Let his posterity be c off; *and* in the H3772
15 that he may c off the memory of them H3772
129: 4 The LORD *is* righteous: he hath c H7112
143:12 And of thy mercy c off mine enemies, H6789
Prv 2:22 But the wicked shall be c off from the H3772
10:31 but the froward tongue shall be c out. H3772
23:18 and thine expectation shall not be c off. H3772
24:14 and thy expectation shall not be c off. H3772
Isa 9:10 the sycomores are c down, but we will H1438
14 Therefore the LORD will c off from H3772
10: 7 to destroy and c off nations not a few. H3772
34 And he shall c down the thickets of the H5362
11:13 of Judah shall be c off: Ephraim shall H3772
14:12 *how* art thou c down to the ground, H1438
22 of hosts, and c off from Babylon the H3772
15: 2 *be* baldness, *and* every beard c off. H1438
18: 5 he shall both c off the sprigs with H3772
5 take away *and* c down the branches. H8456
22:25 removed, and be c down, and fall; and H1438
25 be c off: for the LORD hath spoken *it.* H3772
29:20 and all that watch for iniquity are c off: H3772
33:12 c up shall they be burned in the fire. H3683
37:24 and I will c down the tall cedars H3772
38:12 tent: I have c off like a weaver my H7088
12 my life: he will c me off with pining H1214
45: 2 brass, and c in sunder the bars of iron: H1438
48: 9 I refrain for thee, that I c thee not off. H3772
19 c off nor destroyed from before me. H3772
51: 9 c Rahab, *and* wounded the dragon? H2672
53: 8 for he was c off out of the land of H1504
55:13 everlasting sign *that* shall not be c off. H3772
56: 5 name, that shall not be c off. H3772
66: 3 a lamb, *as if* he c off a dog's neck; he that
Jer 7:28 perished, and is c off from their mouth. H3772
29 C off thine hair, *O Jerusalem,* and cast H1494
9:21 our palaces, to c off the children from H3772
11:19 thereof, and let us c him off from the H3772
16: 6 for them, nor c themselves, nor make H1413
22: 7 and they shall c down thy choice H3772
25:37 And the peaceable habitations are c H1826
34:18 me, when they c the calf in twain, and H3772
36:23 or four leaves, he c it with the penknife, H7167
41: 5 rent, and having c themselves, with H1413
44: 7 your souls, to c off from you man and H3772
8 that ye might c yourselves off, and H3772
11 you for evil, and to c off all Judah. H3772
46:23 They shall c down her forest, saith the H3772
47: 4 Philistines, *and* to c off from Tyrus and H3772
5 upon Gaza; Ashkelon is c off *with* the H1820
5 valley: how long wilt thou c thyself? H1413
48: 2 it; come, and let us c it off from *being* a H3772
2 Also thou shalt be c down, O Madmen; H1826
25 The horn of Moab is c off, and his arm H1438
49:26 of war shall be c off in that day, saith H1826
50:16 C off the sower from Babylon, and him H3772
23 of the whole earth c asunder and H1438
30 be c off in that day, saith the LORD. H1826
51: 6 his soul: be not c off in her iniquity; for H1826
62 this place, to c it off, that none shall H3772
Lam 2: 3 He hath c off in *his* fierce anger all the H1438
3:53 They have c off my life in the dungeon, H6789
54 over mine head; *then* I said, I am c off. H1504
Ezk 6: 6 your images may be c down, and your H1438
14: 8 a proverb, and I will c him off from the H3772
13 it, and will c off man and beast from it: H3772
17 so that I c off man and beast from it: H3772
19 blood, to c off from it man and beast: H3772
21 to c off from it man and beast? H3772
16: 4 thy navel was not c, neither wast thou H3772
17: 9 the roots thereof, and c off the fruit H7082
17 building forts, to c off many persons: H3772
21: 3 his sheath, and will c off from thee the H3772
4 Seeing then that I will c off from thee H3772
Ezk 25: 7 heathen; and I will c thee off from the H3772
13 Edom, and will c off man and beast H3772
16 and I will c off the Cherethims, H3772
29: 8 and c off man and beast out of thee. H3772
30:15 and I will c off the multitude of No. H3772
31:12 of the nations, have c him off, and have H3772
35: 7 desolate, and c off from it him that H3772
37:11 hope is lost: we are c off for our parts. H1504
39:10 the field, neither c down *any* out of the H2404
Dan 2: 5 thereof, ye shall be c in pieces, and H5648
34 Thou sawest till that a stone was c out H1505
45 sawest that the stone was c out of the H1505
3:29 shall be c in pieces, and their H5648
4:14 the tree, and c off his branches, shake H7113
9:26 shall Messiah be c off, but not for H3772
Hos 8: 4 them idols, that they may be c off. H3772
10: 7 *As for* Samaria, her king is c off as the H1820
15 shall the king of Israel utterly be c off. H1820
Joel 1: 5 wine; for it is c off from your mouth. H3772
9 drink offering is c off from the house of H3772
16 Is not the meat c off before our eyes, H3772
Am 1: 5 of Damascus, and c off the inhabitant H3772
8 And I will c off the inhabitant from H3772
2: 3 And I will c off the judge from the H3772
3:14 shall be c off, and fall to the ground. H1438
9: 1 may shake: and c them in the head, all H1214
Oba 5 (how art thou c off!) would they not H1820
9 of Esau may be c off by slaughter. H3772
10 thee, and thou shalt be c off for ever. H3772
14 in the crossway, to c off those of his H3772
Mic 5: 9 and all thine enemies shall be c off. H3772
10 LORD, that I will c off thy horses out of H3772
11 And I will c off the cities of thy land, H3772
12 And I will c off witchcrafts out of thine H3772
13 Thy graven images also will I c off, and H3772
Nah 1:12 yet thus shall they be c down, when he H1494
14 of thy gods will I c off the graven image H3772
15 pass through thee; he is utterly c off. H3772
2:13 lions: and I will c off thy prey from the H3772
3:15 the sword shall c thee off, it shall eat H3772
Hab 3:17 the flock shall be c off from the fold, H1504
Zep 1: 3 wicked; and I will c off man from off H3772
4 and I will c off the remnant of Baal H3772
11 people are c down; all they that bear H1820
11 down; all they that bear silver are c off. H3772
3: 6 I have c off the nations: their towers H3772
7 should not be c off, howsoever I H3772
Zec 5: 3 stealeth shall be c off *as* on this side H5352
3 be c off *as* on that side according to it. H5352
9: 6 I will c off the pride of the Philistines. H3772
10 And I will c off the chariot from H3772
10 bow shall be c off: and he shall speak H3772
11: 8 Three shepherds also I c off in one H3582
9 that that is to be c off, let it be cut off; H3582
9 be cut off, let it be c off; and let the rest H3582
10 And I took my staff, *even* Beauty, and c H1438
14 Then I c asunder mine other staff, *even* H1438
16 visit those that be c off, neither shall H3582
12: 3 with it shall be c in pieces, though all H8295
13: 2 of hosts, *that* I will c off the names of H3772
8 therein shall be c off *and* die; but the H3772
14: 2 people shall not be c off from the city. H3772
Mal 2:12 The LORD will c off the man that doeth H3772
Mt 5:30 And if thy right hand offend thee, c it *G1581*
18: 8 foot offend thee, c them off, and cast *G1581*
21: 8 in the way; others c down branches *G2875*
24:51 And shall c him asunder, and appoint *G1371*
Mk 9:43 And if thy hand offend thee, c it off: it is *G609*
45 And if thy foot offend thee, c it off: it is *G609*
11: 8 way: and others c down branches off *G2875*
14:47 of the high priest, and c off his ear. *G851*
Lk 12:46 aware, and will c him in sunder, and *G1371*
13: 7 tree, and find none: c it down; why *G1581*
9 *then* after that thou shalt c it down. *G1581*
22:50 of the high priest, and c off his right ear. *G851*
Jn 18:10 servant, and c off his right ear. The *G809*
26 whose ear Peter c off, saith, Did not I see *G809*
Act 5:33 When they heard *that,* they were c *to* *G1282*
7:54 things, they were c to the heart, and *G1282*
27:32 Then the soldiers c off the ropes of the *G609*
Ro 9:28 For he will finish the work, and c *it* *G4932*
11:22 otherwise thou also shalt be c off. *G1581*
24 For if thou wert c out of the olive tree *G1581*
2Co 11:12 I will do, that I may c off occasion from *G1581*
Gal 5:12 I would they were even c off which *G609*

CUTH

2Ki 17:30 and the men of C made Nergal, and the H3575

CUTHAH
2Ki 17:24 and from C, and from Ava, and. H3575

CUTTEST
Dt 24:19 When thou c down thine harvest in thy H7114

CUTTETH
Job 28:10 He c out rivers among the rocks; and H1234
Ps 46: 9 the bow, and c the spear in sunder; H7112
141: 7 c and cleaveth *wood* upon the earth. H6398
Prv 26: 6 c off the feet, *and* drinketh damage. H7096
Jer 10: 3 *are* vain: for *one* c a tree out of the H3772
22:14 chambers, and c him out windows; H7167

CUTTING
Ex 31: 5 And in c of stones, to set *them*, and in H2799
35:33 And in the c of stones, to set *them*, and H2799
Isa 38:10 I said in the c off of my days, I shall go H1824
Hab 2:10 to thy house by c off many people, and H7096
Mk 5: 5 crying, and c himself with stones. *G2629*

CUTTINGS
Lev 19:28 Ye shall not make any c in your flesh H8296
21: 5 beard, nor make any c in their flesh. H8296
Jer 48:37 *shall be* c, and upon the loins sackcloth. H1417

CYMBAL
1Co 13: 1 *as* sounding brass, or a tinkling c. *G2950*

CYMBALS
2Sa 6: 5 on timbrels, and on cornets, and on c. H6767
1Ch 13: 8 and with c, and with trumpets. H4700
15:16 and harps and c, sounding, by lifting H4700
19 *appointed* to sound with c of brass; H4700
1Ch 15:28 and with c, making a noise with H4700
16: 5 harps; but Asaph made a sound with c; H4700
42 with trumpets and c for those that H4700
25: 1 and with c: and the number of the H4700
6 of the LORD, with c, psalteries, and H4700
2Ch 5:12 linen, having c and psalteries and H4700
13 the trumpets and c and instruments of H4700
29:25 of the LORD with c, with psalteries, and H4700
Ezr 3:10 of Asaph with c, to praise the LORD, H4700
Neh 12:27 *with* c, psalteries, and with harps. H4700
Ps 150: 5 Praise him upon the loud c: praise him H6767
5 praise him upon the high sounding c. H6767

CYPRESS
Isa 44:14 and taketh the c and the oak, which H8645

CYPRUS
Act 4:36 a Levite, *and* of the country of C, *G2953*
11:19 far as Phenice, and C, and Antioch, *G2954*
20 And some of them were men of C and *G2953*
13: 4 and from thence they sailed to C. *G2954*
15:39 Barnabas took Mark, and sailed unto C; *G2954*
21: 3 Now when we had discovered C, we left *G2954*
16 one Mnason of C, an old disciple, with *G2953*
27: 4 C, because the winds were contrary. *G2954*

CYRENE
Mt 27:32 found a man of C, Simon by name: him *G2956*
Act 2:10 parts of Libya about C, and strangers of *G2957*
11:20 of Cyprus and C, which, when they were *G2956*
13: 1 and Lucius of C, and Manaen, which *G2956*

CYRENIAN
Mk 15:21 And they compel one Simon a C, who *G2956*
Lk 23:26 upon one Simon, a C, coming out of the *G2956*

CYRENIANS
Act 6: 9 Libertines, and C, and Alexandrians, *G2956*

CYRENIUS
Lk 2: 2 made when C was governor of Syria.) *G2958*

CYRUS
2Ch 36:22 Now in the first year of C king of H3566
22 up the spirit of C king of Persia, that H3566
23 Thus saith C king of Persia, All the H3566
Ezr 1: 1 Now in the first year of C king of H3566
1 up the spirit of C king of Persia, that H3566
2 Thus saith C king of Persia, The LORD H3566
7 Also C the king brought forth the H3566
8 Even those did C king of Persia bring H3566
3: 7 grant that they had of C king of Persia. H3566
4: 3 of Israel, as king C the king of Persia H3566
5 all the days of C king of Persia, even H3566
5:13 But in the first year of C the king of H3567
13 *the same* king C made a decree to build H3567
14 those did C the king take out of H3567
17 was made of C the king to build this H3567
6: 3 In the first year of C the king *the same* H3567
3 the king *the same* C the king made a H3567
14 commandment of C, and Darius, and H3567
Isa 44:28 That saith of C, *He is* my shepherd, and H3566
45: 1 to his anointed, to C, whose right hand I H3566
Dan 1:21 *even* unto the first year of king C. H3566
6:28 and in the reign of C the Persian. H3567
10: 1 In the third year of C king of Persia a H3566

D

DABAREH
Jos 21:28 with her suburbs, D with her suburbs, H1705

DABBASHETH
Jos 19:11 and reached to D, and reached to the H1708

DABERATH
Jos 19:12 goeth out to D, and goeth up to Japhia, H1705
1Ch 6:72 with her suburbs, D with her suburbs, H1705

DAGGER
Jdg 3:16 But Ehud made him a d which had two H2719
21 and took the d from his right thigh, H2719
22 not draw the d out of his belly; and H2719

DAGON
Jdg 16:23 great sacrifice unto D their god, and to H1712
1Sa 5: 2 into the house of D, and set it by Dagon. H1712
2 into the house of Dagon, and set it by D. H1712
3 morrow, behold, D *was* fallen upon his H1712
3 took D, and set him in his place again. H1712
4 morning, behold, D *was* fallen upon his H1712
4 and the head of D and both the palms H1712
4 only *the stump of* D was left to him. H1712
5 Therefore neither the priests of D, nor H1712
5 threshold of D in Ashdod unto this day. H1712
7 is sore upon us, and upon D our god. H1712
1Ch 10:10 fastened his head in the temple of D. H1712

DAGON'S
1Sa 5: 5 that come into D house, tread on the H1712

DAILY
Ex 5:13 *your* d tasks, as when there was straw. H3117
19 *ought* from your bricks of your d task. H3117
16: 5 shall be twice as much as they gather d. H3117
Nu 4:16 incense, and the d meat offering, and H8548
28:24 After this manner ye shall offer d, H3117
29: 6 offering, and the d burnt offering, and H8548
Jdg 16:16 she pressed him d with her words, and H3117
2Ki 25:30 him of the king, a d rate for every day, H3117
2Ch 31:16 of the LORD, his d portion for their H3117
Ezr 3: 4 and *offered* the d burnt offerings by H3117
Neh 5:18 *for me* d *was* one ox *and* H3117+H259
Est 3: 4 when they spake d unto him, and he H3117
Ps 13: 2 in my heart d? how long shall mine H3119
42:10 d unto me, Where *is* thy God? H3605+H3117
Ps 56: 1 he fighting d oppresseth me. H3605+H3117
2 Mine enemies would d H3605+H3117
61: 8 ever, that I may d perform my vows. H3117
68:19 Blessed *be* the Lord, *who* d loadeth us H3117
72:15 *and* d shall he be praised. H3605+H3117
74:22 man reproacheth thee d. H3605+H3117
86: 3 O Lord: for I cry unto thee d. H3605+H3117
88: 9 I have called d upon thee, I H3605+H3117
17 They came round about me d H3605+H3117
Prv 8:30 *him*: and I was d *his* delight, rejoicing H3117
34 me, watching d at my gates, waiting H3117
Isa 58: 2 Yet they seek me d, and delight to know H3117
Jer 7:25 d rising up early and sending *them*: H3117
20: 7 d, every one mocketh me. H3605+H3117
8 a reproach unto me, and a derision, d. H3117
37:21 should give him d a piece of bread out H3117
Ezk 30:16 and Noph *shall have* distresses d. H3119
45:23 without blemish d the seven days; and H3117
23 a kid of the goats d *for* a sin offering. H3117
46:13 Thou shalt d prepare a burnt offering H3117
Dan 1: 5 And the king appointed them a d H3117
8:11 and by him the d *sacrifice* was taken H8548
12 *him* against the d *sacrifice* by reason H8548
13 *concerning* the d *sacrifice*, and the H8548
11:31 take away the d *sacrifice*, and they H8548
12:11 And from the time *that* the d *sacrifice* H8548
Hos 12: 1 the east wind: he d increaseth lies and H3117
Mt 6:11 Give us this day our d bread. *G1967*
26:55 to take me? I sat d with you *G2596+G2250*
Mk 14:49 I was d with you in the temple *G2596+G2250*
Lk 9:23 up his cross d, and follow me. *G2596+G2250*
11: 3 Give us day by day our d bread. *G1967*
19:47 And he taught d in the temple. *G2596+G2250*
22:53 When I was d with you in the *G2596+G2250*
Act 2:46 And they, continuing d with *G2596+G2250*
47 d such as should be saved. *G2596+G2250*
3: 2 they laid d at the gate of the *G2596+G2250*
5:42 And d in the temple, and in *G3956+G2250*
6: 1 in the d ministration. *G3956+G2250*
16: 5 and increased in number d. *G2596+G2250*
17:11 the scriptures d, whether those *G2596+G2250*
17 market d with them *G2596+G3956+G2250*
19: 9 disputing d in the school of *G2596+G2250*
1Co 15:31 Christ Jesus our Lord, I die d. *G2596+G2250*
2Co 11:28 d, the care of all the churches. *G2596+G2250*
Heb 3:13 another d, while it is *G2596+G1538+G2250*
7:27 Who needeth not d, as those *G2596+G2250*
10:11 And every priest standeth d *G2596+G2250*
Jas 2:15 sister be naked, and destitute of d food, *G2184*

DAINTIES
Gen 49:20 *shall be* fat, and he shall yield royal d. H4574
Ps 141: 4 iniquity: and let me not eat of their d. H4516
Prv 23: 3 Be not desirous of his d: for they *are* H4303

DAINTY
Job 33:20 abhorreth bread, and his soul d meat. H8378
Prv 23: 6 eye, neither desire thou his d meats: H4303
Rev 18:14 all things which were d and goodly are *G3045*

DALAIAH
1Ch 3:24 and Johanan, and D, and Anani, seven. H1806

DALE
Gen 14:17 valley of Shaveh, which *is* the king's d. H6010
2Sa 18:18 *is* in the king's d: for he said, I have no H6010

DALMANUTHA
Mk 8:10 disciples, and came into the parts of D. *G1148*

DALMATIA
2Ti 4:10 Crescens to Galatia, Titus unto D. *G1149*

DALPHON
Est 9: 7 And Parshandatha, and D, and H1813

DAM
Ex 22:30 d; on the eighth day thou shalt give it me. H517
Lev 22:27 days under the d; and from the eighth H517
Dt 22: 6 ones, or eggs, and the d sitting upon the H517
6 thou shalt not take the d with the young: H517
7 *But* thou shalt in any wise let the d go, H517

DAMAGE
Ezr 4:22 should d grow to the hurt of the kings? H2257
Est 7: 4 could not countervail the king's d. H5143
Prv 26: 6 fool cutteth off the feet, *and* drinketh d. H2555
Dan 6: 2 them, and the king should have no d. H5142
Act 27:10 hurt and much d, not only of the lading *G2209*
2Co 7: 9 ye might receive d by us in nothing. *G2210*

DAMARIS
Act 17:34 named D, and others with them. *G1152*

DAMASCENES
2Co 11:32 kept the city of the D with a garrison, *G1153*

DAMASCUS
Gen 14:15 Hobah, which *is* on the left hand of **D**. H1834
15: 2 steward of my house *is* this Eliezer of **D**? H1834
2Sa 8: 5 And when the Syrians of **D** came to H1834
6 Then David put garrisons in Syria of **D**: H1834
1Ki 11:24 and they went to **D**, and dwelt therein, H1834
24 and dwelt therein, and reigned in **D**. H1834
15:18 king of Syria, that dwelt at **D**, saying, H1834
19:15 to the wilderness of **D**: and when thou H1834
20:34 streets for thee in **D**, as my father made H1834
2Ki 5:12 Pharpar, rivers of **D**, better than all the H1834
8: 7 And Elisha came to **D**; and Ben-hadad H1834
9 good thing of **D**, forty camels' burden, H1834
14:28 and how he recovered **D**, and Hamath, H1834
16: 9 went up against **D**, and took it, and H1834
10 And king Ahaz went to **D** to meet H1834
10 altar that *was* at **D**: and king Ahaz sent H1834
11 had sent from **D**: so Urijah the priest H1834
11 *it* against king Ahaz came from **D**. H1834
12 And when the king was come from **D**, H1834
1Ch 18: 5 And when the Syrians of **D** came to H1834
2Ch 16: 2 king of Syria, that dwelt at **D**, saying, H1834
24:23 all the spoil of them unto the king of **D**. H1834
28: 5 brought *them* to **D**. And he was also H1834
23 For he sacrificed unto the gods of **D**, H1834
Song 7: 4 of Lebanon which looketh toward **D**. H1834
Isa 7: 8 For the head of Syria *is* **D**, and the head H1834
8 and the head of **D** *is* Rezin; and within H1834
8: 4 the riches of **D** and the spoil of Samaria H1834
10: 9 Hamath as Arpad? *is* not Samaria as **D**? H1834
17: 1 The burden of **D**. Behold, Damascus is H1834
1 The burden of Damascus. Behold, **D** is H1834
3 the kingdom from **D**, and the remnant H1834
Jer 49:23 Concerning **D**. Hamath is confounded, H1834
24 **D** is waxed feeble, *and* turneth herself H1834
27 And I will kindle a fire in the wall of **D**, H1834
Ezk 27:18 **D** *was* thy merchant in the multitude of H1834
47:16 the border of **D** and the border of H1834
17 the border of **D**, and the north H1834
18 Hauran, and from **D**, and from Gilead, H1834
48: 1 the border of **D** northward, to the coast H1834
Am 1: 3 transgressions of **D**, and for four, I will H1834
5 I will break also the bar of **D**, and cut H1834
3:12 corner of a bed, and in **D** *in* a couch. H1833
5:27 captivity beyond **D**, saith the LORD, H1834
Zec 9: 1 of Hadrach, and **D** *shall be* the rest H1834
Act 9: 2 And desired of him letters to **D** to the G1154
3 And as he journeyed, he came near **D**: G1154
8 by the hand, and brought *him* into **D**. G1154
10 And there was a certain disciple at **D**, G1154
19 days with the disciples which were at **D**. G1154
22 at **D**, proving that this is very Christ. G1154
27 boldly at **D** in the name of Jesus. G1154
22: 5 and went to **D**, to bring them which G1154
6 was come nigh unto **D** about noon, G1154
10 Arise, and go into **D**; and there it shall G1154
11 them that were with me, I came into **D**. G1154
26:12 Whereupon as I went to **D** with G1154
20 But shewed first unto them of **D**, and at G1154
2Co 11:32 In **D** the governor under Aretas the G1154
Gal 1:17 into Arabia, and returned again unto **D**. G1154

DAMNABLE
2Pt 2: 1 shall bring in **d** heresies, even denying G684

DAMNATION
Mt 23:14 therefore ye shall receive the greater **d**. G2917
33 vipers, how can ye escape the **d** of hell? G2920
Mk 3:29 but is in danger of eternal **d**: G2920
12:40 prayers: these shall receive greater **d**. G2917
Lk 20:47 the same shall receive greater **d**. G2917
Jn 5:29 done evil, unto the resurrection of **d**. G2920
Ro 3: 8 that good may come? whose **d** is just. G2917
13: 2 that resist shall receive to themselves **d**. G2917
1Co 11:29 eateth and drinketh **d** to himself, not G2917
1Ti 5:12 Having **d**, because they have cast off G2917
2Pt 2: 3 not, and their **d** slumbereth not. G684

DAMNED
Mk 16:16 but he that believeth not shall be **d**. G2632
Ro 14:23 And he that doubteth is **d** if he eat, G2632
2Th 2:12 That they all might be **d** who believed G2919

DAMSEL
Gen 24:14 And let it come to pass, that the **d** to H5291
16 And the **d** *was* very fair to look upon, a H5291
28 And the **d** ran, and told *them of* her H5291
55 said, Let the **d** abide with us *a few* H5291
57 And they said, We will call the **d**, and H5291
34: 3 **d**, and spake kindly unto the damsel. H5291
3 damsel, and spake kindly unto the **d**. H5291
4 Hamor, saying, Get me this **d** to wife. H3207
12 say unto me: but give me the **d** to wife. H5291
Dt 22:15 Then shall the father of the **d**, and her H5291
19 the father of the **d**, because he hath H5291
20 *of* virginity be not found for the **d**: H5291
21 Then they shall bring out the **d** to the H5291
23 If a **d** *that is* a virgin be betrothed unto H5291
24 that they die; the **d**, because she cried H5291
25 But if a man find a betrothed **d** in the H5291
26 But unto the **d** thou shalt do nothing; H5291
26 *there is* in the **d** no sin *worthy* of death: H5291
27 *and* the betrothed **d** cried, and *there* H5291
28 If a man find a **d** *that is* a virgin, which H5291
Jdg 5:30 to every man a **d** *or* two; to Sisera a H7356
19: 3 the **d** saw him, he rejoiced to meet him. H5291
Ru 2: 5 set over the reapers, Whose **d** *is* this? H5291
6 It *is* the Moabitish **d** that came back H5291
1Ki 1: 3 So they sought for a fair **d** throughout H5291
4 And the **d** *was* very fair, and cherished H5291
Mt 14:11 the **d**: and she brought *it* to her mother. G2877
26:69 in the palace: and a **d** came unto him, G3814
Mk 5:39 weep? the **d** is not dead, but sleepeth. G3813
40 the mother of the **d**, and them that were G3813
40 and entereth in where the **d** was lying. G3813
41 And he took the **d** by the hand, and G3813
41 interpreted, **D**, I say unto thee, arise. G2877
42 And straightway the **d** arose, and G2877
6:22 the king said unto the **d**, Ask of me G2877
28 **d**: and the damsel gave it to her mother. G2877
28 and the **d** gave it to her mother. G2877
Jn 18:17 Then saith the **d** that kept the door G3814
Act 12:13 a **d** came to hearken, named Rhoda. G3814
16:16 to prayer, a certain **d** possessed with a G3814

DAMSELS
Gen 24:61 And Rebekah arose, and her **d**, and H5291
1Sa 25:42 an ass, with five **d** of hers that went H5291
Ps 68:25 *them were* the **d** playing with timbrels. H5959

DAMSEL'S
Dt 22:15 *the tokens of* the **d** virginity unto the H5291
16 And the **d** father shall say unto the H5291
29 shall give unto the **d** father fifty *shekels* H5291
Jdg 19: 4 And his father in law, the **d** father, H5291
5 up to depart: and the **d** father said unto H5291
6 together: for the **d** father had said unto H5291
8 day to depart: and the **d** father said, H5291
9 his father in law, the **d** father, said unto H5291

DAN
Gen 14:14 eighteen, and pursued *them* unto **D**. H1835
30: 6 a son: therefore called she his name **D**. H1835
35:25 Rachel's handmaid; **D**, and Naphtali: H1835
46:23 And the sons of **D**; Hushim. H1835
49:16 **D** shall judge his people, as one of the H1835
17 **D** shall be a serpent by the way, an H1835
Ex 1: 4 **D**, and Naphtali, Gad, and Asher. H1835
31: 6 of the tribe of **D**: and in the hearts of H1835
35:34 the son of Ahisamach, of the tribe of **D**. H1835
38:23 of the tribe of **D**, an engraver, and a H1835
Lev 24:11 the daughter of Dibri, of the tribe of **D**:) H1835
Nu 1:12 Of **D**; Ahiezer the son of Ammishaddai. H1835
38 Of the children of **D**, by their H1835
39 of the tribe of **D**, *were* threescore and H1835
2:25 The standard of the camp of **D** *shall be* H1835
25 of the children of **D** *shall be* Ahiezer the H1835
31 in the camp of **D** *were* an hundred H1835
7:66 prince of the children of **D**, *offered*: H1835
10:25 of the children of **D** set forward, *which* H1835
13:12 Of the tribe of **D**, Ammiel the son of H1835
26:42 These *are* the sons of **D** after their H1835
42 the families of **D** after their families. H1835
34:22 the children of **D**, Bukki the son of Jogli. H1835
Dt 27:13 Asher, and Zebulun, **D**, and Naphtali. H1835
33:22 And of **D** he said, Dan *is* a lion's whelp: H1835
22 And of Dan he said, **D** *is* a lion's whelp: H1835
34: 1 him all the land of Gilead, unto **D**, H1835
Jos 19:40 of **D** according to their families. H1835
47 And the coast of the children of **D** went H1835
47 the children of **D** went up to fight H1835
47 **D**, after the name of Dan their father. H1835
47 Dan, after the name of **D** their father. H1835
48 of the children of **D** according to their H1835
21: 5 out of the tribe of **D**, and out of the half H1835
23 And out of the tribe of **D**, Eltekeh with H1835
Jdg 1:34 the children of **D** into the mountain: H1835
5:17 and why did **D** remain in ships? Asher H1835
13:25 camp of **D** between Zorah and Eshtaol. H1835
18: 2 And the children of **D** sent of their H1835
16 of **D**, stood by the entering of the gate. H1835
22 and overtook the children of **D**. H1835
23 And they cried unto the children of **D**. H1835
25 And the children of **D** said unto him, H1835
26 And the children of **D** went their way: H1835
29 And they called the name of the city **D**, H1835
29 after the name of **D** their father, who H1835
30 And the children of **D** set up the graven H1835
30 to the tribe of **D** until the day of the H1839
20: 1 together as one man, from **D** even to H1835
1Sa 3:20 And all Israel from **D** even to H1835
2Sa 3:10 over Judah, from **D** even to Beer-sheba. H1835
17:11 unto thee, from **D** even to Beer-sheba, H1835
24: 2 of Israel, from **D** even to Beer-sheba, H1835
15 died of the people from **D** even to H1835
1Ki 4:25 his fig tree, from **D** even to Beersheba, H1835
12:29 in Beth-el, and the other put he in **D**. H1835
30 *to worship* before the one, *even* unto **D**. H1835
15:20 and smote Ijon, and **D**, and H1835
2Ki 10:29 that *were* in Beth-el, and that *were* in **D**. H1835
1Ch 2: 2 **D**, Joseph, and Benjamin, Naphtali, H1835
21: 2 even to **D**; and bring the number H1835
27:22 Of **D**, Azareel the son of Jeroham. These H1835
2Ch 2:14 the daughters of **D**, and his father *was* H1835
16: 4 smote Ijon, and **D**, and Abel-maim, and H1835
30: 5 even to **D**, that they should come H1835
Jer 4:15 For a voice declareth from **D**, and H1835
8:16 was heard from **D**: the whole land H1835
Ezk 27:19 **D** also and Javan going to and fro H1835
48: 1 his sides east *and* west; a *portion for* **D**. H1835
2 And by the border of **D**, from the east H1835
32 one gate of Benjamin, one gate of **D**. H1835
Am 8:14 and say, Thy god, O **D**, liveth; and, The H1835

DANCE
Jdg 21:21 come out to **d** in dances, then come H2342
Job 21:11 ones like a flock, and their children **d**. H7540
Ps 149: 3 Let them praise his name in the **d**: let H4234
150: 4 Praise him with the timbrel and **d**: H4234
Ecc 3: 4 laugh; a time to mourn, and a time to **d**; H7540
Isa 13:21 dwell there, and satyrs shall **d** there. H7540
Jer 31:13 Then shall the virgin rejoice in the **d**, H4234
Lam 5:15 The joy of our heart is ceased; our **d** is H4234

DANCED
Jdg 21:23 of them that **d**, whom they caught: H2342
2Sa 6:14 And David **d** before the LORD with all H3769
Mt 11:17 and ye have not **d**; we have mourned G3738
14: 6 **d** before them, and pleased Herod. G3738
Mk 6:22 came in, and **d**, and pleased Herod G3738
Lk 7:32 and ye have not **d**; we have mourned to G3738

DANCES
Ex 15:20 out after her with timbrels and with **d**. H4246
Jdg 11:34 timbrels and with **d**: and she *was his* H4246
21:21 out to dance in **d**, then come ye out of H4246
1Sa 21:11 another of him in **d**, saying, Saul hath H4246
29: 5 one to another in **d**, saying, Saul slew H4246
Jer 31: 4 forth in the **d** of them that make merry. H4234

DANCING
Ex 32:19 the calf, and the **d**: and Moses' anger H4246
1Sa 18: 6 singing and **d**, to meet king Saul, with H4246
30:16 and drinking, and **d**, because of all the H2287
2Sa 6:16 David leaping and **d** before the LORD; H3769
1Ch 15:29 saw king David **d** and playing: and she H7540
Ps 30:11 my mourning into **d**: thou hast put off H4234
Lk 15:25 to the house, he heard musick and **d**. G5525

DANDLED
Isa 66:12 *her* sides, and be **d** upon *her* knees. H8173

DANGER
Mt 5:21 shall kill shall be in **d** of the judgment: G1777
22 a cause shall be in **d** of the judgment: G1777
22 Raca, shall be in **d** of the council: but G1777
22 say, Thou fool, shall be in **d** of hell fire. G1777
Mk 3:29 but is in **d** of eternal damnation: G1777
Act 19:27 So that not only this our craft is in **d** to G2793
40 For we are in **d** to be called in question G2793

DANGEROUS
Act 27: 9 sailing was now **d**, because the fast was G2000

DANIEL
1Ch 3: 1 second **D**, of Abigail the Carmelitess: H1840

Ezr 8: 2 **D**: of the sons of David; Hattush. H1840
Neh 10: 6 **D**, Ginnethon, Baruch, H1840
Ezk 14:14 Though these three men, Noah, **D**, and H1840
20 Though Noah, **D**, and Job, *were* in it, *as* H1840
28: 3 Behold, thou *art* wiser than **D**; there is H1840
Dan 1: 6 **D**, Hananiah, Mishael, and Azariah: H1840
7 names: for he gave unto **D** *the name* of H1840
8 But **D** purposed in his heart that he H1840
9 Now God had brought **D** into favour H1840
10 eunuchs said unto **D**, I fear my lord the H1840
11 Then said **D** to Melzar, whom the H1840
11 **D**, Hananiah, Mishael, and Azariah, H1840
17 and wisdom: and **D** had understanding H1840
19 found none like **D**, Hananiah, Mishael, H1840
21 And **D** continued *even* unto the first H1840
2:13 sought **D** and his fellows to be slain. H1841
14 Then **D** answered with counsel and H1841
15 Arioch made the thing known to **D**. H1841
16 Then **D** went in, and desired of the king H1841
17 Then **D** went to his house, and made H1841
18 this secret; that **D** and his fellows H1841
19 Then was the secret revealed unto **D** in H1841
19 Then **D** blessed the God of heaven. H1841
20 **D** answered and said, Blessed be the H1841
24 Therefore **D** went in unto Arioch, H1841
25 Then Arioch brought in **D** before the H1841
26 The king answered and said to **D**, H1841
27 **D** answered in the presence of the king, H1841
46 and worshipped **D**, and commanded H1841
47 The king answered unto **D**, and said, Of H1841
48 Then the king made **D** a great man, H1841
49 Then **D** requested of the king, and he H1841
49 but **D** *sat* in the gate of the king. H1841
4: 8 But at the last **D** came in before me, H1841
19 Then **D**, whose name *was* Belteshazzar, H1841
5:12 found in the same **D**, whom the king H1841
12 now let **D** be called, and he will H1841
13 Then was **D** brought in before the king. H1841
13 and said unto **D**, *Art* thou that Daniel, H1841
13 Daniel, *Art* thou that **D**, which *art* of the H1841
17 Then **D** answered and said before the H1841
29 and they clothed **D** with scarlet, and H1841
6: 2 of whom **D** *was* first: that the princes H1841
3 Then this **D** was preferred above the H1841
4 find occasion against **D** concerning the H1841
5 against this **D**, except we find *it* against H1841
10 Now when **D** knew that the writing was H1841
11 and found **D** praying and making H1841
13 before the king, That **D**, which *is* of the H1841
14 set *his* heart on **D** to deliver him: and H1841
16 and they brought **D**, and cast *him* into H1841
16 and said unto **D**, Thy God whom thou H1841
17 might not be changed concerning **D**. H1841
20 voice unto **D**: *and* the king spake H1841
20 spake and said to **D**, O Daniel, servant H1841
20 said to Daniel, O **D**, servant of the living H1841
21 Then said **D** unto the king, O king, live H1841
23 they should take **D** up out of the den. H1841
23 out of the den. So **D** was taken up out H1841
24 had accused **D**, and they cast *them* H1841
26 before the God of **D**: for he *is* the living H1841
27 **D** from the power of the lions. H1841
28 So this **D** prospered in the reign of H1841
7: 1 king of Babylon **D** had a dream and H1841
2 **D** spake and said, I saw in my vision by H1841
15 I **D** was grieved in my spirit in the H1841
28 the matter. As for me **D**, my cogitations H1841
8: 1 me, *even unto* me **D**, after that which H1840
15 And it came to pass, when I, *even* I **D**, H1840
27 And I **D** fainted, and was sick *certain* H1840
9: 2 In the first year of his reign I **D** H1840
22 me, and said, O **D**, I am now come forth H1840
10: 1 was revealed unto **D**, whose name was H1840
2 In those days I **D** was mourning three H1840
7 And I **D** alone saw the vision: for the H1840
11 And he said unto me, O **D**, a man H1840
12 Then said he unto me, Fear not, **D**: for H1840
12: 4 But thou, O **D**, shut up the words, and H1840
5 Then I **D** looked, and, behold, there H1840
9 And he said, Go thy way, **D**: for the H1840
Mt 24:15 spoken of by **D** the prophet, stand *G1158*
Mk 13:14 spoken of by **D** the prophet, standing *G1158*

DANITES
Jdg 13: 2 of the family of the **D**, whose name *was* H1839
18: 1 days the tribe of the **D** sought them an H1839
11 of the family of the **D**, out of Zorah and H1839
1Ch 12:35 And of the **D** expert in war twenty and H1839

DAN-JAAN
2Sa 24: 6 they came to **D**, and about to Zidon, H1842

DANNAH
Jos 15:49 And **D**, and Kirjath-sannah, which *is* H1837

DARA
1Ch 2: 6 and Calcol, and **D**: five of them in all. H1873

DARDA
1Ki 4:31 and Chalcol, and **D**, the sons of Mahol: H1862

DARE
Job 41:10 None *is so* fierce that **d** stir him up: who
Ro 5: 7 a good man some would even **d** to die. *G5111*
15:18 For I will not **d** to speak of any of those *G5111*
1Co 6: 1 **D** any of you, having a matter against *G5111*
2Co 10:12 For we **d** not make ourselves of the *G5111*

DARIUS
Ezr 4: 5 even until the reign of **D** king of Persia. H1867
24 year of the reign of **D** king of Persia. H1868
5: 5 the matter came to **D**: and then they H1868
6 this side the river, sent unto **D** the king: H1868
7 thus; Unto **D** the king, all peace. H1868
6: 1 Then **D** the king made a decree, and H1868
12 which *is* at Jerusalem. I **D** have made a H1868
13 to that which **D** the king had sent, so H1868
14 and **D**, and Artaxerxes king of Persia. H1868
15 the sixth year of the reign of **D** the king. H1868
Neh 12:22 priests, to the reign of **D** the Persian. H1867
Dan 5:31 And **D** the Median took the kingdom, H1868
6: 1 It pleased **D** to set over the kingdom an H1868
6 thus unto him, King **D**, live for ever. H1868
9 Wherefore king **D** signed the writing H1868
25 Then king **D** wrote unto all people, H1868
28 **D**, and in the reign of Cyrus the Persian. H1868
9: 1 In the first year of **D** the son of H1867
11: 1 Also I in the first year of **D** the Mede, H1867
Hag 1: 1 In the second year of **D** the king, in the H1867
15 in the second year of **D** the king. H1867
2:10 the second year of **D**, came the word of H1867
Zec 1: 1 the second year of **D**, came the word of H1867
7 the second year of **D**, came the word of H1867
7: 1 year of king **D**, *that* the word of the H1867

DARK
Gen 15:17 down, and it was **d**, behold a smoking H5939
Lev 13: 6 *be* somewhat **d**, *and* the plague spread H3544
21 but *be* somewhat **d**; then the priest shall H3544
26 but *be* somewhat **d**; then the priest shall H3544
28 but it *be* somewhat **d**; it *is* a rising of the H3544
56 *be* somewhat **d** after the washing of H3544
Nu 12: 8 and not in **d** speeches; and the H2420
Jos 2: 5 gate, when it was **d**, that the men went H2822
2Sa 22:12 **d** waters, *and* thick clouds of the skies. H2841
Neh 13:19 began to be **d** before the sabbath, H6751
Job 3: 9 Let the stars of the twilight thereof be **d**; H2821
12:25 They grope in the **d** without light, and H2822
18: 6 The light shall be **d** in his tabernacle, H2821
22:13 can he judge through the **d** cloud? H6205
24:16 In the **d** they dig through houses, *which* H2822
Ps 18:11 **d** waters *and* thick clouds of the skies. H2824
35: 6 Let their way be **d** and slippery: and let H2822
49: 4 I will open my **d** saying upon the harp. H2420
74:20 covenant: for the **d** places of the earth H4285
78: 2 a parable: I will utter **d** sayings of old: H2420
88:12 Shall thy wonders be known in the **d**? H2822
105:28 He sent darkness, and made it **d**; and H2821
Prv 1: 6 words of the wise, and their **d** sayings. H2420
7: 9 in the evening, in the black and **d** night: H653
Isa 29:15 works are in the **d**, and they say, Who H4285
45:19 I have not spoken in secret, in a **d** place H2822
Jer 13:16 stumble upon the **d** mountains, and, H5399
Lam 3: 6 He hath set me in **d** places, as *they that* H4285
Ezk 8:12 of Israel do in the **d**, every man in the H2822
32: 7 the stars thereof **d**; I will cover the sun H6937
8 heaven will I make **d** over thee, and set H6937
34:12 been scattered in the cloudy and **d** day. H6205
Dan 8:23 **d** sentences, shall stand up. H2420
Joel 2:10 the moon shall be **d**, and the stars shall H6937
Am 5: 8 and maketh the day **d** with night: that H2821
20 even very **d**, and no brightness in it? H651
Mic 3: 6 and it shall be **d** unto you, that ye shall H2821
6 and the day shall be **d** over them. H6937
Zec 14: 6 *that* the light shall not be clear, *nor* **d**: H7087
Lk 11:36 having no part **d**, the whole shall be full *G4652*
Jn 6:17 now **d**, and Jesus was not come to them. *G4653*
20: 1 when it was yet **d**, unto the sepulchre, *G4653*
2Pt 1:19 that shineth in a **d** place, until the day *G850*

DARKEN
Am 8: 9 and I will **d** the earth in the clear day: H2821

DARKENED
Ex 10:15 so that the land was **d**; and they did eat H2821
Ps 69:23 Let their eyes be **d**, that they see not; H2821
Ecc 12: 2 **d**, nor the clouds return after the rain: H2821
3 those that look out of the windows be **d**, H2821
Isa 5:30 the light is **d** in the heavens thereof. H2821
9:19 hosts is the land **d**, and the people shall H6272
13:10 the sun shall be **d** in his going forth, H2821
24:11 all joy is **d**, the mirth of the land is gone. H6150
Ezk 30:18 At Tehaphnehes also the day shall be **d**, H2821
Joel 3:15 The sun and the moon shall be **d**, and H6937
Zec 11:17 up, and his right eye shall be utterly **d**. H3543
Mt 24:29 shall the sun be **d**, and the moon shall *G4654*
Mk 13:24 **d**, and the moon shall not give her light, *G4654*
Lk 23:45 And the sun was **d**, and the veil of the *G4654*
Ro 1:21 and their foolish heart was **d**. *G4654*
11:10 Let their eyes be **d**, that they may not *G4654*
Eph 4:18 Having the understanding **d**, being *G4654*
Rev 8:12 part of them was **d**, and the day shone *G4654*
9: 2 **d** by reason of the smoke of the pit. *G4654*

DARKENETH
Job 38: 2 Who *is* this that **d** counsel by words H2821

DARKISH
Lev 13:39 of their flesh *be* **d** white; it *is* a freckled H3544

DARKLY
1Co 13:12 a glass, **d**; but then face to *G1722+G135*

DARKNESS
Gen 1: 2 and void; and **d** *was* upon the face of H2822
4 and God divided the light from the **d**. H2822
5 And God called the light Day, and the **d** H2822
18 the **d**: and God saw that *it was* good. H2822
15:12 lo, an horror of great **d** fell upon him. H2825
Ex 10:21 that there may be **d** over the land of H2822
21 of Egypt, even **d** *which* may be felt. H2822
22 **d** in all the land of Egypt three days: H2822
14:20 and it was a cloud and **d** *to them*, but it H2822
20:21 near unto the thick **d** where God *was*. H6205
Dt 4:11 with **d**, clouds, and thick darkness. H2822
11 with darkness, clouds, and thick **d**. H6205
5:22 and of the thick **d**, with a great voice: H6205
23 of the midst of the **d**, (for the mountain H2822
28:29 the blind gropeth in **d**, and thou shalt not H653
Jos 24: 7 the LORD, he put **d** between you and H3990
1Sa 2: 9 **d**; for by strength shall no man prevail. H2822
2Sa 22:10 came down; and **d** *was* under his feet. H6205
12 And he made **d** pavilions round about H2822
29 LORD: and the LORD will lighten my **d**. H2822
1Ki 8:12 said that he would dwell in the thick **d**. H6205
2Ch 6: 1 said that he would dwell in the thick **d**. H6205
Job 3: 4 Let that day be **d**; let not God regard it H2822
5 Let **d** and the shadow of death stain it; H2822
6 As *for* that night, let **d** seize upon it; let it H652
5:14 They meet with **d** in the daytime, and H2822
10:21 the land of **d** and the shadow of death; H2822
22 A land of **d**, as darkness *itself; and* of H5890
22 A land of darkness, as **d** *itself; and* of the H652
22 any order, and *where* the light *is* as **d**. H652
12:22 He discovereth deep things out of **d**, H2822
15:22 of **d**, and he is waited for of the sword. H2822
23 that the day of **d** is ready at his hand. H2822
30 He shall not depart out of **d**; the flame H2822
17:12 into day: the light *is* short because of **d**. H2822
13 house: I have made my bed in the **d**. H2822
18:18 He shall be driven from light into **d**, and H2822
19: 8 pass, and he hath set **d** in my paths. H2822
20:26 All **d** *shall be* hid in his secret places: a H2822
22:11 Or **d**, *that* thou canst not see; and H2822
23:17 Because I was not cut off before the **d**, H2822
17 hath he covered the **d** from my face. H652
28: 3 He setteth an end to **d**, and searcheth H2822
3 the stones of **d**, and the shadow of death. H652
29: 3 *when* by his light I walked *through* **d**; H2822
30:26 when I waited for light, there came **d**. H652
34:22 *There is* no **d**, nor shadow of death, H2822
37:19 cannot order *our speech* by reason of **d**. H2822
38: 9 and thick **d** a swaddlingband for it, H6205
19 and *as for* **d**, where *is* the place thereof, H2822
Ps 18: 9 came down: and **d** *was* under his feet. H6205
11 He made **d** his secret place; his H2822
28 the LORD my God will enlighten my **d**. H2822

Ps 82: 5 they walk on in **d**: all the foundations H2825
88: 6 me in the lowest pit, in **d**, in the deeps. H4285
18 me, *and* mine acquaintance into **d**. H4285
91: 6 *Nor* for the pestilence *that* walketh in **d**; H652
97: 2 Clouds and **d** *are* round about him: H6205
104:20 Thou makest **d**, and it is night: wherein H2822
105:28 He sent **d**, and made it dark; and they H2822
107:10 Such as sit in **d** and in the shadow of H2822
14 He brought them out of **d** and the H2822
112: 4 ariseth light in the **d**: *he is* gracious, and H2822
139:11 If I say, Surely the **d** shall cover me; H2822
12 Yea, the **d** hideth not from thee; but the H2822
12 **d** and the light *are* both alike *to thee*. H2825
143: 3 in **d**, as those that have been long dead. H4285
Prv 2:13 of uprightness, to walk in the ways of **d**; H2822
4:19 The way of the wicked *is* as **d**: they know H653
20:20 his lamp shall be put out in obscure **d**. H2822
Ecc 2:13 excelleth folly, as far as light excelleth **d**. H2822
14 but the fool walketh in **d**: and I myself H2822
5:17 All his days also he eateth in **d**, and *he* H2822
6: 4 and departeth in **d**, and his name shall H2822
4 and his name shall be covered with **d**. H2822
11: 8 the days of **d**; for they shall be many. H2822
Isa 5:20 good evil; that put **d** for light, and light H2822
20 light, and light for **d**; that put bitter for H2822
30 the land, behold **d** *and* sorrow, and the H2822
8:22 trouble and **d**, dimness of anguish; H2825
22 of anguish; and *they shall be* driven to **d**. H653
9: 2 The people that walked in **d** have seen H2822
29:18 shall see out of obscurity, and out of **d**. H2822
42: 7 that sit in **d** out of the prison house. H2822
16 I will make **d** light before them, and H4285
45: 3 And I will give thee the treasures of **d**, H2822
7 I form the light, and create **d**: I make H2822
47: 5 Sit thou silent, and get thee into **d**, O H2822
49: 9 to them that *are* in **d**, Shew yourselves. H2822
50:10 that walketh *in* **d**, and hath no light? let H2825
58:10 obscurity, and thy **d** *be* as the noonday: H653
59: 9 for brightness, *but* we walk in **d**. H653
60: 2 For, behold, the **d** shall cover the earth, H2822
2 earth, and gross **d** the people: but the H6205
Jer 2:31 Israel? a land of **d**? wherefore say my H3991
13:16 before he cause **d**, and before your feet H2821
16 shadow of death, *and* make *it* gross **d**. H6205
23:12 *ways* in the **d**: they shall be driven H653
Lam 3: 2 He hath led me, and brought *me into* **d**, H2822
Ezk 32: 8 **d** upon thy land, saith the Lord GOD. H2822
Dan 2:22 the **d**, and the light dwelleth with him. H2816
Joel 2: 2 A day of **d** and of gloominess, a day of H2822
2 and of thick **d**, as the morning spread H6205
31 The sun shall be turned into **d**, and the H2822
Am 4:13 the morning **d**, and treadeth upon H5890
5:18 the day of the LORD *is* **d**, and not light. H2822
20 *Shall* not the day of the LORD *be* **d**, and H2822
Mic 7: 8 in **d**, the LORD *shall be* a light unto me. H2822
Nah 1: 8 and **d** shall pursue his enemies. H2822
Zep 1:15 a day of **d** and gloominess, a day H2822
15 gloominess, a day of clouds and thick **d**, H6205
Mt 4:16 The people which sat in **d** saw great G4655
6:23 shall be full of **d**. If therefore the light G4652
23 in thee be **d**, how great *is* that darkness! G4655
23 in thee be darkness, how great *is* that **d**! G4655
8:12 be cast out into outer **d**: there shall be G4655
10:27 What I tell you in **d**, *that* speak ye in G4653
22:13 *him* into outer **d**; there shall be weeping G4655
25:30 servant into outer **d**: there shall be G4655
27:45 Now from the sixth hour there was **d** G4655
Mk 15:33 come, there was **d** over the whole land G4655
Lk 1:79 To give light to them that sit in **d** and G4655
11:34 *eye* is evil, thy body also *is* full of **d**. G4652
35 that the light which is in thee be not **d**. G4655
12: 3 ye have spoken in **d** shall be heard in G4653
22:53 this is your hour, and the power of **d**. G4655
23:44 and there was a **d** over all the earth G4655
Jn 1: 5 And the light shineth in **d**; and the G4653
5 and the **d** comprehended it not. G4653
3:19 and men loved **d** rather than light, G4655
8:12 walk in **d**, but shall have the light of life. G4653
12:35 ye have the light, lest **d** come upon you: G4653
35 in **d** knoweth not whither he goeth. G4653
46 believeth on me should not abide in **d**. G4653
Act 2:20 The sun shall be turned into **d**, and the G4655
13:11 him a mist and a **d**; and he went about G4655
26:18 to turn *them* from **d** to light, and *from* G4655
Ro 2:19 the blind, a light of them which are in **d**, G4655
13:12 **d**, and let us put on the armour of light. G4655
1Co 4: 5 the hidden things of **d**, and will make G4655
2Co 4: 6 to shine out of **d**, hath shined in our G4655
6:14 and what communion hath light with **d**? G4655
Eph 5: 8 For ye were sometimes **d**, but now *are* G4655
11 works of **d**, but rather reprove *them*. G4655
6:12 the rulers of the **d** of this world, against G4655
Col 1:13 us from the power of **d**, and hath G4655
1Th 5: 4 But ye, brethren, are not in **d**, that that G4655
5 day: we are not of the night, nor of **d**. G4655
Heb 12:18 unto blackness, and **d**, and tempest, G4655
1Pt 2: 9 you out of **d** into his marvellous light: G4655
2Pt 2: 4 of **d**, to be reserved unto judgment; G2217
17 whom the mist of **d** is reserved for ever. G4655
1Jn 1: 5 God is light, and in him is no **d** at all. G4653
6 walk in **d**, we lie, and do not the truth: G4655
2: 8 you: because the **d** is past, and the true G4653
9 his brother, is in **d** even until now. G4653
11 But he that hateth his brother is in **d**, G4653
11 and walketh in **d**, and knoweth not G4653
11 because that **d** hath blinded his eyes. G4653
Jude 6 **d** unto the judgment of the great day. G2217
13 is reserved the blackness of **d** for ever. G4655
Rev 16:10 was full of **d**; and they gnawed their G4656

DARKON

Ezr 2:56 the children of **D**, the children of Giddel, H1874
Neh 7:58 The children of Jaala, the children of **D**, H1874

DARLING

Ps 22:20 Deliver my soul from the sword; my **d** H3173
35:17 their destructions, my **d** from the lions. H3173

DART

Job 41:26 the spear, the **d**, nor the habergeon. H4551
Prv 7:23 Till a **d** strike through his liver; as a H2671
Heb 12:20 be stoned, or thrust through with a **d**: G1002

DARTS

2Sa 18:14 And he took three **d** in his hand, and H7626
2Ch 32: 5 and made **d** and shields in abundance. H7973
Job 41:29 **D** are counted as stubble: he laugheth H8455
Eph 6:16 to quench all the fiery **d** of the wicked. G956

DASH

2Ki 8:12 sword, and wilt **d** their children, and H7376
Ps 2: 9 **d** them in pieces like a potter's vessel. H5310
91:12 lest thou **d** thy foot against a stone. H5062
Isa 13:18 *Their* bows also shall **d** the young men H7376
Jer 13:14 And I will **d** them one against another, H5310
Mt 4: 6 time thou **d** thy foot against a stone. G4350
Lk 4:11 time thou **d** thy foot against a stone. G4350

DASHED

Ex 15: 6 O LORD, hath **d** in pieces the enemy. H7492
Isa 13:16 Their children also shall be **d** to pieces H7376
Hos 10:14 was **d** in pieces upon *her* children. H7376
13:16 infants shall be **d** in pieces, and their H7376
Nah 3:10 children also were **d** in pieces at the top H7376

DASHETH

Ps 137: 9 Happy *shall he be*, that taketh and **d** H5310
Nah 2: 1 He that **d** in pieces is come up before H6327

DATHAN

Nu 16: 1 the son of Levi, and **D** and Abiram, the H1885
12 And Moses sent to call **D** and Abiram, H1885
24 tabernacle of Korah, **D**, and Abiram. H1885
25 And Moses rose up and went unto **D** H1885
27 of Korah, **D**, and Abiram, on every H1885
27 on every side: and **D** and Abiram came H1885
26: 9 And the sons of Eliab; Nemuel, and **D**, H1885
9 This *is that* **D** and Abiram, *which* H1885
Dt 11: 6 And what he did unto **D** and Abiram, H1885
Ps 106:17 The earth opened and swallowed up **D**, H1885

DAUB

Ezk 13:11 Say unto them which **d** *it* with H2902

DAUBED

Ex 2: 3 of bulrushes, and **d** it with slime and H2560
Ezk 13:10 lo, others **d** it with untempered *morter*: H2902
12 *is* the daubing wherewith ye have **d** *it*? H2902
14 wall that ye have **d** with untempered H2902
15 them that have **d** it with untempered H2902
15 wall *is* no *more*, neither they that **d** it; H2902
22:28 And her prophets have **d** them with H2902

DAUBING

Ezk 13:12 *is* the **d** wherewith ye have daubed *it*? H2915

DAUGHTER

Gen 11:29 wife, Milcah, the **d** of Haran, the father H1323
11:31 son, and Sarai his **d** in law, his son H3618
20:12 sister; she *is* the **d** of my father, but not H1323
12 father, but not the **d** of my mother; and H1323
24:23 And said, Whose **d** *art* thou? tell me, I H1323
24 And she said unto him, I *am* the **d** of H1323
47 And I asked her, and said, Whose **d** *art* H1323
47 And she said, The **d** of Bethuel, Nahor's H1323
48 my master's brother's **d** unto his son. H1323
25:20 to wife, the **d** of Bethuel the Syrian H1323
26:34 to wife Judith the **d** of Beeri the Hittite, H1323
34 Bashemath the **d** of Elon the Hittite: H1323
28: 9 he had Mahalath the **d** of Ishmael H1323
29: 6 Rachel his **d** cometh with the sheep. H1323
10 saw Rachel the **d** of Laban his mother's H1323
18 seven years for Rachel thy younger **d**. H1323
23 he took Leah his **d**, and brought her to H1323
24 And Laban gave unto his **d** Leah H1323
28 he gave him Rachel his **d** to wife also. H1323
29 And Laban gave to Rachel his **d** Bilhah H1323
30:21 And afterwards she bare a **d**, and called H1323
34: 1 And Dinah the **d** of Leah, which she H1323
3 And his soul clave unto Dinah the **d** of H1323
5 defiled Dinah his **d**: now his sons were H1323
7 **d**; which thing ought not to be done. H1323
8 your **d**: I pray you give her him to wife. H1323
17 will we take our **d**, and we will be gone. H1323
19 delight in Jacob's **d**: and he *was* more H1323
36: 2 Canaan; Adah the **d** of Elon the Hittite, H1323
2 and Aholibamah the **d** of Anah the H1323
2 of Anah the **d** of Zibeon the Hivite; H1323
3 And Bashemath Ishmael's **d**, sister of H1323
14 of Aholibamah, the **d** of Anah the H1323
14 of Anah the **d** of Zibeon, Esau's wife: H1323
18 the **d** of Anah, Esau's wife. H1323
25 and Aholibamah the **d** of Anah. H1323
39 **d** of Matred, the daughter of Mezahab. H1323
39 daughter of Matred, the **d** of Mezahab. H1323
38: 2 And Judah saw there a **d** of a certain H1323
11 Then said Judah to Tamar his **d** in law, H3618
12 And in process of time the **d** of Shuah H1323
16 not that she *was* his **d** in law.) And she H3618
24 saying, Tamar thy **d** in law hath played H3618
41:45 to wife Asenath the **d** of Poti-pherah H1323
50 Asenath the **d** of Poti-pherah priest H1323
46:15 with his **d** Dinah: all the souls H1323
18 gave to Leah his **d**, and these she bare H1323
20 Asenath the **d** of Poti-pherah priest H1323
25 unto Rachel his **d**, and she bare these H1323
Ex 1:16 him: but if it *be* a **d**, then she shall live. H1323
22 river, and every **d** ye shall save alive. H1323
2: 1 of Levi, and took *to wife* a **d** of Levi. H1323
5 And the **d** of Pharaoh came down to H1323
7 Then said his sister to Pharaoh's **d**, H1323
8 And Pharaoh's **d** said to her, Go. And H1323
9 And Pharaoh's **d** said unto her, Take H1323
10 unto Pharaoh's **d**, and he became her H1323
21 and he gave Moses Zipporah his **d**. H1323
6:23 And Aaron took him Elisheba, **d** of H1323
20:10 thy son, nor thy **d**, thy manservant, nor H1323
21: 7 And if a man sell his **d** to be a H1323
31 son, or have gored a **d**, according to this H1323
Lev 12: 6 for a son, or for a **d**, she shall bring a H1323
18: 9 The nakedness of thy sister, the **d** of H1323
9 of thy father, or **d** of thy mother, H1323
10 The nakedness of thy son's **d**, or of thy H1323
10 or of thy daughter's **d**, *even* their H1323
11 The nakedness of thy father's wife's **d**, H1323
15 the nakedness of thy **d** in law: she *is* thy H3618
17 a woman and her **d**, neither shalt thou H1323
17 thou take her son's **d**, or her daughter's H1323
17 or her daughter's **d**, to uncover her H1323
19:29 Do not prostitute thy **d**, to cause her to H1323
20:12 And if a man lie with his **d** in law, both H3618
17 his sister, his father's **d**, or his mother's H1323
17 daughter, or his mother's **d**, and see her H1323
21: 2 son, and for his **d**, and for his brother, H1323
9 And the **d** of any priest, if she profane H1323
22:12 If the priest's **d** also be *married* unto a H1323
13 But if the priest's **d** be a widow, or H1323
24:11 the **d** of Dibri, of the tribe of Dan:) H1323
Nu 25:15 *was* Cozbi, the **d** of Zur; he *was* head H1323
18 of Cozbi, the **d** of a prince of Midian, H1323
26:46 And the name of the **d** of Asher *was* H1323
59 *was* Jochebed, the **d** of Levi, whom *her* H1323
27: 8 cause his inheritance to pass unto his **d**. H1323
9 And if he have no **d**, then ye shall give H1323
30:16 the father and his **d**, *being yet* in her H1323
36: 8 And every **d**, that possesseth an H1323
Dt 5:14 thy son, nor thy **d**, nor thy manservant, H1323

D

Dt 7: 3 with them; thy **d** thou shalt not give H1323
3 nor his **d** shalt thou take unto thy son. H1323
12:18 thy son, and thy **d**, and thy manservant, H1323
13: 6 or thy son, or thy **d**, or the wife of thy H1323
16:11 thy son, and thy **d**, and thy manservant, H1323
14 thy son, and thy **d**, and thy manservant, H1323
18:10 his son or his **d** to pass through the H1323
22:16 elders, I gave my **d** unto this man to H1323
17 I found not thy **d** a maid; and yet these H1323
27:22 with his sister, the **d** of his father, or H1323
22 his father, or the **d** of his mother. And H1323
28:56 and toward her son, and toward her **d**, H1323
Jos 15:16 to him will I give Achsah my **d** to wife. H1323
17 and he gave him Achsah his **d** to wife. H1323
Jdg 1:12 to him will I give Achsah my **d** to wife. H1323
13 and he gave him Achsah his **d** to wife. H1323
11:34 and, behold, his **d** came out to meet H1323
34 beside her he had neither son nor **d**. H1323
35 said, Alas, my **d**! thou hast brought me H1323
40 yearly to lament the **d** of Jephthah the H1323
19:24 Behold, *here is* my **d** a maiden, and his H1323
21: 1 of us give his **d** unto Benjamin to wife. H1323
Ru 1:22 the Moabitess, her **d** in law, with her, H3618
2: 2 grace. And she said unto her, Go, my **d**. H1323
8 thou not, my **d**? Go not to glean in H1323
20 And Naomi said unto her **d** in law, H3618
22 And Naomi said unto Ruth her **d** in H3618
22 in law, *It is* good, my **d**, that thou go out H1323
3: 1 said unto her, My **d**, shall I not seek rest H1323
10 thou of the LORD, my **d**: *for* thou hast H1323
11 And now, my **d**, fear not; I will do to H1323
16 Who *art* thou, my **d**? And she told her H1323
18 Then said she, Sit still, my **d**, until thou H1323
4:15 old age: for thy **d** in law, which loveth H3618
1Sa 1:16 Count not thine handmaid for a **d** of H1323
4:19 And his **d** in law, Phinehas' wife, was H3618
14:50 *was* Ahinoam, the **d** of Ahimaaz: and H1323
17:25 and will give him his **d**, and make his H1323
18:17 Behold my elder **d** Merab, her will I H1323
19 Merab Saul's **d** should have been given H1323
20 And Michal Saul's **d** loved David: and H1323
27 Saul gave him Michal his **d** to wife. H1323
28 and *that* Michal Saul's **d** loved him. H1323
25:44 But Saul had given Michal his **d**, H1323
2Sa 3: 3 the **d** of Talmai king of Geshur; H1323
7 name *was* Rizpah, the **d** of Aiah: and H1323
13 **d**, when thou comest to see my face. H1323
6:16 Michal Saul's **d** looked through a H1323
20 And Michal the **d** of Saul came out to H1323
23 Therefore Michal the **d** of Saul had no H1323
11: 3 Bath-sheba, the **d** of Eliam, the wife of H1323
12: 3 in his bosom, and was unto him as a **d**. H1323
14:27 three sons, and one **d**, whose name *was* H1323
17:25 in to Abigail the **d** of Nahash, sister to H1323
21: 8 sons of Rizpah the **d** of Aiah, whom she H1323
8 sons of Michal the **d** of Saul, whom she H1323
10 And Rizpah the **d** of Aiah took H1323
11 David what Rizpah the **d** of Aiah, the H1323
1Ki 3: 1 took Pharaoh's **d**, and brought her into H1323
4:11 had Taphath the **d** of Solomon to wife: H1323
15 took Basmath the **d** of Solomon to wife: H1323
7: 8 for Pharaoh's **d**, whom he had taken H1323
9:16 a present unto his **d**, Solomon's wife. H1323
24 But Pharaoh's **d** came up out of the city H1323
11: 1 together with the **d** of Pharaoh, women H1323
15: 2 *was* Maachah, the **d** of Abishalom. H1323
10 *was* Maachah, the **d** of Abishalom. H1323
16:31 to wife Jezebel the **d** of Ethbaal king of H1323
22:42 name *was* Azubah the **d** of Shilhi. H1323
2Ki 8:18 of Ahab: for the **d** of Ahab was his wife: H1323
26 Athaliah, the **d** of Omri king of Israel. H1323
9:34 and bury her: for she *is* a king's **d**. H1323
11: 2 But Jehosheba, the **d** of king Joram, H1323
14: 9 saying, Give thy **d** to my son to wife: H1323
15:33 name *was* Jerusha, the **d** of Zadok. H1323
18: 2 name also *was* Abi, the **d** of Zachariah. H1323
19:21 The virgin the **d** of Zion hath despised H1323
21 thee to scorn; the **d** of Jerusalem hath H1323
21:19 the **d** of Haruz of Jotbah. H1323
22: 1 Jedidah, the **d** of Adaiah of Boscath. H1323
23:10 **d** to pass through the fire to Molech. H1323
31 Hamutal, the **d** of Jeremiah of Libnah. H1323
36 Zebudah, the **d** of Pedaiah of Rumah. H1323
24: 8 the **d** of Elnathan of Jerusalem. H1323
18 Hamutal, the **d** of Jeremiah of Libnah. H1323
1Ch 1:50 **d** of Matred, the daughter of Mezahab. H1323
50 daughter of Matred, the **d** of Mezahab. H1323
2: 3 born unto him of the **d** of Shua the H1323
4 And Tamar his **d** in law bare him H3618
1Ch 2:21 And afterward Hezron went in to the **d** H1323
35 And Sheshan gave his **d** to Jarha his H1323
49 Gibea: and the **d** of Caleb *was* Achsah. H1323
3: 2 son of Maachah the **d** of Talmai king of H1323
5 four, of Bath-shua the **d** of Ammiel: H1323
4:18 the **d** of Pharaoh, which Mered took. H1323
7:24 (And his **d** *was* Sherah, who built H1323
15:29 that Michal the **d** of Saul looking out H1323
2Ch 8:11 And Solomon brought up the **d** of H1323
11:18 him Mahalath the **d** of Jerimoth the H1121
18 Abihail the **d** of Eliab the son of Jesse; H1323
20 And after her he took Maachah the **d** of H1323
21 And Rehoboam loved Maachah the **d** H1323
13: 2 *was* Michaiah the **d** of Uriel of Gibeah. H1323
20:31 name *was* Azubah the **d** of Shilhi. H1323
21: 6 for he had the **d** of Ahab to wife: and H1323
22: 2 name also *was* Athaliah the **d** of Omri. H1323
11 But Jehoshabeath, the **d** of the king, H1323
11 Jehoshabeath, the **d** of king Jehoram, H1323
25:18 saying, Give thy **d** to my son to wife: H1323
27: 1 also *was* Jerushah, the **d** of Zadok. H1323
29: 1 name *was* Abijah, the **d** of Zechariah. H1323
Neh 6:18 **d** of Meshullam the son of Berechiah. H1323
Est 2: 7 Esther, his uncle's **d**: for she had neither H1323
7 mother were dead, took for his own **d**. H1323
15 Now when the turn of Esther, the **d** of H1323
15 taken her for his **d**, was come to go in H1323
9:29 Then Esther the queen, the **d** of H1323
Ps 9:14 **d** of Zion: I will rejoice in thy salvation. H1323
45:10 Hearken, O **d**, and consider, and incline H1323
12 And the **d** of Tyre *shall be there* with a H1323
13 The king's **d** *is* all glorious within: her H1323
137: 8 O **d** of Babylon, who art to be H1323
Song 7: 1 shoes, O prince's **d**! the joints of thy H1323
Isa 1: 8 And the **d** of Zion is left as a cottage in H1323
10:30 Lift up thy voice, O **d** of Gallim: cause it H1323
32 of the **d** of Zion, the hill of Jerusalem. H1004
16: 1 unto the mount of the **d** of Zion. H1323
22: 4 of the spoiling of the **d** of my people. H1323
23:10 Pass through thy land as a river, O **d** of H1323
12 oppressed virgin, **d** of Zidon: arise, H1323
37:22 The virgin, the **d** of Zion, hath despised H1323
22 thee to scorn; the **d** of Jerusalem hath H1323
47: 1 the dust, O virgin **d** of Babylon, sit on H1323
1 *is* no throne, O **d** of the Chaldeans: for H1323
5 into darkness, O **d** of the Chaldeans: H1323
52: 2 bands of thy neck, O captive **d** of Zion. H1323
62:11 Say ye to the **d** of Zion, Behold, thy H1323
Jer 4:11 toward the **d** of my people, not to H1323
31 child, the voice of the **d** of Zion, *that* H1323
6: 2 I have likened the **d** of Zion to a comely H1323
14 They have healed also the hurt *of the* **d** H1323
23 men for war against thee, O **d** of Zion. H1323
26 O **d** of my people, gird *thee* with H1323
8:11 For they have healed the hurt of the **d** H1323
19 Behold the voice of the cry of the **d** of H1323
21 For the hurt of the **d** of my people am I H1323
22 health of the **d** of my people recovered? H1323
9: 1 for the slain of the **d** of my people! H1323
7 how shall I do for the **d** of my people? H1323
14:17 for the virgin **d** of my people is broken H1323
31:22 thou backsliding **d**? for the LORD hath H1323
46:11 O virgin, the **d** of Egypt: in vain shalt H1323
19 O thou **d** dwelling in Egypt, furnish H1323
24 The **d** of Egypt shall be confounded; H1323
48:18 Thou **d** that dost inhabit Dibon, come H1323
49: 4 O backsliding **d**? that trusted in her H1323
50:42 the battle, against thee, O **d** of Babylon. H1323
51:33 God of Israel; The **d** of Babylon *is* like a H1323
52: 1 Hamutal the **d** of Jeremiah of Libnah. H1323
Lam 1: 6 And from the **d** of Zion all her beauty is H1323
15 the **d** of Judah, *as* in a winepress. H1323
2: 1 How hath the Lord covered the **d** of H1323
2 strong holds of the **d** of Judah; he hath H1323
4 tabernacle of the **d** of Zion: he poured H1323
5 **d** of Judah mourning and lamentation. H1323
8 the wall of the **d** of Zion: he hath H1323
10 The elders of the **d** of Zion sit upon the H1323
11 the destruction of the **d** of my people; H1323
13 I liken to thee, O **d** of Jerusalem? what H1323
13 thee, O virgin **d** of Zion? for thy breach H1323
15 wag their head at the **d** of Jerusalem, H1323
18 Lord, O wall of the **d** of Zion, let tears H1323
3:48 the destruction of the **d** of my people. H1323
4: 3 their young ones: the **d** of my people *is* H1323
6 of the iniquity of the **d** of my people is H1323
10 the destruction of the **d** of my people. H1323
21 Rejoice and be glad, O **d** of Edom, that H1323
22 is accomplished, O **d** of Zion; he will no H1323
Lam 4:22 O **d** of Edom; he will discover thy sins. H1323
Ezk 14:20 neither son nor **d**; they shall *but* deliver H1323
16:44 saying, As *is* the mother, *so is* her **d**. H1323
45 Thou *art* thy mother's **d**, that lotheth H1323
22:11 lewdly defiled his **d** in law; and another H3618
11 hath humbled his sister, his father's **d**. H1323
44:25 or for son, or for **d**, for brother, or for H1323
Dan 11: 6 for the king's **d** of the south shall come H1323
17 he shall give him the **d** of women, H1323
Hos 1: 3 So he went and took Gomer the **d** of H1323
6 And she conceived again, and bare a **d**. H1323
Mic 1:13 of the sin to the **d** of Zion: for the H1323
4: 8 strong hold of the **d** of Zion, unto thee H1323
8 shall come to the **d** of Jerusalem. H1323
10 labour to bring forth, O **d** of Zion, like a H1323
13 Arise and thresh, O **d** of Zion: for I will H1323
5: 1 Now gather thyself in troops, O **d** of H1323
7: 6 the father, the **d** riseth up against her H1323
6 her mother, the **d** in law against her H3618
Zep 3:10 *even* the **d** of my dispersed, shall H1323
14 Sing, O **d** of Zion; shout, O Israel; be H1323
14 with all the heart, O **d** of Jerusalem. H1323
Zec 2: 7 that dwellest *with* the **d** of Babylon. H1323
10 Sing and rejoice, O **d** of Zion: for, lo, I H1323
9: 9 Rejoice greatly, O **d** of Zion; shout, O H1323
9 of Zion; shout, O **d** of Jerusalem: H1323
Mal 2:11 hath married the **d** of a strange god. H1323
Mt 9:18 him, saying, My **d** is even now dead: *G2364*
22 saw her, he said, **D**, be of good comfort; *G2364*
10:35 his father, and the **d** against her *G2364*
35 the **d** in law against her mother in law. *G3565*
37 or **d** more than me is not worthy of me. *G2364*
14: 6 was kept, the **d** of Herodias danced *G2364*
15:22 my **d** is grievously vexed with a devil. *G2364*
28 **d** was made whole from that very hour. *G2364*
21: 5 Tell ye the **d** of Sion, Behold, thy King *G2364*
Mk 5:23 saying, My little **d** lieth at the point of *G2365*
34 And he said unto her, **D**, thy faith hath *G2364*
35 *certain* which said, Thy **d** is dead: why *G2364*
6:22 And when the **d** of the said Herodias *G2364*
7:25 For a *certain* woman, whose young **d** *G2365*
26 would cast forth the devil out of her **d**. *G2364*
29 thy way; the devil is gone out of thy **d**. *G2364*
30 gone out, and her **d** laid upon the bed. *G2364*
Lk 2:36 a prophetess, the **d** of Phanuel, of the *G2364*
8:42 For he had one only **d**, about twelve *G2364*
48 And he said unto her, **D**, be of good *G2364*
49 Thy **d** is dead; trouble not the Master. *G2364*
12:53 against the **d**, and the daughter against *G2364*
53 the daughter, and the **d** against the *G2364*
53 in law against her **d** in law, and the *G2364*
53 the **d** in law against her mother in law. *G3565*
13:16 And ought not this woman, being a **d** *G2364*
Jn 12:15 Fear not, **d** of Sion: behold, thy King *G2364*
Act 7:21 And when he was cast out, Pharaoh's **d** *G2364*
Heb 11:24 to be called the son of Pharaoh's **d**; *G2364*

DAUGHTERS

Gen 5: 4 years: and he begat sons and **d**: H1323
7 and seven years, and begat sons and **d**: H1323
10 and fifteen years, and begat sons and **d**: H1323
13 and forty years, and begat sons and **d**: H1323
16 and thirty years, and begat sons and **d**: H1323
19 hundred years, and begat sons and **d**: H1323
22 hundred years, and begat sons and **d**: H1323
26 and two years, and begat sons and **d**: H1323
30 and five years, and begat sons and **d**: H1323
6: 1 the earth, and **d** were born unto them, H1323
2 That the sons of God saw the **d** of men H1323
4 came in unto the **d** of men, and they H1323
11:11 hundred years, and begat sons and **d**. H1323
13 and three years, and begat sons and **d**. H1323
15 and three years, and begat sons and **d**. H1323
17 and thirty years, and begat sons and **d**. H1323
19 and nine years, and begat sons and **d**. H1323
21 and seven years, and begat sons and **d**. H1323
23 hundred years, and begat sons and **d**. H1323
25 nineteen years, and begat sons and **d**. H1323
19: 8 Behold now, I have two **d** which have H1323
12 thy sons, and thy **d**, and whatsoever H1323
14 which married his **d**, and said, Up, get H1323
15 wife, and thy two **d**, which are here; lest H1323
16 the hand of his two **d**; the LORD being H1323
30 and his two **d** with him; for he feared H1323
30 he dwelt in a cave, he and his two **d**. H1323
36 Thus were both the **d** of Lot with child H1323
24: 3 unto my son of the **d** of the Canaanites, H1323
13 of water; and the **d** of the men of the H1323
37 to my son of the **d** of the Canaanites, in H1323

Gen 27:46 life because of the **d** of Heth: if Jacob H1323
46 take a wife of the **d** of Heth, such as H1323
46 *which are* of the **d** of the land, what H1323
28: 1 not take a wife of the **d** of Canaan. H1323
2 of the **d** of Laban thy mother's brother. H1323
6 not take a wife of the **d** of Canaan; H1323
8 And Esau seeing that the **d** of Canaan H1323
29:16 And Laban had two **d**: the name of the H1323
30:13 And Leah said, Happy am I, for the **d** H1323
31:26 my **d**, as captives *taken* with the sword? H1323
28 my sons and my **d**? thou hast now done H1323
31 wouldest take by force thy **d** from me. H1323
41 years for thy two **d**, and six years for H1323
43 unto Jacob, *These* **d** *are* my daughters, H1323
43 daughters *are* my **d**, and *these* children H1323
43 this day unto these my **d**, or unto their H1323
50 If thou shalt afflict my **d**, or if thou shalt H1323
50 wives beside my **d**, no man *is* with us; H1323
55 his sons and his **d**, and blessed them: H1323
34: 1 Jacob, went out to see the **d** of the land. H1323
9 us, *and* give your **d** unto us, and take H1323
9 unto us, and take our **d** unto you. H1323
16 Then will we give our **d** unto you, and H1323
16 we will take your **d** to us, and we will H1323
21 let us take their **d** to us for wives, and H1323
21 us for wives, and let us give them our **d**. H1323
36: 2 Esau took his wives of the **d** of Canaan; H1323
6 his sons, and his **d**, and all the persons H1323
37:35 And all his sons and all his **d** rose up to H1323
46: 7 sons' sons with him, his **d**, and his sons' H1323
7 and his sons' **d**, and all his seed brought H1323
15 sons and his **d** *were* thirty and three. H1323
Ex 2:16 Now the priest of Midian had seven **d**: H1323
20 And he said unto his **d**, And where *is* H1323
3:22 your **d**; and ye shall spoil the Egyptians. H1323
6:25 him *one* of the **d** of Putiel to wife; and H1323
10: 9 our sons and with our **d**, with our flocks H1323
21: 4 born him sons or **d**; the wife and her H1323
9 deal with her after the manner of **d**. H1323
32: 2 and of your **d**, and bring *them* unto me. H1323
34:16 And thou take of their **d** unto thy sons, H1323
16 thy sons, and their **d** go a whoring after H1323
Lev 10:14 thy sons, and thy **d** with thee: for *they* H1323
26:29 and the flesh of your **d** shall ye eat. H1323
Nu 18:11 thy sons and to thy **d** with thee, by a H1323
19 and thy sons and thy **d** with thee, by a H1323
21:29 escaped, and his **d**, into captivity unto H1323
25: 1 commit whoredom with the **d** of Moab. H1323
26:33 had no sons, but **d**: and the names of H1323
33 the names of the **d** of Zelophehad *were* H1323
27: 1 Then came the **d** of Zelophehad, the H1323
1 the names of his **d**; Mahlah, Noah, and H1323
7 The **d** of Zelophehad speak right: thou H1323
36: 2 of Zelophehad our brother unto his **d**. H1323
6 concerning the **d** of Zelophehad, H1323
10 Moses, so did the **d** of Zelophehad: H1323
11 and Noah, the **d** of Zelophehad, were H1323
Dt 12:12 your sons, and your **d**, and your H1323
31 sons and their **d** they have burnt in the H1323
23:17 There shall be no whore of the **d** of H1323
28:32 Thy sons and thy **d** *shall be* given unto H1323
41 Thou shalt beget sons and **d**, but thou H1323
53 sons and of thy **d**, which the LORD thy H1323
32:19 the provoking of his sons, and of his **d**. H1323
Jos 7:24 his sons, and his **d**, and his oxen, and H1323
17: 3 had no sons, but **d**: and these *are* the H1323
3 the names of his **d**, Mahlah, and Noah, H1323
6 Because the **d** of Manasseh had an H1323
Jdg 3: 6 And they took their **d** to be their wives, H1323
6 **d** to their sons, and served their gods. H1323
11:40 *That* the **d** of Israel went yearly to H1323
12: 9 And he had thirty sons, and thirty **d**, H1323
9 and took in thirty **d** from abroad for H1323
14: 1 in Timnath of the **d** of the Philistines. H1323
2 in Timnath of the **d** of the Philistines: H1323
3 among the **d** of thy brethren, or among H1323
21: 7 we will not give them of our **d** to wives? H1323
18 them wives of our **d**: for the children of H1323
21 And see, and, behold, if the **d** of Shiloh H1323
21 his wife of the **d** of Shiloh, and go to H1323
Ru 1: 6 Then she arose with her **d** in law, that H3618
7 was, and her two **d** in law with her; and H3618
8 And Naomi said unto her two **d** in law, H3618
11 And Naomi said, Turn again, my **d**: H1323
12 Turn again, my **d**, go *your way;* for I am H1323
13 nay, my **d**; for it grieveth me much H1323
1Sa 1: 4 and to all her sons and her **d**, portions: H1323
2:21 sons and two **d**. And the child Samuel H1323
8:13 And he will take your **d** *to be* H1323

1Sa 14:49 the names of his two **d** *were these;* the H1323
30: 3 sons, and their **d**, were taken captives. H1323
6 his sons and for his **d**: but David H1323
19 neither sons nor **d**, neither spoil, nor H1323
2Sa 1:20 of Askelon; lest the **d** of the Philistines H1323
20 the **d** of the uncircumcised triumph. H1323
24 Ye **d** of Israel, weep over Saul, who H1323
5:13 were yet sons and **d** born to David. H1323
13:18 were the king's **d** *that were* virgins H1323
19: 5 sons and of thy **d**, and the lives of thy H1323
2Ki 17:17 And they caused their sons and their **d** H1323
1Ch 2:34 Now Sheshan had no sons, but **d**. And H1323
4:27 And Shimei had sixteen sons and six **d**; H1323
7:15 Zelophehad: and Zelophehad had **d**. H1323
14: 3 and David begat more sons and **d**. H1323
23:22 had no sons, but **d**: and their brethren H1323
25: 5 to Heman fourteen sons and three **d**. H1323
2Ch 2:14 The son of a woman of the **d** of Dan, H1323
11:21 and eight sons, and threescore **d**.) H1323
13:21 twenty and two sons, and sixteen **d**. H1323
24: 3 two wives; and he begat sons and **d**. H1323
28: 8 women, sons, and **d**, and took also H1323
29: 9 our sons and our **d** and our wives *are* H1323
31:18 their sons, and their **d**, through all the H1323
Ezr 2:61 took a wife of the **d** of Barzillai the H1323
9: 2 For they have taken of their **d** for H1323
12 Now therefore give not your **d** unto H1323
12 neither take their **d** unto your sons, nor H1323
Neh 3:12 the half part of Jerusalem, he and his **d**. H1323
4:14 your **d**, your wives, and your houses. H1323
5: 2 We, our sons, and our **d**, *are* many: H1323
5 our sons and our **d** to be servants, and H1323
5 and *some* of our **d** are brought unto H1323
7:63 which took *one* of the **d** of Barzillai the H1323
10:28 sons, and their **d**, every one having H1323
30 And that we would not give our **d** unto H1323
30 the land, nor take their **d** for our sons: H1323
13:25 shall not give your **d** unto their sons, H1323
25 **d** unto your sons, or for yourselves. H1323
Job 1: 2 born unto him seven sons and three **d**. H1323
13 his sons and his **d** *were* eating and H1323
18 Thy sons and thy **d** *were* eating and H1323
42:13 He had also seven sons and three **d**. H1323
15 *so* fair as the **d** of Job: and their father H1323
Ps 45: 9 Kings' **d** *were* among thy honourable H1323
48:11 Let mount Zion rejoice, let the **d** of H1323
97: 8 Zion heard, and was glad; and the **d** of H1323
106:37 their sons and their **d** unto devils, H1323
38 their sons and of their **d**, whom they H1323
144:12 youth; *that* our **d** *may be* as corner H1323
Prv 30:15 The horseleach hath two **d**, *crying,* H1323
31:29 Many **d** have done virtuously, but thou H1323
Ecc 12: 4 the **d** of musick shall be brought low; H1323
Song 1: 5 I *am* black, but comely, O ye **d** of H1323
2: 2 thorns, so *is* my love among the **d**. H1323
7 I charge you, O ye **d** of Jerusalem, by H1323
3: 5 I charge you, O ye **d** of Jerusalem, by H1323
10 paved *with* love, for the **d** of Jerusalem. H1323
11 Go forth, O ye **d** of Zion, and behold H1323
5: 8 I charge you, O **d** of Jerusalem, if ye H1323
16 and this *is* my friend, O **d** of Jerusalem. H1323
6: 9 her that bare her. The **d** saw her, and H1323
8: 4 I charge you, O **d** of Jerusalem, that ye H1323
Isa 3:16 LORD saith, Because the **d** of Zion are H1323
17 of the head of the **d** of Zion, and the H1323
4: 4 the filth of the **d** of Zion, and shall have H1323
16: 2 of the nest, *so* the **d** of Moab shall be at H1323
32: 9 ye careless **d**; give ear unto my speech. H1323
43: 6 and my **d** from the ends of the earth; H1323
49:22 **d** shall be carried upon *their* shoulders. H1323
56: 5 of sons and of **d**: I will give them an H1323
60: 4 and thy **d** shall be nursed at *thy* side. H1323
Jer 3:24 and their herds, their sons and their **d**. H1323
5:17 thy sons and thy **d** should eat: they H1323
7:31 sons and their **d** in the fire; which I H1323
9:20 and teach your **d** wailing, and every H1323
11:22 sons and their **d** shall die by famine: H1323
14:16 sons, nor their **d**: for I will pour their H1323
16: 2 shalt thou have sons or **d** in this place. H1323
3 concerning the **d** that are born in this H1323
19: 9 the flesh of their **d**, and they shall eat H1323
29: 6 Take ye wives, and beget sons and **d**; H1323
6 and give your **d** to husbands, that they H1323
6 may bear sons and **d**; that ye may be H1323
32:35 sons and their **d** to pass through *the* H1323
35: 8 we, our wives, our sons, nor our **d**; H1323
41:10 *even* the king's **d**, and all the people H1323
43: 6 and the king's **d**, and every person that H1323
48:46 are taken captives, and thy **d** captives. H1323

Jer 49: 2 heap, and her **d** shall be burned with H1323
3 is spoiled: cry, ye **d** of Rabbah, gird you H1323
Lam 3:51 heart because of all the **d** of my city. H1323
Ezk 13:17 face against the **d** of thy people, which H1323
14:16 neither sons nor **d**; they only shall be H1323
18 neither sons nor **d**, but they only shall H1323
22 *both* sons and **d**: behold, they shall H1323
16:20 thy sons and thy **d**, whom thou hast H1323
27 that hate thee, the **d** of the Philistines, H1323
46 she and her **d** that dwell at thy left H1323
46 at thy right hand, *is* Sodom and her **d**. H1323
48 done, she nor her **d**, as thou hast done, H1323
48 as thou hast done, thou and thy **d**. H1323
49 was in her and in her **d**, neither did she H1323
53 of Sodom and her **d**, and the captivity H1323
53 of Samaria and her **d**, then *will I bring* H1323
55 When thy sisters, Sodom and her **d**, H1323
55 Samaria and her **d** shall return to their H1323
55 **d** shall return to your former estate. H1323
57 reproach of the **d** of Syria, and all *that* H1323
57 about her, the **d** of the Philistines, H1323
61 thee for **d**, but not by thy covenant. H1323
23: 2 were two women, the **d** of one mother: H1323
4 they bare sons and **d**. Thus *were* their H1323
10 her sons and her **d**, and slew her with H1323
25 take thy sons and thy **d**; and thy residue H1323
47 **d**, and burn up their houses with fire. H1323
24:21 sons and your **d** whom ye have left H1323
25 set their minds, their sons and their **d**, H1323
26: 6 And her **d** which *are* in the field shall H1323
8 He shall slay with the sword thy **d** in H1323
30:18 her, and her **d** shall go into captivity. H1323
32:16 lament her: the **d** of the nations shall H1323
18 *even* her, and the **d** of the famous H1323
Hos 4:13 good: therefore your **d** shall commit H1323
14 I will not punish your **d** when they H1323
Joel 2:28 sons and your **d** shall prophesy, your H1323
3: 8 And I will sell your sons and your **d** H1323
Am 7:17 and thy sons and thy **d** shall fall by the H1323
Lk 1: 5 his wife *was* of the **d** of Aaron, and her G2364
23:28 But Jesus turning unto them said, **D** of G2364
Act 2:17 sons and your **d** shall prophesy, and G2364
21: 9 And the same man had four **d**, virgins, G2364
2Co 6:18 sons and **d**, saith the Lord Almighty. G2364
1Pt 3: 6 him lord: whose **d** ye are, as long as ye G5043

DAUGHTER'S

Lev 18:10 or of thy **d** daughter, *even* their H1323
17 son's daughter, or her **d** daughter, to H1323
Dt 22:17 *the tokens of* my **d** virginity. And they H1323

DAVID

Ru 4:17 he *is* the father of Jesse, the father of **D**. H1732
22 Obed begat Jesse, and Jesse begat **D**. H1732
1Sa 16:13 the LORD came upon **D** from that day H1732
19 me **D** thy son, which *is* with the sheep. H1732
20 and sent *them* by **D** his son unto Saul. H1732
21 And **D** came to Saul, and stood before H1732
22 And Saul sent to Jesse, saying, Let **D**, I H1732
23 upon Saul, that **D** took an harp, and H1732
17:12 Now **D** *was* the son of that Ephrathite H1732
14 And **D** *was* the youngest: and the three H1732
15 But **D** went and returned from Saul to H1732
17 And Jesse said unto **D** his son, Take H1732
20 And **D** rose up early in the morning, H1732
22 And **D** left his carriage in the hand of H1732
23 to the same words: and **D** heard *them*. H1732
26 And **D** spake to the men that stood by H1732
28 kindled against **D**, and he said, Why H1732
29 And **D** said, What have I now done? *Is* H1732
31 words were heard which **D** spake, they H1732
32 And **D** said to Saul, Let no man's heart H1732
33 And Saul said to **D**, Thou art not able to H1732
34 And **D** said unto Saul, Thy servant kept H1732
37 **D** said moreover, The LORD that H1732
37 unto **D**, Go, and the LORD be with thee. H1732
38 And Saul armed **D** with his armour, H1732
39 And **D** girded his sword upon his H1732
39 not proved *it*. And **D** said unto Saul, I H1732
39 proved *them*. And **D** put them off him. H1732
41 drew near unto **D**; and the man that H1732
42 about, and saw **D**, he disdained him: H1732
43 And the Philistine said unto **D**, *Am* I a H1732
43 the Philistine cursed **D** by his gods. H1732
44 And the Philistine said to **D**, Come to H1732
45 Then said **D** to the Philistine, Thou H1732
48 drew nigh to meet **D**, that David hasted, H1732
48 to meet David, that **D** hasted, and ran H1732
49 And **D** put his hand in his bag, and H1732

1Sa 17:50 So **D** prevailed over the Philistine with H1732
50 *there was* no sword in the hand of **D**. H1732
51 Therefore **D** ran, and stood upon the H1732
54 And **D** took the head of the Philistine, H1732
55 And when Saul saw **D** go forth against H1732
57 And as **D** returned from the slaughter H1732
58 young man? And **D** answered, I *am* the H1732
18: 1 with the soul of **D**, and Jonathan loved H1732
3 Then Jonathan and **D** made a H1732
4 and gave it to **D**, and his garments, H1732
5 And **D** went out whithersoever Saul H1732
6 they came, when **D** was returned from H1732
7 thousands, and **D** his ten thousands. H1732
8 ascribed unto **D** ten thousands, and H1732
9 And Saul eyed **D** from that day and H1732
10 of the house: and **D** played with his H1732
11 he said, I will smite **D** even to the wall H1732
11 **D** avoided out of his presence twice. H1732
12 And Saul was afraid of **D**, because the H1732
14 And **D** behaved himself wisely in all his H1732
16 But all Israel and Judah loved **D**, H1732
17 And Saul said to **D**, Behold my elder H1732
18 And **D** said unto Saul, Who *am* I? and H1732
19 been given to **D**, that she was given H1732
20 And Michal Saul's daughter loved **D**: H1732
21 Saul said to **D**, Thou shalt this day H1732
22 Commune with **D** secretly, and say, H1732
23 words in the ears of **D**. And David said, H1732
23 of David. And **D** said, Seemeth it to H1732
24 him, saying, On this manner spake **D**. H1732
25 And Saul said, Thus shall ye say to **D**, H1732
25 **D** fall by the hand of the Philistines. H1732
26 And when his servants told **D** these H1732
26 words, it pleased **D** well to be the king's H1732
27 Wherefore **D** arose and went, he and H1732
27 men; and **D** brought their foreskins, H1732
28 the LORD *was* with **D**, and *that* Michal H1732
29 And Saul was yet the more afraid of **D**; H1732
30 went forth, *that* **D** behaved himself H1732
19: 1 all his servants, that they should kill **D**. H1732
2 delighted much in **D**: and Jonathan told H1732
2 and Jonathan told **D**, saying, Saul my H1732
4 And Jonathan spake good of **D** unto H1732
4 servant, against **D**; because he hath not H1732
5 blood, to slay **D** without a cause? H1732
7 And Jonathan called **D**, and Jonathan H1732
7 Jonathan brought **D** to Saul, and he H1732
8 And there was war again: and **D** went H1732
9 his hand: and **D** played with *his* hand. H1732
10 And Saul sought to smite **D** even to the H1732
10 and **D** fled, and escaped that night. H1732
12 So Michal let **D** down through a H1732
14 to take **D**, she said, He *is* sick. H1732
15 *again* to see **D**, saying, Bring him up H1732
18 So **D** fled, and escaped, and came to H1732
19 And it was told Saul, saying, Behold, **D** H1732
20 And Saul sent messengers to take **D**: H1732
22 Where *are* Samuel and **D**? And *one* said, H1732
20: 1 And **D** fled from Naioth in Ramah, and H1732
3 And **D** sware moreover, and said, Thy H1732
4 Then said Jonathan unto **D**, H1732
5 And **D** said unto Jonathan, Behold, to H1732
6 If thy father at all miss me, then say, **D** H1732
10 Then said **D** to Jonathan, Who shall tell H1732
11 And Jonathan said unto **D**, Come, and H1732
12 And Jonathan said unto **D**, O LORD H1732
12 *be* good toward **D**, and I then send not H1732
15 **D** every one from the face of the earth. H1732
16 with the house of **D**, *saying*, Let the H1732
17 And Jonathan caused **D** to swear H1732
18 Then Jonathan said to **D**, To morrow *is* H1732
24 So **D** hid himself in the field: and when H1732
28 And Jonathan answered Saul, **D** H1732
33 was determined of his father to slay **D**. H1732
34 he was grieved for **D**, because his father H1732
35 with **D**, and a little lad with him. H1732
39 only Jonathan and **D** knew the matter. H1732
41 *And* as soon as the lad was gone, **D** H1732
41 one with another, until **D** exceeded. H1732
42 And Jonathan said to **D**, Go in peace, H1732
21: 1 Then came **D** to Nob to Ahimelech the H1732
1 at the meeting of **D**, and said unto him, H1732
2 And **D** said unto Ahimelech the priest, H1732
4 And the priest answered **D**, and said, H1732
5 And **D** answered the priest, and said H1732
8 And **D** said unto Ahimelech, And is H1732
9 that here. And **D** said, *There is* none H1732
10 And **D** arose, and fled that day for fear H1732
11 him, *Is* not this **D** the king of the land? H1732

1Sa 21:11 thousands, and **D** his ten thousands? H1732
12 And **D** laid up these words in his heart, H1732
22: 1 **D** therefore departed thence, and H1732
3 And **D** went thence to Mizpeh of Moab: H1732
4 all the while that **D** was in the hold. H1732
5 And the prophet Gad said unto **D**, H1732
5 of Judah. Then **D** departed, and came H1732
6 When Saul heard that **D** was H1732
14 all thy servants as **D**, which is the king's H1732
17 hand also *is* with **D**, and because they H1732
20 Abiathar, escaped, and fled after **D**. H1732
21 And Abiathar shewed **D** that Saul had H1732
22 And **D** said unto Abiathar, I knew *it* H1732
23: 1 Then they told **D**, saying, Behold, the H1732
2 Therefore **D** inquired of the LORD, H1732
2 LORD said unto **D**, Go, and smite the H1732
4 Then **D** inquired of the LORD yet H1732
5 So **D** and his men went to Keilah, and H1732
5 So **D** saved the inhabitants of Keilah. H1732
6 Ahimelech fled to **D** to Keilah, *that* he H1732
7 And it was told Saul that **D** was come H1732
8 to Keilah, to besiege **D** and his men. H1732
9 And **D** knew that Saul secretly H1732
10 Then said **D**, O LORD God of Israel, thy H1732
12 Then said **D**, Will the men of Keilah H1732
13 Then **D** and his men, *which were* about H1732
13 was told Saul that **D** was escaped from H1732
14 And **D** abode in the wilderness in H1732
15 And **D** saw that Saul was come out to H1732
15 to seek his life: and **D** *was* in the H1732
16 and went to **D** into the wood, and H1732
18 the LORD: and **D** abode in the wood, H1732
19 saying, Doth not **D** hide himself with us H1732
24 before Saul: but **D** and his men *were* in H1732
25 And they told **D**: wherefore he came H1732
25 after **D** in the wilderness of Maon. H1732
26 mountain, and **D** and his men on that H1732
26 the mountain: and **D** made haste to get H1732
26 men compassed **D** and his men round H1732
28 pursuing after **D**, and went against the H1732
29 And **D** went up from thence, and dwelt H1732
24: 1 **D** *is* in the wilderness of En-gedi. H1732
2 and went to seek **D** and his men upon H1732
3 to cover his feet: and **D** and his men H1732
4 And the men of **D** said unto him, H1732
4 unto thee. Then **D** arose, and cut off H1732
7 So **D** stayed his servants with these H1732
8 **D** also arose afterward, and went out H1732
8 behind him, **D** stooped with his face H1732
9 And **D** said to Saul, Wherefore hearest H1732
9 saying, Behold, **D** seeketh thy hurt? H1732
16 And it came to pass, when **D** had made H1732
16 thy voice, my son **D**? And Saul lifted up H1732
17 And he said to **D**, Thou *art* more H1732
22 And **D** sware unto Saul. And Saul went H1732
22 Saul went home; but **D** and his men gat H1732
25: 1 at Ramah. And **D** arose, and went H1732
4 And **D** heard in the wilderness that H1732
5 And **D** sent out ten young men, and H1732
5 young men, and **D** said unto the young H1732
8 unto thy servants, and to thy son **D**. H1732
9 words in the name of **D**, and ceased. H1732
10 and said, Who *is* **D**? and who *is* the son H1732
13 And **D** said unto his men, Gird ye on H1732
13 his sword; and **D** also girded on his H1732
13 went up after **D** about four hundred H1732
14 saying, Behold, **D** sent messengers out H1732
20 hill, and, behold, **D** and his men came H1732
21 Now **D** had said, Surely in vain have I H1732
22 the enemies of **D**, if I leave of all that H1732
23 And when Abigail saw **D**, she hasted, H1732
23 ass, and fell before **D** on her face, and H1732
32 And **D** said to Abigail, Blessed *be* the H1732
35 So **D** received of her hand *that* which H1732
39 And when **D** heard that Nabal was H1732
39 own head. And **D** sent and communed H1732
40 And when the servants of **D** were come H1732
40 unto her, saying, **D** sent us unto thee, H1732
42 messengers of **D**, and became his wife. H1732
43 **D** also took Ahinoam of Jezreel; and H1732
26: 1 saying, Doth not **D** hide himself in the H1732
2 to seek **D** in the wilderness of Ziph. H1732
3 by the way. But **D** abode in the H1732
4 **D** therefore sent out spies, and H1732
5 And **D** arose, and came to the place H1732
5 had pitched: and **D** beheld the place H1732
6 Then answered **D** and said to H1732
7 So **D** and Abishai came to the people H1732
8 Then said Abishai to **D**, God hath H1732

1Sa 26: 9 And **D** said to Abishai, Destroy him H1732
10 **D** said furthermore, *As* the LORD H1732
12 So **D** took the spear and the cruse of H1732
13 Then **D** went over to the other side, and H1732
14 And **D** cried to the people, and to H1732
15 And **D** said to Abner, *Art* not thou a H1732
17 thy voice, my son **D**? And David said, *It* H1732
17 **D** said, *It is* my voice, my lord, O king. H1732
21 return, my son **D**: for I will no more do H1732
22 And **D** answered and said, Behold the H1732
25 Then Saul said to **D**, Blessed *be* thou, H1732
25 *be* thou, my son **D**: thou shalt both do H1732
25 still prevail. So **D** went on his way, and H1732
27: 1 And **D** said in his heart, I shall now H1732
2 And **D** arose, and he passed over with H1732
3 And **D** dwelt with Achish at Gath, he H1732
3 household, *even* **D** with his two wives, H1732
4 And it was told Saul that **D** was fled to H1732
5 And **D** said unto Achish, If I have now H1732
7 And the time that **D** dwelt in the H1732
8 And **D** and his men went up, and H1732
9 And **D** smote the land, and left neither H1732
10 a road to day? And **D** said, Against the H1732
11 And **D** saved neither man nor woman H1732
11 us, saying, So did **D**, and so *will be* his H1732
12 And Achish believed **D**, saying, He hath H1732
28: 1 And Achish said unto **D**, Know thou H1732
2 And **D** said to Achish, Surely thou shalt H1732
2 Achish said to **D**, Therefore will I make H1732
17 given it to thy neighbour, *even* to **D**: H1732
29: 2 and by thousands: but **D** and his men H1732
3 *Is* not this **D**, the servant of Saul H1732
5 *Is* not this **D**, of whom they sang one to H1732
5 thousands, and **D** his ten thousands? H1732
6 Then Achish called **D**, and said unto H1732
8 And **D** said unto Achish, But what have H1732
9 And Achish answered and said to **D**, I H1732
11 So **D** and his men rose up early to H1732
30: 1 And it came to pass, when **D** and his H1732
3 So **D** and his men came to the city, H1732
4 Then **D** and the people that *were* with H1732
6 And **D** was greatly distressed; for the H1732
6 for his daughters: but **D** encouraged H1732
7 And **D** said to Abiathar the priest, H1732
7 brought thither the ephod to **D**. H1732
8 And **D** inquired at the LORD, saying, H1732
9 So **D** went, he and the six hundred men H1732
10 But **D** pursued, he and four hundred H1732
11 brought him to **D**, and gave him bread, H1732
13 And **D** said unto him, To whom H1732
15 And **D** said to him, Canst thou bring H1732
17 And **D** smote them from the twilight H1732
18 And **D** recovered all that the H1732
18 away: and **D** rescued his two wives. H1732
19 had taken to them: **D** recovered all. H1732
20 And **D** took all the flocks and the herds, H1732
21 And **D** came to the two hundred men, H1732
21 they could not follow **D**, whom they had H1732
21 forth to meet **D**, and to meet the people H1732
21 with him: and when **D** came near to the H1732
22 that went with **D**, and said, Because H1732
23 Then said **D**, Ye shall not do so, my H1732
26 And when **D** came to Ziklag, he sent of H1732
31 all the places where **D** himself and his H1732
2Sa 1: 1 of Saul, when **D** was returned from H1732
1 and **D** had abode two days in Ziklag; H1732
2 when he came to **D**, that he fell to the H1732
3 And **D** said unto him, From whence H1732
4 And **D** said unto him, How went the H1732
5 And **D** said unto the young man that H1732
11 Then **D** took hold on his clothes, and H1732
13 And **D** said unto the young man that H1732
14 And **D** said unto him, How wast thou H1732
15 And **D** called one of the young men, H1732
16 And **D** said unto him, Thy blood *be* H1732
17 And **D** lamented with this lamentation H1732
2: 1 And it came to pass after this, that **D** H1732
1 him, Go up. And **D** said, Whither shall H1732
2 So **D** went up thither, and his two wives H1732
3 And his men that *were* with him did **D** H1732
4 they anointed **D** king over the house H1732
4 And they told **D**, saying, *That* the men H1732
5 And **D** sent messengers unto the men H1732
10 But the house of Judah followed **D**. H1732
11 And the time that **D** was king in H1732
13 the servants of **D**, went out, and met H1732
15 of Saul, and twelve of the servants of **D**. H1732
17 men of Israel, before the servants of **D**. H1732
31 But the servants of **D** had smitten of H1732

2Sa 3: 1 and the house of **D**: but David waxed H1732
1 of David: but **D** waxed stronger and H1732
2 And unto **D** were sons born in Hebron: H1732
5 wife. These were born to **D** in Hebron. H1732
6 and the house of **D**, that Abner made H1732
8 into the hand of **D**, that thou chargest H1732
9 hath sworn to **D**, even so I do to him; H1732
10 up the throne of **D** over Israel and over H1732
12 And Abner sent messengers to **D** on his H1732
14 And **D** sent messengers to Ish-bosheth H1732
17 for **D** in times past *to be* king over you: H1732
18 hath spoken of **D**, saying, By the hand H1732
18 of my servant **D** I will save my people H1732
19 in the ears of **D** in Hebron all that H1732
20 So Abner came to **D** to Hebron, and H1732
20 with him. And **D** made Abner and the H1732
21 And Abner said unto **D**, I will arise and H1732
21 desireth. And **D** sent Abner away; and H1732
22 And, behold, the servants of **D** and H1732
22 *was* not with **D** in Hebron; for he had H1732
26 And when Joab was come out from **D**, H1732
26 the well of Sirah: but **D** knew *it* not. H1732
28 And afterward when **D** heard *it*, he H1732
31 And **D** said to Joab, and to all the H1732
31 And king **D** *himself* followed the bier. H1732
35 came to cause **D** to eat meat while it H1732
35 it was yet day, **D** sware, saying, So do H1732
4: 8 of Ish-bosheth unto **D** to Hebron, and H1732
9 And **D** answered Rechab and Baanah H1732
12 And **D** commanded his young men, H1732
5: 1 Then came all the tribes of Israel to **D** H1732
3 to Hebron; and king **D** made a league H1732
3 and they anointed **D** king over Israel. H1732
4 **D** *was* thirty years old when he began H1732
6 which spake unto **D**, saying, Except H1732
6 thinking, **D** cannot come in hither. H1732
7 Nevertheless **D** took the strong hold of H1732
7 hold of Zion: the same *is* the city of **D**. H1732
8 And **D** said on that day, Whosoever H1732
9 So **D** dwelt in the fort, and called it the H1732
9 called it the city of **D**. And David built H1732
9 city of David. And **D** built round about H1732
10 And **D** went on, and grew great, and H1732
11 messengers to **D**, and cedar trees, and H1732
11 masons: and they built **D** an house. H1732
12 And **D** perceived that the LORD had H1732
13 And **D** took *him* more concubines and H1732
13 were yet sons and daughters born to **D**. H1732
17 they had anointed **D** king over Israel, H1732
17 came up to seek **D**; and David heard *of* H1732
17 to seek David; and **D** heard *of it*, and H1732
19 And **D** inquired of the LORD, saying, H1732
19 the LORD said unto **D**, Go up: for I will H1732
20 And **D** came to Baal-perazim, and H1732
20 and **D** smote them there, and H1732
21 And there they left their images, and **D** H1732
23 And when **D** inquired of the LORD, he H1732
25 And **D** did so, as the LORD had H1732
6: 1 Again, **D** gathered together all *the* H1732
2 And **D** arose, and went with all the H1732
5 And **D** and all the house of Israel H1732
8 And **D** was displeased, because the H1732
9 And **D** was afraid of the LORD that H1732
10 So **D** would not remove the ark of the H1732
10 into the city of **D**: but David carried it H1732
10 the city of David: but **D** carried it aside H1732
12 And it was told king **D**, saying, The H1732
12 the ark of God. So **D** went and brought H1732
12 into the city of **D** with gladness. H1732
14 And **D** danced before the LORD with H1732
14 and **D** *was* girded with a linen ephod. H1732
15 So **D** and all the house of Israel brought H1732
16 came into the city of **D**, Michal Saul's H1732
16 and saw king **D** leaping and dancing H1732
17 tabernacle that **D** had pitched for it: H1732
17 had pitched for it: and **D** offered burnt H1732
18 And as soon as **D** had made an end of H1732
20 Then **D** returned to bless his H1732
20 Saul came out to meet **D**, and said, How H1732
21 And **D** said unto Michal, *It was* before H1732
7: 5 Go and tell my servant **D**, Thus saith H1732
8 say unto my servant **D**, Thus saith the H1732
17 this vision, so did Nathan speak unto **D**. H1732
18 Then went king **D** in, and sat before the H1732
20 And what can **D** say more unto thee? H1732
26 servant **D** be established before thee. H1732
8: 1 And after this it came to pass, that **D** H1732
1 them: and **D** took Metheg-ammah H1732
3 **D** smote also Hadadezer, the son of H1732

2Sa 8: 4 And **D** took from him a thousand H1732
4 footmen: and **D** houghed all the chariot H1732
5 king of Zobah, **D** slew of the Syrians H1732
6 Then **D** put garrisons in Syria of H1732
6 servants to **D**, *and* brought gifts. And H1732
6 preserved **D** whithersoever he went. H1732
7 And **D** took the shields of gold that H1732
8 king **D** took exceeding much brass. H1732
9 When Toi king of Hamath heard that **D** H1732
10 his son unto king **D**, to salute him, and H1732
11 Which also king **D** did dedicate unto H1732
13 And **D** gat *him* a name when he H1732
14 preserved **D** whithersoever he went. H1732
15 And **D** reigned over all Israel; and H1732
15 all Israel; and **D** executed judgment H1732
9: 1 And **D** said, Is there yet any that is left H1732
2 called him unto **D**, the king said unto H1732
5 Then king **D** sent, and fetched him out H1732
6 was come unto **D**, he fell on his face, H1732
6 reverence. And **D** said, Mephibosheth. H1732
7 And **D** said unto him, Fear not: for I H1732
10: 2 Then said **D**, I will shew kindness unto H1732
2 unto me. And **D** sent to comfort him H1732
3 thou that **D** doth honour thy father, H1732
3 unto thee? hath not **D** *rather* sent his H1732
5 When they told *it* unto **D**, he sent to H1732
6 that they stank before **D**, the children of H1732
7 And when **D** heard of *it*, he sent Joab, H1732
17 And when it was told **D**, he gathered all H1732
17 array against **D**, and fought with him. H1732
18 before Israel; and **D** slew *the men of* H1732
11: 1 *to battle*, that **D** sent Joab, and his H1732
1 But **D** tarried still at Jerusalem. H1732
2 eveningtide, that **D** arose from off his H1732
3 And **D** sent and inquired after the H1732
4 And **D** sent messengers, and took her; H1732
5 and told **D**, and said, I *am* with child. H1732
6 And **D** sent to Joab, *saying*, Send me H1732
6 the Hittite. And Joab sent Uriah to **D**. H1732
7 come unto him, **D** demanded *of him* H1732
8 And **D** said to Uriah, Go down to thy H1732
10 And when they had told **D**, saying, H1732
10 unto his house, **D** said unto Uriah, H1732
11 And Uriah said unto **D**, The ark, and H1732
12 And **D** said to Uriah, Tarry here to day H1732
13 And when **D** had called him, he did eat H1732
14 in the morning, that **D** wrote a letter to H1732
17 of **D**; and Uriah the Hittite died also. H1732
18 Then Joab sent and told **D** all the H1732
22 **D** all that Joab had sent him for. H1732
23 And the messenger said unto **D**, Surely H1732
25 Then **D** said unto the messenger, Thus H1732
27 And when the mourning was past, **D** H1732
27 that **D** had done displeased the LORD. H1732
12: 1 And the LORD sent Nathan unto **D**. H1732
7 And Nathan said to **D**, Thou *art* the H1732
13 And **D** said unto Nathan, I have sinned H1732
13 Nathan said unto **D**, The LORD also H1732
15 wife bare unto **D**, and it was very sick. H1732
16 **D** therefore besought God for the child; H1732
16 for the child; and **D** fasted, and went H1732
18 the servants of **D** feared to tell him that H1732
19 But when **D** saw that his servants H1732
19 whispered, **D** perceived that the child H1732
19 was dead: therefore **D** said unto his H1732
20 Then **D** arose from the earth, and H1732
24 And **D** comforted Bath-sheba his wife, H1732
27 And Joab sent messengers to **D**, and H1732
29 And **D** gathered all the people together, H1732
31 of Ammon. So **D** and all the people H1732
13: 1 the son of **D** had a fair sister, whose H1732
1 and Amnon the son of **D** loved her. H1732
7 Then **D** sent home to Tamar, saying, H1732
21 But when king **D** heard of all these H1732
30 that tidings came to **D**, saying, Absalom H1732
37 And *D* mourned for his son every day.
39 And *the soul of* king **D** longed to go H1732
15:13 And there came a messenger to **D**, H1732
14 And **D** said unto all his servants that H1732
22 And **D** said to Ittai, Go and pass over. H1732
30 And **D** went up by the ascent of *mount* H1732
31 And *one* told **D**, saying, Ahithophel *is* H1732
31 Absalom. And **D** said, O LORD, I pray H1732
32 And it came to pass, that *when* **D** was H1732
33 Unto whom **D** said, If thou passest on H1732
16: 1 And when **D** was a little past the top *of* H1732
5 And when king **D** came to Bahurim, H1732
6 And he cast stones at **D**, and at all the H1732
6 servants of king **D**: and all the people H1732

2Sa 16:10 unto him, Curse **D**. Who shall then say, H1732
11 And **D** said to Abishai, and to all his H1732
13 And as **D** and his men went by the way, H1732
23 both with **D** and with Absalom. H1732
17: 1 will arise and pursue after **D** this night: H1732
16 Now therefore send quickly, and tell **D**, H1732
17 them; and they went and told king **D**. H1732
21 and told king **D**, and said unto David, H1732
21 David, and said unto **D**, Arise, and pass H1732
22 Then **D** arose, and all the people that H1732
24 Then **D** came to Mahanaim. And H1732
27 And it came to pass, when **D** was come H1732
29 cheese of kine, for **D**, and for the people H1732
18: 1 And **D** numbered the people that *were* H1732
2 And **D** sent forth a third part of the H1732
7 the servants of **D**, and there was there H1732
9 And Absalom met the servants of **D**. H1732
24 And **D** sat between the two gates: and H1732
19:11 And king **D** sent to Zadok and to H1732
16 with the men of Judah to meet king **D**. H1732
22 And **D** said, What have I to do with H1732
43 also more *right* in **D** than ye: why then H1732
20: 1 We have no part in **D**, neither have we H1732
2 up from after **D**, *and* followed Sheba H1732
3 And **D** came to his house at Jerusalem; H1732
6 And **D** said to Abishai, Now shall H1732
11 he that *is* for **D**, *let him go* after Joab. H1732
21 king, *even* against **D**: deliver him only, H1732
26 the Jairite was a chief ruler about **D**. H1732
21: 1 in the days of **D** three years, year after H1732
1 year after year; and **D** inquired of the H1732
3 Wherefore **D** said unto the Gibeonites, H1732
7 **D** and Jonathan the son of Saul. H1732
11 And it was told **D** what Rizpah the H1732
12 And **D** went and took the bones of Saul H1732
15 with Israel; and **D** went down, and his H1732
15 the Philistines: and **D** waxed faint. H1732
16 a new *sword*, thought to have slain **D**. H1732
17 Then the men of **D** sware unto him, H1732
21 of Shimea the brother of **D** slew him. H1732
22 of **D**, and by the hand of his servants. H1732
22: 1 And **D** spake unto the LORD the words H1732
51 unto **D**, and to his seed for evermore. H1732
23: 1 Now these *be* the last words of **D**. David H1732
1 words of David. **D** the son of Jesse said, H1732
8 men whom **D** had: The Tachmonite H1732
9 mighty men with **D**, when they defied H1732
13 and came to **D** in the harvest time H1732
14 And **D** *was* then in an hold, and the H1732
15 And **D** longed, and said, Oh that one H1732
16 *it*, and brought *it* to **D**: nevertheless he H1732
23 three. And **D** set him over his guard. H1732
24: 1 and he moved **D** against them to say, H1732
10 the people. And **D** said unto the LORD, H1732
11 For when **D** was up in the morning, the H1732
12 Go and say unto **D**, Thus saith the H1732
13 So Gad came to **D**, and told him, and H1732
14 And **D** said unto Gad, I am in a great H1732
17 And **D** spake unto the LORD when he H1732
18 And Gad came that day to **D**, and said H1732
19 And **D**, according to the saying of Gad, H1732
21 to his servant? And **D** said, To buy the H1732
22 And Araunah said unto **D**, Let my lord H1732
24 cost me nothing. So **D** bought the H1732
25 And **D** built there an altar unto the H1732
1Ki 1: 1 Now king **D** was old *and* stricken in H1732
8 *belonged* to **D**, were not with Adonijah. H1732
11 reign, and **D** our lord knoweth *it* not? H1732
13 Go and get thee in unto king **D**, and say H1732
28 Then king **D** answered and said, Call H1732
31 said, Let my lord king **D** live for ever. H1732
32 And king **D** said, Call me Zadok the H1732
37 than the throne of my lord king **D**. H1732
43 lord king **D** hath made Solomon king. H1732
47 our lord king **D**, saying, God make the H1732
2: 1 Now the days of **D** drew nigh that he H1732
10 So **D** slept with his fathers, and was H1732
10 fathers, and was buried in the city of **D**. H1732
11 And the days that **D** reigned over Israel H1732
12 Then sat Solomon upon the throne of **D** H1732
24 on the throne of **D** my father, and who H1732
26 the Lord GOD before **D** my father, and H1732
32 the sword, my father **D** not knowing H1732
33 for ever: but upon **D**, and upon his seed, H1732
44 to, that thou didst to **D** my father: H1732
45 blessed, and the throne of **D** shall be H1732
3: 1 her into the city of **D**, until he had made H1732
3 in the statutes of **D** his father: only he H1732
6 unto thy servant **D** my father great H1732

1Ki 3: 7 king instead of D my father: and I *am* H1732
14 as thy father D did walk, then I will H1732
5: 1 father: for Hiram was ever a lover of D. H1732
3 Thou knowest how that D my father H1732
5 LORD spake unto D my father, saying, H1732
7 D a wise son over this great people. H1732
6:12 thee, which I spake unto D thy father: H1732
7:51 in the things which D his father had H1732
8: 1 out of the city of D, which *is* Zion. H1732
15 his mouth unto D my father, and hath H1732
16 I chose D to be over my people Israel. H1732
17 And it was in the heart of D my father H1732
18 And the LORD said unto D my father, H1732
20 up in the room of D my father, and sit H1732
24 Who hast kept with thy servant D my H1732
25 with thy servant D my father that thou H1732
26 spakest unto thy servant D my father. H1732
66 D his servant, and for Israel his people. H1732
9: 4 And if thou wilt walk before me, as D H1732
5 as I promised to D thy father, saying, H1732
24 up out of the city of D unto her house H1732
11: 4 God, as *was* the heart of D his father. H1732
6 after the LORD, as *did* D his father. H1732
12 I will not do it for D thy father's sake: H1732
13 to thy son for D my servant's sake, and H1732
15 For it came to pass, when D was in H1732
21 in Egypt that D slept with his fathers, H1732
24 a band, when D slew them *of Zobah:* H1732
27 the breaches of the city of D his father. H1732
33 and my judgments, as *did* D his father. H1732
34 days of his life for D my servant's sake, H1732
36 one tribe, that D my servant may have H1732
38 as D my servant did; that H1732
38 for D, and will give Israel unto thee. H1732
39 And I will for this afflict the seed of D, H1732
43 buried in the city of D his father: and H1732
12:16 portion have we in D? neither *have we* H1732
16 D. So Israel departed unto their tents. H1732
19 against the house of D unto this day. H1732
20 house of D, but the tribe of Judah only. H1732
26 the kingdom return to the house of D: H1732
13: 2 unto the house of D, Josiah by name; H1732
14: 8 from the house of D, and gave it thee: H1732
8 been as my servant D, who kept my H1732
31 in the city of D. And his mother's name H1732
15: 3 his God, as the heart of D his father. H1732
5 Because D did *that which was* right in H1732
8 D: and Asa his son reigned in his stead. H1732
11 eyes of the LORD, as *did* D his father. H1732
24 fathers in the city of D his father: and H1732
22:50 in the city of D his father: and Jehoram H1732
2Ki 8:19 destroy Judah for D his servant's sake, H1732
24 in the city of D: and Ahaziah his son H1732
9:28 with his fathers in the city of D. H1732
12:21 in the city of D: and Amaziah his son H1732
14: 3 LORD, yet not like D his father: he did H1732
20 with his fathers in the city of D. H1732
15: 7 in the city of D: and Jotham his son H1732
38 in the city of D his father: and Ahaz H1732
16: 2 of the LORD his God, like D his father. H1732
20 in the city of D: and Hezekiah his son H1732
17:21 For he rent Israel from the house of D; H1732
18: 3 according to all that D his father did. H1732
20: 5 LORD, the God of D thy father, I have H1732
21: 7 the LORD said to D, and to Solomon his H1732
22: 2 in all the way of D his father, and H1732
1Ch 2:15 Ozem the sixth, D the seventh: H1732
3: 1 Now these were the sons of D, which H1732
9 *These were* all the sons of D, beside the H1732
4:31 *were* their cities unto the reign of D. H1732
6:31 And these *are they* whom D set over H1732
7: 2 *was* in the days of D two and twenty H1732
9:22 villages, whom D and Samuel the seer H1732
10:14 the kingdom unto D the son of Jesse. H1732
11: 1 themselves to D unto Hebron, saying, H1732
3 to Hebron; and D made a covenant H1732
3 and they anointed D king over Israel, H1732
4 And D and all Israel went to Jerusalem, H1732
5 And the inhabitants of Jebus said to D, H1732
5 Nevertheless D took the castle of Zion, H1732
5 the castle of Zion, which *is* the city of D. H1732
6 And D said, Whosoever smiteth the H1732
7 And D dwelt in the castle; therefore H1732
7 therefore they called it the city of D. H1732
9 So D waxed greater and greater: for the H1732
10 men whom D had, who strengthened H1732
11 men whom D had; Jashobeam, an H1732
13 He was with D at Pas-dammim, and H1732
15 down to the rock to D, into the cave of H1732

1Ch 11:16 And D *was* then in the hold, and the H1732
17 And D longed, and said, Oh that one H1732
18 *it*, and brought *it* to D: but David would H1732
18 *it* to David: but D would not drink *of* H1732
25 three: and D set him over his guard. H1732
12: 1 Now these *are* they that came to D to H1732
8 themselves unto D into the hold to the H1732
16 Benjamin and Judah to the hold unto D. H1732
17 And D went out to meet them, and H1732
18 Thine *are we*, D, and on thy side, thou H1732
18 thee. Then D received them, and H1732
19 And there fell *some* of Manasseh to D, H1732
21 And they helped D against the band *of* H1732
22 day there came to D to help him, until H1732
23 war, *and* came to D to Hebron, to turn H1732
31 by name, to come and make D king. H1732
38 Hebron, to make D king over all Israel: H1732
38 *were* of one heart to make D king. H1732
39 And there they were with D three days, H1732
13: 1 And D consulted with the captains of H1732
2 And D said unto all the congregation of H1732
5 So D gathered all Israel together, from H1732
6 And D went up, and all Israel, to H1732
8 And D and all Israel played before God H1732
11 And D was displeased, because the H1732
12 And D was afraid of God that day, H1732
13 So D brought not the ark *home* to H1732
13 to the city of D, but carried it aside H1732
14: 1 messengers to D, and timber of cedars, H1732
2 And D perceived that the LORD had H1732
3 And D took more wives at Jerusalem: H1732
3 and D begat more sons and daughters. H1732
8 And when the Philistines heard that D H1732
8 went up to seek D. And David heard *of* H1732
8 to seek David. And D heard *of it*, and H1732
10 And D inquired of God, saying, Shall I H1732
11 and D smote them there. Then H1732
11 them there. Then D said, God hath H1732
12 left their gods there, D gave a H1732
14 Therefore D inquired again of God; H1732
16 D therefore did as God commanded H1732
17 And the fame of D went out into all H1732
15: 1 And *D* made him houses in the city of
1 in the city of D, and prepared a place H1732
2 Then D said, None ought to carry the H1732
3 And D gathered all Israel together to H1732
4 And D assembled the children of H1732
11 And D called for Zadok and Abiathar H1732
16 And D spake to the chief of the Levites H1732
25 So D, and the elders of Israel, and the H1732
27 And D *was* clothed with a robe of fine H1732
27 with the singers: D also *had* upon him H1732
29 came to the city of D, that Michal the H1732
29 a window saw king D dancing and H1732
16: 1 of the tent that D had pitched for it: H1732
2 And when D had made an end of H1732
7 Then on that day D delivered first *this* H1732
43 and D returned to bless his house. H1732
17: 1 Now it came to pass, as D sat in his H1732
1 in his house, that D said to Nathan the H1732
2 Then Nathan said unto D, Do all that *is* H1732
4 Go and tell D my servant, Thus saith H1732
7 say unto my servant D, Thus saith the H1732
15 this vision, so did Nathan speak unto D. H1732
16 And D the king came and sat before H1732
18 What can D *speak* more to thee for the H1732
24 and *let* the house of D thy servant *be* H1732
18: 1 Now after this it came to pass, that D H1732
3 And D smote Hadarezer king of Zobah H1732
4 And D took from him a thousand H1732
4 footmen: D also houghed all the H1732
5 king of Zobah, D slew of the Syrians H1732
6 Then D put *garrisons* in H1732
6 preserved D whithersoever he went. H1732
7 And D took the shields of gold that H1732
8 brought D very much brass, wherewith H1732
9 heard how D had smitten all the H1732
10 He sent Hadoram his son to king D, to H1732
11 Them also king D dedicated unto the H1732
13 preserved D whithersoever he went. H1732
14 So D reigned over all Israel, and H1732
17 the sons of D *were* chief about the king. H1732
19: 2 And D said, I will shew kindness unto H1732
2 to me. And D sent messengers to H1732
2 So the servants of D came into the land H1732
3 thou that D doth honour thy father, H1732
5 Then there went *certain*, and told D H1732
6 odious to D, Hanun and the children H1732
8 And when D heard *of it*, he sent Joab, H1732

1Ch 19:17 And it was told D; and he gathered all H1732
17 them. So when D had put the battle in H1732
18 before Israel; and D slew of the Syrians H1732
19 made peace with D, and became his H1732
20: 1 Rabbah. But D tarried at Jerusalem. H1732
2 And D took the crown of their king H1732
3 Even so dealt D with all the cities of H1732
3 of Ammon. And D and all the people H1732
8 of D, and by the hand of his servants. H1732
21: 1 and provoked D to number Israel. H1732
2 And D said to Joab and to the rulers of H1732
5 of the people unto D. And all *they of* H1732
8 And D said unto God, I have sinned H1732
10 Go and tell D, saying, Thus saith the H1732
11 So Gad came to D, and said unto him, H1732
13 And D said unto Gad, I am in a great H1732
16 And D lifted up his eyes, and saw the H1732
16 Jerusalem. Then D and the elders *of* H1732
17 And D said unto God, *Is it* not I *that* H1732
18 Gad to say to D, that David should go H1732
18 say to David, that D should go up, and H1732
19 And D went up at the saying of Gad, H1732
21 And as D came to Ornan, Ornan H1732
21 looked and saw D, and went out of the H1732
21 to D with *his* face to the ground. H1732
22 Then D said to Ornan, Grant me the H1732
23 And Ornan said unto D, Take *it* to thee, H1732
24 And king D said to Ornan, Nay; but I H1732
25 So D gave to Ornan for the place six H1732
26 And D built there an altar unto the H1732
28 At that time when D saw that the H1732
30 But D could not go before it to inquire H1732
22: 1 Then D said, This *is* the house of the H1732
2 And D commanded to gather together H1732
3 And D prepared iron in abundance for H1732
4 of Tyre brought much cedar wood to D. H1732
5 And D said, Solomon my son *is* young H1732
5 for it. So D prepared abundantly H1732
7 And D said to Solomon, My son, as for H1732
17 D also commanded all the princes of H1732
23: 1 So when D was old and full of days, he H1732
5 I made, *said D*, to praise *therewith*. H1732
6 And D divided them into courses H1732
25 For D said, The LORD God of Israel H1732
27 For by the last words of D the Levites H1732
24: 3 And D distributed them, both Zadok of H1732
31 in the presence of D the king, and H1732
25: 1 Moreover D and the captains of the H1732
26:26 things, which D the king, and the chief H1732
31 of the reign of D they were sought for, H1732
32 whom king D made rulers over the H1732
27:18 D: of Issachar, Omri the son of Michael: H1732
23 But D took not the number of them H1732
24 the account of the chronicles of king D. H1732
28: 1 And D assembled all the princes of H1732
2 Then D the king stood up upon his feet, H1732
11 Then D gave to Solomon his son the H1732
19 All *this, said D*, the LORD made me
20 And D said to Solomon his son, Be H1732
29: 1 Furthermore D the king said unto all H1732
9 D the king also rejoiced with great joy. H1732
10 Wherefore D blessed the LORD before H1732
10 congregation: and D said, Blessed *be* H1732
20 And D said to all the congregation, H1732
22 the son of D king the second time, H1732
23 as king instead of D his father, and H1732
24 sons likewise of king D, submitted H1732
26 Thus D the son of Jesse reigned over all H1732
29 Now the acts of D the king, first and H1732
2Ch 1: 1 And Solomon the son of D was H1732
4 But the ark of God had D brought up H1732
4 to *the place which* D had prepared for H1732
8 great mercy unto D my father, and hast H1732
9 let thy promise unto D my father be H1732
2: 3 didst deal with D my father, and didst H1732
7 whom D my father did provide. H1732
12 who hath given to D the king a wise H1732
14 cunning men of my lord D thy father. H1732
17 wherewith D his father had numbered H1732
3: 1 appeared unto D his father, in the H1732
1 in the place that D had prepared in the H1732
5: 1 in *all* the things that D his father had H1732
2 out of the city of D, which *is* Zion. H1732
6: 4 with his mouth to my father D, saying, H1732
6 chosen D to be over my people Israel. H1732
7 Now it was in the heart of D my father H1732
8 But the LORD said to D my father, H1732
10 up in the room of D my father, and am H1732
15 kept with thy servant D my father that H1732

2Ch 6:16 keep with thy servant D my father that H1732
17 thou hast spoken unto thy servant D. H1732
42 the mercies of D thy servant. H1732
7: 6 the LORD, which D the king had made H1732
6 for ever, when D praised by their H1732
10 had shewed unto D, and to Solomon, H1732
17 before me, as D thy father walked, and H1732
18 covenanted with D thy father, saying, H1732
8:11 out of the city of D unto the house that H1732
11 dwell in the house of D king of Israel, H1732
14 to the order of D his father, the courses H1732
14 so had D the man of God commanded. H1732
9:31 buried in the city of D his father: and H1732
10:16 portion have we in D? and *we have* none H1732
16 O Israel: *and* now, D, see to thine own H1732
19 against the house of D unto this day. H1732
11:17 walked in the way of D and Solomon. H1732
18 the son of D to wife, *and* Abihail H1732
12:16 in the city of D: and Abijah his son H1732
13: 5 over Israel to D for ever, *even* to him H1732
6 the son of D, is risen up, and hath H1732
8 hand of the sons of D; and ye *be* a great H1732
14: 1 him in the city of D: and Asa his son H1732
16:14 in the city of D, and laid him in the H1732
17: 3 father D, and sought not unto Baalim; H1732
21: 1 in the city of D. And Jehoram his son H1732
7 the house of D, because of the covenant H1732
7 that he had made with D, and as he H1732
12 the LORD God of D thy father, Because H1732
20 him in the city of D, but not in the H1732
23: 3 as the LORD hath said of the sons of D. H1732
18 the Levites, whom D had distributed in H1732
18 with singing, *as it was ordained* by D. H1732
24:16 And they buried him in the city of D H1732
25 him in the city of D, but they buried H1732
27: 9 him in the city of D: and Ahaz his son H1732
28: 1 the sight of the LORD, like D his father: H1732
29: 2 to all that D his father had done. H1732
25 the commandment of D, and of Gad the H1732
26 of D, and the priests with the trumpets. H1732
27 *ordained* by D king of Israel. H1732
30 with the words of D, and of Asaph the H1732
30:26 the son of D king of Israel *there* H1732
32: 5 Millo *in* the city of D, and made darts H1732
30 west side of the city of D. And Hezekiah H1732
33 of the sons of D: and all Judah and the H1732
33: 7 God had said to D and to Solomon his H1732
14 without the city of D, on the west side of H1732
34: 2 walked in the ways of D his father, and H1732
3 after the God of D his father: and in the H1732
35: 3 the son of D king of Israel did build; H1732
4 to the writing of D king of Israel, and H1732
15 commandment of D, and Asaph, and H1732
Ezr 3:10 after the ordinance of D king of Israel. H1732
8: 2 Daniel: of the sons of D; Hattush. H1732
20 Also of the Nethinims, whom D and the H1732
Neh 3:15 stairs that go down from the city of D. H1732
16 the sepulchres of D, and to the pool that H1732
12:24 commandment of D the man of God, H1732
36 instruments of D the man of God, and H1732
37 of the city of D, at the going up of the H1732
37 D, even unto the water gate eastward. H1732
45 of D, *and* of Solomon his son. H1732
46 For in the days of D and Asaph of old H1732
Ps 3:ttl A Psalm of D, when he fled from H1732
4:ttl Musician on Neginoth, A Psalm of D. H1732
5:ttl Musician upon Nehiloth, A Psalm of D. H1732
6:ttl upon Sheminith, A Psalm of D. H1732
7:ttl Shiggaion of D, which he sang unto the H1732
8:ttl Musician upon Gittith, A Psalm of D. H1732
9:ttl upon Muth-labben, A Psalm of D. H1732
11:ttl To the chief Musician, *A Psalm* of D. H1732
12:ttl upon Sheminith, A Psalm of D. H1732
13:ttl To the chief Musician, A Psalm of D. H1732
14:ttl To the chief Musician, *A Psalm* of D. H1732
15:ttl A Psalm of D. H1732
16:ttl Michtam of D. H1732
17:ttl A Prayer of D. H1732
18:50 to D, and to his seed for evermore. H1732
ttl To the chief Musician, *A Psalm* of D, H1732
19:ttl To the chief Musician, A Psalm of D. H1732
20:ttl To the chief Musician, A Psalm of D. H1732
21:ttl To the chief Musician, A Psalm of D. H1732
22:ttl upon Aijeleth Shahar, A Psalm of D. H1732
23:ttl A Psalm of D. H1732
24:ttl A Psalm of D. H1732
25:ttl *A Psalm* of D. H1732
26:ttl *A Psalm* of D. H1732
27:ttl *A Psalm* of D. H1732

Ps 28:ttl *A Psalm* of D. H1732
29:ttl A Psalm of D. H1732
30:ttl *at* the dedication of the house of D. H1732
31:ttl To the chief Musician, A Psalm of D. H1732
32:ttl *A Psalm* of D, Maschil. H1732
34:ttl *A Psalm* of D, when he changed his H1732
35:ttl *A Psalm* of D. H1732
36:ttl To the chief Musician, *A Psalm* of D H1732
37:ttl *A Psalm* of D. H1732
38:ttl A Psalm of D, to bring to remembrance. H1732
39:ttl *even* to Jeduthun, A Psalm of D. H1732
40:ttl To the chief Musician, A Psalm of D. H1732
41:ttl To the chief Musician, A Psalm of D. H1732
51:ttl To the chief Musician, A Psalm of D, H1732
52:ttl *A Psalm* of D, when Doeg the Edomite H1732
ttl D is come to the house of Ahimelech. H1732
53:ttl upon Mahalath, Maschil, *A Psalm* of D. H1732
54:ttl *A Psalm* of D, when the Ziphims came H1732
ttl Saul, Doth not D hide himself with us? H1732
55:ttl on Neginoth, Maschil, *A Psalm* of D. H1732
56:ttl Michtam of D, when the Philistines H1732
57:ttl D, when he fled from Saul in the cave. H1732
58:ttl Musician, Al-taschith, Michtam of D. H1732
59:ttl Michtam of D; when Saul sent, and H1732
60:ttl Michtam of D, to teach; when he strove H1732
61:ttl Musician upon Neginah, *A Psalm* of D. H1732
62:ttl Musician, to Jeduthun, A Psalm of D. H1732
63:ttl A Psalm of D, when he was in the H1732
64:ttl To the chief Musician, A Psalm of D. H1732
65:ttl chief Musician, A Psalm *and* Song of D. H1732
68:ttl chief Musician, A Psalm *or* Song of D. H1732
69:ttl upon Shoshannim, *A Psalm* of D. H1732
70:ttl To the chief Musician, *A Psalm* of D, to H1732
72:20 The prayers of D the son of Jesse are H1732
78:70 He chose D also his servant, and took H1732
86:ttl A Prayer of D. H1732
89: 3 I have sworn unto D my servant, H1732
20 I have found D my servant; with my H1732
35 by my holiness that I will not lie unto D. H1732
49 thou swarest unto D in thy truth? H1732
101:ttl A Psalm of D. H1732
103:ttl *A Psalm* of D. H1732
108:ttl A Song *or* Psalm of D. H1732
109:ttl To the chief Musician, A Psalm of D. H1732
110:ttl A Psalm of D. H1732
122: 5 judgment, the thrones of the house of D. H1732
ttl A Song of degrees of D. H1732
124:ttl A Song of degrees of D. H1732
131:ttl A Song of degrees of D. H1732
132: 1 LORD, remember D, *and* all his H1732
11 The LORD hath sworn *in* truth unto D; H1732
17 There will I make the horn of D to bud: H1732
133:ttl A Song of degrees of D. H1732
138:ttl *A Psalm* of D. H1732
139:ttl To the chief Musician, A Psalm of D. H1732
140:ttl To the chief Musician, A Psalm of D. H1732
141:ttl A Psalm of D. H1732
142:ttl Maschil of D; A Prayer when he was in H1732
143:ttl A Psalm of D. H1732
144:10 D his servant from the hurtful sword. H1732
ttl *A Psalm* of D. H1732
Prv 1: 1 The proverbs of Solomon the son of D, H1732
Ecc 1: 1 The words of the Preacher, the son of D, H1732
Song 4: 4 Thy neck *is* like the tower of D builded H1732
Isa 7: 2 And it was told the house of D, saying, H1732
13 And he said, Hear ye now, O house of D; H1732
9: 7 the throne of D, and upon his kingdom, H1732
16: 5 in the tabernacle of D, judging, and H1732
22: 9 of the city of D, that they are many: H1732
22 And the key of the house of D will I lay H1732
29: 1 Woe to Ariel, to Ariel, the city *where* D H1732
38: 5 LORD, the God of D thy father, I have H1732
55: 3 with you, *even* the sure mercies of D. H1732
Jer 17:25 the throne of D, riding in chariots and H1732
21:12 O house of D, thus saith the LORD; H1732
22: 2 the throne of D, thou, and thy servants, H1732
4 the throne of D, riding in chariots and H1732
30 of D, and ruling any more in Judah. H1732
23: 5 I will raise unto D a righteous Branch, H1732
29:16 the throne of D, and of all the people H1732
30: 9 their God, and D their king, whom I H1732
33:15 to grow up unto D; and he shall execute H1732
17 For thus saith the LORD; D shall never H1732
21 be broken with D my servant, that he H1732
22 the seed of D my servant, and the H1732
26 the seed of Jacob, and D my servant, *so* H1732
36:30 the throne of D: and his dead body H1732
Ezk 34:23 *even* my servant D; he shall feed them, H1732
24 God, and my servant D a prince among H1732

Ezk 37:24 And D my servant *shall be* king over H1732
25 servant D *shall be* their prince for ever. H1732
Hos 3: 5 their God, and D their king; and shall H1732
Am 6: 5 instruments of musick, like D; H1732
9:11 the tabernacle of D that is fallen, and H1732
Zec 12: 7 of the house of D and the glory of the H1732
8 that day shall be as D; and the house of H1732
8 and the house of D *shall be* as God, as H1732
10 And I will pour upon the house of D, H1732
12 of the house of D apart, and their wives H1732
13: 1 opened to the house of D and to the H1732
Mt 1: 1 the son of D, the son of Abraham. G1138
6 And Jesse begat D the king; and David G1138
6 And Jesse begat David the king; and D G1138
17 from Abraham to D *are* fourteen G1138
17 and from D until the carrying away G1138
20 thou son of D, fear not to take unto G1138
9:27 *Thou* son of D, have mercy on us. G1138
12: 3 ye not read what D did, when he was G1138
23 and said, Is not this the son of D? G1138
15:22 O Lord, *thou* son of D; my daughter is G1138
20:30 mercy on us, O Lord, *thou* son of D. G1138
31 mercy on us, O Lord, *thou* son of D. G1138
21: 9 to the son of D: Blessed *is* he that G1138
15 the son of D; they were sore displeased, G1138
22:42 is he? They say unto him, *The son* of D. G1138
43 He saith unto them, How then doth D G1138
45 If D then call him Lord, how is he his G1138
Mk 2:25 ye never read what D did, when he had G1138
10:47 Jesus, *thou* son of D, have mercy on me. G1138
48 deal, *Thou* son of D, have mercy on me. G1138
11:10 Blessed *be* the kingdom of our father D, G1138
12:35 the scribes that Christ is the son of D? G1138
36 For D himself said by the Holy Ghost, G1138
37 D therefore himself calleth him Lord; G1138
Lk 1:27 of D; and the virgin's name *was* Mary. G1138
32 give unto him the throne of his father D: G1138
69 for us in the house of his servant D; G1138
2: 4 unto the city of D, which is called G1138
4 he was of the house and lineage of D:) G1138
11 D a Saviour, which is Christ the Lord. G1138
3:31 *son* of Nathan, which was *the son* of D, G1138
6: 3 as this, what D did, when himself was G1138
18:38 Jesus, *thou* son of D, have mercy on me. G1138
39 *Thou* son of D, have mercy on me. G1138
20:42 And D himself saith in the book of G1138
44 D therefore calleth him Lord, how is he G1138
Jn 7:42 of the seed of D, and out of the town G1138
42 the town of Bethlehem, where D was? G1138
Act 1:16 Ghost by the mouth of D spake before G1138
2:25 For D speaketh concerning him, I G1138
29 of the patriarch D, that he is both dead G1138
34 For D is not ascended into the heavens: G1138
4:25 Who by the mouth of thy servant D G1138
7:45 face of our fathers, unto the days of D; G1138
13:22 up unto them D to be their king; to G1138
22 said, I have found D the *son* of Jesse, a G1138
34 I will give you the sure mercies of D. G1138
36 For D, after he had served his own G1138
15:16 the tabernacle of D, which is fallen G1138
Ro 1: 3 of the seed of D according to the flesh; G1138
4: 6 Even as D also describeth the G1138
11: 9 And D saith, Let their table be made a G1138
2Ti 2: 8 of the seed of D was raised from the G1138
Heb 4: 7 day, saying in D, To day, after so long G1138
11:32 *of* Jephthae; *of* D also, and Samuel, and G1138
Rev 3: 7 hath the key of D, he that openeth, and G1138
5: 5 of Juda, the Root of D, hath prevailed to G1138
22:16 of D, *and* the bright and morning star. G1138

DAVID'S

1Sa 18:29 and Saul became D enemy continually. H1732
19:11 Saul also sent messengers unto D H1732
11 and Michal D wife told him, saying, H1732
20:16 require *it* at the hand of D enemies. H1732
25 by Saul's side, and D place was empty. H1732
27 of the month, that D place was empty: H1732
23: 3 And D men said unto him, Behold, we H1732
24: 5 And it came to pass afterward, that D H1732
25: 9 And when D young men came, they H1732
10 And Nabal answered D servants, and H1732
12 So D young men turned their way, and H1732
44 his daughter, D wife, to Phalti the son H1732
26:17 And Saul knew D voice, and said, *Is* H1732
30: 5 And D two wives were taken captives, H1732
20 *other* cattle, and said, This *is* D spoil. H1732
2Sa 2:30 D servants nineteen men and Asahel. H1732
3: 5 And the sixth, Ithream, by Eglah D H1732
5: 8 *that are* hated of D soul, *he shall be* H1732

2Sa 8: 2 became **D** servants, *and* brought gifts. H1732
14 of Edom became **D** servants. And the H1732
18 and **D** sons were chief rulers. H1732
10: 2 for his father. And **D** servants came H1732
4 Wherefore Hanun took **D** servants, and H1732
12: 5 And **D** anger was greatly kindled H1732
30 and it was *set* on **D** head. And he H1732
13: 3 the son of Shimeah **D** brother: and H1732
32 And Jonadab, the son of Shimeah **D** H1732
15:12 the Gilonite, **D** counsellor, from his H1732
37 So Hushai **D** friend came into the city, H1732
16:16 the Archite, **D** friend, was come unto H1732
19:41 and all **D** men with him, over Jordan? H1732
24:10 And **D** heart smote him after that he H1732
11 unto the prophet Gad, **D** seer, saying, H1732
1Ki 1:38 **D** mule, and brought him to Gihon. H1732
11:32 tribe for my servant **D** sake, and for H1732
15: 4 Nevertheless for **D** sake did the LORD H1732
2Ki 11:10 priest give king **D** spears and shields, H1732
19:34 own sake, and for my servant **D** sake. H1732
20: 6 own sake, and for my servant **D** sake. H1732
1Ch 18: 2 became **D** servants, *and* brought gifts. H1732
6 the Syrians became **D** servants, *and* H1732
13 Edomites became **D** servants. Thus the H1732
19: 4 Wherefore Hanun took **D** servants, and H1732
20: 2 it was set upon **D** head: and he brought H1732
7 the son of Shimea **D** brother slew him. H1732
21: 9 And the LORD spake unto Gad, **D** seer, H1732
27:31 of the substance which *was* king **D**. H1732
32 Also Jonathan **D** uncle was a H1732
2Ch 23: 9 king **D**, which *were* in the house of God. H1732
Ps 132:10 For thy servant **D** sake turn not away H1732
145:ttl **D** *Psalm* of praise. H1732
Isa 37:35 own sake, and for my servant **D** sake. H1732
Jer 13:13 that sit upon **D** throne, and the priests, H1732
Lk 20:41 How say they that Christ is **D** son? *G1138*

DAWN

Mt 28: 1 as it began to **d** toward the first *day* *G2020*
2Pt 1:19 **d**, and the day star arise in your hearts: *G1306*

DAWNING

Jos 6:15 rose early about the **d** of the day, and H5927
Jdg 19:26 Then came the woman in the **d** of the H6437
Job 3: 9 none; neither let it see the **d** of the day: H6079
7: 4 to and fro unto the **d** of the day. H5399
Ps119:147 I prevented the **d** of the morning, and H5399

DAY

Gen 1: 5 And God called the light **D**, and the H3117
5 and the morning were the first **d**. H3117
8 and the morning were the second **d**. H3117
13 and the morning were the third **d**. H3117
14 to divide the **d** from the night; and H3117
16 light to rule the **d**, and the lesser light H3117
18 And to rule over the **d** and over the H3117
19 and the morning were the fourth **d**. H3117
23 and the morning were the fifth **d**. H3117
31 and the morning were the sixth **d**. H3117
2: 2 And on the seventh **d** God ended his H3117
2 on the seventh **d** from all his work H3117
3 And God blessed the seventh **d**, and H3117
4 created, in the **d** that the LORD God H3117
17 eat of it: for in the **d** that thou eatest H3117
3: 5 For God doth know that in the **d** ye eat H3117
8 in the cool of the **d**: and Adam and his H3117
4:14 Behold, thou hast driven me out this **d** H3117
5: 1 of Adam. In the **d** that God created H3117
2 in the **d** when they were created. H3117
7:11 the seventeenth **d** of the month, the H3117
11 the month, the same **d** were all the H3117
13 In the selfsame **d** entered Noah, and H3117
8: 4 the seventeenth **d** of the month, upon H3117
5 on the first *d* of the month, were H3117
13 *month*, the first *d* of the month, the H3117
14 **d** of the month, was the earth dried. H3117
22 winter, and **d** and night shall not cease. H3117
15:18 In the same **d** the LORD made a H3117
17:23 selfsame **d**, as God had said unto him. H3117
26 In the selfsame **d** was Abraham H3117
18: 1 sat in the tent door in the heat of the **d**; H3117
19:37 *is* the father of the Moabites unto this **d**. H3117
38 of the children of Ammon unto this **d**. H3117
21: 8 the *same* **d** that Isaac was weaned. H3117
26 me, neither yet heard I *of it*, but to **d**. H3117
22: 4 Then on the third **d** Abraham lifted up H3117
14 as it is said *to* this **d**, In the mount of H3117
24:12 good speed this **d**, and shew kindness H3117
42 And I came this **d** unto the well, and H3117
Gen 25:31 And Jacob said, Sell me this **d** thy H3117
33 And Jacob said, Swear to me this **d**; and H3117
26:32 And it came to pass the same **d**, that H3117
33 of the city *is* Beer-sheba unto this **d**. H3117
27: 2 I am old, I know not the **d** of my death: H3117
45 I be deprived also of you both in one **d**? H3117
29: 7 And he said, Lo, *it is* yet high **d**, neither H3117
30:32 I will pass through all thy flock to **d**, H3117
35 And he removed that **d** the he goats H3117
31:22 And it was told Laban on the third **d** H3117
39 *whether* stolen by **d**, or stolen by night. H3117
40 *Thus* I was; in the **d** the drought H3117
43 and what can I do this **d** unto these my H3117
48 me and thee this **d**. Therefore was the H3117
32:24 with him until the breaking of the **d**. H7837
26 And he said, Let me go, for the **d** H7837
32 thigh, unto this **d**: because he touched H3117
33:13 them one **d**, all the flock will die. H3117
16 So Esau returned that **d** on his way H3117
34:25 And it came to pass on the third **d**, H3117
35: 3 me in the **d** of my distress, and H3117
20 the pillar of Rachel's grave unto this **d**. H3117
39:10 she spake to Joseph **d** by day, that he H3117
10 to Joseph day by **d**, that he hearkened H3117
40: 7 saying, Wherefore look ye *so* sadly to **d**? H3117
20 And it came to pass the third **d**, *which* H3117
41: 9 saying, I do remember my faults this **d**: H3117
42:13 *is* this **d** with our father, and one *is* not. H3117
18 And Joseph said unto them the third **d**, H3117
32 youngest *is* this **d** with our father in the H3117
47:23 bought you this **d** and your land for H3117
26 land of Egypt unto this **d**, *that* Pharaoh H3117
48:15 fed me all my life long unto this **d**, H3117
20 And he blessed them that **d**, saying, In H3117
50:20 as *it is* this **d**, to save much people alive. H3117
Ex 2:13 And when he went out the second **d**, H3117
18 How *is it that* ye are come so soon to **d**? H3117
5: 6 And Pharaoh commanded the same **d** H3117
14 both yesterday and to **d**, as heretofore? H3117
6:28 And it came to pass on the **d** *when* the H3117
8:22 And I will sever in that **d** the land of H3117
10: 6 seen, since the **d** that they were upon H3117
6 the earth unto this **d**. And he turned H3117
13 the land all that **d**, and all *that* night; H3117
28 **d** thou seest my face thou shalt die. H3117
12: 3 In the tenth *d* of this month they shall
6 the fourteenth **d** of the same month: H3117
14 And this **d** shall be unto you for a H3117
15 even the first **d** ye shall put away H3117
15 from the first **d** until the seventh day, H3117
15 **d**, that soul shall be cut off from Israel. H3117
16 And in the first **d** *there shall be* an holy H3117
16 and in the seventh **d** there shall be an H3117
17 in this selfsame **d** have I brought your H3117
17 ye observe this **d** in your generations H3117
18 In the first *month*, on the fourteenth **d** H3117
18 and twentieth **d** of the month at even. H3117
41 even the selfsame **d** it came to pass, H3117
51 And it came to pass the selfsame **d**, *that* H3117
13: 3 Remember this **d**, in which ye came out H3117
4 This **d** came ye out in the month Abib. H3117
6 seventh **d** *shall be* a feast to the LORD. H3117
8 And thou shalt shew thy son in that **d**, H3117
21 And the LORD went before them by **d** H3119
21 to give them light; to go by **d** and night: H3119
22 of the cloud by **d**, nor the pillar of fire H3119
14:13 will shew to you to **d**: for the Egyptians H3117
13 ye have seen to **d**, ye shall see them H3117
30 Thus the LORD saved Israel that **d** out H3117
16: 1 on the fifteenth **d** of the second month H3117
4 a certain rate every **d**, that I may prove H3117
5 that on the sixth **d** they shall prepare H3117
22 And it came to pass, *that* on the sixth **d** H3117
23 ye will bake *to d*, and seethe that ye will
25 And Moses said, Eat that to **d**; for to H3117
25 that to day; for to **d** *is* a sabbath unto H3117
25 to **d** ye shall not find it in the field. H3117
26 it; but on the seventh **d**, *which is* the H3117
27 **d** for to gather, and they found none. H3117
29 you on the sixth **d** the bread of two H3117
29 go out of his place on the seventh **d**. H3117
30 So the people rested on the seventh **d**. H3117
19: 1 of Egypt, the same **d** came they *into* the H3117
10 sanctify them to **d** and to morrow, and H3117
11 And be ready against the third **d**: for the H3117
11 day: for the third **d** the LORD will come H3117
15 the third **d**: come not at *your* wives. H3117
16 And it came to pass on the third **d** in H3117
20: 8 Remember the sabbath **d**, to keep it H3117
Ex 20:10 But the seventh **d** *is* the sabbath of the H3117
11 and rested the seventh **d**: wherefore the H3117
11 blessed the sabbath **d**, and hallowed it. H3117
21:21 Notwithstanding, if he continue a **d** or H3117
22:30 on the eighth **d** thou shalt give it me. H3117
23:12 on the seventh **d** thou shalt rest: that H3117
24:16 and the seventh **d** he called unto Moses H3117
29:36 And thou shalt offer every **d** a bullock H3117
38 of the first year **d** by day continually. H3117
38 of the first year day by **d** continually. H3117
31:15 **d**, he shall surely be put to death. H3117
17 seventh **d** he rested, and was refreshed. H3117
32:28 that **d** about three thousand men. H3117
29 yourselves to **d** to the LORD, even H3117
29 may bestow upon you a blessing this **d**. H3117
34 in the **d** when I visit I will visit H3117
34:11 thee this **d**: behold, I drive out before H3117
21 but on the seventh **d** thou shalt rest: in H3117
35: 2 but on the seventh **d** there shall be to H3117
2 be to you an holy **d**, a sabbath of rest to
3 your habitations upon the sabbath **d**. H3117
40: 2 On the first **d** of the first month shalt H3117
17 year, on the first *d* of the month, *that* the
37 not till the **d** that it was taken up. H3117
38 the tabernacle by **d**, and fire was on it H3119
Lev 6: 5 in the **d** of his trespass offering. H3117
20 the LORD in the **d** when he is anointed; H3117
7:15 be eaten the same **d** that it is offered; H3117
16 be eaten the same **d** that he offereth his H3117
17 on the third **d** shall be burnt with fire. H3117
18 eaten at all on the third **d**, it shall not be H3117
35 by fire, in the **d** *when* he presented H3117
36 of Israel, in the **d** that he anointed H3117
38 Sinai, in the **d** that he commanded H3117
8:34 As he hath done this **d**, *so* the LORD H3117
35 of the congregation **d** and night seven H3119
9: 1 And it came to pass on the eighth **d**, H3117
4 for to **d** the LORD will appear unto you. H3117
10:19 Behold, this **d** have they offered their H3117
19 the sin offering to **d**, should it have been H3117
12: 3 And in the eighth **d** the flesh of his H3117
13: 5 him the seventh **d**: and, behold, *if* the H3117
6 again the seventh **d**: and, behold, *if* the H3117
27 him the seventh **d**: *and* if it be spread H3117
32 And in the seventh **d** the priest shall H3117
34 And in the seventh **d** the priest shall H3117
51 plague on the seventh **d**: if the plague be H3117
14: 2 of the leper in the **d** of his cleansing: He H3117
9 But it shall be on the seventh **d**, that he H3117
10 And on the eighth **d** he shall take two H3117
23 on the eighth **d** for his cleansing unto H3117
39 again the seventh **d**, and shall look: H3117
15:14 And on the eighth **d** he shall take to H3117
29 And on the eighth **d** she shall take unto H3117
16:29 on the tenth *d* of the month, ye shall
30 For on that **d** shall *the priest* make an H3117
19: 6 It shall be eaten the same **d** ye offer it, H3117
6 the third **d**, it shall be burnt in the fire. H3117
7 And if it be eaten at all on the third **d**, it H3117
22:27 from the eighth **d** and thenceforth it H3117
28 not kill it and her young both in one **d**. H3117
30 On the same **d** it shall be eaten up; ye H3117
23: 3 but the seventh **d** *is* the sabbath of rest, H3117
5 In the fourteenth *d* of the first month at
6 And on the fifteenth **d** of the same H3117
7 In the first **d** ye shall have an holy H3117
8 in the seventh **d** *is* an holy convocation: H3117
12 And ye shall offer that **d** when ye wave H3117
14 ears, until the selfsame **d** that ye have H3117
15 sabbath, from the **d** that ye brought the H3117
21 on the selfsame **d**, *that* it may be an H3117
24 month, in the first *d* of the month, shall
27 Also on the tenth *d* of this seventh
27 *there shall be* a **d** of atonement: it shall H3117
28 And ye shall do no work in that same **d**: H3117
28 day: for it *is* a **d** of atonement, to make H3117
29 in that same **d**, he shall be cut off from H3117
30 work in that same **d**, the same soul will H3117
32 souls: in the ninth *d* of the month at
34 The fifteenth *d* of this seventh month H3117
35 On the first **d** *shall be* an holy H3117
36 LORD: on the eighth **d** shall be an holy H3117
37 drink offerings, every thing upon his **d**: H3117
39 Also in the fifteenth **d** of the seventh H3117
39 days: on the first **d** *shall be* a sabbath, H3117
39 and on the eighth **d** *shall be* a sabbath. H3117
40 And ye shall take you on the first **d** the H3117
25: 9 to sound on the tenth *d* of the seventh
9 month, in the **d** of atonement shall H3117

Lev 27:23 that **d**, *as* a holy thing unto the LORD. H3117
Nu 1: 1 on the first *d* of the second month,
18 on the first *d* of the second month,
3: 1 and Moses in the **d** *that* the LORD H3117
13 mine; *for* on the **d** that I smote all the H3117
6: 9 his head in the **d** of his cleansing, on H3117
9 on the seventh **d** shall he shave it. H3117
10 And on the eighth **d** he shall bring two H3117
11 and shall hallow his head that same **d**. H3117
7: 1 And it came to pass on the **d** that H3117
10 of the altar in the **d** that it was H3117
11 on his **d**, for the dedicating of the altar. H3117
12 his offering the first **d** was Nahshon the H3117
18 On the second **d** Nethaneel the son of H3117
24 On the third **d** Eliab the son of Helon, H3117
30 On the fourth **d** Elizur the son of H3117
36 On the fifth **d** Shelumiel the son of H3117
42 On the sixth **d** Eliasaph the son of H3117
48 On the seventh **d** Elishama the son of H3117
54 On the eighth **d** *offered* Gamaliel the H3117
60 On the ninth **d** Abidan the son of H3117
66 On the tenth **d** Ahiezer the son of H3117
72 On the eleventh **d** Pagiel the son of H3117
78 On the twelfth **d** Ahira the son of Enan, H3117
84 of the altar, in the **d** when it was H3117
8:17 and beast: on the **d** that I smote every H3117
9: 3 In the fourteenth **d** of this month, at H3117
5 on the fourteenth **d** of the first month H3117
6 the passover on that **d**: and they came H3117
6 Moses and before Aaron on that **d**: H3117
11 The fourteenth **d** of the second month H3117
15 And on the **d** that the tabernacle was H3117
16 So it was alway: the cloud covered it *by d*,
21 whether *it was* by **d** or by night that the H3119
10:10 Also in the **d** of your gladness, and in H3117
11 And it came to pass on the twentieth *d*
34 by **d**, when they went out of the camp. H3119
11:19 Ye shall not eat one **d**, nor two days, H3117
32 And the people stood up all that **d**, and H3117
32 and all the next **d**, and they gathered H3117
14:14 before them, by **d** time in a pillar of a H3119
34 forty days, each **d** for a year, shall ye H3117
15:23 of Moses, from the **d** that the LORD H3117
32 gathered sticks upon the sabbath **d**. H3117
19:12 it on the third **d**, and on the seventh H3117
12 on the seventh **d** he shall be clean: but H3117
12 not himself the third **d**, then the seventh H3117
12 the seventh **d** he shall not be clean. H3117
19 on the third **d**, and on the seventh H3117
19 on the seventh **d**: and on the seventh H3117
19 and on the seventh **d** he shall purify H3117
22:30 thine unto this **d**? was I ever wont to do H3117
25:18 in the **d** of the plague for Peor's sake. H3117
28: 3 first year without spot **d** by day, *for* a H3117
3 day by **d**, *for* a continual burnt offering. H3117
9 And on the sabbath **d** two lambs of the H3117
16 And in the fourteenth **d** of the first H3117
17 And in the fifteenth **d** of this month *is* H3117
18 In the first **d** *shall be* an holy H3117
25 And on the seventh **d** ye shall have an H3117
26 Also in the **d** of the firstfruits, when ye H3117
29: 1 And in the seventh month, on the first *d*
1 a **d** of blowing the trumpets unto you. H3117
7 And ye shall have on the tenth *d* of this
12 And on the fifteenth **d** of the seventh H3117
17 And on the second **d** *ye shall offer* H3117
20 And on the third **d** eleven bullocks, two H3117
23 And on the fourth **d** ten bullocks, two H3117
26 And on the fifth **d** nine bullocks, two H3117
29 And on the sixth **d** eight bullocks, two H3117
32 And on the seventh **d** seven bullocks, H3117
35 On the eighth **d** ye shall have a solemn H3117
30: 5 But if her father disallow her in the **d** H3117
7 peace at her in the **d** that he heard *it*: H3117
8 her on the **d** that he heard *it*; then H3117
12 them void on the **d** he heard *them; then* H3117
14 his peace at her from **d** to day; then he H3117
14 peace at her from day to **d**; then he H3117
14 at her in the **d** that he heard *them*. H3117
31:19 on the third **d**, and on the seventh day. H3117
19 on the third day, and on the seventh **d**. H3117
24 on the seventh **d**, and ye shall be clean, H3117
33: 3 on the fifteenth **d** of the first month; on H3117
38 of Egypt, in the first *d* of the fifth month.
Dt 1: 3 month, on the first *d* of the month, *that*
10 **d** as the stars of heaven for multitude. H3117
33 way ye should go, and in a cloud by **d**. H3119
39 which in that **d** had no knowledge H3117
2:18 through Ar, the coast of Moab, this **d**: H3117
Dt 2:22 dwelt in their stead even unto this **d**: H3117
25 This **d** will I begin to put the dread of H3117
30 him into thy hand, as *appeareth* this **d**. H3117
3:14 name, Bashan-havoth-jair, unto this **d**. H3117
4: 4 God *are* alive every one of you this **d**. H3117
8 this law, which I set before you this **d**? H3117
10 *Specially* the **d** that thou stoodest H3117
15 of similitude on the **d** *that* the LORD H3117
20 a people of inheritance, as *ye are* this **d**. H3117
26 against you this **d**, that ye shall soon H3117
32 thee, since the **d** that God created man H3117
38 land *for* an inheritance, as *it is* this **d**. H3117
39 Know therefore this **d**, and consider *it* H3117
40 thee this **d**, that it may go well with H3117
5: 1 in your ears this **d**, that ye may learn H3117
3 us, who *are* all of us here alive this **d**. H3117
12 Keep the sabbath **d** to sanctify it, as the H3117
14 But the seventh **d** *is* the sabbath of the H3117
15 commanded thee to keep the sabbath **d**. H3117
24 we have seen this **d** that God doth talk H3117
6: 6 thee this **d**, shall be in thine heart: H3117
24 might preserve us alive, as *it is* at this **d**. H3117
7:11 I command thee this **d**, to do them. H3117
8: 1 thee this **d** shall ye observe to do, H3117
11 statutes, which I command thee this **d**: H3117
18 he sware unto thy fathers, as *it is* this **d**. H3117
19 you this **d** that ye shall surely perish. H3117
9: 1 over Jordan this **d**, to go in to possess H3117
3 Understand therefore this **d**, that the H3117
7 from the **d** that thou didst depart H3117
10 of the fire in the **d** of the assembly. H3117
24 the LORD from the **d** that I knew you. H3117
10: 4 of the fire in the **d** of the assembly: and H3117
8 and to bless in his name, unto this **d**. H3117
13 I command thee this **d** for thy good? H3117
15 *even* you above all people, as *it is* this **d**. H3117
11: 2 And know ye this **d**: for *I speak* not with H3117
4 LORD hath destroyed them unto this **d**; H3117
8 you this **d**, that ye may be strong, H3117
13 you this **d**, to love the LORD your H3117
26 Behold, I set before you this **d** a H3117
27 your God, which I command you this **d**: H3117
28 you this **d**, to go after other gods, H3117
32 judgments which I set before you this **d**. H3117
12: 8 that we do here this **d**, every man H3117
13:18 thee this **d**, to do *that which is* right H3117
15: 5 which I command thee this **d**. H3117
15 I command thee this thing to **d**. H3117
16: 3 remember the **d** when thou camest H3117
4 the first **d** at even, remain all H3117
8 and on the seventh **d** *shall be* a solemn H3117
18:16 God in Horeb in the **d** of the assembly, H3117
19: 9 thee this **d**, to love the LORD thy H3117
20: 3 ye approach this **d** unto battle against H3117
21:23 bury him that **d**; (for he that is hanged H3117
24:15 At his **d** thou shalt give *him* his hire, H3117
26: 3 him, I profess this **d** unto the LORD thy H3117
16 This **d** the LORD thy God hath H3117
17 Thou hast avouched the LORD this **d** to H3117
18 thee this **d** to be his peculiar people, H3117
27: 1 which I command you this **d**. H3117
2 And it shall be on the **d** when ye shall H3117
4 you this **d**, in mount Ebal, and H3117
9 O Israel; this **d** thou art become the H3117
10 statutes, which I command thee this **d**. H3117
11 charged the people the same **d**, saying, H3117
28: 1 thee this **d**, that the LORD thy God H3117
13 thee this **d**, to observe and to do *them*: H3117
14 thee this **d**, *to* the right hand, or H3117
15 thee this **d**; that all these curses H3117
32 for them all the **d** long: and *there shall* H3117
66 thou shalt fear **d** and night, and shalt H3119
29: 4 to see, and ears to hear, unto this **d**. H3117
10 Ye stand this **d** all of you before the H3117
12 LORD thy God maketh with thee this **d**: H3117
13 That he may establish thee to **d** for a H3117
15 here with us this **d** before the LORD H3117
15 with *him* that *is* not here with us this **d**: H3117
18 turneth away this **d** from the LORD our H3117
28 them into another land, as *it is* this **d**. H3117
30: 2 thee this **d**, thou and thy children, H3117
8 which I command thee this **d**. H3117
11 thee this **d**, it *is* not hidden from H3117
15 See, I have set before thee this **d** life H3117
16 In that I command thee this **d** to love H3117
18 I denounce unto you this **d**, that ye shall H3117
19 I call heaven and earth to record this **d** H3117
31: 2 years old this **d**; I can no more go out H3117
17 them in that **d**, and I will forsake them, H3117
Dt 31:17 will say in that **d**, Are not these evils H3117
18 And I will surely hide my face in that **d** H3117
22 **d**, and taught it the children of Israel. H3117
27 yet alive with you this **d**, ye have been H3117
32:35 *due* time: for the **d** of their calamity *is* H3117
46 testify among you this **d**, which ye shall H3117
48 unto Moses that selfsame **d**, saying, H3117
33:12 cover him all the **d** long, and he shall H3117
34: 6 knoweth of his sepulchre unto this **d**. H3117
Jos 1: 8 meditate therein **d** and night, that thou H3119
3: 7 And the LORD said unto Joshua, This **d** H3117
4: 9 stood: and they are there unto this **d**. H3117
14 On that **d** the LORD magnified Joshua H3117
19 on the tenth *d* of the first month, and
5: 9 And the LORD said unto Joshua, This **d** H3117
9 of the place is called Gilgal unto this **d**. H3117
10 on the fourteenth **d** of the month at H3117
11 and parched *corn* in the selfsame **d**. H3117
6: 4 and the seventh **d** ye shall compass the H3117
10 **d** I bid you shout; then shall ye shout. H3117
14 And the second **d** they compassed the H3117
15 And it came to pass on the seventh **d**, H3117
15 dawning of the **d**, and compassed the H7837
15 **d** they compassed the city seven times. H3117
25 *even* unto this **d**; because she hid the H3117
7:25 trouble thee this **d**. And all Israel stoned H3117
26 heap of stones unto this **d**. So the LORD H3117
26 called, The valley of Achor, unto this **d**. H3117
8:25 And *so* it was, *that* all that fell that **d**, H3117
28 for ever, *even* a desolation unto this **d**. H3117
29 of stones, *that remaineth* unto this **d**. H3117
9:12 of our houses on the **d** we came forth to H3117
17 cities on the third **d**. Now their cities H3117
27 And Joshua made them that **d** hewers H3117
27 **d**, in the place which he should choose. H3117
10:12 to the LORD in the **d** when the LORD H3117
13 hasted not to go down about a whole **d**. H3117
14 And there was no **d** like that before it H3117
27 mouth, *which remain* until this very **d**. H3117
28 And that **d** Joshua took Makkedah, H3117
32 it on the second **d**, and smote it with the H3117
35 And they took it on that **d**, and smote it H3117
35 destroyed that **d**, according to all that H3117
13:13 dwell among the Israelites until this **d**. H3117
14: 9 And Moses sware on that **d**, saying, H3117
10 *am* this **d** fourscore and five years old. H3117
11 As yet I *am as* strong this **d** as *I was* in H3117
11 day as *I was* in the **d** that Moses sent H3117
12 spake in that **d**; for thou heardest in H3117
12 heardest in that **d** how the Anakims H3117
14 Kenezite unto this **d**, because that he H3117
15:63 of Judah at Jerusalem unto this **d**. H3117
16:10 unto this **d**, and serve under tribute. H3117
22: 3 days unto this **d**, but have kept the H3117
16 to turn away this **d** from following the H3117
16 ye might rebel this **d** against the LORD? H3117
17 not cleansed until this **d**, although there H3117
18 But that ye must turn away this **d** from H3117
18 *seeing* ye rebel to **d** against the LORD, H3117
22 against the LORD, (save us not this **d**,) H3117
29 and turn this **d** from following the H3117
31 of Manasseh, This **d** we perceive that H3117
23: 8 your God, as ye have done unto this **d**. H3117
9 able to stand before you unto this **d**. H3117
14 And, behold, this **d** I *am* going the way H3117
24:15 choose you this **d** whom ye will serve; H3117
25 the people that **d**, and set them a statute H3117
Jdg 1:21 of Benjamin in Jerusalem unto this **d**. H3117
26 which *is* the name thereof unto this **d**. H3117
3:30 So Moab was subdued that **d** under the H3117
4:14 Up; for this *is* the **d** in which the LORD H3117
23 So God subdued on that **d** Jabin the H3117
5: 1 the son of Abinoam on that **d**, saying, H3117
6:24 **d** it *is* yet in Ophrah of the Abi-ezrites. H3117
27 not do it by **d**, that he did *it* by night. H3119
32 Therefore on that **d** he called him H3117
9:18 father's house this **d**, and have slain his H3117
19 with his house this **d**, *then* rejoice ye in H3117
45 the city all that **d**; and he took the city, H3117
10: 4 this **d**, which *are* in the land of Gilead. H3117
15 deliver us only, we pray thee, this **d**. H3117
11:27 be judge this **d** between the children H3117
12: 3 up unto me this **d**, to fight against me? H3117
13: 7 from the womb to the **d** of his death. H3117
10 me, that came unto me the *other* **d**. H3117
14:15 And it came to pass on the seventh **d**, H3117
17 pass on the seventh **d**, that he told her, H3117
18 on the seventh **d** before the sun went H3117
15:19 which *is* in Lehi unto this **d**. H3117

Jdg 16: 2 morning, when it is **d**, we shall kill him. H216
18: 1 in; for unto that **d** *all their* inheritance H3117
12 **d**: behold, *it is* behind Kirjath-jearim. H3117
30 until the **d** of the captivity of the land. H3117
19: 5 And it came to pass on the fourth **d**, H3117
8 on the fifth **d** to depart: and the H3117
9 Behold, now the **d** draweth toward H3117
9 night: behold, the **d** groweth to an end, H3117
11 *And* when they *were* by Jebus, the **d** H3117
25 the **d** began to spring, they let her go. H7837
26 dawning of the **d**, and fell down at the H1242
30 nor seen from the **d** that the children of H3117
30 of Egypt unto this **d**: consider of it, take H3117
20:21 that **d** twenty and two thousand men. H3117
22 they put themselves in array the first **d**. H3117
24 the children of Benjamin the second **d**. H3117
25 of Gibeah the second **d**, and destroyed H3117
26 and fasted that **d** until even, and H3117
30 on the third **d**, and put themselves H3117
35 the Benjamites that **d** twenty and five H3117
46 So that all which fell that **d** of H3117
21: 3 be to **d** one tribe lacking in Israel? H3117
6 is one tribe cut off from Israel this **d**. H3117
Ru 2:19 hast thou gleaned to **d**? and where H3117
19 with whom I wrought to **d** *is* Boaz. H3117
3:18 until he have finished the thing this **d**. H3117
4: 5 Then said Boaz, What **d** thou buyest H3117
9 *are* witnesses this **d**, that I have bought H3117
10 gate of his place: ye *are* witnesses this **d**. H3117
14 not left thee this **d** without a kinsman, H3117
1Sa 2:34 in one **d** they shall die both of them. H3117
3:12 In that **d** I will perform against Eli all H3117
4: 3 smitten us to **d** before the Philistines? H3117
12 to Shiloh the same **d** with his clothes H3117
16 and I fled to **d** out of the army. And H3117
5: 5 of Dagon in Ashdod unto this **d**. H3117
6:15 sacrifices the same **d** unto the LORD. H3117
16 *it*, they returned to Ekron the same **d**. H3117
18 unto this **d** in the field of Joshua, H3117
7: 6 and fasted on that **d**, and said there, We H3117
10 thunder on that **d** upon the Philistines, H3117
8: 8 done since the **d** that I brought them H3117
8 even unto this **d**, wherewith they have H3117
18 And ye shall cry out in that **d** because H3117
18 the LORD will not hear you in that **d**. H3117
9:12 for he came to **d** to the city; for *there* H3117
12 of the people to **d** in the high place: H3117
15 in his ear a **d** before Saul came, saying, H3117
19 eat with me to **d**, and to morrow I will H3117
24 So Saul did eat with Samuel that **d**. H3117
26 the spring of the **d**, that Samuel called H7837
10: 2 When thou art departed from me to **d**, H3117
9 and all those signs came to pass that **d**. H3117
19 And ye have this **d** rejected your God, H3117
11:11 the heat of the **d**: and it came to pass, H3117
13 put to death this **d**: for to day the LORD H3117
13 death this day: for to **d** the LORD hath H3117
12: 2 you from my childhood unto this **d**. H3117
5 *is* witness this **d**, that ye have not found H3117
17 *Is it* not wheat harvest to **d**? I will call H3117
18 and rain that **d**: and all the people H3117
13:22 So it came to pass in the **d** of battle, H3117
14: 1 Now it came to pass upon a **d**, that H3117
23 So the LORD saved Israel that **d**: and H3117
24 distressed that **d**: for Saul had adjured H3117
28 food this **d**. And the people were faint. H3117
30 had eaten freely to **d** of the spoil of H3117
31 And they smote the Philistines that **d** H3117
33 roll a great stone unto me this **d**. H3117
37 Israel? But he answered him not that **d**. H3117
38 see wherein this sin hath been this **d**. H3117
45 with God this **d**. So the people rescued H3117
15:28 from thee this **d**, and hath given it to H3117
35 to see Saul until the **d** of his death: H3117
16:13 David from that **d** forward. So Samuel H3117
17:10 of Israel this **d**; give me a man, that H3117
46 This **d** will the LORD deliver thee into H3117
46 the Philistines this **d** unto the fowls of H3117
18: 2 And Saul took him that **d**, and would let H3117
9 And Saul eyed David from that **d** and H3117
21 Thou shalt this **d** be my son in law in H3117
19:24 naked all that **d** and all that night. H3117
20: 5 in the field unto the third *d* at even.
12 time, *or* the third *d*, and, behold, *if there*
26 not any thing that **d**: for he thought, H3117
27 *was* the second *d* of the month, that
27 to meat, neither yesterday, nor to **d**? H3117
34 meat the second **d** of the month: for he H3117
21: 5 it were sanctified this **d** in the vessel. H3117

1Sa 21: 6 bread in the **d** when it was taken away. H3117
7 *was* there that **d**, detained before the H3117
10 And David arose, and fled that **d** for H3117
22: 8 against me, to lie in wait, as at this **d**? H3117
13 against me, to lie in wait, as at this **d**? H3117
18 and slew on that **d** fourscore and five H3117
22 I knew *it* that **d**, when Doeg the H3117
23:14 sought him every **d**, but God delivered H3117
24: 4 him, Behold the **d** of which the LORD H3117
10 Behold, this **d** thine eyes have seen how H3117
10 delivered thee to **d** into mine hand in H3117
18 And thou hast shewed this **d** how that H3117
19 for that thou hast done unto me this **d**. H3117
25: 8 we come in a good **d**: give, I pray thee, H3117
16 us both by night and **d**, all the while we H3119
32 which sent thee this **d** to meet me: H3117
33 hast kept me this **d** from coming to H3117
26: 8 thine hand this **d**: now therefore let me H3117
10 smite him; or his **d** shall come to die; or H3117
19 driven me out this **d** from abiding in H3117
21 in thine eyes this **d**: behold, I have H3117
23 thee into *my* hand to **d**, but I would not H3117
24 much set by this **d** in mine eyes, so let H3117
27: 1 now perish one **d** by the hand of Saul: H3117
6 Then Achish gave him Ziklag that **d**: H3117
6 unto the kings of Judah unto this **d**. H3117
10 ye made a road to **d**? And David said, H3117
28:18 LORD done this thing unto thee this **d**. H3117
20 no bread all the **d**, nor all the night. H3117
29: 3 in him since he fell *unto me* unto this **d**? H3117
6 in thee since the **d** of thy coming unto H3117
6 unto me unto this **d**: nevertheless the H3117
8 thee unto this **d**, that I may not go fight H3117
30: 1 on the third **d**, that the Amalekites H3117
17 of the next **d**: and there escaped not H4283
25 And it was *so* from that **d** forward, that H3117
25 and an ordinance for Israel unto this **d**. H3117
31: 6 and all his men, that same **d** together. H3117
2Sa 1: 2 It came even to pass on the third **d**, H3117
2:17 And there was a very sore battle that **d**; H3117
32 and they came to Hebron at break of **d**. H215
3: 8 kindness this **d** unto the house of Saul H3117
8 **d** with a fault concerning this woman? H3117
35 while it was yet **d**, David sware, saying, H3117
37 understood that **d** that it was not of the H3117
38 and a great man fallen this **d** in Israel? H3117
39 And I *am* this **d** weak, though anointed H3117
4: 3 and were sojourners there until this **d**.) H3117
5 about the heat of the **d** to the house of H3117
8 the king this **d** of Saul, and of his seed. H3117
5: 8 And David said on that **d**, Whosoever H3117
6: 8 name of the place Perez-uzzah to this **d**. H3117
9 of the LORD that **d**, and said, How shall H3117
20 the king of Israel to **d**, who uncovered H3117
20 himself to **d** in the eyes of the H3117
23 had no child unto the **d** of her death. H3117
7: 6 Egypt, even to this **d**, but have walked H3117
11:12 Tarry here to **d** also, and to morrow H3117
12 in Jerusalem that **d**, and the morrow. H3117
12:18 And it came to pass on the seventh **d**, H3117
13: 4 son, lean from **d** to day? wilt thou not H1242
4 lean from day to **d**? wilt thou not tell H1242
32 the **d** that he forced his sister Tamar. H3117
37 And *David* mourned for his son every **d**. H3117
14:22 king: and Joab said, To **d** thy servant H3117
15:20 should I this **d** make thee go up and H3117
16: 3 for he said, To **d** shall the house of H3117
12 requite me good for his cursing this **d**. H3117
18: 7 that **d** of twenty thousand *men*. H3117
8 people that **d** than the sword devoured. H3117
18 it is called unto this **d**, Absalom's place. H3117
20 bear tidings this **d**, but thou shalt bear H3117
20 tidings another **d**: but this day thou H3117
20 day: but this **d** thou shalt bear no H3117
31 **d** of all them that rose up against thee. H3117
19: 2 And the victory that **d** was *turned* into H3117
2 **d** how the king was grieved for his son. H3117
3 by stealth that **d** into the city, as people H3117
5 hast shamed this **d** the faces of all thy H3117
5 which this **d** have saved thy life, H3117
6 hast declared this **d**, that thou regardest H3117
6 servants: for this **d** I perceive, that if H3117
6 this **d**, then it had pleased thee well. H3117
19 did perversely the **d** that my lord the H3117
20 come the first this **d** of all the house of H3117
22 that ye should this **d** be adversaries H3117
22 put to death this **d** in Israel? for do not H3117
22 know that I *am* this **d** king over Israel? H3117
24 clothes, from the **d** the king departed H3117

2Sa 19:24 until the **d** he came *again* in peace. H3117
35 I *am* this **d** fourscore years old: *and* H3117
20: 3 **d** of their death, living in widowhood. H3117
21:10 by **d**, nor the beasts of the field by night. H3119
22: 1 of this song in the **d** *that* the LORD had H3117
19 They prevented me in the **d** of my H3117
23:10 a great victory that **d**; and the people H3117
24:18 And Gad came that **d** to David, and H3117
1Ki 1:25 For he is gone down this **d**, and hath H3117
30 stead; even so will I certainly do this **d**. H3117
48 throne this **d**, mine eyes even seeing *it*. H3117
51 swear unto me to **d** that he will not slay H3117
2: 8 grievous curse in the **d** when I went to H3117
24 Adonijah shall be put to death this **d**. H3117
37 For it shall be, *that* on the **d** thou goest H3117
42 a certain, on the **d** thou goest out, and H3117
3: 6 a son to sit on his throne, as *it is* this **d**. H3117
18 And it came to pass the third **d** after H3117
4:22 And Solomon's provision for one **d** was H3117
5: 7 *be* the LORD this **d**, which hath given H3117
8: 8 without: and there they are unto this **d**. H3117
16 Since the **d** that I brought forth my H3117
24 *it* with thine hand, as *it is* this **d**. H3117
28 thy servant prayeth before thee to **d**: H3117
29 this house night and **d**, *even* toward the H3117
59 the LORD our God **d** and night, that he H3119
61 keep his commandments, as at this **d**. H3117
64 The same **d** did the king hallow the H3117
66 On the eighth **d** he sent the people H3117
9:13 them the land of Cabul unto this **d**. H3117
21 a tribute of bondservice unto this **d**. H3117
10:12 almug trees, nor were seen unto this **d**. H3117
12: 7 this people this **d**, and wilt serve them, H3117
12 the third **d**, as the king had appointed, H3117
12 saying, Come to me again the third **d**. H3117
19 against the house of David unto this **d**. H3117
32 on the fifteenth **d** of the month, like H3117
33 the fifteenth **d** of the eighth month, H3117
13: 3 And he gave a sign the same **d**, saying, H3117
11 had done that **d** in Beth-el: the words H3117
14:14 Jeroboam that **d**: but what? even now. H3117
16:16 king over Israel that **d** in the camp. H3117
17:14 of oil fail, until the **d** *that* the LORD H3117
18:15 I will surely shew myself unto him to **d**. H3117
36 it be known this **d** that thou *art* God in H3117
20:13 thine hand this **d**; and thou shalt know H3117
29 in the seventh **d** the battle was joined: H3117
29 an hundred thousand footmen in one **d**. H3117
22: 5 pray thee, at the word of the LORD to **d**. H3117
25 shalt see in that **d**, when thou shalt go H3117
35 And the battle increased that **d**: and the H3117
2Ki 2: 3 from thy head to **d**? And he said, Yea, I H3117
5 from thy head to **d**? And he answered, H3117
22 So the waters were healed unto this **d**, H3117
4: 8 And it fell on a **d**, that Elisha passed to H3117
11 And it fell on a **d**, that he came thither, H3117
18 grown, it fell on a **d**, that he went out to H3117
23 thou go to him to **d**? *it is* neither new H3117
6:28 to **d**, and we will eat my son to morrow. H3117
29 her on the next **d**, Give thy son, that we H3117
31 of Shaphat shall stand on him this **d**. H3117
7: 9 We do not well: this **d** *is* a day of good H3117
9 well: this day *is* a **d** of good tidings, and H3117
8: 6 **d** that she left the land, even until now. H3117
22 hand of Judah unto this **d**. Then Libnah H3117
10:27 made it a draught house unto this **d**. H3117
14: 7 the name of it Joktheel unto this **d**. H3117
15: 5 was a leper unto the **d** of his death, and H3117
16: 6 to Elath, and dwelt there unto this **d**. H3117
17:23 of their own land to Assyria unto this **d**. H3117
34 Unto this **d** they do after the former H3117
41 did their fathers, so do they unto this **d**. H3117
19: 3 Hezekiah, This **d** *is* a day of trouble, H3117
3 This day *is* a **d** of trouble, and of H3117
20: 5 thee: on the third **d** thou shalt go up H3117
8 into the house of the LORD the third **d**? H3117
17 in store unto this **d**, shall be carried into H3117
21:15 to anger, since the **d** their fathers came H3117
15 forth out of Egypt, even unto this **d**. H3117
25: 1 month, in the tenth *d* of the month, *that*
3 And on the ninth *d* of the *fourth* month
8 And in the fifth month, on the seventh *d*
27 seven and twentieth *d* of the month, *that*
30 rate for every **d**, all the days of his life. H3117
1Ch 4:41 utterly unto this **d**, and dwelt in their H3117
43 escaped, and dwelt there unto this **d**. H3117
5:26 and to the river Gozan, unto this **d**. H3117
9:33 employed in *that* work **d** and night. H3119
11:22 and slew a lion in a pit in a snowy **d**. H3117

1Ch 12:22 For at *that* time **d** by day there came to H3117
22 For at *that* time day by **d** there came to H3117
13:11 that place is called Perez-uzza to this **d**. H3117
12 And David was afraid of God that **d**, H3117
16: 7 Then on that **d** David delivered first H3117
23 shew forth from **d** to day his salvation. H3117
23 shew forth from day to **d** his salvation. H3117
17: 5 an house since the **d** that I brought up H3117
5 up Israel unto this **d**; but have gone H3117
26:17 northward four a **d**, southward four a H3117
17 a **d**, and toward Asuppim two *and* two. H3117
28: 7 and my judgments, as at this **d**. H3117
29: 5 his service this **d** unto the LORD? H3117
21 morrow after that **d**, *even* a thousand H3117
22 before the LORD on that **d** with great H3117
2Ch 3: 2 And he began to build in the second ***d*** of
5: 9 seen without. And there it is unto this **d**. H3117
6: 5 Since the **d** that I brought forth my H3117
15 *it* with thine hand, as *it is* this **d**. H3117
20 upon this house **d** and night, upon the H3119
7: 9 And in the eighth **d** they made a H3117
10 And on the three and twentieth **d** of the H3117
8: 8 make to pay tribute until this **d**. H3117
13 Even after a certain rate every **d**, H3117
14 as the duty of every **d** required: the H3117
16 prepared unto the **d** of the foundation H3117
10:12 on the third **d**, as the king bade, saying, H3117
12 Come again to me on the third **d**. H3117
19 against the house of David unto this **d**. H3117
18: 4 pray thee, at the word of the LORD to **d**. H3117
24 shalt see on that **d** when thou shalt go H3117
34 And the battle increased that **d**: H3117
20:26 And on the fourth **d** they assembled H3117
26 The valley of Berachah, unto this **d**. H3117
21:10 of Judah unto this **d**. The same time H3117
15 out by reason of the sickness **d** by day. H3117
15 out by reason of the sickness day by **d**. H3117
24:11 Thus they did **d** by day, and gathered H3117
11 **d**, and gathered money in abundance. H3117
26:21 was a leper unto the **d** of his death, and H3117
28: 6 thousand in one **d**, *which were* all H3117
29:17 Now they began on the first ***d*** of the first
17 and on the eighth **d** of the month came H3117
17 **d** of the first month they made an end. H3117
30:15 on the fourteenth ***d*** of the second month:
21 praised the LORD **d** by day, *singing* H3117
21 the LORD day by **d**, *singing* with loud H3117
35: 1 on the fourteenth ***d*** of the first month.
16 the same **d**, to keep the passover, H3117
21 not against thee this **d**, but against the H3117
25 to this **d**, and made them an H3117
Ezr 3: 4 as the duty of every **d** required; H3117
6 From the first **d** of the seventh month H3117
6: 9 it be given them **d** by day without fail: H3118
9 it be given them day by **d** without fail: H3118
15 on the third **d** of the month Adar, H3118
19 upon the fourteenth ***d*** of the first month.
7: 9 For upon the first ***d*** of the first month
9 and on the first ***d*** of the fifth month
8:31 on the twelfth ***d*** of the first month, to
33 Now on the fourth **d** was the silver and H3117
9: 7 great trespass unto this **d**; and for our H3117
7 and to confusion of face, as *it is* this **d**. H3117
15 as *it is* this **d**: behold, we *are* before H3117
10: 9 on the twentieth ***d*** of the month; and all
13 *this* a work of one **d** or two: for we are H3117
16 down in the first **d** of the tenth month H3117
17 wives by the first **d** of the first month. H3117
Neh 1: 6 before thee now, **d** and night, for the H3119
11 thy servant this **d**, and grant him mercy H3117
4: 2 make an end in a **d**? will they revive the H3117
9 them **d** and night, because of them. H3119
22 be a guard to us, and labour on the **d**. H3117
5:11 to them, even this **d**, their lands, their H3117
6:15 twenty and fifth ***d*** of *the month* Elul, in
8: 2 upon the first **d** of the seventh month. H3117
9 all the people, This **d** *is* holy unto the H3117
10 is prepared: for *this* **d** *is* holy unto our H3117
11 for the **d** *is* holy; neither be ye grieved. H3117
13 And on the second **d** were gathered H3117
17 of Nun unto that **d** had not the children H3117
18 Also **d** by day, from the first day unto H3117
18 Also day by **d**, from the first day unto H3117
18 Also day by day, from the first **d** unto H3117
18 day unto the last **d**, he read in the book H3117
18 days; and on the eighth **d** *was* a solemn H3117
9: 1 Now in the twenty and fourth **d** of this H3117
3 fourth part of the **d**; and *another* fourth H3117
10 thou get thee a name, as *it is* this **d**. H3117

Neh 9:12 Moreover thou leddest them in the **d** by H3119
19 not from them by **d**, to lead them in the H3119
32 time of the kings of Assyria unto this **d**. H3117
36 Behold, we *are* servants this **d**, and *for* H3117
10:31 on the sabbath **d** to sell, *that* we would H3117
31 or on the holy **d**: and *that* we would H3117
11:23 be for the singers, due for every **d**. H3117
12:43 Also that **d** they offered great H3117
47 the porters, every **d** his portion: and H3117
13: 1 On that **d** they read in the book of H3117
15 on the sabbath **d**: and I testified *against* H3117
15 in the **d** wherein they sold victuals. H3117
17 that ye do, and profane the sabbath **d**? H3117
19 burden be brought in on the sabbath **d**. H3117
22 the sabbath **d**. Remember me, O my H3117
Est 1:10 On the seventh **d**, when the heart of the H3117
18 and Media say this **d** unto all the king's H3117
2:11 And Mordecai walked every **d** before H3117
3: 7 Haman from **d** to day, and from month H3117
7 from day to **d**, and from month to H3117
12 on the thirteenth **d** of the first month, H3117
13 and women, in one **d**, *even* upon the H3117
13 the thirteenth ***d*** of the twelfth month, H3117
14 they should be ready against that **d**. H3117
4:16 days, night or **d**: I also and my maidens H3117
5: 1 Now it came to pass on the third **d**, that H3117
4 Haman come this **d** unto the banquet H3117
9 Then went Haman forth that **d** joyful H3117
7: 2 on the second **d** at the banquet of wine, H3117
8: 1 On that **d** did the king Ahasuerus give H3117
9 three and twentieth ***d*** thereof; and it was
12 Upon one **d** in all the provinces of king H3117
12 the thirteenth ***d*** of the twelfth month,
13 be ready against that **d** to avenge H3117
17 a feast and a good **d**. And many of the H3117
9: 1 on the thirteenth **d** of the same, when H3117
1 execution, in the **d** that the enemies of H3117
11 On that **d** the number of those that H3117
15 on the fourteenth **d** also of the month H3117
17 On the thirteenth **d** of the month Adar; H3117
17 on the fourteenth **d** of the same rested H3117
17 made it a **d** of feasting and gladness. H3117
18 on the thirteenth ***d*** thereof, and on the
18 and on the fifteenth ***d*** of the same they
18 made it a **d** of feasting and gladness. H3117
19 the fourteenth **d** of the month Adar *a* H3117
19 of the month Adar *a* ***d*** *of* gladness and
19 and a good **d**, and of sending portions
21 the fourteenth **d** of the month Adar, H3117
21 and the fifteenth **d** of the same, yearly, H3117
22 into a good **d**: that they should make H3117
Job 1: 4 every one his **d**; and sent and called H3117
6 Now there was a **d** when the sons of H3117
13 And there was a **d** when his sons and H3117
2: 1 Again there was a **d** when the sons of H3117
3: 1 Job his mouth, and cursed his **d**. H3117
3 Let the **d** perish wherein I was born, H3117
4 Let that **d** be darkness; let not God H3117
5 it; let the blackness of the **d** terrify it. H3117
8 Let them curse it that curse the **d**, who H3117
9 neither let it see the dawning of the **d**: H7837
7: 4 to and fro unto the dawning of the **d**. H5399
14: 6 shall accomplish, as an hireling, his **d**. H3117
15:23 the **d** of darkness is ready at his hand. H3117
17:12 They change the night into **d**: the light H3117
18:20 be astonied at his **d**, as they that went H3117
19:25 shall stand at the latter ***d*** upon the earth:
20:28 shall flow away in the **d** of his wrath. H3117
21:30 That the wicked is reserved to the **d** of H3117
30 shall be brought forth to the **d** of wrath. H3117
23: 2 Even to **d** *is* my complaint bitter: my H3117
26:10 until the **d** and night come to an end. H216
38:23 against the **d** of battle and war? H3117
Ps 1: 2 his law doth he meditate **d** and night. H3119
2: 7 *art* my Son; this **d** have I begotten thee. H3117
7:11 God is angry *with the wicked* every **d**. H3117
18:18 They prevented me in the **d** of my H3117
ttl of this song in the **d** *that* the LORD H3117
19: 2 **D** unto day uttereth speech, and night H3117
2 Day unto **d** uttereth speech, and night H3117
20: 1 The LORD hear thee in the **d** of trouble; H3117
25: 5 my salvation; on thee do I wait all the **d**. H3117
32: 3 old through my roaring all the **d** long. H3117
4 For **d** and night thy hand was heavy H3119
35:28 *and* of thy praise all the **d** long. H3117
37:13 him: for he seeth that his **d** is coming. H3117
38: 6 greatly; I go mourning all the **d** long. H3117
12 and imagine deceits all the **d** long. H3117
42: 3 My tears have been my meat **d** and H3119

Ps 44: 8 In God we boast all the **d** long, and H3117
22 Yea, for thy sake are we killed all the **d** H3117
50:15 And call upon me in the **d** of trouble: I H3117
55:10 **D** and night they go about it upon the H3119
56: 5 Every **d** they wrest my words: all their H3117
59:16 and refuge in the **d** of my trouble. H3117
71: 8 praise *and with* thy honour all the **d**. H3117
15 **d**; for I know not the numbers *thereof*. H3117
24 all the **d** long: for they are confounded, H3117
73:14 For all the **d** long have I been plagued, H3117
74:16 The **d** *is* thine, the night also *is* thine: H3117
77: 2 In the **d** of my trouble I sought the H3117
78: 9 bows, turned back in the **d** of battle. H3117
42 his hand, *nor* the **d** when he delivered H3117
81: 3 time appointed, on our solemn feast **d**. H3117
84:10 For a **d** in thy courts *is* better than a H3117
86: 7 In the **d** of my trouble I will call upon H3117
88: 1 I have cried **d** *and* night before thee: H3117
89:16 In thy name shall they rejoice all the **d**: H3117
91: 5 night; *nor* for the arrow *that* flieth by **d**; H3119
92: ttl A Psalm *or* Song for the sabbath **d**. H3117
95: 7 his hand. To **d** if ye will hear his voice, H3117
8 the **d** of temptation in the wilderness: H3117
96: 2 shew forth his salvation from **d** to day. H3117
2 shew forth his salvation from day to **d**. H3117
102: 2 Hide not thy face from me in the **d** H3117
2 the **d** *when* I call answer me speedily. H3117
8 Mine enemies reproach me all the **d**; H3117
110: 3 Thy people *shall be* willing in the **d** of H3117
5 through kings in the **d** of his wrath. H3117
118:24 This *is* the **d** *which* the LORD hath H3117
119:91 They continue this **d** according to thine H3117
97 I thy law! it *is* my meditation all the **d**. H3117
164 Seven times a **d** do I praise thee H3117
121: 6 The sun shall not smite thee by **d**, nor H3119
136: 8 The sun to rule by **d**: for his mercy H3117
137: 7 of Edom in the **d** of Jerusalem; who H3117
138: 3 In the **d** when I cried thou answeredst H3117
139:12 shineth as the **d**: the darkness and the H3117
140: 7 hast covered my head in the **d** of battle. H3117
145: 2 Every **d** will I bless thee; and I will H3117
146: 4 in that very **d** his thoughts perish. H3117
Prv 4:18 more and more unto the perfect **d**. H3117
6:34 he will not spare in the **d** of vengeance. H3117
7:14 *I have* peace offerings with me; this **d** H3117
20 will come home at the **d** appointed. H3117
11: 4 Riches profit not in the **d** of wrath: but H3117
16: 4 yea, even the wicked for the **d** of evil. H3117
21:26 He coveteth greedily all the **d** long: but H3117
31 The horse *is* prepared against the **d** of H3117
22:19 known to thee this **d**, even to thee. H3117
23:17 in the fear of the LORD all the **d** long. H3117
24:10 *If* thou faint in the **d** of adversity, thy H3117
27: 1 knowest not what a **d** may bring forth. H3117
10 house in the **d** of thy calamity: *for* H3117
15 A continual dropping in a very rainy **d** H3117
Ecc 7: 1 **d** of death than the day of one's birth. H3117
1 day of death than the **d** of one's birth. H3117
14 In the **d** of prosperity be joyful, but in H3117
14 be joyful, but in the **d** of adversity H3117
8: 8 *he* power in the **d** of death: and *there* H3117
16 **d** nor night seeth sleep with his eyes:) H3117
12: 3 In the **d** when the keepers of the house H3117
Song 2:17 Until the **d** break, and the shadows flee H3117
3:11 him in the **d** of his espousals, and H3117
11 in the **d** of the gladness of his heart. H3117
4: 6 Until the **d** break, and the shadows flee H3117
8: 8 in the **d** when she shall be spoken for? H3117
Isa 2:11 LORD alone shall be exalted in that **d**. H3117
12 For the **d** of the LORD of hosts *shall be* H3117
17 LORD alone shall be exalted in that **d**. H3117
20 In that **d** a man shall cast his idols of H3117
3: 7 In that **d** shall he swear, saying, I will H3117
18 In that **d** the Lord will take away the H3117
4: 1 And in that **d** seven women shall take H3117
2 In that **d** shall the branch of the LORD H3117
5 and smoke by **d**, and the shining of a H3119
5:30 And in that **d** they shall roar against H3117
7:17 not come, from the **d** that Ephraim H3117
18 And it shall come to pass in that **d**, *that* H3117
20 In the same **d** shall the Lord shave with H3117
21 And it shall come to pass in that **d**, *that* H3117
23 And it shall come to pass in that **d**, *that* H3117
9: 4 of his oppressor, as in the **d** of Midian. H3117
14 and tail, branch and rush, in one **d**. H3117
10: 3 And what will ye do in the **d** of H3117
17 his thorns and his briers in one **d**; H3117
20 And it shall come to pass in that **d**, *that* H3117
27 And it shall come to pass in that **d**, *that* H3117

Isa 10:32 As yet shall he remain at Nob that **d**: he H3117
11:10 And in that **d** there shall be a root of H3117
11 And it shall come to pass in that **d**, *that* H3117
16 to Israel in the **d** that he came up out H3117
12: 1 And in that **d** thou shalt say, O LORD, I H3117
4 And in that **d** shall ye say, Praise the H3117
13: 6 Howl ye; for the **d** of the LORD *is* at H3117
9 Behold, the **d** of the LORD cometh, H3117
13 hosts, and in the **d** of his fierce anger. H3117
14: 3 And it shall come to pass in the **d** that H3117
17: 4 And in that **d** it shall come to pass, *that* H3117
7 At that **d** shall a man look to his H3117
9 In that **d** shall his strong cities be as a H3117
11 In the **d** shalt thou make thy plant to H3117
11 the **d** of grief and of desperate sorrow. H3117
19:16 In that **d** shall Egypt be like unto H3117
18 In that **d** shall five cities in the land of H3117
19 In that **d** shall there be an altar to the H3117
21 know the LORD in that **d**, and shall do H3117
23 In that **d** shall there be a highway out H3117
24 In that **d** shall Israel be the third with H3117
20: 6 shall say in that **d**, Behold, such *is* our H3117
22: 5 For *it is* a **d** of trouble, and of treading H3117
8 didst look in that **d** to the armour of H3117
12 And in that **d** did the Lord GOD of H3117
20 And it shall come to pass in that **d**, that H3117
25 In that **d**, saith the LORD of hosts, shall H3117
23:15 And it shall come to pass in that **d**, that H3117
24:21 And it shall come to pass in that **d**, *that* H3117
25: 9 And it shall be said in that **d**, Lo, this *is* H3117
26: 1 In that **d** shall this song be sung in the H3117
27: 1 In that **d** the LORD with his sore and H3117
2 In that **d** sing ye unto her, A vineyard H3117
3 *any* hurt it, I will keep it night and **d**. H3117
8 rough wind in the **d** of the east wind. H3117
12 And it shall come to pass in that **d**, *that* H3117
13 And it shall come to pass in that **d**, *that* H3117
28: 5 In that **d** shall the LORD of hosts be for H3117
19 it pass over, by **d** and by night: and it H3117
24 Doth the plowman plow all **d** to sow? H3117
29:18 And in that **d** shall the deaf hear the H3117
30:23 **d** shall thy cattle feed in large pastures. H3117
25 streams of waters in the **d** of the great H3117
26 of seven days, in the **d** that the LORD H3117
31: 7 For in that **d** every man shall cast away H3117
34: 8 For *it is* the **d** of the LORD'S vengeance, H3117
10 It shall not be quenched night nor **d**; the H3119
37: 3 Hezekiah, This **d** *is* a day of trouble, H3117
3 This day *is* a **d** of trouble, and of H3117
38:12 sickness: from **d** *even* to night wilt thou H3117
13 all my bones: from **d** *even* to night wilt H3117
19 thee, as I *do* this **d**: the father to the H3117
39: 6 in store until this **d**, shall be carried to H3117
43:13 Yea, before the **d** *was* I *am* he; and H3117
47: 9 a moment in one **d**, the loss of children, H3117
48: 7 even before the **d** when thou heardest H3117
49: 8 thee, and in a **d** of salvation have I H3117
51:13 continually every **d** because of the fury H3117
52: 5 continually every **d** *is* blasphemed. H3117
6 *shall know* in that **d** that I *am* he that H3117
56:12 be as this **d**, *and* much more abundant. H3117
58: 3 Behold, in the **d** of your fast ye find H3117
4 fast as *ye do this* **d**, to make your voice H3117
5 Is it such a fast that I have chosen? a **d** H3117
5 fast, and an acceptable **d** to the LORD? H3117
13 on my holy **d**; and call the sabbath H3117
60:11 shall not be shut **d** nor night; that *men* H3119
19 The sun shall be no more thy light by **d**; H3119
61: 2 of the LORD, and the **d** of vengeance of H3117
62: 6 hold their peace **d** nor night: ye that H3117
63: 4 For the **d** of vengeance *is* in mine heart, H3117
65: 2 I have spread out my hands all the **d** H3117
5 in my nose, a fire that burneth all the **d**. H3117
66: 8 bring forth in one **d**? *or* shall a nation be H3117
Jer 1:10 See, I have this **d** set thee over the H3117
18 For, behold, I have made thee this **d** a H3117
3:25 even unto this **d**, and have not obeyed H3117
4: 9 And it shall come to pass at that **d**, H3117
6: 4 unto us! for the **d** goeth away, for the H3117
7:22 them in the **d** that I brought them H3117
25 Since the **d** that your fathers came H3117
25 of Egypt unto this **d** I have even sent H3117
9: 1 that I might weep **d** and night for the H3119
11: 4 your fathers in the **d** *that* I brought H3117
5 honey, as *it is* this **d**. Then answered I, H3117
7 your fathers in the **d** *that* I brought H3117
7 Egypt, *even* unto this **d**, rising early and H3117
12: 3 prepare them for the **d** of slaughter. H3117
14:17 with tears night and **d**, and let them not H3119
Jer 15: 9 down while *it was* yet **d**: she hath been H3119
16:13 serve other gods **d** and night; where I H3119
19 and my refuge in the **d** of affliction, the H3117
17:16 desired the woeful **d**; thou knowest: that H3117
17 me: thou *art* my hope in the **d** of evil. H3117
18 upon them the **d** of evil, and destroy H3117
21 on the sabbath **d**, nor bring *it* in by the H3117
22 on the sabbath **d**, neither do ye any H3117
22 **d**, as I commanded your fathers. H3117
24 city on the sabbath **d**, but hallow the H3117
24 the sabbath **d**, to do no work therein; H3117
27 hallow the sabbath **d**, and not to bear a H3117
27 on the sabbath **d**; then will I kindle a H3117
18:17 not the face, in the **d** of their calamity. H3117
20:14 Cursed *be* the **d** wherein I was born: let H3117
14 born: let not the **d** wherein my mother H3117
25: 3 even unto this **d**, that *is* the three and H3117
18 an hissing, and a curse; as *it is* this **d**; H3117
33 shall be at that **d** from *one* end of the H3117
27:22 they be until the **d** that I visit them, H3117
30: 7 Alas! for that **d** *is* great, so that none *is* H3117
8 For it shall come to pass in that **d**, saith H3117
31: 6 For there shall be a **d**, *that* the H3117
32 fathers in the **d** *that* I took them by H3117
35 sun for a light by **d**, *and* the ordinances H3119
32:20 *even* unto this **d**, and in Israel, and H3117
20 hast made thee a name, as at this **d**; H3117
31 of my fury from the **d** that they built it H3117
31 it even unto this **d**; that I should remove H3117
33:20 covenant of the **d**, and my covenant of H3117
20 not be **d** and night in their season; H3119
25 *be* not with **d** and night, *and if* I have H3119
34:13 your fathers in the **d** that I brought H3117
35:14 for unto this **d** they drink none, but H3117
36: 2 nations, from the **d** I spake unto thee, H3117
2 the days of Josiah, even unto this **d**. H3117
6 upon the fasting **d**: and also thou shalt H3117
30 be cast out in the **d** to the heat, and in H3117
38:28 prison until the **d** that Jerusalem was H3117
39: 2 *d* of the month, the city was broken up. H3117
16 be *accomplished* in that **d** before thee. H3117
17 But I will deliver thee in that **d**, saith the H3117
40: 4 And now, behold, I loose thee this **d** H3117
41: 4 And it came to pass the second **d** after H3117
42:19 that I have admonished you this **d**. H3117
21 And *now* I have this **d** declared *it* to H3117
44: 2 Judah; and, behold, this **d** they *are* a H3117
6 are wasted *and* desolate, as at this **d**. H3117
10 They are not humbled *even* unto this **d**, H3117
22 without an inhabitant, as at this **d**. H3117
23 evil is happened unto you, as at this **d**. H3117
46:10 For this *is* the **d** of the Lord GOD of H3117
10 GOD of hosts, a **d** of vengeance, that he H3117
21 stand, because the **d** of their calamity H3117
47: 4 Because of the **d** that cometh to spoil H3117
48:41 in Moab at that **d** shall be as the heart H3117
49:22 and at that **d** shall the heart of the H3117
26 off in that **d**, saith the LORD of hosts. H3117
50:27 **d** is come, the time of their visitation. H3117
30 be cut off in that **d**, saith the LORD. H3117
31 **d** is come, the time *that* I will visit thee. H3117
51: 2 land: for in the **d** of trouble they shall H3117
52: 4 month, in the tenth *d* of the month, *that*
6 And in the fourth month, in the ninth *d*
11 put him in prison till the **d** of his death. H3117
12 Now in the fifth month, in the tenth *d* of
31 five and twentieth *d* of the month, *that*
34 of Babylon, every **d** a portion until the H3117
34 **d** of his death, all the days of his life. H3117
Lam 1:12 afflicted *me* in the **d** of his fierce anger. H3117
13 made me desolate *and* faint all the **d**. H3117
21 *it*: thou wilt bring the **d** *that* thou hast H3117
2: 1 not his footstool in the **d** of his anger! H3117
7 the LORD, as in the **d** of a solemn feast. H3117
16 this *is* the **d** that we looked for; H3117
18 run down like a river **d** and night: give H3119
21 slain *them* in the **d** of thine anger; thou H3117
22 Thou hast called as in a solemn **d** my H3117
22 so that in the **d** of the LORD'S anger H3117
3: 3 turneth his hand *against me* all the **d**. H3117
14 all my people; *and* their song all the **d**. H3117
57 Thou drewest near in the **d** *that* I called H3117
62 and their device against me all the **d**. H3117
Ezk 1: 1 *month*, in the fifth *d* of the month, as I
2 In the fifth *d* of the month, which *was*
28 in the cloud in the **d** of rain, so *was* the H3117
2: 3 against me, *even* unto this very **d**. H3117
4: 6 I have appointed thee each **d** for a year. H3117
10 a **d**: from time to time shalt thou eat it. H3117
Ezk 7: 7 time is come, the **d** of trouble *is* near, H3117
10 Behold the **d**, behold, it is come: the H3117
12 The time is come, the **d** draweth near: H3117
19 them in the **d** of the wrath of the LORD: H3117
8: 1 *month*, in the fifth *d* of the month, *as* I
12: 3 and remove by **d** in their sight; and H3119
4 forth thy stuff by **d** in their sight, as H3119
7 brought forth my stuff by **d**, as stuff for H3119
13: 5 in the battle in the **d** of the LORD. H3117
16: 4 And *as for* thy nativity, in the **d** thou H3117
5 person, in the **d** that thou wast born. H3117
56 by thy mouth in the **d** of thy pride, H3117
20: 1 *month*, the tenth *d* of the month, *that*
5 Lord GOD; In the **d** when I chose Israel, H3117
6 In the **d** *that* I lifted up mine hand unto H3117
29 thereof is called Bamah unto this **d**. H3117
31 even unto this **d**: and shall I be inquired H3117
21:25 prince of Israel, whose **d** is come, when H3117
29 of the wicked, whose **d** is come, when H3117
22:24 rained upon in the **d** of indignation. H3117
23:38 **d**, and have profaned my sabbaths. H3117
39 came the same **d** into my sanctuary to H3117
24: 1 in the tenth *d* of the month, the word
2 the name of the **d**, *even* of this same H3117
2 *even* of this same **d**: the king of Babylon H3117
2 himself against Jerusalem this same **d**. H3117
25 *shall it* not *be* in the **d** when I take from H3117
26 *That* he that escapeth in that **d** shall H3117
27 In that **d** shall thy mouth be opened to H3117
26: 1 year, in the first *d* of the month, *that* the
18 Now shall the isles tremble in the **d** of H3117
27:27 midst of the seas in the **d** of thy ruin. H3117
28:13 in thee in the **d** that thou wast created. H3117
15 in thy ways from the **d** that thou wast H3117
29: 1 in the twelfth *d* of the month, the word
17 *month*, in the first *d* of the month, the
21 In that **d** will I cause the horn of the H3117
30: 2 Lord GOD; Howl ye, Woe worth the **d**! H3117
3 For the **d** *is* near, even the day of the H3117
3 For the day *is* near, even the **d** of the H3117
3 **d**; it shall be the time of the heathen. H3117
9 In that **d** shall messengers go forth H3117
9 as in the **d** of Egypt: for, lo, it cometh. H3117
18 At Tehaphnehes also the **d** shall be H3117
20 in the seventh *d* of the month, *that* the
31: 1 *month*, in the first *d* of the month, *that*
15 Thus saith the Lord GOD; In the **d** H3117
32: 1 month, in the first *d* of the month, *that*
10 man for his own life, in the **d** of thy fall. H3117
17 in the fifteenth *d* of the month, *that* the
33:12 not deliver him in the **d** of his H3117
12 not fall thereby in the **d** that he turneth H3117
12 *righteousness* in the **d** that he sinneth. H3117
21 *month*, in the fifth *d* of the month, *that*
34:12 out his flock in the **d** that he is among H3117
12 scattered in the cloudy and dark **d**. H3117
36:33 Thus saith the Lord GOD; In the **d** that H3117
38:14 Lord GOD; In that **d** when my people of H3117
19 Surely in that **d** there shall be a great H3117
39: 8 this *is* the **d** whereof I have spoken. H3117
11 And it shall come to pass in that **d**, *that* H3117
13 a renown the **d** that I shall be glorified, H3117
22 their God from that **d** and forward. H3117
40: 1 year, in the tenth *d* of the month, in the
1 in the selfsame **d** the hand of the LORD H3117
43:18 of the altar in the **d** when they shall H3117
22 And on the second **d** thou shalt offer a H3117
25 Seven days shalt thou prepare every **d** H3117
27 upon the eighth **d**, and *so* forward, the H3117
44:27 And in the **d** that he goeth into the H3117
45:18 *month*, in the first *d* of the month, thou
20 And so thou shalt do the seventh *d* of the
21 In the first *month*, in the fourteenth **d** H3117
22 And upon that **d** shall the prince H3117
25 In the seventh *month*, in the fifteenth **d** H3117
46: 1 **d** of the new moon it shall be opened. H3117
4 in the sabbath **d** *shall be* six lambs H3117
6 And in the **d** of the new moon *it shall* H3117
12 on the sabbath **d**: then he shall go forth; H3117
48:35 *that* **d** *shall be*, The LORD *is* there. H3117
Dan 6:10 three times a **d**, and prayed, and gave H3118
13 but maketh his petition three times a **d**. H3118
9: 7 of faces, as at this **d**; to the men of H3117
15 renown, as at this **d**; we have sinned, we H3117
10: 4 And in the four and twentieth **d** of the H3117
12 for from the first **d** that thou didst set H3117
Hos 1: 5 And it shall come to pass at that **d**, that H3117
11 land: for great *shall be* the **d** of Jezreel. H3117
2: 3 set her as in the **d** that she was born, H3117

Hos 2:15 and as in the **d** when she came up out H3117
16 And it shall be at that **d**, saith the H3117
18 And in that **d** will I make a covenant H3117
21 And it shall come to pass in that **d**, I H3117
4: 5 Therefore shalt thou fall in the **d**, and H3117
5: 9 Ephraim shall be desolate in the **d** of H3117
6: 2 us: in the third **d** he will raise us up, H3117
7: 5 In the **d** of our king the princes have H3117
9: 5 What will ye do in the solemn **d**, and in H3117
5 and in the **d** of the feast of the LORD? H3117
10:14 Beth-arbel in the **d** of battle: the H3117
Joel 1:15 Alas for the **d**! for the day of the LORD H3117
15 Alas for the day! for the **d** of the LORD H3117
2: 1 tremble: for the **d** of the LORD cometh, H3117
2 A **d** of darkness and of gloominess, a H3117
2 and of gloominess, a **d** of clouds and of H3117
11 his word: for the **d** of the LORD *is* great H3117
31 and the terrible **d** of the LORD come. H3117
3:14 decision: for the **d** of the LORD *is* near H3117
18 And it shall come to pass in that **d**, *that* H3117
Am 1:14 with shouting in the **d** of battle, with a H3117
14 a tempest in the **d** of the whirlwind: H3117
2:16 away naked in that **d**, saith the LORD. H3117
3:14 That in the **d** that I shall visit the H3117
5: 8 and maketh the **d** dark with night: that H3117
18 Woe unto you that desire the **d** of the H3117
18 end *is* it for you? the **d** of the LORD *is* H3117
20 *Shall* not the **d** of the LORD *be* H3117
6: 3 Ye that put far away the evil **d**, and H3117
8: 3 howlings in that **d**, saith the Lord GOD: H3117
9 And it shall come to pass in that **d**, H3117
9 I will darken the earth in the clear **d**: H3117
10 *son*, and the end thereof as a bitter **d**. H3117
13 In that **d** shall the fair virgins and H3117
9:11 In that **d** will I raise up the tabernacle H3117
Oba 8 Shall I not in that **d**, saith the LORD, H3117
11 In the **d** that thou stoodest on the other H3117
11 other side, in the **d** that the strangers H3117
12 looked on the **d** of thy brother in the H3117
12 of thy brother in the **d** that he became a H3117
12 of Judah in the **d** of their destruction; H3117
12 spoken proudly in the **d** of distress. H3117
13 of my people in the **d** of their calamity; H3117
13 affliction in the **d** of their calamity, nor H3117
13 substance in the **d** of their calamity; H3117
14 his that did remain in the **d** of distress. H3117
15 For the **d** of the LORD *is* near upon all H3117
Jna 4: 7 rose the next **d**, and it smote the gourd H4283
Mic 2: 4 In that **d** shall *one* take up a parable H3117
3: 6 and the **d** shall be dark over them. H3117
4: 6 In that **d**, saith the LORD, will I H3117
5:10 And it shall come to pass in that **d**, H3117
7: 4 a thorn hedge: the **d** of thy watchmen H3117
11 *In* the **d** that thy walls are to be built, *in* H3117
11 that **d** shall the decree be far removed. H3117
12 *In* that **d** *also* he shall come even to H3117
Nah 1: 7 strong hold in the **d** of trouble; and he H3117
2: 3 torches in the **d** of his preparation, H3117
3:17 hedges in the cold **d**, *but* when the sun H3117
Hab 3:16 I might rest in the **d** of trouble: when he H3117
Zep 1: 7 Lord GOD: for the **d** of the LORD *is* at H3117
8 And it shall come to pass in the **d** of the H3117
9 In the same **d** also will I punish all H3117
10 And it shall come to pass in that **d**, H3117
14 The great **d** of the LORD *is* near, *it is* H3117
14 *even* the voice of the **d** of the LORD: the H3117
15 That **d** *is* a day of wrath, a day of H3117
15 That day *is* a **d** of wrath, a day of H3117
15 That day *is* a day of wrath, a **d** of H3117
15 and distress, a **d** of wasteness and H3117
15 and desolation, a **d** of darkness and H3117
15 a **d** of clouds and thick darkness, H3117
16 A **d** of the trumpet and alarm against H3117
18 them in the **d** of the LORD'S wrath; H3117
2: 2 forth, *before* the **d** pass as the chaff, H3117
2 **d** of the LORD'S anger come upon you. H3117
3 be hid in the **d** of the LORD'S anger. H3117
4 noon **d**, and Ekron shall be rooted up. H6672
3: 8 LORD, until the **d** that I rise up to the H3117
11 In that **d** shalt thou not be ashamed for H3117
16 In that **d** it shall be said to Jerusalem, H3117
Hag 1: 1 month, in the first **d** of the month, H3117
15 In the four and twentieth **d** of the sixth H3117
2: 1 one and twentieth *d* of the month, came
10 In the four and twentieth *d* of the ninth
15 consider from this **d** and upward, from H3117
18 Consider now from this **d** and upward, H3117
18 and twentieth **d** of the ninth *month,* H3117
18 *even* from the **d** that the foundation H3117

Hag 2:19 forth: from this **d** will I bless *you.* H3117
20 and twentieth *d* of the month, saying,
23 In that **d**, saith the LORD of hosts, will I H3117
Zec 1: 7 Upon the four and twentieth **d** of the H3117
2:11 to the LORD in that **d**, and shall be my H3117
3: 9 the iniquity of that land in one **d**. H3117
10 In that **d**, saith the LORD of hosts, shall H3117
4:10 For who hath despised the **d** of small H3117
6:10 thou the same **d**, and go into the house H3117
7: 1 *d* of the ninth month, *even* in Chisleu;
8: 9 which *were* in the **d** *that* the foundation H3117
9:12 of hope: even to **d** do I declare *that* I H3117
16 save them in that **d** as the flock of his H3117
11:11 And it was broken in that **d**: and so the H3117
12: 3 And in that **d** will I make Jerusalem a H3117
4 In that **d**, saith the LORD, I will smite H3117
6 In that **d** will I make the governors of H3117
8 In that **d** shall the LORD defend the H3117
8 them at that **d** shall be as David; and H3117
9 And it shall come to pass in that **d**, *that* H3117
11 In that **d** shall there be a great H3117
13: 1 In that **d** there shall be a fountain H3117
2 And it shall come to pass in that **d**, H3117
4 And it shall come to pass in that **d**, *that* H3117
14: 1 Behold, the **d** of the LORD cometh, and H3117
3 as when he fought in the **d** of battle. H3117
4 And his feet shall stand in that **d** upon H3117
6 And it shall come to pass in that **d**, *that* H3117
7 But it shall be one **d** which shall be H3117
7 to the LORD, not **d**, nor night: but it H3117
8 And it shall be in that **d**, *that* living H3117
9 the earth: in that **d** shall there be one H3117
13 And it shall come to pass in that **d**, *that* H3117
20 In that **d** shall there be upon the bells H3117
21 and in that **d** there shall be no more H3117
Mal 3: 2 But who may abide the **d** of his H3117
17 of hosts, in that **d** when I make up my H3117
4: 1 For, behold, the **d** cometh, that shall H3117
1 be stubble: and the **d** that cometh shall H3117
3 of your feet in the **d** that I shall do *this,* H3117
5 the great and dreadful **d** of the LORD: H3117
Mt 6:11 Give us this **d** our daily bread. G4594
30 the field, which to **d** is, and to morrow G4594
34 Sufficient unto the **d** *is* the evil thereof. G2250
7:22 Many will say to me in that **d**, Lord, G2250
10:15 in the **d** of judgment, than for that city. G2250
11:22 at the **d** of judgment, than for you. G2250
23 it would have remained until this **d**. G4594
24 in the **d** of judgment, than for thee. G2250
12: 1 At that time Jesus went on the sabbath **d**
2 is not lawful to do upon the sabbath **d**.
8 Son of man is Lord even of the sabbath **d**.
11 pit on the sabbath **d**, will he not lay hold
36 account thereof in the **d** of judgment. G2250
13: 1 The same **d** went Jesus out of the G2250
16: 3 *be* foul weather to **d**: for the sky is red G4594
21 killed, and be raised again the third **d**. G2250
17:23 And they shall kill him, and the third **d** G2250
20: 2 a **d**, he sent them into his vineyard. G2250
6 them, Why stand ye here all the **d** idle? G2250
12 borne the burden and heat of the **d**. G2250
19 *him:* and the third **d** he shall rise again. G2250
21:28 said, Son, go work to **d** in my vineyard. G4594
22:23 The same **d** came to him the G2250
46 **d** forth ask him any more *questions.* G2250
24:20 in the winter, neither on the sabbath **d**:
36 But of that **d** and hour knoweth no G2250
38 the **d** that Noe entered into the ark, G2250
50 shall come in a **d** when he looketh not G2250
25:13 ye know neither the **d** nor the hour G2250
26: 5 But they said, Not on the feast *d*, lest
17 Now the first *d* of the *feast of*
29 of the vine, until that **d** when I drink it G2250
27: 8 called, The field of blood, unto this **d**. G4594
19 this **d** in a dream because of him. G4594
62 Now the next **d**, that followed the day of G1887
62 Now the next day, that followed the **d** of
64 until the third **d**, lest his disciples come G2250
28: 1 toward the first *d* of the week, came
15 reported among the Jews until this **d**. G4594
Mk 1:21 on the sabbath **d** he entered into the
35 a great while before **d**, he went out, and G1773
2:23 fields on the sabbath **d**; and his disciples
24 the sabbath **d** that which is not lawful?
3: 2 sabbath **d**; that they might accuse him.
4:27 And should sleep, and rise night and **d**, G2250
35 And the same **d**, when the even was G2250
5: 5 And always, night and **d**, he was in the G2250
6: 2 And when the sabbath **d** was come, he

Mk 6:11 in the **d** of judgment, than for that city. G2250
21 And when a convenient **d** was come, G2250
35 And when the **d** was now far spent, his G5610
9:31 that he is killed, he shall rise the third **d**. G2250
10:34 him: and the third **d** he shall rise again. G2250
13:32 But of that **d** and *that* hour knoweth no G2250
14: 2 But they said, Not on the feast *d*, lest
12 And the first **d** of unleavened bread, G2250
25 the vine, until that **d** that I drink it new G2250
30 thee, That this **d**, *even* in this night, G4594
15:42 that is, the **d** before the sabbath,
16: 2 And very early in the morning the first *d*
9 was risen early the first *d* of the week, he
Lk 1:20 to speak, until the **d** that these things G2250
59 pass, that on the eighth **d** they came to G2250
80 till the **d** of his shewing unto Israel. G2250
2:11 For unto you is born this **d** in the city of G4594
37 with fastings and prayers night and **d**. G2250
4:16 the sabbath **d**, and stood up for to read. G2250
21 And he began to say unto them, This **d** G4594
42 And when it was **d**, he departed and G2250
5:17 And it came to pass on a certain **d**, as G2250
26 We have seen strange things to **d**. G4594
6: 7 on the sabbath **d**; that they might find
13 And when it was **d**, he called *unto him* G2250
23 Rejoice ye in that **d**, and leap for joy: G2250
7:11 And it came to pass the **d** after, that he G2250
8:22 Now it came to pass on a certain **d**, that G2250
9:12 And when the **d** began to wear away, G2250
22 and be slain, and be raised the third **d**. G2250
37 And it came to pass, that on the next **d**, G2250
10:12 in that **d** for Sodom, than for that city. G2250
11: 3 Give us **d** by day our daily G2596+G2250
3 Give us day by **d** our daily G2596+G2250
12:28 grass, which is to **d** in the field, and to G4594
46 will come in a **d** when he looketh not G2250
13:14 on the sabbath **d**, and said unto the
14 be healed, and not on the sabbath **d**. G2250
16 loosed from this bond on the sabbath **d**? G2250
31 The same **d** there came certain of the G2250
32 and I do cures to **d** and to morrow, and G4594
32 and the third *d* I shall be perfected.
33 Nevertheless I must walk to **d**, and to G4594
33 to morrow, and the *d* following: for it
14: 1 on the sabbath **d**, that they watched him.
3 Is it lawful to heal on the sabbath **d**?
5 pull him out on the sabbath **d**? G2250
16:19 linen, and fared sumptuously every **d**: G2596
17: 4 seven times in a **d**, and seven times in G2250
4 seven times in a **d** turn again to thee, G2250
24 so shall also the Son of man be in his **d**. G2250
27 until the **d** that Noe entered into G2250
29 But the same **d** that Lot went out of G2250
30 Even thus shall it be in the **d** when the G2250
31 In that **d**, he which shall be upon the G2250
18: 7 elect, which cry **d** and night unto him, G2250
33 and the third **d** he shall rise again. G2250
19: 5 for to **d** I must abide at thy house. G4594
9 And Jesus said unto him, This **d** is G4594
42 at least in this thy **d**, the things *which* G2250
21:34 so that **d** come upon you unawares. G2250
37 And in the **d** time he was teaching in G2250
22: 7 Then came the **d** of unleavened bread, G2250
34 shall not crow this **d**, before that thou G4594
66 And as soon as it was **d**, the elders of G2250
23:12 And the same **d** Pilate and Herod were G2250
43 To **d** shalt thou be with me in paradise. G4594
54 And that **d** was the preparation, and G2250
56 **d** according to the commandment.
24: 1 Now upon the first *d* of the week, very
7 be crucified, and the third **d** rise again. G2250
13 went that same **d** to a village called G2250
21 and beside all this, to **d** is the third day G4594
21 third **d** since these things were done. G2250
29 evening, and the **d** is far spent. And he G2250
46 and to rise from the dead the third **d**: G2250
Jn 1:29 The next **d** John seeth Jesus coming G1887
35 Again the next **d** after John stood, and G1887
39 that **d**: for it was about the tenth hour. G2250
43 The **d** following Jesus would go forth G1887
2: 1 And the third **d** there was a marriage G2250
23 in the feast *d*, many believed in his
5: 9 and on the same **d** was the sabbath. G2250
10 It is the sabbath **d**: it is not lawful for
16 had done these things on the sabbath **d**.
6:22 The **d** following, when the people G1887
39 should raise it up again at the last **d**. G2250
40 life: and I will raise him up at the last **d**. G2250
44 and I will raise him up at the last **d**. G2250

Jn 6:54 life; and I will raise him up at the last **d**. G2250
7:22 ye on the sabbath **d** circumcise a man.
23 If a man on the sabbath **d** receive
23 man every whit whole on the sabbath **d**?
37 In the last **d**, that great *day* of the feast, G2250
37 In the last day, that great ***d*** of the feast,
8:56 see my **d**: and he saw *it*, and was glad. G2250
9: 4 sent me, while it is **d**: the night cometh, G2250
14 And it was the sabbath **d** when Jesus
16 not the sabbath **d**. Others said, How can
11: 9 hours in the **d**? If any man walk in G2250
9 man walk in the **d**, he stumbleth not, G2250
24 again in the resurrection at the last **d**. G2250
53 Then from that **d** forth they took G2250
12: 7 the **d** of my burying hath she kept this. G2250
12 On the next **d** much people that were G1887
48 the same shall judge him in the last **d**. G2250
14:20 At that **d** ye shall know that I *am* in my G2250
16:23 And in that **d** ye shall ask me nothing. G2250
26 At that **d** ye shall ask in my name: and G2250
19:31 on the sabbath **d**, (for that sabbath day
31 (for that sabbath **d** was an high day,)
31 day was an high **d**,) besought Pilate that G2250
42 ***d***; for the sepulchre was nigh at hand.
20: 1 The first ***d*** of the week cometh Mary
19 Then the same **d** at evening, being the G2250
19 being the first ***d*** of the week, when the
Act 1: 2 Until the **d** in which he was taken up, G2250
22 unto that same **d** that he was taken up G2250
2: 1 And when the **d** of Pentecost was fully G2250
15 seeing it is *but* the third hour of the **d**. G2250
20 great and notable **d** of the Lord come: G2250
29 and his sepulchre is with us unto this **d**. G2250
41 and the same **d** there were added *unto* G2250
4: 3 unto the next **d**: for it was now eventide. G839
9 If we this **d** be examined of the good G4594
7: 8 him the eighth **d**; and Isaac *begat* G2250
26 And the next **d** he shewed himself unto G2250
9:24 the gates **d** and night to kill him. G2250
10: 3 the ninth hour of the **d** an angel of God G2250
40 Him God raised up the third **d**, and G2250
12:18 Now as soon as it was **d**, there was no G2250
21 And upon a set **d** Herod, arrayed in G2250
13:14 on the sabbath **d**, and sat down. G2250
27 read every sabbath **d**, they have fulfilled
33 art my Son, this **d** have I begotten thee. G4594
44 And the next sabbath **d** came almost the
14:20 **d** he departed with Barnabas to Derbe. G1887
15:21 read in the synagogues every sabbath **d**.
16:11 and the next ***d*** to Neapolis;
35 And when it was **d**, the magistrates sent G2250
17:31 Because he hath appointed a **d**, in the G2250
20: 7 And upon the first ***d*** of the week, when
11 while, even till break of **d**, so he departed. G827
15 and came the next ***d*** over against Chios;
15 and the next ***d*** we arrived at Samos,
15 and the next ***d*** we came to Miletus.
16 to be at Jerusalem the **d** of Pentecost. G2250
18 from the first **d** that I came into Asia, G2250
26 Wherefore I take you to record this **d**, G2250
31 warn every one night and **d** with tears. G2250
21: 1 unto Coos, and the ***d*** following unto
7 brethren, and abode with them one **d**. G2250
8 And the next ***d*** we that were of Paul's
18 And the ***d*** following Paul went in with us
26 Then Paul took the men, and the next **d** G2250
22: 3 zealous toward God, as ye all are this **d**. G4594
23: 1 good conscience before God until this **d**. G2250
12 And when it was **d**, certain of the Jews G2250
24:21 I am called in question by you this **d**. G4594
25: 6 and the next **d** sitting on the judgment G1887
26: 2 for myself this **d** before thee touching G4594
7 serving *God* **d** and night, hope to come. G2250
22 continue unto this **d**, witnessing both to G2250
29 that hear me this **d**, were both almost, G4594
27: 3 And the next ***d*** we touched at Sidon. And
18 the next ***d*** they lightened the ship;
19 And the third ***d*** we cast out with our own
29 out of the stern, and wished for the **d**. G2250
33 And while the **d** was coming on, Paul G2250
33 meat, saying, This **d** is the fourteenth G4594
33 is the fourteenth **d** that ye have tarried G2250
39 And when it was **d**, they knew not the G2250
28:13 and after one **d** the south wind blew, G2250
13 and we came the next **d** to Puteoli: G1206
23 And when they had appointed him a **d**, G2250
Ro 2: 5 wrath against the **d** of wrath and G2250
16 In the **d** when God shall judge the G2250
8:36 we are killed all the **d** long; we are G2250
10:21 But to Israel he saith, All **d** long I have G2250
11: 8 that they should not hear;) unto this **d**. G2250
13:12 The night is far spent, the **d** is at hand: G2250
13 Let us walk honestly, as in the **d**; not in G2250
14: 5 One man esteemeth one **d** above G2250
5 esteemeth every **d** *alike*. Let every man G2250
6 He that regardeth the **d**, regardeth *it* G2250
6 regardeth not the **d**, to the Lord he doth G2250
1Co 1: 8 in the **d** of our Lord Jesus Christ. G2250
3:13 manifest: for the **d** shall declare it, G2250
4:13 the offscouring of all things unto this **d**. G737
5: 5 be saved in the **d** of the Lord Jesus. G2250
10: 8 in one **d** three and twenty thousand. G2250
15: 4 the third **d** according to the scriptures: G2250
16: 2 Upon the first ***d*** of the week let every one
2Co 1:14 also *are* ours in the **d** of the Lord Jesus. G2250
3:14 for until this **d** remaineth the same G4594
15 But even unto this **d**, when Moses is G4594
4:16 the inward *man* is renewed **d** by day. G2250
16 the inward *man* is renewed day by **d**. G2250
6: 2 and in the **d** of salvation have I G2250
2 behold, now *is* the **d** of salvation.) G2250
11:25 a night and a **d** I have been in the deep; G3574
Eph 4:30 ye are sealed unto the **d** of redemption. G2250
6:13 the evil **d**, and having done all, to stand. G2250
Php 1: 5 in the gospel from the first **d** until now; G2250
6 perform *it* until the **d** of Jesus Christ: G2250
10 and without offence till the **d** of Christ; G2250
2:16 I may rejoice in the **d** of Christ, that I G2250
3: 5 Circumcised the eighth **d**, of the stock of G3637
Col 1: 6 in you, since the **d** ye heard *of it*, and G2250
9 For this cause we also, since the **d** we G2250
1Th 2: 9 night and **d**, because we would not G2250
3:10 Night and **d** praying exceedingly that G2250
5: 2 know perfectly that the **d** of the Lord so G2250
4 that **d** should overtake you as a thief. G2250
5 the children of the **d**: we are not of the G2250
8 But let us, who are of the **d**, be sober, G2250
2Th 1:10 among you was believed) in that **d**. G2250
2: 2 us, as that the **d** of Christ is at hand. G2250
3 means: for *that* ***d*** *shall not come*, except
3: 8 travail night and **d**, that we might not G2250
1Ti 5: 5 supplications and prayers night and **d**. G2250
2Ti 1: 3 of thee in my prayers night and **d**; G2250
12 committed unto him against that **d**. G2250
18 of the Lord in that **d**: and in how many G2250
4: 8 give me at that **d**: and not to me only, G2250
Heb 1: 5 art my Son, this **d** have I begotten thee? G4594
3: 7 saith, To **d** if ye will hear his voice, G4594
8 the **d** of temptation in the wilderness: G2250
13 while it is called To **d**; lest any of you be G4594
15 While it is said, To **d** if ye will hear his G4594
4: 4 of the seventh ***d*** on this wise, And God
4 rest the seventh **d** from all his works. G2250
7 Again, he limiteth a certain **d**, saying in G2250
7 in David, To **d**, after so long a time; G4594
7 as it is said, To **d** if ye will hear his G4594
8 afterward have spoken of another **d**. G2250
5: 5 art my Son, to **d** have I begotten thee. G4594
8: 9 fathers in the **d** when I took them by G2250
10:25 the more, as ye see the **d** approaching. G2250
13: 8 same yesterday, and to **d**, and for ever. G4594
Jas 4:13 Go to now, ye that say, To **d** or to G4594
5: 5 your hearts, as in a **d** of slaughter. G2250
1Pt 2:12 glorify God in the **d** of visitation. G2250
2Pt 1:19 place, until the **d** dawn, and the day G2250
19 and the **d** star arise in your hearts: G5459
2: 8 **d** to day with *their* unlawful deeds;) G2250
8 day to **d** with *their* unlawful deeds;) G2250
9 unto the **d** of judgment to be punished: G2250
13 to riot in the **d** time. Spots *they are* G2250
3: 7 unto fire against the **d** of judgment and G2250
8 thing, that one **d** *is* with the Lord as a G2250
8 years, and a thousand years as one **d**. G2250
10 But the **d** of the Lord will come as a G2250
12 the coming of the **d** of God, wherein the G2250
1Jn 4:17 boldness in the **d** of judgment: because G2250
Jude 6 unto the judgment of the great **d**. G2250
Rev 1:10 I was in the Spirit on the Lord's **d**, and G2250
4: 8 and they rest not **d** and night, saying, G2250
6:17 For the great **d** of his wrath is come; G2250
7:15 God, and serve him **d** and night in his G2250
8:12 darkened, and the **d** shone not for a G2250
9:15 for an hour, and a **d**, and a month, and G2250
12:10 them before our God **d** and night. G2250
14:11 and they have no rest **d** nor night, who G2250
16:14 battle of that great **d** of God Almighty. G2250
18: 8 come in one **d**, death, and mourning, G2250
20:10 **d** and night for ever and ever. G2250
21:25 by **d**: for there shall be no night there. G2250

DAYS

Gen 1:14 and for seasons, and for **d**, and years: H3117
3:14 dust shalt thou eat all the **d** of thy life: H3117
17 shalt thou eat *of* it all the **d** of thy life; H3117
5: 4 And the **d** of Adam after he had H3117
5 And all the **d** that Adam lived were H3117
8 And all the **d** of Seth were nine H3117
11 And all the **d** of Enos were nine H3117
14 And all the **d** of Cainan were nine H3117
17 And all the **d** of Mahalaleel were eight H3117
20 And all the **d** of Jared were nine H3117
23 And all the **d** of Enoch were three H3117
27 And all the **d** of Methuselah were nine H3117
31 And all the **d** of Lamech were seven H3117
6: 3 *is* flesh: yet his **d** shall be an hundred H3117
4 the earth in those **d**; and also after that, H3117
7: 4 For yet seven **d**, and I will cause it to H3117
4 the earth forty **d** and forty nights; and H3117
10 And it came to pass after seven **d**, that H3117
12 upon the earth forty **d** and forty nights. H3117
17 And the flood was forty **d** upon the H3117
24 upon the earth an hundred and fifty **d**. H3117
8: 3 and fifty **d** the waters were abated. H3117
6 at the end of forty **d**, that Noah opened H3117
10 And he stayed yet other seven **d**; and H3117
12 And he stayed yet other seven **d**; and H3117
9:29 And all the **d** of Noah were nine H3117
10:25 *was* Peleg; for in his **d** was the earth H3117
11:32 And the **d** of Terah were two hundred H3117
14: 1 And it came to pass in the **d** of H3117
17:12 And he that is eight **d** old shall be H3117
21: 4 **d** old, as God had commanded him. H3117
34 in the Philistines' land many **d**. H3117
24:55 with us *a few* **d**, at the least ten; after H3117
25: 7 And these *are* the **d** of the years of H3117
24 And when her **d** to be delivered were H3117
26: 1 that was in the **d** of Abraham. And H3117
15 had digged in the **d** of Abraham his H3117
18 had digged in the **d** of Abraham his H3117
27:41 in his heart, The **d** of mourning for my H3117
44 And tarry with him a few **d**, until thy H3117
29:20 *but* a few **d**, for the love he had to her. H3117
21 my wife, for my **d** are fulfilled, that I H3117
30:14 And Reuben went in the **d** of wheat H3117
35:28 And the **d** of Isaac were an hundred H3117
29 old and full of **d**: and his sons Esau and H3117
37:34 loins, and mourned for his son many **d**. H3117
40:12 of it: The three branches *are* three **d**: H3117
13 Yet within three **d** shall Pharaoh lift up H3117
18 thereof: The three baskets *are* three **d**: H3117
19 Yet within three **d** shall Pharaoh lift up H3117
42:17 put them all together into ward three **d**. H3117
47: 9 And Jacob said unto Pharaoh, The **d** of H3117
9 and evil have the **d** of the years of my H3117
9 attained unto the **d** of the years of the H3117
9 my fathers in the **d** of their pilgrimage. H3117
49: 1 *that* which shall befall you in the last **d**. H3117
50: 3 And forty **d** were fulfilled for him; for H3117
3 so are fulfilled the **d** of those which are H3117
3 mourned for him threescore and ten **d**. H3117
4 And when the **d** of his mourning were H3117
10 a mourning for his father seven **d**. H3117
Ex 2:11 And it came to pass in those **d**, when H3117
7:25 And seven **d** were fulfilled, after that H3117
10:22 in all the land of Egypt three **d**: H3117
23 his place for three **d**: but all the children H3117
12:15 Seven **d** shall ye eat unleavened bread; H3117
19 Seven **d** shall there be no leaven found H3117
13: 6 Seven **d** thou shalt eat unleavened H3117
7 be eaten seven **d**; and there shall no H3117
15:22 they went three **d** in the wilderness, H3117
16:26 Six **d** ye shall gather it; but on the H3117
29 the bread of two **d**; abide ye every man H3117
20: 9 Six **d** shalt thou labour, and do all thy H3117
11 For *in* six **d** the LORD made heaven H3117
12 mother: that thy **d** may be long upon H3117
22:30 thy sheep: seven **d** it shall be with his H3117
23:12 Six **d** thou shalt do thy work, and on H3117
15 bread seven **d**, as I commanded thee, H3117
26 land: the number of thy **d** I will fulfil. H3117
24:16 covered it six **d**: and the seventh day H3117
18 in the mount forty **d** and forty nights. H3117
29:30 put them on seven **d**, when he cometh H3117
35 seven **d** shalt thou consecrate them. H3117
37 Seven **d** thou shalt make an atonement H3117
31:15 Six **d** may work be done; but in the H3117
17 for ever: for *in* six **d** the LORD made H3117

Ex 34:18 shalt thou keep. Seven **d** thou shalt eat H3117
21 Six **d** thou shalt work, but on the H3117
28 the LORD forty **d** and forty nights; he H3117
35: 2 Six **d** shall work be done, but on the H3117
Lev 8:33 *in* seven **d**, until the days of your H3117
33 days, until the **d** of your consecration H3117
33 for seven **d** shall he consecrate you. H3117
35 and night seven **d**, and keep the charge H3117
12: 2 be unclean seven **d**; according to the H3117
2 according to the **d** of the separation for H3117
4 three and thirty **d**; she shall touch no H3117
4 until the **d** of her purifying be fulfilled. H3117
5 of her purifying threescore and six **d**. H3117
6 And when the **d** of her purifying are H3117
13: 4 up *him that hath* the plague seven **d**: H3117
5 priest shall shut him up seven **d** more: H3117
21 the priest shall shut him up seven **d**: H3117
26 the priest shall shut him up seven **d**: H3117
31 *that hath* the plague of the scall seven **d**: H3117
33 *him that hath* the scall seven **d** more: H3117
46 All the **d** wherein the plague *shall be* in H3117
50 shut up *it that hath* the plague seven **d**: H3117
54 *is*, and he shall shut it up seven **d** more: H3117
14: 8 tarry abroad out of his tent seven **d**. H3117
38 house, and shut up the house seven **d**: H3117
15:13 to himself seven **d** for his cleansing, H3117
19 be put apart seven **d**: and whosoever H3117
24 be unclean seven **d**; and all the bed H3117
25 of her blood many **d** out of the time of H3117
25 separation; all the **d** of the issue of her H3117
25 shall be as the **d** of her separation: she H3117
26 Every bed whereon she lieth all the **d** of H3117
28 **d**, and after that she shall be clean. H3117
22:27 it shall be seven **d** under the dam; and H3117
23: 3 Six **d** shall work be done: but the H3117
6 seven **d** ye must eat unleavened bread. H3117
8 the LORD seven **d**: in the seventh day *is* H3117
16 ye number fifty **d**; and ye shall offer a H3117
34 tabernacles *for* seven **d** unto the LORD. H3117
36 Seven **d** ye shall offer an offering made H3117
39 the LORD seven **d**: on the first day *shall* H3117
40 before the LORD your God seven **d**. H3117
41 the LORD seven **d** in the year. *It shall* H3117
42 Ye shall dwell in booths seven **d**; all that H3117
Nu 6: 4 All the **d** of his separation shall he eat H3117
5 All the **d** of the vow of his separation H3117
5 his head: until the **d** be fulfilled, in the H3117
6 All the **d** that he separateth *himself* H3117
8 All the **d** of his separation he *is* holy H3117
12 the LORD the **d** of his separation, and H3117
12 offering: but the **d** that were before H3117
13 when the **d** of his separation are H3117
9:19 tabernacle many **d**, then the children of H3117
20 cloud was a few **d** upon the tabernacle; H3117
22 Or *whether it were* two **d**, or a month, H3117
10:10 in your solemn **d**, and in the beginnings H4150
11:19 Ye shall not eat one day, nor two **d**, nor H3117
19 **d**, neither ten days, nor twenty days; H3117
19 days, neither ten **d**, nor twenty days; H3117
19 days, neither ten days, nor twenty **d**; H3117
12:14 be ashamed seven **d**? let her be shut out H3117
14 the camp seven **d**, and after that let her H3117
15 from the camp seven **d**: and the people H3117
13:25 from searching of the land after forty **d**. H3117
14:34 After the number of the **d** in which ye H3117
34 land, *even* forty **d**, each day for a year, H3117
19:11 of any man shall be unclean seven **d**. H3117
14 *is* in the tent, shall be unclean seven **d**. H3117
16 or a grave, shall be unclean seven **d**. H3117
20:29 thirty **d**, *even* all the house of Israel. H3117
24:14 shall do to thy people in the latter **d**. H3117
28:17 **d** shall unleavened bread be eaten. H3117
24 the seven **d**, the meat of the sacrifice H3117
29:12 keep a feast unto the LORD seven **d**: H3117
31:19 the camp seven **d**: whosoever hath H3117
Dt 1:46 So ye abode in Kadesh many **d**, H3117
46 unto the **d** that ye abode *there*. H3117
2: 1 and we compassed mount Seir many **d**. H3117
4: 9 thy heart all the **d** of thy life: but teach H3117
10 to fear me all the **d** that they shall live H3117
26 not prolong *your* **d** upon it, but shall H3117
30 *even* in the latter **d**, if thou turn to the H3117
32 For ask now of the **d** that are past, H3117
40 prolong *thy* **d** upon the earth, which H3117
5:13 Six **d** thou shalt labour, and do all thy H3117
16 thee; that thy **d** may be prolonged, H3117
33 **d** in the land which ye shall possess. H3117
6: 2 son's son, all the **d** of thy life; and that H3117
2 life; and that thy **d** may be prolonged. H3117

Dt 9: 9 in the mount forty **d** and forty nights, I H3117
11 at the end of forty **d** and forty nights, H3117
18 as at the first, forty **d** and forty nights: I H3117
25 the LORD forty **d** and forty nights, as H3117
10:10 first time, forty **d** and forty nights; and H3117
11: 9 And that ye may prolong *your* **d** in the H3117
21 That your **d** may be multiplied, and the H3117
21 and the **d** of your children, in H3117
21 as the **d** of heaven upon the earth. H3117
12: 1 it, all the **d** that ye live upon the earth. H3117
16: 3 bread with it; seven **d** shalt thou eat H3117
3 of the land of Egypt all the **d** of thy life. H3117
4 all thy coast seven **d**; neither shall there H3117
8 Six **d** thou shalt eat unleavened bread: H3117
13 of tabernacles seven **d**, after that thou H3117
15 Seven **d** shalt thou keep a solemn feast H3117
17: 9 shall be in those **d**, and inquire; and H3117
19 therein all the **d** of his life: that he may H3117
20 may prolong *his* **d** in his kingdom, he, H3117
19:17 the judges, which shall be in those **d**; H3117
22: 7 and *that* thou mayest prolong *thy* **d**. H3117
19 wife; he may not put her away all his **d**. H3117
29 her, he may not put her away all his **d**. H3117
23: 6 nor their prosperity all thy **d** for ever. H3117
25:15 have: that thy **d** may be lengthened H3117
26: 3 shall be in those **d**, and say unto him, I H3117
30:18 shall not prolong *your* **d** upon the land, H3117
20 the length of thy **d**: that thou mayest H3117
31:14 Behold, thy **d** approach that thou H3117
29 you in the latter **d**; because ye will do H3117
32: 7 Remember the **d** of old, consider the H3117
47 ye shall prolong *your* **d** in the land, H3117
33:25 and as thy **d**, *so shall* thy strength *be*. H3117
34: 8 of Moab thirty **d**: so the days of weeping H3117
8 thirty days: so the **d** of weeping *and* H3117
Jos 1: 5 before thee all the **d** of thy life: as I was H3117
11 for within three **d** ye shall pass over H3117
2:16 there three **d**, until the pursuers be H3117
22 abode there three **d**, until the pursuers H3117
3: 2 And it came to pass after three **d**, that H3117
4:14 they feared Moses, all the **d** of his life. H3117
6: 3 the city once. Thus shalt thou do six **d**. H3117
14 into the camp: so they did six **d**. H3117
9:16 at the end of three **d** after they had H3117
20: 6 shall be in those **d**: then shall the slayer H3117
22: 3 these many **d** unto this day, but have H3117
24:31 And Israel served the LORD all the **d** of H3117
31 Joshua, and all the **d** of the elders that H3117
Jdg 2: 7 the LORD all the **d** of Joshua, and all H3117
7 and all the **d** of the elders that outlived H3117
18 enemies all the **d** of the judge: for it H3117
5: 6 In the **d** of Shamgar the son of Anath, H3117
6 of Anath, in the **d** of Jael, the highways H3117
8:28 forty years in the **d** of Gideon. H3117
11:40 Jephthah the Gileadite four **d** in a year. H3117
14:12 within the seven **d** of the feast, and find H3117
14 not in three **d** expound the riddle. H3117
17 And she wept before him the seven **d**, H3117
15:20 And he judged Israel in the **d** of the H3117
17: 6 In those **d** *there was* no king in Israel, H3117
18: 1 In those **d** *there was* no king in Israel: H3117
1 and in those **d** the tribe of the Danites H3117
19: 1 And it came to pass in those **d**, when H3117
4 with him three **d**: so they did eat and H3117
20:27 covenant of God *was* there in those **d**, H3117
28 before it in those **d**,) saying, Shall I yet H3117
21:25 In those **d** *there was* no king in Israel: H3117
Ru 1: 1 Now it came to pass in the **d** when the H3117
1Sa 1:11 the LORD all the **d** of his life, and there H3117
2:31 Behold, the **d** come, that I will cut off H3117
3: 1 in those **d**; *there was* no open vision. H3117
7:13 the Philistines all the **d** of Samuel. H3117
15 And Samuel judged Israel all the **d** of H3117
9:20 were lost three **d** ago, set not thy mind H3117
10: 8 offerings: seven **d** shalt thou tarry, till H3117
13: 8 And he tarried seven **d**, according to the H3117
11 not within the **d** appointed, and *that* H3117
14:52 Philistines all the **d** of Saul: and when H3117
17:12 men *for* an old man in the **d** of Saul. H3117
16 evening, and presented himself forty **d**. H3117
18:26 son in law: and the **d** were not expired. H3117
20:19 And *when* thou hast stayed three **d**, H8027
21: 5 us about these three **d**, since I came out, H8543
25:10 servants now a **d** that break away H3117
28 hath not been found in thee *all* thy **d**. H3117
38 And it came to pass about ten **d** *after*, H3117
28: 1 And it came to pass in those **d**, that the H3117
29: 3 with me these **d**, or these years, and H3117
30:12 *any* water, three **d** and three nights. H3117

1Sa 30:13 me, because three **d** agone I fell sick. H3117
31:13 a tree at Jabesh, and fasted seven **d**. H3117
2Sa 1: 1 and David had abode two **d** in Ziklag; H3117
7:12 And when thy **d** be fulfilled, and thou H3117
16:23 in those **d**, *was* as if a man had H3117
20: 4 three **d**, and be thou here present. H3117
21: 1 Then there was a famine in the **d** of H3117
9 put to death in the **d** of harvest, in the H3117
9 first *d*, in the beginning of barley harvest.
24: 8 at the end of nine months and twenty **d**. H3117
1Ki 2: 1 Now the **d** of David drew nigh that he H3117
11 And the **d** that David reigned over H3117
38 And Shimei dwelt in Jerusalem many **d**. H3117
3: 2 the name of the LORD, until those **d**. H3117
13 among the kings like unto thee all thy **d**. H3117
14 did walk, then I will lengthen thy **d**. H3117
4:21 and served Solomon all the **d** of his life. H3117
25 to Beersheba, all the **d** of Solomon. H3117
8:40 That they may fear thee all the **d** that H3117
65 **d** and seven days, *even* fourteen days. H3117
65 days and seven **d**, *even* fourteen days. H3117
65 days and seven days, *even* fourteen **d**. H3117
10:21 accounted of in the **d** of Solomon. H3117
11:12 Notwithstanding in thy **d** I will not do H3117
25 to Israel all the **d** of Solomon, beside H3117
34 him prince all the **d** of his life for David H3117
12: 5 yet *for* three **d**, then come again to H3117
14:20 And the **d** which Jeroboam reigned H3117
30 Rehoboam and Jeroboam all *their* **d**. H3117
15: 5 him all the **d** of his life, save only H3117
6 and Jeroboam all the **d** of his life. H3117
14 was perfect with the LORD all his **d**. H3117
16 and Baasha king of Israel all their **d**. H3117
32 and Baasha king of Israel all their **d**. H3117
16:15 Zimri reign seven **d** in Tirzah. And the H3117
34 In his **d** did Hiel the Beth-elite build H3117
17:15 and he, and her house, did eat *many* **d**. H3117
18: 1 And it came to pass *after* many **d**, that H3117
19: 8 of that meat forty **d** and forty nights H3117
20:29 the other seven **d**. And *so* it was, that H3117
21:29 the evil in his **d**: *but* in his son's days H3117
29 **d** will I bring the evil upon his house. H3117
22:46 remained in the **d** of his father Asa, he H3117
2Ki 2:17 they sought three **d**, but found him not. H3117
8:20 In his **d** Edom revolted from under the H3117
10:32 In those **d** the LORD began to cut Israel H3117
12: 2 of the LORD all his **d** wherein Jehoiada H3117
13: 3 the son of Hazael, all *their* **d**. H3117
22 oppressed Israel all the **d** of Jehoahaz. H3117
15:18 not all his **d** from the sins of Jeroboam H3117
29 In the **d** of Pekah king of Israel came H3117
37 In those **d** the LORD began to send H3117
18: 4 for unto those **d** the children of Israel H3117
20: 1 In those **d** was Hezekiah sick unto H3117
6 And I will add unto thy **d** fifteen years; H3117
17 Behold, the **d** come, that all that *is* in H3117
19 not *good*, if peace and truth be in my **d**? H3117
23:22 passover from the **d** of the judges that H3117
22 nor in all the **d** of the kings of Israel, H3117
29 In his **d** Pharaoh-nechoh king of Egypt H3117
24: 1 In his **d** Nebuchadnezzar king of H3117
25:29 before him all the **d** of his life. H3117
30 rate for every day, all the **d** of his life. H3117
1Ch 1:19 because in his **d** the earth was divided: H3117
4:41 name came in the **d** of Hezekiah king H3117
5:10 And in the **d** of Saul they made war H3117
17 genealogies in the **d** of Jotham king of H3117
17 and in the **d** of Jeroboam king of Israel. H3117
7: 2 *was* in the **d** of David two and twenty H3117
22 mourned many **d**, and his brethren H3117
9:25 seven **d** from time to time with them. H3117
10:12 the oak in Jabesh, and fasted seven **d**. H3117
12:39 And there they were with David three **d**, H3117
13: 3 we inquired not at it in the **d** of Saul. H3117
17:11 And it shall come to pass, when thy **d** H3117
21:12 *thee*; or else three **d** the sword of the H3117
22: 9 and quietness unto Israel in his **d**. H3117
23: 1 So when David was old and full of **d**, he H3117
29:15 our fathers: our **d** on the earth *are* as H3117
28 And he died in a good old age, full of **d**, H3117
2Ch 7: 8 the feast seven **d**, and all Israel with H3117
9 altar seven **d**, and the feast seven days. H3117
9 altar seven days, and the feast seven **d**. H3117
9:20 thing accounted of in the **d** of Solomon. H3117
10: 5 after three **d**. And the people departed. H3117
13:20 again in the **d** of Abijah: and the LORD H3117
14: 1 In his **d** the land was quiet ten years. H3117
15:17 the heart of Asa was perfect all his **d**. H3117
20:25 they were three **d** in gathering of the H3117

2Ch 21: 8 In his **d** the Edomites revolted from H3117
24: 2 LORD all the **d** of Jehoiada the priest. H3117
14 LORD continually all the **d** of Jehoiada. H3117
15 old, and was full of **d** when he died; an H3117
26: 5 And he sought God in the **d** of H3117
29:17 of the LORD in eight **d**; and in the H3117
30:21 bread seven **d** with great gladness: H3117
22 the feast seven **d**, offering peace H3117
23 keep other seven **d**: and they kept *other* H3117
23 they kept *other* seven **d** with gladness. H3117
32:24 In those **d** Hezekiah was sick to the H3117
26 not upon them in the **d** of Hezekiah. H3117
34:33 God. *And* all his **d** they departed not H3117
35:17 the feast of unleavened bread seven **d**. H3117
18 kept in Israel from the **d** of Samuel the H3117
36: 9 months and ten **d** in Jerusalem: and he H3117
Ezr 4: 2 him since the **d** of Esar-haddon king H3117
5 their purpose, all the **d** of Cyrus king of H3117
7 And in the **d** of Artaxerxes wrote H3117
6:22 bread seven **d** with joy: for the LORD H3117
8:15 we in tents three **d**: and I viewed the H3117
32 to Jerusalem, and abode there three **d**. H3117
9: 7 Since the **d** of our fathers *have* we *been* H3117
10: 8 come within three **d**, according to the H3117
9 within three **d**. It *was* the ninth month, H3117
Neh 1: 4 and mourned *certain* **d**, and fasted, and H3117
2:11 to Jerusalem, and was there three **d**. H3117
5:18 and once in ten **d** store of all sorts of H3117
6:15 of *the month* Elul, in fifty and two **d**. H3117
17 Moreover in those **d** the nobles of H3117
8:17 for since the **d** of Jeshua the son of H3117
18 the feast seven **d**; and on the eighth day H3117
12: 7 and of their brethren in the **d** of Jeshua. H3117
12 And in the **d** of Joiakim were priests, H3117
22 The Levites in the **d** of Eliashib, Joiada, H3117
23 the **d** of Johanan the son of Eliashib. H3117
26 These *were* in the **d** of Joiakim the son H3117
26 and in the **d** of Nehemiah the governor, H3117
46 For in the **d** of David and Asaph of old H3117
47 And all Israel in the **d** of Zerubbabel, H3117
47 and in the **d** of Nehemiah, gave H3117
13: 6 certain **d** obtained I leave of the king: H3117
15 In those **d** saw I in Judah *some* H3117
23 In those **d** also saw I Jews *that* had H3117
Est 1: 1 Now it came to pass in the **d** of H3117
2 *That* in those **d**, when the king H3117
4 **d**, *even* an hundred and fourscore days. H3117
4 days, *even* an hundred and fourscore **d**. H3117
5 And when these **d** were expired, the H3117
5 and small, seven **d**, in the court of the H3117
2:12 (for so were the **d** of their purifications H3117
21 In those **d**, while Mordecai sat in the H3117
4:11 to come in unto the king these thirty **d**. H3117
16 nor drink three **d**, night or day: I also H3117
9:22 As the **d** wherein the Jews rested from H3117
22 make them **d** of feasting and joy, H3117
26 Wherefore they called these **d** Purim H3117
27 keep these two **d** according to their H3117
28 And *that* these **d** *should be* H3117
28 and *that* these **d** of Purim should not H3117
31 To confirm these **d** of Purim in their H3117
Job 1: 5 And it was so, when the **d** of *their* H3117
2:13 the ground seven **d** and seven nights, H3117
3: 6 be joined unto the **d** of the year, let it H3117
7: 1 his **d** also like the days of an hireling? H3117
1 his days also like the **d** of an hireling? H3117
6 My **d** are swifter than a weaver's H3117
16 let me alone; for my **d** *are* vanity. H3117
8: 9 our **d** upon earth *are* a shadow:) H3117
9:25 Now my **d** are swifter than a post: they H3117
10: 5 *Are* thy **d** as the days of man? *are* thy H3117
5 *Are* thy days as the **d** of man? *are* thy H3117
5 days of man? *are* thy years as man's **d**, H3117
20 *Are* not my **d** few? cease *then, and* let H3117
12:12 and in length of **d** understanding. H3117
14: 1 a woman *is* of few **d**, and full of trouble. H3117
5 Seeing his **d** *are* determined, the H3117
14 he live *again*? all the **d** of my appointed H3117
15:20 with pain all *his* **d**, and the number of H3117
17: 1 My breath is corrupt, my **d** are extinct, H3117
11 My **d** are past, my purposes are broken H3117
21:13 They spend their **d** in wealth, and in a H3117
24: 1 do they that know him not see his **d**? H3117
29: 2 as *in* the **d** *when* God preserved me; H3117
4 As I was in the **d** of my youth, when the H3117
18 and I shall multiply *my* **d** as the sand. H3117
30:16 out upon me; the **d** of affliction have H3117
27 My bowels boiled, and rested not: the **d** H3117
32: 7 I said, **D** should speak, and multitude H3117
Job 33:25 he shall return to the **d** of his youth: H3117
36:11 shall spend their **d** in prosperity, and H3117
38:12 the morning since thy **d**; *and* caused the H3117
21 *because* the number of thy **d** *is* great? H3117
42:17 So Job died, *being* old and full of **d**. H3117
Ps 21: 4 him, *even* length of **d** for ever and ever. H3117
23: 6 follow me all the **d** of my life: and I will H3117
27: 4 the LORD all the **d** of my life, to behold H3117
34:12 loveth *many* **d**, that he may see good? H3117
37:18 The LORD knoweth the **d** of the H3117
19 the **d** of famine they shall be satisfied. H3117
39: 4 measure of my **d**, what it *is; that* I may H3117
5 Behold, thou hast made my **d** *as* an H3117
44: 1 thou didst in their **d**, in the times of old. H3117
49: 5 Wherefore should I fear in the **d** of evil, H3117
55:23 out half their **d**; but I will trust in thee. H3117
72: 7 In his **d** shall the righteous flourish; H3117
77: 5 I have considered the **d** of old, the H3117
78:33 Therefore their **d** did he consume in H3117
89:29 ever, and his throne as the **d** of heaven. H3117
45 The **d** of his youth hast thou shortened: H3117
90: 9 For all our **d** are passed away in thy H3117
10 The **d** of our years *are* threescore years H3117
12 So teach *us* to number our **d**, that we H3117
14 we may rejoice and be glad all our **d**. H3117
15 Make us glad according to the **d** H3117
94:13 him rest from the **d** of adversity, until H3117
102: 3 For my **d** are consumed like smoke, H3117
11 My **d** *are* like a shadow that declineth; H3117
23 strength in the way; he shortened my **d**. H3117
24 away in the midst of my **d**: thy years *are* H3117
103:15 *As for* man, his **d** *are* as grass: as a H3117
109: 8 Let his **d** be few; *and* let another take H3117
119:84 How many *are* the **d** of thy servant? H3117
128: 5 good of Jerusalem all the **d** of thy life. H3117
143: 5 I remember the **d** of old; I meditate on H3117
144: 4 Man is like to vanity: his **d** *are* as a H3117
Prv 3: 2 For length of **d**, and long life, and H3117
16 Length of **d** *is* in her right hand; *and* in H3117
9:11 For by me thy **d** shall be multiplied, H3117
10:27 The fear of the LORD prolongeth **d**: but H3117
15:15 All the **d** of the afflicted *are* evil: but he H3117
28:16 hateth covetousness shall prolong *his* **d**. H3117
31:12 good and not evil all the **d** of her life. H3117
Ecc 2: 3 under the heaven all the **d** of their life. H3117
16 now *is* in the **d** to come shall all be H3117
23 For all his **d** *are* sorrows, and his H3117
5:17 All his **d** also he eateth in darkness, H3117
18 the sun all the **d** of his life, which God H3117
20 For he shall not much remember the **d** H3117
6: 3 years, so that the **d** of his years be H3117
12 man in *this* life, all the **d** of his vain life H3117
7:10 that the former **d** were better than H3117
15 All *things* have I seen in the **d** of my H3117
8:12 times, and his *d* be prolonged, yet surely
13 shall he prolong *his* **d**, *which are* as a H3117
15 of his labour the **d** of his life, which H3117
9: 9 thou lovest all the **d** of the life of thy H3117
9 the sun, all the **d** of thy vanity: for that H3117
11: 1 for thou shalt find it after many **d**. H3117
8 remember the **d** of darkness; for they H3117
9 cheer thee in the **d** of thy youth, and H3117
12: 1 Remember now thy Creator in the **d** of H3117
1 while the evil **d** come not, nor the years H3117
Isa 1: 1 Jerusalem in the **d** of Uzziah, Jotham, H3117
2: 2 And it shall come to pass in the last **d**, H3117
7: 1 And it came to pass in the **d** of Ahaz H3117
17 thy father's house, **d** that have not H3117
13:22 and her **d** shall not be prolonged. H3117
23: 7 *is* of ancient **d**? her own feet shall carry H3117
15 according to the **d** of one king: after the H3117
24:22 and after many **d** shall they be visited. H3117
30:26 the light of seven **d**, in the day that the H3117
32:10 Many **d** and years shall ye be troubled, H3117
38: 1 In those **d** was Hezekiah sick unto H3117
5 I will add unto thy **d** fifteen years. H3117
10 I said in the cutting off of my **d**, I shall H3117
20 **d** of our life in the house of the LORD. H3117
39: 6 Behold, the **d** come, that all that *is* in H3117
8 there shall be peace and truth in my **d**. H3117
51: 9 as in the ancient **d**, in the generations of H3117
53:10 shall prolong *his* **d**, and the pleasure of H3117
60:20 the **d** of thy mourning shall be ended. H3117
63: 9 them, and carried them all the **d** of old. H3117
11 Then he remembered the **d** of old, H3117
65:20 an infant of **d**, nor an old man that H3117
20 hath not filled his **d**: for the child shall H3117
22 eat: for as the **d** of a tree *are* the days H3117
22 of a tree *are* the **d** of my people, and H3117
Jer 1: 2 LORD came in the **d** of Josiah the son H3117
3 It came also in the **d** of Jehoiakim the H3117
2:32 have forgotten me **d** without number. H3117
3: 6 The LORD said also unto me in the **d** of H3117
16 in the land, in those **d**, saith the LORD, H3117
18 In those **d** the house of Judah shall H3117
5:18 Nevertheless in those **d**, saith the H3117
6:11 the aged with *him that is* full of **d**. H3117
7:32 Therefore, behold, the **d** come, saith H3117
9:25 Behold, the **d** come, saith the LORD, H3117
13: 6 And it came to pass after many **d**, that H3117
16: 9 eyes, and in your **d**, the voice of mirth, H3117
14 Therefore, behold, the **d** come, saith H3117
17:11 of his **d**, and at his end shall be a fool. H3117
19: 6 Therefore, behold, the **d** come, saith H3117
20:18 my **d** should be consumed with shame? H3117
22:30 not prosper in his **d**: for no man of his H3117
23: 5 Behold, the **d** come, saith the LORD, H3117
6 In his **d** Judah shall be saved, and H3117
7 Therefore, behold, the **d** come, saith H3117
20 latter **d** ye shall consider it perfectly. H3117
25:34 of the flock: for the **d** of your slaughter H3117
26:18 prophesied in the **d** of Hezekiah king of H3117
30: 3 For, lo, the **d** come, saith the LORD, H3117
24 in the latter **d** ye shall consider it. H3117
31:27 Behold, the **d** come, saith the LORD, H3117
29 In those **d** they shall say no more, The H3117
31 Behold, the **d** come, saith the LORD, H3117
33 Israel; After those **d**, saith the LORD, I H3117
38 Behold, the **d** come, saith the LORD, H3117
32:14 vessel, that they may continue many **d**. H3117
33:14 Behold, the **d** come, saith the LORD, H3117
15 In those **d**, and at that time, will I cause H3117
16 In those **d** shall Judah be saved, and H3117
35: 1 the LORD in the **d** of Jehoiakim the son H3117
7 *any*: but all your **d** ye shall dwell in H3117
7 **d** in the land where ye *be* strangers. H3117
8 no wine all our **d**, we, our wives, our H3117
36: 2 the **d** of Josiah, even unto this day. H3117
37:16 Jeremiah had remained there many **d**; H3117
42: 7 And it came to pass after ten **d**, that the H3117
46:26 as in the **d** of old, saith the LORD. H3117
48:12 Therefore, behold, the **d** come, saith H3117
47 of Moab in the latter **d**, saith the LORD. H3117
49: 2 Therefore, behold, the **d** come, saith H3117
39 But it shall come to pass in the latter **d**, H3117
50: 4 In those **d**, and in that time, saith the H3117
20 In those **d**, and in that time, saith the H3117
51:47 Therefore, behold, the **d** come, that I H3117
52 Wherefore, behold, the **d** come, saith H3117
52:33 bread before him all the **d** of his life. H3117
34 the day of his death, all the **d** of his life. H3117
Lam 1: 7 Jerusalem remembered in the **d** of her H3117
7 that she had in the **d** of old, when her H3117
2:17 in the **d** of old: he hath thrown H3117
4:18 our **d** are fulfilled; for our end is come. H3117
5:21 shall be turned; renew our **d** as of old. H3117
Ezk 3:15 there astonished among them seven **d**. H3117
16 the end of seven **d**, that the word of the H3117
4: 4 the number of the **d** that thou shalt lie H3117
5 the number of the **d**, three hundred and H3117
5 and ninety **d**: so shalt thou bear the H3117
6 of Judah forty **d**: I have appointed thee H3117
8 till thou hast ended the **d** of thy siege. H3117
9 the number of the **d** that thou shalt lie H3117
9 and ninety **d** shalt thou eat thereof. H3117
5: 2 of the city, when the **d** of the siege are H3117
12:22 of Israel, saying, The **d** are prolonged, H3117
23 unto them, The **d** are at hand, and the H3117
25 for in your **d**, O rebellious house, H3117
27 he seeth *is* for many **d** *to come*, and he H3117
16:22 remembered the **d** of thy youth, when H3117
43 not remembered the **d** of thy youth, but H3117
60 with thee in the **d** of thy youth, and I H3117
22: 4 hast caused thy **d** to draw near, and art H3117
14 be strong, in the **d** that I shall deal with H3117
23:19 to remembrance the **d** of her youth, H3117
38: 8 After many **d** thou shalt be visited: in H3117
16 be in the latter **d**, and I will bring thee H3117
17 in those **d** *many* years that I would H3117
43:25 Seven **d** shalt thou prepare every day a H3117
26 Seven **d** shall they purge the altar and H3117
27 And when these **d** are expired, it shall H3117
44:26 they shall reckon unto him seven **d**. H3117
45:21 **d**; unleavened bread shall be eaten. H3117
23 And seven **d** of the feast he shall H3117
23 daily the seven **d**; and a kid of the goats H3117
25 feast of the seven **d**, according to the sin H3117
46: 1 the six working **d**; but on the sabbath H3117

Dan 1:12 I beseech thee, ten **d**; and let them give H3117
14 in this matter, and proved them ten **d**. H3117
15 And at the end of ten **d** their H3117
18 Now at the end of the **d** that the king H3117
2:28 be in the latter **d**. Thy dream, and the H3118
44 And in the **d** of these kings shall the H3118
4:34 And at the end of the **d** I H3118
5:11 gods; and in the **d** of thy father light H3118
6: 7 or man for thirty **d**, save of thee, O king, H3118
12 or man within thirty **d**, save of thee, O H3118
7: 9 and the Ancient of **d** did sit, whose H3118
13 to the Ancient of **d**, and they brought H3118
22 Until the Ancient of **d** came, and H3118
8:14 three hundred **d**; then shall the H6153+H1242
26 up the vision; for it *shall be* for many **d**. H3117
27 was sick *certain* **d**; afterward I rose up, H3117
10: 2 In those **d** I Daniel was mourning three H3117
13 one and twenty **d**: but, lo, Michael, one H3117
14 **d**: for yet the vision *is* for *many* days. H3117
14 days: for yet the vision *is* for *many* **d**. H3117
11:20 but within few **d** he shall be destroyed, H3117
33 by captivity, and by spoil, *many* **d**. H3117
12:11 a thousand two hundred and ninety **d**. H3117
12 three hundred and five and thirty **d**. H3117
13 and stand in thy lot at the end of the **d**. H3117
Hos 1: 1 of Beeri, in the **d** of Uzziah, Jotham, H3117
1 of Judah, and in the **d** of Jeroboam the H3117
2:11 to cease, her feast **d**, her new moons, H2282
13 And I will visit upon her the **d** of H3117
15 there, as in the **d** of her youth, and as H3117
3: 3 for me many **d**; thou shalt not play H3117
4 shall abide many **d** without a king, and H3117
5 LORD and his goodness in the latter **d**. H3117
6: 2 After two **d** will he revive us: in the H3117
9: 7 The **d** of visitation are come, the days H3117
7 The days of visitation are come, the **d** H3117
9 as in the **d** of Gibeah: *therefore* H3117
10: 9 O Israel, thou hast sinned from the **d** of H3117
12: 9 as in the **d** of the solemn feast. H3117
Joel 1: 2 **d**, or even in the days of your fathers? H3117
2 days, or even in the **d** of your fathers? H3117
2:29 in those **d** will I pour out my spirit. H3117
3: 1 For, behold, in those **d**, and in that H3117
Am 1: 1 Israel in the **d** of Uzziah king of Judah, H3117
1 of Judah, and in the **d** of Jeroboam the H3117
4: 2 that, lo, the **d** shall come upon you, H3117
5:21 I hate, I despise your feast **d**, and I will H2282
8:11 Behold, the **d** come, saith the Lord H3117
9:11 and I will build it as in the **d** of old: H3117
13 Behold, the **d** come, saith the LORD, H3117
Jna 1:17 of the fish three **d** and three nights. H3117
3: 4 **d**, and Nineveh shall be overthrown. H3117
Mic 1: 1 Morasthite in the **d** of Jotham, Ahaz, H3117
4: 1 But in the last **d** it shall come to pass, H3117
7:14 Bashan and Gilead, as in the **d** of old. H3117
15 According to the **d** of thy coming out of H3117
20 unto our fathers from the **d** of old. H3117
Hab 1: 5 work a work in your **d**, *which* ye will not H3117
Zep 1: 1 of Hizkiah, in the **d** of Josiah the son of H3117
Hag 2:16 Since those *d* were, when *one* came to an
Zec 8: 6 this people in these **d**, should it also be H3117
9 that hear in these **d** these words by the H3117
10 For before these **d** there was no hire for H3117
11 the former **d**, saith the LORD of hosts. H3117
15 So again have I thought in these **d** to do H3117
23 of hosts; In those **d** *it shall come to* H3117
14: 5 earthquake in the **d** of Uzziah king of H3117
Mal 3: 4 in the **d** of old, and as in former years. H3117
7 Even from the **d** of your fathers ye are H3117
Mt 2: 1 of Judaea in the **d** of Herod the king, *G2250*
3: 1 In those **d** came John the Baptist, *G2250*
4: 2 And when he had fasted forty **d** and *G2250*
9:15 them? but the **d** will come, when the *G2250*
11:12 And from the **d** of John the Baptist *G2250*
12: 5 that on the sabbath **d** the priests in the
10 sabbath **d**? that they might accuse him.
12 it is lawful to do well on the sabbath **d**.
40 For as Jonas was three **d** and three *G2250*
40 of man be three **d** and three nights in *G2250*
15:32 me now three **d**, and have nothing to *G2250*
17: 1 And after six **d** Jesus taketh Peter, *G2250*
23:30 And say, If we had been in the **d** of our *G2250*
24:19 and to them that give suck in those **d**! *G2250*
22 And except those **d** should be *G2250*
22 elect's sake those **d** shall be shortened. *G2250*
29 of those **d** shall the sun be darkened, *G2250*
37 But as the **d** of Noe *were*, so shall also *G2250*
38 For as in the **d** that were before the *G2250*
26: 2 Ye know that after two **d** is *the feast of* *G2250*

Mt 26:61 temple of God, and to build it in three **d**. *G2250*
27:40 and buildest *it* in three **d**, save thyself. If *G2250*
63 yet alive, After three **d** I will rise again. *G2250*
Mk 1: 9 And it came to pass in those **d**, that *G2250*
13 wilderness forty **d**, tempted of Satan; *G2250*
2: 1 after *some* **d**; and it was noised that *G2250*
20 But the **d** will come, when the *G2250*
20 and then shall they fast in those **d**. *G2250*
26 of God in the **d** of Abiathar the high *G1909*
3: 4 on the sabbath **d**, or to do evil? to save
8: 1 In those **d** the multitude being very *G2250*
2 me three **d**, and have nothing to eat: *G2250*
31 be killed, and after three **d** rise again. *G2250*
9: 2 And after six **d** Jesus taketh *with him* *G2250*
13:17 and to them that give suck in those **d**! *G2250*
19 For *in* those **d** shall be affliction, such *G2250*
20 shortened those **d**, no flesh should be *G2250*
20 hath chosen, he hath shortened the **d**. *G2250*
24 But in those **d**, after that tribulation, the *G2250*
14: 1 After two **d** was *the feast of* the *G2250*
58 and within three **d** I will build another *G2250*
15:29 the temple, and buildest *it* in three **d**, *G2250*
Lk 1: 5 There was in the **d** of Herod, the king of *G2250*
23 as soon as the **d** of his ministration *G2250*
24 And after those **d** his wife Elisabeth *G2250*
25 with me in the **d** wherein he looked on *G2250*
39 And Mary arose in those **d**, and went *G2250*
75 before him, all the **d** of our life. *G2250*
2: 1 And it came to pass in those **d**, that *G2250*
6 were there, the **d** were accomplished *G2250*
21 And when eight **d** were accomplished *G2250*
22 And when the **d** of her purification *G2250*
43 And when they had fulfilled the **d**, as *G2250*
46 And it came to pass, that after three **d** *G2250*
4: 2 Being forty **d** tempted of the devil. And *G2250*
2 And in those **d** he did eat nothing: *G2250*
25 in Israel in the **d** of Elias, when the *G2250*
31 and taught them on the sabbath **d**.
5:35 But the **d** will come, when the *G2250*
35 and then shall they fast in those **d**. *G2250*
6: 2 is not lawful to do on the sabbath **d**?
9 on the sabbath **d** to do good, or to do
12 And it came to pass in those **d**, that he *G2250*
9:28 And it came to pass about an eight **d** *G2250*
36 no man in those **d** any of those things *G2250*
13:14 There are six **d** in which men ought *G2250*
15:13 And not many **d** after the younger son *G2250*
17:22 And he said unto the disciples, The **d** *G2250*
22 to see one of the **d** of the Son of man, *G2250*
26 And as it was in the **d** of Noe, so shall it *G2250*
26 it be also in the **d** of the Son of man. *G2250*
28 Likewise also as it was in the **d** of Lot; *G2250*
19:43 For the **d** shall come upon thee, that *G2250*
20: 1 *that* on one of those **d**, as he taught the *G2250*
21: 6 ye behold, the **d** will come, in the which *G2250*
22 For these be the **d** of vengeance, that all *G2250*
23 give suck, in those **d**! for there shall be *G2250*
23:29 For, behold, the **d** are coming, in the *G2250*
24:18 which are come to pass there in these **d**? *G2250*
Jn 2:12 and they continued there not many **d**. *G2250*
19 temple, and in three **d** I will raise it up. *G2250*
20 and wilt thou rear it up in three **d**? *G2250*
4:40 with them: and he abode there two **d**. *G2250*
43 Now after two **d** he departed thence, *G2250*
11: 6 **d** still in the same place where he was. *G2250*
17 he had *lain* in the grave four **d** already. *G2250*
39 stinketh: for he hath been *dead* four **d**. *G5066*
12: 1 Then Jesus six **d** before the passover *G2250*
20:26 And after eight **d** again his disciples *G2250*
Act 1: 3 seen of them forty **d**, and speaking of *G2250*
5 with the Holy Ghost not many **d** hence. *G2250*
15 And in those **d** Peter stood up in the *G2250*
2:17 And it shall come to pass in the last **d**, *G2250*
18 **d** of my Spirit; and they shall prophesy: *G2250*
3:24 have likewise foretold of these **d**. *G2250*
5:36 For before these **d** rose up Theudas, *G2250*
37 of Galilee in the **d** of the taxing, and *G2250*
6: 1 And in those **d**, when the number of the *G2250*
7:41 And they made a calf in those **d**, and *G2250*
45 face of our fathers, unto the **d** of David; *G2250*
9: 9 And he was three **d** without sight, and *G2250*
19 was Saul certain **d** with the disciples *G2250*
23 And after that many **d** were fulfilled, *G2250*
37 And it came to pass in those **d**, that she *G2250*
43 **d** in Joppa with one Simon a tanner. *G2250*
10:30 And Cornelius said, Four **d** ago I was *G2250*
48 prayed they him to tarry certain **d**. *G2250*
11:27 And in these **d** came prophets from *G2250*
28 to pass in the **d** of Claudius Caesar. *G1909*

Act 12: 3 (Then were the **d** of unleavened bread.) *G2250*
13:31 And he was seen many **d** of them *G2250*
41 a work in your **d**, a work which ye shall *G2250*
15:36 And some **d** after Paul said unto *G2250*
16:12 we were in that city abiding certain **d**. *G2250*
18 And this did she many **d**. But Paul, *G2250*
17: 2 and three sabbath **d** reasoned with them
20: 6 from Philippi after the **d** of unleavened *G2250*
6 in five **d**; where we abode seven days. *G2250*
6 in five days; where we abode seven **d**. *G2250*
21: 4 there seven **d**: who said to Paul through *G2250*
5 those **d**, we departed and went *G2250*
10 And as we tarried *there* many **d**, there *G2250*
15 And after those **d** we took up our *G2250*
26 of the **d** of purification, until *G2250*
27 And when the seven **d** were almost *G2250*
38 before these **d** madest an uproar, *G2250*
24: 1 And after five **d** Ananias the high priest *G2250*
11 are yet but twelve **d** since I went up to *G2250*
24 And after certain **d**, when Felix came *G2250*
25: 1 after three **d** he ascended from *G2250*
6 more than ten **d**, he went down unto *G2250*
13 And after certain **d** king Agrippa and *G2250*
14 And when they had been there many **d**, *G2250*
27: 7 And when we had sailed slowly many **d**, *G2250*
20 nor stars in many **d** appeared, and no *G2250*
28: 7 us, and lodged us three **d** courteously. *G2250*
12 at Syracuse, we tarried *there* three **d**. *G2250*
14 seven **d**: and so we went toward Rome. *G2250*
17 And it came to pass, that after three **d** *G2250*
Gal 1:18 see Peter, and abode with him fifteen **d**. *G2250*
4:10 Ye observe **d**, and months, and times, *G2250*
Eph 5:16 Redeeming the time, because the **d** are *G2250*
Col 2:16 or of the new moon, or of the sabbath ***d***:
2Ti 3: 1 This know also, that in the last **d** *G2250*
Heb 1: 2 Hath in these last **d** spoken unto us by *G2250*
5: 7 Who in the **d** of his flesh, when he had *G2250*
7: 3 beginning of **d**, nor end of life; but *G2250*
8: 8 he saith, Behold, the **d** come, saith the *G2250*
10 Israel after those **d**, saith the Lord; I will *G2250*
10:16 them after those **d**, saith the Lord, I will *G2250*
32 But call to remembrance the former **d**, *G2250*
11:30 they were compassed about seven **d**. *G2250*
12:10 For they verily for a few **d** chastened *us* *G2250*
Jas 5: 3 heaped treasure together for the last **d**. *G2250*
1Pt 3:10 For he that will love life, and see good **d**, *G2250*
20 God waited in the **d** of Noah, while the *G2250*
2Pt 3: 3 come in the last **d** scoffers, walking *G2250*
Rev 2:10 tribulation ten **d**: be thou faithful unto *G2250*
13 even in those **d** wherein Antipas *was* *G2250*
9: 6 And in those **d** shall men seek death, *G2250*
10: 7 But in the **d** of the voice of the seventh *G2250*
11: 3 *and* threescore **d**, clothed in sackcloth. *G2250*
6 it rain not in the **d** of their prophecy: *G2250*
9 dead bodies three **d** and an half, and *G2250*
11 And after three **d** and an half the Spirit *G2250*
12: 6 two hundred *and* threescore **d**. *G2250*

DAY'S

Nu 11:31 the camp, as it were a **d** journey on this H3117
31 and as it were a **d** journey on the other H3117
1Ki 19: 4 But he himself went a **d** journey into H3117
1Ch 16:37 as every **d** work required: H3117+H3117
Est 9:13 unto this **d** decree, and let Haman's H3117
Jna 3: 4 into the city a **d** journey, and he cried, H3117
Lk 2:44 company, went a **d** journey; and they *G2250*
Act 1:12 is from Jerusalem a sabbath **d** journey.
19:40 question for this **d** uproar, there being *G4594*

DAYS'

Gen 30:36 And he set three **d** journey betwixt H3117
31:23 after him seven **d** journey; and they H3117
Ex 3:18 beseech thee, three **d** journey into the H3117
5: 3 we pray thee, three **d** journey into the H3117
8:27 We will go three **d** journey into the H3117
Nu 10:33 of the LORD three **d** journey: and the H3117
33 them in the three **d** journey, to search H3117
33: 8 and went three **d** journey in the H3117
Dt 1: 2 (*There are* eleven **d** *journey* from H3117
1Sa 11: 3 Give us seven **d** respite, that we may H3117
2Sa 24:13 that there be three **d** pestilence in thy H3117
2Ki 3: 9 compass of seven **d** journey: and there H3117
Jna 3: 3 exceeding great city of three **d** journey. H3117

DAYSMAN

Job 9:33 Neither is there any **d** betwixt us, *that* H3198

DAYSPRING

Job 38:12 *and* caused the **d** to know his place; H7837

Lk 1:78 the **d** from on high hath visited us, *G395*

DAYSTAR See DAY and STAR.

DAYTIME
Job 5:14 They meet with darkness in the **d**, and H3119
24:16 in the **d**: they know not the light. H3119
Ps 22: 2 O my God, I cry in the **d**, but thou H3119
42: 8 in the **d**, and in the night his H3119
78:14 In the **d** also he led them with a cloud, H3119
Isa 4: 6 a shadow in the **d** from the heat, and H3119
21: 8 watchtower in the **d**, and I am set in my H3119

DEACON
1Ti 3:10 the office of a **d**, being *found* blameless. *G1247*
13 For they that have used the office of a **d** *G1247*

DEACONS
Php 1: 1 are at Philippi, with the bishops and **d**: *G1249*
1Ti 3: 8 Likewise *must* the **d** *be* grave, not *G1249*
12 Let the **d** be the husbands of one wife, *G1249*

DEAD
Gen 20: 3 thou *art but* a **d** man, for the woman H4191
23: 3 up from before his **d**, and spake unto H4191
4 that I may bury my **d** out of my sight. H4191
6 bury thy **d**; none of us shall withhold H4191
6 but that thou mayest bury thy **d**. H4191
8 I should bury my **d** out of my sight; H4191
11 of my people give I it thee: bury thy **d**. H4191
13 *it* of me, and I will bury my **d** there. H4191
15 me and thee? bury therefore thy **d**. H4191
42:38 for his brother is **d**, and he is left alone: H4191
44:20 and his brother is **d**, and he alone is left H4191
50:15 their father was **d**, they said, Joseph will H4191
Ex 4:19 all the men are **d** which sought thy life. H4191
9: 7 of the Israelites **d**. And the heart of H4191
12:30 not a house where *there was* not one **d**. H4191
33 in haste; for they said, We *be* all **d** *men*. H4191
14:30 the Egyptians **d** upon the sea shore. H4191
21:34 of them; and the **d** *beast* shall be his. H4191
35 it; and the **d** *ox* also they shall divide. H4191
36 ox for ox; and the **d** shall be his own. H4191
Lev 11:31 be **d**, shall be unclean until the even. H4194
32 when they are **d**, doth fall, it shall be H4194
19:28 in your flesh for the **d**, nor print any H5315
21: 1 be defiled for the **d** among his people: H5315
11 Neither shall he go in to any **d** body, H4191
22: 4 **d**, or a man whose seed goeth from him; H5315
Nu 5: 2 issue, and whosoever is defiled by the **d**: H5315
6: 6 the LORD he shall come at no **d** body. H4191
11 he sinned by the **d**, and shall hallow his H5315
9: 6 defiled by the **d** body of a man, that H5315
7 We *are* defiled by the **d** body of a man: H5315
10 by reason of a **d** body, or *be* in a H5315
12:12 Let her not be as one **d**, of whom the H4191
16:48 And he stood between the **d** and the H4191
19:11 He that toucheth the **d** body of any H4191
13 Whosoever toucheth the **d** body of any H4191
13 of any man that is **d**, and purifieth not H4191
16 open fields, or a **d** body, or a bone of a H4191
18 bone, or one slain, or one **d**, or a grave: H4191
20:29 that Aaron was **d**, they mourned for H1478
Dt 2:16 and **d** from among the people, H4191
14: 1 baldness between your eyes for the **d**. H4191
8 of their flesh, nor touch their **d** carcase. H5038
25: 5 child, the wife of the **d** shall not marry H4191
6 brother *which is* **d**, that his name be not H4191
26:14 thereof for the **d**: *but* I have hearkened H4191
Jos 1: 2 Moses my servant is **d**; now therefore H4191
Jdg 2:19 the judge was **d**, *that* they returned, H4194
3:25 lord *was* fallen down **d** on the earth. H4191
4: 1 sight of the LORD, when Ehud was **d**. H4191
22 lay **d**, and the nail *was* in his temples. H4191
5:27 where he bowed, there he fell down **d**. H7703
8:33 as Gideon was **d**, that the children of H4191
9:55 Abimelech was **d**, they departed every H4191
16:30 therein. So the **d** which he slew at his H4191
20: 5 have they forced, that she is **d**. H4191
Ru 1: 8 ye have dealt with the **d**, and with me. H4191
2:20 the living and to the **d**. And Naomi said H4191
4: 5 the wife of the **d**, to raise up the name H4191
5 the name of the **d** upon his inheritance. H4191
10 the name of the **d** upon his inheritance, H4191
10 the name of the **d** be not cut off from H4191
1Sa 4:17 are **d**, and the ark of God is taken. H4191
19 her husband were **d**, she bowed herself H4191
17:51 saw their champion was **d**, they fled. H4191
24:14 thou pursue? after a **d** dog, after a flea. H4191
1Sa 25:39 that Nabal was **d**, he said, Blessed *be* H4191
28: 3 Now Samuel was **d**, and all Israel had H4191
31: 5 saw that Saul was **d**, he fell likewise H4191
7 and his sons were **d**, they forsook the H4191
2Sa 1: 4 also are fallen and **d**; and Saul and H4191
4 Saul and Jonathan his son are **d** also. H4191
5 that Saul and Jonathan his son be **d**? H4191
2: 7 master Saul is **d**, and also the house H4191
4: 1 that Abner was **d** in Hebron, his hands H4191
10 Behold, Saul is **d**, thinking to have H4191
9: 8 look upon such a **d** dog as I *am*? H4191
11:21 Thy servant Uriah the Hittite is **d** also. H4191
24 king's servants be **d**, and thy servant H4191
24 thy servant Uriah the Hittite is **d** also. H4191
26 was **d**, she mourned for her husband. H4191
12:18 him that the child was **d**: for they said, H4191
18 himself, if we tell him that the child is **d**? H4191
19 that the child was **d**: therefore David H4191
19 Is the child **d**? And they said, He is dead. H4191
19 the child dead? And they said, He is **d**. H4191
21 was **d**, thou didst rise and eat bread. H4191
23 But now he is **d**, wherefore should I H4191
13:32 sons; for Amnon only is **d**: for by the H4191
33 sons are **d**: for Amnon only is dead. H4191
33 sons are dead: for Amnon only is **d**. H4191
39 concerning Amnon, seeing he was **d**. H4191
14: 2 that had a long time mourned for the **d**: H4191
5 widow woman, and mine husband is **d**. H4191
16: 9 Why should this **d** dog curse my lord H4191
18:20 no tidings, because the king's son is **d**. H4191
19:10 over us, is **d** in battle. Now therefore H4191
28 For all *of* my father's house were but **d** H4194
1Ki 3:20 and laid her **d** child in my bosom. H4191
21 suck, behold, it was **d**: but when I had H4191
22 *is* my son, and the **d** *is* thy son. And H4191
22 said, No; but the **d** *is* thy son, and the H4191
23 and thy son *is* the **d**: and the other H4191
23 son *is* the **d**, and my son *is* the living. H4191
11:21 of the host was **d**, Hadad said to H4191
13:31 When I am **d**, then bury me in the H4191
21:14 saying, Naboth is stoned, and is **d**. H4191
15 stoned, and was **d**, that Jezebel said to H4191
15 money: for Naboth is not alive, but **d**. H4191
16 that Naboth was **d**, that Ahab rose up to H4191
2Ki 3: 5 But it came to pass, when Ahab was **d**, H4194
4: 1 my husband is **d**; and thou knowest H4191
32 the child was **d**, *and* laid upon his bed. H4191
8: 5 he had restored a **d** body to life, that, H4191
11: 1 saw that her son was **d**, she arose and H4191
19:35 behold, they *were* all **d** corpses. H4191
23:30 him in a chariot **d** from Megiddo, and H4191
1Ch 1:44 And when Bela was **d**, Jobab the son of H4191
45 And when Jobab was **d**, Husham of the H4191
46 And when Husham was **d**, Hadad the H4191
47 And when Hadad was **d**, Samlah of H4191
48 And when Samlah was **d**, Shaul of H4191
49 And when Shaul was **d**, Baal-hanan the H4191
50 And when Baal-hanan was **d**, Hadad H4191
2:19 And when Azubah was **d**, Caleb took H4191
24 And after that Hezron was **d** in H4194
10: 5 saw that Saul was **d**, he fell likewise on H4191
7 and his sons were **d**, then they forsook H4191
2Ch 20:24 behold, they *were* **d** bodies fallen to the H6297
25 riches with the **d** bodies, and precious H6297
22:10 saw that her son was **d**, she arose and H4191
Est 2: 7 were **d**, took for his own daughter. H4194
Job 1:19 men, and they are **d**; and I only am H4191
26: 5 **D** *things* are formed from under the H7496
Ps 31:12 I am forgotten as a **d** man out of mind: H4191
76: 6 chariot and horse are cast into a **d** sleep.
79: 2 The **d** bodies of thy servants have they H5033
88: 5 Free among the **d**, like the slain that lie H4191
10 Wilt thou shew wonders to the **d**? shall H4191
10 shall the **d** arise *and* praise thee? Selah. H7496
106:28 and ate the sacrifices of the **d**. H4191
110: 6 *the places* with the **d** bodies; he shall H1472
115:17 The **d** praise not the LORD, neither any H4191
143: 3 as those that have been long **d**. H4191
Prv 2:18 unto death, and her paths unto the **d**. H7496
9:18 But he knoweth not that the **d** *are* H7496
21:16 remain in the congregation of the **d**. H7496
Ecc 4: 2 Wherefore I praised the **d** which are H4191
2 which are already **d** more than the H4191
9: 3 they live, and after that *they go* to the **d**. H4191
4 for a living dog is better than a **d** lion. H4191
5 shall die: but the **d** know not any thing, H4191
10: 1 **D** flies cause the ointment of the H4194
Isa 8:19 unto their God? for the living to the **d**? H4191
14: 9 it stirreth up the **d** for thee, *even* all the H7496
Isa 22: 2 slain with the sword, nor **d** in battle. H4191
26:14 *They are* **d**, they shall not live; *they are* H4191
19 Thy **d** *men* shall live, *together with* my H4191
19 live, *together with* my **d** body shall they H4191
19 herbs, and the earth shall cast out the **d**. H7496
37:36 behold, they *were* all **d** corpses. H4191
59:10 *we are* in desolate places as **d** *men*. H4191
Jer 16: 7 them for the **d**; neither shall *men* give H4191
22:10 Weep ye not for the **d**, neither bemoan H4191
26:23 and cast his **d** body into the graves H5038
31:40 And the whole valley of the **d** bodies, H6297
33: 5 to fill them with the **d** bodies of men, H6297
34:20 their life: and their **d** bodies shall be for H5038
36:30 of David: and his **d** body shall be cast H5038
41: 9 had cast all the **d** bodies of the men, H6297
Lam 3: 6 in dark places, as *they that be* **d** of old. H4191
Ezk 6: 5 And I will lay the **d** carcases of the
24:17 no mourning for the **d**, bind the tire of H4191
44:25 And they shall come at no **d** person to H4191
31 of any thing that is **d** of itself, or torn, H5038
Am 8: 3 *shall be* many **d** bodies in every place; H6297
Hag 2:13 *that is* unclean by a **d** body touch any of
Mt 2:19 But when Herod was **d**, behold, an *G5053*
20 **d** which sought the young child's life. *G2348*
8:22 me; and let the **d** bury their dead. *G3498*
22 me; and let the dead bury their **d**. *G3498*
9:18 is even now **d**: but come and lay thy *G5053*
24 for the maid is not **d**, but sleepeth. And *G599*
10: 8 lepers, raise the **d**, cast out devils: freely *G3498*
11: 5 the deaf hear, the **d** are raised up, and *G3498*
14: 2 he is risen from the **d**; and therefore *G3498*
17: 9 Son of man be risen again from the **d**. *G3498*
22:31 resurrection of the **d**, have ye not read *G3498*
32 is not the God of the **d**, but of the living. *G3498*
23:27 **d** *men's* bones, and of all uncleanness. *G3498*
27:64 He is risen from the **d**: so the last error *G3498*
28: 4 did shake, and became as **d** *men*. *G3498*
7 he is risen from the **d**; and, behold, he *G3498*
Mk 5:35 Thy daughter is **d**: why troublest thou the *G599*
39 weep? the damsel is not **d**, but sleepeth. *G599*
6:14 risen from the **d**, and therefore mighty *G3498*
16 I beheaded: he is risen from the **d**. *G3498*
9: 9 the Son of man were risen from the **d**. *G3498*
10 the rising from the **d** should mean, *G3498*
26 and he was as one **d**; insomuch that *G3498*
26 dead; insomuch that many said, He is **d**. *G599*
12:25 For when they shall rise from the **d**, *G3498*
26 And as touching the **d**, that they rise: *G3498*
27 He is not the God of the **d**, but the God *G3498*
15:44 if he were already **d**: and calling *unto* *G2348*
44 him whether he had been any while **d**. *G599*
Lk 7:12 there was a **d** man carried out, the *G2348*
15 And he that was **d** sat up, and began to *G3498*
22 the deaf hear, the **d** are raised, to the *G3498*
8:49 daughter is **d**; trouble not the Master. *G2348*
52 said, Weep not; she is not **d**, but sleepeth. *G599*
53 him to scorn, knowing that she was **d**. *G599*
9: 7 of some, that John was risen from the **d**; *G3498*
60 Jesus said unto him, Let the **d** bury *G3498*
60 the dead bury their **d**: but go thou and *G3498*
10:30 *him*, and departed, leaving *him* half **d**. *G2253*
15:24 For this my son was **d**, and is alive *G3498*
32 thy brother was **d**, and is alive again; *G3498*
16:30 unto them from the **d**, they will repent. *G3498*
31 persuaded, though one rose from the **d**. *G3498*
20:35 from the **d**, neither marry, nor *G3498*
37 Now that the **d** are raised, even Moses *G3498*
38 For he is not a God of the **d**, but of the *G3498*
24: 5 Why seek ye the living among the **d**? *G3498*
46 and to rise from the **d** the third day: *G3498*
Jn 2:22 was risen from the **d**, his disciples *G3498*
5:21 For as the Father raiseth up the **d**, and *G3498*
25 now is, when the **d** shall hear the voice *G3498*
6:49 eat manna in the wilderness, and are **d**. *G599*
58 manna, and are **d**: he that eateth of this *G599*
8:52 a devil. Abraham is **d**, and the prophets; *G599*
53 Abraham, which is **d**? and the prophets *G599*
53 are **d**: whom makest thou thyself? *G599*
11:14 Jesus unto them plainly, Lazarus is **d**. *G599*
25 in me, though he were **d**, yet shall he live: *G599*
39 of him that was **d**, saith unto him, Lord, *G2348*
39 stinketh: for he hath been *d* four days.
41 *place* where the **d** was laid. And Jesus *G2348*
44 And he that was **d** came forth, bound *G2348*
12: 1 been **d**, whom he raised from the dead. *G2348*
1 been dead, whom he raised from the **d**. *G3498*
9 also, whom he had raised from the **d**. *G3498*
17 and raised him from the **d**, bare record. *G3498*
19:33 was **d** already, they brake not his legs: *G2348*

Jn 20: 9 that he must rise again from the **d**. G3498
21:14 after that he was risen from the **d**. G3498
Act 2:29 that he is both **d** and buried, and his G5053
3:15 from the **d**; whereof we are witnesses. G3498
4: 2 Jesus the resurrection from the **d**. G3498
10 raised from the **d**, *even* by him doth this G3498
5:10 in, and found her **d**, and, carrying *her* G3498
7: 4 his father was **d**, he removed him into G599
10:41 drink with him after he rose from the **d**. G3498
42 of God *to be* the Judge of quick and **d**. G3498
13:30 But God raised him from the **d**: G3498
34 him up from the **d**, *now* no more to G3498
14:19 of the city, supposing he had been **d**. G2348
17: 3 again from the **d**; and that this Jesus, G3498
31 in that he hath raised him from the **d**. G3498
32 the resurrection of the **d**, some mocked: G3498
20: 9 from the third loft, and was taken up **d**. G3498
23: 6 of the **d** I am called in question. G3498
24:15 of the **d**, both of the just and unjust. G3498
21 the resurrection of the **d** I am called in G3498
25:19 was **d**, whom Paul affirmed to be alive. G2348
26: 8 with you, that God should raise the **d**? G3498
23 rise from the **d**, and should shew light G3498
28: 6 or fallen down **d** suddenly: but after G3498
Ro 1: 4 holiness, by the resurrection from the **d**: G3498
4:17 who quickeneth the **d**, and calleth those G3498
19 not his own body now **d**, when he was G3499
24 raised up Jesus our Lord from the **d**; G3498
5:15 of one many be **d**, much more the grace G599
6: 2 God forbid. How shall we, that are **d** to G599
4 raised up from the **d** by the glory of the G3498
7 For he that is **d** is freed from sin. G599
8 Now if we be **d** with Christ, we believe G599
9 raised from the **d** dieth no more; death G3498
11 yourselves to be **d** indeed unto sin, but G3498
13 are alive from the **d**, and your members G3498
7: 2 if the husband be **d**, she is loosed from G599
3 if her husband be **d**, she is free from that G599
4 ye also are become **d** to the law by the G2289
4 who is raised from the **d**, that we should G3498
6 the law, that being **d** wherein we were G599
8 For without the law sin *was* **d**. G3498
8:10 And if Christ *be* in you, the body *is* **d** G3498
11 up Jesus from the **d** dwell in you, he G3498
11 up Christ from the **d** shall also quicken G3498
10: 7 is, to bring up Christ again from the **d**.) G3498
9 him from the **d**, thou shalt be saved. G3498
11:15 receiving *of them be*, but life from the **d**? G3498
14: 9 might be Lord both of the **d** and living. G3498
1Co 7:39 if her husband be **d**, she is at liberty to G2837
15:12 that he rose from the **d**, how say some G3498
12 that there is no resurrection of the **d**? G3498
13 But if there be no resurrection of the **d**, G3498
15 not up, if so be that the **d** rise not. G3498
16 For if the **d** rise not, then is not Christ G3498
20 But now is Christ risen from the **d**, *and* G3498
21 *came* also the resurrection of the **d**. G3498
29 baptized for the **d**, if the dead rise not G3498
29 for the dead, if the **d** rise not at all? why G3498
29 why are they then baptized for the **d**? G3498
32 it me, if the **d** rise not? let us eat and G3498
35 But some *man* will say, How are the **d** G3498
42 So also *is* the resurrection of the **d**. It is G3498
52 shall sound, and the **d** shall be raised G3498
2Co 1: 9 but in God which raiseth the **d**: G3498
5:14 that if one died for all, then were all **d**: G599
Gal 1: 1 the Father, who raised him from the **d**;) G3498
2:19 For I through the law am **d** to the law, G599
21 *come* by the law, then Christ is **d** in vain. G599
Eph 1:20 him from the **d**, and set *him* at his own G3498
2: 1 who were **d** in trespasses and sins; G3498
5 Even when we were **d** in sins, hath G3498
5:14 the **d**, and Christ shall give thee light. G3498
Php 3:11 attain unto the resurrection of the **d**. G3498
Col 1:18 firstborn from the **d**; that in all *things* G3498
2:12 of God, who hath raised him from the **d**. G3498
13 And you, being **d** in your sins and the G3498
20 Wherefore if ye be **d** with Christ from the G599
3: 3 For ye are **d**, and your life is hid with G599
1Th 1:10 he raised from the **d**, *even* Jesus, which G3498
4:16 God: and the **d** in Christ shall rise first: G3498
1Ti 5: 6 But she that liveth in pleasure is **d** G2348
2Ti 2: 8 from the **d** according to my gospel: G3498
11 *It is* a faithful saying: For if we be **d** G4880
4: 1 **d** at his appearing and his kingdom; G3498
Heb 6: 1 from **d** works, and of faith toward God, G3498
2 of the **d**, and of eternal judgment. G3498
9:14 from **d** works to serve the living God? G3498
17 after men are **d**: otherwise it is of no G1909

Heb 11: 4 gifts: and by it he being **d** yet speaketh. G599
12 him as good as **d**, *so many* as the stars G3499
19 up, even from the **d**; from whence also G3498
35 Women received their **d** raised to life G3498
13:20 again from the **d** our Lord Jesus, that G3498
Jas 2:17 Even so faith, if it hath not works, is **d**, G3498
20 vain man, that faith without works is **d**? G3498
26 For as the body without the spirit is **d**, G3498
26 dead, so faith without works is **d** also. G3498
1Pt 1: 3 resurrection of Jesus Christ from the **d**, G3498
21 him up from the **d**, and gave him glory; G3498
2:24 tree, that we, being **d** to sins, should live G581
4: 5 is ready to judge the quick and the **d**. G3498
6 to them that are **d**, that they might be G3498
Jude 12 fruit, twice **d**, plucked up by the roots; G599
Rev 1: 5 begotten of the **d**, and the prince of the G3498
17 I fell at his feet as **d**. And he laid his G3498
18 I *am* he that liveth, and was **d**; and, G3498
2: 8 and the last, which was **d**, and is alive; G3498
3: 1 hast a name that thou livest, and art **d**. G3498
11: 8 And their **d** bodies *shall lie* in the street G4430
9 shall see their **d** bodies three days and G4430
9 their **d** bodies to be put in graves. G4430
18 the time of the **d**, that they should be G3498
14:13 Blessed *are* the **d** which die in the Lord G3498
16: 3 as the blood of a **d** *man*: and every G3498
20: 5 But the rest of the **d** lived not again G3498
12 And I saw the **d**, small and great, stand G3498
12 of life: and the **d** were judged out of G3498
13 And the sea gave up the **d** which were G3498
13 delivered up the **d** which were in them: G3498

DEADLY
1Sa 5:11 people: for there was a **d** destruction H4194
Ps 17: 9 my **d** enemies, *who* compass me about. H5315
Ezk 30:24 with the groanings of a **d** wounded *man*.
Mk 16:18 if they drink any **d** thing, it shall not G2286
Jas 3: 8 *it is* an unruly evil, full of **d** poison. G2287
Rev 13: 3 to death; and his **d** wound was healed: G2288
12 first beast, whose **d** wound was healed. G2288

DEADNESS
Ro 4:19 old, neither yet the **d** of Sarah's womb: G3500

DEAF
Ex 4:11 the dumb, or **d**, or the seeing, or the H2795
Lev 19:14 Thou shalt not curse the **d**, nor put a H2795
Ps 38:13 But I, as a **d** *man*, heard not; and *I was* H2795
58: 4 like the **d** adder *that* stoppeth her ear; H2795
Isa 29:18 And in that day shall the **d** hear the H2795
35: 5 the ears of the **d** shall be unstopped. H2795
42:18 Hear, ye **d**; and look, ye blind, that ye H2795
19 Who *is* blind, but my servant? or **d**, as H2795
43: 8 have eyes, and the **d** that have ears. H2795
Mic 7:16 upon *their* mouth, their ears shall be **d**. H2790
Mt 11: 5 cleansed, and the **d** hear, the dead are G2974
Mk 7:32 unto him one that was **d**, and had an G2974
37 the **d** to hear, and the dumb to speak. G2974
9:25 *Thou* dumb and **d** spirit, I charge thee, G2974
Lk 7:22 are cleansed, the **d** hear, the dead are G2974

DEAL
Gen 19: 9 a judge: now will we **d** worse with thee,
21:23 that thou wilt not **d** falsely with me, nor
24:49 And now if ye will **d** kindly and truly H6213
32: 9 thy kindred, and I will **d** well with thee:
34:31 And they said, Should he **d** with our H6213
47:29 my thigh, and **d** kindly and truly with H6213
Ex 1:10 Come on, let us **d** wisely with them; lest
8:29 let not Pharaoh **d** deceitfully any more
21: 9 his son, he shall **d** with her after the H6213
23:11 thou shalt **d** with thy vineyard, *and* H6213
29:40 And with the one lamb a tenth **d** of flour
Lev 14:21 for him, and one tenth **d** of fine flour
19:11 Ye shall not steal, neither **d** falsely,
Nu 11:15 And if thou **d** thus with me, kill me, I H6213
15: 4 offering of a tenth **d** of flour mingled
28:13 And a several tenth **d** of flour mingled
21 A several tenth **d** shalt thou offer for
29 A several tenth **d** unto one lamb,
29: 4 And one tenth **d** for one lamb,
10 A several tenth **d** for one lamb,
15 And a several tenth **d** to each lamb of
Dt 7: 5 But thus shall ye **d** with them; ye shall H6213
Jos 2:14 we will **d** kindly and truly with thee. H6213
Ru 1: 8 house: the LORD **d** kindly with you, as H6213
1Sa 20: 8 Therefore thou shalt **d** kindly with thy H6213
2Sa 18: 5 and Ittai, saying, *D* gently for my sake
2Ch 2: 3 As thou didst **d** with David my father, H6213

2Ch 2: 3 to dwell therein, *even so* **d** *with me.*
19:11 before you. **D** courageously, and the H6213
Job 42: 8 will I accept: lest I **d** with you *after your* H6213
Ps 75: 4 I said unto the fools, **D** not foolishly: and
105:25 people, to **d** subtilly with his servants.
119:17 **D** bountifully with thy servant, *that* I H1580
124 **D** with thy servant according unto thy H6213
142: 7 for thou shalt **d** bountifully with me. H1580
Prv 12:22 but they that **d** truly *are* his delight. H6213
Isa 26:10 uprightness will he **d** unjustly, and will
33: 1 make an end to **d** treacherously, they
1 they shall **d** treacherously with thee.
48: 8 that thou wouldest **d** very treacherously,
52:13 Behold, my servant shall **d** prudently, he
58: 7 *Is it* not to **d** thy bread to the hungry, H6536
Jer 12: 1 all they happy that **d** very treacherously?
18:23 before thee; **d** *thus* with them in the H6213
21: 2 the LORD will **d** with us according to H6213
Ezk 8:18 Therefore will I also **d** in fury: mine eye H6213
16:59 GOD; I will even **d** with thee as thou H6213
18: 9 my judgments, to **d** truly; he *is* just, he H6213
22:14 the days that I shall **d** with thee? I the H6213
23:25 and they shall **d** furiously with thee: H6213
29 And they shall **d** with thee hatefully, H6213
31:11 he shall surely **d** with him: I have H6213
Dan 1:13 and as thou seest, **d** with thy servants. H6213
11: 7 shall **d** against them, and shall prevail: H6213
Hab 1:13 upon them that **d** treacherously, *and*
Mal 2:10 us? why do we **d** treacherously every
15 your spirit, and let none **d** treacherously
16 your spirit, that ye **d** not treacherously.
Mk 7:36 the more a great **d** they published *it*; G4054
10:48 the more a great **d**, *Thou* son of David, G4183

DEALER
Isa 21: 2 the treacherous **d** dealeth treacherously, H898

DEALERS
Isa 24:16 me! the treacherous **d** have dealt H898
16 **d** have dealt very treacherously. H898

DEALEST
Ex 5:15 **d** thou thus with thy servants? H6213
Isa 33: 1 not spoiled; and **d** treacherously, and

DEALETH
Jdg 18: 4 Thus and thus **d** Micah with me, and H6213
1Sa 23:22 for it is told me *that* he **d** very subtilly.
Prv 10: 4 He becometh poor that **d** *with* a slack H6213
13:16 Every prudent *man* **d** with knowledge: H6213
14:17 *He that is* soon angry **d** foolishly: and a H6213
21:24 *is* his name, who **d** in proud wrath. H6213
Isa 21: 2 treacherous dealer **d** treacherously, and
Jer 6:13 even unto the priest every one **d** falsely. H6213
8:10 even unto the priest every one **d** falsely. H6213
Heb 12: 7 If ye endure chastening, God **d** with G4374

DEALING
Ps 7:16 **d** shall come down upon his own pate.

DEALINGS
1Sa 2:23 I hear of your evil **d** by all this people. H1697
Jn 4: 9 Jews have no **d** with the Samaritans. G4798

DEALS
Lev 14:10 and three tenth **d** of fine flour *for* a meat
23:13 *shall be* two tenth **d** of fine flour mingled
17 loaves of two tenth **d**: they shall be of fine
24: 5 thereof: two tenth **d** shall be in one cake.
Nu 15: 6 offering two tenth **d** of flour mingled H6241
9 of three tenth **d** of flour mingled with H6241
28: 9 and two tenth **d** of flour *for* a meat H6241
12 And three tenth **d** of flour *for* a meat H6241
12 and two tenth **d** of flour *for* a meat H6241
20 oil: three tenth **d** shall ye offer for a H6241
20 a bullock, and two tenth **d** for a ram; H6241
28 oil, three tenth **d** unto one bullock, two H6241
28 one bullock, two tenth **d** unto one ram, H6241
29: 3 oil, three tenth **d** for a bullock, *and* two H6241
3 a bullock, *and* two tenth **d** for a ram, H6241
9 oil, three tenth **d** to a bullock, *and* two H6241
9 a bullock, *and* two tenth **d** to one ram, H6241
14 oil, three tenth **d** unto every bullock of H6241
14 tenth **d** to each ram of the two rams, H6241

DEALT
Gen 16: 6 **d** hardly with her, she fled from her face.
33:11 because God hath **d** graciously with me,
43: 6 And Israel said, Wherefore **d** ye *so* ill

Ex 1:20 Therefore God **d** well with the midwives:
14:11 hast thou **d** thus with us, to carry H6213
18:11 they **d** proudly *he was* above them.
21: 8 seeing he hath **d** deceitfully with her.
Jdg 9:16 and if ye have **d** well with Jerubbaal H6213
19 If ye then have **d** truly and sincerely H6213
23 **d** treacherously with Abimelech: H898
Ru 1: 8 ye have **d** with the dead, and with me. H6213
20 Almighty hath **d** very bitterly with me.
1Sa 24:18 how that thou hast **d** well with me: H6213
25:31 the LORD shall have **d** well with my lord,
2Sa 6:19 And he **d** among all the people, *even* H2505
2Ki 12:15 on workmen: for they **d** faithfully. H6213
21: 6 and **d** with familiar spirits H6213
22: 7 their hand, because they **d** faithfully. H6213
1Ch 16: 3 And he **d** to every one of Israel, both H2505
20: 3 with axes. Even so **d** David with all the H6213
2Ch 6:37 have done amiss, and have **d** wickedly;
11:23 And he **d** wisely, and dispersed of all his
33: 6 witchcraft, and **d** with a familiar spirit, H6213
Neh 1: 7 We have **d** very corruptly against thee,
9:10 knewest that they **d** proudly against
16 But they and our fathers **d** proudly, and
29 unto thy law: yet they **d** proudly, and
Job 6:15 My brethren have **d** deceitfully as a
Ps 13: 6 because he hath **d** bountifully with me.
44:17 have we **d** falsely in thy covenant.
78:57 But turned back, and **d** unfaithfully like
103:10 He hath not **d** with us after our sins; H6213
116: 7 the LORD hath **d** bountifully with thee. H1580
119:65 Thou hast **d** well with thy servant, O H6213
78 Let the proud be ashamed; for they **d**
147:20 He hath not **d** so with any nation: and H6213
Isa 24:16 dealers have **d** treacherously; yea, the
16 dealers have **d** very treacherously.
33: 1 and they **d** not treacherously with
Jer 3:20 so have ye **d** treacherously with me,
5:11 of Judah have **d** very treacherously
12: 6 even they have **d** treacherously with
Lam 1: 2 all her friends have **d** treacherously with
Ezk 22: 7 of thee have they **d** by oppression with H6213
25:12 that Edom hath **d** against the house of H6213
15 Philistines have **d** by revenge, and have H6213
Hos 5: 7 They have **d** treacherously against the
6: 7 have they **d** treacherously against me.
Joel 2:26 God, that hath **d** wondrously with you: H6213
Zec 1: 6 to our doings, so hath he **d** with us. H6213
Mal 2:11 Judah hath **d** treacherously, and an
14 whom thou hast **d** treacherously: yet *is*
Lk 1:25 Thus hath the Lord **d** with me in the *G4160*
2:48 hast thou thus **d** with us? behold, thy *G4160*
Act 7:19 The same **d** subtilly with our kindred,
25:24 of the Jews have **d** with me, both at *G1793*
Ro 12: 3 **d** to every man the measure of faith. *G3307*

DEAR

Jer 31:20 *Is* Ephraim my **d** son? *is he* a pleasant H3357
Lk 7: 2 **d** unto him, was sick, and ready to die. *G1784*
Act 20:24 count I my life **d** unto myself, so that *G5093*
Eph 5: 1 Be ye therefore followers of God, as **d** *G27*
Col 1: 7 As ye also learned of Epaphras our **d** *G27*
13 *us* into the kingdom of his **d** Son: *G26*
1Th 2: 8 own souls, because ye were **d** unto us. *G27*

DEARLY

Jer 12: 7 I have given the **d** beloved of my soul
Ro 12:19 **D** beloved, avenge not yourselves, but
1Co 10:14 Wherefore, my **d** beloved, flee from
2Co 7: 1 Having therefore these promises, **d**
12:19 all things, **d** beloved, for your edifying.
Php 4: 1 Therefore, my brethren **d** beloved and
1 so stand fast in the Lord, *my* **d** beloved.
2Ti 1: 2 To Timothy, *my* **d** beloved son: Grace,
Phlm 1 our **d** beloved, and fellowlabourer,
1Pt 2:11 **D** beloved, I beseech *you* as strangers

DEARTH

Gen 41:54 And the seven years of **d** began to H7458
54 had said: and the **d** was in all lands; H7458
2Ki 4:38 and *there was* a **d** in the land; and the H7458
2Ch 6:28 If there be **d** in the land, if there be H7458
Neh 5: 3 we might buy corn, because of the **d**. H7458
Jer 14: 1 came to Jeremiah concerning the **d**. H1226
Act 7:11 Now there came a **d** over all the land of *G3042*
11:28 should be great **d** throughout all the *G3042*

DEATH

Gen 21:16 Let me not see the **d** of the child. And H4194
24:67 Isaac was comforted after his mother's **d**.
Gen 25:11 And it came to pass after the **d** of H4194
26:11 man or his wife shall surely be put to **d**. H4191
18 them after the **d** of Abraham: and he H4194
27: 2 I am old, I know not the day of my **d**: H4194
7 bless thee before the LORD before my **d**. H4194
10 and that he may bless thee before his **d**. H4194
Ex 10:17 he may take away from me this **d** only. H4194
19:12 the mount shall be surely put to **d**: H4191
21:12 so that he die, shall be surely put to **d**. H4191
15 or his mother, shall be surely put to **d**. H4191
16 in his hand, he shall surely be put to **d**. H4191
17 or his mother, shall surely be put to **d**. H4191
29 and his owner also shall be put to **d**. H4191
22:19 with a beast shall surely be put to **d**. H4191
31:14 surely be put to **d**: for whosoever doeth H4191
15 sabbath day, he shall surely be put to **d**. H4191
35: 2 doeth work therein shall be put to **d**. H4191
Lev 16: 1 Moses after the **d** of the two sons of H4194
19:20 be put to **d**, because she was not free. H4191
20: 2 surely be put to **d**: the people of the land H4191
9 be surely put to **d**: he hath cursed his H4191
10 the adulteress shall surely be put to **d**. H4191
11 to **d**; their blood *shall be* upon them. H4191
12 surely be put to **d**: they have wrought H4191
13 to **d**; their blood *shall be* upon them. H4191
15 be put to **d**: and ye shall slay the beast. H4191
16 to **d**; their blood *shall be* upon them. H4191
27 surely be put to **d**: they shall stone them H4191
24:16 shall surely be put to **d**, *and* all the H4191
16 the name *of the LORD*, shall be put to **d**. H4191
17 killeth any man shall surely be put to **d**. H4191
21 that killeth a man, he shall be put to **d**. H4191
27:29 redeemed; *but* shall surely be put to **d**. H4191
Nu 1:51 that cometh nigh shall be put to **d**. H4191
3:10 that cometh nigh shall be put to **d**. H4191
38 that cometh nigh shall be put to **d**. H4191
15:35 be surely put to **d**: all the congregation H4191
16:29 If these men die the common **d** of all H4194
18: 7 that cometh nigh shall be put to **d**. H4191
23:10 Let me die the **d** of the righteous, and H4194
35:16 the murderer shall surely be put to **d**. H4191
17 the murderer shall surely be put to **d**. H4191
18 the murderer shall surely be put to **d**. H4191
21 surely be put to **d**; *for* he *is* a murderer: H4191
25 in it unto the **d** of the high priest, which H4194
28 refuge until the **d** of the high priest: but H4194
28 but after the **d** of the high priest the H4194
30 shall be put to **d** by the mouth of H7523
31 of **d**: but he shall be surely put to death. H4191
31 of death: but he shall be surely put to **d**. H4191
32 in the land, until the **d** of the priest. H4194
Dt 13: 5 shall be put to **d**; because he hath H4191
9 him to put him to **d**, and afterwards the H4191
17: 6 that is worthy of **d** be put to death; *but* H4191
6 of death be put to **d**; *but* at the mouth of H4191
6 of one witness he shall not be put to **d**. H4191
7 him to put him to **d**, and afterward the H4191
19: 6 he *was* not worthy of **d**, inasmuch as he H4194
21:22 a sin worthy of **d**, and he be to be put H4194
22 put to **d**, and thou hang him on a tree: H4191
22:26 no sin *worthy* of **d**: for as when a man H4194
24:16 The fathers shall not be put to **d** for the H4191
16 the children be put to **d** for the fathers: H4191
16 man shall be put to **d** for his own sin. H4191
30:15 this day life and good, and **d** and evil; H4194
19 you life and **d**, blessing and cursing: H4194
31:27 LORD; and how much more after my **d**? H4194
29 For I know that after my **d** ye will H4194
33: 1 the children of Israel before his **d**. H4194
Jos 1: 1 Now after the **d** of Moses the servant of H4194
18 **d**: only be strong and of a good courage. H4191
2:13 they have, and deliver our lives from **d**. H4194
20: 6 *and* until the **d** of the high priest that H4194
Jdg 1: 1 Now after the **d** of Joshua it came to H4194
5:18 the **d** in the high places of the field. H4191
6:31 him, let him be put to **d** whilst *it is yet* H4191
13: 7 God from the womb to the day of his **d**. H4194
16:16 him, *so* that his soul was vexed unto **d**; H4191
30 he slew at his **d** were more than *they* H4194
20:13 may put them to **d**, and put away evil H4191
21: 5 saying, He shall surely be put to **d**. H4191
Ru 1:17 also, *if aught* but **d** part thee and me. H4194
2:11 in law since the **d** of thine husband: H4194
1Sa 4:20 And about the time of her **d** the women H4191
11:12 the men, that we may put them to **d**. H4191
13 a man be put to **d** this day: for to day H4191
15:32 said, Surely the bitterness of **d** is past. H4194
35 the day of his **d**: nevertheless Samuel H4194
20: 3 *there is* but a step between me and **d**. H4194
1Sa 22:22 *d* of all the persons of thy father's house.
2Sa 1: 1 Now it came to pass after the **d** of Saul, H4194
23 their lives, and in their **d** they were not H4194
6:23 Saul had no child unto the day of her **d**. H4194
8: 2 he to put to **d**, and with one full line H4191
15:21 be, whether in **d** or life, even there also H4194
19:21 Shimei be put to **d** for this, because he H4191
22 any man be put to **d** this day in Israel? H4191
20: 3 the day of their **d**, living in widowhood. H4191
21: 9 and were put to **d** in the days of H4191
22: 5 When the waves of **d** compassed me, H4194
6 about; the snares of **d** prevented me; H4194
1Ki 2: 8 I will not put thee to **d** with the sword. H4191
24 Adonijah shall be put to **d** this day. H4191
26 for thou *art* worthy of **d**: but I will not at H4194
26 time put thee to **d**, because thou barest H4191
11:40 was in Egypt until the **d** of Solomon. H4194
2Ki 1: 1 against Israel after the **d** of Ahab. H4194
2:21 thence any more **d** or barren *land*. H4194
4:40 of God, *there is* **d** in the pot. And they H4194
14: 6 shall not be put to **d** for the children, H4191
6 children be put to **d** for the fathers; but H4191
6 man shall be put to **d** for his own sin. H4191
17 lived after the **d** of Jehoash son of H4194
15: 5 the day of his **d**, and dwelt in a several H4194
20: 1 In those days was Hezekiah sick unto **d**. H4191
1Ch 22: 5 prepared abundantly before his **d**. H4194
2Ch 15:13 should be put to **d**, whether small or H4191
22: 4 the **d** of his father to his destruction. H4194
23: 7 he shall be put to **d**: but be ye with the H4191
24:17 Now after the **d** of Jehoiada came the H4194
25:25 Judah lived after the **d** of Joash son of H4194
26:21 the day of his **d**, and dwelt in a several H4194
32:24 was sick to the **d**, and prayed unto the H4191
33 him honour at his **d**. And Manasseh his H4194
Ezr 7:26 whether *it be* unto **d**, or to banishment, H4193
Est 4:11 of his to put *him* to **d**, except such to H4191
Job 3: 5 Let darkness and the shadow of **d** stain H6757
21 Which long for **d**, but it *cometh* not; H4194
5:20 In famine he shall redeem thee from **d**: H4194
7:15 strangling, *and* **d** rather than my life. H4194
10:21 land of darkness and the shadow of **d**; H6757
22 of the shadow of **d**, without any order, H6757
12:22 bringeth out to light the shadow of **d**. H6757
16:16 and on my eyelids *is* the shadow of **d**; H6757
18:13 firstborn of **d** shall devour his strength. H4194
24:17 as the shadow of **d**: if *one* know *them*, H6757
17 *are in* the terrors of the shadow of **d**. H6757
27:15 in **d**: and his widows shall not weep. H4194
28: 3 of darkness, and the shadow of **d**. H6757
22 Destruction and **d** say, We have heard H4194
30:23 For I know *that* thou wilt bring me *to* **d**, H4194
34:22 *There is* no darkness, nor shadow of **d**, H6757
38:17 Have the gates of **d** been opened unto H4194
17 thou seen the doors of the shadow of **d**? H6757
Ps 6: 5 For in **d** *there is* no remembrance of H4194
7:13 the instruments of **d**; he ordaineth his H4194
9:13 that liftest me up from the gates of **d**: H4194
13: 3 mine eyes, lest I sleep the *sleep of* **d**; H4194
18: 4 The sorrows of **d** compassed me, and H4194
5 about: the snares of **d** prevented me. H4194
22:15 thou hast brought me into the dust of **d**. H4194
23: 4 of the shadow of **d**, I will fear no evil: H6757
33:19 To deliver their soul from **d**, and to H4194
44:19 and covered us with the shadow of **d**. H6757
48:14 ever: he will be our guide *even* unto **d**. H4192
49:14 Like sheep they are laid in the grave; **d** H4194
55: 4 and the terrors of **d** are fallen upon me. H4194
15 Let **d** seize upon them, *and* let them go H4194
56:13 For thou hast delivered my soul from **d**: H4194
68:20 GOD the Lord *belong* the issues from **d**. H4194
73: 4 For *there are* no bands in their **d**: but H4194
78:50 not their soul from **d**, but gave their life H4194
89:48 and shall not see **d**? shall he deliver his H4194
102:20 to loose those that are appointed to **d**; H8546
107:10 of **d**, *being* bound in affliction and iron; H6757
14 of **d**, and brake their bands in sunder. H6757
18 and they draw near unto the gates of **d**. H4194
116: 3 The sorrows of **d** compassed me, and H4194
8 For thou hast delivered my soul from **d**, H4194
15 sight of the LORD *is* the **d** of his saints. H4194
118:18 but he hath not given me over unto **d**. H4194
Prv 2:18 For her house inclineth unto **d**, and her H4194
5: 5 Her feet go down to **d**; her steps take H4194
7:27 hell, going down to the chambers of **d**. H4194
8:36 own soul: all they that hate me love **d**. H4194
10: 2 but righteousness delivereth from **d**. H4194
11: 4 but righteousness delivereth from **d**. H4194
19 pursueth evil *pursueth it* to his own **d**. H4194

Prv 12:28 in the pathway thereof there is no d. H4194
13:14 of life, to depart from the snares of d. H4194
14:12 but the end thereof are the ways of d. H4194
27 of life, to depart from the snares of d. H4194
32 but the righteous hath hope in his d. H4194
16:14 of d: but a wise man will pacify it. H4194
25 but the end thereof are the ways of d. H4194
18:21 D and life are in the power of the H4194
21: 6 tossed to and fro of them that seek d. H4194
24:11 d, and those that are ready to be slain; H4194
26:18 who casteth firebrands, arrows, and d, H4194
Ecc 7: 1 the day of d than the day of one's birth. H4194
26 And I find more bitter than d the H4194
8: 8 power in the day of d: and there is no H4194
Song 8: 6 love is strong as d; jealousy is cruel as H4194
Isa 9: 2 of d, upon them hath the light shined. H6757
25: 8 He will swallow up d in victory; and the H4194
28:15 a covenant with d, and with hell are we H4194
18 And your covenant with d shall be H4194
38: 1 In those days was Hezekiah sick unto d. H4191
18 For the grave cannot praise thee, d can H4194
53: 9 the rich in his d; because he had done H4194
12 poured out his soul unto d: and he was H4194
Jer 2: 6 of the shadow of d, through a land that H6757
8: 3 And d shall be chosen rather than life H4194
9:21 For d is come up into our windows, H4194
13:16 of d, and make it gross darkness. H6757
15: 2 Such as are for d, to death; and such as H4194
2 are for death, to d; and such as are for H4194
18:21 men be put to d; let their young men H4194
21: 8 you the way of life, and the way of d. H4194
26:15 if ye put me to d, ye shall surely bring H4191
19 put him at all to d? did he not fear the H4191
21 to put him to d: but when Urijah heard H4191
24 the hand of the people to put him to d. H4191
38: 4 let this man be put to d: for thus he H4191
15 not surely put me to d? and if I give thee H4191
16 not put thee to d, neither will I give thee H4191
25 to d; also what the king said unto thee: H4191
43: 3 might put us to d, and carry us away H4191
11 such as are for d to death; and such as H4194
11 as are for death to d; and such as are H4194
52:11 put him in prison till the day of his d. H4194
27 and put them to d in Riblah in the land H4191
34 the day of his d, all the days of his life. H4194
Lam 1:20 sword bereaveth, at home there is as d. H4194
Ezk 18:32 For I have no pleasure in the d of him H4194
31:14 all delivered unto d, to the nether parts H4194
33:11 no pleasure in the d of the wicked; but H4194
Hos 13:14 them from d: O death, I will be thy H4194
14 from death: O d, I will be thy plagues; H4194
Am 5: 8 the shadow of d into the morning, and H6757
Jna 4: 9 said, I do well to be angry, even unto d. H4194
Hab 2: 5 as hell, and is as d, and cannot be H4194
Mt 2:15 And was there until the d of Herod: G5054
4:16 and shadow of d light is sprung up. G2288
10:21 up the brother to d, and the father the G2288
21 parents, and cause them to be put to d. G2289
14: 5 And when he would have put him to d, G615
15: 4 father or mother, let him die the d. G2288
16:28 shall not taste of d, till they see the Son G2288
20:18 and they shall condemn him to d, G2288
26:38 d: tarry ye here, and watch with me. G2288
59 witness against Jesus, to put him to d; G2289
66 answered and said, He is guilty of d. G2288
27: 1 counsel against Jesus to put him to d: G2289
Mk 5:23 at the point of d: I pray thee, come and G2079
7:10 father or mother, let him die the d: G2288
9: 1 shall not taste of d, till they have seen G2288
10:33 d, and shall deliver him to the Gentiles: G2288
13:12 the brother to d, and the father the son; G2288
12 and shall cause them to be put to d. G2289
14: 1 take him by craft, and put him to d. G615
34 unto d: tarry ye here, and watch. G2288
55 Jesus to put him to d; and found none. G2289
64 all condemned him to be guilty of d. G2288
Lk 1:79 in the shadow of d, to guide our feet G2288
2:26 d, before he had seen the Lord's Christ. G2288
9:27 of d, till they see the kingdom of God. G2288
18:33 d: and the third day he shall rise again. G615
21:16 of you shall they cause to be put to d. G2289
22:33 go with thee, both into prison, and to d. G2288
23:15 nothing worthy of d is done unto him. G2288
22 have found no cause of d in him: I will G2288
32 malefactors, led with him to be put to d. G337
24:20 to d, and have crucified him. G2288
Jn 4:47 heal his son: for he was at the point of d. G599
5:24 but is passed from d unto life. G2288
8:51 keep my saying, he shall never see d. G2288
Jn 8:52 my saying, he shall never taste of d. G2288
11: 4 is not unto d, but for the glory of G2288
13 Howbeit Jesus spake of his d: but they G2288
53 took counsel together for to put him to d. G615
12:10 that they might put Lazarus also to d; G615
33 This he said, signifying what d he G2288
18:31 is not lawful for us to put any man to d: G615
32 spake, signifying what d he should die. G2288
21:19 This spake he, signifying by what d he G2288
Act 2:24 loosed the pains of d: because it was not G2288
8: 1 And Saul was consenting unto his d. And G336
12:19 should be put to d. And he went down G520
13:28 And though they found no cause of d in G2288
22: 4 And I persecuted this way unto the d, G2288
20 unto his d, and kept the raiment G336
23:29 to his charge worthy of d or of bonds. G2288
25:11 thing worthy of d, I refuse not to die: G2288
25 nothing worthy of d, and that he G2288
26:10 put to d, I gave my voice against them. G337
31 doeth nothing worthy of d or of bonds. G2288
28:18 because there was no cause of d in me. G2288
Ro 1:32 are worthy of d, not only do the same, G2288
5:10 to God by the d of his Son, much more, G2288
12 the world, and d by sin; and so death G2288
12 by sin; and so d passed upon all men, G2288
14 Nevertheless d reigned from Adam to G2288
17 For if by one man's offence d reigned G2288
21 That as sin hath reigned unto d, even so G2288
6: 3 Jesus Christ were baptized into his d? G2288
4 by baptism into d: that like as Christ G2288
5 the likeness of his d, we shall be also in G2288
9 d hath no more dominion over him. G2288
16 d, or of obedience unto righteousness? G2288
21 for the end of those things is d. G2288
23 For the wages of sin is d; but the gift of G2288
7: 5 our members to bring forth fruit unto d. G2288
10 ordained to life, I found to be unto d. G2288
13 Was then that which is good made d G2288
13 sin, working d in me by that which G2288
24 shall deliver me from the body of this d? G2288
8: 2 made me free from the law of sin and d. G2288
6 For to be carnally minded is d; but to be G2288
38 For I am persuaded, that neither d, nor G2288
1Co 3:22 world, or life, or d, or things present, or G2288
4: 9 were appointed to d: for we are made a G1935
11:26 ye do shew the Lord's d till he come. G2288
15:21 For since by man came d, by man came G2288
26 last enemy that shall be destroyed is d. G2288
54 is written, D is swallowed up in victory. G2288
55 O d, where is thy sting? O grave, where G2288
56 The sting of d is sin; and the strength of G2288
2Co 1: 9 But we had the sentence of d in G2288
10 Who delivered us from so great a d, and G2288
2:16 To the one we are the savour of d unto G2288
16 of death unto d; and to the other the G2288
3: 7 But if the ministration of d, written and G2288
4:11 delivered unto d for Jesus' sake, that G2288
12 So then d worketh in us, but life in you. G2288
7:10 but the sorrow of the world worketh d. G2288
Php 1:20 my body, whether it be by life, or by d. G2288
2: 8 unto d, even the death of the cross. G2288
8 unto death, even the d of the cross. G2288
27 For indeed he was sick nigh unto d: but G2288
30 he was nigh unto d, not regarding his G2288
3:10 being made conformable unto his d; G2288
Col 1:22 In the body of his flesh through d, to G2288
2Ti 1:10 hath abolished d, and hath brought life G2288
Heb 2: 9 the suffering of d, crowned with glory G2288
9 of God should taste d for every man. G2288
14 that through d he might destroy him G2288
14 had the power of d, that is, the devil; G2288
15 through fear of d were all their lifetime G2288
5: 7 d, and was heard in that he feared; G2288
7:23 not suffered to continue by reason of d: G2288
9:15 that by means of d, for the redemption G2288
16 of necessity be the d of the testator. G2288
11: 5 he should not see d; and was not found, G2288
Jas 1:15 sin, when it is finished, bringeth forth d. G2288
5:20 d, and shall hide a multitude of sins. G2288
1Pt 3:18 to God, being put to d in the flesh, but G2289
1Jn 3:14 We know that we have passed from d G2288
14 that loveth not his brother abideth in d. G2288
5:16 which is not unto d, he shall ask, and he G2288
16 that sin not unto d. There is a sin unto G2288
16 d: I do not say that he shall pray for it. G2288
17 is sin: and there is a sin not unto d. G2288
Rev 1:18 and have the keys of hell and of d. G2288
2:10 d, and I will give thee a crown of life. G2288
11 shall not be hurt of the second d. G2288
Rev 2:23 And I will kill her children with d; and G2288
6: 8 sat on him was D, and Hell followed G2288
8 with d, and with the beasts of the earth. G2288
9: 6 And in those days shall men seek d, and G2288
6 to die, and d shall flee from them. G2288
12:11 they loved not their lives unto the d. G2288
13: 3 it were wounded to d; and his deadly G2288
18: 8 come in one day, d, and mourning, and G2288
20: 6 such the second d hath no power, but G2288
13 were in it; and d and hell delivered up G2288
14 And d and hell were cast into the lake G2288
14 the lake of fire. This is the second d. G2288
21: 4 shall be no more d, neither sorrow, nor G2288
8 and brimstone: which is the second d. G2288

DEATHS
Jer 16: 4 They shall die of grievous d; they shall H4463
Ezk 28: 8 thou shalt die the d of them that are H4463
10 Thou shalt die the d of the H4194
2Co 11:23 in prisons more frequent, in d oft. G2288

DEBAR See LO-DEBAR.

DEBASE
Isa 57: 9 off, and didst d thyself even unto hell. H8213

DEBATE
Prv 25: 9 D thy cause with thy neighbour H7378
Isa 27: 8 forth, thou wilt d with it: he stayeth his H7378
58: 4 Behold, ye fast for strife and d, and to H4683
Ro 1:29 d, deceit, malignity; whisperers, G2054

DEBATES
2Co 12:20 not: lest there be d, envyings, wraths, G2054

DEBIR
Jos 10: 3 and unto D king of Eglon, saying, H1688
38 with him, to D; and fought against it: H1688
39 so he did to D, and to the king thereof; H1688
11:21 Hebron, from D, from Anab, and from H1688
12:13 The king of D, one; the king of Geder, H1688
13:26 from Mahanaim unto the border of D; H1688
15: 7 And the border went up toward D from H1688
15 to the inhabitants of D: and the name of H1688
15 name of D before was Kirjath-sepher. H1688
49 and Kirjath-sannah, which is D, H1688
21:15 And Holon with her suburbs, and D H1688
Jdg 1:11 the inhabitants of D: and the name of H1688
11 name of D before was Kirjath-sepher: H1688
1Ch 6:58 And Hilen with her suburbs, D with her H1688

DEBORAH
Gen 35: 8 But D Rebekah's nurse died, and she H1683
Jdg 4: 4 And D, a prophetess, the wife of H1683
5 And she dwelt under the palm tree of D H1683
9 of a woman. And D arose, and went H1683
10 at his feet: and D went up with him. H1683
14 And D said unto Barak, Up; for this is H1683
5: 1 Then sang D and Barak the son of H1683
7 D arose, that I arose a mother in Israel. H1683
12 Awake, awake, D: awake, awake, utter H1683
15 were with D; even Issachar, and H1683

DEBT
1Sa 22: 2 one that was in d, and every one that H5378
2Ki 4: 7 oil, and pay thy d, and live thou and thy H5386
Neh 10:31 year, and the exaction of every d. H3027
Mt 18:27 and loosed him, and forgave him the d. G1156
30 him into prison, till he should pay the d. G3784
32 all that d, because thou desiredst me: G3782
Ro 4: 4 reward not reckoned of grace, but of d. G3783

DEBTOR
Ezk 18: 7 hath restored to the d his pledge, hath H2326
Mt 23:16 by the gold of the temple, he is a d! G3784
Ro 1:14 I am d both to the Greeks, and to the G3781
Gal 5: 3 that he is a d to do the whole law. G3781

DEBTORS
Mt 6:12 us our debts, as we forgive our d. G3781
Lk 7:41 which had two d: the one owed five G5533
16: 5 So he called every one of his lord's d G5533
Ro 8:12 Therefore, brethren, we are d, not to the G3781
15:27 It hath pleased them verily; and their d G3781

DEBTS
Prv 22:26 or of them that are sureties for d. H4859
Mt 6:12 And forgive us our d, as we forgive our G3783

DECAPOLIS
Mt 4:25 from Galilee, and *from* **D**, and *from* G1179
Mk 5:20 to publish in **D** how great things Jesus G1179
7:31 through the midst of the coasts of **D**. G1179

DECAY
Lev 25:35 poor, and fallen in **d** with thee; then H4131

DECAYED
Neh 4:10 of burdens is **d**, and *there is* much H3782
Isa 44:26 and I will raise up the **d** places thereof: H2723

DECAYETH
Job 14:11 the sea, and the flood **d** and drieth up: H2717
Ecc 10:18 By much slothfulness the building **d**; H4355
Heb 8:13 Now that which **d** and waxeth old *is* G3822

DECEASE
Lk 9:31 and spake of his **d** which he should G1841
2Pt 1:15 be able after my **d** to have these things G1841

DECEASED
Isa 26:14 not live; *they are* **d**, they shall not rise: H7496
Mt 22:25 married a wife, **d**, and, having no issue, G5053

DECEIT
Job 15:35 vanity, and their belly prepareth **d**. H4820
27: 4 wickedness, nor my tongue utter **d**. H7423
31: 5 vanity, or if my foot hath hasted to **d**; H4820
Ps 10: 7 His mouth is full of cursing and **d** and H4820
36: 3 *are* iniquity and **d**: he hath left off to be H4820
50:19 to evil, and thy tongue frameth **d**. H4820
55:11 Wickedness *is* in the midst thereof: **d** H8496
72:14 He shall redeem their soul from **d** and H8496
101: 7 He that worketh **d** shall not dwell H7423
119:118 thy statutes: for their **d** *is* falsehood. H8649
Prv 12: 5 *but* the counsels of the wicked *are* **d**. H4820
17 righteousness: but a false witness **d**. H4820
20 **D** *is* in the heart of them that imagine H4820
14: 8 his way: but the folly of fools *is* **d**. H4820
20:17 Bread of **d** *is* sweet to a man; but H8267
26:24 his lips, and layeth up **d** within him; H4820
26 *Whose* hatred is covered by **d**, his H4860
Isa 53: 9 neither *was any* **d** in his mouth. H4820
Jer 5:27 their houses full of **d**: therefore they are H4820
8: 5 they hold fast **d**, they refuse to return. H8649
9: 6 Thine habitation *is* in the midst of **d**; H4820
6 of deceit; through **d** they refuse to H4820
8 shot out; it speaketh **d**: *one* speaketh H4820
14:14 of nought, and the **d** of their heart. H8649
23:26 prophets of the **d** of their own heart; H8649
Hos 11:12 of Israel with **d**: but Judah yet ruleth H4820
12: 7 *He is* a merchant, the balances of **d** *are* H4820
Am 8: 5 great, and falsifying the balances by **d**? H4820
Zep 1: 9 masters' houses with violence and **d**. H4820
Mk 7:22 Thefts, covetousness, wickedness, **d**, G1388
Ro 1:29 debate, **d**, malignity; whisperers, G1388
3:13 **d**; the poison of asps *is* under their lips: G1387
Col 2: 8 and vain **d**, after the tradition of G539
1Th 2: 3 For our exhortation *was* not of **d**, nor of G4106

DECEITFUL
Ps 5: 6 will abhor the bloody and **d** man. H4820
35:20 but they devise **d** matters against *them* H4820
43: 1 deliver me from the **d** and unjust man. H4820
52: 4 all devouring words, O *thou* **d** tongue. H4820
55:23 bloody and **d** men shall not live out H4820
78:57 they were turned aside like a **d** bow. H7423
109: 2 the mouth of the **d** are opened against H4820
120: 2 from lying lips, *and* from a **d** tongue. H7423
Prv 11:18 The wicked worketh a **d** work: but to H8267
14:25 A true witness delivereth souls: but a **d** H4820
23: 3 of his dainties: for they *are* **d** meat. H3577
27: 6 friend; but the kisses of an enemy *are* **d**. H6280
29:13 The poor and the **d** man meet together: H8501
31:30 Favour *is* **d**, and beauty *is* vain: *but* a H8267
Jer 17: 9 The heart *is* **d** above all *things*, and H6121
Hos 7:16 they are like a **d** bow: their princes H7423
Mic 6:11 and with the bag of **d** weights? H4820
12 and their tongue *is* **d** in their mouth. H7423
Zep 3:13 neither shall a **d** tongue be found in H8649
2Co 11:13 For such *are* false apostles, **d** workers, G1386
Eph 4:22 which is corrupt according to the **d** lusts; G539

DECEITFULLY
Gen 34:13 Hamor his father **d**, and said, because H4820
Ex 8:29 let not Pharaoh deal **d** any more in not H2048
21: 8 power, seeing he hath dealt **d** with her. H898
Lev 6: 4 which he hath **d** gotten, or that which H6231
Job 6:15 My brethren have dealt **d** as a brook, H898
13: 7 wickedly for God? and talk **d** for him? H7423
Ps 24: 4 up his soul unto vanity, nor sworn **d**. H4820
52: 2 like a sharp razor, working **d**. H7423
Jer 48:10 work of the LORD **d**, and cursed *be* he H7423
Dan 11:23 him he shall work **d**: for he shall come H4820
2Co 4: 2 the word of God **d**; but by manifestation G1389

DECEITFULNESS
Mt 13:22 this world, and the **d** of riches, choke the G539
Mk 4:19 And the cares of this world, and the **d** of G539
Heb 3:13 of you be hardened through the **d** of sin. G539

DECEITS
Ps 38:12 things, and imagine **d** all the day long. H4820
Isa 30:10 unto us smooth things, prophesy **d**: H4123

DECEIVABLENESS
2Th 2:10 And with all **d** of unrighteousness in G539

DECEIVE
2Sa 3:25 that he came to **d** thee, and to know thy H6601
2Ki 4:28 of my lord? did I not say, Do not **d** me? H7952
18:29 Thus saith the king, Let not Hezekiah **d** H5377
19:10 thou trustest **d** thee, saying, Jerusalem H5377
2Ch 32:15 Now therefore let not Hezekiah **d** you, H5377
Prv 24:28 without cause; and **d** *not* with thy lips. H6601
Isa 36:14 Thus saith the king, Let not Hezekiah **d** H5377
37:10 thou trustest, **d** thee, saying, Jerusalem H5377
Jer 9: 5 And they will **d** every one his H2048
29: 8 in the midst of you, **d** you, neither H5377
37: 9 Thus saith the LORD; **D** not yourselves, H5377
Zec 13: 4 shall they wear a rough garment to **d**: H3584
Mt 24: 4 them, Take heed that no man **d** you. G4105
5 saying, I am Christ; and shall **d** many. G4105
11 prophets shall rise, and shall **d** many. G4105
24 possible, they shall **d** the very elect. G4105
Mk 13: 5 to say, Take heed lest any *man* **d** you: G4105
6 saying, I am *Christ*; and shall **d** many. G4105
Ro 16:18 fair speeches **d** the hearts of the simple. G1818
1Co 3:18 Let no man **d** himself. If any man G1818
Eph 4:14 craftiness, whereby they lie in wait to **d**; G3180
5: 6 Let no man **d** you with vain words: for G538
2Th 2: 3 Let no man **d** you by any means: for G1818
1Jn 1: 8 If we say that we have no sin, we **d** G4105
3: 7 Little children, let no man **d** you: he G4105
Rev 20: 3 that he should **d** the nations no more, G4105
8 And shall go out to **d** the nations which G4105

DECEIVED
Gen 31: 7 And your father hath **d** me, and H2048
Lev 6: 2 by violence, or hath **d** his neighbour; H6231
Dt 11:16 your heart be not **d**, and ye turn aside, H6601
1Sa 19:17 Why hast thou **d** me so, and sent away H7411
28:12 Why hast thou **d** me? for thou *art* Saul. H7411
2Sa 19:26 king, my servant **d** me: for thy servant H7411
Job 12:16 wisdom: the **d** and the deceiver *are* his. H7683
15:31 Let not him that is **d** trust in vanity: for H8582
31: 9 If mine heart have been **d** by a woman, H6601
Prv 20: 1 and whosoever is **d** thereby is not wise. H7686
Isa 19:13 of Noph are **d**; they have also seduced H5377
44:20 He feedeth on ashes: a **d** heart hath H2048
Jer 4:10 thou hast greatly **d** this people and H5377
20: 7 O LORD, thou hast **d** me, and I was H6601
7 me, and I was **d**: thou art stronger than H6601
49:16 Thy terribleness hath **d** thee, *and* the H5377
Lam 1:19 I called for my lovers, *but* they **d** me: H7411
Ezk 14: 9 And if the prophet be **d** when he hath H6601
9 I the LORD have **d** that prophet, and I H6601
Oba 3 The pride of thine heart hath **d** thee, H5377
7 with thee have **d** thee, *and* prevailed H5377
Lk 21: 8 And he said, Take heed that ye be not **d**: G4105
Jn 7:47 them the Pharisees, Are ye also **d**? G4105
Ro 7:11 **d** me, and by it slew *me*. G1818
1Co 6: 9 of God? Be not **d**: neither fornicators, G4105
15:33 Be not **d**: evil communications corrupt G4105
Gal 6: 7 Be not **d**; God is not mocked: for G4105
1Ti 2:14 And Adam was not **d**, but the woman G538
14 being **d** was in the transgression. G538
2Ti 3:13 and worse, deceiving, and being **d**. G4105
Tit 3: 3 disobedient, **d**, serving divers lusts G4105
Rev 18:23 for by thy sorceries were all nations **d**. G4105
19:20 with which he **d** them that had received G4105
20:10 And the devil that **d** them was cast into G4105

DECEIVER
Gen 27:12 seem to him as a **d**; and I shall bring a H8591
Job 12:16 wisdom: the deceived and the **d** *are* his. H7686
Mal 1:14 But cursed *be* the **d**, which hath in his H5230
Mt 27:63 Saying, Sir, we remember that that **d** G4108
2Jn 7 the flesh. This is a **d** and an antichrist. G4108

DECEIVERS
2Co 6: 8 and good report: as **d**, and *yet* true; G4108
Tit 1:10 **d**, specially they of the circumcision: G5423
2Jn 7 For many **d** are entered into the world, G4108

DECEIVETH
Prv 26:19 So *is* the man *that* **d** his neighbour, and H7411
Jn 7:12 others said, Nay; but he **d** the people. G4105
Gal 6: 3 when he is nothing, he **d** himself. G5422
Jas 1:26 not his tongue, but **d** his own heart, this G538
Rev 12: 9 and Satan, which **d** the whole world: he G4105
13:14 And **d** them that dwell on the earth by G4105

DECEIVING
2Ti 3:13 and worse, **d**, and being deceived. G4105
Jas 1:22 not hearers only, **d** your own selves. G3884

DECEIVINGS
2Pt 2:13 their own **d** while they feast with you; G539

DECENTLY
1Co 14:40 Let all things be done **d** and in order. G2156

DECIDED
1Ki 20:40 *shall* thy judgment *be;* thyself hast **d** *it.* H2782

DECISION
Joel 3:14 in the valley of **d**: for the day of the H2742
14 of the LORD *is* near in the valley of **d**. H2742

DECK
Job 40:10 **D** thyself now *with* majesty and H5710
Jer 10: 4 They **d** it with silver and with gold; they H3302

DECKED
Prv 7:16 I have **d** my bed with coverings of H7234
Ezk 16:11 I **d** thee also with ornaments, and I put H5710
13 Thus wast thou **d** with gold and silver; H5710
Hos 2:13 to them, and she **d** herself with her H5710
Rev 17: 4 colour, and **d** with gold and precious G5558
18:16 and scarlet, and **d** with gold, and G5558

DECKEDST
Ezk 16:16 didst take, and **d** thy high places with H6213
23:40 thy eyes, and **d** thyself with ornaments, H5710

DECKEST
Jer 4:30 though thou **d** thee with ornaments H5710

DECKETH
Isa 61:10 as a bridegroom **d** *himself* with H3547

DECLARATION
Est 10: 2 his might, and the **d** of the greatness of H6575
Job 13:17 Hear diligently my speech, and my **d** H262
Lk 1: 1 forth in order a **d** of those things which G1335
2Co 8:19 same Lord, and *d of* your ready mind:

DECLARE
Gen 41:24 *there was* none that could **d** *it* to me. H5046
Dt 1: 5 began Moses to **d** this law, saying, H874
Jos 20: 4 of the city, and shall **d** his cause in the H1696
Jdg 14:12 if ye can certainly **d** it me within the H5046
13 But if ye cannot **d** *it* me, then shall ye H5046
15 that he may **d** unto us the riddle, lest H5046
1Ki 22:13 of the prophets *d* good unto the king
1Ch 16:24 **D** his glory among the heathen; his H5608
2Ch 18:12 of the prophets *d* good to the king with
Est 4: 8 Esther, and to **d** *it* unto her, and to H5046
Job 12: 8 the fishes of the sea shall **d** unto thee. H5608
15:17 me; and that *which* I have seen I will **d**; H5608
21:31 Who shall **d** his way to his face? and H5046
28:27 Then did he see it, and **d** it; he H5608
31:37 I would **d** unto him the number of my H5046
38: 4 earth? **d**, if thou hast understanding. H5046
18 of the earth? **d** if thou knowest it all. H5046
40: 7 demand of thee, and **d** thou unto me. H3045
42: 4 demand of thee, and **d** thou unto me. H3045
Ps 2: 7 I will **d** the decree: the LORD hath said H5608
9:11 in Zion: **d** among the people his doings. H5046
19: 1 The heavens **d** the glory of God; and H5608
22:22 I will **d** thy name unto my brethren: in H5608
31 They shall come, and shall **d** his H5046
30: 9 dust praise thee? shall it **d** thy truth? H5046
38:18 For I will **d** mine iniquity; I will be H5046
40: 5 thee: *if* I would **d** and speak *of them*, H5046

Ps 50: 6 And the heavens shall **d** his H5046
16 hast thou to do to **d** my statutes, or H5608
64: 9 And all men shall fear, and shall **d** the H5046
66:16 I will **d** what he hath done for my soul. H5608
73:28 Lord GOD, that I may **d** all thy works. H5608
75: 1 name is near thy wondrous works **d**. H5608
9 But I will **d** for ever; I will sing praises H5046
78: 6 arise and **d** *them* to their children: H5608
96: 3 **D** his glory among the heathen, his H5608
97: 6 The heavens **d** his righteousness, and H5046
102:21 To **d** the name of the LORD in Zion, H5608
107:22 and **d** his works with rejoicing. H5608
118:17 I shall not die, but live, and **d** the works H5608
145: 4 to another, and shall **d** thy mighty acts. H5046
6 terrible acts: and I will **d** thy greatness. H5608
Ecc 9: 1 in my heart even to **d** all this, that the H952
Isa 3: 9 them; and they **d** their sin as Sodom, H5046
12: 4 upon his name, **d** his doings among the H3045
21: 6 a watchman, let him **d** what he seeth. H5046
41:22 end of them; or **d** us things for to come. H8085
42: 9 new things do I **d**: before they spring H5046
12 LORD, and **d** his praise in the islands. H5046
43: 9 among them can **d** this, and shew us H5046
26 **d** thou, that thou mayest be justified. H5608
44: 7 And who, as I, shall call, and shall **d** it, H5046
45:19 righteousness, I **d** things that are right. H5046
48: 6 and will not ye **d** *it*? I have shewed thee H5046
20 a voice of singing **d** ye, tell this, utter it H5046
53: 8 and who shall **d** his generation? for H7878
57:12 I will **d** thy righteousness, and thy H5046
66:19 shall **d** my glory among the Gentiles. H5046
Jer 4: 5 **D** ye in Judah, and publish in H5046
5:20 **D** this in the house of Jacob, and H5046
9:12 that he may **d** it, for what the land H5046
31:10 O ye nations, and **d** *it* in the isles afar H5046
38:15 Zedekiah, If I **d** *it* unto thee, wilt thou H5046
25 and say unto thee, **D** unto us now what H5046
42: 4 answer you, I will **d** *it* unto you; I will H5046
20 say, so **d** unto us, and we will do *it*. H5046
46:14 **D** ye in Egypt, and publish in Migdol, H5046
50: 2 **D** ye among the nations, and publish, H5046
28 of Babylon, to **d** in Zion the vengeance H5046
51:10 come, and let us **d** in Zion the work of H5608
Ezk 12:16 that they may **d** all their abominations H5608
23:36 yea, **d** unto them their abominations; H5046
40: 4 brought hither: **d** all that thou seest to H5046
Dan 4:18 O Belteshazzar, **d** the interpretation H560
Mic 1:10 **D** ye *it* not at Gath, weep ye not at all: H5046
3: 8 and of might, to **d** unto Jacob his H5046
Zec 9:12 I **d** *that* I will render double unto thee; H5046
Mt 13:36 came unto him, saying, **D** unto us the *G5419*
15:15 said unto him, **D** unto us this parable. *G5419*
Jn 17:26 thy name, and will **d** *it*: that the love *G1107*
Act 8:33 and who shall **d** his generation? for *G1334*
13:32 And we **d** unto you glad tidings, how *G2097*
41 believe, though a man **d** it unto you. *G1555*
17:23 ignorantly worship, him **d** I unto you. *G2605*
20:27 For I have not shunned to **d** unto you all *G312*
Ro 3:25 in his blood, to **d** his righteousness for *G1732*
26 To **d**, *I say*, at this time his *G1732*
1Co 3:13 for the day shall **d** it, because it shall be *G1213*
11:17 Now in this that I **d** *unto you* I praise *G3853*
15: 1 Moreover, brethren, I **d** unto you the *G1107*
Col 4: 7 All my state shall Tychicus **d** unto you, *G1107*
Heb 2:12 Saying, I will **d** thy name unto my *G518*
11:14 For they that say such things **d** plainly *G1718*
1Jn 1: 3 That which we have seen and heard **d** *G518*
5 heard of him, and **d** unto you, that God *G312*

DECLARED
Ex 9:16 may be **d** throughout all the earth. H5608
Lev 23:44 And Moses **d** unto the children of H1696
Nu 1:18 month, and they **d** their pedigrees after
15:34 was not **d** what should be done to him. H6567
Dt 4:13 And he **d** unto you his covenant, which H5046
2Sa 19: 6 For thou hast **d** this day, that thou H5046
Neh 8:12 the words that were **d** unto them. H3045
Job 26: 3 hast thou plentifully **d** the thing as it is? H3045
Ps 40:10 my heart; I have **d** thy faithfulness and H559
71:17 hitherto have I **d** thy wondrous works. H5046
77:14 hast **d** thy strength among the people. H3045
88:11 Shall thy lovingkindness be **d** in the H5608
119:13 With my lips have I **d** all the judgments H5608
26 I have **d** my ways, and thou heardest H5608
Isa 21: 2 A grievous vision is **d** unto me; the H5046
10 the God of Israel, have I **d** unto you. H5046
41:26 Who hath **d** from the beginning, that H5046
43:12 I have **d**, and have saved, and I have H5046
44: 8 time, and have **d** *it*? ye *are* even my H5046
Isa 45:21 who hath **d** this from ancient time? H8085
48: 3 I have **d** the former things from the H5046
5 I have even from the beginning **d** *it* to H5046
14 among them hath **d** these *things*? The H5046
Jer 36:13 Then Michaiah **d** unto them all the H5046
42:21 And *now* I have this day **d** *it* to you; but H5046
Lk 8:47 before him, she **d** unto him before all the *G518*
Jn 1:18 the bosom of the Father, he hath **d** *him*. *G1834*
17:26 And I have **d** unto them thy name, and *G1107*
Act 9:27 the apostles, and **d** unto them how he *G1334*
10: 8 And when he had **d** all *these* things *G1834*
12:17 hold their peace, **d** unto them how the *G1334*
15: 4 elders, and they **d** all things that God *G312*
14 Simeon hath **d** how God at the first did *G1834*
21:19 And when he had saluted them, he **d** *G1834*
25:14 many days, Festus **d** Paul's cause unto *G394*
Ro 1: 4 And **d** *to be* the Son of God with power, *G3724*
9:17 might be **d** throughout all the earth. *G1229*
1Co 1:11 For it hath been **d** unto me of you, my *G1213*
2Co 3: 3 *Forasmuch as ye are* manifestly **d** to be *G5319*
Col 1: 8 Who also **d** unto us your love in the *G1213*
Rev 10: 7 he hath **d** to his servants the prophets. *G2097*

DECLARETH
Isa 41:26 *there is* none that **d**, yea, *there is* none H8085
Jer 4:15 For a voice **d** from Dan, and publisheth H5046
Hos 4:12 and their staff **d** unto them: for the H5046
Am 4:13 the wind, and **d** unto man what *is* his H5046

DECLARING
Isa 46:10 **D** the end from the beginning, and H5046
Act 15: 3 and Samaria, **d** the conversion of the *G1555*
12 and Paul, **d** what miracles and *G1834*
1Co 2: 1 **d** unto you the testimony of God. *G2605*

DECLINE
Ex 23: 2 to **d** after many to wrest *judgment*: H5186
Dt 17:11 do: thou shalt not **d** from the sentence H5493
Ps119:157 *yet* do I not **d** from thy testimonies. H5186
Prv 4: 5 neither **d** from the words of my mouth. H5186
7:25 Let not thine heart **d** to her ways, go H7847

DECLINED
2Ch 34: 2 his father, and **d** *neither* to the right H5493
Job 23:11 steps, his way have I kept, and not **d**. H5186
Ps 44:18 neither have our steps **d** from thy way; H5186
119:51 derision: *yet* have I not **d** from thy law. H5186

DECLINETH
Ps 102:11 My days *are* like a shadow that **d**; and I H5186
109:23 I am gone like the shadow when it **d**: I H5186

DECREASE
Ps 107:38 and suffereth not their cattle to **d**. H4591
Jn 3:30 He must increase, but I *must* **d**. *G1642*

DECREASED
Gen 8: 5 And the waters **d** continually until the H2637

DECREE
2Ch 30: 5 So they established a **d** to make H1697
Ezr 5:13 made a **d** to build this house of God. H2942
17 it be *so*, that a **d** was made of Cyrus H2942
6: 1 Then Darius the king made a **d**, and H2942
3 the king made a **d** *concerning* the H2942
8 Moreover I make a **d** what ye shall do H2942
11 Also I have made a **d**, that whosoever H2942
12 made a **d**; let it be done with speed. H2942
7:13 I make a **d**, that all they of the people of H2942
21 king, do make a **d** to all the treasurers H2942
Est 1:20 And when the king's **d** which he shall H6599
2: 8 and his **d** was heard, and when H1881
3:15 and the **d** was given in Shushan H1881
4: 3 and his **d** came, *there was* great H1881
8 of the writing of the **d** that was given at H1881
8:14 the **d** was given at Shushan the palace. H1881
17 and his **d** came, the Jews had H1881
9: 1 and his **d** drew near to be put H1881
13 unto this day's **d**, and let Haman's ten H1881
14 to be done: and the **d** was given at H1881
32 And the **d** of Esther confirmed these H3982
Job 22:28 Thou shalt also **d** a thing, and it shall H1504
28:26 When he made a **d** for the rain, and a H2706
Ps 2: 7 I will declare the **d**: the LORD hath said H2706
148: 6 he hath made a **d** which shall not pass. H2706
Prv 8:15 By me kings reign, and princes **d** H2710
29 When he gave to the sea his **d**, that the H2706
Isa 10: 1 Woe unto them that **d** unrighteous H2710
Jer 5:22 sea by a perpetual **d**, that it cannot pass H2706
Dan 2: 9 *there is but* one **d** for you: for ye have H1882
13 And the **d** went forth that the wise *men* H1882
15 Why *is* the **d** *so* hasty from the king? H1882
3:10 Thou, O king, hast made a **d**, that every H2942
29 Therefore I make a **d**, That every H2942
4: 6 Therefore made I a **d** to bring in all the H2942
17 This matter *is* by the **d** of the watchers, H1510
24 king, and this *is* the **d** of the most High, H1510
6: 7 and to make a firm **d**, that whosoever H633
8 Now, O king, establish the **d**, and sign the H633
9 king Darius signed the writing and the **d**. H633
12 the king's **d**; Hast thou not signed H633
12 thou not signed a **d**, that every man that H633
13 O king, nor the **d** that thou hast signed, H633
15 *is*, That no **d** nor statute which the H633
26 I make a **d**, That in every dominion of H2942
Jna 3: 7 Nineveh by the **d** of the king and his H2940
Mic 7:11 *in* that day shall the **d** be far removed. H2706
Zep 2: 2 Before the **d** bring forth, *before* the day H2706
Lk 2: 1 that there went out a **d** from Caesar *G1378*

DECREED
Est 2: 1 had done, and what was **d** against her. H1504
9:31 and as they had **d** for themselves and H6965
Job 38:10 And brake up for it my **d** *place*, and set H2706
Isa 10:22 **d** shall overflow with righteousness. H2782
1Co 7:37 will, and hath so **d** in his heart that he *G2919*

DECREES
Isa 10: 1 decree unrighteous **d**, and that write H2711
Act 16: 4 them the **d** for to keep, that were *G1378*
17: 7 do contrary to the **d** of Caesar, saying *G1378*

DEDAN
Gen 10: 7 and the sons of Raamah; Sheba, and **D**. H1719
25: 3 And Jokshan begat Sheba, and **D**. And H1719
3 And the sons of **D** were Asshurim, and H1719
1Ch 1: 9 And the sons of Raamah; Sheba, and **D**. H1719
32 And the sons of Jokshan; Sheba, and **D**. H1719
Jer 25:23 **D**, and Tema, and Buz, and all *that are* H1719
49: 8 O inhabitants of **D**; for I will bring the H1719
Ezk 25:13 and they of **D** shall fall by the sword. H1719
27:15 The men of **D** *were* thy merchants; H1719
20 **D** *was* thy merchant in precious clothes H1719
38:13 Sheba, and **D**, and the merchants of H1719

DEDANIM
Isa 21:13 lodge, O ye travelling companies of **D**. H1720

DEDICATE
Dt 20: 5 die in the battle, and another man **d** it. H2596
2Sa 8:11 Which also king David did **d** unto the H6942
1Ch 26:27 **d** to maintain the house of the LORD. H6942
2Ch 2: 4 LORD my God, to **d** *it* to him, *and* to H6942

DEDICATED
Dt 20: 5 and hath not **d** it? let him go and return H2596
Jdg 17: 3 said, I had wholly **d** the silver unto the H6942
2Sa 8:11 had **d** of all nations which he subdued; H6942
1Ki 7:51 his father had **d**; *even* the silver, and H6944
8:63 of Israel **d** the house of the LORD. H2596
15:15 his father had **d**, and the things which H6944
15 which himself had **d**, into the house of H6944
2Ki 12: 4 All the money of the **d** things that is H6944
18 of Judah, had **d**, and his own hallowed H6942
1Ch 18:11 Them also king David **d** unto the H6942
26:20 and over the treasures of the **d** things. H6944
26 treasures of the **d** things, which David H6944
26 and the captains of the host, had **d**. H6942
28 of Zeruiah, had **d**; *and* whosoever had H6942
28 *and* whosoever had **d** *any thing, it was* H6942
28:12 and of the treasuries of the **d** things: H6944
2Ch 5: 1 his father had **d**; and the silver, and H6944
7: 5 and all the people **d** the house of God. H2596
15:18 his father had **d**, and that he himself H6944
18 had **d**, silver, and gold, and vessels. H6944
24: 7 and also all the **d** things of the house H6944
31:12 the tithes and the **d** *things* faithfully: H6944
Ezk 44:29 every **d** thing in Israel shall be theirs. H2764
Heb 9:18 first *testament* was **d** without blood. *G1457*

DEDICATING
Nu 7:10 And the princes offered for **d** of the H2598
11 prince on his day, for the **d** of the altar. H2598

DEDICATION
Nu 7:84 This *was* the **d** of the altar, in the day H2598
88 sixty. This *was* the **d** of the altar, after H2598
2Ch 7: 9 for they kept the **d** of the altar seven H2598

Ezr 6:16 kept the **d** of this house of God with joy, H2597
17 And offered at the **d** of this house of H2597
Neh 12:27 And at the **d** of the wall of Jerusalem H2598
27 to keep the **d** with gladness, both H2598
Ps 30:ttl A Psalm *and* Song *at* the **d** of the house H2598
Dan 3: 2 to come to the **d** of the image which H2597
3 together unto the **d** of the image that H2597
Jn 10:22 the feast of the **d**, and it was winter. *G1456*

DEED

Gen 44:15 And Joseph said unto them, What **d** *is* H4639
Ex 9:16 And in very **d** for this *cause* have I raised H199
Jdg 19:30 was no such **d** done nor seen from H2063
1Sa 25:34 For in very **d**, *as* the LORD God of Israel H199
26: 4 that Saul was come in very **d**. H3559
2Sa 12:14 Howbeit, because by this **d** thou hast H1697
2Ch 6:18 But will God in very **d** dwell with men on H552
Est 1:17 For *this* **d** of the queen shall come H1697
18 have heard of the **d** of the queen. Thus H1697
Lk 23:51 to the counsel and **d** of them;) *he was* *G4234*
24:19 a prophet mighty in **d** and word before *G2041*
Act 4: 9 of the good **d** done to the impotent *G2108*
Ro 15:18 the Gentiles obedient, by word and **d**, *G2041*
1Co 5: 2 hath done this **d** might be taken away *G2041*
3 him that hath so done this **d**, *G5124*
2Co 10:11 *we be* also in **d** when we are present. *G2041*
Col 3:17 And whatsoever ye do in word or **d**, *do* *G2041*
Jas 1:25 work, this man shall be blessed in his **d**. *G4162*
1Jn 3:18 neither in tongue; but in **d** and in truth. *G2041*

DEEDS

Gen 20: 9 **d** unto me that ought not to be done. H4639
1Ch 16: 8 make known his **d** among the people. H5949
2Ch 35:27 And his **d**, first and last, behold, they H1697
Ezr 9:13 upon us for our evil **d**, and for our great H4639
Neh 6:19 Also they reported his good **d** before H2896
13:14 not out my good **d** that I have done for H2617
Ps 28: 4 Give them according to their **d**, and H6467
105: 1 make known his **d** among the people. H5949
Isa 59:18 According to *their* **d**, accordingly he will H1578
Jer 5:28 they overpass the **d** of the wicked: they H1697
25:14 according to their **d**, and according to H6467
Lk 11:48 that ye allow the **d** of your fathers: for *G2041*
23:41 due reward of our **d**: but this man hath *G3739*
Jn 3:19 than light, because their **d** were evil. *G2041*
20 the light, lest his **d** should be reproved. *G2041*
21 to the light, that his **d** may be made *G2041*
8:41 Ye do the **d** of your father. Then said *G2041*
Act 7:22 and was mighty in words and in **d**. *G2041*
19:18 and confessed, and shewed their **d**. *G4234*
24: 2 that very worthy **d** are done unto this *G2735*
Ro 2: 6 render to every man according to his **d**: *G2041*
3:20 Therefore by the **d** of the law there *G2041*
28 by faith without the **d** of the law. *G2041*
8:13 mortify the **d** of the body, ye shall live. *G4234*
2Co 12:12 in signs, and wonders, and mighty **d**. *G1411*
Col 3: 9 ye have put off the old man with his **d**; *G4234*
2Pt 2: 8 from day to day with *their* unlawful **d**;) *G2041*
2Jn 11 him God speed is partaker of his evil **d**. *G2041*
3Jn 10 I will remember his **d** which he doeth, *G2041*
Jude 15 of all their ungodly **d** which they have *G2041*
Rev 2: 6 **d** of the Nicolaitans, which I also hate. *G2041*
22 except they repent of their **d**. *G2041*
16:11 their sores, and repented not of their **d**. *G2041*

DEEMED

Act 27:27 **d** that they drew near to some country; *G5282*

DEEP

Gen 1: 2 the face of the **d**. And the Spirit of God H8415
2:21 And the LORD God caused a **d** sleep to H8639
7:11 of the great **d** broken up, and the H8415
8: 2 The fountains also of the **d** and the H8415
15:12 And when the sun was going down, a **d** H8639
49:25 blessings of the **d** that lieth under, H8415
Dt 33:13 and for the **d** that coucheth beneath, H8415
1Sa 26:12 all asleep; because a **d** sleep from the H8639
Job 4:13 the night, when **d** sleep falleth on men, H8639
12:22 He discovereth **d** things out of H6013
33:15 of the night, when **d** sleep falleth upon H8639
38:30 a stone, and the face of the **d** is frozen. H8415
41:31 He maketh the **d** to boil like a pot: he H4688
32 him; *one* would think the **d** *to be* hoary. H8415
Ps 36: 6 *are* a great **d**: O LORD, thou preservest H8415
42: 7 **D** calleth unto deep at the noise of thy H8415
7 Deep calleth unto **d** at the noise of thy H8415
64: 6 every one *of them*, and the heart, *is* **d**. H6013
69: 2 I sink in **d** mire, where *there is* no H4688
2 I am come into **d** waters, where the H4615
Ps 69:14 that hate me, and out of the **d** waters. H4615
15 me, neither let the **d** swallow me up, H4688
80: 9 it to take **d** root, and it filled the land. H8328
92: 5 thy works! *and* thy thoughts are very **d**. H6009
95: 4 In his hand *are* the **d** places of the H4278
104: 6 Thou coveredst it with the **d** as *with* a H8415
107:24 of the LORD, and his wonders in the **d**. H4688
135: 6 in earth, in the seas, and all **d** places. H8415
140:10 into **d** pits, that they rise not up again. H4113
Prv 8:28 he strengthened the fountains of the **d**: H8415
18: 4 The words of a man's mouth *are as* **d** H6013
19:15 Slothfulness casteth into a **d** sleep; and H8639
20: 5 Counsel in the heart of man *is like* **d** H6013
22:14 The mouth of strange women *is* a **d** pit: H6013
23:27 For a whore *is* a **d** ditch; and a strange H6013
Ecc 7:24 That which is far off, and exceeding **d**, H6013
Isa 29:10 upon you the spirit of **d** sleep, and hath H8639
15 Woe unto them that seek **d** to hide H6009
30:33 he hath made *it* **d** *and* large: the pile H6009
44:27 That saith to the **d**, Be dry, and I will H6683
51:10 of the great **d**; that hath made the H8415
63:13 That led them through the **d**, as an H8415
Jer 49: 8 Flee ye, turn back, dwell **d**, O H6009
30 Flee, get you far off, dwell **d**, O ye H6009
Ezk 23:32 of thy sister's cup **d** and large: thou H6013
26:19 I shall bring up the **d** upon thee, and H8415
31: 4 The waters made him great, the **d** set H8415
15 I covered the **d** for him, and I H8415
32:14 Then will I make their waters **d**, and H8257
34:18 to have drunk of the **d** waters, but ye H4950
Dan 2:22 He revealeth the **d** and secret things: he H5994
8:18 with me, I was in a **d** sleep on my face H7290
10: 9 then was I in a **d** sleep on my face, and H7290
Am 7: 4 the great **d**, and did eat up a part. H8415
Jna 2: 3 For thou hadst cast me into the **d**, in the H4688
Hab 3:10 passed by: the **d** uttered his voice, *and* H8415
Lk 5: 4 **d**, and let down your nets for a draught. *G899*
6:48 an house, and digged **d**, and laid the *G900*
8:31 not command them to go out into the **d**. *G12*
Jn 4:11 and the well is **d**: from whence then hast *G901*
Act 20: 9 being fallen into a **d** sleep: and as Paul *G901*
Ro 10: 7 Or, Who shall descend into the **d**? (that *G12*
1Co 2:10 all things, yea, the **d** things of God. *G899*
2Co 8: 2 their joy and their **d** poverty abounded *G899*
11:25 a night and a day I have been in the **d**; *G1037*

DEEPER

Lev 13: 3 plague in sight *be* **d** than the skin of his H6013
4 in sight *be* not **d** than the skin, and the H6013
25 and it *be in* sight **d** than the skin; it *is* a H6013
30 if it *be* in sight **d** than the skin; *and* H6013
31 it *be* not in sight **d** than the skin, and H6013
32 the scall *be* not in sight **d** than the skin; H6013
34 nor *be* in sight **d** than the skin; then H6013
Job 11: 8 do? **d** than hell; what canst thou know? H6013
Isa 33:19 a people of a **d** speech than thou canst H6012

DEEPLY

Isa 31: 6 the children of Israel have **d** revolted. H6009
Hos 9: 9 They have **d** corrupted *themselves*, as H6009
Mk 8:12 And he sighed **d** in his spirit, and saith, *G389*

DEEPNESS

Mt 13: 5 up, because they had no **d** of earth: *G899*

DEEPS

Neh 9:11 the **d**, as a stone into the mighty waters. H4688
Ps 88: 6 in the lowest pit, in darkness, in the **d**. H4688
148: 7 from the earth, ye dragons, and all **d**: H8415
Zec 10:11 sea, and all the **d** of the river shall dry H4688

DEER

Dt 14: 5 and the fallow **d**, and the wild goat, and H3180

DEFAMED

1Co 4:13 Being **d**, we entreat: we are made as the *G987*

DEFAMING

Jer 20:10 For I heard the **d** of many, fear on H1681

DEFEAT

2Sa 15:34 for me **d** the counsel of Ahithophel. H6565
17:14 had appointed to **d** the good counsel of H6565

DEFENCE

Nu 14: 9 bread for us: their **d** is departed from H6738
2Ch 11: 5 and built cities for **d** in Judah. H4692
Job 22:25 Yea, the Almighty shall be thy **d**, and H1220
Ps 7:10 My **d** *is* of God, which saveth the H4043
Ps 31: 2 rock, for an house of **d** to save me. H4686
59: 9 will I wait upon thee: for God *is* my **d**. H4869
16 **d** and refuge in the day of my trouble. H4869
17 God *is* my **d**, *and* the God of my mercy. H4869
62: 2 *he is* my **d**; I shall not be greatly moved. H4869
6 *he is* my **d**; I shall not be moved. H4869
89:18 For the LORD *is* our **d**; and the Holy H4043
94:22 But the LORD is my **d**; and my God *is* H4869
Ecc 7:12 For wisdom *is* a **d**, *and* money *is* a H6738
12 *and* money *is* a **d**: but the excellency of H6738
Isa 4: 5 night: for upon all the glory *shall be* a **d**. H2646
19: 6 *and* the brooks of **d** shall be H4693+H4692
33:16 He shall dwell on high: his place of **d** H4869
Nah 2: 5 thereof, and the **d** shall be prepared. H5526
Act 19:33 would have made his **d** unto the people. *G626*
22: 1 ye my **d** *which I make* now unto you. *G627*
Php 1: 7 bonds, and in the **d** and confirmation of *G627*
17 that I am set for the **d** of the gospel. *G627*

DEFENCED

Isa 25: 2 city an heap; *of* a **d** city a ruin: a palace H1219
27:10 Yet the **d** city *shall be* desolate, *and* the H1219
36: 1 all the **d** cities of Judah, and took them. H1219
37:26 to lay waste **d** cities *into* ruinous heaps. H1219
Jer 1:18 thee this day a **d** city, and an iron H4013
4: 5 and let us go into the **d** cities. H4013
8:14 us enter into the **d** cities, and let us be H4013
34: 7 **d** cities remained of the cities of Judah. H4013
Ezk 21:20 and to Judah in Jerusalem the **d**. H1219

DEFEND

Jdg 10: 1 And after Abimelech there arose to **d** H3467
2Ki 19:34 For I will **d** this city, to save it, for mine H1598
20: 6 Assyria; and I will **d** this city for mine H1598
Ps 20: 1 the name of the God of Jacob **d** thee; H7682
59: 1 O my God: **d** me from them that H7682
82: 3 **D** the poor and fatherless: do justice to H8199
Isa 31: 5 will the LORD of hosts **d** Jerusalem; H1598
37:35 For I will **d** this city to save it for mine H1598
38: 6 king of Assyria: and I will **d** this city. H1598
Zec 9:15 The LORD of hosts shall **d** them; and H1598
12: 8 In that day shall the LORD **d** the H1598

DEFENDED

2Sa 23:12 of the ground, and **d** it, and slew the H5337
Act 7:24 suffer wrong, he **d** *him*, and avenged *G292*

DEFENDEST

Ps 5:11 joy, because thou **d** them: let them also H5526

DEFENDING

Isa 31: 5 defend Jerusalem; **d** also he will deliver H1598

DEFER

Ecc 5: 4 When thou vowest a vow unto God, **d** H309
Isa 48: 9 For my name's sake will I **d** mine anger, H748
Dan 9:19 hearken and do; **d** not, for thine own H309

DEFERRED

Gen 34:19 And the young man **d** not to do the H309
Prv 13:12 Hope **d** maketh the heart sick: but H4900
Act 24:22 of *that* way, he **d** them, and said, When *G306*

DEFERRETH

Prv 19:11 The discretion of a man **d** his anger; and H748

DEFIED

Nu 23: 8 I defy, *whom* the LORD hath not **d**? H2194
1Sa 17:36 he hath **d** the armies of the living God. H2778
45 the armies of Israel, whom thou hast **d**. H2778
2Sa 21:21 And when he **d** Israel, Jonathan the son H2778
23: 9 David, when they **d** the Philistines *that* H2778
1Ch 20: 7 But when he **d** Israel, Jonathan the son H2778

DEFILE

Lev 11:44 neither shall ye **d** yourselves with any H2930
15:31 **d** my tabernacle that *is* among them. H2930
18:20 neighbour's wife, to **d** thyself with her. H2930
23 with any beast to **d** thyself therewith: H2930
24 **D** not ye yourselves in any of these H2930
28 out also, when ye **d** it, as it spued out H2930
30 you, and that ye **d** not yourselves H2930
20: 3 unto Molech, to **d** my sanctuary, and H2930
21: 4 *But* he shall not **d** himself, *being* a chief H2930
11 dead body, nor **d** himself for his father, H2930
22: 8 to **d** himself therewith: I *am* the LORD. H2930
Nu 5: 3 them; that they **d** not their camps, in H2930
35:34 **D** not therefore the land which ye shall H2930
2Ki 23:13 the children of Ammon, did the king **d**. H2930

Song 5: 3 washed my feet; how shall I **d** them? H2936
Isa 30:22 Ye shall **d** also the covering of thy H2930
Jer 32:34 which is called by my name, to **d** it. H2930
Ezk 7:22 the robbers shall enter into it, and **d** it. H2490
9: 7 And he said unto them, **D** the house, H2930
20: 7 of his eyes, and **d** not yourselves with H2930
18 nor **d** yourselves with their idols: H2930
22: 3 idols against herself to **d** herself. H2930
28: 7 and they shall **d** thy brightness. H2490
33:26 and ye **d** every one his neighbour's H2930
37:23 Neither shall they **d** themselves any H2930
43: 7 of Israel no more **d**, *neither* they, nor H2930
44:25 no dead person to **d** themselves: but for H2930
25 no husband, they may **d** themselves. H2930
Dan 1: 8 that he would not **d** himself with the H1351
8 eunuchs that he might not **d** himself. H1351
Mt 15:18 from the heart; and they **d** the man. *G2840*
20 These are *the things* which **d** a man: *G2840*
Mk 7:15 into him can **d** him: but the things *G2840*
15 of him, those are they that **d** the man. *G2840*
18 entereth into the man, *it* cannot **d** him; *G2840*
23 come from within, and **d** the man. *G2840*
1Co 3:17 If any man **d** the temple of God, him *G5351*
1Ti 1:10 For whoremongers, for them that **d** *G733*
Jude 8 Likewise also these *filthy* dreamers **d** *G3392*

DEFILED
Gen 34: 2 took her, and lay with her, and **d** her. H6031
5 And Jacob heard that he had **d** Dinah H2930
13 because he had **d** Dinah their sister: H2930
27 the city, because they had **d** their sister. H2930
Lev 5: 3 a man shall be **d** withal, and it be hid H2930
11:43 with them, that ye should be **d** thereby. H2930
13:46 in him he shall be **d**; he *is* unclean: he H2930
15:32 goeth from him, and is **d** therewith; H2930
18:24 are **d** which I cast out before you: H2930
25 And the land is **d**: therefore I do visit H2930
27 *were* before you, and the land is **d**;) H2930
19:31 be **d** by them: I *am* the LORD your God. H2930
21: 1 be **d** for the dead among his people: H2930
3 had no husband; for her may he be **d**. H2930
Nu 5: 2 issue, and whosoever is **d** by the dead: H2931
13 close, and she be **d**, and *there be* no H2930
14 his wife, and she be **d**: or if the spirit of H2930
14 be jealous of his wife, and she be not **d**: H2930
20 and if thou be **d**, and some man have H2930
27 *that*, if she be **d**, and have done trespass H2930
28 And if the woman be not **d**, but be H2930
29 instead of her husband, and is **d**; H2930
6: 9 by him, and he hath **d** the head of his H2930
12 be lost, because his separation was **d**. H2930
9: 6 men, who were **d** by the dead body of H2931
7 unto him, We *are* **d** by the dead body of H2931
19:20 because he hath **d** the sanctuary of the H2930
Dt 21:23 thy land be not **d**, which the LORD thy H2930
22: 9 and the fruit of thy vineyard, be **d**. H6942
24: 4 wife, after that she is **d**; for that *is* H2930
2Ki 23: 8 of Judah, and **d** the high places where H2930
10 And he **d** Topheth, which *is* in the H2930
1Ch 5: 1 forasmuch as he **d** his father's bed, his H2490
Neh 13:29 because they have **d** the priesthood, H1352
Job 16:15 my skin, and **d** my horn in the dust. H5953
Ps 74: 7 they have **d** *by casting down* the H2490
79: 1 **d**; they have laid Jerusalem on heaps. H2930
106:39 Thus were they **d** with their own works, H2930
Isa 24: 5 The earth also is **d** under the H2610
59: 3 For your hands are **d** with blood, and H1351
Jer 2: 7 ye entered, ye **d** my land, and made H2930
3: 9 that she **d** the land, and committed H2610
16:18 because they have **d** my land, they H2490
19:13 of Judah, shall be **d** as the place of H2931
Ezk 4:13 of Israel eat their **d** bread among the H2931
5:11 because thou hast **d** my sanctuary with H2930
7:24 and their holy places shall be **d**. H2490+H5157
18: 6 neither hath **d** his neighbour's wife, H2930
11 and **d** his neighbour's wife, H2930
15 Israel, hath not **d** his neighbour's wife, H2930
20:43 ye have been **d**; and ye shall lothe H2930
22: 4 shed; and hast **d** thyself in thine idols H2930
11 hath lewdly **d** his daughter in law; H2930
23: 7 doted: with all their idols she **d** herself. H2930
13 Then I saw that she was **d**, *that* they H2930
17 bed of love, and they **d** her with their H2930
38 me: they have **d** my sanctuary in the H2930
28:18 Thou hast **d** thy sanctuaries by the H2490
36:17 own land, they **d** it by their own way H2930
43: 8 they have even **d** my holy name by H2930
Hos 5: 3 committest whoredom, *and* Israel is **d**. H2930
6:10 the whoredom of Ephraim, Israel is **d**. H2930
Mic 4:11 be **d**, and let our eye look upon Zion. H2610
Mk 7: 2 eat bread with **d**, that is to say, with *G2839*
Jn 18:28 **d**; but that they might eat the passover. *G3392*
1Co 8: 7 and their conscience being weak is **d**. *G3435*
Tit 1:15 them that are **d** and unbelieving *is* *G3392*
15 even their mind and conscience is **d**. *G3392*
Heb 12:15 up trouble *you*, and thereby many be **d**; *G3392*
Rev 3: 4 which have not **d** their garments; and *G3435*
14: 4 These are they which were not **d** with *G3435*

DEFILEDST
Gen 49: 4 then **d** thou *it*: he went up to my couch. H2490

DEFILETH
Ex 31:14 every one that **d** it shall surely be put H2490
Nu 19:13 not himself, **d** the tabernacle of the H2930
35:33 ye *are*: for blood it **d** the land: and the H2610
Mt 15:11 Not that which goeth into the mouth **d** *G2840*
11 cometh out of the mouth, this **d** a man. *G2840*
20 eat with unwashen hands **d** not a man. *G2840*
Mk 7:20 cometh out of the man, that **d** the man. *G2840*
Jas 3: 6 members, that it **d** the whole body, and *G4695*
Rev 21:27 it any thing that **d**, neither *whatsoever* *G2840*

DEFRAUD
Lev 19:13 Thou shalt not **d** thy neighbour, neither H6231
Mk 10:19 **D** not, Honour thy father and mother. *G650*
1Co 6: 8 Nay, ye do wrong, and **d**, and that *your* *G650*
7: 5 **D** ye not one the other, except *it be* with *G650*
1Th 4: 6 That no *man* go beyond and **d** his *G4122*

DEFRAUDED
1Sa 12: 3 taken? or whom have I **d**? whom have I H6231
4 And they said, Thou hast not **d** us, nor H6231
1Co 6: 7 do ye not rather *suffer yourselves to* be **d**? *G650*
2Co 7: 2 corrupted no man, we have **d** no man. *G4122*

DEFY
Nu 23: 7 curse me Jacob, and come, **d** Israel. H2194
8 I **d**, *whom* the LORD hath not defied? H2194
1Sa 17:10 And the Philistine said, I **d** the armies H2778
25 come up? surely to **d** Israel is he come H2778
26 should **d** the armies of the living God? H2778

DEGENERATE
Jer 2:21 the **d** plant of a strange vine unto me? H5494

DEGREE
1Ch 15:18 of the second *d*, Zechariah, Ben, and
17:17 estate of a man of high **d**, O LORD God.
Ps 62: 9 Surely men of low **d** *are* vanity, *and* men
9 *and* men of high **d** *are* a lie: to be laid in
Lk 1:52 *their* seats, and exalted them of low **d**. *G5011*
1Ti 3:13 themselves a good **d**, and great boldness *G898*
Jas 1: 9 Let the brother of low **d** rejoice in that *G5011*

DEGREES
2Ki 20: 9 forward ten **d**, or go back ten degrees? H4609
9 forward ten degrees, or go back ten **d**? H4609
10 to go down ten **d**: nay, but let the H4609
10 let the shadow return backward ten **d**. H4609
11 the shadow ten **d** backward, by which H4609
Ps 120: ttl A Song of **d**. H4609
121: ttl A Song of **d**. H4609
122: ttl A Song of **d** of David. H4609
123: ttl A Song of **d**. H4609
124: ttl A Song of **d** of David. H4609
125: ttl A Song of **d**. H4609
126: ttl A Song of **d**. H4609
127: ttl A Song of **d** for Solomon. H4609
128: ttl A Song of **d**. H4609
129: ttl A Song of **d**. H4609
130: ttl A Song of **d**. H4609
131: ttl A Song of **d** of David. H4609
132: ttl A Song of **d**. H4609
133: ttl A Song of **d** of David. H4609
134: ttl A Song of **d**. H4609
Isa 38: 8 the shadow of the **d**, which is gone H4609
8 dial of Ahaz, ten **d** backward. So the H4609
8 **d**, by which degrees it was gone down. H4609
8 degrees, by which **d** it was gone down. H4609

DEHAVITES
Ezr 4: 9 Susanchites, the **D**, *and* the Elamites, H1723

DEKAR
1Ki 4: 9 The son of **D**, in Makaz, and in H1857

DELAIAH
1Ch 24:18 The three and twentieth to **D**, the four H1806
Ezr 2:60 The children of **D**, the children of H1806
Neh 6:10 the son of **D** the son of Mehetabeel, H1806
7:62 The children of **D**, the children of H1806
Jer 36:12 the scribe, and **D** the son of Shemaiah, H1806
25 Nevertheless Elnathan and **D** and H1806

DELAY
Ex 22:29 Thou shalt not **d** *to offer* the first of thy H309
Act 9:38 that he would not **d** to come to them. *G3635*
25:17 without any **d** on the morrow I sat *G311*

DELAYED
Ex 32: 1 And when the people saw that Moses **d** H954
Ps 119:60 I made haste, and **d** not to keep thy H4102

DELAYETH
Mt 24:48 say in his heart, My lord **d** his coming; *G5549*
Lk 12:45 in his heart, My lord **d** his coming; and *G5549*

DELECTABLE
Isa 44: 9 vanity; and their **d** things shall not H2530

DELICACIES
Rev 18: 3 rich through the abundance of her **d**. *G4764*

DELICATE
Dt 28:54 you, and very **d**, his eye shall be evil H6028
56 The tender and **d** woman among you, H6028
Isa 47: 1 shalt no more be called tender and **d**. H6028
Jer 6: 2 of Zion to a comely and **d** *woman*. H6026
Mic 1:16 Make thee bald, and poll thee for thy **d** H8588

DELICATELY
1Sa 15:32 Agag came unto him **d**. And Agag said, H4574
Prv 29:21 He that **d** bringeth up his servant from H6445
Lam 4: 5 They that did feed **d** are desolate in the H4574
Lk 7:25 and live **d**, are in kings' courts. *G5172*

DELICATENESS
Dt 28:56 the ground for **d** and tenderness, her H6026

DELICATES
Jer 51:34 belly with my **d**, he hath cast me out. H5730

DELICIOUSLY
Rev 18: 7 herself, and lived **d**, so much torment *G4763*
9 and lived **d** with her, shall bewail *G4763*

DELIGHT
Gen 34:19 because he had **d** in Jacob's daughter: H2654
Nu 14: 8 If the LORD **d** in us, then he will bring H2654
Dt 10:15 Only the LORD had a **d** in thy fathers to H2836
21:14 And it shall be, if thou have no **d** in her, H2654
1Sa 15:22 the LORD *as great* **d** in burnt offerings H2656
18:22 the king hath **d** in thee, and all his H2654
2Sa 15:26 But if he thus say, I have no **d** in thee; H2654
24: 3 doth my lord the king **d** in this thing? H2654
Est 6: 6 **d** to do honour more than to myself? H2654
Job 22:26 For then shalt thou have thy **d** in the H6026
27:10 Will he **d** himself in the Almighty? will H6026
34: 9 that he should **d** himself with God. H7521
Ps 1: 2 But his **d** *is* in the law of the LORD; and H2656
16: 3 *to* the excellent, in whom *is* all my **d**. H2656
37: 4 **D** thyself also in the LORD; and he H6026
11 the earth; and shall **d** themselves in the H6026
40: 8 I **d** to do thy will, O my God: yea, thy H2654
62: 4 his excellency: they **d** in lies: they bless H7521
68:30 scatter thou the people *that* **d** in war. H2654
94:19 within me thy comforts **d** my soul. H8173
119:16 I will **d** myself in thy statutes: I will not H8173
24 Thy testimonies also *are* my **d** *and* my H8191
35 thy commandments; for therein do I **d**. H2654
47 And I will **d** myself in thy H8173
70 Their heart is as fat as grease; *but* I **d** H8173
77 me, that I may live: for thy law *is* my **d**. H8191
174 salvation, O LORD; and thy law *is* my **d**. H8191
Prv 1:22 and the scorners **d** in their scorning, H2530
2:14 Who rejoice to do evil, *and* **d** in the H1523
8:30 daily *his* **d**, rejoicing always before him; H8191
11: 1 to the LORD: but a just weight *is* his **d**. H7522
20 *as are* upright in *their* way *are* his **d**. H7522
12:22 LORD: but they that deal truly *are* his **d**. H7522
15: 8 but the prayer of the upright *is* his **d**. H7522
16:13 Righteous lips *are* the **d** of kings; and H7522
18: 2 A fool hath no **d** in understanding, but H2654
19:10 **D** is not seemly for a fool; much less for H8588
24:25 But to them that rebuke *him* shall be **d**, H5276

Prv 29:17 rest; yea, he shall give **d** unto thy soul. H4574
Song 2: 3 **d**, and his fruit *was* sweet to my taste. H2530
Isa 1:11 fed beasts; and I **d** not in the blood of H2654
13:17 and *as for* gold, they shall not **d** in it. H2654
55: 2 and let your soul **d** itself in fatness. H6026
58: 2 Yet they seek me daily, and **d** to know H2654
2 they take **d** in approaching to God. H2654
13 and call the sabbath a **d**, the holy of the H6027
14 Then shalt thou **d** thyself in the LORD; H6026
Jer 6:10 them a reproach; they have no **d** in it. H2654
9:24 for in these *things* I **d**, saith the LORD. H2654
Mal 3: 1 whom ye **d** in: behold, he shall H2655
Ro 7:22 For I **d** in the law of God after the *G4913*

DELIGHTED

1Sa 19: 2 But Jonathan Saul's son **d** much in H2654
2Sa 22:20 he delivered me, because he **d** in me. H2654
1Ki 10: 9 Blessed be the LORD thy God, which **d** H2654
2Ch 9: 8 Blessed be the LORD thy God, which **d** H2654
Neh 9:25 **d** themselves in thy great goodness. H5727
Est 2:14 except the king **d** in her, and that she H2654
Ps 18:19 he delivered me, because he **d** in me. H2654
22: 8 let him deliver him, seeing he **d** in him. H2654
109:17 unto him: as he **d** not in blessing, so let H2654
Isa 65:12 and did choose *that* wherein I **d** not. H2654
66: 4 eyes, and chose *that* in which I **d** not. H2654
11 be **d** with the abundance of her glory. H6026

DELIGHTEST

Ps 51:16 I give *it*: thou **d** not in burnt offering. H7521

DELIGHTETH

Est 6: 6 man whom the king **d** to honour? Now H2654
7 the man whom the king **d** to honour, H2654
9 whom the king **d** to honour, and bring H2654
9 to the man whom the king **d** to honour. H2654
11 the man whom the king **d** to honour. H2654
Ps 37:23 by the LORD: and he **d** in his way. H2654
112: 1 *that* **d** greatly in his commandments. H2654
147:10 He **d** not in the strength of the horse: he H2654
Prv 3:12 even as a father the son *in whom* he **d**. H7521
Isa 42: 1 *in whom* my soul **d**; I have put my spirit H7521
62: 4 for the LORD **d** in thee, and thy land H2654
66: 3 and their soul **d** in their abominations. H2654
Mic 7:18 anger for ever, because he **d** *in* mercy. H2654
Mal 2:17 the LORD, and he **d** in them; or, Where H2654

DELIGHTS

2Sa 1:24 in scarlet, with *other* **d**, who put on H5730
Ps 119:92 Unless thy law *had been* my **d**, I should H8191
143 me: *yet* thy commandments *are* my **d**. H8191
Prv 8:31 and my **d** *were* with the sons of men. H8191
Ecc 2: 8 singers, and the **d** of the sons of men, H8588
Song 7: 6 how pleasant art thou, O love, for **d**! H8588

DELIGHTSOME

Mal 3:12 be a **d** land, saith the LORD of hosts. H2656

DELILAH

Jdg 16: 4 the valley of Sorek, whose name *was* **D**. H1807
6 And **D** said to Samson, Tell me, I pray H1807
10 And **D** said unto Samson, Behold, thou H1807
12 **D** therefore took new ropes, and bound H1807
13 And **D** said unto Samson, Hitherto H1807
18 And when **D** saw that he had told her H1807

DELIVER

Gen 32:11 **D** me, I pray thee, from the hand of my H5337
37:22 hands, to **d** him to his father again. H5337
40:13 and thou shalt **d** Pharaoh's cup into H5414
42:34 true *men*: *so* will I **d** you your brother, H5414
37 him not to thee: **d** him into my hand, H5414
Ex 3: 8 And I am come down to **d** them out of H5337
5:18 you, yet shall ye **d** the tale of bricks. H5414
21:13 And if a man lie not in wait, but God **d** H579
22: 7 If a man shall **d** unto his neighbour H5414
10 If a man **d** unto his neighbour an ass, H5414
26 pledge, thou shalt **d** it unto him by that H7725
23:31 the river: for I will **d** the inhabitants of H5414
Lev 26:26 and they shall **d** *you* your bread again H7725
Nu 21: 2 If thou wilt indeed **d** this people into H5414
35:25 And the congregation shall **d** the slayer H5337
Dt 1:27 land of Egypt, to **d** us into the hand of H5414
2:30 that he might **d** him into thy hand, H5414
3: 2 him not: for I will **d** him, and all his H5414
7: 2 And when the LORD thy God shall **d** H5414
16 thy God shall **d** thee; thine eye shall H5414
23 But the LORD thy God shall **d** them H5414
24 And he shall **d** their kings into thine H5414
Dt 19:12 him thence, and **d** him into the hand of H5414
23:14 of thy camp, to **d** thee, and to give up H5337
15 Thou shalt not **d** unto his master the H5462
24:13 In any case thou shalt **d** him the pledge H7725
25:11 near for to **d** her husband out of H5337
32:39 *is there any* that can **d** out of my hand. H5337
Jos 2:13 they have, and **d** our lives from death. H5337
7: 7 over Jordan, to **d** us into the hand of H5414
8: 7 your God will **d** it into your hand. H5414
11: 6 this time will I **d** them up all slain H5414
20: 5 then they shall not **d** the slayer up into H5462
Jdg 4: 7 and I will **d** him into thine hand. H5414
7: 7 I save you, and **d** the Midianites into H5414
10:11 of Israel, *Did* not *I* **d** *you* from the
13 gods: wherefore I will **d** you no more. H3467
14 **d** you in the time of your tribulation. H3467
15 thee; **d** us only, we pray thee, this day. H5337
11: 9 **d** them before me, shall I be your head? H5414
30 thou shalt without fail **d** the children of H5414
13: 5 and he shall begin to **d** Israel out of the H3467
15:12 thee, that we may **d** thee into the hand H5414
13 thee fast, and **d** thee into their hand: H5414
20:13 Now therefore **d** *us* the men, the H5414
28 morrow I will **d** them into thine hand. H5414
1Sa 4: 8 Woe unto us! who shall **d** us out of the H5337
7: 3 **d** you out of the hand of the Philistines. H5337
14 thereof did Israel **d** out of the hands of H5337
12:10 but now **d** us out of the hand of H5337
21 cannot profit nor **d**; for they *are* vain. H5337
14:37 wilt thou **d** them into the hand H5414
17:37 paw of the bear, he will **d** me out of the H5337
46 This day will the LORD **d** thee into H5462
23: 4 I will **d** the Philistines into thine hand. H5414
11 Will the men of Keilah **d** me up into his H5462
12 the men of Keilah **d** me and my men H5462
12 the LORD said, They will **d** *thee* up. H5462
20 *shall be* to **d** him into the king's hand. H5462
24: 4 thee, Behold, I will **d** thine enemy into H5414
15 my cause, and **d** me out of thine hand. H8199
26:24 and let him **d** me out of all tribulation. H5337
28:19 Moreover the LORD will also **d** Israel H5414
19 the LORD also shall **d** the host of Israel H5414
30:15 kill me, nor **d** me into the hands of H5462
2Sa 3:14 Saul's son, saying, **D** *me* my wife H5414
5:19 wilt thou **d** them into mine hand? H5414
19 **d** the Philistines into thine hand. H5414
14: 7 and they said, **D** him that smote his H5414
16 For the king will hear, to **d** his H5337
20:21 against David: **d** him only, and I will H5414
1Ki 8:46 with them, and **d** them to the enemy, H5414
18: 9 thou wouldest **d** thy servant into the H5414
20: 5 saying, Thou shalt **d** me thy silver, and H5414
13 behold, I will **d** it into thine hand this H5414
28 valleys, therefore will I **d** all this great H5414
22: 6 shall **d** *it* into the hand of the king. H5414
12 LORD shall **d** *it* into the king's hand. H5414
15 shall **d** *it* into the hand of the king. H5414
2Ki 3:10 to **d** them into the hand of Moab! H5414
13 to **d** them into the hand of Moab. H5414
18 **d** the Moabites also into your hand. H5414
12: 7 but **d** it for the breaches of the house. H5414
17:39 fear; and he shall **d** you out of the hand H5337
18:23 Assyria, and I will **d** thee two thousand H5414
29 not be able to **d** you out of his hand: H5337
30 The LORD will surely **d** us, and this city H5337
32 you, saying, The LORD will **d** us. H5337
35 should **d** Jerusalem out of mine hand? H5337
20: 6 years; and I will **d** thee and this city out H5337
21:14 inheritance, and **d** them into the hand H5414
22: 5 And let them **d** it into the hand of the H5414
1Ch 14:10 and wilt thou **d** them into mine hand? H5414
10 up; for I will **d** them into thine hand. H5414
16:35 us together, and **d** us from the heathen, H5337
2Ch 6:36 with them, and **d** them over before H5414
18: 5 for God will **d** *it* into the king's hand. H5414
11 shall **d** *it* into the hand of the king. H5414
25:15 **d** their own people out of thine hand? H5337
20 that he might **d** them into the hand H5414
28:11 Now hear me therefore, and **d** the H7725
32:11 our God shall **d** us out of the hand of H5337
13 able to **d** their lands out of mine hand? H5337
14 that could **d** his people out of mine H5337
14 be able to **d** you out of mine hand? H5337
15 was able to **d** his people out of mine H5337
15 shall your God **d** you out of mine hand? H5337
17 **d** his people out of mine hand. H5337
Ezr 7:19 **d** thou before the God of Jerusalem. H8000
Neh 9:28 thou **d** them according to thy mercies; H5337
Job 5: 4 the gate, neither *is there* any to **d** *them*. H5337
Job 5:19 He shall **d** thee in six troubles: yea, in H5337
6:23 Or, **D** me from the enemy's hand? or, H4422
10: 7 *is* none that can **d** out of thine hand. H5337
22:30 He shall **d** the island of the innocent: H4422
33:24 unto him, and saith, **D** him from going H6308
28 He will **d** his soul from going into the H6299
36:18 then a great ransom cannot **d** thee. H5186
Ps 6: 4 Return, O LORD, **d** my soul: oh save H2502
7: 1 all them that persecute me, and **d** me: H5337
2 *it* in pieces, while *there is* none to **d**. H5337
17:13 cast him down: **d** my soul from the H6403
22: 4 they trusted, and thou didst **d** them. H6403
8 *that* he would **d** him: let him deliver H6403
8 him **d** him, seeing he delighted in him. H5337
20 **D** my soul from the sword; my darling H5337
25:20 O keep my soul, and **d** me: let me not H5337
27:12 **D** me not over unto the will of mine H5414
31: 1 ashamed: **d** me in thy righteousness. H6403
2 Bow down thine ear to me; **d** me H5337
15 My times *are* in thy hand: **d** me from H5337
33:17 shall he **d** *any* by his great strength. H4422
19 To **d** their soul from death, and to keep H5337
37:40 And the LORD shall help them, and **d** H6403
40 them: he shall **d** them from the wicked, H6403
39: 8 **D** me from all my transgressions: make H5337
40:13 Be pleased, O LORD, to **d** me: O LORD, H5337
41: 1 the LORD will **d** him in time of trouble. H4422
2 not **d** him unto the will of his enemies. H5414
43: 1 an ungodly nation: O **d** me from the H6403
50:15 I will **d** thee, and thou shalt glorify me. H2502
22 *you* in pieces, and *there be* none to **d**. H5337
51:14 **D** me from bloodguiltiness, O God, H5337
56:13 *wilt* not *thou* **d** my feet from falling, H5337
59: 1 **D** me from mine enemies, O my God: H5337
2 **D** me from the workers of iniquity, and H5337
69:14 **D** me out of the mire, and let me not H5337
18 it: **d** me because of mine enemies. H6299
70: 1 *Make haste*, O God, to **d** me; make H5337
71: 2 **D** me in thy righteousness, and cause H5337
4 **D** me, O my God, out of the hand of the H6403
11 take him; for *there is* none to **d** *him*. H5337
72:12 For he shall **d** the needy when he H5337
74:19 O **d** not the soul of thy turtledove unto H5414
79: 9 of thy name: and **d** us, and purge away H5337
82: 4 **D** the poor and needy: rid *them* out of H6403
89:48 see death? shall he **d** his soul from the H4422
91: 3 Surely he shall **d** thee from the snare of H5337
14 therefore will I **d** him: I will set him on H6403
15 trouble; I will **d** him, and honour him. H2502
106:43 Many times did he **d** them; but they H5337
109:21 because thy mercy *is* good, **d** thou me. H5337
116: 4 O LORD, I beseech thee, **d** my soul. H4422
119:134 **D** me from the oppression of man: so H6299
153 Consider mine affliction, and **d** me: for H2502
154 Plead my cause, and **d** me: quicken me H1350
170 thee: **d** me according to thy word. H5337
120: 2 **D** my soul, O LORD, from lying lips, H5337
140: 1 **D** me, O LORD, from the evil man: H2502
142: 6 am brought very low: **d** me from my H5337
143: 9 **D** me, O LORD, from mine enemies: I H5337
144: 7 rid me, and **d** me out of great waters, H5337
11 Rid me, and **d** me from the hand of H5337
Prv 2:12 To **d** thee from the way of the evil *man*, H5337
16 To **d** thee from the strange woman, H5337
4: 9 a crown of glory shall she **d** to thee. H4042
6: 3 Do this now, my son, and **d** thyself, H5337
5 **D** thyself as a roe from the hand *of the* H5337
11: 6 of the upright shall **d** them: but H5337
12: 6 the mouth of the upright shall **d** them. H5337
19:19 thou **d** *him*, yet thou must do it again. H5337
23:14 the rod, and shalt **d** his soul from hell. H5337
24:11 If thou forbear to **d** *them that are* H5337
Ecc 8: 8 wickedness **d** those that are given to it. H4422
Isa 5:29 carry *it* away safe, and none shall **d** *it*. H5337
19:20 and a great one, and he shall **d** them. H5337
29:11 is sealed, which *men* **d** to one that is H5414
31: 5 also he will **d** *it; and* passing over H5337
36:14 you: for he shall not be able to **d** you. H5337
15 LORD will surely **d** us: this city shall H5337
18 The LORD will **d** us. Hath any of the H5337
20 should **d** Jerusalem out of my hand? H5337
38: 6 And I will **d** thee and this city out of the H5337
43:13 *is* none that can **d** out of my hand: I H5337
44:17 and saith, **D** me; for thou *art* my god. H5337
20 that he cannot **d** his soul, nor say, *Is* H5337
46: 2 they could not **d** the burden, but H4422
4 bear; even I will carry, and will **d** *you*. H4422
47:14 they shall not **d** themselves from the H5337
50: 2 I no power to **d**? behold, at my rebuke H5337

Isa 57:13 When thou criest, let thy companies **d** H5337
Jer 1: 8 *am* with thee to **d** thee, saith the LORD. H5337
19 with thee, saith the LORD, to **d** thee. H5337
15: 9 of them will I **d** to the sword before H5414
20 thee and to **d** thee, saith the LORD. H5337
21 And I will **d** thee out of the hand of the H5337
18:21 Therefore **d** up their children to the H5414
20: 5 Moreover I will **d** all the strength of this H5414
21: 7 And afterward, saith the LORD, I will **d** H5414
12 the morning, and **d** *him that is* spoiled H5337
22: 3 and **d** the spoiled out of the H5337
24: 9 And I will **d** them to be removed into H5414
29:18 and will **d** them to be removed H5414
21 Behold, I will **d** them into the hand H5414
38:19 lest they **d** me into their hand, H5414
20 But Jeremiah said, They shall not **d** H5414
39:17 But I will **d** thee in that day, saith the H5337
18 For I will surely **d** thee, and thou shalt H4422
42:11 save you, and to **d** you from his hand. H5337
43: 3 against us, for to **d** us into the hand of H5414
11 the land of Egypt, *and* **d** such *as are* for
46:26 And I will **d** them into the hand of H5414
51: 6 Flee out of the midst of Babylon, and **d** H4422
45 midst of her, and **d** ye every man his H4422
Lam 5: 8 none that doth **d** *us* out of their hand. H6561
Ezk 7:19 not be able to **d** them in the day of the H5337
11: 9 the midst thereof, and **d** you into the H5414
13:21 Your kerchiefs also will I tear, and **d** H5337
23 for I will **d** my people out of your H5337
14:14 in it, they should **d** *but* their own souls H5337
16 GOD, they shall **d** neither sons nor H5337
18 GOD, they shall **d** neither sons nor H5337
20 Lord GOD, they shall **d** neither son nor H5337
20 they shall *but* **d** their own souls by their H5337
21:31 of my wrath, and **d** thee into the hand H5414
23:28 Behold, I will **d** thee into the hand *of* H5414
25: 4 Behold, therefore I will **d** thee to the H5414
7 thee, and will **d** thee for a spoil to the H5414
33: 5 he that taketh warning shall **d** his soul. H4422
12 shall not **d** him in the day of his H5337
34:10 more; for I will **d** my flock from their H5337
12 sheep, and will **d** them out of all places H5337
Dan 3:15 God that shall **d** you out of my hands? H7804
17 whom we serve is able to **d** us from the H7804
17 he will **d** *us* out of thine hand, O king. H7804
29 no other God that can **d** after this sort. H5338
6:14 *his* heart on Daniel to **d** him: and he H7804
14 till the going down of the sun to **d** him. H5338
16 thou servest continually, he will **d** thee. H7804
20 able to **d** thee from the lions? H7804
8: 4 *any* that could **d** out of his hand; but H5337
7 that could **d** the ram out of his hand. H5337
Hos 2:10 and none shall **d** her out of mine hand. H5337
11: 8 *how* shall I **d** thee, Israel? how shall H4042
Am 1: 6 whole captivity, to **d** *them* up to Edom: H5462
2:14 neither shall the mighty **d** himself: H4422
15 of foot shall not **d** *himself*: neither shall H4422
15 shall he that rideth the horse **d** himself. H4422
6: 8 I **d** up the city with all that is therein. H5462
Jna 4: 6 over his head, to **d** him from his grief. H5337
Mic 5: 6 thus shall he **d** *us* from the Assyrian, H5337
8 and teareth in pieces, and none can **d**. H5337
6:14 hold, but shalt not **d**; and *that* which H6403
Zep 1:18 shall be able to **d** them in the day of the H5337
Zec 2: 7 **D** thyself, O Zion, that dwellest *with* the H4422
11: 6 but, lo, I will **d** the men every one into H4672
6 and out of their hand I will not **d** *them*. H5337
Mt 5:25 the adversary **d** thee to the judge, and G3860
25 and the judge **d** thee to the officer, and G3860
6:13 And lead us not into temptation, but **d** G4506
10:17 But beware of men: for they will **d** you G3860
19 But when they **d** you up, take no G3860
21 And the brother shall **d** up the brother G3860
20:19 And shall **d** him to the Gentiles to G3860
24: 9 Then shall they **d** you up to be afflicted, G3860
26:15 ye give me, and I will **d** him unto you? G3860
27:43 He trusted in God; let him **d** him now, G4506
Mk 10:33 death, and shall **d** him to the Gentiles: G3860
13: 9 for they shall **d** you up to councils; G3860
11 But when they shall lead *you*, and **d** G3860
Lk 11: 4 not into temptation; but **d** us from evil. G4506
12:58 and the judge **d** thee to the officer, and G3860
20:20 that so they might **d** him unto the G3860
Act 7:25 **d** them: but they understood not. G1325
34 am come down to **d** them. And now G1807
21:11 **d** *him* into the hands of the Gentiles. G3860
25:11 **d** me unto them. I appeal unto Caesar. G5483
16 of the Romans to **d** any man to die, G5483
Ro 7:24 O wretched man that I am! who shall **d** G4506
1Co 5: 5 To **d** such an one unto Satan for the G3860
2Co 1:10 a death, and doth **d**: in whom we trust G4506
10 in whom we trust that he will yet **d** *us*; G4506
Gal 1: 4 that he might **d** us from this present G1807
2Ti 4:18 And the Lord shall **d** me from every G4506
Heb 2:15 And **d** them who through fear of death G525
2Pt 2: 9 The Lord knoweth how to **d** the godly G4506

DELIVERANCE

Gen 45: 7 and to save your lives by a great **d**. H6413
Jdg 15:18 given this great **d** into the hand of thy H8668
2Ki 5: 1 LORD had given **d** unto Syria: he was H8668
13:17 of the LORD'S **d**, and the arrow of H8668
17 and the arrow of **d** from Syria: for thou H8668
1Ch 11:14 and the LORD saved *them* by a great **d**. H8668
2Ch 12: 7 grant them some **d**; and my wrath shall H6413
Ezr 9:13 and hast given us *such* **d** as this; H6413
Est 4:14 enlargement and **d** arise to the Jews H2020
Ps 18:50 Great **d** giveth he to his king; and H3444
32: 7 me about with songs of **d**. Selah. H6405
Isa 26:18 not wrought any **d** in the earth; neither H3444
Joel 2:32 Jerusalem shall be **d**, as the LORD hath H6413
Oba 17 But upon mount Zion shall be **d**, and H6413
Lk 4:18 to preach **d** to the captives, and G859
Heb 11:35 not accepting **d**; that they might obtain G629

DELIVERANCES

Ps 44: 4 Thou art my King, O God: command **d** H3444

DELIVERED

Gen 9: 2 of the sea; into your hand are they **d**. H5414
14:20 God, which hath **d** thine enemies into H4042
25:24 And when her days to be **d** were H3205
32:16 And he **d** *them* into the hand of his H5414
37:21 And Reuben heard *it*, and he **d** him out H5337
Ex 1:19 **d** ere the midwives come in unto them. H3205
2:19 And they said, An Egyptian **d** us out of H5337
5:23 neither hast thou **d** thy people at all. H5337
12:27 Egyptians, and **d** our houses. And the H5337
18: 4 and **d** me from the sword of Pharaoh: H5337
8 by the way, and *how* the LORD **d** them. H5337
9 had **d** out of the hand of the Egyptians. H5337
10 LORD, who hath **d** you out of the hand H5337
10 who hath **d** the people from under H5337
Lev 6: 2 in that which was **d** him to keep, or in H6487
4 or that which was **d** him to keep, or the H6487
26:25 shall be **d** into the hand of the enemy. H5414
Nu 21: 3 of Israel, and **d** up the Canaanites; H5414
34 not: for I have **d** him into thy hand, H5414
31: 5 So there were **d** out of the thousands of H4560
Dt 2:33 And the LORD our God **d** him before H5414
36 for us: the LORD our God **d** all unto us: H5414
3: 3 So the LORD our God **d** into our hands H5414
5:22 tables of stone, and **d** them unto me. H5414
9:10 And the LORD **d** unto me two tables of H5414
20:13 And when the LORD thy God hath **d** it H5414
21:10 thy God hath **d** them into thine hands, H5414
31: 9 And Moses wrote this law, and **d** it H5414
Jos 2:24 the LORD hath **d** into our hands all the H5414
9:26 And so did he unto them, and **d** them H5337
10: 8 not: for I have **d** them into thine hand; H5414
12 day when the LORD **d** up the Amorites H5414
19 your God hath **d** them into your hand. H5414
30 And the LORD **d** it also, and the king H5414
32 And the LORD **d** Lachish into the hand H5414
11: 8 And the LORD **d** them into the hand of H5414
21:44 **d** all their enemies into their hand. H5414
22:31 now ye have **d** the children of Israel H5337
24:10 you still: so I **d** you out of his hand. H5337
11 Jebusites; and I **d** them into your hand. H5414
Jdg 1: 2 behold, I have **d** the land into his hand. H5414
4 And Judah went up; and the LORD **d** H5414
2:14 Israel, and he **d** them into the hands H5414
16 up judges, which **d** them out of the H3467
18 the judge, and **d** them out of the hand H3467
23 **d** he them into the hand of Joshua. H5414
3: 9 of Israel, who **d** them, *even* Othniel H3467
10 and the LORD **d** Chushan-rishathaim H5414
28 for the LORD hath **d** your enemies the H5414
31 with an ox goad: and he also **d** Israel. H3467
4:14 the LORD hath **d** Sisera into thine H5414
5:11 *They that are* **d** from the noise of archers
6: 1 and the LORD **d** them into the hand H5414
9 And I **d** you out of the hand of the H5337
13 **d** us into the hands of the Midianites. H5414
7: 9 the host; for I have **d** it into thine hand. H5414
14 hath God **d** Midian, and all the host. H5414
15 **d** into your hand the host of Midian. H5414
8: 3 God hath **d** into your hands the princes H5414
Jdg 8: 7 the LORD hath **d** Zebah and Zalmunna H5414
22 hast **d** us from the hand of Midian. H3467
34 God, who had **d** them out of the hands H5337
9:17 and **d** you out of the hand of Midian: H5337
10:12 to me, and I **d** you out of their hand. H3467
11:21 And the LORD God of Israel **d** Sihon H5414
32 and the LORD **d** them into his hands. H5414
12: 2 you, ye **d** me not out of their hands. H3467
3 And when I saw that ye **d** *me* not, I put H3467
3 and the LORD **d** them into my hand: H5414
13: 1 and the LORD **d** them into the hand H5414
16:23 **d** Samson our enemy into our hand. H5414
24 Our god hath **d** into our hands our H5414
1Sa 4:19 child, *near* to be **d**: and when she heard H3205
10:18 out of Egypt, and **d** you out of the hand H5337
12:11 and Samuel, and **d** you out of the hand H5337
14:10 up: for the LORD hath **d** them into our H5414
12 hath **d** them into the hand of Israel. H5414
48 the Amalekites, and **d** Israel out of the H5337
17:35 smote him, and **d** *it* out of his mouth: H5337
37 David said moreover, The LORD that **d** H5337
23: 7 said, God hath **d** him into mine hand; H5234
14 day, but God **d** him not into his hand. H5414
24:10 the LORD had **d** thee to day into mine H5414
18 the LORD had **d** me into thine hand, H5462
26: 8 to David, God hath **d** thine enemy into H5462
23 for the LORD **d** thee into *my* hand to H5414
30:23 preserved us, and **d** the company that H5414
2Sa 3: 8 and have not **d** thee into the hand of H4672
10:10 And the rest of the people he **d** into the H5414
12: 7 and I **d** thee out of the hand of Saul; H5337
16: 8 the LORD hath **d** the kingdom into the H5414
18:28 thy God, which hath **d** up the men that H5462
19: 9 enemies, and he **d** us out of the hand of H4422
21: 6 Let seven men of his sons be **d** unto us, H5414
9 And he **d** them into the hands of the H5414
22: 1 the LORD had **d** him out of the hand H5337
18 He **d** me from my strong enemy, *and* H5337
20 he **d** me, because he delighted in me. H2502
44 Thou also hast **d** me from the strivings H6403
49 thou hast **d** me from the violent man. H5337
1Ki 3:17 I was **d** of a child with her in the house. H3205
18 after that I was **d**, that this woman was H3205
18 this woman was **d** also: and we *were* H3205
13:26 the LORD hath **d** him unto the lion, H5414
15:18 king's house, and **d** them into the hand H5414
17:23 the house, and **d** him unto his mother: H5414
2Ki 12:15 whose hand they **d** the money to be H5414
13: 3 Israel, and he **d** them into the hand H5414
17:20 them, and **d** them into the hand H5414
18:30 **d** into the hand of the king of Assyria. H5414
33 Hath any of the gods of the nations **d** at H5337
34 have they **d** Samaria out of mine hand? H5337
35 that have **d** their country out of H5337
19:10 **d** into the hand of the king of Assyria. H5414
11 them utterly: and shalt thou be **d**? H5337
12 Have the gods of the nations **d** them H5337
22: 7 the money that was **d** into their hand, H5414
9 house, and have **d** it into the hand of H5414
10 the priest hath **d** me a book. And H5414
1Ch 5:20 Hagarites were **d** into their hand, and H5414
11:14 of *that* parcel, and **d** it, and slew the H5337
16: 7 Then on that day David **d** first *this* H5414
19:11 And the rest of the people he **d** unto the H5414
2Ch 13:16 Judah: and God **d** them into their hand. H5414
16: 8 the LORD, he **d** them into thine hand. H5414
18:14 and they shall be **d** into your hand. H5414
23: 9 Moreover Jehoiada the priest **d** to the H5414
24:24 and the LORD **d** a very great host into H5414
28: 5 Wherefore the LORD his God **d** him H5414
5 And he was also **d** into the hand of the H5414
9 Judah, he hath **d** them into your hand, H5414
29: 8 and he hath **d** them to trouble, to H5414
32:17 lands have not **d** their people out of H5337
34: 9 high priest, they **d** the money that was H5414
15 And Hilkiah **d** the book to Shaphan. H5414
17 LORD, and have **d** it into the hand of H5414
Ezr 5:14 and they were **d** unto *one*, whose name H3052
8:31 upon us, and he **d** us from the hand of H5337
36 And they **d** the king's commissions H5414
9: 7 our priests, been **d** into the hand of the H5414
Est 6: 9 And let this apparel and horse be **d** to H5414
Job 16:11 God hath **d** me to the ungodly, and H5462
22:30 it is **d** by the pureness of thine hands. H4422
23: 7 should I be **d** for ever from my judge. H6403
29:12 Because I **d** the poor that cried, and the H4422
Ps 7: 4 me; (yea, I have **d** him that without H2502
18:17 He **d** me from my strong enemy, and H5337
19 he **d** me, because he delighted in me. H2502

Ps 18:43 Thou hast **d** me from the strivings of H6403
48 thou hast **d** me from the violent man. H5337
ttl *that* the LORD **d** him from the hand H5337
22: 5 They cried unto thee, and were **d**: they H4422
33:16 mighty man is not **d** by much strength. H5337
34: 4 heard me, and **d** me from all my fears. H5337
54: 7 For he hath **d** me out of all trouble: and H5337
55:18 He hath **d** my soul in peace from the H6299
56:13 For thou hast **d** my soul from death: H5337
60: 5 That thy beloved may be **d**; save *with* H2502
69:14 not sink: let me be **d** from them that H5337
78:42 day when he **d** them from the enemy. H6299
61 And **d** his strength into captivity, and H5414
81: 6 his hands were **d** from the pots. H5674
7 Thou calledst in trouble, and I **d** thee; I H2502
86:13 hast **d** my soul from the lowest hell. H5337
107: 6 *and* he **d** them out of their distresses. H5337
20 and **d** *them* from their destructions. H4422
108: 6 That thy beloved may be **d**: save *with* H2502
116: 8 For thou hast **d** my soul from death, H2502
Prv 11: 8 The righteous is **d** out of trouble, and H2502
9 through knowledge shall the just be **d**. H2502
21 but the seed of the righteous shall be **d**. H4422
28:26 but whoso walketh wisely, he shall be **d**. H4422
Ecc 9:15 he by his wisdom **d** the city; yet no man H4422
Isa 20: 6 we flee for help to be **d** from the king of H5337
29:12 And the book is **d** to him that is not H5414
34: 2 them, he hath **d** them to the slaughter. H5414
36:15 **d** into the hand of the king of Assyria. H5414
18 gods of the nations **d** his land out of the H5337
19 have they **d** Samaria out of my hand? H5337
20 lands, that have **d** their land out of my H5337
37:11 them utterly; and shalt thou be **d**? H5337
12 Have the gods of the nations **d** them H5337
38:17 in love to my soul *d it* from the pit of
49:24 the mighty, or the lawful captive **d**? H4422
25 the terrible shall be **d**: for I will contend H4422
66: 7 pain came, she was **d** of a man child. H4422
Jer 7:10 We are **d** to do all these abominations? H5337
20:13 the LORD: for he hath **d** the soul of the H5337
32: 4 but shall surely be **d** into the hand of H5414
16 Now when I had **d** the evidence of the H5414
36 ye say, It shall be **d** into the hand of the H5414
34: 3 be taken, and **d** into his hand; and H5414
37:17 **d** into the hand of the king of Babylon. H5414
46:24 she shall be **d** into the hand of the H5414
Lam 1:14 to fall, the Lord hath **d** me into *their* H5414
Ezk 3:19 in his iniquity; but thou hast **d** thy soul. H5337
21 he is warned; also thou hast **d** thy soul. H5337
14:16 be **d**, but the land shall be desolate. H5337
18 but they only shall be **d** themselves. H5337
16:21 my children, and **d** them to cause them H5414
27 *food*, and **d** thee unto the will of H5414
17:15 shall he break the covenant, and be **d**? H4422
23: 9 Wherefore I have **d** her into the hand of H5414
31:11 I have therefore **d** him into the hand of H5414
14 for they are all **d** unto death, to the H5414
32:20 the sword: she is **d** to the sword: draw H5414
33: 9 in his iniquity; but thou hast **d** thy soul. H5337
34:27 of their yoke, and **d** them out of the H5337
Dan 3:28 sent his angel, and **d** his servants that H7804
6:27 **d** Daniel from the power of the lions. H7804
12: 1 people shall be **d**, every one that shall H4422
Joel 2:32 the LORD shall be **d**: for in mount Zion H4422
Am 1: 9 because they **d** up the whole captivity H5462
9: 1 he that escapeth of them shall not be **d**. H4422
Oba 14 thou have **d** up those of his that H5462
Mic 4:10 shalt thou be **d**; there the LORD shall H5337
Hab 2: 9 he may be **d** from the power of evil! H5337
Mal 3:15 up; yea, *they that* tempt God are even **d**. H4422
Mt 11:27 All things are **d** unto me of my Father: G3860
18:34 And his lord was wroth, and **d** him to G3860
25:14 servants, and **d** unto them his goods. G3860
27: 2 **d** him to Pontius Pilate the governor. G3860
18 For he knew that for envy they had **d** G3860
26 Jesus, he **d** *him* to be crucified. G3860
58 Pilate commanded the body to be **d**. G591
Mk 7:13 **d**: and many such like things do ye. G3860
9:31 The Son of man is **d** into the hands of G3860
10:33 of man shall be **d** unto the chief priests, G3860
15: 1 carried *him* away, and **d** *him* to Pilate. G3860
10 For he knew that the chief priests had **d** G3860
15 unto them, and **d** Jesus, when he had G3860
Lk 1: 2 Even as they **d** them unto us, which G3860
57 be **d**; and she brought forth a son. G5088
74 us, that we being **d** out of the hand of G4506
2: 6 accomplished that she should be **d**. G5088
4: 6 of them: for that is **d** unto me; and to G3860
17 And there was **d** unto him the book of G1929

Lk 7:15 to speak. And he **d** him to his mother. G1325
9:42 the child, and **d** him again to his father. G591
44 man shall be **d** into the hands of men. G3860
10:22 All things are **d** to me of my Father: G3860
12:58 thou mayest be **d** from him; lest he hale G525
18:32 For he shall be **d** unto the Gentiles, and G3860
19:13 And he called his ten servants, and **d** G1325
23:25 had desired; but he **d** Jesus to their will. G3860
24: 7 Saying, The Son of man must be **d** into G3860
20 and our rulers **d** him to be condemned G3860
Jn 16:21 but as soon as she is **d** of the child, she G1080
18:30 would not have **d** him up unto thee. G3860+
35 **d** thee unto me: what hast thou done? G3860
36 I should not be **d** to the Jews: but now G3860
19:11 **d** me unto thee hath the greater sin. G3860
16 Then **d** he him therefore unto them to G3860
Act 2:23 Him, being **d** by the determinate G1560
3:13 Jesus; whom ye **d** up, and denied him G3860
6:14 change the customs which Moses **d** us. G3860
7:10 And **d** him out of all his afflictions, and G1807
12: 4 *him* in prison, and **d** *him* to four G3860
11 angel, and hath **d** me out of the hand G1807
15:30 multitude together, they **d** the epistle: G1929
16: 4 the cities, they **d** them the decrees for G3860
23:33 to Caesarea, and **d** the epistle to the G325
27: 1 into Italy, they **d** Paul and certain other G3860
28:16 the centurion **d** the prisoners to the G3860
17 our fathers, yet was I **d** prisoner from G3860
Ro 4:25 Who was **d** for our offences, and was G3860
6:17 that form of doctrine which was **d** you. G3860
7: 6 But now we are **d** from the law, that G2673
8:21 itself also shall be **d** from the bondage G1659
32 He that spared not his own Son, but **d** G3860
15:31 That I may be **d** from them that do not G4506
1Co 11: 2 the ordinances, as I **d** *them* to you. G3860
23 that which also I **d** unto you, That the G3860
15: 3 For I **d** unto you first of all that which I G3860
24 he shall have **d** up the kingdom to God, G3860
2Co 1:10 Who **d** us from so great a death, and G4506
4:11 For we which live are alway **d** unto G3860
Col 1:13 Who hath **d** us from the power of G4506
1Th 1:10 which **d** us from the wrath to come. G4506
2Th 3: 2 And that we may be **d** from G4506
1Ti 1:20 whom I have **d** unto Satan, that they G3860
2Ti 3:11 but out of *them* all the Lord **d** me. G4506
4:17 I was **d** out of the mouth of the lion. G4506
Heb 11:11 seed, and was **d** of a child when she G5088
2Pt 2: 4 down to hell, and **d** *them* into chains of G3860
7 And **d** just Lot, vexed with the filthy G4506
21 the holy commandment **d** unto them. G3860
Jude 3 faith which was once **d** unto the saints. G3860
Rev 12: 2 travailing in birth, and pained to be **d**. G5088
4 was ready to be **d**, for to devour her G5088
20:13 and death and hell **d** up the dead which G1325

DELIVEREDST

Neh 9:27 Therefore thou **d** them into the hand of H5414
Mt 25:20 saying, Lord, thou **d** unto me five G3860
22 said, Lord, thou **d** unto me two talents: G3860

DELIVERER

Jdg 3: 9 LORD raised up a **d** to the children of H3467
15 raised them up a **d**, Ehud the son of H3467
18:28 And *there was* no **d**, because it *was* far H5337
2Sa 22: 2 *is* my rock, and my fortress, and my **d**; H6403
Ps 18: 2 my fortress, and my **d**; my God, my H6403
40:17 and my **d**; make no tarrying, O my God. H6403
70: 5 and my **d**; O LORD, make no tarrying. H6403
144: 2 tower, and my **d**; my shield, and *he* in H6403
Act 7:35 *to be* a ruler and a **d** by the hand of the G3086
Ro 11:26 out of Sion the **D**, and shall turn away G4506

DELIVEREST

Ps 35:10 unto thee, which **d** the poor from him H5337
Mic 6:14 thou **d** will I give up to the sword. H6403

DELIVERETH

Job 36:15 He **d** the poor in his affliction, and H2502
Ps 18:48 He **d** me from mine enemies: yea, thou H6403
34: 7 about them that fear him, and **d** them. H2502
17 and **d** them out of all their troubles. H5337
19 but the LORD **d** him out of them all. H5337
97:10 **d** them out of the hand of the wicked. H5337
144:10 unto kings: who **d** David his servant H6475
Prv 10: 2 but righteousness **d** from death. H5337
11: 4 wrath: but righteousness **d** from death. H5337
14:25 A true witness **d** souls: but a deceitful H5337
31:24 *it*; and **d** girdles unto the merchant. H5414
Isa 42:22 **d**; for a spoil, and none saith, Restore. H5337

Dan 6:27 He **d** and rescueth, and he worketh H7804

DELIVERING

Lk 21:12 and persecute *you*, **d** *you* up to the G3860
Act 22: 4 **d** into prisons both men and women. G3860
26:17 **D** thee from the people, and *from* the G1807

DELIVERY

Isa 26:17 the time of her **d**, is in pain, *and* crieth H3205

DELUSION

2Th 2:11 strong **d**, that they should believe a lie: G1753

DELUSIONS

Isa 66: 4 I also will choose their **d**, and will bring H8586

DEMAND

Job 38: 3 I will **d** of thee, and answer thou me. H7592
40: 7 **d** of thee, and declare thou unto me. H7592
42: 4 **d** of thee, and declare thou unto me. H7592
Dan 4:17 watchers, and the **d** by the word of the H7595

DEMANDED

Ex 5:14 were beaten, *and* **d**, Wherefore have ye H559
2Sa 11: 7 unto him, David **d** *of him* how Joab H7592
Dan 2:27 the king hath **d** cannot the wise *men*, H7593
Mt 2: 4 **d** of them where Christ should be born. G4441
Lk 3:14 And the soldiers likewise **d** of him, G1905
17:20 And when he was **d** of the Pharisees, G1905
Act 21:33 **d** who he was, and what he had done. G4441

DEMAS

Col 4:14 Luke, the beloved physician, and **D**, G1214
2Ti 4:10 For **D** hath forsaken me, having loved G1214
Phlm 24 Marcus, Aristarchus, **D**, Lucas, my G1214

DEMETRIUS

Act 19:24 For a certain *man* named **D**, a G1216
38 Wherefore if **D**, and the craftsmen G1216
3Jn 12 **D** hath good report of all *men*, and of G1216

DEMONSTRATION

1Co 2: 4 but in **d** of the Spirit and of power: G585

DEN

Ps 10: 9 as a lion in his **d**: he lieth in wait to H5520
Isa 11: 8 shall put his hand on the cockatrice' **d**. H3975
Jer 7:11 name, become a **d** of robbers in your H4631
9:11 heaps, *and* a **d** of dragons; and I will H4583
10:22 of Judah desolate, *and* a **d** of dragons. H4583
Dan 6: 7 king, he shall be cast into the **d** of lions. H1358
12 be cast into the **d** of lions? The king H1358
16 cast *him* into the **d** of lions. *Now* the H1358
17 the mouth of the **d**; and the king sealed H1358
19 and went in haste unto the **d** of lions. H1358
20 And when he came to the **d**, he cried H1358
23 up out of the **d**. So Daniel was taken H1358
23 up out of the **d**, and no manner of hurt H1358
24 cast *them* into the **d** of lions, them, H1358
24 ever they came at the bottom of the **d**. H1358
Am 3: 4 out of his **d**, if he have taken nothing? H4585
Mt 21:13 but ye have made it a **d** of thieves. G4693
Mk 11:17 but ye have made it a **d** of thieves. G4693
Lk 19:46 but ye have made it a **d** of thieves. G4693

DENIED

Gen 18:15 Then Sarah **d**, saying, I laughed not; for H3584
1Ki 20: 7 and for my gold; and I **d** him not. H4513
Job 31:28 I should have **d** the God *that is* above. H3584
Mt 26:70 But he **d** before *them* all, saying, I know G720
72 And again he **d** with an oath, I do not G720
Mk 14:68 But he **d**, saying, I know not, neither G720
70 And he **d** it again. And a little after, they G720
Lk 8:45 me? When all **d**, Peter and they that were G720
12: 9 men shall be **d** before the angels of God. G533
22:57 And he **d** him, saying, Woman, I know G720
Jn 1:20 And he confessed, and **d** not; but G720
13:38 shall not crow, till thou hast **d** me thrice. G533
18:25 his disciples? He **d** *it*, and said, I am not. G720
27 Peter then **d** again: and immediately the G720
Act 3:13 delivered up, and **d** him in the presence G720
14 But ye **d** the Holy One and the Just, and G720
1Ti 5: 8 **d** the faith, and is worse than an infidel. G720
Rev 2:13 and hast not **d** my faith, even in those G720
3: 8 kept my word, and hast not **d** my name. G720

DENIETH

Lk 12: 9 But he that **d** me before men shall be G720
1Jn 2:22 Who is a liar but he that **d** that Jesus is G720

1Jn 2:22 antichrist, that **d** the Father and the Son. *G720*
23 Whosoever **d** the Son, the same hath not *G720*

DENOUNCE
Dt 30:18 I **d** unto you this day, that ye shall H5046

DENS
Jdg 6: 2 made them the **d** which *are* in the H4492
Job 37: 8 Then the beasts go into **d**, and remain in H695
38:40 When they couch in *their* **d**, *and* abide H4585
Ps 104:22 together, and lay them down in their **d**. H4585
Song 4: 8 **d**, from the mountains of the leopards. H4585
Isa 32:14 towers shall be for **d** for ever, a joy of H4631
Nah 2:12 holes with prey, and his **d** with ravin. H4585
Heb 11:38 and *in* **d** and caves of the earth. *G4693*
Rev 6:15 **d** and in the rocks of the mountains; *G4693*

DENY
Jos 24:27 a witness unto you, lest ye **d** your God. H3584
1Ki 2:16 And now I ask one petition of thee, **d** H7725
Job 8:18 **d** him, *saying*, I have not seen thee. H3584
Prv 30: 7 Two *things* have I required of thee; **d** H4513
9 Lest I be full, and **d** *thee*, and say, Who H3584
Mt 10:33 But whosoever shall **d** me before men, *G720*
33 **d** before my Father which is in heaven. *G720*
16:24 after me, let him **d** himself, and take up *G533*
26:34 the cock crow, thou shalt **d** me thrice. *G533*
35 thee, yet will I not **d** thee. Likewise also *G533*
75 crow, thou shalt **d** me thrice. And he *G533*
Mk 8:34 after me, let him **d** himself, and take up *G533*
14:30 cock crow twice, thou shalt **d** me thrice. *G533*
31 with thee, I will not **d** thee in any wise. *G533*
72 twice, thou shalt **d** me thrice. And when *G533*
Lk 9:23 after me, let him **d** himself, and take up *G533*
20:27 the Sadducees, which **d** that there is any *G483*
22:34 shalt thrice **d** that thou knowest me. *G533*
61 the cock crow, thou shalt **d** me thrice. *G533*
Act 4:16 dwell in Jerusalem; and we cannot **d** *it*. *G720*
2Ti 2:12 *him*: if we **d** *him*, he also will deny us: *G720*
12 *him*: if we deny *him*, he also will **d** us: *G720*
13 he abideth faithful: he cannot **d** himself. *G720*
Tit 1:16 God; but in works they **d** *him*, being *G720*

DENYING
2Ti 3: 5 Having a form of godliness, but **d** the *G720*
Tit 2:12 Teaching us that, **d** ungodliness and *G720*
2Pt 2: 1 heresies, even **d** the Lord that bought *G720*
Jude 4 and **d** the only Lord God, and *G720*

DEPART
Gen 13: 9 the right; or if *thou* **d** to the right hand,
49:10 The sceptre shall not **d** from Judah, nor H5493
Ex 8:11 And the frogs shall **d** from thee, and H5493
29 *of flies* may **d** from Pharaoh, from H5493
18:27 And Moses let his father in law **d**; and H7971
21:22 so that her fruit **d** *from her*, and yet no H3318
33: 1 And the LORD said unto Moses, **D**, *and* H3212
Lev 25:41 And *then* shall he **d** from thee, *both* he H3318
Nu 10:30 not go; but I will **d** to mine own land, H3212
16:26 saying, **D**, I pray you, from the H5493
Dt 4: 9 seen, and lest they **d** from thy heart all H5493
9: 7 day that thou didst **d** out of the land of H3318
Jos 1: 8 This book of the law shall not **d** out of H4185
24:28 So Joshua let the people **d**, every man H7971
Jdg 6:18 **D** not hence, I pray thee, until I come H4185
7: 3 let him return and **d** early from mount H6852
19: 5 that he rose up to **d**: and the damsel's H3212
7 And when the man rose up to **d**, his H3212
8 on the fifth day to **d**: and the damsel's H3212
9 And when the man rose up to **d**, he, and H3212
1Sa 15: 6 And Saul said unto the Kenites, Go, **d**, H5493
22: 5 not in the hold; **d**, and get thee into the H3212
29:10 early in the morning, and have light, **d**. H3212
11 rose up early to **d** in the morning, to H3212
30:22 that they may lead *them* away, and **d**. H3212
2Sa 7:15 But my mercy shall not **d** away from H5493
11:12 I will let thee **d**. So Uriah abode in H7971
12:10 Now therefore the sword shall never **d** H5493
15:14 make speed to **d**, lest he overtake us H3212
20:21 only, and I will **d** from the city. And the H3212
22:23 *for* his statutes, I did not **d** from them. H5493
1Ki 11:21 **d**, that I may go to mine own country. H7971
12: 5 And he said unto them, **D** yet *for* three H3212
24 **d**, according to the word of the LORD. H3212
15:19 king of Israel, that he may **d** from me. H5927
2Ch 16: 3 king of Israel, that he may **d** from him. H5927
18:31 and God moved them *to* **d** from him.
35:15 they might not **d** from their service; for H5493
Job 7:19 How long wilt thou not **d** from me, nor H8159
Job 15:30 He shall not **d** out of darkness; the H5493
20:28 The increase of his house shall **d**, *and* H1540
21:14 Therefore they say unto God, **D** from H5493
22:17 Which said unto God, **D** from us: and H5493
28:28 and to **d** from evil *is* understanding. H5493
Ps 6: 8 **D** from me, all ye workers of iniquity; H5493
34:14 **D** from evil, and do good; seek peace, H5493
37:27 **D** from evil, and do good; and dwell for H5493
55:11 deceit and guile **d** not from her streets. H4185
101: 4 A froward heart shall **d** from me: I will H5493
119:115 **D** from me, ye evildoers: for I will keep H5493
139:19 **d** from me therefore, ye bloody men. H5493
Prv 3: 7 eyes: fear the LORD, and **d** from evil. H5493
21 My son, let not them **d** from thine eyes: H3868
4:21 Let them not **d** from thine eyes; keep H3868
5: 7 **d** not from the words of my mouth. H5493
13:14 of life, to **d** from the snares of death. H5493
19 *is* abomination to fools to **d** from evil. H5493
14:27 of life, to **d** from the snares of death. H5493
15:24 wise, that he may **d** from hell beneath. H5493
16: 6 the fear of the LORD *men* **d** from evil. H5493
17 The highway of the upright *is* to **d** from H5493
17:13 evil shall not **d** from his house. H4185+H4185
22: 6 when he is old, he will not **d** from it. H5493
27:22 *yet* will not his foolishness **d** from him. H5493
Isa 11:13 The envy also of Ephraim shall **d**, and H5493
14:25 then shall his yoke **d** from off them, H5493
25 his burden **d** from off their shoulders. H5493
52:11 **D** ye, depart ye, go ye out from thence, H5493
11 Depart ye, **d** ye, go ye out from thence, H5493
54:10 For the mountains shall **d**, and the hills H4185
10 kindness shall not **d** from thee, neither H4185
59:21 mouth, shall not **d** out of thy mouth, H4185
Jer 6: 8 lest my soul **d** from thee; lest I make H3363
17:13 *and* they that **d** from me shall H5493+H3249
31:36 If those ordinances **d** from before me, H4185
32:40 hearts, that they shall not **d** from me. H5493
37: 9 **d** from us: for they shall not depart. H3212
9 depart from us: for they shall not **d**. H3212
50: 3 they shall **d**, both man and beast. H1980
Lam 4:15 They cried unto them, **D** ye; *it is* H5493
15 ye; *it is* unclean; **d**, depart, touch not: H5493
15 *is* unclean; depart, **d**, touch not: when H5493
Ezk 16:42 my jealousy shall **d** from thee, and I H5493
Hos 9:12 woe also to them when I **d** from them! H5493
Mic 2:10 Arise ye, and **d**; for this *is* not *your* rest: H3212
Zec 10:11 and the sceptre of Egypt shall **d** away. H5493
Mt 7:23 you: **d** from me, ye that work iniquity. *G672*
8:18 commandment to **d** unto the other side. *G565*
34 *him* that he would **d** out of their coasts. *G3327*
10:14 words, when ye **d** out of that house or *G1831*
14:16 They need not **d**; give ye them to eat. *G565*
25:41 on the left hand, **D** from me, ye cursed, *G4198*
Mk 5:17 And they began to pray him to **d** out of *G565*
6:10 there abide till ye **d** from that place. *G1831*
11 hear you, when ye **d** thence, shake off *G1607*
Lk 2:29 Lord, now lettest thou thy servant **d** in *G630*
4:42 him, that he should not **d** from them. *G4198*
5: 8 knees, saying, **D** from me; for I am a *G1831*
8:37 besought him to **d** from them; for they *G565*
9: 4 ye enter into, there abide, and thence **d**. *G1831*
12:59 I tell thee, thou shalt not **d** thence, till *G1831*
13:27 **d** from me, all *ye* workers of iniquity. *G868*
31 and **d** hence: for Herod will kill thee. *G4198*
21:21 are in the midst of it **d** out; and let not *G1633*
Jn 7: 3 said unto him, **D** hence, and go into *G3327*
13: 1 that he should **d** out of this world unto *G3327*
16: 7 you; but if I **d**, I will send him unto you. *G4198*
Act 1: 4 they should not **d** from Jerusalem, but *G5563*
16:36 go: now therefore **d**, and go in peace. *G1831*
39 and desired *them* to **d** out of the city. *G1831*
18: 2 to **d** from Rome:) and came unto them. *G5563*
20: 7 them, ready to **d** on the morrow; and *G1826*
22:21 And he said unto me, **D**: for I will send *G4198*
23:22 let the young man **d**, and charged *him*, *G630*
25: 4 that he himself would **d** shortly *thither*. *G1607*
27:12 part advised to **d** thence also, if by any *G321*
1Co 7:10 Let not the wife **d** from *her* husband: *G5563*
11 But and if she **d**, let her remain *G5563*
15 But if the unbelieving **d**, let him depart. *G5563*
15 But if the unbelieving depart, let him **d**. *G5563*
2Co 12: 8 the Lord thrice, that it might **d** from me. *G868*
Php 1:23 two, having a desire to **d**, and to be with *G360*
1Ti 4: 1 times some shall **d** from the faith, giving *G868*
2Ti 2:19 the name of Christ **d** from iniquity. *G868*
Jas 2:16 And one of you say unto them, **D** in *G5217*

DEPARTED
Gen 12: 4 So Abram **d**, as the LORD had spoken H3212
Gen 12: 4 five years old when he **d** out of Haran. H3318
14:12 dwelt in Sodom, and his goods, and **d**. H3212
21:14 her away: and she **d**, and wandered in H3212
24:10 of his master, and **d**; for all the goods of H3212
26:17 And Isaac **d** thence, and pitched his H3212
31 away, and they **d** from him in peace. H3212
31:40 night; and my sleep **d** from mine eyes. H5074
55 Laban **d**, and returned unto his place. H3212
37:17 And the man said, They are **d** hence; H5265
42:26 their asses with the corn, and **d** thence. H3212
45:24 away, and they **d**: and he said unto H3212
Ex 19: 2 For they were **d** from Rephidim, and H5265
33:11 man, **d** not out of the tabernacle. H4185
35:20 of Israel **d** from the presence of Moses. H3318
Lev 13:58 if the plague be **d** from them, then it H5493
Nu 10:33 And they **d** from the mount of the H5265
12: 9 was kindled against them; and he **d**. H3212
10 And the cloud **d** from off the H5493
14: 9 their defence is **d** from them, and the H5493
44 and Moses, **d** not out of the camp. H4185
22: 7 elders of Midian **d** with the rewards of H3212
33: 3 And they **d** from Rameses in the first H5265
6 And they **d** from Succoth, and pitched H5265
8 And they **d** from before Pi-hahiroth, H5265
13 And they **d** from Dophkah, and H5265
15 And they **d** from Rephidim, and H5265
17 And they **d** from Kibroth-hattaavah, H5265
18 And they **d** from Hazeroth, and pitched H5265
19 And they **d** from Rithmah, and pitched H5265
20 And they **d** from Rimmon-parez, and H5265
27 And they **d** from Tahath, and pitched H5265
30 And they **d** from Hashmonah, and H5265
31 And they **d** from Moseroth, and H5265
35 And they **d** from Ebronah, and H5265
41 And they **d** from mount Hor, and H5265
42 And they **d** from Zalmonah, and H5265
43 And they **d** from Punon, and pitched in H5265
44 And they **d** from Oboth, and pitched in H5265
45 And they **d** from Iim, and pitched in H5265
48 And they **d** from the mountains of H5265
Dt 1:19 And when we **d** from Horeb, we went H5265
24: 2 And when she is **d** out of his house, she H3318
Jos 2:21 away, and they **d**: and she bound the H3212
22: 9 returned, and **d** from the children of H3212
Jdg 6:21 angel of the LORD **d** out of his sight. H1980
9:55 dead, they **d** every man unto his place. H3212
16:20 not that the LORD was **d** from him. H5493
17: 8 And the man **d** out of the city from H3212
18: 7 Then the five men **d**, and came to Laish, H3212
21 So they turned and **d**, and put the little H3212
19:10 but he rose up and **d**, and came over H3212
21:24 And the children of Israel **d** thence at H1980
1Sa 4:21 The glory is **d** from Israel: because H1540
22 And she said, The glory is **d** from H1540
6: 6 they not let the people go, and they **d**? H3212
10: 2 When thou art **d** from me to day, then H3212
15: 6 Kenites **d** from among the Amalekites. H5493
16:14 But the spirit of the LORD **d** from Saul, H5493
23 well, and the evil spirit **d** from him. H5493
18:12 was with him, and was **d** from Saul. H5493
20:42 and **d**: and Jonathan went into the city. H3212
22: 1 David therefore **d** thence, and escaped H3212
5 **d**, and came into the forest of Hareth. H3212
23:13 arose and **d** out of Keilah, and went H3318
28:15 against me, and God is **d** from me, and H5493
16 seeing the LORD is **d** from thee, and is H5493
2Sa 6:19 all the people **d** every one to his house. H3212
11: 8 thy feet. And Uriah **d** out of the king's H3318
12:15 And Nathan **d** unto his house. And the H3212
17:21 And it came to pass, after they were **d**, H3212
19:24 **d** until the day he came *again* in peace. H3212
22:22 and have not wickedly **d** from my God. H7561
1Ki 12: 5 come again to me. And the people **d**. H3212
16 David. So Israel **d** unto their tents. H3212
14:17 And Jeroboam's wife arose, and **d**, and H3212
19:19 So he **d** thence, and found Elisha the H3212
20: 9 **d**, and brought him word again. H3212
36 soon as thou art **d** from me, a lion shall H1980
36 as soon as he was **d** from him, a lion H3212
38 So the prophet **d**, and waited for the H3212
2Ki 1: 4 up, but shalt surely die. And Elijah **d**. H3212
3: 3 made Israel to sin; he **d** not therefrom. H5493
27 Israel: and they **d** from him, and H5265
5: 5 of Israel. And he **d**, and took with him H3212
19 in peace. So he **d** from him a little way. H3212
24 and he let the men go, and they **d**. H3212
8:14 So he **d** from Elisha, and came to his H3212
10:12 And he arose and **d**, and came to H935
15 And when he was **d** thence, he lighted H3212

2Ki 10:29 Israel to sin, Jehu **d** not from after H5493
31 his heart: for he **d** not from the sins of H5493
13: 2 made Israel to sin; he **d** not therefrom. H5493
6 Nevertheless they **d** not from the sins H5493
11 of the LORD; he **d** not from all the sins H5493
14:24 of the LORD: he **d** not from all the sins H5493
15: 9 had done: he **d** not from the sins of H5493
18 of the LORD: he **d** not all his days from H5493
24 of the LORD: he **d** not from the sins of H5493
28 of the LORD: he **d** not from the sins of H5493
17:22 which he did; they **d** not from them; H5493
18: 6 For he clave to the LORD, *and* **d** not H5493
19: 8 had heard that he was **d** from Lachish. H5265
36 So Sennacherib king of Assyria **d**, and H5265
1Ch 16:43 And all the people **d** every man to his H3212
21: 4 Wherefore Joab **d**, and went throughout H3318
2Ch 8:15 And they **d** not from the H5493
10: 5 me after three days. And the people **d**. H3212
20:32 his father, and **d** not from it, doing *that* H5493
21:20 eight years, and **d** without being H3212
24:25 And when they were **d** from him, (for H3212
34:33 all his days they **d** not from following H5493
Ezr 8:31 Then we **d** from the river of Ahava on H5265
Neh 9:19 pillar of the cloud **d** not from them by H5493
Ps 18:21 and have not wickedly **d** from my God. H7561
34:ttl who drove him away, and he **d**. H3212
105:38 Egypt was glad when they **d**: for the fear H3318
119:102 I have not **d** from thy judgments: for H5493
Isa 7:17 **d** from Judah; *even* the king of Assyria. H5493
37: 8 had heard that he was **d** from Lachish. H5265
37 So Sennacherib king of Assyria **d**, and H5265
38:12 Mine age is **d**, and is removed from me H5265
Jer 29: 2 the smiths, were **d** from Jerusalem;) H3318
37: 5 tidings of them, they **d** from Jerusalem. H5927
41:10 and **d** to go over to the Ammonites. H3212
17 And they **d**, and dwelt in the habitation H3212
Lam 1: 6 Zion all her beauty is **d**: her princes are H3318
Ezk 6: 9 heart, which hath **d** from me, and with H5493
10:18 Then the glory of the LORD **d** from off H3318
Dan 4:31 is spoken; The kingdom is **d** from thee. H5709
Hos 10: 5 glory thereof, because it is **d** from it. H1540
Mal 2: 8 But ye are **d** out of the way; ye have H5493
Mt 2: 9 When they had heard the king, they **d**; *G4198*
12 **d** into their own country another way. *G402*
13 And when they were **d**, behold, the angel *G402*
14 his mother by night, and **d** into Egypt: *G402*
4:12 was cast into prison, he **d** into Galilee; *G402*
9: 7 And he arose, and **d** to his house. *G565*
27 And when Jesus **d** thence, two blind *G3855*
31 But they, when they were **d**, spread *G1831*
11: 1 disciples, he **d** thence to teach and *G3327*
7 And as they **d**, Jesus began to say unto *G4198*
12: 9 And when he was **d** thence, he went *G3327*
13:53 finished these parables, he **d** thence. *G3332*
14:13 When Jesus heard *of it*, he **d** thence by *G402*
15:21 Then Jesus went thence, and **d** into the *G402*
29 And Jesus **d** from thence, and came *G3327*
16: 4 prophet Jonas. And he left them, and **d**. *G565*
17:18 And Jesus rebuked the devil; and he **d** *G1831*
19: 1 these sayings, he **d** from Galilee, and *G3332*
15 And he laid *his* hands on them, and **d** *G4198*
20:29 And as they **d** from Jericho, a great *G1607*
24: 1 And Jesus went out, and **d** from the *G4198*
27: 5 and **d**, and went and hanged himself. *G402*
60 stone to the door of the sepulchre, and **d**. *G565*
28: 8 And they **d** quickly from the sepulchre *G1831*
Mk 1:35 **d** into a solitary place, and there prayed. *G565*
42 **d** from him, and he was cleansed. *G565*
5:20 And he **d**, and began to publish in *G565*
6:32 And they **d** into a desert place by ship *G565*
46 And when he had sent them away, he **d** *G565*
8:13 into the ship again **d** to the other side. *G565*
9:30 And they **d** thence, and passed through *G1831*
Lk 1:23 accomplished, he **d** to his own house. *G565*
38 to thy word. And the angel **d** from her. *G565*
2:37 four years, which **d** not from the temple, *G868*
4:13 temptation, he **d** from him for a season. *G868*
42 And when it was day, he **d** and went *G1831*
5:13 immediately the leprosy **d** from him. *G565*
25 and **d** to his own house, glorifying God. *G565*
7:24 of John were **d**, he began to speak unto *G565*
8:35 the devils were **d**, sitting at the feet of *G1831*
38 the devils were **d** besought him that he *G1831*
9: 6 And they **d**, and went through the *G1831*
33 And it came to pass, as they **d** from *G1316*
10:30 *him*, and **d**, leaving *him* half dead. *G565*
35 And on the morrow when he **d**, he took *G1831*
24:12 laid by themselves, and **d**, wondering in *G565*
Jn 4: 3 He left Judaea, and **d** again into Galilee. *G565*
Jn 4:43 Now after two days he **d** thence, and *G1831*
5:15 The man **d**, and told the Jews that it was *G565*
6:15 **d** again into a mountain himself alone. *G402*
12:36 and **d**, and did hide himself from them. *G565*
Act 5:41 And they **d** from the presence of the *G4198*
10: 7 unto Cornelius was **d**, he called two of his *G565*
11:25 Then **d** Barnabas to Tarsus, for to seek *G1831*
12:10 and forthwith the angel **d** from him. *G868*
17 And he **d**, and went into another place. *G1831*
13: 4 by the Holy Ghost, **d** unto Seleucia; and *G2718*
14 But when they **d** from Perga, they came *G1330*
14:20 next day he **d** with Barnabas to Derbe. *G1831*
15:38 him with them, who **d** from them from *G868*
39 them, that they **d** asunder one from the *G673*
40 And Paul chose Silas, and **d**, being *G1831*
16:40 brethren, they comforted them, and **d**. *G1831*
17:15 to come to him with all speed, they **d**. *G1826*
33 So Paul **d** from among them. *G1831*
18: 1 After these things Paul **d** from Athens, *G5563*
7 And he **d** thence, and entered into a *G3327*
23 time *there*, he **d**, and went over *all* the *G1831*
19: 9 the multitude, he **d** from them, and *G868*
12 and the diseases **d** from them, and the *G525*
20: 1 *them*, and **d** for to go into Macedonia. *G1831*
11 while, even till break of day, so he **d**. *G1831*
21: 5 those days, we **d** and went our way; *G1831*
8 of Paul's company **d**, and came unto *G1831*
22:29 Then straightway they **d** from him *G868*
28:10 and when we **d**, they laded *us* with such *G321*
11 And after three months we **d** in a ship of *G321*
25 themselves, they **d**, after that Paul had *G630*
29 these words, the Jews **d**, and had great *G565*
Php 4:15 the gospel, when I **d** from Macedonia, *G1831*
2Ti 4:10 world, and is **d** unto Thessalonica; *G4198*
Phlm 15 For perhaps he therefore **d** for a *G5563*
Rev 6:14 And the heaven **d** as a scroll when it is *G673*
18:14 soul lusted after are **d** from thee, and all *G565*
14 and goodly are **d** from thee, and thou *G565*

DEPARTETH
Job 27:21 him away, and he **d**: and as a storm H3212
Prv 14:16 A wise *man* feareth, and **d** from evil: H5493
Ecc 6: 4 For he cometh in with vanity, and **d** in H3212
Isa 59:15 Yea, truth faileth; and he *that* **d** from H5493
Jer 3:20 Surely *as* a wife treacherously **d** from
17: 5 and whose heart **d** from the LORD. H5493
Nah 3: 1 full of lies *and* robbery; the prey **d** not; H4185
Lk 9:39 and bruising him hardly **d** from him. *G672*

DEPARTING
Gen 35:18 as her soul was in **d**, (for she died) that H3318
Ex 16: 1 after their **d** out of the land of Egypt. H3318
Isa 59:13 the LORD, and **d** away from our God, H5253
Dan 9: 5 rebelled, even by **d** from thy precepts H5493
11 thy law, even by **d**, that they might not H5493
Hos 1: 2 great whoredom, *d* from the LORD.
Mk 6:33 And the people saw them **d**, and many *G5217*
7:31 And again, **d** from the coasts of Tyre *G1831*
Act 13:13 John **d** from them returned to Jerusalem. *G672*
20:29 For I know this, that after my **d** shall *G867*
Heb 3:12 of unbelief, in **d** from the living God. *G868*
11:22 mention of the **d** of the children of *G1841*

DEPARTURE
Ezk 26:18 *are* in the sea shall be troubled at thy **d**. H3318
2Ti 4: 6 offered, and the time of my **d** is at hand. *G359*

DEPOSED
Dan 5:20 in pride, he was **d** from his kingly H5182

DEPRIVED
Gen 27:45 I be **d** also of you both in one day? H7921
Job 39:17 Because God hath **d** her of wisdom, H5382
Isa 38:10 I am **d** of the residue of my years. H6485

DEPTH
Job 28:14 The **d** saith, It *is* not in me: and the sea H8415
38:16 hast thou walked in the search of the **d**? H8415
Ps 33: 7 heap: he layeth up the **d** in storehouses. H8415
Prv 8:27 he set a compass upon the face of the **d**: H8415
25: 3 and the earth for **d**, and the heart of H6011
Isa 7:11 it either in the **d**, or in the height above. H6009
Jna 2: 5 *even* to the soul: the **d** closed me round H8415
Mt 18: 6 he were drowned in the **d** of the sea. *G3989*
Mk 4: 5 sprang up, because it had no **d** of earth: *G899*
Ro 8:39 Nor height, nor **d**, nor any other creature, *G899*
11:33 O the **d** of the riches both of the wisdom *G899*
Eph 3:18 breadth, and length, and **d**, and height; *G899*

DEPTHS
Ex 15: 5 The **d** have covered them: they sank H8415
8 an heap, *and* the **d** were congealed in H8415
Dt 8: 7 **d** that spring out of valleys and hills; H8415
Ps 68:22 *my people* again from the **d** of the sea: H4688
71:20 me up again from the **d** of the earth. H8415
77:16 were afraid: the **d** also were troubled. H8415
78:15 gave *them* drink as *out of* the great **d**. H8415
106: 9 the **d**, as through the wilderness. H8415
107:26 down again to the **d**: their soul is melted H8415
130: 1 Out of the **d** have I cried unto thee, O H4615
Prv 3:20 By his knowledge the **d** are broken up, H8415
8:24 When *there were* no **d**, I was brought H8415
9:18 *and that* her guests *are* in the **d** of hell. H6010
Isa 51:10 hath made the **d** of the sea a way for H4615
Ezk 27:34 by the seas in the **d** of the waters thy H4615
Mic 7:19 cast all their sins into the **d** of the sea. H4688
Rev 2:24 not known the **d** of Satan, as they speak; *G899*

DEPUTED
2Sa 15: 3 *is* no man *d* of the king to hear thee.

DEPUTIES
Est 8: 9 and the **d** and rulers of the provinces H6346
9: 3 and the **d**, and officers of the king, H6346
Act 19:38 are **d**: let them implead one another. *G446*

DEPUTY
1Ki 22:47 *There was* then no king in Edom: a **d** H5324
Act 13: 7 Which was with the **d** of the country, *G446*
8 to turn away the **d** from the faith. *G446*
12 Then the **d**, when he saw what was done, *G446*
18:12 And when Gallio was the **d** of Achaia, *G445*

DERBE
Act 14: 6 unto Lystra and **D**, cities of Lycaonia, *G1191*
20 day he departed with Barnabas to **D**. *G1191*
16: 1 Then came he to **D** and Lystra: and, *G1191*
20: 4 and Gaius of **D**, and Timotheus; and *G1190*

DERIDE
Hab 1:10 them: they shall **d** every strong hold; H7832

DERIDED
Lk 16:14 heard all these things: and they **d** him. *G1592*
23:35 also with them **d** *him*, saying, He saved *G1592*

DERISION
Job 30: 1 than I have me in **d**, whose fathers I H7832
Ps 2: 4 laugh: the Lord shall have them in **d**. H3932
44:13 a **d** to them that are round about us. H7047
59: 8 thou shalt have all the heathen in **d**. H3932
79: 4 and **d** to them that are round about us. H7047
119:51 The proud have had me greatly in **d**: *yet* H3887
Jer 20: 7 I am in **d** daily, every one mocketh me. H7814
8 a reproach unto me, and a **d**, daily. H7047
48:26 in his vomit, and he also shall be in **d**. H7814
27 For was not Israel a **d** unto thee? was H7814
39 shall Moab be a **d** and a dismaying to H7814
Lam 3:14 I was a **d** to all my people; *and* their H7814
Ezk 23:32 scorn and had in **d**; it containeth much. H3933
36: 4 a prey and **d** to the residue of the H3933
Hos 7:16 *shall be* their **d** in the land of Egypt. H3933

DESCEND
Nu 34:11 the border shall **d**, and shall reach unto H3381
1Sa 26:10 or he shall **d** into battle, and perish. H3381
Ps 49:17 away: his glory shall not **d** after him. H3381
Isa 5:14 and he that rejoiceth, shall **d** into it. H3381
Ezk 26:20 with them that **d** into the pit, with the H3381
31:16 with them that **d** into the pit: and all H3381
Mk 15:32 Let Christ the King of Israel **d** now *G2597*
Act 11: 5 A certain vessel **d**, as it had been a great *G2597*
Ro 10: 7 Or, Who shall **d** into the deep? (that is, *G2597*
1Th 4:16 For the Lord himself shall **d** from *G2597*

DESCENDED
Ex 19:18 because the LORD **d** upon it in fire: H3381
33: 9 the cloudy pillar **d**, and stood *at* the H3381
34: 5 And the LORD **d** in the cloud, and H3381
Dt 9:21 into the brook that **d** out of the mount. H3381
Jos 2:23 So the two men returned, and **d** from H3381
17: 9 And the coast **d** unto the river Kanah, H3381
18:13 and the border **d** to Ataroth-adar, near H3381
16 on the north, and **d** to the valley of H3381
16 Jebusi on the south, and **d** to En-rogel, H3381
17 of Adummim, and **d** to the stone of H3381
Ps 133: 3 *as the dew* that **d** upon the mountains H3381
Prv 30: 4 up into heaven, or **d**? who hath gathered H3381

Mt 7:25 And the rain d, and the floods came, G2597
27 And the rain d, and the floods came, G2597
28: 2 angel of the Lord d from heaven, and G2597
Lk 3:22 And the Holy Ghost d in a bodily shape G2597
Act 24: 1 the high priest d with the elders, and G2597
Eph 4: 9 d first into the lower parts of the earth? G2597
10 He that d is the same also that G2597

DESCENDETH
Jas 3:15 This wisdom d not from above, but *is* G2076

DESCENDING
Gen 28:12 angels of God ascending and d on it. H3381
Mt 3:16 d like a dove, and lighting upon him: G2597
Mk 1:10 and the Spirit like a dove d upon him: G2597
Jn 1:32 I saw the Spirit d from heaven like a G2597
33 shalt see the Spirit d, and remaining on G2597
51 ascending and d upon the Son of man. G2597
Act 10:11 a certain vessel d unto him, as it had G2597
Rev 21:10 Jerusalem, d out of heaven from God, G2597

DESCENT
Lk 19:37 nigh, even now at the d of the mount of G2600
Heb 7: 3 mother, without d, having neither G35
6 But he whose d is not counted from G1075

DESCRIBE
Jos 18: 4 the land, and d it according to the H3789
6 Ye shall therefore d the land *into* seven H3789
8 them that went to d the land, saying, H3789
8 the land, and d it, and come again H3789

DESCRIBED
Jos 18: 9 the land, and d it by cities into seven H3789
Jdg 8:14 of him: and he d unto him the princes H3789

DESCRIBETH
Ro 4: 6 Even as David also d the blessedness of G3004
10: 5 For Moses d the righteousness which is G1125

DESCRIPTION
Jos 18: 6 and bring *the* d hither to me, that I may

DESCRY
Jdg 1:23 And the house of Joseph sent to d H8446

DESERT
Ex 3: 1 the backside of the d, and came to the H4057
5: 3 journey into the d, and sacrifice unto H4057
19: 2 were come *to* the d of Sinai, and had H4057
23:31 and from the d unto the river: for I H4057
Nu 20: 1 into the d of Zin in the first month: H4057
27:14 in the d of Zin, in the strife of H4057
33:16 And they removed from the d of Sinai, H4057
Dt 32:10 He found him in a d land, and in the H4057
2Ch 26:10 Also he built towers in the d, and H4057
Job 24: 5 Behold, *as* wild asses in the d, go they H4057
Ps 28: 4 of their hands; render to them their d. H1576
78:40 the wilderness, *and* grieve him in the d! H3452
102: 6 wilderness: I am like an owl of the d. H2723
106:14 wilderness, and tempted God in the d. H3452
Isa 13:21 But wild beasts of the d shall lie there; H6728
21: 1 The burden of the d of the sea. As H4057
1 cometh from the d, from a terrible land. H4057
34:14 The wild beasts of the d shall also meet H6728
35: 1 for them; and the d shall rejoice, and H6160
6 waters break out, and streams in the d. H6160
40: 3 straight in the d a highway for our God. H6160
41:19 I will set in the d the fir tree, *and* the H6160
43:19 in the wilderness, *and* rivers in the d. H3452
20 *and* rivers in the d, to give drink to my H3452
51: 3 like Eden, and her d like the garden of H6160
Jer 17: 6 For he shall be like the heath in the d, H6160
25:24 the mingled people that dwell in the d, H4057
50:12 *be* a wilderness, a dry land, and a d. H6160
39 Therefore the wild beasts of the d with H6728
Ezk 47: 8 go down into the d, and go into the sea: H6160
Mt 14:13 by ship into a d place apart: and when G2048
15 saying, This is a d place, and the time G2048
24:26 he is in the d; go not forth: behold, G2048
Mk 1:45 was without in d places: and they came G2048
6:31 apart into a d place, and rest a while: G2048
32 And they departed into a d place by G2048
35 d place, and now the time *is* far passed: G2048
Lk 4:42 and went into a d place: and the people G2048
9:10 privately into a d place belonging to G2048
12 victuals: for we are here in a d place. G2048
Jn 6:31 Our fathers did eat manna in the d; as it G2048
Act 8:26 from Jerusalem unto Gaza, which is d. G2048

DESERTS
Isa 48:21 led them through the d: he caused the H2723
Jer 2: 6 through a land of d and of pits, H6160
Ezk 7:27 according to their d will I judge them; H4941
13: 4 thy prophets are like the foxes in the d. H2723
Lk 1:80 d till the day of his shewing unto Israel. G2048
Heb 11:38 they wandered in d, and *in* mountains, G2047

DESERVE
Ezr 9:13 than our iniquities *d*, and hast given us

DESERVETH
Job 11: 6 of thee *less* than thine iniquity *d*.

DESERVING
Jdg 9:16 him according to the d of his hands; H1576

DESIRABLE
Ezk 23: 6 and rulers, all of them d young men, H2531
12 upon horses, all of them d young men. H2531
23 with them: all of them d young men, H2531

DESIRE
Gen 3:16 forth children; and thy d *shall be* to thy H8669
4: 7 *be* his d, and thou shalt rule over him. H8669
Ex 10:11 for that ye did d. And they were driven H1245
34:24 shall any man d thy land, when thou H2530
Dt 5:21 Neither shalt thou d thy neighbour's H2530
7:25 fire: thou shalt not d the silver or gold H2530
18: 6 come with all the d of his mind unto the H185
21:11 and hast a d unto her, that thou H2836
Jdg 8:24 And Gideon said unto them, I would d H7592
1Sa 9:20 on whom *is* all the d of Israel? *Is it* not H2532
23:20 according to all the d of thy soul to come H183
2Sa 23: 5 *my* d, although he make *it* not to grow. H2656
1Ki 2:20 Then she said, I d one small petition of H7592
5: 8 I will do all thy d concerning timber of H2656
9 my d, in giving food for my household. H2656
10 trees and fir trees *according to* all his d. H2656
9: 1 d which he was pleased to do, H2837
11 to all his d,) that then king Solomon H2656
10:13 of Sheba all her d, whatsoever she H2656
2Ki 4:28 Then she said, Did I d a son of my lord? H7592
2Ch 9:12 of Sheba all her d, whatsoever she H2656
15:15 with their whole d; and he was found of H7522
Neh 1:11 thy servants, who d to fear thy name: H2655
Job 13: 3 Almighty, and I d to reason with God. H2654
14:15 have a d to the work of thine hands. H3700
21:14 for we d not the knowledge of thy ways. H2654
31:16 If I have withheld the poor from *their* d, H2656
35 me! behold, my d *is*, *that* the Almighty H8420
33:32 me: speak, for I d to justify thee. H2654
34:36 My d *is that* Job may be tried unto the H15
36:20 D not the night, when people are cut off H7602
Ps 10: 3 For the wicked boasteth of his heart's d, H8378
17 LORD, thou hast heard the d of the H8378
21: 2 Thou hast given him his heart's d, and H8378
38: 9 Lord, all my d *is* before thee; and my H8378
40: 6 Sacrifice and offering thou didst not d; H2654
45:11 So shall the king greatly d thy beauty: for H183
54: 7 eye hath seen *his* d upon mine enemies.
59:10 let me see *my* d upon mine enemies.
70: 2 and put to confusion, that d my hurt. H2655
73:25 *is* none upon earth *that* I d beside thee. H2654
78:29 well filled: for he gave them their own d; H8378
92:11 Mine eye also shall see *my* d on mine
11 *d* of the wicked that rise up against me.
112: 8 until he see *his d* upon his enemies.
10 away: the d of the wicked shall perish. H8378
118: 7 shall I see *my* d upon them that hate me.
145:16 satisfiest the d of every living thing. H7522
19 He will fulfil the d of them that fear H7522
Prv 3:15 d are not to be compared unto her. H2656
10:24 the d of the righteous shall be granted. H8378
11:23 The d of the righteous *is* only good: *but* H8378
13:12 *when* the d cometh, *it is* a tree of life. H8378
19 The d accomplished is sweet to the H8378
18: 1 Through d a man, having separated H8378
19:22 The d of a man *is* his kindness: and a H8378
21:25 The d of the slothful killeth him; for his H8378
23: 6 evil eye, neither d thou his dainty meats: H183
24: 1 evil men, neither d to be with them. H183
Ecc 6: 9 wandering of the d: this *is* also vanity H5315
12: 5 be a burden, and d shall fail: because H35
Song 7:10 I *am* my beloved's, and his d *is* toward H8669
Isa 26: 8 for thee; the d of *our* soul *is* to thy H8378
53: 2 *is* no beauty that we should d him. H2530
Jer 22:27 they d to return, thither H5375+H5315
42:22 place whither ye d to go *and* to sojourn. H2654
Jer 44:14 which they have a d to return to dwell H5315
Ezk 24:16 from thee the d of thine eyes with a H4261
21 your strength, the d of your eyes, and H4261
25 of their glory, the d of their eyes, and H4261
Dan 2:18 That they would d mercies of the God H1156
11:37 *fathers*, nor the d of women, nor regard H2532
Hos 10:10 *It is* in my d that I should chastise them; H185
Am 5:18 Woe unto you that d the day of the H183
Mic 7: 3 his mischievous d: so they wrap it up. H5315
Hab 2: 5 who enlargeth his d as hell, and *is* as H5315
Hag 2: 7 And I will shake all nations, and the d H2532
Mk 9:35 them, If any man d to be first, *the same* G2309
10:35 do for us whatsoever we shall d. G154
11:24 things soever ye d, when ye pray, believe G154
15: 8 aloud began to d *him to do* as he had G154
Lk 17:22 when ye shall d to see one of the days G1937
20:46 Beware of the scribes, which d to walk G2309
22:15 And he said unto them, With d I have G1939
Act 23:20 And he said, The Jews have agreed to d G2065
28:22 But we d to hear of thee what thou G515
Ro 10: 1 Brethren, my heart's d and prayer to G2107
15:23 d these many years to come unto you; G1974
1Co 14: 1 Follow after charity, and d spiritual G2206
2Co 7: 7 us your earnest d, your mourning, your G1972
11 *what* vehement d, yea, *what* zeal, yea, G1972
11:12 from them which d occasion; that G2309
12: 6 For though I would d to glory, I shall G2309
Gal 4: 9 ye d again to be in bondage? G2309
20 I d to be present with you now, and to G2309
21 Tell me, ye that d to be under the law, G2309
6:12 As many as d to make a fair shew in G2309
13 keep the law; but d to have you G2309
Eph 3:13 Wherefore I d that ye faint not at my G154
Php 1:23 two, having a d to depart, and to be G1939
4:17 Not because I d a gift: but I desire fruit G1934
17 Not because I desire a gift: but I d fruit G1934
Col 1: 9 for you, and to d that ye might be filled G154
1Th 2:17 to see your face with great d. G1939
1Ti 3: 1 This *is* a true saying, If a man d the G3713
Heb 6:11 And we d that every one of you do G1937
11:16 But now they d a better *country*, that G3713
Jas 4: 2 Ye lust, and have not: ye kill, and d to G2206
1Pt 1:12 which things the angels d to look into. G1937
2: 2 As newborn babes, d the sincere milk G1971
Rev 9: 6 find it; and shall d to die, and death G1937

DESIRED
Gen 3: 6 and a tree to be d to make *one* wise, H2530
1Sa 12:13 *and* whom ye have d! and, behold, the H7592
1Ki 9:19 which Solomon d to build in Jerusalem, H2836
2Ch 8: 6 and all that Solomon d to build in H2836
11:23 in abundance. And he d many wives. H7592
21:20 without being d. Howbeit they buried H2532
Est 2:13 whatsoever she d was given her to go H559
Job 20:20 he shall not save of that which he d. H2530
Ps 19:10 More to be d *are they* than gold, yea, H2530
27: 4 One *thing* have I d of the LORD, that H7592
107:30 he bringeth them unto their d haven. H2656
132:13 Zion; he hath d *it* for his habitation. H183
14 for ever: here will I dwell; for I have d it. H183
Prv 8:11 may be d are not to be compared to it. H2656
21:20 *There is* treasure to be d and oil in the H2530
Ecc 2:10 And whatsoever mine eyes d I kept not H7592
Isa 1:29 oaks which ye have d, and ye shall be H2530
26: 9 With my soul have I d thee in the night; H183
Jer 17:16 thee: neither have I d the woeful day; H183
Dan 2:16 Then Daniel went in, and d of the king H1156
23 me now what we d of thee: for thou H1156
Hos 6: 6 For I d mercy, and not sacrifice; and H2654
Mic 7: 1 to eat: my soul d the firstripe fruit. H183
Zep 2: 1 yea, gather together, O nation not d; H3700
Mt 13:17 *men* have d to see *those things* which G1937
16: 1 and tempting d him that he would G1905
Mk 15: 6 them one prisoner, whomsoever they d. G154
Lk 7:36 And one of the Pharisees d him that he G2065
9: 9 hear such things? And he d to see him. G2212
10:24 and kings have d to see those things G2309
22:15 them, With desire I have d to eat this G1937
31 Satan hath d *to have* you, that he G1809
23:25 had d; but he delivered Jesus to their will. G154
Jn 12:21 d him, saying, Sir, we would see Jesus. G2065
Act 3:14 d a murderer to be granted unto you; G154
7:46 Who found favour before God, and d to G154
8:31 guide me? And he d Philip that he G3870
9: 2 And d of him letters to Damascus to the G154
12:20 their friend, d peace; because their G154
13: 7 Saul, and d to hear the word of God. G1934
21 And afterward they d a king: and God G154
28 yet d they Pilate that he should be slain. G154

D

Act 16:39 and **d** *them* to depart out of the city. *G2065*
18:20 When they **d** *him* to tarry longer time *G2065*
25: 3 And **d** favour against him, that he would *G154*
28:14 Where we found brethren, and were **d** *G3870*
1Co 16:12 Apollos, I greatly **d** him to come unto *G3870*
2Co 8: 6 Insomuch that we **d** Titus, that as he *G3870*
12:18 I **d** Titus, and with *him* I sent a *G3870*
1Jn 5:15 we have the petitions that we **d** of him. *G154*

DESIREDST
Dt 18:16 According to all that thou **d** of the H7592
Mt 18:32 thee all that debt, because thou **d** me: *G3870*

DESIRES
Ps 37: 4 he shall give thee the **d** of thine heart. H4862
140: 8 Grant not, O LORD, the **d** of the H3970
Eph 2: 3 flesh, fulfilling the **d** of the flesh and of *G2307*

DESIREST
Ps 51: 6 Behold, thou **d** truth in the inward H2654
16 For thou **d** not sacrifice; else would I H2654

DESIRETH
Dt 14:26 thy soul **d**: and thou shalt eat there H7592
1Sa 2:16 *as much* as thy soul **d**; then he would H183
18:25 to David, The king **d** not any dowry, H2656
20: 4 thy soul **d**, I will even do *it* for thee. H559
2Sa 3:21 all that thine heart **d**. And David sent H183
1Ki 11:37 thy soul **d**, and shalt be king over Israel. H183
Job 7: 2 As a servant earnestly **d** the shadow, H7602
23:13 and *what* his soul **d**, even *that* he doeth. H183
Ps 34:12 What man *is he that* **d** life, *and* loveth H2655
68:16 *is* the hill *which* God **d** to dwell in; yea, H2530
Prv 12:12 The wicked **d** the net of evil *men*: but H2530
13: 4 The soul of the sluggard **d**, and *hath* H183
21:10 The soul of the wicked **d** evil: his H183
Ecc 6: 2 soul of all that he **d**, yet God giveth him H183
Lk 5:39 **d** new: for he saith, The old is better. *G2309*
14:32 ambassage, and **d** conditions of peace. *G2065*
1Ti 3: 1 office of a bishop, he **d** a good work. *G1937*

DESIRING
Mt 12:46 stood without, **d** to speak with him. *G2212*
47 stand without, **d** to speak with thee. *G2212*
20:20 *him*, and **d** a certain thing of him. *G154*
Lk 8:20 brethren stand without, **d** to see thee. *G2309*
16:21 And **d** to be fed with the crumbs which *G1937*
Act 9:38 him two men, **d** *him* that he would not *G3870*
19:31 sent unto him, **d** *him* that he would not *G3870*
25:15 *me*, **d** *to have* judgment against him. *G154*
2Co 5: 2 For in this we groan, earnestly **d** to be *G1971*
1Th 3: 6 of us always, **d** greatly to see us, as *G1971*
1Ti 1: 7 **D** to be teachers of the law; *G2309*
2Ti 1: 4 Greatly **d** to see thee, being mindful of *G1971*

DESIROUS
Prv 23: 3 Be not **d** of his dainties: for they *are* H183
Lk 23: 8 glad: for he was **d** to see him of a long *G2309*
Jn 16:19 Now Jesus knew that they were **d** to ask *G2309*
2Co 11:32 with a garrison, **d** to apprehend me: *G2309*
Gal 5:26 Let us not be **d** of vain glory, provoking *G2755*
1Th 2: 8 So being affectionately **d** of you, we *G2442*

DESOLATE
Gen 47:19 live, and not die, that the land be not **d**. H3456
Ex 23:29 the land become **d**, and the beast of the H8077
Lev 26:22 number; and your *high* ways shall be **d**. H8074
33 land shall be **d**, and your cities waste. H8077
34 as long as it lieth **d**, and ye *be* in your H8074
35 As long as it lieth **d** it shall rest; H8074
43 while she lieth **d** without them: and H8074
2Sa 13:20 **d** in her brother Absalom's house. H8074
2Ch 36:21 as long as she lay **d** she kept sabbath, H8074
Job 3:14 which built **d** places for themselves; H2723
15:28 And he dwelleth in **d** cities, *and* in H3582
34 *shall be* **d**, and fire shall consume H1565
16: 7 thou hast made **d** all my company. H8074
30: 3 wilderness in former time **d** and waste. H7722
38:27 To satisfy the **d** and waste *ground*; and H7722
Ps 25:16 upon me; for I *am* **d** and afflicted. H3173
34:21 they that hate the righteous shall be **d**. H816
22 none of them that trust in him shall be **d**. H816
40:15 Let them be **d** for a reward of their H8074
69:25 Let their habitation be **d**; *and* let none H8074
109:10 *their bread* also out of their **d** places. H2723
143: 4 within me; my heart within me is **d**. H8074
Isa 1: 7 Your country *is* **d**, your cities *are* H8077
7 and *it is* **d**, as overthrown by strangers. H8077
3:26 she *being* **d** shall sit upon the ground. H5352
Isa 5: 9 houses shall be **d**, *even* great and fair, H8047
6:11 without man, and the land be utterly **d**, H7582
7:19 all of them in the **d** valleys, and in the H1327
13: 9 to lay the land **d**: and he shall destroy H8047
22 shall cry in their **d** houses, and dragons H490
15: 6 For the waters of Nimrim shall be **d**: for H4923
24: 6 that dwell therein are **d**: therefore the H816
27:10 Yet the defenced city *shall be* **d**, *and* the H910
49: 8 to cause to inherit the **d** heritages; H8074
19 For thy waste and thy **d** places, and the H8074
21 my children, and am **d**, a captive, and H1565
54: 1 the children of the **d** than the children H8074
3 and make the **d** cities to be inhabited. H8074
59:10 night; *we are* in **d** places as dead *men*. H820
62: 4 more be termed **D**: but thou shalt be H8077
Jer 2:12 afraid, be ye very **d**, saith the LORD. H2717
4: 7 to make thy land **d**; *and* thy cities shall H8047
27 shall be **d**; yet will I not make a full end. H8077
6: 8 lest I make thee **d**, a land not inhabited. H8077
7:34 of the bride: for the land shall be **d**. H2723
9:11 cities of Judah **d**, without an inhabitant. H8077
10:22 cities of Judah **d**, *and* a den of dragons. H8077
25 him, and have made his habitation **d**. H8074
12:10 my pleasant portion a **d** wilderness. H8077
11 They have made it **d**, *and being* H8076
11 *and being* **d** it mourneth unto me; H8077
11 **d**, because no man layeth *it* to heart. H8074
18:16 To make their land **d**, *and* a perpetual H8047
19: 8 And I will make this city **d**, and an H8047
25:38 lion: for their land is **d** because of the H8047
26: 9 and this city shall be **d** without an H2717
32:43 ye say, *It is* **d** without man or beast; H8077
33:10 ye say *shall be* **d** without man and H2720
10 that are **d**, without man, and without H8074
12 this place, which is **d** without man and H2720
44: 6 they are wasted *and* **d**, as at this day. H8077
46:19 be waste and **d** without an inhabitant. H3341
48: 9 shall be **d**, without any to dwell therein. H8047
34 the waters also of Nimrim shall be **d**. H4923
49: 2 and it shall be a **d** heap, and her H8077
20 make their habitations **d** with them. H8074
50: 3 make her land **d**, and none shall dwell H8047
13 it shall be wholly **d**: every one that goeth H8077
45 make *their* habitation **d** with them. H8074
51:26 shalt be **d** for ever, saith the LORD. H8077
62 nor beast, but that it shall be **d** for ever. H8077
Lam 1: 4 all her gates are **d**: her priests sigh, her H8074
13 hath made me **d** *and* faint all the day. H8074
16 are **d**, because the enemy prevailed. H8074
3:11 me in pieces: he hath made me **d**. H8074
4: 5 They that did feed delicately are **d** in H8074
5:18 Zion, which is **d**, the foxes walk upon it. H8074
Ezk 6: 4 And your altars shall be **d**, and your H8074
6 places shall be **d**; that your altars may H3456
6 waste and made **d**, and your idols may H816
14 make the land **d**, yea, more desolate H8077
14 yea, more **d** than the wilderness H4923
12:19 that her land may be **d** from all that is H3456
20 the land shall be **d**; and ye shall know H8077
14:15 it, so that it be **d**, that no man may pass H8077
16 be delivered, but the land shall be **d**. H8077
15: 8 And I will make the land **d**, because H8077
19: 7 And he knew their **d** palaces, and he laid H490
7 and the land was **d**, and the fulness H3456
20:26 I might make them **d**, to the end that H8074
25: 3 when it was **d**; and against the house H8074
13 and I will make it **d** from Teman; and H2723
26:19 I shall make thee a **d** city, like the cities H2717
20 earth, in places **d** of old, with them that H2723
29: 9 And the land of Egypt shall be **d** and H8077
10 utterly waste *and* **d**, from the tower of H8077
12 And I will make the land of Egypt **d** in H8077
12 the countries *that are* **d**, and her cities H8074
12 laid waste shall be **d** forty years: and I H8077
30: 7 And they shall be **d** in the midst of the H8074
7 countries *that are* **d**, and her cities shall H8074
14 And I will make Pathros **d**, and will set H8074
32:15 When I shall make the land of Egypt **d**, H8077
33:28 For I will lay the land most **d**, H8077+H4923
28 shall be **d**, that none shall pass through. H8074
29 the land most **d** because of all H8077+H4923
35: 3 and I will make thee most **d**. H8077+H4923
4 and thou shalt be **d**, and thou shalt H8077
7 Seir most **d**, and cut off from H8077+H8077
12 They are laid **d**, they are given H8074+H8077
14 earth rejoiceth, I will make thee **d**. H8077
15 because it was **d**, so will I do unto thee: H8074
15 thee: thou shalt be **d**, O mount Seir, and H8077
36: 3 have made *you* **d**, and swallowed you H8074
Ezk 36: 4 the valleys, to the **d** wastes, and to the H8074
34 And the **d** land shall be tilled, whereas H8074
34 lay **d** in the sight of all that passed by. H8077
35 This land that was **d** is become like the H8074
35 and the waste and **d** and ruined cities H8074
36 plant that that was **d**: I the LORD have H8074
38:12 hand upon the **d** places *that are now* H2723
Dan 9:17 sanctuary that is **d**, for the Lord's sake. H8076
27 he shall make *it* **d**, even until the H8074
27 determined shall be poured upon the **d**. H8074
11:31 place the abomination that maketh **d**. H8074
12:11 that maketh **d** set up, *there shall be* H8074
Hos 5: 9 Ephraim shall be **d** in the day of H8047
13:16 Samaria shall become **d**; for she hath H816
Joel 1:17 garners are laid **d**, the barns are broken H8074
18 yea, the flocks of sheep are made **d**. H816
2: 3 behind them a **d** wilderness; yea, and H8077
20 into a land barren and **d**, with his face H8077
3:19 Edom shall be a **d** wilderness, for the H8077
Am 7: 9 And the high places of Isaac shall be **d**, H8074
Mic 1: 7 thereof will I lay **d**: for she gathered *it* of H8077
6:13 in making *thee* **d** because of thy sins. H8074
7:13 Notwithstanding the land shall be **d** H8077
Zep 3: 6 their towers are **d**; I made their streets H8074
Zec 7:14 Thus the land was **d** after them, that no H8074
14 for they laid the pleasant land **d**. H8047
Mal 1: 4 and build the **d** places; thus saith the H2723
Mt 23:38 Behold, your house is left unto you **d**. *G2048*
Lk 13:35 Behold, your house is left unto you **d**: *G2048*
Act 1:20 Let his habitation be **d**, and let no man *G2048*
Gal 4:27 not: for the **d** hath many more children *G2048*
1Ti 5: 5 Now she that is a widow indeed, and **d**, *G3443*
Rev 17:16 shall make her **d** and naked, and shall *G2049*
18:19 for in one hour is she made **d**. *G2049*

DESOLATION
Lev 26:31 sanctuaries unto **d**, and I will not smell H8074
32 And I will bring the land into **d**: and H8074
Jos 8:28 heap for ever, *even* a **d** unto this day. H8077
2Ki 22:19 should become a **d** and a curse, and H8047
2Ch 30: 7 therefore gave them up to **d**, as ye see. H8047
Job 30:14 the **d** they rolled themselves *upon me*. H7722
Ps 73:19 How are they *brought* into **d**, as in a H8047
Prv 1:27 When your fear cometh as **d**, H7722+H7584
3:25 of the **d** of the wicked, when it cometh. H7722
Isa 10: 3 and in the **d** *which* shall come from H7722
17: 9 children of Israel: and there shall be **d**. H8077
24:12 In the city is left **d**, and the gate is H8047
47:11 to put it off: and **d** shall come upon H7722
51:19 be sorry for thee? **d**, and destruction, H7701
64:10 Zion is a wilderness, Jerusalem a **d**. H8077
Jer 22: 5 LORD, that this house shall become a **d**. H2723
25:11 And this whole land shall be a **d**, *and* an H2723
18 to make them a **d**, an astonishment, an H2723
34:22 of Judah a **d** without an inhabitant. H8077
44: 2 *are* a **d**, and no man dwelleth therein, H2723
22 is your land a **d**, and an astonishment, H2723
49:13 shall become a **d**, a reproach, a waste, H8047
17 Also Edom shall be a **d**: every one that H8047
33 for dragons, *and* a **d** for ever: there H8077
50:23 become a **d** among the nations! H8047
51:29 of Babylon a **d** without an inhabitant. H8047
43 Her cities are a **d**, a dry land, and a H8047
Lam 3:47 Fear and a snare is come upon us, **d** H7612
Ezk 7:27 be clothed with **d**, and the hands of the H8077
23:33 **d**, with the cup of thy sister Samaria. H8077
Dan 8:13 the transgression of **d**, to give both the H8074
Hos 12: 1 lies and **d**; and they do make a H7701
Joel 3:19 Egypt shall be a **d**, and Edom shall be a H8077
Mic 6:16 make thee a **d**, and the inhabitants H8047
Zep 1:13 and their houses a **d**: they shall also H8077
15 of wasteness and **d**, a day of darkness H4875
2: 4 and Ashkelon a **d**: they shall drive out H8077
9 and a perpetual **d**: the residue of my H8077
13 Nineveh a **d**, *and* dry like a wilderness. H8077
14 sing in the windows; **d** *shall be* in the H2721
15 is she become a **d**, a place for beasts to H8047
Mt 12:25 itself is brought to **d**; and every city or *G2049*
24:15 abomination of **d**, spoken of by Daniel *G2050*
Mk 13:14 abomination of **d**, spoken of by Daniel *G2050*
Lk 11:17 itself is brought to **d**; and a house *G2049*
21:20 then know that the **d** thereof is nigh. *G2050*

DESOLATIONS
Ezr 9: 9 and to repair the **d** thereof, and to give H2723
Ps 46: 8 what **d** he hath made in the earth. H8047
74: 3 Lift up thy feet unto the perpetual **d**; H4876
Isa 61: 4 up the former **d**, and they shall repair H8074
4 waste cities, the **d** of many generations. H8074

Jer 25: 9 and an hissing, and perpetual **d**. H2723
12 and will make it perpetual **d**. H8077
Ezk 35: 9 I will make thee perpetual **d**, and thy H8077
Dan 9: 2 seventy years in the **d** of Jerusalem. H2723
18 and behold our **d**, and the city which is H8074
26 the end of the war **d** are determined. H8074

DESPAIR
1Sa 27: 1 and Saul shall **d** of me, to seek me any H2976
Ecc 2:20 to cause my heart to **d** of all the labour H2976
2Co 4: 8 *we are* perplexed, but not in **d**; *G1820*

DESPAIRED
2Co 1: 8 insomuch that we **d** even of life: *G1820*

DESPERATE
Job 6:26 of one that is **d**, *which are* as wind? H2976
Isa 17:11 heap in the day of grief and of **d** sorrow. H605

DESPERATELY
Jer 17: 9 *things*, and **d** wicked: who can know it? H605

DESPISE
Lev 26:15 And if ye shall **d** my statutes, or if your H3988
1Sa 2:30 they that **d** me shall be lightly esteemed. H959
2Sa 19:43 why then did ye **d** us, that our advice H7043
Est 1:17 so that they shall **d** their husbands in H959
Job 5:17 therefore **d** not thou the chastening H3988
9:21 I not know my soul: I would **d** my life. H3988
10: 3 that thou shouldest **d** the work of thine H3988
31:13 If I did **d** the cause of my manservant H3988
Ps 51:17 a contrite heart, O God, thou wilt not **d**. H959
73:20 thou awakest, thou shalt **d** their image. H959
102:17 of the destitute, and not **d** their prayer. H959
Prv 1: 7 *but* fools **d** wisdom and instruction. H936
3:11 My son, **d** not the chastening of the H3988
6:30 *Men* do not **d** a thief, if he steal to satisfy H936
23: 9 for he will **d** the wisdom of thy words. H936
22 and **d** not thy mother when she is old. H936
Isa 30:12 of Israel, Because ye **d** this word, and H3988
Jer 4:30 lovers will **d** thee, they will seek thy life. H3988
23:17 They say still unto them that **d** me, The H5006
Lam 1: 8 that honoured her **d** her, because they H2107
Ezk 16:57 Philistines, which **d** thee round about. H7590
28:26 upon all those that **d** them round about H7590
Am 5:21 I hate, I **d** your feast days, and I will H3988
Mal 1: 6 you, O priests, that **d** my name. And ye H959
Mt 6:24 to the one, and **d** the other. Ye cannot *G2706*
18:10 Take heed that ye **d** not one of these *G2706*
Lk 16:13 to the one, and **d** the other. Ye cannot *G2706*
Ro 14: 3 Let not him that eateth **d** him that *G1848*
1Co 11:22 to drink in? or **d** ye the church of God, *G2706*
16:11 Let no man therefore **d** him: but *G1848*
1Th 5:20 **D** not prophesyings. *G1848*
1Ti 4:12 Let no man **d** thy youth; but be thou an *G2706*
6: 2 let them not **d** *them*, because they *G2706*
Tit 2:15 with all authority. Let no man **d** thee. *G4065*
Heb 12: 5 unto children, My son, **d** not thou the *G3643*
2Pt 2:10 of uncleanness, and **d** government. *G2706*
Jude 8 **d** dominion, and speak evil of dignities. *G114*

DESPISED
Gen 16: 4 her mistress was **d** in her eyes. H7043
5 had conceived, I was **d** in her eyes: the H7043
25:34 went his way: thus Esau **d** *his* birthright. H959
Lev 26:43 even because they **d** my judgments, H3988
Nu 11:20 that ye have **d** the LORD which *is* H3988
14:31 shall know the land which ye have **d**. H3988
15:31 Because he hath **d** the word of the H959
Jdg 9:38 that thou hast **d**? go out, I pray now, H3988
1Sa 10:27 save us? And they **d** him, and brought H959
2Sa 6:16 the LORD; and she **d** him in her heart. H959
12: 9 Wherefore hast thou **d** the H959
10 because thou hast **d** me, and hast taken H959
2Ki 19:21 of Zion hath **d** thee, *and* laughed thee H959
1Ch 15:29 and playing: and she **d** him in her heart. H959
2Ch 36:16 of God, and **d** his words, and misused H959
Neh 2:19 us to scorn, and **d** us, and said, What *is* H959
4: 4 Hear, O our God; for we are **d**: and turn H939
Job 12: 5 **d** in the thought of him that is at ease. H937
19:18 Yea, young children **d** me; I arose, and H3988
Ps 22: 6 a reproach of men, and **d** of the people. H959
24 For he hath not **d** nor abhorred the H959
53: 5 to shame, because God hath **d** them. H3988
106:24 Yea, they **d** the pleasant land, they H3988
119:141 I *am* small and **d**: *yet* do not I forget thy H959
Prv 1:30 They would none of my counsel: they **d** H5006
5:12 instruction, and my heart **d** reproof; H5006
12: 8 he that is of a perverse heart shall be **d**. H937
Prv 12: 9 *He that is* **d**, and hath a servant, *is* H7034
Ecc 9:16 *is* **d**, and his words are not heard. H959
Song 8: 1 I would kiss thee; yea, I should not be **d**. H936
Isa 5:24 **d** the word of the Holy One of Israel. H5006
33: 8 hath **d** the cities, he regardeth no man. H3988
37:22 of Zion, hath **d** thee, *and* laughed thee H959
53: 3 He is **d** and rejected of men; a man of H959
3 him; he was **d**, and we esteemed him not. H959
60:14 thee; and all they that **d** thee shall bow H5006
Jer 22:28 *Is* this man Coniah a **d** broken idol? *is he* H959
33:24 thus they have **d** my people, that they H5006
49:15 among the heathen, *and* **d** among men. H959
Lam 2: 6 in Zion, and hath **d** in the indignation H5006
Ezk 16:59 **d** the oath in breaking the covenant. H959
17:16 whose oath he **d**, and whose covenant H959
18 Seeing he **d** the oath by breaking the H959
19 oath that he hath **d**, and my covenant H959
20:13 my statutes, and they **d** my judgments, H3988
16 Because they **d** my judgments, and H3988
24 but had **d** my statutes, and had H3988
22: 8 Thou hast **d** mine holy things, and hast H959
28:24 about them, that **d** them; and they H7590
Am 2: 4 because they have **d** the law of the H3988
Oba 2 among the heathen: thou art greatly **d**. H959
Zec 4:10 For who hath **d** the day of small things? H936
Mal 1: 6 ye say, Wherein have we **d** thy name? H959
Lk 18: 9 that they were righteous, and **d** others: *G1848*
Act 19:27 goddess Diana should be **d**, and her *G1519*
1Co 1:28 things which are **d**, hath God chosen, *G1848*
4:10 strong; ye *are* honourable, but we *are* **d**. *G820*
Gal 4:14 was in my flesh ye **d** not, nor rejected; *G1848*
Heb 10:28 He that **d** Moses' law died without mercy *G114*
Jas 2: 6 But ye have **d** the poor. Do not rich men *G818*

DESPISERS
Act 13:41 Behold, ye **d**, and wonder, and perish: *G2707*
2Ti 3: 3 fierce, **d** of those that are good, *G865*

DESPISEST
Ro 2: 4 Or **d** thou the riches of his goodness *G2706*

DESPISETH
Job 36: 5 Behold, God *is* mighty, and **d** not *any:* H3988
Ps 69:33 For the LORD heareth the poor, and **d** H959
Prv 11:12 He that is void of wisdom **d** his H936
13:13 Whoso **d** the word shall be destroyed: H936
14: 2 but *he that is* perverse in his ways **d** him. H959
21 He that **d** his neighbour sinneth: but he H936
15: 5 A fool **d** his father's instruction: but he H5006
20 father: but a foolish man **d** his mother. H959
32 He that refuseth instruction **d** his own H3988
19:16 soul; *but* he that **d** his ways shall die. H959
30:17 at *his* father, and **d** to obey *his* mother, H936
Isa 33:15 uprightly; he that **d** the gain of H3988
49: 7 to him whom man **d**, to him whom the H960
Lk 10:16 me; and he that **d** you despiseth me; and *G114*
16 he that despiseth you **d** me; and he that *G114*
16 he that **d** me despiseth him that sent me. *G114*
16 he that despiseth me **d** him that sent me. *G114*
1Th 4: 8 He therefore that **d**, despiseth not man, *G114*
8 He therefore that despiseth, **d** not man, *G114*

DESPISING
Heb 12: 2 endured the cross, **d** the shame, and is *G2706*

DESPITE
Ezk 25: 6 with all thy **d** against the land of Israel; H7589
Heb 10:29 hath done **d** unto the Spirit of grace? *G1796*

DESPITEFUL
Ezk 25:15 **d** heart, to destroy *it* for the old hatred; H7589
36: 5 with **d** minds, to cast it out for a prey. H7589
Ro 1:30 Backbiters, haters of God, **d**, proud, *G5197*

DESPITEFULLY
Mt 5:44 which **d** use you, and persecute you; *G1908*
Lk 6:28 and pray for them which **d** use you. *G1908*
Act 14: 5 to use *them* **d**, and to stone them, *G5195*

DESTITUTE
Gen 24:27 who hath not left **d** my master of his H5800
Ps 102:17 He will regard the prayer of the **d**, and H6199
141: 8 in thee is my trust; leave not my soul **d**. H6168
Prv 15:21 Folly *is* joy to *him that is* **d** of wisdom: H2638
Ezk 32:15 the country shall be **d** of that whereof it H8074
1Ti 6: 5 minds, and **d** of the truth, supposing *G650*
Heb 11:37 goatskins; being **d**, afflicted, tormented; *G5302*
Jas 2:15 If a brother or sister be naked, and **d** of *G3007*

DESTROY
Gen 6: 7 And the LORD said, I will **d** man whom H4229
13 behold, I will **d** them with the earth. H7843
17 upon the earth, to **d** all flesh, wherein *is* H7843
7: 4 will I **d** from off the face of the earth. H4229
9:11 any more be a flood to **d** the earth. H7843
15 no more become a flood to **d** all flesh. H7843
18:23 also **d** the righteous with the wicked? H5595
24 city: wilt thou also **d** and not spare the H5595
28 wilt thou **d** all the city for *lack of* H7843
28 find there forty and five, I will not **d** *it.* H7843
31 he said, I will not **d** *it* for twenty's sake. H7843
32 he said, I will not **d** *it* for ten's sake. H7843
19:13 For we will **d** this place, because the cry H7843
13 and the LORD hath sent us to **d** it. H7843
14 for the LORD will **d** this city. But he H7843
Ex 8: 9 for thy people, to **d** the frogs from thee H3772
12:13 **d** *you*, when I smite the land of Egypt. H4889
15: 9 draw my sword, my hand shall **d** them. H3423
23:27 thee, and will **d** all the people to whom H2000
34:13 But ye shall **d** their altars, break their H5422
Lev 23:30 soul will I **d** from among his people. H6
26:22 of your children, and **d** your cattle, and H3772
30 And I will **d** your high places, and cut H8045
44 I abhor them, to **d** them utterly, and to H3615
Nu 21: 2 hand, then I will utterly **d** their cities. H2763
24:17 Moab, and **d** all the children of Sheth. H6979
19 shall **d** him that remaineth of the city. H6
32:15 and ye shall **d** all this people. H7843
33:52 before you, and **d** all their pictures, and H6
52 all their pictures, and **d** all their molten H6
Dt 1:27 into the hand of the Amorites, to **d** us. H8045
2:15 against them, to **d** them from among H2000
4:31 thee, neither **d** thee, nor forget the H7843
6:15 **d** thee from off the face of the earth. H8045
7: 2 them, *and* utterly **d** them; thou shalt H2763
4 against you, and **d** thee suddenly. H8045
5 them; ye shall **d** their altars, and break H5422
10 to their face, to **d** them: he will not be H6
23 thee, and shall **d** them with a mighty H1949
24 and thou shalt **d** their name from under H6
9: 3 fire he shall **d** them, and he shall bring H8045
3 them out, and **d** them quickly, as the H6
14 Let me alone, that I may **d** them, and H8045
19 against you to **d** you. But the LORD H8045
25 the LORD had said he would **d** you. H8045
26 said, O Lord GOD, **d** not thy people and H7843
10:10 also, *and* the LORD would not **d** thee. H7843
12: 2 Ye shall utterly **d** all the places, wherein H6
3 **d** the names of them out of that place. H6
20:17 But thou shalt utterly **d** them; *namely,* H2763
19 it, thou shalt not **d** the trees thereof by H7843
20 meat, thou shalt **d** and cut them down; H7843
28:63 rejoice over you to **d** you, and to bring H6
31: 3 thee, *and* he will **d** these nations from H8045
32:25 within, shall **d** both the young man H7921
33:27 before thee; and shall say, **D** *them.* H8045
Jos 7: 7 of the Amorites, to **d** us? would to God H6
12 ye **d** the accursed from among you. H8045
9:24 the land, and to **d** all the inhabitants of H8045
11:20 that he might **d** them utterly, *and* that H2763
20 but that he might **d** them, as the LORD H8045
22:33 them in battle, to **d** the land wherein H7843
Jdg 6: 5 and they entered into the land to **d** it. H7843
21:11 Ye shall utterly **d** every male, and every H2763
1Sa 15: 3 and utterly **d** all that they have, and H2763
6 Amalekites, lest I **d** you with them: for ye H622
9 would not utterly **d** them: but every H2763
18 said, Go and utterly **d** the sinners the H2763
23:10 to Keilah, to **d** the city for my sake. H7843
24:21 **d** my name out of my father's house. H8045
26: 9 And David said to Abishai, **D** him not: H7843
15 of the people in to **d** the king thy lord. H7843
2Sa 1:14 thine hand to **d** the LORD'S anointed? H7843
14: 7 slew; and we will **d** the heir also: and so H8045
11 of blood to **d** any more, lest they H7843
11 more, lest they **d** my son. And he said, H8045
16 the man *that would* **d** me and my son H8045
20:19 thou seekest to **d** a city and a mother H4191
20 from me, that I should swallow up or **d**. H7843
22:41 that I might **d** them that hate me. H6789
24:16 hand upon Jerusalem to **d** it, the LORD H7843
1Ki 9:21 not able utterly to **d**, upon those did H2763
13:34 to **d** *it* from off the face of the earth. H8045
16:12 Thus did Zimri **d** all the house of H8045
2Ki 8:19 Yet the LORD would not **d** Judah for H7843
10:19 that he might **d** the worshippers of Baal. H6
13:23 and would not **d** them, neither cast he H7843
18:25 this place to **d** it? The LORD said to H7843

2Ki 18:25 to me, Go up against this land, and **d** it. H7843
24: 2 against Judah to **d** it, according to the H6
1Ch 21:15 unto Jerusalem to **d** it: and as he was H7843
2Ch 12: 7 *therefore* I will not **d** them, but I will H7843
12 that he would not **d** *him* altogether: H7843
20:23 utterly to slay and **d** *them:* and when H8045
23 of Seir, every one helped to **d** another. H4889
21: 7 Howbeit the LORD would not **d** the H7843
25:16 determined to **d** thee, because thou H7843
35:21 who *is* with me, that he **d** thee not. H7843
Ezr 6:12 to dwell there **d** all kings and people, H4049
12 to alter *and* to **d** this house of God H2255
Est 3: 6 Haman sought to **d** all the Jews that H8045
13 provinces, to **d**, to kill, and to cause H8045
4: 7 king's treasuries for the Jews, to **d** them. H6
8 at Shushan to **d** them, to shew *it* unto H8045
8: 5 which he wrote to **d** the Jews which *are* H6
11 for their life, to **d**, to slay, and to cause H8045
9:24 against the Jews to **d** them, and had cast H6
24 the lot, to consume them, and to **d** them; H6
Job 2: 3 against him, to **d** him without cause. H1104
6: 9 Even that it would please God to **d** me; H1792
8:18 If he **d** him from his place, then *it* shall H1104
10: 8 round about; yet thou dost **d** me. H1104
19:26 And *though* after my skin *worms* **d** this H5362
Ps 5: 6 Thou shalt **d** them that speak leasing: H6
10 **D** thou them, O God; let them fall by H816
18:40 that I might **d** them that hate me. H6789
21:10 Their fruit shalt thou **d** from the earth, H6
28: 5 he shall **d** them, and not build them up. H2040
40:14 after my soul to **d** it; let them be driven H5595
52: 5 God shall likewise **d** thee for ever, he H5422
55: 9 **D**, O Lord, *and* divide their tongues: for H1104
63: 9 But those *that* seek my soul, to **d** *it*, H7722
69: 4 they that would **d** me, *being* mine H6789
74: 8 They said in their hearts, Let us **d** them H3238
101: 8 I will early **d** all the wicked of the land; H6789
106:23 Therefore he said that he would **d** H8045
23 away his wrath, lest he should **d** *them*. H7843
34 They did not **d** the nations, concerning H8045
118:10 in the name of the LORD will I **d** them. H4135
11 in the name of the LORD I will **d** them. H4135
12 in the name of the LORD I will **d** them. H4135
119:95 The wicked have waited for me to **d** me: H6
143:12 mine enemies, and **d** all them that afflict H6
144: 6 shoot out thine arrows, and **d** them. H2000
145:20 love him: but all the wicked will he **d**. H8045
Prv 1:32 and the prosperity of fools shall **d** them. H6
11: 3 of transgressors shall **d** them. H7703+H7703
15:25 The LORD will **d** the house of the H5255
21: 7 The robbery of the wicked shall **d** H1641
Ecc 5: 6 voice, and **d** the work of thine hands? H2254
7:16 wise: why shouldest thou **d** thyself? H8074
Isa 3:12 *thee* to err, and **d** the way of thy paths. H1104
10: 7 heart to **d** and cut off nations not a few. H8045
11: 9 They shall not hurt nor **d** in all my holy H7843
15 And the LORD shall utterly **d** the H2763
13: 5 of his indignation, to **d** the whole land. H2254
9 he shall **d** the sinners thereof out of it. H8045
19: 3 midst thereof; and I will **d** the counsel H1104
23:11 *city*, to **d** the strong holds thereof. H8045
25: 7 And he will **d** in this mountain the face H1104
32: 7 wicked devices to **d** the poor with lying H2254
36:10 this land to **d** it? the LORD said unto H7843
10 me, Go up against this land, and **d** it. H7843
42:14 I will **d** and devour at once. H5395+H8074
51:13 if he were ready to **d**? and where *is* the H7843
54:16 and I have created the waster to **d**. H2254
65: 8 and *one* saith, **D** it not; for a blessing H7843
8 sakes, that I may not **d** them all. H7843
25 They shall not hurt nor **d** in all my holy H7843
Jer 1:10 pull down, and to **d**, and to throw down, H6
5:10 Go ye up upon her walls, and **d**; but H7843
6: 5 us go by night, and let us **d** her palaces. H7843
11:19 me, *saying*, Let us **d** the tree with the H7843
12:17 up and **d** that nation, saith the LORD. H6
13:14 nor spare, nor have mercy, but **d** them. H7843
15: 3 the beasts of the earth, to devour and **d**. H7843
6 and **d** thee; I am weary with repenting. H7843
7 of children, I will **d** my people, *since* they H6
17:18 and **d** them with double destruction. H7665
18: 7 pluck up, and to pull down, and to **d** *it*; H6
23: 1 Woe be unto the pastors that **d** and H6
25: 9 and will utterly **d** them, and make H2763
31:28 down, and to **d**, and to afflict; so will H6
36:29 come and **d** this land, and shall H7843
46: 8 **d** the city and the inhabitants thereof. H6
48:18 thee, *and* he shall **d** thy strong holds. H7843
49: 9 night, they will **d** till they have enough. H7843
Jer 49:38 in Elam, and will **d** from thence the king H6
50:21 waste and utterly **d** after them, saith H2763
26 **d** her utterly: let nothing of her be left. H2763
51: 3 young men; **d** ye utterly all her host. H2763
11 Babylon, to **d** it; because it *is* the H7843
20 and with thee will I **d** kingdoms; H7843
Lam 2: 8 The LORD hath purposed to **d** the wall H7843
3:66 Persecute and **d** them in anger from H8045
Ezk 5:16 I will send to **d** you: and I will increase H7843
6: 3 upon you, and I will **d** your high places. H6
9: 8 Lord GOD! wilt thou **d** all the residue of H7843
14: 9 him, and will **d** him from the midst H8045
21:31 hand of brutish men, *and* skilful to **d**. H4889
22:27 *and* to **d** souls, to get dishonest gain. H6
30 that I should not **d** it: but I found none. H7843
25: 7 countries: I will **d** thee; and thou shalt H8045
15 heart, to **d** *it* for the old hatred; H4889
16 and **d** the remnant of the sea coast. H6
26: 4 And they shall **d** the walls of Tyrus, H7843
12 thy walls, and **d** thy pleasant houses: H5422
28:16 of God: and I will **d** thee, O covering H6
30:11 be brought to **d** the land: and they shall H7843
13 Thus saith the Lord GOD; I will also **d** H6
32:13 I will **d** also all the beasts thereof from H6
34:16 was sick: but I will **d** the fat and the H8045
43: 3 saw when I came to **d** the city: and the H7843
Dan 2:12 to **d** all the wise *men* of Babylon. H7
24 king had ordained to **d** the wise *men* of H7
24 thus unto him; **D** not the wise *men* of H7
4:23 tree down, and **d** it; yet leave the stump H2255
7:26 to consume and to **d** *it* unto the end. H7
8:24 and he shall **d** wonderfully, and shall H7843
24 shall **d** the mighty and the holy people. H7843
25 and by peace shall **d** many: he shall H7843
9:26 that shall come shall **d** the city and the H7843
11:26 of his meat shall **d** him, and his army H7665
44 to **d**, and utterly to make away many. H8045
Hos 2:12 And I will **d** her vines and her fig trees, H8074
4: 5 in the night, and I will **d** thy mother. H1820
11: 9 I will not return to **d** Ephraim: for I *am* H7843
Am 9: 8 and I will **d** it from off the face of H8045
8 **d** the house of Jacob, saith the LORD. H8045
Oba 8 the LORD, even **d** the wise *men* out of H6
Mic 2:10 **d** *you*, even with a sore destruction. H2254
5:10 midst of thee, and I will **d** thy chariots: H6
14 the midst of thee: so will I **d** thy cities. H8045
Zep 2: 5 **d** thee, that there shall be no inhabitant. H6
13 the north, and **d** Assyria; and will make H6
Hag 2:22 and I will **d** the strength of the H8045
Zec 12: 9 *that* I will seek to **d** all the nations that H8045
Mal 3:11 and he shall not **d** the fruits of your H7843
Mt 2:13 Herod will seek the young child to **d** him. *G622*
5:17 Think not that I am come to **d** the law, *G2647*
17 I am not come to **d**, but to fulfil. *G2647*
10:28 is able to **d** both soul and body in hell. *G622*
12:14 against him, how they might **d** him. *G622*
21:41 They say unto him, He will miserably **d** *G622*
26:61 said, I am able to **d** the temple of God, *G2647*
27:20 they should ask Barabbas, and **d** Jesus. *G622*
Mk 1:24 art thou come to **d** us? I know thee who *G622*
3: 6 against him, how they might **d** him. *G622*
9:22 and into the waters, to **d** him: but if thou *G622*
11:18 how they might **d** him: for they feared *G622*
12: 9 do? he will come and **d** the husbandmen, *G622*
14:58 We heard him say, I will **d** this temple *G2647*
Lk 4:34 art thou come to **d** us? I know thee who *G622*
6: 9 good, or to do evil? to save life, or to **d** *it*? *G622*
9:56 For the Son of man is not come to **d** *G622*
19:47 the chief of the people sought to **d** him, *G622*
20:16 He shall come and **d** these husbandmen, *G622*
Jn 2:19 Jesus answered and said unto them, **D** *G3089*
10:10 and to kill, and to **d**: I am come that they *G622*
Act 6:14 of Nazareth shall **d** this place, and shall *G2647*
Ro 14:15 not charitably. **D** not him with thy meat, *G622*
20 For meat **d** not the work of God. All *G2647*
1Co 1:19 For it is written, I will **d** the wisdom of *G622*
3:17 him shall God **d**; for the temple of God *G5351*
6:13 but God shall **d** both it and them. Now *G2673*
2Th 2: 8 **d** with the brightness of his coming: *G2673*
Heb 2:14 death he might **d** him that had the *G2673*
Jas 4:12 to **d**: who art thou that judgest another? *G622*
1Jn 3: 8 that he might **d** the works of the devil. *G3089*
Rev 11:18 **d** them which destroy the earth. *G1311*
18 destroy them which **d** the earth. *G1311*

DESTROYED

Gen 7:23 And every living substance was **d** H4229
23 and they were **d** from the earth: and H4229
13:10 where, before the LORD **d** Sodom and H7843
Gen 19:29 And it came to pass, when God **d** the H7843
34:30 me; and I shall be **d**, I and my house. H8045
Ex 10: 7 knowest thou not yet that Egypt is **d**? H6
22:20 the LORD only, he shall be utterly **d**. H2763
Nu 21: 3 and they utterly **d** them and their H2763
Dt 1:44 and **d** you in Seir, *even* unto Hormah. H3807
2:12 when they had **d** them from before H8045
21 but the LORD **d** them before them; and H8045
22 in Seir, when he **d** the Horims from H8045
23 **d** them, and dwelt in their stead.) H8045
34 time, and utterly **d** the men, and the H2763
3: 6 And we utterly **d** them, as we did unto H2763
4: 3 thy God hath **d** them from among you. H8045
26 *your* days upon it, but shall utterly be **d**. H8045
7:20 left, and hide themselves from thee, be **d**. H6
23 a mighty destruction, until they be **d**. H8045
24 before thee, until thou have **d** them. H8045
9: 8 was angry with you to have **d** you. H8045
20 Aaron to have **d** him: and I prayed for H8045
11: 4 the LORD hath **d** them unto this day; H6
12:30 after that they be **d** from before thee; H8045
28:20 to do, until thou be **d**, and until thou H8045
24 come down upon thee, until thou be **d**. H8045
45 thee, till thou be **d**; because thou H8045
48 upon thy neck, until he have **d** thee. H8045
51 land, until thou be **d**: which *also* shall H8045
51 flocks of thy sheep, until he have **d** thee. H6
61 LORD bring upon thee, until thou be **d**. H8045
31: 4 and unto the land of them, whom he **d**. H8045
Jos 2:10 Sihon and Og, whom ye utterly **d**. H2763
6:21 And they utterly **d** all that *was* in the H2763
8:26 had utterly **d** all the inhabitants of Ai. H2763
10: 1 and had utterly **d** it; as he had done to H2763
28 thereof he utterly **d**, them, and all the H2763
35 therein he utterly **d** that day, according H2763
37 done to Eglon; but **d** it utterly, and all H2763
39 sword, and utterly **d** all the souls that H2763
40 but utterly **d** all that breathed, as H2763
11:12 *and* he utterly **d** them, as Moses the H2763
14 until they had **d** them, neither left they H8045
21 Joshua **d** them utterly with their cities. H2763
23:15 until he have **d** you from off this good H8045
24: 8 land; and I **d** them from before you. H8045
Jdg 1:17 and utterly **d** it. And the name of H2763
4:24 until they had **d** Jabin king of Canaan. H3772
6: 4 against them, and **d** the increase of the H7843
20:21 forth out of Gibeah, and **d** down to the H7843
25 second day, and **d** down to the ground H7843
35 children of Israel **d** of the Benjamites H7843
42 of the cities they **d** in the midst of them. H7843
21:16 the women are **d** out of Benjamin? H8045
17 that a tribe be not **d** out of Israel. H4229
1Sa 5: 6 of Ashdod, and he **d** them, and smote H8074
15: 8 alive, and utterly **d** all the people with H2763
9 *was* vile and refuse, that they **d** utterly. H2763
15 thy God; and the rest we have utterly **d**. H2763
20 and have utterly **d** the Amalekites. H2763
21 have been utterly **d**, to sacrifice unto the H2764
2Sa 11: 1 all Israel; and they **d** the children of H7843
21: 5 *that* we should be **d** from remaining in H8045
22:38 I have pursued mine enemies, and **d** H8045
24:16 said to the angel that **d** the people, It is H7843
1Ki 15:13 a grove; and Asa **d** her idol, and burnt H3772
29 until he had **d** him, according unto H8045
2Ki 10:17 till he had **d** him, according to the H8045
28 Thus Jehu **d** Baal out of Israel. H8045
11: 1 dead, she arose and **d** all the seed royal. H6
13: 7 king of Syria had **d** them, and had made H6
19:12 which my fathers have **d**; *as* Gozan, and H7843
17 have **d** the nations and their lands, H2717
18 and stone: therefore they have **d** them. H6
21: 3 his father had **d**; and he reared up altars H6
9 LORD **d** before the children of Israel. H8045
1Ch 4:41 found there, and **d** them utterly unto H2763
5:25 of the land, whom God **d** before them. H8045
20: 1 And Joab smote Rabbah, and **d** it. H2040
21:12 months to be **d** before thy foes, while H5595
15 to the angel that **d**, It is enough, stay H7843
2Ch 14:13 for they were **d** before the LORD, and H7665
15: 6 And nation was **d** of nation, and city of H3807
20:10 turned from them, and **d** them not; H8045
22:10 she arose and **d** all the seed royal of H1696
24:23 Jerusalem, and **d** all the princes of the H7843
31: 1 they had utterly **d** them all. Then all the H3615
32:14 my fathers utterly **d**, that could deliver H2763
33: 9 had **d** before the children of Israel. H8045
34:11 houses which the kings of Judah had **d**. H7843
36:19 and **d** all the goodly vessels thereof. H7843
Ezr 4:15 time: for which cause was this city **d**. H2718

Ezr 5:12 the Chaldean, who **d** this house, and H5642
Est 3: 9 that they may be **d**: and I will pay ten H6
4:14 house shall be **d**: and who knoweth H6
7: 4 my people, to be **d**, to be slain, and to H8045
9: 6 the Jews slew and **d** five hundred men. H6
12 have slain and **d** five hundred men in H6
Job 4:20 They are **d** from morning to evening: H3807
19:10 He hath **d** me on every side, and I am H5422
34:25 *them* in the night, so that they are **d**. H1792
Ps 9: 5 heathen, thou hast **d** the wicked, thou H6
6 and thou hast **d** cities; their memorial H5428
11: 3 If the foundations be **d**, what can the H2040
37:38 But the transgressors shall be **d** H8045
73:27 **d** all them that go a whoring from thee. H6789
78:38 *their* iniquity, and **d** *them* not: yea, H7843
45 them; and frogs, which **d** them. H7843
47 He **d** their vines with hail, and their H2026
92: 7 *it is* that they shall be **d** for ever: H8045
137: 8 O daughter of Babylon, who art to be **d**; H7703
Prv 13:13 Whoso despiseth the word shall be **d**: H2254
20 but a companion of fools shall be **d**. H7321
23 there is *that is* **d** for want of judgment. H5595
29: 1 be **d**, and that without remedy. H7665
Isa 9:16 err; and *they that are* led of them *are* **d**. H1104
10:27 shall be **d** because of the anointing. H2254
14:17 a wilderness, and **d** the cities thereof; H2040
20 because thou hast **d** thy land, *and* slain H7843
26:14 thou visited and **d** them, and made all H8045
34: 2 armies: he hath utterly **d** them, he hath H2763
37:12 which my fathers have **d**, *as* Gozan, and H7843
19 and stone: therefore they have **d** them. H6
48:19 have been cut off nor **d** from before me. H8045
Jer 12:10 Many pastors have **d** my vineyard, H7843
22:20 the passages: for all thy lovers are **d**. H7665
48: 4 Moab is **d**; her little ones have caused a H7665
8 shall be **d**, as the LORD hath spoken. H8045
42 And Moab shall be **d** from *being* a H8045
51: 8 Babylon is suddenly fallen and **d**: howl H7665
55 Babylon, and **d** out of her the great H6
Lam 2: 5 her palaces: he hath **d** his strong holds, H7843
6 *of* a garden: he hath **d** his places of the H7843
9 ground; he hath **d** and broken her bars: H6
Ezk 26:17 thee, How art thou **d**, *that wast* inhabited H6
27:32 like the **d** in the midst of the sea? H1822
30: 8 and *when* all her helpers shall be **d**. H7665
32:12 and all the multitude thereof shall be **d**. H8045
Dan 2:44 shall never be **d**: and the kingdom shall H2255
6:26 which shall not be **d**, and his dominion H2255
7:11 body **d**, and given to the burning flame. H7
14 his kingdom *that* which shall not be **d**. H2255
11:20 be **d**, neither in anger, nor in battle. H7665
Hos 4: 6 My people are **d** for lack of knowledge: H1820
10: 8 of Israel, shall be **d**: the thorn and the H8045
13: 9 O Israel, thou hast **d** thyself; but in me H7843
Am 2: 9 Yet **d** I the Amorite before them, whose H8045
9 strong as the oaks; yet I **d** his fruit from H8045
Zep 3: 6 by: their cities are **d**, so that there is no H6658
Mt 22: 7 his armies, and **d** those murderers, and G622
Lk 17:27 ark, and the flood came, and **d** them all. G622
29 brimstone from heaven, and **d** *them* all. G622
Act 3:23 shall be **d** from among the people. G1842
9:21 Is not this he that **d** them which called G4199
13:19 And when he had **d** seven nations in G2507
19:27 should be **d**, whom all Asia and G2507
Ro 6: 6 of sin might be **d**, that henceforth we G2673
1Co 10: 9 also tempted, and were **d** of serpents. G622
10 murmured, and were **d** of the destroyer. G622
15:26 The last enemy *that* shall be **d** *is* death. G2673
2Co 4: 9 but not forsaken; cast down, but not **d**; G622
Gal 1:23 preacheth the faith which once he **d**. G4199
2:18 For if I build again the things which I **d**, G2647
Heb 11:28 that **d** the firstborn should touch them. G3645
2Pt 2:12 to be taken and **d**, speak evil of the G5356
Jude 5 afterward **d** them that believed not. G622
Rev 8: 9 and the third part of the ships were **d**. G1311

DESTROYER
Ex 12:23 will not suffer the **d** to come in unto H7843
Jdg 16:24 enemy, and the **d** of our country, which H2717
Job 15:21 prosperity the **d** shall come upon him. H7703
Ps 17: 4 I have kept *me from* the paths of the **d**. H6530
Prv 28:24 same *is* the companion of a **d**. H376+H7843
Jer 4: 7 thicket, and the **d** of the Gentiles is on H7843
1Co 10:10 and were destroyed of the **d**. G3644

DESTROYERS
Job 33:22 unto the grave, and his life to the **d**. H4191
Isa 49:17 Thy children shall make haste; thy **d** H2040
Jer 22: 7 And I will prepare **d** against thee, every H7843
Jer 50:11 ye rejoiced, O ye **d** of mine heritage, H8154

DESTROYEST
Job 14:19 the earth; and thou **d** the hope of man. H6
Jer 51:25 the LORD, which **d** all the earth: and I H7843
Mt 27:40 And saying, Thou that **d** the temple, G2647
Mk 15:29 saying, Ah, thou that **d** the temple, and G2647

DESTROYETH
Dt 8:20 As the nations which the LORD **d** before H6
Job 9:22 said *it*, He **d** the perfect and the wicked. H3615
12:23 He increaseth the nations, and **d** them: H6
Prv 6:32 he *that* doeth it **d** his own soul. H7843
11: 9 An hypocrite with *his* mouth **d** his H7843
31: 3 nor thy ways to that which **d** kings. H4229
Ecc 7: 7 a wise man mad; and a gift **d** the heart. H6
9:18 of war: but one sinner **d** much good. H6

DESTROYING
Dt 3: 6 of Heshbon, utterly **d** the men, women, H2763
13:15 edge of the sword, **d** it utterly, and all H2763
Jos 11:11 of the sword, utterly **d** *them*: there was H2763
2Ki 19:11 to all lands, by **d** them utterly: and H2763
1Ch 21:12 angel of the LORD **d** throughout all the H7843
15 it: and as he was **d**, the LORD beheld, H7843
Isa 28: 2 of hail *and* a **d** storm, as a flood of H6986
37:11 to all lands by **d** them utterly; and shalt H2763
Jer 2:30 devoured your prophets, like a **d** lion. H7843
51: 1 them that rise up against me, a **d** wind; H7843
25 Behold, I *am* against thee, O **d** H4889
Lam 2: 8 his hand from **d**: therefore he made the H1104
Ezk 9: 1 man *with* his **d** weapon in his hand. H4892
20:17 spared them from **d** them, neither did I H7843

DESTRUCTION
Dt 7:23 a mighty **d**, until they be destroyed. H4103
32:24 and with bitter **d**: I will also send the H6986
1Sa 5: 9 with a very great **d**: and he smote the H4103
11 was a deadly **d** throughout all the city; H4103
1Ki 20:42 I appointed to utter **d**, therefore thy life H2764
2Ch 22: 4 after the death of his father to his **d**. H4889
7 And the **d** of Ahaziah was of God by H8395
26:16 lifted up to *his* **d**: for he transgressed H7843
Est 8: 6 can I endure to see the **d** of my kindred? H13
9: 5 and slaughter, and **d**, and did what they H12
Job 5:21 thou be afraid of **d** when it cometh. H7701
22 At **d** and famine thou shalt laugh: H7701
18:12 and **d** *shall be* ready at his side. H343
21:17 *how oft* cometh their **d** upon them! *God* H343
20 His eyes shall see his **d**, and he shall H3589
30 to the day of **d**? they shall be brought H343
26: 6 Hell *is* naked before him, and **d** hath no H11
28:22 **D** and death say, We have heard the H11
30:12 raise up against me the ways of their **d**. H343
24 to the grave, though they cry in his **d**. H6365
31: 3 *Is* not **d** to the wicked? and a strange H343
12 For it *is* a fire *that* consumeth to **d**, and H11
23 For **d** *from* God *was* a terror to me, and H343
29 If I rejoiced at the **d** of him that hated H6365
Ps 35: 8 Let **d** come upon him at unawares; and H7722
8 himself: into that very **d** let him fall. H7722
55:23 into the pit of **d**: bloody and deceitful H7845
73:18 places: thou castedst them down into **d**. H4876
88:11 in the grave? *or* thy faithfulness in **d**? H11
90: 3 Thou turnest man to **d**; and sayest, H1793
91: 6 *nor* for the **d** *that* wasteth at noonday. H6986
103: 4 Who redeemeth thy life from **d**; who H7845
Prv 1:27 and your **d** cometh as a whirlwind; H343
10:14 but the mouth of the foolish *is* near **d**. H4288
15 city: the **d** of the poor *is* their poverty. H4288
29 **d** *shall be* to the workers of iniquity. H4288
13: 3 that openeth wide his lips shall have **d**. H4288
14:28 want of people *is* the **d** of the prince. H4288
15:11 Hell and **d** *are* before the LORD: how H11
16:18 Pride *goeth* before **d**, and an haughty H7667
17:19 *and* he that exalteth his gate seeketh **d**. H7667
18: 7 A fool's mouth *is* his **d**, and his lips *are* H4288
12 Before **d** the heart of man is haughty, H7667
21:15 **d** *shall be* to the workers of iniquity. H4288
24: 2 For their heart studieth **d**, and their lips H7701
27:20 Hell and **d** are never full; so the eyes H11+H10
31: 8 cause of all such as are appointed to **d**. H2475
Isa 1:28 And the **d** of the transgressors and of H7667
10:25 shall cease, and mine anger in their **d**. H8399
13: 6 it shall come as a **d** from the Almighty. H7701
14:23 the besom of **d**, saith the LORD of hosts. H8045
15: 5 Horonaim they shall raise up a cry of **d**. H7667
19:18 hosts; one shall be called, The city of **d**. H2041
24:12 and the gate is smitten with **d**. H7591
Isa 49:19 the land of thy **d**, shall even now be too H2035
51:19 desolation, and **d**, and the famine, and H7667
59: 7 wasting and **d** *are* in their paths. H7667
60:18 land, wasting nor **d** within thy borders; H7667
Jer 4: 6 bring evil from the north, and a great **d**. H7667
20 **D** upon destruction is cried; for the H7667
20 Destruction upon **d** is cried; for the H7667
6: 1 appeareth out of the north, and great **d**. H7667
17:18 of evil, and destroy them with double **d**. H7670
46:20 Egypt *is like* a very fair heifer, *but* **d** H7171
48: 3 from Horonaim, spoiling and great **d**. H7667
5 the enemies have heard a cry of **d**. H7667
50:22 of battle *is* in the land, and of great **d**. H7667
51:54 great **d** from the land of the Chaldeans: H7667
Lam 2:11 the earth, for the **d** of the daughter of H7667
3:47 is come upon us, desolation and **d**. H7667
48 for the **d** of the daughter of my people. H7667
4:10 in the **d** of the daughter of my people. H7667
Ezk 5:16 shall be for *their* **d**, *and* which I will H4889
7:25 **D** cometh; and they shall seek peace, H7089
32: 9 I shall bring thy **d** among the nations, H7667
Hos 7:13 fled from me: **d** unto them! because H7701
9: 6 For, lo, they are gone because of **d**: H7701
13:14 O grave, I will be thy **d**: repentance shall H6987
Joel 1:15 as a **d** from the Almighty shall it come. H7701
Oba 12 in the day of their **d**; neither shouldest H6
Mic 2:10 it shall destroy *you*, even with a sore **d**. H2256
Zec 14:11 be no more utter **d**; but Jerusalem shall H2764
Mt 7:13 that leadeth to **d**, and many there be G684
Ro 3:16 **D** and misery *are* in their ways: G4938
9:22 the vessels of wrath fitted to **d**: G684
1Co 5: 5 unto Satan for the **d** of the flesh, that G3639
2Co 10: 8 for your **d**, I should not be ashamed: G2506
13:10 given me to edification, and not to **d**. G2506
Php 3:19 Whose end *is* **d**, whose God *is their* belly, G684
1Th 5: 3 then sudden **d** cometh upon them, G3639
2Th 1: 9 with everlasting **d** from the presence of G3639
1Ti 6: 9 which drown men in **d** and perdition. G3639
2Pt 2: 1 them, and bring upon themselves swift **d**. G684
3:16 the other scriptures, unto their own **d**. G684

DESTRUCTIONS
Ps 9: 6 O thou enemy, **d** are come to a H2723
35:17 from their **d**, my darling from the lions. H7722
107:20 them, and delivered *them* from their **d**. H7825

DETAIN
Jdg 13:15 I pray thee, let us **d** thee, until we shall H6113
16 Though thou **d** me, I will not eat of H6113

DETAINED
1Sa 21: 7 there that day, **d** before the LORD; and H6113

DETERMINATE
Act 2:23 Him, being delivered by the **d** counsel G3724

DETERMINATION
Zep 3: 8 up to the prey: for my **d** *is* to gather the H4941

DETERMINE
Ex 21:22 him; and he shall pay as the judges **d**.

DETERMINED
1Sa 20: 7 *then* be sure that evil is **d** by him. H3615
9 that evil were **d** by my father to come H3615
33 that it was **d** of his father to slay David. H3617
25:17 wilt do; for evil is **d** against our master, H3615
2Sa 13:32 this hath been **d** from the day that he H7760
2Ch 2: 1 And Solomon **d** to build an house for the H559
25:16 know that God hath **d** to destroy thee, H3289
Est 7: 7 was evil **d** against him by the king. H3615
Job 14: 5 Seeing his days *are* **d**, the number of his H2782
Isa 10:23 even **d**, in the midst of all the land. H2782
19:17 of hosts, which he hath **d** against it. H3289
28:22 even **d** upon the whole earth. H2782
Dan 9:24 Seventy weeks are **d** upon thy people H2852
26 the end of the war desolations are **d**. H2782
27 **d** shall be poured upon the desolate. H2782
11:36 for that that is **d** shall be done. H2782
Lk 22:22 goeth, as it was **d**: but woe unto that G3724
Act 3:13 of Pilate, when he was **d** to let *him* go. G2919
4:28 and thy counsel **d** before to be done. G4309
11:29 to his ability, **d** to send relief unto the G3724
15: 2 with them, they **d** that Paul and G5021
37 And Barnabas **d** to take with them G1011
17:26 the earth, and hath **d** the times before G3724
19:39 it shall be **d** in a lawful assembly. G1956
20:16 For Paul had **d** to sail by Ephesus, G2919
25:25 to Augustus, I have **d** to send him. G2919

Act 27: 1 And when it was **d** that we should sail *G2919*
1Co 2: 2 For I **d** not to know any thing among *G2919*
2Co 2: 1 But I **d** this with myself, that I would *G2919*
Tit 3:12 Nicopolis: for I have **d** there to winter. *G2919*

DETEST
Dt 7:26 thou shalt utterly **d** it, and thou shalt H8262

DETESTABLE
Jer 16:18 of their **d** and abominable things. H8251
Ezk 5:11 with all thy **d** things, and with all H8251
7:20 *and* of their **d** things therein: therefore H8251
11:18 take away all the **d** things thereof and H8251
21 the heart of their **d** things and their H8251
37:23 nor with their **d** things, nor with any H8251

DEUEL
Nu 1:14 Of Gad; Eliasaph the son of **D.** H1845
7:42 On the sixth day Eliasaph the son of **D,** H1845
47 the offering of Eliasaph the son of **D.** H1845
10:20 of Gad *was* Eliasaph the son of **D.** H1845

DEVICE
2Ch 2:14 to find out every **d** which shall be put to H4284
Est 8: 3 **d** that he had devised against the Jews. H4284
9:25 that his wicked **d**, which he devised H4284
Ps 21:11 **d**, *which* they are not able *to perform.* H4209
140: 8 **d**; *lest* they exalt themselves. Selah. H2162
Ecc 9:10 *is* no work, nor **d**, nor knowledge, nor H2808
Jer 18:11 you, and devise a **d** against you: return H4284
51:11 the Medes: for his **d** *is* against Babylon, H4209
Lam 3:62 me, and their **d** against me all the day. H1902
Act 17:29 or stone, graven by art and man's **d.** *G1761*

DEVICES
Job 5:12 He disappointeth the **d** of the crafty, so H4284
21:27 your thoughts, and the **d** *which* ye H4209
Ps 10: 2 taken in the **d** that they have imagined. H4209
33:10 the **d** of the people of none effect. H4284
37: 7 man who bringeth wicked **d** to pass. H4209
Prv 1:31 own way, and be filled with their own **d.** H4156
12: 2 a man of wicked **d** will he condemn. H4209
14:17 and a man of wicked **d** is hated. H4209
19:21 *There are* many **d** in a man's heart; H4284
Isa 32: 7 deviseth wicked **d** to destroy the poor H2154
Jer 11:19 they had devised **d** against me, *saying,* H4284
18:12 after our own **d**, and we will every one H4284
18 and let us devise **d** against Jeremiah; H4284
Dan 11:24 shall forecast his **d** against the strong H4284
25 for they shall forecast **d** against him. H4284
2Co 2:11 of us: for we are not ignorant of his **d.** *G3540*

DEVIL
Mt 4: 1 the wilderness to be tempted of the **d.** *G1228*
5 Then the **d** taketh him up into the holy *G1228*
8 Again, the **d** taketh him up into an *G1228*
11 Then the **d** leaveth him, and, behold, *G1228*
9:32 to him a dumb man possessed with a **d.** *G1139*
33 And when the **d** was cast out, the dumb *G1140*
11:18 nor drinking, and they say, He hath a **d.** *G1140*
12:22 possessed with a **d**, blind, and dumb: *G1139*
13:39 The enemy that sowed them is the **d**; *G1228*
15:22 daughter is grievously vexed with a **d.** *G1139*
17:18 And Jesus rebuked the **d**; and he *G846*
25:41 fire, prepared for the **d** and his angels: *G1228*
Mk 5:15 with the **d**, and had the legion, *G1139*
16 the **d**, and *also* concerning the swine. *G1139*
18 with the **d** prayed him that he *G1139*
7:26 cast forth the **d** out of her daughter. *G1140*
29 way; the **d** is gone out of thy daughter. *G1140*
30 she found the **d** gone out, and her *G1140*
Lk 4: 2 Being forty days tempted of the **d.** And *G1228*
3 And the **d** said unto him, If thou be the *G1228*
5 And the **d**, taking him up into an high *G1228*
6 And the **d** said unto him, All this power *G1228*
13 And when the **d** had ended all the *G1228*
33 **d**, and cried out with a loud voice, *G1140*
35 And when the **d** had thrown him in *G1140*
7:33 drinking wine; and ye say, He hath a **d.** *G1140*
8:12 then cometh the **d**, and taketh away the *G1228*
29 driven of the **d** into the wilderness.) *G1142*
9:42 And as he was yet a coming, the **d** *G1140*
11:14 And he was casting out a **d**, and it was *G1140*
14 to pass, when the **d** was gone out, the *G1140*
Jn 6:70 you twelve, and one of you is a **d**? *G1228*
7:20 hast a **d**: who goeth about to kill thee? *G1140*
8:44 Ye are of *your* father the **d**, and the lusts *G1228*
48 that thou art a Samaritan, and hast a **d**? *G1140*
49 Jesus answered, I have not a **d**; but I *G1140*
Jn 8:52 that thou hast a **d.** Abraham is dead, *G1140*
10:20 And many of them said, He hath a **d**, *G1140*
21 of him that hath a **d.** Can a devil open *G1139*
21 Can a **d** open the eyes of the blind? *G1140*
13: 2 And supper being ended, the **d** having *G1228*
Act 10:38 of the **d**; for God was with him. *G1228*
13:10 *thou* child of the **d**, *thou* enemy of all *G1228*
Eph 4:27 Neither give place to the **d.** *G1228*
6:11 able to stand against the wiles of the **d.** *G1228*
1Ti 3: 6 he fall into the condemnation of the **d.** *G1228*
7 into reproach and the snare of the **d.** *G1228*
2Ti 2:26 out of the snare of the **d**, who are taken *G1228*
Heb 2:14 had the power of death, that is, the **d**; *G1228*
Jas 4: 7 Resist the **d**, and he will flee from you. *G1228*
1Pt 5: 8 your adversary the **d**, as a roaring lion, *G1228*
1Jn 3: 8 He that committeth sin is of the **d**; for *G1228*
8 of the devil; for the **d** sinneth from the *G1228*
8 he might destroy the works of the **d.** *G1228*
10 the children of the **d**: whosoever doeth *G1228*
Jude 9 with the **d** he disputed about the *G1228*
Rev 2:10 suffer: behold, the **d** shall cast *some* of *G1228*
12: 9 serpent, called the **D**, and Satan, which *G1228*
12 of the sea! for the **d** is come down unto *G1228*
20: 2 which is the **D**, and Satan, and bound *G1228*
10 And the **d** that deceived them was cast *G1228*

DEVILISH
Jas 3:15 from above, but *is* earthly, sensual, **d.** *G1141*

DEVILS
Lev 17: 7 sacrifices unto **d**, after whom they have H8163
Dt 32:17 They sacrificed unto **d**, not to God; to H7700
2Ch 11:15 places, and for the **d**, and for the calves H8163
Ps 106:37 their sons and their daughters unto **d**, H7700
Mt 4:24 possessed with **d**, and those which were *G1139*
7:22 have cast out **d**? and in thy name done *G1140*
8:16 possessed with **d**: and he cast out the *G1139*
28 two possessed with **d**, coming out of the *G1139*
31 So the **d** besought him, saying, If thou *G1142*
33 was befallen to the possessed of the **d.** *G1139*
9:34 out **d** through the prince of the devils. *G1140*
34 out devils through the prince of the **d.** *G1140*
10: 8 **d**: freely ye have received, freely give. *G1140*
12:24 doth not cast out **d**, but by Beelzebub *G1140*
24 but by Beelzebub the prince of the **d.** *G1140*
27 And if I by Beelzebub cast out **d**, by *G1140*
28 But if I cast out **d** by the Spirit of God, *G1140*
Mk 1:32 and them that were possessed with **d.** *G1139*
34 cast out many **d**; and suffered not the *G1140*
34 the **d** to speak, because they knew him. *G1140*
39 throughout all Galilee, and cast out **d.** *G1140*
3:15 to heal sicknesses, and to cast out **d**: *G1140*
22 prince of the **d** casteth he out devils. *G1140*
22 the prince of the devils casteth he out **d.** *G1140*
5:12 And all the **d** besought him, saying, *G1142*
6:13 And they cast out many **d**, and *G1140*
9:38 one casting out **d** in thy name, and he *G1140*
16: 9 out of whom he had cast seven **d.** *G1140*
17 **d**; they shall speak with new tongues; *G1140*
Lk 4:41 And **d** also came out of many, crying *G1140*
8: 2 Magdalene, out of whom went seven **d**, *G1140*
27 man, which had **d** long time, and ware *G1140*
30 because many **d** were entered into him. *G1140*
33 Then went the **d** out of the man, and *G1140*
35 man, out of whom the **d** were departed, *G1140*
36 that was possessed of the **d** was healed. *G1139*
38 Now the man out of whom the **d** were *G1140*
9: 1 over all **d**, and to cure diseases. *G1140*
49 one casting out **d** in thy name; and we *G1140*
10:17 Lord, even the **d** are subject unto us *G1140*
11:15 He casteth out **d** through Beelzebub *G1140*
15 through Beelzebub the chief of the **d.** *G1140*
18 that I cast out **d** through Beelzebub. *G1140*
19 And if I by Beelzebub cast out **d**, by *G1140*
20 But if I with the finger of God cast out **d**, *G1140*
13:32 Behold, I cast out **d**, and I do cures to *G1140*
1Co 10:20 they sacrifice to **d**, and not to God: and *G1140*
20 that ye should have fellowship with **d.** *G1140*
21 Lord, and the cup of **d**: ye cannot be *G1140*
21 of the Lord's table, and of the table of **d.** *G1140*
1Ti 4: 1 to seducing spirits, and doctrines of **d**; *G1140*
Jas 2:19 well: the **d** also believe, and tremble. *G1140*
Rev 9:20 not worship **d**, and idols of gold, and *G1140*
16:14 For they are the spirits of **d**, working *G1142*
18: 2 the habitation of **d**, and the hold of *G1142*

DEVISE
Ex 31: 4 To **d** cunning works, to work in gold, H2803
35:32 And to **d** curious works, to work in H2803
Ex 35:35 and of those that **d** cunning work. H2803
2Sa 14:14 yet doth he **d** means, that his banished H2803
Ps 35: 4 brought to confusion that **d** my hurt. H2803
20 For they speak not peace: but they **d** H2803
41: 7 me: against me do they **d** my hurt. H2803
Prv 3:29 **D** not evil against thy neighbour, H2790
14:22 Do they not err that **d** evil? but mercy H2790
22 and truth *shall be* to them that **d** good. H2790
16:30 He shutteth his eyes to **d** froward H2803
Jer 18:11 evil against you, and **d** a device against H2803
18 Then said they, Come, and let us **d** H2803
Ezk 11: 2 *are* the men that **d** mischief, and give H2803
Mic 2: 1 Woe to them that **d** iniquity, and work H2803
3 this family do I **d** an evil, from which H2803

DEVISED
2Sa 21: 5 us, and that **d** against us *that* we H1819
1Ki 12:33 which he had **d** of his own heart; and H908
Est 8: 3 device that he had **d** against the Jews. H2803
5 reverse the letters **d** by Haman the son H4284
9:24 all the Jews, had **d** against the Jews to H2803
25 device, which he **d** against the Jews, H2803
Ps 31:13 me, they **d** to take away my life. H2161
Jer 11:19 not that they had **d** devices against me, H2803
48: 2 they have **d** evil against it; come, H2803
51:12 LORD hath both **d** and done that which H2161
Lam 2:17 *that* which he had **d**; he hath fulfilled H2161
2Pt 1:16 For we have not followed cunningly **d** *G4679*

DEVISETH
Ps 36: 4 He **d** mischief upon his bed; he setteth H2803
52: 2 Thy tongue **d** mischiefs; like a sharp H2803
Prv 6:14 Frowardness *is* in his heart, he **d** H2790
18 An heart that **d** wicked imaginations, H2790
16: 9 A man's heart **d** his way: but the LORD H2803
24: 8 He that **d** to do evil shall be called a H2803
Isa 32: 7 churl *are* evil: he **d** wicked devices to H3289
8 But the liberal **d** liberal things; and by H3289

DEVOTE
Lev 27:28 that a man shall **d** unto the LORD of all H2763

DEVOTED
Lev 27:21 the LORD, as a field **d**; the possession H2764
28 Notwithstanding no **d** thing, that a H2764
28 **d** thing *is* most holy unto the LORD. H2764
29 None **d**, which shall be devoted of men, H2764
29 None devoted, which shall be **d** of men, H2763
Nu 18:14 Every thing **d** in Israel shall be thine. H2764
Ps 119:38 unto thy servant, who *is* **d** to thy fear.

DEVOTIONS
Act 17:23 For as I passed by, and beheld your **d**, I *G4574*

DEVOUR
Gen 49:27 morning he shall **d** the prey, and at night H398
Dt 32:42 my sword shall **d** flesh; *and that* with H398
Jdg 9:15 bramble, and **d** the cedars of Lebanon. H398
20 Abimelech, and **d** the men of Shechem, H398
20 the house of Millo, and **d** Abimelech. H398
2Sa 2:26 Shall the sword **d** for ever? knowest thou H398
2Ch 7:13 the locusts to **d** the land, or if I send H398
Job 18:13 It shall **d** the strength of his skin: *even* H398
13 firstborn of death shall **d** his strength. H398
Ps 21: 9 in his wrath, and the fire shall **d** them. H398
50: 3 silence: a fire shall **d** before him, and it H398
80:13 and the wild beast of the field doth **d** it. H7462
Prv 30:14 teeth *as* knives, to **d** the poor from off H398
Isa 1: 7 land, strangers **d** it in your presence, H398
9:12 and they shall **d** Israel with open mouth. H398
18 as the fire: it shall **d** the briers and H398
10:17 **d** his thorns and his briers in one day; H398
26:11 the fire of thine enemies shall **d** them. H398
31: 8 of a mean man, shall **d** him: but he shall H398
33:11 stubble: your breath, *as* fire, shall **d** you. H398
42:14 woman; I will destroy and **d** at once. H7602
56: 9 All ye beasts of the field, come to **d**, *yea,* H398
Jer 2: 3 increase: all that **d** him shall offend; evil H398
5:14 this people wood, and it shall **d** them. H398
12: 9 all the beasts of the field, come to **d.** H402
12 of the LORD shall **d** from the *one* end of H398
15: 3 the beasts of the earth, to **d** and destroy. H398
17:27 and it shall **d** the palaces of Jerusalem, H398
21:14 and it shall **d** all things round about it. H398
30:16 Therefore all they that **d** thee shall be H398
46:10 the sword shall **d**, and it shall be satiate H398
14 for the sword shall **d** round about thee. H398
48:45 of Sihon, and shall **d** the corner of Moab, H398
50:32 cities, and it shall **d** all round about him. H398

Ezk 7:15 city, famine and pestilence shall **d** him. H398
15: 7 *another* fire shall **d** them; and ye shall H398
20:47 in thee, and it shall **d** every green tree in H398
23:37 for them through *the fire*, to **d** *them*. H402
28:18 of thee, it shall **d** thee, and I will bring H398
34:28 beast of the land **d** them; but they shall H398
36:14 Therefore thou shalt **d** men no more, H398
Dan 7: 5 said thus unto it, Arise, **d** much flesh. H399
23 and shall **d** the whole earth, and H399
Hos 5: 7 a month **d** them with their portions. H398
8:14 cities, and it shall **d** the palaces thereof. H398
11: 6 **d** *them*, because of their own counsels. H398
13: 8 and there will I **d** them like a lion: the H398
Am 1: 4 which shall **d** the palaces of Ben-hadad. H398
7 Gaza, which shall **d** the palaces thereof: H398
10 Tyrus, which shall **d** the palaces thereof. H398
12 which shall **d** the palaces of Bozrah. H398
14 and it shall **d** the palaces thereof, H398
2: 2 upon Moab, and it shall **d** the palaces of H398
5 and it shall **d** the palaces of Jerusalem. H398
5: 6 of Joseph, and **d** *it*, and *there be* none H398
Oba 18 in them, and **d** them; and there shall H398
Nah 2:13 the sword shall **d** thy young lions: and H398
3:13 thine enemies: the fire shall **d** thy bars. H398
15 There shall the fire **d** thee; the sword H398
Hab 3:14 rejoicing *was* as to **d** the poor secretly. H398
Zec 9:15 and they shall **d**, and subdue with sling H398
11: 1 Lebanon, that the fire may **d** thy cedars. H398
12: 6 and they shall **d** all the people round H398
Mt 23:14 hypocrites! for ye **d** widows' houses, *G2719*
Mk 12:40 Which **d** widows' houses, and for a *G2719*
Lk 20:47 Which **d** widows' houses, and for a *G2719*
2Co 11:20 bondage, if a man **d** *you*, if a man take *G2719*
Gal 5:15 But if ye bite and **d** one another, take *G2719*
Heb 10:27 which shall **d** the adversaries. *G2068*
1Pt 5: 8 about, seeking whom he may **d**: *G2666*
Rev 12: 4 to **d** her child as soon as it was born. *G2719*

DEVOURED
Gen 31:15 us, and hath quite **d** also our money. H398
37:20 evil beast hath **d** him: and we shall see H398
33 coat; an evil beast hath **d** him; Joseph is H398
41: 7 And the seven thin ears **d** the seven H1104
24 And the thin ears **d** the seven good H1104
Lev 10: 2 **d** them, and they died before the LORD. H398
Nu 26:10 what time the fire **d** two hundred and H398
Dt 31:17 and they shall be **d**, and many evils and H398
32:24 *They shall be* burnt with hunger, and **d** H3898
2Sa 18: 8 and the wood **d** more people that day H398
8 more people that day than the sword **d**. H398
22: 9 of his mouth **d**: coals were kindled by it. H398
Ps 18: 8 of his mouth **d**: coals were kindled by it. H398
78:45 them, which **d** them; and frogs, which H398
79: 7 For they have **d** Jacob, and laid waste his H398
105:35 land, and **d** the fruit of their ground. H398
Isa 1:20 But if ye refuse and rebel, ye shall be **d** H398
24: 6 Therefore hath the curse **d** the earth, H398
Jer 2:30 **d** your prophets, like a destroying lion. H398
3:24 For shame hath **d** the labour of our H398
8:16 come, and have **d** the land, and all that H398
10:25 up Jacob, and **d** him, and consumed H398
30:16 thee shall be **d**; and all thine adversaries, H398
50: 7 All that found them have **d** them: and H398
17 king of Assyria hath **d** him; and last this H398
51:34 of Babylon hath **d** me, he hath crushed H398
Lam 4:11 and it hath **d** the foundations thereof. H398
Ezk 15: 5 when the fire hath **d** it, and it is burned? H398
16:20 sacrificed unto them to be **d**. *Is this* of thy H398
19: 3 it learned to catch the prey; it **d** men. H398
6 learned to catch the prey, *and* **d** men. H398
14 *which* hath **d** her fruit, so that she H398
22:25 the prey; they have **d** souls; they have H398
23:25 and thy residue shall be **d** by the fire. H398
33:27 to the beasts to be **d**, and they that *be* in H398
39: 4 sort, and *to* the beasts of the field to be **d**. H402
Dan 7: 7 great iron teeth: it **d** and brake in pieces, H399
19 *of* brass; *which* **d**, brake in pieces, and H399
Hos 7: 7 They are all hot as an oven, and have **d** H398
9 Strangers have **d** his strength, and he H398
Joel 1:19 cry: for the fire hath **d** the pastures of the H398
20 hath **d** the pastures of the wilderness. H398
Am 4: 9 the palmerworm **d** *them*: yet have ye not H398
7: 4 it **d** the great deep, and did eat up a part. H398
Nah 1:10 they shall be **d** as stubble fully dry. H398
Zep 1:18 whole land shall be **d** by the fire of his H398
3: 8 shall be **d** with the fire of my jealousy. H398
Zec 9: 4 in the sea; and she shall be **d** with fire. H398
Mt 13: 4 and the fowls came and **d** them up: *G2719*
Mk 4: 4 the fowls of the air came and **d** it up. *G2719*
Lk 8: 5 down, and the fowls of the air **d** it. *G2719*
15:30 was come, which hath **d** thy living with *G2719*
Rev 20: 9 from God out of heaven, and **d** them. *G2719*

DEVOURER
Mal 3:11 And I will rebuke the **d** for your sakes, H398

DEVOUREST
Ezk 36:13 unto you, Thou *land* **d** up men, and hast H398

DEVOURETH
2Sa 11:25 thee, for the sword **d** one as well as H398
Prv 19:28 and the mouth of the wicked **d** iniquity. H1104
20:25 *It is* a snare to the man *who* **d** *that* H3216
Isa 5:24 Therefore as the fire **d** the stubble, and H398
Lam 2: 3 like a flaming fire, *which* **d** round about. H398
Ezk 15: 4 for fuel; the fire **d** both the ends of it, and H398
Joel 2: 3 A fire **d** before them; and behind them a H398
5 of a flame of fire that **d** the stubble, as a H398
Hab 1:13 when the wicked **d** *the man that is* H1104
Rev 11: 5 their mouth, and **d** their enemies: and *G2719*

DEVOURING
Ex 24:17 of the LORD *was* like **d** fire on the top of H398
Ps 52: 4 Thou lovest all **d** words, O *thou* H1105
Isa 29: 6 and tempest, and the flame of **d** fire. H398
30:27 indignation, and his tongue as a **d** fire: H398
30 and *with* the flame of a **d** fire, *with* H398
33:14 dwell with the **d** fire? who among us H398

DEVOUT
Lk 2:25 man *was* just and **d**, waiting for the *G2126*
Act 2: 5 at Jerusalem Jews, **d** men, out of every *G2126*
8: 2 And **d** men carried Stephen *to his* *G2126*
10: 2 *A* **d** *man*, and one that feared God with *G2152*
7 servants, and a **d** soldier of them that *G2152*
13:50 But the Jews stirred up the **d** and *G4576*
17: 4 and Silas; and of the **d** Greeks a great *G4576*
17 Jews, and with the **d** persons, and in *G4576*
22:12 And one Ananias, a **d** man according *G2152*

DEW
Gen 27:28 Therefore God give thee of the **d** of H2919
39 and of the **d** of heaven from above; H2919
Ex 16:13 the **d** lay round about the host. H2919
14 And when the **d** that lay was gone up, H2919
Nu 11: 9 And when the **d** fell upon the camp in H2919
Dt 32: 2 shall distil as the **d**, as the small rain H2919
33:13 of heaven, for the **d**, and for the deep H2919
28 also his heavens shall drop down **d**. H2919
Jdg 6:37 floor; *and* if the **d** be on the fleece only, H2919
38 **d** out of the fleece, a bowl full of water. H2919
39 and upon all the ground let there be **d**. H2919
40 and there was **d** on all the ground. H2919
2Sa 1:21 *let there be* no **d**, neither *let there be* H2919
17:12 light upon him as the **d** falleth on the H2919
1Ki 17: 1 there shall not be **d** nor rain these H2919
Job 29:19 the **d** lay all night upon my branch. H2919
38:28 or who hath begotten the drops of **d**? H2919
Ps 110: 3 morning: thou hast the **d** of thy youth. H2919
133: 3 As the **d** of Hermon, *and as the dew* H2919
3 As the dew of Hermon, *and as the* **d** that
Prv 3:20 up, and the clouds drop down the **d**. H2919
19:12 but his favour *is* as **d** upon the grass. H2919
Song 5: 2 head is filled with **d**, *and* my locks with H2919
Isa 18: 4 like a cloud of **d** in the heat of harvest. H2919
26:19 in dust: for thy **d** *is as* the dew of herbs, H2919
19 for thy dew *is as* the **d** of herbs, and the H2919
Dan 4:15 it be wet with the **d** of heaven, and *let* H2920
23 it be wet with the **d** of heaven, and *let* H2920
25 shall wet thee with the **d** of heaven, and H2920
33 was wet with the **d** of heaven, till his H2920
5:21 was wet with the **d** of heaven; till he H2920
Hos 6: 4 cloud, and as the early **d** it goeth away. H2919
13: 3 and as the early **d** that passeth away, H2919
14: 5 I will be as the **d** unto Israel: he shall H2919
Mic 5: 7 many people as a **d** from the LORD, as H2919
Hag 1:10 **d**, and the earth is stayed *from* her fruit. H2919
Zec 8:12 shall give their **d**; and I will cause the H2919

DIADEM
Job 29:14 my judgment *was* as a robe and a **d**. H6797
Isa 28: 5 of glory, and for a **d** of beauty, unto the H6843
62: 3 and a royal **d** in the hand of thy God. H6797
Ezk 21:26 GOD; Remove the **d**, and take off the H4701

DIAL
2Ki 20:11 it had gone down in the **d** of Ahaz. H4609
Isa 38: 8 down in the sun **d** of Ahaz, ten degrees H4609

DIAMOND
Ex 28:18 *be* an emerald, a sapphire, and a **d**. H3095
39:11 row, an emerald, a sapphire, and a **d**. H3095
Jer 17: 1 with the point of a **d**: *it is* graven upon H8068
Ezk 28:13 topaz, and the **d**, the beryl, the onyx, H3095

DIANA
Act 19:24 silver shrines for **D**, brought no small *G735*
27 the great goddess **D** should be despised, *G735*
28 out, saying, Great *is* **D** of the Ephesians. *G735*
34 cried out, Great *is* **D** of the Ephesians. *G735*
35 of the great goddess **D**, and of the *image* *G735*

D

DIBLAIM
Hos 1: 3 the daughter of **D**; which conceived, H1691

DIBLATH
Ezk 6:14 toward **D**, in all their habitations: H1689

DIBON
Nu 21:30 even unto **D**, and we have laid them H1769
32: 3 Ataroth, and **D**, and Jazer, and Nimrah, H1769
34 And the children of Gad built **D**, and H1769
Jos 13: 9 and all the plain of Medeba unto **D**; H1769
17 *are* in the plain; **D**, and Bamoth-baal, H1769
Neh 11:25 thereof, and at **D**, and *in* the villages H1769
Isa 15: 2 He is gone up to Bajith, and to **D**, the H1769
Jer 48:18 Thou daughter that dost inhabit **D**, H1769
22 And upon **D**, and upon Nebo, and upon H1769

DIBON-GAD
Nu 33:45 departed from Iim, and pitched in **D**. H1769
46 And they removed from **D**, and H1769

DIBRI
Lev 24:11 the daughter of **D**, of the tribe of Dan:) H1704

DID See the Appendix.

DIDDEST
Act 7:28 Wilt thou kill me, as thou **d** the Egyptian *G337*

DIDST See the Appendix.

DIDYMUS
Jn 11:16 Then said Thomas, which is called **D**, *G1324*
20:24 But Thomas, one of the twelve, called **D**, *G1324*
21: 2 and Thomas called **D**, and Nathanael of *G1324*

DIE
Gen 2:17 thou eatest thereof thou shalt surely **d**. H4191
3: 3 of it, neither shall ye touch it, lest ye **d**. H4191
4 unto the woman, Ye shall not surely **d**: H4191
6:17 every thing that *is* in the earth shall **d**. H1478
19:19 lest some evil take me, and I **d**: H4191
20: 7 surely **d**, thou, and all that *are* thine. H4191
25:32 I *am* at the point to **d**: and what profit H4191
26: 9 him, Because I said, Lest I **d** for her. H4191
27: 4 that my soul may bless thee before I **d**. H4191
30: 1 Jacob, Give me children, or else I **d**. H4191
33:13 them one day, all the flock will **d**. H4191
38:11 peradventure he **d** also, as his brethren H4191
42: 2 thence; that we may live, and not **d**. H4191
20 and ye shall not **d**. And they did so. H4191
43: 8 may live, and not **d**, both we, and thou, H4191
44: 9 both let him **d**, and we also will be H4191
22 leave his father, *his father* would **d**. H4191
31 *us*, that he will **d**: and thy servants shall H4191
45:28 alive: I will go and see him before I **d**. H4191
46:30 Now let me **d**, since I have seen thy H4191
47:15 for why should we **d** in thy presence? H4191
19 Wherefore shall we **d** before thine eyes, H4191
19 and not **d**, that the land be not desolate. H4191
29 that Israel must **d**: and he called his son H4191
48:21 Joseph, Behold, I **d**: but God shall be H4191
50: 5 saying, Lo, I **d**: in my grave which I H4191
24 And Joseph said unto his brethren, I **d**: H4191
Ex 7:18 And the fish that *is* in the river shall **d**, H4191
9: 4 **d** of all *that is* the children's of Israel. H4191
19 down upon them, and they shall **d**. H4191
10:28 day thou seest my face thou shalt **d**. H4191
11: 5 of Egypt shall **d**, from the firstborn of H4191
14:11 taken us away to **d** in the wilderness? H4191
12 that we should **d** in the wilderness. H4191
20:19 but let not God speak with us, lest we **d**. H4191
21:12 He that smiteth a man, so that he **d**, H4191
14 him from mine altar, that he may **d**. H4191
18 fist, and he **d** not, but keepeth *his* bed: H4191
20 with a rod, and he **d** under his hand; he H4191

Ex 21:28 woman, that they **d**: then the ox shall be H4191
35 another's, that he **d**; then they shall sell H4191
22: 2 **d**, *there shall* no blood *be shed* for him. H4191
10 to keep; and it **d**, or be hurt, or driven H4191
14 and it be hurt, or **d**, the owner thereof H4191
28:35 and when he cometh out, that he **d** not. H4191
43 not iniquity, and **d**: *it shall be* a statute H4191
30:20 water, that they **d** not; or when they H4191
21 feet, that they **d** not: and it shall be H4191
Lev 8:35 that ye **d** not: for so I am commanded. H4191
10: 6 clothes; lest ye **d**, and lest wrath come H4191
7 lest ye **d**: for the anointing oil H4191
9 lest ye **d**: *it shall be* a statute H4191
11:39 of which ye may eat, **d**; he that toucheth H4191
15:31 that they **d** not in their uncleanness, H4191
16: 2 the ark; that he **d** not: for I will appear H4191
13 *is* upon the testimony, that he **d** not: H4191
20:20 bear their sin; they shall **d** childless. H4191
22: 9 bear sin for it, and **d** therefore, if they H4191
Nu 4:15 thing, lest they **d**. These *things are* the H4191
19 they may live, and not **d**, when they H4191
20 the holy things are covered, lest they **d**. H4191
6: 7 his sister, when they **d**: because the H4194
9 And if any man **d** very suddenly by H4191
14:35 be consumed, and there they shall **d**. H4191
16:29 If these men **d** the common death of all H4191
17:10 murmurings from me, that they **d** not. H4191
12 Behold, we **d**, we perish, we all perish. H1478
13 **d**: shall we be consumed with dying? H4191
18: 3 altar, that neither they, nor ye also, **d**. H4191
22 congregation, lest they bear sin, and **d**. H4191
32 things of the children of Israel, lest ye **d**. H4191
20: 4 that we and our cattle should **d** there? H4191
26 *unto his people*, and shall **d** there. H4191
21: 5 up out of Egypt to **d** in the wilderness? H4191
23:10 *part* of Israel? Let me **d** the death of the H4191
26:65 They shall surely **d** in the wilderness. H4191
27: 8 saying, If a man **d**, and have no son, H4191
35:12 the manslayer **d** not, until he stand H4191
16 of iron, so that he **d**, he *is* a murderer: H4191
17 wherewith he may **d**, and he die, he *is* a H4191
17 may die, and he **d**, he *is* a murderer: the H4191
18 wherewith he may **d**, and he die, he *is* a H4191
18 may die, and he **d**, he *is* a murderer: the H4191
20 hurl at him by laying of wait, that he **d**; H4191
21 his hand, that he **d**: he that smote *him* H4191
23 a man may **d**, seeing *him* not, and H4191
23 *it* upon him, that he **d**, and *was* not his H4191
30 against any person *to cause him* to **d**. H4191
Dt 4:22 But I must **d** in this land, I must not go H4191
5:25 Now therefore why should we **d**? for this H4191
25 our God any more, then we shall **d**. H4191
13:10 with stones, that he **d**; because he hath H4191
17: 5 shalt stone them with stones, till they **d**. H4191
12 that man shall **d**: and thou shalt put H4191
18:16 this great fire any more, that I **d** not. H4191
20 of other gods, even that prophet shall **d**. H4191
19: 5 neighbour, that he **d**; he shall flee unto H4191
11 he **d**, and fleeth into one of these cities: H4191
12 of the avenger of blood, that he may **d**. H4191
20: 5 to his house, lest he **d** in the battle, and H4191
6 his house, lest he **d** in the battle, and H4191
7 his house, lest he **d** in the battle, and H4191
21:21 stones, that he **d**: so shalt thou put evil H4191
22:21 with stones that she **d**: because she hath H4191
22 shall both of them **d**, *both* the man that H4191
24 stones that they **d**; the damsel, because H4191
25 the man only that lay with her shall **d**: H4191
24: 3 **d**, which took her *to be* his wife; H4191
7 that thief shall **d**; and thou shalt put evil H4191
25: 5 and one of them **d**, and have no child, H4191
31:14 that thou must **d**: call Joshua, and H4191
32:50 And **d** in the mount whither thou goest H4191
33: 6 Let Reuben live, and not **d**; and let *not* H4191
Jos 20: 9 thither, and not **d** by the hand of the H4191
Jdg 6:23 *be* unto thee; fear not: thou shalt not **d**. H4191
30 thy son, that he may **d**: because he hath H4191
13:22 surely **d**, because we have seen God. H4191
15:18 and now shall I **d** for thirst, and fall H4191
16:30 And Samson said, Let me **d** with the H4191
Ru 1:17 Where thou diest, will I **d**, and there will H4191
1Sa 2:33 house shall **d** in the flower of their age. H4191
34 in one day they shall **d** both of them. H4191
12:19 thy God, that we **d** not: for we have H4191
14:39 he shall surely **d**. But *there was* not a H4191
43 *was* in mine hand, *and*, lo, I must **d**. H4191
44 also: for thou shalt surely **d**, Jonathan. H4191
45 Shall Jonathan **d**, who hath wrought H4191
20: 2 thou shalt not **d**: behold, my father will H4191
1Sa 20:14 the kindness of the LORD, that I **d** not: H4191
31 fetch him unto me, for he shall surely **d**. H4191
22:16 And the king said, Thou shalt surely **d**, H4191
26:10 day shall come to **d**; or he shall descend H4191
16 ye *are* worthy to **d**, because ye have not H4194
28: 9 a snare for my life, to cause me to **d**? H4191
2Sa 11:15 him, that he may be smitten, and **d**. H4191
12: 5 that hath done this *thing* shall surely **d**: H4194
13 hath put away thy sin; thou shalt not **d**. H4191
14 *that is* born unto thee shall surely **d**. H4191
14:14 For we must needs **d**, and *are* as water H4191
18: 3 if half of us **d**, will they care for us: H4191
19:23 not **d**. And the king sware unto him. H4191
37 again, that I may **d** in mine own city, H4191
1Ki 1:52 shall be found in him, he shall **d**. H4191
2: 1 nigh that he should **d**; and he charged H4191
30 Nay; but I will **d** here. And Benaiah H4191
37 thou shalt surely **d**: thy blood shall be H4191
42 that thou shalt surely **d**? and thou saidst H4191
14:12 feet enter into the city, the child shall **d**. H4191
17:12 and my son, that we may eat it, and **d**. H4191
19: 4 that he might **d**; and said, It is enough; H4191
21:10 him out, and stone him, that he may **d**. H4191
2Ki 1: 4 but shalt surely **d**. And Elijah departed. H4191
6 thou art gone up, but shalt surely **d**. H4191
16 thou art gone up, but shalt surely **d**. H4191
7: 3 to another, Why sit we here until we **d**? H4191
4 city, and we shall **d** there: and if we sit H4191
4 sit still here, we **d** also. Now therefore H4191
4 live; and if they kill us, we shall but **d**. H4191
8:10 hath shewed me that he shall surely **d**. H4191
18:32 ye may live, and not **d**: and hearken not H4191
20: 1 in order; for thou shalt **d**, and not live. H4191
2Ch 25: 4 The fathers shall not **d** for the children, H4191
4 shall the children **d** for the fathers, but H4191
4 but every man shall **d** for his own sin. H4191
32:11 over yourselves to **d** by famine and by H4191
Job 2: 9 retain thine integrity? curse God, and **d**. H4191
4:21 go away? they **d**, even without wisdom. H4191
12: 2 people, and wisdom shall **d** with you. H4191
14: 8 and the stock thereof **d** in the ground; H4191
14 If a man **d**, shall he live *again*? all the H4191
27: 5 justify you: till I **d** I will not remove H1478
29:18 Then I said, I shall **d** in my nest, and I H1478
34:20 In a moment shall they **d**, and the H4191
36:12 and they shall **d** without knowledge. H1478
14 They **d** in youth, and their life *is* among H4191
Ps 41: 5 When shall he **d**, and his name perish? H4191
49:10 For he seeth *that* wise men **d**, likewise H4191
79:11 thou those that are appointed to **d**; H8546
82: 7 But ye shall **d** like men, and fall like H4191
88:15 I *am* afflicted and ready to **d** from *my* H1478
104:29 breath, they **d**, and return to their dust. H1478
118:17 I shall not **d**, but live, and declare the H4191
Prv 5:23 He shall **d** without instruction; and in H4191
10:21 many: but fools **d** for want of wisdom. H4191
15:10 way: *and* he that hateth reproof shall **d**. H4191
19:16 *but* he that despiseth his ways shall **d**. H4191
23:13 beatest him with the rod, he shall not **d**. H4191
30: 7 of thee; deny me *them* not before I **d**: H4191
Ecc 3: 2 A time to be born, and a time to **d**; a H4191
7:17 why shouldest thou **d** before thy time? H4191
9: 5 For the living know that they shall **d**: H4191
Isa 22:13 eat and drink; for to morrow we shall **d**. H4191
14 till ye **d**, saith the Lord GOD of hosts. H4191
18 there shalt thou **d**, and there the H4191
38: 1 in order: for thou shalt **d**, and not live. H4191
51: 6 dwell therein shall **d** in like manner: H4191
12 of a man *that* shall **d**, and of the son of H4191
14 that he should not **d** in the pit, nor that H4191
65:20 for the child shall **d** an hundred years H4191
66:24 worm shall not **d**, neither shall their fire H4191
Jer 11:21 the LORD, that thou **d** not by our hand: H4191
22 young men shall **d** by the sword; their H4191
22 and their daughters shall **d** by famine: H4191
16: 4 They shall **d** of grievous deaths; they H4191
6 Both the great and the small shall **d** in H4191
20: 6 there thou shalt **d**, and shalt be buried H4191
21: 6 beast: they shall **d** of a great pestilence. H4191
9 He that abideth in this city shall **d** by H4191
22:12 But he shall **d** in the place whither they H4191
26 ye were not born; and there shall ye **d**. H4191
26: 8 took him, saying, Thou shalt surely **d**. H4191
11 This man *is* worthy to **d**; for he hath H4194
16 *is* not worthy to **d**: for he hath spoken H4194
27:13 Why will ye **d**, thou and thy people, by H4191
28:16 year thou shalt **d**, because thou hast H4191
31:30 But every one shall **d** for his own H4191
34: 4 of thee, Thou shalt not **d** by the sword: H4191
Jer 34: 5 *But* thou shalt **d** in peace: and with the H4191
37:20 of Jonathan the scribe, lest I **d** there. H4191
38: 2 in this city shall **d** by the sword, by the H4191
9 and he is like to **d** for hunger in the H4191
10 out of the dungeon, before he **d**. H4191
24 of these words, and thou shalt not **d**. H4191
26 return to Jonathan's house, to **d** there. H4191
42:16 you there in Egypt; and there ye shall **d**. H4191
17 there; they shall **d** by the sword, by the H4191
22 that ye shall **d** by the sword, by the H4191
44:12 famine: they shall **d**, from the least even H4191
Ezk 3:18 Thou shalt surely **d**; and thou givest H4191
18 wicked *man* shall **d** in his iniquity; but H4191
19 way, he shall **d** in his iniquity; but thou H4191
20 him, he shall **d**: because thou hast not H4191
20 warning, he shall **d** in his sin, and his H4191
5:12 A third part of thee shall **d** with the H4191
6:12 He that is far off shall **d** of the H4191
12 is besieged shall **d** by the famine: thus H4191
7:15 *is* in the field shall **d** with the sword; H4191
12:13 he not see it, though he shall **d** there. H4191
13:19 that should not **d**, and to save the souls H4191
17:16 him in the midst of Babylon he shall **d**. H4191
18: 4 is mine: the soul that sinneth, it shall **d**. H4191
13 surely **d**; his blood shall be upon him. H4191
17 he shall not **d** for the iniquity of his H4191
18 lo, even he shall **d** in his iniquity. H4191
20 The soul that sinneth, it shall **d**. The son H4191
21 right, he shall surely live, he shall not **d**. H4191
23 that the wicked should **d**? saith the Lord H4194
24 that he hath sinned, in them shall he **d**. H4191
26 iniquity that he hath done shall he **d**. H4191
28 he shall surely live, he shall not **d**. H4191
31 for why will ye **d**, O house of Israel? H4191
28: 8 pit, and thou shalt **d** the deaths of *them* H4191
10 Thou shalt **d** the deaths of the H4191
33: 8 thou shalt surely **d**; if thou dost not H4191
8 wicked *man* shall **d** in his iniquity; but H4191
9 his way, he shall **d** in his iniquity; but H4191
11 for why will ye **d**, O house of Israel? H4191
13 he hath committed, he shall **d** for it. H4191
14 Thou shalt surely **d**; if he turn from his H4191
15 he shall surely live, he shall not **d**. H4191
18 iniquity, he shall even **d** thereby. H4191
27 in the caves shall **d** of the pestilence. H4191
Am 2: 2 and Moab shall **d** with tumult, with H4191
6: 9 ten men in one house, that they shall **d**. H4191
7:11 For thus Amos saith, Jeroboam shall **d** H4191
17 and thou shalt **d** in a polluted land: H4191
9:10 All the sinners of my people shall **d** by H4191
Jna 4: 3 for *it is* better for me to **d** than to live. H4194
8 in himself to **d**, and said, *It is* better H4191
8 said, *It is* better for me to **d** than to live. H4194
Hab 1:12 One? we shall not **d**. O LORD, thou hast H4191
Zec 11: 9 that dieth, let it **d**; and that that is to be H4191
13: 8 *and* **d**; but the third shall be left therein. H1478
Mt 15: 4 father or mother, let him **d** the death. *G5053*
22:24 Saying, Master, Moses said, If a man **d**, *G599*
26:35 Peter said unto him, Though I should **d** *G599*
Mk 7:10 father or mother, let him **d** the death: *G5053*
12:19 If a man's brother **d**, and leave *his* wife *G599*
14:31 If I should **d** with thee, I will not *G4880*
Lk 7: 2 unto him, was sick, and ready to **d**. *G5053*
20:28 any man's brother **d**, having a wife, and *G599*
28 a wife, and he **d** without children, that *G599*
36 Neither can they **d** any more: for they *G599*
Jn 4:49 unto him, Sir, come down ere my child **d**. *G599*
6:50 that a man may eat thereof, and not **d**. *G599*
8:21 shall seek me, and shall **d** in your sins: *G599*
24 I said therefore unto you, that ye shall **d** *G599*
24 not that I am *he*, ye shall **d** in your sins. *G599*
11:16 Let us also go, that we may **d** with him. *G599*
26 in me shall never **d**. Believest thou this? *G599*
50 one man should **d** for the people, and *G599*
51 that Jesus should **d** for that nation; *G599*
12:24 the ground and **d**, it abideth alone: but *G599*
24 but if it **d**, it bringeth forth much fruit. *G599*
33 said, signifying what death he should **d**. *G599*
18:14 that one man should **d** for the people. *G622*
32 spake, signifying what death he should **d**. *G599*
19: 7 our law he ought to **d**, because he made *G599*
21:23 disciple should not **d**: yet Jesus said not *G599*
23 him, He shall not **d**; but, If I will that he *G599*
Act 21:13 only, but also to **d** at Jerusalem for the *G599*
25:11 I refuse not to **d**: but if there be none *G599*
16 to deliver any man to **d**, before that he *G684*
Ro 5: 7 man will one **d**: yet peradventure for *G599*
7 a good man some would even dare to **d**. *G599*
8:13 For if ye live after the flesh, ye shall **d**: but *G599*

Ro 14: 8 and whether we **d**, we die unto the Lord: *G599*
8 and whether we die, we **d** unto the Lord: *G599*
8 we live therefore, or **d**, we are the Lord's. *G599*
1Co 9:15 better for me to **d**, than that any man *G599*
15:22 For as in Adam all **d**, even so in Christ *G599*
31 I have in Christ Jesus our Lord, I **d** daily. *G599*
32 let us eat and drink; for to morrow we **d**. *G599*
36 thou sowest is not quickened, except it **d**: *G599*
2Co 7: 3 are in our hearts to **d** and live with *you*. *G4880*
Php 1:21 For to me to live *is* Christ, and to **d** *is* *G599*
Heb 7: 8 And here men that **d** receive tithes; but *G599*
9:27 once to **d**, but after this the judgment: *G599*
Rev 3: 2 that are ready to **d**: for I have not found *G599*
9: 6 to **d**, and death shall flee from them. *G599*
14:13 *are* the dead which **d** in the Lord from *G599*

DIED

Gen 5: 5 hundred and thirty years: and he **d**. H4191
8 hundred and twelve years: and he **d**. H4191
11 nine hundred and five years: and he **d**. H4191
14 nine hundred and ten years: and he **d**. H4191
17 ninety and five years: and he **d**. H4191
20 hundred sixty and two years: and he **d**. H4191
27 hundred sixty and nine years: and he **d**. H4191
31 seventy and seven years: and he **d**. H4191
7:21 And all flesh **d** that moved upon the H1478
22 of life, of all that *was* in the dry *land*, **d**. H4191
9:29 nine hundred and fifty years: and he **d**. H4191
11:28 And Haran **d** before his father Terah in H4191
32 and five years: and Terah **d** in Haran. H4191
23: 2 And Sarah **d** in Kirjath-arba; the same H4191
25: 8 up the ghost, and **d** in a good old age, H4191
17 **d**; and was gathered unto his people. H4191
18 he **d** in the presence of all his brethren. H5307
35: 8 But Deborah Rebekah's nurse **d**, and H4191
18 (for she **d**) that she called his name H4191
19 And Rachel **d**, and was buried in the H4191
29 And Isaac gave up the ghost, and **d**, and H4191
36:33 And Bela **d**, and Jobab the son of Zerah H4191
34 And Jobab **d**, and Husham of the land H4191
35 And Husham **d**, and Hadad the son of H4191
36 And Hadad **d**, and Samlah of Masrekah H4191
37 And Samlah **d**, and Saul of Rehoboth *by* H4191
38 And Saul **d**, and Baal-hanan the son of H4191
39 And Baal-hanan the son of Achbor **d**, H4191
38:12 Shuah Judah's wife **d**; and Judah was H4191
46:12 Zerah: but Er and Onan **d** in the land of H4191
48: 7 Padan, Rachel **d** by me in the land of H4191
50:16 did command before he **d**, saying, H4194
26 So Joseph **d**, *being* an hundred and ten H4191
Ex 1: 6 And Joseph **d**, and all his brethren, and H4191
2:23 the king of Egypt **d**: and the children of H4191
7:21 And the fish that *was* in the river **d**; and H4191
8:13 and the frogs **d** out of the houses, out H4191
9: 6 the cattle of Egypt **d**: but of the cattle of H4191
6 of the children of Israel **d** not one. H4191
16: 3 to God we had **d** by the hand of the H4191
Lev 10: 2 them, and they **d** before the LORD. H4191
16: 1 they offered before the LORD, and **d**; H4191
17:15 And every soul that eateth that which **d** H5038
Nu 3: 4 And Nadab and Abihu **d** before the H4191
14: 2 God that we had **d** in the land of Egypt! H4191
2 would God we had **d** in this wilderness! H4191
37 land, **d** by the plague before the LORD. H4191
15:36 he **d**; as the LORD commanded Moses. H4191
16:49 Now they that **d** in the plague were H4191
49 them that **d** about the matter of Korah. H4191
20: 1 Miriam **d** there, and was buried there. H4191
3 God that we had **d** when our brethren H1478
3 when our brethren **d** before the LORD! H1478
28 son; and Aaron **d** there in the top of the H4191
21: 6 the people; and much people of Israel **d**. H4191
25: 9 And those that **d** in the plague were H4191
26:10 that company **d**, what time the fire H4194
11 the children of Korah **d** not. H4191
19 Er and Onan **d** in the land of Canaan. H4191
61 And Nadab and Abihu **d**, when they H4191
27: 3 Our father **d** in the wilderness, and he H4191
3 but **d** in his own sin, and had no sons. H4191
33:38 of the LORD, and **d** there, in the H4191
39 years old when he **d** in mount Hor. H4194
Dt 10: 6 there Aaron **d**, and there he was buried; H4191
32:50 Aaron thy brother **d** in mount Hor, and H4191
34: 5 So Moses the servant of the LORD **d** H4191
7 years old when he **d**: his eye was not H4194
Jos 5: 4 the men of war, **d** in the wilderness by H4191
10:11 Azekah, and they **d**: *they were* more H4191
11 *were* more which **d** with hailstones H4191
24:29 **d**, *being* an hundred and ten years old. H4191
Jos 24:33 And Eleazar the son of Aaron **d**; and H4191
Jdg 1: 7 him to Jerusalem, and there he **d**. H4191
2: 8 **d**, *being* an hundred and ten years old. H4191
21 nations which Joshua left when he **d**: H4191
3:11 years. And Othniel the son of Kenaz **d**. H4191
4:21 he was fast asleep and weary. So he **d**. H4191
8:32 And Gideon the son of Joash **d** in a H4191
9:49 the tower of Shechem **d** also, about a H4191
54 man thrust him through, and he **d**. H4191
10: 2 years, and **d**, and was buried in Shamir. H4191
5 And Jair **d**, and was buried in Camon. H4191
12: 7 Israel six years. Then **d** Jephthah the H4191
10 Then **d** Ibzan, and was buried at H4191
12 And Elon the Zebulonite **d**, and was H4191
15 the Pirathonite **d**, and was buried in H4191
Ru 1: 3 And Elimelech Naomi's husband **d**; and H4191
5 And Mahlon and Chilion **d** also both of H4191
1Sa 4:18 brake, and he **d**: for he was an old man, H4191
5:12 And the men that **d** not were smitten H4191
14:45 people rescued Jonathan, that he **d** not. H4191
25: 1 And Samuel **d**; and all the Israelites H4191
37 that his heart **d** within him, and he H4191
38 that the LORD smote Nabal, that he **d**. H4191
31: 5 upon his sword, and **d** with him. H4191
6 So Saul **d**, and his three sons, and his H4191
2Sa 1:15 upon him. And he smote him that he **d**. H4191
2:23 down there, and **d** in the same place: H4191
23 Asahel fell down and **d** stood still. H4191
31 three hundred and threescore men **d**. H4191
3:27 **d**, for the blood of Asahel his brother. H4191
33 and said, **D** Abner as a fool dieth? H4191
6: 7 error; and there he **d** by the ark of God. H4191
10: 1 of Ammon **d**, and Hanun his son H4191
18 the captain of their host, who **d** there. H4191
11:17 of David; and Uriah the Hittite **d** also. H4191
21 the wall, that he **d** in Thebez? why went H4191
12:18 day, that the child **d**. And the servants H4191
17:23 himself, and **d**, and was buried in the H4191
18:33 **d** for thee, O Absalom, my son, my son! H4191
19: 6 and all we had **d** this day, then it had H4191
20:10 him not again; and he **d**. So Joab and H4191
24:15 and there **d** of the people from Dan H4191
1Ki 2:25 and he fell upon him that he **d**. H4191
46 upon him, that he **d**. And the kingdom H4191
3:19 And this woman's child **d** in the night; H4191
12:18 with stones, that he **d**. Therefore king H4191
14:17 to the threshold of the door, the child **d**; H4191
16:18 king's house over him with fire, and **d**, H4191
22 Ginath: so Tibni **d**, and Omri reigned. H4191
21:13 and stoned him with stones, that he **d**. H4191
22:35 the Syrians, and **d** at even: and the H4191
37 So the king **d**, and was brought to H4191
2Ki 1:17 So he **d** according to the word of the H4191
4:20 sat on her knees till noon, and *then* **d**. H4191
7:17 in the gate, and he **d**, as the man of God H4191
20 trode upon him in the gate, and he **d**. H4191
8:15 he **d**: and Hazael reigned in his stead. H4191
9:27 And he fled to Megiddo, and **d** there. H4191
12:21 him, and he **d**; and they buried him H4191
13:14 whereof he **d**. And Joash the king H4191
20 And Elisha **d**, and they buried him. And H4191
24 So Hazael king of Syria **d**; and H4191
23:34 and he came to Egypt, and **d** there. H4191
25:25 Gedaliah, that he **d**, and the Jews and H4191
1Ch 1:51 Hadad **d** also. And the dukes of Edom H4191
2:30 Appaim: but Seled **d** without children. H4191
32 and Jether **d** without children. H4191
10: 5 he fell likewise on the sword, and **d**. H4191
6 So Saul **d**, and his three sons, and all his H4191
6 sons, and all his house **d** together. H4191
13 So Saul **d** for his transgression which H4191
13:10 to the ark: and there he **d** before God. H4191
19: 1 **d**, and his son reigned in his stead. H4191
23:22 And Eleazar **d**, and had no sons, but H4191
24: 2 But Nadab and Abihu **d** before their H4191
29:28 And he **d** in a good old age, full of days, H4191
2Ch 10:18 stones, that he **d**. But king Rehoboam H4191
13:20 and the LORD struck him, and he **d**. H4191
16:13 And Asa slept with his fathers, and **d** in H4191
18:34 the time of the sun going down he **d**. H4191
21:19 of his sickness: so he **d** of sore diseases. H4191
24:15 full of days when he **d**; an hundred and H4191
15 and thirty years old *was he* when he **d**. H4194
22 son. And when he **d**, he said, The LORD H4194
25 on his bed, and he **d**: and they buried H4191
35:24 Jerusalem, and he **d**, and was buried in H4191
Job 3:11 Why **d** I not from the womb? *why* did I H4191
42:17 So Job **d**, *being* old and full of days. H4191
Isa 6: 1 In the year that king Uzziah **d** I saw H4194
Isa 14:28 In the year that king Ahaz **d** was this H4194
Jer 28:17 So Hananiah the prophet **d** the same H4191
Ezk 11:13 son of Benaiah **d**. Then fell I down upon H4191
24:18 and at even my wife **d**; and I did in the H4191
Hos 13: 1 but when he offended in Baal, he **d**. H4191
Mt 22:27 And last of all the woman **d** also. *G599*
Mk 12:21 And the second took her, and **d**, neither *G599*
22 left no seed: last of all the woman **d** also. *G599*
Lk 16:22 And it came to pass, that the beggar **d**, *G599*
22 the rich man also **d**, and was buried; *G599*
20:29 first took a wife, and **d** without children. *G599*
30 took her to wife, and he **d** childless. *G599*
31 also: and they left no children, and **d**. *G599*
32 Last of all the woman **d** also. *G599*
Jn 11:21 hadst been here, my brother had not **d**. *G2348*
32 hadst been here, my brother had not **d**. *G599*
37 that even this man should not have **d**? *G599*
Act 7:15 So Jacob went down into Egypt, and **d**, *G5053*
9:37 she was sick, and **d**: whom when they *G599*
Ro 5: 6 in due time Christ **d** for the ungodly. *G599*
8 we were yet sinners, Christ **d** for us. *G599*
6:10 For in that he **d**, he died unto sin once: *G599*
10 For in that he died, he **d** unto sin once: *G599*
7: 9 came, sin revived, and I **d**. *G599*
8:34 *It is* Christ that **d**, yea rather, that is risen *G599*
14: 9 For to this end Christ both **d**, and rose, *G599*
15 him with thy meat, for whom Christ **d**. *G599*
1Co 8:11 weak brother perish, for whom Christ **d**? *G599*
15: 3 how that Christ **d** for our sins according *G599*
2Co 5:14 that if one **d** for all, then were all dead: *G599*
15 And *that* he **d** for all, that they which live *G599*
15 him which **d** for them, and rose again. *G599*
1Th 4:14 For if we believe that Jesus **d** and rose *G599*
5:10 Who **d** for us, that, whether we wake or *G599*
Heb 10:28 He that despised Moses' law **d** without *G599*
11:13 These all **d** in faith, not having received *G599*
22 By faith Joseph, when he **d**, made *G5053*
Rev 8: 9 sea, and had life, **d**; and the third part of *G599*
11 and many men **d** of the waters, because *G599*
16: 3 *man*: and every living soul **d** in the sea. *G599*

DIEST

Ru 1:17 Where thou **d**, will I die, and there will I H4191

DIET

Jer 52:34 And *for* his **d**, there was a continual diet H737
34 And *for* his diet, there was a continual **d** H737

DIETH

Lev 7:24 And the fat of the beast that **d** of itself, H5038
22: 8 That which **d** of itself, or is torn *with* H5038
Nu 19:14 This *is* the law, when a man **d** in a tent: H4191
Dt 14:21 Ye shall not eat *of* any thing that **d** of H5038
2Sa 3:33 Abner, and said, Died Abner as a fool **d**? H4194
1Ki 14:11 Him that **d** of Jeroboam in the city H4191
11 eat; and him that **d** in the field shall the H4191
16: 4 Him that **d** of Baasha in the city shall H4191
4 eat; and him that **d** of his in the fields H4191
21:24 Him that **d** of Ahab in the city the dogs H4191
24 eat; and him that **d** in the field shall the H4191
Job 14:10 But man **d**, and wasteth away: yea, H4191
21:23 One **d** in his full strength, being wholly H4191
25 And another **d** in the bitterness of his H4191
Ps 49:17 For when he **d** he shall carry nothing H4194
Prv 11: 7 When a wicked man **d**, *his* expectation H4194
Ecc 2:16 And how **d** the wise *man*? as the fool. H4191
3:19 them: as the one **d**, so dieth the other; H4194
19 the one dieth, so **d** the other; yea, they H4194
Isa 50: 2 *there is* no water, and **d** for thirst. H4191
59: 5 eateth of their eggs **d**, and that which is H4191
Ezk 4:14 of that which **d** of itself, or is torn in H5038
18:26 iniquity, and **d** in them; for his iniquity H4191
32 the death of him that **d**, saith the Lord H4191
Zec 11: 9 feed you: that that **d**, let it die; and that H4191
Mk 9:44 Where their worm **d** not, and the fire is *G5053*
46 Where their worm **d** not, and the fire is *G5053*
48 Where their worm **d** not, and the fire is *G5053*
Ro 6: 9 from the dead **d** no more; death hath *G599*
14: 7 to himself, and no man **d** to himself. *G599*

DIFFER

1Co 4: 7 For who maketh thee to **d** *from* *G1252*

DIFFERENCE

Ex 11: 7 a **d** between the Egyptians and Israel. H6395
Lev 10:10 And that ye may put **d** between holy and H914
11:47 To make a **d** between the unclean and H914
20:25 Ye shall therefore put **d** between clean H914
Ezk 22:26 they have put no **d** between the holy and H914

Ezk 22:26 have they shewed *d* between the unclean
44:23 And they shall teach my people *the d*
Act 15: 9 And put no **d** between us and them, *G1252*
Ro 3:22 all them that believe: for there is no **d**: *G1293*
10:12 For there is no **d** between the Jew and *G1293*
1Co 7:34 There is **d** *also* between a wife and a *G3307*
Jude 22 of some have compassion, making a **d**: *G1252*

DIFFERENCES
1Co 12: 5 And there are **d** of administrations, but *G1243*

DIFFERETH
1Co 15:41 *one* star **d** from *another* star in glory. *G1308*
Gal 4: 1 long as he is a child, **d** nothing from a *G1308*

DIFFERING
Ro 12: 6 Having then gifts **d** according to the *G1313*

DIG
Ex 21:33 or if a man shall **d** a pit, and not cover H3738
Dt 8: 9 out of whose hills thou mayest **d** brass. H2672
23:13 abroad, thou shalt **d** therewith, and H2658
Job 3:21 **d** for it more than for hid treasures; H2658
6:27 and ye **d** *a pit* for your friend. H3738
11:18 yea, thou shalt **d** *about thee, and* thou H2658
24:16 In the dark they **d** through houses, H2864
Ezk 8: 8 Then said he unto me, Son of man, **d** H2864
12: 5 **D** thou through the wall in their sight, H2864
12 forth: they shall **d** through the wall to H2864
Am 9: 2 Though they **d** into hell, thence shall H2864
Lk 13: 8 also, till I shall **d** about it, and dung *it*: *G4626*
16: 3 I cannot **d**; to beg I am ashamed. *G4626*

DIGGED
Gen 21:30 unto me, that I have **d** this well. H2658
26:15 servants had **d** in the days of Abraham H2658
18 And Isaac **d** again the wells of water, H2658
18 water, which they had **d** in the days of H2658
19 And Isaac's servants **d** in the valley, H2658
21 And they **d** another well, and strove for H2658
22 And he removed from thence, and **d** H2658
25 and there Isaac's servants **d** a well. H3738
32 which they had **d**, and said unto him, H2658
49: 6 and in their selfwill they **d** down a wall. H6131
50: 5 which I have **d** for me in the land of H3738
Ex 7:24 And all the Egyptians **d** round about H2658
Nu 21:18 The princes **d** the well, the nobles of the H2658
18 of the people **d** it, by *the direction of* H3738
Dt 6:11 not, and wells **d**, which thou diggedst H2672
2Ki 19:24 I have **d** and drunk strange waters, and H6979
2Ch 26:10 in the desert, and **d** many wells: for he H2672
Neh 9:25 full of all goods, wells **d**, vineyards, and H2672
Ps 7:15 He made a pit, and **d** it, and is fallen H2658
35: 7 without cause they have **d** for my soul. H2658
57: 6 down: they have **d** a pit before me, into H3738
94:13 until the pit be **d** for the wicked. H3738
119:85 The proud have **d** pits for me, which H3738
Isa 5: 6 be pruned, nor **d**; but there shall come H5737
7:25 And *on* all hills that shall be **d** with the H5737
37:25 I have **d**, and drunk water; and with the H6979
51: 1 to the hole of the pit *whence* ye are **d**. H5365
Jer 13: 7 Then I went to Euphrates, and **d**, and H2658
18:20 good? for they have **d** a pit for my soul. H3738
22 for they have **d** a pit to take me, and H3738
Ezk 8: 8 I had **d** in the wall, behold a door. H2864
12: 7 and in the even I **d** through the wall H2864
Mt 21:33 it round about, and **d** a winepress in it, *G3736*
25:18 one went and **d** in the earth, and hid *G3736*
Mk 12: 1 about *it*, and **d** *a place for* the winefat, *G3736*
Lk 6:48 an house, and **d** deep, and laid the *G4626*
Ro 11: 3 thy prophets, and **d** down thine altars; *G2679*

DIGGEDST
Dt 6:11 which thou **d** not, vineyards and H2672

DIGGETH
Prv 16:27 An ungodly man **d** up evil: and in his H3738
26:27 Whoso **d** a pit shall fall therein: and he H3738
Ecc 10: 8 He that **d** a pit shall fall into it; and H2658

DIGNITIES
2Pt 2:10 they are not afraid to speak evil of **d**. *G1391*
Jude 8 despise dominion, and speak evil of **d**. *G1391*

DIGNITY
Gen 49: 3 of **d**, and the excellency of power: H7613
Est 6: 3 And the king said, What honour and **d** H1420
Ecc 10: 6 Folly is set in great **d**, and the rich sit in H4791
Hab 1: 7 their **d** shall proceed of themselves. H7613

DIKLAH
Gen 10:27 And Hadoram, and Uzal, and **D**, H1853
1Ch 1:21 Hadoram also, and Uzal, and **D**, H1853

DILEAN
Jos 15:38 And **D**, and Mizpeh, and Joktheel, H1810

DILIGENCE
Prv 4:23 Keep thy heart with all **d**; for out of it H4929
Lk 12:58 in the way, give **d** that thou mayest be *G2039*
Ro 12: 8 he that ruleth, with **d**; he that sheweth *G4710*
2Co 8: 7 and *in* all **d**, and *in* your love to *G4710*
2Ti 4: 9 Do thy **d** to come shortly unto me: *G4704*
21 Do thy **d** to come before winter. *G4704*
Heb 6:11 you do shew the same **d** to the full *G4710*
2Pt 1: 5 And beside this, giving all **d**, add to *G4710*
10 Wherefore the rather, brethren, give **d** *G4704*
Jude 3 Beloved, when I gave all **d** to write unto *G4710*

DILIGENT
Dt 19:18 And the judges shall make **d** H3190
Jos 22: 5 But take **d** heed to do the H3966
Ps 64: 6 they accomplish a **d** search: both the
77: 6 own heart: and my spirit made **d** search.
Prv 10: 4 but the hand of the **d** maketh rich. H2742
12:24 The hand of the **d** shall bear rule: but H2742
27 the substance of a **d** man *is* precious. H2742
13: 4 but the soul of the **d** shall be made fat. H2742
21: 5 The thoughts of the **d** *tend* only to H2742
22:29 Seest thou a man **d** in his business? he H4106
27:23 Be thou **d** to know the state of thy H3045
2Co 8:22 oftentimes proved **d** in many things, *G4705*
22 but now much more **d**, upon the great *G4707*
Tit 3:12 or Tychicus, be **d** to come unto me to *G4704*
2Pt 3:14 for such things, be **d** that ye may be *G4704*

DILIGENTLY
Ex 15:26 And said, If thou wilt **d** hearken to the H8085
Lev 10:16 And Moses **d** sought the goat of the sin H1875
Dt 4: 9 and keep thy soul **d**, lest thou forget the H3966
6: 7 And thou shalt teach them **d** unto thy H8150
17 Ye shall **d** keep the commandments of H8104
11:13 pass, if ye shall hearken **d** unto my H8085
22 For if ye shall **d** keep all these H8104
13:14 search, and ask **d**; and, behold, *if it be* H3190
17: 4 *of it*, and inquired **d**, and, behold, *it be* H3190
24: 8 that thou observe **d**, and do according H3966
28: 1 shalt hearken **d** unto the voice of the H8085
1Ki 20:33 Now the men did **d** observe whether H5172
Ezr 7:23 of heaven, let it be **d** done for the house H149
Job 13:17 Hear **d** my speech, and my declaration H8085
21: 2 Hear **d** my speech, and let this be your H8085
Ps 37:10 **d** consider his place, and it *shall* not *be*. H995
119: 4 commanded *us* to keep thy precepts **d**. H3966
Prv 7:15 Therefore came I forth to meet thee, **d** H7836
11:27 He that **d** seeketh good procureth H7836
23: 1 a ruler, consider **d** what *is* before thee: H995
Isa 21: 7 and he hearkened **d** with much heed: H7182
55: 2 not? hearken **d** unto me, and eat ye H8085
Jer 2:10 **d**, and see if there be such a thing. H3966
12:16 And it shall come to pass, if they will **d** H3925
17:24 And it shall come to pass, if ye **d** H8085
Zec 6:15 **d** obey the voice of the LORD your God. H8085
Mt 2: 7 of them **d** what time the star appeared. *G198*
8 Go and search **d** for the young child; *G199*
16 he had **d** inquired of the wise men.
Lk 15: 8 the house, and seek **d** till she find *it*? *G1960*
Act 18:25 he spake and taught **d** the things of the *G199*
1Ti 5:10 if she have **d** followed every good work.
2Ti 1:17 he sought me out very **d**, and found *me*. *G4706*
Tit 3:13 **d**, that nothing be wanting unto them. *G4709*
Heb 11: 6 is a rewarder of them that **d** seek him. *G1567*
12:15 Looking **d** lest any man fail of the grace *G1983*
1Pt 1:10 and searched **d**, who prophesied of the *G1830*

DIM
Gen 27: 1 and his eyes were **d**, so that he could H3543
48:10 Now the eyes of Israel were **d** for age, H3513
Dt 34: 7 was not **d**, nor his natural force abated. H3543
1Sa 3: 2 began to wax **d**, *that* he could not see; H3544
4:15 his eyes were **d**, that he could not see. H6965
Job 17: 7 Mine eye also is **d** by reason of sorrow, H3543
Isa 32: 3 see shall not be **d**, and the ears of them H8159
Lam 4: 1 How is the gold become **d**! *how* is the H6004
5:17 is faint; for these *things* our eyes are **d**. H2821

DIMINISH
Ex 5: 8 them; ye shall not **d** *ought* thereof: for H1639
21:10 her duty of marriage, shall he not **d**. H1639
Lev 25:16 of years thou shalt **d** the price of it: for H4591
Dt 4: 2 neither shall ye **d** *ought* from it, that ye H1639
12:32 shalt not add thereto, nor **d** from it. H1639
Jer 26: 2 thee to speak unto them; **d** not a word: H1639
Ezk 5:11 will I also **d** *thee*; neither shall mine H1639
29:15 the nations: for I will **d** them, that they H4591

DIMINISHED
Ex 5:11 it: yet not ought of your work shall be **d**. H1639
Prv 13:11 Wealth *gotten* by vanity shall be **d**: but H4591
Isa 21:17 of Kedar, shall be **d**: for the LORD God H4591
Jer 29: 6 ye may be increased there, and not **d**. H4591
Ezk 16:27 thee, and have **d** thine ordinary *food*, H1639

DIMINISHING
Ro 11:12 the world, and the **d** of them the riches *G2275*

DIMNAH
Jos 21:35 **D** with her suburbs, Nahalal with her H1829

DIMNESS
Isa 8:22 and darkness, **d** of anguish; and *they* H4588
9: 1 Nevertheless the **d** *shall* not *be* such as H4155

DIMON
Isa 15: 9 For the waters of **D** shall be full of H1775
9 bring more upon **D**, lions upon him that H1775

DIMONAH
Jos 15:22 And Kinah, and **D**, and Adadah, H1776

DINAH
Gen 30:21 a daughter, and called her name **D**. H1783
34: 1 And **D** the daughter of Leah, which she H1783
3 And his soul clave unto **D** the daughter H1783
5 And Jacob heard that he had defiled **D** H1783
13 because he had defiled **D** their sister: H1783
26 sword, and took **D** out of Shechem's H1783
46:15 with his daughter **D**: all the souls of his H1783

DINAH'S
Gen 34:25 Simeon and Levi, **D** brethren, took H1783

DINAITES
Ezr 4: 9 their companions; the **D**, the H1784

DINE
Gen 43:16 for *these* men shall **d** with me at noon. H398
Lk 11:37 besought him to **d** with him: and he *G709*
Jn 21:12 Jesus saith unto them, Come *and* **d**. And *G709*

DINED
Jn 21:15 So when they had **d**, Jesus saith to Simon *G709*

DINHABAH
Gen 36:32 Edom: and the name of his city *was* **D**. H1838
1Ch 1:43 of Beor: and the name of his city *was* **D**. H1838

DINNER
Prv 15:17 Better *is* a **d** of herbs where love is, than H737
Mt 22: 4 I have prepared my **d**: my oxen and *my* *G712*
Lk 11:38 that he had not first washed before **d**. *G712*
14:12 thou makest a **d** or a supper, call not *G712*

DIONYSIUS
Act 17:34 the which *was* **D** the Areopagite, and *G1354*

DIOTREPHES
3Jn 9 I wrote unto the church: but **D**, who *G1361*

DIP
Ex 12:22 of hyssop, and **d** *it* in the blood that *is* H2881
Lev 4: 6 And the priest shall **d** his finger in the H2881
17 And the priest shall **d** his finger *in* H2881
14: 6 hyssop, and shall **d** them and the living H2881
16 And the priest shall **d** his right finger in H2881
51 living bird, and **d** them in the blood of H2881
Nu 19:18 take hyssop, and **d** *it* in the water, and H2881
Dt 33:24 brethren, and let him **d** his foot in oil. H2881
Ru 2:14 of the bread, and **d** thy morsel in the H2881
Lk 16:24 that he may **d** the tip of his finger in *G911*

DIPPED
Gen 37:31 the goats, and **d** the coat in the blood; H2881
Lev 9: 9 unto him: and he **d** his finger in the H2881
Jos 3:15 bare the ark were **d** in the brim of the H2881
1Sa 14:27 in his hand, and **d** it in an honeycomb, H2881
2Ki 5:14 Then went he down, and **d** himself H2881
8:15 a thick cloth, and **d** *it* in water, and H2881

Ps 68:23 That thy foot may be **d** in the blood of H4272
Jn 13:26 a sop, when I have **d** *it*. And when he G911
26 And when he had **d** the sop, he gave *it* G1686
Rev 19:13 And he *was* clothed with a vesture **d** in G911

DIPPETH
Mt 26:23 And he answered and said, He that **d** G1686
Mk 14:20 the twelve, that **d** with me in the dish. G1686

DIRECT
Gen 46:28 unto Joseph, to **d** his face unto Goshen; H3384
Ps 5: 3 in the morning will I **d** *my prayer* unto H6186
Prv 3: 6 him, and he shall **d** thy paths. H3474
11: 5 The righteousness of the perfect shall **d** H3474
Ecc 10:10 strength: but wisdom *is* profitable to **d**. H3787
Isa 45:13 and I will **d** all his ways: he shall H3474
61: 8 offering; and I will **d** their work in H5414
Jer 10:23 not in man that walketh to **d** his steps. H3559
1Th 3:11 Lord Jesus Christ, **d** our way unto you. G2720
2Th 3: 5 And the Lord **d** your hearts into the G2720

DIRECTED
Job 32:14 Now he hath not **d** *his* words against H6186
Ps 119: 5 O that my ways were **d** to keep thy H3559
Isa 40:13 Who hath **d** the spirit of the LORD, or H8505

DIRECTETH
Job 37: 3 He **d** it under the whole heaven, and H3474
Prv 16: 9 his way: but the LORD **d** his steps. H3559
21:29 but *as for* the upright, he **d** his way. H3559

DIRECTION
Nu 21:18 digged it, by *the* **d** *of* the lawgiver, with

DIRECTLY
Nu 19: 4 of her blood **d** before the tabernacle H5227
Ezk 42:12 the way, *even* the way **d** before the wall H1903

DIRT
Jdg 3:22 out of his belly; and the **d** came out. H6574
Ps 18:42 cast them out as the **d** in the streets. H2916
Isa 57:20 rest, whose waters cast up mire and **d**. H2916

DISALLOW
Nu 30: 5 But if her father **d** her in the day that H5106

DISALLOWED
Nu 30: 5 forgive her, because her father **d** her. H5106
8 But if her husband **d** her on the day H5106
11 peace at her, *and* **d** her not: then all her H5106
1Pt 2: 4 *unto* a living stone, **d** indeed of men, but G593
7 which the builders **d**, the same is made G593

DISANNUL
Job 40: 8 Wilt thou also **d** my judgment? wilt H6565
Isa 14:27 and who shall **d** *it*? and his hand *is* H6565
Gal 3:17 after, cannot **d**, that it should make G3756

DISANNULLED
Isa 28:18 death shall be **d**, and your agreement H3722

DISANNULLETH
Gal 3:15 confirmed, no man **d**, or addeth thereto. G114

DISANNULLING
Heb 7:18 For there is verily a **d** of the G115

DISAPPOINT
Ps 17:13 Arise, O LORD, **d** him, cast him down: H6923

DISAPPOINTED
Prv 15:22 Without counsel purposes are **d**: but in H6565

DISAPPOINTETH
Job 5:12 He **d** the devices of the crafty, so that H6565

DISCERN
Gen 31:32 our brethren **d** thou what *is* thine with H5234
38:25 and she said, D, I pray thee, whose *are* H5234
2Sa 14:17 my lord the king to **d** good and bad: H8085
19:35 old: *and* can I **d** between good and evil? H3045
1Ki 3: 9 that I may **d** between good and H995
11 thyself understanding to **d** judgment; H8085
Ezr 3:13 So that the people could not **d** the noise H5234
Job 4:16 It stood still, but I could not **d** the form H5234
6:30 cannot my taste **d** perverse things? H995
Ezk 44:23 **d** between the unclean and the clean. H3045
Jna 4:11 that cannot **d** between their right H3045
Mal 3:18 Then shall ye return, and **d** between H7200
Mt 16: 3 hypocrites, ye can **d** the face of the sky; G1252
3 but can ye not ***d*** the signs of the times?
Lk 12:56 *Ye* hypocrites, ye can **d** the face of the G1381
56 but how is it that ye do not **d** this time? G1381
Heb 5:14 exercised to **d** both good and evil. G1253

DISCERNED
Gen 27:23 And he **d** him not, because his hands H5234
1Ki 20:41 **d** him that he *was* of the prophets. H5234
Prv 7: 7 And beheld among the simple ones, I **d** H995
1Co 2:14 *them*, because they are spiritually **d**. G350

DISCERNER
Heb 4:12 marrow, and *is* a **d** of the thoughts and G2924

DISCERNETH
Ecc 8: 5 man's heart **d** both time and judgment. H3045

DISCERNING
1Co 11:29 to himself, not **d** the Lord's body. G1252
12:10 to another **d** of spirits; to another G1253

DISCHARGE
Ecc 8: 8 and *there is* no **d** in *that* war; neither H4917

DISCHARGED
1Ki 5: 9 will cause them to be **d** there, and thou H5310

DISCIPLE
Mt 10:24 The **d** is not above *his* master, nor the G3101
25 It is enough for the **d** that he be as his G3101
42 in the name of a **d**, verily I say unto you, G3101
27:57 Joseph, who also himself was Jesus' **d**: G3100
Lk 6:40 The **d** is not above his master: but G3101
14:26 his own life also, he cannot be my **d**. G3101
27 and come after me, cannot be my **d**. G3101
33 not all that he hath, he cannot be my **d**. G3101
Jn 9:28 art his **d**; but we are Moses' disciples. G3101
18:15 and *so did* another **d**: that disciple was G3101
15 disciple: that **d** was known unto the G3101
16 out that other **d**, which was known unto G3101
19:26 mother, and the **d** standing by, whom G3101
27 Then saith he to the **d**, Behold thy G3101
27 that **d** took her unto his own *home*. G3101
38 being a **d** of Jesus, but secretly G3101
20: 2 and to the other **d**, whom Jesus loved, G3101
3 that other **d**, and came to the sepulchre. G3101
4 and the other **d** did outrun Peter, and G3101
8 Then went in also that other **d**, which G3101
21: 7 Therefore that **d** whom Jesus loved G3101
20 Then Peter, turning about, seeth the **d** G3101
23 brethren, that that **d** should not die: yet G3101
24 This is the **d** which testifieth of these G3101
Act 9:10 And there was a certain **d** at G3101
26 him, and believed not that he was a **d**. G3101
36 Now there was at Joppa a certain **d** G3102
16: 1 behold, a certain **d** was there, named G3101
21:16 an old **d**, with whom we should lodge. G3101

DISCIPLES
Isa 8:16 testimony, seal the law among my **d**. H3928
Mt 5: 1 when he was set, his **d** came unto him: G3101
8:21 And another of his **d** said unto him, G3101
23 entered into a ship, his **d** followed him. G3101
25 And his **d** came to *him*, and awoke G3101
9:10 came and sat down with him and his **d**. G3101
11 *it*, they said unto his **d**, Why eateth your G3101
14 Then came to him the **d** of John, G3101
14 Pharisees fast oft, but thy **d** fast not? G3101
19 and followed him, and *so did* his **d**. G3101
37 Then saith he unto his **d**, The harvest G3101
10: 1 *him* his twelve **d**, he gave them power G3101
11: 1 his twelve **d**, he departed thence G3101
2 the works of Christ, he sent two of his **d**, G3101
12: 1 the corn; and his **d** were an hungred, G3101
2 him, Behold, thy **d** do that which is not G3101
49 hand toward his **d**, and said, Behold my G3101
13:10 And the **d** came, and said unto him, G3101
36 the house: and his **d** came unto him, G3101
14:12 And his **d** came, and took up the body, G3101
15 And when it was evening, his **d** came to G3101
19 *his* **d**, and the disciples to the multitude. G3101
19 disciples, and the **d** to the multitude. G3101
22 constrained his **d** to get into a ship, G3101
26 And when the **d** saw him walking on G3101
15: 2 Why do thy **d** transgress the tradition G3101
12 Then came his **d**, and said unto him, G3101
23 a word. And his **d** came and besought G3101
32 Then Jesus called his **d** *unto him*, and G3101
33 And his **d** say unto him, Whence G3101
36 his **d**, and the disciples to the multitude. G3101
36 disciples, and the **d** to the multitude. G3101
16: 5 And when his **d** were come to the other G3101
13 he asked his **d**, saying, Whom do men G3101
20 Then charged he his **d** that they should G3101
21 to shew unto his **d**, how that he must go G3101
24 Then said Jesus unto his **d**, If any *man* G3101
17: 6 And when the **d** heard *it*, they fell on G3101
10 And his **d** asked him, saying, Why then G3101
13 Then the **d** understood that he spake G3101
16 And I brought him to thy **d**, and they G3101
19 Then came the **d** to Jesus apart, and G3101
18: 1 At the same time came the **d** unto G3101
19:10 His **d** say unto him, If the case of the G3101
13 and pray: and the **d** rebuked them. G3101
23 Then said Jesus unto his **d**, Verily I say G3101
25 When his **d** heard *it*, they were G3101
20:17 took the twelve **d** apart in the way, and G3101
21: 1 mount of Olives, then sent Jesus two **d**, G3101
6 And the **d** went, and did as Jesus G3101
20 And when the **d** saw *it*, they marvelled, G3101
22:16 And they sent out unto him their **d** G3101
23: 1 Jesus to the multitude, and to his **d**, G3101
24: 1 temple: and his **d** came to *him* for to G3101
3 mount of Olives, the **d** came unto him G3101
26: 1 all these sayings, he said unto his **d**, G3101
8 But when his **d** saw *it*, they had G3101
17 bread the **d** came to Jesus, saying G3101
18 the passover at thy house with my **d**. G3101
19 And the **d** did as Jesus had appointed G3101
26 **d**, and said, Take, eat; this is my body. G3101
35 deny thee. Likewise also said all the **d**. G3101
36 and saith unto the **d**, Sit ye here, while I G3101
40 And he cometh unto the **d**, and findeth G3101
45 Then cometh he to his **d**, and saith unto G3101
56 Then all the **d** forsook him, and fled. G3101
27:64 third day, lest his **d** come by night, and G3101
28: 7 And go quickly, and tell his **d** that he is G3101
8 joy; and did run to bring his **d** word. G3101
9 And as they went to tell his **d**, behold, G3101
13 Saying, Say ye, His **d** came by night, G3101
16 Then the eleven **d** went away into G3101
Mk 2:15 with Jesus and his **d**: for there were G3101
16 they said unto his **d**, How is it that he G3101
18 And the **d** of John and of the Pharisees G3101
18 him, Why do the **d** of John and of the G3101
18 of the Pharisees fast, but thy **d** fast not? G3101
23 day; and his **d** began, as they went, G3101
3: 7 But Jesus withdrew himself with his **d** G3101
9 And he spake to his **d**, that a small ship G3101
4:34 alone, he expounded all things to his **d**. G3101
5:31 And his **d** said unto him, Thou seest G3101
6: 1 his own country; and his **d** follow him. G3101
29 And when his **d** heard *of it*, they came G3101
35 now far spent, his **d** came unto him, G3101
41 gave *them* to his **d** to set before them; G3101
45 And straightway he constrained his **d** G3101
7: 2 And when they saw some of his **d** eat G3101
5 Why walk not thy **d** according to the G3101
17 **d** asked him concerning the parable. G3101
8: 1 his **d** *unto him*, and saith unto them, G3101
4 And his **d** answered him, From whence G3101
6 and gave to his **d** to set before *them*; G3101
10 a ship with his **d**, and came into the G3101
14 Now *the* **d** had forgotten to take bread,
27 And Jesus went out, and his **d**, into the G3101
27 way he asked his **d**, saying unto them, G3101
33 and looked on his **d**, he rebuked Peter, G3101
34 *unto him* with his **d** also, he said unto G3101
9:14 And when he came to *his* **d**, he saw a G3101
18 and I spake to thy **d** that they should G3101
28 come into the house, his **d** asked him G3101
31 For he taught his **d**, and said unto G3101
10:10 And in the house his **d** asked him again G3101
13 *his* **d** rebuked those that brought *them*. G3101
23 and saith unto his **d**, How hardly shall G3101
24 And the **d** were astonished at his G3101
46 out of Jericho with his **d** and a great G3101
11: 1 of Olives, he sendeth forth two of his **d**, G3101
14 hereafter for ever. And his **d** heard *it*. G3101
12:43 And he called *unto him* his **d**, and saith G3101
13: 1 the temple, one of his **d** saith unto him, G3101
14:12 the passover, his **d** said unto him, G3101
13 And he sendeth forth two of his **d**, and G3101
14 I shall eat the passover with my **d**? G3101
16 And his **d** went forth, and came into G3101
32 to his **d**, Sit ye here, while I shall pray. G3101
16: 7 But go your way, tell his **d** and Peter G3101

Lk 5:30 against his **d**, saying, Why do ye eat G3101
33 And they said unto him, Why do the **d** G3101
33 and likewise *the d* of the Pharisees; but G3588
6: 1 fields; and his **d** plucked the ears of G3101
13 *unto him* his **d**: and of them he chose G3101
17 the company of his **d**, and a great G3101
20 And he lifted up his eyes on his **d**, and G3101
7:11 his **d** went with him, and much people. G3101
18 And the **d** of John shewed him of all G3101
19 And John calling *unto him* two of his **d** G3101
8: 9 And his **d** asked him, saying, What G3101
22 into a ship with his **d**: and he said unto G3101
9: 1 Then he called his twelve **d** together, G3101
14 And he said to his **d**, Make them sit G3101
16 to the **d** to set before the multitude. G3101
18 alone praying, his **d** were with him: G3101
40 And I besought thy **d** to cast him out; G3101
43 which Jesus did, he said unto his **d**, G3101
54 And when his **d** James and John saw G3101
10:23 And he turned him unto *his* **d**, and said G3101
11: 1 he ceased, one of his **d** said unto him, G3101
1 us to pray, as John also taught his **d**. G3101
12: 1 to say unto his **d** first of all, Beware ye G3101
22 And he said unto his **d**, Therefore I say G3101
16: 1 And he said also unto his **d**, There was G3101
17: 1 Then said he unto the **d**, It is impossible G3101
22 And he said unto the **d**, The days will G3101
18:15 when *his* **d** saw *it*, they rebuked them. G3101
19:29 *mount* of Olives, he sent two of his **d**, G3101
37 multitude of the **d** began to rejoice and G3101
39 said unto him, Master, rebuke thy **d**. G3101
20:45 of all the people he said unto his **d**, G3101
22:11 I shall eat the passover with my **d**? G3101
39 of Olives; and his **d** also followed him. G3101
45 **d**, he found them sleeping for sorrow, G3101
Jn 1:35 day after John stood, and two of his **d**; G3101
37 And the two **d** heard him speak, and G3101
2: 2 And both Jesus was called, and his **d**, to G3101
11 his glory; and his **d** believed on him. G3101
12 brethren, and his **d**: and they continued G3101
17 And his **d** remembered that it was G3101
22 from the dead, his **d** remembered that G3101
3:22 After these things came Jesus and his **d** G3101
25 John's **d** and the Jews about purifying. G3101
4: 1 made and baptized more **d** than John, G3101
2 Jesus himself baptized not, but his **d**,) G3101
8 (For his **d** were gone away unto the city G3101
27 And upon this came his **d**, and G3101
31 In the mean while his **d** prayed him, G3101
33 Therefore said the **d** one to another, G3101
6: 3 a mountain, and there he sat with his **d**. G3101
8 One of his **d**, Andrew, Simon Peter's G3101
11 distributed to the **d**, and the disciples to G3101
11 disciples, and the **d** to them that were G3101
12 filled, he said unto his **d**, Gather up the G3101
16 And when even was *now* come, his **d** G3101
22 one whereinto his **d** were entered, and G3101
22 went not with his **d** into the boat, but G3101
22 but *that* his **d** were gone away alone; G3101
24 not there, neither his **d**, they also took G3101
60 Many therefore of his **d**, when they had G3101
61 When Jesus knew in himself that his **d** G3101
66 From that *time* many of his **d** went G3101
7: 3 into Judaea, that thy **d** also may see the G3101
8:31 in my word, *then* are ye my **d** indeed; G3101
9: 2 And his **d** asked him, saying, Master, G3101
27 ye hear *it* again? will ye also be his **d**? G3101
28 art his disciple; but we are Moses' **d**. G3101
11: 7 Then after that saith he to *his* **d**, Let us G3101
8 *His* **d** say unto him, Master, the Jews of G3101
12 Then said his **d**, Lord, if he sleep, he G3101
54 and there continued with his **d**. G3101
12: 4 Then saith one of his **d**, Judas Iscariot, G3101
16 These things understood not his **d** at G3101
13:22 Then the **d** looked one on another, G3101
23 bosom one of his **d**, whom Jesus loved. G3101
35 are my **d**, if ye have love one to another. G3101
15: 8 ye bear much fruit; so shall ye be my **d**. G3101
16:17 Then said *some* of his **d** among G3101
29 His **d** said unto him, Lo, now speakest G3101
18: 1 forth with his **d** over the brook Cedron, G3101
1 into the which he entered, and his **d**. G3101
2 ofttimes resorted thither with his **d**. G3101
17 *one* of this man's **d**? He saith, I am not. G3101
19 asked Jesus of his **d**, and of his doctrine. G3101
25 his **d**? He denied *it*, and said, I am not. G3101
20:10 Then the **d** went away again unto their G3101
18 Mary Magdalene came and told the **d** G3101
19 shut where the **d** were assembled for G3101
Jn 20:20 the **d** glad, when they saw the Lord. G3101
25 The other **d** therefore said unto him, G3101
26 And after eight days again his **d** were G3101
30 **d**, which are not written in this book: G3101
21: 1 again to the **d** at the sea of Tiberias; G3101
2 *sons* of Zebedee, and two other of his **d**. G3101
4 but the **d** knew not that it was Jesus. G3101
8 And the other **d** came in a little ship; G3101
12 And none of the **d** durst ask him, Who G3101
14 **d**, after that he was risen from the dead. G3101
Act 1:15 up in the midst of the **d**, and said, (the G3101
6: 1 the number of the **d** was multiplied, G3101
2 multitude of the **d** *unto them*, and said, G3101
7 and the number of the **d** multiplied in G3101
9: 1 against the **d** of the Lord, went unto G3101
19 with the **d** which were at Damascus. G3101
25 Then the **d** took him by night, and let G3101
26 join himself to the **d**: but they were all G3101
38 nigh to Joppa, and the **d** had heard that G3101
11:26 much people. And the **d** were called G3101
29 Then the **d**, every man according to his G3101
13:52 And the **d** were filled with joy, and with G3101
14:20 Howbeit, as the **d** stood round about G3101
22 Confirming the souls of the **d**, *and* G3101
28 there they abode long time with the **d**. G3101
15:10 the neck of the **d**, which neither our G3101
18:23 in order, strengthening all the **d**. G3101
27 exhorting the **d** to receive him: who, G3101
19: 1 came to Ephesus: and finding certain **d**, G3101
9 and separated the **d**, disputing daily in G3101
30 unto the people, the **d** suffered him not. G3101
20: 1 unto *him* the **d**, and embraced *them*, G3101
7 the week, when the **d** came together to G3101
30 things, to draw away **d** after them. G3101
21: 4 And finding **d**, we tarried there seven G3101
16 There went with us also *certain* of the **d** G3101

DISCIPLES'
Jn 13: 5 began to wash the **d** feet, and to wipe G3101

DISCIPLINE
Job 36:10 He openeth also their ear to **d**, and H4148

DISCLOSE
Isa 26:21 earth also shall **d** her blood, and shall H1540

DISCOMFITED
Ex 17:13 And Joshua **d** Amalek and his people H2522
Nu 14:45 them, and **d** them, *even* unto Hormah. H3807
Jos 10:10 And the LORD **d** them before Israel, H2000
Jdg 4:15 And the LORD **d** Sisera, and all *his* H2000
8:12 and Zalmunna, and **d** all the host. H2729
1Sa 7:10 Philistines, and **d** them; and they were H2000
2Sa 22:15 scattered them; lightning, and **d** them. H2000
Ps 18:14 and he shot out lightnings, and **d** them. H2000
Isa 31: 8 sword, and his young men shall be **d**. H4522

DISCOMFITURE
1Sa 14:20 his fellow, *and there was* a very great **d**. H4103

DISCONTENTED
1Sa 22: 2 every one *that was* **d**, gathered H4751+H5315

DISCONTINUE
Jer 17: 4 And thou, even thyself, shalt **d** from H8058

DISCORD
Prv 6:14 mischief continually; he soweth **d**. H4066
19 and he that soweth **d** among brethren. H4090

DISCOURAGE
Nu 32: 7 And wherefore **d** ye the heart of the H5106

DISCOURAGED
Nu 21: 4 people was much **d** because of the way. H7114
32: 9 saw the land, they **d** the heart of the H5106
Dt 1:21 said unto thee; fear not, neither be **d**. H2865
28 our brethren have **d** our heart, saying, H4549
Isa 42: 4 He shall not fail nor be **d**, till he have set H7533
Col 3:21 not your children *to anger*, lest they be **d**. G120

DISCOVER
Dt 22:30 father's wife, nor **d** his father's skirt. H1540
1Sa 14: 8 and we will **d** ourselves unto them. H1540
Job 41:13 Who can **d** the face of his garment? *or* H1540
Prv 18: 2 but that his heart may **d** itself. H1540
25: 9 *himself*; and **d** not a secret to another: H1540
Isa 3:17 and the LORD will **d** their secret parts. H6168
Jer 13:26 Therefore will I **d** thy skirts upon thy H2834
Lam 4:22 O daughter of Edom; he will **d** thy sins. H1540
Ezk 16:37 thee, and will **d** thy nakedness unto H1540
Hos 2:10 And now will I **d** her lewdness in the H1540
Mic 1: 6 and I will **d** the foundations thereof. H1540
Nah 3: 5 of hosts; and I will **d** thy skirts upon H1540

DISCOVERED
Ex 20:26 that thy nakedness be not **d** thereon. H1540
Lev 20:18 he hath **d** her fountain, and she H6168
1Sa 14:11 And both of them **d** themselves unto H1540
22: 6 When Saul heard that David was **d**, and H3045
2Sa 22:16 of the world were **d**, at the rebuking of H1540
Ps 18:15 of the world were **d** at thy rebuke, O H1540
Isa 22: 8 And he **d** the covering of Judah, and H1540
57: 8 for thou hast **d** *thyself to another* than H1540
Jer 13:22 thy skirts **d**, *and* thy heels made bare. H1540
Lam 2:14 and they have not **d** thine iniquity, to H1540
Ezk 13:14 thereof shall be **d**, and it shall fall, and H1540
16:36 and thy nakedness **d** through thy H1540
57 Before thy wickedness was **d**, as at the H1540
21:24 transgressions are **d**, so that in all your H1540
22:10 In thee have they **d** their fathers' H1540
23:10 These **d** her nakedness: they took her H1540
18 So she **d** her whoredoms, and H1540
18 whoredoms, and **d** her nakedness: then H1540
29 shall be **d**, both thy lewdness and H1540
Hos 7: 1 of Ephraim was **d**, and the wickedness H1540
Act 21: 3 Now when we had **d** Cyprus, we left it on G398
27:39 not the land: but they **d** a certain creek G2657

DISCOVERETH
Job 12:22 He **d** deep things out of darkness, and H1540
Ps 29: 9 to calve, and **d** the forests: and in his H2834

DISCOVERING
Hab 3:13 **d** the foundation unto the neck. Selah. H6168

DISCREET
Gen 41:33 look out a man **d** and wise, and set him H995
39 *there is* none so **d** and wise as thou *art*: H995
Tit 2: 5 *To be* **d**, chaste, keepers at home, good, G4998

DISCREETLY
Mk 12:34 that he answered **d**, he said unto him, G3562

DISCRETION
Ps 112: 5 lendeth: he will guide his affairs with **d**. H4941
Prv 1: 4 to the young man knowledge and **d**. H4209
2:11 **D** shall preserve thee, understanding H4209
3:21 thine eyes: keep sound wisdom and **d**: H4209
5: 2 That thou mayest regard **d**, and *that* H4209
11:22 *so is* a fair woman which is without **d**. H2940
19:11 The **d** of a man deferreth his anger; H7922
Isa 28:26 For his God doth instruct him to **d**, *and* H4941
Jer 10:12 hath stretched out the heavens by his **d**. H8394

DISDAINED
1Sa 17:42 and saw David, he **d** him: for he was *but* H959
Job 30: 1 **d** to have set with the dogs of my flock. H3988

DISEASE
2Ki 1: 2 Ekron whether I shall recover of this **d**. H2483
8: 8 by him, saying, Shall I recover of this **d**? H2483
9 to thee, saying, Shall I recover of this **d**? H2483
2Ch 16:12 in his feet, until his **d** *was* exceeding H2483
12 *great*: yet in his **d** he sought not to the H2483
21:15 great sickness by **d** of thy bowels, until H4245
18 him in his bowels with an incurable **d**. H2483
Job 30:18 By the great force *of my* **d** is my garment
Ps 38: 7 **d**: and *there is* no soundness in my flesh.
41: 8 An evil **d**, *say they*, cleaveth fast unto H1697
Ecc 6: 2 it: this *is* vanity, and it *is* an evil **d**. H2483
Mt 4:23 and all manner of **d** among the people. G3119
9:35 and every **d** among the people. G3119
10: 1 of sickness and all manner of **d**. G3119
Jn 5: 4 made whole of whatsoever **d** he had. G3553

DISEASED
1Ki 15:23 time of his old age he was **d** in his feet. H2470
2Ch 16:12 of his reign was **d** in his feet, until his H2456
Ezk 34: 4 The **d** have ye not strengthened, H2470
21 and pushed all the **d** with your horns, H2470
Mt 9:20 And, behold, a woman, which was **d**
14:35 unto him all that were **d**; G2560+G2192
Mk 1:32 all that were **d**, and them that G2560+G2192
Jn 6: 2 which he did on them that were **d**. G770

DISEASES
Ex 15:26 put none of these **d** upon thee, which I H4245

Dt 7:15 none of the evil **d** of Egypt, which thou H4064
28:60 upon thee all the **d** of Egypt, which H4064
2Ch 21:19 so he died of sore **d**. And his people H8463
24:25 left him in great **d**,) his own servants H4251
Ps 103: 3 thine iniquities; who healeth all thy **d**; H8463
Mt 4:24 taken with divers **d** and torments, and *G3554*
Mk 1:34 were sick of divers **d**, and cast out many *G3554*
Lk 4:40 sick with divers **d** brought them unto *G3554*
6:17 to hear him, and to be healed of their **d**; *G3554*
9: 1 authority over all devils, and to cure **d**. *G3554*
Act 19:12 or aprons, and the **d** departed from *G3554*
28: 9 **d** in the island, came, and were healed: *G769*

DISFIGURE
Mt 6:16 for they **d** their faces, that they *G853*

DISGRACE
Jer 14:21 sake, do not **d** the throne of thy glory: H5034

DISGUISE
1Ki 14: 2 I pray thee, and **d** thyself, that thou be H8138
22:30 I will **d** myself, and enter into H2664
2Ch 18:29 I will **d** myself, and will go H2664

DISGUISED
1Sa 28: 8 And Saul **d** himself, and put on other H2664
1Ki 20:38 and **d** himself with ashes upon his face. H2664
22:30 **d** himself, and went into the battle. H2664
2Ch 18:29 **d** himself; and they went to the battle. H2664
35:22 from him, but **d** himself, that he might H2664

DISGUISETH
Job 24:15 No eye shall see me: and **d** *his* face. H5643

DISH
Jdg 5:25 she brought forth butter in a lordly **d**. H5602
2Ki 21:13 as *a man* wipeth a **d**, wiping *it*, and H6747
Mt 26:23 me in the **d**, the same shall betray me. *G5165*
Mk 14:20 twelve, that dippeth with me in the **d**. *G5165*

DISHAN
Gen 36:21 And Dishon, and Ezer, and **D**: these *are* H1789
28 The children of **D** *are* these; Uz, and H1789
30 Duke Dishon, duke Ezer, duke **D**: these H1789
1Ch 1:38 Anah, and Dishon, and Ezer, and **D**. H1789
42 Jakan. The sons of **D**; Uz, and Aran. H1789

DISHES
Ex 25:29 And thou shalt make the **d** thereof, and H7086
37:16 upon the table, his **d**, and his spoons, H7086
Nu 4: 7 put thereon the **d**, and the spoons, and H7086

DISHON
Gen 36:21 And **D**, and Ezer, and Dishan: these *are* H1787
25 And the children of Anah *were* these; **D**, H1787
26 And these *are* the children of **D**; H1789
30 Duke **D**, duke Ezer, duke Dishan: these H1787
1Ch 1:38 Anah, and **D**, and Ezer, and Dishan. H1787
41 The sons of Anah; **D**. And the sons of H1787
41 And the sons of **D**; Amram, and H1787

DISHONEST
Ezk 22:13 mine hand at thy **d** gain which thou H1215
27 *and* to destroy souls, to get **d** gain. H1215

DISHONESTY
2Co 4: 2 the hidden things of **d**, not walking in *G152*

DISHONOUR
Ezr 4:14 us to see the king's **d**, therefore have we H6173
Ps 35:26 **d** that magnify *themselves* against me. H3639
69:19 **d**: mine adversaries *are* all before thee. H3639
71:13 *with* reproach and **d** that seek my hurt. H3639
Prv 6:33 A wound and **d** shall he get; and his H7036
Jn 8:49 but I honour my Father, and ye do **d** me. *G818*
Ro 1:24 **d** their own bodies between themselves: *G818*
9:21 vessel unto honour, and another unto **d**? *G819*
1Co 15:43 It is sown in **d**; it is raised in glory: it is *G819*
2Co 6: 8 By honour and **d**, by evil report and good *G819*
2Ti 2:20 and some to honour, and some to **d**. *G819*

DISHONOUREST
Ro 2:23 through breaking the law **d** thou God? *G818*

DISHONOURETH
Mic 7: 6 For the son **d** the father, the daughter H5034
1Co 11: 4 having *his* head covered, **d** his head. *G2617*
5 head uncovered **d** her head: for that is *G2617*

DISINHERIT
Nu 14:12 pestilence, and **d** them, and will make H3423

DISMAYED
Dt 31: 8 forsake thee: fear not, neither be **d**. H2865
Jos 1: 9 neither be thou **d**: for the LORD thy God H2865
8: 1 neither be thou **d**: take all the people of H2865
10:25 Fear not, nor be **d**, be strong and of H2865
1Sa 17:11 they were **d**, and greatly afraid. H2865
2Ki 19:26 power, they were **d** and confounded; H2865
1Ch 22:13 of good courage; dread not, nor be **d**. H2865
28:20 *it*: fear not, nor be **d**: for the LORD God, H2865
2Ch 20:15 Be not afraid nor **d** by reason of this H2865
17 fear not, nor be **d**; to morrow go out H2865
32: 7 be not afraid nor **d** for the king of H2865
Isa 21: 3 hearing *of it*; I was **d** at the seeing *of it*. H926
37:27 power, they were **d** and confounded: H2865
41:10 with thee: be not **d**; for I *am* thy God: I H8159
23 we may be **d**, and behold *it* together. H8159
Jer 1:17 thee: be not **d** at their faces, lest I H2865
8: 9 The wise *men* are ashamed, they are **d** H2865
10: 2 and be not **d** at the signs of heaven; H2865
2 heaven; for the heathen are **d** at them. H2865
17:18 let them be **d**, but let not me be H2865
18 but let not me be **d**: bring upon them H2865
23: 4 no more, nor be **d**, neither shall they be H2865
30:10 LORD; neither be **d**, O Israel: for, lo, I H2865
46: 5 Wherefore have I seen them **d** *and* H2844
27 Jacob, and be not **d**, O Israel: for, H2865
48: 1 taken: Misgab is confounded and **d**. H2865
49:37 For I will cause Elam to be **d** before H2865
50:36 her mighty men; and they shall be **d**. H2865
Ezk 2: 6 words, nor be **d** at their looks, though H2865
3: 9 not, neither be **d** at their looks, though H2865
Oba 9 O Teman, shall be **d**, to the end that H2865

DISMAYING
Jer 48:39 derision and a **d** to all them about him. H4288

DISMISSED
2Ch 23: 8 Jehoiada the priest **d** not the courses. H6362
Act 15:30 So when they were **d**, they came to *G630*
19:41 And when he had thus spoken, he **d** the *G630*

DISOBEDIENCE
Ro 5:19 For as by one man's **d** many were *G3876*
2Co 10: 6 all **d**, when your obedience is fulfilled. *G3876*
Eph 2: 2 that now worketh in the children of **d**: *G543*
5: 6 the wrath of God upon the children of **d**. *G543*
Col 3: 6 of God cometh on the children of **d**: *G543*
Heb 2: 2 transgression and **d** received a just *G3876*

DISOBEDIENT
1Ki 13:26 of God, who was **d** unto the word of the H4784
Neh 9:26 Nevertheless they were **d**, and rebelled H4784
Lk 1:17 children, and the **d** to the wisdom of the *G545*
Act 26:19 Whereupon, O king Agrippa, I was not **d** *G545*
Ro 1:30 inventors of evil things, **d** to parents, *G545*
10:21 hands unto a **d** and gainsaying people. *G544*
1Ti 1: 9 for the lawless and **d**, for the ungodly and *G506*
2Ti 3: 2 **d** to parents, unthankful, unholy, *G545*
Tit 1:16 **d**, and unto every good work reprobate. *G545*
3: 3 sometimes foolish, **d**, deceived, serving *G545*
1Pt 2: 7 them which be **d**, the stone which the *G544*
8 **d**: whereunto also they were appointed. *G544*
3:20 Which sometime were **d**, when once the *G544*

DISOBEYED
1Ki 13:21 as thou hast **d** the mouth of the LORD, H4784

DISORDERLY
2Th 3: 6 brother that walketh **d**, and not after the *G814*
7 we behaved not ourselves **d** among you; *G812*
11 **d**, working not at all, but are busybodies. *G814*

DISPATCH
Ezk 23:47 with stones, and **d** them with their H1254

DISPENSATION
1Co 9:17 a **d** *of the gospel* is committed unto me. *G3622*
Eph 1:10 That in the **d** of the fulness of times he *G3622*
3: 2 If ye have heard of the **d** of the grace of *G3622*
Col 1:25 according to the **d** of God which is *G3622*

DISPERSE
1Sa 14:34 And Saul said, **D** yourselves among the H6327
Prv 15: 7 The lips of the wise **d** knowledge: but H2219
Ezk 12:15 nations, and **d** them in the countries. H2219
20:23 and **d** them through the countries; H2219
22:15 among the heathen, and **d** thee in the H2219
29:12 and will **d** them through the countries. H2219
30:23 and will **d** them through the countries. H2219
26 the nations, and **d** them among the H2219

DISPERSED
2Ch 11:23 And he dealt wisely, and **d** of all his H6555
Est 3: 8 abroad and **d** among the people in H6504
Ps 112: 9 He hath **d**, he hath given to the poor; his H6340
Prv 5:16 Let thy fountains be **d** abroad, *and* H6327
Isa 11:12 together the **d** of Judah from the four H5310
Ezk 36:19 and they were **d** through the countries: H2219
Zep 3:10 of my **d**, shall bring mine offering. H6327
Jn 7:35 him? will he go unto the **d** among the *G1290*
Act 5:37 *even* as many as obeyed him, were **d**. *G1287*
2Co 9: 9 (As it is written, He hath **d** abroad; he *G4650*

DISPERSIONS
Jer 25:34 and of your **d** are accomplished; and H8600

DISPLAYED
Ps 60: 4 it may be **d** because of the truth. Selah. H5127

DISPLEASE
Gen 31:35 And she said to her father, Let it not **d** H2734
Nu 22:34 therefore, if it **d** thee, I will get H7489+H5869
1Sa 29: 7 that thou **d** not the lords of H7451+H5869
2Sa 11:25 not this thing **d** thee, for the H7489+H5869
Prv 24:18 Lest the LORD see *it*, and it **d** H7489+H5869

DISPLEASED
Gen 38:10 And the thing which he did **d** H7489+H5869
48:17 of Ephraim, it **d** him: and he H7489+H5869
Nu 11: 1 complained, it **d** the LORD: and H7451+H241
10 greatly; Moses also was **d**. H7489+H5869
1Sa 8: 6 But the thing **d** Samuel, when H7489+H5869
18: 8 the saying **d** him; and he said, H7489+H5869
2Sa 6: 8 And David was **d**, because the LORD H2734
11:27 David had done **d** the LORD. H7489+H5869
1Ki 1: 6 And his father had not **d** him at any H6087
20:43 heavy and **d**, and came to Samaria. H2198
21: 4 house heavy and **d** because of the word H2198
1Ch 13:11 And David was **d**, because the LORD H2734
21: 7 And God was **d** with this thing; H3415+H5869
Ps 60: 1 hast been **d**; O turn thyself to us again. H599
Isa 59:15 saw *it*, and it **d** him that *there* H3415+H5869
Dan 6:14 words, was sore **d** with himself, and set H888
Jna 4: 1 But it **d** Jonah exceedingly, H7489+H5869
Hab 3: 8 Was the LORD **d** against the rivers? H2734
Zec 1: 2 The LORD hath been sore **d** with your H7107
15 And I am very sore **d** with the heathen H7107
15 for I was but a little **d**, and they helped H7107
Mt 21:15 to the son of David; they were sore **d**, *G23*
Mk 10:14 But when Jesus saw *it*, he was much **d**, *G23*
41 to be much **d** with James and John. *G23*
Act 12:20 And Herod was highly **d** with them of *G2371*

DISPLEASURE
Dt 9:19 For I was afraid of the anger and hot **d**, H2534
Jdg 15: 3 the Philistines, though I do them a **d**. H7451
Ps 2: 5 in his wrath, and vex them in his sore **d**. H2740
6: 1 anger, neither chasten me in thy hot **d**. H2534
38: 1 wrath: neither chasten me in thy hot **d**. H2534

DISPOSED
Job 34:13 earth? or who hath **d** the whole world? H7760
37:15 Dost thou know when God **d** them, and H7760
Act 18:27 And when he was **d** to pass into *G1014*
1Co 10:27 *a feast*, and ye be **d** to go; whatsoever is *G2309*

DISPOSING
Prv 16:33 but the whole **d** thereof *is* of the LORD. H4941

DISPOSITION
Act 7:53 Who have received the law by the **d** of *G1296*

DISPOSSESS
Nu 33:53 And ye shall **d** *the inhabitants* of the H3423
Dt 7:17 *are* more than I; how can I **d** them? H3423

DISPOSSESSED
Nu 32:39 it, and **d** the Amorite which *was* in it. H3423
Jdg 11:23 So now the LORD God of Israel hath **d** H3423

DISPUTATION
Act 15: 2 small dissension and **d** with them, they *G4803*

DISPUTATIONS
Ro 14: 1 faith receive ye, *but* not to doubtful **d**. *G1253*

DISPUTE
Job 23: 7 There the righteous might **d** with him; H3198

DISPUTED
Mk 9:33 that ye **d** among yourselves by the way? *G1260*
34 the way they had **d** among themselves, *G1256*
Act 9:29 Lord Jesus, and **d** against the Grecians: *G4802*
17:17 Therefore **d** he in the synagogue with *G1256*
Jude 9 with the devil he **d** about the body of *G1256*

DISPUTER
1Co 1:20 where *is* the **d** of this world? hath *G4804*

DISPUTING
Act 6: 9 of Cilicia and of Asia, **d** with Stephen. *G4802*
15: 7 And when there had been much **d**, Peter *G4803*
19: 8 of three months, **d** and persuading the *G1256*
9 **d** daily in the school of one Tyrannus. *G1256*
24:12 me in the temple **d** with any man, *G1256*

DISPUTINGS
Php 2:14 all things without murmurings and **d**: *G1261*
1Ti 6: 5 Perverse **d** of men of corrupt minds, *G3859*

DISQUIET
Jer 50:34 land, and **d** the inhabitants of Babylon. H7264

DISQUIETED
1Sa 28:15 Why hast thou **d** me, to bring me up? H7264
Ps 39: 6 surely they are **d** in vain: he heapeth H1993
42: 5 and *why* art thou **d** in me? hope thou in H1993
11 and why art thou **d** within me? hope H1993
43: 5 and why art thou **d** within me? hope in H1993
Prv 30:21 For three *things* the earth is **d**, and for H7264

DISQUIETNESS
Ps 38: 8 roared by reason of the **d** of my heart. H5100

DISSEMBLED
Jos 7:11 also stolen, and **d** also, and they have H3584
Jer 42:20 For ye **d** in your hearts, when ye sent H8582
Gal 2:13 And the other Jews **d** likewise with him; *G4942*

DISSEMBLERS
Ps 26: 4 vain persons, neither will I go in with **d**. H5956

DISSEMBLETH
Prv 26:24 He that hateth **d** with his lips, and H5234

DISSENSION
Act 15: 2 had no small **d** and disputation with *G4714*
23: 7 so said, there arose a **d** between the *G4714*
10 And when there arose a great **d**, the *G4714*

DISSIMULATION
Ro 12: 9 *Let* love be without **d**. Abhor that which *G505*
Gal 2:13 also was carried away with their **d**. *G5272*

DISSOLVE
Dan 5:16 and **d** doubts: now if thou H8271

DISSOLVED
Ps 75: 3 are **d**: I bear up the pillars of it. Selah. H4127
Isa 14:31 Palestina, *art* **d**: for there shall come H4127
24:19 clean **d**, the earth is moved exceedingly. H6565
34: 4 And all the host of heaven shall be **d**, H4743
Nah 2: 6 be opened, and the palace shall be **d**. H4127
2Co 5: 1 tabernacle were **d**, we have a building *G2647*
2Pt 3:11 these things shall be **d**, what manner *of* *G3089*
12 on fire shall be **d**, and the elements *G3089*

DISSOLVEST
Job 30:22 to ride *upon it*, and **d** my substance. H4127

DISSOLVING
Dan 5:12 sentences, and **d** of doubts, were found H8271

DISTAFF
Prv 31:19 the spindle, and her hands hold the **d**. H6418

DISTANT
Ex 36:22 One board had two tenons, equally **d** H7947

DISTIL
Dt 32: 2 my speech shall **d** as the dew, as the H5140
Job 36:28 Which the clouds do drop *and* **d** upon H7491

DISTINCTION
1Co 14: 7 except they give a **d** in the sounds, how *G1293*

DISTINCTLY
Neh 8: 8 in the law of God **d**, and gave the sense, H6567

DISTRACTED
Ps 88:15 up: *while* I suffer thy terrors I am **d**. H6323

DISTRACTION
1Co 7:35 ye may attend upon the Lord without **d**. *G563*

DISTRESS
Gen 35: 3 in the day of my **d**, and was with me in H6869
42:21 hear; therefore is this **d** come upon us. H6869
Dt 2: 9 And the LORD said unto me, **D** not the H6696
19 of Ammon, **d** them not, nor meddle H6696
28:53 wherewith thine enemies shall **d** thee: H6693
55 enemies shall **d** thee in all thy gates. H6693
57 thine enemy shall **d** thee in thy gates. H6693
Jdg 11: 7 ye come unto me now when ye are in **d**? H6887
1Sa 22: 2 And every one *that was* in **d**, and every H4689
2Sa 22: 7 In my **d** I called upon the LORD, and H6862
1Ki 1:29 that hath redeemed my soul out of all **d**, H6869
2Ch 28:22 And in the time of his **d** did he trespass H6887
Neh 2:17 Then said I unto them, Ye see the **d** H7451
9:37 at their pleasure, and we *are* in great **d**. H6869
Ps 4: 1 me *when I was* in **d**; have mercy upon H6862
18: 6 In my **d** I called upon the LORD, and H6862
118: 5 I called upon the LORD in **d**: the LORD H4712
120: 1 In my **d** I cried unto the LORD, and he H6869
Prv 1:27 when **d** and anguish cometh upon you. H6869
Isa 25: 4 to the needy in his **d**, a refuge from the H6862
29: 2 Yet I will **d** Ariel, and there shall be H6693
7 and that **d** her, shall be as a dream H6693
Jer 10:18 will **d** them, that they may find *it so*. H6887
Lam 1:20 Behold, O LORD; for I *am* in **d**: my H6887
Oba 12 have spoken proudly in the day of **d**. H6869
14 of his that did remain in the day of **d**. H6869
Zep 1:15 day of trouble and **d**, a day of wasteness H4691
17 And I will bring **d** upon men, that they H6887
Lk 21:23 for there shall be great **d** in the land, and *G318*
25 and upon the earth **d** of nations, with *G4928*
Ro 8:35 tribulation, or **d**, or persecution, or *G4730*
1Co 7:26 **d**, *I say*, that *it is* good for a man so to be. *G318*
1Th 3: 7 in all our affliction and **d** by your faith: *G318*

DISTRESSED
Gen 32: 7 Then Jacob was greatly afraid and **d**: H3334
Nu 22: 3 was **d** because of the children of Israel. H6973
Jdg 2:15 unto them: and they were greatly **d**. H3334
10: 9 of Ephraim; so that Israel was sore **d**. H3334
1Sa 13: 6 the people were **d**,) then the people did H5065
14:24 And the men of Israel were **d** that day: H5065
28:15 I am sore **d**; for the Philistines make H6887
30: 6 And David was greatly **d**; for the people H3334
2Sa 1:26 I am **d** for thee, my brother Jonathan: H6887
2Ch 28:20 and **d** him, but strengthened him not. H6696
2Co 4: 8 **d**; *we are* perplexed, but not in despair; *G4729*

DISTRESSES
Ps 25:17 enlarged: *O* bring thou me out of my **d**. H4691
107: 6 *and* he delivered them out of their **d**. H4691
13 *and* he saved them out of their **d**. H4691
19 *and* he saveth them out of their **d**. H4691
28 and he bringeth them out of their **d**. H4691
Ezk 30:16 asunder, and Noph *shall have* **d** daily. H6862
2Co 6: 4 in afflictions, in necessities, in **d**, *G4730*
12:10 in persecutions, in **d** for Christ's sake: *G4730*

DISTRIBUTE
Jos 13:32 which Moses did **d** for inheritance in H5157
2Ch 31:14 of God, to **d** the oblations of the H5414
Neh 13:13 office *was* to **d** unto their brethren. H2505
Lk 18:22 thou hast, and **d** unto the poor, and *G1239*
1Ti 6:18 ready to **d**, willing to communicate; *G2130*

DISTRIBUTED
Jos 14: 1 of Israel, **d** for inheritance to them. H5157
1Ch 24: 3 And David **d** them, both Zadok of the H2505
2Ch 23:18 whom David had **d** in the house of the H2505
Jn 6:11 given thanks, he **d** to the disciples, and *G1239*
1Co 7:17 But as God hath **d** to every man, as the *G3307*
2Co 10:13 which God hath **d** to us, a measure to *G3307*

DISTRIBUTETH
Job 21:17 them! *God* **d** sorrows in his anger. H2505

DISTRIBUTING
Ro 12:13 **D** to the necessity of saints; given to *G2841*

DISTRIBUTION
Act 4:35 the apostles' feet: and **d** was made unto *G1239*
2Co 9:13 liberal **d** unto them, and unto all *men*; *G2842*

DITCH
Job 9:31 Yet shalt thou plunge me in the **d**, and H7845
Ps 7:15 and is fallen into the **d** *which* he made. H7845
Prv 23:27 For a whore *is* a deep **d**; and a strange H7745
Isa 22:11 Ye made also a **d** between the two walls H4724
Mt 15:14 lead the blind, both shall fall into the **d**. *G999*
Lk 6:39 blind? shall they not both fall into the **d**? *G999*

DITCHES
2Ki 3:16 the LORD, Make this valley full of **d**. H1356

DIVERS
Dt 22: 9 Thou shalt not sow thy vineyard with **d** H3610
11 Thou shalt not wear a garment of **d** H8162
25:13 Thou shalt not have in thy bag **d**
14 Thou shalt not have in thine house **d**
Jdg 5:30 to Sisera a prey of **d** colours, a prey of H6648
30 divers colours, a prey of **d** colours of H6648
30 colours of needlework, of **d** colours of H6648
2Sa 13:18 And *she had* a garment of **d** colours H6446
19 her garment of **d** colours that *was* on H6446
1Ch 29: 2 stones, and of **d** colours, and all H7553
2Ch 16:14 with sweet odours and **d** kinds *of spices*
21: 4 and *d* also of the princes of Israel.
30:11 Nevertheless **d** of Asher and Manasseh H582
Ps 78:45 He sent **d** sorts of flies among them,
105:31 He spake, and there came **d** sorts of flies,
Prv 20:10 **D** weights, *and* divers measures, both of
10 Divers weights, *and* **d** measures, both of
23 **D** weights *are* an abomination unto the
Ecc 5: 7 *are* also *d* vanities: but fear thou God.
Ezk 16:16 thy high places with **d** colours, and H2921
17: 3 which had **d** colours, came unto H7553
Mt 4:24 that were taken with **d** diseases and *G4164*
24: 7 and earthquakes, in **d** places.
Mk 1:34 And he healed many that were sick of **d** *G4164*
8: 3 the way: for **d** of them came from far. *G5100*
13: 8 be earthquakes in **d** places, and there
Lk 4:40 had any sick with **d** diseases brought *G4164*
21:11 And great earthquakes shall be in **d**
Act 19: 9 But when **d** were hardened, and *G5100*
1Co 12:10 spirits; to another *d* kinds of tongues; to
2Ti 3: 6 laden with sins, led away with **d** lusts, *G4164*
Tit 3: 3 deceived, serving **d** lusts and pleasures, *G4164*
Heb 1: 1 God, who at sundry times and in **d** *G4187*
2: 4 and with **d** miracles, and gifts of *G4164*
9:10 meats and drinks, and **d** washings, and *G1313*
13: 9 Be not carried about with **d** and *G4164*
Jas 1: 2 all joy when ye fall into **d** temptations; *G4164*

DIVERSE
Lev 19:19 gender with a **d** kind: thou shalt not H3610
Est 1: 7 (the vessels being **d** one from another,) H8138
3: 8 and their laws *are* **d** from all people; H8138
Dan 7: 3 up from the sea, **d** one from another. H8133
7 of it: and it *was* **d** from all the beasts H8133
19 beast, which was **d** from all the others, H8133
23 which shall be **d** from all kingdoms, H8133
24 and he shall be **d** from the first, and he H8133

DIVERSITIES
1Co 12: 4 Now there are **d** of gifts, but the same *G1243*
6 And there are **d** of operations, but it is *G1243*
28 helps, governments, **d** of tongues. *G1085*

DIVIDE
Gen 1: 6 and let it **d** the waters from the waters. H914
14 of the heaven to **d** the day from the H914
18 the night, and to **d** the light from the H914
49: 7 it was cruel: I will **d** them in Jacob, and H2505
27 prey, and at night he shall **d** the spoil. H2505
Ex 14:16 over the sea, and **d** it: and the children H1234
15: 9 will overtake, I will **d** the spoil; my lust H2505
21:35 the live ox, and **d** the money of it; and H2673
35 of it; and the dead *ox* also they shall **d**. H2673
26:33 and the vail shall **d** unto you between H914
Lev 1:17 *but* shall not **d** *it* asunder: and the priest H914
5: 8 from his neck, but shall not **d** *it* asunder: H914
11: 4 cud, or of them that **d** the hoof: *as* the H6536
7 And the swine, though he **d** the hoof, H6536
Nu 31:27 And **d** the prey into two parts; between H2673
33:54 And ye shall **d** the land by lot for an H5157
34:17 men which shall **d** the land unto you: H5157
18 tribe, to **d** the land by inheritance. H5157
29 commanded to **d** the inheritance unto H5157

Dt 14: 7 or of them that **d** the cloven hoof; *as* H6536
7 they chew the cud, but **d** not the hoof; H6536
19: 3 Thou shalt prepare thee a way, and **d** the
Jos 1: 6 people shalt thou **d** for an inheritance
13: 6 of Israel: only **d** thou it by lot unto the H5307
7 Now therefore **d** this land for an H2505
18: 5 And they shall **d** it into seven parts: H2505
22: 8 very much raiment: **d** the spoil of your H2505
2Sa 19:29 I have said, Thou and Ziba **d** the land. H2505
1Ki 3:25 And the king said, **D** the living child in H1504
26 it be neither mine nor thine, *but* **d** *it*. H1504
Neh 9:11 And thou didst **d** the sea before them, H1234
22 nations, and didst **d** them into corners: H2505
Job 27:17 on, and the innocent shall **d** the silver. H2505
Ps 55: 9 Destroy, O Lord, *and* **d** their tongues: H6385
60: 6 I will rejoice, I will **d** Shechem, and H2505
74:13 Thou didst **d** the sea by thy strength: H6565
108: 7 I will rejoice, I will **d** Shechem, and H2505
Prv 16:19 than to **d** the spoil with the proud. H2505
Isa 9: 3 as *men* rejoice when they **d** the spoil. H2505
53:12 Therefore will I **d** him *a portion* with H2505
12 great, and he shall **d** the spoil with the H2505
Ezk 5: 1 thee balances to weigh, and **d** the *hair*. H2505
45: 1 Moreover, when ye shall **d** by lot the H5307
47:21 So shall ye **d** this land unto you H2505
22 to pass, *that* ye shall **d** it by lot for an H5307
48:29 This *is* the land which ye shall **d** by lot H5307
Dan 11:39 many, and shall **d** the land for gain. H2505
Lk 12:13 that he **d** the inheritance with me. *G3307*
22:17 Take this, and **d** *it* among yourselves: *G1266*

DIVIDED
Gen 1: 4 and God **d** the light from the darkness. H914
7 And God made the firmament, and **d** the H914
10: 5 By these were the isles of the Gentiles **d** H6504
25 **d**; and his brother's name *was* Joktan. H6385
32 nations **d** in the earth after the flood. H6504
14:15 And he **d** himself against them, he and H2505
15:10 And he took unto him all these, and **d** H1334
10 against another: but the birds **d** he not. H1334
32: 7 distressed: and he **d** the people that H2673
33: 1 men. And he **d** the children unto Leah, H2673
Ex 14:21 the sea dry *land*, and the waters were **d**. H1234
Nu 26:53 Unto these the land shall be **d** for an H2505
55 Notwithstanding the land shall be **d** by H2505
56 thereof be **d** between many and few. H2505
31:42 Moses **d** from the men that warred, H2673
Dt 4:19 thy God hath **d** unto all nations under H2505
32: 8 When the most High **d** to the nations H5157
Jos 14: 5 of Israel did, and they **d** the land. H2505
18:10 and there Joshua **d** the land unto the H2505
19:51 children of Israel, **d** for an inheritance
23: 4 Behold, I have **d** unto you by lot these H5307
Jdg 5:30 Have they not sped? have they *not* **d** H2505
7:16 And he **d** the three hundred men *into* H2673
9:43 And he took the people, and **d** them H2673
19:29 concubine, and **d** her, *together* with her H5408
2Sa 1:23 they were not **d**: they were swifter than H6504
1Ki 16:21 Then were the people of Israel **d** into H2505
18: 6 So they **d** the land between them to H2505
2Ki 2: 8 and they were **d** hither and thither, so H2673
1Ch 1:19 **d**: and his brother's name *was* Joktan. H6385
23: 6 And David **d** them into courses among H2505
24: 4 *thus* were they **d**. Among the sons of H2505
5 Thus were they **d** by lot, one sort with H2505
2Ch 35:13 **d** *them* speedily among all the people. H7323
Job 38:25 Who hath **d** a watercourse for the H6385
Ps 68:12 she that tarried at home **d** the spoil. H2505
78:13 He **d** the sea, and caused them to pass H1234
55 also before them, and **d** them an H5307
136:13 To him which **d** the Red sea into parts: H1504
Isa 33:23 a great spoil **d**; the lame take the prey. H2505
34:17 and his hand hath **d** it unto them by H2505
51:15 But I *am* the LORD thy God, that **d** the H7280
Lam 4:16 The anger of the LORD hath **d** them; he H2505
Ezk 37:22 **d** into two kingdoms any more at all: H2673
Dan 2:41 kingdom shall be **d**; but there shall be in H6386
5:28 PERES; Thy kingdom is **d**, and given to H6537
11: 4 and shall be **d** toward the four winds H2673
Hos 10: 2 Their heart is **d**; now shall they be H2505
Am 7:17 thy land shall be **d** by line; and thou H2505
Mic 2: 4 me! turning away he hath **d** our fields. H2505
Zec 14: 1 thy spoil shall be **d** in the midst of thee. H2505
Mt 12:25 them, Every kingdom **d** against itself is *G3307*
25 house **d** against itself shall not stand: *G3307*
26 And if Satan cast out Satan, he is **d** *G3307*
Mk 3:24 And if a kingdom be **d** against itself, *G3307*
25 And if a house be **d** against itself, that *G3307*
26 be **d**, he cannot stand, but hath an end. *G3307*
Mk 6:41 the two fishes **d** he among them all. *G3307*
Lk 11:17 them, Every kingdom **d** against itself is *G1266*
17 and a house **d** against a house falleth.
18 If Satan also be **d** against himself, how *G1266*
12:52 five in one house **d**, three against two, *G1266*
53 The father shall be **d** against the son, *G1266*
15:12 *to me*. And he **d** unto them *his* living. *G1244*
Act 13:19 he **d** their land to them by lot. *G2624*
14: 4 But the multitude of the city was **d**: and *G4977*
23: 7 Sadducees: and the multitude was **d**. *G4977*
1Co 1:13 Is Christ **d**? was Paul crucified for you? *G3307*
Rev 16:19 And the great city was **d** into three *G1096*

DIVIDER
Lk 12:14 who made me a judge or a **d** over you? *G3312*

DIVIDETH
Lev 11: 4 **d** not the hoof; he *is* unclean unto you. H6536
5 **d** not the hoof; he *is* unclean unto you. H6536
6 **d** not the hoof; he *is* unclean unto you. H6536
26 *The carcases* of every beast which **d** the H6536
Dt 14: 8 And the swine, because it **d** the hoof, H6536
Job 26:12 He **d** the sea with his power, and by his H7280
Ps 29: 7 The voice of the LORD **d** the flames of H2672
Jer 31:35 light by night, which **d** the sea when the H7280
Mt 25:32 a shepherd **d** *his* sheep from the goats: *G873*
Lk 11:22 wherein he trusted, and **d** his spoils. *G1239*

DIVIDING
Jos 19:49 When they had made an end of **d** the
51 So they made an end of **d** the country. H2505
Isa 63:12 his glorious arm, **d** the water before H1234
Dan 7:25 a time and times and the **d** of time. H6387
1Co 12:11 **d** to every man severally as he will. *G1244*
2Ti 2:15 ashamed, rightly **d** the word of truth. *G3718*
Heb 4:12 even to the **d** asunder of soul and *G3311*

DIVINATION
Nu 22: 7 the rewards of **d** in their hand; and H7081
23:23 *is there* any **d** against Israel: according H7081
Dt 18:10 fire, *or* that useth **d**, *or* an observer of H7081
2Ki 17:17 the fire, and used **d** and enchantments, H7081
Jer 14:14 you a false vision and **d**, and a thing of H7081
Ezk 12:24 flattering **d** within the house of Israel. H4738
13: 6 They have seen vanity and lying **d**, H7081
7 ye not spoken a lying **d**, whereas ye say, H4738
21:21 two ways, to use **d**: he made *his* arrows H7081
22 At his right hand was the **d** for H7081
23 And it shall be unto them as a false **d** in H7080
Act 16:16 with a spirit of **d** met us, which brought *G4436*

DIVINATIONS
Ezk 13:23 vanity, nor divine **d**: for I will deliver H7081

DIVINE
Gen 44:15 that such a man as I can certainly **d**? H5172
1Sa 28: 8 he said, I pray thee, **d** unto me by the H7080
Prv 16:10 A **d** sentence *is* in the lips of the king: H7081
Ezk 13: 9 vanity, and that **d** lies: they shall not be H7080
23 no more vanity, nor **d** divinations: for I H7080
21:29 thee, whiles they **d** a lie unto thee, to H7080
Mic 3: 6 that ye shall not **d**; and the sun shall go H7080
11 prophets thereof **d** for money: yet will H7080
Heb 9: 1 of **d** service, and a worldly sanctuary. *G2999*
2Pt 1: 3 According as his **d** power hath given *G2304*
4 be partakers of the **d** nature, having *G2304*

DIVINERS
Dt 18:14 of times, and unto **d**: but as for thee, the H7080
1Sa 6: 2 for the priests and the **d**, saying, What H7080
Isa 44:25 liars, and maketh **d** mad; that turneth H7080
Jer 27: 9 nor to your **d**, nor to your dreamers, H7080
29: 8 your prophets and your **d**, that *be* in the H7080
Mic 3: 7 ashamed, and the **d** confounded: yea, H7080
Zec 10: 2 vanity, and the **d** have seen a lie, and H7080

DIVINETH
Gen 44: 5 he **d**? ye have done evil in so doing. H5172

DIVINING
Ezk 22:28 seeing vanity, and **d** lies unto them, H7080

DIVISION
Ex 8:23 And I will put a **d** between my people H6304
2Ch 35: 5 *after* the **d** of the families of the Levites. H2515
Lk 12:51 on earth? I tell you, Nay; but rather **d**: *G1267*
Jn 7:43 So there was a **d** among the people *G4978*
9:16 And there was a **d** among them. *G4978*
10:19 There was a **d** therefore again among *G4978*

DIVISIONS
Jos 11:23 according to their **d** by their tribes. H4256
12: 7 *for* a possession according to their **d**; H4256
18:10 children of Israel according to their **d**. H4256
Jdg 5:15 the valley. For the **d** of Reuben *there* H6390
16 of the flocks? For the **d** of Reuben *there* H6390
1Ch 24: 1 Now *these are* the **d** of the sons of H4256
26: 1 Concerning the **d** of the porters: Of the H4256
12 Among these *were* the **d** of the porters, H4256
19 These *are* the **d** of the porters among H4256
2Ch 35: 5 according to the **d** of the families of the H6391
12 according to the **d** of the families of the H4653
Ezr 6:18 And they set the priests in their **d**, and H6392
Neh 11:36 And of the Levites *were* **d** *in* Judah, *and* H4256
Ro 16:17 mark them which cause **d** and offences *G1370*
1Co 1:10 *that* there be no **d** among you; but *that* *G4978*
3: 3 **d**, are ye not carnal, and walk as men? *G1370*
11:18 be **d** among you; and I partly believe it. *G4978*

DIVORCE
Jer 3: 8 given her a bill of **d**; yet her treacherous H3748

DIVORCED
Lev 21:14 A widow, or a **d** woman, or profane, *or* H1644
22:13 be a widow, or **d**, and have no child, H1644
Nu 30: 9 and of her that is **d**, wherewith they H1644
Mt 5:32 marry her that is **d** committeth adultery. *G630*

DIVORCEMENT
Dt 24: 1 write her a bill of **d**, and give *it* in her H3748
3 write her a bill of **d**, and giveth *it* in her H3748
Isa 50: 1 of your mother's **d**, whom I have put H3748
Mt 5:31 his wife, let him give her a writing of **d**: *G647*
19: 7 give a writing of **d**, and to put her away? *G647*
Mk 10: 4 to write a bill of **d**, and to put *her* away. *G647*

DIZAHAB
Dt 1: 1 and Laban, and Hazeroth, and **D**. H1774

DO
See the Appendix.

DOCTOR
Act 5:34 named Gamaliel, a **d** of the law, had in *G3547*

DOCTORS
Lk 2:46 in the midst of the **d**, both hearing *G1320*
5:17 Pharisees and **d** of the law sitting by, *G3547*

DOCTRINE
Dt 32: 2 My **d** shall drop as the rain, my speech H3948
Job 11: 4 For thou hast said, My **d** *is* pure, and I H3948
Prv 4: 2 For I give you good **d**, forsake ye not my H3948
Isa 28: 9 to understand **d**? *them that are* weaned H8052
29:24 and they that murmured shall learn **d**. H3948
Jer 10: 8 and foolish: the stock *is* a **d** of vanities. H4148
Mt 7:28 the people were astonished at his **d**: *G1322*
16:12 bread, but of the **d** of the Pharisees and *G1322*
22:33 *this*, they were astonished at his **d**. *G1322*
Mk 1:22 And they were astonished at his **d**: for *G1322*
27 is this? what new **d** *is* this? for with *G1322*
4: 2 parables, and said unto them in his **d**, *G1322*
11:18 all the people was astonished at his **d**. *G1322*
12:38 And he said unto them in his **d**, Beware *G1322*
Lk 4:32 And they were astonished at his **d**: for *G1322*
Jn 7:16 Jesus answered them, and said, My **d** is *G1322*
17 he shall know of the **d**, whether it be of *G1322*
18:19 Jesus of his disciples, and of his **d**. *G1322*
Act 2:42 in the apostles' **d** and fellowship, and *G1322*
5:28 with your **d**, and intend to bring *G1322*
13:12 being astonished at the **d** of the Lord. *G1322*
17:19 this new **d**, whereof thou speakest, *is*? *G1322*
Ro 6:17 form of **d** which was delivered you. *G1322*
16:17 contrary to the **d** which ye have *G1322*
1Co 14: 6 knowledge, or by prophesying, or by **d**? *G1322*
26 a psalm, hath a **d**, hath a tongue, hath *G1322*
Eph 4:14 with every wind of **d**, by the sleight of *G1319*
1Ti 1: 3 charge some that they teach no other **d**, *G2085*
10 other thing that is contrary to sound **d**; *G1319*
4: 6 good **d**, whereunto thou hast attained. *G1319*
13 to reading, to exhortation, to **d**. *G1319*
16 Take heed unto thyself, and unto the **d**; *G1319*
5:17 they who labour in the word and **d**. *G1319*
6: 1 of God and *his* **d** be not blasphemed. *G1319*
3 the **d** which is according to godliness; *G1319*
2Ti 3:10 But thou hast fully known my **d**, *G1319*
16 and *is* profitable for **d**, for reproof, for *G1319*
4: 2 exhort with all longsuffering and **d**. *G1322*
3 not endure sound **d**; but after their own *G1319*
Tit 1: 9 be able by sound **d** both to exhort and *G1319*

Tit 2: 1 thou the things which become sound **d**: *G1319*
7 pattern of good works: in **d** *shewing* *G1319*
10 the **d** of God our Saviour in all things. *G1319*
Heb 6: 1 principles of the **d** of Christ, let us go *G3056*
2 Of the **d** of baptisms, and of laying on *G1322*
2Jn 9 abideth not in the **d** of Christ, hath not *G1322*
9 that abideth in the **d** of Christ, he hath *G1322*
10 and bring not this **d**, receive him not *G1322*
Rev 2:14 them that hold the **d** of Balaam, who *G1322*
15 So hast thou also them that hold the **d** *G1322*
24 as have not this **d**, and which have not *G1322*

DOCTRINES
Mt 15: 9 *for* **d** the commandments of men. *G1319*
Mk 7: 7 *for* **d** the commandments of men. *G1319*
Col 2:22 the commandments and **d** of men? *G1319*
1Ti 4: 1 to seducing spirits, and **d** of devils; *G1319*
Heb 13: 9 and strange **d**. For *it is* a good thing *G1322*

DODAI
1Ch 27: 4 month *was* **D** an Ahohite, and of H1737

DODANIM
Gen 10: 4 Elishah, and Tarshish, Kittim, and **D**. H1721
1Ch 1: 7 Elishah, and Tarshish, Kittim, and **D**. H1721

DODAVAH
2Ch 20:37 Then Eliezer the son of **D** of Mareshah H1735

DODO
Jdg 10: 1 Puah, the son of **D**, a man of Issachar; H1734
2Sa 23: 9 And after him *was* Eleazar the son of **D** H1734
24 Elhanan the son of **D** of Beth-lehem, H1734
1Ch 11:12 And after him *was* Eleazar the son of **D**, H1734
26 Elhanan the son of **D** of Beth-lehem, H1734

DOEG
1Sa 21: 7 and his name *was* **D**, an Edomite, the H1673
22: 9 Then answered **D** the Edomite, which H1673
18 And the king said to **D**, Turn thou, and H1673
18 the priests. And **D** the Edomite turned, H1673
22 *it* that day, when **D** the Edomite *was* H1673
Ps 52: ttl of David, when **D** the Edomite came H1673

DOER
Gen 39:22 they did there, he was the **d** *of it*. H6213
2Sa 3:39 **d** of evil according to his wickedness. H6213
Ps 31:23 and plentifully rewardeth the proud **d**. H6213
Prv 17: 4 A wicked **d** giveth heed to false lips; H7489
2Ti 2: 9 Wherein I suffer trouble, as an evil **d**, *G2557*
Jas 1:23 word, and not a **d**, he is like unto a man *G4163*
25 hearer, but a **d** of the work, this man *G4163*
4:11 thou art not a **d** of the law, but a judge. *G4163*

DOERS
2Ki 22: 5 the hand of the **d** of the work, that have H6213
5 them give it to the **d** of the work which H6213
Job 8:20 *man*, neither will he help the evil **d**:
Ps 26: 5 I have hated the congregation of evil **d**;
101: 8 all wicked **d** from the city of the LORD. H6466
Ro 2:13 but the **d** of the law shall be justified. *G4163*
Jas 1:22 But be ye **d** of the word, and not *G4163*

DOEST See the Appendix.

DOETH See the Appendix.

DOG
Ex 11: 7 of Israel shall not a **d** move his tongue, H3611
Dt 23:18 or the price of a **d**, into the house of the H3611
Jdg 7: 5 his tongue, as a **d** lappeth, him shalt H3611
1Sa 17:43 David, *Am* I a **d**, that thou comest to H3611
24:14 thou pursue? after a dead **d**, after a flea. H3611
2Sa 9: 8 look upon such a dead **d** as I *am?* H3611
16: 9 should this dead **d** curse my lord the H3611
2Ki 8:13 *is* thy servant a **d**, that he should do this H3611
Ps 22:20 my darling from the power of the **d**. H3611
59: 6 like a **d**, and go round about the city. H3611
14 like a **d**, and go round about the city. H3611
Prv 26:11 As a **d** returneth to his vomit, *so* a fool H3611
17 *is like* one that taketh a **d** by the ears. H3611
Ecc 9: 4 for a living **d** is better than a dead lion. H3611
2Pt 2:22 the true proverb, The **d** *is* turned to his *G2965*

DOGS
Ex 22:31 in the field; ye shall cast it to the **d**. H3611
1Ki 14:11 in the city shall the **d** eat; and him that H3611
16: 4 in the city shall the **d** eat; and him that H3611
21:19 In the place where **d** licked the blood of H3611
1Ki 21:19 shall **d** lick thy blood, even thine. H3611
23 **d** shall eat Jezebel by the wall of Jezreel. H3611
24 Him that dieth of Ahab in the city the **d** H3611
22:38 Samaria; and the **d** licked up his blood; H3611
2Ki 9:10 And the **d** shall eat Jezebel in the H3611
36 of Jezreel shall **d** eat the flesh of Jezebel: H3611
Job 30: 1 to have set with the **d** of my flock. H3611
Ps 22:16 For **d** have compassed me: the H3611
68:23 *and* the tongue of thy **d** in the same. H3611
Isa 56:10 they *are* all dumb **d**, they cannot bark; H3611
11 Yea, *they are* greedy **d** *which* can never H3611
Jer 15: 3 to slay, and the **d** to tear, and the fowls H3611
Mt 7: 6 Give not that which is holy unto the **d**, *G2965*
15:26 the children's bread, and to cast *it* to **d**. *G2952*
27 And she said, Truth, Lord: yet the **d** eat *G2952*
Mk 7:27 bread, and to cast *it* unto the **d**. *G2952*
28 Yes, Lord: yet the **d** under the table eat *G2952*
Lk 16:21 the **d** came and licked his sores. *G2965*
Php 3: 2 Beware of **d**, beware of evil workers, *G2965*
Rev 22:15 For without *are* **d**, and sorcerers, and *G2965*

DOG'S
2Sa 3: 8 and said, *Am* I a **d** head, which against H3611
Isa 66: 3 *as if* he cut off a **d** neck; he that offereth H3611

DOING See the Appendix.

DOINGS See the Appendix.

DOLEFUL
Isa 13:21 shall be full of **d** creatures; and owls H255
Mic 2: 4 and lament with a **d** lamentation, *and* H5093

DOMINION
Gen 1:26 and let them have **d** over the fish of the H7287
28 it: and have **d** over the fish of the sea, H7287
27:40 shalt have the **d**, that thou shalt break H7300
37: 8 thou indeed have **d** over us? And they H4910
Nu 24:19 he that shall have **d**, and shall destroy H7287
Jdg 5:13 that remaineth have **d** over the nobles H7287
13 made me have **d** over the mighty. H7287
14: 4 time the Philistines had **d** over Israel. H4910
1Ki 4:24 For he had **d** over all *the region* on this H7287
9:19 in Lebanon, and in all the land of his **d**. H4475
2Ki 20:13 his **d**, that Hezekiah shewed them not. H4475
1Ch 4:22 Saraph, who had the **d** in Moab, and H1166
18: 3 to stablish his **d** by the river Euphrates. H3027
2Ch 8: 6 and throughout all the land of his **d**. H4475
21: 8 from under the **d** of Judah, and made H3027
Neh 9:28 so that they had the **d** over them: yet H7287
37 also they have **d** over our bodies, and H4910
Job 25: 2 **D** and fear *are* with him, he maketh H4910
38:33 thou set the **d** thereof in the earth? H4896
Ps 8: 6 Thou madest him to have **d** over the H4910
19:13 let them not have **d** over me: then shall H4910
49:14 upright shall have **d** over them in the H7287
72: 8 He shall have **d** also from sea to sea, H7287
103:22 of his **d**: bless the LORD, O my soul. H4475
114: 2 was his sanctuary, *and* Israel his **d**. H4475
119:133 let not any iniquity have **d** over me. H7980
145:13 **d** *endureth* throughout all generations. H4475
Isa 26:13 thee have had **d** over us: *but* by thee H1166
39: 2 his **d**, that Hezekiah shewed them not. H4475
Jer 34: 1 of the earth of his **d**, and all the people, H4475
51:28 rulers thereof, and all the land of his **d**. H4475
Dan 4: 3 his **d** *is* from generation to generation. H7985
22 and thy **d** to the end of the earth. H7985
34 for ever, whose **d** *is* an everlasting H7985
34 *is* an everlasting **d**, and his kingdom *is* H7985
6:26 I make a decree, That in every **d** of my H7985
26 and his **d** *shall be even* unto the end. H7985
7: 6 also four heads; and **d** was given to it. H7985
12 they had their **d** taken away: yet their H7985
14 And there was given him **d**, and glory, H7985
14 serve him: his **d** *is* an everlasting H7985
14 *is* an everlasting **d**, which shall not pass H7985
26 take away his **d**, to consume and to H7985
27 And the kingdom and **d**, and the H7985
11: 3 great **d**, and do according to his will. H4474
4 according to his **d** which he ruled: for H4915
5 him, and have **d**; his dominion *shall* H4910
5 his **d** *shall be* a great dominion. H4475
5 his dominion *shall be* a great **d**. H4474
Mic 4: 8 even the first **d**; the kingdom shall come H4475
Zec 9:10 heathen: and his **d** *shall be* from sea H4915
Mt 20:25 Gentiles exercise **d** over them, and they *G2634*
Ro 6: 9 more; death hath no more **d** over him. *G2961*
14 For sin shall not have **d** over you: for ye *G2961*
7: 1 hath **d** over a man as long as he liveth? *G2961*
2Co 1:24 Not for that we have **d** over your faith, *G2961*
Eph 1:21 and might, and **d**, and every name that *G2963*
1Pt 4:11 praise and **d** for ever and ever. Amen. *G2904*
5:11 To him *be* glory and **d** for ever and *G2904*
Jude 8 despise **d**, and speak evil of dignities. *G2963*
25 and majesty, **d** and power, both now *G2904*
Rev 1: 6 *be* glory and **d** for ever and ever. Amen. *G2904*

DOMINIONS
Dan 7:27 and all **d** shall serve and obey him. H7985
Col 1:16 *be* thrones, or **d**, or principalities, or *G2963*

DONE
Gen 3:13 *is* this *that* thou hast **d**? And the woman H6213
14 Because thou hast **d** this, thou *art* H6213
4:10 And he said, What hast thou **d**? the H6213
8:21 any more every thing living, as I have **d**. H6213
9:24 what his younger son had **d** unto him. H6213
12:18 *is* this *that* thou hast **d** unto me? why H6213
18:21 see whether they have **d** altogether H6213
20: 5 innocency of my hands have I **d** this. H6213
9 What hast thou **d** unto us? and what H6213
9 sin? thou hast **d** deeds unto me that H6213
9 deeds unto me that ought not to be **d**. H6213
10 thou, that thou hast **d** this thing? H6213
21:23 that I have **d** unto thee, thou shalt H6213
26 I wot not who hath **d** this thing: neither H6213
22:16 for because thou hast **d** this thing, and H6213
24:15 And it came to pass, before he had **d** H3615
19 And when she had **d** giving him drink, H3615
19 camels also, until they have **d** drinking. H3615
22 as the camels had **d** drinking, that the H3615
45 And before I had **d** speaking in mine H3615
66 told Isaac all things that he had **d**. H6213
26:10 *is* this thou hast **d** unto us? one of the H6213
29 and as we have **d** unto thee nothing but H6213
27:19 firstborn; I have **d** according as thou H6213
45 which thou hast **d** to him: then I will H6213
28:15 **d** *that* which I have spoken to thee of. H6213
29:25 *is* this thou hast **d** unto me? did not I H6213
26 And Laban said, It must not be so **d** in H6213
30:26 my service which I have **d** thee. H5647
31:26 What hast thou **d**, that thou hast stolen H6213
28 thou hast now **d** foolishly in *so* doing. H5528
34: 7 which thing ought not to be **d**. H6213
40:15 here also have I **d** nothing that they H6213
42:28 What *is* this *that* God hath **d** unto us? H6213
44: 5 he divineth? ye have **d** evil in so doing. H7489
15 this that ye have **d**? wot ye not that such H6213
Ex 1:18 Why have ye **d** this thing, and have H6213
2: 4 afar off, to wit what would be **d** to him. H6213
3:16 *seen* that which is **d** to you in Egypt: H6213
5:23 thy name, he hath **d** evil to this people;
10: 2 signs which I have **d** among them; that H7760
12:16 of work shall be **d** in them, save *that* H6213
16 must eat, that only may be **d** of you. H6213
13: 8 day, saying, *This is* **d** because of that
14: 5 Why have we **d** this, that we have let H6213
18: 1 of all that God had **d** for Moses, and for H6213
8 the LORD had **d** unto Pharaoh and to H6213
9 the LORD had **d** to Israel, whom he H6213
21:31 to this judgment shall it be **d** unto him. H6213
31:15 Six days may work be **d**; but in the H6213
34:10 as have not been **d** in all the earth, nor H1254
33 And *till* Moses had **d** speaking with H3615
35: 2 Six days shall work be **d**, but on the H6213
39:43 behold, they had **d** it as the LORD had H6213
43 had they **d** it: and Moses blessed them. H6213
Lev 4: 2 be **d**, and shall do against any of them: H6213
13 and they have **d** *somewhat against* any H6213
13 which should not be **d**, and are guilty; H6213
22 When a ruler hath sinned, and **d** H6213
22 which should not be **d**, and is guilty; H6213
27 which ought not to be **d**, and be guilty; H6213
5:16 harm that he hath **d** in the holy thing,
17 are forbidden to be **d** by the H6213
6: 7 that he hath **d** in trespassing therein. H6213
8: 5 which the LORD commanded to be **d**. H6213
34 As he hath **d** this day, *so* the LORD H6213
11:32 *any* work is **d**, it must be put into water, H6213
18:27 men of the land **d**, which *were* before H6213
19:22 sin which he hath **d**: and the sin which H2398
22 which he hath **d** shall be forgiven him. H2398
23: 3 Six days shall work be **d**: but the H6213
24:19 as he hath **d**, so shall it be done to him; H6213
19 as he hath done, so shall it be **d** to him; H6213
20 in a man, so shall it be **d** to him *again*. H5414
Nu 5: 7 sin which they have **d**: and he shall H6213
27 defiled, and have **d** trespass against her

Nu 12:11 **d** foolishly, and wherein we have sinned.
15:11 Thus shall it be **d** for one bullock, or for H6213
34 not declared what should be **d** to him. H6213
16:28 for *I have* not **d** *them* of mine own mind.
22: 2 all that Israel had **d** to the Amorites. H6213
28 What have I **d** unto thee, that thou H6213
23:11 What hast thou **d** unto me? I took thee H6213
27: 4 of our father be **d** away from among H1639
32:13 that had **d** evil in the sight of the H6213
Dt 3:21 your God hath **d** unto these two kings: H6213
10:21 *is* thy God, that hath **d** for thee these H6213
12:31 hateth, have they **d** unto their gods; for H6213
19:19 thought to have **d** unto his brother: so H6213
20:18 which they have **d** unto their gods; so H6213
25: 9 say, So shall it be **d** unto that man that H6213
26:14 my God, *and* have **d** according to all H6213
29:24 hath the LORD **d** thus unto this land? H6213
32:27 high, and the LORD hath not **d** all this. H6466
Jos 5: 8 And it came to pass, when they had **d** H8552
7:19 what thou hast **d**; hide *it* not from me. H6213
20 of Israel, and thus and thus have I **d**: H6213
9: 3 Joshua had **d** unto Jericho and to Ai, H6213
24 because of you, and have **d** this thing. H6213
10: 1 it; as he had **d** to Jericho and her king, H6213
1 king, so he had **d** to Ai and her king; H6213
32 to all that he had **d** to Libnah. H6213
35 to all that he had **d** to Lachish. H6213
37 to all that he had **d** to Eglon; but H6213
39 as he had **d** to Hebron, so he did H6213
39 had **d** also to Libnah, and to her king. H6213
22:24 And if we have not *rather* **d** it for fear H6213
23: 3 your God hath **d** unto all these nations H6213
8 your God, as ye have **d** unto this day. H6213
24: 7 seen what I have **d** in Egypt: and ye H6213
20 you, after that he hath **d** you good.
31 of the LORD, that he had **d** for Israel. H6213
Jdg 1: 7 table: as I have **d**, so God hath requited H6213
2: 2 obeyed my voice: why have ye **d** this? H6213
10 yet the works which he had **d** for Israel. H6213
3:12 had **d** evil in the sight of the LORD. H6213
6:29 Who hath **d** this thing? And when H6213
29 the son of Joash hath **d** this thing. H6213
8: 2 And he said unto them, What have I **d** H6213
9:16 Now therefore, if ye have **d** truly and H6213
16 house, and have **d** unto him according H6213
24 That the cruelty *d* to the threescore and
48 me do, make haste, *and* do as I *have d*.
11:37 Let this thing be **d** for me: let me alone H6213
14: 6 his father or his mother what he had **d**. H6213
15: 6 Then the Philistines said, Who hath **d** H6213
7 Though ye have **d** this, yet will I be H6213
10 up, to do to him as he hath **d** to us. H6213
11 *is* this *that* thou hast **d** unto us? And he H6213
11 did unto me, so have I **d** unto them. H6213
19:30 was no such deed **d** nor seen from the H1961
20:12 wickedness *is* this that is **d** among you? H1961
Ru 2:11 all that thou hast **d** unto thy mother in H6213
3: 3 he shall have **d** eating and drinking. H3615
16 told her all that the man had **d** to her. H6213
1Sa 4:16 And he said, What is there **d**, my son? H1697
6: 9 *then* he hath **d** us this great evil: but H6213
8: 8 which they have **d** since the day that I H6213
11: 7 so shall it be **d** unto his oxen. And H6213
12:17 which ye have **d** in the sight of the H6213
20 Fear not: ye have **d** all this wickedness: H6213
24 how great *things* he hath **d** for you. H1431
13:11 And Samuel said, What hast thou **d**? H6213
13 And Samuel said to Saul, Thou hast **d**
14:43 what thou hast **d**. And Jonathan told H6213
17:26 What shall be **d** to the man that killeth H6213
27 shall it be **d** to the man that killeth him. H6213
29 And David said, What have I now **d**? *Is* H6213
19:18 all that Saul had **d** to him. And he and H6213
20: 1 What have I **d**? what *is* mine iniquity? H6213
32 shall he be slain? what hath he **d**? H6213
34 because his father had **d** him shame.
24:19 for that thou hast **d** unto me this day. H6213
25:30 the LORD shall have **d** to my lord H6213
26:16 This thing *is* not good that thou hast **d**. H6213
18 have I **d**? or what evil *is* in mine hand? H6213
28: 9 what Saul hath **d**, how he hath cut off H6213
17 And the LORD hath **d** to him, as he H6213
18 LORD **d** this thing unto thee this day. H6213
29: 8 But what have I **d**? and what hast thou H6213
31:11 which the Philistines had **d** to Saul; H6213
2Sa 2: 6 kindness, because ye have **d** this thing. H6213
3:24 What hast thou **d**? behold, Abner came H6213
7:21 own heart, hast thou **d** all these great H6213
11:27 that David had **d** displeased the LORD. H6213

2Sa 12: 5 that hath **d** this *thing* shall surely die: H6213
21 *is* this that thou hast **d**? thou didst fast H6213
13:12 to be **d** in Israel: do not thou this folly. H6213
14:20 thy servant Joab **d** this thing: and my H6213
21 now, I have **d** this thing: go therefore, H6213
15:24 people had **d** passing out of the city. H8552
16:10 then say, Wherefore hast thou **d** so? H6213
21:11 of Aiah, the concubine of Saul, had **d**. H6213
23:20 Kabzeel, who had **d** many acts, he slew H6213
24:10 in that I have **d**: and now, I beseech H6213
10 of thy servant; for I have **d** very foolishly.
17 sinned, and I have **d** wickedly: but these
17 what have they **d**? let thine hand, I pray H6213
1Ki 1: 6 Why hast thou **d** so? and he also *was* H6213
27 Is this thing **d** by my lord the king, and H1961
3:12 Behold, I have **d** according to thy H6213
8:47 sinned, and have **d** perversely, we have
66 the LORD had **d** for David his servant, H6213
9: 8 hath the LORD **d** thus unto this land, H6213
11:11 as this is **d** of thee, and thou hast
13:11 man of God had **d** that day in Beth-el: H6213
14: 9 But hast **d** evil above all that were H6213
22 above all that their fathers had **d**. H6213
15: 3 which he had **d** before him: and his H6213
18:36 I have **d** all these things at thy word. H6213
19: 1 all that Elijah had **d**, and withal how he H6213
20 back again: for what have I **d** to thee? H6213
22:53 according to all that his father had **d**. H6213
2Ki 4:13 care; what *is* to be **d** for thee? wouldest H6213
14 And he said, What then *is* to be **d** for H6213
5:13 thou not have **d** *it*? how much rather H6213
7:12 the Syrians have **d** to us. They know H6213
8: 4 all the great things that Elisha hath **d**. H6213
10:10 for the LORD hath **d** *that* which he H6213
30 Because thou hast **d** well in executing
30 eyes, *and* hast **d** unto the house of H6213
15: 3 to all that his father Amaziah had **d**; H6213
9 as his fathers had **d**: he departed not H6213
34 to all that his father Uzziah had **d**. H6213
17: 4 of Assyria, as *he had* **d** year by year:
19:11 kings of Assyria have **d** to all lands, by H6213
25 long ago *how* I have **d** it, *and* of ancient H6213
20: 3 heart, and have **d** *that which is* good in H6213
21:11 of Judah hath **d** these abominations, H6213
11 *and* hath **d** wickedly above all that H6213
15 Because they have **d** *that which was* H6213
23:17 thou hast **d** against the altar of Beth-el. H6213
19 to all the acts that he had **d** in Beth-el. H6213
32 according to all that his fathers had **d**. H6213
37 according to all that his fathers had **d**. H6213
24: 9 according to all that his father had **d**. H6213
19 according to all that Jehoiakim had **d**. H6213
1Ch 10:11 all that the Philistines had **d** to Saul, H6213
11:22 Kabzeel, who had **d** many acts; he slew
16:12 that he hath **d**, his wonders, and the H6213
17:19 heart, hast thou **d** all this greatness, in H6213
21: 8 because I have **d** this thing: but now, H6213
8 of thy servant; for I have **d** very foolishly.
17 have sinned and **d** evil indeed; but *as for*
17 what have they **d**? let thine hand, I pray H6213
2Ch 6:37 have **d** amiss, and have dealt wickedly;
7:21 hath the LORD **d** thus unto this land, H6213
11: 4 house: for this thing is **d** of me. And they
16: 9 Herein thou hast **d** foolishly: therefore H6213
24:16 because he had **d** good in Israel, both H6213
22 his father had **d** to him, but slew his H6213
25:16 because thou hast **d** this, and hast not H6213
29: 2 to all that David his father had **d**. H6213
6 For our fathers have trespassed, and **d** H6213
36 the people: for the thing was **d** suddenly.
30: 5 for they had not **d** *it* of a long *time in* H6213
32:13 my fathers have **d** unto all the people of H6213
25 to the benefit *d* unto him; for his heart
31 wonder that was *d* in the land, God left
Ezr 6:12 made a decree; let it be **d** with speed. H5648
7:21 shall require of you, it be **d** speedily, H5648
23 let it be diligently **d** for the house of the H5648
9: 1 Now when these things were **d**, the H3615
10: 3 and let it be **d** according to the law. H6213
Neh 5:19 to all that I have **d** for this people. H6213
6: 8 are no such things **d** as thou sayest, but H1961
9 that it be not **d**. Now therefore, *O God*, H6213
8:17 children of Israel **d** so. And there was H6213
9:33 **d** right, but we have done wickedly: H6213
33 hast done right, but we have **d** wickedly:
13:14 deeds that I have **d** for the house of my H6213
Est 1:16 the queen hath not **d** wrong to the king
2: 1 **d**, and what was decreed against her. H6213
4: 1 all that was **d**, Mordecai rent his H6213

Est 6: 3 dignity hath been **d** to Mordecai for H6213
3 unto him, There is nothing **d** for him. H6213
6 What shall be **d** unto the man whom H6213
9 Thus shall it be **d** to the man whom the H6213
11 Thus shall it be **d** unto the man whom H6213
9:12 what have they **d** in the rest of the H6213
12 *is* thy request further? and it shall be **d**. H6213
14 And the king commanded it so to be **d**: H6213
Job 21:31 who shall repay him *what* he hath **d**? H6213
34:29 him? whether *it be* **d** against a nation, or
32 if I have **d** iniquity, I will do no more. H6466
Ps 7: 3 O LORD my God, if I have **d** this; if H6213
14: 1 corrupt, they have **d** abominable works,
22:31 that shall be born, that he hath **d** *this*. H6213
33: 4 *is* right; and all his works *are* **d** in truth.
9 For he spake, and it was *d*; he
40: 5 *which* thou hast **d**, and thy thoughts H6213
50:21 These *things* hast thou **d**, and I kept H6213
51: 4 have I sinned, and **d** *this* evil in thy H6213
52: 9 because thou hast **d** *it*: and I will wait H6213
53: 1 are they, and have **d** abominable
66:16 will declare what he hath **d** for my soul. H6213
71:19 high, who hast **d** great things: O God, H6213
74: 3 enemy hath **d** wickedly in the sanctuary.
78: 4 and his wonderful works that he hath **d**. H6213
98: 1 song; for he hath **d** marvellous things: H6213
105: 5 that he hath **d**; his wonders, and the H6213
106: 6 committed iniquity, we have **d** wickedly.
21 which had **d** great things in Egypt; H6213
109:27 *is* thy hand; *that* thou, LORD, hast **d** it. H6213
111: 8 *and are* **d** in truth and uprightness. H6213
115: 3 he hath **d** whatsoever he hath pleased. H6213
119:121 I have **d** judgment and justice: leave H6213
166 salvation, and **d** thy commandments. H6213
120: 3 shall be **d** unto thee, thou false tongue? H3254
126: 2 LORD hath **d** great things for them. H6213
3 The LORD hath **d** great things for us; H6213
Prv 3:30 cause, if he have **d** thee no harm. H1580
4:16 For they sleep not, except they have **d**
24:29 Say not, I will do so to him as he hath **d** H6213
30:20 and saith, I have **d** no wickedness. H6466
32 If thou hast **d** foolishly in lifting up
31:29 Many daughters have **d** virtuously, but H6213
Ecc 1: 9 and that which is **d** *is* that which shall H6213
9 which shall be **d**: and *there is* no new H6213
13 all *things* that are **d** under heaven: this H6213
14 I have seen all the works that are **d** H6213
2:12 *even* that which hath been already **d**. H6213
4: 1 that are **d** under the sun: and H6213
3 the evil work that is **d** under the sun. H6213
8: 9 every work that is **d** under the sun: H6213
10 where they had so **d**: this *is* also vanity. H6213
14 There is a vanity which is **d** upon the H6213
16 business that is **d** upon the earth: (for H6213
17 out the work that is **d** under the sun: H6213
9: 3 all *things* that are **d** under the sun, that H6213
6 in any *thing* that is **d** under the sun. H6213
Isa 5: 4 What could have been **d** more to my H6213
4 that I have not **d** in it? wherefore, when H6213
10:11 Shall I not, as I have **d** unto Samaria H6213
13 of my hand I have **d** *it*, and by my H6213
12: 5 Sing unto the LORD; for he hath **d** H6213
24:13 gleaning grapes when the vintage is **d**. H3615
25: 1 for thou hast **d** wonderful *things; thy* H6213
33:13 Hear, ye *that are* far off, what I have **d**; H6213
37:11 kings of Assyria have **d** to all lands by H6213
26 ago, *how* I have **d** it; *and* of ancient H6213
38: 3 heart, and have **d** *that which is* good in H6213
15 and himself hath **d** *it*: I shall go softly H6213
41: 4 Who hath wrought and **d** *it*, calling the H6213
20 of the LORD hath **d** this, and the Holy H6213
44:23 for the LORD hath **d** *it*: shout, ye lower H6213
46:10 that are not *yet* **d**, saying, My counsel H6213
48: 5 Mine idol hath **d** them, and my graven H6213
53: 9 because he had **d** no violence, neither H6213
Jer 2:23 know what thou hast **d**: *thou art* a swift H6213
3: 5 and **d** evil things as thou couldest. H6213
6 Israel hath **d**? she is gone up upon H6213
7 And I said after she had **d** all these H6213
16 *it*; neither shall *that* be **d** any more. H6213
5:13 in them: thus shall it be **d** unto them. H6213
7:13 And now, because ye have **d** all these H6213
14 to your fathers, as I have **d** to Shiloh. H6213
30 For the children of Judah have **d** evil in H6213
8: 6 What have I **d**? every one turned to H6213
11:17 which they have **d** against themselves H6213
16:12 And ye have **d** worse than your fathers; H6213
18:13 of Israel hath **d** a very horrible thing. H6213
22: 8 the LORD **d** thus unto this great city? H6213

Jer 30:15 I have **d** these things unto thee. H6213
24 until he have **d** *it*, and until he have H6213
31:37 for all that they have **d**, saith the LORD. H6213
32:23 thy law; they have **d** nothing of all that H6213
30 Judah have only **d** evil before me from H6213
32 which they have **d** to provoke me to H6213
34:15 And ye were now turned, and had **d** H6213
35:10 have obeyed, and **d** according to all H6213
18 his precepts, and **d** according unto all H6213
38: 9 My lord the king, these men have **d** evil
9 in all that they have **d** to Jeremiah the H6213
40: 3 Now the LORD hath brought *it*, and **d** H6213
41:11 Ishmael the son of Nethaniah had **d**, H6213
42:10 me of the evil that I have **d** unto you. H6213
44:17 her, as we have **d**, we, and our fathers, H6213
48:19 her that escapeth, *and* say, What is **d**? H1961
50:15 upon her; as she hath **d**, do unto her. H6213
29 all that she hath **d**, do unto her: for she H6213
51:12 hath both devised and **d** that which he H6213
24 **d** in Zion in your sight, saith the LORD. H6213
35 The violence **d** to me and to my flesh *be*
52: 2 according to all that Jehoiakim had **d**. H6213
Lam 1:12 sorrow, which is **d** unto me, wherewith H5953
21 that thou hast **d** *it*: thou wilt bring the H6213
22 them, as thou hast **d** unto me for all my H5953
2:17 The LORD hath **d** *that* which he had H6213
20 to whom thou hast **d** this. Shall the H5953
Ezk 3:20 which he hath **d** shall not be H6213
5: 7 neither have **d** according to the H6213
9 which I have not **d**, and whereunto I H6213
9: 4 that be **d** in the midst thereof. H6213
11 I have **d** as thou hast commanded me. H6213
11:12 but have **d** after the manners of H6213
12:11 Say, I *am* your sign: like as I have **d**, so H6213
11 done, so shall it be **d** unto them: they H6213
28 spoken shall be **d**, saith the Lord GOD. H6213
14:23 that I have not **d** without cause all that H6213
23 that I have **d** in it, saith the Lord GOD. H6213
16:47 after their ways, nor **d** after their H6213
48 Sodom thy sister hath not **d**, she nor her H6213
48 as thou hast **d**, thou and thy daughters. H6213
51 thine abominations which thou hast **d**. H6213
54 **d**, in that thou art a comfort unto them. H6213
59 with thee as thou hast **d**, which hast H6213
63 all that thou hast **d**, saith the Lord GOD. H6213
17:18 **d** all these *things*, he shall not escape. H6213
24 I the LORD have spoken and have **d** *it*. H6213
18:13 shall not live: he hath **d** all these H6213
14 which he hath **d**, and considereth, and H6213
19 the son hath **d** that which is lawful H6213
19 and hath **d** them, he shall surely live. H6213
22 that he hath **d** he shall live. H6213
24 that he hath **d** shall not be mentioned: H6213
26 his iniquity that he hath **d** shall he die. H6213
23:38 Moreover this they have **d** unto me: H6213
39 have they **d** in the midst of mine house. H6213
24:22 And ye shall do as I have **d**: ye shall not H6213
24 to all that he hath **d** shall ye do: and H6213
33:16 unto him: he hath **d** that which is H6213
39: 8 Behold, it is come, and it is **d**, saith the H1961
24 have I **d** unto them, and hid H6213
43:11 of all that they have **d**, shew them the H6213
44:14 and for all that shall be **d** therein. H6213
Dan 6:22 before thee, O king, have I **d** no hurt. H5648
9: 5 iniquity, and have **d** wickedly, and have
12 **d** as hath been done upon Jerusalem. H6213
12 done as hath been **d** upon Jerusalem. H6213
15 we have sinned, we have **d** wickedly.
11:24 his fathers have not **d**, nor his fathers' H6213
36 for that that is determined shall be **d**. H6213
Hos 2: 5 them hath **d** shamefully: for she said,
Joel 2:20 up, because he hath **d** great things. H6213
Am 3: 6 in a city, and the LORD hath not **d** *it*? H6213
Oba 15 as thou hast **d**, it shall be done unto H6213
15 hast done, it shall be **d** unto thee: thy H6213
Jna 1:10 Why hast thou **d** this? For the men H6213
14 O LORD, hast **d** as it pleased thee. H6213
Mic 6: 3 O my people, what have I **d** unto thee? H6213
Zep 3: 4 they have **d** violence to the law.
Zec 7: 3 as I have **d** these so many years? H6213
Mal 2:13 And this have ye **d** again, covering the H6213
Mt 1:22 Now all this was **d**, that it might be *G1096*
6:10 Thy kingdom come. Thy will be **d** in *G1096*
7:22 in thy name **d** many wonderful works? *G4160*
8:13 believed, *so* be it **d** unto thee. And his *G1096*
11:20 were **d**, because they repented not: *G1096*
21 which were **d** in you, had been done *G1096*
21 in you, had been **d** in Tyre and Sidon, *G1096*
23 which have been **d** in thee, had been *G1096*
Mt 11:23 in thee, had been **d** in Sodom, it would *G1096*
13:28 He said unto them, An enemy hath **d** *G4160*
17:12 knew him not, but have **d** unto him *G4160*
18:19 ask, it shall be **d** for them of my Father *G1096*
31 saw what was **d**, they were very sorry, *G1096*
31 and told unto their lord all that was **d**. *G1096*
21: 4 All this was **d**, that it might be fulfilled *G1096*
21 do this *which is* **d** to the fig tree, but *G1096*
21 be thou cast into the sea; it shall be **d**. *G1096*
23:23 **d**, and not to leave the other undone. *G4160*
25:21 His lord said unto him, Well **d**, *thou* *G2095*
23 His lord said unto him, Well **d**, good *G2095*
40 as ye have **d** *it* unto one of the least *G4160*
40 my brethren, ye have **d** *it* unto me. *G4160*
26:13 hath **d**, be told for a memorial of her. *G4160*
42 from me, except I drink it, thy will be **d**. *G1096*
56 But all this was **d**, that the scriptures of *G1096*
27:23 what evil hath he **d**? But they cried out *G4160*
54 things that were **d**, they feared greatly, *G1096*
28:11 chief priests all the things that were **d**. *G1096*
Mk 4:11 all *these* things are **d** in parables: *G1096*
5:14 went out to see what it was that was **d**. *G1096*
19 the Lord hath **d** for thee, and hath had *G4160*
20 had **d** for him: and all *men* did marvel. *G4160*
32 about to see her that had **d** this thing. *G4160*
33 what was **d** in her, came and fell *G1096*
6:30 they had **d**, and what they had taught. *G4160*
7:37 saying, He hath **d** all things well: he *G4160*
9:13 and they have **d** unto him whatsoever *G4160*
13:30 shall not pass, till all these things be **d**. *G1096*
14: 8 She hath **d** what she could: she is come *G4160*
9 also that she hath **d** shall be spoken of *G4160*
15: 8 *him to do* as he had ever **d** unto them. *G4160*
14 what evil hath he **d**? And they cried out *G4160*
Lk 1:49 For he that is mighty hath **d** to me *G4160*
3:19 and for all the evils which Herod had **d**, *G4160*
4:23 we have heard **d** in Capernaum, do *G1096*
5: 6 And when they had this **d**, they inclosed *G4160*
8:34 saw what was **d**, they fled, and went *G1096*
35 Then they went out to see what was **d**; *G1096*
39 things God hath **d** unto thee. And he *G4160*
39 how great things Jesus had **d** unto him. *G4160*
56 they should tell no man what was **d**. *G1096*
9: 7 of all that was **d** by him: and he was *G1096*
10 all that they had **d**. And he took them, *G4160*
10:13 works had been **d** in Tyre and Sidon, *G1096*
13 which have been **d** in you, they had a *G1096*
11: 2 Thy will be **d**, as in heaven, so in earth. *G1096*
42 **d**, and not to leave the other undone. *G4160*
13:17 the glorious things that were **d** by him. *G1096*
14:22 And the servant said, Lord, it is **d** as *G1096*
16: 8 because he had **d** wisely: for the *G4160*
17:10 So likewise ye, when ye shall have **d** all *G4160*
10 have **d** that which was our duty to do. *G4160*
22:42 not my will, but thine, be **d**. *G1096*
23: 8 to have seen some miracle **d** by him. *G1096*
15 nothing worthy of death is **d** unto him. *G4238*
22 what evil hath he **d**? I have found no *G4160*
31 a green tree, what shall be **d** in the dry? *G1096*
41 but this man hath **d** nothing amiss. *G4238*
47 saw what was **d**, he glorified God, *G1096*
48 **d**, smote their breasts, and returned. *G1096*
24:21 the third day since these things were **d**. *G1096*
35 And they told what things *were* **d** in the
Jn 1:28 These things were **d** in Bethabara *G1096*
5:16 had **d** these things on the sabbath day. *G4160*
29 And shall come forth; they that have **d** *G4160*
29 and they that have **d** evil, unto the *G4238*
7:21 I have **d** one work, and ye all marvel. *G4160*
31 than these which this *man* hath **d**? *G4160*
11:46 and told them what things Jesus had **d**. *G4160*
12:16 *that* they had **d** these things unto him. *G4160*
18 they heard that he had **d** this miracle. *G4160*
37 But though he had **d** so many miracles *G4160*
13:12 them, Know ye what I have **d** to you? *G4160*
15 that ye should do as I have **d** to you. *G4160*
15: 7 what ye will, and it shall be **d** unto you. *G1096*
24 If I had not **d** among them the works *G4160*
18:35 thee unto me: what hast thou **d**? *G4160*
19:36 For these things were **d**, that the *G1096*
Act 2:43 and signs were **d** by the apostles. *G1096*
4: 7 or by what name, have ye **d** this? *G4160*
9 of the good deed **d** to the impotent *G2108*
16 notable miracle hath been **d** by them *is* *G1096*
21 *men* glorified God for that which was **d**. *G1096*
28 thy counsel determined before to be **d**. *G1096*
30 **d** by the name of thy holy child Jesus. *G1096*
5: 7 wife, not knowing what was **d**, came in. *G1096*
8:13 the miracles and signs which were **d**. *G1096*
Act 9:13 he hath **d** to thy saints at Jerusalem: *G4160*
10:16 This was **d** thrice: and the vessel was *G1096*
33 thee; and thou hast well **d** that thou art *G4160*
11:10 And this was **d** three times: and all *G1096*
12: 9 was true which was **d** by the angel; but *G1096*
13:12 he saw what was **d**, believed, being *G1096*
14: 3 and wonders to be **d** by their hands. *G1096*
11 what Paul had **d**, they lifted up their *G4160*
13 would have **d** sacrifice with the people.
18 that they had not **d** sacrifice unto them.
27 all that God had **d** with them, and how *G4160*
15: 4 all things that God had **d** with them. *G4160*
21:14 saying, The will of the Lord be **d**. *G1096*
33 who he was, and what he had **d**. *G4160*
24: 2 **d** unto this nation by thy providence, *G1096*
25:10 I **d** no wrong, as thou very well knowest. *G91*
26:26 for this thing was not **d** in a corner. *G4238*
28: 9 So when this was **d**, others also, which *G1096*
Ro 9:11 neither having **d** any good or evil, that *G4238*
1Co 5: 2 that he that hath **d** this deed might be *G4160*
3 him that hath so **d** this deed, *G2716*
9:15 it should be so **d** unto me: for *it were* *G1096*
13:10 that which is in part shall be **d** away. *G2763*
14:26 Let all things be **d** unto edifying. *G1096*
40 Let all things be **d** decently and in *G1096*
16:14 Let all your things be **d** with charity. *G1096*
2Co 3: 7 which *glory* was to be **d** away: *G2763*
11 For if that which is **d** away *was* *G2763*
14 which *veil* is **d** away in Christ. *G2763*
5:10 may receive the things *d* in *his* body,
10 he hath **d**, whether *it be* good or bad. *G4238*
7:12 his cause that had **d** the wrong, nor for *G91*
Eph 5:12 things which are **d** of them in secret. *G1096*
6:13 the evil day, and having **d** all, to stand. *G2716*
Php 2: 3 *Let* nothing *be* **d** through strife or
4:14 Notwithstanding ye have well **d**, that ye *G4160*
Col 3:25 **d**: and there is no respect of persons. *G91*
4: 9 unto you all things which *are* **d** here.
Tit 3: 5 which we have **d**, but according to his *G4160*
Heb 10:29 hath **d** despite unto the Spirit of grace? *G1796*
36 that, after ye have **d** the will of God, ye *G4160*
Rev 16:17 heaven, from the throne, saying, It is **d**. *G1096*
21: 6 And he said unto me, It is **d**. I am Alpha *G1096*
22: 6 the things which must shortly be **d**. *G1096*

DOOR

Gen 4: 7 sin lieth at the **d**. And unto thee *shall* H6607
6:16 it above; and the **d** of the ark shalt thou H6607
18: 1 sat in the tent **d** in the heat of the day; H6607
2 from the tent **d**, and bowed himself H6607
10 *it* in the tent **d**, which *was* behind him. H6607
19: 6 And Lot went out at the **d** unto them, H6607
6 unto them, and shut the **d** after him, H1817
9 *even* Lot, and came near to break the **d**. H1817
10 the house to them, and shut to the **d**. H1817
11 that *were* at the **d** of the house with H6607
11 they wearied themselves to find the **d**. H6607
43:19 with him at the **d** of the house, H6607
Ex 12: 7 and on the upper **d** post of the houses, H4947
22 at the **d** of his house until the morning. H6607
23 will pass over the **d**, and will not suffer H6607
21: 6 also bring him to the **d**, or unto the door H1817
6 the door, or unto the **d** post; and his H4201
26:36 an hanging for the **d** of the tent, *of* H6607
29: 4 bring unto the **d** of the tabernacle of H6607
11 **d** of the tabernacle of the congregation. H6607
32 **d** of the tabernacle of the congregation. H6607
42 generations *at* the **d** of the tabernacle H6607
33: 8 man *at* his tent **d**, and looked after H6607
9 and stood *at* the **d** of the tabernacle, H6607
10 *at* the tabernacle **d**: and all the people H6607
10 worshipped, every man *in* his tent **d**. H6607
35:15 **d** at the entering in of the tabernacle, H6607
17 and the hanging for the **d** of the court, H8179
36:37 for the tabernacle **d** *of* blue, and H6607
38: 8 **d** of the tabernacle of the congregation. H6607
30 the sockets to the **d** of the tabernacle of H6607
39:38 and the hanging for the tabernacle **d**, H6607
40: 5 the hanging of the **d** to the tabernacle. H6607
6 offering before the **d** of the tabernacle H6607
12 his sons unto the **d** of the tabernacle of H6607
28 And he set up the hanging *at* the **d** of H6607
29 offering *by* the **d** of the tabernacle of H6607
Lev 1: 3 will at the **d** of the tabernacle of H6607
5 **d** of the tabernacle of the congregation. H6607
3: 2 and kill it *at* the **d** of the tabernacle of H6607
4: 4 bullock unto the **d** of the tabernacle of H6607
7 **d** of the tabernacle of the congregation. H6607
18 **d** of the tabernacle of the congregation. H6607

Lev 8: 3 **d** of the tabernacle of the congregation. H6607
4 **d** of the tabernacle of the congregation. H6607
31 the flesh *at* the **d** of the tabernacle of H6607
33 And ye shall not go out of the **d** of the H6607
35 Therefore shall ye abide *at* the **d** of the H6607
10: 7 And ye shall not go out from the **d** of H6607
12: 6 offering, unto the **d** of the tabernacle of H6607
14:11 **d** of the tabernacle of the congregation: H6607
23 priest, unto the **d** of the tabernacle of H6607
38 of the house to the **d** of the house, and H6607
15:14 LORD unto the **d** of the tabernacle of H6607
29 **d** of the tabernacle of the congregation. H6607
16: 7 **d** of the tabernacle of the congregation. H6607
17: 4 And bringeth it not unto the **d** of the H6607
5 LORD, unto the **d** of the tabernacle of H6607
6 of the LORD *at* the **d** of the tabernacle H6607
9 And bringeth it not unto the **d** of the H6607
19:21 LORD, unto the **d** of the tabernacle of H6607
Nu 3:25 **d** of the tabernacle of the congregation, H6607
26 the curtain for the **d** of the court, which H6607
4:25 **d** of the tabernacle of the congregation, H6607
26 the hanging for the **d** of the gate of the H6607
6:10 **d** of the tabernacle of the congregation: H6607
13 **d** of the tabernacle of the congregation: H6607
18 separation *at* the **d** of the tabernacle of H6607
10: 3 **d** of the tabernacle of the congregation. H6607
11:10 every man in the **d** of his tent: and the H6607
12: 5 and stood *in* the **d** of the tabernacle, H6607
16:18 and stood in the **d** of the tabernacle of H6607
19 them unto the **d** of the tabernacle of H6607
27 and stood in the **d** of their tents, and H6607
50 Moses unto the **d** of the tabernacle of H6607
20: 6 assembly unto the **d** of the tabernacle H6607
25: 6 **d** of the tabernacle of the congregation. H6607
27: 2 *by* the **d** of the tabernacle of H6607
Dt 11:20 And thou shalt write them upon the **d** H4201
15:17 his ear unto the **d**, and he shall be thy H1817
22:21 out the damsel to the **d** of her father's H6607
31:15 stood over the **d** of the tabernacle. H6607
Jos 19:51 the LORD, at the **d** of the tabernacle of H6607
Jdg 4:20 Again he said unto her, Stand in the **d** H6607
9:52 the **d** of the tower to burn it with fire. H6607
19:22 *and* beat at the **d**, and spake to the H1817
26 fell down at the **d** of the man's house H6607
27 fallen down *at* the **d** of the house, and H6607
1Sa 2:22 **d** of the tabernacle of the congregation. H6607
2Sa 11: 9 But Uriah slept at the **d** of the king's H6607
13:17 out from me, and bolt the **d** after her. H1817
18 her out, and bolted the **d** after her. H1817
1Ki 6: 8 The **d** for the middle chamber *was* in H6607
33 So also made he for the **d** of the temple H6607
34 leaves of the one **d** *were* folding, and H1817
34 two leaves of the other **d** *were* folding. H1817
14: 6 she came in at the **d**, that he said, Come H6607
17 to the threshold of the **d**, the child died; H1004
27 which kept the **d** of the king's house. H6607
2Ki 4: 4 shalt shut the **d** upon thee and upon H1817
5 So she went from him, and shut the **d** H1817
15 he had called her, she stood in the **d**. H6607
21 and shut *the d* upon him, and went out.
33 He went in therefore, and shut the **d** H1817
5: 9 stood at the **d** of the house of Elisha. H6607
6:32 cometh, shut the **d**, and hold him fast at H1817
32 him fast at the **d**: *is* not the sound of his H1817
9: 3 open the **d**, and flee, and tarry not. H1817
10 *her*. And he opened the **d**, and fled. H1817
12: 9 that kept the **d** put therein all the H5592
22: 4 of the **d** have gathered of the people: H5592
23: 4 the keepers of the **d**, to bring forth out H5592
25:18 priest, and the three keepers of the **d**: H5592
1Ch 9:21 **d** of the tabernacle of the congregation. H6607
Neh 3:20 *of the wall* unto the **d** of the house of H6607
21 piece, from the **d** of the house of H6607
Est 2:21 those which kept the **d**, were wroth, and H5592
6: 2 the keepers of the **d**, who sought to lay H5592
Job 31: 9 *if* I have laid wait at my neighbour's **d**; H6607
34 I kept silence, *and* went not out of the **d**? H6607
Ps 141: 3 my mouth; keep the **d** of my lips. H1817
Prv 5: 8 and come not nigh the **d** of her house: H6607
9:14 For she sitteth at the **d** of her house, on H6607
26:14 *As* the **d** turneth upon his hinges, so H1817
Song 5: 4 **d**, and my bowels were moved for him.
8: 9 and if she *be* a **d**, we will inclose her H1817
Isa 6: 4 And the posts of the **d** moved at the H5592
Jer 35: 4 the son of Shallum, the keeper of the **d**: H5592
52:24 priest, and the three keepers of the **d**: H5592
Ezk 8: 3 to Jerusalem, to the **d** of the inner gate H6607
7 And he brought me to the **d** of the H6607
8 I had digged in the wall, behold a **d**. H6607
Ezk 8:14 Then he brought me to the **d** of the gate H6607
16 behold, at the **d** of the temple of the H6607
10:19 *one* stood at the **d** of the east gate of H6607
11: 1 and behold at the **d** of the gate five and H6607
40:13 five and twenty cubits, **d** against door. H6607
13 five and twenty cubits, door against **d**. H6607
41: 2 And the breadth of the **d** *was* ten H6607
2 the sides of the **d** *were* five cubits on H6607
3 the post of the **d**, two cubits; and the H6607
3 cubits; and the **d**, six cubits; and the H6607
3 and the breadth of the **d**, seven cubits. H6607
11 *that was* left, one **d** toward the north, H6607
11 and another **d** toward the south: and H6607
16 The **d** posts, and the narrow windows, H6607
16 over against the **d**, cieled with wood H5592
17 To that above the **d**, even unto the inner H6607
20 From the ground unto above the **d** H6607
24 **d**, and two leaves for the other *door*. H1817
24 door, and two leaves for the other *d*. H1817
42: 2 **d**, and the breadth *was* fifty cubits. H6607
12 the south *was* a **d** in the head of the H6607
46: 3 worship at the **d** of this gate before the H6607
47: 1 me again unto the **d** of the house; and, H6607
Hos 2:15 of Achor for a **d** of hope: and she shall H6607
Am 9: 1 the lintel of the **d**, that the posts may
Mt 6: 6 thou hast shut thy **d**, pray to thy Father G2374
25:10 to the marriage: and the **d** was shut. G2374
27:60 to the **d** of the sepulchre, and departed. G2374
28: 2 the stone from the **d**, and sat upon it. G2374
Mk 1:33 the city was gathered together at the **d**. G2374
2: 2 **d**: and he preached the word unto them. G2374
11: 4 the colt tied by the **d** without in a place G2374
15:46 a stone unto the **d** of the sepulchre. G2374
16: 3 the stone from the **d** of the sepulchre? G2374
Lk 11: 7 me not: the **d** is now shut, and my G2374
13:25 and hath shut to the **d**, and ye begin to G2374
25 to knock at the **d**, saying, Lord, Lord, G2374
Jn 10: 1 not by the **d** into the sheepfold, but G2374
2 But he that entereth in by the **d** is the G2374
7 I say unto you, I am the **d** of the sheep. G2374
9 I am the **d**: by me if any man enter in, G2374
18:16 But Peter stood at the **d** without. Then G2374
16 that kept the **d**, and brought in Peter. G2377
17 Then saith the damsel that kept the **d** G2377
Act 5: 9 *are* at the **d**, and shall carry thee out. G2374
12: 6 keepers before the **d** kept the prison. G2374
13 And as Peter knocked at the **d** of the G2374
16 *d*, and saw him, they were astonished.
14:27 opened the **d** of faith unto the Gentiles. G2374
1Co 16: 9 For a great **d** and effectual is opened G2374
2Co 2:12 a **d** was opened unto me of the Lord, G2374
Col 4: 3 open unto us a **d** of utterance, to speak G2374
Jas 5: 9 behold, the judge standeth before the **d**. G2374
Rev 3: 8 thee an open **d**, and no man can shut G2374
20 Behold, I stand at the **d**, and knock: if G2374
20 and open the **d**, I will come in to him, G2374
4: 1 After this I looked, and, behold, a **d** G2374

DOORKEEPER
Ps 84:10 I had rather be a **d** in the house of my H5605

DOORKEEPERS
1Ch 15:23 And Berechiah and Elkanah *were* **d** for H7778
24 and Jehiah *were* **d** for the ark. H7778

DOOR-POST See DOOR and POST.

DOORS
Jos 2:19 shall go out of the **d** of thy house into H1817
Jdg 3:23 and shut the **d** of the parlour upon H1817
24 that, behold, the **d** of the parlour *were* H1817
25 he opened not the **d** of the parlour; H1817
11:31 forth of the **d** of my house to meet H1817
16: 3 and took the **d** of the gate of the city, H1817
19:27 and opened the **d** of the house, and H1817
1Sa 3:15 and opened the **d** of the house of the H1817
21:13 scrabbled on the **d** of the gate, and let H1817
1Ki 6:31 oracle he made **d** *of* olive tree: the lintel H1817
32 The two **d** also *were of* olive tree; and H1817
34 And the two **d** *were of* fir tree: the two H1817
7: 5 And all the **d** and posts *were* square, H6607
50 gold, *both* for the **d** of the inner house, H1817
50 the **d** of the house, *to wit*, of the temple. H1817
2Ki 18:16 *the gold from* the **d** of the temple of the H1817
1Ch 22: 3 the nails for the **d** of the gates, and for H1817
2Ch 3: 7 thereof, and the **d** thereof, with gold; H1817
4: 9 great court, and **d** for the court, and H1817
9 and overlaid the **d** of them with brass. H1817
22 house, the inner **d** thereof for the most H1817
2Ch 4:22 *place*, and the **d** of the house of the H1817
23: 4 of the Levites, *shall be* porters of the **d**; H5592
28:24 and shut up the **d** of the house of the H1817
29: 3 opened the **d** of the house of the LORD, H1817
7 Also they have shut up the **d** of the H1817
34: 9 that kept the **d** had gathered of the H5592
Neh 3: 1 it, and set up the **d** of it; even unto the H1817
3 and set up the **d** thereof, the locks H1817
6 and set up the **d** thereof, and the locks H1817
13 it, and set up the **d** thereof, the locks H1817
14 it, and set up the **d** thereof, the locks H1817
15 it, and set up the **d** thereof, the locks H1817
6: 1 I had not set up the **d** upon the gates;) H1817
10 and let us shut the **d** of the temple: for H1817
7: 1 I had set up the **d**, and the porters and H1817
3 let them shut the **d**, and bar *them*: and H1817
Job 3:10 Because it shut not up the **d** of my H1817
31:32 *but* I opened my **d** to the traveller. H1817
38: 8 Or *who* shut up the sea with **d**, when it H1817
10 it my decreed *place*, and set bars and **d**, H1817
17 thou seen the **d** of the shadow of death? H8179
41:14 Who can open the **d** of his face? his H1817
Ps 24: 7 **d**; and the King of glory shall come in. H6607
9 **d**; and the King of glory shall come in. H6607
78:23 above, and opened the **d** of heaven, H1817
Prv 8: 3 of the city, at the coming in at the **d**. H6607
34 my gates, waiting at the posts of my **d**. H6607
Ecc 12: 4 And the **d** shall be shut in the streets, H1817
Isa 26:20 and shut thy **d** about thee: hide thyself H1817
57: 8 Behind the **d** also and the posts hast H1817
Ezk 33:30 walls and in the **d** of the houses, and H6607
41:11 And the **d** of the side chambers *were* H6607
23 temple and the sanctuary had two **d**. H1817
24 And the **d** had two leaves *apiece*, two H1817
25 made on them, on the **d** of the temple, H1817
42: 4 cubit; and their **d** toward the north. H6607
11 their fashions, and according to their **d**. H6607
12 And according to the **d** of the chambers H6607
Mic 7: 5 a guide: keep the **d** of thy mouth from H6607
Zec 11: 1 Open thy **d**, O Lebanon, that the fire H1817
Mal 1:10 would shut the **d** *for nought*? neither H1817
Mt 24:33 know that it is near, *even* at the **d**. G2374
Mk 13:29 pass, know that it is nigh, *even* at the **d**. G2374
Jn 20:19 week, when the **d** were shut where the G2374
26 came Jesus, the **d** being shut, and stood G2374
Act 5:19 **d**, and brought them forth, and said, G2374
23 without before the **d**: but when we had G2374
16:26 all the **d** were opened, and every G2374
27 seeing the prison **d** open, he drew out G2374
21:30 temple: and forthwith the **d** were shut. G2374

DOPHKAH
Nu 33:12 wilderness of Sin, and encamped in **D**. H1850
13 And they departed from **D**, and H1850

DOR
Jos 11: 2 and in the borders of **D** on the west, H1756
12:23 The king of **D** in the coast of Dor, one; H1756
23 The king of Dor in the coast of **D**, one; H1756
17:11 the inhabitants of **D** and her towns, H1756
Jdg 1:27 the inhabitants of **D** and her towns, H1756
1Ki 4:11 in all the region of **D**; which had H1756
1Ch 7:29 and her towns, **D** and her towns. In H1756

DORCAS
Act 9:36 is called **D**: this woman was full G1393
39 **D** made, while she was with them. G1393

DOST See the Appendix.

DOTE
Jer 50:36 and they shall **d**: a sword *is* upon her H2973

DOTED
Ezk 23: 5 was mine; and she **d** on her lovers, on H5689
7 **d**: with all their idols she defiled herself. H5689
9 of the Assyrians, upon whom she **d**. H5689
12 She **d** upon the Assyrians *her* H5689
16 with her eyes, she **d** upon them, and H5689
20 For she **d** upon their paramours, whose H5689

DOTH See the Appendix.

DOTHAN
Gen 37:17 say, Let us go to **D**. And Joseph went H1886
17 his brethren, and found them in **D**. H1886
2Ki 6:13 was told him, saying, Behold, *he is* in **D**. H1886

DOTING
1Ti 6: 4 He is proud, knowing nothing, but **d** *G3552*

DOUBLE
Gen 43:12 And take **d** money in your hand; and H4932
15 and they took **d** money in their hand, H4932
Ex 22: 4 ox, or ass, or sheep; he shall restore **d**. H8147
7 if the thief be found, let him pay **d**. H8147
9 he shall pay **d** unto his neighbour. H8147
26: 9 and shalt **d** the sixth curtain in H3717
39: 9 the breastplate **d**: a span *was* the length H3717
Dt 15:18 he hath been worth a **d** hired servant *to* H4932
21:17 by giving him a **d** portion of all that he H8147
2Ki 2: 9 let a **d** portion of thy spirit be upon me. H8147
1Ch 12:33 keep rank: *they were* not of **d** heart. H3820
Job 11: 6 that *they are* **d** to that which is! Know H3718
41:13 who can come *to him* with his **d** bridle? H3718
Ps 12: 2 lips *and* with a **d** heart do they speak. H3820
Isa 40: 2 of the LORD'S hand **d** for all her sins. H3718
61: 7 For your shame *ye shall have* **d**; and *for* H4932
7 **d**: everlasting joy shall be unto them. H4932
Jer 16:18 and their sin **d**; because they have H4932
17:18 and destroy them with **d** destruction. H4932
Zec 9:12 I declare *that* I will render **d** unto thee; H4932
1Ti 5:17 counted worthy of **d** honour, especially *G1362*
Jas 1: 8 A **d** minded man *is* unstable in all his *G1374*
4: 8 and purify *your* hearts, *ye* **d** minded. *G1374*
Rev 18: 6 you, and **d** unto her double according *G1363*
6 and double unto her **d** according to her *G1362*
6 cup which she hath filled fill to her **d**. *G1362*

DOUBLED
Gen 41:32 And for that the dream was **d** unto H8138
Ex 28:16 Foursquare it shall be *being* **d**; a span H3717
39: 9 and a span the breadth thereof, *being* **d**. H3717
Ezk 21:14 let the sword be **d** the third time, the H3717

DOUBLE-MINDED See DOUBLE and MINDED.

DOUBLETONGUED
1Ti 3: 8 *be* grave, not **d**, not given to much wine, *G1351*

DOUBT
Gen 37:33 him; Joseph is without **d** rent in pieces.
Dt 28:66 And thy life shall hang in **d** before thee;
Job 12: 2 No **d** but ye *are* the people, and wisdom H551
Mt 14:31 of little faith, wherefore didst thou **d**? *G1365*
21:21 If ye have faith, and **d** not, ye shall not *G1252*
Mk 11:23 the sea; and shall not **d** in his heart, but *G1252*
Lk 11:20 **d** the kingdom of God is come upon you. *G687*
Jn 10:24 thou make us to **d**? If thou be the *G142+G5590*
Act 2:12 and were in **d**, saying one to another, *G1280*
28: 4 among themselves, No **d** this man is a *G3843*
1Co 9:10 For our sakes, no **d**, *this* is written: that *G1063*
Gal 4:20 change my voice; for I stand in **d** of you. *G639*
1Jn 2:19 us, they would *no* **d** have continued with

DOUBTED
Mt 28:17 him, they worshipped him: but some **d**. *G1365*
Act 5:24 **d** of them whereunto this would grow. *G1280*
10:17 Now while Peter **d** in himself what this *G1280*
25:20 And because I **d** of such manner of *G639*

DOUBTETH
Ro 14:23 And he that **d** is damned if he eat, *G1252*

DOUBTFUL
Lk 12:29 ye shall drink, neither be ye of **d** mind. *G3349*
Ro 14: 1 receive ye, *but* not to **d** disputations. *G1261*

DOUBTING
Jn 13:22 one on another, **d** of whom he spake. *G639*
Act 10:20 them, **d** nothing: for I have sent them. *G1252*
11:12 them, nothing **d**. Moreover these six *G1252*
1Ti 2: 8 up holy hands, without wrath and **d**. *G1261*

DOUBTLESS
Nu 14:30 **D** ye shall not come into the land, H518
2Sa 5:19 **d** deliver the Philistines into thine hand.
Ps 126: 6 seed, shall **d** come again with rejoicing,
Isa 63:16 **D** thou *art* our father, though Abraham H3588
1Co 9: 2 If I be not an apostle unto others, yet **d** *G1065*
2Co 12: 1 It is not expedient for me **d** to glory. I *G1211*
Php 3: 8 Yea **d**, and I count all things *but* loss for *G3304*

DOUBTS
Dan 5:12 and dissolving of **d**, were found in the H7001
16 and dissolve **d**: now if thou canst read H7001

DOUGH
Ex 12:34 And the people took their **d** before it H1217
39 cakes of the **d** which they brought H1217
Nu 15:20 cake of the first of your **d** *for* an heave H6182
21 Of the first of your **d** ye shall give unto H6182
Neh 10:37 firstfruits of our **d**, and our offerings, H6182
Jer 7:18 knead *their* **d**, to make cakes to the H1217
Ezk 44:30 the first of your **d**, that he may cause H6182
Hos 7: 4 hath kneaded the **d**, until it be leavened. H1217

DOVE
Gen 8: 8 Also he sent forth a **d** from him, to see H3123
9 But the **d** found no rest for the sole of H3123
10 again he sent forth the **d** out of the ark; H3123
11 And the **d** came in to him in the H3123
12 and sent forth the **d**; which returned not H3123
Ps 55: 6 And I said, Oh that I had wings like a **d**! H3123
68:13 *as* the wings of a **d** covered with silver, H3123
Song 2:14 O my **d**, *that art* in the clefts of the rock, H3123
5: 2 my love, my **d**, my undefiled: for my H3123
6: 9 My **d**, my undefiled is *but* one; she *is* H3123
Isa 38:14 I did mourn as a **d**: mine eyes fail *with* H3123
Jer 48:28 and be like the **d** *that* maketh her nest H3123
Hos 7:11 Ephraim also is like a silly **d** without H3123
11:11 of Egypt, and as a **d** out of the land of H3123
Mt 3:16 like a **d**, and lighting upon him: *G4058*
Mk 1:10 Spirit like a **d** descending upon him: *G4058*
Lk 3:22 shape like a **d** upon him, and a voice *G4058*
Jn 1:32 heaven like a **d**, and it abode upon him. *G4058*

DOVES
Song 5:12 His eyes *are as the eyes* of **d** by the H3123
Isa 59:11 and mourn sore like **d**: we look for H3123
60: 8 a cloud, and as the **d** to their windows? H3123
Ezk 7:16 mountains like **d** of the valleys, all of H3123
Nah 2: 7 voice of **d**, tabering upon their breasts. H3123
Mt 10:16 wise as serpents, and harmless as **d**. *G4058*
21:12 and the seats of them that sold **d**, *G4058*
Mk 11:15 and the seats of them that sold **d**; *G4058*
Jn 2:14 **d**, and the changers of money sitting: *G4058*
16 And said unto them that sold **d**, Take *G4058*

DOVE'S
2Ki 6:25 a cab of **d** dung for five *pieces* of silver. H1686

DOVES'
Song 1:15 behold, thou *art* fair; thou *hast* **d** eyes. H3123
4: 1 *art* fair; thou *hast* **d** eyes within thy H3123

DOWN
Gen 11: 5 And the LORD came **d** to see the city H3381
7 Go to, let us go **d**, and there confound H3381
12:10 land: and Abram went **d** into Egypt to H3381
15:11 And when the fowls came **d** upon the H3381
12 And when the sun was going **d**, a deep H935
17 when the sun went **d**, and it was dark, H935
18:21 I will go **d** now, and see whether they H3381
19: 4 But before they lay **d**, the men of the H7901
33 not when she lay **d**, nor when she arose. H7901
35 not when she lay **d**, nor when she arose. H7901
21:16 And she went, and sat her **d** over H3427
23:12 And Abraham bowed **d** himself before H7812
24:11 And he made his camels to kneel **d** H1288
14 I shall say, Let **d** thy pitcher, I pray H5186
16 her: and she went **d** to the well, and H3381
18 hasted, and let **d** her pitcher upon her H3381
26 And the man bowed **d** his head, and H6915
45 and she went **d** unto the well, and drew H3381
46 And she made haste, and let **d** her H3381
48 And I bowed **d** my head, and H6915
26: 2 and said, Go not **d** into Egypt; dwell in H3381
27:29 and nations bow **d** to thee: be lord over H7812
29 sons bow **d** to thee: cursed *be* every H7812
28:11 pillows, and lay **d** in that place to sleep. H7901
37:10 to bow **d** ourselves to thee to the earth? H7812
25 And they sat **d** to eat bread: and they H3427
25 and myrrh, going to carry *it* **d** to Egypt. H3381
35 said, For I will go **d** into the grave unto H3381
38: 1 that Judah went **d** from his brethren, H3381
39: 1 And Joseph was brought **d** to Egypt; H3381
1 which had brought him **d** thither. H3381
42: 2 in Egypt: get you **d** thither, and buy for H3381
3 And Joseph's ten brethren went **d** to H3381
6 came, and bowed **d** themselves before H7812
38 And he said, My son shall not go **d** with H3381
38 go, then shall ye bring **d** my gray hairs H3381
43: 4 with us, we will go **d** and buy thee food: H3381
5 we will not go **d**: for the man said unto H3381
7 that he would say, Bring your brother **d**? H3381
Gen 43:11 vessels, and carry **d** the man a present, H3381
15 **d** to Egypt, and stood before Joseph. H3381
20 And said, O sir, we came indeed **d** at H3381
22 And other money have we brought **d** in H3381
28 **d** their heads, and made obeisance. H6915
44:11 Then they speedily took **d** every man H3381
21 Bring him **d** unto me, that I may H3381
23 brother come **d** with you, ye shall see H3381
26 And we said, We cannot go **d**: if our H3381
26 us, then will we go **d**: for we may not see H3381
29 ye shall bring **d** my gray hairs with H3381
31 shall bring **d** the gray hairs of thy H3381
45: 9 of all Egypt: come **d** unto me, tarry not: H3381
13 haste and bring **d** my father hither. H3381
46: 3 fear not to go **d** into Egypt; for I will H3381
4 I will go **d** with thee into Egypt; and I H3381
49: 6 in their selfwill they digged **d** a wall. H6131
8 children shall bow **d** before thee. H7812
9 up: he stooped **d**, he couched as a lion, H3766
14 Issachar *is* a strong ass couching **d** H7257
50:18 And his brethren also went and fell **d** H5307
Ex 2: 5 And the daughter of Pharaoh came **d** H3381
15 land of Midian: and he sat **d** by a well. H3427
3: 8 And I am come **d** to deliver them out of H3381
7:10 and Aaron cast **d** his rod before H7993
12 For they cast **d** every man his rod, and H7993
9:19 come **d** upon them, and they shall die. H3381
11: 8 And all these thy servants shall come **d** H3381
8 unto me, and bow **d** themselves unto H7812
17:11 he let **d** his hand, Amalek prevailed. H5117
12 were steady until the going **d** of the sun. H935
19:11 LORD will come **d** in the sight of all the H3381
14 And Moses went **d** from the mount H3381
20 And the LORD came **d** upon mount H3381
21 And the LORD said unto Moses, Go **d**, H3381
24 Away, get thee **d**, and thou shalt come H3381
25 So Moses went **d** unto the people, and H3381
20: 5 Thou shalt not bow **d** thyself to them, H7812
22:26 it unto him by that the sun goeth **d**: H935
23:24 Thou shalt not bow **d** to their gods, nor H7812
24 them, and quite break **d** their images. H7665
32: 1 delayed to come **d** out of the mount, H3381
6 and the people sat **d** to eat and to H3427
7 Go, get thee **d**; for thy people, which H3381
15 And Moses turned, and went **d** from H3381
34:13 their images, and cut **d** their groves: H3772
29 when Moses came **d** from mount Sinai H3381
29 when he came **d** from the mount, that H3381
Lev 9:22 them, and came **d** from offering of the H3381
11:35 shall be broken **d**: *for* they *are* unclean, H5422
14:45 And he shall break **d** the house, the H5422
18:23 a beast to lie **d** thereto: it *is* confusion. H7250
19:16 Thou shalt not go up and **d** *as* a
20:16 any beast, and lie **d** thereto, thou shalt H7250
22: 7 And when the sun is **d**, he shall be clean, H935
26: 1 **d** unto it: for I *am* the LORD your God. H7812
6 and ye shall lie **d**, and none shall make H7901
30 places, and cut **d** your images, and cast H3772
Nu 1:51 shall take it **d**: and when the tabernacle H3381
4: 5 they shall take **d** the covering vail, and H3381
10:17 And the tabernacle was taken **d**; and H3381
11:17 And I will come **d** and talk with thee H3381
25 And the LORD came **d** in a cloud, and H3381
12: 5 And the LORD came **d** in the pillar of H3381
13:23 of Eshcol, and cut **d** from thence a H3772
24 the children of Israel cut **d** from thence. H3772
14:45 Then the Amalekites came **d**, and the H3381
16:30 them, and they go **d** quick into the pit; H3381
33 to them, went **d** alive into the pit, and H3381
20:15 How our fathers went **d** into Egypt, and H3381
28 and Eleazar came **d** from the mount. H3381
21:15 brooks that goeth **d** to the dwelling of H5186
22:27 of the LORD, she fell **d** under Balaam: H7257
31 **d** his head, and fell flat on his face. H6915
23:24 lion: he shall not lie **d** until he eat *of* the H7901
24: 9 He couched, he lay **d** as a lion, and as a H7901
25: 2 did eat, and bowed **d** to their gods. H7812
33:52 and quite pluck **d** all their high places: H8045
34:11 And the coast shall go **d** from Shepham H3381
12 And the border shall go **d** to Jordan, H3381
Dt 1:25 and brought *it* **d** unto us, and brought H3381
5: 9 Thou shalt not bow **d** thyself unto H7812
6: 7 thou liest **d**, and when thou risest up. H7901
7: 5 altars, and break **d** their images, and H7665
5 images, and cut **d** their groves, and H1438
9: 3 shall bring them **d** before thy face: so H3665
12 unto me, Arise, get thee **d** quickly from H3381
15 So I turned and came **d** from the H3381
18 And I fell **d** before the LORD, as at the H5307

Dt 9:25 Thus I fell **d** before the LORD forty H5307
25 nights, as I fell **d** *at the first;* because H5307
10: 5 And I turned myself and came **d** from H3381
22 Thy fathers went **d** into Egypt with H3381
11:19 thou liest **d**, and when thou risest up.
30 where the sun goeth **d**, in the land of the H3996
12: 3 and ye shall hew **d** the graven images H1438
16: 6 at even, at the going **d** of the sun, at the H935
19: 5 with the axe to cut **d** the tree, and the H3772
20:19 shalt not cut them **d** (for the tree of the H3772
20 and cut them **d**; and thou shalt build H3772
21: 4 And the elders of that city shall bring **d** H3381
22: 4 ass or his ox fall **d** by the way, and hide H5307
23:11 is **d**, he shall come into the camp *again*. H935
24:13 the sun goeth **d**, that he may sleep in H935
15 shall the sun go **d** upon it; for he *is* poor, H935
19 When thou cuttest **d** thine harvest in H7114
25: 2 cause him to lie **d**, and to be beaten H5307
26: 4 **d** before the altar of the LORD thy God. H3240
5 father, and he went **d** into Egypt, and H3381
15 Look **d** from thy holy habitation, from H8259
28:24 **d** upon thee, until thou be destroyed. H3381
43 high; and thou shalt come **d** very low. H3381
52 and fenced walls come **d**, wherein thou H3381
33: 3 and they sat **d** at thy feet; *every one* H8497
28 also his heavens shall drop **d** dew. H6201
Jos 1: 4 going **d** of the sun, shall be your coast. H3996
2: 8 And before they were laid **d**, she came H7901
15 Then she let them **d** by a cord through H3381
18 thou didst let us **d** by: and thou shalt H3381
3:13 waters that come **d** from above; and H3381
16 That the waters which came **d** from H3381
16 those that came **d** toward the sea of the H3381
4: 8 they lodged, and laid them **d** there. H3240
6: 5 the city shall fall **d** flat, and the people H5307
20 that the wall fell **d** flat, so that the H5307
7: 5 them in the going **d**: wherefore the H4174
8:29 as the sun was **d**, Joshua commanded H935
29 take his carcase **d** from the tree, and H3381
10:11 were in the going **d** to Beth-horon, that H4174
11 that the LORD cast **d** great stones from H7993
13 hasted not to go **d** about a whole day. H935
27 the time of the going **d** of the sun, *that* H935
27 they took them **d** off the trees, and cast H3381
15:10 side, and went **d** to Beth-shemesh, and H3381
16: 3 And goeth **d** westward to the coast of H3381
7 And it went **d** from Janohah to H3381
17:15 *country,* and cut **d** for thyself there in H1254
18 thou shalt cut it **d**: and the outgoings of H1254
18:16 And the border came **d** to the end of H3381
18 northward, and went **d** unto Arabah: H3381
24: 4 and his children went **d** into Egypt. H3381
Jdg 1: 9 of Judah went **d** to fight against the H3381
34 not suffer them to come **d** to the valley: H3381
2: 2 ye shall throw **d** their altars: but ye H5422
19 them, and to bow **d** unto them; they H7812
3:25 lord *was* fallen **d** dead on the earth. H5307
27 of Israel went **d** with him from the H3381
28 And they went **d** after him, and took H3381
4:14 So Barak went **d** from mount Tabor, H3381
15 so that Sisera lighted **d** off *his* chariot, H3381
5:11 people of the LORD go **d** to the gates. H3381
14 of Machir came **d** governors, and out H3381
21 my soul, thou hast trodden **d** strength. H1869
27 At her feet he bowed, he fell, he lay **d**: at H7901
27 where he bowed, there he fell **d** dead. H5307
6:25 old, and throw **d** the altar of Baal that H2040
25 hath, and cut **d** the grove that *is* by it: H3772
26 of the grove which thou shalt cut **d**. H3772
28 of Baal was cast **d**, and the grove was H5422
28 the grove was cut **d** that *was* by it, and H3772
30 he hath cast **d** the altar of Baal, and H5422
30 he hath cut **d** the grove that *was* by it. H3772
31 because *one* hath cast **d** his altar. H5422
32 because he hath thrown **d** his altar. H5422
7: 4 *too* many; bring them **d** unto the water, H3381
5 So he brought **d** the people unto the H3381
5 that boweth **d** upon his knees to drink. H3766
6 **d** upon their knees to drink water. H3766
9 Arise, get thee **d** unto the host; for I H3381
10 But if thou fear to go **d**, go thou with H3381
10 with Phurah thy servant **d** to the host: H3381
11 to go **d** unto the host. Then H3381
11 host. Then went he **d** with Phurah his H3381
24 saying, Come **d** against the Midianites, H3381
8: 9 in peace, I will break **d** this tower. H5422
17 And he beat **d** the tower of Penuel, and H5422
9:36 there come people **d** from the top of the H3381
37 there come people **d** by the middle of H3381
Jdg 9:45 beat **d** the city, and sowed it with salt. H5422
48 his hand, and cut **d** a bough from the H3772
49 And all the people likewise cut **d** every H3772
11:37 that I may go up and **d** upon the H3381
14: 1 And Samson went **d** to Timnath, and H3381
5 Then went Samson **d**, and his father H3381
7 And he went **d**, and talked with the H3381
10 So his father went **d** unto the woman: H3381
18 the sun went **d**, What *is* sweeter than H935
19 him, and he went **d** to Ashkelon, and H3381
15: 8 and he went **d** and dwelt in the top H3381
12 him, We are come **d** to bind thee, that H3381
16:21 and brought him **d** to Gaza, and bound H3381
31 of his father came **d**, and took him, and H3381
19: 6 And they sat **d**, and did eat and drink H3427
14 and the sun went **d** upon them *when* H935
15 in, he sat him **d** in a street of the city: H3427
26 of the day, and fell **d** at the door of the H5307
27 was fallen **d** *at* the door of the house, H5307
20:21 and destroyed **d** to the ground of the
25 day, and destroyed **d** to the ground of
32 They *are* smitten **d** before us, as at the
39 smitten **d** before us, as *in* the first battle.
43 *and* trode them **d** with ease over against
Ru 3: 3 thee, and get thee **d** to the floor: *but* H3381
4 And it shall be, when he lieth **d**, that H7901
4 feet, and lay thee **d**; and he will tell thee H7901
6 And she went **d** unto the floor, and did H3381
7 he went to lie **d** at the end of the heap H7901
7 and uncovered his feet, and laid her **d**. H7901
13 LORD liveth: lie **d** until the morning. H7901
4: 1 gate, and sat him **d** there: and, behold, H3427
1 turn aside, sit **d** here. And he turned H3427
1 here. And he turned aside, and sat **d**. H3427
2 said, Sit ye **d** here. And they sat down. H3427
2 said, Sit ye down here. And they sat **d**. H3427
1Sa 2: 6 **d** to the grave, and bringeth up. H3381
3: 2 when Eli *was* laid **d** in his place, and H7901
3 *was,* and Samuel was laid **d** *to sleep;* H7901
5 lie **d** again. And he went and lay down. H7901
5 lie down again. And he went and lay **d**. H7901
6 I called not, my son; lie **d** again. H7901
9 Samuel, Go, lie **d**: and it shall be, if he H7901
9 So Samuel went and lay **d** in his place. H7901
6:15 And the Levites took **d** the ark of the H3381
18 Abel, whereon they set **d** the ark of the H3240
21 come ye **d**, *and* fetch it up to you. H3381
9:25 And when they were come **d** from the H3381
27 *And* as they were going **d** to the end of H3381
10: 5 prophets coming **d** from the high place H3381
8 And thou shalt go **d** before me to H3381
8 I will come **d** unto thee, to offer burnt H3381
13:12 will come **d** now upon me to Gilgal, H3381
20 But all the Israelites went **d** to the H3381
14:16 they went on beating **d** *one another.* H1986
36 And Saul said, Let us go **d** after the H3381
37 counsel of God, Shall I go **d** after the H3381
15: 6 Go, depart, get you **d** from among the H3381
12 and passed on, and gone **d** to Gilgal. H3381
16:11 for we will not sit **d** till he come hither. H5437
17: 8 man for you, and let him come **d** to me. H3381
28 Why camest thou **d** hither? and with H3381
28 **d** that thou mightest see the battle. H3381
52 of the Philistines fell **d** by the way to H5307
19:12 So Michal let David **d** through a H3381
24 manner, and lay **d** naked all that day H5307
20:19 *then* thou shalt go **d** quickly, and come H3381
24 come, the king sat him **d** to eat meat. H3427
21:13 and let his spittle fall **d** upon his beard. H3381
22: 1 heard *it,* they went **d** thither to him. H3381
23: 4 said, Arise, go **d** to Keilah; for I will H3381
6 he came **d** *with* an ephod in his hand. H3381
8 to war, to go **d** to Keilah, to besiege H3381
11 will Saul come **d**, as thy servant hath H3381
11 And the LORD said, He will come **d**. H3381
20 Now therefore, O king, come **d** H3381
20 of thy soul to come **d**; and our part *shall* H3381
25 he came **d** into a rock, and abode H3381
25: 1 and went **d** to the wilderness of Paran. H3381
20 ass, that she came **d** by the covert of H3381
20 came **d** against her; and she met them. H3381
26: 2 Then Saul arose, and went **d** to the H3381
6 Who will go **d** with me to Saul to the H3381
6 And Abishai said, I will go **d** with thee. H3381
29: 4 and let him not go **d** with us to battle, H3381
30:15 thou bring me **d** to this company? And H3381
15 and I will bring thee **d** to this company. H3381
16 And when he had brought him **d**, H3381
24 his part *is* that goeth **d** to the battle, so H3381
1Sa 31: 1 and fell **d** slain in mount Gilboa. H5307
2Sa 2:13 and they sat **d**, the one on the one side H3427
16 side; so they fell **d** together: wherefore H5307
23 him; and he fell **d** there, and died in the H5307
23 where Asahel fell **d** and died stood still. H5307
24 and the sun went **d** when they were H935
3:35 bread, or ought else, till the sun be **d**. H935
5:17 heard *of it,* and went **d** to the hold. H3381
8: 2 a line, casting them **d** to the ground; H7901
11: 8 And David said to Uriah, Go **d** to thy H3381
9 of his lord, and went not **d** to his house. H3381
10 Uriah went not **d** unto his house, David H3381
10 didst thou not go **d** unto thine house? H3381
13 of his lord, but went not **d** to his house. H3381
13: 5 And Jonadab said unto him, Lay thee **d** H7901
6 So Amnon lay **d**, and made himself H7901
8 and he was laid **d**. And she took flour, H7901
15:20 thee go up and **d** with us? seeing I go H5128
24 God: and they set **d** the ark of God; and H3332
17:18 a well in his court; whither they went **d**. H3381
18:28 is well. And he fell **d** to the earth upon H7812
19:16 hasted and came **d** with the men of H3381
18 son of Gera fell **d** before the king, as he H5307
20 to go **d** to meet my lord the king. H3381
24 son of Saul came **d** to meet the king, H3381
31 And Barzillai the Gileadite came **d** H3381
20:15 Joab battered the wall, to throw it **d**. H5307
21:15 and David went **d**, and his servants H3381
22:10 **d**; and darkness *was* under his feet. H3381
28 *that* thou mayest bring *them* **d**. H8213
48 that bringeth **d** the people under me, H3381
23:13 And three of the thirty chief went **d**, and H3381
20 of Moab: he went **d** also and slew a lion H3381
21 hand; but he went **d** to him with a staff, H3381
1Ki 1:25 For he is gone **d** this day, and hath H3381
33 own mule, and bring him **d** to Gihon: H3381
38 Pelethites, went **d**, and caused Solomon H3381
53 they brought him **d** from the altar. And H3381
2: 6 hoar head go **d** to the grave in peace. H3381
8 but he came **d** to meet me at Jordan, H3381
9 bring thou **d** to the grave with blood. H3381
19 unto her, and sat **d** on his throne, and H3427
5: 9 My servants shall bring *them* **d** from H3381
8:33 When thy people Israel be smitten **d** H5062
17:23 and brought him **d** out of the chamber H3381
18:30 altar of the LORD *that was* broken **d**. H2040
40 brought them **d** to the brook Kishon, H3381
42 he cast himself **d** upon the earth, and H1457
44 get thee **d**, that the rain stop thee not. H3381
19: 4 and came and sat **d** under a juniper H3427
6 eat and drink, and laid him **d** again. H7901
10 covenant, thrown **d** thine altars, and H2040
14 covenant, thrown **d** thine altars, and H2040
21: 4 And he laid him **d** upon his bed, and H7901
16 Ahab rose up to go **d** to the vineyard of H3381
18 Arise, go **d** to meet Ahab king of Israel, H3381
18 whither he is gone **d** to possess it. H3381
22: 2 of Judah came **d** to the king of Israel. H3381
36 about the going **d** of the sun, saying, H935
2Ki 1: 2 And Ahaziah fell **d** through a lattice in H5307
4 shalt not come **d** from that bed on H3381
6 thou shalt not come **d** from that bed on H3381
9 of God, the king hath said, Come **d**. H3381
10 then let fire come **d** from heaven, and H3381
10 And there came **d** fire from heaven, H3381
11 hath the king said, Come **d** quickly. H3381
12 God, let fire come **d** from heaven, and H3381
12 fire of God came **d** from heaven, and H3381
14 Behold, there came fire **d** from heaven, H3381
15 said unto Elijah, Go **d** with him: be not H3381
15 and went **d** with him unto the king. H3381
16 shalt not come **d** off that bed on which H3381
2: 2 leave thee. So they went **d** to Beth-el. H3381
3:12 and the king of Edom went **d** to him. H3381
25 And they beat **d** the cities, and on every H2040
5:14 Then went he **d**, and dipped himself H3381
18 when I bow **d** myself in the house H7812
21 him, he lighted **d** from the chariot to H5307
6: 4 they came to Jordan, they cut **d** wood. H1504
6 place. And he cut **d** a stick, and cast *it* H7094
9 for thither the Syrians are come **d**. H5185
18 And when they came **d** to him, Elisha H3381
33 messenger came **d** unto him: and he H3381
7:17 spake when the king came **d** to him. H3381
8:29 of Judah went **d** to see Joram the son H3381
9:16 king of Judah was come **d** to see Joram. H3381
24 his heart, and he sunk **d** in his chariot. H3766
33 And he said, Throw her **d**. So they threw H8058
33 So they threw her **d**: and *some* of her H8058

2Ki 10:13 and we go **d** to salute the children H3381
27 And they brake **d** the image of Baal, H5422
27 of Baal, and brake **d** the house of Baal, H5422
11: 6 of the house, that it be not broken **d**. H4535
18 Baal, and brake it **d**; his altars and his H5422
19 and they brought **d** the king from the H3381
12:20 house of Millo, which goeth **d** to Silla. H3381
13:14 of Israel came **d** unto him, and wept H3381
21 the man was let **d**, and touched the H3212
14: 9 in Lebanon, and trode **d** the thistle. H7429
13 and brake **d** the wall of Jerusalem H6555
16:17 off them; and took **d** the sea from off H3381
18: 4 the images, and cut **d** the groves, and H3772
19:16 LORD, bow **d** thine ear, and hear: H5186
23 and will cut **d** the tall cedar trees H3772
20:10 the shadow to go **d** ten degrees: nay, H5186
11 which it had gone **d** in the dial of Ahaz. H3381
21:13 dish, wiping *it*, and turning *it* upside **d**. H6440
23: 5 And he put **d** the idolatrous priests, H7673
7 And he brake **d** the houses of the H5422
8 and brake **d** the high places of the H5422
12 did the king beat **d**, and brake *them* H5422
12 and brake *them* **d** from thence, and H7323
14 images, and cut **d** the groves, and filled H3772
15 place he brake **d**, and burned the high H5422
25:10 **d** the walls of Jerusalem round about. H5422
1Ch 5:22 For there fell **d** many slain, because the H5307
7:21 they came **d** to take away their cattle. H3381
10: 1 and fell **d** slain in mount Gilboa. H5307
11:15 Now three of the thirty captains went **d** H3381
22 also he went **d** and slew a lion in a H3381
23 and he went **d** to him with a staff, H3381
29:20 fathers, and bowed **d** their heads, and H6915
2Ch 6:13 and kneeled **d** upon his knees before H1288
7: 1 the fire came **d** from heaven, and the H3381
3 how the fire came **d**, and the glory of H3381
13:17 so there fell **d** slain of Israel five H5307
14: 3 **d** the images, and cut down the groves: H7665
3 down the images, and cut **d** the groves: H1438
15:16 and Asa cut **d** her idol, and stamped H3772
18: 2 And after *certain* years he went **d** to H3381
34 the time of the sun going **d** he died.
20:16 To morrow go ye **d** against them: H3381
22: 6 of Judah went **d** to see Jehoram the son H3381
23:17 of Baal, and brake it **d**, and brake his H5422
20 land, and brought **d** the king from the H3381
25: 8 God hath power to help, and to cast **d**. H3782
12 and cast them **d** from the top of the H7993
14 his gods, and bowed **d** himself before H7812
18 in Lebanon, and trode **d** the thistle. H7429
23 and brake **d** the wall of Jerusalem H6555
26: 6 and brake **d** the wall of Gath, and H6555
31: 1 in pieces, and cut **d** the groves, and H1438
1 the groves, and threw **d** the high places H5422
32:30 brought it straight **d** to the west side of H4295
33: 3 father had broken **d**, and he reared up H5422
34: 4 And they brake **d** the altars of Baalim H5422
4 them, he cut **d**; and the groves, and H1438
7 And when he had broken **d** the altars H5422
7 into powder, and cut **d** all the idols H1438
36: 3 And the king of Egypt put him **d** at H5493
19 house of God, and brake **d** the wall of H5422
Ezr 6:11 timber be pulled **d** from his house, and H5256
9: 3 and of my beard, and sat **d** astonied. H3427
10: 1 casting himself **d** before the house of H5307
16 separated, and sat **d** in the first day of H3427
Neh 1: 3 also *is* broken **d**, and the gates thereof H6555
4 these words, that I sat **d** and wept, and H3427
2:13 were broken **d**, and the gates thereof H6555
3:15 stairs that go **d** from the city of David. H3381
4: 3 he shall even break **d** their stone wall. H6555
6: 3 I cannot come **d**: why should the work H3381
3 whilst I leave it, and come **d** to you? H3381
16 were much cast **d** in their own eyes: for H5307
9:13 Thou camest **d** also upon mount Sinai, H3381
Est 3:15 and Haman sat **d** to drink; but the city H3427
8: 3 the king, and fell **d** at his feet, and H5307
Job 1: 7 earth, and from walking up and **d** in it. H1980
20 **d** upon the ground, and worshipped, H5307
2: 2 earth, and from walking up and **d** in it. H1980
8 withal; and he sat **d** among the ashes. H3427
13 So they sat **d** with him upon the ground H3427
6:21 ye see *my* casting **d**, and are afraid. H2866
7: 4 When I lie **d**, I say, When shall I arise, H7901
9 **d** to the grave shall come up no *more*. H3381
19 let me alone till I swallow **d** my spittle? H1104
8:12 **d**, it withereth before any *other* herb. H6998
11:19 Also thou shalt lie **d**, and none shall H7257
12:14 Behold, he breaketh **d**, and it cannot be H2040

Job 14: 2 a flower, and is cut **d**: he fleeth also as a
7 For there is hope of a tree, if it be cut **d**,
12 So man lieth **d**, and riseth not: till the H7901
17: 3 Lay **d** now, put me in a surety with thee;
16 They shall go **d** to the bars of the pit, H3381
18: 7 and his own counsel shall cast him **d**. H7993
20:11 which shall lie **d** with him in the dust. H7901
15 He hath swallowed **d** riches, and he shall
18 shall not swallow *it* **d**: according to *his*
21:13 and in a moment go **d** to the grave. H5181
26 They shall lie **d** alike in the dust, and H7901
22:16 Which were cut **d** out of time, whose
20 Whereas our substance is not cut **d**, but
29 When *men* are cast **d**, then thou shalt H8213
27:19 The rich man shall lie **d**, but he shall H7901
29:24 light of my countenance they cast not **d**. H5307
31:10 and let others bow **d** upon her. H3766
32:13 wisdom: God thrusteth him **d**, not man.
33:24 **d** to the pit: I have found a ransom. H3381
36:27 **d** rain according to the vapour thereof:
40:12 and tread **d** the wicked in their place.
41: 1 tongue with a cord *which* thou lettest **d**? H8257
9 *one* be cast **d** even at the sight of him? H2904
Ps 3: 5 I laid me **d** and slept; I awaked; for the H7901
4: 8 I will both lay me **d** in peace, and sleep: H7901
7: 5 *it*; yea, let him tread **d** my life upon the H7429
16 shall come **d** upon his own pate. H3381
9:15 The heathen are sunk **d** in the pit *that*
14: 2 The LORD looked **d** from heaven upon H8259
17:11 set their eyes bowing **d** to the earth; H5186
13 him, cast him **d**: deliver my soul from H3766
18: 9 **d**: and darkness *was* under his feet. H3381
27 people; but wilt bring **d** high looks. H8213
20: 8 They are brought **d** and fallen: but we H3766
22:29 all they that go **d** to the dust shall bow H3381
23: 2 He maketh me to lie **d** in green H7257
28: 1 become like them that go **d** into the pit. H3381
30: 3 alive, that I should not go **d** to the pit. H3381
9 blood, when I go **d** to the pit? Shall the H3381
31: 2 Bow **d** thine ear to me; deliver me H5186
35:14 brother: I bowed **d** heavily, as one that H7817
36:12 are cast **d**, and shall not be able to rise. H1760
37: 2 For they shall soon be cut **d** like the H5243
14 bent their bow, to cast **d** the poor and H5307
24 shall not be utterly cast **d**: for the LORD H2904
38: 6 I am troubled; I am bowed **d** greatly; I H7817
42: 5 Why art thou cast **d**, O my soul? and H7817
6 O my God, my soul is cast **d** within me: H7817
11 Why art thou cast **d**, O my soul? and H7817
43: 5 Why art thou cast **d**, O my soul? and H7817
44: 5 Through thee will we push **d** our H5055
25 For our soul is bowed **d** to the dust: our H7743
50: 1 of the sun unto the going **d** thereof. H3996
53: 2 God looked **d** from heaven upon the H8259
55:15 *and* let them go **d** quick into hell: for H3381
23 But thou, O God, shalt bring them **d** H3381
56: 7 in *thine* anger cast **d** the people, O God. H3381
57: 6 my soul is bowed **d**: they have digged a H3721
59:11 and bring them **d**, O Lord our shield. H3381
15 Let them wander up and **d** for meat, and
60:12 he *it is that* shall tread **d** our enemies.
62: 4 They only consult to cast *him* **d** from his
72: 6 He shall come **d** like rain upon the H3381
11 Yea, all kings shall fall **d** before him: all H7812
73:18 thou castedst them **d** into destruction. H5307
74: 6 But now they break **d** the carved work
7 defiled *by casting* **d** the dwelling place of
75: 7 But God *is* the judge: he putteth **d** one, H8213
78:16 and caused waters to run **d** like rivers. H3381
24 And had rained **d** manna upon them to
31 and smote **d** the chosen *men* of Israel. H3766
80:12 Why hast thou *then* broken **d** her
14 O God of hosts: look **d** from heaven, and
16 *It is* burned with fire, *it is* cut **d**: they
85:11 righteousness shall look **d** from heaven.
86: 1 Bow **d** thine ear, O LORD, hear me: for H5186
88: 4 I am counted with them that go **d** into H3381
89:23 And I will beat **d** his foes before his face,
40 Thou hast broken **d** all his hedges; thou
44 and cast his throne **d** to the ground.
90: 6 in the evening it is cut **d**, and withereth.
95: 6 O come, let us worship and bow **d**: let H3766
102:10 for thou hast lifted me up, and cast me **d**.
19 For he hath looked **d** from the height of
104: 8 They go up by the mountains; they go **d** H3381
19 for seasons: the sun knoweth his going **d**.
22 together, and lay them **d** in their dens. H7257
107:12 Therefore he brought **d** their heart with H3665
12 they fell **d**, and *there was* none to help. H3782

Ps 107:23 They that go **d** to the sea in ships, that H3381
26 heaven, they go **d** again to the depths: H3381
108:13 he *it is that* shall tread **d** our enemies.
109:23 I am tossed up and **d** as the locust.
113: 3 the sun unto the going **d** of the same the
115:17 neither any that go **d** into silence. H3381
119:118 Thou hast trodden **d** all them that err
136 Rivers of waters run **d** mine eyes, H3381
133: 2 the head, that ran **d** upon the beard, H3381
2 went **d** to the skirts of his garments; H3381
137: 1 By the rivers of Babylon, there we sat **d**,
139: 3 **d**, and art acquainted *with* all my ways. H7252
143: 3 smitten my life **d** to the ground; he hath
7 be like unto them that go **d** into the pit. H3381
144: 5 Bow thy heavens, O LORD, and come **d**: H3381
145:14 and raiseth up all *those that be* bowed **d**.
146: 8 bowed **d**: the LORD loveth the righteous:
9 way of the wicked he turneth upside **d**.
147: 6 he casteth the wicked **d** to the ground. H8213
Prv 1:12 whole, as those that go **d** into the pit: H3381
3:20 up, and the clouds drop **d** the dew. H7491
24 When thou liest **d**, thou shalt not be H7901
24 shalt lie **d**, and thy sleep shall be sweet. H7901
5: 5 Her feet go **d** to death; her steps take H3381
7:26 For she hath cast **d** many wounded: yea,
27 Her house *is* the way to hell, going **d** to H3381
14: 1 foolish plucketh it **d** with her hands. H8045
18: 8 **d** into the innermost parts of the belly. H3381
21:22 and casteth **d** the strength of the H3381
22:17 Bow **d** thine ear, and hear the words of H5186
23:34 Yea, thou shalt be as he that lieth **d** in H7901
24:31 the stone wall thereof was broken **d**. H2040
25:26 A righteous man falling **d** before the
28 a city *that is* broken **d**, *and* without walls.
26:22 **d** into the innermost parts of the belly. H3381
Ecc 1: 5 and the sun goeth **d**, and hasteth to his
3: 3 a time to break **d**, and a time to build up;
Song 2: 3 the sons. I sat **d** under his shadow with
6: 2 My beloved is gone **d** into his garden, H3381
11 I went **d** into the garden of nuts to see H3381
7: 9 beloved, that goeth ***d*** sweetly, causing
Isa 2: 9 And the mean man boweth **d**, and the H7817
11 shall be bowed **d**, and the LORD alone H7817
17 shall be bowed **d**, and the haughtiness H7817
5: 5 up; *and* break **d** the wall thereof, and
5 wall thereof, and it shall be trodden **d**:
15 And the mean man shall be brought **d**, H7817
9:10 The bricks are fallen **d**, but we will build
10 **d**, but we will change *them into* cedars. H1438
10: 4 Without me they shall bow **d** under the H3766
6 tread them **d** like the mire of the streets.
13 **d** the inhabitants like a valiant *man*: H3381
33 **d**, and the haughty shall be humbled. H1438
34 And he shall cut **d** the thickets of the
11: 6 leopard shall lie **d** with the kid; and the H7257
7 ones shall lie **d** together: and the lion H7257
14: 8 laid **d**, no feller is come up against us. H7901
11 Thy pomp is brought **d** to the grave, H3381
12 *how* art thou cut **d** to the ground, H1438
15 Yet thou shalt be brought **d** to hell, to H3381
19 a sword, that go **d** to the stones of the H3381
30 the needy shall lie **d** in safety: and I will H7257
16: 8 have broken **d** the principal plants
17: 2 lie **d**, and none shall make *them* afraid. H7257
18: 2 **d**, whose land the rivers have spoiled!
5 and take away *and* cut **d** the branches.
21: 3 I was bowed **d** at the hearing *of it*; I
22: 5 and of treading **d**, and of perplexity by
5 of vision, breaking **d** the walls, and of
10 have ye broken **d** to fortify the wall. H5422
19 and from thy state shall he pull thee **d**.
25 and be cut **d**, and fall; and the burden H1438
24: 1 and turneth it upside **d**, and scattereth
10 The city of confusion is broken **d**: every
19 The earth is utterly broken **d**, the earth is
25: 5 Thou shalt bring **d** the noise of H3665
10 shall be trodden **d** under him, even as
10 as straw is trodden **d** for the dunghill.
11 swim: and he shall bring **d** their pride H8213
12 shall he bring **d**, lay low, *and* bring to H7817
26: 5 For he bringeth **d** them that dwell on H7817
6 The foot shall tread it **d**, *even* the feet of
27:10 **d**, and consume the branches thereof. H7257
28: 2 shall cast **d** to the earth with the hand.
18 through, then ye shall be trodden **d** by it.
29: 4 And thou shalt be brought **d**, and shalt H8213
16 Surely your turning of things upside **d**
30: 2 That walk to go **d** into Egypt, and have H3381
30 shew the lighting **d** of his arm, with the H5183

Isa 30:31 be beaten **d**, *which* smote with a rod.
31: 1 Woe to them that go **d** to Egypt for H3381
3 fall **d**, and they all shall fail together.
4 of hosts come **d** to fight for mount H3381
32:19 When it shall hail, coming **d** on the H3381
33: 9 *and* hewn **d**: Sharon is like a wilderness;
20 shall not be taken **d**; not one of the stakes
34: 4 their host shall fall **d**, as the leaf falleth
5 it shall come **d** upon Idumea, and H3381
7 And the unicorns shall come **d** with H3381
37:24 and I will cut **d** the tall cedars thereof,
38: 8 which is gone **d** in the sun dial of Ahaz, H3381
8 by which degrees it was gone **d**. H3381
18 **d** into the pit cannot hope for thy truth. H3381
42:10 earth, ye that go **d** to the sea, and all H3381
43:14 and have brought **d** all their nobles, H3381
17 they shall lie **d** together, they shall not
44:14 He heweth him **d** cedars, and taketh the
15 it a graven image, and falleth **d** thereto. H5456
17 graven image: he falleth **d** unto it, and H5456
19 shall I fall **d** to the stock of a tree? H5456
45: 8 Drop **d**, ye heavens, from above, and let
8 let the skies pour **d** righteousness: let the
14 and they shall fall **d** unto thee, they H7812
46: 1 Bel boweth **d**, Nebo stoopeth, their idols H3766
2 They stoop, they bow **d** together; they H3766
6 it a god: they fall **d**, yea, they worship. H5456
47: 1 Come **d**, and sit in the dust, O virgin H3381
49:23 they shall bow **d** to thee with *their* face H7812
50:11 of mine hand; ye shall lie **d** in sorrow. H7901
51:23 to thy soul, Bow **d**, that we may go over: H7812
52: 2 dust; arise, *and* sit **d**, O Jerusalem: loose
4 My people went **d** aforetime into Egypt H3381
55:10 For as the rain cometh **d**, and the snow H3381
56:10 sleeping, lying **d**, loving to slumber. H7901
58: 5 soul? *is it* to bow **d** his head as a bulrush,
60:14 bow themselves **d** at the soles of thy H7812
20 Thy sun shall no more go **d**; neither shall
63: 6 And I will tread **d** the people in mine
6 will bring **d** their strength to the earth. H3381
14 As a beast goeth **d** into the valley, the H3381
15 Look **d** from heaven, and behold from
18 have trodden **d** thy sanctuary.
64: 1 wouldest come **d**, that the mountains H3381
1 mountains might flow **d** at thy presence,
3 not for, thou camest **d**, the mountains H3381
3 the mountains flowed **d** at thy presence.
65:10 for the herds to lie **d** in, for my people H7257
12 and ye shall all bow **d** to the slaughter: H3766
Jer 1:10 out, and to pull **d**, and to destroy, and
10 and to throw **d**, to build, and to plant. H2040
3:25 We lie **d** in our shame, and our H7901
4:26 were broken **d** at the presence of the H5422
6: 6 of hosts said, Hew ye **d** trees, and cast a
15 they shall be cast **d**, saith the LORD. H3782
8:12 they shall be cast **d**, saith the LORD. H3782
9:18 our eyes may run **d** with tears, and our H3381
13:17 sore, and run **d** with tears, because H3381
18 yourselves, sit **d**: for your principalities
18 come **d**, *even* the crown of your glory. H3381
14:17 Let mine eyes run **d** with tears night H3381
15: 9 her sun is gone **d** while *it was* yet day:
18: 2 Arise, and go **d** to the potter's house, H3381
3 Then I went **d** to the potter's house, H3381
7 pluck up, and to pull **d**, and to destroy *it*;
21:13 Who shall come **d** against us? or who H5181
22: 1 Thus saith the LORD; Go **d** to the house H3381
7 and they shall cut **d** thy choice cedars,
24: 6 and not pull *them* **d**; and I will plant
25:37 And the peaceable habitations are cut **d**
26:10 the LORD, and sat **d** in the entry of the
31:28 up, and to break **d**, and to throw down, H5422
28 and to throw **d**, and to destroy, and H2040
40 up, nor thrown **d** any more for ever. H2040
33: 4 **d** by the mounts, and by the sword; H5422
12 shepherds causing *their* flocks to lie **d**. H7257
36:12 Then he went **d** into the king's house, H3381
15 And they said unto him, Sit **d** now, and H3427
38: 6 and they let **d** Jeremiah with cords. H7971
11 rags, and let them **d** by cords into the H7971
39: 8 and brake **d** the walls of Jerusalem. H5422
42:10 and not pull *you* **d**, and I will plant you, H2040
45: 4 built will I break **d**, and that which I H2040
46: 5 ones are beaten **d**, and are fled apace,
23 They shall cut **d** her forest, saith the
48: 2 Also thou shalt be cut **d**, O Madmen; the
5 up; for in the going **d** of Horonaim the H4174
15 men are gone **d** to the slaughter, saith H3381
18 Dibon, come **d** from *thy* glory, and H3381

Jer 48:20 Moab is confounded; for it is broken **d**:
39 How is it broken **d**! how hath Moab
49:16 thee **d** from thence, saith the LORD. H3381
50:15 her walls are thrown **d**: for it *is* the H2040
27 Slay all her bullocks; let them go **d** to H3381
51:25 thee, and roll thee **d** from the rocks, and
40 I will bring them **d** like lambs to the H3381
52:14 of the guard, brake **d** all the walls of H5422
Lam 1: 9 she came **d** wonderfully: she had H3381
16 eye, mine eye runneth **d** with water, H3381
2: 1 his anger, *and* cast **d** from heaven unto
2 he hath thrown **d** in his wrath the H2040
2 hath brought *them* **d** to the ground: he
10 hang **d** their heads to the ground. H3381
17 he hath thrown **d**, and hath not pitied: H2040
18 of Zion, let tears run **d** like a river day H3381
3:48 Mine eye runneth **d** with rivers of H3381
49 Mine eye trickleth **d**, and ceaseth not,
50 Till the LORD look **d**, and behold from
63 Behold their sitting **d**, and their rising up;
Ezk 1:13 it went up and **d** among the living
24 when they stood, they let **d** their wings. H7503
25 they stood, *and* had let **d** their wings. H7503
6: 4 cast **d** your slain *men* before your idols. H5307
6 **d**, and your works may be abolished. H1438
11:13 died. Then fell I **d** upon my face, and H5307
13:14 So will I break **d** the wall that ye have H2040
14 and bring it **d** to the ground, so that
16:39 they shall throw **d** thine eminent place, H2040
39 and shall break **d** thy high places: they H5422
17:24 have brought **d** the high tree, have H8213
19: 2 A lioness: she lay **d** among lions, she H7257
6 And he went up and **d** among the lions,
12 fury, she was cast **d** to the ground, and
24:16 nor weep, neither shall thy tears run **d**.
26: 4 of Tyrus, and break **d** her towers: I will H2040
9 his axes he shall break **d** thy towers. H5422
11 shall he tread **d** all thy streets: he shall
11 garrisons shall go **d** to the ground. H3381
12 and they shall break **d** thy walls, and H2040
16 of the sea shall come **d** from their H3381
20 When I shall bring thee **d** with them H3381
20 with them that go **d** to the pit, that thou H3381
27:29 sea, shall come **d** from their ships, they H3381
28: 8 They shall bring thee **d** to the pit, and H3381
14 and **d** in the midst of the stones of fire.
30: 4 and her foundations shall be broken **d**. H2040
6 power shall come **d**: from the tower of H3381
25 Pharaoh shall fall **d**; and they shall know
31:12 **d** from his shadow, and have left him. H3381
14 of men, with them that go **d** to the pit. H3381
15 the day when he went **d** to the grave I H3381
16 when I cast him **d** to hell with them H3381
17 They also went **d** into hell with him H3381
18 thou be brought **d** with the trees of H3381
32:18 and cast them **d**, *even* her, and the H3381
18 earth, with them that go **d** into the pit. H3381
19 Whom dost thou pass in beauty? go **d**, H3381
21 they are gone **d**, they lie uncircumcised, H3381
24 which are gone **d** uncircumcised into H3381
24 shame with them that go **d** to the pit. H3381
25 with them that go **d** to the pit: he is put H3381
27 which are gone **d** to hell with their H3381
29 and with them that go **d** to the pit. H3381
30 which are gone **d** with the slain; with H3381
30 shame with them that go **d** to the pit. H3381
34:15 cause them to lie **d**, saith the Lord GOD. H7257
18 but ye must tread **d** with your feet the
26 shower to come **d** in his season; there H3381
37: 1 LORD, and set me **d** in the midst of the
38:20 shall be thrown **d**, and the steep places H2040
39:10 field, neither cut **d** *any* out of the forests;
47: 1 the waters came **d** from under from the H3381
8 country, and go **d** into the desert, and H3381
Dan 3: 5 of musick, ye fall **d** and worship the
6 And whoso falleth not **d** and
7 the languages, fell **d** *and* worshipped the
10 fall **d** and worship the golden image:
11 And whoso falleth not **d** and
15 of musick, ye fall **d** and worship the
23 Abed-nego, fell **d** bound into the midst
4:13 and an holy one came **d** from heaven; H5182
14 He cried aloud, and said thus, Hew **d** the
23 holy one coming **d** from heaven, and H5182
23 Hew the tree **d**, and destroy it; yet leave
5:19 he set up; and whom he would he put **d**. H8214
6:14 the going **d** of the sun to deliver him. H4606
7: 9 I beheld till the thrones were cast **d**, and
23 shall tread it **d**, and break it in pieces.

Dan 8: 7 but he cast him **d** to the ground, and
10 and it cast **d** *some* of the host and H5307
11 and the place of his sanctuary was cast **d**.
12 and it cast **d** the truth to the ground;
11:12 up; and he shall cast **d** *many* ten H5307
26 overflow: and many shall fall **d** slain. H5307
Hos 2:18 and will make them to lie **d** safely. H7901
7:12 I will bring them **d** as the fowls of the H3381
10: 2 **d** their altars, he shall spoil their images.
Joel 1:17 are broken **d**; for the corn is withered. H2040
2:23 will cause to come **d** for you the rain, H3381
3: 2 and will bring them **d** into the valley of H3381
11 thy mighty ones to come **d**, O LORD. H5181
13 come, get you **d**; for the press is full, H3381
18 shall drop **d** new wine, and the hills
Am 2: 8 And they lay *themselves* **d** upon clothes
3:11 and he shall bring **d** thy strength from H3381
5:24 But let judgment run **d** as waters, and
6: 2 the great: then go **d** to Gath of the H3381
8: 9 cause the sun to go **d** at noon, and I will
9: 2 to heaven, thence will I bring them **d**: H3381
Oba 3 Who shall bring me **d** to the ground? H3381
4 will I bring thee **d**, saith the LORD. H3381
16 they shall swallow **d**, and they shall be as
Jna 1: 3 the LORD, and went **d** to Joppa; and he H3381
3 thereof, and went **d** into it, to go with H3381
5 Jonah was gone **d** into the sides of the H3381
2: 6 I went **d** to the bottoms of the H3381
Mic 1: 3 and will come **d**, and tread upon the H3381
4 waters *that are* poured **d** a steep place.
6 and I will pour **d** the stones thereof into
12 but evil came **d** from the LORD unto H3381
3: 6 the sun shall go **d** over the prophets, and
5: 8 both treadeth **d**, and teareth in pieces,
11 land, and throw **d** all thy strong holds: H2040
6:14 and thy casting **d** *shall be* in the midst
7:10 be trodden **d** as the mire of the streets.
Nah 1: 6 and the rocks are thrown **d** by him. H5422
12 shall they be cut **d**, when he shall pass
Zep 1:11 cut **d**; all they that bear silver are cut off.
2: 7 shall they lie **d** in the evening: for the H7257
14 And flocks shall lie **d** in the midst of H7257
15 place for beasts to lie **d** in! every one that
3:13 lie **d**, and none shall make *them* afraid. H7257
Hag 2:22 **d**, every one by the sword of his brother. H3381
Zec 10: 5 *men*, which tread **d** *their enemies* in the
11 shall be brought **d**, and the sceptre of H3381
12 up and **d** in his name, saith the LORD.
11: 2 for the forest of the vintage is come **d**. H3381
Mal 1: 4 but I will throw **d**; and they shall call H2040
11 unto the going **d** of the same my name
4: 3 And ye shall tread **d** the wicked; for they
Mt 2:11 his mother, and fell **d**, and worshipped *G4098*
3:10 fruit is hewn **d**, and cast into the fire. *G1581*
4: 6 God, cast thyself **d**: for it is written, He *G2736*
9 thee, if thou wilt fall **d** and worship me. *G4098*
7:19 fruit is hewn **d**, and cast into the fire. *G1581*
8: 1 When he was come **d** from the *G2597*
11 west, and shall sit **d** with Abraham, and *G347*
32 ran violently **d** a steep place into the *G2596*
9:10 and sat **d** with him and his disciples. *G4873*
11:23 shalt be brought **d** to hell: for if the *G2601*
13:48 to shore, and sat **d**, and gathered the *G2523*
14:19 the multitude to sit **d** on the grass, and *G347*
29 Peter was come **d** out of the ship, he *G2597*
15:29 up into a mountain, and sat **d** there. *G2521*
30 **d** at Jesus' feet; and he healed them: *G4496*
35 the multitude to sit **d** on the ground. *G377*
17: 9 And as they came **d** from the *G2597*
14 man, kneeling **d** to him, and saying, *G1120*
18:26 The servant therefore fell **d**, and *G4098*
29 And his fellowservant fell **d** at his feet, *G4098*
21: 8 way; others cut **d** branches from the *G2875*
24: 2 another, that shall not be thrown **d**. *G2647*
17 **d** to take any thing out of his house: *G2597*
26:20 Now when the even was come, he sat **d** *G345*
27: 5 And he cast **d** the pieces of silver in the *G4496*
19 When he was set **d** on the judgment *G2521*
36 And sitting **d** they watched him there; *G2521*
40 the Son of God, come **d** from the cross. *G2597*
42 let him now come **d** from the cross, *G2597*
Mk 1: 7 am not worthy to stoop **d** and unloose. *G2955*
40 him, and kneeling **d** to him, and saying *G1120*
2: 4 *it* up, they let **d** the bed wherein the *G5465*
3:11 they saw him, fell **d** before him, and
22 And the scribes which came **d** from *G2597*
5:13 herd ran violently **d** a steep place into *G2596*
33 **d** before him, and told him all the truth.
6:39 sit **d** by companies upon the green grass. *G347*

D

Mk 6:40 And they sat **d** in ranks, by hundreds, G377
8: 6 And he commanded the people to sit **d** G377
9: 9 And as they came **d** from the G2597
35 And he sat **d**, and called the twelve, and G2523
11: 8 and others cut **d** branches off the trees, G2875
13: 2 another, that shall not be thrown **d**. G2647
15 the housetop not go **d** into the house, G2597
15:30 Save thyself, and come **d** from the G2597
36 whether Elias will come to take him **d**. G2507
46 and took him **d**, and wrapped him in G2507
Lk 1:52 He hath put **d** the mighty from *their* G2507
2:51 And he went **d** with them, and came to G2597
3: 9 fruit is hewn **d**, and cast into the fire. G1581
4: 9 Son of God, cast thyself **d** from hence: G2736
20 minister, and sat **d**. And the eyes of all G2523
29 that they might cast him **d** headlong. G2630
31 And came **d** to Capernaum, a city of G2718
5: 3 **d**, and taught the people out of the ship. G2523
4 deep, and let **d** your nets for a draught. G5465
5 at thy word I will let **d** the net. G5465
8 When Simon Peter saw *it*, he fell **d** at
19 and let him **d** through the tiling with G2524
29 and of others that sat **d** with them. G2621
6:17 And he came **d** with them, and stood in G2597
38 good measure, pressed **d**, and shaken G4085
7:36 the Pharisee's house, and sat **d** to meat. G347
8: 5 **d**, and the fowls of the air devoured it. G2662
23 and there came **d** a storm of wind on G2597
28 cried out, and fell **d** before him, and with
33 herd ran violently **d** a steep place into G2596
41 and he fell **d** at Jesus' feet, and G4098
47 and falling **d** before him, she declared
9:14 them sit **d** by fifties in a company. G2625
15 And they did so, and made them all sit **d**. G347
37 **d** from the hill, much people met him. G2718
42 devil threw him **d**, and tare *him*. And G4486
44 Let these sayings sink **d** into your ears: G5087
54 fire to come **d** from heaven, and G2597
10:15 to heaven, shalt be thrust **d** to hell. G2601
30 certain *man* went **d** from Jerusalem to G2597
31 And by chance there came **d** a certain G2597
11:37 him: and he went in, and sat **d** to meat. G377
12:18 And he said, This will I do: I will pull **d** G2507
37 and make them to sit **d** to meat, and will G347
13: 7 cut it **d**; why cumbereth it the ground? G1581
9 if not, *then* after that thou shalt cut it **d**. G1581
29 and shall sit **d** in the kingdom of God. G347
14: 8 to a wedding, sit not **d** in the highest G2625
10 But when thou art bidden, go and sit **d** G377
28 tower, sitteth not **d** first, and counteth G2523
31 king, sitteth not **d** first, and consulteth G2523
16: 6 bill, and sit **d** quickly, and write fifty. G2523
17: 7 from the field, Go and sit **d** to meat? G377
16 And fell **d** on *his* face at his feet, giving
31 let him not come **d** to take it away: and G2597
18:14 I tell you, this man went **d** to his house G2597
19: 5 **d**; for to day I must abide at thy house. G2597
6 And he made haste, and came **d**, and G2597
21 **d**, and reapest that thou didst not sow. G5087
22 not **d**, and reaping that I did not sow: G5087
21: 6 another, that shall not be thrown **d**. G2647
24 shall be trodden **d** of the Gentiles, until G3961
22:14 And when the hour was come, he sat **d**, G377
41 stone's cast, and kneeled **d**, and prayed, G5087
44 drops of blood falling **d** to the ground. G2597
55 hall, and were set **d** together, Peter sat G4776
55 together, Peter sat **d** among them. G2521
23:53 And he took it **d**, and wrapped it in G2507
24: 5 And as they were afraid, and bowed **d** G2827
12 and stooping **d**, he beheld the linen G3879
Jn 2:12 After this he went **d** to Capernaum, he, G2597
3:13 but he that came **d** from heaven, *even* G2597
4:47 he would come **d**, and heal his son: for G2597
49 unto him, Sir, come **d** ere my child die. G2597
51 And as he was now going **d**, his G2597
5: 4 For an angel went **d** at a certain season G2597
7 coming, another steppeth **d** before me. G2597
6:10 And Jesus said, Make the men sit **d**. Now G377
10 sat **d**, in number about five thousand. G377
11 them that were set **d**; and likewise of the G345
16 come, his disciples went **d** unto the sea, G2597
33 is he which cometh **d** from heaven, and G2597
38 For I came **d** from heaven, not to do G2597
41 the bread which came **d** from heaven. G2597
42 that he saith, I came **d** from heaven? G2597
50 This is the bread which cometh **d** from G2597
51 I am the living bread which came **d** G2597
58 This is that bread which came **d** from G2597
8: 2 him; and he sat **d**, and taught them. G2523

Jn 8: 6 But Jesus stooped **d**, and with *his* finger G2736
8 And again he stooped **d**, and wrote on G2736
10:15 and I lay **d** my life for the sheep. G5087
17 lay **d** my life, that I might take it again. G5087
18 No man taketh it from me, but I lay it **d** G5087
18 power to lay it **d**, and I have power to G5087
11:32 saw him, she fell **d** at his feet, saying G4098
13:12 and was set **d** again, he said unto them, G377
37 now? I will lay **d** my life for thy sake. G5087
38 Jesus answered him, Wilt thou lay **d** G5087
15:13 that a man lay **d** his life for his friends. G5087
19:13 forth, and sat **d** in the judgment seat G2523
20: 5 And he stooping **d**, *and looking in*, saw G3879
11 **d**, *and looked* into the sepulchre, G3879
Act 4:35 And laid *them* **d** at the apostles' feet: G5087
5: 5 And Ananias hearing these words fell **d**, G4098
10 Then fell she **d** straightway at his feet, G4098
7:15 So Jacob went **d** into Egypt, and died, G2597
34 and am come **d** to deliver them. And G2597
58 the witnesses laid **d** their clothes at a G659
60 And he kneeled **d**, and cried with a loud G5087
8: 5 Then Philip went **d** to the city of G2718
15 Who, when they were come **d**, prayed G2597
26 the way that goeth **d** from Jerusalem G2597
38 and they went **d** both into the water, G2597
9:25 and let *him* **d** by the wall in a basket. G2524
30 they brought him **d** to Caesarea, and G2609
32 *quarters*, he came **d** also to the saints G2718
40 forth, and kneeled **d**, and prayed; and G5087
10:11 the four corners, and let **d** to the earth: G2524
20 Arise therefore, and get thee **d**, and go G2597
21 Then Peter went **d** to the men which G2597
25 fell **d** at his feet, and worshipped *him*. G4098
11: 5 a great sheet, let **d** from heaven by four G2524
12:19 death. And he went **d** from Judaea to G2718
13:14 on the sabbath day, and sat **d**. G2523
29 they took *him* **d** from the tree, and laid G2507
14:11 are come **d** to us in the likeness of men. G2597
25 word in Perga, they went **d** into Attalia: G2597
15: 1 And certain men which came **d** from G2718
16 which is fallen **d**; and I will build again G4098
16: 8 And they passing by Mysia came **d** to G2597
13 made; and we sat **d**, and spake unto the G2523
29 and fell **d** before Paul and Silas,
17: 6 the world upside **d** are come hither also; G387
18:22 the church, he went **d** to Antioch. G2597
19:35 of the *image* which fell **d** from Jupiter?
20: 9 he sunk **d** with sleep, and fell G2702
9 sleep, and fell **d** from the third loft, G2736
10 And Paul went **d**, and fell on him, and G2597
36 he kneeled **d**, and prayed with them all. G5087
21: 5 we kneeled **d** on the shore, and prayed. G5087
10 days, there came **d** from Judaea a G2718
32 and ran **d** unto them: and when G2701
22:30 Paul **d**, and set him before them. G2609
23:10 the soldiers to go **d**, and to take him by G2597
15 captain that he bring him **d** unto you to G2609
20 wouldest bring **d** Paul to morrow into G2609
24:22 shall come **d**, I will know the uttermost G2597
25: 5 you are able, go **d** with *me*, and accuse G4782
6 ten days, he went **d** unto Caesarea; and G2597
7 the Jews which came **d** from Jerusalem G2597
27:27 were driven up and **d** in Adria, about G1308
30 when they had let **d** the boat into the G5465
28: 6 swollen, or fallen **d** dead suddenly: but G2667
Ro 10: 6 (that is, to bring Christ **d** *from above*:) G2609
11: 3 and digged **d** thine altars; and I am G2679
10 not see, and bow **d** their back alway. G4781
16: 4 Who have for my life laid **d** their own G5294
1Co 10: 7 **d** to eat and drink, and rose up to play. G2523
14:25 and so falling **d** on *his* face he will G4098
15:24 **d** all rule and all authority and power. G2673
2Co 4: 9 Persecuted, but not forsaken; cast **d**, G2598
7: 6 **d**, comforted us by the coming of Titus; G5011
10: 4 God to the pulling **d** of strong holds;) G2506
5 Casting **d** imaginations, and every high G2507
11:33 **d** by the wall, and escaped his hands. G5465
Eph 2:14 and hath broken **d** the middle wall of G3089
4:26 let not the sun go **d** upon your wrath: G1931
Heb 1: 3 our sins, sat **d** on the right hand of G2523
10:12 for ever, sat **d** on the right hand of God; G2523
11:30 By faith the walls of Jericho fell **d**, after G4098
12: 2 shame, and is set **d** at the right hand of G2523
12 which hang **d**, and the feeble knees; G3935
Jas 1:17 and cometh **d** from the Father of lights, G2597
5: 4 who have reaped **d** your fields, which is
1Pt 1:12 Holy Ghost sent **d** from heaven; which
2Pt 2: 4 but cast *them* **d** to hell, and delivered
1Jn 3:16 because he laid **d** his life for us: and we

1Jn 3:16 ought to lay **d** *our* lives for the brethren.
Rev 1:13 with a garment **d** to the foot, and girt
3:12 which cometh **d** out of heaven from G2597
21 am set **d** with my Father in his throne. G2523
4:10 The four and twenty elders fall **d** before G4098
5: 8 twenty elders fell **d** before the Lamb, G4098
14 twenty elders fell **d** and worshipped G4098
10: 1 angel come **d** from heaven, clothed G2597
12:10 brethren is cast **d**, which accused them G2598
12 for the devil is come **d** unto you, having G2597
13:13 maketh fire come **d** from heaven on the G2597
18: 1 angel come **d** from heaven, having G2597
21 **d**, and shall be found no more at all. G906
19: 4 the four beasts fell **d** and worshipped G4098
20: 1 And I saw an angel come **d** from G2597
9 city: and fire came **d** from God out of G2597
21: 2 coming **d** from God out of heaven, G2597
22: 8 and seen, I fell **d** to worship before the G4098

DOWNSITTING

Ps 139: 2 Thou knowest my **d** and mine uprising, H3427

DOWNWARD

2Ki 19:30 take root **d**, and bear fruit upward. H4295
Ecc 3:21 of the beast that goeth **d** to the earth? H4295
Isa 37:31 take root **d**, and bear fruit upward: H4295
Ezk 1:27 of his loins even **d**, I saw as it were the H4295
8: 2 of his loins even **d**, fire; and from his H4295

DOWRY

Gen 30:20 me *with* a good **d**; now will my husband H2065
34:12 Ask me never so much **d** and gift, and I H4119
Ex 22:17 money according to the **d** of virgins. H4119
1Sa 18:25 king desireth not any **d**, but an hundred H4119

DRAG

Hab 1:15 **d**: therefore they rejoice and are glad. H4365
16 incense unto their **d**; because by them H4365

DRAGGING

Jn 21: 8 hundred cubits,) **d** the net with fishes. G4951

DRAGON

Neh 2:13 even before the **d** well, and to the dung H8577
Ps 91:13 the **d** shalt thou trample under feet. H8577
Isa 27: 1 he shall slay the **d** that *is* in the sea. H8577
51: 9 hath cut Rahab, *and* wounded the **d**? H8577
Jer 51:34 me up like a **d**, he hath filled his belly H8577
Ezk 29: 3 of Egypt, the great **d** that lieth in the H8577
Rev 12: 3 and behold a great red **d**, having seven G1404
4 to the earth: and the **d** stood before the G1404
7 fought against the **d**; and the dragon G1404
7 and the **d** fought and his angels, G1404
9 And the great **d** was cast out, that old G1404
13 And when the **d** saw that he was cast G1404
16 which the **d** cast out of his mouth. G1404
17 And the **d** was wroth with the woman, G1404
13: 2 of a lion: and the **d** gave him his power, G1404
4 And they worshipped the **d** which gave G1404
11 horns like a lamb, and he spake as a **d**. G1404
16:13 of the mouth of the **d**, and out of the G1404
20: 2 And he laid hold on the **d**, that old G1404

DRAGONS

Dt 32:33 Their wine *is* the poison of **d**, and the H8577
Job 30:29 I am a brother to **d**, and a companion H8577
Ps 44:19 us in the place of **d**, and covered us with H8577
74:13 the heads of the **d** in the waters. H8577
148: 7 Praise the LORD from the earth, ye **d**, H8577
Isa 13:22 houses, and **d** in *their* pleasant palaces: H8577
34:13 an habitation of **d**, *and* a court for owls. H8577
35: 7 in the habitation of **d**, where each lay, H8577
43:20 shall honour me, the **d** and the owls: H8577
Jer 9:11 *and* a den of **d**; and I will make the H8577
10:22 cities of Judah desolate, *and* a den of **d**. H8577
14: 6 up the wind like **d**; their eyes did fail, H8577
49:33 And Hazor shall be a dwelling for **d**, H8577
51:37 a dwellingplace for **d**, an astonishment, H8577
Mic 1: 8 like the **d**, and mourning as the owls. H8577
Mal 1: 3 waste for the **d** of the wilderness. H8568

DRAGON-WELL See DRAGON and WELL.

DRAMS

1Ch 29: 7 and ten thousand **d**, and of silver ten H150
Ezr 2:69 and one thousand **d** of gold, and five H1871
8:27 of a thousand **d**; and two vessels of fine H150
Neh 7:70 a thousand **d** of gold, fifty basons, H1871
71 twenty thousand **d** of gold, and two H1871

Neh 7:72 twenty thousand **d** of gold, and two H1871

DRANK
Gen 9:21 And he **d** of the wine, and was H8354
24:46 **d**, and she made the camels drink also. H8354
27:25 eat: and he brought him wine, and he **d**. H8354
43:34 And they **d**, and were merry with him. H8354
Nu 20:11 congregation **d**, and their beasts *also.* H8354
Dt 32:38 sacrifices, *and* **d** the wine of their drink H8354
2Sa 12: 3 of his own meat, and **d** of his own cup, H8354
1Ki 13:19 eat bread in his house, and **d** water. H8354
17: 6 in the evening; and he **d** of the brook. H8354
Dan 1: 5 of the wine which he **d**: so nourishing H4960
8 with the wine which he **d**: therefore he H4960
5: 1 lords, and **d** wine before the thousand. H8355
3 wives, and his concubines, **d** in them. H8355
4 They **d** wine, and praised the gods of H8355
Mk 14:23 he gave *it* to them: and they all **d** of it. *G4095*
Lk 17:27 They did eat, they **d**, they married *G4095*
28 they did eat, they **d**, they bought, they *G4095*
Jn 4:12 us the well, and **d** thereof himself, and *G4095*
1Co 10: 4 drink: for they **d** of that spiritual Rock *G4095*

DRAUGHT
2Ki 10:27 and made it a **d** house unto this day. H4280
Mt 15:17 into the belly, and is cast out into the **d**? *G856*
Mk 7:19 goeth out into the **d**, purging all meats? *G856*
Lk 5: 4 the deep, and let down your nets for a **d**. *G61*
9 the **d** of the fishes which they had taken: *G61*

DRAUGHT-HOUSE See DRAUGHT and HOUSE.

DRAVE
Ex 14:25 wheels, that they **d** them heavily: so H5090
Jos 16:10 And they **d** not out the Canaanites that H3423
24:12 before you, which **d** them out from H1644
18 And the LORD **d** out from before us all H1644
Jdg 1:19 Judah; and he **d** out *the inhabitants* H3423
6: 9 you, and **d** them out from before H1644
1Sa 30:20 herds, *which* they **d** before those *other* H5090
2Sa 6: 3 the sons of Abinadab, **d** the new cart. H5090
2Ki 16: 6 to Syria, and **d** the Jews from Elath: H5394
17:21 and Jeroboam **d** Israel from following H5071
1Ch 13: 7 and Uzza and Ahio **d** the cart. H5090
Act 7:45 whom God **d** out before the face of *G1856*
18:16 And he **d** them from the judgment seat. *G556*

DRAW
Gen 24:11 the time that women go out to **d** *water.* H7579
13 men of the city come out to **d** water: H7579
19 she said, I will **d** *water* for thy camels H7579
20 to **d** *water,* and drew for all his camels. H7579
43 cometh forth to **d** *water,* and I say to H7579
44 and I will also **d** for thy camels: *let* the H7579
Ex 3: 5 And he said, **D** not nigh hither: put off
12:21 said unto them, **D** out and take you a H4900
15: 9 upon them; I will **d** my sword, my hand H7324
Lev 26:33 heathen, and will **d** out a sword after H7324
Jdg 3:22 so that he could not **d** the dagger out of H8025
4: 6 *saying,* Go and **d** toward mount Tabor, H4900
7 And I will **d** unto thee to the river H4900
9:54 said unto him, **D** thy sword, and slay H8025
19:13 Come, and let us **d** near to one of these
20:32 Let us flee, and **d** them from the city H5423
1Sa 9:11 going out to **d** water, and said unto H7579
14:36 the priest, Let us **d** near hither unto God.
38 And Saul said, **D** ye near hither, all the
31: 4 his armourbearer, **D** thy sword, and H8025
2Sa 17:13 city, and we will **d** it into the river, until H5498
1Ch 10: 4 Then said Saul to his armourbearer, **D** H8025
Job 21:33 every man shall **d** after him, as *there* H4900
40:23 that he can **d** up Jordan into his mouth. H1518
41: 1 Canst thou **d** out leviathan with an H4900
Ps 28: 3 **D** me not away with the wicked, and H4900
35: 3 **D** out also the spear, and stop *the way* H7324
69:18 **D** nigh unto my soul, *and* redeem it:
73:28 But *it is* good for me to **d** near to God: I
85: 5 **d** out thine anger to all generations? H4900
107:18 and they **d** near unto the gates of death.
119:150 They **d** nigh that follow after mischief:
Prv 20: 5 a man of understanding will **d** it out. H1802
Ecc 12: 1 not, nor the years **d** nigh, when thou
Song 1: 4 **D** me, we will run after thee: the king H4900
Isa 5:18 Woe unto them that **d** iniquity with H4900
19 **d** nigh and come, that we may know *it!*
12: 3 Therefore with joy shall ye **d** water out H7579
29:13 as this people **d** near *me* with their
45:20 Assemble yourselves and come; **d** near
57: 3 But **d** near hither, ye sons of the
Isa 57: 4 a wide mouth, *and* **d** out the tongue? *are* H748
58:10 And *if* thou **d** out thy soul to the H6329
66:19 Pul, and Lud, that **d** the bow, *to* Tubal, H4900
Jer 30:21 I will cause him to **d** near, and he shall
46: 3 Order ye the buckler and shield, and **d**
49:20 of the flock shall **d** them out: surely he H5498
50:45 of the flock shall **d** them out: surely he H5498
Lam 4: 3 Even the sea monsters **d** out the breast, H2502
Ezk 5: 2 and I will **d** out a sword after them. H7324
12 and I will **d** out a sword after them. H7324
9: 1 over the city to **d** near, even every man
12:14 and I will **d** out the sword after them. H7324
21: 3 thee, and will **d** forth my sword out H3318
22: 4 caused thy days to **d** near, and art come
28: 7 and they shall **d** their swords against H7324
30:11 and they shall **d** their swords against H7324
32:20 the sword: **d** her and all her multitudes. H4900
Joel 3: 9 men of war **d** near; let them come up:
Nah 3:14 **D** thee waters for the siege, fortify thy H7579
Hag 2:16 the pressfat for to **d** out fifty *vessels* out H2834
Jn 2: 8 And he saith unto them, **D** out now, and *G501*
4: 7 There cometh a woman of Samaria to **d** *G501*
11 hast nothing to **d** with, and the well is *G502*
15 that I thirst not, neither come hither to **d**. *G501*
6:44 hath sent me **d** him: and I will raise *G1670*
12:32 from the earth, will **d** all *men* unto me. *G1670*
21: 6 able to **d** it for the multitude of fishes. *G1670*
Act 20:30 things, to **d** away disciples after them. *G645*
Heb 7:19 *did;* by the which we **d** nigh unto God.
10:22 Let us **d** near with a true heart in full *G4334*
38 but if *any man* **d** back, my soul shall *G5288*
39 But we are not of them who **d** back *G5289*
Jas 2: 6 and **d** you before the judgment seats? *G1670*
4: 8 **D** nigh to God, and he will draw nigh to
8 Draw nigh to God, and he will **d** nigh to

DRAWER
Dt 29:11 of thy wood unto the **d** of thy water: H7579

DRAWERS
Jos 9:21 of wood and **d** of water unto all the H7579
23 **d** of water for the house of my God. H7579
27 hewers of wood and **d** of water for the H7579

DRAWEST See WITHDRAWEST.

DRAWETH
Dt 25:11 the wife of the one **d** near for to deliver
Jdg 19: 9 now the day **d** toward evening, I pray H7503
Job 24:22 He **d** also the mighty with his power: he H4900
33:22 Yea, his soul **d** near unto the grave, and
Ps 10: 9 the poor, when he **d** him into his net. H4900
88: 3 and my life **d** nigh unto the grave.
Isa 26:17 Like as a woman with child, *that* **d** near
Ezk 7:12 The time is come, the day **d** near: let not
Mt 15: 8 This people **d** nigh unto me with their
Lk 21: 8 **d** near: go ye not therefore after them.
28 your heads; for your redemption **d** nigh.
Jas 5: 8 for the coming of the Lord **d** nigh.

DRAWING
Jdg 5:11 in the places of **d** water, there shall H4857
Jn 6:19 on the sea, and **d** nigh unto the ship: *G1096*

DRAWN
Nu 22:23 and his sword **d** in his hand: and the H8025
31 and his sword **d** in his hand: and he H8025
Dt 21: 3 with, *and* which hath not **d** in the yoke; H4900
30:17 hear, but shalt be **d** away, and worship H5080
Jos 5:13 him with his sword **d** in his hand: and H8025
8: 6 us) till we have **d** them from the city; H5423
16 Joshua, and were **d** away from the city. H5423
15: 9 And the border was **d** from the top of H8388
9 **d** to Baalah, which *is* Kirjath-jearim: H8388
11 and the border was **d** to Shicron, and H8388
18:14 And the border was **d** *thence,* and H8388
17 And was **d** from the north, and went H8388
Jdg 20:31 people, *and* were **d** away from the city; H5423
Ru 2: 9 of *that* which the young men have **d**. H7579
1Ch 21:16 heaven, having a **d** sword in his hand H8025
Job 20:25 It is **d**, and cometh out of the body; yea, H8025
Ps 37:14 The wicked have **d** out the sword, and H6605
55:21 softer than oil, yet *were* they **d** swords. H6609
Prv 24:11 *them that are* **d** unto death, and *those* H3947
Isa 21:15 swords, from the **d** sword, and from H5203
28: 9 from the milk, *and* **d** from the breasts. H6267
Jer 22:19 the burial of an ass, and **d** and cast forth H5498
31: 3 with lovingkindness have I **d** thee. H4900
Lam 2: 3 of Israel: he hath **d** back his right hand H7725
Ezk 21: 5 I the LORD have **d** forth my sword out H3318
28 the sword *is* **d**: for the slaughter *it is* H6605
Act 11:10 and all were **d** up again into heaven. *G385*
Jas 1:14 But every man is tempted, when he is **d** *G1828*

DREAD
Gen 9: 2 And the fear of you and the **d** of you H2844
Ex 15:16 Fear and **d** shall fall upon them; by the H6343
Dt 1:29 Then I said unto you, **D** not, neither be H6206
2:25 This day will I begin to put the **d** of thee H6343
11:25 of you and the **d** of you upon all the H4172
1Ch 22:13 good courage; **d** not, nor be dismayed. H3372
Job 13:11 you afraid? and his **d** fall upon you? H6343
21 me: and let not thy **d** make me afraid. H367
Isa 8:13 him *be* your fear, and *let* him *be* your **d**. H6206

DREADFUL
Gen 28:17 And he was afraid, and said, How **d** *is* H3372
Job 15:21 A **d** sound *is* in his ears: in prosperity H6343
Ezk 1:18 that they were **d**; and their rings *were* H3374
Dan 7: 7 a fourth beast, **d** and terrible, and H1763
19 others, exceeding **d**, whose teeth *were of* H1763
9: 4 Lord, the great and **d** God, keeping the H3372
Hab 1: 7 They *are* terrible and **d**: their judgment H3372
Mal 1:14 and my name *is* **d** among the heathen. H3372
4: 5 of the great and **d** day of the LORD: H3372

DREAM
Gen 20: 3 But God came to Abimelech in a **d** by H2472
6 And God said unto him in a **d**, Yea, I H2472
31:10 eyes, and saw in a **d**, and, behold, the H2472
11 **d**, *saying,* Jacob: And I said, Here *am* I. H2472
24 the Syrian in a **d** by night, and said H2472
37: 5 And Joseph dreamed a **d**, and he told *it* H2472
6 pray you, this **d** which I have dreamed: H2472
9 And he dreamed yet another **d**, and told H2472
9 I have dreamed a **d** more; and, behold, H2472
10 unto him, What *is* this **d** that thou hast H2472
40: 5 And they dreamed a **d** both of them, H2472
5 each man his **d** in one night, each man H2472
5 of his **d**, the butler and the baker H2472
8 We have dreamed a **d**, and *there is* no H2472
9 And the chief butler told his **d** to H2472
9 In my **d**, behold, a vine *was* before me; H2472
16 I also *was* in my **d**, and, behold, *I had* H2472
41: 7 Pharaoh awoke, and, behold, *it was* a **d**. H2472
8 told them his **d**; but *there was* none H2472
11 And we dreamed a **d** in one night, I H2472
11 according to the interpretation of his **d**. H2472
12 according to his **d** he did interpret. H2472
15 I have dreamed a **d**, and *there is* none H2472
15 canst understand a **d** to interpret it. H2472
17 Joseph, In my **d**, behold, I stood upon H2472
22 And I saw in my **d**, and, behold, seven H2472
25 And Joseph said unto Pharaoh, The **d** H2472
26 good ears *are* seven years: the **d** *is* one. H2472
32 And for that the **d** was doubled unto H2472
Nu 12: 6 a vision, *and* will speak unto him in a **d**. H2472
Jdg 7:13 a man that told a **d** unto his fellow, and H2472
13 I dreamed a **d**, and, lo, a cake of barley H2472
15 heard the telling of the **d**, and the H2472
1Ki 3: 5 to Solomon in a **d** by night: and God H2472
15 and, behold, *it was* a **d**. And he came to H2472
Job 20: 8 He shall fly away as a **d**, and shall not H2472
33:15 In a **d**, in a vision of the night, when H2472
Ps 73:20 As a **d** when *one* awaketh; *so,* O Lord, H2472
126: 1 of Zion, we were like them that **d**. H2492
Ecc 5: 3 For a **d** cometh through the multitude H2472
Isa 29: 7 her, shall be as a **d** of a night vision. H2472
Jer 23:28 The prophet that hath a **d**, let him tell a H2472
28 let him tell a **d**; and he that hath my H2472
Dan 2: 3 I have dreamed a **d**, and my spirit was H2472
3 my spirit was troubled to know the **d**. H2472
4 **d**, and we will shew the interpretation. H2493
5 unto me the **d**, with the interpretation H2493
6 But if ye shew the **d**, and the H2493
6 the **d**, and the interpretation thereof. H2493
7 his servants the **d**, and we will shew the H2493
9 unto me the **d**, *there is but* one decree H2493
9 tell me the **d**, and I shall know that H2493
26 unto me the **d** which I have seen, and H2493
28 latter days. Thy **d**, and the visions of thy H2493
36 This *is* the **d**; and we will tell the H2493
45 hereafter: and the **d** *is* certain, and the H2493
4: 5 I saw a **d** which made me afraid, and H2493
6 unto me the interpretation of the **d**. H2493
7 and I told the **d** before them; but they H2493
8 and before him I told the **d**, *saying,* H2493
9 me the visions of my **d** that I have seen, H2493

Dan 4:18 This **d** I king Nebuchadnezzar have H2493
19 let not the **d**, or the interpretation H2493
19 said, My lord, the **d** *be* to them that H2493
7: 1 Daniel had a **d** and visions of his head H2493
1 the **d**, *and* told the sum of the matters. H2493
Joel 2:28 old men shall **d** dreams, your young H2492
Mt 1:20 unto him in a **d**, saying, Joseph, thou *G3677*
2:12 And being warned of God in a **d** that *G3677*
13 to Joseph in a **d**, saying, Arise, and take *G3677*
19 appeareth in a **d** to Joseph in Egypt, *G3677*
22 of God in a **d**, he turned aside into *G3677*
27:19 things this day in a **d** because of him. *G3677*
Act 2:17 and your old men shall **d** dreams: *G1797*

DREAMED
Gen 28:12 And he **d**, and behold a ladder set up on H2492
37: 5 And Joseph **d** a dream, and he told *it* H2492
6 I pray you, this dream which I have **d**: H2492
9 And he **d** yet another dream, and told H2492
9 Behold, I have **d** a dream more; and, H2492
10 that thou hast **d**? Shall I and thy mother H2492
40: 5 And they **d** a dream both of them, each H2492
8 And they said unto him, We have **d** a H2492
41: 1 **d**: and, behold, he stood by the river. H2492
5 And he slept and **d** the second time: H2492
11 And we **d** a dream in one night, I and H2492
11 one night, I and he; we **d** each man H2492
15 Joseph, I have **d** a dream, and *there* H2492
42: 9 dreams which he **d** of them, and said H2492
Jdg 7:13 said, Behold, I **d** a dream, and, lo, a H2492
Jer 23:25 name, saying, I have **d**, I have dreamed. H2492
25 name, saying, I have dreamed, I have **d**. H2492
29: 8 to your dreams which ye cause to be **d**. H2492
Dan 2: 1 Nebuchadnezzar **d** dreams, wherewith H2492
3 And the king said unto them, I have **d** a H2492

DREAMER
Gen 37:19 Behold, this **d** cometh. H1167+H2472
Dt 13: 1 a prophet, or a **d** of dreams, and giveth H2492
3 prophet, or that **d** of dreams: for the H2492
5 And that prophet, or that **d** of dreams, H2492

DREAMERS
Jer 27: 9 nor to your **d**, nor to your enchanters, H2472
Jude 8 Likewise also these *filthy* **d** defile the *G1797*

DREAMETH
Isa 29: 8 when an hungry *man* **d**, and, behold, he H2492
8 when a thirsty man **d**, and, behold, he H2492

DREAMS
Gen 37: 8 the more for his **d**, and for his words. H2472
20 we shall see what will become of his **d**. H2472
41:12 to us our **d**; to each man according H2472
42: 9 And Joseph remembered the **d** which H2472
Dt 13: 1 of **d**, and giveth thee a sign or a wonder, H2472
3 or that dreamer of **d**: for the LORD your H2472
5 And that prophet, or that dreamer of **d**, H2472
1Sa 28: 6 by **d**, nor by Urim, nor by prophets. H2472
15 by prophets, nor by **d**: therefore I have H2472
Job 7:14 Then thou scarest me with **d**, and H2472
Ecc 5: 7 For in the multitude of **d** and many H2472
Jer 23:27 my name by their **d** which they tell H2472
32 prophesy false **d**, saith the LORD, and H2472
29: 8 your **d** which ye cause to be dreamed. H2472
Dan 1:17 had understanding in all visions and **d**. H2472
2: 1 dreamed **d**, wherewith his spirit H2472
2 shew the king his **d**. So they came and H2472
5:12 interpreting of **d**, and shewing of hard H2493
Joel 2:28 **d**, your young men shall see visions: H2472
Zec 10: 2 have told false **d**; they comfort in vain: H2472
Act 2:17 and your old men shall dream **d**: *G1798*

DREGS
Ps 75: 8 of the same: but the **d** thereof, all the H8105
Isa 51:17 thou hast drunken the **d** of the cup of H6907
22 *even* the **d** of the cup of my fury; H6907

DRESS
Gen 2:15 garden of Eden to **d** it and to keep it. H5647
18: 7 a young man; and he hasted to **d** it. H6213
Dt 28:39 Thou shalt plant vineyards, and **d** H5647
2Sa 12: 4 of his own herd, to **d** for the wayfaring H6213
13: 5 give me meat, and **d** the meat in my H6213
7 Amnon's house, and **d** him meat. H6213
1Ki 17:12 I may go in and **d** it for me and my son, H6213
18:23 *under:* and I will **d** the other bullock, H6213
25 for yourselves, and **d** *it* first; for ye *are* H6213

DRESSED
Gen 18: 8 calf which he had **d**, and set *it* before H6213
Lev 7: 9 and all that is **d** in the fryingpan, and H6213
1Sa 25:18 five sheep ready **d**, and five measures of H6213
2Sa 12: 4 **d** it for the man that was come to him. H6213
19:24 king, and had neither **d** his feet, nor H6213
1Ki 18:26 them, and they **d** *it*, and called on the H6213
Heb 6: 7 it is **d**, receiveth blessing from God: *G1090*

DRESSER
Lk 13: 7 Then said he unto the **d** of his vineyard, *G289*

DRESSERS
2Ch 26:10 *also*, and vine **d** in the mountains, and H3755

DRESSETH
Ex 30: 7 morning: when he **d** the lamps, he shall H3190

DREW
Gen 18:23 And Abraham **d** near, and said, Wilt
24:20 to draw *water*, and **d** for all his camels. H7579
45 unto the well, and **d** *water*: and I said H7579
37:28 and they **d** and lifted up Joseph H4900
38:29 And it came to pass, as he **d** back his H7725
47:29 And the time **d** nigh that Israel must H7126
Ex 2:10 said, Because I **d** him out of the water. H4871
16 they came and **d** *water*, and filled the H1802
19 and also **d** *water* enough for us, H1802
14:10 And when Pharaoh **d** nigh, the children
20:21 afar off, and Moses **d** near unto the thick
Lev 9: 5 **d** near and stood before the LORD.
Jos 8:11 him, went up, and **d** nigh, and came
26 For Joshua **d** not his hand back, H7725
Jdg 8:10 twenty thousand men that **d** sword. H8025
20 But the youth **d** not his sword: for he H8025
20: 2 thousand footmen that **d** sword. H8025
15 thousand men that **d** sword, beside the H8025
17 **d** sword: all these *were* men of war. H8025
25 thousand men; all these **d** the sword. H8025
35 an hundred men: all these **d** the sword. H8025
37 the liers in wait **d** *themselves* along, H4900
46 men that **d** the sword; all these H8025
Ru 4: 8 Buy *it* for thee. So he **d** off his shoe. H8025
1Sa 7: 6 to Mizpeh, and **d** water, and poured *it* H7579
10 the Philistines **d** near to battle against
9:18 Then Saul **d** near to Samuel in the gate,
17:16 And the Philistine **d** near morning and
40 his hand: and he **d** near to the Philistine.
41 And the Philistine came on and **d** near
48 and came and **d** nigh to meet David,
51 his sword, and **d** it out of the sheath H8025
2Sa 10:13 And Joab **d** nigh, and the people that
18:25 mouth. And he came apace, and **d** near.
22:17 He sent from above, he took me; he **d** H4871
23:16 Philistines, and **d** water out of the well H7579
24: 9 valiant men that **d** the sword; and the H8025
1Ki 2: 1 Now the days of David **d** nigh that he
8: 8 And they **d** out the staves, that the ends H748
22:34 And a *certain* man **d** a bow at a H4900
2Ki 3:26 hundred men that **d** swords, to break H8025
9:24 And Jehu **d** a bow with his full strength,
1Ch 11:18 Philistines, and **d** water out of the well H7579
19:14 that *were* with him **d** nigh before the
16 messengers, and **d** forth the Syrians H3318
21: 5 men that **d** sword: and Judah *was* H8025
5 and ten thousand men that **d** sword. H8025
2Ch 5: 9 And they **d** out the staves *of the ark*, that H748
14: 8 bare shields and **d** bows, two hundred H1869
18:33 And a *certain* man **d** a bow at a H4900
Est 5: 2 hand. So Esther **d** near, and touched the
9: 1 and his decree **d** near to be put in
Ps 18:16 He sent from above, he took me, he **d** H4871
Isa 41: 5 the earth were afraid, **d** near, and came.
Jer 38:13 So they **d** up Jeremiah with cords, and H4900
Hos 11: 4 I **d** them with cords of a man, with H4900
Zep 3: 2 in the LORD; she **d** not near to her God.
Mt 13:48 Which, when it was full, they **d** to shore, *G307*
21: 1 And when they **d** nigh unto Jerusalem,
34 And when the time of the fruit **d** near, he
26:51 out *his* hand, and **d** his sword, and *G645*
Mk 6:53 land of Gennesaret, and **d** to the shore. *G4358*
14:47 And one of them that stood by **d** a *G4685*
Lk 15: 1 Then **d** near unto him all the publicans
25 as he came and **d** nigh to the house, he
22: 1 Now the feast of unleavened bread **d**
47 them, and **d** near unto Jesus to kiss him.
23:54 the preparation, and the sabbath **d** on. *G2020*
24:15 himself **d** near, and went with them.
28 And they **d** nigh unto the village, whither
Jn 2: 9 the servants which **d** the water knew;) *G501*
18:10 Then Simon Peter having a sword **d** it, *G1670*
21:11 Simon Peter went up, and **d** the net to *G1670*
Act 5:37 of the taxing, and **d** away much people *G868*
7:17 But when the time of the promise **d** nigh,
31 sight: and as he **d** near to behold *it*, the *G4334*
10: 9 their journey, and **d** nigh unto the city,
14:19 stoned Paul, **d** *him* out of the city, *G4951*
16:19 Paul and Silas, and **d** *them* into the *G1670*
27 doors open, he **d** out his sword, and *G4685*
17: 6 And when they found them not, they **d** *G4951*
19:33 And they **d** Alexander out of the *G4264*
21:30 took Paul, and **d** him out of the temple: *G1670*
27:27 that they **d** near to some country; *G4317*
Rev 12: 4 And his tail **d** the third part of the stars *G4951*

DREWEST
Lam 3:57 Thou **d** near in the day *that* I called

DRIED
Gen 8: 7 waters were **d** up from off the earth. H3001
13 the waters were **d** up from off the H2717
14 day of the month, was the earth **d**. H3001
Lev 2:14 green ears of corn **d** by the fire, *even* H7033
Nu 6: 3 of grapes, nor eat moist grapes, or **d**. H3002
11: 6 But now our soul *is* **d** away: *there is* H3001
Jos 2:10 For we have heard how the LORD **d** up H3001
4:23 For the LORD your God **d** up the H3001
23 Red sea, which he **d** up from before us, H3001
5: 1 that the LORD had **d** up the waters of H3001
Jdg 16: 7 that were never **d**, then shall I be weak, H2717
8 been **d**, and she bound him with them. H2717
1Ki 13: 4 put forth against him, **d** up, so that he H3001
17: 7 that the brook **d** up, because there had H3001
2Ki 19:24 I **d** up all the rivers of besieged places. H2717
Job 18:16 His roots shall be **d** up beneath, and H3001
28: 4 **d** up, they are gone away from men. H1809
Ps 22:15 My strength is **d** up like a potsherd; H3001
69: 3 I am weary of my crying: my throat is **d**: H2787
106: 9 also, and it was **d** up: so he led them H2717
Isa 5:13 and their multitude **d** up with thirst. H6704
19: 5 and the river shall be wasted and **d** up. H3001
6 **d** up: the reeds and flags shall wither. H2717
37:25 of my feet have I **d** up all the rivers of H2717
51:10 *Art* thou not it which hath **d** the sea, H2717
Jer 23:10 of the wilderness are **d** up, and their H3001
50:38 and they shall be **d** up: for it *is* the land H3001
Ezk 17:24 the low tree, have **d** up the green tree, H3001
19:12 and the east wind **d** up her fruit: her H3001
37:11 Our bones are **d**, and our hope is lost: H3001
Hos 9:16 Ephraim is smitten, their root is **d** up, H3001
13:15 fountain shall be **d** up: he shall spoil H2717
Joel 1:10 new wine is **d** up, the oil languisheth. H3001
12 The vine is **d** up, and the fig tree H3001
20 of waters are **d** up, and the fire hath H3001
Zec 11:17 arm shall be clean **d** up, and his right H3001
Mk 5:29 of her blood was **d** up; and she felt in *G3583*
11:20 saw the fig tree **d** up from the roots. *G3583*
Rev 16:12 water thereof was **d** up, that the way of *G3583*

DRIEDST
Ps 74:15 and the flood: thou **d** up mighty rivers. H3001

DRIETH
Job 14:11 sea, and the flood decayeth and **d** up: H3001
Prv 17:22 but a broken spirit **d** the bones. H3001
Nah 1: 4 it dry, and **d** up all the rivers: Bashan H2717

DRINK
Gen 19:32 Come, let us make our father **d** wine, H8248
33 And they made their father **d** wine that H8248
34 let us make him **d** wine this night also; H8248
35 And they made their father **d** wine that H8248
21:19 bottle with water, and gave the lad **d**. H8248
24:14 thee, that I may **d**; and she shall say, H8354
14 and she shall say, **D**, and I will give thy H8354
14 give thy camels **d** also: *let the same be* H8248
17 pray thee, **d** a little water of thy pitcher. H1572
18 And she said, **D**, my lord: and she H8354
18 pitcher upon her hand, and gave him **d**. H8248
19 And when she had done giving him **d**, H8248
43 thee, a little water of thy pitcher to **d**; H8248
44 And she say to me, Both **d** thou, and I H8354
45 I said unto her, Let me **d**, I pray thee. H8248
46 and said, **D**, and I will give thy camels H8354
46 give thy camels **d** also: so I drank, and H8248
46 and she made the camels **d** also. H8248
54 And they did eat and **d**, he and the men H8354
25:34 he did eat and **d**, and rose up, and went H8354

Gen 26:30 them a feast, and they did eat and **d**. H8354
30:38 the flocks came to **d**, that they should H8354
38 should conceive when they came to **d**. H8354
35:14 and he poured a **d** offering thereon, H5262
Ex 7:18 shall lothe to **d** of the water of the river. H8354
21 could not **d** of the water of the river; H8354
24 river for water to **d**; for they could not H8354
24 could not **d** of the water of the river. H8354
15:23 they could not **d** of the waters of H8354
24 against Moses, saying, What shall we **d**? H8354
17: 1 *there was* no water for the people to **d**. H8354
2 water that we may **d**. And Moses said H8354
6 the people may **d**. And Moses did so in H8354
24:11 also they saw God, and did eat and **d**. H8354
29:40 part of an hin of wine *for* a **d** offering. H5262
41 according to the **d** offering thereof, for H5262
30: 9 shall ye pour **d** offering thereon. H5262
32: 6 to eat and to **d**, and rose up to play. H8354
20 and made the children of Israel **d** *of it*. H8248
34:28 eat bread, nor **d** water. And he wrote H8354
Lev 10: 9 Do not **d** wine nor strong drink, thou, H8354
9 Do not drink wine nor strong **d**, thou, H7941
11:34 unclean: and all **d** that may be drunk H4945
23:13 savour: and the **d** offering thereof *shall* H5262
18 offering, and their **d** offerings, *even* an H5262
37 **d** offerings, every thing upon his day: H5262
Nu 5:24 And he shall cause the woman to **d** the H8248
26 shall cause the woman to **d** the water. H8248
27 And when he hath made her to **d** the H8248
6: 3 wine and strong **d**, and shall drink no H7941
3 drink, and shall **d** no vinegar of wine, H8354
3 or vinegar of strong **d**, neither shall he H7941
3 neither shall he **d** any liquor of grapes, H8354
15 meat offering, and their **d** offerings. H5262
17 his meat offering, and his **d** offering. H5262
20 and after that the Nazarite may **d** wine. H8354
15: 5 hin of wine for a **d** offering shalt thou H5262
7 And for a **d** offering thou shalt offer the H5262
10 And thou shalt bring for a **d** offering H5262
24 offering, and his **d** offering, according H5262
20: 5 neither *is* there any water to **d**. H8354
8 the congregation and their beasts **d**. H8248
17 neither will we **d** *of* the water of the H8354
19 if I and my cattle **d** of thy water, then I H8354
21:22 we will not **d** *of* the waters of the H8354
23:24 the prey, and **d** the blood of the slain. H8354
28: 7 And the **d** offering thereof *shall be* the H5262
7 poured unto the LORD *for* a **d** offering. H5262
8 and as the **d** offering thereof, thou H5262
9 with oil, and the **d** offering thereof: H5262
10 burnt offering, and his **d** offering. H5262
14 And their **d** offerings shall be half an H5262
15 burnt offering, and his **d** offering. H5262
24 burnt offering, and his **d** offering. H5262
31 without blemish) and their **d** offerings. H5262
29: 6 meat offering, and their **d** offerings, H5262
11 offering of it, and their **d** offerings. H5262
16 his meat offering, and his **d** offering. H5262
18 And their meat offering and their **d** H5262
19 offering thereof, and their **d** offerings. H5262
21 And their meat offering and their **d** H5262
22 his meat offering, and his **d** offering. H5262
24 Their meat offering and their **d** H5262
25 his meat offering, and his **d** offering. H5262
27 And their meat offering and their **d** H5262
28 his meat offering, and his **d** offering. H5262
30 And their meat offering and their **d** H5262
31 his meat offering, and his **d** offering. H5262
33 And their meat offering and their **d** H5262
34 his meat offering, and his **d** offering. H5262
37 Their meat offering and their **d** H5262
38 his meat offering, and his **d** offering. H5262
39 and for your **d** offerings, and for your H5262
33:14 where was no water for the people to **d**. H8354
Dt 2: 6 water of them for money, that ye may **d**. H8354
28 **d**: only I will pass through on my feet; H8354
9: 9 I neither did eat bread nor **d** water: H8354
18 eat bread, nor **d** water, because of all H8354
14:26 wine, or for strong **d**, or for whatsoever H7941
28:39 but shalt neither **d** *of* the wine, nor H8354
29: 6 wine or strong **d**: that ye might know H7941
32:14 didst **d** the pure blood of the grape. H8354
38 the wine of their **d** offerings? let them H5257
Jdg 4:19 a little water to **d**; for I am thirsty. And H8248
19 milk, and gave him **d**, and covered him. H8248
7: 5 that boweth down upon his knees to **d**. H8354
6 down upon their knees to **d** water. H8354
9:27 did eat and **d**, and cursed Abimelech. H8354
13: 4 I pray thee, and **d** not wine nor strong H8354

Jdg 13: 4 strong **d**, and eat not any unclean *thing*: H7941
7 a son; and now **d** no wine nor strong H8354
7 no wine nor strong **d**, neither eat any H7941
14 neither let her **d** wine or strong drink, H8354
14 wine or strong **d**, nor eat any unclean H7941
19: 4 so they did eat and **d**, and lodged there. H8354
6 And they sat down, and did eat and **d** H8354
21 washed their feet, and did eat and **d**. H8354
Ru 2: 9 the vessels, and **d** of *that* which the H8354
1Sa 1:15 wine nor strong **d**, but have poured out H7941
30:11 he did eat; and they made him **d** water; H8248
2Sa 11:11 to eat and to **d**, and to lie with my wife? H8354
13 he did eat and **d** before him; and he H8354
16: 2 as be faint in the wilderness may **d**. H8354
19:35 I eat or what I **d**? can I hear any more H8354
23:15 would give me **d** of the water of the well H8248
16 he would not **d** thereof, but poured H8354
17 he would not **d** it. These things did H8354
1Ki 1:25 they eat and **d** before him, and say, H8354
13: 8 I eat bread nor **d** water in this place: H8354
9 Eat no bread, nor **d** water, nor turn H8354
16 nor **d** water with thee in this place: H8354
17 eat no bread nor **d** water there, nor H8354
18 and **d** water. *But* he lied unto him. H8354
22 thee, Eat no bread, and **d** no water; thy H8354
17: 4 And it shall be, *that* thou shalt **d** of the H8354
10 a little water in a vessel, that I may **d**. H8354
18:41 thee up, eat and **d**; for *there is* a sound H8354
42 So Ahab went up to eat and to **d**. And H8354
19: 6 eat and **d**, and laid him down again. H8354
8 And he arose, and did eat and **d**, and H8354
2Ki 3:17 that ye may **d**, both ye, and your cattle, H8354
6:22 may eat and **d**, and go to their master. H8354
7: 8 and did eat and **d**, and carried thence H8354
9:34 in, he did eat and **d**, and said, Go, see H8354
16:13 and poured his **d** offering, and H5262
15 offering, and their **d** offerings; and H5262
18:27 dung, and **d** their own piss with you? H8354
31 **d** ye every one the waters of his cistern: H8354
1Ch 11:17 would give me **d** of the water of the well H8248
18 **d** *of* it, but poured it out to the LORD, H8354
19 this thing: shall I **d** the blood of these H8354
19 he would not **d** it. These things did H8354
29:21 lambs, with their **d** offerings, and H5262
22 And did eat and **d** before the LORD on H8354
2Ch 28:15 gave them to eat and to **d**, and anointed H8248
29:35 offerings, and the **d** offerings for *every* H5262
Ezr 3: 7 and meat, and **d**, and oil, unto them of H4960
7:17 and their **d** offerings, and offer H5261
10: 6 did eat no bread, nor **d** water: for he H8354
Neh 8:10 eat the fat, and **d** the sweet, and send H8354
12 their way to eat, and to **d**, and to send H8354
Est 1: 7 And they gave *them* **d** in vessels of H8248
3:15 **d**; but the city Shushan was perplexed. H8354
4:16 neither eat nor **d** three days, night or H8354
Job 1: 4 three sisters to eat and to **d** with them. H8354
21:20 he shall **d** of the wrath of the Almighty. H8354
22: 7 water to the weary to **d**, and thou hast H8248
Ps 16: 4 another *god*: their **d** offerings of blood H5262
36: 8 them **d** of the river of thy pleasures. H8248
50:13 Will I eat the flesh of bulls, or **d** the H8354
60: 3 made us to **d** the wine of astonishment. H8248
69:21 in my thirst they gave me vinegar to **d**. H8248
75: 8 shall wring *them* out, *and* **d** *them*. H8354
78:15 gave *them* **d** as *out of* the great depths. H8248
44 and their floods, that they could not **d**. H8354
80: 5 them tears to **d** in great measure. H8248
102: 9 and mingled my **d** with weeping, H8249
104:11 They give **d** to every beast of the field: H8248
110: 7 He shall **d** of the brook in the way: H8354
Prv 4:17 wickedness, and **d** the wine of violence. H8354
5:15 **D** waters out of thine own cistern, and H8354
9: 5 Come, eat of my bread, and **d** of the H8354
20: 1 Wine *is* a mocker, strong **d** *is* raging: H7941
23: 7 so *is* he: Eat and **d**, saith he to thee; but H8354
25:21 and if he be thirsty, give him water to **d**: H8248
31: 4 to **d** wine; nor for princes strong drink: H8354
4 to drink wine; nor for princes strong **d**: H7941
5 Lest they **d**, and forget the law, and H8354
6 Give strong **d** unto him that is ready to H7941
7 Let him **d**, and forget his poverty, and H8354
Ecc 2:24 he should eat and **d**, and *that* he should H8354
3:13 should eat and **d**, and enjoy the good H8354
5:18 *for one* to eat and to **d**, and to enjoy the H8354
8:15 than to eat, and to **d**, and to be merry: H8354
9: 7 with joy, and **d** thy wine with a merry H8354
Song 5: 1 **d**, yea, drink abundantly, O beloved. H8354
1 drink, yea, **d** abundantly, O beloved. H7937
8: 2 cause thee to **d** of spiced wine of the H8248

Isa 5:11 may follow strong **d**; that continue until H7941
22 Woe unto *them that are* mighty to **d** H8354
22 and men of strength to mingle strong **d**: H7941
21: 5 the watchtower, eat, **d**: arise, ye princes, H8354
22:13 eat and **d**; for to morrow we shall die. H8354
24: 9 They shall not **d** wine with a song; H8354
9 **d** shall be bitter to them that drink it. H7941
9 drink shall be bitter to them that **d** it. H8354
28: 7 through strong **d** are out of the way; H7941
7 through strong **d**, they are swallowed H7941
7 through strong **d**; they err in vision, H7941
29: 9 they stagger, but not with strong **d**. H7941
32: 6 he will cause the **d** of the thirsty to fail. H4945
36:12 dung, and **d** their own piss with you? H8354
16 of his fig tree, and **d** ye every one the H8354
43:20 to give **d** to my people, my chosen. H8248
51:22 my fury; thou shalt no more **d** it again: H8354
56:12 with strong **d**; and to morrow shall H7941
57: 6 thou poured a **d** offering, thou hast H5262
62: 8 stranger shall not **d** thy wine, for the H8354
9 shall **d** it in the courts of my holiness. H8354
65:11 the **d** offering unto that number. H4469
13 my servants shall **d**, but ye shall be H8354
Jer 2:18 way of Egypt, to **d** the waters of Sihor? H8354
18 of Assyria, to **d** the waters of the river? H8354
7:18 and to pour out **d** offerings unto other H5262
8:14 us water of gall to **d**, because we have H8248
9:15 and give them water of gall to **d**. H8248
16: 7 to **d** for their father or for their mother. H8248
8 to sit with them to eat and to **d**. H8354
19:13 poured out **d** offerings unto other gods. H5262
22:15 thy father eat and **d**, and do judgment H8354
23:15 and make them **d** the water of gall: for H8248
25:15 nations, to whom I send thee, to **d** it. H8248
16 And they shall **d**, and be moved, and be H8354
17 **d**, unto whom the LORD had sent me: H8248
26 the king of Sheshach shall **d** after them. H8354
27 hosts, the God of Israel; **D** ye, and be H8354
28 at thine hand to **d**, then shalt thou say H8354
28 the LORD of hosts; Ye shall certainly **d**. H8354
32:29 and poured out **d** offerings unto other H5262
35: 2 the chambers, and give them wine to **d**. H8248
5 cups, and I said unto them, **D** ye wine. H8354
6 But they said, We will **d** no wine: for H8354
6 saying, Ye shall **d** no wine, *neither ye*, H8354
8 charged us, to **d** no wine all our days, H8354
14 his sons not to **d** wine, are performed; H8354
14 for unto this day they **d** none, but obey H8354
44:17 and to pour out **d** offerings unto her, as H5262
18 and to pour out **d** offerings unto her, H5262
19 and poured out **d** offerings unto her, H5262
19 **d** offerings unto her, without our men? H5262
25 and to pour out **d** offerings unto her: ye H5262
49:12 *was* not to **d** of the cup have assuredly H8354
12 but thou shalt surely **d** *of it*. H8354
Ezk 4:11 Thou shalt **d** also water by measure, H8354
11 an hin: from time to time shalt thou **d**. H8354
16 and they shall **d** water by measure, and H8354
12:18 with quaking, and **d** thy water with H8354
19 carefulness, and **d** their water with H8354
20:28 and poured out there their **d** offerings. H8354
23:32 Thus saith the Lord GOD; Thou shalt **d** H8354
34 Thou shalt even **d** it and suck *it* out, H8354
25: 4 eat thy fruit, and they shall **d** thy milk. H8354
31:14 height, all that **d** water: for they are all H8354
16 of Lebanon, all that **d** water, shall be H8354
34:19 feet; and they **d** that which ye have H8354
39:17 that ye may eat flesh, and **d** blood. H8354
18 of the mighty, and **d** the blood of the H8354
19 And ye shall eat fat till ye be full, and **d** H8354
44:21 Neither shall any priest **d** wine, when H8354
45:17 offerings, and **d** offerings, in the feasts, H5262
Dan 1:10 meat and your **d**: for why should he see H4960
12 give us pulse to eat, and water to **d**. H8354
16 they should **d**; and gave them pulse. H4960
5: 2 and his concubines, might **d** therein. H8355
Hos 2: 5 wool and my flax, mine oil and my **d**. H8250
4:18 Their **d** is sour: they have committed H5435
Joel 1: 9 The meat offering and the **d** offering is H5262
13 meat offering and the **d** offering is H5262
2:14 a **d** offering unto the LORD your God? H5262
3: 3 sold a girl for wine, that they might **d**. H8354
Am 2: 8 every altar, and they **d** the wine of the H8354
12 But ye gave the Nazarites wine to **d**; and H8248
4: 1 say to their masters, Bring, and let us **d**. H8354
8 unto one city, to **d** water; but they were H8354
5:11 but ye shall not **d** wine of them. H8354
6: 6 That **d** wine in bowls, and anoint H8354
9:14 vineyards, and **d** the wine thereof; they H8354

Oba 16 all the heathen **d** continually, yea, they H8354
16 yea, they shall **d**, and they shall swallow H8354
Jna 3: 7 thing: let them not feed, nor **d** water: H8354
Mic 2:11 and of strong **d**; he shall even be the H7941
6:15 and sweet wine, but shalt not **d** wine. H8354
Hab 2:15 his neighbour **d**, that puttest thy bottle H8248
16 Thou art filled with shame for glory: **d** H8354
Zep 1:13 vineyards, but not **d** the wine thereof. H8354
Hag 1: 6 not enough; ye **d**, but ye are not filled H8354
6 are not filled with **d**; ye clothe you, but H7937
Zec 7: 6 and when ye did **d**, did not ye eat *for* H8354
6 *for yourselves*, and **d** *for yourselves*? H8354
9:15 and they shall **d**, *and* make a noise as H8354
Mt 6:25 eat, or what ye shall **d**; nor yet for your *G4095*
31 **d**? or, Wherewithal shall we be clothed? *G4095*
10:42 And whosoever shall give to **d** unto one *G4222*
20:22 ye ask. Are ye able to **d** of the cup that I *G4095*
22 cup that I shall **d** of, and to be baptized *G4095*
23 And he saith unto them, Ye shall **d** *G4095*
24:49 and to eat and **d** with the drunken; *G4095*
25:35 **d**: I was a stranger, and ye took me in: *G4222*
37 fed *thee*? or thirsty, and gave *thee* **d**? *G4222*
42 I was thirsty, and ye gave me no **d**: *G4222*
26:27 gave *it* to them, saying, **D** ye all of it; *G4095*
29 But I say unto you, I will not **d** *G4095*
29 that day when I **d** it new with you in *G4095*
42 from me, except I **d** it, thy will be done. *G4095*
27:34 They gave him vinegar to **d** mingled *G4095*
34 he had tasted *thereof*, he would not **d**. *G4095*
48 and put *it* on a reed, and gave him to **d**. *G4222*
Mk 9:41 you a cup of water to **d** in my name, *G4222*
10:38 ye ask: can ye **d** of the cup that I drink *G4095*
38 of the cup that I **d** of? and be baptized *G4095*
39 Ye shall indeed **d** of the cup that I drink *G4095*
39 of the cup that I **d** of; and with the *G4095*
14:25 Verily I say unto you, I will **d** no more *G4095*
25 that I **d** it new in the kingdom of God. *G4095*
15:23 And they gave him to **d** wine mingled *G4095*
36 and gave him to **d**, saying, Let alone; let *G4222*
16:18 and if they **d** any deadly thing, it *G4095*
Lk 1:15 the Lord, and shall **d** neither wine nor *G4095*
15 wine nor strong **d**; and he shall be filled *G4608*
5:30 eat and **d** with publicans and sinners? *G4095*
33 of the Pharisees; but thine eat and **d**? *G4095*
12:19 take thine ease, eat, **d**, *and* be merry. *G4095*
29 shall **d**, neither be ye of doubtful mind. *G4095*
45 and to eat and **d**, and to be drunken; *G4095*
17: 8 and afterward thou shalt eat and **d**? *G4095*
22:18 For I say unto you, I will not **d** of the *G4095*
30 That ye may eat and **d** at my table in *G4095*
Jn 4: 7 Jesus saith unto her, Give me to **d**. *G4095*
9 a Jew, askest **d** of me, which am a *G4095*
10 to thee, Give me to **d**; thou wouldest *G4095*
6:53 and **d** his blood, ye have no life in you. *G4095*
55 meat indeed, and my blood is **d** indeed. *G4213*
7:37 thirst, let him come unto me, and **d**. *G4095*
18:11 Father hath given me, shall I not **d** it? *G4095*
Act 9: 9 without sight, and neither did eat nor **d**. *G4095*
10:41 **d** with him after he rose from the dead. *G4844*
23:12 eat nor **d** till they had killed Paul. *G4095*
21 neither eat nor **d** till they have killed *G4095*
Ro 12:20 if he thirst, give him **d**: for in so doing *G4222*
14:17 is not meat and **d**; but righteousness, *G4213*
21 *It is* good neither to eat flesh, nor to **d** *G4095*
1Co 9: 4 Have we not power to eat and to **d**? *G4095*
10: 4 And did all **d** the same spiritual drink: *G4095*
4 And did all drink the same spiritual **d**: *G4188*
7 down to eat and **d**, and rose up to play. *G4095*
21 Ye cannot **d** the cup of the Lord, and *G4095*
31 Whether therefore ye eat, or **d**, or *G4095*
11:22 to eat and to **d** in? or despise ye the *G4095*
25 as oft as ye **d** *it*, in remembrance of me. *G4095*
26 For as often as ye eat this bread, and **d** *G4095*
27 this bread, and **d** *this* cup of the Lord, *G4095*
28 eat of *that* bread, and **d** of *that* cup. *G4095*
12:13 have been all made to **d** into one Spirit. *G4222*
15:32 let us eat and **d**; for to morrow we die. *G4095*
Col 2:16 you in meat, or in **d**, or in respect of an *G4213*
1Ti 5:23 **D** no longer water, but use a little wine *G5202*
Rev 14: 8 made all nations **d** of the wine of the *G4222*
10 The same shall **d** of the wine of the *G4095*
16: 6 them blood to **d**; for they are worthy. *G4095*

DRINKERS
Joel 1: 5 and howl, all ye **d** of wine, because of H8354

DRINKETH
Gen 44: 5 *Is* not this *it* in which my lord **d**, and H8354
Dt 11:11 *and* **d** water of the rain of heaven: H8354
Job 6: 4 the poison whereof **d** up my spirit: the H8354
15:16 *is* man, which **d** iniquity like water? H8354
34: 7 What man *is* like Job, *who* **d** up H8354
40:23 Behold, he **d** up a river, *and* hasteth H6231
Prv 26: 6 fool cutteth off the feet, *and* **d** damage. H8354
Isa 29: 8 and, behold, he **d**; but he awaketh, and, H8354
44:12 faileth: he **d** no water, and is faint. H8354
Mk 2:16 and **d** with publicans and sinners? *G4095*
Jn 4:13 **d** of this water shall thirst again: *G4095*
14 But whosoever **d** of the water that I *G4095*
6:54 Whoso eateth my flesh, and **d** my *G4095*
56 He that eateth my flesh, and **d** my *G4095*
1Co 11:29 For he that eateth and **d** unworthily, *G4095*
29 eateth and **d** damnation to himself, *G4095*
Heb 6: 7 For the earth which **d** in the rain that *G4095*

DRINKING
Gen 24:19 thy camels also, until they have done **d**. H8354
22 camels had done **d**, that the man took a H8354
Ru 3: 3 until he shall have done eating and **d**. H8354
1Sa 30:16 the earth, eating and **d**, and dancing, H8354
1Ki 4:20 eating and **d**, and making merry. H8354
10:21 And all king Solomon's **d** vessels *were* H4945
16: 9 as he was in Tirzah, **d** himself drunk in H8354
20:12 as he *was* **d**, he and the kings in H8354
16 Ben-hadad *was* **d** himself drunk in the H8354
1Ch 12:39 days, eating and **d**: for their brethren H8354
2Ch 9:20 And all the **d** vessels of king Solomon H4945
Est 1: 8 And the **d** *was* according to the law; H8360
Job 1:13 **d** wine in their eldest brother's house: H8354
18 **d** wine in their eldest brother's house: H8354
Isa 22:13 eating flesh, and **d** wine: let us eat and H8354
Mt 11:18 For John came neither eating nor **d**, and *G4095*
19 The Son of man came eating and **d**, and *G4095*
24:38 were eating and **d**, marrying and giving *G4095*
Lk 7:33 nor **d** wine; and ye say, He hath a devil. *G4095*
34 The Son of man is come eating and **d**; *G4095*
10: 7 eating and **d** such things as they *G4095*

DRINK-OFFERING See DRINK and OFFERING.

DRINKS
Heb 9:10 *Which stood* only in meats and **d**, and *G4188*

DRIVE
Ex 6: 1 hand shall he **d** them out of his land. H1644
23:28 thee, which shall **d** out the Hivite, the H1644
29 I will not **d** them out from before thee H1644
30 By little and little I will **d** them out H1644
31 and thou shalt **d** them out before thee. H1644
33: 2 thee; and I will **d** out the Canaanite, the H1644
34:11 this day: behold, I **d** out before thee the H1644
Nu 22: 6 and *that* I may **d** them out of the land: H1644
11 to overcome them, and **d** them out. H1644
33:52 Then ye shall **d** out all the inhabitants H3423
55 But if ye will not **d** out the inhabitants H3423
Dt 4:38 To **d** out nations from before thee H3423
9: 3 thy face: so shalt thou **d** them out, and H3423
4 **d** them out from before thee. H3423
5 thy God doth **d** them out from before H3423
11:23 Then will the LORD **d** out all these H3423
18:12 God doth **d** them out from before thee. H3423
Jos 3:10 will without fail **d** out from before you H3423
13: 6 them will I **d** out from before the H3423
14:12 able to **d** them out, as the LORD said. H3423
15:63 of Judah could not **d** them out: but the H3423
17:12 could not **d** out *the inhabitants* H3423
13 tribute; but did not utterly **d** them out. H3423
18 for thou shalt **d** out the Canaanites, H3423
23: 5 before you, and **d** them from out of H3423
13 God will no more **d** out *any of* these H3423
Jdg 1:19 but could not **d** out the inhabitants H3423
21 And the children of Benjamin did not **d** H3423
27 Neither did Manasseh **d** out *the* H3423
28 tribute, and did not utterly **d** them out. H3423
29 Neither did Ephraim **d** out the H3423
30 Neither did Zebulun **d** out the H3423
31 Neither did Asher **d** out the inhabitants H3423
32 of the land: for they did not **d** them out. H3423
33 Neither did Naphtali **d** out the H3423
2: 3 Wherefore I also said, I will not **d** them H1644
21 I also will not henceforth **d** out any H3423
11:24 our God shall **d** out from before us, H3423
2Ki 4:24 to her servant, **D**, and go forward; slack H5090
2Ch 20: 7 *Art* not thou our God, *who* didst **d** out H3423
Job 18:11 every side, and shall **d** him to his feet. H6327
24: 3 They **d** away the ass of the fatherless, H5090
Ps 44: 2 *How* thou didst **d** out the heathen with H3423
68: 2 As smoke is driven away, *so* **d** *them* H5086
Prv 22:15 rod of correction shall **d** it far from him. H7368
Isa 22:19 And I will **d** thee from thy station, and H1920
Jer 24: 9 in all places whither I shall **d** them. H5080
27:10 should **d** you out, and ye should perish. H5080
15 that I might **d** you out, and that ye H5080
46:15 not, because the LORD did **d** them. H1920
Ezk 4:13 the Gentiles, whither I will **d** them. H5080
Dan 4:25 That they shall **d** thee from men, and H2957
32 And they shall **d** thee from men, and H2957
Hos 9:15 their doings I will **d** them out of mine H1644
Joel 2:20 *army*, and will **d** him into a land H5080
Zep 2: 4 they shall **d** out Ashdod at the noon H16444
Act 27:15 not bear up into the wind, we let *her* **d**. *G1929*

DRIVEN
Gen 4:14 Behold, thou hast **d** me out this day H1644
Ex 10:11 were **d** out from Pharaoh's presence. H1644
22:10 or be hurt, or **d** away, no man seeing *it*: H7617
Nu 32:21 **d** out his enemies from before him, H3423
Dt 4:19 shouldest be **d** to worship them, and H5080
30: 1 whither the LORD thy God hath **d** thee, H5080
4 If *any* of thine be **d** out unto the H5080
Jos 23: 9 For the LORD hath **d** out from before H3423
1Sa 26:19 for they have **d** me out this day from H1644
Job 6:13 *Is* not my help in me? and is wisdom **d** H5080
13:25 Wilt thou break a leaf **d** to and fro? and H5086
18:18 He shall be **d** from light into darkness, H1920
30: 5 They were **d** forth from among *men*, H1644
Ps 40:14 it; let them be **d** backward and put to H5472
68: 2 As smoke is **d** away, *so* drive *them* H5086
114: 3 The sea saw *it*, and fled: Jordan was **d** H5437
5 thou Jordan, *that* thou wast **d** back? H5437
Prv 14:32 The wicked is **d** away in his H1760
Isa 8:22 and *they shall be* **d** to darkness. H5080
19: 7 wither, be **d** away, and be no *more*. H5086
41: 2 his sword, *and* as **d** stubble to his bow. H5086
Jer 8: 3 I have **d** them, saith the LORD of hosts. H5080
16:15 whither he had **d** them: and I will bring H5080
23: 2 my flock, and **d** them away, and have H5080
3 whither I have **d** them, and will bring H5080
8 whither I had **d** them; and they shall H5080
12 they shall be **d** on, and fall therein: H1760
29:14 whither I have **d** you, saith the LORD; H5080
18 all the nations whither I have **d** them: H5080
32:37 whither I have **d** them in mine anger, H5080
40:12 whither they were **d**, and came to the H5080
43: 5 been **d**, to dwell in the land of Judah; H5080
46:28 whither I have **d** thee: but I will not H5080
49: 5 and ye shall be **d** out every man right H5080
50:17 the lions have **d** *him* away: first the H5080
Ezk 31:11 I have **d** him out for his wickedness. H1644
34: 4 that which was **d** away, neither have H5080
16 that which was **d** away, and will bind H5080
Dan 4:33 and he was **d** from men, and did H2957
5:21 And he was **d** from the sons of men; H2957
9: 7 whither thou hast **d** them, because of H5080
Hos 13: 3 away, as the chaff *that* is **d** with the H5590
Mic 4: 6 is **d** out, and her that I have afflicted; H5080
Zep 3:19 her that was **d** out; and I will get them H5080
Lk 8:29 was **d** of the devil into the wilderness.) *G1643*
Act 27:17 quicksands, strake sail, and so were **d**. *G5342*
27 come, as we were **d** up and down in *G1308*
Jas 1: 6 of the sea **d** with the wind and tossed. *G416*
3: 4 so great, and *are* **d** of fierce winds, yet *G1643*

DRIVER
1Ki 22:34 he said unto the **d** of his chariot, Turn H7395
Job 39: 7 neither regardeth he the crying of the **d**. H5065

DRIVETH
2Ki 9:20 the son of Nimshi; for he **d** furiously. H5090
Ps 1: 4 like the chaff which the wind **d** away. H5086
Prv 25:23 The north wind **d** away rain: so *doth* H2342
Mk 1:12 And immediately the Spirit **d** him into *G1544*

DRIVING
Jdg 2:23 nations, without **d** them out hastily; H3423
2Ki 9:20 not again: and the **d** *is* like the driving H4491
20 driving *is* like the **d** of Jehu the son of H4491
1Ch 17:21 and terribleness, by **d** out nations from H1644

DROMEDARIES
1Ki 4:28 for the horses and **d** brought they unto H7409
Est 8:10 riders on mules, camels, *and* young **d**: H7424
Isa 60: 6 cover thee, the **d** of Midian and Ephah; H1070

DROMEDARY
Jer 2:23 *thou art* a swift **d** traversing her ways; H1072

DROP
Dt 32: 2 My doctrine shall **d** as the rain, my H6201
33:28 also his heavens shall **d** down dew. H6201
Job 36:28 Which the clouds do **d** *and* distil upon H5140
Ps 65:11 thy goodness; and thy paths **d** fatness. H7491
12 They **d** *upon* the pastures of the H7491
Prv 3:20 up, and the clouds **d** down the dew. H7491
5: 3 For the lips of a strange woman **d** *as* an H5197
Song 4:11 Thy lips, O *my* spouse, **d** *as* the H5197
Isa 40:15 Behold, the nations *are* as a **d** of a H4752
45: 8 **D** down, ye heavens, from above, and H7491
Ezk 20:46 the south, and **d** *thy word* toward the H5197
21: 2 Jerusalem, and **d** *thy word* toward the H5197
Joel 3:18 mountains shall **d** down new wine, and H5197
Am 7:16 Israel, and **d** not *thy word* against H5197
9:13 mountains shall **d** sweet wine, and all H5197

DROPPED
Jdg 5: 4 **d**, the clouds also dropped water. H5197
4 dropped, the clouds also **d** water. H5197
1Sa 14:26 behold, the honey **d**; but no man put his H1982
2Sa 21:10 until water **d** upon them out of heaven, H5413
Job 29:22 again; and my speech **d** upon them. H5197
Ps 68: 8 The earth shook, the heavens also **d** at H5197
Song 5: 5 and my hands **d** *with* myrrh, and my H5197

DROPPETH
Ecc 10:18 of the hands the house **d** through. H1811

DROPPING
Prv 19:13 contentions of a wife *are* a continual **d**. H1812
27:15 A continual **d** in a very rainy day and a H1812
Song 5:13 lips *like* lilies, **d** sweet smelling myrrh. H5197

DROPS
Job 36:27 For he maketh small the **d** of water: H5198
38:28 or who hath begotten the **d** of dew? H96
Song 5: 2 *and* my locks with the **d** of the night. H7447
Lk 22:44 **d** of blood falling down to the ground. *G2361*

DROPSY
Lk 14: 2 man before him which had the **d**. *G5203*

DROSS
Ps119:119 *like* **d**: therefore I love thy testimonies. H5509
Prv 25: 4 Take away the **d** from the silver, and H5509
26:23 *like* a potsherd covered with silver **d**. H5509
Isa 1:22 Thy silver is become **d**, thy wine mixed H5509
25 away thy **d**, and take away all thy tin: H5509
Ezk 22:18 is to me become **d**: all they *are* brass, H5509
18 furnace; they are *even* the **d** of silver. H5509
19 ye are all become **d**, behold, therefore I H5509

DROUGHT
Gen 31:40 *Thus* I was; in the day the **d** consumed H2721
Dt 8:15 scorpions, and **d**, where *there was* no H6774
Job 24:19 **D** and heat consume the snow waters: H6723
Ps 32: 4 is turned into the **d** of summer. Selah. H2725
Isa 58:11 satisfy thy soul in **d**, and make fat thy H6710
Jer 2: 6 through a land of **d**, and of the shadow H6723
17: 8 in the year of **d**, neither shall cease from H1226
50:38 A **d** *is* upon her waters; and they shall H2721
Hos 13: 5 in the wilderness, in the land of great **d**. H8514
Hag 1:11 And I called for a **d** upon the land, and H2721

DROVE
Gen 3:24 So he **d** out the man; and he placed at H1644
15:11 the carcases, Abram **d** them away. H5380
32:16 of his servants, every **d** by themselves; H5739
16 and put a space betwixt **d** and drove. H5739
16 and put a space betwixt drove and **d**. H5739
33: 8 thou by all this **d** which I met? And he H4264
Ex 2:17 And the shepherds came and **d** them H1644
Nu 21:32 and **d** out the Amorites that *were* there. H3423
Jos 15:14 And Caleb **d** thence the three sons of H3423
1Ch 8:13 who **d** away the inhabitants of Gath: H1272
Ps 34:ttl who **d** him away, and he departed. H1644
Hab 3: 6 he beheld, and **d** asunder the nations; H5425
Jn 2:15 of small cords, he **d** them all out of the *G1544*

DROVES
Gen 32:19 all that followed the **d**, saying, On this H5739

DROWN
Song 8: 7 can the floods **d** it: if *a* man would give H7857
1Ti 6: 9 **d** men in destruction and perdition. *G1036*

DROWNED
Ex 15: 4 captains also are **d** in the Red sea. H2883
Am 8: 8 cast out and **d**, as *by* the flood of Egypt. H8257
9: 5 and shall be **d**, as *by* the flood of Egypt. H8257
Mt 18: 6 *that* he were **d** in the depth of the sea. *G2670*
Heb 11:29 the Egyptians assaying to do were **d**. *G2666*

DROWSINESS
Prv 23:21 and **d** shall clothe *a man* with rags. H5124

DRUNK
Lev 11:34 **d** in every *such* vessel shall be unclean. H8354
Dt 29: 6 neither have ye **d** wine or strong drink: H8354
32:42 I will make mine arrows **d** with blood, H7937
Jdg 15:19 and when he had **d**, his spirit came H8354
Ru 3: 7 And when Boaz had eaten and **d**, and H8354
1Sa 1: 9 and after they had **d**. Now Eli the priest H8354
15 spirit: I have **d** neither wine nor strong H8354
30:12 no bread, nor **d** *any* water, three days H8354
2Sa 11:13 and he made him **d**: and at even he H7937
1Ki 13:22 eaten bread and **d** water in the place, H8354
23 and after he had **d**, that he saddled for H8354
16: 9 drinking himself **d** in the house of Arza H7910
20:16 drinking himself **d** in the pavilions, he H7910
2Ki 6:23 had eaten and **d**, he sent them away, H8354
19:24 I have digged and **d** strange waters, H8354
Song 5: 1 my honey; I have **d** my wine with my H8354
Isa 37:25 I have digged, and **d** water; and with H8354
51:17 which hast **d** at the hand of the LORD H8354
63: 6 and make them **d** in my fury, and I will H7937
Jer 46:10 be satiate and made **d** with their blood: H7301
51:57 And I will make **d** her princes, and her H7937
Ezk 34:18 and to have **d** of the deep waters, H8354
Dan 5:23 concubines, have **d** wine in them; and H8355
Oba 16 For as ye have **d** upon my holy H8354
Lk 5:39 No man also having **d** old *wine* *G4095*
13:26 have eaten and **d** in thy presence, and *G4095*
Jn 2:10 men have well **d**, then that which is *G3184*
Eph 5:18 And be not **d** with wine, wherein is *G3182*
Rev 17: 2 **d** with the wine of her fornication. *G3184*
18: 3 For all nations have **d** of the wine of the *G4095*

DRUNKARD
Dt 21:20 obey our voice; *he is* a glutton, and a **d**. H5433
Prv 23:21 For the **d** and the glutton shall come to H5433
26: 9 **d**, so *is* a parable in the mouth of fools. H7910
Isa 24:20 The earth shall reel to and fro like a **d**, H7910
1Co 5:11 or a railer, or a **d**, or an extortioner; *G3183*

DRUNKARDS
Ps 69:12 me; and I *was* the song of the **d**. H8354+H7941
Isa 28: 1 Woe to the crown of pride, to the **d** of H7910
3 The crown of pride, the **d** of Ephraim, H7910
Joel 1: 5 Awake, ye **d**, and weep; and howl, all ye H7910
Nah 1:10 they are drunken *as* **d**, they shall be H5435
1Co 6:10 Nor thieves, nor covetous, nor **d**, nor *G3183*

DRUNKEN
Gen 9:21 And he drank of the wine, and was **d**; H7937
1Sa 1:13 therefore Eli thought she had been **d**. H7910
14 thou be **d**? put away thy wine from thee. H7937
25:36 for he *was* very **d**: wherefore she told H7910
Job 12:25 maketh them to stagger like *a* **d** *man*. H7910
Ps 107:27 like a **d** man, and are at their wits' end. H7910
Isa 19:14 as a **d** *man* staggereth in his vomit. H7910
29: 9 and cry: they are **d**, but not with wine; H7937
49:26 and they shall be **d** with their own H7937
51:17 of his fury; thou hast **d** the dregs of the H8354
21 thou afflicted, and **d**, but not with wine: H7937
Jer 23: 9 shake; I am like a **d** man, and like a H7910
25:27 Drink ye, and be **d**, and spue, and fall, H7937
48:26 Make ye him **d**: for he magnified H7937
49:12 have assuredly **d**; and *art* thou he *that* H8354
51: 7 made all the earth **d**: the nations have H7937
7 the nations have **d** of her wine; H8354
39 and I will make them **d**, that they may H7937
Lam 3:15 he hath made me **d** with wormwood. H7301
4:21 be **d**, and shalt make thyself naked. H7937
5: 4 We have **d** our water for money; our H8354
Ezk 39:19 blood till ye be **d**, of my sacrifice which H7943
Nah 1:10 and while they are **d** *as* drunkards, H5433
3:11 Thou also shalt be **d**: thou shalt be hid, H7937
Hab 2:15 *him*, and makest *him* **d** also, that thou H7937
Mt 24:49 and to eat and drink with the **d**; *G3184*
Lk 12:45 and to eat and drink, and to be **d**; *G3182*
17: 8 I have eaten and **d**; and afterward thou *G4095*
Act 2:15 For these are not **d**, as ye suppose, *G3184*
1Co 11:21 and one is hungry, and another is **d**. *G3184*
1Th 5: 7 they that be **d** are drunken in the night. *G3182*
7 they that be drunken are **d** in the night. *G3184*
Rev 17: 6 And I saw the woman **d** with the blood *G3184*

DRUNKENNESS
Dt 29:19 of mine heart, to add **d** to thirst: H7302
Ecc 10:17 due season, for strength, and not for **d**! H8358
Jer 13:13 all the inhabitants of Jerusalem, with **d**. H7943
Ezk 23:33 Thou shalt be filled with **d** and sorrow, H7943
Lk 21:34 surfeiting, and **d**, and cares of this life, *G3178*
Ro 13:13 not in rioting and **d**, not in chambering *G3178*
Gal 5:21 Envyings, murders, **d**, revellings, and *G3178*

DRUSILLA
Act 24:24 with his wife **D**, which was a Jewess, *G1409*

DRY
Gen 1: 9 let the **d** *land* appear: and it was so. H3004
10 And God called the **d** *land* Earth; and H3004
7:22 life, of all that *was* in the **d** *land*, died. H2724
8:13 behold, the face of the ground was **d**. H2717
Ex 4: 9 pour *it* upon the **d** *land*: and the water H3004
9 shall become blood upon the **d** *land*. H3006
14:16 **d** *ground* through the midst of the sea. H3004
21 **d** *land*, and the waters were divided. H2724
22 of the sea upon the **d** *ground*: and the H3004
29 walked upon **d** *land* in the midst of H3004
15:19 went on **d** *land* in the midst of the sea. H3004
Lev 7:10 with oil, and **d**, shall all the sons of H2720
13:30 unclean: it *is* a **d** scall, *even* a leprosy H5424
Jos 3:17 stood firm on **d** ground in the midst H2724
17 passed over on **d** ground, until all the H2724
4:18 were lifted up unto the **d** land, that the H2724
22 Israel came over this Jordan on **d** land. H3004
9: 5 of their provision was **d** *and* mouldy. H3001
12 now, behold, it is **d**, and it is mouldy: H3001
Jdg 6:37 only, and *it be* **d** upon all the earth H2721
39 let it now be **d** only upon the fleece, H2721
40 And God did so that night: for it was **d** H2721
2Ki 2: 8 that they two went over on **d** ground. H2724
Neh 9:11 of the sea on the **d** land; and their H3004
Job 12:15 waters, and they **d** up: also he sendeth H3001
13:25 fro? and wilt thou pursue the **d** stubble? H3002
15:30 the flame shall **d** up his branches, and H3001
Ps 63: 1 a **d** and thirsty land, where no water is; H6723
66: 6 He turned the sea into **d** *land*: they H3004
68: 6 but the rebellious dwell in a **d** *land*. H6707
95: 5 it: and his hands formed the **d** *land*. H3006
105:41 they ran in the **d** places *like* a river. H6723
107:33 and the watersprings into **d** ground; H6774
35 water, and **d** ground into watersprings. H6723
Prv 17: 1 Better *is* a **d** morsel, and quietness H2720
Isa 25: 5 as the heat in a **d** place; *even* the heat H6724
32: 2 of water in a **d** place, as the shadow H6724
41:18 water, and the **d** land springs of water. H6723
42:15 and hills, and **d** up all their herbs; and H3001
15 rivers islands, and I will **d** up the pools. H3001
44: 3 floods upon the **d** ground: I will pour H3004
27 That saith to the deep, Be **d**, and I will H2717
27 deep, Be dry, and I will **d** up thy rivers: H3001
50: 2 at my rebuke I **d** up the sea, I make the H2717
53: 2 as a root out of a **d** ground: he hath no H6723
56: 3 the eunuch say, Behold, I *am* a **d** tree. H3002
Jer 4:11 and to Jerusalem, A **d** wind of the high H6703
50:12 *be* a wilderness, a **d** land, and a desert. H6723
51:36 for thee; and I will **d** up her sea, and H2717
36 dry up her sea, and make her springs **d**. H3001
43 Her cities are a desolation, a **d** land, H6723
Ezk 17:24 have made the **d** tree to flourish: I the H3002
19:13 wilderness, in a **d** and thirsty ground. H6723
20:47 in thee, and every **d** tree: the flaming H3002
30:12 And I will make the rivers **d**, and sell H2724
37: 2 open valley; and, lo, *they were* very **d**. H3002
4 ye **d** bones, hear the word of the LORD. H3002
Hos 2: 3 like a **d** land, and slay her with thirst. H6723
9:14 a miscarrying womb and **d** breasts. H6784
13:15 shall become **d**, and his fountain shall H954
Jna 1: 9 hath made the sea and the **d** *land*. H3004
2:10 it vomited out Jonah upon the **d** *land*. H3004
Nah 1: 4 He rebuketh the sea, and maketh it **d**, H3001
10 shall be devoured as stubble fully **d**. H3002
Zep 2:13 a desolation, *and* **d** like a wilderness. H6723
Hag 2: 6 the earth, and the sea, and the **d** *land*; H2724
Zec 10:11 of the river shall **d** up: and the pride of H3001
Mt 12:43 **d** places, seeking rest, and findeth none. *G504*
Lk 11:24 walketh through **d** places, seeking rest; *G504*
23:31 green tree, what shall be done in the **d**? *G3584*
Heb 11:29 the Red sea as by **d** *land*: which the *G3584*

DRY-GROUND See DRY and GROUND.

DRY-LAND See DRY and LAND.

DRYSHOD
Isa 11:15 streams, and make *men* go over **d**. H5275

DUE
Lev 10:13 because it *is* thy **d**, and thy sons' due, of H2706
13 due, and thy sons' **d**, of the sacrifices of H2706
14 for *they be* thy **d**, and thy sons' due, H2706
14 due, and thy sons' **d**, *which* are given H2706
26: 4 Then I will give you rain in **d** season,
Nu 28: 2 to offer unto me in their **d** season.
Dt 11:14 of your land in his **d** season, the first
18: 3 And this shall be the priest's **d** from the H4941
32:35 foot shall slide in *d* time: for the day of
1Ch 15:13 that we sought him not after the **d** order.
16:29 Give unto the LORD the glory *d* unto his
Neh 11:23 be for the singers, **d** for every day. H1697
Ps 29: 2 Give unto the LORD the glory **d** unto his
96: 8 Give unto the LORD the glory *d unto* his
104:27 give *them* their meat in **d** season.
145:15 thou givest them their meat in **d** season.
Prv 3:27 to whom it is **d**, when it is in the power H1167
15:23 word *spoken* in **d** season, how good *is it*!
Ecc 10:17 thy princes eat in **d** season, for strength,
Mt 18:34 he should pay all that was **d** unto him. G3784
24:45 to give them meat in **d** season?
Lk 12:42 *them their* portion of meat in **d** season?
23:41 for we receive the **d** reward of our deeds: G514
Ro 5: 6 in **d** time Christ died for the ungodly.
13: 7 to whom tribute *is d*; custom to whom
1Co 7: 3 Let the husband render unto the wife **d** G3784
15: 8 of me also, as of one born out of **d** time.
Gal 6: 9 **d** season we shall reap, if we faint not. G2398
1Ti 2: 6 ransom for all, to be testified in **d** time. G2398
Tit 1: 3 But hath in **d** times manifested his G2398
1Pt 5: 6 of God, that he may exalt you in **d** time:

DUES
Ro 13: 7 Render therefore to all their **d**: tribute G3782

DUG See DIGGED.

DUKE
Gen 36:15 *son* of Esau; **d** Teman, duke Omar, H441
15 **d** Omar, duke Zepho, duke Kenaz, H441
15 duke Omar, **d** Zepho, duke Kenaz, H441
15 duke Omar, duke Zepho, **d** Kenaz, H441
16 **D** Korah, duke Gatam, *and* duke H441
16 Duke Korah, **d** Gatam, *and* duke H441
16 Duke Korah, duke Gatam, *and* **d** H441
17 of Reuel Esau's son; **d** Nahath, duke H441
17 duke Nahath, **d** Zerah, duke Shammah, H441
17 duke Zerah, **d** Shammah, duke Mizzah: H441
17 duke Shammah, **d** Mizzah: these *are* the H441
18 Esau's wife; **d** Jeush, duke Jaalam, H441
18 wife; duke Jeush, **d** Jaalam, duke Korah: H441
18 duke Jaalam, **d** Korah: these *were* the H441
29 of the Horites; **d** Lotan, duke Shobal, H441
29 **d** Shobal, duke Zibeon, duke Anah, H441
29 duke Shobal, **d** Zibeon, duke Anah, H441
29 duke Shobal, duke Zibeon, **d** Anah, H441
30 **D** Dishon, duke Ezer, duke Dishan: these H441
30 Duke Dishon, **d** Ezer, duke Dishan: these H441
30 Duke Dishon, duke Ezer, **d** Dishan: these H441
40 **d** Timnah, duke Alvah, duke Jetheth, H441
40 duke Timnah, **d** Alvah, duke Jetheth, H441
40 duke Timnah, duke Alvah, **d** Jetheth, H441
41 **D** Aholibamah, duke Elah, duke Pinon, H441
41 Duke Aholibamah, **d** Elah, duke Pinon, H441
41 Duke Aholibamah, duke Elah, **d** Pinon, H441
42 **D** Kenaz, duke Teman, duke Mibzar, H441
42 Duke Kenaz, **d** Teman, duke Mibzar, H441
42 Duke Kenaz, duke Teman, **d** Mibzar, H441
43 **D** Magdiel, duke Iram: these *be* the H441
43 Duke Magdiel, **d** Iram: these *be* the H441
1Ch 1:51 **d** Timnah, duke Aliah, duke Jetheth, H441
51 duke Timnah, **d** Aliah, duke Jetheth, H441
51 duke Timnah, duke Aliah, **d** Jetheth, H441
52 **D** Aholibamah, duke Elah, duke Pinon, H441
52 Duke Aholibamah, **d** Elah, duke Pinon, H441
52 Duke Aholibamah, duke Elah, **d** Pinon, H441
53 **D** Kenaz, duke Teman, duke Mibzar, H441
53 Duke Kenaz, **d** Teman, duke Mibzar, H441
53 Duke Kenaz, duke Teman, **d** Mibzar, H441
54 **D** Magdiel, duke Iram. These *are* the H441
54 Duke Magdiel, **d** Iram. These *are* the H441

DUKES
Gen 36:15 These *were* **d** of the sons of Esau: the H441
16 these *are* the **d** *that came* of Eliphaz H441
Gen 36:17 these *are* the **d** *that came* of Reuel in H441
18 Korah: these *were* the **d** *that came* of H441
19 Esau, who *is* Edom, and these *are* their **d**. H441
21 these *are* the **d** of the Horites, the H441
29 These *are* the **d** *that came* of the Horites; H441
30 these *are* the **d** *that came* of Hori, among H441
30 Hori, among their **d** in the land of Seir. H441
40 And these *are* the names of the **d** *that* H441
43 Duke Magdiel, duke Iram: these *be* the **d** H441
Ex 15:15 Then the **d** of Edom shall be amazed; the H441
Jos 13:21 **d** of Sihon, dwelling in the country. H5257
1Ch 1:51 Hadad died also. And the **d** of Edom H441
54 duke Iram. These *are* the **d** of Edom. H441

DULCIMER
Dan 3: 5 sackbut, psaltery, **d**, and all kinds of H5481
10 psaltery, and **d**, and all kinds of musick, H5481
15 psaltery, and **d**, and all kinds of musick, H5481

DULL
Mt 13:15 and *their* ears are **d** of hearing, and their G917
Act 28:27 and their ears are **d** of hearing, and their G917
Heb 5:11 be uttered, seeing ye are **d** of hearing. G3576

DUMAH
Gen 25:14 And Mishma, and **D**, and Massa, H1746
Jos 15:52 Arab, and **D**, and Eshean, H1746
1Ch 1:30 Mishma, and **D**, Massa, Hadad, and H1746
Isa 21:11 The burden of **D**. He calleth to me out of H1746

DUMB
Ex 4:11 or who maketh the **d**, or deaf, or the H483
Ps 38:13 as a **d** man *that* openeth not his mouth. H483
39: 2 I was **d** with silence, I held my peace, H481
9 I was **d**, I opened not my mouth; because H481
Prv 31: 8 Open thy mouth for the **d** in the cause of H483
Isa 35: 6 and the tongue of the **d** sing: for in the H483
53: 7 is **d**, so he openeth not his mouth. H481
56:10 they *are* all **d** dogs, they cannot bark; H483
Ezk 3:26 that thou shalt be **d**, and shalt not be to H481
24:27 and be no more **d**: and thou shalt be a H481
33:22 mouth was opened, and I was no more **d**. H481
Dan 10:15 face toward the ground, and I became **d**. H481
Hab 2:18 work trusteth therein, to make **d** idols? H483
19 Awake; to the **d** stone, Arise, it shall H1748
Mt 9:32 to him a **d** man possessed with a devil. G2974
33 And when the devil was cast out, the **d** G2974
12:22 with a devil, blind, and **d**: and he healed G2974
22 the blind and **d** both spake and saw. G2974
15:30 *were* lame, blind, **d**, maimed, and many G2974
31 when they saw the **d** to speak, the G2974
Mk 7:37 both the deaf to hear, and the **d** to speak. G216
9:17 unto thee my son, which hath a **d** spirit; G216
25 unto him, *Thou* **d** and deaf spirit, I G216
Lk 1:20 And, behold, thou shalt be **d**, and not G4623
11:14 out a devil, and it was **d**. And it came to G2974
14 the **d** spake; and the people wondered. G2974
Act 8:32 and like a lamb **d** before his shearer, so G880
1Co 12: 2 unto these **d** idols, even as ye were led. G880
2Pt 2:16 But was rebuked for his iniquity: the **d** G880

DUNG
Ex 29:14 his skin, and his **d**, shalt thou burn with H6569
Lev 4:11 his legs, and his inwards, and his **d**, H6569
8:17 his flesh, and his **d**, he burnt with fire H6569
16:27 their skins, and their flesh, and their **d**. H6569
Nu 19: 5 her blood, with her **d**, shall he burn: H6569
1Ki 14:10 a man taketh away **d**, till it be all gone. H1557
2Ki 6:25 cab of dove's **d** for five *pieces* of silver. H2755
9:37 And the carcase of Jezebel shall be as **d** H1828
18:27 eat their own **d**, and drink their H2716+H6675
Neh 2:13 well, and to the **d** port, and viewed the H830
3:13 cubits on the wall unto the **d** gate. H830
14 But the **d** gate repaired Malchiah the son H830
12:31 hand upon the wall toward the **d** gate: H830
Job 20: 7 for ever like his own **d**: they which have H1561
Ps 83:10 En-dor: they became *as* **d** for the earth. H1828
Isa 36:12 eat their own **d**, and drink their H2716+H6675
Jer 8: 2 be for **d** upon the face of the earth. H1828
9:22 men shall fall as **d** upon the open field, H1828
16: 4 they shall be as **d** upon the face of the H1828
25:33 they shall be **d** upon the ground. H1828
Ezk 4:12 shalt bake it with **d** that cometh out of H1561
15 given thee cow's **d** for man's dung, and H6832
15 cow's dung for man's **d**, and thou shalt H1561
Zep 1:17 out as dust, and their flesh as the **d**. H1561
Mal 2: 3 seed, and spread **d** upon your faces, H6569
3 faces, *even* the **d** of your solemn feasts; H6569
Lk 13: 8 till I shall dig about it, and **d** *it*: G906+G2874
Php 3: 8 them *but* **d**, that I may win Christ, G4657

DUNGEON
Gen 40:15 that they should put me into the **d**. H953
41:14 him hastily out of the **d**: and he shaved H953
Ex 12:29 **d**; and all the firstborn of cattle. H1004+H953
Jer 37:16 into the **d**, and into the cabins, H1004+H953
38: 6 cast him into the **d** of Malchiah the son H953
6 cords. And in the **d** *there was* no water, H953
7 Jeremiah in the **d**; the king then sitting H953
9 have cast into the **d**; and he is like to die H953
10 the prophet out of the **d**, before he die. H953
11 down by cords into the **d** to Jeremiah. H953
13 took him up out of the **d**: and Jeremiah H953
Lam 3:53 They have cut off my life in the **d**, and H953
55 thy name, O LORD, out of the low **d**. H953

DUNG-GATE See DUNG and GATE.

DUNGHILL
1Sa 2: 8 the beggar from the **d**, to set *them* among H830
Ezr 6:11 and let his house be made a **d** for this. H5122
Ps 113: 7 dust, *and* lifteth the needy out of the **d**; H830
Isa 25:10 even as straw is trodden down for the **d**. H4087
Dan 2: 5 and your houses shall be made a **d**. H5122
3:29 shall be made a **d**: because there is no H5122
Lk 14:35 nor yet for the **d**; *but* men cast it out. G2874

DUNGHILLS
Lam 4: 5 were brought up in scarlet embrace **d**. H830

DURA
Dan 3: 1 plain of **D**, in the province of Babylon. H1757

DURABLE
Prv 8:18 Riches and honour *are* with me; *yea*, **d** H6276
Isa 23:18 to eat sufficiently, and for **d** clothing. H6266

DURETH
Mt 13:21 Yet hath he not root in himself, but **d** G2076

DURST
Est 7: 5 he, that **d** presume in his heart to do so?
Job 32: 6 and **d** not shew you mine opinion. H3372
Mt 22:46 a word, neither **d** any *man* from that G5111
Mk 12:34 man after that **d** ask him *any question*. G5111
Lk 20:40 And after that they **d** not ask him any G5111
Jn 21:12 of the disciples **d** ask him, Who art G5111
Act 5:13 And of the rest **d** no man join himself G5111
7:32 Moses trembled, and **d** not behold. G5111
Jude 9 body of Moses, **d** not bring against him G5111

DUST
Gen 2: 7 man *of* the **d** of the ground, and H6083
3:14 **d** shalt thou eat all the days of thy life: H6083
19 thou taken: for **d** thou *art*, and unto H6083
19 thou *art*, and unto **d** shalt thou return. H6083
13:16 And I will make thy seed as the **d** of the H6083
16 can number the **d** of the earth, *then* H6083
18:27 the Lord, which *am but* **d** and ashes: H6083
28:14 And thy seed shall be as the **d** of the H6083
Ex 8:16 rod, and smite the **d** of the land, that it H6083
17 and smote the **d** of the earth, and it H6083
17 in beast; all the **d** of the land became H6083
9: 9 And it shall become small **d** in all the H80
Lev 14:41 shall pour out the **d** that they scrape off H6083
17:13 the blood thereof, and cover it with **d**. H6083
Nu 5:17 vessel; and of the **d** that is in the floor H6083
23:10 Who can count the **d** of Jacob, and the H6083
Dt 9:21 it was as small as **d**: and I cast the dust H6083
21 and I cast the **d** thereof into the brook H6083
28:24 land powder and **d**: from heaven shall it H6083
32:24 with the poison of serpents of the **d**. H6083
Jos 7: 6 of Israel, and put **d** upon their heads. H6083
1Sa 2: 8 He raiseth up the poor out of the **d**, *and* H6083
2Sa 16:13 and threw stones at him, and cast **d**. H6083
22:43 Then did I beat them as small as the **d** H6083
1Ki 16: 2 thee out of the **d**, and made thee prince H6083
18:38 the stones, and the **d**, and licked up the H6083
20:10 and more also, if the **d** of Samaria shall H6083
2Ki 13: 7 had made them like the **d** by threshing. H6083
23:12 the **d** of them into the brook Kidron. H6083
2Ch 1: 9 like the **d** of the earth in multitude. H6083
34: 4 in pieces, and made **d** *of them*, and H1854
Job 2:12 **d** upon their heads toward heaven. H6083
4:19 **d**, *which* are crushed before the moth? H6083
5: 6 not forth of the **d**, neither doth trouble H6083
7: 5 and clods of **d**; my skin is broken, and H6083
21 shall I sleep in the **d**; and thou shalt H6083

Job 10: 9 and wilt thou bring me into **d** again? H6083
14:19 grow *out* of the **d** of the earth; and thou H6083
16:15 my skin, and defiled my horn in the **d**. H6083
17:16 pit, when *our* rest together *is* in the **d**. H6083
20:11 which shall lie down with him in the **d**. H6083
21:26 They shall lie down alike in the **d**, and H6083
22:24 Then shalt thou lay up gold as **d**, and H6083
27:16 Though he heap up silver as the **d**, and H6083
28: 6 of sapphires: and it hath **d** of gold. H6083
30:19 and I am become like **d** and ashes. H6083
34:15 and man shall turn again unto **d**. H6083
38:38 When the **d** groweth into hardness, H6083
39:14 in the earth, and warmeth them in **d**, H6083
40:13 Hide them in the **d** together; *and* bind H6083
42: 6 *myself*, and repent in **d** and ashes. H6083
Ps 7: 5 and lay mine honour in the **d**. Selah. H6083
18:42 Then did I beat them small as the **d** H6083
22:15 hast brought me into the **d** of death. H6083
29 go down to the **d** shall bow before him: H6083
30: 9 **d** praise thee? shall it declare thy truth? H6083
44:25 For our soul is bowed down to the **d**: H6083
72: 9 him; and his enemies shall lick the **d**. H6083
78:27 He rained flesh also upon them as **d**, H6083
102:14 in her stones, and favour the **d** thereof. H6083
103:14 frame; he remembereth that we *are* **d**. H6083
104:29 breath, they die, and return to their **d**. H6083
113: 7 He raiseth up the poor out of the **d**, *and* H6083
119:25 My soul cleaveth unto the **d**: quicken H6083
Prv 8:26 the highest part of the **d** of the world. H6083
Ecc 3:20 All go unto one place; all are of the **d**, H6083
20 are of the dust, and all turn to **d** again. H6083
12: 7 Then shall the **d** return to the earth as H6083
Isa 2:10 hide thee in the **d**, for fear of the LORD, H6083
5:24 shall go up as **d**: because they have cast H80
25:12 *and* bring to the ground, *even* to the **d**. H6083
26: 5 the ground; he bringeth it *even* to the **d**. H6083
19 ye that dwell in **d**: for thy dew *is as* the H6083
29: 4 be low out of the **d**, and thy voice shall H6083
4 thy speech shall whisper out of the **d**. H6083
5 shall be like small **d**, and the multitude of H80
34: 7 and their **d** made fat with fatness. H6083
9 into pitch, and the **d** thereof into H6083
40:12 the **d** of the earth in a measure, H6083
15 as the small **d** of the balance: behold, H7834
41: 2 gave *them* as the **d** to his sword, *and* as H6083
47: 1 Come down, and sit in the **d**, O virgin H6083
49:23 and lick up the **d** of thy feet; and thou H6083
52: 2 Shake thyself from the **d**; arise, *and* sit H6083
65:25 the bullock: and **d** *shall be* the serpent's H6083
Lam 2:10 they have cast up **d** upon their heads; H6083
3:29 He putteth his mouth in the **d**; if so be H6083
Ezk 24: 7 not upon the ground, to cover it with **d**; H6083
26: 4 also scrape her **d** from her, and make H6083
10 of his horses their **d** shall cover thee: thy H80
12 and thy **d** in the midst of the water. H6083
27:30 and shall cast up **d** upon their heads, H6083
Dan 12: 2 And many of them that sleep in the **d** of H127
Am 2: 7 That pant after the **d** of the earth on H6083
Mic 1:10 house of Aphrah roll thyself in the **d**. H6083
7:17 They shall lick the **d** like a serpent, they H6083
Nah 1: 3 and the clouds *are* the **d** of his feet. H80
3:18 nobles shall dwell *in the d*: thy people is
Hab 1:10 hold; for they shall heap **d**, and take it. H6083
Zep 1:17 out as **d**, and their flesh as the dung. H6083
Zec 9: 3 up silver as the **d**, and fine gold as the H6083
Mt 10:14 or city, shake off the **d** of your feet. *G2868*
Mk 6:11 shake off the **d** under your feet for *G5522*
Lk 9: 5 shake off the very **d** from your feet for a *G2868*
10:11 Even the very **d** of your city, which *G2868*
Act 13:51 But they shook off the **d** of their feet *G2868*
22:23 *their* clothes, and threw **d** into the air, *G2868*
Rev 18:19 And they cast **d** on their heads, and *G5522*

DUTIES
Ezk 18:11 And that doeth not any of those *d*, but

DUTY
Ex 21:10 her **d** of marriage, shall he not diminish.
Dt 25: 5 the **d** of an husband's brother unto her.
7 perform the **d** of my husband's brother.
2Ch 8:14 before the priests, as the **d** of every day H1697
Ezr 3: 4 custom, as the **d** of every day required; H1697
Ecc 12:13 for this *is* the whole *d* of man.
Lk 17:10 have done that which was our **d** to do. *G3784*
Ro 15:27 things, their **d** is also to minister unto *G3784*

DWARF
Lev 21:20 Or crookbackt, or a **d**, or that hath a H1851

DWELL
Gen 4:20 **d** in tents, and *of such as have* cattle. H3427
9:27 and he shall **d** in the tents of Shem; H7931
13: 6 that they might **d** together: for their H3427
6 great, so that they could not **d** together. H3427
16:12 **d** in the presence of all his brethren. H7931
19:30 for he feared to **d** in Zoar: and he dwelt H3427
20:15 *is* before thee: **d** where it pleaseth thee. H3427
24: 3 of the Canaanites, among whom I **d**: H3427
37 of the Canaanites, in whose land I **d**: H3427
26: 2 **d** in the land which I shall tell thee of: H7931
30:20 will my husband **d** with me, because I H2082
34:10 And ye shall **d** with us: and the land H3427
10 be before you; **d** and trade ye therein, H3427
16 to us, and we will **d** with you, and we H3427
21 us; therefore let them **d** in the land, and H3427
22 unto us for to **d** with us, to be one H3427
23 unto them, and they will **d** with us. H3427
35: 1 up to Beth-el, and **d** there: and make H3427
36: 7 that they might **d** together; and the H3427
45:10 And thou shalt **d** in the land of Goshen, H3427
46:34 that ye may **d** in the land of Goshen; H3427
47: 4 thy servants **d** in the land of Goshen. H3427
6 and brethren to **d**; in the land of Goshen H3427
6 Goshen let them **d**: and if thou knowest H3427
49:13 Zebulun shall **d** at the haven of the sea; H7931
Ex 2:21 And Moses was content to **d** with the H3427
8:22 which my people **d**, that no swarms *of* H5975
15:17 made for thee to **d** in, *in* the Sanctuary, H3427
23:33 They shall not **d** in thy land, lest they H3427
25: 8 a sanctuary; that I may **d** among them. H7931
29:45 And I will **d** among the children of H7931
46 Egypt, that I may **d** among them: I *am* H7931
Lev 13:46 unclean: he shall **d** alone; without the H3427
20:22 you to **d** therein, spue you not out. H3427
23:42 Ye shall **d** in booths seven days; all that H3427
42 are Israelites born shall **d** in booths: H3427
43 of Israel to **d** in booths, when I brought H3427
25:18 and ye shall **d** in the land in safety. H3427
19 eat your fill, and **d** therein in safety. H3427
26: 5 to the full, and **d** in your land safely. H3427
32 **d** therein shall be astonished at it. H3427
Nu 5: 3 their camps, in the midst whereof I **d**. H7931
13:19 And what the land *is* that they **d** in, H3427
19 *they be* that they **d** in, whether in tents, H3427
28 *be* strong that **d** in the land, and the H3427
29 The Amalekites **d** in the land of the H3427
29 and the Amorites, **d** in the mountains: H3427
29 the Canaanites **d** by the sea, and by the H3427
14:30 to make you **d** therein, save Caleb H7931
23: 9 the people shall **d** alone, and shall not H7931
32:17 little ones shall **d** in the fenced cities H3427
33:53 of the land, and **d** therein: for I have H3427
55 shall vex you in the land wherein ye **d**. H3427
35: 2 cities to **d** in; and ye shall give H3427
3 And the cities shall they have to **d** in; H3427
32 come again to **d** in the land, until the H3427
34 inhabit, wherein I **d**: for I the LORD H7931
34 LORD **d** among the children of Israel. H7931
Dt 2: 4 of Esau, which **d** in Seir; and they shall H3427
29 (As the children of Esau which **d** in H3427
29 Moabites which **d** in Ar, did unto me;) H3427
11:30 Canaanites, which **d** in the champaign H3427
31 and ye shall possess it, and **d** therein. H3427
12:10 But *when* ye go over Jordan, and **d** in H3427
10 round about, so that ye **d** in safety; H3427
11 cause his name to **d** there; thither shall H7931
13:12 God hath given thee to **d** there, saying, H3427
17:14 it, and shalt **d** therein, and shalt say, H3427
23:16 He shall **d** with thee, *even* among you, H3427
25: 5 If brethren **d** together, and one of them H3427
28:30 and thou shalt not **d** therein: thou shalt H3427
30:20 that thou mayest **d** in the land which H3427
33:12 of the LORD shall **d** in safety by him; H7931
12 and he shall **d** between his shoulders. H7931
28 Israel then shall **d** in safety alone: the H7931
Jos 9: 7 Peradventure ye **d** among us; and how H3427
22 far from you; when ye **d** among us? H3427
10: 6 the Amorites that **d** in the mountains H3427
13:13 **d** among the Israelites until this day. H3427
14: 4 the land, save cities to **d** *in*, with their H3427
15:63 but the Jebusites **d** with the children of H3427
16:10 but the Canaanites **d** among the H3427
17:12 the Canaanites would **d** in that land. H3427
16 the Canaanites that **d** in the land of the H3427
20: 4 a place, that he may **d** among them. H3427
6 And he shall **d** in that city, until he H3427
21: 2 Moses to give us cities to **d** in, with the H3427
24:13 ye built not, and ye **d** in them; of the H3427
Jos 24:15 in whose land ye **d**: but as for me and H3427
Jdg 1:21 but the Jebusites **d** with the children of H3427
27 the Canaanites would **d** in that land. H3427
35 But the Amorites would **d** in mount H3427
6:10 ye **d**: but ye have not obeyed my voice. H3427
9:41 that they should not **d** in Shechem. H3427
17:10 And Micah said unto him, **D** with me, H3427
11 And the Levite was content to **d** with H3427
18: 1 an inheritance to **d** in; for unto that H3427
1Sa 12: 8 Egypt, and made them **d** in this place. H3427
27: 5 that I may **d** there: for why should H3427
5 servant **d** in the royal city with thee? H3427
2Sa 7: 2 See now, I **d** in an house of cedar, H3427
5 thou build me an house for me to **d** in? H3427
10 that they may **d** in a place of their own, H7931
1Ki 2:36 in Jerusalem, and **d** there, and go not H3427
3:17 I and this woman **d** in one house; and I H3427
6:13 And I will **d** among the children of H7931
8:12 that he would **d** in the thick darkness. H7931
13 I have surely built thee an house to **d** H2073
27 But will God indeed **d** on the earth? H3427
17: 9 to Zidon, and **d** there: behold, I have H3427
2Ki 4:13 answered, I **d** among mine own people. H3427
6: 1 we **d** with thee is too strait for us. H3427
2 we may **d**. And he answered, Go ye. H3427
17:27 let them go and **d** there, and let him H3427
25:24 of the Chaldees: **d** in the land, and H3427
1Ch 17: 1 the prophet, Lo, I **d** in an house of H3427
4 shalt not build me an house to **d** in: H3427
9 and they shall **d** in their place, and H7931
23:25 that they may **d** in Jerusalem for ever: H7931
2Ch 2: 3 to **d** therein, *even so deal with me.* H3427
6: 1 that he would **d** in the thick darkness. H7931
18 But will God in very deed **d** with men H3427
8: 2 caused the children of Israel to **d** there. H3427
11 My wife shall not **d** in the house of H3427
19:10 of your brethren that **d** in their cities, H3427
Ezr 4:17 companions that **d** in Samaria, and H3488
6:12 his name to **d** there destroy all kings H7932
Neh 8:14 of Israel should **d** in booths in the feast H3427
11: 1 bring one of ten to **d** in Jerusalem the H3427
1 city, and nine parts *to d* in *other* cities. H3427
2 offered themselves to **d** at Jerusalem. H3427
Job 3: 5 stain it; let a cloud **d** upon it; let the H7931
4:19 How much less *in* them that **d** in H7931
11:14 let not wickedness **d** in thy tabernacles. H7931
18:15 It shall **d** in his tabernacle, because it *is* H7931
19:15 They that **d** in mine house, and my H1481
30: 6 To **d** in the clifts of the valleys, *in* caves H7931
Ps 4: 8 LORD, only makest me **d** in safety. H3427
5: 4 neither shall evil **d** with thee. H1481
15: 1 tabernacle? who shall **d** in thy holy hill? H7931
23: 6 **d** in the house of the LORD for ever. H3427
24: 1 the world, and they that **d** therein. H3427
25:13 His soul shall **d** at ease; and his seed H3885
27: 4 after; that I may **d** in the house of the H3427
37: 3 *so* shalt thou **d** in the land, and verily H7931
27 Depart from evil, and do good; and **d** H7931
29 inherit the land, and **d** therein for ever. H7931
65: 4 *thee, that* he may **d** in thy courts: we H7931
8 They also that **d** in the uttermost parts H3427
68: 6 but the rebellious **d** in a dry *land*. H7931
16 God desireth to **d** in; yea, the LORD will H3427
16 in; yea, the LORD will **d** *in it* for ever. H7931
18 the LORD God might **d** *among them*. H7931
69:25 desolate; *and* let none **d** in their tents. H3427
35 may **d** there, and have it in possession. H3427
36 they that love his name shall **d** therein. H7931
72: 9 They that **d** in the wilderness shall bow
78:55 the tribes of Israel to **d** in their tents. H7931
84: 4 Blessed *are* they that **d** in thy house: H3427
10 than to **d** in the tents of wickedness. H1752
85: 9 fear him; that glory may **d** in our land. H7931
98: 7 the world, and they that **d** therein. H3427
101: 6 land, that they may **d** with me: he that H3427
7 He that worketh deceit shall not **d** H3427
107: 4 solitary way; they found no city to **d** in. H4186
34 the wickedness of them that **d** therein. H3427
36 And there he maketh the hungry to **d**, H3427
120: 5 Mesech, *that* I **d** in the tents of Kedar! H7931
132:14 This *is* my rest for ever: here will I **d**; for H3427
133: 1 *it is* for brethren to **d** together in unity! H3427
139: 9 *and* **d** in the uttermost parts of the sea; H7931
140:13 the upright shall **d** in thy presence. H3427
143: 3 he hath made me to **d** in darkness, as H3427
Prv 1:33 But whoso hearkeneth unto me shall **d** H7931
2:21 For the upright shall **d** in the land, and H7931
8:12 I wisdom **d** with prudence, and find H7931
21: 9 *It is* better to **d** in a corner of the H3427

Prv 21:19 *It is* better to **d** in the wilderness, than H3427
25:24 *It is* better to **d** in the corner of the H3427
Isa 6: 5 unclean lips, and I **d** in the midst of a H3427
9: 2 light: they that **d** in the land of the H3427
11: 6 The wolf also shall **d** with the lamb, H1481
13:21 **d** there, and satyrs shall dance there. H7931
16: 4 Let mine outcasts **d** with thee, Moab; H1481
23:13 it for them that **d** in the wilderness: they
18 be for them that **d** before the LORD, to H3427
24: 6 and they that **d** therein are desolate: H3427
26: 5 For he bringeth down them that **d** on H3427
19 and sing, ye that **d** in dust: for thy dew H7931
30:19 For the people shall **d** in Zion at H3427
32:16 Then judgment shall **d** in the H7931
18 And my people shall **d** in a peaceable H3427
33:14 among us shall **d** with the devouring H1481
14 us shall **d** with everlasting burnings? H1481
16 He shall **d** on high: his place of defence H7931
24 sick: the people that **d** therein *shall be* H3427
34:11 and the raven shall **d** in it: and he shall H7931
17 to generation shall they **d** therein. H7931
40:22 spreadeth them out as a tent to **d** in: H3427
49:20 for me: give place to me that I may **d**. H3427
51: 6 and they that **d** therein shall die in H3427
57:15 name *is* Holy; I **d** in the high and holy H7931
58:12 breach, The restorer of paths to **d** in. H3427
65: 9 it, and my servants shall **d** there. H7931
Jer 4:29 *be* forsaken, and not a man **d** therein. H3427
7: 3 and I will cause you to **d** in this place. H7931
7 Then will I cause you to **d** in this place, H7931
8:16 in it; the city, and those that **d** therein. H3427
19 of them that **d** in a far country: *Is* not
9:26 corners, that **d** in the wilderness: for H3427
12: 4 of them that **d** therein? the beasts H3427
20: 6 And thou, Pashur, and all that **d** in H3427
23: 6 and Israel shall **d** safely: and this *is* his H7931
8 and they shall **d** in their own land. H3427
24: 8 and them that **d** in the land of Egypt: H3427
25: 5 your doings, and **d** in the land that the H3427
24 the mingled people that **d** in the desert, H7931
27:11 and they shall till it, and **d** therein. H3427
29: 5 Build ye houses, and **d** *in them*; and H3427
28 ye houses, and **d** *in them*; and plant H3427
32 shall not have a man to **d** among this H3427
31:24 And there shall **d** in Judah itself, and in H3427
32:37 place, and I will cause them to **d** safely: H3427
33:16 Jerusalem shall **d** safely: and this *is the* H7931
35: 7 all your days ye shall **d** in tents; that ye H3427
9 Nor to build houses for us to **d** in: H3427
11 of the Syrians: so we **d** at Jerusalem. H3427
15 them, and ye shall **d** in the land which I H3427
40: 5 of Judah, and **d** with him among the H3427
9 the Chaldeans: **d** in the land, and serve H3427
10 As for me, behold, I will **d** at Mizpah to H3427
10 and **d** in your cities that ye have taken. H3427
42:13 But if ye say, We will not **d** in this land, H3427
14 hunger of bread; and there will we **d**: H3427
43: 4 of the LORD, to **d** in the land of Judah. H3427
5 been driven, to **d** in the land of Judah; H1481
44: 1 all the Jews which **d** in the land of H3427
1 of Egypt, which **d** at Migdol, and at H3427
8 ye be gone to **d**, that ye might cut H1481
13 For I will punish them that **d** in the H3427
14 a desire to return to **d** there: for none H3427
26 all Judah that **d** in the land of Egypt; H3427
47: 2 and them that **d** therein: then the men H3427
48: 9 be desolate, without any to **d** therein. H3427
28 O ye that **d** in Moab, leave the cities, H3427
28 the cities, and **d** in the rock, and be H7931
49: 1 Gad, and his people **d** in his cities? H3427
8 Flee ye, turn back, **d** deep, O H3427
18 there, neither shall a son of man **d** in it. H1481
30 Flee, get you far off, **d** deep, O ye H3427
31 neither gates nor bars, *which* **d** alone. H7931
33 abide there, nor *any* son of man **d** in it. H1481
50: 3 and none shall **d** therein: they shall H3427
39 the islands shall **d** *there*, and the owls H3427
39 and the owls shall **d** therein: and it H3427
40 neither shall any son of man **d** therein. H1481
51: 1 and against them that **d** in the midst of H3427
Ezk 2: 6 and thou dost **d** among scorpions: be H3427
12:19 the violence of all them that **d** therein. H3427
16:46 daughters that **d** at thy left hand: and H3427
17:23 and under it shall **d** all fowl of every H7931
23 of the branches thereof shall they **d**. H7931
28:25 then shall they **d** in their land that I H3427
26 And they shall **d** safely therein, and H3427
26 yea, they shall **d** with confidence, when H3427
32:15 all them that **d** therein, then shall they H3427
Ezk 34:25 land: and they shall **d** safely in the H3427
28 but they shall **d** safely, and none shall H3427
36:28 And ye shall **d** in the land that I gave to H3427
33 also cause *you* to **d** in the cities, and H3427
37:25 And they shall **d** in the land that I have H3427
25 and they shall **d** therein, *even* they, and H3427
38: 8 and they shall **d** safely all of them. H3427
11 are at rest, that **d** safely, all of them H3427
12 goods, that **d** in the midst of the land. H3427
39: 6 among them that **d** carelessly in the H3427
9 And they that **d** in the cities of Israel H3427
43: 7 feet, where I will **d** in the midst of the H7931
9 I will **d** in the midst of them for ever. H7931
Dan 2:38 And wheresoever the children of men **d**, H1753
4: 1 languages, that **d** in all the earth; Peace H1753
6:25 languages, that **d** in all the earth; Peace H1753
Hos 9: 3 They shall not **d** in the LORD'S land; H3427
12: 9 yet make thee to **d** in tabernacles, as in H3427
14: 7 They that **d** under his shadow shall H3427
Joel 3:20 But Judah shall **d** for ever, and H3427
Am 3:12 be taken out that **d** in Samaria in the H3427
5:11 but ye shall not **d** in them; ye have H3427
9: 5 shall melt, and all that **d** therein shall H3427
Mic 4:10 and thou shalt **d** in the field, and thou H7931
7:13 **d** therein, for the fruit of their doings. H3427
14 thine heritage, which **d** solitarily *in* the H7931
Nah 1: 5 yea, the world, and all that **d** therein. H3427
3:18 thy nobles shall **d** *in the dust*: thy H7931
Hab 2: 8 of the city, and of all that **d** therein. H3427
17 of the city, and of all that **d** therein. H3427
Zep 1:18 riddance of all them that **d** in the land. H3427
Hag 1: 4 *Is it* time for you, O ye, to **d** in your H3427
Zec 2:10 **d** in the midst of thee, saith the LORD. H7931
11 people: and I will **d** in the midst of thee, H7931
8: 3 unto Zion, and will **d** in the midst of H7931
4 men and old women **d** in the streets of H3427
8 And I will bring them, and they shall **d** H7931
9: 6 And a bastard shall **d** in Ashdod, and I H3427
14:11 And *men* shall **d** in it, and there shall H3427
Mt 12:45 they enter in and **d** there: and the last G2730
Lk 11:26 they enter in, and **d** there: and the last G2730
21:35 that **d** on the face of the whole earth. G2521
Act 1:20 and let no man **d** therein: and his G2730
2:14 and all *ye* that **d** at Jerusalem, be this G2730
4:16 **d** in Jerusalem; and we cannot deny *it*. G2730
7: 4 him into this land, wherein ye now **d**. G2730
13:27 For they that **d** at Jerusalem, and their G2730
17:26 of men for to **d** on all the face of the G2730
28:16 was suffered to **d** by himself with a G3306
Ro 8: 9 the Spirit of God **d** in you. Now if any G3611
11 from the dead **d** in you, he that raised G3611
1Co 7:12 **d** with him, let him not put her away. G3611
13 to **d** with her, let her not leave him. G3611
2Co 6:16 hath said, I will **d** in them, and walk in G1774
Eph 3:17 That Christ may **d** in your hearts by G2730
Col 1:19 *Father* that in him should all fulness **d**; G2730
3:16 Let the word of Christ **d** in you richly in G1774
1Pt 3: 7 Likewise, ye husbands, **d** with *them* G4924
1Jn 4:13 Hereby know we that we **d** in him, and G3306
Rev 3:10 to try them that **d** upon the earth. G2730
6:10 our blood on them that **d** on the earth? G2730
7:15 on the throne shall **d** among them. G4637
11:10 And they that **d** upon the earth shall G2730
12:12 and ye that **d** in them. Woe to the G4637
13: 6 tabernacle, and them that **d** in heaven. G4637
8 And all that **d** upon the earth shall G2730
12 and them which **d** therein to worship G2730
14 And deceiveth them that **d** on the earth G2730
14 to them that **d** on the earth, that they G2730
14: 6 unto them that **d** on the earth, and to G2730
17: 8 and they that **d** on the earth shall G2730
21: 3 men, and he will **d** with them, and they G4637

DWELLED

Gen 13: 7 and the Perizzite **d** then in the land. H3427
12 Abram **d** in the land of Canaan, and H3427
12 of Canaan, and Lot **d** in the cities of the H3427
20: 1 country, and **d** between Kadesh and H3427
Ru 1: 4 Ruth: and they **d** there about ten years. H3427
1Sa 12:11 enemies on every side, and ye **d** safe. H3427

DWELLERS

Isa 18: 3 All ye inhabitants of the world, and **d** H7931
Act 1:19 And it was known unto all the **d** at G2730
2: 9 Elamites, and the **d** in Mesopotamia, G2730

DWELLEST

Dt 12:29 succeedest them, and **d** in their land; H3427
19: 1 **d** in their cities, and in their houses; H3427
Dt 26: 1 and possessest it, and **d** therein; H3427
2Ki 19:15 God of Israel, which **d** *between* the H3427
Ps 80: 1 **d** *between* the cherubims, shine forth. H3427
123: 1 eyes, O thou that **d** in the heavens. H3427
Song 8:13 Thou that **d** in the gardens, the H3427
Isa 10:24 O my people that **d** in Zion, be not H3427
37:16 O LORD of hosts, God of Israel, that **d** H3427
47: 8 to pleasures, that **d** carelessly, that H3427
Jer 49:16 heart, O thou that **d** in the clefts of the H7931
51:13 O thou that **d** upon many waters, H7931
Lam 4:21 of Edom, that **d** in the land of Uz; the H3427
Ezk 7: 7 thee, O thou that **d** in the land: the time H3427
12: 2 Son of man, thou **d** in the midst of a H3427
Oba 3 thee, thou that **d** in the clefts of the H7931
Zec 2: 7 Deliver thyself, O Zion, that **d** *with* the H3427
Jn 1:38 interpreted, Master,) where **d** thou? G3306
Rev 2:13 I know thy works, and where thou **d**, G2730

DWELLETH

Lev 19:34 *But* the stranger that **d** with you shall H1481
25:39 And if thy brother *that* **d** by thee be
47 thy brother *that* **d** by him wax poor, and
Nu 13:18 the people that **d** therein, whether they H3427
Dt 33:20 that enlargeth Gad: he **d** as a lion, and H7931
Jos 6:25 she had; and she **d** in Israel *even* unto H3427
22:19 tabernacle **d**, and take possession H7931
1Sa 4: 4 LORD of hosts, which **d** *between* the H3427
27:11 he **d** in the country of the Philistines. H3427
2Sa 6: 2 of hosts that **d** *between* the cherubims. H3427
7: 2 but the ark of God **d** within curtains. H3427
1Ch 13: 6 God the LORD, that **d** *between* the H3427
Job 15:28 And he **d** in desolate cities, *and* in H7931
38:19 Where *is* the way *where* light **d**? and *as* H7931
39:28 She **d** and abideth on the rock, upon H7931
Ps 9:11 Sing praises to the LORD, which **d** in H3427
26: 8 and the place where thine honour **d**. H4908
91: 1 He that **d** in the secret place of the most H3427
113: 5 the LORD our God, who **d** on high, H3427
135:21 **d** at Jerusalem. Praise ye the LORD. H7931
Prv 3:29 seeing he **d** securely by thee. H3427
Isa 8:18 LORD of hosts, which **d** in mount Zion. H7931
33: 5 The LORD is exalted; for he **d** on high: H7931
Jer 29:16 all the people that **d** in this city, *and* of H3427
44: 2 a desolation, and no man **d** therein, H3427
49:31 nation, that **d** without care, saith H3427
51:43 wherein no man **d**, neither doth *any* son H3427
Lam 1: 3 servitude: she **d** among the heathen, H3427
Ezk 16:46 sister, that **d** at thy right hand, *is* H3427
17:16 *where* the king *d* that made him king,
38:14 Israel **d** safely, shalt thou not know *it*? H3427
Dan 2:22 the darkness, and the light **d** with him. H8271
Hos 4: 3 every one that **d** therein shall languish, H3427
Joel 3:21 not cleansed: for the LORD **d** in Zion. H7931
Am 8: 8 one mourn that **d** therein? and it shall H3427
Mt 23:21 by it, and by him that **d** therein. G2730
Jn 6:56 my blood, **d** in me, and I in him. G3306
14:10 that **d** in me, he doeth the works. G3306
17 for he **d** with you, and shall be in you. G3306
Act 7:48 Howbeit the most High **d** not in G2730
17:24 **d** not in temples made with hands; G2730
Ro 7:17 more I that do it, but sin that **d** in me. G3611
18 is, in my flesh,) **d** no good thing: for to G3611
20 more I that do it, but sin that **d** in me. G3611
8:11 bodies by his Spirit that **d** in you. G1774
1Co 3:16 and *that* the Spirit of God **d** in you? G3611
Col 2: 9 For in him **d** all the fulness of the G2730
2Ti 1:14 keep by the Holy Ghost which **d** in us. G1774
Jas 4: 5 The spirit that **d** in us lusteth to envy? G2730
2Pt 3:13 a new earth, wherein **d** righteousness. G2730
1Jn 3:17 him, how **d** the love of God in him? G3306
24 his commandments **d** in him, and he in G3306
4:12 **d** in us, and his love is perfected in us. G3306
15 of God, God **d** in him, and he in God. G3306
16 is love; and he that **d** in love dwelleth in G3306
16 in love **d** in God, and God in him. G3306
2Jn 2 For the truth's sake, which **d** in us, and G3306
Rev 2:13 was slain among you, where Satan **d**. G2730

DWELLING

Gen 10:30 And their **d** was from Mesha, as thou H4186
25:27 and Jacob *was* a plain man, **d** in tents. H3427
27:39 him, Behold, thy **d** shall be the fatness H4186
Lev 25:29 And if a man sell a **d** house in a walled H4186
Nu 21:15 goeth down to the **d** of Ar, and lieth H3427
Jos 13:21 *were* dukes of Sihon, **d** in the country. H3427
1Ki 8:30 in heaven thy **d** place: and when thou H3427
39 Then hear thou in heaven thy **d** place, H3427
43 Hear thou in heaven thy **d** place, and H3427
49 thy **d** place, and maintain their cause, H3427

1Ki 21: 8 that *were* in his city, **d** with Naboth. H3427
2Ki 17:25 the beginning of their **d** there, *that* they H3427
1Ch 6:32 And they ministered before the **d** place H4908
54 Now these *are* their **d** places H4186
2Ch 6: 2 for thee, and a place for thy **d** for ever. H3427
21 hear thou from thy **d** place, *even* from H3427
30 Then hear thou from heaven thy **d** H3427
33 heavens, *even* from thy **d** place, and do H3427
39 *even* from thy **d** place, their prayer and H3427
30:27 to his holy **d** place, *even* unto heaven. H4583
36:15 on his people, and on his **d** place: H4583
Job 8:22 shame; and the **d** place of the wicked H168
21:28 where *are* the **d** places of the wicked? H4908
Ps 49:11 for ever, *and* their **d** places to all H4908
14 shall consume in the grave from their **d**. H2073
52: 5 thee out of *thy* **d** place, and root thee H168
74: 7 the **d** place of thy name to the ground. H4908
76: 2 his tabernacle, and his **d** place in Zion. H4585
79: 7 Jacob, and laid waste his **d** place. H5116
90: 1 Lord, thou hast been our **d** place in all H4583
91:10 neither shall any plague come nigh thy **d**. H168
Prv 21:20 and oil in the **d** of the wise; but a H5116
24:15 *man*, against the **d** of the righteous; H5116
Isa 4: 5 And the LORD will create upon every **d** H4349
18: 4 consider in my **d** place like a clear heat H4349
Jer 46:19 O thou daughter **d** in Egypt, furnish H3427
49:33 And Hazor shall be a **d** for dragons, H4583
Ezk 38:11 safely, all of them **d** without walls, and H3427
48:15 for the city, for **d**, and for suburbs: and H4186
Dan 2:11 the gods, whose **d** is not with flesh. H4070
4:25 men, and thy **d** shall be with the beasts H4070
32 men, and thy **d** *shall be* with the beasts H4070
5:21 the beasts, and his **d** *was* with the wild H4070
Joel 3:17 the LORD your God **d** in Zion, my holy H7931
Nah 2:11 Where *is* the **d** of the lions, and the H4583
Zep 3: 7 so their **d** should not be cut off, H4583
Mk 5: 3 Who had *his* **d** among the tombs; and G2731
Act 2: 5 And there were **d** at Jerusalem Jews, G2730
19:17 and Greeks also **d** at Ephesus; and fear G2730
1Ti 6:16 Who only hath immortality, **d** in the G3611
Heb 11: 9 *in* a strange country, **d** in tabernacles G2730
2Pt 2: 8 (For that righteous man **d** among G1460

DWELLING-HOUSE See DWELLING and HOUSE.

DWELLINGPLACE
Nu 24:21 **d**, and thou puttest thy nest in a rock. H4186
Jer 51:37 And Babylon shall become heaps, a **d** H4583
1Co 4:11 and are buffeted, and have no certain **d**; G790

DWELLINGPLACES
Jer 30:18 have mercy on his **d**; and the city shall H4908
51:30 have burned her **d**; her bars are broken. H4908
Ezk 6: 6 In all your **d** the cities shall be laid H4186
37:23 out of all their **d**, wherein they have H4186
Hab 1: 6 to possess the **d** *that are* not theirs. H4908

DWELLINGS
Ex 10:23 children of Israel had light in their **d**. H4186
Lev 3:17 your **d**, that ye eat neither fat nor blood. H4186
7:26 *be* of fowl or of beast, in any of your **d**. H4186
23: 3 *is* the sabbath of the LORD in all your **d**. H4186
14 your generations in all your **d**. H4186
21 your **d** throughout your generations. H4186
31 your generations in all your **d**. H4186
Nu 35:29 your generations in all your **d**. H4186
Job 18:19 his people, nor any remaining in his **d**. H4033
21 Surely such *are* the **d** of the wicked, H4908
39: 6 wilderness, and the barren land his **d**. H4908
Ps 55:15 *is* in their **d**, *and* among them. H4033
87: 2 of Zion more than all the **d** of Jacob. H4908
Isa 32:18 in sure **d**, and in quiet resting places; H4908
Jer 9:19 land, because our **d** have cast *us* out. H4908
Ezk 25: 4 and make their **d** in thee: they shall eat H4908
Zep 2: 6 And the sea coast shall be **d** *and* H5116

DWELT
Gen 4:16 of the LORD, and **d** in the land of Nod, H3427
11: 2 in the land of Shinar; and they **d** there. H3427
31 they came unto Haran, and **d** there. H3427
13:18 and came and **d** in the plain of Mamre, H3427
14: 7 Amorites, that **d** in Hazezon-tamar. H3427
12 brother's son, who **d** in Sodom, and his H3427
13 the Hebrew; for he **d** in the plain of H7931
16: 3 after Abram had **d** ten years in the H3427
19:29 overthrew the cities in the which Lot **d**. H3427
30 And Lot went up out of Zoar, and **d** in H3427
30 **d** in a cave, he and his two daughters. H3427
21:20 and he grew, and **d** in the wilderness, H3427
Gen 21:21 And he **d** in the wilderness of Paran: H3427
22:19 and Abraham **d** at Beer-sheba. H3427
23:10 And Ephron **d** among the children of H3427
24:62 for he **d** in the south country. H3427
25:11 and Isaac **d** by the well Lahai-roi. H3427
18 And they **d** from Havilah unto Shur, H7931
26: 6 And Isaac **d** in Gerar: H3427
17 tent in the valley of Gerar, and **d** there. H3427
35:22 And it came to pass, when Israel **d** in H7931
36: 8 Thus **d** Esau in mount Seir: Esau *is* H3427
37: 1 And Jacob **d** in the land wherein his H3427
38:11 went and **d** in her father's house. H3427
47:27 And Israel **d** in the land of Egypt, in the H3427
50:22 And Joseph **d** in Egypt, he, and his H3427
Ex 2:15 face of Pharaoh, and **d** in the land of H3427
12:40 of Israel, who **d** in Egypt, *was* four H3427
Lev 18: 3 of Egypt, wherein ye **d**, shall ye not do: H3427
26:35 in your sabbaths, when ye **d** upon it. H3427
Nu 14:25 and the Canaanites **d** in the valley.) To H3427
45 the Canaanites which **d** in that hill, and H3427
20:15 and we have **d** in Egypt a long time; H3427
21: 1 Canaanite, which **d** in the south, heard H3427
25 cities: and Israel **d** in all the cities of H3427
31 Thus Israel **d** in the land of the H3427
34 of the Amorites, which **d** at Heshbon. H3427
31:10 **d**, and all their goodly castles, with fire. H4186
32:40 the son of Manasseh; and he **d** therein. H3427
33:40 And king Arad the Canaanite, which **d** H3427
Dt 1: 4 Amorites, which **d** in Heshbon, and Og H3427
4 Bashan, which **d** at Astaroth in Edrei: H3427
6 Ye have **d** long enough in this mount: H3427
44 And the Amorites, which **d** in that H3427
2: 8 of Esau, which **d** in Seir, through the H3427
10 The Emims **d** therein in times past, a H3427
12 The Horims also **d** in Seir beforetime; H3427
12 before them, and **d** in their stead; as H3427
20 of giants: giants **d** therein in old time; H3427
21 succeeded them, and **d** in their stead: H3427
22 of Esau, which **d** in Seir, when he H3427
22 and **d** in their stead even unto this day: H3427
23 And the Avims which **d** in Hazerim, H3427
23 destroyed them, and **d** in their stead.) H3427
3: 2 of the Amorites, which **d** at Heshbon. H3427
4:46 of the Amorites, who **d** at Heshbon, H3427
8:12 hast built goodly houses, and **d** *therein*; H3427
29:16 (For ye know how we have **d** in the H3427
33:16 will of him that **d** in the bush: let *the* H7931
Jos 2:15 the town wall, and she **d** upon the wall. H3427
7: 7 and **d** on the other side Jordan! H3427
9:16 and *that* they **d** among them. H3427
12: 2 Sihon king of the Amorites, who **d** in H3427
4 that **d** at Ashtaroth and at Edrei, H3427
16:10 the Canaanites that **d** in Gezer: but the H3427
19:47 possessed it, and **d** therein, and called H3427
50 and he built the city, and **d** therein. H3427
21:43 and they possessed it, and **d** therein. H3427
22:33 the children of Reuben and Gad **d**. H3427
24: 2 Your fathers **d** on the other side of H3427
7 ye **d** in the wilderness a long season. H3427
8 the Amorites, which **d** on the other side H3427
18 Amorites which **d** in the land: *therefore* H3427
Jdg 1: 9 the Canaanites, that **d** in the mountain, H3427
10 Canaanites that **d** in Hebron: (now the H3427
16 and they went and **d** among the people. H3427
29 the Canaanites that **d** in Gezer; but the H3427
29 Canaanites **d** in Gezer among them. H3427
30 but the Canaanites **d** among them, and H3427
32 But the Asherites **d** among the H3427
33 but he **d** among the Canaanites, H3427
3: 3 the Hivites that **d** in mount Lebanon, H3427
5 And the children of Israel **d** among the H3427
4: 2 which **d** in Harosheth of the Gentiles. H3427
5 And she **d** under the palm tree of H3427
8:11 way of them that **d** in tents on the east H7931
29 of Joash went and **d** in his own house. H3427
9:21 went to Beer, and **d** there, for fear of H3427
41 And Abimelech **d** at Arumah: and H3427
10: 1 and he **d** in Shamir in mount Ephraim. H3427
11: 3 his brethren, and **d** in the land of Tob: H3427
26 While Israel **d** in Heshbon and her H3427
15: 8 and **d** in the top of the rock Etam. H3427
18: 7 therein, how they **d** careless, after the H3427
28 And they built a city, and **d** therein. H3427
21:23 and repaired the cities, and **d** in them. H3427
Ru 2:23 harvest; and **d** with her mother in law. H3427
1Sa 19:18 he and Samuel went and **d** in Naioth. H3427
22: 4 of Moab: and they **d** with him all the H3427
23:29 And David went up from thence, and **d** H3427
27: 3 And David **d** with Achish at Gath, he H3427
1Sa 27: 7 And the time that David **d** in the H3427
31: 7 the Philistines came and **d** in them. H3427
2Sa 2: 3 and they **d** in the cities of Hebron. H3427
5: 9 So David **d** in the fort, and called it the H3427
7: 6 Whereas I have not **d** in *any* house H3427
9:12 And all that **d** in the house of Ziba H4186
13 So Mephibosheth **d** in Jerusalem: for he H3427
14:28 So Absalom **d** two full years in H3427
1Ki 2:38 And Shimei **d** in Jerusalem many days. H3427
4:25 And Judah and Israel **d** safely, every H3427
7: 8 And his house where he **d** *had* another H3427
9:16 Canaanites that **d** in the city, and given H3427
11:24 **d** therein, and reigned in Damascus. H3427
12: 2 Solomon, and Jeroboam **d** in Egypt;) H3427
17 But *as for* the children of Israel which **d** H3427
25 Ephraim, and **d** therein; and went out H3427
13:11 Now there **d** an old prophet in Beth-el; H3427
25 *it* in the city where the old prophet **d**. H3427
15:18 of Syria, that **d** at Damascus, saying, H3427
21 off building of Ramah, and **d** in Tirzah. H3427
17: 5 for he went and **d** by the brook Cherith, H3427
2Ki 13: 5 of Israel **d** in their tents, as beforetime. H3427
15: 5 of his death, and **d** in a several house. H3427
16: 6 to Elath, and **d** there unto this day. H3427
17:24 Samaria, and **d** in the cities thereof. H3427
28 came and **d** in Beth-el, and taught H3427
29 nation in their cities wherein they **d**. H3427
19:36 went and returned, and **d** at Nineveh. H3427
22:14 (now she **d** in Jerusalem in the H3427
1Ch 2:55 And the families of the scribes which **d** H3427
4:23 and those that **d** among plants and H3427
23 there they **d** with the king for his work. H3427
28 And they **d** at Beer-sheba, and H3427
40 for *they* of Ham had **d** there of old. H3427
41 unto this day, and **d** in their rooms: H3427
43 escaped, and **d** there unto this day. H3427
5: 8 son of Joel, who **d** in Aroer, even unto H3427
10 their hand: and they **d** in their tents H3427
11 And the children of Gad **d** over against H3427
16 And they **d** in Gilead in Bashan, and in H3427
22 **d** in their steads until the captivity. H3427
23 tribe of Manasseh **d** in the land: they H3427
7:29 towns. In these **d** the children of Joseph H3427
8:28 chief *men*. These **d** in Jerusalem. H3427
29 And at Gibeon **d** the father of Gibeon; H3427
32 And these also **d** with their brethren H3427
9: 2 Now the first inhabitants that *d* in their
3 And in Jerusalem **d** of the children of H3427
16 **d** in the villages of the Netophathites. H3427
34 their generations; these **d** at Jerusalem. H3427
35 And in Gibeon **d** the father of Gibeon, H3427
38 And they also **d** with their brethren H3427
10: 7 the Philistines came and **d** in them. H3427
11: 7 And David **d** in the castle; therefore H3427
17: 5 For I have not **d** in an house since the H3427
2Ch 10:17 But *as for* the children of Israel that **d** H3427
11: 5 And Rehoboam **d** in Jerusalem, and H3427
16: 2 of Syria, that **d** at Damascus, saying, H3427
19: 4 And Jehoshaphat **d** at Jerusalem: and H3427
20: 8 And they **d** therein, and have built thee H3427
26: 7 that **d** in Gur-baal, and the Mehunims. H3427
21 of his death, and **d** in a several house, H3427
28:18 the villages thereof: and they **d** there. H3427
30:25 of Israel, and that **d** in Judah, rejoiced. H3427
31: 4 the people that **d** in Jerusalem to give H3427
6 and Judah, that **d** in the cities of Judah, H3427
34:22 (now she **d** in Jerusalem in the H3427
Ezr 2:70 the Nethinims, **d** in their cities, and all H3427
Neh 3:26 Moreover the Nethinims **d** in Ophel, H3427
4:12 the Jews which **d** by them came, they H3427
7:73 and all Israel, **d** in their cities; and H3427
11: 1 And the rulers of the people **d** at H3427
3 the province that **d** in Jerusalem: but in H3427
3 in the cities of Judah **d** every one in his H3427
4 And at Jerusalem **d** *certain* of the H3427
6 All the sons of Perez that **d** at H3427
21 But the Nethinims **d** in Ophel: and Ziha H3427
25 the children of Judah **d** at Kirjath-arba, H3427
30 thereof. And they **d** from Beer-sheba H2583
31 from Geba *d* at Michmash, and Aija,
13:16 There **d** men of Tyre also therein, H3427
Est 9:19 of the villages, that **d** in the unwalled H3427
Job 22: 8 earth; and the honourable man **d** in it. H3427
29:25 and sat chief, and **d** as a king in the H7931
Ps 68:10 Thy congregation hath **d** therein: thou, H3427
74: 2 this mount Zion, wherein thou hast **d**. H7931
94:17 help, my soul had almost **d** in silence. H7931
120: 6 My soul hath long **d** with him that H7931
Isa 13:20 neither shall it be **d** in from generation H7931

Isa 29: 1 city *where* David **d**! add ye year to year; H2583
37:37 went and returned, and **d** at Nineveh. H3427
Jer 2: 6 passed through, and where no man **d**? H3427
35:10 But we have **d** in tents, and have H3427
39:14 him home: so he **d** among the people. H3427
40: 6 to Mizpah; and **d** with him among the H3427
41:17 And they departed, and **d** in the H3427
44:15 even all the people that **d** in the land of H3427
50:39 be **d** in from generation to generation. H7931
Ezk 3:15 at Tel-abib, that **d** by the river of H3427
31: 6 under his shadow **d** all great nations. H3427
17 *were* his arm, *that* **d** under his shadow H3427
36:17 Son of man, when the house of Israel **d** H3427
37:25 your fathers have **d**; and they shall H3427
39:26 me, when they **d** safely in their land, H3427
Dan 4:12 of the heaven **d** in the boughs thereof, H1753
21 beasts of the field **d**, and upon whose H1753
Zep 2:15 This *is* the rejoicing city that **d** H3427
Mt 2:23 And he came and **d** in a city called G2730
4:13 And leaving Nazareth, he came and **d** G2730
Lk 1:65 And fear came on all that **d** round G4039
13: 4 above all men that **d** in Jerusalem? G2730
Jn 1:14 And the Word was made flesh, and **d** G4637
39 and saw where he **d**, and abode with G3306
Act 7: 2 Mesopotamia, before he **d** in Charran, G2730
4 the Chaldaeans, and **d** in Charran: and G2730
9:22 the Jews which **d** at Damascus, proving G2730
32 also to the saints which **d** at Lydda. G2730
35 And all that **d** at Lydda and Saron saw G2730
11:29 unto the brethren which **d** in Judaea: G2730
13:17 people when they **d** as strangers in the G3940
19:10 that all they which **d** in Asia heard the G2730
22:12 report of all the Jews which **d** *there*, G2730
28:30 And Paul **d** two whole years in his own G3306
2Ti 1: 5 that is in thee, which **d** first in thy G1774
Rev 11:10 tormented them that **d** on the earth. G2730

DYED
Ex 25: 5 And rams' skins **d** red, and badgers'
26:14 tent *of* rams' skins **d** red, and a covering
35: 7 And rams' skins **d** red, and badgers'
36:19 tent *of* rams' skins **d** red, and a covering
39:34 And the covering of rams' skins **d** red,
Isa 63: 1 from Edom, with **d** garments from H2556
Ezk 23:15 loins, exceeding in **d** attire upon their H2871

DYING
Nu 17:13 shall die: shall we be consumed with **d**? H1478
Mk 12:20 the first took a wife, and **d** left no seed. G599
Lk 8:42 of age, and she lay a **d**. But as he went the G599
2Co 4:10 Always bearing about in the body the **d** G3500
6: 9 As unknown, and *yet* well known; as **d**, G599
Heb 11:21 By faith Jacob, when he was a **d**, blessed G599

E

EACH
Gen 15:10 the midst, and laid **e** piece one against H376
34:25 brethren, took **e** man his sword, and
40: 5 both of them, **e** man his dream in one
5 in one night, **e** man according to the
41:11 he; we dreamed **e** man according to the
12 to us our dreams; to **e** man according to
45:22 To all of them he gave **e** man changes of
Ex 18: 7 and they asked **e** other of *their* welfare; H376
30:34 of **e** shall there be a like *weight:* H905
Lev 24: 7 frankincense upon **e** row, that it may be
Nu 1:44 **e** one was for the house of his fathers. H376
7: 3 princes, and for **e** one an ox: and they H259
11 offer their offering, **e** prince on his day, H259
85 **E** charger of silver *weighing* an hundred H259
85 and thirty *shekels*, **e** bowl seventy: all the H259
14:34 *even* forty days, **e** day for a year, shall
16:17 also, and Aaron, **e** *of you* his censer. H376
17: 6 a rod apiece, for **e** prince one, according
29:14 two tenth deals to **e** ram of the two rams, H259
15 And a several tenth deal to **e** lamb of the H259
Jos 18: 4 you three men for **e** tribe: and I will send
22:14 And with him ten princes, of **e** chief
14 of Israel; and **e** one *was* an head of the H376
Jdg 8:18 **e** one resembled the children of a king. H259
21:22 we reserved not to **e** man his wife in the H376
Ru 1: 8 in law, Go, return **e** to her mother's H802
9 ye may find rest, **e** *of you* in the house of H802
1Ki 4: 7 and his household: **e** man his month in a H259
6:23 *of* olive tree, **e** ten cubits high.
22:10 king of Judah sat **e** on his throne, having H376
2Ki 9:21 of Judah went out, **e** in his chariot, and H376
15:20 men of wealth, of **e** man fifty shekels of H259
1Ch 20: 6 and twenty, six *on* **e** *hand*, and six *on*
6 *hand*, and six *on* **e** *foot:* and he also was
2Ch 3:15 on the top of **e** of them *was* five cubits.
4:13 pomegranates on **e** wreath, to cover the H259
9:18 and stays on **e** side of the sitting place,
Neh 13:24 according to the language of **e** people.
Ps 85:10 and peace have kissed **e** *other.*
Isa 2:20 which they made **e** *one* for himself to
6: 2 Above it stood the seraphims: **e** one had H259
35: 7 of dragons, where **e** lay, *shall be* grass
57: 2 beds, **e** *one* walking *in* his uprightness.
Ezk 4: 6 I have appointed thee **e** day for a year.
40:16 and upon **e** post *were* palm trees.
48 and measured **e** post of the porch, five
Lk 13:15 hypocrite, doth not **e** one of you on the
Act 2: 3 as of fire, and it sat upon **e** of them. G1538
Php 2: 3 **e** esteem other better than themselves. G1538
2Th 1: 3 one of you all toward **e** other aboundeth; G240
Rev 4: 8 And the four beasts had **e** of them six G303

EAGLE
Lev 11:13 the **e**, and the ossifrage, and the ospray, H5404
18 swan, and the pelican, and the gier **e**, H7360
Dt 14:12 the **e**, and the ossifrage, and the ospray, H5404
17 And the pelican, and the gier **e**, and the H7360
28:49 *as swift* as the **e** flieth; a nation whose H5404
32:11 As an **e** stirreth up her nest, fluttereth H5404
Job 9:26 ships: as the **e** *that* hasteth to the prey. H5404
39:27 Doth the **e** mount up at thy command, H5404
Prv 23: 5 they fly away as an **e** toward heaven. H5404
Prv 30:19 The way of an **e** in the air; the way of a H5404
Jer 48:40 he shall fly as an **e**, and shall spread his H5404
49:16 nest as high as the **e**, I will bring thee H5404
22 come up and fly as the **e**, and spread his H5404
Ezk 1:10 side; they four also had the face of an **e**. H5404
10:14 of a lion, and the fourth the face of an **e**. H5404
17: 3 Lord GOD; A great **e** with great wings, H5404
7 There was also another great **e** with H5404
Hos 8: 1 *shall come* as an **e** against the house of H5404
Oba 4 Though thou exalt *thyself* as the **e**, and H5404
Mic 1:16 baldness as the **e**; for they are gone into H5404
Hab 1: 8 shall fly as the **e** *that* hasteth to eat. H5404
Rev 4: 7 and the fourth beast *was* like a flying **e**. G105
12:14 wings of a great **e**, that she might fly into G105

EAGLES
2Sa 1:23 than **e**, they were stronger than lions. H5404
Prv 30:17 pick it out, and the young **e** shall eat it. H5404
Isa 40:31 up with wings as **e**; they shall run, and H5404
Jer 4:13 than **e**. Woe unto us! for we are spoiled. H5404
Lam 4:19 Our persecutors are swifter than the **e** H5404
Mt 24:28 is, there will the **e** be gathered together. G105
Lk 17:37 *is*, thither will the **e** be gathered together. G105

EAGLE'S
Ps 103: 5 *so that* thy youth is renewed like the **e**. H5404
Dan 7: 4 The first *was* like a lion, and had **e** H5403

EAGLES'
Ex 19: 4 **e** wings, and brought you unto myself. H5404
Dan 4:33 were grown like **e** *feathers*, and his H5403

EAR
Ex 9:31 *was* in the **e**, and the flax *was* bolled. H24
15:26 his sight, and wilt give **e** to his H238
21: 6 shall bore his **e** through with an aul; H241
29:20 the tip of the right **e** of Aaron, and upon H241
20 the tip of the right **e** of his sons, and H241
Lev 8:23 the tip of Aaron's right **e**, and upon the H241
24 tip of their right **e**, and upon the thumbs H241
14:14 the tip of the right **e** of him that is to be H241
17 the tip of the right **e** of him that is to be H241
25 the tip of the right **e** of him that is to be H241
28 the tip of the right **e** of him that is to be H241
Dt 1:45 to your voice, nor give **e** unto you. H238
15:17 *it* through his **e** unto the door, and he H241
32: 1 Give **e**, O ye heavens, and I will speak; H238
Jdg 5: 3 Hear, O ye kings; give **e**, O ye princes; I, H238
1Sa 8:12 *will set them* to **e** his ground, and to H2790
9:15 Now the LORD had told Samuel in his **e** H241
2Ki 19:16 LORD, bow down thine **e**, and hear: H241
2Ch 24:19 against them: but they would not give **e**. H238
Neh 1: 6 Let thine **e** now be attentive, and thine H241
11 O Lord, I beseech thee, let now thine **e** be H241
9:30 they not give **e**: therefore gavest thou H238
Job 4:12 me, and mine **e** received a little thereof. H241
12:11 Doth not the **e** try words? and the mouth H241
13: 1 Lo, mine eye hath seen all *this*, mine **e** H241
29:11 When the **e** heard *me*, then it blessed H241
21 Unto me *men* gave **e**, and waited, and H8085
32:11 Behold, I waited for your words; I gave **e** H238
34: 2 give **e** unto me, ye that have knowledge. H238
3 For the **e** trieth words, as the mouth H241
36:10 He openeth also their **e** to discipline, and H241
Job 42: 5 of the **e**: but now mine eye seeth thee. H241
Ps 5: 1 Give **e** to my words, O LORD, consider H238
10:17 heart, thou wilt cause thine **e** to hear: H241
17: 1 unto my cry, give **e** unto my prayer, *that* H238
6 thine **e** unto me, *and hear* my speech. H241
31: 2 Bow down thine **e** to me; deliver me H241
39:12 Hear my prayer, O LORD, and give **e** H238
45:10 and incline thine **e**; forget also thine own H241
49: 1 Hear this, all *ye* people; give **e**, all *ye* H238
4 I will incline mine **e** to a parable: I will H241
54: 2 Hear my prayer, O God; give **e** to the H238
55: 1 Give **e** to my prayer, O God; and hide not H238
58: 4 like the deaf adder *that* stoppeth her **e**; H241
71: 2 incline thine **e** unto me, and save me. H241
77: 1 with my voice; and he gave **e** unto me. H238
78: 1 Give **e**, O my people, *to* my law: incline H238
80: 1 Give **e**, O Shepherd of Israel, thou that H238
84: 8 my prayer: give **e**, O God of Jacob. Selah. H238
86: 1 Bow down thine **e**, O LORD, hear me: for H241
6 Give **e**, O LORD, unto my prayer; and H238
88: 2 before thee: incline thine **e** unto my cry; H241
94: 9 He that planted the **e**, shall he not hear? H241
102: 2 incline thine **e** unto me: in the day H241
116: 2 Because he hath inclined his **e** unto me, H241
141: 1 **e** unto my voice, when I cry unto thee. H238
143: 1 Hear my prayer, O LORD, give **e** to my H238
Prv 2: 2 So that thou incline thine **e** unto H241
4:20 words; incline thine **e** unto my sayings. H241
5: 1 *and* bow thine **e** to my understanding: H241
13 mine **e** to them that instructed me! H241
15:31 The **e** that heareth the reproof of life H241
17: 4 *and* a liar giveth **e** to a naughty tongue. H238
18:15 and the **e** of the wise seeketh knowledge. H241
20:12 The hearing **e**, and the seeing eye, the H241
22:17 Bow down thine **e**, and hear the words of H241
25:12 *so is* a wise reprover upon an obedient **e**. H241
28: 9 He that turneth away his **e** from hearing H241
Ecc 1: 8 with seeing, nor the **e** filled with hearing. H241
Isa 1: 2 Hear, O heavens, and give **e**, O earth: for H238
10 of Sodom; give **e** unto the law of our H238
8: 9 broken in pieces; and give **e**, all ye of far H238
28:23 Give ye **e**, and hear my voice; hearken, H238
30:24 young asses that **e** the ground shall eat H5647
32: 9 daughters; give **e** unto my speech. H238
37:17 Incline thine **e**, O LORD, and hear; open H241
42:23 Who among you will give **e** to this? *who* H238
48: 8 time *that* thine **e** was not opened: for H241
50: 4 wakeneth mine **e** to hear as the learned. H241
5 The Lord GOD hath opened mine **e**, and I H241
51: 4 Hearken unto me, my people; and give **e** H238
55: 3 Incline your **e**, and come unto me: hear, H241
59: 1 neither his **e** heavy, that it cannot hear: H241
64: 4 perceived by the **e**, neither hath the eye H238
Jer 6:10 hear? behold, their **e** *is* uncircumcised, H241
7:24 nor inclined their **e**, but walked in the H241
26 nor inclined their **e**, but hardened their H241
9:20 and let your **e** receive the word of his H241
11: 8 Yet they obeyed not, nor inclined their **e**, H241
13:15 Hear ye, and give **e**; be not proud: for the H238
17:23 inclined their **e**, but made their neck H241
25: 4 hearkened, nor inclined your **e** to hear. H241
34:14 not unto me, neither inclined their **e**. H241
35:15 inclined your **e**, nor hearkened unto me. H241
44: 5 nor inclined their **e** to turn from their H241

Lam 3:56 not thine e at my breathing, at my cry. H241
Dan 9:18 O my God, incline thine e, and hear; open H241
Hos 5: 1 Israel; and give ye e, O house of the king; H238
Joel 1: 2 Hear this, ye old men, and give e, all ye H238
Am 3:12 or a piece of an e; so shall the children H241
Mt 10:27 e, *that* preach ye upon the housetops. G3775
26:51 of the high priest's, and smote off his e. G5621
Mk 4:28 the e, after that the full corn in the ear. G4719
28 the ear, after that the full corn in the e. G4719
14:47 of the high priest, and cut off his e. G5621
Lk 12: 3 have spoken in the e in closets shall be G3775
22:50 of the high priest, and cut off his right e. G3775
51 And he touched his e, and healed him. G5621
Jn 18:10 e. The servant's name was Malchus. G5621
26 kinsman whose e Peter cut off, saith, G5621
1Co 2: 9 Eye hath not seen, nor e heard, neither G3775
12:16 And if the e shall say, Because I am not G3775
Rev 2: 7 He that hath an e, let him hear what the G3775
11 He that hath an e, let him hear what the G3775
17 He that hath an e, let him hear what the G3775
29 He that hath an e, let him hear what the G3775
3: 6 He that hath an e, let him hear what the G3775
13 He that hath an e, let him hear what the G3775
22 He that hath an e, let him hear what the G3775
13: 9 If any man have an e, let him hear. G3775

EARED

Dt 21: 4 which is neither e nor sown, and shall H5647

EARING

Gen 45: 6 *there shall* neither *be* e nor harvest. H2758
Ex 34:21 in e time and in harvest thou shalt rest. H2758

EARLY

Gen 19: 2 ye shall rise up e, and go on your ways. H7925
27 And Abraham gat up e in the morning H7925
20: 8 Therefore Abimelech rose e in the H7925
21:14 And Abraham rose up e in the H7925
22: 3 And Abraham rose up e in the H7925
28:18 And Jacob rose up e in the morning, H7925
31:55 And e in the morning Laban rose up, H7925
Ex 8:20 Moses, Rise up e in the morning, and H7925
9:13 Moses, Rise up e in the morning, and H7925
24: 4 and rose up e in the morning, and H7925
32: 6 And they rose up e on the morrow, and H7925
34: 4 Moses rose up e in the morning, and H7925
Nu 14:40 And they rose up e in the morning, and H7925
Jos 3: 1 And Joshua rose e in the morning; and H7925
6:12 And Joshua rose e in the morning, and H7925
15 day, that they rose e about the dawning H7925
7:16 So Joshua rose up e in the morning, H7925
8:10 And Joshua rose up e in the morning, H7925
14 and rose up e, and the men of the H7925
Jdg 6:28 And when the men of the city arose e in H7925
38 And it was so: for he rose up e on the H7925
7: 1 with him, rose up e, and pitched beside H7925
3 him return and depart e from mount H6852
9:33 is up, thou shalt rise e, and set upon the H7925
19: 5 when they arose e in the morning, that H7925
8 And he arose e in the morning on the H7925
9 to morrow get you e on your way, that H7925
21: 4 the people rose e, and built there an H7925
1Sa 1:19 And they rose up in the morning e, and H7925
5: 3 And when they of Ashdod arose e on H7925
4 And when they arose e on the morrow H7925
9:26 And they arose e: and it came to pass H7925
15:12 And when Samuel rose e to meet Saul H7925
17:20 And David rose up e in the morning, H7925
29:10 Wherefore now rise up e in the H7925
10 soon as ye be up e in the morning, and H7925
11 So David and his men rose up e to H7925
2Sa 15: 2 And Absalom rose up e, and stood H7925
2Ki 3:22 And they rose up e in the morning, and H7925
6:15 man of God was risen e, and gone forth, H7925
19:35 and when they arose e in the morning, H7925
2Ch 20:20 And they rose e in the morning, and H7925
29:20 Then Hezekiah the king rose e, and H7925
Job 1: 5 them, and rose up e in the morning, H7925
Ps 46: 5 God shall help her, *and that* right e. H1242
57: 8 and harp: I *myself* will awake e. H7837
63: 1 O God, thou *art* my God; e will I seek H7836
78:34 they returned and inquired e after God. H7836
90:14 O satisfy us e with thy mercy; that we H1242
101: 8 I will e destroy all the wicked of the H1242
108: 2 and harp: I *myself* will awake e. H7837
127: 2 *It is* vain for you to rise up e, to sit up H7925
Prv 1:28 seek me e, but they shall not find me: H7836
8:17 and those that seek me e shall find me. H7836
27:14 a loud voice, rising e in the morning, it H7925
Song 7:12 Let us get up e to the vineyards; let us H7925
Isa 5:11 Woe unto them that rise up e in the H7925
26: 9 me will I seek thee e: for when thy H7836
37:36 and when they arose e in the morning, H7925
Jer 7:13 you, rising up e and speaking, but ye H7925
25 daily rising up e and sending *them*: H7925
11: 7 unto this day, rising e and protesting, H7925
25: 3 unto you, rising e and speaking; but ye H7925
4 prophets, rising e and sending *them*; H7925
26: 5 both rising up e, and sending *them*, H7925
29:19 rising up e and sending *them*; H7925
32:33 them, rising up e and teaching *them*, H7925
35:14 unto you, rising e and speaking; but ye H7925
15 rising up e and sending *them*, H7925
44: 4 prophets, rising e and sending *them*, H7925
Dan 6:19 Then the king arose very e in the H8238
Hos 5:15 in their affliction they will seek me e. H7836
6: 4 cloud, and as the e dew it goeth away. H7925
13: 3 cloud, and as the e dew that passeth H7925
Zep 3: 7 rose e, *and* corrupted all their doings. H7925
Mt 20: 1 went out e in the morning to G260+G4404
Mk 16: 2 And very e in the morning the first *day* G4404
9 Now when *Jesus* was risen e the first G4404
Lk 21:38 And all the people came e in the G3719
24: 1 of the week, very e in the morning, they G3722
22 which were e at the sepulchre; G3721
Jn 8: 2 And e in the morning he came again G3722
18:28 and it was e; and they themselves G4405
20: 1 Mary Magdalene e, when it was yet G4404
Act 5:21 into the temple e in the morning, and G3722
Jas 5: 7 it, until he receive the e and latter rain. G4406

EARNEST

Ro 8:19 For the e expectation of the creature G603
2Co 1:22 Who hath also sealed us, and given the e G728
5: 5 hath given unto us the e of the Spirit. G728
7: 7 when he told us your e desire, your G1972
8:16 e care into the heart of Titus for you. G4710
Eph 1:14 Which is the e of our inheritance until G728
Php 1:20 According to my e expectation and *my* G603
Heb 2: 1 Therefore we ought to give the more e G4056

EARNESTLY

Nu 22:37 And Balak said unto Balaam, Did I not e
1Sa 20: 6 then say, David e asked *leave* of me H7592
28 And Jonathan answered Saul, David e H7592
Neh 3:20 After him Baruch the son of Zabbai e H2734
Job 7: 2 As a servant e desireth the shadow, and
Jer 11: 7 For I e protested unto your fathers in H5749
31:20 against him, I do e remember him still: H2142
Mic 7: 3 with both hands e, the prince asketh, H3190
Lk 22:44 he prayed more e: and his sweat was as G1617
56 sat by the fire, and e looked upon him, G816
Act 3:12 or why look ye so e on us, as though by G816
23: 1 And Paul, e beholding the council, said, G816
1Co 12:31 But covet e the best gifts: and yet shew G2206
2Co 5: 2 For in this we groan, e desiring to be G1971
Jas 5:17 and he prayed e that it might not rain: G4335
Jude 3 *you* that ye should e contend for the G1864

EARNETH

Hag 1: 6 warm; and he that e wages earneth H7936
6 e wages *to put it* into a bag with holes. H7936

EARRING

Gen 24:22 took a golden e of half a shekel weight, H5141
30 And it came to pass, when he saw the e H5141
47 him: and I put the e upon her face, and H5141
Job 42:11 of money, and every one an e of gold. H5141
Prv 25:12 *As* an e of gold, and an ornament of H5141

EARRINGS

Gen 35: 4 hand, and *all their* e which *were* in H5141
Ex 32: 2 off the golden e, which *are* in the ears H5141
3 off the golden e which *were* in their H5141
35:22 bracelets, and e, and rings, and tablets, H5141
Nu 31:50 bracelets, rings, e, and tablets, to make H5694
Jdg 8:24 me every man the e of his prey. (For H5141
24 e, because they *were* Ishmaelites.) H5141
25 therein every man the e of his prey. H5141
26 And the weight of the golden e that he H5141
Isa 3:20 headbands, and the tablets, and the e, H3908
Ezk 16:12 thy forehead, and e in thine ears, and a H5694
Hos 2:13 herself with her e and her jewels, and H5141

EARS

Gen 20: 8 in their e: and the men were sore afraid. H241
35: 4 which *were* in their e; and Jacob hid H241
41: 5 behold, seven e of corn came up upon H7641
Gen 41: 6 And, behold, seven thin e and blasted H7641
7 And the seven thin e devoured the H7641
7 rank and full e. And Pharaoh awoke, H7641
22 e came up in one stalk, full and good: H7641
23 And, behold, seven e, withered, thin, H7641
24 And the thin e devoured the seven good H7641
24 the seven good e: and I told *this* unto H7641
26 e *are* seven years: the dream *is* one. H7641
27 the seven empty e blasted with the east H7641
44:18 a word in my lord's e, and let not thine H241
50: 4 I pray you, in the e of Pharaoh, saying, H241
Ex 10: 2 And that thou mayest tell in the e of thy H241
11: 2 Speak now in the e of the people, and let H241
17:14 rehearse *it* in the e of Joshua: for I will H241
32: 2 which *are* in the e of your wives, of your H241
3 in their e, and brought *them* unto Aaron. H241
Lev 2:14 first-fruits green e of corn dried by the H24
14 the fire, *even* corn beaten out of full e. H3759
23:14 corn, nor green e, until the selfsame day H3759
Nu 11:18 for ye have wept in the e of the LORD, H241
14:28 spoken in mine e, so will I do to you: H241
Dt 5: 1 I speak in your e this day, that ye may H241
23:25 mayest pluck the e with thine hand; H4425
29: 4 eyes to see, and e to hear, unto this day. H241
31:28 words in their e, and call heaven and H241
30 And Moses spake in the e of all the H241
32:44 of this song in the e of the people, he, H241
Jos 20: 4 his cause in the e of the elders of that H241
Jdg 7: 3 Now therefore go to, proclaim in the e of H241
9: 2 Speak, I pray you, in the e of all the men H241
3 spake of him in the e of all the men of H241
17: 2 of also in mine e, behold, the silver *is* H241
Ru 2: 2 field, and glean e of corn after *him* in H7641
1Sa 3:11 e of every one that heareth it shall tingle. H241
8:21 he rehearsed them in the e of the LORD. H241
11: 4 the tidings in the e of the people: and all H241
15:14 the sheep in mine e, and the lowing of the H241
18:23 spake those words in the e of David. And H241
2Sa 3:19 And Abner also spake in the e of H241
19 also to speak in the e of David in Hebron H241
7:22 to all that we have heard with our e. H241
22: 7 temple, and my cry *did enter* into his e. H241
2Ki 4:42 of barley, and full e of corn in the husk H3759
18:26 the e of the people that *are* on the wall. H241
19:28 come up into mine e, therefore I will put H241
21:12 heareth of it, both his e shall tingle. H241
23: 2 he read in their e all the words of the H241
1Ch 17:20 to all that we have heard with our e. H241
2Ch 6:40 open, and *let* thine e *be* attent unto the H241
7:15 shall be open, and mine e attent unto the H241
34:30 he read in their e all the words of the H241
Neh 8: 3 and the e of all the people *were* H241
Job 13:17 speech, and my declaration with your e. H241
15:21 A dreadful sound *is* in his e: in prosperity H241
24:24 and cut off as the tops of the e of corn. H7641
28:22 have heard the fame thereof with our e. H241
33:16 Then he openeth the e of men, and H241
36:15 and openeth their e in oppression. H241
Ps 18: 6 my cry came before him, *even* into his e. H241
34:15 and his e *are open* unto their cry. H241
40: 6 not desire; mine e hast thou opened: H241
44: 1 We have heard with our e, O God, our H241
78: 1 incline your e to the words of my mouth. H241
92:11 mine enemies, *and* mine e shall hear *my* H241
115: 6 They have e, but they hear not: noses H241
130: 2 Lord, hear my voice: let thine e be H241
135:17 They have e, but they hear not; neither is H241
Prv 21:13 Whoso stoppeth his e at the cry of the H241
23: 9 Speak not in the e of a fool: for he will H241
12 and thine e to the words of knowledge. H241
26:17 *is like* one that taketh a dog by the e. H241
Isa 5: 9 In mine e *said* the LORD of hosts, Of a H241
6:10 fat, and make their e heavy, and shut H241
10 and hear with their e, and understand H241
11: 3 neither reprove after the hearing of his e: H241
17: 5 and reapeth the e with his arm; and it H7641
5 gathereth e in the valley of Rephaim. H7641
22:14 And it was revealed in mine e by the H241
30:21 And thine e shall hear a word behind H241
32: 3 the e of them that hear shall hearken. H241
33:15 that stoppeth his e from hearing of H241
35: 5 and the e of the deaf shall be unstopped. H241
36:11 the e of the people that *are* on the wall. H241
37:29 come up into mine e, therefore will I put H241
42:20 not; opening the e, but he heareth not. H241
43: 8 that have eyes, and the deaf that have e. H241
49:20 shall say again in thine e, The place *is* too H241
Jer 2: 2 Go and cry in the e of Jerusalem, saying, H241
5:21 and see not; which have e, and hear not: H241

Jer 19: 3 whosoever heareth, his **e** shall tingle. H241
26:11 this city, as ye have heard with your **e**. H241
15 you to speak all these words in your **e**. H241
28: 7 thine **e**, and in the ears of all the people; H241
7 thine ears, and in the **e** of all the people; H241
29:29 letter in the **e** of Jeremiah the prophet. H241
36: 6 of the LORD in the **e** of the people in the H241
6 read them in the **e** of all Judah that come H241
10 LORD'S house, in the **e** of all the people. H241
13 read the book in the **e** of the people. H241
14 thou hast read in the **e** of the people, and H241
15 it in our **e**. So Baruch read *it* in their ears. H241
15 it in our ears. So Baruch read *it* in their **e**. H241
20 told all the words in the **e** of the king. H241
21 read it in the **e** of the king, and in the H241
21 of the king, and in the **e** of all the princes H241
Ezk 3:10 in thine heart, and hear with thine **e**. H241
8:18 they cry in mine **e** with a loud voice, *yet* H241
9: 1 He cried also in mine **e** with a loud H241
12: 2 see not; they have **e** to hear, and hear H241
16:12 earrings in thine **e**, and a beautiful crown H241
23:25 thy nose and thine **e**; and thy remnant H241
24:26 thee, to cause *thee* to hear *it* with *thine* **e**? H241
40: 4 and hear with thine **e**, and set thine heart H241
44: 5 hear with thine **e** all that I say unto thee H241
Mic 7:16 upon *their* mouth, their **e** shall be deaf. H241
Zec 7:11 their **e**, that they should not hear. H241
Mt 11:15 He that hath **e** to hear, let him hear. G3775
12: 1 began to pluck the **e** of corn, and to eat. G4719
13: 9 Who hath **e** to hear, let him hear. G3775
15 gross, and *their* **e** are dull of hearing, G3775
15 and hear with *their* **e**, and should G3775
16 for they see: and your **e**, for they hear. G3775
43 Who hath **e** to hear, let him hear. G3775
28:14 And if this come to the governor's **e**, we G191
Mk 2:23 as they went, to pluck the **e** of corn. G4719
4: 9 And he said unto them, He that hath **e** G3775
23 If any man have **e** to hear, let him hear. G3775
7:16 If any man have **e** to hear, let him hear. G3775
33 **e**, and he spit, and touched his tongue; G3775
35 And straightway his **e** were opened, and G189
8:18 Having eyes, see ye not? and having **e**, G3775
Lk 1:44 **e**, the babe leaped in my womb for joy. G3775
4:21 day is this scripture fulfilled in your **e**. G3775
6: 1 plucked the **e** of corn, and did eat, G4719
8: 8 He that hath **e** to hear, let him hear. G3775
9:44 Let these sayings sink down into your **e**: G3775
14:35 He that hath **e** to hear, let him hear. G3775
Act 7:51 in heart and **e**, ye do always resist G3775
57 **e**, and ran upon him with one accord, G3775
11:22 came unto the **e** of the church which G3775
17:20 things to our **e**: we would know therefore G189
28:27 gross, and their **e** are dull of hearing, G3775
27 hear with *their* **e**, and understand with G3775
Ro 11: 8 not see, and **e** that they should not G3775
2Ti 4: 3 to themselves teachers, having itching **e**; G189
4 And they shall turn away *their* **e** from G189
Jas 5: 4 into the **e** of the Lord of sabaoth. G3775
1Pt 3:12 righteous, and his **e** *are open* unto their G3775

EARTH

Gen 1: 1 God created the heaven and the **e**. H776
2 And the **e** was without form, and void; H776
10 And God called the dry *land* E; and the H776
11 And God said, Let the **e** bring forth H776
11 seed *is* in itself, upon the **e**: and it was so. H776
12 And the **e** brought forth grass, *and* herb H776
15 to give light upon the **e**: and it was so. H776
17 of the heaven to give light upon the **e**, H776
20 the **e** in the open firmament of heaven. H776
22 in the seas, and let fowl multiply in the **e**. H776
24 And God said, Let the **e** bring forth the H776
24 of the **e** after his kind: and it was so. H776
25 And God made the beast of the **e** after H776
25 creepeth upon the **e** after his kind: and H127
26 cattle, and over all the **e**, and over every H776
26 creeping thing that creepeth upon the **e**. H776
28 and replenish the **e**, and subdue it: and H776
28 living thing that moveth upon the **e**. H776
29 the face of all the **e**, and every tree, in the H776
30 And to every beast of the **e**, and to every H776
30 creepeth upon the **e**, wherein *there is* life, H776
2: 1 Thus the heavens and the **e** were H776
4 the heavens and of the **e** when they were H776
4 LORD God made the **e** and the heavens, H776
5 before it was in the **e**, and every herb of H776
5 it to rain upon the **e**, and *there was* not a H776
6 But there went up a mist from the **e**, and H776
4:11 And now *art* thou cursed from the **e**, H127
Gen 4:12 and a vagabond shalt thou be in the **e**. H776
14 the face of the **e**; and from thy face shall H127
14 a vagabond in the **e**; and it shall come to H776
6: 1 **e**, and daughters were born unto them, H127
4 There were giants in the **e** in those days; H776
5 man *was* great in the **e**, and *that* every H776
6 on the **e**, and it grieved him at his heart. H776
7 the face of the **e**; both man, and beast, H127
11 The **e** also was corrupt before God, and H776
11 God, and the **e** was filled with violence. H776
12 And God looked upon the **e**, and, behold, H776
12 flesh had corrupted his way upon the **e**. H776
13 before me; for the **e** is filled with violence H776
13 behold, I will destroy them with the **e**. H776
17 of waters upon the **e**, to destroy all flesh, H776
17 *and* every thing that *is* in the **e** shall die. H776
20 thing of the **e** after his kind, two of H127
7: 3 keep seed alive upon the face of all the **e**. H776
4 it to rain upon the **e** forty days and forty H776
4 will I destroy from off the face of the **e**. H127
6 when the flood of waters was upon the **e**. H776
8 of every thing that creepeth upon the **e**, H127
10 the waters of the flood were upon the **e**. H776
12 And the rain was upon the **e** forty days H776
14 creepeth upon the **e** after his kind, and H776
17 And the flood was forty days upon the **e**; H776
17 up the ark, and it was lift up above the **e**. H776
18 greatly upon the **e**; and the ark went H776
19 upon the **e**; and all the high hills, H776
21 And all flesh died that moved upon the **e**, H776
21 that creepeth upon the **e**, and every man: H776
23 destroyed from the **e**: and Noah only H776
24 And the waters prevailed upon the **e** an H776
8: 1 over the **e**, and the waters asswaged; H776
3 And the waters returned from off the **e** H776
7 the waters were dried up from off the **e**. H776
9 face of the whole **e**: then he put forth his H776
11 the waters were abated from off the **e**. H776
13 up from off the **e**: and Noah removed the H776
14 day of the month, was the **e** dried. H776
17 creepeth upon the **e**; that they may breed H776
17 abundantly in the **e**, and be fruitful, and H776
17 and be fruitful, and multiply upon the **e**. H776
19 creepeth upon the **e**, after their kinds, H776
22 While the **e** remaineth, seedtime and H776
9: 1 and multiply, and replenish the **e**. H776
2 every beast of the **e**, and upon every fowl H776
2 that moveth *upon* the **e**, and upon all the H127
7 in the **e**, and multiply therein. H776
10 of every beast of the **e** with you; from all H776
10 go out of the ark, to every beast of the **e**. H776
11 any more be a flood to destroy the **e**. H776
13 of a covenant between me and the **e**. H776
14 **e**, that the bow shall be seen in the cloud: H776
16 creature of all flesh that *is* upon the **e**. H776
17 me and all flesh that *is* upon the **e**. H776
19 and of them was the whole **e** overspread. H776
10: 8 he began to be a mighty one in the **e**. H776
25 for in his days was the **e** divided; and his H776
32 nations divided in the **e** after the flood. H776
11: 1 And the whole **e** was of one language, H776
4 abroad upon the face of the whole **e**. H776
8 all the **e**: and they left off to build the city. H776
9 language of all the **e**: and from thence did H776
9 them abroad upon the face of all the **e**. H776
12: 3 thee shall all families of the **e** be blessed. H127
13:16 as the dust of the **e**: so that if a man can H776
16 **e**, *then* shall thy seed also be numbered. H776
14:19 high God, possessor of heaven and **e**: H776
22 high God, the possessor of heaven and **e**, H776
18:18 nations of the **e** shall be blessed in him? H776
25 Shall not the Judge of all the **e** do right? H776
19:23 The sun was risen upon the **e** when Lot H776
31 *is* not a man in the **e** to come in unto us H776
31 in unto us after the manner of all the **e**: H776
22:18 the nations of the **e** be blessed; because H776
24: 3 and the God of the **e**, that thou shalt not H776
52 the LORD, *bowing himself* to the **e**. H776
26: 4 shall all the nations of the **e** be blessed; H776
15 stopped them, and filled them with **e**. H6083
27:28 of the **e**, and plenty of corn and wine: H776
39 **e**, and of the dew of heaven from above; H776
28:12 set up on the **e**, and the top of it reached H776
14 And thy seed shall be as the dust of the **e**, H776
14 shall all the families of the **e** be blessed. H127
37:10 to bow down ourselves to thee to the **e**? H776
41:47 And in the seven plenteous years the **e** H776
56 all the face of the **e**: And Joseph opened H776
42: 6 before him *with* their faces to the **e**. H776
Gen 43:26 and bowed themselves to him to the **e**. H776
45: 7 a posterity in the **e**, and to save your lives H776
48:12 he bowed himself with his face to the **e**. H776
16 into a multitude in the midst of the **e**. H776
Ex 8:17 the dust of the **e**, and it became lice in H776
22 that I *am* the LORD in the midst of the **e**. H776
9:14 that *there is* none like me in all the **e**. H776
15 and thou shalt be cut off from the **e**. H776
16 may be declared throughout all the **e**. H776
29 know how that the **e** *is* the LORD'S. H776
33 and the rain was not poured upon the **e**. H776
10: 5 And they shall cover the face of the **e**, H776
5 be able to see the **e**: and they shall eat the H776
6 they were upon the **e** unto this day. And H127
15 For they covered the face of the whole **e**, H776
15:12 thy right hand, the **e** swallowed them. H776
19: 5 me above all people: for all the **e** *is* mine: H776
20: 4 or that *is* in the **e** beneath, or that *is* in H776
4 or that *is* in the water under the **e**: H776
11 made heaven and **e**, the sea, and all that H776
24 An altar of **e** thou shalt make unto me, H127
31:17 made heaven and **e**, and on the seventh H776
32:12 the face of the **e**? Turn from thy fierce H127
33:16 the people that *are* upon the face of the **e**. H127
34: 8 his head toward the **e**, and worshipped. H776
10 done in all the **e**, nor in any nation: and H776
Lev 11: 2 among all the beasts that *are* on the **e**. H776
21 their feet, to leap withal upon the **e**; H776
29 that creep upon the **e**; the weasel, and the H776
41 that creepeth upon the **e** *shall be* an H776
42 creep upon the **e**, them ye shall not eat; H776
44 creeping thing that creepeth upon the **e**. H776
46 every creature that creepeth upon the **e**: H776
15:12 And the vessel of **e**, that he toucheth H2789
26:19 heaven as iron, and your **e** as brass: H776
Nu 11:31 two cubits *high* upon the face of the **e**. H776
12: 3 men which *were* upon the face of the **e**.) H127
14:21 But *as* truly *as* I live, all the **e** shall be H776
16:30 a new thing, and the **e** open her mouth, H127
32 And the **e** opened her mouth, and H776
33 the pit, and the **e** closed upon them: and H776
34 they said, Lest the **e** swallow us up *also*. H776
22: 5 of the **e**, and they abide over against me: H776
11 the face of the **e**: come now, curse me H776
26:10 And the **e** opened her mouth, and H776
Dt 3:24 in heaven or in **e**, that can do according H776
4:10 **e**, and *that* they may teach their children. H127
17 The likeness of any beast that *is* on the **e**, H776
18 fish that *is* in the waters beneath the **e**: H776
26 I call heaven and **e** to witness against H776
32 man upon the **e**, and *ask* from the one H776
36 thee: and upon **e** he shewed thee his H776
39 upon the **e** beneath: *there is* none else. H776
40 *thy* days upon the **e**, which the LORD thy H127
5: 8 or that *is* in the **e** beneath, or that *is* in H776
8 or that *is* in the waters beneath the **e**: H776
6:15 destroy thee from off the face of the **e**. H127
7: 6 all people that *are* upon the face of the **e**. H127
10:14 God, the **e** *also*, with all that therein *is*. H776
11: 6 of Reuben: how the **e** opened her mouth, H776
21 them, as the days of heaven upon the **e**. H776
12: 1 it, all the days that ye live upon the **e**. H127
16 ye shall pour it upon the **e** as water. H776
19 Levite as long as thou livest upon the **e**. H127
24 it; thou shalt pour it upon the **e** as water. H776
13: 7 **e** even unto the *other* end of the earth; H776
7 earth even unto the *other* end of the **e**; H776
14: 2 above all the nations that *are* upon the **e**. H127
26: 2 of all the fruit of the **e**, which thou shalt H127
28: 1 thee on high above all nations of the **e**: H776
10 And all people of the **e** shall see that H776
23 and the **e** that is under thee *shall be* iron. H776
25 removed into all the kingdoms of the **e**. H776
26 the **e**, and no man shall fray *them* away. H776
49 far, from the end of the **e**, *as swift* as the H776
64 the one end of the **e** even unto the other; H776
30:19 I call heaven and **e** to record this day H776
31:28 heaven and **e** to record against them. H776
32: 1 and hear, O **e**, the words of my mouth. H776
13 high places of the **e**, that he might eat the H776
22 shall consume the **e** with her increase, H776
33:16 And for the precious things of the **e** and H776
17 to the ends of the **e**: and they *are* the ten H776
Jos 2:11 God in heaven above, and in **e** beneath. H776
3:11 **e** passeth over before you into Jordan. H776
13 the Lord of all the **e**, shall rest in the H776
4:24 That all the people of the **e** might know H776
5:14 on his face to the **e**, and did worship, and H776
7: 6 and fell to the **e** upon his face before H776

Jos 7: 9 our name from the **e**: and what wilt thou H776
21 they *are* hid in the **e** in the midst of my H776
23:14 the way of all the **e**: and ye know in all H776
Jdg 3:25 their lord *was* fallen down dead on the **e**. H776
5: 4 field of Edom, the **e** trembled, and the H776
6: 4 the increase of the **e**, till thou come unto H776
37 *be* dry upon all the **e** *beside,* then shall I H776
18:10 *is* no want of any thing that *is* in the **e**. H776
1Sa 2: 8 the pillars of the **e** *are* the LORD'S, and H776
10 judge the ends of the **e**; and he shall give H776
4: 5 a great shout, so that the **e** rang again. H776
12 clothes rent, and with **e** upon his head. H127
5: 3 his face to the **e** before the ark of the H776
14:15 trembled, and the **e** quaked: so it was a H776
17:46 the wild beasts of the **e**; that all the earth H776
46 **e** may know that there is a God in Israel. H776
49 and he fell upon his face to the **e**. H776
20:15 of David every one from the face of the **e**. H127
24: 8 with his face to the **e**, and bowed himself. H776
25:41 on *her* face to the **e**, and said, Behold, *let* H776
26: 8 spear even to the **e** at once, and I will not H776
20 my blood fall to the **e** before the face of H776
28:13 Saul, I saw gods ascending out of the **e**. H776
20 all along on the **e**, and was sore afraid, H776
23 arose from the **e**, and sat upon the bed. H776
30:16 upon all the **e**, eating and drinking, H776
2Sa 1: 2 clothes rent, and **e** upon his head: and *so* H127
2 that he fell to the **e**, and did obeisance. H776
4:11 hand, and take you away from the **e**? H776
7: 9 name of the great *men* that *are* in the **e**. H776
23 And what one nation in the **e** *is* like thy H776
12:16 and went in, and lay all night upon the **e**. H776
17 him up from the **e**: but he would not, H776
20 Then David arose from the **e**, and H776
13:31 and lay on the **e**; and all his servants H776
14: 7 *neither* name nor remainder upon the **e**. H127
11 shall not one hair of thy son fall to the **e**. H776
20 God, to know all *things* that *are* in the **e**. H776
15:32 with his coat rent, and **e** upon his head: H127
18: 9 the heaven and the **e**; and the mule that H776
28 he fell down to the **e** upon his face before H776
22: 8 Then the **e** shook and trembled; the H776
43 as the dust of the **e**, I did stamp them as H776
23: 4 out of the **e** by clear shining after rain. H776
1Ki 1:31 with *her* face to the **e**, and did reverence H776
40 that the **e** rent with the sound of them. H776
52 hair of him fall to the **e**: but if wickedness H776
2: 2 I go the way of all the **e**: be thou strong H776
4:34 of the **e**, which had heard of his wisdom. H776
8:23 above, or on **e** beneath, who keepest H776
27 But will God indeed dwell on the **e**? H776
43 all people of the **e** may know thy name, H776
53 all the people of the **e**, *to be* thine H776
60 That all the people of the **e** may know H776
10:23 kings of the **e** for riches and for wisdom. H776
24 And all the **e** sought to Solomon, to hear H776
13:34 to destroy *it* from off the face of the **e**. H127
17:14 *that* the LORD sendeth rain upon the **e**. H127
18: 1 Ahab; and I will send rain upon the **e**. H127
42 the **e**, and put his face between his knees, H776
2Ki 5:15 *is* no God in all the **e**, but in Israel: now H776
17 mules' burden of **e**? for thy servant will H127
10:10 Know now that there shall fall unto the **e** H776
19:15 the **e**; thou hast made heaven and earth. H776
15 the earth; thou hast made heaven and **e**. H776
19 kingdoms of the **e** may know that thou H776
1Ch 1:10 he began to be mighty upon the **e**. H776
19 in his days the **e** was divided: and his H776
16:14 our God; his judgments *are* in all the **e**. H776
23 Sing unto the LORD, all the **e**; shew forth H776
30 Fear before him, all the **e**: the world also H776
31 Let the heavens be glad, and let the **e** H776
33 LORD, because he cometh to judge the **e**. H776
17: 8 name of the great men that *are* in the **e**. H776
21 And what one nation in the **e** *is* like thy H776
21:16 stand between the **e** and the heaven, H776
22: 8 shed much blood upon the **e** in my sight. H776
29:11 heaven and in the **e** *is thine;* thine *is* the H776
15 our days on the **e** *are* as a shadow, and H776
2Ch 1: 9 people like the dust of the **e** in multitude. H776
2:12 made heaven and **e**, who hath given to H776
6:14 the heaven, nor in the **e**; which keepest H776
18 with men on the **e**? behold, heaven and H776
33 all people of the **e** may know thy name, H776
9:22 the kings of the **e** in riches and wisdom. H776
23 And all the kings of the **e** sought the H776
16: 9 the whole **e**, to shew himself strong H776
20:24 bodies fallen to the **e**, and none escaped. H776
32:19 of the people of the **e**, *which were* the H776
2Ch 36:23 kingdoms of the **e** hath the LORD God H776
Ezr 1: 2 kingdoms of the **e**; and he hath charged H776
5:11 God of heaven and **e**, and build the house H772
Neh 9: 1 and with sackclothes, and **e** upon them. H127
6 all their host, the **e**, and all *things* that H776
Job 1: 7 **e**, and from walking up and down in it. H776
8 like him in the **e**, a perfect and an upright H776
2: 2 **e**, and from walking up and down in it. H776
3 like him in the **e**, a perfect and an upright H776
3:14 With kings and counsellors of the **e**, H776
5:10 Who giveth rain upon the **e**, and sendeth H776
22 shalt thou be afraid of the beasts of the **e**. H776
25 and thine offspring as the grass of the **e**. H776
7: 1 time to man upon **e**? *are not* his days also H776
8: 9 because our days upon **e** *are* a shadow:) H776
19 way, and out of the **e** shall others grow. H6083
9: 6 Which shaketh the **e** out of her place, H776
24 The **e** is given into the hand of the H776
11: 9 The measure thereof *is* longer than the **e**, H776
12: 8 Or speak to the **e**, and it shall teach thee: H776
15 them out, and they overturn the **e**. H776
24 of the people of the **e**, and causeth them H776
14: 8 Though the root thereof wax old in the **e**, H776
19 **e**; and thou destroyest the hope of man. H776
15:19 Unto whom alone the **e** was given, and H776
29 the perfection thereof upon the **e**. H776
16:18 O **e**, cover not thou my blood, and let my H776
18: 4 in his anger: shall the **e** be forsaken for H776
17 perish from the **e**, and he shall have no H776
19:25 shall stand at the latter *day* upon the **e**: H6083
20: 4 this of old, since man was placed upon **e**, H776
27 and the **e** shall rise up against him. H776
22: 8 But *as for* the mighty man, he had the **e**; H776
24: 4 poor of the **e** hide themselves together. H776
18 is cursed in the **e**: he beholdeth not the H776
26: 7 place, *and* hangeth the **e** upon nothing. H776
28: 2 Iron is taken out of the **e**, and brass *is* H6083
5 *As for* the **e**, out of it cometh bread: and H776
24 For he looketh to the ends of the **e**, *and* H776
30: 6 *in* caves of the **e**, and *in* the rocks. H6083
8 of base men: they were viler than the **e**. H776
34:13 Who hath given him a charge over the **e**? H776
35:11 the beasts of the **e**, and maketh us wiser H776
37: 3 and his lightning unto the ends of the **e**. H776
6 Be thou *on* the **e**; likewise to the small H776
12 them upon the face of the world in the **e**. H776
17 he quieteth the **e** by the south *wind*? H776
38: 4 **e**? declare, if thou hast understanding. H776
13 hold of the ends of the **e**, that the wicked H776
18 Hast thou perceived the breadth of the **e**? H776
24 scattereth the east wind upon the **e**? H776
26 To cause it to rain on the **e**, *where* no H776
33 thou set the dominion thereof in the **e**? H776
39:14 Which leaveth her eggs in the **e**, and H776
41:33 Upon **e** there is not his like, who is H6083
Ps 2: 2 The kings of the **e** set themselves, and H776
8 parts of the **e** *for* thy possession. H776
10 ye kings: be instructed, ye judges of the **e**. H776
7: 5 my life upon the **e**, and lay mine honour H776
8: 1 *is* thy name in all the **e**! who hast set thy H776
9 how excellent *is* thy name in all the **e**! H776
10:18 the man of the **e** may no more oppress. H776
12: 6 in a furnace of **e**, purified seven times. H776
16: 3 *But* to the saints that *are* in the **e**, and *to* H776
17:11 have set their eyes bowing down to the **e**; H776
18: 7 Then the **e** shook and trembled; the H776
19: 4 Their line is gone out through all the **e**, H776
21:10 Their fruit shalt thou destroy from the **e**, H776
22:29 All *they that be* fat upon **e** shall eat and H776
24: 1 The **e** *is* the LORD'S, and the fulness H776
25:13 at ease; and his seed shall inherit the **e**. H776
33: 5 the **e** is full of the goodness of the LORD. H776
8 Let all the **e** fear the LORD: let all the H776
14 looketh upon all the inhabitants of the **e**. H776
34:16 off the remembrance of them from the **e**. H776
37: 9 upon the LORD, they shall inherit the **e**. H776
11 But the meek shall inherit the **e**; and shall H776
22 him shall inherit the **e**; and *they that be* H776
41: 2 be blessed upon the **e**: and thou wilt not H776
44:25 to the dust: our belly cleaveth unto the **e**. H776
45:16 thou mayest make princes in all the **e**. H776
46: 2 Therefore will not we fear, though the **e** H776
6 he uttered his voice, the **e** melted. H776
8 what desolations he hath made in the **e**. H776
9 unto the end of the **e**; he breaketh the H776
10 the heathen, I will be exalted in the **e**. H776
47: 2 terrible; *he is* a great King over all the **e**. H776
7 For God *is* the King of all the **e**: sing ye H776
9 **e** *belong* unto God: he is greatly exalted. H776
Ps 48: 2 the joy of the whole **e**, *is* mount Zion, *on* H776
10 **e**: thy right hand is full of righteousness. H776
50: 1 and called the **e** from the rising of the H776
4 to the **e**, that he may judge his people. H776
57: 5 heavens; *let* thy glory *be* above all the **e**. H776
11 heavens: *let* thy glory *be* above all the **e**. H776
58: 2 weigh the violence of your hands in the **e**. H776
11 verily he is a God that judgeth in the **e**. H776
59:13 in Jacob unto the ends of the **e**. Selah. H776
60: 2 Thou hast made the **e** to tremble; thou H776
61: 2 From the end of the **e** will I cry unto H776
63: 9 *it,* shall go into the lower parts of the **e**. H776
65: 5 all the ends of the **e**, and of them that are H776
9 Thou visitest the **e**, and waterest it: thou H776
66: 4 All the **e** shall worship thee, and shall H776
67: 2 That thy way may be known upon **e**, thy H776
4 and govern the nations upon **e**. Selah. H776
6 *Then* shall the **e** yield her increase; *and* H776
7 and all the ends of the **e** shall fear him. H776
68: 8 The **e** shook, the heavens also dropped H776
32 Sing unto God, ye kingdoms of the **e**; O H776
69:34 Let the heaven and **e** praise him, the H776
71:20 me up again from the depths of the **e**. H776
72: 6 mown grass: as showers *that* water the **e**. H776
8 and from the river unto the ends of the **e**. H776
16 of corn in the **e** upon the top of the H776
16 the city shall flourish like grass of the **e**. H776
19 and let the whole **e** be filled *with* his H776
73: 9 and their tongue walketh through the **e**. H776
25 *is* none upon **e** *that* I desire beside thee. H776
74:12 working salvation in the midst of the **e**. H776
17 Thou hast set all the borders of the **e**: H776
20 **e** are full of the habitations of cruelty. H776
75: 3 The **e** and all the inhabitants thereof are H776
8 **e** shall wring *them* out, *and* drink *them*. H776
76: 8 from heaven; the **e** feared, and was still, H776
9 to save all the meek of the **e**. Selah. H776
12 *he is* terrible to the kings of the **e**. H776
77:18 the world: the **e** trembled and shook. H776
78:69 the **e** which he hath established for ever. H776
79: 2 of thy saints unto the beasts of the **e**. H776
82: 5 foundations of the **e** are out of course. H776
8 Arise, O God, judge the **e**: for thou shalt H776
83:10 at En-dor: they became *as* dung for the **e**. H127
18 *art* the most high over all the **e**. H776
85:11 Truth shall spring out of the **e**; and H776
89:11 The heavens *are* thine, the **e** also *is* H776
27 firstborn, higher than the kings of the **e**. H776
90: 2 hadst formed the **e** and the world, even H776
94: 2 Lift up thyself, thou judge of the **e**: render H776
95: 4 In his hand *are* the deep places of the **e**: H776
96: 1 new song: sing unto the LORD, all the **e**. H776
9 of holiness: fear before him, all the **e**. H776
11 Let the heavens rejoice, and let the **e** be H776
13 to judge the **e**: he shall judge the world H776
97: 1 The LORD reigneth; let the **e** rejoice; let H776
4 the world: the **e** saw, and trembled. H776
5 at the presence of the Lord of the whole **e**. H776
9 For thou, LORD, *art* high above all the **e**: H776
98: 3 the **e** have seen the salvation of our God. H776
4 the LORD, all the **e**: make a loud noise, H776
9 to judge the **e**: with righteousness shall H776
99: 1 the cherubims; let the **e** be moved. H776
102:15 and all the kings of the **e** thy glory. H776
19 from heaven did the LORD behold the **e**; H776
25 foundation of the **e**: and the heavens *are* H776
103:11 For as the heaven is high above the **e**, *so* H776
104: 5 *Who* laid the foundations of the **e**, *that* it H776
9 that they turn not again to cover the **e**. H776
13 **e** is satisfied with the fruit of thy works. H776
14 that he may bring forth food out of the **e**; H776
24 made them all: the **e** is full of thy riches. H776
30 and thou renewest the face of the **e**. H127
32 He looketh on the **e**, and it trembleth: he H776
35 Let the sinners be consumed out of the **e**, H776
105: 7 our God: his judgments *are* in all the **e**. H776
106:17 The **e** opened and swallowed up Dathan, H776
108: 5 heavens: and thy glory above all the **e**; H776
109:15 cut off the memory of them from the **e**. H776
112: 2 His seed shall be mighty upon **e**: the H776
113: 6 *things that are* in heaven, and in the **e**! H776
114: 7 Tremble, thou **e**, at the presence of the H776
115:15 of the LORD which made heaven and **e**. H776
16 **e** hath he given to the children of men. H776
119:19 I *am* a stranger in the **e**: hide not thy H776
64 The **e**, O LORD, is full of thy mercy: teach H776
87 They had almost consumed me upon **e**; H776
90 hast established the **e**, and it abideth. H776
119 Thou puttest away all the wicked of the **e** H776

Ps 121: 2 the LORD, which made heaven and **e**. H776
124: 8 of the LORD, who made heaven and **e**. H776
134: 3 The LORD that made heaven and **e** bless H776
135: 6 and in **e**, in the seas, and all deep places. H776
7 the ends of the **e**; he maketh lightnings H776
136: 6 To him that stretched out the **e** above H776
138: 4 All the kings of the **e** shall praise thee, O H776
139:15 wrought in the lowest parts of the **e**. H776
140:11 be established in the **e**: evil shall hunt the H776
141: 7 cutteth and cleaveth *wood* upon the **e**. H776
146: 4 **e**; in that very day his thoughts perish. H127
6 Which made heaven, and **e**, the sea, and H776
147: 8 rain for the **e**, who maketh grass to H776
15 *upon* **e**: his word runneth very swiftly. H776
148: 7 Praise the LORD from the **e**, ye dragons, H776
11 Kings of the **e**, and all people; princes, H776
11 people; princes, and all judges of the **e**: H776
13 his glory *is* above the **e** and heaven. H776
Prv 2:22 But the wicked shall be cut off from the **e**, H776
3:19 hath founded the **e**; by understanding H776
8:16 and nobles, *even* all the judges of the **e**. H776
23 from the beginning, or ever the **e** was. H776
26 While as yet he had not made the **e**, nor H776
29 he appointed the foundations of the **e**: H776
31 Rejoicing in the habitable part of his **e**; H776
10:30 but the wicked shall not inhabit the **e**. H776
11:31 **e**: much more the wicked and the sinner. H776
17:24 the eyes of a fool *are* in the ends of the **e**. H776
25: 3 The heaven for height, and the **e** for H776
30: 4 all the ends of the **e**? what *is* his name, H776
14 the **e**, and the needy from *among* men. H776
16 The grave; and the barren womb; the **e** H776
21 For three *things* the **e** is disquieted, and H776
24 upon the **e**, but they *are* exceeding wise: H776
Ecc 1: 4 cometh: but the **e** abideth for ever. H776
3:21 the beast that goeth downward to the **e**? H776
5: 2 upon **e**: therefore let thy words be few. H776
9 Moreover the profit of the **e** is for all: the H776
7:20 For *there is* not a just man upon **e**, that H776
8:14 is done upon the **e**; that there be just H776
16 is done upon the **e**: (for also *there is that* H776
10: 7 princes walking as servants upon the **e**. H776
11: 2 not what evil shall be upon the **e**. H776
3 upon the **e**: and if the tree fall toward H776
12: 7 Then shall the dust return to the **e** as it H776
Song 2:12 The flowers appear on the **e**; the time of H776
Isa 1: 2 Hear, O heavens, and give ear, O **e**: for H776
2:19 the caves of the **e**, for fear of the LORD, H6083
19 when he ariseth to shake terribly the **e**. H776
21 when he ariseth to shake terribly the **e**. H776
4: 2 and the fruit of the **e** *shall be* excellent H776
5: 8 may be placed alone in the midst of the **e**! H776
26 from the end of the **e**: and, behold, they H776
6: 3 of hosts: the whole **e** *is* full of his glory. H776
8:22 And they shall look unto the **e**; and H776
10:14 I gathered all the **e**; and there was none H776
11: 4 for the meek of the **e**: and he shall smite H776
4 he shall smite the **e** with the rod of his H776
9 mountain: for the **e** shall be full of the H776
12 of Judah from the four corners of the **e**. H776
12: 5 things: this *is* known in all the **e**. H776
13:13 heavens, and the **e** shall remove out of H776
14: 7 The whole **e** is at rest, *and* is quiet: they H776
9 chief ones of the **e**; it hath raised up from H776
16 **e** to tremble, that did shake kingdoms; H776
26 upon the whole **e**: and this *is* the hand H776
18: 3 dwellers on the **e**, see ye, when he lifteth H776
6 to the beasts of the **e**: and the fowls shall H776
6 beasts of the **e** shall winter upon them. H776
23: 8 traffickers *are* the honourable of the **e**? H776
9 into contempt all the honourable of the **e**. H776
17 of the world upon the face of the **e**. H127
24: 1 Behold, the LORD maketh the **e** empty, H776
4 The **e** mourneth *and* fadeth away, the H776
4 the haughty people of the **e** do languish. H776
5 The **e** also is defiled under the H776
6 Therefore hath the curse devoured the **e**, H776
6 of the **e** are burned, and few men left. H776
16 From the uttermost part of the **e** have we H776
17 *are* upon thee, O inhabitant of the **e**. H776
18 and the foundations of the **e** do shake. H776
19 The **e** is utterly broken down, the earth is H776
19 The earth is utterly broken down, the **e** is H776
19 dissolved, the **e** is moved exceedingly. H776
20 The **e** shall reel to and fro like a H776
21 and the kings of the **e** upon the earth. H127
21 and the kings of the earth upon the **e**. H127
25: 8 off all the **e**: for the LORD hath spoken *it*. H776
26: 9 *are* in the **e**, the inhabitants of the H776

Isa 26:15 removed *it* far *unto* all the ends of the **e**. H776
18 any deliverance in the **e**; neither have the H776
19 herbs, and the **e** shall cast out the dead. H776
21 inhabitants of the **e** for their iniquity: the H776
21 their iniquity: the **e** also shall disclose H776
28: 2 shall cast down to the **e** with the hand. H776
22 even determined upon the whole **e**. H776
30:23 of the increase of the **e**, and it shall be fat H127
33: 9 The **e** mourneth *and* languisheth: H776
34: 1 ye people: let the **e** hear, and all that is H776
37:16 the **e**: thou hast made heaven and earth. H776
16 the earth: thou hast made heaven and **e**. H776
20 kingdoms of the **e** may know that thou H776
40:12 the dust of the **e** in a measure, and H776
21 from the foundations of the **e**? H776
22 the circle of the **e**, and the inhabitants H776
23 he maketh the judges of the **e** as vanity. H776
24 not take root in the **e**: and he shall also H776
28 of the ends of the **e**, fainteth not, neither H776
41: 5 the **e** were afraid, drew near, and came. H776
9 the ends of the **e**, and called thee from H776
42: 4 the **e**: and the isles shall wait for his law. H776
5 that spread forth the **e**, and that which H776
10 from the end of the **e**, ye that go down to H776
43: 6 and my daughters from the ends of the **e**; H776
44:23 ye lower parts of the **e**: break forth into H776
24 that spreadeth abroad the **e** by myself; H776
45: 8 let the **e** open, and let them bring H776
9 potsherds of the **e**. Shall the clay say to H127
12 I have made the **e**, and created man H776
18 that formed the **e** and made it; he hath H776
19 a dark place of the **e**: I said not unto the H776
22 **e**: for I *am* God, and *there is* none else. H776
48:13 foundation of the **e**, and my right hand H776
20 to the end of the **e**; say ye, The LORD H776
49: 6 be my salvation unto the end of the **e**. H776
8 to establish the **e**, to cause to inherit the H776
13 Sing, O heavens; and be joyful, O **e**; and H776
23 face toward the **e**, and lick up the dust H776
51: 6 and look upon the **e** beneath: for the H776
6 like smoke, and the **e** shall wax old like a H776
13 the foundations of the **e**; and hast feared H776
16 foundations of the **e**, and say unto Zion, H776
52:10 the **e** shall see the salvation of our God. H776
54: 5 God of the whole **e** shall he be called. H776
9 more go over the **e**; so have I sworn that H776
55: 9 For *as* the heavens are higher than the **e**, H776
10 but watereth the **e**, and maketh it bring H776
58:14 high places of the **e**, and feed thee with H776
60: 2 shall cover the **e**, and gross darkness H776
61:11 For as the **e** bringeth forth her bud, and H776
62: 7 till he make Jerusalem a praise in the **e**. H776
63: 6 I will bring down their strength to the **e**. H776
65:16 That he who blesseth himself in the **e** H776
16 sweareth in the **e** shall swear by the God H776
17 new heavens and a new **e**: and the former H776
66: 1 *is* my throne, and the **e** *is* my footstool: H776
8 such things? Shall the **e** be made to bring H776
22 For as the new heavens and the new **e**, H776
Jer 4:23 I beheld the **e**, and, lo, *it was* without H776
28 For this shall the **e** mourn, and the H776
6:19 Hear, O **e**: behold, I will bring evil upon H776
22 shall be raised from the sides of the **e**. H776
7:33 of the **e**; and none shall fray *them* away. H776
8: 2 shall be for dung upon the face of the **e**. H127
9: 3 for the truth upon the **e**; for they proceed H776
24 in the **e**: for in these *things* I delight, H776
10:10 at his wrath the **e** shall tremble, and the H776
11 heavens and the **e**, *even* they shall perish H778
11 the **e**, and from under these heavens. H772
12 He hath made the **e** by his power, he H776
13 the ends of the **e**; he maketh lightnings H776
14: 4 was no rain in the **e**, the plowmen were H776
15: 3 beasts of the **e**, to devour and destroy. H776
4 into all kingdoms of the **e**, because of H776
10 to the whole **e**! I have neither lent on H776
16: 4 upon the face of the **e**: and they shall be H127
4 of heaven, and for the beasts of the **e**. H776
19 the ends of the **e**, and shall say, Surely H776
17:13 be written in the **e**, because they have H776
19: 7 of the heaven, and for the beasts of the **e**. H776
22:29 O **e**, earth, earth, hear the word of the H776
29 O earth, **e**, earth, hear the word of the H776
29 O earth, earth, **e**, hear the word of the H776
23: 5 execute judgment and justice in the **e**. H776
24 not I fill heaven and **e**? saith the LORD. H776
24: 9 kingdoms of the **e** for *their* hurt, *to be* a H776
25:26 upon the face of the **e**: and the king of H127
29 of the **e**, saith the LORD of hosts. H776

Jer 25:30 against all the inhabitants of the **e**. H776
31 to the ends of the **e**; for the LORD hath a H776
32 be raised up from the coasts of the **e**. H776
33 *one* end of the **e** even unto the *other* H776
33 the *other* end of the **e**: they shall not be H776
26: 6 this city a curse to all the nations of the **e**. H776
27: 5 I have made the **e**, the man and the beast H776
28:16 off the face of the **e**: this year thou shalt H127
29:18 kingdoms of the **e**, to be a curse, and an H776
31: 8 the coasts of the **e**, *and* with them the H776
22 in the **e**, A woman shall compass a man. H776
37 the foundations of the **e** searched out H776
32:17 the heaven and the **e** by thy great power H776
33: 9 the nations of the **e**, which shall hear all H776
25 the ordinances of heaven and **e**; H776
34: 1 kingdoms of the **e** of his dominion, and H776
17 removed into all the kingdoms of the **e**. H776
20 of the heaven, and to the beasts of the **e**. H776
44: 8 reproach among all the nations of the **e**? H776
46: 8 *and* will cover the **e**; I will destroy the city H776
49:21 The **e** is moved at the noise of their fall, H776
50:23 How is the hammer of the whole **e** cut H776
41 be raised up from the coasts of the **e**. H776
46 of Babylon the **e** is moved, and the cry H776
51: 7 that made all the **e** drunken: the nations H776
15 He hath made the **e** by his power, he H776
16 the ends of the **e**: he maketh lightnings H776
25 destroyest all the **e**: and I will stretch out H776
41 praise of the whole **e** surprised! how is H776
48 Then the heaven and the **e**, and all that *is* H776
49 at Babylon shall fall the slain of all the **e**. H776
Lam 2: 1 heaven unto the **e** the beauty of Israel, H776
11 is poured upon the **e**, for the destruction H776
15 of beauty, The joy of the whole **e**? H776
3:34 under his feet all the prisoners of the **e**, H776
4:12 The kings of the **e**, and all the inhabitants H776
Ezk 1:15 wheel upon the **e** by the living creatures, H776
19 up from the **e**, the wheels were lifted up. H776
21 were lifted up from the **e**, the wheels were H776
7:21 the **e** for a spoil; and they shall pollute it. H776
8: 3 me up between the **e** and the heaven, H776
12 us not; the LORD hath forsaken the **e**. H776
9: 9 forsaken the **e**, and the LORD seeth not. H776
10:16 to mount up from the **e**, the same wheels H776
19 up from the **e** in my sight: when they H776
26:20 the low parts of the **e**, in places desolate H776
27:33 the kings of the **e** with the multitude of H776
28:18 to ashes upon the **e** in the sight of all H776
31:12 the people of the **e** are gone down from H776
14 nether parts of the **e**, in the midst of the H776
16 be comforted in the nether parts of the **e**. H776
18 nether parts of the **e**: thou shalt lie in the H776
32: 4 fill the beasts of the whole **e** with thee. H776
18 **e**, with them that go down into the pit. H776
24 nether parts of the **e**, which caused their H776
34: 6 all the face of the **e**, and none did search H776
27 yield her fruit, and the **e** shall yield her H776
35:14 **e** rejoiceth, I will make thee desolate. H776
38:20 creep upon the **e**, and all the men that H127
20 upon the face of the **e**, shall shake at my H127
39:14 the face of the **e**, to cleanse it: after the H776
18 of the princes of the **e**, of rams, of lambs, H776
43: 2 waters: and the **e** shined with his glory. H776
Dan 2:10 not a man upon the **e** that can shew the H3007
35 a great mountain, and filled the whole **e**. H772
39 brass, which shall bear rule over all the **e**. H772
4: 1 in all the **e**; Peace be multiplied unto you. H772
10 of the **e**, and the height thereof *was* great. H772
11 the sight thereof to the end of all the **e**: H772
15 of his roots in the **e**, even with a band of H772
15 *be* with the beasts in the grass of the **e**: H772
20 heaven, and the sight thereof to all the **e**; H772
22 and thy dominion to the end of the **e**. H772
23 roots thereof in the **e**, even with a band of H772
35 And all the inhabitants of the **e** *are* H772
35 inhabitants of the **e**: and none can stay H772
6:25 in all the **e**; Peace be multiplied unto you. H772
27 in heaven and in **e**, who hath delivered H772
7: 4 was lifted up from the **e**, and made stand H772
17 four kings, *which* shall arise out of the **e**. H772
23 kingdom upon **e**, which shall be diverse H772
23 devour the whole **e**, and shall tread it H772
8: 5 face of the whole **e**, and touched not the H776
12: 2 in the dust of the **e** shall awake, some H6083
Hos 2:18 **e**, and will make them to lie down safely. H776
21 the heavens, and they shall hear the **e**; H776
22 And the **e** shall hear the corn, and the H776
23 And I will sow her unto me in the **e**; and I H776
6: 3 as the latter *and* former rain unto the **e**. H776

Joel 2:10 The e shall quake before them; the H776
30 e, blood, and fire, and pillars of smoke. H776
3:16 heavens and the e shall shake: but the H776
Am 2: 7 That pant after the dust of the e on the H776
3: 2 all the families of the e: therefore I will H127
5 Can a bird fall in a snare upon the e, H776
5 the e, and have taken nothing at all? H127
4:13 high places of the e, The LORD, The God H776
5: 7 and leave off righteousness in the e, H776
8 the face of the e: The LORD is his name: H776
8: 9 and I will darken the e in the clear day: H776
9: 6 his troop in the e; he that calleth for the H776
6 the face of the e: The LORD is his name. H776
8 off the face of the e; saving that I will not H127
9 shall not the least grain fall upon the e. H776
Jna 2: 6 the mountains; the e with her bars was H776
Mic 1: 2 Hear, all ye people; hearken, O e, and all H776
3 and tread upon the high places of the e. H776
4:13 substance unto the Lord of the whole e. H776
5: 4 shall he be great unto the ends of the e. H776
6: 2 foundations of the e: for the LORD hath a H776
7: 2 The good man is perished out of the e: H776
17 like worms of the e: they shall be afraid H776
Nah 1: 5 the hills melt, and the e is burned at his H776
2:13 thy prey from the e, and the voice of thy H776
Hab 2:14 For the e shall be filled with the H776
20 let all the e keep silence before him. H776
3: 3 heavens, and the e was full of his praise. H776
6 He stood, and measured the e: he beheld, H776
9 Thou didst cleave the e with rivers. H776
Zep 2: 3 Seek ye the LORD, all ye meek of the e, H776
11 all the gods of the e; and men shall H776
3: 8 anger: for all the e shall be devoured H776
20 all people of the e, when I turn back your H776
Hag 1:10 dew, and the e is stayed from her fruit. H776
2: 6 and the e, and the sea, and the dry land; H776
21 I will shake the heavens and the e; H776
Zec 1:10 sent to walk to and fro through the e. H776
11 fro through the e, and, behold, all the H776
11 all the e sitteth still, and is at rest. H776
4:10 run to and fro through the whole e. H776
14 that stand by the Lord of the whole e. H776
5: 3 the face of the whole e: for every one that H776
6 is their resemblance through all the e. H776
9 the ephah between the e and the heaven. H776
6: 5 standing before the Lord of all the e. H776
7 fro through the e: and he said, Get you H776
7 fro through the e. So they walked to and H776
7 So they walked to and fro through the e. H776
9:10 from the river even to the ends of the e. H776
12: 1 the foundation of the e, and formeth the H776
3 of the e be gathered together against it. H776
14: 9 be king over all the e: in that day shall H776
17 the families of the e unto Jerusalem to H776
Mal 4: 6 lest I come and smite the e with a curse. H776
Mt 5: 5 the meek: for they shall inherit the e. G1093
13 Ye are the salt of the e: but if the salt G1093
18 Till heaven and e pass, one jot or one G1093
35 Nor by the e; for it is his footstool: G1093
6:10 Thy will be done in e, as it is in heaven. G1093
19 treasures upon e, where moth and rust G1093
9: 6 hath power on e to forgive sins, (then G1093
10:34 to send peace on e: I came not to send G1093
11:25 of heaven and e, because thou hast hid G1093
12:40 and three nights in the heart of the e. G1093
42 parts of the e to hear the wisdom G1093
13: 5 had not much e: and forthwith they G1093
5 up, because they had no deepness of e: G1093
16:19 thou shalt bind on e shall be bound in G1093
19 loose on e shall be loosed in heaven. G1093
17:25 do the kings of the e take custom or G1093
18:18 ye shall bind on e shall be bound in G1093
18 loose on e shall be loosed in heaven. G1093
19 of you shall agree on e as touching any G1093
23: 9 And call no man your father upon the e: G1093
35 shed upon the e, from the blood of G1093
24:30 all the tribes of the e mourn, and they G1093
35 Heaven and e shall pass away, but my G1093
25:18 in the e, and hid his lord's money. G1093
25 in the e: lo, there thou hast that is thine. G1093
27:51 the e did quake, and the rocks rent; G1093
28:18 is given unto me in heaven and in e. G1093
Mk 2:10 hath power on e to forgive sins, (he G1093
4: 5 it had not much e; and immediately it G1093
5 sprang up, because it had no depth of e: G1093
28 For the e bringeth forth fruit of herself; G1093
31 it is sown in the e, is less than all the G1093
31 is less than all the seeds that be in the e: G1093
9: 3 so as no fuller on e can white them. G1093
Mk 13:27 the e to the uttermost part of heaven. G1093
31 Heaven and e shall pass away: but my G1093
Lk 2:14 Glory to God in the highest, and on e G1093
5:24 hath power upon e to forgive sins, (he G1093
6:49 an house upon the e; against which the G1093
10:21 of heaven and e, that thou hast hid G1093
11: 2 Thy will be done, as in heaven, so in e. G1093
31 parts of the e to hear the wisdom G1093
12:49 I am come to send fire on the e; and G1093
51 on e? I tell you, Nay; but rather division: G1093
56 the sky and of the e; but how is it that ye G1093
16:17 And it is easier for heaven and e to G1093
18: 8 cometh, shall he find faith on the e? G1093
21:25 and upon the e distress of nations, G1093
26 are coming on the e: for the powers of G3625
33 Heaven and e shall pass away: but my G1093
35 that dwell on the face of the whole e. G1093
23:44 over all the e until the ninth hour. G1093
24: 5 their faces to the e, they said unto them, G1093
Jn 3:31 all: he that is of the e is earthly, and G1093
31 speaketh of the e: he that cometh from G1093
12:32 And I, if I be lifted up from the e, will G1093
17: 4 I have glorified thee on the e: I have G1093
Act 1: 8 and unto the uttermost part of the e. G1093
2:19 and signs in the e beneath; blood, and G1093
3:25 all the kindreds of the e be blessed. G1093
4:24 e, and the sea, and all that in them is: G1093
26 The kings of the e stood up, and the G1093
7:49 Heaven is my throne, and e is my G1093
8:33 for his life is taken from the e. G1093
9: 4 And he fell to the e, and heard a voice G1093
8 And Saul arose from the e; and when G1093
10:11 the four corners, and let down to the e: G1093
12 beasts of the e, and wild beasts, and G1093
11: 6 beasts of the e, and wild beasts, and G1093
13:47 be for salvation unto the ends of the e. G1093
14:15 made heaven, and e, and the sea, and G1093
17:24 Lord of heaven and e, dwelleth not in G1093
26 on all the face of the e, and hath G1093
22:22 the e: for it is not fit that he should live. G1093
26:14 And when we were all fallen to the e, I G1093
Ro 9:17 might be declared throughout all the e. G1093
28 work will the Lord make upon the e. G1093
10:18 went into all the e, and their words unto G1093
1Co 8: 5 in heaven or in e, (as there be gods G1093
10:26 For the e is the Lord's, and the fulness G1093
28 e is the Lord's, and the fulness thereof: G1093
15:47 The first man is of the e, earthy: the G1093
Eph 1:10 and which are on e; even in him: G1093
3:15 family in heaven and e is named, G1093
4: 9 first into the lower parts of the e? G1093
6: 3 and thou mayest live long on the e. G1093
Php 2:10 things in e, and things under the earth; G1919
10 things in earth, and things under the e; G2709
Col 1:16 and that are in e, visible and invisible, G1093
20 they be things in e, or things in heaven. G1093
3: 2 on things above, not on things on the e. G1093
5 which are upon the e; fornication, G1093
2Ti 2:20 of wood and of e; and some to honour, G3749
Heb 1:10 foundation of the e; and the heavens G1093
6: 7 For the e which drinketh in the rain G1093
8: 4 For if he were on e, he should not be a G1093
11:13 were strangers and pilgrims on the e. G1093
38 and in dens and caves of the e. G1093
12:25 him that spake on e, much more shall G1093
26 Whose voice then shook the e: but now G1093
26 I shake not the e only, but also heaven. G1093
Jas 5: 5 Ye have lived in pleasure on the e, and G1093
7 fruit of the e, and hath long patience G1093
12 neither by the e, neither by any other G1093
17 it rained not on the e by the space of G1093
18 rain, and the e brought forth her fruit. G1093
2Pt 3: 5 of old, and the e standing out of the G1093
7 But the heavens and the e, which are G1093
10 fervent heat, the e also and the works G1093
13 new e, wherein dwelleth righteousness. G1093
1Jn 5: 8 bear witness in e, the Spirit, and the G1093
Rev 1: 5 of the kings of the e. Unto him that G1093
7 all kindreds of the e shall wail because G1093
3:10 to try them that dwell upon the e. G1093
5: 3 And no man in heaven, nor in e, neither G1093
3 neither under the e, was able to open G1093
6 Spirits of God sent forth into all the e. G1093
10 and priests: and we shall reign on the e. G1093
13 and on the e, and under the earth, G1093
13 and under the e, and such as are in the G1093
6: 4 peace from the e, and that they should G1093
8 fourth part of the e, to kill with sword, G1093
8 with death, and with the beasts of the e. G1093
Rev 6:10 our blood on them that dwell on the e? G1093
13 And the stars of heaven fell unto the e, G1093
15 And the kings of the e, and the great G1093
7: 1 four corners of the e, holding the four G1093
1 the four winds of the e, that the wind G1093
1 the e, nor on the sea, nor on any tree. G1093
2 it was given to hurt the e and the sea, G1093
3 Saying, Hurt not the e, neither the sea, G1093
8: 5 and cast it into the e: and there were G1093
7 cast upon the e: and the third part of G1093
13 the inhabiters of the e by reason of the G1093
9: 1 from heaven unto the e: and to him was G1093
3 locusts upon the e: and unto them was G1093
3 as the scorpions of the e have power. G1093
4 the grass of the e, neither any green G1093
10: 2 upon the sea, and his left foot on the e, G1093
5 the e lifted up his hand to heaven, G1093
6 are, and the e, and the things that G1093
8 standeth upon the sea and upon the e. G1093
11: 4 standing before the God of the e. G1093
6 e with all plagues, as often as they will. G1093
10 And they that dwell upon the e shall G1093
10 tormented them that dwelt on the e. G1093
18 destroy them which destroy the e. G1093
12: 4 did cast them to the e: and the dragon G1093
9 cast out into the e, and his angels were G1093
12 inhabiters of the e and of the sea! for G1093
13 was cast unto the e, he persecuted the G1093
16 And the e helped the woman, and the G1093
16 woman, and the e opened her mouth, G1093
13: 8 And all that dwell upon the e shall G1093
11 up out of the e; and he had two horns G1093
12 him, and causeth the e and them which G1093
13 heaven on the e in the sight of men, G1093
14 And deceiveth them that dwell on the e G1093
14 that dwell on the e, that they should G1093
14: 3 which were redeemed from the e. G1093
6 that dwell on the e, and to every nation, G1093
7 made heaven, and e, and the sea, and G1093
15 to reap; for the harvest of the e is ripe. G1093
16 on the e; and the earth was reaped. G1093
16 on the earth; and the e was reaped. G1093
18 of the e; for her grapes are fully ripe. G1093
19 in his sickle into the e, and gathered the G1093
19 the vine of the e, and cast it into the G1093
16: 1 the vials of the wrath of God upon the e. G1093
2 out his vial upon the e; and there fell a G1093
14 unto the kings of the e and of the whole G1093
18 men were upon the e, so mighty an G1093
17: 2 With whom the kings of the e have G1093
2 inhabitants of the e have been made G1093
5 AND ABOMINATIONS OF THE E. G1093
8 that dwell on the e shall wonder, whose G1093
18 which reigneth over the kings of the e. G1093
18: 1 and the e was lightened with his glory. G1093
3 and the kings of the e have committed G1093
3 the merchants of the e are waxed rich G1093
9 And the kings of the e, who have G1093
11 And the merchants of the e shall weep G1093
23 great men of the e; for by thy sorceries G1093
24 and of all that were slain upon the e. G1093
19: 2 did corrupt the e with her fornication, G1093
19 and the kings of the e, and their armies, G1093
20: 8 quarters of the e, Gog and Magog, to G1093
9 the breadth of the e, and compassed the G1093
11 whose face the e and the heaven fled G1093
21: 1 And I saw a new heaven and a new e: G1093
1 and the first e were passed away; and G1093
24 the kings of the e do bring their glory G1093

EARTHEN

Lev 6:28 But the e vessel wherein it is sodden H2789
11:33 And every e vessel, whereinto any of H2789
14: 5 in an e vessel over running water: H2789
50 birds in an e vessel over running water: H2789
Nu 5:17 holy water in an e vessel; and of the H2789
2Sa 17:28 Brought beds, and basons, and e H3335
Jer 19: 1 and get a potter's e bottle, and take of H2789
32:14 put them in an e vessel, that they may H2789
Lam 4: 2 they esteemed as e pitchers, the work H2789
2Co 4: 7 But we have this treasure in e vessels, G3749

EARTHLY

Jn 3:12 If I have told you e things, and ye G1919
31 is of the earth is e, and speaketh of the G1537
2Co 5: 1 For we know that if our e house of this G1919
Php 3:19 is in their shame, who mind e things.) G1919
Jas 3:15 from above, but is e, sensual, devilish. G1919

EARTHQUAKE
1Ki 19:11 after the wind an **e**; *but* the LORD *was* H7494
11 *but* the LORD *was* not in the **e**: H7494
12 And after the **e** a fire; *but* the LORD H7494
Isa 29: 6 thunder, and with **e**, and great noise, H7494
Am 1: 1 king of Israel, two years before the **e**. H7494
Zec 14: 5 from before the **e** in the days of Uzziah H7494
Mt 27:54 Jesus, saw the **e**, and those things that *G4578*
28: 2 And, behold, there was a great **e**: for the *G4578*
Act 16:26 And suddenly there was a great **e**, so *G4578*
Rev 6:12 there was a great **e**; and the sun became *G4578*
8: 5 thunderings, and lightnings, and an **e**. *G4578*
11:13 And the same hour was there a great **e**, *G4578*
13 city fell, and in the **e** were slain of men *G4578*
19 thunderings, and an **e**, and great hail. *G4578*
16:18 and there was a great **e**, such as was not *G4578*
18 the earth, so mighty an **e**, *and* so great. *G4578*

EARTHQUAKES
Mt 24: 7 and pestilences, and **e**, in divers places. *G4578*
Mk 13: 8 and there shall be **e** in divers places, *G4578*
Lk 21:11 And great **e** shall be in divers places, *G4578*

EARTHY
1Co 15:47 The first man *is* of the earth, **e**: the *G5517*
48 As *is* the **e**, such *are* they also that are *G5517*
48 *are* they also that are **e**: and as *is* the *G5517*
49 the image of the **e**, we shall also bear *G5517*

EASE
Dt 23:13 be, when thou wilt **e** thyself abroad, H3427
28:65 shalt thou find no **e**, neither shall the H7280
Jdg 20:43 them down with **e** over against Gibeah H4496
2Ch 10: 4 now therefore **e** thou somewhat the H7043
9 to me, saying, **E** somewhat the yoke H7043
Job 7:13 me, my couch shall **e** my complaint; H5375
12: 5 in the thought of him that is at **e**. H7600
16:12 I was at **e**, but he hath broken me H7961
21:23 strength, being wholly at **e** and quiet. H7946
Ps 25:13 His soul shall dwell at **e**; and his seed H2896
123: 4 **e**, *and* with the contempt of the proud. H7600
Isa 1:24 One of Israel, Ah, I will **e** me of mine H5162
32: 9 Rise up, ye women that are at **e**; hear H7600
11 Tremble, ye women that are at **e**; be H7600
Jer 46:27 at **e**, and none shall make *him* afraid. H7599
48:11 Moab hath been at **e** from his youth, H7599
Ezk 23:42 And a voice of a multitude being at **e** H7961
Am 6: 1 Woe to them *that are* at **e** in Zion, and H7600
Zec 1:15 *that are* at **e**: for I was but a little H7600
Lk 12:19 take thine **e**, eat, drink, *and* be merry. *G373*

EASED
Job 16: 6 and *though* I forbear, what am I **e**? H1980
2Co 8:13 For *I mean* not that other men be **e**, and *G425*

EASIER
Ex 18:22 so shall it be **e** for thyself, and they H7043
Mt 9: 5 For whether is **e**, to say, *Thy* sins be *G2123*
19:24 And again I say unto you, It is **e** for a *G2123*
Mk 2: 9 Whether is it **e** to say to the sick of the *G2123*
10:25 It is **e** for a camel to go through the eye *G2123*
Lk 5:23 Whether is **e**, to say, Thy sins be *G2123*
16:17 And it is **e** for heaven and earth to *G2123*
18:25 For it is **e** for a camel to go through a *G2123*

EASILY
1Co 13: 5 own, is not **e** provoked, thinketh no evil;
Heb 12: 1 sin which doth so **e** beset *us*, and let us

EAST
Gen 2:14 goeth toward the **e** of Assyria. And the H6926
3:24 he placed at the **e** of the garden of Eden H6924
4:16 in the land of Nod, on the **e** of Eden. H6926
10:30 goest unto Sephar a mount of the **e**. H6924
11: 2 from the **e**, that they found a plain H6924
12: 8 a mountain on the **e** of Beth-el, and H6924
8 and Hai on the **e**: and there he builded H6924
13:11 Jordan; and Lot journeyed **e**: and they H6924
25: 6 yet lived, eastward, unto the **e** country. H6924
28:14 west, and to the **e**, and to the north, and H6924
29: 1 into the land of the people of the **e**. H6924
41: 6 with the **e** wind sprung up after them. H6921
23 with the **e** wind, sprung up after them: H6921
27 **e** wind shall be seven years of famine. H6921
Ex 10:13 LORD brought an **e** wind upon the land H6921
13 the **e** wind brought the locusts. H6921
14:21 *back* by a strong **e** wind all that night, H6921
27:13 And the breadth of the court on the **e** H6924
38:13 And for the **e** side eastward fifty cubits. H6924
Lev 1:16 on the **e** part, by the place of the ashes: H6924
Nu 2: 3 And on the **e** side toward the rising of H6924
3:38 toward the **e**, *even* before the tabernacle H6924
10: 5 that lie on the **e** parts shall go forward. H6924
23: 7 mountains of the **e**, *saying*, Come, curse H6924
34:10 And ye shall point out your **e** border H6924
11 to Riblah, on the **e** side of Ain; and the H6924
35: 5 the city on the **e** side two thousand H6924
Jos 4:19 in Gilgal, in the **e** border of Jericho. H4217
7: 2 Beth-aven, on the **e** side of Beth-el, and H6924
11: 3 *And to* the Canaanite on the **e** and on H4217
12: 1 Hermon, and all the plain on the **e**: H4217
3 Chinneroth on the **e**, and unto the sea of H4217
3 *even* the salt sea on the **e**, the way to H4217
15: 5 And the **e** border *was* the salt sea, *even* H6924
16: 1 of Jericho on the **e**, to the wilderness H4217
5 their inheritance on the **e** side was H4217
6 and passed by it on the **e** to Janohah; H4217
17:10 on the north, and in Issachar on the **e**. H4217
18: 7 Jordan on the **e**, which Moses the H4217
20 border of it on the **e** side. This *was* the H6924
19:13 on along on the **e** to Gittah-hepher, to H6924
Jdg 6: 3 the **e**, even they came up against them; H6924
33 and the children of the **e** were gathered H6924
7:12 all the children of the **e** lay along in the H6924
8:10 of the children of the **e**: for there fell an H6924
11 dwelt in tents on the **e** of Nobah and H6924
11:18 came by the **e** side of the land H4217+H8121
21:19 on the **e** side of the highway H4217+H8121
1Ki 4:30 **e** country, and all the wisdom of Egypt. H6924
7:25 toward the **e**: and the sea *was set* H4217
1Ch 4:39 *even* unto the **e** side of the valley, to H4217
5:10 throughout all the **e** *land* of Gilead. H4217
6:78 by Jericho, on the **e** side of Jordan, H4217
9:24 toward the **e**, west, north, and south. H4217
12:15 *both* toward the **e**, and toward the west. H4217
2Ch 4: 4 toward the **e**: and the sea *was set* H4217
10 of the **e** end, over against the south. H6924
5:12 stood at the **e** end of the altar, and H4217
29: 4 them together into the **e** street, H4217
31:14 the porter toward the **e**, *was* over the H4217
Neh 3:26 the **e**, and the tower that lieth out. H4217
29 of Shechaniah, the keeper of the **e** gate. H4217
Job 1: 3 was the greatest of all the men of the **e**. H6924
15: 2 and fill his belly with the **e** wind? H6921
27:21 The **e** wind carrieth him away, and he H6921
38:24 scattereth the **e** wind upon the earth? H6921
Ps 48: 7 the ships of Tarshish with an **e** wind. H6921
75: 6 neither from the **e**, nor from the west, H4161
78:26 He caused an **e** wind to blow in the H6921
103:12 As far as the **e** is from the west, *so* far H4217
107: 3 lands, from the **e**, and from the west, H4217
Isa 2: 6 from the **e**, and *are* soothsayers H6924
11:14 spoil them of the **e** together: they shall H6924
27: 8 his rough wind in the day of the **e** wind. H6921
41: 2 *man* from the **e**, called him to his foot, H4217
43: 5 the **e**, and gather thee from the west; H4217
46:11 Calling a ravenous bird from the **e**, the H4217
Jer 18:17 I will scatter them as with an **e** wind H6921
19: 2 by the entry of the **e** gate, and proclaim H2777
31:40 gate toward the **e**, *shall be* holy unto the H4217
49:28 up to Kedar, and spoil the men of the **e**. H6924
Ezk 8:16 their faces toward the **e**; and they H6924
16 they worshipped the sun toward the **e**. H6924
10:19 at the door of the **e** gate of the LORD'S H6931
11: 1 me unto the **e** gate of the LORD'S H6931
23 which *is* on the **e** side of the city. H6924
17:10 wither, when the **e** wind toucheth it? it H6921
19:12 ground, and the **e** wind dried up her H6921
25: 4 to the men of the **e** for a possession, H6924
10 Unto the men of the **e** with the H6924
27:26 great waters: the **e** wind hath broken H6921
39:11 passengers on the **e** of the sea: and it H6926
40: 6 toward the **e**, and went up the stairs H6921
22 toward the **e**; and they went up unto H6921
23 and toward the **e**; and he measured H6921
32 court toward the **e**: and he measured H6921
44 one at the side of the **e** gate *having* the H6921
41:14 place toward the **e**, an hundred cubits. H6921
42: 9 the entry on the **e** side, as one goeth H6921
10 the court toward the **e**, over against the H6921
12 toward the **e**, as one entereth into them. H6921
15 the **e**, and measured it round about. H6921
16 He measured the **e** side with the H6921
43: 1 *even* the gate that looketh toward the **e**: H6921
2 the way of the **e**: and his voice *was* like H6921
4 the gate whose prospect *is* toward the **e**. H6921
17 and his stairs shall look toward the **e**. H6921
44: 1 looketh toward the **e**; and it *was* shut. H6921
Ezk 45: 7 and from the **e** side eastward: and H6924
7 from the west border unto the **e** border. H6921
46: 1 toward the **e** shall be shut the six H6921
12 toward the **e**, and he shall prepare H6921
47: 1 *stood toward* the **e**, and the waters H6921
8 out toward the **e** country, and go down H6930
18 And the **e** side ye shall measure from H6921
18 unto the **e** sea. And *this is* the east side. H6931
18 unto the east sea. And *this is* the **e** side. H6921
48: 1 his sides **e** *and* west; a *portion for* Dan. H6921
2 And by the border of Dan, from the **e** H6921
3 And by the border of Asher, from the **e** H6921
4 Naphtali, from the **e** side unto the west H6921
5 from the **e** side unto the west side, H6921
6 Ephraim, from the **e** side even unto the H6921
7 Reuben, from the **e** side unto the west H6921
8 And by the border of Judah, from the **e** H6921
8 parts, from the **e** side unto the west H6921
10 and toward the **e** ten thousand in H6921
16 and on the **e** side four thousand H6921
17 and toward the **e** two hundred and H6921
21 toward the **e** border, and westward H6921
23 As for the rest of the tribes, from the **e** H6921
24 from the **e** side unto the west side, H6921
25 Simeon, from the **e** side unto the west H6921
26 Issachar, from the **e** side unto the west H6921
27 Zebulun, from the **e** side unto the west H6921
32 And at the **e** side four thousand and H6921
Dan 8: 9 the **e**, and toward the pleasant *land*. H4217
11:44 But tidings out of the **e** and out of the H4217
Hos 12: 1 and followeth after the **e** wind: he daily H6921
13:15 *his* brethren, an **e** wind shall come, the H6921
Joel 2:20 face toward the **e** sea, and his hinder H6931
Am 8:12 the north even to the **e**, they shall run to H4217
Jna 4: 5 and sat on the **e** side of the city, and H6924
8 a vehement **e** wind; and the sun beat H6921
Hab 1: 9 shall sup up *as* the **e** wind, and they H6921
Zec 8: 7 **e** country, and from the west country; H4217
14: 4 Jerusalem on the **e**, and the mount of H6924
4 thereof toward the **e** and toward the H4217
Mt 2: 1 came wise men from the **e** to Jerusalem, *G395*
2 in the **e**, and are come to worship him. *G395*
9 they saw in the **e**, went before them, till *G395*
8:11 come from the **e** and west, and shall sit *G395*
24:27 For as the lightning cometh out of the **e**, *G395*
Lk 13:29 And they shall come from the **e**, and *G395*
Rev 7: 2 ascending from the **e**, having the seal of *G395*
16:12 of the kings of the **e** might be prepared. *G395*
21:13 On the **e** three gates; on the north three *G395*

EAST WIND See EAST and WIND.

EASTER
Act 12: 4 after **E** to bring him forth to the people. *G3957*

EAST-SIDE See EAST and SIDE.

EASTWARD
Gen 2: 8 And the LORD God planted a garden **e** H6924
13:14 and southward, and **e**, and westward: H6924
25: 6 he yet lived, **e**, unto the east country. H6924
Ex 27:13 on the east side **e** *shall be* fifty cubits. H4217
38:13 And for the east side **e** fifty cubits. H4217
Lev 16:14 the mercy seat **e**; and before the mercy H6924
Nu 3:38 the congregation **e**, *shall be* Moses, and H4217
32:19 is fallen to us on this side Jordan **e**. H4217
34: 3 be the outmost coast of the salt sea **e**: H6924
11 unto the side of the sea of Chinnereth **e**: H6924
15 *near* Jericho **e**, toward the sunrising. H6924
Dt 3:17 the salt sea, under Ashdoth-pisgah **e**. H4217
27 southward, and **e**, and behold *it* with H4217
4:49 And all the plain on this side Jordan **e**, H4217
Jos 11: 8 the valley of Mizpeh **e**; and they smote H4217
13: 8 beyond Jordan **e**, *even* as Moses the H4217
27 Chinnereth on the other side Jordan **e**. H4217
32 on the other side Jordan, by Jericho, **e**. H4217
16: 6 the border went about **e** unto H4217
19:12 And turned from Sarid **e** toward the H6924
20: 8 Jordan by Jericho **e**, they assigned Bezer H4217
1Sa 13: 5 in Michmash, **e** from Beth-aven. H6926
1Ki 7:39 of the house **e** over against the south. H6924
17: 3 Get thee hence, and turn thee **e**, and H6924
2Ki 10:33 From Jordan **e**, all the land of H4217+H8121
13:17 And he said, Open the window **e**. And H6924
1Ch 5: 9 And **e** he inhabited unto the entering in H4217
7:28 thereof, and **e** Naaran, and westward H4217
9:18 in the king's gate **e**: they *were* porters in H4217
26:14 And the lot **e** fell to Shelemiah. Then H4217
17 **E** *were* six Levites, northward four a H4217

Neh 12:37 of David, even unto the water gate **e**. H4217
Ezk 11: 1 which looketh **e**: and behold at the door H6921
40:10 of the gate **e** *were* three on this H1870+H6921
19 an hundred cubits **e** and northward. H6921
45: 7 and from the east side **e**: and the length H6921
47: 1 of the house **e**: for the forefront of the H6921
2 way that looketh **e**; and, behold, there H6921
3 his hand went forth **e**, he measured a H6921
48:18 *be* ten thousand **e**, and ten thousand H6921

EASY

Prv 14: 6 *is* **e** unto him that understandeth. H7043
Mt 11:30 For my yoke *is* **e**, and my burden is *G5543*
1Co 14: 9 the tongue words **e** to be understood, *G2154*
Jas 3:17 gentle, *and* **e** to be entreated, full *G2133*

EAT

Gen 2:16 tree of the garden thou mayest freely **e**: H398
17 evil, thou shalt not **e** of it: for in the day H398
3: 1 Ye shall not **e** of every tree of the garden? H398
2 **e** of the fruit of the trees of the garden: H398
3 said, Ye shall not **e** of it, neither shall ye H398
5 For God doth know that in the day ye **e** H398
6 thereof, and did **e**, and gave also unto her H398
6 unto her husband with her; and he did **e**. H398
11 thee that thou shouldest not **e**? H398
12 me, she gave me of the tree, and I did **e**. H398
13 The serpent beguiled me, and I did **e**. H398
14 dust shalt thou **e** all the days of thy life: H398
17 Thou shalt not **e** of it: cursed *is* the H398
17 shalt thou **e** *of* it all the days of thy life; H398
18 and thou shalt **e** the herb of the field; H398
19 In the sweat of thy face shalt thou **e** H398
22 of the tree of life, and **e**, and live for ever: H398
9: 4 *which is* the blood thereof, shall ye not **e**. H398
18: 8 by them under the tree, and they did **e**. H398
19: 3 bake unleavened bread, and they did **e**. H398
24:33 And there was set *meat* before him to **e**: H398
33 he said, I will not **e**, until I have told mine H398
54 And they did **e** and drink, he and the H398
25:28 And Isaac loved Esau, because he did **e** H6310
34 lentiles; and he did **e** and drink, and rose H398
26:30 them a feast, and they did **e** and drink. H398
27: 4 *it* to me, that I may **e**; that my soul may H398
7 meat, that I may **e**, and bless thee before H398
10 father, that he may **e**, and that he may H398
19 I pray thee, sit and **e** of my venison, that H398
25 to me, and I will **e** of my son's venison, H398
25 to him, and he did **e**: and he brought him H398
31 father arise, and **e** of his son's venison, H398
28:20 me bread to **e**, and raiment to put on, H398
31:46 and they did **e** there upon the heap. H398
54 his brethren to **e** bread: and they did H398
54 and they did **e** bread, and tarried all H398
32:32 Therefore the children of Israel **e** not *of* H398
37:25 And they sat down to **e** bread: and they H398
39: 6 bread which he did **e**. And Joseph was *a* H398
40:17 **e** them out of the basket upon my head. H398
19 the birds shall **e** thy flesh from off thee. H398
41: 4 kine did **e** up the seven well favoured H398
20 kine did **e** up the first seven fat kine: H398
43:25 heard that they should **e** bread there. H398
32 which did **e** with him, by themselves: H398
32 might not **e** bread with the Hebrews; H398
45:18 Egypt, and ye shall **e** the fat of the land. H398
47:22 Pharaoh, and did **e** their portion which H398
Ex 2:20 the man? call him, that he may **e** bread. H398
10: 5 earth: and they shall **e** the residue of that H398
5 the hail, and shall **e** every tree which H398
12 the land of Egypt, and **e** every herb of the H398
15 and they did **e** every herb of the land, H398
12: 7 of the houses, wherein they shall **e** it. H398
8 And they shall **e** the flesh in that night, H398
8 *and* with bitter *herbs* they shall **e** it. H398
9 **E** not of it raw, nor sodden at all with H398
11 And thus shall ye **e** it; *with* your loins H398
11 **e** it in haste: it *is* the LORD's passover. H398
15 Seven days shall ye **e** unleavened bread; H398
16 must **e**, that only may be done of you. H398
18 at even, ye shall **e** unleavened bread, H398
20 Ye shall **e** nothing leavened; in all your H398
20 habitations shall ye **e** unleavened bread. H398
43 There shall no stranger **e** thereof: H398
44 circumcised him, then shall he **e** thereof. H398
45 and an hired servant shall not **e** thereof. H398
48 no uncircumcised person shall **e** thereof. H398
13: 6 Seven days thou shalt **e** unleavened H398
16: 3 *and* when we did **e** bread to the full; for H398
8 the evening flesh to **e**, and in the morning H398

Ex 16:12 At even ye shall **e** flesh, and in the H398
15 which the LORD hath given you to **e**. H402
25 And Moses said, **E** that to day; for to day H398
35 And the children of Israel did **e** manna H398
35 inhabited; they did **e** manna, until they H398
18:12 elders of Israel, to **e** bread with Moses' H398
22:31 neither shall ye **e** *any* flesh *that is* torn H398
23:11 of thy people may **e**: and what they leave H398
11 of the field shall **e**. In like manner thou H398
15 bread: (thou shalt **e** unleavened bread H398
24:11 also they saw God, and did **e** and drink. H398
29:32 And Aaron and his sons shall **e** the flesh H398
33 And they shall **e** those things wherewith H398
33 not **e** *thereof*, because they *are* holy. H398
32: 6 to **e** and to drink, and rose up to play. H398
34:15 *one* call thee, and thou **e** of his sacrifice; H398
18 days thou shalt **e** unleavened bread, as H398
28 he did neither **e** bread, nor drink water. H398
Lev 3:17 that ye **e** neither fat nor blood. H398
6:16 Aaron and his sons **e**: with unleavened H398
16 of the congregation they shall **e** it. H398
18 of Aaron shall **e** of it. *It shall be* a statute H398
26 The priest that offereth it for sin shall **e** H398
29 All the males among the priests shall **e** H398
7: 6 Every male among the priests shall **e** H398
19 the flesh, all that be clean shall **e** thereof. H398
21 unclean *thing*, and **e** of the flesh of the H398
23 saying, Ye shall **e** no manner of fat, of H398
24 other use: but ye shall in no wise **e** of it. H398
26 Moreover ye shall **e** no manner of blood, H398
8:31 and there **e** it with the bread that H398
31 saying, Aaron and his sons shall **e** it. H398
10:12 made by fire, and **e** it without leaven H398
13 And ye shall **e** it in the holy place, H398
14 shoulder shall ye **e** in a clean place; thou, H398
11: 2 which ye shall **e** among all the beasts H398
3 cud, among the beasts, that shall ye **e**. H398
4 Nevertheless these shall ye not **e** of them H398
8 Of their flesh shall ye not **e**, and their H398
9 These shall ye **e** of all that *are* in the H398
9 seas, and in the rivers, them shall ye **e**. H398
11 you; ye shall not **e** of their flesh, but ye H398
21 Yet these may ye **e** of every flying H398
22 *Even* these of them ye may **e**; the locust H398
39 And if any beast, of which ye may **e**, die; H402
42 shall not **e**; for they *are* an abomination. H398
17:12 soul of you shall **e** blood, neither shall H398
12 that sojourneth among you **e** blood. H398
14 of Israel, Ye shall **e** the blood of no H398
19:25 And in the fifth year shall ye **e** of the H398
26 Ye shall not **e** *any thing* with the blood: H398
21:22 He shall **e** the bread of his God, *both* of H398
22: 4 issue; he shall not **e** of the holy things, H398
6 even, and shall not **e** of the holy things, H398
7 and shall afterward **e** of the holy things; H398
8 *beasts*, he shall not **e** to defile himself H398
10 There shall no stranger **e** *of* the holy H398
10 servant, shall not **e** *of* the holy thing. H398
11 his money, he shall **e** of it, and he that is H398
11 in his house: they shall **e** of his meat. H398
12 not **e** of an offering of the holy things. H398
13 youth, she shall **e** of her father's meat: H398
13 but there shall no stranger **e** thereof. H398
14 And if a man **e** *of* the holy thing H398
16 when they **e** their holy things: for H398
23: 6 seven days ye must **e** unleavened bread. H398
14 And ye shall **e** neither bread, nor H398
24: 9 and they shall **e** it in the holy place: for H398
25:12 **e** the increase thereof out of the field. H398
19 **e** your fill, and dwell therein in safety. H398
20 And if ye shall say, What shall we **e** the H398
22 And ye shall sow the eighth year, and **e** H398
22 fruits come in ye shall **e** *of* the old *store*. H398
26: 5 time: and ye shall **e** your bread to the H398
10 And ye shall **e** old store, and bring forth H398
16 seed in vain, for your enemies shall **e** it. H398
26 and ye shall **e**, and not be satisfied. H398
29 And ye shall **e** the flesh of your sons, and H398
29 and the flesh of your daughters shall ye **e**. H398
38 the land of your enemies shall **e** you up. H398
Nu 6: 3 of grapes, nor **e** moist grapes, or dried. H398
4 All the days of his separation shall he **e** H398
9:11 shall keep it, *and* **e** it with unleavened H398
11: 4 and said, Who shall give us flesh to **e**? H398
5 We remember the fish, which we did **e** in H398
13 me, saying, Give us flesh, that we may **e**. H398
18 and ye shall **e** flesh: for ye have wept H398
18 give us flesh to **e**? for *it was* well with us H398
18 LORD will give you flesh, and ye shall **e**. H398

Nu 11:19 Ye shall not **e** one day, nor two days, nor H398
21 flesh, that they may **e** a whole month. H398
15:19 Then it shall be, that, when ye **e** of the H398
18:10 In the most holy *place* shalt thou **e** it; H398
10 male shall **e** it: it shall be holy unto thee. H398
11 that is clean in thy house shall **e** of it. H398
13 that is clean in thine house shall **e** *of* it. H398
31 And ye shall **e** it in every place, ye and H398
23:24 lie down until he **e** *of* the prey, and drink H398
24: 8 an unicorn: he shall **e** up the nations his H398
25: 2 did **e**, and bowed down to their gods. H398
Dt 2: 6 that ye may **e**; and ye shall also buy H398
28 money, that I may **e**; and give me water H398
4:28 neither see, nor hear, nor **e**, nor smell. H398
8: 9 A land wherein thou shalt **e** bread H398
9: 9 I neither did **e** bread nor drink water: H398
18 I did neither **e** bread, nor drink water, H398
11:15 thy cattle, that thou mayest **e** and be full. H398
12: 7 And there ye shall **e** before the LORD H398
15 Notwithstanding thou mayest kill and **e** H398
15 and the clean may **e** thereof, as of the H398
16 Only ye shall not **e** the blood; ye shall H398
17 Thou mayest not **e** within thy gates the H398
18 But thou must **e** them before the LORD H398
20 shalt say, I will **e** flesh, because thy soul H398
20 thy soul longeth to **e** flesh; thou mayest H398
20 **e** flesh, whatsoever thy soul lusteth after. H398
21 and thou shalt **e** in thy gates whatsoever H398
22 so thou shalt **e** them: the unclean and H398
22 and the clean shall **e** *of* them alike. H398
23 Only be sure that thou **e** not the blood: H398
23 thou mayest not **e** the life with the flesh. H398
24 Thou shalt not **e** it; thou shalt pour it H398
25 Thou shalt not **e** it; that it may go well H398
27 thy God, and thou shalt **e** the flesh. H398
14: 3 Thou shalt not **e** any abominable thing. H398
4 These *are* the beasts which ye shall **e**: the H398
6 the cud among the beasts, that ye shall **e**. H398
7 Nevertheless these ye shall not **e** of them H398
8 unto you: ye shall not **e** of their flesh, nor H398
9 These ye shall **e** of all that *are* in the H398
9 all that have fins and scales shall ye **e**: H398
10 ye may not **e**; it *is* unclean unto you. H398
11 *Of* all clean birds ye shall **e**. H398
12 But these *are they* of which ye shall not **e**: H398
20 *But of* all clean fowls ye may **e**. H398
21 Ye shall not **e** *of* any thing that dieth of H398
21 gates, that he may **e** it; or thou mayest H398
23 And thou shalt **e** before the LORD thy H398
26 and thou shalt **e** there before the LORD H398
29 come, and shall **e** and be satisfied; that H398
15:20 Thou shalt **e** *it* before the LORD thy God H398
22 Thou shalt **e** it within thy gates: the H398
22 the clean *person shall* **e** *it* alike, as the H398
23 Only thou shalt not **e** the blood thereof; H398
16: 3 Thou shalt **e** no leavened bread with it; H398
3 days shalt thou **e** unleavened bread H398
7 And thou shalt roast and **e** *it* in the place H398
8 Six days thou shalt **e** unleavened bread: H398
18: 1 Israel: they shall **e** the offerings of the H398
8 They shall have like portions to **e**, beside H398
20: 6 in the battle, and another man **e** of it. H2490
14 and thou shalt **e** the spoil of thine H398
19 for thou mayest **e** of them, and thou H398
23:24 then thou mayest **e** grapes thy fill at H398
26:12 may **e** within thy gates, and be filled; H398
27: 7 and shalt **e** there, and rejoice before H398
28:31 and thou shalt not **e** thereof: thine ass H398
33 thou knowest not **e** up; and thou shalt be H398
39 *the grapes;* for the worms shall **e** them. H398
51 And he shall **e** the fruit of thy cattle, and H398
53 And thou shalt **e** the fruit of thine own H398
55 whom he shall **e**: because he hath H398
57 bear: for she shall **e** them for want of all H398
32:13 that he might **e** the increase of the fields; H398
38 Which did **e** the fat of their sacrifices, H398
Jos 5:11 And they did **e** of the old corn of the land H398
12 more; but they did **e** of the fruit of the H398
24:13 oliveyards which ye planted not do ye **e**. H398
Jdg 9:27 did **e** and drink, and cursed Abimelech. H398
13: 4 drink, and **e** not any unclean *thing*: H398
7 drink, neither **e** any unclean *thing*: for H398
14 She may not **e** of any *thing* that cometh H398
14 or strong drink, nor **e** any unclean *thing*: H398
16 me, I will not **e** of thy bread: and if thou H398
14: 9 gave them, and they did **e**: but he told not H398
19: 4 they did **e** and drink, and lodged there. H398
6 And they sat down, and did **e** and drink H398
8 afternoon, and they did **e** both of them. H398

Book	Ref	Context	Strong's
Jdg	19:21	washed their feet, and did **e** and drink.	H398
Ru	2:14	thou hither, and **e** of the bread, and dip	H398
	14	and she did **e**, and was sufficed, and left.	H398
1Sa	1: 7	her; therefore she wept, and did not **e**.	H398
	18	**e**, and her countenance was no more *sad*.	H398
	2:36	offices, that I may **e** a piece of bread.	H398
	9:13	to the high place to **e**: for the people will	H398
	13	for the people will not **e** until he come,	H398
	13	afterwards they **e** that be bidden. Now	H398
	19	place; for ye shall **e** with me to day, and	H398
	24	*it* before thee, *and* **e**: for unto this time	H398
	24	So Saul did **e** with Samuel that day.	H398
	14:32	the people did **e** *them* with the blood.	H398
	33	LORD, in that they **e** with the blood. And	H398
	34	*them* here, and **e**; and sin not against the	H398
	20:24	come, the king sat him down to **e** meat.	H398
	34	anger, and did **e** no meat the second	H398
	28:22	before thee; and **e**, that thou mayest have	H398
	23	But he refused, and said, I will not **e**. But	H398
	25	and they did **e**. Then they rose up, and	H398
	30:11	he did **e**; and they made him drink water;	H398
2Sa	3:35	to cause David to **e** meat while it was	H1262
	9: 7	shalt **e** bread at my table continually.	H398
	10	may have food to **e**: but Mephibosheth	H398
	10	master's son shall **e** bread alway at my	H398
	11	**e** at my table, as one of the king's sons.	H398
	13	for he did **e** continually at the king's	H398
	11:11	into mine house, to **e** and to drink, and	H398
	13	called him, he did **e** and drink before	H398
	12: 3	his children; it did **e** of his own meat,	H398
	17	not, neither did he **e** bread with them.	H1262
	20	they set bread before him, and he did **e**.	H398
	21	was dead, thou didst rise and **e** bread.	H398
	13: 5	that I may see *it*, and **e** *it* at her hand.	H398
	6	in my sight, that I may **e** at her hand.	H1262
	9	but he refused to **e**. And Amnon said,	H398
	10	that I may **e** of thine hand. And	H1262
	11	*them* unto him to **e**, he took hold of her,	H398
	16: 2	the young men to **e**; and the wine, that	H398
	17:29	*were* with him, to **e**: for they said, The	H398
	19:28	them that did **e** at thine own table. What	H398
	35	taste what I **e** or what I drink? can	H398
1Ki	1:25	and, behold, they **e** and drink before	H398
	2: 7	be of those that **e** at thy table: for so they	H398
	13: 8	I **e** bread nor drink water in this place:	H398
	9	the LORD, saying, **E** no bread, nor drink	H398
	15	him, Come home with me, and **e** bread.	H398
	16	thee: neither will I **e** bread nor drink	H398
	17	LORD, Thou shalt **e** no bread nor drink	H398
	18	house, that he may **e** bread and drink	H398
	19	So he went back with him, and did **e**	H398
	22	did say to thee, **E** no bread, and drink	H398
	14:11	city shall the dogs **e**; and him that dieth	H398
	11	of the air **e**: for the LORD hath spoken *it*.	H398
	16: 4	city shall the dogs **e**; and him that dieth	H398
	4	in the fields shall the fowls of the air **e**.	H398
	17:12	and my son, that we may **e** it, and die.	H398
	15	and he, and her house, did **e** *many* days.	H398
	18:19	four hundred, which **e** at Jezebel's table.	H398
	41	Ahab, Get thee up, **e** and drink; for *there*	H398
	42	So Ahab went up to **e** and to drink. And	H398
	19: 5	him, and said unto him, Arise *and* **e**.	H398
	6	**e** and drink, and laid him down again.	H398
	7	said, Arise *and* **e**; because the journey	H398
	8	And he arose, and did **e** and drink, and	H398
	21	and they did **e**. Then he arose, and went	H398
	21: 4	away his face, and would **e** no bread.	H398
	7	Israel? arise, *and* **e** bread, and let thine	H398
	23	dogs shall **e** Jezebel by the wall of Jezreel.	H398
	24	city the dogs shall **e**; and him that dieth	H398
	24	in the field shall the fowls of the air **e**.	H398
2Ki	4: 8	constrained him to **e** bread. And *so* it	H398
	8	by, he turned in thither to **e** bread.	H398
	40	So they poured out for the men to **e**. And	H398
	40	in the pot. And they could not **e** *thereof*.	H398
	41	may **e**. And there was no harm in the pot.	H398
	42	Give unto the people, that they may **e**.	H398
	43	that they may **e**: for thus saith the LORD,	H398
	43	They shall **e**, and shall leave *thereof*.	H398
	44	So he set *it* before them, and they did **e**,	H398
	6:22	may **e** and drink, and go to their master.	H398
	28	son, that we may **e** him to day, and we	H398
	28	to day, and we will **e** my son to morrow.	H398
	29	So we boiled my son, and did **e** him: and	H398
	29	we may **e** him: and she hath hid her son.	H398
	7: 2	*it* with thine eyes, but shalt not **e** thereof.	H398
	8	into one tent, and did **e** and drink, and	H398
	19	it with thine eyes, but shalt not **e** thereof.	H398
	9:10	And the dogs shall **e** Jezebel in the	H398
2Ki	9:34	And when he was come in, he did **e** and	H398
	36	of Jezreel shall dogs **e** the flesh of Jezebel:	H398
	18:27	the wall, that they may **e** their own dung,	H398
	31	to me, and *then* **e** ye every man of his	H398
	19:29	sign unto thee, Ye shall **e** this year such	H398
	29	plant vineyards, and **e** the fruits thereof.	H398
	23: 9	but they did **e** of the unleavened bread	H398
	25:29	and he did **e** bread continually before	H398
1Ch	29:22	And did **e** and drink before the LORD on	H398
2Ch	28:15	and gave them to **e** and to drink, and	H398
	30:18	yet did they **e** the passover otherwise	H398
	22	and they did **e** throughout the feast	H398
	31:10	had enough to **e**, and have left plenty:	H398
Ezr	2:63	that they should not **e** of the most holy	H398
	6:21	to seek the LORD God of Israel, did **e**,	H398
	9:12	ye may be strong, and **e** the good of the	H398
	10: 6	thither, he did **e** no bread, nor drink	H398
Neh	5: 2	corn *for them*, that we may **e**, and live.	H398
	7:65	that they should not **e** of the most holy	H398
	8:10	Then he said unto them, Go your way, **e**	H398
	12	And all the people went their way to **e**,	H398
	9:25	so they did **e**, and were filled, and	H398
	36	unto our fathers to **e** the fruit thereof	H398
Est	4:16	ye for me, and neither **e** nor drink three	H398
Job	1: 4	three sisters to **e** and to drink with them.	H398
	3:24	For my sighing cometh before I **e**, and	H3899
	31: 8	*Then* let me sow, and let another **e**; yea,	H398
	42:11	before, and did **e** bread with him in his	H398
Ps	14: 4	knowledge? who **e** up my people *as* they	H398
	4	**e** bread, and call not upon the LORD.	H398
	22:26	The meek shall **e** and be satisfied: they	H398
	29	All *they that be* fat upon earth shall **e**	H398
	27: 2	to **e** up my flesh, they stumbled and fell.	H398
	41: 9	I trusted, which did **e** of my bread, hath	H398
	50:13	Will I **e** the flesh of bulls, or drink the	H398
	53: 4	knowledge? who **e** up my people *as* they	H398
	4	**e** bread: they have not called upon God.	H398
	78:24	upon them to **e**, and had given them	H398
	25	Man did **e** angels' food: he sent them	H398
	29	So they did **e**, and were well filled: for he	H398
	102: 4	like grass; so that I forget to **e** my bread.	H398
	105:35	And did **e** up all the herbs in their land,	H398
	127: 2	to sit up late, to **e** the bread of sorrows:	H398
	128: 2	For thou shalt **e** the labour of thine	H398
	141: 4	and let me not **e** of their dainties.	H3898
Prv	1:31	Therefore shall they **e** of the fruit of their	H398
	4:17	For they **e** the bread of wickedness, and	H3898
	9: 5	Come, **e** of my bread, and drink of the	H3898
	13: 2	A man shall **e** good by the fruit of *his*	H398
	2	soul of the transgressors *shall* **e** violence.	H398
	18:21	they that love it shall **e** the fruit thereof.	H398
	23: 1	When thou sittest to **e** with a ruler,	H3898
	6	**E** thou not the bread of *him that hath*	H3898
	7	his heart, so *is* he: **E** and drink, saith he	H398
	24:13	My son, **e** thou honey, because *it is* good;	H398
	25:16	Hast thou found honey? **e** so much as is	H398
	21	give him bread to **e**; and if he be thirsty,	H398
	27	*It is* not good to **e** much honey: so *for*	H398
	27:18	Whoso keepeth the fig tree shall **e** the	H398
	30:17	it out, and the young eagles shall **e** it.	H398
Ecc	2:24	that he should **e** and drink, and *that*	H398
	25	For who can **e**, or who else can hasten	H398
	3:13	And also that every man should **e** and	H398
	5:11	they are increased that **e** them: and what	H398
	12	*is* sweet, whether he **e** little or much: but	H398
	18	comely *for one* to **e** and to drink, and to	H398
	19	given him power to **e** thereof, and to	H398
	6: 2	giveth him not power to **e** thereof, but a	H398
	8:15	the sun, than to **e**, and to drink, and to	H398
	9: 7	Go thy way, **e** thy bread with joy, and	H398
	10:16	child, and thy princes **e** in the morning!	H398
	17	and thy princes **e** in due season, for	H398
Song	4:16	his garden, and **e** his pleasant fruits.	H398
	5: 1	wine with my milk: **e**, O friends; drink,	H398
Isa	1:19	If ye be willing and obedient, ye shall **e**	H398
	3:10	for they shall **e** the fruit of their doings.	H398
	4: 1	saying, We will **e** our own bread, and	H398
	5:17	places of the fat ones shall strangers **e**.	H398
	7:15	Butter and honey shall he **e**, that he may	H398
	22	shall give he shall **e** butter: for butter	H398
	22	shall every one **e** that is left in the land.	H398
	9:20	and he shall **e** on the left hand, and	H398
	20	**e** every man the flesh of his own arm:	H398
	11: 7	and the lion shall **e** straw like the ox.	H398
	21: 5	in the watchtower, **e**, drink: arise, ye	H398
	22:13	**e** and drink; for to morrow we shall die.	H398
	23:18	**e** sufficiently, and for durable clothing.	H398
	30:24	ear the ground shall **e** clean provender,	H398
	36:12	the wall, that they may **e** their own dung,	H398
Isa	36:16	out to me: and **e** ye every one of his vine,	H398
	37:30	unto thee, Ye shall **e** *this* year such as	H398
	30	plant vineyards, and **e** the fruit thereof.	H398
	50: 9	as a garment; the moth shall **e** them up.	H398
	51: 8	For the moth shall **e** them up like a	H398
	8	and the worm shall **e** them like wool: but	H398
	55: 1	come ye, buy, and **e**; yea, come, buy wine	H398
	2	unto me, and **e** ye *that which is* good,	H398
	61: 6	of our God: ye shall **e** the riches of the	H398
	62: 9	But they that have gathered it shall **e** it,	H398
	65: 4	monuments, which **e** swine's flesh, and	H398
	13	my servants shall **e**, but ye shall be	H398
	21	plant vineyards, and **e** the fruit of them.	H398
	22	plant, and another **e**: for as the days of a	H398
	25	and the lion shall **e** straw like the	H398
Jer	2: 7	country, to **e** the fruit thereof and	H398
	5:17	And they shall **e** up thine harvest, and	H398
	17	daughters should **e**: they shall eat up thy	H398
	17	eat: they shall **e** up thy flocks and thine	H398
	17	herds: they shall **e** up thy vines and thy	H398
	7:21	unto your sacrifices, and **e** flesh.	H398
	15:16	Thy words were found, and I did **e** them;	H398
	16: 8	to sit with them to **e** and to drink.	H398
	19: 9	And I will cause them to **e** the flesh of	H398
	9	and they shall **e** every one the flesh of	H398
	22:15	did not thy father **e** and drink, and do	H398
	22	The wind shall **e** up all thy pastors, and	H7462
	29: 5	plant gardens, and **e** the fruit of them;	H398
	28	plant gardens, and **e** the fruit of them.	H398
	31: 5	and shall **e** *them* as common things.	
	41: 1	they did **e** bread together in Mizpah.	H398
	52:33	he did continually **e** bread before him all	H398
Lam	2:20	this. Shall the women **e** their fruit, *and*	H398
Ezk	2: 8	open thy mouth, and **e** that I give thee.	H398
	3: 1	me, Son of man, **e** that thou findest; eat	H398
	1	eat that thou findest; **e** this roll, and go	H398
	2	mouth, and he caused me to **e** that roll.	H398
	3	cause thy belly to **e**, and fill thy bowels	H398
	3	thee. Then did I **e** *it*; and it was in my	H398
	4: 9	and ninety days shalt thou **e** thereof.	H398
	10	And thy meat which thou shalt **e** *shall be*	H398
	10	a day: from time to time shalt thou **e** it.	H398
	12	And thou shalt **e** it *as* barley cakes, and	H398
	13	children of Israel **e** their defiled bread	H398
	16	and they shall **e** bread by weight, and	H398
	5:10	Therefore the fathers shall **e** the sons in	H398
	10	and the sons shall **e** their fathers; and I	H398
	12:18	Son of man, **e** thy bread with quaking,	H398
	19	of Israel; They shall **e** their bread with	H398
	16:13	work; thou didst **e** fine flour, and honey,	H398
	22: 9	and in thee they **e** upon the mountains:	H398
	24:17	not *thy* lips, and **e** not the bread of men.	H398
	22	cover *your* lips, nor **e** the bread of men.	H398
	25: 4	**e** thy fruit, and they shall drink thy milk.	H398
	33:25	the Lord GOD; Ye **e** with the blood, and	H398
	34: 3	Ye **e** the fat, and ye clothe you with the	H398
	19	And *as for* my flock, they **e** that which	H7462
	39:17	that ye may **e** flesh, and drink blood.	H398
	18	Ye shall **e** the flesh of the mighty, and	H398
	19	And ye shall **e** fat till ye be full, and	H398
	42:13	the LORD shall **e** the most holy things:	H398
	44: 3	he shall sit in it to **e** bread before the	H398
	29	They shall **e** the meat offering, and the	H398
	31	The priests shall not **e** of any thing that	H398
Dan	1:12	give us pulse to **e**, and water to drink.	H398
	13	of the children that **e** of the portion of	H398
	15	did **e** the portion of the king's meat.	H398
	4:25	shall make thee to **e** grass as oxen, and	H2939
	32	shall make thee to **e** grass as oxen, and	H2939
	33	from men, and did **e** grass as oxen, and	H399
Hos	2:12	and the beasts of the field shall **e** them.	H398
	4: 8	They **e** up the sin of my people, and they	H398
	10	For they shall **e**, and not have enough:	H398
	8:13	mine offerings, and **e** *it*; *but* the LORD	H398
	9: 3	they shall **e** unclean *things* in Assyria.	H398
	4	of mourners; all that **e** thereof shall be	H398
Joel	2:26	And ye shall **e** in plenty, and be satisfied,	H398
Am	6: 4	their couches, and **e** the lambs out of the	H398
	7: 4	the great deep, and did **e** up a part.	H398
	12	and there **e** bread, and prophesy there:	H398
	9:14	make gardens, and **e** the fruit of them.	H398
Oba	7	thee; *they that* **e** thy bread have laid a	
Mic	3: 3	Who also **e** the flesh of my people, and	H398
	6:14	Thou shalt **e**, but not be satisfied; and thy	H398
	7: 1	to **e**: my soul desired the firstripe fruit.	H398
Nah	3:15	cut thee off, it shall **e** thee up like the	H398
Hab	1: 8	shall fly as the eagle *that* hasteth to **e**.	H398
Hag	1: 6	and bring in little; ye **e**, but ye have not	H398
Zec	7: 6	And when ye did **e**, and when ye did	H398

Zec 7: 6 drink, did not ye **e** *for yourselves*, and H398
11: 9 the rest **e** every one the flesh of another. H398
16 still: but he shall **e** the flesh of the fat, H398
Mt 6:25 life, what ye shall **e**, or what ye shall G5315
31 What shall we **e**? or, What shall we G5315
12: 1 to pluck the ears of corn, and to **e**. G2068
4 of God, and did **e** the shewbread, which G5315
4 not lawful for him to **e**, neither for them G5315
14:16 They need not depart; give ye them to **e**. G5315
20 And they did all **e**, and were filled: and G5315
15: 2 not their hands when they **e** bread. G2068
20 a man: but to **e** with unwashen hands G5315
27 Lord: yet the dogs **e** of the crumbs G2068
32 have nothing to **e**: and I will not send G5315
37 And they did all **e**, and were filled: and G5315
38 And they that did **e** were four thousand G2068
24:49 and to **e** and drink with the drunken; G2068
26:17 we prepare for thee to **e** the passover? G5315
21 And as they did **e**, he said, Verily I say G2068
26 and said, Take, **e**; this is my body. G5315
Mk 1: 6 and he did **e** locusts and wild honey; G2068
2:16 Pharisees saw him **e** with publicans G2068
26 priest, and did **e** the shewbread, which G5315
26 is not lawful to **e** but for the priests, G5315
3:20 that they could not so much as **e** bread. G5315
5:43 that something should be given her to **e**. G5315
6:31 and they had no leisure so much as to **e**. G5315
36 bread: for they have nothing to **e**. G5315
37 Give ye them to **e**. And they say unto G5315
37 of bread, and give them to **e**? G5315
42 And they did all **e**, and were filled. G5315
44 And they that did **e** of the loaves were G5315
7: 2 of his disciples **e** bread with defiled, G2068
3 wash *their* hands oft, **e** not, holding the G2068
4 they wash, they **e** not. And many other G2068
5 but **e** bread with unwashen hands? G2068
28 the table **e** of the children's crumbs. G2068
8: 1 having nothing to **e**, Jesus called his G5315
2 me three days, and have nothing to **e**: G5315
8 So they did **e**, and were filled: and they G5315
11:14 unto it, No man **e** fruit of thee hereafter G5315
14:12 that thou mayest **e** the passover? G5315
14 shall **e** the passover with my disciples? G5315
18 And as they sat and did **e**, Jesus said, G2068
22 And as they did **e**, Jesus took bread, and G2068
22 and said, Take, **e**: this is my body. G5315
Lk 4: 2 those days he did **e** nothing: and when G5315
5:30 saying, Why do ye **e** and drink with G2068
33 of the Pharisees; but thine **e** and drink? G2068
6: 1 and did **e**, rubbing *them* in *their* hands. G2068
4 and did take and **e** the shewbread, and G5315
4 not lawful to **e** but for the priests alone? G5315
7:36 him that he would **e** with him. And he G5315
9:13 Give ye them to **e**. And they said, We G5315
17 And they did **e**, and were all filled: and G5315
10: 8 you, **e** such things as are set before you: G2068
12:19 take thine ease, **e**, drink, *and* be merry. G5315
22 your life, what ye shall **e**; neither for the G5315
29 And seek not ye what ye shall **e**, or what G5315
45 and to **e** and drink, and to be drunken; G2068
14: 1 the chief Pharisees to **e** bread on the G5315
15 shall **e** bread in the kingdom of God. G5315
15:16 swine did **e**: and no man gave unto him. G2068
23 and kill *it*; and let us **e**, and be merry: G5315
17: 8 and afterward thou shalt **e** and drink? G5315
27 They did **e**, they drank, they married G2068
28 days of Lot; they did **e**, they drank, they G2068
22: 8 prepare us the passover, that we may **e**. G5315
11 shall **e** the passover with my disciples? G5315
15 **e** this passover with you before I suffer: G5315
16 I will not any more **e** thereof, until it be G5315
30 That ye may **e** and drink at my table in G2068
24:43 And he took *it*, and did **e** before them. G5315
Jn 4:31 disciples prayed him, saying, Master, **e**. G5315
32 But he said unto them, I have meat to **e** G5315
33 Hath any man brought him *ought* to **e**? G5315
6: 5 shall we buy bread, that these may **e**? G5315
23 where they did **e** bread, after that the G5315
26 ye did **e** of the loaves, and were filled. G5315
31 Our fathers did **e** manna in the desert; G5315
31 He gave them bread from heaven to **e**. G5315
49 Your fathers did **e** manna in the G5315
50 that a man may **e** thereof, and not die. G5315
51 if any man **e** of this bread, he shall G5315
52 How can this man give us *his* flesh to **e**? G5315
53 you, Except ye **e** the flesh of the Son G5315
58 as your fathers did **e** manna, and are G5315
18:28 but that they might **e** the passover. G5315
Act 2:46 house to house, did **e** their meat with G3335
Act 9: 9 sight, and neither did **e** nor drink. G5315
10:13 a voice to him, Rise, Peter; kill, and **e**. G5315
41 to us, who did **e** and drink with him G4906
11: 3 uncircumcised, and didst **e** with them. G4906
7 saying unto me, Arise, Peter; slay and **e**. G5315
23:12 **e** nor drink till they had killed Paul. G5315
14 will **e** nothing until we have slain Paul. G1089
21 they will neither **e** nor drink till they G5315
27:35 when he had broken *it*, he began to **e**. G2068
Ro 14: 2 For one believeth that he may **e** all G5315
21 *It is* good neither to **e** flesh, nor to G5315
23 And he that doubteth is damned if he **e**, G5315
1Co 5:11 with such an one no not to **e**. G4906
8: 7 the idol unto this hour **e** *it* as a thing G2068
8 for neither, if we **e**, are we the better; G5315
8 neither, if we **e** not, are we the worse. G5315
10 be emboldened to **e** those things which G2068
13 to offend, I will **e** no flesh while the G5315
9: 4 Have we not power to **e** and to drink? G5315
10: 3 And did all **e** the same spiritual meat; G5315
7 to **e** and drink, and rose up to play. G5315
18 are not they which **e** of the sacrifices G2068
25 in the shambles, *that* **e**, asking no G2068
27 is set before you, **e**, asking no question G2068
28 unto idols, **e** not for his sake that G2068
31 Whether therefore ye **e**, or drink, or G2068
11:20 place, *this* is not to **e** the Lord's supper. G5315
22 What? have ye not houses to **e** and to G2068
24 *it*, and said, Take, **e**: this is my body, G5315
26 For as often as ye **e** this bread, and G2068
27 Wherefore whosoever shall **e** this G2068
28 **e** of *that* bread, and drink of *that* cup. G2068
33 together to **e**, tarry one for another. G5315
34 And if any man hunger, let him **e** at G2068
15:32 us **e** and drink; for to morrow we die. G5315
Gal 2:12 James, he did **e** with the Gentiles: but G4906
2Th 3: 8 Neither did we **e** any man's bread for G5315
10 would not work, neither should he **e**. G2068
12 they work, and **e** their own bread. G2068
2Ti 2:17 And their word will **e** as doth a canker: G2192
Heb 13:10 right to **e** which serve the tabernacle. G5315
Jas 5: 3 you, and shall **e** your flesh as it were G5315
Rev 2: 7 will I give to **e** of the tree of life, which G5315
14 of Israel, to **e** things sacrificed unto G5315
17 will I give to **e** of the hidden manna, G5315
20 and to **e** things sacrificed unto idols. G5315
10: 9 me, Take *it*, and **e** it up; and it shall G2719
17:16 shall **e** her flesh, and burn her with fire. G5315
19:18 That ye may **e** the flesh of kings, and G5315

EATEN

Gen 3:11 naked? Hast thou **e** of the tree, whereof I H398
17 thy wife, and hast **e** of the tree, of which H398
6:21 of all food that is **e**, and thou shalt gather H398
14:24 young men have **e**, and the portion of the H398
27:33 *it* me, and I have **e** of all before thou H398
31:38 and the rams of thy flock have I not **e**. H398
41:21 And when they had **e** them up, H935+H7130
21 that they had **e** them; but they H935+H7130
43: 2 And it came to pass, when they had **e** up H398
Ex 12:46 In one house shall it be **e**; thou shalt not H398
13: 3 *place:* there shall no leavened bread be **e**. H398
7 Unleavened bread shall be **e** seven days; H398
21:28 be **e**; but the owner of the ox *shall be* quit. H398
22: 5 or vineyard to be **e**, and shall put in his H1197
29:34 fire: it shall not be **e**, because it *is* holy. H398
Lev 6:16 bread shall it be **e** in the holy place; in H398
23 shall be wholly burnt: it shall not be **e**. H398
26 holy place shall it be **e**, in the court of the H398
30 shall be **e**: it shall be burnt in the fire. H398
7: 6 be **e** in the holy place: it *is* most holy. H398
15 shall be **e** the same day that it H398
16 offering, it shall be **e** the same day that H398
16 also the remainder of it shall be **e**: H398
18 peace offerings be **e** at all on the third H398
19 *thing* shall not be **e**; it shall be burnt with H398
10:17 Wherefore have ye not **e** the sin offering H398
18 **e** it in the holy *place*, as I commanded. H398
19 me: and *if* I had **e** the sin offering to day, H398
11:13 fowls; they shall not be **e**, they *are* an H398
34 Of all meat which may be **e**, *that* on H398
41 *shall be* an abomination; it shall not be **e**. H398
47 **e** and the beast that may not be eaten. H398
47 be eaten and the beast that may not be **e**. H398
17:13 or fowl that may be **e**; he shall even pour H398
19: 6 It shall be **e** the same day ye offer it, and H398
7 And if it be **e** at all on the third day, it *is* H398
23 unto you: it shall not be **e** of. H398
22:30 On the same day it shall be **e** up; ye shall H398
Nu 28:17 seven days shall unleavened bread be **e**. H398
Dt 6:11 not; when thou shalt have **e** and be full; H398
8:10 When thou hast **e** and art full, then thou H398
12 Lest *when* thou hast **e** and art full, and H398
12:22 Even as the roebuck and the hart is **e**, so H398
14:19 *is* unclean unto you: they shall not be **e**. H398
20: 6 and hath not *yet* **e** of it? let him *also* go H2490
26:14 I have not **e** thereof in my mourning, H398
29: 6 Ye have not **e** bread, neither have ye H398
31:20 honey; and they shall have **e** and filled H398
Jos 5:12 after they had **e** of the old corn of the H398
Ru 3: 7 And when Boaz had **e** and drunk, and H398
1Sa 1: 9 So Hannah rose up after they had **e** in H398
14:30 the people had **e** freely to day of the spoil H398
28:20 **e** no bread all the day, nor all the night. H398
30:12 and when he had **e**, his spirit came again H398
12 to him: for he had **e** no bread, nor drunk H398
2Sa 19:42 this matter? have we **e** at all of the king's H398
1Ki 13:22 But camest back, and hast **e** bread and H398
23 And it came to pass, after he had **e** H398
28 had not **e** the carcase, nor torn the ass. H398
2Ki 6:23 and when they had **e** and drunk, he sent H398
Neh 5:14 have not **e** the bread of the governor. H398
Job 6: 6 Can that which is unsavoury be **e** H398
13:28 consumeth, as a garment that is moth **e**. H398
31:17 Or have **e** my morsel myself alone, and H398
17 and the fatherless hath not **e** thereof; H398
39 If I have **e** the fruits thereof without H398
Ps 69: 9 For the zeal of thine house hath **e** me up; H398
102: 9 For I have **e** ashes like bread, and H398
Prv 9:17 Stolen waters are sweet, and bread ***e*** in
23: 8 The morsel *which* thou hast **e** shalt thou H398
Song 5: 1 my spice; I have **e** my honeycomb with H398
Isa 3:14 thereof: for ye have **e** up the vineyard; H398
5: 5 and it shall be **e** up; *and* break down H398
6:13 and shall be **e**: as a teil tree, and as H1197
44:19 roasted flesh, and **e** *it*: and shall I make H398
Jer 10:25 for they have **e** up Jacob, and devoured H398
24: 2 which could not be **e**, they were so bad. H398
3 evil, that cannot be **e**, they are so evil. H398
8 And as the evil figs, which cannot be **e**, H398
29:17 vile figs, that cannot be **e**, they are so evil. H398
31:29 The fathers have **e** a sour grape, and the H398
Ezk 4:14 till now have I not **e** of that which dieth H398
18: 2 The fathers have **e** sour grapes, and the H398
6 *And* hath not **e** upon the mountains, H398
11 but even hath **e** upon the mountains, H398
15 *That* hath not **e** upon the mountains, H398
34:18 unto you to have **e** up the good pasture, H7462
45:21 seven days; unleavened bread shall be **e**. H398
Hos 10:13 iniquity; ye have **e** the fruit of lies: H398
Joel 1: 4 left hath the locust **e**; and that which the H398
4 the cankerworm **e**; and that which the H398
4 hath left hath the caterpiller **e**. H398
2:25 the locust hath **e**, the cankerworm, and H398
Mt 14:21 And they that had **e** were about five G2068
Mk 8: 9 And they that had **e** were about four G5315
Lk 13:26 Then shall ye begin to say, We have **e** G5315
17: 8 me, till I have **e** and drunken; and G5315
Jn 2:17 The zeal of thine house hath **e** me up. G2719
6:13 over and above unto them that had **e**. G977
Act 10:10 and would have **e**: but while they made G1089
14 **e** any thing that is common or unclean. G5315
12:23 was **e** of worms, and gave up the ghost. G4662
20:11 broken bread, and **e**, and talked a long G1089
27:38 And when they had **e** enough, they G2880
Rev 10:10 soon as I had **e** it, my belly was bitter. G5315

EATER

Jdg 14:14 And he said unto them, Out of the **e** H398
Isa 55:10 seed to the sower, and bread to the **e**: H398
Nah 3:12 shall even fall into the mouth of the **e**. H398

EATERS

Prv 23:20 winebibbers; among riotous **e** of flesh: H2151

EATEST

Gen 2:17 that thou **e** thereof thou shalt surely die. H398
1Sa 1: 8 thou? and why **e** thou not? and why is H398
1Ki 21: 5 is thy spirit so sad, that thou **e** no bread? H398

EATETH

Ex 12:15 for whosoever **e** leavened bread from H398
19 for whosoever **e** that which is leavened, H398
Lev 7:18 soul that **e** of it shall bear his iniquity. H398
20 But the soul that **e** *of* the flesh of the H398
25 For whosoever **e** the fat of the beast, of H398
25 that **e** *it* shall be cut off from his people. H398
27 Whatsoever soul *it be* that **e** any manner H398

Lev 11:40 And he that **e** of the carcase of it shall H398
14:47 **e** in the house shall wash his clothes. H398
17:10 among you, that **e** any manner of blood; H398
10 that soul that **e** blood, and will cut him H398
14 thereof: whosoever **e** it shall be cut off. H398
15 And every soul that **e** that which died *of* H398
19: 8 Therefore *every one* that **e** it shall bear H398
Nu 13:32 it, *is* a land that **e** up the inhabitants H398
1Sa 14:24 Cursed *be* the man that **e** *any* food until H398
28 *be* the man that **e** *any* food this day. And H398
Job 5: 5 Whose harvest the hungry **e** up, and H398
21:25 of his soul, and never **e** with pleasure. H398
40:15 I made with thee; he **e** grass as an ox. H398
Ps 106:20 into the similitude of an ox that **e** grass. H398
Prv 13:25 The righteous **e** to the satisfying of his H398
30:20 woman; she **e**, and wipeth her mouth, H398
31:27 and **e** not the bread of idleness. H398
Ecc 4: 5 his hands together, and **e** his own flesh. H398
5:17 All his days also he **e** in darkness, and *he* H398
6: 2 but a stranger **e** it: this *is* vanity, and H398
Isa 28: 4 while it is yet in his hand he **e** it up. H1104
29: 8 and, behold, he **e**; but he awaketh, and H398
44:16 part thereof he **e** flesh; he roasteth roast, H398
59: 5 web: he that **e** of their eggs dieth, and H398
Jer 31:30 every man that **e** the sour grape, his H398
Mt 9:11 his disciples, Why **e** your Master with G2068
Mk 2:16 How is it that he **e** and drinketh with G2068
14:18 you which **e** with me shall betray me. G2068
Lk 15: 2 receiveth sinners, and **e** with them. G4906
Jn 6:54 Whoso **e** my flesh, and drinketh my G5176
56 He that **e** my flesh, and drinketh my G5176
57 he that **e** me, even he shall live by me. G5176
58 that **e** of this bread shall live for ever. G5176
13:18 fulfilled, He that **e** bread with me hath G5176
Ro 14: 2 things: another, who is weak, **e** herbs. G2068
3 Let not him that **e** despise him that G2068
3 despise him that **e** not; and let not him G2068
3 let not him which **e** not judge him that G2068
3 him that **e**: for God hath received him. G2068
6 regard *it*. He that **e**, eateth to the Lord, G2068
6 *it*. He that eateth, **e** to the Lord, for he G2068
6 and he that **e** not, to the Lord he eateth G2068
6 Lord he **e** not, and giveth God thanks. G2068
20 *is* evil for that man who **e** with offence. G2068
23 if he eat, because *he* **e** not of faith: for G2068
1Co 9: 7 a vineyard, and **e** not of the fruit G2068
7 flock, and **e** not of the milk of the flock? G2068
11:29 For he that **e** and drinketh unworthily, G2068
29 unworthily, **e** and drinketh damnation G2068

EATING
Ex 12: 4 his **e** shall make your count for the lamb. H400
16:16 according to his **e**, an omer for every H400
18 gathered every man according to his **e**. H400
21 **e**: and when the sun waxed hot, it melted. H400
Jdg 14: 9 and went on **e**, and came to his father H398
Ru 3: 3 until he shall have done **e** and drinking. H398
1Sa 14:34 the LORD in **e** with the blood. And H398
30:16 upon all the earth, **e** and drinking, and H398
1Ki 1:41 made an end of **e**. And when Joab heard H398
4:20 **e** and drinking, and making merry. H398
2Ki 4:40 pass, as they were **e** of the pottage, that H398
1Ch 12:39 David three days, **e** and drinking: for H398
Job 1:13 his daughters *were* **e** and drinking wine H398
18 thy daughters *were* **e** and drinking wine H398
20:23 and shall rain *it* upon him while he is **e**. H3894
Isa 22:13 and killing sheep, **e** flesh, and drinking H398
66:17 *tree* in the midst, **e** swine's flesh, and the H398
Am 7: 2 made an end of **e** the grass of the land, H398
Mt 11:18 For John came neither **e** nor drinking, G2068
19 The Son of man came **e** and drinking, G2068
24:38 the flood they were **e** and drinking, G5176
26:26 And as they were **e**, Jesus took bread, G2068
Lk 7:33 For John the Baptist came neither **e** G2068
34 The Son of man is come **e** and G2068
10: 7 And in the same house remain, **e** and G2068
1Co 8: 4 As concerning therefore the **e** of those G1035
11:21 For in **e** every one taketh before *other* G5315

EBAL
Gen 36:23 Manahath, and E, Shepho, and Onam. H5858
Dt 11:29 Gerizim, and the curse upon mount **E**. H5858
27: 4 this day, in mount **E**, and thou shalt H5858
13 And these shall stand upon mount **E** to H5858
Jos 8:30 the LORD God of Israel in mount **E**, H5858
33 against mount **E**; as Moses the servant H5858
1Ch 1:22 And **E**, and Abimael, and Sheba, H5858
40 Manahath, and **E**, Shephi, and Onam. H5858

EBED
Jdg 9:26 And Gaal the son of **E** came with his H5651
28 And Gaal the son of **E** said, Who *is* H5651
30 the son of **E**, his anger was kindled. H5651
31 Gaal the son of **E** and his brethren be H5651
35 And Gaal the son of **E** went out, and H5651
Ezr 8: 6 Of the sons also of Adin; **E** the son of H5651

EBED-MELECH
Jer 38: 7 Now when **E** the Ethiopian, one of the H5663
8 **E** went forth out of the king's house, H5663
10 Then the king commanded **E** the H5663
11 So **E** took the men with him, and went H5663
12 And **E** the Ethiopian said unto H5663
39:16 Go and speak to **E** the Ethiopian, H5663

EBEN-EZER
1Sa 4: 1 **E**: and the Philistines pitched in Aphek. H72
5: 1 and brought it from **E** unto Ashdod. H72
7:12 the name of it **E**, saying, Hitherto hath H72

EBER
Gen 10:21 of all the children of **E**, the brother of H5677
24 begat Salah; and Salah begat **E**. H5677
25 And unto **E** were born two sons: the H5677
11:14 Salah lived thirty years, and begat **E**: H5677
15 And Salah lived after he begat **E** four H5677
16 And **E** lived four and thirty years, and H5677
17 And **E** lived after he begat Peleg four H5677
Nu 24:24 **E**, and he also shall perish for ever. H5677
1Ch 1:18 begat Shelah, and Shelah begat **E**. H5677
19 And unto **E** were born two sons: the H5677
25 **E**, Peleg, Reu, H5677
8:12 The sons of Elpaal; **E**, and Misham, and H5677
Neh 12:20 Of Sallai, Kallai; of Amok, **E**; H5677

EBIASAPH
1Ch 6:23 Elkanah his son, and **E** his son, and H43
37 of Assir, the son of **E**, the son of Korah, H43
9:19 of Kore, the son of **E**, the son of Korah, H43

EBONY
Ezk 27:15 thee *for* a present horns of ivory and **e**. H1894

EBRONAH
Nu 33:34 from Jotbathah, and encamped at **E**. H5684
35 And they departed from **E**, and H5684

ED
Jos 22:34 called the altar *E*: for it *shall be* a witness

EDAR
Gen 35:21 spread his tent beyond the tower of **E**. H5740

EDEN
Gen 2: 8 eastward in **E**; and there he put the H5731
10 And a river went out of **E** to water the H5731
15 garden of **E** to dress it and to keep it. H5731
3:23 the garden of **E**, to till the ground from H5731
24 of the garden of **E** Cherubims, and a H5731
4:16 in the land of Nod, on the east of **E**. H5731
2Ki 19:12 children of **E** which *were* in Thelasar? H5729
2Ch 29:12 son of Zimmah, and **E** the son of Joah: H5731
31:15 And next him *were* **E**, and Miniamin, H5731
Isa 37:12 children of **E** which *were* in Telassar? H5729
51: 3 wilderness like **E**, and her desert like H5731
Ezk 27:23 Haran, and Canneh, and **E**, the H5729
28:13 Thou hast been in **E** the garden of God; H5731
31: 9 that all the trees of **E**, that *were* in the H5731
16 pit: and all the trees of **E**, the choice and H5731
18 the trees of **E**? yet shalt thou be brought H5731
18 with the trees of **E** unto the nether H5731
36:35 like the garden of **E**; and the waste and H5731
Joel 2: 3 *is* as the garden of **E** before them, and H5731
Am 1: 5 from the house of **E**: and the people of H5731

EDER
Jos 15:21 were Kabzeel, and **E**, and Jagur, H5740
1Ch 23:23 The sons of Mushi; Mahli, and **E**, and H5740
24:30 The sons also of Mushi; Mahli, and **E**, H5740

EDGE
Gen 34:26 his son with the **e** of the sword, and H6310
Ex 13:20 in Etham, in the **e** of the wilderness. H7097
17:13 and his people with the **e** of the sword. H6310
26: 4 of blue upon the **e** of the one curtain H8193
4 in the uttermost **e** of *another* curtain, H8193
5 thou make in the **e** of the curtain that *is* H7097
10 fifty loops on the **e** of the one curtain H8193
Ex 26:10 fifty loops in the **e** of the curtain which H8193
36:11 And he made loops of blue on the **e** of H8193
12 made he in the **e** of the curtain which H7097
17 the uttermost **e** of the curtain in the H8193
17 made he upon the **e** of the curtain H8193
Nu 21:24 And Israel smote him with the **e** of the H6310
33: 6 which *is* in the **e** of the wilderness. H7097
37 Hor, in the **e** of the land of Edom. H7097
Dt 13:15 of that city with the **e** of the sword, H6310
15 cattle thereof, with the **e** of the sword. H6310
20:13 male thereof with the **e** of the sword: H6310
Jos 6:21 sheep, and ass, with the **e** of the sword. H6310
8:24 all fallen on the **e** of the sword, until H6310
24 and smote it with the **e** of the sword. H6310
10:28 smote it with the **e** of the sword, and H6310
30 smote it with the **e** of the sword, and all H6310
32 smote it with the **e** of the sword, and all H6310
35 smote it with the **e** of the sword, and all H6310
37 smote it with the **e** of the sword, and H6310
39 them with the **e** of the sword, and H6310
11:11 therein with the **e** of the sword, utterly H6310
12 them with the **e** of the sword, *and* he H6310
14 smote with the **e** of the sword, until H6310
13:27 *even* unto the **e** of the sea of Chinnereth H7097
19:47 smote it with the **e** of the sword, and H6310
Jdg 1: 8 **e** of the sword, and set the city on fire. H6310
25 the city with the **e** of the sword; but H6310
4:15 *his* host, with the **e** of the sword before H6310
16 fell upon the **e** of the sword; *and* there H6310
18:27 them with the **e** of the sword, and H6310
20:37 all the city with the **e** of the sword. H6310
48 them with the **e** of the sword, as well H6310
21:10 with the **e** of the sword, with the H6310
1Sa 15: 8 all the people with the **e** of the sword. H6310
22:19 smote he with the **e** of the sword, both H6310
19 and sheep, with the **e** of the sword. H6310
2Sa 15:14 smite the city with the **e** of the sword. H6310
2Ki 10:25 them with the **e** of the sword; and the H6310
Job 1:15 servants with the **e** of the sword; and I H6310
17 servants with the **e** of the sword; and I H6310
Ps 89:43 Thou hast also turned the **e** of his H6697
Ecc 10:10 he do not whet the **e**, then must he put H6440
Jer 21: 7 them with the **e** of the sword; he shall H6310
31:29 and the children's teeth are set on **e**. H6949
30 sour grape, his teeth shall be set on **e**. H6949
Ezk 18: 2 and the children's teeth are set on **e**? H6949
43:13 thereof by the **e** thereof round about H8193
Lk 21:24 And they shall fall by the **e** of the G4750
Heb 11:34 fire, escaped the **e** of the sword, out of G4750

EDGES
Ex 28: 7 joined at the two **e** thereof; and *so* it H7098
39: 4 by the two **e** was it coupled together. H7099
Jdg 3:16 which had two **e**, of a cubit length; and H6366
Rev 2:12 which hath the sharp sword with two **e**; G1366

EDIFICATION
Ro 15: 2 please *his* neighbour for *his* good to **e**. G3619
1Co 14: 3 *to* **e**, and exhortation, and comfort. G3619
2Co 10: 8 hath given us for **e**, and not for your G3619
13:10 given me to **e**, and not to destruction. G3619

EDIFIED
Act 9:31 and were **e**; and walking in the fear G3618
1Co 14:17 thanks well, but the other is not **e**. G3618

EDIFIETH
1Co 8: 1 Knowledge puffeth up, but charity **e**. G3618
14: 4 *unknown* tongue **e** himself; but he that G3618
4 but he that prophesieth **e** the church. G3618

EDIFY
Ro 14:19 things wherewith one may **e** another. G3619
1Co 10:23 are lawful for me, but all things **e** not. G3618
1Th 5:11 and **e** one another, even as also ye do. G3618

EDIFYING
1Co 14: 5 interpret, that the church may receive **e**. G3619
12 that ye may excel to the **e** of the church. G3619
26 Let all things be done unto **e**. G3619
2Co 12:19 *do* all things, dearly beloved, for your **e**. G3619
Eph 4:12 ministry, for the **e** of the body of Christ: G3619
16 of the body unto the **e** of itself in love. G3619
29 is good to the use of **e**, that it may G3619
1Ti 1: 4 than godly **e** which is in faith: *so do*. G3622

EDOM
Gen 25:30 faint: therefore was his name called **E**. H123
32: 3 unto the land of Seir, the country of **E**. H123

Gen 36: 1 *are* the generations of Esau, who *is* **E**. H123
8 dwelt Esau in mount Seir: Esau *is* **E**. H123
16 land of **E**; these *were* the sons of Adah. H123
17 in the land of **E**; these *are* the sons of H123
19 These *are* the sons of Esau, who *is* **E**, and H123
21 the children of Seir in the land of **E**. H123
31 in the land of **E**, before there reigned H123
32 And Bela the son of Beor reigned in **E**: H123
43 *be* the dukes of **E**, according to their H123
Ex 15:15 Then the dukes of **E** shall be amazed; the H123
Nu 20:14 unto the king of **E**, Thus saith thy brother H123
18 And **E** said unto him, Thou shalt not H123
20 go through. And **E** came out against him H123
21 Thus **E** refused to give Israel passage H123
23 Hor, by the coast of the land of **E**, saying, H123
21: 4 the land of **E**: and the soul of the people H123
24:18 And **E** shall be a possession, Seir also H123
33:37 mount Hor, in the edge of the land of **E**. H123
34: 3 by the coast of **E**, and your south border H123
Jos 15: 1 to the border of **E** the wilderness of Zin H123
21 toward the coast of **E** southward were H123
Jdg 5: 4 out of the field of **E**, the earth trembled, H123
11:17 unto the king of **E**, saying, Let me, I pray H123
17 but the king of **E** would not hearken H123
18 the land of **E**, and the land of Moab, H123
1Sa 14:47 and against **E**, and against the kings H123
2Sa 8:14 And he put garrisons in **E**; throughout all H123
14 throughout all **E** put he garrisons, and H123
14 and all they of **E** became David's H123
1Ki 9:26 the shore of the Red sea, in the land of **E**. H123
11:14 Edomite: he *was* of the king's seed in **E**. H123
15 pass, when David was in **E**, and Joab the H123
15 after he had smitten every male in **E**; H123
16 until he had cut off every male in **E**:) H123
22:47 *There was* then no king in **E**: a deputy H123
2Ki 3: 8 The way through the wilderness of **E**. H123
9 and the king of **E**: and they fetched a H123
12 and the king of **E** went down to him. H123
20 **E**, and the country was filled with water. H123
26 unto the king of **E**: but they could not. H123
8:20 In his days **E** revolted from under the H123
22 Yet **E** revolted from under the hand of H123
14: 7 He slew of **E** in the valley of salt ten H123
10 Thou hast indeed smitten **E**, and thine H123
1Ch 1:43 in the land of **E** before *any* king reigned H123
51 Hadad died also. And the dukes of **E** H123
54 duke Iram. These *are* the dukes of **E**. H123
18:11 nations; from **E**, and from Moab, and H123
13 And he put garrisons in **E**; and all the H123
2Ch 8:17 to Eloth, at the sea side in the land of **E**. H123
25:20 because they sought after the gods of **E**. H123
Ps 60: 8 Moab *is* my washpot; over **E** will I cast H123
9 the strong city? who will lead me into **E**? H123
ttl of **E** in the valley of salt twelve thousand. H123
83: 6 The tabernacles of **E**, and the H123
108: 9 Moab *is* my washpot; over **E** will I cast H123
10 the strong city? who will lead me into **E**? H123
137: 7 Remember, O LORD, the children of **E** in H123
Isa 11:14 their hand upon **E** and Moab; and the H123
63: 1 Who *is* this that cometh from **E**, with H123
Jer 9:26 Egypt, and Judah, and **E**, and the H123
25:21 **E**, and Moab, and the children of H123
27: 3 And send them to the king of **E**, and to H123
40:11 and in **E**, and that *were* in all H123
49: 7 Concerning **E**, thus saith the LORD of H123
17 Also **E** shall be a desolation: every one H123
20 hath taken against **E**; and his purposes, H123
22 the mighty men of **E** be as the heart of a H123
Lam 4:21 Rejoice and be glad, O daughter of **E**, H123
22 O daughter of **E**; he will discover thy sins. H123
Ezk 25:12 Thus saith the Lord GOD; Because that **E** H123
13 mine hand upon **E**, and will cut off man H123
14 And I will lay my vengeance upon **E** by H123
14 and they shall do in **E** according to mine H123
32:29 There *is* **E**, her kings, and all her princes, H123
Dan 11:41 of his hand, *even* **E**, and Moab, and the H123
Joel 3:19 Egypt shall be a desolation, and **E** shall H123
Am 1: 6 whole captivity, to deliver *them* up to **E**: H123
9 whole captivity to **E**, and remembered H123
11 transgressions of **E**, and for four, I will H123
2: 1 the bones of the king of **E** into lime: H123
9:12 That they may possess the remnant of **E**, H123
Oba 1 GOD concerning **E**; We have heard a H123
8 wise *men* out of **E**, and understanding H123
Mal 1: 4 Whereas **E** saith, We are impoverished, H123

EDOMITE
Dt 23: 7 Thou shalt not abhor an **E**; for he *is* thy H130
1Sa 21: 7 name *was* Doeg, an **E**, the chiefest of the H130
1Sa 22: 9 Then answered Doeg the **E**, which was H130
18 And Doeg the **E** turned, and he fell upon H130
22 day, when Doeg the **E** *was* there, that he H130
1Ki 11:14 the **E**: he *was* of the king's seed in Edom. H130
Ps 52:ttl when Doeg the **E** came and told Saul, H130

EDOMITES
Gen 36: 9 of Esau the father of the **E** in mount Seir: H123
43 possession: he *is* Esau the father of the **E**. H123
1Ki 11: 1 Ammonites, **E**, Zidonians, *and* Hittites; H130
17 That Hadad fled, he and certain **E** of his H130
2Ki 8:21 and smote the **E** which compassed him H123
1Ch 18:12 **E** in the valley of salt eighteen thousand. H123
13 in Edom; and all the **E** became David's H123
2Ch 21: 8 In his days the **E** revolted from under H123
9 and smote the **E** which compassed him H123
10 So the **E** revolted from under the hand of H123
25:14 slaughter of the **E**, that he brought the H130
19 Thou sayest, Lo, thou hast smitten the **E**; H130
28:17 For again the **E** had come and smitten H130

EDREI
Nu 21:33 he, and all his people, to the battle at **E**. H154
Dt 1: 4 of Bashan, which dwelt at Astaroth in **E**: H154
3: 1 us, he and all his people, to battle at **E**. H154
10 **E**, cities of the kingdom of Og in Bashan. H154
Jos 12: 4 giants, that dwelt at Ashtaroth and at **E**, H154
13:12 Ashtaroth and in **E**, who remained of the H154
31 And half Gilead, and Ashtaroth, and **E**, H154
19:37 And Kedesh, and **E**, and En-hazor, H154

EFFECT
Nu 30: 8 none **e**: and the LORD shall forgive her. H6565
2Ch 34:22 college:) and they spake to her to that *e*.
Ps 33:10 the devices of the people of none **e**. H5106
Isa 32:17 be peace; and the **e** of righteousness H5656
Jer 48:30 *shall* not *be* so; his lies shall not so **e** *it*. H6213
Ezk 12:23 are at hand, and the **e** of every vision. H1697
Mt 15: 6 of God of none **e** by your tradition. *G208*
Mk 7:13 Making the word of God of none **e** *G208*
Ro 3: 3 make the faith of God without **e**? *G2673*
4:14 void, and the promise made of none **e**: *G2673*
9: 6 hath taken none **e**. For they *are* not all *G1601*
1Co 1:17 of Christ should be made of none **e**. *G2758*
Gal 3:17 it should make the promise of none **e**. *G2673*
5: 4 Christ is become of no **e** unto you, *G2673*

EFFECTED
2Ch 7:11 in his own house, he prosperously **e**. H6743

EFFECTUAL
1Co 16: 9 For a great door and **e** is opened unto *G1756*
2Co 1: 6 salvation, which is **e** in the enduring of *G1754*
Eph 3: 7 unto me by the **e** working of his power. *G1753*
4:16 according to the **e** working in the *G1753*
Phlm 6 thy faith may become **e** by the *G1756*
Jas 5:16 be healed. The **e** fervent prayer of a *G1754*

EFFECTUALLY
Gal 2: 8 (For he that wrought **e** in Peter to the *G1754*
1Th 2:13 **e** worketh also in you that believe. *G1754*

EFFEMINATE
1Co 6: 9 nor adulterers, nor **e**, nor abusers of *G3120*

EGG
Job 6: 6 or is there *any* taste in the white of an **e**? H2495
Lk 11:12 Or if he shall ask an **e**, will he offer him *G5609*

EGGS
Dt 22: 6 *be* young ones, or **e**, and the dam sitting H1000
6 or upon the **e**, thou shalt not take H1000
Job 39:14 Which leaveth her **e** in the earth, and H1000
Isa 10:14 as one gathereth **e** *that are* left, have I H1000
59: 5 They hatch cockatrice' **e**, and weave the H1000
5 he that eateth of their **e** dieth, and that H1000
Jer 17:11 *As* the partridge sitteth *on* **e**, and

EGLAH
2Sa 3: 5 And the sixth, Ithream, by **E** David's H5698
1Ch 3: 3 Abital: the sixth, Ithream by **E** his wife. H5698

EGLAIM
Isa 15: 8 thereof unto **E**, and the howling thereof H97

EGLON
Jos 10: 3 and unto Debir king of **E**, saying, H5700
5 the king of **E**, gathered themselves H5700
23 the king of Lachish, *and* the king of **E**. H5700
Jos 10:34 passed unto **E**, and all Israel with him; H5700
36 And Joshua went up from **E**, and all H5700
37 that he had done to **E**; but destroyed it H5700
12:12 The king of **E**, one; the king of Gezer, H5700
15:39 Lachish, and Bozkath, and **E**, H5700
Jdg 3:12 LORD strengthened **E** the king of Moab H5700
14 So the children of Israel served **E** the H5700
15 sent a present unto **E** the king of Moab. H5700
17 And he brought the present unto **E** H5700
17 of Moab: and **E** *was* a very fat man. H5700

EGYPT
Gen 12:10 went down into **E** to sojourn there; for H4714
11 near to enter into **E**, that he said unto H4714
14 was come into **E**, the Egyptians beheld H4714
13: 1 And Abram went up out of **E**, he, and H4714
10 the land of **E**, as thou comest unto Zoar. H4714
15:18 from the river of **E** unto the great river, H4714
21:21 took him a wife out of the land of **E**. H4714
25:18 that *is* before **E**, as thou goest toward H4714
26: 2 Go not down into **E**; dwell in the land H4714
37:25 and myrrh, going to carry *it* down to **E**. H4714
28 silver: and they brought Joseph into **E**. H4714
36 And the Midianites sold him into **E** H4714
39: 1 And Joseph was brought down to **E**; H4714
40: 1 of the king of **E** and *his* baker had H4714
1 had offended their lord the king of **E**. H4714
5 of **E**, which *were* bound in the prison. H4714
41: 8 all the magicians of **E**, and all the wise H4714
19 saw in all the land of **E** for badness: H4714
29 plenty throughout all the land of **E**: H4714
30 in the land of **E**; and the famine shall H4714
33 wise, and set him over the land of **E**. H4714
34 land of **E** in the seven plenteous years. H4714
36 be in the land of **E**; that the land perish H4714
41 I have set thee over all the land of **E**. H4714
43 made him *ruler* over all the land of **E**. H4714
44 up his hand or foot in all the land of **E**. H4714
45 Joseph went out over *all* the land of **E**. H4714
46 Pharaoh king of **E**. And Joseph went out H4714
46 and went throughout all the land of **E**. H4714
48 in the land of **E**, and laid up the food H4714
53 that was in the land of **E**, were ended. H4714
54 but in all the land of **E** there was bread. H4714
55 And when all the land of **E** was H4714
56 the famine waxed sore in the land of **E**. H4714
57 And all countries came into **E** to Joseph H4714
42: 1 there was corn in **E**, Jacob said unto his H4714
2 there is corn in **E**: get you down thither, H4714
3 brethren went down to buy corn in **E**. H4714
43: 2 brought out of **E**, their father said unto H4714
15 down to **E**, and stood before Joseph. H4714
45: 4 your brother, whom ye sold into **E**. H4714
8 and a ruler throughout all the land of **E**. H4714
9 of all **E**: come down unto me, tarry not: H4714
13 of all my glory in **E**, and of all that ye H4714
18 of **E**, and ye shall eat the fat of the land. H4714
19 out of the land of **E** for your little ones, H4714
20 the good of all the land of **E** *is* yours. H4714
23 the good things of **E**, and ten she asses H4714
25 And they went up out of **E**, and came H4714
26 over all the land of **E**. And Jacob's heart H4714
46: 3 to go down into **E**; for I will there make H4714
4 I will go down with thee into **E**; and I H4714
6 into **E**, Jacob, and all his seed with him: H4714
7 all his seed brought he with him into **E**. H4714
8 which came into **E**, Jacob and his sons: H4714
20 And unto Joseph in the land of **E** were H4714
26 with Jacob into **E**, which came out of his H4714
27 were born him in **E**, *were* two souls: all H4714
27 came into **E**, *were* threescore and ten. H4714
47: 6 The land of **E** *is* before thee; in the best H4714
11 in the land of **E**, in the best of the land, H4714
13 so that the land of **E** and *all* the land of H4714
14 in the land of **E**, and in the land of H4714
15 in the land of **E**, and in the land of H4714
20 And Joseph bought all the land of **E** for H4714
21 of **E** even to the *other* end thereof. H4714
26 over the land of **E** unto this day, *that* H4714
27 And Israel dwelt in the land of **E**, in the H4714
28 And Jacob lived in the land of **E** H4714
29 with me; bury me not, I pray thee, in **E**: H4714
30 carry me out of **E**, and bury me in their H4714
48: 5 thee in the land of **E** before I came unto H4714
5 unto thee into **E**, *are* mine; as Reuben H4714
50: 7 and all the elders of the land of **E**, H4714
14 And Joseph returned into **E**, he, and his H4714
22 And Joseph dwelt in **E**, he, and his H4714
26 him, and he was put in a coffin in **E**. H4714

Ex 1: 1 which came into E; every man and his H4714
5 souls: for Joseph was in E *already.* H4714
8 Now there arose up a new king over E, H4714
15 And the king of E spake to the Hebrew H4714
17 not as the king of E commanded them, H4714
18 And the king of E called for the H4714
2:23 time, that the king of E died: and the H4714
3: 7 which *are* in E, and have heard their H4714
10 people the children of Israel out of E. H4714
11 forth the children of Israel out of E? H4714
12 the people out of E, ye shall serve God H4714
16 and *seen* that which is done to you in E: H4714
17 of the affliction of E unto the land of H4714
18 unto the king of E, and ye shall say unto H4714
19 And I am sure that the king of E will H4714
20 hand, and smite E with all my wonders H4714
4:18 which *are* in E, and see whether they H4714
19 Go, return into E: for all the men are H4714
20 to the land of E: and Moses took the H4714
21 to return into E, see that thou do all H4714
5: 4 And the king of E said unto them, H4714
12 of E to gather stubble instead of straw. H4714
6:11 Go in, speak unto Pharaoh king of E, H4714
13 Pharaoh king of E, to bring the children H4714
13 children of Israel out of the land of E. H4714
26 the land of E according to their armies. H4714
27 to Pharaoh king of E, to bring out the H4714
27 E: these *are* that Moses and Aaron. H4714
28 spake unto Moses in the land of E, H4714
29 king of E all that I say unto thee. H4714
7: 3 signs and my wonders in the land of E. H4714
4 lay my hand upon E, and bring forth H4714
4 out of the land of E by great judgments. H4714
5 mine hand upon E, and bring out the H4714
11 the magicians of E, they also did in like H4714
19 the waters of E, upon their streams, H4714
19 all the land of E, both in *vessels of* H4714
21 was blood throughout all the land of E. H4714
22 And the magicians of E did so with H4714
8: 5 frogs to come up upon the land of E. H4714
6 over the waters of E; and the frogs came H4714
6 came up, and covered the land of E. H4714
7 brought up frogs upon the land of E. H4714
16 lice throughout all the land of E. H4714
17 lice throughout all the land of E. H4714
24 and into all the land of E: the land was H4714
9: 4 and the cattle of E: and there shall H4714
6 all the cattle of E died: but of the cattle H4714
9 in all the land of E, and shall be a boil H4714
9 beast, throughout all the land of E. H4714
18 hath not been in E since the foundation H4714
22 hail in all the land of E, upon man, and H4714
22 of the field, throughout the land of E. H4714
23 LORD rained hail upon the land of E. H4714
24 the land of E since it became a nation. H4714
25 all the land of E all that *was* in the H4714
10: 2 I have wrought in E, and my signs H4714
7 thou not yet that E is destroyed? H4714
12 over the land of E for the locusts, that H4714
12 upon the land of E, and eat every herb H4714
13 rod over the land of E, and the LORD H4714
14 all the land of E, and rested in all the H4714
14 in all the coasts of E: very grievous *were* H4714
15 of the field, through all the land of E. H4714
19 not one locust in all the coasts of E. H4714
21 of E, even darkness *which* may be felt. H4714
22 darkness in all the land of E three days: H4714
11: 1 and upon E; afterwards he will let H4714
3 great in the land of E, in the sight of H4714
4 will I go out into the midst of E: H4714
5 And all the firstborn in the land of E H4714
6 all the land of E, such as there was none H4714
9 may be multiplied in the land of E. H4714
12: 1 and Aaron in the land of E, saying, H4714
12 For I will pass through the land of E H4714
12 in the land of E, both man and beast; H4714
12 against all the gods of E I will execute H4714
13 destroy *you,* when I smite the land of E. H4714
17 out of the land of E: therefore shall ye H4714
27 of Israel in E, when he smote the H4714
29 in the land of E, from the firstborn of H4714
30 was a great cry in E; for *there was* not a H4714
39 forth out of E, for it was not leavened; H4714
39 they were thrust out of E, and could not H4714
40 in E, *was* four hundred and thirty years. H4714
41 the LORD went out from the land of E. H4714
42 from the land of E: this *is* that night of H4714
51 out of the land of E by their armies. H4714
13: 3 ye came out from E, out of the house of H4714

Ex 13: 8 did unto me when I came forth out of E. H4714
9 hath the LORD brought thee out of E. H4714
14 out from E, from the house of bondage: H4714
15 in the land of E, both the firstborn of H4714
16 the LORD brought us forth out of E. H4714
17 they see war, and they return to E: H4714
18 went up harnessed out of the land of E. H4714
14: 5 And it was told the king of E that the H4714
7 E, and captains over every one of them. H4714
8 Pharaoh king of E, and he pursued after H4714
11 *were* no graves in E, hast thou taken us H4714
11 thus with us, to carry us forth out of E? H4714
12 that we did tell thee in E, saying, Let us H4714
16: 1 their departing out of the land of E. H4714
3 in the land of E, when we sat by the H4714
6 brought you out from the land of E: H4714
32 I brought you forth from the land of E. H4714
17: 3 us up out of E, to kill us and our H4714
18: 1 the LORD had brought Israel out of E; H4714
19: 1 out of the land of E, the same day came H4714
20: 2 land of E, out of the house of bondage. H4714
22:21 for ye were strangers in the land of E. H4714
23: 9 ye were strangers in the land of E. H4714
15 thou camest out from E: and none shall H4714
29:46 out of the land of E, that I may dwell H4714
32: 1 of E, we wot not what is become of him. H4714
4 brought thee up out of the land of E. H4714
7 land of E, have corrupted *themselves:* H4714
8 brought thee up out of the land of E. H4714
11 out of the land of E with great power, H4714
23 of E, we wot not what is become of him. H4714
33: 1 up out of the land of E, unto the land H4714
34:18 month Abib thou camest out from E. H4714
Lev 11:45 out of the land of E, to be your God: ye H4714
18: 3 After the doings of the land of E, H4714
19:34 the land of E: I *am* the LORD your God. H4714
36 which brought you out of the land of E. H4714
22:33 That brought you out of the land of E, H4714
23:43 the land of E: I *am* the LORD your God. H4714
25:38 out of the land of E, to give you the land H4714
42 of E: they shall not be sold as bondmen. H4714
55 the land of E: I *am* the LORD your God. H4714
26:13 out of the land of E, that ye should not H4714
45 out of the land of E in the sight of the H4714
Nu 1: 1 were come out of the land of E, saying, H4714
3:13 in the land of E I hallowed unto me H4714
8:17 land of E I sanctified them for myself. H4714
9: 1 were come out of the land of E, saying, H4714
11: 5 we did eat in E freely; the cucumbers, H4714
18 well with us in E: therefore the LORD H4714
20 saying, Why came we forth out of E? H4714
13:22 was built seven years before Zoan in E.) H4714
14: 2 died in the land of E! or would God we H4714
3 were it not better for us to return into E? H4714
4 a captain, and let us return into E. H4714
19 this people, from E even until now. H4714
22 which I did in E and in the wilderness, H4714
15:41 out of the land of E, to be your God: I H4714
20: 5 to come up out of E, to bring us in unto H4714
15 How our fathers went down into E, and H4714
15 we have dwelt in E a long time; and the H4714
16 us forth out of E: and, behold, we *are* H4714
21: 5 us up out of E to die in the wilderness? H4714
22: 5 come out from E: behold, they cover the H4714
11 Behold, *there is* a people come out of E, H4714
23:22 God brought them out of E; he hath as it H4714
24: 8 God brought him forth out of E; he hath H4714
26: 4 which went forth out of the land of E. H4714
59 bare to Levi in E: and she bare unto H4714
32:11 came up out of E, from twenty years old H4714
33: 1 out of the land of E with their armies H4714
38 of E, in the first *day* of the fifth month. H4714
34: 5 unto the river of E, and the goings out H4714
Dt 1:27 out of the land of E, to deliver us into H4714
30 he did for you in E before your eyes; H4714
4:20 *even* out of E, to be unto him a people H4714
34 God did for you in E before your eyes? H4714
37 sight with his mighty power out of E; H4714
45 of Israel, after they came forth out of E, H4714
46 after they were come forth out of E: H4714
5: 6 land of E, from the house of bondage. H4714
15 in the land of E, and *that* the LORD H4714
6:12 land of E, from the house of bondage. H4714
21 bondmen in E; and the LORD brought H4714
21 us out of E with a mighty hand: H4714
22 and sore, upon E, upon Pharaoh, and H4714
7: 8 from the hand of Pharaoh king of E. H4714
15 evil diseases of E, which thou knowest, H4714
18 God did unto Pharaoh, and unto all E; H4714

Dt 8:14 land of E, from the house of bondage; H4714
9: 7 out of the land of E, until ye came unto H4714
12 brought forth out of E have corrupted H4714
26 forth out of E with a mighty hand. H4714
10:19 for ye were strangers in the land of E. H4714
22 Thy fathers went down into E with H4714
11: 3 did in the midst of E unto Pharaoh the H4714
3 the king of E, and unto all his land; H4714
4 And what he did unto the army of E, H4714
10 *is* not as the land of E, from whence ye H4714
13: 5 out of the land of E, and redeemed you H4714
10 land of E, from the house of bondage. H4714
15:15 in the land of E, and the LORD thy God H4714
16: 1 brought thee forth out of E by night. H4714
3 out of the land of E in haste: that thou H4714
3 of the land of E all the days of thy life. H4714
6 season that thou camest forth out of E. H4714
12 a bondman in E: and thou shalt observe H4714
17:16 to return to E, to the end that he should H4714
20: 1 brought thee up out of the land of E. H4714
23: 4 came forth out of E; and because they H4714
24: 9 after that ye were come forth out of E. H4714
18 a bondman in E, and the LORD thy God H4714
22 in the land of E: therefore I command H4714
25:17 way, when ye were come forth out of E; H4714
26: 5 he went down into E, and sojourned H4714
8 us forth out of E with a mighty hand, H4714
28:27 thee with the botch of E, and with the H4714
60 all the diseases of E, which thou wast H4714
68 And the LORD shall bring thee into E H4714
29: 2 eyes in the land of E unto Pharaoh, and H4714
16 in the land of E; and how we came H4714
25 brought them forth out of the land of E: H4714
34:11 do in the land of E to Pharaoh, and to H4714
Jos 2:10 ye came out of E; and what ye did unto H4714
5: 4 that came out of E, *that were* males, H4714
4 by the way, after they came out of E. H4714
5 of E, *them* they had not circumcised. H4714
6 which came out of E, were consumed, H4714
9 away the reproach of E from off you. H4714
9: 9 fame of him, and all that he did in E, H4714
13: 3 From Sihor, which *is* before E, even H4714
15: 4 unto the river of E; and the goings out H4714
47 unto the river of E, and the great sea, H4714
24: 4 and his children went down into E. H4714
5 and I plagued E, according to that H4714
6 And I brought your fathers out of E: H4714
7 I have done in E: and ye dwelt in the H4714
14 flood, and in E; and serve ye the LORD. H4714
17 out of the land of E, from the house of H4714
32 brought up out of E, buried they in H4714
Jdg 2: 1 to go up out of E, and have brought you H4714
12 out of the land of E, and followed other H4714
6: 8 you up from E, and brought you forth H4714
13 bring us up from E? but now the LORD H4714
11:13 they came up out of E, from Arnon even H4714
16 But when Israel came up from E, and H4714
19:30 up out of the land of E unto this day: H4714
1Sa 2:27 they were in E in Pharaoh's house? H4714
8: 8 them up out of E even unto this day, H4714
10:18 up Israel out of E, and delivered you out H4714
12: 6 your fathers up out of the land of E. H4714
8 When Jacob was come into E, and your H4714
8 of E, and made them dwell in this place. H4714
15: 2 in the way, when he came up from E. H4714
6 they came up out of E. So the Kenites H4714
7 comest to Shur, that *is* over against E. H4714
27: 8 goest to Shur, even unto the land of E. H4714
30:13 *am* a young man of E, servant to an H4713
2Sa 7: 6 of Israel out of E, even to this day, but H4714
23 E, *from* the nations and their gods? H4714
1Ki 3: 1 Pharaoh king of E, and took Pharaoh's H4714
4:21 and unto the border of E: they brought H4714
30 east country, and all the wisdom of E. H4714
6: 1 out of the land of E, in the fourth year of H4714
8: 9 when they came out of the land of E. H4714
16 Israel out of E, I chose no city out of H4714
21 he brought them out of the land of E. H4714
51 E, from the midst of the furnace of iron: H4714
53 our fathers out of E, O Lord GOD. H4714
65 unto the river of E, before the LORD our H4714
9: 9 out of the land of E, and have taken H4714
16 *For* Pharaoh king of E had gone up, H4714
10:28 brought out of E, and linen yarn: the H4714
29 up and went out of E for six hundred H4714
11:17 go into E; Hadad *being* yet a little child. H4714
18 and they came to E, unto Pharaoh king H4714
18 Pharaoh king of E; which gave him an H4714
21 And when Hadad heard in E that H4714

1Ki 11:40 and fled into E, unto Shishak king of H4714
40 Shishak king of E, and was in Egypt H4714
40 was in E until the death of Solomon. H4714
12: 2 who was yet in E, heard *of it,* (for he H4714
2 Solomon, and Jeroboam dwelt in E;) H4714
28 brought thee up out of the land of E. H4714
14:25 king of E came up against Jerusalem: H4714
2Ki 17: 4 to So king of E, and brought no present H4714
7 up out of the land of E, from under the H4714
7 king of E, and had feared other gods, H4714
36 out of the land of E with great power H4714
18:21 reed, *even* upon E, on which if a man H4714
21 king of E unto all that trust on him. H4714
24 on E for chariots and for horsemen? H4714
21:15 came forth out of E, even unto this day. H4714
23:29 In his days Pharaoh-nechoh king of E H4714
34 away: and he came to E, and died there. H4714
24: 7 And the king of E came not again any H4714
7 taken from the river of E unto the river H4714
7 all that pertained to the king of E. H4714
25:26 E: for they were afraid of the Chaldees. H4714
1Ch 13: 5 from Shihor of E even unto the H4714
17:21 whom thou hast redeemed out of E? H4714
2Ch 1:16 brought out of E, and linen yarn: the H4714
17 forth out of E a chariot for six hundred H4714
5:10 of Israel, when they came out of E. H4714
6: 5 out of the land of E I chose no city H4714
7: 8 in of Hamath unto the river of E. H4714
22 out of the land of E, and laid hold on H4714
9:26 the Philistines, and to the border of E. H4714
28 horses out of E, and out of all lands. H4714
10: 2 of Nebat, who *was* in E, whither he had H4714
2 *it,* that Jeroboam returned out of E. H4714
12: 2 Shishak king of E came up against H4714
3 came with him out of E; the Lubims, the H4714
9 So Shishak king of E came up against H4714
20:10 out of the land of E, but they turned H4714
26: 8 the entering in of E; for he strengthened H4714
35:20 Necho king of E came up to fight H4714
36: 3 And the king of E put him down at H4714
4 And the king of E made Eliakim his H4714
4 his brother, and carried him to E. H4714
Neh 9: 9 of our fathers in E, and heardest their H4714
18 E, and had wrought great provocations; H4714
Ps 68:31 Princes shall come out of E; Ethiopia H4714
78:12 in the land of E, *in* the field of Zoan. H4714
43 How he had wrought his signs in E, and H4714
51 And smote all the firstborn in E; the H4714
80: 8 Thou hast brought a vine out of E: thou H4714
81: 5 the land of E: *where* I heard a language H4714
10 E: open thy mouth wide, and I will fill it. H4714
105:23 Israel also came into E; and Jacob H4714
38 E was glad when they departed: for the H4714
106: 7 thy wonders in E; they remembered not H4714
21 which had done great things in E; H4714
114: 1 When Israel went out of E, the house of H4714
135: 8 Who smote the firstborn of E, both of H4714
9 midst of thee, O E, upon Pharaoh, and H4714
136:10 To him that smote E in their firstborn: H4714
Prv 7:16 with carved *works,* with fine linen of E. H4714
Isa 7:18 of the rivers of E, and for the bee that H4714
10:24 against thee, after the manner of E. H4714
26 shall he lift it up after the manner of E. H4714
11:11 Assyria, and from E, and from Pathros, H4714
16 that he came up out of the land of E. H4714
19: 1 The burden of E. Behold, the LORD H4714
1 shall come into E: and the idols of Egypt H4714
1 and the idols of E shall be moved at his H4714
1 heart of E shall melt in the midst of it. H4714
3 And the spirit of E shall fail in the H4714
12 LORD of hosts hath purposed upon E. H4714
13 have also seduced E, *even they that are* H4714
14 they have caused E to err in every work H4714
15 Neither shall there be *any* work for E, H4714
16 In that day shall E be like unto women: H4714
17 shall be a terror unto E, every one that H4714
18 in the land of E speak the language H4714
19 of the land of E, and a pillar at the H4714
20 in the land of E: for they shall cry unto H4714
21 And the LORD shall be known to E, and H4714
22 And the LORD shall smite E: he shall H4714
23 a highway out of E to Assyria, and the H4714
23 shall come into E, and the Egyptian into H4714
24 be the third with E and with Assyria, H4714
25 saying, Blessed *be* E my people, and H4714
20: 3 wonder upon E and upon Ethiopia; H4714
4 buttocks uncovered, to the shame of E. H4714
5 their expectation, and of E their glory. H4714
23: 5 As at the report concerning E, *so* shall H4714

Isa 27:12 unto the stream of E, and ye shall be H4714
13 in the land of E, and shall worship the H4714
30: 2 That walk to go down into E, and have H4714
2 and to trust in the shadow of E! H4714
3 in the shadow of E *your* confusion. H4714
31: 1 Woe to them that go down to E for H4714
36: 6 broken reed, on E; whereon if a man H4714
6 king of E to all that trust in him. H4714
9 on E for chariots and for horsemen? H4714
43: 3 thy Saviour: I gave E *for* thy ransom, H4714
45:14 Thus saith the LORD, The labour of E, H4714
52: 4 aforetime into E to sojourn there; and H4714
Jer 2: 6 out of the land of E, that led us through H4714
18 thou to do in the way of E, to drink the H4714
36 of E, as thou wast ashamed of Assyria. H4714
7:22 out of the land of E, concerning burnt H4714
25 out of the land of E unto this day I have H4714
9:26 E, and Judah, and Edom, and the H4714
11: 4 forth out of the land of E, from the iron H4714
7 out of the land of E, *even* unto this day, H4714
16:14 children of Israel out of the land of E; H4714
23: 7 children of Israel out of the land of E; H4714
24: 8 and them that dwell in the land of E: H4714
25:19 Pharaoh king of E, and his servants, H4714
26:21 was afraid, and fled, and went into E; H4714
22 sent men into E, *namely,* Elnathan the H4714
22 and *certain* men with him into E. H4714
23 And they fetched forth Urijah out of E, H4714
31:32 out of the land of E; which my covenant H4714
32:20 in the land of E, *even* unto this day, H4714
21 out of the land of E with signs, and H4714
34:13 E, out of the house of bondmen, saying, H4714
37: 5 was come forth out of E: and when the H4714
7 shall return to E into their own land. H4714
41:17 is by Beth-lehem, to go to enter into E, H4714
42:14 go into the land of E, where we shall see H4714
15 to enter into E, and go to sojourn there; H4714
16 there in the land of E, and the famine, H4714
16 you there in E; and there ye shall die. H4714
17 faces to go into E to sojourn there; they H4714
18 ye shall enter into E: and ye shall be an H4714
19 Go ye not into E: know certainly that H4714
43: 2 to say, Go not into E to sojourn there: H4714
7 So they came into the land of E: for they H4714
11 smite the land of E, *and deliver* such *as* H4714
12 of the gods of E; and he shall burn H4714
12 with the land of E, as a shepherd H4714
13 *is* in the land of E; and the houses of the H4714
44: 1 in the land of E, which dwell at Migdol, H4714
8 gods in the land of E, whither ye be H4714
12 go into the land of E to sojourn there, H4714
12 fall in the land of E; they shall *even* be H4714
13 in the land of E, as I have punished H4714
14 into the land of E to sojourn there, H4714
15 in the land of E, in Pathros, answered H4714
24 all Judah that *are* in the land of E: H4714
26 in the land of E; Behold, I have sworn H4714
26 land of E, saying, The Lord GOD liveth. H4714
27 *are* in the land of E shall be consumed H4714
28 out of the land of E into the land of H4714
28 into the land of E to sojourn there, H4714
30 king of E into the hand of his H4714
46: 2 Against E, against the army of H4714
2 king of E, which was by the river H4714
8 E riseth up like a flood, and *his* waters H4714
11 the daughter of E: in vain shalt thou use H4714
13 should come *and* smite the land of E. H4714
14 Declare ye in E, and publish in Migdol, H4714
17 They did cry there, Pharaoh king of E H4714
19 O thou daughter dwelling in E, furnish H4714
20 E *is like* a very fair heifer, *but* H4714
24 The daughter of E shall be confounded; H4714
25 and Pharaoh, and E, with their gods, H4714
Ezk 17:15 his ambassadors into E, that they might H4714
19: 4 him with chains unto the land of E. H4714
20: 5 in the land of E, when I lifted up mine H4714
6 of the land of E into a land that I had H4714
7 the idols of E: I *am* the LORD your God. H4714
8 the idols of E: then I said, I will pour H4714
8 them in the midst of the land of E. H4714
9 bringing them forth out of the land of E. H4714
10 out of the land of E, and brought them H4714
36 of the land of E, so will I plead with H4714
23: 3 And they committed whoredoms in E; H4714
8 *brought* from E: for in her youth they H4714
19 had played the harlot in the land of E. H4714
27 from the land of E: so that thou shalt H4714
27 unto them, nor remember E any more. H4714
27: 7 Fine linen with broidered work from E H4714

Ezk 29: 2 Pharaoh king of E, and prophesy H4714
2 against him, and against all E: H4714
3 Pharaoh king of E, the great dragon H4714
6 And all the inhabitants of E shall know H4714
9 And the land of E shall be desolate and H4714
10 make the land of E utterly waste *and* H4714
12 And I will make the land of E desolate H4714
14 And I will bring again the captivity of E, H4714
19 will give the land of E unto H4714
20 I have given him the land of E *for* his H4714
30: 4 And the sword shall come upon E, and H4714
4 slain shall fall in E, and they shall take H4714
6 also that uphold E shall fall; and the H4714
8 I have set a fire in E, and *when* all her H4714
9 as in the day of E: for, lo, it cometh. H4714
10 the multitude of E to cease by the hand H4714
11 E, and fill the land with the slain. H4714
13 of the land of E: and I will put a fear H4714
13 and I will put a fear in the land of E. H4714
15 E; and I will cut off the multitude of No. H4714
16 And I will set fire in E: Sin shall have H4714
18 there the yokes of E: and the pomp of H4714
19 Thus will I execute judgments in E: and H4714
21 Pharaoh king of E; and, lo, it shall not H4714
22 Pharaoh king of E, and will break his H4714
25 shall stretch it out upon the land of E. H4714
31: 2 unto Pharaoh king of E, and to his H4714
32: 2 Pharaoh king of E, and say unto him, H4714
12 shall spoil the pomp of E, and all the H4714
15 When I shall make the land of E H4714
16 for her, *even* for E, and for all her H4714
18 Son of man, wail for the multitude of E, H4714
Dan 9:15 forth out of the land of E with a mighty H4714
11: 8 And shall also carry captives into E H4714
42 and the land of E shall not escape. H4714
43 precious things of E: and the Libyans H4714
Hos 2:15 when she came up out of the land of E. H4714
7:11 heart: they call to E, they go to Assyria. H4714
16 *shall be* their derision in the land of E. H4714
8:13 visit their sins: they shall return to E. H4714
9: 3 shall return to E, and they shall eat H4714
6 of destruction: E shall gather them up, H4714
11: 1 I loved him, and called my son out of E. H4714
5 He shall not return into the land of E, H4714
11 They shall tremble as a bird out of E, H4714
12: 1 the Assyrians, and oil is carried into E. H4714
9 from the land of E will yet make thee to H4714
13 E, and by a prophet was he preserved. H4714
13: 4 from the land of E, and thou shalt know H4714
Joel 3:19 E shall be a desolation, and Edom shall H4714
Am 2:10 up from the land of E, and led you forty H4714
3: 1 I brought up from the land of E, saying, H4714
9 in the land of E, and say, Assemble H4714
4:10 the manner of E: your young men have H4714
8: 8 out and drowned, as *by* the flood of E. H4714
9: 5 shall be drowned, as *by* the flood of E. H4714
7 out of the land of E? and the Philistines H4714
Mic 6: 4 out of the land of E, and redeemed thee H4714
7:15 out of the land of E will I shew unto H4714
Nah 3: 9 Ethiopia and E *were* her strength, and H4714
Hag 2: 5 when ye came out of E, so my spirit H4714
Zec 10:10 out of the land of E, and gather them H4714
11 and the sceptre of E shall depart away. H4714
14:18 And if the family of E go not up, and H4714
19 This shall be the punishment of E, and H4714
Mt 2:13 and flee into E, and be thou there until G125
14 his mother by night, and departed into E: G125
15 saying, Out of E have I called my son. G125
19 appeareth in a dream to Joseph in E, G125
Act 2:10 Phrygia, and Pamphylia, in E, and in the G125
7: 9 Joseph into E: but God was with him, G125
10 of Pharaoh king of E; and he made him G125
10 him governor over E and all his house. G125
11 over all the land of E and Chanaan, and G125
12 corn in E, he sent out our fathers first. G125
15 So Jacob went down into E, and died, he, G125
17 the people grew and multiplied in E, G125
34 people which is in E, and I have heard G125
34 And now come, I will send thee into E. G125
36 signs in the land of E, and in the Red sea, G125
39 in their hearts turned back again into E, G125
40 of E, we wot not what is become of him. G125
13:17 in the land of E, and with an high arm G125
Heb 3:16 not all that came out of E by Moses. G125
8: 9 them out of the land of E; because they G125
11:26 the treasures in E: for he had respect G125
27 By faith he forsook E, not fearing the G125
Jude 5 out of the land of E, afterward destroyed G125
Rev 11: 8 and E, where also our Lord was crucified. G125

EGYPTIAN

Gen 16: 1 an E, whose name *was* Hagar. H4713
3 her maid the E, after Abram had dwelt H4713
21: 9 And Sarah saw the son of Hagar the E, H4713
25:12 whom Hagar the E, Sarah's handmaid, H4713
39: 1 of the guard, an E, bought him of the H4713
2 he was in the house of his master the E. H4713
Ex 1:19 *are* not as the E women; for they *are* H4713
2:11 and he spied an E smiting an Hebrew, H4713
12 he slew the E, and hid him in the sand. H4713
14 thou killedst the E? And Moses feared, H4713
19 And they said, An E delivered us out of H4713
Lev 24:10 father *was* an E, went out among the H4713
Dt 23: 7 shalt not abhor an E; because thou wast H4713
1Sa 30:11 And they found an E in the field, and H4713
2Sa 23:21 And he slew an E, a goodly man: and H4713
21 man: and the E had a spear in his H4713
1Ch 2:34 a servant, an E, whose name *was* Jarha. H4713
11:23 And he slew an E, a man of *great* H4713
Isa 11:15 the tongue of the E sea; and with his H4714
19:23 Egypt, and the E into Assyria, and the H4714
Act 7:24 that was oppressed, and smote the E: *G124*
28 Wilt thou kill me, as thou diddest the E *G124*
21:38 Art not thou that E, which before these *G124*

EGYPTIANS

Gen 12:12 to pass, when the E shall see thee, that H4713
14 into Egypt, the E beheld the woman H4713
41:55 said unto all the E, Go unto Joseph; H4714
56 and sold unto the E; and the famine H4714
43:32 and for the E, which did eat with him, H4713
32 because the E might not eat bread H4713
32 for that *is* an abomination unto the E. H4714
45: 2 And he wept aloud: and the E and the H4714
46:34 shepherd *is* an abomination unto the E. H4714
47:15 of Canaan, all the E came unto Joseph, H4714
20 Pharaoh; for the E sold every man his H4714
50: 3 and the E mourned for him threescore H4714
11 mourning to the E: wherefore the name H4714
Ex 1:13 And the E made the children of Israel H4714
3: 8 of the hand of the E, and to bring them H4714
9 wherewith the E oppress them. H4714
21 in the sight of the E: and it shall come to H4714
22 your daughters; and ye shall spoil the E. H4714
6: 5 of Israel, whom the E keep in bondage; H4714
6 the burdens of the E, and I will rid you H4714
7 out from under the burdens of the E. H4714
7: 5 And the E shall know that I *am* the H4714
18 stink; and the E shall lothe to drink H4714
21 stank, and the E could not drink of the H4714
24 And all the E digged round about the H4714
8:21 and the houses of the E shall be full of H4714
26 of the E to the LORD our God: H4714
26 of the E before their eyes, and H4714
9:11 upon the magicians, and upon all the E. H4714
10: 6 houses of all the E; which neither thy H4714
11: 3 in the sight of the E. Moreover the man H4714
7 a difference between the E and Israel. H4714
12:23 to smite the E; and when he seeth the H4714
27 when he smote the E, and delivered our H4714
30 and all the E; and there was a great H4714
33 And the E were urgent upon the H4714
35 borrowed of the E jewels of silver, and H4714
36 in the sight of the E, so that they lent H4714
36 *they required.* And they spoiled the E. H4714
14: 4 his host; that the E may know that I *am* H4714
9 But the E pursued after them, all the H4714
10 and, behold, the E marched after them; H4714
12 that we may serve the E? For *it had been* H4714
12 better for us to serve the E, than that we H4714
13 to you to day: for the E whom ye have H4714
17 the hearts of the E, and they shall follow H4714
18 And the E shall know that I *am* the H4714
20 And it came between the camp of the E H4714
23 And the E pursued, and went in after H4714
24 the host of the E through the pillar of H4714
24 cloud, and troubled the host of the E, H4714
25 so that the E said, Let us flee from H4714
25 LORD fighteth for them against the E. H4714
26 again upon the E, upon their chariots, H4714
27 appeared; and the E fled against it; and H4714
27 overthrew the E in the midst of the sea. H4714
30 of the hand of the E; and Israel saw the H4714
30 saw the E dead upon the sea shore. H4714
31 did upon the E: and the people feared H4714
15:26 E: for I *am* the LORD that healeth thee. H4714
18: 8 and to the E for Israel's sake, *and* H4714
9 had delivered out of the hand of the E. H4714
10 out of the hand of the E, and out of the H4714
Ex 18:10 people from under the hand of the E. H4714
19: 4 Ye have seen what I did unto the E, and H4714
32:12 Wherefore should the E speak, and H4714
Nu 14:13 the LORD, Then the E shall hear *it,* (for H4714
20:15 and the E vexed us, and our fathers: H4714
33: 3 an high hand in the sight of all the E. H4714
4 For the E buried all *their* firstborn, H4714
Dt 26: 6 And the E evil entreated us, and H4713
Jos 24: 6 the sea; and the E pursued after your H4714
7 you and the E, and brought the sea H4713
Jdg 6: 9 out of the hand of the E, and out of the H4714
10:11 *you* from the E, and from the Amorites, H4714
1Sa 4: 8 E with all the plagues in the wilderness. H4714
6: 6 your hearts, as the E and Pharaoh H4714
10:18 out of the hand of the E, and out of the H4714
2Ki 7: 6 and the kings of the E, to come upon us. H4714
Ezr 9: 1 the Moabites, the E, and the Amorites. H4713
Isa 19: 2 And I will set the E against the H4714
2 against the E: and they shall fight H4714
4 And the E will I give over into the hand H4714
21 to Egypt, and the E shall know the H4714
23 the E shall serve with the Assyrians. H4714
20: 4 lead away the E prisoners, and the H4714
30: 7 For the E shall help in vain, and to no H4714
31: 3 Now the E *are* men, and not God; and H4714
Jer 43:13 gods of the E shall he burn with fire. H4714
Lam 5: 6 We have given the hand *to* the E, *and to* H4714
Ezk 16:26 with the E thy neighbours, great H4714
23:21 teats by the E for the paps of thy youth. H4714
29:12 I will scatter the E among the nations, H4714
13 will I gather the E from the people H4714
30:23 And I will scatter the E among the H4714
26 And I will scatter the E among the H4714
Act 7:22 the wisdom of the E, and was mighty in *G124*
Heb 11:29 the E assaying to do were drowned. *G124*

EGYPTIAN'S

Gen 39: 5 LORD blessed the E house for Joseph's H4713
2Sa 23:21 spear out of the E hand, and slew him H4713
1Ch 11:23 high; and in the E hand *was* a spear H4713
23 spear out of the E hand, and slew him H4713

EHI

Gen 46:21 and Naaman, E, and Rosh, Muppim, H278

EHUD

Jdg 3:15 them up a deliverer, E the son of Gera, a H164
16 But E made him a dagger which had two H164
20 And E came unto him; and he was H164
20 for himself alone. And E said, I have a H164
21 And E put forth his left hand, and took H164
23 Then E went forth through the porch, H164
26 And E escaped while they tarried, and H164
4: 1 the sight of the LORD, when E was dead. H164
1Ch 7:10 Benjamin, and E, and Chenaanah, and H164
8: 6 And these *are* the sons of E: these are the H261

EIGHT

Gen 5: 4 Seth were e hundred years: and H8083
7 And Seth lived after he begat Enos e H8083
10 And Enos lived after he begat Cainan e H8083
13 begat Mahalaleel e hundred and forty H8083
16 he begat Jared e hundred and thirty H8083
17 And all the days of Mahalaleel were e H8083
19 And Jared lived after he begat Enoch e H8083
17:12 And he that is e days old shall be H8083
21: 4 son Isaac being e days old, as God had H8083
22:23 And Bethuel begat Rebekah: these e H8083
Ex 26: 2 The length of one curtain *shall be* e and H8083
25 And they shall be e boards, and their H8083
36: 9 *was* twenty and e cubits, and the H8083
30 And there were e boards; and their H8083
Nu 2:24 thousand and e thousand and an H8083
3:28 and upward, *were* e thousand and six H8083
4:48 of them, were e thousand and five H8083
7: 8 And four wagons and e oxen he gave H8083
29:29 And on the sixth day e bullocks, two H8083
35: 7 *shall be* forty and e cities: them *shall ye* H8083
Dt 2:14 *was* thirty and e years; until all the H8083
Jos 21:41 forty and e cities with their suburbs. H8083
Jdg 3: 8 served Chushan-rishathaim e years. H8083
12:14 ass colts: and he judged Israel e years. H8083
1Sa 4:15 Now Eli was ninety and e years old; H8083
17:12 Jesse; and he had e sons: and the man H8083
2Sa 23: 8 e hundred, whom he slew at one time. H8083
24: 9 were in Israel e hundred thousand H8083
1Ki 7:10 of ten cubits, and stones of e cubits. H8083
2Ki 8:17 and he reigned e years in Jerusalem. H8083
10:36 in Samaria *was* twenty and e years. H8083
2Ki 22: 1 Josiah *was* e years old when he began H8083
1Ch 12:24 e hundred, ready armed to the war. H8083
30 thousand and e hundred, mighty men H8083
35 and e thousand and six hundred. H8083
16:38 threescore and e; Obed-edom also the H8083
23: 3 by man, was thirty and e thousand. H8083
24: 4 *their* fathers, and e among the sons of H8083
25: 7 was two hundred fourscore and e. H8083
2Ch 11:21 and e sons, and threescore daughters.) H8083
13: 3 against him with e hundred thousand H8083
21: 5 and he reigned e years in Jerusalem. H8083
20 in Jerusalem e years, and departed H8083
29:17 house of the LORD in e days; and in the H8083
34: 1 Josiah *was* e years old when he began H8083
36: 9 Jehoiachin *was* e years old when he H8083
Ezr 2: 6 two thousand e hundred and twelve. H8083
16 of Ater of Hezekiah, ninety and e. H8083
23 of Anathoth, an hundred twenty and e. H8083
41 of Asaph, an hundred twenty and e. H8083
8:11 and with him twenty and e males. H8083
Neh 7:11 thousand and e hundred *and* eighteen. H8083
13 The children of Zattu, e hundred forty H8083
15 of Binnui, six hundred forty and e. H8083
16 of Bebai, six hundred twenty and e. H8083
21 of Ater of Hezekiah, ninety and e. H8083
22 Hashum, three hundred twenty and e. H8083
26 Netophah, an hundred fourscore and e. H8083
27 of Anathoth, an hundred twenty and e. H8083
44 of Asaph, an hundred forty and e. H8083
45 of Shobai, an hundred thirty and e. H8083
11: 6 hundred threescore and e valiant men. H8083
8 Sallai, nine hundred twenty and e. H8083
12 of the house *were* e hundred twenty H8083
14 twenty and e: and their overseer *was* H8083
Ecc 11: 2 Give a portion to seven, and also to e; H8083
Jer 41:15 e men, and went to the Ammonites. H8083
52:29 e hundred thirty and two persons: H8083
Ezk 40: 9 the porch of the gate, e cubits; and the H8083
31 and the going up to it *had* e steps. H8083
34 side: and the going up to it *had* e steps. H8083
37 side: and the going up to it *had* e steps. H8083
41 side of the gate; e tables, whereupon H8083
Mic 5: 5 seven shepherds, and e principal men. H8083
Lk 2:21 And when e days were accomplished *G3638*
9:28 And it came to pass about an e days *G3638*
Jn 5: 5 had an infirmity thirty and e years. *G3638*
20:26 And after e days again his disciples *G3638*
Act 9:33 bed e years, and was sick of the palsy. *G3638*
1Pt 3:20 that is, e souls were saved by water. *G3638*

EIGHT HUNDRED See EIGHT and HUNDRED.

EIGHT THOUSAND See EIGHT and THOUSAND.

EIGHTEEN

Gen 14:14 e, and pursued *them* unto Dan. H8083+H6240
Jdg 3:14 the king of Moab e years. H8083+H6240
10: 8 of Israel: e years, all the H8083+H6240
20:25 of Israel again e thousand H8083+H6240
44 And there fell of Benjamin e H8083+H6240
2Sa 8:13 of salt, *being* e thousand *men.* H8083+H6240
1Ki 7:15 of brass, of e cubits high H8083+H6240
2Ki 24: 8 Jehoiachin *was* e years old H8083+H6240
25:17 one pillar *was* e cubits, and the H8083+H6240
1Ch 12:31 tribe of Manasseh e thousand, H8083+H6240
18:12 in the valley of salt e thousand. H8083+H6240
26: 9 and brethren, strong men, e. H8083+H6240
29: 7 and of brass e thousand H8083+H7239
2Ch 11:21 (for he took e wives, and H8083+H6240
Ezr 8: 9 him two hundred and e males. H8083+H6240
18 his sons and his brethren, e; H8083+H6240
Neh 7:11 and eight hundred *and* e. H8083+H6240
Jer 52:21 one pillar *was* e cubits; and a H8083+H6240
Ezk 48:35 *It was* round about e thousand H8083+H6240
Lk 13: 4 Or those e, upon whom the *G2532+G3638*
11 of infirmity e years, and was *G2532+G3638*
16 lo, these e years, be loosed *G2532+G3638*

EIGHTEEN THOUSAND See EIGHTEEN and THOUSAND.

EIGHTEENTH

1Ki 15: 1 Now in the e year of king H8083+H6240
2Ki 3: 1 in Samaria the e year of H8083+H6240
22: 3 And it came to pass in the e H8083+H6240
23:23 But in the e year of king H8083+H6240
1Ch 24:15 The seventeenth to Hezir, the e H8083+H6240
25:25 The e to Hanani, *he,* his sons, H8083+H6240
2Ch 13: 1 Now in the e year of king H8083+H6240

34: 8 Now in the **e** year of his reign, H8083+H6240
2Ch 35:19 In the **e** year of the reign of H8083+H6240
Jer 32: 1 the **e** year of Nebuchadrezzar. H8083+H6240
52:29 In the **e** year of H8083+H6240

EIGHTH
Ex 22:30 dam; on the **e** day thou shalt give it me. H8066
Lev 9: 1 And it came to pass on the **e** day, *that* H8066
12: 3 And in the **e** day the flesh of his H8066
14:10 And on the **e** day he shall take two he H8066
23 And he shall bring them on the **e** day H8066
15:14 And on the **e** day he shall take to him H8066
29 And on the **e** day she shall take unto H8066
22:27 and from the **e** day and thenceforth H8066
23:36 the LORD: on the **e** day shall be an holy H8066
39 and on the **e** day *shall be* a sabbath. H8066
25:22 And ye shall sow the **e** year, and eat *yet* H8066
Nu 6:10 And on the **e** day he shall bring two H8066
7:54 On the **e** day *offered* Gamaliel the son H8066
29:35 On the **e** day ye shall have a solemn H8066
1Ki 6:38 Bul, which *is* the **e** month, was the H8066
8:66 On the **e** day he sent the people away: H8066
12:32 And Jeroboam ordained a feast in the **e** H8066
33 day of the **e** month, *even* in the H8066
16:29 And in the thirty and **e** year of Asa king H8083
2Ki 15: 8 In the thirty and **e** year of Azariah king H8083
24:12 took him in the **e** year of his reign. H8083
1Ch 12:12 Johanan the **e**, Elzabad the ninth, H8066
24:10 The seventh to Hakkoz, the **e** to Abijah, H8066
25:15 The **e** to Jeshaiah, *he*, his sons, and his H8066
26: 5 Peulthai the **e**: for God blessed him. H8066
27:11 The **e** *captain* for the eighth month *was* H8066
11 The eighth *captain* for the **e** month *was* H8066
2Ch 7: 9 And in the **e** day they made a solemn H8066
29:17 and on the **e** day of the month came H8083
34: 3 For in the **e** year of his reign, while he H8083
Neh 8:18 days; and on the **e** day *was* a solemn H8066
Ezk 43:27 shall be, *that* upon the **e** day, and *so* H8066
Zec 1: 1 In the **e** month, in the second year of H8066
Lk 1:59 And it came to pass, that on the **e** day G3590
Act 7: 8 him the **e** day; and Isaac *begat* G3590
Php 3: 5 Circumcised the **e** day, of the stock of G3637
2Pt 2: 5 saved Noah the **e** *person*, a preacher G3590
Rev 17:11 not, even he is the **e**, and is of the seven, G3590
21:20 chrysolyte; the **e**, beryl; the ninth, a G3590

EIGHTIETH
1Ki 6: 1 the four hundred and **e** year after the H8084

EIGHTY
Gen 5:25 And Methuselah lived an hundred **e** H8084
26 seven hundred **e** and two years, and H8084
28 And Lamech lived an hundred **e** and H8084

EITHER
Gen 31:24 thou speak not to Jacob **e** good or bad.
29 thou speak not to Jacob **e** good or bad.
Lev 10: 1 of Aaron, took **e** of them his censer, and H376
13:49 or in the skin, **e** in the warp, or in the H176
51 in the garment, **e** in the warp, or in the H176
53 in the garment, **e** in the warp, or in the H176
57 And if it appear still in the garment, **e** in H176
58 And the garment, **e** warp, or woof, or H176
59 of woollen or linen, **e** in the warp, or H176
22:23 **E** a bullock or a lamb that hath any
25:49 **E** his uncle, or his uncle's son, may H176
Nu 6: 2 unto them, When **e** man or woman shall H376
22:26 to turn **e** to the right hand or to the left.
24:13 of the LORD, to do *e* good or bad of mine
Dt 17: 3 worshipped them, **e** the sun, or moon, or
28:51 shall not leave thee *e* corn, wine, or oil,
Jdg 9: 2 *is* better for you, **e** that all the sons of
1Sa 20: 2 will do nothing **e** great or small, but that
25:31 unto my lord, **e** that thou hast shed
30: 2 they slew not any, **e** great or small, but
1Ki 7:15 cubits did compass **e** of them about. H8145
10:19 *there were* stays on **e** side on the place of
18:27 for he *is* a god; **e** he is talking, or he is H3588
1Ch 21:12 **E** three years' famine; or three months to H518
2Ch 18: 9 king of Judah sat **e** of them on his H376
Ecc 9: 1 no man knoweth **e** love or hatred *by* all H1571
11: 6 shall prosper, **e** this or that, or whether
Isa 7:11 it **e** in the depth, or in the height above.
17: 8 have made, **e** the groves, or the images.
Ezk 21:16 Go thee one way or other, *e* on the right
Mt 6:24 No man can serve two masters: for **e** he G2228
12:33 **E** make the tree good, and his fruit G2228
Lk 6:42 **E** how canst thou say to thy brother, G2228
15: 8 **E** what woman having ten pieces of G2228
16:13 No servant can serve two masters: for **e** G2228
Jn 19:18 with him, on **e** side one, and G1782+G2532
Act 17:21 **e** to tell, or to hear some new thing.) G2228
1Co 14: 6 shall speak to you **e** by revelation, or by G2228
Php 3:12 Not as though I had already attained, **e** G2228
Jas 3:12 bear olive berries? **e** a vine, figs? so *can* G2228
Rev 22: 2 of it, and on **e** side of the G1782+G2532

EKER
1Ch 2:27 were, Maaz, and Jamin, and **E**. H6134

EKRON
Jos 13: 3 the borders of **E** northward, *which* is H6138
15:11 unto the side of **E** northward: and the H6138
45 **E**, with her towns and her villages: H6138
46 From **E** even unto the sea, all that *lay* H6138
19:43 And Elon, and Thimnathah, and **E**, H6138
Jdg 1:18 thereof, and **E** with the coast thereof. H6138
1Sa 5:10 Therefore they sent the ark of God to **E**. H6138
10 ark of God came to **E**, that the Ekronites H6138
6:16 *it*, they returned to **E** the same day. H6138
17 Askelon one, for Gath one, for **E** one; H6138
7:14 to Israel, from **E** even unto Gath; and H6138
17:52 and to the gates of **E**. And the wounded H6138
52 Shaaraim, even unto Gath, and unto **E**. H6138
2Ki 1: 2 the god of **E** whether I shall recover H6138
3 to inquire of Baal-zebub the god of **E**? H6138
6 the god of **E**? therefore thou shalt H6138
16 the god of **E**, *is it* not because *there* H6138
Jer 25:20 and **E**, and the remnant of Ashdod, H6138
Am 1: 8 hand against **E**: and the remnant of H6138
Zep 2: 4 the noon day, and **E** shall be rooted up. H6138
Zec 9: 5 sorrowful, and **E**; for her expectation H6138
7 governor in Judah, and **E** as a Jebusite. H6138

EKRONITES
Jos 13: 3 the Gittites, and the **E**; also the Avites: H6139
1Sa 5:10 to Ekron, that the **E** cried out, saying, H6139

ELADAH
1Ch 7:20 son, and **E** his son, and Tahath his son, H497

ELAH
Gen 36:41 Duke Aholibamah, duke **E**, duke Pinon, H425
1Sa 17: 2 by the valley of **E**, and set the battle in H425
19 valley of **E**, fighting with the Philistines. H425
21: 9 in the valley of **E**, behold, it *is here* H425
1Ki 4:18 Shimei the son of **E**, in Benjamin: H414
16: 6 and **E** his son reigned in his stead. H425
8 of Judah began **E** the son of Baasha to H425
13 and the sins of **E** his son, by which they H425
14 Now the rest of the acts of **E**, and all that H425
2Ki 15:30 And Hoshea the son of **E** made a H425
17: 1 Hoshea the son of **E** to reign in Samaria H425
18: 1 of Hoshea son of **E** king of Israel, *that* H425
9 of Hoshea son of **E** king of Israel, *that* H425
1Ch 1:52 Duke Aholibamah, duke **E**, duke Pinon, H425
4:15 of Jephunneh; Iru, **E**, and Naam: and the H425
15 Naam: and the sons of **E**, even Kenaz. H425
9: 8 And Ibneiah the son of Jeroham, and **E** H425

ELAM
Gen 10:22 The children of Shem; **E**, and Asshur, H5867
14: 1 king of **E**, and Tidal king of nations; H5867
9 With Chedorlaomer the king of **E**, and H5867
1Ch 1:17 The sons of Shem; **E**, and Asshur, and H5867
8:24 And Hananiah, and **E**, and Antothijah, H5867
26: 3 **E** the fifth, Jehohanan the sixth, H5867
Ezr 2: 7 The children of **E**, a thousand two H5867
31 The children of the other **E**, a thousand H5867
8: 7 And of the sons of **E**; Jeshaiah the son of H5867
10: 2 *one* of the sons of **E**, answered and said H5867
26 And of the sons of **E**; Mattaniah, H5867
Neh 7:12 The children of **E**, a thousand two H5867
34 The children of the other **E**, a thousand H5867
10:14 Parosh, Pahath-moab, **E**, Zatthu, Bani, H5867
12:42 Malchijah, and **E**, and Ezer. And the H5867
Isa 11:11 Cush, and from **E**, and from Shinar, H5867
21: 2 Go up, O **E**: besiege, O Media; all H5867
22: 6 And **E** bare the quiver with chariots of H5867
Jer 25:25 of **E**, and all the kings of the Medes, H5867
49:34 prophet against **E** in the beginning of H5867
35 the bow of **E**, the chief of their might. H5867
36 And upon **E** will I bring the four winds H5867
36 the outcasts of **E** shall not come. H5867
37 For I will cause **E** to be dismayed H5867
38 And I will set my throne in **E**, and will H5867
39 the captivity of **E**, saith the LORD. H5867
Ezk 32:24 There *is* **E** and all her multitude round H5867
Dan 8: 2 *is* in the province of **E**; and I saw in a H5867

ELAMITES
Ezr 4: 9 Susanchites, the Dehavites, *and* the **E**, H5962
Act 2: 9 Parthians, and Medes, and **E**, and the G1639

ELASAH
Ezr 10:22 Ishmael, Nethaneel, Jozabad, and **E**. H501
Jer 29: 3 By the hand of **E** the son of Shaphan, H501

ELATH
Dt 2: 8 way of the plain from **E**, and from H359
2Ki 14:22 He built **E**, and restored it to Judah, after H359
16: 6 of Syria recovered **E** to Syria, and drave H359
6 the Jews from **E**: and the Syrians came H359
6 came to **E**, and dwelt there unto this day. H359

EL-BETH-EL
Gen 35: 7 and called the place **E**: because there God H416

ELDAAH
Gen 25: 4 **E**. All these *were* the children of Keturah. H420
1Ch 1:33 and **E**. All these *are* the sons of Keturah. H420

ELDAD
Nu 11:26 of the one *was* **E**, and the name of the H419
27 **E** and Medad do prophesy in the camp. H419

ELDER
Gen 10:21 the **e**, even to him were *children* born. H1419
25:23 and the **e** shall serve the younger. H7227
27:42 And these words of Esau her **e** son H1419
29:16 the name of the **e** *was* Leah, and the H1419
1Sa 18:17 And Saul said to David, Behold my **e** H1419
1Ki 2:22 for he *is* mine **e** brother; even for him, H1419
Job 15:10 very aged men, much **e** than thy father.
32: 4 because they *were* **e** than he. H2205+H3117
Ezk 16:46 And thine **e** sister *is* Samaria, she and H1419
61 thy sisters, thine **e** and thy younger: H1419
23: 4 *were* Aholah the **e**, and Aholibah her H1419
Lk 15:25 Now his **e** son was in the field: and as G4245
Ro 9:12 It was said unto her, The **e** shall serve G3187
1Ti 5: 1 Rebuke not an **e**, but entreat *him* as a G4245
2 The **e** women as mothers; the younger G4245
19 Against an **e** receive not an accusation, G4245
1Pt 5: 1 who am also an **e**, and a witness of the G4850
5 unto the **e**. Yea, all *of you* be subject G4245
2Jn 1 The **e** unto the elect lady and her G4245
3Jn 1 The **e** unto the wellbeloved Gaius, G4245

ELDERS
Gen 50: 7 of Pharaoh, the **e** of his house, and all H2205
7 and all the **e** of the land of Egypt, H2205
Ex 3:16 Go, and gather the **e** of Israel together, H2205
18 thou and the **e** of Israel, unto the king H2205
4:29 all the **e** of the children of Israel: H2205
12:21 Then Moses called for all the **e** of H2205
17: 5 with thee of the **e** of Israel; and thy rod, H2205
6 did so in the sight of the **e** of Israel. H2205
18:12 came, and all the **e** of Israel, to eat H2205
19: 7 And Moses came and called for the **e** of H2205
24: 1 the **e** of Israel; and worship ye afar off. H2205
9 Abihu, and seventy of the **e** of Israel: H2205
14 And he said unto the **e**, Tarry ye here H2205
Lev 4:15 And the **e** of the congregation shall lay H2205
9: 1 Aaron and his sons, and the **e** of Israel; H2205
Nu 11:16 men of the **e** of Israel, whom thou H2205
16 knowest to be the **e** of the people, and H2205
24 men of the **e** of the people, and set H2205
25 *it* unto the seventy **e**: and it came to H2205
30 into the camp, he and the **e** of Israel. H2205
16:25 and the **e** of Israel followed him. H2205
22: 4 And Moab said unto the **e** of Midian, H2205
7 And the **e** of Moab and the elders of H2205
7 And the elders of Moab and the **e** of H2205
Dt 5:23 all the heads of your tribes, and your **e**; H2205
19:12 Then the **e** of his city shall send and H2205
21: 2 Then thy **e** and thy judges shall come H2205
3 man, even the **e** of that city shall take H2205
4 And the **e** of that city shall bring down H2205
6 And all the **e** of that city, *that are* next H2205
19 him out unto the **e** of his city, and unto H2205
20 And they shall say unto the **e** of his H2205
22:15 unto the **e** of the city in the gate: H2205
16 shall say unto the **e**, I gave my daughter H2205
17 spread the cloth before the **e** of the city. H2205
18 And the **e** of that city shall take that H2205
25: 7 to the gate unto the **e**, and say, My H2205
8 Then the **e** of his city shall call him, H2205

E

9 the presence of the **e**, and loose his shoe H2205
27: 1 And Moses with the **e** of Israel H2205
Dt 29:10 of your tribes, your **e**, and your officers, H2205
31: 9 the LORD, and unto all the **e** of Israel. H2205
28 Gather unto me all the **e** of your tribes, H2205
32: 7 shew thee; thy **e**, and they will tell thee. H2205
Jos 7: 6 he and the **e** of Israel, and put dust H2205
8:10 the **e** of Israel, before the people to Ai. H2205
33 And all Israel, and their **e**, and officers, H2205
9:11 Wherefore our **e** and all the H2205
20: 4 in the ears of the **e** of that city, they H2205
23: 2 *and* for their **e**, and for their heads, H2205
24: 1 and called for the **e** of Israel, and for H2205
31 and all the days of the **e** that overlived H2205
Jdg 2: 7 and all the days of the **e** that outlived H2205
8:14 of Succoth, and the **e** thereof, *even* H2205
16 And he took the **e** of the city, and H2205
11: 5 against Israel, the **e** of Gilead went to H2205
7 And Jephthah said unto the **e** of Gilead, H2205
8 And the **e** of Gilead said unto Jephthah, H2205
9 And Jephthah said unto the **e** of Gilead, H2205
10 And the **e** of Gilead said unto Jephthah, H2205
11 Then Jephthah went with the **e** of H2205
21:16 Then the **e** of the congregation said, H2205
Ru 4: 2 And he took ten men of the **e** of the H2205
4 and before the **e** of my people. If thou H2205
9 And Boaz said unto the **e**, and *unto* all H2205
11 in the gate, and the **e**, said, *We are* H2205
1Sa 4: 3 into the camp, the **e** of Israel said, H2205
8: 4 Then all the **e** of Israel gathered H2205
11: 3 And the **e** of Jabesh said unto him, Give H2205
15:30 thee, before the **e** of my people, and H2205
16: 4 And the **e** of the town trembled H2205
30:26 of the spoil unto the **e** of Judah, *even* to H2205
2Sa 3:17 with the **e** of Israel, saying, Ye H2205
5: 3 So all the **e** of Israel came to the king to H2205
12:17 And the **e** of his house arose, *and went* H2205
17: 4 Absalom well, and all the **e** of Israel. H2205
15 Absalom and the **e** of Israel; and thus H2205
19:11 Speak unto the **e** of Judah, saying, Why H2205
1Ki 8: 1 Then Solomon assembled the **e** of H2205
3 And all the **e** of Israel came, and the H2205
20: 7 Then the king of Israel called all the **e** H2205
8 And all the **e** and all the people said H2205
21: 8 letters unto the **e** and to the nobles that H2205
11 And the men of his city, *even* the **e** and H2205
2Ki 6:32 But Elisha sat in his house, and the **e** H2205
32 to him, he said to the **e**, See ye how this H2205
10: 1 of Jezreel, to the **e**, and to them that H2205
5 *was* over the city, the **e** also, and the H2205
19: 2 the scribe, and the **e** of the priests, H2205
23: 1 all the **e** of Judah and of Jerusalem. H2205
1Ch 11: 3 Therefore came all the **e** of Israel to the H2205
15:25 So David, and the **e** of Israel, and the H2205
21:16 David and the **e** *of Israel, who were* H2205
2Ch 5: 2 Then Solomon assembled the **e** of H2205
4 And all the **e** of Israel came; and the H2205
34:29 all the **e** of Judah and Jerusalem. H2205
Ezr 5: 5 But the eye of their God was upon the **e** H7868
9 Then asked we those **e**, *and* said unto H7868
6: 7 the Jews and the **e** of the Jews build this H7868
8 ye shall do to the **e** of these Jews for the H7868
14 And the **e** of the Jews builded, and they H7868
10: 8 the princes and the **e**, all his substance H2205
14 and with them the **e** of every city, and H2205
Ps 107:32 and praise him in the assembly of the **e**. H2205
Prv 31:23 he sitteth among the **e** of the land. H2205
Isa 37: 2 the scribe, and the **e** of the priests H2205
Jer 26:17 Then rose up certain of the **e** of the H2205
29: 1 the residue of the **e** which were carried H2205
Lam 1:19 priests and mine **e** gave up the ghost in H2205
2:10 The **e** of the daughter of Zion sit upon H2205
4:16 of the priests, they favoured not the **e**. H2205
5:12 hand: the faces of **e** were not honoured. H2205
14 The **e** have ceased from the gate, the H2205
Ezk 8: 1 house, and the **e** of Judah sat before H2205
14: 1 Then came certain of the **e** of Israel H2205
20: 1 *that* certain of the **e** of Israel came to H2205
3 Son of man, speak unto the **e** of Israel, H2205
Joel 1:14 gather the **e** *and* all the inhabitants H2205
2:16 assemble the **e**, gather the children, H2205
Mt 15: 2 the tradition of the **e**? for they wash not *G4245*
16:21 things of the **e** and chief priests and *G4245*
21:23 priests and the **e** of the people came *G4245*
26: 3 scribes, and the **e** of the people, unto *G4245*
47 the chief priests and **e** of the people. *G4245*
57 the scribes and the **e** were assembled. *G4245*
59 Now the chief priests, and **e**, and all the *G4245*
27: 1 chief priests and **e** of the people took *G4245*
3 of silver to the chief priests and **e**, *G4245*
12 priests and **e**, he answered nothing. *G4245*
Mt 27:20 But the chief priests and **e** persuaded *G4245*
41 *him*, with the scribes and **e**, said, *G4245*
28:12 with the **e**, and had taken counsel, *G4245*
Mk 7: 3 eat not, holding the tradition of the **e**. *G4245*
5 **e**, but eat bread with unwashen hands? *G4245*
8:31 and be rejected of the **e**, and *of* the chief *G4245*
11:27 chief priests, and the scribes, and the **e**, *G4245*
14:43 chief priests and the scribes and the **e**. *G4245*
53 chief priests and the **e** and the scribes. *G4245*
15: 1 with the **e** and scribes and the *G4245*
Lk 7: 3 he sent unto him the **e** of the Jews, *G4245*
9:22 be rejected of the **e** and chief priests *G4245*
20: 1 the scribes came upon *him* with the **e**, *G4245*
22:52 temple, and the **e**, which were come to *G4245*
66 And as soon as it was day, the **e** of the *G4244*
Act 4: 5 that their rulers, and **e**, and scribes, *G4245*
8 Ye rulers of the people, and **e** of Israel, *G4245*
23 chief priests and **e** had said unto them. *G4245*
6:12 people, and the **e**, and the scribes, and *G4245*
11:30 Which also they did, and sent it to the **e** *G4245*
14:23 And when they had ordained them **e** in *G4245*
15: 2 the apostles and **e** about this question. *G4245*
4 the apostles and **e**, and they declared all *G4245*
6 And the apostles and **e** came together *G4245*
22 Then pleased it the apostles and **e**, with *G4245*
23 The apostles and **e** and brethren *send* *G4245*
16: 4 and **e** which were at Jerusalem. *G4245*
20:17 Ephesus, and called the **e** of the church. *G4245*
21:18 unto James; and all the **e** were present. *G4245*
22: 5 all the estate of the **e**: from whom also I *G4244*
23:14 chief priests and **e**, and said, We have *G4245*
24: 1 with the **e**, and *with* a certain orator *G4245*
25:15 priests and the **e** of the Jews informed *G4245*
1Ti 5:17 Let the **e** that rule well be counted *G4245*
Tit 1: 5 **e** in every city, as I had appointed thee: *G4245*
Heb 11: 2 For by it the **e** obtained a good report. *G4245*
Jas 5:14 let him call for the **e** of the church; and *G4245*
1Pt 5: 1 The **e** which are among you I exhort, *G4245*
Rev 4: 4 four and twenty **e** sitting, clothed in *G4245*
10 The four and twenty **e** fall down before *G4245*
5: 5 And one of the **e** saith unto me, Weep *G4245*
6 in the midst of the **e**, stood a Lamb as it *G4245*
8 four *and* twenty **e** fell down before the *G4245*
11 the beasts and the **e**: and the number of *G4245*
14 the four *and* twenty **e** fell down and *G4245*
7:11 and *about* the **e** and the four beasts, *G4245*
13 And one of the **e** answered, saying unto *G4245*
11:16 And the four and twenty **e**, which sat *G4245*
14: 3 beasts, and the **e**: and no man could *G4245*
19: 4 And the four and twenty **e** and the four *G4245*

ELDEST

Gen 24: 2 And Abraham said unto his **e** servant H2205
27: 1 he called Esau his **e** son, and said unto H1419
15 raiment of her **e** son Esau, which *were* H1419
44:12 And he searched, *and* began at the **e**, H1419
Nu 1:20 And the children of Reuben, Israel's **e** H1060
26: 5 Reuben, the **e** son of Israel: the H1060
1Sa 17:13 And the three **e** sons of Jesse went *and* H1419
14 and the three **e** followed Saul. H1419
28 And Eliab his **e** brother heard when he H1419
2Ki 3:27 Then he took his **e** son that should H1060
2Ch 22: 1 had slain all the **e**. So Ahaziah the son H7223
Job 1:13 wine in their **e** brother's house: H1060
18 wine in their **e** brother's house: H1060
Jn 8: 9 beginning at the **e**, *even* unto the last: *G4245*

ELEAD

1Ch 7:21 son, and Ezer, and **E**, whom the men of H496

ELEALEH

Nu 32: 3 **E**, and Shebam, and Nebo, and Beon, H500
37 built Heshbon, and **E**, and Kirjathaim, H500
Isa 15: 4 And Heshbon shall cry, and **E**: their voice H500
16: 9 O Heshbon, and **E**: for the shouting for H500
Jer 48:34 From the cry of Heshbon *even* unto **E**, H500

ELEASAH

1Ch 2:39 Azariah begat Helez, and Helez begat **E**, H501
40 And **E** begat Sisamai, and Sisamai begat H501
8:37 *was* his son, **E** his son, Azel his son: H501
9:43 his son, **E** his son, Azel his son. H501

ELEAZAR

Ex 6:23 him Nadab, and Abihu, **E**, and Ithamar. H499
25 And **E** Aaron's son took him *one* of the H499
28: 1 Abihu, **E** and Ithamar, Aaron's sons. H499
Lev 10: 6 And Moses said unto Aaron, and unto **E** H499
12 Aaron, and unto **E** and unto Ithamar, H499
Lev 10:16 he was angry with **E** and Ithamar, the H499
Nu 3: 2 the firstborn, and Abihu, **E**, and Ithamar. H499
4 had no children: and **E** and Ithamar H499
32 And **E** the son of Aaron the priest *shall* H499
4:16 And to the office of **E** the son of Aaron H499
16:37 Speak unto **E** the son of Aaron the H499
39 And **E** the priest took the brasen censers, H499
19: 3 And ye shall give her unto **E** the priest, H499
4 And **E** the priest shall take of her blood H499
20:25 Take Aaron and **E** his son, and bring H499
26 and put them upon **E** his son: and Aaron H499
28 and put them upon **E** his son; and Aaron H499
28 and **E** came down from the mount. H499
25: 7 And when Phinehas, the son of **E**, the son H499
11 Phinehas, the son of **E**, the son of Aaron H499
26: 1 **E** the son of Aaron the priest, saying, H499
3 And Moses and **E** the priest spake with H499
60 born Nadab, and Abihu, **E**, and Ithamar. H499
63 by Moses and **E** the priest, who H499
27: 2 Moses, and before **E** the priest, and H499
19 And set him before **E** the priest, and H499
21 And he shall stand before **E** the priest, H499
22 and set him before **E** the priest, and H499
31: 6 the son of **E** the priest, to the war, H499
12 unto Moses, and **E** the priest, and unto H499
13 And Moses, and **E** the priest, and all the H499
21 And **E** the priest said unto the men of H499
26 of beast, thou, and **E** the priest, and the H499
29 Take *it* of their half, and give it unto **E** H499
31 And Moses and **E** the priest did as the H499
41 offering, unto **E** the priest, as the LORD H499
51 And Moses and **E** the priest took the H499
54 And Moses and **E** the priest took the H499
32: 2 unto Moses, and to **E** the priest, and H499
28 commanded **E** the priest, and Joshua H499
34:17 **E** the priest, and Joshua the son of Nun. H499
Dt 10: 6 he was buried; and **E** his son ministered H499
Jos 14: 1 land of Canaan, which **E** the priest, and H499
17: 4 And they came near before **E** the priest, H499
19:51 These *are* the inheritances, which **E** the H499
21: 1 of the Levites unto **E** the priest, and unto H499
22:13 Gilead, Phinehas the son of **E** the priest, H499
31 And Phinehas the son of **E** the priest H499
32 And Phinehas the son of **E** the priest, H499
24:33 And **E** the son of Aaron died; and they H499
Jdg 20:28 And Phinehas, the son of **E**, the son of H499
1Sa 7: 1 **E** his son to keep the ark of the LORD. H499
2Sa 23: 9 And after him *was* **E** the son of Dodo the H499
1Ch 6: 3 Nadab, and Abihu, **E**, and Ithamar. H499
4 **E** begat Phinehas, Phinehas begat H499
50 And these *are* the sons of Aaron; **E** his H499
9:20 And Phinehas the son of **E** was the ruler H499
11:12 And after him *was* **E** the son of Dodo, H499
23:21 Mushi. The sons of Mahli; **E**, and Kish. H499
22 And **E** died, and had no sons, but H499
24: 1 Nadab, and Abihu, **E**, and Ithamar. H499
2 no children: therefore **E** and Ithamar H499
3 of the sons of **E**, and Ahimelech of the H499
4 found of the sons of **E** than of the sons of H499
4 Among the sons of **E** *there were* sixteen H499
5 the sons of **E**, and of the sons of Ithamar. H499
6 taken for **E**, and *one* taken for Ithamar. H499
28 Of Mahli *came* **E**, who had no sons. H499
Ezr 7: 5 of **E**, the son of Aaron the chief priest: H499
8:33 and with him *was* **E** the son of Phinehas; H499
10:25 and **E**, and Malchijah, and Benaiah. H499
Neh 12:42 And Maaseiah, and Shemaiah, and **E**, H499
Mt 1:15 And Eliud begat **E**; and Eleazar begat *G1648*
15 And Eliud begat Eleazar; and **E** begat *G1648*

ELECT

Isa 42: 1 I uphold; mine **e**, *in whom* my soul H972
45: 4 and Israel mine **e**, I have even called thee H972
65: 9 and mine **e** shall inherit it, and my H972
22 people, and mine **e** shall long enjoy the H972
Mt 24:24 possible, they shall deceive the very **e**. *G1588*
31 together his **e** from the four winds, *G1588*
Mk 13:22 to seduce, if *it were* possible, even the **e**. *G1588*
27 together his **e** from the four winds, *G1588*
Lk 18: 7 And shall not God avenge his own **e**, *G1588*
Ro 8:33 of God's **e**? *It is* God that justifieth. *G1588*
Col 3:12 Put on therefore, as the **e** of God, holy *G1588*
1Ti 5:21 Christ, and the **e** angels, that thou *G1588*
Tit 1: 1 to the faith of God's **e**, and the *G1588*
1Pt 1: 2 **E** according to the foreknowledge of *G1588*
2: 6 a chief corner stone, **e**, precious: and he *G1588*
2Jn 1 The elder unto the **e** lady and her *G1588*

13 The children of thy e sister greet thee. G1588

ELECTED
1Pt 5:13 The church that is at Babylon, e G4899

ELECTION
Ro 9:11 God according to e might stand, not of G1589
11: 5 a remnant according to the e of grace. G1589
7 for; but the e hath obtained it, and G1589
28 as touching the e, they are beloved for G1589
1Th 1: 4 Knowing, brethren beloved, your e of G1589
2Pt 1:10 your calling and e sure: for if ye do G1589

ELECT'S
Mt 24:22 e sake those days shall be shortened. G1588
Mk 13:20 be saved: but for the e sake, whom he G1588
2Ti 2:10 Therefore I endure all things for the e G1588

EL-ELOHE-ISRAEL
Gen 33:20 he erected there an altar, and called it E. H415

ELEMENTS
Gal 4: 3 in bondage under the e of the world: G4747
9 and beggarly e, whereunto ye desire G4747
2Pt 3:10 noise, and the e shall melt with fervent G4747
12 and the e shall melt with fervent heat? G4747

ELEPH
Jos 18:28 And Zelah, E, and Jebusi, which is H507

ELEVEN
Gen 32:22 and his e sons, and passed H259+H6240
37: 9 e stars made obeisance to me. H259+H6240
Ex 26: 7 e curtains shalt thou make. H6249+H6240
8 and the e curtains shall be H6249+H6240
36:14 e curtains he made them. H6249+H6240
15 the e curtains were of one size. H6249+H6240
Nu 29:20 And on the third day e H6249+H6240
Dt 1: 2 (There are e days' journey from H259+H6240
Jos 15:51 Giloh; e cities with their villages: H259+H6240
Jdg 16: 5 of us e hundred pieces of silver. H505+H3967
17: 2 mother, The e hundred shekels H505+H3967
3 And when he had restored the e H505+H3967
2Ki 23:36 reign; and he reigned e years in H259+H6240
24:18 reign, and he reigned e years in H259+H6240
2Ch 36: 5 reign, and he reigned e years in H259+H6240
11 reigned e years in Jerusalem. H259+H6240
Jer 52: 1 reign, and he reigned e years in H259+H6240
Ezk 40:49 the breadth e cubits; and he H6249+H6240
Mt 28:16 Then the e disciples went away into G1733
Mk 16:14 Afterward he appeared unto the e as G1733
Lk 24: 9 things unto the e, and to all the rest. G1733
33 and found the e gathered together, and G1733
Act 1:26 he was numbered with the e apostles. G1733
2:14 But Peter, standing up with the e, lifted G1733

ELEVEN HUNDRED See ELEVEN and HUNDRED.

ELEVENTH
Nu 7:72 On the e day Pagiel the son of H6249+H6240
Dt 1: 3 year, in the e month, on the H6249+H6240
1Ki 6:38 And in the e year, in the month H259+H6240
2Ki 9:29 And in the e year of Joram the H259+H6240
25: 2 the e year of king Zedekiah. H6249+H6240
1Ch 12:13 the tenth, Machbanai the e. H6249+H6240
24:12 The e to Eliashib, the twelfth to H6249+H6240
25:18 The e to Azareel, he, his sons, H6249+H6240
27:14 The e captain for the eleventh H6249+H6240
14 The eleventh captain for the e H6249+H6240
Jer 1: 3 unto the end of the e year of H6249+H6240
39: 2 And in the e year of Zedekiah, H6249+H6240
52: 5 the e year of king Zedekiah. H6249+H6240
Ezk 26: 1 And it came to pass in the e H6249+H6240
30:20 And it came to pass in the e H259+H6240
31: 1 And it came to pass in the e H259+H6240
Zec 1: 7 day of the e month, which is H6249+H6240
Mt 20: 6 And about the e hour he went out, and G1734
9 hired about the e hour, they received G1734
Rev 21:20 e, a jacinth; the twelfth, an amethyst. G1734

ELHANAN
2Sa 21:19 the Philistines, where E the son of H445
23:24 thirty; E the son of Dodo of Beth-lehem, H445
1Ch 11:26 of Joab, E the son of Dodo of Beth-lehem, H445
20: 5 the Philistines; and E the son of Jair slew H445

ELI
1Sa 1: 3 And the two sons of E, Hophni and H5941
9 had drunk. Now E the priest sat upon H5941
12 the LORD, that E marked her mouth. H5941
13 E thought she had been drunken. H5941
1Sa 1:14 And E said unto her, How long wilt H5941
17 Then E answered and said, Go in H5941
25 a bullock, and brought the child to E. H5941
2:11 unto the LORD before E the priest. H5941
12 Now the sons of E were sons of Belial; H5941
20 And E blessed Elkanah and his wife, H5941
22 Now E was very old, and heard all that H5941
27 And there came a man of God unto E, H5941
3: 1 the LORD before E. And the word of the H5941
2 at that time, when E was laid down in H5941
5 And he ran unto E, and said, Here am I; H5941
6 arose and went to E, and said, Here am H5941
8 arose and went to E, and said, Here am H5941
8 didst call me. And E perceived that the H5941
9 Therefore E said unto Samuel, Go, lie H5941
12 In that day I will perform against E all H5941
14 unto the house of E, that the iniquity of H5941
15 Samuel feared to shew E the vision. H5941
16 Then E called Samuel, and said, H5941
4: 4 and the two sons of E, Hophni and H5941
11 of E, Hophni and Phinehas, were slain. H5941
13 And when he came, lo, E sat upon a H5941
14 And when E heard the noise of the H5941
14 the man came in hastily, and told E. H5941
15 Now E was ninety and eight years old; H5941
16 And the man said unto E, I am he that H5941
14: 3 the son of E, the LORD'S priest in H5941
1Ki 2:27 concerning the house of E in Shiloh. H5941
Mt 27:46 voice, saying, E, Eli, lama sabachthani? G2241
46 voice, saying, Eli, E, lama sabachthani? G2241

ELIAB
Nu 1: 9 Of Zebulun; E the son of Helon. H446
2: 7 Then the tribe of Zebulun: and E the son H446
7:24 On the third day E the son of Helon, H446
29 was the offering of E the son of Helon. H446
10:16 of Zebulun was E the son of Helon. H446
16: 1 the sons of E, and On, the son of Peleth, H446
12 of E: which said, We will not come up: H446
26: 8 And the sons of Pallu; E. H446
9 And the sons of E; Nemuel, and Dathan, H446
Dt 11: 6 the sons of E, the son of Reuben: how H446
1Sa 16: 6 that he looked on E, and said, Surely the H446
17:13 to the battle were E the firstborn, and H446
28 And E his eldest brother heard when he H446
1Ch 2:13 And Jesse begat his firstborn E, and H446
6:27 E his son, Jeroham his son, Elkanah his H446
12: 9 Ezer the first, Obadiah the second, E the H446
15:18 Jehiel, and Unni, E, and Benaiah, and H446
20 and Unni, and E, and Maaseiah, and H446
16: 5 and Mattithiah, and E, and Benaiah, and H446
2Ch 11:18 the daughter of E the son of Jesse; H446

ELIAB'S
1Sa 17:28 unto the men; and E anger was kindled H446

ELIADA
2Sa 5:16 And Elishama, and E, and Eliphalet. H450
1Ch 3: 8 And Elishama, and E, and Eliphelet, H450
2Ch 17:17 And of Benjamin; E a mighty man of H450

ELIADAH
1Ki 11:23 Rezon the son of E, which fled from his H450

ELIAH
1Ch 8:27 And Jaresiah, and E, and Zichri, the sons H452
Ezr 10:26 Jehiel, and Abdi, and Jeremoth, and E. H452

ELIAHBA
2Sa 23:32 E the Shaalbonite, of the sons of Jashen, H455
1Ch 11:33 Azmaveth the Baharumite, E the H455

ELIAKIM
2Ki 18:18 came out to them E the son of Hilkiah, H471
26 Then said E the son of Hilkiah, and H471
37 Then came E the son of Hilkiah, which H471
19: 2 And he sent E, which was over the H471
23:34 And Pharaoh-nechoh made E the son of H471
2Ch 36: 4 And the king of Egypt made E his H471
Neh 12:41 And the priests; E, Maaseiah, Miniamin, H471
Isa 22:20 will call my servant E the son of Hilkiah: H471
36: 3 Then came forth unto him E, Hilkiah's H471
11 Then said E and Shebna and Joah unto H471
22 Then came E, the son of Hilkiah, that H471
37: 2 And he sent E, who was over the H471
Mt 1:13 Abiud begat E; and Eliakim begat Azor; G1662
13 begat Eliakim; and E begat Azor; G1662
Lk 3:30 son of Jonan, which was the son of E, G1662

ELIAM
2Sa 11: 3 of E, the wife of Uriah the Hittite? H463
23:34 E the son of Ahithophel the Gilonite, H463

ELIAS
Mt 11:14 And if ye will receive it, this is E, which G2243
16:14 John the Baptist: some, E; and others, G2243
17: 3 them Moses and E talking with him. G2243
4 thee, and one for Moses, and one for E. G2243
10 say the scribes that E must first come? G2243
11 said unto them, E truly shall first come, G2243
12 But I say unto you, That E is come G2243
27:47 heard that, said, This man calleth for E. G2243
49 us see whether E will come to save him. G2243
Mk 6:15 Others said, That it is E. And others G2243
8:28 say, E; and others, One of the prophets. G2243
9: 4 And there appeared unto them E with G2243
5 thee, and one for Moses, and one for E. G2243
11 say the scribes that E must first come? G2243
12 And he answered and told them, E G2243
13 But I say unto you, That E is indeed G2243
15:35 they heard it, said, Behold, he calleth E. G2243
36 whether E will come to take him down. G2243
Lk 1:17 and power of E, to turn the hearts of G2243
4:25 in the days of E, when the heaven was G2243
26 But unto none of them was E sent, save G2243
9: 8 And of some, that E had appeared; and G2243
19 but some say, E; and others say, that G2243
30 him two men, which were Moses and E: G2243
33 one for E: not knowing what he said. G2243
54 and consume them, even as E did? G2243
Jn 1:21 then? Art thou E? And he saith, I am G2243
25 that Christ, nor E, neither that prophet? G2243
Ro 11: 2 the scripture saith of E? how he maketh G2243
Jas 5:17 E was a man subject to like passions as G2243

ELIASAPH
Nu 1:14 Of Gad; E the son of Deuel. H460
2:14 sons of Gad shall be E the son of Reuel. H460
3:24 Gershonites shall be E the son of Lael. H460
7:42 On the sixth day E the son of Deuel, H460
47 was the offering of E the son of Deuel. H460
10:20 children of Gad was E the son of Deuel. H460

ELIASHIB
1Ch 3:24 were, Hodaiah, and E, and Pelaiah, and H475
24:12 The eleventh to E, the twelfth to Jakim, H475
Ezr 10: 6 Johanan the son of E: and when he came H475
24 Of the singers also; E: and of the porters; H475
27 And of the sons of Zattu; Elioenai, E, H475
36 Vaniah, Meremoth, E, H475
Neh 3: 1 Then E the high priest rose up with his H475
20 door of the house of E the high priest. H475
21 of the house of E even to the end of the H475
21 even to the end of the house of E. H475
12:10 also begat E, and Eliashib begat Joiada, H475
10 also begat Eliashib, and E begat Joiada, H475
22 The Levites in the days of E, Joiada, and H475
23 until the days of Johanan the son of E. H475
13: 4 And before this, E the priest, having the H475
7 of the evil that E did for Tobiah, in H475
28 Joiada, the son of E the high priest, was H475

ELIATHAH
1Ch 25: 4 Hanani, E, Giddalti, and Romamti-ezer, H448
27 The twentieth to E, he, his sons, and his H448

ELIDAD
Nu 34:21 Of the tribe of Benjamin, E the son of H449

ELIEL
1Ch 5:24 Epher, and Ishi, and E, and Azriel, and H447
6:34 of Jeroham, the son of E, the son of Toah, H447
8:20 And Elienai, and Zilthai, and E, H447
22 And Ishpan, and Heber, and E, H447
11:46 E the Mahavite, and Jeribai, and H447
47 E, and Obed, and Jasiel the Mesobaite. H447
12:11 Attai the sixth, E the seventh, H447
15: 9 Of the sons of Hebron; E the chief, and H447
11 Joel, Shemaiah, and E, and Amminadab, H447
2Ch 31:13 and Jozabad, and E, and Ismachiah, and H447

ELIENAI
1Ch 8:20 And E, and Zilthai, and Eliel, H462

ELIEZER
Gen 15: 2 of my house is this E of Damascus? H461

Ex 18: 4 And the name of the other *was* E; for the H461
1Ch 7: 8 and Joash, and E, and Elioenai, and H461
1Ch 15:24 and Benaiah, and E, the priests, did blow H461
23:15 sons of Moses *were*, Gershom, and E. H461
17 And the sons of E *were*, Rehabiah the H461
17 the chief. And E had none other sons; H461
26:25 And his brethren by E; Rehabiah his son, H461
27:16 Reubenites *was* E the son of Zichri: of H461
2Ch 20:37 Then E the son of Dodavah of Mareshah H461
Ezr 8:16 Then sent I for E, for Ariel, for Shemaiah, H461
10:18 and E, and Jarib, and Gedaliah. H461
23 same *is* Kelita,) Pethahiah, Judah, and E. H461
31 And *of* the sons of Harim; E, Ishijah, H461
Lk 3:29 was *the son* of E, which was *the son* of *G1663*

ELIHOENAI
Ezr 8: 4 Of the sons of Pahath-moab; E the son of H454

ELIHOREPH
1Ki 4: 3 E and Ahiah, the sons of Shisha, scribes; H456

ELIHU
1Sa 1: 1 the son of E, the son of Tohu, the H453
1Ch 12:20 and Jozabad, and E, and Zilthai, H453
26: 7 *were* strong men, E, and Semachiah. H453
27:18 Of Judah, E, *one* of the brethren of David: H453
Job 32: 2 Then was kindled the wrath of E the son H453
4 Now E had waited till Job had spoken, H453
5 When E saw that *there was* no answer in H453
6 And E the son of Barachel the Buzite H453
34: 1 Furthermore E answered and said, H453
35: 1 E spake moreover, and said, H453
36: 1 E also proceeded, and said, H453

ELIJAH
1Ki 17: 1 And E the Tishbite, *who was* of the H452
13 And E said unto her, Fear not; go *and* do H452
15 to the saying of E: and she, and he, and H452
16 word of the LORD, which he spake by E. H452
18 And she said unto E, What have I to do H452
22 And the LORD heard the voice of E; and H452
23 And E took the child, and brought him H452
23 mother: and E said, See, thy son liveth. H452
24 And the woman said to E, Now by this I H452
18: 1 of the LORD came to E in the third year, H452
2 And E went to shew himself unto Ahab. H452
7 in the way, behold, E met him: and he H452
7 face, and said, *Art* thou that my lord E? H452
8 I *am*: go, tell thy lord, Behold, E *is here*. H452
11 Go, tell thy lord, Behold, E *is here*. H452
14 Behold, E *is here*: and he shall slay me. H452
15 And E said, *As* the LORD of hosts liveth, H452
16 and told him: and Ahab went to meet E. H452
17 And it came to pass, when Ahab saw E, H452
21 And E came unto all the people, and H452
22 Then said E unto the people, I, *even* I H452
25 And E said unto the prophets of Baal, H452
27 And it came to pass at noon, that E H452
30 And E said unto all the people, Come H452
31 And E took twelve stones, according to H452
36 sacrifice, that E the prophet came near, H452
40 And E said unto them, Take the H452
40 took them: and E brought them down H452
41 And E said unto Ahab, Get thee up, eat H452
42 and to drink. And E went up to the top H452
46 And the hand of the LORD was on E; and H452
19: 1 And Ahab told Jezebel all that E had H452
2 Then Jezebel sent a messenger unto E, H452
9 said unto him, What doest thou here, E? H452
13 And it was *so*, when E heard *it*, that he H452
13 him, and said, What doest thou here, E? H452
19 the twelfth: and E passed by him, and H452
20 And he left the oxen, and ran after E, and H452
21 went after E, and ministered unto him. H452
21:17 And the word of the LORD came to E the H452
20 And Ahab said to E, Hast thou found me, H452
28 And the word of the LORD came to E the H452
2Ki 1: 3 But the angel of the LORD said to E the H452
4 up, but shalt surely die. And E departed. H452
8 loins. And he said, It *is* E the Tishbite. H452
10 And E answered and said to the captain H452
12 And E answered and said unto them, If I H452
13 on his knees before E, and besought him, H452
15 And the angel of the LORD said unto E, H452
17 of the LORD which E had spoken. And H452
2: 1 LORD would take up E into heaven by a H452
1 that E went with Elisha from Gilgal. H452
2 And E said unto Elisha, Tarry here, I H452
4 And E said unto him, Elisha, tarry here, H452
6 And E said unto him, Tarry, I pray thee, H452
8 And E took his mantle, and wrapped *it* H452
2Ki 2: 9 gone over, that E said unto Elisha, Ask H452
11 E went up by a whirlwind into heaven. H452
13 He took up also the mantle of E that fell H452
14 And he took the mantle of E that fell H452
14 *is* the LORD God of E? and when he also H452
15 said, The spirit of E doth rest on Elisha. H452
3:11 which poured water on the hands of E. H452
9:36 by his servant E the Tishbite, saying, H452
10:10 *that* which he spake by his servant E. H452
17 saying of the LORD, which he spake to E. H452
2Ch 21:12 And there came a writing to him from E H452
Ezr 10:21 E, and Shemaiah, and Jehiel, and Uzziah. H452
Mal 4: 5 Behold, I will send you E the prophet H452

ELIKA
2Sa 23:25 Shammah the Harodite, E the Harodite, H470

ELIM
Ex 15:27 And they came to E, where *were* twelve H362
16: 1 And they took their journey from E, and H362
1 Sin, which *is* between E and Sinai, on the H362
Nu 33: 9 and came unto E: and in Elim *were* H362
9 came unto Elim: and in E *were* twelve H362
10 And they removed from E, and H362

ELIMELECH
Ru 1: 2 And the name of the man *was* E, and the H458
3 And E Naomi's husband died; and she H458
2: 1 the family of E; and his name *was* Boaz. H458
3 unto Boaz, who *was* of the kindred of E. H458

ELIMELECH'S
Ru 4: 3 parcel of land, which *was* our brother E: H458
9 bought all that *was* E, and all that *was* H458

ELIOENAI
1Ch 3:23 And the sons of Neariah; E, and H454
24 And the sons of E *were*, Hodaiah, and H454
4:36 And E, and Jaakobah, and Jeshohaiah, H454
7: 8 Joash, and Eliezer, and E, and Omri, and H454
26: 3 Elam the fifth, Jehohanan the sixth, E H454
Ezr 10:22 And of the sons of Pashur; E, Maaseiah, H454
27 And of the sons of Zattu; E, Eliashib, H454
Neh 12:41 Michaiah, E, Zechariah, *and* Hananiah, H454

ELIPHAL
1Ch 11:35 Ahiam the son of Sacar the Hararite, E H465

ELIPHALET
2Sa 5:16 And Elishama, and Eliada, and E. H467
1Ch 14: 7 And Elishama, and Beeliada, and E. H467

ELIPHAZ
Gen 36: 4 And Adah bare to Esau E; and H464
10 These *are* the names of Esau's sons; E H464
11 And the sons of E were Teman, Omar, H464
12 And Timna was concubine to E Esau's H464
12 and she bare to E Amalek: these *were* H464
15 Esau: the sons of E the firstborn *son* of H464
16 the dukes *that came* of E in the land of H464
1Ch 1:35 The sons of Esau; E, Reuel, and Jeush, H464
36 The sons of E; Teman, and Omar, Zephi, H464
Job 2:11 from his own place; E the Temanite, and H464
4: 1 Then E the Temanite answered and H464
15: 1 Then answered E the Temanite, and H464
22: 1 Then E the Temanite answered and H464
42: 7 the LORD said to E the Temanite, My H464
9 So E the Temanite and Bildad the H464

ELIPHELEH
1Ch 15:18 Mattithiah, and E, and Mikneiah, and H466
21 And Mattithiah, and E, and Mikneiah, H466

ELIPHELET
2Sa 23:34 E the son of Ahasbai, the son of the H467
1Ch 3: 6 Ibhar also, and Elishama, and E, H467
8 And Elishama, and Eliada, and E, nine. H467
8:39 Jehush the second, and E the third. H467
Ezr 8:13 names *are* these, E, Jeiel, and Shemaiah, H467
10:33 E, Jeremai, Manasseh, *and* Shimei. H467

ELI'S
1Sa 3:14 that the iniquity of E house shall not be H5941

ELISABETH
Lk 1: 5 of Aaron, and her name *was* E. *G1665*
7 And they had no child, because that E *G1665*
13 and thy wife E shall bear thee a son, *G1665*
24 And after those days his wife E *G1665*
Lk 1:36 And, behold, thy cousin E, she hath also *G1665*
40 the house of Zacharias, and saluted E. *G1665*
41 And it came to pass, that, when E *G1665*
41 and E was filled with the Holy Ghost: *G1665*

ELISABETH'S
Lk 1:57 Now E full time came that she should *G1665*

ELISEUS
Lk 4:27 in the time of E the prophet; and none *G1666*

ELISHA
1Ki 19:16 over Israel: and E the son of Shaphat of H477
17 from the sword of Jehu shall E slay. H477
19 So he departed thence, and found E the H477
2Ki 2: 1 that Elijah went with E from Gilgal. H477
2 And Elijah said unto E, Tarry here, I pray H477
2 me to Beth-el. And E said *unto him*, *As* H477
3 came forth to E, and said unto him, H477
4 And Elijah said unto him, E, tarry here, I H477
5 at Jericho came to E, and said unto him, H477
9 Elijah said unto E, Ask what I shall do for H477
9 from thee. And E said, I pray thee, let H477
12 And E saw *it*, and he cried, My father, H477
14 hither and thither: and E went over. H477
15 Elijah doth rest on E. And they came to H477
19 And the men of the city said unto E, H477
22 to the saying of E which he spake. H477
3:11 and said, Here *is* E the son of Shaphat, H477
13 And E said unto the king of Israel, What H477
14 And E said, *As* the LORD of hosts liveth, H477
4: 1 the prophets unto E, saying, Thy servant H477
2 And E said unto her, What shall I do for H477
8 And it fell on a day, that E passed to H477
17 at that season that E had said unto her, H477
32 And when E was come into the house, H477
38 And E came again to Gilgal: and *there* H477
5: 8 And it was *so*, when E the man of God H477
9 and stood at the door of the house of E. H477
10 And E sent a messenger unto him, H477
20 But Gehazi, the servant of E the man of H477
25 before his master. And E said unto him, H477
6: 1 And the sons of the prophets said unto E, H477
12 lord, O king: but E, the prophet that *is* in H477
17 And E prayed, and said, LORD, I pray H477
17 and chariots of fire round about E. H477
18 And when they came down to him, E H477
18 blindness according to the word of E. H477
19 And E said unto them, This *is* not the H477
20 into Samaria, that E said, LORD, open H477
21 And the king of Israel said unto E, when H477
31 me, if the head of E the son of Shaphat H477
32 But E sat in his house, and the elders sat H477
7: 1 Then E said, Hear ye the word of the H477
8: 1 Then spake E unto the woman, whose H477
4 all the great things that E hath done. H477
5 this *is* her son, whom E restored to life. H477
7 And E came to Damascus; and H477
10 And E said unto him, Go, say unto him, H477
13 great thing? And E answered, The LORD H477
14 So he departed from E, and came to his H477
14 said to him, What said E to thee? And he H477
9: 1 And E the prophet called one of the H477
13:14 Now E was fallen sick of his sickness H477
15 And E said unto him, Take bow and H477
16 E put his hands upon the king's hands. H477
17 he opened *it*. Then E said, Shoot. And he H477
20 And E died, and they buried him. And H477
21 the sepulchre of E: and when the man H477
21 of E, he revived, and stood up on his feet. H477

ELISHAH
Gen 10: 4 And the sons of Javan; E, and Tarshish, H473
1Ch 1: 7 And the sons of Javan; E, and Tarshish, H473
Ezk 27: 7 isles of E was that which covered thee. H473

ELISHAMA
Nu 1:10 Of the children of Joseph: of Ephraim; E H476
2:18 Ephraim *shall be* E the son of Ammihud. H476
7:48 On the seventh day E the son of H476
53 the offering of E the son of Ammihud. H476
10:22 over his host *was* E the son of Ammihud. H476
2Sa 5:16 And E, and Eliada, and Eliphalet. H476
2Ki 25:25 the son of E, of the seed royal, came, H476
1Ch 2:41 begat Jekamiah, and Jekamiah begat E. H476
3: 6 Ibhar also, and E, and Eliphelet, H476
8 And E, and Eliada, and Eliphelet, nine. H476

7:26 Laadan his son, Ammihud his son, E his H476
14: 7 And E, and Beeliada, and Eliphalet. H476
2Ch 17: 8 and with them E and Jehoram, priests. H476
Jer 36:12 sat there, *even* E the scribe, and Delaiah H476
20 in the chamber of E the scribe, and told H476
21 he took it out of E the scribe's chamber. H476
41: 1 the son of E, of the seed royal, and H476

ELISHAPHAT
2Ch 23: 1 son of Adaiah, and E the son of Zichri, H478

ELISHEBA
Ex 6:23 And Aaron took him E, daughter of H472

ELISHUA
2Sa 5:15 Ibhar also, and E, and Nepheg, and H474
1Ch 14: 5 And Ibhar, and E, and Elpalet, H474

ELITE See BETH-ELITE.

ELIUD
Mt 1:14 begat Achim; and Achim begat E; *G1664*
15 And E begat Eleazar; and Eleazar begat *G1664*

ELIZABETH See ELISABETH.

ELIZAPHAN
Nu 3:30 Kohathites *shall be* E the son of Uzziel. H469
34:25 of Zebulun, E the son of Parnach. H469
1Ch 15: 8 Of the sons of E; Shemaiah the chief, and H469
2Ch 29:13 And of the sons of E; Shimri, and Jeiel: H469

ELIZUR
Nu 1: 5 *tribe of* Reuben; E the son of Shedeur. H468
2:10 of Reuben *shall be* E the son of Shedeur. H468
7:30 On the fourth day E the son of Shedeur, H468
35 *was* the offering of E the son of Shedeur. H468
10:18 over his host *was* E the son of Shedeur. H468

ELKANAH
Ex 6:24 And the sons of Korah; Assir, and E, and H511
1Sa 1: 1 and his name *was* E, the son of Jeroham, H511
4 And when the time was that E offered, H511
8 Then said E her husband to her, H511
19 to Ramah: and E knew Hannah his wife; H511
21 And the man E, and all his house, went H511
23 And E her husband said unto her, Do H511
2:11 And E went to Ramah to his house. And H511
20 And Eli blessed E and his wife, and said, H511
1Ch 6:23 E his son, and Ebiasaph his son, and H511
25 And the sons of E; Amasai, and H511
26 *As for* E: the sons of Elkanah; Zophai his H511
26 *As for* Elkanah: the sons of E; Zophai his H511
27 Eliab his son, Jeroham his son, E his H511
34 The son of E, the son of Jeroham, the son H511
35 The son of Zuph, the son of E, the son of H511
36 The son of E, the son of Joel, the son of H511
9:16 son of Asa, the son of E, that dwelt in the H511
12: 6 E, and Jesiah, and Azareel, and Joezer, H511
15:23 And Berechiah and E *were* doorkeepers H511
2Ch 28: 7 house, and E *that was* next to the king. H511

ELKOSHITE
Nah 1: 1 The book of the vision of Nahum the E. H512

ELLASAR
Gen 14: 1 Arioch king of E, Chedorlaomer king H495
9 Arioch king of E; four kings with five. H495

ELMODAM
Lk 3:28 *the son* of E, which was *the son* of Er, *G1678*

ELMS
Hos 4:13 and poplars and e, because the shadow H424

ELNAAM
1Ch 11:46 the sons of E, and Ithmah the Moabite, H493

ELNATHAN
2Ki 24: 8 the daughter of E of Jerusalem. H494
Ezr 8:16 Shemaiah, and for E, and for Jarib, and H494
16 for Jarib, and for E, and for Nathan, and H494
16 Joiarib, and for E, men of understanding. H494
Jer 26:22 Egypt, *namely*, E the son of Achbor, and H494
36:12 of Shemaiah, and E the son of Achbor, H494
25 Nevertheless E and Delaiah and H494

ELOHE See EL-ELOHE-ISRAEL.

ELOI
Mk 15:34 loud voice, saying, E, Eloi, lama *G1682*
Mk 15:34 saying, Eloi, E, lama sabachthani? *G1682*

ELON
Gen 26:34 Bashemath the daughter of E the Hittite: H356
36: 2 Adah the daughter of E the Hittite, and H356
46:14 And the sons of Zebulun; Sered, and E, H440
Nu 26:26 of the Sardites: of E, the family of the H440
Jos 19:43 And E, and Thimnathah, and Ekron, H356
Jdg 12:11 And after him E, a Zebulonite, judged H356
12 And E the Zebulonite died, and was H356

ELON-BETH-HANAN
1Ki 4: 9 in Shaalbim, and Beth-shemesh, and E: H358

ELONITES
Nu 26:26 E: of Jahleel, the family of the Jahleelites. H440

ELOQUENT
Ex 4:10 my Lord, I *am* not e, neither heretofore, H1697
Isa 3: 3 the cunning artificer, and the e orator. H995
Act 18:24 at Alexandria, an e man, *and* mighty in *G3052*

ELOTH
1Ki 9:26 which *is* beside E, on the shore of the Red H359
2Ch 8:17 to E, at the sea side in the land of Edom. H359
26: 2 He built E, and restored it to Judah, after H359

ELPAAL
1Ch 8:11 And of Hushim he begat Abitub, and E. H508
12 The sons of E; Eber, and Misham, and H508
18 and Jezliah, and Jobab, the sons of E; H508

ELPALET
1Ch 14: 5 And Ibhar, and Elishua, and E, H467

EL-PARAN
Gen 14: 6 Seir, unto E, which *is* by the wilderness. H364

ELSE
Gen 30: 1 unto Jacob, Give me children, or e I die. H369
42:16 truth in you: or e by the life of Pharaoh H3808
Ex 8:21 E, if thou wilt not let my people go, H3588
10: 4 E, if thou refuse to let my people go, H3588
Nu 20:19 *doing* any thing *e*, go through on my feet.
Dt 4:35 he *is* God; *there is* none e beside him. H5750
39 upon the earth beneath: *there is* none e. H5750
Jos 23:12 E if ye do in any wise go back, and H3588
Jdg 7:14 said, This *is* nothing e save the sword of
2Sa 3:35 bread, or ought e, till the sun be down.
15:14 for we shall not *e* escape from Absalom:
1Ki 8:60 LORD *is* God, *and that there is* none e. H5750
20:39 life, or e thou shalt pay a talent of silver.
21: 6 for money; or e, if it please thee, I will
1Ch 21:12 overtaketh *thee;* or e three days the H518
2Ch 23: 7 and whosoever *e* cometh into the house,
Neh 2: 2 this *is* nothing *e* but sorrow of heart.
Ps 51:16 For thou desirest not sacrifice; e would I
Ecc 2:25 For who can eat, or who e can hasten
Isa 45: 5 I *am* the LORD, and *there is* none e, H5750
6 me. I *am* the LORD, and *there is* none e. H5750
14 and *there is* none e, *there is* no God. H5750
18 I *am* the LORD; and *there is* none e. H5750
21 *there is* no God e beside me; a just God H5750
22 earth: for I *am* God, and *there is* none e. H5750
46: 9 e; *I am* God, and *there is* none like me, H5750
47: 8 I *am*, and none e beside me; I shall not H5750
10 heart, I *am*, and none e beside me. H5750
Joel 2:27 God, and none e: and my people shall H5750
Mt 6:24 love the other; or e he will hold to the
9:17 into old bottles: e the bottles break, *G1490*
12:29 Or e how can one enter into a strong
33 and his fruit good; or e make the tree
Mk 2:21 on an old garment: e the new piece that *G1490*
22 into old bottles: e the new wine doth *G1490*
Lk 5:37 into old bottles; e the new wine will *G1490*
14:32 Or e, while the other is yet a great way *G1490*
16:13 love the other; or e he will hold to the
Jn 14:11 e believe me for the very works' sake. *G1490*
Act 17:21 time in nothing e, but either to tell, or *G2087*
24:20 Or e let these same *here* say, if they have
Ro 2:15 accusing or e excusing one another;) *G2532*
1Co 7:14 by the husband: e were your children *G1893*
14:16 E when thou shalt bless with the spirit, *G1893*
15:29 E what shall they do which are *G1893*
Php 1:27 and see you, or e be absent, I may hear
Rev 2: 5 do the first works; or e I will come unto *G1490*
16 Repent; or e I will come unto thee *G1490*

ELTEKEH
Jos 19:44 And E, and Gibbethon, and Baalath, H514
21:23 And out of the tribe of Dan, E with her H514

ELTEKON
Jos 15:59 And Maarath, and Beth-anoth, and E; H515

ELTOLAD
Jos 15:30 And E, and Chesil, and Hormah, H513
19: 4 And E, and Bethul, and Hormah, H513

ELUL
Neh 6:15 *day* of *the month* E, in fifty and two days. H435

ELUZAI
1Ch 12: 5 E, and Jerimoth, and Bealiah, and H498

E

ELYMAS
Act 13: 8 But E the sorcerer (for so is his name *G1681*

ELZABAD
1Ch 12:12 Johanan the eighth, E the ninth, H443
26: 7 and Obed, E, whose brethren *were* H443

ELZAPHAN
Ex 6:22 And the sons of Uzziel; Mishael, and E, H469
Lev 10: 4 And Moses called Mishael and E, the H469

EMBALM
Gen 50: 2 the physicians to e his father: and the H2590

EMBALMED
Gen 50: 2 his father: and the physicians e Israel. H2590
3 of those which are e: and the Egyptians H2590
26 old: and they e him, and he was put H2590

EMBASSY See AMBASSAGE.

EMBOLDENED
1Co 8:10 which is weak be e to eat those things *G3618*

EMBOLDENETH
Job 16: 3 or what e thee that thou answerest? H4834

EMBRACE
2Ki 4:16 of life, thou shalt e a son. And she said, H2263
Job 24: 8 and e the rock for want of a shelter. H2263
Prv 4: 8 thee to honour, when thou dost e her. H2263
5:20 woman, and e the bosom of a stranger? H2263
Ecc 3: 5 together; a time to e, and a time to H2263
Song 2: 6 my head, and his right hand doth e me. H2263
8: 3 head, and his right hand should e me. H2263
Lam 4: 5 were brought up in scarlet e dunghills. H2263

EMBRACED
Gen 29:13 ran to meet him, and e him, and kissed H2263
33: 4 And Esau ran to meet him, and e him, H2263
48:10 him; and he kissed them, and e them. H2263
Act 20: 1 the disciples, and e *them*, and departed *G782*
Heb 11:13 of *them*, and e *them*, and confessed *G782*

EMBRACING
Ecc 3: 5 embrace, and a time to refrain from e; H2263
Act 20:10 fell on him, and e *him* said, Trouble *G4843*

EMBROIDER
Ex 28:39 And thou shalt e the coat of fine linen, H7660

EMBROIDERER
Ex 35:35 and of the e, in blue, and in purple, H7551
38:23 workman, and an e in blue, and in H7551

EMEK See BETH-EMEK.

EMERALD
Ex 28:18 And the second row *shall be* an e, a H5306
39:11 And the second row, an e, a sapphire, H5306
Ezk 28:13 the sapphire, the e, and the carbuncle, H5306
Rev 4: 3 about the throne, in sight like unto an e. *G4664*
21:19 the third, a chalcedony; the fourth, an e; *G4665*

EMERALDS
Ezk 27:16 occupied in thy fairs with e, purple, and H5306

EMERODS
Dt 28:27 and with the e, and with the scab, and H6076
1Sa 5: 6 e, *even* Ashdod and the coasts thereof. H6076
9 and they had e in their secret parts. H6076
12 smitten with the e: and the cry of the H6076

1Sa 6: 4 Five golden e, and five golden mice, H6076
5 images of your e, and images of your H6076
11 mice of gold and the images of their e. H2914
17 And these *are* the golden e which the H2914

EMIMS
Gen 14: 5 Ham, and the E in Shaveh Kiriathaim, H368
Dt 2:10 The E dwelt therein in times past, a H368
11 Anakims; but the Moabites call them E. H368

EMINENT
Ezk 16:24 *That* thou hast also built unto thee an e H1354
31 In that thou buildest thine e place in H1354
39 throw down thine e place, and shall H1354
17:22 plant *it* upon an high mountain and e: H8524

EMMANUEL
Mt 1:23 shall call his name E, which being G1694

EMMAUS
Lk 24:13 to a village called E, which was from G1695

EMMOR
Act 7:16 of the sons of E *the father* of Sychem. G1697

EMPIRE
Est 1:20 throughout all his e, (for it is great,) all H4438

EMPLOY
Dt 20:19 *life*) to e *them* in the siege: H935+H6440

EMPLOYED
1Ch 9:33 they were e in *that* work day and night. H5921
Ezr 10:15 son of Tikvah were e about this *matter*: H5975

EMPLOYMENT
Ezk 39:14 men of continual e, passing through the H8548

EMPTIED
Gen 24:20 And she hasted, and e her pitcher into H6168
42:35 And it came to pass as they e their H7324
2Ch 24:11 officer came and e the chest, and took H6168
Neh 5:13 he shaken out, and e. And all the H7386
Isa 19: 6 of defence shall be e and dried up: the H1809
24: 3 The land shall be utterly e, and utterly H1238
Jer 48:11 lees, and hath not been e from vessel to H7324
Nah 2: 2 for the emptiers have e them out, and H1238

EMPTIERS
Nah 2: 2 of Israel: for the e have emptied them H1238

EMPTINESS
Isa 34:11 the line of confusion, and the stones of e. H922

EMPTY
Gen 31:42 sent me away now e. God hath seen H7387
37:24 the pit *was* e, *there was* no water in it. H7386
41:27 and the seven e ears blasted with the H7386
Ex 3:21 pass, that, when ye go, ye shall not go e: H7387
23:15 and none shall appear before me e:) H7387
34:20 And none shall appear before me e. H7387
Lev 14:36 that they e the house, before the H6437
Dt 15:13 thee, thou shalt not let him go away e: H7387
16:16 shall not appear before the LORD e: H7387
Jdg 7:16 man's hand, with e pitchers, and lamps H7386
Ru 1:21 me home again e: why *then* call ye me H7387
3:17 to me, Go not e unto thy mother in law. H7387
1Sa 6: 3 of Israel, send it not e; but in any wise H7387
20:18 be missed, because thy seat will be e. H6485
25 by Saul's side, and David's place was e. H6485
27 David's place was e: and Saul said unto H6485
2Sa 1:22 and the sword of Saul returned not e. H7387
2Ki 4: 3 *even* e vessels; borrow not a few. H7386
Job 22: 9 Thou hast sent widows away e, and the H7387
26: 7 He stretcheth out the north over the e H8414
Ecc 11: 3 If the clouds be full of rain, they e H7324
Isa 24: 1 Behold, the LORD maketh the earth e, H1238
29: 8 and his soul is e: or as when a thirsty H7386
32: 6 the LORD, to make e the soul of the H7324
Jer 14: 3 with their vessels e; they were ashamed H7387
48:12 e his vessels, and break their bottles. H7324
51: 2 fan her, and shall e her land: for in the H1238
34 he hath made me an e vessel, he hath H7385
Ezk 24:11 Then set it e upon the coals thereof, H7386
Hos 10: 1 Israel *is* an e vine, he bringeth forth H1238
Nah 2:10 She is e, and void, and waste: and the H950
Hab 1:17 Shall they therefore e their net, and not H7324
Zec 4:12 e the golden *oil* out of themselves? H7324
Mt 12:44 he findeth *it* e, swept, and garnished. G4980
Mk 12: 3 and beat him, and sent *him* away e. G2756
Lk 1:53 and the rich he hath sent e away. G2756
20:10 beat him, and sent *him* away e. G2756
11 *him* shamefully, and sent *him* away e. G2756

EMULATION
Ro 11:14 If by any means I may provoke to e G3863

EMULATIONS
Gal 5:20 Idolatry, witchcraft, hatred, variance, e, G2205

ENABLED
1Ti 1:12 our Lord, who hath e me, for that he G1743

ENAM
Jos 15:34 and En-gannim, Tappuah, and E, H5879

ENAN
Nu 1:15 Of Naphtali; Ahira the son of E. H5881
2:29 of Naphtali *shall be* Ahira the son of E. H5881
7:78 On the twelfth day Ahira the son of E, H5881
83 *was* the offering of Ahira the son of E. H5881
10:27 of Naphtali *was* Ahira the son of E. H5881

ENCAMP
Ex 14: 2 Israel, that they turn and e before H2583
2 before it shall ye e by the sea. H2583
Nu 1:50 and shall e round about the tabernacle. H2583
2:17 of the camp: as they e, so shall they set H2583
27 And those that e by him *shall be* the H2583
3:38 But those that e before the tabernacle H2583
10:31 how we are to e in the wilderness, and H2583
2Sa 12:28 together, and e against the city, and H2583
Job 19:12 me, and e round about my tabernacle. H2583
Ps 27: 3 Though an host should e against me, H2583
Zec 9: 8 And I will e about mine house because H2583

ENCAMPED
Ex 13:20 from Succoth, and e in Etham, in the H2583
15:27 trees: and they e there by the waters. H2583
18: 5 where he e at the mount of God: H2583
Nu 33:10 And they removed from Elim, and e by H2583
11 Red sea, and e in the wilderness of Sin. H2583
12 wilderness of Sin, and e in Dophkah. H2583
13 from Dophkah, and e in Alush. H2583
14 And they removed from Alush, and e at H2583
17 Kibroth-hattaavah, and e at Hazeroth. H2583
24 mount Shapher, and e in Haradah. H2583
26 from Makheloth, and e at Tahath. H2583
30 from Hashmonah, and e at Moseroth. H2583
32 Bene-jaakan, and e at Hor-hagidgad. H2583
34 from Jotbathah, and e at Ebronah. H2583
35 from Ebronah, and e at Ezion-gaber. H2583
46 and e in Almon-diblathaim. H2583
Jos 4:19 first month, and e in Gilgal, in the east H2583
5:10 And the children of Israel e in Gilgal, H2583
10: 5 all their hosts, and e before Gibeon, H2583
31 and e against it, and fought against it: H2583
34 they e against it, and fought against it: H2583
Jdg 6: 4 And they e against them, and H2583
9:50 Then went Abimelech to Thebez, and e H2583
10:17 together, and e in Gilead. And the H2583
17 themselves together, and e in Mizpeh. H2583
20:19 in the morning, and e against Gibeah. H2583
1Sa 11: 1 came up, and e against Jabesh-gilead: H2583
13:16 but the Philistines e in Michmash. H2583
2Sa 11:11 of my lord, are e in the open fields; H2583
1Ki 16:15 the people *were* e against Gibbethon, H2583
16 And the people *that were* e heard say, H2583
1Ch 11:15 Philistines e in the valley of Rephaim. H2583
2Ch 32: 1 into Judah, and e against the fenced H2583

ENCAMPETH
Ps 34: 7 The angel of the LORD e round about H2583
53: 5 bones of him that e *against* thee: thou H2583

ENCAMPING
Ex 14: 9 and overtook them e by the sea, beside H2583

ENCHANTER
Dt 18:10 an observer of times, or an e, or a witch, H5172

ENCHANTERS
Jer 27: 9 nor to your e, nor to your sorcerers, H6049

ENCHANTMENT
Lev 19:26 shall ye use e, nor observe times. H5172
Nu 23:23 Surely *there is* no e against Jacob, H5173
Ecc 10:11 Surely the serpent will bite without e; H3908

ENCHANTMENTS
Ex 7:11 also did in like manner with their e. H3858
22 did so with their e: and Pharaoh's heart H3909
8: 7 And the magicians did so with their e, H3909
18 And the magicians did so with their e H3909
Nu 24: 1 times, to seek for e, but he set his face H5173
2Ki 17:17 divination and e, and sold themselves H5172
21: 6 times, and used e, and dealt with H5172
2Ch 33: 6 times, and used e, and used witchcraft, H5172
Isa 47: 9 *and* for the great abundance of thine e. H2267
12 Stand now with thine e, and with the H2267

ENCLOSINGS See INCLOSINGS.

ENCOUNTERED
Act 17:18 and of the Stoicks, e him. And some G4820

ENCOURAGE
Dt 1:38 shall go in thither: e him: for he shall H2388
3:28 But charge Joshua, and e him, and H2388
2Sa 11:25 city, and overthrow it: and e thou him. H2388
Ps 64: 5 They e themselves *in* an evil matter: H2388

ENCOURAGED
Jdg 20:22 And the people the men of Israel e H2388
1Sa 30: 6 David e himself in the LORD his God. H2388
2Ch 31: 4 they might be e in the law of the LORD. H2388
35: 2 their charges, and e them to the service H2388
Isa 41: 7 So the carpenter e the goldsmith, *and* H2388

END
Gen 6:13 And God said unto Noah, The e of all H7093
8: 3 and after the e of the hundred and H7097
6 And it came to pass at the e of forty H7093
23: 9 which *is* in the e of his field; for as H7097
27:30 had made an e of blessing Jacob, and H3615
41: 1 And it came to pass at the e of two full H7093
47:21 to cities from *one* e of the borders of H7097
21 of Egypt even to the *other* e thereof. H7097
49:33 And when Jacob had made an e of H3615
Ex 8:22 be there; to the e thou mayest know H4616
12:41 And it came to pass at the e of the four H7093
23:16 *which is* in the e of the year, when thou H3318
25:19 And make one cherub on the one e, and H7098
19 on the other e: *even* of the mercy seat H7098
26:28 of the boards shall reach from e to end. H7097
28 of the boards shall reach from end to e. H7097
31:18 he had made an e of communing with H3615
34:22 the feast of ingathering at the year's e. H8622
36:33 the boards from the one e to the other. H7097
37: 8 One cherub on the e on this side, and H7098
8 on the *other* e on that side: out of H7098
Lev 8:33 be at an e: for seven days shall H4390
16:20 And when he hath made an e of H3615
17: 5 To the e that the children of Israel may H4616
Nu 4:15 sons have made an e of covering the H3615
16:31 he had made an e of speaking all these H3615
23:10 righteous, and let my last e be like his! H319
24:20 latter e *shall be* that he perish for ever. H319
Dt 8:16 prove thee, to do thee good at thy latter e; H319
9:11 And it came to pass at the e of forty H7093
11:12 of the year even unto the e of the year. H319
13: 7 thee, from the *one* e of the earth even H7097
7 earth even unto the *other* e of the earth; H7097
14:28 At the e of three years thou shalt bring H7097
15: 1 At the e of *every* seven years thou shalt H7093
17:16 return to Egypt, to the e that he should H4616
20 *to* the left: to the e that he may prolong H4616
20: 9 have made an e of speaking unto the H3615
26:12 When thou hast made an e of tithing H3615
28:49 from far, from the e of the earth, *as* H7097
64 from the one e of the earth even unto H7097
31:10 saying, At the e of *every* seven years, H7093
24 had made an e of writing the words H3615
32:20 will see what their e *shall be*: for they *are* H319
29 *that* they would consider their latter e! H319
45 And Moses made an e of speaking all H3615
Jos 8:24 Israel had made an e of slaying all the H3615
9:16 And it came to pass at the e of three H7097
10:20 had made an e of slaying them with H3615
15: 5 salt sea, *even* to the e of Jordan. And H7097
8 e of the valley of the giants northward: H7097
18:15 And the south quarter *was* from the e H7097
16 And the border came down to the e of H7097
19 e of Jordan: this *was* the south coast. H7097
19:49 When they had made an e of dividing H3615
51 they made an e of dividing the country. H3615
Jdg 3:18 And when he had made an e to offer H3615
6:21 put forth the e of the staff that *was* H7097

Jdg 11:39 And it came to pass at the e of two H7093
15:17 he had made an e of speaking, that he H3615
19: 9 the day groweth to an e, lodge here, that H2583
Ru 2:23 to glean unto the e of barley harvest H3615
3: 7 to lie down at the e of the heap of corn: H7097
10 in the latter e than at the beginning, H314
1Sa 3:12 when I begin, I will also make an e. H3615
9:27 *And* as they were going down to the e H7097
10:13 And when he had made an e of H3615
13:10 he had made an e of offering the burnt H3615
14:27 he put forth the e of the rod that *was* H7097
43 honey with the e of the rod that *was* H7097
18: 1 he had made an e of speaking unto H3615
24:16 had made an e of speaking these words H3615
2Sa 2:23 with the hinder e of the spear smote him H310
26 in the latter e? how long shall it be then, H314
6:18 And as soon as David had made an e of H3615
11:19 hast made an e of telling the matters H3615
13:36 as he had made an e of speaking, that, H3615
14:26 was at every year's e that he polled *it:* H7093
24: 8 the e of nine months and twenty days. H7097
1Ki 1:41 as they had made an e of eating. And H3615
2:39 And it came to pass at the e of three H7093
3: 1 he had made an e of building his own H3615
7:40 Hiram made an e of doing all the work H3615
8:54 had made an e of praying all this H3615
9:10 And it came to pass at the e of twenty H7097
2Ki 8: 3 at the seven years' e, that the woman H7097
10:21 of Baal was full from one e to another. H6310
25 he had made an e of offering the burnt H3615
18:10 And at the e of three years they took it: H7097
21:16 from one e to another; beside his H6310
1Ch 16: 2 And when David had made an e of H3615
2Ch 4:10 side of the east e, over against the south.
5:12 stood at the east e of the altar, and with
7: 1 Now when Solomon had made an e of H3615
8: 1 And it came to pass at the e of twenty H7093
20:16 find them at the e of the brook, before H5490
23 they had made an e of the inhabitants H3615
21:19 of time, after the e of two years, his H7093
24:10 into the chest, until they had made an e. H3615
23 And it came to pass at the e of the year, H8622
29:17 day of the first month they made an e. H3615
29 And when they had made an e of H3615
Ezr 9:11 e to another with their uncleanness. H6310
10:17 And they made an e with all the men H3615
Neh 3:21 even to the e of the house of Eliashib. H8503
4: 2 will they make an e in a day? will they H3615
Job 6:11 *is* mine e, that I should prolong my life? H7093
8: 7 yet thy latter e should greatly increase. H319
16: 3 Shall vain words have an e? or what H7093
18: 2 How long *will it be ere* ye make an e of H7078
26:10 until the day and night come to an e. H8503
28: 3 He setteth an e to darkness, and H7093
34:36 may be tried unto the e because of *his* H5331
42:12 So the LORD blessed the latter e of Job H319
Ps 7: 9 wicked come to an e; but establish the H1584
9: 6 come to a perpetual e: and thou hast H8552
19: 4 their words to the e of the world. In H7097
6 His going forth *is* from the e of the H7097
30:12 To the e that *my* glory may sing praise H4616
37:37 upright: for the e of *that* man *is* peace. H319
38 the e of the wicked shall be cut off. H319
39: 4 LORD, make me to know mine e, and H7093
46: 9 He maketh wars to cease unto the e of H7097
61: 2 From the e of the earth will I cry unto H7097
73:17 of God; *then* understood I their e. H319
102:27 the same, and thy years shall have no e. H8552
107:27 a drunken man, and are at their wits' e. H1104
119:33 statutes; and I shall keep it *unto* the e. H6118
96 I have seen an e of all perfection: *but* H7093
112 thy statutes alway, *even unto* the e. H6118
Prv 5: 4 But her e is bitter as wormwood, sharp H319
14:12 but the e thereof *are* the ways of death. H319
13 and the e of that mirth *is* heaviness. H319
16:25 but the e thereof *are* the ways of death. H319
19:20 that thou mayest be wise in thy latter e. H319
20:21 but the e thereof shall not be blessed. H319
23:18 For surely there is an e; and thine H319
25: 8 *not* what to do in the e thereof, when thy H319
Ecc 3:11 maketh from the beginning to the e. H5490
4: 8 yet *is there* no e of all his labour; H7093
16 *There is* no e of all the people, *even* of H7093
7: 2 for that *is* the e of all men; and the H5490
8 Better *is* the e of a thing than the H319
14 the other, to the e that man should find H1700
10:13 the e of his talk *is* mischievous madness. H319
12:12 books *there is* no e; and much study *is* a H7093
Isa 2: 7 *is there any* e of their treasures; their H7097
Isa 2: 7 neither *is there any* e of their chariots: H7097
5:26 unto them from the e of the earth: and, H7097
7: 3 thy son, at the e of the conduit of the H7097
9: 7 *there shall be* no e, upon the throne of H7093
13: 5 country, from the e of heaven, *even* the H7097
16: 4 extortioner is at an e, the spoiler ceaseth, H656
23:15 of one king: after the e of seventy years H7093
17 And it shall come to pass after the e of H7093
33: 1 shalt make an e to deal treacherously, H5239
38:12 to night wilt thou make an e of me. H7999
13 to night wilt thou make an e of me. H7999
41:22 know the latter e of them; or declare us
42:10 praise from the e of the earth, ye that H7097
45:17 world without e. H5704+H5769+H5703
46:10 Declaring the e from the beginning, and H319
47: 7 neither didst remember the latter e of it.
48:20 utter it *even* to the e of the earth; say H7097
49: 6 be my salvation unto the e of the earth. H7097
62:11 unto the e of the world, Say ye H7097
Jer 1: 3 of Judah, unto the e of the eleventh H8552
3: 5 he keep *it* to the e? Behold, thou hast H5331
4:27 be desolate; yet will I not make a full e. H3617
5:10 but make not a full e: take away her H3617
18 LORD, I will not make a full e with you. H3617
31 so: and what will ye do in the e thereof? H319
12: 4 they said, He shall not see our last e. H319
12 from the *one* e of the land even to the H7097
12 e of the land: no flesh shall have peace. H7097
17:11 of his days, and at his e shall be a fool. H319
25:33 at that day from *one* e of the earth even H7097
33 unto the *other* e of the earth: they shall H7097
26: 8 had made an e of speaking all that H3615
29:11 and not of evil, to give you an expected e. H319
30:11 I make a full e of all nations whither H3617
11 will I not make a full e of thee: but I will H3617
31:17 And there is hope in thine e, saith the H319
34:14 At the e of seven years let ye go every H7093
43: 1 had made an e of speaking unto all H3615
44:27 the famine, until there be an e of them. H3615
46:28 for I will make a full e of all the nations H3617
28 not make a full e of thee, but correct H3617
51:13 in treasures, thine e is come, *and* the H7093
31 Babylon that his city is taken at *one* e, H7097
63 hast made an e of reading this book, H3615
Lam 1: 9 not her last e; therefore she came down H319
4:18 go in our streets: our e is near, our days H7093
18 our days are fulfilled; for our e is come. H7093
Ezk 3:16 And it came to pass at the e of seven H7097
7: 2 the land of Israel; An e, the end is come H7093
2 Israel; An end, the e is come upon the H7093
3 Now *is* the e *come* upon thee, and I will H7093
6 An e is come, the end is come: it H7093
6 An end is come, the e is come: it H7093
11:13 make a full e of the remnant of Israel? H3617
20:17 I make an e of them in the wilderness. H3617
26 desolate, to the e that they might know H4616
21:25 is come, when iniquity *shall have* an e, H7093
29 when their iniquity *shall have* an e. H7093
29:13 Yet thus saith the Lord GOD; At the e of H7093
31:14 To the e that none of all the trees by the H4616
35: 5 in the time *that their* iniquity *had* an e: H7093
39:14 e of seven months shall they search. H7097
41:12 place at the e toward the west *was* H6285
42:15 Now when he had made an e of H3615
43:23 When thou hast made an e of cleansing H3615
48: 1 From the north e to the coast of the H7097
Dan 1: 5 years, that at the e thereof they might H7117
15 And at the e of ten days their H7117
18 Now at the e of the days that the king H7117
4:11 sight thereof to the e of all the earth: H5491
22 and thy dominion to the e of the earth. H5491
29 At the e of twelve months he walked in H7118
34 And at the e of the days I H7118
6:26 his dominion *shall be even* unto the e. H5491
7:26 to consume and to destroy *it* unto the e. H5491
28 Hitherto *is* the e of the matter. As for H5491
8:17 at the time of the e *shall be* the vision. H7093
19 shall be in the last e of the indignation: H319
19 for at the time appointed the e *shall be*. H7093
9:24 and to make an e of sins, and to make H7093
26 and the e thereof *shall be* with H7093
26 and unto the e of the war desolations H7093
11: 6 And in the e of years they shall join H7093
27 yet the e *shall be* at the time appointed. H7093
35 e: because *it is* yet for a time appointed. H7093
40 And at the time of the e shall the king H7093
45 come to his e, and none shall help him. H7093
12: 4 to the time of the e: many shall run to H7093
6 *shall it be to* the e of these wonders? H7093
Dan 12: 8 Lord, what *shall be* the e of these *things*? H319
9 up and sealed till the time of the e. H7093
13 But go thou thy way till the e *be*: for H7093
13 and stand in thy lot at the e of the days. H7093
Am 3:15 houses shall have an e, saith the LORD. H5486
5:18 of the LORD! to what e *is* it for you? the H4100
7: 2 they had made an e of eating the grass H3615
8: 2 LORD unto me, The e is come upon my H7093
10 *son*, and the e thereof as a bitter day. H319
Oba 9 dismayed, to the e that every one of the H4616
Nah 1: 8 he will make an utter e of the place H3617
9 will make an utter e: affliction shall not H3617
2: 9 for *there is* none e of the store *and* H7097
3: 3 and *there is* none e of *their* corpses; H7097
Hab 2: 3 time, but at the e it shall speak, and not H7093
Mt 10:22 that endureth to the e shall be saved. G5056
11: 1 had made an e of commanding his G5055
13:39 the harvest is the e of the world; and G4930
40 fire; so shall it be in the e of this world. G4930
49 So shall it be at the e of the world: the G4930
24: 3 thy coming, and of the e of the world? G4930
6 must come to pass, but the e is not yet. G5056
13 But he that shall endure unto the e, the G5056
14 all nations; and then shall the e come. G5056
31 winds, from one e of heaven to the other. G206
26:58 and sat with the servants, to see the e. G5056
28: 1 In the e of the sabbath, as it began to G3796
20 *even* unto the e of the world. Amen. G4930
Mk 3:26 divided, he cannot stand, but hath an e. G5056
13: 7 needs be; but the e *shall* not *be* yet. G5056
13 unto the e, the same shall be saved. G5056
Lk 1:33 and of his kingdom there shall be no e. G5056
18: 1 unto them *to this* e, that men ought
21: 9 to pass; but the e *is* not by and by. G5056
22:37 for the things concerning me have an e. G5056
Jn 13: 1 in the world, he loved them unto the e. G5056
18:37 am a king. To this e was I born, and for G5124
Act 7:19 children, to the e they might not live. G1519
Ro 1:11 gift, to the e ye may be established; G1519
4:16 *be* by grace; to the e the promise might G1519
6:21 for the e of those things *is* death. G5056
22 holiness, and the e everlasting life. G5056
10: 4 For Christ *is* the e of the law for G5056
14: 9 For to this e Christ both died, and rose, G5124
1Co 1: 8 Who shall also confirm you unto the e, G5056
15:24 Then *cometh* the e, when he shall have G5056
2Co 1:13 trust ye shall acknowledge even to the e; G5056
2: 9 For to this e also did I write, that I G5124
3:13 look to the e of that which is abolished: G5056
11:15 e shall be according to their works. G5056
Eph 3:21 all ages, world without e. Amen. G165
Php 3:19 Whose e *is* destruction, whose God *is* G5056
1Th 3:13 To the e he may stablish your hearts G1519
1Ti 1: 5 Now the e of the commandment is G5056
Heb 3: 6 rejoicing of the hope firm unto the e. G5056
14 of our confidence stedfast unto the e; G5056
6: 8 unto cursing; whose e *is* to be burned. G5056
11 to the full assurance of hope unto the e: G5056
16 *is* to them an e of all strife. G4009
7: 3 of days, nor e of life; but made like G5056
9:26 now once in the e of the world hath he G4930
13: 7 considering the e of *their* conversation. G1545
Jas 5:11 and have seen the e of the Lord; that G5056
1Pt 1: 9 Receiving the e of your faith, *even* the G5056
13 and hope to the e for the grace that is G5049
4: 7 But the e of all things is at hand: be ye G5056
17 at us, what shall the e *be* of them that G5056
2Pt 2:20 the latter e is worse with them G2078
Rev 2:26 my works unto the e, to him will I give G5056
21: 6 the beginning and the e. I will give unto G5056
22:13 and the e, the first and the last. G5056

ENDAMAGE

Ezr 4:13 *so* thou shalt e the revenue of the kings. H5142

ENDANGER

Dan 1:10 ye make *me* e my head to the king. H2325

ENDANGERED

Ecc 10: 9 that cleaveth wood shall be e thereby. H5533

ENDEAVOUR

2Pt 1:15 Moreover I will e that ye may be able G4704

ENDEAVOURED

Act 16:10 vision, immediately we e to go into G2212
1Th 2:17 not in heart, e the more abundantly G4704

ENDEAVOURING
Eph 4: 3 E to keep the unity of the Spirit in the G4704

ENDEAVOURS
Ps 28: 4 of their e: give them after the H4611

ENDED
Gen 2: 2 And on the seventh day God e his work H3615
41:53 that was in the land of Egypt, were e. H3615
47:18 When that year was e, they came unto H8552
Dt 31:30 the words of this song, until they were e. H8552
34: 8 *and* mourning for Moses were e. H8552
Ru 2:21 men, until they have e all my harvest. H3615
2Sa 20:18 at Abel: and so they e *the matter.* H8552
1Ki 7:51 So was e all the work that king H7999
2Ch 29:34 till the work was e, and until the *other* H3615
Job 31:40 of barley. The words of Job are e. H8552
Ps 72:20 prayers of David the son of Jesse are e. H3615
Isa 60:20 and the days of thy mourning shall be e. H7999
Jer 8:20 The harvest is past, the summer is e, H3615
Ezk 4: 8 till thou hast e the days of thy siege. H3615
Mt 7:28 And it came to pass, when Jesus had e G4931
Lk 4: 2 they were e, he afterward hungered. G4931
13 And when the devil had e all the G4931
7: 1 Now when he had e all his sayings in G4137
Jn 13: 2 And supper being e, the devil having G1096
Act 19:21 After these things were e, Paul G4137
21:27 days were almost e, the Jews which G4931

ENDETH
Isa 24: 8 rejoice e, the joy of the harp ceaseth. H2308

ENDING
Rev 1: 8 the beginning and the e, saith the Lord, G5056

ENDLESS
1Ti 1: 4 Neither give heed to fables and e G562
Heb 7:16 but after the power of an e life. G179

ENDOR
Jos 17:11 the inhabitants of E and her towns, H5874

EN-DOR
1Sa 28: 7 woman that hath a familiar spirit at E. H5874
Ps 83:10 *Which* perished at E: they became *as* H5874

ENDOW
Ex 22:16 her, he shall surely e her to be his wife. H4117

ENDS
Ex 25:18 them, in the two e of the mercy seat. H7098
19 the cherubims on the two e thereof. H7098
28:14 And two chains *of* pure gold at the e; *of* H4020
22 at the e *of* wreathen work *of* pure gold. H1383
23 rings on the two e of the breastplate. H7098
24 *which are* on the e of the breastplate. H7098
25 And *the other* two e of the two H7098
26 upon the two e of the breastplate in H7098
37: 7 he them, on the two e of the mercy seat; H7098
8 he the cherubims on the two e thereof. H7098
38: 5 And he cast four rings for the four e of H7099
39:15 at the e, *of* wreathen work *of* pure gold. H1383
16 rings in the two e of the breastplate. H7098
17 two rings on the e of the breastplate. H7098
18 And the two e of the two wreathen H7098
19 *them* on the two e of the breastplate, H7098
Dt 33:17 together to the e of the earth: and they H657
1Sa 2:10 shall judge the e of the earth; and he H657
1Ki 8: 8 And they drew out the staves, that the e H7218
2Ch 5: 9 *of the ark,* that the e of the staves were H7218
Job 28:24 For he looketh to the e of the earth, *and* H7098
37: 3 his lightning unto the e of the earth. H3671
38:13 That it might take hold of the e of the H3671
Ps 19: 6 his circuit unto the e of it: and there is H7098
22:27 All the e of the world shall remember H657
48:10 praise unto the e of the earth: thy right H7099
59:13 in Jacob unto the e of the earth. Selah. H657
65: 5 of all the e of the earth, and of H7099
67: 7 God shall bless us; and all the e of the H657
72: 8 from the river unto the e of the earth. H657
98: 3 of Israel: all the e of the earth have seen H657
135: 7 to ascend from the e of the earth; he H7097
Prv 17:24 eyes of a fool *are* in the e of the earth. H7097
30: 4 established all the e of the earth? what *is* H657
Isa 26:15 *it* far *unto* all the e of the earth. H7099
40:28 LORD, the Creator of the e of the earth, H7098
41: 5 The isles saw *it,* and feared; the e of the H7098
9 *Thou* whom I have taken from the e of H7098
43: 6 my daughters from the e of the earth; H7097
Isa 45:22 Look unto me, and be ye saved, all the e H657
52:10 nations; and all the e of the earth shall H657
Jer 10:13 to ascend from the e of the earth; he H7097
16:19 unto thee from the e of the earth, and H657
25:31 A noise shall come *even* to the e of the H7097
51:16 to ascend from the e of the earth: he H7097
Ezk 15: 4 both the e of it, and the midst H7098
Mic 5: 4 shall he be great unto the e of the earth. H657
Zec 9:10 from the river *even* to the e of the earth. H657
Act 13:47 be for salvation unto the e of the earth. G2078
Ro 10:18 their words unto the e of the world. G4009
1Co 10:11 whom the e of the world are come. G5056

ENDUED
Gen 30:20 And Leah said, God hath e me *with* a H2064
2Ch 2:12 king a wise son, e with prudence and H3045
13 And now I have sent a cunning man, e H3045
Lk 24:49 until ye be e with power from on high. G1746
Jas 3:13 Who *is* a wise man and e with G1990

ENDURE
Gen 33:14 e, until I come unto my lord unto Seir. H7272
Ex 18:23 shalt be able to e, and all this people H5975
Est 8: 6 For how can I e to see the evil that shall H3201
6 e to see the destruction of my kindred? H3201
Job 8:15 he shall hold it fast, but it shall not e. H6965
31:23 by reason of his highness I could not e.
Ps 9: 7 But the LORD shall e for ever: he hath H3427
30: 5 life: weeping may e for a night, but joy H3885
72: 5 moon e, throughout all generations. H6440
17 His name shall e for ever: his name H1961
89:29 His seed also will I make *to* e for ever,
36 His seed shall e for ever, and his throne H1961
102:12 But thou, O LORD, shalt e for ever; and H3427
26 They shall perish, but thou shalt e: yea, H5975
104:31 The glory of the LORD shall e for ever: H1961
Prv 27:24 doth the crown e to every generation?
Ezk 22:14 Can thine heart e, or can thine hands be H5975
Mt 24:13 But he that shall e unto the end, the G5278
Mk 4:17 and so e but for a time: afterward, G1526
13:13 but he that shall e unto the end, the G5278
2Th 1: 4 persecutions and tribulations that ye e: G430
2Ti 2: 3 Thou therefore e hardness, as a good G2553
10 Therefore I e all things for the elect's G5278
4: 3 when they will not e sound doctrine; but G430
5 But watch thou in all things, e G2553
Heb 12: 7 If ye e chastening, God dealeth with G5278
20 (For they could not e that which was G5342
Jas 5:11 Behold, we count them happy which e. G5278
1Pt 2:19 God e grief, suffering wrongfully. G5297

ENDURED
Ps 81:15 but their time should have e for ever. H1961
Ro 9:22 make his power known, e with much G5342
2Ti 3:11 persecutions I e: but out of *them* all the G5297
Heb 6:15 And so, after he had patiently e, he G3114
10:32 ye e a great fight of afflictions; G5278
11:27 for he e, as seeing him who is invisible. G2594
12: 2 set before him e the cross, despising G5278
3 For consider him that e such G5278

ENDURETH
1Ch 16:34 for *he is* good; for his mercy *e* for ever.
41 the LORD, because his mercy *e* for ever;
2Ch 5:13 good; for his mercy *e* for ever: that *then*
7: 3 For *he is* good; for his mercy *e* for ever.
6 because his mercy *e* for ever, when
20:21 the LORD; for his mercy *e* for ever.
Ezr 3:11 *is* good, for his mercy *e* for ever toward
Ps 30: 5 For his anger *e but* a moment; in his
52: 1 man? the goodness of God *e* continually.
72: 7 of peace so long as the moon e. H1097
100: 5 and his truth *e* to all generations.
106: 1 for *he is* good: for his mercy *e* for ever.
107: 1 for *he is* good: for his mercy *e* for ever.
111: 3 and his righteousness e for ever. H5975
10 *commandments*: his praise e for ever. H5975
112: 3 house: and his righteousness e for ever. H5975
9 his righteousness e for ever; his horn H5975
117: 2 the LORD *e* for ever. Praise ye the LORD.
118: 1 *he is* good: because his mercy *e* for ever.
2 Let Israel now say, that his mercy *e* for
3 now say, that his mercy *e* for ever.
4 the LORD say, that his mercy *e* for ever.
29 for *he is* good: for his mercy *e* for ever.
119:160 of thy righteous judgments *e* for ever.
135:13 Thy name, O LORD, *e* for ever; *and* thy
136: 1 for *he is* good: for his mercy *e* for ever.
2 the God of gods: for his mercy *e* for ever.
Ps 136: 3 Lord of lords: for his mercy *e* for ever.
4 great wonders: for his mercy *e* for ever.
5 the heavens: for his mercy *e* for ever.
6 the waters: for his mercy *e* for ever.
7 great lights: for his mercy *e* for ever:
8 The sun to rule by day: for his mercy *e*
9 to rule by night: for his mercy *e* for ever.
10 their firstborn: for his mercy *e* for ever:
11 among them: for his mercy *e* for ever:
12 out arm: for his mercy *e* for ever.
13 sea into parts: for his mercy *e* for ever:
14 the midst of it: for his mercy *e* for ever:
15 in the Red sea: for his mercy *e* for ever.
16 the wilderness: for his mercy *e* for ever.
17 great kings: for his mercy *e* for ever:
18 And slew famous kings: for his mercy *e*
19 of the Amorites: for his mercy *e* for ever:
20 king of Bashan: for his mercy *e* for ever:
21 for an heritage: for his mercy *e* for ever:
22 his servant: for his mercy *e* for ever.
23 our low estate: for his mercy *e* for ever:
24 our enemies: for his mercy *e* for ever.
25 food to all flesh: for his mercy *e* for ever.
26 God of heaven: for his mercy *e* for ever.
138: 8 mercy, O LORD, *e* for ever: forsake not
145:13 dominion *e* throughout all generations.
Jer 33:11 *is* good; for his mercy *e* for ever: *and* of
Mt 10:22 but he that e to the end shall be saved. G5278
Jn 6:27 that meat which e unto everlasting life, G3306
1Co 13: 7 things, hopeth all things, e all things. G5278
Jas 1:12 Blessed *is* the man that e temptation: G5278
1Pt 1:25 But the word of the Lord e for ever. G3306

ENDURING
Ps 19: 9 The fear of the LORD *is* clean, e for H5975
2Co 1: 6 which is effectual in the e of the same G5281
Heb 10:34 in heaven a better and an e substance. G3306

ENEAS See AENEAS.

EN-EGLAIM
Ezk 47:10 En-gedi even unto E; they shall be a H5882

ENEMIES
Gen 14:20 delivered thine e into thy hand. And H6862
22:17 thy seed shall possess the gate of his e; H341
49: 8 *be* in the neck of thine e; thy father's H341
Ex 1:10 join also unto our e, and fight against H8130
23:22 an enemy unto thine e, and an adversary H341
27 all thine e turn their backs unto thee. H341
32:25 naked unto *their* shame among their e:) H6965
Lev 26: 7 And ye shall chase your e, and they shall H341
8 your e shall fall before you by the sword. H341
16 your seed in vain, for your e shall eat it. H341
17 be slain before your e: they that hate you H341
32 and your e which dwell therein H341
36 in the lands of their e; and the sound of a H341
37 have no power to stand before your e. H341
38 and the land of your e shall eat you up. H341
41 into the land of their e; if then their H341
44 in the land of their e, I will not cast them H341
Nu 10: 9 God, and ye shall be saved from your e. H341
35 and let thine e be scattered; and let H341
14:42 you; that ye be not smitten before your e. H341
23:11 thee to curse mine e, and, behold, thou H341
24: 8 eat up the nations his e, and shall break H6862
10 thee to curse mine e, and, behold, thou H341
18 for his e; and Israel shall do valiantly. H341
32:21 hath driven out his e from before him, H341
Dt 1:42 you; lest ye be smitten before your e. H341
6:19 To cast out all thine e from before thee, H341
12:10 e round about, so that ye dwell in safety; H341
20: 1 against thine e, and seest horses, and H341
3 battle against your e: let not your hearts H341
4 fight for you against your e, to save you. H341
14 the spoil of thine e, which the LORD thy H341
21:10 to war against thine e, and the LORD thy H341
23: 9 forth against thine e, then keep thee from H341
14 to give up thine e before thee; therefore H341
25:19 rest from all thine e round about, in the H341
28: 7 The LORD shall cause thine e that rise H341
25 before thine e: thou shalt go out one H341
31 *be* given unto thine e, and thou shalt H341
48 Therefore shalt thou serve thine e which H341
53 wherewith thine e shall distress thee: H341
55 thine e shall distress thee in all thy gates. H341
68 be sold unto your e for bondmen and H341
30: 7 curses upon thine e, and on them that H341
32:31 even our e themselves *being* judges. H341

Dt 32:41 e, and will reward them that hate me. H6862
33: 7 and be thou an help *to him* from his e. H6862
29 and thine e shall be found liars unto H341
Jos 7: 8 Israel turneth their backs before their e! H341
12 not stand before their e, *but* turned *their* H341
12 backs before their e, because they were H341
13 stand before thine e, until ye take away H341
10:13 upon their e. *Is* not this written in H341
19 And stay ye not, *but* pursue after your e, H341
25 do to all your e against whom ye fight. H341
21:44 not a man of all their e before them; the H341
44 delivered all their e into their hand. H341
22: 8 the spoil of your e with your brethren. H341
23: 1 from all their e round about, that Joshua H341
Jdg 2:14 the hands of their e round about, so that H341
14 could not any longer stand before their e. H341
18 of the hand of their e all the days of the H341
3:28 delivered your e the Moabites into your H341
5:31 So let all thine e perish, O LORD: but *let* H341
8:34 of the hands of all their e on every side: H341
11:36 thine e, *even* of the children of Ammon. H341
1Sa 2: 1 mine e; because I rejoice in thy salvation. H341
4: 3 it may save us out of the hand of our e. H341
12:10 the hand of our e, and we will serve thee. H341
11 e on every side, and ye dwelled safe. H341
14:24 e. So none of the people tasted *any* food. H341
30 of the spoil of their e which they found? H341
47 against all his e on every side, against H341
18:25 of the king's e. But Saul thought to make H341
20:15 hath cut off the e of David every one H341
16 even require *it* at the hand of David's e. H341
25:22 So and more also do God unto the e of H341
26 hand, now let thine e, and they that seek H341
29 the souls of thine e, them shall he sling H341
29: 8 fight against the e of my lord the king? H341
30:26 for you of the spoil of the e of the LORD; H341
2Sa 3:18 and out of the hand of all their e. H341
5:20 forth upon mine e before me, as the H341
7: 1 him rest round about from all his e; H341
9 cut off all thine e out of thy sight, and H341
11 to rest from all thine e. Also the LORD H341
12:14 great occasion to the e of the LORD to H341
18:19 that the LORD hath avenged him of his e. H341
32 answered, The e of my lord the king, H341
19: 6 In that thou lovest thine e, and hatest H8130
9 of the hand of our e, and he delivered us H341
22: 1 of all his e, and out of the hand of Saul: H341
4 praised: so shall I be saved from mine e. H341
38 I have pursued mine e, and destroyed H341
41 the necks of mine e, that I might destroy H341
49 And that bringeth me forth from mine e: H341
24:13 before thine e, while they pursue thee? H6862
1Ki 3:11 the life of thine e; but hast asked for H341
8:48 in the land of their e, which led them H341
2Ki 17:39 deliver you out of the hand of all your e. H341
21:14 into the hand of their e; and they shall H341
14 become a prey and a spoil to all their e; H341
1Ch 12:17 betray me to mine e, seeing *there is* no H6862
14:11 in upon mine e by mine hand like the H341
17: 8 cut off all thine e from before thee, and H341
10 subdue all thine e. Furthermore I tell thee H341
21:12 the sword of thine e overtaketh *thee;* or H341
22: 9 rest from all his e round about: for his H341
2Ch 1:11 the life of thine e, neither yet hast asked H8130
6:28 caterpillers; if their e besiege them in the H341
34 war against their e by the way that thou H341
36 over before *their* e, and they carry them H341
20:27 had made them to rejoice over their e. H341
29 the LORD fought against the e of Israel. H341
25:20 the hand *of their e,* because they sought H341
Neh 4:15 And it came to pass, when our e heard H341
5: 9 of the reproach of the heathen our e? H341
6: 1 and the rest of our e, heard that I had H341
16 And it came to pass, that when all our e H341
9:27 the hand of their e, who vexed them: H6862
27 saved them out of the hand of their e. H6862
28 in the hand of their e, so that they had H341
Est 8:13 that day to avenge themselves on their e. H341
9: 1 in the day that the e of the Jews hoped to H341
5 Thus the Jews smote all their e with the H341
16 had rest from their e, and slew of their H341
22 rested from their e, and the month which H341
Job 19:11 counteth me unto him as *one of* his e. H6862
Ps 3: 7 smitten all mine e *upon* the cheek bone; H341
5: 8 because of mine e; make thy way H8324
6: 7 it waxeth old because of all mine e. H6887
10 Let all mine e be ashamed and sore H341
7: 6 the rage of mine e: and awake for me *to* H6887
8: 2 because of thine e, that thou mightest H6887
Ps 9: 3 When mine e are turned back, they shall H341
10: 5 sight: *as for* all his e, he puffeth at them. H6887
17: 9 my deadly e, *who* compass me about. H341
18: 3 praised: so shall I be saved from mine e. H341
37 I have pursued mine e, and overtaken H341
40 the necks of mine e; that I might destroy H341
48 He delivereth me from mine e: yea, thou H341
ttl the hand of all his e, and from the hand H341
21: 8 Thine hand shall find out all thine e: thy H341
23: 5 presence of mine e: thou anointest my H6887
25: 2 let not mine e triumph over me. H341
19 Consider mine e; for they are many; and H341
27: 2 When the wicked, *even* mine e and my H6862
6 lifted up above mine e round about me: H341
11 me in a plain path, because of mine e. H8324
12 the will of mine e: for false witnesses H6862
31:11 I was a reproach among all mine e, but H6887
15 e, and from them that persecute me. H341
35:19 Let not them that are mine e wrongfully H341
37:20 But the wicked shall perish, and the e of H341
38:19 But mine e *are* lively, *and* they are H341
41: 2 wilt not deliver him unto the will of his e. H341
5 Mine e speak evil of me, When shall he H341
42:10 *As* with a sword in my bones, mine e H6887
44: 5 Through thee will we push down our e: H6862
7 But thou hast saved us from our e, and H6862
45: 5 e; *whereby* the people fall under thee. H341
54: 5 He shall reward evil unto mine e: cut H8324
7 eye hath seen *his desire* upon mine e. H341
56: 2 Mine e would daily swallow *me* up: for H8324
9 When I cry *unto thee,* then shall mine e H341
59: 1 Deliver me from mine e, O my God: H341
10 shall let me see *my desire* upon mine e. H8324
60:12 for he *it is that* shall tread down our e. H6862
66: 3 thine e submit themselves unto thee. H341
68: 1 Let God arise, let his e be scattered: let H341
21 But God shall wound the head of his e, H341
23 e, *and* the tongue of thy dogs in the same. H341
69: 4 destroy me, *being* mine e wrongfully, are H341
18 redeem it: deliver me because of mine e. H341
71:10 For mine e speak against me; and they H341
72: 9 before him; and his e shall lick the dust. H341
74: 4 Thine e roar in the midst of thy H6887
23 Forget not the voice of thine e: the H6887
78:53 not: but the sea overwhelmed their e. H341
66 And he smote his e in the hinder parts: H6862
80: 6 and our e laugh among themselves. H341
81:14 I should soon have subdued their e, and H341
83: 2 For, lo, thine e make a tumult: and they H341
89:10 scattered thine e with thy strong arm. H341
42 thou hast made all his e to rejoice. H341
51 Wherewith thine e have reproached, O H341
92: 9 For, lo, thine e, O LORD, for, lo, thine H341
9 LORD, for, lo, thine e shall perish; all the H341
11 see *my desire* on mine e, *and* mine ears H7790
97: 3 and burneth up his e round about. H6862
102: 8 Mine e reproach me all the day; *and* they H341
105:24 and made them stronger than their e. H6862
106:11 And the waters covered their e: there H6862
42 Their e also oppressed them, and they H341
108:13 for he *it is that* shall tread down our e. H6862
110: 1 hand, until I make thine e thy footstool. H341
2 of Zion: rule thou in the midst of thine e. H341
112: 8 until he see *his desire* upon his e. H6862
119:98 than mine e: for they *are* ever with me. H341
139 mine e have forgotten thy words. H6862
157 Many *are* my persecutors and mine e; H6862
127: 5 they shall speak with the e in the gate. H341
132:18 His e will I clothe with shame: but upon H341
136:24 And hath redeemed us from our e: for H6862
138: 7 mine e, and thy right hand shall save me. H341
139:20 *and* thine e take *thy name* in vain. H6145
22 with perfect hatred: I count them mine e. H341
143: 9 Deliver me, O LORD, from mine e: I flee H341
12 And of thy mercy cut off mine e, and H341
Prv 16: 7 even his e to be at peace with him. H341
Isa 1:24 adversaries, and avenge me of mine e: H341
9:11 against him, and join his e together; H341
26:11 the fire of thine e shall devour them. H6862
42:13 yea, roar; he shall prevail against his e. H341
59:18 recompence to his e; to the islands he will H341
62: 8 *to be* meat for thine e; and the sons of the H341
66: 6 that rendereth recompence to his e. H341
14 and *his* indignation toward his e. H341
Jer 12: 7 beloved of my soul into the hand of her e. H341
15: 9 the sword before their e, saith the LORD. H341
14 And I will make *thee* to pass with thine e H341
17: 4 thee to serve thine e in the land which H341
19: 7 sword before their e, and by the hands of H341
Jer 19: 9 wherewith their e, and they that seek H341
20: 4 the sword of their e, and thine eyes shall H341
5 into the hand of their e, which shall spoil H341
21: 7 the hand of their e, and into the hand of H341
34:20 the hand of their e, and into the hand of H341
21 the hand of their e, and into the hand of H341
44:30 the hand of his e, and into the hand of H341
48: 5 the e have heard a cry of destruction. H6862
49:37 before their e, and before them that H341
Lam 1: 2 with her, they are become her e. H341
5 Her adversaries are the chief, her e H341
21 me: all mine e have heard of my trouble; H341
2:16 All thine e have opened their mouth H341
3:46 All our e have opened their mouths H341
52 Mine e chased me sore, like a bird, H341
Ezk 39:23 of their e: so fell they all by the sword. H6862
Dan 4:19 the interpretation thereof to thine e. H6146
Am 9: 4 before their e, thence will I command H341
Mic 4:10 redeem thee from the hand of thine e. H341
5: 9 and all thine e shall be cut off. H341
7: 6 a man's e *are* the men of his own house. H341
Nah 1: 2 and he reserveth *wrath* for his e. H341
8 thereof, and darkness shall pursue his e. H341
3:13 thine e: the fire shall devour thy bars. H341
Zec 10: 5 tread down *their* e in the mire of the
Mt 5:44 But I say unto you, Love your e, bless *G2190*
22:44 hand, till I make thine e thy footstool? *G2190*
Mk 12:36 hand, till I make thine e thy footstool. *G2190*
Lk 1:71 That we should be saved from our e, *G2190*
74 of our e might serve him without fear, *G2190*
6:27 your e, do good to them which hate you, *G2190*
35 But love ye your e, and do good, and *G2190*
19:27 But those mine e, which would not that *G2190*
43 thee, that thine e shall cast a trench *G2190*
20:43 Till I make thine e thy footstool. *G2190*
Ro 5:10 For if, when we were e, we were *G2190*
11:28 As concerning the gospel, *they are* e for *G2190*
1Co 15:25 For he must reign, till he hath put all e *G2190*
Php 3:18 *they are* the e of the cross of Christ: *G2190*
Col 1:21 alienated and e in *your* mind by *G2190*
Heb 1:13 until I make thine e thy footstool? *G2190*
10:13 From henceforth expecting till his e be *G2190*
Rev 11: 5 devoureth their e: and if any man will *G2190*
12 in a cloud; and their e beheld them. *G2190*

ENEMIES'
Lev 26:34 and ye *be* in your e land; *even* then shall H341
39 iniquity in your e lands; and also in the H341
Ezk 39:27 them out of their e lands, and am H341

ENEMY
Ex 15: 6 O LORD, hath dashed in pieces the e. H341
9 The e said, I will pursue, I will overtake, H341
23:22 then I will be an e unto thine enemies, H340
Lev 26:25 shall be delivered into the hand of the e. H341
Nu 10: 9 land against the e that oppresseth you, H6862
35:23 *was* not his e, neither sought his harm: H341
Dt 28:57 thine e shall distress thee in thy gates. H341
32:27 the wrath of the e, lest their adversaries H341
42 the beginning of revenges upon the e. H341
33:27 shall thrust out the e from before thee; H341
Jdg 16:23 delivered Samson our e into our hand. H341
24 into our hands our e, and the destroyer H341
1Sa 2:32 And thou shalt see an e *in my* H6862
18:29 and Saul became David's e continually. H341
19:17 and sent away mine e, that he is escaped? H341
24: 4 I will deliver thine e into thine hand, H341
19 For if a man find his e, will he let him go H341
26: 8 delivered thine e into thine hand this H341
28:16 from thee, and is become thine e? H6145
2Sa 4: 8 son of Saul thine e, which sought thy life; H341
22:18 He delivered me from my strong e, *and* H341
1Ki 8:33 down before the e, because they have H341
37 caterpiller; if their e besiege them in the H341
44 battle against their e, whithersoever thou H341
46 deliver them to the e, so that they carry H341
46 unto the land of the e, far or near; H341
21:20 found me, O mine e? And he answered, I H341
2Ch 6:24 the worse before the e, because they have H341
25: 8 thee fall before the e: for God hath power H341
26:13 power, to help the king against the e. H341
Ezr 8:22 help us against the e in the way: because H341
31 e, and of such as lay in wait by the way. H341
Est 3:10 Hammedatha the Agagite, the Jews' e. H6887
7: 4 although the e could not countervail H6862
6 And Esther said, The adversary and e *is* H341
8: 1 of Haman the Jews' e unto Esther the H6887
9:10 of Hammedatha, the e of the Jews, slew H6887
24 the Agagite, the e of all the Jews, had H6887

Job 13:24 thou thy face, and holdest me for thine **e**? H341
16: 9 mine **e** sharpeneth his eyes upon me. H6862
27: 7 Let mine **e** be as the wicked, and he that H341
33:10 against me, he counteth me for his **e**, H341
Ps 7: 4 him that without cause is mine **e**:) H6887
5 Let the **e** persecute my soul, and take *it*; H341
8: 2 thou mightest still the **e** and the avenger. H341
9: 6 O thou **e**, destructions are come to a H341
13: 2 long shall mine **e** be exalted over me? H341
4 Lest mine **e** say, I have prevailed against H341
18:17 He delivered me from my strong **e**, and H341
31: 8 **e**: thou hast set my feet in a large room. H341
41:11 mine **e** doth not triumph over me. H341
42: 9 because of the oppression of the **e**? H341
43: 2 because of the oppression of the **e**? H341
44:10 back from the **e**: and they which H6862
16 by reason of the **e** and avenger. H341
55: 3 Because of the voice of the **e**, because of H341
12 For *it was* not an **e** *that* reproached me; H341
61: 3 for me, *and* a strong tower from the **e**. H341
64: 1 preserve my life from fear of the **e**. H341
74: 3 **e** hath done wickedly in the sanctuary. H341
10 shall the **e** blaspheme thy name for ever? H341
18 Remember this, *that* the **e** hath H341
78:42 day when he delivered them from the **e**. H6862
89:22 The **e** shall not exact upon him; nor the H341
106:10 redeemed them from the hand of the **e**. H341
107: 2 hath redeemed from the hand of the **e**; H6862
143: 3 For the **e** hath persecuted my soul; he H341
Prv 24:17 Rejoice not when thine **e** falleth, and let H341
25:21 If thine **e** be hungry, give him bread to H8130
27: 6 but the kisses of an **e** *are* deceitful. H8130
Isa 59:19 the sun. When the **e** shall come in like a H6862
63:10 to be their **e**, *and* he fought against them. H341
Jer 6:25 sword of the **e** *and* fear *is* on every side. H341
15:11 I will cause the **e** to entreat thee *well* in H341
18:17 wind before the **e**; I will shew them the H341
30:14 the wound of an **e**, with the chastisement H341
31:16 shall come again from the land of the **e**. H341
44:30 of Babylon, his **e**, and that sought his life. H341
Lam 1: 5 are gone into captivity before the **e**. H6862
7 the hand of the **e**, and none did help H6862
9 for the **e** hath magnified *himself*. H341
16 are desolate, because the **e** prevailed. H341
2: 3 from before the **e**, and he burned against H341
4 He hath bent his bow like an **e**: he stood H341
5 The Lord was as an **e**: he hath swallowed H341
7 into the hand of the **e** the walls of her H341
17 hath caused *thine* **e** to rejoice over thee, H341
22 and brought up hath mine **e** consumed. H341
4:12 adversary and the **e** should have entered H341
Ezk 36: 2 Thus saith the Lord GOD; Because the **e** H341
Hos 8: 3 *that is* good: the **e** shall pursue him. H341
Mic 2: 8 is risen up as an **e**: ye pull off the robe H341
7: 8 Rejoice not against me, O mine **e**: when I H341
10 Then *she that is* mine **e** shall see *it*, and H341
Nah 3:11 also shalt seek strength because of the **e**. H341
Zep 3:15 hath cast out thine **e**: the king of Israel, H341
Mt 5:43 love thy neighbour, and hate thine **e**. *G2190*
13:25 But while men slept, his **e** came and *G2190*
28 He said unto them, An **e** hath done *G2190*
39 The **e** that sowed them is the devil; the *G2190*
Lk 10:19 the power of the **e**: and nothing shall by *G2190*
Act 13:10 of the devil, *thou* **e** of all righteousness, *G2190*
Ro 12:20 Therefore if thine **e** hunger, feed him; if *G2190*
1Co 15:26 The last **e** *that* shall be destroyed *is* *G2190*
Gal 4:16 Am I therefore become your **e**, because *G2190*
2Th 3:15 Yet count *him* not as an **e**, but *G2190*
Jas 4: 4 be a friend of the world is the **e** of God. *G2190*

ENEMY'S
Ex 23: 4 If thou meet thine **e** ox or his ass going H341
Job 6:23 Or, Deliver me from the **e** hand? or, H6862
Ps 78:61 captivity, and his glory into the **e** hand. H6862

ENFLAMING
Isa 57: 5 **E** yourselves with idols under every H2552

ENGAGED
Jer 30:21 who *is* this that **e** his heart to approach H6148

EN-GANNIM
Jos 15:34 And Zanoah, and **E**, Tappuah, and H5873
19:21 And Remeth, and **E**, and En-haddah, H5873
21:29 Jarmuth with her suburbs, **E** with her H5873

EN-GEDI
Jos 15:62 Salt, and **E**; six cities with their villages. H5872
1Sa 23:29 thence, and dwelt in strong holds at **E**. H5872
1Sa 24: 1 Behold, David *is* in the wilderness of **E**. H5872
2Ch 20: 2 they *be* in Hazazontamar, which *is* **E**. H5872
Song 1:14 of camphire in the vineyards of **E**. H5872
Ezk 47:10 upon it from **E** even unto En-eglaim; H5872

ENGINES
2Ch 26:15 And he made in Jerusalem **e**, invented H2810
Ezk 26: 9 And he shall set **e** of war against thy H4239

ENGRAFTED
Jas 1:21 with meekness the **e** word, which is *G1721*

ENGRAVE
Ex 28:11 signet, shalt thou **e** the two stones with H6605
Zec 3: 9 seven eyes: behold, I will **e** the graving H6605

ENGRAVEN
2Co 3: 7 of death, written *and* **e** in stones, was *G1795*

ENGRAVER
Ex 28:11 With the work of an **e** in stone, *like* the H2796
35:35 of work, of the **e**, and of the cunning H2796
38:23 the tribe of Dan, an **e**, and a cunning H2796

ENGRAVINGS
Ex 28:11 in stone, *like* the **e** of a signet, shalt H6603
21 names, *like* the **e** of a signet; every one H6603
36 grave upon it, *like* the **e** of a signet, H6603
39:14 names, *like* the **e** of a signet, every one H6603
30 a writing, *like to* the **e** of a signet, H6603

EN-HADDAH
Jos 19:21 And Remeth, and En-gannim, and **E**, H5876

EN-HAKKORE
Jdg 15:19 **E**, which *is* in Lehi unto this day. H5875

EN-HAZOR
Jos 19:37 And Kedesh, and Edrei, and **E**, H5877

ENJOIN
Phlm 8 to **e** thee that which is convenient, *G2004*

ENJOINED
Est 9:31 the queen had **e** them, and as they had H6965
Job 36:23 Who hath **e** him his way? or who can H6485
Heb 9:20 testament which God hath **e** unto you. *G1781*

ENJOY
Lev 26:34 Then shall the land **e** her sabbaths, as H7521
34 shall the land rest, and **e** her sabbaths. H7521
43 left of them, and shall **e** her sabbaths, H7521
Nu 36: 8 children of Israel may **e** every man the H3423
Dt 28:41 **e** them; for they shall go into captivity. H1961
Jos 1:15 possession, and **e** it, which Moses the H3423
Ecc 2: 1 with mirth, therefore **e** pleasure: and, H7200
24 make his soul **e** good in his labour. H7200
3:13 eat and drink, and **e** the good of all his H7200
5:18 to drink, and to **e** the good of all his H7200
Isa 65:22 shall long **e** the work of their hands. H1086
Act 24: 2 that by thee we **e** great quietness, and *G5177*
1Ti 6:17 God, who giveth us richly all things to **e**; *G619*
Heb 11:25 to **e** the pleasures of sin for a season; *G619*

ENJOYED
2Ch 36:21 until the land had **e** her sabbaths: *for* H7521

ENLARGE
Gen 9:27 God shall **e** Japheth, and he shall dwell H6601
Ex 34:24 before thee, and **e** thy borders: neither H7337
Dt 12:20 When the LORD thy God shall **e** thy H7337
19: 8 And if the LORD thy God **e** thy coast, as H7337
1Ch 4:10 me indeed, and **e** my coast, and that H7235
Ps 119:32 when thou shalt **e** my heart. H7337
Isa 54: 2 **E** the place of thy tent, and let them H7337
Am 1:13 Gilead, that they might **e** their border: H7337
Mic 1:16 delicate children; **e** thy baldness as the H7337
Mt 23: 5 and **e** the borders of their garments, *G3170*

ENLARGED
1Sa 2: 1 my mouth is **e** over mine enemies; H7337
2Sa 22:37 Thou hast **e** my steps under me; so that H7337
Ps 4: 1 thou hast **e** me *when I was* in distress; H7337
18:36 Thou hast **e** my steps under me, that H7337
25:17 The troubles of my heart are **e**: *O* bring H7337
Isa 5:14 Therefore hell hath **e** herself, and H7337
57: 8 gone up; thou hast **e** thy bed, and made H7337
60: 5 heart shall fear, and be **e**; because the H7337
2Co 6:11 mouth is open unto you, our heart is **e**. *G4115*
2Co 6:13 as unto *my* children,) be ye also **e**. *G4115*
10:15 that we shall be **e** by you according to *G3170*

ENLARGEMENT
Est 4:14 *then* shall there **e** and deliverance arise H7305

ENLARGETH
Dt 33:20 Blessed *be* he that **e** Gad: he dwelleth as H7337
Job 12:23 them: he **e** the nations, and straiteneth H7849
Hab 2: 5 at home, who **e** his desire as hell, and H7337

ENLARGING
Ezk 41: 7 And *there was* an **e**, and a winding H7337

ENLIGHTEN
Ps 18:28 the LORD my God will **e** my darkness. H5050

ENLIGHTENED
1Sa 14:27 hand to his mouth; and his eyes were **e**. H215
29 **e**, because I tasted a little of this honey. H215
Job 33:30 the pit, to be **e** with the light of the living. H215
Ps 97: 4 His lightnings **e** the world: the earth saw, H215
Eph 1:18 The eyes of your understanding being **e**; *G5461*
Heb 6: 4 who were once **e**, and have tasted of the *G5461*

ENLIGHTENING
Ps 19: 8 of the LORD *is* pure, **e** the eyes. H215

EN-MISHPAT
Gen 14: 7 And they returned, and came to **E**, H5880

ENMITY
Gen 3:15 And I will put **e** between thee and the H342
Nu 35:21 Or in **e** smite him with his hand, that he H342
22 But if he thrust him suddenly without **e**, H342
Lk 23:12 they were at **e** between themselves. *G2189*
Ro 8: 7 Because the carnal mind *is* **e** against *G2189*
Eph 2:15 Having abolished in his flesh the **e**, *even* *G2189*
16 by the cross, having slain the **e** thereby: *G2189*
Jas 4: 4 of the world is **e** with God? whosoever *G2189*

ENOCH
Gen 4:17 and bare **E**: and he builded a city, H2585
17 of the city, after the name of his son, **E**. H2585
18 And unto **E** was born Irad: and Irad H2585
5:18 sixty and two years, and he begat **E**: H2585
19 And Jared lived after he begat **E** eight H2585
21 And **E** lived sixty and five years, and H2585
22 And **E** walked with God after he begat H2585
23 And all the days of **E** were three H2585
24 And **E** walked with God: and he *was* H2585
Lk 3:37 was *the son* of **E**, which was *the son* of *G1802*
Heb 11: 5 By faith **E** was translated that he *G1802*
Jude 14 And **E** also, the seventh from Adam, *G1802*

ENON See AENON.

ENOS
Gen 4:26 he called his name **E**; then began men to H583
5: 6 an hundred and five years, and begat **E**: H583
7 And Seth lived after he begat **E** eight H583
9 And **E** lived ninety years, and begat H583
10 And **E** lived after he begat Cainan eight H583
11 And all the days of **E** were nine hundred H583
Lk 3:38 Which was *the son* of **E**, which was *the* *G1800*

ENOSH
1Ch 1: 1 Adam, Sheth, **E**, H583

ENOUGH
Gen 24:25 and provender **e**, and room to lodge in. H7227
33: 9 And Esau said, I have **e**, my brother; H7227
11 **e**. And he urged him, and he took *it*. H3605
34:21 behold, *it is* large **e** for them; let us take H3027
45:28 And Israel said, *It is* **e**; Joseph my son *is* H7227
Ex 2:19 *water* **e** for us, and watered the flock. H1802
9:28 Entreat the LORD (for *it is* **e**) that there H7227
36: 5 much more than **e** for the service of the H1767
Dt 1: 6 Ye have dwelt long **e** in this mount: H7227
2: 3 mountain long **e**: turn you northward. H7227
Jos 17:16 said, The hill is not **e** for us: and all the H4672
2Sa 24:16 the people, It is **e**: stay now thine hand. H7227
1Ki 19: 4 die; and said, It is **e**; now, O LORD, take H7227
1Ch 21:15 destroyed, It is **e**, stay now thine hand. H7227
2Ch 31:10 we have had **e** to eat, and have left H7646
Prv 27:27 And *thou shalt have* goats' milk **e** for H1767
28:19 after vain *persons* shall have poverty **e**. H7646
30:15 *yea*, four *things* say not, *It is* **e**: H1952
16 water; and the fire *that* saith not, *It is* **e**. H1952

Isa 56:11 *which* can never have **e**, and they *are* H7654
Jer 49: 9 night, they will destroy till they have **e**. H1767
Hos 4:10 For they shall eat, and not have **e**: they H7646
Oba 5 have stolen till they had **e**? if the H1767
Nah 2:12 The lion did tear in pieces **e** for his H1767
Hag 1: 6 but ye have not **e**; ye drink, but ye are H7654
Mal 3:10 *there shall* not *be room* **e** *to receive it*. H1767
Mt 10:25 It is **e** for the disciple that he be as his G713
25: 9 *so*; lest there be not **e** for us and you: but G714
Mk 14:41 take *your* rest: it is **e**, the hour is come; G566
Lk 15:17 have bread **e** and to spare, and G4052
22:38 swords. And he said unto them, It is **e**. G2425
Act 27:38 And when they had eaten **e**, they G2880

ENQUIRE See INQUIRE.

ENRICH
1Sa 17:25 him, the king will **e** him with great H6238
Ezk 27:33 people; thou didst **e** the kings of the H6238

ENRICHED
1Co 1: 5 That in every thing ye are **e** by him, in G4148
2Co 9:11 Being **e** in every thing to all G4148

ENRICHEST
Ps 65: 9 it: thou greatly **e** it with the river of H6238

EN-RIMMON
Neh 11:29 And at **E**, and at Zareah, and at H5884

ENROGEL
Jos 15: 7 and the goings out thereof were at **E**: H5883

EN-ROGEL
Jos 18:16 on the south, and descended to **E**, H5883
2Sa 17:17 stayed by **E**; for they might not be H5883
1Ki 1: 9 which *is* by **E**, and called all his H5883

ENSAMPLE
Php 3:17 which walk so as ye have us for an **e**. G5179
2Th 3: 9 ourselves an **e** unto you to follow us. G5179
2Pt 2: 6 making *them* an **e** unto those that after G5262

ENSAMPLES
1Co 10:11 unto them for **e**: and they are written G5179
1Th 1: 7 So that ye were **e** to all that believe in G5179
1Pt 5: 3 *God's* heritage, but being **e** to the flock. G5179

EN-SHEMESH
Jos 15: 7 the waters of **E**, and the goings out H5885
18:17 and went forth to **E**, and went forth H5885

ENSIGN
Nu 2: 2 own standard, with the **e** of their father's H226
Isa 5:26 And he will lift up an **e** to the nations H5251
11:10 shall stand for an **e** of the people; to it H5251
12 And he shall set up an **e** for the H5251
18: 3 he lifteth up an **e** on the mountains; H5251
30:17 of a mountain, and as an **e** on an hill. H5251
31: 9 shall be afraid of the **e**, saith the LORD, H5251
Zec 9:16 crown, lifted up as an **e** upon his land. H5264

ENSIGNS
Ps 74: 4 they set up their **e** *for* signs. H226

ENSNARED
Job 34:30 hypocrite reign not, lest the people be **e**. H4170

ENSUE
1Pt 3:11 do good; let him seek peace, and **e** it. G1377

ENTANGLE
Mt 22:15 how they might **e** him in *his* talk. G3802

ENTANGLED
Ex 14: 3 of Israel, They *are* **e** in the land, the H943
Gal 5: 1 not **e** again with the yoke of bondage. G1758
2Pt 2:20 Christ, they are again **e** therein, and G1707

ENTANGLETH
2Ti 2: 4 No man that warreth **e** himself with the G1707

EN-TAP-PUAH
Jos 17: 7 right hand unto the inhabitants of **E**. H5887

ENTER
Gen 12:11 was come near to **e** into Egypt, that he H935
Ex 40:35 And Moses was not able to **e** into the H935
Nu 4: 3 years old, all that **e** into the host, to do H935
4:23 them; all that **e** in to perform the service, H935
5:24 curse shall **e** into her, *and become* bitter. H935
27 the curse shall **e** into her, *and become* H935
20:24 for he shall not **e** into the land which I H935
Dt 23: 1 not **e** into the congregation of the LORD. H935
2 A bastard shall not **e** into the H935
2 not **e** into the congregation of the LORD. H935
3 An Ammonite or Moabite shall not **e** H935
3 shall they not **e** into the congregation H935
8 of them shall **e** into the congregation H935
29:12 That thou shouldest **e** into covenant H5674
Jos 10:19 suffer them not to **e** into their cities: for H935
Jdg 18: 9 to go, *and* to **e** to possess the land. H935
2Sa 22: 7 temple, and my cry *did e* into his ears.
1Ki 14:12 thy feet **e** into the city, the child shall die. H935
22:30 myself, and **e** into the battle; but put H935
2Ki 7: 4 If we say, We will **e** into the city, then the H935
11: 5 part of you that **e** in on the sabbath shall H935
19:23 thereof: and I will **e** into the lodgings of H935
2Ch 7: 2 And the priests could not **e** into the H935
23:19 *was* unclean in any thing should **e** in. H935
30: 8 the LORD, and **e** into his sanctuary, H935
Neh 2: 8 house that I shall **e** into. And the king H935
Est 4: 2 for none *might* **e** into the king's gate H935
Job 22: 4 thee? will he **e** with thee into judgment? H935
34:23 he should **e** into judgment with God. H1980
Ps 37:15 Their sword shall **e** into their own heart, H935
45:15 they shall **e** into the king's palace. H935
95:11 that they should not **e** into my rest. H935
100: 4 **E** into his gates with thanksgiving, *and* H935
118:20 LORD, into which the righteous shall **e**. H935
143: 2 And **e** not into judgment with thy H935
Prv 4:14 **E** not into the path of the wicked, and go H935
18: 6 A fool's lips **e** into contention, and his H935
23:10 Remove not the old landmark; and **e** not H935
Isa 2:10 **E** into the rock, and hide thee in the H935
3:14 The LORD will **e** into judgment with the H935
26: 2 nation which keepeth the truth may **e** in. H935
20 Come, my people, **e** thou into thy H935
37:24 thereof: and I will **e** into the height of his H935
57: 2 He shall **e** into peace: they shall rest in H935
59:14 fallen in the street, and equity cannot **e**. H935
Jer 7: 2 **e** in at these gates to worship the LORD. H935
8:14 and let us **e** into the defenced cities, H935
14:18 the sword! and if I **e** into the city, then H935
16: 5 For thus saith the LORD, **E** not into the H935
17:20 of Jerusalem, that **e** in by these gates: H935
25 Then shall there **e** into the gates of this H935
21:13 us? or who shall **e** into our habitations? H935
22: 2 and thy people that **e** in by these gates: H935
4 then shall there **e** in by the gates of this H935
41:17 is by Beth-lehem, to go to **e** into Egypt, H935
42:15 to **e** into Egypt, and go to sojourn there; H935
18 you, when ye shall **e** into Egypt: and ye H935
Lam 1:10 they should not **e** into thy congregation. H935
3:13 arrows of his quiver to **e** into my reins. H935
Ezk 7:22 the robbers shall **e** into it, and defile it. H935
13: 9 neither shall they **e** into the land of H935
20:38 and they shall not **e** into the land of H935
26:10 when he shall **e** into thy gates, as men H935
10 **e** into a city wherein is made a breach. H935
37: 5 breath to **e** into you, and ye shall live: H935
42:14 When the priests **e** therein, then shall H935
44: 2 and no man shall **e** in by it; because the H935
3 the LORD; he shall **e** by the way of the H935
9 in flesh, shall **e** into my sanctuary, of H935
16 They shall **e** into my sanctuary, and they H935
17 *that* when they **e** in at the gates of the H935
21 wine, when they **e** into the inner court. H935
46: 2 And the prince shall **e** by the way of the H935
8 And when the prince shall **e**, he shall go H935
Dan 11: 7 an army, and shall **e** into the fortress of H935
17 He shall also set his face to **e** with the H935
24 He shall **e** peaceably even upon the H935
40 ships; and he shall **e** into the countries, H935
41 He shall **e** also into the glorious land, H935
Hos 11: 9 of thee: and I will not **e** into the city. H935
Joel 2: 9 shall **e** in at the windows like a thief. H935
Am 5: 5 But seek not Beth-el, nor **e** into Gilgal, H935
Jna 3: 4 And Jonah began to **e** into the city a H935
Zec 5: 4 hosts, and it shall **e** into the house of the H935
Mt 5:20 no case **e** into the kingdom of heaven. G1525
6: 6 But thou, when thou prayest, **e** into thy G1525
7:13 **E** ye in at the strait gate: for wide *is* the G1525
21 Lord, Lord, shall **e** into the kingdom of G1525
10: 5 *any* city of the Samaritans **e** ye not: G1525
11 or town ye shall **e**, inquire who in it is G1525
12:29 Or else how can one **e** into a strong G1525
45 himself, and they **e** in and dwell there: G1525
Mt 18: 3 shall not **e** into the kingdom of heaven. G1525
8 is better for thee to **e** into life halt or G1525
9 is better for thee to **e** into life with one G1525
19:17 **e** into life, keep the commandments. G1525
23 hardly **e** into the kingdom of heaven. G1525
24 rich man to **e** into the kingdom of God. G1525
25:21 things: **e** thou into the joy of thy lord. G1525
23 things: **e** thou into the joy of thy lord. G1525
26:41 Watch and pray, that ye **e** not into G1525
Mk 1:45 no more openly **e** into the city, but was G1525
3:27 No man can **e** into a strong man's G1525
5:12 the swine, that we may **e** into them. G1525
6:10 place soever ye **e** into an house, there G1525
9:25 out of him, and **e** no more into him. G1525
43 is better for thee to **e** into life maimed, G1525
45 is better for thee to **e** halt into life, than G1525
47 better for thee to **e** into the kingdom of G1525
10:15 as a little child, he shall not **e** therein. G1525
23 have riches **e** into the kingdom of God! G1525
24 in riches to **e** into the kingdom of God! G1525
25 rich man to **e** into the kingdom of God. G1525
13:15 the house, neither **e** *therein*, to take G1525
14:38 Watch ye and pray, lest ye **e** into G1525
Lk 7: 6 that thou shouldest **e** under my roof: G1525
8:16 that they which **e** in may see the light. G1531
32 to **e** into them. And he suffered them. G1525
9: 4 And whatsoever house ye **e** into, there G1525
10: 5 And into whatsoever house ye **e**, first G1525
8 And into whatsoever city ye **e**, and they G1525
10 But into whatsoever city ye **e**, and they G1525
11:26 himself; and they **e** in, and dwell there: G1525
13:24 Strive to **e** in at the strait gate: for G1525
24 will seek to **e** in, and shall not be able. G1525
18:17 a little child shall in no wise **e** therein. G1525
24 have riches **e** into the kingdom of God! G1525
25 rich man to **e** into the kingdom of God. G1525
21:21 that are in the countries **e** thereinto. G1525
22:40 Pray that ye **e** not into temptation. G1525
46 rise and pray, lest ye **e** into temptation. G1525
24:26 these things, and to **e** into his glory? G1525
Jn 3: 4 he is old? can he **e** the second time into G1525
5 he cannot **e** into the kingdom of God. G1525
10: 9 I am the door: by me if any man **e** in, G1525
Act 14:22 tribulation **e** into the kingdom of God. G1525
20:29 **e** in among you, not sparing the flock. G1525
Heb 3:11 wrath, They shall not **e** into my rest.) G1525
18 they should not **e** into his rest, but to G1525
19 So we see that they could not **e** in G1525
4: 3 For we which have believed do **e** into G1525
3 my wrath, if they shall **e** into my rest: G1525
5 And in this *place* again, If they shall **e** G1525
6 that some must **e** therein, and they to G1525
11 Let us labour therefore to **e** into that G1525
10:19 **e** into the holiest by the blood of Jesus, G1529
Rev 15: 8 man was able to **e** into the temple, till G1525
21:27 And there shall in no wise **e** into it any G1525
22:14 **e** in through the gates into the city. G1525

ENTERED
Gen 7:13 In the selfsame day **e** Noah, and Shem, H935
19: 3 in unto him, and **e** into his house; and H935
23 upon the earth when Lot **e** into Zoar. H935
31:33 of Leah's tent, and **e** into Rachel's tent. H935
43:30 he **e** into *his* chamber, and wept there. H935
Ex 33: 9 And it came to pass, as Moses **e** into the H935
Jos 2: 3 to thee, which are **e** into thine house: for H935
8:19 his hand: and they **e** into the city, and H935
10:20 remained of them **e** into fenced cities. H935
Jdg 6: 5 and they **e** into the land to destroy it. H935
9:46 heard *that*, they **e** into an hold of the H935
2Sa 10:14 Abishai, and **e** into the city. So Joab H935
2Ki 7: 8 came again, and **e** into another tent, and H935
9:31 And as Jehu **e** in at the gate, she said, H935
1Ch 19:15 his brother, and **e** into the city. Then H935
2Ch 12:11 And when the king **e** into the house of H935
15:12 And they **e** into a covenant to seek the H935
27: 2 did: howbeit he **e** not into the temple of H935
32: 1 of Assyria came, and **e** into Judah, and H935
Neh 2:15 and turned back, and **e** by the gate of the H935
10:29 their nobles, and **e** into a curse, and into H935
Job 38:16 Hast thou **e** into the springs of the sea? H935
22 Hast thou **e** into the treasures of the H935
Jer 2: 7 but when ye **e**, ye defiled my land, and H935
9:21 windows, *and* is **e** into our palaces, to H935
34:10 people, which had **e** into the covenant, H935
37:16 When Jeremiah was **e** into the dungeon, H935
Lam 1:10 *that* the heathen **e** into her sanctuary, H935
4:12 have **e** into the gates of Jerusalem. H935
Ezk 2: 2 And the spirit **e** into me when he spake H935

Ezk 3:24 Then the spirit e into me, and set me H935
16: 8 unto thee, and e into a covenant with H935
36:20 And when they e unto the heathen, H935
41: 6 in order; and they e into the wall which H935
44: 2 hath e in by it, therefore it shall be shut. H935
Oba 11 and foreigners e into his gates, and cast H935
13 Thou shouldest not have e into the gate H935
Hab 3:16 voice: rottenness e into my bones, and I H935
Mt 8: 5 And when Jesus was e into G1525
23 And when he was e into a ship, his G1684
9: 1 And he e into a ship, and passed over, G1684
12: 4 How he e into the house of God, and G1525
24:38 until the day that Noe e into the ark, G1525
Mk 1:21 he e into the synagogue, and taught. G1525
29 the synagogue, they e into the house of G2064
2: 1 And again he e into Capernaum after G1525
3: 1 And he e again into the synagogue; and G1525
4: 1 so that he e into a ship, and sat G1684
5:13 went out, and e into the swine: and G1525
6:56 And whithersoever he e, into villages, or G1531
7:17 And when he was e into the house from G1525
24 and Sidon, and e into an house, and G1525
8:10 And straightway he e into a ship with G1684
11: 2 as soon as ye be e into it, ye shall find G1531
11 And Jesus e into Jerusalem, and into G1525
Lk 1:40 And e into the house of Zacharias, and G1525
4:38 synagogue, and e into Simon's house. G1525
5: 3 And he e into one of the ships, which G1684
6: 6 sabbath, that he e into the synagogue G1525
7: 1 of the people, he e into Capernaum. G1525
44 this woman? I e into thine house, thou G1525
8:30 because many devils were e into him. G1525
33 of the man, and e into the swine: and G1525
9:34 they feared as they e into the cloud. G1525
52 they went, and e into a village of the G1525
10:38 as they went, that he e into a certain G1525
11:52 of knowledge: ye e not in yourselves, G1525
17:12 And as he e into a certain village, there G1525
27 the day that Noe e into the ark, and the G1525
19: 1 And *Jesus* e and passed through G1525
22: 3 Then e Satan into Judas surnamed G1525
10 when ye are e into the city, there shall G1525
24: 3 And they e in, and found not the body G1525
Jn 4:38 and ye are e into their labours. G1525
6:17 And e into a ship, and went over the G1684
22 his disciples were e, and that Jesus went G1684
13:27 And after the sop Satan e into him. G1525
18: 1 into the which he e, and his disciples. G1525
33 Then Pilate e into the judgment hall G1525
21: 3 They went forth, and e into a ship G305
Act 3: 2 alms of them that e into the temple; G1531
8 and walked, and e with them into the G1525
5:21 And when they heard *that*, they e into G1525
9:17 And Ananias went his way, and e into G1525
10:24 And the morrow after they e into G1525
11: 8 hath at any time e into my mouth. G1525
12 me, and we e into the man's house: G1525
16:40 And they went out of the prison, and e G1525
18: 7 And he departed thence, and e into a G2064
19 but he himself e into the synagogue, G1525
19:30 And when Paul would have e in unto G1525
21: 8 Caesarea: and we e into the house of G1525
26 himself with them e into the temple, to G1524
23:16 and e into the castle, and told Paul. G1525
25:23 great pomp, and was e into the place of G1525
28: 8 to whom Paul e in, and prayed, and G1525
Ro 5:12 Wherefore, as by one man sin e into G1525
20 Moreover the law e, that the offence G3922
1Co 2: 9 neither have e into the heart of man, G305
Heb 4: 6 preached e not in because of unbelief: G1525
10 For he that is e into his rest, he also G1525
6:20 Whither the forerunner is for us e, *even* G1525
9:12 his own blood he e in once into the holy G1525
24 For Christ is not e into the holy places G1525
Jas 5: 4 e into the ears of the Lord of sabaoth. G1525
2Jn 7 For many deceivers are e into the G1525
Rev 11:11 of life from God e into them, and they G1525

ENTERETH

Nu 4:30 every one that e into the service, to do H935
35 old, every one that e into the service, for H935
39 old, every one that e into the service, for H935
43 old, every one that e into the service, for H935
2Ch 31:16 every one that e into the house of the H935
Prv 2:10 When wisdom e into thine heart, and H935
17:10 A reproof e more into a wise man than H5181
Ezk 21:14 slain, which e into their privy chambers.
42:12 wall toward the east, as one e into them. H935
46: 9 feasts, he that e in by the way of the H935
Ezk 46: 9 gate; and he that e by the way of the H935
Mt 15:17 that whatsoever e in at the mouth G1531
Mk 5:40 and e in where the damsel was lying. G1531
7:18 e into the man, *it* cannot defile him; G1531
19 Because it e not into his heart, but into G1531
Lk 22:10 him into the house where he e in. G1531
Jn 10: 1 Verily, verily, I say unto you, He that e G1525
2 But he that e in by the door is the G1525
Heb 6:19 and which e into that within the veil; G1525
9:25 as the high priest e into the holy place G1525

ENTERING

Ex 35:15 the door at the e in of the tabernacle, H6607
Jos 8:29 and cast it at the e of the gate of the H6607
13: 5 mount Hermon unto the e into Hamath. H935
20: 4 shall stand at the e of the gate of the H6607
Jdg 3: 3 Baal-hermon unto the e in of Hamath. H935
9:35 out, and stood in the e of the gate of the H6607
40 wounded, *even* unto the e of the gate. H6607
44 and stood in the e of the gate of the H6607
18:16 of Dan, stood by the e of the gate. H6607
17 priest stood in the e of the gate with the H6607
1Sa 23: 7 e into a town that hath gates and bars. H935
2Sa 10: 8 in array at the e in of the gate: and the H6607
11:23 upon them even unto the e of the gate. H6607
1Ki 6:31 And for the e of the oracle he made H6607
8:65 from the e in of Hamath unto the H935
19:13 and stood in the e in of the cave. And, H6607
2Ki 7: 3 men at the e in of the gate: and H6607
10: 8 the e in of the gate until the morning. H6607
14:25 He restored the coast of Israel from the e H935
23: 8 gates that *were* in the e in of the gate of H6607
11 to the sun, at the e in of the house of the H935
1Ch 5: 9 And eastward he inhabited unto the e in H935
13: 5 even unto the e of Hemath, to bring H935
2Ch 7: 8 e in of Hamath unto the river of Egypt. H935
18: 9 in a void place at the e in of the gate of H6607
23: 4 A third part of you e on the sabbath, of H935
13 at his pillar at the e in, and the princes H3996
15 was come to the e of the horse gate by H3996
26: 8 abroad *even* to the e in of Egypt; for he H935
33:14 valley, even to the e in at the fish gate, H935
Isa 23: 1 is no house, no e in: from the land of H935
Jer 1:15 one his throne at the e of the gates of H6607
17:27 bear a burden, even e in at the gates of H935
Ezk 44: 5 and mark well the e in of the house, H3996
Am 6:14 afflict you from the e in of Hemath unto H935
Mt 23:13 suffer ye them that are e to go in. G1525
Mk 4:19 of other things e in, choke the word, G1531
7:15 a man, that e into him can defile G1531
8:13 And he left them, and e into the ship G1684
16: 5 And e into the sepulchre, they saw a G1525
Lk 11:52 and them that were e in ye hindered. G1525
19:30 the which at your e ye shall find a colt G1531
Act 8: 3 of the church, e into every house, and G1531
27: 2 And e into a ship of Adramyttium, we G1910
1Th 1: 9 what manner of e in we had unto you, G1529
Heb 4: 1 being left *us* of e into his rest, any of G1525

ENTERPRISE

Job 5:12 that their hands cannot perform *their* e. H8454

ENTERTAIN

Heb 13: 2 Be not forgetful to e strangers: for G5381

ENTERTAINED

Heb 13: 2 thereby some have e angels unawares. G3579

ENTICE

Ex 22:16 And if a man e a maid that is not H6601
Dt 13: 6 *is* as thine own soul, e thee secretly, H5496
Jdg 14:15 Samson's wife, E thy husband, that he H6601
16: 5 her, and said unto her, E him, and see H6601
2Ch 18:19 And the LORD said, Who shall e Ahab H6601
20 and said, I will e him. And the LORD H6601
21 said, Thou shalt e *him*, and thou shalt H6601
Prv 1:10 My son, if sinners e thee, consent thou H6601

ENTICED

Job 31:27 And my heart hath been secretly e, or H6601
Jer 20:10 he will be e, and we shall prevail H6601
Jas 1:14 he is drawn away of his own lust, and e. G1185

ENTICETH

Prv 16:29 A violent man e his neighbour, and H6601

ENTICING

1Co 2: 4 *was* not with e words of man's wisdom, G3981
Col 2: 4 man should beguile you with e words. G4086

ENTIRE

Jas 1: 4 may be perfect and e, wanting nothing. G3648

ENTRANCE

Nu 34: 8 *border* unto the e of Hamath; and the H935
Jdg 1:24 we pray thee, the e into the city, and we H3996
25 And when he shewed them the e into H3996
1Ki 18:46 and ran before Ahab to the e of Jezreel. H935
22:10 in a void place in the e of the gate of H6607
1Ch 4:39 And they went to the e of Gedor, *even* H3996
2Ch 12:10 that kept the e of the king's house. H6607
Ps119:130 The e of thy words giveth light; it giveth H6608
Ezk 40:15 And from the face of the gate of the e H2978
1Th 2: 1 For yourselves, brethren, know our e in G1529
2Pt 1:11 For so an e shall be ministered unto G1529

ENTRANCES

Mic 5: 6 of Nimrod in the e thereof: thus shall H6607

ENTREAT

Gen 23: 8 e for me to Ephron the son of Zohar, H6293
Ex 8: 8 Aaron, and said, E the LORD, that he H6279
9 me: when shall I e for thee, and for thy H6279
28 ye shall not go very far away: e for me. H6279
29 thee, and I will e the LORD that the H6279
9:28 E the LORD (for *it is* enough) that H6279
10:17 this once, and e the LORD your God, H6279
Ru 1:16 And Ruth said, E me not to leave thee, H6293
1Sa 2:25 the LORD, who shall e for him? H6419
1Ki 13: 6 the man of God, E now the face of the H2470
Ps 45:12 among the people shall e thy favour. H2470
Prv 19: 6 Many will e the favour of the prince: H2470
Jer 15:11 the enemy to e thee *well* in the time H6293
Act 7: 6 and e *them* evil four hundred years. G2559
1Co 4:13 Being defamed, we e: we are made as G3870
Php 4: 3 And I e thee also, true yokefellow, help G2065
1Ti 5: 1 Rebuke not an elder, but e *him* as a G3870

ENTREATED

Gen 12:16 And he e Abram well for her sake: and H3190
25:21 And Isaac e the LORD for his wife, H6279
21 the LORD was e of him, and Rebekah H6279
Ex 5:22 hast thou *so* evil e this people? why *is* it H7489
8:30 out from Pharaoh, and e the LORD. H6279
10:18 And he went out from Pharaoh, and e H6279
Dt 26: 6 And the Egyptians evil e us, and H7489
Jdg 13: 8 Then Manoah e the LORD, and said, O H6279
2Sa 21:14 And after that God was e for the land. H6279
24:25 So the LORD was e for the land, and H6279
1Ch 5:20 battle, and he was e of them; because H6279
2Ch 33:13 And prayed unto him: and he was e of H6279
19 His prayer also, and *how God* was e of H6279
Ezr 8:23 our God for this: and he was e of us. H6279
Job 19:16 *me* no answer; I e him with my mouth. H2603
17 to my wife, though I e for the children's H2589
Ps 119:58 I e thy favour with *my* whole heart: be H2470
Isa 19:22 shall be e of them, and shall heal them. H6279
Mt 22: 6 and e *them* spitefully, and slew *them*. G5195
Lk 15:28 came his father out, and e him. G3870
18:32 and spitefully e, and spitted on: G5195
20:11 beat him also, and e *him* shamefully, G818
Act 7:19 kindred, and evil e our fathers, so that G2559
27: 3 Julius courteously e Paul, and gave *him* G5530
1Th 2: 2 and were shamefully e, as ye know, at G5195
Heb 12:19 they that heard e that the word should G3868
Jas 3:17 *and* easy to be e, full of mercy and good G2138

ENTREATETH

Job 24:21 He evil e the barren *that* beareth not: H7462

ENTREATIES

Prv 18:23 The poor useth e; but the rich H8469

ENTREATY

2Co 8: 4 Praying us with much e that we would G3874

ENTRIES

Ezk 40:38 And the chambers and the e thereof H6607

ENTRY

2Ki 16:18 and the king's e without, turned he H3996
1Ch 9:19 host of the LORD, *were* keepers of the e. H3996
2Ch 4:22 *of* pure gold: and the e of the house, the H6607
Prv 8: 3 She crieth at the gates, at the e of the H6310
Jer 19: 2 which *is* by the e of the east gate, and H6607
26:10 e of the new gate of the LORD'S *house*. H6607
36:10 court, at the e of the new gate of the H6607
38:14 him into the third e that *is* in the house H3996
43: 9 which *is* at the e of Pharaoh's house H6607

Ezk 8: 5 the altar this image of jealousy in the e. H872
27: 3 art situate at the e of the sea, *which art* H3997
40:11 And he measured the breadth of the e H6607
40 one goeth up to the e of the north gate, H6607
42: 9 chambers *was* the e on the east side, as H3996
46:19 After he brought me through the e, H3996

ENVIED
Gen 26:14 of servants: and the Philistines e him. H7065
30: 1 children, Rachel e her sister; and said H7065
37:11 And his brethren e him; but his father H7065
Ps 106:16 They e Moses also in the camp, *and* H7065
Ecc 4: 4 for this a man is e of his neighbour. H7068
Ezk 31: 9 that *were* in the garden of God, e him. H7065

ENVIES
1Pt 2: 1 and e, and all evil speakings, G5355

ENVIEST
Nu 11:29 And Moses said unto him, E thou for H7065

ENVIETH
1Co 13: 4 is kind; charity e not; charity vaunteth G2206

ENVIOUS
Ps 37: 1 thou e against the workers of iniquity. H7065
73: 3 For I was e at the foolish, *when* I saw H7065
Prv 24: 1 Be not thou e against evil men, neither H7065
19 *men*, neither be thou e at the wicked; H7065

ENVIRON
Jos 7: 9 *of it*, and shall e us round, and cut off H5437

ENVY
Job 5: 2 foolish man, and e slayeth the silly one. H7068
Prv 3:31 E thou not the oppressor, and choose H7065
14:30 flesh: but e the rottenness of the bones. H7068
23:17 Let not thine heart e sinners: but *be* H7065
27: 4 but who *is* able to stand before e? H7068
Ecc 9: 6 hatred, and their e, is now perished; H7068
Isa 11:13 The e also of Ephraim shall depart, H7068
13 Ephraim shall not e Judah, and Judah H7065
26:11 ashamed for *their* e at the people; yea, H7068
Ezk 35:11 according to thine e which thou hast H7068
Mt 27:18 For he knew that for e they had G5355
Mk 15:10 chief priests had delivered him for e. G5355
Act 7: 9 And the patriarchs, moved with e, sold G2206
13:45 were filled with e, and spake against G2205
17: 5 not, moved with e, took unto them G2206
Ro 1:29 full of e, murder, debate, deceit, G5355
Php 1:15 Some indeed preach Christ even of e G5355
1Ti 6: 4 e, strife, railings, evil surmisings, G5355
Tit 3: 3 and e, hateful, *and* hating one another. G5355
Jas 4: 5 spirit that dwelleth in us lusteth to e? G5355

ENVYING
Ro 13:13 and wantonness, not in strife and e. G2205
1Co 3: 3 *there is* among you e, and strife, and G2205
Gal 5:26 provoking one another, e one another. G5354
Jas 3:14 But if ye have bitter e and strife in your G2205
16 For where e and strife *is*, there *is* G2205

ENVYINGS
2Co 12:20 lest *there be* debates, e, wraths, strifes, G2205
Gal 5:21 E, murders, drunkenness, revellings, G5355

EPAENETUS
Ro 16: 5 my well beloved E, who is the firstfruits G1866

EPAPHRAS
Col 1: 7 As ye also learned of E our dear G1889
4:12 E, who is *one* of you, a servant of Christ, G1889
Phlm 23 There salute thee E, my fellowprisoner G1889

EPAPHRODITUS
Php 2:25 to send to you E, my brother, and G1891
4:18 having received of E the things *which* G1891

EPENETUS See EPAENETUS.

EPHAH
Gen 25: 4 And the sons of Midian; E, and Epher, H5891
Ex 16:36 Now an omer *is* the tenth *part* of an e. H374
Lev 5:11 the tenth part of an e of fine flour for a H374
6:20 the tenth part of an e of fine flour for a H374
19:36 Just balances, just weights, a just e, and a H374
Nu 5:15 the tenth *part* of an e of barley meal; he H374
28: 5 And a tenth *part* of an e of flour for a H374
Jdg 6:19 cakes of an e of flour: the flesh he H374
Ru 2:17 gleaned: and it was about an e of barley. H374
1Sa 1:24 bullocks, and one e of flour, and a bottle H374
17:17 for thy brethren an e of this parched H374
1Ch 1:33 And the sons of Midian; E, and Epher, H5891
2:46 And E, Caleb's concubine, bare Haran, H5891
47 Ge-shan, and Pelet, and E, and Shaaph. H5891
Isa 5:10 and the seed of an homer shall yield an e. H374
60: 6 of Midian and E; all they from Sheba H5891
Ezk 45:10 Ye shall have just balances, and a just e, H374
11 The e and the bath shall be of one H374
11 an homer, and the e the tenth part of an H374
13 the sixth part of an e of an homer of H374
13 sixth part of an e of an homer of barley: H374
24 a meat offering of an e for a bullock, and H374
24 a bullock, and an e for a ram, and an hin H374
24 for a ram, and an hin of oil for an e. H374
46: 5 And the meat offering *shall be* an e for a H374
5 be able to give, and an hin of oil to an e. H374
7 a meat offering, an e for a bullock, and H374
7 for a bullock, and an e for a ram, and for H374
7 attain unto, and an hin of oil to an e. H374
11 offering shall be an e to a bullock, and H374
11 a bullock, and an e to a ram, and to the H374
11 is able to give, and an hin of oil to an e. H374
14 the sixth part of an e, and the third part H374
Am 8: 5 forth wheat, making the e small, and the H374
Zec 5: 6 he said, This *is* an e that goeth forth. He H374
7 woman that sitteth in the midst of the e. H374
8 the midst of the e; and he cast the weight H374
9 the e between the earth and the heaven. H374
10 with me, Whither do these bear the e? H374

EPHAI
Jer 40: 8 and the sons of E the Netophathite, H5778

EPHER
Gen 25: 4 And the sons of Midian; Ephah, and E, H6081
1Ch 1:33 And the sons of Midian; Ephah, and E, H6081
4:17 and Mered, and E, and Jalon: and she H6081
5:24 their fathers, even E, and Ishi, and Eliel, H6081

EPHES-DAMMIM
1Sa 17: 1 between Shochoh and Azekah, in E. H658

EPHESIAN
Act 21:29 Trophimus an E, whom they supposed G2180

EPHESIANS
Act 19:28 out, saying, Great *is* Diana of the E. G2180
34 hours cried out, Great *is* Diana of the E. G2180
35 that the city of the E is a worshipper of G2180

EPHESUS
Act 18:19 And he came to E, and left them there: G2181
21 you, if God will. And he sailed from E. G2181
24 *and* mighty in the scriptures, came to E. G2181
19: 1 to E: and finding certain disciples, G2181
17 also dwelling at E; and fear fell on them G2181
26 hear, that not alone at E, but almost G2181
35 he said, *Ye* men of E, what man is there G2180
20:16 For Paul had determined to sail by E, G2181
17 And from Miletus he sent to E, and G2181
1Co 15:32 with beasts at E, what advantageth it G2181
16: 8 But I will tarry at E until Pentecost. G2181
Eph 1: 1 at E, and to the faithful in Christ Jesus: G2181
1Ti 1: 3 As I besought thee to abide still at E, G2181
2Ti 1:18 unto me at E, thou knowest very well. G2181
4:12 And Tychicus have I sent to E. G2181
Rev 1:11 are in Asia; unto E, and unto Smyrna, G2181
2: 1 Unto the angel of the church of E write; G2179

EPHLAL
1Ch 2:37 And Zabad begat E, and Ephlal begat H654
37 And Zabad begat Ephlal, and E begat H654

EPHOD
Ex 25: 7 Onyx stones, and stones to be set in the e, H646
28: 4 and an e, and a robe, and a broidered H646
6 And they shall make the e *of* gold, *of* H646
8 And the curious girdle of the e, which *is* H642
12 shoulders of the e *for* stones of memorial H646
15 the work of the e thou shalt make it; *of* H646
25 on the shoulderpieces of the e before it. H646
26 which *is* in the side of the e inward. H646
27 on the two sides of the e underneath, H646
27 thereof, above the curious girdle of the e. H646
28 the rings of the e with a lace of blue, that H646
28 girdle of the e, and that the breastplate H646
28 the breastplate be not loosed from the e. H646
Ex 28:31 And thou shalt make the robe of the e all H646
29: 5 and the robe of the e, and the ephod, and H646
5 the ephod, and the e, and the breastplate, H646
5 gird him with the curious girdle of the e: H646
35: 9 be set for the e, and for the breastplate. H646
27 be set, for the e, and for the breastplate; H646
39: 2 And he made the e *of* gold, blue, and H646
5 And the curious girdle of his e, that *was* H642
7 shoulders of the e, *that they should be* H646
8 like the work of the e; *of* gold, blue, and H646
18 on the shoulderpieces of the e, before it. H646
19 it, which *was* on the side of the e inward. H646
20 on the two sides of the e underneath, H646
20 thereof, above the curious girdle of the e. H646
21 the rings of the e with a lace of blue, that H646
21 girdle of the e, and that the breastplate H646
21 the e; as the LORD commanded Moses. H646
22 And he made the robe of the e *of* woven H646
Lev 8: 7 the robe, and put the e upon him, and he H646
7 the e, and bound *it* unto him therewith. H646
Nu 34:23 of Manasseh, Hanniel the son of E. H641
Jdg 8:27 And Gideon made an e thereof, and put H646
17: 5 gods, and made an e, and teraphim, and H646
18:14 in these houses an e, and teraphim, and H646
17 image, and the e, and the teraphim, and H646
18 carved image, the e, and the teraphim, H646
20 and he took the e, and the teraphim, and H646
1Sa 2:18 *being* a child, girded with a linen e. H646
28 incense, to wear an e before me? and did H646
14: 3 in Shiloh, wearing an e. And the people H646
21: 9 in a cloth behind the e: if thou wilt take H646
22:18 and five persons that did wear a linen e. H646
23: 6 he came down *with* an e in his hand. H646
9 to Abiathar the priest, Bring hither the e. H646
30: 7 thee, bring me hither the e. And Abiathar H646
7 Abiathar brought thither the e to David. H646
2Sa 6:14 and David *was* girded with a linen e. H646
1Ch 15:27 David also *had* upon him an e of linen. H646
Hos 3: 4 and without an e, and *without* teraphim: H646

EPHPHATHA
Mk 7:34 saith unto him, E, that is, Be opened. G2188

EPHRAIM
Gen 41:52 And the name of the second called he E: H669
46:20 Manasseh and E, which Asenath the H669
48: 1 with him his two sons, Manasseh and E. H669
5 And now thy two sons, E and Manasseh, H669
13 And Joseph took them both, E in his H669
17 upon the head of E, it displeased him: H669
20 God make thee as E and as Manasseh: H669
20 and he set E before Manasseh. H669
Nu 1:10 Of the children of Joseph: of E; Elishama H669
32 of the children of E, by their generations, H669
33 E, *were* forty thousand and five hundred. H669
2:18 of the camp of E according to their H669
18 of the sons of E *shall be* Elishama the H669
24 All that were numbered of the camp of E H669
7:48 prince of the children of E, *offered*: H669
10:22 camp of the children of E set forward H669
13: 8 Of the tribe of E, Oshea the son of Nun. H669
26:28 their families *were* Manasseh and E. H669
35 These *are* the sons of E after their H669
37 These *are* the families of the sons of E H669
34:24 of E, Kemuel the son of Shiphtan. H669
Dt 33:17 the ten thousands of E, and they *are* the H669
34: 2 And all Naphtali, and the land of E, and H669
Jos 14: 4 Manasseh and E: therefore they gave no H669
16: 4 Manasseh and E, took their inheritance. H669
5 And the border of the children of E H669
8 of the children of E by their families. H669
9 for the children of E *were* among the H669
17: 8 Manasseh *belonged* to the children of E; H669
9 these cities of E *are* among the cities H669
15 if mount E be too narrow for thee. H669
17 of Joseph, *even* to E and to Manasseh, H669
19:50 in mount E: and he built the city, H669
20: 7 Shechem in mount E, and Kirjatharba, H669
21: 5 of the tribe of E, and out of the tribe of H669
20 the cities of their lot out of the tribe of E. H669
21 suburbs in mount E, *to be* a city of refuge H669
24:30 E, on the north side of the hill of Gaash. H669
33 son, which was given him in mount E. H669
Jdg 1:29 Neither did E drive out the Canaanites H669
2: 9 of E, on the north side of the hill Gaash. H669
3:27 in the mountain of E, and the children of H669
4: 5 Beth-el in mount E: and the children of H669
5:14 Out of E *was there* a root of them against H669
7:24 all mount E, saying, Come down H669

Jdg 7:24 all the men of E gathered themselves H669
8: 1 And the men of E said unto him, Why H669
2 of E better than the vintage of Abi-ezer? H669
10: 1 and he dwelt in Shamir in mount E. H669
9 of E; so that Israel was sore distressed. H669
12: 1 And the men of E gathered themselves H669
4 and fought with E: and the men of Gilead H669
4 of Gilead smote E, because they said, Ye H669
4 Gileadites *are* fugitives of E among the H669
15 of E, in the mount of the Amalekites. H669
17: 1 And there was a man of mount E, whose H669
8 and he came to mount E to the house of H669
18: 2 came to mount E, to the house of Micah, H669
13 And they passed thence unto mount E, H669
19: 1 the side of mount E, who took to him a H669
16 *was* also of mount E; and he sojourned in H669
18 the side of mount E; from thence *am* I: H669
1Sa 1: 1 of mount E, and his name *was* Elkanah, H669
9: 4 And he passed through mount E, and H669
14:22 in mount E, *when* they heard that H669
2Sa 2: 9 Jezreel, and over E, and over Benjamin, H669
13:23 which *is* beside E: and Absalom invited H669
18: 6 and the battle was in the wood of E; H669
20:21 but a man of mount E, Sheba the son of H669
1Ki 4: 8 their names: The son of Hur, in mount E: H669
12:25 Shechem in mount E, and dwelt therein; H669
2Ki 5:22 to me from mount E two young men of H669
14:13 from the gate of E unto the corner gate, H669
1Ch 6:66 cities of their coasts out of the tribe of E. H669
67 Shechem in mount E with her suburbs; H669
7:20 And the sons of E; Shuthelah, and Bered H669
22 And E their father mourned many days, H669
9: 3 and of the children of E, and Manasseh; H669
12:30 And of the children of E twenty H669
27:10 of the children of E: and in his course H669
14 of the children of E: and in his course H669
20 Of the children of E, Hoshea the son of H669
2Ch 13: 4 which *is* in mount E, and said, Hear me, H669
15: 8 taken from mount E, and renewed the H669
9 with them out of E and Manasseh, and H669
17: 2 of E, which Asa his father had taken. H669
19: 4 to mount E, and brought them back H669
25: 7 Israel, *to wit, with* all the children of E. H669
10 come to him out of E, to go home again: H669
23 from the gate of E to the corner gate, H669
28: 7 And Zichri, a mighty man of E, slew H669
12 of the children of E, Azariah the son of H669
30: 1 letters also to E and Manasseh, that H669
10 the country of E and Manasseh even H669
18 people, *even* many of E, and Manasseh, H669
31: 1 and Benjamin, in E also and Manasseh, H669
34: 6 of Manasseh, and E, and Simeon, even H669
9 hand of Manasseh and E, and of all the H669
Neh 8:16 gate, and in the street of the gate of E. H669
12:39 And from above the gate of E, and above H669
Ps 60: 7 Gilead *is* mine, and Manasseh *is* mine; E H669
78: 9 The children of E, *being* armed, *and* H669
67 of Joseph, and chose not the tribe of E: H669
80: 2 Before E and Benjamin and Manasseh H669
108: 8 Gilead *is* mine; Manasseh *is* mine; E also H669
Isa 7: 2 is confederate with E. And his heart was H669
5 Because Syria, E, and the son of H669
8 shall E be broken, that it be not a people. H669
9 And the head of E *is* Samaria, and the H669
17 from the day that E departed from H669
9: 9 And all the people shall know, *even* E H669
21 Manasseh, E; and Ephraim, Manasseh: H669
21 Manasseh, Ephraim; and E, Manasseh: H669
11:13 The envy also of E shall depart, and the H669
13 shall be cut off: E shall not envy Judah, H669
13 envy Judah, and Judah shall not vex E. H669
17: 3 The fortress also shall cease from E, and H669
28: 1 to the drunkards of E, whose glorious H669
3 The crown of pride, the drunkards of E, H669
Jer 4:15 and publisheth affliction from mount E. H669
7:15 your brethren, *even* the whole seed of E. H669
31: 6 upon the mount E shall cry, Arise ye, H669
9 a father to Israel, and E *is* my firstborn. H669
18 I have surely heard E bemoaning H669
20 *Is* E my dear son? *is he* a pleasant child? H669
50:19 be satisfied upon mount E and Gilead. H669
Ezk 37:16 For Joseph, the stick of E, and *for* all the H669
19 *is* in the hand of E, and the tribes of H669
48: 5 side unto the west side, a *portion for* E. H669
6 And by the border of E, from the east H669
Hos 4:17 E *is* joined to idols: let him alone. H669
5: 3 I know E, and Israel is not hid from me: H669
3 from me: for now, O E, thou committest H669
5 shall Israel and E fall in their iniquity; H669

Hos 5: 9 E shall be desolate in the day of rebuke: H669
11 E *is* oppressed *and* broken in judgment, H669
12 Therefore *will* I *be* unto E as a moth, and H669
13 When E saw his sickness, and Judah *saw* H669
13 wound, then went E to the Assyrian, and H669
14 For I *will be* unto E as a lion, and as a H669
6: 4 O E, what shall I do unto thee? O Judah, H669
10 *is* the whoredom of E, Israel is defiled. H669
7: 1 then the iniquity of E was discovered, H669
8 E, he hath mixed himself among the H669
8 the people; E is a cake not turned. H669
11 E also is like a silly dove without heart: H669
8: 9 ass alone by himself: E hath hired lovers. H669
11 Because E hath made many altars to sin, H669
9: 3 the LORD'S land; but E shall return to H669
8 The watchman of E *was* with my God: H669
11 *As for* E, their glory shall fly away like a H669
13 E, as I saw Tyrus, *is* planted in a pleasant H669
13 a pleasant place: but E shall bring forth H669
16 E is smitten, their root is dried up, they H669
10: 6 to king Jareb: E shall receive shame, H669
11 And E *is as* an heifer *that is* taught, *and* H669
11 neck: I will make E to ride; Judah shall H669
11: 3 I taught E also to go, taking them by H669
8 How shall I give thee up, E? *how* shall I H669
9 return to destroy E: for I *am* God, and H669
12 E compasseth me about with lies, and H669
12: 1 E feedeth on wind, and followeth after H669
8 And E said, Yet I am become rich, I have H669
14 E provoked *him* to anger most bitterly: H669
13: 1 When E spake trembling, he exalted H669
12 The iniquity of E *is* bound up; his sin *is* H669
14: 8 E *shall say,* What have I to do any more H669
Oba 19 the fields of E, and the fields of Samaria: H669
Zec 9:10 And I will cut off the chariot from E, and H669
13 filled the bow with E, and raised up thy H669
10: 7 And *they of* E shall be like a mighty H669
Jn 11:54 into a city called E, and there continued *G2187*

EPHRAIMITE
Jdg 12: 5 unto him, *Art* thou an E? If he said, Nay; H673

EPHRAIMITES
Jos 16:10 E unto this day, and serve under tribute. H669
Jdg 12: 4 among the E, *and* among the Manassites. H669
5 of Jordan before the E: and it was *so,* that H669
5 that when those E which were escaped H669
6 time of the E forty and two thousand. H669

EPHRAIM'S
Gen 48:14 and laid *it* upon E head, who *was* the H669
17 it from E head unto Manasseh's head. H669
50:23 And Joseph saw E children of the third H669
Jos 17:10 Southward *it was* E, and northward *it* H669

EPHRAIN
2Ch 13:19 thereof, and E with the towns thereof. H6085

EPHRATAH
Ru 4:11 in E, and be famous in Beth-lehem: H672
1Ch 2:50 of E; Shobal the father of Kirjath-jearim, H672
4: 4 firstborn of E, the father of Beth-lehem. H672
Ps 132: 6 Lo, we heard of it at E: we found it in the H672
Mic 5: 2 But thou, Beth-lehem E, *though* thou be H672

EPHRATH
Gen 35:16 way to come to E: and Rachel travailed, H672
19 in the way to E, which *is* Beth-lehem. H672
48: 7 way to come unto E: and I buried her H672
7 in the way of E; the same *is* Beth-lehem. H672
1Ch 2:19 took unto him E, which bare him Hur. H672

EPHRATHITE
1Sa 1: 1 the son of Tohu, the son of Zuph, an E: H673
17:12 Now David *was* the son of that E of H673
1Ki 11:26 And Jeroboam the son of Nebat, an E of H673

EPHRATHITES
Ru 1: 2 and Chilion, E of Beth-lehem-judah. H673

EPHRON
Gen 23: 8 entreat for me to E the son of Zohar, H6085
10 And E dwelt among the children of H6085
10 of Heth: and E the Hittite answered H6085
13 And he spake unto E in the audience of H6085
14 And E answered Abraham, saying unto H6085
16 And Abraham hearkened unto E; and H6085
16 weighed to E the silver, which he H6085
17 And the field of E, which *was* in H6085

Gen 25: 9 in the field of E the son of Zohar the H6085
49:29 cave that *is* in the field of E the Hittite, H6085
30 with the field of E the Hittite for a H6085
50:13 of E the Hittite, before Mamre. H6085
Jos 15: 9 cities of mount E; and the border was H6085

EPICUREANS
Act 17:18 Then certain philosophers of the E, and *G1946*

EPISTLE
Act 15:30 multitude together, they delivered the e: *G1992*
23:33 and delivered the e to the governor, *G1992*
Ro 16:22 I Tertius, who wrote *this* e, salute you in *G1992*
1Co 5: 9 I wrote unto you in an e not to *G1992*
2Co 3: 2 Ye are our e written in our hearts, *G1992*
3 declared to be the e of Christ *G1992*
7: 8 that the same e hath made you sorry, *G1992*
Col 4:16 And when this e is read among you, *G1992*
16 ye likewise read the *e* from Laodicea.
1Th 5:27 I charge you by the Lord that this e be *G1992*
2Th 2:15 been taught, whether by word, or our e. *G1992*
3:14 our word by this e, note that man, and *G1992*
17 which is the token in every e: so I write. *G1992*
2Pt 3: 1 This second e, beloved, I now write *G1992*

EPISTLES
2Co 3: 1 as some *others,* e of commendation to *G1992*
2Pt 3:16 As also in all *his* e, speaking in them of *G1992*

EQUAL
Job 28:17 The gold and the crystal cannot e it: H6186
19 The topaz of Ethiopia shall not e it, H6186
Ps 17: 2 thine eyes behold the things that are e. H4339
55:13 But *it was* thou, a man mine e, my H6187
Prv 26: 7 The legs of the lame are not e: so *is* a H1809
Isa 40:25 me, or shall I be e? saith the Holy One. H7737
46: 5 me, and make *me* e, and compare me, H7737
Lam 2:13 what shall I e to thee, that I may H7737
Ezk 18:25 Yet ye say, The way of the Lord is not e. H8505
25 my way e? are not your ways unequal? H8505
29 of the Lord is not e. O house of Israel, H8505
29 my ways e? are not your ways unequal? H8505
33:17 of the Lord is not e: but as for them, H8505
17 but as for them, their way is not e. H8505
20 Yet ye say, The way of the Lord is not e. H8505
Mt 20:12 hast made them e unto us, which have *G2470*
Lk 20:36 more: for they are e unto the angels; *G2465*
Jn 5:18 his Father, making himself e with God. *G2470*
Php 2: 6 thought it not robbery to be e with God: *G2470*
Col 4: 1 which is just and e; knowing that ye *G2471*
Rev 21:16 the breadth and the height of it are e. *G2470*

EQUALITY
2Co 8:14 But by an e, *that* now at this time your *G2471*
14 for your want: that there may be e: *G2471*

EQUALLY
Ex 36:22 One board had two tenons, e distant H7947

EQUALS
Gal 1:14 above many my e in mine own nation, *G4915*

EQUITY
Ps 98: 9 judge the world, and the people with e. H4339
99: 4 thou dost establish e, thou executest H4339
Prv 1: 3 wisdom, justice, and judgment, and e; H4339
2: 9 judgment, and e; *yea,* every good path. H4339
17:26 *is* not good, *nor* to strike princes for e. H3476
Ecc 2:21 knowledge, and in e; yet to a man that H3788
Isa 11: 4 and reprove with e for the meek of the H4334
59:14 fallen in the street, and e cannot enter. H5229
Mic 3: 9 that abhor judgment, and pervert all e. H3477
Mal 2: 6 me in peace and e, and did turn many H4334

ER
Gen 38: 3 bare a son; and he called his name E. H6147
6 And Judah took a wife for E his H6147
7 And E, Judah's firstborn, was wicked in H6147
46:12 And the sons of Judah; E, and Onan, H6147
12 and Zerah: but E and Onan died in the H6147
Nu 26:19 The sons of Judah *were* E and Onan: H6147
19 Er and Onan: and E and Onan died in H6147
1Ch 2: 3 The sons of Judah; E, and Onan, and H6147
3 the Canaanitess. And E, the firstborn of H6147
4:21 of Judah *were,* E the father of Lecah, H6147
Lk 3:28 of Elmodam, which was *the son* of E, *G2262*

ERAN
Nu 26:36 of E, the family of the Eranites. H6197

ERANITES
Nu 26:36 Shuthelah: of Eran, the family of the **E**. H6198

ERASTUS
Act 19:22 Timotheus and **E**; but he himself stayed G2037
Ro 16:23 saluteth you. **E** the chamberlain of G2037
2Ti 4:20 **E** abode at Corinth: but Trophimus G2037

ERE
Ex 1:19 **e** the midwives come in unto them. H2962
Nu 11:33 their teeth, **e** it was chewed, the wrath H2962
14:11 how long will it be **e** they believe me, H3808
1Sa 3: 3 And **e** the lamp of God went out in the H2962
2Sa 2:26 shall it be then, **e** thou bid the people H3808
2Ki 6:32 before him: but **e** the messenger came H2962
Job 18: 2 How long *will it be* **e** ye make an end of
Jer 47: 6 how long *will it be* **e** thou be quiet? put H3808
Hos 8: 5 *will it be* **e** they attain to innocency? H3808
Jn 4:49 him, Sir, come down **e** my child die. G4250

ERECH
Gen 10:10 was Babel, and **E**, and Accad, and H751

ERECTED
Gen 33:20 And he **e** there an altar, and called it H5324

ERI
Gen 46:16 and Ezbon, **E**, and Arodi, and Areli. H6179
Nu 26:16 Of Ozni, the family of the Oznites: of **E**, H6179

ERITES
Nu 26:16 the Oznites: of Eri, the family of the **E**: H6180

ERR
2Ch 33: 9 of Jerusalem to **e**, *and* to do worse than H8582
Ps 95:10 *is* a people that do **e** in their heart, and H8582
119:21 which do **e** from thy commandments. H7686
118 all them that **e** from thy statutes: for H7686
Prv 14:22 Do they not **e** that devise evil? but H8582
19:27 to **e** from the words of knowledge. H7686
Isa 3:12 to **e**, and destroy the way of thy paths. H8582
9:16 cause *them* to **e**; and *they that are* led H8582
19:14 have caused Egypt to **e** in every work H8582
28: 7 **e** in vision, they stumble *in* judgment. H7686
30:28 jaws of the people, causing *them* to **e**. H8582
35: 8 men, though fools, shall not **e** *therein*. H8582
63:17 O LORD, why hast thou made us to **e** H8582
Jer 23:13 Baal, and caused my people Israel to **e**. H8582
32 my people to **e** by their lies, and by H8582
Hos 4:12 caused *them* to **e**, and they have gone H8582
Am 2: 4 caused them to **e**, after the which their H8582
Mic 3: 5 make my people **e**, that bite with their H8582
Mt 22:29 unto them, Ye do **e**, not knowing the G4105
Mk 12:24 ye not therefore **e**, because ye know not G4105
27 of the living: ye therefore do greatly **e**. G4105
Heb 3:10 They do alway **e** in *their* heart; and G4105
Jas 1:16 Do not **e**, my beloved brethren. G4105
5:19 Brethren, if any of you do **e** from the G4105

ERRAND
Gen 24:33 told mine **e**. And he said, Speak on. H1697
Jdg 3:19 I have a secret **e** unto thee, O king: who H1697
2Ki 9: 5 he said, I have an **e** to thee, O captain. H1697

ERRED
Lev 5:18 wherein he **e** and wist *it* not, and H7683
Nu 15:22 And if ye have **e**, and not observed all H7686
1Sa 26:21 the fool, and have **e** exceedingly. H7686
Job 6:24 me to understand wherein I have **e**. H7686
19: 4 And be it indeed *that* I have **e**, mine H7686
Ps119:110 for me: yet I **e** not from thy precepts. H8582
Isa 28: 7 But they also have **e** through wine, and H7686
7 and the prophet have **e** through strong H7686
29:24 They also that **e** in spirit shall come to H8582
1Ti 6:10 after, they have **e** from the faith, and G635
21 Which some professing have **e** G795
2Ti 2:18 Who concerning the truth have **e**, saying G795

ERRETH
Prv 10:17 but he that refuseth reproof **e**. H8582
Ezk 45:20 for every one that **e**, and for *him that is* H7686

ERROR
2Sa 6: 7 **e**; and there he died by the ark of God. H7944
Job 19: 4 erred, mine **e** remaineth with myself. H4879
Ecc 5: 6 that it *was* an **e**: wherefore should God H7684
10: 5 an **e** *which* proceedeth from the ruler: H7684
Isa 32: 6 and to utter **e** against the LORD, to H8442
Dan 6: 4 was there any **e** or fault found in him. H7960
Mt 27:64 the last **e** shall be worse than the first. G4106
Ro 1:27 recompence of their **e** which was meet. G4106
Jas 5:20 sinner from the **e** of his way shall save G4106
2Pt 2:18 clean escaped from them who live in **e**. G4106
3:17 led away with the **e** of the wicked, fall G4106
1Jn 4: 6 we the spirit of truth, and the spirit of **e**. G4106
Jude 11 ran greedily after the **e** of Balaam for G4106

ERRORS
Ps 19:12 Who can understand *his* **e**? cleanse thou H7691
Jer 10:15 They *are* vanity, *and* the work of **e**: in H8595
51:18 They *are* vanity, the work of **e**: in the H8595
Heb 9: 7 for himself, and *for* the **e** of the people: G51

ESAIAS
Mt 3: 3 of by the prophet **E**, saying, The voice of G2268
4:14 was spoken by **E** the prophet, saying, G2268
8:17 was spoken by **E** the prophet, saying, G2268
12:17 was spoken by **E** the prophet, saying, G2268
13:14 the prophecy of **E**, which saith, By G2268
15: 7 Ye hypocrites, well did **E** prophesy of G2268
Mk 7: 6 them, Well hath **E** prophesied of you G2268
Lk 3: 4 of the words of **E** the prophet, saying, G2268
4:17 of the prophet **E**. And when he had G2268
Jn 1:23 way of the Lord, as said the prophet **E**. G2268
12:38 That the saying of **E** the prophet might G2268
39 not believe, because that **E** said again, G2268
41 These things said **E**, when he saw his G2268
Act 8:28 in his chariot read **E** the prophet. G2268
30 him read the prophet **E**, and said, G2268
28:25 by **E** the prophet unto our fathers, G2268
Ro 9:27 **E** also crieth concerning Israel, Though G2268
29 And as **E** said before, Except the Lord G2268
10:16 the gospel. For **E** saith, Lord, who hath G2268
20 But **E** is very bold, and saith, I was G2268
15:12 And again, **E** saith, There shall be a G2268

ESAR-HADDON
2Ki 19:37 And **E** his son reigned in his stead. H634
Ezr 4: 2 since the days of **E** king of Assur, which H634
Isa 37:38 and **E** his son reigned in his stead. H634

ESAU
Gen 25:25 garment; and they called his name **E**. H6215
27 And the boys grew: and **E** was a H6215
28 And Isaac loved **E**, because he did eat of H6215
29 And Jacob sod pottage: and **E** came H6215
30 And **E** said to Jacob, Feed me, I pray H6215
32 And **E** said, Behold, I *am* at the point to H6215
34 Then Jacob gave **E** bread and pottage H6215
34 his way: thus **E** despised *his* birthright. H6215
26:34 And **E** was forty years old when he took H6215
27: 1 not see, he called **E** his eldest son, and H6215
5 Isaac spake to **E** his son. And Esau H6215
5 Esau his son. And **E** went to the field to H6215
6 speak unto **E** thy brother, saying, H6215
11 his mother, Behold, **E** my brother *is* a H6215
15 of her eldest son **E**, which *were* with her H6215
19 And Jacob said unto his father, I *am* **E** H6215
21 whether thou *be* my very son **E** or not. H6215
22 voice, but the hands *are* the hands of **E**. H6215
24 And he said, *Art* thou my very son **E**? H6215
30 his father, that **E** his brother came in H6215
32 he said, I *am* thy son, thy firstborn **E**. H6215
34 And when **E** heard the words of his H6215
37 And Isaac answered and said unto **E**, H6215
38 And **E** said unto his father, Hast thou H6215
38 And **E** lifted up his voice, and wept. H6215
41 And **E** hated Jacob because of the H6215
41 blessed him: and **E** said in his heart, H6215
42 And these words of **E** her elder son H6215
42 thy brother **E**, as touching thee, doth H6215
28: 6 When **E** saw that Isaac had blessed H6215
8 And **E** seeing that the daughters of H6215
9 Then went **E** unto Ishmael, and took H6215
32: 3 before him to **E** his brother unto the H6215
4 unto my lord **E**; Thy servant Jacob saith H6215
6 to thy brother **E**, and also he cometh H6215
8 And said, If **E** come to the one H6215
11 from the hand of **E**: for I fear him, lest H6215
13 to his hand a present for **E** his brother; H6215
17 saying, When **E** my brother meeteth H6215
18 **E**: and, behold, also he *is* behind us. H6215
19 ye speak unto **E**, when ye find him. H6215
33: 1 and, behold, **E** came, and with him H6215
4 And **E** ran to meet him, and embraced H6215
9 And **E** said, I have enough, my brother; H6215
15 And **E** said, Let me now leave with thee H6215
16 So **E** returned that day on his way unto H6215
Gen 35: 1 fleddest from the face of **E** thy brother. H6215
29 and his sons **E** and Jacob buried him. H6215
36: 1 Now these *are* the generations of **E**, who H6215
2 **E** took his wives of the daughters of H6215
4 And Adah bare to **E** Eliphaz; and H6215
5 *are* the sons of **E**, which were born unto H6215
6 And **E** took his wives, and his sons, H6215
8 Thus dwelt **E** in mount Seir: Esau *is* H6215
8 Thus dwelt Esau in mount Seir: **E** *is* H6215
9 And these *are* the generations of **E** the H6215
10 of Adah the wife of **E**, Reuel the son of H6215
10 the son of Bashemath the wife of **E**. H6215
14 to **E** Jeush, and Jaalam, and Korah. H6215
15 These *were* dukes of the sons of **E**: the H6215
15 firstborn *son* of **E**; duke Teman, duke H6215
19 These *are* the sons of **E**, who *is* Edom, H6215
40 dukes *that came* of **E**, according to their H6215
43 he *is* **E** the father of the Edomites. H6215
Dt 2: 4 the children of **E**, which dwell in Seir; H6215
5 mount Seir unto **E** *for* a possession. H6215
8 the children of **E**, which dwelt in Seir, H6215
12 but the children of **E** succeeded them, H6215
22 As he did to the children of **E**, which H6215
29 (As the children of **E** which dwell in H6215
Jos 24: 4 And I gave unto Isaac Jacob and **E**: and H6215
4 Esau: and I gave unto **E** mount Seir, to H6215
1Ch 1:34 Isaac. The sons of Isaac; **E** and Israel. H6215
35 The sons of **E**; Eliphaz, Reuel, and H6215
Jer 49: 8 the calamity of **E** upon him, the time H6215
10 But I have made **E** bare, I have H6215
Oba 6 How are *the things* of **E** searched out! H6215
8 understanding out of the mount of **E**? H6215
9 mount of **E** may be cut off by slaughter. H6215
18 and the house of **E** for stubble, and H6215
18 of **E**; for the LORD hath spoken *it*. H6215
19 the mount of **E**; and *they of* the plain H6215
21 the mount of **E**; and the kingdom shall H6215
Mal 1: 2 loved us? *Was* not **E** Jacob's brother? H6215
3 And I hated **E**, and laid his mountains H6215
Ro 9:13 Jacob have I loved, but **E** have I hated. G2269
Heb 11:20 By faith Isaac blessed Jacob and **E** G2269
12:16 person, as **E**, who for one morsel G2269

ESAU'S
Gen 25:26 his hand took hold on **E** heel; and his H6215
27:23 his brother **E** hands: so he blessed him. H6215
28: 5 of Rebekah, Jacob's and **E** mother. H6215
36:10 These *are* the names of **E** sons; Eliphaz H6215
12 to Eliphaz **E** son; and she bare to H6215
12 these *were* the sons of Adah **E** wife. H6215
13 were the sons of Bashemath **E** wife. H6215
14 of Zibeon, **E** wife: and she bare to H6215
17 And these *are* the sons of Reuel **E** son; H6215
17 these *are* the sons of Bashemath **E** wife. H6215
18 of Aholibamah **E** wife; duke Jeush, H6215
18 the daughter of Anah, **E** wife. H6215

ESCAPE
Gen 19:17 that he said, **E** for thy life; look not H4422
17 in all the plain; **e** to the mountain, lest H4422
19 life; and I cannot **e** to the mountain, H4422
20 one: Oh, let me **e** thither, (*is* it not a H4422
22 Haste thee, **e** thither; for I cannot do H4422
32: 8 the other company which is left shall **e**. H6413
Jos 8:22 that they let none of them remain or **e**. H6412
1Sa 27: 1 I should speedily **e** into the land of the H4422
1 of Israel: so shall I **e** out of his hand. H4422
2Sa 15:14 for we shall not *else* **e** from Absalom: H6413
20: 6 lest he get him fenced cities, and **e** us. H5337
1Ki 18:40 not one of them **e**. And they took them: H4422
2Ki 9:15 **e** out of the city to go to tell *it* in Jezreel. H6412
10:24 into your hands **e**, *he that letteth him* H4422
19:31 and they that **e** out of mount Zion: H6413
Ezr 9: 8 us a remnant to **e**, and to give us a nail H6413
Est 4:13 that thou shalt **e** in the king's house, H4422
Job 11:20 and they shall not **e**, and their hope H6+H4498
Ps 55: 8 I would hasten my **e** from the windy H4655
56: 7 Shall they **e** by iniquity? in *thine* anger H6405
71: 2 and cause me to **e**: incline thine ear H6403
141:10 their own nets, whilst that I withal **e**. H5674
Prv 19: 5 and *he that* speaketh lies shall not **e**. H4422
Ecc 7:26 pleaseth God shall **e** from her; but the H4422
Isa 20: 6 the king of Assyria: and how shall we **e**? H4422
37:32 and they that **e** out of mount Zion: H6413
66:19 will send those that **e** of them unto the H6412
Jer 11:11 not be able to **e**; and though they shall H3318
25:35 flee, nor the principal of the flock to **e**. H6413
32: 4 And Zedekiah king of Judah shall not **e** H4422
34: 3 And thou shalt not **e** out of his hand, H4422

Jer 38:18 and thou shalt not **e** out of their hand. H4422
23 and thou shalt not **e** out of their hand, H4422
42:17 shall remain or **e** from the evil that I H6412
44:14 there, shall **e** or remain, that they H6412
14 for none shall return but such as shall **e**. H6405
28 Yet a small number that **e** the sword H6412
46: 6 the mighty man **e**; they shall stumble, H4422
48: 8 and no city shall **e**: the valley also shall H4422
50:28 The voice of them that flee and **e** out of H6412
29 let none thereof **e**: recompense her H6413
Ezk 6: 8 *some* that shall **e** the sword among the H6412
9 And they that **e** of you shall remember H6412
7:16 But they that **e** of them shall escape, H6412
16 But they that escape of them shall **e**, H6403
17:15 he prosper? shall he **e** that doeth such H4422
18 done all these *things*, he shall not **e**. H4422
Dan 11:41 but these shall **e** out of his hand, *even* H4422
42 and the land of Egypt shall not **e**. H6413
Joel 2: 3 yea, and nothing shall **e** them. H6413
Oba 14 of his that did **e**; neither shouldest thou H6412
Mt 23:33 how can ye **e** the damnation of hell? *G5343*
Lk 21:36 worthy to **e** all these things that *G1628*
Act 27:42 any of them should swim out, and **e**. *G1309*
Ro 2: 3 that thou shalt **e** the judgment of God? *G1628*
1Co 10:13 way to **e**, that ye may be able to bear *it*. *G1545*
1Th 5: 3 woman with child; and they shall not **e**. *G1628*
Heb 2: 3 How shall we **e**, if we neglect so great *G1628*
12:25 more *shall not* we **e**, if we turn away *G5343*

ESCAPED

Gen 14:13 And there came one that had **e**, and H6412
Ex 10: 5 of that which is **e**, which remaineth H6413
Nu 21:29 given his sons that **e**, and his daughters, H6412
Dt 23:15 which is **e** from his master unto thee: H5337
Jdg 3:26 And Ehud **e** while they tarried, and H4422
26 the quarries, and **e** unto Seirath. H4422
29 men of valour; and there **e** not a man. H4422
12: 5 which were **e** said, Let me go over; H6412
21:17 for them that be **e** of Benjamin, that a H6413
1Sa 14:41 Jonathan were taken: but the people **e**. H3318
19:10 wall: and David fled, and **e** that night. H4422
12 a window: and he went, and fled, and **e**. H4422
17 mine enemy, that he is **e**? And Michal H4422
18 So David fled, and **e**, and came to H4422
22: 1 David therefore departed thence, and **e** H4422
20 Abiathar, **e**, and fled after David. H4422
23:13 that David was **e** from Keilah; and he H4422
30:17 day: and there **e** not a man of them, H4422
2Sa 1: 3 him, Out of the camp of Israel am I **e**. H4422
4: 6 and Rechab and Baanah his brother **e**. H4422
1Ki 20:20 Syria **e** on an horse with the horsemen. H4422
2Ki 19:30 And the remnant that is **e** of the house H6413
37 the sword: and they **e** into the land of H4422
1Ch 4:43 were **e**, and dwelt there unto this day. H6413
2Ch 16: 7 of the king of Syria **e** out of thine hand. H4422
20:24 bodies fallen to the earth, and none **e**. H6413
30: 6 of you, that are **e** out of the hand of the H6413
36:20 And them that had **e** from the sword H7611
Ezr 9:15 for we remain yet **e**, as *it is* this day: H6413
Neh 1: 2 the Jews that had **e**, which were left of H6413
Job 1:15 and I only am **e** alone to tell thee. H4422
16 them; and I only am **e** alone to tell thee. H4422
17 and I only am **e** alone to tell thee. H4422
19 dead; and I only am **e** alone to tell thee. H4422
19:20 and I am **e** with the skin of my teeth. H4422
Ps 124: 7 Our soul is **e** as a bird out of the snare H4422
7 the snare is broken, and we are **e**. H4422
Isa 4: 2 comely for them that are **e** of Israel. H6413
10:20 and such as are **e** of the house of Jacob, H6413
37:31 And the remnant that is **e** of the house H6413
38 the sword; and they **e** into the land of H4422
45:20 ye *that are* **e** of the nations: they H6412
Jer 41:15 But Ishmael the son of Nethaniah **e** H4422
51:50 Ye that have **e** the sword, go away, H6412
Lam 2:22 anger none **e** nor remained: those H6412
Ezk 24:27 to him which is **e**, and thou shalt speak, H6412
33:21 *that* one that had **e** out of Jerusalem H6412
22 afore he that was **e** came; and had H6412
Jn 10:39 to take him: but he **e** out of their hand, *G1831*
Act 27:44 to pass, that they **e** all safe to land. *G1295*
28: 1 And when they were **e**, then they knew *G1295*
4 though he hath **e** the sea, yet vengeance *G1295*
2Co 11:33 I let down by the wall, and **e** his hands. *G1628*
Heb 11:34 Quenched the violence of fire, **e** the *G5343*
12:25 For if they **e** not who refused him *G5343*
2Pt 1: 4 nature, having **e** the corruption that is *G668*
2:18 clean **e** from them who live in error. *G668*
20 For if after they have **e** the pollutions of *G668*

ESCAPETH

1Ki 19:17 *that* him that **e** the sword of Hazael H4422
17 slay: and him that **e** from the sword of H4422
Isa 15: 9 upon him that **e** of Moab, and upon H6413
Jer 48:19 and her that **e**, *and* say, What is done? H4422
Ezk 24:26 *That* he that **e** in that day shall come H6412
Am 9: 1 he that **e** of them shall not be delivered. H6412

ESCAPING

Ezr 9:14 that *there should be* no remnant nor **e**? H6413

ESCHEW

1Pt 3:11 Let him **e** evil, and do good; let him *G1578*

ESCHEWED

Job 1: 1 and one that feared God, and **e** evil. H5493

ESCHEWETH

Job 1: 8 man, one that feareth God, and **e** evil? H5493
2: 3 that feareth God, and **e** evil? and still he H5493

ESEK

Gen 26:20 well **E**; because they strove with him. H6230

ESHBAAL

1Ch 8:33 and Malchishua, and Abinadab, and **E**. H792
9:39 and Malchishua, and Abinadab, and **E**. H792

ESHBAN

Gen 36:26 Hemdan, and **E**, and Ithran, and Cheran. H790
1Ch 1:41 Amram, and **E**, and Ithran, and Cheran. H790

ESHCOL

Gen 14:13 brother of **E**, and brother of Aner: H812
24 with me, Aner, **E**, and Mamre; let them H812
Nu 13:23 And they came unto the brook of **E**, and H812
24 The place was called the brook **E**, H812
32: 9 up unto the valley of **E**, and saw the land, H812
Dt 1:24 unto the valley of **E**, and searched it out. H812

ESHEAN

Jos 15:52 Arab, and Dumah, and **E**, H824

ESHEK

1Ch 8:39 And the sons of **E** his brother *were*, H6232

ESHKALONITES

Jos 13: 3 Ashdothites, the **E**, the Gittites, and the H832

ESHTAOL

Jos 15:33 *And* in the valley, **E**, and Zoreah, and H847
19:41 was Zorah, and **E**, and Ir-shemesh, H847
Jdg 13:25 the camp of Dan between Zorah and **E**. H847
16:31 Zorah and **E** in the burying-place H847
18: 2 Zorah, and from **E**, to spy out the land, H847
8 to Zorah and **E**: and their brethren said H847
11 of Zorah and out of **E**, six hundred men H847

ESHTAULITES

1Ch 2:53 of them came the Zareathites, and the **E**. H848

ESHTEMOA

Jos 21:14 And Jattir with her suburbs, and **E** with H851
1Sa 30:28 Siphmoth, and to *them* which *were* in **E**, H851
1Ch 4:17 Shammai, and Ishbah the father of **E**. H851
19 the Garmite, and **E** the Maachathite. H851
6:57 and Jattir, and **E**, with their suburbs, H851

ESHTEMOH

Jos 15:50 And Anab, and **E**, and Anim, H851

ESHTON

1Ch 4:11 begat Mehir, which *was* the father of **E**. H850
12 And **E** begat Beth-rapha, and Paseah, H850

ESLI

Lk 3:25 *son* of **E**, which was *the son* of Nagge, *G2069*

ESPECIALLY

Ps 31:11 all mine enemies, but **e** among my H3966
Act 26: 3 **E** *because I know* thee to be expert in *G3122*
Gal 6:10 unto all *men*, **e** unto them who are *G3122*
1Ti 5:17 of double honour, **e** they who labour in *G3122*
2Ti 4:13 and the books, *but* **e** the parchments. *G3122*

ESPIED

Gen 42:27 in the inn, he **e** his money; for, behold, H7200
Ezk 20: 6 a land that I had **e** for them, flowing H8446

ESPOUSALS

Song 3:11 in the day of his **e**, and in the day of the H2861
Jer 2: 2 the love of thine **e**, when thou wentest H3623

ESPOUSED

2Sa 3:14 Michal, which I **e** to me for an hundred H781
Mt 1:18 mother Mary was **e** to Joseph, before *G3423*
Lk 1:27 To a virgin **e** to a man whose name was *G3423*
2: 5 To be taxed with Mary his **e** wife, being *G3423*
2Co 11: 2 godly jealousy: for I have **e** you to one *G718*

ESPY

Jos 14: 7 Kadesh-barnea to **e** out the land; and I H7270
Jer 48:19 by the way, and **e**; ask him that fleeth, H6822

ESROM

Mt 1: 3 Phares begat **E**; and Esrom begat Aram; *G2074*
3 begat Esrom; and **E** begat Aram; *G2074*
Lk 3:33 was *the son* of **E**, which was *the son* of *G2074*

ESTABLISH

Gen 6:18 But with thee will I **e** my covenant; and H6965
9: 9 And I, behold, I **e** my covenant with H6965
11 And I will **e** my covenant with you; H6965
17: 7 And I will **e** my covenant between me H6965
19 Isaac: and I will **e** my covenant with H6965
21 But my covenant will I **e** with Isaac, H6965
Lev 26: 9 you, and **e** my covenant with you. H6965
Nu 30:13 **e** it, or her husband may make it void. H6965
Dt 8:18 that he may **e** his covenant which H6965
28: 9 The LORD shall **e** thee an holy people H6965
29:13 That he may **e** thee to day for a people H6965
1Sa 1:23 him; only the LORD **e** his word. So the H6965
2Sa 7:12 of thy bowels, and I will **e** his kingdom. H3559
25 **e** *it* for ever, and do as thou hast said. H6965
1Ki 9: 5 Then I will **e** the throne of thy kingdom H6965
15: 4 his son after him, and to **e** Jerusalem: H5975
1Ch 17:11 of thy sons; and I will **e** his kingdom. H3559
22:10 his father; and I will **e** the throne of his H3559
28: 7 Moreover I will **e** his kingdom for ever, H3559
2Ch 9: 8 God loved Israel, to **e** them for ever, H5975
Job 36: 7 **e** them for ever, and they are exalted. H3427
Ps 7: 9 come to an end; but **e** the just: for the H3559
48: 8 of our God: God will **e** it for ever. Selah. H3559
87: 5 her: and the highest himself shall **e** her. H3559
89: 2 shalt thou **e** in the very heavens. H3559
4 Thy seed will I **e** for ever, and build up H3559
90:17 be upon us: and **e** thou the work of our H3559
17 us; yea, the work of our hands **e** thou it. H3559
99: 4 thou dost **e** equity, thou executest H3559
Prv 15:25 but he will **e** the border of the widow. H5324
Isa 9: 7 to order it, and to **e** it with judgment H5582
49: 8 of the people, to **e** the earth, to cause to H6965
62: 7 And give him no rest, till he **e**, and till H3559
Jer 33: 2 it, to **e** it; the LORD *is* his name; H3559
Ezk 16:60 **e** unto thee an everlasting covenant. H6965
62 And I will **e** my covenant with thee; H6965
Dan 6: 7 together to **e** a royal statute, and H6966
8 Now, O king, **e** the decree, and sign the H6966
11:14 to **e** the vision; but they shall fall. H5975
Am 5:15 Hate the evil, and love the good, and **e** H3322
Ro 3:31 faith? God forbid: yea, we **e** the law. *G2476*
10: 3 and going about to **e** their own *G2476*
1Th 3: 2 the gospel of Christ, to **e** you, and to *G4741*
Heb 10: 9 the first, that he may **e** the second. *G2476*

ESTABLISHED

Gen 9:17 which I have **e** between me and all H6965
41:32 the thing *is* **e** by God, and God will H3559
Ex 6: 4 And I have also **e** my covenant with H6965
15:17 O Lord, *which* thy hands have **e**. H3559
Lev 25:30 city shall be **e** for ever to him that H6965
Dt 19:15 of three witnesses, shall the matter be **e**. H6965
32: 6 hath he not made thee, and **e** thee? H3559
1Sa 3:20 *was* **e** *to be* a prophet of the LORD. H539
13:13 **e** thy kingdom upon Israel for ever. H3559
20:31 thou shalt not be **e**, nor thy kingdom. H3559
24:20 of Israel shall be **e** in thine hand. H6965
2Sa 5:12 the LORD had **e** him king over Israel, H3559
7:16 kingdom shall be **e** for ever before thee: H539
16 thee: thy throne shall be **e** for ever. H3559
26 of thy servant David be **e** before thee. H3559
1Ki 2:12 father; and his kingdom was **e** greatly. H3559
24 liveth, which hath **e** me, and set me on H3559
45 shall be **e** before the LORD for ever. H3559
46 was **e** in the hand of Solomon. H3559
1Ch 17:14 and his throne shall be **e** for evermore. H3559
23 be **e** for ever, and do as thou hast said. H539
24 Let it even be **e**, that thy name may be H539

1Ch 17:24 of David thy servant *be* **e** before thee. H3559
2Ch 1: 9 David my father be **e**: for thou hast made H539
12: 1 Rehoboam had **e** the kingdom, and H3559
20:20 your God, so shall ye be **e**; believe his H539
25: 3 the kingdom was **e** to him, that he slew H2388
30: 5 So they **e** a decree to make H5975
Job 21: 8 Their seed is **e** in their sight with them, H3559
22:28 and it shall be **e** unto thee: and the light H6965
Ps 24: 2 upon the seas, and **e** it upon the floods. H3559
40: 2 my feet upon a rock, *and* **e** my goings. H3559
78: 5 For he **e** a testimony in Jacob, and H6965
69 like the earth which he hath **e** for ever. H3245
89:21 With whom my hand shall be **e**: mine H3559
37 It shall be **e** for ever as the moon, and H3559
93: 2 Thy throne *is* **e** of old: thou *art* from H3559
96:10 world also shall be **e** that it shall not be H3559
102:28 and their seed shall be **e** before thee. H3559
112: 8 His heart *is* **e**, he shall not be afraid, H5564
119:90 thou hast **e** the earth, and it abideth. H3559
140:11 Let not an evil speaker be **e** in the H3559
Prv 3:19 understanding hath he **e** the heavens. H3559
4:26 of thy feet, and let all thy ways be **e**. H3559
8:28 When he **e** the clouds above: when he H553
12: 3 A man shall not be **e** by wickedness: H3559
19 The lip of truth shall be **e** for ever: but a H3559
15:22 the multitude of counsellors they are **e**. H6965
16: 3 the LORD, and thy thoughts shall be **e**. H3559
12 for the throne is **e** by righteousness. H3559
20:18 *Every* purpose is **e** by counsel: and with H3559
24: 3 builded; and by understanding it is **e**: H3559
25: 5 his throne shall be **e** in righteousness. H3559
29:14 the poor, his throne shall be **e** for ever. H3559
30: 4 who hath **e** all the ends of the earth? H6965
Isa 2: 2 house shall be **e** in the top of the H3559
7: 9 will not believe, surely ye shall not be **e**. H539
16: 5 And in mercy shall the throne be **e**: and H3559
45:18 made it; he hath **e** it, he created it not H3559
54:14 In righteousness shalt thou be **e**: thou H3559
Jer 10:12 by his power, he hath **e** the world by his H3559
30:20 shall be **e** before me, and I will H3559
51:15 by his power, he hath **e** the world by his H3559
Dan 4:36 me; and I was **e** in my kingdom, and H8627
Mic 4: 1 of the LORD shall be **e** in the top of the H3559
Hab 1:12 God, thou hast **e** them for correction. H3245
Zec 5:11 be **e**, and set there upon her own base. H3559
Mt 18:16 or three witnesses every word may be **e**. *G2476*
Act 16: 5 And so were the churches **e** in the faith, *G4732*
Ro 1:11 spiritual gift, to the end ye may be **e**; *G4741*
2Co 13: 1 or three witnesses shall every word be **e**. *G2476*
Heb 8: 6 which was **e** upon better promises. *G3549*
13: 9 that the heart be **e** with grace; not with *G950*
2Pt 1:12 *them*, and be **e** in the present truth. *G4741*

ESTABLISHETH
Nu 30:14 to day; then he **e** all her vows, or all her H6965
Prv 29: 4 The king by judgment **e** the land: but H5975
Dan 6:15 which the king **e** may be changed. H6966

ESTABLISHMENT
2Ch 32: 1 After these things, and the **e** thereof, H571

ESTATE
1Ch 17:17 me according to the **e** of a man of high H8448
Est 1:19 **e** unto another that is better than she. H4438
Ps 136:23 Who remembered us in our low **e**: for H8216
Ecc 1:16 I am come to great **e**, and have gotten H1431
3:18 I said in mine heart concerning the **e** of H1700
Ezk 16:55 to their former **e**, and Samaria and her H6927
55 to their former **e**, then thou and thy H6927
55 daughters shall return to your former **e**. H6927
Dan 11: 7 stand up in his **e**, which shall come with H3653
20 Then shall stand up in his **e** a raiser of H3653
21 And in his **e** shall stand up a vile H3653
38 But in his **e** shall he honour the God of H3653
Lk 1:48 For he hath regarded the low **e** of his
Act 22: 5 witness, and all the **e** of the elders: from
Ro 12:16 low **e**. Be not wise in your own conceits.
Col 4: 8 know your **e**, and comfort your hearts; *G4012*
Jude 6 kept not their first **e**, but left their own

ESTATES
Ezk 36:11 you after your old **e**, and will do better
Mk 6:21 high captains, and chief **e** of Galilee;

ESTEEM
Job 36:19 Will he **e** thy riches? *no*, not gold, nor H6186
Ps119:128 Therefore I **e** all *thy* precepts *concerning*
Isa 53: 4 yet we did **e** him stricken, smitten H2803
Php 2: 3 let each **e** other better than themselves. *G2233*
1Th 5:13 And to **e** them very highly in love for *G2233*

ESTEEMED
Dt 32:15 and lightly **e** the Rock of his salvation. H5034
1Sa 2:30 they that despise me shall be lightly **e**. H7043
18:23 that I *am* a poor man, and lightly **e**? H7034
Job 23:12 of his lips; I have **e** the words of his H6845
Prv 17:28 his lips *is* **e** a man of understanding.
Isa 29:16 down shall be **e** as the potter's clay: H2803
17 the fruitful field shall be **e** as a forest? H2803
53: 3 he was despised, and we **e** him not. H2803
Lam 4: 2 fine gold, how are they **e** as earthen H2803
Lk 16:15 that which is highly **e** among men is *G5308*
1Co 6: 4 to judge who are least **e** in the church. *G1848*

ESTEEMETH
Job 41:27 He **e** iron as straw, *and* brass as rotten H2803
Ro 14: 5 One man **e** one day above another: *G2919*
5 another: another **e** every day *alike*. Let *G2919*
14 itself: but to him that **e** any thing to be *G3049*

ESTEEMING
Heb 11:26 **E** the reproach of Christ greater riches *G2233*

ESTHER
Est 2: 7 And he brought up Hadassah, that *is*, **E**, H635
8 of Hegai, that **E** was brought also unto H635
10 **E** had not shewed her people nor her H635
11 **E** did, and what should become of her. H635
15 Now when the turn of **E**, the daughter of H635
15 appointed. And **E** obtained favour in the H635
16 So **E** was taken unto king Ahasuerus H635
17 And the king loved **E** above all the H635
20 **E** had not *yet* shewed her kindred nor H635
20 had charged her: for **E** did the H635
22 who told *it* unto **E** the queen; and Esther H635
22 the queen; and **E** certified the king H635
4: 5 Then called **E** for Hatach, *one* of the H635
8 to shew *it* unto **E**, and to declare *it* unto H635
9 And Hatach came and told **E** the words H635
10 Again **E** spake unto Hatach, and gave H635
13 Then Mordecai commanded to answer **E**, H635
15 Then **E** bade *them* return Mordecai *this* H635
17 to all that **E** had commanded him. H635
5: 1 on the third day, that **E** put on *her* royal H635
2 And it was so, when the king saw **E** the H635
2 the king held out to **E** the golden sceptre H635
2 *was* in his hand. So **E** drew near, and H635
3 What wilt thou, queen **E**? and what *is* thy H635
4 And **E** answered, If *it seem* good unto H635
5 that he may do as **E** hath said. So the H635
5 to the banquet that **E** had prepared. H635
6 And the king said unto **E** at the banquet H635
7 Then answered **E**, and said, My petition H635
12 Haman said moreover, Yea, **E** the queen H635
6:14 unto the banquet that **E** had prepared. H635
7: 1 came to banquet with **E** the queen. H635
2 And the king said again unto **E** on the H635
2 *is* thy petition, queen **E**? and it shall be H635
3 Then **E** the queen answered and said, If I H635
5 and said unto **E** the queen, Who is he, H635
6 And **E** said, The adversary and enemy *is* H635
7 for his life to **E** the queen; for he saw H635
8 the bed whereon **E** *was*. Then said the H635
8: 1 the Jews' enemy unto **E** the queen. And H635
1 for **E** had told what he *was* unto her. H635
2 Mordecai. And **E** set Mordecai over the H635
3 And **E** spake yet again before the king, H635
4 sceptre toward **E**. So Esther arose, and H635
4 So **E** arose, and stood before the king, H635
7 Then the king Ahasuerus said unto **E** the H635
7 I have given **E** the house of Haman, H635
9:12 And the king said unto **E** the queen, The H635
13 Then said **E**, If it please the king, let it be H635
25 But when *E* came before the king, he
29 Then **E** the queen, the daughter of H635
31 the Jew and **E** the queen had enjoined H635
32 And the decree of **E** confirmed these H635

ESTHER'S
Est 2:18 his servants, *even* **E** feast; and he made H635
4: 4 So **E** maids and her chamberlains came H635
12 And they told to Mordecai **E** words. H635

ESTIMATE
Lev 27:14 the priest shall **e** it, whether it be good H6186
14 as the priest shall **e** it, so shall it stand. H6186

ESTIMATION
Lev 5:15 flocks, with thy **e** by shekels of silver, H6187
18 of the flock, with thy **e**, for a trespass H6187
6: 6 of the flock, with thy **e**, for a trespass H6187
27: 2 persons *shall be* for the LORD by thy **e**. H6187
3 And thy **e** shall be of the male from H6187
3 sixty years old, even thy **e** shall be fifty H6187
4 And if it *be* a female, then thy **e** shall be H6187
5 years old, then thy **e** shall be of the H6187
6 five years old, then thy **e** shall be of the H6187
6 thy **e** *shall be* three shekels of silver. H6187
7 *be* a male, then thy **e** shall be fifteen H6187
8 But if he be poorer than thy **e**, then he H6187
13 shall add a fifth *part* thereof unto thy **e**. H6187
15 of thy **e** unto it, and it shall be his. H6187
16 then thy **e** shall be according to H6187
17 jubile, according to thy **e** it shall stand. H6187
18 jubile, and it shall be abated from thy **e**. H6187
19 the money of thy **e** unto it, and it shall H6187
23 the worth of thy **e**, *even* unto the year of H6187
23 he shall give thine **e** in that day, *as* a H6187
27 *it* according to thine **e**, and shall add a H6187
27 then it shall be sold according to thy **e**. H6187
Nu 18:16 according to thine **e**, for the money of H6187

ESTIMATIONS
Lev 27:25 And all thy **e** shall be according to the H6187

ESTRANGED
Job 19:13 acquaintance are verily **e** from me. H2114
Ps 58: 3 The wicked are **e** from the womb: they H2114
78:30 They were not **e** from their lust. But H2114
Jer 19: 4 me, and have **e** this place, and have H5234
Ezk 14: 5 are all **e** from me through their idols. H2114

ETAM
Jdg 15: 8 down and dwelt in the top of the rock **E**. H5862
11 to the top of the rock **E**, and said to H5862
1Ch 4: 3 And these *were of* the father of **E**; H5862
32 And their villages *were*, **E**, and Ain, H5862
2Ch 11: 6 He built even Beth-lehem, and **E**, and H5862

ETERNAL
Dt 33:27 The **e** God *is thy* refuge, and H6924
Isa 60:15 will make thee an **e** excellency, a joy of H5769
Mt 19:16 thing shall I do, that I may have **e** life? *G166*
25:46 punishment: but the righteous into life **e**. *G166*
Mk 3:29 but is in danger of **e** damnation: *G166*
10:17 what shall I do that I may inherit **e** life? *G166*
30 and in the world to come **e** life. *G166*
Lk 10:25 Master, what shall I do to inherit **e** life? *G166*
18:18 Master, what shall I do to inherit **e** life? *G166*
Jn 3:15 in him should not perish, but have **e** life. *G166*
4:36 fruit unto life **e**: that both he that soweth *G166*
5:39 ye think ye have **e** life: and they are they *G166*
6:54 my blood, hath **e** life; and I will raise *G166*
68 shall we go? thou hast the words of **e** life. *G166*
10:28 And I give unto them **e** life; and they *G166*
12:25 life in this world shall keep it unto life **e**. *G166*
17: 2 **e** life to as many as thou hast given him. *G166*
3 And this is life **e**, that they might know *G166*
Act 13:48 many as were ordained to **e** life believed. *G166*
Ro 1:20 that are made, *even* his **e** power and *G126*
2: 7 and honour and immortality, **e** life: *G166*
5:21 unto **e** life by Jesus Christ our Lord. *G166*
6:23 *is* **e** life through Jesus Christ our Lord. *G166*
2Co 4:17 more exceeding *and* **e** weight of glory; *G166*
18 but the things which are not seen *are* **e**. *G166*
5: 1 not made with hands, **e** in the heavens. *G166*
Eph 3:11 According to the **e** purpose which he *G165*
1Ti 1:17 Now unto the King **e**, immortal, invisible, *G165*
6:12 faith, lay hold on **e** life, whereunto thou *G166*
19 to come, that they may lay hold on **e** life. *G166*
2Ti 2:10 which is in Christ Jesus with **e** glory. *G166*
Tit 1: 2 In hope of **e** life, which God, that cannot *G166*
3: 7 heirs according to the hope of **e** life. *G166*
Heb 5: 9 **e** salvation unto all them that obey him; *G166*
6: 2 of the dead, and of **e** judgment. *G166*
9:12 having obtained **e** redemption *for us*. *G166*
14 who through the **e** Spirit offered himself *G166*
15 receive the promise of **e** inheritance. *G166*
1Pt 5:10 called us unto his **e** glory by Christ Jesus, *G166*
1Jn 1: 2 and shew unto you that **e** life, which was *G166*
2:25 that he hath promised us, *even* **e** life. *G166*
3:15 no murderer hath **e** life abiding in him. *G166*
5:11 to us **e** life, and this life is in his Son. *G166*
13 know that ye have **e** life, and that ye may *G166*
20 Christ. This is the true God, and **e** life. *G166*
Jude 7 suffering the vengeance of **e** fire. *G166*

Jude 21 of our Lord Jesus Christ unto **e** life. G166

ETERNITY
Isa 57:15 that inhabiteth **e**, whose name *is* Holy; H5703

ETHAM
Ex 13:20 in **E**, in the edge of the wilderness. H864
Nu 33: 6 **E**, which *is* in the edge of the wilderness. H864
7 And they removed from **E**, and turned H864
8 wilderness of **E**, and pitched in Marah. H864

ETHAN
1Ki 4:31 For he was wiser than all men; than **E** H387
1Ch 2: 6 And the sons of Zerah; Zimri, and **E**, and H387
8 And the sons of **E**; Azariah. H387
6:42 The son of **E**, the son of Zimmah, the son H387
44 on the left hand: **E** the son of Kishi, the H387
15:17 their brethren, **E** the son of Kushaiah; H387
19 So the singers, Heman, Asaph, and **E**, H387
Ps 89:ttl Maschil of **E** the Ezrahite. H387

ETHANIM
1Ki 8: 2 the month **E**, which *is* the seventh month. H389

ETHBAAL
1Ki 16:31 the daughter of **E** king of the Zidonians, H856

ETHER
Jos 15:42 Libnah, and **E**, and Ashan, H6281
19: 7 Ain, Remmon, and **E**, and Ashan; four H6281

ETHIOPIA
Gen 2:13 it that compasseth the whole land of **E**. H3568
2Ki 19: 9 Tirhakah king of **E**, Behold, he is come H3568
Est 1: 1 India even unto **E**, *over* an hundred and H3568
8: 9 from India unto **E**, an hundred twenty H3568
Job 28:19 The topaz of **E** shall not equal it, H3568
Ps 68:31 Princes shall come out of Egypt; **E** shall H3568
87: 4 Tyre, with **E**; this *man* was born there. H3568
Isa 18: 1 wings, which *is* beyond the rivers of **E**: H3568
20: 3 and wonder upon Egypt and upon **E**; H3568
5 and ashamed of **E** their expectation, H3568
37: 9 Tirhakah king of **E**, He is come forth to H3568
43: 3 *for* thy ransom, **E** and Seba for thee. H3568
45:14 merchandise of **E** and of the Sabeans, H3568
Ezk 29:10 of Syene even unto the border of **E**. H3568
30: 4 pain shall be in **E**, when the slain shall H3568
5 **E**, and Libya, and Lydia, and all the H3568
38: 5 Persia, **E**, and Libya with them; all of H3568
Nah 3: 9 **E** and Egypt *were* her strength, and *it* H3568
Zep 3:10 From beyond the rivers of **E** my H3568
Act 8:27 behold, a man of **E**, an eunuch of great G128

ETHIOPIAN
Nu 12: 1 because of the **E** woman whom he had H3569
1 for he had married an **E** woman. H3569
2Ch 14: 9 them Zerah the **E** with an host of a H3569
Jer 13:23 Can the **E** change his skin, or the H3569
38: 7 Now when Ebed-melech the **E**, one of H3569
10 Ebed-melech the **E**, saying, Take from H3569
12 And Ebed-melech the **E** said unto H3569
39:16 Go and speak to Ebed-melech the **E**, H3569

ETHIOPIANS
2Ch 12: 3 the Lubims, the Sukkiims, and the **E**. H3569
14:12 So the LORD smote the **E** before Asa, H3569
12 Asa, and before Judah; and the **E** fled. H3569
13 Gerar: and the **E** were overthrown, that H3569
16: 8 Were not the **E** and the Lubims a huge H3569
21:16 of the Arabians, that *were* near the **E**: H3569
Isa 20: 4 prisoners, and the **E** captives, young H3568
Jer 46: 9 come forth; the **E** and the Libyans, that H3568
Ezk 30: 9 make the careless **E** afraid, and great H3568
Dan 11:43 Libyans and the **E** *shall be* at his steps. H3569
Am 9: 7 *Are* ye not as children of the **E** unto me, H3569
Zep 2:12 Ye **E** also, ye *shall be* slain by my H3569
Act 8:27 queen of the **E**, who had the charge G128

ETHNAN
1Ch 4: 7 of Helah *were*, Zereth, and Jezoar, and **E**. H869

ETHNI
1Ch 6:41 The son of **E**, the son of Zerah, the son of H867

EUBULUS
2Ti 4:21 before winter. **E** greeteth thee, and G2103

EUNICE
2Ti 1: 5 **E**; and I am persuaded that in thee also. G2131

EUNUCH
Isa 56: 3 let the **e** say, Behold, I *am* a dry tree. H5631
Jer 52:25 He took also out of the city an **e**, which H5631
Act 8:27 of Ethiopia, an **e** of great authority G2135
34 And the **e** answered Philip, and said, I G2135
36 water: and the **e** said, See, *here is* G2135
38 Philip and the **e**; and he baptized him. G2135
39 Philip, that the **e** saw him no more: and G2135

EUNUCHS
2Ki 9:32 there looked out to him two *or* three **e**. H5631
20:18 **e** in the palace of the king of Babylon. H5631
Isa 39: 7 **e** in the palace of the king of Babylon. H5631
56: 4 For thus saith the LORD unto the **e** that H5631
Jer 29: 2 and the queen, and the **e**, the princes of H5631
34:19 of Jerusalem, the **e**, and the priests, and H5631
38: 7 one of the **e** which was in the king's H5631
41:16 the children, and the **e**, whom he had H5631
Dan 1: 3 the master of his **e**, that he should bring H5631
7 Unto whom the prince of the **e** gave H5631
8 the **e** that he might not defile himself. H5631
9 and tender love with the prince of the **e**. H5631
10 And the prince of the **e** said unto H5631
11 the prince of the **e** had set over Daniel, H5631
18 the prince of the **e** brought them in H5631
Mt 19:12 For there are some **e**, which were so G2135
12 and there are some **e**, which were made G2135
12 which were made **e** of men: and there G2134
12 men: and there be **e**, which have made G2135
12 made themselves **e** for the kingdom of G2134

EUODIAS
Php 4: 2 I beseech **E**, and beseech Syntyche, that G2136

EUPHRATES
Gen 2:14 of Assyria. And the fourth river *is* **E**. H6578
15:18 Egypt unto the great river, the river **E**: H6578
Dt 1: 7 unto the great river, the river **E**. H6578
11:24 the river, the river **E**, even unto the H6578
Jos 1: 4 river, the river **E**, all the land of the H6578
2Sa 8: 3 to recover his border at the river **E**. H6578
2Ki 23:29 to the river **E**: and king Josiah went H6578
24: 7 unto the river **E** all that pertained to H6578
1Ch 5: 9 from the river **E**: because their cattle H6578
18: 3 to stablish his dominion by the river **E**. H6578
2Ch 35:20 by **E**: and Josiah went out against him. H6578
Jer 13: 4 **E**, and hide it there in a hole of the rock. H6578
5 So I went, and hid it by **E**, as the LORD H6578
6 me, Arise, go to **E**, and take the girdle H6578
7 Then I went to **E**, and digged, and took H6578
46: 2 was by the river **E** in Carchemish, H6578
6 and fall toward the north by the river **E**. H6578
10 in the north country by the river **E**. H6578
51:63 to it, and cast it into the midst of **E**: H6578
Rev 9:14 which are bound in the great river **E**. G2166
16:12 the great river **E**; and the water thereof G2166

EUROCLYDON
Act 27:14 against it a tempestuous wind, called **E**. G2148

EUTYCHUS
Act 20: 9 man named **E**, being fallen into a deep G2161

EVANGELIST
Act 21: 8 house of Philip the **e**, which was *one* of G2099
2Ti 4: 5 of an **e**, make full proof of thy ministry. G2099

EVANGELISTS
Eph 4:11 **e**; and some, pastors and teachers; G2099

EVE
Gen 3:20 And Adam called his wife's name **E**; H2332
4: 1 And Adam knew **E** his wife; and she H2332
2Co 11: 3 serpent beguiled **E** through his subtilty, G2096
1Ti 2:13 For Adam was first formed, then **E**. G2096

EVEN See the Appendix.

EVENING
Gen 1: 5 **e** and the morning were the first day. H6153
8 Heaven. And the **e** and the morning H6153
13 And the **e** and the morning were the H6153
19 And the **e** and the morning were the H6153
23 And the **e** and the morning were the H6153
31 **e** and the morning were the sixth day. H6153
8:11 And the dove came in to him in the **e**; H6153
24:11 at the time of the **e**, *even* the time that H6153
29:23 And it came to pass in the **e**, that he H6153
30:16 And Jacob came out of the field in the **e**, H6153
Ex 12: 6 of Israel shall kill it in the **e**. H6153
16: 8 give you in the **e** flesh to eat, and in the H6153
18:13 by Moses from the morning unto the **e**. H6153
27:21 shall order it from **e** to morning before H6153
Lev 24: 3 order it from the **e** unto the morning H6153
Dt 23:11 But it shall be, when **e** cometh on, he H6153
Jos 10:26 were hanging upon the trees until the **e**. H6153
Jdg 19: 9 draweth toward **e**, I pray you tarry all H6150
1Sa 14:24 *any* food until **e**, that I may be avenged H6153
17:16 **e**, and presented himself forty days. H6150
30:17 even unto the **e** of the next day: and H6153
1Ki 17: 6 in the **e**; and he drank of the brook. H6153
18:29 the offering of the **e** sacrifice, that *there*
36 the offering of the **e** sacrifice, that Elijah
2Ki 16:15 offering, and the **e** meat offering, and H6153
1Ch 16:40 morning and **e**, and *to do* according H6153
2Ch 2: 4 morning and **e**, on the sabbaths, and H6153
13:11 and every **e** burnt sacrifices and H6153
11 to burn every **e**: for we keep the charge H6153
31: 3 the morning and **e** burnt offerings, and H6153
Ezr 3: 3 *even* burnt offerings morning and **e**. H6153
9: 4 and I sat astonied until the **e** sacrifice. H6153
5 And at the **e** sacrifice I arose up from H6153
Est 2:14 In the **e** she went, and on the morrow H6153
Job 4:20 They are destroyed from morning to **e**: H6153
Ps 55:17 **E**, and morning, and at noon, will I H6153
59: 6 They return at **e**: they make a noise like H6153
14 And at **e** let them return; *and* let them H6153
65: 8 of the morning and **e** to rejoice. H6153
90: 6 in the **e** it is cut down, and withereth. H6153
104:23 his work and to his labour until the **e**. H6153
141: 2 up of my hands *as* the **e** sacrifice. H6153
Prv 7: 9 In the twilight, in the **e**, in the black and H6153
Ecc 11: 6 seed, and in the **e** withhold not thine H6153
Jer 6: 4 the shadows of the **e** are stretched out. H6153
Ezk 33:22 was upon me in the **e**, afore he that was H6153
46: 2 but the gate shall not be shut until the **e**. H6153
Dan 8:26 And the vision of the **e** and the H6153
9:21 me about the time of the **e** oblation. H6153
Hab 1: 8 more fierce than the **e** wolves: and their H6153
Zep 2: 7 lie down in the **e**: for the LORD their H6153
3: 3 her judges *are* **e** wolves; they gnaw not H6153
Zec 14: 7 to pass, *that* at **e** time it shall be light. H6153
Mt 14:15 And when it was **e**, his disciples came to G3798
23 the **e** was come, he was there alone. G3798
16: 2 them, When it is **e**, ye say, *It will be* fair G3798
Mk 14:17 And in the **e** he cometh with the twelve. G3798
Lk 24:29 us: for it is toward **e**, and the day is far G2073
Jn 20:19 Then the same day at **e**, being the first G3798
Act 28:23 *out of* the prophets, from morning till **e**. G2073

EVENINGS
Jer 5: 6 *and* a wolf of the **e** shall spoil them, a H6160

EVENINGTIDE
2Sa 11: 2 And it came to pass in an **e**, H6256+H6153
Isa 17:14 And behold at **e** trouble; *and* H6256+H6153

EVENT
Ecc 2:14 also that one **e** happeneth to them all. H4745
9: 2 to all: *there is* one **e** to the righteous, H4745
3 that *there is* one **e** unto all: yea, also the H4745

EVENTIDE
Gen 24:63 the field at the **e**: and he lifted H6256+H6153
Jos 7: 6 LORD until the **e**, he and the elders of H6153
8:29 on a tree until **e**: and as soon as H6256+H6153
Mk 11:11 and now the **e** was come, he G3798+G5610
Act 4: 3 hold unto the next day: for it was now **e**. G2073

EVER
Gen 3:22 of the tree of life, and eat, and live for **e**: H5769
13:15 thee will I give it, and to thy seed for **e**. H5769
43: 9 thee, then let me bear the blame for **e**: H3117
44:32 shall bear the blame to my father for **e**. H3117
Ex 3:15 this *is* my name for **e**, and this *is* my H5769
12:14 keep it a feast by an ordinance for **e**. H5769
17 your generations by an ordinance for **e**. H5769
24 ordinance to thee and to thy sons for **e**. H5769
14:13 ye shall see them again no more for **e**. H5769
15:18 The LORD shall reign for **e** and ever. H5769
18 The LORD shall reign for ever and **e**. H5703
19: 9 believe thee for **e**. And Moses told the H5769
21: 6 an aul; and he shall serve him for **e**. H5769
27:21 *be* a statute for **e** unto their generations H5769
28:43 for **e** unto him and his seed after him. H5769
29:28 by a statute for **e** from the children of H5769
30:21 be a statute for **e** to them, *even* to him H5769
31:17 of Israel for **e**: for *in* six days the LORD H5769

Ex 32:13 your seed, and they shall inherit *it* for e. H5769
Lev 6:13 The fire shall e be burning upon the H8548
18 *be* a statute for e in your generations H5769
22 it: *it is* a statute for e unto the LORD; it H5769
7:34 for e from among the children of Israel. H5769
36 for e throughout their generations. H5769
10: 9 for e throughout your generations: H5769
15 for e; as the LORD hath commanded. H5769
16:29 And *this* shall be a statute for e unto H5769
31 afflict your souls, by a statute for e. H5769
17: 7 be a statute for e unto them throughout H5769
23:14 *shall be* a statute for e throughout your H5769
21 *be* a statute for e in all your dwellings H5769
31 *shall be* a statute for e throughout your H5769
41 *be* a statute for e in your generations: H5769
24: 3 *be* a statute for e in your generations. H5769
25:23 The land shall not be sold for e: for the H6783
30 be established for e to him that bought H6783
46 be your bondmen for e: but over your H5769
Nu 10: 8 for e throughout your generations. H5769
15:15 an ordinance for e in your generations: H5769
18: 8 and to thy sons, by an ordinance for e. H5769
11 by a statute for e: every one that is clean H5769
19 by a statute for e: it *is* a covenant of salt H5769
19 of salt for e before the LORD unto H5769
23 *shall be* a statute for e throughout your H5769
19:10 among them, for a statute for e. H5769
22:30 thou hast ridden e since *I was* thine H5750
30 unto this day? was I e wont to do so unto
24:20 latter end *shall be* that he perish for e. H5703
24 Eber, and he also shall perish for e. H5703
Dt 4:33 Did *e* people hear the voice of God
40 thy God giveth thee, for e. H3605+H3117
5:29 with them, and with their children for e! H5769
12:28 after thee for e, when thou doest *that* H5769
13:16 an heap for e; it shall not be built again. H5769
15:17 be thy servant for e. And also unto thy H5769
18: 5 LORD, him and his sons for e. H3605+H3117
19: 9 and to walk e in his ways; then H3605+H3117
23: 3 into the congregation of the LORD for e: H5769
6 nor their prosperity all thy days for e. H5769
28:46 for a wonder, and upon thy seed for e. H5769
29:29 to our children for e, that *we* may do all H5769
32:40 my hand to heaven, and say, I live for e. H5769
Jos 4: 7 unto the children of Israel for e. H5769
24 fear the LORD your God for e. H3605+H3117
8:28 for e, *even* a desolation unto this day. H5769
14: 9 thy children's for e, because thou hast H5769
Jdg 11:25 of Moab? did he e strive against Israel, H7378
25 Israel, or did he e fight against them, H3898
1Sa 1:22 before the LORD, and there abide for e. H5769
2:30 walk before me for e: but now the LORD H5769
32 old man in thine house for e. H3605+H3117
35 before mine anointed for e. H3605+H3117
3:13 his house for e for the iniquity which H5769
14 purged with sacrifice nor offering for e. H5769
13:13 thy kingdom upon Israel for e. H5769
20:15 from my house for e: no, not when the H5769
23 the LORD *be* between thee and me for e. H5769
42 and thy seed for e. And he arose and H5769
27:12 therefore he shall be my servant for e. H5769
28: 2 thee keeper of mine head for e. H3605+H3117
2Sa 2:26 sword devour for e? knowest thou not H5331
3:28 the LORD for e from the blood of H5769
7:13 stablish the throne of his kingdom for e. H5769
16 be established for e before thee: thy H5769
16 thy throne shall be established for e. H5769
24 unto thee for e: and thou, LORD, H5769
25 *it* for e, and do as thou hast said. H5769
26 And let thy name be magnified for e, H5769
29 it may continue for e before thee: for H5769
29 house of thy servant be blessed for e. H5769
1Ki 1:31 said, Let my lord king David live for e. H5769
2:33 of his seed for e: but upon David, and H5769
33 there be peace for e from the LORD. H5769
45 be established before the LORD for e. H5769
5: 1 Hiram was e a lover of David. H3605+H3117
8:13 a settled place for thee to abide in for e. H5769
9: 3 my name there for e; and mine eyes and H5769
5 upon Israel for e, as I promised to H5769
10: 9 loved Israel for e, therefore made he H5769
11:39 the seed of David, but not for e. H3605+H3117
12: 7 they will be thy servants for e. H3605+H3117
2Ki 5:27 unto thy seed for e. And he went out H5769
21: 7 tribes of Israel, will I put my name for e: H5769
1Ch 15: 2 of God, and to minister unto him for e. H5769
16:34 *he is* good; for his mercy *endureth* for e. H5769
36 Blessed *be* the LORD God of Israel for e H5769
36 Israel for ever and e. And all the people H5769

1Ch 16:41 because his mercy *endureth* for e; H5769
17:12 and I will stablish his throne for e. H5769
14 my kingdom for e: and his throne shall H5769
22 e; and thou, LORD, becamest their God. H5769
23 for e, and do as thou hast said. H5769
24 be magnified for e, saying, The LORD of H5769
27 be before thee for e: for thou blessest, O H5769
27 O LORD, and *it shall be* blessed for e. H5769
22:10 throne of his kingdom over Israel for e. H5769
23:13 he and his sons for e, to burn incense H5769
13 him, and to bless in his name for e. H5769
25 that they may dwell in Jerusalem for e: H5769
28: 4 over Israel for e: for he hath chosen H5769
7 his kingdom for e, if he be constant to H5769
8 for your children after you for e. H5769
9 forsake him, he will cast thee off for e. H5703
29:10 God of Israel our father, for e and ever. H5769
10 God of Israel our father, for ever and e. H5769
18 keep this for e in the imagination of H5769
2Ch 2: 4 This *is an ordinance* for e to Israel. H5769
5:13 *endureth* for e: that *then* the house H5769
6: 2 thee, and a place for thy dwelling for e. H5769
7: 3 *he is* good; for his mercy *endureth* for e. H5769
6 *endureth* for e, when David praised H5769
16 may be there for e: and mine eyes and H5769
9: 8 establish them for e, therefore made he H5769
10: 7 they will be thy servants for e. H3605+H3117
13: 5 Israel to David for e, *even* to him and to H5769
20: 7 to the seed of Abraham thy friend for e? H5769
21 the LORD; for his mercy *endureth* for e. H5769
21: 7 to him and to his sons for e. H3605+H3117
30: 8 he hath sanctified for e: and serve the H5769
33: 4 In Jerusalem shall my name be for e. H5769
7 tribes of Israel, will I put my name for e: H5865
Ezr 3:11 *endureth* for e toward Israel. And H5769
9:12 or their wealth for e: that ye may be H5769
12 an inheritance to your children for e. H5769
Neh 2: 3 the king live for e: why should not my H5769
9: 5 your God for e and ever: and blessed H5769
5 God for ever and e: and blessed be thy H5769
13: 1 into the congregation of God for e; H5769
Job 4: 7 Remember, I pray thee, who *e* perished,
20 perish for e without any regarding *it*. H5331
14:20 Thou prevailest for e against him, and H5331
19:24 an iron pen and lead in the rock for e! H5703
20: 7 *Yet* he shall perish for e like his own H5331
23: 7 I be delivered for e from my judge. H5331
36: 7 them for e, and they are exalted. H5331
41: 4 wilt thou take him for a servant for e? H5769
Ps 5:11 thee rejoice: let them e shout for joy, H5769
9: 5 hast put out their name for e and ever. H5769
5 hast put out their name for ever and e. H5703
7 But the LORD shall endure for e: he H5769
18 of the poor shall *not* perish for e. H5703
10:16 The LORD *is* King for e and ever: the H5769
16 The LORD *is* King for ever and e: the H5703
12: 7 them from this generation for e. H5769
13: 1 me, O LORD? for e? how long wilt thou H5331
19: 9 enduring for e: the judgments of the H5703
21: 4 him, *even* length of days for e and ever. H5769
4 him, *even* length of days for ever and e. H5703
6 most blessed for e: thou hast made him H5703
22:26 seek him: your heart shall live for e. H5703
23: 6 in the house of the LORD for e. H753+H3117
25: 6 for they *have been* e of old.
15 Mine eyes *are* e toward the LORD; for H8548
28: 9 feed them also, and lift them up for e. H5769
29:10 flood; yea, the LORD sitteth King for e. H5769
30:12 God, I will give thanks unto thee for e. H5769
33:11 The counsel of the LORD standeth for e, H5769
37:18 and their inheritance shall be for e. H5769
26 *He is* e merciful, and lendeth; H3605+H3117
28 are preserved for e: but the seed of the H5769
29 inherit the land, and dwell therein for e. H5703
41:12 and settest me before thy face for e. H5769
44: 8 long, and praise thy name for e. Selah. H5769
23 thou, O Lord? arise, cast *us* not off for e. H5331
45: 2 therefore God hath blessed thee for e. H5769
6 Thy throne, O God, *is* for e and ever: H5769
6 Thy throne, O God, *is* for ever and e: the H5703
17 the people praise thee for e and ever. H5769
17 the people praise thee for ever and e. H5703
48: 8 God: God will establish it for e. Selah. H5769
14 For this God *is* our God for e and ever: H5769
14 For this God *is* our God for ever and e: H5703
49: 8 soul *is* precious, and it ceaseth for e:) H5769
9 That he should still live for e, *and* not H5331
11 *shall continue* for e, *and* their dwelling H5769
51: 3 and my sin *is* e before me. H8548

Ps 52: 5 God shall likewise destroy thee for e, he H5331
8 in the mercy of God for e and ever. H5769
8 trust in the mercy of God for ever and e. H5703
9 I will praise thee for e, because thou H5769
61: 4 I will abide in thy tabernacle for e: I will H5769
7 He shall abide before God for e: O H5769
8 e, that I may daily perform my vows. H5703
66: 7 He ruleth by his power for e; his eyes H5769
68:16 in; yea, the LORD will dwell *in it* for e. H5331
72:17 His name shall endure for e: his name H5769
19 And blessed *be* his glorious name for e: H5769
73:26 of my heart, and my portion for e. H5769
74: 1 O God, why hast thou cast *us* off for e? H5331
10 the enemy blaspheme thy name for e? H5331
19 not the congregation of thy poor for e. H5331
75: 9 But I will declare for e; I will sing H5769
77: 7 Will the Lord cast off for e? and will he H5769
8 Is his mercy clean gone for e? doth *his* H5331
78:69 earth which he hath established for e. H5769
79: 5 for e? shall thy jealousy burn like fire? H5331
13 thee thanks for e: we will shew forth thy H5769
81:15 their time should have endured for e. H5769
83:17 and troubled for e; yea, let them be put H5703
85: 5 Wilt thou be angry with us for e? wilt H5769
89: 1 of the LORD for e: with my mouth will H5769
2 be built up for e: thy faithfulness shalt H5769
4 Thy seed will I establish for e, and build H5769
29 e, and his throne as the days of heaven. H5703
36 His seed shall endure for e, and his H5769
37 It shall be established for e as the H5769
46 for e? shall thy wrath burn like fire? H5331
90: 2 brought forth, or e thou hadst formed
92: 7 *it is* that they shall be destroyed for e: H5703
93: 5 thine house, O LORD, for e. H753+H3117
102:12 But thou, O LORD, shalt endure for e; H5769
103: 9 neither will he keep *his anger* for e. H5769
104: 5 it should not be removed for e. H5769+H5703
31 e: the LORD shall rejoice in his works. H5769
105: 8 his covenant for e, the word *which* he H5769
106: 1 *he is* good: for his mercy *endureth* for e. H5769
107: 1 *he is* good: for his mercy *endureth* for e. H5769
110: 4 for e after the order of Melchizedek. H5769
111: 3 and his righteousness endureth for e. H5703
5 he will e be mindful of his covenant. H5769
8 They stand fast for e and ever, *and are* H5703
8 They stand fast for ever and e, *and are* H5769
9 for e: holy and reverend *is* his name. H5769
10 his praise endureth for e. H5703
112: 3 and his righteousness endureth for e. H5703
6 Surely he shall not be moved for e: the H5769
9 e; his horn shall be exalted with honour. H5703
117: 2 *endureth* for e. Praise ye the LORD. H5769
118: 1 good: because his mercy *endureth* for e. H5769
2 now say, that his mercy *endureth* for e. H5769
3 now say, that his mercy *endureth* for e. H5769
4 say, that his mercy *endureth* for e. H5769
29 *he is* good: for his mercy *endureth* for e. H5769
119:44 So shall I keep thy law continually for e H5769
44 keep thy law continually for ever and e. H5703
89 For e, O LORD, thy word is settled in H5769
98 mine enemies: for they *are* e with me. H5769
111 e: for they *are* the rejoicing of my heart. H5769
152 old that thou hast founded them for e. H5769
160 thy righteous judgments *endureth* for e. H5769
125: 1 cannot be removed, *but* abideth for e. H5769
2 his people from henceforth even for e. H5769
131: 3 in the LORD from henceforth and for e. H5769
132:14 This *is* my rest for e: here will I dwell; H5703
135:13 Thy name, O LORD, *endureth* for e; *and* H5769
136: 1 *he is* good: for his mercy *endureth* for e. H5769
2 of gods: for his mercy *endureth* for e. H5769
3 of lords: for his mercy *endureth* for e. H5769
4 wonders: for his mercy *endureth* for e. H5769
5 heavens: for his mercy *endureth* for e. H5769
6 the waters: for his mercy *endureth* for e. H5769
7 lights: for his mercy *endureth* for e: H5769
8 by day: for his mercy *endureth* for e: H5769
9 by night: for his mercy *endureth* for e. H5769
10 firstborn: for his mercy *endureth* for e: H5769
11 them: for his mercy *endureth* for e: H5769
12 out arm: for his mercy *endureth* for e. H5769
13 into parts: for his mercy *endureth* for e: H5769
14 midst of it: for his mercy *endureth* for e: H5769
15 Red sea: for his mercy *endureth* for e. H5769
16 for his mercy *endureth* for e. H5769
17 kings: for his mercy *endureth* for e: H5769
18 kings: for his mercy *endureth* for e: H5769
19 Amorites: for his mercy *endureth* for e: H5769
20 of Bashan: for his mercy *endureth* for e: H5769

Ps 136:21 heritage: for his mercy *endureth* for **e**: H5769
22 servant: for his mercy *endureth* for **e**. H5769
23 low estate: for his mercy *endureth* for **e**. H5769
24 enemies: for his mercy *endureth* for **e**. H5769
25 to all flesh: for his mercy *endureth* for **e**. H5769
26 of heaven: for his mercy *endureth* for **e**. H5769
138: 8 *endureth* for **e**: forsake not the works H5769
145: 1 I will bless thy name for **e** and ever. H5769
1 and I will bless thy name for ever and **e**. H5703
2 I will praise thy name for **e** and ever. H5769
2 I will praise thy name for ever and **e**. H5703
21 bless his holy name for **e** and ever. H5769
21 flesh bless his holy name for ever and **e**. H5703
146: 6 therein *is*: which keepeth truth for **e**: H5769
10 The LORD shall reign for **e**, *even* thy H5769
148: 6 He hath also stablished them for **e** and H5703
6 them for ever and **e**: he hath made a H5769
Prv 8:23 from the beginning, or **e** the earth was. H6924
12:19 be established for **e**: but a lying tongue H5703
27:24 For riches *are* not for **e**: and doth the H5769
29:14 his throne shall be established for **e**. H5703
Ecc 1: 4 cometh: but the earth abideth for **e**. H5769
2:16 than of the fool for **e**; seeing that which H5769
3:14 it shall be for **e**: nothing can be put H5769
9: 6 more a portion for **e** in any *thing* that H5769
12: 6 Or **e** the silver cord be loosed, or the H3808
Song 6:12 Or **e** I was aware, my soul made me H3808
Isa 9: 7 even for **e**. The zeal of the LORD H5769
26: 4 Trust ye in the LORD for **e**: for in the H5703
28:28 he will not **e** be threshing it, nor H5331
30: 8 be for the time to come for **e** and ever: H5703
8 be for the time to come for ever and **e**: H5769
32:14 be for dens for **e**, a joy of wild asses, a H5769
17 quietness and assurance for **e**. H5769
33:20 thereof shall **e** be removed, neither H5331
34:10 shall go up for **e**: from generation to H5769
10 shall pass through it for **e** and ever. H5331
10 shall pass through it for ever and **e**. H5331
17 shall possess it for **e**, from generation to H5769
40: 8 the word of our God shall stand for **e**. H5769
47: 7 And thou saidst, I shall be a lady for **e**: H5769
51: 6 shall be for **e**, and my righteousness H5769
8 shall be for **e**, and my salvation from H5769
57:16 For I will not contend for **e**, neither will H5769
59:21 the LORD, from henceforth and for **e**. H5769
60:21 inherit the land for **e**, the branch of my H5769
64: 9 iniquity for **e**: behold, see, we beseech H5703
65:18 But be ye glad and rejoice for **e** *in that* H5703
Jer 3: 5 Will he reserve *his anger* for **e**? will he H5769
12 LORD, *and* I will not keep *anger* for **e**. H5769
7: 7 I gave to your fathers, for **e** and ever. H5769
7 I gave to your fathers, for ever and **e**. H5769
17: 4 in mine anger, *which* shall burn for **e**. H5769
25 and this city shall remain for **e**. H5769
25: 5 you and to your fathers for **e** and ever: H5769
5 you and to your fathers for ever and **e**: H5769
31:36 being a nation before me for **e**. H3605+H3117
40 up, nor thrown down any more for **e**. H5769
32:39 fear me for **e**, for the good of H3605+H3117
33:11 *endureth* for **e**: *and* of them that shall H5769
35: 6 no wine, *neither ye*, nor your sons for **e**: H5769
19 a man to stand before me for **e**. H3605+H3117
49:33 a desolation for **e**: there shall no man H5769
50:39 inhabited for **e**; neither shall it be dwelt H5331
51:26 shalt be desolate for **e**, saith the LORD. H5769
62 beast, but that it shall be desolate for **e**. H5769
Lam 3:31 For the Lord will not cast off for **e**: H5769
5:19 Thou, O LORD, remainest for **e**; thy H5769
20 Wherefore dost thou forget us for **e**, *and* H5331
Ezk 37:25 children for **e**: and my servant David H5769
25 David *shall be* their prince for **e**. H5769
43: 7 of Israel for **e**, and my holy name, H5769
9 I will dwell in the midst of them for **e**. H5769
Dan 2: 4 O king, live for **e**: tell thy servants the H5957
20 the name of God for **e** and ever: for H5957
20 and **e**: for wisdom and might are his: H5957
44 these kingdoms, and it shall stand for **e**. H5957
3: 9 king Nebuchadnezzar, O king, live for **e**. H5957
4:34 him that liveth for **e**, whose dominion *is* H5957
5:10 O king, live for **e**: let not thy thoughts H5957
6: 6 thus unto him, King Darius, live for **e**. H5957
21 Daniel unto the king, O king, live for **e**. H5957
24 **e** they came at the bottom of the den. H3809
26 and stedfast for **e**, and his kingdom *that* H5957
7:18 kingdom for **e**, even for ever and ever. H5957
18 kingdom for ever, even for **e** and ever. H5957
18 kingdom for ever, even for ever and **e**. H5957
12: 3 as the stars for **e** and ever. H5769
3 as the stars for ever and **e**. H5703
Dan 12: 7 him that liveth for **e** that *it shall be* for H5769
Hos 2:19 And I will betroth thee unto me for **e**; H5769
Joel 2: 2 hath not been **e** the like, neither shall H5769
3:20 But Judah shall dwell for **e**, and H5769
Am 1:11 perpetually, and he kept his wrath for **e**: H5331
Oba 10 thee, and thou shalt be cut off for **e**. H5769
Jna 2: 6 bars *was* about me for **e**: yet hast thou H5769
Mic 2: 9 have ye taken away my glory for **e**. H5769
4: 5 of the LORD our God for **e** and ever. H5769
5 of the LORD our God for ever and **e**. H5703
7 Zion from henceforth, even for **e**. H5769
7:18 for **e**, because he delighteth *in* mercy. H5703
Zec 1: 5 and the prophets, do they live for **e**? H5769
Mal 1: 4 whom the LORD hath indignation for **e**. H5769
Mt 6:13 the power, and the glory, for **e**. Amen. *G1519*
21:19 henceforward for **e**. And presently the *G1519*
24:21 world to this time, no, nor **e** shall be. *G3364*
Mk 11:14 for **e**. And his disciples heard *it*. *G1519*
15: 8 *him to do* as he had **e** done unto them. *G104*
Lk 1:33 the house of Jacob for **e**; and of his *G1519*
55 to Abraham, and to his seed for **e**. *G1519*
15:31 And he said unto him, Son, thou art **e** *G3842*
Jn 4:29 that **e** I did: is not this the Christ? *G3745*
39 testified, He told me all that **e** I did. *G3745*
6:51 he shall live for **e**: and the bread that I *G1519*
58 that eateth of this bread shall live for **e**. *G1519*
8:35 house for **e**: *but* the Son abideth ever. *G1519*
35 house for ever: *but* the Son abideth **e**. *G1519*
10: 8 All that **e** came before me are thieves *G3745*
12:34 Christ abideth for **e**: and how sayest *G1519*
14:16 that he may abide with you for **e**; *G1519*
18:20 openly to the world; I **e** taught in the *G3842*
Act 23:15 **e** he come near, are ready to kill him. *G4253*
Ro 1:25 the Creator, who is blessed for **e**. Amen. *G1519*
9: 5 is over all, God blessed for **e**. Amen. *G1519*
11:36 things: to whom *be* glory for **e**. Amen. *G1519*
16:27 glory through Jesus Christ for **e**. Amen. *G1519*
2Co 9: 9 poor: his righteousness remaineth for **e**. *G1519*
Gal 1: 5 To whom *be* glory for **e** and ever. Amen. *G165*
5 To whom *be* glory for ever and **e**. Amen. *G165*
Eph 5:29 For no man **e** yet hated his own flesh; *G4218*
Php 4:20 Father *be* glory for **e** and ever. Amen. *G165*
20 our Father *be* glory for ever and **e**. Amen. *G165*
1Th 4:17 air: and so shall we **e** be with the Lord. *G3842*
5:15 unto any *man*; but **e** follow that which *G3842*
1Ti 1:17 honour and glory for **e** and ever. Amen. *G165*
17 honour and glory for ever and **e**. Amen. *G165*
2Ti 3: 7 **E** learning, and never able to come to *G3842*
4:18 to whom *be* glory for **e** and ever. Amen. *G165*
18 to whom *be* glory for ever and **e**. Amen. *G165*
Phlm 15 that thou shouldest receive him for **e**; *G166*
Heb 1: 8 O God, *is* for **e** and ever: a sceptre of *G165*
8 God, *is* for ever and **e**: a sceptre of *G165*
5: 6 for **e** after the order of Melchisedec. *G1519*
6:20 for **e** after the order of Melchisedec. *G1519*
7:17 For he testifieth, Thou *art* a priest for **e** *G1519*
21 for **e** after the order of Melchisedec:) *G1519*
24 But this *man*, because he continueth **e**, *G1519*
25 **e** liveth to make intercession for them. *G3842*
10:12 **e**, sat down on the right hand of God; *G1519*
14 perfected for **e** them that are sanctified. *G1519*
13: 8 same yesterday, and to day, and for **e**. *G1519*
21 to whom *be* glory for **e** and ever. Amen. *G165*
21 to whom *be* glory for ever and **e**. Amen. *G165*
1Pt 1:23 of God, which liveth and abideth for **e**. *G1519*
25 But the word of the Lord endureth for **e**. *G1519*
4:11 and dominion for **e** and ever. Amen. *G165*
11 and dominion for ever and **e**. Amen. *G165*
5:11 To him *be* glory and dominion for **e** and *G165*
11 and dominion for ever and **e**. Amen. *G165*
2Pt 2:17 the mist of darkness is reserved for **e**. *G1519*
3:18 him *be* glory both now and for **e**. Amen. *G1519*
1Jn 2:17 that doeth the will of God abideth for **e**. *G1519*
2Jn 2 in us, and shall be with us for **e**. *G1519*
Jude 13 the blackness of darkness for **e**. *G1519*
25 and power, both now and **e**. Amen. *G1519*
Rev 1: 6 and dominion for **e** and ever. Amen. *G165*
6 and dominion for ever and **e**. Amen. *G165*
4: 9 on the throne, who liveth for **e** and ever, *G165*
9 on the throne, who liveth for ever and **e**, *G165*
10 him that liveth for **e** and ever, and cast *G165*
10 that liveth for ever and **e**, and cast their *G165*
5:13 and unto the Lamb for **e** and ever. *G165*
13 and unto the Lamb for ever and **e**. *G165*
14 him that liveth for **e** and ever. *G165*
14 him that liveth for ever and **e**. *G165*
7:12 *be* unto our God for **e** and ever. Amen. *G165*
12 *be* unto our God for ever and **e**. Amen. *G165*
10: 6 And sware by him that liveth for **e** and *G165*
Rev 10: 6 that liveth for ever and **e**, who created *G165*
11:15 Christ; and he shall reign for **e** and ever. *G165*
15 Christ; and he shall reign for ever and **e**. *G165*
14:11 ascendeth up for **e** and ever: and they *G165*
11 up for ever and **e**: and they have no rest *G165*
15: 7 wrath of God, who liveth for **e** and ever. *G165*
7 wrath of God, who liveth for ever and **e**. *G165*
19: 3 And her smoke rose up for **e** and ever. *G165*
3 And her smoke rose up for ever and **e**. *G165*
20:10 tormented day and night for **e** and ever. *G165*
10 tormented day and night for ever and **e**. *G165*
22: 5 light: and they shall reign for **e** and ever. *G165*
5 light: and they shall reign for ever and **e**. *G165*

EVERLASTING

Gen 9:16 remember the **e** covenant between God H5769
17: 7 generations for an **e** covenant, to be a H5769
8 **e** possession; and I will be their God. H5769
13 shall be in your flesh for an **e** covenant. H5769
19 with him for an **e** covenant, *and* with H5769
21:33 on the name of the LORD, the **e** God. H5769
48: 4 thy seed after thee *for* an **e** possession. H5769
49:26 bound of the **e** hills: they shall be on H5769
Ex 40:15 shall surely be an **e** priesthood H5769
Lev 16:34 And this shall be an **e** statute unto you, H5769
24: 8 the children of Israel by an **e** covenant. H5769
Nu 25:13 *even* the covenant of an **e** priesthood; H5769
Dt 33:27 *are* the **e** arms: and he shall thrust H5769
2Sa 23: 5 made with me an **e** covenant, ordered H5769
1Ch 16:17 a law, *and* to Israel *for* an **e** covenant, H5769
Ps 24: 7 be ye lift up, ye **e** doors; and the King H5769
9 lift *them* up, ye **e** doors; and the King H5769
41:13 **e**, and to everlasting. Amen, and Amen. H5769
13 everlasting, and to **e**. Amen, and Amen. H5769
90: 2 from **e** to everlasting, thou *art* God. H5769
2 from everlasting to **e**, thou *art* God. H5769
93: 2 *is* established of old: thou *art* from **e**. H5769
100: 5 For the LORD *is* good; his mercy *is* **e**; H5769
103:17 But the mercy of the LORD *is* from **e** to H5769
17 everlasting to **e** upon them that fear H5769
105:10 a law, *and* to Israel *for* an **e** covenant: H5769
106:48 God of Israel from **e** to everlasting: and H5769
48 everlasting to **e**: and let all the people H5769
112: 6 righteous shall be in **e** remembrance. H5769
119:142 Thy righteousness *is* an **e** H5769
144 of thy testimonies *is* **e**: give me H5769
139:24 way in me, and lead me in the way **e**. H5769
145:13 Thy kingdom *is* an **e** kingdom, and thy H5769
Prv 8:23 I was set up from **e**, from the beginning, H5769
10:25 but the righteous *is* an **e** foundation. H5769
Isa 9: 6 God, The **e** Father, The Prince of Peace. H5703
24: 5 the ordinance, broken the **e** covenant. H5769
26: 4 in the LORD JEHOVAH *is* **e** strength: H5769
33:14 among us shall dwell with **e** burnings? H5769
35:10 with songs and **e** joy upon their heads: H5769
40:28 not heard, *that* the **e** God, the LORD, H5769
45:17 the LORD with an **e** salvation: ye shall H5769
51:11 unto Zion; and **e** joy *shall be* upon their H5769
54: 8 a moment; but with **e** kindness will I H5769
55: 3 and I will make an **e** covenant with H5769
13 for an **e** sign *that* shall not be cut off. H5769
56: 5 an **e** name, that shall not be cut off. H5769
60:19 thee an **e** light, and thy God thy glory. H5769
20 shall be thine **e** light, and the days of H5769
61: 7 the double: **e** joy shall be unto them. H5769
8 I will make an **e** covenant with them. H5769
63:12 them, to make himself an **e** name? H5769
16 our redeemer; thy name *is* from **e**. H5769
Jer 10:10 living God, and an **e** king: at his wrath H5769
20:11 **e** confusion shall never be forgotten. H5769
23:40 And I will bring an **e** reproach upon H5769
31: 3 loved thee with an **e** love: therefore H5769
32:40 And I will make an **e** covenant with H5769
Ezk 16:60 will establish unto thee an **e** covenant. H5769
37:26 it shall be an **e** covenant with them: H5769
Dan 4: 3 his kingdom *is* an **e** kingdom, and his H5957
34 dominion *is* an **e** dominion, and his H5957
7:14 his dominion *is* an **e** dominion, which H5957
27 kingdom *is* an **e** kingdom, and all H5957
9:24 and to bring in **e** righteousness, and H5769
12: 2 awake, some to **e** life, and some to H5769
2 and some to shame *and* **e** contempt. H5769
Mic 5: 2 forth *have been* from of old, from **e**. H5769
Hab 1:12 *Art* thou not from **e**, O LORD my God, H6924
3: 6 the nations; and the **e** mountains were H5703
6 perpetual hills did bow: his ways *are* **e**. H5769
Mt 18: 8 hands or two feet to be cast into **e** fire. *G166*
19:29 an hundredfold, and shall inherit **e** life. *G166*
25:41 me, ye cursed, into **e** fire, prepared for *G166*

Mt 25:46 And these shall go away into e G166
Lk 16: 9 they may receive you into e habitations. G166
18:30 time, and in the world to come life e. G166
Jn 3:16 in him should not perish, but have e life. G166
36 He that believeth on the Son hath e life: G166
4:14 a well of water springing up into e life. G166
5:24 that sent me, hath e life, and shall not G166
6:27 endureth unto e life, which the Son of G166
40 on him, may have e life: and I will raise G166
47 you, He that believeth on me hath e life. G166
12:50 is life e: whatsoever I speak therefore, G166
Act 13:46 of e life, lo, we turn to the Gentiles. G166
Ro 6:22 fruit unto holiness, and the end e life. G166
16:26 of the e God, made known to G166
Gal 6: 8 to the Spirit shall of the Spirit reap life e. G166
2Th 1: 9 Who shall be punished with e G166
2:16 us, and hath given *us* e consolation and G166
1Ti 1:16 should hereafter believe on him to life e. G166
6:16 to whom *be* honour and power e. Amen. G166
Heb 13:20 through the blood of the e covenant, G166
2Pt 1:11 into the e kingdom of our Lord G166
Jude 6 he hath reserved in e chains under G126
Rev 14: 6 of heaven, having the e gospel to preach G166

EVERMORE
Dt 28:29 e, and no man shall save *thee*. H3605+H3117
2Sa 22:51 unto David, and to his seed for e. H5769
2Ki 17:37 to do for e; and ye shall not H3605+H3117
1Ch 17:14 his throne shall be established for e. H5769
Ps 16:11 thy right hand *there are* pleasures for e. H5331
18:50 to David, and to his seed for e. H5769
37:27 from evil, and do good; and dwell for e. H5769
77: 8 for ever? doth *his* promise fail for e? H1755
86:12 heart: and I will glorify thy name for e. H5769
89:28 My mercy will I keep for him for e, and H5769
52 Blessed *be* the LORD for e. Amen, and H5769
92: 8 But thou, LORD, *art most* high for e. H5769
105: 4 LORD, and his strength: seek his face e. H8548
106:31 unto all generations for e. H5769
113: 2 LORD from this time forth and for e. H5769
115:18 time forth and for e. Praise the LORD. H5769
121: 8 in from this time forth, and even for e. H5769
132:12 shall also sit upon thy throne for e. H5703
133: 3 the blessing, *even* life for e. H5769
Ezk 37:26 sanctuary in the midst of them for e. H5769
28 shall be in the midst of them for e. H5769
Jn 6:34 Then said they unto him, Lord, e give G3842
2Co 11:31 for e, knoweth that I lie not. G3588+G165
1Th 5:16 Rejoice e. G3842
Heb 7:28 Son, who is consecrated for e. G3588+G165
Rev 1:18 I am alive for e, Amen; and have G3588+G165

EVERY See the Appendix.

EVERYONE See EVERY and ONE.

EVERYTHING See EVERY and THING.

EVERYWHERE See EVERY and WHERE.

EVI
Nu 31: 8 slain; *namely,* E, and Rekem, and Zur, H189
Jos 13:21 princes of Midian, E, and Rekem, and H189

EVIDENCE
Jer 32:10 And I subscribed the e, and sealed *it,* H5612
11 So I took the e of the purchase, *both* H5612
12 And I gave the e of the purchase unto H5612
14 evidences, this e of the purchase, both H5612
14 is sealed, and this e which is open; and H5612
16 Now when I had delivered the e of the H5612
Heb 11: 1 hoped for, the e of things not seen. G1650

EVIDENCES
Jer 32:14 Israel; Take these e, this evidence of the H5612
44 and subscribe e, and seal *them,* and H5612

EVIDENT
Job 6:28 me; for *it is* e unto you if I lie. H5921+H6440
Gal 3:11 *it is* e: for, The just shall live by faith. G1212
Php 1:28 is to them an e token of perdition, but G1732
Heb 7:14 For *it is* e that our Lord sprang out of G4271
15 And it is yet far more e: for that after G2612

EVIDENTLY
Act 10: 3 He saw in a vision e about the ninth G5320
Gal 3: 1 been e set forth, crucified among you? G4270

EVIL
Gen 2: 9 the tree of knowledge of good and e. H7451
17 of good and e, thou shalt not eat of H7451
3: 5 shall be as gods, knowing good and e. H7451
22 to know good and e: and now, lest he H7451
6: 5 of his heart *was* only e continually. H7451
8:21 of man's heart *is* e from his youth; H7451
19:19 lest some e take me, and I die: H7451
37: 2 brought unto his father their e report. H7451
20 and we will say, Some e beast hath H7451
33 *is* my son's coat; an e beast hath H7451
44: 4 have ye rewarded e for good? H7451
5 he divineth? ye have done e in so doing. H7489
34 see the e that shall come on my father. H7451
47: 9 years: few and e have the days of the H7451
48:16 me from all e, bless the lads; and let H7451
50:15 us all the e which we did unto him. H7451
17 they did unto thee e: and now, we pray H7451
20 But as for you, ye thought e against H7451
Ex 5:19 see *that* they *were* in e *case,* after it was H7451
22 hast thou *so* e entreated this people? H7489
23 he hath done e to this people; neither H7489
10:10 little ones: look *to it;* for e *is* before you. H7451
23: 2 a multitude to *do* e; neither shalt thou H7451
32:12 and repent of this e against thy people. H7451
14 And the LORD repented of the e which H7451
33: 4 And when the people heard these e H7451
Lev 5: 4 with *his* lips to do e, or to do good, H7489
26: 6 and I will rid e beasts out of the land, H7451
Nu 13:32 And they brought up an e report of the H1681
14:27 How long *shall I bear with* this e H7451
35 do it unto all this e congregation, that H7451
37 Even those men that did bring up the e H7451
20: 5 us in unto this e place? it *is* no place H7451
32:13 that had done e in the sight of the H7451
Dt 1:35 these men of this e generation see that H7451
39 between good and e, they shall go in H7451
4:25 and shall do e in the sight of the LORD H7451
7:15 will put none of the e diseases of Egypt, H7451
13: 5 put the e away from the midst of thee. H7451
15: 9 and thine eye be e against thy poor H7489
17: 7 shalt put the e away from among you. H7451
12 thou shalt put away the e from Israel. H7451
19:19 thou put the e away from among you. H7451
20 no more any such e among you. H7451
21:21 so shalt thou put e away from among H7451
22:14 and bring up an e name upon her, and H7451
19 brought up an e name upon a virgin H7451
21 shalt thou put e away from among you. H7451
22 so shalt thou put away e from Israel. H7451
24 thou shalt put away e from among you. H7451
24: 7 thou shalt put e away from among you. H7451
26: 6 And the Egyptians e entreated us, and H7489
28:54 his eye shall be e toward his brother, H7489
56 her eye shall be e toward the husband H7489
29:21 separate him unto e out of all the tribes H7451
30:15 this day life and good, and death and e; H7451
31:29 you; and e will befall you in the H7451
29 because ye will do e in the sight of the H7451
Jos 23:15 bring upon you all e things, until he H7451
24:15 And if it seem e unto you to serve the H7489
Jdg 2:11 And the children of Israel did e in the H7451
15 against them for e, as the LORD had H7451
3: 7 And the children of Israel did e in the H7451
12 And the children of Israel did e again H7451
12 had done e in the sight of the LORD. H7451
4: 1 And the children of Israel again did e H7451
6: 1 And the children of Israel did e in the H7451
9:23 Then God sent an e spirit between H7451
57 And all the e of the men of Shechem H7451
10: 6 And the children of Israel did e again H7451
13: 1 And the children of Israel did e again H7451
20:13 and put away e from Israel. But the H7451
34 they knew not that e *was* near them. H7451
41 they saw that e was come upon them. H7451
1Sa 2:23 of your e dealings by all this people. H7451
6: 9 done us this great e: but if not, then we H7451
12:19 unto all our sins *this* e, to ask us a king. H7451
15:19 and didst e in the sight of the LORD? H7451
16:14 e spirit from the LORD troubled him. H7451
15 an e spirit from God troubleth thee. H7451
16 to pass, when the e spirit from God is H7451
23 And it came to pass, when the e spirit H7451
23 and the e spirit departed from him. H7451
18:10 the morrow, that the e spirit from God H7451
19: 9 And the e spirit from the LORD was H7451
20: 7 be sure that e is determined by him. H7451
9 certainly that e were determined by H7451
13 father *to do* thee e, then I will shew it H7451
1Sa 24:11 *there is* neither e nor transgression in H7451
17 good, whereas I have rewarded thee e. H7451
25: 3 *was* churlish and e in his doings; and H7451
17 what thou wilt do; for e is determined H7451
21 and he hath requited me e for good. H7451
26 that seek e to my lord, be as Nabal. H7451
28 of the LORD, and e hath not been H7451
39 his servant from e: for the LORD hath H7451
26:18 have I done? or what e *is* in mine hand? H7451
29: 6 I have not found e in thee since the day H7451
2Sa 3:39 doer of e according to his wickedness. H7451
12: 9 of the LORD, to do e in his sight? thou H7451
11 I will raise up e against thee out of H7451
13:16 *is* no cause: this e in sending me away H7451
15:14 and bring e upon us, and smite H7451
17:14 LORD might bring e upon Absalom. H7451
19: 7 thee than all the e that befell thee from H7451
35 between good and e? can thy servant H7451
24:16 him of the e, and said to the angel H7451
1Ki 5: 4 *is* neither adversary nor e occurrent. H7451
9: 9 the LORD brought upon them all this e. H7451
11: 6 And Solomon did e in the sight of the H7451
13:33 not from his e way, but made again H7451
14: 9 But hast done e above all that were H7489
10 Therefore, behold, I will bring e upon H7451
22 And Judah did e in the sight of the H7451
15:26 And he did e in the sight of the LORD, H7451
34 And he did e in the sight of the LORD, H7451
16: 7 even for all the e that he did in the sight H7451
19 For his sins which he sinned in doing e H7451
25 But Omri wrought e in the eyes of the H7451
30 And Ahab the son of Omri did e in the H7451
17:20 thou also brought e upon the widow H7489
21:20 to work e in the sight of the LORD, H7451
21 Behold, I will bring e upon thee, and H7451
29 I will not bring the e in his days: *but* in H7451
29 days will I bring the e upon his house. H7451
22: 8 me, but e. And Jehoshaphat said, H7451
18 prophesy no good concerning me, but e? H7451
23 LORD hath spoken e concerning thee. H7451
52 And he did e in the sight of the LORD, H7451
2Ki 3: 2 And he wrought e in the sight of the H7451
6:33 he said, Behold, this e *is* of the LORD; H7451
8:12 I know the e that thou wilt do unto H7451
18 and he did e in the sight of the LORD. H7451
27 of Ahab, and did e in the sight of the H7451
13: 2 And he did *that which was* e in the H7451
11 And he did *that which was* e in the H7451
14:24 And he did *that which was* e in the H7451
15: 9 And he did *that which was* e in the H7451
18 And he did *that which was* e in the H7451
24 And he did *that which was* e in the H7451
28 And he did *that which was* e in the H7451
17: 2 And he did *that which was* e in the H7451
13 Turn ye from your e ways, and keep H7451
17 themselves to do e in the sight of the H7451
21: 2 And he did *that which was* e in the H7451
9 them to do more e than did the nations H7451
12 I *am* bringing *such* e upon Jerusalem H7451
15 *that which was* e in my sight, and have H7451
16 *which was* e in the sight of the LORD. H7451
20 And he did *that which was* e in the H7451
22:16 I will bring e upon this place, and H7451
20 not see all the e which I will bring upon H7451
23:32 And he did *that which was* e in the H7451
37 And he did *that which was* e in the H7451
24: 9 And he did *that which was* e in the H7451
19 And he did *that which was* e in the H7451
1Ch 2: 3 of Judah, was e in the sight of the H7451
4:10 keep *me* from e, that it may not grieve H7451
7:23 because it went e with his house. H7451
21:15 him of the e, and said to the angel H7451
17 sinned and done e indeed; but *as for* H7489
2Ch 7:22 hath he brought all this e upon them. H7451
12:14 And he did e, because he prepared not H7451
18: 7 me, but always e: the same *is* Micaiah H7451
17 not prophesy good unto me, but e? H7451
22 the LORD hath spoken e against thee. H7451
20: 9 If, *when* e cometh upon us, *as* the H7451
21: 6 *which was* e in the eyes of the LORD. H7451
22: 4 Wherefore he did e in the sight of the H7451
29: 6 done *that which was* e in the eyes of the H7451
33: 2 But did *that which was* e in the sight of H7451
6 he wrought much e in the sight of the H7451
22 But he did *that which was* e in the sight H7451
34:24 I will bring e upon this place, and H7451
28 eyes see all the e that I will bring upon H7451
36: 5 *was* e in the sight of the LORD his God. H7451
9 *which was* e in the sight of the LORD. H7451

2Ch 36:12 And he did that which was e in the H7451
Ezr 9:13 upon us for our e deeds, and for our H7451
Neh 6:13 e report, that they might reproach me. H7451
9:28 But after they had rest, they did e again H7451
13: 7 understood of the e that Eliashib did H7451
17 unto them, What e thing is this that ye H7451
18 God bring all this e upon us, and upon H7451
27 you to do all this great e, to transgress H7451
Est 7: 7 e determined against him by the king. H7451
8: 6 For how can I endure to see the e that H7451
Job 1: 1 one that feared God, and eschewed e. H7451
8 one that feareth God, and escheweth e? H7451
2: 3 and escheweth e? and still he holdeth H7451
10 e? In all this did not Job sin with his lips. H7451
11 heard of all this e that was come upon H7451
5:19 in seven there shall no e touch thee. H7451
8:20 man, neither will he help the e doers: H7489
24:21 He e entreateth the barren that beareth H7462
28:28 and to depart from e is understanding. H7451
30:26 When I looked for good, then e came H7451
31:29 or lifted up myself when e found him: H7451
35:12 answer, because of the pride of e men. H7451
42:11 him over all the e that the LORD had H7451
Ps 5: 4 neither shall e dwell with thee. H7451
7: 4 If I have rewarded e unto him that was H7451
10:15 the wicked and the e man: seek out his H7451
15: 3 tongue, nor doeth e to his neighbour, H7451
21:11 For they intended e against thee: they H7451
23: 4 I will fear no e: for thou art with me; H7451
26: 5 I have hated the congregation of e H7451
34:13 Keep thy tongue from e, and thy lips H7451
14 Depart from e, and do good; seek peace, H7451
16 against them that do e, to cut off the H7451
21 E shall slay the wicked: and they that H7451
35:12 They rewarded me e for good to the H7451
36: 4 that is not good; he abhorreth not e. H7451
37: 8 fret not thyself in any wise to do e. H7489
19 They shall not be ashamed in the e H7451
27 Depart from e, and do good; and dwell H7451
38:20 They also that render e for good are H7451
40:14 and put to shame that wish me e. H7451
41: 5 Mine enemies speak e of me, When H7451
8 An e disease, say they, cleaveth fast H1100
49: 5 Wherefore should I fear in the days of e, H7451
50:19 Thou givest thy mouth to e, and thy H7451
51: 4 and done this e in thy sight: that thou H7451
52: 3 Thou lovest e more than good; and H7451
54: 5 He shall reward e unto mine enemies: H7451
56: 5 all their thoughts are against me for e. H7451
64: 5 They encourage themselves in an e H7451
78:49 by sending e angels among them. H7451
90:15 and the years wherein we have seen e. H7451
91:10 There shall no e befall thee, neither H7451
97:10 Ye that love the LORD, hate e: he H7451
109: 5 And they have rewarded me e for good, H7451
20 of them that speak e against my soul. H7451
112: 7 He shall not be afraid of e tidings: his H7451
119:101 I have refrained my feet from every e H7451
121: 7 from all e: he shall preserve thy soul. H7451
140: 1 Deliver me, O LORD, from the e man: H7451
11 Let not an e speaker be established in
11 in the earth: e shall hunt the violent H7451
141: 4 Incline not my heart to any e thing, to H7451
Prv 1:16 For their feet run to e, and make haste H7451
33 safely, and shall be quiet from fear of e. H7451
2:12 To deliver thee from the way of the e H7451
14 Who rejoice to do e, and delight in the H7451
3: 7 eyes: fear the LORD, and depart from e. H7451
29 Devise not e against thy neighbour, H7451
4:14 wicked, and go not in the way of e men. H7451
27 nor to the left: remove thy foot from e. H7451
5:14 I was almost in all e in the midst of the H7451
6:24 To keep thee from the e woman, from H7451
8:13 The fear of the LORD is to hate e: pride, H7451
13 and the e way, and the froward H7451
11:19 e pursueth it to his own death. H7451
12:12 The wicked desireth the net of e men: H7451
20 e: but to the counsellors of peace is joy. H7451
21 There shall no e happen to the just: but H205
13:19 abomination to fools to depart from e. H7451
21 E pursueth sinners: but to the H7451
14:16 e: but the fool rageth, and is confident. H7451
19 The e bow before the good; and the H7451
22 Do they not err that devise e? but mercy H7451
15: 3 place, beholding the e and the good. H7451
15 All the days of the afflicted are e: but he H7451
28 of the wicked poureth out e things. H7451
16: 4 yea, even the wicked for the day of e. H7451
6 fear of the LORD men depart from e. H7451
Prv 16:17 is to depart from e: he that keepeth his H7451
27 An ungodly man diggeth up e: and in H7451
30 moving his lips he bringeth e to pass. H7451
17:11 An e man seeketh only rebellion: H7451
13 Whoso rewardeth e for good, evil shall H7451
13 Whoso rewardeth evil for good, e shall H7451
19:23 satisfied; he shall not be visited with e. H7451
20: 8 scattereth away all e with his eyes. H7451
22 Say not thou, I will recompense e; but H7451
30 cleanseth away e: so do stripes the H7451
21:10 The soul of the wicked desireth e: his H7451
22: 3 A prudent man foreseeth the e, and H7451
23: 6 him that hath an e eye, neither desire H7451
24: 1 Be not thou envious against e men, H7451
8 He that deviseth to do e shall be called H7489
19 Fret not thyself because of e men, H7489
20 For there shall be no reward to the e H7451
27:12 A prudent man foreseeth the e, and H7451
28: 5 E men understand not judgment: but H7451
10 to go astray in an e way, he shall fall H7451
22 He that hasteth to be rich hath an e H7451
29: 6 In the transgression of an e man there H7451
30:32 e, lay thine hand upon thy mouth. H2161
31:12 She will do him good and not e all the H7451
Ecc 2:21 This also is vanity and a great e. H7451
4: 3 the e work that is done under the sun. H7451
5: 1 for they consider not that they do e. H7451
13 There is a sore e which I have seen H7451
14 But those riches perish by e travail: H7451
16 And this also is a sore e, that in all H7451
6: 1 There is an e which I have seen under H7451
2 it: this is vanity, and it is an e disease. H7451
8: 3 stand not in an e thing; for he doeth H7451
5 shall feel no e thing: and a wise man's H7451
11 Because sentence against an e work is H7451
11 sons of men is fully set in them to do e. H7451
12 Though a sinner do e an hundred H7451
9: 3 This is an e among all things that are H7451
3 of men is full of e, and madness is in H7451
12 are taken in an e net, and as the birds H7451
12 of men snared in an e time, when it H7451
10: 5 There is an e which I have seen under H7451
11: 2 not what e shall be upon the earth. H7451
10 and put away e from thy flesh: for H7451
12: 1 youth, while the e days come not, nor H7451
14 whether it be good, or whether it be e. H7451
Isa 1:16 put away the e of your doings from H7455
16 from before mine eyes; cease to do e; H7489
3: 9 they have rewarded e unto themselves. H7451
5:20 Woe unto them that call e good, and H7451
20 good, and good e; that put darkness for H7451
7: 5 taken e counsel against thee, saying, H7451
15 to refuse the e, and choose the good. H7451
16 know to refuse the e, and choose the H7451
13:11 And I will punish the world for their e, H7451
31: 2 Yet he also is wise, and will bring e, and H7451
32: 7 The instruments also of the churl are e: H7451
33:15 and shutteth his eyes from seeing e; H7451
41:23 yea, do good, or do e, that we may be H7489
45: 7 create e: I the LORD do all these things. H7451
47:11 Therefore shall e come upon thee; thou H7451
56: 2 and keepeth his hand from doing any e. H7451
57: 1 is taken away from the e to come. H7451
59: 7 Their feet run to e, and they make haste H7451
15 that departeth from e maketh himself a H7451
65:12 not hear; but did e before mine eyes, H7451
66: 4 hear: but they did e before mine eyes, H7451
Jer 1:14 of the north an e shall break forth upon H7451
2: 3 him shall offend; e shall come upon H7451
19 see that it is an e thing and bitter, that H7451
3: 5 and done e things as thou couldest. H7451
17 after the imagination of their e heart. H7451
4: 4 it, because of the e of your doings. H7455
6 for I will bring e from the north, and H7451
22 they are wise to do e, but to do good H7489
5:12 not he; neither shall e come upon us; H7451
6: 1 for e appeareth out of the H7451
19 Hear, O earth: behold, I will bring e H7451
7:24 of their e heart, and went backward, H7451
30 For the children of Judah have done e H7451
8: 3 remain of this e family, which remain H7451
9: 3 they proceed from e to evil, and they H7451
3 from evil to e, and they know not me, H7451
10: 5 e, neither also is it in them to do good. H7489
11: 8 of their e heart: therefore I will H7451
11 I will bring e upon them, which they H7451
15 when thou doest e, then thou rejoicest. H7451
17 hath pronounced e against thee, for the H7451
17 thee, for the e of the house of Israel H7451
Jer 11:23 them: for I will bring e upon the men of H7451
12:14 Thus saith the LORD against all mine e H7451
13:10 This e people, which refuse to hear my H7451
23 do good, that are accustomed to do e. H7489
15:11 time of e and in the time of affliction. H7451
16:10 all this great e against us? or what H7451
12 imagination of his e heart, that they H7451
17:17 me: thou art my hope in the day of e. H7451
18 them the day of e, and destroy them H7451
18: 8 turn from their e, I will repent of the H7451
8 of the e that I thought to do unto them. H7451
10 If it do e in my sight, that it obey not H7451
11 Behold, I frame e against you, and H7451
11 every one from his e way, and make H7451
12 one do the imagination of his e heart. H7451
20 Shall e be recompensed for good? for H7451
19: 3 I will bring e upon this place, the H7451
15 all her towns all the e that I have H7451
21:10 this city for e, and not for good, saith H7451
12 it, because of the e of your doings. H7455
23: 2 the e of your doings, saith the LORD. H7455
10 course is e, and their force is not right. H7451
12 for I will bring e upon them, even the H7451
17 own heart, No e shall come upon you. H7451
22 them from their e way, and from the H7451
22 way, and from the e of their doings. H7455
24: 3 figs, very good; and the e, very evil, that H7451
3 e, that cannot be eaten, they are so evil. H7451
3 evil, that cannot be eaten, they are so e. H7455
8 And as the e figs, which cannot be H7451
8 be eaten, they are so e; surely thus saith H7455
25: 5 every one from his e way, and from the H7451
5 evil way, and from the e of your doings, H7455
29 For, lo, I begin to bring e on the city H7489
32 of hosts, Behold, e shall go forth from H7451
26: 3 man from his e way, that I may repent H7451
3 repent me of the e, which I purpose to H7451
3 them because of the e of their doings. H7455
13 e that he hath pronounced against you. H7451
19 him of the e which he had pronounced H7451
19 we procure great e against our souls. H7451
28: 8 of war, and of e, and of pestilence. H7451
29:11 not of e, to give you an expected end. H7451
17 figs, that cannot be eaten, they are so e. H7455
32:23 caused all this e to come upon them: H7451
30 have only done e before me from their H7451
32 Because of all the e of the children of H7451
42 all this great e upon this people, so H7451
35:15 man from his e way, and amend your H7451
17 of Jerusalem all the e that I have H7451
36: 3 will hear all the e which I purpose to do H7451
3 man from his e way; that I may forgive H7451
7 every one from his e way: for great is H7451
31 men of Judah, all the e that I have H7451
38: 9 men have done e in all that they have H7489
39:16 upon this city for e, and not for good; H7451
40: 2 pronounced this e upon this place. H7451
41:11 heard of all the e that Ishmael the son H7451
42: 6 Whether it be good, or whether it be e, H7451
10 me of the e that I have done unto you. H7451
17 from the e that I will bring upon them. H7451
44: 2 have seen all the e that I have brought H7451
7 ye this great e against your souls, H7451
11 you for e, and to cut off all Judah. H7451
17 of victuals, and were well, and saw no e. H7451
22 because of the e of your doings, and H7455
23 e is happened unto you, as at this day. H7451
27 Behold, I will watch over them for e, H7451
29 shall surely stand against you for e: H7451
45: 5 I will bring e upon all flesh, saith H7451
48: 2 they have devised e against it; come, H7451
49:23 for they have heard e tidings: they are H7451
37 and I will bring e upon them, even my H7451
51:24 Chaldea all their e that they have done H7451
60 So Jeremiah wrote in a book all the e H7451
64 not rise from the e that I will bring H7451
52: 2 And he did that which was e in the eyes H7451
Lam 3:38 most High proceedeth not e and good? H7451
Ezk 5:16 When I shall send upon them the e H7451
17 So will I send upon you famine and e H7451
6:10 vain that I would do this e unto them. H7451
11 Alas for all the e abominations of the H7451
7: 5 Thus saith the Lord GOD; An e, an only H7451
5 An evil, an only e, behold, is come. H7451
14:22 concerning the e that I have brought H7451
33:11 turn ye from your e ways; for why will H7451
34:25 and will cause the e beasts to cease out H7451
36:31 Then shall ye remember your own e H7451
38:10 and thou shalt think an e thought: H7451

Dan 9:12 upon us a great **e**: for under the whole H7451
13 of Moses, all this **e** is come upon us: yet H7451
14 watched upon the **e**, and brought it H7451
Joel 2:13 kindness, and repenteth him of the **e**. H7451
Am 3: 6 shall there be **e** in a city, and the LORD H7451
5:13 silence in that time; for it *is* an **e** time. H7451
14 Seek good, and not **e**, that ye may live: H7451
15 Hate the **e**, and love the good, and H7451
6: 3 Ye that put far away the **e** day, and H7451
9: 4 eyes upon them for **e**, and not for good. H7451
10 **e** shall not overtake nor prevent us. H7451
Jna 1: 7 whose cause this **e** *is* upon us. So they H7451
8 whose cause this **e** *is* upon us; What *is* H7451
3: 8 every one from his **e** way, and from the H7451
10 they turned from their **e** way; and God H7451
10 repented of the **e**, that he had said that H7451
4: 2 kindness, and repentest thee of the **e**. H7451
Mic 1:12 for good: but **e** came down from the H7451
2: 1 iniquity, and work **e** upon their beds! H7451
3 do I devise an **e**, from which ye shall H7451
3 shall ye go haughtily: for this time *is* **e**. H7451
3: 2 Who hate the good, and love the **e**; who H7451
11 among us? none **e** can come upon us. H7451
7: 3 That they may do **e** with both hands H7451
Nah 1:11 that imagineth **e** against the LORD, a H7451
Hab 1:13 *Thou art* of purer eyes than to behold **e**, H7451
2: 9 Woe to him that coveteth an **e** H7451
9 may be delivered from the power of **e**! H7451
Zep 1:12 will not do good, neither will he do **e**. H7489
3:15 of thee: thou shalt not see **e** any more. H7451
Zec 1: 4 ye now from your **e** ways, and *from* H7451
4 and *from* your **e** doings: but they did H7451
7:10 **e** against his brother in your heart. H7451
8:17 And let none of you imagine **e** in your H7451
Mal 1: 8 sacrifice, *is it* not **e**? and if ye offer the H7451
8 and sick, *is it* not **e**? offer it now unto H7451
2:17 one that doeth **e** *is* good in the sight H7451
Mt 5:11 all manner of **e** against you G4190+G4487
37 is more than these cometh of **e**. G4190
39 But I say unto you, That ye resist not **e**: G4190
45 sun to rise on the **e** and on the good, G4190
6:13 but deliver us from **e**: For thine is the G4190
23 But if thine eye be **e**, thy whole body G4190
34 Sufficient unto the day *is* the **e** thereof. G2549
7:11 If ye then, being **e**, know how to give G4190
17 but a corrupt tree bringeth forth **e** fruit. G4190
18 A good tree cannot bring forth **e** fruit, G4190
9: 4 Wherefore think ye **e** in your hearts? G4190
12:34 how can ye, being **e**, speak good things? G4190
35 things: and an **e** man out of the evil G4190
35 **e** treasure bringeth forth evil things. G4190
35 evil treasure bringeth forth **e** things. G4190
39 said unto them, An **e** and adulterous G4190
15:19 For out of the heart proceed **e** thoughts, G4190
20:15 own? Is thine eye **e**, because I am good? G4190
24:48 But and if that **e** servant shall say in his G2556
27:23 And the governor said, Why, what **e** G2556
Mk 3: 4 days, or to do **e**? to save life, or to kill? G2554
7:21 of men, proceed **e** thoughts, adulteries, G2556
22 **e** eye, blasphemy, pride, foolishness: G4190
23 All these **e** things come from within, G4190
9:39 name, that can lightly speak **e** of me. G2551
15:14 them, Why, what **e** hath he done? And G2556
Lk 6: 9 or to do **e**? to save life, or to destroy *it*? G2554
22 name as **e**, for the Son of man's sake. G4190
35 kind unto the unthankful and *to* the **e**. G4190
45 is good; and an **e** man out of the evil G4190
45 man out of the **e** treasure of his heart G4190
45 bringeth forth that which is **e**: for of the G4190
7:21 and plagues, and of **e** spirits; and unto G4190
8: 2 been healed of **e** spirits and infirmities, G4190
11: 4 into temptation; but deliver us from **e**. G4190
13 If ye then, being **e**, know how to give G4190
29 to say, This is an **e** generation: they G4190
34 is **e**, thy body also *is* full of darkness. G4190
16:25 likewise Lazarus **e** things: but now he G2556
23:22 time, Why, what **e** hath he done? I have G2556
Jn 3:19 than light, because their deeds were **e**. G4190
20 For every one that doeth **e** hateth the G5337
5:29 **e**, unto the resurrection of damnation. G5337
7: 7 testify of it, that the works thereof are **e**. G4190
17:15 thou shouldest keep them from the **e**. G4190
18:23 Jesus answered him, If I have spoken **e**, G2560
23 the **e**: but if well, why smitest thou me? G2556
Act 7: 6 and entreat *them* **e** four hundred years. G2559
19 with our kindred, and **e** entreated our G2559
9:13 man, how much **e** he hath done to thy G2556
14: 2 minds **e** affected against the brethren. G2559
19: 9 not, but spake **e** of that way before the G2551
Act 19:12 and the **e** spirits went out of them. G4190
13 them which had **e** spirits the name of G4190
15 And the **e** spirit answered and said, G4190
16 And the man in whom the **e** spirit was G4190
23: 5 not speak **e** of the ruler of thy people. G2560
9 We find no **e** in this man: but if a G2556
24:20 have found any **e** doing in me, while I G92
Ro 1:30 of **e** things, disobedient to parents, G2556
2: 9 of man that doeth **e**, of the Jew first, G2556
3: 8 that we say,) Let us do **e**, that good may G2556
7:19 but the **e** which I would not, that I do. G2556
21 I would do good, **e** is present with me. G2556
9:11 done any good or **e**, that the purpose of G2556
12: 9 which is **e**; cleave to that which is good. G4190
17 Recompense to no man **e** for evil. G2556
17 Recompense to no man evil for **e**. G2556
21 Be not overcome of **e**, but overcome evil G2556
21 of evil, but overcome **e** with good. G2556
13: 3 works, but to the **e**. Wilt thou then not G2556
4 thou do that which is **e**, be afraid; for he G2556
4 to *execute* wrath upon him that doeth **e**. G2556
14:16 Let not then your good be **e** spoken of:
20 **e** for that man who eateth with offence. G2556
16:19 which is good, and simple concerning **e**. G2556
1Co 10: 6 lust after **e** things, as they also lusted. G2556
30 a partaker, why am I **e** spoken of for that G987
13: 5 is not easily provoked, thinketh no **e**; G2556
15:33 Be not deceived: **e** communications G2556
2Co 6: 8 By honour and dishonour, by **e** report G1426
13: 7 Now I pray to God that ye do no **e**; not G2556
Gal 1: 4 from this present **e** world, according to G4190
Eph 4:31 and clamour, and **e** speaking, be put G988
5:16 the time, because the days are **e**. G4190
6:13 **e** day, and having done all, to stand. G4190
Php 3: 2 Beware of dogs, beware of **e** workers, G2556
Col 3: 5 affection, **e** concupiscence, and G2556
1Th 5:15 See that none render **e** for evil unto any G2556
15 See that none render evil for **e** unto any G2556
22 Abstain from all appearance of **e**. G4190
2Th 3: 3 shall stablish you, and keep *you* from **e**. G4190
1Ti 6: 4 envy, strife, railings, **e** surmisings, G4190
10 For the love of money is the root of all **e**: G2556
2Ti 2: 9 Wherein I suffer trouble, as an **e** doer, G2557
3:13 But **e** men and seducers shall wax G4190
4:14 did me much **e**: the Lord reward him G2556
18 deliver me from every **e** work, and will G4190
Tit 1:12 *are* alway liars, **e** beasts, slow bellies. G2556
2: 8 having no **e** thing to say of you. G5337
3: 2 To speak **e** of no man, to be no brawlers, G987
Heb 3:12 in any of you an **e** heart of unbelief, in G4190
5:14 exercised to discern both good and **e**. G2556
10:22 sprinkled from an **e** conscience, and G4190
Jas 1:13 with **e**, neither tempteth he any man: G2556
2: 4 and are become judges of **e** thoughts? G4190
3: 8 *it is* an unruly **e**, full of deadly poison. G2556
16 *is*, there *is* confusion and every **e** work. G5337
4:11 Speak not **e** one of another, brethren. G2635
11 He that speaketh **e** of *his* brother, and G2635
11 his brother, speaketh **e** of the law, and G2635
16 in your boastings: all such rejoicing is **e**. G4190
1Pt 2: 1 and envies, and all **e** speakings, G2636
3: 9 Not rendering **e** for evil, or railing for G2556
9 Not rendering evil for **e**, or railing for G2556
10 **e**, and his lips that they speak no guile: G2556
11 Let him eschew **e**, and do good; let him G2556
12 of the Lord *is* against them that do **e**. G2556
16 they speak **e** of you, as of evildoers, G2635
17 suffer for well doing, than for **e** doing. G2554
4: 4 same excess of riot, speaking **e** of *you*: G987
14 on their part he is **e** spoken of, but on G987
2Pt 2: 2 the way of truth shall be **e** spoken of. G987
10 are not afraid to speak **e** of dignities. G987
12 destroyed, speak **e** of the things that they G987
1Jn 3:12 were **e**, and his brother's righteous. G4190
2Jn 11 God speed is partaker of his **e** deeds. G4190
3Jn 11 Beloved, follow not that which is **e**, but G2556
11 but he that doeth **e** hath not seen God. G2554
Jude 8 dominion, and speak **e** of dignities. G987
10 But these speak **e** of those things which G987
Rev 2: 2 them which are **e**: and thou hast tried G2556

EVILDOER
Isa 9:17 an hypocrite and an **e**, and every mouth H7489
1Pt 4:15 *as* a thief, or *as* an **e**, or as a busybody G2555

EVILDOERS
Ps 37: 1 Fret not thyself because of **e**, neither be H7489
9 For **e** shall be cut off: but those that H7489
94:16 Who will rise up for me against the **e**? *or* H7489
Ps119:115 Depart from me, ye **e**: for I will keep the H7489
Isa 1: 4 iniquity, a seed of **e**, children that are H7489
14:20 the seed of **e** shall never be renowned. H7489
31: 2 the house of the **e**, and against the help H7489
Jer 20:13 the soul of the poor from the hand of **e**. H7489
23:14 also the hands of **e**, that none doth H7489
1Pt 2:12 against you as **e**, they may by *your* good G2555
14 the punishment of **e**, and for the praise G2555
3:16 speak evil of you, as of **e**, they may be G2555

EVILFAVOUREDNESS
Dt 17: 1 blemish, *or* any **e**: for that *is* an H7451+H1697

EVIL-MERODACH
2Ki 25:27 of the month, *that* **E** king of Babylon in H192
Jer 52:31 of the month, *that* **E** king of Babylon in H192

EVILS
Dt 31:17 and many **e** and troubles shall befall H7451
17 that day, Are not these **e** come upon us, H7451
18 in that day for all the **e** which they shall H7451
21 pass, when many **e** and troubles are H7451
Ps 40:12 For innumerable **e** have compassed me H7451
Jer 2:13 For my people have committed two **e**; H7451
Ezk 6: 9 themselves for the **e** which they have H7451
20:43 for all your **e** that ye have committed. H7451
Lk 3:19 for all the **e** which Herod had done, G4190

EWE
Gen 21:28 And Abraham set seven **e** lambs of the H3535
29 *mean* these seven **e** lambs which thou H3535
30 And he said, For *these* seven **e** lambs H3535
Lev 14:10 blemish, and one **e** lamb of the first H3535
22:28 And *whether it be* cow or **e**, ye shall not H7716
Nu 6:14 offering, and one **e** lamb of the first H3535
2Sa 12: 3 save one little **e** lamb, which he had H3535

EWE-LAMB See EWE and LAMB.

EWES
Gen 31:38 with thee; thy **e** and thy she goats have H7353
32:14 goats, two hundred **e**, and twenty rams, H7353
Ps 78:71 From following the **e** great with young H5763

EXACT
Dt 15: 2 *it;* he shall not **e** *it* of his neighbour, H5065
3 Of a foreigner thou mayest **e** *it again*: H5065
Neh 5: 7 unto them, Ye **e** usury, every one of H5378
10 servants, might **e** of them money and H5383
11 the wine, and the oil, that ye **e** of them. H5383
Ps 89:22 The enemy shall not **e** upon him; nor H5378
Isa 58: 3 find pleasure, and **e** all your labours. H5065
Lk 3:13 And he said unto them, **E** no more G4238

EXACTED
2Ki 15:20 And Menahem **e** the money of Israel, H3318
23:35 of Pharaoh: he **e** the silver and the gold H5065

EXACTETH
Job 11: 6 therefore that God **e** of thee *less* than H5382

EXACTION
Neh 10:31 seventh year, and the **e** of every debt. H4853

EXACTIONS
Ezk 45: 9 **e** from my people, saith the Lord GOD. H1646

EXACTORS
Isa 60:17 peace, and thine **e** righteousness. H5065

EXALT
Ex 15: 2 my father's God, and I will **e** him. H7311
1Sa 2:10 king, and **e** the horn of his anointed. H7311
Job 17: 4 therefore shalt thou not **e** *them*. H7311
Ps 34: 3 me, and let us **e** his name together. H7311
37:34 way, and he shall **e** thee to inherit the H7311
66: 7 not the rebellious **e** themselves. Selah. H7311
92:10 But my horn shalt thou **e** like *the horn* H7311
99: 5 **E** ye the LORD our God, and worship at H7311
9 **E** the LORD our God, and worship at H7311
107:32 Let them **e** him also in the H7311
118:28 thee: *thou art* my God, I will **e** thee. H7311
140: 8 device; *lest* they **e** themselves. Selah. H7311
Prv 4: 8 **E** her, and she shall promote thee: she H5549
Isa 13: 2 high mountain, **e** the voice unto them, H7311
14:13 into heaven, I will **e** my throne above H7311
25: 1 O LORD, thou *art* my God; I will **e** thee, H7311
Ezk 21:26 not *be* the same: **e** *him that is* low, and H1361
29:15 neither shall it **e** itself any more above H5375

E

Ezk 31:14 by the waters e themselves for their H1361
Dan 11:14 of thy people shall e themselves to H5375
36 his will; and he shall e himself, and H7311
Hos 11: 7 the most High, none at all would e *him*. H7311
Oba 4 Though thou e *thyself* as the eagle, and H1361
Mt 23:12 And whosoever shall e himself shall be *G5312*
2Co 11:20 *of you*, if a man e himself, if a man *G1869*
1Pt 5: 6 of God, that he may e you in due time: *G5312*

EXALTED

Nu 24: 7 than Agag, and his kingdom shall be e. H5375
1Sa 2: 1 mine horn is e in the LORD: my mouth H7311
2Sa 5:12 and that he had e his kingdom for his H5375
22:47 *be* my rock; and e be the God of the H7311
1Ki 1: 5 Then Adonijah the son of Haggith e H5375
14: 7 Forasmuch as I e thee from among the H7311
16: 2 Forasmuch as I e thee out of the dust, H7311
2Ki 19:22 whom hast thou e *thy* voice, and lifted H7311
1Ch 29:11 and thou art e as head above all. H5375
Neh 9: 5 is e above all blessing and praise. H7311
Job 5:11 those which mourn may be e to safety. H7682
24:24 They are e for a little while, but are H7426
36: 7 establish them for ever, and they are e. H1361
Ps 12: 8 every side, when the vilest men are e. H7311
13: 2 long shall mine enemy be e over me? H7311
18:46 and let the God of my salvation be e. H7311
21:13 Be thou e, LORD, in thine own strength: H7311
46:10 that I *am* God: I will be e among the H7311
10 the heathen, I will be e in the earth. H7311
47: 9 earth *belong* unto God: he is greatly e. H5927
57: 5 Be thou e, O God, above the heavens; *let* H7311
11 Be thou e, O God, above the heavens: *let* H7311
75:10 *but* the horns of the righteous shall be e. H7311
89:16 and in thy righteousness shall they be e. H7311
17 and in thy favour our horn shall be e. H7311
19 I have e *one* chosen out of the people. H7311
24 and in my name shall his horn be e. H7311
97: 9 the earth: thou art e far above all gods. H5927
108: 5 Be thou e, O God, above the heavens: H7311
112: 9 ever; his horn shall be e with honour. H7311
118:16 The right hand of the LORD is e: the H7426
Prv 11:11 upright the city is e: but it is overthrown H7311
Isa 2: 2 and shall be e above the hills; and H5375
11 the LORD alone shall be e in that day. H7682
17 the LORD alone shall be e in that day. H7682
5:16 But the LORD of hosts shall be e in H1361
12: 4 make mention that his name is e. H7682
30:18 will he be e, that he may have mercy H7311
33: 5 The LORD is e; for he dwelleth on high: H7682
10 now will I be e; now will I lift up myself. H7426
37:23 whom hast thou e *thy* voice, and lifted H7311
40: 4 Every valley shall be e, and every H5375
49:11 a way, and my highways shall be e. H7311
52:13 be e and extolled, and be very high. H7311
Ezk 17:24 the high tree, have e the low tree, have H1361
19:11 and her stature was e among the thick H1361
31: 5 Therefore his height was e above all the H1361
Hos 13: 1 When Ephraim spake trembling, he e H5375
6 was e; therefore have they forgotten me. H7311
Mic 4: 1 and it shall be e above the hills; and H5375
Mt 11:23 And thou, Capernaum, which art e *G5312*
23:12 he that shall humble himself shall be e. *G5312*
Lk 1:52 *their* seats, and e them of low degree. *G5312*
10:15 And thou, Capernaum, which art e to *G5312*
14:11 and he that humbleth himself shall be e. *G5312*
18:14 and he that humbleth himself shall be e. *G5312*
Act 2:33 the right hand of God e, and having *G5312*
5:31 Him hath God e with his right hand *to* *G5312*
13:17 our fathers, and e the people when they *G5312*
2Co 11: 7 that ye might be e, because I have *G5312*
12: 7 And lest I should be e above measure *G5229*
7 me, lest I should be e above measure. *G5229*
Php 2: 9 Wherefore God also hath highly e him, *G5251*
Jas 1: 9 of low degree rejoice in that he is e: *G5311*

EXALTEST

Ex 9:17 As yet e thou thyself against my people, H5549

EXALTETH

Job 36:22 Behold, God e by his power: who H7682
Ps 148:14 He also e the horn of his people, the H7311
Prv 14:29 but *he that is* hasty of spirit e folly. H7311
34 Righteousness e a nation: but sin *is* a H7311
17:19 he that e his gate seeketh destruction. H1361
Lk 14:11 For whosoever e himself shall be *G5312*
18:14 for every one that e himself shall be *G5312*
2Co 10: 5 every high thing that e itself against the *G1869*
2Th 2: 4 Who opposeth and e himself above all *G5229*

EXAMINATION

Act 25:26 e had, I might have somewhat to write. *G351*

EXAMINE

Ezr 10:16 day of the tenth month to e the matter. H1875
Ps 26: 2 E me, O LORD, and prove me; try my H974
1Co 9: 3 Mine answer to them that do e me is *G350*
11:28 But let a man e himself, and so let him *G1381*
2Co 13: 5 E yourselves, whether ye be in the *G3985*

EXAMINED

Lk 23:14 behold, I, having e *him* before you, have *G350*
Act 4: 9 If we this day be e of the good deed done *G350*
12:19 found him not, he e the keepers, and *G350*
22:24 that he should be e by scourging; that he *G426*
29 which should have e him: and the chief *G426*
28:18 Who, when they had e me, would have *G350*

EXAMINING

Act 24: 8 to come unto thee: by e of whom thyself *G350*

EXAMPLE

Mt 1:19 e, was minded to put her away privily. *G3856*
Jn 13:15 For I have given you an e, that ye *G5262*
1Ti 4:12 but be thou an e of the believers, in *G5179*
Heb 4:11 man fall after the same e of unbelief. *G5262*
8: 5 Who serve unto the e and shadow of *G5262*
Jas 5:10 name of the Lord, for an e of suffering *G5262*
1Pt 2:21 us an e, that ye should follow his steps: *G5261*
Jude 7 flesh, are set forth for an e, suffering the *G1164*

EXAMPLES

1Co 10: 6 Now these things were our e, to the *G5179*

EXCEED

Dt 25: 3 give him, *and* not e: lest, *if* he should H3254
3 lest, *if* he should e, and beat him above H3254
Mt 5:20 shall e *the righteousness* of *G4052*
2Co 3: 9 of righteousness e in glory. *G4052*

EXCEEDED

1Sa 20:41 wept one with another, until David e. H1431
1Ki 10:23 So king Solomon e all the kings of the H1431
Job 36: 9 their transgressions that they have e. H1396

EXCEEDEST

2Ch 9: 6 me: *for* thou e the fame that I heard. H3254

EXCEEDETH

1Ki 10: 7 prosperity e the fame which I heard. H3254

EXCEEDING

Gen 15: 1 I *am* thy shield, *and* thy e great reward. H3966
17: 6 And I will make thee e fruitful, and I H3966
27:34 with a great and e bitter cry, and said H3966
Ex 1: 7 and waxed e mighty; and the land H3966
19:16 of the trumpet e loud; so that all the H3966
Nu 14: 7 through to search it, *is* an e good land. H3966
1Sa 2: 3 Talk no more so e proudly; let *not* H1364
2Sa 8: 8 king David took e much brass. H3966
12: 2 The rich *man* had e many flocks and H3966
1Ki 4:29 understanding e much, and largeness H3966
7:47 because they were e many: neither was H3966
1Ch 20: 2 also e much spoil out of the city. H3966
22: 5 for the LORD *must be* e magnifical, of H4605
2Ch 11:12 made them e strong, having H7235+H3966
14:14 for there was e much spoil in them. H7235
16:12 until his disease *was* e *great:* yet in his H4605
32:27 And Hezekiah had e much riches and H3966
Ps 21: 6 made him e glad with thy countenance. H2302
43: 4 God, unto God my e joy: yea, upon the H8057
119:96 *but* thy commandment *is* e broad. H3966
Prv 30:24 little upon the earth, but they *are* e wise:
Ecc 7:24 That which is far off, and e deep, who
Jer 48:29 of Moab, (he is e proud) his loftiness, H3966
Ezk 9: 9 and Judah *is* e great, and the land H3966
16:13 oil: and thou wast e beautiful, and thou H3966
23:15 Girded with girdles upon their loins, e H5628
37:10 up upon their feet, an e great army. H3966
47:10 as the fish of the great sea, e many. H3966
Dan 3:22 and the furnace e hot, the flame of the H3493
6:23 Then was the king e glad for him, and H7690
7:19 all the others, e dreadful, whose teeth H3493
8: 9 which waxed e great, toward the south, H3499
Jna 3: 3 an e great city of three days' journey. H430
4: 6 grief. So Jonah was e glad of the gourd. H1419
Mt 2:10 the star, they rejoiced with e great joy. *G4970*
16 of the wise men, was e wroth, and sent *G3029*
4: 8 him up into an e high mountain, and *G3029*
5:12 Rejoice, and be e glad: for great *is* your
8:28 out of the tombs, e fierce, so that no *G3029*
17:23 be raised again. And they were e sorry. *G4970*
26:22 And they were e sorrowful, and began *G4970*
38 Then saith he unto them, My soul is e *G4036*
Mk 6:26 And the king was e sorry; *yet* for his *G4036*
9: 3 And his raiment became shining, e *G3029*
14:34 And saith unto them, My soul is e *G4036*
Lk 23: 8 And when Herod saw Jesus, he was e *G3029*
Act 7:20 was born, and was e fair, and *G3588+G2316*
Ro 7:13 might become e sinful. *G2596+G5236*
2Co 4:17 e *and* eternal weight of glory; *G2596+G5236*
7: 4 I am e joyful in all our tribulation. *G5248*
9:14 after you for the e grace of God in you. *G5235*
Eph 1:19 And what *is* the e greatness of his *G5235*
2: 7 he might shew the e riches of his grace *G5235*
3:20 Now unto him that is able to do e *G5228*
1Ti 1:14 And the grace of our Lord was e *G5250*
1Pt 4:13 revealed, ye may be glad also with e joy.
2Pt 1: 4 Whereby are given unto us e great and
Jude 24 the presence of his glory with e joy,
Rev 16:21 hail; for the plague thereof was e great. *G4970*

EXCEEDINGLY

Gen 7:19 And the waters prevailed e upon the H3966
13:13 wicked and sinners before the LORD e. H3966
16:10 multiply thy seed e, that it shall not be H7235
17: 2 me and thee, and will multiply thee e. H3966
20 will multiply him e; twelve princes shall H3966
27:33 And Isaac trembled very e, and said, H1419
30:43 And the man increased e, and had H3966
47:27 therein, and grew, and multiplied e. H3966
1Sa 26:21 I have played the fool, and have erred e. H3966
2Sa 13:15 Then Amnon hated her e; so that the H3966
2Ki 10: 4 But they were e afraid, and said, H3966
1Ch 29:25 And the LORD magnified Solomon e in H4605
2Ch 1: 1 *was* with him, and magnified him e. H4605
17:12 And Jehoshaphat waxed great e; and he H4605
26: 8 of Egypt; for he strengthened *himself* e. H4605
Neh 2:10 *of it*, it grieved them e that there was H1419
Est 4: 4 was the queen e grieved; and she sent H3966
Job 3:22 Which rejoice e, *and* are glad, when H1524
Ps 68: 3 before God: yea, let them e rejoice. H8057
106:14 But lusted e in the wilderness, and H8378
119:167 kept thy testimonies; and I love them e. H3966
123: 3 us: for we are e filled with contempt. H7227
4 Our soul is e filled with the scorning of H7227
Isa 24:19 is clean dissolved, the earth is moved e. H4131
Dan 7: 7 and strong e; and it had great iron H3493
Jna 1:10 Then were the men e afraid, and said H1419
16 Then the men feared the LORD e, and H1419
4: 1 But it displeased Jonah e, and he was H1419
Mt 19:25 When his disciples heard *it*, they were e *G4970*
Mk 4:41 And they feared e, and said one *G5401+G3173*
15:14 they cried out the more e, Crucify him. *G4056*
Act 16:20 men, being Jews, do e trouble our city, *G1613*
26:11 and being e mad against them, *G4057*
27:18 And we being e tossed with a tempest, *G4971*
2Co 7:13 comfort: yea, and e the more joyed we *G4056*
Gal 1:14 being more e zealous of the traditions *G4056*
1Th 3:10 praying e that we *G5228+G1537+G4053*
2Th 1: 3 your faith groweth e, and the charity of
Heb 12:21 *that* Moses said, I e fear and quake:) *G1630*

EXCEL

Gen 49: 4 Unstable as water, thou shalt not e; H3498
1Ch 15:21 with harps on the Sheminith to e. H5329
Ps 103:20 Bless the LORD, ye his angels, that e in H1368
Isa 10:10 did e them of Jerusalem and of Samaria;
1Co 14:12 ye may e to the edifying of the church. *G4052*

EXCELLED

1Ki 4:30 And Solomon's wisdom e the wisdom H7235

EXCELLENCY

Gen 49: 3 of my strength, the e of dignity, and the H3499
3 of dignity, and the e of power: H3499
Ex 15: 7 And in the greatness of thine e thou H1347
Dt 33:26 in thy help, and in his e on the sky. H1346
29 *is* the sword of thy e! and thine enemies H1346
Job 4:21 Doth not their e *which is* in them go H3499
13:11 Shall not his e make you afraid? and H7613
20: 6 Though his e mount up to the heavens, H7863
37: 4 the voice of his e; and he will not stay H1347
40:10 Deck thyself now *with* majesty and e; H1363
Ps 47: 4 the e of Jacob whom he loved. Selah. H1347
62: 4 down from his e: they delight in lies: H7613
68:34 Ascribe ye strength unto God: his e *is* H1346
Ecc 7:12 *is* a defence: but the e of knowledge *is*, H3504

Isa 13:19 of the Chaldees' **e**, shall be as when God H1347
35: 2 be given unto it, the **e** of Carmel and H1926
2 of the LORD, *and* the **e** of our God. H1926
60:15 an eternal **e**, a joy of many generations. H1347
Ezk 24:21 my sanctuary, the **e** of your strength, H1347
Am 6: 8 hosts, I abhor the **e** of Jacob, and hate H1347
8: 7 The LORD hath sworn by the **e** of H1347
Nah 2: 2 For the LORD hath turned away the **e** H1347
2 of Jacob, as the **e** of Israel: for the H1347
1Co 2: 1 you, came not with **e** of speech or of *G5247*
2Co 4: 7 vessels, that the **e** of the power may be *G5236*
Php 3: 8 *but* loss for the **e** of the knowledge of *G5242*

EXCELLENT
Est 1: 4 the honour of his **e** majesty many days, H8597
Job 37:23 find him out: *he is* **e** in power, and in H7689
Ps 8: 1 O LORD our Lord, how **e** *is* thy name in H117
9 O LORD our Lord, how **e** *is* thy name in H117
16: 3 and *to* the **e**, in whom *is* all my delight. H117
36: 7 How **e** *is* thy lovingkindness, O God! H3368
76: 4 Thou *art* more glorious *and* **e** than the H117
141: 5 me; *it shall be* an **e** oil, *which* shall not H7218
148:13 his name alone is **e**; his glory *is* above H7682
150: 2 him according to his **e** greatness. H7230
Prv 8: 6 Hear; for I will speak of **e** things; and H5057
12:26 The righteous *is* more **e** than his H8446
17: 7 **E** speech becometh not a fool: much H3499
27 man of understanding is of an **e** spirit. H7119
22:20 Have not I written to thee **e** things in H7991
Song 5:15 *is* as Lebanon, **e** as the cedars. H977
Isa 4: 2 of the earth *shall be* **e** and comely for H1347
12: 5 Sing unto the LORD; for he hath done **e** H1348
28:29 in counsel, *and* **e** in working. H1431
Ezk 16: 7 and thou art come to **e** ornaments: *thy* H5716
Dan 2:31 brightness *was* **e**, stood before thee; and H3493
4:36 and **e** majesty was added unto me. H3493
5:12 Forasmuch as an **e** spirit, and H3493
14 and **e** wisdom is found in thee. H3493
6: 3 because an **e** spirit *was* in him; and H3493
Lk 1: 3 unto thee in order, most **e** Theophilus, *G2903*
Act 23:26 Claudius Lysias unto the most **e** *G2903*
Ro 2:18 more **e**, being instructed out of the law; *G1308*
1Co 12:31 and yet shew I unto you a more **e** way. *G2596*
Php 1:10 That ye may approve things that are **e**; *G1308*
Heb 1: 4 obtained a more **e** name than they. *G1313*
8: 6 But now hath he obtained a more **e** *G1313*
11: 4 unto God a more **e** sacrifice than Cain, *G4119*
2Pt 1:17 to him from the **e** glory, This is my *G3169*

EXCELLEST
Prv 31:29 done virtuously, but thou **e** them all. H5927

EXCELLETH
Ecc 2:13 Then I saw that wisdom **e** folly, as far H3504
13 folly, as far as light **e** darkness. H3504
2Co 3:10 respect, by reason of the glory that **e**. *G5235*

EXCEPT
Gen 31:42 **E** the God of my father, the God of H3884
32:26 not let thee go, **e** thou bless me. H3588+H518
42:15 go forth hence, **e** your youngest H3588+H518
43: 3 my face, **e** your brother *be* with you. H1115
5 my face, **e** your brother *be* with you. H1115
10 For **e** we had lingered, surely now we H3884
44:23 thy servants, **E** your youngest H518+H3808
26 face, **e** our youngest brother *be* with us. H369
47:26 have the fifth *part*; **e** the land of the H7535
Nu 16:13 in the wilderness, **e** thou make thyself H3588
Dt 32:30 to flight, **e** their Rock H518+H3808+H3588
Jos 7:12 you any more, **e** ye destroy the H518+H3808
1Sa 25:34 hurting thee, **e** thou hadst H3588+H3884
2Sa 3: 9 So do God to Abner, and more also, **e**, H3588
13 see my face, **e** thou first bring H3588+H518
5: 6 David, saying, **E** thou take away H3588+H518
2Ki 4:24 *thy* riding for me, **e** I bid thee. H3588+H518
Est 2:14 the king no more, **e** the king H3588+H518
4:11 to put *him* to death, **e** such to whom the H905
Ps 127: 1 **E** the LORD build the house, H518+H3808
1 that build it: **e** the LORD keep H518+H3808
Prv 4:16 For they sleep not, **e** they have H518+H3808
Isa 1: 9 **E** the LORD of hosts had left unto us a H3884
Dan 2:11 it before the king, **e** the gods, whose H3861
3:28 nor worship any god, **e** their own God. H3861
6: 5 this Daniel, **e** we find *it* against him H3861
Am 3: 3 Can two walk together, **e** they be H1115
Mt 5:20 For I say unto you, That **e** your *G3362*
12:29 and spoil his goods, **e** he first bind the *G3362*
18: 3 And said, Verily I say unto you, **E** ye be *G3362*
19: 9 shall put away his wife, **e** *it be* for *G1508*
24:22 And **e** those days should be shortened, *G1508*
26:42 from me, **e** I drink it, thy will be done. *G3362*
Mk 3:27 spoil his goods, **e** he will first bind the *G3362*
7: 3 For the Pharisees, and all the Jews, **e** *G3362*
4 from the market, **e** they wash, they eat *G3362*
13:20 And **e** that the Lord had shortened *G1508*
Lk 9:13 and two fishes; **e** we should go and buy *G1509*
13: 3 I tell you, Nay: but, **e** ye repent, ye shall *G1437*
5 I tell you, Nay: but, **e** ye repent, ye shall *G1437*
Jn 3: 2 that thou doest, **e** God be with him. *G3362*
3 I say unto thee, **E** a man be born again, *G3362*
5 I say unto thee, **E** a man be born of *G3362*
27 nothing, **e** it be given him from heaven. *G3362*
4:48 Then said Jesus unto him, **E** ye see *G3362*
6:44 No man can come to me, **e** the Father *G3362*
53 I say unto you, **E** ye eat the flesh of the *G3362*
65 **e** it were given unto him of my Father. *G3362*
12:24 Verily, verily, I say unto you, **E** a corn *G3362*
15: 4 bear fruit of itself, **e** it abide in the vine; *G3362*
4 vine; no more can ye, **e** ye abide in me. *G3362*
19:11 *at all* against me, **e** it were given thee *G1508*
20:25 he said unto them, **E** I shall see in his *G3362*
Act 8: 1 of Judaea and Samaria, **e** the apostles. *G4133*
31 And he said, How can I, **e** some man *G3362*
15: 1 *and said*, **E** ye be circumcised after *G3362*
24:21 **E** it be for this one voice, that I cried *G2228*
26:29 altogether such as I am, **e** these bonds. *G3924*
27:31 and to the soldiers, **E** these abide in the *G3362*
Ro 7: 7 had not known lust, **e** the law had said, *G1508*
9:29 And as Esaias said before, **E** the Lord *G1508*
10:15 And how shall they preach, **e** they be *G3362*
1Co 7: 5 Defraud ye not one the other, **e** *it be* *G1509*
14: 5 with tongues, **e** he interpret, *G1622+G1508*
6 shall I profit you, **e** I shall speak to you *G3362*
7 pipe or harp, **e** they give a distinction *G3362*
9 So likewise ye, **e** ye utter by the tongue *G3362*
15:36 thou sowest is not quickened, **e** it die: *G3362*
2Co 12:13 to other churches, **e** *it be* that I myself *G1508*
13: 5 Christ is in you, **e** ye be reprobates? *G1509*
2Th 2: 3 *shall not come*, **e** there come a falling *G3362*
2Ti 2: 5 is he not crowned, **e** he strive lawfully. *G3362*
Rev 2: 5 out of his place, **e** thou repent. *G3362*
22 **e** they repent of their deeds. *G3362*

EXCEPTED
1Co 15:27 is **e**, which did put all things under him. *G1622*

EXCESS
Mt 23:25 within they are full of extortion and **e**. *G192*
Eph 5:18 wherein is **e**; but be filled with the Spirit; *G810*
1Pt 4: 3 lusts, **e** of wine, revellings, *G3632*
4 the same **e** of riot, speaking evil of *you*: *G401*

EXCHANGE
Gen 47:17 gave them bread *in* **e** for horses, and for
Lev 27:10 then it and the **e** thereof shall be holy. H8545
Job 28:17 equal it: and the **e** of it *shall not be for* H8545
Ezk 48:14 And they shall not sell of it, neither **e**, H4171
Mt 16:26 what shall a man give in **e** for his soul? *G465*
Mk 8:37 Or what shall a man give in **e** for his *G465*

EXCHANGERS
Mt 25:27 put my money to the **e**, and *then* at my *G5133*

EXCLUDE
Gal 4:17 would **e** you, that ye might affect them. *G1576*

EXCLUDED
Ro 3:27 Where *is* boasting then? It is **e**. By what *G1576*

EXCUSE
Lk 14:18 began to make **e**. The first said unto *G3868*
Ro 1:20 and Godhead; so that they are without **e**: *G379*
2Co 12:19 Again, think ye that we **e** ourselves unto *G626*

EXCUSED
Lk 14:18 go and see it: I pray thee have me **e**. *G3868*
19 go to prove them: I pray thee have me **e**. *G3868*

EXCUSING
Ro 2:15 while accusing or else **e** one another;) *G626*

EXECRATION
Jer 42:18 Egypt: and ye shall be an **e**, and an H423
44:12 they shall be an **e**, *and* an astonishment, H423

EXECUTE
Ex 12:12 I will **e** judgment: I *am* the LORD. H6213
Nu 5:30 the priest shall **e** upon her all this law. H6213
8:11 they may **e** the service of the LORD. H5647
Dt 10:18 He doth **e** the judgment of the H6213
1Ki 6:12 my statutes, and **e** my judgments, and H6213
Ps 119:84 **e** judgment on them that persecute me? H6213
149: 7 To **e** vengeance upon the heathen, *and* H6213
9 To **e** upon them the judgment written: H6213
Isa 16: 3 Take counsel, **e** judgment; make thy H6213
Jer 7: 5 if ye throughly **e** judgment between a H6213
21:12 thus saith the LORD; **E** judgment in the H1777
22: 3 Thus saith the LORD; **E** ye judgment H6213
23: 5 **e** judgment and justice in the earth. H6213
33:15 David; and he shall **e** judgment and H6213
Ezk 5: 8 thee, and will **e** judgments in the midst H6213
10 fathers; and I will **e** judgments in thee, H6213
15 thee, when I shall **e** judgments in thee H6213
11: 9 and will **e** judgments among you. H6213
16:41 with fire, and **e** judgments upon thee H6213
25:11 And I will **e** judgments upon Moab; H6213
17 And I will **e** great vengeance upon H6213
30:14 in Zoan, and will **e** judgments in No. H6213
19 Thus will I **e** judgments in Egypt: and H6213
45: 9 and spoil, and **e** judgment and justice, H6213
Hos 11: 9 I will not **e** the fierceness of mine H6213
Mic 5:15 And I will **e** vengeance in anger and H6213
7: 9 my cause, and **e** judgment for me: he H6213
Zec 7: 9 of hosts, saying, **E** true judgment, and H8199
8:16 to his neighbour; **e** the judgment of H8199
Jn 5:27 And hath given him authority to **e** *G4160*
Ro 13: 4 to **e** wrath upon him that doeth evil.
Jude 15 To **e** judgment upon all, and to *G4160*

EXECUTED
Nu 33: 4 their gods also the LORD **e** judgments. H6213
Dt 33:21 of the people, he **e** the justice of the H6213
2Sa 8:15 all Israel; and David **e** judgment and H6213
1Ch 6:10 (he *it is* that **e** the priest's office in
18:14 So David reigned over all Israel, and **e** H6213
24: 2 Eleazar and Ithamar **e** the priest's office.
2Ch 24:24 So they **e** judgment against Joash. H6213
Ezr 7:26 let judgment be **e** speedily upon him, H5648
Ps 106:30 Then stood up Phinehas, and **e**
Ecc 8:11 an evil work is not **e** speedily, therefore H6213
Jer 23:20 return, until he have **e**, and till he have H6213
Ezk 11:12 statutes, neither **e** my judgments, but H6213
18: 8 iniquity, hath **e** true judgment between H6213
17 nor increase, hath **e** my judgments, H6213
20:24 Because they had not **e** my judgments, H6213
23:10 for they had **e** judgment upon her. H6213
28:22 when I shall have **e** judgments in her, H6213
26 when I have **e** judgments upon all H6213
39:21 that I have **e**, and my hand that I H6213
Lk 1: 8 And it came to pass, that while he **e** the *G2407*

EXECUTEDST
1Sa 28:18 of the LORD, nor **e** his fierce wrath H6213

EXECUTEST
Ps 99: 4 **e** judgment and righteousness in Jacob. H6213

EXECUTETH
Ps 9:16 *which* he **e**: the wicked is snared H6213
103: 6 The LORD **e** righteousness and H6213
146: 7 Which **e** judgment for the oppressed: H6213
Isa 46:11 east, the man that **e** my counsel from a
Jer 5: 1 if there be *any* that **e** judgment, that H6213
Joel 2:11 *he is* strong that **e** his word: for the day H6213

EXECUTING
2Ki 10:30 hast done well in **e** *that which is* right H6213
2Ch 11:14 from **e** the priest's office unto the LORD:
22: 8 when Jehu was **e** judgment upon the

EXECUTION
Est 9: 1 near to be put in **e**, in the day that the H6213

EXECUTIONER
Mk 6:27 And immediately the king sent an **e**, *G4688*

EXEMPTED
1Ki 15:22 Judah; none *was* **e**: and they took away H5355

EXERCISE
Ps 131: 1 eyes lofty: neither do I **e** myself in great H1980
Jer 9:24 *am* the LORD which **e** lovingkindness, H6213
Mt 20:25 of the Gentiles **e** dominion over them, *G2634*
25 that are great **e** authority upon them. *G2715*
Mk 10:42 over the Gentiles **e** lordship over them; *G2634*
42 their great ones **e** authority upon them. *G2715*
Lk 22:25 of the Gentiles **e** lordship over them; *G2961*

Lk 22:25 and they that e authority upon them G1850
Act 24:16 And herein do I e myself, to have always G778
1Ti 4: 7 and e thyself *rather* unto godliness. G1128
8 For bodily e profiteth little: but G1129

EXERCISED
Ecc 1:13 to the sons of man to be e therewith. H6031
3:10 given to the sons of men to be e in it. H6031
Ezk 22:29 oppression, and e robbery, and have H1497
Heb 5:14 senses e to discern both good and evil. G1128
12:11 unto them which are e thereby. G1128
2Pt 2:14 an heart they have e with covetous G1128

EXERCISETH
Rev 13:12 And he e all the power of the first beast G4160

EXHORT
Act 2:40 words did he testify and e, saying, Save G3870
27:22 And now I e you to be of good cheer: G3867
2Co 9: 5 Therefore I thought it necessary to e G3870
1Th 4: 1 you, brethren, and e *you* by the Lord G3870
5:14 Now we e you, brethren, warn them G3870
2Th 3:12 we command and e by our Lord Jesus G3870
1Ti 2: 1 I e therefore, that, first of all, G3870
6: 2 of the benefit. These things teach and e. G3870
2Ti 4: 2 e with all longsuffering and doctrine. G3870
Tit 1: 9 to e and to convince the gainsayers. G3870
2: 6 Young men likewise e to be sober G3870
9 *E* servants to be obedient unto their own
15 These things speak, and e, and rebuke G3870
Heb 3:13 But e one another daily, while it is G3870
1Pt 5: 1 The elders which are among you I e, G3870
Jude 3 unto you, and e *you* that ye should G3870

EXHORTATION
Lk 3:18 And many other things in his e G3870
Act 13:15 any word of e for the people, say on. G3874
20: 2 them much e, he came into Greece, G3056
Ro 12: 8 Or he that exhorteth, on e: he that G3874
1Co 14: 3 men *to* edification, and e, and comfort. G3874
2Co 8:17 For indeed he accepted the e; but being G3874
1Th 2: 3 For our e *was* not of deceit, nor of G3874
1Ti 4:13 attendance to reading, to e, to doctrine. G3874
Heb 12: 5 And ye have forgotten the e which G3874
13:22 suffer the word of e: for I have written a G3874

EXHORTED
Act 11:23 was glad, and e them all, that with G3870
15:32 also themselves, e the brethren with G3870
1Th 2:11 As ye know how we e and comforted G3870

EXHORTETH
Ro 12: 8 Or he that e, on exhortation: he that G3870

EXHORTING
Act 14:22 the disciples, *and* e them to continue in G3870
18:27 the brethren wrote, e the disciples to G4389
Heb 10:25 of some *is*; but e *one another*: and so G3870
1Pt 5:12 written briefly, e, and testifying that G3870

EXILE
2Sa 15:19 for thou *art* a stranger, and also an e. H1540
Isa 51:14 The captive e hasteneth that he may be H6808

EXORCISTS
Act 19:13 Then certain of the vagabond Jews, e, G1845

EXPECTATION
Ps 9:18 e of the poor shall *not* perish for ever. H8615
62: 5 only upon God; for my e *is* from him. H8615
Prv 10:28 but the e of the wicked shall perish. H8615
11: 7 When a wicked man dieth, *his* e shall H8615
23 good: *but* the e of the wicked *is* wrath. H8615
23:18 For surely there is an end; and thine e H8615
24:14 a reward, and thy e shall not be cut off. H8615
Isa 20: 5 their e, and of Egypt their glory. H4007
6 such *is* our e, whither we flee for help H4007
Zec 9: 5 and Ekron; for her e shall be ashamed; H4007
Lk 3:15 And as the people were in e, and all G4328
Act 12:11 *from* all the e of the people of the Jews. G4329
Ro 8:19 For the earnest e of the creature waiteth G603
Php 1:20 According to my earnest e and *my* hope, G603

EXPECTED
Jer 29:11 and not of evil, to give you an e end. H8615

EXPECTING
Act 3: 5 And he gave heed unto them, e to G4328
Heb 10:13 From henceforth e till his enemies be G1551

EXPEDIENT
Jn 11:50 Nor consider that it is e for us, that one G4851
16: 7 Nevertheless I tell you the truth; It is e G4851
18:14 Jews, that it was e that one man should G4851
1Co 6:12 all things are not e: all things are lawful G4851
10:23 all things are not e: all things are lawful G4851
2Co 8:10 advice: for this is e for you, who have G4851
12: 1 It is not e for me doubtless to glory. I G4851

EXPEL
Jos 23: 5 And the LORD your God, he shall e H1920
Jdg 11: 7 ye hate me, and e me out of my father's H1644

EXPELLED
Jos 13:13 Nevertheless the children of Israel e H3423
Jdg 1:20 and he e thence the three sons of Anak. H3423
2Sa 14:14 that his banished be not e from him. H5080
Act 13:50 and e them out of their coasts. G1544

EXPENSES
Ezr 6: 4 the e be given out of the king's house: H5313
8 river, forthwith e be given unto these H5313

EXPERIENCE
Gen 30:27 I have learned by e that the LORD hath H5172
Ecc 1:16 had great e of wisdom and knowledge. H7200
Ro 5: 4 And patience, e; and experience, hope: G1382
4 And patience, experience; and e, hope: G1382

EXPERIMENT
2Co 9:13 Whiles by the e of this ministration G1382

EXPERT
1Ch 12:33 went forth to battle, e in war, with all H6186
35 And of the Danites e in war twenty and H6186
36 to battle, e in war, forty thousand. H6186
Song 3: 8 They all hold swords, *being* e in war: H3925
Jer 50: 9 e man; none shall return in vain. H7919
Act 26: 3 Especially *because I know* thee to be e G1109

EXPIRED
1Sa 18:26 son in law: and the days were not e. H4390
2Sa 11: 1 after the year was e, at the time when H8666
1Ch 17:11 when thy days be e that thou must go H4390
20: 1 after the year was e, at the time that H8666
2Ch 36:10 And when the year was e, king H8666
Est 1: 5 And when these days were e, the king H4390
Ezk 43:27 And when these days are e, it shall be, H3615
Act 7:30 And when forty years were e, there G4137
Rev 20: 7 And when the thousand years are e, G5055

EXPLOITS
Dan 11:28 he shall do e, and return to his own land.
32 know their God shall be strong, and do e.

EXPOUND
Jdg 14:14 could not in three days e the riddle. H5046

EXPOUNDED
Jdg 14:19 unto them which e the riddle. And his H5046
Mk 4:34 alone, he e all things to his disciples. G1956
Lk 24:27 the prophets, he e unto them in all the G1329
Act 11: 4 and e *it* by order unto them, saying, G1620
18:26 unto *them*, and e unto him the way of G1620
28:23 lodging; to whom he e and testified the G1620

EXPRESS
Heb 1: 3 of *his* glory, and the e image of his G5481

EXPRESSED
Nu 1:17 these men which are e by *their* names: H5344
1Ch 12:31 which were e by name, to come and H5344
16:41 chosen, who were e by name, to give H5344
2Ch 28:15 And the men which were e by name H5344
31:19 the men that were e by name, to give H5344
Ezr 8:20 Nethinims: all of them were e by name. H5344

EXPRESSLY
1Sa 20:21 out the arrows. If I e say unto the lad, H559
Ezk 1: 3 The word of the LORD came e unto
1Ti 4: 1 Now the Spirit speaketh e, that in the G4490

EXTEND
Ps 109:12 Let there be none to e mercy unto him: H4900
Isa 66:12 Behold, I will e peace to her like a river, H5186

EXTENDED
Ezr 7:28 And hath e mercy unto me before the H5186
9: 9 bondage, but hath e mercy unto us in H5186

EXTENDETH
Ps 16: 2 *art* my Lord: my goodness e not to thee;

EXTINCT
Job 17: 1 My breath is corrupt, my days are e, the H2193
Isa 43:17 they are e, they are quenched as tow. H1846

EXTOL
Ps 30: 1 I will e thee, O LORD; for thou hast H7311
68: 4 to his name: e him that rideth upon H5549
145: 1 I will e thee, my God, O king; and I will H7311
Dan 4:37 Now I Nebuchadnezzar praise and e H7313

EXTOLLED
Ps 66:17 mouth, and he was e with my tongue. H7318
Isa 52:13 shall be exalted and e, and be very high. H5375

EXTORTION
Ezk 22:12 thy neighbours by e, and hast forgotten H6233
Mt 23:25 but within they are full of e and excess. G724

EXTORTIONER
Ps 109:11 Let the e catch all that he hath; and let H5383
Isa 16: 4 of the spoiler: for the e is at an end, the H4160
1Co 5:11 or an e; with such an one no not to eat. G727

EXTORTIONERS
Lk 18:11 as other men *are*, e, unjust, adulterers, or G727
1Co 5:10 the covetous, or e, or with idolaters; for G727
6:10 nor e, shall inherit the kingdom of God. G727

EXTREME
Dt 28:22 and with an e burning, and with the H2746

EXTREMITY
Job 35:15 anger; yet he knoweth *it* not in great e: H6580

EYE
Ex 21:24 E for eye, tooth for tooth, hand for H5869
24 Eye for e, tooth for tooth, hand for H5869
26 And if a man smite the e of his servant, H5869
26 his servant, or the e of his maid, that it H5869
Lev 21:20 hath a blemish in his e, or be scurvy, or H5869
24:20 Breach for breach, e for eye, tooth for H5869
20 Breach for breach, eye for e, tooth for H5869
Dt 7:16 deliver thee; thine e shall have no pity H5869
13: 8 neither shall thine e pity him, neither H5869
15: 9 at hand; and thine e be evil against thy H5869
19:13 Thine e shall not pity him, but thou H5869
21 And thine e shall not pity; *but* life *shall* H5869
21 life *shall go* for life, e for eye, tooth for H5869
21 *go* for life, eye for e, tooth for tooth, H5869
25:12 off her hand, thine e shall not pity *her.* H5869
28:54 very delicate, his e shall be evil toward H5869
56 tenderness, her e shall be evil toward H5869
32:10 him, he kept him as the apple of his e. H5869
34: 7 when he died: his e was not dim, nor H5869
1Sa 24:10 kill thee: but *mine* e spared thee; and I
2Sa 22:25 to my cleanness in his e sight. H5869
Ezr 5: 5 But the e of their God was upon the H5870
Job 7: 7 *is* wind: mine e shall no more see good. H5869
8 The e of him that hath seen me shall H5869
10:18 up the ghost, and no e had seen me! H5869
13: 1 Lo, mine e hath seen all *this*, mine ear H5869
16:20 My friends scorn me: *but* mine e H5869
17: 2 mine e continue in their provocation? H5869
7 Mine e also is dim by reason of sorrow, H5869
20: 9 The e also *which* saw him shall *see him* H5869
24:15 The e also of the adulterer waiteth for H5869
15 e shall see me: and disguiseth *his* face. H5869
28: 7 which the vulture's e hath not seen: H5869
10 and his e seeth every precious thing. H5869
29:11 the e saw *me*, it gave witness to me: H5869
42: 5 of the ear: but now mine e seeth thee. H5869
Ps 6: 7 Mine e is consumed because of grief; it H5869
17: 8 Keep me as the apple of the e, hide me H5869
31: 9 in trouble: mine e is consumed with H5869
32: 8 shalt go: I will guide thee with mine e. H5869
33:18 Behold, the e of the LORD *is* upon them H5869
35:19 the e that hate me without a cause. H5869
21 *and* said, Aha, aha, our e hath seen *it.* H5869
54: 7 all trouble: and mine e hath seen *his* H5869
88: 9 Mine e mourneth by reason of H5869
92:11 Mine e also shall see *my desire* on mine H5869
94: 9 he that formed the e, shall he not see? H5869
Prv 7: 2 live; and my law as the apple of thine e. H5869
10:10 He that winketh with the e causeth H5869
20:12 The hearing ear, and the seeing e, the H5869
22: 9 He that hath a bountiful e shall be H5869

Prv 23: 6 **e**, neither desire thou his dainty meats: H5869
28:22 He that hasteth to be rich *hath* an evil **e**, H5869
30:17 The **e** *that* mocketh at *his* father, and H5869
Ecc 1: 8 cannot utter *it*: the **e** is not satisfied H5869
4: 8 neither is his **e** satisfied with riches; H5869
Isa 13:18 womb; their **e** shall not spare children. H5869
52: 8 for they shall see **e** to eye, when the H5869
8 shall see eye to **e**, when the LORD shall H5869
64: 4 neither hath the **e** seen, O God, beside H5869
Jer 13:17 pride; and mine **e** shall weep sore, and H5869
Lam 1:16 For these *things* I weep; mine **e**, mine H5869
16 mine eye, mine **e** runneth down with H5869
2: 4 pleasant to the **e** in the tabernacle of H5869
18 rest; let not the apple of thine **e** cease. H5869
3:48 Mine **e** runneth down with rivers of H5869
49 Mine **e** trickleth down, and ceaseth not, H5869
51 Mine **e** affecteth mine heart because of H5869
Ezk 5:11 **e** spare, neither will I have any pity. H5869
7: 4 And mine **e** shall not spare thee, H5869
9 And mine **e** shall not spare, neither will H5869
8:18 deal in fury: mine **e** shall not spare, H5869
9: 5 not your **e** spare, neither have ye pity: H5869
10 And as for me also, mine **e** shall not H5869
16: 5 None **e** pitied thee, to do any of these H5869
20:17 Nevertheless mine **e** spared them from H5869
Mic 4:11 defiled, and let our **e** look upon Zion. H5869
Zec 2: 8 you toucheth the apple of his **e**. H5869
11:17 and upon his right **e**: his arm shall be H5869
17 his right **e** shall be utterly darkened. H5869
Mt 5:29 And if thy right **e** offend thee, pluck it G3788
38 An **e** for an eye, and a tooth for a tooth: G3788
38 An eye for an **e**, and a tooth for a tooth: G3788
6:22 The light of the body is the **e**: if G3788
22 if therefore thine **e** be single, thy whole G3788
23 But if thine **e** be evil, thy whole body G3788
7: 3 is in thy brother's **e**, but considerest not G3788
3 not the beam that is in thine own **e**? G3788
4 the mote out of thine **e**; and, behold, a G3788
4 and, behold, a beam *is* in thine own **e**? G3788
5 out of thine own **e**; and then shalt thou G3788
5 cast out the mote out of thy brother's **e**. G3788
18: 9 And if thine **e** offend thee, pluck it out, G3788
9 into life with one **e**, rather than having G3442
19:24 to go through the **e** of a needle, than for G5169
20:15 Is thine **e** evil, because I am good? G3788
Mk 7:22 an evil **e**, blasphemy, pride, foolishness: G3788
9:47 And if thine **e** offend thee, pluck it out: G3788
47 of God with one **e**, than having two eyes G3442
10:25 to go through the **e** of a needle, than for G5168
Lk 6:41 is in thy brother's **e**, but perceivest not G3788
41 not the beam that is in thine own **e**? G3788
42 that is in thine **e**, when thou thyself G3788
42 is in thine own **e**? Thou hypocrite, cast G3788
42 out of thine own **e**, and then shalt thou G3788
42 out the mote that is in thy brother's **e**. G3788
11:34 The light of the body is the **e**: therefore G3788
34 when thine **e** is single, thy whole G3788
34 but when *thine* **e** is evil, thy body G3788
18:25 go through a needle's **e**, than for a rich G5168
1Co 2: 9 But as it is written, **E** hath not seen, nor G3788
12:16 I am not the **e**, I am not of the body; G3788
17 If the whole body *were* an **e**, where *were* G3788
21 And the **e** cannot say unto the hand, I G3788
15:52 In a moment, in the twinkling of an **e**, G3788
Rev 1: 7 clouds; and every **e** shall see him, and G3788

EYEBROWS

Lev 14: 9 his beard and his **e**, even all his H1354+H5869

EYED

Gen 29:17 Leah *was* tender **e**; but Rachel was H5869
1Sa 18: 9 And Saul **e** David from that day and H5770

EYELIDS

Job 16:16 and on my **e** *is* the shadow of death; H6079
41:18 his eyes *are* like the **e** of the morning. H6079
Ps 11: 4 behold, his **e** try, the children of men. H6079
132: 4 to mine eyes, *or* slumber to mine **e**, H6079
Prv 4:25 let thine **e** look straight before thee. H6079
6: 4 to thine eyes, nor slumber to thine **e**. H6079
25 neither let her take thee with her **e**. H6079
30:13 are their eyes! and their **e** are lifted up. H6079
Jer 9:18 tears, and our **e** gush out with waters. H6079

EYES

Gen 3: 5 thereof, then your **e** shall be opened, H5869
6 *was* pleasant to the **e**, and a tree to be H5869
7 And the **e** of them both were opened, H5869
6: 8 But Noah found grace in the **e** of the H5869
Gen 13:10 And Lot lifted up his **e**, and beheld all H5869
14 Lift up now thine **e**, and look from the H5869
16: 4 her mistress was despised in her **e**. H5869
5 was despised in her **e**: the LORD judge H5869
18: 2 And he lift up his **e** and looked, and, lo, H5869
19: 8 as *is* good in your **e**: only unto these H5869
20:16 a covering of the **e**, unto all that *are* H5869
21:19 And God opened her **e**, and she saw a H5869
22: 4 up his **e**, and saw the place afar off. H5869
13 And Abraham lifted up his **e**, and H5869
24:63 he lifted up his **e**, and saw, and, behold, H5869
64 And Rebekah lifted up her **e**, and when H5869
27: 1 was old, and his **e** were dim, so that he H5869
30:27 found favour in thine **e**, *tarry: for* I have H5869
41 the rods before the **e** of the cattle in the H5869
31:10 I lifted up mine **e**, and saw in a dream, H5869
12 And he said, Lift up now thine **e**, and H5869
40 and my sleep departed from mine **e**. H5869
33: 1 And Jacob lifted up his **e**, and looked, H5869
5 And he lifted up his **e**, and saw the H5869
34:11 find grace in your **e**, and what ye shall H5869
37:25 they lifted up their **e** and looked, and, H5869
39: 7 wife cast her **e** upon Joseph; and she H5869
41:37 And the thing was good in the **e** of H5869
37 and in the **e** of all his servants. H5869
42:24 Simeon, and bound him before their **e**. H5869
43:29 And he lifted up his **e**, and saw his H5869
44:21 me, that I may set mine **e** upon him. H5869
45:12 And, behold, your **e** see, and the eyes of H5869
12 And, behold, your eyes see, and the **e** of H5869
46: 4 Joseph shall put his hand upon thine **e**. H5869
47:19 Wherefore shall we die before thine **e**, H5869
48:10 Now the **e** of Israel were dim for age, *so* H5869
49:12 His **e** *shall be* red with wine, and his H5869
50: 4 grace in your **e**, speak, I pray you, in H5869
Ex 5:21 be abhorred in the **e** of Pharaoh, and in H5869
21 and in the **e** of his servants, to put H5869
8:26 their **e**, and will they not stone us? H5869
13: 9 between thine **e**, that the LORD'S law H5869
16 between thine **e**: for by strength of hand H5869
14:10 Israel lifted up their **e**, and, behold, the H5869
24:17 mount in the **e** of the children of Israel. H5869
Lev 4:13 be hid from the **e** of the assembly, and H5869
20: 4 ways hide their **e** from the man, when H5869
26:16 shall consume the **e**, and cause sorrow H5869
Nu 5:13 it be hid from the **e** of her husband, H5869
10:31 and thou mayest be to us instead of **e**. H5869
11: 6 at all, beside this manna, *before* our **e**. H5869
15:39 **e**, after which ye use to go a whoring: H5869
16:14 **e** of these men? we will not come up. H5869
20: 8 the rock before their **e**; and it shall give H5869
12 sanctify me in the **e** of the children of H5869
22:31 Then the LORD opened the **e** of H5869
24: 2 And Balaam lifted up his **e**, and he saw H5869
3 the man whose **e** are open hath said: H5869
4 *into a trance,* but having his **e** open: H5869
15 the man whose **e** are open hath said: H5869
16 *into a trance,* but having his **e** open: H5869
27:14 water before their **e**: that *is* the water of H5869
33:55 *be* pricks in your **e**, and thorns in your H5869
Dt 1:30 he did for you in Egypt before your **e**; H5869
3:21 saying, Thine **e** have seen all that the H5869
27 and lift up thine **e** westward, and H5869
27 **e**: for thou shalt not go over this Jordan. H5869
4: 3 Your **e** have seen what the LORD did H5869
9 things which thine **e** have seen, and lest H5869
19 And lest thou lift up thine **e** unto H5869
34 God did for you in Egypt before your **e**? H5869
6: 8 shall be as frontlets between thine **e**. H5869
22 upon all his household, before our **e**: H5869
7:19 The great temptations which thine **e** H5869
9:17 hands, and brake them before your **e**. H5869
10:21 things, which thine **e** have seen. H5869
11: 7 But your **e** have seen all the great acts H5869
12 careth for: the **e** of the LORD thy God H5869
18 may be as frontlets between your **e**. H5869
12: 8 man whatsoever *is* right in his own **e**. H5869
13:18 *is* right in the **e** of the LORD thy God. H5869
14: 1 baldness between your **e** for the dead. H5869
16:19 a gift doth blind the **e** of the wise, and H5869
21: 7 this blood, neither have our **e** seen *it*. H5869
24: 1 find no favour in his **e**, because he hath H5869
28:31 Thine ox *shall be* slain before thine **e**, H5869
32 people, and thine **e** shall look, and fail H5869
34 sight of thine **e** which thou shalt see. H5869
65 and failing of **e**, and sorrow of mind: H5869
67 sight of thine **e** which thou shalt see. H5869
29: 2 did before your **e** in the land of Egypt H5869
3 The great temptations which thine **e** H5869
Dt 29: 4 to perceive, and **e** to see, and ears to H5869
34: 4 **e**, but thou shalt not go over thither. H5869
Jos 5:13 that he lifted up his **e** and looked, and, H5869
23:13 thorns in your **e**, until ye perish from H5869
24: 7 them; and your **e** have seen what I H5869
Jdg 16:21 and put out his **e**, and brought him H5869
28 avenged of the Philistines for my two **e**. H5869
17: 6 did *that which was* right in his own **e**. H5869
19:17 And when he had lifted up his **e**, he saw H5869
21:25 did *that which was* right in his own **e**. H5869
Ru 2: 9 *Let* thine **e** *be* on the field that they do H5869
10 grace in thine **e**, that thou shouldest H5869
1Sa 2:33 to consume thine **e**, and to grieve thine H5869
3: 2 his place, and his **e** began to wax dim, H5869
4:15 his **e** were dim, that he could not see. H5869
6:13 they lifted up their **e**, and saw the ark, H5869
11: 2 out all your right **e**, and lay it *for* a H5869
12: 3 **e** therewith? and I will restore it you. H5869
16 which the LORD will do before your **e**. H5869
14:27 his mouth; and his **e** were enlightened. H5869
29 pray you, how mine **e** have been H5869
20: 3 grace in thine **e**; and he saith, Let not H5869
29 favour in thine **e**, let me get away, I H5869
24:10 Behold, this day thine **e** have seen how H5869
25: 8 favour in thine **e**: for we come in a good H5869
26:21 precious in thine **e** this day: behold, I H5869
24 by this day in mine **e**, so let my life be H5869
24 much set by in the **e** of the LORD, and H5869
27: 5 grace in thine **e**, let them give me a H5869
2Sa 6:20 to day in the **e** of the handmaids of H5869
12:11 thy wives before thine **e**, and give *them* H5869
13:34 watch lifted up his **e**, and looked, and, H5869
15:25 find favour in the **e** of the LORD, he H5869
18:24 and lifted up his **e**, and looked, and H5869
19:27 do therefore *what is* good in thine **e**. H5869
22:28 save: but thine **e** *are* upon the haughty, H5869
24: 3 and that the **e** of my lord the king H5869
1Ki 1:20 And thou, my lord, O king, the **e** of all H5869
48 throne this day, mine **e** even seeing *it*. H5869
8:29 That thine **e** may be open toward this H5869
52 That thine **e** may be open unto the H5869
9: 3 for ever; and mine **e** and mine heart H5869
10: 7 I came, and mine **e** had seen *it*: and, H5869
11:33 *which is* right in mine **e**, and *to keep* my H5869
14: 4 for his **e** were set by reason of his age. H5869
8 do *that* only *which was* right in mine **e**; H5869
15: 5 *was* right in the **e** of the LORD, and H5869
11 **e** of the LORD, as *did* David his father. H5869
16:25 But Omri wrought evil in the **e** of the H5869
20: 6 is pleasant in thine **e**, they shall put *it* in H5869
22:43 *which was* right in the **e** of the LORD: H5869
2Ki 4:34 mouth, and his **e** upon his eyes, and his H5869
34 his eyes upon his **e**, and his hands upon H5869
35 seven times, and the child opened his **e**. H5869
6:17 thee, open his **e**, that he may see. And H5869
17 LORD opened the **e** of the young man; H5869
20 LORD, open the **e** of these *men,* that H5869
20 opened their **e**, and they saw; and, H5869
7: 2 *it* with thine **e**, but shalt not eat thereof. H5869
19 it with thine **e**, but shalt not eat thereof. H5869
10: 5 do thou *that which is* good in thine **e**. H5869
30 *is* right in mine **e**, *and* hast done unto H5869
19:16 open, LORD, thine **e**, and see: and hear H5869
22 and lifted up thine **e** on high? *even* H5869
22:20 peace; and thine **e** shall not see all the H5869
25: 7 before his **e**, and put out the eyes H5869
7 and put out the **e** of Zedekiah, and H5869
1Ch 13: 4 was right in the **e** of all the people. H5869
17:17 thing in thine **e**, O God; for thou hast H5869
21:16 And David lifted up his **e**, and saw the H5869
23 *is* good in his **e**: lo, I give *thee* the oxen H5869
2Ch 6:20 That thine **e** may be open upon this H5869
40 thee, thine **e** be open, and *let* thine H5869
7:15 Now mine **e** shall be open, and mine H5869
16 for ever: and mine **e** and mine heart H5869
9: 6 I came, and mine **e** had seen *it*: and, H5869
14: 2 and right in the **e** of the LORD his God: H5869
16: 9 For the **e** of the LORD run to and fro H5869
20:12 we what to do: but our **e** *are* upon thee. H5869
21: 6 *which was* evil in the **e** of the LORD. H5869
29: 6 *was* evil in the **e** of the LORD our God, H5869
8 and to hissing, as ye see with your **e**. H5869
34:28 neither shall thine **e** see all the evil that H5869
Ezr 3:12 was laid before their **e**, wept with a loud H5869
9: 8 may lighten our **e**, and give us a little H5869
Neh 1: 6 and thine **e** open, that thou mayest H5869
6:16 down in their own **e**: for they perceived H5869
Est 1:17 husbands in their **e**, when it shall be H5869
8: 5 I *be* pleasing in his **e**, let it be written to H5869

Job 2:12 And when they lifted up their **e** afar off, H5869
3:10 womb, nor hid sorrow from mine **e**. H5869
4:16 *was* before mine **e**, *there was* silence, H5869
7: 8 thine **e** *are* upon me, and I *am* not. H5869
10: 4 Hast thou **e** of flesh? or seest thou as H5869
11: 4 *is* pure, and I am clean in thine **e**. H5869
20 But the **e** of the wicked shall fail, and H5869
14: 3 And dost thou open thine **e** upon such H5869
15:12 thee away? and what do thy **e** wink at, H5869
16: 9 mine enemy sharpeneth his **e** upon me. H5869
17: 5 even the **e** of his children shall fail. H5869
19:27 myself, and mine **e** shall behold, and H5869
21: 8 them, and their offspring before their **e**. H5869
20 His **e** shall see his destruction, and he H5869
24:23 resteth; yet his **e** *are* upon their ways. H5869
27:19 he openeth his **e**, and he *is* not. H5869
28:21 Seeing it is hid from the **e** of all living, H5869
29:15 I was **e** to the blind, and feet *was* I to H5869
31: 1 I made a covenant with mine **e**; why H5869
7 walked after mine **e**, and if any blot H5869
16 have caused the **e** of the widow to fail; H5869
32: 1 because he *was* righteous in his own **e**. H5869
34:21 For his **e** *are* upon the ways of man, H5869
36: 7 He withdraweth not his **e** from the H5869
39:29 the prey, *and* her **e** behold afar off. H5869
40:24 He taketh it with his **e**: *his* nose pierceth H5869
41:18 **e** *are* like the eyelids of the morning. H5869
Ps 10: 8 his **e** are privily set against the poor. H5869
11: 4 *is* in heaven: his **e** behold, his eyelids H5869
13: 3 mine **e**, lest I sleep the *sleep of* death; H5869
15: 4 In whose **e** a vile person is contemned; H5869
17: 2 **e** behold the things that are equal. H5869
11 set their **e** bowing down to the earth; H5869
19: 8 of the LORD *is* pure, enlightening the **e**. H5869
25:15 Mine **e** *are* ever toward the LORD; for H5869
26: 3 For thy lovingkindness *is* before mine **e**: H5869
31:22 from before thine **e**: nevertheless thou H5869
34:15 The **e** of the LORD *are* upon the H5869
36: 1 *that there is* no fear of God before his **e**. H5869
2 For he flattereth himself in his own **e**, H5869
38:10 light of mine **e**, it also is gone from me. H5869
50:21 and set *them* in order before thine **e**. H5869
66: 7 He ruleth by his power for ever; his **e** H5869
69: 3 mine **e** fail while I wait for my God. H5869
23 Let their **e** be darkened, that they see H5869
73: 7 Their **e** stand out with fatness: they H5869
77: 4 Thou holdest mine **e** waking: I am so H5869
91: 8 Only with thine **e** shalt thou behold and H5869
101: 3 I will set no wicked thing before mine **e**: H5869
6 Mine **e** *shall be* upon the faithful of the H5869
115: 5 not: **e** have they, but they see not: H5869
116: 8 **e** from tears, *and* my feet from falling. H5869
118:23 LORD'S doing; it *is* marvellous in our **e**. H5869
119:18 Open thou mine **e**, that I may behold H5869
37 Turn away mine **e** from beholding H5869
82 Mine **e** fail for thy word, saying, When H5869
123 Mine **e** fail for thy salvation, and for H5869
136 Rivers of waters run down mine **e**, H5869
148 Mine **e** prevent the *night* watches, that H5869
121: 1 I will lift up mine **e** unto the hills, from H5869
123: 1 Unto thee lift I up mine **e**, O thou that H5869
2 Behold, as the **e** of servants *look* unto H5869
2 *and* as the **e** of a maiden unto the H5869
2 mistress; so our **e** *wait* upon the LORD H5869
131: 1 haughty, nor mine **e** lofty: neither do I H5869
132: 4 I will not give sleep to mine **e**, *or* H5869
135:16 not; **e** have they, but they see not; H5869
139:16 Thine **e** did see my substance, yet being H5869
141: 8 But mine **e** *are* unto thee, O GOD the H5869
145:15 The **e** of all wait upon thee; and thou H5869
146: 8 The LORD openeth *the **e** of* the blind: the
Prv 3: 7 Be not wise in thine own **e**: fear the H5869
21 **e**: keep sound wisdom and discretion: H5869
4:21 Let them not depart from thine **e**; keep H5869
25 Let thine **e** look right on, and let thine H5869
5:21 For the ways of man *are* before the **e** of H5869
6: 4 Give not sleep to thine **e**, nor slumber to H5869
13 He winketh with his **e**, he speaketh with H5869
10:26 as smoke to the **e**, so *is* the sluggard to H5869
12:15 The way of a fool *is* right in his own **e**: H5869
15: 3 The **e** of the LORD *are* in every place, H5869
30 The light of the **e** rejoiceth the heart: H5869
16: 2 **e**; but the LORD weigheth the spirits. H5869
30 He shutteth his **e** to devise froward H5869
17: 8 A gift *is as* a precious stone in the **e** of H5869
24 **e** of a fool *are* in the ends of the earth. H5869
20: 8 scattereth away all evil with his **e**. H5869
13 open thine **e**, *and* thou shalt be satisfied H5869
21: 2 **e**: but the LORD pondereth the hearts. H5869

Prv 21:10 neighbour findeth no favour in his **e**. H5869
22:12 The **e** of the LORD preserve knowledge, H5869
23: 5 Wilt thou set thine **e** upon that which is H5869
26 heart, and let thine **e** observe my ways. H5869
29 without cause? who hath redness of **e**? H5869
33 Thine **e** shall behold strange women, H5869
25: 7 of the prince whom thine **e** have seen. H5869
27:20 full; so the **e** of man are never satisfied. H5869
28:27 hideth his **e** shall have many a curse. H5869
29:13 the LORD lighteneth both their **e**. H5869
30:12 *are* pure in their own **e**, and *yet* is not H5869
13 their **e**! and their eyelids are lifted up. H5869
Ecc 2:10 And whatsoever mine **e** desired I kept H5869
14 The wise man's **e** *are* in his head; but H5869
5:11 the beholding *of them* with their **e**? H5869
6: 9 Better *is* the sight of the **e** than the H5869
8:16 day nor night seeth sleep with his **e**:) H5869
11: 7 *thing it is* for the **e** to behold the sun: H5869
9 the sight of thine **e**: but know thou, that H5869
Song 1:15 behold, thou *art* fair; thou *hast* doves' **e**. H5869
4: 1 thou *hast* doves' **e** within thy locks: thy H5869
9 of thine **e**, with one chain of thy neck. H5869
5:12 His **e** *are* as *the eyes* of doves by the H5869
12 His eyes *are* as *the* **e** of doves by the H5869
6: 5 Turn away thine **e** from me, for they H5869
7: 4 Thy neck *is* as a tower of ivory; thine **e** H5869
8:10 was I in his **e** as one that found favour. H5869
Isa 1:15 I will hide mine **e** from you: yea, when H5869
16 from before mine **e**; cease to do evil; H5869
3: 8 the LORD, to provoke the **e** of his glory. H5869
16 forth necks and wanton **e**, walking and H5869
5:15 and the **e** of the lofty shall be humbled: H5869
21 own **e**, and prudent in their own sight! H5869
6: 5 lips: for mine **e** have seen the King, H5869
10 and shut their **e**; lest they see with their H5869
10 lest they see with their **e**, and hear with H5869
11: 3 the sight of his **e**, neither reprove after H5869
13:16 pieces before their **e**; their houses shall H5869
17: 7 his Maker, and his **e** shall have respect H5869
29:10 hath closed your **e**: the prophets and H5869
18 of the book, and the **e** of the blind shall H5869
30:20 more, but thine **e** shall see thy teachers: H5869
32: 3 And the **e** of them that see shall not be H5869
33:15 and shutteth his **e** from seeing evil; H5869
17 Thine **e** shall see the king in his beauty: H5869
20 solemnities: thine **e** shall see Jerusalem H5869
35: 5 Then the **e** of the blind shall be opened, H5869
37:17 hear; open thine **e**, O LORD, and see: H5869
23 and lifted up thine **e** on high? *even* H5869
38:14 as a dove: mine **e** fail *with looking* H5869
40:26 Lift up your **e** on high, and behold who H5869
42: 7 To open the blind **e**, to bring out the H5869
43: 8 Bring forth the blind people that have **e**, H5869
44:18 he hath shut their **e**, that they cannot H5869
49: 5 I be glorious in the **e** of the LORD, and H5869
18 Lift up thine **e** round about, and H5869
51: 6 Lift up your **e** to the heavens, and look H5869
52:10 holy arm in the **e** of all the nations; and H5869
59:10 grope as if *we had* no **e**: we stumble at H5869
60: 4 Lift up thine **e** round about, and see: all H5869
65:12 evil before mine **e**, and did choose *that* H5869
16 and because they are hid from mine **e**. H5869
66: 4 did evil before mine **e**, and chose *that* in H5869
Jer 3: 2 Lift up thine **e** unto the high places, H5869
5: 3 O LORD, *are* not thine **e** upon the H5869
21 which have **e**, and see not; which have H5869
7:11 den of robbers in your **e**? Behold, even I H5869
9: 1 waters, and mine **e** a fountain of tears, H5869
18 for us, that our **e** may run down with H5869
13:20 Lift up your **e**, and behold them that H5869
14: 6 **e** did fail, because *there was* no grass. H5869
17 them; Let mine **e** run down with tears H5869
16: 9 of this place in your **e**, and in your days, H5869
17 For mine **e** *are* upon all their ways: H5869
17 is their iniquity hid from mine **e**. H5869
20: 4 and thine **e** shall behold *it*: and H5869
22:17 But thine **e** and thine heart *are* not but H5869
24: 6 For I will set mine **e** upon them for H5869
29:21 and he shall slay them before your **e**; H5869
31:16 and thine **e** from tears: for thy work H5869
32: 4 mouth, and his **e** shall behold his eyes; H5869
4 mouth, and his eyes shall behold his **e**; H5869
19 in work: for thine **e** *are* open upon all H5869
34: 3 hand; and thine **e** shall behold the eyes H5869
3 eyes shall behold the **e** of the king of H5869
39: 6 in Riblah before his **e**: also the king of H5869
7 Moreover he put out Zedekiah's **e**, and H5869
42: 2 few of many, as thine **e** do behold us:) H5869
52: 2 And he did *that which was* evil in the **e** H5869

Jer 52:10 before his **e**: he slew also all the princes H5869
11 Then he put out the **e** of Zedekiah; and H5869
Lam 2:11 Mine **e** do fail with tears, my bowels H5869
4:17 As for us, our **e** as yet failed for our H5869
5:17 is faint; for these *things* our **e** are dim. H5869
Ezk 1:18 *were* full of **e** round about them four. H5869
6: 9 from me, and with their **e**, which go a H5869
8: 5 of man, lift up thine **e** now the way H5869
5 So I lifted up mine **e** the way toward H5869
10:12 *were* full of **e** round about, *even* the H5869
12: 2 house, which have **e** to see, and see not; H5869
12 that he see not the ground with *his* **e**. H5869
18: 6 hath lifted up his **e** to the idols of the H5869
12 hath lifted up his **e** to the idols, hath H5869
15 hath lifted up his **e** to the idols of the H5869
20: 7 of his **e**, and defile not yourselves H5869
8 of their **e**, neither did they forsake H5869
24 their **e** were after their fathers' idols. H5869
21: 6 and with bitterness sigh before their **e**. H5869
22:26 and have hid their **e** from my sabbaths, H5869
23:16 saw them with her **e**, she doted upon H5869
27 shalt not lift up thine **e** unto them, nor H5869
40 **e**, and deckedst thyself with ornaments, H5869
24:16 the desire of thine **e** with a stroke: yet H5869
21 the desire of your **e**, and that which H5869
25 glory, the desire of their **e**, and that H5869
33:25 and lift up your **e** toward your idols, H5869
36:23 shall be sanctified in you before their **e**. H5869
37:20 shall be in thine hand before their **e**. H5869
38:16 sanctified in thee, O Gog, before their **e**. H5869
23 will be known in the **e** of many nations, H5869
40: 4 behold with thine **e**, and hear with thine H5869
44: 5 behold with thine **e**, and hear with thine H5869
Dan 4:34 lifted up mine **e** unto heaven, and mine H5870
7: 8 in this horn *were* **e** like the eyes of man, H5870
8 horn *were* eyes like the **e** of man, and a H5870
20 that horn that had **e**, and a mouth that H5870
8: 3 Then I lifted up mine **e**, and saw, and, H5869
5 goat *had* a notable horn between his **e**. H5869
21 that *is* between his **e** *is* the first king. H5869
9:18 and hear; open thine **e**, and behold our H5869
10: 5 Then I lifted up mine **e**, and looked, and H5869
6 of lightning, and his **e** as lamps of fire, H5869
Hos 13:14 repentance shall be hid from mine **e**. H5869
Joel 1:16 Is not the meat cut off before our **e**, *yea*, H5869
Am 9: 4 **e** upon them for evil, and not for good. H5869
8 Behold, the **e** of the Lord GOD *are* upon H5869
Mic 7:10 thy God? mine **e** shall behold her: now H5869
Hab 1:13 *Thou art* of purer **e** than to behold evil, H5869
Zep 3:20 captivity before your **e**, saith the LORD. H5869
Hag 2: 3 your **e** in comparison of it as nothing? H5869
Zec 1:18 Then lifted I up mine **e** again, and saw, and H5869
2: 1 I lifted up mine **e** again, and looked, H5869
3: 9 *shall be* seven **e**: behold, I will engrave H5869
4:10 seven; they *are* the **e** of the LORD, H5869
5: 1 Then I turned, and lifted up mine **e**, and H5869
5 **e**, and see what *is* this that goeth forth. H5869
9 Then lifted I up mine **e**, and looked, H5869
6: 1 And I turned, and lifted up mine **e**, and H5869
8: 6 marvellous in the **e** of the remnant of H5869
6 in mine **e**? saith the LORD of hosts. H5869
9: 1 thereof: when the **e** of man, as of all the H5869
8 more: for now have I seen with mine **e**. H5869
12: 4 I will open mine **e** upon the house of H5869
14:12 feet, and their **e** shall consume away H5869
Mal 1: 5 And your **e** shall see, and ye shall say, H5869
Mt 9:29 Then touched he their **e**, saying, *G3788*
30 And their **e** were opened; and Jesus *G3788*
13:15 hearing, and their **e** they have closed; *G3788*
15 see with *their* **e**, and hear with *their* *G3788*
16 But blessed *are* your **e**, for they see: and *G3788*
17: 8 And when they had lifted up their **e**, *G3788*
18: 9 having two **e** to be cast into hell fire. *G3788*
20:33 They say unto him, Lord, that our **e** *G3788*
34 and touched their **e**: and immediately *G3788*
34 immediately their **e** received sight, and *G3788*
21:42 doing, and it is marvellous in our **e**? *G3788*
26:43 asleep again: for their **e** were heavy. *G3788*
Mk 8:18 Having **e**, see ye not? and having ears, *G3788*
23 he had spit on his **e**, and put his hands *G3659*
25 again upon his **e**, and made him look *G3788*
9:47 having two **e** to be cast into hell fire: *G3788*
12:11 doing, and it is marvellous in our **e**? *G3788*
14:40 again, (for their **e** were heavy,) neither *G3788*
Lk 2:30 For mine **e** have seen thy salvation, *G3788*
4:20 sat down. And the **e** of all them that *G3788*
6:20 And he lifted up his **e** on his disciples, *G3788*
10:23 the **e** which see the things that ye see: *G3788*
16:23 And in hell he lift up his **e**, being in *G3788*

Lk 18:13 up so much as *his* e unto heaven, but G3788
19:42 but now they are hid from thine e. G3788
24:16 But their e were holden that they G3788
31 And their e were opened, and they G3788
Jn 4:35 you, Lift up your e, and look on the G3788
6: 5 When Jesus then lifted up *his* e, and G3788
9: 6 the e of the blind man with the clay, G3788
10 unto him, How were thine e opened? G3788
11 anointed mine e, and said unto me, Go G3788
14 Jesus made the clay, and opened his e. G3788
15 upon mine e, and I washed, and do see. G3788
17 thine e? He said, He is a prophet. G3788
21 hath opened his e, we know not: he is of G3788
26 did he to thee? how opened he thine e? G3788
30 he is, and *yet* he hath opened mine e. G3788
32 the e of one that was born blind. G3788
10:21 Can a devil open the e of the blind? G3788
11:37 which opened the e of the blind, have G3788
41 Jesus lifted up *his* e, and said, Father, I G3788
12:40 He hath blinded their e, and hardened G3788
40 not see with *their* e, nor understand G3788
17: 1 and lifted up his e to heaven, and said, G3788
Act 3: 4 And Peter, fastening his e upon him with G816
9: 8 and when his e were opened, he saw G3788
18 And immediately there fell from his e G3788
40 e: and when she saw Peter, she sat up. G3788
11: 6 I had fastened mine e, I considered, and G816
13: 9 with the Holy Ghost, set his e on him, G816
26:18 To open their e, *and* to turn *them* from G3788
28:27 hearing, and their e have they closed; G3788
27 see with *their* e, and hear with *their* G3788
Ro 3:18 There is no fear of God before their e. G3788
11: 8 the spirit of slumber, e that they should G3788
10 Let their e be darkened, that they may G3788
Gal 3: 1 before whose e Jesus Christ hath been G3788
4:15 your own e, and have given them to me. G3788
Eph 1:18 The e of your understanding being G3788
Heb 4:13 the e of him with whom we have to do. G3788
1Pt 3:12 For the e of the Lord *are* over the G3788
2Pt 2:14 Having e full of adultery, and that G3788
1Jn 1: 1 seen with our e, which we have looked G3788
2:11 that darkness hath blinded his e. G3788
16 and the lust of the e, and the pride of G3788
Rev 1:14 snow; and his e *were* as a flame of fire; G3788
2:18 God, who hath his e like unto a flame G3788
3:18 e with eyesalve, that thou mayest see. G3788
4: 6 four beasts full of e before and behind. G3788
8 *they were* full of e within: and they rest G3788
5: 6 horns and seven e, which are the seven G3788
7:17 shall wipe away all tears from their e. G3788
19:12 His e *were* as a flame of fire, and on his G3788
Rev 21: 4 tears from their e; and there shall be no G3788

EYE'S
Ex 21:26 he shall let him go free for his e sake. H5869

EYESALVE
Rev 3:18 thine eyes with e, that thou mayest see. G2854

EYESERVICE
Eph 6: 6 Not with e, as menpleasers; but as the G3787
Col 3:22 to the flesh; not with e, as menpleasers; G3787

EYESIGHT
Ps 18:24 to the cleanness of my hands in his e. H5869

EYEWITNESSES
Lk 1: 2 were e, and ministers of the word; G845
2Pt 1:16 Jesus Christ, but were e of his majesty. G2030

EZBAI
1Ch 11:37 Hezro the Carmelite, Naarai the son of E, H229

EZBON
Gen 46:16 Shuni, and E, Eri, and Arodi, and Areli. H675
1Ch 7: 7 And the sons of Bela; E, and Uzzi, and H675

EZEKIAS
Mt 1: 9 begat Achaz; and Achaz begat E; G1478
10 And E begat Manasses; and Manasses G1478

EZEKIEL
Ezk 1: 3 expressly unto E the priest, the son of H3168
24:24 Thus E is unto you a sign: according to H3168

EZEL
1Sa 20:19 *in hand,* and shalt remain by the stone E. H237

EZEM
1Ch 4:29 And at Bilhah, and at E, and at Tolad, H6107

EZER
Gen 36:21 And Dishon, and E, and Dishan: these H687
27 The children of E *are* these; Bilhan, and H687
30 Duke Dishon, duke E, duke Dishan: these H687
1Ch 1:38 Anah, and Dishon, and E, and Dishan. H687
42 The sons of E; Bilhan, and Zavan, *and* H687
4: 4 And Penuel the father of Gedor, and E H5829
7:21 his son, and E, and Elead, whom the H5827
12: 9 E the first, Obadiah the second, Eliab H5829
Neh 3:19 And next to him repaired E the son of H5829
12:42 and Elam, and E. And the singers sang H5829

EZION-GABER
Nu 33:35 from Ebronah, and encamped at E. H6100
36 And they removed from E, and pitched H6100
Dt 2: 8 from Elath, and from E, we turned and H6100

EZION-GEBER
1Ki 9:26 a navy of ships in E, which *is* beside H6100
22:48 not; for the ships were broken at E. H6100
2Ch 8:17 Then went Solomon to E, and to Eloth, H6100
20:36 Tarshish: and they made the ships in E. H6100

EZNITE
2Sa 23: 8 *was* Adino the E: *he lift up his spear* H6112

EZRA
1Ch 4:17 And the sons of E *were,* Jether, and H5834
Ezr 7: 1 king of Persia, E the son of Seraiah, H5830
6 This E went up from Babylon; and he H5830
10 For E had prepared his heart to seek H5830
11 gave unto E the priest, the scribe, H5830
12 Artaxerxes, king of kings, unto E the H5831
21 that whatsoever E the priest, the scribe H5831
25 And thou, E, after the wisdom of thy H5831
10: 1 Now when E had prayed, and when he H5830
2 and said unto E, We have trespassed H5830
5 Then arose E, and made the chief H5830
6 Then E rose up from before the house H5830
10 And E the priest stood up, and said H5830
16 did so. And E the priest, *with* certain H5830
Neh 8: 1 they spake unto E the scribe to bring H5830
2 And E the priest brought the law before H5830
4 And E the scribe stood upon a pulpit of H5830
5 And E opened the book in the sight of H5830
6 And E blessed the LORD, the great H5830
9 Tirshatha, and E the priest the scribe, H5830
13 the Levites, unto E the scribe, even to H5830
12: 1 and Jeshua: Seraiah, Jeremiah, E, H5830
13 Of E, Meshullam; of Amariah, H5830
26 and of E the priest, the scribe. H5830
33 And Azariah, E, and Meshullam, H5830
36 of God, and E the scribe before them. H5830

EZRAHITE
1Ki 4:31 men; than Ethan the E, and Heman, and H250
Ps 88:ttl Leannoth, Maschil of Heman the E. H250
89:ttl Maschil of Ethan the E. H250

EZRI
1Ch 27:26 of the ground *was* E the son of Chelub: H5836

EZRITE See ABI-EZRITE.

F

FABLES
1Ti 1: 4 Neither give heed to f and endless G3454
4: 7 But refuse profane and old wives' f, and G3454
2Ti 4: 4 the truth, and shall be turned unto f. G3454
Tit 1:14 Not giving heed to Jewish f, and G3454
2Pt 1:16 cunningly devised f, when we made G3454

FACE
Gen 1: 2 *was* upon the f of the deep. And the H6440
2 of God moved upon the f of the waters. H6440
29 which *is* upon the f of all the earth, and H6440
2: 6 and watered the whole f of the ground. H6440
3:19 In the sweat of thy f shalt thou eat bread, H639
4:14 out this day from the f of the earth; and H6440
14 and from thy f shall I be hid; and I H6440
6: 1 to multiply on the f of the earth, and H6440
7 created from the f of the earth; both H6440
7: 3 seed alive upon the f of all the earth. H6440
4 will I destroy from off the f of the earth. H6440
18 the ark went upon the f of the waters. H6440
23 was upon the f of the ground, both H6440
8: 8 abated from off the f of the ground; H6440
9 waters *were* on the f of the whole earth: H6440
13 behold, the f of the ground was dry. H6440
11: 4 abroad upon the f of the whole earth. H6440
8 thence upon the f of all the earth: and H6440
9 them abroad upon the f of all the earth. H6440
16: 6 hardly with her, she fled from her f. H6440
8 I flee from the f of my mistress Sarai. H6440
17: 3 And Abram fell on his f: and God talked H6440
Gen 17:17 Then Abraham fell upon his f, and H6440
19: 1 himself with his f toward the ground; H639
13 great before the f of the LORD; and the H6440
24:47 her f, and the bracelets upon her hands. H639
30:33 my hire before thy f: every one that *is* H6440
31:21 and set his f *toward* the mount Gilead. H6440
32:20 his f; peradventure he will accept of me. H6440
30 God f to face, and my life is preserved. H6440
30 God face to f, and my life is preserved. H6440
33:10 I have seen thy f, as though I had seen H6440
10 I had seen the f of God, and thou wast H6440
35: 1 fleddest from the f of Esau thy brother. H6440
7 when he fled from the f of his brother. H6440
36: 6 country from the f of his brother Jacob. H6440
38:15 harlot; because she had covered her f. H6440
41:56 And the famine was over all the f of the H6440
43: 3 my f, except your brother *be* with you. H6440
5 my f, except your brother *be* with you. H6440
31 And he washed his f, and went out, and H6440
44:23 with you, ye shall see my f no more. H6440
26 not see the man's f, except our youngest H6440
46:28 to direct his f unto Goshen; and they H6440
30 seen thy f, because thou *art* yet alive. H6440
48:11 thought to see thy f: and, lo, God hath H6440
12 he bowed himself with his f to the earth. H639
50: 1 And Joseph fell upon his father's f, and H6440
18 fell down before his f; and they said, H6440
Ex 2:15 fled from the f of Pharaoh, and dwelt H6440
3: 6 f; for he was afraid to look upon God. H6440
10: 5 And they shall cover the f of the earth, H5869
15 For they covered the f of the whole H5869
Ex 10:28 to thyself, see my f no more; for in *that* H6440
28 *that* day thou seest my f thou shalt die. H6440
29 well, I will see thy f again no more. H6440
14:19 before their f, and stood behind them: H6440
25 Let us flee from the f of Israel; for the H6440
16:14 up, behold, upon the f of the wilderness H6440
32:12 them from the f of the earth? Turn H6440
33:11 And the LORD spake unto Moses f to H6440
11 unto Moses face to f, as a man speaketh H6440
16 people that *are* upon the f of the earth. H6440
20 And he said, Thou canst not see my f: H6440
23 back parts: but my f shall not be seen. H6440
34:29 of his f shone while he talked with him. H6440
30 the skin of his f shone; and they were H6440
33 with them, he put a vail on his f. H6440
35 And the children of Israel saw the f of H6440
35 the skin of Moses' f shone: and Moses H6440
35 the vail upon his f again, until he went H6440
Lev 13:41 his f, he *is* forehead bald: *yet is* he clean. H6440
17:10 I will even set my f against that soul H6440
19:32 and honour the f of the old man, and H6440
20: 3 And I will set my f against that man, H6440
5 Then I will set my f against that man, H6440
6 I will even set my f against that soul, H6440
26:17 And I will set my f against you, and ye H6440
Nu 6:25 The LORD make his f shine upon thee, H6440
11:31 two cubits *high* upon the f of the earth. H6440
12: 3 which *were* upon the f of the earth.) H6440
14 had but spit in her f, should she not be H6440
14:14 LORD art seen f to face, and *that* thy H5869
14 art seen face to f, and *that* thy cloud H5869

Nu 16: 4 when Moses heard *it*, he fell upon his f: H6440
19: 3 camp, and *one* shall slay her before his f:
22: 5 they cover the f of the earth, and they H5869
11 covereth the f of the earth: come now, H5869
31 down his head, and fell flat on his f. H639
24: 1 but he set his f toward the wilderness. H6440
Dt 1:17 not be afraid of the f of man; for the H6440
5: 4 The LORD talked with you f to face in H6440
4 The LORD talked with you face to f in H6440
6:15 destroy thee from off the f of the earth. H6440
7: 6 people that *are* upon the f of the earth. H6440
10 hate him to their f, to destroy them: he H6440
10 hateth him, he will repay him to his f. H6440
8:20 before your f, so shall ye perish; H6440
9: 3 down before thy f: so shalt thou drive H6440
25: 2 be beaten before his f, according to his H6440
9 and spit in his f, and shall answer and H6440
28: 7 smitten before thy f: they shall come out H6440
31 away from before thy f, and shall not be H6440
31: 5 up before your f, that ye may do unto H6440
17 and I will hide my f from them, and H6440
18 And I will surely hide my f in that day H6440
32:20 And he said, I will hide my f from H6440
34:10 Moses, whom the LORD knew f to face, H6440
10 Moses, whom the LORD knew face to f, H6440
Jos 5:14 Joshua fell on his f to the earth, and did H6440
7: 6 to the earth upon his f before the ark of H6440
10 up; wherefore liest thou thus upon thy f? H6440
Jdg 6:22 seen an angel of the LORD f to face. H6440
22 seen an angel of the LORD face to f. H6440
Ru 2:10 Then she fell on her f, and bowed H6440
1Sa 5: 3 fallen upon his f to the earth before the H6440
4 fallen upon his f to the ground before H6440
17:49 and he fell upon his f to the earth. H6440
20:15 David every one from the f of the earth. H6440
41 and fell on his f to the ground, and H639
24: 8 his f to the earth, and bowed himself. H639
25:23 her f, and bowed herself to the ground, H6440
41 herself on *her* f to the earth, and said, H639
26:20 earth before the f of the LORD: for the H6440
28:14 *his* f to the ground, and bowed himself. H639
2Sa 2:22 I hold up my f to Joab thy brother? H6440
3:13 shalt not see my f, except thou first H6440
13 when thou comest to see my f. H6440
9: 6 he fell on his f, and did reverence. And H6440
14: 4 king, she fell on her f to the ground, and H639
22 And Joab fell to the ground on his f, and H6440
24 and let him not see my f. So Absalom H6440
24 his own house, and saw not the king's f. H6440
28 in Jerusalem, and saw not the king's f. H6440
32 me see the king's f; and if there be *any* H6440
33 himself on his f to the ground before H639
18: 8 scattered over the f of all the country: H6440
28 the earth upon his f before the king, and H639
19: 4 But the king covered his f, and the king H6440
24:20 before the king on his f upon the ground. H639
1Ki 1:23 before the king with his f to the ground. H639
31 Then Bath-sheba bowed with *her* f to the H639
8:14 And the king turned his f about, and H6440
13: 6 Entreat now the f of the LORD thy God, H6440
34 to destroy *it* from off the f of the earth. H6440
18: 7 and fell on his f, and said, *Art* thou that H6440
42 earth, and put his f between his knees, H6440
19:13 he wrapped his f in his mantle, and H6440
20:38 disguised himself with ashes upon his f. H5869
41 away from his f; and the king of Israel H5869
21: 4 away his f, and would eat no bread. H6440
2Ki 4:29 and lay my staff upon the f of the child. H6440
31 laid the staff upon the f of the child; but H6440
8:15 spread *it* on his f, so that he died: and H6440
9:30 she painted her f, and tired her head, H5869
32 And he lifted up his f to the window, H6440
37 be as dung upon the f of the field in the H6440
12:17 Hazael set his f to go up to Jerusalem. H6440
13:14 and wept over his f, and said, O my H6440
14: 8 Come, let us look one another in the f. H6440
11 one another in the f at Beth-shemesh, H6440
18:24 How then wilt thou turn away the f of H6440
20: 2 Then he turned his f to the wall, and H6440
1Ch 16:11 and his strength, seek his f continually. H6440
21:21 to David with *his* f to the ground. H639
2Ch 6: 3 And the king turned his f, and blessed H6440
42 O LORD God, turn not away the f of H6440
7:14 and pray, and seek my f, and turn from H6440
20:18 his head with *his* f to the ground: and all H639
25:17 Come, let us see one another in the f. H6440
21 saw one another in the f, *both* he and H6440
30: 9 *his* f from you, if ye return unto him. H6440
32:21 with shame of f to his own land. And H6440

2Ch 35:22 would not turn his f from him, but H6440
Ezr 9: 6 blush to lift up my f to thee, my God: H6440
7 and to confusion of f, as *it is* this day. H6440
Est 1:14 saw the king's f, *and* which sat the first H6440
7: 8 king's mouth, they covered Haman's f. H6440
Job 1:11 he hath, and he will curse thee to thy f. H6440
2: 5 his flesh, and he will curse thee to thy f. H6440
4:15 Then a spirit passed before my f; the H6440
11:15 For then shalt thou lift up thy f without H6440
13:24 Wherefore hidest thou thy f, and H6440
15:27 Because he covereth his f with his H6440
16: 8 rising up in me beareth witness to my f. H6440
16 My f is foul with weeping, and on my H6440
21:31 Who shall declare his way to his f? and H6440
22:26 and shalt lift up thy f unto God. H6440
23:17 he covered the darkness from my f. H6440
24:15 eye shall see me: and disguiseth *his* f. H6440
26: 9 He holdeth back the f of his throne, H6440
30:10 from me, and spare not to spit in my f. H6440
33:26 he shall see his f with joy: for he will H6440
34:29 and when he hideth *his* f, who then can H6440
37:12 upon the f of the world in the earth. H6440
38:30 a stone, and the f of the deep is frozen. H6440
41:13 Who can discover the f of his garment? H6440
14 Who can open the doors of his f? his H6440
Ps 5: 8 make thy way straight before my f. H6440
10:11 he hideth his f; he will never see *it*. H6440
13: 1 how long wilt thou hide thy f from me? H6440
17:15 As for me, I will behold thy f in H6440
21:12 upon thy strings against the f of them. H6440
22:24 hath he hid his f from him; but when H6440
24: 6 him, that seek thy f, O Jacob. Selah. H6440
27: 8 *When thou saidst*, Seek ye my f; my H6440
8 said unto thee, Thy f, LORD, will I seek. H6440
9 Hide not thy f *far* from me; put not thy H6440
30: 7 didst hide thy f, *and* I was troubled. H6440
31:16 Make thy f to shine upon thy servant: H6440
34:16 The f of the LORD *is* against them that H6440
41:12 and settest me before thy f for ever. H6440
44:15 the shame of my f hath covered me, H6440
24 Wherefore hidest thou thy f, *and* H6440
51: 9 Hide thy f from my sins, and blot out H6440
67: 1 *and* cause his f to shine upon us; Selah. H6440
69: 7 reproach; shame hath covered my f. H6440
17 And hide not thy f from thy servant; for H6440
80: 3 Turn us again, O God, and cause thy f H6440
7 thy f to shine; and we shall be saved. H6440
19 thy f to shine; and we shall be saved. H6440
84: 9 and look upon the f of thine anointed. H6440
88:14 soul? *why* hidest thou thy f from me? H6440
89:14 mercy and truth shall go before thy f. H6440
23 his f, and plague them that hate him. H6440
102: 2 Hide not thy f from me in the day *when* H6440
104:15 oil to make *his* f to shine, and bread H6440
29 Thou hidest thy f, they are troubled: H6440
30 and thou renewest the f of the earth. H6440
105: 4 and his strength: seek his f evermore. H6440
119:135 Make thy f to shine upon thy servant; H6440
132:10 turn not away the f of thine anointed. H6440
143: 7 hide not thy f from me, lest I be like H6440
Prv 7:13 *and* with an impudent f said unto him, H6440
15 to seek thy f, and I have found thee. H6440
8:27 set a compass upon the f of the depth: H6440
21:29 A wicked man hardeneth his f: but *as* H6440
24:31 had covered the f thereof, and the H6440
27:19 As in water f *answereth* to face, so the H6440
19 As in water face *answereth* to f, so the H6440
Ecc 8: 1 maketh his f to shine, and the boldness H6440
1 the boldness of his f shall be changed. H6440
Isa 6: 2 he covered his f, and with twain he H6440
8:17 that hideth his f from the house of H6440
14:21 nor fill the f of the world with cities. H6440
16: 4 to them from the f of the spoiler: for the H6440
23:17 of the world upon the f of the earth. H6440
25: 7 this mountain the f of the covering cast H6440
27: 6 and fill the f of the world with fruit. H6440
28:25 When he hath made plain the f thereof, H6440
29:22 neither shall his f now wax pale. H6440
36: 9 How then wilt thou turn away the f of H6440
38: 2 Then Hezekiah turned his f toward the H6440
49:23 to thee with *their* f toward the earth, and H639
50: 6 I hid not my f from shame and spitting. H6440
7 have I set my f like a flint, and I know H6440
54: 8 In a little wrath I hid my f from thee for H6440
59: 2 *his* f from you, that he will not hear. H6440
64: 7 thou hast hid thy f from us, and hast H6440
65: 3 continually to my f; that sacrificeth in H6440
Jer 1:13 and the f thereof *is* toward the north. H6440
2:27 me, and not *their* f: but in the time of H6440

Jer 4:30 thou rentest thy f with painting, in vain H5869
8: 2 be for dung upon the f of the earth. H6440
13:26 upon thy f, that thy shame may appear. H6440
16: 4 be as dung upon the f of the earth: and H6440
17 are not hid from my f, neither is their H6440
18:17 not the f, in the day of their calamity. H6440
21:10 For I have set my f against this city for H6440
22:25 *of them* whose f thou fearest, even into H6440
25:26 *are* upon the f of the earth: and the H6440
28:16 cast thee from off the f of the earth: this H6440
32:31 I should remove it from before my f, H6440
33 the back, and not the f: though I taught H6440
33: 5 I have hid my f from this city. H6440
44:11 I will set my f against you for evil, H6440
Lam 2:19 water before the f of the Lord: lift up H6440
3:35 of a man before the f of the most High, H6440
Ezk 1:10 they four had the f of a man, and the H6440
10 of a man, and the f of a lion, on the H6440
10 they four had the f of an ox on the left H6440
10 they four also had the f of an eagle. H6440
28 f, and I heard a voice of one that spake. H6440
3: 8 Behold, I have made thy f strong H6440
23 the river of Chebar: and I fell on my f. H6440
4: 3 city: and set thy f against it, and it shall H6440
7 Therefore thou shalt set thy f toward H6440
6: 2 Son of man, set thy f toward the H6440
7:22 My f will I turn also from them, and H6440
9: 8 left, that I fell upon my f, and cried, and H6440
10:14 And every one had four faces: the first f H6440
14 first face *was* the f of a cherub, and the H6440
14 and the second f *was* the face of a man, H6440
14 face *was* the f of a man, and the third H6440
14 and the third the f of a lion, and the H6440
14 a lion, and the fourth the f of an eagle. H6440
11:13 I down upon my f, and cried with a loud H6440
12: 6 shalt cover thy f, that thou see not the H6440
12 he shall cover his f, that he see not the H6440
13:17 Likewise, thou son of man, set thy f H6440
14: 3 f: should I be inquired of at all by them? H6440
4 iniquity before his f, and cometh to the H6440
7 iniquity before his f, and cometh to a H6440
8 And I will set my f against that man, H6440
15: 7 And I will set my f against them; they H6440
7 LORD, when I set my f against them. H6440
20:35 and there will I plead with you f to face. H6440
35 and there will I plead with you face to f. H6440
46 Son of man, set thy f toward the south, H6440
21: 2 Son of man, set thy f toward Jerusalem, H6440
16 *or* on the left, whithersoever thy f *is* set. H6440
25: 2 Son of man, set thy f against the H6440
28:21 Son of man, set thy f against Zidon, H6440
29: 2 Son of man, set thy f against Pharaoh H6440
34: 6 upon all the f of the earth, and none H6440
35: 2 Son of man, set thy f against mount H6440
38: 2 Son of man, set thy f against Gog, the H6440
18 GOD, *that* my fury shall come up in my f. H639
20 that *are* upon the f of the earth, shall H6440
39:14 that remain upon the f of the earth, to H6440
23 therefore hid I my f from them, and H6440
24 unto them, and hid my f from them. H6440
29 Neither will I hide my f any more from H6440
40:15 And from the f of the gate of the H6440
15 entrance unto the f of the porch of the H6440
41:14 Also the breadth of the f of the house, H6440
19 So that the f of a man *was* toward the H6440
19 the one side, and the f of a young lion H6440
21 squared, *and* the f of the sanctuary; the H6440
25 planks upon the f of the porch without. H6440
43: 3 the river Chebar; and I fell upon my f. H6440
44: 4 of the LORD: and I fell upon my f. H6440
Dan 2:46 fell upon his f, and worshipped Daniel, H600
8: 5 the west on the f of the whole earth, H6440
17 and fell upon my f: but he said unto me, H6440
18 deep sleep on my f toward the ground: H6440
9: 3 And I set my f unto the Lord God, to H6440
8 O Lord, to us *belongeth* confusion of f, H6440
17 and cause thy f to shine upon thy H6440
10: 6 the beryl, and his f as the appearance H6440
9 my f, and my face toward the ground. H6440
9 my face, and my f toward the ground. H6440
15 unto me, I set my f toward the ground, H6440
11:17 He shall also set his f to enter with the H6440
18 After this shall he turn his f unto the H6440
19 Then he shall turn his f toward the fort H6440
Hos 5: 5 doth testify to his f: therefore shall H6440
15 and seek my f: in their affliction they H6440
7: 2 beset them about; they are before my f. H6440
10 And the pride of Israel testifieth to his f: H6440
Joel 2: 6 Before their f the people shall be much H6440

Joel 2:20 desolate, with his f toward the east sea, H6440
Am 5: 8 f of the earth: The LORD *is* his name: H6440
9: 6 f of the earth: The LORD *is* his name. H6440
8 it from off the f of the earth; saving H6440
Mic 3: 4 will even hide his f from them at that H6440
Nah 2: 1 up before thy f: keep the munition, H6440
3: 5 thy skirts upon thy f, and I will shew the H6440
Zec 5: 3 forth over the f of the whole earth: for H6440
Mt 6:17 anoint thine head, and wash thy f; G4383
11:10 before thy f, which shall prepare G4383
16: 3 ye can discern the f of the sky; but can G4383
17: 2 them: and his f did shine as the sun, G4383
6 they fell on their f, and were sore afraid. G4383
18:10 the f of my Father which is in heaven. G4383
26:39 and fell on his f, and prayed, saying, G4383
67 Then did they spit in his f, and buffeted G4383
Mk 1: 2 before thy f, which shall prepare G4383
14:65 and to cover his f, and to buffet him, G4383
Lk 1:76 the f of the Lord to prepare his ways; G4383
2:31 Which thou hast prepared before the f G4383
5:12 Jesus fell on *his* f, and besought him, G4383
7:27 before thy f, which shall prepare G4383
9:51 stedfastly set his f to go to Jerusalem, G4383
52 And sent messengers before his f: and G4383
53 him, because his f was as though he G4383
10: 1 and two before his f into every city and G4383
12:56 *Ye* hypocrites, ye can discern the f of G4383
17:16 And fell down on *his* f at his feet, giving G4383
21:35 that dwell on the f of the whole earth. G4383
22:64 struck him on the f, and asked him, G4383
Jn 11:44 and his f was bound about with G3799
Act 2:25 Lord always before my f, for he is on my G3450
6:15 his f as it had been the face of an angel. G4383
15 his face as it had been the f of an angel. G4383
7:45 f of our fathers, unto the days of David; G4383
17:26 for to dwell on all the f of the earth, and G4383
20:25 of God, shall see my f no more. G4383
38 they should see his f no more. And they G4383
25:16 have the accusers f to face, and have G4383
16 accusers face to f, and have licence to G2596
1Co 13:12 darkly; but then f to face: now I know G4383
12 but then face to f: now I know in part; G4383
14:25 down on *his* f he will worship God, G4383
2Co 3: 7 behold the f of Moses for the glory G4383
13 put a veil over his f, that the children of G4383
18 But we all, with open f beholding as in G4383
4: 6 the glory of God in the f of Jesus Christ. G4383
11:20 himself, if a man smite you on the f. G4383
Gal 1:22 And was unknown by f unto the G4383
2:11 to the f, because he was to be blamed. G4383
Col 2: 1 as have not seen my f in the flesh; G4383
1Th 2:17 to see your f with great desire. G4383
3:10 we might see your f, and might perfect G4383
Jas 1:23 man beholding his natural f in a glass: G4383
1Pt 3:12 prayers: but the f of the Lord *is* against G4383
2Jn 12 speak f to face, that our joy may be full. G4750
12 speak face to f, that our joy may be full. G4750
3Jn 14 we shall speak f to face. Peace *be* to G4750
14 shall speak face to f. Peace *be* to thee. G4750
Rev 4: 7 third beast had a f as a man, and the G4383
6:16 hide us from the f of him that sitteth on G4383
10: 1 his head, and his f *was* as it were the G4383
12:14 half a time, from the f of the serpent. G4383
20:11 on it, from whose f the earth and the G4383
22: 4 And they shall see his f; and his name G4383

FACED See SHAMEFACEDNESS.

FACES
Gen 9:23 father; and their f *were* backward, and H6440
18:22 And the men turned their f from H6437
30:40 the lambs, and set the f of the flocks H6440
42: 6 before him *with* their f to the earth. H639
Ex 19: 7 laid before their f all these words which H6440
20:20 may be before your f, that ye sin not. H6440
25:20 wings, and their f *shall look* one to H6440
20 seat shall the f of the cherubims be. H6440
37: 9 seat, with their f one to another; *even* H6440
9 seatward were the f of the cherubims. H6440
Lev 9:24 saw, they shouted, and fell on their f. H6440
Nu 14: 5 Then Moses and Aaron fell on their f H6440
16:22 And they fell upon their f, and said, O H6440
45 in a moment. And they fell upon their f. H6440
20: 6 fell upon their f: and the glory of the H6440
Jdg 13:20 on *it*, and fell on their f to the ground. H6440
18:23 And they turned their f, and said unto H6440
2Sa 19: 5 this day the f of all thy servants, which H6440
1Ki 2:15 all Israel set their f on me, that I should H6440
18:39 *it*, they fell on their f: and they said, The H6440
1Ch 12: 8 buckler, whose f *were like* the faces of H6440
8 faces *were like* the f of lions, and *were* H6440
21:16 clothed in sackcloth, fell upon their f. H6440
2Ch 3:13 on their feet, and their f *were* inward. H6440
7: 3 with their f to the ground upon the H639
29: 6 turned away their f from the habitation H6440
Neh 8: 6 the LORD with *their* f to the ground. H639
Job 9:24 he covereth the f of the judges thereof; H6440
40:13 together; *and* bind their f in secret. H6440
Ps 34: 5 and their f were not ashamed. H6440
83:16 Fill their f with shame; that they may H6440
Isa 3:15 and grind the f of the poor? saith the H6440
13: 8 at another; their f *shall be as* flames. H6440
25: 8 tears from off all f; and the rebuke of H6440
53: 3 hid as it were *our* f from him; he was H6440
Jer 1: 8 Be not afraid of their f: for I *am* with H6440
17 their f, lest I confound thee before them. H6440
5: 3 have made their f harder than a rock; H6440
7:19 to the confusion of their own f? H6440
30: 6 and all f are turned into paleness? H6440
42:15 ye wholly set your f to enter into Egypt, H6440
17 men that set their f to go into Egypt to H6440
44:12 that have set their f to go into the land H6440
50: 5 way to Zion with their f thitherward, H6440
51:51 hath covered our f: for strangers are H6440
Lam 5:12 the f of elders were not honoured. H6440
Ezk 1: 6 And every one had four f, and every one H6440
8 they four had their f and their wings. H6440
10 As for the likeness of their f, they four H6440
11 Thus *were* their f: and their wings *were* H6440
15 by the living creatures, with his four f. H6440
3: 8 against their f, and thy forehead strong H6440
7:18 all f, and baldness upon all their heads. H6440
8:16 LORD, and their f toward the east; and H6440
10:14 And every one had four f: the first face H6440
21 Every one had four f apiece, and every H6440
22 And the likeness of their f *was* the H6440
22 *was* the same f which I saw by the river H6440
14: 6 your f from all your abominations. H6440
20:47 quenched, and all f from the south to H6440
41:18 a cherub; and *every* cherub had two f; H6440
Dan 1:10 should he see your f worse liking than H6440
9: 7 us confusion of f, as at this day; to the H6440
Joel 2: 6 pained: all f shall gather blackness. H6440
Nah 2:10 and the f of them all gather blackness. H6440
Hab 1: 9 They shall come all for violence: their f H6440
Mal 2: 3 dung upon your f, *even* the dung of H6440
Mt 6:16 disfigure their f, that they may appear G4383
Lk 24: 5 bowed down *their* f to the earth, they G4383
Rev 7:11 throne on their f, and worshipped God, G4383
9: 7 and their f *were* as the faces of men. G4383
7 and their faces *were* as the f of men. G4383
11:16 fell upon their f, and worshipped God, G4383

FADE
2Sa 22:46 Strangers shall f away, and they shall H5034
Ps 18:45 The strangers shall f away, and be H5034
Isa 64: 6 rags; and we all do f as a leaf; and our H5034
Jer 8:13 and the leaf shall f; and *the things that* H5034
Ezk 47:12 leaf shall not f, neither shall the fruit H5034
Jas 1:11 shall the rich man f away in his ways. G3133

FADETH
Isa 1:30 For ye shall be as an oak whose leaf f, H5034
24: 4 The earth mourneth *and* f away, the H5034
4 languisheth *and* f away, the haughty H5034
40: 7 The grass withereth, the flower f: H5034
8 The grass withereth, the flower f: but H5034
1Pt 1: 4 f not away, reserved in heaven for you, G263
5: 4 receive a crown of glory that f not away. G262

FADING
Isa 28: 1 beauty *is* a f flower, which *are* on H5034
4 fat valley, shall be a f flower, *and* as the H5034

FAIL
Gen 47:16 I will give you for your cattle, if money f. H656
Dt 28:32 shall look, and f *with longing* for them H3616
31: 6 he will not f thee, nor forsake thee. H7503
8 thee, he will not f thee, neither forsake H7503
Jos 1: 5 thee: I will not f thee, nor forsake thee. H7503
3:10 he will without f drive out from before H3423
Jdg 11:30 If thou shalt without f deliver the H5414
1Sa 2:16 unto him, Let them not f to burn the fat H6999
17:32 Let no man's heart f because of him; H5307
20: 5 and I should not f to sit with the king at H3427
30: 8 *them*, and without f recover *all*. H5337
2Sa 3:29 and let there not f from the house of H3772
1Ki 2: 4 there shall not f thee (said he) a man H3772
1Ki 8:25 There shall not f thee a man in my H3772
9: 5 f thee a man upon the throne of Israel. H3772
17:14 the cruse of oil f, until the day *that* the H2637
16 did the cruse of oil f, according to the H2638
1Ch 28:20 with thee; he will not f thee, nor forsake H7503
2Ch 6:16 There shall not f thee a man in my H3772
7:18 not f thee a man *to be* ruler in Israel. H3772
Ezr 4:22 Take heed now that ye f not to do this: H7960
6: 9 it be given them day by day without f: H7960
Est 6:10 nothing f of all that thou hast spoken. H5307
9:27 so as it should not f, that they would H5674
28 of Purim should not f from among the H5674
Job 11:20 But the eyes of the wicked shall f, and H3615
14:11 *As* the waters f from the sea, and the H235
17: 5 even the eyes of his children shall f. H3615
31:16 have caused the eyes of the widow to f; H3615
Ps 12: 1 f from among the children of men. H6461
69: 3 mine eyes f while I wait for my God. H3615
77: 8 ever? doth *his* promise f for evermore? H1584
89:33 him, nor suffer my faithfulness to f. H8266
119:82 Mine eyes f for thy word, saying, When H3615
123 Mine eyes f for thy salvation, and for H3615
Prv 22: 8 vanity: and the rod of his anger shall f. H3615
Ecc 12: 5 and desire shall f: because man goeth H6565
Isa 19: 3 And the spirit of Egypt shall f in the H1238
5 And the waters shall f from the sea, H5405
21:16 and all the glory of Kedar shall f: H3615
31: 3 fall down, and they all shall f together. H3615
32: 6 will cause the drink of the thirsty to f. H2637
10 shall f, the gathering shall not come. H3615
34:16 one of these shall f, none shall want her H5737
38:14 as a dove: mine eyes f *with looking* H1809
42: 4 He shall not f nor be discouraged, till H3543
51:14 in the pit, nor that his bread should f. H2637
57:16 the spirit should f before me, and the H5848
58:11 a spring of water, whose waters f not. H3576
Jer 14: 6 eyes did f, because *there was* no grass. H3615
15:18 unto me as a liar, *and as* waters *that* f? H539
48:33 caused wine to f from the winepresses: H7673
Lam 2:11 Mine eyes do f with tears, my bowels H3615
3:22 because his compassions f not. H3615
Hos 9: 2 them, and the new wine shall f in her. H3584
Am 8: 4 even to make the poor of the land to f, H7673
Hab 3:17 of the olive shall f, and the fields shall H3584
Lk 16: 9 that, when ye f, they may receive you G1587
17 to pass, than one tittle of the law to f. G4098
22:32 for thee, that thy faith f not: and when G1587
1Co 13: 8 they shall f; whether *there be* tongues, G2673
Heb 1:12 art the same, and thy years shall not f. G1587
11:32 say? for the time would f me to tell of G1952
12:15 Looking diligently lest any man f of the G5302

FAILED
Gen 42:28 and their heart f *them*, and they were H3318
47:15 And when money f in the land of H8552
Jos 3:16 *even* the salt sea, f, *and* were cut off: H8552
21:45 There f not ought of any good thing H5307
23:14 that not one thing hath f of all the good H5307
14 you, *and* not one thing hath f thereof. H5307
1Ki 8:56 there hath not f one word of all his H5307
Job 19:14 My kinsfolk have f, and my familiar H2308
Ps 142: 4 refuge f me; no man cared for my soul. H6
Song 5: 6 was gone: my soul f when he spake: I H3318
Jer 51:30 their might hath f; they became as H5405
Lam 4:17 As for us, our eyes as yet f for our vain H3615

FAILETH
Gen 47:15 we die in thy presence? for the money f. H656
Job 21:10 Their bull gendereth, and f not; their H1602
Ps 31:10 my strength f because of mine iniquity, H3782
38:10 My heart panteth, my strength f me: as H5800
40:12 of mine head: therefore my heart f me. H5800
71: 9 age; forsake me not when my strength f. H3615
73:26 My flesh and my heart f: *but* God *is* the H3615
109:24 fasting; and my flesh f of fatness. H3584
143: 7 Hear me speedily, O LORD: my spirit f: H3615
Ecc 10: 3 way, his wisdom f *him*, and he saith to H2638
Isa 15: 6 the grass f, there is no green thing. H3615
40:26 for that *he is* strong in power; not one f. H5737
41:17 none, *and* their tongue f for thirst, I the H5405
44:12 f: he drinketh no water, and is faint. H369
59:15 Yea, truth f; and he *that* departeth from H5737
Ezk 12:22 days are prolonged, and every vision f? H6
Zep 3: 5 to light, he f not; but the unjust H5737
Lk 12:33 in the heavens that f not, where no thief G413
1Co 13: 8 Charity never f: but whether *there be* G1601

FAILING
Dt 28:65 and f of eyes, and sorrow of mind: H3631

F

Lk 21:26 Men's hearts f them for fear, and for *G674*

FAIN
Job 27:22 spare: he would f flee out of his hand. H1272
Lk 15:16 And he would f have filled his belly *G1937*

FAINT
Gen 25:29 Esau came from the field, and he *was* f: H5889
30 f: therefore was his name called Edom. H5889
Dt 20: 3 let not your hearts f, fear not, and do H7401
8 brethren's heart f as well as his heart. H4549
25:18 f and weary; and he feared not God. H5889
Jos 2: 9 of the land f because of you. H4127
24 of the country do f because of us. H4127
Jdg 8: 4 *were* with him, f, yet pursuing *them*. H5889
5 me; for they *be* f, and I am pursuing H5889
1Sa 14:28 food this day. And the people were f. H5774
31 to Aijalon: and the people were very f. H5774
30:10 which were so f that they could not H6296
21 which were so f that they could not H6296
2Sa 16: 2 as be f in the wilderness may drink. H3287
21:15 the Philistines: and David waxed f. H5774
Prv 24:10 *If* thou f in the day of adversity, thy H7503
Isa 1: 5 head is sick, and the whole heart f. H1742
13: 7 Therefore shall all hands be f, and every H7503
29: 8 and, behold, *he is* f, and his soul hath H5889
40:29 He giveth power to the f; and to *them* H3287
30 Even the youths shall f and be weary, H3286
31 weary; *and* they shall walk, and not f. H3286
44:12 faileth: he drinketh no water, and is f. H3286
Jer 8:18 against sorrow, my heart *is* f in me. H1742
51:46 And lest your heart f, and ye fear for the H7401
Lam 1:13 made me desolate *and* f all the day. H1739
22 my sighs *are* many, and my heart *is* f. H1742
2:19 f for hunger in the top of every street. H5848
5:17 For this our heart is f; for these *things* H1739
Ezk 21: 7 every spirit shall f, and all knees shall H3543
15 *their* heart may f, and *their* ruins be H4127
Am 8:13 fair virgins and young men f for thirst. H5968
Mt 15:32 away fasting, lest they f in the way. *G1590*
Mk 8: 3 own houses, they will f by the way: for *G1590*
Lk 18: 1 men ought always to pray, and not to f; *G1573*
2Co 4: 1 as we have received mercy, we f not; *G1573*
16 For which cause we f not; but though *G1573*
Gal 6: 9 in due season we shall reap, if we f not. *G1590*
Eph 3:13 Wherefore I desire that ye f not at my *G1573*
Heb 12: 3 lest ye be wearied and f in your minds. *G1590*
5 nor f when thou art rebuked of him: *G1590*

FAINTED
Gen 45:26 heart f, for he believed them not. H6313
47:13 of Canaan f by reason of the famine. H3856
Ps 27:13 *I had* f, unless I had believed to see the
107: 5 Hungry and thirsty, their soul f in H5848
Isa 51:20 Thy sons have f, they lie at the head of H5968
Jer 45: 3 I f in my sighing, and I find no rest. H3021
Ezk 31:15 and all the trees of the field f for him. H5969
Dan 8:27 And I Daniel f, and was sick *certain* H1961
Jna 2: 7 When my soul f within me I H5848
4: 8 head of Jonah, that he f, and wished in H5968
Mt 9:36 because they f, and were scattered *G2258*
Rev 2: 3 sake hast laboured, and hast not f. *G2577*

FAINTEST
Job 4: 5 thee, and thou f; it toucheth thee, and H3811

FAINTETH
Ps 84: 2 My soul longeth, yea, even f for the H3615
119:81 My soul f for thy salvation: *but* I hope H3615
Isa 10:18 shall be as when a standardbearer f. H4549
40:28 the ends of the earth, f not, neither is H3286

FAINTHEARTED
Dt 20: 8 *is* fearful and f? let him go and H7390+H3824
Isa 7: 4 not, neither be f for the two H7401+H3824
Jer 49:23 tidings: they are f; *there is* sorrow on H4127

FAINTNESS
Lev 26:36 of you I will send a f into their hearts in H4816

FAIR
Gen 6: 2 that they *were* f; and they took them H2896
12:11 that thou *art* a f woman to look upon: H3303
14 beheld the woman that she *was* very f. H3303
24:16 And the damsel *was* very f to look H2896
26: 7 because she *was* f to look upon. H2896
1Sa 17:42 and ruddy, and of a f countenance. H3303
2Sa 13: 1 the son of David had a f sister, whose H3303
14:27 she was a woman of a f countenance. H3303
1Ki 1: 3 So they sought for a f damsel H3303
4 And the damsel *was* very f, and H3303
Est 1:11 her beauty: for she *was* f to look on. H2896
2: 2 Let there be f young virgins H2896+H4758
3 all the f young virgins unto H2896+H4758
7 the maid *was* f and beautiful; H3303+H8389
Job 37:22 F weather cometh out of the north: H2091
42:15 women found *so* f as the daughters of H3303
Prv 7:21 With her much f speech she caused H3948
11:22 a f woman which is without discretion. H3303
26:25 When he speaketh f, believe him not: H2603
Song 1:15 Behold, thou *art* f, my love; behold, H3303
15 thou *art* f; thou *hast* doves' eyes. H3303
16 Behold, thou *art* f, my beloved, yea, H3303
2:10 up, my love, my f one, and come away. H3302
13 my love, my f one, and come away. H3302
4: 1 Behold, thou *art* f, my love; behold, H3303
1 behold, thou *art* f; thou *hast* doves' eyes H3303
7 Thou *art* all f, my love; *there is* no spot H3303
10 How f is thy love, my sister, *my* spouse! H3302
6:10 as the morning, f as the moon, clear as H3303
7: 6 How f and how pleasant art thou, O H3302
Isa 5: 9 *even* great and f, without inhabitant. H2896
54:11 lay thy stones with f colours, and lay H6320
Jer 4:30 shalt thou make thyself f; *thy* lovers will H3302
11:16 A green olive tree, f, *and* of goodly fruit: H3303
12: 6 though they speak f words unto thee. H2896
46:20 Egypt *is like* a very f heifer, *but* H3304
Ezk 16:17 Thou hast also taken thy f jewels of my H8597
39 and shall take thy f jewels, and leave H8597
23:26 thy clothes, and take away thy f jewels. H8597
31: 3 in Lebanon with f branches, and with H3303
7 Thus was he f in his greatness, in the H3302
9 I have made him f by the multitude of H3303
Dan 4:12 The leaves thereof *were* f, and the fruit H8209
21 Whose leaves *were* f, and the fruit H8209
Hos 10:11 over upon her f neck: I will make H2898
Am 8:13 In that day shall the f virgins and H3303
Zec 3: 5 And I said, Let them set a f mitre upon H2889
5 his head. So they set a f mitre upon his H2889
Mt 16: 2 *It will be* f weather: for the sky is red. *G2105*
Act 7:20 and was exceeding f, and nourished up *G791*
27: 8 is called The f havens; nigh whereunto *G2570*
Ro 16:18 good words and f speeches deceive the *G2129*
Gal 6:12 As many as desire to make a f shew in *G2146*

FAIRER
Jdg 15: 2 her younger sister f than she? take her, H2896
Ps 45: 2 Thou art f than the children of men: H3302
Dan 1:15 appeared f and fatter in flesh than H2896

FAIREST
Song 1: 8 If thou know not, O thou f among H3303
5: 9 beloved, O thou f among women? what H3303
6: 1 Whither is thy beloved gone, O thou f H3303

FAIR-HAVENS See FAIR and HAVENS.

FAIRS
Ezk 27:12 iron, tin, and lead, they traded in thy f. H5801
14 f with horses and horsemen and mules. H5801
16 they occupied in thy f with emeralds, H5801
19 fro occupied in thy f: bright iron, cassia, H5801
22 they occupied in thy f with chief of all H5801
27 Thy riches, and thy f, thy merchandise, H5801

FAITH
Dt 32:20 generation, children in whom *is* no f. H529
Hab 2: 4 in him: but the just shall live by his f. H530
Mt 6:30 much more *clothe* you, O ye of little f? *G3640*
8:10 not found so great f, no, not in Israel. *G4102*
26 O ye of little f? Then he arose, and *G3640*
9: 2 Jesus seeing their f said unto the sick of *G4102*
22 of good comfort; thy f hath made thee *G4102*
29 According to your f be it unto you. *G4102*
14:31 of little f, wherefore didst thou doubt? *G3640*
15:28 great *is* thy f: be it unto thee even *G4102*
16: 8 unto them, O ye of little f, why reason ye *G3640*
17:20 you, If ye have f as a grain of mustard *G4102*
21:21 you, If ye have f, and doubt not, ye shall *G4102*
23:23 mercy, and f: these ought ye to have *G4102*
Mk 2: 5 When Jesus saw their f, he said unto the *G4102*
4:40 ye so fearful? how is it that ye have no f? *G4102*
5:34 And he said unto her, Daughter, thy f *G4102*
10:52 him, Go thy way; thy f hath made thee *G4102*
11:22 saith unto them, Have f in God. *G4102*
Lk 5:20 And when he saw their f, he said unto *G4102*
7: 9 not found so great f, no, not in Israel. *G4102*
50 And he said to the woman, Thy f hath *G4102*
Lk 8:25 And he said unto them, Where is your f? *G4102*
48 f hath made thee whole; go in peace. *G4102*
12:28 more *will he clothe* you, O ye of little f? *G3640*
17: 5 said unto the Lord, Increase our f. *G4102*
6 And the Lord said, If ye had f as a *G4102*
19 thy way: thy f hath made thee whole. *G4102*
18: 8 cometh, shall he find f on the earth? *G4102*
42 Receive thy sight: thy f hath saved thee. *G4102*
22:32 But I have prayed for thee, that thy f *G4102*
Act 3:16 And his name through f in his name *G4102*
16 and know: yea, the f which is by him *G4102*
6: 5 a man full of f and of the Holy Ghost, *G4102*
7 of the priests were obedient to the f. *G4102*
8 And Stephen, full of f and power, did *G4102*
11:24 Holy Ghost and of f: and much people *G4102*
13: 8 to turn away the deputy from the f. *G4102*
14: 9 perceiving that he had f to be healed, *G4102*
22 to continue in the f, and that we must *G4102*
27 opened the door of f unto the Gentiles. *G4102*
15: 9 us and them, purifying their hearts by f. *G4102*
16: 5 in the f, and increased in number daily. *G4102*
20:21 and f toward our Lord Jesus Christ. *G4102*
24:24 heard him concerning the f in Christ. *G4102*
26:18 which are sanctified by f that is in me. *G4102*
Ro 1: 5 the f among all nations, for his name: *G4102*
8 for you all, that your f is spoken of *G4102*
12 by the mutual f both of you and me. *G4102*
17 of God revealed from f to faith: as it is *G4102*
17 from faith to f: as it is written, The *G4102*
17 as it is written, The just shall live by f. *G4102*
3: 3 make the f of God without effect? *G4102*
22 of God *which is* by f of Jesus Christ *G4102*
25 through f in his blood, to declare *G4102*
27 law? of works? Nay: but by the law of f. *G4102*
28 by f without the deeds of the law. *G4102*
30 by f, and uncircumcision through faith. *G4102*
30 by faith, and uncircumcision through f. *G4102*
31 f? God forbid: yea, we establish the law. *G4102*
4: 5 his f is counted for righteousness. *G4102*
9 also? for we say that f was reckoned to *G4102*
11 of the f which *he had yet* being *G4102*
12 walk in the steps of that f of our father *G4102*
13 law, but through the righteousness of f. *G4102*
14 of the law *be* heirs, f is made void, and *G4102*
16 Therefore *it is* of f, that *it might be* by *G4102*
16 which is of the f of Abraham; who is *G4102*
19 And being not weak in f, he considered *G4102*
20 but was strong in f, giving glory to God; *G4102*
5: 1 Therefore being justified by f, we have *G4102*
2 By whom also we have access by f into *G4102*
9:30 even the righteousness which is of f. *G4102*
32 *sought it* not by f, but as it were by the *G4102*
10: 6 But the righteousness which is of f *G4102*
8 that is, the word of f, which we preach; *G4102*
17 So then f *cometh* by hearing, and *G4102*
11:20 by f. Be not highminded, but fear: *G4102*
12: 3 dealt to every man the measure of f. *G4102*
6 according to the proportion of f; *G4102*
14: 1 Him that is weak in the f receive ye, *but* *G4102*
22 Hast thou f? have *it* to thyself before *G4102*
23 of f: for whatsoever *is* not of faith is sin. *G4102*
23 of faith: for whatsoever *is* not of f is sin. *G4102*
16:26 to all nations for the obedience of f: *G4102*
1Co 2: 5 That your f should not stand in the *G4102*
12: 9 To another f by the same Spirit; to *G4102*
13: 2 and though I have all f, so that I could *G4102*
13 And now abideth f, hope, charity, these *G4102*
15:14 preaching vain, and your f *is* also vain. *G4102*
17 And if Christ be not raised, your f *is* *G4102*
16:13 Watch ye, stand fast in the f, quit you *G4102*
2Co 1:24 over your f, but are helpers of your *G4102*
24 helpers of your joy: for by f ye stand. *G4102*
4:13 We having the same spirit of f, *G4102*
5: 7 (For we walk by f, not by sight:) *G4102*
8: 7 in every *thing, in* f, and utterance, and *G4102*
10:15 hope, when your f is increased, that we *G4102*
13: 5 ye be in the f; prove your own selves. *G4102*
Gal 1:23 the f which once he destroyed. *G4102*
2:16 of the law, but by the f of Jesus Christ, *G4102*
16 be justified by the f of Christ, and not *G4102*
20 flesh I live by the f of the Son of God, *G4102*
3: 2 works of the law, or by the hearing of f? *G4102*
5 works of the law, or by the hearing of f? *G4102*
7 they which are of f, the same are the *G4102*
8 heathen through f, preached before the *G4102*
9 So then they which be of f are blessed *G4102*
11 *it is* evident: for, The just shall live by f. *G4102*
12 And the law is not of f: but, The man *G4102*
14 the promise of the Spirit through f. *G4102*

Gal 3:22 the promise by **f** of Jesus Christ might G4102
23 But before **f** came, we were kept under G4102
23 **f** which should afterwards be revealed. G4102
24 Christ, that we might be justified by **f**. G4102
25 But after that **f** is come, we are no G4102
26 For ye are all the children of God by **f** in G4102
5: 5 wait for the hope of righteousness by **f**. G4102
6 but **f** which worketh by love. G4102
22 longsuffering, gentleness, goodness, **f**, G4102
6:10 them who are of the household of **f**. G4102
Eph 1:15 Wherefore I also, after I heard of your **f** G4102
2: 8 For by grace are ye saved through **f**; and G4102
3:12 access with confidence by the **f** of him. G4102
17 in your hearts by **f**; that ye, being rooted G4102
4: 5 One Lord, one **f**, one baptism, G4102
13 Till we all come in the unity of the **f**, G4102
6:16 Above all, taking the shield of **f**, G4102
23 and love with **f**, from God the Father G4102
Php 1:25 you all for your furtherance and joy of **f**; G4102
27 striving together for the **f** of the gospel; G4102
2:17 of your **f**, I joy, and rejoice with you all. G4102
3: 9 which is through the **f** of Christ, the G4102
9 the righteousness which is of God by **f**: G4102
Col 1: 4 Since we heard of your **f** in Christ Jesus, G4102
23 If ye continue in the **f** grounded and G4102
2: 5 and the stedfastness of your **f** in Christ. G4102
7 and stablished in the **f**, as ye have been G4102
12 *him* through the **f** of the operation of G4102
1Th 1: 3 your work of **f**, and labour of love, and G4102
8 in every place your **f** to God-ward is G4102
3: 2 and to comfort you concerning your **f**: G4102
5 sent to know your **f**, lest by some means G4102
6 tidings of your **f** and charity, and that G4102
7 all our affliction and distress by your **f**: G4102
10 perfect that which is lacking in your **f**? G4102
5: 8 the breastplate of **f** and love; and for an G4102
2Th 1: 3 meet, because that your **f** groweth G4102
4 for your patience and **f** in all your G4102
11 and the work of **f** with power: G4102
3: 2 and wicked men: for all *men* have not **f**. G4102
1Ti 1: 2 Unto Timothy, *my* own son in the **f**: G4102
4 than godly edifying which is in **f**: *so do.* G4102
5 a good conscience, and *of* **f** unfeigned: G4102
14 with **f** and love which is in Christ Jesus. G4102
19 Holding **f**, and a good conscience; G4102
19 concerning **f** have made shipwreck: G4102
2: 7 a teacher of the Gentiles in **f** and verity. G4102
15 if they continue in **f** and charity and G4102
3: 9 Holding the mystery of the **f** in a pure G4102
13 in the **f** which is in Christ Jesus. G4102
4: 1 shall depart from the **f**, giving heed to G4102
6 up in the words of **f** and of good G4102
12 in charity, in spirit, in **f**, in purity. G4102
5: 8 the **f**, and is worse than an infidel. G4102
12 because they have cast off their first **f**. G4102
6:10 have erred from the **f**, and pierced G4102
11 godliness, **f**, love, patience, meekness. G4102
12 Fight the good fight of **f**, lay hold on G4102
21 the **f**. Grace *be* with thee. Amen. G4102
2Ti 1: 5 the unfeigned **f** that is in thee, which G4102
13 in **f** and love which is in Christ Jesus. G4102
2:18 already; and overthrow the **f** of some. G4102
22 righteousness, **f**, charity, peace, with G4102
3: 8 minds, reprobate concerning the **f**. G4102
10 **f**, longsuffering, charity, patience, G4102
15 through **f** which is in Christ Jesus. G4102
4: 7 finished *my* course, I have kept the **f**: G4102
Tit 1: 1 according to the **f** of God's elect, and G4102
4 after the common **f**: Grace, mercy, *and* G4102
13 that they may be sound in the **f**; G4102
2: 2 sound in **f**, in charity, in patience. G4102
3:15 us in the **f**. Grace *be* with you all. Amen. G4102
Phlm 5 Hearing of thy love and **f**, which thou G4102
6 That the communication of thy **f** may G4102
Heb 4: 2 mixed with **f** in them that heard *it*. G4102
6: 1 from dead works, and of **f** toward God, G4102
12 **f** and patience inherit the promises. G4102
10:22 in full assurance of **f**, having our hearts G4102
23 Let us hold fast the profession of *our* **f** G1680
38 Now the just shall live by **f**: but if *any* G4102
11: 1 Now **f** is the substance of things hoped G4102
3 Through **f** we understand that the G4102
4 By **f** Abel offered unto God a more G4102
5 By **f** Enoch was translated that he G4102
6 But without **f** *it is* impossible to please G4102
7 By **f** Noah, being warned of God of G4102
7 heir of the righteousness which is by **f**. G4102
8 By **f** Abraham, when he was called to G4102
9 By **f** he sojourned in the land of G4102
Heb 11:11 Through **f** also Sara herself received G4102
13 These all died in **f**, not having received G4102
17 By **f** Abraham, when he was tried, G4102
20 By **f** Isaac blessed Jacob and Esau G4102
21 By **f** Jacob, when he was a dying, G4102
22 By **f** Joseph, when he died, made G4102
23 By **f** Moses, when he was born, was hid G4102
24 By **f** Moses, when he was come to G4102
27 By **f** he forsook Egypt, not fearing the G4102
28 Through **f** he kept the passover, and G4102
29 By **f** they passed through the Red sea as G4102
30 By **f** the walls of Jericho fell down, after G4102
31 By **f** the harlot Rahab perished not with G4102
33 Who through **f** subdued kingdoms, G4102
39 through **f**, received not the promise: G4102
12: 2 and finisher of *our* **f**; who for the joy G4102
13: 7 of God: whose **f** follow, considering G4102
Jas 1: 3 Knowing *this*, that the trying of your **f** G4102
6 But let him ask in **f**, nothing wavering. G4102
2: 1 My brethren, have not the **f** of our Lord G4102
5 of this world rich in **f**, and heirs of the G4102
14 a man say he hath **f**, and have not G4102
14 and have not works? can **f** save him? G4102
17 Even so **f**, if it hath not works, is dead, G4102
18 Yea, a man may say, Thou hast **f**, and I G4102
18 shew me thy **f** without thy works, and G4102
18 and I will shew thee my **f** by my works. G4102
20 But wilt thou know, O vain man, that **f** G4102
22 Seest thou how **f** wrought with his G4102
22 and by works was **f** made perfect? G4102
24 a man is justified, and not by **f** only. G4102
26 dead, so **f** without works is dead also. G4102
5:15 And the prayer of **f** shall save the sick, G4102
1Pt 1: 5 of God through **f** unto salvation ready G4102
7 That the trial of your **f**, being much G4102
9 Receiving the end of your **f**, *even* the G4102
21 that your **f** and hope might be in God. G4102
5: 9 Whom resist stedfast in the **f**, knowing G4102
2Pt 1: 1 like precious **f** with us through the G4102
5 your **f** virtue; and to virtue knowledge; G4102
1Jn 5: 4 that overcometh the world, *even* our **f**. G4102
Jude 3 contend for the **f** which was once G4102
20 most holy **f**, praying in the Holy Ghost, G4102
Rev 2:13 hast not denied my **f**, even in those days G4102
19 and service, and **f**, and thy patience, G4102
13:10 is the patience and the **f** of the saints. G4102
14:12 of God, and the **f** of Jesus. G4102

FAITHFUL
Nu 12: 7 My servant Moses *is* not so, who *is* **f** in H539
Dt 7: 9 God, he *is* God, the **f** God, which keepeth H539
1Sa 2:35 And I will raise me up a **f** priest, *that* H539
22:14 and said, And who *is so* **f** among all thy H539
2Sa 20:19 *that are* peaceable *and* **f** in Israel: thou H539
Neh 7: 2 a **f** man, and feared God above many. H571
9: 8 And foundest his heart **f** before thee, and H539
13:13 they were counted **f**, and their office *was* H539
Ps 12: 1 **f** fail from among the children of men. H539
31:23 LORD preserveth the **f**, and plentifully H539
89:37 and *as* a **f** witness in heaven. Selah. H539
101: 6 Mine eyes *shall be* upon the **f** of the land, H539
119:86 All thy commandments *are* **f**: they H530
138 commanded *are* righteous and very **f**. H530
Prv 11:13 that is of a **f** spirit concealeth the matter. H539
13:17 mischief: but a **f** ambassador *is* health. H529
14: 5 A **f** witness will not lie: but a false H529
20: 6 goodness: but a **f** man who can find? H529
25:13 of harvest, *so is* a **f** messenger to them H539
27: 6 **F** *are* the wounds of a friend; but the H539
28:20 A **f** man shall abound with blessings: but H530
Isa 1:21 How is the **f** city become an harlot! it H539
26 The city of righteousness, the **f** city. H539
8: 2 And I took unto me **f** witnesses to H539
49: 7 of the LORD that is **f**, *and* the Holy One of H539
Jer 42: 5 be a true and **f** witness between us, H539
Dan 6: 4 as he *was* **f**, neither was there any H540
Hos 11:12 ruleth with God, and is **f** with the saints. H539
Mt 24:45 Who then is a **f** and wise servant, G4103
25:21 *thou* good and **f** servant: thou hast G4103
21 thou hast been **f** over a few things, I G4103
23 done, good and **f** servant; thou hast G4103
23 thou hast been **f** over a few things, I G4103
Lk 12:42 And the Lord said, Who then is that **f** G4103
16:10 He that is **f** in that which is least is G4103
10 which is least is **f** also in much: and he G4103
11 If therefore ye have not been **f** in the G4103
12 And if ye have not been **f** in that which G4103
19:17 thou hast been **f** in a very little, have G4103
Act 16:15 judged me to be **f** to the Lord, come G4103
1Co 1: 9 God *is* **f**, by whom ye were called unto G4103
4: 2 in stewards, that a man be found **f**. G4103
17 my beloved son, and **f** in the Lord, who G4103
7:25 hath obtained mercy of the Lord to be **f**. G4103
10:13 to man: but God *is* **f**, who will not suffer G4103
Gal 3: 9 be of faith are blessed with **f** Abraham. G4103
Eph 1: 1 at Ephesus, and to the **f** in Christ Jesus: G4103
6:21 brother and **f** minister in the Lord, G4103
Col 1: 2 To the saints and **f** brethren in Christ G4103
7 who is for you a **f** minister of Christ; G4103
4: 7 beloved brother, and a **f** minister and G4103
9 With Onesimus, a **f** and beloved G4103
1Th 5:24 **F** *is* he that calleth you, who also will G4103
2Th 3: 3 But the Lord is **f**, who shall stablish you, G4103
1Ti 1:12 me **f**, putting me into the ministry; G4103
15 This *is* a **f** saying, and worthy of all G4103
3:11 not slanderers, sober, **f** in all things. G4103
4: 9 This *is* a **f** saying and worthy of all G4103
6: 2 service, because they are **f** and beloved, G4103
2Ti 2: 2 commit thou to **f** men, who shall be G4103
11 *It is* a **f** saying: For if we be dead with G4103
13 If we believe not, *yet* he abideth **f**: he G4103
Tit 1: 6 **f** children not accused of riot or unruly. G4103
9 Holding fast the **f** word as he hath been G4103
3: 8 *This is* a **f** saying, and these things I G4103
Heb 2:17 be a merciful and **f** high priest in things G4103
3: 2 Who was **f** to him that appointed him, G4103
2 him, as also Moses *was* **f** in all his house.
5 And Moses verily *was* **f** in all his house, G4103
10:23 wavering; (for he *is* **f** that promised;) G4103
11:11 she judged him **f** who had promised. G4103
1Pt 4:19 *him* in well doing, as unto a **f** Creator. G4103
5:12 By Silvanus, a **f** brother unto you, as I G4103
1Jn 1: 9 If we confess our sins, he is **f** and just G4103
Rev 1: 5 And from Jesus Christ, *who is* the **f** G4103
2:10 ten days: be thou **f** unto death, and I G4103
13 Antipas *was* my **f** martyr, who was G4103
3:14 the Amen, the **f** and true witness, the G4103
17:14 with him *are* called, and chosen, and **f**. G4103
19:11 him *was* called **F** and True, and in G4103
21: 5 Write: for these words are true and **f**. G4103
22: 6 These sayings *are* **f** and true: and the G4103

FAITHFULLY
2Ki 12:15 bestowed on workmen: for they dealt **f**. H530
22: 7 into their hand, because they dealt **f**. H530
2Ch 19: 9 of the LORD, **f**, and with a perfect heart. H530
31:12 dedicated *things* **f**: over which Cononiah H530
34:12 And the men did the work **f**: and the H530
Prv 29:14 The king that **f** judgeth the poor, his H571
Jer 23:28 speak my word **f**. What *is* the chaff to H571
3Jn 5 Beloved, thou doest **f** whatsoever thou G4103

FAITHFULNESS
1Sa 26:23 and his **f**: for the LORD delivered H530
Ps 5: 9 For *there is* no **f** in their mouth; their H3559
36: 5 *and* thy **f** *reacheth* unto the clouds. H530
40:10 I have declared thy **f** and thy salvation: I H530
88:11 in the grave? *or* thy **f** in destruction? H530
89: 1 I make known thy **f** to all generations. H530
2 up for ever: thy **f** shalt thou establish H530
5 **f** also in the congregation of the saints. H530
8 unto thee? or to thy **f** round about thee? H530
24 But my **f** and my mercy *shall be* with H530
33 take from him, nor suffer my **f** to fail. H530
92: 2 in the morning, and thy **f** every night, H530
119:75 and *that* thou in **f** hast afflicted me. H530
90 Thy **f** *is* unto all generations: thou hast H530
143: 1 **f** answer me, *and* in thy righteousness. H530
Isa 11: 5 of his loins, and **f** the girdle of his reins. H530
25: 1 *thy* counsels of old *are* **f** *and* truth. H530
Lam 3:23 *are* new every morning: great *is* thy **f**. H530
Hos 2:20 I will even betroth thee unto me in **f**: and H530

FAITHLESS
Mt 17:17 Then Jesus answered and said, O **f** and G571
Mk 9:19 He answereth him, and saith, O **f** G571
Lk 9:41 And Jesus answering said, O **f** and G571
Jn 20:27 into my side: and be not **f**, but believing. G571

FALL
Gen 2:21 a deep sleep to **f** upon Adam, and he H5307
43:18 against us, and **f** upon us, and take us H5307
45:24 them, See that ye **f** not out by the way. H7264
49:17 so that his rider shall **f** backward. H5307
Ex 5: 3 LORD our God; lest he **f** upon us with H6293
15:16 Fear and dread shall **f** upon them; by H5307
21:33 cover it, and an ox or an ass **f** therein; H5307
Lev 11:32 are dead, doth **f**, it shall be unclean; H5307

Lev 11:37 And if *any part* of their carcase f upon H5307
38 f thereon, it *shall be* unclean unto you. H5307
19:29 lest the land f to whoredom, and the
26: 7 they shall f before you by the sword. H5307
8 shall f before you by the sword. H5307
36 and they shall f when none pursueth. H5307
37 And they shall f one upon another, as it H3782
Nu 11:31 sea, and let *them* f by the camp, as it H5203
14: 3 unto this land, to f by the sword, that H5307
29 Your carcases shall f in this wilderness; H5307
32 carcases, they shall f in this wilderness. H5307
43 before you, and ye shall f by the sword: H5307
34: 2 *is* the land that shall f unto you for an H5307
Dt 22: 4 ass or his ox f down by the way, and H5307
8 thine house, if any man f from thence. H5307
Jos 6: 5 of the city shall f down flat, and the H5307
Jdg 8:21 Rise thou, and f upon us: for as the H6293
15:12 that ye will not f upon me yourselves. H6293
18 f into the hand of the uncircumcised? H5307
Ru 2:16 And let f also *some* of the handfuls of H7997
3:18 the matter will f: for the man will not H5307
1Sa 3:19 let none of his words f to the ground. H5307
14:45 hair of his head f to the ground; for he H5307
18:25 David f by the hand of the Philistines. H5307
21:13 let his spittle f down upon his beard. H3381
22:17 hand to f upon the priests of the LORD. H6293
18 Turn thou, and f upon the priests. And H6293
26:20 Now therefore, let not my blood f to the H5307
2Sa 1:15 said, Go near, *and* f upon him. And he H6293
14:11 not one hair of thy son f to the earth. H5307
24:14 a great strait: let us f now into the hand H5307
14 and let me not f into the hand of man. H5307
1Ki 1:52 not an hair of him f to the earth: but if H5307
2:29 of Jehoiada, saying, Go, f upon him. H6293
31 he hath said, and f upon him, and bury H6293
22:20 he may go up and f at Ramoth-gilead? H5307
2Ki 7: 4 come, and let us f unto the host of the H5307
10:10 Know now that there shall f unto the H5307
14:10 f, *even* thou, and Judah with thee? H5307
19: 7 him to f by the sword in his own land. H5307
1Ch 12:19 saying, He will f to his master Saul to H5307
21:13 great strait: let me f now into the hand H5307
13 but let me not f into the hand of man. H5307
2Ch 18:19 he may go up and f at Ramoth-gilead? H5307
21:15 until thy bowels f out by reason of the H3318
25: 8 shall make thee f before the enemy: for H3782
19 f, *even* thou, and Judah with thee? H5307
Est 6:13 thou hast begun to f, thou shalt not H5307
13 him, but shalt surely f before him. H5307
Job 13:11 you afraid? and his dread f upon you? H5307
31:22 *Then* let mine arm f from my shoulder H5307
Ps 5:10 Destroy thou them, O God; let them f H5307
9: 3 they shall f and perish at thy presence. H3782
10:10 that the poor may f by his strong ones. H5307
35: 8 into that very destruction let him f. H5307
37:24 Though he f, he shall not be utterly cast H5307
45: 5 *whereby* the people f under thee. H5307
63:10 They shall f by the sword: they shall be H5064
64: 8 own tongue to f upon themselves: all H3782
72:11 Yea, all kings shall f down before him: H7812
78:28 And he let *it* f in the midst of their H5307
82: 7 But ye shall die like men, and f like one H5307
91: 7 A thousand shall f at thy side, and ten H5307
118:13 that I might f: but the LORD helped me. H5307
140:10 Let burning coals f upon them: let H4131
141:10 Let the wicked f into their own nets, H5307
145:14 The LORD upholdeth all that f, and H5307
Prv 4:16 away, unless they cause *some* to f. H3782
10: 8 but a prating fool shall f. H3832
10 sorrow: but a prating fool shall f. H3832
11: 5 wicked shall f by his own wickedness. H5307
14 Where no counsel *is*, the people f: but in H5307
28 He that trusteth in his riches shall f: but H5307
16:18 and an haughty spirit before a f. H3783
22:14 is abhorred of the LORD shall f therein. H5307
24:16 but the wicked shall f into mischief. H3782
26:27 Whoso diggeth a pit shall f therein: and H5307
28:10 evil way, he shall f himself into his own H5307
14 his heart shall f into mischief. H5307
18 *is* perverse *in his* ways shall f at once. H5307
29:16 but the righteous shall see their f. H4658
Ecc 4:10 For if they f, the one will lift up his H5307
10: 8 He that diggeth a pit shall f into it; and H5307
11: 3 and if the tree f toward the south, or H5307
Isa 3:25 Thy men shall f by the sword, and thy H5307
8:15 shall stumble, and f, and be broken, H5307
10: 4 and they shall f under the slain. For H5307
34 and Lebanon shall f by a mighty one. H5307
13:15 joined *unto them* shall f by the sword. H5307

Isa 22:25 be cut down, and f; and the burden that H5307
24:18 of the fear shall f into the pit; and he H5307
20 it; and it shall f, and not rise again. H5307
28:13 they might go, and f backward, and be H3782
30:13 as a breach ready to f, swelling out in a H5307
25 the great slaughter, when the towers f. H5307
31: 3 he that helpeth shall f, and he that is H3782
3 f down, and they all shall fail together. H5307
8 Then shall the Assyrian f with the H5307
34: 4 all their host shall f down, as the leaf H5034
37: 7 him to f by the sword in his own land. H5307
40:30 and the young men shall utterly f: H3782
44:19 shall I f down to the stock of a tree? H5456
45:14 and they shall f down unto thee, they H7812
46: 6 a god: they f down, yea, they worship. H5456
47:11 and mischief shall f upon thee; thou H5307
54:15 against thee shall f for thy sake. H5307
Jer 3:12 mine anger to f upon you: for I *am* H5307
6:15 they shall f among them that fall: H5307
15 among them that f: at the time *that* I H5307
21 the sons together shall f upon them; the H3782
8: 4 LORD; Shall they f, and not arise? shall H5307
12 shall they f among them that fall: H5307
12 among them that f: in the time of their H5307
9:22 of men shall f as dung upon the open H5307
15: 8 caused *him* to f upon it suddenly, and H5307
19: 7 I will cause them to f by the sword H5307
20: 4 and they shall f by the sword of their H5307
23:12 be driven on, and f therein: for I will H5307
19 whirlwind: it shall f grievously upon H2342
25:27 and spue, and f, and rise no more, H5307
34 and ye shall f like a pleasant vessel. H5307
30:23 whirlwind: it shall f with pain upon the H2342
37:14 Then said Jeremiah, *It is* false; I f not H5307
39:18 and thou shalt not f by the sword, but H5307
44:12 all be consumed, *and* f in the land of H5307
46: 6 shall stumble, and f toward the north H5307
16 He made many to f, yea, one fell upon H3782
48:44 He that fleeth from the fear shall f into H5307
49:21 the noise of their f, at the cry the noise H5307
26 Therefore her young men shall f in her H5307
50:30 Therefore shall her young men f in the H5307
32 shall stumble and f, and none shall H5307
51: 4 Thus the slain shall f in the land of the H5307
44 him: yea, the wall of Babylon shall f. H5307
47 all her slain shall f in the midst of her. H5307
49 slain of Israel to f, so at Babylon shall H5307
49 shall f the slain of all the earth. H5307
Lam 1:14 made my strength to f, the Lord hath H3782
Ezk 5:12 a third part shall f by the sword round H5307
6: 7 And the slain shall f in the midst of H5307
11 for they shall f by the sword, by the H5307
12 that is near shall f by the sword; and he H5307
11:10 Ye shall f by the sword; I will judge you H5307
13:11 *morter*, that it shall f: there shall be an H5307
11 shall f; and a stormy wind shall rend *it*. H5307
14 and it shall f, and ye shall be consumed H5307
17:21 all his bands shall f by the sword, and H5307
23:25 thy remnant shall f by the sword: they H5307
24: 6 it out piece by piece; let no lot f upon it. H5307
21 whom ye have left shall f by the sword. H5307
25:13 and they of Dedan shall f by the sword. H5307
26:15 at the sound of thy f, when the wounded H4658
18 in the day of thy f; yea, the isles that *are* H4658
27:27 of thee, shall f into the midst of the H5307
34 company in the midst of thee shall f. H5307
29: 5 thy rivers: thou shalt f upon the open H5307
30: 4 the slain shall f in Egypt, and they shall H5307
5 league, shall f with them by the sword. H5307
6 uphold Egypt shall f; and the pride of H5307
6 of Syene shall they f in it by the sword, H5307
17 of Pi-beseth shall f by the sword: and H5307
22 cause the sword to f out of his hand. H5307
25 of Pharaoh shall f down; and they shall H5307
31:16 at the sound of his f, when I cast him H4658
32:10 man for his own life, in the day of thy f. H4658
12 thy multitude to f, the terrible of the H5307
20 They shall f in the midst of *them that* H5307
33:12 he shall not f thereby in the day that H3782
27 in the wastes shall f by the sword, and H5307
35: 8 they f that are slain with the sword. H5307
36:15 to f any more, saith the Lord GOD. H3782
38:20 steep places shall f, and every wall shall H5307
20 and every wall shall f to the ground. H5307
39: 3 thine arrows to f out of thy right hand. H5307
4 Thou shalt f upon the mountains of H5307
5 Thou shalt f upon the open field: for I H5307
44:12 the house of Israel to f into iniquity; H4383
47:14 land shall f unto you for inheritance. H5307

Dan 3: 5 of musick, ye f down and worship the H5308
10 f down and worship the golden image: H5308
15 of musick, ye f down and worship the H5308
11:14 to establish the vision; but they shall f. H3782
19 shall stumble and f, and not be found. H5307
26 overflow: and many shall f down slain. H5307
33 yet they shall f by the sword, and by H3782
34 Now when they shall f, they shall be H3782
35 shall f, to try them, and to purge, H3782
Hos 4: 5 Therefore shalt thou f in the day, and H3782
5 the prophet also shall f with thee in the H3782
14 people *that* doth not understand shall f. H3832
5: 5 and Ephraim f in their iniquity; Judah H3782
5 iniquity; Judah also shall f with them. H3782
7:16 their princes shall f by the sword for H5307
10: 8 Cover us; and to the hills, F on us. H5307
13:16 her God: they shall f by the sword: their H5307
14: 9 but the transgressors shall f therein. H3782
Joel 2: 8 and *when* they f upon the sword, they H5307
Am 3: 5 Can a bird f in a snare upon the earth, H5307
14 shall be cut off, and f to the ground. H5307
7:17 daughters shall f by the sword, and thy H5307
8:14 they shall f, and never rise up again. H5307
9: 9 not the least grain f upon the earth. H5307
Mic 7: 8 enemy: when I f, I shall arise; when I H5307
Nah 3:12 shall even f into the mouth of the eater. H5307
Mt 4: 9 if thou wilt f down and worship me. G4098
7:27 and it fell: and great was the f of it. G4431
10:29 f on the ground without your Father. G4098
12:11 one sheep, and if it f into a pit on the G1706
15:14 the blind, both shall f into the ditch. G4098
27 which f from their masters' table. G4098
21:44 And whosoever shall f on this stone G4098
44 it shall f, it will grind him to powder. G4098
24:29 and the stars shall f from heaven, and G4098
Mk 13:25 And the stars of heaven shall f, and the G1601
Lk 2:34 *child* is set for the f and rising again of G4431
6:39 shall they not both f into the ditch? G4098
8:13 and in time of temptation f away. G868
10:18 Satan as lightning f from heaven. G4098
20:18 Whosoever shall f upon that stone shall G4098
18 it shall f, it will grind him to powder. G4098
21:24 And they shall f by the edge of the G4098
23:30 F on us; and to the hills, Cover us. G4098
Jn 12:24 a corn of wheat f into the ground and G4098
Act 27:17 lest they should f into the quicksands, G1601
32 the ropes of the boat, and let her f off. G1601
34 an hair f from the head of any of you. G4098
Ro 11:11 that they should f? God forbid: but G4098
11 through their f salvation *is come* unto G3900
12 Now if the f of them *be* the riches of the G3900
14:13 or an occasion to f in *his* brother's way. G4625
1Co 10:12 thinketh he standeth take heed lest he f. G4098
1Ti 3: 6 he f into the condemnation of the devil. G1706
7 without; lest he f into reproach and the G1706
6: 9 But they that will be rich f into G1706
Heb 4:11 f after the same example of unbelief. G4098
6: 6 If they shall f away, to renew them G3895
10:31 *It is* a fearful thing to f into the hands G1706
Jas 1: 2 My brethren, count it all joy when ye f G4045
5:12 nay, nay; lest ye f into condemnation. G4098
2Pt 1:10 for if ye do these things, ye shall never f: G4417
3:17 wicked, f from your own stedfastness. G1601
Rev 4:10 The four and twenty elders f down G4098
6:16 and rocks, F on us, and hide us from G4098
9: 1 and I saw a star f from heaven unto the G4098

FALLEN

Gen 4: 6 wroth? and why is thy countenance f? H5307
Lev 13:40 And the man whose hair is f off his H4803
41 And he that hath his hair f off from the H4803
25:35 poor, and f in decay with thee; H4131+H3027
Nu 32:19 is f to us on this side Jordan eastward. H935
Jos 2: 9 that your terror is f upon us, and that H5307
8:24 when they were all f on the edge of the H5307
Jdg 3:25 lord *was* f down dead on the earth. H5307
18: 1 f unto them among the tribes of Israel. H5307
19:27 his concubine was f down *at* the door H5307
1Sa 5: 3 Dagon *was* f upon his face to the H5307
4 Dagon *was* f upon his face to the H5307
26:12 sleep from the LORD was f upon them. H5307
31: 8 and his three sons f in mount Gilboa. H5307
2Sa 1: 4 of the people also are f and dead; and H5307
10 after that he was f: and I took the crown H5307
12 because they were f by the sword. H5307
19 thy high places: how are the mighty f! H5307
25 How are the mighty f in the midst of H5307
27 How are the mighty f, and the weapons H5307
3:38 and a great man f this day in Israel? H5307

2Sa 22:39 not arise: yea, they are f under my feet. H5307
2Ki 13:14 Now Elisha was f sick of his sickness
1Ch 10: 8 Saul and his sons f in mount Gilboa. H5307
2Ch 20:24 f to the earth, and none escaped. H5307
29: 9 For, lo, our fathers have f by the sword, H5307
Est 7: 8 wine; and Haman was f upon the bed H5307
Job 1:16 The fire of God is f from heaven, and H5307
Ps 7:15 He made a pit, and digged it, and is f H5307
16: 6 The lines are f unto me in pleasant H5307
18:38 able to rise: they are f under my feet. H5307
20: 8 They are brought down and f: but we H5307
36:12 There are the workers of iniquity f: they H5307
55: 4 and the terrors of death are f upon me. H5307
57: 6 whereof they are f *themselves*. Selah. H5307
69: 9 that reproached thee are f upon me. H5307
Isa 3: 8 For Jerusalem is ruined, and Judah is f: H5307
9:10 The bricks are f down, but we will build H5307
14:12 How art thou f from heaven, O Lucifer, H5307
16: 9 summer fruits and for thy harvest is f. H5307
21: 9 said, Babylon is f, is fallen; and all the H5307
9 is fallen, is f; and all the graven images H5307
26:18 have the inhabitants of the world f. H5307
59:14 f in the street, and equity cannot enter. H3782
Jer 38:19 of the Jews that are f to the Chaldeans, H5307
46:12 mighty, *and* they are f both together. H5307
48:32 the spoiler is f upon thy summer fruits H5307
50:15 foundations are f, her walls are thrown H5307
51: 8 Babylon is suddenly f and destroyed: H5307
Lam 2:21 my young men are f by the sword; thou H5307
5:16 The crown is f *from* our head: woe unto H5307
Ezk 13:12 Lo, when the wall is f, shall it not be H5307
31:12 his branches are f, and his boughs are H5307
32:22 him: all of them slain, f by the sword: H5307
23 all of them slain, f by the sword, which H5307
24 all of them slain, f by the sword, which H5307
27 mighty *that are* f of the uncircumcised, H5307
Hos 7: 7 all their kings are f: *there is* none H5307
14: 1 God; for thou hast f by thine iniquity. H3782
Am 5: 2 The virgin of Israel is f; she shall no H5307
9:11 of David that is f, and close up the H5307
Zec 11: 2 Howl, fir tree; for the cedar is f; because H5307
Lk 14: 5 an ass or an ox f into a pit, and will not *G1706*
Act 8:16 (For as yet he was f upon none of them: *G1968*
15:16 of David, which is f down; and I will *G4098*
20: 9 Eutychus, being f into a deep sleep: *G2702*
26:14 And when we were all f to the earth, I *G2667*
27:29 Then fearing lest we should have f *G1601*
28: 6 have swollen, or f down dead suddenly: *G2667*
1Co 15: 6 this present, but some are f asleep. *G2837*
18 Then they also which are f asleep in *G2837*
Gal 5: 4 justified by the law; ye are f from grace. *G1601*
Php 1:12 unto me have f out rather unto the *G2064*
Rev 2: 5 whence thou art f, and repent, and do *G1601*
14: 8 saying, Babylon is f, is fallen, that great *G4098*
8 is fallen, is f, that great city, because *G4098*
17:10 And there are seven kings: five are f, *G4098*
18: 2 the great is f, is fallen, and is become *G4098*
2 great is fallen, is f, and is become the *G4098*

FALLEST
Jer 37:13 saying, Thou f away to the Chaldeans. H5307

FALLETH
Ex 1:10 that, when there f out any war, they H7122
Lev 11:33 *any* of them f, whatsoever *is* in it shall H5307
35 *part* of their carcase shall be unclean; H5307
Nu 33:54 place where his lot f; according to the H3318
2Sa 3:29 f on the sword, or that lacketh bread. H5307
34 fetters: as a man f before wicked men, H5307
17:12 him as the dew f on the ground: and H5307
Job 4:13 of the night, when deep sleep f on men, H5307
33:15 night, when deep sleep f upon men, in H5307
Prv 13:17 A wicked messenger f into mischief: H5307
17:20 hath a perverse tongue f into mischief. H5307
24:16 For a just *man* f seven times, and riseth H5307
17 Rejoice not when thine enemy f, and let H5307
Ecc 4:10 *that is* alone when he f; for *he hath* not H5307
9:12 time, when it f suddenly upon them. H5307
11: 3 place where the tree f, there it shall be. H5307
Isa 34: 4 down, as the leaf f off from the vine, H5034
44:15 it a graven image, and f down thereto. H5456
17 graven image: he f down unto it, and H5456
Jer 21: 9 goeth out, and f to the Chaldeans that H5307
Dan 3: 6 And whoso f not down and H5308
11 And whoso f not down and H5308
Mt 17:15 he f into the fire, and oft into the water. *G4098*
Lk 11:17 and a house *divided* against a house f. *G4098*
15:12 of goods that f *to me*. And he divided *G1911*
Ro 14: 4 he standeth or f. Yea, he shall be holden *G4098*
Jas 1:11 the flower thereof f, and the grace of the *G1601*
1Pt 1:24 and the flower thereof f away: *G1601*

FALLIBLE See INFALLIBLE.

FALLING
Nu 24: 4 of the Almighty, f *into a trance,* but H5307
16 of the Almighty, f *into a trance,* but H5307
Job 4: 4 upholden him that was f, and thou hast H3782
14:18 And surely the mountain f cometh to H5307
Ps 56:13 my feet from f, that I may walk before H1762
116: 8 eyes from tears, *and* my feet from f. H1762
Prv 25:26 A righteous man f down before H4131+H3027
Isa 34: 4 the vine, and as a f *fig* from the fig tree. H5034
Lk 8:47 trembling, and f down before him, she *G4363*
22:44 drops of blood f down to the ground. *G2597*
Act 1:18 of iniquity; and f headlong, he burst *G1096*
27:41 And f into a place where two seas met, *G4045*
1Co 14:25 manifest; and so f down on *his* face he *G4098*
2Th 2: 3 there come a f away first, and that *G646*
Jude 24 to keep you from f, and to present *you* *G679*

FALLOW
Dt 14: 5 The hart, and the roebuck, and the f H3180
Jer 4: 3 f ground, and sow not among thorns. H5215
Hos 10:12 break up your f ground: for *it is* time H5215

FALLOWDEER
1Ki 4:23 and roebucks, and f, and fatted fowl. H3180

FALLOW-GROUND See FALLOW and GROUND.

FALSE
Ex 20:16 Thou shalt not bear f witness against H8267
23: 1 Thou shalt not raise a f report: put not H7723
7 Keep thee far from a f matter; and the H8267
Dt 5:20 Neither shalt thou bear f witness H7723
19:16 If a f witness rise up against any man H2555
18 *if* the witness *be* a f witness, *and* hath H8267
2Ki 9:12 And they said, *It is* f; tell us now. And H8267
Prv 6:19 A f witness *that* speaketh lies, and he H8267
11: 1 A f balance *is* abomination to the H4820
12:17 righteousness: but a f witness deceit. H8267
14: 5 A faithful witness will not lie: but a f H8267
17: 4 A wicked doer giveth heed to f lips; *and* H205
19: 5 A f witness shall not be unpunished, H8267
9 A f witness shall not be unpunished, H8267
20:23 the LORD; and a f balance *is* not good. H4820
21:28 A f witness shall perish: but the man H3577
25:14 Whoso boasteth himself of a f gift *is* H8267
18 A man that beareth f witness against H8267
Mt 7:15 Beware of f prophets, which come to *G5578*
15:19 thefts, f witness, blasphemies: *G5577*
19:18 not steal, Thou shalt not bear f witness, *G5576*
24:11 And many f prophets shall rise, and *G5578*
24 For there shall arise f Christs, and false
24 For there shall arise false Christs, and f *G5578*
26:59 council, sought f witness against Jesus, *G5580*
60 But found none: yea, though many f *G5575*
60 none. At the last came two f witnesses, *G5575*
Mk 10:19 steal, Do not bear f witness, Defraud *G5576*
13:22 For f Christs and false prophets shall *G5580*
22 For false Christs and f prophets shall *G5578*
14:56 For many bare f witness against him, *G5576*
57 And there arose certain, and bare f *G5576*
Lk 6:26 so did their fathers to the f prophets. *G5578*
18:20 steal, Do not bear f witness, Honour *G5576*
19: 8 by f accusation, I restore *him* fourfold. *G4811*
Act 6:13 And set up f witnesses, which said, *G5571*
13: 6 a certain sorcerer, a f prophet, a Jew, *G5578*
Ro 13: 9 shalt not bear f witness, Thou shalt *G5576*
1Co 15:15 Yea, and we are found f witnesses of *G5575*
2Co 11:13 For such *are* f apostles, deceitful *G5570*
26 in the sea, *in* perils among f brethren; *G5569*
Gal 2: 4 And that because of f brethren *G5569*
2Ti 3: 3 trucebreakers, f accusers, incontinent, *G1228*
Tit 2: 3 holiness, not f accusers, not given *G1228*
2Pt 2: 1 But there were f prophets also among *G5578*
1 as there shall be f teachers among you, *G5572*
1Jn 4: 1 f prophets are gone out into the world. *G5578*
Rev 16:13 and out of the mouth of the f prophet. *G5578*
19:20 taken, and with him the f prophet that *G5578*
20:10 the beast and the f prophet *are,* and *G5578*

FALSE-APOSTLES See FALSE and APOSTLES.

FALSE-BRETHREN See FALSE and BRETHREN.

FALSE-CHRISTS See FALSE and CHRISTS.

FALSE-PROPHET See FALSE and PROPHET.

FALSE-TEACHER See FALSE and TEACHER.

FALSE-WITNESS See FALSE and WITNESS.

FALSEHOOD
2Sa 18:13 Otherwise I should have wrought f H8267
Job 21:34 in your answers there remaineth f? H4604
Ps 7:14 conceived mischief, and brought forth f. H8267
119:118 from thy statutes: for their deceit *is* f. H8267
144: 8 and their right hand *is* a right hand of f. H8267
11 and their right hand *is* a right hand of f: H8267
Isa 28:15 and under f have we hid ourselves: H8267
57: 4 children of transgression, a seed of f, H8267
59:13 and uttering from the heart words of f. H8267
Jer 10:14 *is* f, and *there is* no breath in them. H8267
13:25 thou hast forgotten me, and trusted in f. H8267
51:17 *is* f, and *there is* no breath in them. H8267
Hos 7: 1 for they commit f; and the thief cometh H8267
Mic 2:11 If a man walking in the spirit and f do H8267

FALSELY
Gen 21:23 thou wilt not deal f with me, nor with H8266
Lev 6: 3 it, and sweareth f; in any of all these H8267
5 Or all that about which he hath sworn f; H8267
19:11 Ye shall not steal, neither deal f, neither H3584
12 And ye shall not swear by my name f, H8267
Dt 19:18 *and* hath testified f against his brother; H8267
Ps 44:17 neither have we dealt f in thy covenant. H8266
Jer 5: 2 The LORD liveth; surely they swear f. H8267
31 The prophets prophesy f, and the H8267
6:13 even unto the priest every one dealeth f. H8267
7: 9 and swear f, and burn incense unto H8267
8:10 even unto the priest every one dealeth f. H8267
29: 9 For they prophesy f unto you in my H8267
40:16 thing: for thou speakest f of Ishmael. H8267
43: 2 Thou speakest f: the LORD our God H8267
Hos 10: 4 They have spoken words, swearing f in H7723
Zec 5: 4 him that sweareth f by my name: and it H8267
Mt 5:11 of evil against you f, for my sake. *G5574*
Lk 3:14 *any* f; and be content with your wages. *G4811*
1Ti 6:20 and oppositions of science f so called: *G5581*
1Pt 3:16 may be ashamed that f accuse your good

FALSIFYING
Am 8: 5 great, and f the balances by deceit? H5791

FAME
Gen 45:16 And the f thereof was heard in H6963
Nu 14:15 heard the f of thee will speak, saying, H8088
Jos 6:27 So the LORD was with Joshua; and his f H8089
9: 9 f of him, and all that he did in Egypt, H8089
1Ki 4:31 his f was in all nations round about. H8034
10: 1 of Sheba heard of the f of Solomon H8088
7 exceedeth the f which I heard. H8052
1Ch 14:17 And the f of David went out into all H8034
22: 5 exceeding magnifical, of f and of glory H8034
2Ch 9: 1 of Sheba heard of the f of Solomon, she H8088
6 *for* thou exceedest the f that I heard. H8052
Est 9: 4 house, and his f went out throughout H8089
Job 28:22 have heard the f thereof with our ears. H8088
Isa 66:19 have not heard my f, neither have seen H8088
Jer 6:24 We have heard the f thereof: our hands H8089
Zep 3:19 them praise and f in every land where H8034
Mt 4:24 And his f went throughout all Syria: and *G189*
9:26 And the f hereof went abroad into all *G5345*
31 spread abroad his f in all that country. *G1310*
14: 1 the tetrarch heard of the f of Jesus, *G189*
Mk 1:28 And immediately his f spread abroad *G189*
Lk 4:14 there went out a f of him through all *G5345*
37 And the f of him went out into every *G2279*
5:15 But so much the more went there a f *G3056*

FAMILIAR
Lev 19:31 Regard not them that have f spirits,
20: 6 after such as have f spirits, and after
27 A man also or woman that hath a f
Dt 18:11 Or a charmer, or a consulter with f
1Sa 28: 3 those that had f spirits, and the wizards,
7 woman that hath a f spirit, that I may go
7 a woman that hath a f spirit at En-dor.
8 unto me by the f spirit, and bring me
9 cut off those that have f spirits, and the
2Ki 21: 6 and dealt with f spirits and wizards:
23:24 Moreover the *workers with* f spirits, and
1Ch 10:13 of *one that had* a f spirit, to inquire *of it;*
2Ch 33: 6 and dealt with a f spirit, and with
Job 19:14 My kinsfolk have failed, and my f H3045

Ps 41: 9 Yea, mine own f friend, in whom I H7965
Isa 8:19 unto them that have f spirits, and unto
19: 3 that have f spirits, and to the wizards.
29: 4 as of one that hath a f spirit, out of the

FAMILIARS
Jer 20:10 will report it. All my f watched for my H7965

FAMILIAR-SPIRIT See FAMILIAR and SPIRIT.

FAMILIES
Gen 10: 5 his tongue, after their f, in their nations. H4940
18 the f of the Canaanites spread abroad. H4940
20 These *are* the sons of Ham, after their f, H4940
31 Shem, after their f, after their tongues, H4940
32 These *are* the f of the sons of Noah, H4940
12: 3 thee shall all f of the earth be blessed. H4940
28:14 shall all the f of the earth be blessed. H4940
36:40 according to their f, after their places, H4940
47:12 with bread, according to *their* f. H2945
Ex 6:14 and Carmi: these *be* the f of Reuben. H4940
15 woman: these *are* the f of Simeon. H4940
17 Libni, and Shimi, according to their f. H4940
19 f of Levi according to their generations. H4940
24 these *are* the f of the Korhites. H4940
25 of the Levites according to their f. H4940
12:21 to your f, and kill the passover. H4940
Lev 25:45 ye buy, and of their f that *are* with you, H4940
Nu 1: 2 Israel, after their f, by the house of their H4940
18 after their f, by the house of their H4940
20 after their f, by the house of their H4940
22 after their f, by the house of their H4940
24 after their f, by the house of their H4940
26 after their f, by the house of their H4940
28 after their f, by the house of their H4940
30 after their f, by the house of their H4940
32 after their f, by the house of their H4940
34 after their f, by the house of their H4940
36 after their f, by the house of their H4940
38 after their f, by the house of their H4940
40 after their f, by the house of their H4940
42 after their f, by the house of their H4940
2:34 one after their f, according to the house H4940
3:15 fathers, by their f: every male from a H4940
18 Gershon by their f; Libni, and Shimei. H4940
19 And the sons of Kohath by their f; H4940
20 And the sons of Merari by their f; H4940
20 These *are* the f of the Levites according H4940
21 these *are* the f of the Gershonites. H4940
23 The f of the Gershonites shall pitch H4940
27 these *are* the f of the Kohathites. H4940
29 The f of the sons of Kohath shall pitch H4940
30 of the father of the f of the Kohathites H4940
33 the Mushites: these *are* the f of Merari. H4940
35 of the father of the f of Merari *was* H4940
39 throughout their f, all the males from a H4940
4: 2 their f, by the house of their fathers, H4940
18 Cut ye not off the tribe of the f of the H4940
22 the houses of their fathers, by their f; H4940
24 This *is* the service of the f of the H4940
28 This *is* the service of the f of the sons of H4940
29 their f, by the house of their fathers; H4940
33 This *is* the service of the f of the sons of H4940
34 f, and after the house of their fathers, H4940
36 of them by their f were two thousand H4940
37 numbered of the f of the Kohathites, all H4940
38 f, and by the house of their fathers, H4940
40 throughout their f, by the house of their H4940
41 were numbered of the f of the sons of H4940
42 And those that were numbered of the f H4940
42 their f, by the house of their fathers, H4940
44 of them after their f, were three H4940
45 were numbered of the f of the sons of H4940
46 f, and after the house of their fathers, H4940
11:10 throughout their f, every man in the H4940
26: 7 These *are* the f of the Reubenites: and H4940
12 The sons of Simeon after their f: of H4940
14 These *are* the f of the Simeonites, H4940
15 The children of Gad after their f: of H4940
18 These *are* the f of the children of Gad H4940
20 And the sons of Judah after their f H4940
22 These *are* the f of Judah according to H4940
23 *Of* the sons of Issachar after their f: *of* H4940
25 These *are* the f of Issachar according to H4940
26 *Of* the sons of Zebulun after their f: of H4940
27 These *are* the f of the Zebulunites H4940
28 The sons of Joseph after their f *were* H4940
34 These *are* the f of Manasseh, and those H4940
35 after their f: of Shuthelah, the family H4940
Nu 26:37 These *are* the f of the sons of Ephraim H4940
37 *are* the sons of Joseph after their f. H4940
38 The sons of Benjamin after their f: of H4940
41 after their f: and they that were H4940
42 These *are* the sons of Dan after their f: H4940
42 *are* the f of Dan after their families. H4940
42 *are* the families of Dan after their f. H4940
43 All the f of the Shuhamites, according H4940
44 *Of* the children of Asher after their f: of H4940
47 These *are* the f of the sons of Asher H4940
48 *Of* the sons of Naphtali after their f: of H4940
50 These *are* the f of Naphtali according H4940
50 according to their f: and they that were H4940
57 the Levites after their f: of Gershon, the H4940
58 These *are* the f of the Levites: the H4940
27: 1 Manasseh, of the f of Manasseh the son H4940
33:54 among your f: *and* to the more ye shall H4940
36: 1 And the chief fathers of the f of the H4940
1 of Manasseh, of the f of the sons of H4940
12 *And* they were married into the f of the H4940
Jos 7:14 according to the f *thereof*; and the H4940
13:15 Reuben *inheritance* according to their f. H4940
23 f, the cities and the villages thereof. H4940
24 the children of Gad according to their f. H4940
28 their f, the cities, and their villages. H4940
29 of the children of Manasseh by their f. H4940
31 half of the children of Machir by their f. H4940
15: 1 of Judah by their f; *even* to the border of H4940
12 Judah round about according to their f. H4940
20 children of Judah according to their f. H4940
16: 5 according to their f was *thus*: even the H4940
8 of the children of Ephraim by their f. H4940
17: 2 Manasseh by their f; for the children of H4940
2 Manasseh the son of Joseph by their f. H4940
18:11 up according to their f: and the coast of H4940
20 round about, according to their f. H4940
21 according to their f were Jericho, and H4940
28 of Benjamin according to their f. H4940
19: 1 Simeon according to their f: and their H4940
8 children of Simeon according to their f. H4940
10 according to their f: and the border of H4940
16 to their f, these cities with their villages. H4940
17 of Issachar according to their f. H4940
23 to their f, the cities and their villages. H4940
24 children of Asher according to their f. H4940
31 to their f, these cities with their villages. H4940
32 of Naphtali according to their f. H4940
39 to their f, the cities and their villages. H4940
40 the children of Dan according to their f. H4940
48 to their f, these cities with their villages. H4940
21: 4 And the lot came out for the f of the H4940
5 *had* by lot out of the f of the tribe of H4940
6 *had* by lot out of the f of the tribe of H4940
7 The children of Merari by their f *had* H4940
10 *being* of the f of the Kohathites, *who* H4940
20 And the f of the children of Kohath, the H4940
26 their suburbs for the f of the children of H4940
27 of Gershon, of the f of the Levites, out H4940
33 according to their f *were* thirteen cities H4940
34 And unto the f of the children of H4940
40 of Merari by their f, which were H4940
40 remaining of the f of the Levites, were H4940
1Sa 9:21 the least of all the f of the tribe of H4940
10:21 come near by their f, the family of Matri H4940
1Ch 2:53 And the f of Kirjath-jearim; the H4940
55 And the f of the scribes which dwelt at H4940
4: 2 These *are* the f of the Zorathites. H4940
8 and the f of Aharhel the son of Harum. H4940
21 and the f of the house of them H4940
38 princes in their f: and the house of their H4940
5: 7 And his brethren by their f, when the H4940
6:19 And these *are* the f of the Levites H4940
54 of Aaron, of the f of the Kohathites: for H4940
60 throughout their f *were* thirteen cities. H4940
62 throughout their f out of the tribe of H4940
63 throughout their f, out of the tribe of H4940
66 And *the residue* of the f of the sons of H4940
7: 5 And their brethren among all the f of H4940
2Ch 35: 5 divisions of the f of the fathers of your H1004
5 the division of the f of the Levites. H1+H1004
12 divisions of the f of the people, to H1+H1004
Neh 4:13 people after their f with their swords, H4940
Job 31:34 the contempt of f terrify me, that I kept H4940
Ps 68: 6 God setteth the solitary in f: he bringeth H1004
107:41 and maketh *him* f like a flock. H4940
Jer 1:15 For, lo, I will call all the f of the H4940
2: 4 and all the f of the house of Israel: H4940
10:25 not, and upon the f that call not on thy H4940
25: 9 Behold, I will send and take all the f of H4940
Jer 31: 1 f of Israel, and they shall be my people. H4940
33:24 saying, The two f which the LORD hath H4940
Ezk 20:32 the heathen, as the f of the countries, to H4940
Am 3: 2 You only have I known of all the f of H4940
Nah 3: 4 and f through her witchcrafts. H4940
Zec 12:14 All the f that remain, every family H4940
14:17 come up of *all* the f of the earth unto H4940

FAMILY
Lev 20: 5 and against his f, and will cut him off, H4940
25:10 ye shall return every man unto his f. H4940
41 unto his own f, and unto the possession H4940
47 thee, or to the stock of the stranger's f: H4940
49 unto him of his f may redeem him; or H4940
Nu 3:21 Of Gershon *was* the f of the Libnites, H4940
21 the Libnites, and the f of the Shimites: H4940
27 And of Kohath *was* the f of the H4940
27 and the f of the Izeharites, and H4940
27 Izeharites, and the f of the Hebronites, H4940
27 and the f of the Uzzielites: these H4940
33 Of Merari *was* the f of the Mahlites, H4940
33 the Mahlites, and the f of the Mushites: H4940
26: 5 *whom cometh* the f of the Hanochites: H4940
5 of Pallu, the f of the Palluites: H4940
6 Of Hezron, the f of the Hezronites: of H4940
6 of Carmi, the f of the Carmites. H4940
12 of Nemuel, the f of the Nemuelites: of H4940
12 of Jamin, the f of the Jaminites: of H4940
12 of Jachin, the f of the Jachinites: H4940
13 Of Zerah, the f of the Zarhites: of Shaul, H4940
13 of Shaul, the f of the Shaulites. H4940
15 of Zephon, the f of the Zephonites: of H4940
15 of Haggi, the f of the Haggites: of H4940
15 of Shuni, the f of the Shunites: H4940
16 Of Ozni, the f of the Oznites: of Eri, the H4940
16 of the Oznites: of Eri, the f of the Erites: H4940
17 Of Arod, the f of the Arodites: of Areli, H4940
17 Arodites: of Areli, the f of the Arelites. H4940
20 of Shelah, the f of the Shelanites: of H4940
20 of Pharez, the f of the Pharzites: of H4940
20 of Zerah, the f of the Zarhites. H4940
21 of Hezron, the f of the Hezronites: of H4940
21 of Hamul, the f of the Hamulites. H4940
23 *of* Tola, the f of the Tolaites: of Pua, H4940
23 Tolaites: of Pua, the f of the Punites: H4940
24 Of Jashub, the f of the Jashubites: of H4940
24 of Shimron, the f of the Shimronites. H4940
26 of Sered, the f of the Sardites: of Elon, H4940
26 of Elon, the f of the Elonites: of Jahleel, H4940
26 of Jahleel, the f of the Jahleelites. H4940
29 of Machir, the f of the Machirites: and H4940
29 of Gilead *come* the f of the Gileadites. H4940
30 *of* Jeezer, the f of the Jeezerites: of H4940
30 of Helek, the f of the Helekites: H4940
31 And *of* Asriel, the f of the Asrielites: H4940
31 *of* Shechem, the f of the Shechemites: H4940
32 And *of* Shemida, the f of the H4940
32 and *of* Hepher, the f of the Hepherites. H4940
35 of Shuthelah, the f of the Shuthalhites: H4940
35 of Becher, the f of the Bachrites: of H4940
35 of Tahan, the f of the Tahanites. H4940
36 of Eran, the f of the Eranites. H4940
38 of Bela, the f of the Belaites: of Ashbel, H4940
38 of Ashbel, the f of the Ashbelites: of H4940
38 of Ahiram, the f of the Ahiramites: H4940
39 Of Shupham, the f of the Shuphamites: H4940
39 of Hupham, the f of the Huphamites. H4940
40 *of Ard,* the f of the Ardites: *and* of H4940
40 *and* of Naaman, the f of the Naamites. H4940
42 of Shuham, the f of the Shuhamites. H4940
44 of Jimna, the f of the Jimnites: of Jesui, H4940
44 of Jesui, the f of the Jesuites: of Beriah, H4940
44 Jesuites: of Beriah, the f of the Beriites. H4940
45 Of the sons of Beriah: of Heber, the f of H4940
45 of Malchiel, the f of the Malchielites. H4940
48 of Jahzeel, the f of the Jahzeelites: of H4940
48 of Guni, the f of the Gunites: H4940
49 Of Jezer, the f of the Jezerites: of H4940
49 of Shillem, the f of the Shillemites. H4940
57 of Gershon, the f of the Gershonites: of H4940
57 of Kohath, the f of the Kohathites: of H4940
57 of Merari, the f of the Merarites. H4940
58 of the Levites: the f of the Libnites, the H4940
58 of the Libnites, the f of the Hebronites, H4940
58 Hebronites, the f of the Mahlites, the H4940
58 the Mahlites, the f of the Mushites, the H4940
58 of the Mushites, the f of the Korathites. H4940
27: 4 from among his f, because he hath no H4940
11 is next to him of his f, and he shall H4940

Nu 36: 6 best; only to the f of the tribe of their H4940
8 wife unto one of the f of the tribe of her H4940
12 in the tribe of the f of their father. H4940
Dt 29:18 or woman, or f, or tribe, whose heart H4940
Jos 7:14 *thereof;* and the f which the LORD shall H4940
17 And he brought the f of Judah; and he H4940
17 and he took the f of the Zarhites: and H4940
17 he brought the f of the Zarhites man H4940
Jdg 1:25 but they let go the man and all his f. H4940
6:15 save Israel? behold, my f *is* poor in H504
9: 1 and with all the f of the house of his H4940
13: 2 of Zorah, of the f of the Danites, whose H4940
17: 7 of the f of Judah, who *was* a H4940
18: 2 And the children of Dan sent of their f H4940
11 And there went from thence of the f of H4940
19 a priest unto a tribe and a f in Israel? H4940
21:24 his tribe and to his f, and they went out H4940
Ru 2: 1 f of Elimelech; and his name *was* Boaz. H4940
1Sa 9:21 of Israel? and my f the least of all the H4940
10:21 their families, the f of Matri was taken, H4940
18:18 my life, *or* my father's f in Israel, that I H4940
20: 6 *is* a yearly sacrifice there for all the f. H4940
29 I pray thee; for our f hath a sacrifice in H4940
2Sa 14: 7 And, behold, the whole f is risen H4940
16: 5 out a man of the f of the house of Saul, H4940
1Ch 4:27 f multiply, like to the children of Judah. H4940
6:61 *were* left of the f of that tribe, *were* H4940
70 f of the remnant of the sons of Kohath. H4940
71 *given* out of the f of the half tribe of H4940
13:14 And the ark of God remained with the f H1004
Est 9:28 generation, every f, every province, and H4940
Jer 3:14 two of a f, and I will bring you to Zion: H4940
8: 3 remain of this evil f, which remain in all H4940
Am 3: 1 against the whole f which I brought up H4940
Mic 2: 3 against this f do I devise an evil, from H4940
Zec 12:12 And the land shall mourn, every f H4940
12 every family apart; the f of the house of H4940
12 their wives apart; the f of the house of H4940
13 The f of the house of Levi apart, and H4940
13 wives apart; the f of Shimei apart, and H4940
14 All the families that remain, every f H4940
14:18 And if the f of Egypt go not up, and H4940
Eph 3:15 Of whom the whole f in heaven and *G3965*

FAMINE

Gen 12:10 And there was a f in the land: and H7458
10 for the f *was* grievous in the land. H7458
26: 1 And there was a f in the land, beside H7458
1 beside the first f that was in the days H7458
41:27 the east wind shall be seven years of f. H7458
30 seven years of f; and all the plenty shall H7458
30 and the f shall consume the land; H7458
31 f following; for it *shall be* very grievous. H7458
36 the seven years of f, which shall be in H7458
36 that the land perish not through the f. H7458
50 sons before the years of f came, which H7458
56 And the f was over all the face of the H7458
56 the f waxed sore in the land of Egypt. H7458
57 that the f was *so* sore in all lands. H7458
42: 5 for the f was in the land of Canaan. H7458
19 ye, carry corn for the f of your houses: H7459
33 the f of your households, and be gone: H7459
43: 1 And the f *was* sore in the land. H7458
45: 6 For these two years *hath* the f *been* in H7458
11 *are* five years of f; lest thou, and thy H7458
47: 4 flocks; for the f *is* sore in the land of H7458
13 the land; for the f *was* very sore, so that H7458
13 of Canaan fainted by reason of the f. H7458
20 his field, because the f prevailed over H7458
Ru 1: 1 that there was a f in the land. And a H7458
2Sa 21: 1 Then there was a f in the days of David H7458
24:13 seven years of f come unto thee in thy H7458
1Ki 8:37 If there be in the land f, if there be H7458
18: 2 And *there was* a sore f in Samaria. H7458
2Ki 6:25 And there was a great f in Samaria: H7458
7: 4 the city, then the f *is* in the city, and we H7458
8: 1 hath called for a f; and it shall also H7458
25: 3 *fourth* month the f prevailed in the city, H7458
1Ch 21:12 Either three years' f; or three months to H7458
2Ch 20: 9 or pestilence, or f, we stand before this H7458
32:11 to die by f and by thirst, saying, H7458
Job 5:20 In f he shall redeem thee from death: H7458
22 At destruction and f thou shalt laugh: H3720
30: 3 For want and f *they were* solitary; H3720
Ps 33:19 from death, and to keep them alive in f. H7458
37:19 in the days of f they shall be satisfied. H7459
105:16 Moreover he called for a f upon the H7458
Isa 14:30 with f, and he shall slay thy remnant. H7458
51:19 and the f, and the sword: by whom H7458
Jer 5:12 us; neither shall we see sword nor f: H7458
11:22 sons and their daughters shall die by f: H7458
14:12 and by the f, and by the pestilence. H7458
13 shall ye have f; but I will give you H7458
15 say, Sword and f shall not be in this H7458
15 f shall those prophets be consumed. H7458
16 because of the f and the sword; and H7458
18 them that are sick with f! yea, both the H7458
15: 2 such as *are* for the f, to the famine; and H7458
2 the famine, to the f; and such as *are* for H7458
16: 4 the sword, and by f; and their carcases H7458
18:21 children to the f, and pour out their H7458
21: 7 sword, and from the f, into the hand of H7458
9 the sword, and by the f, and by the H7458
24:10 And I will send the sword, the f, and the H7458
27: 8 and with the f, and with the pestilence, H7458
13 by the sword, by the f, and by the H7458
29:17 the sword, the f, and the pestilence, and H7458
18 the sword, with the f, and with the H7458
32:24 the sword, and of the f, and of the H7458
36 and by the f, and by the pestilence; H7458
34:17 and to the f; and I will make you H7458
38: 2 by the sword, by the f, and by the H7458
42:16 of Egypt, and the f, whereof ye were H7458
17 by the sword, by the f, and by the H7458
22 by the sword, by the f, and by the H7458
44:12 sword *and* by the f: they shall die, from H7458
12 sword and by the f: and they shall be an H7458
13 sword, by the f, and by the pestilence: H7458
18 consumed by the sword and by the f. H7458
27 by the f, until there be an end of them. H7458
52: 6 of the month, the f was sore in the city, H7458
Lam 5:10 like an oven because of the terrible f. H7458
Ezk 5:12 and with f shall they be consumed H7458
16 the evil arrows of f, which shall be for H7458
16 I will increase the f upon you, and will H7458
17 So will I send upon you f and evil H7458
6:11 sword, by the f, and by the pestilence. H7458
12 shall die by the f: thus will I accomplish H7458
7:15 pestilence and the f within: he that *is* in H7458
15 city, f and pestilence shall devour him. H7458
12:16 the sword, from the f, and from the H7458
14:13 and will send f upon it, and will cut H7458
21 the sword, and the f, and the noisome H7458
36:29 will increase it, and lay no f upon you. H7458
30 more reproach of f among the heathen. H7458
Am 8:11 that I will send a f in the land, not a H7458
11 in the land, not a f of bread, nor a H7458
Lk 4:25 great f was throughout all the land; *G3042*
15:14 arose a mighty f in that land; and he *G3042*
Ro 8:35 or f, or nakedness, or peril, or sword? *G3042*
Rev 18: 8 and mourning, and f; and she shall be *G3042*

FAMINES

Mt 24: 7 and there shall be f, and pestilences, *G3042*
Mk 13: 8 and there shall be f and troubles: these *G3042*
Lk 21:11 in divers places, and f, and pestilences; *G3042*

FAMISH

Prv 10: 3 soul of the righteous to f: but he casteth H7456
Zep 2:11 them: for he will f all the gods of the H7329

FAMISHED

Gen 41:55 And when all the land of Egypt was f, H7456
Isa 5:13 men *are* f, and their multitude H7458

FAMOUS

Nu 16: 2 f in the congregation, men of renown: H7148
26: 9 *which were* f in the congregation, H7121
Ru 4:11 and be f in Beth-lehem: H7121+H8034
14 that his name may be f in Israel. H7121
1Ch 5:24 men of valour, f men, *and* heads of the H8034
12:30 f throughout the house of their fathers. H8034
Ps 74: 5 *A man* was f according as he had lifted H3045
136:18 And slew f kings: for his mercy *endureth* H117
Ezk 23:10 and she became f among women; for H8034
32:18 the daughters of the f nations, unto the H117

FAN

Isa 30:24 with the shovel and with the f. H4214
41:16 Thou shalt f them, and the wind shall H2219
Jer 4:11 of my people, not to f, nor to cleanse, H2219
15: 7 And I will f them with a fan in the gates H2219
7 And I will fan them with a f in the gates H4214
51: 2 fanners, that shall f her, and shall H2219
Mt 3:12 Whose f *is* in his hand, and he will *G4425*
Lk 3:17 Whose f *is* in his hand, and he will *G4425*

FANNERS

Jer 51: 2 And will send unto Babylon f, that shall H2114

FAR

Gen 18:25 That be f from thee to do after this H2486
25 as the wicked, that be f from thee: Shall H2486
44: 4 city, *and* not *yet* f off, Joseph said unto H7368
Ex 8:28 shall not go very f away: entreat for me. H7368
23: 7 Keep thee f from a false matter; and H7368
Nu 2: 2 their father's house: f off about the H5048
Dt 12:21 his name there be too f from thee, then H7368
13: 7 nigh unto thee, or f off from thee, from H7350
14:24 *or* if the place be too f from thee, which H7368
20:15 *which are* very f off from thee, which H7350
28:49 against thee from f, from the end of the H7350
29:22 that shall come from a f land, shall say, H7350
30:11 not hidden from thee, neither *is* it f off. H7350
Jos 3:16 up upon an heap very f from the city H7368
8: 4 very f from the city, but be ye all ready: H7368
9: 6 We be come from a f country: now H7350
9 And they said unto him, From a very f H7350
22 f from you; when ye dwell among us? H7350
Jdg 9:17 adventured his life f, and delivered you H5048
18: 7 and they *were* f from the Zidonians, H7350
28 because it *was* f from Zidon, and they H7350
19:11 by Jebus, the day was f spent; and the H3966
1Sa 2:30 LORD saith, Be it f from me; for them H2486
20: 9 And Jonathan said, F be it from thee: H2486
22:15 God for him? be it f from me: let not the H2486
2Sa 15:17 and tarried in a place that was f off. H4801
20:20 And Joab answered and said, F be it, H2486
20 and said, Far be it, f be it from me, that H2486
23:17 And he said, Be it f from me, O LORD, H2486
1Ki 8:41 out of a f country for thy name's sake; H7350
46 unto the land of the enemy, f or near; H7350
2Ki 20:14 from a f country, *even* from Babylon. H7350
2Ch 6:32 but is come from a f country for thy H7350
36 away captives unto a land f off or near; H7350
26:15 his name spread f abroad; for he was H7350
Ezr 6: 6 beyond the river, be ye f from thence: H7352
Neh 4:19 upon the wall, one f from another. H7350
Est 9:20 of the king Ahasuerus, *both* nigh and f, H7350
Job 5: 4 His children are f from safety, and they H7368
11:14 If iniquity *be* in thine hand, put it f H7368
13:21 Withdraw thine hand f from me: and H7368
19:13 He hath put my brethren f from me, H7368
21:16 the counsel of the wicked is f from me. H7368
22:18 the counsel of the wicked is f from me. H7368
23 away iniquity f from thy tabernacles. H7368
30:10 They abhor me, they flee f from me, H7368
34:10 of understanding: f be it from God, *that* H2486
Ps 10: 5 thy judgments *are* f above out of his H5048
22: 1 *why art thou so* f from helping me, *and* H7350
11 Be not f from me; for trouble *is* near; H7368
19 But be not thou f from me, O LORD: O H7368
27: 9 Hide not thy face *f* from me; put not thy
35:22 not silence: O Lord, be not f from me. H7368
38:21 O LORD: O my God, be not f from me. H7368
55: 7 Lo, *then* would I wander f off, *and* H7368
71:12 O God, be not f from me: O my God, H7368
73:27 For, lo, they that are f from thee shall H7369
88: 8 acquaintance f from me; thou hast H7368
18 Lover and friend hast thou put f from H7368
97: 9 earth: thou art exalted f above all gods. H3966
103:12 As f as the east is from the west, *so* far H7350
12 As far as the east is from the west, *so* f H7350
109:17 not in blessing, so let it be f from him. H7368
119:150 after mischief: they are f from thy law. H7368
155 Salvation *is* f from the wicked: for they H7350
Prv 4:24 and perverse lips put f from thee. H7368
5: 8 Remove thy way f from her, and come H7368
15:29 The LORD *is* f from the wicked: but he H7350
19: 7 more do his friends go f from him? he H7368
22: 5 doth keep his soul shall be f from them. H7368
15 of correction shall drive it f from him. H7368
25:25 soul, so *is* good news from a f country. H4801
27:10 *that is* near than a brother f off. H7350
30: 8 Remove f from me vanity and lies: give H7368
31:10 woman? for her price *is* f above rubies. H7350
Ecc 2:13 folly, as f as light excelleth darkness. H7350
7:23 I will be wise; but it *was* f from me. H7350
24 That which is f off, and exceeding H7350
Isa 5:26 to the nations from f, and will hiss unto H7350
6:12 And the LORD have removed men f H7368
8: 9 and give ear, all ye of f countries: gird H4801
10: 3 shall come from f? to whom will ye flee H4801
13: 5 They come from a f country, from the H4801
17:13 and they shall flee f off, and shall be H4801
19: 6 And they shall turn the rivers f away;

F

Isa 22: 3 bound together, *which* have fled from f. H7350
26:15 *it* f *unto* all the ends of the earth. H7368
29:13 their heart f from me, and their H7368
30:27 cometh from f, burning *with* his anger, H4801
33:13 Hear, ye *that are* f off, what I have H7350
17 shall behold the land that is very f off. H4801
39: 3 f country unto me, *even* from Babylon. H7350
43: 6 my sons from f, and my daughters from H7350
46:11 my counsel from a f country: yea, I H4801
12 that *are* f from righteousness: H7350
13 it shall not be f off, and my salvation H7368
49: 1 ye people, from f; The LORD hath called H7350
12 Behold, these shall come from f: and, lo, H7350
19 that swallowed thee up shall be f away. H7368
54:14 thou shalt be f from oppression; for H7368
57: 9 thy messengers f off, and didst debase H7350
19 to *him that is* f off, and to *him that* H7350
59: 9 Therefore is judgment f from us, H7368
11 for salvation, *but* it is f off from us. H7368
60: 4 shall come from f, and thy daughters H7350
9 thy sons from f, their silver and their H7350
Jer 2: 5 that they are gone f from me, and have H7368
4:16 come from a f country, and give out H4801
5:15 upon you from f, O house of Israel, H4801
6:20 the sweet cane from a f country? your H4801
8:19 that dwell in a f country: *Is* not the H4801
12: 2 in their mouth, and f from their reins. H7350
25:26 And all the kings of the north, f and H7350
27:10 to remove you f from your land; and H7368
48:24 the cities of the land of Moab, f or near. H7350
47 LORD. Thus f *is* the judgment of Moab. H2008
49:30 Flee, get you f off, dwell deep, O ye H3966
51:64 Thus f *are* the words of Jeremiah. H2008
Lam 1:16 should relieve my soul is f from me: my H7368
3:17 And thou hast removed my soul f off H2186
Ezk 6:12 He that is f off shall die of the H7350
7:20 therefore have I set it f from them. H5079
8: 6 here, that I should go f off from my H7368
11:15 have said, Get you f from the LORD: H7368
16 I have cast them f off among the H7368
12:27 prophesieth of the times *that are* f off. H7350
22: 5 *Those that be* near, and *those that be* f H7350
23:40 for men to come from f, unto whom a H4801
43: 9 of their kings, f from me, and I will H7368
44:10 And the Levites that are gone away f H7368
Dan 9: 7 near, and *that are* f off, through all the H7350
11: 2 the fourth shall be f richer than *they* H1419
Joel 2:20 But I will remove f off from you the H7368
3: 6 remove them f from their border. H7368
8 f off: for the LORD hath spoken *it*. H7350
Am 6: 3 Ye that put f away the evil day, and
Mic 4: 7 her that was cast f off a strong nation:
7:11 that day shall the decree be f removed. H7368
Hab 1: 8 shall come from f; they shall fly as the H7350
Zec 6:15 And they *that are* f off shall come and H7350
10: 9 remember me in f countries; and they H4801
Mt 15: 8 *their* lips; but their heart is f from me. G4206
16:22 him, saying, Be it f from thee, Lord: G2436
21:33 husbandmen, and went into a f country:
25:14 travelling into a f country, *who* called
Mk 6:35 And when the day was now f spent, his G4183
35 place, and now the time *is* f passed: G4183
7: 6 *their* lips, but their heart is f from me. G568
8: 3 the way: for divers of them came from f. G3113
12: 1 husbandmen, and went into a f country.
34 him, Thou art not f from the kingdom G3112
13:34 as a man taking a f journey, who left his
Lk 7: 6 he was now not f from the house, the G3112
15:13 his journey into a f country, and there G3117
19:12 went into a f country to receive for G3117
20: 9 went into a f country for a long time.
22:51 Suffer ye thus f. And he touched his G2193
24:29 and the day is f spent. And he went in
50 And he led them out as f as to Bethany, G2193
Jn 21: 8 (for they were not f from land, but as it G3112
Act 11:19 travelled as f as Phenice, and Cyprus, G2193
22 that he should go as f as Antioch. G2193
17:27 he be not f from every one of us: G3112
22:21 will send thee f hence unto the Gentiles. G3112
28:15 came to meet us as f as Appii forum, G891
Ro 13:12 The night is f spent, the day is at hand:
2Co 4:17 for us a f more exceeding G1519+G5236
10:14 for we are come as f as to you also in G891
Eph 1:21 F above all principality, and power, G5231
2:13 sometimes were f off are made nigh by G3112
4:10 that ascended up f above all heavens, G5231
Php 1:23 with Christ; which is f better: G4183+G3123
Heb 7:15 And it is yet f more evident: for that G4054

FARE
1Sa 17:18 thy brethren f, and take their pledge. H7965
Jna 1: 3 so he paid the f thereof, and went down H7939
Act 15:29 yourselves, ye shall do well. F ye well. G4517

FARED
Lk 16:19 linen, and f sumptuously every day: G2165

FAREWELL
Lk 9:61 them f, which are at home at my house. G657
Act 18:21 But bade them f, saying, I must by all G657
23:30 thee what *they had* against him. F. G4517
2Co 13:11 Finally, brethren, f. Be perfect, be of G5463

FARM
Mt 22: 5 one to his f, another to his merchandise: G68

FARTHER
Mt 26:39 And he went a little f, and fell on his G4281
Mk 1:19 And when he had gone a little f thence, G4260
10: 1 of Judaea by the f side of Jordan: and G4008

FARTHING
Mt 5:26 till thou hast paid the uttermost f. G2835
10:29 Are not two sparrows sold for a f? and G787
Mk 12:42 she threw in two mites, which make a f. G2835

FARTHINGS
Lk 12: 6 Are not five sparrows sold for two f, and G787

FASHION
Gen 6:15 And this *is the f* which thou shalt make
Ex 26:30 according to the f thereof which was H4941
37:19 Three bowls made after the f of almonds
1Ki 6:38 to all the f of it. So was he seven H4941
2Ki 16:10 the priest the f of the altar, and the H1823
Job 31:15 him? and did not one f us in the womb? H3559
Ezk 43:11 of the house, and the f thereof, and the H8498
Mk 2:12 God, saying, We never saw it on this f. G3779
Lk 9:29 And as he prayed, the f of his G1491
Act 7:44 it according to the f that he had seen. G5179
1Co 7:31 *it*: for the f of this world passeth away. G4976
Php 2: 8 And being found in f as a man, he G4976
Jas 1:11 the grace of the f of it perisheth: so also G4383

FASHIONED
Ex 32: 4 at their hand, and f it with a graving H3335
Job 10: 8 Thine hands have made me and f me H6213
Ps 119:73 Thy hands have made me and f me: H3559
139:16 f, when *as yet there was* none of them. H3335
Isa 22:11 had respect unto him that f it long ago. H3335
Ezk 16: 7 *thy* breasts are f, and thine hair is H3559
Php 3:21 that it may be f like unto his glorious G4832

FASHIONETH
Ps 33:15 He f their hearts alike; he considereth H3335
Isa 44:12 in the coals, and f it with hammers, H3335
45: 9 say to him that f it, What makest thou? H3335

FASHIONING
1Pt 1:14 As obedient children, not f yourselves G4964

FASHIONS
Ezk 42:11 to their f, and according to their doors. H4941

FAST
Gen 20:18 For the LORD had f closed up all the H6113
Jdg 4:21 he was f asleep and weary. So he died.
15:13 we will bind thee f, and deliver thee into H631
16:11 And he said unto her, If they bind me f H631
Ru 2: 8 hence, but abide here f by my maidens: H1692
21 Thou shalt keep f by my young men, H1692
23 So she kept f by the maidens of Boaz to H1692
2Sa 12:21 done? thou didst f and weep for the H6684
23 wherefore should I f? can I bring him H6684
1Ki 21: 9 saying, Proclaim a f, and set Naboth on H6685
12 They proclaimed a f, and set Naboth on H6685
2Ki 6:32 and hold him f at the door: *is* not the H3905
2Ch 20: 3 proclaimed a f throughout all Judah. H6685
Ezr 5: 8 f on, and prospereth in their hands. H629
8:21 Then I proclaimed a f there, at the river H6685
Est 4:16 in Shushan, and f ye for me, and H6684
16 my maidens will f likewise; and so will H6684
Job 2: 3 evil? and still he holdeth f his integrity,
8:15 he shall hold it f, but it shall not endure.
27: 6 My righteousness I hold f, and will not let
38:38 and the clods cleave f together?
Ps 33: 9 *done*; he commanded, and it stood f. H5975
38: 2 For thine arrows stick f in me, and thy H5181
Ps 41: 8 An evil disease, *say they*, cleaveth f H3332
65: 6 Which by his strength setteth f the H3559
89:28 and my covenant shall stand f with him. H539
111: 8 They stand f for ever and ever, *and are* H5564
Prv 4:13 Take f hold of instruction; let *her* not go:
Isa 58: 3 in the day of your f ye find pleasure, H6685
4 Behold, ye f for strife and debate, and H6684
4 ye shall not f as *ye do this* day, to H6684
5 Is it such a f that I have chosen? a day H6685
5 a f, and an acceptable day to the LORD? H6685
6 *Is* not this the f that I have chosen? to H6685
Jer 8: 5 they hold f deceit, they refuse to return.
14:12 When they f, I will not hear their cry; H6684
36: 9 they proclaimed a f before the LORD to H6685
46:14 say ye, Stand f, and prepare thee; for H3320
48:16 to come, and his affliction hasteth f. H3966
50:33 held them f; they refused to let them go.
Joel 1:14 Sanctify ye a f, call a solemn assembly, H6685
2:15 Blow the trumpet in Zion, sanctify a f, H6685
Jna 1: 5 of the ship; and he lay, and was f asleep.
3: 5 God, and proclaimed a f, and put on H6685
Zec 7: 5 did ye at all f unto me, *even* to me? H6684
8:19 Thus saith the LORD of hosts; The f of H6685
19 *month*, and the f of the fifth, and the H6685
19 the fifth, and the f of the seventh, and H6685
19 seventh, and the f of the tenth, shall be H6685
Mt 6:16 Moreover when ye f, be not, as the G3522
16 unto men to f. Verily I say unto you, G3522
18 That thou appear not unto men to f, but G3522
9:14 f oft, but thy disciples fast not? G3522
14 fast oft, but thy disciples f not? G3522
15 taken from them, and then shall they f. G3522
26:48 I shall kiss, that same is he: hold him f. G2902
Mk 2:18 Pharisees used to f: and they come and G3522
18 Pharisees f, but thy disciples fast not? G3522
18 Pharisees fast, but thy disciples f not? G3522
19 of the bridechamber f, while the G3522
19 bridegroom with them, they cannot f. G3522
20 and then shall they f in those days. G3522
Lk 5:33 the disciples of John f often, and make G3522
34 f, while the bridegroom is with them? G3522
35 and then shall they f in those days. G3522
18:12 I f twice in the week, I give tithes of all G3522
Act 16:24 and made their feet f in the stocks. G805
27: 9 because the f was now already past, G3521
41 and the forepart stuck f, and remained G2043
1Co 16:13 Watch ye, stand f in the faith, quit you G4739
Gal 5: 1 Stand f therefore in the liberty G4739
Php 1:27 that ye stand f in one spirit, with one G4739
4: 1 stand f in the Lord, *my* dearly beloved. G4739
1Th 3: 8 For now we live, if ye stand f in the G4739
5:21 Prove all things; hold f that which is G2722
2Th 2:15 Therefore, brethren, stand f, and hold G4739
2Ti 1:13 Hold f the form of sound words, which G2192
Tit 1: 9 Holding f the faithful word as he hath G472
Heb 3: 6 are we, if we hold f the confidence and G2722
4:14 Son of God, let us hold f *our* profession. G2902
10:23 Let us hold f the profession of *our* faith G2722
Rev 2:13 and thou holdest f my name, and hast G2902
25 But that which ye have *already* hold f G2902
3: 3 and heard, and hold f, and repent. If G5083
11 Behold, I come quickly: hold that f G2902

FASTED
Jdg 20:26 the LORD, and f that day until even, H6684
1Sa 7: 6 the LORD, and f on that day, and said H6684
31:13 a tree at Jabesh, and f seven days. H6684
2Sa 1:12 And they mourned, and wept, and f H6684
12:16 child; and David f, and went in, and lay H6684
22 was yet alive, I f and wept: for I said, H6684
1Ki 21:27 f, and lay in sackcloth, and went softly. H6684
1Ch 10:12 the oak in Jabesh, and f seven days. H6684
Ezr 8:23 So we f and besought our God for this: H6684
Neh 1: 4 f, and prayed before the God of heaven, H6684
Isa 58: 3 Wherefore have we f, *say they*, and thou H6684
Zec 7: 5 saying, When ye f and mourned in the H6684
Mt 4: 2 And when he had f forty days and forty G3522
Act 13: 2 As they ministered to the Lord, and f, G3522
3 And when they had f and prayed, and G3522

FASTEN
Ex 28:14 f the wreathen chains to the ouches. H5414
25 *chains* thou shalt f in the two ouches, H5414
39:31 And they tied unto it a lace of blue, to f H5414
Isa 22:23 And I will f him *as* a nail in a sure H8628
Jer 10: 4 with gold; they f it with nails and with H2388

FASTENED
Ex 39:18 chains they f in the two ouches, and H5414

Ex 40:18 tabernacle, and f his sockets, and set H5414
Jdg 4:21 his temples, and f it into the ground: H6795
16:14 And she f *it* with the pin, and said unto H8628
1Sa 31:10 f his body to the wall of Beth-shan. H8628
2Sa 20: 8 *with* a sword f upon his loins in the H6775
1Ki 6: 6 should not be f in the walls of the house. H270
1Ch 10:10 and f his head in the temple of Dagon. H8628
2Ch 9:18 of gold, *which were* f to the throne, and H270
Est 1: 6 blue, *hangings*, f with cords of fine linen H270
Job 38: 6 f? or who laid the corner stone thereof; H2883
Ecc 12:11 goads, and as nails f *by* the masters of H5193
Isa 22:25 the nail that is f in the sure place be H8628
41: 7 sodering: and he f it with nails, *that* it H2388
Ezk 40:43 an hand broad, f round about: and H3559
Lk 4:20 were in the synagogue were f on him. *G816*
Act 11: 6 Upon the which when I had f mine eyes, *G816*
28: 3 viper out of the heat, and f on his hand. *G2510*

FASTENING
Act 3: 4 And Peter, f his eyes upon him with *G816*

FASTEST
Mt 6:17 But thou, when thou f, anoint thine *G3522*

FASTING
Neh 9: 1 assembled with f, and with sackclothes, H6685
Est 4: 3 the Jews, and f, and weeping, and H6685
Ps 35:13 my soul with f; and my prayer returned H6685
69:10 soul with f, that was to my reproach. H6685
109:24 My knees are weak through f; and my H6685
Jer 36: 6 house upon the f day: and also thou H6685
Dan 6:18 and passed the night f: neither were H2908
9: 3 with f, and sackcloth, and ashes: H6685
Joel 2:12 heart, and with f, and with weeping, H6685
Mt 15:32 them away f, lest they faint in the way. *G3523*
17:21 kind goeth not out but by prayer and f. *G3521*
Mk 8: 3 And if I send them away f to their own *G3523*
9:29 forth by nothing, but by prayer and f. *G3521*
Act 10:30 days ago I was f until this hour; and *G3522*
14:23 had prayed with f, they commended *G3521*
27:33 and continued f, having taken nothing. *G777*
1Co 7: 5 give yourselves to f and prayer; and *G3521*

FASTINGS
Est 9:31 seed, the matters of the f and their cry. H6685
Lk 2:37 *God* with f and prayers night and day. *G3521*
2Co 6: 5 tumults, in labours, in watchings, in f; *G3521*
11:27 in f often, in cold and nakedness. *G3521*

FASTNESS See STEDFASTNESS.

FAT
Gen 4: 4 his flock and of the f thereof. And the H2459
41: 4 and f kine. So Pharaoh awoke. H1277
20 kine did eat up the first seven f kine: H1277
45:18 Egypt, and ye shall eat the f of the land. H2459
49:20 Out of Asher his bread *shall be* f, and he H8082
Ex 23:18 neither shall the f of my sacrifice H2459
29:13 And thou shalt take all the f that H2459
13 kidneys, and the f that *is* upon them, H2459
22 Also thou shalt take of the ram the f H2459
22 the rump, and the f that covereth the H2459
22 kidneys, and the f that *is* upon them, H2459
Lev 1: 8 the head, and the f, in order upon the H6309
12 his head and his f: and the priest shall H6309
3: 3 unto the LORD; the f that covereth the H2459
3 and all the f that *is* upon the inwards, H2459
4 And the two kidneys, and the f that *is* H2459
9 the LORD; the f thereof, *and* the whole H2459
9 backbone; and the f that covereth the H2459
9 and all the f that *is* upon the inwards, H2459
10 And the two kidneys, and the f that *is* H2459
14 unto the LORD; the f that covereth the H2459
14 and all the f that *is* upon the inwards, H2459
15 And the two kidneys, and the f that *is* H2459
16 a sweet savour: all the f *is* the LORD'S. H2459
17 that ye eat neither f nor blood. H2459
4: 8 And he shall take off from it all the f of H2459
8 the sin offering; the f that covereth the H2459
8 and all the f that *is* upon the inwards, H2459
9 And the two kidneys, and the f that *is* H2459
19 And he shall take all his f from him, H2459
26 And he shall burn all his f upon the H2459
26 the altar, as the f of the sacrifice of H2459
31 And he shall take away all the f thereof, H2459
31 fat thereof, as the f is taken away from H2459
35 And he shall take away all the f thereof, H2459
35 fat thereof, as the f of the lamb is taken H2459
6:12 thereon the f of the peace offerings. H2459
Lev 7: 3 And he shall offer of it all the f thereof; H2459
3 and the f that covereth the inwards, H2459
4 And the two kidneys, and the f that *is* H2459
23 of f, of ox, or of sheep, or of goat. H2459
24 And the f of the beast that dieth of H2459
24 of itself, and the f of that which is torn H2459
25 For whosoever eateth the f of the beast, H2459
30 made by fire, the f with the breast, it H2459
31 And the priest shall burn the f upon the H2459
33 offerings, and the f, shall have the right H2459
8:16 And he took all the f that *was* upon the H2459
16 f, and Moses burned *it* upon the altar. H2459
20 the head, and the pieces, and the f. H6309
25 And he took the f, and the rump, and all H2459
25 rump, and all the f that *was* upon the H2459
25 and their f, and the right shoulder: H2459
26 on the f, and upon the right shoulder: H2459
9:10 But the f, and the kidneys, and the caul H2459
19 And the f of the bullock and of the ram, H2459
20 And they put the f upon the breasts, H2459
20 and he burnt the f upon the altar: H2459
24 offering and the f: *which* when all the H2459
10:15 made by fire of the f, to wave *it for* a H2459
16:25 And the f of the sin offering shall he H2459
17: 6 the f for a sweet savour unto the LORD. H2459
Nu 13:20 And what the land *is*, whether it *be* f or H8082
18:17 shalt burn their f *for* an offering made H2459
Dt 31:20 and waxen f; then will they turn unto H1878
32:14 Butter of kine, and milk of sheep, with f H2459
14 goats, with the f of kidneys of wheat; H2459
15 But Jeshurun waxed f, and kicked: thou H8080
15 thou art waxen f, thou art grown thick, H8080
38 Which did eat the f of their sacrifices, H2459
Jdg 3:17 of Moab: and Eglon *was* a very f man. H1277
22 the blade; and the f closed upon the H2459
1Sa 2:15 Also before they burnt the f, the priest's H2459
16 not fail to burn the f presently, and H2459
29 make yourselves f with the chiefest of H1254
15:22 *and* to hearken than the f of rams. H2459
28:24 And the woman had a f calf in the H4770
2Sa 1:22 From the blood of the slain, from the f H2459
1Ki 1: 9 and oxen and f cattle by the stone of H4806
19 And he hath slain oxen and f cattle and H4806
25 slain oxen and f cattle and sheep in H4806
4:23 Ten f oxen, and twenty oxen out of the H1277
8:64 meat offerings, and the f of the peace H2459
64 and the f of the peace offerings. H2459
1Ch 4:40 And they found f pasture and good, H8082
2Ch 7: 7 burnt offerings, and the f of the peace H2459
7 and the meat offerings, and the f. H2459
29:35 with the f of the peace offerings, H2459
35:14 burnt offerings and the f until night; H2459
Neh 8:10 your way, eat the f, and drink the sweet, H4924
9:25 And they took strong cities, and a f H8082
25 were filled, and became f, and delighted H8080
35 and in the large and f land which thou H8082
Job 15:27 and maketh collops of f on *his* flanks. H6371
Ps 17:10 They are inclosed in their own f: with H2459
22:29 All *they that be* f upon earth shall eat H1879
37:20 *shall be* as the f of lambs: they shall H3368
92:14 old age; they shall be f and flourishing; H1879
119:70 Their heart is as f as grease; *but* I H2954
Prv 11:25 The liberal soul shall be made f: and he H1878
13: 4 the soul of the diligent shall be made f. H1878
15:30 *and* a good report maketh the bones f. H1878
28:25 his trust in the LORD shall be made f. H1878
Isa 1:11 of rams, and the f of fed beasts; and I H2459
5:17 places of the f ones shall strangers eat. H4220
6:10 Make the heart of this people f, and H8080
10:16 send among his f ones leanness; and H4924
25: 6 all people a feast of f things, a feast of H8081
6 on the lees, of f things full of marrow, H8081
28: 1 on the head of the f valleys of them that H8081
4 *is* on the head of the f valley, shall be a H8081
30:23 and it shall be f and plenteous: in that H1879
34: 6 blood, it is made f with fatness, *and* H1878
6 goats, with the f of the kidneys of rams: H2459
7 and their dust made f with fatness. H1878
43:24 filled me with the f of thy sacrifices: but H2459
58:11 and make f thy bones: and thou H2502
Jer 5:28 They are waxen f, they shine: yea, they H8080
50:11 ye are grown f as the heifer at grass, H6335
Ezk 34: 3 Ye eat the f, and ye clothe you with the H2459
14 good fold, and *in* a f pasture shall they H8082
16 I will destroy the f and the strong; I will H8082
20 the f cattle and between the lean cattle. H1274
39:19 And ye shall eat f till ye be full, and H2459
44: 7 my bread, the f and the blood, and H2459
15 f and the blood, saith the Lord GOD: H2459
Ezk 45:15 out of the f pastures of Israel; for H4945
Am 5:22 the peace offerings of your f beasts. H4806
Hab 1:16 portion *is* f, and their meat plenteous. H8082
Zec 11:16 of the f, and tear their claws in pieces. H1277

FATFLESHED
Gen 41: 2 kine and f; and they fed in a meadow. H1277
18 river seven kine, f and well favoured; H1277

FATHER
Gen 2:24 Therefore shall a man leave his f and his H1
4:20 And Adah bare Jabal: he was the f of H1
21 Jubal: he was the f of all such as handle H1
9:18 Japheth: and Ham *is* the f of Canaan. H1
22 And Ham, the f of Canaan, saw the H1
22 his f, and told his two brethren without. H1
23 nakedness of their f; and their faces *were* H1
10:21 Unto Shem also, the f of all the children H1
11:28 And Haran died before his f Terah in the H1
29 the f of Milcah, and the father of Iscah. H1
29 the father of Milcah, and the f of Iscah. H1
17: 4 and thou shalt be a f of many nations. H1
5 a f of many nations have I made thee. H1
19:31 the younger, Our f *is* old, and *there is* not H1
32 Come, let us make our f drink wine, and H1
32 him, that we may preserve seed of our f. H1
33 And they made their f drink wine that H1
33 in, and lay with her f; and he perceived H1
34 with my f: let us make him drink H1
34 him, that we may preserve seed of our f. H1
35 And they made their f drink wine that H1
36 the daughters of Lot with child by their f. H1
37 *is* the f of the Moabites unto this day. H1
38 the same *is* the f of the children of H1
20:12 *is* the daughter of my f, but not the H1
22: 7 And Isaac spake unto Abraham his f, H1
7 and said, My f: and he said, Here *am* H1
21 his brother, and Kemuel the f of Aram, H1
26: 3 oath which I sware unto Abraham thy f; H1
15 of Abraham his f, the Philistines had H1
18 of Abraham his f; for the Philistines had H1
18 names by which his f had called them. H1
24 of Abraham thy f: fear not, for I *am* with H1
27: 6 f speak unto Esau thy brother, saying, H1
9 savoury meat for thy f, such as he loveth: H1
10 And thou shalt bring *it* to thy f, that he H1
12 My f peradventure will feel me, and I H1
14 made savoury meat, such as his f loved. H1
18 And he came unto his f, and said, My H1
18 and said, My f: and he said, Here *am* H1
19 And Jacob said unto his f, I *am* Esau thy H1
22 And Jacob went near unto Isaac his f; H1
26 And his f Isaac said unto him, Come H1
30 of Isaac his f, that Esau his brother H1
31 brought it unto his f, and said unto his H1
31 and said unto his f, Let my father arise, H1
31 his father, Let my f arise, and eat of his H1
32 And Isaac his f said unto him, Who *art* H1
34 And when Esau heard the words of his f, H1
34 f, Bless me, *even* me also, O my father. H1
34 father, Bless me, *even* me also, O my f. H1
38 And Esau said unto his f, Hast thou but H1
38 but one blessing, my f? bless me, *even* me H1
38 f. And Esau lifted up his voice, and wept. H1
39 And Isaac his f answered and said unto H1
41 wherewith his f blessed him: and Esau H1
41 mourning for my f are at hand; then will H1
28: 2 thy mother's f; and take thee a wife H1
7 And that Jacob obeyed his f and his H1
8 of Canaan pleased not Isaac his f; H1
13 of Abraham thy f, and the God of Isaac: H1
29:12 son: and she ran and told her f. H1
31: 5 but the God of my f hath been with me. H1
6 with all my power I have served your f. H1
7 And your f hath deceived me, and H1
9 cattle of your f, and given *them* to me. H1
16 taken from our f, that *is* ours, and our H1
18 to go to Isaac his f in the land of Canaan. H1
29 but the God of your f spake unto me H1
35 And she said to her f, Let it not displease H1
42 Except the God of my f, the God of H1
53 the God of their f, judge betwixt us. And H1
53 Jacob sware by the fear of his f Isaac. H1
32: 9 And Jacob said, O God of my f Abraham, H1
9 and God of my f Isaac, the LORD which H1
33:19 f, for an hundred pieces of money. H1
34: 4 And Shechem spake unto his f Hamor, H1
6 And Hamor the f of Shechem went out H1
11 And Shechem said unto her f and unto H1

Gen 34:13 and Hamor his **f** deceitfully, and said, H1
19 honourable than all the house of his **f**. H1
35:18 Ben-oni: but his **f** called him Benjamin. H1
27 And Jacob came unto Isaac his **f** unto H1
36: 9 the **f** of the Edomites in mount Seir: H1
24 as he fed the asses of Zibeon his **f**. H1
43 he *is* Esau the **f** of the Edomites. H1
37: 1 **f** was a stranger, in the land of Canaan. H1
2 brought unto his **f** their evil report. H1
4 And when his brethren saw that their **f** H1
10 And he told *it* to his **f**, and to his H1
10 his brethren: and his **f** rebuked him, and H1
11 And his brethren envied him; but his **f** H1
22 their hands, to deliver him to his **f** again. H1
32 brought *it* to their **f**; and said, This have H1
35 son mourning. Thus his **f** wept for him. H1
38:13 saying, Behold thy **f** in law goeth up to H2524
25 she sent to her **f** in law, saying, By the H2524
42:13 *is* this day with our **f**, and one *is* not. H1
29 And they came unto Jacob their **f** unto H1
32 We *be* twelve brethren, sons of our **f**; one H1
32 day with our **f** in the land of Canaan. H1
35 *both* they and their **f** saw the bundles of H1
36 And Jacob their **f** said unto them, Me H1
37 And Reuben spake unto his **f**, saying, H1
43: 2 out of Egypt, their **f** said unto them, Go H1
7 saying, *Is* your **f** yet alive? have ye H1
8 And Judah said unto Israel his **f**, Send the H1
11 And their **f** Israel said unto them, If *it* H1
23 and the God of your **f**, hath given you H1
27 and said, *Is* your **f** well, the old man of H1
28 And they answered, Thy servant our **f** *is* H1
44:17 for you, get you up in peace unto your **f**. H1
19 saying, Have ye a **f**, or a brother? H1
20 And we said unto my lord, We have a **f**, H1
20 left of his mother, and his **f** loveth him. H1
22 cannot leave his **f**: for *if* he should leave H1
22 should leave his **f**, *his father* would die. H1
22 should leave his father, *his* **f** would die.
24 my **f**, we told him the words of my lord. H1
25 And our **f** said, Go again, *and* buy us a H1
27 And thy servant my **f** said unto us, Ye H1
30 to thy servant my **f**, and the lad *be* not H1
31 servant our **f** with sorrow to the grave. H1
32 for the lad unto my **f**, saying, If I bring H1
32 I shall bear the blame to my **f** for ever. H1
34 For how shall I go up to my **f**, and the lad H1
34 I see the evil that shall come on my **f**. H1
45: 3 *am* Joseph; doth my **f** yet live? And his H1
8 he hath made me a **f** to Pharaoh, and H1
9 Haste ye, and go up to my **f**, and say unto H1
13 And ye shall tell my **f** of all my glory in H1
13 shall haste and bring down my **f** hither. H1
18 And take your **f** and your households, H1
19 your wives, and bring your **f**, and come. H1
23 And to his **f** he sent after this *manner*; H1
23 and bread and meat for his **f** by the way. H1
25 the land of Canaan unto Jacob their **f**, H1
27 him, the spirit of Jacob their **f** revived: H1
46: 1 sacrifices unto the God of his **f** Isaac. H1
3 And he said, I *am* God, the God of thy **f**: H1
5 carried Jacob their **f**, and their little ones, H1
29 up to meet Israel his **f**, to Goshen, and H1
47: 1 and said, My **f** and my brethren, and H1
5 **f** and thy brethren are come unto thee: H1
6 of the land make thy **f** and brethren to H1
7 And Joseph brought in Jacob his **f**, and H1
11 And Joseph placed his **f** and his H1
12 And Joseph nourished his **f**, and his H1
48: 1 Joseph, Behold, thy **f** *is* sick: and he took H1
9 And Joseph said unto his **f**, They *are* my H1
17 And when Joseph saw that his **f** laid his H1
18 And Joseph said unto his **f**, Not so, my H1
18 his father, Not so, my **f**: for this *is* the H1
19 And his **f** refused, and said, I know *it*, H1
49: 2 of Jacob; and hearken unto Israel your **f**. H1
25 *Even* by the God of thy **f**, who shall help H1
26 The blessings of thy **f** have prevailed H1
28 this *is it* that their **f** spake unto them, H1
50: 2 **f**: and the physicians embalmed Israel. H1
5 My **f** made me swear, saying, Lo, I die: H1
5 and bury my **f**, and I will come again. H1
6 And Pharaoh said, Go up, and bury thy **f**, H1
7 And Joseph went up to bury his **f**: and H1
10 made a mourning for his **f** seven days. H1
14 bury his **f**, after he had buried his father. H1
14 bury his father, after he had buried his **f**. H1
15 saw that their **f** was dead, they said, H1
16 **f** did command before he died, saying, H1

Gen 50:17 of the God of thy **f**. And Joseph wept H1
Ex 2:18 And when they came to Reuel their **f**, he H1
3: 1 flock of Jethro his **f** in law, the priest of H2859
6 Moreover he said, I *am* the God of thy **f**, H1
4:18 to Jethro his **f** in law, and said unto H2859
18: 1 of Midian, Moses' **f** in law, heard of all H2859
2 Then Jethro, Moses' **f** in law, took H2859
4 for the God of my **f**, *said he, was* mine H1
5 And Jethro, Moses' **f** in law, came with H2859
6 And he said unto Moses, I thy **f** in law H2859
7 And Moses went out to meet his **f** in H2859
8 And Moses told his **f** in law all that the H2859
12 And Jethro, Moses' **f** in law, took a H2859
12 bread with Moses' **f** in law before God. H2859
14 And when Moses' **f** in law saw all that H2859
15 And Moses said unto his **f** in law, H2859
17 And Moses' **f** in law said unto him, The H2859
24 **f** in law, and did all that he had said. H2859
27 And Moses let his **f** in law depart; and H2859
20:12 Honour thy **f** and thy mother: that thy H1
21:15 And he that smiteth his **f**, or his mother, H1
17 And he that curseth his **f**, or his mother, H1
22:17 If her **f** utterly refuse to give her unto H1
40:15 thou didst anoint their **f**, that they may H1
Lev 18: 7 The nakedness of thy **f**, or the nakedness H1
9 the daughter of thy **f**, or daughter of thy H1
11 begotten of thy **f**, she *is* thy sister, thou H1
19: 3 man his mother, and his **f**, and keep my H1
20: 9 For every one that curseth his **f** or his H1
9 he hath cursed his **f** or his mother; his H1
21: 2 his mother, and for his **f**, and for his son, H1
9 her **f**: she shall be burnt with fire. H1
11 defile himself for his **f**, or for his mother; H1
24:10 woman, whose **f** *was* an Egyptian, went H1121
Nu 3: 4 priest's office in the sight of Aaron their **f**. H1
24 And the chief of the house of the **f** of the H1
30 And the chief of the house of the **f** of the H1
35 And the chief of the house of the **f** of the H1
6: 7 unclean for his **f**, or for his mother, for H1
10:29 the Midianite, Moses' **f** in law, We are H2859
11:12 as a nursing **f** beareth the sucking H539
12:14 And the LORD said unto Moses, If her **f** H1
18: 2 the tribe of thy **f**, bring thou with thee, H1
27: 3 Our **f** died in the wilderness, and he was H1
4 Why should the name of our **f** be done H1
4 a possession among the brethren of our **f**. H1
7 inheritance of their **f** to pass unto them. H1
11 And if his **f** have no brethren, then ye H1
30: 4 And her **f** hear her vow, and her bond H1
4 her soul, and her **f** shall hold his peace H1
5 But if her **f** disallow her in the day that H1
5 forgive her, because her **f** disallowed her. H1
16 his wife, between the **f** and his daughter, H1
36: 6 of the tribe of their **f** shall they marry. H1
8 of the tribe of her **f**, that the children of H1
12 in the tribe of the family of their **f**. H1
Dt 5:16 Honour thy **f** and thy mother, as the H1
21:13 and bewail her **f** and her mother a full H1
18 obey the voice of his **f**, or the voice of his H1
19 Then shall his **f** and his mother lay hold H1
22:15 Then shall the **f** of the damsel, and her H1
16 And the damsel's **f** shall say unto the H1
19 and give *them* unto the **f** of the damsel, H1
29 unto the damsel's **f** fifty *shekels* of silver, H1
26: 5 to perish *was* my **f**, and he went down H1
27:16 Cursed *be* he that setteth light by his **f** or H1
22 the daughter of his **f**, or the daughter of H1
32: 6 *is* not he thy **f** *that* hath bought thee? H1
7 ask thy **f**, and he will shew thee; H1
33: 9 Who said unto his **f** and to his mother, I H1
Jos 2:13 And *that* ye will save alive my **f**, and my H1
18 shalt bring thy **f**, and thy mother, and H1
6:23 out Rahab, and her **f**, and her mother, H1
15:13 Arba the **f** of Anak, which *city is* Hebron. H1
18 him to ask of her **f** a field: and she H1
17: 1 of Manasseh, the **f** of Gilead: because he H1
4 among the brethren of their **f**. H1
19:47 Dan, after the name of Dan their **f**. H1
21:11 And they gave them the city of Arba the **f** H1
24: 2 *even* Terah, the **f** of Abraham, and the H1
2 **f** of Nachor: and they served other gods. H1
3 And I took your **f** Abraham from the H1
32 sons of Hamor the **f** of Shechem for an H1
Jdg 1:14 him to ask of her **f** a field: and she H1
16 And the children of the Kenite, Moses' **f** H2859
4:11 of Hobab the **f** in law of Moses, had H2859
6:25 of Baal that thy **f** hath, and cut down the H1
8:32 Joash his **f**, in Ophrah of the Abi-ezrites. H1
9: 1 of the house of his mother's **f**, saying, H1

Jdg 9:17 (For my **f** fought for you, and H1
28 men of Hamor the **f** of Shechem: for why H1
56 his **f**, in slaying his seventy brethren: H1
11:36 And she said unto him, My **f**, *if* thou hast H1
37 And she said unto her **f**, Let this thing be H1
39 she returned unto her **f**, who did with her H1
14: 2 And he came up, and told his **f** and his H1
3 Then his **f** and his mother said unto H1
3 said unto his **f**, Get her for me; for she H1
4 But his **f** and his mother knew not that it H1
5 Then went Samson down, and his **f** and H1
6 his **f** or his mother what he had done. H1
9 and came to his **f** and mother, and he H1
10 So his **f** went down unto the woman: and H1
16 **f** nor my mother, and shall I tell *it* thee? H1
15: 1 But her **f** would not suffer him to go in. H1
2 And her **f** said, I verily thought that thou H1
6 up, and burnt her and her **f** with fire. H1
16:31 all the house of his **f** came down, and H1
31 his **f**. And he judged Israel twenty years. H1
17:10 and be unto me a **f** and a priest, and I H1
18:19 with us, and be to us a **f** and a priest: *is it* H1
29 name of Dan their **f**, who was born unto H1
19: 3 and when the **f** of the damsel saw him, H1
4 And his **f** in law, the damsel's father, H2859
4 And his father in law, the damsel's **f**, H1
5 and the damsel's **f** said unto his son in H1
6 for the damsel's **f** had said unto the H1
7 up to depart, his **f** in law urged him: H2859
8 and the damsel's **f** said, Comfort thine H1
9 his servant, his **f** in law, the damsel's H2859
9 in law, the damsel's **f**, said unto him, H1
Ru 2:11 thou hast left thy **f** and thy mother, and H1
4:17 he *is* the **f** of Jesse, the father of David. H1
17 he *is* the father of Jesse, the **f** of David. H1
1Sa 2:25 **f**, because the LORD would slay them. H1
27 the house of thy **f**, when they were in H1
28 the house of thy **f** all the offerings made H1
30 the house of thy **f**, should walk before me H1
4:19 and that her **f** in law and her husband H2524
21 of her **f** in law and her husband. H2524
9: 3 And the asses of Kish Saul's **f** were lost. H1
5 us return; lest my **f** leave *caring* for the H1
10: 2 found: and, lo, thy **f** hath left the care of H1
12 But who *is* their **f**? Therefore it became H1
14: 1 *is* on the other side. But he told not his **f**. H1
27 But Jonathan heard not when his **f** H1
28 and said, Thy **f** straitly charged the H1
29 Then said Jonathan, My **f** hath troubled H1
51 And Kish *was* the **f** of Saul; and Ner the H1
51 Ner the **f** of Abner *was* the son of Abiel. H1
19: 2 saying, Saul my **f** seeketh to kill thee: H1
3 And I will go out and stand beside my **f** H1
3 commune with my **f** of thee; and what I H1
4 unto Saul his **f**, and said unto him, Let H1
20: 1 sin before thy **f**, that he seeketh my life? H1
2 not die: behold, my **f** will do nothing H1
2 my **f** hide this thing from me? it *is* not *so*. H1
3 and said, Thy **f** certainly knoweth that H1
6 If thy **f** at all miss me, then say, David H1
8 for why shouldest thou bring me to thy **f**? H1
9 determined by my **f** to come upon thee, H1
10 me? or what *if* thy **f** answer thee roughly? H1
12 I have sounded my **f** about to morrow H1
13 but if it please my **f** *to do* thee evil, then I H1
13 be with thee, as he hath been with my **f**. H1
32 And Jonathan answered Saul his **f**, and H1
33 it was determined of his **f** to slay David. H1
34 because his **f** had done him shame. H1
22: 3 of Moab, Let my **f** and my mother, I pray H1
15 unto all the house of my **f**: for thy servant H1
23:17 the hand of Saul my **f** shall not find thee; H1
17 thee; and that also Saul my **f** knoweth. H1
24:11 Moreover, my **f**, see, yea, see the skirt of H1
2Sa 2:32 in the sepulchre of his **f**, which *was in* H1
3: 8 house of Saul thy **f**, to his brethren, and H1
6:21 me before thy **f**, and before all his house, H1
7:14 I will be his **f**, and he shall be my son. If H1
9: 7 the land of Saul thy **f**; and thou shalt eat H1
10: 2 son of Nahash, as his **f** shewed kindness H1
2 of his servants for his **f**. And David's H1
3 doth honour thy **f**, that he hath sent H1
13: 5 sick: and when thy **f** cometh to see thee, H1
16: 3 of Israel restore me the kingdom of my **f**. H1
21 thou art abhorred of thy **f**: then shall the H1
17: 8 For, said Hushai, thou knowest thy **f** and H1
8 in the field: and thy **f** *is* a man of war, H1
10 knoweth that thy **f** *is* a mighty man, and H1
23 and was buried in the sepulchre of his **f**. H1

2Sa 19:37 by the grave of my f and of my mother. H1
21:14 of Kish his f: and they performed H1
1Ki 1: 6 And his f had not displeased him at any H1
2:12 throne of David his f; and his kingdom H1
24 the throne of David my f, and who hath H1
26 before David my f, and because thou hast H1
26 in all wherein my f was afflicted. H1
31 from me, and from the house of my f. H1
32 with the sword, my f David not knowing H1
44 didst to David my f: therefore the LORD H1
3: 3 of David his f: only he sacrificed and H1
6 thy servant David my f great mercy, H1
7 of David my f: and I *am but* a little H1
14 as thy f David did walk, then H1
5: 1 f: for Hiram was ever a lover of David. H1
3 Thou knowest how that David my f H1
5 unto David my f, saying, Thy son, whom H1
6:12 thee, which I spake unto David thy f: H1
7:14 Naphtali, and his f *was* a man of Tyre, a H1
51 which David his f had dedicated; *even* H1
8:15 unto David my f, and hath with his hand H1
17 And it was in the heart of David my f to H1
18 And the LORD said unto David my f, H1
20 room of David my f, and sit on the throne H1
24 servant David my f that thou promisedst H1
25 servant David my f that thou promisedst H1
26 spakest unto thy servant David my f. H1
9: 4 me, as David thy f walked, in integrity of H1
5 to David thy f, saying, There shall not H1
11: 4 his God, as *was* the heart of David his f. H1
6 fully after the LORD, as *did* David his f. H1
27 the breaches of the city of David his f. H1
33 and my judgments, as *did* David his f. H1
43 the city of David his f: and Rehoboam his H1
12: 4 Thy f made our yoke grievous: now H1
4 service of thy f, and his heavy yoke which H1
6 before Solomon his f while he yet lived, H1
9 yoke which thy f did put upon us lighter? H1
10 thee, saying, Thy f made our yoke heavy, H1
11 And now whereas my f did lade you with H1
11 to your yoke: my f hath chastised you H1
14 men, saying, My f made your yoke H1
14 to your yoke: my f *also* chastised you H1
13:11 the king, them they told also to their f. H1
12 And their f said unto them, What way H1
15: 3 And he walked in all the sins of his f, H1
3 his God, as the heart of David his f. H1
11 the eyes of the LORD, as *did* David his f. H1
15 And he brought in the things which his f H1
19 thee, *and* between my f and thy father: H1
19 my father and thy f: behold, I have sent H1
24 city of David his f: and Jehoshaphat his H1
26 walked in the way of his f, and in his sin H1
19:20 I pray thee, kiss my f and my mother, H1
20:34 cities, which my f took from thy father, H1
34 took from thy f, I will restore; and thou H1
34 in Damascus, as my f made in Samaria. H1
22:43 the ways of Asa his f; he turned not aside H1
46 days of his f Asa, he took out of the land. H1
50 city of David his f: and Jehoram his son H1
52 in the way of his f, and in the way of his H1
53 according to all that his f had done. H1
2Ki 2:12 And Elisha saw *it*, and he cried, My f, my H1
12 My father, my f, the chariot of Israel, H1
3: 2 but not like his f, and like his mother: H1
2 the image of Baal that his f had made. H1
13 the prophets of thy f, and to the prophets H1
4:18 that he went out to his f to the reapers. H1
19 And he said unto his f, My head, my H1
5:13 him, and said, My f, *if* the prophet had H1
6:21 f, shall I smite *them*? shall I smite *them*? H1
9:25 f, the LORD laid this burden upon him; H1
13:14 and said, O my f, my father, the chariot H1
14 O my father, my f, the chariot of Israel, H1
25 of Jehoahaz his f by war. Three times H1
14: 3 not like David his f: he did according to H1
3 according to all things as Joash his f did. H1
5 servants which had slain the king his f. H1
21 made him king instead of his f Amaziah. H1
15: 3 to all that his f Amaziah had done; H1
34 to all that his f Uzziah had done. H1
38 f: and Ahaz his son reigned in his stead. H1
16: 2 of the LORD his God, like David his f. H1
18: 3 according to all that David his f did. H1
20: 5 the God of David thy f, I have heard thy H1
21: 3 which Hezekiah his f had destroyed; and H1
20 of the LORD, as his f Manasseh did. H1
21 And he walked in all the way that his f H1
21 that his f served, and worshipped them: H1
2Ki 22: 2 way of David his f, and turned not aside H1
23:34 the room of Josiah his f, and turned his H1
24: 9 according to all that his f had done. H1
1Ch 2:17 And Abigail bare Amasa: and the f of H1
21 of Machir the f of Gilead, whom he H1
23 *to* the sons of Machir the f of Gilead. H1
24 wife bare him Ashur the f of Tekoa. H1
42 which was the f of Ziph; and the sons H1
42 the sons of Mareshah the f of Hebron. H1
44 And Shema begat Raham, the f of H1
45 Maon: and Maon *was* the f of Beth-zur. H1
49 She bare also Shaaph the f of H1
49 Sheva the f of Machbenah, and the H1
49 and the f of Gibea: and the daughter H1
50 Ephratah; Shobal the f of Kirjath-jearim, H1
51 Salma the f of Beth-lehem, Hareph the H1
51 Beth-lehem, Hareph the f of Beth-gader. H1
52 And Shobal the f of Kirjath-jearim had H1
55 of Hemath, the f of the house of Rechab. H1
4: 3 And these *were of* the f of Etam; Jezreel, H1
4 And Penuel the f of Gedor, and Ezer the H1
4 and Ezer the f of Hushah. These *are* H1
4 of Ephratah, the f of Beth-lehem. H1
5 And Ashur the f of Tekoa had two wives, H1
11 begat Mehir, which *was* the f of Eshton. H1
12 and Tehinnah the f of Irnahash. These H1
14 Seraiah begat Joab, the f of the valley of H1
17 and Ishbah the f of Eshtemoa. H1
18 And his wife Jehudijah bare Jered the f H1
18 and Heber the f of Socho, and Jekuthiel H1
18 and Jekuthiel the f of Zanoah. And these H1
19 of Naham, the f of Keilah the Garmite, H1
21 of Judah *were*, Er the f of Lecah, and H1
21 and Laadah the f of Mareshah, and the H1
7:14 Aramitess bare Machir the f of Gilead: H1
22 And Ephraim their f mourned many H1
31 and Malchiel, who *is* the f of Birzavith. H1
8:29 And at Gibeon dwelt the f of Gibeon; H1
9:19 of the house of his f, the Korahites, *were* H1
35 And in Gibeon dwelt the f of Gibeon, H1
17:13 I will be his f, and he shall be my son: H1
19: 2 because his f shewed kindness to me. H1
2 him concerning his f. So the servants of H1
3 doth honour thy f, that he hath sent H1
22:10 and I *will be* his f; and I will establish the H1
24: 2 But Nadab and Abihu died before their f, H1
19 under Aaron their f, as the LORD God of H1
25: 3 under the hands of their f Jeduthun, who H1
6 All these *were* under the hands of their f H1
26: 6 f: for they *were* mighty men of valour. H1
10 firstborn, yet his f made him the chief;) H1
28: 4 all the house of my f to be king over H1
4 the house of my f; and among the sons H1
4 the sons of my f he liked me to make H1
6 him *to be* my son, and I will be his f. H1
9 thou the God of thy f, and serve him with H1
29:10 God of Israel our f, for ever and ever. H1
23 of David his f, and prospered; and H1
2Ch 1: 8 f, and hast made me to reign in his stead. H1
9 unto David my f be established: for thou H1
2: 3 deal with David my f, and didst send him H1
7 whom David my f did provide. H1
14 of Dan, and his f *was* a man of Tyre, H1
14 the cunning men of my lord David thy f. H1
17 David his f had numbered them; H1
3: 1 unto David his f, in the place that David H1
4:16 did Huram his f make to king Solomon H1
5: 1 that David his f had dedicated; and the H1
6: 4 with his mouth to my f David, saying, H1
7 Now it was in the heart of David my f to H1
8 But the LORD said to David my f, H1
10 room of David my f, and am set on the H1
15 servant David my f that which thou hast H1
16 servant David my f that which thou hast H1
7:17 before me, as David thy f walked, and do H1
18 with David thy f, saying, There shall not H1
8:14 order of David his f, the courses of the H1
9:31 the city of David his f: and Rehoboam his H1
10: 4 Thy f made our yoke grievous: now H1
4 servitude of thy f, and his heavy yoke H1
6 before Solomon his f while he yet lived, H1
9 the yoke that thy f did put upon us? H1
10 thee, saying, Thy f made our yoke heavy, H1
11 For whereas my f put a heavy yoke upon H1
11 to your yoke: my f chastised you with H1
14 men, saying, My f made your yoke H1
14 will add thereto: my f chastised you with H1
15:18 the things that his f had dedicated, and H1
16: 3 *there was* between my f and thy father: H1
2Ch 16: 3 my father and thy f: behold, I have sent H1
17: 2 of Ephraim, which Asa his f had taken. H1
3 his f David, and sought not unto Baalim; H1
4 But sought to the LORD God of his f, and H1
20:32 And he walked in the way of Asa his f, H1
21: 3 And their f gave them great gifts of H1
4 to the kingdom of his f, he strengthened H1
12 God of David thy f, Because thou hast not H1
12 f, nor in the ways of Asa king of Judah, H1
22: 4 after the death of his f to his destruction. H1
24:22 which Jehoiada his f had done to him, H1
25: 3 his servants that had killed the king his f. H1
26: 1 him king in the room of his f Amaziah. H1
4 according to all that his f Amaziah did. H1
27: 2 to all that his f Uzziah did: howbeit H1
28: 1 in the sight of the LORD, like David his f: H1
29: 2 to all that David his f had done. H1
33: 3 which Hezekiah his f had broken down, H1
22 did Manasseh his f: for Amon sacrificed H1
22 his f had made, and served them; H1
23 as Manasseh his f had humbled himself; H1
34: 2 ways of David his f, and declined *neither* H1
3 the God of David his f: and in the twelfth H1
Est 2: 7 for she had neither f nor mother, and the H1
7 when her f and mother were dead, H1
Job 15:10 very aged men, much elder than thy f. H1
17:14 I have said to corruption, Thou *art* my f: H1
29:16 I *was* a f to the poor: and the cause H1
31:18 with me, as *with* a f, and I have guided H1
38:28 Hath the rain a f? or who hath begotten H1
42:15 of Job: and their f gave them inheritance H1
Ps 27:10 When my f and my mother forsake me, H1
68: 5 A f of the fatherless, and a judge of the H1
89:26 He shall cry unto me, Thou *art* my f, my H1
103:13 Like as a f pitieth *his* children, *so* the H1
Prv 1: 8 My son, hear the instruction of thy f, and H1
3:12 as a f the son *in whom* he delighteth. H1
4: 1 Hear, ye children, the instruction of a f, H1
10: 1 son maketh a glad f: but a foolish son *is* H1
15:20 A wise son maketh a glad f: but a foolish H1
17:21 sorrow: and the f of a fool hath no joy. H1
25 A foolish son *is* a grief to his f, and H1
19:13 A foolish son *is* the calamity of his f: and H1
26 He that wasteth *his* f, *and* chaseth away H1
20:20 Whoso curseth his f or his mother, his H1
23:22 Hearken unto thy f that begat thee, and H1
24 The f of the righteous shall greatly H1
25 Thy f and thy mother shall be glad, and H1
28: 7 companion of riotous *men* shameth his f. H1
24 Whoso robbeth his f or his mother, and H1
29: 3 Whoso loveth wisdom rejoiceth his f: but H1
30:11 *There is* a generation *that* curseth their f, H1
17 The eye *that* mocketh at *his* f, and H1
Isa 3: 6 of the house of his f, *saying*, Thou hast H1
8: 4 to cry, My f, and my mother, the H1
9: 6 The everlasting F, The Prince of Peace. H1
22:21 and he shall be a f to the inhabitants of H1
38: 5 the God of David thy f, I have heard thy H1
19 as I *do* this day: the f to the children H1
43:27 Thy first f hath sinned, and thy teachers H1
45:10 Woe unto him that saith unto *his* f, What H1
51: 2 Look unto Abraham your f, and unto H1
58:14 of Jacob thy f: for the mouth of the H1
63:16 Doubtless thou *art* our f, though H1
16 O LORD, *art* our f, our redeemer; thy H1
64: 8 But now, O LORD, thou *art* our f; we *are* H1
Jer 2:27 Saying to a stock, Thou *art* my f; and to a H1
3: 4 me, My f, thou *art* the guide of my youth? H1
19 My f; and shalt not turn away from me. H1
12: 6 the house of thy f, even they have dealt H1
16: 7 to drink for their f or for their mother. H1
20:15 tidings to my f, saying, A man child H1
22:11 of Josiah his f, which went forth out H1
15 in cedar? did not thy f eat and drink, and H1
31: 9 f to Israel, and Ephraim *is* my firstborn. H1
35: 6 the son of Rechab our f commanded us, H1
8 son of Rechab our f in all that he hath H1
10 to all that Jonadab our f commanded us. H1
16 of their f, which he commanded H1
18 of Jonadab your f, and kept all his H1
Ezk 16: 3 of Canaan; thy f *was* an Amorite, and H1
45 *was* an Hittite, and your f an Amorite. H1
18: 4 as the soul of the f, so also the soul of the H1
17 the iniquity of his f, he shall surely live. H1
18 *As for* his f, because he cruelly H1
19 the iniquity of the f? When the son hath H1
20 bear the iniquity of the f, neither shall the H1
20 neither shall the f bear the iniquity of the H1
22: 7 In thee have they set light by f and H1

Ezk 44:25 themselves: but for f, or for mother, or H1
Dan 5: 2 vessels which his f Nebuchadnezzar had H2
11 and in the days of thy f light and H2
11 thy f, the king, *I say*, thy father, H2
11 the king, *I say*, thy f, made master of the H2
13 the king my f brought out of Jewry? H2
18 thy f a kingdom, and majesty, H2
Am 2: 7 and a man and his f will go in unto the H1
Mic 7: 6 For the son dishonoureth the f, the H1
Zec 13: 3 prophesy, then his f and his mother that H1
3 the LORD: and his f and his mother that H1
Mal 1: 6 A son honoureth *his* f, and a servant his H1
6 if then I *be* a f, where *is* mine honour? H1
2:10 Have we not all one f? hath not one God H1
Mt 2:22 in the room of his f Herod, he was G3962
3: 9 Abraham to *our* f: for I say unto you, G3962
4:21 ship with Zebedee their f, mending their G3962
22 the ship and their f, and followed him. G3962
5:16 and glorify your F which is in heaven. G3962
45 That ye may be the children of your F G3962
48 Be ye therefore perfect, even as your F G3962
6: 1 no reward of your F which is in heaven. G3962
4 be in secret: and thy F which seeth in G3962
6 door, pray to thy F which is in secret; G3962
6 is in secret; and thy F which seeth in G3962
8 them: for your F knoweth what things G3962
9 pray ye: Our F which art in heaven, G3962
14 your heavenly F will also forgive you: G3962
15 will your F forgive your trespasses. G3962
18 fast, but unto thy F which is in secret: G3962
18 is in secret: and thy F, which seeth in G3962
26 yet your heavenly F feedeth them. Are G3962
32 for your heavenly F knoweth that ye G3962
7:11 more shall your F which is in heaven G3962
21 the will of my F which is in heaven. G3962
8:21 suffer me first to go and bury my f. G3962
10:20 Spirit of your F which speaketh in you. G3962
21 to death, and the f the child: and the G3962
29 not fall on the ground without your F. G3962
32 also before my F which is in heaven. G3962
33 deny before my F which is in heaven. G3962
35 against his f, and the daughter against G3962
37 He that loveth f or mother more than G3962
11:25 I thank thee, O F, Lord of heaven and G3962
26 Even so, F: for so it seemed good in thy G3962
27 unto me of my F: and no man knoweth G3962
27 the Son, but the F; neither knoweth any G3962
27 any man the F, save the Son, and *he* G3962
12:50 For whosoever shall do the will of my F G3962
13:43 F. Who hath ears to hear, let him hear. G3962
15: 4 Honour thy f and mother: and, He G3962
4 f or mother, let him die the death. G3962
5 But ye say, Whosoever shall say to *his* f G3962
6 And honour not his f or his mother, *he* G3962
13 F hath not planted, shall be rooted up. G3962
16:17 unto thee, but my F which is in heaven. G3962
27 in the glory of his F with his angels; G3962
18:10 the face of my F which is in heaven. G3962
14 Even so it is not the will of your F G3962
19 for them of my F which is in heaven. G3962
35 So likewise shall my heavenly F do also G3962
19: 5 shall a man leave f and mother, and G3962
19 Honour thy f and *thy* mother: and, G3962
29 or sisters, or f, or mother, or wife, or G3962
20:23 *them* for whom it is prepared of my F. G3962
21:31 did the will of *his* f? They say unto him, G3962
23: 9 And call no *man* your f upon the earth: G3962
9 for one is your F, which is in heaven. G3962
24:36 the angels of heaven, but my F only. G3962
25:34 ye blessed of my F, inherit the kingdom G3962
26:39 saying, O my F, if it be possible, let G3962
42 saying, O my F, if this cup may not G3962
53 cannot now pray to my F, and he shall G3962
28:19 in the name of the F, and of the Son, G3962
Mk 1:20 and they left their f Zebedee in the ship G3962
5:40 out, he taketh the f and the mother of G3962
7:10 For Moses said, Honour thy f and thy G3962
10 f or mother, let him die the death: G3962
11 But ye say, If a man shall say to his f or G3962
12 to do ought for his f or his mother; G3962
8:38 the glory of his F with the holy angels. G3962
9:21 And he asked his f, How long is it ago G3962
24 And straightway the f of the child cried G3962
10: 7 For this cause shall a man leave his f G3962
19 Defraud not, Honour thy f and mother. G3962
29 or sisters, or f, or mother, or wife, or G3962
11:10 Blessed *be* the kingdom of our f David, G3962
25 any: that your F also which is in G3962
26 neither will your F which is in heaven G3962

Mk 13:12 brother to death, and the f the son; and G3962
32 in heaven, neither the Son, but the F. G3962
14:36 And he said, Abba, F, all things *are* G3962
15:21 of the country, the f of Alexander and G3962
Lk 1:32 give unto him the throne of his f David: G3962
59 him Zacharias, after the name of his f. G3962
62 And they made signs to his f, how he G3962
67 And his f Zacharias was filled with the G3962
73 The oath which he sware to our f G3962
2:48 thy f and I have sought thee sorrowing. G3962
3: 8 Abraham to *our* f: for I say unto you, G3962
6:36 Be ye therefore merciful, as your F also G3962
8:51 the f and the mother of the maiden. G3962
9:42 child, and delivered him again to his f. G3962
59 suffer me first to go and bury my f. G3962
10:21 I thank thee, O F, Lord of heaven and G3962
21 so, F; for so it seemed good in thy sight. G3962
22 All things are delivered to me of my F: G3962
22 who the Son is, but the F; and who the G3962
22 and who the F is, but the Son, and G3962
11: 2 When ye pray, say, Our F which art in G3962
11 any of you that is a f, will he give him a G3962
13 *your* heavenly F give the Holy Spirit G3962
12:30 after: and your F knoweth that ye have G3962
53 The f shall be divided against the son, G3962
53 son against the f; the mother against G3962
14:26 me, and hate not his f, and mother, and G3962
15:12 And the younger of them said to *his* f, G3962
12 said to *his* father, F, give me the portion G3962
18 I will arise and go to my f, and will say G3962
18 and will say unto him, F, I have sinned G3962
20 And he arose, and came to his f. But G3962
20 a great way off, his f saw him, and had G3962
21 And the son said unto him, F, I have G3962
22 But the f said to his servants, Bring G3962
27 is come; and thy f hath killed the fatted G3962
28 came his f out, and entreated him. G3962
29 And he answering said to *his* f, Lo, G3962
16:24 And he cried and said, F Abraham, G3962
27 Then he said, I pray thee therefore, f, G3962
30 And he said, Nay, f Abraham: but if G3962
18:20 witness, Honour thy f and thy mother. G3962
22:29 as my F hath appointed unto me; G3962
42 Saying, F, if thou be willing, remove this G3962
23:34 Then said Jesus, F, forgive them; for G3962
46 loud voice, he said, F, into thy hands I G3962
24:49 the promise of my F upon you: but G3962
Jn 1:14 of the F,) full of grace and truth. G3962
18 bosom of the F, he hath declared *him*. G3962
3:35 The F loveth the Son, and hath given G3962
4:12 Art thou greater than our f Jacob, G3962
21 nor yet at Jerusalem, worship the F. G3962
23 shall worship the F in spirit and in G3962
23 for the F seeketh such to worship him. G3962
53 So the f knew that *it was* at the same G3962
5:17 But Jesus answered them, My F G3962
18 his F, making himself equal with God. G3962
19 what he seeth the F do: for what things G3962
20 For the F loveth the Son, and sheweth G3962
21 For as the F raiseth up the dead, and G3962
22 For the F judgeth no man, but hath G3962
23 they honour the F. He that honoureth G3962
23 not the F which hath sent him. G3962
26 For as the F hath life in himself; so G3962
30 the will of the F which hath sent me. G3962
36 the works which the F hath given me to G3962
36 witness of me, that the F hath sent me. G3962
37 And the F himself, which hath sent me, G3962
45 accuse you to the F: there is *one* that G3962
6:27 you: for him hath God the F sealed. G3962
32 heaven; but my F giveth you the true G3962
37 All that the F giveth me shall come to G3962
42 son of Joseph, whose f and mother we G3962
44 No man can come to me, except the F G3962
45 hath learned of the F, cometh unto me. G3962
46 Not that any man hath seen the F, save G3962
46 he which is of God, he hath seen the F. G3962
57 As the living F hath sent me, and I live G3962
57 and I live by the F: so he that eateth me, G3962
65 except it were given unto him of my F. G3962
8:16 not alone, but I and the F that sent me. G3962
18 F that sent me beareth witness of me. G3962
19 him, Where is thy F? Jesus answered, Ye G3962
19 know me, nor my F: if ye had known G3962
19 me, ye should have known my F also. G3962
27 not that he spake to them of the F. G3962
28 F hath taught me, I speak these things. G3962
29 And he that sent me is with me: the F G3962
38 I have seen with my F: and ye do that G3962

Jn 8:38 do that which ye have seen with your f. G3962
39 him, Abraham is our f. Jesus saith unto G3962
41 Ye do the deeds of your f. Then said G3962
41 of fornication; we have one F, *even* God. G3962
42 If God were your F, ye would love me: G3962
44 Ye are of *your* f the devil, and the lusts G3962
44 the lusts of your f ye will do. He was a G3962
44 his own: for he is a liar, and the f of it. G3962
49 honour my F, and ye do dishonour me. G3962
53 Art thou greater than our f Abraham, G3962
54 is nothing: it is my F that honoureth G3962
56 Your f Abraham rejoiced to see my G3962
10:15 As the F knoweth me, even so know I G3962
15 F: and I lay down my life for the sheep. G3962
17 Therefore doth my F love me, because I G3962
18 commandment have I received of my F. G3962
29 My F, which gave *them* me, is greater G3962
30 I and *my* F are one. G3962
32 you from my F; for which of those G3962
36 Say ye of him, whom the F hath G3962
37 If I do not the works of my F, believe me G3962
38 that the F *is* in me, and I in him. G3962
11:41 F, I thank thee that thou hast heard me. G3962
12:26 man serve me, him will *my* F honour. G3962
27 what shall I say? F, save me from this G3962
28 F, glorify thy name. Then came there a G3962
49 of myself; but the F which sent me, he G3962
50 even as the F said unto me, so I speak. G3962
13: 1 world unto the F, having loved his own G3962
3 Jesus knowing that the F had given all G3962
14: 6 no man cometh unto the F, but by me. G3962
7 have known my F also: and from G3962
8 Lord, shew us the F, and it sufficeth us. G3962
9 me hath seen the F; and how sayest G3962
9 how sayest thou *then*, Shew us the F? G3962
10 Believest thou not that I am in the F, G3962
10 Father, and the F in me? the words that G3962
10 not of myself: but the F that dwelleth in G3962
11 Believe me that I *am* in the F, and the G3962
11 Father, and the F in me: or else believe G3962
12 shall he do; because I go unto my F. G3962
13 that the F may be glorified in the Son. G3962
16 And I will pray the F, and he shall give G3962
20 *am* in my F, and ye in me, and I in you. G3962
21 be loved of my F, and I will love him, G3962
23 words: and my F will love him, and we G3962
26 Ghost, whom the F will send in my G3962
28 the F: for my Father is greater than I. G3962
28 the Father: for my F is greater than I. G3962
31 that I love the F; and as the Father gave G3962
31 the Father; and as the F gave me G3962
15: 1 I am the true vine, and my F is the G3962
8 Herein is my F glorified, that ye bear G3962
9 As the F hath loved me, so have I loved G3962
15 of my F I have made known unto you. G3962
16 the F in my name, he may give it you. G3962
23 He that hateth me hateth my F also. G3962
24 both seen and hated both me and my F. G3962
26 unto you from the F, *even* the Spirit of G3962
26 from the F, he shall testify of me: G3962
16: 3 they have not known the F, nor me. G3962
10 Of righteousness, because I go to my F, G3962
15 All things that the F hath are mine: G3962
16 ye shall see me, because I go to the F. G3962
17 shall see me: and, Because I go to the F? G3962
23 the F in my name, he will give *it* you. G3962
25 but I shall shew you plainly of the F. G3962
26 unto you, that I will pray the F for you: G3962
27 For the F himself loveth you, because G3962
28 I came forth from the F, and am come G3962
28 again, I leave the world, and go to the F. G3962
32 am not alone, because the F is with me. G3962
17: 1 heaven, and said, F, the hour is come; G3962
5 And now, O F, glorify thou me with G3962
11 to thee. Holy F, keep through thine G3962
21 That they all may be one; as thou, F, *art* G3962
24 F, I will that they also, whom thou hast G3962
25 O righteous F, the world hath not G3962
18:11 F hath given me, shall I not drink it? G3962
13 first; for he was f in law to Caiaphas, G3995
20:17 yet ascended to my F: but go to my G3962
17 I ascend unto my F, and your Father; G3962
17 your F; and *to* my God, and your God. G3962
21 *my* F hath sent me, even so send I you. G3962
Act 1: 4 F, which, *saith he*, ye have heard of me. G3962
7 which the F hath put in his own power. G3962
2:33 received of the F the promise of the G3962
7: 2 appeared unto our f Abraham, when G3962
4 from thence, when his f was dead, he G3962

Act 7:14 Then sent Joseph, and called his f G3962
16 of the sons of Emmor *the f* of Sychem.
16: 1 and believed; but his f *was* a Greek: G3962
3 for they knew all that his f was a Greek. G3962
28: 8 And it came to pass, that the f of G3962
Ro 1: 7 God our F, and the Lord Jesus Christ. G3962
4: 1 f, as pertaining to the flesh, hath found? G3962
11 that he might be the f of all them that G3962
12 And the f of circumcision to them who G3962
12 of that faith of our f Abraham, which G3962
16 faith of Abraham; who is the f of us all, G3962
17 (As it is written, I have made thee a f of G3962
18 might become the f of many nations, G3962
6: 4 by the glory of the F, even so we also G3962
8:15 of adoption, whereby we cry, Abba, F. G3962
9:10 conceived by one, *even* by our f Isaac; G3962
15: 6 even the F of our Lord Jesus Christ. G3962
1Co 1: 3 our F, and *from* the Lord Jesus Christ. G3962
8: 6 But to us *there is but* one God, the F, of G3962
15:24 to God, even the F; when he shall have G3962
2Co 1: 2 our F, and *from* the Lord Jesus Christ. G3962
3 Blessed *be* God, even the F of our Lord G3962
3 Jesus Christ, the F of mercies, and the G3962
6:18 And will be a F unto you, and ye shall G3962
11:31 The God and F of our Lord Jesus G3962
Gal 1: 1 the F, who raised him from the dead;) G3962
3 the F, and *from* our Lord Jesus Christ, G3962
4 according to the will of God and our F: G3962
4: 2 until the time appointed of the f. G3962
6 Son into your hearts, crying, Abba, F. G3962
Eph 1: 2 our F, and *from* the Lord Jesus Christ. G3962
3 Blessed *be* the God and F of our Lord G3962
17 Jesus Christ, the F of glory, may give G3962
2:18 have access by one Spirit unto the F. G3962
3:14 unto the F of our Lord Jesus Christ, G3962
4: 6 One God and F of all, who *is* above all, G3962
5:20 F in the name of our Lord Jesus Christ; G3962
31 For this cause shall a man leave his f G3962
6: 2 Honour thy f and mother; which is the G3962
23 God the F and the Lord Jesus Christ. G3962
Php 1: 2 our F, and *from* the Lord Jesus Christ. G3962
2:11 Christ *is* Lord, to the glory of God the F. G3962
22 f, he hath served with me in the gospel. G3962
4:20 Now unto God and our F *be* glory for G3962
Col 1: 2 God our F and the Lord Jesus Christ. G3962
3 We give thanks to God and the F of our G3962
12 Giving thanks unto the F, which hath G3962
19 For it pleased *the F* that in him should G3962
2: 2 of God, and of the F, and of Christ; G3962
3:17 giving thanks to God and the F by him. G3962
1Th 1: 1 *is* in God the F and *in* the Lord Jesus G3962
1 God our F, and the Lord Jesus Christ. G3962
3 Christ, in the sight of God and our F; G3962
2:11 one of you, as a f *doth* his children, G3962
3:11 Now God himself and our F, and our G3962
13 God, even our F, at the coming of our G3962
2Th 1: 1 in God our F and the Lord Jesus Christ: G3962
2 God our F and the Lord Jesus Christ. G3962
2:16 and God, even our F, which hath loved G3962
1Ti 1: 2 God our F and Jesus Christ our Lord. G3962
5: 1 a f; *and* the younger men as brethren; G3962
2Ti 1: 2 God the F and Christ Jesus our Lord. G3962
Tit 1: 4 from God the F and the Lord Jesus G3962
Phlm 3 God our F and the Lord Jesus Christ. G3962
Heb 1: 5 to him a F, and he shall be to me a Son? G3962
7: 3 Without f, without mother, without G540
10 For he was yet in the loins of his f, when G3962
12: 7 son is he whom the f chasteneth not? G3962
9 unto the F of spirits, and live? G3962
Jas 1:17 down from the F of lights, with whom G3962
27 God and the F is this, To visit the G3962
2:21 Was not Abraham our f justified by G3962
3: 9 Therewith bless we God, even the F; and G3962
1Pt 1: 2 of God the F, through sanctification G3962
3 Blessed *be* the God and F of our Lord G3962
17 And if ye call on the F, who without G3962
2Pt 1:17 For he received from God the F honour G3962
1Jn 1: 2 the F, and was manifested unto us;) G3962
3 the F, and with his Son Jesus Christ. G3962
2: 1 with the F, Jesus Christ the righteous: G3962
13 children, because ye have known the F. G3962
15 world, the love of the F is not in him. G3962
16 life, is not of the F, but is of the world. G3962
22 that denieth the F and the Son. G3962
23 the same hath not the F: *but* he that G3962
23 acknowledgeth the Son hath the F also.
24 shall continue in the Son, and in the F. G3962
3: 1 Behold, what manner of love the F hath G3962
4:14 do testify that the F sent the Son *to be* G3962
1Jn 5: 7 in heaven, the F, the Word, and the G3962
2Jn 3 from God the F, and from the Lord G3962
3 the Son of the F, in truth and love. G3962
4 received a commandment from the F. G3962
9 Christ, he hath both the F and the Son. G3962
Jude 1 by God the F, and preserved in Jesus G3962
Rev 1: 6 unto God and his F; to him *be* glory and G3962
2:27 to shivers: even as I received of my F. G3962
3: 5 before my F, and before his angels. G3962
21 am set down with my F in his throne. G3962

FATHER-IN-LAW See FATHER and LAW.

FATHERLESS

Ex 22:22 Ye shall not afflict any widow, or f H3490
24 shall be widows, and your children f. H3490
Dt 10:18 He doth execute the judgment of the f H3490
14:29 the stranger, and the f, and the widow, H3490
16:11 stranger, and the f, and the widow, that H3490
14 stranger, and the f, and the widow, that H3490
24:17 f; nor take a widow's raiment to pledge: H3490
19 stranger, for the f, and for the widow: H3490
20 stranger, for the f, and for the widow. H3490
21 stranger, for the f, and for the widow. H3490
26:12 the stranger, the f, and the widow, that H3490
13 the stranger, to the f, and to the widow, H3490
27:19 of the stranger, f, and widow. And all H3490
Job 6:27 Yea, ye overwhelm the f, and ye dig *a* H3490
22: 9 the arms of the f have been broken. H3490
24: 3 They drive away the ass of the f, they H3490
9 They pluck the f from the breast, and H3490
29:12 f, and *him that had* none to help him. H3490
31:17 alone, and the f hath not eaten thereof; H3490
21 If I have lifted up my hand against the f, H3490
Ps 10:14 unto thee; thou art the helper of the f. H3490
18 To judge the f and the oppressed, that H3490
68: 5 A father of the f, and a judge of the H3490
82: 3 Defend the poor and f: do justice to the H3490
94: 6 and the stranger, and murder the f. H3490
109: 9 Let his children be f, and his wife a H3490
12 let there be any to favour his f children. H3490
146: 9 he relieveth the f and widow: but the H3490
Prv 23:10 and enter not into the fields of the f: H3490
Isa 1:17 judge the f, plead for the widow. H3490
23 they judge not the f, neither doth the H3490
9:17 mercy on their f and widows: for every H3490
10: 2 their prey, and *that* they may rob the f! H3490
Jer 5:28 the cause of the f, yet they prosper; and H3490
7: 6 *If* ye oppress not the stranger, the f, and H3490
22: 3 to the stranger, the f, nor the widow, H3490
49:11 Leave thy f children, I will preserve H3490
Lam 5: 3 We are orphans and f, our mothers H369+H1
Ezk 22: 7 have they vexed the f and the widow. H3490
Hos 14: 3 gods: for in thee the f findeth mercy. H3490
Zec 7:10 And oppress not the widow, nor the f, H3490
Mal 3: 5 widow, and the f, and that turn aside H3490
Jas 1:27 is this, To visit the f and widows in G3737

FATHERS

Gen 15:15 And thou shalt go to thy f in peace; thou H1
31: 3 the land of thy f, and to thy kindred; and H1
46:34 we, *and* also our f: that ye may dwell in H1
47: 3 *are* shepherds, both we, *and* also our f. H1
9 of my f in the days of their pilgrimage. H1
30 But I will lie with my f, and thou shalt H1
48:15 before whom my f Abraham and Isaac H1
16 the name of my f Abraham and Isaac; H1
21 bring you again unto the land of your f. H1
49:29 bury me with my f in the cave that *is* in H1
Ex 3:13 The God of your f hath sent me unto H1
15 The LORD God of your f, the God of H1
16 The LORD God of your f, the God of H1
4: 5 the LORD God of their f, the God of H1
6:25 these *are* the heads of the f of the Levites H1
10: 6 which neither thy f, nor thy fathers' H1
6 nor thy fathers' f have seen, since the H1
12: 3 the house of *their* f, a lamb for an house: H1
13: 5 he sware unto thy f to give thee, a land H1
11 thee and to thy f, and shall give it thee, H1
20: 5 the iniquity of the f upon the children H1
34: 7 the iniquity of the f upon the children, H1
Lev 25:41 the possession of his f shall he return. H1
26:39 of their f shall they pine away with them. H1
40 the iniquity of their f, with their trespass H1
Nu 1: 2 the house of their f, with the number of H1
4 tribe; every one head of the house of his f. H1
16 of their f, heads of thousands in Israel. H1
18 by the house of their f, according to the H1
20 by the house of their f, according to the H1
Nu 1:22 by the house of their f, those that were H1
24 by the house of their f, according to the H1
26 by the house of their f, according to the H1
28 by the house of their f, according to the H1
30 by the house of their f, according to the H1
32 by the house of their f, according to the H1
34 by the house of their f, according to the H1
36 by the house of their f, according to the H1
38 by the house of their f, according to the H1
40 by the house of their f, according to the H1
42 by the house of their f, according to the H1
44 men: each one was for the house of his f. H1
45 by the house of their f, from twenty years H1
47 But the Levites after the tribe of their f H1
2:32 by the house of their f: all those that were H1
34 according to the house of their f. H1
3:15 the house of their f, by their families: H1
20 Levites according to the house of their f. H1
4: 2 their families, by the house of their f, H1
22 the houses of their f, by their families; H1
29 their families, by the house of their f; H1
34 families, and after the house of their f, H1
38 their families, and by the house of their f, H1
40 the house of their f, were two thousand H1
42 their families, by the house of their f, H1
46 families, and after the house of their f, H1
7: 2 the house of their f, who *were* the princes H1
11:12 the land which thou swarest unto their f? H1
13: 2 every tribe of their f shall ye send a man, H1
14:18 the iniquity of the f upon the children H1
23 I sware unto their f, neither shall any of H1
17: 2 to the house of *their* f, of all their princes H1
2 to the house of their f twelve rods: write H1
3 *be* for the head of the house of their f. H1
20:15 How our f went down into Egypt, and we H1
15 and the Egyptians vexed us, and our f: H1
26:55 of the tribes of their f they shall inherit. H1
31:26 and the chief f of the congregation: H1
32: 8 Thus did your f, when I sent them from H1
28 f of the tribes of the children of Israel: H1
33:54 to the tribes of your f ye shall inherit. H1
34:14 to the house of their f, and the tribe of the H1
14 to the house of their f, have received *their* H1
36: 1 And the chief f of the families of the H1
1 the chief f of the children of Israel: H1
3 inheritance of our f, and shall be put to H1
4 from the inheritance of the tribe of our f. H1
7 to the inheritance of the tribe of his f. H1
8 enjoy every man the inheritance of his f. H1
Dt 1: 8 swear unto your f, Abraham, Isaac, and H1
11 (The LORD God of your f make you a H1
21 LORD God of thy f hath said unto thee; H1
35 land, which I sware to give unto your f, H1
4: 1 the LORD God of your f giveth you. H1
31 of thy f which he sware unto them. H1
37 And because he loved thy f, therefore he H1
5: 3 covenant with our f, but with us, *even* us, H1
9 the iniquity of the f upon the children H1
6: 3 LORD God of thy f hath promised thee, H1
10 he sware unto thy f, to Abraham, to H1
18 land which the LORD sware unto thy f, H1
23 us the land which he sware unto our f. H1
7: 8 had sworn unto your f, hath the LORD H1
12 and the mercy which he sware unto thy f: H1
13 which he sware unto thy f to give thee. H1
8: 1 land which the LORD sware unto your f. H1
3 not, neither did thy f know; that he H1
16 manna, which thy f knew not, that he H1
18 he sware unto thy f, as *it is* this day. H1
9: 5 unto thy f, Abraham, Isaac, and Jacob. H1
10:11 I sware unto their f to give unto them. H1
15 Only the LORD had a delight in thy f to H1
22 Thy f went down into Egypt with H1
11: 9 sware unto your f to give unto them and H1
21 sware unto your f to give them, as the H1
12: 1 LORD God of thy f giveth thee to possess H1
13: 6 thou hast not known, thou, nor thy f; H1
17 thee, as he hath sworn unto thy f; H1
19: 8 sworn unto thy f, and give thee all the H1
8 which he promised to give unto thy f; H1
24:16 The f shall not be put to death for the H1
16 put to death for the f: every man shall be H1
26: 3 the LORD sware unto our f for to give us. H1
7 LORD God of our f, the LORD heard our H1
15 swarest unto our f, a land that floweth H1
27: 3 LORD God of thy f hath promised thee. H1
28:11 the LORD sware unto thy f to give thee. H1
36 thou nor thy f have known; and there H1
64 thy f have known, *even* wood and stone. H1

Dt 29:13 thy f, to Abraham, to Isaac, and to Jacob. H1
25 LORD God of their f, which he made with H1
30: 5 the land which thy f possessed, and thou H1
5 thee good, and multiply thee above thy f. H1
9 thee for good, as he rejoiced over thy f: H1
20 sware unto thy f, to Abraham, to Isaac, H1
31: 7 sworn unto their f to give them; and H1
16 shalt sleep with thy f; and this people will H1
20 I sware unto their f, that floweth with H1
32:17 came newly up, whom your f feared not. H1
Jos 1: 6 which I sware unto their f to give them. H1
4: 6 your children ask *their f* in time to come,
21 shall ask their f in time to come, saying, H1
5: 6 sware unto their f that he would give us, H1
14: 1 and the heads of the f of the tribes of the H1
18: 3 the LORD God of your f hath given you? H1
19:51 and the heads of the f of the tribes of the H1
21: 1 Then came near the heads of the f of the H1
1 f of the tribes of the children of Israel; H1
43 to give unto their f; and they possessed it, H1
44 he sware unto their f: and there stood not H1
22:14 of their f among the thousands of Israel. H1
28 LORD, which our f made, not for burnt H1
24: 2 God of Israel, Your f dwelt on the other H1
6 And I brought your f out of Egypt: and H1
6 pursued after your f with chariots and H1
14 gods which your f served on the other H1
15 gods which your f served that *were* on H1
17 us up and our f out of the land of Egypt, H1
Jdg 2: 1 I sware unto your f; and I said, I will H1
10 gathered unto their f: and there arose H1
12 LORD God of their f, which brought them H1
17 way which their f walked in, obeying the H1
19 more than their f, in following other gods H1
20 f, and have not hearkened unto my voice; H1
22 therein, as their f did keep *it*, or not. H1
3: 4 their f by the hand of Moses. H1
6:13 miracles which our f told us of, saying, H1
21:22 And it shall be, when their f or their H1
1Sa 12: 6 your f up out of the land of Egypt. H1
7 LORD, which he did to you and to your f. H1
8 Egypt, and your f cried unto the LORD, H1
8 brought forth your f out of Egypt, and H1
15 be against you, as *it was* against your f. H1
2Sa 7:12 shalt sleep with thy f, I will set up thy H1
1Ki 1:21 shall sleep with his f, that I and my son H1
2:10 So David slept with his f, and was buried H1
8: 1 the chief of the f of the children of Israel, H1
21 he made with our f, when he brought H1
34 the land which thou gavest unto their f. H1
40 in the land which thou gavest unto our f. H1
48 gavest unto their f, the city which thou H1
53 our f out of Egypt, O Lord GOD. H1
57 our f: let him not leave us, nor forsake us: H1
58 judgments, which he commanded our f. H1
9: 9 brought forth their f out of the land of H1
11:21 slept with his f, and that Joab the captain H1
43 And Solomon slept with his f, and was H1
13:22 not come unto the sepulchre of thy f. H1
14:15 he gave to their f, and shall scatter them H1
20 f, and Nadab his son reigned in his stead. H1
22 above all that their f had done. H1
31 And Rehoboam slept with his f, and was H1
31 and was buried with his f in the city of H1
15: 8 And Abijam slept with his f; and they H1
12 all the idols that his f had made. H1
24 And Asa slept with his f, and was buried H1
24 was buried with his f in the city of David H1
16: 6 So Baasha slept with his f, and was H1
28 So Omri slept with his f, and was buried H1
19: 4 my life; for I *am* not better than my f. H1
21: 3 give the inheritance of my f unto thee. H1
4 the inheritance of my f. And he laid him H1
22:40 So Ahab slept with his f; and Ahaziah his H1
50 And Jehoshaphat slept with his f, and H1
50 was buried with his f in the city of David H1
2Ki 8:24 And Joram slept with his f, and was H1
24 and was buried with his f in the city of H1
9:28 sepulchre with his f in the city of David. H1
10:35 And Jehu slept with his f: and they buried H1
12:18 and Ahaziah, his f, kings of Judah, had H1
21 him with his f in the city of David: H1
13: 9 And Jehoahaz slept with his f; and they H1
13 And Joash slept with his f; and Jeroboam H1
14: 6 saying, The f shall not be put to death H1
6 put to death for the f; but every man shall H1
16 And Jehoash slept with his f, and was H1
20 Jerusalem with his f in the city of David. H1
22 Judah, after that the king slept with his f. H1
2Ki 14:29 And Jeroboam slept with his f, *even* with H1
15: 7 So Azariah slept with his f; and they H1
7 him with his f in the city of David: H1
9 sight of the LORD, as his f had done: he H1
22 And Menahem slept with his f; and H1
38 And Jotham slept with his f, and was H1
38 was buried with his f in the city of David H1
16:20 And Ahaz slept with his f, and was H1
20 and was buried with his f in the city of H1
17:13 I commanded your f, and which I sent to H1
14 to the neck of their f, that did not believe H1
15 he made with their f, and his testimonies H1
41 as did their f, so do they unto this day. H1
19:12 them which my f have destroyed; *as* H1
20:17 and that which thy f have laid up in H1
21 And Hezekiah slept with his f: and H1
21: 8 land which I gave their f; only if they will H1
15 since the day their f came forth out of H1
18 And Manasseh slept with his f, and was H1
22 And he forsook the LORD God of his f, H1
22:13 us, because our f have not hearkened H1
20 gather thee unto thy f, and thou shalt be H1
23:32 according to all that his f had done. H1
37 according to all that his f had done. H1
24: 6 So Jehoiakim slept with his f: and H1
1Ch 4:38 the house of their f increased greatly. H1
5:13 And their brethren of the house of their f H1
15 son of Guni, chief of the house of their f. H1
24 the house of their f, even Epher, and Ishi, H1
24 men, *and* heads of the house of their f. H1
25 the God of their f, and went a whoring H1
6:19 of the Levites according to their f. H1
7: 4 after the house of their f, *were* bands of H1
7 of the house of *their* f, mighty men of H1
9 of the house of their f, mighty men of H1
11 by the heads of their f, mighty men of H1
8: 6 are the heads of the f of the inhabitants H1
10 These *were* his sons, heads of the f. H1
13 *were* heads of the f of the inhabitants of H1
28 These *were* heads of the f, by their H1
9: 9 of the f in the house of their fathers. H1
9 chief of the fathers in the house of their f. H1
13 of the house of their f, a thousand and H1
19 and their f, *being* over the host of H1
33 And these *are* the singers, chief of the f H1
34 These chief f of the Levites *were* chief H1
12:17 God of our f look *thereon*, and rebuke *it*. H1
30 famous throughout the house of their f. H1
15:12 Ye *are* the chief of the f of the Levites: H1
17:11 go *to be* with thy f, that I will raise up thy H1
23: 9 These *were* the chief of the f of Laadan. H1
24 the house of their f; *even* the chief of the H1
24 the chief of the f, as they were counted H1
24: 4 the house of *their* f, and eight among the H1
4 Ithamar according to the house of their f. H1
6 *before* the chief of the f of the priests and H1
30 of the Levites after the house of their f. H1
31 and the chief of the f of the priests and H1
31 f over against their younger brethren. H1
26:13 to the house of their f, for every gate. H1
21 Laadan, chief f, *even* of Laadan the H1
26 king, and the chief f, the captains over H1
31 generations of his f. In the fortieth year H1
32 hundred chief f, whom king David made H1
27: 1 *to wit*, the chief f and captains of H1
29: 6 Then the chief of the f and princes of the H1
15 as *were* all our f: our days on the earth H1
18 and of Israel, our f, keep this for ever in H1
20 LORD God of their f, and bowed down H1
2Ch 1: 2 governor in all Israel, the chief of the f. H1
5: 2 the chief of the f of the children of Israel, H1
6:25 which thou gavest to them and to their f. H1
31 in the land which thou gavest unto our f. H1
38 gavest unto their f, and *toward* the city H1
7:22 LORD God of their f, which brought them H1
9:31 And Solomon slept with his f, and he was H1
11:16 to sacrifice unto the LORD God of their f. H1
12:16 And Rehoboam slept with his f, and was H1
13:12 God of your f; for ye shall not prosper. H1
18 they relied upon the LORD God of their f. H1
14: 1 So Abijah slept with his f, and they H1
4 LORD God of their f, and to do the law H1
15:12 LORD God of their f with all their heart H1
16:13 And Asa slept with his f, and died in the H1
17:14 to the house of their f: Of Judah, the H1
19: 4 them back unto the LORD God of their f. H1
8 and of the chief of the f of Israel, for the H1
20: 6 And said, O LORD God of our f, *art* not H1
33 their hearts unto the God of their f. H1
2Ch 21: 1 Now Jehoshaphat slept with his f, and H1
1 and was buried with his f in the city of H1
10 he had forsaken the LORD God of his f. H1
19 burning for him, like the burning of his f. H1
23: 2 f of Israel, and they came to Jerusalem. H1
24:18 LORD God of their f, and served groves H1
24 the LORD God of their f. So they executed H1
25: 4 saying, The f shall not die for the H1
4 f, but every man shall die for his own sin. H1
5 to the houses of *their* f, throughout all H1
28 him with his f in the city of Judah. H1
26: 2 Judah, after that the king slept with his f. H1
12 The whole number of the chief of the f of H1
23 So Uzziah slept with his f, and they H1
23 him with his f in the field of the burial H1
27: 9 And Jotham slept with his f, and they H1
28: 6 had forsaken the LORD God of their f. H1
9 the LORD God of your f was wroth with H1
25 provoked to anger the LORD God of his f. H1
27 And Ahaz slept with his f, and they H1
29: 5 LORD God of your f, and carry forth the H1
6 For our f have trespassed, and done *that* H1
9 For, lo, our f have fallen by the sword, H1
30: 7 And be not ye like your f, and like your H1
7 LORD God of their f, *who* therefore gave H1
8 Now be ye not stiffnecked, as your f H1
19 the LORD God of his f, though *he be* not H1
22 confession to the LORD God of their f. H1
31:17 the house of their f, and the Levites from H1
32:13 Know ye not what I and my f have done H1
14 nations that my f utterly destroyed, that H1
15 of the hand of my f: how much less shall H1
33 And Hezekiah slept with his f, and they H1
33: 8 appointed for your f; so that they will H1
12 himself greatly before the God of his f, H1
20 So Manasseh slept with his f, and they H1
34:21 us, because our f have not kept the word H1
28 Behold, I will gather thee to thy f, and H1
32 to the covenant of God, the God of their f. H1
33 following the LORD, the God of their f. H1
35: 4 the houses of your f, after your courses, H1
5 the families of the f of your brethren the H1
24 the sepulchres of his f. And all Judah and H1
36:15 And the LORD God of their f sent to H1
Ezr 1: 5 Then rose up the chief of the f of Judah H1
2:68 And *some* of the chief of the f, when they H1
3:12 and chief of the f, *who were* ancient men, H1
4: 2 to the chief of the f, and said unto them, H1
3 of the chief of the f of Israel, said unto H1
15 the records of thy f: so shalt thou find in H2
5:12 But after that our f had provoked the H2
7:27 Blessed *be* the LORD God of our f, which H1
8: 1 These *are* now the chief of their f, and H1
28 offering unto the LORD God of your f. H1
29 and chief of the f of Israel, at Jerusalem, H1
9: 7 Since the days of our f *have* we *been* in a H1
10:11 LORD God of your f, and do his pleasure: H1
16 certain chief of the f, after the house of H1
16 the house of their f, and all of them by H1
Neh 7:70 And some of the chief of the f gave unto H1
71 And *some* of the chief of the f gave to the H1
8:13 the chief of the f of all the people, the H1
9: 2 their sins, and the iniquities of their f. H1
9 And didst see the affliction of our f in H1
16 But they and our f dealt proudly, and H1
23 f, that they should go in to possess *it*. H1
32 and on our f, and on all thy people, H1
34 our priests, nor our f, kept thy law, nor H1
36 gavest unto our f to eat the fruit thereof H1
10:34 the houses of our f, at times appointed H1
11:13 And his brethren, chief of the f, two H1
12:12 the chief of the f: of Seraiah, Meraiah; H1
22 chief of the f: also the priests, to the H1
23 The sons of Levi, the chief of the f, *were* H1
13:18 Did not your f thus, and did not our God H1
Job 8: 8 prepare thyself to the search of their f: H1
15:18 Which wise men have told from their f, H1
30: 1 me in derision, whose f I would have H1
Ps 22: 4 Our f trusted in thee: they trusted, and H1
39:12 thee, *and* a sojourner, as all my f *were*. H1
44: 1 our ears, O God, our f have told us, *what* H1
45:16 Instead of thy f shall be thy children, H1
49:19 He shall go to the generation of his f; they H1
78: 3 and known, and our f have told us. H1
5 commanded our f, that they should make H1
8 And might not be as their f, a stubborn H1
12 in the sight of their f, in the land of Egypt, H1
57 like their f: they were turned aside H1
95: 9 When your f tempted me, proved me, H1

Ps 106: 6 We have sinned with our f, we have H1
7 Our f understood not thy wonders in H1
109:14 Let the iniquity of his f be remembered H1
Prv 17: 6 men; and the glory of children *are* their f. H1
19:14 House and riches *are* the inheritance of f: H1
22:28 ancient landmark, which thy f have set. H1
Isa 14:21 for the iniquity of their f; that they do not H1
37:12 them which my f have destroyed, *as* H1
39: 6 and *that* which thy f have laid up in H1
49:23 And kings shall be thy nursing f, and H539
64:11 house, where our f praised thee, is H1
65: 7 the iniquities of your f together, saith the H1
Jer 2: 5 iniquity have your f found in me, that H1
3:18 given for an inheritance unto your f. H1
24 the labour of our f from our youth; their H1
25 God, we and our f, from our youth even H1
6:21 people, and the f and the sons together H1
7: 7 that I gave to your f, for ever and ever. H1
14 and to your f, as I have done to Shiloh. H1
18 The children gather wood, and the f H1
22 For I spake not unto your f, nor H1
25 Since the day that your f came forth out H1
26 their neck: they did worse than their f. H1
9:14 after Baalim, which their f taught them: H1
16 they nor their f have known: and I will H1
11: 4 Which I commanded your f in the day H1
5 sworn unto your f, to give them a land H1
7 For I earnestly protested unto your f in H1
10 my covenant which I made with their f. H1
13:14 against another, even the f and the sons H1
14:20 of our f: for we have sinned against thee. H1
16: 3 their f that begat them in this land; H1
11 Because your f have forsaken me, saith H1
12 And ye have done worse than your f; for, H1
13 *neither* ye nor your f; and there shall ye H1
15 into their land that I gave unto their f. H1
19 say, Surely our f have inherited lies, H1
17:22 the sabbath day, as I commanded your f. H1
19: 4 they nor their f have known, nor the H1
23:27 their f have forgotten my name for Baal. H1
39 your f, *and cast you* out of my presence: H1
24:10 land that I gave unto them and to their f. H1
25: 5 unto you and to your f for ever and ever: H1
30: 3 I gave to their f, and they shall possess it. H1
31:29 say no more, The f have eaten a sour H1
32 I made with their f in the day *that* I took H1
32:18 the iniquity of the f into the bosom of H1
22 didst swear to their f to give them, a land H1
34: 5 the burnings of thy f, the former kings H1
13 a covenant with your f in the day that I H1
14 from thee: but your f hearkened not unto H1
35:15 to you and to your f: but ye have not H1
44: 3 knew not, *neither* they, ye, nor your f. H1
9 wickedness of your f, and the wickedness H1
10 that I set before you and before your f. H1
17 done, we, and our f, our kings, and our H1
21 ye, and your f, your kings, and your H1
47: 3 of his wheels, the f shall not look back to H1
50: 7 even the LORD, the hope of their f. H1
Lam 5: 7 Our f have sinned, *and are* not; and we H1
Ezk 2: 3 me: they and their f have transgressed H1
5:10 Therefore the f shall eat the sons in the H1
10 sons shall eat their f; and I will execute H1
18: 2 of Israel, saying, The f have eaten sour H1
20: 4 to know the abominations of their f: H1
18 in the statutes of your f, neither observe H1
27 Yet in this your f have blasphemed me, H1
30 the manner of your f? and commit ye H1
36 Like as I pleaded with your f in the H1
42 I lifted up mine hand to give it to your f. H1
36:28 that I gave to your f; and ye shall be my H1
37:25 wherein your f have dwelt; and they H1
47:14 to give it unto your f: and this land shall H1
Dan 2:23 O thou God of my f, who hast given me H2
9: 6 our f, and to all the people of the land. H1
8 f, because we have sinned against thee. H1
16 the iniquities of our f, Jerusalem and thy H1
11:24 do *that* which his f have not done, nor H1
24 nor his fathers' f; he shall scatter among H1
37 Neither shall he regard the God of his f, H1
38 and a god whom his f knew not shall he H1
Hos 9:10 I saw your f as the firstripe in the H1
Joel 1: 2 your days, or even in the days of your f? H1
Am 2: 4 err, after the which their f have walked: H1
Mic 7:20 sworn unto our f from the days of old. H1
Zec 1: 2 hath been sore displeased with your f. H1
4 Be ye not as your f, unto whom the H1
5 Your f, where *are* they? and the prophets, H1
6 not take hold of your f? and they returned H1
Zec 8:14 you, when your f provoked me to wrath, H1
Mal 2:10 by profaning the covenant of our f? H1
3: 7 Even from the days of your f ye are gone H1
4: 6 And he shall turn the heart of the f to the H1
6 children to their f, lest I come and smite H1
Mt 23:30 in the days of our f, we would not have G3962
32 Fill ye up then the measure of your f. G3962
Lk 1:17 the hearts of the f to the children, and G3962
55 As he spake to our f, to Abraham, and G3962
72 f, and to remember his holy covenant; G3962
6:23 manner did their f unto the prophets. G3962
26 for so did their f to the false prophets. G3962
11:47 of the prophets, and your f killed them. G3962
48 the deeds of your f: for they indeed G3962
Jn 4:20 Our f worshipped in this mountain; G3962
6:31 Our f did eat manna in the desert; as it G3962
49 Your f did eat manna in the G3962
58 not as your f did eat manna, and G3962
7:22 of Moses, but of the f;) and ye on the G3962
Act 3:13 the God of our f, hath glorified his Son G3962
22 For Moses truly said unto the f, A G3962
25 made with our f, saying unto Abraham, G3962
5:30 The God of our f raised up Jesus, whom G3962
7: 2 And he said, Men, brethren, and f, G3962
11 and our f found no sustenance. G3962
12 corn in Egypt, he sent out our f first. G3962
15 into Egypt, and died, he, and our f, G3962
19 evil entreated our f, so that they cast G3962
32 *Saying,* I *am* the God of thy f, the God of G3962
38 Sina, and *with* our f: who received the G3962
39 To whom our f would not obey, but G3962
44 Our f had the tabernacle of witness in G3962
45 Which also our f that came after G3962
45 the face of our f, unto the days of David; G3962
51 the Holy Ghost: as your f *did,* so *do* ye. G3962
52 Which of the prophets have not your f G3962
13:17 of Israel chose our f, and exalted the G3962
32 the promise which was made unto the f, G3962
36 was laid unto his f, and saw corruption: G3962
15:10 neither our f nor we were able to bear? G3962
22: 1 Men, brethren, and f, hear ye my G3962
3 of the law of the f, and was zealous G3971
14 And he said, The God of our f hath G3962
24:14 I the God of my f, believing all things G3971
26: 6 of the promise made of God unto our f: G3962
28:17 or customs of our f, yet was I delivered G3971
25 Ghost by Esaias the prophet unto our f, G3962
Ro 9: 5 Whose *are* the f, and of whom as G3962
15: 8 confirm the promises *made* unto the f: G3962
1Co 4:15 *have ye* not many f: for in Christ Jesus I G3962
10: 1 how that all our f were under the cloud, G3962
Gal 1:14 zealous of the traditions of my f. G3967
Eph 6: 4 And, ye f, provoke not your children to G3962
Col 3:21 F, provoke not your children *to anger,* G3962
1Ti 1: 9 for murderers of f and murderers of G3964
Heb 1: 1 in time past unto the f by the prophets, G3962
3: 9 When your f tempted me, proved me, G3962
8: 9 I made with their f in the day when I G3962
12: 9 Furthermore we have had f of our flesh G3962
1Pt 1:18 *received* by tradition from your f; G3970
2Pt 3: 4 for since the f fell asleep, all things G3962
1Jn 2:13 I write unto you, f, because ye have G3962
14 I have written unto you, f, because ye G3962

FATHER'S

Gen 9:23 and they saw not their f nakedness. H1
12: 1 and from thy f house, unto a land that H1
20:13 to wander from my f house, that I said H1
24: 7 took me from my f house, and from the H1
23 room *in* thy f house for us to lodge in? H1
38 But thou shalt go unto my f house, and H1
40 son of my kindred, and of my f house: H1
26:15 For all the wells which his f servants had H1
28:21 So that I come again to my f house in H1
29: 9 with her f sheep: for she kept them. H1
12 And Jacob told Rachel that he *was* her f H1
31: 1 all that *was* our f; and of *that* which *was* H1
1 *was* our f hath he gotten all this glory. H1
5 And said unto them, I see your f H1
14 or inheritance for us in our f house? H1
19 had stolen the images that *were* her f. H1
30 longedst after thy f house, *yet* wherefore H1
35:22 and lay with Bilhah his f concubine: and H1
37: 2 sons of Zilpah, his f wives: and Joseph H1
12 And his brethren went to feed their f H1
38:11 a widow at thy f house, till Shelah my H1
11 Tamar went and dwelt in her f house. H1
41:51 me forget all my toil, and all my f house. H1
46:31 and unto his f house, I will go up, and H1
Gen 46:31 brethren, and my f house, which *were* in H1
47:12 and all his f household, with bread, H1
48:17 and he held up his f hand, to remove it H1
49: 4 wentest up to thy f bed; then defiledst H1
8 f children shall bow down before thee. H1
50: 1 And Joseph fell upon his f face, and wept H1
8 brethren, and his f house: only their little H1
22 And Joseph dwelt in Egypt, he, and his f H1
Ex 2:16 filled the troughs to water their f flock. H1
6:20 And Amram took him Jochebed his f H1733
15: 2 my f God, and I will exalt him. H1
Lev 16:32 priest's office in his f stead, shall make H1
18: 8 The nakedness of thy f wife shalt thou H1
8 thou not uncover: it *is* thy f nakedness. H1
11 The nakedness of thy f wife's daughter, H1
12 the nakedness of thy f sister: she *is* thy H1
12 sister: she *is* thy f near kinswoman. H1
14 nakedness of thy f brother, thou shalt H1
20:11 And the man that lieth with his f wife H1
11 hath uncovered his f nakedness: both of H1
17 And if a man shall take his sister, his f H1
19 mother's sister, nor of thy f sister: for he H1
22:13 is returned unto her f house, as in her H1
13 she shall eat of her f meat: but there H1
Nu 2: 2 the ensign of their f house: far off about H1
18: 1 thy sons and thy f house with thee shall H1
27: 7 among their f brethren; and thou shalt H1
10 give his inheritance unto his f brethren. H1
30: 3 bond, *being* in her f house in her youth; H1
16 *being yet* in her youth in her f house. H1
36:11 married unto their f brothers' sons: H1730
Dt 22:21 to the door of her f house, and the men H1
21 the whore in her f house: so shalt thou H1
30 A man shall not take his f wife, nor H1
30 his father's wife, nor discover his f skirt. H1
27:20 Cursed *be* he that lieth with his f wife; H1
20 he uncovereth his f skirt. And all the H1
Jos 2:12 my f house, and give me a true token: H1
18 and all thy f household, home unto thee. H1
6:25 alive, and her f household, and all that H1
Jdg 6:15 and I *am* the least in my f house. H1
25 unto him, Take thy f young bullock, even H1
27 he feared his f household, and the men H1
9: 5 And he went unto his f house at Ophrah, H1
18 And ye are risen up against my f house H1
11: 2 not inherit in our f house; for thou *art* H1
7 expel me out of my f house? and why are H1
14:15 burn thee and thy f house with fire: have H1
19 kindled, and he went up to his f house. H1
19: 2 away from him unto her f house to H1
3 him into her f house: and when the H1
1Sa 2:31 and the arm of thy f house, that there H1
9:20 *Is it* not on thee, and on all thy f house? H1
17:15 Saul to feed his f sheep at Beth-lehem. H1
25 and make his f house free in Israel. H1
34 servant kept his f sheep, and there came H1
18: 2 let him go no more home to his f house. H1
18 *is* my life, *or* my f family in Israel, that H1
22: 1 and all his f house heard *it,* they H1
11 of Ahitub, and all his f house, the priests H1
16 Ahimelech, thou, and all thy f house. H1
22 *death* of all the persons of thy f house. H1
24:21 not destroy my name out of my f house. H1
2Sa 3: 7 hast thou gone in unto my f concubine? H1
29 Joab, and on all his f house; and let there H1
9: 7 for Jonathan thy f sake, and will restore H1
14: 9 on me, and on my f house: and the king H1
15:34 *as* I *have been* thy f servant hitherto, so H1
16:19 f presence, so will I be in thy presence. H1
21 Go in unto thy f concubines, which he H1
22 his f concubines in the sight of all Israel. H1
19:28 For all *of* my f house were but dead men H1
24:17 be against me, and against my f house. H1
1Ki 11:12 do it for David thy f sake: *but* I will rend H1
17 Edomites of his f servants with him, to H1
12:10 *finger* shall be thicker than my f loins. H1
18:18 but thou, and thy f house, in that ye have H1
2Ki 10: 3 and set *him* on his f throne, and fight for H1
23:30 him, and made him king in his f stead. H1
24:17 Mattaniah his f brother king in his H1730
1Ch 5: 1 as he defiled his f bed, his birthright was H1
7: 2 heads of their f house, *to wit,* of Tola: H1
40 Asher, heads of *their* f house, choice *and* H1
12:28 of his f house twenty and two captains. H1
21:17 be on me, and on my f house; but not on H1
23:11 reckoning, according to *their* f house. H1
2Ch 2:13 with understanding, of Huram my f, H1
10:10 *finger* shall be thicker than my f loins. H1
21:13 f house, *which were* better than thyself: H1

2Ch 36: 1 him king in his f stead in Jerusalem. H1
Ezr 2:59 not shew their f house, and their seed, H1
Neh 1: 6 thee: both I and my f house have sinned. H1
7:61 not shew their f house, nor their seed, H1
Est 4:14 place; but thou and thy f house shall be H1
Ps 45:10 also thine own people, and thy f house; H1
Prv 4: 3 For I was my f son, tender and only H1
6:20 My son, keep thy f commandment, and H1
13: 1 A wise son *heareth* his f instruction: but H1
15: 5 A fool despiseth his f instruction: but he H1
27:10 Thine own friend, and thy f friend, H1
Isa 7:17 and upon thy f house, days that have H1
22:23 be for a glorious throne to his f house. H1
24 all the glory of his f house, the offspring H1
Jer 35:14 none, but obey their f commandment: H1
Ezk 18:14 that seeth all his f sins which he hath H1
22:11 hath humbled his sister, his f daughter. H1
Mt 26:29 it new with you in my F kingdom. *G3962*
Lk 2:49 that I must be about my F business? *G3962*
9:26 and *in his* F, and of the holy angels. *G3962*
12:32 Fear not, little flock; for it is your F *G3962*
15:17 servants of my f have bread enough *G3962*
16:27 thou wouldest send him to my f house: *G3962*
Jn 2:16 my F house an house of merchandise. *G3962*
5:43 I am come in my F name, and ye *G3962*
6:39 And this is the F will which hath sent *G3962*
10:25 in my F name, they bear witness of me. *G3962*
29 is able to pluck *them* out of my F hand. *G3962*
14: 2 In my F house are many mansions: if *it* *G3962*
24 is not mine, but the F which sent me. *G3962*
15:10 as I have kept my F commandments, *G3962*
Act 7:20 up in his f house three months: *G3962*
1Co 5: 1 that one should have his f wife. *G3962*
Rev 14: 1 his F name written in their foreheads. *G3962*

FATHERS'
Ex 6:14 These *be* the heads of their f houses: The H1
10: 6 thy fathers, nor thy f fathers have seen, H1
Nu 17: 6 according to their f houses, *even* twelve H1
26: 2 throughout their f house, all that are H1
32:14 And, behold, ye are risen up in your f H1
Neh 2: 3 the place of my f sepulchres, *lieth* waste, H1
5 of my f sepulchres, that I may build it. H1
Ezk 20:24 and their eyes were after their f idols. H1
22:10 In thee have they discovered their f H1
Dan 11:24 have not done, nor his f fathers; he shall H1
Ro 11:28 *they are* beloved for the f sakes. *G3962*

FATHOMS
Act 27:28 And sounded, and found *it* twenty f: *G3712*
28 sounded again, and found *it* fifteen f. *G3712*

FATLING
Isa 11: 6 the young lion and the f together; and a H4806

FATLINGS
1Sa 15: 9 oxen, and of the f, and the lambs, and H4932
2Sa 6:13 gone six paces, he sacrificed oxen and f. H4806
Ps 66:15 burnt sacrifices of f, with the incense of H4220
Ezk 39:18 of bullocks, all of them f of Bashan. H4806
Mt 22: 4 my oxen and *my* f *are* killed, and all *G4619*

FATNESS
Gen 27:28 of heaven, and the f of the earth, and H4924
39 shall be the f of the earth, and of H4924
Dt 32:15 art covered *with f*; then he forsook God
Jdg 9: 9 Should I leave my f, wherewith by me H1880
Job 15:27 Because he covereth his face with his f, H2459
36:16 be set on thy table *should be* full of f. H1880
Ps 36: 8 satisfied with the f of thy house; and H1880
63: 5 *with* marrow and f; and my mouth shall H1880
65:11 thy goodness; and thy paths drop f. H1880
73: 7 Their eyes stand out with f: they have H2459
109:24 fasting; and my flesh faileth of f. H8081
Isa 17: 4 and the f of his flesh shall wax lean. H4924
34: 6 it is made fat with f, *and* with the blood H2459
7 blood, and their dust made fat with f. H2459
55: 2 and let your soul delight itself in f. H1880
Jer 31:14 soul of the priests with f, and my people H1880
Ro 11:17 of the root and f of the olive tree; *G4096*

FATS
Joel 2:24 the f shall overflow with wine and oil. H3342
3:13 the press is full, the f overflow; for their H3342

FATTED
1Ki 4:23 roebucks, and fallowdeer, and f fowl. H75
Jer 46:21 the midst of her like f bullocks; for they H4770
Lk 15:23 And bring hither the f calf, and kill *it*; *G4618*
Lk 15:27 hath killed the f calf, because he hath *G4618*
30 thou hast killed for him the f calf. *G4618*

FATTER
Dan 1:15 fairer and f in flesh than all the H1277

FATTEST
Ps 78:31 upon them, and slew the f of them, and H4924
Dan 11:24 even upon the f places of the province; H4924

FAULT
Ex 5:16 beaten; but the f *is* in thine own people. H2398
Dt 25: 2 according to his f, by a certain number. H7564
1Sa 29: 3 I have found no f in him since he fell H3972
2Sa 3: 8 to day with a f concerning this woman? H5771
Ps 59: 4 *my* f: awake to help me, and behold. H5771
Dan 6: 4 none occasion nor f; forasmuch as he H7844
4 was there any error or f found in him. H7844
Mt 18:15 go and tell him his f between thee and *G1651*
Mk 7: 2 with unwashen, hands, they found f. *G3201*
Lk 23: 4 and *to* the people, I find no f in this man. *G158*
14 before you, have found no f in this man *G158*
Jn 18:38 saith unto them, I find in him no f *at all*. *G156*
19: 4 that ye may know that I find no f in him. *G156*
6 and crucify *him*: for I find no f in him. *G156*
Ro 9:19 find f? For who hath resisted his will? *G3201*
1Co 6: 7 Now therefore there is utterly a f *G2275*
Gal 6: 1 Brethren, if a man be overtaken in a f, *G3900*
Heb 8: 8 For finding f with them, he saith, *G3201*
Rev 14: 5 are without f before the throne of God. *G299*

FAULTLESS
Heb 8: 7 For if that first *covenant* had been f, then *G273*
Jude 24 and to present *you* f before the presence *G299*

FAULTS
Gen 41: 9 saying, I do remember my f this day: H2399
Ps 19:12 *his* errors? cleanse thou me from secret *f*.
Jas 5:16 Confess *your* f one to another, and *G3900*
1Pt 2:20 be buffeted for your f, ye shall take it *G264*

FAULTY
2Sa 14:13 as one which is f, in that the king doth H818
Hos 10: 2 now shall they be found f: he shall break H816

FAVOUR
Gen 18: 3 if now I have found f in thy sight, pass H2580
30:27 if I have found f in thine eyes, *tarry:* H2580
39:21 and gave him f in the sight of the H2580
Ex 3:21 And I will give this people f in the sight H2580
11: 3 And the LORD gave the people f in the H2580
12:36 And the LORD gave the people f in the H2580
Nu 11:11 have I not found f in thy sight, that H2580
15 if I have found f in thy sight; and let H2580
Dt 24: 1 that she find no f in his eyes, because H2580
28:50 of the old, nor shew f to the young: H2603
33:23 satisfied with f, and full with the H7522
Jos 11:20 they might have no f, but that he might H8467
Ru 2:13 Then she said, Let me find f in thy H2580
1Sa 2:26 on, and was in f both with the LORD, H2896
16:22 me; for he hath found f in my sight. H2580
20:29 if I have found f in thine eyes, let me H2580
25: 8 young men find f in thine eyes: for we H2580
29: 6 day: nevertheless the lords f thee not. H2896
2Sa 15:25 city: if I shall find f in the eyes of the H2580
1Ki 11:19 And Hadad found great f in the sight of H2580
Neh 2: 5 have found f in thy sight, that thou H3190
Est 2:15 And Esther obtained f in the sight of all H2580
17 grace and f in his sight more than H2617
5: 2 *that* she obtained f in his sight: and the H2580
8 If I have found f in the sight of the king, H2580
7: 3 If I have found f in thy sight, O king, H2580
8: 5 if I have found f in his sight, and the H2580
Job 10:12 Thou hast granted me life and f, and H2617
Ps 5:12 the righteous; with f wilt thou compass H7522
30: 5 a moment; in his f *is* life: weeping may H7522
7 LORD, by thy f thou hast made my H7522
35:27 and be glad, that f my righteous cause: H2655
44: 3 because thou hadst a f unto them. H7521
45:12 among the people shall entreat thy f. H6440
89:17 and in thy f our horn shall be exalted. H7522
102:13 time to f her, yea, the set time, is come. H2603
14 in her stones, and f the dust thereof. H2603
106: 4 Remember me, O LORD, with the f *that* H7522
109:12 there be any to f his fatherless children. H2603
112: 5 A good man sheweth f, and lendeth: he H2603
119:58 I entreated thy f with *my* whole heart: H6440
Prv 3: 4 So shalt thou find f and good H2580
8:35 life, and shall obtain f of the LORD. H7522
Prv 11:27 good procureth f: but he that seeketh H7522
12: 2 A good *man* obtaineth f of the LORD: H7522
13:15 Good understanding giveth f: but the H2580
14: 9 sin: but among the righteous *there is* f. H7522
35 The king's f *is* toward a wise servant: H7522
16:15 and his f *is* as a cloud of the latter rain. H7522
18:22 *thing*, and obtaineth f of the LORD. H7522
19: 6 Many will entreat the f of the prince: H6440
12 lion; but his f *is* as dew upon the grass. H7522
21:10 his neighbour findeth no f in his eyes. H2603
22: 1 loving f rather than silver and gold. H2580
28:23 shall find more f than he that flattereth H2580
29:26 Many seek the ruler's f; but *every* man's H6440
31:30 F *is* deceitful, and beauty *is* vain: *but* a H2580
Ecc 9:11 nor yet f to men of skill; but time H2580
Song 8:10 was I in his eyes as one that found f. H7965
Isa 26:10 Let f be shewed to the wicked, *yet* will H2603
27:11 that formed them will shew them no f. H2603
60:10 but in my f have I had mercy on thee. H7522
Jer 16:13 and night; where I will not shew you f. H2594
Dan 1: 9 Now God had brought Daniel into f H2617
Lk 1:30 Mary: for thou hast found f with God. *G5485*
2:52 stature, and in f with God and man. *G5485*
Act 2:47 Praising God, and having f with all the *G5485*
7:10 and gave him f and wisdom in the sight *G5485*
46 Who found f before God, and desired *G5485*
25: 3 And desired f against him, that he *G5485*

FAVOURABLE
Jdg 21:22 say unto them, Be f unto them for our H2603
Job 33:26 He shall pray unto God, and he will be f H7521
Ps 77: 7 off for ever? and will he be f no more? H7521
85: 1 LORD, thou hast been f unto thy land: H7521

FAVOURED
Gen 29:17 but Rachel was beautiful and well f. H4758
39: 6 Joseph was *a* goodly *person*, and well f. H4758
41: 2 river seven well f kine and fatfleshed; H4758
3 out of the river, ill f and leanfleshed; H4758
4 And the ill f and leanfleshed kine did H4758
4 well f and fat kine. So Pharaoh awoke. H4758
18 and well f; and they fed in a meadow: H8389
19 poor and very ill f and leanfleshed, H8389
20 And the lean and the ill f kine did eat H7451
21 ill f, as at the beginning. So I awoke. H4758
27 And the seven thin and ill f kine that H7451
Lam 4:16 of the priests, they f not the elders. H2603
Dan 1: 4 no blemish, but well f, and skilful in all H4758
Lk 1:28 *that art* highly f, the Lord *is* with thee: *G5487*

FAVOUREST
Ps 41:11 By this I know that thou f me, because H2654

FAVOURETH
2Sa 20:11 and said, He that f Joab, and he that *is* H2654

FEAR
Gen 9: 2 And the f of you and the dread of you H4172
15: 1 in a vision, saying, F not, Abram: I *am* H3372
20:11 Surely the f of God *is* not in this H3374
21:17 aileth thee, Hagar? f not; for God hath H3372
26:24 thy father: f not, for I *am* with thee, H3372
31:42 Abraham, and the f of Isaac, had been H6343
53 Jacob sware by the f of his father Isaac. H6343
32:11 hand of Esau: for I f him, lest he will H3373
35:17 F not; thou shalt have this son also. H3372
42:18 third day, This do, and live; *for* I f God: H3373
43:23 And he said, Peace *be* to you, f not: H3372
46: 3 God of thy father: f not to go down into H3372
50:19 And Joseph said unto them, F not: for H3372
21 Now therefore f ye not: I will nourish H3372
Ex 9:30 that ye will not yet f the LORD God. H3372
14:13 And Moses said unto the people, F ye H3372
15:16 F and dread shall fall upon them; by the H367
18:21 able men, such as f God, men of truth, H3373
20:20 And Moses said unto the people, F not: H3372
20 you, and that his f may be before your H3374
23:27 I will send my f before thee, and will H367
Lev 19: 3 Ye shall f every man his mother, and H3372
14 but shalt f thy God: I *am* the LORD. H3372
32 man, and f thy God: I *am* the LORD. H3372
25:17 f thy God: for I *am* the LORD your God. H3372
36 him, or increase: but f thy God; that thy H3372
43 him with rigour; but shalt f thy God. H3372
Nu 14: 9 the LORD, neither f ye the people of the H3372
9 and the LORD *is* with us: f them not. H3372
21:34 And the LORD said unto Moses, F him H3372
Dt 1:21 thee; f not, neither be discouraged. H3372
2:25 dread of thee and the f of thee upon the H3374

Dt 3: 2 And the LORD said unto me, F him H3372
22 Ye shall not f them: for the LORD your H3372
4:10 they may learn to f me all the days that H3372
5:29 that they would f me, and keep all my H3372
6: 2 That thou mightest f the LORD thy H3372
13 Thou shalt f the LORD thy God, and H3372
24 these statutes, to f the LORD our God, H3372
8: 6 God, to walk in his ways, and to f him. H3372
10:12 of thee, but to f the LORD thy God, to H3372
20 Thou shalt f the LORD thy God; him H3372
11:25 God shall lay the f of you and the dread H6343
13: 4 your God, and f him, and keep his H3372
11 And all Israel shall hear, and f, and H3372
14:23 learn to f the LORD thy God always. H3372
17:13 And all the people shall hear, and f, and H3372
19 he may learn to f the LORD his God, to H3372
19:20 shall hear, and f, and shall henceforth H3372
20: 3 not your hearts faint, f not, and do not H3372
21:21 you; and all Israel shall hear, and f. H3372
28:58 that thou mayest f this glorious and H3372
66 and thou shalt f day and night, and H6342
67 were morning! for the f of thine heart H6343
67 thou shalt f, and for the sight of H6342
31: 6 Be strong and of a good courage, f not, H3372
8 thee: f not, neither be dismayed. H3372
12 may learn, and f the LORD your God, H3372
13 hear, and learn to f the LORD your H3372
Jos 4:24 ye might f the LORD your God for ever. H3372
8: 1 And the LORD said unto Joshua, F not, H3372
10: 8 And the LORD said unto Joshua, F H3372
25 And Joshua said unto them, F not, nor H3372
22:24 And if we have not *rather* done it for f H1674
24:14 Now therefore f the LORD, and serve H3372
Jdg 4:18 turn in to me; f not. And when he had H3372
6:10 LORD your God; f not the gods of the H3372
23 *be* unto thee; f not: thou shalt not die. H3372
7:10 But if thou f to go down, go thou with H3373
9:21 there, for f of Abimelech his brother. H6440
Ru 3:11 And now, my daughter, f not; I will do H3372
1Sa 4:20 her said unto her, F not; for thou hast H3372
11: 7 his oxen. And the f of the LORD fell on H6343
12:14 If ye will f the LORD, and serve him, H3372
20 And Samuel said unto the people, F H3372
24 Only f the LORD, and serve him in H3372
21:10 fled that day for f of Saul, and went to H6440
22:23 Abide thou with me, f not: for he that H3372
23:17 And he said unto him, F not: for the H3372
26 to get away for f of Saul; for Saul and H6440
2Sa 9: 7 And David said unto him, F not: for I H3372
13:28 Amnon; then kill him, f not: have not I H3372
23: 3 *must be* just, ruling in the f of God. H3374
1Ki 8:40 That they may f thee all the days that H3372
43 know thy name, to f thee, as *do* thy H3372
17:13 And Elijah said unto her, F not; go *and* H3372
18:12 thy servant f the LORD from my youth. H3372
2Ki 4: 1 thy servant did f the LORD: and the H3373
6:16 And he answered, F not: for they that H3372
17:28 them how they should f the LORD. H3372
34 manners: they f not the LORD, neither H3373
35 Ye shall not f other gods, nor bow H3372
36 arm, him shall ye f, and him shall ye H3372
37 evermore; and ye shall not f other gods. H3372
38 not forget; neither shall ye f other gods. H3372
39 But the LORD your God ye shall f; and H3372
25:24 and said unto them, F not to be the H3372
1Ch 14:17 brought the f of him upon all nations. H6343
16:30 F before him, all the earth: the world H2342
28:20 good courage, and do *it:* f not, nor be H3372
2Ch 6:31 That they may f thee, to walk in thy H3372
33 know thy name, and f thee, as *doth* thy H3372
14:14 Gerar; for the f of the LORD came upon H6343
17:10 And the f of the LORD fell upon all the H6343
19: 7 Wherefore now let the f of the LORD be H6343
9 Thus shall ye do in the f of the LORD, H3374
20:17 and Jerusalem: f not, nor be dismayed; H3372
29 And the f of God was on all the H6343
Ezr 3: 3 upon his bases; for f *was* upon them H367
Neh 1:11 who desire to f thy name: and prosper, H3372
5: 9 not to walk in the f of our God because H3374
15 so did not I, because of the f of God. H3374
6:14 prophets, that would have put me in f. H3372
19 *And* Tobiah sent letters to put me in f. H3372
Est 8:17 for the f of the Jews fell upon them. H6343
9: 2 for the f of them fell upon all people. H6343
3 the f of Mordecai fell upon them. H6343
Job 1: 9 and said, Doth Job f God for nought? H3372
4: 6 *Is* not *this* thy f, thy confidence, thy H3374
14 F came upon me, and trembling, which H6343
6:14 but he forsaketh the f of the Almighty. H3374

Job 9:34 from me, and let not his f terrify me: H367
35 *Then* would I speak, and not f him; but H3372
11:15 thou shalt be stedfast, and shalt not f: H3372
15: 4 Yea, thou castest off f, and restrainest H3374
21: 9 Their houses *are* safe from f, neither *is* H6343
22: 4 Will he reprove thee for f of thee? will H3374
10 thee, and sudden f troubleth thee; H6343
25: 2 Dominion and f *are* with him, he H6343
28:28 And unto man he said, Behold, the f of H3374
31:34 Did I f a great multitude, or did the H6206
37:24 Men do therefore f him: he respecteth H3372
39:16 not hers: her labour is in vain without f; H6343
22 He mocketh at f, and is not affrighted; H6343
41:33 is not his like, who is made without f. H2844
Ps 2:11 Serve the LORD with f, and rejoice with H3374
5: 7 f will I worship toward thy holy temple. H3374
9:20 Put them in f, O LORD: *that* the nations H4172
14: 5 There were they in great f: for God *is* in H6342
15: 4 them that f the LORD. *He that* H3373
19: 9 The f of the LORD *is* clean, enduring H3374
22:23 Ye that f the LORD, praise him; all ye H3373
23 him; and f him, all ye the seed of Israel. H1481
25 pay my vows before them that f him. H3373
23: 4 of death, I will f no evil: for thou *art* H3372
25:14 *is* with them that f him; and he will H3373
27: 1 whom shall I f? the LORD *is* the strength H3372
3 my heart shall not f: though war should H3372
31:11 my neighbours, and a f to mine H6343
13 For I have heard the slander of many: f H4032
19 laid up for them that f thee; *which* thou H3373
33: 8 Let all the earth f the LORD: let all the H3372
18 *is* upon them that f him, upon them H3373
34: 7 them that f him, and delivereth them. H3373
9 O f the LORD, ye his saints: for *there is* H3372
9 for *there is* no want to them that f him. H3373
11 me: I will teach you the f of the LORD. H3374
36: 1 *that there is* no f of God before his eyes. H6343
40: 3 *it*, and f, and shall trust in the LORD. H3372
46: 2 Therefore will not we f, though the H3372
48: 6 F took hold upon them there, *and* pain, H7461
49: 5 Wherefore should I f in the days of evil, H3372
52: 6 The righteous also shall see, and f, and H3372
53: 5 There were they in great f, *where* no H6342
5 fear, *where* no f was: for God hath H6343
55:19 no changes, therefore they f not God. H3372
56: 4 I will not f what flesh can do unto me. H3372
60: 4 to them that f thee, that it may be H3373
61: 5 the heritage of those that f thy name. H3373
64: 1 preserve my life from f of the enemy. H6343
4 do they shoot at him, and f not. H3372
9 And all men shall f, and shall declare H3372
66:16 Come *and* hear, all ye that f God, and I H3373
67: 7 all the ends of the earth shall f him. H3372
72: 5 They shall f thee as long as the sun and H3372
85: 9 Surely his salvation *is* nigh them that f H3373
86:11 thy truth: unite my heart to f thy name. H3372
90:11 even according to thy f, *so is* thy wrath. H3374
96: 9 of holiness: f before him, all the earth. H2342
102:15 So the heathen shall f the name of the H3372
103:11 is his mercy toward them that f him. H3373
13 *so* the LORD pitieth them that f him. H3373
17 upon them that f him, and his H3373
105:38 for the f of them fell upon them. H6343
111: 5 He hath given meat unto them that f H3373
10 The f of the LORD *is* the beginning of H3374
115:11 Ye that f the LORD, trust in the LORD: H3373
13 He will bless them that f the LORD, H3373
118: 4 Let them now that f the LORD say, that H3373
6 The LORD *is* on my side; I will not f: H3372
119:38 thy servant, who *is devoted* to thy f. H3374
39 Turn away my reproach which I f: for H3025
63 I *am* a companion of all *them* that f H3372
74 They that f thee will be glad when they H3373
79 Let those that f thee turn unto me, and H3373
120 My flesh trembleth for f of thee; and I H6343
135:20 ye that f the LORD, bless the LORD. H3373
145:19 He will fulfil the desire of them that f H3373
147:11 f him, in those that hope in his mercy. H3373
Prv 1: 7 The f of the LORD *is* the beginning of H3374
26 I will mock when your f cometh; H6343
27 When your f cometh as desolation, and H6343
29 and did not choose the f of the LORD: H3374
33 safely, and shall be quiet from f of evil. H6343
2: 5 Then shalt thou understand the f of the H3374
3: 7 Be not wise in thine own eyes: f the H3372
25 Be not afraid of sudden f, neither of the H6343
8:13 The f of the LORD *is* to hate evil: pride, H3374
9:10 The f of the LORD *is* the beginning of H3374
10:24 The f of the wicked, it shall come upon H4034

Prv 10:27 The f of the LORD prolongeth days: but H3374
14:26 In the f of the LORD *is* strong H3374
27 The f of the LORD *is* a fountain of life, H3374
15:16 Better *is* little with the f of the LORD H3374
33 The f of the LORD *is* the instruction of H3374
16: 6 f of the LORD *men* depart from evil. H3374
19:23 The f of the LORD *tendeth* to life: and H3374
20: 2 The f of a king *is* as the roaring of a lion: H367
22: 4 By humility *and* the f of the LORD *are* H3374
23:17 in the f of the LORD all the day long. H3374
24:21 My son, f thou the LORD and the king: H3372
29:25 The f of man bringeth a snare: but H2731
Ecc 3:14 doeth *it*, that *men* should f before him. H3372
5: 7 *are* also *divers* vanities: but f thou God. H3372
8:12 them that f God, which fear before him: H3373
12 them that fear God, which f before him: H3372
12:13 the whole matter: F God, and keep his H3372
Song 3: 8 upon his thigh because of f in the night. H6343
Isa 2:10 in the dust, for f of the LORD, and for H6343
19 of the earth, for f of the LORD, and for H6343
21 ragged rocks, for f of the LORD, and for H6343
7: 4 heed, and be quiet; f not, neither be H3372
25 come thither the f of briers and thorns: H3374
8:12 neither f ye their fear, nor be afraid. H3372
12 neither fear ye their f, nor be afraid. H4172
13 *be* your f, and *let* him *be* your dread. H4172
11: 2 of knowledge and of the f of the LORD; H3374
3 in the f of the LORD: and he H3374
14: 3 and from thy f, and from the hard H7267
19:16 it shall be afraid and f because of the H6342
21: 4 pleasure hath he turned into f unto me. H2731
24:17 F, and the pit, and the snare, *are* upon H6343
18 the noise of the f shall fall into the pit; H6343
25: 3 city of the terrible nations shall f thee. H3372
29:13 me, and their f toward me is taught H3374
23 of Jacob, and shall f the God of Israel. H6206
31: 9 to his strong hold for f, and his princes H4032
33: 6 the f of the LORD *is* his treasure. H3374
35: 4 heart, Be strong, f not: behold, your H3372
41:10 F thou not; for I *am* with thee: be not H3372
13 saying unto thee, F not; I will help thee. H3372
14 F not, thou worm Jacob, *and* ye men of H3372
43: 1 formed thee, O Israel, F not: for I have H3372
5 F not: for I *am* with thee: I will bring H3372
44: 2 *which* will help thee; F not, O Jacob, my H3372
8 F ye not, neither be afraid: have not I H6342
11 f, *and* they shall be ashamed together. H6342
51: 7 heart *is* my law; f ye not the reproach H3372
54: 4 F not; for thou shalt not be ashamed: H3372
14 for thou shalt not f: and from terror; for H3372
59:19 So shall they f the name of the LORD H3372
60: 5 and thine heart shall f, and be enlarged; H6342
63:17 our heart from thy f? Return for thy H3374
Jer 2:19 God, and that my f *is* not in thee, saith H6345
5:22 F ye not me? saith the LORD: will ye H3372
24 heart, Let us now f the LORD our God, H3372
6:25 of the enemy *and* f *is* on every side. H4032
10: 7 Who would not f thee, O King of H3372
20:10 For I heard the defaming of many, f on H4032
23: 4 them: and they shall f no more, nor be H3372
26:19 to death? did he not f the LORD, and H3373
30: 5 of trembling, of f, and not of peace. H6343
10 Therefore f thou not, O my servant H3372
32:39 that they may f me for ever, for the H3372
40 but I will put my f in their hearts, that H3374
33: 9 and they shall f and tremble for all the H6342
35:11 go to Jerusalem for f of the army of the H6440
11 and for f of the army of the Syrians: H6440
37:11 Jerusalem for f of Pharaoh's army, H6440
40: 9 to their men, saying, F not to serve the H3372
41: 9 king had made for f of Baasha king of H6440
46: 5 *for* f *was* round about, saith the LORD. H4032
27 But f not thou, O my servant Jacob, H3372
28 F thou not, O Jacob my servant, saith H3372
48:43 F, and the pit, and the snare, *shall be* H6343
44 He that fleeth from the f shall fall into H6343
49: 5 Behold, I will bring a f upon thee, saith H6343
24 herself to flee, and f hath seized on *her*: H7374
29 shall cry unto them, F *is* on every side. H4032
50:16 time of harvest: for f of the oppressing H6440
51:46 And lest your heart faint, and ye f for H3372
Lam 3:47 F and a snare is come upon us, H6343
57 I called upon thee: thou saidst, F not. H3372
Ezk 3: 9 thy forehead: f them not, neither be H3372
30:13 and I will put a f in the land of Egypt. H3374
Dan 1:10 said unto Daniel, I f my lord the king, H3373
6:26 men tremble and f before the God of H1763
10:12 Then said he unto me, F not, Daniel: H3372
19 And said, O man greatly beloved, f not: H3372

Hos 3: 5 king; and shall f the LORD and his H6342
10: 5 The inhabitants of Samaria shall f H1481
Joel 2:21 F not, O land; be glad and rejoice: for H3372
Am 3: 8 The lion hath roared, who will not f? the H3372
Jna 1: 9 an Hebrew; and I f the LORD, the God H3373
Mic 7:17 our God, and shall f because of thee. H3372
Zep 3: 7 I said, Surely thou wilt f me, thou wilt H3372
16 be said to Jerusalem, F thou not: *and to* H3372
Hag 1:12 and the people did f before the LORD. H3372
2: 5 spirit remaineth among you: f ye not. H3372
Zec 8:13 f not, *but* let your hands be strong. H3372
15 and to the house of Judah: f ye not. H3372
9: 5 Ashkelon shall see *it*, and f; Gaza also H3372
Mal 1: 6 where *is* my f? saith the LORD of hosts H4172
2: 5 to him *for* the f wherewith he feared H4172
3: 5 and f not me, saith the LORD of hosts. H3372
4: 2 But unto you that f my name shall the H3373
Mt 1:20 thou son of David, f not to take unto G5399
10:26 F them not therefore: for there is G5399
28 And f not them which kill the body, but G5399
28 soul: but rather f him which is able to G5399
31 F ye not therefore, ye are of more value G5399
14:26 It is a spirit; and they cried out for f. G5401
21:26 But if we shall say, Of men; we f the G5399
28: 4 And for f of him the keepers did shake, G5401
5 unto the women, F not ye: for I know G5399
8 the sepulchre with f and great joy; and G5401
Lk 1:12 he was troubled, and f fell upon him. G5401
13 But the angel said unto him, F not, G5399
30 And the angel said unto her, F not, G5399
50 And his mercy *is* on them that f him G5399
65 And f came on all that dwelt round G5401
74 our enemies might serve him without f, G870
2:10 And the angel said unto them, F not: G5399
5:10 Jesus said unto Simon, F not; from G5399
26 were filled with f, saying, We have seen G5401
7:16 And there came a f on all: and they G5401
8:37 taken with great f: and he went up into G5401
50 him, saying, F not: believe only, and G5399
12: 5 But I will forewarn you whom ye shall f: G5399
5 ye shall fear: F him, which after he G5399
5 into hell; yea, I say unto you, F him. G5399
7 are all numbered. F not therefore: ye G5399
32 F not, little flock; for it is your Father's G5399
18: 4 Though I f not God, nor regard man; G5399
21:26 Men's hearts failing them for f, and for G5401
23:40 Dost not thou f God, seeing thou art G5399
Jn 7:13 spake openly of him for f of the Jews. G5401
12:15 F not, daughter of Sion: behold, thy G5399
19:38 but secretly for f of the Jews, besought G5401
20:19 assembled for f of the Jews, came Jesus G5401
Act 2:43 And f came upon every soul: and many G5401
5: 5 the ghost: and great f came on all them G5401
11 And great f came upon all the church, G5401
9:31 and walking in the f of the Lord, and in G5401
13:16 Israel, and ye that f God, give audience. G5399
19:17 at Ephesus; and f fell on them all, and G5401
27:24 Saying, F not, Paul; thou must be G5399
Ro 3:18 There is no f of God before their eyes. G5401
8:15 of bondage again to f; but ye have G5401
11:20 by faith. Be not highminded, but f: G5399
13: 7 to whom custom; f to whom fear; G5401
7 to whom f; honour to whom honour. G5401
1Co 2: 3 and in f, and in much trembling. G5401
16:10 be with you without f: for he worketh the G870
2Co 7: 1 perfecting holiness in the f of God. G5401
11 yea, *what* f, yea, *what* vehement G5401
15 with f and trembling ye received him. G5401
11: 3 But I f, lest by any means, as the G5399
12:20 For I f, lest, when I come, I shall not G5399
Eph 5:21 one to another in the f of God. G5401
6: 5 to the flesh, with f and trembling, in G5401
Php 1:14 more bold to speak the word without f. G870
2:12 own salvation with f and trembling. G5401
1Ti 5:20 before all, that others also may f. G5401
2Ti 1: 7 For God hath not given us the spirit of f; G1167
Heb 2:15 And deliver them who through f of G5401
4: 1 Let us therefore f, lest, a promise being G5399
11: 7 as yet, moved with f, prepared an ark to G2125
12:21 Moses said, I exceedingly f and quake:) G1630
28 acceptably with reverence and godly f: G2124
13: 6 I will not f what man shall do unto me. G5399
1Pt 1:17 the time of your sojourning *here* in f: G5401
2:17 brotherhood. F God. Honour the king. G5399
18 masters with all f; not only to the good G5401
3: 2 chaste conversation *coupled* with f. G5401
15 that is in you with meekness and f: G5401
1Jn 4:18 There is no f in love; but perfect love G5401
18 love casteth out f: because fear hath G5401
1Jn 4:18 out fear: because f hath torment. He G5401
Jude 12 themselves without f: clouds *they are* G870
23 And others save with f, pulling *them* G5401
Rev 1:17 me, F not; I am the first and the last: G5399
2:10 F none of those things which thou shalt G5399
11:11 great f fell upon them which saw them. G5401
18 and them that f thy name, small and G5399
14: 7 Saying with a loud voice, F God, and G5399
15: 4 Who shall not f thee, O Lord, and G5399
18:10 Standing afar off for the f of her G5401
15 f of her torment, weeping and wailing, G5401
19: 5 ye that f him, both small and great. G5399

FEARED
Gen 19:30 with him; for he f to dwell in Zoar: and H3372
26: 7 *is* my sister: for he f to say, *She is* my H3372
Ex 1:17 But the midwives f God, and did not as H3372
21 f God, that he made them houses. H3372
2:14 f, and said, Surely this thing is known. H3372
9:20 He that f the word of the LORD among H3373
14:31 and the people f the LORD, and H3372
Dt 25:18 *wast* faint and weary; and he f not God. H3373
32:17 newly up, whom your fathers f not. H8175
27 Were it not that I f the wrath of the H1481
Jos 4:14 all Israel; and they f him, as they feared H3372
14 as they f Moses, all the days of his life. H3372
10: 2 That they f greatly, because Gibeon H3372
Jdg 6:27 *so* it was, because he f his father's H3372
8:20 for he f, because he *was* yet a youth. H3372
1Sa 3:15 And Samuel f to shew Eli the vision. H3372
12:18 people greatly f the LORD and Samuel. H3372
14:26 to his mouth: for the people f the oath. H3372
15:24 I f the people, and obeyed their voice. H3372
2Sa 3:11 Abner a word again, because he f him. H3372
10:19 So the Syrians f to help the children H3372
12:18 servants of David f to tell him that the H3372
1Ki 1:50 And Adonijah f because of Solomon, H3372
3:28 judged; and they f the king: for they H3372
18: 3 (Now Obadiah f the LORD greatly: H3373
2Ki 17: 7 king of Egypt, and had f other gods, H3372
25 there, *that* they f not the LORD: H3372
32 So they f the LORD, and made unto H3373
33 They f the LORD, and served their own H3373
41 So these nations f the LORD, and H3373
1Ch 16:25 he also *is* to be f above all gods. H3372
2Ch 20: 3 And Jehoshaphat f, and set himself to H3372
Neh 7: 2 a faithful man, and f God above many. H3372
Job 1: 1 and one that f God, and eschewed evil. H3373
3:25 For the thing which I greatly f is come H6342
Ps 76: 7 Thou, *even* thou, *art* to be f: and who H3372
8 from heaven; the earth f, and was still, H3372
11 presents unto him that ought to be f. H4172
78:53 on safely, so that they f not: but the sea H6342
89: 7 God is greatly to be f in the assembly of H6206
96: 4 be praised: he *is* to be f above all gods. H3372
130: 4 with thee, that thou mayest be f. H3372
Isa 41: 5 The isles saw *it*, and f; the ends of the H3372
51:13 earth; and hast f continually every day H6342
57:11 been afraid or f, that thou hast lied, H3372
Jer 3: 8 sister Judah f not, but went and played H3372
42:16 sword, which ye f, shall overtake you H3373
44:10 neither have they f, nor walked in my H3372
Ezk 11: 8 Ye have f the sword; and I will bring a H3372
Dan 5:19 trembled and f before him: whom he H1763
Hos 10: 3 king, because we f not the LORD; what H3372
Jna 1:16 Then the men f the LORD exceedingly, H3372
Mal 2: 5 f me, and was afraid before my name. H3372
3:16 Then they that f the LORD spake often H3373
16 him for them that f the LORD, and that H3373
Mt 14: 5 put him to death, he f the multitude, G5399
21:46 on him, they f the multitude, because G5399
27:54 were done, they f greatly, saying, Truly G5399
Mk 4:41 And they f exceedingly, and said one to G5399
6:20 For Herod f John, knowing that he was G5399
11:18 him: for they f him, because all the G5399
32 But if we shall say, Of men; they f the G5399
12:12 hold on him, but f the people: for they G5399
Lk 9:34 they f as they entered into the cloud. G5399
45 and they f to ask him of that saying. G5399
18: 2 f not God, neither regarded man: G5399
19:21 For I f thee, because thou art an G5399
20:19 on him; and they f the people: for they G5399
22: 2 might kill him; for they f the people. G5399
Jn 9:22 because they f the Jews: for the Jews G5399
Act 5:26 violence: for they f the people, lest they G5399
10: 2 *A* devout *man*, and one that f God with G5399
16:38 and they f, when they heard that G5399
Heb 5: 7 from death, and was heard in that he f; G575

FEAREST
Gen 22:12 I know that thou f God, seeing thou H3373
Isa 57:11 peace even of old, and thou f me not? H3372
Jer 22:25 whose face thou f, even into the hand of H3016

FEARETH
1Ki 1:51 Behold, Adonijah f king Solomon: for, H3372
Job 1: 8 one that f God, and escheweth evil? H3373
2: 3 man, one that f God, and escheweth H3373
Ps 25:12 What man *is* he that f the LORD? him H3373
112: 1 *is* the man *that* f the LORD, *that* H3372
128: 1 Blessed *is* every one that f the LORD; H3373
4 the man be blessed that f the LORD. H3373
Prv 13:13 f the commandment shall be rewarded. H3373
14: 2 He that walketh in his uprightness f the H3373
16 A wise *man* f, and departeth from evil: H3373
28:14 Happy *is* the man that f alway: but he H6342
31:30 *that* f the LORD, she shall be praised. H3373
Ecc 7:18 that f God shall come forth of them all. H3373
8:13 a shadow; because he f not before God. H3373
9: 2 he that sweareth, as *he* that f an oath. H3373
Isa 50:10 Who *is* among you that f the LORD, H3373
Act 10:22 man, and one that f God, and of good G5399
35 But in every nation he that f him, and G5399
13:26 among you f God, to you is the word G5399
1Jn 4:18 He that f is not made perfect in love. G5399

FEARFUL
Ex 15:11 holiness, f *in* praises, doing wonders? H3372
Dt 20: 8 *is there that is* f and fainthearted? let H3373
28:58 and f name, THE LORD THY GOD; H3372
Jdg 7: 3 Whosoever *is* f and afraid, let him H3373
Isa 35: 4 Say to them *that are* of a f heart, Be H4116
Mt 8:26 And he saith unto them, Why are ye f, O G1169
Mk 4:40 And he said unto them, Why are ye so f? G1169
Lk 21:11 and pestilences; and f sights and great G5400
Heb 10:27 But a certain f looking for of judgment G5398
31 *It is* a f thing to fall into the hands of G5398
Rev 21: 8 But the f, and unbelieving, and the G1169

FEARFULLY
Ps 139:14 I will praise thee; for I am f *and* H3372

FEARFULNESS
Ps 55: 5 F and trembling are come upon me, H3374
Isa 21: 4 My heart panted, f affrighted me: the H6427
33:14 The sinners in Zion are afraid; f hath H7461

FEARING
Jos 22:25 our children cease from f the LORD: H3372
Mk 5:33 But the woman f and trembling, G5399
Act 23:10 the chief captain, f lest Paul should G2125
27:17 the ship; and, f lest they should fall G5399
29 Then f lest we should have fallen upon G5399
Gal 2:12 f them which were of the circumcision. G5399
Col 3:22 but in singleness of heart, f God: G5399
Heb 11:27 By faith he forsook Egypt, not f the G5399

FEARS
Ps 34: 4 me, and delivered me from all my f. H4035
Ecc 12: 5 *which is* high, and f *shall be* in the way, H2849
Isa 66: 4 will bring their f upon them; because H4035
2Co 7: 5 without *were* fightings, within *were* f. G5401

FEAST
Gen 19: 3 and he made them a f, and did bake H4960
21: 8 f the *same* day that Isaac was weaned. H4960
26:30 And he made them a f, and they did eat H4960
29:22 all the men of the place, and made a f. H4960
40:20 that he made a f unto all his servants: H4960
Ex 5: 1 may hold a f unto me in the wilderness. H2287
10: 9 for we *must hold* a f unto the LORD. H2282
12:14 and ye shall keep it a f to the LORD H2282
14 keep it a f by an ordinance for ever. H2287
17 And ye shall observe *the* f *of* unleavened
13: 6 seventh day *shall be* a f to the LORD. H2282
23:14 Three times thou shalt keep a f unto H2287
15 Thou shalt keep the f of unleavened H2282
16 And the f of harvest, the firstfruits of H2282
16 in the field: and the f of ingathering, H2282
32: 5 said, To morrow *is* a f to the LORD. H2282
34:18 The f of unleavened bread shalt thou H2282
22 And thou shalt observe the f of weeks, H2282
22 the f of ingathering at the year's end. H2282
25 the sacrifice of the f of the passover be H2282
Lev 23: 6 the same month *is* the f of unleavened H2282
34 month *shall be* the f of tabernacles *for* H2282
39 ye shall keep a f unto the LORD seven H2282
41 And ye shall keep it a f unto the LORD H2282

Nu 28:17 of this month *is* the f: seven days shall H2282
29:12 keep a f unto the LORD seven days: H2282
Dt 16:10 And thou shalt keep the f of weeks unto H2282
13 Thou shalt observe the f of tabernacles H2282
14 And thou shalt rejoice in thy f, thou, H2282
15 Seven days shalt thou keep a solemn f H2287
16 choose; in the f of unleavened bread, H2282
16 bread, and in the f of weeks, and in the H2282
16 weeks, and in the f of tabernacles: and H2282
31:10 year of release, in the f of tabernacles, H2282
Jdg 14:10 a f; for so used the young men to do. H4960
12 seven days of the f, and find *it* out, then H4960
17 days, while their f lasted: and it came H4960
21:19 Then they said, Behold, *there is* a f of H2282
1Sa 25:36 behold, he held a f in his house, like the H4960
36 in his house, like the f of a king; and H4960
2Sa 3:20 and the men that *were* with him a f. H4960
1Ki 3:15 and made a f to all his servants. H4960
8: 2 king Solomon at the f in the month H2282
65 And at that time Solomon held a f, and H2282
12:32 And Jeroboam ordained a f in the H2282
32 like unto the f that *is* in Judah, and H2282
33 and ordained a f unto the children of H2282
2Ch 5: 3 the f which *was* in the seventh month. H2282
7: 8 Solomon kept the f seven days, and all H2282
9 altar seven days, and the f seven days. H2282
8:13 year, *even* in the f of unleavened bread, H2282
13 bread, and in the f of weeks, and in the H2282
13 of weeks, and in the f of tabernacles. H2282
30:13 people to keep the f of unleavened H2282
21 at Jerusalem kept the f of unleavened H2282
22 did eat throughout the f seven days, H4150
35:17 the f of unleavened bread seven days. H2282
Ezr 3: 4 They kept also the f of tabernacles, as *it* H2282
6:22 And kept the f of unleavened bread H2282
Neh 8:14 in booths in the f of the seventh month: H2282
18 And they kept the f seven days; and on H2282
Est 1: 3 reign, he made a f unto all his princes H4960
5 the king made a f unto all the people H4960
9 Also Vashti the queen made a f for the H4960
2:18 Then the king made a great f unto all H4960
18 *even* Esther's f; and he made a release H4960
8:17 and gladness, a f and a good day. And H4960
Ps 81: 3 time appointed, on our solemn f day. H2282
Prv 15:15 is of a merry heart *hath* a continual f. H4960
Ecc 10:19 A f is made for laughter, and wine H3899
Isa 25: 6 unto all people a f of fat things, a feast H4960
6 of fat things, a f of wines on the lees, H4960
Lam 2: 7 the LORD, as in the day of a solemn f. H4150
Ezk 45:21 have the passover, a f of seven days; H2282
23 And seven days of the f he shall H2282
25 he do the like in the f of the seven days, H2282
Dan 5: 1 Belshazzar the king made a great f to a H3900
Hos 2:11 her mirth to cease, her f days, her new H2282
9: 5 and in the day of the f of the LORD? H2282
12: 9 as in the days of the solemn f. H4150
Am 5:21 I hate, I despise your f days, and I will H2282
Zec 14:16 hosts, and to keep the f of tabernacles. H2282
18 not up to keep the f of tabernacles. H2282
19 not up to keep the f of tabernacles. H2282
Mt 26: 2 Ye know that after two days is *the f of*
5 But they said, Not on the f *day*, lest G1859
17 Now the first *day* of the *f of* unleavened
27:15 Now at *that* f the governor was wont to G1859
Mk 14: 1 After two days was *the f of* the passover,
2 But they said, Not on the f *day*, lest G1859
15: 6 Now at *that* f he released unto them G1859
Lk 2:41 every year at the f of the passover. G1859
42 to Jerusalem after the custom of the f. G1859
5:29 And Levi made him a great f in his own G1403
14:13 But when thou makest a f, call the poor, G1403
22: 1 Now the f of unleavened bread drew G1859
23:17 he must release one unto them at the f.) G1859
Jn 2: 8 the governor of the f. And they bare *it*. G755
9 When the ruler of the f had tasted the G755
9 governor of the f called the bridegroom, G755
23 passover, in the f *day*, many believed G1859
4:45 the f: for they also went unto the feast. G1859
45 the feast: for they also went unto the f. G1859
5: 1 After this there was a f of the Jews; and G1859
6: 4 And the passover, a f of the Jews, was G1859
7: 2 Now the Jews' f of tabernacles was at G1859
8 Go ye up unto this f: I go not up yet unto G1859
8 this f; for my time is not yet full come. G1859
10 f, not openly, but as it were in secret. G1859
11 Then the Jews sought him at the f, and G1859
14 Now about the midst of the f Jesus G1859
37 In the last day, that great *day* of the f, G1859
10:22 And it was at Jerusalem the f of the G1456
Jn 11:56 think ye, that he will not come to the f? G1859
12:12 were come to the f, when they heard G1859
20 them that came up to worship at the f: G1859
13: 1 Now before the f of the passover, when G1859
29 of against the f; or, that he should give G1859
Act 18:21 all means keep this f that cometh in G1859
1Co 5: 8 Therefore let us keep the f, not with old G1858
10:27 not bid you *to a f*, and ye be disposed to
2Pt 2:13 own deceivings while they f with you; G4910
Jude 12 charity, when they f with you, feeding G4910

FEAST-DAY See FEAST and DAY.

FEASTED
Job 1: 4 And his sons went and f *in* H4960+H6213

FEASTING
Est 9:17 and made it a day of f and gladness. H4960
18 and made it a day of f and gladness. H4960
19 *of* gladness and f, and a good day, and H4960
22 them days of f and joy, and of sending H4960
Job 1: 5 And it was so, when the days of *their* f H4960
Ecc 7: 2 go to the house of f: for that *is* the end H4960
Jer 16: 8 of f, to sit with them to eat and to drink. H4960

FEASTS
Lev 23: 2 *Concerning* the f of the LORD, which H4150
2 holy convocations, *even* these *are* my f. H4150
4 These *are* the f of the LORD, *even* holy H4150
37 These *are* the f of the LORD, which ye H4150
44 the children of Israel the f of the LORD. H4150
Nu 15: 3 or in your solemn f, to make a sweet H4150
29:39 LORD in your set f, beside your vows, H4150
1Ch 23:31 and on the set f, by number, according H4150
2Ch 2: 4 and on the solemn f of the LORD our H4150
8:13 and on the solemn f, three times in the H4150
31: 3 f, as *it is* written in the law of the LORD. H4150
Ezr 3: 5 and of all the set f of the LORD that H4150
Neh 10:33 moons, for the set f, and for the holy H4150
Ps 35:16 With hypocritical mockers in f, they H4580
Isa 1:14 Your new moons and your appointed f H4150
5:12 wine, are in their f: but they regard not H4960
Jer 51:39 In their heat I will make their f, and I H4960
Lam 1: 4 come to the solemn f: all her gates are H4150
2: 6 caused the solemn f and sabbaths to be H4150
Ezk 36:38 in her solemn f; so shall the waste cities H4150
45:17 drink offerings, in the f, and in the new H2282
46: 9 in the solemn f, he that entereth in by H4150
11 And in the f and in the solemnities the H2282
Hos 2:11 and her sabbaths, and all her solemn f. H4150
Am 8:10 And I will turn your f into mourning, H2282
Nah 1:15 keep thy solemn f, perform thy vows: H2282
Zec 8:19 f; therefore love the truth and peace. H4150
Mal 2: 3 f; and *one* shall take you away with it. H2282
Mt 23: 6 And love the uppermost rooms at f, and G1173
Mk 12:39 and the uppermost rooms at f: G1173
Lk 20:46 synagogues, and the chief rooms at f; G1173
Jude 12 These are spots in your f of charity,

FEATHERED
Ps 78:27 and f fowls like as the sand of the sea: H3671
Ezk 39:17 Speak unto every f fowl, and to every H3671

FEATHERS
Lev 1:16 his crop with his f, and cast it beside the H5133
Job 39:13 or wings and f unto the ostrich? H2624
Ps 68:13 with silver, and her f with yellow gold. H84
91: 4 He shall cover thee with his f, and under H84
Ezk 17: 3 longwinged, full of f, which had divers H5133
7 wings and many f: and, behold, this H5133
Dan 4:33 eagles' *f*, and his nails like birds' *claws*.

FED
Gen 30:36 and Jacob f the rest of Laban's flocks. H7462
36:24 as he f the asses of Zibeon his father. H7462
41: 2 and fatfleshed; and they f in a meadow. H7462
18 well favoured; and they f in a meadow: H7462
47:17 the asses: and he f them with bread for H5095
48:15 f me all my life long unto this day, H7462
Ex 16:32 wherewith I have f you in the wilderness, H398
Dt 8: 3 thee to hunger, and f thee with manna, H398
16 Who f thee in the wilderness with H398
2Sa 20: 3 them in ward, and f them, but went not H3557
1Ki 18: 4 and f them with bread and water.) H3557
13 cave, and f them with bread and water? H3557
1Ch 27:29 And over the herds that f in Sharon H7462
Ps 37: 3 in the land, and verily thou shalt be f. H7462
78:72 So he f them according to the integrity H7462
81:16 He should have f them also with the H398
Isa 1:11 and the fat of f beasts; and I delight H4806
Jer 5: 7 gods: when I had f them to the full, they
8 They were *as* f horses in the morning: H2109
Ezk 16:19 and honey, *wherewith* I f thee, thou hast H398
34: 3 that are f: *but* ye feed not the flock. H1277
8 f themselves, and fed not my flock; H7462
8 fed themselves, and f not my flock; H7462
Dan 4:12 boughs thereof, and all flesh was f of it. H2110
5:21 wild asses: they f him with grass like H2939
Zec 11: 7 other I called Bands; and I f the flock. H7462
Mt 25:37 f *thee*? or thirsty, and gave *thee* drink? G5142
Mk 5:14 And they that f the swine fled, and told G1006
Lk 8:34 When they that f *them* saw what was G1006
16:21 And desiring to be f with the crumbs G5526
1Co 3: 2 I have f you with milk, and not with G4222

FEEBLE
Gen 30:42 But when the cattle were f, he put *them* H5848
Dt 25:18 *even* all *that were* f behind thee, when H2826
1Sa 2: 5 she that hath many children is waxed f. H535
2Sa 4: 1 f, and all the Israelites were troubled. H7503
2Ch 28:15 and carried all the f of them upon H3782
Neh 4: 2 What do these f Jews? will they fortify H537
Job 4: 4 and thou hast strengthened the f knees. H3766
Ps 38: 8 I am f and sore broken: I have roared H6313
105:37 not one f *person* among their tribes. H3782
Prv 30:26 The conies *are but* a f folk, yet H3808+H6099
Isa 16:14 *shall be* very small *and* f. H3808+H3524
35: 3 weak hands, and confirm the f knees. H3782
Jer 6:24 our hands wax f: anguish hath taken H7503
49:24 Damascus is waxed f, *and* turneth H7503
50:43 his hands waxed f: anguish took hold of H7503
Ezk 7:17 All hands shall be f, and all knees shall H7503
21: 7 and all hands shall be f, and every spirit H7503
Zec 12: 8 and he that is f among them at that H3782
1Co 12:22 which seem to be more f, are necessary: G772
Heb 12:12 which hang down, and the f knees; G3886

FEEBLEMINDED
1Th 5:14 comfort the f, support the weak, be G3642

FEEBLENESS
Jer 47: 3 back to *their* children for f of hands; H7510

FEEBLER
Gen 30:42 *them* not in: so the f were Laban's, and H5848

FEED
Gen 25:30 And Esau said to Jacob, F me, I pray H3938
29: 7 water ye the sheep, and go *and* f *them*. H7462
30:31 me, I will again f *and* keep thy flock: H7462
37:12 And his brethren went to f their H7462
13 Do not thy brethren f *the flock* in H7462
16 I pray thee, where they f *their flocks*. H7462
46:32 trade hath been to f cattle; and they have
Ex 22: 5 his beast, and shall f in another man's H1197
34: 3 flocks nor herds f before that mount. H7462
1Sa 17:15 to f his father's sheep at Beth-lehem. H7462
2Sa 5: 2 to thee, Thou shalt f my people Israel, H7462
7: 7 I commanded to f my people Israel, H7462
19:33 and I will f thee with me in Jerusalem. H3557
1Ki 17: 4 commanded the ravens to f thee there. H3557
22:27 in the prison, and f him with bread of H398
1Ch 11: 2 thee, Thou shalt f my people Israel, H7462
17: 6 I commanded to f my people, saying, H7462
2Ch 18:26 in the prison, and f him with bread of H398
Job 24: 2 take away flocks, and f *thereof*. H7462
20 the worm shall f sweetly on him; he shall
Ps 28: 9 f them also, and lift them up for ever. H7462
49:14 grave; death shall f on them; and the H7462
78:71 he brought him to f Jacob his people, H7462
Prv 10:21 The lips of the righteous f many: but H7462
30: 8 f me with food convenient for me: H2963
Song 1: 8 f thy kids beside the shepherds' tents. H7462
4: 5 that are twins, which f among the lilies. H7462
6: 2 to f in the gardens, and to gather lilies. H7462
Isa 5:17 Then shall the lambs f after their H7462
11: 7 And the cow and the bear shall f; their H7462
14:30 And the firstborn of the poor shall f, H7462
27:10 there shall the calf f, and there shall he H7462
30:23 day shall thy cattle f in large pastures. H7462
40:11 He shall f his flock like a shepherd: he H7462
49: 9 They shall f in the ways, and their H7462
26 And I will f them that oppress thee with H398
58:14 of the earth, and f thee with the heritage H398
61: 5 And strangers shall stand and f your H7462
65:25 The wolf and the lamb shall f together, H7462
Jer 3:15 mine heart, which shall f you with H7462
6: 3 they shall f every one in his place. H7462

Jer 9:15 Behold, I will f them, *even* this people, H398
23: 2 the pastors that f my people; Ye have H7462
4 them which shall f them: and they shall H7462
15 Behold, I will f them with wormwood, H398
50:19 and he shall f on Carmel and Bashan, H7462
Lam 4: 5 They that did f delicately are desolate in H398
Ezk 34: 2 of Israel that do f themselves! should H7462
2 should not the shepherds f the flocks? H7462
3 them that are fed: *but* ye f not the flock. H7462
10 the shepherds f themselves any more; H7462
13 their own land, and f them upon the H7462
14 I will f them in a good pasture, and H7462
14 they f upon the mountains of Israel. H7462
15 I will f my flock, and I will cause them H7462
16 the strong; I will f them with judgment. H7462
23 them, and he shall f them, *even* my H7462
23 f them, and he shall be their shepherd. H7462
Dan 11:26 Yea, they that f of the portion of his H398
Hos 4:16 will f them as a lamb in a large place. H7462
9: 2 The floor and the winepress shall not f H7462
Jna 3: 7 thing: let them not f, nor drink water: H7462
Mic 5: 4 And he shall stand and f in the strength H7462
7:14 F thy people with thy rod, the flock of H7462
14 of Carmel: let them f *in* Bashan and H7462
Zep 2: 7 of Judah; they shall f thereupon: in the H7462
3:13 for they shall f and lie down, and none H7462
Zec 11: 4 Thus saith the LORD my God; F the H7462
7 And I will f the flock of slaughter, *even* H7462
9 Then said I, I will not f you: that that H7462
16 that is broken, nor f that that standeth H3557
Lk 15:15 he sent him into his fields to f swine. *G1006*
Jn 21:15 thee. He saith unto him, F my lambs. *G1006*
16 thee. He saith unto him, F my sheep. *G4165*
17 thee. Jesus saith unto him, F my sheep. *G1006*
Act 20:28 you overseers, to f the church of God, *G4165*
Ro 12:20 Therefore if thine enemy hunger, f him; *G5595*
1Co 13: 3 And though I bestow all my goods to f *G5595*
1Pt 5: 2 F the flock of God which is among you, *G4165*
Rev 7:17 of the throne shall f them, and shall *G4165*
12: 6 that they should f her there a thousand *G5142*

FEEDEST
Ps 80: 5 Thou f them with the bread of tears; and H398
Song 1: 7 soul loveth, where thou f, where thou H7462

FEEDETH
Prv 15:14 but the mouth of fools f on foolishness. H7462
Song 2:16 My beloved *is* mine, and I *am* his: he f H7462
6: 3 beloved *is* mine: he f among the lilies. H7462
Isa 44:20 He f on ashes: a deceived heart hath H7462
Hos 12: 1 Ephraim f on wind, and followeth after H7462
Mt 6:26 heavenly Father f them. Are ye not *G5142*
Lk 12:24 nor barn; and God f them: how much *G5142*
1Co 9: 7 thereof? or who f a flock, and eateth *G4165*

FEEDING
Gen 37: 2 years old, was f the flock with his H7462
Job 1:14 plowing, and the asses f beside them: H7462
Ezk 34:10 to cease from f the flock; neither shall H7462
Mt 8:30 off from them an herd of many swine f. *G1006*
Mk 5:11 the mountains a great herd of swine f. *G1006*
Lk 8:32 of many swine f on the mountain: and *G1006*
17: 7 a servant plowing or f cattle, will say *G4165*
Jude 12 feast with you, f themselves without *G4165*

FEEDINGPLACE
Nah 2:11 the lions, and the f of the young lions, H4829

FEEL
Gen 27:12 My father peradventure will f me, and I H4959
21 pray thee, that I may f thee, my son, H4184
Jdg 16:26 me that I may f the pillars whereupon H4184
Job 20:20 Surely he shall not f quietness in his H3045
Ps 58: 9 Before your pots can f the thorns, he H995
Ecc 8: 5 shall f no evil thing: and a H3045
Act 17:27 haply they might f after him, and find *G5584*

FEELING
Eph 4:19 Who being past f have given themselves *G524*
Heb 4:15 be touched with the f of our infirmities; *G4834*

FEET
Gen 18: 4 f, and rest yourselves under the tree: H7272
19: 2 and wash your f, and ye shall rise up H7272
24:32 water to wash his f, and the men's feet H7272
32 and the men's f that *were* with him. H7272
43:24 f; and he gave their asses provender. H7272
49:10 from between his f, until Shiloh come; H7272
33 he gathered up his f into the bed, and H7272
Ex 3: 5 thy shoes from off thy f, for the place H7272
4:25 and cast *it* at his f, and said, Surely a H7272
12:11 shoes on your f, and your staff in your H7272
24:10 *was* under his f as it were a paved work H7272
25:26 corners that *are* on the four f thereof. H7272
30:19 wash their hands and their f thereat: H7272
21 hands and their f, that they die not: and H7272
37:13 corners that *were* in the four f thereof. H7272
40:31 washed their hands and their f thereat: H7272
Lev 8:24 great toes of their right f: and Moses H7272
11:21 their f, to leap withal upon the earth; H7272
23 f, *shall be* an abomination unto you. H7272
42 hath more f among all creeping H7272
Nu 20:19 any thing *else*, go through on my f. H7272
Dt 2:28 drink: only I will pass through on my f; H7272
11:24 Every place whereon the soles of your f H7272
28:57 out from between her f, and toward her H7272
33: 3 f; *every one* shall receive of thy words. H7272
Jos 3:13 as the soles of the f of the priests that H7272
15 Jordan, and the f of the priests that H7272
4: 3 where the priests' f stood firm, twelve H7272
9 place where the f of the priests which H7272
18 of the priests' f were lifted up unto H7272
9: 5 And old shoes and clouted upon their f, H7272
10:24 near, put your f upon the necks of these H7272
24 and put their f upon the necks of them. H7272
14: 9 land whereon thy f have trodden shall H7272
Jdg 3:24 covereth his f in his summer chamber. H7272
4:10 at his f: and Deborah went up with him. H7272
15 off *his* chariot, and fled away on his f. H7272
17 Howbeit Sisera fled away on his f to the H7272
5:27 At her f he bowed, he fell, he lay down: H7272
27 he lay down: at her f he bowed, he fell: H7272
19:21 washed their f, and did eat and drink. H7272
Ru 3: 4 and uncover his f, and lay thee down; H4772
7 and uncovered his f, and laid her down. H4772
8 and, behold, a woman lay at his f. H4772
14 And she lay at his f until the morning: H4772
1Sa 2: 9 He will keep the f of his saints, and the H7272
14:13 and upon his f, and his armourbearer H7272
24: 3 in to cover his f: and David and his men H7272
25:24 And fell at his f, and said, Upon me, my H7272
41 to wash the f of the servants of my lord. H7272
2Sa 3:34 Thy hands *were* not bound, nor thy f H7272
4: 4 *was* lame of *his* f. He was five years old H7272
12 hands and their f, and hanged *them* up H7272
9: 3 hath yet a son, *which is* lame on *his* f. H7272
13 king's table; and was lame on both his f. H7272
11: 8 and wash thy f. And Uriah departed H7272
19:24 dressed his f, nor trimmed his beard, H7272
22:10 down; and darkness *was* under his f. H7272
34 He maketh my f like hinds' *feet*: and H7272
34 He maketh my feet like hinds' *f*: and H7272
37 under me; so that my f did not slip. H7166
39 arise: yea, they are fallen under my f. H7272
1Ki 2: 5 and in his shoes that *were* on his f. H7272
5: 3 LORD put them under the soles of his f. H7272
14: 6 the sound of her f, as she came in at the H7272
12 f enter into the city, the child shall die. H7272
15:23 of his old age he was diseased in his f. H7272
2Ki 4:27 caught him by the f: but Gehazi came H7272
37 Then she went in, and fell at his f, and H7272
6:32 the sound of his master's f behind him? H7272
9:35 and the f, and the palms of *her* hands. H7272
13:21 he revived, and stood up on his f. H7272
19:24 with the sole of my f have I dried up all H6471
21: 8 Neither will I make the f of Israel move H7272
1Ch 28: 2 stood up upon his f, and said, Hear me, H7272
2Ch 3:13 on their f, and their faces *were* inward. H7272
16:12 diseased in his f, until his disease *was* H7272
Neh 9:21 waxed not old, and their f swelled not. H7272
Est 8: 3 fell down at his f, and besought him H7272
Job 12: 5 He that is ready to slip with *his* f *is as* a H7272
13:27 Thou puttest my f also in the stocks, H7272
27 settest a print upon the heels of my f. H7272
18: 8 For he is cast into a net by his own f, H7272
11 every side, and shall drive him to his f. H7272
29:15 I was eyes to the blind, and f *was* I to H7272
30:12 they push away my f, and they raise up H7272
33:11 He putteth my f in the stocks, he H7272
Ps 8: 6 thou hast put all *things* under his f: H7272
18: 9 down: and darkness *was* under his f. H7272
33 He maketh my f like hinds' *feet*, and H7272
33 He maketh my feet like hinds' *f*, and H7272
36 steps under me, that my f did not slip. H7166
38 able to rise: they are fallen under my f. H7272
22:16 me: they pierced my hands and my f. H7272
25:15 for he shall pluck my f out of the net. H7272
31: 8 thou hast set my f in a large room. H7272
Ps 40: 2 clay, and set my f upon a rock, *and* H7272
47: 3 under us, and the nations under our f. H7272
56:13 *thou deliver* my f from falling, that I H7272
58:10 wash his f in the blood of the wicked. H6471
66: 9 and suffereth not our f to be moved. H7272
73: 2 But as for me, my f were almost gone; H7272
74: 3 Lift up thy f unto the perpetual H6471
91:13 the dragon shalt thou trample under f. H7429
105:18 Whose f they hurt with fetters: he was H7272
115: 7 they handle not: f have they, but they H7272
116: 8 eyes from tears, *and* my f from falling. H7272
119:59 I thought on my ways, and turned my f H7272
101 I have refrained my f from every evil H7272
105 Thy word *is* a lamp unto my f, and a H7272
122: 2 Our f shall stand within thy gates, O H7272
Prv 1:16 For their f run to evil, and make haste H7272
4:26 Ponder the path of thy f, and let all thy H7272
5: 5 Her f go down to death; her steps take H7272
6:13 with his f, he teacheth with his fingers; H7272
18 f that be swift in running to mischief, H7272
28 Can one go upon hot coals, and his f H7272
7:11 (She *is* loud and stubborn; her f abide H7272
19: 2 and he that hasteth with *his* f sinneth. H7272
26: 6 cutteth off the f, *and* drinketh damage. H7272
29: 5 his neighbour spreadeth a net for his f. H6471
Song 5: 3 washed my f; how shall I defile them? H7272
7: 1 How beautiful are thy f with shoes, O H6471
Isa 3:16 go, and making a tinkling with their f: H7272
18 *about their f*, and *their* cauls, and
6: 2 covered his f, and with twain he did fly. H7272
7:20 f: and it shall also consume the beard. H7272
14:19 of the pit; as a carcase trodden under f. H947
23: 7 f shall carry her afar off to sojourn. H7272
26: 6 The foot shall tread it down, *even* the f H7272
28: 3 of Ephraim, shall be trodden under f: H7272
32:20 forth *thither* the f of the ox and the ass. H7272
37:25 with the sole of my f have I dried up all H6471
41: 3 the way *that* he had not gone with his f. H7272
49:23 lick up the dust of thy f; and thou shalt H7272
52: 7 the mountains are the f of him that H7272
59: 7 Their f run to evil, and they make haste H7272
60:13 I will make the place of my f glorious. H7272
14 at the soles of thy f; and they shall call H7272
Jer 13:16 and before your f stumble upon the H7272
14:10 have not refrained their f, therefore the H7272
18:22 pit to take me, and hid snares for my f. H7272
38:22 against thee: thy f are sunk in the mire, H7272
Lam 1:13 a net for my f, he hath turned me back: H7272
3:34 To crush under his f all the prisoners of H7272
Ezk 1: 7 And their f *were* straight feet; and the H7272
7 And their feet *were* straight f; and the H7272
7 the sole of their f *was* like the sole of a H7272
2: 1 upon thy f, and I will speak unto thee. H7272
2 f, that I heard him that spake unto me. H7272
3:24 set me upon my f, and spake with me, H7272
16:25 and hast opened thy f to every one that H7272
24:17 shoes upon thy f, and cover not *thy* lips, H7272
23 shoes upon your f: ye shall not mourn H7272
25: 6 and stamped with the f, and rejoiced in H7272
32: 2 with thy f, and fouledst their rivers. H7272
34:18 down with your f the residue of your H7272
18 but ye must foul the residue with your f? H7272
19 trodden with your f; and they drink that H7272
19 that which ye have fouled with your f. H7272
37:10 upon their f, an exceeding great army. H7272
43: 7 of the soles of my f, where I will dwell in H7272
Dan 2:33 His legs of iron, his f part of iron and H7271
34 image upon his f that *were* of iron and H7271
41 And whereas thou sawest the f and H7271
42 And *as* the toes of the f *were* part of H7271
7: 4 stand upon the f as a man, and a man's H7271
7 the residue with the f of it: and it *was* H7271
19 and stamped the residue with his f; H7271
10: 6 and his arms and his f like in colour to H4772
Nah 1: 3 and the clouds *are* the dust of his f. H7272
15 Behold upon the mountains the f of H7272
Hab 3: 5 and burning coals went forth at his f. H7272
19 he will make my f like hinds' *feet*, and H7272
19 my feet like hinds' *f*, and he will make H7272
Zec 14: 4 And his f shall stand in that day upon H7272
12 stand upon their f, and their eyes shall H7272
Mal 4: 3 the soles of your f in the day that I shall H7272
Mt 7: 6 their f, and turn again and rend you. *G4228*
10:14 or city, shake off the dust of your f. *G4228*
15:30 down at Jesus' f; and he healed them: *G4228*
18: 8 or two f to be cast into everlasting fire. *G4228*
29 And his fellowservant fell down at his f, *G4228*
28: 9 held him by the f, and worshipped him. *G4228*
Mk 5:22 and when he saw him, he fell at his f, *G4228*

Mk 6:11 the dust under your f for a testimony G4228
7:25 heard of him, and came and fell at his f: G4228
9:45 than having two f to be cast into hell, G4228
Lk 1:79 to guide our f into the way of peace. G4228
7:38 And stood at his f behind *him* weeping, G4228
38 began to wash his f with tears, and did G4228
38 and kissed his f, and anointed *them* G4228
44 no water for my f: but she hath washed G4228
44 she hath washed my f with tears, and G4228
45 I came in hath not ceased to kiss my f. G4228
46 hath anointed my f with ointment. G4228
8:35 sitting at the f of Jesus, clothed, and G4228
41 fell down at Jesus' f, and besought him G4228
9: 5 your f for a testimony against them. G4228
10:39 also sat at Jesus' f, and heard his word. G4228
15:22 a ring on his hand, and shoes on *his* f: G4228
17:16 And fell down on *his* face at his f, giving G4228
24:39 Behold my hands and my f, that it is I G4228
40 he shewed them *his* hands and *his* f. G4228
Jn 11: 2 and wiped his f with her hair, whose G4228
32 she fell down at his f, saying unto him, G4228
12: 3 and anointed the f of Jesus, and wiped G4228
3 and wiped his f with her hair: and the G4228
13: 5 wash the disciples' f, and to wipe *them* G4228
6 unto him, Lord, dost thou wash my f? G4228
8 never wash my f. Jesus answered him, G4228
9 f only, but also *my* hands and *my* head. G4228
10 not save to wash *his* f, but is clean every G4228
12 So after he had washed their f, and had G4228
14 have washed your f; ye also ought to G4228
14 ye also ought to wash one another's f. G4228
20:12 the f, where the body of Jesus had lain. G4228
Act 3: 7 his f and ankle bones received strength. G939
4:35 And laid *them* down at the apostles' f: G4228
37 the money, and laid *it* at the apostles' f. G4228
5: 2 part, and laid *it* at the apostles' f. G4228
9 Lord? behold, the f of them which have G4228
10 Then fell she down straightway at his f, G4228
7:33 thy shoes from thy f: for the place where G4228
58 a young man's f, whose name was Saul. G4228
10:25 fell down at his f, and worshipped *him*. G4228
13:25 shoes of *his* f I am not worthy to loose. G4228
51 But they shook off the dust of their f G4228
14: 8 impotent in his f, being a cripple from G4228
10 on thy f. And he leaped and walked. G4228
16:24 and made their f fast in the stocks. G4228
21:11 own hands and f, and said, Thus saith G4228
22: 3 up in this city at the f of Gamaliel, *and* G4228
26:16 But rise, and stand upon thy f: for I G4228
Ro 3:15 Their f *are* swift to shed blood: G4228
10:15 beautiful are the f of them that preach G4228
16:20 Satan under your f shortly. The grace G4228
1Co 12:21 the head to the f, I have no need of you. G4228
15:25 till he hath put all enemies under his f. G4228
27 For he hath put all things under his f. G4228
Eph 1:22 And hath put all *things* under his f, and G4228
6:15 And your f shod with the preparation G4228
1Ti 5:10 washed the saints' f, if she have relieved G4228
Heb 2: 8 under his f. For in that he put all G4228
12:13 And make straight paths for your f, lest G4228
Rev 1:15 And his f like unto fine brass, as if they G4228
17 And when I saw him, I fell at his f as G4228
2:18 of fire, and his f *are* like fine brass; G4228
3: 9 f, and to know that I have loved thee. G4228
10: 1 were the sun, and his f as pillars of fire: G4228
11:11 stood upon their f; and great fear fell G4228
12: 1 moon under her f, and upon her head G4228
13: 2 a leopard, and his f were as *the feet* of a G4228
2 his feet were as *the* f of a bear, and his G4228
19:10 And I fell at his f to worship him. And G4228
22: 8 worship before the f of the angel which G4228

FEIGN
2Sa 14: 2 unto her, I pray thee, f thyself to be a
1Ki 14: 5 shall f herself *to be* another *woman*. H5234
Lk 20:20 which should f themselves just men, G5271

FEIGNED
1Sa 21:13 before them, and f himself mad in their
Ps 17: 1 my prayer, *that goeth* not out of f lips. H4820
2Pt 2: 3 shall they with f words make G4112

FEIGNEDLY
Jer 3:10 her whole heart, but f, saith the LORD. H8267

FEIGNEST
1Ki 14: 6 of Jeroboam; why f thou thyself *to be* H5234
Neh 6: 8 but thou f them out of thine own heart. H908

FELIX
Act 23:24 bring *him* safe unto F the governor. G5344
26 excellent governor F *sendeth* greeting. G5344
24: 3 most noble F, with all thankfulness. G5344
22 And when F heard these things, having G5344
24 And after certain days, when F came G5344
25 to come, F trembled, and answered, G5344
27 Felix' room: and F, willing to shew the G5344
25:14 is a certain man left in bonds by F: G5344

FELIX'
Act 24:27 Festus came into F room: and Felix, G5344

FELL
Gen 4: 5 was very wroth, and his countenance f. H5307
14:10 fled, and f there; and they that H5307
15:12 a deep sleep f upon Abram; and, lo, H5307
12 horror of great darkness f upon him. H5307
17: 3 And Abram f on his face: and God H5307
17 Then Abraham f upon his face, and H5307
33: 4 him, and f on his neck, and kissed H5307
44:14 and they f before him on the ground. H5307
45:14 And he f upon his brother Benjamin's H5307
46:29 unto him; and he f on his neck, and H5307
50: 1 And Joseph f upon his father's face, H5307
18 And his brethren also went and f down H5307
Ex 32:28 of Moses: and there f of the people that H5307
Lev 9:24 saw, they shouted, and f on their faces. H5307
16: 9 lot f, and offer him *for* a sin offering. H5927
10 But the goat, on which the lot f to be H5927
Nu 11: 4 *was* among them f a lusting: and the
9 And when the dew f upon the camp in H3381
9 camp in the night, the manna f upon it. H3381
14: 5 Then Moses and Aaron f on their faces H5307
16: 4 And when Moses heard *it*, he f upon H5307
22 And they f upon their faces, and said, H5307
45 a moment. And they f upon their faces. H5307
20: 6 and they f upon their faces: and H5307
22:27 angel of the LORD, she f down under H7257
31 down his head, and f flat on his face. H7812
Dt 9:18 And I f down before the LORD, as at H5307
25 Thus I f down before the LORD forty H5307
25 forty nights, as I f down *at the first;* H5307
Jos 5:14 come. And Joshua f on his face to the H5307
6:20 that the wall f down flat, so that the H5307
7: 6 And Joshua rent his clothes, and f to H5307
8:25 And *so* it was, *that* all that f that day, H5307
11: 7 suddenly; and they f upon them. H5307
16: 1 And the lot of the children of Joseph f H3318
17: 5 And there f ten portions to Manasseh, H5307
22:20 accursed thing, and wrath f on all the H1961
Jdg 4:16 the host of Sisera f upon the edge of the H5307
5:27 At her feet he bowed, he f, he lay down: H5307
27 feet he bowed, he f: where he bowed, H5307
27 where he bowed, there he f down dead. H5307
7:13 smote it that it f, and overturned it, that H5307
8:10 of the east: for there f an hundred and H5307
12: 6 Jordan: and there f at that time of the H5307
13:20 *it*, and f on their faces to the ground. H5307
16:30 and the house f upon the lords, and H5307
19:26 of the day, and f down at the door of H5307
20:44 And there f of Benjamin eighteen H5307
46 So that all which f that day of H5307
Ru 2:10 Then she f on her face, and bowed H5307
1Sa 4:10 f of Israel thirty thousand footmen. H5307
18 ark of God, that he f from off the seat H5307
11: 7 fear of the LORD f on the people, and H5307
14:13 him: and they f before Jonathan; and H5307
17:49 and he f upon his face to the earth. H5307
52 of the Philistines f down by the way to H5307
20:41 the south, and f on his face to the H5307
22:18 turned, and he f upon the priests, and H6293
25:23 off the ass, and f before David on her H5307
24 And f at his feet, and said, Upon me, H5307
28:20 Then Saul f straightway all along on H5307
29: 3 him since he f *unto me* unto this day? H5307
30:13 me, because three days agone I f sick.
31: 1 and f down slain in mount Gilboa. H5307
4 Saul took a sword, and f upon it. H5307
5 Saul was dead, he f likewise upon his H5307
2Sa 1: 2 he f to the earth, and did obeisance. H5307
2:16 fellow's side; so they f down together: H5307
23 him; and he f down there, and died H5307
23 Asahel f down and died stood still. H5307
4: 4 to flee, that he f, and became lame. And H5307
9: 6 unto David, he f on his face, and did H5307
11:17 Joab: and there f *some* of the people of H5307
13: 2 And Amnon was so vexed, that he f sick
14: 4 to the king, she f on her face to the H5307
2Sa 14:22 And Joab f to the ground on his face, H5307
18:28 All is well. And he f down to the earth H7812
19:18 the son of Gera f down before the king, H5307
20: 8 thereof; and as he went forth it f out. H5307
21: 9 LORD: and they f *all* seven together, H5307
22 the giant in Gath, and f by the hand of H5307
1Ki 2:25 and he f upon him that he died. H6293
32 his own head, who f upon two men H6293
34 went up, and f upon him, and slew H6293
46 went out, and f upon him, that he died. H6293
14: 1 time Abijah the son of Jeroboam f sick.
17:17 of the house, f sick; and his sickness
18: 7 he knew him, and f on his face, and H5307
38 Then the fire of the LORD f, and H5307
39 And when all the people saw *it*, they f H5307
20:30 and *there* a wall f upon twenty and H5307
2Ki 1: 2 And Ahaziah f down through a lattice H3766
13 up, and came and f on his knees before H3766
2:13 of Elijah that f from him, and went H5307
14 And he took the mantle of Elijah that f H5307
3:19 city, and shall f every good tree, and H5307
4: 8 And it f on a day, that Elisha passed to H1961
11 And it f on a day, that he came thither, H1961
18 And when the child was grown, it f on a H1961
37 Then she went in, and f at his feet, and H5307
6: 5 the axe head f into the water: and H5307
6 And the man of God said, Where f it? H5307
7:20 And so it f out unto him: for the people H1961
25:11 the fugitives that f away to the king of H5307
1Ch 5:10 the Hagarites, who f by their hand: and H5307
22 For there f down many slain, because H5307
10: 1 and f down slain in mount Gilboa. H5307
4 So Saul took a sword, and f upon it. H5307
5 he f likewise on the sword, and died. H5307
12:19 And there f *some* of Manasseh to H5307
20 As he went to Ziklag, there f to him of H5307
20: 8 giant in Gath; and they f by the hand of H5307
21:14 there f of Israel seventy thousand men. H5307
16 clothed in sackcloth, f upon their faces. H5307
26:14 And the lot eastward f to Shelemiah. H5307
27:24 not, because there f wrath for it against H1961
2Ch 13:17 great slaughter: so there f down slain of H5307
15: 9 Simeon: for they f to him out of Israel H5307
17:10 And the fear of the LORD f upon all the H1961
20:18 of Jerusalem f before the LORD, H5307
21:19 years, his bowels f out by reason of his H3318
25:13 with him to battle, f upon the cities of H6584
Ezr 9: 5 and my mantle, I f upon my knees, and H3766
Est 8: 3 the king, and f down at his feet, and H5307
17 for the fear of the Jews f upon them. H5307
9: 2 for the fear of them f upon all people. H5307
3 the fear of Mordecai f upon them. H5307
Job 1:15 And the Sabeans f *upon them*, and H5307
17 three bands, and f upon the camels, H6584
19 of the house, and it f upon the young H5307
20 his head, and f down upon the ground, H5307
Ps 27: 2 to eat up my flesh, they stumbled and f. H5307
78:64 Their priests f by the sword; and their H5307
105:38 for the fear of them f upon them. H5307
107:12 f down, and *there was* none to help. H3782
Jer 39: 9 and those that f away, that fell to him, H5307
9 that fell away, that f to him, with the H5307
46:16 He made many to fall, yea, one f upon H5307
52:15 and those that f away, that fell to the H5307
15 that fell away, that f to the king of H5307
Lam 1: 7 when her people f into the hand of the H5307
5:13 and the children f under the wood. H3782
Ezk 1:28 when I saw *it*, I f upon my face, and I H5307
3:23 the river of Chebar: and I f on my face. H5307
8: 1 hand of the Lord GOD f there upon me. H5307
9: 8 I was left, that I f upon my face, and H5307
11: 5 And the Spirit of the LORD f upon me, H5307
13 died. Then f I down upon my face, H5307
39:23 enemies: so f they all by the sword. H5307
43: 3 the river Chebar; and I f upon my face. H5307
44: 4 of the LORD: and I f upon my face. H5307
Dan 2:46 Then the king Nebuchadnezzar f upon H5308
3: 7 the languages, f down *and* worshipped H5308
23 and Abed-nego, f down bound into the H5308
4:31 mouth, there f a voice from heaven, H5308
7:20 before whom three f; even *of* that horn H5308
8:17 I was afraid, and f upon my face: but H5307
10: 7 a great quaking f upon them, so that H5307
Jna 1: 7 they cast lots, and the lot f upon Jonah. H5307
Mt 2:11 Mary his mother, and f down, and G4098
7:25 it f not: for it was founded upon a rock. G4098
27 and it f: and great was the fall of it. G4098
13: 4 And when he sowed, some *seeds* f by G4098
5 Some f upon stony places, where they G4098

F

Mt 13: 7 And some f among thorns; and the G4098
8 But other f into good ground, and G4098
17: 6 And when the disciples heard *it*, they f G4098
18:26 The servant therefore f down, and G4098
29 And his fellowservant f down at his G4098
26:39 And he went a little farther, and f on G4098
Mk 3:11 they saw him, f down before him, and G4363
4: 4 as he sowed, some f by the way side, G4098
5 And some f on stony ground, where it G4098
7 And some f among thorns, and the G4098
8 And other f on good ground, and did G4098
5:22 and when he saw him, he f at his feet, G4098
33 in her, came and f down before him, G4363
7:25 of him, and came and f at his feet: G4363
9:20 tare him; and he f on the ground, and G4098
14:35 And he went forward a little, and f on G4098
Lk 1:12 he was troubled, and fear f upon him. G1968
5: 8 When Simon Peter saw *it*, he f down at G4363
12 who seeing Jesus f on *his* face, and G4098
6:49 f; and the ruin of that house was great. G4098
8: 5 as he sowed, some f by the way side; G4098
6 And some f upon a rock; and as soon G4098
7 And some f among thorns; and the G4098
8 And other f on good ground, and G4098
14 And that which f among thorns are G4098
23 But as they sailed he f asleep: and there
28 When he saw Jesus, he cried out, and f G4363
41 the synagogue: and he f down at Jesus' G4098
10:30 to Jericho, and f among thieves, which G4045
36 unto him that f among the thieves? G1706
13: 4 tower in Siloam f, and slew them, think G4098
15:20 ran, and f on his neck, and kissed him. G1968
16:21 the crumbs which f from the rich man's G4098
17:16 And f down on *his* face at his feet, G4098
Jn 11:32 and saw him, she f down at his feet, G4098
18: 6 went backward, and f to the ground. G4098
Act 1:25 f, that he might go to his own place. G3845
26 lots; and the lot f upon Matthias; and G4098
5: 5 And Ananias hearing these words f G4098
10 Then f she down straightway at his G4098
7:60 And when he had said this, he f asleep.
9: 4 And he f to the earth, and heard a voice G4098
18 And immediately there f from his eyes G634
10:10 they made ready, he f into a trance, G1968
25 met him, and f down at his feet, and G4098
44 f on all them which heard the word. G1968
11:15 f on them, as on us at the beginning. G1968
12: 7 And his chains f off from *his* hands. G1601
13:11 immediately there f on him a mist and G1968
36 by the will of God, f on sleep, and was
16:29 and f down before Paul and Silas, G4363
19:17 at Ephesus; and fear f on them all, and G1968
35 the *image* which f down from Jupiter? G1356
20: 9 with sleep, and f down from the third G4098
10 And Paul went down, and f on him, G1968
37 And they all wept sore, and f on Paul's G1968
22: 7 And I f unto the ground, and heard a G4098
Ro 11:22 on them which f, severity; but toward G4098
15: 3 of them that reproached thee f on me. G1968
1Co 10: 8 committed, and f in one day three and G4098
Heb 3:17 whose carcases f in the wilderness? G4098
11:30 By faith the walls of Jericho f down, G4098
2Pt 3: 4 for since the fathers f asleep, all things
Rev 1:17 And when I saw him, I f at his feet as G4098
5: 8 *and* twenty elders f down before the G4098
14 four *and* twenty elders f down and G4098
6:13 And the stars of heaven f unto the G4098
7:11 four beasts, and f before the throne on G4098
8:10 and there f a great star from heaven, G4098
10 a lamp, and it f upon the third part G4098
11:11 fear f upon them which saw them. G4098
13 part of the city f, and in the earthquake G4098
16 God on their seats, f upon their faces, G4098
16: 2 the earth; and there f a noisome and G1096
19 of the nations f: and great Babylon G4098
21 And there f upon men a great hail out G2597
19: 4 the four beasts f down and worshipped G4098
10 And I f at his feet to worship him. And G4098
22: 8 heard and seen, I f down to worship G4098

FELLED
2Ki 3:25 wells of water, and f all the good trees: H5307

FELLER
Isa 14: 8 laid down, no f is come up against us. H3772

FELLEST
2Sa 3:34 wicked men, *so* f thou. And all the H5307

FELLING
2Ki 6: 5 But as one was f a beam, the axe head H5307

FELLOES
1Ki 7:33 f, and their spokes, *were* all molten. H2839

FELLOW
Gen 19: 9 *again*, This one *f* came in to sojourn, H7453
Ex 2:13 wrong, Wherefore smitest thou thy f? H7453
Jdg 7:13 a dream unto his f, and said, Behold, I H7453
14 And his f answered and said, This *is* H7453
22 sword against his f, even throughout all H7453
1Sa 14:20 was against his f, *and there was* a very H7453
21:15 have brought this *f* to play the mad man
15 shall this *f* come into my house?
25:21 have I kept all that this *f* hath in the
29: 4 him, Make this f return, that he may go H376
2Sa 2:16 And they caught every one his f by the H7453
1Ki 22:27 And say, Thus saith the king, Put this *f*
2Ki 9:11 came this mad *f* to thee? And he said
2Ch 18:26 And say, Thus saith the king, Put this *f*
Ecc 4:10 For if they fall, the one will lift up his f: H2270
Isa 34:14 shall cry to his f; the screech owl also H7453
Jna 1: 7 And they said every one to his f, Come, H7453
Zec 13: 7 the man *that is* my f, saith the LORD of H5997
Mt 12:24 *it*, they said, This *f* doth not cast out
26:61 And said, This *f* said, I am able to
71 This *f* was also with Jesus of Nazareth.
Lk 22:59 Of a truth this *f* also was with him: for
23: 2 We found this *f* perverting the nation,
Jn 9:29 this *f*, we know not from whence he is.
Act 18:13 Saying, This *f* persuadeth men to
22:22 Away with such a *f* from the earth: for it
24: 5 For we have found this man *a* pestilent *f*,

FELLOWCITIZENS
Eph 2:19 foreigners, but f with the saints, and G4847

FELLOWDISCIPLES
Jn 11:16 Didymus, unto his f, Let us also go, that G4827

FELLOWHEIRS
Eph 3: 6 That the Gentiles should be f, and of the G4789

FELLOWHELPER
2Co 8:23 *is* my partner and f concerning you: or G4904

FELLOWHELPERS
3Jn 8 such, that we might be f to the truth. G4904

FELLOWLABOURER
1Th 3: 2 of God, and our f in the gospel of G4904
Phlm 1 Philemon our dearly beloved, and f, G4904

FELLOWLABOURERS
Php 4: 3 f, whose names *are* in the book of life. G4904
Phlm 24 Aristarchus, Demas, Lucas, my f. G4904

FELLOWPRISONER
Col 4:10 Aristarchus my f saluteth you, and G4869
Phlm 23 There salute thee Epaphras, my f in G4869

FELLOWPRISONERS
Ro 16: 7 my kinsmen, and my f, who are of note G4869

FELLOWS
Jdg 11:37 and bewail my virginity, I and my f. H7464
18:25 us, lest angry f run upon thee, and thou H582
2Sa 6:20 vain f shamelessly uncovereth himself!
Ps 45: 7 thee with the oil of gladness above thy f. H2270
Isa 44:11 Behold, all his f shall be ashamed: and H2270
Ezk 37:19 tribes of Israel his f, and will put them H2270
Dan 2:13 they sought Daniel and his f to be slain. H2269
18 Daniel and his f should not perish with H2269
7:20 whose look *was* more stout than his f. H2273
Zec 3: 8 thou, and thy f that sit before thee: H7453
Mt 11:16 in the markets, and calling unto their f, G2083
Act 17: 5 them certain lewd f of the baser sort, G435
Heb 1: 9 thee with the oil of gladness above thy f. G3353

FELLOW'S
2Sa 2:16 his sword in his f side; so they fell down H7453

FELLOWSERVANT
Mt 18:29 And his f fell down at his feet, and G4889
33 on thy f, even as I had pity on thee? G4889
Col 1: 7 of Epaphras our dear f, who is for you a G4889
4: 7 a faithful minister and f in the Lord: G4889
Rev 19:10 *do it* not: I am thy f, and of thy brethren G4889
22: 9 *it* not: for I am thy f, and of thy brethren G4889

FELLOWSERVANTS
Mt 18:28 found one of his f, which owed him an G4889
31 So when his f saw what was done, they G4889
24:49 And shall begin to smite *his* f, and to G4889
Rev 6:11 little season, until their f also and their G4889

FELLOWSHIP
Lev 6: 2 him to keep, or in f, or in a thing taken H8667
Ps 94:20 Shall the throne of iniquity have f with H2266
Act 2:42 doctrine and f, and in breaking of G2842
1Co 1: 9 the f of his Son Jesus Christ our Lord. G2842
10:20 not that ye should have f with devils. G2844
2Co 6:14 for what f hath righteousness G3352
8: 4 *us* the f of the ministering to the saints. G2842
Gal 2: 9 the right hands of f; that we *should go* G2842
Eph 3: 9 And to make all *men* see what *is* the f G2842
5:11 And have no f with the unfruitful G4790
Php 1: 5 For your f in the gospel from the first G2842
2: 1 of love, if any f of the Spirit, if any G2842
3:10 and the f of his sufferings, being G2842
1Jn 1: 3 ye also may have f with us: and truly G2842
3 us: and truly our f *is* with the Father, G2842
6 If we say that we have f with him, and G2842
7 in the light, we have f one with another, G2842

FELLOWSOLDIER
Php 2:25 in labour, and f, but your messenger, G4961
Phlm 2 our f, and to the church in thy house: G4961

FELLOWWORKERS
Col 4:11 These only *are my* f unto the kingdom G4904

FELT
Gen 27:22 his father; and he f him, and said, The H4959
Ex 10:21 of Egypt, even darkness *which* may be f. H4959
Prv 23:35 beaten me, *and* I f *it* not: when shall I H3045
Mk 5:29 dried up; and she f in *her* body that she G1097
Act 28: 5 the beast into the fire, and f no harm. G3958

FEMALE
Gen 1:27 he him; male and f created he them. H5347
5: 2 Male and f created he them; and H5347
6:19 alive with thee; they shall be male and f. H5347
7: 2 the male and his f: and of beasts that *are* H802
2 *are* not clean by two, the male and his f. H802
3 the male and the f; to keep seed alive H5347
9 the f, as God had commanded Noah. H5347
16 went in male and f of all flesh, as God H5347
Lev 3: 1 *it be* a male or f, he shall offer it without H5347
6 or f, he shall offer it without blemish. H5347
4:28 a kid of the goats, a f without blemish, H5347
32 he shall bring it a f without blemish. H5347
5: 6 he hath sinned, a f from the flock, a H5347
12: 7 law for her that hath born a male or a f. H5347
27: 4 And if it *be* a f, then thy estimation H5347
5 shekels, and for the f ten shekels. H5347
6 silver, and for the f thy estimation *shall* H5347
7 shekels, and for the f ten shekels. H5347
Nu 5: 3 Both male and f shall ye put out, H5347
Dt 4:16 of any figure, the likeness of male or f, H5347
7:14 not be male or f barren among you, H5347
Mt 19: 4 at the beginning made them male and f, G2338
Mk 10: 6 creation God made them male and f. G2338
Gal 3:28 nor f: for ye are all one in Christ Jesus. G2338

FENCE
Ps 62: 3 wall *shall ye be, and as* a tottering f. H1447

FENCED
Nu 32:17 shall dwell in the f cities because of the H4013
36 And Beth-nimrah, and Beth-haran, f H4013
Dt 3: 5 All these cities *were* f with high walls, H1219
9: 1 thyself, cities great and f up to heaven, H1219
28:52 until thy high and f walls come down, H1219
Jos 10:20 remained of them entered into f cities. H4013
14:12 *were* great *and* f: if so be the LORD *will* H1219
19:35 And the f cities *are* Ziddim, Zer, and H4013
1Sa 6:18 the five lords, *both* of f cities, and of H4013
2Sa 20: 6 lest he get him f cities, and escape us. H1219
23: 7 them must be f with iron and the staff H4390
2Ki 3:19 And ye shall smite every f city, and H4013
10: 2 and horses, a f city also, and armour; H4013
17: 9 the tower of the watchmen to the f city. H4013
18: 8 the tower of the watchmen to the f city. H4013
13 all the f cities of Judah, and took them. H1219
19:25 to lay waste f cities *into* ruinous heaps. H1219
2Ch 8: 5 f cities, with walls, gates, and bars; H4692

2Ch 11:10 *are* in Judah and in Benjamin f cities. H4694
23 unto every f city: and he gave them H4694
12: 4 And he took the f cities which H4694
14: 6 And he built f cities in Judah: for the H4694
17: 2 And he placed forces in all the f cities H1219
19 put in the f cities throughout all Judah. H4013
19: 5 all the f cities of Judah, city by city, H1219
21: 3 things, with f cities in Judah: but the H4694
32: 1 against the f cities, and thought to H1219
33:14 of war in all the f cities of Judah. H1219
Job 10:11 and hast f me with bones and sinews. H7753
19: 8 He hath f up my way that I cannot H1443
Isa 2:15 high tower, and upon every f wall, H1219
5: 2 And he f it, and gathered out the stones H5823
Jer 5:17 impoverish thy f cities, wherein thou H4013
15:20 unto this people a f brasen wall: and H1219
Ezk 36:35 cities *are become* f, *and* are inhabited. H1219
Dan 11:15 and take the most f cities: and the arms H4013
Hos 8:14 hath multiplied f cities: but I will send H1219
Zep 1:16 f cities, and against the high towers. H1219

FENCED-CITY See FENCED and CITY.

FENCED-WALL See FENCED and WALL.

FENS
Job 40:21 trees, in the covert of the reed, and f. H1207

FERRET
Lev 11:30 And the f, and the chameleon, and the H604

FERRY
2Sa 19:18 And there went over a f boat to carry H5679

FERRY-BOAT See FERRY and BOAT.

FERVENT
Act 18:25 Lord; and being f in the spirit, he spake *G2204*
Ro 12:11 Not slothful in business; f in spirit; *G2204*
2Co 7: 7 mourning, your f mind toward me; so *G2205*
Jas 5:16 The effectual f prayer of a righteous *G1754*
1Pt 4: 8 And above all things have f charity *G1618*
2Pt 3:10 shall melt with f heat, the earth also and
12 and the elements shall melt with f heat?

FERVENTLY
Col 4:12 always labouring f for you in prayers, *G75*
1Pt 1:22 *ye* love one another with a pure heart f: *G1619*

FESTUS
Act 24:27 But after two years Porcius F came into *G5347*
25: 1 Now when F was come into the *G5347*
4 But F answered, that Paul should be *G5347*
9 But F, willing to do the Jews a pleasure, *G5347*
12 Then F, when he had conferred with the *G5347*
13 Bernice came unto Caesarea to salute F. *G5347*
14 there many days, F declared Paul's *G5347*
22 Then Agrippa said unto F, I would also *G5347*
24 And F said, King Agrippa, and all men *G5347*
26:24 And as he thus spake for himself, F *G5347*
25 mad, most noble F; but speak forth the *G5347*
32 Then said Agrippa unto F, This man *G5347*

FESTUS'
Act 25:23 men of the city, at F commandment *G5347*

FETCH
Gen 18: 5 And I will f a morsel of bread, and H3947
27: 9 Go now to the flock, and f me from H3947
13 only obey my voice, and go f me *them*. H3947
45 I will send, and f thee from thence: why H3947
42:16 Send one of you, and let him f your H3947
Ex 2: 5 the flags, she sent her maid to f it. H3947
Nu 20:10 must we f you water out of this rock? H3318
34: 5 And the border shall f a compass from
Dt 19:12 city shall send and f him thence, and H3947
24:10 not go into his house to f his pledge. H5670
19 not go again to f it: it shall be for the H3947
30: 4 thee, and from thence will he f thee: H3947
Jdg 11: 5 to f Jephthah out of the land of Tob: H3947
20:10 of ten thousand, to f victual for the H3947
1Sa 4: 3 the Philistines? Let us f the ark of the H3947
6:21 come ye down, *and* f it up to you. H5927
16:11 Jesse, Send and f him: for we will not H3947
20:31 f him unto me, for he shall surely die. H3947
26:22 of the young men come over and f it. H3947
2Sa 5:23 shalt not go up; *but* f a compass behind
14:13 doth not f home again his banished. H7725
20 To f about this form of speech hath thy H5437
1Ki 17:10 to her, and said, F me, I pray thee, a H3947
11 And as she was going to f *it*, he called H3947
2Ki 6:13 I may send and f him. And it was told H3947
2Ch 18: 8 said, F quickly Micaiah the son of Imla.
Neh 8:15 the mount, and f olive branches, and H935
Job 36: 3 I will f my knowledge from afar, and H5375
Isa 56:12 Come ye, *say they*, I will f wine, and we H3947
Jer 36:21 So the king sent Jehudi to f the roll: and H3947
Act 16:37 let them come themselves and f us out. *G1806*

FETCHED
Gen 18: 4 Let a little water, I pray you, be f, and H3947
27:14 And he went, and f, and brought *them* H3947
Jos 15: 3 up to Adar, and f a compass to Karkaa:
Jdg 18:18 house, and f the carved image, the H3947
1Sa 7: 1 came, and f up the ark of the LORD, H5927
10:23 And they ran and f him thence: and H3947
2Sa 4: 6 they would have f wheat; and they H3947
9: 5 Then king David sent, and f him out of H3947
11:27 David sent and f her to his house, and H622
14: 2 And Joab sent to Tekoah, and f thence H3947
1Ki 7:13 And king Solomon sent and f Hiram H3947
9:28 And they came to Ophir, and f from H3947
2Ki 3: 9 of Edom: and they f a compass of seven
11: 4 year Jehoiada sent and f the rulers over H3947
2Ch 1:17 And they f up, and brought forth out of H5927
12:11 guard came and f them, and brought H5375
Jer 26:23 And they f forth Urijah out of Egypt, H3318
Act 28:13 And from thence we f a compass, and

FETCHETH
Dt 19: 5 and his hand f a stroke with the axe H5080

FETCHT
Gen 18: 7 And Abraham ran unto the herd, and f H3947

FETTERS
Jdg 16:21 bound him with f of brass; and he did H5178
2Sa 3:34 nor thy feet put into f: as a man falleth H5178
2Ki 25: 7 f of brass, and carried him to Babylon. H5178
2Ch 33:11 him with f, and carried him to Babylon. H5178
36: 6 him in f, to carry him to Babylon. H5178
Job 36: 8 And if *they be* bound in f, *and* be H2131
Ps 105:18 Whose feet they hurt with f: he was laid H3525
149: 8 chains, and their nobles with f of iron; H3525
Mk 5: 4 often bound with f and chains, and the *G3976*
4 by him, and the f broken in pieces: *G3976*
Lk 8:29 with chains and in f; and he brake the *G3976*

FEVER
Dt 28:22 consumption, and with a f, and with an H6920
Mt 8:14 his wife's mother laid, and sick of a f. *G4445*
15 And he touched her hand, and the f left *G4446*
Mk 1:30 of a f, and anon they tell him of her. *G4445*
31 and immediately the f left her, and she *G4446*
Lk 4:38 great f; and they besought him for her. *G4446*
39 and rebuked the f; and it left her: and *G4446*
Jn 4:52 at the seventh hour the f left him. *G4446*
Act 28: 8 lay sick of a f and of a bloody flux: *G4446*

FEW
Gen 24:55 abide with us *a f* days, at the least ten; H3117
27:44 And tarry with him a f days, until thy H259
29:20 *but* a f days, for the love he had to her. H259
34:30 and I *being* f in number, they shall H4962
47: 9 and thirty years: f and evil have the H4592
Lev 25:52 And if there remain but f years unto H4592
26:22 and make you f in number; and your H4591
Nu 9:20 And *so* it was, when the cloud was a f H4557
13:18 they *be* strong or weak, f or many; H4592
26:54 and to f thou shalt give the less H4592
56 thereof be divided between many and f. H4592
35: 8 from *them that have* f ye shall give few: H4592
8 few ye shall give f: every one shall give H4591
Dt 4:27 and ye shall be left f in number among H4962
26: 5 there with a f, and became there a H4592
28:62 And ye shall be left f in number, H4592
33: 6 and not die; and let *not* his men be f. H4557
Jos 7: 3 to labour thither; for they *are but* f. H4592
1Sa 14: 6 to the LORD to save by many or by f. H4592
17:28 hast thou left those f sheep in the H4592
2Ki 4: 3 *even* empty vessels; borrow not a f. H4591
1Ch 16:19 When ye were but f, even a few, and H4962
19 When ye were but few, even a f, and H4592
2Ch 29:34 But the priests were too f, so that they H4592
Neh 2:12 And I arose in the night, I and some f H4592
7: 4 but the people *were* f therein, and the H4592
Job 10:20 *Are* not my days f? cease *then*, *and* let H4592
14: 1 Man *that is* born of a woman *is* of f H7116
16:22 When a f years are come, then I shall H4557
Ps 105:12 When they were *but* a f men in H4962
12 number; yea, very f, and strangers in it. H4592
109: 8 Let his days be f; *and* let another take H4592
Ecc 5: 2 upon earth: therefore let thy words be f. H4592
9:14 *There was* a little city, and f men H4592
12: 3 because they are f, and those that look H4591
Isa 10: 7 to destroy and cut off nations not a f. H4592
19 shall be f, that a child may write them. H4557
24: 6 of the earth are burned, and f men left. H4213
Jer 30:19 and they shall not be f; I will also glorify H4591
42: 2 f of many, as thine eyes do behold us:) H4592
Ezk 5: 3 Thou shalt also take thereof a f in H4592
12:16 But I will leave a f men of them from H4557
Dan 11:20 but within f days he shall be destroyed, H259
Mt 7:14 unto life, and f there be that find it. *G3641*
9:37 *is* plenteous, but the labourers *are* f; *G3641*
15:34 they said, Seven, and a f little fishes. *G3641*
20:16 last: for many be called, but f chosen. *G3641*
22:14 For many are called, but f *are* chosen. *G3641*
25:21 faithful over a f things, I will make thee *G3641*
23 faithful over a f things, I will make thee *G3641*
Mk 6: 5 upon a f sick folk, and healed *them*. *G3641*
8: 7 And they had a f small fishes: and he *G3641*
Lk 10: 2 the labourers *are* f: pray ye therefore *G3641*
12:48 shall be beaten with f *stripes*. For unto *G3641*
13:23 f that be saved? And he said unto them, *G3641*
Act 17: 4 and of the chief women not a f. *G3641*
12 which were Greeks, and of men, not a f. *G3641*
24: 4 hear us of thy clemency a f words. *G4935*
Eph 3: 3 mystery; (as I wrote afore in f words, *G3641*
Heb 12:10 For they verily for a f days chastened *G3641*
13:22 written a letter unto you in f words. *G1024*
1Pt 3:20 wherein f, that is, eight souls were *G3641*
Rev 2:14 But I have a f things against thee, *G3641*
20 Notwithstanding I have a f things *G3641*
3: 4 Thou hast a f names even in Sardis *G3641*

FEWER
Nu 33:54 and to the f ye shall give the less H4592

FEWEST
Dt 7: 7 people; for ye *were* the f of all people: H4592

FEWNESS
Lev 25:16 according to the f of years thou shalt H4591

FIDELITY
Tit 2:10 Not purloining, but shewing all good f; *G4102*

FIELD
Gen 2: 5 And every plant of the f before it was in H7704
5 every herb of the f before it grew: for H7704
19 every beast of the f, and every fowl of H7704
20 every beast of the f; but for Adam there H7704
3: 1 any beast of the f which the LORD God H7704
14 every beast of the f; upon thy belly shalt H7704
18 and thou shalt eat the herb of the f; H7704
4: 8 they were in the f, that Cain rose up H7704
23: 9 *is* in the end of his f; for as much money H7704
11 Nay, my lord, hear me: the f give I thee, H7704
13 thee money for the f; take *it* of me, and I H7704
17 And the f of Ephron, which *was* in H7704
17 *was* before Mamre, the f, and the cave H7704
17 that *were* in the f, that *were* in all the H7704
19 in the cave of the f of Machpelah before H7704
20 And the f, and the cave that *is* therein, H7704
24:63 And Isaac went out to meditate in the f H7704
65 that walketh in the f to meet us? And H7704
25: 9 Machpelah, in the f of Ephron the son H7704
10 The f which Abraham purchased of the H7704
27 a man of the f; and Jacob *was* a plain H7704
29 Esau came from the f, and he *was* faint: H7704
27: 3 out to the f, and take me *some* venison; H7704
5 f to hunt *for* venison, *and* to bring *it*. H7704
27 of a f which the LORD hath blessed: H7704
29: 2 a well in the f, and, lo, there *were* three H7704
30:14 mandrakes in the f, and brought them H7704
16 And Jacob came out of the f in the H7704
31: 4 Rachel and Leah to the f unto his flock, H7704
33:19 And he bought a parcel of a f, where he H7704
34: 5 his cattle in the f: and Jacob held his H7704
7 And the sons of Jacob came out of the f H7704
28 in the city, and that which *was* in the f, H7704
36:35 Midian in the f of Moab, reigned in H7704
37: 7 sheaves in the f, and, lo, my sheaf H7704
15 wandering in the f: and the man asked H7704
39: 5 that he had in the house, and in the f. H7704
41:48 the food of the f, which *was* round H7704

Gen 47:20 sold every man his f, because the H7704
24 for seed of the f, and for your food, and H7704
49:29 that *is* in the f of Ephron the Hittite, H7704
30 In the cave that *is* in the f of H7704
30 bought with the f of Ephron the Hittite H7704
32 The purchase of the f and of the cave H7704
50:13 him in the cave of the f of Machpelah, H7704
13 bought with the f for a possession of a H7704
Ex 1:14 of service in the f: all their service, H7704
9: 3 which *is* in the f, upon the horses, upon H7704
19 thou hast in the f; *for upon* every man H7704
19 shall be found in the f, and shall not be H7704
21 left his servants and his cattle in the f. H7704
22 of the f, throughout the land of Egypt. H7704
25 all that *was* in the f, both man and H7704
25 the f, and brake every tree of the field. H7704
25 the field, and brake every tree of the f. H7704
10: 5 tree which groweth for you out of the f: H7704
15 of the f, through all the land of Egypt. H7704
16:25 to day ye shall not find it in the f. H7704
22: 5 If a man shall cause a f or vineyard to H7704
5 in another man's f; of the best of his H7704
5 the best of his own f, and of the best of H7704
6 corn, or the f, be consumed *therewith;* H7704
31 in the f; ye shall cast it to the dogs. H7704
23:11 the beasts of the f shall eat. In like H7704
16 thou hast sown in the f: and the feast of H7704
16 hast gathered in thy labours out of the f. H7704
29 the beast of the f multiply against thee. H7704
Lev 14: 7 let the living bird loose into the open f. H7704
17: 5 offer in the open f, even that they may H7704
19: 9 the corners of thy f, neither shalt thou H7704
19 shalt not sow thy f with mingled seed: H7704
23:22 the corners of thy f when thou reapest, H7704
25: 3 Six years thou shalt sow thy f, and six H7704
4 sow thy f, nor prune thy vineyard. H7704
12 eat the increase thereof out of the f. H7704
34 But the f of the suburbs of their cities H7704
26: 4 the trees of the f shall yield their fruit. H7704
27:16 *some part* of a f of his possession, then H7704
17 If he sanctify his f from the year of H7704
18 But if he sanctify his f after the jubile, H7704
19 And if he that sanctified the f will in H7704
20 And if he will not redeem the f, or if he H7704
20 if he have sold the f to another man, it H7704
21 But the f, when it goeth out in the jubile, H7704
21 unto the LORD, as a f devoted; the H7704
22 unto the LORD a f which he hath H7704
24 In the year of the jubile the f shall H7704
28 beast, and of the f of his possession, H7704
Nu 22: 4 up the grass of the f. And Balak the son H7704
23 and went into the f: and Balaam smote H7704
23:14 And he brought him into the f of H7704
Dt 5:21 house, his f, or his manservant, H7704
7:22 the beasts of the f increase upon thee. H7704
14:22 that the f bringeth forth year by year. H7704
20:19 (for the tree of the f *is* man's *life*) to H7704
21: 1 it, lying in the f, *and* it be not known H7704
22:25 damsel in the f, and the man force her, H7704
27 For he found her in the f, *and* the H7704
24:19 harvest in thy f, and hast forgot a sheaf H7704
19 a sheaf in the f, thou shalt not go again H7704
28: 3 city, and blessed *shalt* thou *be* in the f. H7704
16 city, and cursed *shalt* thou *be* in the f. H7704
38 seed out into the f, and shalt gather *but* H7704
Jos 8:24 of Ai in the f, in the wilderness wherein H7704
15:18 ask of her father a f: and she lighted off H7704
Jdg 1:14 to ask of her father a f: and she lighted H7704
5: 4 out of the f of Edom, the earth H7704
18 the death in the high places of the f. H7704
9:32 that *is* with thee, and lie in wait in the f: H7704
42 out into the f; and they told Abimelech. H7704
43 and laid wait in the f, and looked, and, H7704
13: 9 as she sat in the f: but Manoah her H7704
19:16 his work out of the f at even, which *was* H7704
20:31 in the f, about thirty men of Israel. H7704
Ru 2: 2 me now go to the f, and glean ears of H7704
3 and gleaned in the f after the reapers: H7704
3 on a part of the f *belonging* unto Boaz, H7704
8 to glean in another f, neither go from H7704
9 *Let* thine eyes *be* on the f that they do H7704
17 So she gleaned in the f until even, and H7704
22 that they meet thee not in any other f. H7704
4: 5 thou buyest the f of the hand of Naomi, H7704
1Sa 4: 2 in the f about four thousand men. H7704
6:14 And the cart came into the f of Joshua, H7704
18 in the f of Joshua, the Beth-shemite. H7704
11: 5 the herd out of the f; and Saul said, H7704
14:15 in the host, in the f, and among all the H7704
1Sa 17:44 of the air, and to the beasts of the f. H7704
19: 3 my father in the f where thou *art,* and H7704
20: 5 in the f unto the third *day* at even. H7704
11 us go out into the f. And they went out H7704
11 they went out both of them into the f. H7704
24 So David hid himself in the f: and when H7704
35 Jonathan went out into the f at the time H7704
30:11 And they found an Egyptian in the f, H7704
2Sa 10: 8 Maacah, *were* by themselves in the f. H7704
11:23 unto us into the f, and we were upon H7704
14: 6 together in the f, and *there was* none H7704
30 See, Joab's f is near mine, and he H2513
30 Absalom's servants set the f on fire. H2513
31 have thy servants set my f on fire? H2513
17: 8 her whelps in the f: and thy father *is* a H7704
18: 6 So the people went out into the f H7704
20:12 the highway into the f, and cast a cloth H7704
21:10 by day, nor the beasts of the f by night. H7704
1Ki 11:29 and they two *were* alone in the f: H7704
14:11 that dieth in the f shall the fowls of the H7704
21:24 in the f shall the fowls of the air eat. H7704
2Ki 4:39 And one went out into the f to gather H7704
7:12 themselves in the f, saying, When they H7704
8: 6 all the fruits of the f since the day that H7704
9:25 in the portion of the f of Naboth the H7704
37 upon the face of the f in the portion of H7704
18:17 which *is* in the highway of the fuller's f. H7704
19:26 *as* the grass of the f, and *as* the green H7704
1Ch 1:46 Midian in the f of Moab, reigned in H7704
19: 9 were come *were* by themselves in the f. H7704
27:26 did the work of the f for tillage of the H7704
2Ch 26:23 his fathers in the f of the burial which H7704
31: 5 the increase of the f; and the tithe of all H7704
Neh 13:10 the work, were fled every one to his f. H7704
Job 5:23 the stones of the f: and the beasts of the H7704
23 of the f shall be at peace with thee. H7704
24: 6 They reap *every one* his corn in the f: H7704
40:20 food, where all the beasts of the f play. H7704
Ps 8: 7 and oxen, yea, and the beasts of the f; H7704
50:11 and the wild beasts of the f *are* mine. H7704
78:12 in the land of Egypt, *in* the f of Zoan. H7704
43 and his wonders in the f of Zoan: H7704
80:13 the wild beast of the f doth devour it. H7704
96:12 Let the f be joyful, and all that *is* H7704
103:15 as a flower of the f, so he flourisheth. H7704
104:11 They give drink to every beast of the f: H7704
Prv 24:27 the f; and afterwards build thine house. H7704
30 I went by the f of the slothful, and by H7704
27:26 and the goats *are* the price of the f. H7704
31:16 She considereth a f, and buyeth it: with H7704
Ecc 5: 9 all: the king *himself* is served by the f. H7704
Song 2: 7 by the hinds of the f, that ye stir not up, H7704
3: 5 by the hinds of the f, that ye stir not up, H7704
7:11 into the f; let us lodge in the villages. H7704
Isa 5: 8 to house, *that* lay f to field, till *there be* H7704
8 *that* lay field to f, till *there be* no place, H7704
7: 3 pool in the highway of the fuller's f; H7704
10:18 and of his fruitful f, both soul and body: H3759
16:10 out of the plentiful f; and in the vineyards
29:17 into a fruitful f, and the fruitful field
17 fruitful f shall be esteemed as a forest?
32:15 be a fruitful f, and the fruitful field
15 and the fruitful f be counted for a forest.
16 righteousness remain in the fruitful f.
36: 2 pool in the highway of the fuller's f. H7704
37:27 *as* the grass of the f, and *as* the green H7704
40: 6 thereof *is* as the flower of the f: H7704
43:20 The beast of the f shall honour me, the H7704
55:12 the trees of the f shall clap *their* hands. H7704
56: 9 All ye beasts of the f, come to devour, H7704
Jer 4:17 As keepers of a f, are they against her H7704
6:25 Go not forth into the f, nor walk by the H7704
7:20 the trees of the f, and upon the fruit of H7704
9:22 upon the open f, and as the handful H7704
12: 4 and the herbs of every f wither, for the H7704
9 all the beasts of the f, come to devour. H7704
14: 5 Yea, the hind also calved in the f, and H7704
18 If I go forth into the f, then behold the H7704
17: 3 O my mountain in the f, I will give thy H7704
18:14 from the rock of the f? *or* shall the cold H7704
26:18 be plowed *like* a f, and Jerusalem shall H7704
27: 6 f have I given him also to serve him. H7704
28:14 have given him the beasts of the f also. H7704
32: 7 Buy thee my f that *is* in Anathoth: H7704
8 unto me, Buy my f, I pray thee, that *is* H7704
9 And I bought the f of Hanameel my H7704
25 GOD, Buy thee the f for money, and H7704
35: 9 have we vineyard, nor f, nor seed: H7704
41: 8 have treasures in the f, of wheat, and of H7704
Jer 48:33 from the plentiful f, and from the land H3759
Lam 4: 9 through for *want of* the fruits of the f. H7704
Ezk 7:15 he that *is* in the f shall die with the H7704
16: 5 out in the open f, to the lothing of thy H7704
7 as the bud of the f, and thou hast H7704
17: 5 it in a fruitful f; he placed *it* by great H7704
24 And all the trees of the f shall know H7704
20:46 against the forest of the south f; H7704
26: 6 And her daughters which *are* in the f H7704
8 daughters in the f: and he shall make a H7704
29: 5 of the f and to the fowls of the heaven. H776
31: 4 her little rivers unto all the trees of the f. H7704
5 all the trees of the f, and his boughs H7704
6 all the beasts of the f bring forth their H7704
13 of the f shall be upon his branches: H7704
15 all the trees of the f fainted for him. H7704
32: 4 upon the open f, and will cause all the H7704
33:27 that *is* in the open f will I give to the H7704
34: 5 of the f, when they were scattered. H7704
8 every beast of the f, because *there was* H7704
27 And the tree of the f shall yield her H7704
36:30 and the increase of the f, that ye shall H7704
38:20 and the beasts of the f, and all creeping H7704
39: 4 *to* the beasts of the f to be devoured. H7704
5 Thou shalt fall upon the open f: for I H7704
10 no wood out of the f, neither cut down H7704
17 to every beast of the f, Assemble H7704
Dan 2:38 the beasts of the f and the fowls of the H1251
4:12 the beasts of the f had shadow under it, H1251
15 tender grass of the f; and let it be wet H1251
21 the beasts of the f dwelt, and upon H1251
23 tender grass of the f; and let it be wet H1251
23 of the f, till seven times pass over him; H1251
25 the beasts of the f, and they shall make H1251
32 the beasts of the f: they shall make thee H1251
Hos 2:12 and the beasts of the f shall eat them. H7704
18 the beasts of the f, and with the fowls of H7704
4: 3 the beasts of the f, and with the fowls of H7704
10: 4 up as hemlock in the furrows of the f. H7704
Joel 1:10 The f is wasted, the land mourneth; for H7704
11 because the harvest of the f is perished. H7704
12 *even* all the trees of the f, are withered: H7704
19 flame hath burned all the trees of the f. H7704
20 The beasts of the f cry also unto thee: H7704
2:22 Be not afraid, ye beasts of the f: for the H7704
Mic 1: 6 as an heap of the f, *and* as plantings of H7704
3:12 be plowed *as* a f, and Jerusalem shall H7704
4:10 shalt dwell in the f, and thou shalt go H7704
Zec 10: 1 of rain, to every one grass in the f. H7704
Mal 3:11 time in the f, saith the LORD of hosts. H7704
Mt 6:28 the lilies of the f, how they grow; they *G68*
30 the grass of the f, which to day is, and *G68*
13:24 a man which sowed good seed in his f: *G68*
27 in thy f? from whence then hath it tares? *G68*
31 which a man took, and sowed in his f: *G68*
36 unto us the parable of the tares of the f. *G68*
38 The f is the world; the good seed are the *G68*
44 treasure hid in a f; the which when a man *G68*
44 selleth all that he hath, and buyeth that f. *G68*
24:18 Neither let him which is in the f return *G68*
40 Then shall two be in the f; the one shall *G68*
27: 7 them the potter's f, to bury strangers in. *G68*
8 Wherefore that f was called, The field of *G68*
8 Wherefore that field was called, The f of *G68*
10 And gave them for the potter's f, as the *G68*
Mk 13:16 And let him that is in the f not turn back *G68*
Lk 2: 8 f, keeping watch over their flock by night. *G63*
12:28 is to day in the f, and to morrow is cast *G68*
15:25 Now his elder son was in the f: and as he *G68*
17: 7 from the f, Go and sit down to meat? *G68*
31 in the f, let him likewise not return back. *G68*
36 Two *men* shall be in the f; the one shall *G68*
Act 1:18 Now this man purchased a f with the *G5564*
19 insomuch as that f is called in their *G5564*
19 that is to say, The f of blood. *G5564*

FIELDS

Ex 8:13 out of the villages, and out of the f. H7704
Lev 14:53 the city into the open f, and make an H7704
25:31 be counted as the f of the country: they H7704
27:22 which *is* not of the f of his possession; H7704
Nu 16:14 us inheritance of f and vineyards: wilt H7704
19:16 sword in the open f, or a dead body, or H7704
20:17 not pass through the f, or through the H7704
21:22 will not turn into the f, or into the H7704
Dt 11:15 And I will send grass in thy f for thy H7704
32:13 the increase of the f; and he made him H7704
32 Sodom, and of the f of Gomorrah: their H7709
Jos 21:12 But the f of the city, and the villages H7704

Jdg 9:27 And they went out into the f, and H7704
44 that *were* in the f, and slew them. H7704
1Sa 8:14 And he will take your f, and your H7704
22: 7 every one of you f and vineyards, *and* H7704
25:15 with them, when we were in the f: H7704
2Sa 1:21 upon you, nor f of offerings: for there H7704
11:11 in the open f; shall I then go into mine H7704
1Ki 2:26 unto thine own f; for thou *art* worthy H7704
16: 4 his in the f shall the fowls of the air eat. H7704
2Ki 23: 4 Jerusalem in the f of Kidron, and H7709
1Ch 6:56 But the f of the city, and the villages H7704
16:32 let the f rejoice, and all that *is* therein. H7704
27:25 storehouses in the f, in the cities, and in H7704
2Ch 31:19 *which were* in the f of the suburbs of H7704
Neh 11:25 And for the villages, with their f, *some* H7704
30 Lachish, and the f thereof, at Azekah, H7704
12:29 and out of the f of Geba and Azmaveth: H7704
44 into them out of the f of the cities the H7704
Job 5:10 earth, and sendeth waters upon the f: H2351
Ps 107:37 And sow the f, and plant vineyards, H7704
132: 6 we found it in the f of the wood. H7704
Prv 8:26 the earth, nor the f, nor the highest part H2351
23:10 enter not into the f of the fatherless: H7704
Isa 16: 8 For the f of Heshbon languish, *and* the H7709
32:12 for the pleasant f, for the fruitful vine. H7704
Jer 6:12 others, *with their* f and wives together: H7704
8:10 others, *and* their f to them that shall H7704
13:27 on the hills in the f. Woe unto thee, O H7704
31:40 ashes, and all the f unto the brook of H8309
32:15 of Israel; Houses and f and vineyards H7704
43 And f shall be bought in this land, H7704
44 Men shall buy f for money, and H7704
39:10 them vineyards and f at the same time. H3010
40: 7 which *were* in the f, *even* they and their H7704
13 in the f, came to Gedaliah to Mizpah, H7704
Ezk 29: 5 fall upon the open f; thou shalt not be H7704
Hos 12:11 *are* as heaps in the furrows of the f. H7704
Oba 19 shall possess the f of Ephraim, and the H7704
19 of Ephraim, and the f of Samaria: and H7704
Mic 2: 2 And they covet f, and take *them* by H7704
4 me! turning away he hath divided our f. H7704
Hab 3:17 shall fail, and the f shall yield no meat; H7709
Mk 2:23 through the corn f on the sabbath day; G4702
Lk 6: 1 through the corn f; and his disciples G4702
15:15 and he sent him into his f to feed swine. G68
Jn 4:35 f; for they are white already to harvest. G5561
Jas 5: 4 reaped down your f, which is of you G5561

FIERCE

Gen 49: 7 Cursed *be* their anger, for *it was* f; and H5794
Ex 32:12 Turn from thy f wrath, and repent of H2740
Nu 25: 4 the sun, that the f anger of the LORD H2740
32:14 the f anger of the LORD toward Israel. H2740
Dt 28:50 A nation of f countenance, which shall H5794
1Sa 20:34 So Jonathan arose from the table in f H2750
28:18 LORD, nor executedst his f wrath upon H2740
2Ch 28:11 the f wrath of the LORD *is* upon you. H2740
13 and *there is* f wrath against Israel. H2740
29:10 his f wrath may turn away from us. H2740
Ezr 10:14 thereof, until the f wrath of our God for H2740
Job 4:10 the voice of the f lion, and the teeth of H7826
10:16 huntest me as a f lion: and again thou H7826
28: 8 trodden it, nor the f lion passed by it. H7826
41:10 None *is so* f that dare stir him up: who H393
Ps 88:16 Thy f wrath goeth over me; thy terrors
Isa 7: 4 firebrands, for the f anger of Rezin H2750
13: 9 with wrath and f anger, to lay the land H2740
13 of hosts, and in the day of his f anger. H2740
19: 4 a cruel lord; and a f king shall rule over H5794
33:19 Thou shalt not see a f people, a people H3267
Jer 4: 8 and howl: for the f anger of the LORD H2740
26 of the LORD, *and* by his f anger. H2740
12:13 because of the f anger of the LORD. H2740
25:37 because of the f anger of the LORD. H2740
38 oppressor, and because of his f anger. H2740
30:24 The f anger of the LORD shall not H2740
49:37 them, *even* my f anger, saith the LORD; H2740
51:45 his soul from the f anger of the LORD. H2740
Lam 1:12 afflicted *me* in the day of his f anger. H2740
2: 3 He hath cut off in *his* f anger all the H2750
4:11 hath poured out his f anger, and hath H2740
Dan 8:23 to the full, a king of f countenance, and H5794
Jna 3: 9 from his f anger, that we perish not? H2740
Hab 1: 8 and are more f than the evening H2300
Zep 2: 2 chaff, before the f anger of the LORD H2740
3: 8 *even* all my f anger: for all the earth H2740
Mt 8:28 the tombs, exceeding f, so that no man G5467
Lk 23: 5 And they were the more f, saying, He G2001
2Ti 3: 3 f, despisers of those that are good, G434
Jas 3: 4 and *are* driven of f winds, yet are they G4642

FIERCENESS

Dt 13:17 may turn from the f of his anger, and H2740
Jos 7:26 LORD turned from the f of his anger. H2740
2Ki 23:26 not from the f of his great wrath, H2740
2Ch 30: 8 f of his wrath may turn away from you. H2740
Job 39:24 He swalloweth the ground with f and H7494
Ps 78:49 He cast upon them the f of his anger, H2740
85: 3 turned *thyself* from the f of thine anger. H2740
Jer 25:38 because of the f of the oppressor, and H2740
Hos 11: 9 I will not execute the f of mine anger, I H2740
Nah 1: 6 can abide in the f of his anger? his fury H2740
Rev 16:19 the cup of the wine of the f of his wrath. G2372
19:15 of the f and wrath of Almighty God. G2372

FIERCER

2Sa 19:43 f than the words of the men of Israel. H7185

FIERY

Nu 21: 6 And the LORD sent f serpents among H8314
8 Make thee a f serpent, and set it upon H8314
Dt 8:15 *wherein were* f serpents, and H8314
33: 2 his right hand *went* a f law for them. H799
Ps 21: 9 Thou shalt make them as a f oven in the H784
Isa 14:29 and his fruit *shall be* a f flying serpent. H8314
30: 6 lion, the viper and f flying serpent, they H8314
Dan 3: 6 into the midst of a burning f furnace. H5135
11 into the midst of a burning f furnace. H5135
15 midst of a burning f furnace; and who H5135
17 from the burning f furnace, and he will H5135
20 to cast *them* into the burning f furnace. H5135
21 into the midst of the burning f furnace. H5135
23 into the midst of the burning f furnace. H5135
26 of the burning f furnace, *and* spake, H5135
7: 9 f flame, *and* his wheels *as* burning fire. H5135
10 A f stream issued and came forth from H5135
Eph 6:16 to quench all the f darts of the wicked. G4448
Heb 10:27 of judgment and f indignation, which G4442
1Pt 4:12 concerning the f trial which is to try G4451

FIFTEEN

Gen 5:10 eight hundred and f years, and H2568+H6240
7:20 F cubits upward did the waters H2568+H6240
25: 7 threescore and f years. H7657+H2568
Ex 27:14 *the gate shall be* f cubits: their H2568+H6240
15 *be* hangings f *cubits*: their H2568+H6240
38:14 *of the gate were* f cubits; their H2568+H6240
15 *were* hangings of f cubits; their H2568+H6240
25 and f shekels, after the H7657+H2568
Lev 27: 7 shall be f shekels, and for H2568+H6240
Nu 31:37 hundred and threescore and f. H7657+H2568
Jdg 8:10 them, about f thousand *men*, H2568+H6240
2Sa 9:10 f sons and twenty servants. H2568+H6240
19:17 of Saul, and his f sons and his H2568+H6240
1Ki 7: 3 on forty five pillars, f *in* a row. H2568+H6240
2Ki 14:17 Jehoahaz king of Israel f years. H2568+H6240
20: 6 And I will add unto thy days f H2568+H6240
2Ch 25:25 Jehoahaz king of Israel f years. H2568+H6240
Isa 38: 5 will add unto thy days f years. H2568+H6240
Ezk 45:12 f shekels, shall be your maneh. H2568+H6235
Hos 3: 2 So I bought her to me for f H6240+H2568
Jn 11:18 unto Jerusalem, about f furlongs off: G1178
Act 7:14 threescore and f souls. G1440+G4002
27:28 sounded again, and found *it* f fathoms. G1178
Gal 1:18 see Peter, and abode with him f days. G1178

FIFTEENTH

Ex 16: 1 and Sinai, on the f day of the H2568+H6240
Lev 23: 6 And on the f day of the same H2568+H6240
34 Israel, saying, The f day of this H2568+H6240
39 Also in the f day of the seventh H2568+H6240
Nu 28:17 And in the f day of this month H2568+H6240
29:12 And on the f day of the seventh H2568+H6240
33: 3 month, on the f day of the first H2568+H6240
1Ki 12:32 month, on the f day of the H2568+H6240
33 in Beth-el the f day of the H2568+H6240
2Ki 14:23 In the f year of Amaziah the H2568+H6240
1Ch 24:14 The f to Bilgah, the sixteenth H2568+H6240
25:22 The f to Jeremoth, *he*, his sons, H2568+H6240
2Ch 15:10 the f year of the reign of Asa. H2568+H6240
Est 9:18 and on the f *day* of the same H2568+H6240
21 the f day of the same, yearly, H2568+H6240
Ezk 32:17 year, in the f *day* of the month, H2568+H6240
45:25 In the seventh *month*, in the f H2568+H6240
Lk 3: 1 Now in the f year of the reign of G4003

FIFTH

Gen 1:23 and the morning were the f day. H2549
30:17 conceived, and bare Jacob the f son. H2549
41:34 and take up the f part of the land of H2567
47:24 ye shall give the f *part* unto Pharaoh, H2549
26 should have the f *part*; except the land H2569
Lev 5:16 and shall add the f part thereto, and H2549
6: 5 and shall add the f part more thereto, H2549
19:25 And in the f year shall ye eat of the fruit H2549
22:14 he shall put the f *part* thereof unto it, H2549
27:13 a f *part* thereof unto thy estimation. H2549
15 he shall add the f *part* of the money of H2549
19 he shall add the f *part* of the money of H2549
27 and shall add a f *part* of it thereto: or H2549
31 he shall add thereto the f *part* thereof. H2549
Nu 5: 7 add unto it the f *part* thereof, and give H2549
7:36 On the f day Shelumiel the son of H2549
29:26 And on the f day nine bullocks, two H2549
33:38 of Egypt, in the first *day* of the f month. H2549
Jos 19:24 And the f lot came out for the tribe of H2549
Jdg 19: 8 morning on the f day to depart: and the H2549
2Sa 2:23 him under the f *rib*, that the spear H2570
3: 4 and the f, Shephatiah the son of Abital; H2549
27 there under the f *rib*, that he died, for H2570
4: 6 him under the f *rib*: and Rechab and H2570
20:10 therewith in the f *rib*, and shed out his H2570
1Ki 6:31 *and* side posts *were* a f part *of the wall*. H2549
14:25 And it came to pass in the f year of H2549
2Ki 8:16 And in the f year of Joram the son of H2568
25: 8 And in the f month, on the seventh *day* H2549
1Ch 2:14 Nethaneel the fourth, Raddai the f, H2549
3: 3 The f, Shephatiah of Abital: the sixth, H2549
8: 2 Nohah the fourth, and Rapha the f. H2549
12:10 Mishmannah the fourth, Jeremiah the f, H2549
24: 9 The f to Malchijah, the sixth to H2549
25:12 The f to Nethaniah, *he*, his sons, and H2549
26: 3 Elam the f, Jehohanan the sixth, H2549
4 Sacar the fourth, and Nethaneel the f, H2549
27: 8 The f captain for the fifth month *was* H2549
8 The fifth captain for the f month *was* H2549
2Ch 12: 2 And it came to pass, *that* in the f year H2549
Ezr 7: 8 And he came to Jerusalem in the f H2549
9 the first *day* of the f month came he to H2549
Neh 6: 5 f time with an open letter in his hand; H2549
15 in the twenty and f *day of the month* H2568
Jer 1: 3 of Jerusalem captive in the f month. H2549
28: 1 fourth year, *and* in the f month, *that* H2549
36: 9 And it came to pass in the f year of H2549
52:12 Now in the f month, in the tenth *day* of H2549
Ezk 1: 1 *month*, in the f *day* of the month, as H2568
2 In the f *day* of the month, which *was* H2568
2 the f year of king Jehoiachin's captivity, H2549
8: 1 *month*, in the f *day* of the month, *as* H2568
20: 1 year, in the f *month*, the tenth *day* H2549
33:21 *month*, in the f *day* of the month, *that* H2568
Zec 7: 3 I weep in the f month, separating H2549
5 mourned in the f and seventh *month*, H2549
8:19 and the fast of the f, and the fast of the H2549
Rev 6: 9 And when he had opened the f seal, I G3991
9: 1 And the f angel sounded, and I saw a G3991
16:10 And the f angel poured out his vial G3991
21:20 The f, sardonyx; the sixth, sardius; the G3991

FIFTIES

Ex 18:21 hundreds, rulers of f, and rulers of tens: H2572
25 hundreds, rulers of f, and rulers of tens. H2572
Dt 1:15 and captains over f, and captains over H2572
1Sa 8:12 and captains over f; and *will set them* to H2572
2Ki 1:14 of the former f with their fifties: H2572
14 fifties with their f: therefore let my life H2572
Mk 6:40 down in ranks, by hundreds, and by f. G4004
Lk 9:14 them sit down by f in a company. G4004

FIFTIETH

Lev 25:10 And ye shall hallow the f year, and H2572
11 A jubile shall that f year be unto you: H2572
2Ki 15:23 In the f year of Azariah king of Judah H2572
27 In the two and f year of Azariah king of H2572

FIFTY

Gen 6:15 the breadth of it f cubits, and the H2572
7:24 upon the earth an hundred and f days. H2572
8: 3 and f days the waters were abated. H2572
9:28 the flood three hundred and f years. H2572
29 nine hundred and f years: and he died. H2572
18:24 Peradventure there be f righteous H2572
24 for the f righteous that *are* therein? H2572
26 And the LORD said, If I find in Sodom f H2572
28 lack five of the f righteous: wilt thou H2572
Ex 26: 5 F loops shalt thou make in the one H2572
5 the one curtain, and f loops shalt thou H2572

Ex 26: 6 And thou shalt make f taches of gold, H2572
10 And thou shalt make f loops on the H2572
10 the coupling, and f loops in the edge of H2572
11 And thou shalt make f taches of brass, H2572
27:12 *be* hangings of f cubits: their pillars H2572
13 the east side eastward *shall be* f cubits. H2572
18 and the breadth f every where, and the H2572
30:23 *even* two hundred and f *shekels*, and of H2572
23 calamus two hundred and f *shekels*, H2572
36:12 F loops made he in one curtain, and H2572
12 one curtain, and f loops made he in the H2572
13 And he made f taches of gold, and H2572
17 And he made f loops upon the H2572
17 in the coupling, and f loops made he H2572
18 And he made f taches *of* brass to H2572
38:12 *were* hangings of f cubits, their pillars H2572
13 And for the east side eastward f cubits. H2572
26 thousand and five hundred and f *men*. H2572
Lev 23:16 shall ye number f days; and ye shall H2572
27: 3 shall be f shekels of silver, after H2572
16 *shall be valued* at f shekels of silver. H2572
Nu 1:23 of Simeon, *were* f and nine thousand H2572
25 and five thousand six hundred and f. H2572
29 f and four thousand and four hundred. H2572
31 of Zebulun, *were* f and seven thousand H2572
43 of Naphtali, *were* f and three thousand H2572
46 three thousand and five hundred and f. H2572
2: 6 f and four thousand and four hundred. H2572
8 thereof, *were* f and seven thousand H2572
13 of them, *were* f and nine thousand H2572
15 five thousand and six hundred and f. H2572
16 thousand and f and one thousand and H2572
16 four hundred and f, throughout their H2572
30 of them, *were* f and three thousand H2572
31 thousand and f and seven thousand H2572
32 three thousand and five hundred and f. H2572
4: 3 upward even until f years old, all that H2572
23 and upward until f years old shalt thou H2572
30 and upward even unto f years old shalt H2572
35 upward even unto f years old, every H2572
36 two thousand seven hundred and f. H2572
39 upward even unto f years old, every H2572
43 upward even unto f years old, every H2572
47 upward even unto f years old, every H2572
8:25 And from the age of f years they shall H2572
16: 2 Israel, two hundred and f princes of the H2572
17 two hundred and f censers; thou also, H2572
35 and f men that offered incense. H2572
26:10 and f men: and they became a sign. H2572
34 of them, f and two thousand and H2572
47 of them; *who were* f and three H2572
31:30 one portion of f, of the persons, of the H2572
47 one portion of f, *both* of man and of H2572
52 thousand seven hundred and f shekels. H2572
Dt 22:29 damsel's father f *shekels* of silver, and H2572
Jos 7:21 and a wedge of gold of f shekels weight, H2572
1Sa 6:19 smote of the people f thousand and H2572
2Sa 15: 1 horses, and f men to run before him. H2572
24:24 and the oxen for f shekels of silver. H2572
1Ki 1: 5 and f men to run before him. H2572
7: 2 breadth thereof f cubits, and the height H2572
6 the length thereof *was* f cubits, and the H2572
9:23 five hundred and f, which bare rule H2572
10:29 for an hundred and f: and so for all the H2572
18: 4 and hid them by f in a cave, and fed H2572
13 prophets by f in a cave, and fed them H2572
19 four hundred and f, and the prophets of H2572
22 prophets *are* four hundred and f men. H2572
2Ki 1: 9 him a captain of f with his fifty. And he H2572
9 of fifty with his f. And he went up to H2572
10 to the captain of f, If I *be* a man of God, H2572
10 thee and thy f. And there came down H2572
10 heaven, and consumed him and his f. H2572
11 another captain of f with his fifty. And H2572
11 of fifty with his f. And he answered and H2572
12 thee and thy f. And the fire of God H2572
12 heaven, and consumed him and his f. H2572
13 of the third f with his fifty. And the H2572
13 the third fifty with his f. And the third H2572
13 third captain of f went up, and came H2572
13 f thy servants, be precious in thy sight. H2572
2: 7 And f men of the sons of the prophets H2572
16 be with thy servants f strong men; let H2572
17 sent therefore f men; and they sought H2572
13: 7 to Jehoahaz but f horsemen, and ten H2572
15: 2 reigned two and f years in Jerusalem. H2572
20 of each man f shekels of silver, to H2572
25 and with him f men of the Gileadites: H2572
21: 1 to reign, and reigned f and five years in H2572
1Ch 5:21 of their camels f thousand, and of H2572
21 two hundred and f thousand, and of H2572
8:40 f. All these *are* of the sons of Benjamin. H2572
9: 9 nine hundred and f and six. All these H2572
12:33 of war, f thousand, which could H2572
2Ch 1:17 an hundred and f: and so brought they H2572
2:17 an hundred and f thousand and three H2572
3: 9 And the weight of the nails *was* f H2572
8:10 and f, that bare rule over the people. H2572
18 four hundred and f talents of gold, and H2572
26: 3 and he reigned f and two years in H2572
33: 1 reigned f and five years in Jerusalem: H2572
Ezr 2: 7 a thousand two hundred f and four. H2572
14 The children of Bigvai, two thousand f H2572
15 The children of Adin, four hundred f H2572
22 The men of Netophah, f and six. H2572
29 The children of Nebo, f and two. H2572
30 The children of Magbish, an hundred f H2572
31 a thousand two hundred f and four. H2572
37 The children of Immer, a thousand f H2572
60 of Nekoda, six hundred f and two. H2572
8: 3 of the males an hundred and f. H2572
6 son of Jonathan, and with him f males. H2572
26 six hundred and f talents of silver, and H2572
Neh 5:17 table an hundred and f of the Jews and H2572
6:15 of *the month* Elul, in f and two days. H2572
7:10 The children of Arah, six hundred f H2572
12 a thousand two hundred f and four. H2572
20 The children of Adin, six hundred f H2572
33 The men of the other Nebo, f and two. H2572
34 a thousand two hundred f and four. H2572
40 The children of Immer, a thousand f H2572
70 drams of gold, f basons, five hundred H2572
Est 5:14 be made of f cubits high, and to H2572
7: 9 also, the gallows f cubits high, which H2572
Isa 3: 3 The captain of f, and the honourable H2572
Ezk 40:15 porch of the inner gate *were* f cubits. H2572
21 the length thereof *was* f cubits, and the H2572
25 the length *was* f cubits, and the breadth H2572
29 about: *it was* f cubits long, and five H2572
33 about: *it was* f cubits long, and five H2572
36 the length *was* f cubits, and the breadth H2572
42: 2 door, and the breadth *was* f cubits. H2572
7 the length thereof *was* f cubits. H2572
8 in the utter court *was* f cubits: and, lo, H2572
45: 2 round about; and f cubits round about H2572
48:17 two hundred and f, and toward the H2572
17 two hundred and f, and toward the east H2572
17 two hundred and f, and toward the west H2572
17 and toward the west two hundred and f. H2572
Hag 2:16 for to draw out f *vessels* out of the H2572
Lk 7:41 five hundred pence, and the other f. G4004
16: 6 bill, and sit down quickly, and write f. G4004
Jn 8:57 Thou art not yet f years old, and hast G4004
21:11 an hundred and f and three: and for all G4004
Act 13:20 and f years, until Samuel the prophet. G4004
19:19 *it* f thousand *pieces* of silver. G4002+G3461

FIG

Gen 3: 7 and they sewed f leaves together, and H8384
Dt 8: 8 barley, and vines, and f trees, and H8384
Jdg 9:10 And the trees said to the f tree, Come H8384
11 But the f tree said unto them, Should I H8384
1Ki 4:25 his vine and under his f tree, from Dan H8384
2Ki 18:31 and every one of his f tree, and drink ye H8384
Ps 105:33 He smote their vines also and their f H8384
Prv 27:18 Whoso keepeth the f tree shall eat the H8384
Song 2:13 The f tree putteth forth her green figs, H8384
Isa 34: 4 vine, and as a falling *f* from the fig tree. H8384
4 vine, and as a falling *fig* from the f tree. H8384
36:16 and every one of his f tree, and drink ye H8384
Jer 5:17 up thy vines and thy f trees: they shall H8384
8:13 nor figs on the f tree, and the leaf shall H8384
Hos 2:12 And I will destroy her vines and her f H8384
9:10 as the firstripe in the f tree at her first H8384
Joel 1: 7 and barked my f tree: he hath made it H8384
12 The vine is dried up, and the f tree H8384
2:22 her fruit, the f tree and the vine do H8384
Am 4: 9 and your f trees and your olive H8384
Mic 4: 4 his vine and under his f tree; and none H8384
Nah 3:12 All thy strong holds *shall be like* f trees H8384
Hab 3:17 Although the f tree shall not blossom, H8384
Hag 2:19 yet the vine, and the f tree, and the H8384
Zec 3:10 under the vine and under the f tree. H8384
Mt 21:19 And when he saw a f tree in the way, he G4800
19 And presently the f tree withered away. G4800
20 How soon is the f tree withered away! G4800
21 *is done* to the f tree, but also if ye shall G4800
24:32 Now learn a parable of the f tree; When G4800
Mk 11:13 And seeing a f tree afar off having G4800
20 saw the f tree dried up from the roots. G4800
21 behold, the f tree which thou cursedst G4800
13:28 Now learn a parable of the f tree; When G4800
Lk 13: 6 certain *man* had a f tree planted in his G4800
7 fruit on this f tree, and find none: G4800
21:29 Behold the f tree, and all the trees; G4800
Jn 1:48 thou wast under the f tree, I saw thee. G4800
50 thee under the f tree, believest thou? G4800
Jas 3:12 Can the f tree, my brethren, bear olive G4800
Rev 6:13 the earth, even as a f tree casteth her G4800

FIGHT

Ex 1:10 our enemies, and f against us, and *so* H3898
14:14 The LORD shall f for you, and ye shall H3898
17: 9 out men, and go out, f with Amalek: to H3898
Dt 1:30 you, he shall f for you, according to H3898
41 we will go up and f, according to all that H3898
42 Go not up, neither f; for I *am* not among H3898
2:32 us, he and all his people, to f at Jahaz. H4421
3:22 the LORD your God he shall f for you. H3898
20: 4 that goeth with you, to f for you against H3898
10 When thou comest nigh unto a city to f H3898
Jos 9: 2 together, to f with Joshua and with H3898
10:25 to all your enemies against whom ye f. H3898
11: 5 waters of Merom, to f against Israel. H3898
19:47 of Dan went up to f against Leshem, H3898
Jdg 1: 1 the Canaanites first, to f against them? H3898
3 my lot, that we may f against the H3898
9 went down to f against the Canaanites, H3898
8: 1 thou wentest to f with the Midianites? H3898
9:38 go out, I pray now, and f with them. H3898
10: 9 over Jordan to f also against Judah, H3898
18 that will begin to f against the children H3898
11: 6 we may f with the children of Ammon. H3898
8 go with us, and f against the children H3898
9 bring me home again to f against the H3898
12 art come against me to f in my land? H3898
25 Israel, or did he ever f against them, H3898
32 of Ammon to f against them; and the H3898
12: 1 thou over to f against the children H3898
3 up unto me this day, to f against me? H3898
20:20 in array to f against them at Gibeah. H4421
1Sa 4: 9 to you: quit yourselves like men, and f. H3898
8:20 and go out before us, and f our battles. H3898
13: 5 together to f with Israel, thirty H3898
15:18 f against them until they be consumed. H3898
17: 9 If he be able to f with me, and to kill H3898
10 give me a man, that we may f together. H3898
20 forth to the f, and shouted for the battle. H4634
32 will go and f with this Philistine. H3898
33 this Philistine to f with him: for thou H3898
18:17 for me, and f the LORD'S battles. H3898
23: 1 the Philistines f against Keilah, and H3898
28: 1 for warfare, to f with Israel. And H3898
29: 8 that I may not go f against the enemies H3898
2Sa 11:20 city when ye did f? knew ye not that they H3898
1Ki 12:21 were warriors, to f against the house of H3898
24 not go up, nor f against your brethren H3898
20:23 than we; but let us f against them in the H3898
25 and we will f against them in the H3898
26 went up to Aphek, to f against Israel. H4421
22:31 chariots, saying, F neither with small H3898
32 they turned aside to f against him: and H3898
2Ki 3:21 were come up to f against them, they H3898
10: 3 throne, and f for your master's house. H3898
19: 9 he is come out to f against thee: he sent H3898
2Ch 11: 1 were warriors, to f against Israel, that H3898
4 not go up, nor f against your brethren: H3898
13:12 O children of Israel, f ye not against the H3898
18:30 with him, saying, F ye not with small or H3898
31 about him to f: but Jehoshaphat cried H3898
20:17 Ye shall not *need* to f in this *battle:* set H3898
32: 2 was purposed to f against Jerusalem, H4421
8 to help us, and to f our battles. And the H3898
35:20 Egypt came up to f against Carchemish H3898
22 himself, that he might f with him, and H3898
22 and came to f in the valley of Megiddo. H3898
Neh 4: 8 to f against Jerusalem, and to hinder it. H3898
14 and terrible, and f for your brethren, H3898
20 thither unto us: our God shall f for us. H3898
Ps 35: 1 f against them that fight against me. H3898
1 fight against them that f against me. H3898
56: 2 that f against me, O thou most High. H3898
144: 1 my hands to war, *and* my fingers to f: H4421
Isa 19: 2 and they shall f every one against his H3898
29: 7 the nations that f against Ariel, even all H6633
7 Ariel, even all that f against her and H6638
8 nations be, that f against mount Zion. H6633

Isa 30:32 in battles of shaking will he f with it. H3898
31: 4 come down to f for mount Zion, and H6633
Jer 1:19 And they shall f against thee; but they H3898
15:20 and they shall f against thee, but they H3898
21: 4 wherewith ye f against the king of H3898
5 And I myself will f against you with an H3898
32: 5 LORD: though ye f with the Chaldeans, H3898
24 Chaldeans, that f against it, because of H3898
29 And the Chaldeans, that f against this H3898
33: 5 They come to f with the Chaldeans, but H3898
34:22 this city; and they shall f against it, and H3898
37: 8 come again, and f against this city, and H3898
10 Chaldeans that f against you, and there H3898
41:12 men, and went to f with Ishmael the H3898
51:30 have forborn to f, they have remained H3898
Dan 10:20 now will I return to f with the prince of H3898
11:11 come forth and f with him, *even* with H3898
Zec 10: 5 and they shall f, because the LORD *is* H3898
14: 3 Then shall the LORD go forth, and f H3898
14 And Judah also shall f at Jerusalem; H3898
Jn 18:36 would my servants f, that I should not be *G75*
Act 5:39 ye be found even to f against God. *G2314*
23: 9 spoken to him, let us not f against God. *G2313*
1Co 9:26 so f I, not as one that beateth the air: *G4438*
1Ti 6:12 F the good fight of faith, lay hold on *G75*
12 Fight the good f of faith, lay hold on *G73*
2Ti 4: 7 I have fought a good f, I have finished *my* *G73*
Heb 10:32 ye endured a great f of afflictions; *G119*
11:34 waxed valiant in f, turned to flight the *G4171*
Jas 4: 2 and cannot obtain: ye f and war, yet ye *G3164*
Rev 2:16 quickly, and will f against them with *G4170*

FIGHTETH
Ex 14:25 LORD f for them against the Egyptians. H3898
Jos 23:10 that f for you, as he hath promised you. H3898
1Sa 25:28 because my lord f the battles of the H3898

FIGHTING
1Sa 17:19 the valley of Elah, f with the Philistines. H3898
2Ch 26:11 Moreover Uzziah had an host of f men, H4421
Ps 56: 1 me up; he f daily oppresseth me. H3898

FIGHTINGS
2Co 7: 5 side; without *were* f, within *were* fears. *G3163*
Jas 4: 1 From whence *come* wars and f among *G3163*

FIG-LEAVES See FIG and LEAVES.

FIGS
Nu 13:23 of the pomegranates, and of the f. H8384
20: 5 place of seed, or of f, or of vines, or of H8384
1Sa 25:18 cakes of f, and laid *them* on asses.
30:12 And they gave him a piece of a cake of f,
2Ki 20: 7 And Isaiah said, Take a lump of f. And H8384
1Ch 12:40 meal, cakes of f, and bunches of raisins,
Neh 13:15 wine, grapes, and f, and all *manner of* H8384
Song 2:13 The fig tree putteth forth her green f, H6291
Isa 38:21 take a lump of f, and lay *it* for a plaister H8384
Jer 8:13 on the vine, nor f on the fig tree, and H8384
24: 1 two baskets of f *were* set before the H8384
2 One basket *had* very good f, *even* like H8384
2 figs, *even* like the f *that are* first ripe: H8384
2 *had* very naughty f, which could not be H8384
3 And I said, F; the good figs, very good; H8384
3 Figs; the good f, very good; and the evil, H8384
5 Like these good f, so will I acknowledge H8384
8 And as the evil f, which cannot be H8384
29:17 f, that cannot be eaten, they are so evil. H8384
Nah 3:12 with the firstripe f: if they be shaken, H1061
Mt 7:16 gather grapes of thorns, or f of thistles? *G4810*
Mk 11:13 but leaves; for the time of f was not *yet*. *G4810*
Lk 6:44 men do not gather f, nor of a bramble *G4810*
Jas 3:12 either a vine, f? so *can* no fountain both *G4810*
Rev 6:13 f, when she is shaken of a mighty wind. *G3653*

FIG-TREE See FIG and TREE.

FIGURE
Dt 4:16 of any f, the likeness of male or female, H5566
Isa 44:13 and maketh it after the f of a man, H8403
Ro 5:14 who is the f of him that was to come. *G5179*
1Co 4: 6 I have in a f transferred to myself *G3345*
Heb 9: 9 Which *was* a f for the time then *G3850*
11:19 whence also he received him in a f. *G3850*
1Pt 3:21 The like f whereunto *even* baptism doth *G499*

FIGURES
1Ki 6:29 about with carved f of cherubims and H4734
Act 7:43 your god Remphan, f which ye made to *G5179*

Heb 9:24 *which are* the f of the true; but into *G499*

FILE
1Sa 13:21 Yet they had a f for the H6477+H6310

FILL
Gen 1:22 and multiply, and f the waters in the H4390
42:25 Then Joseph commanded to f their H4390
44: 1 of his house, saying, F the men's sacks H4390
Ex 10: 6 And they shall f thy houses, and the H4390
16:32 commandeth, F an omer of it to be H4393
Lev 25:19 eat your f, and dwell therein in safety. H7648
Dt 23:24 eat grapes thy f at thine own pleasure; H7648
1Sa 16: 1 over Israel? f thine horn with oil, H4390
1Ki 18:33 the wood, and said, F four barrels with H4390
Job 8:21 Till he f thy mouth with laughing, and H4390
15: 2 and f his belly with the east wind? H4390
20:23 *When* he is about to f his belly, *God* H4390
23: 4 him, and f my mouth with arguments. H4390
38:39 or f the appetite of the young lions, H4390
41: 7 Canst thou f his skin with barbed H4390
Ps 81:10 open thy mouth wide, and I will f it. H4390
83:16 F their faces with shame; that they may H4390
110: 6 heathen, he shall f *the places* with the H4390
Prv 1:13 we shall f our houses with spoil: H4390
7:18 Come, let us take our f of love until the H7301
8:21 substance; and I will f their treasures. H4390
Isa 8: 8 f the breadth of thy land, O Immanuel. H4393
14:21 nor f the face of the world with cities. H4390
27: 6 and f the face of the world with fruit. H4390
56:12 fetch wine, and we will f ourselves with H5433
Jer 13:13 Behold, I will f all the inhabitants of H4390
23:24 I f heaven and earth? saith the LORD. H4392
33: 5 but *it is* to f them with the dead H4390
51:14 Surely I will f thee with men, as with H4390
Ezk 3: 3 belly to eat, and f thy bowels with this H4390
7:19 their souls, neither f their bowels: H4390
9: 7 the house, and f the courts with the H4390
10: 2 the cherub, and f thine hand with coals H4390
24: 4 the shoulder; f *it* with the choice bones. H4390
30:11 Egypt, and f the land with the slain. H4390
32: 4 thee, and I will f the beasts of the whole H7646
5 and f the valleys with thy height. H4390
35: 8 And I will f his mountains with his H4390
Zep 1: 9 the threshold, which f their masters' H4390
Hag 2: 7 come: and I will f this house with glory, H4390
Mt 9:16 which is put in to f it up taketh from *G4138*
15:33 wilderness, as to f so great a multitude? *G5526*
23:32 F ye up then the measure of your *G4137*
Jn 2: 7 Jesus saith unto them, F the waterpots *G1072*
Ro 15:13 Now the God of hope f you with all joy *G4137*
Eph 4:10 all heavens, that he might f all things.) *G4137*
Col 1:24 for you, and f up that which is behind *G466*
1Th 2:16 might be saved, to f up their sins alway: *G378*
Rev 18: 6 which she hath filled f to her double. *G2767*

FILLED
Gen 6:11 God, and the earth was f with violence. H4390
13 for the earth is f with violence through H4390
21:19 and she went, and f the bottle with H4390
24:16 well, and f her pitcher, and came up. H4390
26:15 stopped them, and f them with earth. H4390
Ex 1: 7 mighty; and the land was f with them. H4390
2:16 drew *water*, and f the troughs to water H4390
16:12 ye shall be f with bread; and ye shall H7646
28: 3 whom I have f with the spirit of H4390
31: 3 And I have f him with the spirit of God, H4390
35:31 And he hath f him with the spirit of H4390
35 Them hath he f with wisdom of heart, H4390
40:34 the glory of the LORD f the tabernacle. H4390
35 the glory of the LORD f the tabernacle. H4390
Nu 14:21 shall be f with the glory of the LORD. H4390
Dt 26:12 they may eat within thy gates, and be f; H7646
31:20 shall have eaten and f themselves, and H7646
Jos 9:13 And these bottles of wine, which we f, H4390
1Ki 7:14 brass: and he was f with wisdom, and H4390
8:10 that the cloud f the house of the LORD, H4390
11 the LORD had f the house of the LORD. H4390
18:35 and he f the trench also with water. H4390
20:27 of kids; but the Syrians f the country. H4390
2Ki 3:17 that valley shall be f with water, that ye H4390
20 and the country was f with water. H4390
25 his stone, and f it; and they stopped H4390
21:16 much, till he had f Jerusalem from one H4390
23:14 f their places with the bones of men. H4390
24: 4 that he shed: for he f Jerusalem with H4390
2Ch 5:13 the house was f with a cloud, *even* the H4390
14 of the LORD had f the house of God. H4390
7: 1 and the glory of the LORD f the house. H4390

2Ch 7: 2 of the LORD had f the LORD'S house. H4390
16:14 the bed which was f with sweet odours H4390
Ezr 9:11 which have f it from one end to another H4390
Neh 9:25 did eat, and were f, and became fat, H7646
Job 3:15 Or with princes that had gold, who f H4390
16: 8 And thou hast f me with wrinkles, H7059
22:18 Yet he f their houses with good *things*: H4390
Ps 38: 7 For my loins are f with a loathsome H4390
71: 8 Let my mouth be f *with* thy praise *and* H4390
72:19 be f *with* his glory; Amen, and Amen. H4390
78:29 So they did eat, and were well f: for he H7646
80: 9 it to take deep root, and it f the land. H4390
104:28 thine hand, they are f with good. H7646
123: 3 for we are exceedingly f with contempt. H7646
4 Our soul is exceedingly f with the H7646
126: 2 Then was our mouth f with laughter, H4390
Prv 1:31 way, and be f with their own devices. H7646
3:10 So shall thy barns be f with plenty, and H4390
5:10 Lest strangers be f with thy wealth; and H7646
12:21 but the wicked shall be f with mischief. H4390
14:14 The backslider in heart shall be f with H7646
18:20 the increase of his lips shall he be f. H7646
20:17 his mouth shall be f with gravel. H4390
24: 4 f with all precious and pleasant riches. H4390
25:16 lest thou be f therewith, and vomit it. H7646
30:16 earth *that* is not f with water; and the H7646
22 and a fool when he is f with meat; H7646
Ecc 1: 8 with seeing, nor the ear f with hearing. H4390
6: 3 his soul be not f with good, and also H7646
7 his mouth, and yet the appetite is not f. H4390
Song 5: 2 for my head is f with dew, *and* my H4390
Isa 6: 1 lifted up, and his train f the temple. H4390
4 cried, and the house was f with smoke. H4390
21: 3 Therefore are my loins f with pain: H4390
33: 5 on high: he hath f Zion with judgment H4390
34: 6 The sword of the LORD is f with blood, H4390
43:24 neither hast thou f me with the fat of H7301
65:20 man that hath not f his days: for the H4390
Jer 13:12 bottle shall be f with wine: and they H4390
12 that every bottle shall be f with wine? H4390
15:17 for thou hast f me with indignation. H4390
16:18 land, they have f mine inheritance with H4390
19: 4 f this place with the blood of innocents; H4390
41: 9 f it with *them that were* slain. H4390
46:12 and thy cry hath f the land: for the H4390
51: 5 their land was f with sin against the H4390
34 a dragon, he hath f his belly with my H4390
Lam 3:15 He hath f me with bitterness, he hath H7646
30 smiteth him: he is f full with reproach. H7646
Ezk 8:17 here? for they have f the land with H4390
10: 3 in; and the cloud f the inner court. H4390
4 and the house was f with the cloud, H4390
11: 6 have f the streets thereof with the slain. H4390
23:33 Thou shalt be f with drunkenness and H4390
28:16 they have f the midst of thee with H4390
36:38 the waste cities be f with flocks of men: H4392
39:20 Thus ye shall be f at my table with H7646
43: 5 the glory of the LORD f the house. H4390
44: 4 the glory of the LORD f the house of the H4390
Dan 2:35 great mountain, and f the whole earth. H4391
Hos 13: 6 so were they f; they were filled, and H7646
6 filled; they were f, and their heart was H7646
Nah 2:12 his lionesses, and f his holes with prey, H4390
Hab 2:14 For the earth shall be f with the H4390
16 Thou art f with shame for glory: drink H7646
Hag 1: 6 but ye are not f with drink; ye clothe
Zec 9:13 When I have bent Judah for me, f the H4390
15 and they shall be f like bowls, *and* as H4390
Mt 5: 6 after righteousness: for they shall be f. *G5526*
14:20 And they did all eat, and were f: and *G5526*
15:37 And they did all eat, and were f: and *G5526*
27:48 a spunge, and f *it* with vinegar, and *G4130*
Mk 2:21 the new piece that f it up taketh away *G4138*
6:42 And they did all eat, and were f. *G5526*
7:27 children first be f: for it is not meet to *G5526*
8: 8 So they did eat, and were f: and they *G5526*
15:36 And one ran and f a spunge full of *G1072*
Lk 1:15 and he shall be f with the Holy Ghost, *G4130*
41 Elisabeth was f with the Holy Ghost: *G4130*
53 He hath f the hungry with good things; *G1705*
67 And his father Zacharias was f with the *G4130*
2:40 strong in spirit, f with wisdom: and the *G4137*
3: 5 Every valley shall be f, and every *G4137*
4:28 heard these things, were f with wrath, *G4130*
5: 7 they came, and f both the ships, so that *G4130*
26 God, and were f with fear, saying, We *G4130*
6:11 And they were f with madness; and *G4130*
21 for ye shall be f. Blessed *are ye* that *G5526*
8:23 f *with water*, and were in jeopardy. *G4845*

Lk 9:17 And they did eat, and were all f: and G5526
14:23 to come in, that my house may be f. G1072
15:16 And he would fain have f his belly with G1072
Jn 2: 7 water. And they f them up to the brim. G1072
6:12 When they were f, he said unto his G1705
13 together, and f twelve baskets with G1072
26 ye did eat of the loaves, and were f. G5526
12: 3 was f with the odour of the ointment. G4137
16: 6 unto you, sorrow hath f your heart. G4137
19:29 of vinegar: and they f a spunge with G4130
Act 2: 2 f all the house where they were sitting. G4137
4 And they were all f with the Holy G4130
3:10 and they were f with wonder and G4130
4: 8 Then Peter, f with the Holy Ghost, said G4130
31 and they were all f with the Holy Ghost, G4130
5: 3 why hath Satan f thine heart to lie to G4137
17 and were f with indignation, G4130
28 behold, ye have f Jerusalem with your G4137
9:17 thy sight, and be f with the Holy Ghost. G4130
13: 9 Then Saul, (who also *is called* Paul,) f G4130
45 they were f with envy, and spake G4130
52 And the disciples were f with joy, and G4137
19:29 And the whole city was f with G4130
Ro 1:29 Being f with all unrighteousness, G4137
15:14 full of goodness, f with all knowledge, G4137
24 I be somewhat f with your *company*. G1705
2Co 7: 4 of you: I am f with comfort, I am G4137
Eph 3:19 might be f with all the fulness of God. G4137
5:18 is excess; but be f with the Spirit; G4137
Php 1:11 Being f with the fruits of righteousness, G4137
Col 1: 9 that ye might be f with the knowledge G4137
2Ti 1: 4 of thy tears, that I may be f with joy; G4137
Jas 2:16 be *ye* warmed and f; notwithstanding G5526
Rev 8: 5 And the angel took the censer, and f it G1072
15: 1 for in them is f up the wrath of God. G5055
8 And the temple was f with smoke from G1072
18: 6 cup which she hath f fill to her double. G2767
19:21 and all the fowls were f with their flesh. G5526

FILLEDST
Dt 6:11 *things*, which thou f not, and wells H4390
Ezk 27:33 of the seas, thou f many people; thou H7646

FILLEST
Ps 17:14 and whose belly thou f with thy hid H4390

FILLET
Jer 52:21 cubits; and a f of twelve cubits did H2339

FILLETED
Ex 27:17 the court *shall be* f with silver; their H2836
38:17 pillars of the court *were* f with silver. H2836
28 overlaid their chapiters, and f them. H2836

FILLETH
Job 9:18 my breath, but f me with bitterness. H7646
Ps 84: 6 make it a well; the rain also f the pools. H5844
107: 9 For he satisfieth the longing soul, and f H4390
129: 7 Wherewith the mower f not his hand; H4390
147:14 He maketh peace *in* thy borders, *and* f H7646
Eph 1:23 body, the fulness of him that f all in all. G4137

FILLETS
Ex 27:10 the pillars and their f *shall be of* silver. H2838
11 hooks of the pillars and their f *of* silver. H2838
36:38 and their f with gold: but their H2838
38:10 of the pillars and their f *were of* silver. H2838
11 hooks of the pillars and their f *of* silver. H2838
12 hooks of the pillars and their f *of* silver. H2838
17 the pillars and their f *of* silver; and the H2838
19 of their chapiters and their f *of* silver. H2838

FILLING
Act 14:17 f our hearts with food and gladness. G1705

FILTH
Isa 4: 4 washed away the f of the daughters of H6675
Nah 3: 6 And I will cast abominable f upon thee, H8251
1Co 4:13 are made as the f of the world, *and are* G4027
1Pt 3:21 away of the f of the flesh, but the G4509

FILTHINESS
2Ch 29: 5 carry forth the f out of the holy *place*. H5079
Ezr 6:21 them from the f of the heathen of the H2932
9:11 land with the f of the people of the H5079
Prv 30:12 eyes, and *yet* is not washed from their f. H6675
Isa 28: 8 For all tables are full of vomit *and* f, *so* H6675
Lam 1: 9 Her f *is* in her skirts; she remembereth H2932
Ezk 16:36 Thus saith the Lord GOD; Because thy f H5178
22:15 and will consume thy f out of thee. H2932
24:11 burn, and *that* the f of it may be molten H2932
13 In thy f *is* lewdness: because I have H2932
13 purged from thy f any more, till I have H2932
36:25 from all your f, and from all your idols, H2932
2Co 7: 1 ourselves from all f of the flesh and G3436
Eph 5: 4 Neither f, nor foolish talking, nor jesting, G151
Jas 1:21 Wherefore lay apart all f and G4507
Rev 17: 4 abominations and f of her fornication: G168

FILTHY
Job 15:16 How much more abominable and f *is* H444
Ps 14: 3 *all* together become f: *there is* none that H444
53: 3 altogether become f; *there is* none that H444
Isa 64: 6 *are* as f rags; and we all do fade H5708
Zep 3: 1 Woe to her that is f and polluted, to the H4754
Zec 3: 3 Now Joshua was clothed with f H6674
4 Take away the f garments from him. H6674
Col 3: 8 f communication out of your mouth. G148
1Ti 3: 3 not greedy of f lucre; but patient, not
8 to much wine, not greedy of f lucre;
Tit 1: 7 to wine, no striker, not given to f lucre; G150
11 which they ought not, for f lucre's sake. G150
1Pt 5: 2 not for f lucre, but of a ready mind; G147
2Pt 2: 7 And delivered just Lot, vexed with the f G766
Jude 8 Likewise also these *f* dreamers defile the
Rev 22:11 and he which is f, let him be filthy still: G4510
11 is filthy, let him be f still: and he that is G4510

FINALLY
2Co 13:11 F, brethren, farewell. Be perfect, be of G3063
Eph 6:10 F, my brethren, be strong in the Lord, G3063
Php 3: 1 F, my brethren, rejoice in the Lord. To G3063
4: 8 F, brethren, whatsoever things are true, G3063
2Th 3: 1 F, brethren, pray for us, that the word G3063
1Pt 3: 8 F, *be ye* all of one mind, having G5056

FIND
Gen 18:26 And the LORD said, If I f in Sodom fifty H4672
28 And he said, If I f there forty and five, H4672
30 said, I will not do *it*, if I f thirty there. H4672
19:11 they wearied themselves to f the door. H4672
32: 5 my lord, that I may f grace in thy sight. H4672
19 ye speak unto Esau, when ye f him. H4672
33: 8 *are* to f grace in the sight of my lord. H4672
15 it? let me f grace in the sight of my lord. H4672
34:11 brethren, Let me f grace in your eyes, H4672
38:22 and said, I cannot f her; and also the H4672
41:38 servants, Can we f *such a one* as this *is*, H4672
47:25 our lives: let us f grace in the sight of H4672
Ex 5:11 Go ye, get you straw where ye can f it: H4672
16:25 to day ye shall not f it in the field. H4672
33:13 thee, that I may f grace in thy sight: H4672
Nu 32:23 and be sure your sin will f you out. H4672
35:27 And the revenger of blood f him H4672
Dt 4:29 God, thou shalt f *him*, if thou seek him H4672
22:23 a man f her in the city, and lie with her; H4672
25 But if a man f a betrothed damsel in H4672
28 If a man f a damsel *that is* a virgin, H4672
24: 1 to pass that she f no favour in his eyes, H4672
28:65 And among these nations shalt thou f no
Jdg 9:33 do to them as thou shalt f occasion. H4672
14:12 of the feast, and f *it* out, then I will give H4672
17: 8 where he could f *a place*: and he came H4672
9 I go to sojourn where I may f *a place*. H4672
Ru 1: 9 The LORD grant you that ye may f rest, H4672
2: 2 in whose sight I shall f grace. And she H4672
13 Then she said, Let me f favour in thy H4672
1Sa 1:18 And she said, Let thine handmaid f H4672
9:13 ye shall straightway f him, before he go H4672
13 up; for about this time ye shall f him. H4672
10: 2 then thou shalt f two men by Rachel's H4672
20:21 a lad, *saying*, Go, f out the arrows. If I H4672
36 And he said unto his lad, Run, f out H4672
23:17 father shall not f thee; and thou shalt H4672
24:19 For if a man f his enemy, will he let H4672
25: 8 let the young men f favour in thine H4672
2Sa 15:25 the city: if I shall f favour in the eyes of H4672
16: 4 f grace in thy sight, my lord, O king. H4672
17:20 not f *them*, they returned to Jerusalem. H4672
1Ki 18: 5 we may f grass to save the horses H4672
12 and he cannot f thee, he shall slay me: H4672
2Ch 2:14 of graving, and to f out every device H2803
20:16 of Ziz; and ye shall f them at the end of H4672
30: 9 your children *shall f* compassion before
32: 4 of Assyria come, and f much water? H4672
Ezr 4:15 so shalt thou f in the book of the H7912
7:16 that thou canst f in all the province of H7912
Job 3:22 are glad, when they can f the grave? H4672
11: 7 Canst thou by searching f out God? H4672
7 f out the Almighty unto perfection? H4672
17:10 I cannot f *one* wise *man* among you. H4672
23: 3 Oh that I knew where I might f him! H4672
34:11 every man to f according to *his* ways. H4672
37:23 *Touching* the Almighty, we cannot f H4672
Ps 10:15 out his wickedness *till* thou f none. H4672
17: 3 me, *and* shalt f nothing; I am purposed H4672
21: 8 Thine hand shall f out all thine H4672
8 hand shall f out those that hate thee. H4672
132: 5 Until I f out a place for the LORD, an H4672
Prv 1:13 We shall f all precious substance, we H4672
28 seek me early, but they shall not f me: H4672
2: 5 the LORD, and f the knowledge of God. H4672
3: 4 So shalt thou f favour and good H4672
4:22 For they *are* life unto those that f them, H4672
8: 9 and right to them that f knowledge. H4672
12 I wisdom dwell with prudence, and f H4672
17 and those that seek me early shall f me. H4672
16:20 He that handleth a matter wisely shall f H4672
19: 8 keepeth understanding shall f good. H4672
20: 6 goodness: but a faithful man who can f? H4672
28:23 afterwards shall f more favour than he H4672
31:10 Who can f a virtuous woman? for her H4672
Ecc 3:11 so that no man can f out the work that H4672
7:14 that man should f nothing after him. H4672
24 and exceeding deep, who can f it out? H4672
26 And I f more bitter than death the H4672
27 one by one, to f out the account: H4672
28 Which yet my soul seeketh, but I f not: H4672
8:17 that a man cannot f out the work that H4672
17 yet he shall not f *it*; yea further; though H4672
17 know *it*, yet shall he not be able to f *it*. H4672
11: 1 for thou shalt f it after many days. H4672
12:10 The preacher sought to f out acceptable H4672
Song 5: 6 but I could not f him; I called him, but H4672
8 of Jerusalem, if ye f my beloved, that ye H4672
8: 1 *when* I should f thee without, I would H4672
Isa 34:14 there, and f for herself a place of rest. H4672
41:12 Thou shalt seek them, and shalt not f H4672
58: 3 f pleasure, and exact all your labours. H4672
Jer 2:24 in her month they shall f her. H4672
5: 1 thereof, if ye can f a man, if there be H4672
6:16 and ye shall f rest for your souls. But H4672
10:18 will distress them, that they may f *it so*. H4672
29:13 And ye shall seek me, and f *me*, when H4672
45: 3 I fainted in my sighing, and I f no rest. H4672
Lam 1: 6 like harts *that* f no pasture, and they H4672
2: 9 also f no vision from the LORD. H4672
Dan 6: 4 princes sought to f occasion against H7912
4 but they could f none occasion nor H7912
5 Then said these men, We shall not f H7912
5 this Daniel, except we f *it* against him H7912
Hos 2: 6 a wall, that she shall not f her paths. H4672
7 but shall not f *them*: then shall she H4672
5: 6 LORD; but they shall not f *him*; he hath H4672
12: 8 f none iniquity in me that *were* sin. H4672
Am 8:12 word of the LORD, and shall not f *it*. H4672
Mt 7: 7 seek, and ye shall f; knock, and it shall G2147
14 unto life, and few there be that f it. G2147
10:39 that loseth his life for my sake shall f it. G2147
11:29 and ye shall f rest unto your souls. G2147
16:25 will lose his life for my sake shall f it. G2147
17:27 mouth, thou shalt f a piece of money: G2147
18:13 And if so be that he f it, verily I say G2147
21: 2 ye shall f an ass tied, and a colt G2147
22: 9 many as ye shall f, bid to the marriage. G2147
24:46 lord when he cometh shall f so doing. G2147
Mk 11: 2 into it, ye shall f a colt tied, whereon G2147
13 if haply he might f any thing thereon: G2147
13:36 Lest coming suddenly he f you G2147
Lk 2:12 unto you; Ye shall f the babe wrapped G2147
5:19 And when they could not f by what *way* G2147
6: 7 might f an accusation against him. G2147
11: 9 seek, and ye shall f; knock, and it shall G2147
12:37 he cometh shall f watching: verily I say G2147
38 f *them* so, blessed are those servants. G2147
43 lord when he cometh shall f so doing. G2147
13: 7 on this fig tree, and f none: cut it down; G2147
15: 4 go after that which is lost, until he f it? G2147
8 house, and seek diligently till she f *it*? G2147
18: 8 cometh, shall he f faith on the earth? G2147
19:30 entering ye shall f a colt tied, whereon G2147
48 And could not f what they might do: for G2147
23: 4 *to* the people, I f no fault in this man. G2147
Jn 7:34 Ye shall seek me, and shall not f *me*: G2147
35 that we shall not f him? will he go unto G2147
36 me, and shall not f *me*: and where I G2147
10: 9 and shall go in and out, and f pasture. G2147

Jn 18:38 unto them, I f in him no fault *at all.* G2147
19: 4 ye may know that I f no fault in him. G2147
6 and crucify *him*: for I f no fault in him. G2147
21: 6 ship, and ye shall f. They cast therefore, G2147
Act 7:46 to f a tabernacle for the God of Jacob. G2147
17:27 feel after him, and f him, though he be G2147
23: 9 strove, saying, We f no evil in this man: G2147
Ro 7:18 to perform that which is good I f not. G2147
21 I f then a law, that, when I would do G2147
9:19 f fault? For who hath resisted his will?
2Co 9: 4 with me, and f you unprepared, we G2147
12:20 when I come, I shall not f you such as I G2147
2Ti 1:18 The Lord grant unto him that he may f G2147
Heb 4:16 and f grace to help in time of need. G2147
Rev 9: 6 and shall not f it; and shall desire to G2147
18:14 and thou shalt f them no more at all. G2147

FINDEST
Gen 31:32 With whomsoever thou f thy gods, let H4672
Ezk 3: 1 of man, eat that thou f; eat this roll, and H4672

FINDETH
Gen 4:14 *that* every one that f me shall slay me. H4672
Job 33:10 Behold, he f occasions against me, he H4672
Ps119:162 I rejoice at thy word, as one that f great H4672
Prv 3:13 Happy *is* the man *that* f wisdom, and H4672
8:35 For whoso f me findeth life, and shall H4672
35 For whoso findeth me f life, and shall H4672
14: 6 A scorner seeketh wisdom, and *f it* not: H4672
17:20 He that hath a froward heart f no good: H4672
18:22 *Whoso* f a wife findeth a good *thing*, H4672
22 *Whoso* findeth a wife f a good *thing*, H4672
21:10 his neighbour f no favour in his eyes.
21 f life, righteousness, and honour. H4672
Ecc 9:10 Whatsoever thy hand f to do, do *it* with H4672
Lam 1: 3 the heathen, she f no rest: all her H4672
Hos 14: 3 gods: for in thee the fatherless f mercy.
Mt 7: 8 and he that seeketh f; and to him that G2147
10:39 He that f his life shall lose it: and he G2147
12:43 dry places, seeking rest, and f none. G2147
44 he f *it* empty, swept, and garnished. G2147
26:40 the disciples, and f them asleep, and G2147
Mk 14:37 And he cometh, and f them sleeping, G2147
Lk 11:10 and he that seeketh f; and to him that G2147
25 And when he cometh, he f *it* swept and G2147
Jn 1:41 He first f his own brother Simon, and G2147
43 into Galilee, and f Philip, and saith G2147
45 Philip f Nathanael, and saith unto him, G2147
5:14 Afterward Jesus f him in the temple, G2147

FINDING
Gen 4:15 Cain, lest any f him should kill him. H4672
Job 9:10 Which doeth great things past f out; H2714
Isa 58:13 own ways, nor f thine own pleasure, H4672
Lk 11:24 seeking rest; and f none, he saith, I will G2147
Act 4:21 they let them go, f nothing how they G2147
19: 1 to Ephesus: and f certain disciples, G2147
21: 2 And f a ship sailing over unto Phenicia, G2147
4 And f disciples, we tarried there seven G429
Ro 11:33 his judgments, and his ways past f out! G421
Heb 8: 8 For f fault with them, he saith, Behold,

FINE
Gen 18: 6 three measures of f meal, knead *it*, and H5560
41:42 him in vestures of f linen, and put a H8336
Ex 25: 4 And blue, and purple, and scarlet, and f
26: 1 *with* ten curtains *of* f twined linen, and
31 purple, and scarlet, and f twined linen of
36 and scarlet, and f twined linen, wrought
27: 9 for the court *of* f twined linen of an
16 and scarlet, and f twined linen, wrought
18 five cubits *of* f twined linen, and their
28: 5 and purple, and scarlet, and f linen.
6 and f twined linen, with cunning work.
8 purple, and scarlet, and f twined linen.
15 and *of* f twined linen, shalt thou make it.
39 And thou shalt embroider the coat of f
39 make the mitre *of* f linen, and thou shalt
35: 6 And blue, and purple, and scarlet, and f
23 and scarlet, and f linen, and goats' *hair*,
25 of purple, *and* of scarlet, *and* of f linen.
35 in scarlet, and in f linen, and of the
36: 8 ten curtains *of* f twined linen, and blue,
35 and scarlet, and f twined linen: *with*
37 and f twined linen, of needlework;
38: 9 *of* f twined linen, an hundred cubits:
16 round about *were* of f twined linen.
18 and scarlet, and f twined linen: and
23 and in purple, and in scarlet, and f linen.
Ex 39: 2 purple, and scarlet, and f twined linen.
3 and in the f linen, *with* cunning work.
5 and scarlet, and f twined linen; as the
8 purple, and scarlet, and f twined linen.
27 And they made coats *of* f linen *of* woven
28 And a mitre *of* f linen, and goodly
28 and goodly bonnets *of* f linen, and linen
28 and linen breeches *of* f twined linen,
29 And a girdle *of* f twined linen, and blue,
Lev 2: 1 offering shall be *of* f flour; and he shall H5560
4 cakes of f flour mingled with oil, H5560
5 *of* f flour unleavened, mingled with oil. H5560
7 it shall be made *of* f flour with oil. H5560
5:11 of an ephah of f flour for a sin offering; H5560
6:20 part of an ephah of f flour for a meat H5560
7:12 cakes mingled with oil, of f flour, fried. H5560
14:10 three tenth deals of f flour *for* a meat H5560
21 one tenth deal of f flour mingled with H5560
23:13 two tenth deals of f flour mingled with H5560
17 they shall be of f flour; they shall be H5560
24: 5 And thou shalt take f flour, and bake H5560
Nu 6:15 bread, cakes of f flour mingled with oil, H5560
7:13 them *were* full of f flour mingled with H5560
19 of them full of f flour mingled with oil H5560
25 of them full of f flour mingled with oil H5560
31 of them full of f flour mingled with oil H5560
37 of them full of f flour mingled with oil H5560
43 of them full of f flour mingled with oil H5560
49 of them full of f flour mingled with oil H5560
55 of them full of f flour mingled with oil H5560
61 of them full of f flour mingled with oil H5560
67 of them full of f flour mingled with oil H5560
73 of them full of f flour mingled with oil H5560
79 of them full of f flour mingled with oil H5560
8: 8 offering, *even* f flour mingled with oil, H5560
1Ki 4:22 was thirty measures of f flour, and
2Ki 7: 1 *shall* a measure of f flour *be sold* for a
16 So a measure of f flour was *sold* for a
18 and a measure of f flour for a shekel,
1Ch 4:21 wrought f linen, of the house of Ashbea,
9:29 sanctuary, and the f flour, and the wine,
15:27 And David *was* clothed with a robe of f
23:29 Both for the shewbread, and for the f
2Ch 2:14 in blue, and in f linen, and in crimson;
3: 5 he overlaid with f gold, and set thereon H2896
8 he overlaid it with f gold, *amounting* to H2896
14 f linen, and wrought cherubims thereon.
Ezr 8:27 two vessels of f copper, precious as gold.
Est 1: 6 with cords of f linen and purple to silver
8:15 with a garment of f linen and purple:
Job 28: 1 and a place for gold *where* they f *it*. H2212
17 of it *shall not be for* jewels of f gold.
31:24 to the f gold, *Thou art* my confidence;
Ps 19:10 yea, than much f gold: sweeter also than
119:127 above gold; yea, above f gold.
Prv 3:14 silver, and the gain thereof than f gold.
7:16 with carved *works*, with f linen of Egypt.
8:19 My fruit *is* better than gold, yea, than f
25:12 and an ornament of f gold, *so is* a wise
31:24 She maketh f linen, and selleth *it*; and
Song 5:11 His head *is as* the most f gold, his locks
15 marble, set upon sockets of f gold: his
Isa 3:23 The glasses, and the f linen, and the
13:12 I will make a man more precious than f
19: 9 Moreover they that work in f flax, and H8305
Lam 4: 1 dim! *how* is the most f gold changed! the
2 Zion, comparable to f gold, how are they
Ezk 16:10 with f linen, and I covered thee with silk.
13 thy raiment *was of* f linen, and silk, and
13 thou didst eat f flour, and honey, and
19 My meat also which I gave thee, f flour,
27: 7 F linen with broidered work from Egypt
16 work, and f linen, and coral, and agate.
46:14 oil, to temper with the f flour; a meat
Dan 2:32 This image's head *was* of f gold, his H2869
10: 5 loins *were* girded with f gold of Uphaz:
Zec 9: 3 and f gold as the mire of the streets.
Mk 15:46 And he bought f linen, and took him
Lk 16:19 clothed in purple and f linen, and fared
Rev 1:15 And his feet like unto f brass, as if they
2:18 flame of fire, and his feet *are* like f brass;
18:12 and of pearls, and f linen, and purple,
13 wine, and oil, and f flour, and wheat,
16 that was clothed in f linen, and purple,
19: 8 be arrayed in f linen, clean and white:
8 the f linen is the righteousness of saints.
14 clothed in f linen, white and clean.

FINER
Prv 25: 4 there shall come forth a vessel for the f. H6884

FINEST
Ps 81:16 He should have fed them also with the f H2459
147:14 *and* filleth thee with the f of the wheat. H2459

FINGER
Ex 8:19 This *is* the f of God: and Pharaoh's H676
29:12 of the altar with thy f, and pour all the H676
31:18 tables of stone, written with the f of God. H676
Lev 4: 6 And the priest shall dip his f in the H676
17 And the priest shall dip his f *in some* of H676
25 offering with his f, and put *it* upon the H676
30 thereof with his f, and put *it* upon the H676
34 offering with his f, and put *it* upon the H676
8:15 about with his f, and purified the altar, H676
9: 9 and he dipped his f in the blood, and put H676
14:16 And the priest shall dip his right f in the H676
16 with his f seven times before the LORD: H676
27 with his right f *some* of the oil that *is* H676
16:14 sprinkle *it* with his f upon the mercy seat H676
14 of the blood with his f seven times. H676
19 blood upon it with his f seven times, and H676
Nu 19: 4 her blood with his f, and sprinkle of her H676
Dt 9:10 written with the f of God; and on them H676
1Ki 12:10 *f* shall be thicker than my father's loins.
2Ch 10:10 *f* shall be thicker than my father's loins.
Isa 58: 9 forth of the f, and speaking vanity; H676
Lk 11:20 But if I with the f of God cast out devils, G1147
16:24 dip the tip of his f in water, and cool G1147
Jn 8: 6 and with *his* f wrote on the ground, G1147
20:25 nails, and put my f into the print of the G1147
27 Reach hither thy f, and behold my G1147

FINGERS
2Sa 21:20 on every hand six f, and on every foot six H676
1Ch 20: 6 stature, whose f and toes *were* four and H676
Ps 8: 3 the work of thy f, the moon and the stars, H676
144: 1 my hands to war, *and* my f to fight: H676
Prv 6:13 with his feet, he teacheth with his f; H676
7: 3 Bind them upon thy f, write them upon H676
Song 5: 5 myrrh, and my f *with* sweet smelling H676
Isa 2: 8 that which their own f have made: H676
17: 8 *that* which his f have made, either the H676
59: 3 blood, and your f with iniquity; your lips H676
Jer 52:21 thereof *was* four f: *it was* hollow. H676
Dan 5: 5 In the same hour came forth f of a man's H677
Mt 23: 4 will not move them with one of their f. G1147
Mk 7:33 and put his f into his ears, and he G1147
Lk 11:46 not the burdens with one of your f. G1147

FINING
Prv 17: 3 The f pot *is* for silver, and the furnace H4715
27:21 *As* the f pot for silver, and the furnace H4715

FINISH
Gen 6:16 in a cubit shalt thou f it above; and the H3615
Dan 9:24 thy holy city, to f the transgression, H3607
Zec 4: 9 his hands shall also f it; and thou shalt H1214
Lk 14:28 cost, whether he have *sufficient* to f *it*? G535
29 and is not able to f *it*, all that behold *it* G1615
30 began to build, and was not able to f. G1615
Jn 4:34 of him that sent me, and to f his work. G5048
5:36 hath given me to f, the same works that G5048
Act 20:24 so that I might f my course with joy, G5048
Ro 9:28 For he will f the work, and cut *it* short G4931
2Co 8: 6 also f in you the same grace also. G2005

FINISHED
Gen 2: 1 Thus the heavens and the earth were f, H3615
Ex 39:32 the congregation f: and the children of H3615
40:33 of the court gate. So Moses f the work. H3615
Dt 31:24 of this law in a book, until they were f, H8552
Jos 4:10 until every thing was f that the LORD H8552
Ru 3:18 rest, until he have f the thing this day. H3615
1Ki 6: 9 So he built the house, and f it; and H3615
14 So Solomon built the house, and f it. H3615
22 gold, until he had f all the house: also H8552
38 was the house f throughout all the H3615
7: 1 thirteen years, and he f all his house. H3615
22 work: so was the work of the pillars f. H8552
9: 1 when Solomon had f the building of the H3615
25 before the LORD. So he f the house. H3615
1Ch 27:24 to number, but he f not, because there H3615
28:20 until thou hast f all the work for the H3615
2Ch 4:11 And Huram f the work that he was H3615
5: 1 house of the LORD was f: and Solomon H3615
7:11 Thus Solomon f the house of the LORD, H3615

2Ch 8:16 and until it was f. *So* the house of the H3615
24:14 And when they had f *it*, they brought H3615
29:28 *continued* until the burnt offering was f. H3615
31: 1 Now when all this was f, all Israel that H3615
7 and f *them* in the seventh month. H3615
Ezr 5:16 it been in building, and *yet* it is not f. H8000
6:14 they builded, and f *it*, according to the H3635
15 And this house was f on the third day H3319
Neh 6:15 So the wall was f in the twenty and fifth H7999
Dan 5:26 hath numbered thy kingdom, and f it. H8000
12: 7 holy people, all these *things* shall be f. H3615
Mt 13:53 f these parables, he departed thence. *G5055*
19: 1 *that* when Jesus had f these sayings, he *G5055*
26: 1 And it came to pass, when Jesus had f *G5055*
Jn 17: 4 f the work which thou gavest me to do. *G5048*
19:30 he said, It is f: and he bowed his head, *G5055*
Act 21: 7 And when we had f *our* course from *G1274*
2Ti 4: 7 I have fought a good fight, I have f *my* *G5055*
Heb 4: 3 f from the foundation of the world. *G1096*
Jas 1:15 and sin, when it is f, bringeth forth death. *G658*
Rev 10: 7 of God should be f, as he hath declared *G5055*
11: 7 And when they shall have f their *G5055*
20: 5 were f. This *is* the first resurrection. *G5055*

FINISHER
Heb 12: 2 Looking unto Jesus the author and f of *G5051*

FINITE See INFINITE.

FINS
Lev 11: 9 whatsoever hath f and scales in the H5579
10 And all that have not f and scales in the H5579
12 Whatsoever hath no f nor scales in the H5579
Dt 14: 9 all that have f and scales shall ye eat: H5579
10 And whatsoever hath not f and scales H5579

FIR
2Sa 6: 5 *made of* f wood, even on harps, H1265
1Ki 5: 8 of cedar, and concerning timber of f. H1265
10 and f trees *according to* all his desire. H1265
6:15 the floor of the house with planks of f. H1265
34 And the two doors *were of* f tree: the H1265
9:11 cedar trees and f trees, and with gold, H1265
2Ki 19:23 *and* the choice f trees thereof: and I H1265
2Ch 2: 8 Send me also cedar trees, f trees, and H1265
3: 5 And the greater house he cieled with f H1265
Ps 104:17 *for* the stork, the f trees *are* her house. H1265
Song 1:17 house *are* cedar, *and* our rafters of f. H1266
Isa 14: 8 Yea, the f trees rejoice at thee, *and* the H1265
37:24 *and* the choice f trees thereof: and I H1265
41:19 set in the desert the f tree, *and* the pine, H1265
55:13 Instead of the thorn shall come up the f H1265
60:13 unto thee, the f tree, the pine tree, and H1265
Ezk 27: 5 They have made all thy *ship* boards of f H1265
31: 8 not hide him: the f trees were not like H1265
Hos 14: 8 f tree. From me is thy fruit found. H1265
Nah 2: 3 and the f trees shall be terribly shaken. H1265
Zec 11: 2 Howl, f tree; for the cedar is fallen; H1265

FIRE
Gen 19:24 and f from the LORD out of heaven; H784
22: 6 son; and he took the f in his hand, and a H784
7 he said, Behold the f and the wood: but H784
Ex 3: 2 him in a flame of f out of the midst of a H784
2 with f, and the bush *was* not consumed. H784
9:23 and hail, and the f ran along upon the H784
24 So there was hail, and f mingled with the H784
12: 8 that night, roast with f, and unleavened H784
9 but roast *with* f; his head with his legs, H784
10 it until the morning ye shall burn with f. H784
13:21 night in a pillar of f, to give them light; to H784
22 of f by night, *from* before the people. H784
14:24 the pillar of f and of the cloud, and H784
19:18 upon it in f: and the smoke thereof H784
22: 6 If f break out, and catch in thorns, so H784
6 the f shall surely make restitution. H1200
24:17 *was* like devouring f on the top of the H784
29:14 f without the camp: it *is* a sin offering. H784
18 an offering made by f unto the LORD. H801
25 *is* an offering made by f unto the LORD. H801
34 f: it shall not be eaten, because it *is* holy. H784
41 an offering made by f unto the LORD. H801
30:20 burn offering made by f unto the LORD: H801
32:20 and burnt *it* in the f, and ground *it* to H784
24 it into the f, and there came out this calf. H784
35: 3 Ye shall kindle no f throughout your H784
40:38 by day, and f was on it by night, in H784
Lev 1: 7 the priest shall put f upon the altar, and H784
7 and lay the wood in order upon the f: H784
Lev 1: 8 that *is* on the f which *is* upon the altar: H784
9 by f, of a sweet savour unto the LORD. H801
12 that *is* on the f which *is* upon the altar: H784
13 by f, of a sweet savour unto the LORD. H801
17 that *is* upon the f: it *is* a burnt sacrifice, H784
17 by f, of a sweet savour unto the LORD. H801
2: 2 by f, of a sweet savour unto the LORD: H801
3 of the offerings of the LORD made by f. H801
9 by f, of a sweet savour unto the LORD. H801
10 of the offerings of the LORD made by f. H801
11 in any offering of the LORD made by f. H801
14 by the f, *even* corn beaten out of full ears. H784
16 *is* an offering made by f unto the LORD. H801
3: 3 offering made by f unto the LORD; the H801
5 the wood that *is* on the f: *it is* an offering H784
5 by f, of a sweet savour unto the LORD. H801
9 offering made by f unto the LORD; the H801
11 of the offering made by f unto the LORD. H801
14 offering made by f unto the LORD; the H801
16 offering made by f for a sweet savour: all H801
4:12 on the wood with f: where the ashes are H784
35 offerings made by f unto the LORD; and H801
5:12 by f unto the LORD: it *is* a sin offering. H801
6: 9 the f of the altar shall be burning in it. H784
10 up the ashes which the f hath consumed H784
12 And the f upon the altar shall be burning H784
13 The f shall ever be burning upon the H784
17 offerings made by f; it *is* most holy, as *is* H801
18 of the LORD made by f: every one that H801
30 shall be eaten: it shall be burnt in the f. H784
7: 5 f unto the LORD: it *is* a trespass offering. H801
17 on the third day shall be burnt with f. H784
19 shall be burnt with f: and as for the flesh, H784
25 offering made by f unto the LORD, even H801
30 of the LORD made by f, the fat with the H801
35 the LORD made by f, in the day *when* he H801
8:17 he burnt with f without the camp; as H784
21 an offering made by f unto the LORD; as H801
28 *is* an offering made by f unto the LORD. H801
32 and of the bread shall ye burn with f. H784
9:11 hide he burnt with f without the camp. H784
24 And there came a f out from before the H784
10: 1 his censer, and put f therein, and put H784
1 offered strange f before the LORD, which H784
2 And there went out f from the LORD, H784
12 the LORD made by f, and eat it without H801
13 made by f: for so I am commanded. H801
15 offerings made by f of the fat, to wave *it* H801
13:52 fretting leprosy; it shall be burnt in the f. H784
55 shalt burn it in the f; it *is* fret inward, H784
57 burn that wherein the plague *is* with f. H784
16:12 of burning coals of f from off the altar H784
13 And he shall put the incense upon the f H784
27 shall burn in the f their skins, and their H784
18:21 pass through *the f* to Molech, neither
19: 6 the third day, it shall be burnt in the f. H784
20:14 shall be burnt with f, both he and they; H784
21: 6 of the LORD made by f, *and* the bread of H801
9 her father: she shall be burnt with f. H784
21 the LORD made by f: he hath a blemish; H801
22:22 f of them upon the altar unto the LORD. H801
27 an offering made by f unto the LORD. H801
23: 8 But ye shall offer an offering made by f H801
13 offering made by f unto the LORD *for* a H801
18 by f, of sweet savour unto the LORD. H801
25 an offering made by f unto the LORD. H801
27 an offering made by f unto the LORD. H801
36 an offering made by f unto the LORD: on H801
36 offering made by f unto the LORD: it *is* H801
37 an offering made by f unto the LORD, a H801
24: 7 an offering made by f unto the LORD. H801
9 LORD made by f by a perpetual statute. H801
Nu 3: 4 offered strange f before the LORD, in H784
6:18 and put *it* in the f which *is* under the H784
9:15 the appearance of f, until the morning. H784
16 *by day*, and the appearance of f by night. H784
11: 1 kindled; and the f of the LORD burnt H784
2 unto the LORD, the f was quenched. H784
3 the f of the LORD burnt among them. H784
14:14 of a cloud, and in a pillar of f by night. H784
15: 3 And will make an offering by f unto the H801
10 by f, of a sweet savour unto the LORD. H801
13 by f, of a sweet savour unto the LORD. H801
14 an offering made by f, of a sweet savour H801
25 a sacrifice made by f unto the LORD, H801
16: 7 And put f therein, and put incense in H784
18 his censer, and put f in them, and laid H784
35 And there came out a f from the LORD, H784
37 thou the f yonder; for they are hallowed. H784
Nu 16:46 a censer, and put f therein from off the H784
18: 9 *reserved* from the f: every oblation of H784
17 by f, for a sweet savour unto the LORD. H801
21:28 For there is a f gone out of Heshbon, a H784
26:10 died, what time the f devoured two H784
61 they offered strange f before the LORD. H784
28: 2 sacrifices made by f, *for* a sweet savour H801
3 offering made by f which ye shall offer H801
6 a sacrifice made by f unto the LORD. H801
8 by f, of a sweet savour unto the LORD. H801
13 a sacrifice made by f unto the LORD. H801
19 But ye shall offer a sacrifice made by f H801
24 the sacrifice made by f, of a sweet savour H801
29: 6 a sacrifice made by f unto the LORD. H801
13 a sacrifice made by f, of a sweet savour H801
36 a sacrifice made by f, of a sweet savour H801
31:10 dwelt, and all their goodly castles, with f. H784
23 Every thing that may abide the f, ye shall H784
23 *it* go through the f, and it shall be clean: H784
23 the f ye shall make go through the water. H784
Dt 1:33 your tents *in*, in f by night, to shew you H784
4:11 burned with f unto the midst of heaven, H784
12 of the midst of the f: ye heard the voice of H784
15 you in Horeb out of the midst of the f: H784
24 For the LORD thy God *is* a consuming f, H784
33 of the f, as thou hast heard, and live? H784
36 thee his great f; and thou heardest his H784
36 his words out of the midst of the f. H784
5: 4 in the mount out of the midst of the f, H784
5 by reason of the f, and went not up into H784
22 of the midst of the f, of the cloud, and of H784
23 did burn with f,) that ye came near unto H784
24 of the midst of the f: we have seen this H784
25 die? for this great f will consume us: if H784
26 the midst of the f, as we *have*, and lived? H784
7: 5 and burn their graven images with f. H784
25 shall ye burn with f: thou shalt not desire H784
9: 3 *as* a consuming f he shall destroy them, H784
10 midst of the f in the day of the assembly. H784
15 mount burned with f: and the two tables H784
21 and burnt it with f, and stamped it, *and* H784
10: 4 out of the midst of the f in the day of the H784
12: 3 burn their groves with f; and ye shall hew H784
31 they have burnt in the f to their gods. H784
13:16 and shalt burn with f the city, and all the H784
18: 1 the LORD made by f, and his inheritance. H801
10 to pass through the f, *or* that useth H784
16 see this great f any more, that I die not. H784
32:22 For a f is kindled in mine anger, and H784
22 on f the foundations of the mountains. H3857
Jos 6:24 And they burnt the city with f, and all H784
7:15 shall be burnt with f, he and all that he H784
25 f, after they had stoned them with stones. H784
8: 8 ye shall set the city on f: according to the H784
19 took it, and hasted and set the city on f. H784
11: 6 horses, and burn their chariots with f. H784
9 horses, and burnt their chariots with f. H784
11 to breathe: and he burnt Hazor with f. H784
13:14 of Israel made by f *are* their inheritance, H801
Jdg 1: 8 edge of the sword, and set the city on f. H784
6:21 and there rose up f out of the rock, and H784
9:15 and if not, let f come out of the bramble, H784
20 But if not, let f come out from H784
20 of Millo; and let f come out from the H784
49 and set the hold on f upon them; so that H784
52 the door of the tower to burn it with f. H784
12: 1 will burn thine house upon thee with f. H784
14:15 father's house with f: have ye called us to H784
15: 5 And when he had set the brands on f, he H784
6 up, and burnt her and her father with f. H784
14 was burnt with f, and his bands loosed H784
16: 9 the f. So his strength was not known. H784
18:27 of the sword, and burnt the city with f. H784
20:48 set on f all the cities that they came to. H784
1Sa 2:28 made by f of the children of Israel? H801
30: 1 and smitten Ziklag, and burned it with f; H784
3 *it was* burned with f; and their wives, and H784
14 of Caleb; and we burned Ziklag with f. H784
2Sa 14:30 there; go and set it on f. And Absalom's H784
30 And Absalom's servants set the field on f. H784
31 have thy servants set my field on f? H784
22: 9 out of his nostrils, and f out of his mouth H784
13 before him were coals of f kindled. H784
23: 7 utterly burned with f in the *same* place. H784
1Ki 9:16 Gezer, and burnt it with f, and slain the H784
16:18 king's house over him with f, and died, H784
18:23 on wood, and put no f *under:* and I will H784
23 and lay *it* on wood, and put no f *under:* H784
24 that answereth by f, let him be God. And H784

1Ki 18:25 name of your gods, but put no f *under.* H784
38 Then the f of the LORD fell, and H784
19:12 And after the earthquake a f; *but* the H784
12 the f: and after the fire a still small voice. H784
12 the fire: and after the f a still small voice. H784
2Ki 1:10 man of God, then let f come down from H784
10 there came down f from heaven, and H784
12 *be* a man of God, let f come down from H784
12 thy fifty. And the f of God came down H784
14 Behold, there came f down from heaven, H784
2:11 a chariot of f, and horses of fire, and H784
11 of fire, and horses of f, and parted them H784
6:17 and chariots of f round about Elisha. H784
8:12 wilt thou set on f, and their young men H784
16: 3 to pass through the f, according to the H784
17:17 daughters to pass through the f, and used H784
31 their children in f to Adrammelech and H784
19:18 And have cast their gods into the f: for H784
21: 6 And he made his son pass through the f, H784
23:10 to pass through the f to Molech. H784
11 and burned the chariots of the sun with f. H784
25: 9 every great *man's* house burnt he with f. H784
1Ch 14:12 and they were burned with f. H784
21:26 by f upon the altar of burnt offering. H784
2Ch 7: 1 an end of praying, the f came down from H784
3 Israel saw how the f came down, and the H784
28: 3 burnt his children in the f, after the H784
33: 6 to pass through the f in the valley of the H784
35:13 And they roasted the passover with f H784
36:19 thereof with f, and destroyed all the H784
Neh 1: 3 and the gates thereof are burned with f. H784
2: 3 the gates thereof are consumed with f? H784
13 the gates thereof were consumed with f. H784
17 are burned with f: come, and let us build H784
9:12 night by a pillar of f, to give them light in H784
19 neither the pillar of f by night, to shew H784
Job 1:16 and said, The f of God is fallen from H784
15:34 *be* desolate, and f shall consume the H784
18: 5 and the spark of his f shall not shine. H784
20:26 in his secret places: a f not blown shall H784
22:20 the remnant of them the f consumeth. H784
28: 5 and under it is turned up as it were f. H784
31:12 For it *is* a f *that* consumeth to H784
41:19 burning lamps, *and* sparks of f leap out. H784
Ps 11: 6 Upon the wicked he shall rain snares, f H784
18: 8 out of his nostrils, and f out of his mouth H784
12 clouds passed, hail *stones* and coals of f. H784
13 gave his voice; hail *stones* and coals of f. H784
21: 9 his wrath, and the f shall devour them. H784
29: 7 of the LORD divideth the flames of f. H784
39: 3 f burned: *then* spake I with my tongue, H784
46: 9 in sunder; he burneth the chariot in the f. H784
50: 3 not keep silence: a f shall devour before H784
57: 4 that are set on f, *even* the sons of men, H3857
66:12 we went through f and through water: H784
68: 2 melteth before the f, *so* let the wicked H784
74: 7 They have cast f into thy sanctuary, they H784
78:14 a cloud, and all the night with a light of f. H784
21 was wroth: so a f was kindled against H784
63 The f consumed their young men; and H784
79: 5 for ever? shall thy jealousy burn like f? H784
80:16 *It is* burned with f, *it is* cut down: they H784
83:14 As the f burneth a wood, and as the H784
14 as the flame setteth the mountains on f; H3857
89:46 for ever? shall thy wrath burn like f? H784
97: 3 A f goeth before him, and burneth up his H784
104: 4 angels spirits; his ministers a flaming f: H784
105:32 He gave them hail for rain, *and* flaming f H784
39 He spread a cloud for a covering; and f H784
106:18 And a f was kindled in their company; H784
118:12 quenched as the f of thorns: for in the H784
140:10 be cast into the f; into deep pits, that they H784
148: 8 F, and hail; snow, and vapour; stormy H784
Prv 6:27 Can a man take f in his bosom, and his H784
16:27 and in his lips *there is* as a burning f. H784
25:22 For thou shalt heap coals of f upon his H1513
26:20 Where no wood is, *there* the f goeth out: H784
21 f; so *is* a contentious man to kindle strife. H784
30:16 and the f *that* saith not, *It is* enough. H784
Song 8: 6 of f, *which hath* a most vehement flame. H784
Isa 1: 7 *are* burned with f: your land, strangers H784
4: 5 of a flaming f by night: for upon all H784
5:24 Therefore as the f devoureth the stubble, H784
9: 5 *this* shall be with burning *and* fuel of f. H784
18 For wickedness burneth as the f: it shall H784
19 of the f: no man shall spare his brother. H784
10:16 kindle a burning like the burning of a f. H784
17 And the light of Israel shall be for a f, and H784
26:11 the f of thine enemies shall devour them. H784
Isa 27:11 *and* set them on f: for it *is* a people of no H215
29: 6 tempest, and the flame of devouring f. H784
30:14 of it a sherd to take f from the hearth, or H784
27 and his tongue as a devouring f: H784
30 of a devouring f, *with* scattering, and H784
33 the pile thereof *is* f and much wood; the H784
31: 9 the LORD, whose f *is* in Zion, and his H217
33:11 your breath, *as* f, shall devour you. H784
12 cut up shall they be burned in the f. H784
14 with the devouring f? who among us shall H784
37:19 And have cast their gods into the f: for H784
42:25 it hath set him on f round about, yet he H3857
43: 2 through the f, thou shalt not be burned; H784
44:16 He burneth part thereof in the f; with H784
16 saith, Aha, I am warm, I have seen the f: H217
19 part of it in the f; yea, also I have baked H784
47:14 Behold, they shall be as stubble; the f H784
14 a coal to warm at, *nor* f to sit before it. H217
50:11 Behold, all ye that kindle a f, that H784
11 in the light of your f, and in the sparks H784
54:16 the coals in the f, and that bringeth forth H784
64: 2 As *when* the melting f burneth, the fire H784
2 As *when* the melting fire burneth, the f H784
11 is burned up with f: and all our pleasant H784
65: 5 in my nose, a f that burneth all the day. H784
66:15 For, behold, the LORD will come with f, H784
15 fury, and his rebuke with flames of f. H784
16 For by f and by his sword will the LORD H784
24 neither shall their f be quenched; and H784
Jer 4: 4 come forth like f, and burn that none can H784
5:14 in thy mouth f, and this people wood, H784
6: 1 and set up a sign of f in Beth-haccerem:
29 is consumed of the f; the founder melteth H784
7:18 the fathers kindle the f, and the women H784
31 daughters in the f; which I commanded H784
11:16 tumult he hath kindled f upon it, and the H784
15:14 knowest not: for a f is kindled in mine H784
17: 4 ye have kindled a f in mine anger, *which* H784
27 then will I kindle a f in the gates thereof, H784
19: 5 their sons with f *for* burnt offerings unto H784
20: 9 mine heart as a burning f shut up in my H784
21:10 of Babylon, and he shall burn it with f. H784
12 my fury go out like f, and burn that none H784
14 and I will kindle a f in the forest thereof, H784
22: 7 choice cedars, and cast *them* into the f. H784
23:29 *Is* not my word like as a f? saith the H784
29:22 the king of Babylon roasted in the f; H784
32:29 shall come and set f on this city, and H784
35 to pass through *the f* unto Molech; H784
34: 2 of Babylon, and he shall burn it with f: H784
22 it, and burn it with f: and I will make the H784
36:22 *a f* on the hearth burning before him.
23 and cast *it* into the f that *was* on the H784
23 in the f that *was* on the hearth. H784
32 had burned in the f: and there were H784
37: 8 this city, and take it, and burn it with f. H784
10 man in his tent, and burn this city with f. H784
38:17 f; and thou shalt live, and thine house: H784
18 shall burn it with f, and thou shalt not H784
23 shalt cause this city to be burned with f. H784
39: 8 f, and brake down the walls of Jerusalem. H784
43:12 And I will kindle a f in the houses of the H784
13 of the Egyptians shall he burn with f. H784
48:45 of the force: but a f shall come forth out H784
49: 2 be burned with f: then shall Israel be heir H784
27 And I will kindle a f in the wall of H784
50:32 and I will kindle a f in his cities, and it H784
51:32 with f, and the men of war are affrighted. H784
58 be burned with f; and the people shall H784
58 the folk in the f, and they shall be weary. H784
52:13 of the great *men*, burned he with f: H784
Lam 1:13 From above hath he sent f into my H784
2: 3 flaming f, *which* devoureth round about. H784
4 of Zion: he poured out his fury like f. H784
4:11 and hath kindled a f in Zion, and it hath H784
Ezk 1: 4 great cloud, and a f infolding itself, and H784
4 colour of amber, out of the midst of the f. H784
13 like burning coals of f, *and* like the H784
13 creatures; and the f was bright, and out H784
13 and out of the f went forth lightning. H784
27 the appearance of f round about within H784
27 of f, and it had brightness round about. H784
5: 2 Thou shalt burn with f a third part in the H217
4 the midst of the f, and burn them in the H784
4 burn them in the f; *for* thereof shall a fire H784
4 f come forth into all the house of Israel. H784
8: 2 the appearance of f: from the appearance H784
2 even downward, f; and from his loins H784
10: 2 hand with coals of f from between the H784
Ezk 10: 6 linen, saying, Take f from between the H784
7 unto the f that *was* between the H784
15: 4 Behold, it is cast into the f for fuel; the H784
4 the fire for fuel; the f devoureth both the H784
5 the f hath devoured it, and it is burned? H784
6 I have given to the f for fuel, so will I give H784
7 go out from *one* f, and *another* fire shall H784
7 fire, and *another* f shall devour them; H784
16:21 them to pass through *the f* for them?
41 And they shall burn thine houses with f, H784
19:12 and withered; the f consumed them. H784
14 And f is gone out of a rod of her H784
20:26 to pass through *the f* all that openeth the
31 sons to pass through the f, ye pollute H784
47 I will kindle a f in thee, and it shall H784
21:31 against thee in the f of my wrath, and H784
32 Thou shalt be for fuel to the f; thy blood H784
22:20 to blow the f upon it, to melt *it*; so H784
21 upon you in the f of my wrath, and ye H784
31 them with the f of my wrath: their own H784
23:25 thy residue shall be devoured by the f. H784
37 for them through *the f*, to devour *them*.
47 and burn up their houses with f. H784
24: 9 city! I will even make the pile for f great.
10 Heap on wood, kindle the f, consume the H784
12 out of her: her scum *shall be* in the f. H784
28:14 and down in the midst of the stones of f. H784
16 cherub, from the midst of the stones of f. H784
18 will I bring forth a f from the midst of H784
30: 8 when I have set a f in Egypt, and *when* H784
14 and will set f in Zoan, and will execute H784
16 And I will set f in Egypt: Sin shall have H784
36: 5 GOD; Surely in the f of my jealousy have H784
38:19 For in my jealousy *and* in the f of my H784
22 and great hailstones, f, and brimstone. H784
39: 6 And I will send a f on Magog, and H784
9 forth, and shall set on f and burn the H1197
9 they shall burn them with f seven years: H784
10 the weapons with f: and they shall spoil H784
Dan 3:22 the flame of the f slew those men that H5135
24 the midst of the f? They answered and H5135
25 in the midst of the f, and they have no H5135
26 came forth of the midst of the f. H5135
27 whose bodies the f had no power, nor H5135
27 nor the smell of f had passed on them. H5135
7: 9 fiery flame, *and* his wheels *as* burning f. H5135
10: 6 eyes as lamps of f, and his arms and his H784
Hos 7: 6 in the morning it burneth as a flaming f. H784
8:14 but I will send a f upon his cities, and it H784
Joel 1:19 O LORD, to thee will I cry: for the f hath H784
20 dried up, and the f hath devoured the H784
2: 3 A f devoureth before them; and behind H784
5 noise of a flame of f that devoureth the H784
30 earth, blood, and f, and pillars of smoke. H784
Am 1: 4 But I will send a f into the house of H784
7 But I will send a f on the wall of Gaza, H784
10 But I will send a f on the wall of Tyrus, H784
12 But I will send a f upon Teman, which H784
14 But I will kindle a f in the wall of H784
2: 2 But I will send a f upon Moab, and it H784
5 But I will send a f upon Judah, and it H784
5: 6 lest he break out like f in the house of H784
7: 4 to contend by f, and it devoured the great H784
Oba 18 And the house of Jacob shall be a f, and H784
Mic 1: 4 as wax before the f, *and* as the waters H784
7 be burned with the f, and all the idols H784
Nah 1: 6 f, and the rocks are thrown down by him. H784
3:13 enemies: the f shall devour thy bars. H784
15 There shall the f devour thee; the sword H784
Hab 2:13 labour in the very f, and the people shall H784
Zep 1:18 be devoured by the f of his jealousy: for H784
3: 8 be devoured with the f of my jealousy. H784
Zec 2: 5 be unto her a wall of f round about, and H784
3: 2 *is* not this a brand plucked out of the f? H784
9: 4 the sea; and she shall be devoured with f. H784
11: 1 Open thy doors, O Lebanon, that the f H784
12: 6 like an hearth of f among the wood, and H784
6 and like a torch of f in a sheaf; and they H784
13: 9 part through the f, and will refine them H784
Mal 1:10 do ye kindle *f* on mine altar for nought.
3: 2 *is* like a refiner's f, and like fullers' soap: H784
Mt 3:10 fruit is hewn down, and cast into the f. *G4442*
11 you with the Holy Ghost, and *with* f: *G4442*
12 burn up the chaff with unquenchable f. *G4442*
5:22 Thou fool, shall be in danger of hell f. *G4442*
7:19 fruit is hewn down, and cast into the f. *G4442*
13:40 f; so shall it be in the end of this world. *G4442*
42 And shall cast them into a furnace of f: *G4442*
50 them into the furnace of f: there shall be *G4442*

F

Mt 17:15 falleth into the f, and oft into the water. G4442
18: 8 or two feet to be cast into everlasting f. G4442
9 having two eyes to be cast into hell f. G4442
25:41 f, prepared for the devil and his angels: G4442
Mk 9:22 And ofttimes it hath cast him into the f, G4442
43 into the f that never shall be quenched: G4442
44 Where their worm dieth not, and the f G4442
45 into the f that never shall be quenched: G4442
46 Where their worm dieth not, and the f G4442
47 having two eyes to be cast into hell f: G4442
48 Where their worm dieth not, and the f G4442
49 For every one shall be salted with f, and G4442
14:54 servants, and warmed himself at the f. G5457
Lk 3: 9 fruit is hewn down, and cast into the f. G4442
16 you with the Holy Ghost and with f: G4442
17 chaff he will burn with f unquenchable. G4442
9:54 thou that we command f to come down G4442
12:49 I am come to send f on the earth; and G4442
17:29 out of Sodom it rained f and brimstone G4442
22:55 And when they had kindled a f in the G4442
56 as he sat by the f, and earnestly looked G5457
Jn 15: 6 *them* into the f, and they are burned. G4442
18:18 who had made a f of coals; for it was
21: 9 to land, they saw a f of coals there, and
Act 2: 3 as of f, and it sat upon each of them. G4442
19 blood, and f, and vapour of smoke: G4442
7:30 of the Lord in a flame of f in a bush. G4442
28: 2 for they kindled a f, and received us G4443
3 laid *them* on the f, there came a viper G4443
5 And he shook off the beast into the f, G4442
Ro 12:20 thou shalt heap coals of f on his head. G4442
1Co 3:13 be revealed by f; and the fire shall try G4442
13 by fire; and the f shall try every man's G4442
15 he himself shall be saved; yet so as by f. G4442
2Th 1: 8 In flaming f taking vengeance on them G4442
Heb 1: 7 spirits, and his ministers a flame of f. G4442
11:34 Quenched the violence of f, escaped the G4442
12:18 that burned with f, nor unto blackness, G4442
29 For our God *is* a consuming f. G4442
Jas 3: 5 how great a matter a little f kindleth! G4442
6 And the tongue *is* a f, a world of G4442
6 and setteth on f the course of nature; G5394
6 of nature; and it is set on f of hell. G5394
5: 3 your flesh as it were f. Ye have heaped G4442
1Pt 1: 7 it be tried with f, might be found unto G4442
2Pt 3: 7 reserved unto f against the day of G4442
12 heavens being on f shall be dissolved, G4448
Jude 7 suffering the vengeance of eternal f. G4442
23 *them* out of the f; hating even the G4442
Rev 1:14 snow; and his eyes *were* as a flame of f; G4442
2:18 of f, and his feet *are* like fine brass; G4442
3:18 gold tried in the f, that thou mayest be G4442
4: 5 seven lamps of f burning before the G4442
8: 5 and filled it with f of the altar, and cast G4442
7 followed hail and f mingled with blood, G4442
8 burning with f was cast into the sea: G4442
9:17 breastplates of f, and of jacinth, and G4447
17 issued f and smoke and brimstone. G4442
18 men killed, by the f, and by the smoke, G4442
10: 1 were the sun, and his feet as pillars of f: G4442
11: 5 And if any man will hurt them, f G4442
13:13 so that he maketh f come down from G4442
14:10 be tormented with f and brimstone in G4442
18 had power over f; and cried with a loud G4442
15: 2 glass mingled with f: and them that had G4442
16: 8 given unto him to scorch men with f. G4442
17:16 shall eat her flesh, and burn her with f. G4442
18: 8 burned with f: for strong *is* the Lord G4442
19:12 His eyes *were* as a flame of f, and on his G4442
20 into a lake of f burning with brimstone. G4442
20: 9 the beloved city: and f came down from G4442
10 into the lake of f and brimstone, where G4442
14 the lake of f. This is the second death. G4442
15 book of life was cast into the lake of f. G4442
21: 8 burneth with f and brimstone: which G4442

FIREBRAND
Jdg 15: 4 put a f in the midst between two tails. H3940
Am 4:11 and ye were as a f plucked out of the H181

FIREBRANDS
Jdg 15: 4 foxes, and took f, and turned tail to tail, H3940
Prv 26:18 As a mad *man* who casteth f, arrows, H2131
Isa 7: 4 of these smoking f, for the fierce anger of H181

FIREPANS
Ex 27: 3 and his f: all the vessels thereof H4289
38: 3 and the f: all the vessels thereof H4289
2Ki 25:15 And the f, and the bowls, *and* such H4289
Jer 52:19 And the basons, and the f, and the H4289

FIRES
Isa 24:15 Wherefore glorify ye the LORD in the f, H217

FIRKINS
Jn 2: 6 Jews, containing two or three f apiece. G3355

FIRM
Jos 3:17 of the LORD stood f on dry ground in H3559
4: 3 priests' feet stood f, twelve stones, and H3559
Job 41:23 f in themselves; they cannot be moved. H3332
24 His heart is as f as a stone; yea, as hard H3332
Ps 73: 4 in their death: but their strength *is* f. H1277
Dan 6: 7 and to make a f decree, that whosoever H8631
Heb 3: 6 the rejoicing of the hope f unto the end. G949

FIRMAMENT
Gen 1: 6 And God said, Let there be a f in the H7549
7 And God made the f, and divided the H7549
7 *were* under the f from the waters which H7549
7 which *were* above the f: and it was so. H7549
8 And God called the f Heaven. And the H7549
14 be lights in the f of the heaven to divide H7549
15 And let them be for lights in the f of the H7549
17 And God set them in the f of the heaven H7549
20 above the earth in the open f of heaven. H7549
Ps 19: 1 God; and the f sheweth his handywork. H7549
150: 1 praise him in the f of his power. H7549
Ezk 1:22 And the likeness of the f upon the H7549
23 And under the f *were* their wings H7549
25 And there was a voice from the f that H7549
26 And above the f that *was* over their H7549
10: 1 Then I looked, and, behold, in the f H7549
Dan 12: 3 brightness of the f; and they that turn H7549

FIRST
Gen 1: 5 evening and the morning were the f day. H259
2:11 The name of the f *is* Pison: that *is* it H259
8: 5 *month*, on the f *day* of the month, were H259
13 the six hundredth and f year, in the first H259
13 first year, in the f *month*, the first *day* H7223
13 the first *month*, the f *day* of the month, H259
13: 4 made there at the f: and there Abram H7223
25:25 And the f came out red, all over like an H7223
26: 1 land, beside the f famine that was in H7223
28:19 of that city *was called* Luz at the f. H7223
38:28 scarlet thread, saying, This came out f. H7223
41:20 kine did eat up the f seven fat kine: H7223
43:18 in our sacks at the f time are we H8462
20 indeed down at the f time to buy food: H8462
Ex 4: 8 to the voice of the f sign, that they will H7223
12: 2 *shall be* the f month of the year to you. H7223
5 a male of the f year: ye shall take *it* H1121
15 bread; even the f day ye shall put away H7223
15 bread from the f day until the seventh H7223
16 And in the f day *there shall be* an holy H7223
18 In the f *month*, on the fourteenth day H7223
22:29 Thou shalt not delay *to offer* the f of H4935
23:19 The f of the firstfruits of thy land thou H7225
28:17 four rows of stones: *the f* row *shall be* a
17 and a carbuncle: *this shall be* the f row. H259
29:38 of the f year day by day continually. H1121
34: 1 of stone like unto the f: and I will write H7223
1 in the f tables, which thou brakest. H7223
4 stone like unto the f; and Moses rose up H7223
26 The f of the firstfruits of thy land thou H7225
39:10 rows of stones: *the f* row *was* a sardius, a
10 and a carbuncle: this *was* the f row. H259
40: 2 On the f day of the first month shalt thou H259
2 On the first day of the f month shalt H7223
17 And it came to pass in the f month in H7223
17 second year, on the f *day* of the month, H259
Lev 4:21 as he burned the f bullock: it *is* a sin H7223
5: 8 for the sin offering f, and wring off his H7223
9: 3 a lamb, *both* of the f year, without H1121
15 slew it, and offered it for sin, as the f. H7223
12: 6 bring a lamb of the f year for a burnt H1121
14:10 ewe lamb of the f year without blemish, H1323
23: 5 In the fourteenth *day* of the f month at H7223
7 In the f day ye shall have an holy H7223
12 blemish of the f year for a burnt H1121
18 blemish of the f year, and one young H1121
19 f year for a sacrifice of peace offerings. H1121
24 month, in the f *day* of the month, shall H259
35 On the f day *shall be* an holy H7223
39 seven days: on the f day *shall be* a H7223
40 And ye shall take you on the f day the H7223
Nu 1: 1 on the f *day* of the second month, H259
1:18 together on the f *day* of the second H259
2: 9 their armies. These shall f set forth. H7223
6:12 bring a lamb of the f year for a trespass H1121
14 one he lamb of the f year without H1121
14 ewe lamb of the f year without blemish H1323
7:12 And he that offered his offering the f H7223
15 lamb of the f year, for a burnt offering: H1121
17 five lambs of the f year: this *was* the H1121
21 lamb of the f year, for a burnt offering: H1121
23 five lambs of the f year: this *was* the H1121
27 lamb of the f year, for a burnt offering: H1121
29 five lambs of the f year: this *was* the H1121
33 lamb of the f year, for a burnt offering: H1121
35 five lambs of the f year: this *was* the H1121
39 lamb of the f year, for a burnt offering: H1121
41 five lambs of the f year: this *was* the H1121
45 lamb of the f year, for a burnt offering: H1121
47 five lambs of the f year: this *was* the H1121
51 lamb of the f year, for a burnt offering: H1121
53 five lambs of the f year: this *was* the H1121
57 lamb of the f year, for a burnt offering: H1121
59 five lambs of the f year: this *was* the H1121
63 lamb of the f year, for a burnt offering: H1121
65 five lambs of the f year: this *was* the H1121
69 lamb of the f year, for a burnt offering: H1121
71 five lambs of the f year: this *was* the H1121
75 lamb of the f year, for a burnt offering: H1121
77 five lambs of the f year: this *was* the H1121
81 lamb of the f year, for a burnt offering: H1121
83 five lambs of the f year: this *was* the H1121
87 the lambs of the f year twelve, with H1121
88 the lambs of the f year sixty. This *was* H1121
9: 1 of Sinai, in the f month of the second H7223
5 day of the f month at even in the H7223
10:13 And they f took their journey according H7223
14 In the f *place* went the standard of the H7223
15:20 Ye shall offer up a cake of the f of your H7225
21 Of the f of your dough ye shall give H7225
27 she goat of the f year for a sin offering. H1323
18:13 *And* whatsoever is f ripe in the land, H1061
20: 1 desert of Zin in the f month: and the H7223
24:20 Amalek *was* the f of the nations; but H7225
28: 3 two lambs of the f year without spot H1121
9 two lambs of the f year without spot, H1121
11 seven lambs of the f year without spot; H1121
16 And in the fourteenth day of the f H7223
18 In the f day *shall be* an holy H7223
19 seven lambs of the f year: they shall be H1121
27 one ram, seven lambs of the f year; H1121
29: 1 And in the seventh month, on the f *day* H259
2 lambs of the f year without blemish: H1121
8 seven lambs of the f year; they shall be H1121
13 f year; they shall be without blemish: H1121
17 lambs of the f year without spot: H1121
20 lambs of the f year without blemish; H1121
23 lambs of the f year without blemish: H1121
26 lambs of the f year without spot: H1121
29 lambs of the f year without blemish: H1121
32 lambs of the f year without blemish: H1121
36 lambs of the f year without blemish: H1121
33: 3 from Rameses in the f month, on the H7223
3 day of the f month; on the morrow H7223
38 of Egypt, in the f *day* of the fifth month. H259
Dt 1: 3 month, on the f *day* of the month, *that* H259
9:18 LORD, as at the f, forty days and forty H7223
25 as I fell down *at the f*; because the LORD
10: 1 stone like unto the f, and come up unto H7223
2 that were in the f tables which thou H7223
3 stone like unto the f, and went up into H7223
4 according to the f writing, the ten H7223
10 according to the f time, forty days and H7223
11:14 his due season, the f rain and the latter H3138
13: 9 hand shall be f upon him to put him H7223
16: 4 sacrificedst the f day at even, remain H7223
17: 7 The hands of the witnesses shall be f H7223
18: 4 of thine oil, and the f of the fleece of thy H7225
26: 2 That thou shalt take of the f of all the H7225
33:21 And he provided the f part for himself, H7225
Jos 4:19 the tenth *day* of the f month, and H7223
8: 5 as at the f, that we will flee before them, H7223
6 the f: therefore we will flee before them. H7223
21:10 of Levi, had: for theirs was the f lot. H7223
Jdg 1: 1 the Canaanites f, to fight against them? H8462
18:29 the name of the city *was* Laish at the f. H7223
20:18 of us shall go up f to the battle against H8462
18 And the LORD said, Judah *shall go up* f. H8462
22 they put themselves in array the f day. H7223
32 before us, as at the f. But the children of H7223
39 down before us, as *in* the f battle. H7223

1Sa 14:14 And that f slaughter, which Jonathan H7223
35 the f altar that he built unto the LORD. H2490
2Sa 3:13 face, except thou f bring Michal Saul's H6440
17: 9 be overthrown at the f, that whosoever H8462
19:20 I am come the f this day of all the H7223
43 should not be f had in bringing back H7223
21: 9 days of harvest, in the f *days*, in the H7223
23:19 howbeit he attained not unto the *f* three.
23 attained not to the *f* three. And David set
1Ki 16:23 In the thirty and f year of Asa king of H259
17:13 a little cake f, and bring *it* unto me, H7223
18:25 and dress *it* f; for ye *are* many; and H7223
20: 9 to thy servant at the f I will do: but this H7223
17 went out f; and Ben-hadad sent H7223
1Ch 9: 2 Now the f inhabitants that *dwelt* in H7223
11: 6 the Jebusites f shall be chief and H7223
6 of Zeruiah went f up, and was chief. H7223
21 howbeit he attained not to the *f* three.
25 attained not to the *f* three: and David set
12: 9 Ezer the f, Obadiah the second, Eliab H7218
15 over Jordan in the f month, when it H7223
15:13 For because ye *did it* not at the f, the H7223
16: 7 Then on that day David delivered f *this* H7218
23:19 Of the sons of Hebron; Jeriah the f, H7218
20 Of the sons of Uzziel; Michah the f, and H7218
24: 7 Now the f lot came forth to Jehoiarib, H7223
21 the sons of Rehabiah, the f *was* Isshiah. H7218
23 And the sons *of Hebron;* Jeriah *the f,*
25: 9 Now the f lot came forth for Asaph to H7223
27: 2 Over the f course for the first month H7223
2 Over the first course for the f month H7223
3 captains of the host for the f month. H7223
29:29 Now the acts of David the king, f and H7223
2Ch 3: 3 by cubits after the f measure *was* H7223
9:29 Now the rest of the acts of Solomon, f H7223
12:15 Now the acts of Rehoboam, f and last, H7223
16:11 And, behold, the acts of Asa, f and last, H7223
17: 3 he walked in the f ways of his father H7223
20:34 of Jehoshaphat, f and last, behold, they H7223
25:26 Now the rest of the acts of Amaziah, f H7223
26:22 Now the rest of the acts of Uzziah, f H7223
28:26 of all his ways, f and last, behold, they H7223
29: 3 He in the f year of his reign, in the first H7223
3 He in the first year of his reign, in the f H7223
17 Now they began on the f *day* of the first H259
17 Now they began on the first *day* of the f H7223
17 day of the f month they made an end. H7223
35: 1 on the fourteenth *day* of the f month. H7223
27 And his deeds, f and last, behold, they H7223
36:22 Now in the f year of Cyrus king of Persia, H259
Ezr 1: 1 Now in the f year of Cyrus king of Persia, H259
3: 6 From the f day of the seventh month H259
12 that had seen the f house, when the H7223
5:13 But in the f year of Cyrus the king of H2298
6: 3 In the f year of Cyrus the king *the same* H2298
19 the fourteenth *day* of the f month. H7223
7: 9 For upon the f *day* of the first month H259
9 For upon the first *day* of the f month H7223
9 and on the f *day* of the fifth month H259
8:31 twelfth *day* of the f month, to go unto H7223
10:16 sat down in the f day of the tenth month H259
17 wives by the f day of the first month. H259
17 wives by the first day of the f month. H7223
Neh 7: 5 up at the f, and found written therein, H7223
8: 2 upon the f day of the seventh month. H259
18 Also day by day, from the f day unto H7223
Est 1:14 *and* which sat the f in the kingdom;) H7223
3: 7 In the f month, that *is*, the month H7223
12 day of the f month, and there was H7223
Job 15: 7 *Art* thou the f man *that* was born? or H7223
42:14 And he called the name of the f, Jemima; H259
Prv 18:17 *He that is* f in his own cause *seemeth* H7223
Isa 1:26 And I will restore thy judges as at the f, H7223
9: 1 when at the f he lightly afflicted the H7223
41: 4 LORD, the f, and with the last; I *am* he. H7223
27 The f *shall say* to Zion, Behold, behold H7223
43:27 Thy f father hath sinned, and thy H7223
44: 6 of hosts; I *am* the f, and I *am* the last; H7223
48:12 I *am* he; I *am* the f, I also *am* the last. H7223
60: 9 the ships of Tarshish f, to bring thy sons H7223
Jer 4:31 bringeth forth her f child, the voice of H1069
7:12 my name at the f, and see what I did to H7223
16:18 And f I will recompense their iniquity H7223
24: 2 the figs *that are* f ripe: and the other H1073
25: 1 that *was* the f year of Nebuchadrezzar H7224
33: 7 return, and will build them, as at the f. H7223
11 of the land, as at the f, saith the LORD. H7223
36:28 that were in the f roll, which Jehoiakim H7223
50:17 driven *him* away: f the king of Assyria H7223

Jer 52:31 of Babylon in the *f* year of his reign lifted
Ezk 10:14 And every one had four faces: the f face H259
26: 1 year, in the f *day* of the month, *that* H259
29:17 year, in the f *month*, in the first *day* H7223
17 first *month*, in the f *day* of the month, H259
30:20 year, in the f *month*, in the seventh H7223
31: 1 third *month*, in the f *day* of the month, H259
32: 1 month, in the f *day* of the month, *that* H259
40:21 the measure of the f gate: the length H7223
44:30 And the f of all the firstfruits of all H7225
30 unto the priest the f of your dough, that H7225
45:18 Thus saith the Lord GOD; In the f H259
18 first *month*, in the f *day* of the month, H7223
21 In the f *month*, in the fourteenth day of H7223
46:13 *of* a lamb of the f year without blemish: H1121
Dan 1:21 And Daniel continued *even* unto the f H259
6: 2 of whom Daniel *was* f: that the princes H2298
7: 1 In the f year of Belshazzar king of H2298
4 The f *was* like a lion, and had eagle's H6933
8 were three of the f horns plucked up by H6933
24 the f, and he shall subdue three kings. H6933
8: 1 that which appeared unto me at the f. H8462
21 that *is* between his eyes *is* the f king. H7223
9: 1 In the f year of Darius the son of H259
2 In the f year of his reign I Daniel H259
10: 4 day of the f month, as I was by the H7223
12 for from the f day that thou didst H7223
11: 1 Also I in the f year of Darius the Mede, H259
Hos 2: 7 and return to my f husband; for then H7223
9:10 the fig tree at her f time: *but* they went H7225
Joel 2:23 rain, and the latter rain in the f *month*. H7223
Am 6: 7 captive with the f that go captive, and H7218
Mic 4: 8 shall it come, even the f dominion; the H7223
Hag 1: 1 sixth month, in the f day of the month, H259
2: 3 this house in her f glory? and how do ye H7223
Zec 6: 2 In the f chariot *were* red horses; and in H7223
12: 7 the tents of Judah f, that the glory of the H7223
14:10 the place of the f gate, unto the corner H7223
Mt 5:24 and go thy way; f be reconciled to thy *G4412*
6:33 But seek ye f the kingdom of God, and *G4412*
7: 5 Thou hypocrite, f cast out the beam out *G4412*
8:21 suffer me f to go and bury my father. *G4412*
10: 2 are these; The f, Simon, who is called *G4413*
12:29 his goods, except he f bind the strong *G4412*
45 is worse than the f. Even so shall it be *G4413*
13:30 Gather ye together f the tares, and bind *G4412*
17:10 say the scribes that Elias must f come? *G4412*
11 shall f come, and restore all things. *G4412*
27 up the fish that f cometh up; and when *G4413*
19:30 But many *that are* f shall be last; and *G4413*
30 first shall be last; and the last *shall be* f. *G4413*
20: 8 hire, beginning from the last unto the f. *G4413*
10 But when the f came, they supposed *G4413*
16 So the last shall be f, and the first last: *G4413*
16 So the last shall be first, and the f last: *G4413*
21:28 he came to the f, and said, Son, go work *G4413*
31 say unto him, The f. Jesus saith unto *G4413*
36 the f: and they did unto them likewise. *G4413*
22:25 seven brethren: and the f, when he had *G4413*
38 This is the f and great commandment. *G4413*
23:26 *Thou* blind Pharisee, cleanse f that *G4412*
26:17 Now the f *day* of the *feast of* *G4413*
27:64 the last error shall be worse than the f. *G4413*
28: 1 to dawn toward the f *day* of the week, *G3391*
Mk 3:27 except he will f bind the strong man; *G4412*
4:28 fruit of herself; f the blade, then the *G4412*
7:27 Let the children f be filled: for it is not *G4412*
9:11 say the scribes that Elias must f come? *G4412*
12 verily cometh f, and restoreth all things; *G4412*
35 man desire to be f, *the same* shall be *G4413*
10:31 But many *that are* f shall be last; and *G4413*
31 *that are* first shall be last; and the last f. *G4413*
12:20 f took a wife, and dying left no seed. *G4413*
28 Which is the f commandment of all? *G4413*
29 And Jesus answered him, The f of all *G4413*
30 strength: this *is* the f commandment. *G4413*
13:10 And the gospel must f be published *G4412*
14:12 And the f day of unleavened bread, *G4413*
16: 2 And very early in the morning the f *day* *G3391*
9 Now when *Jesus* was risen early the f *G4413*
9 the week, he appeared f to Mary *G4412*
Lk 1: 3 from the very f, to write unto thee in *G509*
2: 2 (*And* this taxing was f made when *G4413*
6: 1 second sabbath after the f, that he went *G1207*
42 hypocrite, cast out f the beam out of *G4412*
9:59 suffer me f to go and bury my father. *G4412*
61 thee; but let me f go bid them farewell, *G4412*
10: 5 And into whatsoever house ye enter, f *G4412*
11:26 *state* of that man is worse than the f. *G4413*

Lk 11:38 that he had not f washed before dinner. *G4412*
12: 1 unto his disciples f of all, Beware ye of *G4412*
13:30 f, and there are first which shall be last. *G4413*
30 first, and there are f which shall be last. *G4413*
14:18 to make excuse. The f said unto him, I *G4413*
28 sitteth not down f, and counteth the *G4412*
31 king, sitteth not down f, and consulteth *G4412*
16: 5 f, How much owest thou unto my lord? *G4413*
17:25 But f must he suffer many things, and *G4412*
19:16 Then came the f, saying, Lord, thy *G4413*
20:29 brethren: and the f took a wife, and *G4413*
21: 9 these things must f come to pass; but *G4412*
24: 1 Now upon the f *day* of the week, very *G3391*
Jn 1:41 He f findeth his own brother Simon, *G4413*
5: 4 whosoever then f after the troubling of *G4413*
8: 7 you, let him f cast a stone at her. *G4413*
10:40 John at f baptized; and there he abode. *G4412*
12:16 not his disciples at the f: but when Jesus *G4412*
18:13 And led him away to Annas f; for he *G4412*
19:32 the legs of the f, and of the other which *G4413*
39 which at the f came to Jesus by night, *G4412*
20: 1 The f *day* of the week cometh Mary *G3391*
4 Peter, and came f to the sepulchre. *G4413*
8 which came f to the sepulchre, and *G4413*
19 at evening, being the f *day* of the week, *G3391*
Act 3:26 Unto you f God, having raised up his *G4412*
7:12 corn in Egypt, he sent out our fathers f. *G4412*
11:26 were called Christians f in Antioch. *G4412*
12:10 When they were past the f and the *G4413*
13:24 When John had f preached before his
46 of God should f have been spoken to *G4412*
15:14 Simeon hath declared how God at the f *G4412*
20: 7 And upon the f *day* of the week, when *G3391*
18 Ye know, from the f day that I came *G4413*
26: 4 which was at the f among mine own *G746*
20 But shewed f unto them of Damascus, *G4412*
23 he should be the f that should rise from *G4413*
27:43 f *into the sea*, and get to land: *G4413*
Ro 1: 8 F, I thank my God through Jesus Christ *G4412*
16 to the Jew f, and also to the Greek. *G4412*
2: 9 evil, of the Jew f, and also of the Gentile; *G4412*
10 to the Jew f, and also to the Gentile: *G4412*
10:19 But I say, Did not Israel know? F Moses *G4413*
11:35 Or who hath f given to him, and it shall *G4273*
15:24 by you, if f I be somewhat filled *G4412*
1Co 11:18 For f of all, when ye come together in *G4412*
12:28 And God hath set some in the church, f *G4412*
14:30 that sitteth by, let the f hold his peace. *G4413*
15: 3 For I delivered unto you f of all *G1722+G4413*
45 And so it is written, The f man Adam *G4413*
46 Howbeit that *was* not f which is *G4412*
47 The f man *is* of the earth, earthy: the *G4413*
16: 2 Upon the f *day* of the week let every *G2596*
2Co 8: 5 not as we hoped, but f gave their own *G4412*
12 For if there be f a willing mind, *it is* *G4295*
Gal 4:13 I preached the gospel unto you at the f. *G4386*
Eph 1:12 of his glory, who f trusted in Christ. *G4276*
4: 9 f into the lower parts of the earth? *G4412*
6: 2 is the f commandment with promise; *G4413*
Php 1: 5 in the gospel from the f day until now; *G4413*
1Th 4:16 God: and the dead in Christ shall rise f: *G4412*
2Th 2: 3 a falling away f, and that man of sin *G4412*
1Ti 1:16 mercy, that in me f Jesus Christ might *G4413*
2: 1 I exhort therefore, that, f of all, *G4412*
13 For Adam was f formed, then Eve. *G4413*
3:10 And let these also f be proved; then let *G4412*
5: 4 let them learn f to shew piety at home, *G4412*
12 because they have cast off their f faith. *G4413*
2Ti 1: 5 thee, which dwelt f in thy grandmother *G4412*
2: 6 must be f partaker of the fruits. *G4413*
4:16 At my f answer no man stood with me, *G4413*
Tit 3:10 A man that is an heretick after the f *G3391*
Heb 2: 3 which at the f began to be spoken by *G746*
4: 6 to whom it was f preached entered not *G4386*
5:12 again which *be* the f principles of the *G746*
7: 2 gave a tenth part of all; f being by *G4412*
27 to offer up sacrifice, f for his own sins, *G4386*
8: 7 For if that f *covenant* had been *G4413*
13 he hath made the f old. Now that which *G4413*
9: 1 Then verily the f *covenant* had also *G4413*
2 For there was a tabernacle made; the f, *G4413*
6 went always into the f tabernacle, *G4413*
8 as the f tabernacle was yet standing: *G4413*
15 *were* under the f testament, they which *G4413*
18 Whereupon neither the f *testament* *G4413*
10: 9 the f, that he may establish the second. *G4413*
Jas 3:17 But the wisdom that is from above is f *G4412*
1Pt 4:17 of God: and if *it* f *begin* at us, what *G4412*
2Pt 1:20 Knowing this f, that no prophecy of the *G4412*

2Pt 3: 3 Knowing this f, that there shall come in G4412
1Jn 4:19 We love him, because he f loved us. G4413
Jude 6 And the angels which kept not their f G746
Rev 1: 5 witness, *and* the f begotten of the dead, G4416
11 Saying, I am Alpha and Omega, the f G4413
17 me, Fear not; I am the f and the last: G4413
2: 4 thee, because thou hast left thy f love. G4413
5 repent, and do the f works; or else I will G4413
8 things saith the f and the last, which G4413
19 and the last *to be* more than the f. G4413
4: 1 in heaven: and the f voice which I G4413
7 And the f beast *was* like a lion, and the G4413
8: 7 The f angel sounded, and there G4413
13:12 And he exerciseth all the power of the f G4413
12 to worship the f beast, whose deadly G4413
16: 2 And the f went, and poured out his vial G4413
20: 5 finished. This *is* the f resurrection. G4413
6 hath part in the f resurrection: on such G4413
21: 1 new earth: for the f heaven and the first G4413
1 heaven and the f earth were passed G4413
19 stones. The f foundation *was* jasper; G4413
22:13 and the end, the f and the last. G4413

FIRSTBEGOTTEN
Heb 1: 6 And again, when he bringeth in the f G4416

FIRSTBORN
Gen 10:15 And Canaan begat Sidon his f, and H1060
19:31 And the f said unto the younger, Our H1067
33 that night: and the f went in, and lay H1067
34 the morrow, that the f said unto the H1067
37 And the f bare a son, and called his H1067
22:21 Huz his f, and Buz his brother, and H1060
25:13 their generations: the f of Ishmael, H1060
27:19 I *am* Esau thy f; I have done according H1060
32 And he said, I *am* thy son, thy f Esau. H1060
29:26 to give the younger before the f. H1067
35:23 The sons of Leah; Reuben, Jacob's f, H1060
36:15 sons of Eliphaz the f *son* of Esau; duke H1060
38: 6 And Judah took a wife for Er his f, H1060
7 And Er, Judah's f, was wicked in the H1060
41:51 And Joseph called the name of the f H1060
43:33 And they sat before him, the f H1060
46: 8 Jacob and his sons: Reuben, Jacob's f. H1060
48:14 wittingly; for Manasseh *was* the f. H1060
18 the f; put thy right hand upon his head. H1060
49: 3 Reuben, thou *art* my f, my might, and H1060
Ex 4:22 the LORD, Israel *is* my son, *even* my f: H1060
23 behold, I will slay thy son, *even* thy f. H1060
6:14 of Reuben the f of Israel; Hanoch, and H1060
11: 5 And all the f in the land of Egypt shall H1060
5 shall die, from the f of Pharaoh that H1060
5 even unto the f of the maidservant H1060
5 behind the mill; and all the f of beasts. H1060
12:12 will smite all the f in the land of Egypt, H1060
29 smote all the f in the land of Egypt, H1060
29 of Egypt, from the f of Pharaoh that sat H1060
29 his throne unto the f of the captive that H1060
29 in the dungeon; and all the f of cattle. H1060
13: 2 Sanctify unto me all the f, whatsoever H1060
13 neck: and all the f of man among thy H1060
15 the LORD slew all the f in the land of H1060
15 of Egypt, both the f of man, and the H1060
15 of man, and the f of beast: therefore I H1060
15 but all the f of my children I redeem. H1060
22:29 f of thy sons shalt thou give unto me. H1060
34:20 his neck. All the f of thy sons thou shalt H1060
Nu 3: 2 the f, and Abihu, Eleazar, and Ithamar. H1060
12 instead of all the f that openeth the H1060
13 Because all the f *are* mine; *for* on the H1060
13 day that I smote all the f in the land of H1060
13 unto me all the f in Israel, both man H1060
40 Number all the f of the males of the H1060
41 instead of all the f among the children H1060
42 all the f among the children of Israel. H1060
43 And all the f males by the number of H1060
45 Take the Levites instead of all the f H1060
46 and thirteen of the f of the children of H1060
50 Of the f of the children of Israel took he H1060
8:16 *even instead of* the f of all the children H1060
17 For all the f of the children of Israel *are* H1060
17 that I smote every f in the land of Egypt H1060
18 for all the f of the children of Israel. H1060
18:15 nevertheless the f of man shalt thou H1060
33: 4 For the Egyptians buried all *their* f, H1060
Dt 21:15 and *if* the f son be hers that was hated: H1060
16 son of the beloved f before the son of H1069
16 son of the hated, *which is indeed* the f: H1060
17 of the hated *for* the f, by giving him a H1060
Dt 21:17 of his strength; the right of the f *is* his. H1062
25: 6 And it shall be, *that* the f which she H1060
Jos 6:26 thereof in his f, and in his youngest H1060
17: 1 for he *was* the f of Joseph; *to wit,* for H1060
1 *wit,* for Machir the f of Manasseh, the H1060
Jdg 8:20 And he said unto Jether his f, Up, *and* H1060
1Sa 8: 2 Now the name of his f was Joel; and the H1060
14:49 the name of the f Merab, and the name H1067
17:13 *were* Eliab the f, and next unto him H1060
2Sa 3: 2 in Hebron: and his f was Amnon, of H1060
1Ki 16:34 in Abiram his f, and set up the gates H1060
1Ch 1:13 And Canaan begat Zidon his f, and H1060
29 These *are* their generations: The f of H1060
2: 3 And Er, the f of Judah, was evil in H1060
13 And Jesse begat his f Eliab, and H1060
25 And the sons of Jerahmeel the f of H1060
25 were, Ram the f, and Bunah, and Oren, H1060
27 And the sons of Ram the f of Jerahmeel H1060
42 *were,* Mesha his f, which was the father H1060
50 Caleb the son of Hur, the f of Ephratah; H1060
3: 1 in Hebron; the f Amnon, of Ahinoam H1060
15 And the sons of Josiah *were,* the f H1060
4: 4 f of Ephratah, the father of Beth-lehem. H1060
5: 1 Now the sons of Reuben the f of Israel, H1060
1 (for he *was* the f; but, forasmuch as he H1060
3 The sons, *I say,* of Reuben the f of H1060
6:28 And the sons of Samuel; the f Vashni, H1060
8: 1 Now Benjamin begat Bela his f, Ashbel H1060
30 And his f son Abdon, and Zur, and H1060
39 *were,* Ulam his f, Jehush the second, H1060
9: 5 And of the Shilonites; Asaiah the f, and H1060
31 who *was* the f of Shallum the Korahite, H1060
36 And his f son Abdon, then Zur, and H1060
26: 2 Zechariah the f, Jediael the second, H1060
4 Shemaiah the f, Jehozabad the second, H1060
10 the f, yet his father made him the chief;) H1060
2Ch 21: 3 he to Jehoram; because he *was* the f. H1060
Neh 10:36 Also the f of our sons, and of our cattle, H1060
Job 18:13 the f of death shall devour his strength. H1060
Ps 78:51 And smote all the f in Egypt; the chief H1060
89:27 Also I will make him *my* f, higher than H1060
105:36 He smote also all the f in their land, the H1060
135: 8 Who smote the f of Egypt, both of man H1060
136:10 To him that smote Egypt in their f: for H1060
Isa 14:30 And the f of the poor shall feed, and the H1060
Jer 31: 9 a father to Israel, and Ephraim *is* my f. H1060
Mic 6: 7 of oil? shall I give my f *for* my H1060
Zec 12:10 as one that is in bitterness for *his* f. H1060
Mt 1:25 f son: and he called his name JESUS. G4416
Lk 2: 7 And she brought forth her f son, and G4416
Ro 8:29 might be the f among many brethren. G4416
Col 1:15 invisible God, the f of every creature: G4416
18 the beginning, the f from the dead; that G4416
Heb 11:28 that destroyed the f should touch them. G4416
12:23 and church of the f, which are written G4416

FIRSTFRUIT
Dt 18: 4 The f *also* of thy corn, of thy wine, and H7225
Ro 11:16 For if the f *be* holy, the lump *is* also *holy*: G536

FIRSTFRUITS
Ex 23:16 And the feast of harvest, the f of thy H1061
19 The first of the f of thy land thou shalt H1061
34:22 of weeks, of the f of wheat harvest, and H1061
26 The first of the f of thy land thou shalt H1061
Lev 2:12 As for the oblation of the f, ye shall offer H7225
14 offering of thy f unto the LORD, thou H1061
23:10 of the f of your harvest unto the priest: H7225
17 leaven; *they are* the f unto the LORD. H1061
20 the bread of the f *for* a wave offering H1061
Nu 18:12 of the wheat, the f of them which they H7225
28:26 Also in the day of the f, when ye bring a H1061
Dt 26:10 And now, behold, I have brought the f H7725
2Ki 4:42 of God bread of the f, twenty loaves of H1061
2Ch 31: 5 in abundance the f of corn, wine, and H7225
Neh 10:35 And to bring the f of our ground, and H1061
35 ground, and the f of all fruit of all trees, H1061
37 And *that* we should bring the f of our H7225
13:31 f. Remember me, O my God, for good. H1061
Prv 3: 9 and with the f of all thine increase: H7225
Jer 2: 3 the LORD, *and* the f of his increase: all H7225
Ezk 20:40 offerings, and the f of your oblations, H7225
44:30 And the first of all the f of all *things,* H1061
48:14 nor alienate the f of the land: for *it is* H7225
Ro 8:23 which have the f of the Spirit, even we G536
16: 5 who is the f of Achaia unto Christ. G536
1Co 15:20 *and* become the f of them that slept. G536
23 order: Christ the f; afterward they that G536
16:15 that it is the f of Achaia, and *that* they G536
Jas 1:18 we should be a kind of f of his creatures. G536
Rev 14: 4 *being* the f unto God and to the Lamb. G536

FIRST-FRUITS
Lev 2:14 offering of thy f green ears of corn H1061
Neh 12:44 offerings, for the f, and for the tithes, to H7225

FIRSTLING
Ex 13:12 matrix, and every f that cometh of a H6363
13 And every f of an ass thou shalt redeem H6363
34:19 *is* mine; and every f among thy cattle, H6363
20 But the f of an ass thou shalt redeem H6363
Lev 27:26 Only the f of the beasts, which should H1060
26 be the LORD'S f, no man shall sanctify H1069
Nu 18:15 f of unclean beasts shalt thou redeem. H1060
17 But the f of a cow, or the firstling of a H1060
17 But the firstling of a cow, or the f of a H1060
17 of a sheep, or the f of a goat, thou shalt H1060
Dt 15:19 All the f males that come of thy herd H1060
19 no work with the f of thy bullock, nor H1060
19 bullock, nor shear the f of thy sheep. H1060
33:17 His glory *is like* the f of his bullock, and H1060

FIRSTLINGS
Gen 4: 4 And Abel, he also brought of the f of H1062
Nu 3:41 instead of all the f among the cattle of H1060
Dt 12: 6 the f of your herds and of your flocks: H1062
17 or of thy oil, or the f of thy herds or of H1062
14:23 thine oil, and the f of thy herds and of H1062
Neh 10:36 in the law, and the f of our herds and of H1062

FIRSTRIPE
Nu 13:20 the time *was* the time of the f grapes. H1061
Hos 9:10 your fathers as the f in the fig tree at H1063
Mic 7: 1 to eat: my soul desired the f fruit. H1063
Nah 3:12 *like* fig trees with the f figs: if they be H1063

FIR-TREE See FIR and TREE.

FIR-WOOD See FIR and WOOD.

FISH
Gen 1:26 dominion over the f of the sea, and H1710
28 dominion over the f of the sea, and H1710
Ex 7:18 And the f that *is* in the river shall die, H1710
21 And the f that *was* in the river died; H1710
Nu 11: 5 We remember the f, which we did eat in H1710
22 or shall all the f of the sea be gathered H1709
Dt 4:18 the likeness of any f that *is* in the H1710
2Ch 33:14 the entering in at the f gate, and H1709
Neh 3: 3 But the f gate did the sons of H1709
12:39 and above the f gate, and the tower H1709
13:16 which brought f, and all manner of H1709
Job 41: 7 irons? or his head with f spears? H1709
Ps 8: 8 The fowl of the air, and the f of the sea, H1709
105:29 their waters into blood, and slew their f. H1710
Isa 19:10 all that make sluices *and* ponds for f. H5315
50: 2 a wilderness: their f stinketh, because H1710
Jer 16:16 and they shall f them; and after will H1770
Ezk 29: 4 I will cause the f of thy rivers to stick H1710
4 rivers, and all the f of thy rivers shall H1710
5 thee and all the f of thy rivers: thou H1710
47: 9 very great multitude of f, because these H1710
10 forth nets; their f shall be according to H1710
10 the f of the great sea, exceeding many. H1710
Jna 1:17 Now the LORD had prepared a great f H1709
17 of the f three days and three nights. H1709
2:10 And the LORD spake unto the f, and it H1709
Zep 1:10 of a cry from the f gate, and an howling H1709
Mt 7:10 Or if he ask a f, will he give him a G2486
17:27 and take up the f that first cometh up; G2486
Lk 11:11 a f, will he for a fish give him a serpent? G2486
11 a fish, will he for a f give him a serpent? G2486
24:42 And they gave him a piece of a broiled f, G2486
Jn 21: 9 there, and f laid thereon, and bread. G3795
10 Jesus saith unto them, Bring of the f G3795
13 bread, and giveth them, and f likewise. G3795

FISHERMEN
Lk 5: 2 by the lake: but the f were gone out of G231

FISHERS
Isa 19: 8 The f also shall mourn, and all they H1771
Jer 16:16 Behold, I will send for many f, saith the H1728
Ezk 47:10 And it shall come to pass, *that* the f H1728
Mt 4:18 casting a net into the sea: for they were f. G231
19 Follow me, and I will make you f of men. G231
Mk 1:16 casting a net into the sea: for they were f. G231
17 and I will make you to become f of men. G231

FISHER'S
Jn 21: 7 Lord, he girt *his* f coat *unto him*, (for G1903

FISHES
Gen 9: 2 and upon all the f of the sea; into your H1709
1Ki 4:33 of fowl, and of creeping things, and of f. H1709
Job 12: 8 the f of the sea shall declare unto thee. H1709
Ecc 9:12 his time: as the f that are taken in an H1709
Ezk 38:20 So that the f of the sea, and the fowls of H1709
Hos 4: 3 f of the sea also shall be taken away. H1709
Hab 1:14 And makest men as the f of the sea, as H1709
Zep 1: 3 heaven, and the f of the sea, and the H1709
Mt 14:17 We have here but five loaves, and two f. G2486
19 loaves, and the two f, and looking up to G2486
15:34 And they said, Seven, and a few little f. G2485
36 And he took the seven loaves and the f, G2486
Mk 6:38 they knew, they say, Five, and two f. G2486
41 loaves and the two f, he looked up to G2486
41 the two f divided he among them all. G2486
43 full of the fragments, and of the f. G2486
8: 7 And they had a few small f: and he G2485
Lk 5: 6 multitude of f: and their net brake. G2486
9 draught of the f which they had taken: G2486
9:13 loaves and two f; except we should go G2486
16 loaves and the two f, and looking up to G2486
Jn 6: 9 f: but what are they among so many? G3795
11 likewise of the f as much as they would. G3795
21: 6 able to draw it for the multitude of f. G2486
8 cubits,) dragging the net with f. G2486
11 land full of great f, an hundred and fifty G2486
1Co 15:39 another of f, *and* another of birds. G2486

FISH-GATE
See FISH and GATE.

FISHHOOKS
Am 4: 2 and your posterity with f. H1729+H5518

FISHING
Jn 21: 3 Simon Peter saith unto them, I go a f. G232

FISHPOOLS
Song 7: 4 thine eyes *like* the f in Heshbon, by the H1295

FISH'S
Jna 2: 1 the LORD his God out of the f belly, H1710

FIST
Ex 21:18 *his* f, and he die not, but keepeth *his* bed: H106
Isa 58: 4 and to smite with the f of wickedness: ye H106

FISTS
Prv 30: 4 the wind in his f? who hath bound the H2651

FIT
Lev 16:21 hand of a f man into the wilderness: H6261
1Ch 7:11 *soldiers*, f to go out for war *and* battle.
12: 8 *and* men of war *f* for the battle, that
Job 34:18 *Is it f* to say to a king, *Thou art* wicked?
Prv 24:27 and make it f for thyself in the field; H6257
Lk 9:62 back, is f for the kingdom of God. G2111
14:35 It is neither f for the land, nor yet for G2111
Act 22:22 earth: for it is not f that he should live. G2520
Col 3:18 your own husbands, as it is f in the Lord. G433

FITCHES
Isa 28:25 not cast abroad the f, and scatter the H7100
27 For the f are not threshed with a H7100
27 cummin; but the f are beaten out with H7100
Ezk 4: 9 and millet, and f, and put them in one H3698

FITLY
Prv 25:11 A word f spoken *is like* apples of H5921+H655
Song 5:12 washed with milk, *and* f set. H5921+H4402
Eph 2:21 In whom all the building f framed G4883
4:16 From whom the whole body f joined G4883

FITTED
1Ki 6:35 *them* with gold f upon the carved work. H3474
Prv 22:18 thee; they shall withal be f in thy lips. H3559
Ro 9:22 the vessels of wrath f to destruction: G2675

FITTETH
Isa 44:13 out with a line; he f it with planes, and H6213

FIVE
Gen 5: 6 And Seth lived an hundred and f years, H2568
11 nine hundred and f years: and he died. H2568
15 And Mahalaleel lived sixty and f years, H2568
17 ninety and f years: and he died. H2568
Gen 5:21 And Enoch lived sixty and f years, and H2568
23 were three hundred sixty and f years: H2568
30 he begat Noah f hundred ninety and H2568
30 f years, and begat sons and daughters: H2568
32 And Noah was f hundred years old: H2568
11:11 begat Arphaxad f hundred years, and H2568
12 And Arphaxad lived f and thirty years, H2568
32 and f years: and Terah died in Haran. H2568
12: 4 *was* seventy and f years old when he H2568
14: 9 Arioch king of Ellasar; four kings with f. H2568
18:28 Peradventure there shall lack f of the H2568
28 all the city for *lack of f*? And he said, If I H2568
28 there forty and f, I will not destroy *it*. H2568
43:34 mess was f times so much as any H2568
45: 6 and yet *there are* f years, in the which H2568
11 for yet *there are* f years of famine; lest H2568
22 of silver, and f changes of raiment. H2568
47: 2 of his brethren, *even* f men, and H2568
Ex 22: 1 it; he shall restore f oxen for an ox, and H2568
26: 3 The f curtains shall be coupled together H2568
3 another; and *other* f curtains *shall be* H2568
9 And thou shalt couple f curtains by H2568
26 *of* shittim wood; f for the boards of the H2568
27 And f bars for the boards of the other H2568
27 tabernacle, and f bars for the boards H2568
37 And thou shalt make for the hanging f H2568
37 shalt cast f sockets of brass for them. H2568
27: 1 *of* shittim wood, f cubits long, and five H2568
1 five cubits long, and f cubits broad; the H2568
18 and the height f cubits *of* fine twined H2568
30:23 of pure myrrh f hundred *shekels*, and H2568
24 And of cassia f hundred *shekels*, after H2568
36:10 And he coupled the f curtains one unto H2568
10 f curtains he coupled one unto another. H2568
16 And he coupled f curtains by H2568
31 And he made bars of shittim wood; f H2568
32 And f bars for the boards of the other H2568
32 tabernacle, and f bars for the boards H2568
38 And the f pillars of it with their hooks: H2568
38 gold: but their f sockets *were of* brass. H2568
38: 1 *of* shittim wood: f cubits *was* the length H2568
1 length thereof, and f cubits the breadth H2568
18 in the breadth *was* f cubits, answerable H2568
26 thousand and f hundred and fifty *men*. H2568
28 seventy and f shekels he made hooks H2568
Lev 26: 8 And f of you shall chase an hundred, H2568
27: 5 And if *it be* from f years old even unto H2568
6 old even unto f years old, then thy H2568
6 be of the male f shekels of silver, and H2568
Nu 1:21 forty and six thousand and f hundred. H2568
25 and f thousand six hundred and fifty. H2568
33 *were* forty thousand and f hundred. H2568
37 and f thousand and four hundred. H2568
41 forty and one thousand and f hundred. H2568
46 thousand and f hundred and fifty. H2568
2:11 forty and six thousand and f hundred. H2568
15 f thousand and six hundred and fifty. H2568
19 *were* forty thousand and f hundred. H2568
23 and f thousand and four hundred. H2568
28 forty and one thousand and f hundred. H2568
32 thousand and f hundred and fifty. H2568
3:22 *were* seven thousand and f hundred. H2568
47 Thou shalt even take f shekels apiece H2568
50 and threescore and f *shekels*, after the H2568
4:48 thousand and f hundred and fourscore. H2568
7:17 two oxen, f rams, five he goats, H2568
17 oxen, five rams, f he goats, five lambs H2568
17 five he goats, f lambs of the first year: H2568
23 two oxen, f rams, five he goats, H2568
23 oxen, five rams, f he goats, five lambs H2568
23 five he goats, f lambs of the first year: H2568
29 two oxen, f rams, five he goats, H2568
29 oxen, five rams, f he goats, five lambs H2568
29 five he goats, f lambs of the first year: H2568
35 two oxen, f rams, five he goats, H2568
35 oxen, five rams, f he goats, five lambs H2568
35 five he goats, f lambs of the first year: H2568
41 two oxen, f rams, five he goats, H2568
41 oxen, five rams, f he goats, five lambs H2568
41 five he goats, f lambs of the first year: H2568
47 two oxen, f rams, five he goats, H2568
47 oxen, five rams, f he goats, five lambs H2568
47 five he goats, f lambs of the first year: H2568
53 two oxen, f rams, five he goats, H2568
53 oxen, five rams, f he goats, five lambs H2568
53 five he goats, f lambs of the first year: H2568
59 two oxen, f rams, five he goats, H2568
59 oxen, five rams, f he goats, five lambs H2568
59 five he goats, f lambs of the first year: H2568
Nu 7:65 two oxen, f rams, five he goats, H2568
65 oxen, five rams, f he goats, five lambs H2568
65 five he goats, f lambs of the first year: H2568
71 two oxen, f rams, five he goats, H2568
71 oxen, five rams, f he goats, five lambs H2568
71 five he goats, f lambs of the first year: H2568
77 two oxen, f rams, five he goats, H2568
77 oxen, five rams, f he goats, five lambs H2568
77 five he goats, f lambs of the first year: H2568
83 two oxen, f rams, five he goats, H2568
83 oxen, five rams, f he goats, five lambs H2568
83 five he goats, f lambs of the first year: H2568
8:24 from twenty and f years old and H2568
11:19 nor two days, nor f days, neither ten H2568
18:16 for the money of f shekels, after the H2568
26:18 of them, forty thousand and f hundred. H2568
22 and sixteen thousand and f hundred. H2568
27 threescore thousand and f hundred. H2568
37 two thousand and f hundred. These *are* H2568
41 forty and f thousand and six hundred. H2568
50 and f thousand and four hundred. H2568
31: 8 and Hur, and Reba, f kings of Midian: H2568
28 to battle: one soul of f hundred, *both* of H2568
32 thousand and f thousand sheep, H2568
36 thirty thousand and f hundred sheep: H2568
39 thousand and f hundred; of which the H2568
43 seven thousand and f hundred sheep, H2568
45 And thirty thousand asses and f H2568
Jos 8:12 And he took about f thousand men, H2568
10: 5 Therefore the f kings of the Amorites, H2568
16 But these f kings fled, and hid H2568
17 And it was told Joshua, saying, The f H2568
22 those f kings unto me out of the cave. H2568
23 forth those f kings unto him out H2568
26 hanged them on f trees: and they were H2568
13: 3 counted to the Canaanite: f lords of the H2568
14:10 these forty and f years, even since the H2568
10 I *am* this day fourscore and f years old. H2568
Jdg 3: 3 *Namely*, f lords of the Philistines, and H2568
18: 2 of their family f men from their coasts, H2568
7 Then the f men departed, and came to H2568
14 Then answered the f men that went to H2568
17 And the f men that went to spy out the H2568
20:35 that day twenty and f thousand and an H2568
45 in the highways f thousand men; and H2568
46 were twenty and f thousand men that H2568
1Sa 6: 4 They answered, F golden emerods, and H2568
4 emerods, and f golden mice, *according* H2568
16 And when the f lords of the Philistines H2568
18 *belonging* to the f lords, *both* of fenced H2568
17: 5 coat *was* f thousand shekels of brass. H2568
40 and chose him f smooth stones out of H2568
21: 3 hand? give *me* f *loaves of* bread in H2568
22:18 f persons that did wear a linen ephod. H2568
25:18 of wine, and f sheep ready dressed, H2568
18 dressed, and f measures of parched H2568
42 upon an ass, with f damsels of hers H2568
2Sa 4: 4 of *his* feet. He was f years old when the H2568
21: 8 and the f sons of Michal the daughter H2568
24: 9 Judah *were* f hundred thousand men. H2568
1Ki 4:32 and his songs were a thousand and f. H2568
6: 6 The nethermost chamber *was* f cubits H2568
10 all the house, f cubits high: and they H2568
24 And f cubits *was* the one wing of the H2568
24 of the cherub, and f cubits the other H2568
7: 3 *lay* on forty f pillars, fifteen *in* a row. H2568
16 the one chapiter *was* f cubits, and the H2568
16 of the other chapiter *was* f cubits: H2568
23 and his height *was* f cubits: and a line H2568
39 And he put f bases on the right side of H2568
39 of the house, and f on the left side of H2568
49 And the candlesticks of pure gold, f on H2568
49 the right *side*, and f on the left, before H2568
9:23 Solomon's work, f hundred and fifty, H2568
22:42 Jehoshaphat *was* thirty and f years old H2568
42 twenty and f years in Jerusalem. H2568
2Ki 6:25 cab of dove's dung for f *pieces* of silver. H2568
7:13 take, I pray thee, f of the horses that H2568
13:19 have smitten f or six times; then hadst H2568
14: 2 He was twenty and f years old when he H2568
15:33 F and twenty years old was he when he H2568
18: 2 Twenty and f years old was he when he H2568
19:35 fourscore and f thousand: and when H2568
21: 1 reigned fifty and f years in Jerusalem. H2568
23:36 Jehoiakim *was* twenty and f years old H2568
25:19 the men of war, and f men of them that H2568
1Ch 2: 4 and Zerah. All the sons of Judah *were* f. H2568
6 and Calcol, and Dara: f of them in all. H2568
3:20 and Hasadiah, Jushabhesed, f. H2568

1Ch 4:32 and Tochen, and Ashan, **f** cities: H2568
42 sons of Simeon, **f** hundred men, went H2568
7: 3 Joel, Ishiah, **f**: all of them chief men. H2568
7 Jerimoth, and Iri, **f**; heads of the house H2568
11:23 of *great* stature, **f** cubits high; and in H2568
29: 7 of God of gold **f** thousand talents and H2568
2Ch 3:11 *one cherub was* **f** cubits, reaching to H2568
11 wing *was likewise* **f** cubits, reaching to H2568
12 And *one* wing of the other cherub *was* **f** H2568
12 other wing *was* **f** cubits *also*, joining H2568
15 of thirty and **f** cubits high, and the H2568
15 on the top of each of them *was* **f** cubits. H2568
4: 2 in compass, and **f** cubits the height H2568
6 He made also ten lavers, and put **f** on H2568
6 right hand, and **f** on the left, to wash H2568
7 **f** on the right hand, and five on the left. H2568
7 five on the right hand, and **f** on the left. H2568
8 in the temple, **f** on the right side, and H2568
8 the right side, and **f** on the left. And he H2568
6:13 a brasen scaffold, of **f** cubits long, and H2568
13 cubits long, and **f** cubits broad, and H2568
13:17 Israel **f** hundred thousand chosen men. H2568
15:19 And there was no *more* war unto the **f** H2568
20:31 *he was* thirty and **f** years old when he H2568
31 twenty and **f** years in Jerusalem. H2568
25: 1 Amaziah *was* twenty and **f** years old H2568
26:13 thousand and **f** hundred, that made H2568
27: 1 Jotham *was* twenty and **f** years old H2568
8 He was **f** and twenty years old when he H2568
29: 1 Hezekiah began to reign *when he was* **f** H2568
33: 1 reigned fifty and **f** years in Jerusalem: H2568
35: 9 for passover offerings **f** thousand *small* H2568
9 *small cattle,* and **f** hundred oxen. H2568
36: 5 Jehoiakim *was* twenty and **f** years old H2568
Ezr 1:11 and of silver *were* **f** thousand and four H2568
2: 5 of Arah, seven hundred seventy and **f**. H2568
8 of Zattu, nine hundred forty and **f**. H2568
20 The children of Gibbar, ninety and **f**. H2568
33 and Ono, seven hundred twenty and **f**. H2568
34 of Jericho, three hundred forty and **f**. H2568
66 their mules, two hundred forty and **f**; H2568
67 Their camels, four hundred thirty and **f**; H2568
69 of gold, and **f** thousand pound of H2568
Neh 7:13 of Zattu, eight hundred forty and **f**. H2568
20 of Adin, six hundred fifty and **f**. H2568
25 The children of Gibeon, ninety and **f**. H2568
36 of Jericho, three hundred forty and **f**. H2568
67 and **f** singing men and singing women. H2568
68 their mules, two hundred forty and **f**: H2568
69 *Their* camels, four hundred thirty and **f**: H2568
70 **f** hundred and thirty priests' garments. H2568
Est 9: 6 slew and destroyed **f** hundred men. H2568
12 slain and destroyed **f** hundred men in H2568
16 foes seventy and **f** thousand, but they H2568
Job 1: 3 camels, and **f** hundred yoke of oxen, H2568
3 yoke of oxen, and **f** hundred she asses, H2568
Isa 7: 8 threescore and **f** years shall Ephraim H2568
17: 6 bough, four *or* **f** in the outmost fruitful H2568
19:18 In that day shall **f** cities in the land of H2568
30:17 at the rebuke of **f** shall ye flee: till ye be H2568
37:36 and fourscore and **f** thousand: and H2568
Jer 52:22 one chapiter *was* **f** cubits, with network H2568
30 hundred forty and **f** persons: all the H2568
31 month, in the **f** and twentieth *day* of H2568
Ezk 8:16 the altar, *were* about **f** and twenty men, H2568
11: 1 the door of the gate **f** and twenty men; H2568
40: 1 In the **f** and twentieth year of our H2568
7 little chambers *were* **f** cubits; and the H2568
13 **f** and twenty cubits, door against door. H2568
21 and the breadth **f** and twenty cubits. H2568
25 and the breadth **f** and twenty cubits. H2568
29 long, and **f** and twenty cubits broad. H2568
30 And the arches round about *were* **f** and H2568
30 twenty cubits long, and **f** cubits broad. H2568
33 long, and **f** and twenty cubits broad. H2568
36 and the breadth **f** and twenty cubits. H2568
48 post of the porch, **f** cubits on this side, H2568
48 on this side, and **f** cubits on that side: H2568
41: 2 of the door *were* **f** cubits on the one H2568
2 the one side, and **f** cubits on the other H2568
9 without, *was* **f** cubits: and *that* which H2568
11 that was left *was* **f** cubits round about. H2568
12 of the building *was* **f** cubits thick round H2568
42:16 measuring reed, **f** hundred reeds, with H2568
17 He measured the north side, **f** hundred H2568
18 He measured the south side, **f** hundred H2568
19 *and* measured **f** hundred reeds with H2568
20 a wall round about, **f** hundred *reeds* H2568
20 *reeds* long, and **f** hundred broad, to H2568
Ezk 45: 1 *be* the length of **f** and twenty thousand H2568
2 Of this there shall be for the sanctuary **f** H2568
2 *in length,* with **f** hundred *in breadth,* H2568
3 the length of **f** and twenty thousand, H2568
5 And the **f** and twenty thousand of H2568
6 of the city **f** thousand broad, and H2568
6 broad, and **f** and twenty thousand H2568
12 twenty shekels, **f** and twenty shekels, H2568
48: 8 ye shall offer of **f** and twenty thousand H2568
9 the LORD *shall be* of **f** and twenty H2568
10 toward the north **f** and twenty H2568
10 and toward the south **f** and twenty H2568
13 the Levites *shall have* **f** and twenty H2568
13 all the length *shall be* **f** and twenty H2568
15 And the **f** thousand, that are left in the H2568
15 breadth over against the **f** and twenty H2568
16 four thousand and **f** hundred, and the H2568
16 four thousand and **f** hundred, and on H2568
16 four thousand and **f** hundred, and the H2568
16 west side four thousand and **f** hundred. H2568
20 All the oblation *shall be* **f** and twenty H2568
20 thousand by **f** and twenty thousand: H2568
21 over against the **f** and twenty thousand H2568
21 over against the **f** and twenty thousand H2568
30 thousand and **f** hundred measures. H2568
32 side four thousand and **f** hundred: and H2568
33 side four thousand and **f** hundred H2568
34 At the west side four thousand and **f** H2568
Dan 12:12 three hundred and **f** and thirty days. H2568
Mt 14:17 have here but **f** loaves, and two fishes. G4002
19 and took the **f** loaves, and the two G4002
21 And they that had eaten were about **f** G4000
16: 9 remember the **f** loaves of the five G4002
9 five loaves of the **f** thousand, and how G4000
25: 2 And **f** of them were wise, and five *were* G4002
2 And five of them were wise, and **f** *were* G4002
15 And unto one he gave **f** talents, to G4002
16 Then he that had received the **f** talents G4002
16 same, and made *them* other **f** talents. G4002
20 And so he that had received **f** talents G4002
20 and brought other **f** talents, saying, G4002
20 unto me **f** talents: behold, I have G4002
20 gained beside them **f** talents more. G4002
Mk 6:38 they knew, they say, **F**, and two fishes. G4002
41 And when he had taken the **f** loaves G4002
44 the loaves were about **f** thousand men. G4000
8:19 When I brake the **f** loaves among five G4002
19 When I brake the five loaves among **f** G4000
Lk 1:24 and hid herself **f** months, saying, G4002
7:41 **f** hundred pence, and the other fifty. G4001
9:13 We have no more but **f** loaves and two G4002
14 For they were about **f** thousand men. G4000
16 Then he took the **f** loaves and the two G4002
12: 6 Are not **f** sparrows sold for two G4002
52 For from henceforth there shall be **f** in G4002
14:19 And another said, I have bought **f** yoke G4002
16:28 For I have **f** brethren; that he may G4002
19:18 Lord, thy pound hath gained **f** pounds. G4002
19 to him, Be thou also over **f** cities. G4002
Jn 4:18 For thou hast had **f** husbands; and he G4002
5: 2 tongue Bethesda, having **f** porches. G4002
6: 9 There is a lad here, which hath **f** barley G4002
10 sat down, in number about **f** thousand. G4000
13 fragments of the **f** barley loaves, which G4002
19 So when they had rowed about **f** and G4002
Act 4: 4 of the men was about **f** thousand. G4002
20: 6 in **f** days; where we abode seven days. G4002
24: 1 And after **f** days Ananias the high G4002
1Co 14:19 Yet in the church I had rather speak **f** G4002
15: 6 After that, he was seen of above **f** G4001
2Co 11:24 Of the Jews **f** times received I forty G3999
Rev 9: 5 be tormented **f** months: and their G4002
10 their power *was* to hurt men **f** months. G4002
17:10 And there are seven kings: **f** are fallen, G4002

FIVE-HUNDRED See FIVE and HUNDRED.

FIVE-THOUSAND See FIVE and THOUSAND.

FIVE-TIMES See FIVE and TIMES.

FIXED
Ps 57: 7 My heart is **f**, O God, my heart is fixed: I H3559
7 My heart is fixed, O God, my heart is **f**: I H3559
108: 1 O God, my heart is **f**; I will sing and give H3559
112: 7 his heart is **f**, trusting in the LORD. H3559
Lk 16:26 there is a great gulf **f**: so that they which G4741

FLAG
Job 8:11 mire? can the **f** grow without water? H260

FLAGON
2Sa 6:19 *of flesh,* and a **f** *of wine.* So all the people H809
1Ch 16: 3 a good piece of flesh, and a **f** *of wine.* H809

FLAGONS
Song 2: 5 Stay me with **f**, comfort me with apples: H809
Isa 22:24 of cups, even to all the vessels of **f**. H5035
Hos 3: 1 look to other gods, and love **f** of wine. H809

FLAGS
Ex 2: 3 she laid *it* in the **f** by the river's brink. H5488
5 the **f**, she sent her maid to fetch it. H5488
Isa 19: 6 dried up: the reeds and **f** shall wither. H5488

FLAKES
Job 41:23 The **f** of his flesh are joined together: H4651

FLAME
Ex 3: 2 unto him in a **f** of fire out of the midst H3827
Nu 21:28 out of Heshbon, a **f** from the city of H3852
Jdg 13:20 For it came to pass, when the **f** went up H3851
20 ascended in the **f** of the altar. And H3851
20:38 **f** with smoke rise up out of the city. H4864
40 But when the **f** began to arise up out of H4864
40 the **f** of the city ascended up to heaven. H3632
Job 15:30 out of darkness; the **f** shall dry up his H7957
41:21 His breath kindleth coals, and a **f** goeth H3851
Ps 83:14 As the fire burneth a wood, and as the **f** H3852
106:18 company; the **f** burned up the wicked. H3852
Song 8: 6 of fire, *which hath a* most vehement **f**. H7957
Isa 5:24 stubble, and the **f** consumeth the chaff, H3852
10:17 his Holy One for a **f**: and it shall burn H3852
29: 6 tempest, and the **f** of devouring fire. H3851
30:30 and *with* the **f** of a devouring fire, H3851
43: 2 neither shall the **f** kindle upon thee. H3852
47:14 the power of the **f**: *there shall* not *be* a H3852
Jer 48:45 of Heshbon, and a **f** from the midst of H3852
Ezk 20:47 dry tree: the flaming **f** shall not be H7957
Dan 3:22 exceeding hot, the **f** of the fire slew H7631
7: 9 fiery **f**, *and* his wheels *as* burning fire. H7631
11 destroyed, and given to the burning **f**. H785
11:33 **f**, by captivity, and by spoil, *many* days. H3852
Joel 1:19 **f** hath burned all the trees of the field. H3852
2: 3 behind them a **f** burneth: the land *is* H3852
5 leap, like the noise of a **f** of fire that H3851
Oba 18 house of Joseph a **f**, and the house of H3852
Lk 16:24 my tongue; for I am tormented in this **f**. G5395
Act 7:30 angel of the Lord in a **f** of fire in a bush. G5395
Heb 1: 7 spirits, and his ministers a **f** of fire. G5395
Rev 1:14 snow; and his eyes *were* as a **f** of fire; G5395
2:18 **f** of fire, and his feet *are* like fine brass; G5395
19:12 His eyes *were* as a **f** of fire, and on his G5395

FLAMES
Ps 29: 7 The voice of the LORD divideth the **f** of H3852
Isa 13: 8 one at another; their faces *shall be as* **f**. H3851
66:15 with fury, and his rebuke with **f** of fire. H3851

FLAMING
Gen 3:24 Eden Cherubims, and a **f** sword which H3858
Ps 104: 4 his angels spirits; his ministers a **f** fire: H3857
105:32 He gave them hail for rain, *and* **f** fire in H3852
Isa 4: 5 the shining of a **f** fire by night: for upon H3852
Lam 2: 3 a **f** fire, *which* devoureth round about. H3852
Ezk 20:47 every dry tree: the **f** flame shall not be H3852
Hos 7: 6 in the morning it burneth as a **f** fire. H3852
Nah 2: 3 *shall be* with **f** torches in the day of H784
2Th 1: 8 In **f** fire taking vengeance on them that G5395

FLANKS
Lev 3: 4 which *is* by the **f**, and the caul above H3689
10 which *is* by the **f**, and the caul above H3689
15 which *is* by the **f**, and the caul above H3689
4: 9 which *is* by the **f**, and the caul above H3689
7: 4 which *is* by the **f**, and the caul *that is* H3689
Job 15:27 and maketh collops of fat on *his* **f**. H3689

FLASH
Ezk 1:14 as the appearance of a **f** of lightning. H965

FLAT
Lev 21:18 hath a **f** nose, or any thing superfluous, H2673
Nu 22:31 down his head, and fell **f** on his face.
Jos 6: 5 the city shall fall down **f**, and the people H8478
20 the wall fell down **f**, so that the people H8478

FLATTER
Ps 5: 9 sepulchre; they f with their tongue. H2505
78:36 Nevertheless they did f him with their H6601

FLATTERETH
Ps 36: 2 For he f himself in his own eyes, until H2505
Prv 2:16 the stranger *which* f with her words; H2505
7: 5 the stranger *which* f with her words. H2505
20:19 not with him that f with his lips. H6601
28:23 favour than he that f with the tongue. H2505
29: 5 A man that f his neighbour spreadeth a H2505

FLATTERIES
Dan 11:21 and obtain the kingdom by f. H2519
32 shall he corrupt by f: but the people that H2514
34 but many shall cleave to them with f. H2519

FLATTERING
Job 32:21 neither let me give f titles unto man. H3655
22 For I know not to give f titles; *in so* H3655
Ps 12: 2 his neighbour: *with* f lips *and* with a H2513
3 The LORD shall cut off all f lips, *and* H2513
Prv 7:21 with the f of her lips she forced him. H2506
26:28 by it; and a f mouth worketh ruin. H2509
Ezk 12:24 f divination within the house of Israel. H2509
1Th 2: 5 For neither at any time used we f *G2850*

FLATTERY
Job 17: 5 He that speaketh f to *his* friends, even H2506
Prv 6:24 the f of the tongue of a strange woman. H2513

FLAX
Ex 9:31 And the f and the barley was smitten: H6594
31 *was* in the ear, and the f *was* bolled. H6594
Jos 2: 6 with the stalks of f, which she had laid H6593
Jdg 15:14 arms became as f that was burnt with H6593
Prv 31:13 She seeketh wool, and f, and worketh H6593
Isa 19: 9 Moreover they that work in fine f, and H6593
42: 3 and the smoking f shall he not quench: H6594
Ezk 40: 3 brass, with a line of f in his hand, and a H6593
Hos 2: 5 wool and my f, mine oil and my drink. H6593
9 and my f *given* to cover her nakedness. H6593
Mt 12:20 and smoking f shall he not quench, *G3043*

FLAY
Lev 1: 6 And he shall f the burnt offering, and H6584
2Ch 29:34 they could not f all the burnt offerings: H6584
Mic 3: 3 of my people, and f their skin from off H6584

FLAYED
2Ch 35:11 their hands, and the Levites f *them.* H6584

FLEA
1Sa 24:14 thou pursue? after a dead dog, after a f. H6550
26:20 come out to seek a f, as when one doth H6550

FLED
Gen 14:10 and Gomorrah f, and fell there; and H5127
10 they that remained f to the mountain. H5127
16: 6 hardly with her, she f from her face. H1272
31:20 Syrian, in that he told him not that he f. H1272
21 So he f with all that he had; and he rose H1272
22 Laban on the third day that Jacob was f. H1272
35: 7 when he f from the face of his brother. H1272
39:12 in her hand, and f, and got him out. H5127
13 garment in her hand, and was f forth, H5127
15 with me, and f, and got him out. H5127
18 he left his garment with me, and f out. H5127
Ex 2:15 Moses. But Moses f from the face of H1272
4: 3 a serpent; and Moses f from before it. H5127
14: 5 Egypt that the people f: and the heart of H1272
27 and the Egyptians f against it; and the H5127
Nu 16:34 round about them f at the cry of them: H5127
35:25 whither he was f: and he shall abide in H5127
26 the city of his refuge, whither he was f; H5127
32 for him that is f to the city of his refuge, H5127
Jos 7: 4 men: and they f before the men of Ai. H5127
8:15 and f by the way of the wilderness. H5127
20 and the people that f to the wilderness H5127
10:11 And it came to pass, as they f from H5127
16 But these five kings f, and hid H5127
20: 6 house, unto the city from whence he f. H5127
Jdg 1: 6 But Adoni-bezek f; and they pursued H5127
4:15 off *his* chariot, and f away on his feet. H5127
17 Howbeit Sisera f away on his feet to the H5127
7:21 and all the host ran, and cried, and f. H5127
22 host: and the host f to Beth-shittah in H5127
8:12 And when Zebah and Zalmunna f, he H5127
9:21 And Jotham ran away, and f, and went H1272
Jdg 9:40 And Abimelech chased him, and he f H5127
51 the city, and thither f all the men and H5127
11: 3 Then Jephthah f from his brethren, and H1272
20:45 And they turned and f toward the H5127
47 But six hundred men turned and f to H5127
1Sa 4:10 smitten, and they f every man into his H5127
16 of the army, and I f to day out of the H5127
17 and said, Israel is f before the H5127
14:22 that the Philistines f, even they also H5127
17:24 man, f from him, and were sore afraid. H5127
51 saw their champion was dead, they f. H5127
19: 8 a great slaughter; and they f from him. H5127
10 and David f, and escaped that night. H5127
12 and he went, and f, and escaped. H1272
18 So David f, and escaped, and came to H1272
20: 1 And David f from Naioth in Ramah, H1272
21:10 And David arose, and f that day for H1272
22:17 knew when he f, and did not shew it H1272
20 Abiathar, escaped, and f after David. H1272
23: 6 son of Ahimelech f to David to Keilah, H1272
27: 4 And it was told Saul that David was f to H1272
30:17 men, which rode upon camels, and f. H5127
31: 1 and the men of Israel f from before the H5127
7 the men of Israel f, and that Saul and H5127
7 the cities, and f; and the Philistines H5127
2Sa 1: 4 the people are f from the battle, and H5127
4: 3 And the Beerothites f to Gittaim, and H1272
4 took him up, and f: and it came to pass, H5127
10:13 the Syrians: and they f before him. H5127
14 the Syrians were f, then fled they also H5127
14 were fled, then f they also before H5127
18 And the Syrians f before Israel; and H5127
13:29 man gat him up upon his mule, and f. H5127
34 But Absalom f. And the young man that H1272
37 But Absalom f, and went to Talmai, the H1272
38 So Absalom f, and went to Geshur, and H1272
18:17 and all Israel f every one to his tent. H5127
19: 8 for Israel had f every man to his tent. H5127
9 now he is f out of the land for Absalom. H1272
23:11 and the people f from the Philistines. H5127
1Ki 2: 7 I f because of Absalom thy brother. H1272
28 And Joab f unto the tabernacle H5127
29 that Joab was f unto the tabernacle H5127
11:17 That Hadad f, he and certain Edomites H1272
23 son of Eliadah, which f from his lord H1272
40 arose, and f into Egypt, unto Shishak H1272
12: 2 *of it,* (for he was f from the presence of H1272
20:20 and the Syrians f; and Israel pursued H5127
30 But the rest f to Aphek, into the city; H5127
30 And Ben-hadad f, and came into the H5127
2Ki 3:24 so that they f before them: but they H5127
7: 7 Wherefore they arose and f in the H5127
7 the camp as it *was*, and f for their life. H5127
8:21 and the people f into their tents. H5127
9:10 *her.* And he opened the door, and f. H5127
23 And Joram turned his hands, and f, and H5127
27 of Judah saw *this*, he f by the way of the H5127
27 And he f to Megiddo, and died there. H5127
14:12 and they f every man to their tents. H5127
19 in Jerusalem: and he f to Lachish; but H5127
25: 4 all the men of war *f* by night by the way
1Ch 10: 1 and the men of Israel f from before the H5127
7 saw that they f, and that Saul and his H5127
7 their cities, and f: and the Philistines H5127
11:13 the people f from before the Philistines. H5127
19:14 unto the battle; and they f before him. H5127
15 the Syrians were f, they likewise fled H5127
15 fled, they likewise f before Abishai his H5127
18 But the Syrians f before Israel; and H5127
2Ch 10: 2 whither he had f from the presence of H1272
13:16 And the children of Israel f before H5127
14:12 and before Judah; and the Ethiopians f. H5127
25:22 Israel, and they f every man to his tent. H5127
27 in Jerusalem; and he f to Lachish: but H5127
Neh 13:10 the work, were f every one to his field. H1272
Ps 3:ttl A Psalm of David, when he f from H1272
31:11 they that did see me without f from me. H5074
57:ttl David, when he f from Saul in the cave. H1272
104: 7 At thy rebuke they f; at the voice of thy H5127
114: 3 The sea saw *it*, and f: Jordan was driven H5127
Isa 10:29 Ramah is afraid; Gibeah of Saul is f. H5127
21:14 prevented with their bread him that f. H5074
15 For they f from the swords, from the H5074
22: 3 All thy rulers are f together, they are H5074
3 bound together, *which* have f from far. H1272
33: 3 At the noise of the tumult the people f; H5074
Jer 4:25 and all the birds of the heavens were f. H5074
9:10 and the beast are f; they are gone. H5074
26:21 was afraid, and f, and went into Egypt; H1272
Jer 39: 4 of war, then they f, and went forth out H1272
46: 5 down, and are f apace, and look not H5127
21 back, *and* are f away together: they H5127
48:45 They that f stood under the shadow of H5127
52: 7 all the men of war f, and went forth out H1272
Lam 4:15 not: when they f away and wandered, H5132
Dan 10: 7 them, so that they f to hide themselves. H1272
Hos 7:13 Woe unto them! for they have f from H5074
12:12 And Jacob f into the country of Syria, H1272
Jna 1:10 men knew that he f from the presence H1272
4: 2 Therefore I f before unto Tarshish: H1272
Zec 14: 5 shall flee, like as ye f from before the H5127
Mt 8:33 And they that kept them f, and went *G5343*
26:56 all the disciples forsook him, and f. *G5343*
Mk 5:14 And they that fed the swine f, and told *it* *G5343*
14:50 And they all forsook him, and f. *G5343*
52 And he left the linen cloth, and f from *G5343*
16: 8 And they went out quickly, and f from *G5343*
Lk 8:34 was done, they f, and went and told *it* *G5343*
Act 7:29 Then f Moses at this saying, and was a *G5343*
14: 6 They were ware of *it*, and f unto Lystra *G2703*
16:27 that the prisoners had been f. *G1628*
19:16 them, so that they f out of that house *G1628*
Heb 6:18 who have f for refuge to lay hold *G2703*
Rev 12: 6 And the woman f into the wilderness, *G5343*
16:20 And every island f away, and the *G5343*
20:11 and the heaven f away; and there was *G5343*

FLEDDEST
Gen 35: 1 f from the face of Esau thy brother. H1272
Ps 114: 5 What *ailed* thee, O thou sea, that thou f? H5127

FLEE
Gen 16: 8 I f from the face of my mistress Sarai. H1272
19:20 Behold now, this city *is* near to f unto, H5127
27:43 f thou to Laban my brother to Haran; H1272
31:27 Wherefore didst thou f away secretly, H1272
Ex 9:20 and his cattle f into the houses: H5127
14:25 said, Let us f from the face of Israel; H5127
21:13 appoint thee a place whither he shall f. H5127
Lev 26:17 and ye shall f when none pursueth you. H5127
36 them; and they shall f, as fleeing from a H5127
Nu 10:35 let them that hate thee f before thee. H5127
24:11 Therefore now f thou to thy place: I H1272
35: 6 that he may f thither: and to them H5127
11 the slayer may f thither, which killeth H5127
15 any person unawares may f thither. H5127
Dt 4:42 That the slayer might f thither, which H5127
19: 3 parts, that every slayer may f thither. H5127
4 the slayer, which shall f thither, that he H5127
5 shall f unto one of those cities, and live: H5127
28: 7 one way, and f before thee seven ways. H5127
25 against them, and f seven ways before H5127
Jos 8: 5 at the first, that we will f before them, H5127
6 they will say, They f before us, as at the H5127
6 first: therefore we will f before them. H5127
20 had no power to f this way or that way: H5127
20: 3 *and* unwittingly may f thither: and they H5127
4 And when he that doth f unto one of H5127
9 at unawares might f thither, and not H5127
Jdg 20:32 of Israel said, Let us f, and draw them H5127
2Sa 4: 4 as she made haste to f, that he fell, and H5127
15:14 Arise, and let us f; for we shall not *else* H1272
17: 2 shall f; and I will smite the king only: H5127
18: 3 go forth: for if we f away, they will not H5127
19: 3 steal away when they f in battle. H5127
24:13 thy land? or wilt thou f three months H5127
1Ki 12:18 him up to his chariot, to f to Jerusalem. H5127
2Ki 9: 3 open the door, and f, and tarry not. H5127
2Ch 10:18 him up to *his* chariot, to f to Jerusalem. H5127
Neh 6:11 And I said, Should such a man as I f? H1272
Job 9:25 a post: they f away, they see no good. H1272
20:24 He shall f from the iron weapon, *and* H1272
27:22 spare: he would fain f out of his hand. H1272
30:10 They abhor me, they f far from me, and H7368
41:28 The arrow cannot make him f: H1272
Ps 11: 1 my soul, F *as* a bird to your mountain? H5110
64: 8 all that see them shall f away. H5074
68: 1 them also that hate him f before him. H5127
12 Kings of armies did f apace: and she H5074
139: 7 or whither shall I f from thy presence? H1272
143: 9 mine enemies: I f unto thee to hide me. H3680
Prv 28: 1 The wicked f when no man pursueth: H5127
17 shall f to the pit; let no man stay him. H5127
Song 2:17 Until the day break, and the shadows f H5127
4: 6 Until the day break, and the shadows f H5127
Isa 10: 3 to whom will ye f for help? and where H5127
31 of Gebim gather themselves to f.
13:14 and f every one into his own land. H5127

Isa 15: 5 his fugitives *shall f* unto Zoar, an heifer
17:13 and they shall f far off, and shall be H5127
20: 6 whither we f for help to be delivered H5127
30:16 But ye said, No; for we will f upon H5127
16 therefore shall ye f: and, We will ride H5127
17 One thousand *shall f* at the rebuke of
17 of five shall ye f: till ye be left as a H5127
31: 8 him: but he shall f from the sword, and H5127
35:10 and sorrow and sighing shall f away. H5127
48:20 Go ye forth of Babylon, f ye from the H1272
51:11 sorrow and mourning shall f away. H5127
Jer 4:29 The whole city shall f for the noise of H1272
6: 1 yourselves to f out of the midst of H5756
25:35 have no way to f, nor the principal of H4498
46: 6 Let not the swift f away, nor the mighty H5127
48: 6 F, save your lives, and be like the heath H5127
9 Give wings unto Moab, that it may f H5323
49: 8 F ye, turn back, dwell deep, O H5127
24 turneth herself to f, and fear hath seized H5127
30 F, get you far off, dwell deep, O ye H5127
50:16 they shall f every one to his own land. H5127
28 The voice of them that f and escape out H5127
51: 6 F out of the midst of Babylon, and H5127
Am 2:16 the mighty shall f away naked in that H5127
5:19 As if a man did f from a lion, and a H5127
7:12 O thou seer, go, f thee away into the H1272
9: 1 of them shall not f away, and he that H5127
Jna 1: 3 But Jonah rose up to f unto Tarshish H1272
Nah 2: 8 yet they shall f away. Stand, stand, H5127
3: 7 upon thee shall f from thee, and say, H5074
17 sun ariseth they f away, and their place H5074
Zec 2: 6 Ho, ho, *come forth*, and f from the land H5127
14: 5 And ye shall f *to* the valley of the H5127
5 Azal: yea, ye shall f, like as ye fled from H5127
Mt 2:13 his mother, and f into Egypt, and be *G5343*
3: 7 you to f from the wrath to come? *G5343*
10:23 you in this city, f ye into another: for *G5343*
24:16 Then let them which be in Judaea f into *G5343*
Mk 13:14 that be in Judaea f to the mountains: *G5343*
Lk 3: 7 you to f from the wrath to come? *G5343*
21:21 Then let them which are in Judaea f to *G5343*
Jn 10: 5 not follow, but will f from him: for they *G5343*
Act 27:30 And as the shipmen were about to f out *G5343*
1Co 6:18 F fornication. Every sin that a man *G5343*
10:14 Wherefore, my dearly beloved, f from *G5343*
1Ti 6:11 But thou, O man of God, f these things; *G5343*
2Ti 2:22 F also youthful lusts: but follow *G5343*
Jas 4: 7 Resist the devil, and he will f from you. *G5343*
Rev 9: 6 to die, and death shall f from them. *G5343*

FLEECE

Dt 18: 4 the f of thy sheep, shalt thou give him. H1488
Jdg 6:37 Behold, I will put a f of wool in the H1492
37 if the dew be on the f only, and *it be* dry H1492
38 and thrust the f together, and wringed H1492
38 the dew out of the f, a bowl full of water. H1492
39 but this once with the f; let it now be dry H1492
39 be dry only upon the f, and upon all the H1492
40 was dry upon the f only, and there was H1492
Job 31:20 *not* warmed with the f of my sheep; H1488

FLEEING

Lev 26:36 they shall flee, as f from a sword; and H4499
Dt 4:42 f unto one of these cities he might live: H5127
Job 30: 3 *they were* solitary; f into the wilderness H6207

FLEETH

Dt 19:11 he die, and f into one of these cities: H5127
Job 14: 2 f also as a shadow, and continueth not. H1272
Isa 24:18 And it shall come to pass, *that* he who f H5127
Jer 48:19 and espy; ask him that f, and her that H5127
44 He that f from the fear shall fall into H5211
Am 9: 1 the sword: he that f of them shall not H5127
Jn 10:12 the sheep, and f: and the wolf catcheth *G5343*
13 The hireling f, because he is an hireling, *G5343*

FLESH

Gen 2:21 and closed up the f instead thereof; H1320
23 of my bones, and f of my flesh: she H1320
23 and flesh of my f: she shall be called H1320
24 unto his wife: and they shall be one f. H1320
6: 3 for that he also *is* f: yet his days shall be H1320
12 corrupt; for all f had corrupted his way H1320
13 The end of all f is come before me; for H1320
17 to destroy all f, wherein *is* the breath H1320
19 And of every living thing of all f, two of H1320
7:15 two of all f, wherein *is* the breath of life. H1320
16 male and female of all f, as God had H1320
21 And all f died that moved upon the H1320
Gen 8:17 *is* with thee, of all f, *both* of fowl, and of H1320
9: 4 But f with the life thereof, *which is* the H1320
11 neither shall all f be cut off any more H1320
15 creature of all f; and the waters shall H1320
15 no more become a flood to destroy all f. H1320
16 creature of all f that *is* upon the earth. H1320
17 me and all f that *is* upon the earth. H1320
17:11 And ye shall circumcise the f of your H1320
13 in your f for an everlasting covenant. H1320
14 man child whose f of his foreskin is not H1320
23 circumcised the f of their foreskin in H1320
24 circumcised in the f of his foreskin. H1320
25 circumcised in the f of his foreskin. H1320
29:14 my bone and my f. And he abode with H1320
37:27 our f. And his brethren were content. H1320
40:19 the birds shall eat thy f from off thee. H1320
Ex 4: 7 it was turned again as his *other* f. H1320
12: 8 And they shall eat the f in that night, H1320
46 forth ought of the f abroad out of the H1320
16: 3 we sat by the f pots, *and* when we did H1320
8 you in the evening f to eat, and in the H1320
12 even ye shall eat f, and in the morning H1320
21:28 stoned, and his f shall not be eaten; but H1320
22:31 shall ye eat *any* f *that is* torn of beasts H1320
29:14 But the f of the bullock, and his skin, H1320
31 and seethe his f in the holy place. H1320
32 And Aaron and his sons shall eat the f H1320
34 And if ought of the f of the H1320
30:32 Upon man's f shall it not be poured, H1320
Lev 4:11 and all his f, with his head, and with H1320
6:10 he put upon his f, and take up the ashes H1320
27 Whatsoever shall touch the f thereof H1320
7:15 And the f of the sacrifice of his peace H1320
17 But the remainder of the f of the H1320
18 And if *any* of the f of the sacrifice of his H1320
19 And the f that toucheth any unclean H1320
19 the f, all that be clean shall eat thereof. H1320
20 But the soul that eateth *of* the f of the H1320
21 and eat of the f of the sacrifice of peace H1320
8:17 But the bullock, and his hide, his f, and H1320
31 to his sons, Boil the f *at* the door of the H1320
32 And that which remaineth of the f and H1320
9:11 And the f and the hide he burnt with H1320
11: 8 Of their f shall ye not eat, and their H1320
11 not eat of their f, but ye shall have their H1320
12: 3 And in the eighth day the f of his H1320
13: 2 in the skin of his f a rising, a scab, or H1320
2 be in the skin of his f *like* the plague of H1320
3 in the skin of the f: and *when* the hair in H1320
3 the skin of his f, it *is* a plague of leprosy: H1320
4 in the skin of his f, and in sight *be* not H1320
10 and *there be* quick raw f in the rising; H1320
11 It *is* an old leprosy in the skin of his f, H1320
13 covered all his f, he shall pronounce H1320
14 But when raw f appeareth in him, he H1320
15 And the priest shall see the raw f, and H1320
15 *for* the raw f *is* unclean: it *is* a leprosy. H1320
16 Or if the raw f turn again, and be H1320
18 The f also, in which, *even* in the skin H1320
24 Or if there be *any* f, in the skin whereof H1320
24 and the quick *f* that burneth have a
38 f bright spots, *even* white bright spots; H1320
39 in the skin of their f *be* darkish white; it H1320
43 leprosy appeareth in the skin of the f; H1320
14: 9 his f in water, and he shall be clean. H1320
15: 2 his f, *because of* his issue he *is* unclean. H1320
3 issue: whether his f run with his issue, H1320
3 his issue, or his f be stopped from his H1320
7 And he that toucheth the f of him that H1320
13 f in running water, and shall be clean. H1320
16 he shall wash all his f in water, and be H1320
19 her issue in her f be blood, she shall be H1320
16: 4 breeches upon his f, and shall be girded H1320
4 his f in water, and *so* put them on. H1320
24 And he shall wash his f with water in H1320
26 and bathe his f in water, and afterward H1320
27 their skins, and their f, and their dung. H1320
28 and bathe his f in water, and afterward H1320
17:11 For the life of the f *is* in the blood: and I H1320
14 For *it is* the life of all f; the blood of it *is* H1320
14 of no manner of f: for the life of all flesh H1320
14 for the life of all f *is* the blood thereof: H1320
16 But if he wash *them* not, nor bathe his f; H1320
19:28 any cuttings in your f for the dead, nor H1320
21: 5 beard, nor make any cuttings in their f. H1320
22: 6 things, unless he wash his f with water. H1320
26:29 And ye shall eat the f of your sons, and H1320
29 and the f of your daughters shall ye eat. H1320
Nu 8: 7 shave all their f, and let them wash H1320
Nu 11: 4 and said, Who shall give us f to eat? H1320
13 Whence should I have f to give unto all H1320
13 me, saying, Give us f, that we may eat. H1320
18 and ye shall eat f: for ye have wept in H1320
18 Who shall give us f to eat? for *it was* H1320
18 LORD will give you f, and ye shall eat. H1320
21 f, that they may eat a whole month. H1320
33 And while the f *was* yet between their H1320
12:12 dead, of whom the f is half consumed H1320
16:22 of the spirits of all f, shall one man sin, H1320
18:15 the matrix in all f, which they bring H1320
18 And the f of them shall be thine, as the H1320
19: 5 her skin, and her f, and her blood, with H1320
7 and he shall bathe his f in water, and H1320
8 and bathe his f in water, and shall be H1320
27:16 all f, set a man over the congregation, H1320
Dt 5:26 For who *is there of* all f, that hath heard H1320
12:15 mayest kill and eat f in all thy gates, H1320
20 shalt say, I will eat f, because thy soul H1320
20 soul longeth to eat f; thou mayest eat H1320
20 eat f, whatsoever thy soul lusteth after. H1320
23 thou mayest not eat the life with the f. H1320
27 offerings, the f and the blood, upon H1320
27 LORD thy God, and thou shalt eat the f. H1320
14: 8 of their f, nor touch their dead carcase. H1320
16: 4 there *any thing* of the f, which thou H1320
28:53 own body, the f of thy sons and of thy H1320
55 to any of them of the f of his children H1320
32:42 shall devour f; *and that* with the blood H1320
Jdg 6:19 ephah of flour: the f he put in a basket, H1320
20 him, Take the f and the unleavened H1320
21 and touched the f and the unleavened H1320
21 rock, and consumed the f and the H1320
8: 7 I will tear your f with the thorns of the H1320
9: 2 also that I *am* your bone and your f. H1320
1Sa 2:13 came, while the f was in seething, with H1320
15 sacrificed, Give f to roast for the priest; H1320
15 will not have sodden f of thee, but raw. H1320
17:44 and I will give thy f unto the fowls of H1320
25:11 my water, and my f that I have killed H2878
2Sa 5: 1 Behold, we *are* thy bone and thy f. H1320
6:19 and a good piece *of f*, and a flagon *of* H829
19:12 my bones and my f: wherefore then are H1320
13 bone, and of my f? God do so to me, and H1320
1Ki 17: 6 him bread and f in the morning, and H1320
6 and bread and f in the evening; and H1320
19:21 and boiled their f with the instruments H1320
21:27 sackcloth upon his f, and fasted, and H1320
2Ki 4:34 and the f of the child waxed warm. H1320
5:10 times, and thy f shall come again to H1320
14 of God: and his f came again like unto H1320
14 the f of a little child, and he was clean. H1320
6:30 *he had* sackcloth within upon his f. H1320
9:36 of Jezreel shall dogs eat the f of Jezebel: H1320
1Ch 11: 1 Behold, we *are* thy bone and thy f. H1320
16: 3 a good piece of f, and a flagon *of wine*. H829
2Ch 32: 8 With him *is* an arm of f; but with us *is* H1320
Neh 5: 5 Yet now our f *is* as the flesh of our H1320
5 Yet now our flesh *is* as the f of our H1320
Job 2: 5 his f, and he will curse thee to thy face. H1320
4:15 my face; the hair of my f stood up: H1320
6:12 strength of stones? or *is* my f of brass? H1320
7: 5 My f is clothed with worms and clods H1320
10: 4 Hast thou eyes of f? or seest thou as H1320
11 Thou hast clothed me with skin and f, H1320
13:14 Wherefore do I take my f in my teeth, H1320
14:22 But his f upon him shall have pain, and H1320
19:20 my skin and to my f, and I am escaped H1320
22 as God, and are not satisfied with my f? H1320
26 this *body*, yet in my f shall I see God: H1320
21: 6 and trembling taketh hold on my f. H1320
31:31 we had of his f! we cannot be satisfied. H1320
33:21 His f is consumed away, that it cannot H1320
25 His f shall be fresher than a child's: he H1320
34:15 All f shall perish together, and man H1320
41:23 The flakes of his f are joined together: H1320
Ps 16: 9 rejoiceth: my f also shall rest in hope. H1320
27: 2 to eat up my f, they stumbled and fell. H1320
38: 3 *There is* no soundness in my f because H1320
7 and *there is* no soundness in my f. H1320
50:13 Will I eat the f of bulls, or drink the H1320
56: 4 I will not fear what f can do unto me. H1320
63: 1 for thee, my f longeth for thee in a H1320
65: 2 prayer, unto thee shall all f come. H1320
73:26 My f and my heart faileth: *but* God *is* H7607
78:20 also? can he provide f for his people? H7607
27 He rained f also upon them as dust, H7607
39 that they *were but* f; a wind that H1320
79: 2 of the heaven, the f of thy saints unto H1320

Ps 84: 2 and my f crieth out for the living God. H1320
109:24 fasting; and my f faileth of fatness. H1320
119:120 My f trembleth for fear of thee; and I H1320
136:25 Who giveth food to all f: for his mercy H1320
145:21 f bless his holy name for ever and ever. H1320
Prv 4:22 that find them, and health to all their f. H1320
5:11 And thou mourn at the last, when thy f H1320
11:17 but *he that is* cruel troubleth his own f. H7607
14:30 A sound heart *is* the life of the f: but H1320
23:20 winebibbers; among riotous eaters of f: H1320
Ecc 4: 5 hands together, and eateth his own f. H1320
5: 6 Suffer not thy mouth to cause thy f to H1320
11:10 f: for childhood and youth *are* vanity. H1320
12:12 and much study *is* a weariness of the f. H1320
Isa 9:20 eat every man the f of his own arm: H1320
17: 4 and the fatness of his f shall wax lean. H1320
22:13 sheep, eating f, and drinking wine: H1320
31: 3 and their horses f, and not spirit. When H1320
40: 5 revealed, and all f shall see *it* together: H1320
6 shall I cry? All f *is* grass, and all the H1320
44:16 thereof he eateth f; he roasteth roast, H1320
19 I have roasted f, and eaten *it*: and shall H1320
49:26 thee with their own f; and they shall be H1320
26 wine: and all f shall know that I the H1320
58: 7 thou hide not thyself from thine own f? H1320
65: 4 which eat swine's f, and broth of H1320
66:16 plead with all f: and the slain of the H1320
17 eating swine's f, and the abomination, H1320
23 to another, shall all f come to worship H1320
24 they shall be an abhorring unto all f. H1320
Jer 7:21 offerings unto your sacrifices, and eat f. H1320
11:15 and the holy f is passed from thee? H1320
12:12 end of the land: no f shall have peace. H1320
17: 5 man, and maketh f his arm, and whose H1320
19: 9 And I will cause them to eat the f of H1320
9 their sons and the f of their daughters, H1320
9 eat every one the f of his friend in the H1320
25:31 he will plead with all f; he will give them H1320
32:27 Behold, I *am* the LORD, the God of all f: H1320
45: 5 bring evil upon all f, saith the LORD: H1320
51:35 The violence done to me and to my f *be* H7607
Lam 3: 4 My f and my skin hath he made old; he H1320
Ezk 4:14 there abominable f into my mouth. H1320
11: 3 this *city is* the caldron, and we *be* the f. H1320
7 of it, they *are* the f, and this *city is* the H1320
11 shall ye be the f in the midst thereof; H1320
19 f, and will give them an heart of flesh: H1320
19 flesh, and will give them an heart of f: H1320
16:26 great of f; and hast increased H1320
20:48 And all f shall see that I the LORD have H1320
21: 4 all f from the south to the north: H1320
5 That all f may know that I the LORD H1320
23:20 paramours, whose f *is as* the flesh of H1320
20 flesh *is as* the f of asses, and whose H1320
24:10 the fire, consume the f, and spice it well, H1320
32: 5 And I will lay thy f upon the H1320
36:26 f, and I will give you an heart of flesh. H1320
26 flesh, and I will give you an heart of f. H1320
37: 6 and will bring up f upon you, and cover H1320
8 lo, the sinews and the f came up upon H1320
39:17 that ye may eat f, and drink blood. H1320
18 Ye shall eat the f of the mighty, and H1320
40:43 the tables *was* the f of the offering. H1320
44: 7 and uncircumcised in f, to be in my H1320
9 uncircumcised in f, shall enter into my H1320
Dan 1:15 fairer and fatter in f than all the H1320
2:11 the gods, whose dwelling is not with f. H1321
4:12 boughs thereof, and all f was fed of it. H1321
7: 5 said thus unto it, Arise, devour much f. H1321
10: 3 I ate no pleasant bread, neither came f H1320
Hos 8:13 They sacrifice f *for* the sacrifices of H1320
Joel 2:28 my spirit upon all f; and your sons and H1320
Mic 3: 2 them, and their f from off their bones; H7607
3 Who also eat the f of my people, and H7607
3 for the pot, and as f within the caldron. H1320
Zep 1:17 out as dust, and their f as the dung. H3894
Hag 2:12 If one bear holy f in the skirt of his H1320
Zec 2:13 Be silent, O all f, before the LORD: for H1320
11: 9 the rest eat every one the f of another. H1320
16 but he shall eat the f of the fat, and tear H1320
14:12 Jerusalem; Their f shall consume away H1320
Mt 16:17 Barjona: for f and blood hath not *G4561*
19: 5 his wife: and they twain shall be one f? *G4561*
6 twain, but one f. What therefore God *G4561*
24:22 there should no f be saved: but for the *G4561*
26:41 indeed *is* willing, but the f *is* weak. *G4561*
Mk 10: 8 And they twain shall be one f: so then *G4561*
8 then they are no more twain, but one f. *G4561*
13:20 those days, no f should be saved: but *G4561*

Mk 14:38 spirit truly *is* ready, but the f *is* weak. *G4561*
Lk 3: 6 And all f shall see the salvation of God. *G4561*
24:39 not f and bones, as ye see me have. *G4561*
Jn 1:13 the f, nor of the will of man, but of God. *G4561*
14 And the Word was made f, and dwelt *G4561*
3: 6 That which is born of the f is flesh; and *G4561*
6 That which is born of the flesh is f; and *G4561*
6:51 I will give is my f, which I will give for *G4561*
52 How can this man give us *his* f to eat? *G4561*
53 Except ye eat the f of the Son of man, *G4561*
54 Whoso eateth my f, and drinketh my *G4561*
55 For my f is meat indeed, and my blood *G4561*
56 He that eateth my f, and drinketh my *G4561*
63 It is the spirit that quickeneth; the f *G4561*
8:15 Ye judge after the f; I judge no man. *G4561*
17: 2 As thou hast given him power over all f, *G4561*
Act 2:17 my Spirit upon all f: and your sons and *G4561*
26 moreover also my f shall rest in hope: *G4561*
30 according to the f, he would raise up *G4561*
31 in hell, neither his f did see corruption. *G4561*
Ro 1: 3 of the seed of David according to the f; *G4561*
2:28 circumcision, which is outward in the f: *G4561*
3:20 law there shall no f be justified in his *G4561*
4: 1 as pertaining to the f, hath found? *G4561*
6:19 the infirmity of your f: for as ye have *G4561*
7: 5 For when we were in the f, the motions *G4561*
18 For I know that in me (that is, in my f,) *G4561*
25 of God; but with the f the law of sin. *G4561*
8: 1 walk not after the f, but after the Spirit. *G4561*
3 weak through the f, God sending his *G4561*
3 the likeness of sinful f, and for sin, *G4561*
3 and for sin, condemned sin in the f: *G4561*
4 walk not after the f, but after the Spirit. *G4561*
5 For they that are after the f do mind *G4561*
5 the things of the f; but they that are *G4561*
8 So then they that are in the f cannot *G4561*
9 But ye are not in the f, but in the Spirit, *G4561*
12 not to the f, to live after the flesh. *G4561*
12 not to the flesh, to live after the f. *G4561*
13 For if ye live after the f, ye shall die: but *G4561*
9: 3 my kinsmen according to the f: *G4561*
5 as concerning the f Christ *came*, who is *G4561*
8 the children of the f, these *are* not the *G4561*
11:14 *are* my f, and might save some of them. *G4561*
13:14 for the f, to *fulfil* the lusts *thereof*. *G4561*
14:21 *It is* good neither to eat f, nor to drink *G2907*
1Co 1:26 wise men after the f, not many mighty, *G4561*
29 That no f should glory in his presence. *G4561*
5: 5 destruction of the f, that the spirit may *G4561*
6:16 body? for two, saith he, shall be one f. *G4561*
7:28 have trouble in the f: but I spare you. *G4561*
8:13 I will eat no f while the world standeth, *G2907*
10:18 Behold Israel after the f: are not they *G4561*
15:39 All f *is* not the same flesh: but *there is* *G4561*
39 All flesh *is* not the same f: but *there is* *G4561*
39 *is* one *kind of* f of men, another flesh *G4561*
39 of men, another f of beasts, another of *G4561*
50 Now this I say, brethren, that f and *G4561*
2Co 1:17 according to the f, that with me there *G4561*
4:11 be made manifest in our mortal f. *G4561*
5:16 no man after the f: yea, though we have *G4561*
16 Christ after the f, yet now henceforth *G4561*
7: 1 from all filthiness of the f and spirit, *G4561*
5 Macedonia, our f had no rest, but we *G4561*
10: 2 of us as if we walked according to the f. *G4561*
3 For though we walk in the f, we do not *G4561*
3 in the flesh, we do not war after the f: *G4561*
11:18 Seeing that many glory after the f, I will *G4561*
12: 7 to me a thorn in the f, the messenger of *G4561*
Gal 1:16 I conferred not with f and blood: *G4561*
2:16 works of the law shall no f be justified. *G4561*
20 I now live in the f I live by the faith of *G4561*
3: 3 Spirit, are ye now made perfect by the f? *G4561*
4:13 Ye know how through infirmity of the f *G4561*
14 And my temptation which was in my f *G4561*
23 was born after the f; but he of the *G4561*
29 But as then he that was born after the f *G4561*
5:13 to the f, but by love serve one another. *G4561*
16 and ye shall not fulfil the lust of the f. *G4561*
17 For the f lusteth against the Spirit, and *G4561*
17 the Spirit against the f: and these are *G4561*
19 Now the works of the f are manifest, *G4561*
24 the f with the affections and lusts. *G4561*
6: 8 For he that soweth to his f shall of the *G4561*
8 flesh shall of the f reap corruption; but *G4561*
12 a fair shew in the f, they constrain you *G4561*
13 that they may glory in your f. *G4561*
Eph 2: 3 in the lusts of our f, fulfilling the desires *G4561*
3 the desires of the f and of the mind; *G4561*

Eph 2:11 past Gentiles in the f, who are called *G4561*
11 Circumcision in the f made by hands; *G4561*
15 Having abolished in his f the enmity, *G4561*
5:29 For no man ever yet hated his own f; *G4561*
30 of his body, of his f, and of his bones. *G4561*
31 his wife, and they two shall be one f. *G4561*
6: 5 according to the f, with fear and *G4561*
12 For we wrestle not against f and blood, *G4561*
Php 1:22 But if I live in the f, this *is* the fruit of *G4561*
24 Nevertheless to abide in the f *is* more *G4561*
3: 3 Jesus, and have no confidence in the f. *G4561*
4 confidence in the f. If any other man *G4561*
4 whereof he might trust in the f, I more: *G4561*
Col 1:22 In the body of his f through death, to *G4561*
24 of Christ in my f for his body's sake, *G4561*
2: 1 many as have not seen my face in the f; *G4561*
5 For though I be absent in the f, yet am I *G4561*
11 of the f by the circumcision of Christ: *G4561*
13 of your f, hath he quickened together *G4561*
23 in any honour to the satisfying of the f. *G4561*
3:22 according to the f; not with eyeservice, *G4561*
1Ti 3:16 manifest in the f, justified in the Spirit, *G4561*
Phlm 16 thee, both in the f, and in the Lord? *G4561*
Heb 2:14 are partakers of f and blood, he also *G4561*
5: 7 Who in the days of his f, when he had *G4561*
9:13 sanctifieth to the purifying of the f: *G4561*
10:20 us, through the veil, that is to say, his f; *G4561*
12: 9 had fathers of our f which corrected *us*, *G4561*
Jas 5: 3 and shall eat your f as it were fire. Ye *G4561*
1Pt 1:24 For all f *is* as grass, and all the glory of *G4561*
3:18 in the f, but quickened by the Spirit: *G4561*
21 of the filth of the f, but the answer of a *G4561*
4: 1 for us in the f, arm yourselves likewise *G4561*
1 suffered in the f hath ceased from sin; *G4561*
2 of *his* time in the f to the lusts of men, *G4561*
6 f, but live according to God in the spirit. *G4561*
2Pt 2:10 But chiefly them that walk after the f in *G4561*
18 through the lusts of the f, *through much* *G4561*
1Jn 2:16 the lust of the f, and the lust of the eyes, *G4561*
4: 2 Jesus Christ is come in the f is of God: *G4561*
3 is come in the f is not of God: and this *G4561*
2Jn 7 f. This is a deceiver and an antichrist. *G4561*
Jude 7 going after strange f, are set forth for an *G4561*
8 defile the f, despise dominion, and *G4561*
23 even the garment spotted by the f. *G4561*
Rev 17:16 shall eat her f, and burn her with fire. *G4561*
19:18 That ye may eat the f of kings, and the *G4561*
18 of kings, and the f of captains, and the *G4561*
18 captains, and the f of mighty men, and *G4561*
18 men, and the f of horses, and of them *G4561*
18 on them, and the f of all *men, both* free *G4561*
21 and all the fowls were filled with their f. *G4561*

FLESHHOOK

1Sa 2:13 with a f of three teeth in his hand; H4207
14 or pot; all that the f brought up the H4207

FLESHHOOKS

Ex 27: 3 basons, and his f, and his firepans: all H4207
38: 3 basons, *and* the f, and the firepans: all H4207
Nu 4:14 the censers, the f, and the shovels, and H4207
1Ch 28:17 Also pure gold for the f, and the bowls, H4207
2Ch 4:16 the shovels, and the f, and all their H4207

FLESHLY

2Co 1:12 sincerity, not with f wisdom, but by the *G4559*
Col 2:18 seen, vainly puffed up by his f mind, *G4561*
1Pt 2:11 f lusts, which war against the soul; *G4559*

FLESH-POTS See FLESH and POTS.

FLESHY

2Co 3: 3 of stone, but in f tables of the heart. *G4560*

FLEW

1Sa 14:32 And the people f upon the spoil, and H6213
Isa 6: 6 Then f one of the seraphims unto me, H5774

FLIES

Ex 8:21 send swarms *of* f upon thee, and upon
21 *f*, and also the ground whereon they *are*.
22 that no swarms *of* f shall be there; to the
24 a grievous swarm *of* f into the house of
24 corrupted by reason of the swarm *of* f.
29 that the swarms *of* f may depart from
31 the swarms *of* f from Pharaoh, from
Ps 78:45 He sent divers sorts of f among them, H6157
105:31 sorts of f, *and* lice in all their coasts. H6157
Ecc 10: 1 Dead f cause the ointment of the H2070

FLIETH
Dt 4:17 of any winged fowl that f in the air, H5774
14:19 And every creeping thing that f *is* H5775
28:49 *as swift* as the eagle f; a nation whose H1675
Ps 91: 5 night; *nor* for the arrow *that* f by day; H5774
Nah 3:16 the cankerworm spoileth, and f away. H5774

FLIGHT
Lev 26: 8 put ten thousand to f: and your enemies H7291
Dt 32:30 ten thousand to f, except their Rock had H5127
1Ch 12:15 and they put to f all *them* of the valleys, H1272
Isa 52:12 haste, nor go by f: for the LORD will go H4499
Am 2:14 Therefore the f shall perish from the H4498
Mt 24:20 But pray ye that your f be not in the *G5437*
Mk 13:18 And pray ye that your f be not in the *G5437*
Heb 11:34 turned to f the armies of the aliens. *G2827*

FLINT
Dt 8:15 thee forth water out of the rock of f; H2496
Ps 114: 8 water, the f into a fountain of waters. H2496
Isa 5:28 like f, and their wheels like a whirlwind: H6862
50: 7 I set my face like a f, and I know that I H2496
Ezk 3: 9 As an adamant harder than f have I H6864

FLINTY
Dt 32:13 of the rock, and oil out of the f rock; H2496

FLOATS
1Ki 5: 9 them by sea in f unto the place that H1702
2Ch 2:16 bring it to thee in f by sea to Joppa; and H7513

FLOCK
Gen 4: 4 of the firstlings of his f and of the fat H6629
21:28 seven ewe lambs of the f by themselves. H6629
27: 9 Go now to the f, and fetch me from H6629
29:10 the f of Laban his mother's brother. H6629
30:31 for me, I will again feed *and* keep thy f: H6629
32 I will pass through all thy f to day, H6629
40 the brown in the f of Laban; and he put H6629
31: 4 Rachel and Leah to the field unto his f, H6629
38 and the rams of thy f have I not eaten. H6629
33:13 them one day, all the f will die. H6629
37: 2 old, was feeding the f with his brethren; H6629
12 to feed their father's f in Shechem. H6629
13 brethren feed *the f* in Shechem? come,
38:17 *thee* a kid from the f. And she said, Wilt H6629
Ex 2:16 the troughs to water their father's f. H6629
17 and helped them, and watered their f. H6629
19 *water* enough for us, and watered the f. H6629
3: 1 Now Moses kept the f of Jethro his H6629
1 and he led the f to the backside of the H6629
Lev 1: 2 the cattle, *even* of the herd, and of the f. H6629
3: 6 the LORD *be* of the f; male or female, he H6629
5: 6 a female from the f, a lamb or a kid of H6629
18 without blemish out of the f, with thy H6629
6: 6 without blemish out of the f, with thy H6629
27:32 the herd, or of the f, *even* of whatsoever H6629
Nu 15: 3 unto the LORD, of the herd, or of the f: H6629
Dt 12:17 of thy herds or of thy f, nor any of thy H6629
21 herd and of thy f, which the LORD hath H6629
15:14 him liberally out of thy f, and out of thy H6629
19 thy herd and of thy f thou shalt sanctify H6629
16: 2 thy God, of the f and the herd, in the H6629
1Sa 17:34 a bear, and took a lamb out of the f: H5739
2Sa 12: 4 to take of his own f and of his own H6629
2Ch 35: 7 And Josiah gave to the people, of the f, H6629
Ezr 10:19 *offered* a ram of the f for their trespass. H6629
Job 21:11 They send forth their little ones like a f, H6629
30: 1 to have set with the dogs of my f. H6629
Ps 77:20 Thou leddest thy people like a f by the H6629
78:52 guided them in the wilderness like a f. H5739
80: 1 Joseph like a f; thou that dwellest H6629
107:41 and maketh *him* families like a f. H6629
Song 1: 7 thou makest *thy f* to rest at noon: for
8 the footsteps of the f, and feed thy kids H6629
4: 1 thy hair *is* as a f of goats, that appear H5739
2 Thy teeth *are* like a f *of sheep that are* H5739
6: 5 as a f of goats that appear from Gilead. H5739
6 Thy teeth *are* as a f of sheep which go H5739
Isa 40:11 He shall feed his f like a shepherd: he H5739
63:11 shepherd of his f? where *is* he that put H6629
Jer 13:17 the LORD'S f is carried away captive. H5739
20 the north: where *is* the f *that* was given H5739
20 *that* was given thee, thy beautiful f? H6629
23: 2 have scattered my f, and driven them H6629
3 And I will gather the remnant of my f H6629
25:34 ye principal of the f: for the days of your H6629
35 flee, nor the principal of the f to escape. H6629
36 principal of the f, *shall be heard*: for the H6629
Jer 31:10 and keep him, as a shepherd *doth* his f. H5739
12 the young of the f and of the herd: and H6629
49:20 the least of the f shall draw them out: H6629
50:45 the least of the f shall draw them out: H6629
51:23 shepherd and his f; and with thee will I H5739
Ezk 24: 5 Take the choice of the f, and burn also H6629
34: 3 them that are fed: *but* ye feed not the f. H6629
6 high hill: yea, my f was scattered upon H6629
8 surely because my f became a prey, H6629
8 a prey, and my f became meat to every H6629
8 search for my f, but the shepherds fed H6629
8 fed themselves, and fed not my f; H6629
10 I will require my f at their hand, and H6629
10 from feeding the f; neither shall the H6629
10 for I will deliver my f from their mouth, H6629
12 As a shepherd seeketh out his f in the H5739
15 I will feed my f, and I will cause them to H6629
17 And *as for* you, O my f, thus saith the H6629
19 And *as for* my f, they eat that which ye H6629
22 Therefore will I save my f, and they H6629
31 And ye my f, the flock of my pasture, H6629
31 And ye my flock, the f of my pasture, H6629
36:37 I will increase them with men like a f. H6629
38 As the holy f, as the flock of Jerusalem H6629
38 As the holy flock, as the f of Jerusalem H6629
43:23 and a ram out of the f without blemish. H6629
25 and a ram out of the f, without blemish. H6629
45:15 And one lamb out of the f, out of two H6629
Am 6: 4 lambs out of the f, and the calves out of H6629
7:15 as I followed the f, and the LORD said H6629
Jna 3: 7 nor beast, herd nor f, taste any thing: let H6629
Mic 2:12 of Bozrah, as the f in the midst of their H5739
4: 8 And thou, O tower of the f, the strong H5739
7:14 Feed thy people with thy rod, the f of H6629
Hab 3:17 yield no meat; the f shall be cut off H6629
Zec 9:16 in that day as the f of his people: for H6629
10: 2 their way as a f, they were troubled, H6629
3 hath visited his f the house of Judah, H5739
11: 4 my God; Feed the f of the slaughter; H6629
7 And I will feed the f of slaughter, *even* H6629
7 you, O poor of the f. And I took unto me H6629
7 the other I called Bands; and I fed the f. H6629
11 so the poor of the f that waited upon H6629
17 that leaveth the f! the sword *shall be* H6629
Mal 1:14 which hath in his f a male, and voweth, H5739
Mt 26:31 of the f shall be scattered abroad. *G4167*
Lk 2: 8 keeping watch over their f by night. *G4167*
12:32 Fear not, little f; for it is your Father's *G4168*
Act 20:28 and to all the f, over the which the Holy *G4168*
29 enter in among you, not sparing the f. *G4168*
1Co 9: 7 or who feedeth a f, and eateth not of the *G4167*
7 flock, and eateth not of the milk of the f? *G4167*
1Pt 5: 2 Feed the f of God which is among you, *G4168*
3 heritage, but being ensamples to the f. *G4168*

FLOCKS
Gen 13: 5 Abram, had f, and herds, and tents. H6629
24:35 and he hath given him f, and herds, and H6629
26:14 For he had possession of f, and H6629
29: 2 there *were* three f of sheep lying by it; H5739
2 they watered the f: and a great stone H5739
3 And thither were all the f gathered: and H5739
8 until all the f be gathered together, H5739
30:36 and Jacob fed the rest of Laban's f. H6629
38 pilled before the f in the gutters in the H6629
38 troughs when the f came to drink, that H6629
39 And the f conceived before the rods, H6629
40 and set the faces of the f toward the H6629
40 he put his own f by themselves, and H5739
32: 5 And I have oxen, and asses, f, and H6629
7 with him, and the f, and herds, and the H6629
33:13 tender, and the f and herds with young H6629
37:14 and well with the f; and bring me word H6629
16 me, I pray thee, where they feed *their f*.
45:10 f, and thy herds, and all that thou hast: H6629
46:32 have brought their f, and their herds, H6629
47: 1 and their f, and their herds, and H6629
4 pasture for their f; for the famine *is* sore H6629
17 horses, and for the f, and for the cattle H6629
50: 8 ones, and their f, and their herds, they H6629
Ex 10: 9 with our f and with our herds H6629
24 only let your f and your herds be H6629
12:32 Also take your f and your herds, as ye H6629
38 and f, and herds, *even* very much cattle. H6629
34: 3 the f nor herds feed before that mount. H6629
Lev 1:10 And if his offering *be* of the f, *namely*, H6629
5:15 blemish out of the f, with thy estimation H6629
Nu 11:22 Shall the f and the herds be slain for H6629
31: 9 and all their f, and all their goods. H4735
Nu 31:30 the asses, and of the f, of all manner of H6629
32:26 Our little ones, our wives, our f, and all H4735
Dt 7:13 thy kine, and the f of thy sheep, in the H6251
8:13 And *when* thy herds and thy f multiply, H6629
12: 6 firstlings of your herds and of your f: H6629
14:23 thy herds and of thy f; that thou mayest H6629
28: 4 of thy kine, and the f of thy sheep. H6251
18 of thy kine, and the f of thy sheep. H6251
51 of thy kine, or f of thy sheep, until he H6251
Jdg 5:16 bleatings of the f? For the divisions of H5739
1Sa 30:20 And David took all the f and the herds, H6629
2Sa 12: 2 The rich *man* had exceeding many f H6629
1Ki 20:27 them like two little f of kids; but the H2835
1Ch 4:39 of the valley, to seek pasture for their f. H6629
41 *there was* pasture there for their f. H6629
27:31 And over the f *was* Jaziz the Hagerite. H6629
2Ch 17:11 brought him f, seven thousand and H6629
32:28 for all manner of beasts, and cotes for f. H5739
29 and possessions of f and herds in H6629
Neh 10:36 herds and of our f, to bring to the house H6629
Job 24: 2 violently take away f, and feed *thereof*. H5739
Ps 65:13 The pastures are clothed with f; the H6629
78:48 hail, and their f to hot thunderbolts. H4735
Prv 27:23 state of thy f, *and* look well to thy herds. H6629
Song 1: 7 aside by the f of thy companions? H5739
Isa 17: 2 they shall be for f, which shall lie down, H5739
32:14 ever, a joy of wild asses, a pasture of f; H5739
60: 7 All the f of Kedar shall be gathered H6629
61: 5 and feed your f, and the sons of the H6629
65:10 And Sharon shall be a fold of f, and the H6629
Jer 3:24 our youth; their f and their herds, their H6629
5:17 shall eat up thy f and thine herds: they H6629
6: 3 The shepherds with their f shall come H5739
10:21 and all their f shall be scattered. H4830
31:24 and they *that* go forth with f. H5739
33:12 shepherds causing *their* f to lie down. H6629
13 of Judah, shall the f pass again under H6629
49:29 Their tents and their f shall they take H6629
50: 8 and be as the he goats before the f. H6629
Ezk 25: 5 a couchingplace for f: and ye shall know H6629
34: 2 should not the shepherds feed the f? H6629
36:38 cities be filled with f of men: and they H6629
Hos 5: 6 They shall go with their f and with their H6629
Joel 1:18 yea, the f of sheep are made desolate. H5739
Mic 5: 8 lion among the f of sheep: who, if he H5739
Zep 2: 6 cottages for shepherds, and folds for f. H6629
14 And f shall lie down in the midst of her, H5739

FLOOD
Gen 6:17 And, behold, I, even I, do bring a f of H3999
7: 6 the f of waters was upon the earth. H3999
7 the ark, because of the waters of the f. H3999
10 the waters of the f were upon the earth. H3999
17 And the f was forty days upon the H3999
9:11 by the waters of a f; neither shall there H3999
11 any more be a f to destroy the earth. H3999
15 no more become a f to destroy all flesh. H3999
28 And Noah lived after the f three H3999
10: 1 unto them were sons born after the f. H3999
32 nations divided in the earth after the f. H3999
11:10 begat Arphaxad two years after the f: H3999
Jos 24: 2 the other side of the f in old time, *even* H5104
3 the other side of the f, and led him H5104
14 f, and in Egypt; and serve ye the LORD. H5104
15 the other side of the f, or the gods of the H5104
Job 14:11 sea, and the f decayeth and drieth up: H5104
22:16 foundation was overflown with a f: H5104
28: 4 The f breaketh out from the inhabitant; H5158
Ps 29:10 The LORD sitteth upon the f; yea, the H3999
66: 6 f on foot: there did we rejoice in him. H5104
74:15 and the f: thou driedst up mighty rivers. H5158
90: 5 Thou carriest them away as with a f; H2229
Isa 28: 2 storm, as a f of mighty waters H2230
59:19 come in like a f, the Spirit of the LORD H5104
Jer 46: 7 Who *is* this *that* cometh up as a f, H2975
8 Egypt riseth up like a f, and *his* waters H2975
47: 2 be an overflowing f, and shall overflow H5158
Dan 9:26 *shall be* with a f, and unto the end of H7858
11:22 And with the arms of a f shall they be H7858
Am 8: 8 rise up wholly as a f; and it shall be cast H216
8 out and drowned, as *by* the f of Egypt. H2975
9: 5 rise up wholly like a f; and shall be H2975
5 shall be drowned, as *by* the f of Egypt. H2975
Nah 1: 8 But with an overrunning f he will make H7858
Mt 24:38 For as in the days that were before the f *G2627*
39 And knew not until the f came, and *G2627*
Lk 6:48 and when the f arose, the stream beat *G4132*
17:27 the f came, and destroyed them all. *G2627*
2Pt 2: 5 in the f upon the world of the ungodly; *G2627*

Rev 12:15 mouth water as a f after the woman, G4215
15 cause her to be carried away of the f. G4216
16 swallowed up the f which the dragon G4215

FLOODS

Ex 15: 8 together, the f stood upright as an H5140
2Sa 22: 5 the f of ungodly men made me afraid; H5158
Job 20:17 He shall not see the rivers, the f, the H5104
28:11 He bindeth the f from overflowing; and H5104
Ps 18: 4 the f of ungodly men made me afraid. H5158
24: 2 the seas, and established it upon the f. H5104
32: 6 surely in the f of great waters they H7858
69: 2 deep waters, where the f overflow me. H7641
78:44 and their f, that they could not drink. H5140
93: 3 The f have lifted up, O LORD, the H5104
3 up, O LORD, the f have lifted up their H5104
3 up their voice; the f lift up their waves. H5104
98: 8 Let the f clap *their* hands: let the hills H5104
Song 8: 7 neither can the f drown it: if *a* man H5104
Isa 44: 3 him that is thirsty, and f upon the dry H5140
Ezk 31:15 I restrained the f thereof, and the great H5104
Jna 2: 3 of the seas; and the f compassed me H5104
Mt 7:25 And the rain descended, and the f G4215
27 And the rain descended, and the f G4215

FLOOR

Gen 50:11 mourning in the f of Atad, they said, H1637
Nu 5:17 dust that is in the f of the tabernacle H7172
Dt 15:14 flock, and out of thy f, and out of thy H1637
Jdg 6:37 of wool in the f; *and* if the dew be on H1637
Ru 3: 3 thee down to the f: *but* make not thyself H1637
6 And she went down unto the f, and did H1637
14 known that a woman came into the f. H1637
1Ki 6:15 of cedar, both the f of the house, and H7172
15 the f of the house with planks of fir. H7172
16 the house, both the f and the walls with H7172
30 And the f of the house he overlaid with H7172
7: 7 from one side of the f to the other. H7172
2Ch 34:11 couplings, and to f the houses which H7136
Isa 21:10 O my threshing, and the corn of my f: H1637
Hos 9: 2 The f and the winepress shall not feed H1637
13: 3 f, and as the smoke out of the chimney. H1637
Mic 4:12 gather them as the sheaves into the f. H1637
Mt 3:12 purge his f, and gather his wheat G257
Lk 3:17 purge his f, and will gather the wheat G257

FLOORS

Joel 2:24 And the f shall be full of wheat, and the H1637

FLOUR

Ex 29: 2 oil: *of* wheaten f shalt thou make them. H5560
40 And with the one lamb a tenth deal of f H5560
Lev 2: 1 shall be *of* fine f; and he shall pour oil H5560
2 his handful of the f thereof, and of the H5560
4 cakes of fine f mingled with oil, or H5560
5 *of* fine f unleavened, mingled with oil. H5560
7 it shall be made *of* fine f with oil. H5560
5:11 of an ephah of fine f for a sin offering; H5560
6:15 it his handful, of the f of the meat H5560
20 of an ephah of fine f for a meat offering H5560
7:12 cakes mingled with oil, of fine f, fried. H5560
14:10 tenth deals of fine f *for* a meat offering, H5560
21 tenth deal of fine f mingled with oil for H5560
23:13 tenth deals of fine f mingled with oil, H5560
17 shall be of fine f; they shall be baken H5560
24: 5 And thou shalt take fine f, and bake H5560
Nu 6:15 cakes of fine f mingled with oil, and H5560
7:13 f mingled with oil for a meat offering: H5560
19 f mingled with oil for a meat offering: H5560
25 f mingled with oil for a meat offering: H5560
31 f mingled with oil for a meat offering: H5560
37 f mingled with oil for a meat offering: H5560
43 f mingled with oil for a meat offering: H5560
49 f mingled with oil for a meat offering: H5560
55 f mingled with oil for a meat offering: H5560
61 f mingled with oil for a meat offering: H5560
67 f mingled with oil for a meat offering: H5560
73 f mingled with oil for a meat offering: H5560
79 f mingled with oil for a meat offering: H5560
8: 8 offering, *even* fine f mingled with oil, H5560
15: 4 of a tenth deal of f mingled with the H5560
6 two tenth deals of f mingled with the H5560
9 of f mingled with half an hin of oil. H5560
28: 5 And a tenth *part* of an ephah of f for a H5560
9 two tenth deals of f *for* a meat offering, H5560
12 And three tenth deals of f *for* a meat H5560
12 two tenth deals of f *for* a meat offering, H5560
13 And a several tenth deal of f mingled H5560
20 And their meat offering *shall be of* f H5560
Nu 28:28 And their meat offering of f mingled H5560
29: 3 And their meat offering *shall be of* f H5560
9 And their meat offering *shall be of* f H5560
14 And their meat offering *shall be of* f H5560
Jdg 6:19 of an ephah of f: the flesh he put in a H7058
1Sa 1:24 and one ephah of f, and a bottle of H7058
28:24 killed it, and took f, and kneaded *it*, and H7058
2Sa 13: 8 And she took f, and kneaded *it*, and H1217
17:28 and barley, and f, and parched *corn*, H7058
1Ki 4:22 fine f, and threescore measures of meal, H5560
2Ki 7: 1 a measure of fine f *be sold* for a shekel, H5560
16 So a measure of fine f was *sold* for a H5560
18 a measure of fine f for a shekel, shall be H5560
1Ch 9:29 and the fine f, and the wine, and the H5560
23:29 and for the fine f for meat offering, and H5560
Ezk 16:13 thou didst eat fine f, and honey, and oil: H5560
19 My meat also which I gave thee, fine f, H5560
46:14 temper with the fine f; a meat offering H5560
Rev 18:13 and oil, and fine f, and wheat, and G4585

FLOURISH

Ps 72: 7 In his days shall the righteous f; and H6524
16 of the city shall f like grass of the earth. H6692
92: 7 of iniquity do f; *it is* that they shall be H6692
12 The righteous shall f like the palm tree: H6524
13 LORD shall f in the courts of our God. H6524
132:18 but upon himself shall his crown f. H6692
Prv 11:28 but the righteous shall f as a branch. H6524
14:11 but the tabernacle of the upright shall f. H6524
Ecc 12: 5 the almond tree shall f, and the H5006
Song 7:12 us see if the vine f, *whether* the tender H6524
Isa 17:11 make thy seed to f: *but* the harvest *shall* H6524
66:14 your bones shall f like an herb: and the H6524
Ezk 17:24 made the dry tree to f: I the LORD have H6524

FLOURISHED

Song 6:11 vine f, *and* the pomegranates budded. H6524
Php 4:10 care of me hath f again; wherein ye were G330

FLOURISHETH

Ps 90: 6 In the morning it f, and groweth up; in H6692
103:15 as grass: as a flower of the field, so he f. H6692

FLOURISHING

Ps 92:14 fruit in old age; they shall be fat and f; H7488
Dan 4: 4 rest in mine house, and f in my palace: H7487

FLOW

Job 20:28 shall f away in the day of his wrath. H5064
Ps 147:18 his wind to blow, *and* the waters f. H5140
Song 4:16 the spices thereof may f out. Let my H5140
Isa 2: 2 the hills; and all nations shall f unto it. H5102
48:21 the waters to f out of the rock for them: H5140
60: 5 Then thou shalt see, and f together, H5102
64: 1 might f down at thy presence, H2151
Jer 31:12 of Zion, and shall f together to the H5102
51:44 nations shall not f together any more H5102
Joel 3:18 and the hills shall f with milk, and all H3212
18 of Judah shall f with waters, and a H3212
Mic 4: 1 the hills; and people shall f unto it. H5102
Jn 7:38 of his belly shall f rivers of living water. G4482

FLOWED

Jos 4:18 f over all his banks, as *they did* before. H3212
Isa 64: 3 the mountains f down at thy presence. H2151
Lam 3:54 Waters f over mine head; *then* I said, I H6687

FLOWER

Ex 25:33 *with* a knop and a f in one branch; and H6525
33 *with* a knop and a f: so in the six H6525
37:19 a knop and a f; and three bowls made H6525
19 a knop and a f: so throughout the six H6525
1Sa 2:33 thine house shall die in the f of their age. H582
Job 14: 2 He cometh forth like a f, and is cut H6731
15:33 and shall cast off his f as the olive. H5328
Ps 103:15 *As for* man, his days *are* as grass: as a f H6731
Isa 18: 5 is ripening in the f, he shall both cut off H5328
28: 1 beauty *is* a fading f, which *are* on the H6731
4 shall be a fading f, *and* as the hasty fruit H6733
40: 6 thereof *is* as the f of the field: H6731
7 The grass withereth, the f fadeth: H6731
8 The grass withereth, the f fadeth: but H6731
Nah 1: 4 and the f of Lebanon languisheth. H6525
1Co 7:36 if she pass the f of *her* age, and need G5230
Jas 1:10 as the f of the grass he shall pass away. G438
11 the grass, and the f thereof falleth, and G438
1Pt 1:24 glory of man as the f of grass. The grass G438
24 withereth, and the f thereof falleth away: G438

FLOWERS

Ex 25:31 knops, and his f, shall be of the same. H6525
34 almonds, *with* their knops and their f. H6525
37:17 his knops, and his f, were of the same: H6525
20 like almonds, his knops, and his f: H6525
Lev 15:24 her at all, and her f be upon him, he H5079
33 And of her that is sick of her f, and of H5079
Nu 8: 4 thereof, unto the f thereof, *was* beaten H6525
1Ki 6:18 knops and open f: all *was* cedar; there H6731
29 trees and open f, within and without. H6731
32 trees and open f, and overlaid *them* H6731
35 trees and open f: and covered *them* H6731
7:26 of a cup, with f of lilies: it contained H6525
49 f, and the lamps, and the tongs *of* gold, H6525
2Ch 4: 5 of a cup, with f of lilies; *and* it received H6525
21 And the f, and the lamps, and the tongs, H6525
Song 2:12 The f appear on the earth; the time of H5339
5:13 of spices, *as* sweet f: his lips *like* lilies, H4026

FLOWETH

Lev 20:24 it, a land that f with milk and honey: H2100
Nu 13:27 us, and surely it f with milk and honey; H2100
14: 8 us; a land which f with milk and honey. H2100
16:13 up out of a land that f with milk and H2100
14 us into a land that f with milk and H2100
Dt 6: 3 in the land that f with milk and honey. H2100
11: 9 a land that f with milk and honey. H2100
26: 9 *even* a land that f with milk and honey. H2100
15 a land that f with milk and honey. H2100
27: 3 thee, a land that f with milk and honey; H2100
31:20 unto their fathers, that f with milk and H2100
Jos 5: 6 us, a land that f with milk and honey. H2100

FLOWING

Ex 3: 8 a large, unto a land f with milk and H2100
17 unto a land f with milk and honey. H2100
13: 5 to give thee, a land f with milk and H2100
33: 3 Unto a land f with milk and honey: for H2100
Prv 18: 4 the wellspring of wisdom *as* a f brook. H5042
Isa 66:12 the Gentiles like a f stream: then shall H7857
Jer 11: 5 to give them a land f with milk and H2100
18:14 *or* shall the cold f waters that come H5140
32:22 them, a land f with milk and honey; H2100
49: 4 thou in the valleys, thy f valley, O H2100
Ezk 20: 6 espied for them, f with milk and honey, H2100
15 I had given *them*, f with milk and H2100

FLUTE

Dan 3: 5 of the cornet, f, harp, sackbut, psaltery, H4953
7 of the cornet, f, harp, sackbut, psaltery, H4953
10 of the cornet, f, harp, sackbut, psaltery, H4953
15 of the cornet, f, harp, sackbut, psaltery, H4953

FLUTTERETH

Dt 32:11 As an eagle stirreth up her nest, f over H7363

FLUX

Act 28: 8 and of a bloody f: to whom Paul entered G1420

FLY

Gen 1:20 and fowl *that* may f above the earth in H5774
1Sa 15:19 LORD, but didst f upon the spoil, and H5860
2Sa 22:11 And he rode upon a cherub, and did f: H5774
Job 5: 7 unto trouble, as the sparks f upward. H5774
20: 8 He shall f away as a dream, and shall H5774
39:26 Doth the hawk f by thy wisdom, *and* H82
Ps 18:10 And he rode upon a cherub, and did f: H5774
10 he did f upon the wings of the wind. H1675
55: 6 *for then* would I f away, and be at rest. H5774
90:10 for it is soon cut off, and we f away. H5774
Prv 23: 5 they f away as an eagle toward heaven. H5774
Isa 6: 2 his feet, and with twain he did f. H5774
7:18 LORD shall hiss for the f that *is* in the H2070
11:14 But they shall f upon the shoulders of H5774
60: 8 Who *are* these *that* f as a cloud, and as H5774
Jer 48:40 Behold, he shall f as an eagle, and shall H1675
49:22 Behold, he shall come up and f as the H1675
Ezk 13:20 to make *them* f, and I will tear them H6524
20 the souls that ye hunt to make *them* f. H6524
Dan 9:21 being caused to f swiftly, touched me H3286
Hos 9:11 *As for* Ephraim, their glory shall f away H5774
Hab 1: 8 shall f as the eagle *that* hasteth to eat. H5774
Rev 12:14 that she might f into the wilderness, G4072
14: 6 And I saw another angel f in the midst G4072
19:17 to all the fowls that f in the midst of G4072

FLYING

Lev 11:21 Yet these may ye eat of every f creeping H5775
23 But all *other* f creeping things, which H5775

F

Ps 148:10 all cattle; creeping things, and f fowl: H3671
Prv 26: 2 f, so the curse causeless shall not come. H5774
Isa 14:29 and his fruit *shall be* a fiery f serpent. H5774
30: 6 the viper and fiery f serpent, they will H5774
31: 5 As birds f, so will the LORD of hosts H5774
Zec 5: 1 eyes, and looked, and behold a f roll. H5774
2 I answered, I see a f roll; the length H5774
Rev 4: 7 and the fourth beast *was* like a f eagle. G4072
8:13 And I beheld, and heard an angel f G4072

FOAL
Gen 49:11 Binding his f unto the vine, and his H5895
Zec 9: 9 an ass, and upon a colt the f of an ass. H1121
Mt 21: 5 upon an ass, and a colt the f of an ass. G5207

FOALS
Gen 32:15 ten bulls, twenty she asses, and ten f. H5895

FOAM
Hos 10: 7 king is cut off as the f upon the water. H7110

FOAMETH
Mk 9:18 him: and he f, and gnasheth with his G875
Lk 9:39 teareth him that he f again, and bruising G876

FOAMING
Mk 9:20 he fell on the ground, and wallowed f. G875
Jude 13 Raging waves of the sea, f out their G1890

FODDER
Job 6: 5 hath grass? or loweth the ox over his f? H1098

FOES
1Ch 21:12 before thy f, while that the sword H6862
Est 9:16 and slew of their f seventy and five H8130
Ps 27: 2 enemies and my f, came upon me to eat H341
30: 1 hast not made my f to rejoice over me. H341
89:23 And I will beat down his f before his H6862
Mt 10:36 And a man's f *shall be* they of his own G2190
Act 2:35 Until I make thy f thy footstool. G2190

FOLD
Isa 13:20 shall the shepherds make their f there. H7257
65:10 And Sharon shall be a f of flocks, and H5116
Ezk 34:14 of Israel shall their f be: there shall they H5116
14 they lie in a good f, and *in* a fat pasture H5116
Mic 2:12 in the midst of their f: they shall make H1699
Hab 3:17 be cut off from the f, and *there shall be* H4356
Jn 10:16 are not of this f: them also I must bring, G833
16 there shall be one f, *and* one shepherd. G4167
Heb 1:12 And as a vesture shalt thou f them up, G1667

FOLDEN
Nah 1:10 For while *they be* f together *as* thorns, H5440

FOLDETH
Ecc 4: 5 The fool f his hands together, and H2263

FOLDING
1Ki 6:34 the one door *were* f, and the two leaves H1550
34 the two leaves of the other door *were* f. H1550
Prv 6:10 slumber, a little f of the hands to sleep: H2264
24:33 slumber, a little f of the hands to sleep: H2264

FOLDS
Nu 32:24 little ones, and f for your sheep; and H1448
36 fenced cities: and f for sheep. H1448
Ps 50: 9 of thy house, *nor* he goats out of thy f. H4356
Jer 23: 3 them again to their f; and they shall be H5116
Zep 2: 6 cottages for shepherds, and f for flocks. H1448

FOLK
Gen 33:15 thee *some* of the f that *are* with me. H5971
Prv 30:26 The conies *are but* a feeble f, yet make H5971
Jer 51:58 f in the fire, and they shall be weary. H3816
Mk 6: 5 upon a few sick f, and healed *them*. G732
Jn 5: 3 of impotent f, of blind, halt, withered, G770

FOLKS
Act 5:16 bringing sick f, and them which were G772

FOLLOW
Gen 24: 5 be willing to f me unto this land: H3212+H310
8 be willing to f thee, then thou H3212+H310
39 the woman will not f me. H3212+H310
44: 4 his steward, Up, f after the men; and H7291
Ex 11: 8 all the people that f thee: and after that H7272
14: 4 heart, that he shall f after them; and I H7291
17 and they shall f them: and I will get me H935
Ex 21:22 and yet no mischief f: he shall be surely H1961
23 And if *any* mischief f, then thou shalt H1961
23: 2 Thou shalt not f a multitude to H1961+H310
Dt 16:20 just shalt thou f, that thou mayest live, H7291
18:22 LORD, if the thing f not, nor come to H1961
Jdg 3:28 And he said unto them, F after me: for H7291
8: 5 the people that f me; for they *be* faint, H7272
9: 3 hearts inclined to f Abimelech; for they H310
1Sa 25:27 the young men that f my lord. H1980+H7272
30:21 they could not f David, whom they had H7291
2Sa 17: 9 among the people that f Absalom. H310
1Ki 18:21 LORD *be* God, f him: but if Baal, H3212+H310
21 but if Baal, *then* f him. And the H3212+H310
19:20 and *then* I will f thee. And he H3212+H310
20:10 handfuls for all the people that f me. H7272
2Ki 6:19 *is* this the city: f me, and I will H3212+H310
Ps 23: 6 Surely goodness and mercy shall f me H7291
38:20 because I f *the thing that* good *is*. H7291
45:14 that f her shall be brought unto thee. H310
94:15 and all the upright in heart shall f it. H310
119:150 They draw nigh that f after mischief: H7291
Isa 5:11 *that* they may f strong drink; that H7291
51: 1 Hearken to me, ye that f after H7291
Jer 17:16 *being* a pastor to f thee: neither have I H310
42:16 were afraid, shall f close after you there H1692
Ezk 13: 3 prophets, that f their own spirit, H1980+H310
Hos 2: 7 And she shall f after her lovers, but she H7291
6: 3 Then shall we know, *if* we f on to know H7291
Mt 4:19 And he saith unto them, F me, and I G1205
8:19 I will f thee whithersoever thou goest. G190
22 But Jesus said unto him, F me; and let G190
9: 9 F me. And he arose, and followed him. G190
16:24 himself, and take up his cross, and f me. G190
19:21 treasure in heaven: and come *and* f me. G190
Mk 2:14 F me. And he arose and followed him. G190
5:37 And he suffered no man to f him, save G4870
6: 1 his own country; and his disciples f him. G190
8:34 himself, and take up his cross, and f me. G190
10:21 and come, take up the cross, and f me. G190
14:13 a man bearing a pitcher of water: f him. G190
16:17 And these signs shall f them that G3877
Lk 5:27 of custom: and he said unto him, F me. G190
9:23 and take up his cross daily, and f me. G190
57 I will f thee whithersoever thou goest. G190
59 And he said unto another, F me. But he G190
61 And another also said, Lord, I will f thee; G190
17:23 see there: go not after *them*, nor f *them*. G1377
18:22 treasure in heaven: and come, f me. G190
22:10 a pitcher of water; f him into the house G190
49 saw what would f, they said unto him, G2071
Jn 1:43 findeth Philip, and saith unto him, F me. G190
10: 4 the sheep f him: for they know his voice. G190
5 And a stranger will they not f, but will G190
27 voice, and I know them, and they f me: G190
12:26 If any man serve me, let him f me; and G190
13:36 I go, thou canst not f me now; but thou G190
36 me now; but thou shalt f me afterwards. G190
37 Lord, why cannot I f thee now? I will lay G190
21:19 spoken this, he saith unto him, F me. G190
22 I come, what *is that* to thee? f thou me. G190
Act 3:24 and those that f after, as many as have G2517
12: 8 Cast thy garment about thee, and f me. G190
Ro 14:19 Let us therefore f after the things which G1377
1Co 14: 1 F after charity, and desire spiritual G1377
Php 3:12 perfect: but I f after, if that I may G1377
1Th 5:15 any *man*; but ever f that which is good, G1377
2Th 3: 7 For yourselves know how ye ought to f G3401
9 ourselves an ensample unto you to f us. G3401
1Ti 5:24 judgment; and some *men* they f after. G1872
6:11 these things; and f after righteousness, G1377
2Ti 2:22 Flee also youthful lusts: but f G1377
Heb 12:14 F peace with all *men*, and holiness, G1377
13: 7 God: whose faith f, considering the end G3401
1Pt 1:11 of Christ, and the glory that should f. G3326
2:21 an example, that ye should f his steps: G1872
2Pt 2: 2 And many shall f their pernicious G1811
3Jn 11 Beloved, f not that which is evil, but G3401
Rev 14: 4 are they which f the Lamb whithersoever G190
13 their labours; and their works do f them. G190

FOLLOWED
Gen 24:61 camels, and f the man: and the H3212+H310
32:19 and all that f the droves, saying, H1980+H310
Nu 14:24 with him, and hath f me fully, him will I H310
16:25 and the elders of Israel f him. H3212+H310
32:11 because they have not wholly f me: H310
12 of Nun: for they have wholly f the LORD. H310
Dt 1:36 because he hath wholly f the LORD. H310
4: 3 all the men that f Baal-peor, the H1980+H310
Jos 6: 8 of the covenant of the LORD f them. H1980
14: 8 melt: but I wholly f the LORD my God. H310
9 thou hast wholly f the LORD my God. H310
14 that he wholly f the LORD God of Israel. H310
Jdg 2:12 of Egypt, and f other gods, of the H3212+H310
9: 4 and light persons, which f him. H3212+H310
49 his bough, and f Abimelech, and H3212+H310
1Sa 13: 7 and all the people f him trembling. H310
14:22 also f hard after them in the battle. H1692
17:13 of Jesse went *and* f Saul to the H1980+H310
14 and the three eldest f Saul. H1980+H310
31: 2 And the Philistines f hard upon Saul H1692
2Sa 1: 6 and horsemen f hard after him. H1692
2:10 years. But the house of Judah f David. H310
3:31 king David *himself* f the bier. H1980+H310
11: 8 and there f him a mess *of meat* H3318+H310
17:23 counsel was not f, he saddled *his* ass, H6213
20: 2 from after David, *and* f Sheba the son of H310
1Ki 12:20 was none that f the house of David, but H310
14: 8 and who f me with all his heart, H1980+H310
16:21 of the people f Tibni the son of H1961+H310
21 to make him king; and half f Omri. H310
22 But the people that f Omri prevailed H310
22 the people that f Tibni the son of Ginath: H310
18:18 LORD, and thou hast f Baalim. H3212+H310
20:19 of the city, and the army which f them. H310
2Ki 3: 9 the host, and for the cattle that f them. H7272
4:30 thee. And he arose, and f her. H3212+H310
5:21 So Gehazi f after Naaman. And when H7291
9:27 house. And Jehu f after him, and said, H7291
13: 2 of the LORD, and f the sins of H3212+H310
17:15 them; and they f vanity, and H3212+H310
1Ch 10: 2 And the Philistines f hard after Saul, H1692
Neh 4:23 of the guard which f me, none of us put H310
Ps 68:25 on instruments *f* after; among *them*
Ezk 10:11 looked they f it; they turned not H3212+H310
Am 7:15 And the LORD took me as I f the flock, H310
Mt 4:20 straightway left *their* nets, and f him. G190
22 left the ship and their father, and f him. G190
25 And there f him great multitudes of G190
8: 1 the mountain, great multitudes f him. G190
10 said to them that f, Verily I say unto you, G190
23 entered into a ship, his disciples f him. G190
9: 9 Follow me. And he arose, and f him. G190
19 And Jesus arose, and f him, and *so did* G190
27 two blind men f him, crying, and saying, G190
12:15 f him, and he healed them all; G190
14:13 they f him on foot out of the cities. G190
19: 2 And great multitudes f him; and he G190
27 and f thee; what shall we have therefore? G190
28 you, That ye which have f me, in the G190
20:29 from Jericho, a great multitude f him. G190
34 their eyes received sight, and they f him. G190
21: 9 before, and that f, cried, saying, Hosanna G190
26:58 But Peter f him afar off unto the high G190
27:55 afar off, which f Jesus from Galilee, G190
62 Now the next day, that f the day of the G2076
Mk 1:18 they forsook their nets, and f him. G190
36 they that were with him f after him. G2614
2:14 him, Follow me. And he arose and f him. G190
15 for there were many, and they f him. G190
3: 7 from Galilee f him, and from Judaea, G190
5:24 much people f him, and thronged him. G190
10:28 him, Lo, we have left all, and have f thee. G190
32 and as they f, they were afraid. And G190
52 received his sight, and f Jesus in the way. G190
11: 9 and they that f, cried, saying, Hosanna; G190
14:51 And there f him a certain young man, G190
54 And Peter f him afar off, even into the G190
15:41 (Who also, when he was in Galilee, f G190
Lk 5:11 to land, they forsook all, and f him. G190
28 And he left all, rose up, and f him. G190
7: 9 the people that f him, I say unto you, G190
9:11 And the people, when they knew *it*, f G190
18:28 said, Lo, we have left all, and f thee. G190
43 his sight, and f him, glorifying God: G190
22:39 of Olives; and his disciples also f him. G190
54 high priest's house. And Peter f afar off. G190
23:27 And there f him a great company of G190
49 and the women that f him from Galilee, G4870
55 him from Galilee, f after, and beheld G2628
Jn 1:37 heard him speak, and they f Jesus. G190
40 John *speak*, and f him, was Andrew, G190
6: 2 And a great multitude f him, because G190
11:31 and went out, f her, saying, She goeth G190
18:15 And Simon Peter f Jesus, and *so did* G190
Act 12: 9 And he went out, and f him; and wist not G190
13:43 and religious proselytes f Paul and G190
16:17 The same f Paul and us, and cried, G2628

Act 21:36 For the multitude of the people f after, G190
Ro 9:30 the Gentiles, which f not after G1377
31 But Israel, which f after the law of G1377
1Co 10: 4 that f them: and that Rock was Christ. G190
1Ti 5:10 if she have diligently f every good work. G1872
2Pt 1:16 For we have not f cunningly devised G1811
Rev 6: 8 Death, and Hell f with him. And power G190
8: 7 The first angel sounded, and there f G1096
14: 8 And there f another angel, saying, G190
9 And the third angel f them, saying with a G190
19:14 And the armies *which were* in heaven f G190

FOLLOWEDST
Ru 3:10 as thou f not young men, H3212+H310

FOLLOWERS
1Co 4:16 Wherefore I beseech you, be ye f of me. G3402
11: 1 Be ye f of me, even as I also *am* of G3402
Eph 5: 1 Be ye therefore f of God, as dear G3402
Php 3:17 Brethren, be f together of me, and G4831
1Th 1: 6 And ye became f of us, and of the Lord, G3402
2:14 For ye, brethren, became f of the G3402
Heb 6:12 That ye be not slothful, but f of them G3402
1Pt 3:13 you, if ye be f of that which is good? G3402

FOLLOWETH
2Ki 11:15 and him that f her kill with the H935+H310
2Ch 23:14 and whoso f her, let him be slain H935+H310
Ps 63: 8 My soul f hard after thee: thy right H1692
Prv 12:11 bread: but he that f vain *persons is* H7291
15: 9 loveth him that f after righteousness. H7291
21:21 He that f after righteousness and H7291
28:19 bread: but he that f after vain *persons* H7291
Isa 1:23 loveth gifts, and f after rewards: they H7291
Ezk 16:34 whereas none f thee to commit H310
Hos 12: 1 Ephraim feedeth on wind, and f after H7291
Mt 10:38 And he that taketh not his cross, and f G190
Mk 9:38 in thy name, and he f not us: and we G190
38 and we forbad him, because he f not us. G190
Lk 9:49 we forbad him, because he f not with us. G190
Jn 8:12 the world: he that f me shall not walk in G190

FOLLOWING
Gen 41:31 f; for it *shall be* very grievous. H310+H3651
Dt 7: 4 For they will turn away thy son from f H310
12:30 be not snared by f them, after that they H310
Jos 22:16 away this day from f the LORD, in that H310
18 away this day from f the LORD? and it H310
23 an altar to turn from f the LORD; or if to H310
29 turn this day from f the LORD, to build H310
Jdg 2:19 fathers, in f other gods to serve H3212+H310
Ru 1:16 *or* to return from f after thee: for whither H310
1Sa 12:14 over you continue f the LORD your God: H310
20 yet turn not aside from f the LORD, but H310
14:46 Then Saul went up from f the Philistines: H310
15:11 is turned back from f me, and hath not H310
24: 1 was returned from f the Philistines, that H310
2Sa 2:19 right hand nor to the left from f Abner. H310
21 would not turn aside from f of him. H310
22 thee aside from f me: wherefore should H310
26 the people return from f their brethren? H310
27 gone up every one from f his brother. H310
30 And Joab returned from f Abner: and H310
7: 8 sheepcote, from f the sheep, to be ruler H310
1Ki 1: 7 priest: and they f Adonijah helped *him*. H310
9: 6 *But* if ye shall at all turn from f me, ye or H310
21:26 And he did very abominably in f H3212+H310
2Ki 17:21 drave Israel from f the LORD, and made H310
18: 6 departed not from f him, but kept his H310
1Ch 17: 7 *even* from f the sheep, that thou H310
2Ch 25:27 did turn away from f the LORD they H310
34:33 f the LORD, the God of their fathers. H310
Ps 48:13 that ye may tell *it* to the generation f. H314
78:71 From f the ewes great with young he H310
109:13 f let their name be blotted out. H312
Mk 16:20 the word with signs f. Amen. G1872
Lk 13:33 and the *day* f: for it cannot be that G2192
Jn 1:38 Then Jesus turned, and saw them f, and G190
43 The day f Jesus would go forth into G1887
6:22 The day f, when the people which stood G1887
20: 6 Then cometh Simon Peter f him, and G190
21:20 whom Jesus loved f; which also leaned on G190
Act 21: 1 Coos, and the *day* f unto Rhodes, and G1836
18 And the *day* f Paul went in with us unto G1966
23:11 And the night f the Lord stood by him, G1966
2Pt 2:15 are gone astray, f the way of Balaam G1811

FOLLY
Gen 34: 7 he had wrought f in Israel in lying with H5039
Dt 22:21 she hath wrought f in Israel, to play the H5039
Jos 7:15 because he hath wrought f in Israel. H5039
Jdg 19:23 is come into mine house, do not this f. H5039
20: 6 committed lewdness and f in Israel. H5039
10 the f that they have wrought in Israel. H5039
1Sa 25:25 *is* his name, and f *is* with him: but I H5039
2Sa 13:12 to be done in Israel: do not thou this f. H5039
Job 4:18 and his angels he charged with f: H8417
24:12 crieth out: yet God layeth not f *to them*. H8604
42: 8 with you *after your* f, in that ye have not H5039
Ps 49:13 This their way *is* their f: yet their H3689
85: 8 saints: but let them not turn again to f. H3690
Prv 5:23 the greatness of his f he shall go astray. H200
13:16 knowledge: but a fool layeth open *his* f. H200
14: 8 his way: but the f of fools *is* deceit. H200
18 The simple inherit f: but the prudent are H200
24 riches: *but* the foolishness of fools *is* f. H200
29 but *he that is* hasty of spirit exalteth f. H200
15:21 F *is* joy to *him that is* destitute of H200
16:22 hath it: but the instruction of fools *is* f. H200
17:12 meet a man, rather than a fool in his f. H200
18:13 he heareth *it*, it *is* f and shame unto him. H200
26: 4 Answer not a fool according to his f, lest H200
5 Answer a fool according to his f, lest he H200
11 to his vomit, *so* a fool returneth to his f. H200
Ecc 1:17 madness and f: I perceived that this H5531
2: 3 and to lay hold on f, till I might see H5531
12 and madness, and f: for what *can* the H5531
13 Then I saw that wisdom excelleth f, as H5531
7:25 of f, even of foolishness *and* madness: H3689
10: 1 savour: *so doth* a little f him that is in H5531
6 F is set in great dignity, and the rich sit H5529
Isa 9:17 mouth speaketh f. For all this his anger H5039
Jer 23:13 And I have seen f in the prophets of H8604
2Co 11: 1 a little in *my* f: and indeed bear with me. G877
2Ti 3: 9 no further: for their f shall be manifest G454

FOOD
Gen 2: 9 and good for f; the tree of life also in H3978
3: 6 the tree *was* good for f, and that it *was* H3978
6:21 And take thou unto thee of all f that is H3978
21 it shall be for f for thee, and for them. H402
41:35 And let them gather all the f of those H400
35 and let them keep f in the cities. H400
36 And that f shall be for store to the land H400
48 And he gathered up all the f of the seven H400
48 and laid up the f in the cities: the food H400
48 in the cities: the f of the field, which *was* H400
42: 7 said, From the land of Canaan to buy f. H400
10 lord, but to buy f are thy servants come. H400
33 with me, and take *f for* the famine of
43: 2 unto them, Go again, buy us a little f. H400
4 with us, we will go down and buy thee f: H400
20 indeed down at the first time to buy f: H400
22 in our hands to buy f: we cannot tell who H400
44: 1 men's sacks *with* f, as much as they can H400
25 said, Go again, *and* buy us a little f. H400
47:24 field, and for your f, and for them of your H400
24 households, and for f for your little ones. H398
Ex 21:10 If he take him another *wife*; her f, her H7607
Lev 3:11 the altar: *it is* the f of the offering made H3899
16 the altar: *it is* the f of the offering made H3899
19:23 of trees for f, then ye shall count the H3978
22: 7 eat of the holy things; because it *is* his f. H3899
Dt 10:18 stranger, in giving him f and raiment. H3899
1Sa 14:24 that eateth *any* f until evening, that I H3899
24 So none of the people tasted *any* f. H3899
28 f this day. And the people were faint. H3899
2Sa 9:10 master's son may have f to eat: but H3899
1Ki 5: 9 desire, in giving f for my household. H3899
11 of wheat *for* f to his household, and H4361
Job 23:12 of his mouth more than my necessary *f*.
24: 5 f for them *and* for *their* children. H3899
38:41 Who provideth for the raven his f? when H6718
40:20 Surely the mountains bring him forth f, H944
Ps 78:25 Man did eat angels' f: he sent them H3899
104:14 he may bring forth f out of the earth; H3899
136:25 Who giveth f to all flesh: for his mercy H3899
146: 7 which giveth f to the hungry. The H3899
147: 9 He giveth to the beast his f, *and* to the H3899
Prv 6: 8 *and* gathereth her f in the harvest. H3978
13:23 Much f *is in* the tillage of the poor: but H400
27:27 milk enough for thy f, for the food of thy H3899
27 for thy food, for the f of thy household, H3899
28: 3 *like* a sweeping rain which leaveth no f. H3899
30: 8 feed me with f convenient for me: H3899
31:14 ships; she bringeth her f from afar. H3899
Ezk 16:27 thine ordinary *f*, and delivered thee unto
48:18 be for f unto them that serve the city. H3899
Act 14:17 filling our hearts with f and gladness. G5160
2Co 9:10 bread for *your* f, and multiply your seed G1035
1Ti 6: 8 And having f and raiment let us be G1305
Jas 2:15 sister be naked, and destitute of daily f, G5160

FOOL
1Sa 26:21 the f, and have erred exceedingly. H5528
2Sa 3:33 and said, Died Abner as a f dieth? H5036
Ps 14: 1 The f hath said in his heart, *There is* no H5036
49:10 men die, likewise the f and the brutish H3684
53: 1 The f hath said in his heart, *There is* no H5036
92: 6 not; neither doth a f understand this. H3684
Prv 7:22 or as a f to the correction of the stocks; H191
10: 8 but a prating f shall fall. H191
10 causeth sorrow: but a prating f shall fall. H191
18 and he that uttereth a slander, *is* a f. H3684
23 *It is* as sport to a f to do mischief: but a H3684
11:29 the f *shall be* servant to the wise of heart. H191
12:15 The way of a f *is* right in his own eyes: H191
13:16 but a f layeth open *his* folly. H3684
14:16 evil: but the f rageth, and is confident. H3684
15: 5 A f despiseth his father's instruction: but H191
17: 7 Excellent speech becometh not a f: H5036
10 man than an hundred stripes into a f. H3684
12 meet a man, rather than a f in his folly. H3684
16 in the hand of a f to get wisdom, seeing H3684
21 He that begetteth a f *doeth it* to his H3684
21 and the father of a f hath no joy. H5036
24 eyes of a f *are* in the ends of the earth. H3684
28 Even a f, when he holdeth his peace, is H191
18: 2 A f hath no delight in understanding, H3684
19: 1 *he that is* perverse in his lips, and is a f. H3684
10 Delight is not seemly for a f; much less H3684
20: 3 from strife: but every f will be meddling. H191
23: 9 Speak not in the ears of a f: for he will H3684
24: 7 Wisdom *is* too high for a f: he openeth H191
26: 1 harvest, so honour is not seemly for a f. H3684
4 Answer not a f according to his folly, H3684
5 Answer a f according to his folly, lest H3684
6 by the hand of a f cutteth off the feet, H3684
8 sling, so *is* he that giveth honour to a f. H3684
10 the f, and rewardeth transgressors. H3684
11 As a dog returneth to his vomit, *so* a f H3684
12 *there is* more hope of a f than of him. H3684
27:22 Though thou shouldest bray a f in a H191
28:26 He that trusteth in his own heart is a f: H3684
29:11 A f uttereth all his mind: but a wise H3684
20 *there is* more hope of a f than of him. H3684
30:22 For a servant when he reigneth; and a f H5036
Ecc 2:14 his head; but the f walketh in darkness: H3684
15 happeneth to the f, so it happeneth even H3684
16 more than of the f for ever; seeing that H3684
16 And how dieth the wise *man*? as the f. H3684
19 be a wise *man* or a f? yet shall he have H5530
4: 5 The f foldeth his hands together, and H3684
6: 8 For what hath the wise more than the f? H3684
7: 6 the laughter of the f: this also *is* vanity. H3684
10: 3 Yea also, when he that is a f walketh by H5530
3 and he saith to every one *that* he *is* a f. H5530
12 the lips of a f will swallow up himself. H3684
14 A f also is full of words: a man cannot H5530
Jer 17:11 of his days, and at his end shall be a f. H5036
Hos 9: 7 *it*: the prophet *is* a f, the spiritual man *is* H191
Mt 5:22 Thou f, shall be in danger of hell fire. G3474
Lk 12:20 But God said unto him, *Thou* f, this night G878
1Co 3:18 let him become a f, that he may be wise. G3474
15:36 *Thou* f, that which thou sowest is not G878
2Co 11:16 I say again, Let no man think me a f; if G878
16 if otherwise, yet as a f receive me, that I G878
23 (I speak as a f) I *am* more; in labours G3912
12: 6 I shall not be a f; for I will say the truth: G878
11 I am become a f in glorying; ye have G878

FOOLISH
Dt 32: 6 Do ye thus requite the LORD, O f H5036
21 provoke them to anger with a f nation. H5036
Job 2:10 as one of the f women speaketh. What? H5039
5: 2 For wrath killeth the f man, and envy H191
3 I have seen the f taking root: but H191
Ps 5: 5 The f shall not stand in thy sight: thou H1984
39: 8 make me not the reproach of the f. H5036
73: 3 For I was envious at the f, *when* I saw H1984
22 So f *was* I, and ignorant: I was *as* a H1198
74:18 f people have blasphemed thy name. H5036
22 how the f man reproacheth thee daily. H5036
Prv 9: 6 Forsake the f, and live; and go in the H6612
13 A f woman *is* clamorous: *she is* simple, H3687
10: 1 a f son *is* the heaviness of his mother. H3684
14 the mouth of the f *is* near destruction. H191

Prv 14: 1 the f plucketh it down with her hands. H200
3 In the mouth of the f *is* a rod of pride: H191
7 Go from the presence of a f man, when H3684
15: 7 but the heart of the f *doeth* not so. H3684
20 but a f man despiseth his mother. H3684
17:25 A f son *is* a grief to his father, and H3684
19:13 A f son *is* the calamity of his father: H3684
21:20 of the wise; but a f man spendeth it up. H3684
29: 9 *If* a wise man contendeth with a f man, H191
Ecc 4:13 than an old and f king, who will no H3684
7:17 neither be thou f: why shouldest thou H5530
10:15 The labour of the f wearieth every one H3684
Isa 44:25 and maketh their knowledge f; H5528
Jer 4:22 For my people *is* f, they have not known H191
5: 4 *are* poor; they are f: for they know not H2973
21 Hear now this, O f people, and without H5530
10: 8 But they are altogether brutish and f: H3688
Lam 2:14 Thy prophets have seen vain and f H8602
Ezk 13: 3 Woe unto the f prophets, that follow H5036
Zec 11:15 thee yet the instruments of a f shepherd. H196
Mt 7:26 be likened unto a f man, which built G3474
25: 2 five of them were wise, and five *were* f. G3474
3 They that *were* f took their lamps, and G3474
8 And the f said unto the wise, Give us of G3474
Ro 1:21 and their f heart was darkened. G801
2:20 An instructor of the f, a teacher of babes, G878
10:19 *and* by a f nation I will anger you. G801
1Co 1:20 God made f the wisdom of this world? G3471
27 But God hath chosen the f things of the G3474
Gal 3: 1 O f Galatians, who hath bewitched you, G453
3 Are ye so f? having begun in the Spirit, G453
Eph 5: 4 Neither filthiness, nor f talking, nor G3473
1Ti 6: 9 and *into* many f and hurtful lusts, which G453
2Ti 2:23 But f and unlearned questions avoid, G3474
Tit 3: 3 For we ourselves also were sometimes f, G453
9 But avoid f questions, and genealogies, G3474
1Pt 2:15 put to silence the ignorance of f men: G878

FOOLISHLY

Gen 31:28 thou hast now done f in *so* doing. H5528
Nu 12:11 done f, and wherein we have sinned. H2973
1Sa 13:13 Thou hast done f: thou hast not kept the H5528
2Sa 24:10 of thy servant; for I have done very f. H5528
1Ch 21: 8 of thy servant; for I have done very f. H5528
2Ch 16: 9 Herein thou hast done f: therefore from H5528
Job 1:22 this Job sinned not, nor charged God f. H8604
Ps 75: 4 I said unto the fools, Deal not f: and to H1984
Prv 14:17 *He that is* soon angry dealeth f: and a H200
30:32 If thou hast done f in lifting up thyself, H5034
2Co 11:17 it were f, in this confidence of boasting. G1722
21 any is bold, (I speak f,) I am bold also. G1722

FOOLISHNESS

2Sa 15:31 turn the counsel of Ahithophel into f. H5528
Ps 38: 5 stink *and* are corrupt because of my f. H200
69: 5 O God, thou knowest my f; and my sins H200
Prv 12:23 but the heart of fools proclaimeth f. H200
14:24 *is* their riches: *but* the f of fools *is* folly. H200
15: 2 but the mouth of fools poureth out f. H200
14 but the mouth of fools feedeth on f. H200
19: 3 The f of man perverteth his way: and his H200
22:15 F *is* bound in the heart of a child; *but* the H200
24: 9 The thought of f *is* sin: and the scorner *is* H200
27:22 pestle, *yet* will not his f depart from him. H200
Ecc 7:25 of folly, even of f *and* madness: H5531
10:13 of his mouth *is* f: and the end of his talk H5531
Mk 7:22 an evil eye, blasphemy, pride, f: G877
1Co 1:18 to them that perish f; but unto us which G3472
21 God by the f of preaching to save G3472
23 stumblingblock, and unto the Greeks f; G3472
25 Because the f of God is wiser than men; G3474
2:14 of God: for they are f unto him: neither G3472
3:19 For the wisdom of this world is f with G3472

FOOLS

2Sa 13:13 shalt be as one of the f in Israel. Now H5036
Job 12:17 away spoiled, and maketh the judges f. H1984
30: 8 *They were* children of f, yea, children of H5036
Ps 75: 4 I said unto the f, Deal not foolishly: and H1984
94: 8 people: and *ye* f, when will ye be wise? H3684
107:17 F because of their transgression, and H191
Prv 1: 7 *but* f despise wisdom and instruction. H191
22 their scorning, and f hate knowledge? H3684
32 the prosperity of f shall destroy them. H3684
3:35 but shame shall be the promotion of f. H3684
8: 5 ye f, be ye of an understanding heart. H3684
10:21 feed many: but f die for want of wisdom. H191
12:23 the heart of f proclaimeth foolishness. H3684
13:19 *is* abomination to f to depart from evil. H3684
Prv 13:20 a companion of f shall be destroyed. H3684
14: 8 his way: but the folly of f *is* deceit. H3684
9 F make a mock at sin: but among the H191
24 riches: *but* the foolishness of f *is* folly. H3684
33 *is* in the midst of f is made known. H3684
15: 2 the mouth of f poureth out foolishness. H3684
14 the mouth of f feedeth on foolishness. H3684
16:22 hath it: but the instruction of f *is* folly. H191
19:29 scorners, and stripes for the back of f. H3684
26: 7 equal: so *is* a parable in the mouth of f. H3684
9 so *is* a parable in the mouth of f. H3684
Ecc 5: 1 f: for they consider not that they do evil. H3684
4 in f: pay that which thou hast vowed. H3684
7: 4 the heart of f *is* in the house of mirth. H3684
5 than for a man to hear the song of f. H3684
9 for anger resteth in the bosom of f. H3684
9:17 than the cry of him that ruleth among f. H3684
Isa 19:11 Surely the princes of Zoan *are* f, the H191
13 The princes of Zoan are become f, the H2973
35: 8 men, though f, shall not err *therein*. H191
Mt 23:17 *Ye* f and blind: for whether is greater, G3474
19 *Ye* f and blind: for whether *is* greater, G3474
Lk 11:40 *Ye* f, did not he that made that which is G878
24:25 Then he said unto them, O f, and slow of G453
Ro 1:22 themselves to be wise, they became f, G3471
1Co 4:10 We *are* f for Christ's sake, but ye *are* G3474
2Co 11:19 For ye suffer f gladly, seeing ye G878
Eph 5:15 walk circumspectly, not as f, but as wise, G781

FOOL'S

Prv 12:16 A f wrath is presently known: but a H191
18: 6 A f lips enter into contention, and his H3684
7 A f mouth *is* his destruction, and his H3684
26: 3 for the ass, and a rod for the f back. H3684
27: 3 but a f wrath *is* heavier than them both. H191
Ecc 5: 3 f voice *is known* by multitude of words. H3684
10: 2 his right hand; but a f heart at his left. H3684

FOOT

Gen 8: 9 for the sole of her f, and she returned H7272
41:44 his hand or f in all the land of Egypt. H7272
Ex 12:37 on f *that were* men, beside children. H7273
21:24 for tooth, hand for hand, f for foot, H7272
24 for tooth, hand for hand, foot for f, H7272
29:20 toe of their right f, and sprinkle the H7272
30:18 *of* brass, and his f *also of* brass, to H3653
28 all his vessels, and the laver and his f. H3653
31: 9 all his furniture, and the laver and his f, H3653
35:16 and all his vessels, the laver and his f, H3653
38: 8 *of* brass, and the f of it *of* brass, of the H3653
39:39 and all his vessels, the laver and his f, H3653
40:11 the laver and his f, and sanctify it. H3653
Lev 8:11 the laver and his f, to sanctify them. H3653
23 and upon the great toe of his right f. H7272
13:12 to his f, wheresoever the priest looketh; H7272
14:14 and upon the great toe of his right f: H7272
17 toe of his right f, upon the blood of the H7272
25 and upon the great toe of his right f: H7272
28 toe of his right f, upon the place of the H7272
Nu 22:25 crushed Balaam's f against the wall: H7272
Dt 2: 5 not so much as a f breadth; because I H7272
8: 4 did thy f swell, these forty years. H7272
11:10 *it* with thy f, as a garden of herbs: H7272
19:21 for tooth, hand for hand, f for foot. H7272
21 for tooth, hand for hand, foot for f. H7272
25: 9 shoe from off his f, and spit in his face, H7272
28:35 sole of thy f unto the top of thy head. H7272
56 set the sole of her f upon the ground for H7272
65 shall the sole of thy f have rest: but the H7272
29: 5 thy shoe is not waxen old upon thy f. H7272
32:35 recompence; their f shall slide in *due* H7272
33:24 brethren, and let him dip his f in oil. H7272
Jos 1: 3 Every place that the sole of your f shall H7272
5:15 thy shoe from off thy f; for the place H7272
Jdg 5:15 he was sent on f into the valley. For the H7272
2Sa 2:18 Asahel *was as* light of f as a wild roe. H7272
14:25 the sole of his f even to the crown of H7272
21:20 and on every f six toes, four and twenty H7272
2Ki 9:33 on the horses: and he trode her under f. H7272
1Ch 20: 6 *f:* and he also was the son of the giant.
2Ch 33: 8 Neither will I any more remove the f of H7272
Job 2: 7 from the sole of his f unto his crown. H7272
23:11 My f hath held his steps, his way have I H7272
28: 4 forgotten of the f: they are dried up, H7272
31: 5 If I have walked with vanity, or if my f H7272
39:15 And forgetteth that the f may crush H7272
Ps 9:15 net which they hid is their own f taken. H7272
26:12 My f standeth in an even place: in the H7272
36:11 Let not the f of pride come against me, H7272
Ps 38:16 over me: when my f slippeth, they H7272
66: 6 flood on f: there did we rejoice in him. H7272
68:23 That thy f may be dipped in the blood H7272
91:12 lest thou dash thy f against a stone. H7272
94:18 When I said, My f slippeth; thy mercy, H7272
121: 3 He will not suffer thy f to be moved: he H7272
Prv 1:15 them; refrain thy f from their path: H7272
3:23 way safely, and thy f shall not stumble. H7272
26 and shall keep thy f from being taken. H7272
4:27 nor to the left: remove thy f from evil. H7272
25:17 Withdraw thy f from thy neighbour's H7272
19 *like* a broken tooth, and a f out of joint. H7272
Ecc 5: 1 Keep thy f when thou goest to the H7272
Isa 1: 6 From the sole of the f even unto the H7272
14:25 tread him under f: then shall his yoke H947
18: 7 trodden under f, whose land the rivers H4001
20: 2 off thy shoe from thy f. And he did so, H7272
26: 6 The f shall tread it down, *even* the feet H7272
41: 2 called him to his f, gave the nations H7272
58:13 If thou turn away thy f from the H7272
Jer 2:25 Withhold thy f from being unshod, and H7272
12:10 my portion under f, they have made my H947
Lam 1:15 The Lord hath trodden under f all my H5541
Ezk 1: 7 the sole of a calf's f: and they sparkled H7272
6:11 stamp with thy f, and say, Alas for all H7272
29:11 No f of man shall pass through it, nor H7272
11 through it, nor f of beast shall pass H7272
32:13 neither shall the f of man trouble them H7272
Dan 8:13 and the host to be trodden under f? H4823
Am 2:15 and *he that is* swift of f shall not deliver H7272
Mt 4: 6 time thou dash thy f against a stone. G4228
5:13 out, and to be trodden under f of men. G2662
14:13 they followed him on f out of the cities. G3979
18: 8 Wherefore if thy hand or thy f offend G4228
22:13 him hand and f, and take him away, G4228
Mk 9:45 And if thy f offend thee, cut it off: it is G4228
Lk 4:11 time thou dash thy f against a stone. G4228
Jn 11:44 bound hand and f with graveclothes: G4228
Act 7: 5 *much as* to set his f on: yet he promised G4228
1Co 12:15 If the f shall say, Because I am not the G4228
Heb 10:29 trodden under f the Son of God, and G2662
Rev 1:13 down to the f, and girt about the paps G4158
10: 2 he set his right f upon the sea, and *his* G4228
2 upon the sea, and *his* left *f* on the earth,
11: 2 tread under f forty *and* two months. G3961

FOOTMEN

Nu 11:21 six hundred thousand f; and thou hast H7273
Jdg 20: 2 thousand f that drew sword. H376+H7273
1Sa 4:10 for there fell of Israel thirty thousand f. H7273
15: 4 f, and ten thousand men of Judah. H7273
22:17 And the king said unto the f that stood H7323
2Sa 8: 4 thousand f: and David houghed H376+H7273
10: 6 twenty thousand f, and of king Maacah H7273
1Ki 20:29 an hundred thousand f in one day. H7273
2Ki 13: 7 and ten thousand f; for the king of Syria H7273
1Ch 18: 4 thousand f: David also houghed H376+H7273
19:18 and forty thousand f, and killed H376+H7273
Jer 12: 5 If thou hast run with the f, and they H7273

FOOTSTEPS

Ps 17: 5 goings in thy paths, *that* my f slip not. H6471
77:19 great waters, and thy f are not known. H6119
89:51 reproached the f of thine anointed. H6119
Song 1: 8 way forth by the f of the flock, and feed H6119

FOOTSTOOL

1Ch 28: 2 and for the f of our God, and H1916+H7272
2Ch 9:18 the throne, with a f of gold, *which were* H3534
Ps 99: 5 worship at his f; *for* he *is* holy. H1916+H7272
110: 1 I make thine enemies thy f. H1916+H7272
132: 7 we will worship at his f. H1916+H7272
Isa 66: 1 the earth *is* my f: where *is* the H1916+H7272
Lam 2: 1 his f in the day of his anger! H1916+H7272
Mt 5:35 Nor by the earth; for it is his f: G5286+G4228
22:44 till I make thine enemies thy f? G5286+G4228
Mk 12:36 till I make thine enemies thy f. G5286+G4228
Lk 20:43 Till I make thine enemies thy f. G5286+G4228
Act 2:35 Until I make thy foes thy f. G5286+G4228
7:49 earth *is* my f: what house will G5286+G4228
Heb 1:13 I make thine enemies thy f? G5286+G4228
10:13 till his enemies be made his f. G5286+G4228
Jas 2: 3 Stand thou there, or sit here under my f: G5286

FOR See the Appendix.

FORASMUCH

Gen 41:39 And Pharaoh said unto Joseph, F as God H310
Nu 10:31 I pray thee; f as thou H3588+H5921+H3651

Dt 12:12 within your gates; f as he hath no part H3588
17:16 multiply horses: f as the LORD hath said
Jos 17:14 I *am* a great people, f as the LORD hath H5704
Jdg 11:36 of thy mouth; f as the LORD hath H310+H834
1Sa 20:42 David, Go in peace, f as we have sworn
24:18 well with me: f as when the LORD H854+H834
2Sa 19:30 let him take all, f as my lord the H310+H834
1Ki 11:11 unto Solomon, F as this is done H3282+H834
13:21 saith the LORD, F as thou hast H3282+H834
14: 7 God of Israel, F as I exalted thee H3282+H834
16: 2 F as I exalted thee out of the H3282+H834
2Ki 1:16 the LORD, F as thou hast sent H3282+H834
1Ch 5: 1 *was* the firstborn; but, f as he defiled his
2Ch 6: 8 But the LORD said to David my father, F
Ezr 7:14 F as thou art sent of H3606+H6903+H1768
Isa 8: 6 F as this people refuseth the H3282+H365
29:13 Wherefore the Lord said, F as H3282+H365
Jer 10: 6 F as *there is* none like unto thee, O
7 doth it appertain: f as among all the wise
Dan 2:40 as iron: f as iron H3606+H6903+H1768
41 of the iron, f as thou H3606+H6903+H1768
45 F as thou sawest that H3606+H6903+H1768
4:18 thereof, f as all the H3606+H6903+H1768
5:12 F as an excellent H3606+H6903+H1768
6: 4 nor fault; f as he *was* H3606+H6903+H1768
22 hurt me: f as before H3606+H6903+H1768
Am 5:11 F therefore as your treading *is* upon H3282
Mt 18:25 But f as he had not to pay, his lord
Lk 1: 1 F as many have taken in hand to set G1895
Act 9:38 And f as Lydda was nigh to Joppa, and G5607
11:17 F then as God gave them the like gift as G1487
15:24 F as we have heard, that certain which G1894
17:29 F then as we are the offspring of God, we
24:10 speak, answered, F as I know that thou
1Co 11: 7 to cover *his* head, f as he is the image
14:12 Even so ye, f as ye are zealous of G1893
15:58 work of the Lord, f as ye know that your
2Co 3: 3 *F as ye are* manifestly declared to be the
Heb 2:14 F then as the children are partakers of G1893
1Pt 1:18 F as ye know that ye were not redeemed
4: 1 F then as Christ hath suffered for us in

FORBAD
Dt 2:37 whatsoever the LORD our God f us. H6680
Mt 3:14 But John f him, saying, I have need to G1254
Mk 9:38 we f him, because he followeth not us. G2967
Lk 9:49 in thy name; and we f him, because he G2967
2Pt 2:16 voice f the madness of the prophet. G2967

FORBARE
1Sa 23:13 from Keilah; and he f to go forth. H2308
2Ch 25:16 Then the prophet f, and said, I know H2308
Jer 41: 8 of honey. So he f, and slew them not H2308

FORBEAR
Ex 23: 5 and wouldest f to help him, thou shalt H2308
Dt 23:22 But if thou shalt f to vow, it shall be no H2308
1Ki 22: 6 to battle, or shall I f? And they said, Go H2308
15 to battle, or shall we f? And he answered H2308
2Ch 18: 5 to battle, or shall I f? And they said, Go H2308
14 to battle, or shall I f? And he said, Go ye H2308
25:16 of the king's counsel? f; why shouldest H2308
35:21 me to make haste: f thee from H2308
Neh 9:30 Yet many years didst thou f them, and H4900
Job 16: 6 and *though* I f, what am I eased? H2308
Prv 24:11 If thou f to deliver *them that are* drawn H2820
Jer 40: 4 me into Babylon, f: behold, all the land H2308
Ezk 2: 5 or whether they will f, (for they *are* a H2308
7 they will f: for they *are* most rebellious. H2308
3:11 they will hear, or whether they will f. H2308
27 him f: for they *are* a rebellious house. H2308
24:17 F to cry, make no mourning for the H1826
Zec 11:12 price; and if not, f. So they weighed for H2308
1Co 9: 6 have not we power to f working? G3361
2Co 12: 6 truth: but *now* I f, lest any man should G5339
1Th 3: 1 Wherefore when we could no longer f, G4722
5 For this cause, when I could no longer f, G4722

FORBEARANCE
Ro 2: 4 of his goodness and f and longsuffering; G463
3:25 sins that are past, through the f of God; G463

FORBEARETH
Nu 9:13 not in a journey, and f to keep the H2308
Ezk 3:27 hear; and he that f, let him forbear: for H2310

FORBEARING
Prv 25:15 By long f is a prince persuaded, and a H639
Jer 20: 9 I was weary with f, and I could not *stay.* H3557

Eph 4: 2 with longsuffering, f one another in love; G430
6: 9 same things unto them, f threatening: G447
Col 3:13 F one another, and forgiving one G430

FORBID
Gen 44: 7 these words? God f that thy servants H2486
17 And he said, God f that I should do so: H2486
Nu 11:28 and said, My lord Moses, f them. H3607
Jos 22:29 God f that we should rebel against the H2486
24:16 and said, God f that we should forsake H2486
1Sa 12:23 Moreover as for me, God f that I should H2486
14:45 in Israel? God f: *as* the LORD liveth, H2486
20: 2 And he said unto him, God f; thou shalt H2486
24: 6 And he said unto his men, The LORD f H2486
26:11 The LORD f that I should stretch forth H2486
1Ki 21: 3 And Naboth said to Ahab, The LORD f H2486
1Ch 11:19 And said, My God f it me, that I should H2486
Job 27: 5 God f that I should justify you: till I die H2486
Mt 19:14 little children, and f them not, to come G2967
Mk 9:39 But Jesus said, F him not: for there is G2967
10:14 unto me, and f them not: for of such G2967
Lk 6:29 thy cloak f not *to take thy* coat also. G2967
9:50 And Jesus said unto him, F *him* not: for G2967
18:16 unto me, and f them not: for of such G2967
20:16 they heard *it,* they said, God f. G3361+G1096
Act 10:47 Can any man f water, that these should G2967
24:23 liberty, and that he should f none of his G2967
Ro 3: 4 God f: yea, let God be true, but G3361+G1096
6 God f: for then how shall God G3361+G1096
31 f: yea, we establish the law. G3361+G1096
6: 2 God f. How shall we, that are G3361+G1096
15 the law, but under grace? God f. G3361+G1096
7: 7 law sin? God f. Nay, I had not G3361+G1096
13 unto me? God f. But sin, that it G3361+G1096
9:14 with God? God f. G3361+G1096
11: 1 people? God f. For I also am an G3361+G1096
11 fall? God f: but *rather* through G3361+G1096
1Co 6:15 members of an harlot? God f. G3361+G1096
14:39 and f not to speak with tongues. G2967
Gal 2:17 the minister of sin? God f. G3361+G1096
3:21 of God? God f: for if there had G3361+G1096
6:14 But God f that I should glory, G3361+G1096

FORBIDDEN
Lev 5:17 things which are f to be done by the H3808
Dt 4:23 which the LORD thy God hath f thee. H6680
Act 16: 6 Galatia, and were f of the Holy Ghost to G2967

FORBIDDETH
3Jn 10 the brethren, and f them that would, G2967

FORBIDDING
Lk 23: 2 the nation, and f to give tribute to G2967
Act 28:31 with all confidence, no man f him. G209
1Th 2:16 F us to speak to the Gentiles that they G2967
1Ti 4: 3 F to marry, *and commanding* to G2967

FORBORE See FORBARE.

FORBORN
Jer 51:30 The mighty men of Babylon have f to H2308

FORCE
Gen 31:31 take by f thy daughters from me. H1497
Dt 22:25 field, and the man f her, and lie with H2388
34: 7 was not dim, nor his natural f abated. H3893
1Sa 2:16 *it me* now: and if not, I will take *it* by f. H2394
2Sa 13:12 my brother, do not f me; for no such H6031
Ezr 4:23 and made them to cease by f and power. H153
Est 7: 8 the king, Will he f the queen also before H3533
Job 30:18 By the great f *of my disease* is my H3581
40:16 and his f *is* in the navel of his belly. H202
Jer 18:21 their *blood* by the f of the sword; and H3027
23:10 course is evil, and their f *is* not right. H1369
48:45 because of the f: but a fire shall come H3581
Ezk 34: 4 f and with cruelty have ye ruled them. H2394
35: 5 of Israel by the f of the sword in the H3027
Am 2:14 not strengthen his f, neither shall the H3581
Mt 11:12 violence, and the violent take it by f. G726
Jn 6:15 and take him by f, to make him a king, G726
Act 23:10 and to take him by f from among them, G726
Heb 9:17 For a testament *is* of f after men are G949

FORCED
Jdg 1:34 And the Amorites f the children of Dan H3905
20: 5 concubine have they f, that she is dead. H6031
1Sa 13:12 unto the LORD: I f myself therefore, and H662
2Sa 13:14 than she, f her, and lay with her. H6031
22 because he had f his sister Tamar. H6031

2Sa 13:32 from the day that he f his sister Tamar. H6031
Prv 7:21 with the flattering of her lips she f him. H5080

FORCES
2Ch 17: 2 And he placed f in all the fenced cities H2428
Job 36:19 *no,* not gold, nor all the f of strength. H3981
Isa 60: 5 f of the Gentiles shall come unto thee. H2428
11 unto thee the f of the Gentiles, and H2428
Jer 40: 7 Now when all the captains of the f H2428
13 all the captains of the f that *were* in the H2428
41:11 all the captains of the f that *were* with H2428
13 all the captains of the f that *were* with H2428
16 all the captains of the f that *were* with H2428
42: 1 Then all the captains of the f, and H2428
8 the captains of the f which *were* with H2428
43: 4 the captains of the f, and all the people, H2428
5 all the captains of the f, took all the H2428
Dan 11:10 a multitude of great f: and *one* shall H2428
38 honour the God of f: and a god whom H4581
Oba 11 away captive his f, and foreigners H2428

FORCIBLE
Job 6:25 How f are right words! but what doth H4834

FORCING
Dt 20:19 trees thereof by f an axe against them: H5080
Prv 30:33 so the f of wrath bringeth forth strife. H4330

FORD
Gen 32:22 sons, and passed over the f Jabbok. H4569

FORDS
Jos 2: 7 way to Jordan unto the f: and as soon as H4569
Jdg 3:28 him, and took the f of Jordan toward H4569
Isa 16: 2 of Moab shall be at the f of Arnon. H4569

FORECAST
Dan 11:24 *yea,* and he shall f his devices against H2803
25 for they shall f devices against him. H2803

FOREFATHERS
Jer 11:10 of their f, which refused to hear H7223+H1
2Ti 1: 3 I thank God, whom I serve from *my* f G4269

FOREFRONT
Ex 26: 9 in the f of the tabernacle. H4136+H6440
28:37 the f of the mitre it shall be. H4136+H6440
Lev 8: 9 *even* upon his f, did he put the H4136+H6440
1Sa 14: 5 The f of the one *was* situate northward H8127
2Sa 11:15 ye Uriah in the f of the hottest H4136+H6440
2Ki 16:14 LORD, from the f of the house, from H6440
2Ch 20:27 in the f of them, to go again H7218
Ezk 40:19 the breadth from the f of the lower gate H6440
19 lower gate unto the f of the inner court H6440
47: 1 eastward: for the f of the house *stood* H6440

FOREHEAD
Ex 28:38 And it shall be upon Aaron's f, that H4696
38 be always upon his f, that they may be H4696
Lev 13:41 his face, he *is* f bald: *yet is* he clean. H1371
42 the bald head, or bald f, a white reddish H1372
42 up in his bald head, or his bald f. H1372
43 head, or in his bald f, as the leprosy H1372
1Sa 17:49 Philistine in his f, that the stone sunk H4696
49 f; and he fell upon his face to the earth. H4696
2Ch 26:19 even rose up in his f before the priests H4696
20 he *was* leprous in his f, and they thrust H4696
Jer 3: 3 f, thou refusedst to be ashamed. H4696
Ezk 3: 8 thy f strong against their foreheads. H4696
9 flint have I made thy f: fear them not, H4696
16:12 And I put a jewel on thy f, and earrings H639
Rev 14: 9 receive *his* mark in his f, or in his hand, G3359
17: 5 And upon her f *was* a name written, G3359

FOREHEADS
Ezk 3: 8 and thy forehead strong against their f. H4696
9: 4 a mark upon the f of the men that sigh H4696
Rev 7: 3 sealed the servants of our God in their f. G3359
9: 4 have not the seal of God in their f. G3359
13:16 a mark in their right hand, or in their f: G3359
14: 1 his Father's name written in their f. G3359
20: 4 *his* mark upon their f, or in their hands; G3359
22: 4 face; and his name *shall be* in their f. G3359

FOREIGNER
Ex 12:45 A f and an hired servant shall not eat H8453
Dt 15: 3 Of a f thou mayest exact *it again*: but H5237

FOREIGNERS
Oba 11 his forces, and f entered into his gates, H5237
Eph 2:19 strangers and f, but fellowcitizens with *G3941*

FOREKNEW
Ro 11: 2 people which he f. Wot ye not what the *G4267*

FOREKNOW
Ro 8:29 For whom he did f, he also did *G4267*

FOREKNOWLEDGE
Act 2:23 counsel and f of God, ye have taken, *G4268*
1Pt 1: 2 Elect according to the f of God the *G4268*

FOREMOST
Gen 32:17 And he commanded the f, saying, H7223
33: 2 and their children f, and Leah and her H7223
2Sa 18:27 the running of the f is like the running H7223

FOREORDAINED
1Pt 1:20 Who verily was f before the foundation *G4267*

FOREPART
Ex 28:27 toward the f thereof, over against H6440
39:20 toward the f of it, over against the H6440
1Ki 6:20 And the oracle in the f *was* twenty H6440
Ezk 42: 7 utter court on the f of the chambers, H6440
Act 27:41 ship aground; and the f stuck fast, and *G4408*

FORERUNNER
Heb 6:20 Whither the f is for us entered, *even* *G4274*

FORESAW
Act 2:25 For David speaketh concerning him, I f *G4308*

FORESEEING
Gal 3: 8 And the scripture, f that God would *G4275*

FORESEETH
Prv 22: 3 A prudent *man* f the evil, and hideth H7200
27:12 A prudent *man* f the evil, *and* hideth H7200

FORESHIP
Act 27:30 would have cast anchors out of the f, *G4408*

FORESKIN
Gen 17:11 the flesh of your f; and it shall be a H6190
14 whose flesh of his f is not circumcised, H6190
23 the flesh of their f in the selfsame day, H6190
24 he was circumcised in the flesh of his f. H6190
25 he was circumcised in the flesh of his f. H6190
Ex 4:25 and cut off the f of her son, and cast H6190
Lev 12: 3 And in the eighth day the flesh of his f H6190
Dt 10:16 Circumcise therefore the f of your H6190
Hab 2:16 also, and let thy f be uncovered: the H6188

FORESKINS
Jos 5: 3 the children of Israel at the hill of the f. H6190
1Sa 18:25 but an hundred f of the Philistines, to H6190
27 brought their f, and they gave them H6190
2Sa 3:14 me for an hundred f of the Philistines. H6190
Jer 4: 4 and take away the f of your heart, ye H6190

FOREST
1Sa 22: 5 and came into the f of Hareth. H3293
1Ki 7: 2 He built also the house of the f of H3293
10:17 them in the house of the f of Lebanon. H3293
21 of the house of the f of Lebanon *were of* H3293
2Ki 19:23 borders, *and into* the f of his Carmel. H3293
2Ch 9:16 them in the house of the f of Lebanon. H3293
20 of the house of the f of Lebanon *were of* H3293
Neh 2: 8 of the king's f, that he may give me H6508
Ps 50:10 For every beast of the f *is* mine, *and* the H3293
104:20 all the beasts of the f do creep *forth*. H3293
Isa 9:18 in the thickets of the f, and they shall H3293
10:18 And shall consume the glory of his f, H3293
19 And the rest of the trees of his f shall be H3293
34 the thickets of the f with iron, and H3293
21:13 The burden upon Arabia. In the f in H3293
22: 8 day to the armour of the house of the f. H3293
29:17 fruitful field shall be esteemed as a f? H3293
32:15 and the fruitful field be counted for a f. H3293
19 down on the f; and the city shall be H3293
37:24 of his border, *and* the f of his Carmel. H3293
44:14 the trees of the f: he planteth an ash, H3293
23 ye mountains, O f, and every tree H3293
56: 9 to devour, *yea*, all ye beasts in the f. H3293
Jer 5: 6 Wherefore a lion out of the f shall slay H3293
10: 3 a tree out of the f, the work of the hands H3293
12: 8 unto me as a lion in the f; it crieth out H3293
21:14 kindle a fire in the f thereof, and it shall H3293
26:18 of the house as the high places of a f. H3293
46:23 They shall cut down her f, saith the H3293
Ezk 15: 2 which is among the trees of the f? H3293
6 the trees of the f, which I have given to H3293
20:46 against the f of the south field; H3293
47 And say to the f of the south, Hear the H3293
Hos 2:12 I will make them a f, and the beasts of H3293
Am 3: 4 Will a lion roar in the f, when he hath H3293
Mic 3:12 of the house as the high places of the f. H3293
5: 8 the beasts of the f, as a young lion H3293
Zec 11: 2 for the f of the vintage is come down. H3293

FORESTS
2Ch 27: 4 and in the f he built castles and towers. H2793
Ps 29: 9 and discovereth the f: and in his temple H3295
Ezk 39:10 *any* out of the f; for they shall burn the H3293

FORETELL
2Co 13: 2 I told you before, and f you, as if I were *G4302*

FORETOLD
Mk 13:23 But take ye heed: behold, I have f you *G4280*
Act 3:24 spoken, have likewise f of these days. *G4293*

FOREVER See EVER.

FOREWARN
Lk 12: 5 But I will f you whom ye shall fear: *G5263*

FOREWARNED
1Th 4: 6 as we also have f you and testified. *G4277*

FORFEITED
Ezr 10: 8 should be f, and himself separated H2763

FORGAT
Gen 40:23 butler remember Joseph, but f him. H7911
Jdg 3: 7 of the LORD, and f the LORD their H7911
1Sa 12: 9 And when they f the LORD their God, H7911
Ps 78:11 And f his works, and his wonders that H7911
106:13 They soon f his works; they waited not H7911
21 They f God their saviour, which had H7911
Lam 3:17 soul far off from peace: I f prosperity. H5382
Hos 2:13 her lovers, and f me, saith the LORD. H7911

FORGAVE
Ps 78:38 But he, *being* full of compassion, f *their* H3722
Mt 18:27 and loosed him, and f him the debt. *G863*
32 wicked servant, I f thee all that debt, *G863*
Lk 7:42 to pay, he frankly f them both. Tell me *G5483*
43 *he*, to whom he f most. And he said *G5483*
2Co 2:10 also: for if I f any thing, to whom *G5483*
10 any thing, to whom I f *it*, for your sakes *G5483*
10 your sakes *f I it* in the person of Christ;
Col 3:13 any: even as Christ f you, so also *do* ye. *G5483*

FORGAVEST
Ps 32: 5 and thou f the iniquity of my sin. Selah. H5375
99: 8 wast a God that f them, though thou H5375

FORGED
Ps 119:69 The proud have f a lie against me: *but* I H2950

FORGERS
Job 13: 4 But ye *are* f of lies, ye *are* all physicians H2950

FORGET
Gen 27:45 from thee, and he f *that* which thou H7911
41:51 f all my toil, and all my father's house. H5382
Dt 4: 9 lest thou f the things which thine H7911
23 Take heed unto yourselves, lest ye f the H7911
31 destroy thee, nor f the covenant of thy H7911
6:12 *Then* beware lest thou f the LORD, H7911
8:11 Beware that thou f not the LORD thy H7911
14 lifted up, and thou f the LORD thy God, H7911
19 And it shall be, if thou do at all f the H7911
9: 7 Remember, *and* f not, how thou H7911
25:19 from under heaven; thou shalt not f *it*. H7911
1Sa 1:11 me, and not f thine handmaid, but H7911
2Ki 17:38 not f; neither shall ye fear other gods. H7911
Job 8:13 So *are* the paths of all that f God; and H7911
9:27 If I say, I will f my complaint, I will H7911
11:16 Because thou shalt f *thy* misery, *and* H7911
24:20 The womb shall f him; the worm shall H7911
Ps 9:17 into hell, *and* all the nations that f God. H7913
10:12 lift up thine hand: f not the humble. H7911
13: 1 How long wilt thou f me, O LORD? for H7911
45:10 and incline thine ear; f also thine own H7911
50:22 Now consider this, ye that f God, lest I H7911
59:11 Slay them not, lest my people f: scatter H7911
74:19 *of the wicked*: f not the congregation H7911
23 F not the voice of thine enemies: the H7911
78: 7 in God, and not f the works of God, but H7911
102: 4 like grass; so that I f to eat my bread. H7911
103: 2 Bless the LORD, O my soul, and f not H7911
119:16 in thy statutes: I will not f thy word. H7911
83 in the smoke; *yet* do I not f thy statutes. H7911
93 I will never f thy precepts: for with H7911
109 in my hand: yet do I not f thy law. H7911
141 I *am* small and despised: *yet* do not I f H7911
153 and deliver me: for I do not f thy law. H7911
176 for I do not f thy commandments. H7911
137: 5 If I f thee, O Jerusalem, let my right H7911
5 let my right hand f *her cunning*. H7911
Prv 3: 1 My son, f not my law; but let thine H7911
4: 5 Get wisdom, get understanding: f *it* H7911
31: 5 Lest they drink, and f the law, and H7911
7 Let him drink, and f his poverty, and H7911
Isa 49:15 Can a woman f her sucking child, that H7911
15 they may f, yet will I not forget thee. H7911
15 they may forget, yet will I not f thee. H7911
54: 4 for thou shalt f the shame of thy youth, H7911
65:11 the LORD, that f my holy mountain, H7913
Jer 2:32 Can a maid f her ornaments, *or* a bride H7911
23:27 Which think to cause my people to f H7911
39 I, even I, will utterly f you, and I will H5382
Lam 5:20 Wherefore dost thou f us for ever, *and* H7911
Hos 4: 6 of thy God, I will also f thy children. H7911
Am 8: 7 Surely I will never f any of their works. H7911
Heb 6:10 For God *is* not unrighteous to f your *G1950*
13:16 But to do good and to communicate f *G1950*

FORGETFUL
Heb 13: 2 Be not f to entertain strangers: for *G1950*
Jas 1:25 he being not a f hearer, but a doer of *G1953*

FORGETFULNESS
Ps 88:12 and thy righteousness in the land of f? H5388

FORGETTEST
Ps 44:24 Wherefore hidest thou thy face, *and* f H7911
Isa 51:13 And f the LORD thy maker, that hath H7911

FORGETTETH
Job 39:15 And f that the foot may crush them, or H7911
Ps 9:12 them: he f not the cry of the humble. H7911
Prv 2:17 youth, and f the covenant of her God. H7911
Jas 1:24 f what manner of man he was. *G1950*

FORGETTING
Php 3:13 *this* one thing *I do*, f those things which *G1950*

FORGIVE
Gen 50:17 So shall ye say unto Joseph, F, I pray H5375
17 now, we pray thee, f the trespass of the H5375
Ex 10:17 Now therefore f, I pray thee, my sin H5375
32:32 Yet now, if thou wilt f their sin—; and if H5375
Nu 30: 5 and the LORD shall f her, because her H5545
8 none effect: and the LORD shall f her. H5545
12 them void; and the LORD shall f her. H5545
Jos 24:19 not f your transgressions nor your sins. H5375
1Sa 25:28 I pray thee, f the trespass of thine H5375
1Ki 8:30 place: and when thou hearest, f. H5545
34 Then hear thou in heaven, and f the sin H5545
36 Then hear thou in heaven, and f the sin H5545
39 place, and f, and do, and give to H5545
50 And f thy people that have sinned H5545
2Ch 6:21 from heaven; and when thou hearest, f. H5545
25 the heavens, and f the sin of thy people H5545
27 Then hear thou from heaven, and f the H5545
30 place, and f, and render unto every H5545
39 their cause, and f thy people which H5545
7:14 will f their sin, and will heal their land. H5545
Ps 25:18 and my pain; and f all my sins. H5375
86: 5 For thou, Lord, *art* good, and ready to f; H5546
Isa 2: 9 humbleth himself: therefore f them not. H5375
Jer 18:23 me to slay *me*: f not their iniquity, H3722
31:34 LORD: for I will f their iniquity, and I H5545
36: 3 that I may f their iniquity and their sin. H5545
Dan 9:19 O Lord, hear; O Lord, f; O Lord, hearken H5545
Am 7: 2 I said, O Lord GOD, f, I beseech thee: by H5545
Mt 6:12 And f us our debts, as we forgive our *G863*
12 And forgive us our debts, as we f our *G863*
14 For if ye f men their trespasses, your *G863*
14 your heavenly Father will also f you: *G863*
15 But if ye f not men their trespasses, *G863*

Mt 6:15 will your Father f your trespasses. G863
9: 6 power on earth to f sins, (then saith he G863
18:21 against me, and I f him? till seven times? G863
35 ye from your hearts f not every one his G863
Mk 2: 7 who can f sins but God only? G863
10 f sins, (he saith to the sick of the palsy,) G863
11:25 And when ye stand praying, f, if ye have G863
25 is in heaven may f you your trespasses. G863
26 But if ye do not f, neither will your Father G863
26 which is in heaven f your trespasses. G863
Lk 5:21 Who can f sins, but God alone? G863
24 upon earth to f sins, (he said unto the G863
6:37 condemned: f, and ye shall be forgiven: G630
11: 4 And f us our sins; for we also forgive G863
4 And forgive us our sins; for we also f G863
17: 3 thee, rebuke him; and if he repent, f him. G863
4 thee, saying, I repent; thou shalt f him. G863
23:34 Then said Jesus, Father, f them; for they G863
2Co 2: 7 ye *ought* rather to f *him*, and comfort G5483
10 To whom ye f any thing, I *forgive* also: G5483
10 To whom ye forgive any thing, I *f* also: G5483
12:13 burdensome to you? f me this wrong. G5483
1Jn 1: 9 faithful and just to f us *our* sins, and to G863

FORGIVEN
Lev 4:20 for them, and it shall be f them. H5545
26 his sin, and it shall be f him. H5545
31 for him, and it shall be f him. H5545
35 hath committed, and it shall be f him. H5545
5:10 he hath sinned, and it shall be f him. H5545
13 and it shall be f him: and *the remnant* H5545
16 trespass offering, and it shall be f him. H5545
18 and wist *it* not, and it shall be f him. H5545
6: 7 and it shall be f him for any thing of H5545
19:22 sin which he hath done shall be f him. H5545
Nu 14:19 and as thou hast f this people, from H5375
15:25 Israel, and it shall be f them; for it *is* H5545
26 And it shall be f all the congregation of H5545
28 for him; and it shall be f him. H5545
Dt 21: 8 charge. And the blood shall be f them. H3722
Ps 32: 1 Blessed *is he whose* transgression *is* f, H5375
85: 2 Thou hast f the iniquity of thy people, H5375
Isa 33:24 dwell therein *shall be* f *their* iniquity. H5375
Mt 9: 2 Son, be of good cheer; thy sins be f thee. G863
5 sins be f thee; or to say, Arise, and walk? G863
12:31 blasphemy shall be f unto men: but the G863
31 the *Holy* Ghost shall not be f unto men. G863
32 of man, it shall be f him: but whosoever G863
32 it shall not be f him, neither in this G863
Mk 2: 5 sick of the palsy, Son, thy sins be f thee. G863
9 palsy, *Thy* sins be f thee; or to say, Arise, G863
3:28 Verily I say unto you, All sins shall be f G863
4:12 and *their* sins should be f them. G863
Lk 5:20 said unto him, Man, thy sins are f thee. G863
23 Whether is easier, to say, Thy sins be f G863
6:37 be condemned: forgive, and ye shall be f: G630
7:47 are many, are f; for she loved much: G863
47 to whom little is f, *the same* loveth little. G863
48 And he said unto her, Thy sins are f. G863
12:10 of man, it shall be f him: but unto him G863
10 against the Holy Ghost it shall not be f. G863
Act 8:22 the thought of thine heart may be f thee. G863
Ro 4: 7 are f, and whose sins are covered. G863
Eph 4:32 as God for Christ's sake hath f you. G5483
Col 2:13 with him, having f you all trespasses; G5483
Jas 5:15 have committed sins, they shall be f him. G863
1Jn 2:12 your sins are f you for his name's sake. G863

FORGIVENESS
Ps 130: 4 But *there is* f with thee, that thou H5547
Mk 3:29 f, but is in danger of eternal damnation: G859
Act 5:31 give repentance to Israel, and f of sins. G859
13:38 man is preached unto you the f of sins: G859
26:18 that they may receive f of sins, and G859
Eph 1: 7 his blood, the f of sins, according to G859
Col 1:14 through his blood, *even* the f of sins: G859

FORGIVENESSES
Dan 9: 9 f, though we have rebelled against him; H5547

FORGIVETH
Ps 103: 3 Who f all thine iniquities; who healeth H5545
Lk 7:49 themselves, Who is this that f sins also? G863

FORGIVING
Ex 34: 7 Keeping mercy for thousands, f H5375
Nu 14:18 and of great mercy, f iniquity and H5375
Eph 4:32 tenderhearted, f one another, even as G5483
Col 3:13 Forbearing one another, and f one G5483

FORGOT
Dt 24:19 thy field, and hast f a sheaf in the field, H7911

FORGOTTEN
Gen 41:30 all the plenty shall be f in the land of H7911
Dt 26:13 commandments, neither have I f *them*: H7911
31:21 for it shall not be f out of the mouths of H7911
32:18 and hast f God that formed thee. H7911
Job 19:14 and my familiar friends have f me. H7911
28: 4 *even the waters* f of the foot: they are H7911
Ps 9:18 For the needy shall not alway be f: the H7911
10:11 He hath said in his heart, God hath f: he H7911
31:12 I am f as a dead man out of mind: I am H7911
42: 9 rock, Why hast thou f me? why go I H7911
44:17 yet have we not f thee, neither have we H7911
20 If we have f the name of our God, or H7911
77: 9 Hath God f to be gracious? hath he in H7911
119:61 robbed me: *but* I have not f thy law. H7911
139 mine enemies have f thy words. H7911
Ecc 2:16 to come shall all be f. And how dieth the H7911
8:10 and they were f in the city where they H7911
9: 5 a reward; for the memory of them is f. H7911
Isa 17:10 Because thou hast f the God of thy H7911
23:15 day, that Tyre shall be f seventy years, H7911
16 that hast been f; make sweet melody, H7911
44:21 O Israel, thou shalt not be f of me. H5382
49:14 forsaken me, and my Lord hath f me. H7911
65:16 troubles are f, and because they are H7911
Jer 2:32 have f me days without number. H7911
3:21 *and* they have f the LORD their God. H7911
13:25 hast f me, and trusted in falsehood. H7911
18:15 Because my people hath f me, they H7911
20:11 everlasting confusion shall never be f. H7911
23:27 their fathers have f my name for Baal. H7911
40 a perpetual shame, which shall not be f. H7911
30:14 All thy lovers have f thee; they seek H7911
44: 9 Have ye f the wickedness of your H7911
50: 5 a perpetual covenant *that* shall not be f. H7911
6 to hill, they have f their restingplace. H7911
Lam 2: 6 and sabbaths to be f in Zion, and hath H7911
Ezk 22:12 and hast f me, saith the Lord GOD. H7911
23:35 Because thou hast f me, and cast me H7911
Hos 4: 6 seeing thou hast f the law of thy God, I H7911
8:14 For Israel hath f his Maker, and H7911
13: 6 was exalted; therefore have they f me. H7911
Mt 16: 5 the other side, they had f to take bread. G1950
Mk 8:14 Now *the disciples* had f to take bread, G1950
Lk 12: 6 and not one of them is f before God? G1950
Heb 12: 5 And ye have f the exhortation which G1585
2Pt 1: 9 f that he was purged from his old sins. G3024

FORKS
1Sa 13:21 and for the f, and for the axes, H7969+H7053

FORM
Gen 1: 2 And the earth was without f, and void; H8414
1Sa 28:14 And he said unto her, What f *is* he of? H8389
2Sa 14:20 To fetch about this f of speech hath thy H6440
2Ch 4: 7 according to their f, and set *them* in the H4941
Job 4:16 not discern the f thereof: an image *was* H4758
Isa 45: 7 I f the light, and create darkness: I H3335
52:14 and his f more than the sons of men: H8389
53: 2 he hath no f nor comeliness; and H8389
Jer 4:23 lo, *it was* without f, and void; and the H8414
Ezk 8: 3 And he put forth the f of an hand, and H8403
10 and behold every f of creeping things, H8403
10: 8 f of a man's hand under their wings. H8403
43:11 shew them the f of the house, and the H6699
11 keep the whole f thereof, and all the H6699
Dan 2:31 thee; and the f thereof *was* terrible. H7299
3:19 full of fury, and the f of his visage was H6755
25 f of the fourth is like the Son of God. H7299
Mk 16:12 After that he appeared in another f G3444
Ro 2:20 which hast the f of knowledge and of G3446
6:17 f of doctrine which was delivered you. G5179
Php 2: 6 Who, being in the f of God, thought it G3444
7 took upon him the f of a servant, and G3444
2Ti 1:13 Hold fast the f of sound words, which G5296
3: 5 Having a f of godliness, but denying G3446

FORMED
Gen 2: 7 And the LORD God f man *of* the dust of H3335
8 there he put the man whom he had f. H3335
19 And out of the ground the LORD God f H3335
Dt 32:18 and hast forgotten God that f thee. H2342
2Ki 19:25 times that I have f it? now have I H3335
Job 26: 5 Dead *things* are f from under the H2342
13 his hand hath f the crooked serpent. H2342
33: 6 God's stead: I also am f out of the clay. H7169
Ps 90: 2 or ever thou hadst f the earth and the H2342
94: 9 hear? he that f the eye, shall he not see? H3335
95: 5 made it: and his hands f the dry *land*. H3335
Prv 26:10 The great *God* that f all *things* both H2342
Isa 27:11 that f them will shew them no favour. H3335
37:26 times, that I have f it? now have I H3335
43: 1 Jacob, and he that f thee, O Israel, Fear H3335
7 I have f him; yea, I have made him. H3335
10 God f, neither shall there be after me. H3335
21 This people have I f for myself; they H3335
44: 2 made thee, and f thee from the womb, H3335
10 Who hath f a god, or molten a graven H3335
21 my servant: I have f thee; thou *art* my H3335
24 and he that f thee from the womb, H3335
45:18 God himself that f the earth and made H3335
18 it not in vain, he f it to be inhabited: I H3335
49: 5 And now, saith the LORD that f me H3335
54:17 No weapon that is f against thee shall H3335
Jer 1: 5 Before I f thee in the belly I knew thee; H3335
33: 2 the LORD that f it, to establish it; the H3335
Am 7: 1 and, behold, he f grasshoppers in the H3335
Ro 9:20 Shall the thing f say to him that formed G4110
20 that f *it*, Why hast thou made me thus? G4111
Gal 4:19 in birth again until Christ be f in you, G3445
1Ti 2:13 For Adam was first f, then Eve. G4111

FORMER
Gen 40:13 f manner when thou wast his butler. H7223
Nu 21:26 fought against the f king of Moab, and H7223
Dt 24: 4 Her f husband, which sent her away, H7223
Ru 4: 7 Now this *was the manner* in f time in H6440
1Sa 17:30 him again after the f manner. H7223
2Ki 1:14 captains of the f fifties with their fifties: H7223
17:34 Unto this day they do after the f H7223
40 but they did after their f manner. H7223
Neh 5:15 But the f governors that *had been* H7223
Job 8: 8 For inquire, I pray thee, of the f age, H7223
30: 3 wilderness in f time desolate and waste. H570
Ps 79: 8 O remember not against us f iniquities: H7223
89:49 Lord, where *are* thy f lovingkindnesses, H7223
Ecc 1:11 *There is* no remembrance of f *things*; H7223
7:10 is *the cause* that the f days were better H7223
Isa 41:22 let them shew the f things, what they H7223
42: 9 Behold, the f things are come to pass, H7223
43: 9 this, and shew us f things? let them H7223
18 Remember ye not the f things, neither H7223
46: 9 Remember the f things of old: for I *am* H7223
48: 3 I have declared the f things from the H7223
61: 4 shall raise up the f desolations, and H7223
65: 7 measure their f work into their bosom. H7223
16 of truth; because the f troubles are H7223
17 a new earth: and the f shall not be H7223
Jer 5:24 rain, both the f and the latter, in his H3138
10:16 them: for he *is* the f of all *things*; and H3335
34: 5 of thy fathers, the f kings which were H7223
36:28 write in it all the f words that were in H7223
51:19 them; for he *is* the f of all things: and H3335
Ezk 16:55 return to their f estate, and Samaria H6927
55 return to their f estate, then thou and H6927
55 daughters shall return to your f estate. H6927
Dan 11:13 greater than the f, and shall certainly H7223
29 it shall not be as the f, or as the latter. H7223
Hos 6: 3 as the latter *and* f rain unto the earth. H3138
Joel 2:23 hath given you the f rain moderately, H4175
23 you the rain, the f rain, and the latter H4175
Hag 2: 9 greater than of the f, saith the LORD of H7223
Zec 1: 4 unto whom the f prophets have cried, H7223
7: 7 hath cried by the f prophets, when H7223
12 in his spirit by the f prophets: therefore H7223
8:11 in the f days, saith the LORD of hosts. H7223
14: 8 them toward the f sea, and half of them H6931
Mal 3: 4 as in the days of old, and as in f years. H6931
Act 1: 1 The f treatise have I made, O G4413
Eph 4:22 That ye put off concerning the f G4387
Heb 10:32 But call to remembrance the f days, in G4386
1Pt 1:14 to the f lusts in your ignorance: G4386
Rev 21: 4 pain: for the f things are passed away. G4413

FORMETH
Am 4:13 For, lo, he that f the mountains, and H3335
Zec 12: 1 and f the spirit of man within him. H3335

FORMS
Ezk 43:11 and all the f thereof, and all the H6699
11 and all the f thereof, and all the H6699

FORNICATION
2Ch 21:11 commit f, and compelled Judah *thereto*. H2181
Isa 23:17 hire, and shall commit f with all the H2181

Ezk 16:26 Thou hast also committed f with the H2181
29 Thou hast moreover multiplied thy f in H8457
Mt 5:32 saving for the cause of f, causeth her to G4202
19: 9 wife, except *it be* for f, and shall marry G4202
Jn 8:41 of f; we have one Father, *even* God. G4202
Act 15:20 of idols, and *from* f, and *from* things G4202
29 and from f: from which if ye keep G4202
21:25 blood, and from strangled, and from f. G4202
Ro 1:29 Being filled with all unrighteousness, f, G4202
1Co 5: 1 It is reported commonly *that there is* f G4202
1 you, and such f as is not so much as G4202
6:13 the body *is* not for f, but for the Lord; G4202
18 Flee f. Every sin that a man doeth is G4202
18 f sinneth against his own body. G4203
7: 2 Nevertheless, *to avoid* f, let every man G4202
10: 8 Neither let us commit f, as some of G4203
2Co 12:21 uncleanness and f and lasciviousness G4202
Gal 5:19 f, uncleanness, lasciviousness, G4202
Eph 5: 3 But f, and all uncleanness, or G4202
Col 3: 5 are upon the earth; f, uncleanness, G4202
1Th 4: 3 that ye should abstain from f: G4202
Jude 7 themselves over to f, and going after G1608
Rev 2:14 sacrificed unto idols, and to commit f. G4203
20 to commit f, and to eat things sacrificed G4203
21 And I gave her space to repent of her f; G4202
9:21 nor of their f, nor of their thefts. G4202
14: 8 drink of the wine of the wrath of her f. G4202
17: 2 have committed f, and the inhabitants G4203
2 been made drunk with the wine of her f. G4202
4 of abominations and filthiness of her f: G4202
18: 3 of the wrath of her f, and the kings of G4202
3 have committed f with her, and the G4203
9 have committed f and lived deliciously G4203
19: 2 the earth with her f, and hath avenged G4202

FORNICATIONS
Ezk 16:15 pouredst out thy f on every one that H8457
Mt 15:19 f, thefts, false witness, blasphemies: G4202
Mk 7:21 evil thoughts, adulteries, f, murders, G4202

FORNICATOR
1Co 5:11 a brother be a f, or covetous, or an G4205
Heb 12:16 Lest there *be* any f, or profane person, G4205

FORNICATORS
1Co 5: 9 you in an epistle not to company with f: G4205
10 Yet not altogether with the f of this G4205
6: 9 deceived: neither f, nor idolaters, nor G4205

FORSAKE
Dt 4:31 God;) he will not f thee, neither destroy H7503
12:19 Take heed to thyself that thou f not the H5800
14:27 thou shalt not f him; for he hath no H5800
31: 6 thee; he will not fail thee, nor f thee. H5800
8 f thee: fear not, neither be dismayed. H5800
16 them, and will f me, and break my H5800
17 day, and I will f them, and I will hide H5800
Jos 1: 5 with thee: I will not fail thee, nor f thee. H5800
24:16 should f the LORD, to serve other gods; H5800
20 If ye f the LORD, and serve strange H5800
Jdg 9:11 them, Should I f my sweetness, and my H2308
1Sa 12:22 For the LORD will not f his people for H5203
1Ki 6:13 Israel, and will not f my people Israel. H5800
8:57 fathers: let him not leave us, nor f us: H5203
2Ki 21:14 And I will f the remnant of mine H5203
1Ch 28: 9 thou f him, he will cast thee off for ever. H5800
20 not fail thee, nor f thee, until thou hast H5800
2Ch 7:19 But if ye turn away, and f my statutes H5800
15: 2 you; but if ye f him, he will forsake you. H5800
2 you; but if ye forsake him, he will f you. H5800
Ezr 8:22 his wrath *is* against all them that f him. H5800
Neh 9:31 them, nor f them; for thou *art* a H5800
10:39 and we will not f the house of our God. H5800
Job 20:13 *Though* he spare it, and f it not; but H5800
Ps 27: 9 neither f me, O God of my salvation. H5800
10 When my father and my mother f me, H5800
37: 8 Cease from anger, and f wrath: fret not H5800
38:21 F me not, O LORD: O my God, be not H5800
71: 9 Cast me not off in the time of old age; f H5800
18 O God, f me not; until I have H5800
89:30 If his children f my law, and walk not H5800
94:14 people, neither will he f his inheritance. H5800
119: 8 I will keep thy statutes: O f me not H5800
53 because of the wicked that f thy law. H5800
138: 8 f not the works of thine own hands. H7503
Prv 1: 8 father, and f not the law of thy mother: H5203
3: 3 Let not mercy and truth f thee: bind H5800
4: 2 For I give you good doctrine, f ye not H5800
6 F her not, and she shall preserve thee: H5800
Prv 6:20 and f not the law of thy mother: H5203
9: 6 F the foolish, and live; and go in the H5800
27:10 thy father's friend, f not; neither go into H5800
28: 4 They that f the law praise the wicked: H5800
Isa 1:28 that f the LORD shall be consumed. H5800
41:17 I the God of Israel will not f them. H5800
42:16 will I do unto them, and not f them. H5800
55: 7 Let the wicked f his way, and the H5800
65:11 But ye *are* they that f the LORD, that H5800
Jer 17:13 O LORD, the hope of Israel, all that f H5800
23:33 I will even f you, saith the LORD. H5203
39 you, and I will f you, and the city that H5203
51: 9 she is not healed: f her, and let us go H5800
Lam 5:20 us for ever, *and* f us so long time? H5800
Ezk 20: 8 neither did they f the idols of Egypt: H5800
Dan 11:30 with them that f the holy covenant. H5800
Jna 2: 8 They that observe lying vanities f their H5800
Act 21:21 the Gentiles to f Moses, saying that they G646
Heb 13: 5 said, I will never leave thee, nor f thee. G1459

FORSAKEN
Dt 28:20 of thy doings, whereby thou hast f me. H5800
29:25 Because they have f the covenant of the H5800
Jdg 6:13 the LORD hath f us, and delivered us H5203
10:10 f our God, and also served Baalim. H5800
13 Yet ye have f me, and served other H5800
1Sa 8: 8 they have f me, and served other H5800
12:10 because we have f the LORD, and have H5800
1Ki 11:33 Because that they have f me, and have H5800
18:18 in that ye have f the commandments H5800
19:10 of Israel have f thy covenant, thrown H5800
14 of Israel have f thy covenant, thrown H5800
2Ki 22:17 Because they have f me, and have H5800
2Ch 12: 5 the LORD, Ye have f me, and therefore H5800
13:10 and we have not f him; and the priests, H5800
11 the LORD our God; but ye have f him. H5800
21:10 he had f the LORD God of his fathers. H5800
24:20 f the LORD, he hath also forsaken you. H5800
20 forsaken the LORD, he hath also f you. H5800
24 because they had f the LORD God of H5800
28: 6 had f the LORD God of their fathers. H5800
29: 6 our God, and have f him, and have H5800
34:25 Because they have f me, and have H5800
Ezr 9: 9 our God hath not f us in our bondage, H5800
10 this? for we have f thy commandments, H5800
Neh 13:11 the house of God f? And I gathered them H5800
Job 18: 4 shall the earth be f for thee? and shall H5800
20:19 Because he hath oppressed *and* hath f H5800
Ps 9:10 LORD, hast not f them that seek thee. H5800
22: 1 My God, my God, why hast thou f me? H5800
37:25 righteous f, nor his seed begging bread. H5800
71:11 Saying, God hath f him: persecute and H5800
Isa 1: 4 they have f the LORD, they have H5800
2: 6 Therefore thou hast f thy people the H5203
7:16 abhorrest shall be f of both her kings. H5800
17: 2 The cities of Aroer *are* f: they shall be H5800
9 strong cities be as a f bough, and an H5800
27:10 *and* the habitation f, and left like a H7971
32:14 Because the palaces shall be f; the H5203
49:14 But Zion said, The LORD hath f me, H5800
54: 6 thee as a woman f and grieved in spirit, H5800
7 For a small moment have I f thee; but H5800
60:15 Whereas thou hast been f and hated, H5800
62: 4 Thou shalt no more be termed F; H5800
12 shalt be called, Sought out, A city not f. H5800
Jer 1:16 who have f me, and have burned H5800
2:13 evils; they have f me the fountain of H5800
17 in that thou hast f the LORD thy God, H5800
19 that thou hast f the LORD thy God, and H5800
4:29 *shall be* f, and not a man dwell therein. H5800
5: 7 thy children have f me, and sworn by H5800
19 them, Like as ye have f me, and served H5800
7:29 and f the generation of his wrath. H5203
9:13 Because they have f my law which I set H5800
19 because we have f the land, because H5800
12: 7 I have f mine house, I have left mine H5800
15: 6 Thou hast f me, saith the LORD, thou H5203
16:11 your fathers have f me, saith the H5800
11 have f me, and have not kept my law; H5800
17:13 because they have f the LORD, the H5800
18:14 that come from another place be f? H5428
19: 4 Because they have f me, and have H5800
22: 9 Because they have f the covenant of the H5800
25:38 He hath f his covert, as the lion: for H5800
51: 5 For Israel *hath* not *been* f, nor Judah of H488
Ezk 8:12 seeth us not; the LORD hath f the earth. H5800
9: 9 f the earth, and the LORD seeth not. H5800
36: 4 to the cities that are f, which became a H5800
Am 5: 2 more rise: she is f upon her land; *there* H5203
Zep 2: 4 For Gaza shall be f, and Ashkelon a H5800
Mt 19:27 Behold, we have f all, and followed thee; G863
29 And every one that hath f houses, or G863
27:46 My God, my God, why hast thou f me? G1459
Mk 15:34 My God, my God, why hast thou f me? G1459
2Co 4: 9 Persecuted, but not f; cast down, but G1459
2Ti 4:10 For Demas hath f me, having loved this G1459
2Pt 2:15 Which have f the right way, and are G2641

FORSAKETH
Job 6:14 but he f the fear of the Almighty. H5800
Ps 37:28 For the LORD loveth judgment, and f H5800
Prv 2:17 Which f the guide of her youth, and H5800
15:10 Correction *is* grievous unto him that f H5800
28:13 and f *them* shall have mercy. H5800
Lk 14:33 he be of you that f not all that he hath, G657

FORSAKING
Isa 6:12 *be* a great f in the midst of the land. H5805
Heb 10:25 Not f the assembling of ourselves G1459

FORSOMUCH
Lk 19: 9 house, f as he also is a son of Abraham. G2530

FORSOOK
Dt 32:15 *with fatness*; then he f God *which* made H5203
Jdg 2:12 And they f the LORD God of their H5800
13 And they f the LORD, and served Baal H5800
10: 6 and f the LORD, and served not him. H5800
1Sa 31: 7 were dead, they f the cities, and fled; H5800
1Ki 9: 9 And they shall answer, Because they f H5800
12: 8 But he f the counsel of the old men, H5800
13 roughly, and f the old men's counsel H5800
2Ki 21:22 And he f the LORD God of his fathers, H5800
1Ch 10: 7 dead, then they f their cities, and fled: H5800
2Ch 7:22 Because they f the LORD God of their H5800
10: 8 But he f the counsel which the old men H5800
13 f the counsel of the old men, H5800
12: 1 himself, he f the law of the LORD, H5800
Ps 78:60 So that he f the tabernacle of Shiloh, H5203
119:87 me upon earth; but I f not thy precepts. H5800
Isa 58: 2 and f not the ordinance of H5800
Jer 14: 5 and f *it*, because there was no grass. H5800
Mt 26:56 Then all the disciples f him, and fled. G863
Mk 1:18 And straightway they f their nets, and G863
14:50 And they all f him, and fled. G863
Lk 5:11 to land, they f all, and followed him. G863
2Ti 4:16 me, but all *men* f me: *I pray God* that G1459
Heb 11:27 By faith he f Egypt, not fearing the G2641

FORSOOKEST
Neh 9:17 and of great kindness, and f them not. H5800
19 Yet thou in thy manifold mercies f H5800

FORSWEAR
Mt 5:33 time, Thou shalt not f thyself, but shalt G1964

FORT
2Sa 5: 9 So David dwelt in the f, and called it the H4686
Isa 25:12 And the fortress of the high f of thy H4869
Ezk 4: 2 And lay siege against it, and build a f H1785
21:22 gates, to cast a mount, *and* to build a f. H1785
26: 8 he shall make a f against thee, and cast H1785
Dan 11:19 Then he shall turn his face toward the f H4581

FORTH
Gen 1:11 And God said, Let the earth bring f H1876
12 And the earth brought f grass, *and* H3318
20 And God said, Let the waters bring f H8317
21 the waters brought f abundantly, after H8317
24 And God said, Let the earth bring f the H3318
3:16 thou shalt bring f children; and thy H3205
18 Thorns also and thistles shall it bring f H6779
22 now, lest he put f his hand, and take H7971
23 Therefore the LORD God sent him f H7971
8: 7 And he sent f a raven, which went forth H7971
7 And he sent forth a raven, which went f H3318
8 Also he sent f a dove from him, to see if H7971
9 earth: then he put f his hand, and took H7971
10 again he sent f the dove out of the ark; H7971
12 seven days; and sent f the dove; which H7971
16 Go f of the ark, thou, and thy wife, and H3318
17 Bring f with thee every living thing that H3318
18 And Noah went f, and his sons, and his H3318
19 after their kinds, went f out of the ark. H3318
9: 7 and multiply; bring f abundantly in the H8317
18 And the sons of Noah, that went f of H3318
10:11 Out of that land went f Asshur, and H3318
11:31 and they went f with them from Ur of H3318

Gen 12: 5 and they went f to go into the land of H3318
14:18 of Salem brought f bread and wine: H3318
15: 4 he that shall come f out of thine own H3318
5 And he brought him f abroad, and H3318
19:10 But the men put f their hand, and H7971
16 him f, and set him without the city. H3318
17 had brought them f abroad, that he H3318
22:10 And Abraham stretched f his hand, H7971
24:43 the virgin cometh f to draw *water*, and H3318
45 Rebekah came f with her pitcher on H3318
53 And the servant brought f jewels of H3318
30:39 rods, and brought f cattle ringstraked, H3205
38:24 said, Bring her f, and let her be burnt. H3318
25 When she *was* brought f, she sent to her H3318
29 hast thou broken f? *this* breach *be* upon H6555
39:13 his garment in her hand, and was fled f, H2351
40:10 her blossoms shot f; and the clusters H5927
10 clusters thereof brought f ripe grapes: H1310
41:47 years the earth brought f by handfuls. H6213
42:15 ye shall not go f hence, except your H3318
Ex 3:10 that thou mayest bring f my people the H3318
11 f the children of Israel out of Egypt? H3318
12 thou hast brought f the people out of H3318
4: 4 And the LORD said unto Moses, Put f H7971
4 tail. And he put f his hand, and caught H7971
14 behold, he cometh f to meet thee: and H3318
5:20 the way, as they came f from Pharaoh: H3318
7: 4 Egypt, and bring f mine armies, *and* H3318
5 when I stretch f mine hand upon H5186
8: 3 And the river shall bring f frogs H8317
5 Aaron, Stretch f thine hand with thy H5186
18 to bring f lice, but they could not: H3318
20 lo, he cometh f to the water; and say H3318
9: 9 be a boil breaking f *with* blains upon H6524
10 a boil breaking f *with* blains upon H6524
22 Moses, Stretch f thine hand toward H5186
23 And Moses stretched f his rod toward H5186
10:13 And Moses stretched f his rod over the H5186
22 And Moses stretched f his hand toward H5186
12:31 Rise up, *and* get you f from among my H3318
39 they brought f out of Egypt, for it was H3318
46 thou shalt not carry f ought of the flesh H3318
13: 8 unto me when I came f out of Egypt. H3318
16 the LORD brought us f out of Egypt. H3318
14:11 thus with us, to carry us f out of Egypt? H3318
27 And Moses stretched f his hand over H5186
15: 7 thee: thou sentest f thy wrath, *which* H7971
13 Thou in thy mercy hast led f the people H5148
16: 3 have brought us f into this wilderness, H3318
32 I brought you f from the land of Egypt. H3318
19: 1 of Israel were gone f out of the land of H3318
17 And Moses brought f the people out of H3318
22 lest the LORD break f upon them. H6555
24 the LORD, lest he break f upon them. H6555
25:20 And the cherubims shall stretch f *their* H6566
29:46 that brought them f out of the land of H3318
32:11 thou hast brought f out of the land of H3318
Lev 4:12 Even the whole bullock shall he carry f H3318
21 And he shall carry f the bullock without H3318
6:11 and carry f the ashes without the H3318
14: 3 And the priest shall go f out of the H3318
45 f out of the city into an unclean place. H3318
16:24 and come f, and offer his burnt H3318
27 shall *one* carry f without the camp; and H3318
22:27 or a goat, is brought f, then it shall be H3205
24:14 Bring f him that hath cursed without H3318
23 that they should bring f him that had H3318
25:21 and it shall bring f fruit for three years. H6213
38 which brought you f out of the land of H3318
42 which I brought f out of the land of H3318
55 whom I brought f out of the land of H3318
26:10 And ye shall eat old store, and bring f H3318
13 which brought you f out of the land of H3318
45 whom I brought f out of the land of H3318
Nu 1: 3 all that are able to go f to war in Israel: H3318
20 all that were able to go f to war; H3318
22 all that were able to go f to war; H3318
24 all that were able to go f to war; H3318
26 all that were able to go f to war; H3318
28 all that were able to go f to war; H3318
30 all that were able to go f to war; H3318
32 all that were able to go f to war; H3318
34 all that were able to go f to war; H3318
36 all that were able to go f to war; H3318
38 all that were able to go f to war; H3318
40 all that were able to go f to war; H3318
42 all that were able to go f to war; H3318
45 that were able to go f to war in Israel; H3318
2: 9 their armies. These shall first set f. H5265

Nu 2:16 And they shall set f in the second rank. H5265
11:20 saying, Why came we f out of Egypt? H3318
31 And there went f a wind from the H5265
12: 5 and Miriam: and they both came f. H3318
17: 8 and brought f buds, and bloomed H3318
19: 3 he may bring her f without the camp, H3318
20: 8 and it shall give f his water, and thou H5414
8 thou shalt bring f to them water out of H3318
16 hath brought us f out of Egypt: and, H3318
24: 6 As the valleys are they spread f, as H5186
8 God brought him f out of Egypt; he H3318
26: 4 which went f out of the land of Egypt. H3318
31:13 went f to meet them without the camp. H3318
33: 1 Israel, which went f out of the land of H3318
34: 4 to Zin: and the going f thereof shall be H8444
8 f of the border shall be to Zedad: H8444
Dt 1:27 he hath brought us f out of the land of H3318
2:23 which came f out of Caphtor, destroyed H3318
4:20 you, and brought you f out of the iron H3318
45 of Israel, after they came f out of Egypt, H3318
46 after they were come f out of Egypt: H3318
6:12 brought thee f out of the land of Egypt, H3318
8:14 brought thee f out of the land of Egypt, H3318
15 thee f water out of the rock of flint; H3318
9:12 thou hast brought f out of Egypt have H3318
26 f out of Egypt with a mighty hand. H3318
14:22 that the field bringeth f year by year. H3318
28 thou shalt bring f all the tithe of thine H3318
16: 1 brought thee f out of Egypt by night. H3318
3 for thou camest f out of the land of H3318
3 when thou camest f out of the land of H3318
6 season that thou camest f out of Egypt. H3318
17: 5 Then shalt thou bring f that man or H3318
21: 2 thy judges shall come f, and they shall H3318
10 When thou goest f to war against thine H3318
22:15 take and bring f *the tokens of* the H3318
23: 4 way, when ye came f out of Egypt; and H3318
9 When the host goeth f against thine H3318
12 camp, whither thou shalt go f abroad: H3318
24: 9 after that ye were come f out of Egypt. H3318
25:11 him, and putteth f her hand, and H7971
17 way, when ye were come f out of Egypt; H3318
26: 8 And the LORD brought us f out of H3318
29:25 them f out of the land of Egypt: H3318
33: 2 them; he shined f from mount Paran, H3313
14 And for the precious fruits *brought f* by H3318
14 the precious things put f by the moon, H1645
Jos 2: 3 saying, Bring f the men that are come H3318
5: 5 way as they came f out of Egypt, *them* H3318
8: 9 Joshua therefore sent them f: and they H7971
9:12 the day we came f to go unto you; but H3318
10:23 And they did so, and brought f those H3318
18:11 of their lot came f between the children H3318
17 north, and went f to En-shemesh, and H3318
17 and went f toward Geliloth, which H3318
19: 1 And the second lot came f to Simeon, H3318
Jdg 1:24 And the spies saw a man come f out of H3318
3:21 And Ehud put f his left hand, and took H7971
23 Then Ehud went f through the porch, H3318
5:25 she brought f butter in a lordly dish. H7126
31 sun when he goeth f in his might. And H3318
6: 8 you f out of the house of bondage; H3318
18 thee, and bring f my present, and set H3318
21 Then the angel of the LORD put f the H7971
9: 8 The trees went f *on a time* to anoint a H1980
43 people *were* come f out of the city; and H3318
11:31 cometh f of the doors of my house H3318
14:12 I will now put f a riddle unto you: if H2330
13 Put f thy riddle, that we may hear it. H2330
14 of the eater came f meat, and out of the H3318
14 of the strong came f sweetness. And H3318
16 not: thou hast put f a riddle unto the H2330
15:15 of an ass, and put f his hand, and took H7971
19:22 saying, Bring f the man that came into H3318
25 and brought her f unto them; and they H2351
20:21 And the children of Benjamin came f H3318
25 And Benjamin went f against them out H3318
33 wait of Israel came f out of their places, H1518
Ru 1: 7 Wherefore she went f out of the place H3318
2:18 and she brought f, and gave to her that H3318
1Sa 11: 7 cometh not f after Saul and after H3318
12: 8 which brought f your fathers out of H3318
14:11 the Hebrews come f out of the holes H3318
27 wherefore he put f the end of the rod H7971
17:20 as the host was going f to the fight, and H3318
55 And when Saul saw David go f against H3318
18:30 Philistines went f: and it came to pass, H3318
30 after they went f, *that* David behaved H3318
22: 3 I pray thee, come f, *and be* with you, till H3318

1Sa 22:17 would not put f their hand to fall upon H7971
23:13 from Keilah; and he forbare to go f. H3318
24: 6 to stretch f mine hand against him, H7971
10 said, I will not put f mine hand against H7971
26: 9 who can stretch f his hand against the H7971
11 The LORD forbid that I should stretch f H7971
23 I would not stretch f mine hand against H7971
30:21 and they went f to meet David, and H3318
2Sa 1:14 afraid to stretch f thine hand to destroy H7971
5:20 hath broken f upon mine enemies H6555
6: 6 Uzzah put f *his hand* to the ark H7971
11: 1 when kings go f *to battle*, that David H3318
12:30 And he brought f the spoil of the city H3318
31 And he brought f the people that *were* H3318
13:39 David longed to go f unto Absalom: for H3318
15: 5 obeisance, he put f his hand, and took H7971
16 And the king went f, and all his H3318
17 And the king went f, and all the people H3318
16: 5 he came f, and cursed still as he came. H3318
11 my son, which came f of my bowels, H3318
18: 2 And David sent f a third part of the H7971
2 I will surely go f with you myself also. H3318
3 Thou shalt not go f: for if we flee away, H3318
12 would I not put f mine hand against H7971
19: 7 Now therefore arise, go f, and speak H3318
7 if thou go not f, there will not tarry one H3318
20: 8 thereof; and as he went f it fell out. H3318
22:20 He brought me f also into a large place: H3318
49 And that bringeth me f from mine H4161
1Ki 2:30 the king, Come f. And he said, Nay; but H3318
36 there, and go not f thence any whither. H3318
6:27 and they stretched f the wings of the H6566
8: 7 For the cherubims spread f *their* two
16 Since the day that I brought f my H3318
19 that shall come f out of thy loins, he H3318
22 and spread f his hands toward heaven: H6566
38 spread f his hands toward this house: H6566
51 thou broughtest f out of Egypt, from H3318
9: 9 God, who brought f their fathers out of H3318
13: 4 that he put f his hand from the altar, H7971
4 which he put f against him, dried up, H7971
19:11 And he said, Go f, and stand upon the H3318
20:33 Then Ben-hadad came f to him; and he H3318
21:13 they carried him f out of the city, and H3318
22:21 And there came f a spirit, and stood H3318
22 he said, I will go f, and I will be a lying H3318
22 *him*, and prevail also: go f, and do so. H3318
2Ki 2: 3 at Beth-el came f to Elisha, and said H3318
21 And he went f unto the spring of the H3318
23 way, there came f little children out of H3318
24 And there came f two she bears out of H3318
6:15 risen early, and gone f, behold, an host H3318
8: 3 and she went f to cry unto the king H3318
9:11 Then Jehu came f to the servants of his H3318
15 *then* let none go f *nor* escape out of the H3318
10:22 the vestry, Bring f vestments for all the H3318
22 And he brought them f vestments. H3318
25 let none come f. And they smote them H3318
26 And they brought f the images out of H3318
11: 7 And two parts of all you that go f on H3318
12 And he brought f the king's son, and H3318
15 them, Have her f without the ranges: H3318
18: 7 he went f: and he rebelled against H3318
19: 3 and *there is* not strength to bring f. H3205
31 For out of Jerusalem shall go f a H3318
21:15 came f out of Egypt, even unto this day. H3318
23: 4 the door, to bring f out of the temple of H3318
1Ch 12:33 Of Zebulun, such as went f to battle, H3318
36 And of Asher, such as went f to battle, H3318
13: 9 Chidon, Uzza put f his hand to hold the H7971
14:11 like the breaking f of waters: therefore H6556
15 for God is gone f before thee to smite H3318
16:23 shew f from day to day his salvation. H1319
19:16 and drew f the Syrians that *were* H3318
20: 1 out *to battle*, Joab led f the power of the H5090
24: 7 Now the first lot came f to Jehoiarib, H3318
25: 9 Now the first lot came f for Asaph to H3318
26:16 To Shuppim and Hosah *the lot came f*
2Ch 1:17 And they fetched up, and brought f out H3318
3:13 spread themselves f twenty cubits: and H6566
5: 8 For the cherubims spread f *their* wings H6566
6: 5 Since the day that I brought f my H3318
9 which shall come f out of thy loins, he H3318
12 of Israel, and spread f his hands: H6566
13 and spread f his hands toward heaven, H6566
29 shall spread f his hands in this house: H6566
7:22 which brought them f out of the land of H3318
20:20 and went f into the wilderness H3318
20 and as they went f, Jehoshaphat stood H3318

2Ch 21: 9 Then Jehoram went f with his princes, H5674
23:14 them, Have her f of the ranges: and H3318
25: 5 *men, able* to go f to war, that could H3318
11 himself, and led f his people, and went H5090
26: 6 And he went f and warred against the H3318
29: 5 f the filthiness out of the holy *place.* H3318
23 And they brought f the he goats *for* the H5066
32:21 they that came f of his own bowels slew H3329
Ezr 1: 7 Also Cyrus the king brought f the H3318
7 had brought f out of Jerusalem, and H3318
8 king of Persia bring f by the hand of H3318
6: 5 took f out of the temple which H5312
Neh 4:16 And it came to pass from that time f, *that*
8:15 saying, Go f unto the mount, and H3318
16 So the people went f, and brought *them,* H3318
9: 7 and broughtest him f out of Ur of the H3318
15 and broughtest f water for them out of H3318
13: 8 therefore I cast f all the household stuff H7993
21 f came they no *more* on the sabbath.
Est 4: 6 So Hatach went f to Mordecai unto the H3318
5: 9 Then went Haman f that day joyful H3318
Job 1:11 But put f thine hand now, and touch all H7971
12 himself put not f thine hand. So Satan H7971
12 went f from the presence of the LORD. H3318
2: 5 But put f thine hand now, and touch H7971
7 So went Satan f from the presence of H3318
5: 6 Although affliction cometh not f of the H3318
8:16 his branch shooteth f in his garden. H3318
10:18 Wherefore then hast thou brought me f H3318
11:17 shine f, thou shalt be as the morning.
14: 2 He cometh f like a flower, and is cut H3318
9 bud, and bring f boughs like a plant. H6213
15:35 They conceive mischief, and bring f H3205
21:11 They send f their little ones like a flock, H7971
30 shall be brought f to the day of wrath. H2986
23:10 he hath tried me, I shall come f as gold. H3318
24: 5 in the desert, go they f to their work; H3318
28: 9 He putteth f his hand upon the rock; he H7971
11 *thing that is* hid bringeth he f to light. H3318
30: 5 They were driven f from among *men,* H1644
38: 8 f, *as if* it had issued out of the womb? H1518
27 the bud of the tender herb to spring f? H6779
32 Canst thou bring f Mazzaroth in his H3318
39: 1 of the rock bring f? *or* canst thou mark H3205
2 thou the time when they bring f? H3205
3 They bow themselves, they bring f their H6398
4 they go f, and return not unto them. H3318
40:20 Surely the mountains bring him f food, H5375
Ps 1: 3 that bringeth f his fruit in his season; H5414
7:14 mischief, and brought f falsehood. H3205
9: 1 I will shew f all thy marvellous works. H5608
14 That I may shew f all thy praise in the H5608
17: 2 Let my sentence come f from thy H3318
18:19 He brought me f also into a large place; H3318
19: 6 His going f *is* from the end of the H4161
37: 6 And he shall bring f thy righteousness H3318
44: 9 and goest not f with our armies. H3318
51:15 and my mouth shall shew f thy praise. H5046
55:20 He hath put f his hands against such as H7971
57: 3 God shall send f his mercy and his truth.
66: 2 Sing f the honour of his name: make H2167
68: 7 O God, when thou wentest f before thy H3318
71:15 My mouth shall shew f thy H5608
78:52 But made his own people to go f like H5265
79:13 shew f thy praise to all generations. H5608
80: 1 *between* the cherubims, shine f. H3313
88: 8 *I am* shut up, and I cannot come f. H3318
90: 2 Before the mountains were brought f, or H3205
92: 2 To shew f thy lovingkindness in the H5046
14 They shall still bring f fruit in old age; H5107
96: 2 shew f his salvation from day to day. H1319
104:14 he may bring f food out of the earth; H3318
20 all the beasts of the forest do creep *f.*
23 Man goeth f unto his work and to his H3318
30 Thou sendest f thy spirit, they are
105:30 Their land brought f frogs in H8317
37 He brought them f also with silver and H3318
43 And he brought f his people with joy, H3318
106: 2 LORD? *who* can shew f all his praise? H8085
107: 7 And he led them f by the right way, H1869
108:11 not thou, O God, go f with our hosts? H3318
113: 2 from this time f and for evermore. H6258
115:18 f and for evermore. Praise the LORD.
121: 8 from this time f, and even for evermore.
125: 3 put f their hands unto iniquity. H7971
5 shall lead them f with the workers of
126: 6 He that goeth f and weepeth, bearing H1980
138: 7 thou shalt stretch f thine hand against H7971
141: 2 Let my prayer be set f before thee *as* H3559

Ps 143: 6 I stretch f my hands unto thee: my soul H6566
144: 6 Cast f lightning, and scatter them: H1299
13 sheep may bring f thousands and ten
146: 4 His breath goeth f, he returneth to his H3318
147:15 He sendeth f his commandment *upon* H7971
17 He casteth f his ice like morsels: who H7993
Prv 7:15 Therefore came I f to meet thee, H3318
8: 1 cry? and understanding put f her voice? H5414
24 I was brought f; when *there were* no H2342
25 settled, before the hills was I brought f: H2342
9: 3 She hath sent f her maidens: she crieth H7971
10:31 The mouth of the just bringeth f H5107
12:17 *He that* speaketh truth sheweth f H5046
25: 4 there shall come f a vessel for the finer. H3318
6 Put not f thyself in the presence of the H1921
8 Go not f hastily to strive, lest *thou* H3318
27: 1 knowest not what a day may bring f. H3205
30:27 The locusts have no king, yet go they f H3318
33 Surely the churning of milk bringeth f H3318
33 of the nose bringeth f blood: so the H3318
33 so the forcing of wrath bringeth f strife. H3318
31:20 she reacheth f her hands to the needy. H7971
Ecc 2: 6 the wood that bringeth f trees: H6779
5:15 As he came f of his mother's womb, H3318
7:18 feareth God shall come f of them all. H3318
10: 1 to send f a stinking savour: *so* H5042
Song 1: 3 f, therefore do the virgins love thee. H7324
8 go thy way f by the footsteps of the H3318
12 spikenard sendeth f the smell thereof. H5414
2: 9 our wall, he looketh f at the windows,
13 The fig tree putteth f her green figs, and H2590
3:11 Go f, O ye daughters of Zion, and H3318
6:10 Who *is* she *that* looketh f as the H8259
7:11 Come, my beloved, let us go f into the H3318
12 bud f: there will I give thee my loves. H5132
8: 5 brought thee f: there she brought thee H2254
5 there she brought thee f *that* bare thee. H2254
Isa 1:15 And when ye spread f your hands, I H6566
2: 3 of Zion shall go f the law, and the word H3318
3:16 with stretched f necks and wanton H5186
5: 2 it should bring f grapes, and it brought H6213
2 grapes, and it brought f wild grapes. H6213
4 f grapes, brought it forth wild grapes? H6213
4 forth grapes, brought it f wild grapes? H6213
25 he hath stretched f his hand against H5186
7: 3 Then said the LORD unto Isaiah, Go f H3318
25 be for the sending f of oxen, and for the H4916
11: 1 And there shall come f a rod out of the H3318
13:10 in his going f, and the moon shall H3318
14: 7 *and* is quiet: they break f into singing. H6476
29 root shall come f a cockatrice, and his H3318
23: 4 not, nor bring f children, neither do H3205
25:11 And he shall spread f his hands in the H6566
11 spreadeth f *his hands* to swim: and H6566
26:18 as it were brought f wind; we have not H3205
27: 8 In measure, when it shooteth f, thou H7971
28:19 From the time that it goeth f it shall H5674
29 This also cometh f from the LORD of H3318
31: 4 is called f against him, *he* will H7121
32:20 f *thither* the feet of the ox and the ass. H7971
33:11 Ye shall conceive chaff, ye shall bring f H3205
34: 1 world, and all things that come f of it. H6631
36: 3 Then came f unto him Eliakim, H3318
37: 3 and *there is* not strength to bring f. H3205
9 He is come f to make war with thee. H3318
32 For out of Jerusalem shall go f a H3318
36 Then the angel of the LORD went f, and H3318
41:21 the LORD; bring f your strong *reasons,* H5066
22 Let them bring *them* f, and shew us H5066
42: 1 shall bring f judgment to the Gentiles. H3318
3 he shall bring f judgment unto truth. H3318
5 out; he that spread f the earth, and that H7554
9 before they spring f I tell you of them. H6779
13 The LORD shall go f as a mighty man, H3318
43: 8 Bring f the blind people that have eyes, H3318
9 let them bring f their witnesses, that H5414
17 Which bringeth f the chariot and H3318
19 now it shall spring f; shall ye not know H6779
21 for myself; they shall shew f my praise. H5608
44:23 of the earth: break f into singing, ye H6476
24 that stretcheth f the heavens alone; H5186
45: 8 and let them bring f salvation, and let H6509
10 the woman, What hast thou brought f? H2342
48: 1 and are come f out of the waters of H3318
3 and they went f out of my mouth, and H3318
20 Go ye f of Babylon, flee ye from the H3318
49: 9 the prisoners, Go f; to them that *are* in H3318
13 O earth; and break f into singing, O H6476
17 that made thee waste shall go f of thee. H3318

Isa 51: 5 salvation is gone f, and mine arms shall H3318
13 hath stretched f the heavens, and laid H5186
18 she hath brought f; neither *is there any* H3205
52: 9 Break f into joy, sing together, ye waste
54: 1 not bear; break f into singing, and cry H6476
2 let them stretch f the curtains of thine H5186
3 For thou shalt break f on the right H6555
16 and that bringeth f an instrument for H3318
55:10 maketh it bring f and bud, that it may H3205
11 So shall my word be that goeth f out of H3318
12 with joy, and be led f with peace: the H2986
12 the hills shall break f before you into H6476
58: 8 Then shall thy light break f as the H1234
8 health shall spring f speedily: and thy H6779
9 f of the finger, and speaking vanity; H7971
59: 4 conceive mischief, and bring f iniquity. H3205
60: 6 shall shew f the praises of the LORD. H1319
61:11 For as the earth bringeth f her bud, and H3318
11 in it to spring f; so the Lord GOD will H6779
11 praise to spring f before all the nations. H6779
62: 1 thereof go f as brightness, and the H3318
65: 9 And I will bring f a seed out of Jacob, H3318
23 in vain, nor bring f for trouble; for they H3205
66: 7 Before she travailed, she brought f; H3205
8 be made to bring f in one day? *or* shall H2342
8 travailed, she brought f her children. H3205
9 not cause to bring f? saith the LORD: H3205
9 f, and shut *the womb*? saith thy God. H3205
24 And they shall go f, and look upon the H3318
Jer 1: 5 before thou camest f out of the womb I H3318
9 Then the LORD put f his hand, and H7971
14 f upon all the inhabitants of the land. H6605
2:27 hast brought me f: for they have turned H3205
37 Yea, thou shalt go f from him, and H3318
4: 4 lest my fury come f like fire, and burn H3318
7 his way; he is gone f from his place to H3318
31 of her that bringeth f her first child, the
6:25 Go not f into the field, nor walk by the H3318
7:25 Since the day that your fathers came f H3318
10:13 bringeth f the wind out of his treasures. H3318
20 children are gone f of me, and they *are* H3318
20 *is* none to stretch f my tent any more, H5186
11: 4 *that* I brought them f out of the land of H3318
12: 2 yea, they bring f fruit: thou *art* near in H6213
14:18 If I go f into the field, then behold the H3318
15: 1 *them* out of my sight, and let them go f. H3318
2 shall we go f? then thou shalt tell them, H3318
19 and if thou take f the precious from the H3318
17:22 Neither carry f a burden out of your H3318
19: 2 And go f unto the valley of the son of H3318
20: 3 Pashur brought f Jeremiah out of the H3318
18 Wherefore came I f out of the womb to H3318
22:11 father, which went f out of this place; H3318
19 cast f beyond the gates of Jerusalem. H7993
23:15 is profaneness gone f into all the land. H3318
19 of the LORD is gone f in fury, even a H3318
25:32 evil shall go f from nation to nation, H3318
26:23 And they fetched f Urijah out of Egypt, H3318
29:16 are not gone f with you into captivity; H3318
30:23 of the LORD goeth f with fury, a H3318
31: 4 and shalt go f in the dances of them H3318
24 and they *that* go f with flocks. H5265
39 And the measuring line shall yet go f H3318
32:21 And hast brought f thy people Israel H3318
34:13 that I brought them f out of the land of H3318
37: 5 Then Pharaoh's army was come f out H3318
7 army, which is come f to help you, shall H3318
12 Then Jeremiah went f out of Jerusalem H3318
38: 2 but he that goeth f to the Chaldeans H3318
8 Ebed-melech went f out of the king's H3318
17 wilt assuredly go f unto the king of H3318
18 But if thou wilt not go f to the king of H3318
21 But if thou refuse to go f, this *is* the H3318
22 house *shall be* brought f to the king of H3318
39: 4 fled, and went f out of the city by night, H3318
41: 6 of Nethaniah went f from Mizpah to H3318
42:18 fury hath been poured f upon the H5413
18 my fury be poured f upon you, when ye H5413
43:12 and he shall go f from thence in peace. H3318
44: 6 anger was poured f, and was kindled in H5413
17 thing goeth f out of our own mouth, H3318
46: 4 and stand f with *your* helmets; furbish H3320
9 mighty men come f; the Ethiopians and H3318
48: 7 Chemosh shall go f into captivity *with* H3318
45 a fire shall come f out of Heshbon, and H3318
49: 5 every man right f; and none shall gather H6440
50: 8 of Babylon, and go f out of the land of H3318
25 and hath brought f the weapons of his H3318
51:10 The LORD hath brought f our H3318

Jer 51:16 bringeth f the wind out of his treasures. H3318
44 and I will bring f out of his mouth that H3318
52: 7 war fled, and went f out of the city by H3318
31 Judah, and brought him f out of prison, H3318
Lam 1:17 Zion spreadeth f her hands, *and there* H6566
Ezk 1:13 and out of the fire went f lightning. H3318
22 stretched f over their heads above. H5186
3:22 unto me, Arise, go f into the plain, and H3318
23 Then I arose, and went f into the plain: H3318
5: 4 a fire come f into all the house of Israel. H3318
7:10 the morning is gone f; the rod hath H3318
8: 3 And he put f the form of an hand, and H7971
9: 7 the slain: go ye f. And they went forth, H3318
7 And they went f, and slew in the city. H3318
10: 7 And *one* cherub stretched f his hand H7971
11: 7 I will bring you f out of the midst of it. H3318
12: 4 Then shalt thou bring f thy stuff by day H3318
4 and thou shalt go f at even in their H3318
4 sight, as they that go f into captivity. H4161
6 *and* carry *it* f in the twilight: thou H3318
7 I brought f my stuff by day, as stuff H3318
7 hand; I brought *it* f in the twilight, *and* H3318
12 and shall go f: they shall dig through H3318
14:22 that shall be brought f, *both* sons and H3318
22 they shall come f unto you, and ye shall H3318
16:14 And thy renown went f among the H3318
17: 2 Son of man, put f a riddle, and speak a H2330
6 f branches, and shot forth sprigs. H6213
6 forth branches, and shot f sprigs. H7971
7 him, and shot f her branches toward H7971
8 that it might bring f branches, and that H6213
23 it: and it shall bring f boughs, and bear H5375
18: 8 He *that* hath not given f upon usury,
13 Hath given f upon usury, and hath taken
20: 6 to bring them f of the land of Egypt H3318
9 them f out of the land of Egypt. H3318
10 Wherefore I caused them to go f out of H3318
22 in whose sight I brought them f. H3318
38 I will bring them f out of the country H3318
21: 3 and will draw f my sword out of his H3318
4 shall my sword go f out of his sheath H3318
5 LORD have drawn f my sword out of H3318
19 twain shall come f out of one land: and H3318
24:12 scum went not f out of her: her scum H3318
27: 7 thou spreadest f to be thy sail; blue and H4666
10 in thee; they set f thy comeliness. H5414
33 When thy wares went f out of the seas, H3318
28:18 will I bring f a fire from the midst H3318
29:21 of Israel to bud f, and I will give thee the H6779
30: 9 In that day shall messengers go f from H3318
31: 5 the multitude of waters, when he shot f. H7971
6 of the field bring f their young, and H3205
32: 2 and thou camest f with thy rivers, and H1518
4 I will cast thee f upon the open field, H2904
33:30 the word that cometh f from the LORD. H3318
36: 8 ye shall shoot f your branches, and H5414
20 LORD, and are gone f out of his land. H3318
38: 4 I will bring thee f, and all thine army, H3318
8 but it is brought f out of the nations, H3318
39: 9 of Israel shall go f, and shall set on fire H3318
42: 1 Then he brought me f into the utter H3318
15 he brought me f toward the gate whose H3318
44: 5 with every going f of the sanctuary. H4161
19 And when they go f into the utter court, H3318
46: 2 then he shall go f; but the gate shall not H3318
8 and he shall go f by the way thereof. H3318
9 south gate shall go f by the way of the H3318
9 came in, but shall go f over against it. H3318
10 go in; and when they go f, shall go forth. H3318
10 go in; and when they go forth, shall go f. H3318
12 then he shall go f; and after his going H3318
12 after his going f *one* shall shut the gate. H3318
21 Then he brought me f into the utter H3318
47: 3 line in his hand went f eastward, he H3318
8 *being* brought f into the sea, the waters H3318
10 a *place* to spread f nets; their fish shall H4894
12 it shall bring f new fruit according
Dan 2:13 And the decree went f that the wise H5312
14 gone f to slay the wise *men* of Babylon: H5312
3:26 high God, come f, and come *hither*. H5312
26 came f of the midst of the fire. H5312
5: 5 In the same hour came f fingers of a H5312
7:10 A fiery stream issued and came f from H5312
8: 9 And out of one of them came f a little H3318
9:15 thy people f out of the land of Egypt H3318
22 f to give thee skill and understanding. H3318
23 came f, and I am come to shew H3318
25 from the going f of the commandment H4161
10:20 f, lo, the prince of Grecia shall come. H3318

Dan 11:11 and shall come f and fight with him, H3318
11 and he shall set f a great multitude; but H5975
13 and shall set f a multitude greater H5975
42 He shall stretch f his hand also upon H7971
44 he shall go f with great fury to destroy, H3318
Hos 6: 3 LORD: his going f is prepared as the H4161
5 judgments *are as* the light *that* goeth f. H3318
9:13 bring f his children to the murderer. H3318
16 though they bring f, yet will I slay *even* H3205
10: 1 Israel *is* an empty vine, he bringeth f H7737
13:13 *the place of* the breaking f of children. H4866
14: 5 lily, and cast f his roots as Lebanon. H5221
Joel 2:16 let the bridegroom go f of his chamber, H3318
3:18 shall come f of the house of the LORD, H3318
Am 5: 3 that which went f *by* an hundred shall H3318
7:17 surely go into captivity f of his land. H5921
8: 3 they shall cast *them* f with silence. H7993
5 that we may set f wheat, making the H6605
Jna 1: 5 his god, and cast f the wares that *were* H2904
12 up, and cast me f into the sea; so shall H2904
15 So they took up Jonah, and cast him f H2904
Mic 1: 3 For, behold, the LORD cometh f out of H3318
11 Zaanan came not f in the mourning of H3318
4: 2 the law shall go f of Zion, and the word H3318
10 Be in pain, and labour to bring f, O H1518
10 now shalt thou go f out of the city, and H3318
5: 2 thee shall he come f unto me *that is* to H3318
2 whose goings f *have been* from of old, H4163
3 hath brought f: then the remnant of H3205
7: 9 me: he will bring me f to the light, *and* I H3318
Hab 1: 4 doth never go f: for the wicked doth H3318
3: 5 and burning coals went f at his feet. H3318
13 Thou wentest f for the salvation of thy H3318
Zep 2: 2 Before the decree bring f, *before* the day H3205
Hag 1:11 ground bringeth f, and upon men, and H3318
2:19 brought f: from this day will I bless *you*. H5375
Zec 1:16 shall be stretched f upon Jerusalem. H5186
2: 3 with me went f, and another angel went H3318
6 Ho, ho, *come f*, and flee from the land of
3: 8 I will bring f my servant the BRANCH. H935
4: 7 and he shall bring f the headstone H3318
5: 3 curse that goeth f over the face of the H3318
4 I will bring it f, saith the LORD of hosts, H3318
5 with me went f, and said unto me, Lift H3318
5 eyes, and see what *is* this that goeth f. H3318
6 ephah that goeth f. He said moreover, H3318
6: 5 the heavens, which go f from standing H3318
6 The black horses which *are* therein go f H3318
6 and the white go f after them; and the H3318
6 grisled go f toward the south country. H3318
7 And the bay went f, and sought to go H3318
9:11 I have sent f thy prisoners out of H7971
14 his arrow shall go f as the lightning: H3318
10: 4 Out of him came f the corner, out of H3318
12: 1 which stretcheth f the heavens, and H5186
14: 2 of the city shall go f into captivity, and H3318
3 Then shall the LORD go f, and fight H3318
Mal 4: 2 go f, and grow up as calves of the stall. H3318
Mt 1:21 And she shall bring f a son, and thou *G5088*
23 and shall bring f a son, and they shall *G5088*
25 And knew her not till she had brought f *G5088*
2:16 wroth, and sent f, and slew all the *G649*
3: 8 Bring f therefore fruits meet for *G4160*
10 bringeth not f good fruit is hewn down, *G4160*
7:17 Even so every good tree bringeth f good *G4160*
17 but a corrupt tree bringeth f evil fruit. *G4160*
18 A good tree cannot bring f evil fruit, *G4160*
18 *can* a corrupt tree bring f good fruit. *G4160*
19 Every tree that bringeth not f good fruit *G4160*
8: 3 And Jesus put f *his* hand, and touched *G1614*
9: 9 And as Jesus passed f from thence, he *G3855*
25 But when the people were put f, he went *G1544*
38 will send f labourers into his harvest. *G1544*
10: 5 These twelve Jesus sent f, and *G649*
16 Behold, I send you f as sheep in the *G649*
12:13 Then saith he to the man, Stretch f *G1614*
13 he stretched *it* f; and it was restored *G1614*
20 till he send f judgment unto victory. *G1544*
35 of the heart bringeth f good things: and *G1544*
35 the evil treasure bringeth f evil things. *G1544*
49 And he stretched f his hand toward his *G1614*
13: 3 saying, Behold, a sower went f to sow; *G1831*
8 ground, and brought f fruit, some an *G1325*
23 beareth fruit, and bringeth f, some an *G4160*
24 Another parable put he f unto them, *G3908*
26 f fruit, then appeared the tares also. *G4160*
31 Another parable put he f unto them, *G3908*
41 The Son of man shall send f his angels, *G649*
43 Then shall the righteous shine f as the *G1584*

Mt 13:49 the angels shall come f, and sever the *G1831*
52 which bringeth f out of his treasure *G1544*
14: 2 works do shew f themselves in him. *G1754*
14 And Jesus went f, and saw a great *G1831*
31 And immediately Jesus stretched f *his* *G1614*
15:18 of the mouth come f from the heart; *G1831*
16:21 From that time f began Jesus to shew *G5119*
21:43 to a nation bringing f the fruits thereof. *G4160*
22: 3 And sent f his servants to call them that *G649*
4 Again, he sent f other servants, saying, *G649*
7 wroth: and he sent f his armies, and *G3992*
46 that day f ask him any more *questions*.
24:26 the desert; go not f: behold, *he is* in the *G1831*
32 f leaves, ye know that summer *is* nigh: *G1631*
25: 1 and went f to meet the bridegroom. *G1831*
Mk 1:38 preach there also: for therefore came I f. *G1831*
41 with compassion, put f *his* hand, and *G1614*
2:12 up the bed, and went f before them all; *G1831*
13 And he went f again by the sea side; *G1831*
3: 3 hand, Stand f. *G1519+G3588+G3319*
5 the man, Stretch f thine hand. And he *G1614*
6 And the Pharisees went f, and *G1831*
14 and that he might send them f to preach, *G649*
4: 8 and brought f, some thirty, and some *G5342*
20 *it*, and bring f fruit, some thirtyfold, *G2592*
28 For the earth bringeth f fruit of herself; *G2592*
29 But when the fruit is brought f, *G3860*
6: 7 to send them f by two and two; and *G649*
14 works do shew f themselves in him. *G1754*
17 For Herod himself had sent f and laid *G649*
24 And she went f, and said unto her *G1831*
7:26 cast f the devil out of her daughter. *G1544*
8:11 And the Pharisees came f, and began to *G1831*
9:29 f by nothing, but by prayer and fasting. *G1831*
10:17 And when he was gone f into the way, *G1607*
11: 1 Olives, he sendeth f two of his disciples, *G649*
13:28 f leaves, ye know that summer is near: *G1631*
14:13 And he sendeth f two of his disciples, *G649*
16 And his disciples went f, and came into *G1831*
16:20 And they went f, and preached every *G1831*
Lk 1: 1 in hand to set f in order a declaration *G392*
31 f a son, and shalt call his name JESUS. *G5088*
57 be delivered; and she brought f a son. *G1080*
2: 7 And she brought f her firstborn son, *G5088*
3: 7 that came f to be baptized of him, *G1607*
8 Bring f therefore fruits worthy of *G4160*
9 bringeth not f good fruit is hewn down, *G4160*
5:13 And he put f *his* hand, and touched *G1614*
27 And after these things he went f, and *G1831*
6: 8 Rise up, and stand f in the midst. And *G2476*
8 in the midst. And he arose and stood f. *G2476*
10 the man, Stretch f thy hand. And he did *G1614*
43 For a good tree bringeth not f corrupt *G2076*
43 doth a corrupt tree bring f good fruit. *G4160*
45 his heart bringeth f that which is good; *G4393*
45 his heart bringeth f that which is evil: *G4393*
7:17 And this rumour of him went f *G1831*
8:14 have heard, go f, and are choked with *G4198*
15 keep *it*, and bring f fruit with patience.
22 side of the lake. And they launched f. *G321*
27 And when he went f to land, there met *G1831*
10: 2 send f labourers into his harvest. *G1544*
3 Go your ways: behold, I send you f as *G649*
12:16 certain rich man brought f plentifully: *G2164*
37 meat, and will come f and serve them. *G3928*
14: 7 And he put f a parable to those which *G3004*
15:22 his servants, Bring f the best robe, and *G1627*
20: 9 and let it f to husbandmen, and *G1554*
20 And they watched *him*, and sent f spies, *G649*
21:30 When they now shoot f, ye see and *G4261*
22:53 ye stretched f no hands against me: *G1614*
Jn 1:43 The day following Jesus would go f into *G1831*
2:10 the beginning doth set f good wine; and *G5087*
11 and manifested f his glory; and his *G5319*
5:29 And shall come f; they that have done *G1607*
8:42 for I proceeded f and came from God; *G1831*
10: 4 And when he putteth f his own sheep, *G1544*
11:43 with a loud voice, Lazarus, come f. *G1854*
44 And he that was dead came f, bound *G1831*
53 Then from that day f they took counsel
12:13 trees, and went f to meet him, and *G1831*
24 but if it die, it bringeth f much fruit. *G5342*
15: 2 it, that it may bring f more fruit. *G5342*
5 the same bringeth f much fruit: for *G5342*
6 If a man abide not in me, he is cast f as *G1854*
16 go and bring f fruit, and *that* your *G5342*
16:28 I came f from the Father, and am come *G1831*
30 believe that thou camest f from God. *G1831*
18: 1 words, he went f with his disciples over *G1831*

Jn 18: 4 f, and said unto them, Whom seek ye? G1831
19: 4 Pilate therefore went f again, and saith G1854
4 I bring him f to you, that ye may G1854
5 Then came Jesus f, wearing the crown G1854
13 he brought Jesus f, and sat down in the G1854
17 And he bearing his cross went f into a G1831
20: 3 Peter therefore went f, and that other G1831
21: 3 thee. They went f, and entered into a G1831
18 old, thou shalt stretch f thy hands, and G1614
Act 1:26 And they gave f their lots; and the lot G1325
2:33 shed f this, which ye now see and hear. G1632
4:30 By stretching f thine hand to heal; and G1614
5:10 *her* f, buried *her* by her husband. G1627
15 Insomuch that they brought f the sick G1627
19 doors, and brought them f, and said, G1806
34 to put the apostles f a little space; G1854
7: 7 they come f, and serve me in this place. G1831
9:30 to Caesarea, and sent him f to Tarsus. G1821
40 But Peter put them all f, and kneeled G1854
11:22 and they sent f Barnabas, that he G1821
12: 1 f *his* hands to vex certain of the church. G1911
4 after Easter to bring him f to the people. G321
6 have brought him f, the same night G4254
13: 4 So they, being sent f by the Holy Ghost, G1599
16: 3 Him would Paul have to go f with him; G1831
17:18 to be a setter f of strange gods: because G2604
21: 2 unto Phenicia, we went aboard, and set f. G321
23:28 him, I brought him f into their council: G2609
24: 2 And when he was called f, Tertullus G2564
25:17 commanded the man to be brought f. G71
23 commandment Paul was brought f. G71
26 I have brought him f before you, and G4254
26: 1 f the hand, and answered for himself: G1614
25 f the words of truth and soberness. G669
27:21 But after long abstinence Paul stood f G2476
Ro 3:25 Whom God hath set f *to be* a G4388
7: 4 that we should bring f fruit unto God.
5 our members to bring f fruit unto death.
10:21 I have stretched f my hands unto a G1600
1Co 4: 9 For I think that God hath set f us the G584
16:11 but conduct him f in peace, that he G4311
Gal 3: 1 evidently set f, crucified among you? G4270
4: 4 come, God sent f his Son, made of a G1821
6 God hath sent f the Spirit of his Son G1821
27 bearest not; break f and cry, thou that G4486
Php 2:16 Holding f the word of life; that I may G1907
3:13 f unto those things which are before, G1901
Col 1: 6 and bringeth f fruit, as *it doth* also in
1Ti 1:16 Christ might shew f all longsuffering, G1731
Heb 1:14 spirits, sent f to minister for them G649
6: 7 it, and bringeth f herbs meet for them G5088
13:13 Let us go f therefore unto him without G1831
Jas 1:15 it bringeth f sin: and sin, when it G5088
15 sin, when it is finished, bringeth f death. G616
3:11 Doth a fountain send f at the same G1032
5:18 rain, and the earth brought f her fruit. G985
1Pt 2: 9 that ye should shew f the praises of him G1804
3Jn 7 went f, taking nothing of the Gentiles. G1831
Jude 7 flesh, are set f for an example, suffering G4295
Rev 5: 6 Spirits of God sent f into all the earth. G649
6: 2 he went f conquering, and to conquer. G1831
12: 5 And she brought f a man child, who G5088
13 woman which brought f the man *child*. G5088
16:14 miracles, *which* go f unto the kings of G1607

FORTHWITH
Ezr 6: 8 beyond the river, f expenses be given H629
Mt 13: 5 not much earth: and f they sprung up, G2112
26:49 And f he came to Jesus, and said, Hail, G2112
Mk 1:29 And f, when they were come out of the G2112
43 And he straitly charged him, and f sent G2112
5:13 And f Jesus gave them leave. And the G2112
Jn 19:34 and f came there out blood and water. G2117
Act 9:18 sight f, and arose, and was baptized. G3916
12:10 and f the angel departed from him. G2112
21:30 the temple: and f the doors were shut. G2112

FORTIETH
Nu 33:38 and died there, in the f year after the H705
Dt 1: 3 And it came to pass in the f year, in the H705
1Ch 26:31 of his fathers. In the f year of the reign of H705
2Ch 16:13 died in the one and f year of his reign. H705

FORTIFIED
2Ch 11:11 And he f the strong holds, and put H2388
26: 9 at the turning *of the wall*, and f them. H2388
Neh 3: 8 they f Jerusalem unto the broad wall. H5800
Mic 7:12 and *from* the f cities, and from the H4692

FORTIFY
Jdg 9:31 behold, they f the city against thee. H6696
Neh 4: 2 Jews? will they f themselves? will they H5800
Isa 22:10 have ye broken down to f the wall. H1219
Jer 51:53 though she should f the height of her H1219
Nah 2: 1 *thy* loins strong, f *thy* power mightily. H553
3:14 Draw thee waters for the siege, f thy H2388

FORTRESS
2Sa 22: 2 *is* my rock, and my f, and my deliverer; H4686
Ps 18: 2 The LORD *is* my rock, and my f, and H4686
31: 3 For thou *art* my rock and my f; H4686
71: 3 save me; for thou *art* my rock and my f. H4686
91: 2 and my f: my God; in him will I trust. H4686
144: 2 My goodness, and my f; my high tower, H4686
Isa 17: 3 The f also shall cease from Ephraim, H4013
25:12 And the f of the high fort of thy walls H4013
Jer 6:27 I have set thee *for* a tower *and* a f H4013
10:17 out of the land, O inhabitant of the f. H4692
16:19 O LORD, my strength, and my f, and H4581
Dan 11: 7 shall enter into the f of the king of the H4581
10 return, and be stirred up, *even* to his f. H4581
Am 5: 9 the spoiled shall come against the f. H4013
Mic 7:12 and from the f even to the river, and H4693

FORTRESSES
Isa 34:13 brambles in the f thereof: and it shall H4013
Hos 10:14 people, and all thy f shall be spoiled, as H4013

FORTS
2Ki 25: 1 and they built f against it round about. H1785
Isa 29: 3 a mount, and I will raise f against thee. H4694
32:14 shall be left; the f and towers shall be H6076
Jer 52: 4 it, and built f against it round about. H1785
Ezk 17:17 and building f, to cut off many persons: H1785
33:27 they that *be* in the f and in the caves H4679

FORTUNATUS
1Co 16:17 of Stephanas and F and Achaicus: for G5415

FORTY
Gen 5:13 f years, and begat sons and daughters: H705
7: 4 to rain upon the earth f days and forty H705
4 forty days and f nights; and every living H705
12 And the rain was upon the earth f days H705
12 upon the earth forty days and f nights. H705
17 And the flood was f days upon the earth; H705
8: 6 And it came to pass at the end of f days, H705
18:28 find there f and five, I will not destroy *it*. H705
29 there shall be f found there. And he H705
25:20 And Isaac was f years old when he took H705
26:34 And Esau was f years old when he took H705
32:15 Thirty milch camels with their colts, f H705
47:28 Jacob was an hundred f and seven years. H705
50: 3 And f days were fulfilled for him; for so H705
Ex 16:35 did eat manna f years, until they came H705
24:18 in the mount f days and forty nights. H705
18 in the mount forty days and f nights. H705
26:19 And thou shalt make f sockets of silver H705
21 And their f sockets *of* silver; two sockets H705
34:28 And he was there with the LORD f days H705
28 forty days and f nights; he did neither H705
36:24 And f sockets of silver he made under H705
26 And their f sockets of silver; two sockets H705
Lev 25: 8 years shall be unto thee f and nine years. H705
Nu 1:21 f and six thousand and five hundred. H705
25 tribe of Gad, *were* f and five thousand H705
33 *were* f thousand and five hundred. H705
41 f and one thousand and five hundred. H705
2:11 f and six thousand and five hundred. H705
15 of them, *were* f and five thousand and H705
19 them, *were* f thousand and five hundred. H705
28 f and one thousand and five hundred. H705
13:25 from searching of the land after f days. H705
14:33 in the wilderness f years, and bear your H705
34 the land, *even* f days, each day for a H705
34 your iniquities, *even* f years, and ye shall H705
26: 7 of them were f and three thousand H705
18 of them, f thousand and five hundred. H705
41 f and five thousand and six hundred. H705
50 f and five thousand and four hundred. H705
32:13 in the wilderness f years, until all the H705
35: 6 to them ye shall add f and two cities. H705
7 to the Levites *shall be* f and eight cities: H705
Dt 2: 7 wilderness: these f years the LORD thy H705
8: 2 thy God led thee these f years in the H705
4 neither did thy foot swell, these f years. H705
9: 9 in the mount f days and forty nights, H705
9 forty days and f nights, I neither did H705
9:11 And it came to pass at the end of f days H705
11 of forty days and f nights, *that* the LORD H705
18 as at the first, f days and forty nights: H705
18 forty days and f nights: I did neither H705
25 Thus I fell down before the LORD f days H705
25 forty days and f nights, as I fell down H705
10:10 to the first time, f days and forty nights; H705
10 forty days and f nights; and the LORD H705
25: 3 F stripes he may give him, *and* not H705
29: 5 And I have led you f years in the H705
Jos 4:13 About f thousand prepared for war H705
5: 6 For the children of Israel walked f years H705
14: 7 F years old *was* I when Moses the H705
10 as he said, these f and five years, even H705
21:41 f and eight cities with their suburbs. H705
Jdg 3:11 And the land had rest f years. And H705
5: 8 spear seen among f thousand in Israel? H705
31 his might. And the land had rest f years. H705
8:28 quietness f years in the days of Gideon. H705
12: 6 of the Ephraimites f and two thousand. H705
14 And he had f sons and thirty nephews, H705
13: 1 into the hand of the Philistines f years. H705
1Sa 4:18 heavy. And he had judged Israel f years. H705
17:16 evening, and presented himself f days. H705
2Sa 2:10 Ish-bosheth Saul's son *was* f years old H705
5: 4 began to reign, *and* he reigned f years. H705
10:18 chariots of the Syrians, and f thousand H705
15: 7 And it came to pass after f years, that H705
1Ki 2:11 over Israel *were* f years: seven years H705
4:26 And Solomon had f thousand stalls of H705
6:17 *is*, the temple before it, was f cubits *long*. H705
7: 3 that *lay* on f five pillars, fifteen *in* a row. H705
38 laver contained f baths: *and* every laver H705
11:42 in Jerusalem over all Israel *was* f years. H705
14:21 Rehoboam *was* f and one years old H705
15:10 And f and one years reigned he in H705
19: 8 of that meat f days and forty nights H705
8 f nights unto Horeb the mount of God. H705
2Ki 2:24 and tare f and two children of them. H705
8: 9 thing of Damascus, f camels' burden, H705
10:14 and f men; neither left he any of them. H705
12: 1 began to reign; and f years reigned he in H705
14:23 in Samaria, *and reigned* f and one years. H705
1Ch 5:18 in war, *were* four and f thousand seven H705
12:36 forth to battle, expert in war, f thousand. H705
19:18 *in* chariots, and f thousand footmen, H705
29:27 over Israel *was* f years; seven years H705
2Ch 9:30 in Jerusalem over all Israel f years. H705
12:13 *was* one and f years old when he began H705
22: 2 F and two years old *was* Ahaziah when H705
24: 1 and he reigned f years in Jerusalem. His H705
Ezr 2: 8 The children of Zattu, nine hundred f H705
10 The children of Bani, six hundred f and H705
24 The children of Azmaveth, f and two. H705
25 seven hundred and f and three. H705
34 The children of Jericho, three hundred f H705
38 a thousand two hundred f and seven. H705
64 together *was* f and two H702+H7239
66 six; their mules, two hundred f and five; H705
Neh 5:15 and wine, beside f shekels of silver; yea, H705
7:13 The children of Zattu, eight hundred f H705
15 The children of Binnui, six hundred f H705
28 The men of Beth-azmaveth, f and two. H705
29 and Beeroth, seven hundred f and three. H705
36 The children of Jericho, three hundred f H705
41 a thousand two hundred f and seven. H705
44 of Asaph, an hundred f and eight. H705
62 of Nekoda, six hundred f and two. H705
66 together *was* f and two H702+H7239
67 had two hundred f and five singing men H705
68 six: their mules, two hundred f and five: H705
9:21 Yea, f years didst thou sustain them in H705
11:13 two hundred f and two: and Amashai H705
Job 42:16 After this lived Job an hundred and f H705
Ps 95:10 F years long was I grieved with *this* H705
Jer 52:30 seven hundred f and five persons: all H705
Ezk 4: 6 of the house of Judah f days: I have H705
29:11 it, neither shall it be inhabited f years. H705
12 waste shall be desolate f years: and I will H705
13 GOD; At the end of f years will I gather H705
41: 2 f cubits: and the breadth, twenty cubits. H705
46:22 courts joined of f *cubits* long and thirty H705
Am 2:10 of Egypt, and led you f years through the H705
5:25 the wilderness f years, O house of Israel? H705
Jna 3: 4 cried, and said, Yet f days, and Nineveh H705
Mt 4: 2 And when he had fasted f days and G5062
2 f nights, he was afterward an hungred. G5062
Mk 1:13 And he was there in the wilderness f G5062
Lk 4: 2 Being f days tempted of the devil. And G5062

Jn 2:20 Then said the Jews, F and six years was *G5062*
Act 1: 3 proofs, being seen of them f days, and *G5062*
4:22 For the man was above f years old, on *G5062*
7:23 And when he was full f years old, it *G5063*
30 And when f years were expired, there *G5062*
36 Red sea, and in the wilderness f years. *G5062*
42 *the space of* f years in the wilderness? *G5062*
13:18 And about the time of f years suffered *G5063*
21 of Benjamin, by the space of f years. *G5062*
23:13 And they were more than f which had *G5062*
21 of them more than f men, which have *G5062*
2Co 11:24 Of the Jews five times received I f *G5062*
Heb 3: 9 proved me, and saw my works f years. *G5062*
17 But with whom was he grieved f years? *G5062*
Rev 7: 4 an hundred *and* f *and* four thousand of *G5062*
11: 2 tread under foot f *and* two months. *G5062*
13: 5 him to continue f *and* two months. *G5062*
14: 1 him an hundred f *and* four thousand, *G5062*
3 the hundred *and* f *and* four thousand, *G5062*
21:17 an hundred *and* f *and* four cubits, *G5062*

FORTY'S
Gen 18:29 And he said, I will not do *it* for f sake. H705

FORTY-THOUSAND See FORTY and THOUSAND.

FORUM
Act 28:15 meet us as far as Appii f, and The three *G5410*

FORWARD
Gen 26:13 And the man waxed great, and went f, H1980
Ex 14:15 the children of Israel, that they go f: H5265
Nu 1:51 And when the tabernacle setteth f, the H5265
2:17 shall set f with the camp of the H5265
17 so shall they set f, every man in his H5265
24 And they shall go f in the third rank. H5265
34 and so they set f, every one after their H5265
4: 5 And when the camp setteth f, Aaron H5265
15 the camp is to set f; after that, the sons H5265
10: 5 that lie on the east parts shall go f. H5265
17 of Merari set f, bearing the tabernacle. H5265
18 camp of Reuben set f according to their H5265
21 And the Kohathites set f, bearing the H5265
22 of Ephraim set f according to their H5265
25 of Dan set f, *which was* the rearward H5265
28 to their armies, when they set f. H5265
35 And it came to pass, when the ark set f, H5265
21:10 And the children of Israel set f, and H5265
22: 1 And the children of Israel set f, and H5265
32:19 yonder side Jordan, or f; because our H1973
Jdg 9:44 with him, rushed f, and stood in the H6584
1Sa 10: 3 Then shalt thou go on f from thence, H1973
16:13 from that day f. So Samuel rose up, H4605
18: 9 Saul eyed David from that day and f. H1973
30:25 And it was *so* from that day f, that he H4605
2Ki 3:24 but they went f smiting the Moabites, H5221
4:24 Drive, and go f; slack not *thy* riding for
20: 9 f ten degrees, or go back ten degrees? H1980
1Ch 23: 4 *were* to set f the work of the house H5329
2Ch 34:12 to set *it* f; and *other of* the Levites, H5329
Ezr 3: 8 f the work of the house of the LORD. H5329
9 together, to set f the workmen in the H5329
Job 23: 8 Behold, I go f, but he *is* not *there*; and H6924
30:13 They mar my path, they set f my H3276
Jer 7:24 heart, and went backward, and not f. H6440
Ezk 1: 9 went; they went every one straight f. H6440
12 And they went every one straight f: H6440
10:22 they went every one straight f. H6440
39:22 LORD their God from that day and f. H1973
43:27 eighth day, and *so* f, the priests shall H1973
Zec 1:15 and they helped f the affliction.
Mk 14:35 And he went f a little, and fell on the *G4281*
Act 19:33 the Jews putting him f. And Alexander *G4261*
2Co 8:10 only to do, but also to be f a year ago. *G2309*
17 f, of his own accord he went unto you. *G4707*
Gal 2:10 poor; the same which I also was f to do. *G4704*
3Jn 6 if thou bring f on their journey after *G4311*

FORWARDNESS
2Co 8: 8 by occasion of the f of others, and to *G4710*
9: 2 For I know the f of your mind, for *G4288*

FOUGHT
Ex 17: 8 Then came Amalek, and f with Israel H3898
10 said to him, and f with Amalek: and H3898
Nu 21: 1 the spies; then he f against Israel, and H3898
23 he came to Jahaz, and f against Israel. H3898
26 who had f against the former king H3898
Jos 10:14 of a man: for the LORD f for Israel. H3898
10:29 unto Libnah, and f against Libnah: H3898
31 encamped against it, and f against it: H3898
34 encamped against it, and f against it: H3898
36 unto Hebron; and they f against it: H3898
38 with him, to Debir; and f against it: H3898
42 the LORD God of Israel f for Israel. H3898
23: 3 your God *is* he that hath f for you. H3898
24: 8 Jordan; and they f with you: and I gave H3898
11 the men of Jericho f against you, the H3898
Jdg 1: 5 in Bezek: and they f against him, and H3898
8 Now the children of Judah had f H3898
5:19 The kings came *and* f, then fought the H3898
19 The kings came *and* fought, then f the H3898
20 They f from heaven; the stars in their H3898
20 stars in their courses f against Sisera. H3898
9:17 (For my father f for you, and H3898
39 of Shechem, and f with Abimelech. H3898
45 And Abimelech f against the city all H3898
52 the tower, and f against it, and went H3898
11:20 pitched in Jahaz, and f against Israel. H3898
12: 4 of Gilead, and f with Ephraim: and H3898
1Sa 4:10 And the Philistines f, and Israel was H3898
12: 9 king of Moab, and they f against them. H3898
14:47 over Israel, and f against all his H3898
19: 8 went out, and f with the Philistines, H3898
23: 5 to Keilah, and f with the Philistines, H3898
31: 1 Now the Philistines f against Israel: H3898
2Sa 2:28 no more, neither f they any more. H3898
8:10 because he had f against Hadadezer, H3898
10:17 in array against David, and f with him. H3898
11:17 And the men of the city went out, and f H3898
12:26 And Joab f against Rabbah of the H3898
27 and said, I have f against Rabbah, and H3898
29 to Rabbah, and f against it, and took it. H3898
21:15 with him, and f against the Philistines: H3898
2Ki 8:29 Ramah, when he f against Hazael king H3898
9:15 him, when he f with Hazael king of H3898
12:17 Syria went up, and f against Gath, and H3898
13:12 wherewith he f against Amaziah king H3898
14:15 his might, and how he f with Amaziah H3898
1Ch 10: 1 Now the Philistines f against Israel; H3898
18:10 because he had f against Hadarezer, H3898
19:17 against the Syrians, they f with him. H3898
18 *men which f in* chariots, and forty H3898
2Ch 20:29 LORD f against the enemies of Israel. H3898
22: 6 Ramah, when he f with Hazael king of H3898
27: 5 He f also with the king of the H3898
Ps 109: 3 and f against me without a cause. H3898
Isa 20: 1 and f against Ashdod, and took it; H3898
63:10 be their enemy, *and* he f against them. H3898
Jer 34: 1 and all the people, f against Jerusalem, H3898
7 When the king of Babylon's army f H3898
Zec 14: 3 as when he f in the day of battle. H3898
12 people that have f against Jerusalem; H6633
1Co 15:32 If after the manner of men I have f with *G2341*
2Ti 4: 7 I have f a good fight, I have finished *my* *G75*
Rev 12: 7 and his angels f against the dragon; *G4170*
7 and the dragon f and his angels, *G4170*

FOUL
Job 16:16 My face is f with weeping, and on my H2560
Ezk 34:18 ye must f the residue with your feet? H7515
Mt 16: 3 And in the morning, *It will be* f weather *G5494*
Mk 9:25 he rebuked the f spirit, saying unto him, *G169*
Rev 18: 2 the hold of every f spirit, and a cage of *G169*

FOULED
Ezk 34:19 that which ye have f with your feet. H4833

FOULEDST
Ezk 32: 2 waters with thy feet, and f their rivers. H7515

FOUND
Gen 2:20 there was not f an help meet for him. H4672
6: 8 But Noah f grace in the eyes of the H4672
8: 9 But the dove f no rest for the sole of her H4672
11: 2 the east, that they f a plain in the land H4672
16: 7 And the angel of the LORD f her by a H4672
18: 3 And said, My Lord, if now I have f H4672
29 there shall be forty f there. And he said, H4672
30 shall thirty be f there. And he said, I H4672
31 shall be twenty f there. And he said, I H4672
32 ten shall be f there. And he said, I H4672
19:19 Behold now, thy servant hath f grace in H4672
26:19 and f there a well of springing water. H4672
32 and said unto him, We have f water. H4672
27:20 *is it* that thou hast f *it* so quickly, my H4672
30:14 harvest, and f mandrakes in the field, H4672
27 I pray thee, if I have f favour in thine H4672
Gen 31:33 tents; but he f *them* not. Then went H4672
34 searched all the tent, but f *them* not. H4672
35 And he searched, but f not the images. H4672
37 what hast thou f of all thy household H4672
33:10 thee, if now I have f grace in thy sight, H4672
36:24 *was that* Anah that f the mules in the H4672
37:15 And a certain man f him, and, behold, H4672
17 his brethren, and f them in Dothan. H4672
32 said, This have we f: know now whether H4672
38:20 the woman's hand: but he f her not. H4672
23 I sent this kid, and thou hast not f her. H4672
39: 4 And Joseph f grace in his sight, and he H4672
44: 8 Behold, the money, which we f in our H4672
9 of thy servants it be f, both let him die, H4672
10 words: he with whom it is f shall be my H4672
12 and the cup was f in Benjamin's sack. H4672
16 God hath f out the iniquity of thy H4672
16 we, and *he* also with whom the cup is f. H4672
17 whose hand the cup is f, he shall be my H4672
47:14 money that was f in the land of Egypt, H4672
29 him, If now I have f grace in thy sight, H4672
50: 4 If now I have f grace in your eyes, H4672
Ex 9:19 which shall be f in the field, and shall H4672
12:19 Seven days shall there be no leaven f in H4672
15:22 days in the wilderness, and f no water. H4672
16:27 day for to gather, and they f none. H4672
21:16 him, or if he be f in his hand, he shall H4672
22: 2 If a thief be f breaking up, and be H4672
4 If the theft be certainly f in his hand H4672
7 if the thief be f, let him pay double. H4672
8 If the thief be not f, then the master of H4672
33:12 and thou hast also f grace in my sight. H4672
13 Now therefore, I pray thee, if I have f H4672
16 thy people have f grace in thy sight? *is* H4672
17 for thou hast f grace in my sight, and H4672
34: 9 And he said, If now I have f grace in H4672
35:23 And every man, with whom was f blue, H4672
24 with whom was f shittim wood for any H4672
Lev 6: 3 Or have f that which was lost, and lieth H4672
4 him to keep, or the lost thing which he f, H4672
Nu 11:11 have I not f favour in thy sight, H4672
15 of hand, if I have f favour in thy sight; H4672
15:32 wilderness, they f a man that gathered H4672
33 And they that f him gathering sticks H4672
32: 5 Wherefore, said they, if we have f grace H4672
Dt 17: 2 If there be f among you, within any of H4672
18:10 There shall not be f among you *any one* H4672
20:11 all the people *that is* f therein shall be H4672
21: 1 If *one* be f slain in the land which the H4672
22: 3 hath lost, and thou hast f, shalt thou do H4672
14 when I came to her, I f her not a maid: H4672
17 *her*, saying, I f not thy daughter a H4672
20 *of* virginity be not f for the damsel: H4672
22 If a man be f lying with a woman H4672
27 For he f her in the field, *and* the H4672
28 on her, and lie with her, and they be f; H4672
24: 1 because he hath f some uncleanness in H4672
7 If a man be f stealing any of his H4672
32:10 He f him in a desert land, and in the H4672
33:29 enemies shall be f liars unto thee; and
Jos 2:22 throughout all the way, but f *them* not. H4672
10:17 kings are f hid in a cave at Makkedah. H4672
Jdg 1: 5 And they f Adoni-bezek in Bezek: and H4672
6:17 And he said unto him, If now I have f H4672
14:18 my heifer, ye had not f out my riddle. H4672
15:15 And he f a new jawbone of an ass, and H4672
21:12 And they f among the inhabitants of H4672
Ru 2:10 him, Why have I f grace in thine eyes, H4672
1Sa 9: 4 Shalisha, but they f *them* not: then they H4672
4 of the Benjamites, but they f *them* not. H4672
11 to the city, they f young maidens going H4672
20 them; for they are f. And on whom *is* all H4672
10: 2 to seek are f: and, lo, thy father hath H4672
16 the asses were f. But of the matter of H4672
21 they sought him, he could not be f. H4672
12: 5 that ye have not f ought in my hand. H4672
13:19 Now there was no smith f throughout H4672
22 sword nor spear f in the hand of any of H4672
22 and with Jonathan his son was there f. H4672
14:30 which they f? for had there not been H4672
16:22 me; for he hath f favour in my sight. H4672
20: 3 that I have f grace in thine eyes; H4672
29 and now, if I have f favour in thine H4672
25:28 evil hath not been f in thee *all* thy days. H4672
27: 5 If I have now f grace in thine eyes, H4672
29: 3 years, and I have f no fault in him since H4672
6 for I have not f evil in thee since the H4672
8 what hast thou f in thy servant so long H4672
30:11 And they f an Egyptian in the field, and H4672

1Sa 31: 8 the slain, that they f Saul and his three H4672
2Sa 7:27 hath thy servant f in his heart to pray H4672
14:22 that I have f grace in thy sight, my H4672
17:12 where he shall be f, and we will light H4672
13 there be not one small stone f there. H4672
1Ki 1: 3 of Israel, and f Abishag a Shunammite, H4672
52 shall be f in him, he shall die. H4672
7:47 was the weight of the brass f out. H2713
11:19 And Hadad f great favour in the sight H4672
29 the Shilonite f him in the way; and H4672
13:14 And went after the man of God, and f H4672
28 And he went and f his carcase cast in H4672
14:13 in him there is f *some* good thing H4672
18:10 and nation, that they f thee not. H4672
19:19 So he departed thence, and f Elisha the H4672
20:36 from him, a lion f him, and slew him. H4672
37 Then he f another man, and said, H4672
21:20 And Ahab said to Elijah, Hast thou f H4672
20 answered, I have f *thee:* because thou H4672
2Ki 2:17 they sought three days, but f him not. H4672
4:39 to gather herbs, and f a wild vine, and H4672
9:35 And they went to bury her: but they f H4672
12: 5 wheresoever any breach shall be f. H4672
10 that was f in the house of the LORD. H4672
18 the gold *that was* f in the treasures of H4672
14:14 vessels that were f in the house of the H4672
16: 8 and gold that was f in the house of the H4672
17: 4 And the king of Assyria f conspiracy in H4672
18:15 the silver that was f in the house of the H4672
19: 8 So Rab-shakeh returned, and f the king H4672
20:13 and all that was f in his treasures: there H4672
22: 8 the scribe, I have f the book of the law H4672
9 the money that was f in the house, and H4672
13 of this book that is f: for great *is* the H4672
23: 2 which was f in the house of the LORD. H4672
24 the priest f in the house of the LORD. H4672
25:19 which were f in the city, and the H4672
19 of the land *that were* f in the city: H4672
1Ch 4:40 And they f fat pasture and good, and H4672
41 that were f there, and destroyed H4672
10: 8 the slain, that they f Saul and his sons H4672
17:25 hath f *in his heart* to pray before thee. H4672
20: 2 off his head, and f it to weigh a talent H4672
24: 4 And there were more chief men f of the H4672
26:31 and there were f among them mighty H4672
28: 9 him, he will be f of thee; but if thou H4672
29: 8 stones were f gave *them* to the treasure H4672
2Ch 2:17 and they were f an hundred and fifty H4672
4:18 weight of the brass could not be f out. H2713
15: 2 seek him, he will be f of you; but if ye H4672
4 and sought him, he was f of them. H4672
15 desire; and he was f of them: and the H4672
19: 3 Nevertheless there are good things f in H4672
20:25 the spoil of them, they f among them in H4672
21:17 that was f in the king's house, H4672
22: 8 of Ahab, and f the princes of Judah, H4672
25: 5 and above, and f them three hundred H4672
24 vessels that were f in the house of God H4672
29:16 that they f in the temple of the H4672
34:14 Hilkiah the priest f a book of the law of H4672
15 the scribe, I have f the book of the law H4672
17 money that was f in the house of the H4672
21 of the book that is f: for great *is* the H4672
30 that was f in the house of the LORD. H4672
36: 8 that which was f in him, behold, they H4672
Ezr 2:62 but they were not f: therefore were they, H4672
4:19 made, and it is f that this city of old H7912
6: 2 And there was f at Achmetha, in the H7912
8:15 and f there none of the sons of Levi. H4672
10:18 the priests there were f that had taken H4672
Neh 2: 5 if thy servant have f favour in thy sight,
5: 8 their peace, and f nothing *to answer.* H4672
7: 5 by genealogy. And I f a register of the H4672
5 up at the first, and f written therein, H4672
64 but it was not f: therefore were they, H4672
8:14 And they f written in the law which the H4672
13: 1 and therein was f written, that the H4672
Est 2:23 the matter, it was f out; therefore they H4672
5: 8 If I have f favour in the sight of the H4672
6: 2 And it was f written, that Mordecai H4672
7: 3 and said, If I have f favour in thy sight, H4672
8: 5 king, and if I have f favour in his sight, H4672
Job 19:28 seeing the root of the matter is f in me? H4672
20: 8 and shall not be f: yea, he shall be H4672
28:12 But where shall wisdom be f? and where H4672
13 neither is it f in the land of the living. H4672
31:29 me, or lifted up myself when evil f him: H4672
32: 3 because they had f no answer, and *yet* H4672
13 Lest ye should say, We have f out H4672

Job 33:24 down to the pit: I have f a ransom. H4672
42:15 And in all the land were no women f *so* H4672
Ps 32: 6 thou mayest be f: surely in the floods H4672
36: 2 until his iniquity be f to be hateful. H4672
37:36 yea, I sought him, but he could not be f. H4672
69:20 none; and for comforters, but I f none. H4672
76: 5 of the men of might have f their hands. H4672
84: 3 Yea, the sparrow hath f an house, and H4672
89:20 I have f David my servant; with my H4672
107: 4 solitary way; they f no city to dwell in. H4672
116: 3 hold upon me: I f trouble and sorrow. H4672
132: 6 Lo, we heard of it at Ephratah: we f it H4672
Prv 6:31 But *if* he be f, he shall restore sevenfold; H4672
7:15 to seek thy face, and I have f thee. H4672
10:13 wisdom is f: but a rod *is* for the back H4672
16:31 *if* it be f in the way of righteousness. H4672
24:14 when thou hast f *it,* then there shall be H4672
25:16 Hast thou f honey? eat so much as is H4672
30: 6 lest he reprove thee, and thou be f a liar. H4672
10 lest he curse thee, and thou be f guilty.
Ecc 7:27 Behold, this have I f, saith the preacher, H4672
28 a thousand have I f; but a woman H4672
28 a woman among all those have I not f. H4672
29 Lo, this only have I f, that God hath H4672
9:15 Now there was f in it a poor wise man, H4672
Song 3: 1 loveth: I sought him, but I f him not. H4672
2 loveth: I sought him, but I f him not. H4672
3 The watchmen that go about the city f H4672
4 from them, but I f him whom my soul H4672
5: 7 about the city f me, they smote me, H4672
8:10 was I in his eyes as one that f favour. H4672
Isa 10:10 As my hand hath f the kingdoms of the H4672
14 And my hand hath f as a nest the H4672
13:15 Every one that is f shall be thrust H4672
22: 3 archers: all that are f in thee are bound H4672
30:14 there shall not be f in the bursting of it H4672
35: 9 it shall not be f there; but the redeemed H4672
37: 8 So Rabshakeh returned, and f the king H4672
39: 2 and all that was f in his treasures: there H4672
51: 3 and gladness shall be f therein, H4672
55: 6 Seek ye the LORD while he may be f, H4672
57:10 is no hope: thou hast f the life of thine H4672
65: 1 not *for me;* I am f of *them that* sought H4672
8 As the new wine is f in the cluster, and H4672
Jer 2: 5 have your fathers f in me, that they are H4672
26 As the thief is ashamed when he is f, so H4672
34 Also in thy skirts is f the blood of the H4672
34 f it by secret search, but upon all these. H4672
5:26 For among my people are f wicked H4672
11: 9 A conspiracy is f among the men of H4672
14: 3 came to the pits, *and* f no water; they H4672
15:16 Thy words were f, and I did eat them; H4672
23:11 I f their wickedness, saith the LORD. H4672
29:14 And I will be f of you, saith the LORD: H4672
31: 2 *were* left of the sword f grace in the H4672
41: 3 that were f there, *and* the men of war. H4672
8 But ten men were f among them that H4672
12 of Nethaniah, and f him by the great H4672
48:27 unto thee? was he f among thieves? for H4672
50: 7 All that f them have devoured them: H4672
20 and they shall not be f: for I will pardon H4672
24 not aware: thou art f, and also caught, H4672
52:25 which were f in the city; and the H4672
25 that were f in the midst of the city. H4672
Lam 2:16 looked for; we have f, we have seen *it.* H4672
Ezk 22:30 I should not destroy it: but I f none. H4672
26:21 never be f again, saith the Lord GOD. H4672
28:15 wast created, till iniquity was f in thee. H4672
Dan 1:19 among them all was f none like Daniel, H4672
20 of them, he f them ten times better H4672
2:25 thus unto him, I have f a man of the H7912
35 that no place was f for them: and the H7912
5:11 of the gods, was f in him; whom the H7912
12 of doubts, were f in the same Daniel, H7912
14 and excellent wisdom is f in thee. H7912
27 in the balances, and art f wanting. H7912
6: 4 was there any error or fault f in him. H7912
11 Then these men assembled, and f H7912
22 innocency was f in me; and also before H7912
23 of hurt was f upon him, because H7912
11:19 he shall stumble and fall, and not be f. H4672
12: 1 one that shall be f written in the book. H4672
Hos 9:10 I f Israel like grapes in the wilderness; I H4672
10: 2 now shall they be f faulty: he shall break
12: 4 unto him: he f him *in* Beth-el, and H4672
8 rich, I have f me out substance: *in* H4672
14: 8 a green fir tree. From me is thy fruit f. H4672
Jna 1: 3 down to Joppa; and he f a ship going to H4672
Mic 1:13 transgressions of Israel were f in thee. H4672

Zep 3:13 tongue be f in their mouth: for they H4672
Zec 10:10 and *place* shall not be f for them. H4672
Mal 2: 6 iniquity was not f in his lips: he walked H4672
Mt 1:18 she was f with child of the Holy Ghost. *G2147*
2: 8 and when ye have f *him,* bring me *G2147*
8:10 not f so great faith, no, not in Israel. *G2147*
13:44 when a man hath f, he hideth, and for *G2147*
46 Who, when he had f one pearl of great *G2147*
18:28 But the same servant went out, and f *G2147*
20: 6 he went out, and f others standing idle, *G2147*
21:19 he came to it, and f nothing thereon, *G2147*
22:10 as many as they f, both bad and good: *G2147*
26:43 And he came and f them asleep again: *G2147*
60 But f none: yea, though many false *G2147*
60 came, *yet* f they none. At the last
27:32 And as they came out, they f a man of *G2147*
Mk 1:37 And when they had f him, they said *G2147*
7: 2 say, with unwashen, hands, they f fault.
30 to her house, she f the devil gone out, *G2147*
11: 4 And they went their way, and f the colt *G2147*
13 he came to it, he f nothing but leaves; *G2147*
14:16 into the city, and f as he had said unto *G2147*
40 And when he returned, he f them *G2147*
55 Jesus to put him to death; and f none. *G2147*
Lk 1:30 Mary: for thou hast f favour with God. *G2147*
2:16 And they came with haste, and f Mary, *G429*
45 And when they f him not, they turned *G2147*
46 three days they f him in the temple, *G2147*
4:17 he f the place where it was written, *G2147*
7: 9 not f so great faith, no, not in Israel. *G2147*
10 f the servant whole that had been sick. *G2147*
8:35 came to Jesus, and f the man, out of *G2147*
9:36 past, Jesus was f alone. And they kept *G2147*
13: 6 and sought fruit thereon, and f none. *G2147*
15: 5 And when he hath f *it,* he layeth *it* on *G2147*
6 for I have f my sheep which was lost. *G2147*
9 And when she hath f *it,* she calleth *her* *G2147*
9 for I have f the piece which I had lost. *G2147*
24 and is f. And they began to be merry. *G2147*
32 is alive again; and was lost, and is f. *G2147*
17:18 There are not f that returned to give *G2147*
19:32 and f even as he had said unto them. *G2147*
22:13 And they went, and f as he had said *G2147*
45 he f them sleeping for sorrow, *G2147*
23: 2 him, saying, We f this *fellow* perverting *G2147*
14 before you, have f no fault in this man *G2147*
22 he done? I have f no cause of death in *G2147*
24: 2 And they f the stone rolled away from *G2147*
3 And they entered in, and f not the body *G2147*
23 And when they f not his body, they *G2147*
24 to the sepulchre, and f *it* even so as the *G2147*
33 to Jerusalem, and f the eleven gathered *G2147*
Jn 1:41 him, We have f the Messias, which *G2147*
45 him, We have f him, of whom Moses *G2147*
2:14 And f in the temple those that sold *G2147*
6:25 And when they had f him on the other *G2147*
9:35 and when he had f him, he said unto *G2147*
11:17 Then when Jesus came, he f that he had *G2147*
12:14 And Jesus, when he had f a young ass, *G2147*
Act 5:10 men came in, and f her dead, and, *G2147*
22 But when the officers came, and f them *G2147*
23 Saying, The prison truly f we shut with *G2147*
23 we had opened, we f no man within. *G2147*
39 haply ye be f even to fight against God. *G2147*
7:11 and our fathers f no sustenance. *G2147*
46 Who f favour before God, and desired *G2147*
8:40 But Philip was f at Azotus: and passing *G2147*
9: 2 that if he f any of this way, whether *G2147*
33 And there he f a certain man named *G2147*
10:27 and f many that were come together. *G2147*
11:26 And when he had f him, he brought *G2147*
12:19 for him, and f him not, he examined *G2147*
13: 6 unto Paphos, they f a certain sorcerer, *G2147*
22 and said, I have f David the *son* of *G2147*
28 And though they f no cause of death *in* *G2147*
17: 6 And when they f them not, they drew *G2147*
23 your devotions, I f an altar with this *G2147*
18: 2 And f a certain Jew named Aquila, *G2147*
19:19 and f *it* fifty thousand *pieces* of silver. *G2147*
24: 5 For we have f this man *a* pestilent *G2147*
12 And they neither f me in the temple *G2147*
18 Whereupon certain Jews from Asia f *G2147*
20 say, if they have f any evil doing in me, *G2147*
25:25 But when I f that he had committed *G2638*
27: 6 And there the centurion f a ship of *G2147*
28 And sounded, and f *it* twenty fathoms: *G2147*
28 sounded again, and f *it* fifteen fathoms. *G2147*
28:14 Where we f brethren, and were desired *G2147*
Ro 4: 1 father, as pertaining to the flesh, hath f? *G2147*

Ro 7:10 *ordained* to life, I f *to be* unto death. G2147
10:20 and saith, I was f of them that sought G2147
1Co 4: 2 in stewards, that a man be f faithful. G2147
15:15 Yea, and we are f false witnesses of G2147
2Co 2:13 I had no rest in my spirit, because I f G2147
5: 3 being clothed we shall not be f naked. G2147
7:14 which *I made* before Titus, is f a truth. G1096
11:12 they glory, they may be f even as we. G2147
12:20 and *that* I shall be f unto you such as ye G2147
Gal 2:17 ourselves also are f sinners, *is* therefore G2147
Php 2: 8 And being f in fashion as a man, he G2147
3: 9 And be f in him, not having mine own G2147
1Ti 3:10 the office of a deacon, being *f* blameless.
2Ti 1:17 me out very diligently, and f *me*. G2147
Heb 11: 5 death; and was not f, because God had G2147
12:17 was rejected: for he f no place of G2147
1Pt 1: 7 with fire, might be f unto praise and G2147
2:22 Who did no sin, neither was guile f in G2147
2Pt 3:14 that ye may be f of him in peace, G2147
2Jn 4 I rejoiced greatly that I f of thy children G2147
Rev 2: 2 and are not, and hast f them liars: G2147
3: 2 not f thy works perfect before God. G2147
5: 4 no man was f worthy to open and G2147
12: 8 was their place f any more in heaven. G2147
14: 5 And in their mouth was f no guile: for G2147
16:20 away, and the mountains were not f. G2147
18:21 down, and shall be f no more at all. G2147
22 *he be*, shall be f any more in thee; and G2147
24 And in her was f the blood of prophets, G2147
20:11 and there was f no place for them. G2147
15 And whosoever was not f written in the G2147

FOUNDATION
Ex 9:18 since the f thereof even until now. H3117
Jos 6:26 Jericho: he shall lay the f thereof in his H3245
1Ki 5:17 hewed stones, to lay the f of the house. H3245
6:37 In the fourth year was the f of the H3245
7: 9 even from the f unto the coping, and H4527
10 And the f *was of* costly stones, even H3245
16:34 Jericho: he laid the f thereof in Abiram H3245
2Ch 8:16 unto the day of the f of the house of the H4143
23: 5 at the gate of the f: and all the people H3247
31: 7 began to lay the f of the heaps, and H3245
Ezr 3: 6 the LORD. But the f of the temple of the H3245
10 And when the builders laid the f of the H3245
11 the f of the house of the LORD was laid. H3245
12 house, when the f of this house was H3245
5:16 *and* laid the f of the house of God which H787
Job 4:19 of clay, whose f *is* in the dust, *which* H3247
22:16 whose f was overflown with a flood: H3247
Ps 87: 1 His f *is* in the holy mountains. H3248
102:25 Of old hast thou laid the f of the earth: H3245
137: 7 Rase *it*, rase *it*, *even* to the f thereof. H3247
Prv 10:25 but the righteous *is* an everlasting f. H3247
Isa 28:16 I lay in Zion for a f a stone, a tried H3248
16 *stone*, a sure f: he that believeth shall H4143
44:28 and to the temple, Thy f shall be laid. H3245
48:13 Mine hand also hath laid the f of the H3245
Ezk 13:14 ground, so that the f thereof shall be H3247
Hab 3:13 discovering the f unto the neck. Selah. H3247
Hag 2:18 the day that the f of the LORD'S temple H3245
Zec 4: 9 have laid the f of this house; his hands H3245
8: 9 in the day *that* the f of the house of the H3245
12: 1 and layeth the f of the earth, and H3245
Mt 13:35 kept secret from the f of the world. G2602
25:34 for you from the f of the world: G2602
Lk 6:48 deep, and laid the f on a rock: and G2310
49 that without a f built an house upon G2310
11:50 was shed from the f of the world, may G2602
14:29 Lest haply, after he hath laid the f, and G2310
Jn 17:24 lovedst me before the f of the world. G2602
Ro 15:20 I should build upon another man's f: G2310
1Co 3:10 I have laid the f, and another buildeth G2310
11 For other f can no man lay than that is G2310
12 Now if any man build upon this f gold, G2310
Eph 1: 4 in him before the f of the world, that we G2602
2:20 And are built upon the f of the apostles G2310
1Ti 6:19 themselves a good f against the time to G2310
2Ti 2:19 Nevertheless the f of God standeth G2310
Heb 1:10 hast laid the f of the earth; and the G2311
4: 3 were finished from the f of the world. G2602
6: 1 laying again the f of repentance from G2310
9:26 suffered since the f of the world: but G2602
1Pt 1:20 before the f of the world, but was G2602
Rev 13: 8 the Lamb slain from the f of the world. G2602
17: 8 of life from the f of the world, when G2602
21:19 stones. The first f *was* jasper; the G2310

FOUNDATIONS
Dt 32:22 and set on fire the f of the mountains. H4144
2Sa 22: 8 and trembled; the f of heaven moved H4146
16 sea appeared, the f of the world were H4146
Ezr 4:12 set up the walls *thereof*, and joined the f. H787
6: 3 and let the f thereof be strongly laid; H787
Job 38: 4 Where wast thou when I laid the f of H3245
6 Whereupon are the f thereof fastened? or H134
Ps 11: 3 If the f be destroyed, what can the H8356
18: 7 and trembled; the f also of the hills H4146
15 were seen, and the f of the world were H4146
82: 5 all the f of the earth are out of course. H4144
104: 5 *Who* laid the f of the earth, *that* it H4349
Prv 8:29 when he appointed the f of the earth: H4144
Isa 16: 7 shall howl: for the f of Kir-hareseth shall H808
24:18 open, and the f of the earth do shake. H4146
40:21 not understood from the f of the earth? H4146
51:13 and laid the f of the earth; and hast H3245
16 and lay the f of the earth, and say H3245
54:11 colours, and lay thy f with sapphires. H3245
58:12 thou shalt raise up the f of many H4146
Jer 31:37 be measured, and the f of the earth H4146
50:15 given her hand: her f are fallen, her walls H803
51:26 nor a stone for f; but thou shalt be H4146
Lam 4:11 and it hath devoured the f thereof. H3247
Ezk 30: 4 and her f shall be broken down. H3247
41: 8 round about: the f of the side chambers H4328
Mic 1: 6 valley, and I will discover the f thereof. H3247
6: 2 and ye strong f of the earth: for the H4146
Act 16:26 so that the f of the prison were shaken: G2310
Heb 11:10 For he looked for a city which hath f, G2310
Rev 21:14 And the wall of the city had twelve f, G2310
19 And the f of the wall of the city *were* G2310

FOUNDED
Ps 24: 2 For he hath f it upon the seas, and H3245
89:11 the fulness thereof, thou hast f them. H3245
104: 8 the place which thou hast f for them. H3245
119:152 of old that thou hast f them for ever. H3245
Prv 3:19 The LORD by wisdom hath f the earth; H3245
Isa 14:32 the LORD hath f Zion, and the poor of H3245
23:13 *till* the Assyrian f it for them that dwell H3245
Am 9: 6 the heaven, and hath f his troop in the H3245
Mt 7:25 and it fell not: for it was f upon a rock. G2311
Lk 6:48 not shake it: for it was f upon a rock. G2311

FOUNDER
Jdg 17: 4 gave them to the f, who made thereof a H6884
Jer 6:29 of the fire; the f melteth in vain: for H6884
10: 9 of the hands of the f: blue and purple *is* H6884
14 knowledge: every f is confounded by H6884
51:17 knowledge; every f is confounded by H6884

FOUNDEST
Neh 9: 8 And f his heart faithful before thee, and H4672

FOUNTAIN
Gen 16: 7 LORD found her by a f of water in the H5869
7 wilderness, by the f in the way to Shur. H5869
Lev 11:36 Nevertheless a f or pit, *wherein there is* H4599
20:18 hath discovered her f, and she hath H4726
18 uncovered the f of her blood: and both H4726
Dt 33:28 in safety alone: the f of Jacob *shall be* H5869
Jos 15: 9 top of the hill unto the f of the water of H4599
1Sa 29: 1 pitched by a f which *is* in Jezreel. H5869
Neh 2:14 Then I went on to the gate of the f, and H5869
3:15 But the gate of the f repaired Shallun H5869
12:37 And at the f gate, which was over H5869
Ps 36: 9 For with thee *is* the f of life: in thy light H4726
68:26 *even* the Lord, from the f of Israel. H4726
74:15 Thou didst cleave the f and the flood: H4599
114: 8 water, the flint into a f of waters. H4599
Prv 5:18 Let thy f be blessed: and rejoice with H4726
13:14 The law of the wise *is* a f of life, to H4726
14:27 The fear of the LORD *is* a f of life, to H4726
25:26 *is as* a troubled f, and a corrupt spring. H4599
Ecc 12: 6 the f, or the wheel broken at the cistern. H4002
Song 4:12 *my* spouse; a spring shut up, a f sealed. H4599
15 A f of gardens, a well of living waters, H4599
Jer 2:13 forsaken me the f of living waters, *and* H4726
6: 7 As a f casteth out her waters, so she H953
9: 1 and mine eyes a f of tears, that I might H4726
17:13 the LORD, the f of living waters. H4726
Hos 13:15 dry, and his f shall be dried up: he H4599
Joel 3:18 with waters, and a f shall come forth of H4599
Zec 13: 1 In that day there shall be a f opened to H4726
Mk 5:29 And straightway the f of her blood was G4077
Jas 3:11 Doth a f send forth at the same place G4077
12 *can* no f both yield salt water and fresh. G4077
Rev 21: 6 athirst of the f of the water of life freely. G4077

FOUNTAINS
Gen 7:11 day were all the f of the great deep H4599
8: 2 The f also of the deep and the windows H4599
Nu 33: 9 in Elim *were* twelve f of water, and H5869
Dt 8: 7 of brooks of water, of f and depths that H5869
1Ki 18: 5 the land, unto all f of water, and unto H4599
2Ch 32: 3 the waters of the f which *were* without H5869
4 stopped all the f, and the brook that ran H4599
Prv 5:16 Let thy f be dispersed abroad, *and* H4599
8:24 *there were* no f abounding with water. H4599
28 when he strengthened the f of the deep: H5869
Isa 41:18 I will open rivers in high places, and f H4599
Rev 7:17 them unto living f of waters: and God G4077
8:10 of the rivers, and upon the f of waters; G4077
14: 7 earth, and the sea, and the f of waters. G4077
16: 4 f of waters; and they became blood. G4077

FOUR
Gen 2:10 it was parted, and became into f heads. H702
11:13 after he begat Salah f hundred and three H702
15 And Salah lived after he begat Eber f H702
16 And Eber lived f and thirty years, and H702
17 And Eber lived after he begat Peleg f H702
14: 9 Arioch king of Ellasar; f kings with five. H702
15:13 they shall afflict them f hundred years; H702
23:15 the land *is worth* f hundred shekels of H702
16 of the sons of Heth, f hundred shekels of H702
32: 6 meet thee, and f hundred men with him. H702
33: 1 and with him f hundred men. And he H702
47:24 unto Pharaoh, and f parts shall be your H702
Ex 12:40 in Egypt, *was* f hundred and thirty years. H702
41 And it came to pass at the end of the f H702
22: 1 oxen for an ox, and f sheep for a sheep. H702
25:12 And thou shalt cast f rings of gold for it, H702
12 put *them* in the f corners thereof; and H702
26 And thou shalt make for it f rings of H702
26 put the rings in the f corners that *are* on H702
26 corners that *are* on the f feet thereof. H702
34 And in the candlestick *shall be* f bowls H702
26: 2 of one curtain f cubits: and every one H702
8 of one curtain f cubits: and the eleven H702
32 And thou shalt hang it upon f pillars of H702
32 *be of* gold, upon the f sockets of silver. H702
27: 2 of it upon the f corners thereof: his horns H702
4 net shalt thou make f brasen rings in the H702
4 brasen rings in the f corners thereof. H702
16 pillars *shall be* f, and their sockets four. H702
16 pillars *shall be* four, and their sockets f. H702
28:17 of stones, *even* f rows of stones: *the first* H702
36: 9 f cubits: the curtains *were* all of one size. H702
15 *was* thirty cubits, and f cubits *was* the H702
36 And he made thereunto f pillars *of* H702
36 and he cast for them f sockets of silver. H702
37: 3 And he cast for it f rings of gold, *to be set* H702
3 *to be set* by the f corners of it; even two H702
13 And he cast for it f rings of gold, and put H702
13 the rings upon the f corners that *were* in H702
13 corners that *were* in the f feet thereof. H702
20 And in the candlestick *were* f bowls H702
38: 2 And he made the horns thereof on the f H702
5 And he cast f rings for the four ends of H702
5 And he cast four rings for the f ends of H702
19 And their pillars *were* f, and their sockets H702
19 sockets *of* brass f; their hooks *of* silver, H702
29 two thousand and f hundred shekels. H702
39:10 And they set in it f rows of stones: *the* H702
Lev 11:20 All fowls that creep, going upon *all* f, H702
21 that goeth upon *all* f, which have legs H702
23 f feet, *shall be* an abomination unto you. H702
27 that go on *all* f, those *are* unclean unto H702
42 goeth upon *all* f, or whatsoever hath H702
Nu 1:29 fifty and f thousand and four hundred. H702
29 fifty and four thousand and f hundred. H702
31 fifty and seven thousand and f hundred. H702
37 thirty and five thousand and f hundred. H702
43 fifty and three thousand and f hundred. H702
2: 6 fifty and f thousand and four hundred. H702
6 fifty and four thousand and f hundred. H702
8 fifty and seven thousand and f hundred. H702
9 six thousand and f hundred, throughout H702
16 one thousand and f hundred and fifty, H702
23 thirty and five thousand and f hundred. H702
30 fifty and three thousand and f hundred. H702
7: 7 Two wagons and f oxen he gave unto the H702
8 And f wagons and eight oxen he gave H702
85 two thousand and f hundred *shekels*, H702
88 *were* twenty and f bullocks, the rams H702

Nu 25: 9 the plague were twenty and f thousand. H702
26:25 and f thousand and three hundred. H702
43 and f thousand and four hundred. H702
43 and four thousand and f hundred. H702
47 fifty and three thousand and f hundred. H702
50 forty and five thousand and f hundred. H702
Dt 3:11 length thereof, and f cubits the breadth H702
22:12 Thou shalt make thee fringes upon the f H702
Jos 19: 7 Ain, Remmon, and Ether, and Ashan; f H702
21:18 and Almon with her suburbs; f cities. H702
22 Beth-horon with her suburbs; f cities. H702
24 Gath-rimmon with her suburbs; f cities. H702
29 En-gannim with her suburbs; f cities. H702
31 and Rehob with her suburbs; f cities. H702
35 Nahalal with her suburbs; f cities. H702
37 and Mephaath with her suburbs; f cities. H702
39 Jazer with her suburbs; f cities in all. H702
Jdg 9:34 wait against Shechem in f companies. H702
11:40 Jephthah the Gileadite f days in a year. H702
19: 2 and was there f whole months. H702
20: 2 the people of God, f hundred thousand H702
17 were numbered f hundred thousand H702
47 abode in the rock Rimmon f months. H702
21:12 of Jabesh-gilead f hundred young virgins, H702
1Sa 4: 2 army in the field about f thousand men. H702
22: 2 were with him about f hundred men. H702
25:13 after David about f hundred men; and H702
27: 7 Philistines was a full year and f months. H702
30:10 But David pursued, he and f hundred H702
17 a man of them, save f hundred young H702
2Sa 21:20 on every foot six toes, f and twenty in H702
22 These f were born to the giant in Gath, H702
1Ki 6: 1 And it came to pass in the f hundred and H702
7: 2 thirty cubits, upon f rows of cedar H702
19 *were* of lily work in the porch, f cubits. H702
27 And he made ten bases of brass; f cubits H702
27 of one base, and f cubits the breadth H702
30 And every base had f brasen wheels, and H702
30 of brass: and the f corners thereof had H702
32 And under the borders *were* f wheels; H702
34 And *there were* f undersetters to the four H702
34 And *there were* four undersetters to the f H702
38 every laver was f cubits: *and* upon every H702
42 And f hundred pomegranates for the H702
9:28 from thence gold, f hundred and twenty H702
10:26 a thousand and f hundred chariots, and H702
15:33 all Israel in Tirzah, twenty and f years. H702
18:19 the prophets of Baal f hundred and fifty, H702
19 f hundred, which eat at Jezebel's table. H702
22 prophets *are* f hundred and fifty men. H702
33 and said, Fill f barrels with water, and H702
22: 6 together, about f hundred men, and said H702
2Ki 7: 3 And there were f leprous men at the H702
14:13 unto the corner gate, f hundred cubits. H702
1Ch 3: 5 f, of Bath-shua the daughter of Ammiel: H702
5:18 skilful in war, *were* f and forty thousand H702
7: 1 Tola, and Puah, Jashub, and Shimron, f. H702
7 and two thousand and thirty and f. H702
9:24 In f quarters were the porters, toward H702
26 For these Levites, the f chief porters, H702
12:26 Of the children of Levi f thousand and H702
20: 6 and toes *were* f and twenty, six *on each* H702
21: 5 and Judah *was* f hundred threescore H702
20 the angel; and his f sons with him hid H702
23: 4 Of which, twenty and f thousand *were* to H702
5 Moreover f thousand *were* porters; and H702
5 *were* porters; and f thousand praised the H702
10 Beriah. These f *were* the sons of Shimei. H702
12 Amram, Izhar, Hebron, and Uzziel, f. H702
24:18 The three and twentieth to Delaiah, the f H702
25:31 The f and twentieth to Romamti-ezer, H702
26:17 Eastward *were* six Levites, northward f a H702
17 a day, southward f a day, and toward H702
18 At Parbar westward, f at the causeway, H702
27: 1 course *were* twenty and f thousand. H702
2 his course *were* twenty and f thousand. H702
4 likewise *were* twenty and f thousand. H702
5 his course *were* twenty and f thousand. H702
7 his course *were* twenty and f thousand. H702
8 his course *were* twenty and f thousand. H702
9 his course *were* twenty and f thousand. H702
10 his course *were* twenty and f thousand. H702
11 his course *were* twenty and f thousand. H702
12 his course *were* twenty and f thousand. H702
13 his course *were* twenty and f thousand. H702
14 his course *were* twenty and f thousand. H702
15 his course *were* twenty and f thousand. H702
2Ch 1:14 a thousand and f hundred chariots, and H702
4:13 And f hundred pomegranates on the two H702
2Ch 8:18 and took thence f hundred and fifty H702
9:25 And Solomon had f thousand stalls for H702
13: 3 men of war, *even* f hundred thousand H702
18: 5 of prophets f hundred men, and said H702
25:23 to the corner gate, f hundred cubits. H702
Ezr 1:10 of a second *sort* f hundred and ten, *and* H702
11 five thousand and f hundred. All *these* H702
2: 7 a thousand two hundred fifty and f. H702
15 The children of Adin, f hundred fifty and H702
15 of Adin, four hundred fifty and f. H702
31 a thousand two hundred fifty and f. H702
40 the children of Hodaviah, seventy and f. H702
67 Their camels, f hundred thirty and five; H702
6:17 two hundred rams, f hundred lambs; H703
Neh 6: 4 Yet they sent unto me f times after this H702
7:12 a thousand two hundred fifty and f. H702
23 of Bezai, three hundred twenty and f. H702
34 a thousand two hundred fifty and f. H702
43 the children of Hodevah, seventy and f. H702
69 *Their* camels, f hundred thirty and five: H702
11: 6 at Jerusalem *were* f hundred threescore H702
18 city *were* two hundred fourscore and f. H702
Job 1:19 and smote the f corners of the house, H702
42:16 and his sons' sons, *even* f generations. H702
Prv 30:15 *yea*, f *things* say not, *It is* enough: H702
18 for me, yea, f which I know not: H702
21 and for f *which* it cannot bear: H702
24 There be f *things which are* little upon H702
29 which go well, yea, f are comely in going: H702
Isa 11:12 of Judah from the f corners of the earth. H702
17: 6 the uppermost bough, f *or* five in the H702
Jer 15: 3 And I will appoint over them f kinds, H702
36:23 had read three or f leaves, he cut it with H702
49:36 And upon Elam will I bring the f winds H702
36 winds from the f quarters of heaven, and H702
52:21 thereof *was* f fingers: *it was* hollow. H702
30 *were* f thousand and six hundred. H702
Ezk 1: 5 the likeness of f living creatures. And H702
6 And every one had f faces, and every one H702
6 four faces, and every one had f wings. H702
8 wings on their f sides; and they four H702
8 they f had their faces and their wings. H702
10 As for the likeness of their faces, they f H702
10 right side: and they f had the face of an H702
10 side; they f also had the face of an eagle. H702
15 by the living creatures, with his f faces. H702
16 of a beryl: and they f had one likeness: H702
17 When they went, they went upon their f H702
18 *were* full of eyes round about them f. H702
7: 2 is come upon the f corners of the land. H702
10: 9 And when I looked, behold the f wheels H702
10 And *as for* their appearances, they f had H702
11 When they went, they went upon their f H702
12 about, *even* the wheels that they f had. H702
14 And every one had f faces: the first face H702
21 Every one had f faces apiece, and every H702
21 and every one f wings; and the likeness H702
14:21 when I send my f sore judgments upon H702
37: 9 Come from the f winds, O breath, and H702
40:41 F tables *were* on this side, and four H702
41 Four tables *were* on this side, and f H702
42 And the f tables *were* of hewn stone for H702
41: 5 side chamber, f cubits, round about H702
42:20 He measured it by the f sides: it had a H702
43:14 *be* f cubits, and the breadth *one* cubit. H702
15 So the altar *shall be* f cubits; and from H702
15 the altar and upward *shall be* f horns. H702
16 broad, square in the f squares thereof. H702
17 broad in the f squares thereof; and H702
20 and put *it* on the f horns of it, and on the H702
20 of it, and on the f corners of the settle, H702
45:19 and upon the f corners of the settle H702
46:21 me to pass by the f corners of the court; H702
22 In the f corners of the court *there were* H702
22 these f corners *were* of one measure. H702
23 round about them f, and *it was* made H702
48:16 the north side f thousand and five H702
16 and the south side f thousand and five H702
16 and on the east side f thousand and five H702
16 west side f thousand and five hundred. H702
30 f thousand and five hundred measures. H702
32 And at the east side f thousand and five H702
33 And at the south side f thousand and H702
34 At the west side f thousand and five H702
Dan 1:17 As for these f children, God gave them H702
3:25 He answered and said, Lo, I see f men H703
7: 2 and, behold, the f winds of the heaven H703
3 And f great beasts came up from the sea, H703
6 upon the back of it f wings of a fowl; the H703
Dan 7: 6 f heads; and dominion was given to it. H703
17 These great beasts, which are f, *are* four H703
17 These great beasts, which are four, *are* f H703
8: 8 and for it came up f notable ones toward H702
8 ones toward the f winds of heaven. H702
22 Now that being broken, whereas f stood H702
22 four stood up for it, f kingdoms shall H702
10: 4 And in the f and twentieth day of the H702
11: 4 be divided toward the f winds of heaven; H702
Am 1: 3 Damascus, and for f, I will not turn away H702
6 of Gaza, and for f, I will not turn away H702
9 of Tyrus, and for f, I will not turn away H702
11 of Edom, and for f, I will not turn away H702
13 of Ammon, and for f, I will not turn away H702
2: 1 of Moab, and for f, I will not turn away H702
4 of Judah, and for f, I will not turn away H702
6 of Israel, and for f, I will not turn away H702
Hag 1:15 In the f and twentieth day of the sixth H702
2:10 In the f and twentieth *day* of the ninth H702
18 upward, from the f and twentieth day of H702
20 unto Haggai in the f and twentieth *day* H702
Zec 1: 7 Upon the f and twentieth day of the H702
18 mine eyes, and saw, and behold f horns. H702
20 And the LORD shewed me f carpenters. H702
2: 6 f winds of the heaven, saith the LORD. H702
6: 1 behold, there came f chariots out from H702
5 unto me, These *are* the f spirits of the H702
Mt 15:38 And they that did eat were f thousand *G5070*
16:10 Neither the seven loaves of the f *G5070*
24:31 his elect from the f winds, from one *G5064*
Mk 2: 3 sick of the palsy, which was borne of f. *G5064*
8: 9 And they that had eaten were about f *G5070*
20 And when the seven among f *G5070*
13:27 his elect from the f winds, from the *G5064*
Lk 2:37 fourscore and f years, which departed *G5064*
Jn 4:35 Say not ye, There are yet f months, and *G5072*
11:17 he had *lain* in the grave f days already. *G5064*
39 stinketh: for he hath been *dead* f days. *G5066*
19:23 and made f parts, to every soldier *G5064*
Act 5:36 of men, about f hundred, joined *G6071*
7: 6 and entreat *them* evil f hundred years. *G6071*
10:11 the f corners, and let down to the earth: *G5064*
30 And Cornelius said, F days ago I was *G5067*
11: 5 by f corners; and it came even to me: *G5064*
12: 4 and delivered *him* to f quaternions of *G5064*
13:20 about the space of f hundred and fifty *G5071*
21: 9 And the same man had f daughters, *G5064*
23 have f men which have a vow on them; *G5064*
38 f thousand men that were murderers? *G5070*
27:29 rocks, they cast f anchors out of the *G5064*
Gal 3:17 law, which was f hundred and thirty *G5071*
Rev 4: 4 And round about the throne *were* f and *G5064*
4 the seats I saw f and twenty elders *G5064*
6 f beasts full of eyes before and behind. *G5064*
8 And the f beasts had each of them six *G5064*
10 The f and twenty elders fall down *G5064*
5: 6 throne and of the f beasts, and in the *G5064*
8 And when he had taken the book, the f *G5064*
8 four beasts and f *and* twenty elders fell *G5064*
14 And the f beasts said, Amen. And the *G5064*
14 Amen. And the f *and* twenty elders fell *G5064*
6: 1 of the f beasts saying, Come and see. *G5064*
6 voice in the midst of the f beasts say, A *G5064*
7: 1 And after these things I saw f angels *G5064*
1 standing on the f corners of the earth, *G5064*
1 earth, holding the f winds of the earth, *G5064*
2 a loud voice to the f angels, to whom it *G5064*
4 *and* forty *and* f thousand of all the *G5064*
11 the elders and the f beasts, and fell *G5064*
9:13 a voice from the f horns of the golden *G5064*
14 Loose the f angels which are bound *G5064*
15 And the f angels were loosed, which *G5064*
11:16 And the f and twenty elders, which sat *G5064*
14: 1 hundred forty *and* f thousand, having *G5064*
3 and before the f beasts, and the elders: *G5064*
3 *and* forty *and* f thousand, which were *G5064*
15: 7 And one of the f beasts gave unto the *G5064*
19: 4 And the f and twenty elders and the *G5064*
4 elders and the f beasts fell down and *G5064*
20: 8 which are in the f quarters of the earth, *G5064*
21:17 *and* forty *and* f cubits, *according to* *G5064*

FOUR HUNDRED See FOUR and HUNDRED.

FOUR THOUSAND See FOUR and THOUSAND.

FOURFOLD
2Sa 12: 6 And he shall restore the lamb f, because H706
Lk 19: 8 by false accusation, I restore *him* f. *G5073*

FOURFOOTED
Act 10:12 Wherein were all manner of f beasts of *G5074*
11: 6 and saw f beasts of the earth, *G5074*
Ro 1:23 and f beasts, and creeping things. *G5074*

FOURSCORE
Gen 16:16 And Abram *was* f and six years old, H8084
35:28 of Isaac were an hundred and f years. H8084
Ex 7: 7 And Moses *was* f years old, and Aaron H8084
7 old, and Aaron f and three years old, H8084
Nu 2: 9 thousand and f thousand and six H8084
4:48 eight thousand and five hundred and f. H8084
Jos 14:10 lo, I *am* this day f and five years old. H8084
Jdg 3:30 of Israel. And the land had rest f years. H8084
1Sa 22:18 slew on that day f and five persons that H8084
2Sa 19:32 aged man, *even* f years old: and he had H8084
35 I *am* this day f years old: *and* can I H8084
1Ki 5:15 f thousand hewers in the mountains; H8084
12:21 an hundred and f thousand chosen H8084
2Ki 6:25 head was *sold* for f *pieces* of silver, and H8084
10:24 Jehu appointed f men without, and H8084
19:35 an hundred f and five thousand: and H8084
1Ch 7: 5 genealogies f and seven thousand. H8084
15: 9 Eliel the chief, and his brethren f: H8084
25: 7 cunning, was two hundred f and eight. H8084
2Ch 2: 2 bear burdens, and f thousand to hew in H8084
18 of burdens, and f thousand *to be* H8084
11: 1 an hundred and f thousand chosen H8084
14: 8 two hundred and f thousand: all these H8084
17:15 with him two hundred and f thousand. H8084
18 f thousand ready prepared for the war. H8084
26:17 after him, and with him f priests of the H8084
Ezr 8: 8 son of Michael, and with him f males. H8084
Neh 7:26 and Netophah, an hundred f and eight. H8084
11:18 holy city *were* two hundred f and four. H8084
Est 1: 4 days, *even* an hundred and f days. H8084
Ps 90:10 of strength *they be* f years, yet *is* their H8084
Song 6: 8 There are threescore queens, and f H8084
Isa 37:36 a hundred and f and five thousand: H8084
Jer 41: 5 from Samaria, *even* f men, having their H8084
Lk 2:37 And she *was* a widow of about f and *G3589*
16: 7 unto him, Take thy bill, and write f. *G3589*

FOURSCORE THOUSAND See FOURSCORE and THOUSAND.

FOURSQUARE
Ex 27: 1 the altar shall be f: and the height H7251
28:16 F it shall be *being* doubled; a span *shall* H7251
30: 2 breadth thereof; f shall it be: and two H7251
37:25 of it a cubit; *it was* f; and two cubits *was* H7251
38: 1 f; and three cubits the height thereof. H7251
39: 9 It was f; they made the breastplate H7251
1Ki 7:31 with their borders, f, not round. H7251
Ezk 40:47 cubits broad, f; and the altar *that was* H7251
48:20 f, with the possession of the city. H7243
Rev 21:16 And the city lieth f, and the length is as *G5068*

FOURTEEN
Gen 31:41 I served thee f years for thy two H702+H6240
46:22 to Jacob: all the souls *were* f. H702+H6240
Nu 1:27 f thousand and six hundred. H702+H7657
2: 4 f thousand and six hundred. H702+H7657
16:49 the plague were f thousand and H702+H7657
29:13 two rams, *and* f lambs of the H702+H6240
15 deal to each lamb of the f lambs: H702+H6240
17 two rams, f lambs of the first H702+H6240
20 two rams, f lambs of the first H702+H6240
23 two rams, *and* f lambs of the H702+H6240
26 two rams, *and* f lambs of the H702+H6240
29 two rams, *and* f lambs of the H702+H6240
32 two rams, *and* f lambs of the H702+H6240
Jos 15:36 f cities with their villages: H702+H6240
18:28 *and* Kirjath; f cities with their H702+H6240
1Ki 8:65 and seven days, *even* f days. H702+H6240
1Ch 25: 5 f sons and three daughters. H702+H6240
2Ch 13:21 and married f wives, and begat H702+H6240
Job 42:12 for he had f thousand sheep, H702+H6240
Ezk 43:17 And the settle *shall be* f *cubits* H702+H6240
17 long and f broad in the four H702+H6240
Mt 1:17 to David *are* f generations; and from *G1180*
17 into Babylon *are* f generations; and *G1180*
17 Babylon unto Christ *are* f generations. *G1180*
2Co 12: 2 I knew a man in Christ above f years *G1180*
Gal 2: 1 Then f years after I went up again to *G1180*

FOURTEEN THOUSAND See FOURTEEN and THOUSAND.

FOURTEENTH
Gen 14: 5 And in the f year came H702+H6240
Ex 12: 6 it up until the f day of the same H702+H6240
18 In the first *month,* on the f day H702+H6240
Lev 23: 5 In the f *day* of the first month at H702+H6240
Nu 9: 3 In the f day of this month, at H702+H6240
5 on the f day of the first month H702+H6240
11 The f day of the second month H702+H6240
28:16 And in the f day of the first H702+H6240
Jos 5:10 on the f day of the month H702+H6240
2Ki 18:13 Now in the f year of king H702+H6240
1Ch 24:13 The thirteenth to Huppah, the f H702+H6240
25:21 The f to Mattithiah, *he,* his sons, H702+H6240
2Ch 30:15 on the f *day* of the second H702+H6240
35: 1 on the f *day* of the first month. H702+H6240
Ezr 6:19 the f *day* of the first month. H702+H6240
Est 9:15 together on the f day also of the H702+H6240
17 and on the f day of the same H702+H6240
18 and on the f thereof; and on the H702+H6240
19 made the f day of the month H702+H6240
21 keep the f day of the month H702+H6240
Isa 36: 1 Now it came to pass in the f H702+H6240
Ezk 40: 1 month, in the f year after that H702+H6240
45:21 In the first *month,* in the f day H702+H6240
Act 27:27 But when the f night was come, as we *G5065*
33 This day is the f day that ye have *G5065*

FOURTH
Gen 1:19 and the morning were the f day. H7243
2:14 of Assyria. And the f river *is* Euphrates. H7243
15:16 But in the f generation they shall come H7243
Ex 20: 5 and f *generation* of them that hate me; H7256
28:20 And the f row a beryl, and an onyx, H7243
29:40 mingled with the f part of an hin of H7253
40 of beaten oil; and the f part of an hin of H7243
34: 7 unto the third and to the f *generation.* H7256
39:13 And the f row, a beryl, an onyx, and a H7243
Lev 19:24 But in the f year all the fruit thereof H7243
23:13 *shall be* of wine, the f *part* of an hin. H7243
Nu 7:30 On the f day Elizur the son of Shedeur, H7243
14:18 unto the third and f *generation.* H7256
15: 4 mingled with the f *part* of an hin of oil. H7243
5 And the f *part* of an hin of wine for a H7243
23:10 the number of the f *part* of Israel? Let H7255
28: 5 with the f *part* of an hin of beaten oil. H7243
7 *shall be* the f *part* of an hin for the H7243
14 unto a ram, and a f *part* of an hin unto H7243
29:23 And on the f day ten bullocks, two H7243
Dt 5: 9 and f *generation* of them that hate me, H7256
Jos 19:17 *And* the f lot came out to Issachar, for H7243
Jdg 19: 5 And it came to pass on the f day, when H7243
1Sa 9: 8 here at hand the f part of a shekel of H7253
2Sa 3: 4 And the f, Adonijah the son of Haggith; H7243
1Ki 6: 1 of Egypt, in the f year of Solomon's H7243
33 posts *of* olive tree, a f part *of the wall.* H7243
37 In the f year was the foundation of the H7243
22:41 in the f year of Ahab king of Israel. H702
2Ki 6:25 of silver, and the f part of a cab of H7255
10:30 thy children of the f *generation* shall sit H7243
15:12 f *generation.* And so it came to pass. H7243
18: 9 And it came to pass in the f year of H7243
25: 3 And on the ninth *day* of the *f* month the
1Ch 2:14 Nethaneel the f, Raddai the fifth, H7243
3: 2 the f, Adonijah the son of Haggith: H7243
15 the third Zedekiah, the f Shallum. H7243
8: 2 Nohah the f, and Rapha the fifth. H7243
12:10 Mishmannah the f, Jeremiah the fifth, H7243
23:19 Jahaziel the third, and Jekameam the f. H7243
24: 8 The third to Harim, the f to Seorim, H7243
23 Jahaziel the third, Jekameam the f. H7243
25:11 The f to Izri, *he,* his sons, and his H7243
26: 2 Zebadiah the third, Jathniel the f, H7243
4 and Sacar the f, and Nethaneel the fifth, H7243
11 third, Zechariah the f: all the sons and H7243
27: 7 The f *captain* for the fourth month *was* H7243
7 The fourth *captain* for the f month *was* H7243
2Ch 3: 2 second month, in the f year of his reign. H702
20:26 And on the f day they assembled H7243
Ezr 8:33 Now on the f day was the silver and the H7243
Neh 9: 1 Now in the twenty and f day of this H702
3 their God *one* f part of the day; and H7243
3 day; and *another* f part they confessed, H7243
Jer 25: 1 of Judah in the f year of Jehoiakim the H7243
28: 1 of Judah, in the f year, *and* in the fifth H7243
36: 1 And it came to pass in the f year of H7243
39: 2 of Zedekiah, in the f month, the ninth H7243
45: 1 of Jeremiah, in the f year of Jehoiakim H7243
46: 2 smote in the f year of Jehoiakim the H7243
51:59 Babylon in the f year of his reign. And H7243
52: 6 And in the f month, in the ninth *day* of H7243
Ezk 1: 1 year, in the f *month,* in the fifth *day* H7243
Ezk 10:14 of a lion, and the f the face of an eagle. H7243
Dan 2:40 And the f kingdom shall be strong as H7244
3:25 the form of the f is like the Son of God. H7244
7: 7 and behold a f beast, dreadful and H7244
19 Then I would know the truth of the f H7244
23 Thus he said, The f beast shall be the H7244
23 beast shall be the f kingdom upon H7244
11: 2 in Persia; and the f shall be far richer H7243
Zec 6: 3 in the f chariot grisled and bay horses. H7243
7: 1 And it came to pass in the f year of king H702
1 unto Zechariah in the f *day* of the ninth H702
8:19 The fast of the f *month,* and the fast H7243
Mt 14:25 And in the f watch of the night Jesus *G5067*
Mk 6:48 and about the f watch of the night he *G5067*
Rev 4: 7 and the f beast *was* like a flying eagle. *G5067*
6: 7 And when he had opened the f seal, I *G5067*
7 voice of the f beast say, Come and see. *G5067*
8 them over the f part of the earth, to *G5067*
8:12 And the f angel sounded, and the third *G5067*
16: 8 And the f angel poured out his vial *G5067*
21:19 third, a chalcedony; the f, an emerald; *G5067*

FOWL
Gen 1:20 that hath life, and f *that* may fly above H5775
21 and every winged f after his kind: and H5775
22 the seas, and let f multiply in the earth. H5775
26 sea, and over the f of the air, and over H5775
28 sea, and over the f of the air, and over H5775
30 earth, and to every f of the air, and to H5775
2:19 the field, and every f of the air; and H5775
20 all cattle, and to the f of the air, and to H5775
7:14 f after his kind, every bird of every sort. H5775
21 the earth, both of f, and of cattle, and of H5775
23 things, and the f of the heaven; and H5775
8:17 of all flesh, *both* of f, and of cattle, and H5775
19 thing, and every f, *and* whatsoever H5775
20 and of every clean f, and offered burnt H5775
9: 2 and upon every f of the air, upon all H5775
10 *is* with you, of the f, of the cattle, and of H5775
Lev 7:26 f or of beast, in any of your dwellings. H5775
11:46 beasts, and of the f, and of every living H5775
17:13 any beast or f that may be eaten; he H5775
20:25 by beast, or by f, or by any manner of H5775
Dt 4:17 of any winged f that flieth in the air, H6833
1Ki 4:23 roebucks, and fallowdeer, and fatted f. H1257
33 f, and of creeping things, and of fishes. H5775
Job 28: 7 *There is* a path which no f knoweth, H5861
Ps 8: 8 The f of the air, and the fish of the sea, H6833
148:10 all cattle; creeping things, and flying f: H6833
Jer 9:10 the cattle; both the f of the heavens and H5775
Ezk 17:23 it shall dwell all f of every wing; in the H6833
39:17 every feathered f, and to every beast of H6833
44:31 itself, or torn, whether it be f or beast. H5775
Dan 7: 6 of it four wings of a f; the beast had also H5776

FOWLER
Ps 91: 3 the f, *and* from the noisome pestilence. H3353
Prv 6: 5 and as a bird from the hand of the f. H3353
Hos 9: 8 *is* a snare of a f in all his ways, *and* H3352

FOWLERS
Ps 124: 7 of the snare of the f: the snare is broken, H3369

FOWLS
Gen 6: 7 thing, and the f of the air; for it H5775
20 Of f after their kind, and of cattle after H5775
7: 3 Of f also of the air by sevens, the male H5775
8 not clean, and of f, and of every thing H5775
15:11 And when the f came down upon the H5861
Lev 1:14 to the LORD *be* of f, then he shall bring H5775
11:13 among the f; they shall not be eaten, H5775
20 All f that creep, going upon *all* four, H5775
20:25 between unclean f and clean: and ye H5775
Dt 14:20 *But of* all clean f ye may eat. H5775
28:26 And thy carcase shall be meat unto all f H5775
1Sa 17:44 thy flesh unto the f of the air, and to the H5775
46 this day unto the f of the air, and to the H5775
1Ki 14:11 the field shall the f of the air eat: for the H5775
16: 4 his in the fields shall the f of the air eat. H5775
21:24 in the field shall the f of the air eat. H5775
Neh 5:18 choice sheep; also f were prepared for H6833
Job 12: 7 the f of the air, and they shall tell thee: H5775
28:21 and kept close from the f of the air. H5775
35:11 maketh us wiser than the f of heaven? H5775
Ps 50:11 I know all the f of the mountains: and H5775
78:27 feathered f like as the sand of the sea: H5775
79: 2 *to be* meat unto the f of the heaven, the H5775
104:12 By them shall the f of the heaven have H5775
Isa 18: 6 They shall be left together unto the f of H5861

Isa 18: 6 the earth: and the f shall summer upon H5861
Jer 7:33 be meat for the f of the heaven, and for H5775
15: 3 to tear, and the f of the heaven, and the H5775
16: 4 be meat for the f of heaven, and for the H5775
19: 7 to be meat for the f of the heaven, and H5775
34:20 for meat unto the f of the heaven, and H5775
Ezk 29: 5 of the field and to the f of the heaven. H5775
31: 6 All the f of heaven made their nests in H5775
13 Upon his ruin shall all the f of the H5775
32: 4 and will cause all the f of the heaven to H5775
38:20 So that the fishes of the sea, and the f H5775
Dan 2:38 of the field and the f of the heaven hath H5776
4:12 under it, and the f of the heaven dwelt H6853
14 under it, and the f from his branches: H6853
21 f of the heaven had their habitation: H6853
Hos 2:18 the field, and with the f of heaven, and H5775
4: 3 field, and with the f of heaven; yea, the H5775
7:12 them down as the f of the heaven; I will H5775
Zep 1: 3 I will consume the f of the heaven, and H5775
Mt 6:26 Behold the f of the air: for they sow not, *G4071*
13: 4 and the f came and devoured them up: *G4071*
Mk 4: 4 f of the air came and devoured it up. *G4071*
32 so that the f of the air may lodge *G4071*
Lk 8: 5 down, and the f of the air devoured it. *G4071*
12:24 how much more are ye better than the f? *G4071*
13:19 f of the air lodged in the branches of it. *G4071*
Act 10:12 and creeping things, and f of the air. *G4071*
11: 6 and creeping things, and f of the air. *G4071*
Rev 19:17 saying to all the f that fly in the midst *G3732*
21 and all the f were filled with their flesh. *G3732*

FOX
Neh 4: 3 they build, if a f go up, he shall even H7776
Lk 13:32 Go ye, and tell that f, Behold, I cast out *G258*

FOXES
Jdg 15: 4 three hundred f, and took firebrands, H7776
Ps 63:10 the sword: they shall be a portion for f. H7776
Song 2:15 Take us the f, the little foxes, that spoil H7776
15 Take us the foxes, the little f, that spoil H7776
Lam 5:18 which is desolate, the f walk upon it. H7776
Ezk 13: 4 O Israel, thy prophets are like the f in H7776
Mt 8:20 And Jesus saith unto him, The f have *G258*
Lk 9:58 And Jesus said unto him, F have holes, *G258*

FRAGMENTS
Mt 14:20 the f that remained twelve baskets full. *G2801*
Mk 6:43 baskets full of the f, and of the fishes. *G2801*
8:19 baskets full of f took ye up? They say *G2801*
20 of f took ye up? And they said, Seven. *G2801*
Lk 9:17 f that remained to them twelve baskets. *G2801*
Jn 6:12 the f that remain, that nothing be lost. *G2801*
13 baskets with the f of the five barley *G2801*

FRAIL
Ps 39: 4 what it *is; that* I may know how f I *am*. H2310

FRAME
Jdg 12: 6 for he could not f to pronounce *it* right. H3559
Ps 103:14 For he knoweth our f; he remembereth H3336
Jer 18:11 LORD; Behold, I f evil against you, and H3335
Ezk 40: 2 *was* as the f of a city on the south. H4011
Hos 5: 4 They will not f their doings to turn unto H5414

FRAMED
Isa 29:16 not? or shall the thing f say of him that H3336
16 that f it, He had no understanding? H3335
Eph 2:21 In whom all the building fitly f together *G4883*
Heb 11: 3 the worlds were f by the word of God, *G2675*

FRAMETH
Ps 50:19 mouth to evil, and thy tongue f deceit. H6775
94:20 with thee, which f mischief by a law? H3335

FRANKINCENSE
Ex 30:34 f: of each shall there be a like *weight:* H3828
Lev 2: 1 pour oil upon it, and put f thereon: H3828
2 with all the f thereof; and the priest H3828
15 And thou shalt put oil upon it, and lay f H3828
16 with all the f thereof: *it is* an offering H3828
5:11 *any* f thereon: for it *is* a sin offering. H3828
6:15 and all the f which *is* upon the meat H3828
24: 7 And thou shalt put pure f upon *each* H3828
Nu 5:15 oil upon it, nor put f thereon; for it *is* H3828
1Ch 9:29 and the oil, and the f, and the spices. H3828
Neh 13: 5 meat offerings, the f, and the vessels, H3828
9 of God, with the meat offering and the f. H3828
Song 3: 6 f, with all powders of the merchant? H3828
4: 6 mountain of myrrh, and to the hill of f. H3828
Song 4:14 with all trees of f; myrrh and aloes, with H3828
Mt 2:11 unto him gifts; gold, and f, and myrrh. *G3030*
Rev 18:13 ointments, and f, and wine, and oil, and *G3030*

FRANKLY
Lk 7:42 And when they had nothing to pay, he f *G5435*

FRAUD
Ps 10: 7 and deceit and f: under his tongue *is* H8496
Jas 5: 4 is of you kept back by f, crieth: and the *G650*

FRAY
Dt 28:26 earth, and no man shall f *them* away. H2729
Jer 7:33 the earth; and none shall f *them* away. H2729
Zec 1:21 these are come to f them, to cast out H2729

FRECKLED
Lev 13:39 white; it *is* a f spot *that* groweth in H933

FREE
Ex 21: 2 seventh he shall go out f for nothing. H2670
5 and my children; I will not go out f: H2670
11 then shall she go out f without money. H2600
26 he shall let him go f for his eye's sake. H2670
27 he shall let him go f for his tooth's sake. H2670
36: 3 yet unto him f offerings every morning. H5071
Lev 19:20 be put to death, because she was not f. H2666
Nu 5:19 thy husband, be thou f from this bitter H5352
28 she shall be f, and shall conceive seed. H5352
Dt 15:12 year thou shalt let him go f from thee. H2670
13 And when thou sendest him out f from H2670
18 sendest him away f from thee; for he H2670
24: 5 *but* he shall be f at home one year, and H5355
1Sa 17:25 and make his father's house f in Israel. H2670
1Ch 9:33 the chambers *were* f: for they were H6362
2Ch 29:31 as were of a f heart burnt offerings. H5081
Job 3:19 and the servant *is* f from his master. H2670
39: 5 Who hath sent out the wild ass f? or H2670
Ps 51:12 and uphold me *with thy* f spirit. H5081
88: 5 F among the dead, like the slain that lie H2670
105:20 the ruler of the people, and let him go f. H6605
Isa 58: 6 go f, and that ye break every yoke? H2670
Jer 34: 9 or an Hebrewess, go f; that none should H2670
10 his maidservant, go f, that none should H2670
11 they had let go f, to return, and brought H2670
14 shalt let him go f from thee: but your H2670
Am 4: 5 *and* publish the f offerings: for this H2670
Mt 15: 6 mother, *he shall be f*. Thus have ye made
17:26 saith unto him, Then are the children f. *G1658*
Mk 7:11 mightest be profited by me; *he shall be f*.
Jn 8:32 truth, and the truth shall make you f. *G1659*
33 how sayest thou, Ye shall be made f? *G1658*
36 If the Son therefore shall make you f, ye *G1659*
36 make you free, ye shall be f indeed. *G1658*
Act 22:28 And Paul said, But I was *f* born.
Ro 5:15 But not as the offence, so also *is* the f *G5486*
16 but the f gift *is* of many offences *G5486*
18 of one *the f gift came* upon all men
6:18 Being then made f from sin, ye became *G1659*
20 of sin, ye were f from righteousness. *G1658*
22 But now being made f from sin, and *G1659*
7: 3 be dead, she is f from that law; so that *G1658*
8: 2 me f from the law of sin and death. *G1659*
1Co 7:21 if thou mayest be made f, use *it* rather. *G1658*
22 is called, *being* f, is Christ's servant. *G1658*
9: 1 Am I not an apostle? am I not f? have I *G1658*
19 For though I be f from all *men*, yet *G1658*
12:13 *we be* bond or f; and have been all *G1658*
Gal 3:28 neither bond nor f, there is neither male *G1658*
4:26 But Jerusalem which is above is f, *G1658*
31 of the bondwoman, but of the f. *G1658*
5: 1 hath made us f, and be not entangled *G1659*
Eph 6: 8 of the Lord, whether *he be* bond or f. *G1658*
Col 3:11 bond *nor* f: but Christ is all, and in all. *G1658*
2Th 3: 1 of the Lord may have *f* course, and be
1Pt 2:16 As f, and not using *your* liberty for a *G1658*
Rev 6:15 and every f man, hid themselves *G1658*
13:16 rich and poor, f and bond, to receive *G1658*
19:18 *both* f and bond, both small and great. *G1658*

FREE-BORN See FREE and BORN.

FREED
Jos 9:23 none of you be f from being bondmen, H3772
Ro 6: 7 For he that is dead is f from sin. *G1344*

FREEDOM
Lev 19:20 all redeemed, nor f given her; she shall H2668
Act 22:28 f. And Paul said, But I was *free* born. *G4174*

FREELY
Gen 2:16 tree of the garden thou mayest f eat: H398
Nu 11: 5 did eat in Egypt f; the cucumbers, and H2600
1Sa 14:30 people had eaten f to day of the spoil of H398
Ezr 2:68 at Jerusalem, offered f for the house of H5068
7:15 counsellors have f offered unto the God
Ps 54: 6 I will f sacrifice unto thee: I will praise H5071
Hos 14: 4 I will love them f: for mine anger is H5071
Mt 10: 8 devils: f ye have received, freely give. *G1432*
8 devils: freely ye have received, f give. *G1432*
Act 2:29 Men *and* brethren, let me f speak unto *G3326*
26:26 before whom also I speak f: for I am *G3955*
Ro 3:24 Being justified f by his grace through *G1432*
8:32 he not with him also f give us all things?
1Co 2:12 the things that are f given to us of God.
2Co 11: 7 preached to you the gospel of God f? *G1432*
Rev 21: 6 of the fountain of the water of life f. *G1432*
22:17 will, let him take the water of life f. *G1432*

FREEMAN
1Co 7:22 is the Lord's f: likewise also he that *G558*

FREEWILL
Lev 22:18 and for all his f offerings, which they H5071
21 *his* vow, or a f offering in beeves or H5071
23 thou offer *for* a f offering; but for a vow H5071
23:38 beside all your f offerings, which ye H5071
Nu 15: 3 a vow, or in a f offering, or in your H5071
29:39 vows, and your f offerings, for your H5071
Dt 12: 6 vows, and your f offerings, and the H5071
17 vowest, nor thy f offerings, or heave H5071
16:10 with a tribute of a f offering of thine H5071
23:23 perform; *even* a f offering, according H5071
2Ch 31:14 east, *was* over the f offerings of God, to H5071
Ezr 1: 4 with beasts, beside the f offering for the H5071
3: 5 offered a f offering unto the LORD. H5071
7:13 f to go up to Jerusalem, go with thee. H5069
16 of Babylon, with the f offering of the H5069
8:28 and the gold *are* a f offering unto the H5071
Ps119:108 Accept, I beseech thee, the f offerings of H5071

FREEWOMAN
Gal 4:22 the one by a bondmaid, the other by a f. *G1658*
23 flesh; but he of the f *was* by promise. *G1658*
30 shall not be heir with the son of the f. *G1658*

FREEZE See FROZEN.

FREQUENT
2Co 11:23 in prisons more f, in deaths oft. *G4056*

FRESH
Nu 11: 8 the taste of it was as the taste of f oil. H3955
Job 29:20 My glory *was* f in me, and my bow was H2319
Ps 92:10 unicorn: I shall be anointed with f oil. H7488
Jas 3:12 no fountain both yield salt water and f. *G1099*

FRESHER
Job 33:25 His flesh shall be f than a child's: he H7375

FRET
Lev 13:55 it in the fire; it *is* f inward, *whether* it H6356
1Sa 1: 6 for to make her f, because the LORD H7481
Ps 37: 1 F not thyself because of evildoers, H2734
7 patiently for him: f not thyself because H2734
8 Cease from anger, and forsake wrath: f H2734
Prv 24:19 F not thyself because of evil *men*, H2734
Isa 8:21 be hungry, they shall f themselves, and H7107

FRETTED
Ezk 16:43 youth, but hast f me in all these *things*; H7264

FRETTETH
Prv 19: 3 way: and his heart f against the LORD. H2196

FRETTING
Lev 13:51 the plague *is* a f leprosy; it *is* unclean. H3992
52 a f leprosy; it shall be burnt in the fire. H3992
14:44 *is* a f leprosy in the house: it *is* unclean. H3992

FRIED
Lev 7:12 cakes mingled with oil, of fine flour, f. H7246
1Ch 23:29 for that which is f, and for all manner of H7246

FRIEND
Gen 38:12 he and his f Hirah the Adullamite. H7453
20 by the hand of his f the Adullamite, to H7453
Ex 33:11 man speaketh unto his f. And he turned H7453
Dt 13: 6 of thy bosom, or thy f, which *is* as thine H7453

Jdg 14:20 companion, whom he had used as his f. H7462
2Sa 13: 3 But Amnon had a f, whose name *was* H7453
15:37 So Hushai David's f came into the city, H7463
16:16 the Archite, David's f, was come unto H7463
17 f? why wentest thou not with thy friend? H7453
17 friend? why wentest thou not with thy f? H7453
1Ki 4: 5 *was* principal officer, *and* the king's f: H7463
2Ch 20: 7 it to the seed of Abraham thy f for ever? H157
Job 6:14 *shewed* from his f; but he forsaketh the H7453
27 fatherless, and ye dig *a pit* for your f. H7453
Ps 35:14 *he had been* my f *or* brother: I bowed H7453
41: 9 Yea, mine own familiar f, in whom I
88:18 Lover and f hast thou put far from me, H7453
Prv 6: 1 My son, if thou be surety for thy f, *if* H7453
3 the hand of thy f; go, humble thyself, H7453
3 go, humble thyself, and make sure thy f. H7453
17:17 A f loveth at all times, and a brother is H7453
18 becometh surety in the presence of his f. H7453
18:24 is a f *that* sticketh closer than a brother. H157
19: 6 man *is* a f to him that giveth gifts. H7453
22:11 grace of his lips the king *shall be* his f. H7453
27: 6 Faithful *are* the wounds of a f; but the H157
9 of a man's f by hearty counsel. H7453
10 Thine own f, and thy father's friend, H7453
10 Thine own friend, and thy father's f, H7453
14 He that blesseth his f with a loud voice, H7453
17 sharpeneth the countenance of his f. H7453
Song 5:16 this *is* my f, O daughters of Jerusalem. H7453
Isa 41: 8 I have chosen, the seed of Abraham my f. H157
Jer 6:21 the neighbour and his f shall perish. H7453
19: 9 one the flesh of his f in the siege and H7453
Hos 3: 1 beloved of *her* f, yet an adulteress, H7453
Mic 7: 5 Trust ye not in a f, put ye not H7453
Mt 11:19 and a winebibber, a f of publicans and G5384
20:13 one of them, and said, F, I do thee no G2083
22:12 And he saith unto him, F, how camest G2083
26:50 And Jesus said unto him, F, wherefore G2083
Lk 7:34 a f of publicans and sinners! G5384
11: 5 of you shall have a f, and shall go unto G5384
5 say unto him, F, lend me three loaves; G5384
6 For a f of mine in his journey is come G5384
8 because he is his f, yet because of his G5384
14:10 may say unto thee, F, go up higher: then G5384
Jn 3:29 but the f of the bridegroom, which G5384
11:11 unto them, Our f Lazarus sleepeth; but G5384
19:12 art not Caesar's f: whosoever maketh G5384
Act 12:20 chamberlain their f, desired peace; G3982
Jas 2:23 and he was called the F of God. G5384
4: 4 be a f of the world is the enemy of God. G5384

FRIENDLY
Jdg 19: 3 after her, to speak f unto her, *and* to H3820
Ru 2:13 that thou hast spoken f unto thine H3820
Prv 18:24 must shew himself f: and there is a H7489

FRIENDS
Gen 26:26 one of his f, and Phichol the chief H4828
1Sa 30:26 of Judah, *even* to his f, saying, Behold a H7453
2Sa 3: 8 and to his f, and have not delivered H4828
19: 6 and hatest thy f. For thou hast declared H157
1Ki 16:11 neither of his kinsfolks, nor of his f. H7453
Est 5:10 and called for his f, and Zeresh his wife. H157
14 Then said Zeresh his wife and all his f H157
6:13 his wife and all his f every *thing* that had H157
Job 2:11 Now when Job's three f heard of all this H7453
16:20 My f scorn me: *but* mine eye poureth H7453
17: 5 He that speaketh flattery to *his* f, even H7453
19:14 and my familiar f have forgotten me. H3045
19 All my inward f abhorred me: and they H4962
21 f; for the hand of God hath touched me. H7453
32: 3 Also against his three f was his wrath H7453
42: 7 and against thy two f: for ye have not H7453
10 he prayed for his f: also the LORD gave H7453
Ps 38:11 My lovers and my f stand aloof from H7453
Prv 14:20 own neighbour: but the rich *hath* many f. H157
16:28 strife: and a whisperer separateth chief f. H441
17: 9 that repeateth a matter separateth *very* f. H441
18:24 A man *that hath* f must shew himself H7453
19: 4 Wealth maketh many f; but the poor is H7453
7 much more do his f go far from him? H4828
Song 5: 1 with my milk: eat, O f; drink, yea, drink H7453
Jer 20: 4 and to all thy f: and they shall fall by H157
6 thy f, to whom thou hast prophesied lies. H157
38:22 shall say, Thy f have set thee on, H605+H7965
Lam 1: 2 *her:* all her f have dealt treacherously H7453
Zec 13: 6 I was wounded *in* the house of my f. H157
Mk 3:21 And when his f heard *of it*, they went G3844
5:19 Go home to thy f, and tell them how G4674
Lk 7: 6 the centurion sent f to him, saying unto G5384
12: 4 And I say unto you my f, Be not afraid G5384
14:12 call not thy f, nor thy brethren, neither G5384
15: 6 together *his* f and neighbours, saying G5384
9 *it*, she calleth *her* f and *her* neighbours G5384
29 kid, that I might make merry with my f: G5384
16: 9 to yourselves f of the mammon of G5384
21:16 and kinsfolks, and f; and *some* of you G5384
23:12 Herod were made f together: for before G5384
Jn 15:13 that a man lay down his life for his f. G5384
14 Ye are my f, if ye do whatsoever I G5384
15 I have called you f; for all things that I G5384
Act 10:24 called together his kinsmen and near f. G5384
19:31 Asia, which were his f, sent unto him, G5384
27: 3 to go unto his f to refresh himself. G5384
3Jn 14 *be* to thee. *Our* f salute thee. Greet the G5384
14 salute thee. Greet the f by name. G5384

FRIENDSHIP
Prv 22:24 Make no f with an angry man; and H7462
Jas 4: 4 ye not that the f of the world is enmity G5373

FRIGHT See AFFRIGHT.

FRINGE
Nu 15:38 the f of the borders a ribband of blue: H6734
39 And it shall be unto you for a f, that ye H6734

FRINGES
Nu 15:38 that they make them f in the borders of H6734
Dt 22:12 Thou shalt make thee f upon the four H1434

FRO
Gen 8: 7 went forth to and f, until the waters H7725
2Ki 4:35 house to and f; and went up, and H259+H2008
2Ch 16: 9 For the eyes of the LORD run to and f H7751
Job 1: 7 From going to and f in the earth, and H7751
2: 2 From going to and f in the earth, and H7751
7: 4 to and f unto the dawning of the day. H5076
13:25 Wilt thou break a leaf driven to and f? H5086
Ps 107:27 They reel to and f, and stagger like a H2287
Prv 21: 6 tossed to and f of them that seek death. H5086
Isa 24:20 The earth shall reel to and f like a H5128
33: 4 f of locusts shall he run upon them. H4944
49:21 and removing to and f? and who hath H5493
Jer 5: 1 Run ye to and f through the streets of H7751
49: 3 and run to and f by the hedges; for H7751
Ezk 27:19 Dan also and Javan going to and f H235
Dan 12: 4 f, and knowledge shall be increased. H7751
Joel 2: 9 They shall run to and f in the city; they H8264
Am 8:12 shall run to and f to seek the word of H7751
Zec 1:10 sent to walk to and f through the earth.
11 walked to and f through the earth, and, H1980
4:10 run to and f through the whole earth. H7751
6: 7 might walk to and f through the earth: H1980
7 hence, walk to and f through the earth. H1980
7 they walked to and f through the earth. H1980
Eph 4:14 tossed to and f, and carried about with G2831

FROGS
Ex 8: 2 I will smite all thy borders with f: H6854
3 And the river shall bring forth f H6854
4 And the f shall come up both on thee, H6854
5 f to come up upon the land of Egypt. H6854
6 of Egypt; and the f came up, and H6854
7 brought up f upon the land of Egypt. H6854
8 he may take away the f from me, and H6854
9 to destroy the f from thee and thy H6854
11 And the f shall depart from thee, and H6854
12 because of the f which he had brought H6854
13 of Moses; and the f died out of the H6854
Ps 78:45 them; and f, which destroyed them. H6854
105:30 Their land brought forth f in H6854
Rev 16:13 And I saw three unclean spirits like f G944

FROM See the Appendix.

FRONT
2Sa 10: 9 When Joab saw that the f of the battle H6440
2Ch 3: 4 And the porch that *was* in the f *of the* H6440

FRONTIERS
Ezk 25: 9 cities *which are* on his f, the glory of the H7097

FRONTLETS
Ex 13:16 hand, and for f between thine eyes: H2903
Dt 6: 8 they shall be as f between thine eyes. H2903
11:18 they may be as f between your eyes. H2903

FROST
Gen 31:40 me, and the f by night; and my sleep H7140
Ex 16:14 *as* small as the hoar f on the ground. H3713
Job 37:10 By the breath of God f is given: and the H7140
38:29 f of heaven, who hath gendered it? H3713
Ps 78:47 hail, and their sycomore trees with f. H2602
Jer 36:30 day to the heat, and in the night to the f. H7140

FROWARD
Dt 32:20 *be:* for they *are* a very f generation, H8419
2Sa 22:27 the f thou wilt shew thyself unsavoury. H6141
Job 5:13 the counsel of the f is carried headlong. H6617
Ps 18:26 the f thou wilt shew thyself froward. H6141
26 the froward thou wilt shew thyself f. H6617
101: 4 A f heart shall depart from me: I will H6141
Prv 2:12 from the man that speaketh f things; H8419
15 Whose ways *are* crooked, and *they* f in H3868
3:32 For the f *is* abomination to the LORD: H3868
4:24 Put away from thee a f mouth, and H6143
6:12 a wicked man, walketh with a f mouth. H6143
8: 8 *there is* nothing f or perverse in them. H6617
13 evil way, and the f mouth, do I hate. H8419
10:31 but the f tongue shall be cut out. H8419
11:20 They that are of a f heart *are* H6141
16:28 A f man soweth strife: and a whisperer H8419
30 He shutteth his eyes to devise f things: H8419
17:20 He that hath a f heart findeth no good: H6141
21: 8 The way of man *is* f and strange: but *as* H2019
22: 5 in the way of the f: he that doth keep his H6141
1Pt 2:18 to the good and gentle, but also to the f. G4646

FROWARDLY
Isa 57:17 he went on f in the way of his heart. H7726

FROWARDNESS
Prv 2:14 evil, *and* delight in the f of the wicked; H8419
6:14 F *is* in his heart, he deviseth mischief H8419
10:32 but the mouth of the wicked *speaketh* f. H8419

FROZEN
Job 38:30 a stone, and the face of the deep is f. H3920

FRUIT
Gen 1:11 seed, *and* the f tree yielding fruit after H6529
11 the fruit tree yielding f after his kind, H6529
12 the tree yielding f, whose seed *was* in H6529
29 in the which *is* the f of a tree yielding H6529
3: 2 eat of the f of the trees of the garden: H6529
3 But of the f of the tree which *is* in the H6529
6 she took of the f thereof, and did eat, H6529
4: 3 Cain brought of the f of the ground an H6529
30: 2 withheld from thee the f of the womb? H6529
Ex 10:15 land, and all the f of the trees which the H6529
21:22 child, so that her f depart *from her,* H3206
Lev 19:23 then ye shall count the f thereof as H6529
24 But in the fourth year all the f thereof H6529
25 And in the fifth year shall ye eat of the f H6529
23:39 gathered in the f of the land, ye shall H8393
25: 3 vineyard, and gather in the f thereof; H8393
19 And the land shall yield her f, and ye H6529
21 it shall bring forth f for three years. H8393
22 and eat *yet* of old f until the ninth year; H8393
26: 4 the trees of the field shall yield their f. H6529
27:30 of the land, *or* of the f of the tree, *is* the H6529
Nu 13:20 and bring of the f of the land. Now the H6529
26 and shewed them the f of the land. H6529
27 milk and honey; and this *is* the f of it. H6529
Dt 1:25 And they took of the f of the land in H6529
7:13 will also bless the f of thy womb, and H6529
13 of thy womb, and the f of thy land, thy H6529
11:17 land yield not her f; and *lest* ye perish H2981
22: 9 seeds: lest the f of thy seed which thou H4395
9 and the f of thy vineyard, be defiled. H8393
26: 2 the first of all the f of the earth, which H6529
28: 4 Blessed *shall be* the f of thy body, and H6529
4 thy body, and the f of thy ground, and H6529
4 thy ground, and the f of thy cattle, the H6529
11 in goods, in the f of thy body, and in H6529
11 body, and in the f of thy cattle, and in H6529
11 cattle, and in the f of thy ground, in the H6529
18 Cursed *shall be* the f of thy body, and H6529
18 of thy body, and the f of thy land, the H6529
33 The f of thy land, and all thy labours, H6529
40 the oil; for thine olive shall cast *his f.*
42 All thy trees and f of thy land shall the H6529
51 And he shall eat the f of thy cattle, and H6529
51 of thy cattle, and the f of thy land, until H6529
53 And thou shalt eat the f of thine own H6529
30: 9 thine hand, in the f of thy body, and in H6529

F

Dt 30: 9 body, and in the **f** of thy cattle, and in H6529
9 thy cattle, and in the **f** of thy land, for H6529
Jos 5:12 of the **f** of the land of Canaan that year. H8393
Jdg 9:11 **f**, and go to be promoted over the trees? H8570
2Sa 16: 2 bread and summer **f** for the young men
2Ki 19:30 root downward, and bear **f** upward. H6529
Neh 9:25 oliveyards, and **f** trees in abundance: H3978
36 fathers to eat the **f** thereof and the good H6529
10:35 the firstfruits of all **f** of all trees, year by H6529
37 our offerings, and the **f** of all manner of H6529
Ps 1: 3 bringeth forth his **f** in his season; his H6529
21:10 Their **f** shalt thou destroy from the H6529
72:16 mountains; the **f** thereof shall shake H6529
92:14 They shall still bring forth **f** in old age; H5107
104:13 is satisfied with the **f** of thy works. H6529
105:35 and devoured the **f** of their ground. H6529
127: 3 *and* the **f** of the womb *is his* reward. H6529
132:11 **f** of thy body will I set upon thy throne. H6529
Prv 1:31 Therefore shall they eat of the **f** of their H6529
8:19 My **f** *is* better than gold, yea, than fine H6529
10:16 to life: the **f** of the wicked to sin. H8393
11:30 The **f** of the righteous *is* a tree of life; H6529
12:12 but the root of the righteous yieldeth *f*.
14 with good by the **f** of *his* mouth: and H6529
13: 2 A man shall eat good by the **f** of *his* H6529
18:20 satisfied with the **f** of his mouth; *and* H6529
21 they that love it shall eat the **f** thereof. H6529
27:18 fig tree shall eat the **f** thereof: so he that H6529
31:16 **f** of her hands she planteth a vineyard. H6529
31 Give her of the **f** of her hands; and let H6529
Song 2: 3 and his **f** *was* sweet to my taste. H6529
8:11 every one for the **f** thereof was to bring H6529
12 that keep the **f** thereof two hundred. H6529
Isa 3:10 for they shall eat the **f** of their doings. H6529
4: 2 glorious, and the **f** of the earth *shall be* H6529
10:12 I will punish the **f** of the stout heart of H6529
13:18 no pity on the **f** of the womb; their eye H6529
14:29 and his **f** *shall be* a fiery flying serpent. H6529
27: 6 bud, and fill the face of the world with **f**. H8570
9 and this *is* all the **f** to take away his sin; H6529
28: 4 *and* as the hasty **f** before the summer; H1061
37:30 plant vineyards, and eat the **f** thereof. H6529
31 root downward, and bear **f** upward: H6529
57:19 I create the **f** of the lips; Peace, peace to H5108
65:21 plant vineyards, and eat the **f** of them. H6529
Jer 2: 7 country, to eat the **f** thereof and the H6529
6:19 this people, *even* the **f** of their thoughts, H6529
7:20 and upon the **f** of the ground; and it H6529
11:16 fair, *and* of goodly **f**: with the noise of a H6529
19 the tree with the **f** thereof, and let us H3899
12: 2 they bring forth **f**: thou *art* near in their H6529
17: 8 neither shall cease from yielding **f**. H6529
10 *and* according to the **f** of his doings. H6529
21:14 But I will punish you according to the **f** H6529
29: 5 plant gardens, and eat the **f** of them; H6529
28 plant gardens, and eat the **f** of them. H6529
32:19 and according to the **f** of his doings: H6529
Lam 2:20 the women eat their **f**, *and* children of a H6529
Ezk 17: 8 bear **f**, that it might be a goodly vine. H6529
9 and cut off the **f** thereof, that it wither? H6529
23 boughs, and bear **f**, and be a goodly H6529
19:12 wind dried up her **f**: her strong rods H6529
14 hath devoured her **f**, so that she hath no H6529
25: 4 eat thy **f**, and they shall drink thy milk. H6529
34:27 And the tree of the field shall yield her **f**, H6529
36: 8 and yield your **f** to my people of Israel; H6529
11 increase and bring **f**: and I will settle H6509
30 And I will multiply the **f** of the tree, and H6529
47:12 fade, neither shall the **f** thereof be H6529
12 shall bring forth new **f** according to his H1069
12 sanctuary: and the **f** thereof shall be for H6529
Dan 4:12 The leaves thereof *were* fair, and the **f** H4
14 and scatter his **f**: let the beasts get away H4
21 Whose leaves *were* fair, and the **f** thereof H4
Hos 9:16 they shall bear no **f**: yea, though they H6529
16 I slay *even* the beloved *f* of their womb.
10: 1 vine, he bringeth forth **f** unto himself: H6529
1 multitude of his **f** he hath increased the H6529
13 ye have eaten the **f** of lies: because thou H6529
14: 8 a green fir tree. From me is thy **f** found. H6529
Joel 2:22 tree beareth her **f**, the fig tree and the H6529
Am 2: 9 yet I destroyed his **f** from above, and H6529
6:12 the **f** of righteousness into hemlock: H6529
7:14 herdman, and a gatherer of sycomore **f**: H8256
8: 1 me: and behold a basket of summer **f**. H7019
2 A basket of summer **f**. Then said the H7019
9:14 make gardens, and eat the **f** of them. H6529
Mic 6: 7 the **f** of my body *for* the sin of my soul? H6529
7: 1 to eat: my soul desired the firstripe **f**. H1063

Mic 7:13 dwell therein, for the **f** of their doings. H6529
Hab 3:17 neither *shall* **f** *be* in the vines; the H2981
Hag 1:10 dew, and the earth is stayed *from* her **f**. H2981
Zec 8:12 the vine shall give her **f**, and the ground H6529
Mal 1:12 *is* polluted; and the **f** thereof, *even* his H5108
3:11 your vine cast her **f** before the time in H7920
Mt 3:10 **f** is hewn down, and cast into the fire. G2590
7:17 forth good **f**; but a corrupt tree bringeth G2590
17 but a corrupt tree bringeth forth evil **f**. G2590
18 A good tree cannot bring forth evil **f**, G2590
18 *can* a corrupt tree bring forth good **f**. G2590
19 **f** is hewn down, and cast into the fire. G2590
12:33 Either make the tree good, and his **f** G2590
33 corrupt, and his **f** corrupt: for the tree G2590
33 corrupt: for the tree is known by *his* **f**. G2590
13: 8 ground, and brought forth **f**, some an G2590
23 also beareth **f**, and bringeth forth, G2592
26 forth **f**, then appeared the tares also. G2590
21:19 and said unto it, Let no **f** grow on thee G2590
34 And when the time of the **f** drew near, G2590
26:29 henceforth of this **f** of the vine, until G1081
Mk 4: 7 up, and choked it, and it yielded no **f**. G2590
8 and did yield **f** that sprang up and G2590
20 *it*, and bring forth **f**, some thirtyfold, G2592
28 For the earth bringeth forth **f** of herself; G2592
29 But when the **f** is brought forth, G2590
11:14 it, No man eat **f** of thee hereafter for G2590
12: 2 husbandmen of the **f** of the vineyard. G2590
14:25 no more of the **f** of the vine, until that G1081
Lk 1:42 and blessed *is* the **f** of thy womb. G2590
3: 9 **f** is hewn down, and cast into the fire. G2590
6:43 not forth corrupt **f**; neither doth a G2590
43 doth a corrupt tree bring forth good **f**. G2590
44 For every tree is known by his own **f**. G2590
8: 8 up, and bare **f** an hundredfold. And G2590
14 of *this* life, and bring no **f** to perfection. G5062
15 keep *it*, and bring forth **f** with patience. G2592
13: 6 and sought **f** thereon, and found none. G2590
7 I come seeking **f** on this fig tree, and G2590
9 And if it bear **f**, *well*: and if not, *then* G2590
20:10 give him of the **f** of the vineyard: but G2590
22:18 not drink of the **f** of the vine, until the G1081
Jn 4:36 and gathereth **f** unto life eternal: that G2590
12:24 but if it die, it bringeth forth much **f**. G2590
15: 2 Every branch in me that beareth not **f** G2590
2 that beareth **f**, he purgeth it, that it G2590
2 it, that it may bring forth more **f**. G2590
4 cannot bear **f** of itself, except it abide G2590
5 **f**: for without me ye can do nothing. G2590
8 bear much **f**; so shall ye be my disciples. G2590
16 go and bring forth **f**, and *that* your fruit G2590
16 and *that* your **f** should remain: that G2590
Act 2:30 oath to him, that of the **f** of his loins, G2590
Ro 1:13 I might have some **f** among you also, G2590
6:21 What **f** had ye then in those things G2590
22 God, ye have your **f** unto holiness, and G2590
7: 4 that we should bring forth **f** unto God. G2592
5 members to bring forth **f** unto death. G2592
15:28 this **f**, I will come by you into Spain. G2590
1Co 9: 7 and eateth not of the **f** thereof? or who G2590
Gal 5:22 But the **f** of the Spirit is love, joy, peace, G2590
Eph 5: 9 (For the **f** of the Spirit *is* in all goodness G2590
Php 1:22 But if I live in the flesh, this *is* the **f** of G2590
4:17 **f** that may abound to your account. G2590
Col 1: 6 and bringeth forth **f**, as *it doth* also in G2592
Heb 12:11 the peaceable **f** of righteousness unto G2590
13:15 **f** of *our* lips giving thanks to his name. G2590
Jas 3:18 And the **f** of righteousness is sown in G2590
5: 7 for the precious **f** of the earth, and hath G2590
18 rain, and the earth brought forth her **f**. G2590
Jude 12 winds; trees whose **f** withereth, without G5352
12 **f**, twice dead, plucked up by the roots; G175
Rev 22: 2 *and* yielded her **f** every month: and the G2590

FRUITFUL
Gen 1:22 And God blessed them, saying, Be **f**, H6509
28 said unto them, Be **f**, and multiply, and H6509
8:17 and be **f**, and multiply upon the earth. H6509
9: 1 **f**, and multiply, and replenish the earth. H6509
7 And you, be ye **f**, and multiply; bring H6509
17: 6 And I will make thee exceeding **f**, and I H6509
20 and will make him **f**, and will multiply H6509
26:22 for us, and we shall be **f** in the land. H6509
28: 3 and make thee **f**, and multiply thee, H6509
35:11 *am* God Almighty: be **f** and multiply; a H6509
41:52 me to be **f** in the land of my affliction. H6509
48: 4 I will make thee **f**, and multiply thee, H6509
49:22 Joseph *is* a **f** bough, *even* a fruitful H6509
22 Joseph *is* a fruitful bough, *even* a **f** H6509

Ex 1: 7 And the children of Israel were **f**, and H6509
Lev 26: 9 and make you **f**, and multiply you, and H6509
Ps 107:34 A **f** land into barrenness, for the H6529
128: 3 Thy wife *shall be* as a **f** vine by the H6509
148: 9 Mountains, and all hills; **f** trees, and all H6529
Isa 5: 1 hath a vineyard in a very **f** hill: H1121+H8081
10:18 forest, and of his **f** field, both soul and H3759
17: 6 five in the outmost **f** branches thereof, H6509
29:17 be turned into a **f** field, and the fruitful H3759
17 the **f** field shall be esteemed as a forest? H3759
32:12 for the pleasant fields, for the **f** vine. H6509
15 wilderness be a **f** field, and the fruitful H3759
15 and the **f** field be counted for a forest. H3759
16 and righteousness remain in the **f** field. H3759
Jer 4:26 I beheld, and, lo, the **f** place *was* a H3759
23: 3 folds; and they shall be **f** and increase. H6509
Ezk 17: 5 and planted it in a **f** field; he placed *it* H2233
19:10 waters: she was **f** and full of branches H6509
Hos 13:15 Though he be **f** among *his* brethren, an H6500
Act 14:17 from heaven, and **f** seasons, filling our G2593
Col 1:10 unto all pleasing, being **f** in every good G2592

FRUITS
Gen 43:11 take of the best **f** in the land in your H2173
Ex 22:29 the first of thy ripe **f**, and of thy liquors: H4395
23:10 land, and shalt gather in the **f** thereof: H8393
Lev 25:15 of years of the **f** he shall sell unto thee: H8393
16 *the years* of the **f** doth he sell unto thee. H8393
22 **f** come in ye shall eat *of* the old *store*. H8393
26:20 shall the trees of the land yield their **f**. H6529
Dt 33:14 And for the precious **f** *brought forth* by H8393
2Sa 9:10 shalt bring in *the f*, that thy master's son
16: 1 of summer **f**, and a bottle of wine.
2Ki 8: 6 hers, and all the **f** of the field since the H8393
19:29 plant vineyards, and eat the **f** thereof. H6529
Job 31:39 If I have eaten the **f** thereof without H3581
Ps 107:37 which may yield **f** of increase. H6529
Ecc 2: 5 I planted trees in them of all *kind of* **f**: H6529
Song 4:13 pleasant **f**; camphire, with spikenard, H6529
16 into his garden, and eat his pleasant **f**. H6529
6:11 of nuts to see the **f** of the valley, *and* to H3
7:13 of pleasant *f*, new and old, *which* I
Isa 16: 9 summer **f** and for thy harvest is fallen.
33: 9 and Bashan and Carmel shake off *their f*.
Jer 40:10 ye wine, and summer **f**, and oil, and put H7019
12 wine and summer **f** very much. H7019
48:32 thy summer **f** and upon thy vintage. H7019
Lam 4: 9 through for *want of* the **f** of the field. H8570
Mic 7: 1 the summer **f**, as the grapegleanings H7019
Mal 3:11 shall not destroy the **f** of your ground; H6529
Mt 3: 8 Bring forth therefore **f** meet for G2590
7:16 Ye shall know them by their **f**. Do men G2590
20 Wherefore by their **f** ye shall know G2590
21:34 that they might receive the **f** of it. G2590
41 shall render him the **f** in their seasons. G2590
43 to a nation bringing forth the **f** thereof. G2590
Lk 3: 8 Bring forth therefore **f** worthy of G2590
12:17 I have no room where to bestow my **f**? G2590
18 will I bestow all my **f** and my goods. G1081
2Co 9:10 increase the **f** of your righteousness;) G1081
Php 1:11 Being filled with the **f** of righteousness, G2590
2Ti 2: 6 must be first partaker of the **f**. G2590
Jas 3:17 of mercy and good **f**, without partiality, G2590
Rev 18:14 And the **f** that thy soul lusted after are G3703
22: 2 twelve *manner of* **f**, *and* yielded her G2590

FRUIT-TREE See FRUIT and TREE.

FRUSTRATE
Ezr 4: 5 against them, to **f** their purpose, all the H6565
Gal 2:21 I do not **f** the grace of God: for if G114

FRUSTRATETH
Isa 44:25 That **f** the tokens of the liars, and H6565

FRYINGPAN
Lev 2: 7 **f**, it shall be made *of* fine flour with oil. H4802
7: 9 is dressed in the **f**, and in the pan, shall H4802

FUEL
Isa 9: 5 *this* shall be with burning *and* **f** of fire. H3980
19 shall be as the **f** of the fire: no man H3980
Ezk 15: 4 Behold, it is cast into the fire for **f**; the fire H402
6 given to the fire for **f**, so will I give the H402
21:32 Thou shalt be for **f** to the fire; thy blood H402

FUGITIVE
Gen 4:12 her strength; a **f** and a vagabond shalt H5128
14 and I shall be a **f** and a vagabond in the H5128

FUGITIVES

Jdg 12: 4 Ye Gileadites *are* f of Ephraim among H6412
2Ki 25:11 in the city, and the f that fell away to H5307
Isa 15: 5 My heart shall cry out for Moab; his f H1280
Ezk 17:21 And all his f with all his bands shall fall H4015

FULFIL

Gen 29:27 F her week, and we will give thee this H4390
Ex 5:13 *them,* saying, F your works, *your* daily H3615
23:26 thy land: the number of thy days I will f. H4390
1Ki 2:27 that he might f the word of the LORD, H4390
1Ch 22:13 thou takest heed to f the statutes and H6213
2Ch 36:21 To f the word of the LORD by the H4390
21 sabbath, to f threescore and ten years. H4390
Job 39: 2 months *that* they f? or knowest thou the H4390
Ps 20: 4 thine own heart, and f all thy counsel. H4390
5 banners: the LORD f all thy petitions. H4390
145:19 He will f the desire of them that fear H6213
Mt 3:15 it becometh us to f all righteousness. G4137
5:17 I am not come to destroy, but to f. G4137
Act 13:22 own heart, which shall f all my will. G4160
Ro 2:27 is by nature, if it f the law, judge thee, G5055
13:14 for the flesh, to *f* the lusts *thereof.*
Gal 5:16 and ye shall not f the lust of the flesh. G5055
6: 2 Bear ye one another's burdens, and so f G378
Php 2: 2 F ye my joy, that ye be likeminded, G4137
Col 1:25 to me for you, to f the word of God; G4137
4:17 hast received in the Lord, that thou f it. G4137
2Th 1:11 of *this* calling, and f all the good G4137
Jas 2: 8 If ye f the royal law according to the G5055
Rev 17:17 For God hath put in their hearts to f his G4160

FULFILLED

Gen 25:24 be delivered were f, behold, *there were* H4390
29:21 my days are f, that I may go in unto her. H4390
28 And Jacob did so, and f her week: and H4390
50: 3 And forty days were f for him; for so H4390
3 for him; for so are f the days of those H4390
Ex 5:14 have ye not f your task in making H3615
7:25 And seven days were f, after that the H4390
Lev 12: 4 until the days of her purifying be f. H4390
6 of her purifying are f, for a son, or for a H4390
Nu 6: 5 until the days be f, in the which he H4390
13 his separation are f: he shall be brought H4390
2Sa 7:12 And when thy days be f, and thou shalt H4390
14:22 king hath f the request of his servant. H6213
1Ki 8:15 and hath with his hand f *it,* saying, H4390
24 f *it* with thine hand, as *it is* this day. H4390
2Ch 6: 4 with his hands f *that* which he spake H4390
15 f *it* with thine hand, as *it is* this day. H4390
Ezr 1: 1 Jeremiah might be f, the LORD stirred H3615
Job 36:17 But thou hast f the judgment of the H4390
Jer 44:25 your mouths, and f with your hand, H4390
Lam 2:17 devised; he hath f his word that he had H1214
4:18 our days are f; for our end is come. H4390
Ezk 5: 2 of the siege are f: and thou shalt take H4390
Dan 4:33 The same hour was the thing f upon H5487
10: 3 at all, till three whole weeks were f. H4390
Mt 1:22 that it might be f which was spoken of G4137
2:15 that it might be f which was spoken of G4137
17 Then was f that which was spoken by G4137
23 that it might be f which was spoken by G4137
4:14 That it might be f which was spoken by G4137
5:18 in no wise pass from the law, till all be f. G1096
8:17 That it might be f which was spoken by G4137
12:17 That it might be f which was spoken by G4137
13:14 And in them is f the prophecy of Esaias, G378
35 That it might be f which was spoken by G4137
21: 4 All this was done, that it might be f G4137
24:34 shall not pass, till all these things be f. G1096
26:54 But how then shall the scriptures be f, G4137
56 the prophets might be f. Then all the G4137
27: 9 Then was f that which was spoken by G4137
35 that it might be f which was spoken by G4137
Mk 1:15 And saying, The time is f, and the G4137
13: 4 the sign when all these things shall be f? G4931
14:49 me not: but the scriptures must be f. G4137
15:28 And the scripture was f, which saith, G4137
Lk 1:20 words, which shall be f in their season. G4137
2:43 And when they had f the days, as they G5048
4:21 This day is this scripture f in your ears. G4137
21:22 all things which are written may be f. G4137
24 until the times of the Gentiles be f. G4137
32 shall not pass away, till all be f. G1096
22:16 until it be f in the kingdom of God. G4137
24:44 all things must be f, which were written G4137
Jn 3:29 voice: this my joy therefore is f. G4137
12:38 the prophet might be f, which he spake, G4137
13:18 scripture may be f, He that eateth bread G4137
Jn 15:25 the word might be f that is written in G4137
17:12 perdition; that the scripture might be f. G4137
13 they might have my joy f in themselves. G4137
18: 9 That the saying might be f, which he G4137
32 That the saying of Jesus might be f, G4137
19:24 scripture might be f, which saith, They G4137
28 the scripture might be f, saith, I thirst. G5048
36 be f, A bone of him shall not be broken. G4137
Act 1:16 must needs have been f, which the Holy G4137
3:18 that Christ should suffer, he hath so f. G4137
9:23 And after that many days were f, the G4137
12:25 when they had f *their* ministry, and G4137
13:25 And as John f his course, he said, G4137
27 they have f *them* in condemning *him.* G4137
29 And when they had f all that was G5055
33 God hath f the same unto us their G1603
14:26 grace of God for the work which they f. G4137
Ro 8: 4 the law might be f in us, who walk not G4137
13: 8 he that loveth another hath f the law. G4137
2Co 10: 6 disobedience, when your obedience is f. G4137
Gal 5:14 For all the law is f in one word, *even* in G4137
Jas 2:23 And the scripture was f which saith, G4137
Rev 6:11 be killed as they *were,* should be f. G4137
15: 8 plagues of the seven angels were f. G5055
17:17 beast, until the words of God shall be f. G5055
20: 3 years should be f: and after that he G5055

FULFILLING

Ps 148: 8 and vapour; stormy wind f his word: H6213
Ro 13:10 therefore love *is* the f of the law. G4138
Eph 2: 3 the lusts of our flesh, f the desires of the G4160

FULL

Gen 14:10 And the vale of Siddim *was f of*
15:16 the iniquity of the Amorites *is* not yet f. H8003
25: 8 an old man, and f *of years;* and was H7649
35:29 *being* old and f of days: and his sons H7649
41: 1 And it came to pass at the end of two f H3117
7 seven rank and f ears. And Pharaoh H4392
22 ears came up in one stalk, f and good: H4392
43:21 our money in f weight: and we have H4948
Ex 8:21 Egyptians shall be f of swarms *of flies,* H4390
16: 3 eat bread to the f; for ye have brought H7648
8 bread to the f; for that the LORD H7646
33 and put an omer f of manna therein, H4393
22: 3 he should make f restitution; if he have H7999
Lev 2:14 the fire, *even* corn beaten out of f ears. H3759
16:12 And he shall take a censer f of burning H4393
12 and his hands f of sweet incense beaten H4393
19:29 and the land become f of wickedness. H4390
25:29 sold; *within* a f year may he redeem it. H3117
30 the space of a f year, then the house H8549
26: 5 to the f, and dwell in your land safely. H7648
Nu 7:13 both of them *were* f of fine flour H4392
14 One spoon of ten *shekels* of gold, f of H4392
19 both of them f of fine flour mingled H4392
20 One spoon of gold of ten *shekels,* f of H4392
25 both of them f of fine flour mingled H4392
26 One golden spoon of ten *shekels,* f of H4392
31 both of them f of fine flour mingled H4392
32 One golden spoon of ten *shekels,* f of H4392
37 both of them f of fine flour mingled H4392
38 One golden spoon of ten *shekels,* f of H4392
43 both of them f of fine flour mingled H4392
44 One golden spoon of ten *shekels,* f of H4392
49 both of them f of fine flour mingled H4392
50 One golden spoon of ten *shekels,* f of H4392
55 both of them f of fine flour mingled H4392
56 One golden spoon of ten *shekels,* f of H4392
61 both of them f of fine flour mingled H4392
62 One golden spoon of ten *shekels,* f of H4392
67 both of them f of fine flour mingled H4392
68 One golden spoon of ten *shekels,* f of H4392
73 both of them f of fine flour mingled H4392
74 One golden spoon of ten *shekels,* f of H4392
79 both of them f of fine flour mingled H4392
80 One golden spoon of ten *shekels,* f of H4392
86 The golden spoons *were* twelve, f of H4392
22:18 give me his house f of silver and gold, I H4393
24:13 If Balak would give me his house f of H4393
Dt 6:11 And houses f of all good *things,* which H4392
11 when thou shalt have eaten and be f; H7646
8:10 When thou hast eaten and art f, then H7646
12 Lest *when* thou hast eaten and art f, H7646
11:15 cattle, that thou mayest eat and be f. H7646
21:13 and her mother a f month: and after H3117
33:23 with favour, and f with the blessing of H4392
34: 9 And Joshua the son of Nun was f of the H4392
Jdg 6:38 dew out of the fleece, a bowl f of water. H4393
Jdg 16:27 Now the house was f of men and H4390
Ru 1:21 I went out f, and the LORD hath H4392
2:12 thy work, and a f reward be given thee H8003
1Sa 2: 5 *They that were* f have hired out H7649
18:27 and they gave them in f tale to the king, H4390
27: 7 was a f year and four months. H3117
2Sa 8: 2 and with one f line to keep alive. And H4393
13:23 And it came to pass after two f years, H3117
14:28 So Absalom dwelt two f years in H3117
23:11 a piece of ground f of lentiles: and the H4392
2Ki 3:16 the LORD, Make this valley f of ditches.
4: 4 and thou shalt set aside that which is f. H4392
6 the vessels were f, that she said unto her H4390
39 gourds his lap f, and came and shred H4393
42 of barley, and f ears of corn in the husk
6:17 the mountain *was* f of horses and H4390
7:15 lo, all the way *was* f of garments and H4392
9:24 And Jehu drew a bow with his f H4390
10:21 of Baal was f from one end to another. H4390
15:13 and he reigned a f month in Samaria. H3117
1Ch 11:13 a parcel of ground f of barley; and the H4392
21:22 shalt grant it me for the f price: that the H4392
24 buy it for the f price: for I will not take H4392
23: 1 So when David was old and f of days, H7646
29:28 And he died in a good old age, f of H7649
2Ch 24:15 But Jehoiada waxed old, and was f of H7646
Neh 9:25 possessed houses f of all goods, wells H4392
Est 3: 5 reverence, then was Haman f of wrath. H4390
5: 9 was f of indignation against Mordecai. H4390
Job 5:26 Thou shalt come to *thy* grave in a f age, H3624
7: 4 be gone? and I am f of tossings to and H7646
10:15 lift up my head. *I am* f of confusion; H7649
11: 2 and should a man f of talk be justified?
14: 1 woman *is* of few days, and f of trouble. H7649
20:11 His bones are f *of the sin* of his youth, H4390
21:23 One dieth in his f strength, being H8537
24 His breasts are f of milk, and his bones H4390
32:18 For I am f of matter, the spirit within H4390
36:16 set on thy table *should be* f of fatness. H4390
42:17 So Job died, *being* old and f of days. H7649
Ps 10: 7 His mouth is f of cursing and deceit H4390
17:14 hid *treasure:* they are f of children, and H7646
26:10 and their right hand is f of bribes. H4390
29: 4 the voice of the LORD *is* f of majesty.
33: 5 earth is f of the goodness of the LORD. H4390
48:10 thy right hand is f of righteousness. H4390
65: 9 river of God, *which* is f of water: thou H4390
69:20 my heart; and I am f of heaviness: and I
73:10 of a f *cup* are wrung out to them. H4392
74:20 earth are f of the habitations of cruelty. H4390
75: 8 wine is red; it is f of mixture; and he H4392
78:25 angels' food: he sent them meat to the f. H7648
38 But he, *being* f of compassion, forgave
86:15 But thou, O Lord, *art* a God f of
88: 3 For my soul is f of troubles: and my life H7646
104:16 The trees of the LORD are f *of sap;* the H7646
24 them all: the earth is f of thy riches. H4390
111: 4 LORD *is* gracious and f of compassion.
112: 4 and f of compassion, and righteous.
119:64 The earth, O LORD, is f of thy mercy: H4390
127: 5 Happy *is* the man that hath his quiver f H4390
144:13 *That* our garners *may be* f, affording all H4392
145: 8 The LORD *is* gracious, and f of
Prv 17: 1 than an house f of sacrifices *with* strife. H4392
27: 7 The f soul loatheth an honeycomb; but H7649
20 Hell and destruction are never f; so the H7646
30: 9 Lest I be f, and deny *thee,* and say, Who H7646
Ecc 1: 7 yet the sea *is* not f; unto the place from H4392
8 All things *are* f of labour; man cannot
4: 6 f *with* travail and vexation of spirit. H4393
9: 3 of the sons of men is f of evil, and H4390
10:14 A fool also is f of words: a man cannot H7235
11: 3 If the clouds be f of rain, they empty H4390
Isa 1:11 the LORD: I am f of the burnt offerings H7646
15 will not hear: your hands are f of blood. H4390
21 become an harlot! it was f of judgment; H4392
2: 7 Their land also is f of silver and gold, H4390
7 their land is also f of horses, neither *is* H4390
8 Their land also is f of idols; they H4390
6: 3 hosts: the whole earth *is* f of his glory. H4393
11: 9 the earth shall be f of the knowledge of H4390
13:21 houses shall be f of doleful creatures; H4390
15: 9 For the waters of Dimon shall be f of H4390
22: 2 Thou that art f of stirs, a tumultuous H4392
7 valleys shall be f of chariots, and the H4390
25: 6 lees, of fat things f of marrow, *of* wines
28: 8 For all tables are f of vomit *and* H4390
30:27 heavy: his lips are f of indignation, and H4390
51:20 bull in a net: they are f of the fury of the H4392

Jer 4:12 *Even* a f wind from those *places* shall H4392
27 be desolate; yet will I not make a f end.
5: 7 fed them to the f, they then committed H7646
10 but make not a f end: take away her
18 LORD, I will not make a f end with you.
27 As a cage is f of birds, so *are* their H4392
27 so *are* their houses f of deceit: therefore H4392
6:11 Therefore I am f of the fury of the H4390
11 the aged with *him that is* f of days. H4392
23:10 For the land is f of adulterers; for H4390
28: 3 Within two f years will I bring again H3117
11 within the space of two f years. And the H3117
30:11 though I make a f end of all nations
11 will I not make a f end of thee: but I will
35: 5 the Rechabites pots f of wine, and cups, H4392
46:28 for I will make a f end of all the nations
28 but I will not make a f end of thee, but
Lam 1: 1 sit solitary, *that was* f of people! *how* is H7227
3:30 him: he is filled f with reproach. H7646
Ezk 1:18 *were* f of eyes round about them four. H4392
7:23 Make a chain: for the land is f of H4390
23 crimes, and the city is f of violence. H4390
9: 9 and the land is f of blood, and the city H4390
9 of blood, and the city f of perverseness: H4390
10: 4 f of the brightness of the LORD'S glory. H4390
12 the wheels, *were* f of eyes round about, H4392
11:13 make a f end of the remnant of Israel?
17: 3 longwinged, f of feathers, which had H4392
19:10 f of branches by reason of many waters.
28:12 f of wisdom, and perfect in beauty. H4392
32: 6 and the rivers shall be f of thee. H4390
15 whereof it was f, when I shall smite all H4393
37: 1 of the valley which *was* f of bones, H4392
39:19 And ye shall eat fat till ye be f, and H7654
41: 8 *were* a f reed of six great cubits. H4393
Dan 3:19 Then was Nebuchadnezzar f of fury, H4391
8:23 are come to the f, a king of fierce H8552
10: 2 I Daniel was mourning three f weeks. H3117
Joel 2:24 And the floors shall be f of wheat, and H4390
3:13 for the press is f, the fats overflow; for H4390
Am 2:13 as a cart is pressed *that is* f of sheaves. H4392
Mic 3: 8 But truly I am f of power by the spirit H4390
6:12 For the rich men thereof are f of H4390
Nah 3: 1 Woe to the bloody city! it *is* all f of lies H4392
Hab 3: 3 and the earth was f of his praise. H4390
Zec 8: 5 And the streets of the city shall be f of H4390
Mt 6:22 thy whole body shall be f of light. *G5460*
23 body shall be f of darkness. If therefore
13:48 Which, when it was f, they drew to *G4137*
14:20 that remained twelve baskets f. *G4134*
15:37 *meat* that was left seven baskets f. *G4134*
23:25 they are f of extortion and excess. *G1073*
27 but are within f of dead *men's* bones, *G1073*
28 ye are f of hypocrisy and iniquity. *G3324*
Mk 4:28 the ear, after that the f corn in the ear. *G4134*
37 beat into the ship, so that it was now f. *G1072*
6:43 And they took up twelve baskets f of *G4134*
7: 9 And he said unto them, F well ye reject
8:19 how many baskets f of fragments took *G4134*
20 how many baskets f of fragments took *G4138*
15:36 And one ran and filled a spunge f of *G1072*
Lk 1:57 Now Elisabeth's f time came that she *G4130*
4: 1 And Jesus being f of the Holy Ghost *G4134*
5:12 city, behold a man f of leprosy: who *G4134*
6:25 Woe unto you that are f! for ye shall *G1705*
11:34 whole body also is f of light; but when *G5460*
34 *eye* is evil, thy body also *is* f of darkness.
36 If thy whole body therefore *be* f of light, *G5460*
36 the whole shall be f of light, as when *G5460*
39 part is f of ravening and wickedness. *G1073*
16:20 which was laid at his gate, f of sores,
Jn 1:14 of the Father,) f of grace and truth. *G4134*
7: 8 this feast; for my time is not yet f come. *G4137*
15:11 in you, and *that* your joy might be f. *G4137*
16:24 ye shall receive, that your joy may be f. *G4137*
19:29 Now there was set a vessel f of vinegar: *G3324*
21:11 drew the net to land f of great fishes, an *G3324*
Act 2:13 Others mocking said, These men are f *G3325*
28 make me f of joy with thy countenance. *G4137*
6: 3 of honest report, f of the Holy Ghost *G4134*
5 Stephen, a man f of faith and of the *G4134*
8 And Stephen, f of faith and power, did *G4134*
7:23 And when he was f forty years old, it *G4137*
55 But he, being f of the Holy Ghost, *G4134*
9:36 this woman was f of good works and *G4134*
11:24 For he was a good man, and f of the *G4134*
13:10 And said, O f of all subtilty and all *G4134*
19:28 *sayings*, they were f of wrath, and cried *G4134*
Ro 1:29 maliciousness; f of envy, murder, *G3324*
3:14 Whose mouth *is* f of cursing and *G1073*
15:14 that ye also are f of goodness, filled *G3324*
1Co 4: 8 Now ye are f, now ye are rich, ye have *G2880*
Php 2:26 For he longed after you all, and was f of
4:12 both to be f and to be hungry, both *G5526*
18 But I have all, and abound: I am f, *G4137*
Col 2: 2 unto all riches of the f assurance of *G4136*
2Ti 4: 5 make f proof of thy ministry. *G4135*
Heb 5:14 to them that are of f age, *even* those *G5046*
6:11 to the f assurance of hope unto the end: *G4186*
10:22 Let us draw near with a true heart in f *G4186*
Jas 3: 8 *it is* an unruly evil, f of deadly poison. *G3324*
17 to be entreated, f of mercy and good *G3324*
1Pt 1: 8 with joy unspeakable and f of glory:
2Pt 2:14 Having eyes f of adultery, and that *G3324*
1Jn 1: 4 we unto you, that your joy may be f. *G4137*
2Jn 8 but that we receive a f reward. *G4134*
12 face to face, that our joy may be f. *G4137*
Rev 4: 6 four beasts f of eyes before and behind. *G1073*
8 and *they were* f of eyes within: and they *G1073*
5: 8 and golden vials f of odours, which are *G1073*
15: 7 seven golden vials f of the wrath of *G1073*
16:10 his kingdom was f of darkness; and they
17: 3 scarlet coloured beast, f of names of *G1073*
4 cup in her hand f of abominations and *G1073*
21: 9 had the seven vials f of the seven last *G1073*

FULLER
Mk 9: 3 so as no f on earth can white them. *G1102*

FULLER'S
2Ki 18:17 which *is* in the highway of the f field. H3526
Isa 7: 3 upper pool in the highway of the f field; H3526
36: 2 upper pool in the highway of the f field. H3526

FULLERS'
Mal 3: 2 *is* like a refiner's fire, and like f soap: H3526

FULLY
Nu 7: 1 that Moses had f set up the tabernacle, H3615
14:24 hath followed me f, him will I bring into H4390
Ru 2:11 unto her, It hath f been shewed me, all H5046
1Ki 11: 6 and went not f after the LORD, as *did* H4390
Ecc 8:11 sons of men is f set in them to do evil. H4390
Nah 1:10 they shall be devoured as stubble f dry. H4390
Act 2: 1 And when the day of Pentecost was f *G4845*
Ro 4:21 And being f persuaded that, what he *G4135*
14: 5 man be f persuaded in his own mind. *G4135*
15:19 I have f preached the gospel of Christ. *G4137*
2Ti 3:10 But thou hast f known my doctrine, *G3877*
4:17 might be f known, and *that* all *G4135*
Rev 14:18 of the earth; for her grapes are f ripe.

FULNESS
Nu 18:27 and as the f of the winepress. H4395
Dt 33:16 of the earth and f thereof, and *for* the H4393
1Ch 16:32 Let the sea roar, and the f thereof: let H4393
Job 20:22 In the f of his sufficiency he shall be in H4390
Ps 16:11 in thy presence *is* f of joy; at thy right H7648
24: 1 The earth *is* the LORD'S, and the f H4393
50:12 for the world *is* mine, and the f thereof. H4393
89:11 the f thereof, thou hast founded them. H4393
96:11 glad; let the sea roar, and the f thereof. H4393
98: 7 Let the sea roar, and the f thereof; the H4393
Ezk 16:49 sister Sodom, pride, f of bread, and H7653
19: 7 f thereof, by the noise of his roaring. H4393
Jn 1:16 And of his f have all we received, and *G4138*
Ro 11:12 of the Gentiles; how much more their f? *G4138*
25 until the f of the Gentiles be come in. *G4138*
15:29 f of the blessing of the gospel of Christ. *G4138*
1Co 10:26 For the earth *is* the Lord's, and the f *G4138*
28 earth *is* the Lord's, and the f thereof: *G4138*
Gal 4: 4 But when the f of the time was come, *G4138*
Eph 1:10 That in the dispensation of the f of *G4138*
23 Which is his body, the f of him that *G4138*
3:19 ye might be filled with all the f of God. *G4138*
4:13 of the stature of the f of Christ: *G4138*
Col 1:19 *Father* that in him should all f dwell; *G4138*
2: 9 For in him dwelleth all the f of the *G4138*

FURBISH
Jer 46: 4 with *your* helmets; f the spears, *and* H4838

FURBISHED
Ezk 21: 9 sword, a sword is sharpened, and also f: H4803
10 sore slaughter; it is f that it may glitter: H4803
11 And he hath given it to be f, that it may H4803
11 is f, to give it into the hand of the slayer. H4803
28 f, to consume because of the glittering: H4803

FURIOUS
Prv 22:24 and with a f man thou shalt not go: H2534
29:22 An angry man stirreth up strife, and a f H2534
Ezk 5:15 f rebukes. I the LORD have spoken *it*. H2534
25:17 upon them with f rebukes; and they H2534
Dan 2:12 angry and very f, and commanded to H7108
Nah 1: 2 and *is* f; the LORD will take H1167+H2534

FURIOUSLY
2Ki 9:20 Jehu the son of Nimshi; for he driveth f. H7697
Ezk 23:25 and they shall deal f with thee: they H2534

FURLONGS
Lk 24:13 was from Jerusalem *about* threescore f. *G4712*
Jn 6:19 and twenty or thirty f, they see Jesus *G4712*
11:18 nigh unto Jerusalem, about fifteen f off: *G4712*
Rev 14:20 space of a thousand *and* six hundred f. *G4712*
21:16 twelve thousand f. The length and the *G4712*

FURNACE
Gen 15:17 behold a smoking f, and a burning H8574
19:28 the country went up as the smoke of a f. H3536
Ex 9: 8 of ashes of the f, and let Moses sprinkle H3536
10 And they took ashes of the f, and stood H3536
19:18 f, and the whole mount quaked greatly. H3536
Dt 4:20 out of the iron f, *even* out of Egypt, to H3564
1Ki 8:51 Egypt, from the midst of the f of iron: H3564
Ps 12: 6 in a f of earth, purified seven times. H5948
Prv 17: 3 The fining pot *is* for silver, and the f for H3564
27:21 *As* the fining pot for silver, and the f for H3564
Isa 31: 9 fire *is* in Zion, and his f in Jerusalem. H8574
48:10 I have chosen thee in the f of affliction. H3564
Jer 11: 4 from the iron f, saying, Obey my voice, H3564
Ezk 22:18 of the f; they are *even* the dross of silver. H3564
20 the midst of the f, to blow the fire upon H3564
22 As silver is melted in the midst of the f, H3564
Dan 3: 6 be cast into the midst of a burning fiery f. H861
11 be cast into the midst of a burning fiery f. H861
15 of a burning fiery f; and who *is* that God H861
17 the burning fiery f, and he will deliver *us* H861
19 should heat the f one seven times more H861
20 *and* to cast *them* into the burning fiery f. H861
21 cast into the midst of the burning fiery f. H861
22 was urgent, and the f exceeding hot, the H861
23 into the midst of the burning fiery f. H861
26 of the burning fiery f, *and* spake, and H861
Mt 13:42 And shall cast them into a f of fire: *G2575*
50 And shall cast them into the f of fire: *G2575*
Rev 1:15 as if they burned in a f; and his voice as *G2575*
9: 2 smoke of a great f; and the sun and the *G2575*

FURNACES
Neh 3:11 the other piece, and the tower of the f. H8574
12:38 tower of the f even unto the broad wall; H8574

FURNISH
Dt 15:14 Thou shalt f him liberally out of thy H6059
Ps 78:19 Can God f a table in the wilderness? H6186
Isa 65:11 f the drink offering unto that number. H4390
Jer 46:19 O thou daughter dwelling in Egypt, f H6213

FURNISHED
1Ki 9:11 *(Now* Hiram the king of Tyre had f H5375
Prv 9: 2 her wine; she hath also f her table. H6186
Mt 22:10 and the wedding was f with guests. *G4130*
Mk 14:15 large upper room f *and* prepared: there *G4766*
Lk 22:12 a large upper room f: there make ready. *G4766*
2Ti 3:17 throughly f unto all good works. *G1822*

FURNITURE
Gen 31:34 in the camel's f, and sat upon them. H3733
Ex 31: 7 and all the f of the tabernacle, H3627
8 And the table and his f, and the pure H3627
8 with all his f, and the altar of incense, H3627
9 with all his f, and the laver and his foot, H3627
35:14 the light, and his f, and his lamps, with H3627
39:33 the tent, and all his f, his taches, his H3627
Nah 2: 9 store *and* glory out of all the pleasant f. H3627

FURROW
Job 39:10 his band in the f? or will he harrow the H8525

FURROWS
Job 31:38 If my land cry against me, or that the f H8525
Ps 65:10 thou settlest the f thereof: thou makest H1417
129: 3 upon my back: they made long their f. H4618
Ezk 17: 7 water it by the f of her plantation. H6170
10 it? it shall wither in the f where it grew. H6170
Hos 10: 4 up as hemlock in the f of the field. H8525

Hos 10:10 shall bind themselves in their two f. H5869
12:11 altars *are* as heaps in the f of the fields. H8525

FURTHER
Nu 22:26 And the angel of the LORD went f, and H3254
Dt 20: 8 And the officers shall speak f unto the H3254
1Sa 10:22 Therefore they inquired of the LORD f, H5750
Est 9:12 *is* thy request f? and it shall be done. H5750
Job 38:11 thou come, but no f: and here shall thy H3254
40: 5 yea, twice; but I will proceed no f. H3254
Ps 140: 8 of the wicked: f not his wicked device; H6329
Ecc 8:17 shall not find *it*; yea f; though a wise *man*
12:12 And f, by these, my son, be H3148
Mt 26:65 blasphemy; what f need have we of G2089
Mk 5:35 why troublest thou the Master any f? G2089
14:63 saith, What need we any f witnesses? G2089
Lk 22:71 And they said, What need we any f G2089
24:28 made as though he would have gone f. G4208
Act 4:17 But that it spread no f among the G1909
21 So when they had f threatened them,
12: 3 Jews, he proceeded f to take Peter also. G4369
21:28 this place: and f brought Greeks also G2089
24: 4 Notwithstanding, that I be not f G4119
27:28 had gone a little f, they sounded again, G1024
2Ti 3: 9 But they shall proceed no f: for their G1909
Heb 7:11 the law,) what f need *was there* that G2089

FURTHERANCE
Php 1:12 out rather unto the f of the gospel; G4297
25 with you all for your f and joy of faith; G4297

FURTHERED
Ezr 8:36 they f the people, and the house of God. H5375

FURTHERMORE
Ex 4: 6 And the LORD said f unto him, Put H5750
Dt 4:21 F the LORD was angry with me for your
9:13 F the LORD spake unto me, saying, I
1Sa 26:10 David said f, *As* the LORD liveth, the
1Ch 17:10 all thine enemies. F I tell thee that the
27:16 F over the tribes of Israel: the ruler of the
1Ch 29: 1 F David the king said unto all the
2Ch 4: 9 F he made the court of the priests, and
Job 34: 1 F Elihu answered and said,
Ezk 8: 6 He said f unto me, Son of man, seest
23:40 And f, that ye have sent for men to come H637
2Co 2:12 F, when I came to Troas to *preach* G1161
1Th 4: 1 F then we beseech you, brethren, and G3063
Heb 12: 9 F we have had fathers of our flesh G1534

FURY
Gen 27:44 days, until thy brother's f turn away; H2534
Lev 26:28 unto you also in f; and I, even I, will H2534
Job 20:23 *God* shall cast the f of his wrath upon H2740
Isa 27: 4 F *is* not in me: who would set the briers H2534
34: 2 all nations, and *his* f upon all their H2534
42:25 upon him the f of his anger, and the H2534
51:13 day because of the f of the oppressor, H2534
13 and where *is* the f of the oppressor? H2534
17 the cup of his f; thou hast drunken the H2534
20 of the f of the LORD, the rebuke of thy God. H2534
22 my f; thou shalt no more drink it again: H2534
59:18 he will repay, f to his adversaries, H2534
63: 3 them in my f; and their blood shall H2534
5 unto me; and my f, it upheld me. H2534
6 them drunk in my f, and I will bring H2534
66:15 f, and his rebuke with flames of fire. H2534
Jer 4: 4 of Jerusalem: lest my f come forth like H2534
6:11 Therefore I am full of the f of the H2534
7:20 anger and my f shall be poured out H2534
10:25 Pour out thy f upon the heathen that H2534
21: 5 in anger, and in f, and in great wrath. H2534
12 the oppressor, lest my f go out like fire, H2534
23:19 LORD is gone forth in f, even a grievous H2534
25:15 the wine cup of this f at my hand, and H2534
30:23 LORD goeth forth with f, a continuing H2534
32:31 anger and of my f from the day that H2534
37 anger, and in my f, and in great wrath; H2534
33: 5 anger and in my f, and for all whose H2534
36: 7 the anger and the f that the LORD hath H2534
42:18 anger and my f hath been poured forth H2534
18 so shall my f be poured forth upon H2534
Jer 44: 6 Wherefore my f and mine anger was H2534
Lam 2: 4 of Zion: he poured out his f like fire. H2534
4:11 The LORD hath accomplished his f; he H2534
Ezk 5:13 I will cause my f to rest upon them, and H2534
13 I have accomplished my f in them. H2534
15 thee in anger and in f and in furious H2534
6:12 thus will I accomplish my f upon them. H2534
7: 8 Now will I shortly pour out my f upon H2534
8:18 Therefore will I also deal in f: mine eye H2534
9: 8 pouring out of thy f upon Jerusalem? H2534
13:13 wind in my f; and there shall be an H2534
13 great hailstones in *my* f to consume *it*. H2534
14:19 and pour out my f upon it in blood, to H2534
16:38 I will give thee blood in f and jealousy. H2534
42 So will I make my f toward thee to rest, H2534
19:12 But she was plucked up in f, she was H2534
20: 8 said, I will pour out my f upon them, to H2534
13 would pour out my f upon them in the H2534
21 would pour out my f upon them, to H2534
33 with f poured out, will I rule over you: H2534
34 out arm, and with f poured out. H2534
21:17 my f to rest: I the LORD have said *it*. H2534
22:20 anger and in my f, and I will leave *you* H2534
22 LORD have poured out my f upon you. H2534
24: 8 That it might cause f to come up to H2534
13 I have caused my f to rest upon thee. H2534
25:14 according to my f; and they shall know H2534
30:15 And I will pour my f upon Sin, the H2534
36: 6 and in my f, because ye have borne H2534
18 Wherefore I poured my f upon them H2534
38:18 *that* my f shall come up in my face. H2534
Dan 3:13 Then Nebuchadnezzar in *his* rage and f H2528
19 Then was Nebuchadnezzar full of f, and H2528
8: 6 and ran unto him in the f of his power. H2534
9:16 anger and thy f be turned away from H2534
11:44 go forth with great f to destroy, and H2534
Mic 5:15 in anger and f upon the heathen, such H2534
Nah 1: 6 of his anger? his f is poured out like H2534
Zec 8: 2 and I was jealous for her with great f. H2534

G

GAAL
Jdg 9:26 And G the son of Ebed came with his H1603
28 And G the son of Ebed said, Who *is* H1603
30 the words of G the son of Ebed, his H1603
31 saying, Behold, G the son of Ebed and H1603
35 And G the son of Ebed went out, and H1603
36 And when G saw the people, he said to H1603
37 And G spake again and said, See there H1603
39 And G went out before the men of H1603
41 Zebul thrust out G and his brethren, H1603

GAASH
Jos 24:30 on the north side of the hill of G. H1608
Jdg 2: 9 Ephraim, on the north side of the hill G. H1608
2Sa 23:30 Pirathonite, Hiddai of the brooks of G, H1608
1Ch 11:32 Hurai of the brooks of G, Abiel the H1608

GABA
Jos 18:24 and G; twelve cities with their villages: H1387
Ezr 2:26 The children of Ramah and G, six H1387

GABBAI
Neh 11: 8 And after him G, Sallai, nine hundred H1373

GABBATHA
Jn 19:13 the Pavement, but in the Hebrew, G. G1042

GABER See EZION-GABER.

GABRIEL
Dan 8:16 called, and said, G, make this *man* to H1403
9:21 even the man G, whom I had seen in H1403
Lk 1:19 said unto him, I am G, that stand in the G1043
26 And in the sixth month the angel G was G1043

GAD
Gen 30:11 cometh: and she called his name G. H1410
35:26 Leah's handmaid; G, and Asher: these H1410
46:16 And the sons of G; Ziphion, and Haggi, H1410
Gen 49:19 G, a troop shall overcome him: but he H1410
Ex 1: 4 Dan, and Naphtali, G, and Asher. H1410
Nu 1:14 Of G; Eliasaph the son of Deuel. H1410
24 Of the children of G, by their H1410
25 of the tribe of G, *were* forty and five H1410
2:14 Then the tribe of G: and the captain of H1410
14 of G *shall be* Eliasaph the son of Reuel. H1410
7:42 prince of the children of G, *offered*: H1410
10:20 of G *was* Eliasaph the son of Deuel. H1410
13:15 Of the tribe of G, Geuel the son of H1410
26:15 The children of G after their families: H1410
18 of the children of G according to those H1410
32: 1 and the children of G had a very great H1410
2 The children of G and the children of H1410
6 And Moses said unto the children of G H1410
25 And the children of G and the children H1410
29 If the children of G and the children of H1410
31 And the children of G and the children H1410
33 to the children of G, and to the children H1410
34 And the children of G built Dibon, and H1410
34:14 of the children of G according to the H1425
Dt 27:13 to curse; Reuben, G, and Asher, and H1410
33:20 And of G he said, Blessed *be* he that H1410
20 *be* he that enlargeth G: he dwelleth as a H1410
Jos 4:12 the children of G, and half the tribe of H1410
13:24 unto the tribe of G, *even* unto the H1410
24 of G according to their families. H1410
28 of the children of G after their families, H1410
18: 7 inheritance: and G, and Reuben, and H1410
20: 8 out of the tribe of G, and Golan in H1410
21: 7 out of the tribe of G, and out of the tribe H1410
38 And out of the tribe of G, Ramoth in H1410
22: 9 the children of G and the half tribe of H1410
10 the children of G and the half tribe of H1410
11 the children of G and the half tribe of H1410
13 to the children of G, and to the half tribe H1410
15 to the children of G, and to the half tribe H1410
21 the children of G and the half tribe of H1410
25 and children of G; ye have no part in H1410
30 the children of G and the children of H1410
Jos 22:31 to the children of G, and to the children H1410
32 the children of G, out of the land of H1410
33 the children of Reuben and G dwelt. H1410
34 the children of G called the altar *Ed*: H1410
1Sa 13: 7 to the land of G and Gilead. As for Saul, H1410
22: 5 And the prophet G said unto David, H1410
2Sa 24: 5 of the river of G, and toward Jazer: H1410
11 the prophet G, David's seer, saying, H1410
13 So G came to David, and told him, and H1410
14 And David said unto G, I am in a great H1410
18 And G came that day to David, and H1410
19 G, went up as the LORD commanded. H1410
1Ch 2: 2 and Benjamin, Naphtali, G, and Asher. H1410
5:11 And the children of G dwelt over H1410
6:63 out of the tribe of G, and out of the tribe H1410
80 And out of the tribe of G; Ramoth in H1410
12:14 These *were* of the sons of G, captains of H1410
21: 9 And the LORD spake unto G, David's H1410
11 So G came to David, and said unto H1410
13 And David said unto G, I am in a great H1410
18 commanded G to say to David, that H1410
19 And David went up at the saying of G, H1410
29:29 prophet, and in the book of G the seer, H1410
2Ch 29:25 of David, and of G the king's seer, and H1410
Jer 49: 1 G, and his people dwell in his cities? H1410
Ezk 48:27 side unto the west side, G a *portion*. H1410
28 And by the border of G, at the south H1410
34 gates; one gate of G, one gate of Asher, H1410
Rev 7: 5 tribe of G *were* sealed twelve thousand. G1045

GADARENES
Mk 5: 1 of the sea, into the country of the G. G1046
Lk 8:26 of the G, which is over against Galilee. G1046
37 of the country of the G round about G1046

GADDAH See HAZAR-GADDAH.

GADDEST
Jer 2:36 Why g thou about so much to change H235

GADDI
Nu 13:11 tribe of Manasseh, **G** the son of Susi. H1426

GADDIEL
Nu 13:10 Of the tribe of Zebulun, **G** the son of H1427

GADER
See BETH-GADER.

GADI
2Ki 15:14 For Menahem the son of **G** went up H1424
17 the son of **G** to reign over Israel, H1424

GADITE
2Sa 23:36 the son of Nathan of Zobah, Bani the **G**, H1425

GADITES
Dt 3:12 gave I unto the Reubenites and to the **G**. H1425
16 and unto the **G** I gave from Gilead H1425
4:43 in Gilead, of the **G**; and Golan in H1425
29: 8 **G**, and to the half tribe of Manasseh. H1425
Jos 1:12 And to the Reubenites, and to the **G**, H1425
12: 6 the **G**, and the half tribe of Manasseh. H1425
13: 8 With whom the Reubenites and the **G** H1425
22: 1 the **G**, and the half tribe of Manasseh, H1425
2Ki 10:33 the land of Gilead, the **G**, and the H1425
1Ch 5:18 The sons of Reuben, and the **G**, and half H1425
26 and the **G**, and the half tribe of H1425
12: 8 And of the **G** there separated H1425
37 and the **G**, and of the half tribe H1425
26:32 Reubenites, the **G**, and the half tribe of H1425

GAHAM
Gen 22:24 and **G**, and Thahash, and Maachah. H1514

GAHAR
Ezr 2:47 children of **G**, the children of Reaiah, H1515
Neh 7:49 the children of Giddel, the children of **G**, H1515

GAIN
Jdg 5:19 of Megiddo; they took no **g** of money. H1215
Job 22: 3 righteous? or *is it* **g** *to him*, that thou H1215
Prv 1:19 that is greedy of **g**; *which* taketh away H1215
3:14 silver, and the **g** thereof than fine gold. H8393
15:27 He that is greedy of **g** troubleth his own H1215
28: 8 He that by usury and unjust **g** H8636
Isa 33:15 he that despiseth the **g** of oppressions, H1215
56:11 every one for his **g**, from his quarter. H1215
Ezk 22:13 at thy dishonest **g** which thou hast H1215
27 *and* to destroy souls, to get dishonest **g**. H1215
Dan 2: 8 that ye would **g** the time, because ye H2084
11:39 many, and shall divide the land for **g**. H4242
Mic 4:13 consecrate their **g** unto the LORD, and H1215
Mt 16:26 For what is a man profited, if he shall **g** G2770
Mk 8:36 a man, if he shall **g** the whole world, G2770
Lk 9:25 For what is a man advantaged, if he **g** G2770
Act 16:16 her masters much **g** by soothsaying: G2039
19:24 brought no small **g** unto the craftsmen; G2039
1Co 9:19 unto all, that I might **g** the more. G2770
20 a Jew, that I might **g** the Jews; to them G2770
20 I might **g** them that are under the law; G2770
21 I might **g** them that are without law. G2770
22 as weak, that I might **g** the weak: I am G2770
2Co 12:17 Did I make a **g** of you by any of them G4122
18 Did Titus make a **g** of you? walked we G4122
Php 1:21 to me to live *is* Christ, and to die *is* **g**. G2771
3: 7 But what things were **g** to me, those I G2771
1Ti 6: 5 supposing that **g** is godliness: from G4200
6 godliness with contentment is great **g**. G4200
Jas 4:13 a year, and buy and sell, and get **g**: G2770

GAINED
Job 27: 8 hath **g**, when God taketh away his soul? H1214
Ezk 22:12 thou hast greedily **g** of thy neighbours H1214
Mt 18:15 shall hear thee, thou hast **g** thy brother. G2770
25:17 *had received* two, he also **g** other two. G2770
20 I have **g** beside them five talents more. G2770
22 I have **g** two other talents beside them. G2770
Lk 19:15 how much every man had **g** by trading. G1281
16 Lord, thy pound hath **g** ten pounds. G4333
18 Lord, thy pound hath **g** five pounds. G4160
Act 27:21 and to have **g** this harm and loss. G2770

GAINS
Act 16:19 that the hope of their **g** was gone, they G2039

GAINSAY
Lk 21:15 shall not be able to **g** nor resist. G471

GAINSAYERS
Tit 1: 9 both to exhort and to convince the **g**. G483

GAINSAYING
Act 10:29 Therefore came I *unto you* without **g**, as G369
Ro 10:21 hands unto a disobedient and **g** people. G483
Jude 11 reward, and perished in the **g** of Core. G485

GAIUS
Act 19:29 having caught **G** and Aristarchus, men G1050
20: 4 and Secundus; and **G** of Derbe, and G1050
Ro 16:23 **G** mine host, and of the whole church, G1050
1Co 1:14 none of you, but Crispus and **G**; G1050
3Jn 1 The elder unto the wellbeloved **G**, G1050

GALAL
1Ch 9:15 And Bakbakkar, Heresh, and **G**, and H1559
16 the son of **G**, the son of Jeduthun, H1559
Neh 11:17 the son of **G**, the son of Jeduthun. H1559

GALATIA
Act 16: 6 and the region of **G**, and were forbidden G1054
18:23 over *all* the country of **G** and Phrygia in G1054
1Co 16: 1 to the churches of **G**, even so do ye. G1053
Gal 1: 2 are with me, unto the churches of **G**: G1053
2Ti 4:10 Crescens to **G**, Titus unto Dalmatia. G1053
1Pt 1: 1 **G**, Cappadocia, Asia, and Bithynia, G1053

GALATIANS
Gal 3: 1 O foolish **G**, who hath bewitched you, G1052

GALBANUM
Ex 30:34 and onycha, and **g**; *these* sweet spices H2464

GALEED
Gen 31:47 Jegar-sahadutha: but Jacob called it **G**. H1567
48 Therefore was the name of it called **G**; H1567

GALILAEAN
Mk 14:70 art a **G**, and thy speech agreeth *thereto*. G1057
Lk 22:59 *fellow* also was with him: for he is a **G**. G1057
23: 6 he asked whether the man were a **G**. G1057

GALILAEANS
Lk 13: 1 told him of the **G**, whose blood Pilate G1057
2 ye that these **G** were sinners above G1057
2 **G**, because they suffered such things? G1057
Jn 4:45 into Galilee, the **G** received him, having G1057
Act 2: 7 Behold, are not all these which speak **G**? G1057

GALILEE
Jos 20: 7 And they appointed Kedesh in **G** in H1551
21:32 Kedesh in **G** with her suburbs, *to* H1551
1Ki 9:11 Hiram twenty cities in the land of **G**. H1551
2Ki 15:29 and Gilead, and **G**, all the land of H1551
1Ch 6:76 Kedesh in **G** with her suburbs, and H1551
Isa 9: 1 sea, beyond Jordan, in **G** of the nations. H1551
Mt 2:22 he turned aside into the parts of **G**: G1056
3:13 Then cometh Jesus from **G** to Jordan G1056
4:12 cast into prison, he departed into **G**; G1056
15 sea, beyond Jordan, **G** of the Gentiles; G1056
18 And Jesus, walking by the sea of **G**, saw G1056
23 And Jesus went about all **G**, teaching in G1056
25 of people from **G**, and *from* Decapolis, G1056
15:29 unto the sea of **G**; and went up into a G1056
17:22 And while they abode in **G**, Jesus said G1056
19: 1 he departed from **G**, and came into the G1056
21:11 is Jesus the prophet of Nazareth of **G**. G1056
26:32 risen again, I will go before you into **G**. G1056
69 saying, Thou also wast with Jesus of **G**. G1057
27:55 Jesus from **G**, ministering unto him: G1056
28: 7 before you into **G**; there shall ye see G1056
10 go into **G**, and there shall they see me. G1056
16 went away into **G**, into a mountain G1056
Mk 1: 9 **G**, and was baptized of John in Jordan. G1056
14 Jesus came into **G**, preaching the gospel G1056
16 Now as he walked by the sea of **G**, he G1056
28 all the region round about **G**. G1056
39 throughout all **G**, and cast out devils. G1056
3: 7 from **G** followed him, and from Judaea, G1056
6:21 high captains, and chief *estates* of **G**; G1056
7:31 unto the sea of **G**, through the midst of G1056
9:30 passed through **G**; and he would not G1056
14:28 I am risen, I will go before you into **G**. G1056
15:41 (Who also, when he was in **G**, followed G1056
16: 7 before you into **G**: there shall ye see G1056
Lk 1:26 God unto a city of **G**, named Nazareth, G1056
2: 4 And Joseph also went up from **G**, out of G1056
39 into **G**, to their own city Nazareth. G1056
Lk 3: 1 being tetrarch of **G**, and his brother G1056
4:14 of the Spirit into **G**: and there went out G1056
31 a city of **G**, and taught them on G1056
44 he preached in the synagogues of **G**. G1056
5:17 out of every town of **G**, and Judaea, and G1056
8:26 the Gadarenes, which is over against **G**. G1056
17:11 through the midst of Samaria and **G**. G1056
23: 5 Jewry, beginning from **G** to this place. G1056
6 When Pilate heard of **G**, he asked G1056
49 him from **G**, stood afar off, beholding G1056
55 with him from **G**, followed after, and G1056
24: 6 spake unto you when he was yet in **G**, G1056
Jn 1:43 go forth into **G**, and findeth Philip, G1056
2: 1 of **G**; and the mother of Jesus was there: G1056
11 did Jesus in Cana of **G**, and manifested G1056
4: 3 left Judaea, and departed again into **G**. G1056
43 he departed thence, and went into **G**. G1056
45 Then when he was come into **G**, the G1056
46 So Jesus came again into Cana of **G**, G1056
47 out of Judaea into **G**, he went unto him, G1056
54 when he was come out of Judaea into **G**. G1056
6: 1 sea of **G**, which is *the sea* of Tiberias. G1056
7: 1 After these things Jesus walked in **G**: for G1056
9 words unto them, he abode *still* in **G**. G1056
41 some said, Shall Christ come out of **G**? G1056
52 Art thou also of **G**? Search, and look: for G1056
52 look: for out of **G** ariseth no prophet. G1056
12:21 was of Bethsaida of **G**, and desired him, G1056
21: 2 of Cana in **G**, and the *sons* of Zebedee, G1056
Act 1:11 Which also said, Ye men of **G**, why G1057
5:37 After this man rose up Judas of **G** in the G1057
9:31 all Judaea and **G** and Samaria, and G1056
10:37 and began from **G**, after the baptism G1056
13:31 up with him from **G** to Jerusalem, who G1056

GALL
Dt 29:18 a root that beareth **g** and wormwood; H7219
32:32 *are* grapes of **g**, their clusters *are* bitter: H7219
Job 16:13 he poureth out my **g** upon the ground. H4845
20:14 is turned, *it is* the **g** of asps within him. H4846
25 out of his **g**: terrors *are* upon him. H4846
Ps 69:21 They gave me also **g** for my meat; and H7219
Jer 8:14 given us water of **g** to drink, because H7219
9:15 and give them water of **g** to drink. H7219
23:15 them drink the water of **g**: for from the H7219
Lam 3: 5 and compassed *me* with **g** and travail. H7219
19 my misery, the wormwood and the **g**. H7219
Am 6:12 turned judgment into **g**, and the fruit of H7219
Mt 27:34 mingled with **g**: and when he had tasted G5521
Act 8:23 For I perceive that thou art in the **g** of G5521

GALLANT
Isa 33:21 oars, neither shall **g** ship pass thereby. H117

GALLERIES
Song 7: 5 like purple; the king *is* held in the **g**. H7298
Ezk 41:15 behind it, and the **g** thereof on the one H862
16 windows, and the **g** round about on their H862
42: 5 shorter: for the **g** were higher than these, H862

GALLERY
Ezk 42: 3 *was* **g** against gallery in three *stories*. H862
3 *was* gallery against **g** in three *stories*. H862

GALLEY
Isa 33:21 shall go no **g** with oars, neither shall H590

GALLIM
1Sa 25:44 Phalti the son of Laish, which *was* of **G**. H1554
Isa 10:30 Lift up thy voice, O daughter of **G**: cause H1554

GALLIO
Act 18:12 And when **G** was the deputy of Achaia, G1058
14 open *his* mouth, **G** said unto the Jews, G1058
17 And **G** cared for none of those things. G1058

GALLOWS
Est 5:14 unto him, Let a **g** be made of fifty H6086
14 and he caused the **g** to be made. H6086
6: 4 on the **g** that he had prepared for him. H6086
7: 9 Behold also, the **g** fifty cubits high, H6086
10 So they hanged Haman on the **g** that he H6086
8: 7 hanged upon the **g**, because he laid his H6086
9:13 ten sons be hanged upon the **g**. H6086
25 and his sons should be hanged on the **g**. H6086

GAMALIEL
Nu 1:10 of Manasseh; **G** the son of Pedahzur. H1583
2:20 *shall be* **G** the son of Pedahzur. H1583

Nu 7:54 On the eighth day *offered* **G** the son of H1583
59 the offering of **G** the son of Pedahzur. H1583
10:23 Manasseh *was* **G** the son of Pedahzur. H1583
Act 5:34 Pharisee, named **G**, a doctor of the law, G1059
22: 3 this city at the feet of **G**, *and* taught G1059

GAMMADIMS
Ezk 27:11 about, and the **G** were in thy towers: H1575

GAMUL
1Ch 24:17 to Jachin, the two and twentieth to **G**, H1577

GANNIM See EN-GANNIM.

GAP
Ezk 22:30 and stand in the **g** before me for the H6556

GAPED
Job 16:10 They have **g** upon me with their mouth; H6473
Ps 22:13 They **g** upon me *with* their mouths, *as* H6475

GAPS
Ezk 13: 5 Ye have not gone up into the **g**, neither H6556

GARDEN
Gen 2: 8 And the LORD God planted a **g** H1588
9 also in the midst of the **g**, and the tree of H1588
10 Eden to water the **g**; and from thence it H1588
15 the **g** of Eden to dress it and to keep it. H1588
16 tree of the **g** thou mayest freely eat: H1588
3: 1 Ye shall not eat of every tree of the **g**? H1588
2 may eat of the fruit of the trees of the **g**: H1588
3 in the midst of the **g**, God hath said, Ye H1588
8 walking in the **g** in the cool of the day: H1588
8 LORD God amongst the trees of the **g**. H1588
10 And he said, I heard thy voice in the **g**, H1588
23 him forth from the **g** of Eden, to till the H1588
24 at the east of the **g** of Eden Cherubims, H1588
13:10 *even* as the **g** of the LORD, like the H1588
Dt 11:10 *it* with thy foot, as a **g** of herbs: H1588
1Ki 21: 2 I may have it for a **g** of herbs, because H1588
2Ki 9:27 by the way of the **g** house. And Jehu H1588
21:18 was buried in the **g** of his own house, in H1588
18 own house, in the **g** of Uzza: and Amon H1588
26 sepulchre in the **g** of Uzza: and Josiah H1588
25: 4 *is* by the king's **g**: (now the Chaldees H1588
Neh 3:15 by the king's **g**, and unto the stairs H1588
Est 1: 5 the court of the **g** of the king's palace; H1594
7: 7 into the palace **g**: and Haman stood up H1594
8 out of the palace **g** into the place of the H1594
Job 8:16 and his branch shooteth forth in his **g**. H1593
Song 4:12 A **g** inclosed *is* my sister, *my* spouse; a H1588
16 blow upon my **g**, *that* the spices thereof H1588
16 into his **g**, and eat his pleasant fruits. H1588
5: 1 I am come into my **g**, my sister, *my* H1588
6: 2 My beloved is gone down into his **g**, to H1588
11 I went down into the **g** of nuts to see H1594
Isa 1: 8 in a **g** of cucumbers, as a besieged city.
30 fadeth, and as a **g** that hath no water. H1593
51: 3 her desert like the **g** of the LORD; joy H1588
58:11 be like a watered **g**, and like a spring of H1588
61:11 bud, and as the **g** causeth the things H1593
Jer 31:12 be as a watered **g**; and they shall not H1588
39: 4 way of the king's **g**, by the gate betwixt H1588
52: 7 *was* by the king's **g**; (now the Chaldeans H1588
Lam 2: 6 as *if it were of* a **g**: he hath destroyed his H1588
Ezk 28:13 Thou hast been in Eden the **g** of God; H1588
31: 8 The cedars in the **g** of God could not H1588
8 nor any tree in the **g** of God was like H1588
9 that *were* in the **g** of God, envied him. H1588
36:35 is become like the **g** of Eden; and the H1588
Joel 2: 3 the land *is* as the **g** of Eden before H1588
Lk 13:19 and cast into his **g**; and it grew, and G2779
Jn 18: 1 where was a **g**, into the which he G2779
26 Did not I see thee in the **g** with him? G2779
19:41 there was a **g**; and in the garden a G2779
41 a garden; and in the **g** a new sepulchre, G2779

GARDENER
Jn 20:15 him to be the **g**, saith unto him, Sir, G2780

GARDENS
Nu 24: 6 spread forth, as **g** by the river's side, as H1593
Ecc 2: 5 I made me **g** and orchards, and I H1593
Song 4:15 A fountain of **g**, a well of living waters, H1588
6: 2 to feed in the **g**, and to gather lilies. H1588
8:13 Thou that dwellest in the **g**, the H1588
Isa 1:29 for the **g** that ye have chosen. H1593
65: 3 face; that sacrificeth in **g**, and burneth H1593
66:17 themselves in the **g** behind one *tree* in H1593
Jer 29: 5 and plant **g**, and eat the fruit of them; H1593
28 and plant **g**, and eat the fruit of them. H1593
Am 4: 9 when your **g** and your vineyards H1593
9:14 also make **g**, and eat the fruit of them. H1593

GAREB
2Sa 23:38 Ira an Ithrite, **G** an Ithrite, H1619
1Ch 11:40 Ira the Ithrite, **G** the Ithrite, H1619
Jer 31:39 **G**, and shall compass about to Goath. H1619

GARLANDS
Act 14:13 brought oxen and **g** unto the gates, and G4725

GARLICK
Nu 11: 5 the leeks, and the onions, and the **g**: H7762

GARMENT
Gen 9:23 And Shem and Japheth took a **g**, and H8071
25:25 hairy **g**; and they called his name Esau. H155
39:12 And she caught him by his **g**, saying, Lie H899
12 **g** in her hand, and fled, and got him out. H899
13 left his **g** in her hand, and was fled forth, H899
15 his **g** with me, and fled, and got him out. H899
16 And she laid up his **g** by her, until his H899
18 that he left his **g** with me, and fled out. H899
Lev 6:10 And the priest shall put on his linen **g**, H4055
27 thereof upon any **g**, thou shalt wash that H899
13:47 The **g** also that the plague of leprosy is H899
47 *it be* a woollen **g**, or a linen garment; H899
47 *it be* a woollen garment, or a linen **g**; H899
49 or reddish in the **g**, or in the skin, either H899
51 be spread in the **g**, either in the warp, or H899
52 He shall therefore burn that **g**, whether H899
53 not spread in the **g**, either in the warp, or H899
56 rend it out of the **g**, or out of the skin, or H899
57 And if it appear still in the **g**, either in the H899
58 And the **g**, either warp, or woof, or H899
59 of leprosy in a **g** of woollen or linen, H899
14:55 And for the leprosy of a **g**, and of a H899
15:17 And every **g**, and every skin, whereon is H899
19:19 neither shall a **g** mingled of linen and H899
Dt 22: 5 put on a woman's **g**: for all that do so H8071
11 Thou shalt not wear a **g** of divers sorts, H8162
Jos 7:21 a goodly Babylonish **g**, and two hundred H155
24 the silver, and the **g**, and the wedge of H155
Jdg 8:25 *them*. And they spread a **g**, and did cast H8071
2Sa 13:18 And *she had* a **g** of divers colours upon H3801
19 head, and rent her **g** of divers colours H3801
20: 8 them. And Joab's **g** that he had put on H4055
1Ki 11:29 **g**; and they two *were* alone in the field: H8008
30 And Ahijah caught the new **g** that *was* H8008
2Ki 9:13 took every man his **g**, and put *it* under H899
Ezr 9: 3 And when I heard this thing, I rent my **g** H899
5 having rent my **g** and my mantle, I fell H899
Est 8:15 of gold, and with a **g** of fine linen and H8509
Job 13:28 consumeth, as a **g** that is moth eaten. H899
30:18 By the great force of *my disease* is my **g** H3830
38: 9 When I made the cloud the **g** thereof, H3830
14 clay *to* the seal; and they stand as a **g**. H3830
41:13 Who can discover the face of his **g**? *or* H3830
Ps 69:11 I made sackcloth also my **g**; and I H3830
73: 6 a chain; violence covereth them *as* a **g**. H7897
102:26 shall wax old like a **g**; as a vesture shalt H899
104: 2 light as *with* a **g**: who stretchest out the H8008
6 the deep as *with* a **g**: the waters stood H3830
109:18 like as with his **g**, so let it come into his H4055
19 Let it be unto him as the **g** *which* H899
Prv 20:16 Take his **g** that is surety *for* a stranger: H899
25:20 *As* he that taketh away a **g** in cold H899
27:13 Take his **g** that is surety for a stranger, H899
30: 4 the waters in a **g**? who hath established H8071
Isa 50: 9 old as a **g**; the moth shall eat them up. H899
51: 6 shall wax old like a **g**, and they that dwell H899
8 For the moth shall eat them up like a **g**, H899
61: 3 joy for mourning, the **g** of praise for the H4594
Jer 43:12 putteth on his **g**; and he shall go forth H899
Ezk 18: 7 and hath covered the naked with a **g**; H899
16 and hath covered the naked with a **g**, H899
Dan 7: 9 did sit, whose **g** *was* white as snow, H3831
Mic 2: 8 the robe with the **g** from them that pass H8008
Hag 2:12 If one bear holy flesh in the skirt of his **g**, H899
Zec 13: 4 shall they wear a rough **g** to deceive: H155
Mal 2:16 violence with his **g**, saith the LORD of H3830
Mt 9:16 cloth unto an old **g**, for that which is put G2440
16 from the **g**, and the rent is made worse. G2440
20 *him*, and touched the hem of his **g**: G2440
21 I may but touch his **g**, I shall be whole. G2440
14:36 touch the hem of his **g**: and as many as G2440
22:11 a man which had not on a wedding **g**: G1742
12 a wedding **g**? And he was speechless. G1742
Mk 2:21 cloth on an old **g**: else the new piece G2440
5:27 in the press behind, and touched his **g**. G2440
6:56 but the border of his **g**: and as many as G2440
10:50 And he, casting away his **g**, rose, and G2440
13:16 not turn back again for to take up his **g**. G2440
16: 5 long white **g**; and they were affrighted. G4749
Lk 5:36 a piece of a new **g** upon an old; if G2440
8:44 the border of his **g**: and immediately G2440
22:36 sword, let him sell his **g**, and buy one. G2440
Act 12: 8 Cast thy **g** about thee, and follow me. G2440
Heb 1:11 and they all shall wax old as doth a **g**; G2440
Jude 23 hating even the **g** spotted by the flesh. G5509
Rev 1:13 clothed with a **g** down to the foot, and G1746

GARMENTS
Gen 35: 2 you, and be clean, and change your **g**: H8071
38:14 And she put her widow's **g** off from her, H899
19 her, and put on the **g** of her widowhood. H899
49:11 vine; he washed his **g** in wine, and his H3830
Ex 28: 2 And thou shalt make holy **g** for Aaron H899
3 may make Aaron's **g** to consecrate him, H899
4 And these *are* the **g** which they shall H899
4 shall make holy **g** for Aaron thy brother, H899
29: 5 And thou shalt take the **g**, and put upon H899
21 and upon his **g**, and upon his sons, and H899
21 his sons, and upon the **g** of his sons with H899
21 be hallowed, and his **g**, and his sons, and H899
21 and his sons, and his sons' **g** with him. H899
29 And the holy **g** of Aaron shall be his H899
31:10 And the cloths of service, and the holy **g** H899
10 the priest, and the **g** of his sons, to H899
35:19 the holy *place*, the holy **g** for Aaron the H899
19 the priest, and the **g** of his sons, to H899
21 and for all his service, and for the holy **g**. H899
39: 1 and made the holy **g** for Aaron; as the H899
41 holy *place*, and the holy **g** for Aaron the H899
41 sons' **g**, to minister in the priest's office. H899
40:13 Aaron the holy **g**, and anoint him, and H899
Lev 6:11 And he shall put off his **g**, and put on H899
11 and put on other **g**, and carry forth the H899
8: 2 with him, and the **g**, and the anointing H899
30 *and* upon his **g**, and upon his sons, and H899
30 sons, and upon his sons' **g** with him; and H899
30 Aaron, *and* his **g**, and his sons, and his H899
30 and his sons, and his sons' **g** with him. H899
16: 4 these *are* holy **g**; therefore shall he wash H899
23 put off the linen **g**, which he put on when H899
24 and put on his **g**, and come forth, and H899
32 put on the linen clothes, *even* the holy **g**: H899
21:10 to put on the **g**, shall not uncover his H899
Nu 15:38 in the borders of their **g** throughout their H899
20:26 And strip Aaron of his **g**, and put them H899
28 And Moses stripped Aaron of his **g**, and H899
Jos 9: 5 their feet, and old **g** upon them; and all H8008
13 rent: and these our **g** and our shoes are H8008
Jdg 14:12 you thirty sheets and thirty change of **g**: H899
13 thirty change of **g**. And they said unto H899
19 and gave change of **g** unto them which
1Sa 18: 4 it to David, and his **g**, even to his sword, H4055
2Sa 10: 4 and cut off their **g** in the middle, *even* H4063
13:31 Then the king arose, and tare his **g**, and H899
1Ki 10:25 of gold, and **g**, and armour, and spices, H8008
2Ki 5:22 a talent of silver, and two changes of **g**. H899
23 two changes of **g**, and laid *them* upon H899
26 and to receive **g**, and oliveyards, and H899
7:15 the way *was* full of **g** and vessels, which H899
25:29 And changed his prison **g**: and he did eat H899
1Ch 19: 4 and cut off their **g** in the midst hard by H4063
Ezr 2:69 of silver, and one hundred priests' **g**. H3801
Neh 7:70 five hundred and thirty priests' **g**. H3801
72 and threescore and seven priests' **g**. H3801
Job 37:17 How thy **g** *are* warm, when he quieteth H899
Ps 22:18 They part my **g** among them, and cast H899
45: 8 All thy **g** *smell* of myrrh, and aloes, *and* H899
133: 2 that went down to the skirts of his **g**; H4060
Ecc 9: 8 Let thy **g** be always white; and let thy H899
Song 4:11 of thy **g** *is* like the smell of Lebanon. H8008
Isa 9: 5 noise, and **g** rolled in blood; but H8071
52: 1 on thy beautiful **g**, O Jerusalem, the holy H899
59: 6 Their webs shall not become **g**, neither H899
17 and he put on the **g** of vengeance *for* H899
61:10 me with the **g** of salvation, he hath H899
63: 1 Edom, with dyed **g** from Bozrah? this H899
2 **g** like him that treadeth in the winefat? H899
3 my **g**, and I will stain all my raiment. H899
Jer 36:24 Yet they were not afraid, nor rent their **g**, H899
52:33 And changed his prison **g**: and he did H899

Lam 4:14 so that men could not touch their g. H3830
Ezk 16:16 And of thy g thou didst take, and H899
18 And tookest thy broidered g, and H899
26:16 put off their broidered g: they shall clothe H899
42:14 there they shall lay their g wherein they H899
14 shall put on other g, and shall approach H899
44:17 be clothed with linen g; and no wool shall H899
19 they shall put off their g wherein they H899
19 shall put on other g; and they shall not H899
19 shall not sanctify the people with their g. H899
Dan 3:21 and their *other* g, and were cast into the H3831
Joel 2:13 And rend your heart, and not your g, and H899
Zec 3: 3 Now Joshua was clothed with filthy g, H899
4 away the filthy g from him. And unto H899
5 g. And the angel of the LORD stood by. H899
Mt 21: 8 spread their g in the way; others cut G2440
23: 5 and enlarge the borders of their g, G2440
27:35 and parted his g, casting lots: that it G2440
35 They parted my g among them, and G2440
Mk 11: 7 their g on him; and he sat upon him. G2440
8 And many spread their g in the way: G2440
15:24 him, they parted his g, casting lots upon G2440
Lk 19:35 and they cast their g upon the colt, and G2440
24: 4 two men stood by them in shining g: G2067
Jn 13: 4 g; and took a towel, and girded himself. G2440
12 and had taken his g, and was set down G2440
19:23 Jesus, took his g, and made four parts, G2440
Act 9:39 the coats and g which Dorcas made, G2440
Jas 5: 2 Your riches are corrupted, and your g G2440
Rev 3: 4 not defiled their g; and they shall walk G2440
16:15 and keepeth his g, lest he walk naked, G2440

GARMITE
1Ch 4:19 the G, and Eshtemoa the Maachathite. H1636

GARNER
Mt 3:12 his wheat into the g; but he will burn up G596
Lk 3:17 the wheat into his g; but the chaff he will G596

GARNERS
Ps 144:13 *That* our g *may be* full, affording all H4200
Joel 1:17 their clods, the g are laid desolate, the H214

GARNISH
Mt 23:29 and g the sepulchres of the righteous, G2885

GARNISHED
2Ch 3: 6 And he g the house with precious H6823
Job 26:13 By his spirit he hath g the heavens; his H8235
Mt 12:44 come, he findeth *it* empty, swept, and g. G2885
Lk 11:25 he cometh, he findeth *it* swept and g. G2885
Rev 21:19 of the city *were* g with all manner of G2885

GARRISON
1Sa 10: 5 of God, where *is* the g of the Philistines: H5333
13: 3 And Jonathan smote the g of the H5333
4 had smitten a g of the Philistines, and H5333
23 And the g of the Philistines went out to H4673
14: 1 to the Philistines' g, that *is* on the other H4673
4 the Philistines' g, *there was* a sharp H4673
6 us go over unto the g of these H4673
11 unto the g of the Philistines: and H4673
12 And the men of the g answered H4675
15 all the people: the g, and the spoilers, H4673
2Sa 23:14 in an hold, and the g of the Philistines H4673
1Ch 11:16 Philistines' g *was* then at Beth-lehem. H5333
2Co 11:32 with a g, desirous to apprehend me: G5432

GARRISONS
2Sa 8: 6 Then David put g in Syria of H5333
14 And he put g in Edom; throughout all H5333
14 all Edom put he g, and all they of Edom H5333
1Ch 18: 6 Then David put g in Syria-damascus;
13 And he put g in Edom; and all the H5333
2Ch 17: 2 cities of Judah, and set g in the land of H5333
Ezk 26:11 strong g shall go down to the ground. H4676

GASHMU
Neh 6: 6 the heathen, and G saith *it, that* thou H1654

GAT
Gen 19:27 And Abraham g up early in the morning
Ex 24:18 of the cloud, and g him up into the H5927
Nu 11:30 And Moses g him into the camp, he and H622
14:40 in the morning, and g them up into the H5927
16:27 So they g up from the tabernacle of H5927
Jdg 9:48 And Abimelech g him up to mount H5927
51 and g them up to the top of the tower. H5927
19:28 man rose up, and g him unto his place. H3212
1Sa 13:15 And Samuel arose, and g him up from H5927
24:22 and his men g them up unto the hold. H5927
26:12 bolster; and they g them away, and no H3212
2Sa 4: 7 and took his head, and g them away H3212
8:13 And David g *him* a name when he H6213
13:29 man g him up upon his mule, and fled. H7392
17:23 ass, and arose, and g him home to his H3212
19: 3 And the people g them by stealth that H935
1Ki 1: 1 him with clothes, but he g no heat.
Ps 116: 3 the pains of hell g hold upon me: I found
Ecc 2: 8 of the provinces: I g me men singers H6213
Lam 5: 9 We g our bread with *the peril of* our lives H935

GATAM
Gen 36:11 Omar, Zepho, and G, and Kenaz. H1609
16 Duke Korah, duke G, *and* duke Amalek: H1609
1Ch 1:36 and G, Kenaz, and Timna, and Amalek. H1609

GATE
Gen 19: 1 and Lot sat in the g of Sodom: and Lot H8179
22:17 seed shall possess the g of his enemies; H8179
23:10 that went in at the g of his city, saying, H8179
18 all that went in at the g of his city. H8179
24:60 possess the g of those which hate them. H8179
28:17 of God, and this *is* the g of heaven. H8179
34:20 son came unto the g of their city, and H8179
24 went out of the g of his city; and every H8179
24 all that went out of the g of his city. H8179
Ex 27:14 The hangings of one side *of the g shall*
16 And for the g of the court *shall be* an H8179
32:26 Then Moses stood in the g of the camp, H8179
27 in and out from g to gate throughout H8179
27 and out from gate to g throughout the H8179
38:14 The hangings of the one side *of the g*
15 And for the other side of the court g, on H8179
18 And the hanging for the g of the court H8179
31 of the court g, and all the pins of the H8179
39:40 for the court g, his cords, and his pins, H8179
40: 8 and hang up the hanging at the court g. H8179
33 the court g. So Moses finished the work. H8179
Nu 4:26 for the door of the g of the court, which H8179
Dt 21:19 of his city, and unto the g of his place; H8179
22:15 unto the elders of the city in the g: H8179
24 both out unto the g of that city, and ye H8179
25: 7 wife go up to the g unto the elders, and H8179
Jos 2: 5 of shutting of the g, when it was dark, H8179
7 them were gone out, they shut the g. H8179
7: 5 *from* before the g *even* unto Shebarim, H8179
8:29 at the entering of the g of the city, and H8179
20: 4 at the entering of the g of the city, and H8179
Jdg 9:35 in the entering of the g of the city: and H8179
40 *even* unto the entering of the g. H8179
44 the entering of the g of the city: and the H8179
16: 2 all night in the g of the city, and were H8179
3 the doors of the g of the city, and the H8179
18:16 of Dan, stood by the entering of the g. H8179
17 in the entering of the g with the six H8179
Ru 4: 1 Then went Boaz up to the g, and sat H8179
10 g of his place: ye *are* witnesses this day. H8179
11 And all the people that *were* in the g, H8179
1Sa 4:18 by the side of the g, and his neck brake, H8179
9:18 Then Saul drew near to Samuel in the g, H8179
21:13 the doors of the g, and let his spittle fall H8179
2Sa 3:27 him aside in the g to speak with him H8179
10: 8 entering in of the g: and the Syrians of H8179
11:23 them even unto the entering of the g. H8179
15: 2 the way of the g: and it was *so*, that H8179
18: 4 the king stood by the g side, and all the H8179
24 to the roof over the g unto the wall, and H8179
33 chamber over the g, and wept: and as H8179
19: 8 Then the king arose, and sat in the g. H8179
8 king doth sit in the g. And all the people H8179
23:15 well of Beth-lehem, which *is* by the g! H8179
16 that *was* by the g, and took *it*, and H8179
1Ki 17:10 he came to the g of the city, behold, the H6607
22:10 entrance of the g of Samaria; and all H8179
2Ki 7: 1 barley for a shekel, in the g of Samaria. H8179
3 entering in of the g: and they said one H8179
17 the charge of the g: and the people trode H8179
17 upon him in the g, and he died, as the H8179
18 about this time in the g of Samaria: H8179
20 trode upon him in the g, and he died. H8179
9:31 And as Jehu entered in at the g, she H8179
10: 8 entering in of the g until the morning. H8179
11: 6 And a third part *shall be* at the g of H8179
6 a third part at the g behind the guard: H8179
19 by the way of the g of the guard to the H8179
14:13 from the g of Ephraim unto the H8179
13 unto the corner g, four hundred cubits. H8179
2Ki 15:35 the higher g of the house of the LORD. H8179
23: 8 the entering in of the g of Joshua the H8179
8 on a man's left hand at the g of the city. H8179
25: 4 by the way of the g between two walls, H8179
1Ch 9:18 Who hitherto *waited* in the king's g H8179
11:17 the well of Beth-lehem, that *is* at the g! H8179
18 that *was* by the g, and took *it*, and H8179
19: 9 in array before the g of the city: and the H6607
26:13 to the house of their fathers, for every g. H8179
16 with the g Shallecheth, by the H8179
2Ch 8:14 courses at every g: for so had David the H8179
18: 9 entering in of the g of Samaria; and all H8179
23: 5 a third part at the g of the foundation: H8179
15 of the horse g by the king's house, H8179
20 came through the high g into the king's H8179
24: 8 at the g of the house of the LORD. H8179
25:23 from the g of Ephraim to the corner H8179
23 to the corner g, four hundred cubits. H8179
26: 9 at the corner g, and at the valley gate, H8179
9 and at the valley g, and at the turning *of* H8179
27: 3 He built the high g of the house of the H8179
32: 6 in the street of the g of the city, and H8179
33:14 in at the fish g, and compassed about H8179
35:15 *waited* at every g; they might not depart H8179
Neh 2:13 And I went out by night by the g of the H8179
14 Then I went on to the g of the fountain, H8179
15 by the g of the valley, and *so* returned. H8179
3: 1 builded the sheep g; they sanctified it, H8179
3 But the fish g did the sons of H8179
6 Moreover the old g repaired Jehoiada H8179
13 The valley g repaired Hanun, and the H8179
13 cubits on the wall unto the dung g. H8179
14 But the dung g repaired Malchiah the H8179
15 But the g of the fountain repaired H8179
26 against the water g toward the east, H8179
28 From above the horse g repaired the H8179
29 of Shechaniah, the keeper of the east g. H8179
31 over against the g Miphkad, and to the H8179
32 corner unto the sheep g repaired the H8179
8: 1 before the water g; and they spake unto H8179
3 before the water g from the morning H8179
16 street of the water g, and in the street of H8179
16 and in the street of the g of Ephraim. H8179
12:31 hand upon the wall toward the dung g: H8179
37 And at the fountain g, which was over H8179
37 David, even unto the water g eastward. H8179
39 And from above the g of Ephraim, and H8179
39 and above the old g, and above the fish H8179
39 and above the fish g, and the tower of H8179
39 g: and they stood still in the prison gate. H8179
39 gate: and they stood still in the prison g. H8179
Est 2:19 time, then Mordecai sat in the king's g. H8179
21 sat in the king's g, two of the king's H8179
3: 2 that *were* in the king's g, bowed, and H8179
3 which *were* in the king's g, said unto H8179
4: 2 And came even before the king's g: for H8179
2 into the king's g clothed with sackcloth. H8179
6 the city, which *was* before the king's g. H8179
5: 1 house, over against the g of the house. H6607
9 in the king's g, that he stood not up, H8179
13 Mordecai the Jew sitting at the king's g. H8179
6:10 at the king's g: let nothing fail of all H8179
12 again to the king's g. But Haman hasted H8179
Job 5: 4 g, neither *is there* any to deliver *them*. H8179
29: 7 When I went out to the g through the H8179
31:21 fatherless, when I saw my help in the g: H8179
Ps 69:12 They that sit in the g speak against me; H8179
118:20 This g of the LORD, into which the H8179
127: 5 shall speak with the enemies in the g. H8179
Prv 17:19 that exalteth his g seeketh destruction. H6607
22:22 neither oppress the afflicted in the g: H8179
24: 7 fool: he openeth not his mouth in the g. H8179
Song 7: 4 Heshbon, by the g of Bath-rabbim: thy H8179
Isa 14:31 Howl, O g; cry, O city; thou, whole H8179
22: 7 shall set themselves in array at the g. H8179
24:12 In the city is left desolation, and the g H8179
28: 6 to them that turn the battle to the g. H8179
29:21 reproveth in the g, and turn aside the H8179
Jer 7: 2 Stand in the g of the LORD'S house, H8179
17:19 and stand in the g of the children of the H8179
19: 2 entry of the east g, and proclaim there H8179
20: 2 *were* in the high g of Benjamin, which H8179
26:10 entry of the new g of the LORD'S *house*. H8179
31:38 of Hananeel unto the g of the corner. H8179
40 of the horse g toward the east, *shall* H8179
36:10 entry of the new g of the LORD'S house, H8179
37:13 And when he was in the g of Benjamin, H8179
38: 7 king then sitting in the g of Benjamin; H8179
39: 3 and sat in the middle g, *even* H8179

Jer 39: 4 garden, by the g betwixt the two walls: H8179
52: 7 by the way of the g between the two H8179
Lam 5:14 The elders have ceased from the g, the H8179
Ezk 8: 3 door of the inner g that looketh toward H8179
5 northward at the g of the altar this H8179
14 me to the door of the g of the LORD'S H8179
9: 2 way of the higher g, which lieth toward H8179
10:19 door of the east g of the LORD'S house; H8179
11: 1 me unto the east g of the LORD'S H8179
1 at the door of the g five and twenty H8179
40: 3 a measuring reed; and he stood in the g. H8179
6 Then came he unto the g which looketh H8179
6 threshold of the g, *which was* one reed H8179
6 *of the g, which was* one reed broad.
7 threshold of the g by the porch of the H8179
7 the porch of the g within *was* one reed. H8179
8 He measured also the porch of the g H8179
9 Then measured he the porch of the g, H8179
9 and the porch of the g *was* inward. H8179
10 And the little chambers of the g H8179
11 of the entry of the g, ten cubits; *and* the H8179
11 *and* the length of the g, thirteen cubits. H8179
13 He measured then the g from the roof H8179
14 the post of the court round about the g. H8179
15 And from the face of the g of the H8179
15 porch of the inner g *were* fifty cubits. H8179
16 posts within the g round about, and H8179
19 of the lower g unto the forefront of H8179
20 And the g of the outward court that H8179
21 of the first g: the length thereof *was* H8179
22 after the measure of the g that looketh H8179
23 And the g of the inner court *was* over H8179
23 over against the g toward the north, H8179
23 from g to gate an hundred cubits. H8179
23 from gate to g an hundred cubits. H8179
24 and behold a g toward the south: and H8179
27 And *there was* a g in the inner court H8179
27 he measured from g to gate toward the H8179
27 g toward the south an hundred cubits. H8179
28 court by the south g: and he measured H8179
28 south g according to these measures; H8179
32 the g according to these measures. H8179
35 And he brought me to the north g, and H8179
39 And in the porch of the g *were* two H8179
40 entry of the north g, *were* two tables; H8179
40 at the porch of the g, *were* two tables. H8179
41 side, by the side of the g; eight tables, H8179
44 And without the inner g *were* the H8179
44 side of the north g; and their prospect H8179
44 at the side of the east g *having* the H8179
48 the breadth of the g *was* three cubits on H8179
42:15 forth toward the g whose prospect *is* H8179
43: 1 Afterward he brought me to the g, *even* H8179
1 *even* the g that looketh toward the east: H8179
4 g whose prospect *is* toward the east. H8179
44: 1 back the way of the g of the outward H8179
2 Then said the LORD unto me; This g H8179
3 the porch of *that* g, and shall go out by H8179
4 the way of the north g before the house: H8179
45:19 the posts of the g of the inner court. H8179
46: 1 Thus saith the Lord GOD; The g of the H8179
2 of the porch of *that* g without, and shall H8179
2 by the post of the g, and the priests shall H8179
2 the threshold of the g: then he shall go H8179
2 g shall not be shut until the evening. H8179
3 at the door of this g before the LORD in H8179
8 the porch of *that* g, and he shall go forth H8179
9 way of the north g to worship shall go H8179
9 way of the south g; and he that entereth H8179
9 way of the south g shall go forth by the H8179
9 way of the north g: he shall not return H8179
9 by the way of the g whereby he came H8179
12 shall then open him the g that looketh H8179
12 his going forth *one* shall shut the g. H8179
19 *was* at the side of the g, into the holy H8179
47: 2 of the way of the g northward, and led H8179
2 unto the utter g by the way that looketh H8179
48:31 northward; one g of Reuben, one gate H8179
31 one g of Judah, one gate of Levi. H8179
31 one gate of Judah, one g of Levi. H8179
32 gates; and one g of Joseph, one gate H8179
32 one g of Benjamin, one gate of Dan. H8179
32 one gate of Benjamin, one g of Dan. H8179
33 three gates; one g of Simeon, one gate H8179
33 one g of Issachar, one gate of Zebulun. H8179
33 one gate of Issachar, one g of Zebulun. H8179
34 three gates; one g of Gad, one gate of H8179
34 one g of Asher, one gate of Naphtali. H8179
34 one gate of Asher, one g of Naphtali. H8179
Dan 2:49 but Daniel *sat* in the g of the king. H8651
Am 5:10 They hate him that rebuketh in the g, H8179
12 aside the poor in the g *from their right.* H8179
15 judgment in the g: it may be that the H8179
Oba 13 entered into the g of my people in the H8179
Mic 1: 9 the g of my people, *even* to Jerusalem. H8179
12 the LORD unto the g of Jerusalem. H8179
2:13 through the g, and are gone out by H8179
Zep 1:10 of a cry from the fish g, and an howling H8179
Zec 14:10 from Benjamin's g unto the place of the H8179
10 place of the first g, unto the corner gate, H8179
10 unto the corner g, and *from* the tower H8179
Mt 7:13 Enter ye in at the strait g: for wide *is* the G4439
13 for wide *is* the g, and broad *is* the way, G4439
14 Because strait *is* the g, and narrow *is* G4439
Lk 7:12 Now when he came nigh to the g of the G4439
13:24 Strive to enter in at the strait g: for G4439
16:20 which was laid at his g, full of sores, G4440
Act 3: 2 laid daily at the g of the temple which G2374
10 at the Beautiful g of the temple: and G4439
10:17 Simon's house, and stood before the g, G4440
12:10 unto the iron g that leadeth unto the G4439
13 at the door of the g, a damsel came to G4440
14 opened not the g for gladness, but ran G4440
14 and told how Peter stood before the g. G4440
Heb 13:12 his own blood, suffered without the g. G4439
Rev 21:21 every several g was of one pearl: and G4440

GATES
Ex 20:10 nor thy stranger that *is* within thy g: H8179
Dt 3: 5 with high walls, g, and bars; beside H1817
5:14 stranger that *is* within thy g; that thy H8179
6: 9 the posts of thy house, and on thy g. H8179
11:20 posts of thine house, and upon thy g: H8179
12:12 that *is* within your g; forasmuch as he H8179
15 eat flesh in all thy g, whatsoever thy H8179
17 Thou mayest not eat within thy g the H8179
18 that *is* within thy g: and thou shalt H8179
21 thy g whatsoever thy soul lusteth after. H8179
14:21 that *is* in thy g, that he may eat it; or H8179
27 And the Levite that *is* within thy g; thou H8179
28 year, and shalt lay *it* up within thy g: H8179
29 *are* within thy g, shall come, and shall H8179
15: 7 within any of thy g in thy land which H8179
22 Thou shalt eat it within thy g: the H8179
16: 5 g, which the LORD thy God giveth thee: H8179
11 that *is* within thy g, and the stranger, H8179
14 and the widow, that *are* within thy g. H8179
18 thee in all thy g, which the LORD thy H8179
17: 2 within any of thy g which the LORD thy H8179
5 thing, unto thy g, *even* that man or that H8179
8 within thy g: then shalt thou arise, H8179
18: 6 And if a Levite come from any of thy g H8179
23:16 in one of thy g, where it liketh him H8179
24:14 that *are* in thy land within thy g: H8179
26:12 they may eat within thy g, and be filled; H8179
28:52 And he shall besiege thee in all thy g, H8179
52 thee in all thy g throughout all thy H8179
55 enemies shall distress thee in all thy g. H8179
57 thine enemy shall distress thee in thy g. H8179
31:12 that *is* within thy g, that they may hear, H8179
Jos 6:26 youngest *son* shall he set up the g of it. H1817
Jdg 5: 8 *was* war in the g: was there a shield or H8179
11 people of the LORD go down to the g. H8179
1Sa 17:52 valley, and to the g of Ekron. And the H8179
23: 7 into a town that hath g and bars. H1817
2Sa 18:24 And David sat between the two g: and H8179
1Ki 16:34 and set up the g thereof in his youngest H1817
2Ki 23: 8 the high places of the g that *were* in the H8179
1Ch 9:19 keepers of the g of the tabernacle: and H5592
22 to be porters in the g *were* two hundred H5592
23 oversight of the g of the house of the H8179
22: 3 the doors of the g, and for the joinings; H8179
2Ch 8: 5 fenced cities, with walls, g, and bars; H1817
14: 7 walls, and towers, g, and bars, *while* the H1817
23:19 And he set the porters at the g of the H8179
31: 2 praise in the g of the tents of the LORD. H8179
Neh 1: 3 and the g thereof are burned with fire. H8179
2: 3 the g thereof are consumed with fire? H8179
8 beams for the g of the palace which H8179
13 the g thereof were consumed with fire. H8179
17 waste, and the g thereof are burned H8179
6: 1 I had not set up the doors upon the g;) H8179
7: 3 And I said unto them, Let not the g of H8179
11:19 g, *were* an hundred seventy and two. H8179
12:25 the ward at the thresholds of the g. H8179
30 the people, and the g, and the wall. H8179
13:19 And it came to pass, that when the g of H8179
19 that the g should be shut, and H1817
Neh 13:19 set I at the g, *that* there should no H8179
22 *and* keep the g, to sanctify the sabbath H8179
Job 38:17 Have the g of death been opened unto H8179
Ps 9:13 that liftest me up from the g of death: H8179
14 all thy praise in the g of the daughter of H8179
24: 7 Lift up your heads, O ye g; and be ye lift H8179
9 Lift up your heads, O ye g; even lift H8179
87: 2 The LORD loveth the g of Zion more H8179
100: 4 Enter into his g with thanksgiving, *and* H8179
107:16 For he hath broken the g of brass, and H1817
18 and they draw near unto the g of death. H8179
118:19 Open to me the g of righteousness: I H8179
122: 2 Our feet shall stand within thy g, O H8179
147:13 the bars of thy g; he hath blessed thy H8179
Prv 1:21 the openings of the g: in the city she H8179
8: 3 She crieth at the g, at the entry of the H8179
34 my g, waiting at the posts of my doors. H1817
14:19 the wicked at the g of the righteous. H8179
31:23 Her husband is known in the g, when he H8179
31 let her own works praise her in the g. H8179
Song 7:13 a smell, and at our g *are* all manner of H6607
Isa 3:26 And her g shall lament and mourn; H6607
13: 2 they may go into the g of the nobles. H6607
26: 2 Open ye the g, that the righteous nation H8179
38:10 I shall go to the g of the grave: I am H8179
45: 1 g; and the gates shall not be shut; H1817
1 gates; and the g shall not be shut; H8179
2 in pieces the g of brass, and cut in H1817
54:12 of agates, and thy g of carbuncles, and H8179
60:11 Therefore thy g shall be open H8179
18 thy walls Salvation, and thy g Praise. H8179
62:10 Go through, go through the g; prepare H8179
Jer 1:15 the entering of the g of Jerusalem, and H8179
7: 2 in at these g to worship the LORD. H8179
14: 2 Judah mourneth, and the g thereof H8179
15: 7 And I will fan them with a fan in the g H8179
17:19 go out, and in all the g of Jerusalem; H8179
20 of Jerusalem, that enter in by these g: H8179
21 nor bring *it* in by the g of Jerusalem; H8179
24 burden through the g of this city on the H8179
25 Then shall there enter into the g of this H8179
27 entering in at the g of Jerusalem on the H8179
27 I kindle a fire in the g thereof, and it H8179
22: 2 and thy people that enter in by these g: H8179
4 enter in by the g of this house kings H8179
19 cast forth beyond the g of Jerusalem. H8179
49:31 neither g nor bars, *which* dwell alone. H1817
51:58 and her high g shall be burned with H8179
Lam 1: 4 feasts: all her g are desolate: her priests H8179
2: 9 Her g are sunk into the ground; he hath H8179
4:12 have entered into the g of Jerusalem. H8179
Ezk 21:15 against all their g, that *their* heart may H8179
22 g, to cast a mount, *and* to build a fort. H8179
26: 2 *that was* the g of the people: she is H1817
10 enter into thy g, as men enter into a H8179
38:11 walls, and having neither bars nor g, H1817
40:18 And the pavement by the side of the g H8179
18 of the g *was* the lower pavement. H8179
38 by the posts of the g, where they washed H8179
44:11 charge at the g of the house, and H8179
17 enter in at the g of the inner court, they H8179
17 in the g of the inner court, and within. H8179
48:31 And the g of the city *shall be* after the H8179
31 of Israel: three g northward; one gate H8179
32 and three g; and one gate of Joseph, H8179
33 and three g; one gate of Simeon, H8179
34 *with* their three g; one gate of Gad, one H8179
Oba 11 entered into his g, and cast lots upon H8179
Nah 2: 6 The g of the rivers shall be opened, and H8179
3:13 *are* women: the g of thy land shall be H8179
Zec 8:16 judgment of truth and peace in your g: H8179
Mt 16:18 the g of hell shall not prevail against it. G4439
Act 9:24 the g day and night to kill him. G4439
14:13 garlands unto the g, and would have G4440
Rev 21:12 high, *and* had twelve g, and at the gates G4440
12 gates, and at the g twelve angels, and G4440
13 On the east three g; on the north three G4440
13 on the north three g; on the south three G4440
13 three g; and on the west three gates. G4440
13 three gates; and on the west three g. G4440
15 and the g thereof, and the wall thereof. G4440
21 And the twelve g *were* twelve pearls; G4440
25 And the g of it shall not be shut at all G4440
22:14 enter in through the g into the city. G4440

GATH
Jos 11:22 in G, and in Ashdod, there remained. H1661
1Sa 5: 8 about unto G. And they carried the H1661
6:17 Askelon one, for G one, for Ekron one; H1661

1Sa 7:14 from Ekron even unto **G**; and the coasts H1661
17: 4 named Goliath, of **G**, whose height *was* H1661
23 the Philistine of **G**, Goliath by name, out H1661
52 even unto **G**, and unto Ekron. H1661
21:10 Saul, and went to Achish the king of **G**. H1661
12 was sore afraid of Achish the king of **G**. H1661
27: 2 Achish, the son of Maoch, king of **G**. H1661
3 And David dwelt with Achish at **G**, he H1661
4 David was fled to **G**: and he sought no H1661
11 to bring *tidings* to **G**, saying, Lest they H1661
2Sa 1:20 Tell *it* not in **G**, publish *it* not in the H1661
15:18 him from **G**, passed on before the king. H1661
21:20 And there was yet a battle in **G**, where H1661
22 These four were born to the giant in **G**, H1661
1Ki 2:39 of Maachah king of **G**. And they told H1661
39 saying, Behold, thy servants *be* in **G**. H1661
40 ass, and went to **G** to Achish to seek his H1661
40 went, and brought his servants from **G**. H1661
41 Jerusalem to **G**, and was come again. H1661
2Ki 12:17 and fought against **G**, and took it: and H1661
1Ch 7:21 whom the men of **G** *that were* born in H1661
8:13 who drove away the inhabitants of **G**: H1661
18: 1 them, and took **G** and her towns out of H1661
20: 6 And yet again there was war at **G**, H1661
8 These were born unto the giant in **G**; H1661
2Ch 11: 8 And **G**, and Mareshah, and Ziph, H1661
26: 6 down the wall of **G**, and the wall of H1661
Ps 56:ttl when the Philistines took him in **G**. H1661
Am 6: 2 then go down to **G** of the Philistines: *be* H1661
Mic 1:10 Declare ye *it* not at **G**, weep ye not at all: H1661

GATHER
Gen 6:21 and thou shalt **g** *it* to thee; and it shall H622
31:46 And Jacob said unto his brethren, **G** H3950
34:30 in number, they shall **g** themselves H622
41:35 And let them **g** all the food of those H6908
49: 1 unto his sons, and said, **G** yourselves H622
2 **G** yourselves together, and hear, ye H6908
Ex 3:16 Go, and **g** the elders of Israel together, H622
5: 7 let them go and **g** straw for themselves. H7197
12 of Egypt to **g** stubble instead of straw. H7197
9:19 Send therefore now, *and* **g** thy cattle, H5756
16: 4 shall go out and **g** a certain rate every H3950
5 shall be twice as much as they **g** daily. H3950
16 hath commanded, **G** of it every man H3950
26 Six days ye shall **g** it; but on the H3950
27 day for to **g**, and they found none. H3950
23:10 land, and shalt **g** in the fruits thereof: H622
Lev 8: 3 And **g** thou all the congregation H6950
19: 9 thou **g** the gleanings of thy harvest. H3950
10 neither shalt thou **g** *every* grape of thy H3950
23:22 neither shalt thou **g** any gleaning of thy H3950
25: 3 thy vineyard, and **g** in the fruit thereof; H622
5 not reap, neither **g** the grapes of thy H1219
11 **g** *the grapes* in it of thy vine undressed. H1219
20 we shall not sow, nor **g** in our increase: H622
Nu 8: 9 and thou shalt **g** the whole assembly H6950
10: 4 of Israel, shall **g** themselves unto thee. H3259
11:16 And the LORD said unto Moses, **G** unto H622
19: 9 And a man *that is* clean shall **g** up the H622
20: 8 Take the rod, and **g** thou the assembly H6950
21:16 LORD spake unto Moses, **G** the people H622
Dt 4:10 LORD said unto me, **G** me the people H6950
11:14 that thou mayest **g** in thy corn, and thy H622
13:16 And thou shalt **g** all the spoil of it into H6908
28:30 and shalt not **g** the grapes thereof. H2490
38 the field, and shalt **g** *but* little in; for the H622
39 *of* the wine, nor **g** *the grapes;* for the H103
30: 3 and will return and **g** thee from all the H6908
4 will the LORD thy God **g** thee, and from H6908
31:12 **G** the people together, men, and H6950
28 **G** unto me all the elders of your tribes, H6950
Ru 2: 7 you, let me glean and **g** after the reapers H622
1Sa 7: 5 And Samuel said, **G** all Israel to H6908
2Sa 3:21 and go, and will **g** all Israel unto my H6908
12:28 Now therefore **g** the rest of the people H622
1Ki 18:19 Now therefore send, *and* **g** to me all H6908
2Ki 4:39 And one went out into the field to **g** H3950
22:20 Behold therefore, I will **g** thee unto thy H622
1Ch 13: 2 that they may **g** themselves unto us: H6908
16:35 of our salvation, and **g** us together, and H6908
22: 2 And David commanded to **g** together H3664
2Ch 24: 5 of Judah, and **g** of all Israel money to H6908
34:28 Behold, I will **g** thee to thy fathers, and H622
Ezr 10: 7 **g** themselves together unto Jerusalem; H6908
Neh 1: 9 heaven, *yet* will I **g** them from thence, H6908
7: 5 And my God put into mine heart to **g** H6908
12:44 for the tithes, to **g** into them out of the H3664
Est 2: 3 that they may **g** together all the fair H6908
Est 4:16 Go, **g** together all the Jews that are H3664
8:11 in every city to **g** themselves together, H6905
Job 11:10 If he cut off, and shut up, or **g** together, H6905
24: 6 and they **g** the vintage of the wicked. H3953
34:14 If he set his heart upon man, *if* he **g** unto H622
39:12 home thy seed, and **g** *it into* thy barn? H622
Ps 26: 9 **G** not my soul with sinners, nor my life H622
39: 6 and knoweth not who shall **g** them. H622
50: 5 **G** my saints together unto me; those that H622
56: 6 They **g** themselves together, they hide H1481
94:21 They **g** themselves together against the H1413
104:22 The sun ariseth, they **g** themselves H622
28 *That* thou givest them they **g**: thou H3950
106:47 Save us, O LORD our God, and **g** us H6908
Prv 28: 8 shall **g** it for him that will pity the poor. H6908
Ecc 2:26 giveth travail, to **g** and to heap up, that H622
3: 5 and a time to **g** stones together; a time H3664
Song 6: 2 to feed in the gardens, and to **g** lilies. H3950
Isa 10:31 of Gebim **g** themselves to flee. H5756
11:12 of Israel, and **g** together the dispersed H6908
34:15 and hatch, and **g** under her shadow: H1716
40:11 shepherd: he shall **g** the lambs with his H6908
43: 5 the east, and **g** thee from the west; H6908
49:18 behold: all these **g** themselves together, H6908
54: 7 but with great mercies will I **g** thee. H6908
15 Behold, they shall surely **g** together, *but* H1481
15 whosoever shall **g** together against thee H1481
56: 8 saith, Yet will I **g** *others* to him, beside H6908
60: 4 and see: all they **g** themselves together, H6908
62:10 up the highway; **g** out the stones; lift up H5619
66:18 shall come, that I will **g** all nations and H6908
Jer 4: 5 in the land: cry, **g** together, and say, H4390
6: 1 O ye children of Benjamin, **g** yourselves H5756
7:18 The children **g** wood, and the fathers H3950
9:22 the harvestman, and none shall **g** *them*. H622
10:17 **G** up thy wares out of the land, O H622
23: 3 And I will **g** the remnant of my flock H6908
29:14 and I will **g** you from all the nations, H6908
31: 8 country, and **g** them from the coasts H6908
10 Israel will **g** him, and keep him, H6908
32:37 Behold, I will **g** them out of all H6908
40:10 unto us: but ye, **g** ye wine, and summer H622
49: 5 none shall **g** up him that wandereth. H6908
14 the heathen, *saying*, **G** ye together, and H6908
51:11 Make bright the arrows; **g** the shields: H4390
Ezk 11:17 GOD; I will even **g** you from the people, H6908
16:37 Behold, therefore I will **g** all thy lovers, H6908
37 hated; I will even **g** them round about H6908
20:34 the people, and will **g** you out of the H6908
41 from the people, and **g** you out of the H6908
22:19 I will **g** you into the midst of Jerusalem. H6908
20 *As* they **g** silver, and brass, and iron, H6910
20 to melt *it*; so will I **g** *you* in mine anger H6908
21 Yea, I will **g** you, and blow upon you in H3664
24: 4 **G** the pieces thereof into it, *even* every H622
29:13 forty years will I **g** the Egyptians from H6908
34:13 from the people, and **g** them from the H6908
36:24 the heathen, and **g** you out of all H6908
37:21 be gone, and will **g** them on every side, H6908
39:17 and come; **g** yourselves on every H622
Dan 3: 2 the king sent to **g** together the princes, H3673
Hos 8:10 nations, now will I **g** them, and they H6908
9: 6 Egypt shall **g** them up, Memphis H6908
Joel 1:14 solemn assembly, **g** the elders *and* all the H622
2: 6 pained: all faces shall **g** blackness. H6908
16 **G** the people, sanctify the congregation, H622
16 the elders, **g** the children, and those H622
3: 2 I will also **g** all nations, and will bring H6908
11 ye heathen, and **g** yourselves together H6908
Mic 2:12 of thee; I will surely **g** the remnant of H6908
4: 6 halteth, and I will **g** her that is driven H6908
12 **g** them as the sheaves into the floor. H6908
5: 1 Now **g** thyself in troops, O daughter of H1413
Nah 2:10 and the faces of them all **g** blackness. H6908
Hab 1: 9 they shall **g** the captivity as the sand. H622
15 in their net, and **g** them in their drag: H622
Zep 2: 1 **G** yourselves together, yea, gather H7197
1 Gather yourselves together, yea, **g** H7197
3: 8 determination *is* to **g** the nations, that I H622
18 I will **g** *them that are* sorrowful for the H622
19 that halteth, and **g** her that was driven H6908
20 in the time that I **g** you: for I will make H6908
Zec 10: 8 I will hiss for them, and **g** them; for I H6908
10 the land of Egypt, and **g** them out of H6908
14: 2 For I will **g** all nations against Jerusalem H622
Mt 3:12 his floor, and **g** his wheat into the *G4863*
6:26 do they reap, nor **g** into barns; yet your *G4863*
7:16 **g** grapes of thorns, or figs of thistles? *G4816*
13:28 thou then that we go and **g** them up? *G4816*
Mt 13:29 But he said, Nay; lest while ye **g** up the *G4816*
30 say to the reapers, **G** ye together first *G4816*
30 them: but **g** the wheat into my barn. *G4863*
41 and they shall **g** out of his kingdom *G4816*
24:31 and they shall **g** together his elect from *G1996*
25:26 not, and **g** where I have not strawed: *G4863*
Mk 13:27 his angels, and shall **g** together his elect *G1996*
Lk 3:17 his floor, and will **g** the wheat into his *G4863*
6:44 of thorns men do not **g** figs, nor of a *G4816*
44 nor of a bramble bush **g** they grapes. *G5166*
13:34 as a hen *doth* **g** her brood under *her*
Jn 6:12 unto his disciples, **G** up the fragments *G4863*
11:52 also he should **g** together in one the *G4863*
15: 6 and men **g** them, and cast *them* *G4863*
Eph 1:10 of times he might **g** together in one all *G346*
Rev 14:18 sharp sickle, and **g** the clusters of the *G5166*
16:14 whole world, to **g** them to the battle of *G4863*
19:17 of heaven, Come and **g** yourselves *G4863*
20: 8 Gog and Magog, to **g** them together to *G4863*

GATHERED
Gen 1: 9 the heaven be **g** together unto one H6960
12: 5 that they had **g**, and the souls that they H7408
25: 8 full *of years;* and was **g** to his people. H622
17 and died; and was **g** unto his people. H622
29: 3 And thither were all the flocks **g**: and H622
7 cattle should be **g** together: water ye the H622
8 all the flocks be **g** together, and *till* they H622
22 And Laban **g** together all the men of the H622
35:29 and died, and was **g** unto his people, H622
41:48 And he **g** up all the food of the seven H6908
49 And Joseph **g** corn as the sand of the H6651
47:14 And Joseph **g** up all the money that H3950
49:29 them, I am to be **g** unto my people: bury H622
33 his sons, he **g** up his feet into the bed, H622
33 up the ghost, and was **g** unto his people. H622
Ex 4:29 And Moses and Aaron went and **g** H622
8:14 And they **g** them together upon heaps: H6651
15: 8 the waters were **g** together, the floods H6192
16:17 And the children of Israel did so, and **g**, H3950
18 an omer, he that **g** much had nothing
18 over, and he that **g** little had no lack;
18 **g** every man according to his eating. H3950
21 And they **g** it every morning, every H3950
22 on the sixth day they **g** twice as much H3950
23:16 hast **g** in thy labours out of the field. H622
32: 1 the mount, the people **g** themselves H6950
26 of Levi **g** themselves together unto him. H622
35: 1 And Moses **g** all the congregation of H6950
Lev 8: 4 the assembly was **g** together unto the H6950
23:39 when ye have **g** in the fruit of the land, H622
26:25 and when ye are **g** together within your H622
Nu 10: 7 But when the congregation is to be **g** H6950
11: 8 *And* the people went about, and **g** *it,* H3950
22 be **g** together for them, to suffice them? H622
24 of the LORD, and **g** the seventy men of H622
32 next day, and they **g** the quails: he that H622
32 the quails: he that **g** least gathered ten H4591
32 he that gathered least **g** ten homers: and H622
14:35 that are **g** together against me: H3259
15:32 that **g** sticks upon the sabbath day. H7197
16: 3 And they **g** themselves together against H6950
11 thy company *are* **g** together against the H3259
19 And Korah **g** all the congregation H6950
42 congregation was **g** against Moses and H6950
20: 2 and they **g** themselves together H6950
10 And Moses and Aaron **g** the H6950
24 Aaron shall be **g** unto his people: for he H622
26 be **g** *unto his people,* and shall die there. H622
21:23 his border: but Sihon **g** all his people H622
27: 3 of them that **g** themselves together H3259
13 thou also shalt be **g** unto thy people, as H622
13 thy people, as Aaron thy brother was **g**. H622
31: 2 shalt thou be **g** unto thy people. H622
Dt 16:13 thou hast **g** in thy corn and thy wine: H622
32:50 goest up, and be **g** unto thy people; as H622
50 mount Hor, and was **g** unto his people: H622
33: 5 *and* the tribes of Israel were **g** together. H622
Jos 9: 2 That they **g** themselves together, to H6908
10: 5 the king of Eglon, **g** themselves together, H622
6 mountains are **g** together against us. H6908
22:12 children of Israel **g** themselves together H6950
24: 1 And Joshua **g** all the tribes of Israel to H622
Jdg 1: 7 great toes cut off, **g** *their meat* under H3950
2:10 And also all that generation were **g** unto H622
3:13 And he **g** unto him the children of H622
4:13 And Sisera **g** together all his chariots, H2199
6:33 of the east were **g** together, and went H622
34 trumpet; and Abi-ezer was **g** after him. H2199

Jdg 6:35 who also was g after him: and he sent H2199
7:23 And the men of Israel g themselves H6817
24 men of Ephraim g themselves together, H6817
9: 6 And all the men of Shechem g together, H622
27 And they went out into the fields, and g H1219
47 the tower of Shechem were g together. H6908
10:17 Then the children of Ammon were g H6817
11: 3 and there were g vain men to Jephthah, H3950
20 his coast: but Sihon g all his people H622
12: 1 And the men of Ephraim g themselves H6817
4 Then Jephthah g together all the men H6908
16:23 Then the lords of the Philistines g them H622
18:22 house were g together, and overtook H2199
20: 1 the congregation was g together as one H6950
11 So all the men of Israel were g against H622
14 But the children of Benjamin g H622
1Sa 5: 8 They sent therefore and g all the lords of H622
11 So they sent and g together all the lords H622
7: 6 And they g together to Mizpeh, and H6908
7 of Israel were g together to Mizpeh, H6908
8: 4 Then all the elders of Israel g H6908
13: 5 And the Philistines g themselves H622
11 g themselves together at Michmash; H622
14:48 And he g an host, and smote the H6213
15: 4 And Saul g the people together, and H8085
17: 1 Now the Philistines g together their H622
1 armies to battle, and were g together at H622
2 And Saul and the men of Israel were g H622
20:38 Jonathan's lad g up the arrows, and H3950
22: 2 *was* discontented, g themselves unto H6908
25: 1 all the Israelites were g together, and H6908
28: 1 the Philistines g their armies together H6908
4 And the Philistines g themselves H6908
4 Shunem: and Saul g all Israel together, H6908
29: 1 Now the Philistines g together all their H6908
2Sa 2:25 And the children of Benjamin g H6908
30 and when he had g all the people H6908
6: 1 Again, David g together all *the* chosen H3254
10:15 before Israel, they g themselves together. H622
17 And when it was told David, he g all H622
12:29 And David g all the people together, and H622
14:14 which cannot be g up again; neither H622
17:11 Israel be generally g unto thee, from Dan H622
20:14 g together, and went also after him. H7035
21:13 g the bones of them that were hanged. H622
23: 9 *that* were there g together to battle, and H622
11 Philistines were g together into a troop, H622
1Ki 10:26 And Solomon g together chariots and H622
11:24 And he g men unto him, and became H6908
18:20 of Israel, and g the prophets together H6908
20: 1 And Ben-hadad the king of Syria g all H6908
22: 6 Then the king of Israel g the prophets H6908
2Ki 3:21 against them, they g all that were able H6817
4:39 a wild vine, and g thereof wild gourds H3950
6:24 king of Syria g all his host, and went H6908
10:18 And Jehu g all the people together, and H6908
22: 4 keepers of the door have g of the people: H622
9 Thy servants have g the money that H5413
20 and thou shalt be g into thy grave in H622
23: 1 And the king sent, and they g unto him H622
1Ch 11: 1 Then all Israel g themselves to David H6908
13 the Philistines were g together to battle, H622
13: 5 So David g all Israel together, from H6950
15: 3 And David g all Israel together to H6950
19: 7 of Ammon g themselves together H622
17 And it was told David; and he g all H622
23: 2 And he g together all the princes of H622
2Ch 1:14 And Solomon g chariots and horsemen: H622
11: 1 come to Jerusalem, he g of the house of H6950
12: 5 princes of Judah, that were g together to H622
13: 7 And there are g unto him vain men, the H6908
15: 9 And he g all Judah and Benjamin, and H6908
10 So they g themselves together at H6908
18: 5 Therefore the king of Israel g together H6908
20: 4 And Judah g themselves together, to H6908
23: 2 And they went about in Judah, and g H6908
24: 5 And he g together the priests and the H6908
11 day by day, and g money in abundance. H622
25: 5 Moreover Amaziah g Judah together, H6908
28:24 And Ahaz g together the vessels of the H622
29: 4 and g them together into the east street, H622
15 And they g their brethren, and sanctified H622
20 Then Hezekiah the king rose early, and g H622
30: 3 g themselves together to Jerusalem. H622
32: 4 So there was g much people together, H6908
6 the people, and g them together to him H6908
34: 9 that kept the doors had g of the hand of H622
17 And they have g together the money H5413
28 and thou shalt be g to thy grave in H622
2Ch 34:29 Then the king sent and g together all the H622
Ezr 3: 1 cities, the people g themselves together H622
7:28 upon me, and I g together out of Israel H6908
8:15 And I g them together to the river that H6908
10: 9 and Benjamin g themselves together H6908
Neh 5:16 servants *were* g thither unto the work. H6908
8: 1 And all the people g themselves together H622
13 And on the second day were g together H622
12:28 And the sons of the singers g themselves H622
13:11 forsaken? And I g them together, and H6908
Est 2: 8 maidens were g together unto Shushan H6908
19 And when the virgins were g together H6908
9: 2 The Jews g themselves together in their H6950
15 For the Jews that *were* in Shushan g H6950
16 king's provinces g themselves together, H6950
Job 16:10 have g themselves together against me. H4390
27:19 be g: he openeth his eyes, and he *is* not. H622
30: 7 under the nettles they were g together. H5596
Ps 35:15 they rejoiced, and g themselves together: H622
15 *yea*, the abjects g themselves together H622
47: 9 The princes of the people are g together, H622
59: 3 the mighty are g against me; not *for* H1481
102:22 When the people are g together, and H6908
107: 3 And g them out of the lands, from the H6908
140: 2 continually are they g together *for* war. H1481
Prv 27:25 itself, and herbs of the mountains are g. H622
30: 4 who hath g the wind in his fists? H622
Ecc 2: 8 I g me also silver and gold, and the H3664
Song 5: 1 *my* spouse: I have g my myrrh with my H717
Isa 5: 2 And he fenced it, and g out the stones
10:14 *that are* left, have I g all the earth; and H622
13: 4 of nations g together: the LORD of H622
22: 9 g together the waters of the lower pool. H6908
24:22 And they shall be g together, *as* H622
22 *as* prisoners are g in the pit, and shall H626
27:12 be g one by one, O ye children of Israel. H3950
33: 4 And your spoil shall be g *like* the H622
34:15 also be g, every one with her mate. H6908
16 and his spirit it hath g them. H6908
43: 9 Let all the nations be g together, and let H6908
44:11 let them all be g together, let them H6908
49: 5 Israel be not g, yet shall I be glorious H622
56: 8 him, beside those that are g unto him. H6908
60: 7 All the flocks of Kedar shall be g H6908
62: 9 But they that have g it shall eat it, and H622
Jer 3:17 nations shall be g unto it, to the name H6960
8: 2 they shall not be g, nor be buried; they H622
25:33 be lamented, neither g, nor buried; they H622
26: 9 all the people were g against Jeremiah H6950
40:12 g wine and summer fruits very much. H622
15 the Jews which are g unto thee should H6908
Ezk 28:25 When I shall have g the house of Israel H6908
29: 5 together, nor g: I have given thee for H6908
38: 8 the sword, *and is* g out of many people, H6908
12 the people *that are* g out of the nations, H622
13 a spoil? hast thou g thy company to H6950
39:27 the people, and g them out of their H6908
28 but I have g them unto their own H3664
Dan 3: 3 the provinces, were g together unto the H3673
27 counsellors, being g together, saw these H3673
Hos 1:11 of Israel be g together, and appoint H6908
10:10 the people shall be g against them, when H622
Mic 1: 7 desolate: for she g *it* of the hire of an H6908
4:11 Now also many nations are g against H622
7: 1 Woe is me! for I am as when they have g H625
Zec 12: 3 of the earth be g together against it. H622
14:14 about shall be g together, gold, and H622
Mt 2: 4 And when he had g all the chief priests G4863
13: 2 And great multitudes were g together G4863
40 As therefore the tares are g and burned G4816
47 cast into the sea, and g of every kind: G4863
48 and sat down, and g the good into G4816
18:20 For where two or three are g together G4863
22:10 into the highways, and g together all as G4863
34 to silence, they were g together. G4863
41 While the Pharisees were g together, G4863
23:37 how often would I have g thy children G1996
24:28 is, there will the eagles be g together. G4863
25:32 And before him shall be g all nations: G4863
27:17 Therefore when they were g together, G4863
27 g unto him the whole band *of soldiers*. G4863
Mk 1:33 And all the city was g together at the G1996
2: 2 And straightway many were g together, G4863
4: 1 side: and there was g unto him a great G4863
5:21 side, much people g unto him: and he G4863
6:30 And the apostles g themselves together G4863
Lk 8: 4 And when much people were g G4896
11:29 And when the people were g thick G1865
12: 1 In the mean time, when there were g G1996
Lk 13:34 how often would I have g thy children G1996
15:13 the younger son g all together, and G4863
17:37 *is*, thither will the eagles be g together. G4863
24:33 found the eleven g together, and them G4867
Jn 6:13 Therefore they g *them* together, and G4863
11:47 Then g the chief priests and the G4863
Act 4: 6 priest, were g together at Jerusalem. G4863
26 the rulers were g together against the G4863
27 the people of Israel, were g together, G4863
12:12 where many were g together praying. G4863
14:27 And when they were come, and had g G4863
15:30 and when they had g the multitude G4863
17: 5 baser sort, and g a company, and set G3792
20: 8 chamber, where they were g together. G4863
28: 3 And when Paul had g a bundle of G4962
1Co 5: 4 when ye are g together, and my spirit, G4863
2Co 8:15 As it is written, He that *had* g much had
15 and he that *had* g little had no lack.
Rev 14:19 into the earth, and g the vine of the G5166
16:16 And he g them together into a place G4863
19:19 and their armies, g together to make G4863

GATHERER
Am 7:14 an herdman, and a g of sycomore fruit: H1103

GATHEREST
Dt 24:21 When thou g the grapes of thy H1219

GATHERETH
Nu 19:10 And he that g the ashes of the heifer H622
Ps 33: 7 He g the waters of the sea together as H3664
41: 6 vanity: his heart g iniquity to itself; H6908
147: 2 he g together the outcasts of Israel. H3664
Prv 6: 8 summer, *and* g her food in the harvest. H103
10: 5 He that g in summer *is* a wise son: *but* H103
13:11 but he that g by labour shall increase. H6908
Isa 10:14 people: and as one g eggs *that are* left, H622
17: 5 the harvestman g the corn, and reapeth H622
5 he that g ears in the valley of Rephaim. H3950
56: 8 The Lord GOD which g the outcasts of H6908
Nah 3:18 the mountains, and no man g *them*. H6908
Hab 2: 5 be satisfied, but g unto him all nations, H622
Mt 12:30 that g not with me scattereth abroad. G4863
23:37 even as a hen g her chickens under G1996
Lk 11:23 and he that g not with me scattereth. G4863
Jn 4:36 wages, and g fruit unto life eternal: G4863

GATHERING
Gen 1:10 Earth; and the g together of the waters H4723
49:10 unto him *shall* the g of the people *be*. H3349
Nu 15:33 And they that found him g sticks H7197
1Ki 17:10 woman *was* there g of sticks: and he H7197
12 and, behold, I *am* g two sticks, that I H7197
2Ch 20:25 days in g of the spoil, it was so much. H962
Isa 32:10 vintage shall fail, the g shall not come. H625
33: 4 gathered *like* the g of the caterpiller: as H625
Mt 25:24 and g where thou hast not strawed: G4863
Act 16:10 assuredly g that the Lord had called G4822
2Th 2: 1 Christ, and *by* our g together unto him, G1997

GATHERINGS
1Co 16: 2 him, that there be no g when I come. G3048

GATH-HEPHER
2Ki 14:25 of Amittai, the prophet, which *was* of G. H1662

GATH-RIMMON
Jos 19:45 And Jehud, and Bene-berak, and G, H1667
21:24 Aijalon with her suburbs, G with her H1667
25 and G with her suburbs; two cities. H1667
1Ch 6:69 And Aijalon with her suburbs, and G H1667

GAVE
Gen 2:20 And Adam g names to all cattle, and to H7121
3: 6 and did eat, and g also unto her H5414
12 me, she g me of the tree, and I did eat. H5414
14:20 thy hand. And he g him tithes of all. H5414
16: 3 of Canaan, and g her to her husband H5414
18: 7 and good, and g *it* unto a young man; H5414
20:14 and g *them* unto Abraham, H5414
21:14 of water, and g *it* unto Hagar, putting H5414
19 bottle with water, and g the lad drink. H8248
27 and oxen, and g them unto Abimelech; H5414
24:18 pitcher upon her hand, and g him drink.
32 his camels, and g straw and provender H5414
53 and raiment, and g *them* to Rebekah: H5414
53 to Rebekah: he g also to her brother H5414
25: 5 And Abraham g all that he had unto H5414
6 had, Abraham g gifts, and sent them H5414

Gen 25: 8 Then Abraham **g** up the ghost, and died
17 years: and he **g** up the ghost and died;
34 Then Jacob **g** Esau bread and pottage H5414
27:17 And she **g** the savoury meat and the H5414
28: 4 stranger, which God **g** unto Abraham. H5414
6 as he blessed him he **g** him a charge,
29:24 And Laban **g** unto his daughter Leah H5414
28 **g** him Rachel his daughter to wife also. H5414
29 And Laban **g** to Rachel his daughter H5414
30: 4 And she **g** him Bilhah her handmaid to H5414
9 her maid, and **g** her Jacob to wife. H5414
35 and **g** *them* into the hand of his sons. H5414
35: 4 And they **g** unto Jacob all the strange H5414
12 And the land which I **g** Abraham and H5414
29 And Isaac **g** up the ghost, and died, and
38:18 hand. And he **g** *it* her, and came in H5414
26 I; because that I **g** her not to Shelah my H5414
39:21 him mercy, and **g** him favour in the H5414
40:11 and I **g** the cup into Pharaoh's hand. H5414
21 and he **g** the cup into Pharaoh's hand: H5414
41:45 and he **g** him to wife Asenath H5414
43:24 house, and **g** *them* water, and they H5414
24 feet; and he **g** their asses provender. H5414
45:21 did so: and Joseph **g** them wagons, H5414
21 and **g** them provision for the way. H5414
22 To all of them he **g** each man changes H5414
22 to Benjamin he **g** three hundred *pieces* H5414
46:18 whom Laban **g** to Leah his daughter, H5414
25 Bilhah, which Laban **g** unto Rachel his H5414
47:11 his brethren, and **g** them a possession H5414
17 and Joseph **g** them bread *in exchange* H5414
22 which Pharaoh **g** them: wherefore they H5414
Ex 2:21 and he **g** Moses Zipporah his daughter. H5414
6:13 unto Aaron, and **g** them a charge unto
11: 3 And the LORD **g** the people favour in H5414
12:36 And the LORD **g** the people favour in H5414
14:20 *to them,* but it **g** light by night *to these:*
31:18 And he **g** unto Moses, when he had H5414
32:24 *it* off. So they **g** *it* me: then I cast it into H5414
34:32 Israel came nigh: and he **g** them in
36: 6 And Moses **g** commandment, and they
Nu 3:51 And Moses **g** the money of them that H5414
7: 6 the oxen, and **g** them unto the Levites. H5414
7 Two wagons and four oxen he **g** unto H5414
8 And four wagons and eight oxen he **g** H5414
9 But unto the sons of Kohath he **g** none: H5414
11:25 upon him, and **g** *it* unto the seventy H5414
17: 6 of their princes **g** him a rod apiece, for H5414
27:23 And he laid his hands upon him, and **g**
31:41 And Moses **g** the tribute, *which was* the H5414
47 man and of beast, and **g** them unto the H5414
32:33 And Moses **g** unto them, *even* to the H5414
38 and Shibmah: and **g** other names unto H7121
40 And Moses **g** Gilead unto Machir the H5414
Dt 2:12 which the LORD **g** unto them. H5414
3:12 and the cities thereof, **g** I unto the H5414
13 kingdom of Og, **g** I unto the half tribe H5414
15 And I **g** Gilead unto Machir. H5414
16 unto the Gadites I **g** from Gilead even H5414
9:11 *that* the LORD **g** me the two tables of H5414
10: 4 and the LORD **g** them unto me. H5414
22:16 unto the elders, I **g** my daughter unto H5414
29: 8 And we took their land, and **g** it for an H5414
31:23 And he **g** Joshua the son of Nun a
Jos 1:14 land which Moses **g** you on this side H5414
15 the LORD'S servant **g** you on this side H5414
11:23 and Joshua **g** it for an inheritance H5414
12: 6 of the LORD **g** it *for* a possession unto H5414
7 Seir; which Joshua **g** unto the tribes of H5414
13: 8 which Moses **g** them, beyond Jordan H5414
8 Moses the servant of the LORD **g** them; H5414
14 Only unto the tribe of Levi he **g** none H5414
15 And Moses **g** unto the tribe of the H5414
24 And Moses **g** *inheritance* unto the tribe H5414
29 And Moses **g** *inheritance* unto the half H5414
33 But unto the tribe of Levi Moses **g** not H5414
14: 3 he **g** none inheritance among them. H5414
4 therefore they **g** no part unto the H5414
13 And Joshua blessed him, and **g** unto H5414
15:13 of Jephunneh he **g** a part among the H5414
17 he **g** him Achsah his daughter to wife. H5414
19 of water. And he **g** her the upper H5414
17: 4 of the LORD he **g** them an inheritance H5414
18: 7 Moses the servant of the LORD **g** them. H5414
19:49 children of Israel **g** an inheritance to H5414
50 of the LORD they **g** him the city which H5414
21: 3 And the children of Israel **g** unto the H5414
8 And the children of Israel **g** by lot unto H5414
9 And they **g** out of the tribe of the H5414
Jos 21:11 And they **g** them the city of Arba the H5414
12 villages thereof, **g** they to Caleb the son H5414
13 Thus they **g** to the children of Aaron H5414
21 For they **g** them Shechem with her H5414
27 of Manasseh *they* **g** Golan in Bashan H5414
43 And the LORD **g** unto Israel all the land H5414
44 And the LORD **g** them rest round about,
22: 4 LORD **g** you on the other side Jordan. H5414
7 *other* half thereof **g** Joshua among their H5414
24: 3 multiplied his seed, and **g** him Isaac. H5414
4 And I **g** unto Isaac Jacob and Esau: H5414
4 and Esau: and I **g** unto Esau mount H5414
8 with you: and I **g** them into your hand, H5414
Jdg 1:13 he **g** him Achsah his daughter to wife. H5414
15 of water. And Caleb **g** her the upper H5414
20 And they **g** Hebron unto Caleb, as H5414
3: 6 be their wives, and **g** their daughters to H5414
4:19 milk, and **g** him drink, and covered him.
5:25 He asked water, *and* she **g** *him* milk; H5414
6: 9 from before you, and **g** you their land; H5414
9: 4 And they **g** him threescore and ten H5414
14: 9 mother, and he **g** them, and they did H5414
19 their spoil, and **g** change of garments H5414
15: 2 her; therefore I **g** her to thy companion: H5414
17: 4 of silver, and **g** them to the founder, H5414
19:21 So he brought him into his house, and **g**
20:36 for the men of Israel **g** place to the H5414
21:14 time; and they **g** them wives which they H5414
Ru 2:18 she brought forth, and **g** to her that she H5414
3:17 of barley **g** he me; for he said to H5414
4: 7 off his shoe, and **g** *it* to his neighbour: H5414
13 **g** her conception, and she bare a son. H5414
17 And the women her neighbours **g** it a H7121
1Sa 1: 4 offered, he **g** to Peninnah his wife, H5414
5 But unto Hannah he **g** a worthy H5414
23 **g** her son suck until she weaned him.
9:23 portion which I **g** thee, of which I said H5414
10: 9 from Samuel, God **g** him another heart:
18: 4 upon him, and **g** it to David, and his H5414
27 foreskins, and they **g** them in full tale to
27 Saul **g** him Michal his daughter to wife. H5414
20:40 And Jonathan **g** his artillery unto his H5414
21: 6 So the priest **g** him hallowed *bread:* for H5414
22:10 for him, and **g** him victuals, and gave H5414
10 him victuals, and **g** him the sword of H5414
27: 6 Then Achish **g** him Ziklag that day: H5414
30:11 him to David, and **g** him bread, and he H5414
12 And they **g** him a piece of a cake of figs, H5414
2Sa 12: 8 And I **g** thee thy master's house, and H5414
8 into thy bosom, and **g** thee the house of H5414
18: 5 when the king **g** all the captains charge
24: 9 And Joab **g** up the sum of the number H5414
1Ki 4:29 And God **g** Solomon wisdom and H5414
5:10 So Hiram **g** Solomon cedar trees and H5414
11 And Solomon **g** Hiram twenty H5414
11 thus **g** Solomon to Hiram year by year. H5414
12 And the LORD **g** Solomon wisdom, as H5414
9:11 king Solomon **g** Hiram twenty cities H5414
10:10 And she **g** the king an hundred and H5414
10 the queen of Sheba **g** to king Solomon. H5414
13 And king Solomon **g** unto the queen of H5414
13 *that* which Solomon **g** her of his royal H5414
11:18 of Egypt; which **g** him an house, and H5414
18 him victuals, and **g** him land. H5414
19 so that he **g** him to wife the sister H5414
12:13 the old men's counsel that they **g** him; H3289
13: 3 And he **g** a sign the same day, saying, H5414
14: 8 of David, and **g** it thee: and *yet* thou H5414
15 land, which he **g** to their fathers, and H5414
19:21 of the oxen, and **g** unto the people, and H5414
2Ki 10:15 hand. And he **g** *him* his hand; and he H5414
11:12 upon him, and **g** *him* the testimony; and
12:11 And they **g** the money, being told, into H5414
14 But they **g** that to the workmen, and H5414
13: 5 (And the LORD **g** Israel a saviour, so H5414
15:19 and Menahem **g** Pul a thousand talents H5414
17: 3 his servant, and **g** him presents. H7725
18:15 And Hezekiah **g** *him* all the silver that H5414
16 overlaid, and **g** it to the king of Assyria. H5414
21: 8 the land which I **g** their fathers; only if H5414
22: 8 **g** the book to Shaphan, and he read it. H5414
23:35 And Jehoiakim **g** the silver and the gold H5414
25: 6 Riblah; and they **g** judgment upon him. H1696
1Ch 2:35 And Sheshan **g** his daughter to Jarha H5414
6:55 And they **g** them Hebron in the land of H5414
56 they **g** to Caleb the son of Jephunneh. H5414
57 And to the sons of Aaron they **g** the H5414
64 And the children of Israel **g** to the H5414
65 And they **g** by lot out of the tribe of the H5414
1Ch 6:67 And they **g** unto them, *of* the cities of H5414
67 *they* **g** also Gezer with her suburbs,
14:12 gods there, David **g** a commandment,
21: 5 And Joab **g** the sum of the number of H5414
25 So David **g** to Ornan for the place six H5414
25: 5 up the horn. And God **g** to Heman H5414
28:11 Then David **g** to Solomon his son the H5414
14 *He* **g** of gold by weight for *things* of gold,
16 And by weight *he* **g** gold for the tables of
17 golden basons *he* **g** *gold* by weight for
29: 7 And **g** for the service of the house of H5414
8 stones were found **g** *them* to the H5414
2Ch 9: 9 And she **g** the king an hundred and H5414
9 as the queen of Sheba **g** king Solomon. H5414
12 And king Solomon **g** to the queen of H5414
10: 8 which the old men **g** him, and took H3289
11:23 fenced city: and he **g** them victual in H5414
13: 5 God of Israel **g** the kingdom over Israel H5414
15 Then the men of Judah **g** a shout: and as
15:15 and the LORD **g** them rest round about.
20:30 for his God **g** him rest round about.
21: 3 And their father **g** them great gifts of H5414
3 but the kingdom **g** he to Jehoram; H5414
23:11 the crown, and **g** *him* the testimony, and
24:12 And the king and Jehoiada **g** it to such H5414
26: 8 And the Ammonites **g** gifts to Uzziah: H5414
27: 5 of Ammon **g** him the same year an H5414
28:15 and shod them, and **g** them to eat and to
21 of the princes, and **g** *it* unto the king of H5414
30: 7 **g** them up to desolation, as ye see. H5414
24 and the princes **g** to the congregation
32:24 spake unto him, and he **g** him a sign. H5414
34:10 LORD, and they **g** it to the workmen H5414
11 Even to the artificers and builders **g** H5414
35: 7 And Josiah **g** to the people, of the flock, H7311
8 And his princes **g** willingly unto the H7311
8 the house of God, **g** unto the priests for H5414
9 of the Levites, **g** unto the Levites for H7311
36:17 for age: he **g** *them* all into his hand. H5414
Ezr 2:69 They **g** after their ability unto the H5414
3: 7 They **g** money also unto the masons, H5414
5:12 unto wrath, he **g** them into the hand H3052
7:11 king Artaxerxes **g** unto Ezra the priest, H5414
10:19 And they **g** their hands that they would H5414
Neh 2: 1 up the wine, and **g** *it* unto the king. H5414
9 the river, and **g** them the king's letters. H5414
7: 2 That I **g** my brother Hanani, and
70 And some of the chief of the fathers **g** H5414
70 work. The Tirshatha **g** to the treasure a H5414
71 And *some* of the chief of the fathers **g** H5414
72 And *that* which the rest of the people **g** H5414
8: 8 distinctly, and **g** the sense, and caused H7760
12:31 *of them that* **g** thanks, *whereof one*
38 And the other *company of them that* **g**
40 *of them that* **g** thanks in the house
47 days of Nehemiah, **g** the portions of the H5414
Est 1: 7 And they **g** *them* drink in vessels of gold,
2: 9 and he speedily **g** her her things for H5414
18 the provinces, and **g** gifts, according to H5414
3:10 his hand, and **g** it unto Haman the son H5414
4: 5 upon her, and **g** him a commandment
8 Also he **g** him the copy of the writing of H5414
10 Again Esther spake unto Hatach, and **g**
8: 2 from Haman, and **g** it unto Mordecai. H5414
Job 1:21 thither: the LORD **g**, and the LORD hath H5414
19:16 I called my servant, and he **g** *me* no
29:11 when the eye saw *me,* it **g** witness to me:
21 Unto me *men* **g** ear, and waited, and
32:11 Behold, I waited for your words; I **g** ear
42:10 **g** Job twice as much as he had before. H3254
11 every man also **g** him a piece of money, H5414
15 and their father **g** them inheritance H5414
Ps 18:13 **g** his voice; hail *stones* and coals of fire. H5414
68:11 The Lord **g** the word: great *was* the H5414
69:21 They **g** me also gall for my meat; and in H5414
21 in my thirst they **g** me vinegar to drink.
77: 1 with my voice; and he **g** ear unto me.
78:15 **g** *them* drink as *out of* the great depths.
29 filled: for he **g** them their own desire; H935
46 He **g** also their increase unto the H5414
48 He **g** up their cattle also to the hail, and H5462
50 but **g** their life over to the pestilence; H5462
62 He **g** his people over also unto the H5462
81:12 So I **g** them up unto their own hearts' H7971
99: 7 and the ordinance *that* he **g** them. H5414
105:32 He **g** them hail for rain, *and* flaming H5414
44 And **g** them the lands of the heathen: H5414
106:15 And he **g** them their request; but sent H5414
41 And he **g** them into the hand of the H5414

Ps 135:12 And g their land *for* an heritage, an H5414
136:21 And g their land for an heritage: for his H5414
Prv 8:29 When he g to the sea his decree, that H7760
Ecc 1:13 And I g my heart to seek and search H5414
17 And I g my heart to know wisdom, and H5414
12: 7 spirit shall return unto God who g it. H5414
9 knowledge; yea, he g good heed, and
Song 5: 6 I called him, but he g me no answer.
Isa 41: 2 him to his foot, g the nations before H5414
2 rule over kings? he g *them* as the dust H5414
42:24 Who g Jacob for a spoil, and Israel to H5414
43: 3 thy Saviour: I g Egypt *for* thy ransom, H5414
50: 6 I g my back to the smiters, and my H5414
Jer 7: 7 I g to your fathers, for ever and ever. H5414
14 the place which I g to you and to your H5414
16:15 their land that I g unto their fathers. H5414
17: 4 heritage that I g thee; and I will cause H5414
23:39 you, and the city that I g you and your H5414
24:10 that I g unto them and to their fathers. H5414
30: 3 to the land that I g to their fathers, and H5414
32:12 And I g the evidence of the purchase H5414
36:32 Then took Jeremiah another roll, and g H5414
39: 5 where he g judgment upon him. H1696
10 land of Judah, and g them vineyards H5414
11 Now Nebuchadrezzar king of Babylon g
40: 5 of the guard g him victuals and a H5414
44:30 seek his life; as I g Zedekiah king of H5414
52: 9 where he g judgment upon him. H1696
Lam 1:19 and mine elders g up the ghost in the
Ezk 16:19 My meat also which I g thee, fine flour, H5414
20:11 And I g them my statutes, and shewed H5414
12 Moreover also I g them my sabbaths, H5414
25 Wherefore I g them also statutes *that* H5414
36:28 And ye shall dwell in the land that I g H5414
39:23 from them, and g them into the hand H5414
Dan 1: 2 And the Lord g Jehoiakim king of H5414
7 Unto whom the prince of the eunuchs g H7760
7 names: for he g unto Daniel *the name* H7760
16 they should drink; and g them pulse. H5414
17 As for these four children, God g them H5414
2:48 a great man, and g him many great H3052
5:18 O thou king, the most high God g H3052
19 And for the majesty that he g him, all H3052
6:10 day, and prayed, and g thanks before his
Hos 2: 8 For she did not know that I g her corn, H5414
13:11 I g thee a king in mine anger, and took H5414
Am 2:12 But ye g the Nazarites wine to drink; and
Mal 2: 5 and peace; and I g them to him *for* the H5414
Mt 8:18 about him, he g commandment to G2753
10: 1 disciples, he g them power *against* G1325
14:19 and brake, and g the loaves to *his* G1325
15:36 and the fishes, and g thanks, and brake G1325
36 brake *them*, and g to his disciples, and G1325
21:23 things? and who g thee this authority? G1325
25:15 And unto one he g five talents, to G1325
35 For I was an hungred, and ye g me G1325
35 was thirsty, and ye g me drink: I was a G4222
37 fed *thee*? or thirsty, and g *thee* drink? G4222
42 For I was an hungred, and ye g me no G1325
42 I was thirsty, and ye g me no drink: G4222
26:26 and brake *it*, and g *it* to the disciples, G1325
27 And he took the cup, and g thanks, and G1325
27 g *it* to them, saying, Drink ye all of it; G1325
48 Now he that betrayed him g them a G1325
27:10 And g them for the potter's field, as the G1325
34 They g him vinegar to drink mingled G1325
48 put *it* on a reed, and g him to drink. G4222
28:12 they g large money unto the soldiers, G1325
Mk 2:26 g also to them which were with him? G1325
5:13 And forthwith Jesus g them leave. And G2010
6: 7 and g them power over unclean spirits; G1325
28 in a charger, and g it to the damsel: G1325
28 and the damsel g it to her mother. G1325
41 the loaves, and g *them* to his disciples G1325
8: 6 seven loaves, and g thanks, and brake, G1325
6 and brake, and g to his disciples to set G1325
11:28 g thee this authority to do these things? G1325
13:34 left his house, and g authority to his G1325
14:22 and brake *it*, and g to them, and said, G1325
23 he g *it* to them: and they all drank of it. G1325
15:23 And they g him to drink wine mingled G1325
36 *it* on a reed, and g him to drink, saying, G4222
37 And Jesus cried with a loud voice, and g
39 so cried out, and g up the ghost, he said,
45 the centurion, he g the body to Joseph. G1433
Lk 2:38 And she coming in that instant g thanks G437
4:20 And he closed the book, and he g *it* G591
6: 4 the shewbread, and g also to them that G1325
7:21 unto many *that were* blind he g sight. G5483
Lk 9: 1 together, and g them power and G1325
16 and brake, and g to the disciples to set G1325
10:35 two pence, and g *them* to the host, and G1325
15:16 swine did eat: and no man g unto him. G1325
18:43 when they saw *it*, g praise unto God. G1325
20: 2 or who is he that g thee this authority? G1325
22:17 And he took the cup, and g thanks, and
19 And he took bread, and g thanks, and
19 and brake *it*, and g unto them, saying, G1325
23:24 And Pilate g sentence that it should be
29 bare, and the paps which never g suck.
46 and having said thus, he g up the ghost.
24:30 blessed *it*, and brake, and g to them. G1929
42 And they g him a piece of a broiled G1929
Jn 1:12 But as many as received him, to them g G1325
3:16 For God so loved the world, that he g G1325
4: 5 ground that Jacob g to his son Joseph. G1325
12 Jacob, which g us the well, and drank G1325
6:31 He g them bread from heaven to eat. G1325
32 unto you, Moses g you not that bread G1325
7:22 Moses therefore g unto you G1325
10:29 My Father, which g *them* me, is greater G1325
12:49 Father which sent me, he g me a G1325
13:26 g *it* to Judas Iscariot, *the son* of Simon. G1325
14:31 and as the Father g me commandment, G1781
18:14 Now Caiaphas was he, which g counsel G4823
19: 9 art thou? But Jesus g him no answer. G1325
30 he bowed his head, and g up the ghost. G3860
38 Jesus: and Pilate g *him* leave. He came G2010
Act 1:26 And they g forth their lots; and the lot G1325
2: 4 tongues, as the Spirit g them utterance. G1325
3: 5 And he g heed unto them, expecting to G1907
4:33 And with great power g the apostles G591
5: 5 fell down, and g up the ghost: and great
7: 5 And he g him none inheritance in it, G1325
8 And he g him the covenant of G1325
10 all his afflictions, and g him favour and G1325
42 Then God turned, and g them up to G3860
8: 6 And the people with one accord g heed G4337
10 To whom they all g heed, from the least G4337
9:41 And he g her *his* hand, and lifted her G1325
10: 2 all his house, which g much alms to the G4160
11:17 Forasmuch then as God g them the like G1325
12:22 And the people g a shout, *saying, It is*
23 him, because he g not God the glory: G1325
23 was eaten of worms, and g up the ghost.
13:20 And after that he g *unto them* judges G1325
21 a king: and God g unto them Saul the G1325
22 to whom also he g testimony, and said, G3140
14: 3 in the Lord, which g testimony unto the G3140
17 that he did good, and g us rain from G1325
15:12 kept silence, and g audience to
24 to whom we g no *such* commandment: G1291
22:22 And they g him audience unto this word, G191
23:30 to thee, and g commandment to his
26:10 to death, I g my voice against *them*. G2702
27: 3 Paul, and g *him* liberty to go unto G2010
35 he took bread, and g thanks to God in
Ro 1:24 Wherefore God also g them up to G3860
26 For this cause God g them up unto vile G3860
28 *their* knowledge, God g them over to a G3860
1Co 3: 5 even as the Lord g to every man? G1325
6 Apollos watered; but God g the increase.
2Co 8: 5 we hoped, but first g their own selves to G1325
Gal 1: 4 Who g himself for our sins, that he G1325
2: 5 To whom we g place by subjection, no, G1502
9 unto me, they g to me and Barnabas G1325
20 who loved me, and g himself for me. G3860
3:18 but God g *it* to Abraham by promise. G5483
Eph 1:22 his feet, and g him *to be* the head over G1325
4: 8 captivity captive, and g gifts unto men. G1325
11 And he g some, apostles; and some, G1325
5:25 loved the church, and g himself for it; G3860
1Th 4: 2 we g you by the Lord Jesus. G1325
1Ti 2: 6 Who g himself a ransom for all, to be G1325
Tit 2:14 Who g himself for us, that he might G1325
Heb 7: 2 To whom also Abraham g a tenth part G3307
4 Abraham g the tenth of the spoils. G1325
13 no man g attendance at the altar. G4337
11:22 g commandment concerning his bones.
12: 9 *us*, and we g *them* reverence: shall G1788
Jas 5:18 And he prayed again, and the heaven g G1325
1Pt 1:21 the dead, and g him glory; that your G1325
1Jn 3:23 another, as he g us commandment. G1325
5:10 not the record that God g of his Son. G3140
Jude 3 Beloved, when I g all diligence to write G4160
Rev 1: 1 Christ, which God g unto him, to shew G1325
2:21 And I g her space to repent of her G1325
11:13 and g glory to the God of heaven. G1325
Rev 13: 2 and the dragon g him his power, and G1325
4 the dragon which g power unto the G1325
15: 7 And one of the four beasts g unto the G1325
20:13 And the sea g up the dead which were G1325

GAVEST

Gen 3:12 whom thou g *to be* with me, she gave H5414
1Ki 8:34 land which thou g unto their fathers. H5414
40 the land which thou g unto our fathers. H5414
48 land, which thou g unto their fathers, H5414
2Ch 6:25 thou g to them and to their fathers. H5414
31 the land which thou g unto our fathers. H5414
38 land, which thou g unto their fathers, H5414
20: 7 thy people Israel, and g it to the seed of H5414
Neh 9: 7 and g him the name of Abraham; H7760
13 them from heaven, and g them right H5414
15 And g them bread from heaven for H5414
20 Thou g also thy good spirit to instruct H5414
20 and g them water for their thirst. H5414
22 Moreover thou g them kingdoms and H5414
24 the Canaanites, and g them into their H5414
27 mercies thou g them saviours, who H5414
30 give ear: therefore g thou them into the H5414
35 that thou g them, and in the large H5414
35 land which thou g before them, neither H5414
36 the land that thou g unto our fathers to H5414
Job 39:13 *G thou* the goodly wings unto the
Ps 21: 4 He asked life of thee, *and* thou g *it* him, H5414
74:14 in pieces, *and* g him *to be* meat to the H5414
Lk 7:44 thine house, thou g me no water for my G1325
45 Thou g me no kiss: but this woman G1325
15:29 yet thou never g me a kid, that I might G1325
19:23 Wherefore then g not thou my money G1325
Jn 17: 4 the work which thou g me to do. G1325
6 men which thou g me out of the world: G1325
6 were, and thou g them me; and they G1325
8 words which thou g me; and they have G1325
12 those that thou g me I have kept, and G1325
22 And the glory which thou g me I have G1325
18: 9 them which thou g me have I lost none. G1325

GAY

Jas 2: 3 that weareth the g clothing, and say G2986

GAZA

Gen 10:19 to Gerar, unto G; as thou goest, unto H5804
Jos 10:41 even unto G, and all the country H5804
11:22 of Israel: only in G, in Gath, and in H5804
15:47 and her villages, G with her towns and H5804
Jdg 1:18 Also Judah took G with the coast H5804
6: 4 till thou come unto G, and left no H5804
16: 1 Then went Samson to G, and saw there H5804
21 him down to G, and bound him with H5804
1Sa 6:17 for Ashdod one, for G one, for Askelon H5804
2Ki 18: 8 He smote the Philistines, *even* unto G, H5804
1Ch 7:28 thereof, unto G and the towns thereof: H5804
Jer 47: 1 before that Pharaoh smote G. H5804
5 Baldness is come upon G; Ashkelon is H5804
Am 1: 6 transgressions of G, and for four, I will H5804
7 But I will send a fire on the wall of G, H5804
Zep 2: 4 For G shall be forsaken, and Ashkelon H5804
Zec 9: 5 Ashkelon shall see *it*, and fear; G also H5804
5 G, and Ashkelon shall not be inhabited. H5804
Act 8:26 from Jerusalem unto G, which is desert. G1048

GAZATHITES

Jos 13: 3 Philistines; the G, and the Ashdothites, H5841

GAZE

Ex 19:21 LORD to g, and many of them perish. H7200

GAZER

2Sa 5:25 from Geba until thou come to G. H1507
1Ch 14:16 the Philistines from Gibeon even to G. H1507

GAZEZ

1Ch 2:46 Moza, and G: and Haran begat Gazez. H1495
46 Moza, and Gazez: and Haran begat G. H1495

GAZING

Act 1:11 why stand ye g up into heaven? this G1689

GAZINGSTOCK

Heb 10:33 Partly, whilst ye were made a g both by G2301

GAZING-STOCK

Nah 3: 6 make thee vile, and will set thee as a g. H7210

GAZITES
Jdg 16: 2 *And it was told* the **G**, saying, Samson is H5841

GAZZAM
Ezr 2:48 children of Nekoda, the children of **G**, H1502
Neh 7:51 The children of **G**, the children of Uzza, H1502

GEBA
Jos 21:17 with her suburbs, **G** with her suburbs, H1387
1Sa 13: 3 that *was* in **G**, and the Philistines H1387
2Sa 5:25 from **G** until thou come to Gazer. H1387
1Ki 15:22 with them **G** of Benjamin, and Mizpah. H1387
2Ki 23: 8 incense, from **G** to Beer-sheba, and H1387
1Ch 6:60 And out of the tribe of Benjamin; **G** H1387
8: 6 the inhabitants of **G**, and they removed H1387
2Ch 16: 6 and he built therewith **G** and Mizpah. H1387
Neh 7:30 The men of Ramah and **G**, six hundred H1387
11:31 The children also of Benjamin from **G** H1387
12:29 out of the fields of **G** and Azmaveth: for H1387
Isa 10:29 up their lodging at **G**; Ramah is afraid; H1387
Zec 14:10 as a plain from **G** to Rimmon south of H1387

GEBAL
Ps 83: 7 **G**, and Ammon, and Amalek; the H1381
Ezk 27: 9 The ancients of **G** and the wise *men* H1380

GEBER
1Ki 4:13 The son of **G**, in Ramoth-gilead; to him H1127
19 **G** the son of Uri *was* in the country of H1398

GEBIM
Isa 10:31 of **G** gather themselves to flee. H1374

GEDALIAH
2Ki 25:22 them he made **G** the son of Ahikam, H1436
23 had made **G** governor, there came H1436
23 there came to **G** to Mizpah, even H1436
24 And **G** sware to them, and to their H1436
25 him, and smote **G**, that he died, and the H1436
1Ch 25: 3 Of Jeduthun: the sons of Jeduthun; **G**, H1436
9 the second to **G**, who with his brethren H1436
Ezr 10:18 and Eliezer, and Jarib, and **G**. H1436
Jer 38: 1 of Mattan, and **G** the son of Pashur, H1436
39:14 him unto **G** the son of Ahikam the H1436
40: 5 Go back also to **G** the son of Ahikam H1436
6 Then went Jeremiah unto **G** the son of H1436
7 had made **G** the son of Ahikam H1436
8 Then they came to **G** to Mizpah, even H1436
9 And **G** the son of Ahikam the son of H1436
11 had set over them **G** the son of Ahikam H1436
12 land of Judah, to **G**, unto Mizpah, and H1436
13 *were* in the fields, came to **G** to Mizpah, H1436
14 to slay thee? But **G** the son of Ahikam H1436
15 Kareah spake to **G** in Mizpah secretly, H1436
16 But **G** the son of Ahikam said unto H1436
41: 1 him, came unto **G** the son of Ahikam to H1436
2 him, and smote **G** the son of Ahikam H1436
3 him, *even* with **G**, at Mizpah, and the H1436
4 he had slain **G**, and no man knew *it*, H1436
6 them, Come to **G** the son of Ahikam. H1436
9 slain because of **G**, *was* it which Asa the H1436
10 guard had committed to **G** the son of H1436
16 *that* he had slain **G** the son of Ahikam, H1436
18 had slain **G** the son of Ahikam, H1436
43: 6 had left with **G** the son of Ahikam the H1436
Zep 1: 1 Cushi, the son of **G**, the son of Amariah, H1436

GEDEON
Heb 11:32 fail me to tell of **G**, and *of* Barak, and *of* *G1066*

GEDER
Jos 12:13 The king of Debir, one; the king of **G**, H1445

GEDERAH
Jos 15:36 And Sharaim, and Adithaim, and **G**, H1449

GEDERATHITE
1Ch 12: 4 and Johanan, and Josabad the **G**, H1452

GEDERITE
1Ch 27:28 **G**: and over the cellars of oil *was* Joash: H1451

GEDEROTH
Jos 15:41 And **G**, Beth-dagon, and Naamah, and H1450
2Ch 28:18 and Ajalon, and **G**, and Shocho with the H1450

GEDEROTHAIM
Jos 15:36 **G**; fourteen cities with their villages: H1453

GEDI
See EN-GEDI.

GEDOR
Jos 15:58 Halhul, Beth-zur, and **G**, H1446
1Ch 4: 4 And Penuel the father of **G**, and Ezer H1446
18 Jered the father of **G**, and Heber the H1446
39 And they went to the entrance of **G**, H1446
8:31 And **G**, and Ahio, and Zacher. H1446
9:37 And **G**, and Ahio, and Zechariah, and H1446
12: 7 Zebadiah, the sons of Jeroham of **G**. H1446

GEHAZI
2Ki 4:12 And he said to **G** his servant, Call this H1522
14 done for her? And **G** answered, Verily H1522
25 afar off, that he said to **G** his servant, H1522
27 by the feet: but **G** came near to thrust H1522
29 Then he said to **G**, Gird up thy loins, H1522
31 And **G** passed on before them, and laid H1522
36 And he called **G**, and said, Call this H1522
5:20 But **G**, the servant of Elisha the man of H1522
21 So **G** followed after Naaman. And H1522
25 *comest thou*, **G**? And he said, Thy H1522
8: 4 And the king talked with **G** the servant H1522
5 for her land. And **G** said, My lord, O H1522

GELILOTH
Jos 18:17 and went forth toward **G**, which *is* over H1553

GEMALLI
Nu 13:12 the tribe of Dan, Ammiel the son of **G**. H1582

GEMARIAH
Jer 29: 3 of Shaphan, and **G** the son of Hilkiah, H1587
36:10 LORD, in the chamber of **G** the son of H1587
11 When Michaiah the son of **G**, the son of H1587
12 of Achbor, and **G** the son of Shaphan, H1587
25 Elnathan and Delaiah and **G** had made H1587

GENDER
Lev 19:19 not let thy cattle **g** with a diverse kind: H7250
2Ti 2:23 avoid, knowing that they do **g** strifes. *G1080*

GENDERED
Job 38:29 hoary frost of heaven, who hath **g** it? H3205

GENDERETH
Job 21:10 Their bull **g**, and faileth not; their cow H5674
Gal 4:24 which **g** to bondage, which is Agar. *G1080*

GENEALOGIES
1Ch 5:17 All these were reckoned by **g** in the H3187
7: 5 their **g** fourscore and seven thousand. H3187
7 reckoned by their **g** twenty and two H3187
9: 1 So all Israel were reckoned by **g**; and, H3187
2Ch 12:15 seer concerning **g**? And *there were* wars H3187
31:19 were reckoned by **g** among the Levites. H3187
1Ti 1: 4 to fables and endless **g**, which minister *G1076*
Tit 3: 9 But avoid foolish questions, and **g**, and *G1076*

GENEALOGY
1Ch 4:33 *were* their habitations, and their **g**. H3187
5: 1 son of Israel: and the **g** is not to be H3188
7 their families, when the **g** of their H3187
7: 9 And the number of them, after their **g** H3187
40 throughout the **g** of them that were apt H3187
9:22 reckoned by their **g** in their villages, H3187
2Ch 31:16 Beside their **g** of males, from three H3187
17 Both to the **g** of the priests by the house H3187
18 And to the **g** of all their little ones, their H3187
Ezr 2:62 were reckoned by **g**, but they were not H3187
8: 1 and *this is* the **g** of them that went up H3187
3 by **g** of the males an hundred and fifty. H3187
Neh 7: 5 be reckoned by **g**. And I found a register H3187
5 a register of the **g** of them which came H3188
64 that were reckoned by **g**, but it was not H3187

GENERAL
1Ch 27:34 and the **g** of the king's army *was* Joab. H8269
Heb 12:23 To the **g** assembly and church of the *G3831*

GENERALLY
2Sa 17:11 Therefore I counsel that all Israel be **g** H622
Jer 48:38 *There shall be* lamentation **g** upon all H3605

GENERATION
Gen 7: 1 I seen righteous before me in this **g**. H1755
15:16 But in the fourth **g** they shall come H1755
50:23 of the third **g**: the children also of H8029
Ex 1: 6 and all his brethren, and all that **g**. H1755
17:16 war with Amalek from **g** to generation. H1755
16 war with Amalek from generation to **g**. H1755
20: 5 third and fourth **g** of them that hate me;
34: 7 unto the third and to the fourth **g**.
Nu 14:18 the children unto the third and fourth **g**.
32:13 years, until all the **g**, that had done evil H1755
Dt 1:35 men of this evil **g** see that good land, H1755
2:14 years; until all the **g** of the men of war H1755
5: 9 third and fourth **g** of them that hate me,
23: 2 even to his tenth **g** shall he not enter H1755
3 even to their tenth **g** shall they not H1755
8 of the LORD in their third **g**. H1755
29:22 So that the **g** to come of your children H1755
32: 5 *they are* a perverse and crooked **g**. H1755
20 froward **g**, children in whom *is* no faith. H1755
Jdg 2:10 And also all that **g** were gathered unto H1755
10 there arose another **g** after them, which H1755
2Ki 10:30 fourth **g** shall sit on the throne of Israel.
15:12 unto the fourth **g**. And so it came to pass.
Est 9:28 throughout every **g**, every family, every H1755
Ps 12: 7 preserve them from this **g** for ever. H1755
14: 5 for God *is* in the **g** of the righteous. H1755
22:30 it shall be accounted to the Lord for a **g**. H1755
24: 6 This *is* the **g** of them that seek him, that H1755
48:13 that ye may tell *it* to the **g** following. H1755
49:19 He shall go to the **g** of his fathers; they H1755
71:18 strength unto *this* **g**, *and* thy power to H1755
73:15 offend *against* the **g** of thy children. H1755
78: 4 shewing to the **g** to come the praises H1755
6 That the **g** to come might know *them*, H1755
8 and rebellious **g**; a generation *that* set H1755
8 generation; a **g** *that* set not their heart H1755
95:10 I grieved with *this* **g**, and said, It *is* a H1755
102:18 This shall be written for the **g** to come: H1755
109:13 Let his posterity be cut off; *and* in the **g** H1755
112: 2 the **g** of the upright shall be blessed. H1755
145: 4 One **g** shall praise thy works to H1755
Prv 27:24 and doth the crown *endure* to every **g**? H1755
30:11 *There is* a **g** *that* curseth their father, H1755
12 *There is* a **g** *that are* pure in their own H1755
13 *There is* a **g**, O how lofty are their eyes! H1755
14 *There is* a **g**, whose teeth *are as* swords, H1755
Ecc 1: 4 *One* **g** passeth away, and *another* H1755
4 and *another* **g** cometh: but the earth H1755
Isa 13:20 it be dwelt in from **g** to generation: H1755
20 from generation to **g**: neither shall the H1755
34:10 go up for ever: from **g** to generation it H1755
10 generation to **g** it shall lie waste; none H1755
17 **g** to generation shall they dwell therein. H1755
17 generation to **g** shall they dwell therein. H1755
51: 8 and my salvation from **g** to generation. H1755
8 and my salvation from generation to **g**. H1755
53: 8 shall declare his **g**? for he was cut off out H1755
Jer 2:31 O **g**, see ye the word of the LORD. Have H1755
7:29 and forsaken the **g** of his wrath. H1755
50:39 it be dwelt in from **g** to generation. H1755
39 shall it be dwelt in from generation to **g**. H1755
Lam 5:19 ever; thy throne from **g** to generation. H1755
19 ever; thy throne from generation to **g**. H1755
Dan 4: 3 his dominion *is* from **g** to generation. H1859
3 his dominion *is* from generation to **g**. H1859
34 his kingdom *is* from **g** to generation: H1859
34 his kingdom *is* from generation to **g**: H1859
Joel 1: 3 children, and their children another **g**. H1755
3:20 and Jerusalem from **g** to generation. H1755
20 and Jerusalem from generation to **g**. H1755
Mt 1: 1 The book of the **g** of Jesus Christ, the *G1078*
3: 7 said unto them, O **g** of vipers, who hath *G1081*
11:16 But whereunto shall I liken this **g**? It is *G1074*
12:34 O **g** of vipers, how can ye, being evil, *G1081*
39 and adulterous **g** seeketh after a sign; *G1074*
41 with this **g**, and shall condemn *G1074*
42 with this **g**, and shall condemn *G1074*
45 so shall it be also unto this wicked **g**. *G1074*
16: 4 A wicked and adulterous **g** seeketh *G1074*
17:17 and perverse **g**, how long shall I be *G1074*
23:33 *Ye* serpents, *ye* **g** of vipers, how can ye *G1081*
36 All these things shall come upon this **g**. *G1074*
24:34 Verily I say unto you, This **g** shall not *G1074*
Mk 8:12 Why doth this **g** seek after a sign? verily *G1074*
12 There shall no sign be given unto this **g**. *G1074*
38 and sinful **g**; of him also shall the *G1074*
9:19 saith, O faithless **g**, how long shall I be *G1074*
13:30 Verily I say unto you, that this **g** shall *G1074*
Lk 1:50 that fear him from **g** to generation. *G1074*
50 that fear him from generation to **g**. *G1074*
3: 7 be baptized of him, O **g** of vipers, who *G1081*
7:31 men of this **g**? and to what are they like? *G1074*
9:41 and perverse **g**, how long shall I be *G1074*

Lk 11:29 to say, This is an evil g: they seek a sign; G1074
30 so shall also the Son of man be to this g. G1074
31 the men of this g, and condemn them: G1074
32 with this g, and shall condemn G1074
50 of the world, may be required of this g; G1074
51 unto you, It shall be required of this g. G1074
16: 8 their g wiser than the children of light. G1074
17:25 many things, and be rejected of this g. G1074
21:32 Verily I say unto you, This g shall not G1074
Act 2:40 Save yourselves from this untoward g. G1074
8:33 his g? for his life is taken from the earth. G1074
13:36 served his own g by the will of God, fell G1074
Heb 3:10 Wherefore I was grieved with that g, G1074
1Pt 2: 9 But ye *are* a chosen g, a royal G1085

GENERATIONS

Gen 2: 4 These *are* the g of the heavens and of H8435
5: 1 This *is* the book of the g of Adam. In H8435
6: 9 These *are* the g of Noah: Noah was a H8435
9 in his g, *and* Noah walked with God. H1755
9:12 that *is* with you, for perpetual g: H1755
10: 1 Now these *are* the g of the sons of H8435
32 Noah, after their g, in their nations: and H8435
11:10 These *are* the g of Shem: Shem *was* an H8435
27 Now these *are* the g of Terah: Terah H8435
17: 7 after thee in their g for an everlasting H1755
9 thou, and thy seed after thee in their g. H1755
12 man child in your g, he that is born in H1755
25:12 Now these *are* the g of Ishmael, H8435
13 according to their g: the firstborn of H8435
19 And these *are* the g of Isaac, H8435
36: 1 Now these *are* the g of Esau, who *is* H8435
9 And these *are* the g of Esau the father H8435
37: 2 These *are* the g of Jacob. Joseph, *being* H8435
Ex 3:15 and this *is* my memorial unto all g. H1755
6:16 Levi according to their g; Gershon, and H8435
19 the families of Levi according to their g. H8435
12:14 throughout your g; ye shall keep it a H1755
17 day in your g by an ordinance for ever. H1755
42 of all the children of Israel in their g. H1755
16:32 to be kept for your g; that they may see H1755
33 before the LORD, to be kept for your g. H1755
27:21 g on the behalf of the children of Israel. H1755
29:42 throughout your g *at* the door of the H1755
30: 8 before the LORD throughout your g. H1755
10 your g: it *is* most holy unto the LORD. H1755
21 him and to his seed throughout their g. H1755
31 oil unto me throughout your g. H1755
31:13 throughout your g; that *ye* may know H1755
16 their g, *for* a perpetual covenant. H1755
40:15 priesthood throughout their g. H1755
Lev 3:17 *It shall be* a perpetual statute for your g H1755
6:18 for ever in your g concerning the H1755
7:36 *by* a statute for ever throughout their g. H1755
10: 9 *be* a statute for ever throughout your g: H1755
17: 7 for ever unto them throughout their g. H1755
21:17 *be* of thy seed in their g that hath *any* H1755
22: 3 seed among your g, that goeth unto the H1755
23:14 your g in all your dwellings. H1755
21 in all your dwellings throughout your g. H1755
31 your g in all your dwellings. H1755
41 for ever in your g: ye shall celebrate it H1755
43 That your g may know that I made the H1755
24: 3 *it shall be* a statute for ever in your g. H1755
25:30 his g: it shall not go out in the jubile. H1755
Nu 1:20 son, by their g, after their families, H8435
22 Of the children of Simeon, by their g, H8435
24 Of the children of Gad, by their g, after H8435
26 Of the children of Judah, by their g, H8435
28 Of the children of Issachar, by their g, H8435
30 Of the children of Zebulun, by their g, H8435
32 Ephraim, by their g, after their families, H8435
34 Of the children of Manasseh, by their g, H8435
36 Of the children of Benjamin, by their g, H8435
38 Of the children of Dan, by their g, after H8435
40 Of the children of Asher, by their g, H8435
42 throughout their g, after their families, H8435
3: 1 These also *are* the g of Aaron and H8435
10: 8 ordinance for ever throughout your g. H1755
15:14 you in your g, and will offer an offering H1755
15 for ever in your g: as ye *are*, so shall the H1755
21 the LORD an heave offering in your g. H1755
23 and henceforward among your g; H1755
38 throughout their g, and that they put H1755
18:23 ever throughout your g, that among the H1755
35:29 your g in all your dwellings. H1755
Dt 7: 9 his commandments to a thousand g; H1755
32: 7 the years of many g: ask thy father, and H1755
Jos 22:27 us, and you, and our g after us, that we H1755
Jos 22:28 *so* say to us or to our g in time to come, H1755
Jdg 3: 2 Only that the g of the children of Israel H1755
Ru 4:18 Now these *are* the g of Pharez: Pharez H8435
1Ch 1:29 These *are* their g: The firstborn of H8435
5: 7 the genealogy of their g was reckoned, H8435
7: 2 of might in their g; whose number *was* H8435
4 And with them, by their g, after the H8435
9 genealogy by their g, heads of the house H8435
8:28 g, chief *men*. These dwelt in Jerusalem. H8435
9: 9 And their brethren, according to their g, H8435
34 their g; these dwelt at Jerusalem. H8435
16:15 *which* he commanded to a thousand g; H1755
26:31 according to the g of his fathers. In the H8435
Job 42:16 sons, and his sons' sons, *even* four g. H1755
Ps 33:11 ever, the thoughts of his heart to all g. H1755
45:17 remembered in all g: therefore shall the H1755
49:11 places to all g; they call *their* lands H1755
61: 6 the king's life: *and* his years as many g. H1755
72: 5 sun and moon endure, throughout all g. H1755
79:13 we will shew forth thy praise to all g. H1755
85: 5 wilt thou draw out thine anger to all g? H1755
89: 1 I make known thy faithfulness to all g. H1755
4 and build up thy throne to all g. Selah. H1755
90: 1 hast been our dwelling place in all g. H1755
100: 5 and his truth *endureth* to all g. H1755
102:12 ever; and thy remembrance unto all g. H1755
24 my days: thy years *are* throughout all g. H1755
105: 8 *which* he commanded to a thousand g. H1755
106:31 righteousness unto all g for evermore. H1755
119:90 Thy faithfulness *is* unto all g: thou hast H1755
135:13 memorial, O LORD, throughout all g. H1755
145:13 dominion *endureth* throughout all g. H1755
146:10 O Zion, unto all g. Praise ye the LORD. H1755
Isa 41: 4 and done *it*, calling the g from the H1755
51: 9 days, in the g of old. *Art* thou not H1755
58:12 of many g; and thou shalt be called, H1755
60:15 an eternal excellency, a joy of many g. H1755
61: 4 waste cities, the desolations of many g. H1755
Joel 2: 2 after it, *even* to the years of many g. H1755
Mt 1:17 So all the g from Abraham to David *are* G1074
17 *are* fourteen g; and from David until G1074
17 *are* fourteen g; and from the carrying G1074
17 into Babylon unto Christ *are* fourteen g. G1074
Lk 1:48 henceforth all g shall call me blessed. G1074
Col 1:26 from ages and from g, but now is made G1074

GENNESARET

Mt 14:34 gone over, they came into the land of G. G1082
Mk 6:53 the land of G, and drew to the shore. G1082
Lk 5: 1 word of God, he stood by the lake of G, G1082

GENTILE

Ro 2: 9 evil, of the Jew first, and also of the G; G1672
10 good, to the Jew first, and also to the G: G1672

GENTILES

Gen 10: 5 By these were the isles of the G divided H1471
Jdg 4: 2 which dwelt in Harosheth of the G. H1471
13 of the G unto the river of Kishon. H1471
16 Harosheth of the G: and all the host of H1471
Isa 11:10 G seek: and his rest shall be glorious. H1471
42: 1 he shall bring forth judgment to the G. H1471
6 of the people, for a light of the G; H1471
49: 6 for a light to the G, that thou mayest be H1471
22 up mine hand to the G, and set up my H1471
54: 3 seed shall inherit the G, and make the H1471
60: 3 And the G shall come to thy light, and H1471
5 forces of the G shall come unto thee. H1471
11 G, and *that* their kings *may be* brought. H1471
16 Thou shalt also suck the milk of the G, H1471
61: 6 eat the riches of the G, and in their glory H1471
9 be known among the G, and their H1471
62: 2 And the G shall see thy righteousness, H1471
66:12 the glory of the G like a flowing stream: H1471
19 shall declare my glory among the G. H1471
Jer 4: 7 destroyer of the G is on his way; he is H1471
14:22 the vanities of the G that can cause H1471
16:19 of affliction, the G shall come unto thee H1471
46: 1 to Jeremiah the prophet against the G; H1471
Lam 2: 9 *are* among the G: the law *is* no *more*; H1471
Ezk 4:13 among the G, whither I will drive them. H1471
Hos 8: 8 G as a vessel wherein *is* no pleasure. H1471
Joel 3: 9 Proclaim ye this among the G; Prepare H1471
Mic 5: 8 be among the G in the midst of many H1471
Zec 1:21 the horns of the G, which lifted up *their* H1471
Mal 1:11 great among the G; and in every place H1471
Mt 4:15 the sea, beyond Jordan, Galilee of the G; G1484
6:32 (For after all these things do the G G1484
10: 5 the way of the G, and into *any* city of G1484
Mt 10:18 for a testimony against them and the G. G1484
12:18 and he shall shew judgment to the G. G1484
21 And in his name shall the G trust. G1484
20:19 And shall deliver him to the G to mock, G1484
25 the princes of the G exercise dominion G1484
Mk 10:33 to death, and shall deliver him to the G: G1484
42 to rule over the G exercise lordship G1484
Lk 2:32 A light to lighten the G, and the glory of G1484
18:32 For he shall be delivered unto the G, G1484
21:24 down of the G, until the times of the G1484
24 until the times of the G be fulfilled. G1484
22:25 The kings of the G exercise lordship G1484
Jn 7:35 among the G, and teach the Gentiles? G1672
35 among the Gentiles, and teach the G? G1672
Act 4:27 Pilate, with the G, and the people of G1484
7:45 possession of the G, whom God drave G1484
9:15 G, and kings, and the children of Israel: G1484
10:45 that on the G also was poured out G1484
11: 1 G had also received the word of God. G1484
18 to the G granted repentance unto life. G1484
13:42 synagogue, the G besought that these G1484
46 of everlasting life, lo, we turn to the G. G1484
47 thee to be a light of the G, that thou G1484
48 And when the G heard this, they were G1484
14: 2 stirred up the G, and made their minds G1484
5 made both of the G, and also of the Jews G1484
27 had opened the door of faith unto the G. G1484
15: 3 conversion of the G: and they caused G1484
7 us, that the G by my mouth should G1484
12 had wrought among the G by them. G1484
14 first did visit the G, to take out of them G1484
17 the Lord, and all the G, upon whom my G1484
19 from among the G are turned to God: G1484
23 the G in Antioch and Syria and Cilicia: G1484
18: 6 from henceforth I will go unto the G. G1484
21:11 deliver *him* into the hands of the G. G1484
19 wrought among the G by his ministry. G1484
21 are among the G to forsake Moses, G1484
25 As touching the G which believe, we G1484
22:21 for I will send thee far hence unto the G. G1484
26:17 the G, unto whom now I send thee, G1484
20 and *then* to the G, that they should G1484
23 light unto the people, and to the G. G1484
28:28 unto the G, and *that* they will hear it. G1484
Ro 1:13 you also, even as among other G. G1484
2:14 For when the G, which have not the law, G1484
24 the G through you, as it is written. G1484
3: 9 Jews and G, that they are all under sin; G1672
29 also of the G? Yes, of the Gentiles also: G1484
29 also of the Gentiles? Yes, of the G also: G1484
9:24 not of the Jews only, but also of the G? G1484
30 What shall we say then? That the G, G1484
11:11 the G, for to provoke them to jealousy. G1484
12 of the G; how much more their fulness? G1484
13 For I speak to you G, inasmuch as I am G1484
13 apostle of the G, I magnify mine office: G1484
25 until the fulness of the G be come in. G1484
15: 9 And that the G might glorify God for G1484
9 among the G, and sing unto thy name. G1484
10 And again he saith, Rejoice, ye G, with G1484
11 And again, Praise the Lord, all ye G; G1484
12 the G; in him shall the Gentiles trust. G1484
12 the Gentiles; in him shall the G trust. G1484
16 of Jesus Christ to the G, ministering the G1484
16 the offering up of the G might be G1484
18 the G obedient, by word and deed, G1484
27 they are. For if the G have been made G1484
16: 4 but also all the churches of the G. G1484
1Co 5: 1 as named among the G, that one should G1484
10:20 But I *say*, that the things which the G G1484
32 nor to the G, nor to the church of God: G1672
12: 2 Ye know that ye were G, carried away G1484
13 *we be* Jews or G, whether *we be* bond G1672
Gal 2: 2 I preach among the G, but privately to G1484
8 same was mighty in me toward the G:) G1484
12 did eat with the G: but when they were G1484
14 after the manner of G, and not as do the G1483
14 thou the G to live as do the Jews? G1484
15 by nature, and not sinners of the G, G1484
3:14 come on the G through Jesus Christ; G1484
Eph 2:11 *being* in time past G in the flesh, who G1484
3: 1 the prisoner of Jesus Christ for you G, G1484
6 That the G should be fellowheirs, and G1484
8 the G the unsearchable riches of Christ; G1484
4:17 G walk, in the vanity of their mind, G1484
Col 1:27 among the G; which is Christ in you, G1484
1Th 2:16 Forbidding us to speak to the G that G1484
4: 5 even as the G which know not God: G1484
1Ti 2: 7 a teacher of the G in faith and verity. G1484

G

1Ti 3:16 preached unto the **G**, believed on in the *G1484*
2Ti 1:11 and an apostle, and a teacher of the **G**. *G1484*
4:17 and *that* all the **G** might hear: and I *G1484*
1Pt 2:12 honest among the **G**: that, whereas they *G1484*
4: 3 the will of the **G**, when we walked in *G1484*
3Jn 7 they went forth, taking nothing of the **G**. *G1484*
Rev 11: 2 it is given unto the **G**: and the holy city *G1484*

GENTLE
1Th 2: 7 But we were **g** among you, even as a *G2261*
2Ti 2:24 be **g** unto all *men*, apt to teach, patient, *G2261*
Tit 3: 2 **g**, shewing all meekness unto all men. *G1933*
Jas 3:17 pure, then peaceable, **g**, *and* easy to be *G1933*
1Pt 2:18 the good and **g**, but also to the froward. *G1933*

GENTLENESS
2Sa 22:36 and thy **g** hath made me great. H6031
Ps 18:35 me up, and thy **g** hath made me great. H6037
2Co 10: 1 the meekness and **g** of Christ, who in *G1932*
Gal 5:22 peace, longsuffering, **g**, goodness, faith, *G5544*

GENTLY
2Sa 18: 5 Ittai, saying, *Deal* **g** for my sake with the H328
Isa 40:11 shall **g** lead those that are with young.

GENUBATH
1Ki 11:20 And the sister of Tahpenes bare him **G** H1592
20 house: and **G** was in Pharaoh's H1592

GERA
Gen 46:21 and Ashbel, **G**, and Naaman, Ehi, and H1617
Jdg 3:15 Ehud the son of **G**, a Benjamite, a man H1617
2Sa 16: 5 Shimei, the son of **G**: he came forth, and H1617
19:16 And Shimei the son of **G**, a Benjamite, H1617
18 Shimei the son of **G** fell down before H1617
1Ki 2: 8 thee Shimei the son of **G**, a Benjamite of H1617
1Ch 8: 3 Bela were, Addar, and **G**, and Abihud, H1617
5 And **G**, and Shephuphan, and Huram. H1617
7 And Naaman, and Ahiah, and **G**, he H1617

GERAHS
Ex 30:13 (a shekel *is* twenty **g**:) an half shekel H1626
Lev 27:25 sanctuary: twenty **g** shall be the shekel. H1626
Nu 3:47 thou take *them*: (the shekel *is* twenty **g**:) H1626
18:16 of the sanctuary, which *is* twenty **g**. H1626
Ezk 45:12 And the shekel *shall be* twenty **g**: twenty H1626

GERAR
Gen 10:19 as thou comest to **G**, unto Gaza; as thou H1642
20: 1 Kadesh and Shur, and sojourned in **G**. H1642
2 king of **G** sent, and took Sarah. H1642
26: 1 king of the Philistines unto **G**. H1642
6 And Isaac dwelt in **G**: H1642
17 tent in the valley of **G**, and dwelt there. H1642
20 And the herdmen of **G** did strive with H1642
26 Then Abimelech went to him from **G**, H1642
2Ch 14:13 them unto **G**: and the Ethiopians H1642
14 cities round about **G**; for the fear of the H1642

GERGESENES
Mt 8:28 the country of the **G**, there met him two *G1086*

GERIZIM
Dt 11:29 **G**, and the curse upon mount Ebal. H1630
27:12 These shall stand upon mount **G** to H1630
Jos 8:33 against mount **G**, and half of them over H1630
Jdg 9: 7 in the top of mount **G**, and lifted up his H1630

GERSHOM
Ex 2:22 he called his name **G**: for he said, I have H1647
18: 3 of the one *was* **G**; for he said, I have H1647
Jdg 18:30 the son of **G**, the son of Manasseh, H1647
1Ch 6:16 The sons of Levi; **G**, Kohath, and H1647
17 of the sons of **G**; Libni, and Shimei. H1647
20 Of **G**; Libni his son, Jahath his son, H1647
43 The son of Jahath, the son of **G**, the son H1647
62 And to the sons of **G** throughout their H1647
71 Unto the sons of **G** *were given* out of H1647
15: 7 Of the sons of **G**; Joel the chief, and his H1647
23:15 The sons of Moses *were*, **G**, and Eliezer. H1647
16 Of the sons of **G**, Shebuel *was* the chief. H1647
26:24 And Shebuel the son of **G**, the son of H1647
Ezr 8: 2 Of the sons of Phinehas; **G**: of the sons H1647

GERSHON
Gen 46:11 And the sons of Levi; **G**, Kohath, and H1648
Ex 6:16 their generations; **G**, and Kohath, and H1648
17 The sons of **G**; Libni, and Shimi, H1648
Nu 3:17 names; **G**, and Kohath, and Merari. H1648
Nu 3:18 **G** by their families; Libni, and Shimei. H1648
21 Of **G** *was* the family of the Libnites, and H1648
25 And the charge of the sons of **G** in the H1648
4:22 Take also the sum of the sons of **G**, H1648
28 of the sons of **G** in the tabernacle of H1649
38 of the sons of **G**, throughout their H1648
41 of the sons of **G**, of all that might do H1648
7: 7 the sons of **G**, according to their service: H1648
10:17 and the sons of **G** and the sons of H1648
26:57 their families: of **G**, the family of the H1648
Jos 21: 6 And the children of **G** *had* by lot out of H1648
27 And unto the children of **G**, of the H1648
1Ch 6: 1 The sons of Levi; **G**, Kohath, and H1648
23: 6 of Levi, *namely*, **G**, Kohath, and Merari. H1648

GERSHONITE
1Ch 26:21 the sons of the **G** Laadan, chief fathers, H1649
21 *even* of Laadan the **G**, *were* Jehieli. H1649
29: 8 the LORD, by the hand of Jehiel the **G**. H1649

GERSHONITES
Nu 3:21 Shimites: these *are* the families of the **G**. H1649
23 The families of the **G** shall pitch behind H1649
24 the **G** *shall be* Eliasaph the son of Lael. H1649
4:24 of the **G**, to serve, and for burdens: H1649
27 of the sons of the **G**, in all their burdens, H1649
26:57 the family of the **G**: of Kohath, the H1649
Jos 21:33 All the cities of the **G** according to their H1649
1Ch 23: 7 Of the **G** *were*, Laadan, and Shimei. H1649
2Ch 29:12 and of the **G**; Joah the son of Zimmah, H1649

GE-SHAN
1Ch 2:47 **G**, and Pelet, and Ephah, and Shaaph. H1529

GESHEM
Neh 2:19 Ammonite, and **G** the Arabian, heard H1654
6: 1 and Tobiah, and **G** the Arabian, and H1654
2 That Sanballat and **G** sent unto me, H1654

GESHUR
2Sa 3: 3 the daughter of Talmai king of **G**; H1650
13:37 of Ammihud, king of **G**. And *David* H1650
38 So Absalom fled, and went to **G**, and H1650
14:23 So Joab arose and went to **G**, and H1650
32 am I come from **G**? *it had been* good for H1650
15: 8 while I abode at **G** in Syria, saying, If H1650
1Ch 2:23 And he took **G**, and Aram, with the H1650
3: 2 of Talmai king of **G**: the fourth, H1650

GESHURI
Dt 3:14 unto the coasts of **G** and Maachathi; H1651
Jos 13: 2 the borders of the Philistines, and all **G**, H1651

GESHURITES
Jos 12: 5 unto the border of the **G** and the H1651
13:11 And Gilead, and the border of the **G** H1651
13 Israel expelled not the **G**, nor the H1651
13 but the **G** and the Maachathites H1650
1Sa 27: 8 up, and invaded the **G**, and the Gezrites, H1651

GET
Gen 12: 1 had said unto Abram, **G** thee out of thy H3212
19:14 and said, Up, **g** you out of this place; H3318
22: 2 thou lovest, and **g** thee into the land of H3212
31:13 me: now arise, **g** thee out from this H3318
34: 4 saying, **G** me this damsel to wife. H3947
10 therein, and **g** you possessions therein.
42: 2 is corn in Egypt: **g** you down thither, H3381
44:17 **g** you up in peace unto your father. H5927
45:17 and go, **g** you unto the land of Canaan; H935
Ex 1:10 us, and *so* **g** them up out of the land. H5927
5: 4 their works? **g** you unto your burdens. H3212
11 Go ye, **g** you straw where ye can find it: H3947
7:15 **G** thee unto Pharaoh in the morning; H3212
10:28 And Pharaoh said unto him, **G** thee H3212
11: 8 unto me, saying, **G** thee out, and all the H3318
12:31 and said, Rise up, *and* **g** you forth from H3318
14:17 them: and I will **g** me honour upon H3513
19:24 And the LORD said unto him, Away, **g** H3381
32: 7 And the LORD said unto Moses, Go, **g** H3381
Lev 14:21 And if he *be* poor, and cannot **g** so H5381
22 as he is able to **g**; and the one shall be H5381
30 of the young pigeons, such as he can **g**; H5381
31 *Even* such as he is able to **g**, the one *for* H5381
32 whose hand is not able to **g** *that which* H5381
Nu 6:21 his hand shall **g**: according to the vow H5381
13:17 and said unto them, **G** you up this *way* H5927
14:25 turn you, and **g** you into the wilderness H5265
16:24 Speak unto the congregation, saying, **G** H5927
Nu 16:45 **G** you up from among this H7426
22:13 princes of Balak, **G** you into your land: H3212
34 it displease thee, I will **g** me back again.
27:12 And the LORD said unto Moses, **G** thee H5927
Dt 2:13 Now rise up, *said I*, and **g** you over the H5674
3:27 **G** thee up into the top of Pisgah, and H5927
5:30 Go say to them, **G** you into your tents H7725
8:18 thee power to **g** wealth, that he may H6213
9:12 And the LORD said unto me, Arise, **g** H3381
17: 8 thou arise, and **g** thee up into the place H5927
28:43 The stranger that *is* within thee shall **g** H5927
32:49 **G** thee up into this mountain Abarim, H5927
Jos 2:16 And she said unto them, **G** you to the H3212
7:10 And the LORD said unto Joshua, **G** thee H6965
17:15 a great people, *then* **g** thee up to the H5927
22: 4 return ye, and **g** you unto your tents, H3212
Jdg 7: 9 unto him, Arise, **g** thee down unto the H3381
14: 2 now therefore **g** her for me to wife. H3947
3 **G** her for me; for she pleaseth me well. H3947
19: 9 and to morrow **g** you early on your way,
Ru 3: 3 upon thee, and **g** thee down to the H3381
1Sa 9:13 Now therefore **g** you up; for about this H5927
15: 6 Go, depart, **g** you down from among H3381
20:29 thine eyes, let me **g** away, I pray thee, H4422
22: 5 hold; depart, and **g** thee into the land of H935
23:26 made haste to **g** away for fear of Saul; H3212
25: 5 the young men, **G** you up to Carmel, H5927
2Sa 20: 6 he **g** him fenced cities, and escape us. H4672
1Ki 1: 2 that my lord the king may **g** heat.
13 Go and **g** thee in unto king David, and H935
2:26 said the king, **G** thee to Anathoth, unto H3212
12:18 made speed to **g** him up to his chariot, H5927
14: 2 wife of Jeroboam; and **g** thee to Shiloh: H1980
12 Arise thou therefore, **g** thee to thine H3212
17: 3 **G** thee hence, and turn thee eastward, H3212
9 Arise, **g** thee to Zarephath, which H3212
18:41 And Elijah said unto Ahab, **G** thee up, H5927
44 *thy chariot*, and **g** thee down, that the H3381
2Ki 3:13 I to do with thee? **g** thee to the prophets H3212
7:12 catch them alive, and **g** into the city. H935
2Ch 10:18 made speed to **g** him up to *his* chariot, H5927
Neh 9:10 thou **g** thee a name, as *it is* this day. H6213
Ps119:104 Through thy precepts I **g** understanding:
Prv 4: 5 **G** wisdom, get understanding: forget *it* H7069
5 Get wisdom, **g** understanding: forget *it* H7069
7 thing; *therefore* **g** wisdom: and with all H7069
7 with all thy getting **g** understanding. H7069
6:33 A wound and dishonour shall he **g**; and H4672
16:16 How much better *is it* to **g** wisdom than H7069
16 than gold! and to **g** understanding H7069
17:16 **g** wisdom, seeing *he hath* no heart *to it*? H7069
22:25 Lest thou learn his ways, and **g** a snare H3947
Ecc 3: 6 A time to **g**, and a time to lose; a time to H1245
Song 4: 6 flee away, I will **g** me to the mountain H3212
7:12 Let us **g** up early to the vineyards; let us
Isa 22:15 Thus saith the Lord GOD of hosts, Go, **g** H935
30:11 **G** you out of the way, turn aside out of H5493
22 thou shalt say unto it, **G** thee hence. H3318
40: 9 O Zion, that bringest good tidings, **g** H5927
47: 5 Sit thou silent, and **g** thee into darkness, H935
Jer 5: 5 I will **g** me unto the great men, and will H3212
13: 1 unto me, Go and **g** thee a linen girdle, H7069
19: 1 Thus saith the LORD, Go and **g** a H7069
46: 4 Harness the horses; and **g** up, ye H5927
48: 9 it may flee and **g** away: for the cities H3318
49:30 Flee, **g** you far off, dwell deep, O ye H5110
31 Arise, **g** you up unto the wealthy H5927
Lam 3: 7 **g** out: he hath made my chain heavy. H3318
Ezk 3: 4 And he said unto me, Son of man, go, **g** H935
11 And go, **g** thee to them of the captivity, H935
11:15 have said, **G** you far from the LORD:
22:27 to destroy souls, to **g** dishonest gain. H1214
Dan 4:14 fruit: let the beasts **g** away from under H5111
Joel 3:13 is ripe: come, **g** you down; for the press H3381
Zep 3:19 out; and I will **g** them praise and fame H7760
Zec 6: 7 and he said, **G** you hence, walk to H3212
Mt 4:10 Then saith Jesus unto him, **G** thee *G5217*
14:22 his disciples to **g** into a ship, and to go *G1684*
16:23 But he turned, and said unto Peter, **G** *G5217*
Mk 6:45 his disciples to **g** into the ship, and to *G1684*
8:33 Peter, saying, **G** thee behind me, Satan: *G5217*
Lk 4: 8 and said unto him, **G** thee behind me, *G5217*
9:12 and lodge, and **g** victuals: for we are *G2147*
13:31 saying unto him, **G** thee out, and *G1831*
Act 7: 3 And said unto him, **G** thee out of thy *G1831*
10:20 Arise therefore, and **g** thee down, and *G2597*
22:18 Make haste, and **g** thee quickly out of *G1831*
27:43 first *into the sea*, and **g** to land: *G1826*
2Co 2:11 Lest Satan should **g** an advantage of *G4122*

Jas 4:13 a year, and buy and sell, and g gain:

GETHER
Gen 10:23 Aram; Uz, and Hul, and G, and Mash. H1666
1Ch 1:17 and Uz, and Hul, and G, and Meshech. H1666

GETHSEMANE
Mt 26:36 a place called G, and saith unto the G1068
Mk 14:32 which was named G: and he saith to his G1068

GETTETH
2Sa 5: 8 day, Whosoever g up to the gutter, and H5060
Prv 3:13 and the man *that* g understanding. H6329
9: 7 He that reproveth a scorner g to H3947
7 rebuketh a wicked *man* g himself a blot.
15:32 that heareth reproof g understanding. H7069
18:15 The heart of the prudent g knowledge; H7069
19: 8 He that g wisdom loveth his own soul: H7069
Jer 17:11 not; *so* he that g riches, and not by H6213
48:44 pit; and he that g up out of the pit shall H5927

GETTING
Gen 31:18 the cattle of his g, which he had gotten H7075
Prv 4: 7 and with all thy g get understanding. H7075
21: 6 The g of treasures by a lying tongue *is* a H6467

GEUEL
Nu 13:15 Of the tribe of Gad, G the son of Machi. H1345

GEZER
Jos 10:33 Then Horam king of G came up to help H1507
12:12 The king of Eglon, one; the king of G, H1507
16: 3 the nether, and to G: and the goings out H1507
10 that dwelt in G: but the Canaanites H1507
21:21 for the slayer; and G with her suburbs, H1507
Jdg 1:29 that dwelt in G; but the Canaanites H1507
29 Canaanites dwelt in G among them. H1507
1Ki 9:15 and Hazor, and Megiddo, and G. H1507
16 up, and taken G, and burnt it with fire, H1507
17 And Solomon built G, and Beth-horon H1507
1Ch 6:67 *they gave* also G with her suburbs, H1507
7:28 and westward G, with the towns H1507
20: 4 that there arose war at G with the H1507

GEZRITES
1Sa 27: 8 and the G, and the Amalekites: H1511

GHOST
Gen 25: 8 Then Abraham gave up the g, and died H1478
17 and he gave up the g and died; and was H1478
35:29 And Isaac gave up the g, and died, and H1478
49:33 g, and was gathered unto his people. H1478
Job 3:11 up the g when I came out of the belly? H1478
10:18 given up the g, and no eye had seen me! H1478
11:20 hope *shall be as* the giving up of the g. H5315
13:19 if I hold my tongue, I shall give up the g. H1478
14:10 man giveth up the g, and where *is* he? H1478
Jer 15: 9 she hath given up the g; her sun is gone H5315
Lam 1:19 elders gave up the g in the city, while H1478
Mt 1:18 she was found with child of the Holy G. G4151
20 is conceived in her is of the Holy G. G4151
3:11 you with the Holy G, and *with* fire: G4151
12:31 *Holy* G shall not be forgiven unto men. G4151
32 against the Holy G, it shall not be G4151
27:50 with a loud voice, yielded up the g. G4151
28:19 and of the Son, and of the Holy G: G4151
Mk 1: 8 he shall baptize you with the Holy G. G4151
3:29 against the Holy G hath never G4151
12:36 For David himself said by the Holy G, G4151
13:11 it is not ye that speak, but the Holy G. G4151
15:37 with a loud voice, and gave up the g. G1606
39 and gave up the g, he said, Truly this G1606
Lk 1:15 Holy G, even from his mother's womb. G4151
35 her, The Holy G shall come upon thee, G4151
41 Elisabeth was filled with the Holy G: G4151
67 the Holy G, and prophesied, saying, G4151
2:25 Israel: and the Holy G was upon him. G4151
26 him by the Holy G, that he should not G4151
3:16 you with the Holy G and with fire: G4151
22 And the Holy G descended in a bodily G4151
4: 1 And Jesus being full of the Holy G G4151
12:10 the Holy G it shall not be forgiven. G4151
12 For the Holy G shall teach you in the G4151
23:46 and having said thus, he gave up the g. G1606
Jn 1:33 is he which baptizeth with the Holy G. G4151
7:39 for the Holy G was not yet *given*; G4151
14:26 But the Comforter, *which is* the Holy G, G4151
19:30 he bowed his head, and gave up the g. G4151
20:22 saith unto them, Receive ye the Holy G: G4151
Act 1: 2 he through the Holy G had given G4151
5 with the Holy G not many days hence. G4151
8 after that the Holy G is come upon you: G4151
16 which the Holy G by the mouth of G4151
2: 4 And they were all filled with the Holy G, G4151
33 of the Holy G, he hath shed forth this, G4151
38 ye shall receive the gift of the Holy G. G4151
4: 8 Then Peter, filled with the Holy G, said G4151
31 with the Holy G, and they spake the G4151
5: 3 to lie to the Holy G, and to keep back G4151
5 and gave up the g: and great fear came G1634
10 and yielded up the g: and the young G1634
32 *so is* also the Holy G, whom God hath G4151
6: 3 full of the Holy G and wisdom, whom G4151
5 faith and of the Holy G, and Philip, and G4151
7:51 Holy G: as your fathers *did*, so *do* ye. G4151
55 But he, being full of the Holy G, looked G4151
8:15 that they might receive the Holy G: G4151
17 on them, and they received the Holy G. G4151
18 G was given, he offered them money, G4151
19 I lay hands, he may receive the Holy G. G4151
9:17 thy sight, and be filled with the Holy G. G4151
31 comfort of the Holy G, were multiplied. G4151
10:38 with the Holy G and with power: who G4151
44 these words, the Holy G fell on all them G4151
45 was poured out the gift of the Holy G. G4151
47 have received the Holy G as well as we? G4151
11:15 And as I began to speak, the Holy G fell G4151
16 ye shall be baptized with the Holy G. G4151
24 and full of the Holy G and of faith: and G4151
12:23 was eaten of worms, and gave up the g. G1634
13: 2 fasted, the Holy G said, Separate me G4151
4 So they, being sent forth by the Holy G, G4151
9 with the Holy G, set his eyes on him, G4151
52 filled with joy, and with the Holy G. G4151
15: 8 the Holy G, even as *he did* unto us; G4151
28 For it seemed good to the Holy G, and G4151
16: 6 the Holy G to preach the word in Asia, G4151
19: 2 received the Holy G since ye believed? G4151
2 as heard whether there be any Holy G. G4151
6 them, the Holy G came on them; and G4151
20:23 Save that the Holy G witnesseth in G4151
28 the which the Holy G hath made you G4151
21:11 saith the Holy G, So shall the Jews at G4151
28:25 spake the Holy G by Esaias the prophet G4151
Ro 5: 5 by the Holy G which is given unto us. G4151
9: 1 also bearing me witness in the Holy G, G4151
14:17 and peace, and joy in the Holy G. G4151
15:13 hope, through the power of the Holy G. G4151
16 being sanctified by the Holy G. G4151
1Co 2:13 which the Holy G teacheth; comparing G4151
6:19 temple of the Holy G *which is* in you, G4151
12: 3 Jesus is the Lord, but by the Holy G. G4151
2Co 6: 6 by the Holy G, by love unfeigned, G4151
13:14 of the Holy G, *be* with you all. Amen. G4151
1Th 1: 5 power, and in the Holy G, and in much G4151
6 much affliction, with joy of the Holy G: G4151
2Ti 1:14 by the Holy G which dwelleth in us. G4151
Tit 3: 5 and renewing of the Holy G; G4151
Heb 2: 4 of the Holy G, according to his own will? G4151
3: 7 Wherefore (as the Holy G saith, To day G4151
6: 4 and were made partakers of the Holy G, G4151
9: 8 The Holy G this signifying, that the way G4151
10:15 *Whereof* the Holy G also is a witness to G4151
1Pt 1:12 you with the Holy G sent down from G4151
2Pt 1:21 *as they were* moved by the Holy G. G4151
1Jn 5: 7 and the Holy G: and these three are one. G4151
Jude 20 most holy faith, praying in the Holy G, G4151

GIAH
2Sa 2:24 that *lieth* before G by the way of the H1520

GIANT
2Sa 21:16 of the sons of the g, the weight of whose H7497
18 Saph, which *was* of the sons of the g. H7497
20 number; and he also was born to the g. H7497
22 These four were born to the g in Gath, H7497
1Ch 20: 4 of the g: and they were subdued. H7497
6 *foot:* and he also was the son of the g. H7497
8 These were born unto the g in Gath; H7497
Job 16:14 breach, he runneth upon me like a g. H1368

GIANTS
Gen 6: 4 There were g in the earth in those days; H5303
Nu 13:33 And there we saw the g, the sons of H5303
33 *which come* of the g: and we were in our H5303
Dt 2:11 Which also were accounted g, as the H7497
20 (That also was accounted a land of g: H7497
20 a land of giants: g dwelt therein in old H7497
Dt 3:11 of the remnant of g; behold, his H7497
13 Bashan, which was called the land of g. H7497
Jos 12: 4 g, that dwelt at Ashtaroth and at Edrei, H7497
13:12 of the remnant of the g: for these did H7497
15: 8 end of the valley of the g northward: H7497
17:15 and of the g, if mount Ephraim be H7497
18:16 in the valley of the g on the north, and H7497

GIBBAR
Ezr 2:20 The children of G, ninety and five. H1402

GIBBETHON
Jos 19:44 And Eltekeh, and G, and Baalath, H1405
21:23 with her suburbs, G with her suburbs, H1405
1Ki 15:27 smote him at G, which *belonged* to the H1405
27 for Nadab and all Israel laid siege to G. H1405
16:15 G, which *belonged* to the Philistines. H1405
17 And Omri went up from G, and all H1405

GIBEA
1Ch 2:49 and the father of G: and the daughter of H1388

G

GIBEAH
Jos 15:57 Cain, G, and Timnah; ten cities with H1390
Jdg 19:12 of Israel; we will pass over to G. H1390
13 to lodge all night, in G, or in Ramah. H1390
14 by G, which *belongeth* to Benjamin. H1390
15 in *and* to lodge in G: and when he went H1390
16 he sojourned in G: but the men of the H1390
20: 4 said, I came into G that *belongeth* to H1390
5 And the men of G rose against me, and H1390
9 do to G; *we will go up* by lot against it; H1390
10 they come to G of Benjamin, according H1387
13 which *are* in G, that we may put them H1390
14 of the cities unto G, to go out to battle H1390
15 beside the inhabitants of G, which were H1390
19 the morning, and encamped against G. H1390
20 in array to fight against them at G. H1390
21 came forth out of G, and destroyed H1390
25 them out of G the second day, and H1390
29 Israel set liers in wait round about G. H1390
30 in array against G, as at other times. H1390
31 and the other to G in the field, about H1390
33 places, *even* out of the meadows of G. H1387
34 And there came against G ten H1390
36 in wait which they had set beside G. H1390
37 and rushed upon G; and the liers in H1390
43 over against G toward the sunrising. H1390
1Sa 10:26 And Saul also went home to G; and H1390
11: 4 Then came the messengers to G of H1390
13: 2 with Jonathan in G of Benjamin: and H1390
15 from Gilgal unto G of Benjamin. And H1390
16 them, abode in G of Benjamin: but the H1387
14: 2 the uttermost part of G under a H1390
5 the other southward over against G. H1387
16 And the watchmen of Saul in G of H1390
15:34 Saul went up to his house to G of Saul. H1390
22: 6 Saul abode in G under a tree in Ramah, H1390
23:19 Then came up the Ziphites to Saul to G, H1390
26: 1 And the Ziphites came unto Saul to G, H1390
2Sa 6: 3 that *was* in G: and Uzzah and Ahio, H1390
4 which *was* at G, accompanying the H1390
21: 6 unto the LORD in G of Saul, *whom* the H1390
23:29 out of G of the children of Benjamin, H1390
1Ch 11:31 Ithai the son of Ribai of G, *that* H1390
2Ch 13: 2 of Uriel of G. And there was war H1390
Isa 10:29 Ramah is afraid; G of Saul is fled. H1390
Hos 5: 8 Blow ye the cornet in G, *and* the H1390
9: 9 as in the days of G: *therefore* he will H1390
10: 9 from the days of G: there they stood: the H1390
9 the battle in G against the children H1390

GIBEATH
Jos 18:28 *is* Jerusalem, G, *and* Kirjath; fourteen H1394

GIBEATHITE
1Ch 12: 3 of Shemaah the G; and Jeziel, and Pelet, H1395

GIBEON
Jos 9: 3 And when the inhabitants of G heard H1391
17 their cities *were* G, and Chephirah, and H1391
10: 1 the inhabitants of G had made peace H1391
2 That they feared greatly, because G H1391
4 that we may smite G: for it hath made H1391
5 before G, and made war against it. H1391
6 And the men of G sent unto Joshua to H1391
10 a great slaughter at G, and chased them H1391
12 thou still upon G; and thou, Moon, in H1391
41 all the country of Goshen, even unto G. H1391

Jos 11:19 of **G**: all *other* they took in battle. H1391
18:25 **G**, and Ramah, and Beeroth, H1391
21:17 And out of the tribe of Benjamin, **G** H1391
2Sa 2:12 of Saul, went out from Mahanaim to **G**. H1391
13 by the pool of **G**: and they sat down, H1391
16 Helkath-hazzurim, which *is* in **G**. H1391
24 Giah by the way of the wilderness of **G**. H1391
3:30 their brother Asahel at **G** in the battle. H1391
20: 8 stone which *is* in **G**, Amasa went before H1391
1Ki 3: 4 And the king went to **G** to sacrifice H1391
5 In **G** the LORD appeared to Solomon in H1391
9: 2 as he had appeared unto him at **G**. H1391
1Ch 8:29 And at **G** dwelt the father of Gibeon; H1391
29 And at Gibeon dwelt the father of **G**; H1391
9:35 And in **G** dwelt the father of Gibeon, H1391
35 And in Gibeon dwelt the father of **G**, H1391
14:16 of the Philistines from **G** even to Gazer. H1391
16:39 LORD in the high place that *was* at **G**, H1391
21:29 at that season in the high place at **G**. H1391
2Ch 1: 3 place that *was* at **G**; for there was the H1391
13 place that *was* at **G** to Jerusalem, from H1391
Neh 3: 7 the men of **G**, and of Mizpah, unto H1391
7:25 The children of **G**, ninety and five. H1391
Isa 28:21 as *in* the valley of **G**, that he may do his H1391
Jer 28: 1 which *was* of **G**, spake unto me in the H1391
41:12 him by the great waters that *are* in **G**. H1391
16 whom he had brought again from **G**: H1391

GIBEONITE
1Ch 12: 4 And Ismaiah the **G**, a mighty man H1393
Neh 3: 7 repaired Melatiah the **G**, and Jadon the H1393

GIBEONITES
2Sa 21: 1 bloody house, because he slew the **G**. H1393
2 And the king called the **G**, and said H1393
2 unto them; (now the **G** *were* not of the H1393
3 Wherefore David said unto the **G**, What H1393
4 And the **G** said unto him, We will have H1393
9 the hands of the **G**, and they hanged H1393

GIBLITES
Jos 13: 5 And the land of the **G**, and all Lebanon, H1382

GIDDALTI
1Ch 25: 4 Hananiah, Hanani, Eliathah, **G**, and H1437
29 The two and twentieth to **G**, *he*, his H1437

GIDDEL
Ezr 2:47 The children of **G**, the children of H1435
56 children of Darkon, the children of **G**, H1435
Neh 7:49 the children of **G**, the children of Gahar, H1435
58 children of Darkon, the children of **G**, H1435

GIDEON
Jdg 6:11 and his son **G** threshed wheat by the H1439
13 And **G** said unto him, Oh my Lord, if H1439
19 And **G** went in, and made ready a kid, H1439
22 And when **G** perceived that he *was* an H1439
22 of the LORD, **G** said, Alas, O Lord GOD! H1439
24 Then **G** built an altar there unto the H1439
27 Then **G** took ten men of his servants, H1439
29 **G** the son of Joash hath done this thing. H1439
34 the LORD came upon **G**, and he blew a H1439
36 And **G** said unto God, If thou wilt save H1439
39 And **G** said unto God, Let not thine H1439
7: 1 Then Jerubbaal, who *is* **G**, and all the H1439
2 And the LORD said unto **G**, The people H1439
4 And the LORD said unto **G**, The people H1439
5 the LORD said unto **G**, Every one that H1439
7 And the LORD said unto **G**, By the three H1439
13 And when **G** was come, behold, *there* H1439
14 save the sword of **G** the son of Joash, a H1439
15 And it was *so*, when **G** heard the telling H1439
18 say, *The sword* of the LORD, and of **G**. H1439
19 So **G**, and the hundred men that *were* H1439
20 cried, The sword of the LORD, and of **G**. H1439
24 And **G** sent messengers throughout all H1439
25 and Zeeb to **G** on the other side Jordan. H1439
8: 4 And **G** came to Jordan, *and* passed H1439
7 And **G** said, Therefore when the LORD H1439
11 And **G** went up by the way of them that H1439
13 And **G** the son of Joash returned from H1439
21 *is* his strength. And **G** arose, and slew H1439
22 Then the men of Israel said unto **G**, H1439
23 And **G** said unto them, I will not rule H1439
24 And **G** said unto them, I would desire a H1439
27 And **G** made an ephod thereof, and put H1439
27 a snare unto **G**, and to his house. H1439
28 in quietness forty years in the days of **G**. H1439
Jdg 8:30 And **G** had threescore and ten sons of H1439
32 And **G** the son of Joash died in a good H1439
33 And it came to pass, as soon as **G** was H1439
35 *namely*, **G**, according to all the H1439

GIDEONI
Nu 1:11 Of Benjamin; Abidan the son of **G**. H1441
2:22 Benjamin *shall be* Abidan the son of **G**. H1441
7:60 On the ninth day Abidan the son of **G**, H1441
65 *was* the offering of Abidan the son of **G**. H1441
10:24 of Benjamin *was* Abidan the son of **G**. H1441

GIDOM
Jdg 20:45 **G**, and slew two thousand men of them. H1440

GIER
Lev 11:18 swan, and the pelican, and the **g** eagle, H7360
Dt 14:17 And the pelican, and the **g** eagle, and H7360

GIER-EAGLE See GIER and EAGLE.

GIFT
Gen 34:12 Ask me never so much dowry and **g**, H4976
Ex 23: 8 And thou shalt take no **g**: for the gift H7810
8 And thou shalt take no gift: for the **g** H7810
Nu 8:19 And I have given the Levites *as* a **g** to H5414
18: 6 *they are* given *as* a **g** for the LORD, to H4979
7 *you* as a service of **g**: and the stranger H4979
11 offering of their **g**, with all the wave H4976
Dt 16:19 neither take a **g**: for a gift doth blind H7810
19 take a gift: for a **g** doth blind the eyes H7810
2Sa 19:42 king's *cost*? or hath he given us any **g**? H5379
Ps 45:12 *be there* with a **g**; *even* the rich among H4503
Prv 17: 8 A **g** *is as* a precious stone in the eyes of H7810
23 A wicked *man* taketh a **g** out of the H7810
18:16 A man's **g** maketh room for him, and H4976
21:14 A **g** in secret pacifieth anger: and a H4976
25:14 Whoso boasteth himself of a false **g** *is* H4991
Ecc 3:13 good of all his labour, it *is* the **g** of God. H4991
5:19 in his labour; this *is* the **g** of God. H4991
7: 7 mad; and a **g** destroyeth the heart. H4979
Ezk 46:16 If the prince give a **g** unto any of his H4979
17 But if he give a **g** of his inheritance to H4979
Mt 5:23 Therefore if thou bring thy **g** to the *G1435*
24 Leave there thy **g** before the altar, and *G1435*
24 brother, and then come and offer thy **g**. *G1435*
8: 4 priest, and offer the **g** that Moses *G1435*
15: 5 *his* mother, *It is* a **g**, by whatsoever thou *G1435*
23:18 by the **g** that is upon it, he is guilty. *G1435*
19 **g**, or the altar that sanctifieth the gift? *G1435*
19 gift, or the altar that sanctifieth the **g**? *G1435*
Mk 7:11 that is to say, a **g**, by whatsoever thou *G1435*
Jn 4:10 thou knewest the **g** of God, and who it *G1431*
Act 2:38 ye shall receive the **g** of the Holy Ghost. *G1431*
8:20 hast thought that the **g** of God may be *G1431*
10:45 was poured out the **g** of the Holy Ghost. *G1431*
11:17 gave them the like **g** as *he did* unto us, *G1431*
Ro 1:11 **g**, to the end ye may be established; *G5486*
5:15 so also *is* the free **g**. For if through the *G5486*
15 of God, and the **g** by grace, *which is* by *G1431*
16 sinned, *so is* the **g**: for the judgment *was* *G1434*
16 **g** *is* of many offences unto justification. *G5486*
17 of grace and of the **g** of righteousness *G1431*
18 of one *the free* **g** *came* upon all men unto
6:23 For the wages of sin *is* death; but the **g** *G5486*
1Co 1: 7 So that ye come behind in no **g**; waiting *G5486*
7: 7 hath his proper **g** of God, one after this *G5486*
13: 2 And though I have *the* **g** *of* prophecy,
2Co 1:11 for us, that for the **g** *bestowed* upon us *G5486*
8: 4 would receive the **g**, and *take upon us* *G5485*
9:15 *be* unto God for his unspeakable **g**. *G1431*
Eph 2: 8 that not of yourselves: *it is* the **g** of God: *G1435*
3: 7 according to the **g** of the grace of God *G1431*
4: 7 to the measure of the **g** of Christ. *G1431*
Php 4:17 Not because I desire a **g**: but I desire *G1390*
1Ti 4:14 Neglect not the **g** that is in thee, which *G5486*
2Ti 1: 6 thou stir up the **g** of God, which is in *G5486*
Heb 6: 4 tasted of the heavenly **g**, and were made *G1431*
Jas 1:17 Every good **g** and every perfect gift is *G1394*
17 Every good gift and every perfect **g** is *G1434*
1Pt 4:10 As every man hath received the **g**, *even* *G5486*

GIFTS
Gen 25: 6 Abraham gave **g**, and sent them away H4979
Ex 28:38 in all their holy **g**; and it shall be always H4979
Lev 23:38 and beside your **g**, and beside all your H4979
Nu 18:29 Out of all your **g** ye shall offer every H4979
2Sa 8: 2 David's servants, *and* brought **g**. H4503
6 David, *and* brought **g**. And the LORD H4503
1Ch 18: 2 David's servants, *and* brought **g**. H4503
6 *and* brought **g**. Thus the LORD H4503
2Ch 19: 7 nor respect of persons, nor taking of **g**. H7810
21: 3 And their father gave them great **g** of H4979
26: 8 And the Ammonites gave **g** to Uzziah: H4503
32:23 And many brought **g** unto the LORD to H4503
Est 2:18 **g**, according to the state of the king. H4864
9:22 one to another, and **g** to the poor. H4979
Ps 68:18 thou hast received **g** for men; yea, *for* H4979
72:10 the kings of Sheba and Seba shall offer **g**. H814
Prv 6:35 content, though thou givest many **g**. H7810
15:27 house; but he that hateth **g** shall live. H4979
19: 6 man *is* a friend to him that giveth **g**. H4976
29: 4 but he that receiveth **g** overthroweth it. H8641
Isa 1:23 every one loveth **g**, and followeth after H7810
Ezk 16:33 They give **g** to all whores: but thou H5078
33 thou givest thy **g** to all thy lovers, and H5083
20:26 And I polluted them in their own **g**, in H4979
31 For when ye offer your **g**, when ye make H4979
39 more with your **g**, and with your idols. H4979
22:12 In thee have they taken **g** to shed H7810
Dan 2: 6 shall receive of me **g** and rewards and H4978
48 him many great **g**, and made him ruler H4978
5:17 the king, Let thy **g** be to thyself, and H4978
Mt 2:11 **g**; gold, and frankincense, and myrrh. *G1435*
7:11 how to give good **g** unto your children, *G1390*
Lk 11:13 how to give good **g** unto your children: *G1390*
21: 1 men casting their **g** into the treasury. *G1435*
5 with goodly stones and **g**, he said, *G334*
Ro 11:29 For the **g** and calling of God *are* *G5486*
12: 6 Having then **g** differing according to *G5486*
1Co 12: 1 Now concerning spiritual **g**, brethren, I
4 Now there are diversities of **g**, but the *G5486*
9 the **g** of healing by the same Spirit; *G5486*
28 that miracles, then **g** of healings, helps, *G5486*
30 Have all the **g** of healing? do all speak *G5486*
31 But covet earnestly the best **g**: and yet *G5486*
14: 1 **g**, but rather that ye may prophesy.
12 zealous of spiritual **g**, seek that ye may
Eph 4: 8 captivity captive, and gave **g** unto men. *G1390*
Heb 2: 4 miracles, and **g** of the Holy Ghost, *G3311*
5: 1 may offer both **g** and sacrifices for sins: *G1435*
8: 3 is ordained to offer **g** and sacrifices: *G1435*
4 that offer **g** according to the law: *G1435*
9: 9 were offered both **g** and sacrifices, that *G1435*
11: 4 **g**: and by it he being dead yet speaketh. *G1435*
Rev 11:10 merry, and shall send **g** one to another; *G1435*

GIHON
Gen 2:13 And the name of the second river *is* **G**: H1521
1Ki 1:33 own mule, and bring him down to **G**: H1521
38 David's mule, and brought him to **G**. H1521
45 him king in **G**: and they are come up H1521
2Ch 32:30 upper watercourse of **G**, and brought it H1521
33:14 on the west side of **G**, in the valley, even H1521

GILALAI
Neh 12:36 Azarael, Milalai, **G**, Maai, Nethaneel, H1562

GILBOA
1Sa 28: 4 Israel together, and they pitched in **G**. H1533
31: 1 and fell down slain in mount **G**. H1533
8 and his three sons fallen in mount **G**. H1533
2Sa 1: 6 upon mount **G**, behold, Saul leaned H1533
21 Ye mountains of **G**, *let there be* no dew, H1533
21:12 when the Philistines had slain Saul in **G**: H1533
1Ch 10: 1 and fell down slain in mount **G**. H1533
8 Saul and his sons fallen in mount **G**. H1533

GILEAD
Gen 31:21 and set his face *toward* the mount **G**. H1568
23 and they overtook him in the mount **G**. H1568
25 his brethren pitched in the mount of **G**. H1568
37:25 came from **G** with their camels bearing H1568
Nu 26:29 and Machir begat **G**: of Gilead *come* the H1568
29 of **G** *come* the family of the Gileadites. H1568
30 These *are* the sons of **G**: *of* Jeezer, the H1568
27: 1 Hepher, the son of **G**, the son of Machir, H1568
32: 1 and the land of **G**, that, behold, the H1568
26 cattle, shall be there in the cities of **G**: H1568
29 them the land of **G** for a possession: H1568
39 of Manasseh went to **G**, and took it, and H1568
40 And Moses gave **G** unto Machir the son H1568
36: 1 of the children of **G**, the son of Machir, H1568
Dt 2:36 river, even unto **G**, there was not one H1568
3:10 All the cities of the plain, and all **G**, and H1568
12 Arnon, and half mount **G**, and the cities H1568
13 And the rest of **G**, and all Bashan, *being* H1568
15 And I gave **G** unto Machir. H1568

Dt 3:16 I gave from **G** even unto the river H1568
4:43 and Ramoth in **G**, of the Gadites; and H1568
34: 1 shewed him all the land of **G**, unto Dan, H1568
Jos 12: 2 and from half **G**, even unto the river H1568
5 **G**, the border of Sihon king of Heshbon. H1568
13:11 And **G**, and the border of the Geshurites H1568
25 all the cities of **G**, and half the land of H1568
31 And half **G**, and Ashtaroth, and Edrei, H1568
17: 1 the father of **G**: because he was a man H1568
1 of war, therefore he had **G** and Bashan. H1568
3 Hepher, the son of **G**, the son of Machir, H1568
5 beside the land of **G** and Bashan, which H1568
6 of Manasseh's sons had the land of **G**. H1568
20: 8 and Ramoth in **G** out of the tribe of H1568
21:38 Gad, Ramoth in **G** with her suburbs, *to* H1568
22: 9 the country of **G**, to the land of their H1568
13 into the land of **G**, Phinehas the son of H1568
15 of **G**, and they spake with them, saying, H1568
32 out of the land of **G**, unto the land of H1568
Jdg 5:17 **G** abode beyond Jordan: and why did H1568
7: 3 depart early from mount **G**. And there H1568
10: 4 this day, which *are* in the land of **G**. H1568
8 the land of the Amorites, which *is* in **G**. H1568
17 and encamped in **G**. And the children of H1568
18 And the people *and* princes of **G** said H1568
18 be head over all the inhabitants of **G**. H1568
11: 1 son of an harlot: and **G** begat Jephthah. H1568
5 the elders of **G** went to fetch Jephthah H1568
7 And Jephthah said unto the elders of **G**, H1568
8 And the elders of **G** said unto Jephthah, H1568
8 our head over all the inhabitants of **G**. H1568
9 And Jephthah said unto the elders of **G**, H1568
10 And the elders of **G** said unto Jephthah, H1568
11 with the elders of **G**, and the people H1568
29 he passed over **G**, and Manasseh, and H1568
29 over Mizpeh of **G**, and from Mizpeh of H1568
29 from Mizpeh of **G** he passed over *unto* H1568
12: 4 all the men of **G**, and fought with H1568
4 and the men of **G** smote Ephraim, H1568
5 that the men of **G** said unto him, *Art* H1568
7 and was buried in *one of* the cities of **G**. H1568
20: 1 land of **G**, unto the LORD in Mizpeh. H1568
1Sa 13: 7 land of Gad and **G**. As for Saul, he *was* H1568
2Sa 2: 9 And made him king over **G**, and over H1568
17:26 and Absalom pitched in the land of **G**. H1568
24: 6 Then they came to **G**, and to the land of H1568
1Ki 4:13 which *are* in **G**; to him *also pertained* H1568
19 in the country of **G**, *in* the country of H1568
17: 1 of the inhabitants of **G**, said unto Ahab, H1568
22: 3 ye that Ramoth in **G** is ours, and we *be* H1568
2Ki 10:33 all the land of **G**, the Gadites, and the H1568
33 by the river Arnon, even **G** and Bashan. H1568
15:29 and Hazor, and **G**, and Galilee, all the H1568
1Ch 2:21 the father of **G**, whom he married when H1568
22 three and twenty cities in the land of **G**. H1568
23 *to* the sons of Machir the father of **G**. H1568
5: 9 cattle were multiplied in the land of **G**. H1568
10 tents throughout all the east *land* of **G**. H1568
14 Jaroah, the son of **G**, the son of Michael, H1568
16 And they dwelt in **G** in Bashan, and in H1568
6:80 of Gad; Ramoth in **G** with her suburbs, H1568
7:14 Aramitess bare Machir the father of **G**: H1568
17 *were* the sons of **G**, the son of Machir, H1568
26:31 mighty men of valour at Jazer of **G**. H1568
27:21 Of the half *tribe* of Manasseh in **G**, Iddo H1568
Ps 60: 7 **G** *is* mine, and Manasseh *is* mine; H1568
108: 8 **G** *is* mine; Manasseh *is* mine; Ephraim H1568
Song 4: 1 of goats, that appear from mount **G**. H1568
6: 5 as a flock of goats that appear from **G**. H1568
Jer 8:22 *Is there* no balm in **G**; *is there* no H1568
22: 6 of Judah; Thou *art* **G** unto me, *and* the H1568
46:11 Go up into **G**, and take balm, O virgin, H1568
50:19 satisfied upon mount Ephraim and **G**. H1568
Ezk 47:18 and from **G**, and from the land of H1568
Hos 6: 8 **G** *is* a city of them that work iniquity, H1568
12:11 *Is there* iniquity *in* **G**? surely they are H1568
Am 1: 3 **G** with threshing instruments of iron: H1568
13 **G**, that they might enlarge their border: H1568
Oba 19 Samaria: and Benjamin *shall possess* **G**. H1568
Mic 7:14 *in* Bashan and **G**, as in the days of old. H1568
Zec 10:10 into the land of **G** and Lebanon; and H1568

GILEADITE
Jdg 10: 3 And after him arose Jair, a **G**, and H1569
11: 1 Now Jephthah the **G** was a mighty man H1569
40 of Jephthah the **G** four days in a year. H1569
12: 7 died Jephthah the **G**, and was buried in H1569
2Sa 17:27 and Barzillai the **G** of Rogelim, H1569
19:31 And Barzillai the **G** came down from H1569
1Ki 2: 7 of Barzillai the **G**, and let them be of H1569
Ezr 2:61 the **G**, and was called after their name: H1569
Neh 7:63 of Barzillai the **G** to wife, and was H1569

GILEADITES
Nu 26:29 of Gilead *come* the family of the **G**. H1569
Jdg 12: 4 because they said, Ye **G** *are* fugitives of H1568
5 And the **G** took the passages of Jordan H1568
2Ki 15:25 fifty men of the **G**: and he killed him, H1568

GILEAD'S
Jdg 11: 2 And **G** wife bare him sons; and his H1568

GILGAL
Dt 11:30 against **G**, beside the plains of Moreh? H1537
Jos 4:19 in **G**, in the east border of Jericho. H1537
20 out of Jordan, did Joshua pitch in **G**. H1537
5: 9 of the place is called **G** unto this day. H1537
10 encamped in **G**, and kept the passover H1537
9: 6 unto the camp at **G**, and said unto him, H1537
10: 6 to the camp to **G**, saying, Slack not thy H1537
7 So Joshua ascended from **G**, he, and all H1537
9 *and* went up from **G** all night. H1537
15 all Israel with him, unto the camp to **G**. H1537
43 all Israel with him, unto the camp to **G**. H1537
12:23 one; the king of the nations of **G**, one; H1537
14: 6 unto Joshua in **G**: and Caleb the son of H1537
15: 7 looking toward **G**, that *is* before the H1537
Jdg 2: 1 came up from **G** to Bochim, and said, H1537
3:19 that *were* by **G**, and said, I have a secret H1537
1Sa 7:16 to Beth-el, and **G**, and Mizpeh, and H1537
10: 8 And thou shalt go down before me to **G**; H1537
11:14 go to **G**, and renew the kingdom there. H1537
15 And all the people went to **G**; and there H1537
15 before the LORD in **G**; and there they H1537
13: 4 were called together after Saul to **G**. H1537
7 Saul, he *was* yet in **G**, and all the people H1537
8 came not to **G**; and the people were H1537
12 now upon me to **G**, and I have not made H1537
15 and gat him up from **G** unto Gibeah of H1537
15:12 and passed on, and gone down to **G**. H1537
21 sacrifice unto the LORD thy God in **G**. H1537
33 Agag in pieces before the LORD in **G**. H1537
2Sa 19:15 Judah came to **G**, to go to meet the king, H1537
40 Then the king went on to **G**, and H1537
2Ki 2: 1 that Elijah went with Elisha from **G**. H1537
4:38 And Elisha came again to **G**: and *there* H1537
Neh 12:29 Also from the house of **G**, and out of the H1537
Hos 4:15 come not ye unto **G**, neither go ye up to H1537
9:15 All their wickedness *is* in **G**: for there I H1537
12:11 bullocks in **G**; yea, their altars *are* H1537
Am 4: 4 Come to Beth-el, and transgress; at **G** H1537
5: 5 But seek not Beth-el, nor enter into **G**, H1537
5 to Beer-sheba: for **G** shall surely go into H1537
Mic 6: 5 from Shittim unto **G**; that ye may know H1537

GILOH
Jos 15:51 And Goshen, and Holon, and **G**; eleven H1542
2Sa 15:12 his city, *even* from **G**, while he offered H1542

GILONITE
2Sa 15:12 And Absalom sent for Ahithophel the **G**, H1526
23:34 Eliam the son of Ahithophel the **G**, H1526

GIMZO
2Ch 28:18 villages thereof, **G** also and the villages H1579

GIN
Job 18: 9 The **g** shall take *him* by the heel, *and* H6341
Isa 8:14 of Israel, for a **g** and for a snare to the H6341
Am 3: 5 earth, where no **g** *is* for him? shall *one* H4170

GINATH
1Ki 16:21 Tibni the son of **G**, to make him king; H1527
22 of **G**: so Tibni died, and Omri reigned. H1527

GINNETHO
Neh 12: 4 Iddo, **G**, Abijah, H1599

GINNETHON
Neh 10: 6 Daniel, **G**, Baruch, H1599
12:16 Of Iddo, Zechariah; of **G**, Meshullam; H1599

GINS
Ps 140: 5 wayside; they have set **g** for me. Selah. H4170
141: 9 and the **g** of the workers of iniquity. H4170

GIRD
Ex 29: 5 breastplate, and **g** him with the curious H640
29: 9 And thou shalt **g** them with girdles, H2296
Jdg 3:16 cubit length; and he did **g** it under his H2296
1Sa 25:13 And David said unto his men, **G** ye on H2296
2Sa 3:31 your clothes, and **g** you with sackcloth, H2296
2Ki 4:29 Then he said to Gehazi, **G** up thy loins, H2296
9: 1 said unto him, **G** up thy loins, and take H2296
Job 38: 3 **G** up now thy loins like a man; for I will H247
40: 7 **G** up thy loins now like a man: I will H247
Ps 45: 3 **G** thy sword upon *thy* thigh, O *most* H2296
Isa 8: 9 ye of far countries: **g** yourselves, and ye H247
9 be broken in pieces; **g** yourselves, and ye H247
15: 3 In their streets they shall **g** themselves H2296
32:11 bare, and **g** *sackcloth* upon *your* loins. H2290
Jer 1:17 Thou therefore **g** up thy loins, and H2296
4: 8 For this **g** you with sackcloth, lament H2296
6:26 O daughter of my people, **g** *thee* with H2296
49: 3 of Rabbah, **g** you with sackcloth; H2296
Ezk 7:18 They shall also **g** *themselves* with H2296
27:31 utterly bald for thee, and **g** them with H2296
44:18 they shall not **g** *themselves* with any H2296
Joel 1:13 **G** yourselves, and lament, ye priests: H2296
Lk 12:37 you, that he shall **g** himself, and make *G4024*
17: 8 I may sup, and **g** thyself, and serve me, *G4024*
Jn 21:18 and another shall **g** thee, and carry *G2224*
Act 12: 8 And the angel said unto him, **G** thyself, *G4042*
1Pt 1:13 Wherefore **g** up the loins of your mind, *G328*

GIRDED
Ex 12:11 it; *with* your loins **g**, your shoes on your H2296
Lev 8: 7 And he put upon him the coat, and **g** H2296
7 ephod upon him, and he **g** him with the H2296
13 upon them, and **g** them with girdles, H2296
16: 4 flesh, and shall be **g** with a linen girdle, H2296
Dt 1:41 And when ye had **g** on every man his H2296
1Sa 2: 4 they that stumbled are **g** with strength. H247
18 *being* a child, **g** with a linen ephod. H2296
17:39 And David **g** his sword upon his H2296
25:13 his sword. And they **g** on every man his H2296
13 and David also **g** on his sword: and H2296
2Sa 6:14 and David *was* **g** with a linen ephod. H2296
20: 8 that he had put on was **g** unto him, and H2296
21:16 in weight, he being **g** with a new *sword*, H2296
22:40 For thou hast **g** me with strength to H247
1Ki 18:46 on Elijah; and he **g** up his loins, and H2296
20:32 So they **g** sackcloth on their loins, and H2296
Neh 4:18 one had his sword **g** by his side, and *so* H631
Ps 18:39 For thou hast **g** me with strength unto H247
30:11 my sackcloth, and **g** me with gladness; H247
65: 6 fast the mountains; *being* **g** with power: H247
93: 1 *wherewith* he hath **g** himself: the world H247
109:19 a girdle wherewith he is **g** continually. H2296
Isa 45: 5 **g** thee, though thou hast not known me: H247
Lam 2:10 heads; they have **g** themselves with H2296
Ezk 16:10 skin, and I **g** thee about with fine H2280
23:15 **G** with girdles upon their loins, H2289
Dan 10: 5 loins *were* **g** with fine gold of Uphaz: H2296
Joel 1: 8 Lament like a virgin **g** with sackcloth H2296
Lk 12:35 Let your loins be **g** about, and *your* *G4024*
Jn 13: 4 and took a towel, and **g** himself. *G1241*
5 with the towel wherewith he was **g**. *G1241*
Rev 15: 6 their breasts **g** with golden girdles. *G4024*

GIRDEDST
Jn 21:18 thou wast young, thou **g** thyself, and *G2224*

GIRDETH
1Ki 20:11 Let not him that **g** on *his harness* boast H2296
Job 12:18 He looseth the bond of kings, and **g** their H631
Ps 18:32 *It is* God that **g** me with strength, and H247
Prv 31:17 She **g** her loins with strength, and H2296

GIRDING
Isa 3:24 of a stomacher a **g** of sackcloth; *and* H4228
22:12 to baldness, and to **g** with sackcloth: H2296

GIRDLE
Ex 28: 4 a mitre, and a **g**: and they shall make H73
8 And the curious **g** of the ephod, which H2805
27 above the curious **g** of the ephod. H2805
28 above the curious **g** of the ephod, and H2805
39 thou shalt make the **g** *of* needlework. H73
29: 5 him with the curious **g** of the ephod: H2805
39: 5 And the curious **g** of his ephod, that H2805
20 above the curious **g** of the ephod. H2805
21 above the curious **g** of the ephod, and H2805
29 And a **g** *of* fine twined linen, and blue, H73
Lev 8: 7 him with the **g**, and clothed him with H73
7 with the curious **g** of the ephod, and H2805
16: 4 girded with a linen **g**, and with the linen H73

G

1Sa 18: 4 his sword, and to his bow, and to his **g**. H2289
2Sa 18:11 given thee ten *shekels* of silver, and a **g**. H2290
20: 8 unto him, and upon it a **g** *with* a sword H2289
1Ki 2: 5 of war upon his **g** that *was* about his H2290
2Ki 1: 8 and girt with a **g** of leather about his H232
Job 12:18 of kings, and girdeth their loins with a **g**. H232
Ps 109:19 a **g** wherewith he is girded continually. H4206
Isa 3:24 and instead of a **g** a rent; and instead H2290
5:27 sleep; neither shall the **g** of their loins be H232
11: 5 And righteousness shall be the **g** of his H232
5 loins, and faithfulness the **g** of his reins. H232
22:21 him with thy **g**, and I will commit thy H73
Jer 13: 1 get thee a linen **g**, and put it upon thy H232
2 So I got a **g** according to the word of the H232
4 Take the **g** that thou hast got, which *is* H232
6 and take the **g** from thence, which I H232
7 and took the **g** from the place where H232
7 it: and, behold, the **g** was marred, it was H232
10 be as this **g**, which is good for nothing. H232
11 For as the **g** cleaveth to the loins of a H232
Mt 3: 4 and a leathern **g** about his loins; and *G2223*
Mk 1: 6 hair, and with a **g** of a skin about his *G2223*
Act 21:11 us, he took Paul's **g**, and bound his own *G2223*
11 that owneth this **g**, and shall deliver *G2223*
Rev 1:13 and girt about the paps with a golden **g**. *G2223*

GIRDLES
Ex 28:40 make for them **g**, and bonnets shalt thou H73
29: 9 And thou shalt gird them with **g**, Aaron H73
Lev 8:13 and girded them with **g**, and put bonnets H73
Prv 31:24 *it;* and delivereth **g** unto the merchant. H2289
Ezk 23:15 Girded with **g** upon their loins, H232
Rev 15: 6 their breasts girded with golden **g**. *G2223*

GIRGASHITE
1Ch 1:14 also, and the Amorite, and the **G**, H1622

GIRGASHITES
Gen 15:21 and the **G**, and the Jebusites. H1622
Dt 7: 1 Hittites, and the **G**, and the Amorites, H1622
Jos 3:10 **G**, and the Amorites, and the Jebusites. H1622
24:11 Hittites, and the **G**, the Hivites, and the H1622
Neh 9: 8 Jebusites, and the **G**, to give *it, I say,* to H1622

GIRGASITE
Gen 10:16 Jebusite, and the Amorite, and the **G**, H1622

GIRL
Joel 3: 3 a **g** for wine, that they might drink. H3207

GIRLS
Zec 8: 5 and **g** playing in the streets thereof. H3207

GIRT
2Ki 1: 8 *was* an hairy man, and **g** with a girdle of H247
Jn 21: 7 it was the Lord, he **g** *his* fisher's coat *G1241*
Eph 6:14 Stand therefore, having your loins **g** *G4024*
Rev 1:13 **g** about the paps with a golden girdle. *G4024*

GISPA
Neh 11:21 Ziha and **G** *were* over the Nethinims. H1658

GITTAH-HEPHER
Jos 19:13 on the east to **G**, to Ittah-kazin, and H1662

GITTAIM
2Sa 4: 3 And the Beerothites fled to **G**, and were H1664
Neh 11:33 Hazor, Ramah, **G**, H1664

GITTITE
2Sa 6:10 into the house of Obed-edom the **G**. H1663
11 of Obed-edom the **G** three months: and H1663
15:19 Then said the king to Ittai the **G**, H1663
22 over. And Ittai the **G** passed over, and H1663
18: 2 hand of Ittai the **G**. And the king said H1663
21:19 *of* Goliath the **G**, the staff of whose H1663
1Ch 13:13 into the house of Obed-edom the **G**. H1663
20: 5 of Goliath the **G**, whose spear staff *was* H1663

GITTITES
Jos 13: 3 **G**, and the Ekronites; also the Avites: H1663
2Sa 15:18 and all the **G**, six hundred men which H1663

GITTITH
Ps 8:ttl To the chief Musician upon **G**, A Psalm H1665
81:ttl To the chief Musician upon **G**, *A Psalm* H1665
84:ttl To the chief Musician upon **G**, A Psalm H1665

GIVE
Gen 1:15 to **g** light upon the earth: and it was so. H215
17 of the heaven to **g** light upon the earth, H215
12: 7 thy seed will I **g** this land: and there H5414
13:15 thee will I **g** it, and to thy seed for ever. H5414
17 breadth of it; for I will **g** it unto thee. H5414
14:21 said unto Abram, **G** me the persons, H5414
15: 2 GOD, what wilt thou **g** me, seeing I go H5414
7 to **g** thee this land to inherit it. H5414
17: 8 And I will **g** unto thee, and to thy seed H5414
16 And I will bless her, and **g** thee a son H5414
23: 4 with you: **g** me a possession of H5414
9 That he may **g** me the cave of H5414
9 as it is worth he shall **g** it me for a H5414
11 Nay, my lord, hear me: the field **g** I H5414
11 cave that *is* therein, I **g** it thee; in the H5414
11 of my people **g** I it thee: bury thy dead. H5414
13 But if thou *wilt* **g** *it,* I pray thee, hear me:
13 hear me: I will **g** thee money for the H5414
24: 7 thy seed will I **g** this land; he shall send H5414
14 Drink, and I will **g** thy camels drink H8248
41 and if they **g** not thee *one,* thou shalt H5414
43 and I say to her, **G** me, I pray thee, a
46 Drink, and I will **g** thy camels drink H8248
26: 3 thy seed, I will **g** all these countries, H5414
4 of heaven, and will **g** unto thy seed all H5414
27:28 Therefore God **g** thee of the dew of H5414
28: 4 And **g** thee the blessing of Abraham, to H5414
13 liest, to thee will I **g** it, and to thy seed; H5414
20 that I go, and will **g** me bread to eat, H5414
22 of all that thou shalt **g** me I will surely H5414
22 me I will surely **g** the tenth unto thee. H6237
29:19 And Laban said, *It is* better that I **g** her H5414
19 **g** her to another man: abide with me. H5414
21 And Jacob said unto Laban, **G** *me* my H3051
26 to **g** the younger before the firstborn. H5414
27 Fulfil her week, and we will **g** thee this H5414
30: 1 unto Jacob, **G** me children, or else I die. H3051
14 said to Leah, **G** me, I pray thee, of thy H5414
26 **G** *me* my wives and my children, for H5414
28 Appoint me thy wages, and I will **g** *it.* H5414
31 And he said, What shall I **g** thee? And H5414
31 Thou shalt not **g** me any thing: if thou H5414
34: 8 daughter: I pray you **g** her him to wife. H5414
9 And make ye marriages with us, *and* **g** H5414
11 and what ye shall say unto me I will **g**. H5414
12 and gift, and I will **g** according as ye H5414
12 unto me: but **g** me the damsel to wife. H5414
14 do this thing, to **g** our sister to one that H5414
16 Then will we **g** our daughters unto you, H5414
21 wives, and let us **g** them our daughters. H5414
35:12 to thee I will **g** it, and to thy seed after H5414
12 to thy seed after thee will I **g** the land. H5414
38: 9 that he should **g** seed to his brother. H5414
16 What wilt thou **g** me, that thou mayest H5414
17 thou **g** *me* a pledge, till thou send *it?* H5414
18 And he said, What pledge shall I **g** H5414
41:16 shall **g** Pharaoh an answer of peace. H6030
42:25 his sack, and to **g** them provision for H5414
27 opened his sack to **g** his ass provender H5414
43:14 And God Almighty **g** you mercy before H5414
45:18 me: and I will **g** you the good of the H5414
47:15 Joseph, and said, **G** us bread: for why H3051
16 And Joseph said, **G** your cattle; and I H3051
16 will **g** you for your cattle, if money fail. H5414
19 Pharaoh: and **g** *us* seed, that we may H5414
24 that ye shall **g** the fifth *part* unto H5414
48: 4 of people; and will **g** this land to thy H5414
Ex 2: 9 for me, and I will **g** *thee* thy wages. And H5414
3:21 And I will **g** this people favour in the H5414
5: 7 Ye shall no more **g** the people straw to H5414
10 saith Pharaoh, I will not **g** you straw. H5414
6: 4 with them, to **g** them the land of H5414
8 I did swear to **g** it to Abraham, to H5414
8 **g** it you for an heritage: I *am* the LORD. H5414
10:25 And Moses said, Thou must **g** us also H5414
12:25 the LORD will **g** you, according as he H5414
13: 5 sware unto thy fathers to **g** thee, a land H5414
11 and to thy fathers, and shall **g** it thee, H5414
21 to **g** them light; to go by day and night:
15:26 in his sight, and wilt **g** ear to his
16: 8 the LORD shall **g** you in the evening H5414
17: 2 Moses, and said, **G** us water that we H5414
18:19 Hearken now unto my voice, I will **g** thee
21:23 follow, then thou shalt **g** life for life, H5414
30 then he shall **g** for the ransom of his H5414
32 he shall **g** unto their master thirty H5414
34 make *it* good, *and* **g** money unto the H7725
22:17 If her father utterly refuse to **g** her unto H5414

Ex 22:29 of thy sons shalt thou **g** unto me. H5414
30 on the eighth day thou shalt **g** it me. H5414
24:12 and be there: and I will **g** thee tables of H5414
25:16 ark the testimony which I shall **g** thee. H5414
21 put the testimony that I shall **g** thee. H5414
22 all *things* which I will **g** thee in
37 that they may **g** light over against it.
30:12 then shall they **g** every man a ransom H5414
13 This they shall **g**, every one that passeth H5414
14 shall **g** an offering unto the LORD. H5414
15 The rich shall not **g** more, and the poor
15 and the poor shall not **g** less than half a
15 a shekel, when *they* **g** an offering unto H5414
32:13 spoken of will I **g** unto your seed, and H5414
33: 1 Jacob, saying, Unto thy seed will I **g** it: H5414
14 shall go *with thee,* and I will **g** thee rest.
Lev 5:16 part thereto, and **g** it unto the priest: H5414
6: 5 part more thereto, *and* **g** it unto him to H5414
7:32 And the right shoulder shall ye **g** unto H5414
14:34 of Canaan, which I **g** to you for a H5414
15:14 and **g** them unto the priest: H5414
20:24 land, and I will **g** it unto you to possess H5414
22:14 **g** *it* unto the priest with the holy thing. H5414
23:10 the land which I **g** unto you, and shall H5414
38 offerings, which ye **g** unto the LORD. H5414
25: 2 the land which I **g** you, then shall the H5414
37 Thou shalt not **g** him thy money upon H5414
38 the land of Egypt, to **g** you the land of H5414
51 unto them he shall **g** again the price of H7725
52 his years shall he **g** him again the price H7725
26: 4 Then I will **g** you rain in due season, H5414
6 And I will **g** peace in the land, and ye H5414
27:23 and he shall **g** thine estimation in H5414
Nu 3: 9 And thou shalt **g** the Levites unto H5414
48 And thou shalt **g** the money, wherewith H5414
5: 7 *part* thereof, and **g** *it* unto *him* against H5414
6:26 upon thee, and **g** thee peace. H7760
7: 5 and thou shalt **g** them unto the Levites, H5414
8: 2 shall **g** light over against the candlestick. H215
10:29 LORD said, I will **g** it you: come thou H5414
11: 4 and said, Who shall **g** us flesh to eat?
13 Whence should I have flesh to **g** unto H5414
13 me, saying, **G** us flesh, that we may eat. H5414
18 saying, Who shall **g** us flesh to eat? for *it*
18 LORD will **g** you flesh, and ye shall eat. H5414
21 hast said, I will **g** them flesh, that they H5414
13: 2 Canaan, which I **g** unto the children of H5414
14: 8 into this land, and **g** it us; a land which H5414
15: 2 your habitations, which I **g** unto you, H5414
21 Of the first of your dough ye shall **g** H5414
18:28 and ye shall **g** thereof the LORD'S H5414
19: 3 And ye shall **g** her unto Eleazar the H5414
20: 8 eyes; and it shall **g** forth his water, and
8 rock: so thou shalt **g** the congregation
21 Thus Edom refused to **g** Israel passage H5414
21:16 together, and I will **g** them water. H5414
22:13 refuseth to **g** me leave to go with you. H5414
18 If Balak would **g** me his house full of H5414
24:13 If Balak would **g** me his house full of H5414
25:12 Wherefore say, Behold, I **g** unto him H5414
26:54 To many thou shalt **g** the more
54 to few thou shalt **g** the less inheritance:
27: 4 he hath no son? **G** unto us *therefore* a H5414
7 thou shalt surely **g** them a possession H5414
9 **g** his inheritance unto his brethren. H5414
10 then ye shall **g** his inheritance unto H5414
11 then ye shall **g** his inheritance unto H5414
19 and **g** him a charge in their sight.
31:29 Take *it* of their half, and **g** it unto H5414
30 of beasts, and **g** them unto the Levites, H5414
32:29 you; then ye shall **g** them the land of H5414
33:54 the more ye shall **g** the more inheritance,
54 the fewer ye shall **g** the less inheritance:
34:13 commanded to **g** unto the nine tribes, H5414
35: 2 of Israel, that they **g** unto the Levites of H5414
2 in; and ye shall **g** *also* unto the Levites H5414
4 which ye shall **g** unto the Levites, *shall* H5414
6 And among the cities which ye shall **g** H5414
7 *So* all the cities which ye shall **g** to the H5414
7 cities: them *shall ye* **g** with their suburbs.
8 And the cities which ye shall **g** *shall be* H5414
8 *have* many ye shall **g** many; but from
8 *have* few ye shall **g** few: every one shall
8 every one shall **g** of his cities unto the H5414
13 And of these cities which ye shall **g** six H5414
14 Ye shall **g** three cities on this side H5414
14 cities shall ye **g** in the land of Canaan, H5414
36: 2 my lord to **g** the land for an inheritance H5414
2 by the LORD to **g** the inheritance of H5414

Dt 1: 8 and Jacob, to **g** unto them and to their H5414
20 the LORD our God doth **g** unto us. H5414
25 which the LORD our God doth **g** us. H5414
35 which I sware to **g** unto your fathers, H5414
36 it, and to him will I **g** the land that he H5414
39 will I **g** it, and they shall possess it. H5414
45 to your voice, nor **g** ear unto you. H238
2: 5 Meddle not with them; for I will not **g** H5414
9 for I will not **g** thee of their land *for* H5414
19 them: for I will not **g** thee of the land of H5414
28 I may eat; and **g** me water for money, H5414
31 I have begun to **g** Sihon and his land H5414
4:38 to bring thee in, to **g** thee their land *for* H5414
5:31 in the land which I **g** them to possess it. H5414
6:10 Isaac, and to Jacob, to **g** thee great and H5414
23 bring us in, to **g** us the land which he H5414
7: 3 thou shalt not **g** unto his son, nor his H5414
13 he sware unto thy fathers to **g** thee. H5414
10:11 unto their fathers to **g** unto them. H5414
11: 9 your fathers to **g** unto them and to H5414
14 That I will **g** *you* the rain of your land H5414
21 your fathers to **g** them, as the days of H5414
14:21 dieth of itself: thou shalt **g** it unto the H5414
15:10 Thou shalt surely **g** him, and thine H5414
14 blessed thee thou shalt **g** unto him. H5414
16:10 which thou shalt **g** *unto the LORD thy* H5414
17 Every man *shall* **g** as he is able,
18: 3 and they shall **g** unto the priest the H5414
4 fleece of thy sheep, shalt thou **g** him. H5414
19: 8 unto thy fathers, and **g** thee all the land H5414
8 he promised to **g** unto thy fathers; H5414
20:16 thy God doth **g** thee *for* an inheritance, H5414
22:14 And **g** occasions of speech against her, H7760
19 of silver, and **g** *them* unto the father H5414
29 Then the man that lay with her shall **g** H5414
23:14 thee, and to **g** up thine enemies before H5414
24: 1 divorcement, and **g** *it* in her hand, and H5414
15 At his day thou shalt **g** *him* his hire, H5414
25: 3 Forty stripes he may **g** him, *and* not
26: 3 sware unto our fathers for to **g** us. H5414
28:11 LORD sware unto thy fathers to **g** thee. H5414
12 the heaven to **g** the rain unto thy land H5414
55 So that he will not **g** to any of them of H5414
65 the LORD shall **g** thee there a trembling H5414
30:20 to Isaac, and to Jacob, to **g** them. H5414
31: 5 And the LORD shall **g** them up before H5414
7 their fathers to **g** them; and thou shalt H5414
14 that I may **g** him a charge. And Moses
32: 1 **G** ear, O ye heavens, and I will speak; H238
49 Canaan, which I **g** unto the children of H5414
52 land which I **g** the children of Israel. H5414
34: 4 saying, I will **g** it unto thy seed: I have H5414
Jos 1: 2 land which I do **g** to them, *even* to the H5414
6 I sware unto their fathers to **g** them. H5414
2:12 father's house, and **g** me a true token: H5414
5: 6 that he would **g** us, a land that floweth H5414
7:19 Achan, My son, **g**, I pray thee, glory to H7760
8:18 Ai; for I will **g** it into thine hand. And H5414
9:24 his servant Moses to **g** you all the land, H5414
14:12 Now therefore **g** me this mountain, H5414
15:16 will I **g** Achsah my daughter to wife. H5414
19 Who answered, **G** me a blessing; for H5414
19 me a south land; **g** me also springs of H5414
17: 4 Moses to **g** us an inheritance among H5414
18: 4 **G** out from among you three men for H3051
20: 4 unto them, and **g** him a place, that he H5414
21: 2 hand of Moses to **g** us cities to dwell in, H5414
43 which he sware to **g** unto their fathers; H5414
Jdg 1:12 will I **g** Achsah my daughter to wife. H5414
15 And she said unto him, **G** me a H3051
15 me a south land; **g** me also springs of H5414
4:19 And he said unto her, **G** me, I pray thee,
5: 3 Hear, O ye kings; **g** ear, O ye princes; I, H238
7: 2 many for me to **g** the Midianites into H5414
8: 5 And he said unto the men of Succoth, **G**, H5414
6 we should **g** bread unto thine army? H5414
15 **g** bread unto thy men *that are* weary? H5414
24 you, that ye would **g** me every man the H5414
25 And they answered, We will willingly **g** H5414
14:12 *it* out, then I will **g** you thirty sheets H5414
13 me, then shall ye **g** me thirty sheets and H5414
16: 5 him: and we will **g** thee every one of us H5414
17:10 a priest, and I will **g** thee ten *shekels* of H5414
20: 7 Behold, ye *are* all children of Israel; **g** H3051
21: 1 **g** his daughter unto Benjamin to wife. H5414
7 not **g** them of our daughters to wives? H5414
18 Howbeit we may not **g** them wives of H5414
22 war: for ye did not **g** unto them at this H5414
Ru 4:12 shall **g** thee of this young woman. H5414

1Sa 1:11 but wilt **g** unto thine handmaid H5414
11 child, then I will **g** him unto the LORD H5414
2:10 earth; and he shall **g** strength unto his H5414
15 that sacrificed, **G** flesh to roast for the H5414
16 but thou shalt **g** *it me* now: and if not, H5414
20 and said, The LORD **g** thee seed of this H7760
28 me? and did I **g** unto the house of thy H5414
32 which *God* shall **g** Israel: and there H3190
6: 5 land; and ye shall **g** glory unto the God H5414
8: 6 when they said, **G** us a king to judge us. H5414
14 *of them,* and **g** *them* to his servants. H5414
15 **g** to his officers, and to his servants. H5414
9: 8 *is* to **g** to the man of God, to tell us our way. H5414
10: 4 And they will salute thee, and **g** thee H5414
11: 3 said unto him, **G** us seven days' respite,
14:41 God of Israel, **G** a perfect *lot.* And Saul H3051
17:10 of Israel this day; **g** me a man, that we H5414
25 riches, and will **g** him his daughter, H5414
44 to me, and I will **g** thy flesh unto the H5414
46 thee; and I will **g** the carcases of the H5414
47 and he will **g** you into our hands. H5414
18:17 Merab, her will I **g** thee to wife: only be H5414
21 And Saul said, I will **g** him her, that she H5414
21: 3 is under thine hand? **g** *me five loaves of* H5414
9 said, *There is* none like that; **g** it me. H5414
22: 7 will the son of Jesse **g** every one of you H5414
25: 8 come in a good day: **g**, I pray thee, H5414
11 my shearers, and **g** *it* unto men, whom H5414
27: 5 eyes, let them **g** me a place in some H5414
30:22 with us, we will not **g** them *ought* of the H5414
2Sa 12:11 before thine eyes, and **g** *them* unto thy H5414
13: 5 Tamar come, and **g** me meat, and H1262
14: 8 and I will **g** charge concerning thee.
16:20 Then said Absalom to Ahithophel, **G** H3051
21: 6 And the king said, I will **g** *them.* H5414
22:50 Therefore I will **g** thanks unto thee, O
23:15 Oh that one would **g** me drink of the
24:23 *as* a king, **g** unto the king. And H5414
1Ki 1:12 let me, I pray thee, **g** thee counsel, that
2:17 **g** me Abishag the Shunammite to wife. H5414
3: 5 and God said, Ask what I shall **g** thee. H5414
9 **G** therefore thy servant an H5414
21 And when I rose in the morning to **g** my
25 **g** half to the one, and half to the other. H5414
26 said, O my lord, **g** her the living child, H5414
27 Then the king answered and said, **G** H5414
5: 6 unto thee will I **g** hire for thy servants H5414
8:32 **g** him according to his righteousness. H5414
36 should walk, and **g** rain upon thy land, H5414
39 and do, and **g** to every man according H5414
50 against thee, and **g** them compassion H5414
11:11 from thee, and will **g** it to thy servant. H5414
13 kingdom; *but* will **g** one tribe to thy son H5414
31 Solomon, and will **g** ten tribes to thee: H5414
35 and will **g** it unto thee, *even* ten tribes. H5414
36 And unto his son will I **g** one tribe, that H5414
38 for David, and will **g** Israel unto thee. H5414
12: 9 And he said unto them, What counsel **g** H3289
13: 7 thyself, and I will **g** thee a reward. H5414
8 king, If thou wilt **g** me half thine house, H5414
14:16 And he shall **g** Israel up because of the H5414
15: 4 did the LORD his God **g** him a lamp in H5414
17:19 And he said unto her, **G** me thy son. H5414
18:23 Let them therefore **g** us two bullocks; H5414
21: 2 Naboth, saying, **G** me thy vineyard, H5414
2 house: and I will **g** thee for it a better H5414
2 I will **g** thee the worth of it in money. H5414
3 it me, that I should **g** the inheritance of H5414
4 he had said, I will not **g** thee the H5414
6 said unto him, **G** me thy vineyard for H5414
6 it please thee, I will **g** thee *another* H5414
6 I will not **g** thee my vineyard. H5414
7 be merry: I will **g** thee the vineyard of H5414
15 he refused to **g** thee for money: for H5414
2Ki 4:42 **G** unto the people, that they may eat. H5414
43 He said again, **G** the people, that they H5414
5:22 of the prophets: **g** them, I pray thee, a H5414
6:28 said unto me, **G** thy son, that we may H5414
29 on the next day, **G** thy son, that we may H5414
8:19 promised him to **g** him alway a light, H5414
10:15 It is. If it be, **g** *me* thine hand. And H5414
11:10 did the priest **g** king David's spears H5414
14: 9 Lebanon, saying, **G** thy daughter to my H5414
15:20 of silver, to **g** to the king of Assyria. H5414
18:23 Now therefore, I pray thee, **g** pledges to
22: 5 and let them **g** it to the doers of the H5414
23:35 he taxed the land to **g** the money H5414
35 taxation, to **g** *it* unto Pharaoh-nechoh. H5414
1Ch 11:17 Oh that one would **g** me drink of the

1Ch 16: 8 **G** thanks unto the LORD, call upon his
18 Saying, Unto thee will I **g** the land of H5414
28 **G** unto the LORD, ye kindreds of the H3051
28 **g** unto the LORD glory and strength. H3051
29 **G** unto the LORD the glory *due* unto his H3051
34 O **g** thanks unto the LORD; for *he is*
35 that we may **g** thanks to thy holy name,
41 by name, to **g** thanks to the LORD,
21:23 in his eyes: lo, I **g** *thee* the oxen *also* for H5414
23 wheat for the meat offering; I **g** it all. H5414
22: 9 of rest; and I will **g** him rest from all his
9 and I will **g** peace and quietness H5414
12 Only the LORD **g** thee wisdom and H5414
12 and **g** thee charge concerning
25: 3 to **g** thanks and to praise the LORD.
29:12 to make great, and to **g** strength unto all.
19 And **g** unto Solomon my son a perfect H5414
2Ch 1: 7 said unto him, Ask what I shall **g** thee. H5414
10 **G** me now wisdom and knowledge, that H5414
12 unto thee; and I will **g** thee riches, and H5414
2:10 And, behold, I will **g** to thy servants, H5414
10: 6 What counsel **g** ye *me* to return answer H3289
9 And he said unto them, What advice **g** H3289
21: 7 **g** a light to him and to his sons for ever. H5414
24:19 against them: but they would not **g** ear.
25: 9 is able to **g** thee much more than this. H5414
18 Lebanon, saying, **G** thy daughter to my H5414
30:12 Also in Judah the hand of God was to **g** H5414
24 For Hezekiah king of Judah did **g** to the H7311
31: 2 to minister, and to **g** thanks, and to
4 in Jerusalem to **g** the portion of the H5414
15 *their* set office, to **g** to their brethren by H5414
19 by name, to **g** portions to all the males H5414
32:11 Doth not Hezekiah persuade you to **g** H5414
35:12 that they might **g** according to the H5414
Ezr 4:21 **G** ye now commandment to cause H7761
9: 8 to escape, and to **g** us a nail in his holy H5414
8 **g** us a little reviving in our bondage. H5414
9 kings of Persia, to **g** us a reviving, to set H5414
9 **g** us a wall in Judah and in Jerusalem. H5414
12 Now therefore **g** not your daughters H5414
Neh 2: 8 that he may **g** me timber to make H5414
4: 4 own head, and **g** them for a prey in the H5414
9: 8 covenant with him to **g** the land of the H5414
8 and the Girgashites, to **g** *it, I say,* to his H5414
12 a pillar of fire, to **g** them light in the way
15 which thou hadst sworn to **g** them. H5414
30 yet would they not **g** ear: therefore
10:30 And that we would not **g** our daughters H5414
12:24 to praise *and* to **g** thanks, according to
13:25 Ye shall not **g** your daughters unto H5414
Est 1:19 and let the king **g** her royal estate unto H5414
20 all the wives shall **g** to their husbands H5414
8: 1 On that day did the king Ahasuerus **g** H5414
Job 2: 4 all that a man hath will he **g** for his life. H5414
3:11 *why* did I *not* **g** up the ghost when I H1478
6:22 Did I say, Bring unto me? or, **G** a reward
13:19 I hold my tongue, I shall **g** up the ghost. H1478
32:21 let me **g** flattering titles unto man.
22 For I know not to **g** flattering titles; *in so*
34: 2 Hear my words, O ye wise *men;* and **g**
Ps 2: 8 Ask of me, and I shall **g** *thee* the H5414
5: 1 **G** ear to my words, O LORD, consider
6: 5 in the grave who shall **g** thee thanks?
17: 1 unto my cry, **g** ear unto my prayer,
18:49 Therefore will I **g** thanks unto thee, O
28: 4 **G** them according to their deeds, and H5414
4 of their endeavours: **g** them after the H5414
29: 1 **G** unto the LORD, O ye mighty, give H3051
1 Give unto the LORD, O ye mighty, **g** H3051
2 **G** unto the LORD the glory due unto his H3051
11 The LORD will **g** strength unto his H5414
30: 4 ye saints of his, and **g** thanks at the
12 God, I will **g** thanks unto thee for ever.
35:18 I will **g** thee thanks in the great
37: 4 shall **g** thee the desires of thine heart. H5414
39:12 Hear my prayer, O LORD, and **g** ear
49: 1 Hear this, all *ye* people; **g** ear, all *ye*
7 nor **g** to God a ransom for him: H5414
51:16 else would I **g** *it*: thou delightest not H5414
54: 2 Hear my prayer, O God; **g** ear to the
55: 1 **G** ear to my prayer, O God; and hide not
57: 7 heart is fixed: I will sing and **g** praise.
60:11 **G** us help from trouble: for vain *is* the H3051
72: 1 **G** the king thy judgments, O God, and H5414
75: 1 Unto thee, O God, do we **g** thanks, *unto*
1 *unto thee* do we **g** thanks: for *that* thy
78: 1 **G** ear, O my people, *to* my law: incline
20 can he **g** bread also? can he provide H5414

Ps 79:13 of thy pasture will **g** thee thanks for ever:
80: 1 **G** ear, O Shepherd of Israel, thou that
84: 8 O LORD God of hosts, hear my prayer: **g**
11 the LORD will **g** grace and glory: no H5414
85:12 Yea, the LORD shall **g** *that which is* H5414
86: 6 **G** ear, O LORD, unto my prayer; and
16 mercy upon me; **g** thy strength unto H5414
91:11 For he shall **g** his angels charge over
92: 1 *It is a* good *thing* to **g** thanks unto the
94:13 That thou mayest **g** him rest from the
96: 7 **G** unto the LORD, O ye kindreds of the H3051
7 **g** unto the LORD glory and strength. H3051
8 **G** unto the LORD the glory *due unto* his H3051
97:12 Rejoice in the LORD, ye righteous; and **g**
104:11 They **g** drink to every beast of the field:
27 **g** *them* their meat in due season. H5414
105: 1 O **g** thanks unto the LORD; call upon his
11 Saying, Unto thee will I **g** the land of H5414
39 covering; and fire to **g** light in the night.
106: 1 Praise ye the LORD. O **g** thanks unto the
47 the heathen, to **g** thanks unto thy holy
107: 1 O **g** thanks unto the LORD, for *he is*
108: 1 sing and **g** praise, even with my glory.
12 **G** us help from trouble: for vain *is* the H3051
109: 4 adversaries: but I **g** *myself unto* prayer.
111: 6 **g** them the heritage of the heathen. H5414
115: 1 us, but unto thy name **g** glory, for thy H5414
118: 1 O **g** thanks unto the LORD; for *he is*
29 O **g** thanks unto the LORD; for *he is*
119:34 **G** me understanding, and I shall keep
62 At midnight I will rise to **g** thanks unto
73 and fashioned me: **g** me understanding,
125 I *am* thy servant; **g** me understanding,
144 **g** me understanding, and I shall live.
169 thee, O LORD: **g** me understanding
122: 4 to **g** thanks unto the name of the LORD.
132: 4 I will not **g** sleep to mine eyes, *or* H5414
136: 1 O **g** thanks unto the LORD; for *he is*
2 O **g** thanks unto the God of gods: for his
3 O **g** thanks to the Lord of lords: for his
26 O **g** thanks unto the God of heaven: for
140:13 Surely the righteous shall **g** thanks unto
141: 1 haste unto me; **g** ear unto my voice,
143: 1 Hear my prayer, O LORD, **g** ear to my
Prv 1: 4 To **g** subtilty to the simple, to the H5414
3:28 I will **g**; when thou hast it by thee. H5414
4: 2 For I **g** you good doctrine, forsake ye H5414
9 She shall **g** to thine head an ornament H5414
5: 9 Lest thou **g** thine honour unto others, H5414
6: 4 **G** not sleep to thine eyes, nor slumber H5414
31 shall **g** all the substance of his house. H5414
9: 9 **G** *instruction* to a wise *man*, and he H5414
23:26 My son, **g** me thine heart, and let thine H5414
25:21 If thine enemy be hungry, **g** him bread to
21 if he be thirsty, **g** him water to drink:
29:15 The rod and reproof **g** wisdom: but a H5414
17 Correct thy son, and he shall **g** thee rest;
17 yea, he shall **g** delight unto thy soul. H5414
30: 8 Remove far from me vanity and lies: **g** H5414
15 daughters, *crying*, **G**, give. There are H3051
15 *crying*, Give, **g**. There are three *things* H3051
31: 3 **G** not thy strength unto women, nor H5414
6 **G** strong drink unto him that is ready H5414
31 **G** her of the fruit of her hands; and let H5414
Ecc 2: 3 I sought in mine heart to **g** myself unto H4900
26 up, that he may **g** to *him that is* good H5414
5: 1 to hear, than to **g** the sacrifice of fools: H5414
11: 2 **G** a portion to seven, and also to eight; H5414
Song 2:13 the tender grape **g** a *good* smell. Arise, H5414
7:12 bud forth: there will I **g** thee my loves. H5414
13 The mandrakes **g** a smell, and at our H5414
8: 7 it: if *a* man would **g** all the substance of H5414
Isa 1: 2 Hear, O heavens, and **g** ear, O earth: for
10 ye rulers of Sodom; **g** ear unto the law of
3: 4 And I will **g** children *to be* their H5414
7:14 Therefore the Lord himself shall **g** you H5414
22 *that* they shall **g** he shall eat butter: for H6213
8: 9 broken in pieces; and **g** ear, all ye of far
10: 6 of my wrath will I **g** him a charge, to
13:10 thereof shall not **g** their light: the sun H1984
14: 3 that the LORD shall **g** thee rest from thy
19: 4 And the Egyptians will I **g** over into the H5534
28:23 **G** ye ear, and hear my voice; hearken,
30:20 And *though* the Lord **g** you the bread of H5414
23 Then shall he **g** the rain of thy seed, H5414
32: 9 daughters; **g** ear unto my speech.
36: 8 Now therefore **g** pledges, I pray thee, to
8 Assyria, and I will **g** thee two thousand H5414
41:27 them: and I will **g** to Jerusalem one that H5414
Isa 42: 6 keep thee, and **g** thee for a covenant H5414
8 my glory will I not **g** to another, neither H5414
12 Let them **g** glory unto the LORD, and H7760
23 Who among you will **g** ear to this? *who*
43: 4 I **g** men for thee, and people for thy life. H5414
6 I will say to the north, **G** up; and to the
20 the owls: because I **g** waters in the H5414
20 to **g** drink to my people, my chosen.
45: 3 And I will **g** thee the treasures of H5414
48:11 and I will not **g** my glory unto another. H5414
49: 6 Israel: I will also **g** thee for a light to the H5414
8 will preserve thee, and **g** thee for a H5414
20 for me: **g** place to me that I may dwell.
51: 4 Hearken unto me, my people; and **g** ear
55:10 bud, that it may **g** seed to the sower, H5414
56: 5 Even unto them will I **g** in mine house H5414
5 daughters: I will **g** them an everlasting H5414
60:19 shall the moon **g** light unto thee: but the
61: 3 mourn in Zion, to **g** unto them beauty H5414
62: 7 And **g** him no rest, till he establish, and H5414
8 I will no more **g** thy corn *to be* meat H5414
Jer 3:15 And I will **g** you pastors according to H5414
19 the children, and **g** thee a pleasant H5414
4:12 also will I **g** sentence against them. H1696
16 a far country, and **g** out their voice H5414
6:10 To whom shall I speak, and **g** warning,
8:10 Therefore will I **g** their wives unto H5414
9:15 and **g** them water of gall to drink.
11: 5 your fathers, to **g** them a land flowing H5414
13:15 Hear ye, and **g** ear; be not proud: for the
16 **G** glory to the LORD your God, before H5414
14:13 I will **g** you assured peace in this place. H5414
22 or can the heavens **g** showers? *art* not H5414
15:13 and thy treasures will I **g** to the spoil H5414
16: 7 neither shall *men* **g** them the cup of
17: 3 O my mountain in the field, I will **g** thy H5414
10 try the reins, even to **g** every man H5414
18:18 and let us not **g** heed to any of his words.
19 **G** heed to me, O LORD, and hearken to
19: 7 their carcases will I **g** to be meat for the H5414
20: 4 *it*: and I will **g** all Judah into the hand H5414
5 of Judah will I **g** into the hand of their H5414
22:25 And I will **g** thee into the hand of them H5414
24: 7 And I will **g** them an heart to know me, H5414
8 LORD, So will I **g** Zedekiah the king of H5414
25:30 he shall **g** a shout, as they that H6030
31 all flesh; he will **g** them *that are* wicked H5414
26:24 they should not **g** him into the hand of H5414
29: 6 for your sons, and **g** your daughters to H5414
11 not of evil, to **g** you an expected end. H5414
30:16 that prey upon thee will I **g** for a prey. H5414
32: 3 Behold, I will **g** this city into the hand H5414
19 sons of men: to **g** every one according H5414
22 swear to their fathers to **g** them, a land H5414
28 Behold, I will **g** this city into the hand H5414
39 And I will **g** them one heart, and one H5414
34: 2 Behold, I will **g** this city into the hand H5414
18 And I will **g** the men that have H5414
20 I will even **g** them into the hand of their H5414
21 and his princes will I **g** into the hand of H5414
35: 2 the chambers, and **g** them wine to drink.
37:21 that they should **g** him daily a piece of H5414
38:15 me to death? and if I **g** thee counsel, wilt
16 neither will I **g** thee into the hand of H5414
44:30 Thus saith the LORD; Behold, I will **g** H5414
45: 5 but thy life will I **g** unto thee for a prey H5414
48: 9 **G** wings unto Moab, that it may flee H5414
50:34 cause, that he may **g** rest to the land,
Lam 2:18 day and night: **g** thyself no rest; let not H5414
3:65 **G** them sorrow of heart, thy curse unto H5414
4: 3 out the breast, they **g** suck to their young
Ezk 2: 8 open thy mouth, and eat that I **g** thee. H5414
3: 3 this roll that I **g** thee. Then did I eat H5414
17 mouth, and **g** them warning from me.
7:21 And I will **g** it into the hands of the H5414
11: 2 and **g** wicked counsel in this city: H3289
17 and I will **g** you the land of Israel. H5414
19 And I will **g** them one heart, and I will H5414
19 flesh, and will **g** them an heart of flesh: H5414
15: 6 so will I **g** the inhabitants of Jerusalem. H5414
16:33 They **g** gifts to all whores: but thou H5414
36 which thou didst **g** unto them; H5414
38 I will **g** thee blood in fury and jealousy. H5414
39 And I will also **g** thee into their hand, H5414
41 and thou also shalt **g** no hire any more. H5414
61 and I will **g** them unto thee for H5414
17:15 that they might **g** him horses and much H5414
20:28 up mine hand to **g** it to them, then they H5414
42 up mine hand to **g** it to your fathers. H5414
Ezk 21:11 to **g** it into the hand of the slayer. H5414
27 whose right it is; and I will **g** it *him*. H5414
23:31 will I **g** her cup into thine hand. H5414
46 will **g** them to be removed and spoiled. H5414
25:10 and will **g** them in possession, H5414
29:19 Behold, I will **g** the land of Egypt unto H5414
21 forth, and I will **g** thee the opening of H5414
32: 7 and the moon shall not **g** her light. H215
33:15 *If* the wicked restore the pledge, **g** H7999
27 the open field will I **g** to the beasts to be H5414
36:26 A new heart also will I **g** you, and a H5414
26 flesh, and I will **g** you an heart of flesh. H5414
39: 4 that *is* with thee: I will **g** thee unto the H5414
11 day, *that* I will **g** unto Gog a place there H5414
43:19 And thou shalt **g** to the priests the H5414
44:28 and ye shall **g** them no possession H5414
30 ye shall also **g** unto the priest the first H5414
45: 8 *of* the land shall they **g** to the house of H5414
13 wheat, and ye shall **g** the sixth part of an
16 All the people of the land shall **g** H1961+H413
17 And it shall be the prince's part *to* **g**
46: 5 able to **g**, and an hin of oil to an ephah. H4991
11 able to **g**, and an hin of oil to an ephah. H4991
16 GOD; If the prince **g** a gift unto any of H5414
17 But if he **g** a gift of his inheritance to H5414
18 *but* he shall **g** his sons inheritance
47:14 up mine hand to **g** it unto your fathers: H5414
23 there shall ye **g** *him* his inheritance, H5414
Dan 1:12 **g** us pulse to eat, and water to drink. H5414
2:16 that he would **g** him time, and that H5415
5:17 gifts be to thyself, and **g** thy rewards to H3052
6: 2 that the princes might **g** accounts unto H3052
8:13 of desolation, to **g** both the sanctuary H5414
9:22 forth to **g** thee skill and understanding.
11:17 do: and he shall **g** him the daughter of H5414
21 they shall not **g** the honour of the H5414
Hos 2: 5 my lovers, that **g** *me* my bread and my H5414
15 And I will **g** her her vineyards from H5414
4:18 her rulers *with* shame do love, **G** ye. H3051
5: 1 of Israel; and **g** ye ear, O house of the
9:14 **G** them, O LORD: what wilt thou give? H5414
14 Give them, O LORD: what wilt thou **g**? H5414
14 wilt thou give? **g** them a miscarrying H5414
11: 8 How shall I **g** thee up, Ephraim? *how* H5414
13:10 thou saidst, **G** me a king and princes? H5414
Joel 1: 2 Hear this, ye old men, and **g** ear, all ye
2:17 O LORD, and **g** not thine heritage to H5414
Mic 1:14 Therefore shalt thou **g** presents to H5414
5: 3 Therefore will he **g** them up, until the H5414
6: 7 of oil? shall I **g** my firstborn *for* my H5414
14 thou deliverest will I **g** up to the sword. H5414
Hag 2: 9 will I **g** peace, saith the LORD of hosts. H5414
Zec 3: 7 courts, and I will **g** thee places to walk H5414
8:12 the vine shall **g** her fruit, and the H5414
12 the ground shall **g** her increase, and the H5414
12 the heavens shall **g** their dew; and I will H5414
10: 1 bright clouds, and **g** them showers of H5414
11:12 If ye think good, **g** *me* my price; and if H3051
Mal 2: 2 not lay *it* to heart, to **g** glory unto my H5414
Mt 4: 6 is written, He shall **g** his angels charge *G1781*
9 All these things will I **g** thee, if thou wilt *G1325*
5:31 let him **g** her a writing of divorcement: *G1325*
42 **G** to him that asketh thee, and from *G1325*
6:11 **G** us this day our daily bread. *G1325*
7: 6 **G** not that which is holy unto the dogs, *G1325*
9 son ask bread, will he **g** him a stone? *G3361*
10 Or if he ask a fish, will he **g** him a *G3361*
11 If ye then, being evil, know how to **g** *G1325*
11 **g** good things to them that ask him? *G1325*
9:24 He said unto them, **G** place: for the maid *G402*
10: 8 devils: freely ye have received, freely **g**. *G1325*
42 And whosoever shall **g** to drink unto *G4222*
11:28 are heavy laden, and I will **g** you rest. *G373*
12:36 speak, they shall **g** account thereof in the *G591*
14: 7 to **g** her whatsoever she would ask. *G1325*
8 of her mother, said, **G** me here John *G1325*
16 They need not depart; **g** ye them to eat. *G1325*
16:19 And I will **g** unto thee the keys of the *G1325*
26 shall a man **g** in exchange for his soul? *G1325*
17:27 take, and **g** unto them for me and thee. *G1325*
19: 7 Moses then command to **g** a writing of *G1325*
21 thou hast, and **g** to the poor, and thou *G1325*
20: 4 I will **g** you. And they went their way. *G1325*
8 Call the labourers, and **g** them *their* hire, *G591*
14 I will **g** unto this last, even as unto thee. *G1325*
23 my left, is not mine to **g**, but *it shall be* *G1325*
28 and to **g** his life a ransom for many. *G1325*
22:17 lawful to **g** tribute unto Caesar, or not? *G1325*
24:19 and to them that **g** suck in those days!

Mt 24:29 the moon shall not **g** her light, and the *G1325*
45 to **g** them meat in due season? *G1325*
25: 8 And the foolish said unto the wise, **G** us *G1325*
28 **g** *it* unto him which hath ten talents. *G1325*
26:15 And said *unto them*, What will ye **g** *G1325*
53 and he shall presently **g** me more than *G3936*
Mk 6:22 thou wilt, and I will **g** *it* thee. *G1325*
23 **g** *it* thee, unto the half of my kingdom. *G1325*
25 I will that thou **g** me by and by in a *G1325*
37 He answered and said unto them, **G** ye *G1325*
37 of bread, and **g** them to eat? *G1325*
8:37 Or what shall a man **g** in exchange for *G1325*
9:41 For whosoever shall **g** you a cup of *G4222*
10:21 thou hast, and **g** to the poor, and thou *G1325*
40 is not mine to **g**; but *it shall be given* *G1325*
45 and to **g** his life a ransom for many. *G1325*
12: 9 and will **g** the vineyard unto others. *G1325*
14 it lawful to **g** tribute to Caesar, or not? *G1325*
15 Shall we **g**, or shall we not give? But he, *G1325*
15 Shall we give, or shall we not **g**? But he, *G1325*
13:17 and to them that **g** suck in those days!
24 and the moon shall not **g** her light, *G1325*
14:11 and promised to **g** him money. And he *G1325*
Lk 1:32 and the Lord God shall **g** unto him the *G1325*
77 To **g** knowledge of salvation unto his *G1325*
79 To **g** light to them that sit in darkness *G2014*
4: 6 this power will I **g** thee, and the glory of *G1325*
6 me; and to whomsoever I will I **g** it. *G1325*
10 For it is written, He shall **g** his angels *G1781*
6:30 **G** to every man that asketh of thee; and *G1325*
38 **G**, and it shall be given unto you; good *G1325*
38 over, shall men **g** into your bosom. For *G1325*
8:55 and he commanded to **g** her meat. *G1325*
9:13 But he said unto them, **G** ye them to *G1325*
10: 7 such things as they **g**: for the labourer is *G3844*
19 Behold, I **g** unto you power to tread on *G1325*
11: 3 **G** us day by day our daily bread. *G1325*
7 me in bed; I cannot rise and **g** thee. *G1325*
8 will not rise and **g** him, because he is *G1325*
8 rise and **g** him as many as he needeth. *G1325*
11 is a father, will he **g** him a stone? or if *G1929*
11 a fish, will he for a fish **g** him a serpent? *G1929*
13 If ye then, being evil, know how to **g** *G1325*
13 **g** the Holy Spirit to them that ask him? *G1325*
36 shining of a candle doth **g** thee light. *G5461*
41 But rather **g** alms of such things as ye *G1325*
12:32 good pleasure to **g** you the kingdom. *G1325*
33 Sell that ye have, and **g** alms; provide *G1325*
42 his household, to **g** *them their* portion *G1325*
51 Suppose ye that I am come to **g** peace *G1325*
58 *art* in the way, **g** diligence that thou *G1325*
14: 9 and say to thee, **G** this man place; and *G1325*
15:12 *his* father, Father, **g** me the portion of *G1325*
16: 2 I hear this of thee? **g** an account of thy *G591*
12 shall **g** you that which is your own? *G1325*
17:18 There are not found that returned to **g** *G1325*
18:12 I fast twice in the week, I **g** tithes of all
19: 8 half of my goods I **g** to the poor; and if I *G1325*
24 and **g** *it* to him that hath ten pounds. *G1325*
20:10 that they should **g** him of the fruit of *G1325*
16 and shall **g** the vineyard to others. *G1325*
22 Is it lawful for us to **g** tribute unto *G1325*
21:15 For I will **g** you a mouth and wisdom, *G1325*
23 and to them that **g** suck, in those days!
22: 5 glad, and covenanted to **g** him money. *G1325*
23: 2 and forbidding to **g** tribute to Caesar, *G1325*
Jn 1:22 thou? that we may **g** an answer to them *G1325*
4: 7 Jesus saith unto her, **G** me to drink. *G1325*
10 that saith to thee, **G** me to drink; thou *G1325*
14 the water that I shall **g** him shall never *G1325*
14 water that I shall **g** him shall be in him *G1325*
15 The woman saith unto him, Sir, **g** me *G1325*
6:27 Son of man shall **g** unto you: for him *G1325*
34 him, Lord, evermore **g** us this bread. *G1325*
51 bread that I will **g** is my flesh, which I *G1325*
51 which I will **g** for the life of the world. *G1325*
52 How can this man **g** us *his* flesh to eat? *G1325*
7:19 Did not Moses **g** you the law, and *yet* *G1325*
9:24 said unto him, **G** God the praise: we *G1325*
10:28 And I **g** unto them eternal life; and they *G1325*
11:22 thou wilt ask of God, God will **g** *it* thee. *G1325*
13:26 is, to whom I shall **g** a sop, when I have *G1929*
29 that he should **g** something to the poor. *G1325*
34 A new commandment I **g** unto you, *G1325*
14:16 and he shall **g** you another Comforter, *G1325*
27 Peace I leave with you, my peace I **g** *G1325*
27 the world giveth, **g** I unto you. Let not *G1325*
15:16 Father in my name, he may **g** it you. *G1325*
16:23 the Father in my name, he will **g** *it* you. *G1325*

Jn 17: 2 that he should **g** eternal life to as many *G1325*
Act 3: 6 but such as I have **g** I thee: In the name *G1325*
5:31 a Saviour, for to **g** repentance to Israel, *G1325*
6: 4 But we will **g** ourselves continually to
7: 5 that he would **g** it to him for a *G1325*
38 received the lively oracles to **g** unto us: *G1325*
8:19 Saying, **G** me also this power, that on *G1325*
10:43 To him **g** all the prophets witness, that *G3140*
13:16 Israel, and ye that fear God, **g** audience.
34 I will **g** you the sure mercies of David. *G1325*
19:40 we may **g** an account of this concourse. *G591*
20:32 you up, and to **g** you an inheritance *G1325*
35 It is more blessed to **g** than to receive. *G1325*
Ro 8:32 not with him also freely **g** us all things? *G5483*
12:19 but *rather* **g** place unto wrath: for *G1325*
20 him; if he thirst, **g** him drink: for in so *G4222*
14:12 So then every one of us shall **g** account *G1325*
16: 4 whom not only I **g** thanks, but also all
1Co 7: 5 a time, that ye may **g** yourselves to *G4980*
25 of the Lord: yet I **g** my judgment, as *G1325*
10:30 spoken of for that for which I **g** thanks?
32 **G** none offence, neither to the Jews, nor *G1096*
12: 3 Wherefore I **g** you to understand, that *G1107*
13: 3 and though I **g** my body to be burned, *G3860*
14: 7 harp, except they **g** a distinction in the *G1325*
8 For if the trumpet **g** an uncertain *G1325*
2Co 4: 6 shined in our hearts, to **g** the light of the
5:12 unto you, but **g** you occasion to glory *G1325*
8:10 And herein I **g** *my* advice: for this is *G1325*
9: 7 heart, *so let him* **g**; not grudgingly, or of
Eph 1:16 Cease not to **g** thanks for you, making
17 of glory, may **g** unto you the spirit of *G1325*
4:27 Neither **g** place to the devil. *G1325*
28 he may have to **g** to him that needeth. *G3330*
5:14 the dead, and Christ shall **g** thee light. *G2017*
Col 1: 3 We **g** thanks to God and the Father of
4: 1 Masters, **g** unto *your* servants that *G3930*
1Th 1: 2 We **g** thanks to God always for you all,
5:18 In every thing **g** thanks: for this is the
2Th 2:13 But we are bound to **g** thanks alway to
3:16 Now the Lord of peace himself **g** you *G1325*
1Ti 1: 4 Neither **g** heed to fables and endless
4:13 Till I come, **g** attendance to reading, to
15 Meditate upon these things; **g** thyself *G2468*
5: 7 And these things **g** in charge, that they
14 guide the house, **g** none occasion to the *G1325*
6:13 I **g** thee charge in the sight of God, who *G3853*
2Ti 1:16 The Lord **g** mercy unto the house of *G1325*
2: 7 Consider what I say; and the Lord **g** *G1325*
25 peradventure will **g** them repentance to *G1325*
4: 8 judge, shall **g** me at that day: and *G591*
Heb 2: 1 Therefore we ought to **g** the more *G4337*
13:17 as they that must **g** account, that they *G591*
Jas 2:16 ye **g** them not those things *G1325*
1Pt 3:15 *be* ready always to **g** an answer to every
4: 5 Who shall **g** account to him that is ready *G591*
2Pt 1:10 Wherefore the rather, brethren, **g**
1Jn 5:16 ask, and he shall **g** him life for them *G1325*
Rev 2: 7 overcometh will I **g** to eat of the tree of *G1325*
10 death, and I will **g** thee a crown of life. *G1325*
17 overcometh will I **g** to eat of the hidden *G1325*
17 manna, and will **g** him a white stone, *G1325*
23 hearts: and I will **g** unto every one of *G1325*
26 to him will I **g** power over the nations: *G1325*
28 And I will **g** him the morning star. *G1325*
4: 9 And when those beasts **g** glory and *G1325*
10: 9 said unto him, **G** me the little book. *G1325*
11: 3 And I will **g** *power* unto my two *G1325*
17 Saying, We **g** thee thanks, O Lord God *G2168*
18 that thou shouldest **g** reward unto thy *G1325*
13:15 And he had power to **g** life unto the *G1325*
14: 7 Fear God, and **g** glory to him; for the *G1325*
16: 9 and they repented not to **g** him glory. *G1325*
19 before God, to **g** unto her the cup of *G1325*
17:13 These have one mind, and shall **g** their *G1239*
17 and to agree, and **g** their kingdom unto *G1325*
18: 7 and sorrow **g** her: for she saith in *G1325*
19: 7 Let us be glad and rejoice, and **g** *G1325*
21: 6 and the end. I will **g** unto him that is *G1325*
22:12 is with me, to **g** every man according *G591*

GIVEN

Gen 1:29 And God said, Behold, I have **g** you *H5414*
30 *there is* life, *I have* **g** every green herb for
9: 3 the green herb have I **g** you all things. *H5414*
15: 3 to me thou hast **g** no seed: and, lo, one *H5414*
18 thy seed have I **g** this land, from the *H5414*
16: 5 upon thee: I have **g** my maid into thy *H5414*
20:16 said, Behold, I have **g** thy brother a *H5414*

Gen 21: 7 Sarah should have **g** children suck? for I
24:35 great: and he hath **g** him flocks, and *H5414*
36 unto him hath he **g** all that he hath. *H5414*
27:37 brethren have I **g** to him for servants; *H5414*
29:33 he hath therefore **g** me this *son* also: *H5414*
30: 6 voice, and hath **g** me a son: therefore *H5414*
18 And Leah said, God hath **g** me my hire, *H5414*
18 because I have **g** my maiden to my *H5414*
31: 9 cattle of your father, and **g** *them* to me. *H5414*
33: 5 God hath graciously **g** thy servant. *H2603*
38:14 and she was not **g** unto him to wife. *H5414*
43:23 your father, hath **g** you treasure in your *H5414*
48: 9 whom God hath **g** me in this *place*. And *H5414*
22 Moreover I have **g** to thee one portion *H5414*
Ex 5:16 There is no straw **g** unto thy servants, *H5414*
18 shall no straw be **g** you, yet shall ye *H5414*
16:15 which the LORD hath **g** you to eat. *H5414*
29 See, for that the LORD hath **g** you the *H5414*
21: 4 If his master have **g** him a wife, and *H5414*
31: 6 And I, behold, I have **g** with him *H5414*
Lev 6:17 leaven. I have **g** it *unto them for* their *H5414*
7:34 and have **g** them unto Aaron the *H5414*
36 Which the LORD commanded to be **g** *H5414*
10:14 due, *which* are **g** out of the sacrifices *H5414*
17 holy, and *God* hath **g** it you to bear the *H5414*
17:11 blood: and I have **g** it to you upon the *H5414*
19:20 nor freedom **g** her; she shall be *H5414*
20: 3 because he hath **g** of his seed unto *H5414*
Nu 3: 9 **g** unto him out of the children of Israel. *H5414*
8:16 For they *are* wholly **g** unto me from *H5414*
19 And I have **g** the Levites *as* a gift to *H5414*
16:14 and honey, or **g** us inheritance of fields *H5414*
18: 6 to you *they are* **g** *as* a gift for the LORD, *H5414*
7 shall serve: I have **g** your priest's office *H5414*
8 I also have **g** thee the charge of mine *H5414*
8 unto thee have I **g** them by reason of *H5414*
11 of Israel: I have **g** them unto thee, and *H5414*
12 unto the LORD, them have I **g** thee. *H5414*
19 the LORD, have I **g** thee, and thy sons *H5414*
21 And, behold, I have **g** the children of *H5414*
24 the LORD, I have **g** to the Levites to *H5414*
26 which I have **g** you from them for your *H5414*
20:12 into the land which I have **g** them. *H5414*
24 land which I have **g** unto the children *H5414*
21:29 of Chemosh: he hath **g** his sons that *H5414*
26:54 his inheritance be **g** according to those *H5414*
62 **g** them among the children of Israel. *H5414*
27:12 I have **g** unto the children of Israel. *H5414*
32: 5 let this land be **g** unto thy servants for *H5414*
7 the land which the LORD hath **g** them? *H5414*
9 the land which the LORD had **g** them. *H5414*
33:53 for I have **g** you the land to possess it. *H5414*
Dt 1: 3 had **g** him in commandment unto them;
2: 5 because I have **g** mount Seir unto Esau *H5414*
9 because I have **g** Ar unto the children *H5414*
19 because I have **g** it unto the children *H5414*
24 behold, I have **g** into thine hand Sihon *H5414*
3:18 LORD your God hath **g** you this land to *H5414*
19 abide in your cities which I have **g** you; *H5414*
20 Until the LORD have **g** rest unto your
20 your God hath **g** them beyond Jordan: *H5414*
20 his possession, which I have **g** you. *H5414*
8:10 for the good land which he hath **g** thee. *H5414*
9:23 the land which I have **g** you; then ye *H5414*
12:15 which he hath **g** thee: the unclean and *H5414*
21 which the LORD hath **g** thee, as I have *H5414*
13:12 God hath **g** thee to dwell there, saying, *H5414*
16:17 LORD thy God which he hath **g** thee. *H5414*
20:14 which the LORD thy God hath **g** thee. *H5414*
22:17 And, lo, he hath **g** occasions of speech *H7760*
25:19 thy God hath **g** thee rest from all thine
26: 9 place, and hath **g** us this land, *even* a *H5414*
10 O LORD, hast **g** me. And thou shalt *H5414*
11 thy God hath **g** unto thee, and unto *H5414*
12 of tithing, and hast **g** *it* unto the Levite, *H5414*
13 and also have **g** them unto the Levite, *H5414*
14 unclean *use*, nor **g** *ought* thereof for the *H5414*
15 which thou hast **g** us, as thou swarest *H5414*
28:31 thee: thy sheep *shall be* **g** unto thine *H5414*
32 Thy sons and thy daughters *shall be* **g** *H5414*
52 which the LORD thy God hath **g** thee. *H5414*
53 thy God hath **g** thee, in the siege, and *H5414*
29: 4 Yet the LORD hath not **g** you an heart *H5414*
26 and *whom* he had not **g** unto them: *H2505*
Jos 1: 3 I **g** unto you, as I said unto Moses. *H5414*
13 **g** you rest, and hath given you this land.
13 you rest, and hath **g** you this land. *H5414*
15 Until the LORD have **g** your brethren *H5117*
15 rest, as *he hath* **g** you, and they also

Jos 2: 9 the LORD hath g you the land, and that H5414
14 the LORD hath g us the land, that we H5414
6: 2 See, I have g into thine hand Jericho, H5414
16 for the LORD hath g you the city. H5414
8: 1 up to Ai: see, I have g into thy hand the H5414
14: 3 For Moses had g the inheritance of two H5414
15:19 for thou hast g me a south land; give H5414
17:14 Why hast thou g me *but* one lot and H5414
18: 3 LORD God of your fathers hath g you? H5414
22: 4 And now the LORD your God hath g H5117
7 Moses had g *possession* in Bashan: H5414
23: 1 the LORD had g rest unto Israel from H5117
13 which the LORD your God hath g you. H5414
15 which the LORD your God hath g you. H5414
16 good land which he hath g unto you. H5414
24:13 And I have g you a land for which ye H5414
33 which was g him in mount Ephraim. H5414
Jdg 1:15 for thou hast g me a south land; give H5414
14:20 But Samson's wife was g to his
15: 6 his wife, and g her to his companion. H5414
18 said, Thou hast g this great deliverance H5414
18:10 land: for God hath g it into your hands; H5414
Ru 2:12 a full reward be g thee of the LORD God
1Sa 1:27 g me my petition which I asked of him: H5414
15:28 this day, and hath g it to a neighbour H5414
18:19 should have been g to David, that she H5414
19 g unto Adriel the Meholathite to wife. H5414
22:13 in that thou hast g him bread, and a H5414
25:27 my lord, let it even be g unto the young H5414
44 But Saul had g Michal his daughter, H5414
28:17 g it to thy neighbour, *even* to David: H5414
30:23 which the LORD hath g us, who hath H5414
2Sa 4:10 have g him a reward for his tidings: H5414
7: 1 and the LORD had g him rest round
9: 9 unto him, I have g unto thy master's H5414
12: 8 have g unto thee such and such things. H3254
14 this deed thou hast g great occasion to
17: 7 hath g *is* not good at this time. H3289
18:11 and I would have g thee ten *shekels* of H5414
19:42 the king's *cost*? or hath he g us any gift? H5375
22:36 Thou hast also g me the shield of thy H5414
41 Thou hast also g me the necks of mine H5414
1Ki 1:48 of Israel, which hath g *one* to sit on my H5414
2:21 be g to Adonijah thy brother to wife. H5414
3: 6 that thou hast g him a son to sit on his H5414
12 words: lo, I have g thee a wise and an H5414
13 And I have also g thee that which thou H5414
5: 4 But now the LORD my God hath g me
7 day, which hath g unto David a wise H5414
8:36 hast g to thy people for an inheritance. H5414
56 Blessed *be* the LORD, that hath g rest H5414
9: 7 the land which I have g them; and this H5414
12 had g him; and they pleased him not. H5414
13 which thou hast g me, my brother? And H5414
16 in the city, and g it *for* a present unto H5414
12: 8 which they had g him, and consulted H3289
13: 5 of God had g by the word of the LORD. H5414
18:26 And they took the bullock which was g H5414
2Ki 5: 1 him the LORD had g deliverance unto H5414
17 I pray thee, be g to thy servant two H5414
8:29 the Syrians had g him at Ramah, when H5221
9:15 the Syrians had g him, when he fought H5221
23:11 kings of Judah had g to the sun, at the H5414
25:30 allowance g him of the king, a daily H5414
1Ch 5: 1 his birthright was g unto the sons of H5414
6:61 tribe, *were cities* g out of the half tribe,
63 Unto the sons of Merari *were* g by lot,
71 Unto the sons of Gershom *were* g out of
77 of Merari *were* g out of the tribe of
78 of Jordan, *were* g *them* out of the tribe
22:18 and hath he *not* g you rest on every side?
18 side? for he hath g the inhabitants of H5414
23:25 God of Israel hath g rest unto his people,
28: 5 the LORD hath g me many sons,) he H5414
29: 3 *which* I have g to the house of my God, H5414
14 thee, and of thine own have we g thee. H5414
2Ch 2:12 earth, who hath g to David the king a H5414
6:27 g unto thy people for an inheritance. H5414
7:20 my land which I have g them; and this H5414
14: 6 years; because the LORD had g him rest.
7 *him*, and he hath g us rest on every side.
20:11 which thou hast g us to inherit.
22: 6 which were g him at Ramah, when H5221
25: 9 which I have g to the army of Israel? H5414
32:29 God had g him substance very much. H5414
34:14 book of the law of the LORD g by Moses.
18 the priest hath g me a book. And H5414
36:23 LORD God of heaven g me; and he hath H5414
Ezr 1: 2 of heaven hath g me all the kingdoms H5414

Ezr 4:21 commandment shall be g from me. H7761
6: 4 expenses be g out of the king's house: H3052
8 expenses be g unto these men, that H3052
9 let it be g them day by day without fail: H3052
7: 6 LORD God of Israel had g: and the king H5414
19 The vessels also that are g thee for the H3052
9:13 and hast g us *such* deliverance as this; H5414
Neh 2: 7 the king, let letters be g me to the H5414
10:29 law, which was g by Moses the servant H5414
13: 5 commanded *to be* g to the Levites, and
10 had not been g *them*: for the Levites H5414
Est 2: 3 their things for purification be g *them*: H5414
9 *were* meet to be g her, out of the king's H5414
13 she desired was g her to go with her out H5414
3:11 The silver *is* g to thee, the people also, H5414
14 to be g in every province was H5414
15 the decree was g in Shushan the palace. H5414
4: 8 the decree that was g at Shushan to H5414
5: 3 even g thee to the half of the kingdom. H5414
7: 3 king, let my life be g me at my petition, H5414
8: 7 Behold, I have g Esther the house of H5414
13 to be g in every province *was* H5414
14 the decree was g at Shushan the palace. H5414
9:14 the decree was g at Shushan; and they H5414
Job 3:20 Wherefore is light g to him that is in H5414
23 *Why is light* g to a man whose way is
9:24 The earth is g into the hand of the H5414
10:18 Oh that I had g up the ghost, and no H1478
15:19 Unto whom alone the earth was g, and H5414
22: 7 Thou hast not g water to the weary to
24:23 *Though* it be g him *to be* in safety, H5414
33: 4 breath of the Almighty hath g me life.
34:13 Who hath g him a charge over the earth?
37:10 By the breath of God frost is g: and the H5414
38:36 who hath g understanding to the heart? H5414
39:19 Hast thou g the horse strength? hast H5414
Ps 16: 7 I will bless the LORD, who hath g me
18:35 Thou hast also g me the shield of thy H5414
40 Thou hast also g me the necks of mine H5414
21: 2 Thou hast g him his heart's desire, and H5414
44:11 Thou hast g us like sheep *appointed* for H5414
60: 4 Thou hast g a banner to them that fear H5414
61: 5 vows: thou hast g *me* the heritage of H5414
71: 3 resort: thou hast g commandment to
72:15 And he shall live, and to him shall be g H5414
78:24 and had g them of the corn of heaven. H5414
63 their maidens were not g to marriage.
79: 2 servants have they g *to be* meat unto H5414
111: 5 He hath g meat unto them that fear H5414
112: 9 He hath dispersed, he hath g to the H5414
115:16 earth hath he g to the children of men. H5414
118:18 but he hath not g me over unto death.
120: 3 What shall be g unto thee? or what H5414
124: 6 Blessed *be* the LORD, who hath not g H5414
Prv 19:17 which he hath g will he pay him again. H1576
23: 2 throat, if thou *be* a man g to appetite. H1167
24:21 not with them that are g to change:
Ecc 1:13 travail hath God g to the sons of man H5414
3:10 which God hath g to the sons of men to H5414
5:19 Every man also to whom God hath g H5414
19 and wealth, and hath g him power to eat
6: 2 A man to whom God hath g riches, H5414
8: 8 deliver those that are g to it. H1167
9: 9 which he hath g thee under the sun, H5414
12:11 *which* are g from one shepherd. H5414
Isa 3:11 the reward of his hands shall be g him. H6213
8:18 the LORD hath g me *are* for signs and H5414
9: 6 unto us a son is g: and the government H5414
23:11 the LORD hath g a commandment
33:16 shall be g him; his waters *shall be* sure. H5414
35: 2 of Lebanon shall be g unto it, the H5414
37:10 g into the hand of the king of Assyria. H5414
43:28 and have g Jacob to the curse, and H5414
47: 6 inheritance, and g them into thine H5414
8 Therefore hear now this, *thou that art* g
50: 4 The Lord GOD hath g me the tongue of H5414
55: 4 Behold, I have g him *for* a witness to H5414
Jer 3: 8 had put her away, and g her a bill of H5414
18 g for an inheritance unto your fathers.
6:13 of them every one *is* g to covetousness; H1214
8:10 the greatest is g to covetousness, from H1214
13 g them shall pass away from them. H5414
14 us to silence, and g us water of gall to
11:18 And the LORD hath g me knowledge *of*
12: 7 heritage; I have g the dearly beloved of H5414
13:20 *that* was g thee, thy beautiful flock? H5414
15: 9 she hath g up the ghost; her sun H5301
21:10 LORD: it shall be g into the hand of the H5414
25: 5 the LORD hath g unto you and to your H5414

Jer 27: 5 arm, and have g it unto whom it H5414
6 And now have I g all these lands into H5414
6 the field have I g him also to serve him. H5414
28:14 I have g him the beasts of the field also. H5414
32:22 And hast g them this land, which thou H5414
24 it; and the city is g into the hand of the H5414
25 city is g into the hand of the Chaldeans. H5414
43 it is g into the hand of the Chaldeans. H5414
35:15 land which I have g to you and to your H5414
38: 3 city shall surely be g into the hand of H5414
18 shall this city be g into the hand of the H5414
39:17 thou shalt not be g into the hand of the H5414
44:20 which had g him *that* answer, saying,
47: 7 the LORD hath g it a charge against
50:15 round about: she hath g her hand: her H5414
52:34 a continual diet g him of the king of H5414
Lam 1:11 bread; they have g their pleasant things H5414
2: 7 he hath g up into the hand of H5462
5: 6 We have g the hand *to* the Egyptians, H5414
Ezk 3:20 thou hast not g him warning, he shall
4:15 Then he said unto me, Lo, I have g thee H5414
11:15 unto us is this land g in possession. H5414
15: 6 which I have g to the fire for fuel, so H5414
16:17 silver, which I had g thee, and madest H5414
34 and no reward is g unto thee, therefore H5414
17:18 when, lo, he had g his hand, and hath H5414
18: 7 by violence, hath g his bread to the H5414
8 He *that* hath not g forth upon usury, H5414
13 Hath g forth upon usury, and hath H5414
16 by violence, *but* hath g his bread to the H5414
20:15 land which I had g *them*, flowing with H5414
21:11 And he hath g it to be furbished, that it H5414
28:25 land that I have g to my servant Jacob. H5414
29: 5 gathered: I have g thee for meat to the H5414
20 I have g him the land of Egypt *for* his H5414
33:24 many; the land is g us for inheritance. H5414
35:12 laid desolate, they are g us to consume. H5414
37:25 the land that I have g unto Jacob my H5414
47:11 not be healed; they shall be g to salt. H5414
Dan 2:23 my fathers, who hast g me wisdom and H3052
37 God of heaven hath g thee a kingdom, H3052
38 heaven hath he g into thine hand, and H3052
4:16 a beast's heart be g unto him; and let H3052
5:28 PERES; Thy kingdom is divided, and g H3052
7: 4 a man, and a man's heart was g to it. H3052
6 four heads; and dominion was g to it. H3052
11 destroyed, and g to the burning flame. H3052
14 And there was g him dominion, and H3052
22 and judgment was g to the saints of the H3052
25 and they shall be g into his hand until a H3052
27 heaven, shall be g to the people of the H3052
8:12 And an host was g *him* against the H5414
11: 6 but she shall be g up, and they that H5414
11 the multitude shall be g into his hand. H5414
Hos 2: 9 and my flax g to cover her nakedness.
12 my lovers have g me: and I will make H5414
Joel 2:23 God: for he hath g you the former rain H5414
3: 3 people; and have g a boy for an harlot, H5414
Am 4: 6 And I also have g you cleanness of H5414
9:15 I have g them, saith the LORD thy God. H5414
Nah 1:14 And the LORD hath g a commandment
Mt 7: 7 Ask, and it shall be g you; seek, and ye *G1325*
9: 8 which had g such power unto men. *G1325*
10:19 for it shall be g you in that same hour *G1325*
12:39 shall no sign be g to it, but the sign of *G1325*
13:11 Because it is g unto you to know the *G1325*
11 of heaven, but to them it is not g. *G1325*
12 For whosoever hath, to him shall be g, *G1325*
14: 9 at meat, he commanded *it* to be g *her*. *G1325*
11 in a charger, and g to the damsel: and *G1325*
16: 4 shall no sign be g unto it, but the sign *G1325*
19:11 this saying, save *they* to whom it is g. *G1325*
20:23 give, but *it shall be* g *to them* for whom
21:43 from you, and g to a nation bringing *G1325*
22:30 marry, nor are g in marriage, but are *G1547*
25:29 For unto every one that hath shall be g, *G1325*
26: 9 been sold for much, and g to the poor. *G1325*
28:18 is g unto me in heaven and in earth. *G1325*
Mk 4:11 And he said unto them, Unto you it is g *G1325*
24 and unto you that hear shall more be g. *G4369*
25 For he that hath, to him shall be g: and *G1325*
5:43 that something should be g her to eat. *G1325*
6: 2 *is* this which is g unto him, that even *G1325*
8:12 shall no sign be g unto this generation. *G1325*
10:40 *be* g *to them* for whom it is prepared.
12:25 marry, nor are g in marriage; but are
13:11 shall be g you in that hour, that *G1325*
14: 5 and have been g to the poor. And they *G1325*
23 And he took the cup, and when he had g

Mk 14:44 And he that betrayed him had **g** them a G1325
Lk 6:38 Give, and it shall be **g** unto you; good G1325
8:10 And he said, Unto you it is **g** to know G1325
18 to him shall be **g**; and whosoever hath G1325
11: 9 and it shall be **g** you; seek, and ye shall G1325
29 **g** it, but the sign of Jonas the prophet. G1325
12:48 much is **g**, of him shall be much G1325
17:27 wives, they were **g** in marriage, until the
19:15 to whom he had **g** the money, that he G1325
26 hath shall be **g**; and from him that hath G1325
20:34 this world marry, and are **g** in marriage:
35 neither marry, nor are **g** in marriage:
22:19 my body which is **g** for you: this do in G1325
Jn 1:17 For the law was **g** by Moses, *but* grace G1325
3:27 except it be **g** him from heaven. G1325
35 The Father loveth the Son, and hath **g** G1325
4:10 and he would have **g** thee living water. G1325
5:26 he **g** to the Son to have life in himself; G1325
27 And hath **g** him authority to execute G1325
36 the Father hath **g** me to finish, the G1325
6:11 loaves; and when he had **g** thanks, he
23 bread, after that the Lord had **g** thanks:)
39 of all which he hath **g** me I should lose G1325
65 except it were **g** unto him of my Father. G1325
7:39 Ghost was not yet **g**; because that Jesus
11:57 the Pharisees had **g** a commandment, G1325
12: 5 hundred pence, and **g** to the poor? G1325
13: 3 Jesus knowing that the Father had **g** all G1325
15 For I have **g** you an example, that ye G1325
17: 2 As thou hast **g** him power over all flesh, G1325
2 life to as many as thou hast **g** him. G1325
7 whatsoever thou hast **g** me are of thee. G1325
8 For I have **g** unto them the words G1325
9 thou hast **g** me; for they are thine. G1325
11 **g** me, that they may be one, as we *are*. G1325
14 I have **g** them thy word; and the world G1325
22 gavest me I have **g** them; that they may G1325
24 also, whom thou hast **g** me, be with me G1325
24 which thou hast **g** me: for thou lovedst G1325
18:11 Father hath **g** me, shall I not drink it? G1325
19:11 me, except it were **g** thee from above: G1325
Act 1: 2 the Holy Ghost had **g** commandments
3:16 which is by him hath **g** him this perfect G1325
4:12 under heaven **g** among men, whereby G1325
5:32 God hath **g** to them that obey him. G1325
8:18 Ghost was **g**, he offered them money, G1325
17:16 he saw the city wholly **g** to idolatry.
31 *whereof* he hath **g** assurance unto all G3930
20: 2 those parts, and had **g** them much G3870
21:40 And when he had **g** him licence, Paul G2010
24:26 should have been **g** him of Paul, that he G1325
27:24 hath **g** thee all them that sail with thee. G5483
Ro 5: 5 by the Holy Ghost which is **g** unto us. G1325
11: 8 (According as it is written, God hath **g** G1325
35 Or who hath first **g** to him, and it shall G4272
12: 3 For I say, through the grace **g** unto me, G1325
6 to the grace that is **g** to us, whether G1325
13 Distributing to the necessity of saints; **g** G1377
15:15 of the grace that is **g** to me of God, G1325
1Co 1: 4 of God which is **g** you by Jesus Christ; G1325
2:12 the things that are freely **g** to us of God. G5483
3:10 of God which is **g** unto me, as a wise G1325
11:15 her: for *her* hair is **g** her for a covering. G1325
24 And when he had **g** thanks, he brake *it*,
12: 7 But the manifestation of the Spirit is **g** G1325
8 For to one is **g** by the Spirit the word of G1325
24 together, having **g** more abundant G1325
16: 1 saints, as I have **g** order to the churches
2Co 1:11 may be **g** by many on our behalf. G2168
22 Who hath also sealed us, and **g** the G1325
5: 5 hath **g** unto us the earnest of the Spirit. G1325
18 **g** to us the ministry of reconciliation; G1325
9: 9 abroad; he hath **g** to the poor: his G1325
10: 8 the Lord hath **g** us for edification, and G1325
12: 7 there was **g** to me a thorn in the G1325
13:10 the Lord hath **g** me to edification, and G1325
Gal 2: 9 the grace that was **g** unto me, they gave G1325
3:21 had been a law **g** which could have G1325
21 given which could have **g** life, verily G2227
22 Christ might be **g** to them that believe. G1325
4:15 your own eyes, and have **g** them to me. G1325
Eph 3: 2 of God which is **g** me to you-ward: G1325
7 of the grace of God **g** unto me by the G1325
8 is this grace **g**, that I should preach G1325
4: 7 But unto every one of us is **g** grace G1325
19 Who being past feeling have **g** G3860
5: 2 loved us, and hath **g** himself for us an G3860
6:19 And for me, that utterance may be **g** G1325
Php 1:29 For unto you it is **g** in the behalf of G5483
Php 2: 9 exalted him, and **g** him a name which G5483
Col 1:25 of God which is **g** to me for you, to fulfil G1325
1Th 4: 8 who hath also **g** unto us his holy Spirit. G1325
2Th 2:16 loved us, and hath **g** *us* everlasting G1325
1Ti 3: 2 behaviour, **g** to hospitality, apt to teach;
3 Not **g** to wine, no striker, not greedy of G3943
8 not **g** to much wine, not greedy G4337
4:14 in thee, which was **g** thee by prophecy, G1325
2Ti 1: 7 For God hath not **g** us the spirit of fear; G1325
9 grace, which was **g** us in Christ Jesus G1325
3:16 All scripture *is* **g** by inspiration of God,
Tit 1: 7 soon angry, not **g** to wine, no striker, G3943
7 to wine, no striker, not **g** to filthy lucre;
2: 3 not false accusers, not **g** to much wine, G1402
Phlm 22 your prayers I shall be **g** unto you. G5483
Heb 2:13 and the children which God hath **g** me. G1325
4: 8 For if Jesus had **g** them rest, then G2664
Jas 1: 5 upbraideth not; and it shall be **g** him. G1325
2Pt 1: 3 According as his divine power hath **g** G1433
4 Whereby are **g** unto us exceeding great G1433
3:15 **g** unto him hath written unto you; G1325
1Jn 3:24 in us, by the Spirit which he hath **g** us. G1325
4:13 in us, because he hath **g** us of his Spirit. G1325
5:11 And this is the record, that God hath **g** G1325
20 God is come, and hath **g** us an G1325
Rev 6: 2 and a crown was **g** unto him: and he G1325
4 red: and *power* was **g** to him that sat G1325
4 there was **g** unto him a great sword. G1325
8 And power was **g** unto them over the G1325
11 And white robes were **g** unto every one G1325
7: 2 it was **g** to hurt the earth and the sea, G1325
8: 2 and to them were **g** seven trumpets. G1325
3 censer; and there was **g** unto him much G1325
9: 1 him was **g** the key of the bottomless pit. G1325
3 and unto them was **g** power, as the G1325
5 And to them it was **g** that they should G1325
11: 1 And there was **g** me a reed like unto a G1325
2 it not; for it is **g** unto the Gentiles: and G1325
12:14 And to the woman were **g** two wings of G1325
13: 5 And there was **g** unto him a mouth G1325
5 and power was **g** unto him to continue G1325
7 And it was **g** unto him to make war G1325
7 and power was **g** him over all kindreds, G1325
16: 6 and thou hast **g** them blood to drink; G1325
8 **g** unto him to scorch men with fire. G1325
20: 4 and judgment was **g** unto them: and *I* G1325

GIVER

Isa 24: 2 of usury, so with the **g** of usury to him.
2Co 9: 7 of necessity: for God loveth a cheerful **g**. G1395

GIVEST

Dt 15: 9 brother, and thou **g** him nought; and H5414
10 grieved when thou **g** unto him: because H5414
Job 35: 7 If thou be righteous, what **g** thou him? H5414
Ps 50:19 Thou **g** thy mouth to evil, and thy H7971
80: 5 **g** them tears to drink in great measure.
104:28 *That* thou **g** them they gather: thou H5414
145:15 thou **g** them their meat in due season. H5414
Prv 6:35 rest content, though thou **g** many gifts.
Ezk 3:18 die; and thou **g** him not warning, nor
16:33 They give gifts to all whores: but thou **g** H5414
34 and in that thou **g** a reward, and no H5414
1Co 14:17 For thou verily **g** thanks well, but the

GIVETH

Gen 49:21 Naphtali *is* a hind let loose: he **g** goodly H5414
Ex 16:29 therefore he **g** you on the sixth day H5414
20:12 land which the LORD thy God **g** thee. H5414
25: 2 of every man that **g** it willingly with his
Lev 20: 2 in Israel, that **g** *any* of his seed unto H5414
4 the man, when he **g** of his seed unto H5414
27: 9 **g** of such unto the LORD shall be holy. H5414
Nu 5:10 any man **g** the priest, it shall be his. H5414
Dt 2:29 the land which the LORD our God **g** us. H5414
4: 1 the LORD God of your fathers **g** you. H5414
21 thy God **g** thee *for* an inheritance: H5414
40 the LORD thy God **g** thee, for ever. H5414
5:16 land which the LORD thy God **g** thee. H5414
8:18 God: for *it is* he that **g** thee power to get H5414
9: 6 the LORD thy God **g** thee not this good H5414
11:17 the good land which the LORD **g** you. H5414
31 the LORD your God **g** you, and ye shall H5414
12: 1 God of thy fathers **g** thee to possess it, H5414
9 which the LORD your God **g** you. H5414
10 the LORD your God **g** you to inherit, and
10 and *when* he **g** you rest from all your
13: 1 dreams, and **g** thee a sign or a wonder, H5414
15: 4 **g** thee *for* an inheritance to possess it: H5414
Dt 15: 7 the LORD thy God **g** thee, thou shalt H5414
16: 5 gates, which the LORD thy God **g** thee: H5414
18 the LORD thy God **g** thee, throughout H5414
20 land which the LORD thy God **g** thee. H5414
17: 2 the LORD thy God **g** thee, man or H5414
14 the LORD thy God **g** thee, and shalt H5414
18: 9 the LORD thy God **g** thee, thou shalt H5414
19: 1 the LORD thy God **g** thee, and thou H5414
2 the LORD thy God **g** thee to possess it. H5414
3 the LORD thy God **g** thee to inherit, into
10 which the LORD thy God **g** thee *for* an H5414
14 the LORD thy God **g** thee to possess it. H5414
21: 1 the LORD thy God **g** thee to possess it, H5414
23 thy God **g** thee *for* an inheritance. H5414
24: 3 divorcement, and **g** *it* in her hand, and H5414
4 thy God **g** thee *for* an inheritance. H5414
25:15 land which the LORD thy God **g** thee. H5414
19 which the LORD thy God **g** thee *for* an H5414
26: 1 which the LORD thy God **g** thee *for* an H5414
2 the LORD thy God **g** thee, and shalt put H5414
27: 2 the LORD thy God **g** thee, that thou H5414
3 the LORD thy God **g** thee, a land that H5414
28: 8 land which the LORD thy God **g** thee. H5414
Jos 1:11 the LORD your God **g** you to possess it. H5414
15 LORD your God **g** them: then ye shall H5414
Jdg 11:24 Chemosh thy god **g** thee to possess? So H5414
21:18 Cursed *be* he that **g** a wife to Benjamin. H5414
Job 5:10 Who **g** rain upon the earth, and H5414
14:10 man **g** up the ghost, and where *is* he? H1478
32: 8 of the Almighty **g** them understanding.
33:13 he **g** not account of any of his matters.
34:29 When he **g** quietness, who then can
35:10 my maker, who **g** songs in the night; H5414
12 There they cry, but none **g** answer,
36: 6 of the wicked: but **g** right to the poor. H5414
31 For by them judgeth he the people; he **g** H5414
Ps 18:50 Great deliverance **g** he to his king; and
37:21 but the righteous sheweth mercy, and **g**. H5414
68:35 God of Israel *is* he that **g** strength and H5414
119:130 The entrance of thy words **g** light; it
130 it **g** understanding unto the simple.
127: 2 sorrows: *for* so he **g** his beloved sleep. H5414
136:25 Who **g** food to all flesh: for his mercy H5414
144:10 *It is he* that **g** salvation unto kings: who H5414
146: 7 oppressed: which **g** food to the hungry. H5414
147: 9 He **g** to the beast his food, *and* to the H5414
16 He **g** snow like wool: he scattereth the H5414
Prv 2: 6 For the LORD **g** wisdom: out of his H5414
3:34 scorners: but he **g** grace unto the lowly. H5414
13:15 Good understanding **g** favour: but the H5414
17: 4 A wicked doer **g** heed to false lips; *and* a
4 *and* a liar **g** ear to a naughty tongue.
19: 6 every man *is* a friend to him that **g** gifts.
21:26 but the righteous **g** and spareth not. H5414
22: 9 for he **g** of his bread to the poor. H5414
16 **g** to the rich, *shall* surely *come* to want. H5414
23:31 it is red, when it **g** his colour in the cup, H5414
24:26 *Every man* shall kiss *his* lips that **g** a H7725
26: 8 a sling, so *is* he that **g** honour to a fool. H5414
28:27 He that **g** unto the poor shall not lack: H5414
31:15 while it is yet night, and **g** meat to her H5414
Ecc 2:26 For *God* **g** to a man that *is* good in his H5414
26 to the sinner he **g** travail, to gather and H5414
5:18 which God **g** him: for it *is* his portion. H5414
6: 2 desireth, yet God **g** him not power to eat
7:12 *that* wisdom **g** life to them that have it.
8:15 life, which God **g** him under the sun. H5414
Isa 40:29 He **g** power to the faint; and to *them* H5414
42: 5 out of it; he that **g** breath unto the H5414
Jer 5:24 our God, that **g** rain, both the former H5414
22:13 wages, and **g** him not for his work; H5414
31:35 Thus saith the LORD, which **g** the sun H5414
Lam 3:30 He **g** *his* cheek to him that smiteth him: H5414
Dan 2:21 up kings: he **g** wisdom unto the wise, H3052
4:17 of men, and **g** it to whomsoever he H5415
25 of men, and **g** it to whomsoever he will. H5415
32 of men, and **g** it to whomsoever he will. H5415
Hab 2:15 Woe unto him that **g** his neighbour
Mt 5:15 it **g** light unto all that are in the house.
Jn 3:34 **g** not the Spirit by measure *unto him*. G1325
6:32 **g** you the true bread from heaven. G1325
33 from heaven, and **g** life unto the world. G1325
37 All that the Father **g** me shall come to G1325
10:11 good shepherd **g** his life for the sheep. G5087
14:27 not as the world **g**, give I unto you. Let G1325
21:13 bread, and **g** them, and fish likewise. G1325
Act 17:25 **g** to all life, and breath, and all things; G1325
Ro 12: 8 he that **g**, *let him do it* with simplicity; G3330
14: 6 to the Lord, for he **g** God thanks; and G2168

Ro 14: 6 Lord he eateth not, and g God thanks. G2168
1Co 3: 7 watereth; but God that g the increase.
7:38 So then he that g *her* in marriage doeth
38 that g *her* not in marriage doeth better. G1547
15:38 But God g it a body as it hath pleased G1325
57 But thanks *be* to God, which g us the G1325
2Co 3: 6 for the letter killeth, but the spirit g life.
1Ti 6:17 God, who g us richly all things to enjoy; G3930
Jas 1: 5 ask of God, that g to all *men* liberally, G1325
4: 6 But he g more grace. Wherefore he G1325
6 proud, but g grace unto the humble. G1325
1Pt 4:11 the ability which God g: that God in all G5524
5: 5 the proud, and g grace to the humble. G1325
Rev 22: 5 for the Lord God g them light: and they G5461

GIVING
Gen 24:19 And when she had done g him drink, she
Dt 10:18 stranger, in g him food and raiment. H5414
21:17 *for* the firstborn, by g him a double H5414
Ru 1: 6 had visited his people in g them bread. H5414
1Ki 5: 9 my desire, in g food for my household. H5414
2Ch 6:23 g him according to his righteousness. H5414
Ezr 3:11 in praising and g thanks unto the LORD;
Job 11:20 hope *shall be as* the g up of the ghost. H4646
Mt 24:38 marrying and g in marriage, until the
Lk 17:16 And fell down on *his* face at his feet, g G2168
Act 8: 9 g out that himself was some great one: G3004
15: 8 them witness, g them the Holy Ghost, G1325
Ro 4:20 but was strong in faith, g glory to God; G1325
9: 4 and the g of the law, and the service G3548
1Co 14: 7 And even things without life g sound, G1325
16 say Amen at thy g of thanks, seeing he
2Co 6: 3 G no offence in any thing, that the G1325
Eph 5: 4 not convenient: but rather g of thanks.
20 G thanks always for all things unto God
Php 4:15 g and receiving, but ye only. G1394
Col 1:12 G thanks unto the Father, which hath
3:17 g thanks to God and the Father by him.
1Ti 2: 1 *and* g of thanks, be made for all men;
4: 1 depart from the faith, g heed to seducing
Tit 1:14 Not g heed to Jewish fables, and
Heb 13:15 the fruit of *our* lips g thanks to his name.
1Pt 3: 7 to knowledge, g honour unto the wife, G632
2Pt 1: 5 And beside this, g all diligence, add to G3923
Jude 7 in like manner, g themselves over to

GIZONITE
1Ch 11:34 The sons of Hashem the G, Jonathan H1493

GLAD
Ex 4:14 he seeth thee, he will be g in his heart. H8055
Jdg 18:20 And the priest's heart was g, and he H3190
1Sa 11: 9 *it* to the men of Jabesh; and they were g. H8055
1Ki 8:66 tents joyful and g of heart for all the H2896
1Ch 16:31 Let the heavens be g, and let the earth H8055
2Ch 7:10 into their tents, g and merry in heart H8056
Est 5: 9 day joyful and with a g heart: but when H2896
8:15 the city of Shushan rejoiced and was g. H8056
Job 3:22 Which rejoice exceedingly, *and* are g, H7797
22:19 The righteous see *it*, and are g: and the H8055
Ps 9: 2 I will be g and rejoice in thee: I will sing H8055
14: 7 Jacob shall rejoice, *and* Israel shall be g. H8055
16: 9 Therefore my heart is g, and my glory H8055
21: 6 him exceeding g with thy countenance. H8057
31: 7 I will be g and rejoice in thy mercy: for H1523
32:11 Be g in the LORD, and rejoice, ye H8055
34: 2 the humble shall hear *thereof*, and be g. H8055
35:27 Let them shout for joy, and be g, that H8055
40:16 rejoice and be g in thee: let such as love H8055
45: 8 whereby they have made thee g. H8055
46: 4 shall make g the city of God, the H8055
48:11 Judah be g, because of thy judgments. H1523
53: 6 Jacob shall rejoice, *and* Israel shall be g. H8055
64:10 The righteous shall be g in the LORD, H8055
67: 4 O let the nations be g and sing for joy: H8055
68: 3 But let the righteous be g; let them H8055
69:32 The humble shall see *this, and* be g: and H8055
70: 4 rejoice and be g in thee: and let such H8055
90:14 we may rejoice and be g all our days. H8055
15 Make us g according to the days H8055
92: 4 For thou, LORD, hast made me g H8055
96:11 let the earth be g; let the sea roar, and H1523
97: 1 let the multitude of isles be g *thereof*. H8055
8 Zion heard, and was g; and the H8055
104:15 And wine *that* maketh g the heart of H8055
34 shall be sweet: I will be g in the LORD. H8055
105:38 Egypt was g when they departed: for H8055
107:30 Then are they g because they be quiet; H8055
118:24 made; we will rejoice and be g in it. H8055
Ps 119:74 They that fear thee will be g when they H8055
122: 1 I was g when they said unto me, Let us H8055
126: 3 great things for us; *whereof* we are g. H8056
Prv 10: 1 A wise son maketh a g father: but a H8055
12:25 it stoop: but a good word maketh it g. H8055
15:20 A wise son maketh a g father: but a H8055
17: 5 *and* he that is g at calamities shall not H8056
23:25 Thy father and thy mother shall be g, H8055
24:17 thine heart be g when he stumbleth: H1523
27:11 My son, be wise, and make my heart g, H8055
Song 1: 4 we will be g and rejoice in thee, H1523
Isa 25: 9 will be g and rejoice in his salvation. H1523
35: 1 place shall be g for them; and the H7797
39: 2 And Hezekiah was g of them, and H8055
65:18 But be ye g and rejoice for ever *in that* H7797
66:10 Rejoice ye with Jerusalem, and be g H1523
Jer 20:15 is born unto thee; making him very g. H8055
41:13 that *were* with him, then they were g. H8055
50:11 Because ye were g, because ye rejoiced, H8055
Lam 1:21 trouble; they are g that thou hast done H7797
4:21 Rejoice and be g, O daughter of Edom, H8055
Dan 6:23 Then was the king exceeding g for him, H2868
Hos 7: 3 They make the king g with their H8055
Joel 2:21 Fear not, O land; be g and rejoice: for H1523
23 Be g then, ye children of Zion, and H1523
Jna 4: 6 So Jonah was exceeding g of the gourd. H8055
Hab 1:15 drag: therefore they rejoice and are g. H1523
Zep 3:14 shout, O Israel; be g and rejoice with all H8055
Zec 10: 7 g; their heart shall rejoice in the LORD. H8055
Mt 5:12 Rejoice, and be exceeding g: for great *is* G21
Mk 14:11 And when they heard *it*, they were g, G5463
Lk 1:19 thee, and to shew thee these g tidings. G2097
8: 1 and shewing the g tidings of the G2097
15:32 merry, and be g: for this thy brother G5463
22: 5 And they were g, and covenanted to G5463
23: 8 he was exceeding g: for he was desirous G5463
Jn 8:56 to see my day: and he saw *it*, and was g. G5463
11:15 And I am g for your sakes that I was G5463
20:20 the disciples g, when they saw the Lord. G5463
Act 2:26 my tongue was g; moreover also my flesh G21
11:23 grace of God, was g, and exhorted them G5463
13:32 And we declare unto you g tidings, how G2097
48 this, they were g, and glorified the word G5463
Ro 10:15 and bring g tidings of good things! G2097
16:19 unto all *men*. I am g therefore on your G5463
1Co 16:17 I am g of the coming of Stephanas and G5463
2Co 2: 2 that maketh me g, but the same which G2165
13: 9 For we are g, when we are weak, and ye G5463
1Pt 4:13 ye may be g also with exceeding joy. G5463
Rev 19: 7 Let us be g and rejoice, and give G5463

GLADLY
Mk 6:20 he did many things, and heard him g. G2234
12:37 And the common people heard him g. G2234
Lk 8:40 the people g received him: for they
Act 2:41 Then they that g received his word were G780
21:17 to Jerusalem, the brethren received us g. G780
2Co 11:19 For ye suffer fools g, seeing ye G2234
12: 9 in weakness. Most g therefore will I G2236
15 And I will very g spend and be spent G2236

GLADNESS
Nu 10:10 Also in the day of your g, and in your H8057
Dt 28:47 and with g of heart, for the abundance H2898
2Sa 6:12 into the city of David with g. H8057
1Ch 16:27 strength and g *are* in his place. H2304
29:22 that day with great g. And they made H8057
2Ch 29:30 sang praises with g, and they bowed H8057
30:21 days with great g: and the Levites and H8057
23 and they kept *other* seven days with g. H8057
Neh 8:17 done so. And there was very great g. H8057
12:27 the dedication with g, both with H8057
Est 8:16 The Jews had light, and g, and joy, and H8057
17 Jews had joy and g, a feast and a good H8342
9:17 and made it a day of feasting and g. H8057
18 and made it a day of feasting and g. H8057
19 Adar *a day of* g and feasting, and a H8057
Ps 4: 7 Thou hast put g in my heart, more than H8057
30:11 off my sackcloth, and girded me with g; H8057
45: 7 thee with the oil of g above thy fellows. H8342
15 With g and rejoicing shall they be H8057
51: 8 Make me to hear joy and g; *that* the H8057
97:11 Light is sown for the righteous, and g H8057
100: 2 Serve the LORD with g: come before his H8057
105:43 people with joy, *and* his chosen with g: H7440
106: 5 may rejoice in the g of thy nation, that H8057
Prv 10:28 The hope of the righteous *shall be* g: but H8057
Song 3:11 and in the day of the g of his heart. H8057
Isa 16:10 And g is taken away, and joy out of the H8057
Isa 22:13 And behold joy and g, slaying oxen, and H8057
30:29 is kept; and g of heart, as when one H8057
35:10 shall obtain joy and g, and sorrow and H8057
51: 3 of the LORD; joy and g shall be found H8057
11 they shall obtain g and joy; *and* sorrow H8342
Jer 7:34 and the voice of g, the voice of the H8057
16: 9 and the voice of g, the voice of the H8057
25:10 and the voice of g, the voice of the H8057
31: 7 For thus saith the LORD; Sing with g H8057
33:11 The voice of joy, and the voice of g, the H8057
48:33 And joy and g is taken from the H1524
Joel 1:16 joy and g from the house of our God? H1524
Zec 8:19 of Judah joy and g, and cheerful feasts; H8057
Mk 4:16 the word, immediately receive it with g; G5479
Lk 1:14 And thou shalt have joy and g; and many G20
Act 2:46 meat with g and singleness of heart, G20
12:14 not the gate for g, but ran in, and told G5479
14:17 filling our hearts with food and g. G2167
Php 2:29 with all g; and hold such in reputation: G5479
Heb 1: 9 thee with the oil of g above thy fellows. G20

GLASS
Job 37:18 *is* strong, *and* as a molten looking g? H7209
1Co 13:12 For now we see through a g, darkly; but G2072
2Co 3:18 face beholding as in a g the glory of the G2734
Jas 1:23 a man beholding his natural face in a g: G2072
Rev 4: 6 *there was* a sea of g like unto crystal: G5193
15: 2 And I saw as it were a sea of g mingled G5193
2 on the sea of g, having the harps of God. G5193
21:18 the city *was* pure gold, like unto clear g. G5194
21 *was* pure gold, as it were transparent g. G5194

GLASSES
Isa 3:23 The g, and the fine linen, and the H1549

GLEAN
Lev 19:10 And thou shalt not g thy vineyard, H5953
Dt 24:21 thou shalt not g *it* afterward: it shall H5953
Ru 2: 2 go to the field, and g ears of corn after H3950
7 And she said, I pray you, let me g and H3950
8 Go not to g in another field, neither H3950
15 And when she was risen up to g, Boaz H3950
15 men, saying, Let her g even among the H3950
16 she may g *them*, and rebuke her not. H3950
23 of Boaz to g unto the end of barley H3950
Jer 6: 9 shall throughly g the remnant of Israel H5953

GLEANED
Jdg 20:45 and they g of them in the highways H5953
Ru 2: 3 And she went, and came, and g in the H3950
17 So she g in the field until even, and H3950
17 g: and it was about an ephah of barley. H3950
18 saw what she had g: and she brought H3950
19 Where hast thou g to day? and where H3950

GLEANING
Lev 23:22 thou gather any g of thy harvest: thou H3951
Jdg 8: 2 of you? *Is* not the g of the grapes of H5955
Isa 17: 6 Yet g grapes shall be left in it, as the H5955
24:13 the g grapes when the vintage is done. H5955
Jer 49: 9 not leave *some* g grapes? if thieves by H5955

GLEANING-GRAPES
See GLEANING and GRAPES.

GLEANINGS
Lev 19: 9 shalt thou gather the g of thy harvest. H3951

GLEDE
Dt 14:13 And the g, and the kite, and the vulture H7201

GLISTERING
1Ch 29: 2 *stones* to be set, g stones, and of divers H6320
Lk 9:29 and his raiment *was* white *and* g. G1823

GLITTER
Ezk 21:10 that it may g: should we then make H1300

GLITTERING
Dt 32:41 If I whet my g sword, and mine hand H1300
Job 20:25 the body; yea, the g sword cometh out H1300
39:23 The quiver rattleth against him, the g H3851
Ezk 21:28 furbished, to consume because of the g: H1300
Nah 3: 3 sword and the g spear: and *there is* a H1300
Hab 3:11 went, *and* at the shining of thy g spear. H1300

GLOOMINESS
Joel 2: 2 A day of darkness and of g, a day of H653
Zep 1:15 g, a day of clouds and thick darkness, H653

GLORIEST
Jer 49: 4 Wherefore **g** thou in the valleys, thy H1984

GLORIETH
Jer 9:24 But let him that **g** glory in this, that he H1984
1Co 1:31 He that **g**, let him glory in the Lord. *G2744*
2Co 10:17 But he that **g**, let him glory in the Lord. *G2744*

GLORIFIED
Lev 10: 3 I will be **g**. And Aaron held his peace. H3513
Isa 26:15 nation: thou art **g**: thou hadst removed H3513
44:23 Jacob, and **g** himself in Israel. H6286
49: 3 servant, O Israel, in whom I will be **g**. H6286
55: 5 Holy One of Israel; for he hath **g** thee. H6286
60: 9 One of Israel, because he hath **g** thee. H6286
21 the work of my hands, that I may be **g**. H6286
61: 3 of the LORD, that he might be **g**. H6286
66: 5 Let the LORD be **g**: but he shall appear H3513
Ezk 28:22 and I will be **g** in the midst of thee: H3513
39:13 that I shall be **g**, saith the Lord GOD. H3513
Dan 5:23 whose *are* all thy ways, hast thou not **g**: H1922
Hag 1: 8 in it, and I will be **g**, saith the LORD. H3513
Mt 9: 8 marvelled, and **g** God, which had given *G1392*
15:31 to see: and they **g** the God of Israel. *G1392*
Mk 2:12 all amazed, and **g** God, saying, We *G1392*
Lk 4:15 in their synagogues, being **g** of all. *G1392*
5:26 And they were all amazed, and they **g** *G1392*
7:16 on all: and they **g** God, saying, That a *G1392*
13:13 she was made straight, and **g** God. *G1392*
17:15 back, and with a loud voice **g** God, *G1392*
23:47 saw what was done, he **g** God, saying, *G1392*
Jn 7:39 *given*; because that Jesus was not yet **g**.) *G1392*
11: 4 that the Son of God might be **g** thereby. *G1392*
12:16 when Jesus was **g**, then remembered *G1392*
23 come, that the Son of man should be **g**. *G1392*
28 have both **g** *it*, and will glorify *it* again. *G1392*
13:31 of man **g**, and God is glorified in him. *G1392*
31 of man glorified, and God is **g** in him. *G1392*
32 If God be **g** in him, God shall also *G1392*
14:13 do, that the Father may be **g** in the Son. *G1392*
15: 8 Herein is my Father **g**, that ye bear *G1392*
17: 4 I have **g** thee on the earth: I have *G1392*
10 thine are mine; and I am **g** in them. *G1392*
Act 3:13 our fathers, hath **g** his Son Jesus; whom *G1392*
4:21 all *men* **g** God for that which was done. *G1392*
11:18 their peace, and **g** God, saying, Then *G1392*
13:48 were glad, and **g** the word of the Lord: *G1392*
21:20 And when they heard *it*, they **g** the *G1392*
Ro 1:21 they knew God, they **g** *him* not as God, *G1392*
8:17 *him*, that we may be also **g** together. *G4888*
30 and whom he justified, them he also **g**. *G1392*
Gal 1:24 And they **g** God in me. *G1392*
2Th 1:10 When he shall come to be **g** in his *G1740*
12 Christ may be **g** in you, and ye in him, *G1740*
3: 1 course, and be **g**, even as *it is* with you: *G1392*
Heb 5: 5 So also Christ **g** not himself to be made *G1392*
1Pt 4:11 in all things may be **g** through Jesus *G1392*
14 evil spoken of, but on your part he is **g**. *G1392*
Rev 18: 7 How much she hath **g** herself, and lived *G1392*

GLORIFIETH
Ps 50:23 Whoso offereth praise **g** me: and to H3513

GLORIFY
Ps 22:23 the seed of Jacob, **g** him; and fear him, H3513
50:15 I will deliver thee, and thou shalt **g** me. H3513
86: 9 thee, O Lord; and shall **g** thy name. H3513
12 and I will **g** thy name for evermore. H3513
Isa 24:15 Wherefore **g** ye the LORD in the fires, H3513
25: 3 Therefore shall the strong people **g** H3513
60: 7 and I will **g** the house of my glory. H6286
Jer 30:19 **g** them, and they shall not be small. H3513
Mt 5:16 and **g** your Father which is in heaven. *G1392*
Jn 12:28 Father, **g** thy name. Then came there a *G1392*
28 both glorified *it*, and will **g** *it* again. *G1392*
13:32 God shall also **g** him in himself, and *G1392*
32 himself, and shall straightway **g** him. *G1392*
16:14 He shall **g** me: for he shall receive of *G1392*
17: 1 the hour is come; **g** thy Son, that thy *G1392*
1 thy Son, that thy Son also may **g** thee: *G1392*
5 And now, O Father, **g** thou me with *G1392*
21:19 death he should **g** God. And when he *G1392*
Ro 15: 6 *and* one mouth **g** God, even the Father *G1392*
9 And that the Gentiles might **g** God for *G1392*
1Co 6:20 a price: therefore **g** God in your body, *G1392*
2Co 9:13 this ministration they **g** God for your *G1392*
1Pt 2:12 behold, **g** God in the day of visitation. *G1392*
4:16 but let him **g** God on this behalf. *G1392*
Rev 15: 4 Who shall not fear thee, O Lord, and **g** *G1392*

GLORIFYING
Lk 2:20 And the shepherds returned, **g** and *G1392*
5:25 and departed to his own house, **g** God. *G1392*
18:43 and followed him, **g** God: and all the *G1392*

GLORIOUS
Ex 15: 6 Thy right hand, O LORD, is become **g** in H142
11 who *is* like thee, **g** in holiness, fearful *in* H142
Dt 28:58 mayest fear this **g** and fearful name, H3513
2Sa 6:20 and said, How **g** was the king of Israel H3513
1Ch 29:13 we thank thee, and praise thy **g** name. H8597
Neh 9: 5 and blessed be thy **g** name, which is H3519
Est 1: 4 When he shewed the riches of his **g** H3519
Ps 45:13 The king's daughter *is* all **g** within: her H3520
66: 2 honour of his name: make his praise **g**. H3519
72:19 And blessed *be* his **g** name for ever: H3519
76: 4 Thou *art* more **g** *and* excellent than the H215
87: 3 **G** things are spoken of thee, O city of H3513
111: 3 His work *is* honourable and **g**: and his H1926
145: 5 I will speak of the **g** honour of thy H3519
12 acts, and the **g** majesty of his kingdom. H3519
Isa 4: 2 be beautiful and **g**, and the fruit of the H3519
11:10 the Gentiles seek: and his rest shall be **g**. H3519
22:23 be for a **g** throne to his father's house. H3519
28: 1 of Ephraim, whose **g** beauty *is* a fading H6643
4 And the **g** beauty, which *is* on the head H6643
30:30 And the LORD shall cause his **g** voice H1935
33:21 But there the **g** LORD *will be* unto us a H117
49: 5 yet shall I be **g** in the eyes of the LORD, H3513
60:13 and I will make the place of my feet **g**. H3513
63: 1 this *that is* **g** in his apparel, travelling H1921
12 of Moses with his **g** arm, dividing the H8597
14 thy people, to make thyself a **g** name. H8597
Jer 17:12 A **g** high throne from the beginning *is* H3519
Ezk 27:25 made very **g** in the midst of the seas. H3513
Dan 11:16 shall stand in the **g** land, which by his H6643
41 He shall enter also into the **g** land, and H6643
45 the seas in the **g** holy mountain; yet H6643
Lk 13:17 all the **g** things that were done by him. *G1741*
Ro 8:21 into the **g** liberty of the children of God. *G1391*
2Co 3: 7 in stones, was **g**, so that the children *G1722*
8 ministration of the spirit be rather **g**? *G1722*
10 For even that which was made **g** had *G1392*
11 For if that which is done away *was* **g**, *G1223*
11 much more that which remaineth *is* **g**. *G1722*
4: 4 lest the light of the **g** gospel of Christ, *G1391*
Eph 5:27 That he might present it to himself a **g** *G1741*
Php 3:21 like unto his **g** body, according to *G1391*
Col 1:11 according to his **g** power, unto all *G1391*
1Ti 1:11 According to the **g** gospel of the blessed *G1391*
Tit 2:13 hope, and the **g** appearing of the great *G1391*

GLORIOUSLY
Ex 15: 1 he hath triumphed **g**: the horse and his H1342
21 he hath triumphed **g**; the horse and his H1342
Isa 24:23 in Jerusalem, and before his ancients **g**. H3519

GLORY
Gen 31: 1 our father's hath he gotten all this **g**. H3519
45:13 And ye shall tell my father of all my **g** H3519
Ex 8: 9 And Moses said unto Pharaoh, **G** over H6286
16: 7 ye shall see the **g** of the LORD; for that H3519
10 **g** of the LORD appeared in the cloud. H3519
24:16 And the **g** of the LORD abode upon H3519
17 And the sight of the **g** of the LORD *was* H3519
28: 2 Aaron thy brother for **g** and for beauty. H3519
40 make for them, for **g** and for beauty. H3519
29:43 *tabernacle* shall be sanctified by my **g**. H3519
33:18 he said, I beseech thee, shew me thy **g**. H3519
22 And it shall come to pass, while my **g** H3519
40:34 the **g** of the LORD filled the tabernacle. H3519
35 the **g** of the LORD filled the tabernacle. H3519
Lev 9: 6 **g** of the LORD shall appear unto you. H3519
23 the people: and the **g** of the LORD H3519
Nu 14:10 with stones. And the **g** of the LORD H3519
21 shall be filled with the **g** of the LORD. H3519
22 have seen my **g**, and my miracles, H3519
16:19 and the **g** of the LORD appeared H3519
42 it, and the **g** of the LORD appeared. H3519
20: 6 the **g** of the LORD appeared unto them. H3519
Dt 5:24 shewed us his **g** and his greatness, and H3519
33:17 His **g** *is like* the firstling of his bullock, H1926
Jos 7:19 give, I pray thee, **g** to the LORD God of H3519
1Sa 2: 8 the throne of **g**: for the pillars of the H3519
4:21 saying, The **g** is departed from Israel: H3519
22 And she said, The **g** is departed from H3519
6: 5 and ye shall give **g** unto the God of H3519
1Ki 8:11 of the cloud: for the **g** of the LORD had H3519
2Ki 14:10 lifted thee up: **g** *of this*, and tarry at H3513
1Ch 16:10 **G** ye in his holy name: let the heart of H1984
24 Declare his **g** among the heathen; his H3519
27 **G** and honour *are* in his presence; H1935
28 give unto the LORD **g** and strength. H3519
29 Give unto the LORD the **g** *due* unto his H3519
35 to thy holy name, *and* **g** in thy praise. H7623
22: 5 of fame and of **g** throughout all H8597
29:11 power, and the **g**, and the victory, and H8597
2Ch 5:14 of the cloud: for the **g** of the LORD had H3519
7: 1 and the **g** of the LORD filled the house. H3519
2 because the **g** of the LORD had filled H3519
3 down, and the **g** of the LORD upon the H3519
Est 5:11 And Haman told them of the **g** of his H3519
Job 19: 9 He hath stripped me of my **g**, and taken H3519
29:20 My **g** *was* fresh in me, and my bow was H3519
39:20 the **g** of his nostrils *is* terrible. H1935
40:10 and array thyself with **g** and beauty. H1935
Ps 3: 3 my **g**, and the lifter up of mine head. H3519
4: 2 *will ye turn* my **g** into shame? *how long* H3519
8: 1 who hast set thy **g** above the heavens. H1935
5 hast crowned him with **g** and honour. H3519
16: 9 Therefore my heart is glad, and my **g** H3519
19: 1 The heavens declare the **g** of God; and H3519
21: 5 His **g** *is* great in thy salvation: honour H3519
24: 7 doors; and the King of **g** shall come in. H3519
8 Who *is* this King of **g**? The LORD strong H3519
9 doors; and the King of **g** shall come in. H3519
10 Who is this King of **g**? The LORD of H3519
10 of hosts, he *is* the King of **g**. Selah. H3519
29: 1 give unto the LORD **g** and strength. H3519
2 Give unto the LORD the **g** due unto his H3519
3 waters: the God of **g** thundereth: the H3519
9 temple doth every one speak of *his* **g**. H3519
30:12 To the end that *my* **g** may sing praise H3519
45: 3 mighty, with thy **g** and thy majesty. H1935
49:16 when the **g** of his house is increased; H3519
17 away: his **g** shall not descend after him. H3519
57: 5 *let* thy **g** *be* above all the earth. H3519
8 Awake up, my **g**; awake, psaltery and H3519
11 *let* thy **g** *be* above all the earth. H3519
62: 7 In God *is* my salvation and my **g**: the H3519
63: 2 To see thy power and thy **g**, so *as* I have H3519
11 by him shall **g**: but the mouth of them H1984
64:10 him; and all the upright in heart shall **g**. H1984
72:19 be filled *with* his **g**; Amen, and Amen. H3519
73:24 counsel, and afterward receive me *to* **g**. H3519
78:61 and his **g** into the enemy's hand. H8597
79: 9 salvation, for the **g** of thy name: and H3519
84:11 will give grace and **g**: no good *thing* will H3519
85: 9 fear him; that **g** may dwell in our land. H3519
89:17 For thou *art* the **g** of their strength: and H8597
44 Thou hast made his **g** to cease, and H2892
90:16 servants, and thy **g** unto their children. H1926
96: 3 Declare his **g** among the heathen, his H3519
7 give unto the LORD **g** and strength. H3519
8 Give unto the LORD the **g** *due unto* his H3519
97: 6 and all the people see his **g**. H3519
102:15 and all the kings of the earth thy **g**. H3519
16 build up Zion, he shall appear in his **g**. H3519
104:31 The **g** of the LORD shall endure for H3519
105: 3 **G** ye in his holy name: let the heart of H1984
106: 5 that I may **g** with thine inheritance. H1984
20 Thus they changed their **g** into the H3519
108: 1 sing and give praise, even with my **g**. H3519
5 heavens: and thy **g** above all the earth; H3519
113: 4 nations, *and* his **g** above the heavens. H3519
115: 1 thy name give **g**, for thy mercy, *and* for H3519
138: 5 LORD: for great *is* the **g** of the LORD. H3519
145:11 They shall speak of the **g** of thy H3519
148:13 his **g** *is* above the earth and heaven. H1935
149: 5 Let the saints be joyful in **g**: let them H3519
Prv 3:35 The wise shall inherit **g**: but shame H3519
4: 9 a crown of **g** shall she deliver to thee. H8597
16:31 The hoary head *is* a crown of **g**, *if* it be H8597
17: 6 and the **g** of children *are* their fathers. H8597
19:11 *it is* his **g** to pass over a transgression. H8597
20:29 The **g** of young men *is* their strength: H8597
25: 2 *It is* the **g** of God to conceal a thing: but H3519
27 *men* to search their own **g** *is not* glory. H3519
27 *men* to search their own glory *is not* **g**. H3519
28:12 *there is* great **g**: but when the wicked H8597
Isa 2:10 the LORD, and for the **g** of his majesty. H1926
19 the LORD, and for the **g** of his majesty, H1926
21 the LORD, and for the **g** of his majesty, H1926
3: 8 the LORD, to provoke the eyes of his **g**. H3519
4: 5 for upon all the **g** *shall be* a defence. H3519
5:14 and their **g**, and their multitude, H1926
6: 3 of hosts: the whole earth *is* full of his **g**. H3519
8: 7 and all his **g**: and he shall come up H3519

Isa 10: 3 for help? and where will ye leave your **g**? H3519
12 of Assyria, and the **g** of his high looks. H8597
16 and under his **g** he shall kindle a H3519
18 And shall consume the **g** of his forest, H3519
13:19 And Babylon, the **g** of kingdoms, the H6643
14:18 lie in **g**, every one in his own house. H3519
16:14 an hireling, and the **g** of Moab shall be H3519
17: 3 they shall be as the **g** of the children of H3519
4 to pass, *that* the **g** of Jacob shall be H3519
20: 5 their expectation, and of Egypt their **g**. H8597
21:16 and all the **g** of Kedar shall fail: H3519
22:18 the chariots of thy **g** *shall be* the shame H3519
24 And they shall hang upon him all the **g** H3519
23: 9 stain the pride of all **g**, *and* to bring into H6643
24:16 heard songs, *even* **g** to the righteous. H6643
28: 5 be for a crown of **g**, and for a diadem of H6643
35: 2 and singing: the **g** of Lebanon shall be H3519
2 they shall see the **g** of the LORD, *and* H3519
40: 5 And the **g** of the LORD shall be H3519
41:16 *and* shalt **g** in the Holy One of Israel. H1984
42: 8 *is* my name: and my **g** will I not give to H3519
12 Let them give **g** unto the LORD, and H3519
43: 7 him for my **g**, I have formed him; H3519
45:25 seed of Israel be justified, and shall **g**. H1984
46:13 place salvation in Zion for Israel my **g**. H8597
48:11 and I will not give my **g** unto another. H3519
58: 8 **g** of the LORD shall be thy rearward. H3519
59:19 the west, and his **g** from the rising of H3519
60: 1 the **g** of the LORD is risen upon thee. H3519
2 thee, and his **g** shall be seen upon thee. H3519
7 and I will glorify the house of my **g**. H8597
13 The **g** of Lebanon shall come unto thee, H3519
19 an everlasting light, and thy God thy **g**. H8597
61: 6 and in their **g** shall ye boast yourselves. H3519
62: 2 and all kings thy **g**: and thou shalt be H3519
3 Thou shalt also be a crown of **g** in the H8597
63:15 and of thy **g**: where *is* thy zeal and H8597
66:11 delighted with the abundance of her **g**. H3519
12 a river, and the **g** of the Gentiles like a H3519
18 and they shall come, and see my **g**. H3519
19 have seen my **g**; and they shall declare H3519
19 shall declare my **g** among the Gentiles. H3519
Jer 2:11 their **g** for *that which* doth not profit. H3519
4: 2 in him, and in him shall they **g**. H1984
9:23 Let not the wise *man* **g** in his wisdom, H1984
23 the mighty *man* **g** in his might, let not H1984
23 let not the rich *man* **g** in his riches: H1984
24 But let him that glorieth **g** in this, that H1984
13:11 and for a **g**: but they would not hear. H8597
16 Give **g** to the LORD your God, before he H3519
18 come down, *even* the crown of your **g**. H8597
14:21 the throne of thy **g**: remember, break H3519
22:18 for him, *saying*, Ah lord! or, Ah his **g**! H1935
48:18 down from *thy* **g**, and sit in thirst; for H3519
Ezk 1:28 the likeness of the **g** of the LORD. And H3519
3:12 *be* the **g** of the LORD from his place. H3519
23 and, behold, the **g** of the LORD stood H3519
23 stood there, as the **g** which I saw by the H3519
8: 4 And, behold, the **g** of the God of Israel H3519
9: 3 And the **g** of the God of Israel was gone H3519
10: 4 Then the **g** of the LORD went up from H3519
4 full of the brightness of the LORD'S **g**. H3519
18 Then the **g** of the LORD departed from H3519
19 house; and the **g** of the God of Israel H3519
11:22 them; and the **g** of the God of Israel H3519
23 And the **g** of the LORD went up from H3519
20: 6 and honey, which *is* the **g** of all lands: H6643
15 and honey, which *is* the **g** of all lands; H6643
24:25 the joy of their **g**, the desire of their H8597
25: 9 on his frontiers, the **g** of the country, H6643
26:20 I shall set **g** in the land of the living; H6643
31:18 To whom art thou thus like in **g** and in H3519
39:21 And I will set my **g** among the heathen, H3519
43: 2 And, behold, the **g** of the God of Israel H3519
2 waters: and the earth shined with his **g**. H3519
4 And the **g** of the LORD came into the H3519
5 the **g** of the LORD filled the house. H3519
44: 4 and, behold, the **g** of the LORD filled H3519
Dan 2:37 a kingdom, power, and strength, and **g**. H3367
4:36 me; and for the **g** of my kingdom, mine H3367
5:18 and majesty, and **g**, and honour: H3367
20 throne, and they took his **g** from him: H3367
7:14 dominion, and **g**, and a kingdom, that H3367
11:20 of taxes *in* the **g** of the kingdom: but H1925
39 *and* increase with **g**: and he shall cause H3519
Hos 4: 7 will I change their **g** into shame. H3519
9:11 *As for* Ephraim, their **g** shall fly away H3519
10: 5 on it, for the **g** thereof, because it is H3519
Mic 1:15 come unto Adullam the **g** of Israel. H3519
Mic 2: 9 have ye taken away my **g** for ever. H1926
Nah 2: 9 *and* **g** out of all the pleasant furniture. H3519
Hab 2:14 knowledge of the **g** of the LORD, as the H3519
16 Thou art filled with shame for **g**: drink H3519
16 and shameful spewing *shall be* on thy **g**. H3519
3: 3 mount Paran. Selah. His **g** covered the H1935
Hag 2: 3 house in her first **g**? and how do ye see it H3519
7 house with **g**, saith the LORD of hosts. H3519
9 The **g** of this latter house shall be H3519
Zec 2: 5 and will be the **g** in the midst of her. H3519
8 of hosts; After the **g** hath he sent me H3519
6:13 he shall bear the **g**, and shall sit and H1935
11: 3 for their **g** is spoiled: a voice of H155
12: 7 first, that the **g** of the house of David H8597
7 of David and the **g** of the inhabitants of H8597
Mal 2: 2 lay *it* to heart, to give **g** unto my name, H3519
Mt 4: 8 of the world, and the **g** of them; *G1391*
6: 2 they may have **g** of men. Verily I say *G1392*
13 the power, and the **g**, for ever. Amen. *G1391*
29 his **g** was not arrayed like one of these. *G1391*
16:27 For the Son of man shall come in the **g** *G1391*
19:28 the throne of his **g**, ye also shall sit upon *G1391*
24:30 of heaven with power and great **g**. *G1391*
25:31 shall come in his **g**, and all the holy *G1391*
31 shall he sit upon the throne of his **g**: *G1391*
Mk 8:38 the **g** of his Father with the holy angels. *G1391*
10:37 and the other on thy left hand, in thy **g**. *G1391*
13:26 in the clouds with great power and **g**. *G1391*
Lk 2: 9 upon them, and the **g** of the Lord shone *G1391*
14 **G** to God in the highest, and on earth *G1391*
32 A light to lighten the Gentiles, and the **g** *G1391*
4: 6 give thee, and the **g** of them: for that is *G1391*
9:26 come in his own **g**, and *in his* Father's, *G1391*
31 Who appeared in **g**, and spake of his *G1391*
32 **g**, and the two men that stood with him. *G1391*
12:27 his **g** was not arrayed like one of these. *G1391*
17:18 to give **g** to God, save this stranger. *G1391*
19:38 peace in heaven, and **g** in the highest. *G1391*
21:27 in a cloud with power and great **g**. *G1391*
24:26 these things, and to enter into his **g**? *G1391*
Jn 1:14 we beheld his **g**, the glory as of the only *G1391*
14 his glory, the **g** as of the only begotten *G1391*
2:11 his **g**; and his disciples believed on him. *G1391*
7:18 seeketh his own **g**: but he that seeketh *G1391*
18 he that seeketh his **g** that sent him, the *G1391*
8:50 And I seek not mine own **g**: there is one *G1391*
11: 4 death, but for the **g** of God, that the Son *G1391*
40 thou shouldest see the **g** of God? *G1391*
12:41 when he saw his **g**, and spake of him. *G1391*
17: 5 own self with the **g** which I had with *G1391*
22 And the **g** which thou gavest me I have *G1391*
24 they may behold my **g**, which thou hast *G1391*
Act 7: 2 The God of **g** appeared unto our *G1391*
55 and saw the **g** of God, and Jesus *G1391*
12:23 gave not God the **g**: and he was eaten of *G1391*
22:11 And when I could not see for the **g** of *G1391*
Ro 1:23 And changed the **g** of the uncorruptible *G1391*
2: 7 well doing seek for **g** and honour and *G1391*
10 But **g**, honour, and peace, to every man *G1391*
3: 7 **g**; why yet am I also judged as a sinner? *G1391*
23 sinned, and come short of the **g** of God; *G1391*
4: 2 hath *whereof* to **g**; but not before God. *G2745*
20 but was strong in faith, giving **g** to God; *G1391*
5: 2 and rejoice in hope of the **g** of God. *G1391*
3 And not only *so*, but we **g** in *G2744*
6: 4 the dead by the **g** of the Father, even so *G1391*
8:18 the **g** which shall be revealed in us. *G1391*
9: 4 adoption, and the **g**, and the covenants, *G1391*
23 the riches of his **g** on the vessels of *G1391*
23 which he had afore prepared unto **g**, *G1391*
11:36 things: to whom *be* **g** for ever. Amen. *G1391*
15: 7 Christ also received us to the **g** of God. *G1391*
17 I have therefore whereof I may **g** *G2746*
16:27 To God only wise, *be* **g** through Jesus *G1391*
1Co 1:29 That no flesh should **g** in his presence. *G2744*
31 He that glorieth, let him **g** in the Lord. *G2744*
2: 7 ordained before the world unto our **g**: *G1391*
8 would not have crucified the Lord of **g**. *G1391*
3:21 Therefore let no man **g** in men. For all *G2744*
4: 7 thou **g**, as if thou hadst not received *it*? *G2744*
9:16 I have nothing to **g** of: for necessity is *G2745*
10:31 ye do, do all to the **g** of God. *G1391*
11: 7 he is the image and **g** of God: but the *G1391*
7 but the woman is the **g** of the man. *G1391*
15 But if a woman have long hair, it is a **g** *G1391*
15:40 terrestrial: but the **g** of the celestial *is* *G1391*
40 and the **g** of the terrestrial *is* another. *G1391*
41 *There is* one **g** of the sun, and another *G1391*
41 sun, and another **g** of the moon, and *G1391*
1Co 15:41 and another **g** of the stars: for *one* *G1391*
41 star differeth from *another* star in **g**. *G1391*
43 It is sown in dishonour; it is raised in **g**: *G1391*
2Co 1:20 in him Amen, unto the **g** of God by us. *G1391*
3: 7 of Moses for the **g** of his countenance; *G1391*
7 which **g** was to be done away: *G1391*
9 of condemnation *be* **g**, much more doth *G1391*
9 of righteousness exceed in **g**. *G1391*
10 glorious had no **g** in this respect, by *G1392*
10 by reason of the **g** that excelleth. *G1391*
18 as in a glass the **g** of the Lord, are *G1391*
18 same image from **g** to glory, *even* as by *G1391*
18 to **g**, *even* as by the Spirit of the Lord. *G1391*
4: 6 the **g** of God in the face of Jesus Christ. *G1391*
15 of many redound to the **g** of God. *G1391*
17 more exceeding *and* eternal weight of **g**; *G1391*
5:12 you occasion to **g** on our behalf, that ye *G2745*
12 **g** in appearance, and not in heart. *G2744*
8:19 by us to the **g** of the same Lord, and *G1391*
23 of the churches, *and* the **g** of Christ. *G1391*
10:17 But he that glorieth, let him **g** in the *G2744*
11:12 they **g**, they may be found even as we. *G2744*
18 Seeing that many **g** after the flesh, I will *G2744*
18 many glory after the flesh, I will **g** also. *G2744*
30 If I must needs **g**, I will glory of the *G2744*
30 If I must needs glory, I will **g** of the *G2744*
12: 1 It is not expedient for me doubtless to **g**. *G2744*
5 Of such an one will I **g**: yet of myself I *G2744*
5 I will not **g**, but in mine infirmities. *G2744*
6 For though I would desire to **g**, I shall *G2744*
9 will I rather **g** in my infirmities, that *G2744*
Gal 1: 5 To whom *be* **g** for ever and ever. Amen. *G1391*
5:26 Let us not be desirous of vain **g**, *G2755*
6:13 that they may **g** in your flesh. *G2744*
14 But God forbid that I should **g**, save in *G2744*
Eph 1: 6 To the praise of the **g** of his grace, *G1391*
12 That we should be to the praise of his **g**, *G1391*
14 possession, unto the praise of his **g**. *G1391*
17 the Father of **g**, may give unto you the *G1391*
18 of the **g** of his inheritance in the saints, *G1391*
3:13 my tribulations for you, which is your **g**. *G1391*
16 to the riches of his **g**, to be strengthened *G1391*
21 Unto him *be* **g** in the church by Christ *G1391*
Php 1:11 Christ, unto the **g** and praise of God. *G1391*
2:11 *is* Lord, to the **g** of God the Father. *G1391*
3:19 belly, and *whose* **g** *is* in their shame, *G1391*
4:19 to his riches in **g** by Christ Jesus. *G1391*
20 Now unto God and our Father *be* **g** for *G1391*
Col 1:27 *is* the riches of the **g** of this mystery *G1391*
27 which is Christ in you, the hope of **g**: *G1391*
3: 4 then shall ye also appear with him in **g**. *G1391*
1Th 2: 6 Nor of men sought we **g**, neither of you, *G1391*
12 called you unto his kingdom and **g**. *G1391*
20 For ye are our **g** and joy. *G1391*
2Th 1: 4 So that we ourselves **g** in you in the *G2744*
9 the Lord, and from the **g** of his power; *G1391*
2:14 of the **g** of our Lord Jesus Christ. *G1391*
1Ti 1:17 honour and **g** for ever and ever. Amen. *G1391*
3:16 on in the world, received up into **g**. *G1391*
2Ti 2:10 which is in Christ Jesus with eternal **g**. *G1391*
4:18 to whom *be* **g** for ever and ever. Amen. *G1391*
Heb 1: 3 Who being the brightness of *his* **g**, and *G1391*
2: 7 him with **g** and honour, and didst *G1391*
9 crowned with **g** and honour; that he *G1391*
10 many sons unto **g**, to make the captain *G1391*
3: 3 counted worthy of more **g** than Moses, *G1391*
9: 5 And over it the cherubims of **g** *G1391*
13:21 to whom *be* **g** for ever and ever. Amen. *G1391*
Jas 2: 1 *the Lord* of **g**, with respect of persons. *G1391*
3:14 **g** not, and lie not against the truth. *G2620*
1Pt 1: 7 and **g** at the appearing of Jesus Christ: *G1391*
8 with joy unspeakable and full of **g**: *G1392*
11 of Christ, and the **g** that should follow. *G1391*
21 and gave him **g**; that your faith and *G1391*
24 For all flesh *is* as grass, and all the **g** of *G1391*
2:20 For what **g** *is it*, if, when ye be buffeted *G2811*
4:13 that, when his **g** shall be revealed, ye *G1391*
14 *ye*; for the spirit of **g** and of God resteth *G1391*
5: 1 partaker of the **g** that shall be revealed: *G1391*
4 a crown of **g** that fadeth not away. *G1391*
10 us unto his eternal **g** by Christ Jesus, *G1391*
11 To him *be* **g** and dominion for ever and *G1391*
2Pt 1: 3 him that hath called us to **g** and virtue: *G1391*
17 honour and **g**, when there came such *G1391*
17 from the excellent **g**, This is my beloved *G1391*
3:18 him *be* **g** both now and for ever. Amen. *G1391*
Jude 24 presence of his **g** with exceeding joy, *G1391*
25 To the only wise God our Saviour, *be* **g** *G1391*
Rev 1: 6 Father; to him *be* **g** and dominion for *G1391*

Rev 4: 9 And when those beasts give **g** and G1391
11 Thou art worthy, O Lord, to receive **g** G1391
5:12 and honour, and **g**, and blessing. G1391
13 and honour, and **g**, and power, *be* unto G1391
7:12 Saying, Amen: Blessing, and **g**, and G1391
11:13 and gave **g** to the God of heaven. G1391
14: 7 God, and give **g** to him; for the hour G1391
15: 8 smoke from the **g** of God, and from his G1391
16: 9 and they repented not to give him **g**. G1391
18: 1 and the earth was lightened with his **g**. G1391
19: 1 Salvation, and **g**, and honour, and G1391
21:11 Having the **g** of God: and her light *was* G1391
23 shine in it: for the **g** of God did lighten G1391
24 do bring their **g** and honour into it. G1391
26 And they shall bring the **g** and honour G1391

GLORYING
1Co 5: 6 Your **g** *is* not good. Know ye not that a G2745
9:15 that any man should make my **g** void. G2745
2Co 7: 4 you, great *is* my **g** of you: I am filled G2746
12:11 I am become a fool in **g**; ye have G2744

GLUTTON
Dt 21:20 our voice; *he is* a **g**, and a drunkard. H2151
Prv 23:21 For the drunkard and the **g** shall come H2151

GLUTTONOUS
Mt 11:19 say, Behold a man **g**, and a winebibber, G5314
Lk 7:34 and ye say, Behold a **g** man, and a G5314

GNASH
Ps 112:10 grieved; he shall **g** with his teeth, and H2786
Lam 2:16 thee: they hiss and **g** the teeth: they say, H2786

GNASHED
Ps 35:16 feasts, they **g** upon me with their teeth. H2786
Act 7:54 and they **g** on him with *their* teeth. G1031

GNASHETH
Job 16: 9 who hateth me: he **g** upon me with his H2786
Ps 37:12 the just, and **g** upon him with his teeth. H2786
Mk 9:18 he foameth, and **g** with his teeth, and G5149

GNASHING
Mt 8:12 there shall be weeping and **g** of teeth. G1030
13:42 there shall be wailing and **g** of teeth. G1030
50 there shall be wailing and **g** of teeth. G1030
22:13 there shall be weeping and **g** of teeth. G1030
24:51 there shall be weeping and **g** of teeth. G1030
25:30 there shall be weeping and **g** of teeth. G1030
Lk 13:28 There shall be weeping and **g** of teeth, G1030

GNAT
Mt 23:24 *Ye* blind guides, which strain at a **g**, and G2971

GNAW
Zep 3: 3 they **g** not the bones till the morrow. H1633

GNAWED
Rev 16:10 and they **g** their tongues for pain, G3145

GO
Gen 3:14 belly shalt thou **g**, and dust shalt thou H3212
8:16 **G** forth of the ark, thou, and thy wife, H3318
9:10 you; from all that **g** out of the ark, to H3318
11: 3 And they said one to another, **G** to, let H3051
4 And they said, **G** to, let us build us a H3051
7 **G** to, let us go down, and there H3051
7 Go to, let us **g** down, and there H3381
31 Ur of the Chaldees, to **g** into the land of H3212
12: 5 they went forth to **g** into the land of H3212
19 thy wife, take *her,* and **g** thy way. H3212
13: 9 hand, then I will **g** to the right; or if *thou*
9 to the right hand, then I will **g** to the left.
15: 2 give me, seeing I **g** childless, and the H1980
15 And thou shalt **g** to thy fathers in peace; H935
16: 2 I pray thee, **g** in unto my maid; it may H935
8 whither wilt thou **g**? And she said, I flee H3212
18:21 I will **g** down now, and see whether H3381
19: 2 rise up early, and **g** on your ways. And H1980
34 this night also; and **g** thou in, *and* lie H935
22: 5 and I and the lad will **g** yonder and H3212
24: 4 But thou shalt **g** unto my country, and H3212
11 time that women **g** out to draw *water.* H3318
38 But thou shalt **g** unto my father's H3212
42 now thou do prosper my way which I **g**: H1980
51 thee, take *her,* and **g**, and let her be thy H3212
55 at the least ten; after that she shall **g**. H3212
56 me away that I may **g** to my master. H3212
Gen 24:58 her, Wilt thou **g** with this man? And H3212
58 go with this man? And she said, I will **g**. H3212
26: 2 him, and said, **G** not down into Egypt; H3381
16 And Abimelech said unto Isaac, **G** H3212
27: 3 and thy bow, and **g** out to the field, and H3318
9 **G** now to the flock, and fetch me from H3212
13 obey my voice, and **g** fetch me *them.* H3212
28: 2 Arise, **g** to Padan-aram, to the house of H3212
20 me in this way that I **g**, and will give me H1980
29: 7 ye the sheep, and **g** *and* feed *them.* H3212
21 are fulfilled, that I may **g** in unto her. H935
30: 3 And she said, Behold my maid Bilhah, **g** H935
25 me away, that I may **g** unto mine own H3212
26 thee, and let me **g**: for thou knowest my H3212
31:18 for to **g** to Isaac his father in H935
32:26 And he said, Let me **g**, for the day H7971
26 will not let thee **g**, except thou bless me. H7971
33:12 and let us **g**, and I will go before thee. H3212
12 and let us go, and I will **g** before thee. H3212
35: 1 And God said unto Jacob, Arise, **g** up to H5927
3 And let us arise, and **g** up to Beth-el; H5927
37:14 And he said to him, **G**, I pray thee, see H3212
17 them say, Let us **g** to Dothan. And H3212
30 The child *is* not; and I, whither shall I **g**? H935
35 he said, For I will **g** down into the grave H3381
38: 8 And Judah said unto Onan, **G** in unto H935
16 the way, and said, **G** to, I pray thee, let H3051
41:55 all the Egyptians, **G** unto Joseph; what H3212
42:15 ye shall not **g** forth hence, except H3318
19 of your prison: **g** ye, carry corn for the H3212
38 And he said, My son shall not **g** down H3381
38 in the which ye **g**, then shall ye bring H3212
43: 2 them, **G** again, buy us a little food. H7725
4 us, we will **g** down and buy thee food: H3381
5 *him,* we will not **g** down: for the man H3381
8 we will arise and **g**; that we may live, H3212
13 Take also your brother, and arise, **g** H6965
44:25 And our father said, **G** again, *and* buy H7725
26 And we said, We cannot **g** down: if our H3381
26 us, then will we **g** down: for we may not H3381
33 and let the lad **g** up with his brethren. H5927
34 For how shall I **g** up to my father, and H5927
45: 1 every man to **g** out from me. And there H3318
9 Haste ye, and **g** up to my father, and H5927
17 and **g**, get you unto the land of Canaan; H3212
28 alive: I will **g** and see him before I die. H3212
46: 3 father: fear not to **g** down into Egypt; H3381
4 I will **g** down with thee into Egypt; and H3381
31 house, I will **g** up, and shew Pharaoh, H5927
50: 5 therefore let me **g** up, I pray thee, and H5927
6 And Pharaoh said, **G** up, and bury thy H5927
Ex 2: 7 daughter, Shall I **g** and call to thee a H3212
8 And Pharaoh's daughter said to her, **G**. H3212
3:11 *am* I, that I should **g** unto Pharaoh, H3212
16 **G**, and gather the elders of Israel H3212
18 us: and now let us **g**, we beseech thee, H3212
19 not let you **g**, no, not by a mighty hand. H1980
20 thereof: and after that he will let you **g**. H7971
21 that, when ye **g**, ye shall not go empty: H3212
21 that, when ye go, ye shall not **g** empty: H3212
4:12 Now therefore **g**, and I will be with thy H3212
18 unto him, Let me **g**, I pray thee, and H3212
18 And Jethro said to Moses, **G** in peace. H3212
19 Moses in Midian, **G**, return into Egypt: H3212
21 heart, that he shall not let the people **g**. H7971
23 And I say unto thee, Let my son **g**, that H7971
23 refuse to let him **g**, behold, I will slay H7971
26 So he let him **g**: then she said, A bloody H7503
27 And the LORD said to Aaron, **G** into H3212
5: 1 Let my people **g**, that they may hold H7971
2 his voice to let Israel **g**? I know not the H7971
2 not the LORD, neither will I let Israel **g**. H7971
3 met with us: let us **g**, we pray thee, three H3212
7 **g** and gather straw for themselves. H3212
8 Let us **g** *and* sacrifice to our God. H3212
11 **G** ye, get you straw where ye can find H3212
17 Let us **g** *and* do sacrifice to the LORD. H3212
18 **G** therefore now, *and* work; for there H3212
6: 1 shall he let them **g**, and with a strong H7971
11 **G** in, speak unto Pharaoh king of Egypt, H935
11 the children of Israel **g** out of his land. H7971
7:14 he refuseth to let the people **g**. H7971
16 Let my people **g**, that they may serve H7971
8: 1 And the LORD spake unto Moses, **G** H935
1 my people **g**, that they may serve me. H7971
2 And if thou refuse to let *them* **g**, behold, H7971
3 which shall **g** up and come into thine H5927
8 I will let the people **g**, that they may do H7971
20 my people **g**, that they may serve me. H7971
Ex 8:21 Else, if thou wilt not let my people **g**, H7971
25 **G** ye, sacrifice to your God in the land. H3212
27 We will **g** three days' journey into the H3212
28 And Pharaoh said, I will let you **g**, that H7971
28 not **g** very far away: entreat for me. H3212
29 And Moses said, Behold, I **g** out from H3318
29 the people **g** to sacrifice to the LORD. H7971
32 also, neither would he let the people **g**. H7971
9: 1 Then the LORD said unto Moses, **G** in H935
1 my people **g**, that they may serve me. H7971
2 For if thou refuse to let *them* **g**, and wilt H7971
7 and he did not let the people **g**. H7971
13 my people **g**, that they may serve me. H7971
17 my people, that thou wilt not let them **g**? H7971
28 let you **g**, and ye shall stay no longer. H7971
35 **g**; as the LORD had spoken by Moses. H7971
10: 1 And the LORD said unto Moses, **G** in H935
3 let my people **g**, that they may serve me. H7971
4 Else, if thou refuse to let my people **g**, H7971
7 us? let the men **g**, that they may serve H7971
8 said unto them, **G**, serve the LORD your H3212
8 your God: *but* who *are* they that shall **g**? H1980
9 And Moses said, We will **g** with our H3212
9 our herds will we **g**; for we *must hold* a H3212
10 as I will let you **g**, and your little ones: H7971
11 Not so: **g** now ye *that are* men, and H3212
20 he would not let the children of Israel **g**. H7971
24 Moses, and said, **G** ye, serve the LORD; H3212
24 let your little ones also **g** with you. H3212
26 Our cattle also shall **g** with us; there H3212
27 heart, and he would not let them **g**. H7971
11: 1 he will let you **g** hence: when he shall H7971
1 he shall let *you* **g**, he shall surely thrust H7971
4 will I **g** out into the midst of Egypt: H3318
8 after that I will **g** out. And he went out H3318
10 the children of Israel **g** out of his land. H7971
12:22 none of you shall **g** out at the door of H3318
31 and **g**, serve the LORD, as ye have said. H3212
13:15 hardly let us **g**, that the LORD slew H7971
17 had let the people **g**, that God led them H7971
21 give them light; to **g** by day and night: H3212
14: 5 we have let Israel **g** from serving us? H7971
15 children of Israel, that they **g** forward: H5265
16 of Israel shall **g** on dry *ground* through H935
21 caused the sea to **g** *back* by a strong H3212
16: 4 and the people shall **g** out and gather a H3318
29 **g** out of his place on the seventh day. H3318
17: 5 And the LORD said unto Moses, **G** on H5674
5 the river, take in thine hand, and **g**. H1980
9 us out men, and **g** out, fight with H3318
18:23 shall also **g** to their place in peace. H935
19:10 And the LORD said unto Moses, **G** unto H3212
12 to yourselves, *that ye* **g** *not* up into the H5927
21 And the LORD said unto Moses, **G** H3381
20:26 Neither shalt thou **g** up by steps unto H5927
21: 2 seventh he shall **g** out free for nothing. H3318
3 If he came in by himself, he shall **g** out H3318
3 then his wife shall **g** out with him. H3318
4 master's, and he shall **g** out by himself. H3318
5 and my children; I will not **g** out free: H3318
7 shall not **g** out as the menservants do. H3318
11 shall she **g** out free without money. H3318
26 he shall let him **g** free for his eye's sake. H7971
27 shall let him **g** free for his tooth's sake. H7971
23:23 For mine Angel shall **g** before thee, and H3212
24: 2 neither shall the people **g** up with him. H5927
30:20 When they **g** into the tabernacle of the H935
32: 1 gods, which shall **g** before us; for *as for* H3212
7 And the LORD said unto Moses, **G**, get H3212
23 gods, which shall **g** before us: for *as for* H3212
27 by his side, *and* **g** in and out from gate H5674
30 sin: and now I will **g** up unto the LORD; H5927
34 Therefore now **g**, lead the people unto H3212
34 behold, mine Angel shall **g** before thee: H3212
33: 1 Depart, *and* **g** up hence, thou and H5927
3 for I will not **g** up in the midst of thee; H5927
14 And he said, My presence shall **g** *with* H3212
15 And he said unto him, If thy presence **g** H1980
34: 9 Lord, I pray thee, **g** among us; for it *is* a H3212
15 of the land, and they **g** a whoring after
16 their daughters **g** a whoring after their
16 thy sons **g** a whoring after their gods.
24 when thou shalt **g** up to appear before H5927
Lev 6:13 upon the altar; it shall never **g** out. H3518
8:33 And ye shall not **g** out of the door of the H3318
9: 7 And Moses said unto Aaron, **G** unto H7126
10: 7 And ye shall not **g** out from the door of H3318
9 with thee, when ye **g** into the tabernacle H935
11:27 of beasts that **g** on *all* four, those *are* H1980

Lev 14: 3 And the priest shall **g** forth out of the H3318
36 before the priest **g** *into it* to see the H935
36 the priest shall **g** in to see the house: H935
38 Then the priest shall **g** out of the house H3318
53 But he shall let **g** the living bird out of H7971
15:16 And if any man's seed of copulation **g** H3318
16:10 **g** for a scapegoat into the wilderness. H7971
18 And he shall **g** out unto the altar that *is* H3318
22 he shall let **g** the goat in the wilderness. H7971
26 And he that let **g** the goat for the H7971
19:16 Thou shalt not **g** up and down *as* a H3212
20: 5 off, and all that **g** a whoring after him,
6 after wizards, to **g** a whoring after them,
21:11 Neither shall he **g** in to any dead body, H935
12 Neither shall he **g** out of the sanctuary, H3318
23 Only he shall not **g** in unto the vail, nor H935
25:28 in the jubile it shall **g** out, and he shall H3318
30 it shall not **g** out in the jubile. H3318
31 and they shall **g** out in the jubile. H3318
33 his possession, shall **g** out in *the year of* H3318
54 then he shall **g** out in the year of jubile, H3318
26: 6 shall the sword **g** through your land. H5674
13 of your yoke, and made you **g** upright. H3212
Nu 1: 3 all that are able to **g** forth to war in H3318
20 all that were able to **g** forth to war; H3318
22 all that were able to **g** forth to war; H3318
24 all that were able to **g** forth to war; H3318
26 all that were able to **g** forth to war; H3318
28 all that were able to **g** forth to war; H3318
30 all that were able to **g** forth to war; H3318
32 all that were able to **g** forth to war; H3318
34 all that were able to **g** forth to war; H3318
36 all that were able to **g** forth to war; H3318
38 all that were able to **g** forth to war; H3318
40 all that were able to **g** forth to war; H3318
42 all that were able to **g** forth to war; H3318
45 were able to **g** forth to war in Israel; H3318
2:24 they shall **g** forward in the third rank. H5265
31 shall **g** hindmost with their standards. H5265
4:19 and his sons shall **g** in, and appoint H935
20 But they shall not **g** in to see when the H935
5:12 If any man's wife **g** aside, and commit H7847
22 the curse shall **g** into thy bowels, to H935
8:15 And after that shall the Levites **g** in to do H935
24 upward they shall **g** in to wait upon the H935
10: 5 lie on the east parts shall **g** forward. H5265
9 And if ye **g** to war in your land against H935
30 And he said unto him, I will not **g**; but I H3212
32 And it shall be, if thou **g** with us, yea, it H3212
13:17 and **g** up into the mountain: H5927
30 and said, Let us **g** up at once, and H5927
31 said, We be not able to **g** up against the H5927
14:40 we *be here*, and will **g** up unto the place H5927
42 **G** not up, for the LORD *is* not among H5927
44 But they presumed to **g** up unto the hill H5927
15:39 eyes, after which ye use to **g** a whoring:
16:30 them, and they **g** down quick into the H3381
46 put on incense, and **g** quickly unto the H3212
20:17 of the wells: we will **g** by the king's *high* H3212
19 unto him, We will **g** by the high way: H5927
19 any thing *else*, **g** through on my feet. H5674
20 And he said, Thou shalt not **g** through. H5674
21:22 well: *but* we will **g** along by the king's H3212
22:12 Thou shalt not **g** with them; thou shalt H3212
13 refuseth to give me leave to **g** with you. H1980
18 and gold, I cannot **g** beyond the word H5674
20 thee, rise up, *and* **g** with them; but yet H3212
35 said unto Balaam, **G** with the men: but H3212
23: 3 offering, and I will **g**: peradventure the H3212
16 said, **G** again unto Balak, and say thus. H7725
24:13 silver and gold, I cannot **g** beyond the H5674
14 And now, behold, I **g** unto my people: H1980
26: 2 all that are able to **g** to war in Israel. H3318
27:17 Which may **g** out before them, and H3318
17 and which may **g** in before them, and H935
21 word shall they **g** out, and at his word H3318
31: 3 the war, and let them **g** against the H1961
23 ye shall make *it* **g** through the fire, and H5674
23 fire ye shall make **g** through the water. H5674
32: 6 brethren **g** to war, and shall ye sit here? H935
9 they should not **g** into the land which H935
17 But we ourselves will **g** ready armed
20 ye will **g** armed before the LORD to war,
21 And will **g** all of you armed over Jordan H5674
34: 4 and shall **g** on to Hazar-addar, H3318
9 And the border shall **g** on to Ziphron, H3318
11 And the coast shall **g** down from H3381
12 And the border shall **g** down to Jordan, H3381
Dt 1: 7 Turn you, and take your journey, and **g** H935

Dt 1: 8 Behold, I have set the land before you: **g** H935
21 land before thee: **g** up *and* possess *it*, as H5927
22 what way we must **g** up, and into what H5927
26 Notwithstanding ye would not **g** up, H5927
28 Whither shall we **g** up? our brethren H5927
33 way ye should **g**, and in a cloud by day. H3212
37 saying, Thou also shalt not **g** in thither. H935
38 thee, he shall **g** in thither: encourage H935
39 and evil, they shall **g** in thither, and unto H935
41 the LORD, we will **g** up and fight, H5927
41 war, ye were ready to **g** up into the hill. H5927
42 Say unto them, **G** not up, neither fight; H5927
2:27 Let me pass through thy land: I will **g** H3212
3:25 I pray thee, let me **g** over, and see the H5674
27 for thou shalt not **g** over this Jordan. H5674
28 him: for he shall **g** over before this H5674
4: 1 ye may live, and **g** in and possess the H935
5 so in the land whither ye **g** to possess it. H935
14 the land whither ye **g** over to possess it. H5674
21 that I should not **g** over Jordan, and H5674
21 and that I should not **g** in unto that good H935
22 But I must die in this land, I must not **g** H5674
22 **g** over, and possess that good land. H5674
26 the land whereunto ye **g** over Jordan to H5674
34 Or hath God assayed to **g** *and* take him a H935
40 day, that it may **g** well with thee, and H3190
5:16 and that it may **g** well with thee, in the H3190
27 **G** thou near, and hear all that the H7126
30 **G** say to them, Get you into your tents H3212
6: 1 in the land whither ye **g** to possess it: H5674
14 Ye shall not **g** after other gods, of the H3212
18 that thou mayest **g** in and possess the H935
8: 1 and multiply, and **g** in and possess the H935
9: 1 over Jordan this day, to **g** in to possess H935
5 heart, dost thou **g** to possess their land: H935
23 saying, **G** up and possess the H5927
10:11 that they may **g** in and possess the land, H935
11: 8 may be strong, and **g** in and possess the H935
8 the land, whither ye **g** to possess it; H5674
11 But the land, whither ye **g** to possess it, H5674
28 you this day, to **g** after other gods, H3212
31 For ye shall pass over Jordan to **g** in to H935
12:10 But *when* ye **g** over Jordan, and dwell H5674
25 Thou shalt not eat it; that it may **g** well
26 shalt take, and **g** unto the place which H935
28 thee, that it may **g** well with thee, and
13: 2 saying, Let us **g** after other gods, which H3212
6 saying, Let us **g** and serve other gods, H3212
13 city, saying, Let us **g** and serve other H3212
14:25 hand, and shalt **g** unto the place which H1980
15:12 year thou shalt let him **g** free from thee. H7971
13 thou shalt not let him **g** away empty: H7971
16 unto thee, I will not **g** away from thee; H3318
16: 7 in the morning, and **g** unto thy tents. H1980
19:13 Israel, that it may **g** well with thee. H2895
21 pity; *but* life *shall* **g** for life, eye for eye,
20: 5 it? let him **g** and return to his house, H3212
6 of it? let him *also* **g** and return unto his H3212
7 taken her? let him **g** and return unto H3212
8 let him **g** and return unto his H3212
21:13 that thou shalt **g** in unto her, and be her H935
14 thou shalt let her **g** whither she will; but H7971
22: 1 ox or his sheep **g** astray, and hide thyself
7 *But* thou shalt in any wise let the dam **g**, H7971
13 If any man take a wife, and **g** in unto H935
23:10 then shall he **g** abroad out of the camp, H3318
12 whither thou shalt **g** forth abroad: H3318
24: 2 she may **g** and be another man's *wife*. H1980
5 wife, he shall not **g** out to war, neither H3318
10 not **g** into his house to fetch his pledge. H935
15 shall the sun **g** down upon it; for he H935
19 thou shalt not **g** again to fetch it: it H7725
20 tree, thou shalt not **g** over the boughs
25: 5 brother shall **g** in unto her, and take H935
7 his brother's wife **g** up to the gate unto H5927
26: 2 a basket, and shalt **g** unto the place H1980
3 And thou shalt **g** unto the priest that H935
27: 3 over, that thou mayest **g** in unto the land H935
28:14 And thou shalt not **g** aside from any of H5493
14 left, to **g** after other gods to serve them. H3212
25 thou shalt **g** out one way against H3318
41 them; for they shall **g** into captivity. H3212
29:18 LORD our God, to **g** *and* serve the gods H3212
30:12 say, Who shall **g** up for us to heaven, H5927
13 say, Who shall **g** over the sea for us, H5674
18 passest over Jordan to **g** to possess it. H935
31: 2 I can no more **g** out and come in: also H3318
2 me, Thou shalt not **g** over this Jordan. H5674
3 The LORD thy God, he will **g** over H5674

Dt 31: 3 Joshua, he shall **g** over before thee, as H5674
6 he *it is* that doth **g** with thee; he will not H1980
7 for thou must **g** with this people unto H935
8 And the LORD, he *it is* that doth **g** H1980
13 whither ye **g** over Jordan to possess it. H5674
16 will rise up, and **g** a whoring after the
16 land, whither they **g** *to be* among them, H935
21 which they **g** about, even now, before H6213
32:47 whither ye **g** over Jordan to possess it. H5674
52 but thou shalt not **g** thither unto the land H935
34: 4 eyes, but thou shalt not **g** over thither. H5674
Jos 1: 2 now therefore arise, **g** over this Jordan, H5674
11 over this Jordan, to **g** in to possess the H935
16 thou sendest us, we will **g**. H3212
2: 1 secretly, saying, **G** view the land, even H3212
16 and afterward may ye **g** your way. H3212
19 And it shall be, *that* whosoever shall **g** H3318
3: 3 remove from your place, and **g** after it. H1980
4 way by which ye must **g**: for ye have not H3212
6: 3 men of war, *and* **g** round about the city H5362
22 spied out the country, **G** into the harlot's H935
7: 2 unto them, saying, **G** up and view the H5927
3 not all the people **g** up; but let about H5927
3 thousand men **g** up and smite Ai; *and* H5927
8: 1 thee, and arise, **g** up to Ai: see, I have H5927
3 people of war, to **g** up against Ai: and H5927
4 behind the city: **g** not very far from the H7368
9:11 the journey, and **g** to meet them, and H3212
12 we came forth to **g** unto you; but now, H3212
10:13 hasted not to **g** down about a whole day. H935
14:11 for war, both to **g** out, and to come in. H3318
18: 3 long *are* ye slack to **g** to possess the land, H935
4 shall rise, and **g** through the land, and H1980
8 the land, saying, **G** and walk through H3212
22: 9 land of Canaan, to **g** unto the country H3212
12 at Shiloh, to **g** up to war against them. H5927
33 did not intend to **g** up against them in H5927
23:12 Else if ye do in any wise **g** back, and H7725
12 and **g** in unto them, and they to you: H935
Jdg 1: 1 saying, Who shall **g** up for us against H5927
2 And the LORD said, Judah shall **g** up: H5927
3 and I likewise will **g** with thee into thy H1980
25 they let **g** the man and all his family. H7971
2: 1 I made you to **g** up out of Egypt, and H5927
6 And when Joshua had let the people **g**, H7971
4: 6 *saying*, **G** and draw toward mount H3212
8 And Barak said unto her, If thou wilt **g** H3212
8 me, then I will **g**: but if thou wilt not H1980
8 wilt not **g** with me, *then* I will not go. H3212
8 wilt not go with me, *then* I will not **g**. H3212
9 And she said, I will surely **g** with thee: H3212
5:11 of the LORD **g** down to the gates. H3381
6:14 him, and said, **G** in this thy might, and H3212
7: 3 Now therefore **g** to, proclaim in the H4994
4 thee, This shall **g** with thee, the same H3212
4 thee, the same shall **g** with thee; and of H3212
4 not **g** with thee, the same shall not go. H3212
4 not go with thee, the same shall not **g**. H3212
7 people **g** every man unto his place. H3212
10 But if thou fear to **g** down, go thou with H3381
10 But if thou fear to go down, **g** thou with H3381
11 be strengthened to **g** down unto the H3381
9: 9 and **g** to be promoted over the trees? H1980
11 and **g** to be promoted over the trees? H1980
13 and **g** to be promoted over the trees? H1980
38 **g** out, I pray now, and fight with them. H3318
10:14 **G** and cry unto the gods which ye have H3212
11: 8 that thou mayest **g** with us, and fight H1980
35 unto the LORD, and I cannot **g** back. H7725
37 that I may **g** up and down upon H3212
38 And he said, **G**. And he sent her away H3212
12: 1 didst not call us to **g** with thee? we will H3212
5 said, Let me **g** over; that the men of H5674
15: 1 and he said, I will **g** in to my wife into H935
1 her father would not suffer him to **g** in. H935
5 on fire, he let *them* **g** into the standing H7971
16:17 my strength will **g** from me, and I shall H5493
20 and said, I will **g** out as at other times H3318
17: 9 I **g** to sojourn where I may find *a place*. H1980
18: 2 said unto them, **G**, search the land: who H3212
5 way which we **g** shall be prosperous. H1980
6 And the priest said unto them, **G** in H3212
6 the LORD *is* your way wherein ye **g**. H3212
9 And they said, Arise, that we may **g** up H5927
9 to **g**, *and* to enter to possess the land. H3212
10 When ye **g**, ye shall come unto a people H935
19 thy mouth, and **g** with us, and be to us H3212
19: 5 of bread, and afterward **g** your way. H3212
9 on your way, that thou mayest **g** home. H1980

Jdg 19:15 And they turned aside thither, to **g** in H935
25 the day began to spring, they let her **g**. H7971
27 and went out to **g** his way: and, behold, H3212
20: 8 will not any *of us* **g** to his tent, neither H3212
9 to Gibeah; *we will* **g** *up* by lot against it;
14 unto Gibeah, to **g** out to battle against H3318
18 Which of us shall **g** up first to the battle H5927
18 the LORD said, Judah *shall* **g** *up* first.
23 saying, Shall I **g** up again to battle H5066
23 And the LORD said, **G** up against him.) H5927
28 Shall I yet again **g** out to battle against H3318
28 the LORD said, **G** up; for to morrow I H5927
21:10 them, saying, **G** and smite the H3212
20 **G** and lie in wait in the vineyards; H3212
21 Shiloh, and **g** to the land of Benjamin. H1980
Ru 1: 8 daughters in law, **G**, return each to her H3212
11 why will ye **g** with me? *are* there yet H3212
12 Turn again, my daughters, **g** *your way;* H3212
16 thou goest, I will **g**; and where thou H3212
18 minded to **g** with her, then she left H3212
2: 2 Let me now **g** to the field, and glean H3212
2 And she said unto her, **G**, my daughter. H3212
8 not, my daughter? **G** not to glean in H3212
8 field, neither **g** from hence, but abide H5674
9 they do reap, and **g** thou after them: H1980
9 thou art athirst, **g** unto the vessels, and H1980
22 that thou **g** out with his maidens, H3318
3: 4 lie, and thou shalt **g** in, and uncover his H935
17 me, **G** not empty unto thy mother in law. H935
1Sa 1:17 Then Eli answered and said, **G** in H3212
22 husband, *I will not* **g** *up* until the child
3: 9 Therefore Eli said unto Samuel, **G**, lie H3212
5:11 of Israel, and let it **g** again to his own H7725
6: 6 not let the people **g**, and they departed? H7971
8 thereof; and send it away, that it may **g**. H1980
20 and to whom shall he **g** up from us? H5927
8:20 **g** out before us, and fight our battles. H3318
22 of Israel, **G** ye every man unto his city. H3212
9: 3 with thee, and arise, **g** seek the asses. H3212
6 surely to pass: now let us **g** thither; H3212
6 can shew us our way that we should **g**. H1980
7 But, behold, *if* we **g**, what shall we bring H3212
9 Come, and let us **g** to the seer: for *he* H3212
10 said; come, let us **g**. So they went unto H3212
13 him, before he **g** up to the high place H5927
14 them, for to **g** up to the high place. H5927
19 I *am* the seer: **g** up before me unto the H5927
19 I will let thee **g**, and will tell thee all H7971
10: 3 Then shalt thou **g** on forward from H2498
8 And thou shalt **g** down before me to H3381
9 turned his back to **g** from Samuel, God H3212
11:14 Come, and let us **g** to Gilgal, and renew H3212
12:21 for *then should ye* **g** after vain *things,*
14: 1 armour, Come, and let us **g** over to the H5674
4 sought to **g** over unto the Philistines' H5674
6 Come, and let us **g** over unto the H5674
9 our place, and will not **g** up unto them. H5927
10 us; then we will **g** up: for the LORD H5927
36 And Saul said, Let us **g** down after the H3381
37 counsel of God, Shall I **g** down after the H3381
15: 3 Now **g** and smite Amalek, and utterly H3212
6 And Saul said unto the Kenites, **G**, H3212
18 a journey, and said, **G** and utterly H3212
27 And as Samuel turned about to **g** away, H3212
16: 1 horn with oil, and **g**, I will send thee to H3212
2 And Samuel said, How can I **g**? if Saul H3212
17:32 will **g** and fight with this Philistine. H3212
33 art not able to **g** against this Philistine H3212
37 David, **G**, and the LORD be with thee. H3212
39 and he assayed to **g**; for he had not H3212
39 Saul, I cannot **g** with these; for I have H3212
55 And when Saul saw David **g** forth H3318
18: 2 **g** no more home to his father's house. H7725
19: 3 And I will **g** out and stand beside my H3318
17 me, Let me **g**; why should I kill thee? H7971
20: 5 at meat: but let me **g**, that I may hide H7971
11 Come, and let us **g** out into the field. H3318
13 that thou mayest **g** in peace: and the H1980
19 *then* thou shalt **g** down quickly, and H3381
21 a lad, *saying,* **G**, find out the arrows. H3212
22 *are* beyond thee; **g** thy way: for the H3212
28 asked *leave* of me *to* **g** to Beth-lehem:
29 And he said, Let me **g**, I pray thee; for H7971
40 said unto him, **G**, carry *them* to the city. H3212
42 And Jonathan said to David, **G** in H3212
23: 2 LORD, saying, Shall I **g** and smite these H3212
2 said unto David, **G**, and smite the H3212
4 and said, Arise, **g** down to Keilah; for H3381
8 together to war, to **g** down to Keilah, to H3381

1Sa 23:13 they could **g**. And it was told Saul H1980
13 from Keilah; and he forbare to **g** forth. H3318
22 **G**, I pray you, prepare yet, and know H3212
23 and I will **g** with you: and it shall H1980
24:19 will he let him **g** well away? wherefore H7971
25: 5 **g** to Nabal, and greet him in my name: H935
19 And she said unto her servants, **G** on H5674
35 and said unto her, **G** up in peace to H5927
26: 6 saying, Who will **g** down with me to H3381
6 Abishai said, I will **g** down with thee. H3381
11 and the cruse of water, and let us **g**. H3212
19 the LORD, saying, **G**, serve other gods. H3212
28: 1 that thou shalt **g** out with me to battle, H3318
7 spirit, that I may **g** to her, and inquire H3212
29: 4 that he may **g** again to his place which H7725
4 him, and let him not **g** down with us to H3381
7 Wherefore now return, and **g** in peace, H3212
8 day, that I may not **g** fight against the H935
9 He shall not **g** up with us to the battle. H5927
30:10 they could not **g** over the brook Besor. H5674
2Sa 1:15 men, and said, **G** near, *and* fall upon H5066
2: 1 saying, Shall I **g** up into any of the H5927
1 said unto him, **G** up. And David said, H5927
1 shall I **g** up? And he said, Unto Hebron. H5927
3:16 unto him, **G**, return. And he returned. H3212
21 I will arise and **g**, and will gather all H3212
5:19 saying, Shall I **g** up to the Philistines? H3212
19 LORD said unto David, **G** up: for I will H3212
23 said, Thou shalt not **g** up; *but* fetch a H3212
24 shall the LORD **g** out before thee, to H3318
7: 3 And Nathan said to the king, **G**, do all H3212
5 **G** and tell my servant David, Thus H3212
11: 1 time when kings **g** forth *to battle,* that H3318
8 And David said to Uriah, **G** down to H3381
10 thou not **g** down unto thine house? H3381
11 fields; shall I then **g** into mine house, to H935
12:23 **g** to him, but he shall not return to me. H1980
13: 7 to Tamar, saying, **G** now to thy brother H3212
13 my shame to **g**? and as for thee, thou H3212
24 and his servants **g** with thy servant. H3212
25 son, let us not all now **g**, lest we be H3212
25 he would not **g**, but blessed him. H3212
26 brother Amnon **g** with us. And the king H3212
26 unto him, Why should he **g** with thee? H3212
27 and all the king's sons **g** with him. H7971
39 And *the soul of* king David longed to **g** H3318
14: 8 And the king said unto the woman, **G** H3212
21 done this thing: **g** therefore, bring the H3212
30 hath barley there; **g** and set it on fire. H3212
15: 7 I pray thee, let me **g** and pay my vow, H3212
9 And the king said unto him, **G** in H3212
20 day make thee **g** up and down with us? H3212
20 down with us? seeing I **g** whither I may, H1980
22 And David said to Ittai, **G** and pass H3212
16: 9 the king? let me **g** over, I pray thee, and H5674
21 And Ahithophel said unto Absalom, **G** in H935
17:11 thou **g** to battle in thine own person. H1980
18: 2 will surely **g** forth with you myself also. H3318
3 Thou shalt not **g** forth: for if we flee H3318
21 Then said Joab to Cushi, **G** tell the king H3212
19: 7 Now therefore arise, **g** forth, and speak H3318
7 the LORD, if thou **g** not forth, there will H3318
15 came to Gilgal, to **g** to meet the king, to H3212
20 to **g** down to meet my lord the king. H3381
26 ride thereon, and **g** to the king; because H3212
34 **g** up with the king unto Jerusalem? H5927
36 Thy servant will **g** a little way over H5674
37 Chimham; let him **g** over with my lord H5674
38 Chimham shall **g** over with me, and I H5674
20:11 he that *is* for David, *let him* **g** after Joab.
21:17 saying, Thou shalt **g** no more out with H3318
24: 1 to say, **G**, number Israel and Judah. H3212
2 *was* with him, **G** now through all the H7751
12 **G** and say unto David, Thus saith the H1980
18 said unto him, **G** up, rear an altar unto H5927
1Ki 1:13 **G** and get thee in unto king David, and H3212
53 said unto him, **G** to thine house. H3212
2: 2 I **g** the way of all the earth: be thou H1980
6 head **g** down to the grave in peace. H3381
29 of Jehoiada, saying, **G**, fall upon him. H3212
36 and **g** not forth thence any whither. H3318
3: 7 I know not *how* to **g** out or come in. H3318
8:44 If thy people **g** out to battle against H3318
9: 6 set before you, but **g** and serve other H1980
11: 2 Israel, Ye shall not **g** in to them, neither H935
10 that he should not **g** after other gods: H3212
17 with him, to **g** into Egypt; Hadad *being* H935
21 that I may **g** to mine own country. H3212
22 thou seekest to **g** to thine own country? H3212

1Ki 11:22 Nothing: howbeit let me **g** in any wise. H7971
12:24 Thus saith the LORD, Ye shall not **g** up, H5927
27 If this people **g** up to do sacrifice in the H5927
27 **g** again to Rehoboam king of Judah. H5927
28 too much for you to **g** up to Jerusalem: H5927
13: 8 house, I will not **g** in with thee, neither H935
16 with thee, nor **g** in with thee: neither H935
17 again to **g** by the way that thou camest. H3212
14: 3 of honey, and **g** to him: he shall tell thee H935
7 **G**, tell Jeroboam, Thus saith the LORD H3212
15:17 **g** out or come in to Asa king of Judah. H3318
17:12 sticks, that I may **g** in and dress it for me H935
13 And Elijah said unto her, Fear not; **g** *and* H935
18: 1 third year, saying, **G**, shew thyself unto H3212
5 And Ahab said unto Obadiah, **G** into H3212
8 And he answered him, I *am:* **g**, tell thy H3212
11 And now thou sayest, **G**, tell thy lord, H3212
14 And now thou sayest, **G**, tell thy lord, H3212
43 And said to his servant, **G** up now, look H5927
43 And he said, **G** again seven times. H7725
44 And he said, **G** up, say unto Ahab, H5927
19:11 And he said, **G** forth, and stand upon H3318
15 And the LORD said unto him, **G**, return H3212
20 he said unto him, **G** back again: for H3212
20:22 said unto him, **G**, strengthen thyself, H3212
31 our heads, and **g** out to the king of H3318
33 Then he said, **G** ye, bring him. Then H935
42 thou hast let **g** out of *thy* hand a man H7971
42 thy life shall **g** for his life, and thy H1961
21:16 Ahab rose up to **g** down to the vineyard H3381
18 Arise, **g** down to meet Ahab king of H3381
22: 4 Wilt thou **g** with me to battle to H3212
6 said unto them, Shall I **g** against H3212
6 And they said, **G** up; for the Lord shall H5927
12 so, saying, **G** up to Ramoth-gilead, H5927
15 him, Micaiah, shall we **g** against H3212
15 he answered him, **G**, and prosper: for H5927
20 Ahab, that he may **g** up and fall at H5927
22 And he said, I will **g** forth, and I will be H3318
22 and prevail also: **g** forth, and do so. H3318
25 **g** into an inner chamber to hide thyself. H935
48 of Tharshish to **g** to Ophir for gold: but H3212
49 Let my servants **g** with thy servants in H3212
2Ki 1: 2 and said unto them, **G**, inquire of H3212
3 the Tishbite, Arise, **g** up to meet the H5927
3 God in Israel, *that* ye **g** to inquire of H1980
6 and said unto us, **G**, turn again unto the H3212
15 said unto Elijah, **G** down with him: be H3381
2:16 men; let them **g**, we pray thee, and seek H3212
18 them, Did I not say unto you, **G** not? H3212
23 said unto him, **G** up, thou bald head; H5927
23 thou bald head; **g** up, thou bald head. H5927
3: 7 me: wilt thou **g** with me against Moab H3212
7 And he said, I will **g** up: I *am* as thou H5927
8 And he said, Which way shall we **g** up? H5927
4: 3 Then he said, **G**, borrow thee vessels H3212
7 of God. And he said, **G**, sell the oil, and H3212
23 And he said, Wherefore wilt thou **g** to H1980
24 Drive, and **g** forward; slack not *thy* H3212
29 in thine hand, and **g** thy way: if thou H3212
5: 5 And the king of Syria said, **G** to, go, H3212
5 And the king of Syria said, Go to, **g**, and I H935
10 unto him, saying, **G** and wash in H1980
19 And he said unto him, **G** in peace. So H3212
24 he let the men **g**, and they departed. H7971
6: 2 Let us **g**, we pray thee, unto Jordan, and H3212
2 we may dwell. And he answered, **G** ye. H3212
3 I pray thee, and **g** with thy servants. H3212
3 thy servants. And he answered, I will **g**. H3212
13 And he said, **G** and spy where he *is,* H3212
22 eat and drink, and **g** to their master. H3212
7: 5 And they rose up in the twilight, to **g** H935
9 we may **g** and tell the king's household. H935
14 host of the Syrians, saying, **G** and see. H3212
8: 1 life, saying, Arise, and **g** thou and thine H3212
8 in thine hand, and **g**, meet the man of H3212
10 And Elisha said unto him, **G**, say unto H3212
9: 1 in thine hand, and **g** to Ramothgilead: H3212
2 son of Nimshi, and **g** in, and make him H935
15 *then* let none **g** forth *nor* escape out H3318
15 out of the city to **g** to tell *it* in Jezreel. H3212
34 drink, and said, **G**, see now this cursed H6485
10:13 Ahaziah; and we **g** down to salute the H3381
24 *him* **g**, his life *shall be* for the life of him.
25 to the captains, **G** in, *and* slay them; let H935
11: 7 And two parts of all you that **g** forth on H3318
9 them that should **g** out on the sabbath, H3318
12:17 set his face to **g** up to Jerusalem. H5927
17:27 and let them **g** and dwell there, and H3212

2Ki 18:21 if a man lean, it will **g** into his hand, and H935
25 **G** up against this land, and destroy it. H5927
19:31 For out of Jerusalem shall **g** forth a H3318
20: 5 shalt **g** up unto the house of the LORD. H5927
8 and that I shall **g** up into the house of H5927
9 spoken: shall the shadow **g** forward ten H1980
9 ten degrees, or **g** back ten degrees? H7725
10 for the shadow to **g** down ten degrees: H5186
22: 4 **G** up to Hilkiah the high priest, that he H5927
13 **G** ye, inquire of the LORD for me, and H3212
1Ch 7:11 *soldiers,* fit to **g** out for war *and* battle. H3318
14:10 God, saying, Shall I **g** up against the H5927
10 said unto him, **G** up; for I will deliver H5927
14 said unto him, **G** not up after them; H5927
15 then thou shalt **g** out to battle: for God H3318
17: 4 **G** and tell David my servant, Thus H3212
11 that thou must **g** *to be* with thy fathers, H3212
20: 1 time that kings **g** out *to battle,* Joab led H3318
21: 2 of the people, **G**, number Israel from H3212
10 **G** and tell David, saying, Thus saith the H3212
18 that David should **g** up, and set up an H5927
30 But David could not **g** before it to H3212
2Ch 1:10 that I may **g** out and come in before H3318
6:34 If thy people **g** out to war against their H3318
7:19 you, and shall **g** and serve other gods, H1980
11: 4 Thus saith the LORD, Ye shall not **g** up, H5927
14:11 in thy name we **g** against this multitude. H935
16: 1 **g** out or come in to Asa king of Judah. H3318
3 silver and gold; **g**, break thy league with H3212
18: 2 to **g** up *with him* to Ramoth-gilead. H5927
3 of Judah, Wilt thou **g** with me to H3212
5 them, Shall we **g** to Ramoth-gilead to H3212
5 And they said, **G** up; for God will H5927
11 so, saying, **G** up to Ramoth-gilead, H5927
14 Micaiah, shall we **g** to Ramoth-gilead H3212
14 And he said, **G** ye up, and prosper, H5927
19 Israel, that he may **g** up and fall at H5927
21 And he said, I will **g** out, and be a lying H3318
21 also prevail: **g** out, and do *even* so. H3318
24 **g** into an inner chamber to hide thyself. H935
29 myself, and will **g** to the battle; but put H935
20:16 To morrow **g** ye down against them: H3381
17 to morrow **g** out against them: for H3318
27 of them, to **g** again to Jerusalem H7725
36 to make ships to **g** to Tarshish: and H3212
37 they were not able to **g** to Tarshish. H3212
21:13 of Jerusalem to **g** a whoring, like to the H935
23: 6 the Levites; they shall **g** in, for they *are* H3318
8 them that were to **g** *out* on the sabbath: H3318
24: 5 and said to them, **G** out unto the cities H3318
25: 5 *men, able* to **g** forth to war, that could H3318
7 not the army of Israel **g** with thee; for the H935
8 But if thou wilt **g**, do *it,* be strong for the H935
10 him out of Ephraim, to **g** home again: H3212
13 they should not **g** with him to battle, H3212
26:18 to burn incense: **g** out of the sanctuary; H3318
20 hasted also to **g** out, because the LORD H3318
34:21 **G**, inquire of the LORD for me, and for H3212
36:23 his God *be* with him, and let him **g** up. H5927
Ezr 1: 3 him, and let him **g** up to Jerusalem, H5927
5 God had raised, to **g** up to build the H5927
5:15 And said unto him, Take these vessels, **g**, H236
7: 9 began he to **g** up from Babylon, and H4609
13 to **g** up to Jerusalem, go with thee. H1946
13 to go up to Jerusalem, **g** with thee. H1946
28 out of Israel chief men to **g** up with me. H5927
8:31 of the first month, to **g** unto Jerusalem: H3212
9:11 land, unto which ye **g** to possess it, is an H935
Neh 3:15 that **g** down from the city of David. H3381
4: 3 they build, if a fox **g** up, he shall even H5927
6:11 as I *am,* would **g** into the temple to save H935
11 the temple to save his life? I will not **g** in. H935
8:10 Then he said unto them, **G** your way, H3212
15 in Jerusalem, saying, **G** forth unto the H3318
9:12 light in the way wherein they should **g**. H3212
15 that they should **g** in to possess the land H935
19 and the way wherein they should **g**. H3212
23 that they should **g** in to possess *it.* H935
Est 1:19 If it please the king, let there **g** a royal H3318
2:12 maid's turn was come to **g** in to king H935
13 was given her to **g** with her out of the H935
15 was come to **g** in unto the king, she H935
4: 8 her that she should **g** in unto the king, to H935
16 **G**, gather together all the Jews that are H3212
16 and so will I **g** in unto the king, which H935
5:14 thereon: then **g** thou in merrily with H935
Job 4:21 **g** away? they die, even without wisdom. H5265
6:18 aside; they **g** to nothing, and perish. H5927
10:21 Before I **g** *whence* I shall not return, H3212
Job 15:13 lettest *such* words **g** out of thy mouth? H3318
30 breath of his mouth shall he **g** away. H5493
16:22 **g** the way *whence* I shall not return. H1980
17:16 They shall **g** down to the bars of the pit, H3381
20:26 him; it shall **g** ill with him that is left
21:13 and in a moment **g** down to the grave. H5181
29 Have ye not asked them that **g** by the H5674
23: 8 Behold, I **g** forward, but he *is* not *there;* H1980
24: 5 Behold, *as* wild asses in the desert, **g** H3318
10 They cause *him* to **g** naked without H1980
27: 6 and will not let it **g**: my heart shall not H7503
31:37 as a prince would I **g** near unto him. H7126
37: 8 Then the beasts **g** into dens, and remain H935
38:35 may **g**, and say unto thee, Here we *are?* H3212
39: 4 they **g** forth, and return not unto them. H3318
41:19 Out of his mouth **g** burning lamps, *and* H1980
42: 8 seven rams, and **g** to my servant Job, H3212
Ps 22:29 all they that **g** down to the dust shall H3381
26: 4 neither will I **g** in with dissemblers. H935
28: 1 like them that **g** down into the pit. H3381
30: 3 that I should not **g** down to the pit. H3381
9 in my blood, when I **g** down to the pit? H3381
32: 8 shalt **g**: I will guide thee with mine eye. H3212
38: 6 greatly; I **g** mourning all the day long. H1980
39:13 before I **g** hence, and be no more. H3212
42: 9 thou forgotten me? why **g** I mourning H3212
43: 2 cast me off? why **g** I mourning because H1980
4 Then will I **g** unto the altar of God, unto H935
48:12 Walk about Zion, and **g** round about H5362
49:19 He shall **g** to the generation of his H935
55:10 Day and night they **g** about it upon the H5437
15 *and* let them **g** down quick into hell: H3381
58: 3 the womb: they **g** astray as soon as H8582
59: 6 like a dog, and **g** round about the city. H5437
14 like a dog, and **g** round about the city. H5437
60:10 *which* didst not **g** out with our armies? H3318
63: 9 shall **g** into the lower parts of the earth. H935
66:13 I will **g** into thy house with burnt H935
71:16 I will **g** in the strength of the Lord GOD: I H935
73:27 all them that **g** a whoring from thee.
78:52 But made his own people to **g** forth like H5265
80:18 So will not we **g** back from thee: H5472
84: 7 They **g** from strength to strength, *every* H3212
85:13 Righteousness shall **g** before him; and H1980
88: 4 I am counted with them that **g** down H3381
89:14 mercy and truth shall **g** before thy face. H6923
104: 8 They **g** up by the mountains; they go H5927
8 They go up by the mountains; they **g** H3381
26 There **g** the ships: *there is* that H1980
105:20 ruler of the people, and let him **g** free.
107: 7 they might **g** to a city of habitation. H3212
23 They that **g** down to the sea in ships, H3381
26 They mount up to the heaven, they **g** H3381
108:11 not thou, O God, **g** forth with our hosts? H3318
115:17 neither any that **g** down into silence. H3381
118:19 **g** into them, *and* I will praise the LORD: H935
119:35 Make me to **g** in the path of thy H1869
122: 1 Let us **g** into the house of the LORD. H3212
4 Whither the tribes **g** up, the tribes of H5927
129: 8 Neither do they which **g** by say, The H5674
132: 3 of my house, nor **g** up into my bed; H5927
7 We will **g** into his tabernacles: we will H935
139: 7 Whither shall I **g** from thy spirit? or H3212
143: 7 like unto them that **g** down into the pit. H3381
Prv 1:12 as those that **g** down into the pit: H3381
2:19 None that **g** unto her return again, H935
3:28 Say not unto thy neighbour, **G**, and H3212
4:13 let *her* not **g**: keep her; for she *is* thy life. H7503
14 wicked, and **g** not in the way of evil *men.* H833
5: 5 Her feet **g** down to death; her steps take H3381
23 greatness of his folly he shall **g** astray. H7686
6: 3 of thy friend; **g**, humble thyself, and H3212
6 **G** to the ant, thou sluggard; consider H3212
28 Can one **g** upon hot coals, and his feet H1980
7:25 to her ways, **g** not astray in her paths. H8582
9: 6 Forsake the foolish, and live; and **g** in H833
15 To call passengers who **g** right on their
14: 7 **G** from the presence of a foolish man, H3212
15:12 him: neither will he **g** unto the wise. H3212
18: 8 as wounds, and they **g** down into the H3381
19: 7 more do his friends **g** far from him? he H7368
22: 6 Train up a child in the way he should **g**: H6310
10 contention shall **g** out; yea, strife and H3318
24 and with a furious man thou shalt not **g**: H935
23:30 the wine; they that **g** to seek mixed wine. H935
25: 8 **G** not forth hastily to strive, lest *thou* H3318
26:22 as wounds, and they **g** down into the H3381
27:10 not; neither **g** into thy brother's house H935
28:10 Whoso causeth the righteous to **g** H7686
Prv 30:27 The locusts have no king, yet **g** they H3318
29 There be three *things* which **g** well, yea, H6806
Ecc 2: 1 I said in mine heart, **G** to now, I will H3212
3:20 All **g** unto one place; all are of the dust, H1980
5:15 shall he return to **g** as he came, and H3212
16 he came, so shall he **g**: and what profit H3212
6: 6 seen no good: do not all **g** to one place? H1980
7: 2 *It is* better to **g** to the house of H3212
2 of mourning, than to **g** to the house of H3212
8: 3 Be not hasty to **g** out of his sight: stand H3212
9: 3 live, and after that *they* **g** to the dead.
7 **G** thy way, eat thy bread with joy, and H3212
10:15 he knoweth not how to **g** to the city. H3212
12: 5 and the mourners **g** about the streets: H5437
Song 1: 8 among women, **g** thy way forth by the H3318
3: 2 I will rise now, and **g** about the city in H5437
3 The watchmen that **g** about the city H5437
4 would not let him **g**, until I had brought H7503
11 **G** forth, O ye daughters of Zion, and H3318
6: 6 of sheep which **g** up from the washing, H5927
7: 8 I said, I will **g** up to the palm tree, I will H5927
11 Come, my beloved, let us **g** forth into H3318
Isa 2: 3 And many people shall **g** and say, H1980
3 ye, and let us **g** up to the mountain H5927
3 out of Zion shall **g** forth the law, and H3318
19 And they shall **g** into the holes of the H935
21 To **g** into the clefts of the rocks, and into H935
3:16 **g**, and making a tinkling with their feet: H3212
5: 5 And now **g** to; I will tell you what I will
24 blossom shall **g** up as dust: because H5927
6: 8 and who will **g** for us? Then said I, H3212
9 And he said, **G**, and tell this people, H3212
7: 3 Then said the LORD unto Isaiah, **G** H3318
6 Let us **g** up against Judah, and vex it, H5927
8: 6 of Shiloah that **g** softly, and rejoice in H1980
7 his channels, and **g** over all his banks: H1980
8 he shall overflow and **g** over, he shall H5674
11:15 and make *men* **g** over dryshod. H1869
13: 2 they may **g** into the gates of the nobles. H935
14:19 with a sword, that **g** down to the stones H3381
15: 5 weeping shall they **g** it up; for in the H5927
18: 2 waters, *saying,* **G**, ye swift messengers, H3212
20: 2 son of Amoz, saying, **G** and loose the H3212
21: 2 the spoiler spoileth. **G** up, O Elam: H5927
6 For thus hath the Lord said unto me, **G**, H3212
22:15 Thus saith the Lord GOD of hosts, **G**, H3212
23:16 Take an harp, **g** about the city, thou H5437
27: 4 me in battle? I would **g** through them, I H6585
28:13 that they might **g**, and fall backward, H3212
30: 2 That walk to **g** down into Egypt, and H3381
8 Now **g**, write it before them in a table, H935
31: 1 Woe to them that **g** down to Egypt for H3381
33:21 wherein shall **g** no galley with oars, H3212
34:10 smoke thereof shall **g** up for ever: from H5927
35: 9 beast shall **g** up thereon, it shall H5927
36: 6 if a man lean, it will **g** into his hand, and H935
10 **G** up against this land, and destroy it. H5927
37:32 For out of Jerusalem shall **g** forth a H3318
38: 5 **G**, and say to Hezekiah, Thus saith the H1980
10 of my days, I shall **g** to the gates of the H3212
15 done *it:* I shall **g** softly all my years in H1718
18 thee: they that **g** down into the pit H3381
22 I shall **g** up to the house of the LORD? H5927
42:10 of the earth, ye that **g** down to the sea, H3381
13 The LORD shall **g** forth as a mighty H3318
45: 2 I will **g** before thee, and make the H3212
13 and he shall let **g** my captives, not for H7971
16 all of them: they shall **g** to confusion H1980
48:17 thee by the way *that* thou should-est **g**. H3212
20 **G** ye forth of Babylon, flee ye from the H3318
49: 9 to the prisoners, **G** forth; to them that H3318
17 made thee waste shall **g** forth of thee. H3318
51:23 that we may **g** over: and thou hast H5674
52:11 Depart ye, depart ye, **g** ye out from H3318
11 no unclean *thing;* **g** ye out of the midst H3318
12 For ye shall not **g** out with haste, nor go H3318
12 For ye shall not go out with haste, nor **g** H3212
12 for the LORD will **g** before you; and the H1980
54: 9 should no more **g** over the earth; so H5674
55:12 For ye shall **g** out with joy, and be led H3318
58: 6 **g** free, and that ye break every yoke? H7971
8 shall **g** before thee; the glory H1980
60:20 Thy sun shall no more **g** down; neither H935
62: 1 thereof **g** forth as brightness, H3318
10 **G** through, go through the gates; H5674
10 Go through, **g** through the gates; H5674
66:24 And they shall **g** forth, and look upon H3318
Jer 1: 7 for thou shalt **g** to all that I shall send H3212
2: 2 **G** and cry in the ears of Jerusalem, H1980

Jer 2:25 loved strangers, and after them will I **g**. H3212
37 Yea, thou shalt **g** forth from him, and H3318
3: 1 away his wife, and she **g** from him, and H1980
12 **G** and proclaim these words toward the H1980
4: 5 and let us **g** into the defenced cities. H935
29 they shall **g** into thickets, and climb H935
5:10 **G** ye up upon her walls, and destroy; H5927
6: 4 her; arise, and let us **g** up at noon. Woe H5927
5 Arise, and let us **g** by night, and let us H5927
25 **G** not forth into the field, nor walk by H3318
7:12 But **g** ye now unto my place which *was* H3212
9: 2 my people, and **g** from them! for they H3212
10: 5 they cannot **g**. Be not afraid of them; H6805
11:12 of Jerusalem **g**, and cry unto the gods H1980
13: 1 Thus saith the LORD unto me, **G** and H1980
4 loins, and arise, **g** to Euphrates, and H3212
6 unto me, Arise, **g** to Euphrates, and H3212
14:18 If I **g** forth into the field, then behold H3318
18 **g** about into a land that they know not. H5503
15: 1 out of my sight, and let them **g** forth. H3318
2 Whither shall we **g** forth? then thou H3318
5 shall **g** aside to ask how thou doest? H5493
16: 5 of mourning, neither **g** to lament nor H3212
8 Thou shalt not also **g** into the house of H935
17:19 Thus said the LORD unto me; **G** and H1980
19 **g** out, and in all the gates of Jerusalem; H3318
18: 2 Arise, and **g** down to the potter's H3381
11 Now therefore **g** to, speak to the men of H4994
19: 1 Thus saith the LORD, **G** and get a H1980
2 And **g** forth unto the valley of the son H3318
10 in the sight of the men that **g** with thee, H1980
20: 6 thine house shall **g** into captivity: and H3212
21: 2 works, that he may **g** up from us. H5927
12 lest my fury **g** out like fire, and burn H3318
22: 1 Thus saith the LORD; **G** down to the H3381
20 **G** up to Lebanon, and cry; and lift up H5927
22 thy lovers shall **g** into captivity: surely H3212
25: 6 And **g** not after other gods to serve H3212
32 Behold, evil shall **g** forth from nation to H3318
27:18 and at Jerusalem, **g** not to Babylon. H935
28:13 **G** and tell Hananiah, saying, Thus H1980
29:12 me, and ye shall **g** and pray unto me, H1980
30:16 one of them, shall **g** into captivity; and H3212
31: 4 tabrets, and shalt **g** forth in the dances H3318
6 **g** up to Zion unto the LORD our God. H5927
22 How long wilt thou **g** about, O thou H2559
24 and they *that* **g** forth with flocks. H5265
39 And the measuring line shall yet **g** H3318
34: 2 the God of Israel; **G** and speak to H1980
3 to mouth, and thou shalt **g** to Babylon. H935
9 or an Hebrewess, **g** free; that none H7971
10 one his maidservant, **g** free, that none H7971
10 more, then they obeyed, and let *them* **g**. H7971
11 whom they had let **g** free, to return, H7971
14 At the end of seven years let ye **g** every H7971
14 thou shalt let him **g** free from thee: but H7971
35: 2 **G** unto the house of the Rechabites, H1980
11 Come, and let us **g** to Jerusalem for fear H935
13 the God of Israel; **G** and tell the men of H1980
15 your doings, and **g** not after other gods H3212
36: 5 I cannot **g** into the house of the LORD: H935
6 Therefore **g** thou, and read in the roll, H935
19 Then said the princes unto Baruch, **G**, H3212
37:12 out of Jerusalem to **g** into the land of H3212
38:17 wilt assuredly **g** forth unto the king H3318
18 But if thou wilt not **g** forth to the king H3318
21 But if thou refuse to **g** forth, this *is* the H3318
39:16 **G** and speak to Ebed-melech the H1980
40: 1 the guard had let him **g** from Ramah, H7971
4 and convenient for thee to **g**, thither go. H3212
4 and convenient for thee to go, thither **g**. H3212
5 back, *he said*, **G** back also to Gedaliah H7725
5 the people: or **g** wheresoever it seemeth H3212
5 unto thee to **g**. So the captain of the H3212
5 victuals and a reward, and let him **g**. H7971
15 saying, Let me **g**, I pray thee, and I will H3212
41:10 departed to **g** over to the Ammonites. H5674
17 by Beth-lehem, to **g** to enter into Egypt, H3212
42:14 Saying, No; but we will **g** into the land of H935
15 enter into Egypt, and **g** to sojourn there; H935
17 set their faces to **g** into Egypt to sojourn H935
19 remnant of Judah; **G** ye not into Egypt: H935
22 whither ye desire to **g** *and* to sojourn. H935
43: 2 to say, **G** not into Egypt to sojourn there: H935
12 he shall **g** forth from thence in peace. H3318
44:12 set their faces to **g** into the land of Egypt H935
46: 8 and he saith, I will **g** up, *and* will cover H5927
11 **G** up into Gilead, and take balm, O H5927
16 Arise, and let us **g** again to our own H7725

Jer 46:19 furnish thyself to **g** into captivity: for H3212
22 The voice thereof shall **g** like a serpent; H3212
48: 5 weeping shall **g** up; for in the going H5927
7 Chemosh shall **g** forth into captivity H3318
49: 3 for their king shall **g** into captivity, *and* H3212
12 *that* shall altogether **g** unpunished? thou
12 thou shalt not **g** unpunished, but thou
28 the LORD; Arise ye, **g** up to Kedar, and H5927
50: 4 shall **g**, and seek the LORD their God. H3212
6 caused them to **g** astray, they have H8582
8 of Babylon, and **g** forth out of the land H3318
21 **G** up against the land of Merathaim, H5927
27 Slay all her bullocks; let them **g** down H3381
33 them fast; they refused to let them **g**. H7971
51: 9 her, and let us **g** every one into his own H3212
45 My people, **g** ye out of the midst of her, H3318
50 Ye that have escaped the sword, **g** H1980
Lam 4:18 They hunt our steps, that we cannot **g** H3212
Ezk 1:12 the spirit was to **g**, they went; *and* they H3212
20 Whithersoever the spirit was to **g**, they H3212
20 *was their* spirit to **g**; and the wheels H3212
3: 1 and **g** speak unto the house of Israel. H3212
4 And he said unto me, Son of man, **g**, get H3212
11 And **g**, get thee to them of the captivity, H3212
22 unto me, Arise, **g** forth into the plain, H3318
24 me, **G**, shut thyself within thine house. H935
25 and thou shalt not **g** out among them: H3318
6: 9 their eyes, which **g** a whoring after their
8: 6 here, that I should **g** far off from my H7368
9 And he said unto me, **G** in, and behold H935
9: 4 And the LORD said unto him, **G** H5674
5 said in mine hearing, **G** ye after him H5674
7 with the slain: **g** ye forth. And they H3318
10: 2 linen, and said, **G** in between the wheels, H935
12: 4 and thou shalt **g** forth at even in their H3318
4 sight, as they that **g** forth into captivity. H4161
11 they shall remove *and* **g** into captivity. H3212
12 twilight, and shall **g** forth: they shall H3318
13:20 will let the souls **g**, *even* the souls that H7971
14:11 That the house of Israel may **g** no more H8582
17 and say, Sword, **g** through the land; so H5674
15: 7 them; they shall **g** out from *one* fire, H3318
20:10 Wherefore I caused them to **g** forth out H3318
29 high place whereunto ye **g**? And the name H935
39 the Lord GOD; **G** ye, serve ye every one H3212
21: 4 shall my sword **g** forth out of his sheath H3318
16 **G** thee one way or other, *either* on the H258
23:44 Yet they went in unto her, as they **g** in H935
24:14 do *it*; I will not **g** back, neither will I H6544
26:11 garrisons shall **g** down to the ground. H3381
20 with them that **g** down to the pit, that H3381
30: 9 In that day shall messengers **g** forth H3318
17 and these *cities* shall **g** into captivity. H3212
18 her daughters shall **g** into captivity. H3212
31:14 men, with them that **g** down to the pit. H3381
32:18 with them that **g** down into the pit. H3381
19 Whom dost thou pass in beauty? **g** H3381
24 with them that **g** down to the pit. H3381
25 with them that **g** down to the pit: he is H3381
29 and with them that **g** down to the pit. H3381
30 with them that **g** down to the pit. H3381
38:11 And thou shalt say, I will **g** up to the H5927
11 villages; I will **g** to them that are at rest, H935
39: 9 of Israel shall **g** forth, and shall set H3318
40:26 And *there were* seven steps to **g** up to H5930
42:14 then shall they not **g** out of the holy H3318
44: 3 and shall **g** out by the way of the same. H3318
19 And when they **g** forth into the utter H3318
46: 2 gate: then he shall **g** forth; but the gate H3318
8 shall enter, he shall **g** in by the way of H935
8 and he shall **g** forth by the way thereof. H3318
9 to worship shall **g** out by the way of the H3318
9 south gate shall **g** forth by the way of H3318
9 in, but shall **g** forth over against it. H3318
10 of them, when they **g** in, shall go in; and H935
10 they go in, shall **g** in; and when they go H3318
10 and when they **g** forth, shall go forth. H3318
10 and when they go forth, shall **g** forth. H3318
12 day: then he shall **g** forth; and after his H3318
47: 8 the east country, and **g** down into the H3318
8 into the desert, and **g** into the sea: *which* H935
15 the way of Hethlon, as men **g** to Zedad; H935
Dan 11:44 therefore he shall **g** forth with great H3318
12: 9 And he said, **G** thy way, Daniel: for the H3212
13 But **g** thou thy way till the end *be*: for H3212
Hos 1: 2 said to Hosea, **G**, take unto thee a wife H3212
2: 5 for she said, I will **g** after my lovers, H3212
7 she say, I will **g** and return to my first H3212
3: 1 Then said the LORD unto me, **G** yet, H3212

Hos 4:15 Gilgal, neither **g** ye up to Beth-aven, H5927
5: 6 They shall **g** with their flocks and with H3212
14 *even* I, will tear and **g** away; I will take H3212
15 I will **g** *and* return to my place, till they H3212
7:11 they call to Egypt, they **g** to Assyria. H1980
12 When they shall **g**, I will spread my net H3212
11: 3 I taught Ephraim also to **g**, taking them H7270
Joel 2:16 let the bridegroom **g** forth of his H3318
Am 1: 5 of Syria shall **g** into captivity unto Kir,
15 And their king shall **g** into captivity, he H1980
2: 7 and his father will **g** in unto the *same* H3212
4: 3 And ye shall **g** out at the breaches, H3318
5: 5 Gilgal shall surely **g** into captivity, and
27 Therefore will I cause you to **g** into
6: 2 and from thence **g** ye to Hamath the H3212
2 the great: then **g** down to Gath of the H3381
7 Therefore now shall they **g** captive with
7 with the first that **g** captive, and the
7:12 O thou seer, **g**, flee thee away into H3212
15 me, **G**, prophesy unto my people Israel. H3212
17 surely **g** into captivity forth of his land.
8: 9 cause the sun to **g** down at noon, and I H935
9: 4 And though they **g** into captivity before H3212
Jna 1: 2 Arise, **g** to Nineveh, that great city, and H3212
3 went down into it, to **g** with them unto H935
3: 2 Arise, **g** unto Nineveh, that great city, H3212
Mic 1: 8 Therefore I will wail and howl, I will **g** H3212
2: 3 ye **g** haughtily: for this time *is* evil. H3212
3: 6 and the sun shall **g** down over the H935
4: 2 Come, and let us **g** up to the mountain H5927
2 for the law shall **g** forth of Zion, and H3318
10 for now shalt thou **g** forth out of the H3318
10 and thou shalt **g** *even* to Babylon; there H935
5: 8 of sheep: who, if he **g** through, both H5674
Nah 3:14 thy strong holds: **g** into clay, and tread H935
Hab 1: 4 doth never **g** forth: for the wicked H3318
Hag 1: 8 **G** up to the mountain, and bring wood, H5927
Zec 6: 5 heavens, which **g** forth from standing H3318
6 The black horses which *are* therein **g** H3318
6 and the white **g** forth after them; and H3318
6 **g** forth toward the south country. H3318
7 and sought to **g** that they might walk H3212
8 Behold, these that **g** toward the north H3318
10 the same day, and **g** into the house of H935
8:21 And the inhabitants of one *city* shall **g** H1980
21 saying, Let us **g** speedily to pray before H3212
21 to seek the LORD of hosts: I will **g** also. H3212
23 saying, We will **g** with you: for we have H3212
9:14 his arrow shall **g** forth as the lightning: H3318
14 shall **g** with whirlwinds of the south. H1980
14: 2 of the city shall **g** forth into captivity, H3318
3 Then shall the LORD **g** forth, and fight H3318
8 *that* living waters shall **g** out from H3318
16 shall even **g** up from year to year H5927
18 And if the family of Egypt **g** not up, and H5927
Mal 4: 2 and ye shall **g** forth, and grow up H3318
Mt 2: 8 and said, **G** and search diligently *G4198*
20 and his mother, and **g** into the land of *G4198*
22 Herod, he was afraid to **g** thither: *G565*
5:24 before the altar, and **g** thy way; first be *G5217*
41 And whosoever shall compel thee to **g** a *G29*
41 thee to go a mile, **g** with him twain. *G5217*
7:13 and many there be which **g** in thereat: *G1525*
8: 4 tell no man; but **g** thy way, shew thyself *G5217*
9 I say to this *man*, **G**, and he goeth; and *G4198*
13 And Jesus said unto the centurion, **G** *G5217*
21 suffer me first to **g** and bury my father. *G565*
31 us to **g** away into the herd of swine. *G565*
32 And he said unto them, **G**. And when *G5217*
9: 6 up thy bed, and **g** unto thine house. *G5217*
13 But **g** ye and learn what *that* meaneth, *G4198*
10: 5 them, saying, **G** not into the way of the *G565*
6 But **g** rather to the lost sheep of the *G4198*
7 And as ye **g**, preach, saying, The *G4198*
11 worthy; and there abide till ye **g** thence. *G1831*
11: 4 Jesus answered and said unto them, **G** *G4198*
13:28 thou then that we **g** and gather them up? *G565*
14:15 that they may **g** into the villages, and *G565*
22 into a ship, and to **g** before him unto *G4254*
29 he walked on the water, to **g** to Jesus. *G2064*
16:21 how that he must **g** unto Jerusalem, and *G565*
17:27 offend them, **g** thou to the sea, and *G4198*
18:15 against thee, **g** and tell him his fault *G5217*
19:21 wilt be perfect, **g** *and* sell that thou *G5217*
24 for a camel to **g** through the eye of a *G1330*
20: 4 And said unto them; **G** ye also into the *G5217*
7 He saith unto them, **G** ye also into the *G5217*
14 Take *that* thine *is*, and **g** thy way: I will *G5217*
18 Behold, we **g** up to Jerusalem; and the *G305*

Mt 21: 2 Saying unto them, G into the village G4198
28 Son, g work to day in my vineyard. G5217
30 answered and said, I g, sir: and went not. G565
31 g into the kingdom of God before you. G4254
22: 9 G ye therefore into the highways, and G4198
23:13 for ye neither g in *yourselves*, neither G1525
13 suffer ye them that are entering to g in. G1525
24:26 he is in the desert; g not forth: behold, G1831
25: 6 cometh; g ye out to meet him. G1831
9 for us and you: but g ye rather to them G4198
46 And these shall g away into everlasting G565
26:18 And he said, G into the city to such a G5217
32 But after I am risen again, I will g G4254
36 Sit ye here, while I g and pray yonder. G565
27:65 g your way, make *it* as sure as ye can. G5217
28: 7 And g quickly, and tell his disciples G4198
10 Be not afraid: g tell my brethren that G5217
10 my brethren that they g into Galilee, and G565
19 G ye therefore, and teach all nations, G4198
Mk 1:38 And he said unto them, Let us g into the G71
44 to any man: but g thy way, shew thyself G5217
2:11 bed, and g thy way into thine house. G5217
5:19 saith unto him, G home to thy friends, G5217
34 g in peace, and be whole of thy plague. G5217
6:36 Send them away, that they may g into G565
37 say unto him, Shall we g and buy two G565
38 loaves have ye? g and see. And when G5217
45 into the ship, and to g to the other side G4254
7:29 And he said unto her, For this saying g G5217
8:26 saying, Neither g into the town, nor tell G1525
9:43 two hands to g into hell, into the fire G565
10:21 One thing thou lackest: g thy way, sell G5217
25 It is easier for a camel to g through the G1525
33 *Saying*, Behold, we g up to Jerusalem; G305
52 And Jesus said unto him, G thy way; G5217
11: 2 And saith unto them, G your way into G5217
6 had commanded: and they let them g. G863
12:38 which love to g in long clothing, and G4043
13:15 on the housetop not g down into the G2597
14:12 wilt thou that we g and prepare that G565
13 saith unto them, G ye into the city, and G5217
14 And wheresoever he shall g in, say ye G1525
28 But after that I am risen, I will g before G4254
42 Rise up, let us g; lo, he that betrayeth me G71
16: 7 But g your way, tell his disciples and G5217
15 And he said unto them, G ye into all G4198
Lk 1:17 And he shall g before him in the spirit G4281
76 for thou shalt g before the face of the G4313
2:15 Let us now g even unto Bethlehem, G1330
5:14 to tell no man: but g, and shew thyself to G565
24 up thy couch, and g into thine house. G4198
7: 8 I say unto one, G, and he goeth; and to G4198
22 said unto them, G your way, and tell G4198
50 Thy faith hath saved thee; g in peace. G4198
8:14 when they have heard, g forth, and are G4198
22 unto them, Let us g over unto the other G1330
31 command them to g out into the deep. G565
48 faith hath made thee whole; g in peace. G4198
51 no man to g in, save Peter, and James, G1525
9: 5 you, when ye g out of that city, shake G1831
12 that they may g into the towns and G565
13 g and buy meat for all this people. G4198
51 stedfastly set his face to g to Jerusalem, G4198
53 was as though he would g to Jerusalem. G4198
59 suffer me first to g and bury my father. G565
60 g thou and preach the kingdom of God. G565
61 thee; but let me first g bid them farewell,
10: 3 G your ways: behold, I send you forth G4198
7 of his hire. G not from house to house. G3327
10 receive you not, g your ways out into G1831
37 unto him, G, and do thou likewise. G4198
11: 5 have a friend, and shall g unto him at G4198
13:32 And he said unto them, G ye, and tell G4198
14: 4 took *him*, and healed him, and let him g; G630
10 But when thou art bidden, g and sit G4198
10 say unto thee, Friend, g up higher: then G4320
18 and I must needs g and see it: I pray G1831
19 of oxen, and I g to prove them: I pray G4198
21 to his servant, G out quickly into the G1831
23 And the lord said unto the servant, G G1831
15: 4 wilderness, and g after that which is G4198
18 I will arise and g to my father, and will G4198
28 And he was angry, and would not g in: G1525
17: 7 from the field, G and sit down to meat? G3928
14 he said unto them, G shew yourselves G4198
19 And he said unto him, Arise, g thy way: G4198
23 there: g not after *them*, nor follow *them*. G565
18:25 For it is easier for a camel to g through G1525
31 them, Behold, we g up to Jerusalem, and G305

Lk 19:30 Saying, G ye into the village over G5217
21: 8 near: g ye not therefore after them. G4198
22: 8 And he sent Peter and John, saying, G G4198
33 I am ready to g with thee, both into G4198
68 *you*, ye will not answer me, nor let *me* g. G630
23:22 will therefore chastise him, and let *him* g. G630
Jn 1:43 The day following Jesus would g forth G1831
4: 4 And he must needs g through Samaria. G1330
16 Jesus saith unto her, G, call thy G5217
50 Jesus saith unto him, G thy way; thy G4198
6:67 unto the twelve, Will ye also g away? G5217
68 we g? thou hast the words of eternal life. G565
7: 3 Depart hence, and g into Judaea, that G5217
8 G ye up unto this feast: I go not up yet G305
8 Go ye up unto this feast: I g not up yet G305
19 the law? Why g ye about to kill me? G2212
33 and *then* I g unto him that sent me. G5217
35 Whither will he g, that we shall not find G4198
35 find him? will he g unto the dispersed G4198
8:11 do I condemn thee: g, and sin no more. G4198
14 and whither I g; but ye cannot tell G5217
14 tell whence I come, and whither I g. G5217
21 Then said Jesus again unto them, I g G5217
21 your sins: whither I g, ye cannot come. G5217
22 he saith, Whither I g, ye cannot come. G5217
9: 7 And said unto him, G, wash in the pool G5217
11 eyes, and said unto me, G to the pool of G5217
10: 9 shall g in and out, and find pasture. G1525
11: 7 *his* disciples, Let us g into Judaea again. G71
11 I g, that I may awake him out of sleep. G4198
15 believe; nevertheless let us g unto him. G71
16 Let us also g, that we may die with him. G71
44 unto them, Loose him, and let him g. G5217
13:33 g, ye cannot come; so now I say to you. G5217
36 him, Whither I g, thou canst not follow G5217
14: 2 told you. I g to prepare a place for you. G4198
3 And if I g and prepare a place for you, I G4198
4 And whither I g ye know, and the way G5217
12 he do; because I g unto my Father. G4198
28 Ye have heard how I said unto you, I g G5217
28 because I said, I g unto the Father: for G4198
31 even so I do. Arise, let us g hence. G71
15:16 that ye should g and bring forth fruit, G5217
16: 5 But now I g my way to him that sent G5217
7 for you that I g away: for if I go not G565
7 that I go away: for if I g not away, the G565
10 Of righteousness, because I g to my G5217
16 shall see me, because I g to the Father. G5217
17 see me: and, Because I g to the Father? G5217
28 I leave the world, and g to the Father. G4198
18: 8 ye seek me, let these g their way: G5217
19:12 If thou let this man g, thou art not G630
20:17 to my Father: but g to my brethren, G4198
21: 3 Simon Peter saith unto them, I g a G5217
3 unto him, We also g with thee. They G2064
Act 1:11 as ye have seen him g into heaven. G4198
25 fell, that he might g to his own place. G4198
3: 3 Who seeing Peter and John about to g G1524
13 when he was determined to let *him* g. G630
4:15 them to g aside out of the council, G565
21 they let them g, finding nothing how G630
23 And being let g, they went to their own G630
5:20 G, stand and speak in the temple to the G4198
40 in the name of Jesus, and let them g. G630
7:40 Saying unto Aaron, Make us gods to g G4313
8:26 saying, Arise, and g toward the south G4198
29 Then the Spirit said unto Philip, G G4334
9: 6 him, Arise, and g into the city, and it G1525
11 him, Arise, and g into the street which G4198
15 But the Lord said unto him, G thy way: G4198
10:20 thee down, and g with them, doubting G4198
11:12 And the Spirit bade me g with them, G4905
22 that he should g as far as Antioch. G1330
12:17 And he said, G shew these things unto
15: 2 of them, should g up to Jerusalem unto G305
33 space, they were let g in peace from the G630
36 Barnabas, Let us g again and visit our G1994
16: 3 Him would Paul have to g forth with G1831
7 they assayed to g into Bithynia: but the G4198
10 we endeavoured to g into Macedonia, G1831
35 the serjeants, saying, Let those men g. G630
36 g: now therefore depart, and go in peace. G630
36 now therefore depart, and g in peace. G4198
17: 9 Jason, and of the other, they let them g. G630
14 sent away Paul to g as it were to the G4198
18: 6 henceforth I will g unto the Gentiles. G4198
19:21 and Achaia, to g to Jerusalem, saying, G4198
20: 1 and departed for to g into Macedonia. G4198
13 appointed, minding himself to g afoot.

Act 20:22 And now, behold, I g bound in the G4198
21: 4 that he should not g up to Jerusalem. G305
12 besought him not to g up to Jerusalem. G305
22:10 me, Arise, and g into Damascus; and G4198
23:10 the soldiers to g down, and to take him G2597
23 hundred soldiers to g to Caesarea, and G4198
32 g with him, and returned to the castle: G4198
24:25 and answered, G thy way for this time; G4198
25: 5 you are able, g down with *me*, and G4782
9 and said, Wilt thou g up to Jerusalem, G305
12 unto Caesar? unto Caesar shalt thou g. G4198
20 whether he would g to Jerusalem, and G4198
27: 3 to g unto his friends to refresh himself. G4198
28:18 would have let *me* g, because there was G630
26 Saying, G unto this people, and say, G4198
Ro 15:25 But now I g unto Jerusalem to minister G4198
1Co 5:10 then must ye needs g out of the world. G1831
6: 1 against another, g to law before the
7 among you, because ye g to law one with
10:27 ye be disposed to g; whatsoever is set G4198
16: 4 And if it be meet that I g also, they G4198
4 that I go also, they shall g with me. G4198
6 me on my journey whithersoever I g. G4198
2Co 9: 5 that they would g before unto you, and G4281
Gal 2: 9 that we *should* g unto the heathen, and
Eph 4:26 not the sun g down upon your wrath: G1931
Php 2:23 soon as I shall see how it will g with me.
1Th 4: 6 That no *man* g beyond and defraud his G5233
Heb 6: 1 of Christ, let us g on unto perfection; G5342
11: 8 when he was called to g out into a place G1831
13:13 Let us g forth therefore unto him G1831
Jas 4:13 G to now, ye that say, To day or to G33
13 or to morrow we will g into such a city, G4198
5: 1 G to now, *ye* rich men, weep and howl G33
Rev 3:12 God, and he shall g no more out: and I G1831
10: 8 again, and said, G *and* take the little G5217
13:10 He that leadeth into captivity shall g G5217
16: 1 to the seven angels, G your ways, and G5217
14 miracles, *which* g forth unto the kings G1607
17: 8 pit, and g into perdition: and G5217
20: 8 And shall g out to deceive the nations G1831

GOAD
Jdg 3:31 an ox g: and he also delivered Israel. H4451

GOADS
1Sa 13:21 and for the axes, and to sharpen the g. H1861
Ecc 12:11 The words of the wise *are* as g, and as H1861

GOAT
Gen 15: 9 old, and a she g of three years old, and H5795
Lev 3:12 And if his offering *be* a g, then he shall H5795
4:24 the head of the g, and kill it in the place H8163
7:23 manner of fat, of ox, or of sheep, or of g. H5795
9:15 and took the g, which *was* the sin H8163
10:16 And Moses diligently sought the g of H8163
16: 9 And Aaron shall bring the g upon H8163
10 But the g, on which the lot fell to be the H8163
15 Then shall he kill the g of the sin H8163
18 of the blood of the g, and put *it* upon H8163
20 and the altar, he shall bring the live g: H8163
21 head of the live g, and confess over him H8163
21 the head of the g, and shall send *him* H8163
22 And the g shall bear upon him all their H8163
22 he shall let go the g in the wilderness. H8163
26 And he that let go the g for the H8163
27 offering, and the g *for* the sin offering, H8163
17: 3 an ox, or lamb, or g, in the camp, or H5795
22:27 When a bullock, or a sheep, or a g, is H5795
Nu 15:27 she g of the first year for a sin offering. H5795
18:17 or the firstling of a g, thou shalt not H5795
28:22 And one g *for* a sin offering, to make H8163
29:22 And one g *for* a sin offering; beside the H8163
28 And one g *for* a sin offering; beside the H8163
31 And one g *for* a sin offering; beside the H8163
34 And one g *for* a sin offering; beside the H8163
38 And one g *for* a sin offering; beside the H8163
Dt 14: 4 ye shall eat: the ox, the sheep, and the g, H5795
5 deer, and the wild g, and the pygarg, and H689
Prv 30:31 A greyhound; an he g also; and a king, H8495
Ezk 43:25 every day a g *for* a sin offering: they H8163
Dan 8: 5 behold, an he g came from the west H5795
5 g *had* a notable horn between his eyes. H6842
8 Therefore the he g waxed very great: H5795
21 And the rough g *is* the king of Grecia: H6842

GOATH
Jer 31:39 Gareb, and shall compass about to G. H1601

GOATS

Gen 27: 9 good kids of the **g**; and I will make them H5795
16 of the kids of the **g** upon his hands, and H5795
30:32 the **g**: and *of such* shall be my hire. H5795
33 among the **g**, and brown among the H5795
35 And he removed that day the he **g** that H8495
35 and all the she **g** that were speckled H5795
31:38 ewes and thy she **g** have not cast their H5795
32:14 Two hundred she **g**, and twenty he H5795
14 **g**, two hundred ewes, and twenty rams, H8495
37:31 the **g**, and dipped the coat in the blood; H5795
Ex 12: 5 *it* out from the sheep, or from the **g**: H5795
Lev 1:10 sheep, or of the **g**, for a burnt sacrifice; H5795
4:23 a kid of the **g**, a male without blemish: H5795
28 a kid of the **g**, a female without blemish, H5795
5: 6 or a kid of the **g**, for a sin offering; and H5795
9: 3 ye a kid of the **g** for a sin offering; and H5795
16: 5 two kids of the **g** for a sin offering, and H5795
7 And he shall take the two **g**, and present H8163
8 cast lots upon the two **g**; one lot for the H8163
22:19 of the beeves, of the sheep, or of the **g**. H5795
23:19 Then ye shall sacrifice one kid of the **g** H5795
Nu 7:16 One kid of the **g** for a sin offering: H5795
17 five rams, five he **g**, five lambs of the H6260
22 One kid of the **g** for a sin offering: H5795
23 five rams, five he **g**, five lambs of the H6260
28 One kid of the **g** for a sin offering: H5795
29 five rams, five he **g**, five lambs of the H6260
34 One kid of the **g** for a sin offering: H5795
35 five rams, five he **g**, five lambs of the H6260
40 One kid of the **g** for a sin offering: H5795
41 five rams, five he **g**, five lambs of the H6260
46 One kid of the **g** for a sin offering: H5795
47 five rams, five he **g**, five lambs of the H6260
52 One kid of the **g** for a sin offering: H5795
53 five rams, five he **g**, five lambs of the H6260
58 One kid of the **g** for a sin offering: H5795
59 five rams, five he **g**, five lambs of the H6260
64 One kid of the **g** for a sin offering: H5795
65 five rams, five he **g**, five lambs of the H6260
70 One kid of the **g** for a sin offering: H5795
71 five rams, five he **g**, five lambs of the H6260
76 One kid of the **g** for a sin offering: H5795
77 five rams, five he **g**, five lambs of the H6260
82 One kid of the **g** for a sin offering: H5795
83 five rams, five he **g**, five lambs of the H6260
87 the kids of the **g** for sin offering twelve. H5795
88 rams sixty, the he **g** sixty, the lambs of H6260
15:24 and one kid of the **g** for a sin offering. H5795
28:15 And one kid of the **g** for a sin offering H5795
30 *And* one kid of the **g**, to make an H5795
29: 5 And one kid of the **g** *for* a sin offering, H5795
11 One kid of the **g** *for* a sin offering; H5795
16 And one kid of the **g** *for* a sin offering; H5795
19 And one kid of the **g** *for* a sin offering; H5795
25 And one kid of the **g** *for* a sin offering; H5795
Dt 32:14 breed of Bashan, and **g**, with the fat of H6260
1Sa 24: 2 his men upon the rocks of the wild **g**. H3277
25: 2 and a thousand **g**: and he was shearing H5795
2Ch 17:11 thousand and seven hundred he **g**. H8495
29:21 and seven he **g**, for a sin offering for H5795
23 And they brought forth the he **g** *for* the H8163
Ezr 6:17 all Israel, twelve he **g**, according to the H5796
8:35 lambs, twelve he **g** *for* a sin offering: all H6842
Job 39: 1 Knowest thou the time when the wild **g** H3277
Ps 50: 9 of thy house, *nor* he **g** out of thy folds. H6260
13 flesh of bulls, or drink the blood of **g**? H6260
66:15 rams; I will offer bullocks with **g**. Selah. H6260
104:18 the wild **g**; *and* the rocks for the conies. H3277
Prv 27:26 and the **g** *are* the price of the field. H6260
Song 4: 1 of **g**, that appear from mount Gilead. H5795
6: 5 as a flock of **g** that appear from Gilead. H5795
Isa 1:11 of bullocks, or of lambs, or of he **g**. H6260
34: 6 blood of lambs and **g**, with the fat of the H6260
Jer 50: 8 and be as the he **g** before the flocks. H6260
51:40 to the slaughter, like rams with he **g**. H6260
Ezk 27:21 **g**: in these *were they* thy merchants. H6260
34:17 cattle, between the rams and the he **g**. H6260
39:18 of lambs, and of **g**, of bullocks, all of H6260
43:22 offer a kid of the **g** without blemish for H5795
45:23 a kid of the **g** daily *for* a sin offering. H5795
Zec 10: 3 I punished the **g**: for the LORD of hosts H6260
Mt 25:32 shepherd divideth *his* sheep from the **g**: G2056
33 on his right hand, but the **g** on the left. G2055
Heb 9:12 Neither by the blood of **g** and calves, G5131
13 For if the blood of bulls and of **g**, and G5131
19 of calves and of **g**, with water, and G5131
10: 4 of bulls and of **g** should take away sins. G5131

GOATS'

Ex 25: 4 and scarlet, and fine linen, and **g** *hair,* H5795
26: 7 And thou shalt make curtains *of* **g** *hair* H5795
35: 6 and scarlet, and fine linen, and **g** *hair,* H5795
23 fine linen, and **g** *hair,* and red skins H5795
26 stirred them up in wisdom spun **g** *hair.* H5795
36:14 And he made curtains *of* **g** *hair* for the H5795
Nu 31:20 of **g** *hair,* and all things made of wood. H5795
1Sa 19:13 put a pillow of **g** *hair* for his bolster, H5795
16 with a pillow of **g** *hair* for his bolster. H5795
Prv 27:27 And *thou shalt have* **g** milk enough for H5795

GOATS'-HAIR See GOATS' and HAIR.

GOATSKINS

Heb 11:37 **g**; being destitute, afflicted, tormented; *G122*

GOB

2Sa 21:18 the Philistines at **G**: then Sibbechai the H1359
19 And there was again a battle in **G** with H1359

GOBLET

Song 7: 2 Thy navel *is like* a round **g**, *which* H101

GOD

Gen 1: 1 In the beginning **G** created the heaven H430
2 of **G** moved upon the face of the waters. H430
3 And **G** said, Let there be light: and there H430
4 And **G** saw the light, that *it was* good: H430
4 **G** divided the light from the darkness. H430
5 And **G** called the light Day, and the H430
6 And **G** said, Let there be a firmament in H430
7 And **G** made the firmament, and divided H430
8 And **G** called the firmament Heaven. H430
9 And **G** said, Let the waters under the H430
10 And **G** called the dry *land* Earth; and the H430
10 he Seas: and **G** saw that *it was* good. H430
11 And **G** said, Let the earth bring forth H430
12 his kind: and **G** saw that *it was* good. H430
14 And **G** said, Let there be lights in the H430
16 And **G** made two great lights; the greater H430
17 And **G** set them in the firmament of the H430
18 darkness: and **G** saw that *it was* good. H430
20 And **G** said, Let the waters bring forth H430
21 And **G** created great whales, and every H430
21 his kind: and **G** saw that *it was* good. H430
22 And **G** blessed them, saying, Be fruitful, H430
24 And **G** said, Let the earth bring forth the H430
25 And **G** made the beast of the earth after H430
25 his kind: and **G** saw that *it was* good. H430
26 And **G** said, Let us make man in our H430
27 So **G** created man in his *own* image, in H430
27 in the image of **G** created he him; male H430
28 And **G** blessed them, and God said unto H430
28 And God blessed them, and **G** said unto H430
29 And **G** said, Behold, I have given you H430
31 And **G** saw every thing that he had H430
2: 2 And on the seventh day **G** ended his H430
3 And **G** blessed the seventh day, and H430
3 all his work which **G** created and made. H430
4 **G** made the earth and the heavens, H430
5 for the LORD **G** had not caused it to H430
7 And the LORD **G** formed man *of* the dust H430
8 And the LORD **G** planted a garden H430
9 And out of the ground made the LORD **G** H430
15 And the LORD **G** took the man, and put H430
16 And the LORD **G** commanded the man, H430
18 And the LORD **G** said, *It is* not good that H430
19 And out of the ground the LORD **G** H430
21 And the LORD **G** caused a deep sleep to H430
22 And the rib, which the LORD **G** had H430
3: 1 which the LORD **G** had made. And he H430
1 woman, Yea, hath **G** said, Ye shall not H430
3 of the garden, **G** hath said, Ye shall not H430
5 For **G** doth know that in the day ye eat H430
8 And they heard the voice of the LORD **G** H430
8 **G** amongst the trees of the garden. H430
9 And the LORD **G** called unto Adam, and H430
13 And the LORD **G** said unto the woman, H430
14 And the LORD **G** said unto the serpent, H430
21 his wife did the LORD **G** make coats of H430
22 And the LORD **G** said, Behold, the man H430
23 Therefore the LORD **G** sent him forth H430
4:25 his name Seth: For **G**, *said she,* hath H430
5: 1 In the day that **G** created man, in the H430
1 man, in the likeness of **G** made he him; H430
22 And Enoch walked with **G** after he begat H430
24 And Enoch walked with **G**: and he *was* H430
24 God: and he *was* not; for **G** took him. H430

Gen 6: 2 That the sons of **G** saw the daughters of H430
4 when the sons of **G** came in unto the H430
5 And **G** saw that the wickedness of man H3068
9 generations, *and* Noah walked with **G**. H430
11 The earth also was corrupt before **G**, and H430
12 And **G** looked upon the earth, and, H430
13 And **G** said unto Noah, The end of all H430
22 Thus did Noah; according to all that **G** H430
7: 9 the female, as **G** had commanded Noah. H430
16 of all flesh, as **G** had commanded him: H430
8: 1 And **G** remembered Noah, and every H430
1 in the ark: and **G** made a wind to pass H430
15 And **G** spake unto Noah, saying, H430
9: 1 And **G** blessed Noah and his sons, and H430
6 for in the image of **G** made he man. H430
8 And **G** spake unto Noah, and to his sons H430
12 And **G** said, This *is* the token of the H430
16 covenant between **G** and every living H430
17 And **G** said unto Noah, This *is* the token H430
26 And he said, Blessed *be* the LORD **G** of H430
27 **G** shall enlarge Japheth, and he shall H430
14:18 and he *was* the priest of the most high **G**. H410
19 high **G**, possessor of heaven and earth: H410
20 And blessed be the most high **G**, which H410
22 **G**, the possessor of heaven and earth, H410
15: 2 And Abram said, Lord **G**, what wilt H3069
8 And he said, Lord **G**, whereby shall I H3069
16:13 unto her, Thou **G** seest me: for she said, H410
17: 1 **G**; walk before me, and be thou perfect. H410
3 And Abram fell on his face: and **G** talked H430
7 a **G** unto thee, and to thy seed after thee. H430
8 possession; and I will be their **G**. H430
9 And **G** said unto Abraham, Thou shalt H430
15 And **G** said unto Abraham, As for Sarai H430
18 And Abraham said unto **G**, O that H430
19 And **G** said, Sarah thy wife shall bear H430
22 And he left off talking with him, and **G** H430
23 selfsame day, as **G** had said unto him. H430
19:29 And it came to pass, when **G** destroyed H430
29 cities of the plain, that **G** remembered H430
20: 3 But **G** came to Abimelech in a dream by H430
6 And **G** said unto him in a dream, Yea, I H430
11 Surely the fear of **G** *is* not in this place; H430
13 And it came to pass, when **G** caused me H430
17 So Abraham prayed unto **G**: and God H430
17 So Abraham prayed unto God: and **G** H430
21: 2 set time of which **G** had spoken to him. H430
4 days old, as **G** had commanded him. H430
6 And Sarah said, **G** hath made me to H430
12 And **G** said unto Abraham, Let it not be H430
17 And **G** heard the voice of the lad; and the H430
17 and the angel of **G** called to Hagar out H430
17 fear not; for **G** hath heard the voice H430
19 And **G** opened her eyes, and she saw a H430
20 And **G** was with the lad; and he grew, H430
22 **G** *is* with thee in all that thou doest: H430
23 Now therefore swear unto me here by **G** H430
33 the name of the LORD, the everlasting **G**. H410
22: 1 these things, that **G** did tempt Abraham, H430
3 unto the place of which **G** had told him. H430
8 And Abraham said, My son, **G** will H430
9 And they came to the place which **G** had H430
12 that thou fearest **G**, seeing thou hast not H430
24: 3 by the LORD, the **G** of heaven, and the H430
3 of heaven, and the **G** of the earth, that H430
7 The LORD **G** of heaven, which took me H430
12 And he said, O LORD **G** of my master H430
27 And he said, Blessed *be* the LORD **G** of H430
42 well, and said, O LORD **G** of my master H430
48 and blessed the LORD **G** of my master H430
25:11 of Abraham, that **G** blessed his son H430
26:24 and said, I *am* the **G** of Abraham thy H430
27:20 the LORD thy **G** brought *it* to me. H430
28 Therefore **G** give thee of the dew of H430
28: 3 And **G** Almighty bless thee, and make H410
4 a stranger, which **G** gave unto Abraham. H430
12 of **G** ascending and descending on it. H430
13 I *am* the LORD **G** of Abraham thy father, H430
13 thy father, and the **G** of Isaac: the land H430
17 house of **G**, and this *is* the gate of heaven. H430
20 And Jacob vowed a vow, saying, If **G** will H430
21 in peace; then shall the LORD be my **G**: H430
30: 6 And Rachel said, **G** hath judged me, and H430
17 And **G** hearkened unto Leah, and she H430
18 And Leah said, **G** hath given me my hire, H430
20 And Leah said, **G** hath endued me *with* a H430
22 And **G** remembered Rachel, and God H430
22 And God remembered Rachel, and **G** H430
23 said, **G** hath taken away my reproach: H430

G

Gen 31: 5 the **G** of my father hath been with me. H430
7 but **G** suffered him not to hurt me. H430
9 Thus **G** hath taken away the cattle of H430
11 And the angel of **G** spake unto me in a H430
13 I *am* the **G** of Beth-el, where thou H410
16 For all the riches which **G** hath taken H430
16 whatsoever **G** hath said unto thee, do. H430
24 And **G** came to Laban the Syrian in a H430
29 you hurt: but the **G** of your father spake H430
42 Except the **G** of my father, the God of H430
42 Except the God of my father, the **G** of H430
42 me away now empty. **G** hath seen mine H430
50 see, **G** *is* witness betwixt me and thee. H430
53 The **G** of Abraham, and the God of H430
53 The God of Abraham, and the **G** of H430
53 the God of Nahor, the **G** of their father, H430
32: 1 on his way, and the angels of **G** met him. H430
9 And Jacob said, O **G** of my father H430
9 Abraham, and **G** of my father Isaac, the H430
28 **G** and with men, and hast prevailed. H430
30 **G** face to face, and my life is preserved. H430
33: 5 **G** hath graciously given thy servant. H430
10 face of **G**, and thou wast pleased with me. H430
11 to thee; because **G** hath dealt graciously H430
35: 1 And **G** said unto Jacob, Arise, go up to H430
1 there an altar unto **G**, that appeared unto H410
3 there an altar unto **G**, who answered me H410
5 And they journeyed: and the terror of **G** H430
7 because there **G** appeared unto him, H430
9 And **G** appeared unto Jacob again, when H430
10 And **G** said unto him, Thy name *is* H430
11 And **G** said unto him, I *am* God H430
11 And God said unto him, I *am* **G** H410
13 And **G** went up from him in the place H430
15 place where **G** spake with him, Beth-el. H430
39: 9 this great wickedness, and sin against **G**? H430
40: 8 *belong* to **G**? tell me *them*, I pray you. H430
41:16 *It is* not in me: **G** shall give Pharaoh an H430
25 dream of Pharaoh *is* one: **G** hath shewed H430
28 unto Pharaoh: What **G** *is* about to do he H430
32 **G**, and God will shortly bring it to pass. H430
32 God, and **G** will shortly bring it to pass. H430
38 this *is*, a man in whom the spirit of **G** *is*? H430
39 Forasmuch as **G** hath shewed thee all H430
51 Manasseh: For **G**, *said he*, hath made me H430
52 he Ephraim: For **G** hath caused me to be H430
42:18 third day, This do, and live; *for* I fear **G**: H430
28 What *is* this *that* **G** hath done unto us? H430
43:14 And **G** Almighty give you mercy before H410
23 to you, fear not: your **G**, and the God of H430
23 your God, and the **G** of your father, hath H430
29 he said, **G** be gracious unto thee, my son. H430
44: 7 my lord these words? **G** forbid that thy H2486
16 we clear ourselves? **G** hath found out the H430
17 And he said, **G** forbid that I should do H2486
45: 5 sold me hither: for **G** did send me before H430
7 And **G** sent me before you to preserve H430
8 sent me hither, but **G**: and he hath made H430
9 thy son Joseph, **G** hath made me lord of H430
46: 1 sacrifices unto the **G** of his father Isaac. H430
2 And **G** spake unto Israel in the visions of H430
3 And he said, I *am* **G**, the God of thy H410
3 And he said, I *am* God, the **G** of thy H430
48: 3 And Jacob said unto Joseph, **G** Almighty H410
9 my sons, whom **G** hath given me in this H430
11 and, lo, **G** hath shewed me also thy seed. H430
15 And he blessed Joseph, and said, **G**, H430
15 Isaac did walk, the **G** which fed me all H430
20 bless, saying, **G** make thee as Ephraim H430
21 Behold, I die: but **G** shall be with you, H430
49:24 of the mighty **G** of Jacob; (from thence
25 *Even* by the **G** of thy father, who shall H410
50:17 the servants of the **G** of thy father. And H430
19 them, Fear not: for *am* I in the place of **G**? H430
20 against me; *but* **G** meant it unto good, H430
24 I die: and **G** will surely visit you, H430
25 of Israel, saying, **G** will surely visit you, H430
Ex 1:17 But the midwives feared **G**, and did not H430
20 Therefore **G** dealt well with the H430
21 feared **G**, that he made them houses. H430
2:23 up unto **G** by reason of the bondage. H430
24 And **G** heard their groaning, and God H430
24 And God heard their groaning, and **G** H430
25 And **G** looked upon the children of H430
25 of Israel, and **G** had respect unto *them*. H430
3: 1 to the mountain of **G**, *even* to Horeb. H430
4 aside to see, **G** called unto him out H430
6 Moreover he said, I *am* the **G** of thy H430
6 of thy father, the **G** of Abraham, the God H430

Ex 3: 6 of Abraham, the **G** of Isaac, and the God H430
6 of Isaac, and the **G** of Jacob. And Moses H430
6 face; for he was afraid to look upon **G**. H430
11 And Moses said unto **G**, Who *am* I, that I H430
12 ye shall serve **G** upon this mountain. H430
13 And Moses said unto **G**, Behold, *when* I H430
13 unto them, The **G** of your fathers hath H430
14 And **G** said unto Moses, I AM THAT I H430
15 And **G** said moreover unto Moses, Thus H430
15 Israel, The LORD **G** of your fathers, the H430
15 of your fathers, the **G** of Abraham, the H430
15 of Abraham, the **G** of Isaac, and the God H430
15 of Isaac, and the **G** of Jacob, hath sent H430
16 them, The LORD **G** of your fathers, the H430
16 of your fathers, the **G** of Abraham, of H430
18 him, The LORD **G** of the Hebrews hath H430
18 that we may sacrifice to the LORD our **G**. H430
4: 5 That they may believe that the LORD **G** H430
5 of their fathers, the **G** of Abraham, the H430
5 of Abraham, the **G** of Isaac, and the God H430
5 the **G** of Jacob, hath appeared unto thee. H430
16 and thou shalt be to him instead of **G**. H430
20 and Moses took the rod of **G** in his hand. H430
27 him in the mount of **G**, and kissed him. H430
5: 1 Thus saith the LORD **G** of Israel, Let my H430
3 And they said, The **G** of the Hebrews H430
3 unto the LORD our **G**; lest he fall upon us H430
8 saying, Let us go *and* sacrifice to our **G**. H430
6: 2 And **G** spake unto Moses, and said unto H430
3 by *the name of* **G** Almighty, but by my H410
7 I will be to you a **G**: and ye shall know H430
7 *am* the LORD your **G**, which bringeth you H430
7: 1 I have made thee a **g** to Pharaoh: and H430
16 him, The LORD **G** of the Hebrews hath H430
8:10 *there is* none like unto the LORD our **G**. H430
19 *is* the finger of **G**: and Pharaoh's heart H430
25 Go ye, sacrifice to your **G** in the land. H430
26 to the LORD our **G**: lo, shall we sacrifice H430
27 LORD our **G**, as he shall command us. H430
28 to the LORD your **G** in the wilderness; H430
9: 1 saith the LORD **G** of the Hebrews, Let H430
13 saith the LORD **G** of the Hebrews, Let H430
30 that ye will not yet fear the LORD **G**. H430
10: 3 saith the LORD **G** of the Hebrews, How H430
7 the LORD their **G**: knowest thou not yet H430
8 your **G**: *but* who *are* they that shall go? H430
16 the LORD your **G**, and against you. H430
17 the LORD your **G**, that he may take away H430
25 we may sacrifice unto the LORD our **G**. H430
26 the LORD our **G**; and we know not with H430
13:17 let the people go, that **G** led them not H430
17 although that *was* near; for **G** said, Lest H430
18 But **G** led the people about, *through* the H430
19 of Israel, saying, **G** will surely visit you; H430
14:19 And the angel of **G**, which went before H430
15: 2 salvation: he *is* my **G**, and I will prepare H410
2 my father's **G**, and I will exalt him. H430
26 voice of the LORD thy **G**, and wilt do that H430
16: 3 them, Would to **G** we had died by the
12 shall know that I *am* the LORD your **G**. H430
17: 9 the hill with the rod of **G** in mine hand. H430
18: 1 heard of all that **G** had done for Moses, H430
4 *was* Eliezer; for the **G** of my father, *said* H430
5 where he encamped at the mount of **G**: H430
12 and sacrifices for **G**: and Aaron came, H430
12 bread with Moses' father in law before **G**. H430
15 the people come unto me to inquire of **G**: H430
16 know the statutes of **G**, and his laws. H430
19 thee counsel, and **G** shall be with thee: H430
19 thou mayest bring the causes unto **G**: H430
21 men, such as fear **G**, men of truth, hating H430
23 If thou shalt do this thing, and **G** H430
19: 3 And Moses went up unto **G**, and the H430
17 camp to meet with **G**; and they stood at H430
19 spake, and **G** answered him by a voice. H430
20: 1 And **G** spake all these words, saying, H430
2 I *am* the LORD thy **G**, which have H430
5 for I the LORD thy **G** *am* a jealous God, H430
5 God *am* a jealous **G**, visiting the iniquity H410
7 of the LORD thy **G** in vain; for the LORD H430
10 of the LORD thy **G**: *in it* thou shalt not do H430
12 land which the LORD thy **G** giveth thee. H430
19 but let not **G** speak with us, lest we die. H430
20 Fear not: for **G** is come to prove you, H430
21 unto the thick darkness where **G** *was*. H430
21:13 And if a man lie not in wait, but **G** H430
22:20 He that sacrificeth unto *any* **g**, save unto H430
23:17 males shall appear before the Lord **G**. H3068
19 of the LORD thy **G**. Thou shalt not seethe H430

Ex 23:25 And ye shall serve the LORD your **G**, and H430
24:10 And they saw the **G** of Israel: and *there* H430
11 also they saw **G**, and did eat and drink. H430
13 and Moses went up into the mount of **G**. H430
29:45 the children of Israel, and will be their **G**. H430
46 *am* the LORD their **G**, that brought them H430
46 among them: I *am* the LORD their **G**. H430
31: 3 And I have filled him with the spirit of **G**, H430
18 of stone, written with the finger of **G**. H430
32:11 And Moses besought the LORD his **G**, H430
16 And the tables *were* the work of **G**, and H430
16 the writing of **G**, graven upon the tables. H430
27 saith the LORD **G** of Israel, Put every H430
34: 6 The LORD, The LORD **G**, merciful and H410
14 For thou shalt worship no other **g**: for the H410
14 whose name *is* Jealous, *is* a jealous **G**: H410
23 before the Lord **G**, the God of Israel. H3068
23 before the Lord GOD, the **G** of Israel. H430
24 before the LORD thy **G** thrice in the year. H430
26 of the LORD thy **G**. Thou shalt not seethe H430
35:31 him with the spirit of **G**, in wisdom, in H430
Lev 2:13 covenant of thy **G** to be lacking from thy H430
4:22 of the LORD his **G** *concerning things* H430
10:17 it *is* most holy, and **G** hath given it you
11:44 For I *am* the LORD your **G**: ye shall H430
45 Egypt, to be your **G**: ye shall therefore be H430
18: 2 say unto them, I am the LORD your **G**. H430
4 to walk therein: I *am* the LORD your **G**. H430
21 the name of thy **G**: I *am* the LORD. H430
30 therein: I *am* the LORD your **G**. H430
19: 2 be holy: for I the LORD your **G** *am* holy. H430
3 my sabbaths: I *am* the LORD your **G**. H430
4 molten gods: I *am* the LORD your **G**. H430
10 and stranger: I *am* the LORD your **G**. H430
12 the name of thy **G**: I *am* the LORD. H430
14 but shalt fear thy **G**: I *am* the LORD. H430
25 increase thereof: I *am* the LORD your **G**. H430
31 defiled by them: I *am* the LORD your **G**. H430
32 old man, and fear thy **G**: I *am* the LORD. H430
34 the land of Egypt: I *am* the LORD your **G**. H430
36 *am* the LORD your **G**, which brought you H430
20: 7 be ye holy: for I *am* the LORD your **G**. H430
24 I *am* the LORD your **G**, which have H430
21: 6 They shall be holy unto their **G**, and not H430
6 the name of their **G**: for the offerings of H430
6 *and* the bread of their **G**, they do offer: H430
7 her husband: for he *is* holy unto his **G**. H430
8 the bread of thy **G**: he shall be holy unto H430
12 sanctuary of his **G**; for the crown of the H430
12 oil of his **G** *is* upon him: I *am* the LORD. H430
17 not approach to offer the bread of his **G**. H430
21 not come nigh to offer the bread of his **G**. H430
22 He shall eat the bread of his **G**, *both* of H430
22:25 offer the bread of your **G** of any of these; H430
33 of Egypt, to be your **G**: I *am* the LORD. H430
23:14 offering unto your **G**: *it shall be* a statute H430
22 to the stranger: I *am* the LORD your **G**. H430
28 for you before the LORD your **G**. H430
40 before the LORD your **G** seven days. H430
43 the land of Egypt: I *am* the LORD your **G**. H430
24:15 curseth his **G** shall bear his sin. H430
22 own country: for I *am* the LORD your **G**. H430
25:17 fear thy **G**: for I *am* the LORD your God. H430
17 fear thy God: for I *am* the LORD your **G**. H430
36 **G**; that thy brother may live with thee. H430
38 I *am* the LORD your **G**, which brought H430
38 the land of Canaan, *and* to be your **G**. H430
43 him with rigour; but shalt fear thy **G**. H430
55 the land of Egypt: I *am* the LORD your **G**. H430
26: 1 down unto it: for I *am* the LORD your **G**. H430
12 will be your **G**, and ye shall be my people. H430
13 I *am* the LORD your **G**, which brought H430
44 with them: for I *am* the LORD their **G**. H430
45 that I might be their **G**: I *am* the LORD. H430
Nu 6: 7 consecration of his **G** *is* upon his head. H430
10: 9 the LORD your **G**, and ye shall be saved H430
10 before your **G**: I *am* the LORD your God. H430
10 before your God: I *am* the LORD your **G**. H430
11:29 my sake? would **G** that all the LORD'S H5414
12:13 Heal her now, O **G**, I beseech thee. H410
14: 2 unto them, Would **G** that we had died in
2 **G** we had died in this wilderness! H3863
15:40 and be holy unto your **G**. H430
41 I *am* the LORD your **G**, which brought H430
41 to be your **G**: I *am* the LORD your God. H430
41 to be your God: I *am* the LORD your **G**. H430
16: 9 thing unto you, that the **G** of Israel hath H430
22 their faces, and said, O **G**, the God of the H410
22 said, O God, the **G** of the spirits of all H430

Nu 20: 3 saying, Would **G** that we had died when
21: 5 And the people spake against **G**, and H430
22: 9 And **G** came unto Balaam, and said, H430
10 And Balaam said unto **G**, Balak the son H430
12 And **G** said unto Balaam, Thou shalt not H430
18 of the LORD my **G**, to do less or more. H430
20 And **G** came unto Balaam at night, and H430
38 the word that **G** putteth in my mouth, H430
23: 4 And **G** met Balaam: and he said unto H430
8 How shall I curse, whom **G** hath not H410
19 **G** *is* not a man, that he should lie; H410
21 the LORD his **G** *is* with him, and the H430
22 **G** brought them out of Egypt; he hath as H410
23 and of Israel, What hath **G** wrought! H410
27 it will please **G** that thou mayest curse H430
24: 2 and the spirit of **G** came upon him. H430
4 heard the words of **G**, which saw the H410
8 **G** brought him forth out of Egypt; he H410
16 heard the words of **G**, and knew the H410
23 Alas, who shall live when **G** doeth this! H410
25:13 he was zealous for his **G**, and made an H430
27:16 Let the LORD, the **G** of the spirits of all H430
Dt 1: 6 The LORD our **G** spake unto us in H430
10 The LORD your **G** hath multiplied you, H430
11 (The LORD **G** of your fathers make you H430
19 as the LORD our **G** commanded us; and H430
20 the LORD our **G** doth give unto us. H430
21 Behold, the LORD thy **G** hath set the H430
21 *it*, as the LORD **G** of thy fathers hath H430
25 land which the LORD our **G** doth give us. H430
26 the commandment of the LORD your **G**: H430
30 The LORD your **G** which goeth before H430
31 that the LORD thy **G** bare thee, as a man H430
32 thing ye did not believe the LORD your **G**, H430
41 all that the LORD our **G** commanded us. H430
2: 7 For the LORD thy **G** hath blessed thee in H430
7 the LORD thy **G** *hath been* with thee; H430
29 land which the LORD our **G** giveth us. H430
30 for the LORD thy **G** hardened his spirit, H430
33 And the LORD our **G** delivered him H430
36 us: the LORD our **G** delivered all unto us: H430
37 whatsoever the LORD our **G** forbad us. H430
3: 3 So the LORD our **G** delivered into our H430
18 The LORD your **G** hath given you this H430
20 which the LORD your **G** hath given them H430
21 the LORD your **G** hath done unto these H430
22 the LORD your **G** he shall fight for you. H430
24 O Lord **G**, thou hast begun to shew thy H3069
24 hand: for what **G** *is there* in heaven or H410
4: 1 the LORD **G** of your fathers giveth you. H430
2 the LORD your **G** which I command you. H430
3 **G** hath destroyed them from among you. H430
4 **G** *are* alive every one of you this day. H430
5 as the LORD my **G** commanded me, that H430
7 *so* great, who *hath* **G** *so* nigh unto them, H430
7 as the LORD our **G** *is* in all *things that* H430
10 the LORD thy **G** in Horeb, when the H430
19 the LORD thy **G** hath divided unto all H430
21 thy **G** giveth thee *for* an inheritance: H430
23 of the LORD your **G**, which he made with H430
23 the LORD thy **G** hath forbidden thee. H430
24 For the LORD thy **G** *is* a consuming fire, H430
24 *is* a consuming fire, *even* a jealous **G**. H410
25 LORD thy **G**, to provoke him to anger: H430
29 seek the LORD thy **G**, thou shalt find H430
30 **G**, and shalt be obedient unto his voice; H430
31 (For the LORD thy **G** *is* a merciful God;) H430
31 (For the LORD thy God *is* a merciful **G**;) H410
32 since the day that **G** created man upon H430
33 Did *ever* people hear the voice of **G** H430
34 Or hath **G** assayed to go *and* take him a H430
34 **G** did for you in Egypt before your eyes? H430
35 he *is* **G**; *there is* none else beside him. H430
39 the LORD he *is* **G** in heaven above, and H430
40 the LORD thy **G** giveth thee, for ever. H430
5: 2 The LORD our **G** made a covenant with H430
6 I *am* the LORD thy **G**, which brought thee H430
9 for I the LORD thy **G** *am* a jealous God, H430
9 God *am* a jealous **G**, visiting the iniquity H410
11 of the LORD thy **G** in vain: for the LORD H430
12 the LORD thy **G** hath commanded thee. H430
14 of the LORD thy **G**: *in it* thou shalt not do H430
15 *that* the LORD thy **G** brought thee out H430
15 the LORD thy **G** commanded thee to H430
16 as the LORD thy **G** hath commanded H430
16 land which the LORD thy **G** giveth thee. H430
24 And ye said, Behold, the LORD our **G** H430
24 that **G** doth talk with man, and he liveth. H430
25 LORD our **G** any more, then we shall die. H430
Dt 5:26 voice of the living **G** speaking out of the H430
27 all that the LORD our **G** shall say: and H430
27 all that the LORD our **G** shall speak unto H430
32 as the LORD your **G** hath commanded H430
33 the LORD your **G** hath commanded you, H430
6: 1 the LORD your **G** commanded to teach H430
2 That thou mightest fear the LORD thy **G**, H430
3 as the LORD **G** of thy fathers hath H430
4 Hear, O Israel: The LORD our **G** *is* one H430
5 And thou shalt love the LORD thy **G** with H430
10 And it shall be, when the LORD thy **G** H430
13 Thou shalt fear the LORD thy **G**, and H430
15 (For the LORD thy **G** *is* a jealous God H430
15 (For the LORD thy God *is* a jealous **G** H410
15 of the LORD thy **G** be kindled against H430
16 Ye shall not tempt the LORD your **G**, as H430
17 of the LORD your **G**, and his testimonies, H430
20 the LORD our **G** hath commanded you? H430
24 to fear the LORD our **G**, for our good H430
25 LORD our **G**, as he hath commanded us. H430
7: 1 When the LORD thy **G** shall bring thee H430
2 And when the LORD thy **G** shall deliver H430
6 unto the LORD thy **G**: the LORD thy God H430
6 God: the LORD thy **G** hath chosen thee H430
9 Know therefore that the LORD thy **G**, he H430
9 thy God, he *is* **G**, the faithful God, which H430
9 he *is* God, the faithful **G**, which keepeth H410
12 that the LORD thy **G** shall keep unto thee H430
16 the LORD thy **G** shall deliver thee; thine H430
18 **G** did unto Pharaoh, and unto all Egypt; H430
19 the LORD thy **G** brought thee out: so H430
19 so shall the LORD thy **G** do unto all the H430
20 Moreover the LORD thy **G** will send the H430
21 for the LORD thy **G** *is* among you, a H430
21 *is* among you, a mighty **G** and terrible. H410
22 And the LORD thy **G** will put out those H430
23 But the LORD thy **G** shall deliver them H430
25 it *is* an abomination to the LORD thy **G**. H430
8: 2 the LORD thy **G** led thee these forty H430
5 son, *so* the LORD thy **G** chasteneth thee. H430
6 **G**, to walk in his ways, and to fear him. H430
7 For the LORD thy **G** bringeth thee into a H430
10 bless the LORD thy **G** for the good land H430
11 not the LORD thy **G**, in not keeping his H430
14 the LORD thy **G**, which brought thee H430
18 the LORD thy **G**: for *it is* he that giveth H430
19 the LORD thy **G**, and walk after other H430
20 unto the voice of the LORD your **G**. H430
9: 3 that the LORD thy **G** *is* he which goeth H430
4 that the LORD thy **G** hath cast them out H430
5 the LORD thy **G** doth drive them out H430
6 that the LORD thy **G** giveth thee not this H430
7 the LORD thy **G** to wrath in the H430
10 with the finger of **G**; and on them *was* H430
16 the LORD your **G**, *and* had made you a H430
23 of the LORD your **G**, and ye believed him H430
26 and said, O Lord **G**, destroy not thy H3069
10: 9 as the LORD thy **G** promised him. H430
12 doth the LORD thy **G** require of thee, but H430
12 to fear the LORD thy **G**, to walk in all his H430
12 **G** with all thy heart and with all thy soul, H430
14 **G**, the earth *also*, with all that therein *is*. H430
17 For the LORD your **G** *is* God of gods, and H430
17 For the LORD your God *is* **G** of gods, and H430
17 Lord of lords, a great **G**, a mighty, and a H410
20 Thou shalt fear the LORD thy **G**; him H430
21 He *is* thy praise, and he *is* thy **G**, that H430
22 now the LORD thy **G** hath made thee as H430
11: 1 shalt love the LORD thy **G**, and keep his H430
2 of the LORD your **G**, his greatness, his H430
12 A land which the LORD thy **G** careth for: H430
12 of the LORD thy **G** *are* always upon it, H430
13 the LORD your **G**, and to serve him with H430
22 the LORD your **G**, to walk in all his ways, H430
25 *for* the LORD your **G** shall lay the fear of H430
27 your **G**, which I command you this day: H430
28 of the LORD your **G**, but turn aside out of H430
29 the LORD thy **G** hath brought thee in H430
31 the LORD your **G** giveth you, and ye H430
12: 1 which the LORD **G** of thy fathers giveth H430
4 Ye shall not do so unto the LORD your **G**. H430
5 the LORD your **G** shall choose out of all H430
7 the LORD your **G**, and ye shall rejoice H430
7 the LORD thy **G** hath blessed thee. H430
9 which the LORD your **G** giveth you. H430
10 the LORD your **G** giveth you to inherit, H430
11 the LORD your **G** shall choose to cause H430
12 the LORD your **G**, ye, and your sons, and H430
15 of the LORD thy **G** which he hath given H430
Dt 12:18 the LORD thy **G** in the place which the H430
18 the LORD our **G** shall choose, thou, and H430
18 the LORD thy **G** in all that thou puttest H430
20 When the LORD thy **G** shall enlarge thy H430
21 If the place which the LORD thy **G** hath H430
27 of the LORD thy **G**: and the blood of thy H430
27 LORD thy **G**, and thou shalt eat the flesh. H430
28 and right in the sight of the LORD thy **G**. H430
29 When the LORD thy **G** shall cut off the H430
31 so unto the LORD thy **G**: for every H430
13: 3 for the LORD your **G** proveth you, to H430
3 the LORD your **G** with all your heart and H430
4 Ye shall walk after the LORD your **G**, and H430
5 the LORD your **G**, which brought you out H430
5 the LORD thy **G** commanded thee to H430
10 from the LORD thy **G**, which brought H430
12 **G** hath given thee to dwell there, saying, H430
16 for the LORD thy **G**: and it shall be an H430
18 voice of the LORD thy **G**, to keep all his H430
18 *is* right in the eyes of the LORD thy **G**. H430
14: 1 Ye *are* the children of the LORD your **G**: H430
2 unto the LORD thy **G**, and the LORD hath H430
21 unto the LORD thy **G**. Thou shalt not H430
23 the LORD thy **G**, in the place which he H430
23 learn to fear the LORD thy **G** always. H430
24 the LORD thy **G** shall choose to set his H430
24 when the LORD thy **G** hath blessed thee: H430
25 which the LORD thy **G** shall choose: H430
26 the LORD thy **G**, and thou shalt rejoice, H430
29 that the LORD thy **G** may bless thee in H430
15: 4 which the LORD thy **G** giveth thee *for* an H430
5 of the LORD thy **G**, to observe to do all H430
6 For the LORD thy **G** blesseth thee, as he H430
7 the LORD thy **G** giveth thee, thou shalt H430
10 the LORD thy **G** shall bless thee in all H430
14 the LORD thy **G** hath blessed thee thou H430
15 and the LORD thy **G** redeemed thee: H430
18 **G** shall bless thee in all that thou doest. H430
19 unto the LORD thy **G**: thou shalt do no H430
20 Thou shalt eat *it* before the LORD thy **G** H430
21 not sacrifice it unto the LORD thy **G**. H430
16: 1 unto the LORD thy **G**: for in the month of H430
1 Abib the LORD thy **G** brought thee forth H430
2 unto the LORD thy **G**, of the flock and the H430
5 gates, which the LORD thy **G** giveth thee: H430
6 But at the place which the LORD thy **G** H430
7 the LORD thy **G** shall choose: and thou H430
8 thy **G**: thou shalt do no work *therein*. H430
10 unto the LORD thy **G** with a tribute of a H430
10 *unto the LORD thy* **G**, according as the
10 as the LORD thy **G** hath blessed thee: H430
11 the LORD thy **G**, thou, and thy son, and H430
11 **G** hath chosen to place his name there. H430
15 unto the LORD thy **G** in the place which H430
15 the LORD thy **G** shall bless thee in all H430
16 the LORD thy **G** in the place which he H430
17 LORD thy **G** which he hath given thee. H430
18 the LORD thy **G** giveth thee, throughout H430
20 land which the LORD thy **G** giveth thee. H430
21 LORD thy **G**, which thou shalt make thee. H430
22 image; which the LORD thy **G** hateth. H430
17: 1 unto the LORD thy **G** *any* bullock, or H430
1 *is* an abomination unto the LORD thy **G**. H430
2 the LORD thy **G** giveth thee, man or H430
2 thy **G**, in transgressing his covenant, H430
8 which the LORD thy **G** shall choose; H430
12 the LORD thy **G**, or unto the judge, even H430
14 the LORD thy **G** giveth thee, and shalt H430
15 the LORD thy **G** shall choose: *one* from H430
19 to fear the LORD his **G**, to keep all the H430
18: 5 For the LORD thy **G** hath chosen him out H430
7 of the LORD his **G**, as all his brethren the H430
9 the LORD thy **G** giveth thee, thou shalt H430
12 **G** doth drive them out from before thee. H430
13 shalt be perfect with the LORD thy **G**. H430
14 thy **G** hath not suffered thee so *to do*. H430
15 The LORD thy **G** will raise up unto thee a H430
16 of the LORD thy **G** in Horeb in the day H430
16 of the LORD my **G**, neither let me see this H430
19: 1 When the LORD thy **G** hath cut off the H430
1 land the LORD thy **G** giveth thee, and H430
2 the LORD thy **G** giveth thee to possess it. H430
3 the LORD thy **G** giveth thee to inherit, H430
8 And if the LORD thy **G** enlarge thy coast, H430
9 love the LORD thy **G**, and to walk ever in H430
10 which the LORD thy **G** giveth thee *for* an H430
14 the LORD thy **G** giveth thee to possess it. H430
20: 1 for the LORD thy **G** *is* with thee, which H430
4 For the LORD your **G** *is* he that goeth H430

Dt 20:13 And when the LORD thy G hath H430
14 which the LORD thy G hath given thee. H430
16 the LORD thy G doth give thee *for* an H430
17 the LORD thy G hath commanded thee: H430
18 should ye sin against the LORD your G. H430
21: 1 the LORD thy G giveth thee to possess H430
5 the LORD thy G hath chosen to minister H430
10 and the LORD thy G hath delivered them H430
23 *is* accursed of G;) that thy land be not H430
23 thy G giveth thee *for* an inheritance. H430
22: 5 *are* abomination unto the LORD thy G. H430
23: 5 Nevertheless the LORD thy G would not H430
5 but the LORD thy G turned the curse H430
5 because the LORD thy G loved thee. H430
14 For the LORD thy G walketh in the midst H430
18 of the LORD thy G for any vow: for even H430
18 *are* abomination unto the LORD thy G. H430
20 that the LORD thy G may bless thee in H430
21 vow unto the LORD thy G, thou shalt not H430
21 for the LORD thy G will surely require it H430
23 unto the LORD thy G, which thou hast H430
24: 4 thy G giveth thee *for* an inheritance. H430
9 Remember what the LORD thy G did H430
13 unto thee before the LORD thy G. H430
18 and the LORD thy G redeemed thee H430
19 that the LORD thy G may bless thee in H430
25:15 land which the LORD thy G giveth thee. H430
16 an abomination unto the LORD thy G. H430
18 faint and weary; and he feared not G. H430
19 the LORD thy G hath given thee rest H430
19 which the LORD thy G giveth thee *for* an H430
26: 1 which the LORD thy G giveth thee *for* an H430
2 that the LORD thy G giveth thee, and H430
2 G shall choose to place his name there. H430
3 day unto the LORD thy G, that I am come H430
4 down before the altar of the LORD thy G. H430
5 the LORD thy G, A Syrian ready to perish H430
7 And when we cried unto the LORD G of H430
10 the LORD thy G, and worship before H430
10 and worship before the LORD thy G: H430
11 the LORD thy G hath given unto thee, H430
13 the LORD thy G, I have brought away H430
14 voice of the LORD my G, *and* have done H430
16 This day the LORD thy G hath H430
17 this day to be thy G, and to walk in his H430
19 unto the LORD thy G, as he hath spoken. H430
27: 2 the LORD thy G giveth thee, that thou H430
3 the LORD thy G giveth thee, a land that H430
3 G of thy fathers hath promised thee. H430
5 unto the LORD thy G, an altar of stones: H430
6 of the LORD thy G of whole stones: and H430
6 offerings thereon unto the LORD thy G: H430
7 there, and rejoice before the LORD thy G. H430
9 art become the people of the LORD thy G. H430
10 voice of the LORD thy G, and do his H430
28: 1 of the LORD thy G, to observe *and* to do H430
1 that the LORD thy G will set thee on high H430
2 unto the voice of the LORD thy G. H430
8 land which the LORD thy G giveth thee. H430
9 of the LORD thy G, and walk in his ways. H430
13 of the LORD thy G, which I command H430
15 of the LORD thy G, to observe to do all H430
45 voice of the LORD thy G, to keep his H430
47 not the LORD thy G with joyfulness, and H430
52 which the LORD thy G hath given thee. H430
53 the LORD thy G hath given thee, in the H430
58 and fearful name, THE LORD THY G; H430
62 not obey the voice of the LORD thy G. H430
67 shalt say, Would G it were even! and at H5414
67 shalt say, Would G it were morning! for H5414
29: 6 might know that I *am* the LORD your G. H430
10 the LORD your G; your captains of your H430
12 with the LORD thy G, and into his oath, H430
12 LORD thy G maketh with thee this day: H430
13 he may be unto thee a G, as he hath said H430
15 the LORD our G, and also with *him* that H430
18 the LORD our G, to go *and* serve the gods H430
25 of the LORD G of their fathers, which H430
29 unto the LORD our G: but those *things* H430
30: 1 the LORD thy G hath driven thee, H430
2 And shalt return unto the LORD thy G, H430
3 That then the LORD thy G will turn thy H430
3 the LORD thy G hath scattered thee. H430
4 will the LORD thy G gather thee, and H430
5 And the LORD thy G will bring thee into H430
6 And the LORD thy G will circumcise H430
6 love the LORD thy G with all thine heart, H430
7 And the LORD thy G will put all these H430
9 And the LORD thy G will make thee H430

Dt 30:10 voice of the LORD thy G, to keep his H430
10 turn unto the LORD thy G with all thine H430
16 love the LORD thy G, to walk in his ways, H430
16 and the LORD thy G shall bless thee in H430
20 That thou mayest love the LORD thy G, H430
31: 3 The LORD thy G, he will go over before H430
6 for the LORD thy G, he *it is* that doth go H430
11 the LORD thy G in the place which he H430
12 the LORD your G, and observe to do all H430
13 the LORD your G, as long as ye live in H430
17 upon us, because our G *is* not among us? H430
26 of the LORD your G, that it may be there H430
32: 3 LORD: ascribe ye greatness unto our G. H430
4 *are* judgment: a G of truth and without H410
12 and *there was* no strange g with him. H410
15 then he forsook G *which* made him, and H433
17 They sacrificed unto devils, not to G; to H433
18 and hast forgotten G that formed thee. H410
21 *that which is* not G; they have provoked H410
39 he, and *there is* no g with me: I kill, and I H430
33: 1 Moses the man of G blessed the children H430
26 *There is* none like unto the G of H410
27 The eternal G *is thy* refuge, and H430
Jos 1: 9 G *is* with thee whithersoever thou goest. H430
11 LORD your G giveth you to possess it. H430
13 The LORD your G hath given you rest, H430
15 the LORD your G giveth them: then ye H430
17 G be with thee, as he was with Moses. H430
2:11 for the LORD your G, he *is* G in heaven H430
11 your God, he *is* G in heaven above, and H430
3: 3 of the LORD your G, and the priests the H430
9 and hear the words of the LORD your G. H430
10 that the living G *is* among you, and *that* H410
4: 5 ark of the LORD your G into the midst of H430
23 For the LORD your G dried up the H430
23 as the LORD your G did to the Red sea, H430
24 ye might fear the LORD your G for ever. H430
7: 7 And Joshua said, Alas, O Lord G, H3069
7 us? would to G we had been content, H3863
13 saith the LORD G of Israel, *There is* an H430
19 glory to the LORD G of Israel, and make H430
20 against the LORD G of Israel, and thus H430
8: 7 your G will deliver it into your hand. H430
30 the LORD G of Israel in mount Ebal, H430
9: 9 of the LORD thy G: for we have heard the H430
18 them by the LORD G of Israel. And all H430
19 unto them by the LORD G of Israel: now H430
23 drawers of water for the house of my G. H430
24 that the LORD thy G commanded his H430
10:19 G hath delivered them into your hand. H430
40 as the LORD G of Israel commanded. H430
42 the LORD G of Israel fought for Israel. H430
13:14 of the LORD G of Israel made by fire H430
33 the LORD G of Israel *was* their H430
14: 6 Moses the man of G concerning me and H430
8 but I wholly followed the LORD my G. H430
9 hast wholly followed the LORD my G. H430
14 he wholly followed the LORD G of Israel. H430
18: 3 LORD G of your fathers hath given you? H430
6 lots for you here before the LORD our G. H430
22: 3 the commandment of the LORD your G. H430
4 And now the LORD your G hath given H430
5 the LORD your G, and to walk in all his H430
16 against the G of Israel, to turn away H430
19 altar beside the altar of the LORD our G. H430
22 The LORD G of gods, the LORD God of H410
22 The LORD God of gods, the LORD G of H410
24 have ye to do with the LORD G of Israel? H430
29 G forbid that we should rebel against the
29 our G that *is* before his tabernacle. H430
33 of Israel blessed G, and did not intend to H430
34 a witness between us that the LORD *is* G. H430
23: 3 that the LORD your G hath done unto all H430
3 your G *is* he that hath fought for you. H430
5 And the LORD your G, he shall expel H430
5 LORD your G hath promised unto you. H430
8 But cleave unto the LORD your G, as ye H430
10 for the LORD your G, he *it is* that fighteth H430
11 yourselves, that ye love the LORD your G. H430
13 the LORD your G will no more drive out H430
13 which the LORD your G hath given you. H430
14 the LORD your G spake concerning you; H430
15 the LORD your G promised you; so shall H430
15 which the LORD your G hath given you. H430
16 covenant of the LORD your G, which he H430
24: 1 and they presented themselves before G. H430
2 saith the LORD G of Israel, Your fathers H430
16 And the people answered and said, G
17 For the LORD our G, he *it is* that brought H430

Jos 24:18 we also serve the LORD; for he *is* our G. H430
19 for he *is* an holy G; he *is* a jealous God; H430
19 he *is* a jealous G; he will not forgive your H410
23 your heart unto the LORD G of Israel. H430
24 The LORD our G will we serve, and his H430
26 the book of the law of G, and took a great H430
27 a witness unto you, lest ye deny your G. H430
Jdg 1: 7 as I have done, so G hath requited me. H430
2:12 And they forsook the LORD G of their H430
3: 7 G, and served Baalim and the groves. H430
20 a message from G unto thee. And he H430
4: 6 not the LORD G of Israel commanded, H430
23 So G subdued on that day Jabin the king H430
5: 3 I will sing *praise* to the LORD G of Israel. H430
5 Sinai from before the LORD G of Israel. H430
6: 8 saith the LORD G of Israel, I brought H430
10 *am* the LORD your G; fear not the gods of H430
20 And the angel of G said unto him, Take H430
22 said, Alas, O Lord G! for because I have H3069
26 And build an altar unto the LORD thy G H430
31 morning: if he *be* a g, let him plead for H430
36 And Gideon said unto G, If thou wilt save H430
39 And Gideon said unto G, Let not thine H430
40 And G did so that night: for it was dry H430
7:14 G delivered Midian, and all the host. H430
8: 3 G hath delivered into your hands the H430
33 Baalim, and made Baal-berith their g. H430
34 not the LORD their G, who had delivered H430
9: 7 Shechem, that G may hearken unto you. H430
9 by me they honour G and man, and go H430
13 which cheereth G and man, and go to H430
23 Then G sent an evil spirit between H430
27 into the house of their g, and did eat and H430
29 And would to G this people were under H5414
46 into an hold of the house of the g Berith. H410
56 Thus G rendered the wickedness of H430
57 men of Shechem did G render upon their H430
10:10 forsaken our G, and also served Baalim. H430
11:21 And the LORD G of Israel delivered H430
23 So now the LORD G of Israel hath H430
24 Chemosh thy g giveth thee to possess? H430
24 the LORD our G shall drive out from H430
13: 5 be a Nazarite unto G from the womb: H430
6 saying, A man of G came unto me, and H430
6 of an angel of G, very terrible: but I asked H430
7 G from the womb to the day of his death. H430
8 let the man of G which thou didst send H430
9 And G hearkened to the voice of H430
9 and the angel of G came again unto the H430
22 shall surely die, because we have seen G. H430
15:19 But G clave an hollow place that *was* in H430
16:17 a Nazarite unto G from my mother's H430
23 unto Dagon their g, and to rejoice: for H430
23 for they said, Our g hath delivered H430
24 they praised their g: for they said, Our H430
24 for they said, Our g hath delivered into H430
28 and said, O Lord G, remember me, I H3069
28 only this once, O G, that I may be at once H430
18: 5 we pray thee, of G, that we may know H430
10 to a large land: for G hath given it into H430
31 time that the house of G was in Shiloh. H430
20: 2 of the people of G, four hundred H430
18 up to the house of G, and asked counsel H1008
18 asked counsel of G, and said, Which of H430
26 unto the house of G, and wept, and sat H1008
27 covenant of G *was* there in those days, H430
31 up to the house of G, and the other to H1008
21: 2 And the people came to the house of G, H1008
2 till even before G, and lifted up their H430
3 And said, O LORD G of Israel, why is H430
Ru 1:16 *shall be* my people, and thy G my God: H430
16 *shall be* my people, and thy God my G: H430
2:12 thee of the LORD G of Israel, under H430
1Sa 1:17 in peace: and the G of Israel grant *thee* H430
2: 2 thee: neither *is there* any rock like our G. H430
3 for the LORD *is* a G of knowledge, and H410
27 And there came a man of G unto Eli, and H430
30 Wherefore the LORD G of Israel saith, I H430
32 *the wealth* which G shall give Israel: and
3: 3 And ere the lamp of G went out in the H430
3 where the ark of G *was*, and Samuel was H430
17 hide *it* not from me: G do so to thee, and H430
4: 4 there with the ark of the covenant of G. H430
7 for they said, G is come into the camp. H430
11 And the ark of G was taken; and the two H430
13 for the ark of G. And when the man came H430
17 are dead, and the ark of G is taken. H430
18 of the ark of G, that he fell from off H430
19 that the ark of G was taken, and that H430

1Sa 4:21 because the ark of G was taken, and H430
22 from Israel: for the ark of G is taken. H430
5: 1 And the Philistines took the ark of G, and H430
2 When the Philistines took the ark of G, H430
7 The ark of the G of Israel shall not abide H430
7 is sore upon us, and upon Dagon our g. H430
8 with the ark of the G of Israel? And they H430
8 Let the ark of the G of Israel be carried H430
8 the ark of the G of Israel about *thither.* H430
10 Therefore they sent the ark of G to H430
10 pass, as the ark of G came to Ekron, that H430
10 the ark of the G of Israel to us, to slay H430
11 away the ark of the G of Israel, and let it H430
11 city; the hand of G was very heavy there. H430
6: 3 away the ark of the G of Israel, send it H430
5 shall give glory unto the G of Israel: H430
20 G? and to whom shall he go up from us? H430
7: 8 unto the LORD our G for us, that he will H430
9: 6 in this city a man of G, and *he is* an H430
7 to bring to the man of G: what have we? H430
8 I give to the man of G, to tell us our way. H430
9 man went to inquire of G, thus he spake, H430
10 unto the city where the man of G *was.* H430
27 that I may shew thee the word of G. H430
10: 3 three men going up to G to Beth-el, one H430
5 After that thou shalt come to the hill of G, H430
7 as occasion serve thee; for G *is* with thee. H430
9 to go from Samuel, G gave him another H430
10 and the spirit of G came upon him, and H430
18 saith the LORD G of Israel, I brought up H430
19 And ye have this day rejected your G, H430
24 shouted, and said, G save the king.
26 of men, whose hearts G had touched. H430
11: 6 And the spirit of G came upon Saul H430
12: 9 And when they forgat the LORD their G, H430
12 when the LORD your G *was* your king. H430
14 you continue following the LORD your G: H430
19 unto the LORD thy G, that we die not: for H430
23 Moreover as for me, G forbid that I
13:13 of the LORD thy G, which he commanded H430
14:18 hither the ark of G. For the ark of God H430
18 of God. For the ark of G was at that time H430
36 priest, Let us draw near hither unto G. H430
37 And Saul asked counsel of G, Shall I go H430
41 Therefore Saul said unto the LORD G of H430
44 And Saul answered, G do so and more H430
45 great salvation in Israel? G forbid: *as* the
45 he hath wrought with G this day. So the H430
15:15 G; and the rest we have utterly destroyed. H430
21 sacrifice unto the LORD thy G in Gilgal. H430
30 me, that I may worship the LORD thy G. H430
16:15 now, an evil spirit from G troubleth thee. H430
16 the evil spirit from G is upon thee, that H430
23 the *evil* spirit from G was upon Saul, H430
17:26 he should defy the armies of the living G? H430
36 he hath defied the armies of the living G. H430
45 the LORD of hosts, the G of the armies of H430
46 may know that there is a G in Israel. H430
18:10 the evil spirit from G came upon Saul, H430
19:20 over them, the spirit of G was upon the H430
23 and the spirit of G was upon him also, H430
20: 2 And he said unto him, G forbid; thou
12 David, O LORD G of Israel, when I have H430
22: 3 you, till I know what G will do for me. H430
13 and hast inquired of G for him, that he H430
15 Did I then begin to inquire of G for him? H430
23: 7 And Saul said, G hath delivered him into H430
10 Then said David, O LORD G of Israel, H430
11 heard? O LORD G of Israel, I beseech H430
14 but G delivered him not into his hand. H430
16 wood, and strengthened his hand in G. H430
25:22 So and more also do G unto the enemies H430
29 life with the LORD thy G; and the souls of H430
32 *be* the LORD G of Israel, which sent H430
34 For in very deed, *as* the LORD G of Israel H430
26: 8 Then said Abishai to David, G hath H430
28:15 against me, and G is departed from me, H430
29: 9 as an angel of G: notwithstanding the H430
30: 6 encouraged himself in the LORD his G. H430
15 said, Swear unto me by G, that thou wilt H430
2Sa 2:27 And Joab said, *As* G liveth, unless thou H430
3: 9 So do G to Abner, and more also, except, H430
35 saying, So do G to me, and more also, H430
5:10 and the LORD G of hosts *was* with him. H430
6: 2 thence the ark of G, whose name is called H430
3 And they set the ark of G upon a new H430
4 ark of G: and Ahio went before the ark. H430
6 *hand* to the ark of G, and took hold of it; H430
7 Uzzah; and G smote him there for H430

2Sa 6: 7 error; and there he died by the ark of G. H430
12 of the ark of G. So David went and H430
12 up the ark of G from the house of H430
7: 2 the ark of G dwelleth within curtains. H430
18 Who *am* I, O Lord G? and what *is* my H3069
19 in thy sight, O Lord G; but thou hast H3069
19 *is* this the manner of man, O Lord G? H3069
20 for thou, Lord G, knowest thy servant. H3069
22 Wherefore thou art great, O LORD G: for H430
22 *is there any* G beside thee, according H430
23 like Israel, whom G went to redeem for a H430
24 and thou, LORD, art become their G. H430
25 And now, O LORD G, the word that thou H430
26 of hosts *is* the G over Israel: and let the H430
27 For thou, O LORD of hosts, G of Israel, H430
28 And now, O Lord G, thou *art* that God, H3069
28 And now, O Lord GOD, thou *art* that G, H430
29 for thou, O Lord G, hast spoken *it:* and H3069
9: 3 the kindness of G unto him? And Ziba H430
10:12 for the cities of our G: and the LORD do H430
12: 7 saith the LORD G of Israel, I anointed H430
16 David therefore besought G for the child; H430
22 can tell *whether* G will be gracious to H3068
14:11 the LORD thy G, that thou wouldest not H430
13 the people of G? for the king doth speak H430
14 neither doth G respect *any* person: H430
16 son together out of the inheritance of G. H430
17 for as an angel of G, so *is* my lord the H430
17 the LORD thy G will be with thee. H430
20 of an angel of G, to know all *things* that H430
15:24 of the covenant of G: and they set down H430
24 set down the ark of G; and Abiathar went H430
25 back the ark of G into the city: if I shall H430
29 carried the ark of G again to Jerusalem: H430
32 he worshipped G, behold, Hushai the H430
16:16 G save the king, God save the king.
16 God save the king, G save the king.
23 at the oracle of G: so *was* all the counsel H430
18:28 *be* the LORD thy G, which hath delivered H430
33 Absalom! would G I had died for thee, O
19:13 and of my flesh? G do so to me, and H430
27 *is* as an angel of G: do therefore *what is* H430
21:14 after that G was entreated for the land. H430
22: 3 The G of my rock; in him will I trust: *he* H430
7 and cried to my G: and he did hear my H430
22 have not wickedly departed from my G. H430
30 troop: by my G have I leaped over a wall. H430
31 *As for* G, his way *is* perfect; the word of H410
32 For who *is* G, save the LORD? and who *is* H410
32 the LORD? and who *is* a rock, save our G? H430
33 G *is* my strength *and* power: and he H410
47 be the G of the rock of my salvation. H430
48 It *is* G that avengeth me, and that H410
23: 1 the anointed of the G of Jacob, and the H430
3 The G of Israel said, the Rock of Israel H430
3 men *must be* just, ruling in the fear of G. H430
5 Although my house *be* not so with G; yet H410
24: 3 king, Now the LORD thy G add unto the H430
23 the king, The LORD thy G accept thee. H430
24 unto the LORD my G of that which doth H430
1Ki 1:17 swarest by the LORD thy G unto thine H430
25 him, and say, G save king Adonijah.
30 thee by the LORD G of Israel, saying, H430
34 trumpet, and say, G save king Solomon.
36 LORD G of my lord the king say so *too.* H430
39 all the people said, G save king Solomon.
47 king David, saying, G make the name of H430
48 *be* the LORD G of Israel, which hath H430
2: 3 And keep the charge of the LORD thy G, H430
23 by the LORD, saying, G do so to me, and H430
26 the ark of the Lord G before David my H3069
3: 5 and G said, Ask what I shall give thee. H430
7 And now, O LORD my G, thou hast made H430
11 And G said unto him, Because thou hast H430
28 of G *was* in him, to do judgment. H430
4:29 And G gave Solomon wisdom and H430
5: 3 of the LORD his G for the wars which H430
4 But now the LORD my G hath given me H430
5 of the LORD my G, as the LORD spake H430
8:15 And he said, Blessed *be* the LORD G of H430
17 for the name of the LORD G of Israel. H430
20 for the name of the LORD G of Israel. H430
23 And he said, LORD G of Israel, *there is* H430
23 Israel, *there is* no G like thee, in heaven H430
25 Therefore now, LORD G of Israel, keep H430
26 And now, O G of Israel, let thy word, I H430
27 But will G indeed dwell on the earth? H430
28 O LORD my G, to hearken unto the H430
53 our fathers out of Egypt, O Lord G. H3069

1Ki 8:57 The LORD our G be with us, as he was H430
59 unto the LORD our G day and night, that H430
60 LORD *is* G, *and that there is* none else. H430
61 with the LORD our G, to walk in his H430
65 the LORD our G, seven days and seven H430
9: 9 the LORD their G, who brought forth H430
10: 9 Blessed be the LORD thy G, which H430
24 wisdom, which G had put in his heart. H430
11: 4 G, as *was* the heart of David his father. H430
9 from the LORD G of Israel, which had H430
23 And G stirred him up *another* adversary, H430
31 the LORD, the G of Israel, Behold, I will H430
33 Chemosh the g of the Moabites, and H430
33 and Milcom the g of the children of H430
12:22 But the word of G came unto Shemaiah H430
22 unto Shemaiah the man of G, saying, H430
13: 1 And, behold, there came a man of G out H430
4 of the man of G, which had cried against H430
5 of G had given by the word of the LORD. H430
6 unto the man of G, Entreat now the face H430
6 of the LORD thy G, and pray for me, that H430
6 And the man of G besought the LORD, H430
7 And the king said unto the man of G, H430
8 And the man of G said unto the king, If H430
11 that the man of G had done that day in H430
12 man of G went, which came from Judah. H430
14 And went after the man of G, and found H430
14 *Art* thou the man of G that camest from H430
21 And he cried unto the man of G that H430
21 which the LORD thy G commanded thee, H430
26 It *is* the man of G, who was disobedient H430
29 of the man of G, and laid it upon the H430
31 the man of G *is* buried; lay my bones H430
14: 7 saith the LORD G of Israel, Forasmuch H430
13 G of Israel in the house of Jeroboam. H430
15: 3 his G, as the heart of David his father. H430
4 did the LORD his G give him a lamp in H430
30 provoked the LORD G of Israel to anger. H430
16:13 G of Israel to anger with their vanities. H430
26 G of Israel to anger with their vanities. H430
33 to provoke the LORD G of Israel to anger H430
17: 1 *As* the LORD G of Israel liveth, before H430
12 And she said, *As* the LORD thy G liveth, H430
14 For thus saith the LORD G of Israel, The H430
18 O thou man of G? art thou come unto H430
20 and said, O LORD my G, hast thou also H430
21 said, O LORD my G, I pray thee, let this H430
24 thou *art* a man of G, *and* that the word of H430
18:10 *As* the LORD thy G liveth, there is no H430
21 if the LORD *be* G, follow him: but if Baal, H430
24 the LORD: and the G that answereth by H430
24 by fire, let him be G. And all the people H430
27 aloud: for he *is* a g; either he is talking, or H430
36 and said, LORD G of Abraham, Isaac, H430
36 day that thou *art* G in Israel, and *that* I H430
37 thou *art* the LORD G, and *that* thou hast H430
39 he *is* the G; the LORD, he *is* the God. H430
39 he *is* the God; the LORD, he *is* the G. H430
19: 8 forty nights unto Horeb the mount of G. H430
10 for the LORD G of hosts: for the children H430
14 for the LORD G of hosts: because the H430
20:28 And there came a man of G, and spake H430
28 said, The LORD *is* G of the hills, but he *is* H430
28 the hills, but he *is* not G of the valleys, H430
21:10 didst blaspheme G and the king. And H430
13 did blaspheme G and the king. Then H430
22:53 to anger the LORD G of Israel, according H430
2Ki 1: 2 of Baal-zebub the g of Ekron whether I H430
3 *there is* not a G in Israel, *that* ye go to H430
3 to inquire of Baal-zebub the g of Ekron? H430
6 *there is* not a G in Israel, *that* thou H430
6 of Baal-zebub the g of Ekron? therefore H430
9 of G, the king hath said, Come down. H430
10 fifty, If I *be* a man of G, then let fire come H430
11 him, O man of G, thus hath the king said, H430
12 If I *be* a man of G, let fire come down H430
12 fifty. And the fire of G came down from H430
13 him, O man of G, I pray thee, let my life, H430
16 of Baalzebub the g of Ekron, *is it* not H430
16 because *there is* no G in Israel to inquire H430
2:14 *is* the LORD G of Elijah? and when H430
4: 7 Then she came and told the man of G. H430
9 of G, which passeth by us continually. H430
16 of G, do not lie unto thine handmaid. H430
21 bed of the man of G, and shut *the door* H430
22 run to the man of G, and come again. H430
25 So she went and came unto the man of G H430
25 when the man of G saw her afar off, that H430
27 And when she came to the man of G to H430

G

2Ki 4:27 And the man of **G** said, Let her alone; for H430
40 O *thou* man of **G**, *there is* death in the H430
42 the man of **G** bread of the firstfruits, H430
5: 3 mistress, Would **G** my lord *were* with the H305
7 and said, *Am* I **G**, to kill and to make H430
8 And it was *so*, when Elisha the man of **G** H430
11 of the LORD his **G**, and strike his hand H430
14 of the man of **G**: and his flesh came again H430
15 And he returned to the man of **G**, he and H430
15 that *there is* no **G** in all the earth, but in H430
20 of Elisha the man of **G**, said, Behold, my H430
6: 6 And the man of **G** said, Where fell it? H430
9 And the man of **G** sent unto the king of H430
10 place which the man of **G** told him and H430
15 And when the servant of the man of **G** H430
31 Then he said, **G** do so and more also to H430
7: 2 the man of **G**, and said, Behold, *if* H430
17 he died, as the man of **G** had said, who H430
18 And it came to pass as the man of **G** had H430
19 And that lord answered the man of **G**, H430
8: 2 of the man of **G**: and she went with her H430
4 of the man of **G**, saying, Tell me, I pray H430
7 saying, The man of **G** is come hither. H430
8 go, meet the man of **G**, and inquire of the H430
11 was ashamed: and the man of **G** wept. H430
9: 6 Thus saith the LORD **G** of Israel, I have H430
10:31 law of the LORD **G** of Israel with all his H430
11:12 their hands, and said, **G** save the king.
13:19 And the man of **G** was wroth with him, H430
14:25 word of the LORD **G** of Israel, which he H430
16: 2 of the LORD his **G**, like David his father. H430
17: 7 the LORD their **G**, which had brought H430
9 the LORD their **G**, and they built them H430
14 that did not believe in the LORD their **G**. H430
16 of the LORD their **G**, and made them H430
19 of the LORD their **G**, but walked in the H430
26 not the manner of the **G** of the land: H430
26 not the manner of the **G** of the land. H430
27 them the manner of the **G** of the land. H430
39 But the LORD your **G** ye shall fear; and H430
18: 5 He trusted in the LORD **G** of Israel; so H430
12 of the LORD their **G**, but transgressed his H430
22 in the LORD our **G**: *is* not that he, whose H430
19: 4 It may be the LORD thy **G** will hear all H430
4 to reproach the living **G**; and will reprove H430
4 the LORD thy **G** hath heard: wherefore H430
10 saying, Let not thy **G** in whom thou H430
15 and said, O LORD **G** of Israel, which H430
15 thou art the **G**, *even* thou alone, of all H430
16 hath sent him to reproach the living **G**. H430
19 Now therefore, O LORD our **G**, I beseech H430
19 thou *art* the LORD **G**, *even* thou only. H430
20 saith the LORD **G** of Israel, *That* which H430
37 of Nisroch his **g**, that Adrammelech and H430
20: 5 the LORD, the **G** of David thy father, H430
21:12 Therefore thus saith the LORD **G** of H430
22 And he forsook the LORD **G** of his H430
22:15 saith the LORD **G** of Israel, Tell the man H430
18 saith the LORD **G** of Israel, *As touching* H430
23:16 which the man of **G** proclaimed, who H430
17 of the man of **G**, which came from Judah, H430
21 the LORD your **G**, as *it is* written in the H430
1Ch 4:10 And Jabez called on the **G** of Israel, H430
10 **G** granted him that which he requested. H430
5:20 for they cried to **G** in the battle, and he H430
22 the war *was* of **G**. And they dwelt in their H430
25 And they transgressed against the **G** of H430
25 land, whom **G** destroyed before them. H430
26 And the **G** of Israel stirred up the spirit H430
6:48 of the tabernacle of the house of **G**. H430
49 the servant of **G** had commanded. H430
9:11 son of Ahitub, the ruler of the house of **G**; H430
13 the work of the service of the house of **G**. H430
26 and treasuries of the house of **G**. H430
27 about the house of **G**, because the charge H430
11: 2 and the LORD thy **G** said unto thee, H430
19 And said, My **G** forbid it me, that I H430
12:17 in mine hands, the **G** of our fathers look H430
18 helpers; for thy **G** helpeth thee. Then H430
22 *it was* a great host, like the host of **G**. H430
13: 2 *be* of the LORD our **G**, let us send abroad H430
3 And let us bring again the ark of our **G** H430
5 bring the ark of **G** from Kirjath-jearim. H430
6 up thence the ark of **G** the LORD, that H430
7 And they carried the ark of **G** in a new H430
8 And David and all Israel played before **G** H430
10 to the ark: and there he died before **G**. H430
12 And David was afraid of **G** that day, H430
12 shall I bring the ark of **G** *home* to me? H430

1Ch 13:14 And the ark of **G** remained with the H430
14:10 And David inquired of **G**, saying, Shall I H430
11 Then David said, **G** hath broken in upon H430
14 Therefore David inquired again of **G**; and H430
14 again of God; and **G** said unto him, Go H430
15 shalt go out to battle: for **G** is gone forth H430
16 David therefore did as **G** commanded H430
15: 1 for the ark of **G**, and pitched for it a tent. H430
2 to carry the ark of **G** but the Levites: for H430
2 of **G**, and to minister unto him for ever. H430
12 the ark of the LORD **G** of Israel unto *the* H430
13 the first, the LORD our **G** made a breach H430
14 bring up the ark of the LORD **G** of Israel. H430
15 bare the ark of **G** upon their shoulders H430
24 before the ark of **G**: and Obed-edom and H430
26 And it came to pass, when **G** helped the H430
16: 1 So they brought the ark of **G**, and set it in H430
1 sacrifices and peace offerings before **G**. H430
4 thank and praise the LORD **G** of Israel: H430
6 before the ark of the covenant of **G**. H430
14 He *is* the LORD our **G**; his judgments *are* H430
35 And say ye, Save us, O **G** of our H430
36 Blessed *be* the LORD **G** of Israel for ever H430
42 instruments of **G**. And the sons of H430
17: 2 that *is* in thine heart; for **G** *is* with thee. H430
3 the word of **G** came to Nathan, saying, H430
16 Who *am* I, O LORD **G**, and what *is* mine H430
17 in thine eyes, O **G**; for thou hast *also* H430
17 of a man of high degree, O LORD **G**. H430
20 *is there any* **G** beside thee, according H430
21 Israel, whom **G** went to redeem *to be* H430
22 ever; and thou, LORD, becamest their **G**. H430
24 of hosts *is* the **G** of Israel, *even* a God H430
24 of Israel, *even* a **G** to Israel: and *let* the H430
25 For thou, O my **G**, hast told thy servant H430
26 And now, LORD, thou art **G**, and hast H430
19:13 for the cities of our **G**: and let the LORD H430
21: 7 And **G** was displeased with this thing; H430
8 And David said unto **G**, I have sinned H430
15 And **G** sent an angel unto Jerusalem to H430
17 And David said unto **G**, *Is it* not I *that* H430
17 thee, O LORD my **G**, be on me, and on H430
30 before it to inquire of **G**: for he was afraid H430
22: 1 house of the LORD **G**, and this *is* the altar H430
2 wrought stones to build the house of **G**. H430
6 build an house for the LORD **G** of Israel. H430
7 house unto the name of the LORD my **G**: H430
11 the LORD thy **G**, as he hath said of thee. H430
12 mayest keep the law of the LORD thy **G**. H430
18 *Is* not the LORD your **G** with you? and H430
19 the LORD your **G**; arise therefore, and H430
19 of the LORD **G**, to bring the ark of the H430
19 the holy vessels of **G**, into the house that H430
23:14 Now *concerning* Moses the man of **G**, his H430
25 For David said, The LORD **G** of Israel H430
28 the work of the service of the house of **G**; H430
24: 5 *of the house* of **G**, were of the sons of H430
19 LORD **G** of Israel had commanded him. H430
25: 5 in the words of **G**, to lift up the horn. And H430
5 lift up the horn. And **G** gave to Heman H430
6 of the house of **G**, according to the king's H430
26: 5 Peulthai the eighth: for **G** blessed him. H430
20 of the house of **G**, and over the treasures H430
32 pertaining to **G**, and affairs of the king. H430
28: 2 **G**, and had made ready for the building: H430
3 But **G** said unto me, Thou shalt not build H430
4 Howbeit the LORD **G** of Israel chose me H430
8 audience of our **G**, keep and seek for all H430
8 of the LORD your **G**: that ye may possess H430
9 son, know thou the **G** of thy father, and H430
12 of the house of **G**, and of the treasuries H430
20 for the LORD **G**, *even* my God, *will be* H430
20 God, *even* my **G**, *will be* with thee; he H430
21 of the house of **G**: and *there shall be* with H430
29: 1 son, whom alone **G** hath chosen, *is yet* H430
1 *is* not for man, but for the LORD **G**. H430
2 the house of my **G** the gold for *things to* H430
3 to the house of my **G**, I have of mine own H430
3 to the house of my **G**, over and above all H430
7 of the house of **G** of gold five thousand H430
10 **G** of Israel our father, for ever and ever. H430
13 Now therefore, our **G**, we thank thee, and H430
16 O LORD our **G**, all this store that we have H430
17 I know also, my **G**, that thou triest the H430
18 O LORD **G** of Abraham, Isaac, and of H430
20 bless the LORD your **G**. And all the H430
20 blessed the LORD **G** of their fathers, and H430
2Ch 1: 1 and the LORD his **G** *was* with him, and H430
3 the congregation of **G**, which Moses the H430

2Ch 1: 4 But the ark of **G** had David brought up H430
7 In that night did **G** appear unto H430
8 And Solomon said unto **G**, Thou hast H430
9 Now, O LORD **G**, let thy promise unto H430
11 And **G** said to Solomon, Because this H430
2: 4 of the LORD my **G**, to dedicate *it* to him, H430
4 **G**. This *is an ordinance* for ever to Israel. H430
5 *is* great: for great *is* our **G** above all gods. H430
12 *be* the LORD **G** of Israel, that made H430
3: 3 of the house of **G**. The length by cubits H430
4:11 for king Solomon for the house of **G**; H430
19 *for* the house of **G**, the golden altar also, H430
5: 1 he among the treasures of the house of **G**. H430
14 of the LORD had filled the house of **G**. H430
6: 4 And he said, Blessed *be* the LORD **G** of H430
7 for the name of the LORD **G** of Israel. H430
10 for the name of the LORD **G** of Israel. H430
14 And said, O LORD **G** of Israel, *there is* no H430
14 of Israel, *there is* no **G** like thee in the H430
16 Now therefore, O LORD **G** of Israel, keep H430
17 Now then, O LORD **G** of Israel, let thy H430
18 But will **G** in very deed dwell with men H430
19 O LORD my **G**, to hearken unto the H430
40 Now, my **G**, let, I beseech thee, thine eyes H430
41 Now therefore arise, O LORD **G**, into thy H430
41 thy priests, O LORD **G**, be clothed with H430
42 O LORD **G**, turn not away the face of H430
7: 5 all the people dedicated the house of **G**. H430
22 they forsook the LORD **G** of their fathers, H430
8:14 so had David the man of **G** commanded. H430
9: 8 Blessed be the LORD thy **G**, which H430
8 for the LORD thy **G**: because thy God H430
8 thy God: because thy **G** loved Israel, to H430
23 his wisdom, that **G** had put in his heart. H430
10:15 the cause was of **G**, that the LORD might H430
11: 2 came to Shemaiah the man of **G**, saying, H430
16 to seek the LORD **G** of Israel came to H430
16 unto the LORD **G** of their fathers. H430
13: 5 Ought ye not to know that the LORD **G** H430
10 But as for us, the LORD *is* our **G**, and we H430
11 LORD our **G**; but ye have forsaken him. H430
12 And, behold, **G** himself *is* with us for *our* H430
12 against the LORD **G** of your fathers; for H430
15 it came to pass, that **G** smote Jeroboam H430
16 and **G** delivered them into their hand. H430
18 relied upon the LORD **G** of their fathers. H430
14: 2 and right in the eyes of the LORD his **G**: H430
4 to seek the LORD **G** of their fathers, and H430
7 the LORD our **G**, we have sought *him*, H430
11 And Asa cried unto the LORD his **G**, and H430
11 us, O LORD our **G**; for we rest on thee, H430
11 our **G**; let not man prevail against thee. H430
15: 1 And the spirit of **G** came upon Azariah H430
3 *been* without the true **G**, and without a H430
4 unto the LORD **G** of Israel, and sought H430
6 for **G** did vex them with all adversity. H430
9 saw that the LORD his **G** *was* with him. H430
12 to seek the LORD **G** of their fathers with H430
13 not seek the LORD **G** of Israel should be H430
18 And he brought into the house of **G** the H430
16: 7 on the LORD thy **G**, therefore is the host H430
17: 4 But sought to the *LORD* **G** of his father, H430
18: 5 for **G** will deliver *it* into the king's hand. H430
13 even what my **G** saith, that will I speak. H430
31 and **G** moved them *to depart* from him. H430
19: 3 and hast prepared thine heart to seek **G**. H430
4 back unto the LORD **G** of their fathers. H430
7 with the LORD our **G**, nor respect of H430
20: 6 And said, O LORD **G** of our fathers, *art* H430
6 *art* not thou **G** in heaven? and rulest H430
7 *Art* not thou our **G**, *who* didst drive out H430
12 O our **G**, wilt thou not judge them? for we H430
19 **G** of Israel with a loud voice on high. H430
20 in the LORD your **G**, so shall ye be H430
29 And the fear of **G** was on all the H430
30 for his **G** gave him rest round about. H430
33 their hearts unto the **G** of their fathers. H430
21:10 had forsaken the LORD **G** of his fathers. H430
12 saith the LORD **G** of David thy father, H430
22: 7 And the destruction of Ahaziah was of **G** H430
12 them hid in the house of **G** six years: and H430
23: 3 in the house of **G**. And he said unto them, H430
9 David's, which *were* in the house of **G**. H430
11 anointed him, and said, **G** save the king.
24: 5 the house of your **G** from year to year, H430
7 broken up the house of **G**; and also all the H430
9 of **G** *laid* upon Israel in the wilderness. H430
13 of **G** in his state, and strengthened it. H430
16 both toward **G**, and toward his house. H430

2Ch 24:18 And they left the house of the LORD G of H430
20 And the spirit of G came upon Zechariah H430
20 them, Thus saith G, Why transgress ye H430
24 the LORD G of their fathers. So they H430
27 of the house of G, behold, they *are* H430
25: 7 But there came a man of G to him, H430
8 for the battle: G shall make thee fall H430
8 G hath power to help, and to cast down. H430
9 And Amaziah said to the man of G, But H430
9 And the man of G answered, The LORD H430
16 said, I know that G hath determined to H430
20 not hear; for it *came* of G, that he might H430
24 in the house of G with Obed-edom, and H430
26: 5 And he sought G in the days of H430
5 in the visions of G: and as long as he H430
5 the LORD, G made him to prosper. H430
7 And G helped him against the H430
16 the LORD his G, and went into the H430
18 *it be* for thine honour from the LORD G. H430
27: 6 his ways before the LORD his G. H430
28: 5 Wherefore the LORD his G delivered H430
6 forsaken the LORD G of their fathers. H430
9 because the LORD G of your fathers was H430
10 with you, sins against the LORD your G? H430
24 of the house of G, and cut in pieces the H430
24 of the house of G, and shut up the doors H430
25 to anger the LORD G of his fathers. H430
29: 5 the house of the LORD G of your fathers, H430
6 of the LORD our G, and have forsaken H430
7 in the holy *place* unto the G of Israel. H430
10 with the LORD G of Israel, that his fierce H430
36 all the people, that G had prepared the H430
30: 1 the passover unto the LORD G of Israel. H430
5 unto the LORD G of Israel at Jerusalem: H430
6 unto the LORD G of Abraham, Isaac, H430
7 against the LORD G of their fathers, *who* H430
8 the LORD your G, that the fierceness of H430
9 for the LORD your G *is* gracious and H430
12 Also in Judah the hand of G was to give H430
16 Moses the man of G: the priests sprinkled H430
19 *That* prepareth his heart to seek G, the H430
19 God, the LORD G of his fathers, though H430
22 to the LORD G of their fathers. H430
31: 6 LORD their G, and laid *them* by heaps. H430
13 and Azariah the ruler of the house of G. H430
14 offerings of G, to distribute the oblations H430
20 right and truth before the LORD his G. H430
21 of the house of G, and in the law, and H430
21 to seek his G, he did *it* with all his H430
32: 8 us *is* the LORD our G to help us, and to H430
11 The LORD our G shall deliver us out of H430
14 mine hand, that your G should be able to H430
15 yet believe him: for no g of any nation or H433
15 your G deliver you out of mine hand? H430
16 G, and against his servant Hezekiah. H430
17 to rail on the LORD G of Israel, and to H430
17 so shall not the G of Hezekiah deliver H430
19 And they spake against the G of H430
21 the house of his g, they that came forth H430
29 G had given him substance very much. H430
31 *done* in the land, G left him, to try him, H430
33: 7 in the house of G, of which God had said H430
7 of God, of which G had said to David H430
12 the LORD his G, and humbled himself H430
12 greatly before the G of his fathers, H430
13 Manasseh knew that the LORD he *was* G. H430
16 Judah to serve the LORD G of Israel. H430
17 places, *yet* unto the LORD their G only. H430
18 his prayer unto his G, and the words of H430
18 name of the LORD G of Israel, behold, H430
19 His prayer also, and *how* G was
34: 3 to seek after the G of David his father: H430
8 to repair the house of the LORD his G. H430
9 into the house of G, which the Levites H430
23 saith the LORD G of Israel, Tell ye the H430
26 saith the LORD G of Israel *concerning* H430
27 thyself before G, when thou heardest H430
32 covenant of G, the God of their fathers. H430
32 covenant of God, the G of their fathers. H430
33 the LORD their G. *And* all his days they H430
33 the LORD, the G of their fathers. H430
35: 3 the LORD your G, and his people Israel, H430
8 of the house of G, gave unto the priests H430
21 I have war: for G commanded me to H430
21 *meddling with* G, who *is* with me, that H430
22 from the mouth of G, and came to fight H430
36: 5 *was* evil in the sight of the LORD his G. H430
12 of the LORD his G, *and* humbled not H430
13 him swear by G: but he stiffened his H430

2Ch 36:13 from turning unto the LORD G of Israel. H430
15 And the LORD G of their fathers sent to H430
16 But they mocked the messengers of G, H430
18 And all the vessels of the house of G, H430
19 And they burnt the house of G, and brake H430
23 hath the LORD G of heaven given me; H430
23 his G *be* with him, and let him go up. H430
Ezr 1: 2 of Persia, The LORD G of heaven hath H430
3 all his people? his G be with him, and let H430
3 house of the LORD G of Israel, (he *is* the H430
3 Israel, (he *is* the G,) which *is* in Jerusalem. H430
4 for the house of G that *is* in Jerusalem. H430
5 *them* whose spirit G had raised, to go up H430
2:68 the house of G to set it up in his place: H430
3: 2 the altar of the G of Israel, to offer burnt H430
2 written in the law of Moses the man of G. H430
8 unto the house of G at Jerusalem, in the H430
9 in the house of G: the sons of Henadad, H430
4: 1 the temple unto the LORD G of Israel; H430
2 for we seek your G, as ye *do*; and we do H430
3 an house unto our G; but we ourselves H430
3 unto the LORD G of Israel, as king Cyrus H430
24 Then ceased the work of the house of G H426
5: 1 name of the G of Israel, *even* unto them. H426
2 to build the house of G which *is* at H426
2 *were* the prophets of G helping them. H426
5 But the eye of their G was upon the H426
8 the house of the great G, which is builded H426
11 are the servants of the G of heaven and H426
12 had provoked the G of heaven unto H426
13 made a decree to build this house of G. H426
14 of the house of G, which Nebuchadnezzar H426
15 let the house of G be builded in his place. H426
16 of the house of G which *is* in Jerusalem: H426
17 build this house of G at Jerusalem, and H426
6: 3 the house of G at Jerusalem, Let the H426
5 of the house of G, which Nebuchadnezzar H426
5 place, and place *them* in the house of G. H426
7 Let the work of this house of G alone; let H426
7 Jews build this house of G in his place. H426
8 of this house of G: that of the king's H426
9 offerings of the G of heaven, wheat, salt, H426
10 savours unto the G of heaven, and pray H426
12 And the G that hath caused his name to H426
12 this house of G which *is* at Jerusalem. H426
14 of the G of Israel, and according H426
16 dedication of this house of G with joy, H426
17 of this house of G an hundred bullocks, H426
18 courses, for the service of G, which *is* at H426
21 to seek the LORD G of Israel, did eat, H430
22 work of the house of G, the God of Israel. H430
22 work of the house of God, the G of Israel. H430
7: 6 which the LORD G of Israel had given: H430
6 to the hand of the LORD his G upon him. H430
9 to the good hand of his G upon him. H430
12 of the law of the G of heaven, perfect H426
14 the law of thy G which *is* in thine hand; H426
15 freely offered unto the G of Israel, whose H426
16 house of their G which *is* in Jerusalem: H426
17 house of your G which *is* in Jerusalem. H426
18 the gold, that do after the will of your G. H426
19 of the house of thy G, *those* deliver thou H426
19 deliver thou before the G of Jerusalem. H426
20 the house of thy G, which thou shalt have H426
21 scribe of the law of the G of heaven, shall H426
23 Whatsoever is commanded by the G of H426
23 for the house of the G of heaven: for why H426
24 of this house of G, it shall not be lawful H426
25 after the wisdom of thy G, that *is* in thine H426
25 the laws of thy G; and teach ye them that H426
26 do the law of thy G, and the law of the H426
27 Blessed *be* the LORD G of our fathers, H430
28 of the LORD my G *was* upon me, and I H430
8:17 unto us ministers for the house of our G. H430
18 And by the good hand of our G upon us H430
21 before our G, to seek of him a right H430
22 The hand of our G *is* upon all them for H430
23 So we fasted and besought our G for H430
25 of the house of our G, which the king, H430
28 unto the LORD G of your fathers. H430
30 to Jerusalem unto the house of our G. H430
31 the hand of our G was upon us, and he H430
33 in the house of our G by the hand of H430
35 offerings unto the G of Israel, twelve H430
36 furthered the people, and the house of G. H430
9: 4 at the words of the G of Israel, because H430
5 out my hands unto the LORD my G, H430
6 And said, O my G, I am ashamed and H430
6 face to thee, my G: for our iniquities are H430

Ezr 9: 8 the LORD our G, to leave us a remnant H430
8 place, that our G may lighten our eyes, H430
9 For we *were* bondmen; yet our G hath H430
9 up the house of our G, and to repair the H430
10 And now, O our G, what shall we say H430
13 that thou our G hast punished us less H430
15 O LORD G of Israel, thou *art* righteous: H430
10: 1 before the house of G, there assembled H430
2 against our G, and have taken strange H430
3 covenant with our G to put away all the H430
3 G; and let it be done according to the law. H430
6 before the house of G, and went into the H430
9 of the house of G, trembling because of H430
11 unto the LORD G of your fathers, and H430
14 our G for this matter be turned from us. H430
Neh 1: 4 and prayed before the G of heaven, H430
5 And said, I beseech thee, O LORD G of H430
5 the great and terrible G, that keepeth H410
2: 4 request? So I prayed to the G of heaven. H430
8 to the good hand of my G upon me. H430
12 *any* man what my G had put in my heart H430
18 Then I told them of the hand of my G H430
20 said unto them, The G of heaven, he will H430
4: 4 Hear, O our G; for we are despised: and H430
9 our prayer unto our G, and set a watch H430
15 known unto us, and G had brought their H430
20 thither unto us: our G shall fight for us. H430
5: 9 walk in the fear of our G because of the H430
13 Also I shook my lap, and said, So G H430
15 but so did not I, because of the fear of G. H430
19 Think upon me, my G, for good, H430
6: 9 therefore, *O G*, strengthen my hands.
10 in the house of G, within the temple, and H430
12 And, lo, I perceived that G had not sent H430
14 My G, think thou upon Tobiah and H430
16 that this work was wrought of our G. H430
7: 2 faithful man, and feared G above many. H430
5 And my G put into mine heart to gather H430
8: 6 And Ezra blessed the LORD, the great G. H430
8 So they read in the book in the law of G H430
9 the LORD your G; mourn not, nor weep. H430
16 of the house of G, and in the street of the H430
18 book of the law of G. And they kept the H430
9: 3 of the LORD their G *one* fourth part of H430
3 and worshipped the LORD their G. H430
4 with a loud voice unto the LORD their G. H430
5 the LORD your G for ever and ever: and H430
7 Thou *art* the LORD the G, who didst H430
17 but thou *art* a G ready to pardon, H433
18 said, This *is* thy G that brought thee up H430
31 for thou *art* a gracious and merciful G. H410
32 Now therefore, our G, the great, the H430
32 and the terrible G, who keepest covenant H410
10:28 unto the law of G, their wives, their sons, H430
29 the servant of G, and to observe and H430
32 for the service of the house of our G; H430
33 *for* all the work of the house of our G. H430
34 the house of our G, after the houses of H430
34 LORD our G, as *it is* written in the law: H430
36 to the house of our G, unto the priests H430
36 that minister in the house of our G: H430
37 of the house of our G; and the tithes of H430
38 the house of our G, to the chambers, into H430
39 we will not forsake the house of our G. H430
11:11 of Ahitub, *was* the ruler of the house of G. H430
16 the outward business of the house of G. H430
22 *were* over the business of the house of G. H430
12:24 the man of G, ward over against ward. H430
36 of G, and Ezra the scribe before them. H430
40 in the house of G, and I, and the half of H430
43 and rejoiced: for G had made them H430
45 the ward of their G, and the ward of the H430
46 songs of praise and thanksgiving unto G. H430
13: 1 come into the congregation of G for ever; H430
2 our G turned the curse into a blessing. H430
4 house of our G, *was* allied unto Tobiah: H430
7 chamber in the courts of the house of G. H430
9 of the house of G, with the meat offering H430
11 Why is the house of G forsaken? And I H430
14 Remember me, O my G, concerning this, H430
14 of my G, and for the offices thereof. H430
18 and did not our G bring all this evil upon H430
22 me, O my G, *concerning* this also, H430
25 them swear by G, *saying*, Ye shall not H430
26 was beloved of his G, and God made him H430
26 of his God, and G made him king over H430
27 our G in marrying strange wives? H430
29 Remember them, O my G, because they H430
31 Remember me, O my G, for good. H430

Job 1: 1 one that feared G, and eschewed evil. H430
5 sinned, and cursed G in their hearts. H430
6 Now there was a day when the sons of G H430
8 one that feareth G, and escheweth evil? H430
9 and said, Doth Job fear G for nought? H430
16 said, The fire of G is fallen from heaven, H430
22 In all this Job sinned not, nor charged G H430
2: 1 day when the sons of G came to present H430
3 one that feareth G, and escheweth evil? H430
9 retain thine integrity? curse G, and die. H430
10 at the hand of G, and shall we not receive H430
3: 4 Let that day be darkness; let not G H433
23 way is hid, and whom G hath hedged in? H433
4: 9 By the blast of G they perish, and by the H433
17 Shall mortal man be more just than G? H433
5: 8 I would seek unto G, and unto God would H410
8 I would seek unto God, and unto G H430
17 Behold, happy *is* the man whom G H433
6: 4 G do set themselves in array against me. H433
8 request; and that G would grant *me* the H433
9 Even that it would please G to destroy H433
8: 3 Doth G pervert judgment? or doth the H410
5 If thou wouldest seek unto G betimes, H410
13 So *are* the paths of all that forget G; and H410
20 Behold, G will not cast away a perfect H410
9: 2 but how should man be just with G? H410
13 *If* G will not withdraw his anger, the H433
10: 2 I will say unto G, Do not condemn me; H433
11: 5 But oh that G would speak, and open his H433
6 therefore that G exacteth of thee *less* H433
7 Canst thou by searching find out G? canst H433
12: 4 who calleth upon G, and he answereth H433
6 and they that provoke G are secure; into H410
6 into whose hand G bringeth *abundantly*. H433
13: 3 Almighty, and I desire to reason with G. H410
7 Will ye speak wickedly for G? and talk H410
8 accept his person? will ye contend for G? H410
15: 4 off fear, and restrainest prayer before G. H410
8 Hast thou heard the secret of G? and dost H433
11 *Are* the consolations of G small with H410
13 That thou turnest thy spirit against G, H410
25 For he stretcheth out his hand against G, H410
16:11 G hath delivered me to the ungodly, and H410
20 *but* mine eye poureth out *tears* unto G. H433
21 O that one might plead for a man with G, H433
18:21 *is* the place *of him that* knoweth not G. H410
19: 6 Know now that G hath overthrown me, H433
21 for the hand of G hath touched me. H433
22 Why do ye persecute me as G, and are H410
26 this *body*, yet in my flesh shall I see G: H433
20:15 again: G shall cast them out of his belly. H410
23 *When* he is about to fill his belly, G shall
29 a wicked man from G, and the heritage H430
29 the heritage appointed unto him by G. H410
21: 9 fear, neither *is* the rod of G upon them. H433
14 Therefore they say unto G, Depart from H410
17 G distributeth sorrows in his anger.
19 G layeth up his iniquity for his children: H433
22 Shall *any* teach G knowledge? seeing he H410
22: 2 Can a man be profitable unto G, as he H410
12 *Is* not G in the height of heaven? and H433
13 And thou sayest, How doth G know? can H410
17 Which said unto G, Depart from us: and H410
26 and shalt lift up thy face unto G. H433
23:16 For G maketh my heart soft, and the H410
24:12 crieth out: yet G layeth not folly *to them*. H433
25: 4 How then can man be justified with G? or H410
27: 2 *As* G liveth, *who* hath taken away my H410
3 me, and the spirit of G *is* in my nostrils; H433
5 G forbid that I should justify you: till I
8 gained, when G taketh away his soul? H433
9 Will G hear his cry when trouble cometh H410
10 Almighty? will he always call upon G? H433
11 I will teach you by the hand of G: *that* H410
13 a wicked man with G, and the heritage of H410
22 For G shall cast upon him, and not
28:23 G understandeth the way thereof, and he H430
29: 2 as *in* the days *when* G preserved me; H433
4 the secret of G *was* upon my tabernacle; H433
31: 2 For what portion of G *is there* from H433
6 that G may know mine integrity. H433
14 What then shall I do when G riseth up? H410
23 For destruction *from* G *was* a terror to H410
28 I should have denied the G *that is* above. H410
32: 2 he justified himself rather than G. H430
13 G thrusteth him down, not man. H410
33: 4 The Spirit of G hath made me, and the H410
12 answer thee, that G is greater than man. H433
14 For G speaketh once, yea twice, *yet man* H410

Job 33:26 He shall pray unto G, and he will be H433
29 Lo, all these *things* worketh G oftentimes H410
34: 5 For Job hath said, I am righteous: and G H410
9 that he should delight himself with G. H430
10 far be it from G, *that he should do* H410
12 Yea, surely G will not do wickedly, H410
23 he should enter into judgment with G. H410
31 Surely it is meet to be said unto G, I have H410
37 us, and multiplieth his words against G. H410
35:10 But none saith, Where *is* G my maker, H433
13 Surely G will not hear vanity, neither will H410
36: 5 Behold, G *is* mighty, and despiseth not H410
22 Behold, G exalteth by his power: who H410
26 Behold, G *is* great, and we know *him* H410
37: 5 G thundereth marvellously with his H410
10 By the breath of G frost is given: and the H410
14 and consider the wondrous works of G. H410
15 Dost thou know when G disposed them, H433
22 of the north: with G *is* terrible majesty. H433
38: 7 and all the sons of G shouted for joy? H430
41 cry unto G, they wander for lack of meat. H410
39:17 Because G hath deprived her of wisdom, H433
40: 2 he that reproveth G, let him answer it. H433
9 Hast thou an arm like G? or canst thou H410
19 He *is* the chief of the ways of G: he that H410
Ps 3: 2 soul, *There is* no help for him in G. Selah. H430
7 Arise, O LORD; save me, O my G: for H430
4: 1 Hear me when I call, O G of my H430
5: 2 King, and my G: for unto thee will I pray. H430
4 For thou *art* not a G that hath pleasure H410
10 Destroy thou them, O G; let them fall by H430
7: 1 O LORD my G, in thee do I put my trust: H430
3 O LORD my G, if I have done this; if there H430
9 righteous G trieth the hearts and reins. H430
10 My defence *is* of G, which saveth the H430
11 G judgeth the righteous, and God is H430
11 God judgeth the righteous, and G is H410
9:17 hell, *and* all the nations that forget G. H430
10: 4 *after* G: God is not in all his thoughts.
4 *after God*: G *is* not in all his thoughts. H430
11 He hath said in his heart, G hath H410
12 Arise, O LORD; O G, lift up thine hand: H410
13 Wherefore doth the wicked contemn G? H430
13: 3 Consider *and* hear me, O LORD my G: H430
14: 1 heart, *There is* no G. They are corrupt, H430
2 any that did understand, *and* seek G. H430
5 There were they in great fear: for G *is* in H430
16: 1 Preserve me, O G: for in thee do I put my H410
4 *after* another *g*: their drink offerings
17: 6 wilt hear me, O G: incline thine ear unto H410
18: 2 and my deliverer; my G, my strength, in H410
6 and cried unto my G: he heard my voice H430
21 have not wickedly departed from my G. H430
28 LORD my G will enlighten my darkness. H430
29 and by my G have I leaped over a wall. H430
30 *As for* G, his way *is* perfect: the word of H410
31 For who *is* G save the LORD? or who *is* a H433
31 the LORD? or who *is* a rock save our G? H430
32 *It is* G that girdeth me with strength, and H410
46 and let the G of my salvation be exalted. H430
47 *It is* G that avengeth me, and subdueth H410
19: 1 The heavens declare the glory of G; and H410
20: 1 the name of the G of Jacob defend thee; H430
5 in the name of our G we will set up *our* H430
7 remember the name of the LORD our G. H430
22: 1 My G, my God, why hast thou forsaken H410
1 My God, my G, why hast thou forsaken H410
2 O my G, I cry in the daytime, but thou H430
10 thou *art* my G from my mother's belly. H410
24: 5 from the G of his salvation. H430
25: 2 O my G, I trust in thee: let me not be H430
5 for thou *art* the G of my salvation; on H430
22 Redeem Israel, O G, out of all his H430
27: 9 neither forsake me, O G of my salvation. H430
29: 3 the waters: the G of glory thundereth: H410
30: 2 O LORD my G, I cried unto thee, and H430
12 G, I will give thanks unto thee for ever. H430
31: 5 hast redeemed me, O LORD G of truth. H410
14 in thee, O LORD: I said, Thou *art* my G. H430
33:12 Blessed *is* the nation whose G *is* the H430
35:23 *even* unto my cause, my G and my Lord. H430
24 Judge me, O LORD my G, according to H430
36: 1 *that there is* no fear of G before his eyes. H430
7 How excellent *is* thy lovingkindness, O G! H430
37:31 The law of his G *is* in his heart; none of H430
38:15 do I hope: thou wilt hear, O Lord my G. H430
21 Forsake me not, O LORD: O my G, be not H430
40: 3 praise unto our G: many shall see *it*, and H430
5 Many, O LORD my G, *are* thy wonderful H430

Ps 40: 8 I delight to do thy will, O my G: yea, thy H430
17 my deliverer; make no tarrying, O my G. H430
41:13 Blessed *be* the LORD G of Israel from H430
42: 1 so panteth my soul after thee, O G. H430
2 My soul thirsteth for G, for the living H430
2 God, for the living G: when shall I come H410
2 when shall I come and appear before G? H430
3 continually say unto me, Where *is* thy G? H430
4 to the house of G, with the voice of joy H430
5 me? hope thou in G: for I shall yet praise H430
6 O my G, my soul is cast down within me: H430
8 me, *and* my prayer unto the G of my life. H410
9 I will say unto G my rock, Why hast thou H410
10 they say daily unto me, Where *is* thy G? H430
11 me? hope thou in G: for I shall yet praise H430
11 the health of my countenance, and my G. H430
43: 1 Judge me, O G, and plead my cause H430
2 For thou *art* the G of my strength: why H430
4 Then will I go unto the altar of G, unto H430
4 altar of God, unto G my exceeding joy: H410
4 the harp will I praise thee, O G my God. H430
4 the harp will I praise thee, O God my G. H430
5 within me? hope in G: for I shall yet H430
5 the health of my countenance, and my G. H430
44: 1 We have heard with our ears, O G, our H430
4 Thou art my King, O G: command H430
8 In G we boast all the day long, and H430
20 If we have forgotten the name of our G, H430
20 or stretched out our hands to a strange g; H410
21 Shall not G search this out? for he H430
45: 2 therefore G hath blessed thee for ever. H430
6 Thy throne, O G, *is* for ever and ever: the H430
7 therefore G, thy God, hath anointed H430
7 therefore God, thy G, hath anointed thee H430
46: 1 G *is* our refuge and strength, a very H430
4 glad the city of G, the holy *place* of the H430
5 G *is* in the midst of her; she shall not be H430
5 G shall help her, *and that* right early. H430
7 The LORD of hosts *is* with us; the G of H430
10 Be still, and know that I *am* G: I will be H430
11 The LORD of hosts *is* with us; the G of H430
47: 1 shout unto G with the voice of triumph. H430
5 G is gone up with a shout, the LORD H430
6 Sing praises to G, sing praises: sing H430
7 For G *is* the King of all the earth: sing ye H430
8 G reigneth over the heathen: God sitteth H430
8 God reigneth over the heathen: G sitteth H430
9 the people of the G of Abraham: for the H430
9 earth *belong* unto G: he is greatly exalted. H430
48: 1 of our G, *in* the mountain of his holiness. H430
3 G is known in her palaces for a refuge. H430
8 G: God will establish it for ever. Selah. H430
8 God: G will establish it for ever. Selah. H430
9 O G, in the midst of thy temple. H430
10 According to thy name, O G, so *is* thy H430
14 For this G *is* our God for ever and ever: H430
14 For this God *is* our G for ever and ever: H430
49: 7 brother, nor give to G a ransom for him: H430
15 But G will redeem my soul from the H430
50: 1 The mighty G, *even* the LORD, hath H410
2 Out of Zion, the perfection of beauty, G H430
3 Our G shall come, and shall not keep H430
6 for G *is* judge himself. Selah. H430
7 against thee: I *am* G, *even* thy God. H430
7 against thee: I *am* God, *even* thy G. H430
14 Offer unto G thanksgiving; and pay thy H430
16 But unto the wicked G saith, What hast H430
22 Now consider this, ye that forget G, lest I H433
23 *aright* will I shew the salvation of G. H430
51: 1 Have mercy upon me, O G, according to H430
10 Create in me a clean heart, O G; and H430
14 Deliver me from bloodguiltiness, O G, H430
14 O God, thou G of my salvation: *and* H430
17 The sacrifices of G *are* a broken spirit: a H430
17 contrite heart, O G, thou wilt not despise. H430
52: 1 the goodness of G *endureth* continually. H410
5 G shall likewise destroy thee for ever, he H410
7 Lo, *this is* the man *that* made not G his H430
8 tree in the house of G: I trust in the mercy H430
8 trust in the mercy of G for ever and ever. H430
53: 1 his heart, *There is* no G. Corrupt are they, H430
2 G looked down from heaven upon the H430
2 *any* that did understand, that did seek G. H430
4 eat bread: they have not called upon G. H430
5 no fear was: for G hath scattered the H430
5 shame, because G hath despised them. H430
6 out of Zion! When G bringeth back the H430
54: 1 Save me, O G, by thy name, and judge me H430
2 Hear my prayer, O G; give ear to the H430

Ps 54: 3 they have not set G before them. Selah. H430
4 Behold, G *is* mine helper: the Lord *is* H430
55: 1 Give ear to my prayer, O G; and hide not H430
14 walked unto the house of G in company. H430
16 As for me, I will call upon G; and the H430
19 G shall hear, and afflict them, even he H410
19 no changes, therefore they fear not G. H430
23 But thou, O G, shalt bring them down H430
56: 1 Be merciful unto me, O G: for man would H430
4 In G I will praise his word, in God I have H430
4 In God I will praise his word, in G I have H430
7 in *thine* anger cast down the people, O G. H430
9 turn back: this I know; for G *is* for me. H430
10 In G will I praise *his* word: in the LORD H430
11 In G have I put my trust: I will not be H430
12 Thy vows *are* upon me, O G: I will render H430
13 walk before G in the light of the living? H430
57: 1 Be merciful unto me, O G, be merciful H430
2 I will cry unto G most high; unto God H430
2 I will cry unto God most high; unto G H410
3 me up. Selah. G shall send forth his H430
5 Be thou exalted, O G, above the heavens; H430
7 My heart is fixed, O G, my heart is fixed: I H430
11 Be thou exalted, O G, above the heavens: H430
58: 6 Break their teeth, O G, in their mouth: H430
11 verily he is a G that judgeth in the earth. H430
59: 1 Deliver me from mine enemies, O my G: H430
5 Thou therefore, O LORD G of hosts, the H430
5 God of hosts, the G of Israel, awake to H430
9 I wait upon thee: for G *is* my defence. H430
10 The G of my mercy shall prevent me: H430
10 shall prevent me: G shall let me see *my* H430
13 and let them know that G ruleth in Jacob H430
17 will I sing: for G *is* my defence, *and* the H430
17 *is* my defence, *and* the G of my mercy. H430
60: 1 O G, thou hast cast us off, thou hast H430
6 G hath spoken in his holiness; I will H430
10 *Wilt* not thou, O G, *which* hadst cast us H430
10 us off? and *thou*, O G, *which* didst not go H430
12 Through G we shall do valiantly: for he *it* H430
61: 1 Hear my cry, O G; attend unto my prayer. H430
5 For thou, O G, hast heard my vows: thou H430
7 He shall abide before G for ever: O H430
62: 1 Truly my soul waiteth upon G: from him H430
5 My soul, wait thou only upon G; for my H430
7 In G *is* my salvation and my glory: the H430
7 of my strength, *and* my refuge, *is* in G. H430
8 before him: G *is* a refuge for us. Selah. H430
11 G hath spoken once; twice have I heard H430
11 heard this; that power *belongeth* unto G. H430
63: 1 O G, thou *art* my God; early will I seek H430
1 O God, thou *art* my G; early will I seek H410
11 But the king shall rejoice in G; every one H430
64: 1 Hear my voice, O G, in my prayer: H430
7 But G shall shoot at them *with* an arrow; H430
9 shall declare the work of G; for they shall H430
65: 1 Praise waiteth for thee, O G, in Sion: and H430
5 thou answer us, O G of our salvation; H430
9 it with the river of G, *which* is full of H430
66: 1 Make a joyful noise unto G, all ye lands: H430
3 Say unto G, How terrible *art thou in* thy H430
5 Come and see the works of G: *he is* H430
8 O bless our G, ye people, and make the H430
10 For thou, O G, hast proved us: thou hast H430
16 Come *and* hear, all ye that fear G, and I H430
19 *But* verily G hath heard *me*; he hath H430
20 Blessed *be* G, which hath not turned H430
67: 1 G be merciful unto us, and bless us; *and* H430
3 Let the people praise thee, O G; let all the H430
5 Let the people praise thee, O G; let all the H430
6 *and* G, *even* our own God, shall bless us. H430
6 *and* God, *even* our own G, shall bless us. H430
7 G shall bless us; and all the ends of the H430
68: 1 Let G arise, let his enemies be scattered: H430
2 let the wicked perish at the presence of G. H430
3 G: yea, let them exceedingly rejoice. H430
4 Sing unto G, sing praises to his name: H430
5 the widows, *is* G in his holy habitation. H430
6 G setteth the solitary in families: he H430
7 O G, when thou wentest forth before thy H430
8 at the presence of G: *even* Sinai itself *was* H430
8 at the presence of G, the God of Israel. H430
8 at the presence of God, the G of Israel. H430
9 Thou, O G, didst send a plentiful rain, H430
10 therein: thou, O G, hast prepared of thy H430
15 The hill of G *is as* the hill of Bashan; an H430
16 *is* the hill *which* G desireth to dwell in; H430
17 The chariots of G *are* twenty thousand, H430
18 the LORD G might dwell *among them*. H430

Ps 68:19 *even* the G of our salvation. Selah. H410
20 *He that is* our G *is* the God of salvation; H410
20 *He that is* our God *is* the G of salvation; H410
20 and unto G the Lord *belong* the H3069
21 But G shall wound the head of his H430
24 They have seen thy goings, O G; *even* the H430
24 of my G, my King, in the sanctuary. H410
26 Bless ye G in the congregations, *even* the H430
28 Thy G hath commanded thy strength: H430
28 O G, that which thou hast wrought for us. H430
31 shall soon stretch out her hands unto G. H430
32 Sing unto G, ye kingdoms of the earth; O H430
34 Ascribe ye strength unto G: his excellency H430
35 O G, *thou art* terrible out of thy holy H430
35 thy holy places: the G of Israel *is* he that H410
35 and power unto *his* people. Blessed *be* G. H430
69: 1 Save me, O G; for the waters are come in H430
3 mine eyes fail while I wait for my G. H430
5 O G, thou knowest my foolishness; and H430
6 on thee, O Lord G of hosts, be ashamed H3069
6 confounded for my sake, O G of Israel. H430
13 acceptable time: O G, in the multitude of H430
29 let thy salvation, O G, set me up on high. H430
30 I will praise the name of G with a song, H430
32 and your heart shall live that seek G. H430
35 For G will save Zion, and will build the H430
70: 1 *Make haste*, O G, to deliver me; make H430
4 say continually, Let G be magnified. H430
5 haste unto me, O G: thou *art* my help and H430
71: 4 Deliver me, O my G, out of the hand of H430
5 For thou *art* my hope, O Lord G: *thou* H3069
11 Saying, G hath forsaken him: persecute H430
12 O G, be not far from me: O my God, make H430
12 O God, be not far from me: O my G, make H430
16 I will go in the strength of the Lord G: I H3069
17 O G, thou hast taught me from my youth: H430
18 old and grayheaded, O G, forsake me not; H430
19 Thy righteousness also, O G, *is* very high, H430
19 great things: O G, who *is* like unto thee! H430
22 thy truth, O my G: unto thee will I sing H430
72: 1 Give the king thy judgments, O G, and H430
18 Blessed *be* the LORD G, the God of Israel, H430
18 Blessed *be* the LORD God, the G of H430
73: 1 Truly G *is* good to Israel, *even* to such as H430
11 And they say, How doth G know? and is H410
17 Until I went into the sanctuary of G; *then* H410
26 My flesh and my heart faileth: *but* G is H430
28 But *it is* good for me to draw near to G: I H430
28 G, that I may declare all thy works. H3069
74: 1 O G, why hast thou cast *us* off for ever? H430
8 up all the synagogues of G in the land. H410
10 O G, how long shall the adversary H430
12 For G *is* my King of old, working H430
22 Arise, O G, plead thine own cause: H430
75: 1 Unto thee, O G, do we give thanks, *unto* H430
7 But G *is* the judge: he putteth down one, H430
9 ever; I will sing praises to the G of Jacob. H430
76: 1 In Judah *is* G known: his name *is* great H430
6 At thy rebuke, O G of Jacob, both the H430
9 When G arose to judgment, to save all H430
11 Vow, and pay unto the LORD your G: let H430
77: 1 I cried unto G with my voice, *even* unto H430
1 voice, *even* unto G with my voice; and he H430
3 I remembered G, and was troubled: I H430
9 Hath G forgotten to be gracious? hath he H410
13 Thy way, O G, *is* in the sanctuary: who *is* H430
13 who *is so* great a G as *our* God? H410
13 who *is so* great a God as *our* G? H430
14 Thou *art* the G that doest wonders: thou H410
16 The waters saw thee, O G, the waters saw H430
78: 7 That they might set their hope in G, and H430
7 of G, but keep his commandments: H410
8 and whose spirit was not stedfast with G. H410
10 They kept not the covenant of G, and H430
18 And they tempted G in their heart by H410
19 Yea, they spake against G; they said, Can H430
19 Can G furnish a table in the wilderness? H410
22 Because they believed not in G, and H430
31 The wrath of G came upon them, and H430
34 they returned and inquired early after G. H410
35 And they remembered that G *was* their H430
35 rock, and the high G their redeemer. H410
41 Yea, they turned back and tempted G, H410
56 high G, and kept not his testimonies: H430
59 When G heard *this*, he was wroth, and H430
79: 1 O G, the heathen are come into thine H430
9 Help us, O G of our salvation, for the H430
10 say, Where *is* their G? let him be known H430
80: 3 Turn us again, O G, and cause thy face to H430

Ps 80: 4 O LORD G of hosts, how long wilt thou H430
7 Turn us again, O G of hosts, and cause H430
14 Return, we beseech thee, O G of hosts: H430
19 Turn us again, O LORD G of hosts, cause H430
81: 1 Sing aloud unto G our strength: make a H430
1 make a joyful noise unto the G of Jacob. H430
4 for Israel, *and* a law of the G of Jacob. H430
9 There shall no strange g be in thee; H410
9 neither shalt thou worship any strange g. H410
10 I *am* the LORD thy G, which brought thee H430
82: 1 G standeth in the congregation of the H430
8 Arise, O G, judge the earth: for thou shalt H430
83: 1 Keep not thou silence, O G: hold not thy H430
1 hold not thy peace, and be not still, O G. H410
12 ourselves the houses of G in possession. H430
13 O my G, make them like a wheel; as the H430
84: 2 and my flesh crieth out for the living G. H410
3 O LORD of hosts, my King, and my G. H430
7 *one of them* in Zion appeareth before G. H430
8 O LORD G of hosts, hear my prayer: give H430
8 my prayer: give ear, O G of Jacob. Selah. H430
9 Behold, O G our shield, and look upon H430
10 in the house of my G, than to dwell in the H430
11 For the LORD G *is* a sun and shield: the H430
85: 4 Turn us, O G of our salvation, and cause H430
8 I will hear what G the LORD will speak: H410
86: 2 G, save thy servant that trusteth in thee. H430
10 doest wondrous things: thou *art* G alone. H430
12 I will praise thee, O Lord my G, with all H430
14 O G, the proud are risen against me, and H430
15 But thou, O Lord, *art* a G full of H410
87: 3 are spoken of thee, O city of G. Selah. H430
88: 1 O LORD G of my salvation, I have cried H430
89: 7 G is greatly to be feared in the assembly H410
8 O LORD G of hosts, who *is* a strong H430
26 my G, and the rock of my salvation. H410
90: 2 everlasting to everlasting, thou *art* G. H410
17 And let the beauty of the LORD our G be H430
ttl A Prayer of Moses the man of G. H430
91: 2 and my fortress: my G; in him will I trust. H430
92:13 shall flourish in the courts of our G. H430
94: 1 O LORD G, to whom vengeance H410
1 belongeth; O G, to whom vengeance H410
7 neither shall the G of Jacob regard *it*. H430
22 But the LORD is my defence; and my G H430
23 *yea*, the LORD our G shall cut them off. H430
95: 3 For the LORD *is* a great G, and a great H410
7 For he *is* our G; and we *are* the people of H430
98: 3 earth have seen the salvation of our G. H430
99: 5 Exalt ye the LORD our G, and worship at H430
8 Thou answeredst them, O LORD our G: H430
8 God: thou wast a G that forgavest them, H410
9 Exalt the LORD our G, and worship at his H430
9 his holy hill; for the LORD our G *is* holy. H430
100: 3 Know ye that the LORD he *is* G: *it is* he H430
102:24 I said, O my G, take me not away in the H410
104: 1 soul. O LORD my G, thou art very great; H430
21 their prey, and seek their meat from G. H410
33 praise to my G while I have my being. H430
105: 7 He *is* the LORD our G: his judgments *are* H430
106:14 wilderness, and tempted G in the desert. H410
21 They forgat G their saviour, which had H410
47 Save us, O LORD our G, and gather us H430
48 Blessed *be* the LORD G of Israel from H430
107:11 the words of G, and contemned the H410
108: 1 O G, my heart is fixed; I will sing and give H430
5 Be thou exalted, O G, above the heavens: H430
7 G hath spoken in his holiness; I will H430
11 *Wilt* not *thou*, O G, *who* hast cast us off? H430
11 not thou, O G, go forth with our hosts? H430
13 Through G we shall do valiantly: for he *it* H430
109: 1 Hold not thy peace, O G of my praise; H430
21 But do thou for me, O G the Lord, for H3069
26 Help me, O LORD my G: O save me H430
113: 5 Who *is* like unto the LORD our G, who H430
114: 7 Lord, at the presence of the G of Jacob; H433
115: 2 the heathen say, Where *is* now their G? H430
3 But our G *is* in the heavens: he hath H430
116: 5 and righteous; yea, our G *is* merciful. H430
118:27 G *is* the LORD, which hath shewed us H410
28 Thou *art* my G, and I will praise thee: H410
28 thee: *thou art* my G, I will exalt thee. H430
119:115 I will keep the commandments of my G. H430
122: 9 Because of the house of the LORD our G H430
123: 2 our G, until that he have mercy upon us. H430
132: 2 *and* vowed unto the mighty G of Jacob;
5 an habitation for the mighty G of Jacob.
135: 2 in the courts of the house of our G, H430
136: 2 O give thanks unto the G of gods: for his H430

Ps 136:26 O give thanks unto the **G** of heaven: for H410
139:17 me, O **G**! how great is the sum of them! H410
19 Surely thou wilt slay the wicked, O **G**: H433
23 Search me, O **G**, and know my heart: try H410
140: 6 I said unto the LORD, Thou *art* my **G**: H410
7 O **G** the Lord, the strength of my H3069
141: 8 But mine eyes *are* unto thee, O **G** the H3069
143:10 for thou *art* my **G**: thy spirit *is* good; lead H430
144: 9 I will sing a new song unto thee, O **G**: H430
15 *is that* people, whose **G** *is* the LORD. H430
145: 1 I will extol thee, my **G**, O king; and I will H430
146: 2 unto my **G** while I have any being. H430
5 Happy *is he* that *hath* the **G** of Jacob for H410
5 help, whose hope *is* in the LORD his **G**: H430
10 for ever, *even* thy **G**, O Zion, unto all H430
147: 1 **G**; for *it is* pleasant; *and* praise is comely. H430
7 sing praise upon the harp unto our **G**: H430
12 LORD, O Jerusalem; praise thy **G**, O Zion. H430
149: 6 *Let* the high *praises* of **G** *be* in their H410
150: 1 Praise ye the LORD. Praise **G** in his H410
Prv 2: 5 the LORD, and find the knowledge of **G**. H430
17 and forgetteth the covenant of her **G**. H430
3: 4 in the sight of **G** and man. H430
21:12 of the wicked: *but* **G** overthroweth the
25: 2 *It is* the glory of **G** to conceal a thing: but H430
26:10 The great **G** that formed all *things* both
30: 5 Every word of **G** *is* pure: he *is* a shield H433
9 and take the name of my **G** *in vain*. H430
Ecc 1:13 sore travail hath **G** given to the sons of H430
2:24 I saw, that it *was* from the hand of **G**. H430
26 For **G** giveth to a man that *is* good in his
26 *that is* good before **G**. This also *is* vanity H430
3:10 I have seen the travail, which **G** hath H430
11 **G** maketh from the beginning to the end. H430
13 good of all his labour, it *is* the gift of **G**. H430
14 I know that, whatsoever **G** doeth, it shall H430
14 taken from it: and **G** doeth *it*, that *men* H430
15 been; and **G** requireth that which is past. H430
17 I said in mine heart, **G** shall judge the H430
18 the sons of men, that **G** might manifest H430
5: 1 to the house of **G**, and be more ready to H430
2 *any* thing before **G**: for God *is* in heaven, H430
2 before God: for **G** *is* in heaven, and thou H430
4 When thou vowest a vow unto **G**, defer H430
6 wherefore should **G** be angry at thy H430
7 *are* also *divers* vanities: but fear thou **G**. H430
18 which **G** giveth him: for it *is* his portion. H430
19 Every man also to whom **G** hath given H430
19 rejoice in his labour; this *is* the gift of **G**. H430
20 **G** answereth *him* in the joy of his heart. H430
6: 2 A man to whom **G** hath given riches, H430
2 he desireth, yet **G** giveth him not power H430
7:13 Consider the work of **G**: for who can H430
14 of adversity consider: **G** also hath set the H430
18 feareth **G** shall come forth of them all. H430
26 whoso pleaseth **G** shall escape from her; H430
29 Lo, this only have I found, that **G** hath H430
8: 2 and *that* in regard of the oath of **G**. H430
12 them that fear **G**, which fear before him: H430
13 shadow; because he feareth not before **G**. H430
15 life, which **G** giveth him under the sun. H430
17 Then I beheld all the work of **G**, that a H430
9: 1 *are* in the hand of **G**: no man knoweth H430
7 heart; for **G** now accepteth thy works. H430
11: 5 not the works of **G** who maketh all. H430
9 *things* **G** will bring thee into judgment. H430
12: 7 spirit shall return unto **G** who gave it. H430
13 the whole matter: Fear **G**, and keep his H430
14 For **G** shall bring every work into H430
Isa 1:10 the law of our **G**, ye people of Gomorrah. H430
2: 3 to the house of the **G** of Jacob; and he H430
3:15 of the poor? saith the Lord **G** of hosts. H3069
5:16 in judgment, and **G** that is holy shall be H410
7: 7 Thus saith the Lord **G**, It shall not H3069
11 Ask thee a sign of the LORD thy **G**; ask it H430
13 weary men, but will ye weary my **G** also? H430
8:10 and it shall not stand: for **G** *is* with us. H410
19 unto their **G**? for the living to the dead? H430
21 their king and their **G**, and look upward. H430
9: 6 The mighty **G**, The everlasting Father, H410
10:21 the remnant of Jacob, unto the mighty **G**. H410
23 For the Lord **G** of hosts shall make a H3069
24 Therefore thus saith the Lord **G** of H3069
12: 2 Behold, **G** *is* my salvation; I will trust, H410
13:19 **G** overthrew Sodom and Gomorrah. H430
14:13 above the stars of **G**: I will sit also upon H410
17: 6 thereof, saith the LORD **G** of Israel. H430
10 Because thou hast forgotten the **G** of thy H430
13 many waters: but **G** shall rebuke them,

Isa 21:10 the **G** of Israel, have I declared unto you. H430
17 for the LORD **G** of Israel hath spoken *it*. H430
22: 5 by the Lord **G** of hosts in the valley H3069
12 And in that day did the Lord **G** of hosts H3069
14 you till ye die, saith the Lord **G** of hosts. H3069
15 Thus saith the Lord **G** of hosts, Go, get H3069
24:15 LORD **G** of Israel in the isles of the sea. H430
25: 1 O LORD, thou *art* my **G**; I will exalt thee, H430
8 and the Lord **G** will wipe away tears H3069
9 day, Lo, this *is* our **G**; we have waited for H430
26: 1 will **G** appoint *for* walls and bulwarks.
13 O LORD our **G**, *other* lords beside thee H430
28:16 Therefore thus saith the Lord **G**, H3069
22 heard from the Lord **G** of hosts a H3069
26 For his **G** doth instruct him to H430
29:23 of Jacob, and shall fear the **G** of Israel. H430
30:15 For thus saith the Lord **G**, the Holy One H3069
18 for the LORD *is* a **G** of judgment: blessed H430
31: 3 Now the Egyptians *are* men, and not **G**; H410
35: 2 of the LORD, *and* the excellency of our **G**. H430
4 fear not: behold, your **G** will come *with* H430
4 vengeance, *even* **G** *with* a recompence; H430
36: 7 in the LORD our **G**: *is it* not he, whose H430
37: 4 It may be the LORD thy **G** will hear the H430
4 to reproach the living **G**, and will reprove H430
4 the LORD thy **G** hath heard: wherefore H430
10 saying, Let not thy **G**, in whom thou H430
16 O LORD of hosts, **G** of Israel, that H430
16 thou *art* the **G**, *even* thou alone, of all H430
17 which hath sent to reproach the living **G**. H430
20 Now therefore, O LORD our **G**, save us H430
21 saith the LORD **G** of Israel, Whereas H430
38 of Nisroch his **g**, that Adrammelech and H430
38: 5 the LORD, the **G** of David thy father, H430
40: 1 ye, comfort ye my people, saith your **G**. H430
3 in the desert a highway for our **G**. H430
8 the word of our **G** shall stand for ever. H430
9 unto the cities of Judah, Behold your **G**! H430
10 Behold, the Lord **G** will come with H3069
18 To whom then will ye liken **G**? or what H410
27 my judgment is passed over from my **G**? H430
28 the everlasting **G**, the LORD, the Creator H430
41:10 for I *am* thy **G**: I will strengthen thee; H430
13 For I the LORD thy **G** will hold thy right H430
17 I the **G** of Israel will not forsake them. H430
42: 5 Thus saith **G** the LORD, he that created H410
43: 3 For I *am* the LORD thy **G**, the Holy One of H430
10 me there was no **G** formed, neither shall H410
12 *was* no strange **g** among you: therefore
12 witnesses, saith the LORD, that I *am* **G**. H410
44: 6 *am* the last; and beside me *there is* no **G**. H430
8 Is there a **G** beside me? yea, *there* H433
8 me? yea, *there is* no **G**; I know not *any*. H6697
10 Who hath formed a **g**, or molten a graven H410
15 yea, he maketh a **g**, and worshippeth *it*; H410
17 And the residue thereof he maketh a **g**, H410
17 and saith, Deliver me; for thou *art* my **g**. H410
45: 3 call *thee* by thy name, *am* the **G** of Israel. H430
5 else, *there is* no **G** beside me: I girded H430
14 *saying*, Surely **G** *is* in thee; and *there* H410
14 thee; and *there is* none else, *there is* no **G**. H430
15 Verily thou *art* a **G** that hidest thyself, O H410
15 hidest thyself, O **G** of Israel, the Saviour. H430
18 the heavens; **G** himself that formed H430
20 and pray unto a **g** *that* cannot save. H410
21 and *there is* no **G** else beside me; a just H430
21 beside me; a just **G** and a Saviour; *there* H410
22 earth: for I *am* **G**, and *there is* none else. H410
46: 6 it a **g**: they fall down, yea, they worship. H410
9 of old: for I *am* **G**, and *there is* none else; H410
9 else; *I am* **G**, and *there is* none like me, H430
48: 1 mention of the **G** of Israel, *but* not in H430
2 upon the **G** of Israel; The LORD H430
16 the Lord **G**, and his Spirit, hath sent me. H3069
17 I *am* the LORD thy **G** which teacheth H430
49: 4 with the LORD, and my work with my **G**. H430
5 LORD, and my **G** shall be my strength. H430
22 Thus saith the Lord **G**, Behold, I will lift H3069
50: 4 The Lord **G** hath given me the tongue H3069
5 The Lord **G** hath opened mine ear, and H3069
7 For the Lord **G** will help me; therefore H3069
9 Behold, the Lord **G** will help me; who *is* H3069
10 name of the LORD, and stay upon his **G**. H430
51:15 But I *am* the LORD thy **G**, that divided H430
20 the fury of the LORD, the rebuke of thy **G**. H430
22 the LORD, and thy **G** *that* pleadeth the H430
52: 4 For thus saith the Lord **G**, My people H3069
7 that saith unto Zion, Thy **G** reigneth! H430
10 the earth shall see the salvation of our **G**. H430

Isa 52:12 the **G** of Israel *will be* your rearward. H430
53: 4 him stricken, smitten of **G**, and afflicted. H430
54: 5 **G** of the whole earth shall he be called. H430
6 when thou wast refused, saith thy **G**. H430
55: 5 of the LORD thy **G**, and for the Holy One H430
7 to our **G**, for he will abundantly pardon. H430
56: 8 The Lord **G** which gathereth the H3069
57:21 *There is* no peace, saith my **G**, to the H430
58: 2 ordinance of their **G**: they ask of me the H430
2 they take delight in approaching to **G**. H430
59: 2 you and your **G**, and your sins have hid H430
13 away from our **G**, speaking oppression H430
60: 9 of the LORD thy **G**, and to the Holy One H430
19 an everlasting light, and thy **G** thy glory. H430
61: 1 The Spirit of the Lord **G** *is* upon me; H3069
2 of our **G**; to comfort all that mourn; H430
6 Ministers of our **G**: ye shall eat the riches H430
10 be joyful in my **G**; for he hath clothed me H430
11 spring forth; so the Lord **G** will cause H3069
62: 3 and a royal diadem in the hand of thy **G**. H430
5 bride, *so* shall thy **G** rejoice over thee. H430
64: 4 the eye seen, O **G**, beside thee, *what* he H430
65:13 Therefore thus saith the Lord **G**, H3069
15 for the Lord **G** shall slay thee, and H3069
16 himself in the **G** of truth; and he that H430
16 shall swear by the **G** of truth; because H430
66: 9 forth, and shut *the womb*? saith thy **G**. H430
Jer 1: 6 Then said I, Ah, Lord **G**! behold, I H3069
2:17 thy **G**, when he led thee by the way? H430
19 the LORD thy **G**, and that my fear *is* not H430
19 *is* not in thee, saith the Lord **G** of hosts. H3069
22 is marked before me, saith the Lord **G**. H3069
3:13 the LORD thy **G**, and hast scattered thy H430
21 they have forgotten the LORD their **G**. H430
22 unto thee; for thou *art* the LORD our **G**. H430
23 LORD our **G** *is* the salvation of Israel. H430
25 the LORD our **G**, we and our fathers, H430
25 not obeyed the voice of the LORD our **G**. H430
4:10 Then said I, Ah, Lord **G**! surely thou H3069
5: 4 of the LORD, *nor* the judgment of their **G**. H430
5 the judgment of their **G**: but these have H430
14 Wherefore thus saith the LORD **G** of H430
19 the LORD our **G** all these *things* unto H430
24 fear the LORD our **G**, that giveth rain, H430
7: 3 Thus saith the LORD of hosts, the **G** of H430
20 Therefore thus saith the Lord **G**; H3069
21 Thus saith the LORD of hosts, the **G** of H430
23 and I will be your **G**, and ye shall be my H430
28 voice of the LORD their **G**, nor receiveth H430
8:14 there: for the LORD our **G** hath put us to H430
9:15 LORD of hosts, the **G** of Israel; Behold, I H430
10:10 But the LORD *is* the true **G**, he *is* the H430
10 God, he *is* the living **G**, and an everlasting H430
11: 3 saith the LORD **G** of Israel; Cursed *be* H430
4 ye be my people, and I will be your **G**: H430
13:12 saith the LORD **G** of Israel, Every bottle H430
16 Give glory to the LORD your **G**, before he H430
14:13 Then said I, Ah, Lord **G**! behold, the H3069
22 he, O LORD our **G**? therefore we will wait H430
15:16 called by thy name, O LORD **G** of hosts. H430
16: 9 For thus saith the LORD of hosts, the **G** H430
10 have committed against the LORD our **G**? H430
19: 3 LORD of hosts, the **G** of Israel; Behold, I H430
15 Thus saith the LORD of hosts, the **G** of H430
21: 4 Thus saith the LORD **G** of Israel; Behold, H430
22: 9 of the LORD their **G**, and worshipped H430
23: 2 Therefore thus saith the LORD **G** of H430
23 *Am* I a **G** at hand, saith the LORD, and H430
23 saith the LORD, and not a **G** afar off? H430
36 living **G**, of the LORD of hosts our God. H430
36 living God, of the LORD of hosts our **G**. H430
24: 5 Thus saith the LORD, the **G** of Israel; H430
7 and I will be their **G**: for they shall return H430
25:15 For thus saith the LORD **G** of Israel unto H430
27 LORD of hosts, the **G** of Israel; Drink ye, H430
26:13 of the LORD your **G**; and the LORD will H430
16 to us in the name of the LORD our **G**. H430
27: 4 the LORD of hosts, the **G** of Israel; Thus H430
21 Yea, thus saith the LORD of hosts, the **G** H430
28: 2 Thus speaketh the LORD of hosts, the **G** H430
14 For thus saith the LORD of hosts, the **G** H430
29: 4 Thus saith the LORD of hosts, the **G** of H430
8 For thus saith the LORD of hosts, the **G** H430
21 Thus saith the LORD of hosts, the **G** of H430
25 Thus speaketh the LORD of hosts, the **G** H430
30: 2 Thus speaketh the LORD **G** of Israel, H430
9 But they shall serve the LORD their **G**, H430
22 shall be my people, and I will be your **G**. H430
31: 1 LORD, will I be the **G** of all the families H430

Jer 31: 6 let us go up to Zion unto the LORD our **G**. H430
18 be turned; for thou *art* the LORD my **G**. H430
23 Thus saith the LORD of hosts, the **G** of H430
33 be their **G**, and they shall be my people. H430
32:14 Thus saith the LORD of hosts, the **G** of H430
15 For thus saith the LORD of hosts, the **G** H430
17 Ah Lord **G**! behold, thou hast made the H3069
18 **G**, the LORD of hosts, *is* his name, H410
25 And thou hast said unto me, O Lord **G**, H3069
27 Behold, I *am* the LORD, the **G** of all H430
36 the LORD, the **G** of Israel, concerning H430
38 shall be my people, and I will be their **G**: H430
33: 4 For thus saith the LORD, the **G** of Israel, H430
34: 2 Thus saith the LORD, the **G** of Israel; Go H430
13 Thus saith the LORD, the **G** of Israel; I H430
35: 4 of Igdaliah, a man of **G**, which *was* by the H430
13 Thus saith the LORD of hosts, the **G** of H430
17 Therefore thus saith the LORD **G** of H430
17 God of hosts, the **G** of Israel; Behold, I H430
18 LORD of hosts, the **G** of Israel; Because H430
19 LORD of hosts, the **G** of Israel; Jonadab H430
37: 3 Pray now unto the LORD our **G** for us. H430
7 Thus saith the LORD, the **G** of Israel; H430
38:17 the LORD, the **G** of hosts, the God of H430
17 God of hosts, the **G** of Israel; If thou wilt H430
39:16 LORD of hosts, the **G** of Israel; Behold, I H430
40: 2 The LORD thy **G** hath pronounced this H430
42: 2 us unto the LORD thy **G**, *even* for all this H430
3 That the LORD thy **G** may shew us the H430
4 unto the LORD your **G** according to your H430
5 the LORD thy **G** shall send thee to us. H430
6 of the LORD our **G**, to whom we send H430
6 we obey the voice of the LORD our **G**. H430
9 the LORD, the **G** of Israel, unto whom H430
13 obey the voice of the LORD your **G**, H430
15 the LORD of hosts, the **G** of Israel; If ye H430
18 For thus saith the LORD of hosts, the **G** H430
20 the LORD your **G**, saying, Pray for us H430
20 us unto the LORD our **G**; and according H430
20 all that the LORD our **G** shall say, so H430
21 of the LORD your **G**, nor any *thing* for the H430
43: 1 of the LORD their **G**, for which the LORD H430
1 the LORD their **G** had sent him to them, H430
2 the LORD our **G** hath not sent thee to H430
10 LORD of hosts, the **G** of Israel; Behold, I H430
44: 2 Thus saith the LORD of hosts, the **G** of H430
7 the LORD, the **G** of hosts, the God of H430
7 God of hosts, the **G** of Israel; Wherefore H430
11 LORD of hosts, the **G** of Israel; Behold, I H430
25 Thus saith the LORD of hosts, the **G** of H430
26 of Egypt, saying, The Lord **G** liveth. H3069
45: 2 Thus saith the LORD, the **G** of Israel, H430
46:10 For this *is* the day of the Lord **G** of H3069
10 for the Lord **G** of hosts hath a sacrifice H3069
25 The LORD of hosts, the **G** of Israel, saith; H430
48: 1 LORD of hosts, the **G** of Israel; Woe unto H430
49: 5 saith the Lord **G** of hosts, from all those H3069
50: 4 they shall go, and seek the LORD their **G**. H430
18 LORD of hosts, the **G** of Israel; Behold, I H430
25 **G** of hosts in the land of the Chaldeans. H3069
28 our **G**, the vengeance of his temple. H430
31 saith the Lord **G** of hosts: for thy day H3069
40 As **G** overthrew Sodom and Gomorrah H430
51: 5 nor Judah of his **G**, of the LORD of hosts; H430
10 in Zion the work of the LORD our **G**. H430
33 For thus saith the LORD of hosts, the **G** H430
56 **G** of recompences shall surely requite. H410
Lam 3:41 with *our* hands unto **G** in the heavens. H410
Ezk 1: 1 were opened, and I saw visions of **G**. H430
2: 4 say unto them, Thus saith the Lord **G**. H3069
3:11 saith the Lord **G**; whether they will hear, H3069
27 saith the Lord **G**; He that heareth, let H3069
4:14 Then said I, Ah Lord **G**! behold, my soul H3069
5: 5 Thus saith the Lord **G**; This *is* H3069
7 Therefore thus saith the Lord **G**; H3069
8 Therefore thus saith the Lord **G**; H3069
11 Wherefore, *as* I live, saith the Lord **G**; H3069
6: 3 word of the Lord **G**; Thus saith the Lord H3069
3 saith the Lord **G** to the mountains, and H3069
11 Thus saith the Lord **G**; Smite with thine H3069
7: 2 saith the Lord **G** unto the land of Israel; H3069
5 Thus saith the Lord **G**; An evil, an only H3069
8: 1 hand of the Lord **G** fell there upon me. H3069
3 in the visions of **G** to Jerusalem, to the H430
4 And, behold, the glory of the **G** of Israel H430
9: 3 And the glory of the **G** of Israel was gone H430
8 and said, Ah Lord **G**! wilt thou destroy H3069
10: 5 of the Almighty **G** when he speaketh. H410
19 of the **G** of Israel *was* over them above. H430

Ezk 10:20 I saw under the **G** of Israel by the river H430
11: 7 Therefore thus saith the Lord **G**; Your H3069
8 a sword upon you, saith the Lord **G**. H3069
13 and said, Ah Lord **G**! wilt thou make a H3069
16 Therefore say, Thus saith the Lord **G**; H3069
17 Therefore say, Thus saith the Lord **G**; I H3069
20 shall be my people, and I will be their **G**. H430
21 upon their own heads, saith the Lord **G**. H3069
22 of the **G** of Israel *was* over them above. H430
24 by the Spirit of **G** into Chaldea, to them H430
12:10 Thus saith the Lord **G**; This burden H3069
19 saith the Lord **G** of the inhabitants of H3069
23 Thus saith the Lord **G**; I will make this H3069
25 and will perform it, saith the Lord **G**. H3069
28 saith the Lord **G**; There shall none of H3069
28 spoken shall be done, saith the Lord **G**. H3069
13: 3 Thus saith the Lord **G**; Woe unto the H3069
8 Therefore thus saith the Lord **G**; H3069
8 I *am* against you, saith the Lord **G**. H3069
9 and ye shall know that I *am* the Lord **G**. H3069
13 Therefore thus saith the Lord **G**; I will H3069
16 and *there is* no peace, saith the Lord **G**. H3069
18 And say, Thus saith the Lord **G**; Woe to H3069
20 Wherefore thus saith the Lord **G**; H3069
14: 4 Thus saith the Lord **G**; Every man of the H3069
6 Thus saith the Lord **G**; Repent, and turn H3069
11 I may be their **G**, saith the Lord GOD. H430
11 I may be their God, saith the Lord **G**. H3069
14 by their righteousness, saith the Lord **G**. H3069
16 live, saith the Lord **G**, they shall deliver H3069
18 live, saith the Lord **G**, they shall deliver H3069
20 live, saith the Lord **G**, they shall deliver H3069
21 For thus saith the Lord **G**; How much H3069
23 that I have done in it, saith the Lord **G**. H3069
15: 6 Therefore thus saith the Lord **G**; As the H3069
8 committed a trespass, saith the Lord **G**. H3069
16: 3 And say, Thus saith the Lord **G** unto H3069
8 the Lord **G**, and thou becamest mine. H3069
14 I had put upon thee, saith the Lord **G**. H3069
19 and *thus* it was, saith the Lord **G**. H3069
23 (woe, woe unto thee! saith the Lord **G**;) H3069
30 saith the Lord **G**, seeing thou doest all H3069
36 Thus saith the Lord **G**; Because thy H3069
43 saith the Lord **G**: and thou shalt not H3069
48 *As* I live, saith the Lord **G**, Sodom thy H3069
59 For thus saith the Lord **G**; I will even H3069
63 that thou hast done, saith the Lord **G**. H3069
17: 3 And say, Thus saith the Lord **G**; A great H3069
9 Say thou, Thus saith the Lord **G**; Shall it H3069
16 *As* I live, saith the Lord **G**, surely in the H3069
19 Therefore thus saith the Lord **G**; *As* I H3069
22 Thus saith the Lord **G**; I will also take of H3069
18: 3 *As* I live, saith the Lord **G**, ye shall not H3069
9 he shall surely live, saith the Lord **G**. H3069
23 saith the Lord **G**: *and* not that he should H3069
30 saith the Lord **G**. Repent, and turn H3069
32 dieth, saith the Lord **G**: wherefore turn H3069
20: 3 saith the Lord **G**; Are ye come to inquire H3069
3 Lord **G**, I will not be inquired of by you. H3069
5 saith the Lord **G**; In the day when I H3069
5 them, saying, I *am* the LORD your **G**; H430
7 the idols of Egypt: I *am* the LORD your **G**. H430
19 I *am* the LORD your **G**; walk in my H430
20 ye may know that I *am* the LORD your **G**. H430
27 Thus saith the Lord **G**; Yet in this your H3069
30 saith the Lord **G**; Are ye polluted after H3069
31 Lord **G**, I will not be inquired of by you. H3069
33 *As* I live, saith the Lord **G**, surely with a H3069
36 will I plead with you, saith the Lord **G**. H3069
39 saith the Lord **G**; Go ye, serve ye every H3069
40 saith the Lord **G**, there shall all the H3069
44 O ye house of Israel, saith the Lord **G**. H3069
47 saith the Lord **G**; Behold, I will kindle H3069
49 Then said I, Ah Lord **G**! they say of me, H3069
21: 7 be brought to pass, saith the Lord **G**. H3069
13 it shall be no *more*, saith the Lord **G**. H3069
24 Therefore thus saith the Lord **G**; H3069
26 Thus saith the Lord **G**; Remove the H3069
28 Thus saith the Lord **G** concerning the H3069
22: 3 Then say thou, Thus saith the Lord **G**, H3069
12 and hast forgotten me, saith the Lord **G**. H3069
19 Therefore thus saith the Lord **G**; H3069
28 **G**, when the LORD hath not spoken. H3069
31 upon their heads, saith the Lord **G**. H3069
23:22 saith the Lord **G**; Behold, I will raise H3069
28 For thus saith the Lord **G**; Behold, I will H3069
32 Thus saith the Lord **G**; Thou shalt drink H3069
34 for I have spoken *it*, saith the Lord **G**. H3069
35 Therefore thus saith the Lord **G**; H3069

Ezk 23:46 For thus saith the Lord **G**; I will bring H3069
49 and ye shall know that I *am* the Lord **G**. H3069
24: 3 saith the Lord **G**; Set on a pot, set *it* on, H3069
6 Wherefore thus saith the Lord **G**; Woe H3069
9 Therefore thus saith the Lord **G**; Woe to H3069
14 shall they judge thee, saith the Lord **G**. H3069
21 saith the Lord **G**; Behold, I will profane H3069
24 ye shall know that I *am* the Lord **G**. H3069
25: 3 word of the Lord **G**; Thus saith the Lord H3069
3 saith the Lord **G**; Because thou saidst, H3069
6 For thus saith the Lord **G**; Because thou H3069
8 Thus saith the Lord **G**; Because that H3069
12 Thus saith the Lord **G**; Because that H3069
13 Therefore thus saith the Lord **G**; I will H3069
14 know my vengeance, saith the Lord **G**. H3069
15 Thus saith the Lord **G**; Because the H3069
16 Therefore thus saith the Lord **G**; H3069
26: 3 Therefore thus saith the Lord **G**; H3069
5 *it*, saith the Lord **G**: and it shall become H3069
7 For thus saith the Lord **G**; Behold, I will H3069
14 LORD have spoken *it*, saith the Lord **G**. H3069
15 Thus saith the Lord **G** to Tyrus; Shall H3069
19 For thus saith the Lord **G**; When I shall H3069
21 never be found again, saith the Lord **G**. H3069
27: 3 saith the Lord **G**; O Tyrus, thou hast H3069
28: 2 saith the Lord **G**; Because thine heart H3069
2 hast said, I *am* a **G**, I sit *in* the seat of H410
2 I sit *in* the seat of **G**, in the midst of the H430
2 *art* a man, and not **G**, though thou set H410
2 thou set thine heart as the heart of **G**: H430
6 Therefore thus saith the Lord **G**; H3069
6 hast set thine heart as the heart of **G**; H430
9 slayeth thee, I *am* **G**? but thou *shalt be* a H430
9 **G**, in the hand of him that slayeth thee. H410
10 for I have spoken *it*, saith the Lord **G**. H3069
12 saith the Lord **G**; Thou sealest up the H3069
13 Thou hast been in Eden the garden of **G**; H430
14 holy mountain of **G**; thou hast walked up H430
16 of the mountain of **G**: and I will destroy H430
22 And say, Thus saith the Lord **G**; Behold, H3069
24 they shall know that I *am* the Lord **G**. H3069
25 Thus saith the Lord **G**; When I shall H3069
26 shall know that I *am* the LORD their **G**. H430
29: 3 Speak, and say, Thus saith the Lord **G**; H3069
8 Therefore thus saith the Lord **G**; H3069
13 Yet thus saith the Lord **G**; At the end of H3069
16 they shall know that I *am* the Lord **G**. H3069
19 Therefore thus saith the Lord **G**; H3069
20 they wrought for me, saith the Lord **G**. H3069
30: 2 Lord **G**; Howl ye, Woe worth the day! H3069
6 fall in it by the sword, saith the Lord **G**. H3069
10 Thus saith the Lord **G**; I will also make H3069
13 Thus saith the Lord **G**; I will also H3069
22 Therefore thus saith the Lord **G**; H3069
31: 8 The cedars in the garden of **G** could not H430
8 of **G** was like unto him in his beauty. H430
9 that *were* in the garden of **G**, envied him. H430
10 Therefore thus saith the Lord **G**; H3069
15 Thus saith the Lord **G**; In the day when H3069
18 and all his multitude, saith the Lord **G**. H3069
32: 3 Thus saith the Lord **G**; I will therefore H3069
8 upon thy land, saith the Lord **G**. H3069
11 For thus saith the Lord **G**; The sword of H3069
14 rivers to run like oil, saith the Lord **G**. H3069
16 for all her multitude, saith the Lord **G**. H3069
31 slain by the sword, saith the Lord **G**. H3069
32 and all his multitude, saith the Lord **G**. H3069
33:11 saith the Lord **G**, I have no pleasure in H3069
25 saith the Lord **G**; Ye eat with the blood, H3069
27 saith the Lord **G**; *As* I live, surely they H3069
34: 2 saith the Lord **G** unto the shepherds; H3069
8 *As* I live, saith the Lord **G**, surely H3069
10 Thus saith the Lord **G**; Behold, I *am* H3069
11 For thus saith the Lord **G**; Behold, I, H3069
15 them to lie down, saith the Lord **G**. H3069
17 thus saith the Lord **G**; Behold, I judge H3069
20 Therefore thus saith the Lord **G** unto H3069
24 And I the LORD will be their **G**, and my H430
30 I the LORD their **G** *am* with them, and H430
30 Israel, *are* my people, saith the Lord **G**. H3069
31 *and* I *am* your **G**, saith the Lord GOD. H430
31 *and* I *am* your God, saith the Lord **G**. H3069
35: 3 And say unto it, Thus saith the Lord **G**; H3069
6 Therefore, *as* I live, saith the Lord **G**, I H3069
11 Therefore, *as* I live, saith the Lord **G**, I H3069
14 Thus saith the Lord **G**; When the whole H3069
36: 2 Thus saith the Lord **G**; Because the H3069
3 saith the Lord **G**; Because they have H3069
4 word of the Lord **G**; Thus saith the Lord H3069

Ezk 36: 4 saith the Lord **G** to the mountains, and H3069
5 Therefore thus saith the Lord **G**; Surely H3069
6 saith the Lord **G**; Behold, I have spoken H3069
7 Therefore thus saith the Lord **G**; I have H3069
13 Thus saith the Lord **G**; Because they say H3069
14 thy nations any more, saith the Lord **G**. H3069
15 to fall any more, saith the Lord **G**. H3069
22 saith the Lord **G**; I do not *this* for your H3069
23 LORD, saith the Lord **G**, when I shall be H3069
28 shall be my people, and I will be your **G**. H430
32 saith the Lord **G**, be it known unto you: H3069
33 Thus saith the Lord **G**; In the day that I H3069
37 Thus saith the Lord **G**; I will yet *for* this H3069
37: 3 I answered, O Lord **G**, thou knowest. H3069
5 Thus saith the Lord **G** unto these H3069
9 saith the Lord **G**; Come from the four H3069
12 saith the Lord **G**; Behold, O my people, H3069
19 Say unto them, Thus saith the Lord **G**; H3069
21 saith the Lord **G**; Behold, I will take the H3069
23 they be my people, and I will be their **G**. H430
27 be their **G**, and they shall be my people. H430
38: 3 And say, Thus saith the Lord **G**; Behold, H3069
10 Thus saith the Lord **G**; It shall also H3069
14 saith the Lord **G**; In that day when my H3069
17 Thus saith the Lord **G**; *Art* thou he of H3069
18 saith the Lord **G**, *that* my fury shall H3069
21 saith the Lord **G**: every man's sword H3069
39: 1 saith the Lord **G**; Behold, I *am* against H3069
5 for I have spoken *it*, saith the Lord **G**. H3069
8 saith the Lord **G**; this *is* the day whereof H3069
10 that robbed them, saith the Lord **G**. H3069
13 I shall be glorified, saith the Lord **G**. H3069
17 thus saith the Lord **G**; Speak unto every H3069
20 with all men of war, saith the Lord **G**. H3069
22 their **G** from that day and forward. H430
25 Therefore thus saith the Lord **G**; Now H3069
28 *am* the LORD their **G**, which caused them H430
29 the house of Israel, saith the Lord **G**. H3069
40: 2 In the visions of **G** brought he me into H430
43: 2 And, behold, the glory of the **G** of Israel H430
18 thus saith the Lord **G**; These *are* the H3069
19 **G**, a young bullock for a sin offering. H3069
27 and I will accept you, saith the Lord **G**. H3069
44: 2 the LORD, the **G** of Israel, hath entered H430
6 saith the Lord **G**; O ye house of Israel, H3069
9 Thus saith the Lord **G**; No stranger, H3069
12 **G**, and they shall bear their iniquity. H3069
15 the fat and the blood, saith the Lord **G**: H3069
27 offer his sin offering, saith the Lord **G**. H3069
45: 9 Thus saith the Lord **G**; Let it suffice you, H3069
9 from my people, saith the Lord **G**. H3069
15 for them, saith the Lord **G**. H3069
18 Thus saith the Lord **G**; In the first H3069
46: 1 Thus saith the Lord **G**; The gate of the H3069
16 Thus saith the Lord **G**; If the prince give H3069
47:13 Thus saith the Lord **G**; This *shall be* the H3069
23 *him* his inheritance, saith the Lord **G**. H3069
48:29 *are* their portions, saith the Lord **G**. H3069
Dan 1: 2 of the house of **G**: which he carried into H430
2 to the house of his **g**; and he brought the H430
2 vessels into the treasure house of his **g**. H430
9 Now **G** had brought Daniel into favour H430
17 As for these four children, **G** gave them H430
2:18 That they would desire mercies of the **G** H426
19 Then Daniel blessed the **G** of heaven. H426
20 be the name of **G** for ever and ever: for H426
23 I thank thee, and praise thee, O thou **G** H426
28 But there is a **G** in heaven that revealeth H426
37 of kings: for the **G** of heaven hath given H426
44 these kings shall the **G** of heaven set up a H426
45 the gold; the great **G** hath made known H426
47 *it is*, that your **G** *is* a God of gods, and H426
47 that your God *is* a **G** of gods, and a Lord H426
3:15 **G** that shall deliver you out of my hands? H426
17 If it be *so*, our **G** whom we serve is able H426
25 the form of the fourth is like the Son of **G**. H426
26 of the most high **G**, come forth, and come H426
28 Blessed *be* the **G** of Shadrach, Meshach, H426
28 nor worship any **g**, except their own God. H426
28 nor worship any god, except their own **G**. H426
29 thing amiss against the **G** of Shadrach, H426
29 other **G** that can deliver after this sort. H426
4: 2 the high **G** hath wrought toward me. H426
8 to the name of my **g**, and in whom *is* the H426
5: 3 temple of the house of **G** which *was* at H426
18 O thou king, the most high **G** gave H426
21 knew that the most high **G** ruled in the H426
23 nor know: and the **G** in whose hand thy H426
26 the thing: MENE; **G** hath numbered thy H426

Dan 6: 5 against him concerning the law of his **G**. H426
7 ask a petition of any **G** or man for thirty H426
10 thanks before his **G**, as he did aforetime. H426
11 and making supplication before his **G**. H426
12 *a petition* of any **G** or man within thirty H426
16 unto Daniel, Thy **G** whom thou servest H426
20 of the living **G**, is thy God, whom thou H426
20 living God, is thy **G**, whom thou servest H426
22 My **G** hath sent his angel, and hath shut H426
23 upon him, because he believed in his **G**. H426
26 and fear before the **G** of Daniel: for he *is* H426
26 for he *is* the living **G**, and stedfast for H426
9: 3 And I set my face unto the Lord **G**, to H430
4 And I prayed unto the LORD my **G**, and H430
4 the great and dreadful **G**, keeping the H410
9 To the Lord our **G** *belong* mercies and H430
10 of the LORD our **G**, to walk in his laws, H430
11 **G**, because we have sinned against him. H430
13 the LORD our **G**, that we might turn from H430
14 for the LORD our **G** *is* righteous in all his H430
15 And now, O Lord our **G**, that hast H430
17 Now therefore, O our **G**, hear the prayer H430
18 O my **G**, incline thine ear, and hear; open H430
19 own sake, O my **G**: for thy city and thy H430
20 my **G** for the holy mountain of my God; H430
20 my God for the holy mountain of my **G**; H430
10:12 thyself before thy **G**, thy words were H430
11:32 their **G** shall be strong, and do *exploits*. H430
36 himself above every **g**, and shall speak H410
36 things against the **G** of gods, and shall H410
37 Neither shall he regard the **G** of his H430
37 **g**: for he shall magnify himself above all. H433
38 But in his estate shall he honour the **G** of H433
38 of forces: and a **g** whom his fathers knew H433
39 holds with a strange **g**, whom he shall H433
Hos 1: 6 a daughter. And *G* said unto him, Call
7 by the LORD their **G**, and will not save H430
9 Then said *G*, Call his name Lo-ammi: for
9 not my people, and I will not be your *G*.
10 them, *Ye are* the sons of the living **G**. H410
2:23 and they shall say, *Thou art* my **G**. H430
3: 5 the LORD their **G**, and David their king; H430
4: 1 mercy, nor knowledge of **G** in the land. H430
6 of thy **G**, I will also forget thy children. H430
12 have gone a whoring from under their **G**. H430
5: 4 to turn unto their **G**: for the spirit of H430
6: 6 of **G** more than burnt offerings. H430
7:10 LORD their **G**, nor seek him for all this. H430
8: 2 Israel shall cry unto me, My **G**, we know H430
6 it; therefore it *is* not **G**: but the calf of H430
9: 1 a whoring from thy **G**, thou hast loved a H430
8 *was* with my **G**: *but* the prophet *is* a H430
8 ways, *and* hatred in the house of his **G**. H430
17 My **G** will cast them away, because they H430
11: 9 Ephraim: for I *am* **G**, and not man; the H410
12 with **G**, and is faithful with the saints. H410
12: 3 and by his strength he had power with **G**: H430
5 Even the LORD **G** of hosts; the LORD *is* H430
6 Therefore turn thou to thy **G**: keep mercy H430
6 and wait on thy **G** continually. H430
9 And I *that am* the LORD thy **G** from the H430
13: 4 Yet I *am* the LORD thy **G** from the land H430
4 thou shalt know no **g** but me: for *there is* H430
16 against her **G**: they shall fall by the H430
14: 1 O Israel, return unto the LORD thy **G**; for H430
Joel 1:13 ye ministers of my **G**: for the meat H430
13 is withholden from the house of your **G**. H430
14 LORD your **G**, and cry unto the LORD, H430
16 and gladness from the house of our **G**? H430
2:13 the LORD your **G**: for he *is* gracious and H430
14 a drink offering unto the LORD your **G**? H430
17 say among the people, Where *is* their **G**? H430
23 in the LORD your **G**: for he hath given H430
26 of the LORD your **G**, that hath dealt H430
27 *am* the LORD your **G**, and none else: and H430
3:17 I *am* the LORD your **G** dwelling in Zion, H430
Am 1: 8 shall perish, saith the Lord **G**. H3069
2: 8 of the condemned *in* the house of their **g**. H430
3: 7 Surely the Lord **G** will do nothing, but H3069
8 **G** hath spoken, who can but prophesy? H3069
11 Therefore thus saith the Lord **G**; An H3069
13 saith the Lord **G**, the God of hosts, H3069
13 saith the Lord GOD, the **G** of hosts, H430
4: 2 The Lord **G** hath sworn by his holiness, H3069
5 O ye children of Israel, saith the Lord **G**. H3069
11 I have overthrown *some* of you, as **G** H430
12 thee, prepare to meet thy **G**, O Israel. H430
13 The LORD, The **G** of hosts, *is* his name. H430
5: 3 For thus saith the Lord **G**; The city that H3069

Am 5:14 and so the LORD, the **G** of hosts, shall be H430
15 may be that the LORD **G** of hosts will be H430
16 Therefore the LORD, the **G** of hosts, the H430
26 of your **g**, which ye made to yourselves. H430
27 LORD, whose name *is* The **G** of hosts. H430
6: 8 The Lord **G** hath sworn by himself, H3069
8 saith the LORD the **G** of hosts, I abhor H430
14 saith the LORD the **G** of hosts; and they H430
7: 1 Thus hath the Lord **G** shewed unto me; H3069
2 I said, O Lord **G**, forgive, I beseech thee: H3069
4 Thus hath the Lord **G** shewed unto me: H3069
4 behold, the Lord **G** called to contend by H3069
5 Then said I, O Lord **G**, cease, I beseech H3069
6 This also shall not be, saith the Lord **G**. H3069
8: 1 Thus hath the Lord **G** shewed unto me: H3069
3 saith the Lord **G**: *there shall be* many H3069
9 saith the Lord **G**, that I will cause the H3069
11 saith the Lord **G**, that I will send a H3069
14 and say, Thy **g**, O Dan, liveth; and, The H430
9: 5 And the Lord **G** of hosts *is* he that H3069
8 Behold, the eyes of the Lord **G** *are* upon H3069
15 I have given them, saith the LORD thy **G**. H430
Oba 1 saith the Lord **G** concerning Edom; We H3069
Jna 1: 5 every man unto his **g**, and cast forth the H430
6 arise, call upon thy **G**, if so be that God H430
6 **G** will think upon us, that we perish not. H430
9 I fear the LORD, the **G** of heaven, which H430
2: 1 Then Jonah prayed unto the LORD his **G** H430
6 my life from corruption, O LORD my **G**. H430
3: 5 So the people of Nineveh believed **G**, and H430
8 cry mightily unto **G**: yea, let them turn H430
9 Who can tell *if* **G** will turn and repent, H430
10 And **G** saw their works, that they turned H430
10 their evil way; and **G** repented of the evil, H430
4: 2 thou *art* a gracious **G**, and merciful, slow H410
6 And the LORD **G** prepared a gourd, and H430
7 But **G** prepared a worm when the H430
8 the sun did arise, that **G** prepared a H430
9 And **G** said to Jonah, Doest thou well to H430
Mic 1: 2 and let the Lord **G** be witness against H3069
3: 7 their lips; for *there is* no answer of **G**. H430
4: 2 to the house of the **G** of Jacob; and he H430
5 in the name of his **g**, and we will walk in H430
5 of the LORD our **G** for ever and ever. H430
5: 4 of the LORD his **G**; and they shall abide: H430
6: 6 before the high **G**? shall I come before H430
8 mercy, and to walk humbly with thy **G**? H430
7: 7 **G** of my salvation: my God will hear me. H430
7 God of my salvation: my **G** will hear me. H430
10 Where is the LORD thy **G**? mine eyes shall H430
17 our **G**, and shall fear because of thee. H430
18 Who *is* a **G** like unto thee, that H410
Nah 1: 2 **G** *is* jealous, and the LORD revengeth; H410
Hab 1:11 *imputing* this his power unto his **g**. H433
12 O LORD my **G**, mine Holy One? we shall H430
12 and, O mighty **G**, thou hast established H6697
3: 3 **G** came from Teman, and the Holy One H433
18 LORD, I will joy in the **G** of my salvation. H430
19 The LORD **G** *is* my strength, and he will H136
Zep 1: 7 of the Lord **G**: for the day of the LORD H3069
2: 7 for the LORD their **G** shall visit them, H430
9 the LORD of hosts, the **G** of Israel, Surely H430
3: 2 in the LORD; she drew not near to her **G**. H430
17 The LORD thy **G** in the midst of thee *is* H430
Hag 1:12 of the LORD their **G**, and the words of H430
12 as the LORD their **G** had sent him, and H430
14 the house of the LORD of hosts, their **G**, H430
Zec 6:15 obey the voice of the LORD your **G**. H430
7: 2 When they had sent unto the house of **G** H410
8: 8 be their **G**, in truth and in righteousness. H430
23 for we have heard *that* **G** is with you. H430
9: 7 he, *shall be* for our **G**, and he shall be as a H430
14 and the Lord **G** shall blow the trumpet, H3069
16 And the LORD their **G** shall save them in H430
10: 6 the LORD their **G**, and will hear them. H430
11: 4 Thus saith the LORD my **G**; Feed the H430
12: 5 my strength in the LORD of hosts their **G**. H430
8 **G**, as the angel of the LORD before them. H430
13: 9 and they shall say, The LORD *is* my **G**. H430
14: 5 and the LORD my **G** shall come, *and* all H430
Mal 1: 9 And now, I pray you, beseech **G** that he H410
2:10 hath not one **G** created us? why do we H410
11 hath married the daughter of a strange **g**. H410
16 For the LORD, the **G** of Israel, saith that H430
17 in them; or, Where *is* the **G** of judgment? H430
3: 8 Will a man rob **G**? Yet ye have robbed H430
14 Ye have said, It *is* vain to serve **G**: and H430
15 *they that* tempt **G** are even delivered. H430
18 serveth **G** and him that serveth him not. H430

Mt 1:23 which being interpreted is, G with us. G2316
2:12 And being warned of G in a dream that G5537
22 being warned of G in a dream, he G5537
3: 9 I say unto you, that G is able of these G2316
16 he saw the Spirit of G descending like a G2316
4: 3 If thou be the Son of G, command that G2316
4 that proceedeth out of the mouth of G. G2316
6 thou be the Son of G, cast thyself down: G2316
7 Thou shalt not tempt the Lord thy G. G2316
10 thy G, and him only shalt thou serve. G2316
5: 8 the pure in heart: for they shall see G. G2316
9 they shall be called the children of G. G2316
6:24 Ye cannot serve G and mammon. G2316
30 Wherefore, if G so clothe the grass of G2316
33 But seek ye first the kingdom of G, and G2316
8:29 Jesus, thou Son of G? art thou come G2316
9: 8 and glorified G, which had given such G2316
12: 4 How he entered into the house of G, and G2316
28 But if I cast out devils by the Spirit of G, G2316
28 the kingdom of G is come unto you. G2316
14:33 saying, Of a truth thou art the Son of G. G2316
15: 3 commandment of G by your tradition? G2316
4 For G commanded, saying, Honour thy G2316
6 of G of none effect by your tradition. G2316
31 see: and they glorified the G of Israel. G2316
16:16 art the Christ, the Son of the living G. G2316
23 that be of G, but those that be of men. G2316
19: 6 What therefore G hath joined together, G2316
17 but one, *that is*, G: but if thou wilt enter G2316
24 man to enter into the kingdom of G. G2316
26 but with G all things are possible. G2316
21:12 And Jesus went into the temple of G, G2316
31 go into the kingdom of G before you. G2316
43 The kingdom of G shall be taken from G2316
22:16 the way of G in truth, neither carest G2316
21 and unto G the things that are God's. G2316
29 the scriptures, nor the power of G. G2316
30 but are as the angels of G in heaven. G2316
31 was spoken unto you by G, saying, G2316
32 I am the G of Abraham, and the God of G2316
32 I am the God of Abraham, and the G of G2316
32 of Isaac, and the G of Jacob? God is not G2316
32 the God of Jacob? G is not the God of G2316
32 not the G of the dead, but of the living. G2316
37 love the Lord thy G with all thy heart, G2316
23:22 of G, and by him that sitteth thereon. G2316
26:61 of G, and to build it in three days. G2316
63 thee by the living G, that thou tell us G2316
63 thou be the Christ, the Son of G. G2316
27:40 Son of G, come down from the cross. G2316
43 He trusted in G; let him deliver him G2316
43 have him: for he said, I am the Son of G. G2316
46 G, my God, why hast thou forsaken me? G2316
46 God, my G, why hast thou forsaken me? G2316
54 saying, Truly this was the Son of G. G2316
Mk 1: 1 the gospel of Jesus Christ, the Son of G; G2316
14 the gospel of the kingdom of G, G2316
15 the kingdom of G is at hand: repent ye, G2316
24 thee who thou art, the Holy One of G. G2316
2: 7 who can forgive sins but G only? G2316
12 and glorified G, saying, We never saw G2316
26 How he went into the house of G in the G2316
3:11 cried, saying, Thou art the Son of G. G2316
35 For whosoever shall do the will of G, the G2316
4:11 of the kingdom of G: but unto them that G2316
26 And he said, So is the kingdom of G, as G2316
30 liken the kingdom of G? or with what G2316
5: 7 Son of the most high G? I adjure thee by G2316
7 thee by G, that thou torment me not. G2316
7: 8 the commandment of G, ye hold the G2316
9 G, that ye may keep your own tradition. G2316
13 Making the word of G of none effect G2316
8:33 be of G, but the things that be of men. G2316
9: 1 the kingdom of G come with power. G2316
47 the kingdom of G with one eye, than G2316
10: 6 G made them male and female. G2316
9 What therefore G hath joined together, G2316
14 not: for of such is the kingdom of G. G2316
15 the kingdom of G as a little child, he G2316
18 *there is* none good but one, *that is*, G. G2316
23 have riches enter into the kingdom of G! G2316
24 in riches to enter into the kingdom of G! G2316
25 man to enter into the kingdom of G. G2316
27 G: for with God all things are possible. G2316
27 God: for with G all things are possible. G2316
11:22 saith unto them, Have faith in G. G2316
12:14 the way of G in truth: Is it lawful G2316
17 Caesar's, and to G the things that are G2316
24 the scriptures, neither the power of G? G2316
Mk 12:26 how in the bush G spake unto him, G2316
26 saying, I *am* the G of Abraham, and G2316
26 the G of Isaac, and the God of Jacob? G2316
26 the God of Isaac, and the G of Jacob? G2316
27 He is not the G of the dead, but the God G2316
27 He is not the God of the dead, but the G G2316
29 O Israel; The Lord our G is one Lord: G2316
30 And thou shalt love the Lord thy G with G2316
32 is one G; and there is none other but he: G2316
34 the kingdom of G. And no man after G2316
13:19 the creation which G created unto this G2316
14:25 that I drink it new in the kingdom of G. G2316
15:34 G, my God, why hast thou forsaken me? G2316
34 God, my G, why hast thou forsaken me? G2316
39 said, Truly this man was the Son of G. G2316
43 the kingdom of G, came, and went in G2316
16:19 heaven, and sat on the right hand of G. G2316
Lk 1: 6 And they were both righteous before G, G2316
8 before G in the order of his course, G2316
16 Israel shall he turn to the Lord their G. G2316
19 in the presence of G; and am sent to G2316
26 was sent from G unto a city of Galilee, G2316
30 for thou hast found favour with G. G2316
32 and the Lord G shall give unto him G2316
35 born of thee shall be called the Son of G. G2316
37 For with G nothing shall be impossible. G2316
47 And my spirit hath rejoiced in G my G2316
64 *loosed*, and he spake, and praised G. G2316
68 Blessed *be* the Lord G of Israel; for he G2316
78 Through the tender mercy of our G; G2316
2:13 heavenly host praising G, and saying, G2316
14 Glory to G in the highest, and on earth G2316
20 and praising G for all the things that G2316
28 up in his arms, and blessed G, and said, G2316
37 temple, but served G with fastings and
40 and the grace of G was upon him. G2316
52 stature, and in favour with G and man. G2316
3: 2 the word of G came unto John the G2316
6 all flesh shall see the salvation of G. G2316
8 unto you, That G is able of these stones G2316
38 *son* of Adam, which was *the son* of G. G2316
4: 3 If thou be the Son of G, command this G2316
4 by bread alone, but by every word of G. G2316
8 thy G, and him only shalt thou serve. G2316
9 Son of G, cast thyself down from hence: G2316
12 Thou shalt not tempt the Lord thy G. G2316
34 thee who thou art; the Holy One of G. G2316
41 art Christ the Son of G. And he rebuking G2316
43 the kingdom of G to other cities also: G2316
5: 1 of G, he stood by the lake of Gennesaret, G2316
21 Who can forgive sins, but G alone? G2316
25 departed to his own house, glorifying G. G2316
26 and they glorified G, and were filled G2316
6: 4 How he went into the house of G, and G2316
12 and continued all night in prayer to G. G2316
20 *ye* poor: for yours is the kingdom of G. G2316
7:16 all: and they glorified G, saying, That a G2316
16 us; and, That G hath visited his people. G2316
28 in the kingdom of G is greater than he. G2316
29 justified G, being baptized with G2316
30 the counsel of G against themselves, G2316
8: 1 of G: and the twelve *were* with him, G2316
10 of the kingdom of G: but to others in G2316
11 is this: The seed is the word of G. G2316
21 which hear the word of G, and do it. G2316
28 thee, Jesus, *thou* Son of G most high? I G2316
39 how great things G hath done unto G2316
9: 2 the kingdom of G, and to heal the sick. G2316
11 of the kingdom of G, and healed them G2316
20 Peter answering said, The Christ of G. G2316
27 of death, till they see the kingdom of G. G2316
43 the mighty power of G. But while they G2316
60 go thou and preach the kingdom of G. G2316
62 back, is fit for the kingdom of G. G2316
10: 9 kingdom of G is come nigh unto you. G2316
11 kingdom of G is come nigh unto you. G2316
27 love the Lord thy G with all thy heart, G2316
11:20 But if I with the finger of G cast out G2316
20 the kingdom of G is come upon you. G2316
28 that hear the word of G, and keep it. G2316
42 and the love of G: these ought ye to have G2316
49 Therefore also said the wisdom of G, I G2316
12: 6 not one of them is forgotten before G? G2316
8 man also confess before the angels of G: G2316
9 shall be denied before the angels of G. G2316
20 But G said unto him, *Thou* fool, this G2316
21 for himself, and is not rich toward G. G2316
24 nor barn; and G feedeth them: how G2316
28 If then G so clothe the grass, which is to G2316
Lk 12:31 But rather seek ye the kingdom of G; G2316
13:13 she was made straight, and glorified G. G2316
18 what is the kingdom of G like? and G2316
20 shall I liken the kingdom of G? G2316
28 of G, and you *yourselves* thrust out. G2316
29 and shall sit down in the kingdom of G. G2316
14:15 shall eat bread in the kingdom of G. G2316
15:10 of G over one sinner that repenteth. G2316
16:13 Ye cannot serve G and mammon. G2316
15 before men; but G knoweth your G2316
15 men is abomination in the sight of G. G2316
16 time the kingdom of G is preached, and G2316
17:15 back, and with a loud voice glorified G, G2316
18 to give glory to G, save this stranger. G2316
20 the kingdom of G should come, he G2316
20 of G cometh not with observation: G2316
21 behold, the kingdom of G is within you. G2316
18: 2 feared not G, neither regarded man: G2316
4 Though I fear not G, nor regard man; G2316
7 And shall not G avenge his own elect, G2316
11 thus with himself, G, I thank thee, that I G2316
13 saying, G be merciful to me a sinner. G2316
16 not: for of such is the kingdom of G. G2316
17 the kingdom of G as a little child shall G2316
19 good? none *is* good, save one, *that is*, G. G2316
24 have riches enter into the kingdom of G! G2316
25 man to enter into the kingdom of G. G2316
27 with men are possible with G. G2316
43 him, glorifying G: and all the people, G2316
43 when they saw *it*, gave praise unto G. G2316
19:11 of G should immediately appear. G2316
37 rejoice and praise G with a loud voice G2316
20:16 heard *it*, they said, G forbid. G3361+G1096
21 *of any*, but teachest the way of G truly: G2316
25 and unto G the things which be God's. G2316
36 are the children of G, being the children G2316
37 the Lord the G of Abraham, and the G2316
37 the G of Isaac, and the God of Jacob. G2316
37 the God of Isaac, and the G of Jacob. G2316
38 For he is not a G of the dead, but of the G2316
21: 4 the offerings of G: but she of her penury G2316
31 that the kingdom of G is nigh at hand. G2316
22:16 until it be fulfilled in the kingdom of G. G2316
18 until the kingdom of G shall come. G2316
69 sit on the right hand of the power of G. G2316
70 then the Son of G? And he said unto G2316
23:35 himself, if he be Christ, the chosen of G. G2316
40 Dost not thou fear G, seeing thou art in G2316
47 done, he glorified G, saying, Certainly G2316
51 himself waited for the kingdom of G. G2316
24:19 and word before G and all the people: G2316
53 temple, praising and blessing G. Amen. G2316
Jn 1: 1 was with G, and the Word was God. G2316
1 was with God, and the Word was G. G2316
2 The same was in the beginning with G. G2316
6 There was a man sent from G, whose G2316
12 the sons of G, *even* to them that believe G2316
13 flesh, nor of the will of man, but of G. G2316
18 No man hath seen G at any time; the G2316
29 the Lamb of G, which taketh away G2316
34 bare record that this is the Son of G. G2316
36 walked, he saith, Behold the Lamb of G! G2316
49 the Son of G; thou art the King of Israel. G2316
51 and the angels of G ascending and G2316
3: 2 come from G: for no man can do these G2316
2 that thou doest, except G be with him. G2316
3 again, he cannot see the kingdom of G. G2316
5 he cannot enter into the kingdom of G. G2316
16 For G so loved the world, that he gave G2316
17 For G sent not his Son into the world to G2316
18 the name of the only begotten Son of G. G2316
21 manifest, that they are wrought in G. G2316
33 hath set to his seal that G is true. G2316
34 For he whom G hath sent speaketh the G2316
34 the words of G: for God giveth not the G2316
34 the words of God: for G giveth not the G2316
36 life; but the wrath of G abideth on him. G2316
4:10 knewest the gift of G, and who it is that G2316
24 G *is* a Spirit: and they that worship him G2316
5:18 but said also that G was his Father, G2316
18 Father, making himself equal with G. G2316
25 Son of G: and they that hear shall live. G2316
42 that ye have not the love of G in you. G2316
44 the honour that *cometh* from G only? G2316
6:27 you: for him hath G the Father sealed. G2316
28 do, that we might work the works of G? G2316
29 This is the work of G, that ye believe on G2316
33 For the bread of G is he which cometh G2316
45 be all taught of G. Every man therefore G2316

G

Jn 6:46 which is of G, he hath seen the Father. G2316
69 art that Christ, the Son of the living G. G2316
7:17 it be of G, or *whether* I speak of myself. G2316
8:40 have heard of G: this did not Abraham. G2316
41 we have one Father, *even* G. G2316
42 Jesus said unto them, If G were your G2316
42 and came from G; neither came I of G2316
47 He that is of G heareth God's words: ye G2316
47 hear *them* not, because ye are not of G. G2316
54 me; of whom ye say, that he is your G: G2316
9: 3 of G should be made manifest in him. G2316
16 This man is not of G, because he G2316
24 unto him, Give G the praise: we know G2316
29 We know that G spake unto Moses: *as* G2316
31 Now we know that G heareth not G2316
31 of G, and doeth his will, him he heareth. G2318
33 If this man were not of G, he could do G2316
35 him, Dost thou believe on the Son of G? G2316
10:33 thou, being a man, makest thyself G. G2316
35 whom the word of G came, and the G2316
36 because I said, I am the Son of G? G2316
11: 4 for the glory of G, that the Son of God G2316
4 the Son of G might be glorified thereby. G2316
22 thou wilt ask of G, God will give *it* thee. G2316
22 thou wilt ask of God, G will give *it* thee. G2316
27 of G, which should come into the world. G2316
40 thou shouldest see the glory of G? G2316
52 of G that were scattered abroad. G2316
12:43 of men more than the praise of G. G2316
13: 3 he was come from G, and went to God; G2316
3 he was come from God, and went to G; G2316
31 glorified, and G is glorified in him. G2316
32 If G be glorified in him, God shall also G2316
32 If God be glorified in him, G shall also G2316
14: 1 ye believe in G, believe also in me. G2316
16: 2 you will think that he doeth G service. G2316
27 have believed that I came out from G. G2316
30 believe that thou camest forth from G. G2316
17: 3 thee the only true G, and Jesus Christ, G2316
19: 7 because he made himself the Son of G. G2316
20:17 Father; and *to* my G, and your God. G2316
17 Father; and *to* my God, and your G. G2316
28 and said unto him, My Lord and my G. G2316
31 Christ, the Son of G; and that believing G2316
21:19 he should glorify G. And when he had G2316
Act 1: 3 things pertaining to the kingdom of G: G2316
2:11 our tongues the wonderful works of G. G2316
17 last days, saith G, I will pour out of my G2316
22 a man approved of G among you by G2316
22 and signs, which G did by him in the G2316
23 foreknowledge of G, ye have taken, and G2316
24 Whom G hath raised up, having loosed G2316
30 and knowing that G had sworn with an G2316
32 This Jesus hath G raised up, whereof G2316
33 Therefore being by the right hand of G G2316
36 assuredly, that G hath made that same G2316
39 as many as the Lord our G shall call. G2316
47 Praising G, and having favour with all G2316
3: 8 walking, and leaping, and praising G. G2316
9 saw him walking and praising G: G2316
13 The G of Abraham, and of Isaac, and G2316
13 and of Jacob, the G of our fathers, hath G2316
15 And killed the Prince of life, whom G G2316
18 But those things, which G before had G2316
21 all things, which G hath spoken by the G2316
22 the Lord your G raise up unto you of G2316
25 the covenant which G made with our G2316
26 Unto you first G, having raised up his G2316
4:10 ye crucified, whom G raised from the G2316
19 in the sight of G to hearken unto you G2316
19 unto you more than unto G, judge ye. G2316
21 glorified G for that which was done. G2316
24 up their voice to G with one accord, G2316
24 said, Lord, thou *art* G, which hast made G2316
31 spake the word of G with boldness. G2316
5: 4 hast not lied unto men, but unto G. G2316
29 We ought to obey G rather than men. G2316
30 The G of our fathers raised up Jesus, G2316
31 Him hath G exalted with his right hand G2316
32 G hath given to them that obey him. G2316
39 But if it be of G, ye cannot overthrow it; G2316
39 ye be found even to fight against G. G2314
6: 2 leave the word of G, and serve tables. G2316
7 And the word of G increased; and the G2316
11 words against Moses, and *against* G. G2316
7: 2 hearken; The G of glory appeared unto G2316
6 And G spake on this wise, That his seed G2316
7 will I judge, said G: and after that shall G2316
9 Joseph into Egypt: but G was with him, G2316

Act 7:17 drew nigh, which G had sworn to G2316
25 how that G by his hand would deliver G2316
32 *Saying*, I *am* the G of thy fathers, the G2316
32 of thy fathers, the G of Abraham, and G2316
32 Abraham, and the G of Isaac, and the G2316
32 God of Isaac, and the G of Jacob. Then G2316
35 the same did G send *to be* a ruler and G2316
37 the Lord your G raise up unto you of G2316
42 Then G turned, and gave them up to G2316
43 the star of your g Remphan, figures G2316
45 Gentiles, whom G drave out before the G2316
46 Who found favour before G, and G2316
46 to find a tabernacle for the G of Jacob. G2316
55 saw the glory of G, and Jesus standing G2316
55 Jesus standing on the right hand of G, G2316
56 of man standing on the right hand of G. G2316
59 And they stoned Stephen, calling upon *G*,
8:10 This man is the great power of G. G2316
12 the kingdom of G, and the name of G2316
14 G, they sent unto them Peter and John: G2316
20 of G may be purchased with money. G2316
21 thy heart is not right in the sight of G. G2316
22 and pray G, if perhaps the thought G2316
37 believe that Jesus Christ is the Son of G. G2316
9:20 the synagogues, that he is the Son of G. G2316
10: 2 *A* devout *man*, and one that feared G G2316
2 to the people, and prayed to G alway. G2316
3 the day an angel of G coming in to him, G2316
4 are come up for a memorial before G. G2316
15 time, What G hath cleansed, *that* G2316
22 one that feareth G, and of good report G2316
22 was warned from G by an holy angel to G5537
28 nation; but G hath shewed me that G2316
31 had in remembrance in the sight of G. G2316
33 present before G, to hear all things that G2316
33 things that are commanded thee of G. G2316
34 that G is no respecter of persons: G2316
36 The word which *G* sent unto the children
38 How G anointed Jesus of Nazareth with G2316
38 of the devil; for G was with him. G2316
40 Him G raised up the third day, and G2316
41 chosen before of G, *even* to us, who did G2316
42 of G *to be* the Judge of quick and dead. G2316
46 and magnify G. Then answered Peter, G2316
11: 1 had also received the word of G. G2316
9 heaven, What G hath cleansed, *that* G2316
17 Forasmuch then as G gave them the G2316
17 what was I, that I could withstand G? G2316
18 and glorified G, saying, Then hath God G2316
18 God, saying, Then hath G also to the G2316
23 had seen the grace of G, was glad, and G2316
12: 5 ceasing of the church unto G for him. G2316
22 *It is* the voice of a g, and not of a man. G2316
23 he gave not G the glory: and he was G2316
24 But the word of G grew and multiplied. G2316
13: 5 the word of G in the synagogues of G2316
7 Saul, and desired to hear the word of G. G2316
16 and ye that fear G, give audience. G2316
17 The G of this people of Israel chose our G2316
21 a king: and G gave unto them Saul G2316
23 Of this man's seed hath G according to G2316
26 you feareth G, to you is the word of G2316
30 But G raised him from the dead: G2316
33 G hath fulfilled the same unto us their G2316
36 by the will of G, fell on sleep, and was G2316
37 But he, whom G raised again, saw no G2316
43 them to continue in the grace of G. G2316
44 city together to hear the word of G. G2316
46 that the word of G should first have G2316
14:15 unto the living G, which made heaven, G2316
22 tribulation enter into the kingdom of G. G2316
26 of G for the work which they fulfilled. G2316
27 they rehearsed all that G had done with G2316
15: 4 all things that G had done with them. G2316
7 that a good while ago G made choice G2316
8 And G, which knoweth the hearts, bare G2316
10 Now therefore why tempt ye G, to put a G2316
12 and wonders G had wrought among G2316
14 Simeon hath declared how G at the G2316
18 Known unto G are all his works from G2316
19 among the Gentiles are turned to G: G2316
40 by the brethren unto the grace of G. G2316
16:14 worshipped G, heard *us*: whose heart G2316
17 of the most high G, which shew unto us G2316
25 unto G: and the prisoners heard them. G2316
34 believing in G with all his house. G2316
17:13 that the word of G was preached of G2316
23 THE UNKNOWN G. Whom therefore ye G2316
24 G that made the world and all things G2316

Act 17:29 the offspring of G, we ought not to think G2316
30 And the times of this ignorance G G2316
18: 7 that worshipped G, whose house joined G2316
11 teaching the word of G among them. G2316
13 men to worship G contrary to the law. G2316
21 if G will. And he sailed from Ephesus. G2316
26 unto him the way of G more perfectly. G2316
19: 8 things concerning the kingdom of G. G2316
11 And G wrought special miracles by the G2316
20 So mightily grew the word of G and G2962
20:21 toward G, and faith toward our G2316
24 to testify the gospel of the grace of G. G2316
25 of G, shall see my face no more. G2316
27 to declare unto you all the counsel of G. G2316
28 to feed the church of G, which he hath G2316
32 I commend you to G, and to the word of G2316
21:19 what things G had wrought among G2316
22: 3 zealous toward G, as ye all are this day. G2316
14 And he said, The G of our fathers hath G2316
23: 1 conscience before G until this day. G2316
3 Then said Paul unto him, G shall smite G2316
9 to him, let us not fight against G. G2313
24:14 so worship I the G of my fathers, G2316
15 And have hope toward G, which they G2316
16 of offence toward G, and *toward* men. G2316
26: 6 promise made of G unto our fathers: G2316
7 instantly serving G day and night, hope
8 with you, that G should raise the dead? G2316
18 of Satan unto G, that they may receive G2316
20 G, and do works meet for repentance. G2316
22 Having therefore obtained help of G, I G2316
29 And Paul said, I would to G, that not G2316
27:23 of G, whose I am, and whom I serve, G2316
24 Caesar: and, lo, G hath given thee all G2316
25 G, that it shall be even as it was told me. G2316
35 gave thanks to G in presence of them G2316
28: 6 their minds, and said that he was a g. G2316
15 saw, he thanked G, and took courage. G2316
23 the kingdom of G, persuading them G2316
28 that the salvation of G is sent unto the G2316
31 Preaching the kingdom of G, and G2316
Ro 1: 1 apostle, separated unto the gospel of G, G2316
4 And declared *to be* the Son of G with G2316
7 To all that be in Rome, beloved of G, G2316
7 and peace from G our Father, and the G2316
8 First, I thank my G through Jesus G2316
9 For G is my witness, whom I serve with G2316
10 by the will of G to come unto you. G2316
16 it is the power of G unto salvation to G2316
17 For therein is the righteousness of G G2316
18 For the wrath of G is revealed from G2316
19 Because that which may be known of G G2316
19 them; for G hath shewed *it* unto them. G2316
21 Because that, when they knew G, they G2316
21 *him* not as G, neither were thankful; G2316
23 of the uncorruptible G into an image G2316
24 Wherefore G also gave them up to G2316
25 Who changed the truth of G into a lie, G2316
26 For this cause G gave them up unto vile G2316
28 not like to retain G in *their* knowledge, G2316
28 *their* knowledge, G gave them over to a G2316
30 Backbiters, haters of G, despiteful, G2319
32 Who knowing the judgment of G, that G2316
2: 2 But we are sure that the judgment of G G2316
3 thou shalt escape the judgment of G? G2316
4 of G leadeth thee to repentance? G2316
5 of the righteous judgment of G; G2316
11 there is no respect of persons with G. G2316
13 law *are* just before G, but the doers of G2316
16 In the day when G shall judge the G2316
17 in the law, and makest thy boast of G, G2316
23 breaking the law dishonourest thou G? G2316
24 For the name of G is blasphemed G2316
29 whose praise *is* not of men, but of G. G2316
3: 2 them were committed the oracles of G. G2316
3 make the faith of G without effect? G2316
4 G forbid: yea, let God be true, G3361+G1096
4 God forbid: yea, let G be true, but every G2316
5 righteousness of G, what shall we say? G2316
5 shall we say? *Is* G unrighteous who G2316
6 G forbid: for then how shall G3361+G1096
6 God forbid: for then how shall G judge G2316
7 For if the truth of G hath more G2316
11 there is none that seeketh after G. G2316
18 There is no fear of G before their eyes. G2316
19 the world may become guilty before G. G2316
21 But now the righteousness of G without G2316
22 Even the righteousness of G *which is* by G2316
23 and come short of the glory of G; G2316

Ro 3:25 Whom G hath set forth *to be* a G2316
25 are past, through the forbearance of G; G2316
29 *Is he* the G of the Jews only? *is he* not G2316
30 Seeing *it is* one G, which shall justify the G2316
31 through faith? G forbid: yea, G3361+G1096
4: 2 hath *whereof* to glory; but not before G. G2316
3 believed G, and it was counted G2316
6 the man, unto whom G imputeth G2316
17 he believed, *even* G, who quickeneth the G2316
20 He staggered not at the promise of G G2316
20 was strong in faith, giving glory to G; G2316
5: 1 with G through our Lord Jesus Christ: G2316
2 and rejoice in hope of the glory of G. G2316
5 the love of G is shed abroad in our G2316
8 But G commendeth his love toward us, G2316
10 were reconciled to G by the death of his G2316
11 And not only *so*, but we also joy in G G2316
15 more the grace of G, and the gift by G2316
6: 2 G forbid. How shall we, that G3361+G1096
10 but in that he liveth, he liveth unto G. G2316
11 unto G through Jesus Christ our Lord. G2316
13 yourselves unto G, as those that are G2316
13 *as* instruments of righteousness unto G. G2316
15 law, but under grace? G forbid. G3361+G1096
17 But G be thanked, that ye were the G2316
22 servants to G, ye have your fruit unto G2316
23 but the gift of G *is* eternal life through G2316
7: 4 that we should bring forth fruit unto G. G2316
7 *Is* the law sin? G forbid. Nay, I G3361+G1096
13 unto me? G forbid. But sin, G3361+G1096
22 For I delight in the law of G after the G2316
25 I thank G through Jesus Christ our G2316
25 of G; but with the flesh the law of sin. G2316
8: 3 through the flesh, G sending his own G2316
7 *is* enmity against G: for it is not subject G2316
7 to the law of G, neither indeed can be. G2316
8 that are in the flesh cannot please G. G2316
9 that the Spirit of G dwell in you. Now if G2316
14 the Spirit of G, they are the sons of God. G2316
14 the Spirit of God, they are the sons of G. G2316
16 our spirit, that we are the children of G: G2316
17 And if children, then heirs; heirs of G, G2316
19 for the manifestation of the sons of G. G2316
21 the glorious liberty of the children of G. G2316
27 for the saints according to *the will of* G. G2316
28 to them that love G, to them who are G2316
31 If G *be* for us, who *can be* against us? G2316
33 of God's elect? *It is* G that justifieth. G2316
34 G, who also maketh intercession for us. G2316
39 of G, which is in Christ Jesus our Lord. G2316
9: 4 and the service *of* G, and the promises;
5 is over all, G blessed for ever. Amen. G2316
6 Not as though the word of G hath taken G2316
8 not the children of G: but the children of G2316
11 the purpose of G according to election G2316
14 unrighteousness with G? God forbid. G2316
14 with God? G forbid. G3361+G1096
16 runneth, but of G that sheweth mercy. G2316
20 that repliest against G? Shall the thing G2316
22 *What* if G, willing to shew *his* wrath, G2316
26 be called the children of the living G. G2316
10: 1 and prayer to G for Israel is, that they G2316
2 of G, but not according to knowledge. G2316
3 themselves unto the righteousness of G. G2316
9 in thine heart that G hath raised him G2316
17 hearing, and hearing by the word of G. G2316
11: 1 I say then, Hath G cast away his G2316
1 his people? G forbid. For I also G3361+G1096
2 G hath not cast away his people which G2316
2 intercession to G against Israel, saying, G2316
4 But what saith the answer of G unto G5538
8 (According as it is written, G hath G2316
11 they should fall? G forbid: but G3361+G1096
21 For if G spared not the natural G2316
22 and severity of G: on them which fell, G2316
23 in: for G is able to graff them in again. G2316
29 For the gifts and calling of G *are* G2316
30 past have not believed G, yet have now G2316
32 For G hath concluded them all in G2316
33 and knowledge of G! how unsearchable G2316
12: 1 by the mercies of G, that ye present G2316
1 G, *which is* your reasonable service. G2316
2 and acceptable, and perfect, will of G. G2316
3 according as G hath dealt to every G2316
13: 1 is no power but of G: the powers that be G2316
1 the powers that be are ordained of G. G2316
2 the ordinance of G: and they that resist G2316
4 For he is the minister of G to thee for G2316
4 he is the minister of G, a revenger to G2316

Ro 14: 3 that eateth: for G hath received him. G2316
4 up: for G is able to make him stand. G2316
6 for he giveth G thanks; and he that G2316
6 he eateth not, and giveth G thanks. G2316
11 me, and every tongue shall confess to G. G2316
12 of us shall give account of himself to G. G2316
17 For the kingdom of G is not meat and G2316
18 acceptable to G, and approved of men. G2316
20 For meat destroy not the work of G. All G2316
22 *it* to thyself before G. Happy *is* he that G2316
15: 5 Now the G of patience and consolation G2316
6 one mouth glorify G, even the Father of G2316
7 Christ also received us to the glory of G. G2316
8 for the truth of G, to confirm the G2316
9 And that the Gentiles might glorify G G2316
13 Now the G of hope fill you with all joy G2316
15 of the grace that is given to me of G, G2316
16 the gospel of G, that the offering up G2316
17 in those things which pertain to G. G2316
19 power of the Spirit of G; so that from G2316
30 with me in *your* prayers to G for me; G2316
32 of G, and may with you be refreshed. G2316
33 Now the G of peace *be* with you all. G2316
16:20 And the G of peace shall bruise Satan G2316
26 of the everlasting G, made known to all G2316
27 To G only wise, *be* glory through Jesus G2316
1Co 1: 1 will of G, and Sosthenes *our* brother, G2316
2 Unto the church of G which is at G2316
3 Grace *be* unto you, and peace, from G G2316
4 I thank my G always on your behalf, G2316
4 of G which is given you by Jesus Christ; G2316
9 G *is* faithful, by whom ye were called G2316
14 I thank G that I baptized none of you, G2316
18 us which are saved it is the power of G. G2316
20 this world? hath not G made foolish the G2316
21 For after that in the wisdom of G the G2316
21 wisdom knew not G, it pleased God by G2316
21 God, it pleased G by the foolishness of G2316
24 the power of G, and the wisdom of God. G2316
24 the power of God, and the wisdom of G. G2316
25 Because the foolishness of G is wiser G2316
25 weakness of G is stronger than men. G2316
27 But G hath chosen the foolish things of G2316
27 the wise; and G hath chosen the weak G2316
28 are despised, hath G chosen, *yea*, and G2316
30 Christ Jesus, who of G is made unto us G2316
2: 1 declaring unto you the testimony of G. G2316
5 wisdom of men, but in the power of G. G2316
7 But we speak the wisdom of G in a G2316
7 *wisdom*, which G ordained before the G2316
9 the things which G hath prepared for G2316
10 But G hath revealed *them* unto us by G2316
10 all things, yea, the deep things of G. G2316
11 so the things of G knoweth no man, but G2316
11 knoweth no man, but the Spirit of G. G2316
12 spirit which is of G; that we might know G2316
12 things that are freely given to us of G. G2316
14 things of the Spirit of G: for they are G2316
3: 6 I have planted, Apollos watered; but G G2316
7 but G that giveth the increase. G2316
9 For we are labourers together with G: ye G2316
10 According to the grace of G which is G2316
16 Know ye not that ye are the temple of G, G2316
16 *that* the Spirit of G dwelleth in you? G2316
17 If any man defile the temple of G, him G2316
17 of God, him shall G destroy; for the G2316
17 of G is holy, which *temple* ye are. G2316
19 is foolishness with G. For it is written, G2316
4: 1 and stewards of the mysteries of G. G2316
5 then shall every man have praise of G. G2316
8 us: and I would to G ye did reign, that G3785
9 For I think that G hath set forth us the G2316
20 For the kingdom of G *is* not in word, G2316
5:13 But them that are without G judgeth. G2316
6: 9 the kingdom of G? Be not deceived: G2316
10 shall inherit the kingdom of G. G2316
11 Lord Jesus, and by the Spirit of our G. G2316
13 for meats: but G shall destroy both it G2316
14 And G hath both raised up the Lord, G2316
15 of an harlot? G forbid. G3361+G1096
19 ye have of G, and ye are not your own? G2316
20 therefore glorify G in your body, and in G2316
7: 7 hath his proper gift of G, one after this G2316
15 *cases*: but G hath called us to peace. G2316
17 But as G hath distributed to every man, G2316
19 the keeping of the commandments of G. G2316
24 he is called, therein abide with G. G2316
40 I think also that I have the Spirit of G. G2316
8: 3 But if any man love G, the same is G2316

1Co 8: 4 and that *there is* none other G but one. G2316
6 But to us *there is but* one G, the Father, G2316
8 But meat commendeth us not to G: for G2316
9: 9 the corn. Doth G take care for oxen? G2316
21 not without law to G, but under the law G2316
10: 5 But with many of them G was not well G2316
13 to man: but G *is* faithful, who will G2316
20 to devils, and not to G: and I would not G2316
31 ye do, do all to the glory of G. G2316
32 to the Gentiles, nor to the church of G: G2316
11: 3 *is* the man; and the head of Christ *is* G. G2316
7 and glory of G: but the woman is the G2316
12 also by the woman; but all things of G. G2316
13 that a woman pray unto G uncovered? G2316
16 such custom, neither the churches of G. G2316
22 ye the church of G, and shame them G2316
12: 3 speaking by the Spirit of G calleth Jesus G2316
6 is the same G which worketh all in all. G2316
18 But now hath G set the members every G2316
24 have no need: but G hath tempered the G2316
28 And G hath set some in the church, G2316
14: 2 unto men, but unto G: for no man G2316
18 I thank my G, I speak with tongues G2316
25 he will worship G, and report that God G2316
25 and report that G is in you of a truth. G2316
28 and let him speak to himself, and to G. G2316
33 For G is not *the author* of confusion, G2316
36 What? came the word of G out from G2316
15: 9 because I persecuted the church of G. G2316
10 But by the grace of G I am what I am: G2316
10 but the grace of G which was with me. G2316
15 false witnesses of G; because we have G2316
15 we have testified of G that he raised up G2316
24 up the kingdom to G, even the Father; G2316
28 under him, that G may be all in all. G2316
34 of G: I speak *this* to your shame. G2316
38 But G giveth it a body as it hath G2316
50 inherit the kingdom of G; neither doth G2316
57 But thanks *be* to G, which giveth us the G2316
16: 2 lay by him in store, as G hath prospered
2Co 1: 1 Christ by the will of G, and Timothy *our* G2316
1 unto the church of G which is at G2316
2 Grace *be* to you and peace from G our G2316
3 Blessed *be* G, even the Father of our G2316
3 of mercies, and the G of all comfort; G2316
4 we ourselves are comforted of G. G2316
9 but in G which raiseth the dead: G2316
12 but by the grace of G, we have had our G2316
18 But *as* G *is* true, our word toward you G2316
19 For the Son of G, Jesus Christ, who was G2316
20 For all the promises of G in him *are* G2316
20 in him Amen, unto the glory of G by us. G2316
21 in Christ, and hath anointed us, *is* G; G2316
23 Moreover I call G for a record upon my G2316
2:14 Now thanks *be* unto G, which always G2316
15 For we are unto G a sweet savour of G2316
17 the word of G: but as of sincerity, but G2316
17 sincerity, but as of G, in the sight of God G2316
17 in the sight of G speak we in Christ. G2316
3: 3 the Spirit of the living G; not in tables of G2316
5 of ourselves; but our sufficiency *is* of G; G2316
4: 2 the word of G deceitfully; but by G2316
2 man's conscience in the sight of G. G2316
4 In whom the g of this world hath G2316
4 the image of G, should shine unto them. G2316
6 For G, who commanded the light to G2316
6 glory of G in the face of Jesus Christ. G2316
7 of the power may be of G, and not of us. G2316
15 of many redound to the glory of G. G2316
5: 1 we have a building of G, an house not G2316
5 selfsame thing *is* G, who also hath given G2316
11 manifest unto G; and I trust also are G2316
13 ourselves, *it is* to G: or whether we be G2316
18 And all things *are* of G, who hath G2316
19 To wit, that G was in Christ, G2316
20 Christ, as though G did beseech *you* by G2316
20 in Christ's stead, be ye reconciled to G. G2316
21 be made the righteousness of G in him. G2316
6: 1 ye receive not the grace of G in vain. G2316
4 as the ministers of G, in much patience, G2316
7 By the word of truth, by the power of G, G2316
16 hath the temple of G with idols? for ye G2316
16 of the living G; as God hath said, I G2316
16 of the living God; as G hath said, I will G2316
16 be their G, and they shall be my people. G2316
7: 1 perfecting holiness in the fear of G. G2316
6 Nevertheless G, that comforteth those G2316
12 the sight of G might appear unto you. G2316
8: 1 to wit of the grace of G bestowed on the G2316

2Co 8: 5 the Lord, and unto us by the will of G. G2316
16 But thanks be to G, which put the same G2316
9: 7 necessity: for G loveth a cheerful giver. G2316
8 And G is able to make all grace abound G2316
11 causeth through us thanksgiving to G. G2316
12 also by many thanksgivings unto G; G2316
13 they glorify G for your professed G2316
14 you for the exceeding grace of G in you. G2316
15 Thanks be unto G for his unspeakable G2316
10: 4 G to the pulling down of strong holds;) G2316
5 the knowledge of G, and bringing into G2316
13 of the rule which G hath distributed to G2316
11: 1 Would to G ye could bear with me a G3785
7 preached to you the gospel of G freely? G2316
11 Wherefore? because I love you not? G G2316
31 The G and Father of our Lord Jesus G2316
12: 2 I cannot tell: G knoweth;) such an G2316
3 of the body, I cannot tell: G knoweth;) G2316
19 we speak before G in Christ: but we do G2316
21 And lest, when I come again, my G will G2316
13: 4 by the power of G. For we also are weak G2316
4 him by the power of G toward you. G2316
7 Now I pray to G that ye do no evil; not G2316
11 G of love and peace shall be with you. G2316
14 and the love of G, and the communion G2316
Gal 1: 1 by Jesus Christ, and G the Father, who G2316
3 Grace be to you and peace from G the G2316
4 to the will of G and our Father: G2316
10 For do I now persuade men, or G? or do G2316
13 the church of G, and wasted it: G2316
15 But when it pleased G, who separated G2316
20 unto you, behold, before G, I lie not. G2316
24 And they glorified G in me. G2316
2: 6 no matter to me: G accepteth no man's G2316
17 the minister of sin? G forbid. G3361+G1096
19 to the law, that I might live unto G. G2316
20 faith of the Son of G, who loved me, and G2316
21 I do not frustrate the grace of G: for if G2316
3: 6 Even as Abraham believed G, and it G2316
8 And the scripture, foreseeing that G G2316
11 law in the sight of G, it is evident: for, G2316
17 before of G in Christ, the law, which G2316
18 but G gave it to Abraham by promise. G2316
20 is not a mediator of one, but G is one. G2316
21 the promises of G? God forbid: for if G2316
21 of God? G forbid: for if there G3361+G1096
26 For ye are all the children of G by faith G2316
4: 4 time was come, G sent forth his Son, G2316
6 And because ye are sons, G hath sent G2316
7 a son, then an heir of G through Christ. G2316
8 Howbeit then, when ye knew not G, ye G2316
9 But now, after that ye have known G, or G2316
9 are known of G, how turn ye again to G2316
14 as an angel of G, even as Christ Jesus. G2316
5:21 shall not inherit the kingdom of G. G2316
6: 7 Be not deceived; G is not mocked: for G2316
14 But G forbid that I should G3361+G1096
16 and mercy, and upon the Israel of G. G2316
Eph 1: 1 by the will of G, to the saints which G2316
2 Grace be to you, and peace, from G our G2316
3 Blessed be the G and Father of our G2316
17 That the G of our Lord Jesus Christ, the G2316
2: 4 But G, who is rich in mercy, for his G2316
8 that not of yourselves: it is the gift of G: G2316
10 works, which G hath before ordained G2316
12 no hope, and without G in the world: G112
16 both unto G in one body by the cross, G2316
19 the saints, and of the household of G; G2316
22 an habitation of G through the Spirit. G2316
3: 2 of G which is given me to you-ward: G2316
7 gift of the grace of G given unto me by G2316
9 hath been hid in G, who created all G2316
10 the church the manifold wisdom of G, G2316
19 might be filled with all the fulness of G. G2316
4: 6 One G and Father of all, who is above G2316
13 of the Son of G, unto a perfect man, G2316
18 alienated from the life of G through the G2316
24 new man, which after G is created in G2316
30 And grieve not the holy Spirit of G, G2316
32 G for Christ's sake hath forgiven you. G2316
5: 1 Be ye therefore followers of G, as dear G2316
2 to G for a sweetsmelling savour. G2316
5 in the kingdom of Christ and of G. G2316
6 of G upon the children of disobedience. G2316
20 for all things unto G and the Father in G2316
21 one to another in the fear of G. G2316
6: 6 doing the will of G from the heart; G2316
11 Put on the whole armour of G, that ye G2316
13 whole armour of G, that ye may be able G2316

Eph 6:17 of the Spirit, which is the word of G: G2316
23 G the Father and the Lord Jesus Christ. G2316
Php 1: 2 Grace be unto you, and peace, from G G2316
3 I thank my G upon every remembrance G2316
8 For G is my record, how greatly I long G2316
11 Christ, unto the glory and praise of G. G2316
28 but to you of salvation, and that of G. G2316
2: 6 Who, being in the form of G, thought it G2316
6 it not robbery to be equal with G: G2316
9 Wherefore G also hath highly exalted G2316
11 is Lord, to the glory of G the Father. G2316
13 For it is G which worketh in you both G2316
15 the sons of G, without rebuke, in the G2316
27 unto death: but G had mercy on him; G2316
3: 3 which worship G in the spirit, and G2316
9 righteousness which is of G by faith: G2316
14 of the high calling of G in Christ Jesus. G2316
15 G shall reveal even this unto you. G2316
19 Whose end is destruction, whose G is G2316
4: 6 your requests be made known unto G. G2316
7 And the peace of G, which passeth all G2316
9 and the G of peace shall be with you. G2316
18 sacrifice acceptable, wellpleasing to G. G2316
19 But my G shall supply all your need G2316
20 Now unto G and our Father be glory for G2316
Col 1: 1 will of G, and Timotheus our brother, G2316
2 G our Father and the Lord Jesus Christ. G2316
3 We give thanks to G and the Father of G2316
6 of it, and knew the grace of G in truth: G2316
10 and increasing in the knowledge of G; G2316
15 Who is the image of the invisible G, the G2316
25 dispensation of G which is given to me G2316
25 to me for you, to fulfil the word of G; G2316
27 To whom G would make known what G2316
2: 2 of G, and of the Father, and of Christ; G2316
12 G, who hath raised him from the dead. G2316
19 increaseth with the increase of G. G2316
3: 1 Christ sitteth on the right hand of G. G2316
3 and your life is hid with Christ in G. G2316
6 For which things' sake the wrath of G G2316
12 Put on therefore, as the elect of G, holy G2316
15 And let the peace of G rule in your G2316
17 thanks to G and the Father by him. G2316
22 but in singleness of heart, fearing G: G2316
4: 3 Withal praying also for us, that G G2316
11 G, which have been a comfort unto me. G2316
12 perfect and complete in all the will of G. G2316
1Th 1: 1 which is in G the Father and in the G2316
1 and peace, from G our Father, and the G2316
2 We give thanks to G always for you all, G2316
3 Christ, in the sight of G and our Father; G2316
4 brethren beloved, your election of G. G2316
9 how ye turned to G from idols to serve G2316
9 idols to serve the living and true G; G2316
2: 2 were bold in our G to speak unto you G2316
2 the gospel of G with much contention. G2316
4 But as we were allowed of G to be put G2316
4 men, but G, which trieth our hearts. G2316
5 a cloak of covetousness; G is witness: G2316
8 not the gospel of G only, but also our G2316
9 we preached unto you the gospel of G. G2316
10 Ye are witnesses, and G also, how G2316
12 That ye would walk worthy of G, who G2316
13 For this cause also thank we G without G2316
13 the word of G which ye heard of us, G2316
13 truth, the word of G, which effectually G2316
14 of the churches of G which in Judaea G2316
15 not G, and are contrary to all men: G2316
3: 2 brother, and minister of G, and our G2316
9 For what thanks can we render to G G2316
9 we joy for your sakes before our G; G2316
11 Now G himself and our Father, and our G2316
13 in holiness before G, even our Father, at G2316
4: 1 G, so ye would abound more and more. G2316
3 For this is the will of G, even your G2316
5 even as the Gentiles which know not G: G2316
7 For G hath not called us unto G2316
8 not man, but G, who hath also given G2316
9 are taught of G to love one another. G2312
14 sleep in Jesus will G bring with him. G2316
16 G: and the dead in Christ shall rise first: G2316
5: 9 For G hath not appointed us to wrath, G2316
18 of G in Christ Jesus concerning you. G2316
23 And the very G of peace sanctify you G2316
23 wholly; and I pray G your whole spirit
2Th 1: 1 G our Father and the Lord Jesus Christ: G2316
2 Grace unto you, and peace, from G our G2316
3 We are bound to thank G always for G2316
4 in the churches of G for your patience G2316

2Th 1: 5 judgment of G, that ye may be counted G2316
5 kingdom of G, for which ye also suffer: G2316
6 Seeing it is a righteous thing with G to G2316
8 that know not G, and that obey not the G2316
11 for you, that our G would count you G2316
12 of our G and the Lord Jesus Christ. G2316
2: 4 above all that is called G, or that is G2316
4 so that he as G sitteth in the temple G2316
4 of G, shewing himself that he is God. G2316
4 of God, shewing himself that he is G. G2316
11 And for this cause G shall send them G2316
13 thanks alway to G for you, brethren G2316
13 of the Lord, because G hath from the G2316
16 himself, and G, even our Father, which G2316
3: 5 into the love of G, and into the patient G2316
1Ti 1: 1 commandment of G our Saviour, and G2316
2 and peace, from G our Father and G2316
11 G, which was committed to my trust. G2316
17 the only wise G, be honour and glory G2316
2: 3 in the sight of G our Saviour; G2316
5 For there is one G, and one mediator G2316
5 G and men, the man Christ Jesus; G2316
3: 5 shall he take care of the church of G?) G2316
15 in the house of G, which is the church G2316
15 G, the pillar and ground of the truth. G2316
16 of godliness: G was manifest in the G2316
4: 3 from meats, which G hath created to be G2316
4 For every creature of G is good, and G2316
5 For it is sanctified by the word of G and G2316
10 trust in the living G, who is the Saviour G2316
5: 4 that is good and acceptable before G. G2316
5 trusteth in G, and continueth in G2316
21 I charge thee before G, and the Lord G2316
6: 1 G and his doctrine be not blasphemed. G2316
11 But thou, O man of G, flee these things; G2316
13 I give thee charge in the sight of G, who G2316
17 but in the living G, who giveth us richly G2316
2Ti 1: 1 Christ by the will of G, according to the G2316
2 G the Father and Christ Jesus our Lord. G2316
3 I thank G, whom I serve from my G2316
6 stir up the gift of G, which is in thee by G2316
7 For G hath not given us the spirit of G2316
8 the gospel according to the power of G; G2316
2: 9 bonds; but the word of G is not bound. G2316
15 Study to shew thyself approved unto G, G2316
19 Nevertheless the foundation of G G2316
25 themselves; if G peradventure will give G2316
3: 4 of pleasures more than lovers of G; G5377
16 by inspiration of G, and is profitable for G2315
17 That the man of G may be perfect, G2316
4: 1 I charge thee therefore before G, and G2316
16 G that it may not be laid to their charge.
Tit 1: 1 Paul, a servant of G, and an apostle of G2316
2 In hope of eternal life, which G, that G2316
3 to the commandment of G our Saviour; G2316
4 and peace, from G the Father and the G2316
7 as the steward of G; not selfwilled, not G2316
16 They profess that they know G; but in G2316
2: 5 that the word of G be not blasphemed. G2316
10 doctrine of G our Saviour in all things. G2316
11 For the grace of G that bringeth G2316
13 great G and our Saviour Jesus Christ; G2316
3: 4 G our Saviour toward man appeared, G2316
8 have believed in G might be careful to G2316
Phlm 3 Grace to you, and peace, from G our G2316
4 I thank my G, making mention of thee G2316
Heb 1: 1 G, who at sundry times and in divers G2316
6 And let all the angels of G worship him. G2316
8 Thy throne, O G, is for ever and ever: G2316
9 iniquity; therefore G, even thy God, G2316
9 God, even thy G, hath anointed thee G2316
2: 4 G also bearing them witness, both with G2316
9 of G should taste death for every man. G2316
13 the children which G hath given me. G2316
17 pertaining to G, to make reconciliation G2316
3: 4 man; but he that built all things is G. G2316
12 unbelief, in departing from the living G. G2316
4: 4 on this wise, And G did rest the seventh G2316
9 therefore a rest to the people of G. G2316
10 from his own works, as G did from his. G2316
12 For the word of G is quick, and G2316
14 Son of G, let us hold fast our profession. G2316
5: 1 pertaining to G, that he may offer both G2316
4 but he that is called of G, as was Aaron. G2316
10 Called of G an high priest after the G2316
12 of the oracles of G; and are become G2316
6: 1 dead works, and of faith toward G, G2316
3 And this will we do, if G permit. G2316
5 And have tasted the good word of G, G2316

Heb 6: 6 the Son of G afresh, and put *him* *G2316*
7 it is dressed, receiveth blessing from G: *G2316*
10 For G *is* not unrighteous to forget your *G2316*
13 For when G made promise to *G2316*
17 Wherein G, willing more abundantly to *G2316*
18 impossible for G to lie, we might have *G2316*
7: 1 of the most high G, who met Abraham *G2316*
3 Son of G; abideth a priest continually. *G2316*
19 *did*; by the which we draw nigh unto G. *G2316*
25 that come unto G by him, seeing he *G2316*
8: 5 admonished of G when he was about *G5537*
10 a G, and they shall be to me a people: *G2316*
9: 6 accomplishing the service *of* G.
14 himself without spot to G, purge your *G2316*
14 from dead works to serve the living G? *G2316*
20 which G hath enjoined unto you. *G2316*
24 to appear in the presence of G for us: *G2316*
10: 7 it is written of me,) to do thy will, O G. *G2316*
9 to do thy will, O G. He taketh away the *G2316*
12 ever, sat down on the right hand of G; *G2316*
21 an high priest over the house of G; *G2316*
29 foot the Son of G, and hath counted the *G2316*
31 to fall into the hands of the living G. *G2316*
36 will of G, ye might receive the promise. *G2316*
11: 3 by the word of G, so that things which *G2316*
4 By faith Abel offered unto G a more *G2316*
4 he was righteous, G testifying of his *G2316*
5 found, because G had translated him: *G2316*
5 had this testimony, that he pleased G. *G2316*
6 he that cometh to G must believe that *G2316*
7 By faith Noah, being warned of G of *G5537*
10 whose builder and maker *is* G. *G2316*
16 wherefore G is not ashamed to be *G2316*
16 G: for he hath prepared for them a city. *G2316*
19 Accounting that G *was* able to raise *G2316*
25 with the people of G, than to enjoy the *G2316*
40 G having provided some better thing *G2316*
12: 2 at the right hand of the throne of G. *G2316*
7 If ye endure chastening, G dealeth with *G2316*
15 fail of the grace of G; lest any root of *G2316*
22 the city of the living G, the heavenly *G2316*
23 in heaven, and to G the Judge of all, *G2316*
28 we may serve G acceptably with *G2316*
29 For our G *is* a consuming fire. *G2316*
13: 4 and adulterers G will judge. *G2316*
7 you the word of G: whose faith follow, *G2316*
15 of praise to G continually, that is, *G2316*
16 with such sacrifices G is well pleased. *G2316*
20 Now the G of peace, that brought again *G2316*
Jas 1: 1 James, a servant of G and of the Lord *G2316*
5 let him ask of G, that giveth to all *men* *G2316*
13 I am tempted of G: for God cannot be *G2316*
13 of God: for G cannot be tempted *G2316*
20 worketh not the righteousness of G. *G2316*
27 Pure religion and undefiled before G *G2316*
2: 5 Hath not G chosen the poor of *G2316*
19 Thou believest that there is one G; thou *G2316*
23 believed G, and it was imputed *G2316*
23 and he was called the Friend of G. *G2316*
3: 9 Therewith bless we G, even the Father; *G2316*
9 are made after the similitude of G. *G2316*
4: 4 is enmity with G? whosoever therefore *G2316*
4 a friend of the world is the enemy of G. *G2316*
6 he saith, G resisteth the proud, *G2316*
7 Submit yourselves therefore to G. Resist *G2316*
8 Draw nigh to G, and he will draw nigh *G2316*
1Pt 1: 2 foreknowledge of G the Father, through *G2316*
3 Blessed *be* the G and Father of our *G2316*
5 Who are kept by the power of G *G2316*
21 Who by him do believe in G, that raised *G2316*
21 that your faith and hope might be in G. *G2316*
23 of G, which liveth and abideth for ever. *G2316*
2: 4 of men, but chosen of G, *and* precious, *G2316*
5 acceptable to G by Jesus Christ. *G2316*
10 *are* now the people of G: which had not *G2316*
12 glorify G in the day of visitation. *G2316*
15 For so is the will of G, that with well *G2316*
16 maliciousness, but as the servants of G. *G2316*
17 brotherhood. Fear G. Honour the king. *G2316*
19 G endure grief, suffering wrongfully. *G2316*
20 it patiently, this *is* acceptable with G. *G2316*
3: 4 which is in the sight of G of great price. *G2316*
5 who trusted in G, adorned themselves, *G2316*
15 But sanctify the Lord G in your hearts: *G2316*
17 For *it is* better, if the will of G be so, *G2316*
18 might bring us to G, being put to death *G2316*
20 longsuffering of G waited in the days of *G2316*
21 G,) by the resurrection of Jesus Christ: *G2316*
22 on the right hand of G; angels and *G2316*

1Pt 4: 2 to the lusts of men, but to the will of G. *G2316*
6 but live according to G in the spirit. *G2316*
10 stewards of the manifold grace of G. *G2316*
11 as the oracles of G; if any man minister, *G2316*
11 the ability which G giveth: that God in *G2316*
11 God giveth: that G in all things may be *G2316*
14 of glory and of G resteth upon you: on *G2316*
16 but let him glorify G on this behalf. *G2316*
17 at the house of G: and if *it* first *begin* *G2316*
17 of them that obey not the gospel of G? *G2316*
19 to the will of G commit the keeping *G2316*
5: 2 Feed the flock of G which is among *G2316*
5 with humility: for G resisteth the *G2316*
6 of G, that he may exalt you in due time: *G2316*
10 But the G of all grace, who hath called *G2316*
12 is the true grace of G wherein ye stand. *G2316*
2Pt 1: 1 of G and our Saviour Jesus Christ: *G2316*
2 knowledge of G, and of Jesus our Lord, *G2316*
17 For he received from G the Father *G2316*
21 but holy men of G spake *as they were* *G2316*
2: 4 For if G spared not the angels that *G2316*
3: 5 by the word of G the heavens were of *G2316*
12 of the day of G, wherein the heavens *G2316*
1Jn 1: 5 unto you, that G is light, and in him *G2316*
2: 5 is the love of G perfected: hereby know *G2316*
14 and the word of G abideth in you, and *G2316*
17 doeth the will of G abideth for ever. *G2316*
3: 1 called the sons of G: therefore the world *G2316*
2 Beloved, now are we the sons of G, and *G2316*
8 the Son of G was manifested, that *G2316*
9 Whosoever is born of G doth not *G2316*
9 he cannot sin, because he is born of G. *G2316*
10 In this the children of G are manifest, *G2316*
10 is not of G, neither he that loveth *G2316*
16 Hereby perceive we the love *of* G, because
17 him, how dwelleth the love of G in him? *G2316*
20 For if our heart condemn us, G is *G2316*
21 not, *then* have we confidence toward G. *G2316*
4: 1 they are of G: because many false *G2316*
2 Hereby know ye the Spirit of G: Every *G2316*
2 Jesus Christ is come in the flesh is of G: *G2316*
3 in the flesh is not of G: and this is that *G2316*
4 Ye are of G, little children, and have *G2316*
6 We are of G: he that knoweth God *G2316*
6 We are of God: he that knoweth G *G2316*
6 us; he that is not of G heareth not us. *G2316*
7 for love is of G; and every one that *G2316*
7 loveth is born of G, and knoweth God. *G2316*
7 loveth is born of God, and knoweth G. *G2316*
8 He that loveth not knoweth not G; for *G2316*
8 not knoweth not God; for G is love. *G2316*
9 In this was manifested the love of G *G2316*
9 toward us, because that G sent his only *G2316*
10 Herein is love, not that we loved G, but *G2316*
11 Beloved, if G so loved us, we ought also *G2316*
12 No man hath seen G at any time. If we *G2316*
12 love one another, G dwelleth in us, and *G2316*
15 G, God dwelleth in him, and he in God. *G2316*
15 God, G dwelleth in him, and he in God. *G2316*
15 God, God dwelleth in him, and he in G. *G2316*
16 the love that G hath to us. God is love; *G2316*
16 God hath to us. G is love; and he that *G2316*
16 in love dwelleth in G, and God in him. *G2316*
16 in love dwelleth in God, and G in him. *G2316*
20 If a man say, I love G, and hateth his *G2316*
20 can he love G whom he hath not seen? *G2316*
21 he who loveth G love his brother also. *G2316*
5: 1 Christ is born of G: and every one that *G2316*
2 the children of G, when we love God, *G2316*
2 love G, and keep his commandments. *G2316*
3 For this is the love of G, that we keep his *G2316*
4 For whatsoever is born of G *G2316*
5 that believeth that Jesus is the Son of G? *G2316*
9 the witness of G is greater: for this is *G2316*
9 of G which he hath testified of his Son. *G2316*
10 He that believeth on the Son of G hath *G2316*
10 that believeth not G hath made him a *G2316*
10 not the record that G gave of his Son. *G2316*
11 And this is the record, that G hath *G2316*
12 that hath not the Son of G hath not life. *G2316*
13 of the Son of G; that ye may know that *G2316*
13 believe on the name of the Son of G. *G2316*
18 We know that whosoever is born of G *G2316*
18 that is begotten of G keepeth himself, *G2316*
19 *And* we know that we are of G, and the *G2316*
20 And we know that the Son of G is *G2316*
20 This is the true G, and eternal life. *G2316*
2Jn 3 *and* peace, from G the Father, and *G2316*
9 of Christ, hath not G. He that abideth in *G2316*

2Jn 10 *your* house, neither bid him G speed:
11 For he that biddeth him G speed is
3Jn 11 doeth good is of G: but he that doeth *G2316*
11 but he that doeth evil hath not seen G. *G2316*
Jude 1 that are sanctified by G the Father, and *G2316*
4 the grace of our G into lasciviousness, *G2316*
4 only Lord G, and our Lord Jesus Christ. *G2316*
21 Keep yourselves in the love of G, *G2316*
25 To the only wise G our Saviour, *be* *G2316*
Rev 1: 1 The Revelation of Jesus Christ, which G *G2316*
2 Who bare record of the word of G, and *G2316*
6 and priests unto G and his Father; to *G2316*
9 G, and for the testimony of Jesus Christ. *G2316*
2: 7 is in the midst of the paradise of G. *G2316*
18 saith the Son of G, who hath his eyes *G2316*
3: 1 seven Spirits of G, and the seven stars; *G2316*
2 not found thy works perfect before G. *G2316*
12 the temple of my G, and he shall go no *G2316*
12 the name of my G, and the name of the *G2316*
12 name of the city of my G, *which is* new *G2316*
12 of heaven from my G: and *I will write* *G2316*
14 the beginning of the creation of G; *G2316*
4: 5 throne, which are the seven Spirits of G. *G2316*
8 holy, holy, Lord G Almighty, which *G2316*
5: 6 Spirits of G sent forth into all the earth. *G2316*
9 redeemed us to G by thy blood out of *G2316*
10 And hast made us unto our G kings *G2316*
6: 9 for the word of G, and for the testimony *G2316*
7: 2 seal of the living G: and he cried with a *G2316*
3 servants of our G in their foreheads. *G2316*
10 Salvation to our G which sitteth upon *G2316*
11 on their faces, and worshipped G, *G2316*
12 *be* unto our G for ever and ever. Amen. *G2316*
15 the throne of G, and serve him day *G2316*
17 of waters: and G shall wipe away all *G2316*
8: 2 stood before G; and to them were given *G2316*
4 up before G out of the angel's hand. *G2316*
9: 4 not the seal of G in their foreheads. *G2316*
13 of the golden altar which is before G, *G2316*
10: 7 the mystery of G should be finished, *G2316*
11: 1 the temple of G, and the altar, and them *G2316*
4 standing before the G of the earth. *G2316*
11 Spirit of life from G entered into them, *G2316*
13 and gave glory to the G of heaven. *G2316*
16 which sat before G on their seats, fell *G2316*
16 fell upon their faces, and worshipped G, *G2316*
17 Saying, We give thee thanks, O Lord G *G2316*
19 And the temple of G was opened in *G2316*
12: 5 caught up unto G, and *to* his throne. *G2316*
6 a place prepared of G, that they should *G2316*
10 kingdom of our G, and the power of his *G2316*
10 them before our G day and night. *G2316*
17 of G, and have the testimony *G2316*
13: 6 against G, to blaspheme his name, *G2316*
14: 4 the firstfruits unto G and to the Lamb. *G2316*
5 are without fault before the throne of G. *G2316*
7 Saying with a loud voice, Fear G, and *G2316*
10 of the wrath of G, which is poured out *G2316*
12 of G, and the faith of Jesus. *G2316*
19 the great winepress of the wrath of G. *G2316*
15: 1 for in them is filled up the wrath of G. *G2316*
2 the sea of glass, having the harps of G. *G2316*
3 the servant of G, and the song of the *G2316*
3 thy works, Lord G Almighty; just and *G2316*
7 wrath of G, who liveth for ever and ever. *G2316*
8 smoke from the glory of G, and from his *G2316*
16: 1 vials of the wrath of G upon the earth. *G2316*
7 say, Even so, Lord G Almighty, true *G2316*
9 the name of G, which hath power over *G2316*
11 And blasphemed the G of heaven *G2316*
14 battle of that great day of G Almighty. *G2316*
19 before G, to give unto her the *G2316*
21 and men blasphemed G because of the *G2316*
17:17 For G hath put in their hearts to fulfil *G2316*
17 until the words of G shall be fulfilled. *G2316*
18: 5 and G hath remembered her iniquities. *G2316*
8 strong *is* the Lord G who judgeth her. *G2316*
20 for G hath avenged you on her. *G2316*
19: 1 and power, unto the Lord our G: *G2316*
4 down and worshipped G that sat on the *G2316*
5 saying, Praise our G, all ye his servants, *G2316*
6 for the Lord G omnipotent reigneth. *G2316*
9 me, These are the true sayings of G. *G2316*
10 of Jesus: worship G: for the testimony of *G2316*
13 and his name is called The Word of G. *G2316*
15 the fierceness and wrath of Almighty G. *G2316*
17 together unto the supper of the great G; *G2316*
20: 4 for the word of G, and which had not *G2316*
6 shall be priests of G and of Christ, and *G2316*

Rev 20: 9 G out of heaven, and devoured them. G2316
12 stand before G; and the books were G2316
21: 2 down from G out of heaven, prepared G2316
3 the tabernacle of G is with men, and he G2316
3 be his people, and G himself shall be G2316
3 shall be with them, and be their G. G2316
4 And G shall wipe away all tears from G2316
7 I will be his G, and he shall be my son. G2316
10 descending out of heaven from G, G2316
11 Having the glory of G: and her light was G2316
22 for the Lord G Almighty and the Lamb G2316
23 it: for the glory of G did lighten it, and G2316
22: 1 out of the throne of G and of the Lamb. G2316
3 but the throne of G and of the Lamb G2316
5 sun; for the Lord G giveth them light: G2316
6 and true: and the Lord G of the holy G2316
9 the sayings of this book: worship G. G2316
18 unto these things, G shall add unto him G2316
19 of this prophecy, G shall take away his G2316

GODDESS

1Ki 11: 5 For Solomon went after Ashtoreth the g H430
33 Ashtoreth the g of the Zidonians, H430
Act 19:27 temple of the great g Diana should be G2299
35 of the great g Diana, and of the image G2299
37 nor yet blasphemers of your g. G2299

GODHEAD

Act 17:29 to think that the G is like unto gold, or G2304
Ro 1:20 and G; so that they are without excuse: G2305
Col 2: 9 dwelleth all the fulness of the G bodily. G2320

GODLINESS

1Ti 2: 2 and peaceable life in all g and honesty. G2150
10 women professing g) with good works. G2317
3:16 is the mystery of g: God was manifest in G2150
4: 7 and exercise thyself rather unto g. G2150
8 For bodily exercise profiteth little: but g G2150
6: 3 to the doctrine which is according to g; G2150
5 gain is g: from such withdraw thyself. G2150
6 But g with contentment is great gain. G2150
11 g, faith, love, patience, meekness. G2150
2Ti 3: 5 Having a form of g, but denying the G2150
Tit 1: 1 of the truth which is after g; G2150
2Pt 1: 3 unto life and g, through the knowledge G2150
6 temperance patience; and to patience g; G2150
7 And to g brotherly kindness; and to G2150
3:11 ye to be in all holy conversation and g, G2150

GODLY

Ps 4: 3 set apart him that is g for himself: the H2623
12: 1 Help, LORD; for the g man ceaseth; for H2623
32: 6 For this shall every one that is g pray H2623
Mal 2:15 he might seek a g seed. Therefore take H430
2Co 1:12 in simplicity and g sincerity, not with G2316
7: 9 sorry after a g manner, that ye G2596+G2316
10 For g sorrow worketh G2596+G2316
11 after a g sort, what carefulness G2596+G2316
11: 2 For I am jealous over you with g G2316
1Ti 1: 4 than g edifying which is in faith: so do. G2316
2Ti 3:12 Yea, and all that will live g in Christ G2153
Tit 2:12 and g, in this present world; G2153
Heb 12:28 acceptably with reverence and g fear:
2Pt 2: 9 The Lord knoweth how to deliver the g G2152
3Jn 6 after a g sort, thou shalt do well: G2316

GODS

Gen 3: 5 ye shall be as g, knowing good and evil. H430
31:30 yet wherefore hast thou stolen my g? H430
32 With whomsoever thou findest thy g, let H430
35: 2 away the strange g that are among you, H430
4 all the strange g which were in their H430
Ex 12:12 and against all the g of Egypt I will H430
15:11 O LORD, among the g? who is like thee, H410
18:11 is greater than all g: for in the thing H430
20: 3 Thou shalt have no other g before me. H430
23 Ye shall not make with me g of silver, H430
23 neither shall ye make unto you g of gold. H430
22:28 Thou shalt not revile the g, nor curse the H430
23:13 of the name of other g, neither let it be H430
24 Thou shalt not bow down to their g, nor H430
32 no covenant with them, nor with their g. H430
33 their g, it will surely be a snare unto thee. H430
32: 1 unto him, Up, make us g, which shall go H430
4 they said, These be thy g, O Israel, which H430
8 said, These be thy g, O Israel, which have H430
23 For they said unto me, Make us g, which H430
31 great sin, and have made them g of gold. H430
34:15 a whoring after their g, and do sacrifice H430
Ex 34:15 sacrifice unto their g, and one call thee, H430
16 whoring after their g, and make thy sons H430
16 make thy sons go a whoring after their g. H430
17 Thou shalt make thee no molten g. H430
Lev 19: 4 molten g: I am the LORD your God. H430
Nu 25: 2 sacrifices of their g: and the people did H430
2 did eat, and bowed down to their g. H430
33: 4 g also the LORD executed judgments. H430
Dt 4:28 And there ye shall serve g, the work of H430
5: 7 Thou shalt have none other g before me. H430
6:14 Ye shall not go after other g, of the gods H430
14 Ye shall not go after other gods, of the g H430
7: 4 may serve other g: so will the anger of the H430
16 their g; for that will be a snare unto thee. H430
25 The graven images of their g shall ye H430
8:19 walk after other g, and serve them, and H430
10:17 For the LORD your God is God of g, and H430
11:16 and serve other g, and worship them; H430
28 after other g, which ye have not known. H430
12: 2 served their g, upon the high mountains, H430
3 images of their g, and destroy the names H430
30 not after their g, saying, How did these H430
30 serve their g? even so will I do likewise. H430
31 done unto their g; for even their sons and H430
31 they have burnt in the fire to their g. H430
13: 2 us go after other g, which thou hast not H430
6 go and serve other g, which thou hast not H430
7 Namely, of the g of the people which are H430
13 serve other g, which ye have not known; H430
17: 3 And hath gone and served other g, and H430
18:20 of other g, even that prophet shall die. H430
20:18 have done unto their g; so should ye sin H430
28:14 the left, to go after other g to serve them. H430
36 shalt thou serve other g, wood and stone. H430
64 shalt serve other g, which neither thou H430
29:18 to go and serve the g of these nations; H430
26 For they went and served other g, and H430
26 worshipped them, g whom they knew H430
30:17 and worship other g, and serve them; H430
31:16 a whoring after the g of the strangers of H430
18 in that they are turned unto other g. H430
20 turn unto other g, and serve them, and H430
32:16 with strange g, with abominations
17 not to God; to g whom they knew not, H430
17 knew not, to new g that came newly up,
37 And he shall say, Where are their g, their H430
Jos 22:22 The LORD God of g, the LORD God of H430
22 the LORD God of g, he knoweth, and H430
23: 7 of the name of their g, nor cause to swear H430
16 gone and served other g, and bowed H430
24: 2 of Nachor: and they served other g. H430
14 and put away the g which your fathers H430
15 serve; whether the g which your fathers H430
15 of the flood, or the g of the Amorites, in H430
16 forsake the LORD, to serve other g; H430
20 and serve strange g, then he will turn and H430
23 he, the strange g which are among you, H430
Jdg 2: 3 and their g shall be a snare unto you. H430
12 and followed other g, of the gods of the H430
12 other gods, of the g of the people that H430
17 after other g, and bowed themselves H430
19 in following other g to serve them, and H430
3: 6 to their sons, and served their g. H430
5: 8 They chose new g; then was war in the H430
6:10 God; fear not the g of the Amorites, in H430
10: 6 Ashtaroth, and the g of Syria, and the H430
6 of Syria, and the g of Zidon, and the H430
6 of Zidon, and the g of Moab, and the H430
6 of Moab, and the g of the children of H430
6 of Ammon, and the g of the Philistines, H430
13 g: wherefore I will deliver you no more. H430
14 Go and cry unto the g which ye have H430
16 And they put away the strange g from H430
17: 5 And the man Micah had an house of g, H430
18:24 And he said, Ye have taken away my g H430
Ru 1:15 her g: return thou after thy sister in law. H430
1Sa 4: 8 of these mighty G? these are the Gods that H430
8 these are the G that smote the Egyptians H430
6: 5 from off your g, and from off your land. H430
7: 3 away the strange g and Ashtaroth from H430
8: 8 served other g, so do they also unto thee. H430
17:43 And the Philistine cursed David by his g. H430
26:19 of the LORD, saying, Go, serve other g. H430
28:13 Saul, I saw g ascending out of the earth. H430
2Sa 7:23 from Egypt, from the nations and their g? H430
1Ki 9: 6 go and serve other g, and worship them: H430
9 hold upon other g, and have worshipped H430
11: 2 their g: Solomon clave unto these in love. H430
4 heart after other g: and his heart was not H430
1Ki 11: 8 burnt incense and sacrificed unto their g. H430
10 not go after other g: but he kept not that H430
12:28 behold thy g, O Israel, which brought H430
14: 9 made thee other g, and molten images, H430
18:24 And call ye on the name of your g, and I H430
25 the name of your g, but put no fire under. H430
19: 2 saying, So let the g do to me, and more H430
20:10 him, and said, The g do so unto me, and H430
23 unto him, Their g are gods of the hills; H430
23 Their gods are g of the hills; therefore H430
2Ki 5:17 unto other g, but unto the LORD. H430
17: 7 king of Egypt, and had feared other g, H430
29 Howbeit every nation made g of their H430
31 and Anammelech, the g of Sepharvaim. H430
33 served their own g, after the manner of H430
35 shall not fear other g, nor bow yourselves H430
37 evermore; and ye shall not fear other g. H430
38 not forget; neither shall ye fear other g. H430
18:33 Hath any of the g of the nations H430
34 Where are the g of Hamath, and of H430
34 where are the g of Sepharvaim, Hena, H430
35 Who are they among all the g of the H430
19:12 Have the g of the nations delivered them H430
18 And have cast their g into the fire: for H430
18 for they were no g, but the work of men's H430
22:17 incense unto other g, that they might H430
1Ch 5:25 a whoring after the g of the people of the H430
10:10 in the house of their g, and fastened his H430
14:12 And when they had left their g there, H430
16:25 he also is to be feared above all g. H430
26 For all the g of the people are idols: but H430
2Ch 2: 5 is great: for great is our God above all g. H430
7:19 go and serve other g, and worship them; H430
22 and laid hold on other g, and worshipped H430
13: 8 calves, which Jeroboam made you for g. H430
9 may be a priest of them that are no g. H430
14: 3 of the strange g, and the high places,
25:14 that he brought the g of the children of H430
14 set them up to be his g, and bowed down H430
15 sought after the g of the people, which H430
20 because they sought after the g of Edom. H430
28:23 For he sacrificed unto the g of H430
23 said, Because the g of the kings of Syria H430
25 incense unto other g, and provoked to H430
32:13 lands? were the g of the nations of those H430
14 Who was there among all the g of those H430
17 him, saying, As the g of the nations of H430
19 as against the g of the people of the H430
33:15 And he took away the strange g, and the H430
34:25 incense unto other g, that they might H430
Ezr 1: 7 and had put them in the house of his g; H430
Ps 82: 1 of the mighty; he judgeth among the g. H430
6 I have said, Ye are g; and all of you are H430
86: 8 Among the g there is none like unto thee, H430
95: 3 a great God, and a great King above all g. H430
96: 4 be praised: he is to be feared above all g. H430
5 For all the g of the nations are idols: but H430
97: 7 of idols: worship him, all ye g. H430
9 the earth: thou art exalted far above all g. H430
135: 5 is great, and that our Lord is above all g. H430
136: 2 O give thanks unto the God of g: for his H430
138: 1 before the g will I sing praise unto thee. H430
Isa 21: 9 of her g he hath broken unto the ground. H430
36:18 us. Hath any of the g of the nations H430
19 Where are the g of Hamath and Arphad? H430
19 where are the g of Sepharvaim? and H430
20 Who are they among all the g of these H430
37:12 Have the g of the nations delivered them H430
19 And have cast their g into the fire: for H430
19 for they were no g, but the work of men's H430
41:23 know that ye are g: yea, do good, or do H430
42:17 say to the molten images, Ye are our g. H430
Jer 1:16 incense unto other g, and worshipped the H430
2:11 Hath a nation changed their g, which are H430
11 which are yet no g? but my people have H430
28 But where are thy g that thou hast made H430
28 number of thy cities are thy g, O Judah. H430
5: 7 them that are no g: when I had fed them H430
19 and served strange g in your land, so H430
7: 6 neither walk after other g to your hurt: H430
9 walk after other g whom ye know not; H430
18 g, that they may provoke me to anger. H430
10:11 Thus shall ye say unto them, The g that H426
11:10 they went after other g to serve them: the H430
12 and cry unto the g unto whom they offer H430
13 of thy cities were thy g, O Judah; and H430
13:10 walk after other g, to serve them, and to H430
16:11 walked after other g, and have served H430
13 shall ye serve other g day and night; H430

Jer 16:20 Shall a man make **g** unto himself, and H430
20 gods unto himself, and they *are* no **g**? H430
19: 4 in it unto other **g**, whom neither they nor H430
13 poured out drink offerings unto other **g**. H430
22: 9 worshipped other **g**, and served them. H430
25: 6 And go not after other **g** to serve them, H430
32:29 unto other **g**, to provoke me to anger. H430
35:15 go not after other **g** to serve them, and ye H430
43:12 in the houses of the **g** of Egypt; and he H430
13 the houses of the **g** of the Egyptians shall H430
44: 3 *and* to serve other **g**, whom they knew H430
5 to burn no incense unto other **g**. H430
8 incense unto other **g** in the land of H430
15 incense unto other **g**, and all the women H430
46:25 Egypt, with their **g**, and their kings; even H430
48:35 and him that burneth incense to his **g**. H430
Dan 2:11 the **g**, whose dwelling is not with flesh. H426
47 God *is* a God of **g**, and a Lord of kings, H426
3:12 they serve not thy **g**, nor worship the H426
14 do not ye serve my **g**, nor worship the H426
18 we will not serve thy **g**, nor worship the H426
4: 8 spirit of the holy **g**: and before him I told H426
9 the spirit of the holy **g** *is* in thee, and no H426
18 able; for the spirit of the holy **g** *is* in thee. H426
5: 4 They drank wine, and praised the **g** of H426
11 spirit of the holy **g**; and in the days of thy H426
11 the wisdom of the **g**, was found in him; H426
14 that the spirit of the **g** *is* in thee, and *that* H426
23 hast praised the **g** of silver, and gold, of H426
11: 8 into Egypt their **g**, with their princes, *and* H430
36 against the God of **g**, and shall prosper H410
Hos 3: 1 look to other **g**, and love flagons of wine. H430
14: 3 our hands, *Ye are* our **g**: for in thee the H430
Nah 1:14 out of the house of thy **g** will I cut off the H430
Zep 2:11 he will famish all the **g** of the earth; and H430
Jn 10:34 not written in your law, I said, Ye are **g**? *G2316*
35 If he called them **g**, unto whom the *G2316*
Act 7:40 Saying unto Aaron, Make us **g** to go *G2316*
14:11 of Lycaonia, The **g** are come down to *G2316*
17:18 forth of strange **g**: because he preached *G1140*
19:26 be no **g**, which are made with hands: *G2316*
1Co 8: 5 For though there be that are called **g**, *G2316*
5 (as there be **g** many, and lords many,) *G2316*
Gal 4: 8 unto them which by nature are no **g**. *G2316*

GOD'S

Gen 28:22 a pillar, shall be **G** house: and of all that H430
30: 2 and he said, *Am* I in **G** stead, who hath H430
32: 2 he said, This *is* **G** host: and he called the H430
Nu 22:22 And **G** anger was kindled because he H430
Dt 1:17 for the judgment *is* **G**: and the cause that H430
2Ch 20:15 for the battle *is* not yours, but **G**. H430
Neh 10:29 an oath, to walk in **G** law, which was H430
Job 33: 6 Behold, I *am* according to thy wish in **G** H410
35: 2 saidst, My righteousness *is* more than **G**? H410
36: 2 thee that *I have* yet to speak on **G** behalf. H433
Mt 5:34 neither by heaven; for it is **G** throne: *G2316*
22:21 and unto God the things that are **G**. *G2316*
Mk 12:17 that are **G**. And they marvelled at him. *G2316*
Lk 18:29 or children, for the kingdom of **G** sake, *G2316*
20:25 and unto God the things which be **G**. *G2316*
Jn 8:47 He that is of God heareth **G** words: ye *G2316*
Act 23: 4 by said, Revilest thou **G** high priest? *G2316*
Ro 8:33 of **G** elect? *It is* God that justifieth. *G2316*
10: 3 For they being ignorant of **G** *G2316*
13: 6 tribute also: for they are **G** ministers, *G2316*
1Co 3: 9 **G** husbandry, *ye are* God's building. *G2316*
9 God's husbandry, *ye are* **G** building. *G2316*
23 And ye are Christ's; and Christ *is* **G**. *G2316*
6:20 body, and in your spirit, which are **G**. *G2316*
Tit 1: 1 to the faith of **G** elect, and the *G2316*
1Pt 5: 3 Neither as being lords over **G** heritage, *G2316*

GOD-WARD

Ex 18:19 for the people to **G**, that thou mayest H4136
2Co 3: 4 such trust have we through Christ to **G**: *G2316*
1Th 1: 8 place your faith to **G** is spread abroad; *G2316*

GOEST

Gen 10:19 unto Gaza; as thou **g**, unto Sodom, and H935
30 thou **g** unto Sephar a mount of the east. H935
25:18 Egypt, as thou **g** toward Assyria: *and* H935
28:15 whither thou **g**, and will bring thee H3212
32:17 thou? and whither **g** thou? and whose H3212
Ex 4:21 When thou **g** to return into Egypt, H3212
33:16 *it* not in that thou **g** with us? so shall we H3212
34:12 land whither thou **g**, lest it be for a snare H935
Nu 14:14 and *that* thou **g** before them, by day H1980
Dt 7: 1 land whither thou **g** to possess it, and H935
11:10 For the land, whither thou **g** in to H935
29 land whither thou **g** to possess it, that H935
12:29 thee, whither thou **g** to possess them, H935
20: 1 When thou **g** out to battle against thine H3318
21:10 When thou **g** forth to war against thine H3318
23:20 in the land whither thou **g** to possess it. H935
28: 6 blessed *shalt* thou *be* when thou **g** out. H3318
19 cursed *shalt* thou *be* when thou **g** out. H3318
21 off the land, whither thou **g** to possess it. H935
63 off the land whither thou **g** to possess it. H935
30:16 in the land whither thou **g** to possess it. H935
32:50 And die in the mount whither thou **g** H5927
Jos 1: 7 mayest prosper whithersoever thou **g**. H3212
9 God *is* with thee whithersoever thou **g**. H3212
Jdg 14: 3 people, that thou **g** to take a wife of the H1980
19:17 **g** thou? and whence comest thou? H3212
Ru 1:16 for whither thou **g**, I will go; and where H3212
1Sa 27: 8 **g** to Shur, even unto the land of Egypt. H935
28:22 have strength, when thou **g** on thy way. H3212
2Sa 15:19 Gittite, Wherefore **g** thou also with us? H3212
1Ki 2:37 For it shall be, *that* on the day thou **g** H3318
42 on the day thou **g** out, and walkest H3318
Ps 44: 9 and **g** not forth with our armies. H3318
Prv 4:12 When thou **g**, thy steps shall not be H3212
6:22 When thou **g**, it shall lead thee; when H1980
Ecc 5: 1 Keep thy foot when thou **g** to the house H3212
9:10 wisdom, in the grave, whither thou **g**. H1980
Jer 45: 5 for a prey in all places whither thou **g**. H3212
Zec 2: 2 Then said I, Whither **g** thou? And he H1980
Mt 8:19 I will follow thee whithersoever thou **g**. *G565*
Lk 9:57 I will follow thee whithersoever thou **g**. *G565*
12:58 When thou **g** with thine adversary to *G5217*
Jn 11: 8 to stone thee; and **g** thou thither again? *G5217*
13:36 Lord, whither **g** thou? Jesus answered *G5217*
14: 5 thou **g**; and how can we know the way? *G5217*
16: 5 of you asketh me, Whither **g** thou? *G5217*

GOETH

Gen 2:14 that *is* it which **g** toward the east of H1980
32:20 with the present that **g** before me, and H1980
33:14 as the cattle that **g** before me and the
38:13 law **g** up to Timnath to shear his sheep. H5927
Ex 7:15 morning; lo, he **g** out unto the water; H3318
22:26 it unto him by that the sun **g** down: H935
28:29 his heart, when he **g** in unto the holy H935
30 heart, when he **g** in before the LORD: H935
35 be heard when he **g** in unto the holy H935
Lev 11:21 thing that **g** upon *all* four, which H1980
27 And whatsoever **g** upon his paws, H1980
42 Whatsoever **g** upon the belly, and H1980
42 and whatsoever **g** upon *all* four, or H1980
14:46 Moreover he that **g** into the house all the H935
15:32 **g** from him, and is defiled therewith; H3318
16:17 when he **g** in to make an atonement H935
22: 3 your generations, that **g** unto the holy H7126
4 dead, or a man whose seed **g** from him; H3318
27:21 But the field, when it **g** out in the jubile, H3318
Nu 5:29 when a wife **g** aside *to another* instead H7847
21:15 And at the stream of the brooks that **g** H5186
Dt 1:30 The LORD your God which **g** before H1980
9: 3 God *is* he which **g** over before thee; *as* H5674
11:30 way where the sun **g** down, in the land H3996
19: 5 As when a man **g** into the wood with his H935
20: 4 For the LORD your God *is* he that **g** H1980
23: 9 When the host **g** forth against thine H3318
24:13 when the sun **g** down, that he may sleep H935
Jos 10:10 along the way that **g** up to Beth-horon, H4609
11:17 *Even* from the mount Halak, that **g** up H5927
12: 7 mount Halak, that **g** up to Seir; which H5927
16: 1 the wilderness that **g** up from Jericho H5927
2 And **g** out from Beth-el to Luz, and H3318
3 And **g** down westward to the coast of H3381
19:12 and then **g** out to Daberath, and H3318
12 out to Daberath, and **g** up to Japhia, H5927
13 and **g** out to Remmonmethoar to Neah; H3318
27 and **g** out to Cabul on the left hand, H3318
34 Aznothtabor, and **g** out from thence to H3318
Jdg 5:31 as the sun when he **g** forth in his might. H3318
20:31 of which one **g** up to the house of God, H5927
21:19 the highway that **g** up from Beth-el to H5927
1Sa 6: 9 And see, if it **g** up by the way of his own H5927
22:14 son in law, and **g** at thy bidding, and H5493
30:24 as his part *is* that **g** down to the battle, H3381
2Ki 5:18 *that* when my master **g** into the house of H935
11: 8 king as he **g** out and as he cometh in. H3318
12:20 house of Millo, which **g** down to Silla. H3381
2Ch 23: 7 when he cometh in, and when he **g** out. H3318
Ezr 5: 8 and this work **g** fast on, and prospereth H5648
Job 7: 9 away: so he that **g** down to the grave H3381
9:11 Lo, he **g** by me, and I see *him* not: he H5674
34: 8 Which **g** in company with the workers of H732
37: 2 and the sound *that* **g** out of his mouth. H3318
39:21 he **g** on to meet the armed men. H3318
41:20 Out of his nostrils **g** smoke, as *out* of a H3318
21 coals, and a flame **g** out of his mouth. H3318
Ps 17: 1 my prayer, *that* **g** not out of feigned lips.
41: 6 to itself; *when* he **g** abroad, he telleth *it*. H3318
68:21 an one as **g** on still in his trespasses. H1980
88:16 Thy fierce wrath **g** over me; thy terrors H5674
97: 3 A fire **g** before him, and burneth up his H3212
104:23 Man **g** forth unto his work and to his H3318
126: 6 He that **g** forth and weepeth, bearing H3212
146: 4 His breath **g** forth, he returneth to his H3318
Prv 6:29 So he that **g** in to his neighbour's wife; H935
7:22 He **g** after her straightway, as an ox H1980
22 as an ox **g** to the slaughter, or as H935
11:10 When it **g** well with the righteous, the
16:18 Pride **g** before destruction, and an
20:19 He that **g** about *as* a talebearer H1980
26: 9 *As* a thorn **g** up into the hand of a H5927
20 Where no wood is, *there* the fire **g** out: H3518
31:18 *is* good: her candle **g** not out by night. H3518
Ecc 1: 5 The sun also ariseth, and the sun **g** H935
6 The wind **g** toward the south, and H1980
3:21 Who knoweth the spirit of man that **g** H5927
21 beast that **g** downward to the earth? H3381
12: 5 fail: because man **g** to his long home, H1980
Song 7: 9 for my beloved, that **g** *down* sweetly, H1980
Isa 28:19 From the time that it **g** forth it shall H5674
30:29 as when one **g** with a pipe to come H1980
55:11 So shall my word be that **g** forth out of H3318
59: 8 **g** therein shall not know peace. H1869
63:14 As a beast **g** down into the valley, the H3318
Jer 5: 6 every one that **g** out thence shall be H3318
6: 4 us! for the day **g** away, for the shadows H6437
21: 9 but he that **g** out, and falleth to the H3318
22:10 sore for him that **g** away: for he shall H1980
30:23 Behold, the whirlwind of the LORD **g** H3318
38: 2 but he that **g** forth to the Chaldeans H3318
44:17 do whatsoever thing **g** forth out of our H3318
49:17 every one that **g** by it shall be H5674
50:13 every one that **g** by Babylon shall be H5674
Ezk 7:14 ready; but none **g** to the battle: for my H1980
33:31 their heart **g** after their covetousness. H1980
40:40 And at the side without, as one **g** up to H5927
42: 9 as one **g** into them from the utter court. H935
44:27 And in the day that he **g** into the H935
48: 1 way of Hethlon, as one **g** to Hamath, H935
Hos 6: 4 cloud, and as the early dew it **g** away. H1980
5 judgments *are as* the light *that* **g** forth. H3318
Zec 5: 3 *is* the curse that **g** forth over the face of H3318
5 eyes, and see what *is* this that **g** forth. H3318
6 This *is* an ephah that **g** forth. He said H3318
Mt 8: 9 this *man*, Go, and he **g**; and to another, *G4198*
12:45 Then **g** he, and taketh with himself *G4198*
13:44 and for joy thereof **g** and selleth all that *G5217*
15:11 Not that which **g** into the mouth *G1525*
17 in at the mouth **g** into the belly, and is *G5562*
17:21 Howbeit this kind **g** not out but by *G1607*
18:12 and nine, and **g** into the mountains, *G4198*
26:24 The Son of man **g** as it is written of *G5217*
28: 7 dead; and, behold, he **g** before you into *G4254*
Mk 3:13 And he **g** up into a mountain, and *G305*
7:19 but into the belly, and **g** out into the *G1607*
14:21 The Son of man indeed **g**, as it is *G5217*
45 And as soon as he was come, he **g** *G4334*
16: 7 and Peter that he **g** before you into *G4254*
Lk 7: 8 unto one, Go, and he **g**; and to another, *G4198*
11:26 Then **g** he, and taketh *to him* seven *G4198*
22:22 And truly the Son of man **g**, as it was *G4198*
Jn 3: 8 and whither it **g**: so is every one that *G5217*
7:20 hast a devil: who **g** about to kill thee? *G2212*
10: 4 his own sheep, he **g** before them, and *G4198*
11:31 She **g** unto the grave to weep there. *G5217*
12:35 in darkness knoweth not whither he **g**. *G5217*
Act 8:26 south unto the way that **g** down from *G2597*
1Co 6: 6 But brother **g** to law with brother, and
9: 7 Who **g** a warfare any time at his own
Jas 1:24 For he beholdeth himself, and **g** his way, *G565*
1Jn 2:11 not whither he **g**, because that darkness *G5217*
Rev 14: 4 Lamb whithersoever he **g**. These were *G5217*
17:11 is of the seven, and **g** into perdition. *G5217*
19:15 And out of his mouth **g** a sharp sword, *G1607*

GOG

1Ch 5: 4 The sons of Joel; Shemaiah his son, **G** H1463
Ezk 38: 2 Son of man, set thy face against **G**, the H1463
3 *am* against thee, O **G**, the chief prince of H1463

Ezk 38:14 and say unto **G**, Thus saith the Lord H1463
16 in thee, O **G**, before their eyes. H1463
18 same time when **G** shall come against H1463
39: 1 prophesy against **G**, and say, Thus saith H1463
1 *am* against thee, O **G**, the chief prince of H1463
11 *that* I will give unto **G** a place there of H1463
11 shall they bury **G** and all his multitude: H1463
Rev 20: 8 of the earth, **G** and Magog, to gather G1136

GOING
Gen 12: 9 And Abram journeyed, **g** on still H1980
15:12 And when the sun was **g** down, a deep H935
37:25 and myrrh, **g** to carry *it* down to Egypt. H1980
Ex 17:12 were steady until the **g** down of the sun. H935
23: 4 ox or his ass **g** astray, thou shalt surely H8582
37:18 And six branches **g** out of the sides H3318
19 six branches **g** out of the candlestick. H3318
21 to the six branches **g** out of it. H3318
Lev 11:20 All fowls that creep, **g** upon *all* four, H1980
Nu 32: 7 of Israel from **g** over into the land H5674
34: 4 on to Zin: and the **g** forth thereof shall H8444
Dt 16: 6 at even, at the **g** down of the sun, at the H935
33:18 in thy **g** out; and, Issachar, in thy tents. H3318
Jos 1: 4 **g** down of the sun, shall be your coast. H3996
6: 9 **g** on, and blowing with the trumpets. H1980
11 the city, **g** about *it* once: and they H5362
13 **g** on, and blowing with the trumpets. H1980
7: 5 smote them in the **g** down: wherefore H4174
10:11 *and* were in the **g** down to Beth-horon, H4174
27 And it came to pass at the time of the **g** H935
15: 7 that *is* before the **g** up to Adummim, H4608
18:17 *is* over against the **g** up of Adummim, H4608
23:14 And, behold, this day I *am* **g** the way of H1980
Jdg 1:36 *was* from the **g** up to Akrabbim, from H4608
19:18 but I *am now* **g** to the house of the H1980
28 Up, and let us be **g**. But none answered. H3212
1Sa 9:11 young maidens **g** out to draw water, H3318
27 *And* as they were **g** down to the end of H3381
10: 3 thee three men **g** up to God to Beth-el, H5927
17:20 as the host was **g** forth to the fight, and H3318
29: 6 upright, and thy **g** out and thy coming H3318
2Sa 2:19 Abner; and in **g** he turned not to the H3212
3:25 and to know thy **g** out and thy coming H4161
5:24 the sound of a **g** in the tops of the H6807
1Ki 17:11 And as she was **g** to fetch *it*, he called H3212
22:36 the host about the **g** down of the sun, H935
2Ki 2:23 and as he was **g** up by the way, there H5927
9:27 *they did so* at the **g** up to Gur, which *is* H4608
19:27 But I know thy abode, and thy **g** out, H3318
1Ch 14:15 hear a sound of **g** in the tops of the H6807
26:16 of the **g** up, ward against ward. H5927
2Ch 11: 4 and returned from **g** against Jeroboam. H3212
18:34 the time of the sun **g** down he died. H935
Neh 3:19 over against the **g** up to the armoury at H5927
31 Miphkad, and to the **g** up of the corner. H5944
32 And between the **g** up of the corner H5944
12:37 of David, at the **g** up of the wall, above H4608
Job 1: 7 and said, From **g** to and fro in the H7751
2: 2 and said, From **g** to and fro in the H7751
33:24 Deliver him from **g** down to the pit: I H3381
28 He will deliver his soul from **g** into the H5674
Ps 19: 6 His **g** forth *is* from the end of the H4161
50: 1 of the sun unto the **g** down thereof. H3996
104:19 seasons: the sun knoweth his **g** down. H3996
113: 3 From the rising of the sun unto the **g** H3996
121: 8 The LORD shall preserve thy **g** out and H3318
144:14 breaking in, nor **g** out; that *there be* no H3318
Prv 7:27 Her house *is* the way to hell, **g** down to H3381
14:15 the prudent *man* looketh well to his **g**. H838
30:29 which go well, yea, four are comely in **g**: H3212
Isa 13:10 be darkened in his **g** forth, and the H3318
37:28 But I know thy abode, and thy **g** out, H3318
Jer 48: 5 For in the **g** up of Luhith continual H4608
5 go up; for in the **g** down of Horonaim H4174
50: 4 of Judah together, **g** and weeping: they H1980
Ezk 27:19 Dan also and Javan **g** to and fro H235
40:31 and the **g** up to it *had* eight steps. H4608
34 side: and the **g** up to it *had* eight steps. H4608
37 side: and the **g** up to it *had* eight steps. H4608
44: 5 with every **g** forth of the sanctuary. H4161
46:12 after his **g** forth *one* shall shut the gate. H3318
Dan 6:14 the **g** down of the sun to deliver him. H4606
9:25 understand, *that* from the **g** forth of the H4161
Hos 6: 3 the LORD: his **g** forth is prepared as H4161
Jna 1: 3 he found a ship **g** to Tarshish: so he paid H935
Mal 1:11 sun even unto the **g** down of the same H3996
Mt 4:21 And **g** on from thence, he saw other G4260
20:17 And Jesus **g** up to Jerusalem took the G305
26:46 Rise, let us be **g**: behold, he is at hand G71
Mt 28:11 Now when they were **g**, behold, some of G4198
Mk 6:31 many coming and **g**, and they had no G5217
10:32 And they were in the way **g** up to G305
Lk 14:31 Or what king, **g** to make war against G4198
Jn 4:51 And as he was now **g** down, his G2597
8:59 out of the temple, **g** through the midst G1330
Act 9:28 And he was with them coming in and **g** G1607
20: 5 These **g** before tarried for us at Troas. G4281
Ro 10: 3 and **g** about to establish their G2212
1Ti 5:24 are open beforehand, **g** before to G4254
Heb 7:18 the commandment **g** before for the G4254
1Pt 2:25 For ye were as sheep **g** astray; but are G4105
Jude 7 to fornication, and **g** after strange flesh, G565

GOINGS
Nu 33: 2 And Moses wrote their **g** out according H4161
2 their journeys according to their **g** out. H4161
34: 5 and the **g** out of it shall be at the sea. H8444
8 **g** forth of the border shall be to Zedad: H8444
9 Ziphron, and the **g** out of it shall be at H8444
12 to Jordan, and the **g** out of it shall be at H8444
Jos 15: 4 of Egypt; and the **g** out of that coast H8444
7 and the **g** out thereof were at Enrogel: H8444
11 the **g** out of the border were at the sea. H8444
16: 3 and the **g** out thereof are at the sea. H8444
8 Kanah; and the **g** out thereof were at H8444
18:12 westward; and the **g** out thereof were at H8444
14 and the **g** out thereof were at H8444
Job 34:21 the ways of man, and he seeth all his **g**. H6806
Ps 17: 5 Hold up my **g** in thy paths, *that* my H838
40: 2 feet upon a rock, *and* established my **g**. H838
68:24 They have seen thy **g**, O God; *even* the H1979
24 O God; *even* the **g** of my God, my King, H1979
140: 4 who have purposed to overthrow my **g**. H6471
Prv 5:21 of the LORD, and he pondereth all his **g**. H4570
20:24 Man's **g** *are* of the LORD; how can a H4703
Isa 59: 8 no judgment in their **g**: they have made H4570
Ezk 42:11 as they: and all their **g** out *were* both H4161
43:11 thereof, and the **g** out thereof, and the H4161
48:30 And these *are* the **g** out of the city on H8444
Mic 5: 2 in Israel; whose **g** forth *have been* from H4163

GOLAN
Dt 4:43 and **G** in Bashan, of the Manassites. H1474
Jos 20: 8 tribe of Gad, and **G** in Bashan out of H1474
21:27 *they gave* **G** in Bashan with her H1474
1Ch 6:71 of Manasseh, **G** in Bashan with her H1474

GOLD
Gen 2:11 whole land of Havilah, where *there is* **g**; H2091
12 And the **g** of that land *is* good: there *is* H2091
13: 2 very rich in cattle, in silver, and in **g**. H2091
24:22 for her hands of ten *shekels* weight of **g**; H2091
35 and silver, and **g**, and menservants, H2091
53 and jewels of **g**, and raiment, and gave H2091
41:42 linen, and put a **g** chain about his neck; H2091
44: 8 steal out of thy lord's house silver or **g**? H2091
Ex 3:22 and jewels of **g**, and raiment: and ye H2091
11: 2 jewels of silver, and jewels of **g**. H2091
12:35 of silver, and jewels of **g**, and raiment: H2091
20:23 shall ye make unto you gods of **g**. H2091
25: 3 take of them; **g**, and silver, and brass, H2091
11 And thou shalt overlay it with pure **g**, H2091
11 upon it a crown of **g** round about. H2091
12 And thou shalt cast four rings of **g** for H2091
13 shittim wood, and overlay them with **g**. H2091
17 a mercy seat *of* pure **g**: two cubits and a H2091
18 two cherubims *of* **g**, *of* beaten work H2091
24 And thou shalt overlay it with pure **g**, H2091
24 thereto a crown of **g** round about. H2091
26 for it four rings of **g**, and put the rings H2091
28 overlay them with **g**, that the table may H2091
29 withal: *of* pure **g** shalt thou make them. H2091
31 *of* pure **g**: *of* beaten work shall H2091
36 all it *shall be* one beaten work *of* pure **g**. H2091
38 snuffdishes thereof, *shall be of* pure **g**. H2091
39 *Of* a talent of pure **g** shall he make it, H2091
26: 6 And thou shalt make fifty taches of **g**, H2091
29 the boards with **g**, and make their rings H2091
29 their rings *of* **g** *for* places for the bars: H2091
29 and thou shalt overlay the bars with **g**. H2091
32 overlaid with **g**: their hooks *shall be* H2091
32 *be of* **g**, upon the four sockets of silver. H2091
37 overlay them with **g**, *and* their hooks H2091
37 hooks *shall be of* **g**: and thou shalt cast H2091
28: 5 And they shall take **g**, and blue, and H2091
6 And they shall make the ephod *of* **g**, *of* H2091
8 thereof; *even of* **g**, *of* blue, and purple, H2091
11 make them to be set in ouches of **g**. H2091
Ex 28:13 And thou shalt make ouches *of* **g**; H2091
14 And two chains *of* pure **g** at the ends; H2091
15 thou shalt make it; *of* **g**, *of* blue, and *of* H2091
20 they shall be set in **g** in their inclosings. H2091
22 at the ends *of* wreathen work *of* pure **g**. H2091
23 two rings of **g**, and shalt put the two H2091
24 *chains* of **g** in the two rings *which* H2091
26 And thou shalt make two rings of **g**, and H2091
27 And two *other* rings of **g** thou shalt H2091
33 bells of **g** between them round about: H2091
36 And thou shalt make a plate *of* pure **g**, H2091
30: 3 And thou shalt overlay it with pure **g**, H2091
3 make unto it a crown of **g** round about. H2091
5 shittim wood, and overlay them with **g**. H2091
31: 4 To devise cunning works, to work in **g**, H2091
32:24 hath any **g**, let them break *it* off. H2091
31 sin, and have made them gods of **g**. H2091
35: 5 of the LORD; **g**, and silver, and brass, H2091
22 all jewels of **g**: and every man that H2091
22 *offered* an offering of **g** unto the LORD. H2091
32 to work in **g**, and in silver, and in brass, H2091
36:13 And he made fifty taches of **g**, and H2091
34 And he overlaid the boards with **g**, and H2091
34 their rings *of* **g** *to be* places for the H2091
34 the bars, and overlaid the bars with **g**. H2091
36 them with **g**: their hooks *were of* H2091
36 hooks *were of* **g**; and he cast for them H2091
38 **g**: but their five sockets *were of* brass. H2091
37: 2 And he overlaid it with pure **g** within H2091
2 made a crown of **g** to it round about. H2091
3 And he cast for it four rings of **g**, *to be* H2091
4 shittim wood, and overlaid them with **g**. H2091
6 And he made the mercy seat *of* pure **g**: H2091
7 And he made two cherubims *of* **g**, H2091
11 And he overlaid it with pure **g**, and H2091
11 thereunto a crown of **g** round about. H2091
12 of **g** for the border thereof round about. H2091
13 And he cast for it four rings of **g**, and H2091
15 overlaid them with **g**, to bear the table. H2091
16 his covers to cover withal, *of* pure **g**. H2091
17 And he made the candlestick *of* pure **g**: H2091
22 all of it *was* one beaten work *of* pure **g**. H2091
23 snuffers, and his snuffdishes, *of* pure **g**. H2091
24 *Of* a talent of pure **g** made he it, and all H2091
26 And he overlaid it with pure **g**, *both* the H2091
26 made unto it a crown of **g** round about. H2091
27 And he made two rings of **g** for it under H2091
28 shittim wood, and overlaid them with **g**. H2091
38:24 All the **g** that was occupied for the H2091
24 *place*, even the **g** of the offering, was H2091
39: 2 And he made the ephod *of* **g**, blue, and H2091
3 And they did beat the **g** into thin H2091
5 the work thereof; *of* **g**, blue, and purple, H2091
6 in ouches of **g**, graven, as signets are H2091
8 of the ephod; *of* **g**, blue, and purple, and H2091
13 in ouches of **g** in their inclosings. H2091
15 at the ends, *of* wreathen work *of* pure **g**. H2091
16 And they made two ouches *of* **g**, and H2091
16 *of* gold, and two **g** rings; and put the H2091
17 chains of **g** in the two rings on H2091
19 And they made two rings of **g**, and put H2091
25 And they made bells *of* pure **g**, and put H2091
30 crown *of* pure **g**, and wrote upon it a H2091
40: 5 And thou shalt set the altar of **g** for the H2091
Nu 7:14 One spoon of ten *shekels* of **g**, full of H2091
20 One spoon of **g** of ten *shekels*, full of H2091
84 twelve silver bowls, twelve spoons of **g**: H2091
86 sanctuary: all the **g** of the spoons *was* H2091
8: 4 *was of* beaten **g**, unto the shaft thereof, H2091
22:18 full of silver and **g**, I cannot go beyond H2091
24:13 full of silver and **g**, I cannot go beyond H2091
31:22 Only the **g**, and the silver, the brass, the H2091
50 hath gotten, of jewels of **g**, chains, and H2091
51 the **g** of them, *even* all wrought jewels. H2091
52 And all the **g** of the offering that they H2091
54 the priest took the **g** of the captains of H2091
Dt 7:25 desire the silver or **g** *that is* on them, H2091
8:13 thy silver and thy **g** is multiplied, and H2091
17:17 greatly multiply to himself silver and **g**. H2091
29:17 silver and **g**, which *were* among them:) H2091
Jos 6:19 But all the silver, and **g**, and vessels of H2091
24 the silver, and the **g**, and the vessels of H2091
7:21 and a wedge of **g** of fifty shekels weight, H2091
24 and the wedge of **g**, and his sons, and H2091
22: 8 silver, and with **g**, and with brass, and H2091
Jdg 8:26 *shekels* of **g**; beside ornaments, and H2091
1Sa 6: 8 put the jewels of **g**, which ye return him H2091
11 of **g** and the images of their emerods. H2091
15 the jewels of **g** *were*, and put *them* H2091

2Sa 1:24 on ornaments of **g** upon your apparel. H2091
8: 7 And David took the shields of **g** that H2091
10 and vessels of **g**, and vessels of brass: H2091
11 LORD, with the silver and **g** that he had H2091
12:30 *was* a talent of **g** with the precious H2091
21: 4 have no silver nor **g** of Saul, nor of his H2091
1Ki 6:20 it with pure **g**; and *so* covered the H2091
21 within with pure **g**: and he made a H2091
21 by the chains of **g** before the oracle; H2091
21 the oracle; and he overlaid it with **g**. H2091
22 And the whole house he overlaid with **g**, H2091
22 *was* by the oracle he overlaid with **g**. H2091
28 And he overlaid the cherubims with **g**. H2091
30 he overlaid with **g**, within and without. H2091
32 *them* with **g**, and spread gold upon H2091
32 with gold, and spread **g** upon the H2091
35 with **g** fitted upon the carved work. H2091
7:48 LORD: the altar of **g**, and the table of H2091
48 of **g**, whereupon the shewbread *was*, H2091
49 And the candlesticks of pure **g**, five on H2091
49 and the lamps, and the tongs *of* **g**, H2091
50 the censers *of* pure **g**; and the hinges *of* H2091
50 and the hinges *of* **g**, *both* for the doors H2091
51 the silver, and the **g**, and the vessels, H2091
9:11 fir trees, and with **g**, according to all his H2091
14 sent to the king sixscore talents of **g**. H2091
28 from thence **g**, four hundred and twenty H2091
10: 2 and very much **g**, and precious stones: H2091
10 twenty talents of **g**, and of spices very H2091
11 that brought **g** from Ophir, brought H2091
14 Now the weight of **g** that came to H2091
14 hundred threescore and six talents of **g**, H2091
16 targets *of* beaten **g**: six hundred *shekels* H2091
16 *shekels* of **g** went to one target. H2091
17 shields *of* beaten **g**; three pound of gold H2091
17 three pound of **g** went to one shield: H2091
18 of ivory, and overlaid it with the best **g**. H2091
21 vessels *were of* **g**, and all the vessels of H2091
21 *were of* pure **g**; none *were of* silver: H2091
22 bringing **g**, and silver, ivory, and H2091
25 and vessels of **g**, and garments, and H2091
12:28 two calves *of* **g**, and said unto them, H2091
14:26 shields of **g** which Solomon had made. H2091
15:15 of the LORD, silver, and **g**, and vessels. H2091
18 Then Asa took all the silver and the **g** H2091
19 of silver and **g**; come and break thy H2091
20: 3 Thy silver and thy **g** *is* mine; thy wives H2091
5 thy **g**, and thy wives, and thy children; H2091
7 and for my **g**; and I denied him not. H2091
22:48 to go to Ophir for **g**: but they went not; H2091
2Ki 5: 5 *pieces* of **g**, and ten changes of raiment. H2091
7: 8 thence silver, and **g**, and raiment, and H2091
12:13 any vessels of **g**, or vessels of silver, H2091
18 things, and all the **g** *that was* found in H2091
14:14 And he took all the **g** and silver, and all H2091
16: 8 And Ahaz took the silver and **g** that H2091
18:14 talents of silver and thirty talents of **g**. H2091
16 At that time did Hezekiah cut off *the* **g**
20:13 the silver, and the **g**, and the spices, and H2091
23:33 talents of silver, and a talent of **g**. H2091
35 the silver and the **g** to Pharaoh; but he H2091
35 the silver and the **g** of the people of the H2091
24:13 all the vessels of **g** which Solomon king H2091
25:15 such things as *were* of **g**, *in* gold, and of H2091
15 as *were* of gold, *in* **g**, and of silver, *in* H2091
1Ch 18: 7 And David took the shields of **g** that H2091
10 of vessels of **g** and silver and brass. H2091
11 the silver and the **g** that he brought H2091
20: 2 to weigh a talent of **g**, and *there were* H2091
21:25 six hundred shekels of **g** by weight. H2091
22:14 talents of **g**, and a thousand thousand H2091
16 Of the **g**, the silver, and the brass, and H2091
28:14 *He gave* of **g** by weight for *things* of H2091
14 for *things* of **g**, for all instruments H2091
15 for the candlesticks of **g**, and for their H2091
15 for their lamps of **g**, by weight for every H2091
16 And by weight *he gave* **g** for the tables H2091
17 Also pure **g** for the fleshhooks, and the H2091
17 basons *he gave* **g** by weight for every
18 And for the altar of incense refined **g** H2091
18 by weight; and **g** for the pattern of the H2091
29: 2 of my God the **g** for *things to be made* H2091
2 *to be made* of **g**, and the silver for H2091
3 proper good, of **g** and silver, *which* I H2091
4 *Even* three thousand talents of **g**, of the H2091
4 of gold, of the **g** of Ophir, and seven H2091
5 The **g** for *things* of gold, and the silver H2091
5 The gold for *things* of **g**, and the silver H2091
7 house of God of **g** five thousand talents H2091

2Ch 1:15 And the king made silver and **g** at H2091
2: 7 to work in **g**, and in silver, and in H2091
14 skilful to work in **g**, and in silver, in H2091
3: 4 and he overlaid it within with pure **g**. H2091
5 he overlaid with fine **g**, and set thereon H2091
6 beauty: and the **g** *was* gold of Parvaim. H2091
6 beauty: and the gold *was* **g** of Parvaim. H2091
7 **g**; and graved cherubims on the walls. H2091
8 **g**, *amounting* to six hundred talents. H2091
9 fifty shekels of **g**. And he overlaid the H2091
9 he overlaid the upper chambers with **g**. H2091
10 image work, and overlaid them with **g**. H2091
4: 7 And he made ten candlesticks of **g** H2091
8 And he made an hundred basons of **g**. H2091
20 the manner before the oracle, of pure **g**; H2091
21 *made he of* **g**, *and* that perfect gold; H2091
21 *made he of* gold, *and* that perfect **g**; H2091
22 censers, *of* pure **g**: and the entry of the H2091
22 of the house of the temple, *were of* **g**. H2091
5: 1 and the silver, and the **g**, and all the H2091
8:18 **g**, and brought *them* to king Solomon. H2091
9: 1 bare spices, and **g** in abundance, and H2091
9 twenty talents of **g**, and of spices great H2091
10 which brought **g** from Ophir, brought H2091
13 Now the weight of **g** that came to H2091
13 and threescore and six talents of **g**; H2091
14 brought **g** and silver to Solomon. H2091
15 targets *of* beaten **g**: six hundred *shekels* H2091
15 *shekels* of beaten **g** went to one target. H2091
16 *made he of* beaten **g**: three hundred H2091
16 *shekels* of **g** went to one shield. H2091
17 of ivory, and overlaid it with pure **g**. H2091
18 throne, with a footstool of **g**, *which were* H2091
20 Solomon *were of* **g**, and all the vessels of H2091
20 *were of* pure **g**: none *were of* silver; H2091
21 Tarshish bringing **g**, and silver, ivory, H2091
24 and vessels of **g**, and raiment, harness, H2091
12: 9 shields of **g** which Solomon had made. H2091
13:11 and the candlestick of **g** with the lamps H2091
15:18 dedicated, silver, and **g**, and vessels. H2091
16: 2 Then Asa brought out silver and **g** out H2091
3 thee silver and **g**; go, break thy league H2091
21: 3 gifts of silver, and of **g**, and of precious H2091
24:14 and vessels of **g** and silver. And they H2091
25:24 And *he took* all the **g** and the silver, H2091
32:27 for silver, and for **g**, and for precious H2091
36: 3 talents of silver and a talent of **g**. H2091
Ezr 1: 4 silver, and with **g**, and with goods, and H2091
6 of silver, with **g**, with goods, and with H2091
9 them: thirty chargers of **g**, a thousand H2091
10 Thirty basons of **g**, silver basons of a H2091
11 All the vessels of **g** and of silver *were* H2091
2:69 drams of **g**, and five thousand pound H2091
5:14 And the vessels also of **g** and silver of H1722
7:15 And to carry the silver and **g**, which the H1722
16 And all the silver and **g** that thou canst H1722
18 the **g**, that do after the will of your God. H1722
8:25 the silver, and the **g**, and the vessels, H2091
26 talents, *and* of **g** an hundred talents; H2091
27 Also twenty basons of **g**, of a thousand H2091
27 vessels of fine copper, precious as **g**. H2091
28 and the silver and the **g** *are* a freewill H2091
30 the silver, and the **g**, and the vessels, to H2091
33 was the silver and the **g** and the vessels H2091
Neh 7:70 drams of **g**, fifty basons, five hundred H2091
71 drams of **g**, and two thousand and H2091
72 drams of **g**, and two thousand pound H2091
Est 1: 6 the beds *were of* **g** and silver, upon a H2091
7 drink in vessels of **g**, (the vessels being H2091
8:15 a great crown of **g**, and with a garment H2091
Job 3:15 Or with princes that had **g**, who filled H2091
22:24 Then shalt thou lay up **g** as dust, and H1220
24 **g** of Ophir as the stones of the brooks.
23:10 hath tried me, I shall come forth as **g**. H2091
28: 1 and a place for **g** *where* they fine *it*. H2091
6 place of sapphires: and it hath dust of **g**. H2091
15 It cannot be gotten for **g**, neither shall H5458
16 It cannot be valued with the **g** of Ophir, H3800
17 The **g** and the crystal cannot equal it: H2091
17 of it *shall not be for* jewels of fine **g**. H6337
19 it, neither shall it be valued with pure **g**. H3800
31:24 If I have made **g** my hope, or have said H2091
24 to the fine **g**, *Thou art* my confidence; H3800
36:19 Will he esteem thy riches? *no*, not **g**, nor H1222
42:11 money, and every one an earring of **g**. H2091
Ps 19:10 More to be desired *are they* than **g**, yea, H2091
10 than much fine **g**: sweeter also than H6337
21: 3 settest a crown of pure **g** on his head. H6337
45: 9 hand did stand the queen in **g** of Ophir. H3800

Ps 45:13 within: her clothing *is* of wrought **g**. H2091
68:13 silver, and her feathers with yellow **g**. H2742
72:15 be given of the **g** of Sheba: prayer also H2091
105:37 with silver and **g**: and *there was* not one H2091
115: 4 Their idols *are* silver and **g**, the work of H2091
119:72 me than thousands of **g** and silver. H2091
127 above **g**; yea, above fine gold. H2091
127 above gold; yea, above fine **g**. H6337
135:15 silver and **g**, the work of men's hands. H2091
Prv 3:14 silver, and the gain thereof than fine **g**. H2742
8:10 and knowledge rather than choice **g**. H2742
19 My fruit *is* better than **g**, yea, than fine H2742
19 **g**; and my revenue than choice silver. H6337
11:22 *As* a jewel of **g** in a swine's snout, *so is* H2091
16:16 to get wisdom than **g**! and to get H2742
17: 3 for **g**: but the LORD trieth the hearts. H2091
20:15 There is **g**, and a multitude of rubies: H2091
22: 1 loving favour rather than silver and **g**. H2091
25:11 A word fitly spoken *is like* apples of **g** H2091
12 *As* an earring of **g**, and an ornament of H2091
12 ornament of fine **g**, *so is* a wise reprover H3800
27:21 furnace for **g**; so *is* a man to his praise. H2091
Ecc 2: 8 I gathered me also silver and **g**, and the H2091
Song 1:10 rows *of jewels*, thy neck with chains *of* **g**.
11 We will make thee borders of **g** with H2091
3:10 bottom thereof *of* **g**, the covering of it *of* H2091
5:11 His head *is as* the most fine **g**, his locks H6337
14 His hands *are as* **g** rings set with the H2091
15 sockets of fine **g**: his countenance *is* as H6337
Isa 2: 7 Their land also is full of silver and **g**, H2091
20 and his idols of **g**, which they made H2091
13:12 precious than fine **g**; even a man than H6337
17 and *as for* **g**, they shall not delight in it. H2091
30:22 thy molten images of **g**: thou shalt cast H2091
31: 7 and his idols of **g**, which your own H2091
39: 2 the silver, and the **g**, and the spices, and H2091
40:19 it over with **g**, and casteth silver chains. H2091
46: 6 They lavish **g** out of the bag, and weigh H2091
60: 6 they shall bring **g** and incense; and H2091
9 silver and their **g** with them, unto the H2091
17 For brass I will bring **g**, and for iron I H2091
Jer 4:30 thee with ornaments of **g**, though thou H2091
10: 4 They deck it with silver and with **g**; they H2091
9 Tarshish, and **g** from Uphaz, the work H2091
52:19 *that* which *was* of **g** *in* gold, and *that* H2091
19 *was* of gold *in* **g**, and *that* which *was* H2091
Lam 4: 1 How is the **g** become dim! *how* is the H2091
1 is the most fine **g** changed! the stones H3800
2 to fine **g**, how are they esteemed H6337
Ezk 7:19 streets, and their **g** shall be removed: H2091
19 silver and their **g** shall not be able to H2091
16:13 Thus wast thou decked with **g** and H2091
17 thy fair jewels of my **g** and of my silver, H2091
27:22 and with all precious stones, and **g**. H2091
28: 4 gotten **g** and silver into thy treasures: H2091
13 carbuncle, and **g**: the workmanship of H2091
38:13 away silver and **g**, to take away cattle H2091
Dan 2:32 This image's head *was* of fine **g**, his H1722
35 the silver, and the **g**, broken to pieces H1722
38 over them all. Thou *art* this head of **g**. H1722
45 the silver, and the **g**; the great God hath H1722
3: 1 made an image of **g**, whose height *was* H1722
5: 4 the gods of **g**, and of silver, of brass, H1722
7 *have* a chain of **g** about his neck, and H1722
16 *have* a chain of **g** about thy neck, and H1722
23 the gods of silver, and **g**, of brass, iron, H1722
29 and *put* a chain of **g** about his neck, H1722
10: 5 loins *were* girded with fine **g** of Uphaz: H3800
11: 8 of silver and of **g**; and he shall continue H2091
38 he honour with **g**, and silver, and with H2091
43 the treasures of **g** and of silver, and H2091
Hos 2: 8 and **g**, *which* they prepared for Baal. H2091
8: 4 silver and their **g** have they made them H2091
Joel 3: 5 my silver and my **g**, and have carried H2091
Nah 2: 9 take the spoil of **g**: for *there is* none end H2091
Hab 2:19 it *is* laid over with **g** and silver, and H2091
Zep 1:18 Neither their silver nor their **g** shall be H2091
Hag 2: 8 The silver *is* mine, and the **g** *is* mine, H2091
Zec 4: 2 a candlestick all *of* **g**, with a bowl upon H2091
6:11 Then take silver and **g**, and make H2091
9: 3 and fine **g** as the mire of the streets. H2742
13: 9 will try them as **g** is tried: they shall call H2091
14:14 be gathered together, **g**, and silver, and H2091
Mal 3: 3 purge them as **g** and silver, that they H2091
Mt 2:11 gifts; **g**, and frankincense, and myrrh. *G5557*
10: 9 Provide neither **g**, nor silver, nor brass *G5557*
23:16 by the **g** of the temple, he is a debtor! *G5557*
17 is greater, the **g**, or the temple that *G5557*
17 or the temple that sanctifieth the **g**? *G5557*

G

Act 3: 6 Then Peter said, Silver and **g** have I G5553
17:29 is like unto **g**, or silver, or stone, graven G5557
20:33 I have coveted no man's silver, or **g**, or G5553
1Co 3:12 upon this foundation **g**, silver, precious G5557
1Ti 2: 9 hair, or **g**, or pearls, or costly array; G5557
2Ti 2:20 not only vessels of **g** and of silver, but G5552
Heb 9: 4 round about with **g**, wherein *was* the G5553
Jas 2: 2 a man with a **g** ring, in goodly apparel, G5554
5: 3 Your **g** and silver is cankered; and the G5557
1Pt 1: 7 more precious than of **g** that perisheth, G5553
18 things, *as* silver and **g**, from your vain G5553
3: 3 of **g**, or of putting on of apparel; G5553
Rev 3:18 I counsel thee to buy of me **g** tried in G5553
4: 4 they had on their heads crowns of **g**. G5552
9: 7 were crowns like **g**, and their faces *were* G5557
20 and idols of **g**, and silver, and brass, G5552
17: 4 and decked with **g** and precious stones G5557
18:12 The merchandise of **g**, and silver, and G5557
16 with **g**, and precious stones, and pearls! G5557
21:18 city *was* pure **g**, like unto clear glass. G5553
21 *was* pure **g**, as it were transparent glass. G5553

GOLDEN
Gen 24:22 that the man took a **g** earring of half a H2091
Ex 25:25 and thou shalt make a **g** crown to the H2091
28:34 A **g** bell and a pomegranate, a golden H2091
34 A golden bell and a pomegranate, a **g** H2091
30: 4 And two **g** rings shalt thou make to it H2091
32: 2 Break off the **g** earrings, which *are* H2091
3 And all the people brake off the **g** H2091
39:20 And they made two *other* **g** rings, and H2091
38 And the **g** altar, and the anointing oil, H2091
40:26 And he put the **g** altar in the tent of the H2091
Lev 8: 9 did he put the **g** plate, the holy crown; H2091
Nu 4:11 And upon the **g** altar they shall spread H2091
7:26 One **g** spoon of ten *shekels*, full of H2091
32 One **g** spoon of ten *shekels*, full of H2091
38 One **g** spoon of ten *shekels*, full of H2091
44 One **g** spoon of ten *shekels*, full of H2091
50 One **g** spoon of ten *shekels*, full of H2091
56 One **g** spoon of ten *shekels*, full of H2091
62 One **g** spoon of ten *shekels*, full of H2091
68 One **g** spoon of ten *shekels*, full of H2091
74 One **g** spoon of ten *shekels*, full of H2091
80 One **g** spoon of ten *shekels*, full of H2091
86 The **g** spoons *were* twelve, full of H2091
Jdg 8:24 (For they had **g** earrings, because they H2091
26 And the weight of the **g** earrings that he H2091
1Sa 6: 4 answered, Five **g** emerods, and five H2091
4 emerods, and five **g** mice, *according to* H2091
17 And these *are* the **g** emerods which the H2091
18 And the **g** mice, *according to* the H2091
2Ki 10:29 them, *to wit*, the **g** calves that *were* in H2091
1Ch 28:17 cups: and for the **g** basons *he gave gold* H2091
2Ch 4:19 house of God, the **g** altar also, and the H2091
13: 8 and *there are* with you **g** calves, which H2091
Ezr 6: 5 And also let the **g** and silver vessels of H1722
Est 4:11 shall hold out the **g** sceptre, that he H2091
5: 2 out to Esther the **g** sceptre that *was* in H2091
8: 4 Then the king held out the **g** sceptre H2091
Ecc 12: 6 be loosed, or the **g** bowl be broken, or H2091
Isa 13:12 even a man than the **g** wedge of Ophir. H3800
14: 4 the oppressor ceased! the **g** city ceased! H4062
Jer 51: 7 Babylon *hath been* a **g** cup in the H2091
Dan 3: 5 down and worship the **g** image that H1722
7 *and* worshipped the **g** image that H1722
10 fall down and worship the **g** image: H1722
12 the **g** image which thou hast set up. H1722
14 the **g** image which I have set up? H1722
18 the **g** image which thou hast set up. H1722
5: 2 to bring the **g** and silver vessels which H1722
3 Then they brought the **g** vessels that H1722
Zec 4:12 through the two **g** pipes empty the H2091
12 empty the **g** *oil* out of themselves? H2091
Heb 9: 4 Which had the **g** censer, and the ark of G5552
4 wherein *was* the **g** pot that had manna, G5552
Rev 1:12 turned, I saw seven **g** candlesticks; G5552
13 and girt about the paps with a **g** girdle. G5552
20 and the seven **g** candlesticks. The seven G5552
2: 1 the midst of the seven **g** candlesticks; G5552
5: 8 them harps, and **g** vials full of odours, G5552
8: 3 the altar, having a **g** censer; and there G5552
3 **g** altar which was before the throne. G5552
9:13 of the **g** altar which is before God, G5552
14:14 on his head a **g** crown, and in his hand G5552
15: 6 their breasts girded with **g** girdles. G5552
7 angels seven **g** vials full of the wrath G5552
17: 4 pearls, having a **g** cup in her hand full G5552
21:15 And he that talked with me had a **g** G5552

GOLDSMITH
Isa 40:19 image, and the **g** spreadeth it over with H6884
41: 7 So the carpenter encouraged the **g**, *and* H6884
46: 6 *and* hire a **g**; and he maketh it a H6884

GOLDSMITHS
Neh 3: 8 Harhaiah, of the **g**. Next unto him also H6884
32 gate repaired the **g** and the merchants. H6884

GOLDSMITH'S
Neh 3:31 After him repaired Malchiah the **g** son H6885

GOLGOTHA
Mt 27:33 **G**, that is to say, a place of a skull, G1115
Mk 15:22 And they bring him unto the place **G**, G1115
Jn 19:17 a skull, which is called in the Hebrew **G**: G1115

GOLIATH
1Sa 17: 4 named **G**, of Gath, whose height H1555
23 Philistine of Gath, **G** by name, out of H1555
21: 9 And the priest said, The sword of **G** the H1555
22:10 gave him the sword of **G** the Philistine. H1555
2Sa 21:19 *the brother of* **G** the Gittite, the staff H1555
1Ch 20: 5 the brother of **G** the Gittite, whose H1555

GOMER
Gen 10: 2 The sons of Japheth; **G**, and Magog, and H1586
3 And the sons of **G**; Ashkenaz, and H1586
1Ch 1: 5 The sons of Japheth; **G**, and Magog, and H1586
6 And the sons of **G**; Ashchenaz, and H1586
Ezk 38: 6 **G**, and all his bands; the house of H1586
Hos 1: 3 So he went and took **G** the daughter of H1586

GOMORRAH
Gen 10:19 unto Sodom, and **G**, and Admah, and H6017
13:10 Sodom and **G**, *even* as the garden H6017
14: 2 with Birsha king of **G**, Shinab king of H6017
8 and the king of **G**, and the king of H6017
10 of Sodom and **G** fled, and fell there; H6017
11 of Sodom and **G**, and all their victuals, H6017
18:20 the cry of Sodom and **G** is great, and H6017
19:24 Sodom and upon **G** brimstone and fire H6017
28 And he looked toward Sodom and **G**, H6017
Dt 29:23 of Sodom, and **G**, Admah, and Zeboim, H6017
32:32 and of the fields of **G**: their grapes *are* H6017
Isa 1: 9 *and* we should have been like unto **G**. H6017
10 unto the law of our God, ye people of **G**. H6017
13:19 as when God overthrew Sodom and **G**. H6017
Jer 23:14 and the inhabitants thereof as **G**. H6017
49:18 As in the overthrow of Sodom and **G** H6017
50:40 As God overthrew Sodom and **G** and H6017
Am 4:11 Sodom and **G**, and ye were as a H6017
Zep 2: 9 of Ammon as **G**, *even* the breeding of H6017

GOMORRHA
Mt 10:15 land of Sodom and **G** in the day of G1116
Mk 6:11 tolerable for Sodom and **G** in the day of G1116
Ro 9:29 as Sodoma, and been made like unto **G**. G1116
2Pt 2: 6 And turning the cities of Sodom and **G** G1116
Jude 7 Even as Sodom and **G**, and the cities G1116

GONE
Gen 27:30 was yet scarce **g** out from the presence H3318
28: 7 his mother, and was **g** to Padan-aram; H3212
31:30 wouldest needs be **g**, because thou sore H1980
34:17 we take our daughter, and we will be **g**. H1980
42:33 famine of your households, and be **g**: H3212
44: 4 *And* when they were **g** out of the city, H3318
49: 9 prey, my son, thou art **g** up: he stooped H5927
Ex 9:29 As soon as I am **g** out of the city, I will H3318
12:32 have said, and be **g**; and bless me also. H3212
16:14 And when the dew that lay was **g** up, H5927
19: 1 of Israel were **g** forth out of the land H3318
33: 8 until he was **g** into the tabernacle. H935
Lev 17: 7 whom they have **g** a whoring. This shall
Nu 5:19 if thou hast not **g** aside to uncleanness H7847
20 But if thou hast **g** aside *to another* H7847
7:89 And when Moses was **g** into the H935
13:32 which we have **g** to search it, *is* a land H5674
16:46 for there is wrath **g** out from the LORD; H3318
21:28 For there is a fire **g** out of Heshbon, a H3318
Dt 9: 9 When I was **g** up into the mount to H5927
13:13 of Belial, are **g** out from among you, H3318
17: 3 And hath **g** and served other gods, and H3212
23:23 That which is **g** out of thy lips thou H4161
27: 4 Therefore it shall be when ye be **g** over H5674
32:36 is **g**, and *there is* none shut up, or left. H235
Jos 2: 7 them were **g** out, they shut the gate. H3318
4:23 from before us, until we were **g** over: H5674
Jos 23:16 you, and have **g** and served other gods, H1980
Jdg 3:24 When he was **g** out, his servants came; H3318
4:12 of Abinoam was **g** up to mount Tabor. H5927
14 is not the LORD **g** out before thee? So H3318
18:24 the priest, and ye are **g** away: and what H3212
20: 3 of Israel were **g** up to Mizpeh.) Then H5927
Ru 1:13 hand of the LORD is **g** out against me. H3318
15 thy sister in law is **g** back unto her H7725
1Sa 14: 3 people knew not that Jonathan was **g**. H1980
17 and see who is **g** from us. And when H1980
15:12 up a place, and is **g** about, and passed H5437
12 and passed on, and **g** down to Gilgal. H3381
20 LORD, and have **g** the way which the H3212
20:41 *And* as soon as the lad was **g**, David H935
25:37 the wine was **g** out of Nabal, and his H3318
2Sa 2:27 the people had **g** up every one from H9527
3: 7 thou **g** in unto my father's concubine? H935
22 sent him away, and he was **g** in peace. H3212
23 sent him away, and he is **g** in peace. H3212
24 hast sent him away, and he is quite **g**? H3212
6:13 ark of the LORD had **g** six paces, he H6805
13:15 And Amnon said unto her, Arise, be **g**. H3212
17:20 unto them, They be **g** over the brook of H5674
22 one of them that was not **g** over Jordan. H5674
23: 9 and the men of Israel were **g** away: H5927
24: 8 So when they had **g** through all the H7751
1Ki 1:25 For he is **g** down this day, and hath H3381
2:41 that Shimei had **g** from Jerusalem to H1980
9:16 *For* Pharaoh king of Egypt had **g** up, H5927
11:15 of the host was **g** up to bury the slain, H5927
13:24 And when he was **g**, a lion met him by H3212
14: 9 thee: for thou hast **g** and made thee H3212
10 a man taketh away dung, till it be all **g**. H8552
18:12 *as soon as* I am **g** from thee, that the H3212
20:40 here and there, he was **g**. And the king of H369
21:18 whither he is **g** down to possess it. H3381
22:13 And the messenger that was **g** to call H1980
2Ki 1: 4 on which thou art **g** up, but shalt surely H5927
6 thou art **g** up, but shalt surely die. H5927
16 thou art **g** up, but shalt surely die. H5927
2: 9 And it came to pass, when they were **g** H5674
5: 2 And the Syrians had **g** out by H3318
6:15 risen early, and **g** forth, behold, an host H3318
7:12 therefore are they **g** out of the camp to H3318
20: 4 And it came to pass, afore Isaiah was **g** H3318
11 it had **g** down in the dial of Ahaz. H3381
1Ch 14:15 battle: for God is **g** forth before thee to H3318
17: 5 this day; but have **g** from tent to tent, H1961
Job 1: 5 of *their* feasting were **g** about, that Job H5362
7: 4 and the night be **g**? and I am full of H4059
19:10 side, and I am **g**: and mine hope hath H3212
23:12 Neither have I **g** back from the H4185
24:24 a little while, but are **g** and brought low; H369
28: 4 dried up, they are **g** away from men. H5128
Ps 14: 3 They are all **g** aside, they are *all* H5493
19: 4 Their line is **g** out through all the earth, H3318
38: 4 For mine iniquities are **g** over mine H5674
10 light of mine eyes, it also is **g** from me. H369
42: 4 in me: for I had **g** with the multitude, H5674
7 waves and thy billows are **g** over me. H5674
47: 5 God is **g** up with a shout, the LORD H5927
51:ttl him, after he had **g** in to Bath-sheba. H935
53: 3 Every one of them is **g** back: they are H5472
73: 2 But as for me, my feet were almost **g**; H5186
77: 8 Is his mercy clean **g** for ever? doth *his* H656
89:34 alter the thing that is **g** out of my lips. H4161
103:16 For the wind passeth over it, and it is **g**; H369
109:23 I am **g** like the shadow when it H1980
119:176 I have **g** astray like a lost sheep; seek H8552
124: 4 us, the stream had **g** over our soul: H5674
5 Then the proud waters had **g** over our H5674
Prv 7:19 For the goodman *is* not at home, he is **g** H1980
20:14 when he is **g** his way, then he boasteth. H235
Ecc 8:10 had come and **g** from the place of the H1980
Song 2:11 the winter is past, the rain is over *and* **g**; H1980
5: 6 himself, *and* was **g**: my soul failed when H5674
6: 1 Whither is thy beloved **g**, O thou fairest H1980
2 My beloved is **g** down into his garden, H3381
Isa 1: 4 unto anger, they are **g** away backward. H2114
5:13 Therefore my people are **g** into captivity,
10:29 They are **g** over the passage: they have H5674
15: 2 He is **g** up to Bajith, and to Dibon, the H5927
8 For the cry is **g** round about the H5362
16: 8 stretched out, they are **g** over the sea. H5674
22: 1 thou art wholly **g** up to the housetops? H5927
24:11 is darkened, the mirth of the land is **g**. H1540
38: 8 the degrees, which is **g** down in the sun H3381
8 by which degrees it was **g** down. H3381
41: 3 the way *that* he had not **g** with his feet. H935

Isa 45:23 I have sworn by myself, the word is **g** H3318
46: 2 but themselves are **g** into captivity. H1980
51: 5 my salvation is **g** forth, and mine arms H3318
53: 6 All we like sheep have **g** astray; we H8552
57: 8 than me, and art **g** up; thou hast H5927
Jer 2: 5 in me, that they are **g** far from me, and
23 I have not **g** after Baalim? see thy H1980
3: 6 hath done? she is **g** up upon every high H1980
4: 7 is on his way; he is **g** forth from his H3318
5:23 heart; they are revolted and **g**. H3212
9:10 and the beast are fled; they are **g**. H1980
10:20 my children are **g** forth of me, and they H3318
14: 2 and the cry of Jerusalem is **g** up. H5927
15: 6 LORD, thou art **g** backward: therefore H3212
9 ghost; her sun is **g** down while *it was* yet H935
23:15 is profaneness **g** forth into all the land. H3318
19 Behold, a whirlwind of the LORD is **g** H3318
29:16 are not **g** forth with you into captivity; H3318
34:21 army, which are **g** up from you. H5927
40: 5 Now while he was not yet **g** back, *he* H7725
44: 8 whither ye be **g** to dwell, that ye might H935
14 Judah, which are **g** into the land of Egypt H935
28 of Judah, that are **g** into the land of H935
48:11 vessel, neither hath he **g** into captivity: H1980
15 Moab is spoiled, and **g** up *out of* her H5927
15 chosen young men are **g** down to the H3381
32 thy plants are **g** over the sea, they reach H5674
50: 6 they have **g** from mountain to hill, H1980
Lam 1: 3 Judah is **g** into captivity because of
5 are **g** into captivity before the enemy. H1980
6 **g** without strength before the pursuer. H3212
18 and my young men are **g** into captivity. H1980
Ezk 7:10 the morning is **g** forth; the rod hath H3318
9: 3 And the glory of the God of Israel was **g** H5927
13: 5 Ye have not **g** up into the gaps, neither H5927
19:14 And fire is **g** out of a rod of her H3318
23:30 because thou hast **g** a whoring after the
24: 6 whose scum is not **g** out of it! bring it H3318
31:12 people of the earth are **g** down from his H3381
32:21 that help him: they are **g** down, they lie H3381
24 the sword, which are **g** down H3381
27 which are **g** down to hell with their H3381
30 which are **g** down with the slain; H3381
36:20 LORD, and are **g** forth out of his land. H3318
37:21 whither they be **g**, and will gather them H1980
44:10 And the Levites that are **g** away far from
Dan 2: 5 The thing is **g** from me: if ye will not H230
8 because ye see the thing is **g** from me. H230
14 **g** forth to slay the wise *men* of Babylon: H5312
10:20 and when I am **g** forth, lo, the prince H3318
Hos 4:12 have **g** a whoring from under their God.
8: 9 For they are **g** up to Assyria, a wild ass H5927
9: 1 for thou hast **g** a whoring from thy
6 For, lo, they are **g** because of H1980
Am 8: 5 Saying, When will the new moon be **g**, H5674
Jna 1: 5 But Jonah was **g** down into the sides H3381
Mic 1:16 for they are **g** into captivity from thee.
2:13 the gate, and are **g** out by it: and their H3318
Mal 3: 7 your fathers ye are **g** away from mine H5493
Mt 10:23 Ye shall not have **g** over the cities of G5055
12:43 When the unclean spirit is **g** out of a G1831
14:34 And when they were **g** over, they came G1276
18:12 one of them be **g** astray, doth he not G4105
12 and seeketh that which is **g** astray?
25: 8 us of your oil; for our lamps are **g** out. G4570
26:71 And when he was **g** out into the porch, G1831
Mk 1:19 And when he had **g** a little farther G4260
5:30 that virtue had **g** out of him, turned G1831
7:29 way; the devil is **g** out of thy daughter. G1831
30 found the devil **g** out, and her daughter G1831
10:17 And when he was **g** forth into the way, G1607
Lk 2:15 And it came to pass, as the angels were **g** G565
5: 2 the fishermen were **g** out of them, and G576
8:46 for I perceive that virtue is **g** out of me. G1831
11:14 the devil was **g** out, the dumb spake; G1831
24 When the unclean spirit is **g** out of a G1831
19: 7 That he was **g** to be guest with a man G1525
24:28 as though he would have **g** further. G4198
Jn 4: 8 (For his disciples were **g** away unto the G565
6:22 but *that* his disciples were **g** away alone; G565
7:10 But when his brethren were **g** up, then G305
12:19 behold, the world is **g** after him. G565
13:31 Therefore, when he was **g** out, Jesus G1831
Act 13: 6 And when they had **g** through the isle G1330
42 And when the Jews were **g** out of the G1826
16: 6 Now when they had **g** throughout G1330
19 of their gains was **g**, they caught Paul G1831
18:22 at Caesarea, and **g** up, and saluted the G305
20: 2 And when he had **g** over those parts, G1330
Act 20:25 whom I have **g** preaching the kingdom G1330
24: 6 Who also hath **g** about to profane the G3985
26:31 And when they were **g** aside, they talked G402
27:28 when they had **g** a little further, they G1339
Ro 3:12 They are all **g** out of the way, they are G1578
1Pt 3:22 Who is **g** into heaven, and is on the G4198
2Pt 2:15 right way, and are **g** astray, following G4105
1Jn 4: 1 false prophets are **g** out into the world. G1831
Jude 11 Woe unto them! for they have **g** in the G4198

GOOD

Gen 1: 4 And God saw the light, that *it was* **g**: H2896
10 he Seas: and God saw that *it was* **g**. H2896
12 his kind: and God saw that *it was* **g**. H2896
18 darkness: and God saw that *it was* **g**. H2896
21 his kind: and God saw that *it was* **g**. H2896
25 his kind: and God saw that *it was* **g**. H2896
31 *it was* very **g**. And the evening and H2896
2: 9 to the sight, and **g** for food; the tree of H2896
9 and the tree of knowledge of **g** and evil. H2896
12 And the gold of that land *is* **g**: there *is* H2896
17 But of the tree of the knowledge of **g** H2896
18 And the LORD God said, *It is* not **g** that H2896
3: 5 ye shall be as gods, knowing **g** and evil. H2896
6 that the tree *was* **g** for food, and that it H2896
22 one of us, to know **g** and evil: and now, H2896
15:15 thou shalt be buried in a **g** old age. H2896
18: 7 a calf tender and **g**, and gave *it* unto a H2896
19: 8 do ye to them as *is* **g** in your eyes: only H2896
21:16 against *him* a **g** way off, as it were a H7368
24:12 pray thee, send me **g** speed this day, and
50 we cannot speak unto thee bad or **g**. H2896
25: 8 and died in a **g** old age, an old man, H2896
26:29 thee nothing but **g**, and have sent thee H2896
27: 9 me from thence two **g** kids of the goats; H2896
46 of the land, what **g** shall my life do me? H4100
30:20 endued me *with* a **g** dowry; now will H2896
31:24 thou speak not to Jacob either **g** or bad. H2896
29 thou speak not to Jacob either **g** or bad. H2896
32:12 And thou saidst, I will surely do thee **g**, H3190
40:16 the interpretation was **g**, he said unto H2896
41: 5 came up upon one stalk, rank and **g**. H2896
22 ears came up in one stalk, full and **g**: H2896
24 And the thin ears devoured the seven **g** H2896
26 The seven **g** kine *are* seven years; and H2896
26 and the seven **g** ears *are* seven years: H2896
35 all the food of those **g** years that come, H2896
37 And the thing was **g** in the eyes of H3190
43:28 our father *is* in **g** health, he *is* yet alive. H7965
44: 4 Wherefore have ye rewarded evil for **g**? H2896
45:18 and I will give you the **g** of the land of H2898
20 Also regard not your stuff; for the **g** of H2898
23 laden with the **g** things of Egypt, and H2898
46:29 neck, and wept on his neck a **g** while. H5750
49:15 And he saw that rest *was* **g**, and the H2896
50:20 God meant it unto **g**, to bring to pass, as H2896
Ex 3: 8 of that land unto a **g** land and a large, H2896
18:17 him, The thing that thou doest *is* not **g**. H2896
21:34 The owner of the pit shall make *it* **g**, H7999
22:11 *thereof,* and he shall not make *it* **g**. H7999
13 shall not make **g** that which was torn. H7999
14 not with it, he shall surely make *it* **g**. H7999
15 he shall not make *it* **g**: if it *be* an hired H7999
Lev 5: 4 to do evil, or to do **g**, whatsoever *it be* H3190
24:18 a beast shall make it **g**; beast for beast. H7999
27:10 He shall not alter it, nor change it, a **g** H2896
10 a bad, or a bad for a **g**: and if he shall at H2896
12 value it, whether it be **g** or bad: as thou H2896
14 it, whether it be **g** or bad: as the priest H2896
33 He shall not search whether it be **g** or H2896
Nu 10:29 we will do thee **g**: for the LORD hath H2895
29 LORD hath spoken **g** concerning Israel. H2896
13:19 in, whether it *be* **g** or bad; and what H2896
20 not. And be ye of **g** courage, and bring of
14: 7 to search it, *is* an exceeding **g** land. H2896
23:19 he spoken, and shall he not make it **g**? H6965
24:13 to do *either* **g** or bad of mine own H2896
Dt 1:14 thou hast spoken *is* **g** *for us* to do. H2896
25 and said, *It is* a **g** land which the LORD H2896
35 see that **g** land, which I sware H2896
39 between **g** and evil, they shall H2896
2: 4 ye **g** heed unto yourselves therefore: H3966
3:25 over, and see the **g** land that *is* beyond H2896
4:15 Take ye therefore **g** heed unto H3966
21 go in unto that **g** land, which the LORD H2896
22 shall go over, and possess that **g** land. H2896
6:11 And houses full of all **g** *things,* which H2898
18 *which is* right and **g** in the sight of the H2896
18 go in and possess the **g** land which the H2896
Dt 6:24 our God, for our **g** always, that he H2896
8: 7 thee into a **g** land, a land of brooks H2896
10 for the **g** land which he hath given thee. H2896
16 thee, to do thee **g** at thy latter end; H3190
9: 6 thee not this **g** land to possess it for H2896
10:13 I command thee this day for thy **g**? H2896
11:17 the **g** land which the LORD giveth you. H2896
12:28 *that which is* **g** and right in the sight H2896
26:11 And thou shalt rejoice in every **g** *thing* H2896
28:12 The LORD shall open unto thee his **g** H2896
63 over you to do you **g**, and to multiply H3190
30: 5 **g**, and multiply thee above thy fathers. H3190
9 fruit of thy land, for **g**: for the LORD will H2896
9 for **g**, as he rejoiced over thy fathers: H2896
15 this day life and **g**, and death and evil; H2896
31: 6 Be strong and of a **g** courage, fear not,
7 Be strong and of a **g** courage: for thou
23 Be strong and of a **g** courage: for thou
33:16 and *for* the **g** will of him that dwelt H7522
Jos 1: 6 Be strong and of a **g** courage: for unto
8 and then thou shalt have **g** success.
9 Be strong and of a **g** courage; be not
18 death: only be strong and of a **g** courage.
9:25 **g** and right unto thee to do unto us, do. H2896
10:25 be strong and of **g** courage: for thus shall
21:45 There failed not ought of any **g** thing H2896
23:11 Take **g** heed therefore unto yourselves, H3966
13 from off this **g** land which the LORD H2896
14 hath failed of all the **g** things which the H2896
15 to pass, *that* as all **g** things are come H2896
15 you from off this **g** land which the H2896
16 **g** land which he hath given unto you. H2896
24:20 you, after that he hath done you **g**. H3190
Jdg 8:32 And Gideon the son of Joash died in a **g** H2896
9:11 and my **g** fruit, and go to be promoted H2896
10:15 seemeth **g** unto thee; deliver us H2896
17:13 **g**, seeing I have a Levite to *my* priest. H3190
18: 9 behold, it *is* very **g**: and *are* ye still? be H2896
22 *And* when they were a **g** way from the H7368
19:24 what seemeth **g** unto you: but unto this H2896
Ru 2:22 in law, *It is* **g**, my daughter, that thou H2896
1Sa 1:23 what seemeth thee **g**; tarry until thou H2896
2:24 Nay, my sons; for *it is* no **g** report that I H2896
3:18 LORD: let him do what seemeth him **g**. H2896
11:10 do with us all that seemeth **g** unto you. H2896
12:23 I will teach you the **g** and the right way: H2896
14:36 seemeth **g** unto thee. Then said H2896
40 Saul, Do what seemeth **g** unto thee. H2896
15: 9 and all *that was* **g**, and would not H2896
19: 4 And Jonathan spake **g** of David unto H2896
4 works *have been* to thee-ward very **g**: H2896
20:12 behold, *if there be* **g** toward David, and H2895
24: 4 him as it shall seem **g** unto thee. Then H3190
17 **g**, whereas I have rewarded thee evil. H2896
19 LORD reward thee **g** for that thou hast H2896
25: 3 *was* a woman of **g** understanding, and H2896
8 for we come in a **g** day: give, I pray H2896
15 But the men *were* very **g** unto us, and H2896
21 him: and he hath requited me evil for **g**. H2896
30 to all the **g** that he hath spoken H2896
26:16 This thing *is* not **g** that thou hast done. H2896
29: 6 me in the host *is* **g** in my sight: for I H2896
9 that thou *art* **g** in my sight, as an angel H2896
2Sa 3:19 all that seemed **g** to Israel, and that H2896
19 **g** to the whole house of Benjamin.
4:10 to have brought **g** tidings, I took hold H1319
6:19 of bread, and a **g** piece *of flesh,* and a
10:12 Be of **g** courage, and let us play the men
12 the LORD do that which seemeth him **g**. H2896
13:22 Amnon neither **g** nor bad: for Absalom H2896
14:17 the king to discern **g** and bad: therefore H2896
32 *it had been* **g** for me *to have been* H2896
15: 3 thy matters *are* **g** and right; but *there* H2896
26 him do to me as seemeth **g** unto him. H2896
16:12 requite me **g** for his cursing this day. H2896
17: 7 hath given *is* not **g** at this time. H2896
14 to defeat the **g** counsel of Ahithophel, H2896
18:27 **g** man, and cometh with good tidings. H2896
27 good man, and cometh with **g** tidings. H2896
19:18 what he thought **g**. And Shimei the son H2896
27 do therefore *what is* **g** in thine eyes. H2896
35 I discern between **g** and evil? can thy H2896
37 do to him what shall seem **g** unto thee. H2896
38 that which shall seem **g** unto thee: and H2896
24:22 up what *seemeth* **g** unto him: behold, H2896
1Ki 1:42 a valiant man, and bringest **g** tidings. H2896
2:38 The saying *is* **g**: as my lord the king H2896
42 me, The word *that* I have heard *is* **g**. H2896
3: 9 discern between **g** and bad: for who is H2896

1Ki 8:36 teach them the **g** way wherein they H2896
56 one word of all his **g** promise, which he H2896
12: 7 them, and speak **g** words to them, then H2896
14:13 there is found *some* **g** thing toward the H2896
15 Israel out of this **g** land, which he gave H2896
21: 2 it; *or,* if it seem **g** to thee, I will give thee H2896
22: 8 he doth not prophesy **g** concerning me, H2896
13 prophets *declare* **g** unto the king with H2896
13 one of them, and speak *that which is* **g**. H2896
18 prophesy no **g** concerning me, but evil? H2896
2Ki 3:19 shall fell every **g** tree, and stop all wells H2896
19 mar every **g** piece of land with stones. H2896
25 and on every **g** piece of land cast every H2896
25 water, and felled all the **g** trees: only in H2896
7: 9 this day *is* a day of **g** tidings, and we
8: 9 with him, even of every **g** thing of H2898
10: 5 do thou *that which is* **g** in thine eyes. H2896
20: 3 **g** in thy sight. And Hezekiah wept sore. H2896
19 Then said Hezekiah unto Isaiah, **G** *is* H2896
19 *it* not **g**, if peace and truth be in my days?
1Ch 4:40 And they found fat pasture and **g**, and H2896
13: 2 of Israel, If *it seem* **g** unto you, and *that* H2895
16: 3 a **g** piece of flesh, and a flagon *of wine.*
34 *he is* **g**; for his mercy *endureth* for ever. H2896
19:13 Be of **g** courage, and let us behave
13 LORD do *that which is* **g** in his sight. H2896
21:23 do *that which is* **g** in his eyes: lo, I give H2896
22:13 **g** courage; dread not, nor be dismayed.
28: 8 ye may possess this **g** land, and leave *it* H2896
20 Be strong and of **g** courage, and do *it:*
29: 3 mine own proper **g**, of gold and silver, H5459
28 And he died in a **g** old age, full of days, H7868
2Ch 5:13 LORD, *saying,* For *he is* **g**; for his mercy H2896
6:27 taught them the **g** way, wherein they H2896
7: 3 *he is* **g**; for his mercy *endureth* for ever. H2896
10: 7 them, and speak **g** words to them, they H2896
14: 2 And Asa did *that which was* **g** and H2896
18: 7 he never prophesied **g** unto me, but H2896
12 prophets *declare* **g** to the king with one H2896
12 be like one of theirs, and speak thou **g**. H2896
17 not prophesy **g** unto me, but evil? H2896
19: 3 Nevertheless there are **g** things found H2896
11 and the LORD shall be with the **g**. H2896
24:16 he had done **g** in Israel, both toward H2896
30:18 saying, The **g** LORD pardon every one H2896
22 that taught the **g** knowledge of the H2896
31:20 *that which was* **g** and right and truth H2896
Ezr 3:11 because *he is* **g**, for his mercy *endureth* H2896
5:17 Now therefore, if *it seem* **g** to the king, H2869
7: 9 to the **g** hand of his God upon him. H2896
18 And whatsoever shall seem **g** to thee, H3191
8:18 And by the **g** hand of our God upon us H2896
22 upon all them for **g** that seek him; but H2896
9:12 and eat the **g** of the land, and leave H2898
10: 4 *be* with thee: be of **g** courage, and do *it.*
Neh 2: 8 to the **g** hand of my God upon me. H2896
18 God which was **g** upon me; as also the H2896
18 their hands for *this* **g** *work.* H2896
5: 9 Also I said, It *is* not **g** that ye do: ought H2896
19 Think upon me, my God, for **g**, H2896
6:19 Also they reported his **g** deeds before H2896
9:13 laws, **g** statutes and commandments: H2896
20 Thou gavest also thy **g** spirit to instruct H2896
36 **g** thereof, behold, we *are* servants in it: H2898
13:14 wipe not out my **g** deeds that I have H2617
31 Remember me, O my God, for **g**. H2896
Est 3:11 to do with them as it seemeth **g** to thee. H2896
5: 4 And Esther answered, If *it seem* **g** unto H2895
7: 9 who had spoken **g** for the king, H2896
8:17 a feast and a **g** day. And many of the H2896
9:19 feasting, and a **g** day, and of sending H2896
22 from mourning into a **g** day: that they H2896
Job 2:10 shall we receive **g** at the hand of God, H2896
5:27 it *is*; hear it, and know thou *it* for thy **g**.
7: 7 *is* wind: mine eye shall no more see **g**. H2896
9:25 a post: they flee away, they see no **g**. H2896
10: 3 *Is it* **g** unto thee that thou shouldest H2895
13: 9 Is it **g** that he should search you out? or H2895
15: 3 speeches wherewith he can do no **g**? H3276
21:16 Lo, their **g** *is* not in their hand: the H2898
22:18 Yet he filled their houses with **g** *things*: H2896
21 peace: thereby **g** shall come unto thee. H2896
24:21 not: and doeth not **g** to the widow. H3190
30:26 When I looked for **g**, then evil came H2896
34: 4 let us know among ourselves what *is* **g**. H2896
39: 4 Their young ones are in **g** liking, they H2492
Ps 4: 6 will shew us *any* **g**? LORD, lift thou up H2896
14: 1 works, *there is* none that doeth **g**. H2896
3 *there is* none that doeth **g**, no, not one. H2896

Ps 25: 8 **G** and upright *is* the LORD: therefore H2896
27:14 Wait on the LORD: be of **g** courage, and
31:24 Be of **g** courage, and he shall strengthen
34: 8 O taste and see that the LORD *is* **g**: H2896
10 the LORD shall not want any **g** *thing*. H2896
12 loveth *many* days, that he may see **g**? H2896
14 Depart from evil, and do **g**; seek peace, H2896
35:12 They rewarded me evil for **g** *to* the H2896
36: 3 he hath left off to be wise, *and* to do **g**. H3190
4 way *that is* not **g**; he abhorreth not evil. H2896
37: 3 Trust in the LORD, and do **g**; *so* shalt H2896
23 The steps of a **g** man are ordered by the
27 Depart from evil, and do **g**; and dwell H2896
38:20 They also that render evil for **g** are H2896
20 because I follow *the thing that* **g** *is*. H2896
39: 2 from **g**; and my sorrow was stirred. H2896
45: 1 My heart is inditing a **g** matter: I speak H2896
51:18 Do **g** in thy good pleasure unto Zion: H3190
18 Do good in thy **g** pleasure unto Zion:
52: 3 Thou lovest evil more than **g**; *and* lying H2896
9 thy name; for *it is* **g** before thy saints. H2896
53: 1 iniquity: *there is* none that doeth **g**. H2896
3 *there is* none that doeth **g**, no, not one. H2896
54: 6 praise thy name, O LORD; for *it is* **g**. H2896
69:16 thy lovingkindness *is* **g**: turn unto me H2896
73: 1 Truly God *is* **g** to Israel, *even* to such as H2896
28 But *it is* **g** for me to draw near to God: I H2896
84:11 and glory: no **g** *thing* will he withhold H2896
85:12 **g**; and our land shall yield her increase. H2896
86: 5 For thou, Lord, *art* **g**, and ready to H2896
17 Shew me a token for **g**; that they which H2896
92: 1 *It is a* **g** *thing* to give thanks unto the H2896
100: 5 For the LORD *is* **g**; his mercy *is* H2896
103: 5 Who satisfieth thy mouth with **g** H2896
104:28 thine hand, they are filled with **g**. H2896
106: 1 *he is* **g**: for his mercy *endureth* for ever. H2896
5 That I may see the **g** of thy chosen, that H2896
107: 1 *he is* **g**: for his mercy *endureth* for ever. H2896
109: 5 And they have rewarded me evil for **g**, H2896
21 because thy mercy *is* **g**, deliver thou me. H2896
111:10 of wisdom: a **g** understanding have H2896
112: 5 A **g** man sheweth favour, and lendeth: H2896
118: 1 **g**: because his mercy *endureth* for ever. H2896
29 *he is* **g**: for his mercy *endureth* for ever. H2896
119:39 which I fear: for thy judgments *are* **g**. H2896
66 Teach me **g** judgment and knowledge: H2898
68 Thou *art* **g**, and doest good; teach me H2896
68 Thou *art* good, and doest **g**; teach me H2895
71 *It is* **g** for me that I have been afflicted; H2896
122 Be surety for thy servant for **g**: let not H2896
122: 9 of the LORD our God I will seek thy **g**. H2896
125: 4 Do **g**, O LORD, unto *those that be* good, H2895
4 Do good, O LORD, unto *those that be* **g**, H2896
128: 5 **g** of Jerusalem all the days of thy life. H2898
133: 1 Behold, how **g** and how pleasant *it is* H2896
135: 3 Praise the LORD; for the LORD *is* **g**: H2896
136: 1 *he is* **g**: for his mercy *endureth* for ever. H2896
143:10 **g**; lead me into the land of uprightness. H2896
145: 9 The LORD *is* **g** to all: and his tender H2896
147: 1 Praise ye the LORD: for *it is* **g** to sing H2896
Prv 2: 9 and equity; *yea*, every **g** path. H2896
20 That thou mayest walk in the way of **g** H2896
3: 4 So shalt thou find favour and **g** H2896
27 Withhold not **g** from them to whom it H2896
4: 2 For I give you **g** doctrine, forsake ye not H2896
11:17 The merciful man doeth **g** to his own H1580
23 The desire of the righteous *is* only **g**: *but* H2896
27 He that diligently seeketh **g** procureth H2896
12: 2 A **g** *man* obtaineth favour of the LORD: H2896
14 A man shall be satisfied with **g** by the H2896
25 it stoop: but a **g** word maketh it glad. H2896
13: 2 A man shall eat **g** by the fruit of *his* H2896
15 **G** understanding giveth favour: but the H2896
21 but to the righteous **g** shall be repayed. H2896
22 A **g** *man* leaveth an inheritance to his H2896
14:14 a **g** man *shall be satisfied* from himself. H2896
19 The evil bow before the **g**; and the H2896
22 and truth *shall be* to them that devise **g**. H2896
15: 3 place, beholding the evil and the **g**. H2896
23 word *spoken* in due season, how **g** *is it!* H2896
30 *and* a **g** report maketh the bones fat. H2896
16:20 wisely shall find **g**: and whoso trusteth H2896
29 leadeth him into the way *that is* not **g**. H2896
17:13 Whoso rewardeth evil for **g**, evil shall H2896
20 heart findeth no **g**: and he that hath a H2896
22 A merry heart doeth **g** *like* a medicine: H3190
26 Also to punish the just *is* not **g**, *nor* to H2896
18: 5 *It is* not **g** to accept the person of the H2896
22 *Whoso* findeth a wife findeth a **g** *thing*, H2896

Prv 19: 2 *it is* not **g**; and he that hasteth H2896
8 that keepeth understanding shall find **g**. H2896
20:18 by counsel: and with **g** advice make war.
23 the LORD; and a false balance *is* not **g**. H2896
22: 1 A **g** name *is* rather to be chosen than
24:13 My son, eat thou honey, because *it is* **g**; H2896
23 to the wise. *It is* not **g** to have respect of H2896
25 and a **g** blessing shall come upon them. H2896
25:25 *As* cold waters to a thirsty soul, so *is* **g** H2896
27 *It is* not **g** to eat much honey: so *for* H2896
28:10 shall have **g** *things* in possession. H2896
21 To have respect of persons *is* not **g**: for H2896
31:12 She will do him **g** and not evil all the H2896
18 *is* **g**: her candle goeth not out by night. H2896
Ecc 2: 3 see what *was* that **g** for the sons of H2896
24 his soul enjoy **g** in his labour. This also H2896
26 For *God* giveth to a man that *is* **g** in his H2896
26 give to *him that is* **g** before God. This H2896
3:12 I know that *there is* no **g** in them, but H2896
12 *a man* to rejoice, and to do **g** in his life. H2896
13 **g** of all his labour, it *is* the gift of God. H2896
4: 8 my soul of **g**? This *is* also vanity, H2896
9 they have a **g** reward for their labour. H2896
5:11 them: and what **g** *is there* to the owners H3788
18 Behold *that* which I have seen: *it is* **g** H2896
18 and to enjoy the **g** of all his labour that H2896
6: 3 be not filled with **g**, and also *that* he H2896
6 he seen no **g**: do not all go to one place? H2896
12 For who knoweth what *is* **g** for man in H2896
7: 1 A **g** name *is* better than precious
11 Wisdom *is* **g** with an inheritance: and H2896
18 *It is* **g** that thou shouldest take hold of H2896
20 earth, that doeth **g**, and sinneth not. H2896
9: 2 to the wicked; to the **g** and to the clean, H2896
2 not: as *is* the **g**, so *is* the sinner; *and* H2896
18 war: but one sinner destroyeth much **g**. H2896
11: 6 or whether they both *shall be* alike **g**. H2896
12: 9 yea, he gave **g** heed, and sought out,
14 whether *it be* **g**, or whether *it be* evil. H2896
Song 1: 3 Because of the savour of thy **g** H2896
2:13 tender grape give a **g** smell. Arise, my
Isa 1:19 obedient, ye shall eat the **g** of the land: H2898
5:20 Woe unto them that call evil **g**, and H2896
20 that call evil good, and **g** evil; that put H2896
7:15 to refuse the evil, and choose the **g**. H2896
16 and choose the **g**, the land that thou H2896
38: 3 **g** in thy sight. And Hezekiah wept sore. H2896
39: 8 Then said Hezekiah to Isaiah, **G** *is* the H2896
40: 9 O Zion, that bringest **g** tidings, get thee H1319
9 that bringest **g** tidings, lift up thy voice H1319
41: 6 *one* said to his brother, Be of **g** courage.
23 *are* gods: yea, do **g**, or do evil, that we H3190
27 Jerusalem one that bringeth **g** tidings. H1319
52: 7 of him that bringeth **g** tidings, that H1319
7 that bringeth **g** tidings of good, that H2896
7 good tidings of **g**, that publisheth H2896
55: 2 eat ye *that which is* **g**, and let your soul H2896
61: 1 me to preach **g** tidings unto the meek; H1319
65: 2 *that was* not **g**, after their own thoughts; H2896
Jer 4:22 but to do **g** they have no knowledge. H3190
5:25 have withholden **g** *things* from you. H2896
6:16 where *is* the **g** way, and walk therein, H2896
8:15 We looked for peace, but no **g** *came;* H2896
10: 5 do evil, neither also *is it* in them to do **g**. H3190
13:10 be as this girdle, which is **g** for nothing. H6743
23 do **g**, that are accustomed to do evil. H3190
14:11 me, Pray not for this people for *their* **g**. H2896
19 and *there is* no **g**; and for the time of H2896
17: 6 shall not see when **g** cometh; but shall H2896
18: 4 as seemed **g** to the potter to make *it*. H3474
10 I will repent of the **g**, wherewith I said I H2896
11 and make your ways and your doings **g**. H3190
20 Shall evil be recompensed for **g**? for they H2896
20 thee to speak **g** for them, *and* to turn H2896
21:10 for evil, and not for **g**, saith the LORD: it H2896
24: 2 One basket *had* very **g** figs, *even* like H2896
3 I said, Figs; the **g** figs, very good; and H2896
3 the good figs, very **g**; and the evil, very H2896
5 of Israel; Like these **g** figs, so will I H2896
5 the land of the Chaldeans for *their* **g**. H2896
6 For I will set mine eyes upon them for **g**, H2896
26:14 me as seemeth **g** and meet unto you. H2896
29:10 and perform my **g** word toward you, in H2896
32 he behold the **g** that I will do for my H2896
32:39 for ever, for the **g** of them, and of their H2896
40 them, to do them **g**; but I will put my H3190
41 over them to do them **g**, and I will plant H2895
42 all the **g** that I have promised them. H2896
33: 9 shall hear all the **g** that I do unto them: H2896

Jer 33:11 hosts: for the LORD *is* g; for his mercy H2896
14 I will perform that g thing which I have H2896
39:16 for evil, and not for g; and they shall be H2896
40: 4 hand. If it seem g unto thee to come H2896
4 whither it seemeth g and convenient H2896
42: 6 Whether *it be* g, or whether *it be* evil, H2896
44:27 evil, and not for g: and all the men of H2896
Lam 3:25 The LORD *is* g unto them that wait for H2896
26 *It is* g that *a man* should both hope and H2896
27 *It is* g for a man that he bear the yoke H2896
38 most High proceedeth not evil and g? H2896
Ezk 16:50 therefore I took them away as I saw g.
17: 8 It was planted in a g soil by great H2896
18:18 *that* which *is* not g among his people, H2896
20:25 statutes *that were* not g, and judgments H2896
24: 4 into it, *even* every g piece, the thigh, H2896
34:14 I will feed them in a g pasture, and H2896
14 shall they lie in a g fold, and *in* a fat H2896
18 to have eaten up the g pasture, but ye H2896
36:31 doings that *were* not g, and shall lothe H2896
Dan 4: 2 I thought it g to shew the signs and H8232
Hos 4:13 the shadow thereof *is* g: therefore your H2896
8: 3 Israel hath cast off *the thing that is* g: H2896
Am 5:14 Seek g, and not evil, that ye may live: H2896
15 Hate the evil, and love the g, and H2896
9: 4 eyes upon them for evil, and not for g. H2896
Mic 1:12 carefully for g: but evil came down H2896
2: 7 do g to him that walketh uprightly? H3190
3: 2 Who hate the g, and love the evil; who H2896
6: 8 He hath shewed thee, O man, what *is* g; H2896
7: 2 The g *man* is perished out of the earth: H2623
Nah 1: 7 The LORD *is* g, a strong hold in the day H2896
15 of him that bringeth g tidings, that H1319
Zep 1:12 will not do g, neither will he do evil. H3190
Zec 1:13 *with* g words *and* comfortable words. H2896
11:12 And I said unto them, If ye think g, give H2896
Mal 2:13 or receiveth *it* with g will at your hand. H7522
17 that doeth evil *is* g in the sight of the H2896
Mt 3:10 bringeth not forth g fruit is hewn down, G2570
5:13 it is thenceforth g for nothing, but to be G2480
16 they may see your g works, and glorify G2570
44 that curse you, do g to them that hate G2573
45 the evil and on the g, and sendeth rain on G18
7:11 If ye then, being evil, know how to give g G18
11 give g things to them that ask him? G18
17 Even so every g tree bringeth forth good G18
17 tree bringeth forth g fruit; but a corrupt G2570
18 A g tree cannot bring forth evil fruit, G18
18 *can* a corrupt tree bring forth g fruit. G2570
19 Every tree that bringeth not forth g G2570
8:30 And there was a g way off from them G3112
9: 2 be of g cheer; thy sins be forgiven thee.
22 Daughter, be of g comfort; thy faith hath
11:26 Even so, Father: for so it seemed g in G2107
12:33 Either make the tree g, and his fruit G2570
33 good, and his fruit g; or else make the G2570
34 being evil, speak g things? for out of the G18
35 A g man out of the good treasure of the G18
35 A good man out of the g treasure of the G18
35 bringeth forth g things: and an evil man G18
13: 8 But other fell into g ground, and G2570
23 But he that received seed into the g G2570
24 a man which sowed g seed in his field: G2570
27 didst not thou sow g seed in thy field? G2570
37 soweth the g seed is the Son of man; G2570
38 The field is the world; the g seed are the G2570
48 g into vessels, but cast the bad away. G2570
14:27 Be of g cheer; it is I; be not afraid.
17: 4 Jesus, Lord, it is g for us to be here: if G2570
19:10 be so with *his* wife, it is not g to marry. G4851
16 and said unto him, G Master, what good G18
16 Good Master, what g thing shall I do, G18
17 callest thou me g? *there is* none good but G18
17 me good? *there is* none g but one, *that is*, G18
20:15 own? Is thine eye evil, because I am g? G18
22:10 both bad and g: and the wedding was G18
25:21 Well done, *thou* g and faithful servant: G18
23 His lord said unto him, Well done, g and G18
26:10 she hath wrought a g work upon me. G2570
24 g for that man if he had not been born. G2570
Mk 3: 4 Is it lawful to do g on the sabbath days, G15
4: 8 And other fell on g ground, and did G2570
20 are sown on g ground; such as hear G2570
6:50 them, Be of g cheer: it is I; be not afraid.
9: 5 Jesus, Master, it is g for us to be here: G2570
50 Salt *is* g: but if the salt have lost his G2570
10:17 and asked him, G Master, what shall I G18
18 callest thou me g? *there is* none good but G18
18 *there is* none g but one, *that is*, God. G18

Mk 10:49 Be of g comfort, rise; he calleth thee.
14: 6 her? she hath wrought a g work on me. G2570
7 do them g: but me ye have not always. G2095
21 man is betrayed! g were it for that man G2570
Lk 1: 3 It seemed g to me also, having had G1380
53 He hath filled the hungry with g things; G18
2:10 I bring you g tidings of great joy, G2097
14 and on earth peace, g will toward men. G2107
3: 9 bringeth not forth g fruit is hewn down, G2570
6: 9 the sabbath days to do g, or to do evil? to G15
27 enemies, do g to them which hate you, G2573
33 And if ye do g to them which do good to G15
33 And if ye do good to them which do g to G15
35 But love ye your enemies, and do g, and G15
38 Give, and it shall be given unto you; g G2570
43 For a g tree bringeth not forth corrupt G2570
43 doth a corrupt tree bring forth g fruit. G2570
45 A g man out of the good treasure of his G18
45 A good man out of the g treasure of his G18
45 forth that which is g; and an evil man out G18
8: 8 And other fell on g ground, and sprang G18
15 But that on the g ground are they, G2570
15 in an honest and g heart, having heard G18
48 And he said unto her, Daughter, be of g
9:33 Jesus, Master, it is g for us to be here: G2570
10:21 Father; for so it seemed g in thy sight. G2107
42 hath chosen that g part, which shall not G18
11:13 If ye then, being evil, know how to give g G18
12:32 g pleasure to give you the kingdom.
14:34 Salt *is* g: but if the salt have lost his G2570
16:25 receivedst thy g things, and likewise G18
18:18 And a certain ruler asked him, saying, G G18
19 g? none *is* good, save one, *that is*, God. G18
19 good? none *is* g, save one, *that is*, God. G18
19:17 And he said unto him, Well, thou g G18
23:50 *and he was* a g man, and a just: G18
Jn 1:46 him, Can there any g thing come out of G18
2:10 doth set forth g wine; and when men G2570
10 thou hast kept the g wine until now. G2570
5:29 that have done g, unto the resurrection G18
7:12 some said, He is a g man: others said, G18
10:11 I am the g shepherd: the good shepherd G2570
11 I am the good shepherd: the g shepherd G2570
14 I am the g shepherd, and know my G2570
32 Jesus answered them, Many g works G2570
33 The Jews answered him, saying, For a g G2570
16:33 be of g cheer; I have overcome the world.
Act 4: 9 If we this day be examined of the g G2108
9:36 of g works and almsdeeds which she did. G18
10:22 feareth God, and of g report among all G18
38 went about doing g, and healing all that G2109
11:24 For he was a g man, and full of the Holy G18
14:17 in that he did g, and gave us rain from G15
15: 7 know how that a g while ago God made
25 It seemed g unto us, being assembled G1380
28 For it seemed g to the Holy Ghost, and G1380
38 But Paul thought not g to take him with G515
18:18 And Paul *after this* tarried *there* yet a g G2425
22:12 the law, having a g report of all the Jews
23: 1 g conscience before God until this day. G18
11 and said, Be of g cheer, Paul: for as thou
27:22 And now I exhort you to be of g cheer:
25 Wherefore, sirs, be of g cheer: for I
36 Then were they all of g cheer, and they
Ro 2:10 g, to the Jew first, and also to the Gentile: G18
3: 8 g may come? whose damnation is just. G18
12 there is none that doeth g, no, not one. G5544
5: 7 a g man some would even dare to die. G18
7:12 the commandment holy, and just, and g. G18
13 Was then that which is g made death G18
13 me by that which is g; that sin by the G18
16 not, I consent unto the law that *it is* g. G2570
18 flesh,) dwelleth no g thing: for to will is G18
18 to perform that which is g I find not. G2570
19 For the g that I would I do not: but the G18
21 I would do g, evil is present with me. G2570
8:28 work together for g to them that love G18
9:11 having done any g or evil, that the G18
10:15 peace, and bring glad tidings of g things! G18
11:24 to nature into a g olive tree: how much G2565
12: 2 prove what *is* that g, and acceptable, and G18
9 which is evil; cleave to that which is g. G18
21 of evil, but overcome evil with g. G18
13: 3 For rulers are not a terror to g works, G18
3 do that which is g, and thou shalt have G18
4 For he is the minister of God to thee for g. G18
14:16 Let not then your g be evil spoken of: G18
21 *It is* g neither to eat flesh, nor to drink G2570
15: 2 *his* neighbour for *his* g to edification. G18

Ro 16:18 own belly; and by g words and fair G5542
19 which is g, and simple concerning evil. G18
1Co 5: 6 Your glorying *is* not g. Know ye not that G2570
7: 1 *It is* g for a man not to touch a woman. G2570
8 It is g for them if they abide even as I. G2570
26 I suppose therefore that this is g for the G2570
26 *I say*, that *it is* g for a man so to be. G2570
15:33 communications corrupt g manners. G5543
2Co 5:10 he hath done, whether *it be* g or bad. G18
6: 8 and g report: as deceivers, and *yet* true; G2162
9: 8 all *things*, may abound to every g work: G18
13:11 Be perfect, be of g comfort, be of one
Gal 4:18 But *it is* g to be zealously affected G2570
18 always in *a* g *thing*, and not only G2570
6: 6 unto him that teacheth in all g things. G18
10 let us do g unto all *men*, especially G18
Eph 1: 5 according to the g pleasure of his will,
9 according to his g pleasure which he
2:10 in Christ Jesus unto g works, which God G18
4:28 the thing which is g, that he may have to G18
29 but that which is g to the use of edifying, G18
6: 7 With g will doing service, as to the G2133
8 Knowing that whatsoever g thing any G18
Php 1: 6 hath begun a g work in you will perform G18
15 envy and strife; and some also of g will: G2107
2:13 both to will and to do of *his* g pleasure.
19 be of g comfort, when I know your state.
4: 8 things *are* of g report; if *there be* any G2163
Col 1:10 fruitful in every g work, and increasing G18
1Th 3: 1 thought it g to be left at Athens alone; G2106
6 and brought us g tidings of your faith G2097
6 and that ye have g remembrance of us G18
5:15 that which is g, both among yourselves, G18
21 all things; hold fast that which is g. G2570
2Th 1:11 calling, and fulfil all the g pleasure of *his*
2:16 consolation and g hope through grace, G18
17 stablish you in every g word and work. G18
1Ti 1: 5 *of* a g conscience, and *of* faith unfeigned: G18
8 But we know that the law *is* g, if a man G2570
18 thou by them mightest war a g warfare; G2570
19 Holding faith, and a g conscience; which G18
2: 3 For this *is* g and acceptable in the sight G2570
10 professing godliness) with g works. G18
3: 1 office of a bishop, he desireth a g work. G2570
2 vigilant, sober, of g behaviour, given to
7 Moreover he must have a g report of G2570
13 to themselves a g degree, and great G2570
4: 4 For every creature of God *is* g, and G2570
6 thou shalt be a g minister of Jesus G2570
6 of faith and of g doctrine, whereunto G2570
5: 4 for that is g and acceptable before God. G2570
10 Well reported of for g works; if she G2570
10 have diligently followed every g work. G18
25 Likewise also the g works *of some* are G2570
6:12 Fight the g fight of faith, lay hold on G2570
12 a g profession before many witnesses. G2570
13 Pilate witnessed a g confession; G2570
18 That they do g, that they be rich in good G14
18 that they be rich in g works, ready to G2570
19 Laying up in store for themselves a g G2570
2Ti 1:14 That g thing which was committed G2570
2: 3 Thou therefore endure hardness, as a g G2570
21 use, *and* prepared unto every g work. G18
3: 3 fierce, despisers of those that are g, G865
17 throughly furnished unto all g works. G18
4: 7 I have fought a g fight, I have finished G2570
Tit 1: 8 But a lover of hospitality, a lover of g G5358
16 and unto every g work reprobate. G18
2: 3 to much wine, teachers of g things; G2567
5 keepers at home, g, obedient to their own G18
7 thyself a pattern of g works: in doctrine G2570
10 Not purloining, but shewing all g G18
14 a peculiar people, zealous of g works. G2570
3: 1 magistrates, to be ready to every g work, G18
8 to maintain g works. These things G2570
8 things are g and profitable unto men. G2570
14 And let ours also learn to maintain g G2570
Phlm 6 g thing which is in you in Christ Jesus. G18
Heb 5:14 exercised to discern both g and evil. G2570
6: 5 And have tasted the g word of God, G2570
9:11 But Christ being come an high priest of g G18
10: 1 For the law having a shadow of g things G18
24 to provoke unto love and to g works: G2570
11: 2 For by it the elders obtained a g report.
12 of one, and him as g as dead, *so many* as
39 And these all, having obtained a g report
13: 9 For *it is* a g thing that the heart G2570
16 But to do g and to communicate forget G2140
18 Pray for us: for we trust we have a g G2570

Heb 13:21 Make you perfect in every g work to do G18
Jas 1:17 Every g gift and every perfect gift is from G18
2: 3 Sit thou here in a g place; and say to G2573
3:13 him shew out of a g conversation his G2570
17 full of mercy and g fruits, without G18
4:17 Therefore to him that knoweth to do g, G2570
1Pt 2:12 they may by your g works, which they G2570
18 the g and gentle, but also to the froward. G18
3:10 For he that will love life, and see g days, G18
11 Let him eschew evil, and do g; let him G18
13 you, if ye be followers of that which is g? G18
16 Having a g conscience; that, whereas G18
16 accuse your g conversation in Christ. G18
21 but the answer of a g conscience toward G18
4:10 one to another, as g stewards of the G2570
1Jn 3:17 But whoso hath this world's g, and seeth G979
3Jn 11 but that which is g. He that doeth good is G18
11 He that doeth g is of God: but he that G15
12 Demetrius hath g report of all men, and

GOODLIER
1Sa 9: 2 of Israel a g person than he: from H2896

GOODLIEST
1Sa 8:16 and your g young men, and your H2896
1Ki 20: 3 and thy children, even the g, are mine. H2896

GOODLINESS
Isa 40: 6 g thereof is as the flower of the field: H2617

GOODLY
Gen 27:15 And Rebekah took g raiment of her H2532
39: 6 a g person, and well favoured. H3303+H8389
49:21 Naphtali is a hind let loose: he giveth g H8233
Ex 2: 2 a g child, she hid him three months. H2896
39:28 And a mitre of fine linen, and g H6287
Lev 23:40 day the boughs of g trees, branches of H1926
Nu 24: 5 How g are thy tents, O Jacob, and thy H2895
31:10 dwelt, and all their g castles, with fire.
Dt 3:25 Jordan, that g mountain, and Lebanon. H2896
6:10 and g cities, which thou buildedst not, H2896
8:12 hast built g houses, and dwelt therein; H2896
Jos 7:21 When I saw among the spoils a g H2896
1Sa 9: 2 young man, and a g: and there was not H2896
16:12 countenance, and g to look to. And the H2896
2Sa 23:21 And he slew an Egyptian, a g man: and H4758
1Ki 1: 6 and he also was a very g man; and his H2896
2Ch 36:10 Babylon, with the g vessels of the house H2532
19 and destroyed all the g vessels thereof. H4261
Job 39:13 Gavest thou the g wings unto the H7443
Ps 16: 6 places; yea, I have a g heritage. H8231
80:10 boughs thereof were like the g cedars. H410
Jer 3:19 thee a pleasant land, a g heritage of the H6643
11:16 tree, fair, and of g fruit: with the noise H8389
Ezk 17: 8 bear fruit, that it might be a g vine. H155
23 bear fruit, and be a g cedar: and under it H117
Hos 10: 1 of his land they have made g images. H2895
Joel 3: 5 your temples my g pleasant things: H2896
Zec 10: 3 made them as his g horse in the battle. H1935
11:13 it unto the potter: a g price that I was H145
Mt 13:45 a merchant man, seeking g pearls: G2570
Lk 21: 5 with g stones and gifts, he said, G2570
Jas 2: 2 a gold ring, in g apparel, and there G2986
Rev 18:14 were dainty and g are departed from G2986

GOODMAN
Prv 7:19 For the g is not at home, he is gone a H376
Mt 20:11 murmured against the g of the house, G3617
24:43 But know this, that if the g of the house G3617
Mk 14:14 go in, say ye to the g of the house, The G3617
Lk 12:39 And this know, that if the g of the G3617
22:11 And ye shall say unto the g of the G3617

GOODNESS
Ex 18: 9 And Jethro rejoiced for all the g which H2896
33:19 And he said, I will make all my g pass H2898
34: 6 and abundant in g and truth, H2617
Nu 10:32 shall be, that what g the LORD shall do H2896
Jdg 8:35 the g which he had shewed unto Israel. H2896
2Sa 7:28 hast promised this g unto thy servant: H2896
1Ki 8:66 of heart for all the g that the LORD had H2896
1Ch 17:26 hast promised this g unto thy servant: H2896
2Ch 6:41 salvation, and let thy saints rejoice in g. H2896
7:10 in heart for the g that the LORD had H2896
32:32 of Hezekiah, and his g, behold, they are H2617
35:26 of Josiah, and his g, according to that H2617
Neh 9:25 and delighted themselves in thy great g. H2898
35 and in thy great g that thou gavest H2898
Ps 16: 2 my Lord: my g extendeth not to thee; H2896
21: 3 the blessings of g: thou settest a crown H2896
23: 6 Surely g and mercy shall follow me all H2896
27:13 g of the LORD in the land of the living. H2898
31:19 Oh how great is thy g, which thou hast H2898
33: 5 the earth is full of the g of the LORD. H2617
52: 1 the g of God endureth continually. H2617
65: 4 g of thy house, even of thy holy temple. H2898
11 Thou crownest the year with thy g; and H2896
68:10 hast prepared of thy g for the poor. H2896
107: 8 praise the LORD for his g, and for his H2617
9 soul, and filleth the hungry soul with g. H2896
15 praise the LORD for his g, and for his H2617
21 praise the LORD for his g, and for his H2617
31 praise the LORD for his g, and for his H2617
144: 2 My g, and my fortress; my high tower, H2617
145: 7 g, and shall sing of thy righteousness. H2898
Prv 20: 6 own g: but a faithful man who can find? H2617
Isa 63: 7 us, and the great g toward the house of H2898
Jer 2: 7 thereof and the g thereof; but when ye H2898
31:12 flow together to the g of the LORD, for H2898
14 be satisfied with my g, saith the LORD. H2898
33: 9 and tremble for all the g and for all the H2896
Hos 3: 5 the LORD and his g in the latter days. H2898
6: 4 thee? for your g is as a morning cloud, H2617
10: 1 according to the g of his land they have H2896
Zec 9:17 For how great is his g, and how great is H2898
Ro 2: 4 Or despisest thou the riches of his g G5544
4 g of God leadeth thee to repentance? G5543
11:22 Behold therefore the g and severity of G5544
22 but toward thee, g, if thou continue in G5544
22 g: otherwise thou also shalt be cut off. G5544
15:14 that ye also are full of g, filled with all G19
Gal 5:22 peace, longsuffering, gentleness, g, faith, G19
Eph 5: 9 (For the fruit of the Spirit is in all g and G19
2Th 1:11 his g, and the work of faith with power: G19

GOODNESS'
Ps 25: 7 thou me for thy g sake, O LORD. H2898

GOODS
Gen 14:11 And they took all the g of Sodom and H7399
12 in Sodom, and his g, and departed. H7399
16 And he brought back all the g, and also H7399
16 g, and the women also, and the people. H7399
21 the persons, and take the g to thyself. H7399
24:10 for all the g of his master were in H2898
31:18 his cattle, and all his g which he had H7399
46: 6 And they took their cattle, and their g, H7399
Ex 22: 8 put his hand unto his neighbour's g. H4399
11 his neighbour's g; and the owner of it H4399
Nu 16:32 appertained unto Korah, and all their g. H7399
31: 9 and all their flocks, and all their g. H2428
35: 3 and for their g, and for all their beasts. H7399
Dt 28:11 thee plenteous in g, in the fruit of thy H2896
2Ch 21:14 children, and thy wives, and all thy g: H7399
Ezr 1: 4 with gold, and with g, and with beasts, H7399
6 with gold, with g, and with beasts, and H7399
6: 8 that of the king's g, even of the tribute H5232
7:26 confiscation of g, or to imprisonment. H5232
Neh 9:25 houses full of all g, wells digged, H2898
Job 20:10 poor, and his hands shall restore their g. H202
21 therefore shall no man look for his g. H2898
28 g shall flow away in the day of his wrath.
Ecc 5:11 When g increase, they are increased H2896
Ezk 38:12 g, that dwell in the midst of the land. H7075
13 away cattle and g, to take a great spoil? H7075
Zep 1:13 Therefore their g shall become a booty, H2428
Mt 12:29 and spoil his g, except he first bind G4632
24:47 he shall make him ruler over all his g. G5224
25:14 servants, and delivered unto them his g. G5224
Mk 3:27 and spoil his g, except he will first bind G4632
Lk 6:30 taketh away thy g ask them not again. G4674
11:21 keepeth his palace, his g are in peace: G5224
12:18 there will I bestow all my fruits and my g. G18
19 Soul, thou hast much g laid up for many G18
15:12 me the portion of g that falleth to me. G3776
16: 1 unto him that he had wasted his g. G5224
19: 8 the half of my g I give to the poor; and G5224
Act 2:45 And sold their possessions and g, and G5223
1Co 13: 3 And though I bestow all my g to feed G5224
Heb 10:34 the spoiling of your g, knowing in G5224
Rev 3:17 and increased with g, and have need of G4147

GOPHER
Gen 6:14 Make thee an ark of g wood; rooms H1613

GOPHER-WOOD
See GOPHER and WOOD.

GORE
Ex 21:28 If an ox g a man or a woman, that they H5055

GORED
Ex 21:31 Whether he have g a son, or have gored H5055
31 Whether he have gored a son, or have g H5055

GORGEOUS
Lk 23:11 a g robe, and sent him again to Pilate. G2986

GORGEOUSLY
Ezk 23:12 clothed most g, horsemen riding upon H4358
Lk 7:25 they which are g apparelled, and live G1741

GOSHEN
Gen 45:10 And thou shalt dwell in the land of G, H1657
46:28 his face unto G; and they came into H1657
28 and they came into the land of G. H1657
29 his father, to G, and presented himself H1657
34 in the land of G; for every shepherd H1657
47: 1 and, behold, they are in the land of G. H1657
4 let thy servants dwell in the land of G. H1657
6 in the land of G let them dwell: and H1657
27 Egypt, in the country of G; and they had H1657
50: 8 their herds, they left in the land of G. H1657
Ex 8:22 day the land of G, in which my people H1657
9:26 Only in the land of G, where the H1657
Jos 10:41 all the country of G, even unto Gibeon. H1657
11:16 and all the land of G, and the valley, H1657
15:51 And G, and Holon, and Giloh; eleven H1657

GOSPEL
Mt 4:23 and preaching the g of the kingdom, G2098
9:35 and preaching the g of the kingdom, G2098
11: 5 the poor have the g preached to them. G2098
24:14 And this g of the kingdom shall be G2098
26:13 Wheresoever this g shall be preached G2098
Mk 1: 1 The beginning of the g of Jesus Christ, G2098
14 preaching the g of the kingdom of God, G2098
15 is at hand: repent ye, and believe the g. G2098
13:10 And the g must first be published G2098
14: 9 Wheresoever this g shall be preached G2098
16:15 and preach the g to every creature. G2098
Lk 4:18 me to preach the g to the poor; he hath G2097
7:22 raised, to the poor the g is preached. G2097
9: 6 the g, and healing every where. G2097
20: 1 and preached the g, the chief priests G2097
Act 8:25 g in many villages of the Samaritans. G2097
14: 7 And there they preached the g. G2258
21 And when they had preached the g to G2097
15: 7 hear the word of the g, and believe. G2098
16:10 called us for to preach the g unto them. G2097
20:24 to testify the g of the grace of God. G2098
Ro 1: 1 apostle, separated unto the g of God, G2098
9 with my spirit in the g of his Son, that G2098
15 the g to you that are at Rome also. G2097
16 For I am not ashamed of the g of G2098
2:16 men by Jesus Christ according to my g. G2098
10:15 that preach the g of peace, and bring G2097
16 But they have not all obeyed the g. For G2098
11:28 As concerning the g, they are enemies G2098
15:16 ministering the g of God, that the G2098
19 I have fully preached the g of Christ. G2098
20 Yea, so have I strived to preach the g, G2097
29 of the blessing of the g of Christ. G2098
16:25 according to my g, and the preaching of G2098
1Co 1:17 but to preach the g: not with wisdom of G2097
4:15 Jesus I have begotten you through the g. G2098
9:12 lest we should hinder the g of Christ. G2098
14 preach the g should live of the gospel. G2098
14 preach the gospel should live of the g. G2098
16 For though I preach the g, I have G2097
16 woe is unto me, if I preach not the g! G2097
17 of the g is committed unto me.
18 when I preach the g, I may make the G2097
18 I may make the g of Christ without G2098
18 that I abuse not my power in the g. G2098
15: 1 unto you the g which I preached unto G2098
2Co 2:12 to preach Christ's g, and a door was G2098
4: 3 But if our g be hid, it is hid to them that G2098
4 of the glorious g of Christ, who is the G2098
8:18 is in the g throughout all the churches; G2098
9:13 unto the g of Christ, and for your G2098
10:14 to you also in preaching the g of Christ: G2098
16 To preach the g in the regions beyond G2097
11: 4 or another g, which ye have not G2098
7 preached to you the g of God freely? G2098
Gal 1: 6 into the grace of Christ unto another g: G2098
7 you, and would pervert the g of Christ. G2098

Gal 1: 8 preach any other g unto you than that G2097
9 preach any other g unto you than that G2097
11 But I certify you, brethren, that the g G2098
2: 2 unto them that g which I preach G2098
5 truth of the g might continue with you. G2098
7 when they saw that the g of the G2098
7 *the* g of the circumcision *was* unto Peter;
14 to the truth of the g, I said unto Peter G2098
3: 8 before the g unto Abraham, *saying*, G4283
4:13 I preached the g unto you at the first. G2097
Eph 1:13 word of truth, the g of your salvation: G2098
3: 6 of his promise in Christ by the g: G2098
6:15 with the preparation of the g of peace; G2098
19 to make known the mystery of the g, G2098
Php 1: 5 For your fellowship in the g from the G2098
7 the g, ye all are partakers of my grace. G2098
12 out rather unto the furtherance of the g; G2098
17 that I am set for the defence of the g. G2098
27 be as it becometh the g of Christ: that G2098
27 striving together for the faith of the g; G2098
2:22 father, he hath served with me in the g. G2098
4: 3 with me in the g, with Clement also, G2098
15 the beginning of the g, when I departed G2098
Col 1: 5 before in the word of the truth of the g; G2098
23 the hope of the g, which ye have heard, G2098
1Th 1: 5 For our g came not unto you in word G2098
2: 2 you the g of God with much contention. G2098
4 in trust with the g, even so we speak; G2098
8 unto you, not the g of God only, but G2098
9 we preached unto you the g of God. G2098
3: 2 in the g of Christ, to establish G2098
2Th 1: 8 obey not the g of our Lord Jesus Christ: G2098
2:14 Whereunto he called you by our g, to G2098
1Ti 1:11 According to the glorious g of the G2098
2Ti 1: 8 of the g according to the power of God; G2098
10 and immortality to light through the g: G2098
2: 8 raised from the dead according to my g: G2098
Phlm 13 unto me in the bonds of the g: G2098
Heb 4: 2 For unto us was the g preached, as well G2097
1Pt 1:12 have preached the g unto you with the G2097
25 which by the g is preached unto you. G2097
4: 6 For for this cause was the g preached G2097
17 *be* of them that obey not the g of God? G2098
Rev 14: 6 the everlasting g to preach unto them G2098

GOSPEL'S
Mk 8:35 sake and the g, the same shall save it. G2098
10:29 or lands, for my sake, and the g, G2098
1Co 9:23 And this I do for the g sake, that I G2098

GOT
Gen 36: 6 which he had g in the land of Canaan; H7408
39:12 in her hand, and fled, and g him out. H3318
15 with me, and fled, and g him out. H3318
Ps 44: 3 For they g not the land in possession by H3423
Ecc 2: 7 I g *me* servants and maidens, and had H7069
Jer 13: 2 So I g a girdle according to the word of H7069
4 Take the girdle that thou hast g, which H7069

GOTTEN
Gen 4: 1 said, I have g a man from the LORD. H7069
12: 5 that they had g in Haran; and they H6213
31: 1 *was* our father's hath he g all this glory. H6213
18 which he had g, the cattle of his getting, H7408
18 which he had g in Padan-aram, for H7408
46: 6 goods, which they had g in the land of H7408
Ex 14:18 when I have g me honour upon Pharaoh,
Lev 6: 4 he hath deceitfully g, or that which was H6231
Nu 31:50 every man hath g, of jewels of gold, H4672
Dt 8:17 of *mine* hand hath g me this wealth. H6213
2Sa 17:13 Moreover, if he be g into a city, then H622
Job 28:15 It cannot be g for gold, neither shall H5414
31:25 and because mine hand had g much; H4672
Ps 98: 1 and his holy arm, hath g him the victory.
Prv 13:11 Wealth g by vanity shall be diminished:
20:21 An inheritance *may be* g hastily at the
Ecc 1:16 estate, and have g more wisdom than H3254
Isa 15: 7 Therefore the abundance they have g, H6213
Jer 48:36 the riches *that* he hath g are perished. H6213
Ezk 28: 4 thou hast g thee riches, and hast H6213
4 g gold and silver into thy treasures: H6213
38:12 which have g cattle and goods, that H6213
Dan 9:15 hand, and hast g thee renown, as at H6213
Act 21: 1 And it came to pass, that after we were g G645
Rev 15: 2 and them that had g the victory over the

GOURD
Jna 4: 6 And the LORD God prepared a g, and H7021
6 So Jonah was exceeding glad of the g. H7021
7 day, and it smote the g that it withered. H7021
9 to be angry for the g? And he said, I do H7021
10 had pity on the g, for the which thou H7021

GOURDS
2Ki 4:39 thereof wild g his lap full, and came H6498

GOVERN
1Ki 21: 7 Dost thou now g the kingdom of Israel? H6213
Job 34:17 Shall even he that hateth right g? and H2280
Ps 67: 4 and g the nations upon earth. Selah. H5148

GOVERNMENT
Isa 9: 6 is given: and the g shall be upon his H4951
7 Of the increase of *his* g and peace *there* H4951
22:21 I will commit thy g into his hand: and H4475
2Pt 2:10 and despise g. Presumptuous *are they*, G2963

GOVERNMENTS
1Co 12:28 helps, g, diversities of tongues. G2941

GOVERNOR
Gen 42: 6 And Joseph *was* the g over the land, H7989
45:26 yet alive, and he *is* g over all the land of H4910
1Ki 18: 3 which *was* the g of *his* house. (Now H5921
22:26 unto Amon the g of the city, and to H8269
2Ki 23: 8 gate of Joshua the g of the city, which H8269
25:23 had made Gedaliah g, there came to H6485
1Ch 29:22 *to be* the chief g, and Zadok *to be* priest. H5057
2Ch 1: 2 g in all Israel, the chief of the fathers. H5387
18:25 back to Amon the g of the city, and to H8269
28: 7 and Azrikam the g of the house, and H5057
34: 8 and Maaseiah the g of the city, and H8269
Ezr 5: 3 to them Tatnai, g on this side the river, H6347
6 The copy of the letter that Tatnai, g on H6347
14 Sheshbazzar, whom he had made g; H6347
6: 6 Now *therefore*, Tatnai, g beyond the H6347
7 God alone; let the g of the Jews and the H6347
13 Then Tatnai, g on this side the river, H6347
Neh 3: 7 throne of the g on this side the river. H6346
5:14 to be their g in the land of Judah, H6346
14 have not eaten the bread of the g. H6346
18 not I the bread of the g, because the H6346
12:26 the g, and of Ezra the priest, the scribe. H6346
Ps 22:28 and he *is* the g among the nations. H4910
Jer 20: 1 who *was* also chief g in the house of the H6496
30:21 and their g shall proceed from H4910
40: 5 hath made g over the cities of Judah, H6485
7 the son of Ahikam g in the land, and H6485
41: 2 of Babylon had made g over the land. H6485
18 the king of Babylon made g in the land. H6485
Hag 1: 1 the son of Shealtiel, g of Judah, and to H6346
14 the son of Shealtiel, g of Judah, and the H6346
2: 2 the son of Shealtiel, g of Judah, and to H6346
21 Speak to Zerubbabel, g of Judah, H6346
Zec 9: 7 as a g in Judah, and Ekron as a Jebusite. H441
Mal 1: 8 it now unto thy g; will he be pleased H6346
Mt 2: 6 a G, that shall rule my people Israel. G2233
27: 2 delivered him to Pontius Pilate the g. G2232
11 And Jesus stood before the g: and the G2232
11 governor: and the g asked him, saying, G2232
14 insomuch that the g marvelled greatly. G2232
15 Now at *that* feast the g was wont to G2232
21 The g answered and said unto them, G2232
23 And the g said, Why, what evil hath he G2232
27 Then the soldiers of the g took Jesus G2232
Lk 2: 2 made when Cyrenius was g of Syria.) G2230
3: 1 Pilate being g of Judaea, and Herod G2230
20:20 unto the power and authority of the g. G2232
Jn 2: 8 unto the g of the feast. And they bare *it*. G755
9 the g of the feast called the bridegroom, G755
Act 7:10 him g over Egypt and all his house. G2233
23:24 on, and bring *him* safe unto Felix the g. G2232
26 most excellent g Felix *sendeth* greeting. G2232
33 the g, presented Paul also before him. G2232
34 And when the g had read *the letter*, he G2232
24: 1 who informed the g against Paul. G2232
10 Then Paul, after that the g had G2232
26:30 rose up, and the g, and Bernice, and G2232
2Co 11:32 In Damascus the g under Aretas the G1481
Jas 3: 4 small helm, whithersoever the g listeth. G3730

GOVERNORS
Jdg 5: 9 My heart *is* toward the g of Israel, that H2710
14 came down g, and out of Zebulun H2710
1Ki 10:15 of Arabia, and of the g of the country. H6346
1Ch 24: 5 another; for the g of the sanctuary, and H8269
5 sanctuary, and g *of the house* of God, H8269
2Ch 9:14 of Arabia and g of the country brought H6346
23:20 nobles, and the g of the people, and all H4910
Ezr 8:36 and to the g on this side the river: H6346
Neh 2: 7 be given me to the g beyond the river, H6346
9 Then I came to the g beyond the river, H6346
5:15 But the former g that *had been* before H6346
Est 3:12 and to the g that *were* over every H6346
Dan 2:48 the g over all the wise *men* of Babylon. H5460
3: 2 the princes, the g, and the captains, the H5460
3 Then the princes, the g, and captains, H5460
27 And the princes, g, and captains, and H5460
6: 7 All the presidents of the kingdom, the g, H5460
Zec 12: 5 And the g of Judah shall say in their H441
6 In that day will I make the g of Judah H441
Mt 10:18 And ye shall be brought before g and G2232
Gal 4: 2 But is under tutors and g until the time G3623
1Pt 2:14 Or unto g, as unto them that are sent by G2232

GOVERNOR'S
Mt 28:14 And if this come to the g ears, we will G2232

GOZAN
2Ki 17: 6 of G, and in the cities of the Medes. H1470
18:11 of G, and in the cities of the Medes: H1470
19:12 have destroyed; *as* G, and Haran, and H1470
1Ch 5:26 Hara, and to the river G, unto this day. H1470
Isa 37:12 have destroyed, *as* G, and Haran, and H1470

GRACE
Gen 6: 8 But Noah found g in the eyes of the H2580
19:19 Behold now, thy servant hath found g H2580
32: 5 my lord, that I may find g in thy sight. H2580
33: 8 *are* to find g in the sight of my lord. H2580
10 if now I have found g in thy sight, then H2580
15 it? let me find g in the sight of my lord. H2580
34:11 Let me find g in your eyes, and what H2580
39: 4 And Joseph found g in his sight, and he H2580
47:25 our lives: let us find g in the sight of my H2580
29 If now I have found g in thy sight, put, I H2580
50: 4 now I have found g in your eyes, speak, H2580
Ex 33:12 and thou hast also found g in my sight. H2580
13 if I have found g in thy sight, shew me H2580
13 thee, that I may find g in thy sight: and H2580
16 people have found g in thy sight? *is it* H2580
17 for thou hast found g in my sight, and I H2580
34: 9 And he said, If now I have found g in H2580
Nu 32: 5 if we have found g in thy sight, let this H2580
Jdg 6:17 If now I have found g in thy sight, then H2580
Ru 2: 2 sight I shall find g. And she said unto H2580
10 Why have I found g in thine eyes, that H2580
1Sa 1:18 handmaid find g in thy sight. So the H2580
20: 3 that I have found g in thine eyes; and H2580
27: 5 If I have now found g in thine eyes, let H2580
2Sa 14:22 that I have found g in thy sight, my H2580
16: 4 find g in thy sight, my lord, O king. H2580
Ezr 9: 8 And now for a little space g hath been H8467
Est 2:17 and she obtained g and favour in his H2580
Ps 45: 2 children of men: g is poured into thy H2580
84:11 the LORD will give g and glory: no H2580
Prv 1: 9 For they *shall be* an ornament of g H2580
3:22 So shall they be life unto thy soul, and g H2580
34 but he giveth g unto the lowly. H2580
4: 9 an ornament of g: a crown of glory shall H2580
22:11 g of his lips the king *shall be* his friend. H2580
Jer 31: 2 of the sword found g in the wilderness; H2580
Zec 4: 7 *with* shoutings, *crying*, G, grace unto it. H2580
7 *with* shoutings, *crying*, Grace, g unto it. H2580
12:10 the spirit of g and of supplications: H2580
Lk 2:40 and the g of God was upon him. G5485
Jn 1:14 of the Father,) full of g and truth. G5485
16 have all we received, and g for grace. G5485
16 have all we received, and grace for g. G5485
17 For the law was given by Moses, *but* g G5485
Act 4:33 Jesus: and great g was upon them all. G5485
11:23 and had seen the g of God, was glad, G5485
13:43 them to continue in the g of God. G5485
14: 3 the word of his g, and granted signs and G5485
26 to the g of God for the work G5485
15:11 But we believe that through the g of the G5485
40 by the brethren unto the g of God. G5485
18:27 much which had believed through g: G5485
20:24 to testify the gospel of the g of God. G5485
32 to the word of his g, which is able to G5485
Ro 1: 5 By whom we have received g and G5485
7 *to be* saints: G to you and peace from G5485
3:24 Being justified freely by his g through G5485
4: 4 reward not reckoned of g, but of debt. G5485
16 that *it might be* by g; to the end the G5485
5: 2 by faith into this g wherein we stand, G5485
15 much more the g of God, and the gift G5485

Ro 5:15 and the gift by **g**, *which is* by one man, G5485
17 abundance of **g** and of the gift of G5485
20 abounded, **g** did much more abound: G5485
21 death, even so might **g** reign through G5485
6: 1 we continue in sin, that **g** may abound? G5485
14 ye are not under the law, but under **g**. G5485
15 under the law, but under **g**? God forbid. G5485
11: 5 remnant according to the election of **g**. G5485
6 And if by **g**, then *is it* no more of works: G5485
6 of works: otherwise **g** is no more grace. G5485
6 grace is no more **g**. But if *it be* of works, G5485
6 **g**: otherwise work is no more work. G5485
12: 3 For I say, through the **g** given unto me, G5485
6 according to the **g** that is given to us, G5485
15:15 of the **g** that is given to me of God, G5485
16:20 feet shortly. The **g** of our Lord Jesus G5485
24 The **g** of our Lord Jesus Christ *be* with G5485
1Co 1: 3 **G** *be* unto you, and peace, from God G5485
4 behalf, for the **g** of God which is given G5485
3:10 According to the **g** of God which is G5485
10:30 For if I by **g** be a partaker, why am I G5485
15:10 But by the **g** of God I am what I am: G5485
10 I am: and his **g** which *was bestowed* G5485
10 I, but the **g** of God which was with me. G5485
16:23 The **g** of our Lord Jesus Christ *be* with G5485
2Co 1: 2 **G** *be* to you and peace from God our G5485
12 but by the **g** of God, we have had G5485
4:15 that the abundant **g** might through the G5485
6: 1 that ye receive not the **g** of God in vain. G5485
8: 1 you to wit of the **g** of God bestowed on G5485
6 also finish in you the same **g** also. G5485
7 to us, *see* that ye abound in this **g** also. G5485
9 For ye know the **g** of our Lord Jesus G5485
19 travel with us with this **g**, which is G5485
9: 8 And God *is* able to make all **g** abound G5485
14 you for the exceeding **g** of God in you. G5485
12: 9 And he said unto me, My **g** is sufficient G5485
13:14 The **g** of the Lord Jesus Christ, and the G5485
Gal 1: 3 **G** *be* to you and peace from God the G5485
6 the **g** of Christ unto another gospel: G5485
15 mother's womb, and called *me* by his **g**, G5485
2: 9 perceived the **g** that was given unto G5485
21 I do not frustrate the **g** of God: for if G5485
5: 4 justified by the law; ye are fallen from **g**. G5485
6:18 Brethren, the **g** of our Lord Jesus Christ G5485
Eph 1: 2 **G** *be* to you, and peace, from God our G5485
6 To the praise of the glory of his **g**, G5485
7 of sins, according to the riches of his **g**; G5485
2: 5 with Christ, (by **g** ye are saved;) G5485
7 riches of his **g** in *his* kindness toward G5485
8 For by **g** are ye saved through faith; G5485
3: 2 of the **g** of God which is given G5485
7 to the gift of the **g** of God given unto me G5485
8 least of all saints, is this **g** given, that I G5485
4: 7 But unto every one of us is given **g** G5485
29 that it may minister **g** unto the hearers. G5485
6:24 **G** *be* with all them that love our Lord G5485
Php 1: 2 **G** *be* unto you, and peace, from God G5485
7 the gospel, ye all are partakers of my **g**. G5485
4:23 The **g** of our Lord Jesus Christ *be* with G5485
Col 1: 2 are at Colosse: **G** *be* unto you, and G5485
6 *of it*, and knew the **g** of God in truth: G5485
3:16 with **g** in your hearts to the Lord. G5485
4: 6 Let your speech *be* alway with **g**, G5485
18 my bonds. **G** *be* with you. Amen. G5485
1Th 1: 1 Lord Jesus Christ: **G** *be* unto you, and G5485
5:28 The **g** of our Lord Jesus Christ *be* with G5485
2Th 1: 2 **G** unto you, and peace, from God our G5485
12 **g** of our God and the Lord Jesus Christ. G5485
2:16 consolation and good hope through **g**, G5485
3:18 The **g** of our Lord Jesus Christ *be* with G5485
1Ti 1: 2 son in the faith: **G**, mercy, *and* peace, G5485
14 And the **g** of our Lord was exceeding G5485
6:21 the faith. **G** *be* with thee. Amen. G5485
2Ti 1: 2 To Timothy, *my* dearly beloved son: **G**, G5485
9 own purpose and **g**, which was given us G5485
2: 1 strong in the **g** that is in Christ Jesus. G5485
4:22 with thy spirit. **G** *be* with you. Amen. G5485
Tit 1: 4 the common faith: **G**, mercy, *and* peace, G5485
2:11 For the **g** of God that bringeth salvation G5485
3: 7 That being justified by his **g**, we should G5485
15 us in the faith. **G** *be* with you all. Amen. G5485
Phlm 3 **G** to you, and peace, from God our G5485
25 The **g** of our Lord Jesus Christ *be* with G5485
Heb 2: 9 that he by the **g** of God should taste G5485
4:16 boldly unto the throne of **g**, that we may G5485
16 and find **g** to help in time of need. G5485
10:29 hath done despite unto the Spirit of **g**? G5485
12:15 man fail of the **g** of God; lest any root G5485
Heb 12:28 moved, let us have **g**, whereby we may G5485
13: 9 be established with **g**; not with meats, G5485
25 **G** *be* with you all. Amen. G5485
Jas 1:11 falleth, and the **g** of the fashion of it G2143
4: 6 But he giveth more **g**. Wherefore he G5485
6 proud, but giveth **g** unto the humble. G5485
1Pt 1: 2 **G** unto you, and peace, be multiplied. G5485
10 of the **g** *that should come* unto you: G5485
13 hope to the end for the **g** that is to be G5485
3: 7 heirs together of the **g** of life; that your G5485
4:10 stewards of the manifold **g** of God. G5485
5: 5 the proud, and giveth **g** to the humble. G5485
10 But the God of all **g**, who hath called us G5485
12 is the true **g** of God wherein ye stand. G5485
2Pt 1: 2 **G** and peace be multiplied unto you G5485
3:18 But grow in **g**, and *in* the knowledge of G5485
2Jn 3 **G** be with you, mercy, *and* peace, from G5485
Jude 4 men, turning the **g** of our God into G5485
Rev 1: 4 which are in Asia: **G** *be* unto you, and G5485
22:21 The **g** of our Lord Jesus Christ *be* with G5485

GRACIOUS
Gen 43:29 he said, God be **g** unto thee, my son. H2603
Ex 22:27 unto me, that I will hear; for I *am* **g**. H2587
33:19 thee; and will be **g** to whom I will be H2603
19 to whom I will be **g**, and will shew H2603
34: 6 God, merciful and **g**, longsuffering, and H2587
Nu 6:25 shine upon thee, and be **g** unto thee: H2603
2Sa 12:22 will be **g** to me, that the child may live? H2603
2Ki 13:23 And the LORD was **g** unto them, and H2603
2Ch 30: 9 LORD your God *is* **g** and merciful, and H2587
Neh 9:17 ready to pardon, **g** and merciful, slow H2587
31 for thou *art* a **g** and merciful God. H2587
Job 33:24 Then he is **g** unto him, and saith, H2603
Ps 77: 9 Hath God forgotten to be **g**? hath he in H2589
86:15 compassion, and **g**, longsuffering, and H2587
103: 8 The LORD *is* merciful and **g**, slow to H2587
111: 4 the LORD *is* **g** and full of compassion. H2587
112: 4 in the darkness: *he is* **g**, and full of H2587
116: 5 **G** *is* the LORD, and righteous; yea, our H2587
145: 8 The LORD *is* **g**, and full of compassion; H2587
Prv 11:16 A **g** woman retaineth honour: and H2580
Ecc 10:12 The words of a wise man's mouth *are* **g**; H2580
Isa 30:18 wait, that he may be **g** unto you, and H2603
19 he will be very **g** unto thee at the voice H2603
33: 2 O LORD, be **g** unto us; we have waited H2603
Jer 22:23 in the cedars, how **g** shalt thou be when H2603
Joel 2:13 your God: for he *is* **g** and merciful, slow H2587
Am 5:15 will be **g** unto the remnant of Joseph. H2603
Jna 4: 2 that thou *art* a **g** God, and merciful, H2587
Mal 1: 9 that he will be **g** unto us: this hath been H2603
Lk 4:22 and wondered at the **g** words which G5485
1Pt 2: 3 If so be ye have tasted that the Lord *is* **g**. G5543

GRACIOUSLY
Gen 33: 5 which God hath **g** given thy servant. H2603
11 God hath dealt **g** with me, and because H2603
Ps 119:29 way of lying: and grant me thy law **g**. H2603
Hos 14: 2 and receive *us* **g**: so will we render the H2896

GRAFF
Ro 11:23 in: for God is able to **g** them in again. G1461

GRAFFED
Ro 11:17 olive tree, wert **g** in among them, and G1461
19 were broken off, that I might be **g** in. G1461
23 unbelief, shall be **g** in: for God is able to G1461
24 nature, and wert **g** contrary to nature G1461
24 be **g** into their own olive tree? G1461

GRAFT See GRAFF.

GRAIN
Am 9: 9 shall not the least **g** fall upon the earth. H6872
Mt 13:31 of heaven is like to a **g** of mustard seed, G2848
17:20 ye have faith as a **g** of mustard seed, ye G2848
Mk 4:31 *It is* like a **g** of mustard seed, which, G2848
Lk 13:19 It is like a **g** of mustard seed, which a G2848
17: 6 And the Lord said, If ye had faith as a **g** G2848
1Co 15:37 shall be, but bare **g**, it may chance of G2848
37 may chance of wheat, or of some other **g**:

GRANDMOTHER
2Ti 1: 5 which dwelt first in thy **g** Lois, and thy G3125

GRANT
Lev 25:24 ye shall **g** a redemption for the land. H5414
Ru 1: 9 The LORD **g** you that ye may find rest, H5414
1Sa 1:17 the God of Israel **g** *thee* thy petition H5414
1Ch 21:22 Then David said to Ornan, **G** me the H5414
22 the LORD: thou shalt **g** it me for the full H5414
2Ch 12: 7 destroy them, but I will **g** them some H5414
Ezr 3: 7 **g** that they had of Cyrus king of Persia. H7558
Neh 1:11 this day, and **g** him mercy in the sight H5414
Est 5: 8 please the king to **g** my petition, and to H5414
Job 6: 8 would **g** *me* the thing that I long for! H5414
Ps 20: 4 **G** thee according to thine own heart, H5414
85: 7 Shew us thy mercy, O LORD, and **g** us H5414
119:29 Remove from me the way of lying: and **g**
140: 8 **G** not, O LORD, the desires of the H5414
Mt 20:21 saith unto him, **G** that these my two G2036
Mk 10:37 They said unto him, **G** unto us that we G1325
Lk 1:74 That he would **g** unto us, that we being G1325
Act 4:29 threatenings: and **g** unto thy servants, G1325
Ro 15: 5 and consolation **g** you to be likeminded G1325
Eph 3:16 That he would **g** you, according to the G1325
2Ti 1:18 The Lord **g** unto him that he may find G1325
Rev 3:21 To him that overcometh will I **g** to sit G1325

GRANTED
1Ch 4:10 And God **g** him that which he requested. H935
2Ch 1:12 Wisdom and knowledge *is* **g** unto thee; H5414
Ezr 7: 6 and the king **g** him all his request, H5414
Neh 2: 8 into. And the king **g** me, according to H5414
Est 5: 6 and it shall be **g** thee: and what *is* thy H5414
7: 2 and it shall be **g** thee: and what *is* thy H5414
8:11 Wherein the king **g** the Jews which H5414
9:12 and it shall be **g** thee: or what *is* thy H5414
13 the king, let it be **g** to the Jews which H5414
Job 10:12 Thou hast **g** me life and favour, and thy H6213
Prv 10:24 the desire of the righteous shall be **g**. H5414
Act 3:14 desired a murderer to be **g** unto you; G5483
11:18 to the Gentiles **g** repentance unto life. G1325
14: 3 of his grace, and **g** signs and wonders G1325
Rev 19: 8 And to her was **g** that she should be G1325

GRAPE
Lev 19:10 thou gather *every* **g** of thy vineyard; H6528
Dt 32:14 thou didst drink the pure blood of the **g**. H6025
Job 15:33 He shall shake off his unripe **g** as the H1154
Song 2:13 *with* the tender **g** give a *good* smell. H5563
7:12 *whether* the tender **g** appear, *and* the H5563
Isa 18: 5 and the sour **g** is ripening in the flower, H1155
Jer 31:29 have eaten a sour **g**, and the children's H1155
30 the sour **g**, his teeth shall be set on edge. H1155

GRAPEGATHERER
Jer 6: 9 back thine hand as a **g** into the baskets. H1219

GRAPEGATHERERS
Jer 49: 9 If **g** come to thee, would they not leave H1219
Oba 5 they had enough? if the **g** came to thee, H1219

GRAPEGLEANINGS
Mic 7: 1 fruits, as the **g** of the vintage: *there* H5955

GRAPES
Gen 40:10 the clusters thereof brought forth ripe **g**: H6025
11 and I took the **g**, and pressed them into H6025
49:11 wine, and his clothes in the blood of **g**: H6025
Lev 25: 5 reap, neither gather the **g** of thy vine H6025
11 gather *the* **g** in it of thy vine undressed.
Nu 6: 3 of **g**, nor eat moist grapes, or dried. H6025
3 of grapes, nor eat moist **g**, or dried. H6025
13:20 the time *was* the time of the firstripe **g**. H6025
23 with one cluster of **g**, and they bare it H6025
24 of the cluster of **g** which the children of H811
Dt 23:24 thou mayest eat **g** thy fill at thine own H6025
24:21 When thou gatherest the **g** of thy
28:30 and shalt not gather the **g** thereof. H2490
39 *the* **g**; for the worms shall eat them.
32:32 of Gomorrah: their **g** *are* grapes of gall, H6025
32 *are* **g** of gall, their clusters *are* bitter: H6025
Jdg 8: 2 the gleaning of the **g** of Ephraim better
9:27 and trode *the* **g**, and made merry, and
Neh 13:15 asses; as also wine, and **g**, and figs, and all H6025
Song 2:15 the vines: for our vines *have* tender **g**. H5563
7: 7 tree, and thy breasts to clusters *of* **g**.
Isa 5: 2 **g**, and it brought forth wild grapes. H6025
2 forth grapes, and it brought forth wild **g**. H891
4 forth **g**, brought it forth wild grapes? H6025
4 forth grapes, brought it forth wild **g**? H891
17: 6 Yet gleaning **g** shall be left in it, as the H5955
24:13 gleaning **g** when the vintage is done. H5955
Jer 8:13 *there shall be* no **g** on the vine, nor figs H6025
25:30 **g**, against all the inhabitants of the earth.
49: 9 *some* gleaning **g**? if thieves by night, H5955
Ezk 18: 2 have eaten sour **g**, and the children's H1155

Hos 9:10 I found Israel like **g** in the wilderness; I H6025
Am 9:13 and the treader of **g** him that soweth H6025
Oba 5 to thee, would they not leave *some* **g**? H5955
Mt 7:16 gather **g** of thorns, or figs of thistles? G4718
Lk 6:44 nor of a bramble bush gather they **g**. G4718
Rev 14:18 of the earth; for her **g** are fully ripe. G4718

GRASS
Gen 1:11 the earth bring forth **g**, the herb yielding H1877
12 And the earth brought forth **g**, *and* herb H1877
Nu 22: 4 the ox licketh up the **g** of the field. And H3418
Dt 11:15 And I will send **g** in thy fields for thy H6212
29:23 beareth, nor any **g** groweth therein, like H6212
32: 2 herb, and as the showers upon the **g**: H6212
2Sa 23: 4 *as* the tender **g** *springing* out of the H1877
1Ki 18: 5 we may find **g** to save the horses and H2682
2Ki 19:26 they were *as* the **g** of the field, and *as* H6212
26 green herb, *as* the **g** on the housetops, H2682
Job 5:25 thine offspring as the **g** of the earth. H6212
6: 5 Doth the wild ass bray when he hath **g**? H1877
40:15 I made with thee; he eateth **g** as an ox. H2682
Ps 37: 2 like the **g**, and wither as the green herb. H2682
72: 6 mown **g**: as showers *that* water the earth.
16 the city shall flourish like **g** of the earth. H6212
90: 5 *they are* like **g** *which* groweth up. H2682
92: 7 When the wicked spring as the **g**, and H6212
102: 4 like **g**; so that I forget to eat my bread. H6212
11 that declineth; and I am withered like **g**. H6212
103:15 *As for* man, his days *are* as **g**: as a H2682
104:14 He causeth the **g** to grow for the cattle, H2682
106:20 the similitude of an ox that eateth **g**. H6212
129: 6 Let them be as the **g** *upon* the H2682
147: 8 maketh **g** to grow upon the mountains. H2682
Prv 19:12 but his favour *is* as dew upon the **g**. H6212
27:25 The hay appeareth, and the tender **g** H1877
Isa 15: 6 the **g** faileth, there is no green thing. H1877
35: 7 lay, *shall be* **g** with reeds and rushes. H2682
37:27 they were *as* the **g** of the field, and *as* H6212
27 green herb, *as* the **g** on the housetops, H2682
40: 6 shall I cry? All flesh *is* **g**, and all the H2682
7 The **g** withereth, the flower fadeth: H2682
7 bloweth upon it: surely the people *is* **g**. H2682
8 The **g** withereth, the flower fadeth: but H2682
44: 4 the **g**, as willows by the water courses. H2682
51:12 son of man *which* shall be made *as* **g**; H2682
Jer 14: 5 and forsook *it*, because there was no **g**. H1877
6 eyes did fail, because *there was* no **g**. H6212
50:11 as the heifer at **g**, and bellow as bulls; H1877
Dan 4:15 in the tender **g** of the field; and let H1883
15 *be* with the beasts in the **g** of the earth: H6211
23 in the tender **g** of the field; and let H1883
25 make thee to eat **g** as oxen, and they H6211
32 make thee to eat **g** as oxen, and seven H6211
33 men, and did eat **g** as oxen, and his H6211
5:21 they fed him with **g** like oxen, and his H6211
Am 7: 2 end of eating the **g** of the land, then I H6212
Mic 5: 7 showers upon the **g**, that tarrieth not for H6212
Zec 10: 1 of rain, to every one **g** in the field. H6212
Mt 6:30 Wherefore, if God so clothe the **g** of the G5528
14:19 to sit down on the **g**, and took the five G5528
Mk 6:39 down by companies upon the green **g**. G5528
Lk 12:28 If then God so clothe the **g**, which is to G5528
Jn 6:10 there was much **g** in the place. So the G5528
Jas 1:10 the flower of the **g** he shall pass away. G5528
11 but it withereth the **g**, and the flower G5528
1Pt 1:24 For all flesh *is* as **g**, and all the glory of G5528
24 as the flower of **g**. The grass withereth, G5528
24 of grass. The **g** withereth, and the G5528
Rev 8: 7 burnt up, and all green **g** was burnt up. G5528
9: 4 not hurt the **g** of the earth, neither G5528

GRASSHOPPER
Lev 11:22 after his kind, and the **g** after his kind. H2284
Job 39:20 Canst thou make him afraid as a **g**? the H697
Ecc 12: 5 flourish, and the **g** shall be a burden, H2284

GRASSHOPPERS
Nu 13:33 sight as **g**, and so we were in their sight. H2284
Jdg 6: 5 and they came as **g** for multitude; *for* H697
7:12 in the valley like **g** for multitude; and H697
Isa 40:22 thereof *are* as **g**; that stretcheth out the H2284
Jer 46:23 more than the **g**, and *are* innumerable. H697
Am 7: 1 behold, he formed **g** in the beginning of H1462
Nah 3:17 as the great **g**, which camp in the H1462

GRATE
Ex 27: 4 And thou shalt make for it a **g** of H4345
35:16 with his brasen **g**, his staves, and all his H4345
38: 4 And he made for the altar a brasen **g** of H4345
Ex 38: 5 **g** of brass, *to be* places for the staves. H4345
30 **g** for it, and all the vessels of the altar, H4345
39:39 The brasen altar, and his **g** of brass, his H4345

GRAVE
Gen 35:20 And Jacob set a pillar upon her **g**: that H6900
20 *is* the pillar of Rachel's **g** unto this day. H6900
37:35 will go down into the **g** unto my son H7585
42:38 my gray hairs with sorrow to the **g**. H7585
44:29 my gray hairs with sorrow to the **g**. H7585
31 servant our father with sorrow to the **g**. H7585
50: 5 Lo, I die: in my **g** which I have digged H6913
Ex 28: 9 onyx stones, and **g** on them the names H6605
36 *of* pure gold, and **g** upon it, *like* the H6605
Nu 19:16 or a **g**, shall be unclean seven days. H6913
18 a bone, or one slain, or one dead, or a **g**: H6913
1Sa 2: 6 down to the **g**, and bringeth up. H7585
2Sa 3:32 the **g** of Abner; and all the people wept. H6913
19:37 *be buried* by the **g** of my father and of H6913
1Ki 2: 6 hoar head go down to the **g** in peace. H7585
9 bring thou down to the **g** with blood. H7585
13:30 And he laid his carcase in his own **g**; H6913
14:13 shall come to the **g**, because in him H6913
2Ki 22:20 gathered into thy **g** in peace; and thine H6913
2Ch 2: 7 and that can skill to **g** with the cunning H6603
14 in crimson; also to **g** any manner of H6605
34:28 be gathered to thy **g** in peace, neither H6913
Job 3:22 *and* are glad, when they can find the **g**? H6913
5:26 Thou shalt come to *thy* **g** in a full age, H6913
7: 9 down to the **g** shall come up no *more*. H7585
10:19 been carried from the womb to the **g**. H6913
14:13 O that thou wouldest hide me in the **g**, H7585
17:13 If I wait, the **g** *is* mine house: I have H7585
21:13 and in a moment go down to the **g**. H7585
32 Yet shall he be brought to the **g**, and H6913
24:19 *so doth* the **g** *those which* have sinned. H7585
30:24 **g**, though they cry in his destruction. H1164
33:22 Yea, his soul draweth near unto the **g**, H7845
Ps 6: 5 in the **g** who shall give thee thanks? H7585
30: 3 my soul from the **g**: thou hast kept me H7585
31:17 *and* let them be silent in the **g**. H7585
49:14 Like sheep they are laid in the **g**; death H7585
14 consume in the **g** from their dwelling. H7585
15 of the **g**: for he shall receive me. Selah. H7585
88: 3 and my life draweth nigh unto the **g**. H7585
5 the slain that lie in the **g**, whom thou H6913
11 the **g**? *or* thy faithfulness in destruction? H6913
89:48 his soul from the hand of the **g**? Selah. H7585
Prv 1:12 Let us swallow them up alive as the **g**; H7585
30:16 The **g**; and the barren womb; the earth H7585
Ecc 9:10 wisdom, in the **g**, whither thou goest. H7585
Song 8: 6 *is* cruel as the **g**: the coals thereof *are* H7585
Isa 14:11 Thy pomp is brought down to the **g**, H7585
19 But thou art cast out of thy **g** like an H6913
38:10 go to the gates of the **g**: I am deprived of H7585
18 For the **g** cannot praise thee, death can H7585
53: 9 And he made his **g** with the wicked, H6913
Jer 20:17 have been my **g**, and her womb *to be* H6913
Ezk 31:15 he went down to the **g** I caused a H7585
32:23 is round about her **g**: all of them slain, H6900
24 round about her **g**, all of them slain, H6900
Hos 13:14 the power of the **g**; I will redeem them H7585
14 will be thy plagues; O **g**, I will be thy H7585
Nah 1:14 I will make thy **g**; for thou art vile. H6913
Jn 11:17 he had *lain* in the **g** four days already. G3419
31 She goeth unto the **g** to weep there. G3419
38 **g**. It was a cave, and a stone lay upon it. G3419
12:17 Lazarus out of his **g**, and raised him G3419
1Co 15:55 O death, where *is* thy sting? O **g**, where *is* G86
1Ti 3: 8 Likewise *must* the deacons *be* **g**, not G4586
11 Even so *must their* wives *be* **g**, not G4586
Tit 2: 2 That the aged men be sober, **g**, G4586

GRAVECLOTHES
Jn 11:44 and foot with **g**: and his face was bound G2750

GRAVED
1Ki 7:36 thereof, he **g** cherubims, lions, and H6605
2Ch 3: 7 gold; and **g** cherubims on the walls. H6605

GRAVEL
Prv 20:17 his mouth shall be filled with **g**. H2687
Isa 48:19 thy bowels like the **g** thereof; his name H4579
Lam 3:16 He hath also broken my teeth with **g** H2687

GRAVEN
Ex 20: 4 Thou shalt not make unto thee any **g** H6459
32:16 the writing of God, **g** upon the tables. H2801
39: 6 in ouches of gold, **g**, as signets are H6605
Ex 39: 6 as signets are **g**, with the names of the H6603
Lev 26: 1 Ye shall make you no idols nor **g** H6459
Dt 4:16 and make you a **g** image, the similitude H6459
23 you, and make you a **g** image, *or* the H6459
25 and make a **g** image, *or* the likeness H6459
5: 8 Thou shalt not make thee *any* **g** image, H6459
7: 5 and burn their **g** images with fire. H6456
25 The **g** images of their gods shall ye H6456
12: 3 hew down the **g** images of their gods, H6456
27:15 Cursed *be* the man that maketh *any* **g** H6459
Jdg 17: 3 for my son, to make a **g** image and a H6459
4 made thereof a **g** image and a molten H6459
18:14 teraphim, and a **g** image, and a molten H6459
17 *and* took the **g** image, and the ephod, H6459
20 teraphim, and the **g** image, and went H6459
30 And the children of Dan set up the **g** H6459
31 And they set them up Micah's **g** image, H6459
2Ki 17:41 and served their **g** images, both their H6456
21: 7 And he set a **g** image of the grove that H6459
2Ch 33:19 set up groves and **g** images, before he H6456
34: 7 had beaten the **g** images into powder, H6456
Job 19:24 That they were **g** with an iron pen and H2672
Ps 78:58 him to jealousy with their **g** images. H6456
97: 7 Confounded be all they that serve **g** H6459
Isa 10:10 the idols, and whose **g** images did excel H6456
21: 9 fallen; and all the **g** images of her gods H6456
30:22 Ye shall defile also the covering of thy **g** H6456
40:19 The workman melteth a **g** image, and H6459
20 a **g** image, *that* shall not be moved. H6459
42: 8 another, neither my praise to **g** images. H6456
17 that trust in **g** images, that say to H6459
44: 9 They that make a **g** image *are* all of H6459
10 Who hath formed a god, or molten a **g** H6459
15 it a **g** image, and falleth down thereto. H6459
17 a god, *even* his **g** image: he falleth H6459
45:20 up the wood of their **g** image, and pray H6459
48: 5 them, and my **g** image, and my molten H6459
49:16 Behold, I have **g** thee upon the palms of H2710
Jer 8:19 **g** images, *and* with strange vanities? H6456
10:14 by the **g** image: for his molten H6459
17: 1 of a diamond: *it is* **g** upon the table of H2790
50:38 for it *is* the land of **g** images, and they H6456
51:17 by the **g** image: for his molten H6459
47 upon the **g** images of Babylon: H6456
52 upon her **g** images: and through H6456
Hos 11: 2 and burned incense to **g** images. H6456
Mic 1: 7 And all the **g** images thereof shall be H6456
5:13 Thy **g** images also will I cut off, and thy H6456
Nah 1:14 gods will I cut off the **g** image and the H6459
Hab 2:18 What profiteth the **g** image that the H6459
18 thereof hath **g** it; the molten image, H6458
Act 17:29 or stone, **g** by art and man's device. G5480

GRAVES
Ex 14:11 *there were* no **g** in Egypt, hast thou H6913
2Ki 23: 6 the **g** of the children of the people. H6913
2Ch 34: 4 strowed *it* upon the **g** of them that had H6913
Job 17: 1 are extinct, the **g** *are ready* for me. H6913
Isa 65: 4 Which remain among the **g**, and lodge H6913
Jer 8: 1 inhabitants of Jerusalem, out of their **g**: H6913
26:23 body into the **g** of the common people. H6913
Ezk 32:22 her company: his **g** *are* about him: all H6913
23 Whose **g** are set in the sides of the pit, H6913
25 her multitude: her **g** *are* round about H6913
26 her multitude: her **g** *are* round about H6913
37:12 I will open your **g**, and cause you to H6913
12 **g**, and bring you into the land of Israel. H6913
13 I have opened your **g**, O my people, and H6913
13 and brought you up out of your **g**, H6913
39:11 a place there of **g** in Israel, the valley H6913
Mt 27:52 And the **g** were opened; and many G3419
53 And came out of the **g** after his G3419
Lk 11:44 for ye are as **g** which appear not, and G3419
Jn 5:28 all that are in the **g** shall hear his voice, G3419
Rev 11: 9 suffer their dead bodies to be put in **g**. G3418

GRAVE'S
Ps 141: 7 Our bones are scattered at the **g** H7585

GRAVETH
Isa 22:16 **g** an habitation for himself in a rock? H2710

GRAVING
Ex 32: 4 it with a **g** tool, after he had made H2747
2Ch 2:14 any manner of **g**, and to find out every H6603
Zec 3: 9 I will engrave the **g** thereof, saith the H6603

GRAVINGS
1Ki 7:31 mouth of it *were* **g** with their borders, H4734

G

GRAVING-TOOL See GRAVING and TOOL.

GRAVITY
1Ti 3: 4 his children in subjection with all **g**; *G4587*
Tit 2: 7 *shewing* uncorruptness, **g**, sincerity, *G4587*

GRAY
Gen 42:38 my **g** hairs with sorrow to the grave. H7872
44:29 my **g** hairs with sorrow to the grave. H7872
31 bring down the **g** hairs of thy servant H7872
Dt 32:25 suckling *also* with the man of **g** hairs. H7872
Prv 20:29 the beauty of old men *is* the **g** head. H7872
Hos 7: 9 *it* not: yea, **g** hairs are here and there H7872

GRAYHEADED
1Sa 12: 2 and I am old and **g**; and, behold, my H7867
Job 15:10 With us *are* both the **g** and very aged H7867
Ps 71:18 Now also when I am old and **g**, O God, H7872

GREASE
Ps 119:70 Their heart is as fat as **g**; *but* I delight in H2459

GREAT
Gen 1:16 And God made two **g** lights; the greater H1419
21 And God created **g** whales, and every H1419
6: 5 of man *was* **g** in the earth, and *that* H7227
7:11 fountains of the **g** deep broken up, and H7227
10:12 and Calah: the same *is* a **g** city. H1419
12: 2 And I will make of thee a **g** nation, and H1419
2 name **g**; and thou shalt be a blessing: H1431
17 his house with **g** plagues because of H1419
13: 6 **g**, so that they could not dwell together. H7227
15: 1 thy shield, *and* thy exceeding **g** reward. H7235
12 an horror of **g** darkness fell upon him. H1419
14 shall they come out with **g** substance. H1419
18 unto the **g** river, the river Euphrates: H1419
17:20 beget, and I will make him a **g** nation. H1419
18:18 surely become a **g** and mighty nation, H1419
20 and Gomorrah is **g**, and because their H7227
19:11 both small and **g**: so that they wearied H1419
13 of them is waxen **g** before the face of H1431
20: 9 on my kingdom a **g** sin? thou hast done H1419
21: 8 Abraham made a **g** feast the *same* day H1419
18 hand; for I will make him a **g** nation. H1419
24:35 and he is become **g**: and he hath given H1431
26:13 And the man waxed **g**, and went H1431
13 and grew until he became very **g**: H1431
14 of herds, and **g** store of servants: and H7227
27:34 he cried with a **g** and exceeding bitter H1419
29: 2 a **g** stone *was* upon the well's mouth. H1419
30: 8 And Rachel said, With **g** wrestlings have H430
39: 9 this **g** wickedness, and sin against God? H1419
41:29 Behold, there come seven years of **g** H1419
45: 7 to save your lives by a **g** deliverance. H1419
46: 3 for I will there make of thee a **g** nation: H1419
48:19 he also shall be **g**: but truly his younger H1431
50: 9 and it was a very **g** company. H3515
10 they mourned with a **g** and very sore H1419
Ex 3: 3 this **g** sight, why the bush is not burnt. H1419
6: 6 out arm, and with **g** judgments: H1419
7: 4 of the land of Egypt by **g** judgments. H1419
11: 3 Moses *was* very **g** in the land of Egypt, H1419
6 And there shall be a **g** cry throughout H1419
8 he went out from Pharaoh in a **g** anger. H2750
12:30 and there was a **g** cry in Egypt; for H1419
14:31 And Israel saw that **g** work which the H1419
18:22 be, *that* every **g** matter they shall bring H1419
29:20 and upon the **g** toe of their right foot,
32:10 and I will make of thee a **g** nation. H1419
11 with **g** power, and with a mighty hand? H1419
21 hast brought so **g** a sin upon them? H1419
30 Ye have sinned a **g** sin: and now I will H1419
31 have sinned a **g** sin, and have made H1419
Lev 8:23 and upon the **g** toe of his right foot.
24 and upon the **g** toes of their right feet:
11:17 owl, and the cormorant, and the **g** owl, H3244
14:14 and upon the **g** toe of his right foot:
17 and upon the **g** toe of his right foot,
25 and upon the **g** toe of his right foot:
28 and upon the **g** toe of his right foot,
Nu 11:33 smote the people with a very **g** plague. H7227
13:28 walled, *and* very **g**: and moreover we H1419
32 that we saw in it *are* men of a **g** stature. H4060
14:17 of my Lord be **g**, according as thou hast H1431
18 The LORD *is* longsuffering, and of **g** H7227
22:17 For I will promote thee unto very **g** H3513
23:24 Behold, the people shall rise up as a **g** H3833
24: 9 as a lion, and as a **g** lion: who shall stir H3833
11 to promote thee unto **g** honour; but, lo, H3513
Nu 32: 1 of Gad had a very **g** multitude of cattle: H6099
34: 6 even have the **g** sea for a border: this H1419
7 border: from the **g** sea ye shall point H1419
Dt 1: 7 unto the **g** river, the river Euphrates. H1419
17 as well as the **g**; ye shall not be afraid H1419
19 went through all that **g** and terrible H1419
28 we; the cities *are* **g** and walled up to H1419
2: 7 through this **g** wilderness: these forty H1419
10 **g**, and many, and tall, as the Anakims; H1419
21 A people **g**, and many, and tall, as the H1419
3: 5 bars; beside unwalled towns a **g** many. H3966
4: 6 say, Surely this **g** nation *is* a wise and H1419
7 For what nation *is there so* **g**, who *hath* H1419
8 And what nation *is there so* **g**, that hath H1419
32 **g** thing *is*, or hath been heard like it? H1419
34 out arm, and by **g** terrors, according to H1419
36 he shewed thee his **g** fire; and thou H1419
5:22 darkness, with a **g** voice: and he added H1419
25 we die? for this **g** fire will consume us: H1419
6:10 Jacob, to give thee **g** and goodly cities, H1419
22 and wonders, **g** and sore, upon Egypt, H1419
7:19 The **g** temptations which thine eyes H1419
8:15 Who led thee through that **g** and H1419
9: 1 cities **g** and fenced up to heaven, H1419
2 A people **g** and tall, the children of the H1419
10:17 Lord of lords, a **g** God, a mighty, and H1419
21 for thee these **g** and terrible things, H1419
11: 7 But your eyes have seen all the **g** acts of H1419
14:16 The little owl, and the **g** owl, and the H3244
18:16 see this **g** fire any more, that I die not. H1419
25:13 thy bag divers weights, a **g** and a small. H1419
14 divers measures, a **g** and a small. H1419
26: 5 a nation, **g**, mighty, and populous: H1419
8 arm, and with **g** terribleness, and with H1419
27: 2 shalt set thee up **g** stones, and plaister H1419
28:59 of thy seed, *even* **g** plagues, and of long H1419
29: 3 The **g** temptations which thine eyes H1419
3 seen, the signs, and those **g** miracles: H1419
24 what *meaneth* the heat of this **g** anger? H1419
28 in wrath, and in **g** indignation, and H1419
34:12 and in all the **g** terror which Moses H1419
Jos 1: 4 even unto the **g** river, the river H1419
4 and unto the **g** sea toward the going H1419
6: 5 shall shout with a **g** shout; and the wall H1419
20 shouted with a **g** shout, that the wall H1419
7: 9 what wilt thou do unto thy **g** name? H1419
26 And they raised over him a **g** heap of H1419
8:29 raise thereon a **g** heap of stones, *that* H1419
9: 1 all the coasts of the **g** sea over against H1419
10: 2 Gibeon *was* a **g** city, as one of the royal H1419
10 slew them with a **g** slaughter at Gibeon, H1419
11 LORD cast down **g** stones from heaven H1419
18 And Joshua said, Roll **g** stones upon H1419
20 them with a very **g** slaughter, till they H1419
27 been hid, and laid **g** stones in the cave's H1419
11: 8 chased them unto **g** Zidon, and unto H7227
14:12 the cities *were* **g** *and* fenced: if so be H1419
15 *which Arba was* a **g** man among the H1419
15:12 And the west border *was* to the **g** sea, H1419
47 and the **g** sea, and the border *thereof*. H1419
17:14 seeing I *am* a **g** people, forasmuch H7227
15 them, If thou *be* a **g** people, *then* get H7227
17 saying, Thou *art* a **g** people, and hast H7227
17 people, and hast **g** power: thou shalt H1419
19:28 and Kanah, *even* unto **g** Zidon; H7227
22:10 an altar by Jordan, a **g** altar to see to. H1419
23: 4 cut off, even unto the **g** sea westward. H1419
9 from before you **g** nations and strong: H1419
24:17 which did those **g** signs in our sight, H1419
26 of God, and took a **g** stone, and set it H1419
Jdg 1: 6 and cut off his thumbs and his **g** toes.
7 thumbs and their **g** toes cut off, gathered
2: 7 had seen all the **g** works of the LORD, H1419
5:15 Reuben *there were* **g** thoughts of heart. H1419
16 *there were* **g** searchings of heart. H1419
11:33 with a very **g** slaughter. Thus the H1419
12: 2 and my people were at **g** strife with the H3966
15: 8 and thigh with a **g** slaughter: and he H1419
18 hast given this **g** deliverance into the H1419
16: 5 see wherein his **g** strength *lieth*, and by H1419
6 thee, wherein thy **g** strength *lieth*, and H1419
15 told me wherein thy **g** strength *lieth*. H1419
23 for to offer a **g** sacrifice unto Dagon H1419
20:38 should make a **g** flame with smoke rise H7235
21: 5 For they had made a **g** oath concerning H1419
1Sa 2:17 men was very **g** before the LORD: for H1419
4: 5 a **g** shout, so that the earth rang again. H1419
6 the noise of this **g** shout in the camp of H1419
10 there was a very **g** slaughter; for there H1419
1Sa 4:17 hath been also a **g** slaughter among the H1419
5: 9 city with a very **g** destruction: and he H1419
9 city, both small and **g**, and they had H1419
6: 9 hath done us this **g** evil: but if not, then H1419
14 where *there was* a **g** stone: and they H1419
15 put *them* on the **g** stone: and the men H1419
18 even unto the **g** *stone of* Abel, whereon H1419
19 *many* of the people with a **g** slaughter. H1419
7:10 thundered with a **g** thunder on that day H1419
12:16 Now therefore stand and see this **g** H1419
17 wickedness *is* **g**, which ye have done H7227
22 his people for his **g** name's sake: H1419
24 how **g** *things* he hath done for you. H1431
14:15 quaked: so it was a very **g** trembling. H430
20 *and there was* a very **g** discomfiture. H1419
33 roll a **g** stone unto me this day. H1419
45 hath wrought this **g** salvation in Israel? H1419
15:22 And Samuel said, Hath the LORD *as* **g**
17:25 enrich him with **g** riches, and will give H1419
19: 5 the LORD wrought a **g** salvation for all H1419
8 a **g** slaughter; and they fled from him. H1419
22 and came to a **g** well that *is* in Sechu: H1419
20: 2 do nothing either **g** or small, but that H1419
23: 5 and smote them with a **g** slaughter. So H1419
25: 2 the man *was* very **g**, and he had three H1419
26:13 afar off; a **g** space *being* between them: H7227
25 thou shalt both do **g** *things*, and also H6213
30: 2 not any, either **g** or small, but carried H1419
16 because of all the **g** spoil that they had H1419
19 neither small nor **g**, neither sons nor H1419
2Sa 3:22 and brought in a **g** spoil with them: but H7227
38 and a **g** man fallen this day in Israel? H1419
5:10 And David went on, and grew **g**, and H1419
7: 9 have made thee a **g** name, like unto the H1419
9 of the **g** *men* that *are* in the earth. H1419
19 house for a **g** while to come. And H7350
21 done all these **g** things, to make thy H1420
22 Wherefore thou art **g**, O LORD God: for H1431
23 and to do for you **g** things and terrible, H1420
12:14 deed thou hast given **g** occasion to the H5006
30 the spoil of the city in **g** abundance. H3966
18: 7 there was there a **g** slaughter that day H1419
9 thick boughs of a **g** oak, and his head H1419
17 cast him into a **g** pit in the wood, and H1419
17 and laid a very **g** heap of stones upon H1419
29 a **g** tumult, but I knew not what *it was*. H1419
19:32 at Mahanaim; for he *was* a very **g** man. H1419
20: 8 When they *were* at the **g** stone which *is* H1419
21:20 was a man of **g** stature, that had on
22:36 and thy gentleness hath made me **g**. H7235
23:10 the LORD wrought a **g** victory that day; H1419
12 and the LORD wrought a **g** victory. H1419
24:14 And David said unto Gad, I am in a **g** H3966
14 for his mercies *are* **g**: and let me not fall H7227
1Ki 1:40 and rejoiced with **g** joy, so that the H1419
3: 4 there; for that *was* the **g** high place: a H1419
6 David my father **g** mercy, according as H1419
6 kept for him this **g** kindness, that thou H1419
8 hast chosen, a **g** people, that cannot H7227
9 is able to judge this thy so **g** a people? H3515
4:13 **g** cities with walls and brasen bars: H1419
5: 7 David a wise son over this **g** people. H7227
17 and they brought **g** stones, costly H1419
7: 9 *so* on the outside toward the **g** court. H1419
10 costly stones, even **g** stones, stones of H1419
12 And the **g** court round about *was* with H1419
8:42 (For they shall hear of thy **g** name, and H1419
65 Israel with him, a **g** congregation, from H1419
10: 2 with a very **g** train, with camels that H3515
10 and of spices very **g** store, and precious H7235
11 in from Ophir **g** plenty of almug trees, H3966
18 Moreover the king made a **g** throne of H1419
11:19 And Hadad found **g** favour in the sight H3966
18:32 about the altar, as **g** as would contain H1004
45 and there was a **g** rain. And Ahab rode, H1419
19: 7 because the journey *is* too **g** for thee. H7227
11 passed by, and a **g** and strong wind H1419
20:13 thou seen all this **g** multitude? behold, H1419
21 slew the Syrians with a **g** slaughter. H1419
28 I deliver all this **g** multitude into thine H1419
22:31 nor **g**, save only with the king of Israel. H1419
2Ki 3:27 And there was **g** indignation against H1419
4: 8 where *was* a **g** woman; and she H1419
38 his servant, Set on the **g** pot, and seethe H1419
5: 1 of Syria, was a **g** man with his master, H1419
13 had bid thee *do some* **g** thing, wouldest H1419
6:14 chariots, and a **g** host: and they came H3515
23 And he prepared **g** provision for them: H1419
25 And there was a **g** famine in Samaria: H1419

2Ki 7: 6 *even* the noise of a g host: and they H1419
8: 4 all the g things that Elisha hath done. H1419
13 he should do this g thing? And Elisha H1419
10: 6 *were* with the g men of the city, which H1419
11 in Jezreel, and all his g men, and his H1419
19 for I have a g sacrifice *to do* to Baal; H1419
16:15 saying, Upon the g altar burn the H1419
17:21 the LORD, and made them sin a g sin. H1419
36 the land of Egypt with g power and a H1419
18:17 king Hezekiah with a g host against H3515
19 Thus saith the g king, the king of H1419
28 word of the g king, the king of Assyria: H1419
22:13 that is found: for g *is* the wrath of the H1419
23: 2 both small and g: and he read in their H1419
26 fierceness of his g wrath, wherewith his H1419
25: 9 every g *man's* house burnt he with fire. H1419
26 And all the people, both small and g, H1419
1Ch 11:14 LORD saved *them* by a g deliverance. H1419
23 And he slew an Egyptian, a man of g
12:22 *it was* a g host, like the host of God. H1419
16:25 For g *is* the LORD, and greatly to be H1419
17: 8 of the g men that *are* in the earth. H1419
17 house for a g while to come, and H7350
19 in making known all *these* g things. H1420
20: 6 was a man of g stature, whose fingers
21:13 And David said unto Gad, I am in a g H3966
13 LORD; for very g *are* his mercies: but H7227
22: 8 and hast made g wars: thou shalt not H1419
25: 8 as the g, the teacher as the scholar. H1419
26:13 well the small as the g, according to the H1419
29: 1 and the work *is* g: for the palace *is* not H1419
9 David the king also rejoiced with g joy. H1419
12 to make g, and to give strength unto all. H1431
22 on that day with g gladness. And they H1419
2Ch 1: 8 Thou hast shewed g mercy unto David H1419
10 can judge this thy people, *that is so* g? H1419
2: 5 And the house which I build *is* g: for H1419
5 *is* great: for g *is* our God above all gods. H1419
9 am about to build *shall be* wonderful g. H1419
4: 9 priests, and the g court, and doors for H1419
18 all these vessels in g abundance: for the H3966
6:32 far country for thy g name's sake, and H1419
7: 8 with him, a very g congregation, from H1419
9: 1 with a very g company, and camels H3515
9 gold, and of spices g abundance, and H3966
17 Moreover the king made a g throne of H1419
13: 8 of David; and ye *be* a g multitude, and H7227
17 slew them with a g slaughter: so there H7227
15: 5 him that came in, but g vexations *were* H7227
13 small or g, whether man or woman. H1419
16:12 *was* exceeding g: yet in his disease he
14 they made a very g burning for him. H1419
17:12 And Jehoshaphat waxed g exceedingly; H1432
18:30 or g, save only with the king of Israel. H1419
20: 2 There cometh a g multitude against H7227
12 no might against this g company that H7227
15 by reason of this g multitude; for the H7227
21: 3 And their father gave them g gifts of H7227
14 Behold, with a g plague will the LORD H1419
15 And thou *shalt have* g sickness by H7227
24:24 delivered a very g host into their hand, H7230
25 they left him in g diseases,) his own H7227
25:10 and they returned home in g anger. H2750
26:15 shoot arrows and g stones withal. And H1419
28: 5 carried away a g multitude of them H1419
5 who smote him with a g slaughter. H1419
13 for our trespass is g, and *there is* fierce H7227
30:13 second month, a very g congregation. H7230
21 seven days with g gladness: and the H1419
24 sheep: and a g number of priests H7230
26 So there was g joy in Jerusalem: for H1419
31:10 and that which is left *is* this g store.
15 courses, as well to the g as to the small: H1419
33:14 and raised it up a very g height, and put
34:21 that is found: for g *is* the wrath of the H1419
30 and all the people, g and small: and he H1419
36:18 the house of God, g and small, and the H1419
Ezr 3:11 shouted with a g shout, when they H1419
4:10 And the rest of the nations whom the g H7229
5: 8 to the house of the g God, which is H7229
8 is builded with g stones, and timber H1560
11 a g king of Israel builded and set up. H7229
6: 4 *With* three rows of g stones, and a row H1560
9: 7 *have we been* in a g trespass unto this H1419
13 deeds, and for our g trespass, seeing H1419
10: 1 of Israel a very g congregation of men H7227
9 of *this* matter, and for the g rain.
Neh 1: 3 the province *are* in g affliction and H1419
5 of heaven, the g and terrible God, that H1419

Neh 1:10 thy g power, and by thy strong hand. H1419
3:27 over against the g tower that lieth out, H1419
4: 1 g indignation, and mocked the Jews. H7235
14 the Lord, *which is* g and terrible, and H1419
19 The work *is* g and large, and we are H7235
5: 1 And there was a g cry of the people and H1419
7 And I set a g assembly against them. H1419
6: 3 I *am* doing a g work, so that I cannot H1419
7: 4 Now the city *was* large and g: but the H1419
8: 6 And Ezra blessed the LORD, the g God. H1419
12 and to make g mirth, because they H1419
17 so. And there was very g gladness. H1419
9:17 of g kindness, and forsookest them not. H7227
18 and had wrought g provocations; H1419
25 delighted themselves in thy g goodness. H1419
26 thee, and they wrought g provocations. H1419
31 Nevertheless for thy g mercies' sake H7227
32 Now therefore, our God, the g, the H1419
35 and in thy g goodness that thou H7227
37 their pleasure, and we *are* in g distress. H1419
11:14 Zabdiel, the son of *one of* the g men. H1419
12:31 appointed two g *companies of them* H1419
43 Also that day they offered g sacrifices, H1419
43 them rejoice with g joy: the wives also H1419
13: 5 And he had prepared for him a g H1419
27 you to do all this g evil, to transgress H1419
Est 1: 5 palace, both unto g and small, seven H1419
20 empire, (for it is g,) all the wives shall H7227
20 husbands honour, both to g and small. H1419
2:18 Then the king made a g feast unto all H1419
4: 3 came, *there was* g mourning among H1419
8:15 white, and with a g crown of gold, and H1419
9: 4 For Mordecai *was* g in the king's H1419
10: 3 Ahasuerus, and g among the Jews, and H1419
Job 1: 3 asses, and a very g household; so that H7227
19 And, behold, there came a g wind from H1419
2:13 for they saw that *his* grief was very g. H1431
3:19 The small and g are there; and the H1419
5: 9 Which doeth g things and H1419
25 thy seed *shall be* g, and thine offspring H7227
9:10 Which doeth g things past finding out; H1419
22: 5 *Is* not thy wickedness g? and thine H7227
23: 6 Will he plead against me with *his* g H7230
30:18 By the g force *of my disease* is my H7230
31:25 If I rejoiced because my wealth *was* g, H7227
34 Did I fear a g multitude, or did the H7227
32: 9 G men are not *always* wise: neither do H7227
35:15 yet he knoweth *it* not in g extremity: H3966
36:18 then a g ransom cannot deliver thee. H7230
26 Behold, God *is* g, and we know *him* not, H7689
37: 5 with his voice; g things doeth he, which H1419
6 rain, and to the g rain of his strength. H4306
38:21 or *because* the number of thy days *is* g? H7227
39:11 g? or wilt thou leave thy labour to him? H7227
Ps 14: 5 There were they in g fear: for God *is* in H6343
18:35 up, and thy gentleness hath made me g. H7235
50 G deliverance giveth he to his king; and H1431
19:11 in keeping of them *there is* g reward. H7227
13 be innocent from the g transgression. H7227
21: 5 His glory *is* g in thy salvation: honour H1419
22:25 My praise *shall be* of thee in the g H7227
25:11 LORD, pardon mine iniquity; for it *is* g. H7227
31:19 *Oh* how g *is* thy goodness, which thou H7227
32: 6 in the floods of g waters they shall not H7227
33:17 shall he deliver *any* by his g strength. H7230
35:18 I will give thee thanks in the g H7227
36: 6 Thy righteousness *is* like the g H410
6 judgments *are* a g deep: O LORD, thou H7227
37:35 I have seen the wicked in g power, and
40: 9 I have preached righteousness in the g H7227
10 and thy truth from the g congregation. H7227
47: 2 *he is* a g King over all the earth. H1419
48: 1 G *is* the LORD, and greatly to be H1419
2 of the north, the city of the g King. H7227
53: 5 There were they in g fear, *where* no H6343
57:10 For thy mercy *is* g unto the heavens, H1419
58: 6 the g teeth of the young lions, O LORD. H4459
68:11 The Lord gave the word: g *was* the H7227
71:19 g things: O God, who *is* like unto thee! H1419
20 *Thou*, which hast shewed me g and H7227
76: 1 In Judah *is* God known: his name *is* g H1419
77:13 who *is so* g a God as *our* God? H1419
19 and thy path in the g waters, and thy H7227
78:15 gave *them* drink as *out of* the g depths. H7227
71 From following the ewes g with young he
80: 5 them tears to drink in g measure. H7991
86:10 For thou *art* g, and doest wondrous H1419
13 For g *is* thy mercy toward me: and thou H1419
92: 5 O LORD, how g are thy works! *and* thy H1431

Ps 95: 3 For the LORD *is* a g God, and a great H1419
3 For the LORD *is* a great God, and a g H1419
96: 4 For the LORD *is* g, and greatly to be H1419
99: 2 The LORD *is* g in Zion; and he *is* high H1419
3 Let them praise thy g and terrible H1419
103:11 the earth, *so* g is his mercy toward H1396
104: 1 God, thou art very g; thou art clothed H1431
25 *So is* this g and wide sea, wherein *are* H1419
25 innumerable, both small and g beasts. H1419
106:21 which had done g things in Egypt; H1419
107:23 in ships, that do business in g waters; H7227
108: 4 For thy mercy *is* g above the heavens: H1419
111: 2 The works of the LORD *are* g, sought H1419
115:13 that fear the LORD, *both* small and g. H1419
117: 2 For his merciful kindness is g toward H1396
119:156 G *are* thy tender mercies, O LORD: H7227
162 at thy word, as one that findeth g spoil. H7227
165 G peace have they which love thy law: H7227
126: 2 The LORD hath done g things for them. H1431
3 The LORD hath done g things for us; H1431
131: 1 g matters, or in things too high for me. H1419
135: 5 For I know that the LORD *is* g, and *that* H1419
10 Who smote g nations, and slew mighty H7227
136: 4 To him who alone doeth g wonders: for H1419
7 To him that made g lights: for his H1419
17 To him which smote g kings: for his H1419
138: 5 LORD: for g *is* the glory of the LORD. H1419
139:17 me, O God! how g is the sum of them! H6105
144: 7 deliver me out of g waters, from the H7227
145: 3 G *is* the LORD, and greatly to be H1419
7 the memory of thy g goodness, and H7227
8 slow to anger, and of g mercy. H1419
147: 5 G *is* our Lord, and of great power: his H1419
5 Great *is* our Lord, and of g power: his H7227
Prv 13: 7 maketh himself poor, yet *hath* g riches. H7227
14:29 *He that is* slow to wrath *is* of g H7227
15:16 than g treasure and trouble therewith. H7227
16: 8 than g revenues without right. H7230
18: 9 is brother to him that is a g waster. H1167
16 him, and bringeth him before g men. H1419
19:19 A man of g wrath shall suffer
22: 1 to be chosen than g riches, *and* loving H7227
25: 6 and stand not in the place of g *men*: H1419
26:10 The g *God* that formed all *things* both H7227
28:12 do rejoice, *there is* g glory: but when H7227
16 *is* also a g oppressor: *but* he that H7227
Ecc 1:16 Lo, I am come to g estate, and have H1431
16 yea, my heart had g experience of H7235
2: 4 I made me g works; I builded me H1431
7 house; also I had g possessions of great H7235
7 possessions of g and small cattle above H1241
9 So I was g, and increased more than all H1431
21 portion. This also *is* vanity and a g evil. H7227
8: 6 the misery of man *is* g upon him. H7227
9:13 the sun, and it *seemed* g unto me: H1419
14 and there came a g king against it, and H1419
14 it, and built g bulwarks against it: H1419
10: 4 place; for yielding pacifieth g offences. H1419
6 Folly is set in g dignity, and the rich sit H7227
Song 2: 3 his shadow with g delight, and his fruit
Isa 2: 9 down, and the g man humbleth himself:
5: 9 *even* g and fair, without inhabitant. H1419
6:12 a g forsaking in the midst of the land. H7227
8: 1 me, Take thee a g roll, and write in it H1419
9: 2 have seen a g light: they that dwell H1419
12: 6 of Zion: for g *is* the Holy One of Israel H1419
13: 4 like as of a g people; a tumultuous H7227
16:14 with all that g multitude; and the H7227
19:20 and a g one, and he shall deliver them. H7227
23: 3 And by g waters the seed of Sihor, the H7227
27: 1 with his sore and g and strong sword H1419
13 in that day, *that* the g trumpet shall be H1419
29: 6 earthquake, and g noise, with storm H1419
30:25 of the g slaughter, when the towers fall. H7227
32: 2 the shadow of a g rock in a weary land. H3515
33:23 g spoil divided; the lame take the prey. H4766
34: 6 a g slaughter in the land of Idumea. H1419
15 There shall the g owl make her nest, H7091
36: 2 Hezekiah with a g army. And he stood H3515
4 Thus saith the g king, the king of H1419
13 words of the g king, the king of Assyria. H1419
38:17 Behold, for peace I had g bitterness: but
47: 9 g abundance of thine enchantments. H3966
51:10 sea, the waters of the g deep; that hath H7227
53:12 *a portion* with the g, and he shall divide H7227
54: 7 but with g mercies will I gather thee. H1419
13 and g *shall be* the peace of thy children. H7227
63: 7 on us, and the g goodness toward the H7227
Jer 4: 6 from the north, and a g destruction. H1419

Jer 5: 5 I will get me unto the g men, and will H1419
27 they are become g, and waxen rich. H1431
6: 1 out of the north, and g destruction. H1419
22 country, and a g nation shall be raised H1419
10: 6 *art* g, and thy name *is* great in might. H1419
6 *art* great, and thy name *is* g in might. H1419
22 is come, and a g commotion out of the H1419
11:16 with the noise of a g tumult he hath H1419
13: 9 of Judah, and the g pride of Jerusalem. H7227
14:17 a g breach, with a very grievous blow. H1419
16: 6 Both the g and the small shall die in H1419
10 all this g evil against us? or what H1419
20:17 and her womb *to be* always g *with me*. H2030
21: 5 in anger, and in fury, and in g wrath. H1419
6 beast: they shall die of a g pestilence. H1419
22: 8 the LORD done thus unto this g city? H1419
25:14 For many nations and g kings shall H1419
32 to nation, and a g whirlwind shall be H1419
26:19 we procure g evil against our souls. H1419
27: 5 the ground, by my g power and by my H1419
7 g kings shall serve themselves of him. H1419
28: 8 and against g kingdoms, of war, and H1419
30: 7 Alas! for that day *is* g, so that none *is* H1419
31: 8 a g company shall return thither. H1419
32:17 the earth by thy g power and stretched H1419
18 after them: the G, the Mighty God, the H1419
19 G in counsel, and mighty in work: for H1419
21 a stretched out arm, and with g terror; H1419
37 in my fury, and in g wrath; and I will H1419
42 brought all this g evil upon this people, H1419
33: 3 and shew thee g and mighty things, H1419
36: 7 his evil way: for g *is* the anger and the H1419
41:12 him by the g waters that *are* in Gibeon. H7227
43: 9 Take g stones in thine hand, and hide H1419
44: 7 commit ye *this* g evil against your H1419
15 that stood by, a g multitude, even all H1419
26 I have sworn by my g name, saith the H1419
45: 5 And seekest thou g things for thyself? H1419
48: 3 Horonaim, spoiling and g destruction. H1419
50: 9 an assembly of g nations from the H1419
22 *is* in the land, and of g destruction. H1419
41 the north, and a g nation, and many H1419
51:54 Babylon, and g destruction from the H1419
55 out of her the g voice; when her waves H1419
55 waves do roar like g waters, a noise of H7227
52:13 of the g *men*, burned he with fire: H1419
Lam 1: 1 she *that was* g among the nations, H7227
3 and because of g servitude: she H7230
2:13 *is* g like the sea: who can heal thee? H1419
3:23 *They are* new every morning: g *is* thy H7227
Ezk 1: 4 out of the north, a g cloud, and a fire H1419
24 like the noise of g waters, as the voice H7227
3:12 me a voice of a g rushing, *saying*, H1419
13 them, and a noise of a g rushing. H1419
8: 6 they do? *even* the g abominations that H1419
9: 9 *is* exceeding g, and the land is full H1419
13:11 shower; and ye, O g hailstones, shall fall; H417
13 g hailstones in *my* fury to consume *it*. H417
16: 7 and waxen g, and thou art come to H1431
26 thy neighbours, g of flesh; and hast H1432
17: 3 And say, Thus saith the Lord GOD; A g H1419
3 A great eagle with g wings, longwinged, H1419
5 by g waters, *and* set it *as* a willow tree. H7227
7 There was also another g eagle with H1419
7 great eagle with g wings and many H1419
8 It was planted in a good soil by g H7227
9 even without g power or many people H1419
17 mighty army and g company make for H7227
21:14 *is* the sword of the g *men that are* slain, H1419
23:23 and rulers, g lords and renowned, H7991
24: 9 city! I will even make the pile for fire g. H1431
12 with lies, and her g scum went not H7227
25:17 And I will execute g vengeance upon H1419
26:19 thee, and g waters shall cover thee; H7227
27:26 Thy rowers have brought thee into g H7227
28: 5 By thy g wisdom *and* by thy traffick H7230
29: 3 king of Egypt, the g dragon that lieth in H1419
18 army to serve a g service against Tyrus: H1419
30: 4 come upon Egypt, and g pain shall be in
9 afraid, and g pain shall come upon
16 Sin shall have g pain, and No shall be H2342
31: 4 The waters made him g, the deep set H1431
6 under his shadow dwelt all g nations. H7227
7 branches: for his root was by g waters. H7227
15 thereof, and the g waters were stayed: H7227
32:13 from beside the g waters; neither shall H7227
36:23 And I will sanctify my g name, which H1419
37:10 upon their feet, an exceeding g army. H1419
38: 4 *of armour, even* a g company *with* H7227
Ezk 38:13 cattle and goods, to take a g spoil? H1419
15 a g company, and a mighty army: H1419
19 be a g shaking in the land of Israel; H1419
22 and g hailstones, fire, and brimstone. H417
39:17 for you, *even* a g sacrifice upon the H1419
41: 8 chambers *were* a full reed of six g cubits. H679
47: 9 there shall be a very g multitude of fish, H7227
10 the fish of the g sea, exceeding many. H1419
15 north side, from the g sea, the way of H1419
19 the river to the g sea. And *this is* the H1419
20 The west side also *shall be* the g sea H1419
48:28 *and* to the river toward the g sea. H1419
Dan 2: 6 and rewards and g honour: therefore H7690
31 Thou, O king, sawest, and behold a g H7690
31 a great image. This g image, whose H7229
35 g mountain, and filled the whole earth. H7229
45 and the gold; the g God hath made H7229
48 Then the king made Daniel a g man, H7236
48 gave him many g gifts, and made him H7260
4: 3 How g *are* his signs! and how mighty H7260
10 the earth, and the height thereof *was* g. H7690
30 The king spake, and said, Is not this g H7229
5: 1 Belshazzar the king made a g feast to a H7229
7: 2 of the heaven strove upon the g sea. H7229
3 And four g beasts came up from the H7260
7 and it had g iron teeth: it devoured H7260
8 man, and a mouth speaking g things. H7260
11 of the voice of the g words which the H7260
17 These g beasts, which are four, *are* four H7260
20 that spake very g things, whose look H7260
25 And he shall speak g words against the
8: 4 did according to his will, and became g. H1431
8 Therefore the he goat waxed very g: and H1431
8 he was strong, the g horn was broken; H1419
9 waxed exceeding g, toward the south, H1431
10 And it waxed g, *even* to the host of H1431
21 king of Grecia: and the g horn that *is* H1419
9: 4 said, O Lord, the g and dreadful God, H1419
12 upon us a g evil: for under the whole H1419
18 righteousnesses, but for thy g mercies. H7227
10: 4 side of the g river, which *is* Hiddekel; H1419
7 the vision; but a g quaking fell upon H1419
8 alone, and saw this g vision, and there H1419
11: 3 that shall rule with g dominion, and do H7227
5 his dominion *shall be* a g dominion. H7227
10 a multitude of g forces: and *one* shall H7227
11 he shall set forth a g multitude; but the H7227
13 with a g army and with much riches. H1419
25 of the south with a g army; and the H1419
25 battle with a very g and mighty army; H1419
28 into his land with g riches; and his H1419
44 he shall go forth with g fury to destroy, H1419
12: 1 stand up, the g prince which standeth H1419
Hos 1: 2 land hath committed g whoredom, H2181
11 land: for g *shall be* the day of Jezreel. H1419
8:12 I have written to him the g things of my H7239
9: 7 of thine iniquity, and the g hatred. H7227
10:15 you because of your g wickedness: in a H7451
13: 5 wilderness, in the land of g drought. H8514
Joel 1: 6 and he hath the cheek teeth of a g lion. H3833
2: 2 upon the mountains: a g people and a H7227
11 his camp *is* very g: for *he is* strong that H7227
11 of the LORD *is* g and very terrible; and H1419
13 slow to anger, and of g kindness, and H7227
20 up, because he hath done g things. H1431
21 rejoice: for the LORD will do g things. H1431
25 my g army which I sent among you. H1419
31 blood, before the g and the terrible day H1419
3:13 fats overflow; for their wickedness *is* g. H7227
Am 3: 9 and behold the g tumults in the midst H7227
15 perish, and the g houses shall have an H7227
6: 2 go ye to Hamath the g: then go down to H7227
11 and he will smite the g house with H1419
7: 4 the g deep, and did eat up a part. H7227
8: 5 g, and falsifying the balances by deceit? H1431
Jna 1: 2 Arise, go to Nineveh, that g city, and H1419
4 But the LORD sent out a g wind into H1419
12 for my sake this g tempest *is* upon you. H1419
17 Now the LORD had prepared a g fish to H1419
3: 2 Arise, go unto Nineveh, that g city, and H1419
3 exceeding g city of three days' journey. H1419
4: 2 slow to anger, and of g kindness, and H7227
11 And should not I spare Nineveh, that g H1419
Mic 2:12 they shall make g noise by reason of *the*
5: 4 shall he be g unto the ends of the earth. H1431
7: 3 a reward; and the g *man*, he uttereth H1419
Nah 1: 3 The LORD *is* slow to anger, and g in H1419
3: 3 of slain, and a g number of carcases; H3514
10 all her g men were bound in chains. H1419
Nah 3:17 captains as the g grasshoppers, which H1462
Hab 3:15 horses, *through* the heap of g waters. H7227
Zep 1:10 second, and a g crashing from the hills. H1419
14 The g day of the LORD *is* near, *it is* H1419
Zec 1:14 and for Zion with a g jealousy. H1419
4: 7 Who *art* thou, O g mountain? before H1419
7:12 a g wrath from the LORD of hosts. H1419
8: 2 for Zion with g jealousy, and I was H1419
2 and I was jealous for her with g fury. H1419
9:17 For how g *is* his goodness, and how
17 goodness, and how g *is* his beauty! corn
12:11 In that day shall there be a g mourning H1431
14: 4 *shall be* a very g valley; and half of the H1419
13 in that day, *that* a g tumult from the H7227
14 silver, and apparel, in g abundance. H3966
Mal 1:11 same my name *shall be* g among the H1419
11 for my name *shall be* g among the H1419
14 thing: for I *am* a g King, saith the H1419
4: 5 of the g and dreadful day of the LORD: H1419
Mt 2:10 star, they rejoiced with exceeding g joy. G3173
18 and weeping, and g mourning, Rachel G4183
4:16 The people which sat in darkness saw g G3173
25 And there followed him g multitudes of G4183
5:12 Rejoice, and be exceeding glad: for g *is* G4183
19 be called g in the kingdom of heaven. G3173
35 for it is the city of the g King. G3173
6:23 be darkness, how g *is* that darkness! G4214
7:27 and it fell: and g was the fall of it. G3173
8: 1 mountain, g multitudes followed him. G4183
10 not found so g faith, no, not in Israel. G5118
18 Now when Jesus saw g multitudes G4183
24 And, behold, there arose a g tempest in G3173
26 and the sea; and there was a g calm. G3173
12:15 from thence: and g multitudes followed G4183
13: 2 And g multitudes were gathered G4183
46 Who, when he had found one pearl of g G4186
14:14 And Jesus went forth, and saw a g G4183
15:28 her, O woman, g *is* thy faith: be it unto G3173
30 And g multitudes came unto him, G4183
33 wilderness, as to fill so g a multitude? G5118
19: 2 And g multitudes followed him; and he G4183
22 sorrowful: for he had g possessions. G4183
20:25 are g exercise authority upon them. G3173
26 g among you, let him be your minister; G3173
29 And as they departed from Jericho, a g G4183
21: 8 And a very g multitude spread their G4118
22:36 Master, which *is* the g commandment G3173
38 This is the first and g commandment. G3173
24:21 For then shall be g tribulation, such as G3173
24 and shall shew g signs and wonders; G3173
30 of heaven with power and g glory. G4183
31 And he shall send his angels with a g G3173
26:47 came, and with him a g multitude with G4183
27:60 and he rolled a g stone to the door of G3173
28: 2 And, behold, there was a g earthquake: G3173
8 with fear and g joy; and did run to G3173
Mk 1:35 And in the morning, rising up a g while G3029
3: 7 to the sea: and a g multitude from G4183
8 Tyre and Sidon, a g multitude, when G4183
8 what g things he did, came unto him. G3745
4: 1 unto him a g multitude, so that he G4183
32 and shooteth out g branches; so that G3173
37 And there arose a g storm of wind, and G3173
39 wind ceased, and there was a g calm. G3173
5:11 mountains a g herd of swine feeding. G3173
19 and tell them how g things the Lord G3745
20 in Decapolis how g things Jesus had G3745
42 astonished with a g astonishment. G3173
7:36 the more a g deal they published *it*; G3123
8: 1 being very g, and having nothing G3827
9:14 disciples, he saw a g multitude about G4183
10:22 away grieved: for he had g possessions. G4183
42 g ones exercise authority upon them. G3173
43 be g among you, shall be your minister: G3173
46 his disciples and a g number of people, G2425
48 he cried the more a g deal, *Thou* son of G4183
13: 2 Seest thou these g buildings? there shall G3173
26 in the clouds with g power and glory. G4183
14:43 and with him a g multitude with G4183
16: 4 stone was rolled away: for it was very g. G3173
Lk 1:15 For he shall be g in the sight of the G3173
32 He shall be g, and shall be called the G3173
49 For he that is mighty hath done to me g G3167
58 Lord had shewed g mercy upon her; G3170
2: 5 his espoused wife, being g with child.
10 of g joy, which shall be to all people. G3173
36 Aser: she was of a g age, and had lived G4183
4:25 g famine was throughout all the land; G3173
38 g fever; and they besought him for her. G3173

Lk 5: 6 they inclosed a g multitude of fishes: G4183
15 of him: and g multitudes came together G4183
29 And Levi made him a g feast in his own G3173
29 house: and there was a g company of G4183
6:17 disciples, and a g multitude of people G4183
23 your reward *is* g in heaven: for in the G4183
35 reward shall be g, and ye shall be the G4183
49 it fell; and the ruin of that house was g. G3173
7: 9 not found so g faith, no, not in Israel. G5118
16 saying, That a g prophet is risen up G3173
8:37 were taken with g fear: and he went up G3173
39 and shew how g things God hath done G3745
39 how g things Jesus had done unto him. G3745
9:48 among you all, the same shall be g. G3173
10: 2 harvest truly *is* g, but the labourers *are* G4183
13 done in you, they had a g while ago G3819
13:19 and waxed a g tree; and the fowls of G3173
14:16 man made a g supper, and bade many: G3173
25 And there went g multitudes with him: G4183
32 Or else, while the other is yet a g way off,
15:20 when he was yet a g way off, his father G3112
16:26 and you there is a g gulf fixed: so that G3173
21:11 And g earthquakes shall be in divers G3173
11 and g signs shall there be from heaven. G3173
23 for there shall be g distress in the land, G3173
27 in a cloud with power and g glory. G4183
22:44 was as it were g drops of blood falling
23:27 And there followed him a g company of G4183
24:52 and returned to Jerusalem with g joy: G3173
Jn 5: 3 In these lay a g multitude of impotent G4183
6: 2 And a g multitude followed him, G4183
5 eyes, and saw a g company come unto G4183
18 And the sea arose by reason of a g G3173
7:37 In the last day, that g *day* of the feast, G3173
21:11 net to land full of g fishes, an hundred G3173
Act 2:20 g and notable day of the Lord come: G3173
4:33 And with g power gave the apostles G3173
33 Jesus: and g grace was upon them all. G3173
5: 5 up the ghost: and g fear came on all G3173
11 And g fear came upon all the church, G3173
6: 7 greatly; and a g company of the priests G4183
8 faith and power, did g wonders and G3173
7:11 and Chanaan, and g affliction: and our G3173
8: 1 time there was a g persecution against G3173
2 and made g lamentation over him. G3173
8 And there was g joy in that city. G3173
9 giving out that himself was some g one: G3173
10 saying, This man is the g power of God. G3173
27 an eunuch of g authority under Candace
9:16 For I will shew him how g things he G3745
10:11 as it had been a g sheet knit at the four G3173
11: 5 as it had been a g sheet, let down from G3173
21 with them: and a g number believed, G4183
28 there should be g dearth throughout all G3173
14: 1 so spake, that a g multitude both of the G4183
15: 3 they caused g joy unto all the brethren. G3173
16:26 And suddenly there was a g G3173
17: 4 devout Greeks a g multitude, and of the G4183
19:27 that the temple of the g goddess Diana G3173
28 saying, G *is* Diana of the Ephesians. G3173
34 cried out, G *is* Diana of the Ephesians. G3173
35 a worshipper of the g goddess Diana, G3173
21:40 there was made a g silence, he spake G4183
22: 6 from heaven a g light round about me. G2425
28 answered, With a g sum obtained I this G4183
23: 9 And there arose a g cry: and the scribes G3173
10 And when there arose a g dissension, G4183
14 ourselves under a g curse, that we will
24: 2 by thee we enjoy g quietness, and that G4183
7 *upon us*, and with g violence took *him* G4183
25:23 and Bernice, with g pomp, and was G4183
26:22 both to small and g, saying none other G3173
28: 6 they had looked a g while, and saw no G4183
29 had g reasoning among themselves. G4183
Ro 9: 2 That I have g heaviness and continual G3173
15:23 and having a g desire these many years G1974
1Co 9:11 things, *is it* a g thing if we shall reap G3173
16: 9 For a g door and effectual is opened G3173
2Co 1:10 Who delivered us from so g a death, G5082
3:12 hope, we use g plainness of speech: G4183
7: 4 G *is* my boldness of speech toward you, G4183
4 toward you, g *is* my glorying of you: G4183
8: 2 How that in a g trial of affliction the G4183
22 the g confidence which *I have* in you. G4183
11:15 Therefore *it is* no g thing if his G3173
Eph 2: 4 But God, who is rich in mercy, for his g G4183
5:32 This is a g mystery: but I speak G3173
Col 2: 1 For I would that ye knew what g G2245
4:13 For I bear him record, that he hath a g G4183

1Th 2:17 to see your face with g desire. G4183
1Ti 3:13 a good degree, and g boldness in the G4183
16 And without controversy g is the G3173
6: 6 But godliness with contentment is g G3173
2Ti 2:20 But in a g house there are not only G3173
Tit 2:13 the g God and our Saviour Jesus Christ; G3173
Phlm 7 For we have g joy and consolation in G4183
Heb 2: 3 How shall we escape, if we neglect so g G5082
4:14 Seeing then that we have a g high G3173
7: 4 Now consider how g this man *was*, G4080
10:32 ye endured a g fight of afflictions; G4183
35 which hath g recompence of reward.
12: 1 about with so g a cloud of witnesses, G5118
13:20 our Lord Jesus, that g shepherd of the G3173
Jas 3: 4 though *they be* so g, and *are* driven of G5082
5 and boasteth g things. Behold, how G3166
5 how g a matter a little fire kindleth! G2245
1Pt 3: 4 which is in the sight of God of g price. G4185
2Pt 1: 4 Whereby are given unto us exceeding g G3176
2:18 For when they speak g swelling *words* G5246
3:10 shall pass away with a g noise, and the
Jude 6 unto the judgment of the g day. G3173
16 their mouth speaketh g swelling *words*, G5246
Rev 1:10 behind me a g voice, as of a trumpet, G3173
2:22 with her into g tribulation, except they G3173
6: 4 there was given unto him a g sword. G3173
12 lo, there was a g earthquake; and the G3173
15 And the kings of the earth, and the g G3175
17 For the g day of his wrath is come; and G3173
7: 9 After this I beheld, and, lo, a g G4183
14 which came out of g tribulation, and G3173
8: 8 and as it were a g mountain burning G3173
10 and there fell a g star from heaven, G3173
9: 2 as the smoke of a g furnace; and the G3173
14 are bound in the g river Euphrates. G3173
11: 8 *lie* in the street of the g city, which G3173
11 g fear fell upon them which saw them. G3173
12 And they heard a g voice from heaven G3173
13 And the same hour was there a g G3173
15 and there were g voices in heaven, G3173
17 to thee thy g power, and hast reigned. G3173
18 thy name, small and g; and shouldest G3173
19 and an earthquake, and g hail. G3173
12: 1 And there appeared a g wonder in G3173
3 and behold a g red dragon, having G3173
9 And the g dragon was cast out, that old G3173
12 unto you, having g wrath, because he G3173
14 two wings of a g eagle, that she might G3173
13: 2 power, and his seat, and g authority. G3173
5 him a mouth speaking g things and G3173
13 And he doeth g wonders, so that he G3173
16 And he causeth all, both small and g, G3173
14: 2 as the voice of a g thunder: and I heard G3173
8 is fallen, that g city, because she made G3173
19 the g winepress of the wrath of God. G3173
15: 1 And I saw another sign in heaven, g G3173
3 of the Lamb, saying, G and marvellous G3173
16: 1 And I heard a g voice out of the temple G3173
9 And men were scorched with g heat, G3173
12 out his vial upon the g river Euphrates; G3173
14 battle of that g day of God Almighty. G3173
17 air; and there came a g voice out of the G3173
18 and there was a g earthquake, such as G3173
18 so mighty an earthquake, *and* so g. G3173
19 And the g city was divided into three G3173
19 the nations fell: and g Babylon came in G3173
21 And there fell upon men a g hail out of G3173
21 for the plague thereof was exceeding g. G3173
17: 1 g whore that sitteth upon many waters: G3173
5 BABYLON THE G, THE MOTHER OF G3173
6 her, I wondered with g admiration. G3173
18 sawest is that g city, which reigneth G3173
18: 1 heaven, having g power; and the earth G3173
2 Babylon the g is fallen, is fallen, and G3173
10 Alas, alas that g city Babylon, that G3173
16 And saying, Alas, alas, that g city, that G3173
17 For in one hour so g riches is come to G5118
18 What *city is* like unto this g city! G3173
19 Alas, alas, that g city, wherein were G3173
21 up a stone like a g millstone, and cast G3173
21 violence shall that g city Babylon be G3173
23 were the g men of the earth; for G3175
19: 1 And after these things I heard a g voice G3173
2 he hath judged the g whore, which did G3173
5 and ye that fear him, both small and g. G3173
6 And I heard as it were the voice of a g G4183
17 together unto the supper of the g God; G3173
18 *both* free and bond, both small and g. G3173
20: 1 pit and a g chain in his hand. G3173

Rev 20:11 And I saw a g white throne, and him G3173
12 And I saw the dead, small and g, stand G3173
21: 3 And I heard a g voice out of heaven G3173
10 in the spirit to a g and high mountain, G3173
10 and shewed me that g city, the holy G3173
12 And had a wall g and high, *and* had G3173

GREATER

Gen 1:16 And God made two great lights; the g H1419
4:13 My punishment *is* g than I can bear. H1419
39: 9 *There is* none g in this house than I; H1419
41:40 only in the throne will I be g than thou. H1431
48:19 brother shall be g than he, and his seed H1431
Ex 18:11 Now I know that the LORD *is* g than all H1419
Nu 14:12 thee a g nation and mightier than they. H1419
Dt 1:28 The people *is* g and taller than we; H1419
4:38 To drive out nations from before thee g H1419
7: 1 nations g and mightier than thou; H7227
9: 1 to possess nations g and mightier than H1419
14 thee a nation mightier and g than they. H7227
11:23 ye shall possess g nations and mightier H1419
Jos 10: 2 because it *was* g than Ai, and all the H1419
1Sa 14:30 g slaughter among the Philistines? H7235
2Sa 13:15 he hated her *was* g than the love H1419
16 me away *is* g than the other that H1419
1Ki 1:37 make his throne g than the throne of H1431
47 and make his throne g than thy throne. H1431
1Ch 11: 9 So David waxed g and greater: for the H1980
9 So David waxed greater and g: for the H1419
2Ch 3: 5 And the g house he cieled with fir tree, H1419
Est 9: 4 man Mordecai waxed g and greater. H1980
4 man Mordecai waxed greater and g. H1419
Job 33:12 answer thee, that God is g than man. H7235
Lam 4: 6 of my people is g than the punishment H1431
Ezk 8: 6 *and* thou shalt see g abominations. H1419
13 shalt see g abominations that they do. H1419
15 shalt see g abominations than these. H1419
43:14 settle *even* to the g settle *shall be* four H1419
Dan 11:13 set forth a multitude g than the former, H7227
Am 6: 2 or their border g than your border? H7227
Hag 2: 9 The glory of this latter house shall be g H1419
Mt 11:11 there hath not risen a g than John the G3187
11 in the kingdom of heaven is g than he. G3187
12: 6 in this place is *one* g than the temple. G3187
41 and, behold, a g than Jonas *is* here. G4119
42 and, behold, a g than Solomon *is* here. G4119
23:14 ye shall receive the g damnation. G4055
17 *Ye* fools and blind: for whether is g, the G3187
19 *Ye* fools and blind: for whether *is* g, the G3187
Mk 4:32 up, and becometh g than all herbs, and G3187
12:31 other commandment g than these. G3187
40 these shall receive g damnation. G4055
Lk 7:28 there is not a g prophet than John the G3187
28 in the kingdom of God is g than he. G3187
11:31 and, behold, a g than Solomon *is* here. G4119
32 and, behold, a g than Jonas *is* here. G4119
12:18 my barns, and build g; and there will I G3187
20:47 the same shall receive g damnation. G4055
22:27 For whether *is* g, he that sitteth at meat, G3187
Jn 1:50 thou shalt see g things than these. G3187
4:12 Art thou g than our father Jacob, which G3187
5:20 he will shew him g works than these, G3187
36 But I have g witness than *that* of John: G3187
8:53 Art thou g than our father Abraham, G3187
10:29 My Father, which gave *them* me, is g G3187
13:16 you, The servant is not g than his lord; G3187
16 he that is sent g than he that sent him. G3187
14:12 he do also; and g *works* than these G3187
28 the Father: for my Father is g than I. G3187
15:13 G love hath no man than this, that a G3187
20 The servant is not g than his lord. If G3187
19:11 delivered me unto thee hath the g sin. G3187
Act 15:28 g burden than these necessary things; G4119
1Co 14: 5 that ye prophesied: for g *is* he that G3187
15: 6 once; of whom the g part remain unto G4119
Heb 6:13 swear by no g, he sware by himself,
16 For men verily swear by the g: and an G3187
9:11 things to come, by a g and more perfect G3187
11:26 Esteeming the reproach of Christ g G3187
Jas 3: 1 we shall receive the g condemnation. G3187
2Pt 2:11 Whereas angels, which are g in power G3187
1Jn 3:20 For if our heart condemn us, God is g G3187
4: 4 them: because g is he that is in you, G3187
5: 9 the witness of God is g: for this is the G3187
3Jn 4 I have no g joy than to hear that my G3186

GREATEST

1Ch 12:14 hundred, and the g over a thousand. H1419
29 for hitherto the g part of them had kept H4768

Job 1: 3 was the g of all the men of the east. H1419
Jer 6:13 even unto the g of them every one is H1419
8:10 least even unto the g is given to H1419
31:34 of them unto the g of them, saith the H1419
42: 1 the least even unto the g, came near, H1419
8 the people from the least even to the g, H1419
44:12 even unto the g, by the sword and by H1419
Jna 3: 5 the g of them even to the least of them. H1419
Mt 13:32 it is grown, it is the g among herbs, and G3187
18: 1 Who is the g in the kingdom of heaven? G3187
4 same is g in the kingdom of heaven. G3187
23:11 But he that is g among you shall be G3187
Mk 9:34 themselves, who should be the g. G3187
Lk 9:46 them, which of them should be the g. G3187
22:24 of them should be accounted the g. G3187
26 But ye shall not be so: but he that is g G3187
Act 8:10 the least to the g, saying, This man is G3173
1Co 13:13 these three; but the g of these is charity. G3187
Heb 8:11 shall know me, from the least to the g. G3173

GREATLY
Gen 3:16 Unto the woman he said, I will g H7235
7:18 were increased g upon the earth; and H3966
19: 3 And he pressed upon them g; and they H3966
24:35 blessed my master g; and he is become H3966
32: 7 Then Jacob was g afraid and H3966
Ex 19:18 and the whole mount quaked g. H3966
Nu 11:10 kindled g; Moses also was displeased. H3966
14:39 of Israel: and the people mourned g. H3966
Dt 15: 4 for the LORD shall g bless thee in the H1288
17:17 g multiply to himself silver and gold. H3966
Jos 10: 2 That they feared g, because Gibeon was H3966
Jdg 2:15 unto them: and they were g distressed. H3966
6: 6 And Israel was g impoverished H3966
1Sa 11: 6 tidings, and his anger was kindled g. H3966
15 Saul and all the men of Israel rejoiced g. H3966
12:18 people g feared the LORD and Samuel. H3966
16:21 g; and he became his armourbearer. H3966
17:11 they were dismayed, and g afraid. H3966
28: 5 was afraid, and his heart g trembled. H3966
30: 6 And David was g distressed; for the H3966
2Sa 10: 5 the men were g ashamed: and the king H3966
12: 5 And David's anger was g kindled H3966
24:10 I have sinned g in that I have done: H3966
1Ki 2:12 and his kingdom was established g. H3966
5: 7 that he rejoiced g, and said, Blessed be H3966
18: 3 (Now Obadiah feared the LORD g: H3966
1Ch 4:38 the house of their fathers increased g. H7230
16:25 For great is the LORD, and g to be H3966
19: 5 for the men were g ashamed. And the H3966
21: 8 I have sinned g, because I have done H3966
2Ch 25:10 their anger was g kindled against H3966
33:12 himself g before the God of his fathers, H3966
Job 3:25 For the thing which I g feared is come H6343
8: 7 yet thy latter end should g increase. H3966
Ps 21: 1 in thy salvation how g shall he rejoice! H3966
28: 7 therefore my heart g rejoiceth; and with H3966
38: 6 I am troubled; I am bowed down g; I go H3966
45:11 So shall the king g desire thy beauty: for
47: 9 earth belong unto God: he is g exalted. H3966
48: 1 Great is the LORD, and g to be praised H3966
62: 2 is my defence; I shall not be g moved. H7227
65: 9 waterest it: thou g enrichest it with the H7227
71:23 My lips shall g rejoice when I sing unto
78:59 he was wroth, and g abhorred Israel: H3966
89: 7 God is g to be feared in the assembly of H7227
96: 4 For the LORD is great, and g to be H3966
105:24 And he increased his people g; and H3966
107:38 are multiplied g; and suffereth not their H3966
109:30 I will g praise the LORD with my H3966
112: 1 delighteth g in his commandments. H3966
116:10 have I spoken: I was g afflicted: H3966
119:51 The proud have had me g in derision: H3966
145: 3 Great is the LORD, and g to be praised; H3966
Prv 23:24 The father of the righteous shall g H1524
Isa 42:17 back, they shall be g ashamed, that H1322
61:10 I will g rejoice in the LORD, my soul H7797
Jer 3: 1 not that land be g polluted? but thou H2610
4:10 surely thou hast g deceived this people H5377
9:19 are we spoiled! we are g confounded, H3966
20:11 they shall be g ashamed; for they shall H3966
Ezk 20:13 my sabbaths they g polluted: then I H3966
25:12 and hath g offended, and revenged H816
Dan 5: 9 Then was king Belshazzar g troubled, H7690
9:23 thee; for thou art g beloved: therefore
10:11 And he said unto me, O Daniel, a man g
19 And said, O man g beloved, fear not:
Oba 2 the heathen: thou art g despised. H3966
Zep 1:14 is near, and hasteth g, even the voice of H3966
Zec 9: 9 Rejoice g, O daughter of Zion; shout, O H3966
Mt 27:14 that the governor marvelled g. G3029
54 g, saying, Truly this was the Son of God. G4970
Mk 5:23 And besought him g, saying, My little G4183
38 and them that wept and wailed g. G4183
9:15 they beheld him, were g amazed, and G1568
12:27 God of the living: ye therefore do g err. G4183
Jn 3:29 heareth him, rejoiceth g because of the G5479
Act 3:11 that is called Solomon's, g wondering. G1569
6: 7 in Jerusalem g; and a great company G4970
1Co 16:12 As touching our brother Apollos, I g G4183
Php 1: 8 For God is my record, how g I long G1971
4:10 But I rejoiced in the Lord g, that now at G3171
1Th 3: 6 g to see us, as we also to see you: G1971
2Ti 1: 4 G desiring to see thee, being mindful of G1971
4:15 for he hath g withstood our words. G3029
1Pt 1: 6 Wherein ye g rejoice, though now for a
2Jn 4 I rejoiced g that I found of thy children G3029
3Jn 3 For I rejoiced g, when the brethren G3029

GREATNESS
Ex 15: 7 And in the g of thine excellency thou H7230
16 upon them; by the g of thine arm they H1419
Nu 14:19 unto the g of thy mercy, and as H1433
Dt 3:24 thy servant thy g, and thy mighty hand: H1433
5:24 his glory and his g, and we have heard H1433
9:26 through thy g, which thou hast brought H1433
11: 2 your God, his g, his mighty hand, and H1433
32: 3 the LORD: ascribe ye g unto our God. H1433
1Ch 17:19 thou done all this g, in making known H1420
21 thee a name of g and terribleness, by H1420
29:11 Thine, O LORD, is the g, and the power, H1420
2Ch 9: 6 the one half of the g of thy wisdom was H4768
24:27 Now concerning his sons, and the g of H7230
Neh 13:22 me according to the g of thy mercy. H7230
Est 10: 2 the declaration of the g of Mordecai, H1420
Ps 66: 3 through the g of thy power shall thine H7230
71:21 Thou shalt increase my g, and comfort H1420
79:11 thee; according to the g of thy power H1433
145: 3 be praised; and his g is unsearchable. H1420
6 terrible acts: and I will declare thy g. H1420
150: 2 praise him according to his excellent g. H1433
Prv 5:23 in the g of his folly he shall go astray. H7230
Isa 40:26 by names by the g of his might, for that H7230
57:10 Thou art wearied in the g of thy way; H7230
63: 1 travelling in the g of his strength? I that H7230
Jer 13:22 upon me? For the g of thine iniquity are H7230
Ezk 31: 2 multitude; Whom art thou like in thy g? H1433
7 Thus was he fair in his g, in the length H1433
18 in glory and in g among the trees of H1433
Dan 4:22 strong: for thy g is grown, and reacheth H7238
7:27 dominion, and the g of the kingdom H7238
Eph 1:19 And what is the exceeding g of his G3174

GREAT-OWL See GREAT and OWL.

GREAVES
1Sa 17: 6 And he had g of brass upon his legs, H4697

GRECIA
Dan 8:21 And the rough goat is the king of G: and H3120
10:20 forth, lo, the prince of G shall come. H3120
11: 2 shall stir up all against the realm of G. H3120

GRECIANS
Joel 3: 6 have ye sold unto the G, that ye might H3125
Act 6: 1 a murmuring of the G against the G1675
9:29 the G: but they went about to slay him. G1675
11:20 unto the G, preaching the Lord Jesus. G1675

GREECE
Zec 9:13 thy sons, O G, and made thee as the H3120
Act 20: 2 much exhortation, he came into G, G1671

GREEDILY
Prv 21:26 He coveteth g all the day long: but the H8378
Ezk 22:12 increase, and thou hast g gained of thy
Jude 11 of Cain, and ran g after the error of G1632

GREEDINESS
Eph 4:19 to work all uncleanness with g. G4124

GREEDY
Ps 17:12 Like as a lion that is g of his prey, and H3700
Prv 1:19 So are the ways of every one that is g of H1214
15:27 He that is g of gain troubleth his own H1214
Isa 56:11 Yea, they are g dogs which can H5794+H5315
1Ti 3: 3 Not given to wine, no striker, not g of G866
8 given to much wine, not g of filthy lucre; G146

GREEK
Mk 7:26 The woman was a G, a Syrophenician G1674
Lk 23:38 over him in letters of G, and Latin, and G1673
Jn 19:20 written in Hebrew, and G, and Latin. G1676
Act 16: 1 and believed; but his father was a G: G1672
3 they knew all that his father was a G. G1672
21:37 thee? Who said, Canst thou speak G? G1676
Ro 1:16 to the Jew first, and also to the G. G1672
10:12 the Jew and the G: for the same Lord G1672
Gal 2: 3 a G, was compelled to be circumcised: G1672
3:28 There is neither Jew nor G, there is G1672
Col 3:11 Where there is neither G nor Jew, G1672
Rev 9:11 the G tongue hath his name Apollyon. G1673

GREEKS
Jn 12:20 And there were certain G among them G1672
Act 14: 1 of the Jews and also of the G believed. G1672
17: 4 and of the devout G a great multitude, G1672
12 which were G, and of men, not a few. G1674
18: 4 and persuaded the Jews and the G. G1672
17 Then all the G took Sosthenes, the chief G1672
19:10 of the Lord Jesus, both Jews and G. G1672
17 to all the Jews and G also dwelling at G1672
20:21 and also to the G, repentance toward G1672
21:28 further brought G also into the temple, G1672
Ro 1:14 I am debtor both to the G, and to the G1672
1Co 1:22 For the Jews require a sign, and the G G1672
23 and unto the G foolishness; G1672
24 both Jews and G, Christ the power of G1672

GREEN
Gen 1:30 every g herb for meat: and it was so. H3418
9: 3 the g herb have I given you all things. H3418
30:37 And Jacob took him rods of g poplar, H3892
Ex 10:15 remained not any g thing in the trees, H3418
Lev 2:14 of thy first-fruits g ears of corn dried by
23:14 nor parched corn, nor g ears, until the
Dt 12: 2 upon the hills, and under every g tree: H7488
Jdg 16: 7 me with seven g withs that were never H3892
8 up to her seven g withs which had not H3892
1Ki 14:23 every high hill, and under every g tree. H7488
2Ki 16: 4 on the hills, and under every g tree. H7488
17:10 every high hill, and under every g tree: H7488
19:26 field, and as the g herb, as the grass on H3419
2Ch 28: 4 on the hills, and under every g tree. H7488
Est 1: 6 Where were white, g, and blue, H3768
Job 8:16 He is g before the sun, and his branch H7373
15:32 his time, and his branch shall not be g. H7488
39: 8 and he searcheth after every g thing. H3387
Ps 23: 2 He maketh me to lie down in g H1877
37: 2 like the grass, and wither as the g herb. H3418
35 and spreading himself like a g bay tree. H7488
52: 8 But I am like a g olive tree in the house H7488
Song 1:16 beloved, yea, pleasant: also our bed is g. H7488
2:13 The fig tree putteth forth her g figs, and H6291
Isa 15: 6 the grass faileth, there is no g thing. H3418
37:27 field, and as the g herb, as the grass on H3419
57: 5 idols under every g tree, slaying the H7488
Jer 2:20 and under every g tree thou wanderest, H7488
3: 6 and under every g tree, and there hath H7488
13 under every g tree, and ye have not H7488
11:16 The LORD called thy name, A g olive H7488
17: 2 by the g trees upon the high hills. H7488
8 but her leaf shall be g; and shall not be H7488
Ezk 6:13 and under every g tree, and under H7488
17:24 tree, have dried up the g tree, and have H3892
20:47 it shall devour every g tree in thee, and H3892
Hos 14: 8 a g fir tree. From me is thy fruit found. H7488
Mk 6:39 down by companies upon the g grass. G5515
Lk 23:31 For if they do these things in a g tree, G5200
Rev 8: 7 burnt up, and all g grass was burnt up. G5515
9: 4 earth, neither any g thing, neither any G5515

GREENISH
Lev 13:49 And if the plague be g or reddish in the H3422
14:37 hollow strakes, g or reddish, which in H3422

GREENNESS
Job 8:12 Whilst it is yet in his g, and not cut down, H3

GREET
1Sa 25: 5 Nabal, and g him in my name: H7592+H7965
Ro 16: 3 G Priscilla and Aquila my helpers in G782
5 Likewise g the church that is in their
6 G Mary, who bestowed much labour on G782
8 G Amplias my beloved in the Lord. G782
11 Salute Herodion my kinsman. G them G782
1Co 16:20 All the brethren g you. Greet ye one G782
20 All the brethren greet you. G ye one G782

2Co 13:12 G one another with an holy kiss. G782
Php 4:21 The brethren which are with me g you. G782
Col 4:14 beloved physician, and Demas, g you. G782
1Th 5:26 G all the brethren with an holy kiss. G782
Tit 3:15 All that are with me salute thee. G them G782
1Pt 5:14 G ye one another with a kiss of charity. G782
2Jn 13 The children of thy elect sister g thee. G782
3Jn 14 salute thee. G the friends by name. G782

GREETETH
2Ti 4:21 winter. Eubulus g thee, and Pudens, and G782

GREETING
Act 15:23 and brethren *send* g unto the brethren G5463
23:26 excellent governor Felix *sendeth* g. G5463
Jas 1:1 tribes which are scattered abroad, g. G5463

GREETINGS
Mt 23:7 And g in the markets, and to be called of G783
Lk 11:43 in the synagogues, and g in the markets. G783
20:46 robes, and love g in the markets, and G783

GREW
Gen 2:5 the field before it g: for the LORD God H6779
19:25 and that which g upon the ground. H6780
21:8 And the child g, and was weaned: and H1431
20 And God was with the lad; and he g, H1431
25:27 And the boys g: and Esau was a H1431
26:13 and g until he became very great: H1432
47:27 and g, and multiplied exceedingly. H6509
Ex 1:12 multiplied and g. And they were grieved H6555
2:10 And the child g, and she brought him H1431
Jdg 11:2 his wife's sons g up, and they thrust H1431
13:24 the child g, and the LORD blessed him. H1431
1Sa 2:21 the child Samuel g before the LORD. H1431
26 And the child Samuel g on, and was in H1432
3:19 And Samuel g, and the LORD was with H1431
2Sa 5:10 And David went on, and g great, and the
12:3 up: and it g up together with him, H1431
Ezk 17:6 And it g, and became a spreading vine H6779
10 it shall wither in the furrows where it g. H6780
Dan 4:11 The tree g, and was strong, and the H7236
20 The tree that thou sawest, which g, and H7236
Mk 4:7 and the thorns g up, and choked it, and G305
5:26 nothing bettered, but rather g worse, G2064
Lk 1:80 And the child g, and waxed strong in G837
2:40 And the child g, and waxed strong in G837
13:19 his garden; and it g, and waxed a great G837
Act 7:17 the people g and multiplied in Egypt, G837
12:24 But the word of God g and multiplied. G837
19:20 So mightily g the word of God and G837

GREYHOUND
Prv 30:31 A g; an he goat also; and a H2223+H4975

GRIEF
Gen 26:35 Which were a g of mind unto Isaac and H4786
1Sa 1:16 and g have I spoken hitherto. H3708
25:31 That this shall be no g unto thee, nor H6330
2Ch 6:29 sore and his own g, and shall spread H4341
Job 2:13 for they saw that *his* g was very great. H3511
6:2 Oh that my g were throughly weighed, H3708
16:5 of my lips should asswage *your g.*
6 Though I speak, my g is not asswaged: H3511
Ps 6:7 Mine eye is consumed because of g; it H3708
31:9 with g, *yea,* my soul and my belly. H3708
10 For my life is spent with g, and my H3015
69:26 g of those whom thou hast wounded. H4341
Prv 17:25 A foolish son *is* a g to his father, and H3708
Ecc 1:18 For in much wisdom *is* much g: and he H3708
2:23 and his travail g; yea, his heart taketh H3708
Isa 17:11 the day of g and of desperate sorrow. H2470
53:3 and acquainted with g: and we hid as it H2483
10 he hath put *him* to g: when thou shalt H2470
Jer 6:7 before me continually *is* g and wounds. H2483
10:19 Truly this *is* a g, and I must bear it. H2483
45:3 the LORD hath added g to my sorrow; I H3015
Lam 3:32 But though he cause g, yet will he have H3013
Jna 4:6 him from his g. So Jonah was exceeding H7451
2Co 2:5 But if any have caused g, he hath not G3076
Heb 13:17 with g: for that *is* unprofitable for you. G4727
1Pt 2:19 God endure g, suffering wrongfully. G3077

GRIEFS
Isa 53:4 Surely he hath borne our g, and carried H2483

GRIEVANCE
Hab 1:3 cause *me* to behold g? for spoiling and H5999

GRIEVE
1Sa 2:33 thine eyes, and to g thine heart: and all H109
1Ch 4:10 that it may not g me! And God granted H6087
Ps 78:40 the wilderness, *and* g him in the desert! H6087
Lam 3:33 For he doth not afflict willingly nor g H3013
Eph 4:30 And g not the holy Spirit of God, G3076

GRIEVED
Gen 6:6 on the earth, and it g him at his heart. H6087
34:7 and the men were g, and they were very H6087
45:5 Now therefore be not g, nor angry with H6087
49:23 The archers have sorely g him, and H4843
Ex 1:12 were g because of the children of Israel. H6973
Dt 15:10 heart shall not be g when thou givest H7489
Jdg 10:16 his soul was g for the misery of Israel. H7114
1Sa 1:8 g? *am* not I better to thee than ten sons? H3415
15:11 And it g Samuel; and he cried H2734
20:3 this, lest he be g: but truly *as* the LORD H6087
34 month: for he was g for David, because H6087
30:6 all the people was g, every man for his H4843
2Sa 19:2 day how the king was g for his son. H6087
Neh 2:10 heard *of it,* it g them exceedingly that H3415
8:11 for the day *is* holy; neither be ye g. H6087
13:8 And it g me sore: therefore I cast forth H3415
Est 4:4 the queen exceedingly g; and she sent H2342
Job 4:2 with thee, wilt thou be g? but who can H3811
30:25 was *not* my soul g for the poor? H5701
Ps 73:21 Thus my heart was g, and I was pricked H2556
95:10 Forty years long was I g with *this* H6962
112:10 The wicked shall see *it,* and be g; he H3707
119:158 I beheld the transgressors, and was g; H6962
139:21 I g with those that rise up against thee? H6962
Isa 54:6 forsaken and g in spirit, and a wife H6087
57:10 thine hand; therefore thou wast not g. H2470
Jer 5:3 them, but they have not g; thou hast H2342
Dan 7:15 I Daniel was g in my spirit in the midst H3735
11:30 he shall be g, and return, and have H3512
Am 6:6 are not g for the affliction of Joseph. H2470
Mk 3:5 with anger, being g for the hardness of G4818
10:22 away g: for he had great possessions. G3076
Jn 21:17 me? Peter was g because he said unto G3076
Act 4:2 Being g that they taught the people, G1278
16:18 But Paul, being g, turned and said to G1278
Ro 14:15 But if thy brother be g with *thy* meat, G3076
2Co 2:4 that ye should be g, but that ye might G3076
5 grief, he hath not g me, but in part: G3076
Heb 3:10 Wherefore I was g with that G4360
17 But with whom was he g forty years? G4360

GRIEVETH
Ru 1:13 daughters; for it g me much for your H4843
Prv 26:15 it g him to bring it again to his mouth. H3811

GRIEVING
Ezk 28:24 of Israel, nor *any* g thorn of all *that are* H3510

GRIEVOUS
Gen 12:10 there; for the famine *was* g in the land. H3515
18:20 is great, and because their sin is very g; H3513
21:11 And the thing was very g in Abraham's H3415
12 Let it not be g in thy sight because H3415
41:31 famine following; for it *shall be* very g. H3515
50:11 they said, This *is* a g mourning to the H3515
Ex 8:24 and there came a g swarm *of flies* into H3515
9:3 sheep: *there shall be* a very g murrain. H3515
18 it to rain a very g hail, such as hath not H3515
24 with the hail, very g, such as there was H3515
10:14 of Egypt: very g *were they;* before them H3515
1Ki 2:8 cursed me with a g curse in the day H4834
12:4 Thy father made our yoke g: now H7185
4 make thou the g service of thy father, H7186
2Ch 10:4 Thy father made our yoke g: now H7185
4 somewhat the g servitude of thy father, H7186
Ps 10:5 His ways are always g; thy judgments H2342
31:18 which speak g things proudly and H6277
Prv 15:1 away wrath: but g words stir up anger. H6089
10 Correction *is* g unto him that forsaketh H7451
Ecc 2:17 under the sun *is* g unto me: for all *is* H7451
Isa 15:4 cry out; his life shall be g unto him. H3415
21:2 A g vision is declared unto me; the H7186
Jer 6:28 They *are* all g revolters, walking with H5493
10:19 Woe is me for my hurt! my wound is g: H2470
14:17 with a great breach, with a very g blow. H2470
16:4 They shall die of g deaths; they shall H8463
23:19 in fury, even a g whirlwind: it shall fall H2342
30:12 bruise *is* incurable, *and* thy wound *is* g. H2470
Nah 3:19 thy wound is g: all that hear the bruit H2470
Mt 23:4 For they bind heavy burdens and g to G1418
Lk 11:46 men with burdens g to be borne, and G1418

Act 20:29 my departing shall g wolves enter in G926
25:7 and laid many and g complaints against G926
Php 3:1 me indeed *is* not g, but for you *it is* safe. G3636
Heb 12:11 to be joyous, but g: nevertheless G3077
1Jn 5:3 and his commandments are not g. G926
Rev 16:2 fell a noisome and g sore upon the men G4190

GRIEVOUSLY
Isa 9:1 did more g afflict *her by* the way H3513
Jer 23:19 shall fall g upon the head of the wicked. H2342
Lam 1:8 Jerusalem hath g sinned; therefore she H2399
20 me; for I have g rebelled: abroad the H4784
Ezk 14:13 me by trespassing g, then will I stretch H4604
Mt 8:6 at home sick of the palsy, g tormented. G1171
15:22 my daughter is g vexed with a devil. G2560

GRIEVOUSNESS
Isa 10:1 write g *which* they have prescribed; H5999
21:15 the bent bow, and from the g of war. H3514

GRIND
Jdg 16:21 brass; and he did g in the prison house. H2912
Job 31:10 *Then* let my wife g unto another, and H2912
Isa 3:15 to pieces, and g the faces of the poor? H2912
47:2 Take the millstones, and g meal: H2912
Lam 5:13 They took the young men to g, and the H2911
Mt 21:44 it shall fall, it will g him to powder. G3039
Lk 20:18 it shall fall, it will g him to powder. G3039

GRINDERS
Ecc 12:3 and the g cease because they H2912

GRINDING
Ecc 12:4 the sound of the g is low, and he shall H2913
Mt 24:41 Two *women shall be* g at the mill; the G229
Lk 17:35 Two *women* shall be g together; the one G229

GRISLED
Gen 31:10 *were* ringstraked, speckled, and g. H1261
12 speckled, and g: for I have seen all that H1261
Zec 6:3 in the fourth chariot g and bay horses. H1261
6 g go forth toward the south country. H1261

GROAN
Job 24:12 Men g from out of the city, and the soul H5008
Jer 51:52 through all her land the wounded shall g. H602
Ezk 30:24 arms, and he shall g before him with H5008
Joel 1:18 How do the beasts g! the herds of cattle H584
Ro 8:23 even we ourselves g within ourselves, G4727
2Co 5:2 For in this we g, earnestly desiring to be G4727
4 For we that are in *this* tabernacle do g, G4727

GROANED
Jn 11:33 he g in the spirit, and was troubled, G1690

GROANETH
Ro 8:22 For we know that the whole creation g G4959

GROANING
Ex 2:24 And God heard their g, and God H5009
6:5 And I have also heard the g of the H5009
Job 23:2 bitter: my stroke is heavier than my g. H585
Ps 6:6 I am weary with my g; all the night make H585
38:9 thee; and my g is not hid from thee. H585
102:5 By reason of the voice of my g my bones H585
20 To hear the g of the prisoner; to loose H603
Jn 11:38 Jesus therefore again g in himself G1690
Act 7:34 and I have heard their g, and am come G4726

GROANINGS
Jdg 2:18 because of their g by reason of them H5009
Ezk 30:24 with the g of a deadly wounded *man.* H5009
Ro 8:26 for us with g which cannot be uttered. G4726

GROPE
Dt 28:29 And thou shalt g at noonday, as the H4959
Job 5:14 and g in the noonday as in the night. H4959
12:25 They g in the dark without light, and he H4959
Isa 59:10 We g for the wall like the blind, and we H1659
10 like the blind, and we g as if *we had* no H1659

GROPETH
Dt 28:29 as the blind g in darkness, and thou H4959

GROSS
Isa 60:2 the earth, and g darkness the people: H6205
Jer 13:16 of death, *and* make *it* g darkness. H6205
Mt 13:15 For this people's heart is waxed g, and G3975
Act 28:27 For the heart of this people is waxed g, G3975

GROUND
Gen 2: 5 and *there was* not a man to till the **g**. H127
6 and watered the whole face of the **g**. H127
7 *of* the dust of the **g**, and breathed into his H127
9 And out of the **g** made the LORD God to H127
19 And out of the **g** the LORD God formed H127
3:17 eat of it: cursed *is* the **g** for thy sake; in H127
19 return unto the **g**; for out of it wast thou H127
23 to till the **g** from whence he was taken. H127
4: 2 of sheep, but Cain was a tiller of the **g**. H127
3 fruit of the **g** an offering unto the LORD. H127
10 blood crieth unto me from the **g**. H127
12 When thou tillest the **g**, it shall not H127
5:29 of the **g** which the LORD hath cursed. H127
7:23 the face of the **g**, both man, and cattle, H127
8: 8 were abated from off the face of the **g**; H127
13 and, behold, the face of the **g** was dry. H127
21 will not again curse the **g** any more for H127
18: 2 door, and bowed himself toward the **g**, H776
19: 1 bowed himself with his face toward the **g**; H776
25 cities, and that which grew upon the **g**. H127
33: 3 himself to the **g** seven times, until he H776
38: 9 he spilled *it* on the **g**, lest that he should H776
44:11 to the **g**, and opened every man his sack. H776
14 there: and they fell before him on the **g**. H776
Ex 3: 5 place whereon thou standest *is* holy **g**. H127
4: 3 And he said, Cast it on the **g**. And he cast H776
3 And he cast it on the **g**, and it became a H776
8:21 *of flies*, and also the **g** whereon they *are*. H127
9:23 fire ran along upon the **g**; and the LORD H776
14:16 go on dry **g** through the midst of the sea.
22 sea upon the dry **g**: and the waters *were*
16:14 thing, *as* small as the hoar frost on the **g**. H776
32:20 *it* in the fire, and **g** *it* to powder, and H2912
Lev 20:25 creepeth on the **g**, which I have separated H127
Nu 11: 8 gathered *it*, and **g** *it* in mills, or beat *it* H2912
16:31 **g** clave asunder that *was* under them: H127
Dt 4:18 creepeth on the **g**, the likeness of any fish H127
9:21 stamped it, *and* **g** *it* very small, *even* H2912
15:23 thou shalt pour it upon the **g** as water. H776
22: 6 in any tree, or on the **g**, *whether they be* H776
28: 4 and the fruit of thy **g**, and the fruit of thy H127
11 in the fruit of thy **g**, in the land which the H127
56 her foot upon the **g** for delicateness and H776
Jos 3:17 stood firm on dry **g** in the midst of H2724
17 over on dry **g**, until all the people were H2724
24:32 in a parcel of **g** which Jacob bought H7704
Jdg 4:21 and fastened it into the **g**: for he was fast H776
6:39 and upon all the **g** let there be dew. H776
40 only, and there was dew on all the **g**. H776
13:20 on *it*, and fell on their faces to the **g**. H776
20:21 down to the **g** of the Israelites that H776
25 down to the **g** of the children of Israel H776
Ru 2:10 herself to the **g**, and said unto him, Why H776
1Sa 3:19 and did let none of his words fall to the **g**. H776
5: 4 his face to the **g** before the ark of the H776
8:12 *set them* to ear his **g**, and to reap his H2758
14:25 wood; and there was honey upon the **g**. H7704
32 slew *them* on the **g**: and the people did H776
45 his head fall to the **g**; for he hath wrought H776
20:31 Jesse liveth upon the **g**, thou shalt not be H127
41 on his face to the **g**, and bowed himself H776
25:23 on her face, and bowed herself to the **g**, H776
26: 7 his spear stuck in the **g** at his bolster: but H776
28:14 with *his* face to the **g**, and bowed himself. H776
2Sa 2:22 I smite thee to the **g**? how then should I H776
8: 2 them down to the **g**; even with two lines H776
14: 4 on her face to the **g**, and did obeisance, H776
14 as water spilt on the **g**, which cannot be H776
22 And Joab fell to the **g** on his face, and H776
33 on his face to the **g** before the king: and H776
17:12 dew falleth on the **g**: and of him and of H127
19 and spread **g** corn thereon; and the H7383
18:11 him there to the **g**? and I would have H776
20:10 his bowels to the **g**, and struck him not H776
23:11 was a piece of **g** full of lentiles: and the H7704
12 But he stood in the midst of the **g**, and H2513
24:20 before the king on his face upon the **g**. H776
1Ki 1:23 before the king with his face to the **g**. H776
7:46 the clay **g** between Succoth and Zarthan. H127
2Ki 2: 8 so that they two went over on dry **g**. H2724
15 bowed themselves to the **g** before him. H776
19 the water *is* naught, and the **g** barren. H776
4:37 the **g**, and took up her son, and went out. H776
9:26 *of* **g**, according to the word of the LORD.
13:18 the **g**. And he smote thrice, and stayed. H776
1Ch 11:13 was a parcel of **g** full of barley; and the H7704
21:21 himself to David with *his* face to the **g**. H776
27:26 of the **g** *was* Ezri the son of Chelub: H127
2Ch 4:17 clay **g** between Succoth and Zeredathah. H127
7: 3 their faces to the **g** upon the pavement, H776
20:18 with *his* face to the **g**: and all Judah and H776
Neh 8: 6 the LORD with *their* faces to the **g**. H776
10:35 And to bring the firstfruits of our **g**, and H127
37 the tithes of our **g** unto the Levites, that H127
Job 1:20 fell down upon the **g**, and worshipped, H776
2:13 So they sat down with him upon the **g** H776
5: 6 neither doth trouble spring out of the **g**; H127
14: 8 earth, and the stock thereof die in the **g**; H6083
16:13 spare; he poureth out my gall upon the **g**. H776
18:10 The snare *is* laid for him in the **g**, and a H776
38:27 To satisfy the desolate and waste **g**; and
39:24 He swalloweth the **g** with fierceness and H776
Ps 74: 7 the dwelling place of thy name to the **g**. H776
89:39 profaned his crown *by casting it* to the **g**. H776
44 cease, and cast his throne down to the **g**. H776
105:35 land, and devoured the fruit of their **g**. H127
107:33 and the watersprings into dry **g**; H6774
35 water, and dry **g** into watersprings. H776
143: 3 my life down to the **g**; he hath made me H776
147: 6 he casteth the wicked down to the **g**. H776
Isa 3:26 she *being* desolate shall sit upon the **g**. H776
14:12 to the **g**, which didst weaken the nations! H776
21: 9 of her gods he hath broken unto the **g**. H776
25:12 low, *and* bring to the **g**, *even* to the dust. H776
26: 5 to the **g**; he bringeth it *even* to the dust. H776
28:24 he open and break the clods of his **g**? H127
29: 4 speak out of the **g**, and thy speech shall H776
4 spirit, out of the **g**, and thy speech shall H776
30:23 thou shalt sow the **g** withal; and bread of H127
24 young asses that ear the **g** shall eat clean H127
35: 7 And the parched **g** shall become a pool, H8273
44: 3 upon the dry **g**: I will pour my spirit H3004
47: 1 Babylon, sit on the **g**: *there is* no throne, H776
51:23 thy body as the **g**, and as the street, to H776
53: 2 a root out of a dry **g**: he hath no form nor H776
Jer 4: 3 fallow **g**, and sow not among thorns. H5215
7:20 the fruit of the **g**; and it shall burn, and H127
14: 2 **g**; and the cry of Jerusalem is gone up. H776
4 Because the **g** is chapt, for there was no H127
25:33 buried; they shall be dung upon the **g**. H127
27: 5 that *are* upon the **g**, by my great power H776
Lam 2: 2 *them* down to the **g**: he hath polluted the H776
9 Her gates are sunk into the **g**; he hath H776
10 of Zion sit upon the **g**, *and* keep silence: H776
10 hang down their heads to the **g**. H776
21 The young and the old lie on the **g** in the H776
Ezk 12: 6 thou see not the **g**: for I have set thee *for* H776
12 face, that he see not the **g** with *his* eyes. H776
13:14 it down to the **g**, so that the foundation H776
19:12 was cast down to the **g**, and the east wind H776
13 in the wilderness, in a dry and thirsty **g**. H776
24: 7 it not upon the **g**, to cover it with dust; H776
26:11 strong garrisons shall go down to the **g**. H776
16 shall sit upon the **g**, and shall tremble at H776
28:17 I will cast thee to the **g**, I will lay thee H776
38:20 fall, and every wall shall fall to the **g**. H776
41:16 and from the **g** up to the windows, and H776
20 From the **g** unto above the door *were* H776
42: 6 lowest and the middlemost from the **g**. H776
43:14 And from the bottom *upon* the **g** *even* to H776
Dan 8: 5 touched not the **g**: and the goat *had* a H776
7 him down to the **g**, and stamped upon H776
10 stars to the **g**, and stamped upon them. H776
12 to the **g**; and it practised, and prospered. H776
18 my face toward the **g**: but he touched me, H776
10: 9 on my face, and my face toward the **g**. H776
15 face toward the **g**, and I became dumb. H776
Hos 2:18 things of the **g**: and I will break the H127
10:12 up your fallow **g**: for *it is* time to seek H5215
Am 3:14 the altar shall be cut off, and fall to the **g**. H776
Oba 3 heart, Who shall bring me down to the **g**? H776
Hag 1:11 *that* which the **g** bringeth forth, and H127
Zec 8:12 give her fruit, and the **g** shall give her H776
Mal 3:11 the fruits of your **g**; neither shall your H127
Mt 10:29 not fall on the **g** without your Father. *G1093*
13: 8 But other fell into good **g**, and brought *G1093*
23 seed into the good **g** is he that heareth *G1093*
15:35 the multitude to sit down on the **g**. *G1093*
Mk 4: 5 And some fell on stony **g**, where it had *G4075*
8 And other fell on good **g**, and did yield *G1093*
16 are sown on stony **g**; who, when they *G4075*
20 are sown on good **g**; such as hear the *G1093*
26 as if a man should cast seed into the **g**; *G1093*
8: 6 to sit down on the **g**: and he took the *G1093*
9:20 he fell on the **g**, and wallowed foaming. *G1093*
14:35 and fell on the **g**, and prayed that, if it *G1093*
Lk 8: 8 And other fell on good **g**, and sprang *G1093*
8:15 But that on the good **g** are they, which *G1093*
12:16 them, saying, The **g** of a certain rich *G5561*
13: 7 cut it down; why cumbereth it the **g**? *G1093*
14:18 bought a piece of **g**, and I must needs go *G68*
19:44 And shall lay thee even with the **g**, and *G1474*
22:44 drops of blood falling down to the **g**. *G1093*
Jn 4: 5 of **g** that Jacob gave to his son Joseph. *G5564*
8: 6 on the **g**, *as though he heard them not*. *G1093*
8 he stooped down, and wrote on the **g**. *G1093*
9: 6 he spat on the **g**, and made clay of the *G5476*
12:24 wheat fall into the **g** and die, it abideth *G1093*
18: 6 they went backward, and fell to the **g**. *G5476*
Act 7:33 the place where thou standest is holy **g**. *G1093*
22: 7 And I fell unto the **g**, and heard a voice *G1475*
1Ti 3:15 living God, the pillar and **g** of the truth. *G1477*

GROUNDED
Isa 30:32 And *in* every place where the **g** staff H4145
Eph 3:17 that ye, being rooted and **g** in love, *G2311*
Col 1:23 If ye continue in the faith **g** and settled, *G2311*

GROVE
Gen 21:33 And *Abraham* planted a **g** in H815
Dt 16:21 Thou shalt not plant thee a **g** of any trees H842
Jdg 6:25 hath, and cut down the **g** that *is* by it: H842
26 of the **g** which thou shalt cut down. H842
28 cast down, and the **g** was cut down that H842
30 he hath cut down the **g** that *was* by it. H842
1Ki 15:13 made an idol in a **g**; and Asa destroyed H842
16:33 And Ahab made a **g**; and Ahab did more H842
2Ki 13: 6 there remained the **g** also in Samaria.) H842
17:16 calves, and made a **g**, and worshipped all H842
21: 3 Baal, and made a **g**, as did Ahab king of H842
7 And he set a graven image of the **g** that H842
23: 4 Baal, and for the **g**, and for all the host of H842
6 And he brought out the **g** from the house H842
7 the women wove hangings for the **g**. H842
15 *it* small to powder, and burned the **g**. H842
2Ch 15:16 made an idol in a **g**: and Asa cut down H842

GROVES
Ex 34:13 break their images, and cut down their **g**: H842
Dt 7: 5 and cut down their **g**, and burn their H842
12: 3 and burn their **g** with fire; and ye shall H842
Jdg 3: 7 their God, and served Baalim and the **g**. H842
1Ki 14:15 their **g**, provoking the LORD to anger. H842
23 and images, and **g**, on every high hill, H842
18:19 and the prophets of the **g** four hundred, H842
2Ki 17:10 And they set them up images and **g** in H842
18: 4 and cut down the **g**, and brake in pieces H842
23:14 and cut down the **g**, and filled their H842
2Ch 14: 3 down the images, and cut down the **g**: H842
17: 6 away the high places and **g** out of Judah. H842
19: 3 taken away the **g** out of the land, and H842
24:18 fathers, and served **g** and idols: and H842
31: 1 and cut down the **g**, and threw down the H842
33: 3 Baalim, and made **g**, and worshipped all H842
19 places, and set up **g** and graven images, H842
34: 3 places, and the **g**, and the carved images, H842
4 he cut down; and the **g**, and the carved H842
7 the altars and the **g**, and had beaten the H842
Isa 17: 8 have made, either the **g**, or the images. H842
27: 9 the **g** and images shall not stand up. H842
Jer 17: 2 **g** by the green trees upon the high hills. H842
Mic 5:14 And I will pluck up thy **g** out of the midst H842

GROW
Gen 2: 9 the LORD God to **g** every tree that is H6779
48:16 and let them **g** into a multitude in H1711
Nu 6: 5 let the locks of the hair of his head **g**. H1431
Jdg 16:22 Howbeit the hair of his head began to **g** H6779
2Sa 23: 5 *my* desire, although he make *it* not to **g**. H6779
2Ki 19:29 such things as **g** of themselves, and H5599
Ezr 4:22 damage **g** to the hurt of the kings? H7680
Job 8:11 Can the rush **g** up without mire? can H1342
11 mire? can the flag **g** without water? H7685
19 way, and out of the earth shall others **g**. H6779
14:19 the things which **g** *out* of the dust of the H5599
31:40 Let thistles **g** instead of wheat, and H3318
39: 4 good liking, they **g** up with corn; they H7235
Ps 92:12 tree: he shall **g** like a cedar in Lebanon. H7685
104:14 He causeth the grass to **g** for the cattle, H6779
147: 8 maketh grass to **g** upon the mountains. H6779
Ecc 11: 5 how the bones *do* **g** in the womb of her
Isa 11: 1 and a Branch shall **g** out of his roots: H6509
17:11 make thy plant to **g**, and in the morning H7735
53: 2 For he shall **g** up before him as a H5927
Jer 12: 2 taken root: they **g**, yea, they bring forth H3212
33:15 righteousness to **g** up unto David; and H6779

Ezk 44:20 g long; they shall only poll their heads. H7971
47:12 on that side, shall g all trees for meat, H5927
Hos 14: 5 Israel: he shall g as the lily, and cast H6524
7 as the corn, and g as the vine: the scent H6524
Jna 4:10 neither madest it g; which came up in a H1431
Zec 6:12 and he shall g up out of his place, H6779
Mal 4: 2 go forth, and g up as calves of the stall. H6335
Mt 6:28 they g; they toil not, neither do they spin: G837
13:30 Let both g together until the harvest: G4886
21:19 it, Let no fruit g on thee henceforward G1096
Mk 4:27 spring and g up, he knoweth not how. G3373
Lk 12:27 Consider the lilies how they g: they toil G837
Act 5:24 of them whereunto this would g. G1096
Eph 4:15 But speaking the truth in love, may g up G837
1Pt 2: 2 milk of the word, that ye may g thereby: G837
2Pt 3:18 But g in grace, and in the knowledge of G837

GROWETH
Ex 10: 5 tree which g for you out of the field: H6779
Lev 13:39 spot that g in the skin; he is clean. H6524
25: 5 That which g of its own accord of thy H5599
11 reap that which g of itself in it, nor H5599
Dt 29:23 nor any grass g therein, like the H5927
Jdg 19: 9 behold, the day g to an end, lodge here, H2583
Job 38:38 When the dust g into hardness, and the H3332
Ps 90: 5 morning they are like grass which g up. H2498
6 In the morning it flourisheth, and g up; H2498
129: 6 which withereth afore it g up: H8025
Isa 37:30 eat this year such as g of itself; and the H5599
Mk 4:32 But when it is sown, it g up, and G305
Eph 2:21 g unto an holy temple in the Lord: G837
2Th 1: 3 that your faith g exceedingly, and the G5232

GROWN
Gen 38:11 till Shelah my son be g: for he said, Lest H1431
14 saw that Shelah was g, and she was not H1431
Ex 2:11 when Moses was g, that he went out H1431
9:32 were not smitten: for they were not g up. H648
Lev 13:37 that there is black hair g up therein; the H6779
Dt 32:15 art waxen fat, thou art g thick, thou art
Ru 1:13 Would ye tarry for them till they were g? H1431
2Sa 10: 5 until your beards be g, and then return. H6779
1Ki 12: 8 men that were g up with him, and H1431
10 And the young men that were g up with H1431
2Ki 4:18 And when the child was g, it fell on a H1431
19:26 and as corn blasted before it be g up. H6965
1Ch 19: 5 until your beards be g, and then return. H6779
Ezr 9: 6 our trespass is g up unto the heavens. H1431
Ps 144:12 That our sons may be as plants g up in H1431
Prv 24:31 And, lo, it was all g over with thorns, H5927
Isa 37:27 and as corn blasted before it be g up. H6965
Jer 50:11 because ye are g fat as the heifer at H6335
Ezk 16: 7 is g, whereas thou wast naked and bare. H6779
Dan 4:22 It is thou, O king, that art g and H7236
22 thy greatness is g, and reacheth unto H7236
33 till his hairs were g like eagles' feathers, H7236
Mt 13:32 but when it is g, it is the greatest among G837

GROWTH
Am 7: 1 up of the latter g; and, lo, it was the H3954
1 the latter g after the king's mowings. H3954

GRUDGE
Lev 19:18 Thou shalt not avenge, nor bear any g H5201
Ps 59:15 for meat, and g if they be not satisfied. H3885
Jas 5: 9 G not one against another, brethren, G4727

GRUDGING
1Pt 4: 9 hospitality one to another without g. G1112

GRUDGINGLY
2Co 9: 7 so let him give; not g, or of necessity: for G1537

GUARD
Gen 37:36 of Pharaoh's, and captain of the g. H2876
39: 1 captain of the g, an Egyptian, bought H2876
40: 3 the captain of the g, into the prison, the H2876
4 And the captain of the g charged H2876
41:12 to the captain of the g; and we told him, H2876
2Sa 23:23 three. And David set him over his g. H4928
1Ki 14:27 of the chief of the g, which kept the door H7323
28 the LORD, that the g bare them, and H7323
28 brought them back into the g chamber. H7323
2Ki 10:25 Jehu said to the g and to the captains, H7323
25 the sword; and the g and the captains H7323
11: 4 captains and the g, and brought them H7323
6 gate behind the g: so shall ye keep the H7323
11 And the g stood, every man with his H7323
13 the noise of the g and of the people, she H7323
2Ki 11:19 captains, and the g, and all the people H7323
19 of the gate of the g to the king's house. H7323
25: 8 captain of the g, a servant of the king H2876
10 the captain of the g, brake down the H2876
11 the captain of the g carry away. H2876
12 But the captain of the g left of the poor H2876
15 silver, the captain of the g took away. H2876
18 And the captain of the g took Seraiah H2876
20 And Nebuzar-adan captain of the g H2876
1Ch 11:25 first three: and David set him over his g. H4928
2Ch 12:10 hands of the chief of the g, that kept the H7323
11 of the LORD, the g came and fetched H7323
11 them again into the g chamber. H7323
Neh 4:22 be a g to us, and labour on the day. H4929
23 nor the men of the g which followed H4929
Jer 39: 9 the captain of the g carried away H2876
10 But Nebuzar-adan the captain of the g H2876
11 the captain of the g, saying, H2876
13 So Nebuzar-adan the captain of the g H2876
40: 1 the captain of the g had let him go H2876
2 And the captain of the g took Jeremiah, H2876
5 the captain of the g gave him victuals H2876
41:10 the captain of the g had committed to H2876
43: 6 the captain of the g had left with H2876
52:12 captain of the g, which served the king H2876
14 the captain of the g, brake down all the H2876
15 the captain of the g carried away H2876
16 But Nebuzar-adan the captain of the g H2876
19 silver, took the captain of the g away. H2876
24 And the captain of the g took Seraiah H2876
26 So Nebuzar-adan the captain of the g H2876
30 the captain of the g carried away H2876
Ezk 38: 7 unto thee, and be thou a g unto them. H4929
Dan 2:14 of the king's g, which was gone forth H2877
Act 28:16 to the captain of the g: but Paul was G4759

GUARD'S
Gen 41:10 g house, both me and the chief baker: H2876

GUDGODAH
Dt 10: 7 From thence they journeyed unto G; H1412
7 G to Jotbath, a land of rivers of waters. H1412

GUEST
Lk 19: 7 to be g with a man that is a sinner. G2647

GUESTCHAMBER
Mk 14:14 Where is the g, where I shall eat the G2646
Lk 22:11 thee, Where is the g, where I shall eat G2646

GUESTS
1Ki 1:41 And Adonijah and all the g that were H7121
49 And all the g that were with Adonijah H7121
Prv 9:18 and that her g are in the depths of hell. H7121
Zep 1: 7 prepared a sacrifice, he hath bid his g. H7121
Mt 22:10 and the wedding was furnished with g. G345
11 And when the king came in to see the g, G345

GUIDE
Job 38:32 or canst thou g Arcturus with his sons? H5148
Ps 25: 9 The meek will he g in judgment: and H1869
31: 3 for thy name's sake lead me, and g me. H5095
32: 8 shalt go: I will g thee with mine eye. H3289
48:14 ever: he will be our g even unto death. H5090
55:13 But it was thou, a man mine equal, my g, H441
73:24 Thou shalt g me with thy counsel, and H5148
112: 5 he will g his affairs with discretion. H3557
Prv 2:17 Which forsaketh the g of her youth, and H441
6: 7 Which having no g, overseer, or ruler, H7101
11: 3 The integrity of the upright shall g H5148
23:19 Hear thou, my son, and be wise, and g H833
Isa 49:10 by the springs of water shall he g them. H5095
51:18 There is none to g her among all the H5095
58:11 And the LORD shall g thee continually, H5148
Jer 3: 4 My father, thou art the g of my youth? H441
Mic 7: 5 not confidence in a g: keep the doors of H441
Lk 1:79 to g our feet into the way of peace. G2720
Jn 16:13 is come, he will g you into all truth: for G3594
Act 1:16 which was g to them that took Jesus. G3595
8:31 except some man should g me? And he G3594
Ro 2:19 thou thyself art a g of the blind, a light G3595
1Ti 5:14 bear children, g the house, give none G3616

GUIDED
Ex 15:13 thou hast g them in thy strength H5095
2Ch 32:22 of all other, and g them on every side. H5095
Job 31:18 I have g her from my mother's womb;) H5148
Ps 78:52 g them in the wilderness like a flock. H5090
72 g them by the skilfulness of his hands. H5148

GUIDES
Mt 23:16 Woe unto you, ye blind g, which say, G3595
24 Ye blind g, which strain at a gnat, and G3595

GUIDING
Gen 48:14 upon Manasseh's head, g his hands H7919

GUILE
Ex 21:14 to slay him with g; thou shalt take him H6195
Ps 32: 2 and in whose spirit there is no g. H7423
34:13 from evil, and thy lips from speaking g. H4820
55:11 and g depart not from her streets. H4820
Jn 1:47 an Israelite indeed, in whom is no g! G1388
2Co 12:16 being crafty, I caught you with g. G1388
1Th 2: 3 of deceit, nor of uncleanness, nor in g: G1388
1Pt 2: 1 all malice, and all g, and hypocrisies, G1388
22 Who did no sin, neither was g found in G1388
3:10 evil, and his lips that they speak no g: G1388
Rev 14: 5 And in their mouth was found no g: for G1388

GUILT
Dt 19:13 shalt put away the g of innocent blood
21: 9 So shalt thou put away the g of innocent

GUILTINESS
Gen 26:10 thou shouldest have brought g upon us. H817

GUILTLESS
Ex 20: 7 him g that taketh his name in vain. H5352
Nu 5:31 Then shall the man be g from iniquity, H5352
32:22 return, and be g before the LORD, and H5355
Dt 5:11 him g that taketh his name in vain. H5352
Jos 2:19 and we will be g: and whosoever shall H5355
1Sa 26: 9 against the LORD'S anointed, and be g? H5352
2Sa 3:28 my kingdom are g before the LORD for H5355
14: 9 house: and the king and his throne be g. H5355
1Ki 2: 9 Now therefore hold him not g: for thou H5352
Mt 12: 7 ye would not have condemned the g. G338

GUILTY
Gen 42:21 We are verily g concerning our brother, H818
Ex 34: 7 no means clear the g; visiting the iniquity H816
Lev 4:13 which should not be done, and are g; H816
22 which should not be done, and is g; H816
27 which ought not to be done, and be g; H816
5: 2 him; he also shall be unclean, and g. H816
3 when he knoweth of it, then he shall be g. H816
4 of it, then he shall be g in one of these. H816
5 And it shall be, when he shall be g in one H816
17 yet is he g, and shall bear his iniquity. H816
6: 4 he hath sinned, and is g, that he shall H816
Nu 5: 6 against the LORD, and that person be g; H816
14:18 means clearing the g, visiting the iniquity
35:27 kill the slayer; he shall not be g of blood:
31 which is g of death: but he shall H7563
Jdg 21:22 them at this time, that ye should be g. H816
Ezr 10:19 wives; and being g, they offered a ram of H818
Prv 30:10 lest he curse thee, and thou be found g. H816
Ezk 22: 4 Thou art become g in thy blood that H816
Zec 11: 5 themselves not g: and they that sell them H816
Mt 23:18 by the gift that is upon it, he is g. G3784
26:66 answered and said, He is g of death. G1777
Mk 14:64 all condemned him to be g of death. G1777
Ro 3:19 the world may become g before God. G5267
1Co 11:27 be g of the body and blood of the Lord. G1777
Jas 2:10 yet offend in one point, he is g of all. G1777

GULF
Lk 16:26 you there is a great g fixed: so that they G5490

GUNI
Gen 46:24 Jahzeel, and G, and Jezer, and Shillem. H1476
Nu 26:48 of G, the family of the Gunites: H1476
1Ch 5:15 Ahi the son of Abdiel, the son of G, chief H1476
7:13 The sons of Naphtali; Jahziel, and G, H1476

GUNITES
Nu 26:48 Jahzeelites: of Guni, the family of the G: H1477

GUR
2Ki 9:27 so at the going up to G, which is by H1483

GUR-BAAL
2Ch 26: 7 that dwelt in G, and the Mehunims. H1485

GUSH
Jer 9:18 and our eyelids g out with waters. H5140

GUSHED
1Ki 18:28 lancets, till the blood **g** out upon them. H8210
Ps 78:20 that the waters **g** out, and the streams H2100
105:41 He opened the rock, and the waters **g** H2100
Isa 48:21 the rock also, and the waters **g** out. H2100
Act 1:18 in the midst, and all his bowels **g** out. *G1632*

GUTTER
2Sa 5: 8 getteth up to the **g**, and smiteth the H6794

GUTTERS
Gen 30:38 the flocks in the **g** in the watering H7298
41 of the cattle in the **g**, that they might H7298

H

HA
Job 39:25 He saith among the trumpets, **H**, ha; H1889
25 He saith among the trumpets, Ha, **h**; H1889

HAAHASHTARI
1Ch 4: 6 and **H**. These *were* the sons of Naarah. H326

HAAMMONAI See CHEPHAR-HAAMMONAI.

HABAIAH
Ezr 2:61 the children of **H**, the children of Koz, H2252
Neh 7:63 And of the priests: the children of **H**, the H2252

HABAKKUK
Hab 1: 1 The burden which **H** the prophet did H2265
3: 1 A prayer of **H** the prophet upon H2265

HABAZINIAH
Jer 35: 3 the son of **H**, and his brethren, and H2262

HABERGEON
Ex 28:32 were the hole of an **h**, that it be not rent. H8473
39:23 as the hole of an **h**, *with* a band round H8473
Job 41:26 hold: the spear, the dart, nor the **h**. H8302

HABERGEONS
2Ch 26:14 **h**, and bows, and slings *to cast* stones. H8302
Neh 4:16 the bows, and the **h**; and the rulers *were* H8302

HABITABLE
Prv 8:31 Rejoicing in the **h** part of his earth; and H8398

HABITATION
Ex 15: 2 **h**; my father's God, and I will exalt him. H5115
13 *them* in thy strength unto thy holy **h**. H5116
Lev 13:46 alone; without the camp *shall* his **h** *be*. H4186
Dt 12: 5 *even* unto his **h** shall ye seek, and H7933
26:15 Look down from thy holy **h**, from H4583
1Sa 2:29 *in my* **h**; and honourest thy sons H4583
32 And thou shalt see an enemy *in my* **h**, H4583
2Sa 15:25 again, and shew me *both* it, and his **h**: H5116
2Ch 6: 2 But I have built an house of **h** for thee, H2073
29: 6 **h** of the LORD, and turned *their* backs. H4908
Ezr 7:15 God of Israel, whose **h** *is* in Jerusalem, H4907
Job 5: 3 taking root: but suddenly I cursed his **h**. H5116
24 thou shalt visit thy **h**, and shalt not sin. H5116
8: 6 the **h** of thy righteousness prosperous. H5116
18:15 brimstone shall be scattered upon his **h**. H5116
Ps 26: 8 LORD, I have loved the **h** of thy house, H4583
33:14 From the place of his **h** he looketh H3427
68: 5 of the widows, *is* God in his holy **h**. H4583
69:25 Let their **h** be desolate; *and* let none H2918
71: 3 Be thou my strong **h**, whereunto I may H4583
89:14 Justice and judgment *are* the **h** of thy H4349
91: 9 *is* my refuge, *even* the most High, thy **h**; H4583
97: 2 and judgment *are* the **h** of his throne. H4349
104:12 their **h**, *which* sing among the branches. H7931
107: 7 way, that they might go to a city of **h**. H4186
36 that they may prepare a city for **h**; H4186
132: 5 an **h** for the mighty *God* of Jacob. H4908
13 Zion; he hath desired *it* for his **h**. H4186
Prv 3:33 but he blesseth the **h** of the just. H5116
Isa 22:16 that graveth an **h** for himself in a rock? H4908
27:10 desolate, *and* the **h** forsaken, and left H5116
32:18 in a peaceable **h**, and in sure dwellings, H5116
33:20 Jerusalem a quiet **h**, a tabernacle *that* H5116
34:13 an **h** of dragons, *and* a court for owls. H5116
35: 7 of water: in the **h** of dragons, where H5116
63:15 behold from the **h** of thy holiness and H2073
Jer 9: 6 Thine **h** *is* in the midst of deceit; H3427
10:25 him, and have made his **h** desolate. H5116
25:30 from his holy **h**; he shall mightily roar H4583
30 roar upon his **h**; he shall give a shout, H5116
31:23 **h** of justice, *and* mountain of holiness. H5116
33:12 shall be an **h** of shepherds causing H5116
41:17 And they departed, and dwelt in the **h** H1628
49:19 Jordan against the **h** of the strong: but I H5116
50: 7 the LORD, the **h** of justice, even the H5116
19 And I will bring Israel again to his **h**, H5116
44 of Jordan unto the **h** of the strong: but I H5116
45 shall make *their* **h** desolate with them. H5116
Ezk 29:14 the land of their **h**; and they shall be H4351
Dan 4:21 the fowls of the heaven had their **h**: H7932
Oba 3 of the rock, whose **h** *is* high; that saith H3427
Hab 3:11 The sun *and* moon stood still in their **h**: H2073
Zec 2:13 for he is raised up out of his holy **h**. H4583
Act 1:20 of Psalms, Let his **h** be desolate, and let *G1886*
17:26 appointed, and the bounds of their **h**; *G2733*
Eph 2:22 for an **h** of God through the Spirit. *G2732*
Jude 6 but left their own **h**, he hath reserved in *G3613*
Rev 18: 2 and is become the **h** of devils, and the *G2732*

HABITATIONS
Gen 36:43 according to their **h** in the land of their H4186
49: 5 instruments of cruelty *are in* their **h**. H4380
Ex 12:20 your **h** shall ye eat unleavened bread. H4186
35: 3 your **h** upon the sabbath day. H4186
Lev 23:17 Ye shall bring out of your **h** two wave H4186
Nu 15: 2 land of your **h**, which I give unto you, H4186
1Ch 4:33 These *were* their **h**, and their genealogy. H4186
41 tents, and the **h** that were found there, H4583
7:28 And their possessions and **h** *were*, H4186
Ps 74:20 of the earth are full of the **h** of cruelty. H4999
78:28 of their camp, round about their **h**. H4908
Isa 54: 2 curtains of thine **h**: spare not, lengthen H4908
Jer 9:10 and for the **h** of the wilderness a H4999
21:13 us? or who shall enter into our **h**? H4585
25:37 And the peaceable **h** are cut down H4999
49:20 shall make their **h** desolate with them. H5116
Lam 2: 2 The Lord hath swallowed up all the **h** H4999
Ezk 6:14 in all their **h**: and they shall know H4186
Am 1: 2 and the **h** of the shepherds shall H4999
Lk 16: 9 they may receive you into everlasting **h**. *G4633*

HABOR
2Ki 17: 6 them in Halah and in **H** *by* the river of H2249
18:11 them in Halah and in **H** *by* the river of H2249
1Ch 5:26 unto Halah, and **H**, and Hara, and to H2249

HACCEREM See BETH-HACCEREM.

HACHALIAH
Neh 1: 1 The words of Nehemiah the son of **H**. H2446
10: 1 Tirshatha, the son of **H**, and Zidkijah, H2446

HACHILAH
1Sa 23:19 of **H**, which *is* on the south of Jeshimon? H2444
26: 1 the hill of **H**, *which is* before Jeshimon? H2444
3 And Saul pitched in the hill of **H**, which H2444

HACHMONI
1Ch 27:32 the son of **H** *was* with the king's sons: H2453

HACHMONITE
1Ch 11:11 had; Jashobeam, an **H**, the chief of the H2453

HAD See the Appendix.

HADAD
Gen 36:35 And Husham died, and **H** the son of H1908
36 And **H** died, and Samlah of Masrekah H1908
1Ki 11:14 unto Solomon, **H** the Edomite: he *was* H1908
17 That **H** fled, he and certain Edomites of H111
17 go into Egypt; **H** *being* yet a little child. H1908
19 And **H** found great favour in the sight H1908
21 And when **H** heard in Egypt that David H1908
21 host was dead, **H** said to Pharaoh, Let H1908
25 beside the mischief that **H** *did*: and he H1908
1Ch 1:30 Mishma, and Dumah, Massa, **H**, and H2301
46 And when Husham was dead, **H** the H1908
47 And when **H** was dead, Samlah of H1908
50 And when Baal-hanan was dead, **H** H1908
51 **H** died also. And the dukes of Edom H1908

HADADEZER
2Sa 8: 3 David smote also **H**, the son of Rehob, H1909
5 came to succour **H** king of Zobah, H1909
7 of **H**, and brought them to Jerusalem. H1909
8 Berothai, cities of **H**, king David took H1909
9 David had smitten all the host of **H**, H1909
10 fought against **H**, and smitten him: for H1909
10 smitten him: for **H** had wars with Toi. H1909
12 spoil of **H**, son of Rehob, king of Zobah. H1909
1Ki 11:23 fled from his lord **H** king of Zobah: H1909

HADADRIMMON
Zec 12:11 of **H** in the valley of Megiddon. H1910

HADAR
Gen 25:15 **H**, and Tema, Jetur, Naphish, and H2316
36:39 of Achbor died, and **H** reigned in his H1924

HADAREZER
2Sa 10:16 And **H** sent, and brought out the H1928
16 of the host of **H** *went* before them. H1928
19 *were* servants to **H** saw that they were H1928
1Ch 18: 3 And David smote **H** king of Zobah unto H1928
5 came to help **H** king of Zobah, David H1928
7 of **H**, and brought them to Jerusalem. H1928
8 Chun, cities of **H**, brought David very H1928
9 smitten all the host of **H** king of Zobah; H1928
10 fought against **H**, and smitten him; (for H1928
10 smitten him; (for **H** had war with Tou;) H1928
19:16 of the host of **H** *went* before them. H1928
19 And when the servants of **H** saw that H1928

HADASHAH
Jos 15:37 Zenan, and **H**, and Migdal-gad, H2322

HADASSAH
Est 2: 7 And he brought up **H**, that *is*, Esther, H1919

HADATTAH
Jos 15:25 And Hazor, **H**, and Kerioth, *and* H2675

HADDAH See EN-HADDAH.

HADDON See ESAR-HADDON.

HADID
Ezr 2:33 The children of Lod, **H**, and Ono, seven H2307
Neh 7:37 The children of Lod, **H**, and Ono, seven H2307
11:34 **H**, Zeboim, Neballat, H2307

HADLAI
2Ch 28:12 Amasa the son of **H**, stood up against H2311

HADORAM
Gen 10:27 And **H**, and Uzal, and Diklah, H1913
1Ch 1:21 **H** also, and Uzal, and Diklah, H1913
18:10 He sent **H** his son to king David, to H1913
2Ch 10:18 Then king Rehoboam sent **H** that *was* H1913

HADRACH
Zec 9: 1 in the land of **H**, and Damascus *shall* H2317

HADST
Gen 30:30 For *it was* little which thou **h** before I
31:42 me, surely thou **h** sent me away now
Jdg 15: 2 thought that thou **h** utterly hated her;
1Sa 25:34 thee, except thou **h** hasted and come to
2Sa 2:27 liveth, unless thou **h** spoken, surely then
2Ki 13:19 or six times; then **h** thou smitten Syria
19 Syria till thou **h** consumed *it*: whereas
Ezr 9:14 with us till thou **h** consumed *us*, so that
Neh 9:15 land which thou **h** sworn to give them. H5375
23 which thou **h** promised to their fathers,
Ps 44: 3 because thou **h** a favour unto them.
60:10 *Wilt* not thou, O God, *which* **h** cast us
90: 2 forth, or ever thou **h** formed the earth
Isa 26:15 art glorified: thou **h** removed *it* far *unto*

Isa 48:18 O that thou **h** hearkened to my
Jer 3: 3 rain; and thou **h** a whore's forehead, H1961
Jna 2: 3 For thou **h** cast me into the deep, in the
Lk 19:42 Saying, If thou **h** known, even thou, at
Jn 11:21 **h** been here, my brother had not died.
32 **h** been here, my brother had not died.
1Co 4: 7 thou glory, as if thou **h** not received *it*? *G2983*
Heb 10: 8 not, neither **h** pleasure *therein*; which

HAFT
Jdg 3:22 And the **h** also went in after the blade; H5325

HAGAB
Ezr 2:46 The children of **H**, the children of H2285

HAGABA
Neh 7:48 children of **H**, the children of Shalmai, H2286

HAGABAH
Ezr 2:45 children of **H**, the children of Akkub, H2286

HAGAR
Gen 16: 1 an Egyptian, whose name *was* **H**. H1904
3 And Sarai Abram's wife took **H** her H1904
4 And he went in unto **H**, and she H1904
8 And he said, **H**, Sarai's maid, whence H1904
15 And **H** bare Abram a son: and Abram H1904
15 his son's name, which **H** bare, Ishmael. H1904
16 old, when **H** bare Ishmael to Abram. H1904
21: 9 And Sarah saw the son of **H** the H1904
14 and gave *it* unto **H**, putting *it* on her H1904
17 of God called to **H** out of heaven, and H1904
17 What aileth thee, **H**? fear not; for God H1904
25:12 son, whom **H** the Egyptian, Sarah's H1904

HAGARENES
Ps 83: 6 the Ishmaelites; of Moab, and the **H**; H1905

HAGARITES
1Ch 5:10 war with the **H**, who fell by their hand: H1905
19 And they made war with the **H**, with H1905
20 them, and the **H** were delivered into H1905

HAGERITE
1Ch 27:31 And over the flocks *was* Jaziz the **H**. All H1905

HAGGAI
Ezr 5: 1 Then the prophets, **H** the prophet, and H2292
6:14 the prophesying of **H** the prophet and H2292
Hag 1: 1 of the LORD by **H** the prophet unto H2292
3 Then came the word of the LORD by **H** H2292
12 and the words of **H** the prophet, as the H2292
13 Then spake **H** the LORD'S messenger H2292
2: 1 of the LORD by the prophet **H**, saying, H2292
10 of the LORD by **H** the prophet, saying, H2292
13 Then said **H**, If *one that is* unclean by a H2292
14 Then answered **H**, and said, So *is* this H2292
20 the LORD came unto **H** in the four and H2292

HAGGERI
1Ch 11:38 brother of Nathan, Mibhar the son of **H**, H1905

HAGGI
Gen 46:16 And the sons of Gad; Ziphion, and **H**, H2291
Nu 26:15 the Zephonites: of **H**, the family of the H2291

HAGGIAH
1Ch 6:30 Shimea his son, **H** his son, Asaiah his H2293

HAGGITES
Nu 26:15 **H**: of Shuni, the family of the Shunites: H2291

HAGGITH
2Sa 3: 4 And the fourth, Adonijah the son of **H**; H2294
1Ki 1: 5 Then Adonijah the son of **H** exalted H2294
11 the son of **H** doth reign, and David H2294
2:13 And Adonijah the son of **H** came to H2294
1Ch 3: 2 the fourth, Adonijah the son of **H**: H2294

HAHIROTH See PI-HAHIROTH.

HAI
Gen 12: 8 on the west, and **H** on the east: and H5857
13: 3 the beginning, between Beth-el and **H**; H5857

HAIL
Ex 9:18 a very grievous **h**, such as hath not been H1259
19 brought home, the **h** shall come down H1259
22 that there may be **h** in all the land of H1259
Ex 9:23 sent thunder and **h**, and the fire ran H1259
23 LORD rained **h** upon the land of Egypt. H1259
24 So there was **h**, and fire mingled with H1259
24 mingled with the **h**, very grievous, such H1259
25 And the **h** smote throughout all the H1259
25 and beast; and the **h** smote every herb H1259
26 children of Israel *were*, was there no **h**. H1259
28 thunderings and **h**; and I will let you go, H1259
29 there be any more **h**; that thou mayest H1259
33 and the thunders and **h** ceased, and the H1259
34 the rain and the **h** and the thunders H1259
10: 5 unto you from the **h**, and shall eat every H1259
12 of the land, *even* all that the **h** hath left. H1259
15 the trees which the **h** had left: and there H1259
Job 38:22 or hast thou seen the treasures of the **h**, H1259
Ps 18:12 passed, **h** *stones* and coals of fire. H1259
13 his voice; **h** *stones* and coals of fire. H1259
78:47 He destroyed their vines with **h**, and H1259
48 He gave up their cattle also to the **h**, H1259
105:32 He gave them **h** for rain, *and* flaming H1259
148: 8 Fire, and **h**; snow, and vapour; stormy H1259
Isa 28: 2 as a tempest of **h** *and* a destroying H1259
17 plummet: and the **h** shall sweep away H1259
32:19 When it shall **h**, coming down on the H1258
Hag 2:17 mildew and with **h** in all the labours of H1259
Mt 26:49 and said, **H**, master; and kissed him. *G5463*
27:29 him, saying, **H**, King of the Jews! *G5463*
28: 9 them, saying, All **h**. And they came and *G5463*
Mk 15:18 And began to salute him, **H**, King of the *G5463*
Lk 1:28 her, and said, **H**, *thou that art* highly *G5463*
Jn 19: 3 And said, **H**, King of the Jews! and they *G5463*
Rev 8: 7 there followed **h** and fire mingled with *G5464*
11:19 and an earthquake, and great **h**. *G5464*
16:21 And there fell upon men a great **h** out *G5464*
21 of the plague of the **h**; for the plague *G5464*

HAILSTONES
Jos 10:11 died with **h** than *they* whom H68+H1259
Isa 30:30 scattering, and tempest, and **h**. H68+H1259
Ezk 13:11 and ye, O great **h**, shall fall; and a H68+H417
13 great **h** in *my* fury to consume *it*. H68+H417
38:22 and great **h**, fire, and brimstone. H68+H417

HAIR
Ex 25: 4 and scarlet, and fine linen, and goats' *h*,
26: 7 And thou shalt make curtains *of* goats' *h*
35: 6 and scarlet, and fine linen, and goats' *h*,
23 fine linen, and goats' *h*, and red skins of
26 stirred them up in wisdom spun goats' *h*.
36:14 And he made curtains *of* goats' *h* for the
Lev 13: 3 and *when* the **h** in the plague is turned H8181
4 than the skin, and the **h** thereof be not H8181
10 it have turned the **h** white, and *there be* H8181
20 the skin, and the **h** thereof be turned H8181
25 and, behold, *if* the **h** in the bright spot H8181
26 *there be* no white **h** in the bright spot, H8181
30 in it a yellow thin **h**; then the priest shall H8181
31 *there is* no black **h** in it; then the priest H8181
32 be in it no yellow **h**, and the scall *be* not H8181
36 not seek for yellow **h**; he *is* unclean. H8181
37 *that* there is black **h** grown up therein; H8181
40 And the man whose **h** is fallen off his H4803
41 And he that hath his **h** fallen off from H4803
14: 8 shave off all his **h**, and wash himself in H8181
9 he shall shave all his **h** off his head and H8181
9 even all his **h** he shall shave off: and H8181
Nu 6: 5 let the locks of the **h** of his head grow. H8181
18 and shall take the **h** of the head of his H8181
19 after *the* **h** *of* his separation is shaven:
31:20 of goats' *h*, and all things made of wood.
Jdg 16:22 Howbeit the **h** of his head began to H8181
20:16 stones at an **h** *breadth*, and not miss. H8185
1Sa 14:45 there shall not one **h** of his head fall to H8185
19:13 a pillow of goats' *h* for his bolster, and
16 with a pillow of goats' *h* for his bolster.
2Sa 14:11 not one **h** of thy son fall to the earth. H8185
26 *it*: because *the* **h** was heavy on him,
26 it:) he weighed the **h** of his head at two H8181
1Ki 1:52 there shall not an **h** of him fall to the H8185
Ezr 9: 3 plucked off the **h** of my head and of my H8181
Neh 13:25 and plucked off their **h**, and made them H4803
Job 4:15 my face; the **h** of my flesh stood up: H8185
Song 4: 1 thy locks: thy **h** *is* as a flock of goats, H8181
6: 5 overcome me: thy **h** *is* as a flock of H8181
7: 5 Carmel, and the **h** of thine head like H1803
Isa 3:24 and instead of well set **h** baldness; and H4748
7:20 the head, and the **h** of the feet: and it H8181
50: 6 that plucked off the **h**: I hid not my face H4803
Jer 7:29 Cut off thine **h**, *O Jerusalem*, and cast *it* H5145
Ezk 5: 1 thee balances to weigh, and divide the *h*.
16: 7 and thine **h** is grown, whereas thou H8181
Dan 3:27 no power, nor was an **h** of their head H8177
7: 9 as snow, and the **h** of his head like the H8177
Mt 3: 4 of camel's **h**, and a leathern girdle *G2359*
5:36 canst not make one **h** white or black. *G2359*
Mk 1: 6 And John was clothed with camel's **h**, *G2359*
Lk 21:18 But there shall not an **h** of your head *G2359*
Jn 11: 2 her **h**, whose brother Lazarus was sick.) *G2359*
12: 3 his feet with her **h**: and the house was *G2359*
Act 27:34 an **h** fall from the head of any of you. *G2359*
1Co 11:14 have long **h**, it is a shame unto him? *G2863*
15 But if a woman have long **h**, it is a glory *G2863*
15 for *her* **h** is given her for a covering. *G2864*
1Ti 2: 9 **h**, or gold, or pearls, or costly array; *G4117*
1Pt 3: 3 of plaiting the **h**, and of wearing of gold, *G2359*
Rev 6:12 of **h**, and the moon became as blood; *G5155*
9: 8 And they had **h** as the hair of women, *G2359*
8 And they had hair as the **h** of women, *G2359*

HAIR-BREADTH See HAIR and BREADTH.

HAIRS
Gen 42:38 my gray **h** with sorrow to the grave. H7872
44:29 my gray **h** with sorrow to the grave. H7872
31 down the gray **h** of thy servant our H7872
Lev 13:21 *there be* no white **h** therein, and *if* it *be* H8181
Dt 32:25 suckling *also* with the man of gray **h**. H7872
Ps 40:12 they are more than the **h** of mine head: H8185
69: 4 are more than the **h** of mine head: they H8185
Isa 46: 4 and *even* to hoar **h** will I carry *you*: I H7872
Dan 4:33 of heaven, till his **h** were grown like H8177
Hos 7: 9 *it* not: yea, gray **h** are here and there H7872
Mt 10:30 But the very **h** of your head are all *G2359*
Lk 7:38 *them* with the **h** of her head, and kissed *G2359*
44 and wiped *them* with the **h** of her head. *G2359*
12: 7 But even the very **h** of your head are all *G2359*
Rev 1:14 His head and *his* **h** *were* white like *G2359*

HAIRY
Gen 25:25 all over like an **h** garment; and they H8181
27:11 *is* a **h** man, and I *am* a smooth man: H8163
23 his hands were **h**, as his brother Esau's H8163
2Ki 1: 8 And they answered him, *He was* an **h** H8181
Ps 68:21 his enemies, *and* the **h** scalp of such an H8181

HAKKATAN
Ezr 8:12 the son of **H**, and with him an hundred H6997

HAKKORE See EN-HAKKORE.

HAKKOZ
1Ch 24:10 The seventh to **H**, the eighth to Abijah, H6976

HAKUPHA
Ezr 2:51 children of **H**, the children of Harhur, H2709
Neh 7:53 children of **H**, the children of Harhur, H2709

HALAH
2Ki 17: 6 placed them in **H** and in Habor *by* the H2477
18:11 and put them in **H** and in Habor *by* the H2477
1Ch 5:26 them unto **H**, and Habor, and Hara, H2477

HALAK
Jos 11:17 *Even* from the mount **H**, that goeth up H2510
12: 7 unto the mount **H**, that goeth up to Seir; H2510

HALE
Lk 12:58 from him; lest he **h** thee to the judge, *G2694*

HALF
Gen 24:22 a golden earring of **h** a shekel weight, H1235
Ex 24: 6 And Moses took **h** of the blood, and put H2677
6 **h** of the blood he sprinkled on the altar. H2677
25:10 two cubits and a **h** *shall be* the length H2677
10 and a cubit and a **h** the breadth H2677
10 and a cubit and a **h** the height thereof. H2677
17 two cubits and a **h** *shall be* the length H2677
17 a cubit and a **h** the breadth thereof. H2677
23 and a cubit and a **h** the height thereof. H2677
26:12 curtains of the tent, the **h** curtain that H2677
16 a **h** *shall be* the breadth of one board. H2677
30:13 that are numbered, **h** a shekel after the H4276
13 twenty gerahs:) an **h** shekel *shall be* the H4276
15 not give less than **h** a shekel, when *they* H4276
23 sweet cinnamon **h** so much, *even* two H4276
36:21 breadth of a board one cubit and a **h**. H2677
37: 1 two cubits and a **h** *was* the length of it, H2677
1 it, and a cubit and a **h** the breadth of it, H2677

Ex 37: 1 it, and a cubit and a **h** the height of it: H2677
6 gold: two cubits and a **h** *was* the length H2677
6 one cubit and a **h** the breadth thereof. H2677
10 and a cubit and a **h** the height thereof: H2677
38:26 A bekah for every man, *that is*, **h** a H4276
Lev 6:20 perpetual, **h** of it in the morning, H4276
20 in the morning, and **h** thereof at night. H4276
Nu 12:12 whom the flesh is **h** consumed when he H2677
15: 9 of flour mingled with **h** an hin of oil. H2677
10 a drink offering **h** an hin of wine, *for* H2677
28:14 And their drink offerings shall be **h** an H2677
31:29 Take *it* of their **h**, and give it unto H4276
30 And of the children of Israel's **h**, thou H4276
36 And the **h**, *which was* the portion of H4275
42 And of the children of Israel's **h**, which H4276
43 (Now the **h** *that pertained unto* the H4275
47 Even of the children of Israel's **h**, Moses H4276
32:33 of Reuben, and unto **h** the tribe of H2677
34:13 unto the nine tribes, and to the **h** tribe: H2677
14 *their inheritance*; and **h** the tribe of H2677
15 The two tribes and the **h** tribe have H2677
Dt 3:12 river Arnon, and **h** mount Gilead, and H2677
13 gave I unto the **h** tribe of Manasseh; H2677
16 the river Arnon **h** the valley, and the H8432
29: 8 and to the **h** tribe of Manasseh. H2677
Jos 1:12 the Gadites, and to **h** the tribe of H2677
4:12 of Gad, and **h** the tribe of Manasseh, H2677
8:33 among them; **h** of them over against H2677
33 Gerizim, and **h** of them over against H2677
12: 2 river, and from **h** Gilead, even unto the H2677
5 and **h** Gilead, the border of H2677
6 Gadites, and the **h** tribe of Manasseh. H2677
13: 7 tribes, and the **h** tribe of Manasseh, H2677
25 cities of Gilead, and **h** the land of the H2677
29 And Moses gave *inheritance* unto the **h** H2677
29 *possession* of the **h** tribe of the children H2677
31 And **h** Gilead, and Ashtaroth, and H2677
31 *even* to the one **h** of the children of H2677
14: 2 for the nine tribes, and *for* the **h** tribe. H2677
3 two tribes and an **h** tribe on the other H2677
18: 7 Gad, and Reuben, and **h** the tribe of H2677
21: 5 of the **h** tribe of Manasseh, ten cities. H2677
6 and out of the **h** tribe of Manasseh in H2677
25 And out of the **h** tribe of Manasseh, H4276
27 out of the *other* **h** tribe of Manasseh H2677
22: 1 Gadites, and the **h** tribe of Manasseh, H2677
7 Now to the *one* **h** of the tribe of H2677
7 but unto the *other* **h** thereof gave H2677
9 of Gad and the **h** tribe of Manasseh H2677
10 of Gad and the **h** tribe of Manasseh H2677
11 of Gad and the **h** tribe of Manasseh H2677
13 of Gad, and to the **h** tribe of Manasseh, H2677
15 of Gad, and to the **h** tribe of Manasseh, H2677
21 of Gad and the **h** tribe of Manasseh H2677
1Sa 14:14 as it were an **h** acre of land, *which* H2677
2Sa 10: 4 shaved off the one **h** of their beards, H2677
18: 3 for us; neither if **h** of us die, will they H2677
19:40 king, and also **h** the people of Israel. H2677
1Ki 3:25 give **h** to the one, and half to the other. H2677
25 give half to the one, and **h** to the other. H2677
7:31 a cubit and an **h**: and also upon the H2677
32 of a wheel *was* a cubit and **h** a cubit. H2677
35 a round compass of **h** a cubit high: and H2677
10: 7 and, behold, the **h** was not told me: thy H2677
13: 8 If thou wilt give me **h** thine house, I will H2677
16: 9 And his servant Zimri, captain of **h** *his* H4276
21 into two parts: **h** of the people followed H2677
21 make him king; and **h** followed Omri. H2677
1Ch 2:52 Haroeh, *and* **h** of the Manahethites. H2677
54 and **h** of the Manahethites, the Zorites. H2677
5:18 and the Gadites, and **h** the tribe of H2677
23 And the children of the **h** tribe of H2677
26 Gadites, and the **h** tribe of Manasseh, H2677
6:61 *given* out of the **h** tribe, *namely, out of* H2677
61 **h** *tribe* of Manasseh, by lot, ten cities. H4276
70 And out of the **h** tribe of Manasseh; H4276
71 the family of the **h** tribe of Manasseh, H2677
12:31 And of the **h** tribe of Manasseh H2677
37 and of the **h** tribe of Manasseh, H2677
26:32 Gadites, and the **h** tribe of Manasseh, H2677
27:20 of Azaziah: of the **h** tribe of Manasseh, H2677
21 Of the **h** *tribe* of Manasseh in Gilead, H2677
2Ch 9: 6 behold, the one **h** of the greatness of H2677
Neh 3: 9 the ruler of the **h** part of Jerusalem. H2677
12 the ruler of the **h** part of Jerusalem, he H2677
16 the ruler of the **h** part of Beth-zur, unto H2677
17 ruler of the **h** part of Keilah, in his part. H2677
18 the ruler of the **h** part of Keilah. H2677
4: 6 together unto the **h** thereof: for the H2677
Neh 4:16 time forth, *that* the **h** of my servants H2677
16 and the other **h** of them held both the H2677
21 So we laboured in the work: and **h** of H2677
12:32 And after them went Hoshaiah, and **h** H2677
38 them, and the **h** of the people upon H2677
40 and I, and the **h** of the rulers with me: H2677
13:24 And their children spake **h** in the H2677
Est 5: 3 given thee to the **h** of the kingdom. H2677
6 **h** of the kingdom it shall be performed. H2677
7: 2 *even* to the **h** of the kingdom. H2677
Ps 55:23 out **h** their days; but I will trust in thee. H2673
Ezk 16:51 Neither hath Samaria committed **h** of H2677
40:42 of a cubit and an **h** long, and a cubit H2677
42 a cubit and an **h** broad, and one cubit H2677
43:17 about it *shall be* **h** a cubit; and the H2677
Dan 12: 7 times, and an **h**; and when he shall have H2677
Hos 3: 2 of barley, and an **h** homer of barley: H2677
Zec 14: 2 ravished; and **h** of the city shall go H2677
4 great valley; and **h** of the mountain H2677
4 the north, and **h** of it toward the south. H2677
8 from Jerusalem; **h** of them toward the H2677
8 former sea, and **h** of them toward the H2677
Mk 6:23 give *it* thee, unto the **h** of my kingdom. *G2255*
Lk 10:30 and departed, leaving *him* **h** dead. *G2253*
19: 8 Behold, Lord, the **h** of my goods I give *G2255*
Rev 8: 1 in heaven about the space of **h** an hour. *G2256*
11: 9 three days and an **h**, and shall not *G2255*
11 And after three days and an **h** the *G2255*
12:14 **h** a time, from the face of the serpent. *G2255*

HALF-DEAD See HALF and DEAD.

HALF-HOMER See HALF and HOMER.

HALHUL
Jos 15:58 **H**, Beth-zur, and Gedor, H2478

HALI
Jos 19:25 And their border was Helkath, and **H**, H2482

HALING
Act 8: 3 every house, and **h** men and women *G4951*

HALL
Mt 27:27 into the common **h**, and gathered unto *G4232*
Mk 15:16 And the soldiers led him away into the **h**, *G833*
Lk 22:55 in the midst of the **h**, and were set down *G833*
Jn 18:28 Caiaphas unto the **h** of judgment: and *G4232*
28 into the judgment **h**, lest they should be *G4232*
33 into the judgment **h** again, and called *G4232*
19: 9 And went again into the judgment **h**, *G4232*
Act 23:35 him to be kept in Herod's judgment **h**. *G4232*

HALLELUJAH See ALLELUIA.

HALLOHESH
Neh 10:24 **H**, Pileha, Shobek, H3873

HALLOW
Ex 28:38 of Israel shall **h** in all their holy gifts; H6942
29: 1 do unto them to **h** them, to minister H6942
40: 9 *is* therein, and shalt **h** it, and all the H6942
Lev 16:19 and cleanse it, and **h** it from the H6942
22: 2 which they **h** unto me: I *am* the LORD. H6942
3 the children of Israel **h** unto the LORD, H6942
32 of Israel: I *am* the LORD which **h** you, H6942
25:10 And ye shall **h** the fiftieth year, and H6942
Nu 6:11 and shall **h** his head that same day. H6942
1Ki 8:64 The same day did the king **h** the H6942
Jer 17:22 ye any work, but **h** ye the sabbath day, H6942
24 sabbath day, but **h** the sabbath day, to H6942
27 But if ye will not hearken unto me to **h** H6942
Ezk 20:20 And **h** my sabbaths; and they shall be a H6942
44:24 and they shall **h** my sabbaths. H6942

HALLOWED
Ex 20:11 blessed the sabbath day, and **h** it. H6942
29:21 and he shall be **h**, and his garments, H6942
Lev 12: 4 she shall touch no **h** thing, nor come H6944
19: 8 hath profaned the **h** thing of the LORD: H6944
22:32 but I will be **h** among the children H6942
Nu 3:13 in the land of Egypt I **h** unto me all the H6942
5:10 And every man's **h** things shall be his: H6944
16:37 thou the fire yonder; for they are **h**. H6942
38 therefore they are **h**: and they shall be a H6942
18: 8 heave offerings of all the **h** things of the H6944
29 *even* the **h** part thereof out of it. H4720
Dt 26:13 brought away the **h** things out of *mine* H6944
1Sa 21: 4 hand, but there is **h** bread; if the young H6944
1Sa 21: 6 So the priest gave him **h** *bread*: for H6944
1Ki 9: 3 before me: I have **h** this house, which H6942
7 which I have **h** for my name, will I H6942
2Ki 12:18 of Judah took all the **h** things that H6944
18 and his own **h** things, and all the gold H6944
2Ch 7: 7 Moreover Solomon **h** the middle of the H6942
36:14 the LORD which he had **h** in Jerusalem. H6942
Mt 6: 9 which art in heaven, **H** be thy name. *G37*
Lk 11: 2 which art in heaven, **H** be thy name. Thy *G37*

HALOHESH
Neh 3:12 the son of **H**, the ruler of the half H3873

HALT
1Ki 18:21 and said, How long **h** ye between two H6452
Ps 38:17 For I *am* ready to **h**, and my sorrow *is* H6761
Mt 18: 8 to enter into life **h** or maimed, rather *G5560*
Mk 9:45 for thee to enter **h** into life, than having *G5560*
Lk 14:21 the maimed, and the **h**, and the blind. *G5560*
Jn 5: 3 folk, of blind, **h**, withered, waiting for *G5560*

HALTED
Gen 32:31 upon him, and he **h** upon his thigh. H6760
Mic 4: 7 And I will make her that **h** a remnant, H6760

HALTETH
Mic 4: 6 I assemble her that **h**, and I will gather H6760
Zep 3:19 I will save her that **h**, and gather her H6760

HALTING
Jer 20:10 watched for my **h**, *saying*, Peradventure H6761

HAM
Gen 5:32 and Noah begat Shem, **H**, and Japheth. H2526
6:10 And Noah begat three sons, Shem, **H**, H2526
7:13 and Shem, and **H**, and Japheth, the H2526
9:18 were Shem, and **H**, and Japheth: and H2526
18 Japheth: and **H** *is* the father of Canaan. H2526
22 And **H**, the father of Canaan, saw the H2526
10: 1 of Noah, Shem, **H**, and Japheth: and H2526
6 And the sons of **H**; Cush, and Mizraim, H2526
20 These *are* the sons of **H**, after their H2526
14: 5 and the Zuzims in **H**, and the Emims in H1990
1Ch 1: 4 Noah, Shem, **H**, and Japheth. H2526
8 The sons of **H**; Cush, and Mizraim, Put, H2526
4:40 for *they* of **H** had dwelt there of old. H2526
Ps 78:51 of *their* strength in the tabernacles of **H**: H2526
105:23 and Jacob sojourned in the land of **H**. H2526
27 them, and wonders in the land of **H**. H2526
106:22 Wondrous works in the land of **H**, *and* H2526

HAMAN
Est 3: 1 promote **H** the son of Hammedatha H2001
2 and reverenced **H**: for the king had so H2001
4 them, that they told **H**, to see whether H2001
5 And when **H** saw that Mordecai bowed H2001
5 reverence, then was **H** full of wrath. H2001
6 wherefore **H** sought to destroy all H2001
7 *is*, the lot, before **H** from day to day, H2001
8 And **H** said unto king Ahasuerus, H2001
10 hand, and gave it unto **H** the son of H2001
11 And the king said unto **H**, The silver *is* H2001
12 to all that **H** had commanded unto H2001
15 And the king and **H** sat down to drink; H2001
4: 7 of the money that **H** had promised to H2001
5: 4 let the king and **H** come this day unto H2001
5 Then the king said, Cause **H** to make H2001
5 So the king and **H** came to the banquet H2001
8 let the king and **H** come to the banquet H2001
9 Then went **H** forth that day joyful and H2001
9 heart: but when **H** saw Mordecai in the H2001
10 Nevertheless **H** refrained himself: and H2001
11 And **H** told them of the glory of his H2001
12 **H** said moreover, Yea, Esther the H2001
14 the thing pleased **H**; and he caused the H2001
6: 4 in the court? Now **H** was come into the H2001
5 unto him, Behold, **H** standeth in the H2001
6 So **H** came in. And the king said unto H2001
6 to honour? Now **H** thought in his heart, H2001
7 And **H** answered the king, For the man H2001
10 Then the king said to **H**, Make haste, H2001
11 Then took **H** the apparel and the horse, H2001
12 king's gate. But **H** hasted to his house H2001
13 And **H** told Zeresh his wife and all his H2001
14 hasted to bring **H** unto the banquet H2001
7: 1 So the king and **H** came to banquet H2001
6 *is* this wicked **H**. Then Haman was H2001
6 Haman. Then **H** was afraid before the H2001
7 palace garden: and **H** stood up to make H2001

Est 7: 8 of wine; and **H** was fallen upon the H2001
9 fifty cubits high, which **H** had made for H2001
9 in the house of **H**. Then the king said, H2001
10 So they hanged **H** on the gallows that H2001
8: 1 give the house of **H** the Jews' enemy H2001
2 he had taken from **H**, and gave it unto H2001
2 set Mordecai over the house of **H**. H2001
3 the mischief of **H** the Agagite, and his H2001
5 the letters devised by **H** the son of H2001
7 the house of **H**, and him they have H2001
9:10 The ten sons of **H** the son of H2001
12 the ten sons of **H**; what have they done H2001
24 Because **H** the son of Hammedatha, H2001

HAMAN'S
Est 7: 8 the king's mouth, they covered **H** face. H2001
9:13 decree, and let **H** ten sons be hanged H2001
14 Shushan; and they hanged **H** ten sons. H2001

HAMATH
Nu 13:21 of Zin unto Rehob, as men come to **H**. H2574
34: 8 the entrance of **H**; and the goings forth H2574
Jos 13: 5 Hermon unto the entering into **H**. H2574
Jdg 3: 3 Baal-hermon unto the entering in of **H**. H2574
2Sa 8: 9 When Toi king of **H** heard that David H2574
1Ki 8:65 the entering in of **H** unto the river of H2574
2Ki 14:25 the entering of **H** unto the sea of the H2574
28 Damascus, and **H**, *which belonged* to H2574
17:24 from Ava, and from **H**, and from H2574
30 and the men of **H** made Ashima, H2574
18:34 Where *are* the gods of **H**, and of Arpad? H2574
19:13 Where *is* the king of **H**, and the king of H2574
23:33 in the land of **H**, that he might not reign H2574
25:21 in the land of **H**. So Judah was carried H2574
1Ch 18: 3 of Zobah unto **H**, as he went to stablish H2574
9 Now when Tou king of **H** heard how H2574
2Ch 7: 8 entering in of **H** unto the river of Egypt. H2574
8: 4 all the store cities, which he built in **H**. H2574
Isa 10: 9 *Is* not Calno as Carchemish? *is* not **H** as H2574
11:11 from **H**, and from the islands of the sea. H2574
36:19 Where *are* the gods of **H** and Arphad? H2574
37:13 Where *is* the king of **H**, and the king of H2574
Jer 39: 5 **H**, where he gave judgment upon him. H2574
49:23 Concerning Damascus. **H** is H2574
52: 9 **H**; where he gave judgment upon him. H2574
27 Riblah in the land of **H**. Thus Judah was H2574
Ezk 47:16 **H**, Berothah, Sibraim, which *is* between H2574
16 and the border of **H**; Hazar-hatticon, H2574
17 border of **H**. And *this is* the north side. H2574
20 over against **H**. This *is* the west side. H2574
48: 1 as one goeth to **H**, Hazar-enan, the H2574
1 to the coast of **H**; for these are his sides H2574
Am 6: 2 thence go ye to **H** the great: then go H2579
Zec 9: 2 And **H** also shall border thereby; Tyrus, H2574

HAMATHITE
Gen 10:18 the Zemarite, and the **H**: and afterward H2577
1Ch 1:16 Arvadite, and the Zemarite, and the **H**. H2577

HAMATH-ZOBAH
2Ch 8: 3 And Solomon went to **H**, and prevailed H2578

HAMMAHLEKOTH See SELA-HAMMAHLEKOTH.

HAM-MATH
Jos 19:35 Zer, and **H**, Rakkath, and Chinnereth, H2575

HAMMEDATHA
Est 3: 1 Haman the son of **H** the Agagite, and H4099
10 son of **H** the Agagite, the Jews' enemy. H4099
8: 5 Haman the son of **H** the Agagite, which H4099
9:10 The ten sons of Haman the son of **H**, H4099
24 Because Haman the son of **H**, the H4099

HAMMELECH
Jer 36:26 the son of **H**, and Seraiah the son H4428
38: 6 the son of **H**, that *was* in the court H4428

HAMMER
Jdg 4:21 tent, and took an **h** in her hand, and H4718
5:26 hand to the workmen's **h**; and with the H1989
26 and with the **h** she smote Sisera, she
1Ki 6: 7 there was neither **h** nor axe *nor* any H4717
Isa 41: 7 *with* the **h** him that smote the H6360
Jer 23:29 a **h** *that* breaketh the rock in pieces? H6360
50:23 How is the **h** of the whole earth cut H6360

HAMMERS
Ps 74: 6 work thereof at once with axes and **h**. H3597
Isa 44:12 and fashioneth it with **h**, and worketh it H4717
Jer 10: 4 with nails and with **h**, that it move not. H4717

HAMMOLEKETH
1Ch 7:18 And his sister **H** bare Ishod, and H4447

HAMMON
Jos 19:28 And Hebron, and Rehob, and **H**, and H2540
1Ch 6:76 her suburbs, and **H** with her suburbs, H2540

HAMMOTH-DOR
Jos 21:32 for the slayer; and **H** with her suburbs, H2576

HAMON See BAAL-HAMON and HAMON-GOG.

HAMONAH
Ezk 39:16 *be* **H**. Thus shall they cleanse the land. H1997

HAMON-GOG
Ezk 39:11 and they shall call *it* The valley of **H**. H1996
15 buriers have buried it in the valley of **H**. H1996

HAMOR
Gen 33:19 of the children of **H**, Shechem's father, H2544
34: 2 And when Shechem the son of **H** the H2544
4 And Shechem spake unto his father **H**, H2544
6 And **H** the father of Shechem went out H2544
8 And **H** communed with them, saying, H2544
13 Shechem and **H** his father deceitfully, H2544
18 And their words pleased **H**, and H2544
20 And **H** and Shechem his son came unto H2544
24 And unto **H** and unto Shechem his son H2544
26 And they slew **H** and Shechem his son H2544
Jos 24:32 of the sons of **H** the father of Shechem H2544
Jdg 9:28 officer? serve the men of **H** the father of H2544

HAMOR'S
Gen 34:18 pleased Hamor, and Shechem **H** son. H2544

HAMUEL
1Ch 4:26 And the sons of Mishma; **H** his son, H2536

HAMUL
Gen 46:12 the sons of Pharez were Hezron and **H**. H2538
Nu 26:21 of **H**, the family of the Hamulites. H2538
1Ch 2: 5 The sons of Pharez; Hezron, and **H**. H2538

HAMULITES
Nu 26:21 of Hamul, the family of the **H**. H2539

HAMUTAL
2Ki 23:31 **H**, the daughter of Jeremiah of Libnah. H2537
24:18 **H**, the daughter of Jeremiah of Libnah. H2537
Jer 52: 1 **H** the daughter of Jeremiah of Libnah. H2537

HANAMEEL
Jer 32: 7 Behold, **H** the son of Shallum thine H2601
8 So **H** mine uncle's son came to me in H2601
9 And I bought the field of **H** my uncle's H2601
12 in the sight of **H** mine uncle's *son*, and H2601

HANAN
1Ch 8:23 And Abdon, and Zichri, and **H**, H2605
38 and **H**. All these *were* the sons of Azel. H2605
9:44 and **H**: these *were* the sons of Azel. H2605
11:43 **H** the son of Maachah, and Joshaphat H2605
Ezr 2:46 children of Shalmai, the children of **H**, H2605
Neh 7:49 The children of **H**, the children of H2605
8: 7 Azariah, Jozabad, **H**, Pelaiah, and the H2605
10:10 Shebaniah, Hodijah, Kelita, Pelaiah, **H**, H2605
22 Pelatiah, **H**, Anaiah, H2605
26 And Ahijah, **H**, Anan, H2605
13:13 next to them *was* **H** the son of Zaccur, H2605
Jer 35: 4 of the sons of **H**, the son of Igdaliah, H2605

HANANEEL
Neh 3: 1 they sanctified it, unto the tower of **H**. H2606
12:39 and the tower of **H**, and the tower of H2606
Jer 31:38 tower of **H** unto the gate of the corner. H2606
Zec 14:10 tower of **H** unto the king's winepresses. H2606

HANANI
1Ki 16: 1 the son of **H** against Baasha, saying, H2607
7 Jehu the son of **H** came the word of the H2607
1Ch 25: 4 Hananiah, **H**, Eliathah, Giddalti, H2607
25 The eighteenth to **H**, *he*, his sons, and H2607
2Ch 16: 7 And at that time **H** the seer came to H2607
19: 2 And Jehu the son of **H** the seer went out H2607
20:34 of Jehu the son of **H**, who *is* mentioned H2607
Ezr 10:20 And of the sons of Immer; **H**, and H2607
Neh 1: 2 That **H**, one of my brethren, came, he H2607
7: 2 That I gave my brother **H**, and H2607
12:36 and Judah, **H**, with the musical H2607

HANANIAH
1Ch 3:19 and **H**, and Shelomith their sister: H2608
21 And the sons of **H**; Pelatiah, and H2608
8:24 And **H**, and Elam, and Antothijah, H2608
25: 4 and Jerimoth, **H**, Hanani, Eliathah, H2608
23 The sixteenth to **H**, *he*, his sons, and his H2608
2Ch 26:11 hand of **H**, *one* of the king's captains. H2608
Ezr 10:28 Of the sons also of Bebai; Jehohanan, **H**, H2608
Neh 3: 8 him also repaired **H** the son of *one of* H2608
30 After him repaired **H** the son of H2608
7: 2 That I gave my brother Hanani, and **H** H2608
10:23 Hoshea, **H**, Hashub, H2608
12:12 of Seraiah, Meraiah; of Jeremiah, **H**; H2608
41 Zechariah, *and* **H**, with trumpets; H2608
Jer 28: 1 fifth month, *that* **H** the son of Azur the H2608
5 unto the prophet **H** in the presence of H2608
10 Then **H** the prophet took the yoke from H2608
11 And **H** spake in the presence of all the H2608
12 after that **H** the prophet had broken H2608
13 Go and tell **H**, saying, Thus saith the H2608
15 Then said the prophet Jeremiah unto **H** H2608
15 Hear now, **H**; The LORD hath not H2608
17 So **H** the prophet died the same year in H2608
36:12 the son of **H**, and all the princes. H2608
37:13 the son of **H**; and he took Jeremiah H2608
Dan 1: 6 Judah, Daniel, **H**, Mishael, and Azariah: H2608
7 and to **H**, of Shadrach; and to H2608
11 over Daniel, **H**, Mishael, and Azariah, H2608
19 found none like Daniel, **H**, Mishael, and H2608
2:17 the thing known to **H**, Mishael, and H2608

HAND
Gen 3:22 he put forth his **h**, and take also of the H3027
4:11 receive thy brother's blood from thy **h**; H3027
8: 9 he put forth his **h**, and took her, and H3027
9: 2 the sea; into your **h** are they delivered. H3027
5 I require; at the **h** of every beast will I H3027
5 it, and at the **h** of man; at the hand H3027
5 of man; at the **h** of every man's brother H3027
13: 9 *wilt take* the left **h**, then I will go to the H8040
9 to the right **h**, then I will go to the left. H3225
14:15 which *is* on the left **h** of Damascus. H8040
20 into thy **h**. And he gave him tithes of all. H3027
22 I have lift up mine **h** unto the LORD, H3027
16: 6 thy maid *is* in thy **h**; do to her as it H3027
12 And he will be a wild man; his **h** *will be* H3027
12 and every man's **h** against him; and he H3027
19:10 But the men put forth their **h**, and H3027
16 men laid hold upon his **h**, and upon the H3027
16 and upon the **h** of his wife, and upon H3027
16 and upon the **h** of his two daughters; H3027
21:18 **h**; for I will make him a great nation. H3027
30 thou take of my **h**, that they may be a H3027
22: 6 took the fire in his **h**, and a knife; and H3027
10 And Abraham stretched forth his **h**, H3027
12 And he said, Lay not thine **h** upon the H3027
24: 2 Put, I pray thee, thy **h** under my thigh: H3027
9 And the servant put his **h** under the H3027
10 master *were* in his **h**: and he arose, and H3027
18 pitcher upon her **h**, and gave him drink. H3027
49 I may turn to the right **h**, or to the left. H3225
25:26 out, and his **h** took hold on Esau's H3027
27:17 prepared, into the **h** of her son Jacob. H3027
41 at **h**; then will I slay my brother Jacob. H7126
30:35 and gave *them* into the **h** of his sons. H3027
31:29 It is in the power of my **h** to do you H3027
39 loss of it; of my **h** didst thou require it, H3027
32:11 Deliver me, I pray thee, from the **h** of H3027
11 brother, from the **h** of Esau: for I fear H3027
13 to his **h** a present for Esau his brother; H3027
16 And he delivered *them* into the **h** of his H3027
33:10 my present at my **h**: for therefore I have H3027
19 his tent, at the **h** of the children of H3027
35: 4 *were* in their **h**, and *all their* earrings H3027
37:22 and lay no **h** upon him; that he might H3027
27 and let not our **h** be upon him; for he H3027
38:18 that *is* in thine **h**. And he gave *it* her, H3027
20 And Judah sent the kid by the **h** of his H3027
20 the woman's **h**: but he found her not. H3027
28 *one* put out *his* **h**: and the midwife took H3027
28 and bound upon his **h** a scarlet thread, H3027
29 as he drew back his **h**, that, behold, his H3027
30 his **h**: and his name was called Zarah. H3027
39: 3 made all that he did to prosper in his **h**. H3027

H

Gen 39: 4 and all *that* he had he put into his **h**. H3027
6 And he left all that he had in Joseph's **h**; H3027
8 committed all that he hath to my **h**; H3027
12 in her **h**, and fled, and got him out. H3027
13 garment in her **h**, and was fled forth, H3027
22 to Joseph's **h** all the prisoners that H3027
23 *that was* under his **h**; because the LORD H3027
40:11 And Pharaoh's cup *was* in my **h**: and I H3027
11 and I gave the cup into Pharaoh's **h**. H3709
13 cup into his **h**, after the former manner H3027
21 and he gave the cup into Pharaoh's **h**: H3709
41:35 up corn under the **h** of Pharaoh, and let H3027
42 off his ring from his **h**, and put it upon H3027
42 it upon Joseph's **h**, and arrayed him in H3027
44 up his **h** or foot in all the land of Egypt. H3027
42:37 **h**, and I will bring him to thee again. H3027
43: 9 I will be surety for him; of my **h** shalt H3027
12 And take double money in your **h**; and H3027
12 **h**; peradventure it *was* an oversight: H3027
15 money in their **h**, and Benjamin; and H3027
21 and we have brought it again in our **h**. H3027
26 which *was* in their **h** into the house, H3027
44:17 the man in whose **h** the cup is found, H3027
46: 4 Joseph shall put his **h** upon thine eyes. H3027
47:29 I pray thee, thy **h** under my thigh, and H3027
48:13 in his right **h** toward Israel's left H3225
13 Israel's left **h**, and Manasseh in his H8040
13 in his left **h** toward Israel's right H8040
13 **h**, and brought *them* near unto him. H3225
14 And Israel stretched out his right **h**, and H3225
14 and his left **h** upon Manasseh's head, H8040
17 father laid his right **h** upon the head of H3027
17 held up his father's **h**, to remove it from H3027
18 put thy right **h** upon his head. H3225
22 I took out of the **h** of the Amorite with H3027
49: 8 shall praise: thy **h** *shall be* in the neck H3027
Ex 2:19 us out of the **h** of the shepherds, and H3027
3: 8 them out of the **h** of the Egyptians, and H3027
19 not let you go, no, not by a mighty **h**. H3027
20 And I will stretch out my **h**, and smite H3027
4: 2 *is* that in thine **h**? And he said, A rod. H3027
4 Put forth thine **h**, and take it by the tail. H3027
4 he put forth his **h**, and caught it, and it H3027
4 caught it, and it became a rod in his **h**: H3709
6 Put now thine **h** into thy bosom. And H3027
6 And he put his **h** into his bosom: and H3027
6 out, behold, his **h** *was* leprous as snow. H3027
7 And he said, Put thine **h** into thy H3027
7 And he put his **h** into his bosom again; H3027
13 by the **h** *of him whom* thou wilt send. H3027
17 And thou shalt take this rod in thine **h**, H3027
20 and Moses took the rod of God in his **h**. H3027
21 I have put in thine **h**: but I will harden H3027
5:21 to put a sword in their **h** to slay us. H3027
6: 1 for with a strong **h** shall he let them go, H3027
1 **h** shall he drive them out of his land. H3027
7: 4 that I may lay my **h** upon Egypt, and H3027
5 I stretch forth mine **h** upon Egypt, and H3027
15 to a serpent shalt thou take in thine **h**. H3027
17 rod that *is* in mine **h** upon the waters H3027
19 stretch out thine **h** upon the waters of H3027
8: 5 Stretch forth thine **h** with thy rod over H3027
6 And Aaron stretched out his **h** over the H3027
17 stretched out his **h** with his rod, and H3027
9: 3 Behold, the **h** of the LORD is upon thy H3027
15 For now I will stretch out my **h**, that I H3027
22 Stretch forth thine **h** toward heaven, H3027
10:12 Stretch out thine **h** over the land of H3027
21 Stretch out thine **h** toward heaven, that H3027
22 And Moses stretched forth his **h** H3027
12:11 your staff in your **h**; and ye shall eat it H3027
13: 3 for by strength of **h** the LORD brought H3027
9 thee upon thine **h**, and for a memorial H3027
9 for with a strong **h** hath the LORD H3027
14 By strength of **h** the LORD brought us H3027
16 And it shall be for a token upon thine **h**, H3027
16 for by strength of **h** the LORD brought H3027
14: 8 of Israel went out with an high **h**. H3027
16 stretch out thine **h** over the sea, and H3027
21 And Moses stretched out his **h** over the H3027
22 them on their right **h**, and on their left. H3225
26 Stretch out thine **h** over the sea, that H3027
27 And Moses stretched forth his **h** over H3027
29 them on their right **h**, and on their left. H3225
30 that day out of the **h** of the Egyptians; H3027
15: 6 Thy right **h**, O LORD, is become H3225
6 in power: thy right **h**, O LORD, hath H3225
9 my sword, my **h** shall destroy them. H3027
12 Thou stretchedst out thy right **h**, the H3225

Ex 15:20 a timbrel in her **h**; and all the women H3027
16: 3 had died by the **h** of the LORD in the H3027
17: 5 the river, take in thine **h**, and go. H3027
9 of the hill with the rod of God in mine **h**. H3027
11 when Moses held up his **h**, that Israel H3027
11 he let down his **h**, Amalek prevailed. H3027
18: 9 delivered out of the **h** of the Egyptians. H3027
10 you out of the **h** of the Egyptians, and H3027
10 and out of the **h** of Pharaoh, who hath H3027
10 from under the **h** of the Egyptians. H3027
19:13 There shall not an **h** touch it, but he H3027
21:13 *him* into his **h**; then I will appoint thee H3027
16 in his **h**, he shall surely be put to death. H3027
20 his **h**; he shall be surely punished. H3027
24 Eye for eye, tooth for tooth, **h** for hand, H3027
24 Eye for eye, tooth for tooth, hand for **h**, H3027
22: 4 If the theft be certainly found in his **h** H3027
8 put his **h** unto his neighbour's goods. H3027
11 hath not put his **h** unto his neighbour's H3027
23: 1 put not thine **h** with the wicked to be H3027
31 of the land into your **h**; and thou shalt H3027
24:11 he laid not his **h**: also they saw God, H3027
25:25 unto it a border of an **h** breadth round H2948
29:20 of their right **h**, and upon the great H3027
32: 4 And he received *them* at their **h**, and H3027
11 with great power, and with a mighty **h**? H3027
15 *were* in his **h**: the tables *were* written H3027
33:22 cover thee with my **h** while I pass by: H3709
23 And I will take away mine **h**, and thou H3709
34: 4 took in his **h** the two tables of stone. H3027
29 in Moses' **h**, when he came down H3027
35:29 to be made by the **h** of Moses. H3027
38:15 court gate, on this **h** and that hand, *were*
15 this hand and that **h**, *were* hangings of
21 **h** of Ithamar, son to Aaron the priest. H3027
Lev 1: 4 And he shall put his **h** upon the head of H3027
3: 2 And he shall lay his **h** upon the head of H3027
8 And he shall lay his **h** upon the head of H3027
13 And he shall lay his **h** upon the head of H3027
4: 4 and shall lay his **h** upon the bullock's H3027
24 And he shall lay his **h** upon the head of H3027
29 And he shall lay his **h** upon the head of H3027
33 And he shall lay his **h** upon the head of H3027
8:23 the thumb of his right **h**, and upon the H3027
36 LORD commanded by the **h** of Moses. H3027
9:22 And Aaron lifted up his **h** toward the H3027
10:11 spoken unto them by the **h** of Moses. H3027
14:14 the thumb of his right **h**, and upon the H3027
15 pour *it* into the palm of his own left **h**:
16 that *is* in his left **h**, and shall sprinkle of H3709
17 And of the rest of the oil that *is* in his **h** H3709
17 the thumb of his right **h**, and upon the H3027
18 *is* in the priest's **h** he shall pour upon H3709
25 the thumb of his right **h**, and upon the H3027
26 of the oil into the palm of his own left **h**: H8042
27 his left **h** seven times before the LORD: H3709
28 oil that *is* in his **h** upon the tip of the H3709
28 the thumb of his right **h**, and upon the H3027
29 *is* in the priest's **h** he shall put upon the H3709
32 of leprosy, whose **h** is not able to get H3027
16:21 the **h** of a fit man into the wilderness: H3027
22:25 Neither from a stranger's **h** shall ye H3027
25:14 **h**, ye shall not oppress one another: H3027
28 shall remain in the **h** of him that hath H3027
26:25 be delivered into the **h** of the enemy. H3027
46 in mount Sinai by the **h** of Moses. H3027
Nu 4:28 *shall be* under the **h** of Ithamar the son H3027
33 under the **h** of Ithamar the son H3027
37 of the LORD by the **h** of Moses. H3027
45 word of the LORD by the **h** of Moses. H3027
49 numbered by the **h** of Moses, every one H3027
5:18 shall have in his **h** the bitter water that H3027
25 of the woman's **h**, and shall wave the H3027
6:21 *that* that his **h** shall get: according H3027
7: 8 service, under the **h** of Ithamar the son H3027
9:23 of the LORD by the **h** of Moses. H3027
10:13 of the LORD by the **h** of Moses. H3027
11:15 me, I pray thee, out of **h**, if I have found H2026
23 Is the LORD'S **h** waxed short? thou H3027
15:23 you by the **h** of Moses, from the H3027
16:40 LORD said to him by the **h** of Moses. H3027
20:11 And Moses lifted up his **h**, and with his H3027
17 turn to the right **h** nor to the left, until H3225
20 with much people, and with a strong **h**. H3027
21: 2 **h**, then I will utterly destroy their cities. H3027
26 his land out of his **h**, even unto Arnon. H3027
34 him into thy **h**, and all his people, and H3027
22: 7 of divination in their **h**; and they came H3027
23 drawn in his **h**: and the ass turned H3027

Nu 22:26 turn either to the right **h** or to the left. H3225
29 in mine **h**, for now would I kill thee. H3027
31 drawn in his **h**: and he bowed down H3027
25: 7 and took a javelin in his **h**; H3027
27:18 *is* the spirit, and lay thine **h** upon him; H3027
23 LORD commanded by the **h** of Moses. H3027
31: 6 and the trumpets to blow in his **h**. H3027
33: 1 under the **h** of Moses and Aaron. H3027
3 high **h** in the sight of all the Egyptians. H3027
35:18 Or *if* he smite him with an **h** weapon of H3027
21 Or in enmity smite him with his **h**, that H3027
25 slayer out of the **h** of the revenger of H3027
36:13 by the **h** of Moses unto the children H3027
Dt 1:27 the **h** of the Amorites, to destroy us. H3027
2: 7 all the works of thy **h**: he knoweth thy H3027
15 For indeed the **h** of the LORD was H3027
24 given into thine **h** Sihon the Amorite, H3027
27 turn unto the right **h** nor to the left. H3225
30 him into thy **h**, as *appeareth* this day. H3027
3: 2 his land, into thy **h**; and thou shalt do H3027
8 And we took at that time out of the **h** of H3027
24 and thy mighty **h**: for what God *is there* H3027
4:34 and by a mighty **h**, and by a stretched H3027
5:15 through a mighty **h** and by a stretched H3027
32 turn aside to the right **h** or to the left. H3225
6: 8 a sign upon thine **h**, and they shall be as H3027
21 us out of Egypt with a mighty **h**: H3027
7: 8 out with a mighty **h**, and redeemed you H3027
8 from the **h** of Pharaoh king of Egypt. H3027
19 and the mighty **h**, and the stretched out H3027
24 their kings into thine **h**, and thou shalt H3027
8:17 of *mine* **h** hath gotten me this wealth. H3027
9:26 forth out of Egypt with a mighty **h**. H3027
10: 3 mount, having the two tables in mine **h**. H3027
11: 2 his mighty **h**, and his stretched out arm, H3027
18 a sign upon your **h**, that they may be as H3027
12: 6 offerings of your **h**, and your vows, and H3027
7 all that ye put your **h** unto, ye and your H3027
11 offering of your **h**, and all your choice H3027
17 offerings, or heave offering of thine **h**: H3027
13: 9 But thou shalt surely kill him; thine **h** H3027
9 and afterwards the **h** of all the people. H3027
17 thing to thine **h**: that the LORD may H3027
14:25 money in thine **h**, and shalt go unto the H3027
29 the work of thine **h** which thou doest. H3027
15: 3 with thy brother thine **h** shall release; H3027
7 nor shut thine **h** from thy poor brother: H3027
8 But thou shalt open thine **h** wide unto H3027
9 of release, is at **h**; and thine eye be evil H7126
10 in all that thou puttest thine **h** unto. H3027
11 Thou shalt open thine **h** wide unto thy H3027
16:10 offering of thine **h**, which thou shalt H3027
17:11 shew thee, *to* the right **h**, nor *to* the left. H3225
20 *to* the right **h**, or *to* the left: to the H3225
19: 5 wood, and his **h** fetcheth a stroke with H3027
12 him into the **h** of the avenger of blood, H3027
21 for tooth, **h** for hand, foot for foot. H3027
21 tooth for tooth, hand for **h**, foot for foot. H3027
23:20 that thou settest thine **h** to in the land H3027
25 the ears with thine **h**; but thou shalt not H3027
24: 1 in her **h**, and send her out of his house. H3027
3 giveth *it* in her **h**, and sendeth her out H3027
25:11 out of the **h** of him that smiteth H3027
11 her **h**, and taketh him by the secrets: H3027
12 Then thou shalt cut off her **h**, thine eye H3709
26: 4 out of thine **h**, and set it down before H3027
8 Egypt with a mighty **h**, and with an H3027
28: 8 thou settest thine **h** unto; and he shall H3027
12 the work of thine **h**: and thou shalt lend H3027
14 day, *to* the right **h**, or *to* the left, to go H3225
20 thou settest thine **h** unto for to do, until H3027
32 and *there shall be* no might in thine **h**. H3027
30: 9 work of thine **h**, in the fruit of thy body, H3027
32:27 they should say, Our **h** *is* high, and the H3027
35 calamity *is* at **h**, and the things that H7138
39 *there any* that can deliver out of my **h**. H3027
40 For I lift up my **h** to heaven, and say, I H3027
41 sword, and mine **h** take hold on H3027
33: 2 his right **h** *went* a fiery law for them. H3225
3 saints *are* in thy **h**: and they sat down at H3027
34:12 And in all that mighty **h**, and in all the H3027
Jos 1: 7 from it *to* the right **h** or *to* the left, that H3225
2:19 *be* on our head, if *any* **h** be upon him. H3027
4:24 might know the **h** of the LORD, that it H3027
5:13 drawn in his **h**: and Joshua went unto H3027
6: 2 given into thine **h** Jericho, and the king H3027
7: 7 deliver us into the **h** of the Amorites, to H3027
8: 1 given into thy **h** the king of Ai, and his H3027
7 your God will deliver it into your **h**. H3027

Jos 8:18 that *is* in thy **h** toward Ai; for I will H3027
18 will give it into thine **h**. And Joshua H3027
18 that *he had* in his **h** toward the city. H3027
19 stretched out his **h**: and they entered H3027
26 For Joshua drew not his **h** back, H3027
9:25 And now, behold, we *are* in thine **h**: as H3027
26 them out of the **h** of the children of H3027
10: 6 Slack not thy **h** from thy servants; H3027
8 them into thine **h**; there shall not a man H3027
19 God hath delivered them into your **h**. H3027
30 king thereof, into the **h** of Israel; and he H3027
32 Lachish into the **h** of Israel, which took H3027
11: 8 them into the **h** of Israel, who smote H3027
14: 2 by the **h** of Moses, for the nine H3027
17: 7 **h** unto the inhabitants of En-tap-puah. H3225
19:27 and goeth out to Cabul on the left **h**, H8040
20: 2 I spake unto you by the **h** of Moses: H3027
5 slayer up into his **h**; because he smote H3027
9 and not die by the **h** of the avenger of H3027
21: 2 by the **h** of Moses to give us H3027
8 LORD commanded by the **h** of Moses. H3027
44 delivered all their enemies into their **h**. H3027
22: 9 word of the LORD by the **h** of Moses. H3027
31 of Israel out of the **h** of the LORD. H3027
23: 6 therefrom *to* the right **h** or *to* the left; H3225
24: 8 them into your **h**, that ye might possess H3027
10 you still: so I delivered you out of his **h**. H3027
11 and I delivered them into your **h**. H3027
Jdg 1: 2 I have delivered the land into his **h**. H3027
4 into their **h**: and they slew of them H3027
35 in Shaalbim: yet the **h** of the house of H3027
2:15 Whithersoever they went out, the **h** of H3027
16 out of the **h** of those that spoiled them. H3027
18 them out of the **h** of their enemies all H3027
23 delivered he them into the **h** of Joshua. H3027
3: 4 their fathers by the **h** of Moses. H3027
8 he sold them into the **h** of H3027
10 into his **h**; and his hand prevailed H3027
10 his hand; and his **h** prevailed against H3027
21 And Ehud put forth his left **h**, and took H3027
28 into your **h**. And they went down H3027
30 that day under the **h** of Israel. And the H3027
4: 2 And the LORD sold them into the **h** of H3027
7 and I will deliver him into thine **h**. H3027
9 sell Sisera into the **h** of a woman. And H3027
14 Sisera into thine **h**: is not the LORD H3027
21 an hammer in her **h**, and went softly H3027
24 And the **h** of the children of Israel H3027
5:26 She put her **h** to the nail, and her right H3027
26 nail, and her right **h** to the workmen's H3225
6: 1 them into the **h** of Midian seven years. H3027
2 And the **h** of Midian prevailed against H3027
9 And I delivered you out of the **h** of the H3027
9 and out of the **h** of all that oppressed H3027
14 Israel from the **h** of the Midianites: H3709
21 that *was* in his **h**, and touched the flesh H3027
36 save Israel by mine **h**, as thou hast said, H3027
37 save Israel by mine **h**, as thou hast said. H3027
7: 2 saying, Mine own **h** hath saved me. H3027
6 *putting* their **h** to their mouth, were H3027
7 into thine **h**: and let all the *other* H3027
8 So the people took victuals in their **h**, H3027
9 host; for I have delivered it into thine **h**. H3027
14 Israel: *for* into his **h** hath God delivered H3027
15 into your **h** the host of Midian. H3027
16 in every man's **h**, with empty pitchers, H3027
8: 6 now in thine **h**, that we should give H3027
7 into mine **h**, then I will tear your H3027
15 now in thine **h**, that we should give H3027
22 hast delivered us from the **h** of Midian. H3027
9:17 delivered you out of the **h** of Midian: H3027
29 were under my **h**! then would I remove H3027
48 took an axe in his **h**, and cut down a H3027
10:12 me, and I delivered you out of their **h**. H3027
11:21 his people into the **h** of Israel, and they H3027
12: 3 them into my **h**: wherefore then are H3027
13: 1 into the **h** of the Philistines forty years. H3027
5 Israel out of the **h** of the Philistines. H3027
14: 6 *had* nothing in his **h**: but he told not his H3027
15:12 thee into the **h** of the Philistines. And H3027
13 thee into their **h**: but surely we will not H3027
15 and put forth his **h**, and took it, and H3027
17 **h**, and called that place Ramath-lehi. H3027
18 into the **h** of thy servant: and H3027
18 fall into the **h** of the uncircumcised? H3027
16:18 unto her, and brought money in their **h**. H3027
23 Samson our enemy into our **h**. H3027
26 held him by the **h**, Suffer me that I may H3027
29 his right **h**, and of the other with his left. H3225

Jdg 17: 3 LORD from my **h** for my son, to make H3027
18:19 peace, lay thine **h** upon thy mouth, and H3027
20:28 morrow I will deliver them into thine **h**. H3027
48 all that came to **h**: also they set on fire H4672
Ru 1:13 **h** of the LORD is gone out against me. H3027
4: 5 the field of the **h** of Naomi, thou must H3027
9 and Mahlon's, of the **h** of Naomi. H3027
1Sa 2:13 with a fleshhook of three teeth in his **h**; H3027
4: 3 save us out of the **h** of our enemies. H3709
8 us out of the **h** of these mighty Gods? H3027
5: 6 But the **h** of the LORD was heavy upon H3027
7 with us: for his **h** is sore upon us, and H3027
9 it about, the **h** of the LORD was against H3027
11 city; the **h** of God was very heavy there. H3027
6: 3 why his **h** is not removed from you. H3027
5 he will lighten his **h** from off you, and H3027
9 that *it is* not his **h** *that* smote us: it *was* H3027
12 aside *to* the right **h** or *to* the left; and H3225
7: 3 you out of the **h** of the Philistines. H3027
8 save us out of the **h** of the Philistines. H3027
13 of Israel: and the **h** of the LORD was H3027
9: 8 I have here at **h** the fourth part of a H3027
16 people out of the **h** of the Philistines: H3027
10:18 you out of the **h** of the Egyptians, and H3027
18 and out of the **h** of all kingdoms, *and* H3027
12: 3 or of whose **h** have I received *any* H3027
4 hast thou taken ought of any man's **h**. H3027
5 **h**. And they answered, *He is* witness. H3027
9 sold them into the **h** of Sisera, captain H3027
9 and into the **h** of the Philistines, and H3027
9 and into the **h** of the king of Moab, H3027
10 us out of the **h** of our enemies, and H3027
11 you out of the **h** of your enemies on H3027
15 then shall the **h** of the LORD be against H3027
13:22 nor spear found in the **h** of any of the H3027
14:10 our **h**: and this *shall be* a sign unto us. H3027
12 delivered them into the **h** of Israel. H3027
19 said unto the priest, Withdraw thine **h**. H3027
26 no man put his **h** to his mouth: for the H3027
27 that *was* in his **h**, and dipped it in an H3027
27 and put his **h** to his mouth; and his H3027
37 deliver them into the **h** of Israel? But he H3027
43 that *was* in mine **h**, *and*, lo, I must die. H3027
16:16 play with his **h**, and thou shalt be well. H3027
23 and played with his **h**: so Saul was H3027
17:22 And David left his carriage in the **h** of H3027
37 me out of the **h** of this Philistine. And H3027
40 And he took his staff in his **h**, and chose H3027
40 **h**: and he drew near to the Philistine. H3027
46 thee into mine **h**; and I will smite thee, H3027
49 And David put his **h** in his bag, and H3027
50 *there was* no sword in the **h** of David. H3027
57 with the head of the Philistine in his **h**. H3027
18:10 played with his **h**, as at other times: and H3027
10 and *there was* a javelin in Saul's **h**. H3027
17 said, Let not mine **h** be upon him, but H3027
17 let the **h** of the Philistines be upon him. H3027
21 to him, and that the **h** of the Philistines H3027
25 David fall by the **h** of the Philistines. H3027
19: 5 For he did put his life in his **h**, and slew H3709
9 his **h**: and David played with *his* hand. H3027
9 his hand: and David played with *his* **h**. H3027
20:16 require *it* at the **h** of David's enemies. H3027
19 *in* **h**, and shalt remain by the stone Ezel.
21: 3 Now therefore what is under thine **h**? H3027
3 in mine **h**, or what there is present. H3027
4 bread under mine **h**, but there is H3027
8 here under thine **h** spear or sword? for H3027
22: 6 his spear in his **h**, and all his servants H3027
17 because their **h** also *is* with David, and H3027
17 **h** to fall upon the priests of the LORD. H3027
23: 4 I will deliver the Philistines into thine **h**. H3027
6 he came down *with* an ephod in his **h**. H3027
7 him into mine **h**; for he is shut in, by H3027
11 me up into his **h**? will Saul come down, H3027
12 and my men into the **h** of Saul? And the H3027
14 but God delivered him not into his **h**. H3027
16 wood, and strengthened his **h** in God. H3027
17 Fear not: for the **h** of Saul my father H3027
20 *shall be* to deliver him into the king's **h**. H3027
24: 4 enemy into thine **h**, that thou mayest do H3027
6 to stretch forth mine **h** against him, H3027
10 thee to day into mine **h** in the cave: and H3027
10 not put forth mine **h** against my lord; H3027
11 of thy robe in my **h**: for in that I cut off H3027
11 in mine **h**, and I have not sinned H3027
12 thee: but mine **h** shall not be upon thee. H3027
13 but mine **h** shall not be upon thee. H3027
15 my cause, and deliver me out of thine **h**. H3027

1Sa 24:18 me into thine **h**, thou killedst me not. H3027
20 of Israel shall be established in thine **h**. H3027
25: 8 cometh to thine **h** unto thy servants, H3027
26 thyself with thine own **h**, now let thine H3027
33 from avenging myself with mine own **h**. H3027
35 So David received of her **h** *that* which H3027
39 reproach from the **h** of Nabal, and hath H3027
26: 8 thine enemy into thine **h** this day: now H3027
9 stretch forth his **h** against the LORD'S H3027
11 should stretch forth mine **h** against the H3027
18 have I done? or what evil *is* in mine **h**? H3027
23 thee into *my* **h** to day, but I would H3027
23 mine **h** against the LORD'S anointed. H3027
27: 1 perish one day by the **h** of Saul: *there is* H3027
1 of Israel: so shall I escape out of his **h**. H3027
28:17 out of thine **h**, and given it to thy H3027
19 with thee into the **h** of the Philistines: H3027
19 of Israel into the **h** of the Philistines. H3027
21 have put my life in my **h**, and have H3709
30:23 that came against us into our **h**. H3027
2Sa 1:14 **h** to destroy the LORD'S anointed? H3027
2:19 **h** nor to the left from following Abner. H3225
21 aside to thy right **h** or to thy left, and H3225
3: 8 thee into the **h** of David, that thou H3027
12 and, behold, my **h** *shall be* with thee, to H3027
18 saying, By the **h** of my servant David H3027
18 Israel out of the **h** of the Philistines, H3027
18 and out of the **h** of all their enemies. H3027
4:11 **h**, and take you away from the earth? H3027
5:19 them into mine **h**? And the LORD said H3027
19 deliver the Philistines into thine **h**. H3027
6: 6 put forth *his* **h** to the ark of God, and
8: 1 out of the **h** of the Philistines. H3027
10: 2 him by the **h** of his servants for his H3027
10 he delivered into the **h** of Abishai his H3027
11:14 to Joab, and sent *it* by the **h** of Uriah. H3027
12: 7 I delivered thee out of the **h** of Saul; H3027
25 And he sent by the **h** of Nathan the H3027
13: 5 that I may see *it*, and eat *it* at her **h**. H3027
6 in my sight, that I may eat at her **h**. H3027
10 I may eat of thine **h**. And Tamar took H3027
19 her **h** on her head, and went on crying. H3027
14:16 out of the **h** of the man *that would* H3709
19 And the king said, *Is not* the **h** of Joab H3027
19 turn to the right **h** or to the left from H3231
15: 5 his **h**, and took him, and kissed him. H3027
16: 6 men *were* on his right **h** and on his left. H3225
8 the kingdom into the **h** of Absalom thy H3027
18: 2 people under the **h** of Joab, and a third H3027
2 part under the **h** of Abishai the son of H3027
2 part under the **h** of Ittai the Gittite. H3027
12 of silver in mine **h**, *yet* would I not put H3709
12 not put forth mine **h** against the king's H3027
14 three darts in his **h**, and thrust them H3709
28 up their **h** against my lord the king. H3027
19: 9 us out of the **h** of our enemies, and H3709
9 us out of the **h** of the Philistines; and H3709
20: 9 the beard with the right **h** to kiss him. H3027
10 that *was* in Joab's **h**: so he smote him H3027
21 hath lifted up his **h** against the king, H3027
21:20 that had on every **h** six fingers, and on H3027
22 and fell by the **h** of David, and by the H3027
22 of David, and by the **h** of his servants. H3027
22: 1 him out of the **h** of all his enemies, and H3709
1 his enemies, and out of the **h** of Saul: H3709
23:10 until his **h** was weary, and his H3027
10 weary, and his **h** clave unto the sword: H3027
21 had a spear in his **h**; but he went down H3027
21 **h**, and slew him with his own spear. H3027
24:14 fall now into the **h** of the LORD; for his H3027
14 and let me not fall into the **h** of man. H3027
16 And when the angel stretched out his **h** H3027
16 stay now thine **h**. And the angel of the H3027
17 done? let thine **h**, I pray thee, be against H3027
1Ki 2:19 mother; and she sat on his right **h**. H3225
25 And king Solomon sent by the **h** of H3027
46 was established in the **h** of Solomon. H3027
7:26 And it *was* an **h** breadth thick, and the H2947
8:15 and hath with his **h** fulfilled *it*, saying, H3027
24 fulfilled *it* with thine **h**, as *it is* this day. H3027
42 and of thy strong **h**, and of thy stretched H3027
53 spakest by the **h** of Moses thy servant, H3027
56 by the **h** of Moses his servant. H3027
11:12 *but* I will rend it out of the **h** of thy son. H3027
26 even he lifted up *his* **h** against the king. H3027
27 that he lifted up *his* **h** against the king: H3027
31 out of the **h** of Solomon, and will H3027
34 out of his **h**: but I will make him H3027
35 out of his son's **h**, and will give it unto H3027

1Ki 13: 4 that he put forth his **h** from the altar, H3027
4 on him. And his **h**, which he put forth H3027
6 for me, that my **h** may be restored me H3027
6 and the king's **h** was restored him H3027
14:18 the **h** of his servant Ahijah the prophet. H3027
15:18 them into the **h** of his servants: and H3027
16: 7 And also by the **h** of the prophet Jehu H3027
17:11 pray thee, a morsel of bread in thine **h**. H3027
18: 9 servant into the **h** of Ahab, to slay me? H3027
44 sea, like a man's **h**. And he said, Go up, H3709
46 And the **h** of the LORD was on Elijah; H3027
20: 6 shall put *it* in their **h**, and take *it* away. H3027
13 it into thine **h** this day; and thou shalt H3027
28 into thine **h**, and ye shall know that H3027
42 hast let go out of *thy* **h** a man whom I H3027
22: 3 it not out of the **h** of the king of Syria? H3027
6 shall deliver *it* into the **h** of the king. H3027
12 LORD shall deliver *it* into the king's **h**. H3027
15 shall deliver *it* into the **h** of the king. H3027
19 by him on his right **h** and on his left. H3225
34 Turn thine **h**, and carry me out of H3027
2Ki 3:10 to deliver them into the **h** of Moab! H3027
13 to deliver them into the **h** of Moab. H3027
15 that the **h** of the LORD came upon him. H3027
18 deliver the Moabites also into your **h**. H3027
4:29 my staff in thine **h**, and go thy way: if H3027
5:11 **h** over the place, and recover the leper. H3027
18 he leaneth on my **h**, and I bow myself in H3027
24 *them* from their **h**, and bestowed *them* H3027
6: 7 thee. And he put out his **h**, and took it. H3027
7: 2 Then a lord on whose **h** the king leaned H3027
17 the lord on whose **h** he leaned to have H3027
8: 8 a present in thine **h**, and go, meet the H3027
20 from under the **h** of Judah, and made H3027
22 Yet Edom revolted from under the **h** of H3027
9: 1 oil in thine **h**, and go to Ramothgilead: H3027
7 of the LORD, at the **h** of Jezebel. H3027
10:15 it be, give *me* thine **h**. And he gave *him* H3027
15 he gave *him* his **h**; and he took him up H3027
11: 8 with his weapons in his **h**: and he that H3027
11 his weapons in his **h**, round about the H3027
12:15 men, into whose **h** they delivered the H3027
13: 3 them into the **h** of Hazael king of Syria, H3027
3 Syria, and into the **h** of Ben-hadad the H3027
5 from under the **h** of the Syrians: and H3027
16 of Israel, Put thine **h** upon the bow. H3027
16 And he put his **h** *upon it:* and Elisha H3027
25 again out of the **h** of Ben-hadad the H3027
25 had taken out of the **h** of Jehoahaz his H3027
14: 5 was confirmed in his **h**, that he slew his H3027
25 he spake by the **h** of his servant Jonah, H3027
27 by the **h** of Jeroboam the son of Joash. H3027
15:19 of silver, that his **h** might be with him H3027
19 him to confirm the kingdom in his **h**. H3027
16: 7 and save me out of the **h** of the king of H3709
7 and out of the **h** of the king of Israel, H3709
17: 7 from under the **h** of Pharaoh king of H3027
20 them into the **h** of spoilers, until he H3027
39 you out of the **h** of all your enemies. H3027
18:21 it will go into his **h**, and pierce it: so *is* H3709
29 not be able to deliver you out of his **h**: H3027
30 into the **h** of the king of Assyria. H3027
33 land out of the **h** of the king of Assyria? H3027
34 they delivered Samaria out of mine **h**? H3027
35 out of mine **h**, that the LORD should H3027
35 should deliver Jerusalem out of mine **h**? H3027
19:10 into the **h** of the king of Assyria. H3027
14 the letter of the **h** of the messengers, H3027
19 save thou us out of his **h**, that all the H3027
20: 6 and this city out of the **h** of the king of H3709
21:14 them into the **h** of their enemies; and H3027
22: 2 not aside to the right **h** or to the left. H3225
5 And let them deliver it into the **h** of the H3027
7 their **h**, because they dealt faithfully. H3027
9 it into the **h** of them that do the H3027
23: 8 on a man's left **h** at the gate of the city. H8040
13 *were* on the right **h** of the mount of H3225
1Ch 4:10 and that thine **h** might be with me, and H3027
5:10 who fell by their **h**: and they dwelt in H3027
20 into their **h**, and all that *were* with H3027
6:15 Jerusalem by the **h** of Nebuchadnezzar. H3027
39 stood on his right **h**, *even* Asaph the son H3225
44 *stood* on the left **h**: Ethan the son of H8040
11:23 in the Egyptian's **h** *was* a spear like a H3027
23 **h**, and slew him with his own spear. H3027
12: 2 use both the right **h** and the left in H3231
13: 9 Uzza put forth his **h** to hold the ark; for H3027
10 because he put his **h** to the ark: and H3027
14:10 them into mine **h**? And the LORD said H3027

1Ch 14:10 up; for I will deliver them into thine **h**. H3027
11 enemies by mine **h** like the breaking H3027
16: 7 into the **h** of Asaph and his brethren. H3027
18: 1 towns out of the **h** of the Philistines. H3027
19:11 he delivered unto the **h** of Abishai his H3027
20: 6 twenty, six *on each h*, and six *on each*
8 they fell by the **h** of David, and by the H3027
8 of David, and by the **h** of his servants. H3027
21:13 me fall now into the **h** of the LORD; for H3027
13 but let me not fall into the **h** of man. H3027
15 stay now thine **h**. And the angel of the H3027
16 sword in his **h** stretched out over H3027
17 done? let thine **h**, I pray thee, O LORD H3027
22:18 of the land into mine **h**; and the land is H3027
26:28 the **h** of Shelomith, and of his brethren. H3027
28:19 in writing by *his* **h** upon me, *even* all H3027
29: 8 by the **h** of Jehiel the Gershonite. H3027
12 all; and in thine **h** *is* power and might; H3027
12 and in thine **h** *it is* to make great, H3027
16 *cometh* of thine **h**, and *is* all thine own. H3027
2Ch 3:17 one on the right **h**, and the other on the H3225
17 of that on the right **h** Jachin, and the
4: 6 five on the right **h**, and five on the left, H3225
7 five on the right **h**, and five on the left. H3225
6:15 fulfilled *it* with thine **h**, as *it is* this day. H3027
32 and thy mighty **h**, and thy stretched out H3027
10:15 which he spake by the **h** of Ahijah the H3027
12: 5 have I also left you in the **h** of Shishak. H3027
7 upon Jerusalem by the **h** of Shishak. H3027
13: 8 of the LORD in the **h** of the sons of H3027
16 and God delivered them into their **h**. H3027
16: 7 the king of Syria escaped out of thine **h**. H3027
8 LORD, he delivered them into thine **h**. H3027
17: 5 kingdom in his **h**; and all Judah brought H3027
18: 5 for God will deliver *it* into the king's **h**. H3027
11 shall deliver *it* into the **h** of the king. H3027
14 and they shall be delivered into your **h**. H3027
18 standing on his right **h** and *on* his left. H3225
33 man, Turn thine **h**, that thou mayest H3027
20: 6 and in thine **h** *is there not* power and H3027
21:10 from under the **h** of Judah unto this H3027
10 revolt from under his **h**; because he had H3027
23: 7 his weapons in his **h**; and whosoever H3027
10 his weapon in his **h**, from the right side H3027
18 of the LORD by the **h** of the priests the H3027
24:11 office by the **h** of the Levites, and when H3027
24 great host into their **h**, because they had H3027
25:15 deliver their own people out of thine **h**? H3027
20 them into the **h** *of their enemies,* H3027
26:11 account by the **h** of Jeiel the scribe and H3027
11 ruler, under the **h** of Hananiah, *one* of H3027
13 And under their **h** *was* an army, three H3027
19 a censer in his **h** to burn incense: and H3027
28: 5 him into the **h** of the king of Syria; H3027
5 also delivered into the **h** of the king of H3027
9 them into your **h**, and ye have slain H3027
30: 6 out of the **h** of the kings of Assyria. H3709
12 Also in Judah the **h** of God was to give H3027
16 *they received* of the **h** of the Levites. H3027
31:13 under the **h** of Cononiah and Shimei H3027
32:11 us out of the **h** of the king of Assyria? H3709
13 able to deliver their lands out of mine **h**? H3027
14 out of mine **h**, that your God should H3027
14 be able to deliver you out of mine **h**? H3027
15 out of mine **h**, and out of the hand H3027
15 and out of the **h** of my fathers: how H3027
15 your God deliver you out of mine **h**? H3027
17 out of mine **h**, so shall not the God H3027
17 deliver his people out of mine **h**. H3027
22 from the **h** of Sennacherib the H3027
22 and from the **h** of all *other,* and guided H3027
33: 8 and the ordinances by the **h** of Moses. H3027
34: 2 *neither* to the right **h**, nor to the left. H3225
9 had gathered of the **h** of Manasseh and H3027
10 And they put *it* in the **h** of the workmen H3027
17 it into the **h** of the overseers, and H3027
17 overseers, and to the **h** of the workmen. H3027
35: 6 word of the LORD by the **h** of Moses. H3027
36:17 for age: he gave *them* all into his **h**. H3027
Ezr 1: 8 bring forth by the **h** of Mithredath the H3027
5:12 them into the **h** of Nebuchadnezzar H3028
6:12 that shall put to their **h** to alter *and* to H3028
7: 6 to the **h** of the LORD his God upon him. H3027
9 to the good **h** of his God upon him. H3027
14 the law of thy God which *is* in thine **h**; H3028
25 that *is* in thine **h**, set magistrates and H3028
28 as the **h** of the LORD my God H3027
8:18 And by the good **h** of our God upon us H3027
22 king, saying, The **h** of our God *is* upon H3027

Ezr 8:26 I even weighed unto their **h** six H3027
31 and the **h** of our God was upon H3027
31 us from the **h** of the enemy, and of H3709
33 of our God by the **h** of Meremoth the H3027
9: 2 lands: yea, the **h** of the princes and H3027
7 delivered into the **h** of the kings of the H3027
Neh 1:10 by thy great power, and by thy strong **h**. H3027
2: 8 to the good **h** of my God upon me. H3027
18 Then I told them of the **h** of my God H3027
4:17 and with the other *h* held a weapon.
6: 5 fifth time with an open letter in his **h**; H3027
8: 4 on his right **h**; and on his left hand, H3225
4 and on his left **h**, Pedaiah, and Mishael, H8040
9:14 laws, by the **h** of Moses thy servant: H3027
27 them into the **h** of their enemies, who H3027
27 them out of the **h** of their enemies. H3027
28 thou them in the **h** of their enemies, so H3027
30 into the **h** of the people of the lands. H3027
11:24 **h** in all matters concerning the people. H3027
12:31 **h** upon the wall toward the dung gate: H3225
Est 2:21 sought to lay **h** on the king Ahasuerus. H3027
3:10 And the king took his ring from his **h**, H3027
5: 2 that *was* in his **h**. So Esther drew near, H3027
6: 2 sought to lay **h** on the king Ahasuerus. H3027
9 horse be delivered to the **h** of one of the H3027
8: 7 because he laid his **h** upon the Jews. H3027
9: 2 Ahasuerus, to lay **h** on such as sought H3027
10 but on the spoil laid they not their **h**. H3027
15 but on the prey they laid not their **h**. H3027
Job 1:11 But put forth thine **h** now, and touch H3027
12 put not forth thine **h**. So Satan went H3027
2: 5 But put forth thine **h** now, and touch H3027
6 Behold, he *is* in thine **h**; but save his life. H3027
10 receive good at the **h** of God, and shall H854
5:15 mouth, and from the **h** of the mighty. H3027
6: 9 he would let loose his **h**, and cut me off! H3027
23 Or, Deliver me from the enemy's **h**? or, H3027
23 Redeem me from the **h** of the mighty? H3027
9:24 The earth is given into the **h** of the H3027
33 us, *that* might lay his **h** upon us both. H3027
10: 7 *is* none that can deliver out of thine **h**. H3027
11:14 If iniquity *be* in thine **h**, put it far away, H3027
12: 6 into whose **h** God bringeth *abundantly.* H3027
9 Who knoweth not in all these that the **h** H3027
10 In whose **h** *is* the soul of every living H3027
13:14 in my teeth, and put my life in mine **h**? H3709
21 Withdraw thine **h** far from me: and let H3709
15:23 the day of darkness is ready at his **h**. H3027
25 For he stretcheth out his **h** against God, H3027
19:21 for the **h** of God hath touched me. H3027
20:22 **h** of the wicked shall come upon him. H3027
21: 5 and lay *your* **h** upon *your* mouth. H3027
16 Lo, their good *is* not in their **h**: the H3027
23: 9 On the left **h**, where he doth work, but I H8040
9 on the right **h**, that I cannot see *him*: H3225
26:13 his **h** hath formed the crooked serpent. H3027
27:11 I will teach you by the **h** of God: *that* H3027
22 spare: he would fain flee out of his **h**. H3027
28: 9 He putteth forth his **h** upon the rock; he H3027
29: 9 and laid *their* **h** on their mouth. H3709
20 me, and my bow was renewed in my **h**. H3027
30:12 Upon *my* right *h* rise the youth; they
21 **h** thou opposest thyself against me. H3027
24 Howbeit he will not stretch out *his* **h** to H3027
31:21 If I have lifted up my **h** against the H3027
25 and because mine **h** had gotten much; H3027
27 enticed, or my mouth hath kissed my **h**: H3027
33: 7 neither shall my **h** be heavy upon thee. H405
34:20 mighty shall be taken away without **h**. H3027
35: 7 him? or what receiveth he of thine **h**? H3027
37: 7 He sealeth up the **h** of every man; that H3027
40: 4 thee? I will lay mine **h** upon my mouth. H3027
14 that thine own right **h** can save thee. H3225
41: 8 Lay thine **h** upon him, remember the H3709
Ps 10:12 Arise, O LORD; O God, lift up thine **h**: H3027
14 to requite *it* with thy **h**: the poor H3027
16: 8 *he is* at my right **h**, I shall not be moved. H3225
11 **h** *there are* pleasures for evermore. H3225
17: 7 savest by thy right **h** them which put H3225
14 From men *which are* thy **h**, O LORD, H3027
18:35 and thy right **h** hath holden me up, H3225
ttl him from the **h** of all his enemies, and H3709
ttl and from the **h** of Saul: And he said, H3027
20: 6 with the saving strength of his right **h**. H3225
21: 8 Thine **h** shall find out all thine H3027
8 **h** shall find out those that hate thee. H3225
26:10 and their right **h** is full of bribes. H3225
31: 5 Into thine **h** I commit my spirit: thou H3027
8 And hast not shut me up into the **h** of H3027

Ps 31:15 My times *are* in thy **h**: deliver me from H3027
15 me from the **h** of mine enemies, and H3027
32: 4 For day and night thy **h** was heavy H3027
36:11 let not the **h** of the wicked remove me. H3027
37:24 for the LORD upholdeth *him with* his **h**. H3027
33 The LORD will not leave him in his **h**, H3027
38: 2 fast in me, and thy **h** presseth me sore. H3027
39:10 I am consumed by the blow of thine **h**. H3027
44: 2 heathen with thy **h**, and plantedst them; H3027
3 but thy right **h**, and thine arm, and H3225
45: 4 right **h** shall teach thee terrible things. H3225
9 **h** did stand the queen in gold of Ophir. H3225
48:10 thy right **h** is full of righteousness. H3225
60: 5 save *with* thy right **h**, and hear me. H3225
63: 8 after thee: thy right **h** upholdeth me. H3225
71: 4 Deliver me, O my God, out of the **h** of H3027
4 **h** of the unrighteous and cruel man. H3709
73:23 thou hast holden *me* by my right **h**. H3027
74:11 Why withdrawest thou thy **h**, even thy H3027
11 thy right **h**? pluck *it* out of thy bosom. H3225
75: 8 For in the **h** of the LORD *there is* a cup, H3027
77:10 years of the right **h** of the most High. H3225
20 a flock by the **h** of Moses and Aaron. H3027
78:42 They remembered not his **h**, *nor* the H3027
54 *which* his right **h** had purchased. H3225
61 and his glory into the enemy's **h**. H3027
80:15 And the vineyard which thy right **h** H3225
17 Let thy **h** be upon the man of thy right H3027
17 man of thy right **h**, upon the son of man H3225
81:14 turned my **h** against their adversaries. H3027
82: 4 rid *them* out of the **h** of the wicked. H3027
88: 5 more: and they are cut off from thy **h**. H3027
89:13 is thy **h**, *and* high is thy right hand. H3027
13 is thy hand, *and* high is thy right **h**. H3225
21 With whom my **h** shall be established: H3027
25 I will set his **h** also in the sea, and his H3027
25 in the sea, and his right **h** in the rivers. H3225
42 Thou hast set up the right **h** of his H3225
48 his soul from the **h** of the grave? Selah. H3027
91: 7 right **h**; *but* it shall not come nigh thee. H3225
95: 4 In his **h** *are* the deep places of the H3027
7 of his **h**. To day if ye will hear his voice, H3027
97:10 them out of the **h** of the wicked. H3027
98: 1 things: his right **h**, and his holy arm, H3225
104:28 thine **h**, they are filled with good. H3027
106:10 And he saved them from the **h** of him H3027
10 them from the **h** of the enemy. H3027
26 Therefore he lifted up his **h** against H3027
41 And he gave them into the **h** of the H3027
42 brought into subjection under their **h**. H3027
107: 2 redeemed from the **h** of the enemy; H3027
108: 6 save *with* thy right **h**, and answer me. H3225
109: 6 him: and let Satan stand at his right **h**. H3225
27 That they may know that this *is* thy **h**; H3027
31 For he shall stand at the right **h** of the H3225
110: 1 thou at my right **h**, until I make thine H3225
5 The Lord at thy right **h** shall strike H3225
118:15 the right **h** of the LORD doeth valiantly. H3225
16 The right **h** of the LORD is exalted: the H3225
16 the right **h** of the LORD doeth valiantly. H3225
119:109 My soul *is* continually in my **h**: yet do I H3709
173 Let thine **h** help me; for I have chosen H3027
121: 5 the LORD *is* thy shade upon thy right **h**. H3027
123: 2 *look* unto the **h** of their masters, *and* H3027
2 a maiden unto the **h** of her mistress; so H3027
127: 4 As arrows *are* in the **h** of a mighty H3027
129: 7 Wherewith the mower filleth not his **h**; H3709
136:12 With a strong **h**, and with a stretched H3027
137: 5 let my right **h** forget *her cunning*. H3225
138: 7 stretch forth thine **h** against the wrath H3027
7 enemies, and thy right **h** shall save me. H3225
139: 5 and before, and laid thine **h** upon me. H3709
10 Even there shall thy **h** lead me, and thy H3027
10 lead me, and thy right **h** shall hold me. H3225
142: 4 I looked on *my* right **h**, and beheld, but H3225
144: 7 Send thine **h** from above; rid me, and H3027
7 waters, from the **h** of strange children; H3027
8 right **h** *is* a right hand of falsehood. H3225
8 right hand *is* a right **h** of falsehood. H3225
11 Rid me, and deliver me from the **h** of H3027
11 right **h** *is* a right hand of falsehood: H3225
11 right hand *is* a right **h** of falsehood: H3225
145:16 Thou openest thine **h**, and satisfiest the H3027
149: 6 and a twoedged sword in their **h**; H3027
Prv 1:24 out my **h**, and no man regarded; H3027
3:16 Length of days *is* in her right **h**; *and* in H3225
16 *and* in her left **h** riches and honour. H8040
27 it is in the power of thine **h** to do *it*. H3027
4:27 Turn not to the right **h** nor to the left: H3225

Prv 6: 1 hast stricken thy **h** with a stranger, H3709
3 art come into the **h** of thy friend; go, H3709
5 Deliver thyself as a roe from the **h** *of* H3027
5 and as a bird from the **h** of the fowler. H3027
10: 4 *with* a slack **h**: but the hand of the H3709
4 but the **h** of the diligent maketh rich. H3027
11:21 *Though* **h** *join* in hand, the wicked H3027
21 *Though* hand *join* in **h**, the wicked shall H3027
12:24 The **h** of the diligent shall bear rule: but H3027
16: 5 to the LORD: *though* **h** *join* in hand, he H3027
5 *join* in **h**, he shall not be unpunished. H3027
17:16 Wherefore *is there* a price in the **h** of a H3027
19:24 A slothful *man* hideth his **h** in *his* H3027
21: 1 The king's heart *is* in the **h** of the H3027
26: 6 He that sendeth a message by the **h** of a H3027
9 *As* a thorn goeth up into the **h** of a H3027
15 The slothful hideth his **h** in *his* bosom; H3027
27:16 of his right **h**, *which* bewrayeth *itself*. H3225
30:32 evil, *lay* thine **h** upon thy mouth. H3027
31:20 She stretcheth out her **h** to the poor; H3709
Ecc 2:24 I saw, that it *was* from the **h** of God. H3027
5:14 a son, and *there is* nothing in his **h**. H3027
15 which he may carry away in his **h**. H3027
7:18 not thine **h**: for he that feareth God H3027
9: 1 works, *are* in the **h** of God: no man H3027
10 Whatsoever thy **h** findeth to do, do *it* H3027
10: 2 A wise man's heart *is* at his right **h**; but H3225
11: 6 withhold not thine **h**: for thou knowest H3027
Song 2: 6 His left **h** *is* under my head, and his H8040
6 head, and his right **h** doth embrace me. H3225
5: 4 My beloved put in his **h** by the hole *of* H3027
8: 3 His left **h** *should be* under my head, H8040
3 and his right **h** should embrace me. H3225
Isa 1:12 this at your **h**, to tread my courts? H3027
25 And I will turn my **h** upon thee, and H3027
3: 6 ruler, and *let* this ruin *be* under thy **h**: H3027
5:25 stretched forth his **h** against them, and H3027
25 away, but his **h** *is* stretched out still. H3027
6: 6 a live coal in his **h**, *which* he had taken H3027
8:11 me with a strong **h**, and instructed me H3027
9:12 away, but his **h** *is* stretched out still. H3027
17 away, but his **h** *is* stretched out still. H3027
20 And he shall snatch on the right **h**, and H3225
20 eat on the left **h**, and they shall not be H8040
21 away, but his **h** *is* stretched out still. H3027
10: 4 away, but his **h** *is* stretched out still. H3027
5 the staff in their **h** is mine indignation. H3027
10 As my **h** hath found the kingdoms of H3027
13 For he saith, By the strength of my **h** I H3027
14 And my **h** hath found as a nest the H3027
32 he shall shake his **h** *against* the mount H3027
11: 8 shall put his **h** on the cockatrice' den. H3027
11 Lord shall set his **h** again the second H3027
14 they shall lay their **h** upon Edom and H3027
15 shall he shake his **h** over the river, and H3027
13: 2 them, shake the **h**, that they may go H3027
6 Howl ye; for the day of the LORD *is* at **h**; H7138
14:26 and this *is* the **h** that is stretched out H3027
27 *it*? and his **h** *is* stretched out, and H3027
19: 4 give over into the **h** of a cruel lord; and H3027
16 of the shaking of the **h** of the LORD of H3027
22:21 into his **h**: and he shall be a father H3027
23:11 He stretched out his **h** over the sea, he H3027
25:10 For in this mountain shall the **h** of the H3027
26:11 LORD, *when* thy **h** is lifted up, they will H3027
28: 2 shall cast down to the earth with the **h**. H3027
4 while it is yet in his **h** he eateth it up. H3709
30:21 the right **h**, and when ye turn to the left. H3709
31: 3 stretch out his **h**, both he that helpeth H3027
34:17 for them, and his **h** hath divided it unto H3027
36: 6 it will go into his **h**, and pierce it: so *is* H3709
15 into the **h** of the king of Assyria. H3027
18 land out of the **h** of the king of Assyria? H3027
19 they delivered Samaria out of my **h**? H3027
20 land out of my **h**, that the LORD should H3027
20 should deliver Jerusalem out of my **h**? H3027
37:10 given into the **h** of the king of Assyria. H3027
14 the letter from the **h** of the messengers, H3027
20 God, save us from his **h**, that all the H3027
38: 6 and this city out of the **h** of the king of H3709
40: 2 of the LORD'S **h** double for all her sins. H3027
10 come with strong *h*, and his arm shall
12 in the hollow of his **h**, and meted out H8168
41:10 with the right **h** of my righteousness. H3225
13 will hold thy right **h**, saying unto thee, H3225
20 together, that the **h** of the LORD hath H3027
42: 6 will hold thine **h**, and will keep thee, H3027
43:13 my **h**: I will work, and who shall let it? H3027
44: 5 subscribe *with* his **h** unto the LORD, H3027

Isa 44:20 nor say, *Is there* not a lie in my right **h**? H3225
45: 1 whose right **h** I have holden, to subdue H3225
47: 6 them into thine **h**: thou didst shew them H3027
48:13 Mine **h** also hath laid the foundation of H3027
13 earth, and my right **h** hath spanned the H3225
49: 2 in the shadow of his **h** hath he hid me, H3027
22 I will lift up mine **h** to the Gentiles, and H3027
50: 2 to answer? Is my **h** shortened at all, H3027
11 of mine **h**; ye shall lie down in sorrow. H3027
51:16 shadow of mine **h**, that I may plant the H3027
17 hast drunk at the **h** of the LORD the H3027
18 taketh her by the **h** of all the sons *that* H3027
22 have taken out of thine **h** the cup of H3027
23 But I will put it into the **h** of them that H3027
53:10 of the LORD shall prosper in his **h**. H3027
54: 3 forth on the right **h** and on the left; and H3225
56: 2 and keepeth his **h** from doing any evil. H3027
57:10 thine **h**; therefore thou wast not grieved. H3027
59: 1 Behold, the LORD'S **h** is not shortened, H3027
62: 3 of glory in the **h** of the LORD, and a H3027
3 and a royal diadem in the **h** of thy God. H3709
8 The LORD hath sworn by his right **h**, H3225
63:12 That led *them* by the right **h** of Moses H3225
64: 8 potter; and we all *are* the work of thy **h**. H3027
66: 2 For all those *things* hath mine **h** made, H3027
14 an herb: and the **h** of the LORD shall be H3027
Jer 1: 9 Then the LORD put forth his **h**, and H3027
6: 9 **h** as a grapegatherer into the baskets. H3027
12 stretch out my **h** upon the inhabitants H3027
11:21 of the LORD, that thou die not by our **h**: H3027
12: 7 of my soul into the **h** of her enemies. H3709
15: 6 I stretch out my **h** against thee, and H3027
17 because of thy **h**: for thou hast filled me H3027
21 And I will deliver thee out of the **h** of H3027
21 redeem thee out of the **h** of the terrible. H3709
16:21 to know mine **h** and my might; and H3027
18: 4 was marred in the **h** of the potter: so he H3027
6 *is* in the potter's **h**, so *are* ye in mine H3027
6 so *are* ye in mine **h**, O house of Israel. H3027
20: 4 give all Judah into the **h** of the king of H3027
5 will I give into the **h** of their enemies, H3027
13 soul of the poor from the **h** of evildoers. H3027
21: 5 an outstretched **h** and with a strong H3027
7 famine, into the **h** of Nebuchadrezzar H3027
7 and into the **h** of their enemies, and H3027
7 and into the **h** of those that seek their H3027
10 shall be given into the **h** of the king of H3027
12 *is* spoiled out of the **h** of the oppressor, H3027
22: 3 spoiled out of the **h** of the oppressor: H3027
24 right **h**, yet would I pluck thee thence; H3027
25 And I will give thee into the **h** of them H3027
25 life, and into the **h** *of them* whose face H3027
25 even into the **h** of Nebuchadrezzar H3027
25 and into the **h** of the Chaldeans. H3027
23:23 *Am* I a God at **h**, saith the LORD, and H7138
25:15 of this fury at my **h**, and cause all the H3027
17 Then took I the cup at the LORD'S **h**, H3027
28 the cup at thine **h** to drink, then shalt H3027
26:14 As for me, behold, I *am* in your **h**: do H3027
24 Nevertheless the **h** of Ahikam the son H3027
24 the **h** of the people to put him to death. H3027
27: 3 of Zidon, by the **h** of the messengers H3027
6 lands into the **h** of Nebuchadrezzar H3027
8 until I have consumed them by his **h**. H3027
29: 3 By the **h** of Elasah the son of Shaphan, H3027
21 them into the **h** of Nebuchadrezzar H3027
31:11 the **h** of *him that was* stronger than he. H3027
32 I took them by the **h** to bring them out H3027
32: 3 give this city into the **h** of the king of H3027
4 escape out of the **h** of the Chaldeans, H3027
4 be delivered into the **h** of the king of H3027
21 and with a strong **h**, and with a H3027
24 is given into the **h** of the Chaldeans, H3027
25 is given into the **h** of the Chaldeans. H3027
28 this city into the **h** of the Chaldeans, H3027
28 and into the **h** of Nebuchadrezzar H3027
36 be delivered into the **h** of the king of H3027
43 it is given into the **h** of the Chaldeans. H3027
34: 2 give this city into the **h** of the king of H3027
3 And thou shalt not escape out of his **h**, H3027
3 delivered into his **h**; and thine eyes shall H3027
20 I will even give them into the **h** of their H3027
20 and into the **h** of them that seek their H3027
21 will I give into the **h** of their enemies, H3027
21 and into the **h** of them that seek their H3027
21 their life, and into the **h** of the king of H3027
36:14 Take in thine **h** the roll wherein thou H3027
14 the roll in his **h**, and came unto them. H3027
37:17 into the **h** of the king of Babylon. H3027

Jer 38: 3 surely be given into the **h** of the king of H3027
5 he *is* in your **h**: for the king *is* not *he* H3027
16 the **h** of these men that seek thy life. H3027
18 be given into the **h** of the Chaldeans, H3027
18 and thou shalt not escape out of their **h**. H3027
19 me into their **h**, and they mock me. H3027
23 escape out of their **h**, but shalt be taken H3027
23 shalt be taken by the **h** of the king of H3027
39:17 **h** of the men of whom thou *art* afraid. H3027
40: 4 *were* upon thine **h**. If it seem good unto H3027
41: 5 incense in their **h**, to bring *them* to the H3027
42:11 save you, and to deliver you from his **h**. H3027
43: 3 deliver us into the **h** of the Chaldeans, H3027
9 Take great stones in thine **h**, and hide H3027
44:25 fulfilled with your **h**, saying, We will H3027
30 of Egypt into the **h** of his enemies, and H3027
30 and into the **h** of them that seek his H3027
30 of Judah into the **h** of Nebuchadrezzar H3027
46:24 into the **h** of the people of the north. H3027
26 And I will deliver them into the **h** of H3027
26 lives, and into the **h** of Nebuchadrezzar H3027
26 and into the **h** of his servants: and H3027
50:15 she hath given her **h**: her foundations H3027
51: 7 cup in the LORD'S **h**, that made all the H3027
25 stretch out mine **h** upon thee, and roll H3027
Lam 1: 7 people fell into the **h** of the enemy, and H3027
10 The adversary hath spread out his **h** H3027
14 is bound by his **h**: they are wreathed, H3027
2: 3 back his right **h** from before the enemy, H3225
4 with his right **h** as an adversary, and H3225
7 given up into the **h** of the enemy the H3027
8 not withdrawn his **h** from destroying: H3027
3: 3 he turneth his **h** *against me* all the day. H3027
5: 6 We have given the **h** *to* the Egyptians, H3027
8 none that doth deliver *us* out of their **h**. H3027
12 Princes are hanged up by their **h**: the H3027
Ezk 1: 3 the **h** of the LORD was there upon him. H3027
2: 9 And when I looked, behold, an **h** *was* H3027
3:14 the **h** of the LORD was strong upon me. H3027
18 but his blood will I require at thine **h**. H3027
20 but his blood will I require at thine **h**. H3027
22 And the **h** of the LORD was there upon H3027
6:11 Smite with thine **h**, and stamp with thy H3709
14 So will I stretch out my **h** upon them, H3027
8: 1 **h** of the Lord GOD fell there upon me. H3027
3 And he put forth the form of an **h**, and H3027
11 **h**; and a thick cloud of incense went up. H3027
9: 1 *with* his destroying weapon in his **h**. H3027
2 weapon in his **h**; and one man among H3027
10: 2 and fill thine **h** with coals of fire from H2651
7 And *one* cherub stretched forth his **h** H3027
8 form of a man's **h** under their wings. H3027
12: 7 the wall with mine **h**; I brought *it* forth H3027
23 are at **h**, and the effect of every vision. H7126
13: 9 And mine **h** shall be upon the prophets H3027
21 people out of your **h**, and they shall be H3027
21 no more in your **h** to be hunted; and ye H3027
23 people out of your **h**: and ye shall know H3027
14: 9 stretch out my **h** upon him, and will H3027
13 I stretch out mine **h** upon it, and will H3027
16:27 stretched out my **h** over thee, and have H3027
39 And I will also give thee into their **h**, H3027
46 that dwell at thy left **h**: and thy younger H8040
46 right **h**, *is* Sodom and her daughters. H3225
49 strengthen the **h** of the poor and needy. H3027
17:18 lo, he had given his **h**, and hath done all H3027
18: 8 withdrawn his **h** from iniquity, hath H3027
17 *That* hath taken off his **h** from the H3027
20: 5 and lifted up mine **h** unto the seed of H3027
5 I lifted up mine **h** unto them, saying, H3027
6 In the day *that* I lifted up mine **h** unto H3027
15 Yet also I lifted up my **h** unto them in H3027
22 Nevertheless I withdrew mine **h**, and H3027
23 I lifted up mine **h** unto them also in the H3027
28 I lifted up mine **h** to give it to them, H3027
33 with a mighty **h**, and with a stretched H3027
34 with a mighty **h**, and with a stretched H3027
42 up mine **h** to give it to your fathers. H3027
21:11 to give it into the **h** of the slayer. H3027
16 *either* on the right **h**, *or* on the left, H3231
22 At his right **h** was the divination for H3225
24 ye shall be taken with the **h**. H3709
31 thee into the **h** of brutish men, *and* H3027
22:13 smitten mine **h** at thy dishonest gain H3709
23: 9 her into the **h** of her lovers, into the H3027
9 her lovers, into the **h** of the Assyrians, H3027
28 thee into the **h** *of them* whom thou H3027
28 hatest, into the **h** *of them* from whom H3027
31 therefore will I give her cup into thine **h**. H3027
Ezk 25: 7 stretch out mine **h** upon thee, and will H3027
13 stretch out mine **h** upon Edom, and H3027
14 upon Edom by the **h** of my people H3027
16 stretch out mine **h** upon the Philistines, H3027
27:15 of thine **h**: they brought thee *for* H3027
28: 9 God, in the **h** of him that slayeth thee. H3027
10 by the **h** of strangers: for I have H3027
29: 7 When they took hold of thee by thy **h**, H3709
30:10 **h** of Nebuchadrezzar king of Babylon. H3027
12 the land into the **h** of the wicked: and I H3027
12 is therein, by the **h** of strangers: I the H3027
22 will cause the sword to fall out of his **h**. H3027
24 put my sword in his **h**: but I will break H3027
25 put my sword into the **h** of the king of H3027
31:11 him into the **h** of the mighty one of H3027
33: 6 will I require at the watchman's **h**. H3027
8 but his blood will I require at thine **h**. H3027
22 Now the **h** of the LORD was upon me in H3027
34:10 my flock at their **h**, and cause them to H3027
27 them out of the **h** of those that served H3027
35: 3 stretch out mine **h** against thee, and I H3027
36: 7 lifted up mine **h**, Surely the heathen H3027
8 of Israel; for they are at **h** to come. H7126
37: 1 The **h** of the LORD was upon me, and H3027
17 and they shall become one in thine **h**. H3027
19 which *is* in the **h** of Ephraim, and the H3027
19 stick, and they shall be one in mine **h**. H3027
20 shall be in thine **h** before their eyes. H3027
38:12 prey; to turn thine **h** upon the desolate H3027
39: 3 thy bow out of thy left **h**, and will cause H3027
3 thine arrows to fall out of thy right **h**. H3027
21 and my **h** that I have laid upon them. H3027
23 them into the **h** of their enemies: so H3027
40: 1 the selfsame day the **h** of the LORD was H3027
3 a line of flax in his **h**, and a measuring H3027
5 and in the man's **h** a measuring reed of H3027
5 by the cubit and an **h** breadth: so he H2948
43 And within *were* hooks, an **h** broad, H2948
43:13 *is* a cubit and an **h** breadth; even the H2948
44:12 I lifted up mine **h** against them, saith H3027
46: 7 according as his **h** shall attain unto, H3027
47: 3 that had the line in his **h** went forth H3027
14 I lifted up mine **h** to give it unto your H3027
Dan 1: 2 king of Judah into his **h**, with part of the H3027
2:38 given into thine **h**, and hath made thee H3028
3:17 he will deliver *us* out of thine **h**, O king. H3028
4:35 **h**, or say unto him, What doest thou? H3028
5: 5 fingers of a man's **h**, and wrote over H3028
5 king saw the part of the **h** that wrote. H3028
23 the God in whose **h** thy breath *is*, and H3028
24 Then was the part of the **h** sent from H3028
7:25 be given into his **h** until a time and H3028
8: 4 could deliver out of his **h**; but he did H3027
7 that could deliver the ram out of his **h**. H3027
25 craft to prosper in his **h**; and he shall H3027
25 but he shall be broken without **h**. H3027
9:15 with a mighty **h**, and hast gotten thee H3027
10:10 And, behold, an **h** touched me, which H3027
11:11 the multitude shall be given into his **h**. H3027
16 which by his **h** shall be consumed. H3027
41 escape out of his **h**, *even* Edom, and H3027
42 He shall stretch forth his **h** also upon H3027
12: 7 he held up his right **h** and his left hand H3225
7 hand and his left **h** unto heaven, and H8040
Hos 2:10 none shall deliver her out of mine **h**. H3027
7: 5 he stretched out his **h** with scorners. H3027
12: 7 deceit *are* in his **h**: he loveth to oppress. H3027
Joel 1:15 day of the LORD *is* at **h**, and as a H7138
2: 1 of the LORD cometh, for *it is* nigh at **h**; H7138
3: 8 daughters into the **h** of the children of H3027
Am 1: 8 I will turn mine **h** against Ekron: and H3027
5:19 **h** on the wall, and a serpent bit him. H3027
7: 7 a plumbline, with a plumbline in his **h**. H3027
9: 2 thence shall mine **h** take them; though H3027
Jna 4:11 their right **h** and their left hand; H3225
11 and their left **h**; and *also* much cattle? H8040
Mic 2: 1 it, because it is in the power of their **h**. H3027
4:10 thee from the **h** of thine enemies. H3709
5: 9 Thine **h** shall be lifted up upon thine H3027
12 out of thine **h**; and thou shalt have H3027
7:16 they shall lay *their* **h** upon *their* mouth, H3027
Hab 2:16 the LORD'S right **h** shall be turned unto H3225
3: 4 *coming* out of his **h**: and there *was* the H3027
Zep 1: 4 I will also stretch out mine **h** upon H3027
7 of the LORD *is* at **h**: for the LORD hath H7138
2:13 And he will stretch out his **h** against H3027
15 passeth by her shall hiss, *and* wag his **h**. H3027
Zec 2: 1 a man with a measuring line in his **h**. H3027
9 For, behold, I will shake mine **h** upon H3027
Zec 3: 1 standing at his right **h** to resist him. H3225
4:10 plummet in the **h** of Zerubbabel *with* H3027
8: 4 man with his staff in his **h** for very age. H3027
11: 6 his neighbour's **h**, and into the hand of H3027
6 hand, and into the **h** of his king: and H3027
6 out of their **h** I will not deliver *them*. H3027
12: 6 on the right **h** and on the left: and H3225
13: 7 I will turn mine **h** upon the little ones. H3027
14:13 every one on the **h** of his neighbour, H3027
13 and his **h** shall rise up against H3027
13 rise up against the **h** of his neighbour. H3027
Mal 1:10 will I accept an offering at your **h**. H3027
13 I accept this of your **h**? saith the LORD. H3027
2:13 or receiveth *it* with good will at your **h**. H3027
Mt 3: 2 ye: for the kingdom of heaven is at **h**. *G1448*
12 Whose fan *is* in his **h**, and he will *G5495*
4:17 for the kingdom of heaven is at **h**. *G1448*
5:30 And if thy right **h** offend thee, cut it off, *G5495*
6: 3 left **h** know what thy right hand doeth: *G710*
3 left hand know what thy right **h** doeth: *G1188*
8: 3 And Jesus put forth *his* **h**, and touched *G5495*
15 And he touched her **h**, and the fever left *G5495*
9:18 lay thy **h** upon her, and she shall live. *G5495*
25 took her by the **h**, and the maid arose. *G5495*
10: 7 saying, The kingdom of heaven is at **h**. *G1448*
12:10 which had *his* **h** withered. And they *G5495*
13 Stretch forth thine **h**. And he stretched *G5495*
49 And he stretched forth his **h** toward his *G5495*
14:31 stretched forth *his* **h**, and caught him, *G5495*
18: 8 Wherefore if thy **h** or thy foot offend *G5495*
20:21 one on thy right **h**, and the other on the *G1188*
23 to sit on my right **h**, and on my left, is *G1188*
22:13 Bind him **h** and foot, and take him *G5495*
44 Sit thou on my right **h**, till I make thine *G1188*
25:33 on his right **h**, but the goats on the left. *G1188*
34 them on his right **h**, Come, ye blessed of *G1188*
41 them on the left **h**, Depart from me, ye *G2176*
26:18 My time is at **h**; I will keep the passover *G1451*
23 that dippeth *his* **h** with me in the dish, *G5495*
45 the hour is at **h**, and the Son of man *G1448*
46 Rise, let us be going: behold, he is at **h** *G1448*
51 stretched out *his* **h**, and drew his sword, *G5495*
64 sitting on the right **h** of power, and *G1188*
27:29 a reed in his right **h**: and they bowed *G1188*
38 on the right **h**, and another on the left. *G1188*
Mk 1:15 at **h**: repent ye, and believe the gospel. *G1448*
31 And he came and took her by the **h**, and *G5495*
41 put forth *his* **h**, and touched him, and *G5495*
3: 1 a man there which had a withered **h**. *G5495*
3 which had the withered **h**, Stand forth. *G5495*
5 Stretch forth thine **h**. And he stretched *G5495*
5 his **h** was restored whole as the other. *G5495*
5:41 And he took the damsel by the **h**, and *G5495*
7:32 beseech him to put his **h** upon him. *G5495*
8:23 And he took the blind man by the **h**, *G5495*
9:27 But Jesus took him by the **h**, and lifted *G5495*
43 And if thy **h** offend thee, cut it off: it is *G5495*
10:37 one on thy right **h**, and the other on thy *G1188*
37 and the other on thy left **h**, in thy glory. *G2176*
40 But to sit on my right **h** and on my left *G1188*
40 and on my left **h** is not mine to give; *G2176*
12:36 Sit thou on my right **h**, till I make thine *G1188*
14:42 us go; lo, he that betrayeth me is at **h**. *G1448*
62 sitting on the right **h** of power, and *G1188*
15:27 on his right **h**, and the other on his left. *G1188*
16:19 heaven, and sat on the right **h** of God. *G1188*
Lk 1: 1 Forasmuch as many have taken in **h** to *G2021*
66 be! And the **h** of the Lord was with him. *G5495*
71 and from the **h** of all that hate us; *G5495*
74 out of the **h** of our enemies might *G5495*
3:17 Whose fan *is* in his **h**, and he will *G5495*
5:13 And he put forth *his* **h**, and touched *G5495*
6: 6 was a man whose right **h** was withered. *G5495*
8 had the withered **h**, Rise up, and stand *G5495*
10 Stretch forth thy **h**. And he did so: and *G5495*
10 his **h** was restored whole as the other. *G5495*
8:54 the **h**, and called, saying, Maid, arise. *G5495*
9:62 having put his **h** to the plough, and *G5495*
15:22 a ring on his **h**, and shoes on *his* feet: *G5495*
20:42 unto my Lord, Sit thou on my right **h**, *G1188*
21:30 selves that summer is now nigh at **h**. *G1451*
31 ye that the kingdom of God is nigh at **h**. *G1451*
22:21 But, behold, the **h** of him that betrayeth *G5495*
69 sit on the right **h** of the power of God. *G1188*
23:33 on the right **h**, and the other on the left. *G1188*
Jn 2:13 And the Jews' passover was at **h**, and *G1451*
3:35 and hath given all things into his **h**. *G5495*
7: 2 the Jews' feast of tabernacles was at **h**. *G1451*
10:28 shall any *man* pluck them out of my **h**. *G5495*

Jn 10:29 able to pluck *them* out of my Father's **h**. G5495
39 take him: but he escaped out of their **h**, G5495
11:44 came forth, bound **h** and foot with G5495
55 And the Jews' passover was nigh at **h**: G1451
18:22 the palm of his **h**, saying, Answerest G1325
19:42 *day*; for the sepulchre was nigh at **h**. G1451
20:25 my **h** into his side, I will not believe. G5495
27 reach hither thy **h**, and thrust *it* into my G5495
Act 2:25 my right **h**, that I should not be moved: G1188
33 Therefore being by the right **h** of God G1188
34 unto my Lord, Sit thou on my right **h**, G1188
3: 7 And he took him by the right **h**, and G5495
4:28 For to do whatsoever thy **h** and thy G5495
30 By stretching forth thine **h** to heal; and G5495
5:31 Him hath God exalted with his right **h** G1188
7:25 that God by his **h** would deliver them: G5495
35 a deliverer by the **h** of the angel which G5495
50 Hath not my **h** made all these things? G5495
55 Jesus standing on the right **h** of God, G1188
56 of man standing on the right **h** of God. G1188
9: 8 the **h**, and brought *him* into Damascus. G5496
12 in, and putting *his* **h** on him, that he G5495
41 And he gave her *his* **h**, and lifted her up, G5495
11:21 And the **h** of the Lord was with them: G5495
12:11 me out of the **h** of Herod, and *from* G5495
17 But he, beckoning unto them with the **h** G5495
13:11 And now, behold, the **h** of the Lord *is* G5495
11 seeking some to lead him by the **h**. G5497
16 with *his* **h** said, Men of Israel, G5495
19:33 beckoned with the **h**, and would have G5495
21: 3 left it on the left **h**, and sailed into Syria, G2176
40 beckoned with the **h** unto the people. G5495
22:11 being led by the **h** of them that were G5496
23:19 took him by the **h**, and went *with him* G5495
26: 1 forth the **h**, and answered for himself: G5495
28: 3 out of the heat, and fastened on his **h**. G5495
4 beast hang on his **h**, they said among G5495
Ro 8:34 is even at the right **h** of God, who also G1188
13:12 The night is far spent, the day is at **h**: let G1448
1Co 12:15 I am not the **h**, I am not of the body; G5495
21 And the eye cannot say unto the **h**, I G5495
16:21 salutation of *me* Paul with mine own **h**. G5495
2Co 6: 7 on the right **h** and on the left, G1188
10:16 line of things made ready to our **h**. G2092
Gal 3:19 by angels in the **h** of a mediator. G5495
6:11 have written unto you with mine own **h**. G5495
Eph 1:20 his own right **h** in the heavenly *places*, G1188
Php 4: 5 known unto all men. The Lord *is* at **h**. G1451
Col 3: 1 Christ sitteth on the right **h** of God. G1188
4:18 The salutation by the **h** of me Paul. G5495
2Th 2: 2 from us, as that the day of Christ is at **h**. G1764
3:17 The salutation of Paul with mine own **h**, G5495
2Ti 4: 6 and the time of my departure is at **h**. G2186
Phlm 19 I Paul have written *it* with mine own **h**, G5495
Heb 1: 3 on the right **h** of the Majesty on high; G1188
13 Sit on my right **h**, until I make thine G1188
8: 1 is set on the right **h** of the throne of the G1188
9 I took them by the **h** to lead them out of G5495
10:12 ever, sat down on the right **h** of God; G1188
12: 2 at the right **h** of the throne of God. G1188
1Pt 3:22 and is on the right **h** of God; angels and G1188
4: 7 But the end of all things is at **h**: be ye G1448
5: 6 under the mighty **h** of God, that he may G5495
Rev 1: 3 are written therein: for the time *is* at **h**. G1451
16 And he had in his right **h** seven stars: G5495
17 And he laid his right **h** upon me, saying G5495
20 sawest in my right **h**, and the seven G1188
2: 1 stars in his right **h**, who walketh in the G1188
5: 1 And I saw in the right **h** of him that sat G1188
7 right **h** of him that sat upon the throne. G1188
6: 5 on him had a pair of balances in his **h**. G5495
8: 4 up before God out of the angel's **h**. G5495
10: 2 And he had in his **h** a little book open: G5495
5 the earth lifted up his **h** to heaven, G5495
8 is open in the **h** of the angel which G5495
10 out of the angel's **h**, and ate it up; and it G5495
13:16 in their right **h**, or in their foreheads: G5495
14: 9 *his* mark in his forehead, or in his **h**, G5495
14 crown, and in his **h** a sharp sickle. G5495
17: 4 a golden cup in her **h** full of G5495
19: 2 the blood of his servants at her **h**. G5495
20: 1 pit and a great chain in his **h**. G5495
22:10 of this book: for the time is at **h**. G1451

HANDBREADTH

Ex 37:12 a border of an **h** round about; and H2948
2Ch 4: 5 And the thickness of it *was* an **h**, and H2947
Ps 39: 5 my days *as* an **h**; and mine age *is* as H2947

HANDED

2Sa 17: 2 he *is* weary and weak **h**, and will make H3027

HANDFUL

Lev 2: 2 take thereout his **h** of the flour H4393+H7062
5:12 shall take his **h** of it, *even* a H4393+H7062
6:15 And he shall take of it his **h**, of the flour H7062
9:17 and took an **h** thereof, and H4390+H3709
Nu 5:26 And the priest shall take an **h** of the H7061
1Ki 17:12 a cake, but an **h** of meal in a H4393+H3709
Ps 72:16 There shall be an **h** of corn in the earth H6451
Ecc 4: 6 Better *is* an **h** *with* quietness, H4393+H3709
Jer 9:22 open field, and as the **h** after the H5995

HANDFULS

Gen 41:47 years the earth brought forth by **h**. H7062
Ex 9: 8 Take to you **h** of ashes of the H4393+H2651
Ru 2:16 And let fall also *some* of the **h** of H6653
1Ki 20:10 for **h** for all the people that follow me. H8168
Ezk 13:19 my people for **h** of barley and for H8168

HANDIWORK See HANDYWORK.

HANDKERCHIEFS

Act 19:12 unto the sick **h** or aprons, and the G4676

HANDLE

Gen 4:21 of all such as **h** the harp and organ. H8610
Jdg 5:14 they that **h** the pen of the writer. H4900
1Ch 12: 8 battle, that could **h** shield and buckler, H6186
2Ch 25: 5 to war, that could **h** spear and shield. H270
Ps 115: 7 They have hands, but they **h** not: feet H4184
Jer 2: 8 and they that **h** the law knew me not: H8610
46: 9 the Libyans, that **h** the shield; and the H8610
9 the Lydians, that **h** *and* bend the bow. H8610
Ezk 27:29 And all that **h** the oar, the mariners, H8610
Lk 24:39 that it is I myself: **h** me, and see; for a G5584
Col 2:21 (Touch not; taste not; **h** not; G2345

HANDLED

Ezk 21:11 that it may be **h**: this sword is H3709+H8610
Mk 12: 4 head, and sent *him* away shamefully **h**. G821
1Jn 1: 1 our hands have **h**, of the Word of life; G5584

HANDLES

Song 5: 5 smelling myrrh, upon the **h** of the lock. H3709

HANDLETH

Prv 16:20 He that **h** a matter wisely shall find H5921
Jer 50:16 and him that **h** the sickle in the time H8610
Am 2:15 Neither shall he stand that **h** the bow; H8610

HANDLING

Ezk 38: 4 and shields, all of them **h** swords: H8610
2Co 4: 2 in craftiness, nor **h** the word of God G1389

HANDMAID

Gen 16: 1 and she had an **h**, an Egyptian, whose H8198
25:12 Sarah's **h**, bare unto Abraham: H8198
29:24 daughter Leah Zilpah his maid *for* an **h**. H8198
29 daughter Bilhah his **h** to be her maid. H8198
30: 4 And she gave him Bilhah her **h** to wife: H8198
35:25 And the sons of Bilhah, Rachel's **h**; Dan, H8198
26 And the sons of Zilpah, Leah's **h**; Gad, H8198
Ex 23:12 **h**, and the stranger, may be refreshed. H519
Jdg 19:19 for me, and for thy **h**, and for the young H519
Ru 2:13 unto thine **h**, though I be not like H8198
3: 9 I *am* Ruth thine **h**: spread therefore thy H519
9 thine **h**; for thou *art* a near kinsman. H519
1Sa 1:11 affliction of thine **h**, and remember me, H519
11 and not forget thine **h**, but wilt give unto H519
11 give unto thine **h** a man child, then I will H519
16 Count not thine **h** for a daughter of H519
18 And she said, Let thine **h** find grace in H8198
25:24 *be*: and let thine **h**, I pray thee, speak in H519
24 audience, and hear the words of thine **h**. H519
25 him: but I thine **h** saw not the young H519
27 And now this blessing which thine **h** H8198
28 the trespass of thine **h**: for the LORD will H519
31 with my lord, then remember thine **h**. H519
41 Behold, *let* thine **h** *be* a servant to wash H519
28:21 him, Behold, thine **h** hath obeyed thy H8198
22 the voice of thine **h**, and let me set a H8198
2Sa 14: 6 And thy **h** had two sons, and they two H8198
7 against thine **h**, and they said, Deliver H8198
12 Then the woman said, Let thine **h**, I H8198
15 afraid: and thy **h** said, I will now speak H8198
15 the king will perform the request of his **h**. H519
16 For the king will hear, to deliver his **h** H519
2Sa 14:17 Then thine **h** said, The word of my lord H8198
19 all these words in the mouth of thine **h**: H8198
20:17 of thine **h**. And he answered, I do hear. H519
1Ki 1:13 swear unto thine **h**, saying, Assuredly H519
17 thy God unto thine **h**, *saying*, Assuredly H519
3:20 me, while thine **h** slept, and laid it in her H519
2Ki 4: 2 she said, Thine **h** hath not any thing in H8198
16 man of God, do not lie unto thine **h**. H8198
Ps 86:16 thy servant, and save the son of thine **h**. H519
116:16 of thine **h**: thou hast loosed my bonds. H519
Prv 30:23 and an **h** that is heir to her mistress. H8198
Jer 34:16 and every man his **h**, whom ye had set H8198
Lk 1:38 And Mary said, Behold the **h** of the G1399

HANDMAIDEN

Lk 1:48 the low estate of his **h**: for, behold, from G1399

HANDMAIDENS

Gen 33: 6 Then the **h** came near, they and their H8198
Ru 2:13 though I be not like unto one of thine **h**. H8198
Act 2:18 And on my servants and on my **h** I will G1399

HANDMAIDS

Gen 33: 1 and unto Rachel, and unto the two **h**. H8198
2 And he put the **h** and their children H8198
2Sa 6:20 in the eyes of the **h** of his servants, as H519
Isa 14: 2 for servants and **h**: and they shall take H8198
Jer 34:11 servants and the **h**, whom they had let H8198
11 into subjection for servants and for **h**. H8198
16 to be unto you for servants and for **h**. H8198
Joel 2:29 and upon the **h** in those days will I H8198

HANDS

Gen 5:29 and toil of our **h**, because of the ground H3027
16: 9 and submit thyself under her **h**. H3027
20: 5 innocency of my **h** have I done this. H3709
24:22 for her **h** of ten *shekels* weight of gold; H3027
30 upon his sister's **h**, and when he heard H3027
47 her face, and the bracelets upon her **h**. H3027
27:16 his **h**, and upon the smooth of his neck: H3027
22 voice, but the **h** *are* the hands of Esau. H3027
22 voice, but the hands *are* the **h** of Esau. H3027
23 not, because his **h** were hairy, as his H3027
23 his brother Esau's **h**: so he blessed him. H3027
31:42 of my **h**, and rebuked *thee* yesternight. H3709
37:21 of their **h**; and said, Let us not kill him. H3027
22 **h**, to deliver him to his father again. H3027
39: 1 bought him of the **h** of the Ishmeelites, H3027
43:22 down in our **h** to buy food: we cannot H3027
48:14 head, guiding his **h** wittingly; for H3027
49:24 the arms of his **h** were made strong by H3027
24 strong by the **h** of the mighty *God* of H3027
Ex 9:29 spread abroad my **h** unto the LORD; H3709
33 spread abroad his **h** unto the LORD: H3709
15:17 O Lord, *which* thy **h** have established. H3027
17:12 But Moses' **h** *were* heavy; and they took H3027
12 Hur stayed up his **h**, the one on the one H3027
12 other side; and his **h** were steady until H3027
29:10 their **h** upon the head of the bullock. H3027
15 put their **h** upon the head of the ram. H3027
19 put their **h** upon the head of the ram. H3027
24 And thou shalt put all in the **h** of H3709
24 of Aaron, and in the **h** of his sons; and H3709
25 And thou shalt receive them of their **h**, H3027
30:19 wash their **h** and their feet thereat: H3027
21 So they shall wash their **h** and their H3027
32:19 **h**, and brake them beneath the mount. H3027
35:25 did spin with their **h**, and brought that H3027
40:31 washed their **h** and their feet thereat: H3027
Lev 4:15 shall lay their **h** upon the head of the H3027
7:30 His own **h** shall bring the offerings of H3027
8:14 his sons laid their **h** upon the head of H3027
18 laid their **h** upon the head of the ram. H3027
22 laid their **h** upon the head of the ram. H3027
24 of their right **h**, and upon the great H3027
27 And he put all upon Aaron's **h**, and H3709
27 upon his sons' **h**, and waved them *for* H3709
28 And Moses took them from off their **h**, H3709
15:11 not rinsed his **h** in water, he shall wash H3027
16:12 the LORD, and his **h** full of sweet H2651
21 And Aaron shall lay both his **h** upon H3027
24:14 *him* lay their **h** upon his head, and H3027
Nu 5:18 memorial in her **h**, which *is* the jealousy H3709
6:19 put *them* upon the **h** of the Nazarite, H3709
8:10 shall put their **h** upon the Levites: H3027
12 And the Levites shall lay their **h** upon H3027
24:10 and he smote his **h** together: and Balak H3709
27:23 And he laid his **h** upon him, and gave H3027
Dt 1:25 of the land in their **h**, and brought *it* H3027

H

Dt 3: 3 delivered into our **h** Og also, the king of H3027
4:28 the work of men's **h**, wood and stone, H3027
9:15 of the covenant *were* in my two **h**. H3027
17 two **h**, and brake them before your eyes. H3027
12:18 in all that thou puttest thine **h** unto. H3027
16:15 **h**, therefore thou shalt surely rejoice. H3027
17: 7 The **h** of the witnesses shall be first H3027
7 and afterward the **h** of all the people. H3027
20:13 it into thine **h**, thou shalt smite every H3027
21: 6 shall wash their **h** over the heifer that H3027
7 And they shall answer and say, Our **h** H3027
10 **h**, and thou hast taken them captive, H3027
24:19 bless thee in all the work of thine **h**. H3027
27:15 the work of the **h** of the craftsman, and H3027
31:29 to anger through the work of your **h**. H3027
33: 7 his people: let his **h** be sufficient for H3027
11 the work of his **h**: smite through the H3027
34: 9 had laid his **h** upon him: and the H3027
Jos 2:24 delivered into our **h** all the land; for H3027
Jdg 2:14 them into the **h** of spoilers that spoiled H3027
14 he sold them into the **h** of their enemies H3027
6:13 us into the **h** of the Midianites. H3709
7: 2 into their **h**, lest Israel vaunt themselves H3027
11 shall thine **h** be strengthened to H3027
19 brake the pitchers that *were* in their **h**. H3027
20 lamps in their left **h**, and the trumpets H3027
20 in their right **h** to blow *withal*: and H3027
8: 3 God hath delivered into your **h** the H3027
6 said, *Are* the **h** of Zebah and Zalmunna H3709
15 me, saying, *Are* the **h** of Zebah and H3709
34 the **h** of all their enemies on every side: H3027
9:16 him according to the deserving of his **h**; H3027
10: 7 sold them into the **h** of the Philistines, H3027
7 into the **h** of the children of Ammon. H3027
11:30 the children of Ammon into mine **h**, H3027
32 the LORD delivered them into his **h**. H3027
12: 2 you, ye delivered me not out of their **h**. H3027
3 I put my life in my **h**, and passed over H3709
13:23 offering at our **h**, neither would he have H3027
14: 9 And he took thereof in his **h**, and went H3709
15:14 and his bands loosed from off his **h**. H3027
16:24 delivered into our **h** our enemy, and H3027
18:10 given it into your **h**; a place where *there* H3027
19:27 and her **h** *were* upon the threshold. H3027
1Sa 5: 4 the palms of his **h** *were* cut off upon the H3027
7:14 deliver out of the **h** of the Philistines. H3027
10: 4 which thou shalt receive of their **h**. H3027
11: 7 coasts of Israel by the **h** of messengers, H3027
14:13 And Jonathan climbed up upon his **h** H3027
48 out of the **h** of them that spoiled them. H3027
17:47 LORD'S, and he will give you into our **h**. H3027
21:13 mad in their **h**, and scrabbled on the H3027
30:15 me into the **h** of my master, and I H3027
2Sa 2: 7 Therefore now let your **h** be H3027
3:34 Thy **h** *were* not bound, nor thy feet put H3027
4: 1 in Hebron, his **h** were feeble, and all H3027
12 and cut off their **h** and their feet, and H3027
16:21 the **h** of all that *are* with thee be strong. H3027
21: 9 And he delivered them into the **h** of the H3027
22:21 of my **h** hath he recompensed me. H3027
35 He teacheth my **h** to war; so that a bow H3027
23: 6 because they cannot be taken with **h**: H3027
1Ki 8:22 and spread forth his **h** toward heaven: H3709
38 spread forth his **h** toward this house: H3709
54 knees with his **h** spread up to heaven. H3709
14:27 *them* unto the **h** of the chief of the H3027
16: 7 with the work of his **h**, in being like the H3027
2Ki 3:11 which poured water on the **h** of Elijah. H3027
4:34 his eyes, and his **h** upon his hands: and H3709
34 his hands upon his **h**: and he stretched H3709
5:20 not receiving at his **h** that which he H3027
9:23 And Joram turned his **h**, and fled, and H3027
35 and the feet, and the palms of *her* **h**. H3027
10:24 brought into your **h** escape, *he that* H3027
11:12 their **h**, and said, God save the king. H3709
16 And they laid **h** on her; and she went H3027
12:11 told, into the **h** of them that did the H3027
13:16 Elisha put his **h** upon the king's hands. H3027
16 Elisha put his hands upon the king's **h**. H3027
19:18 the work of men's **h**, wood and stone: H3027
22:17 the works of their **h**; therefore my wrath H3027
1Ch 12:17 *is* no wrong in mine **h**, the God of our H3709
25: 2 of Asaph under the **h** of Asaph, which H3027
3 six, under the **h** of their father H3027
6 All these *were* under the **h** of their H3027
29: 5 *to be made* by the **h** of artificers. And H3027
2Ch 6: 4 who hath with his **h** fulfilled *that* which H3027
12 of Israel, and spread forth his **h**: H3709
13 and spread forth his **h** toward heaven, H3709

2Ch 6:29 shall spread forth his **h** in this house: H3709
8:18 And Huram sent him by the **h** of his H3027
12:10 *them* to the **h** of the chief of the guard, H3027
15: 7 and let not your **h** be weak: for your H3027
23:15 So they laid **h** on her; and when she H3027
29:23 and they laid their **h** upon them: H3027
32:19 *which were* the work of the **h** of man. H3027
34:25 the works of their **h**; therefore my wrath H3027
35:11 their **h**, and the Levites flayed *them*. H3027
Ezr 1: 6 strengthened their **h** with vessels of H3027
4: 4 weakened the **h** of the people of Judah, H3027
5: 8 goeth fast on, and prospereth in their **h**. H3028
6:22 to strengthen their **h** in the work of the H3027
9: 5 out my **h** unto the LORD my God, H3709
10:19 And they gave their **h** that they would H3027
Neh 2:18 their **h** for *this* good *work*. H3027
4:17 with one of his **h** wrought in the work, H3027
6: 9 saying, Their **h** shall be weakened from H3027
9 Now therefore, *O God*, strengthen my **h**. H3027
8: 6 lifting up their **h**: and they bowed their H3027
9:24 them into their **h**, with their kings, and H3027
13:21 *so* again, I will lay **h** on you. From that H3027
Est 3: 6 And he thought scorn to lay **h** on H3027
9 of silver to the **h** of those that have the H3027
9:16 but they laid not their **h** on the prey, H3027
Job 1:10 the work of his **h**, and his substance is H3027
4: 3 and thou hast strengthened the weak **h**. H3027
5:12 **h** cannot perform *their* enterprise. H3027
18 he woundeth, and his **h** make whole. H3027
9:30 water, and make my **h** never so clean; H3709
10: 3 the work of thine **h**, and shine upon the H3709
8 Thine **h** have made me and fashioned H3027
11:13 and stretch out thine **h** toward him; H3709
14:15 wilt have a desire to the work of thine **h**. H3027
16:11 me over into the **h** of the wicked. H3027
17 Not for *any* injustice in mine **h**: also my H3709
17: 3 who *is* he *that* will strike **h** with me? H3027
9 clean **h** shall be stronger and stronger. H3027
20:10 and his **h** shall restore their goods. H3027
22:30 is delivered by the pureness of thine **h**. H3709
27:23 *Men* shall clap their **h** at him, and shall H3709
30: 2 strength of their **h** *profit* me, in whom H3027
31: 7 and if any blot hath cleaved to mine **h**; H3709
34:19 poor? for they all *are* the work of his **h**. H3027
37 his sin, he clappeth *his* **h** among us, and H3709
Ps 7: 3 done this; if there be iniquity in my **h**; H3709
8: 6 the works of thy **h**; thou hast put all H3027
9:16 the work of his own **h**. Higgaion. Selah. H3709
18:20 of my **h** hath he recompensed me. H3027
24 to the cleanness of my **h** in his eyesight. H3027
34 He teacheth my **h** to war, so that a bow H3027
22:16 me: they pierced my **h** and my feet. H3027
24: 4 He that hath clean **h**, and a pure heart; H3709
26: 6 I will wash mine **h** in innocency: so will H3709
10 In whose **h** *is* mischief, and their right H3027
28: 2 I lift up my **h** toward thy holy oracle. H3027
4 of their **h**; render to them their desert. H3027
5 the operation of his **h**, he shall destroy H3027
44:20 or stretched out our **h** to a strange god; H3709
47: 1 O clap your **h**, all ye people; shout unto H3709
55:20 He hath put forth his **h** against such as H3027
58: 2 the violence of your **h** in the earth. H3027
63: 4 I live: I will lift up my **h** in thy name. H3709
68:31 shall soon stretch out her **h** unto God. H3027
73:13 vain, and washed my **h** in innocency. H3709
76: 5 of the men of might have found their **h**. H3027
78:72 guided them by the skilfulness of his **h**. H3709
81: 6 his **h** were delivered from the pots. H3709
88: 9 I have stretched out my **h** unto thee. H3709
90:17 the work of our **h** upon us; yea, the H3027
17 yea, the work of our **h** establish thou it. H3027
91:12 They shall bear thee up in *their* **h**, lest H3709
92: 4 I will triumph in the works of thy **h**. H3027
95: 5 made it: and his **h** formed the dry *land*. H3027
98: 8 Let the floods clap *their* **h**: let the hills H3709
102:25 and the heavens *are* the work of thy **h**. H3027
111: 7 The works of his **h** *are* verity and H3027
115: 4 *are* silver and gold, the work of men's **h**. H3027
7 They have **h**, but they handle not: feet H3027
119:48 My **h** also will I lift up unto thy H3709
73 Thy **h** have made me and fashioned H3027
125: 3 put forth their **h** unto iniquity. H3027
128: 2 For thou shalt eat the labour of thine **h**: H3709
134: 2 Lift up your **h** *in* the sanctuary, and H3027
135:15 *are* silver and gold, the work of men's **h**. H3027
138: 8 forsake not the works of thine own **h**. H3027
140: 4 Keep me, O LORD, from the **h** of the H3027
141: 2 up of my **h** *as* the evening sacrifice. H3709
143: 5 thy works; I muse on the work of thy **h**. H3027

Ps 143: 6 I stretch forth my **h** unto thee: my soul H3027
144: 1 my **h** to war, *and* my fingers to fight: H3027
Prv 6:10 a little folding of the **h** to sleep: H3027
17 A proud look, a lying tongue, and **h** H3027
12:14 a man's **h** shall be rendered unto him. H3027
14: 1 the foolish plucketh it down with her **h**. H3027
17:18 striketh **h**, *and* becometh surety H3709
21:25 killeth him; for his **h** refuse to labour. H3027
22:26 Be not thou *one* of them that strike **h**, *or* H3709
24:33 a little folding of the **h** to sleep: H3027
30:28 The spider taketh hold with her **h**, and H3027
31:13 flax, and worketh willingly with her **h**. H3709
16 fruit of her **h** she planteth a vineyard. H3709
19 She layeth her **h** to the spindle, and her H3027
19 the spindle, and her **h** hold the distaff. H3709
20 she reacheth forth her **h** to the needy. H3027
31 Give her of the fruit of her **h**; and let her H3027
Ecc 2:11 the works that my **h** had wrought, and H3027
4: 5 The fool foldeth his **h** together, and H3027
6 than both the **h** full *with* travail and H2651
5: 6 voice, and destroy the work of thine **h**? H3027
7:26 and nets, *and* her **h** *as* bands: whoso H3027
10:18 of the **h** the house droppeth through. H3027
Song 5: 5 my beloved; and my **h** dropped *with* H3027
14 His **h** *are as* gold rings set with the H3027
7: 1 work of the **h** of a cunning workman. H3027
Isa 1:15 And when ye spread forth your **h**, I will H3709
15 I will not hear: your **h** are full of blood. H3027
2: 8 work of their own **h**, that which their H3027
3:11 the reward of his **h** shall be given him. H3027
5:12 neither consider the operation of his **h**. H3027
13: 7 Therefore shall all **h** be faint, and every H3027
17: 8 the work of his **h**, neither shall respect H3027
19:25 of my **h**, and Israel mine inheritance. H3027
25:11 And he shall spread forth his **h** in the H3027
11 spreadeth forth *his* **h** to swim: and he
11 pride together with the spoils of their **h**. H3027
29:23 the work of mine **h**, in the midst of him, H3027
31: 7 own **h** have made unto you *for* a sin. H3027
33:15 that shaketh his **h** from holding of H3709
35: 3 Strengthen ye the weak **h**, and confirm H3027
37:19 the work of men's **h**, wood and stone: H3027
45: 9 thou? or thy work, He hath no **h**? H3027
11 the work of my **h** command ye me. H3027
12 it: I, *even* my **h**, have stretched out the H3027
49:16 **h**; thy walls *are* continually before me. H3709
55:12 the trees of the field shall clap *their* **h**. H3709
59: 3 For your **h** are defiled with blood, and H3709
6 and the act of violence *is* in their **h**. H3709
60:21 work of my **h**, that I may be glorified. H3027
65: 2 I have spread out my **h** all the day unto H3027
22 shall long enjoy the work of their **h**. H3027
Jer 1:16 worshipped the works of their own **h**. H3027
2:37 him, and thine **h** upon thine head: for H3027
4:31 *that* spreadeth her **h**, *saying*, Woe *is* me H3709
6:24 We have heard the fame thereof: our **h** H3027
10: 3 of the **h** of the workman, with the axe. H3027
9 and of the **h** of the founder: blue H3027
19: 7 and by the **h** of them that seek their H3027
21: 4 that *are* in your **h**, wherewith ye fight H3027
23:14 also the **h** of evildoers, that none H3027
25: 6 of your **h**; and I will do you no hurt. H3027
7 the works of your **h** to your own hurt. H3027
14 according to the works of their own **h**. H3027
30: 6 every man with his **h** on his loins, as a H3027
32:30 the work of their **h**, saith the LORD. H3027
33:13 again under the **h** of him that telleth H3027
38: 4 he weakeneth the **h** of the men of war H3027
4 this city, and the **h** of all the people, in H3027
44: 8 the works of your **h**, burning incense H3027
47: 3 to *their* children for feebleness of **h**; H3027
48:37 upon all the **h** *shall be* cuttings, and H3027
50:43 report of them, and his **h** waxed feeble: H3027
Lam 1:14 **h**, *from whom* I am not able to rise up. H3027
17 Zion spreadeth forth her **h**, *and there is* H3027
2:15 All that pass by clap *their* **h** at thee; H3709
19 Lord: lift up thy **h** toward him for the H3709
3:41 Let us lift up our heart with *our* **h** unto H3709
64 LORD, according to the work of their **h**. H3027
4: 2 the work of the **h** of the potter! H3027
6 in a moment, and no **h** stayed on her. H3027
10 The **h** of the pitiful women have H3027
Ezk 1: 8 And *they had* the **h** of a man under H3027
7:17 All **h** shall be feeble, and all knees shall H3027
21 And I will give it into the **h** of the H3027
27 and the **h** of the people of the H3027
10: 7 and put *it* into the **h** of *him that was* H2651
12 backs, and their **h**, and their wings, and H3027
21 the **h** of a man *was* under their wings. H3027

Ezk 11: 9 you into the **h** of strangers, and will H3027
13:22 strengthened the **h** of the wicked, that H3027
16:11 upon thy **h**, and a chain on thy neck. H3027
21: 7 shall melt, and all **h** shall be feeble, and H3027
14 and smite *thine* **h** together, and let the H3709
17 I will also smite mine **h** together, and I H3709
22:14 Can thine heart endure, or can thine **h** H3027
23:37 blood *is* in their **h**, and with their idols H3027
42 upon their **h**, and beautiful crowns H3027
45 *are* adulteresses, and blood *is* in their **h**. H3027
25: 6 hast clapped *thine* **h**, and stamped with H3027
Dan 2:34 was cut out without **h**, which smote the H3028
45 mountain without **h**, and that it brake H3028
3:15 God that shall deliver you out of my **h**? H3028
10:10 my knees and *upon* the palms of my **h**. H3027
Hos 14: 3 to the work of our **h**, *Ye are* our gods: H3027
Oba 13 nor have laid **h** on their substance in
Jna 3: 8 and from the violence that *is* in their **h**. H3709
Mic 5:13 no more worship the work of thine **h**. H3027
7: 3 That they may do evil with both **h** H3709
Nah 3:19 thee shall clap the **h** over thee: for upon H3709
Hab 3:10 his voice, *and* lifted up his **h** on high. H3027
Zep 3:16 *and to* Zion, Let not thine **h** be slack. H3027
Hag 1:11 cattle, and upon all the labour of the **h**. H3709
2:14 work of their **h**; and that which they H3027
17 labours of your **h**; yet ye *turned* not to H3027
Zec 4: 9 The **h** of Zerubbabel have laid the H3027
9 of this house; his **h** shall also finish it; H3027
8: 9 of hosts; Let your **h** be strong, ye that H3027
13 fear not, *but* let your **h** be strong. H3027
13: 6 these wounds in thine **h**? Then he shall H3027
Mt 4: 6 thee: and in *their* **h** they shall bear thee *G5495*
15: 2 wash not their **h** when they eat bread. *G5495*
20 with unwashen **h** defileth not a man. *G5495*
17:22 shall be betrayed into the **h** of men: *G5495*
18: 8 than having two **h** or two feet to be cast *G5495*
28 pence: and he laid **h** on him, and took *G2902*
19:13 he should put *his* **h** on them, and pray: *G5495*
15 And he laid *his* **h** on them, and *G5495*
21:46 But when they sought to lay **h** on him, *G2902*
26:45 man is betrayed into the **h** of sinners. *G5495*
50 and laid **h** on Jesus, and took him. *G5495*
67 smote *him* with the palms of their **h**, *G4474*
27:24 and washed *his* **h** before the multitude, *G5495*
Mk 5:23 come and lay thy **h** on her, that she *G5495*
6: 2 mighty works are wrought by his **h**? *G5495*
5 that he laid his **h** upon a few sick folk, *G5495*
7: 2 say, with unwashen, **h**, they found fault. *G5495*
3 they wash *their* **h** oft, eat not, holding *G5495*
5 elders, but eat bread with unwashen **h**? *G5495*
8:23 eyes, and put his **h** upon him, he asked *G5495*
25 After that he put *his* **h** again upon his *G5495*
9:31 is delivered into the **h** of men, and they *G5495*
43 than having two **h** to go into hell, into *G5495*
10:16 put *his* **h** upon them, and blessed them. *G5495*
14:41 man is betrayed into the **h** of sinners. *G5495*
46 And they laid their **h** on him, and took *G5495*
58 that is made with **h**, and within three *G5499*
58 days I will build another made without **h**. *G886*
65 did strike him with the palms of their **h**. *G4475*
16:18 **h** on the sick, and they shall recover. *G5495*
Lk 4:11 And in *their* **h** they shall bear thee up, *G5495*
40 and he laid his **h** on every one of them, *G5495*
6: 1 and did eat, rubbing *them* in *their* **h**. *G5495*
9:44 shall be delivered into the **h** of men. *G5495*
13:13 And he laid *his* **h** on her: and *G5495*
20:19 hour sought to lay **h** on him; and they *G5495*
21:12 these, they shall lay their **h** on you, and *G5495*
22:53 ye stretched forth no **h** against me: but *G5495*
23:46 said, Father, into thy **h** I commend my *G5495*
24: 7 delivered into the **h** of sinful men, and *G5495*
39 Behold my **h** and my feet, that it is I *G5495*
40 he shewed them *his* **h** and *his* feet. *G5495*
50 he lifted up his **h**, and blessed them. *G5495*
Jn 7:30 but no man laid **h** on him, because his *G5495*
44 taken him; but no man laid **h** on him. *G5495*
8:20 and no man laid **h** on him; for his hour *G4084*
13: 3 all things into his **h**, and that he was *G5495*
9 feet only, but also *my* **h** and *my* head. *G5495*
19: 3 Jews! and they smote him with their **h**. *G1325*
20:20 unto them *his* **h** and his side. Then *G5495*
25 I shall see in his **h** the print of the nails, *G5495*
27 and behold my **h**; and reach hither thy *G5495*
21:18 stretch forth thy **h**, and another shall *G5495*
Act 2:23 by wicked **h** have crucified and slain: *G5495*
4: 3 And they laid **h** on them, and put *them* *G5495*
5:12 And by the **h** of the apostles were many *G5495*
18 And laid their **h** on the apostles, and *G5495*
6: 6 had prayed, they laid *their* **h** on them. *G5495*
Act 7:41 rejoiced in the works of their own **h**. *G5495*
48 made with **h**; as saith the prophet, *G5499*
8:17 Then laid they *their* **h** on them, and *G5495*
18 on of the apostles' **h** the Holy Ghost *G5495*
19 I lay **h**, he may receive the Holy Ghost. *G5495*
9:17 and putting his **h** on him said, Brother *G5495*
11:30 elders by the **h** of Barnabas and Saul. *G5495*
12: 1 forth *his* **h** to vex certain of the church. *G5495*
7 And his chains fell off from *his* **h**. *G5495*
13: 3 *their* **h** on them, they sent *them* away. *G5495*
14: 3 and wonders to be done by their **h**. *G5495*
17:24 dwelleth not in temples made with **h**; *G5499*
25 Neither is worshipped with men's **h**, as *G5495*
19: 6 And when Paul had laid *his* **h** upon *G5495*
11 special miracles by the **h** of Paul: *G5495*
26 be no gods, which are made with **h**: *G5495*
20:34 Yea, ye yourselves know, that these **h** *G5495*
21:11 bound his own **h** and feet, and said, *G5495*
11 deliver *him* into the **h** of the Gentiles. *G5495*
27 up all the people, and laid **h** on him, *G5495*
24: 7 violence took *him* away out of our **h**, *G5495*
27:19 with our own **h** the tackling of the ship. *G849*
28: 8 and laid his **h** on him, and healed him. *G5495*
17 Jerusalem into the **h** of the Romans. *G5495*
Ro 10:21 have stretched forth my **h** unto a *G5495*
1Co 4:12 And labour, working with our own **h**: *G5495*
2Co 5: 1 not made with **h**, eternal in the heavens. *G886*
11:33 let down by the wall, and escaped his **h**. *G5495*
Gal 2: 9 the right **h** of fellowship; that we *G1188*
Eph 2:11 Circumcision in the flesh made by **h**; *G5499*
4:28 working with *his* **h** the thing which is *G5495*
Col 2:11 made without **h**, in putting off the body *G886*
1Th 4:11 your own **h**, as we commanded you; *G5495*
1Ti 2: 8 up holy **h**, without wrath and doubting. *G5495*
4:14 the laying on of the **h** of the presbytery. *G5495*
5:22 Lay **h** suddenly on no man, neither be *G5495*
2Ti 1: 6 is in thee by the putting on of my **h**. *G5495*
Heb 1:10 the heavens are the works of thine **h**: *G5495*
2: 7 didst set him over the works of thy **h**: *G5495*
6: 2 of laying on of **h**, and of resurrection *G5495*
9:11 **h**, that is to say, not of this building; *G5499*
24 holy places made with **h**, *which are* the *G5499*
10:31 *It is* a fearful thing to fall into the **h** of *G5495*
12:12 Wherefore lift up the **h** which hang *G5495*
Jas 4: 8 to you. Cleanse *your* **h**, *ye* sinners; and *G5495*
1Jn 1: 1 our **h** have handled, of the Word of life; *G5495*
Rev 7: 9 with white robes, and palms in their **h**; *G5495*
9:20 of the works of their **h**, that they should *G5495*
20: 4 or in their **h**; and they lived and reigned *G5495*

HANDSTAVES
Ezk 39: 9 and the **h**, and the spears, H4731+H3027

HAND-WEAPON
See HAND and WEAPON.

HANDWRITING
Col 2:14 Blotting out the **h** of ordinances that *G5498*

HANDYWORK
Ps 19: 1 the firmament sheweth his **h**. H4640+H3027

HANES
Isa 30: 4 Zoan, and his ambassadors came to **H**. H2609

HANG
Gen 40:19 off thee, and shall **h** thee on a tree; and H8518
Ex 26:12 **h** over the backside of the tabernacle. H5628
13 of the tent, it shall **h** over the sides of H5628
32 And thou shalt **h** it upon four pillars of H5414
33 And thou shalt **h** up the vail under the H5414
40: 8 and **h** up the hanging at the court gate. H5414
Nu 25: 4 of the people, and **h** them up before the H3363
Dt 21:22 put to death, and thou **h** him on a tree: H8518
28:66 And thy life shall **h** in doubt before H8511
2Sa 21: 6 us, and we will **h** them up unto the H3363
Est 6: 4 unto the king to **h** Mordecai on the H8518
7: 9 Then the king said, **H** him thereon. H8518
Song 4: 4 whereon there **h** a thousand bucklers, H8518
Isa 22:24 And they shall **h** upon him all the glory H8518
Lam 2:10 **h** down their heads to the ground. H3381
Ezk 15: 3 take a pin of it to **h** any vessel thereon? H8518
Mt 22:40 On these two commandments **h** all the *G2910*
Act 28: 4 *venomous* beast **h** on his hand, they *G2910*
Heb 12:12 Wherefore lift up the hands which **h** *G3935*

HANGED
Gen 40:22 But he **h** the chief baker: as Joseph had H8518
41:13 unto mine office, and him he **h**. H8518
Dt 21:23 that day; (for he that is **h** *is* accursed of H8518
Jos 8:29 And the king of Ai he **h** on a tree until H8518
10:26 slew them, and **h** them on five trees: H8518
2Sa 4:12 and their feet, and **h** *them* up over the H8518
17:23 in order, and **h** himself, and died, and H2614
18:10 Behold, I saw Absalom **h** in an oak. H8518
21: 9 and they **h** them in the hill before H3363
12 the Philistines had **h** them, when the H8511
13 gathered the bones of them that were **h**. H3363
Ezr 6:11 set up, let him be **h** thereon; and let his H4223
Est 2:23 they were both **h** on a tree: and it was H8518
5:14 Mordecai may be **h** thereon: then go H8518
7:10 So they **h** Haman on the gallows that H8518
8: 7 and him they have **h** upon the gallows, H8518
9:13 ten sons be **h** upon the gallows. H8518
14 Shushan; and they **h** Haman's ten sons. H8518
25 his sons should be **h** on the gallows. H8518
Ps 137: 2 We **h** our harps upon the willows in the H8518
Lam 5:12 Princes are **h** up by their hand: the H8518
Ezk 27:10 thy men of war: they **h** the shield and H8518
11 in thy towers: they **h** their shields upon H8518
Mt 18: 6 a millstone were **h** about his neck, and *G2910*
27: 5 and departed, and went and **h** himself. *G519*
Mk 9:42 a millstone were **h** about his neck, and *G4029*
Lk 17: 2 a millstone were **h** about his neck, and *G4029*
23:39 which were **h** railed on him, saying, *G2910*
Act 5:30 Jesus, whom ye slew and **h** on a tree. *G2910*
10:39 whom they slew and **h** on a tree: *G2910*

HANGETH
Job 26: 7 place, *and* **h** the earth upon nothing. H8518
Gal 3:13 Cursed *is* every one that **h** on a tree: *G2910*

HANGING
Ex 26:36 And thou shalt make an **h** for the door H4539
37 And thou shalt make for the **h** five H4539
27:16 court *shall be* an **h** of twenty cubits, *of* H4539
35:15 incense, and the **h** for the door at the H4539
17 and the **h** for the door of the court, H4539
36:37 And he made an **h** for the tabernacle H4539
38:18 And the **h** for the gate of the court *was* H4539
39:38 and the **h** for the tabernacle door, H4539
40 sockets, and the **h** for the court gate, H4539
40: 5 put the **h** of the door to the tabernacle. H4539
8 and hang up the **h** at the court gate. H4539
28 And he set up the **h** *at* the door of the H4539
33 and set up the **h** of the court gate. So H4539
Nu 3:25 thereof, and the **h** for the door of the H4539
31 and the **h**, and all the service thereof. H4539
4:25 upon it, and the **h** for the door of the H4539
26 the court, and the **h** for the door of the H4539
Jos 10:26 were **h** upon the trees until the evening. H8518

HANGINGS
Ex 27: 9 *there shall be* **h** for the court *of* fine H7050
11 *there shall be* **h** of an hundred *cubits* H7050
12 west side *shall be* **h** of fifty cubits: their H7050
14 The **h** of one side *of the gate shall be* H7050
15 And on the other side *shall be* **h** fifteen H7050
35:17 The **h** of the court, his pillars, and their H7050
38: 9 southward the **h** of the court *were of* H7050
11 And for the north side *the* **h** *were* an
12 And for the west side *were* **h** of fifty H7050
14 The **h** of the one side *of the gate were* H7050
15 and that hand, *were* **h** of fifteen cubits; H7050
16 All the **h** of the court round about *were* H7050
18 cubits, answerable to the **h** of the court. H7050
39:40 The **h** of the court, his pillars, and his H7050
Nu 3:26 And the **h** of the court, and the curtain H7050
4:26 And the **h** of the court, and the hanging H7050
2Ki 23: 7 where the women wove **h** for the grove. H1004
Est 1: 6 *Where were* white, green, and blue, *h*,

HANIEL
1Ch 7:39 And the sons of Ulla; Arah, and **H**, and H2592

HANNAH
1Sa 1: 2 of the one *was* **H**, and the name of the H2584
2 had children, but **H** had no children. H2584
5 But unto **H** he gave a worthy portion; H2584
5 for he loved **H**: but the LORD had shut H2584
8 husband to her, **H**, why weepest thou? H2584
9 So **H** rose up after they had eaten in H2584
13 Now **H**, she spake in her heart; only her H2584
15 And **H** answered and said, No, my H2584
19 and Elkanah knew **H** his wife; and the H2584
20 come about after **H** had conceived, that H2584
22 But **H** went not up; for she said unto H2584
2: 1 And **H** prayed, and said, My heart H2584
21 And the LORD visited **H**, so that she H2584

HANNATHON
Jos 19:14 the north side to H: and the outgoings H2615

HANNIEL
Nu 34:23 of Manasseh, H the son of Ephod. H2592

HANOCH
Gen 25: 4 and Epher, and H, and Abida, and H2585
46: 9 And the sons of Reuben; H, and Phallu, H2585
Ex 6:14 the firstborn of Israel; H, and Pallu, H2585
Nu 26: 5 of Reuben; H, *of whom cometh* the H2585
1Ch 5: 3 *were*, H, and Pallu, Hezron, and Carmi. H2585

HANOCHITES
Nu 26: 5 H: of Pallu, the family of the Palluites: H2599

HANUN
2Sa 10: 1 and H his son reigned in his stead. H2586
2 kindness unto H the son of Nahash, H2586
3 of Ammon said unto H their lord, H2586
4 Wherefore H took David's servants, H2586
1Ch 19: 2 kindness unto H the son of Nahash, H2586
2 of Ammon to H, to comfort him. H2586
3 of Ammon said to H, Thinkest thou H2586
4 Wherefore H took David's servants, H2586
6 odious to David, H and the children of H2586
Neh 3:13 The valley gate repaired H, and the H2586
30 of Shelemiah, and H the sixth son of H2586

HAP
Ru 2: 3 the reapers: and her **h** was to light on a H4745

HAPHARAIM
Jos 19:19 And H, and Shion, and Anaharath, H2663

HAPLY
1Sa 14:30 How much more, if **h** the people had H3863
Mk 11:13 leaves, he came, if **h** he might find any *G686*
Lk 14:29 Lest **h**, after he hath laid the *G3379*
Act 5:39 overthrow it; lest **h** ye be found even to *G3379*
17:27 That they should seek the Lord, if **h** they *G686*
2Co 9: 4 Lest **h** if they of Macedonia come with *G3381*

HAPPEN
1Sa 28:10 no punishment **h** to thee for this thing. H7136
Prv 12:21 There shall no evil **h** to the just: but the H579
Isa 41:22 shew us what shall **h**: let them shew the H7136
Mk 10:32 them what things should **h** unto him, *G4819*

HAPPENED
1Sa 6: 9 smote us: it *was* a chance *that* **h** to us. H1961
2Sa 1: 6 told him said, As I **h** by chance upon H7136
20: 1 And there **h** to be there a man of Belial, H7122
Est 4: 7 him of all that had **h** unto him, and of H7136
Jer 44:23 this evil is **h** unto you, as at this day. H7122
Lk 24:14 together of all these things which had **h**. *G4819*
Act 3:10 at that which had **h** unto him. *G4819*
Ro 11:25 in part is **h** to Israel, until the fulness *G1096*
1Co 10:11 Now all these things **h** unto them for *G4819*
Php 1:12 the things *which* **h** unto me have fallen
1Pt 4:12 though some strange thing **h** unto you: *G4819*
2Pt 2:22 But it is **h** unto them according to the *G4819*

HAPPENETH
Ecc 2:14 also that one event **h** to them all. H7136
15 Then said I in my heart, As it **h** to the H4745
15 to the fool, so it **h** even to me; and why H7136
8:14 unto whom it **h** according to the work H5060
14 *men*, to whom it **h** according to the H5060
9:11 but time and chance **h** to them all. H7136

HAPPIER
1Co 7:40 But she is **h** if she so abide, after my *G3107*

HAPPUCH See KEREN-HAPPUCH.

HAPPY
Gen 30:13 And Leah said, H am I, for the H837
Dt 33:29 H *art* thou, O Israel: who *is* like unto H835
1Ki 10: 8 H *are* thy men, happy *are* these thy H835
8 Happy *are* thy men, **h** *are* these thy H835
2Ch 9: 7 H *are* thy men, and happy *are* these thy H835
7 Happy *are* thy men, and **h** *are* these thy H835
Job 5:17 Behold, **h** *is* the man whom God H835
Ps 127: 5 H *is* the man that hath his quiver full of H835
128: 2 of thine hands: **h** *shalt* thou *be*, and *it* H835
137: 8 art to be destroyed; **h** *shall he be*, that H835
9 H *shall he be*, that taketh and dasheth H835
144:15 H *is that* people, that is in such a case: H835
Ps 144:15 **h** *is that* people, whose God *is* the LORD. H835
146: 5 H *is he* that *hath* the God of Jacob for his H835
Prv 3:13 H *is* the man *that* findeth wisdom, and H835
18 and **h** *is every one* that retaineth her. H833
14:21 he that hath mercy on the poor, **h** *is* he. H835
16:20 and whoso trusteth in the LORD, **h** *is* he. H835
28:14 H *is* the man that feareth alway: but he H835
29:18 but he that keepeth the law, **h** *is* he. H835
Jer 12: 1 all they **h** that deal very treacherously? H7951
Mal 3:15 And now we call the proud **h**; yea, they H833
Jn 13:17 If ye know these things, **h** are ye if ye *G3107*
Act 26: 2 I think myself **h**, king Agrippa, because *G3107*
Ro 14:22 before God. H *is* he that condemneth *G3107*
Jas 5:11 Behold, we count them **h** which *G3106*
1Pt 3:14 sake, **h** *are ye*: and be not afraid *G3107*
4:14 name of Christ, **h** *are ye*; for the spirit *G3107*

HARA
1Ch 5:26 and Habor, and H, and to the river H2024

HARADAH
Nu 33:24 mount Shapher, and encamped in H. H2732
25 And they removed from H, and pitched H2732

HARAN
Gen 11:26 years, and begat Abram, Nahor, and H. H2039
27 Nahor, and H; and Haran begat Lot. H2039
27 Nahor, and Haran; and H begat Lot. H2039
28 And H died before his father Terah in H2039
29 the daughter of H, the father of Milcah, H2039
31 and Lot the son of H his son's son, and H2039
31 and they came unto H, and dwelt there. H2771
32 and five years: and Terah died in H. H2771
12: 4 years old when he departed out of H. H2771
5 they had gotten in H; and they went H2771
27:43 flee thou to Laban my brother to H; H2771
28:10 from Beer-sheba, and went toward H. H2771
29: 4 *be* ye? And they said, Of H *are* we. H2771
2Ki 19:12 *as* Gozan, and H, and Rezeph, and the H2771
1Ch 2:46 And Ephah, Caleb's concubine, bare H, H2771
46 Moza, and Gazez: and H begat Gazez. H2771
23: 9 and Haziel, and H, three. These *were* H2039
Isa 37:12 *as* Gozan, and H, and Rezeph, and the H2771
Ezk 27:23 H, and Canneh, and Eden, the H2771

HARARITE
2Sa 23:11 son of Agee the H. And the Philistines H2043
33 Shammah the H, Ahiam the son of H2043
33 Ahiam the son of Sharar the H, H2043
1Ch 11:34 Jonathan the son of Shage the H, H2043
35 Ahiam the son of Sacar the H, Eliphal H2043

HARBONA
Est 1:10 Biztha, H, Bigtha, and Abagtha, H2726

HARBONAH
Est 7: 9 And H, one of the chamberlains, said H2726

HARD
Gen 18:14 Is any thing too **h** for the LORD? At the H6381
35:16 Rachel travailed, and she had **h** labour. H7185
17 And it came to pass, when she was in **h** H7185
Ex 1:14 And they made their lives bitter with **h** H7186
18:26 people at all seasons: the **h** causes they H7186
Lev 3: 9 it shall he take off **h** by the backbone; H5980
Dt 1:17 cause that is too **h** for you, bring *it* unto H7185
15:18 It shall not seem **h** unto thee, when H7185
17: 8 If there arise a matter too **h** for thee in H6381
26: 6 us, and laid upon us **h** bondage: H7186
Jdg 9:52 it, and went **h** unto the door of the H5066
20:45 men; and pursued **h** after them unto H1692
1Sa 14:22 also followed **h** after them in the battle. H1692
31: 2 And the Philistines followed **h** upon H1692
2Sa 1: 6 and horsemen followed **h** after him. H1692
3:39 of Zeruiah *be* too **h** for me: the LORD H7186
13: 2 it **h** for him to do any thing to her. H6381
1Ki 10: 1 came to prove him with **h** questions. H2420
21: 1 **h** by the palace of Ahab king of Samaria. H681
2Ki 2:10 And he said, Thou hast asked a **h** H7185
1Ch 10: 2 And the Philistines followed **h** after H1692
19: 4 **h** by their buttocks, and sent them away.
2Ch 9: 1 prove Solomon with **h** questions at H2420
Job 41:24 His heart is as firm as a stone; yea, as **h** H3332
Ps 60: 3 Thou hast shewed thy people **h** things: H7186
63: 8 My soul followeth **h** after thee: thy right H1692
88: 7 Thy wrath lieth **h** upon me, and thou H5564
94: 4 *How long* shall they utter *and* speak **h** H6277
Prv 13:15 favour: but the way of transgressors *is* **h**. H386
Isa 14: 3 fear, and from the **h** bondage wherein H7186
Jer 32:17 *and* there is nothing too **h** for thee: H6381
27 flesh: is there any thing too **h** for me? H6381
Ezk 3: 5 **h** language, *but* to the house of Israel; H3515
6 speech and of an **h** language, whose H3515
Dan 5:12 and shewing of **h** sentences, and H2802
Jna 1:13 Nevertheless the men rowed **h** to bring *it*
Mt 25:24 that thou art an **h** man, reaping where *G4642*
Mk 10:24 Children, how **h** is it for them that trust *G1422*
Jn 6:60 This is an **h** saying; who can hear it? *G4642*
Act 9: 5 *is* **h** for thee to kick against the pricks. *G4642*
18: 7 whose house joined **h** to the synagogue. *G2258*
26:14 *is* **h** for thee to kick against the pricks. *G4642*
Heb 5:11 things to say, and **h** to be uttered, *G1421*
2Pt 3:16 are some things **h** to be understood, *G1425*
Jude 15 and of all their **h** *speeches* which *G4642*

HARDEN
Ex 4:21 hand: but I will **h** his heart, that he H2388
7: 3 And I will **h** Pharaoh's heart, and H7185
14: 4 And I will **h** Pharaoh's heart, that he H2388
17 And I, behold, I will **h** the hearts of the H2388
Dt 15: 7 thou shalt not **h** thine heart, nor shut H553
Jos 11:20 For it was of the LORD to **h** their H2388
1Sa 6: 6 Wherefore then do ye **h** your hearts, as H3513
Job 6:10 yea, I would **h** myself in sorrow: let H5539
Ps 95: 8 H not your heart, as in the H7185
Heb 3: 8 H not your hearts, as in the *G4645*
15 will hear his voice, **h** not your hearts, *G4645*
4: 7 will hear his voice, **h** not your hearts. *G4645*

HARDENED
Ex 7:13 And he **h** Pharaoh's heart, that he H2388
14 *is* **h**, he refuseth to let the people go. H3515
22 heart was **h**, neither did he hearken H2388
8:15 there was respite, he **h** his heart, and H3513
19 heart was **h**, and he hearkened not H2388
32 And Pharaoh **h** his heart at this time H3513
9: 7 was **h**, and he did not let the people go. H3513
12 And the LORD **h** the heart of Pharaoh, H2388
34 and **h** his heart, he and his servants. H3513
35 And the heart of Pharaoh was **h**, neither H2388
10: 1 for I have **h** his heart, and the heart H3513
20 But the LORD **h** Pharaoh's heart, so H2388
27 But the LORD **h** Pharaoh's heart, and H2388
11:10 and the LORD **h** Pharaoh's heart, so H2388
14: 8 And the LORD **h** the heart of Pharaoh H2388
Dt 2:30 for the LORD thy God **h** his spirit, and H7185
1Sa 6: 6 and Pharaoh **h** their hearts? when he H3513
2Ki 17:14 not hear, but **h** their necks, like to the H7185
2Ch 36:13 his neck, and **h** his heart from turning H553
Neh 9:16 dealt proudly, and **h** their necks, and H7185
17 among them; but **h** their necks, and in H7185
29 and **h** their neck, and would not hear. H7185
Job 9: 4 who hath **h** *himself* against him, H7185
39:16 She is **h** against her young ones, as H7188
Isa 63:17 thy ways, *and* **h** our heart from thy H7188
Jer 7:26 their ear, but **h** their neck: they did H7185
19:15 it, because they have **h** their necks, that H7185
Dan 5:20 up, and his mind **h** in pride, he was H8631
Mk 6:52 of the loaves: for their heart was **h**. *G4456*
8:17 understand? have ye your heart yet **h**? *G4456*
Jn 12:40 He hath blinded their eyes, and **h** their *G4456*
Act 19: 9 But when divers were **h**, and believed *G4645*
Heb 3:13 be **h** through the deceitfulness of sin. *G4645*

HARDENETH
Prv 21:29 A wicked man **h** his face: but *as for* the H5810
28:14 that **h** his heart shall fall into mischief. H7185
29: 1 He, that being often reproved **h** *his* H7185
Ro 9:18 will *have mercy*, and whom he will he **h**. *G4645*

HARDER
Prv 18:19 A brother offended *is* **h** *to be won* than a
Jer 5: 3 made their faces **h** than a rock; they H2388
Ezk 3: 9 As an adamant **h** than flint have I H2389

HARDHEARTED
Ezk 3: 7 of Israel *are* impudent and **h**. H7186+H3820

HARDLY
Gen 16: 6 dealt **h** with her, she fled from her face. H6031
Ex 13:15 Pharaoh would **h** let us go, that the H7185
Isa 8:21 And they shall pass through it, **h** H7185
Mt 19:23 **h** enter into the kingdom of heaven. *G1423*
Mk 10:23 his disciples, How **h** shall they that *G1423*
Lk 9:39 bruising him **h** departeth from him. *G3425*
18:24 he said, How **h** shall they that have *G1423*
Act 27: 8 And, **h** passing it, came unto a place *G3433*

HARDNESS
Job 38:38 When the dust groweth into **h**, and the H4165
Mt 19: 8 because of the **h** of your hearts suffered G4641
Mk 3: 5 grieved for the **h** of their hearts, he G4457
10: 5 them, For the **h** of your heart he wrote G4641
16:14 their unbelief and **h** of heart, because G4641
Ro 2: 5 But after thy **h** and impenitent heart G4643
2Ti 2: 3 Thou therefore endure **h**, as a good G2553

HARE
Lev 11: 6 And the **h**, because he cheweth the cud, H768
Dt 14: 7 the camel, and the **h**, and the coney: for H768

HAREPH
1Ch 2:51 Salma the father of Beth-lehem, **H** the H2780

HARESHA See TEL-HARESHA.

HARETH
1Sa 22: 5 departed, and came into the forest of **H**. H2802

HARHAIAH
Neh 3: 8 Uzziel the son of **H**, of the goldsmiths. H2736

HARHAS
2Ki 22:14 of Tikvah, the son of **H**, keeper of the H2745

HARHUR
Ezr 2:51 children of Hakupha, the children of **H**, H2744
Neh 7:53 children of Hakupha, the children of **H**, H2744

HARIM
1Ch 24: 8 The third to **H**, the fourth to Seorim, H2766
Ezr 2:32 The children of **H**, three hundred and H2766
39 The children of **H**, a thousand and H2766
10:21 And of the sons of **H**; Maaseiah, and H2766
31 And *of* the sons of **H**; Eliezer, Ishijah, H2766
Neh 3:11 Malchijah the son of **H**, and Hashub the H2766
7:35 The children of **H**, three hundred and H2766
42 The children of **H**, a thousand and H2766
10: 5 **H**, Meremoth, Obadiah, H2766
27 Malluch, **H**, Baanah. H2766
12:15 Of **H**, Adna; of Meraioth, Helkai; H2766

HARIPH
Neh 7:24 The children of **H**, an hundred and H2756
10:19 **H**, Anathoth, Nebai, H2756

HARLOT
Gen 34:31 he deal with our sister as with an **h**? H2181
38:15 an **h**; because she had covered her face. H2181
21 Where *is* the **h**, that *was* openly by H6948
21 they said, There was no **h** in this *place*. H6948
22 said, *that* there was no **h** in this *place*. H6948
24 hath played the **h**; and also, behold, she H2181
Lev 21:14 or profane, *or* an **h**, these shall he not H2181
Jos 6:17 only Rahab the **h** shall live, she and all H2181
25 And Joshua saved Rahab the **h** alive, H2181
Jdg 11: 1 son of an **h**: and Gilead begat Jephthah. H2181
16: 1 saw there an **h**, and went in unto her. H2181
Prv 7:10 the attire of an **h**, and subtil of heart. H2181
Isa 1:21 How is the faithful city become an **h**! it H2181
23:15 of seventy years shall Tyre sing as an **h**. H2181
16 Take an harp, go about the city, thou **h** H2181
Jer 2:20 tree thou wanderest, playing the **h**. H2181
3: 1 hast played the **h** with many lovers; yet H2181
6 green tree, and there hath played the **h**. H2181
8 not, but went and played the **h** also. H2181
Ezk 16:15 and playedst the **h** because of thy H2181
16 and playedst the **h** thereupon: *the like* H2181
28 hast played the **h** with them, and yet H2181
31 been as an **h**, in that thou scornest hire; H2181
35 Wherefore, O **h**, hear the word of the H2181
41 from playing the **h**, and thou also shalt H2181
23: 5 And Aholah played the **h** when she was H2181
19 had played the **h** in the land of Egypt. H2181
44 that playeth the **h**: so went they in unto H2181
Hos 2: 5 For their mother hath played the **h**: she H2181
3: 3 shalt not play the **h**, and thou shalt not H2181
4:15 Though thou, Israel, play the **h**, *yet* let H2181
Joel 3: 3 given a boy for an **h**, and sold a girl for H2181
Am 7:17 wife shall be an **h** in the city, and thy H2181
Mic 1: 7 *it* of the hire of an **h**, and they shall H2181
7 and they shall return to the hire of an **h**. H2181
Nah 3: 4 of the wellfavoured **h**, the mistress of H2181
1Co 6:15 *them* the members of an **h**? God forbid. G4204
16 is joined to an **h** is one body? for two, G4204
Heb 11:31 By faith the **h** Rahab perished not with G4204
Jas 2:25 Likewise also was not Rahab the **h** G4204

HARLOTS
1Ki 3:16 **h**, unto the king, and stood before him. H2181
Prv 29: 3 with **h** spendeth *his* substance. H2181
Hos 4:14 and they sacrifice with **h**: therefore the H6948
Mt 21:31 the publicans and the **h** go into the G4204
32 publicans and the **h** believed him: and G4204
Lk 15:30 thy living with **h**, thou hast killed for G4204
Rev 17: 5 MOTHER OF **H** AND ABOMINATIONS G4204

HARLOT'S
Jos 2: 1 and came into an **h** house, named H2181
6:22 Go into the **h** house, and bring out H2181

HARLOTS'
Jer 5: 7 themselves by troops in the **h** houses. H2181

HARM
Gen 31:52 this heap and this pillar unto me, for **h**. H7451
Lev 5:16 And he shall make amends for the **h** H2398
Nu 35:23 not his enemy, neither sought his **h**: H7451
1Sa 26:21 will no more do thee **h**, because my soul H7489
2Sa 20: 6 Bichri do us more **h** than *did* Absalom: H3415
2Ki 4:41 And there was no **h** in the pot. H1697+H7451
1Ch 16:22 anointed, and do my prophets no **h**. H7489
Ps 105:15 anointed, and do my prophets no **h**. H7489
Prv 3:30 cause, if he have done thee no **h**. H7451
Jer 39:12 and do him no **h**; but do unto him even H7451
Act 16:28 Do thyself no **h**: for we are all here. G2556
27:21 and to have gained this **h** and loss. G5196
28: 5 off the beast into the fire, and felt no **h**. G2556
6 while, and saw no **h** come to him, they G824
21 came shewed or spake any **h** of thee. G4190
1Pt 3:13 And who *is* he that will **h** you, if ye be G2559

HARMLESS
Mt 10:16 wise as serpents, and **h** as doves. G185
Php 2:15 That ye may be blameless and **h**, the sons G185
Heb 7:26 us, *who is* holy, **h**, undefiled, separate G172

HARNEPHER
1Ch 7:36 The sons of Zophah; Suah, and **H**, and H2774

HARNESS
1Ki 20:11 *h* boast himself as he that putteth it off.
22:34 the joints of the **h**: wherefore he said H8302
2Ch 9:24 and raiment, **h**, and spices, horses, H5402
18:33 the joints of the **h**: therefore he said to H8302
Jer 46: 4 **H** the horses; and get up, ye horsemen, H631

HARNESSED
Ex 13:18 went up **h** out of the land of Egypt. H2571

HAROD
Jdg 7: 1 beside the well of **H**: so that the host of H5878

HARODITE
2Sa 23:25 Shammah the **H**, Elika the Harodite, H2733
25 Shammah the Harodite, Elika the **H**, H2733

HAROEH
1Ch 2:52 sons; **H**, *and* half of the Manahethites. H7204

HARORITE
1Ch 11:27 Shammoth the **H**, Helez the Pelonite, H2033

HAROSHETH
Jdg 4: 2 which dwelt in **H** of the Gentiles. H2800
13 with him, from **H** of the Gentiles unto H2800
16 the host, unto **H** of the Gentiles: and H2800

HARP
Gen 4:21 of all such as handle the **h** and organ. H3658
31:27 and with songs, with tabret, and with **h**? H3658
1Sa 10: 5 and a pipe, and a **h**, before them; and H3658
16:16 player on an **h**: and it shall come to H3658
23 David took an **h**, and played with his H3658
1Ch 25: 3 prophesied with a **h**, to give thanks and H3658
Job 21:12 They take the timbrel and **h**, and rejoice H3658
30:31 My **h** also is *turned* to mourning, and H3658
Ps 33: 2 Praise the LORD with **h**: sing unto him H3658
43: 4 the **h** will I praise thee, O God my God. H3658
49: 4 I will open my dark saying upon the **h**. H3658
57: 8 and **h**: I *myself* will awake early. H3658
71:22 with the **h**, O thou Holy One of Israel. H3658
81: 2 the pleasant **h** with the psaltery. H3658
92: 3 upon the **h** with a solemn sound. H3658
98: 5 Sing unto the LORD with the **h**; with the H3658
5 with the **h**, and the voice of a psalm. H3658
108: 2 Awake, psaltery and **h**: I *myself* will H3658
147: 7 sing praise upon the **h** unto our God: H3658
149: 3 unto him with the timbrel and **h**. H3658
150: 3 praise him with the psaltery and **h**. H3658
Isa 5:12 And the **h**, and the viol, the tabret, and H3658
16:11 sound like an **h** for Moab, and mine H3658
23:16 Take an **h**, go about the city, thou H3658
24: 8 rejoice endeth, the joy of the **h** ceaseth. H3658
Dan 3: 5 of the cornet, flute, **h**, sackbut, psaltery, H7030
7 of the cornet, flute, **h**, sackbut, psaltery, H7030
10 of the cornet, flute, **h**, sackbut, psaltery, H7030
15 of the cornet, flute, **h**, sackbut, psaltery, H7030
1Co 14: 7 whether pipe or **h**, except they give a G2788

HARPED
1Co 14: 7 shall it be known what is piped or **h**? G2789

HARPERS
Rev 14: 2 the voice of **h** harping with their harps: G2790
18:22 And the voice of **h**, and musicians, and G2790

HARPING
Rev 14: 2 the voice of harpers **h** with their harps: G2789

HARPS
2Sa 6: 5 fir wood, even on **h**, and on psalteries, H3658
1Ki 10:12 the king's house, **h** also and psalteries H3658
1Ch 13: 8 singing, and with **h**, and with psalteries, H3658
15:16 musick, psalteries and **h** and cymbals, H3658
21 with **h** on the Sheminith to excel. H3658
28 making a noise with psalteries and **h**. H3658
16: 5 and with **h**; but Asaph made a sound H3658
25: 1 prophesy with **h**, with psalteries, and H3658
6 psalteries, and **h**, for the service of the H3658
2Ch 5:12 and psalteries and **h**, stood at the east H3658
9:11 king's palace, and **h** and psalteries for H3658
20:28 psalteries and **h** and trumpets unto H3658
29:25 psalteries, and with **h**, according to the H3658
Neh 12:27 *with* cymbals, psalteries, and with **h**. H3658
Ps 137: 2 We hanged our **h** upon the willows in H3658
Isa 30:32 be with tabrets and **h**: and in battles of H3658
Ezk 26:13 sound of thy **h** shall be no more heard. H3658
Rev 5: 8 every one of them **h**, and golden vials G2788
14: 2 voice of harpers harping with their **h**: G2788
15: 2 on the sea of glass, having the **h** of God. G2788

HARROW
Job 39:10 or will he **h** the valleys after thee? H7702

HARROWS
2Sa 12:31 saws, and under **h** of iron, and under H2757
1Ch 20: 3 with saws, and with **h** of iron, and with H2757

HARSA See TEL-HARSA.

HARSHA
Ezr 2:52 children of Mehida, the children of **H**, H2797
Neh 7:54 children of Mehida, the children of **H**, H2797

HART
Dt 12:15 as of the roebuck, and as of the **h**. H354
22 Even as the roebuck and the **h** is eaten, H354
14: 5 The **h**, and the roebuck, and the fallow H354
15:22 *eat it* alike, as the roebuck, and as the **h**. H354
Ps 42: 1 As the **h** panteth after the water brooks, H354
Song 2: 9 My beloved is like a roe or a young **h**: H354
17 young **h** upon the mountains of Bether. H354
8:14 a young **h** upon the mountains of spices. H354
Isa 35: 6 Then shall the lame *man* leap as an **h**, H354

HARTS
1Ki 4:23 sheep, beside **h**, and roebucks, and H354
Lam 1: 6 are become like **h** *that* find no pasture, H354

HARUM
1Ch 4: 8 the families of Aharhel the son of **H**. H2037

HARUMAPH
Neh 3:10 Jedaiah the son of **H**, even over against H2739

HARUPHITE
1Ch 12: 5 and Shemariah, and Shephatiah the **H**, H2741

HARUZ
2Ki 21:19 the daughter of **H** of Jotbah. H2743

HARVEST
Gen 8:22 seedtime and **h**, and cold and heat, H7105
30:14 in the days of wheat **h**, and found H7105
45: 6 *there shall* neither *be* earing nor **h**. H7105

Ex 23:16 And the feast of **h**, the firstfruits of thy H7105
34:21 in earing time and in **h** thou shalt rest. H7105
22 of wheat **h**, and the feast of ingathering H7105
Lev 19: 9 And when ye reap the **h** of your land, H7105
9 shalt thou gather the gleanings of thy **h**. H7105
23:10 and shall reap the **h** thereof, then ye H7105
10 the firstfruits of your **h** unto the priest: H7105
22 And when ye reap the **h** of your land, H7105
22 gleaning of thy **h**: thou shalt leave them H7105
25: 5 its own accord of thy **h** thou shalt not H7105
Dt 24:19 When thou cuttest down thine **h** in thy H7105
Jos 3:15 all his banks all the time of **h**,) H7105
Jdg 15: 1 in the time of wheat **h**, that Samson H7105
Ru 1:22 in the beginning of barley **h**. H7105
2:21 men, until they have ended all my **h**. H7105
23 unto the end of barley **h** and of wheat H7105
23 **h**; and dwelt with her mother in law. H7105
1Sa 6:13 their wheat **h** in the valley: and they H7105
8:12 and to reap his **h**, and to make his H7105
12:17 *Is it* not wheat **h** to day? I will call unto H7105
2Sa 21: 9 in the days of **h**, in the first *days*, in H7105
9 first *days*, in the beginning of barley **h**. H7105
10 the beginning of **h** until water dropped H7105
23:13 to David in the **h** time unto the cave of H7105
Job 5: 5 Whose **h** the hungry eateth up, and H7105
Prv 6: 8 *and* gathereth her food in the **h**. H7105
10: 5 in **h** *is* a son that causeth shame. H7105
20: 4 shall he beg in **h**, and *have* nothing. H7105
25:13 As the cold of snow in the time of **h**, *so* H7105
26: 1 As snow in summer, and as rain in **h**, H7105
Isa 9: 3 to the joy in **h**, *and* as *men* rejoice H7105
16: 9 summer fruits and for thy **h** is fallen. H7105
17:11 to flourish: *but* the **h** *shall be* a heap in H7105
18: 4 *and* like a cloud of dew in the heat of **h**. H7105
5 For afore the **h**, when the bud is perfect, H7105
23: 3 seed of Sihor, the **h** of the river, *is* her H7105
Jer 5:17 And they shall eat up thine **h**, and thy H7105
24 unto us the appointed weeks of the **h**. H7105
8:20 The **h** is past, the summer is ended, H7105
50:16 sickle in the time of **h**: for fear of the H7105
51:33 while, and the time of her **h** shall come. H7105
Hos 6:11 Also, O Judah, he hath set an **h** for H7105
Joel 1:11 because the **h** of the field is perished. H7105
3:13 Put ye in the sickle, for the **h** is ripe: H7105
Am 4: 7 months to the **h**: and I caused it to rain H7105
Mt 9:37 Then saith he unto his disciples, The **h** G2326
38 Pray ye therefore the Lord of the **h**, that G2326
38 he will send forth labourers into his **h**. G2326
13:30 Let both grow together until the **h**: and G2326
30 and in the time of **h** I will say to the G2326
39 them is the devil; the **h** is the end of the G2326
Mk 4:29 in the sickle, because the **h** is come. G2326
Lk 10: 2 Therefore said he unto them, The **h** G2326
2 the Lord of the **h**, that he would send G2326
2 would send forth labourers into his **h**. G2326
Jn 4:35 and *then* cometh **h**? behold, I say unto G2326
35 fields; for they are white already to **h**. G2326
Rev 14:15 to reap; for the **h** of the earth is ripe. G2326

HARVESTMAN
Isa 17: 5 And it shall be as when the **h** gathereth H7105
Jer 9:22 after the **h**, and none shall gather *them*. H7114

HASADIAH
1Ch 3:20 Berechiah, and **H**, Jushabhesed, five. H2619

HASENUAH
1Ch 9: 7 the son of Hodaviah, the son of **H**, H5574

HASHABIAH
1Ch 6:45 The son of **H**, the son of Amaziah, the H2811
9:14 the son of **H**, of the sons of Merari; H2811
25: 3 and Jeshaiah, **H**, and Mattithiah, six, H2811
19 The twelfth to **H**, *he*, his sons, and his H2811
26:30 *And* of the Hebronites, **H** and his H2811
27:17 Of the Levites, **H** the son of Kemuel: of H2811
2Ch 35: 9 his brethren, and **H** and Jeiel and H2811
Ezr 8:19 And **H**, and with him Jeshaiah of the H2811
24 **H**, and ten of their brethren with them, H2811
Neh 3:17 unto him repaired **H**, the ruler of the H2811
10:11 Micha, Rehob, **H**, H2811
11:15 the son of **H**, the son of Bunni; H2811
22 son of Bani, the son of **H**, the son of H2811
12:21 Of Hilkiah, **H**; of Jedaiah, Nethaneel. H2811
24 And the chief of the Levites: **H**, H2811

HASHABNAH
Neh 10:25 Rehum, **H**, Maaseiah, H2812

HASHABNIAH
Neh 3:10 him repaired Hattush the son of **H**. H2813
9: 5 Kadmiel, Bani, **H**, Sherebiah, Hodijah, H2813

HASHBADANA
Neh 8: 4 and **H**, Zechariah, *and* Meshullam. H2806

HASHEM
1Ch 11:34 The sons of **H** the Gizonite, Jonathan H2044

HASHMONAH
Nu 33:29 went from Mithcah, and pitched in **H**. H2832
30 And they departed from **H**, and H2832

HASHUB
Neh 3:11 Malchijah the son of Harim, and **H** the H2815
23 After him repaired Benjamin and **H** H2815
10:23 Hoshea, Hananiah, **H**, H2815
11:15 the son of **H**, the son of Azrikam, H2815

HASHUBAH
1Ch 3:20 And **H**, and Ohel, and Berechiah, and H2807

HASHUM
Ezr 2:19 The children of **H**, two hundred twenty H2828
10:33 Of the sons of **H**; Mattenai, Mattathah, H2828
Neh 7:22 The children of **H**, three hundred H2828
8: 4 Malchiah, and **H**, and Hashbadana, H2828
10:18 Hodijah, **H**, Bezai, H2828

HASHUPHA
Neh 7:46 children of **H**, the children of Tabbaoth, H2817

HASRAH
2Ch 34:22 the son of **H**, keeper of the wardrobe; H2641

HASSENAAH
Neh 3: 3 But the fish gate did the sons of **H** H5570

HASSHUB
1Ch 9:14 the son of **H**, the son of Azrikam, H2815

HAST
See the Appendix.

HASTE
Gen 19:22 **H** thee, escape thither; for I cannot do H4116
24:46 And she made **h**, and let down her H4116
43:30 And Joseph made **h**; for his bowels did H4116
45: 9 **H** ye, and go up to my father, and say H4116
13 **h** and bring down my father hither. H4116
Ex 10:16 and Aaron in **h**; and he said, I have H4116
12:11 eat it in **h**: it *is* the LORD'S passover. H2649
33 in **h**; for they said, We *be* all dead *men*. H4116
34: 8 And Moses made **h**, and bowed his H4116
Dt 16: 3 the land of Egypt in **h**: that thou mayest H2649
32:35 that shall come upon them make **h**. H2363
Jdg 9:48 me do, make **h**, *and* do as I *have done*. H4116
13:10 And the woman made **h**, and ran, and H4116
1Sa 9:12 before you: make **h** now, for he came to H4116
20:38 the lad, Make speed, **h**, stay not. And H2363
21: 8 because the king's business required **h**. H5169
23:26 and David made **h** to get away for fear H2648
27 unto Saul, saying, **H** thee, and come; H4116
25:18 Then Abigail made **h**, and took two H4116
2Sa 4: 4 pass, as she made **h** to flee, that he fell, H2648
2Ki 7:15 had cast away in their **h**. And the H2648
2Ch 35:21 me to make **h**: forbear thee from H926
Ezr 4:23 they went up in **h** to Jerusalem unto the H924
Est 5: 5 Haman to make **h**, that he may do as H4116
6:10 Then the king said to Haman, Make **h**, H4116
Job 20: 2 me to answer, and for *this* I make **h**. H2363
Ps 22:19 O my strength, **h** thee to help me. H2363
31:22 For I said in my **h**, I am cut off from H2648
38:22 Make **h** to help me, O Lord my H2363
40:13 me: O LORD, make **h** to help me. H2363
70: 1 *Make* **h**, O God, to deliver me; make
1 me; make **h** to help me, O LORD. H2363
5 But I *am* poor and needy: make **h** unto H2363
71:12 me: O my God, make **h** for my help. H2439
116:11 I said in my **h**, All men *are* liars. H2648
119:60 I made **h**, and delayed not to keep thy H2363
141: 1 LORD, I cry unto thee: make **h** unto H2363
Prv 1:16 For their feet run to evil, and make **h** to H4116
28:20 **h** to be rich shall not be innocent. H213
Song 8:14 Make **h**, my beloved, and be thou like to H1272
Isa 28:16 he that believeth shall not make **h**. H2363
49:17 Thy children shall make **h**; thy H4116
52:12 For ye shall not go out with **h**, nor go by H2649
59: 7 Their feet run to evil, and they make **h** H4116
Jer 9:18 And let them make **h**, and take up a H4116
Dan 2:25 before the king in **h**, and said thus unto H927
3:24 and rose up in **h**, *and* spake, and said H927
6:19 and went in **h** unto the den of lions. H927
Nah 2: 5 they shall make **h** to the wall thereof, H4116
Mk 6:25 And she came in straightway with **h** G4710
Lk 1:39 hill country with **h**, into a city of Juda; G4710
2:16 And they came with **h**, and found Mary, G4692
19: 5 Zacchaeus, make **h**, and come down; G4692
6 And he made **h**, and came down, and G4692
Act 22:18 And saw him saying unto me, Make **h**, G4692

HASTED
Gen 18: 7 unto a young man; and he **h** to dress it. H4116
24:18 my lord: and she **h**, and let down her H4116
20 And she **h**, and emptied her pitcher into H4116
Ex 5:13 And the taskmasters **h** *them*, saying, H213
Jos 4:10 and the people **h** and passed over. H4116
8:14 Ai saw *it*, that they **h** and rose up early, H4116
19 took it, and **h** and set the city on fire. H4116
10:13 and **h** not to go down about a whole day. H213
Jdg 20:37 And the liers in wait **h**, and rushed H2363
1Sa 17:48 David, that David **h**, and ran toward H4116
25:23 And when Abigail saw David, she **h**, H4116
34 except thou hadst **h** and come to meet H4116
42 And Abigail **h**, and arose, and rode H4116
28:24 the house; and she **h**, and killed it, and H4116
2Sa 19:16 *was* of Bahurim, **h** and came down H4116
1Ki 20:41 And he **h**, and took the ashes away H4116
2Ki 9:13 Then they **h**, and took every man his H4116
2Ch 26:20 yea, himself **h** also to go out, because H1765
Est 6:12 king's gate. But Haman **h** to his house H1765
14 chamberlains, and **h** to bring Haman H926
Job 31: 5 vanity, or if my foot hath **h** to deceit; H2363
Ps 48: 5 they were troubled, *and* **h** away. H2648
104: 7 at the voice of thy thunder they **h** away. H2648
Act 20:16 in Asia: for he **h**, if it were possible for G4692

HASTEN
1Ki 22: 9 **H** *hither* Micaiah the son of Imlah. H4116
2Ch 24: 5 and see that ye **h** the matter. Howbeit H4116
Ps 16: 4 be multiplied *that* **h** *after* another *god*: H4116
55: 8 I would **h** my escape from the windy H2363
Ecc 2:25 For who can eat, or who else can **h** H2363
Isa 5:19 That say, Let him make speed, *and* **h** H2363
60:22 nation: I the LORD will **h** it in his time. H2363
Jer 1:12 seen: for I will **h** my word to perform it. H8245

HASTENED
Gen 18: 6 And Abraham **h** into the tent unto H4116
19:15 then the angels **h** Lot, saying, Arise, take H213
2Ch 24: 5 matter. Howbeit the Levites **h** *it* not. H4116
Est 3:15 The posts went out, being **h** by the H1765
8:14 went out, being **h** and pressed on by the H926
Jer 17:16 As for me, I have not **h** from *being* a H213

HASTENETH
Isa 51:14 The captive exile **h** that he may be H4116

HASTETH
Job 9:26 ships: as the eagle *that* **h** to the prey. H2907
40:23 Behold, he drinketh up a river, *and* **h** H2648
Prv 7:23 his liver; as a bird **h** to the snare, and H4116
19: 2 good; and he that **h** with *his* feet sinneth. H213
28:22 He that **h** to be rich *hath* an evil eye, and H926
Ecc 1: 5 and **h** to his place where he arose. H7602
Jer 48:16 near to come, and his affliction **h** fast. H4116
Hab 1: 8 they shall fly as the eagle *that* **h** to eat. H2363
Zep 1:14 *it is* near, and **h** greatly, *even* the voice H4118

HASTILY
Gen 41:14 they brought him **h** out of the dungeon: H7323
Jdg 2:23 driving them out **h**; neither delivered he H4118
9:54 Then he called **h** unto the young man H4120
1Sa 4:14 And the man came in **h**, and told Eli. H4116
1Ki 20:33 from him, and did **h** catch *it*: and they H4116
Prv 20:21 An inheritance *may be* gotten **h** at the H973
25: 8 Go not forth **h** to strive, lest *thou know* H4118
Jn 11:31 Mary, that she rose up **h** and went out, G5030

HASTING
Isa 16: 5 judgment, and **h** righteousness. H4106
2Pt 3:12 Looking for and **h** unto the coming of G4692

HASTY
Prv 14:29 but *he that is* **h** of spirit exalteth folly. H7116
21: 5 but of every one *that is* **h** only to want. H213
29:20 Seest thou a man *that is* **h** in his words? H213
Ecc 5: 2 not thine heart be **h** to utter *any* thing H4116

Ecc 7: 9 Be not **h** in thy spirit to be angry: for H926
8: 3 Be not **h** to go out of his sight: stand not H926
Isa 28: 4 flower, *and* as the **h** fruit before the H1061
Dan 2:15 *is* the decree *so* **h** from the king? Then H2685
Hab 1: 6 *that* bitter and **h** nation, which shall H4116

HASUPHA
Ezr 2:43 children of **H**, the children of Tabbaoth, H2817

HATACH
Est 4: 5 Then called Esther for **H**, *one* of the H2047
6 So **H** went forth to Mordecai unto the H2047
9 And **H** came and told Esther the words H2047
10 Again Esther spake unto **H**, and gave H2047

HATCH
Isa 34:15 nest, and lay, and **h**, and gather under H1234
59: 5 They **h** cockatrice' eggs, and weave the H1234

HATCHETH
Jer 17:11 *As* the partridge sitteth *on eggs*, and **h** H3205

HATE
Gen 24:60 possess the gate of those which **h** them. H8130
26:27 ye to me, seeing ye **h** me, and have sent H8130
50:15 Joseph will peradventure **h** us, and will H7852
Ex 20: 5 fourth *generation* of them that **h** me; H8130
Lev 19:17 Thou shalt not **h** thy brother in thine H8130
26:17 enemies: they that **h** you shall reign H8130
Nu 10:35 let them that **h** thee flee before thee. H8130
Dt 5: 9 fourth *generation* of them that **h** me, H8130
7:10 And repayeth them that **h** him to their H8130
15 will lay them upon all *them* that **h** thee. H8130
19:11 But if any man **h** his neighbour, and lie H8130
22:13 a wife, and go in unto her, and **h** her, H8130
24: 3 And *if* the latter husband **h** her, and H8130
30: 7 that **h** thee, which persecuted thee. H8130
32:41 and will reward them that **h** me. H8130
33:11 that **h** him, that they rise not again. H8130
Jdg 11: 7 Gilead, Did not ye **h** me, and expel me H8130
14:16 Thou dost but **h** me, and lovest me not: H8130
2Sa 22:41 that I might destroy them that **h** me. H8130
1Ki 22: 8 of the LORD: but I **h** him; for he doth H8130
2Ch 18: 7 of the LORD: but I **h** him; for he never H8130
19: 2 love them that **h** the LORD? therefore H8130
Job 8:22 They that **h** thee shall be clothed with H8130
Ps 9:13 of them that **h** me, thou that liftest H8130
18:40 that I might destroy them that **h** me. H8130
21: 8 hand shall find out those that **h** thee. H8130
25:19 many; and they **h** me with cruel hatred. H8130
34:21 that **h** the righteous shall be desolate. H8130
35:19 with the eye that **h** me without a cause. H8130
38:19 that **h** me wrongfully are multiplied. H8130
41: 7 All that **h** me whisper together against H8130
44:10 they which **h** us spoil for themselves. H8130
55: 3 upon me, and in wrath they **h** me. H7852
68: 1 them also that **h** him flee before him. H8130
69: 4 They that **h** me without a cause are H8130
14 that **h** me, and out of the deep waters. H8130
83: 2 they that **h** thee have lifted up the head. H8130
86:17 that they which **h** me may see *it*, and H8130
89:23 his face, and plague them that **h** him. H8130
97:10 Ye that love the LORD, **h** evil: he H8130
101: 3 mine eyes: I **h** the work of them that H8130
105:25 He turned their heart to **h** his people, to H8130
118: 7 I see *my desire* upon them that **h** me. H8130
119:104 therefore I **h** every false way. H8130
113 I **h** *vain* thoughts: but thy law do I love. H8130
128 *to be* right; *and* I **h** every false way. H8130
163 I **h** and abhor lying: *but* thy law do I H8130
129: 5 and turned back that **h** Zion. H8130
139:21 Do not I **h** them, O LORD, that hate H8130
21 Do not I hate them, O LORD, that **h** H8130
22 I **h** them with perfect hatred: I count H8130
Prv 1:22 their scorning, and fools **h** knowledge? H8130
6:16 These six *things* doth the LORD **h**: yea, H8130
8:13 The fear of the LORD *is* to **h** evil: pride, H8130
13 way, and the froward mouth, do I **h**. H8130
36 own soul: all they that **h** me love death. H8130
9: 8 Reprove not a scorner, lest he **h** thee: H8130
19: 7 All the brethren of the poor do **h** him: H8130
25:17 lest he be weary of thee, and *so* **h** thee. H8130
29:10 The bloodthirsty **h** the upright: but the H8130
Ecc 3: 8 A time to love, and a time to **h**; a time of H8130
Isa 61: 8 For I the LORD love judgment, I **h** H8130
Jer 44: 4 do not this abominable thing that I **h**. H8130
Ezk 16:27 will of them that **h** thee, the daughters H8130
Dan 4:19 dream *be* to them that **h** thee, and the H8131
Am 5:10 They **h** him that rebuketh in the gate, H8130
Am 5:15 **H** the evil, and love the good, and H8130
21 I **h**, I despise your feast days, and I will H8130
6: 8 of Jacob, and **h** his palaces: therefore H8130
Mic 3: 2 Who **h** the good, and love the evil; who H8130
Zec 8:17 *are things* that I **h**, saith the LORD. H8130
Mt 5:43 love thy neighbour, and **h** thine enemy. G3404
44 good to them that **h** you, and pray for G3404
6:24 for either he will **h** the one, and love the G3404
24:10 one another, and shall **h** one another. G3404
Lk 1:71 and from the hand of all that **h** us; G3404
6:22 Blessed are ye, when men shall **h** you, G3404
27 enemies, do good to them which **h** you, G3404
14:26 If any *man* come to me, and **h** not his G3404
16:13 for either he will **h** the one, and love the G3404
Jn 7: 7 The world cannot **h** you; but me it G3404
15:18 If the world **h** you, ye know that it G3404
Ro 7:15 that do I not; but what I **h**, that do I. G3404
1Jn 3:13 Marvel not, my brethren, if the world **h** G3404
Rev 2: 6 deeds of the Nicolaitans, which I also **h**. G3404
15 of the Nicolaitans, which thing I **h**. G3404
17:16 the beast, these shall **h** the whore, and G3404

HATED
Gen 27:41 And Esau **h** Jacob because of the H7852
29:31 saw that Leah *was* **h**, he opened her H8130
33 heard that I *was* **h**, he hath therefore H8130
37: 4 his brethren, they **h** him, and could not H8130
5 brethren: and they **h** him yet the more. H8130
8 over us? And they **h** him yet the more H8130
49:23 him, and shot *at him*, and **h** him: H7852
Dt 1:27 said, Because the LORD **h** us, he hath H8135
4:42 unawares, and **h** him not in times past; H8130
9:28 them, and because he **h** them, he hath H8135
19: 4 whom he **h** not in time past; H8130
6 inasmuch as he **h** him not in time past. H8130
21:15 and another **h**, and they have born H8130
15 beloved and the **h**; and *if* the firstborn H8130
15 *if* the firstborn son be hers that was **h**: H8146
16 of the **h**, *which is indeed* the firstborn: H8130
17 the son of the **h** *for* the firstborn, by H8130
Jos 20: 5 unwittingly, and **h** him not beforetime. H8130
Jdg 15: 2 thou hadst utterly **h** her; therefore I H8130
2Sa 5: 8 the blind, *that are* **h** of David's soul, *he* H8130
13:15 Then Amnon **h** her exceedingly; so that H8130
15 wherewith he **h** her *was* greater than H8130
22 bad: for Absalom **h** Amnon, because he H8130
22:18 **h** me: for they were too strong for me. H8130
Est 9: 1 Jews had rule over them that **h** them;) H8130
5 they would unto those that **h** them. H8130
Job 31:29 of him that **h** me, or lifted up myself H8130
Ps 18:17 **h** me: for they were too strong for me. H8130
26: 5 I have **h** the congregation of evil doers; H8130
31: 6 I have **h** them that regard lying H8130
44: 7 and hast put them to shame that **h** us. H8130
55:12 *was it* he that **h** me *that* did magnify H8130
106:10 the hand of him that **h** *them*, and H8130
41 and they that **h** them ruled over them. H8130
Prv 1:29 For that they **h** knowledge, and did not H8130
5:12 And say, How have I **h** instruction, and H8130
14:17 and a man of wicked devices is **h**. H8130
20 The poor is **h** even of his own H8130
Ecc 2:17 Therefore I **h** life; because the work H8130
18 Yea, I **h** all my labour which I had H8130
Isa 60:15 been forsaken and **h**, so that no man H8130
66: 5 brethren that **h** you, that cast you out H8130
Jer 12: 8 out against me: therefore have I **h** it. H8130
Ezk 16:37 that thou hast **h**; I will even gather them H8130
35: 6 **h** blood, even blood shall pursue thee. H8130
Hos 9:15 in Gilgal: for there I **h** them: for the H8130
Mal 1: 3 And I **h** Esau, and laid his mountains H8130
Mt 10:22 And ye shall be **h** of all *men* for my G3404
24: 9 be **h** of all nations for my name's sake. G3404
Mk 13:13 And ye shall be **h** of all *men* for my G3404
Lk 19:14 But his citizens **h** him, and sent a G3404
21:17 And ye shall be **h** of all *men* for my G3404
Jn 15:18 If the world hate you, ye know that it **h** G3404
18 ye know that it hated me before *it* **h** you.
24 seen and **h** both me and my Father. G3404
25 their law, They **h** me without a cause. G3404
17:14 the world hath **h** them, because they G3404
Ro 9:13 Jacob have I loved, but Esau have I **h**. G3404
Eph 5:29 For no man ever yet **h** his own flesh; G3404
Heb 1: 9 Thou hast loved righteousness, and **h** G3404

HATEFUL
Ps 36: 2 eyes, until his iniquity be found to be **h**. H8130
Tit 3: 3 and envy, **h**, *and* hating one another. G4767
Rev 18: 2 and a cage of every unclean and **h** bird. G3404

HATEFULLY
Ezk 23:29 And they shall deal with thee **h**, and H8135

HATERS
Ps 81:15 The **h** of the LORD should have H8130
Ro 1:30 Backbiters, **h** of God, despiteful, proud, G2319

HATEST
2Sa 19: 6 enemies, and **h** thy friends. For thou H8130
Ps 5: 5 thy sight: thou **h** all workers of iniquity. H8130
45: 7 Thou lovest righteousness, and **h** H8130
50:17 Seeing thou **h** instruction, and castest H8130
Ezk 23:28 *of them* whom thou **h**, into the hand *of* H8130
Rev 2: 6 But this thou hast, that thou **h** the G3404

HATETH
Ex 23: 5 If thou see the ass of him that **h** thee H8130
Dt 7:10 **h** him, he will repay him to his face. H8130
12:31 LORD, which he **h**, have they done unto H8130
16:22 *any* image; which the LORD thy God **h**. H8130
22:16 unto this man to wife, and he **h** her; H8130
Job 16: 9 He teareth *me* in his wrath, who **h** me: H7852
34:17 Shall even he that **h** right govern? and H8130
Ps 11: 5 and him that loveth violence his soul **h**. H8130
120: 6 hath long dwelt with him that **h** peace. H8130
Prv 11:15 *for it*: and he that **h** suretiship is sure. H8130
12: 1 but he that **h** reproof *is* brutish. H8130
13: 5 A righteous *man* **h** lying: but a wicked H8130
24 He that spareth his rod **h** his son: but H8130
15:10 way: *and* he that **h** reproof shall die. H8130
27 own house; but he that **h** gifts shall live. H8130
26:24 He that **h** dissembleth with his lips, H8130
28 A lying tongue **h** *those that are* afflicted H8130
28:16 **h** covetousness shall prolong *his* days. H8130
29:24 Whoso is partner with a thief **h** his own H8130
Isa 1:14 feasts my soul **h**: they are a trouble unto H8130
Mal 2:16 saith that he **h** putting away: for *one* H8130
Jn 3:20 For every one that doeth evil **h** the G3404
7: 7 The world cannot hate you; but me it **h**, G3404
12:25 lose it; and he that **h** his life in this G3404
15:19 of the world, therefore the world **h** you. G3404
23 He that **h** me hateth my Father also. G3404
23 He that hateth me **h** my Father also. G3404
1Jn 2: 9 He that saith he is in the light, and **h** G3404
11 But he that **h** his brother is in darkness, G3404
3:15 Whosoever **h** his brother is a murderer: G3404
4:20 If a man say, I love God, and **h** his G3404

HATH See the Appendix.

HATHATH
1Ch 4:13 and Seraiah: and the sons of Othniel; **H**. H2867

HATING
Ex 18:21 God, men of truth, **h** covetousness; and H8130
Tit 3: 3 and envy, hateful, *and* **h** one another. G3404
Jude 23 out of the fire; **h** even the garment G3404

HATIPHA
Ezr 2:54 children of Neziah, the children of **H**. H2412
Neh 7:56 children of Neziah, the children of **H**. H2412

HATITA
Ezr 2:42 the children of **H**, the children of H2410
Neh 7:45 the children of **H**, the children of H2410

HATRED
Nu 35:20 But if he thrust him of **h**, or hurl at him H8135
2Sa 13:15 so that the **h** wherewith he hated H8135
Ps 25:19 many; and they hate me with cruel **h**. H8135
109: 3 about also with words of **h**; and fought H8135
5 me evil for good, and **h** for my love. H8135
139:22 I hate them with perfect **h**: I count them H8135
Prv 10:12 **H** stirreth up strifes: but love covereth H8135
18 He that hideth **h** *with* lying lips, and he H8135
15:17 is, than a stalled ox and **h** therewith. H8135
26:26 *Whose* **h** is covered by deceit, his H8135
Ecc 9: 1 love or **h** *by* all *that is* before them. H8135
6 Also their love, and their **h**, and their H8135
Ezk 25:15 heart, to destroy *it* for the old **h**; H342
35: 5 Because thou hast had a perpetual **h**, and H342
11 used out of thy **h** against them; and I H8135
Hos 9: 7 of thine iniquity, and the great **h**. H4895
8 his ways, *and* **h** in the house of his God. H4895
Gal 5:20 Idolatry, witchcraft, **h**, variance, G2189

HATS
Dan 3:21 their hosen, and their **h**, and their *other* H3737

HATTAAVAH See KIBROTH-HATTAAVAH.

HATTICON See HAZAR-HATTICON.

HATTIL
Ezr 2:57 the children of **H**, the children of H2411
Neh 7:59 the children of **H**, the children of H2411

HATTUSH
1Ch 3:22 the sons of Shemaiah; **H**, and Igeal, and H2407
Ezr 8: 2 Daniel: of the sons of David; **H**. H2407
Neh 3:10 him repaired **H** the son of Hashabniah. H2407
10: 4 **H**, Shebaniah, Malluch, H2407
12: 2 Amariah, Malluch, **H**, H2407

HAUGHTILY
Mic 2: 3 shall ye go **h**: for this time *is* evil. H7317

HAUGHTINESS
Isa 2:11 be humbled, and the **h** of men shall be H7312
17 down, and the **h** of men shall be made H7312
13:11 and will lay low the **h** of the terrible. H1346
16: 6 proud: *even* of his **h**, and his pride, and H1346
Jer 48:29 and his pride, and the **h** of his heart. H7312

HAUGHTY
2Sa 22:28 **h**, *that* thou mayest bring *them* down. H7311
Ps 131: 1 LORD, my heart is not **h**, nor mine eyes H1361
Prv 16:18 and an **h** spirit before a fall. H1363
18:12 is **h**, and before honour *is* humility. H1361
21:24 Proud *and* **h** scorner *is* his name, who H3093
Isa 3:16 of Zion are **h**, and walk with stretched H1361
10:33 down, and the **h** shall be humbled. H1364
24: 4 the **h** people of the earth do languish. H4791
Ezk 16:50 And they were **h**, and committed H1361
Zep 3:11 be **h** because of my holy mountain. H1361

HAUNT
1Sa 23:22 place where his **h** is, *and* who hath seen H7272
30:31 himself and his men were wont to **h**. H1980
Ezk 26:17 cause their terror *to be* on all that **h** it! H3427

HAURAN
Ezk 47:16 which *is* by the coast of H. H2362
18 measure from **H**, and from Damascus, H2362

HAVE See the Appendix.

HAVEN
Gen 49:13 Zebulun shall dwell at the **h** of the sea; H2348
13 he *shall be* for an **h** of ships; and his H2348
Ps 107:30 he bringeth them unto their desired **h**. H4231
Act 27:12 And because the **h** was not *G3040*
12 *which is* an **h** of Crete, and lieth toward *G3040*

HAVENS
Act 27: 8 **h**; nigh whereunto was the city *of* Lasea. *G3040*

HAVILAH
Gen 2:11 the whole land of **H**, where *there is* gold; H2341
10: 7 And the sons of Cush; Seba, and **H**, and H2341
29 And Ophir, and **H**, and Jobab: all these H2341
25:18 And they dwelt from **H** unto Shur, that H2341
1Sa 15: 7 And Saul smote the Amalekites from **H** H2341
1Ch 1: 9 And the sons of Cush; Seba, and **H**, and H2341
23 And Ophir, and **H**, and Jobab. All these H2341

HAVING See the Appendix.

HAVOCK
Act 8: 3 As for Saul, he made **h** of the church, *G3075*

HAVOTH-JAIR
Nu 32:41 small towns thereof, and called them **H**. H2334
Jdg 10: 4 which are called **H** unto this day, which H2334

HAWK
Lev 11:16 And the owl, and the night **h**, and the H8464
16 the cuckow, and the **h** after his kind, H5322
Dt 14:15 And the owl, and the night **h**, and the H8464
15 the cuckow, and the **h** after his kind, H5322
Job 39:26 Doth the **h** fly by thy wisdom, *and* H5322

HAY
Prv 27:25 The **h** appeareth, and the tender grass H2682
Isa 15: 6 be desolate: for the **h** is withered away, H2682
1Co 3:12 precious stones, wood, **h**, stubble; *G5528*

HAZAEL
1Ki 19:15 comest, anoint **H** *to be* king over Syria: H2371
17 the sword of **H** shall Jehu slay: and H2371
2Ki 8: 8 And the king said unto **H**, Take a H2371
9 So **H** went to meet him, and took a H2371
12 And **H** said, Why weepeth my lord? H2371
13 And **H** said, But what, *is* thy servant a H2371
15 he died: and **H** reigned in his stead. H2371
28 to the war against **H** king of Syria in H2371
29 he fought against **H** king of Syria. And H2371
9:14 all Israel, because of **H** king of Syria. H2371
15 he fought with **H** king of Syria.) And H2371
10:32 **H** smote them in all the coasts of Israel; H2371
12:17 Then **H** king of Syria went up, and H2371
17 **H** set his face to go up to Jerusalem. H2371
18 and sent *it* to **H** king of Syria: and he H2371
13: 3 into the hand of **H** king of Syria, and H2371
3 Ben-hadad the son of **H**, all *their* days. H2371
22 But **H** king of Syria oppressed Israel all H2371
24 So **H** king of Syria died; and H2371
25 the son of **H** the cities, which he H2371
2Ch 22: 5 Israel to war against **H** king of Syria at H2371
6 he fought with **H** king of Syria. And H2371
Am 1: 4 But I will send a fire into the house of **H**, H2371

HAZAIAH
Neh 11: 5 the son of **H**, the son of Adaiah, the H2382

HAZAR-ADDAR
Nu 34: 4 shall go on to **H**, and pass on to Azmon: H2692

HAZARDED
Act 15:26 Men that have **h** their lives for the *G3860*

HAZAR-ENAN
Nu 34: 9 be at **H**: this shall be your north border. H2704
10 your east border from **H** to Shepham: H2704
Ezk 47:17 And the border from the sea shall be **H**, H2703
48: 1 one goeth to Hamath, **H**, the border of H2704

HAZAR-GADDAH
Jos 15:27 And **H**, and Heshmon, and Beth-palet, H2693

HAZAR-HATTICON
Ezk 47:16 **H**, which *is* by the coast of Hauran. H2694

HAZARMAVETH
Gen 10:26 and Sheleph, and **H**, and Jerah, H2700
1Ch 1:20 and Sheleph, and **H**, and Jerah, H2700

HAZAR-SHUAL
Jos 15:28 And **H**, and Beer-sheba, and Bizjothjah, H2705
19: 3 And **H**, and Balah, and Azem, H2705
1Ch 4:28 at Beer-sheba, and Moladah, and **H**, H2705
Neh 11:27 And at **H**, and at Beer-sheba, and *in* the H2705

HAZAR-SUSAH
Jos 19: 5 Ziklag, and Beth-marcaboth, and **H**, H2701

HAZAR-SUSIM
1Ch 4:31 And at Beth-marcaboth, and **H**, and at H2702

HAZAZONTAMAR
2Ch 20: 2 behold, they *be* in **H**, which *is* En-gedi. H2688

HAZEL
Gen 30:37 poplar, and of the **h** and chesnut tree; H3869

HAZELELPONI
1Ch 4: 3 and the name of their sister *was* **H**: H6753

HAZERIM
Dt 2:23 And the Avims which dwelt in **H**, *even* H2699

HAZEROTH
Nu 11:35 unto **H**; and abode at Hazeroth. H2698
35 unto Hazeroth; and abode at **H**. H2698
12:16 removed from **H**, and pitched in the H2698
33:17 and encamped at **H**. H2698
18 And they departed from **H**, and pitched H2698
Dt 1: 1 and Laban, and **H**, and Dizahab. H2698

HAZEZON-TAMAR
Gen 14: 7 and also the Amorites, that dwelt in **H**. H2688

HAZIEL
1Ch 23: 9 The sons of Shimei; Shelomith, and **H**, H2381

HAZO
Gen 22:22 And Chesed, and **H**, and Pildash, and H2375

HAZOR
Jos 11: 1 Jabin king of **H** had heard *those things*, H2674
10 back, and took **H**, and smote the king H2674
10 the sword: for **H** beforetime was the H2674
11 to breathe: and he burnt **H** with fire. H2674
13 save **H** only; *that* did Joshua burn. H2674
12:19 The king of Madon, one; the king of **H**, H2674
15:23 And Kedesh, and **H**, and Ithnan, H2674
25 And **H**, Hadattah, and Kerioth, *and* H2674
25 and Kerioth, *and* Hezron, which *is* **H**, H2674
19:36 And Adamah, and Ramah, and **H**, H2674
Jdg 4: 2 that reigned in **H**; the captain of whose H2674
17 of **H** and the house of Heber the Kenite. H2674
1Sa 12: 9 of the host of **H**, and into the hand of H2674
1Ki 9:15 and **H**, and Megiddo, and Gezer. H2674
2Ki 15:29 and Kedesh, and **H**, and Gilead, and H2674
Neh 11:33 **H**, Ramah, Gittaim, H2674
Jer 49:28 concerning the kingdoms of **H**, which H2674
30 ye inhabitants of **H**, saith the LORD; for H2674
33 And **H** shall be a dwelling for dragons, H2674

HAZZURIM See HELKATH-HAZZURIM.

HE See the Appendix.

HEAD
Gen 3:15 thy **h**, and thou shalt bruise his heel. H7218
24:26 And the man bowed down his **h**, and H6915
48 And I bowed down my **h**, and H6915
40:13 lift up thine **h**, and restore thee unto H7218
16 *I had* three white baskets on my **h**: H7218
17 eat them out of the basket upon my **h**. H7218
19 lift up thy **h** from off thee, and shall H7218
20 he lifted up the **h** of the chief butler and H7218
47:31 Israel bowed himself upon the bed's **h**. H7218
48:14 laid *it* upon Ephraim's **h**, who *was* the H7218
14 upon Manasseh's **h**, guiding his hands H7218
17 right hand upon the **h** of Ephraim, it H7218
17 Ephraim's **h** unto Manasseh's head. H7218
17 Ephraim's head unto Manasseh's **h**. H7218
18 firstborn; put thy right hand upon his **h**. H7218
49:26 shall be on the **h** of Joseph, and on the H7218
26 on the crown of the **h** of him that was H6936
Ex 12: 9 roast *with* fire; his **h** with his legs, and H7218
27 people bowed the **h** and worshipped. H6915
26:24 together above the **h** of it unto one ring: H7218
29: 6 the mitre upon his **h**, and put the holy H7218
7 and pour *it* upon his **h**, and anoint him. H7218
10 their hands upon the **h** of the bullock. H7218
15 put their hands upon the **h** of the ram. H7218
17 *them* unto his pieces, and unto his **h**. H7218
19 put their hands upon the **h** of the ram. H7218
34: 8 **h** toward the earth, and worshipped. H6915
36:29 together at the **h** thereof, to one ring: H7218
Lev 1: 4 And he shall put his hand upon the **h** of H7218
8 lay the parts, the **h**, and the fat, in order H7218
12 pieces, with his **h** and his fat: and the H7218
15 and wring off his **h**, and burn *it* on the H7218
3: 2 And he shall lay his hand upon the **h** of H7218
8 And he shall lay his hand upon the **h** of H7218
13 And he shall lay his hand upon the **h** of H7218
4: 4 **h**, and kill the bullock before the LORD. H7218
11 his flesh, with his **h**, and with his legs, H7218
15 hands upon the **h** of the bullock before H7218
24 And he shall lay his hand upon the **h** of H7218
29 And he shall lay his hand upon the **h** of H7218
33 And he shall lay his hand upon the **h** of H7218
5: 8 and wring off his **h** from his neck, but H7218
8: 9 And he put the mitre upon his **h**; also H7218
12 **h**, and anointed him, to sanctify him. H7218
14 the **h** of the bullock for the sin offering. H7218
18 laid their hands upon the **h** of the ram. H7218
20 burnt the **h**, and the pieces, and the fat. H7218
22 laid their hands upon the **h** of the ram. H7218
9:13 **h**: and he burnt *them* upon the altar. H7218
13:12 the plague from his **h** even to his foot, H7218
29 have a plague upon the **h** or the beard; H7218
30 *even* a leprosy upon the **h** or beard. H7218
40 off his **h**, he *is* bald; *yet is* he clean. H7218
41 the part of his **h** toward his face, he H7218
42 And if there be in the bald **h**, or bald H7146
42 up in his bald **h**, or his bald forehead. H7146
43 in his bald **h**, or in his bald forehead, H7146
44 utterly unclean; his plague *is* in his **h**. H7218
45 be rent, and his **h** bare, and he shall H7218
14: 9 all his hair off his **h** and his beard and H7218

Lev 14:18 pour upon the **h** of him that is to be H7218
29 shall put upon the **h** of him that is to be H7218
16:21 hands upon the **h** of the live goat, and H7218
21 them upon the **h** of the goat, and shall H7218
19:32 Thou shalt rise up before the hoary **h**, H7872
21: 5 upon their **h**, neither shall they shave H7218
10 upon whose **h** the anointing oil was H7218
10 not uncover his **h**, nor rend his clothes; H7218
24:14 their hands upon his **h**, and let all the H7218
Nu 1: 4 every one **h** of the house of his fathers. H7218
5:18 the woman's **h**, and put the offering H7218
6: 5 razor come upon his **h**: until the days be H7218
5 let the locks of the hair of his **h** grow. H7218
7 consecration of his God *is* upon his **h**. H7218
9 hath defiled the **h** of his consecration; H7218
9 he shall shave his **h** in the day of his H7218
11 and shall hallow his **h** that same day. H7218
18 And the Nazarite shall shave the **h** of H7218
18 the hair of the **h** of his separation, and H7218
17: 3 for the **h** of the house of their fathers. H7218
22:31 down his **h**, and fell flat on his face. H6915
25:15 of Zur; he *was* **h** over a people, *and* of H7218
Dt 19: 5 the tree, and the **h** slippeth from the H1270
21:12 shall shave her **h**, and pare her nails; H7218
28:13 And the LORD shall make thee the **h**, H7218
23 And thy heaven that *is* over thy **h** shall H7218
35 the sole of thy foot unto the top of thy **h**. H6936
44 shall be the **h**, and thou shalt be the tail. H7218
33:16 come upon the **h** of Joseph, and upon H7218
16 upon the top of the **h** of him *that was* H6936
20 teareth the arm with the crown of the **h**. H6936
Jos 2:19 *shall be* upon his **h**, and we *will be* H7218
19 *be* on our **h**, if *any* hand be upon him. H7218
11:10 was the **h** of all those kingdoms. H7218
22:14 each one *was* an **h** of the house of their H7218
Jdg 5:26 she smote off his **h**, when she had H7218
9:53 **h**, and all to brake his skull. H7218
10:18 be **h** over all the inhabitants of Gilead. H7218
11: 8 our **h** over all the inhabitants of Gilead. H7218
9 them before me, shall I be your **h**? H7218
11 people made him **h** and captain over H7218
13: 5 shall come on his **h**: for the child shall H7218
16:13 the seven locks of my **h** with the web. H7218
17 a razor upon mine **h**; for I *have been* a H7218
19 seven locks of his **h**; and she began to H7218
22 Howbeit the hair of his **h** began to grow H7218
1Sa 1:11 there shall no razor come upon his **h**. H7218
4:12 clothes rent, and with earth upon his **h**. H7218
5: 4 of the LORD; and the **h** of Dagon and H7218
10: 1 poured *it* upon his **h**, and kissed him, H7218
14:45 not one hair of his **h** fall to the ground; H7218
15:17 thou not *made* the **h** of the tribes of H7218
17: 5 of brass upon his **h**, and he *was* armed H7218
7 and his spear's **h** *weighed* six hundred H3852
38 of brass upon his **h**; also he armed him H7218
46 and take thine **h** from thee; and I will H7218
51 and cut off his **h** therewith. And when H7218
54 And David took the **h** of the Philistine, H7218
57 with the **h** of the Philistine in his hand. H7218
25:39 upon his own **h**. And David sent and H7218
28: 2 I make thee keeper of mine **h** for ever. H7218
31: 9 And they cut off his **h**, and stripped off H7218
2Sa 1: 2 earth upon his **h**: and *so* it was, when H7218
10 that *was* upon his **h**, and the bracelet H7218
16 blood *be* upon thy **h**; for thy mouth hath H7218
2:16 his fellow by the **h**, and *thrust* his sword H7218
3: 8 and said, *Am* I a dog's **h**, which against H7218
29 Let it rest on the **h** of Joab, and on all H7218
4: 7 him, and took his **h**, and gat them away H7218
8 And they brought the **h** of Ish-bosheth H7218
8 king, Behold the **h** of Ish-bosheth the H7218
12 But they took the **h** of Ish-bosheth, and H7218
12:30 king's crown from off his **h**, the weight H7218
30 it was *set* on David's **h**. And he brought H7218
13:19 And Tamar put ashes on her **h**, and H7218
19 her hand on her **h**, and went on crying. H7218
14:25 of his **h** there was no blemish in him. H6936
26 And when he polled his **h**, (for it was at H7218
26 the hair of his **h** at two hundred shekels H7218
15:30 up, and had his **h** covered, and he went H7218
30 every man his **h**, and they went up, H7218
32 with his coat rent, and earth upon his **h**: H7218
16: 9 go over, I pray thee, and take off his **h**. H7218
18: 9 great oak, and his **h** caught hold of the H7218
20:21 **h** shall be thrown to thee over the wall. H7218
22 they cut off the **h** of Sheba the son of H7218
22:44 hast kept me to *be* **h** of the heathen: a H7218
1Ki 2: 6 hoar **h** go down to the grave in peace. H7872
9 him; but his hoar **h** bring thou down to H7872

1Ki 2:32 upon his own **h**, who fell upon two men H7218
33 return upon the **h** of Joab, and upon H7218
33 and upon the **h** of his seed for ever: H7218
37 thy blood shall be upon thine own **h**. H7218
44 thy wickedness upon thine own **h**; H7218
8:32 his way upon his **h**; and justifying the H7218
19: 6 of water at his **h**. And he did eat and H4763
2Ki 2: 3 master from thy **h** to day? And he said, H7218
5 thy master from thy **h** to day? And he H7218
23 up, thou bald **h**; go up, thou bald head. H7142
23 up, thou bald head; go up, thou bald **h**. H7142
4:19 And he said unto his father, My **h**, my H7218
19 My head, my **h**. And he said to a lad, H7218
6: 5 a beam, the axe **h** fell into the water: H1270
25 besieged it, until an ass's **h** was *sold* for H7218
31 also to me, if the **h** of Elisha the son of H7218
32 to take away mine **h**? look, when the H7218
9: 3 oil, and pour *it* on his **h**, and say, Thus H7218
6 the oil on his **h**, and said unto him, H7218
30 tired her **h**, and looked out at a window. H7218
19:21 of Jerusalem hath shaken her **h** at thee. H7218
25:27 did lift up the **h** of Jehoiachin king of H7218
1Ch 10: 9 him, they took his **h**, and his armour, H7218
10 fastened his **h** in the temple of Dagon. H1538
20: 2 their king from off his **h**, and found it to H7218
2 set upon David's **h**: and he brought also H7218
29:11 and thou art exalted as **h** above all. H7218
2Ch 6:23 way upon his own **h**; and by justifying H7218
20:18 And Jehoshaphat bowed his **h** with *his* H6915
Ezr 9: 3 off the hair of my **h** and of my beard, H7218
6 over *our* **h**, and our trespass is H7218
Neh 4: 4 upon their own **h**, and give them for a H7218
Est 2:17 crown upon her **h**, and made her queen H7218
6: 8 the crown royal which is set upon his **h**: H7218
12 mourning, and having his **h** covered. H7218
9:25 upon his own **h**, and that he and his H7218
Job 1:20 and shaved his **h**, and fell down upon H7218
10:15 I not lift up my **h**. *I am* full of confusion; H7218
16: 4 against you, and shake mine **h** at you. H7218
19: 9 glory, and taken the crown *from* my **h**. H7218
20: 6 and his **h** reach unto the clouds; H7218
29: 3 When his candle shined upon my **h**, H7218
41: 7 barbed irons? or his **h** with fish spears? H7218
Ps 3: 3 my glory, and the lifter up of mine **h**. H7218
7:16 upon his own **h**, and his violent dealing H7218
18:43 hast made me the **h** of the heathen: a H7218
21: 3 settest a crown of pure gold on his **h**. H7218
22: 7 out the lip, they shake the **h**, *saying*, H7218
23: 5 my **h** with oil; my cup runneth over. H7218
27: 6 And now shall mine **h** be lifted up H7218
38: 4 gone over mine **h**: as an heavy burden H7218
40:12 mine **h**: therefore my heart faileth me. H7218
44:14 a shaking of the **h** among the people. H7218
60: 7 of mine **h**; Judah *is* my lawgiver; H7218
68:21 But God shall wound the **h** of his H7218
69: 4 the hairs of mine **h**: they that would H7218
83: 2 they that hate thee have lifted up the **h**. H7218
108: 8 of mine **h**; Judah *is* my lawgiver; H7218
110: 7 the way: therefore shall he lift up the **h**. H7218
118:22 is become the **h** *stone* of the corner. H7218
133: 2 upon the **h**, that ran down upon H7218
140: 7 hast covered my **h** in the day of battle. H7218
9 *As for* the **h** of those that compass me H7218
141: 5 not break my **h**: for yet my prayer also H7218
Prv 1: 9 unto thy **h**, and chains about thy neck. H7218
4: 9 She shall give to thine **h** an ornament H7218
10: 6 Blessings *are* upon the **h** of the just: but H7218
11:26 *be* upon the **h** of him that selleth *it*. H7218
16:31 The hoary **h** *is* a crown of glory, *if* it be H7872
20:29 and the beauty of old men *is* the gray **h**. H7872
25:22 his **h**, and the LORD shall reward thee. H7218
Ecc 2:14 The wise man's eyes *are* in his **h**; but the H7218
9: 8 white; and let thy **h** lack no ointment. H7218
Song 2: 6 His left hand *is* under my **h**, and his H7218
5: 2 undefiled: for my **h** is filled with dew, H7218
11 His **h** *is as* the most fine gold, his locks H7218
7: 5 Thine **h** upon thee *is* like Carmel, and H7218
5 the hair of thine **h** like purple; the king H7218
8: 3 His left hand *should be* under my **h**, H7218
Isa 1: 5 **h** is sick, and the whole heart faint. H7218
6 the foot even unto the **h** *there is* no H7218
3:17 the crown of the **h** of the daughters of H6936
7: 8 For the **h** of Syria *is* Damascus, and the H7218
8 and the **h** of Damascus *is* Rezin; H7218
9 And the **h** of Ephraim *is* Samaria, and H7218
9 *is* Samaria, and the **h** of Samaria *is* H7218
20 of Assyria, the **h**, and the hair of the H7218
9:14 cut off from Israel **h** and tail, branch H7218
15 he *is* the **h**; and the prophet that H7218

Isa 19:15 the **h** or tail, branch or rush, may do. H7218
28: 1 which *are* on the **h** of the fat valleys of H7218
4 which *is* on the **h** of the fat valley, shall H7218
37:22 of Jerusalem hath shaken her **h** at thee. H7218
51:11 *shall be* upon their **h**: they shall obtain H7218
20 Thy sons have fainted, they lie at the **h** H7218
58: 5 *it* to bow down his **h** as a bulrush, and H7218
59:17 salvation upon his **h**; and he put on the H7218
Jer 2:16 have broken the crown of thy **h**. H6936
37 hands upon thine **h**: for the LORD hath H7218
9: 1 Oh that my **h** were waters, and mine H7218
18:16 shall be astonished, and wag his **h**. H7218
22: 6 unto me, *and* the **h** of Lebanon: *yet* H7218
23:19 grievously upon the **h** of the wicked. H7218
30:23 fall with pain upon the **h** of the wicked. H7218
48:37 For every **h** *shall be* bald, and every H7218
45 crown of the **h** of the tumultuous ones. H6936
52:31 reign lifted up the **h** of Jehoiachin king H7218
Lam 2:15 hiss and wag their **h** at the daughter of H7218
3:54 Waters flowed over mine **h**; *then* I said, H7218
5:16 The crown is fallen *from* our **h**: woe H7218
Ezk 5: 1 *it* to pass upon thine **h** and upon thy H7218
8: 3 by a lock of mine **h**; and the spirit lifted H7218
9:10 will recompense their way upon their **h**. H7218
10: 1 was above the **h** of the cherubims there H7218
11 the place whither the **h** looked they H7218
13:18 kerchiefs upon the **h** of every stature to H7218
16:12 and a beautiful crown upon thine **h**. H7218
25 place at every **h** of the way, and hast H7218
31 place in the **h** of every way, and makest H7218
43 way upon *thine* **h**, saith the Lord GOD: H7218
17:19 it will I recompense upon his own **h**. H7218
21:19 choose *it* at the **h** of the way to the city. H7218
21 of the way, at the **h** of the two ways, to H7218
24:17 the tire of thine **h** upon thee, and put H6287
29:18 Tyrus: every **h** *was* made bald, and H7218
33: 4 his blood shall be upon his own **h**. H7218
42:12 *was* a door in the **h** of the way, *even* the H7218
Dan 1:10 ye make *me* endanger my **h** to the king. H7218
2:28 of thy **h** upon thy bed, are these; H7217
32 This image's **h** *was* of fine gold, his H7217
38 over them all. Thou *art* this **h** of gold. H7217
3:27 an hair of their **h** singed, neither were H7217
4: 5 and the visions of my **h** troubled me. H7217
10 Thus *were* the visions of mine **h** in my H7217
13 I saw in the visions of my **h** upon my H7217
7: 1 and visions of his **h** upon his bed: then H7217
9 and the hair of his **h** like the pure wool: H7217
15 and the visions of my **h** troubled me. H7217
20 And of the ten horns that *were* in his **h**, H7217
Hos 1:11 themselves one **h**, and they shall come H7218
Joel 3: 4 your recompence upon your own **h**; H7218
7 your recompence upon your own **h**: H7218
Am 2: 7 of the earth on the **h** of the poor, and H7218
8:10 upon every **h**; and I will make it as H7218
9: 1 cut them in the **h**, all of them; and I will H7218
Oba 15 reward shall return upon thine own **h**. H7218
Jna 2: 5 the weeds were wrapped about my **h**. H7218
4: 6 be a shadow over his **h**, to deliver him H7218
8 sun beat upon the **h** of Jonah, that he H7218
Mic 2:13 them, and the LORD on the **h** of them. H7218
Hab 3:13 woundedst the **h** out of the house of the H7218
14 with his staves the **h** of his villages: H7218
Zec 1:21 no man did lift up his **h**: but these are H7218
3: 5 fair mitre upon his **h**. So they set a fair H7218
5 mitre upon his **h**, and clothed him with H7218
6:11 set *them* upon the **h** of Joshua the son H7218
Mt 5:36 Neither shalt thou swear by thy **h**, G2776
6:17 anoint thine **h**, and wash thy face; G2776
8:20 Son of man hath not where to lay *his* **h**. G2776
10:30 But the very hairs of your **h** are all G2776
14: 8 me here John Baptist's **h** in a charger. G2776
11 And his **h** was brought in a charger, G2776
21:42 is become the **h** of the corner: this is G2776
26: 7 poured it on his **h**, as he sat *at meat*. G2776
27:29 put *it* upon his **h**, and a reed in his right G2776
30 took the reed, and smote him on the **h**. G2776
37 And set up over his **h** his accusation G2776
Mk 6:24 And she said, The **h** of John the Baptist. G2776
25 in a charger the **h** of John the Baptist. G2776
27 commanded his **h** to be brought: and G2776
28 And brought his **h** in a charger, and G2776
12: 4 *him* in the **h**, and sent *him* away G2775
10 rejected is become the **h** of the corner: G2776
14: 3 brake the box, and poured *it* on his **h**. G2776
15:17 a crown of thorns, and put it about his *h*,
19 And they smote him on the **h** with a G2776
Lk 7:38 the hairs of her **h**, and kissed his feet, G2776
44 and wiped *them* with the hairs of her **h**. G2776

H

Lk 7:46 My **h** with oil thou didst not anoint: but *G2776*
9:58 Son of man hath not where to lay his **h**. *G2776*
12: 7 But even the very hairs of your **h** are all *G2776*
20:17 the same is become the **h** of the corner? *G2776*
21:18 But there shall not an hair of your **h** *G2776*
Jn 13: 9 feet only, but also *my* hands and *my* **h**. *G2776*
19: 2 **h**, and they put on him a purple robe, *G2776*
30 he bowed his **h**, and gave up the ghost. *G2776*
20: 7 And the napkin, that was about his **h**, *G2776*
12 the one at the **h**, and the other at the *G2776*
Act 4:11 which is become the **h** of the corner. *G2776*
18:18 *his* **h** in Cenchrea: for he had a vow. *G2776*
27:34 an hair fall from the **h** of any of you. *G2776*
Ro 12:20 thou shalt heap coals of fire on his **h**. *G2776*
1Co 11: 3 But I would have you know, that the **h** *G2776*
3 is Christ; and the **h** of the woman *is* the *G2776*
3 *is* the man; and the **h** of Christ *is* God. *G2776*
4 *his* **h** covered, dishonoureth his head. *G2776*
4 *his* head covered, dishonoureth his **h**. *G2776*
5 with *her* **h** uncovered dishonoureth *G2776*
5 dishonoureth her **h**: for that is even all *G2776*
7 not to cover *his* **h**, forasmuch as he is *G2776*
10 power on *her* **h** because of the angels. *G2776*
12:21 the **h** to the feet, I have no need of you. *G2776*
Eph 1:22 *to be* the **h** over all *things* to the church, *G2776*
4:15 in all things, which is the **h**, *even* Christ: *G2776*
5:23 For the husband is the **h** of the wife, *G2776*
23 as Christ is the **h** of the church: and he *G2776*
Col 1:18 And he is the **h** of the body, the church: *G2776*
2:10 is the **h** of all principality and power: *G2776*
19 And not holding the **H**, from which all *G2776*
1Pt 2: 7 the same is made the **h** of the corner, *G2776*
Rev 1:14 His **h** and *his* hairs *were* white like *G2776*
10: 1 *was* upon his **h**, and his face *was* as *G2776*
12: 1 and upon her **h** a crown of twelve stars: *G2776*
14:14 having on his **h** a golden crown, and *G2776*
19:12 of fire, and on his **h** *were* many crowns; *G2776*

HEADBANDS
Isa 3:20 the **h**, and the tablets, and the earrings, H7196

HEADLONG
Job 5:13 the counsel of the froward is carried **h**. H4116
Lk 4:29 built, that they might cast him down **h**. *G2630*
Act 1:18 and falling **h**, he burst asunder in *G4248*

HEADS
Gen 2:10 it was parted, and became into four **h**. H7218
43:28 down their **h**, and made obeisance. H6915
Ex 4:31 they bowed their **h** and worshipped. H6915
6:14 These *be* the **h** of their fathers' houses: H7218
25 these *are* the **h** of the fathers of the H7218
18:25 and made them **h** over the people, H7218
Lev 10: 6 Uncover not your **h**, neither rend your H7218
19:27 the corners of your **h**, neither shalt thou H7218
Nu 1:16 their fathers, **h** of thousands in Israel. H7218
7: 2 That the princes of Israel, **h** of the H7218
8:12 hands upon the **h** of the bullocks: and H7218
10: 4 princes, *which are* **h** of the thousands H7218
13: 3 men *were* **h** of the children of Israel. H7218
25: 4 Take all the **h** of the people, and hang H7218
30: 1 And Moses spake unto the **h** of the H7218
Dt 1:15 and made them **h** over you, captains H7218
5:23 all the **h** of your tribes, and your elders; H7218
33: 5 when the **h** of the people *and* the H7218
21 he came with the **h** of the people, he H7218
Jos 7: 6 of Israel, and put dust upon their **h**. H7218
14: 1 of Nun, and the **h** of the fathers of the H7218
19:51 of Nun, and the **h** of the fathers of the H7218
21: 1 Then came near the **h** of the fathers of H7218
1 of Nun, and unto the **h** of the fathers of H7218
22:21 unto the **h** of the thousands of Israel, H7218
30 congregation and **h** of the thousands of H7218
23: 2 and for their **h**, and for their judges, H7218
24: 1 and for their **h**, and for their judges, H7218
Jdg 7:25 and brought the **h** of Oreb and Zeeb to H7218
8:28 they lifted up their **h** no more. And the H7218
9:57 render upon their **h**: and upon them H7218
1Sa 29: 4 *it* not *be* with the **h** of these men? H7218
1Ki 8: 1 of Israel, and all the **h** of the tribes, the H7218
20:31 and ropes upon our **h**, and go out to the H7218
32 *put* ropes on their **h**, and came to the H7218
2Ki 10: 6 my voice, take ye the **h** of the men your H7218
7 and put their **h** in baskets, and sent H7218
8 have brought the **h** of the king's sons. H7218
1Ch 5:24 And these *were* the **h** of the house of H7218
24 *and* **h** of the house of their fathers. H7218
7: 2 and Shemuel, **h** of their father's house, H7218
7 and Iri, five; **h** of the house of *their* H7218
1Ch 7: 9 by their generations, **h** of the house of H7218
11 All these the sons of Jediael, by the **h** of H7218
40 All these *were* the children of Asher, **h** H7218
8: 6 these are the **h** of the fathers of the H7218
10 These *were* his sons, **h** of the fathers. H7218
13 Beriah also, and Shema, who *were* **h** of H7218
28 These *were* **h** of the fathers, by their H7218
9:13 And their brethren, **h** of the house of H7218
12:19 his master Saul to *the jeopardy of* our **h**. H7218
32 ought to do; the **h** of them *were* two H7218
29:20 bowed down their **h**, and worshipped H6915
2Ch 3:16 put *them* on the **h** of the pillars; and H7218
5: 2 of Israel, and all the **h** of the tribes, the H7218
28:12 Then certain of the **h** of the children of H7218
29:30 they bowed their **h** and worshipped. H6915
Neh 8: 6 they bowed their **h**, and worshipped the H6915
Job 2:12 dust upon their **h** toward heaven. H7218
Ps 24: 7 Lift up your **h**, O ye gates; and be ye lift H7218
9 Lift up your **h**, O ye gates; even lift *them* H7218
66:12 to ride over our **h**; we went through fire H7218
74:13 the **h** of the dragons in the waters. H7218
14 Thou brakest the **h** of leviathan in H7218
109:25 looked upon me they shaked their **h**. H7218
110: 6 wound the **h** over many countries. H7218
Isa 15: 2 on all their **h** *shall be* baldness, *and* H7218
35:10 joy upon their **h**: they shall obtain joy H7218
Jer 14: 3 and confounded, and covered their **h**. H7218
4 were ashamed, they covered their **h**. H7218
Lam 2:10 up dust upon their **h**; they have girded H7218
10 hang down their **h** to the ground. H7218
Ezk 1:22 upon the **h** of the living creature H7218
22 stretched forth over their **h** above. H7218
25 *was* over their **h**, when they stood, *and* H7218
26 *was* over their **h** *was* the likeness of H7218
7:18 all faces, and baldness upon all their **h**. H7218
11:21 upon their own **h**, saith the Lord GOD. H7218
22:31 upon their **h**, saith the Lord GOD. H7218
23:15 attire upon their **h**, all of them princes H7218
42 and beautiful crowns upon their **h**. H7218
24:23 And your tires *shall be* upon your **h**, H7218
27:30 up dust upon their **h**, they shall wallow H7218
32:27 under their **h**, but their iniquities H7218
44:18 upon their **h**, and shall have linen H7218
20 Neither shall they shave their **h**, nor H7218
20 grow long; they shall only poll their **h**. H7218
Dan 7: 6 four **h**; and dominion was given to it. H7217
Mic 3: 1 And I said, Hear, I pray you, O **h** of H7218
9 Hear this, I pray you, ye **h** of the house H7218
11 The **h** thereof judge for reward, and the H7218
Mt 27:39 passed by reviled him, wagging their **h**, *G2776*
Mk 15:29 wagging their **h**, and saying, Ah, thou *G2776*
Lk 21:28 **h**; for your redemption draweth nigh. *G2776*
Act 18: 6 *be* upon your own **h**; I *am* clean: from *G2776*
21:24 may shave *their* **h**: and all may know *G2776*
Rev 4: 4 and they had on their **h** crowns of gold. *G2776*
9: 7 and on their **h** *were* as it were crowns *G2776*
17 and the **h** of the horses *were* as *G2776*
17 horses *were* as the **h** of lions; and out of *G2776*
19 and had **h**, and with them they do hurt. *G2776*
12: 3 having seven **h** and ten horns, and *G2776*
3 horns, and seven crowns upon his **h**. *G2776*
13: 1 sea, having seven **h** and ten horns, and *G2776*
1 upon his **h** the name of blasphemy. *G2776*
3 And I saw one of his **h** as it were *G2776*
17: 3 having seven **h** and ten horns. *G2776*
7 which hath the seven **h** and ten horns. *G2776*
9 The seven **h** are seven mountains, *G2776*
18:19 And they cast dust on their **h**, and cried, *G2776*

HEADSTONE
Zec 4: 7 bring forth the **h** *thereof with* H68+H7222

HEADY
2Ti 3: 4 Traitors, **h**, highminded, lovers of *G4312*

HEAL
Nu 12:13 **H** her now, O God, I beseech thee. H7495
Dt 32:39 I wound, and I **h**: neither *is there any* H7495
2Ki 20: 5 behold, I will **h** thee: on the third day H7495
8 the LORD will **h** me, and that I shall H7495
2Ch 7:14 forgive their sin, and will **h** their land. H7495
Ps 6: 2 O LORD, **h** me; for my bones are vexed. H7495
41: 4 I said, LORD, be merciful unto me: **h** H7495
60: 2 **h** the breaches thereof; for it shaketh. H7495
Ecc 3: 3 A time to kill, and a time to **h**; a time to H7495
Isa 19:22 he shall smite and **h** *it*: and they shall H7495
22 be entreated of them, and shall **h** them. H7495
57:18 I have seen his ways, and will **h** him: I H7495
19 near, saith the LORD; and I will **h** him. H7495
Jer 3:22 *and* I will **h** your backslidings. Behold, H7495
17:14 **H** me, O LORD, and I shall be healed; H7495
30:17 thee, and I will **h** thee of thy wounds, H7495
Lam 2:13 *is* great like the sea: who can **h** thee? H7495
Hos 5:13 not **h** you, nor cure you of your wound. H7495
6: 1 torn, and he will **h** us; he hath smitten, H7495
14: 4 I will **h** their backsliding, I will love H7495
Zec 11:16 young one, nor **h** that that is broken, H7495
Mt 8: 7 saith unto him, I will come and **h** him. *G2323*
10: 1 cast them out, and to **h** all manner of *G2323*
8 **H** the sick, cleanse the lepers, raise the *G2323*
12:10 Is it lawful to **h** on the sabbath days? *G2323*
13:15 be converted, and I should **h** them. *G2390*
Mk 3: 2 him, whether he would **h** him on the *G2323*
15 And to have power to **h** sicknesses, and *G2323*
Lk 4:18 poor; he hath sent me to **h** the *G2390*
23 Physician, **h** thyself: whatsoever *G2323*
5:17 of the Lord was *present* to **h** them. *G2390*
6: 7 whether he would **h** on the sabbath *G2323*
7: 3 that he would come and **h** his servant. *G1295*
9: 2 the kingdom of God, and to **h** the sick. *G2390*
10: 9 And **h** the sick that are therein, and say *G2323*
14: 3 Is it lawful to **h** on the sabbath day? *G2323*
Jn 4:47 come down, and **h** his son: for he was *G2390*
12:40 and be converted, and I should **h** them. *G2390*
Act 4:30 By stretching forth thine hand to **h**; and *G2392*
28:27 be converted, and I should **h** them. *G2390*

HEALED
Gen 20:17 God: and God **h** Abimelech, and his H7495
Ex 21:19 and shall cause *him* to be thoroughly **h**. H7495
Lev 13:18 in the skin thereof, was a boil, and is **h**, H7495
37 the scall is **h**, he *is* clean: and the H7495
14: 3 the plague of leprosy be **h** in the leper; H7495
48 house clean, because the plague is **h**. H7495
Dt 28:27 the itch, whereof thou canst not be **h**. H7495
35 that cannot be **h**, from the sole of thy H7495
1Sa 6: 3 then ye shall be **h**, and it shall be known H7495
2Ki 2:21 the LORD, I have **h** these waters; there H7495
22 So the waters were **h** unto this day, H7495
8:29 And king Joram went back to be **h** in H7495
9:15 But king Joram was returned to be **h** in H7495
2Ch 22: 6 And he returned to be **h** in Jezreel H7495
30:20 to Hezekiah, and **h** the people. H7495
Ps 30: 2 I cried unto thee, and thou hast **h** me. H7495
107:20 He sent his word, and **h** them, and H7495
Isa 6:10 with their heart, and convert, and be **h**. H7495
53: 5 upon him; and with his stripes we are **h**. H7495
Jer 6:14 They have **h** also the hurt *of the* H7495
8:11 For they have **h** the hurt of the H7495
15:18 refuseth to be **h**? wilt thou be altogether H7495
17:14 Heal me, O LORD, and I shall be **h**; save H7495
51: 8 balm for her pain, if so be she may be **h**. H7495
9 We would have **h** Babylon, but she is H7495
9 but she is not **h**: forsake her, and let H7495
Ezk 30:21 be bound up to be **h**, to put a roller to H7499
34: 4 neither have ye **h** that which was sick, H7495
47: 8 forth into the sea, the waters shall be **h**. H7495
9 for they shall be **h**; and every thing shall H7495
11 not be **h**; they shall be given to salt. H7495
Hos 7: 1 When I would have **h** Israel, then the H7495
11: 3 arms; but they knew not that I **h** them. H7495
Mt 4:24 that had the palsy; and he **h** them. *G2323*
8: 8 word only, and my servant shall be **h**. *G2390*
13 his servant was **h** in the selfsame hour. *G2390*
16 with *his* word, and **h** all that were sick: *G2323*
12:15 followed him, and he **h** them all; *G2323*
22 and dumb: and he **h** him, insomuch *G2323*
14:14 toward them, and he **h** their sick. *G2323*
15:30 down at Jesus' feet; and he **h** them: *G2323*
19: 2 followed him; and he **h** them there. *G2323*
21:14 to him in the temple; and he **h** them. *G2323*
Mk 1:34 And he **h** many that were sick of divers *G2323*
3:10 For he had **h** many; insomuch that they *G2323*
5:23 that she may be **h**; and she shall live. *G4982*
29 *her* body that she was **h** of that plague. *G2390*
6: 5 upon a few sick folk, and **h** *them*. *G2323*
13 oil many that were sick, and **h** *them*. *G2323*
Lk 4:40 on every one of them, and **h** them. *G2323*
5:15 and to be **h** by him of their infirmities. *G2323*
6:17 hear him, and to be **h** of their diseases; *G2390*
18 with unclean spirits: and they were **h**. *G2323*
19 went virtue out of him, and **h** *them* all. *G2390*
7: 7 in a word, and my servant shall be **h**. *G2390*
8: 2 And certain women, which had been **h** *G2323*
36 that was possessed of the devils was **h**. *G4982*
43 physicians, neither could be **h** of any, *G2323*
47 him, and how she was **h** immediately. *G2390*
9:11 and **h** them that had need of healing. *G2390*

Lk 9:42 spirit, and **h** the child, and delivered G2390
13:14 that Jesus had **h** on the sabbath day, G2323
14 and be **h**, and not on the sabbath day. G2323
14: 4 took *him*, and **h** him, and let him go; G2390
17:15 he saw that he was **h**, turned back, and G2390
22:51 far. And he touched his ear, and **h** him. G2390
Jn 5:13 And he that was **h** wist not who it was: G2390
Act 3:11 And as the lame man which was **h** held G2390
4:14 And beholding the man which was **h** G2323
5:16 spirits: and they were **h** every one. G2323
8: 7 palsies, and that were lame, were **h**. G2323
14: 9 and perceiving that he had faith to be **h**, G4982
28: 8 and laid his hands on him, and **h** him. G2390
9 in the island, came, and were **h**: G2323
Heb 12:13 out of the way; but let it rather be **h**. G2390
Jas 5:16 that ye may be **h**. The effectual fervent G2390
1Pt 2:24 by whose stripes ye were **h**. G2390
Rev 13: 3 deadly wound was **h**: and all the world G2323
12 first beast, whose deadly wound was **h**. G2323

HEALER
Isa 3: 7 I will not be an **h**; for in my house *is* H2280

HEALETH
Ex 15:26 for I *am* the LORD that **h** thee. H7495
Ps 103: 3 thine iniquities; who **h** all thy diseases; H7495
147: 3 He **h** the broken in heart, and bindeth H7495
Isa 30:26 and **h** the stroke of their wound. H7495

HEALING
Jer 14:19 us, and *there is* no **h** for us? we looked H4832
19 for the time of **h**, and behold trouble! H4832
30:13 bound up: thou hast no **h** medicines. H8585
Nah 3:19 *There is* no **h** of thy bruise; thy wound H3545
Mal 4: 2 arise with **h** in his wings; and ye H4832
Mt 4:23 of the kingdom, and **h** all manner of G2323
9:35 the kingdom, and **h** every sickness and G2323
Lk 9: 6 the gospel, and **h** every where. G2323
11 and healed them that had need of **h**. G2322
Act 4:22 on whom this miracle of **h** was shewed. G2392
10:38 about doing good, and **h** all that were G2390
1Co 12: 9 the gifts of **h** by the same Spirit; G2386
30 Have all the gifts of **h**? do all speak with G2386
Rev 22: 2 of the tree *were* for the **h** of the nations. G2322

HEALINGS
1Co 12:28 then gifts of **h**, helps, governments, G2386

HEALTH
Gen 43:28 father *is* in good **h**, he *is* yet alive. And H7965
2Sa 20: 9 And Joab said to Amasa, *Art* thou in **h**, H7965
Ps 42:11 the **h** of my countenance, and my God. H3444
43: 5 the **h** of my countenance, and my God. H3444
67: 2 earth, thy saving **h** among all nations. H3444
Prv 3: 8 It shall be **h** to thy navel, and marrow H7500
4:22 that find them, and **h** to all their flesh. H4832
12:18 a sword: but the tongue of the wise *is* **h**. H4832
13:17 but a faithful ambassador *is* **h**. H4832
16:24 sweet to the soul, and **h** to the bones. H4832
Isa 58: 8 and thine **h** shall spring forth speedily: H724
Jer 8:15 *and* for a time of **h**, and behold trouble! H4832
22 why then is not the **h** of the daughter of H724
30:17 For I will restore **h** unto thee, and I will H724
33: 6 Behold, I will bring it **h** and cure, and I H724
Act 27:34 for this is for your **h**: for there shall not G4991
3Jn 2 be in **h**, even as thy soul prospereth. G5198

HEAP
Gen 31:46 **h**: and they did eat there upon the heap. H1530
46 heap: and they did eat there upon the **h**. H1530
48 And Laban said, This **h** *is* a witness H1530
51 And Laban said to Jacob, Behold this **h**, H1530
52 This **h** *be* witness, and *this* pillar *be* H1530
52 not pass over this **h** to thee, and that H1530
52 **h** and this pillar unto me, for harm. H1530
Ex 15: 8 upright as an **h**, *and* the depths were H5067
Dt 13:16 an **h** for ever; it shall not be built again. H8510
32:23 I will **h** mischiefs upon them; I will H5595
Jos 3:13 above; and they shall stand upon an **h**. H5067
16 rose up upon an **h** very far from the H5067
7:26 And they raised over him a great **h** of H1530
8:28 And Joshua burnt Ai, and made it an **h** H8510
29 raise thereon a great **h** of stones, *that* H1530
Ru 3: 7 at the end of the **h** of corn: and she H6194
2Sa 18:17 laid a very great **h** of stones upon him: H1530
Job 8:17 His roots are wrapped about the **h**, *and* H1530
16: 4 stead, I could **h** up words against you, H2266
27:16 Though he **h** up silver as the dust, and H6651
36:13 But the hypocrites in heart **h** up wrath: H7760
Ps 33: 7 sea together as an **h**: he layeth up the H5067
78:13 he made the waters to stand as an **h**. H5067
Prv 25:22 For thou shalt **h** coals of fire upon his H2846
Ecc 2:26 to gather and to **h** up, that he may give H3664
Song 7: 2 *like* an **h** of wheat set about with lilies. H6194
Isa 17: 1 *being* a city, and it shall be a ruinous **h**. H4596
11 harvest *shall be* a **h** in the day of grief H5067
25: 2 For thou hast made of a city an **h**; *of* a H1530
Jer 30:18 upon her own **h**, and the palace shall H8510
49: 2 shall be a desolate **h**, and her daughters H8510
Ezk 24:10 **H** on wood, kindle the fire, consume H7235
Mic 1: 6 Therefore I will make Samaria as an **h** H5856
Hab 1:10 hold; for they shall **h** dust, and take it. H6651
3:15 horses, *through* the **h** of great waters. H2563
Hag 2:16 *one* came to an **h** of twenty *measures*, H6194
Ro 12:20 thou shalt **h** coals of fire on his head. G4987
2Ti 4: 3 own lusts shall they **h** to themselves G2002

HEAPED
Zec 9: 3 a strong hold, and **h** up silver as the H6651
Jas 5: 3 **h** treasure together for the last days. G2343

HEAPETH
Ps 39: 6 in vain: he **h** up *riches*, and knoweth H6651
Hab 2: 5 all nations, and **h** unto him all people: H6908

HEAPS
Ex 8:14 together upon **h**: and the land stank. H2563
Jdg 15:16 jawbone of an ass, **h** upon heaps, with H2565
16 an ass, heaps upon **h**, with the jaw of an H2565
2Ki 10: 8 ye them in two **h** at the entering in of H6652
19:25 to lay waste fenced cities *into* ruinous **h**. H1530
2Ch 31: 6 LORD their God, and laid *them* by **h**. H6194
7 foundation of the **h**, and finished *them* H6194
8 came and saw the **h**, they blessed the H6194
9 and the Levites concerning the **h**. H6194
Neh 4: 2 the **h** of the rubbish which are burned? H6194
Job 15:28 which are ready to become **h**. H1530
Ps 79: 1 defiled; they have laid Jerusalem on **h**. H5856
Isa 37:26 waste defenced cities *into* ruinous **h**. H1530
Jer 9:11 And I will make Jerusalem **h**, *and* a den H1530
26:18 shall become **h**, and the mountain of H5856
31:21 make thee high **h**: set thine heart H8564
50:26 cast her up as **h**, and destroy her H6194
51:37 And Babylon shall become **h**, a H1530
Hos 12:11 *are* as **h** in the furrows of the fields. H1530
Mic 3:12 shall become **h**, and the mountain of H5856

HEAR
Gen 4:23 Adah and Zillah, **H** my voice; ye wives H8085
21: 6 *so that* all that **h** will laugh with me. H8085
23: 6 **H** us, my lord: thou *art* a mighty prince H8085
8 out of my sight; **h** me, and entreat for H8085
11 Nay, my lord, **h** me: the field give I H8085
13 *give it*, I pray thee, **h** me: I will give thee H8085
37: 6 And he said unto them, **H**, I pray you, H8085
42:21 us, and we would not **h**; therefore is this H8085
22 and ye would not **h**? therefore, behold, H8085
49: 2 Gather yourselves together, and **h**, ye H8085
Ex 6:12 **h** me, who *am* of uncircumcised lips? H8085
7:16 behold, hitherto thou wouldest not **h**. H8085
15:14 The people shall **h**, *and* be afraid: H8085
19: 9 the people may **h** when I speak with H8085
20:19 us, and we will **h**: but let not God speak H8085
22:23 at all unto me, I will surely **h** their cry; H8085
27 unto me, that I will **h**; for I *am* gracious. H8085
32:18 *but* the noise of *them that* sing do I **h**. H8085
Lev 5: 1 And if a soul sin, and **h** the voice of H8085
Nu 9: 8 still, and I will **h** what the LORD will H8085
12: 6 And he said, **H** now my words: If there H8085
14:13 the Egyptians shall **h** *it*, (for thou H8085
16: 8 And Moses said unto Korah, **H**, I pray H8085
20:10 said unto them, **H** now, ye rebels; must H8085
23:18 **h**; hearken unto me, thou son of Zippor: H8085
30: 4 And her father **h** her vow, and her H8085
Dt 1:16 that time, saying, **H** *the causes* between H8085
17 *but* ye shall **h** the small as well as H8085
17 for you, bring *it* unto me, and I will **h** it. H8085
43 and ye would not **h**, but rebelled against H8085
2:25 heaven, who shall **h** report of thee, and H8085
3:26 and would not **h** me: and the LORD H8085
4: 6 which shall **h** all these statutes, and H8085
10 I will make them **h** my words, that they H8085
28 neither see, nor **h**, nor eat, nor smell. H8085
33 Did *ever* people **h** the voice of God H8085
36 Out of heaven he made thee to **h** his H8085
5: 1 said unto them, **H**, O Israel, the statutes H8085
25 will consume us: if we **h** the voice of the H8085
27 Go thou near, and **h** all that the LORD H8085
Dt 5:27 unto thee; and we will **h** *it*, and do *it*. H8085
6: 3 **H** therefore, O Israel, and observe to do H8085
4 **H**, O Israel: The LORD our God *is* one H8085
9: 1 **H**, O Israel: Thou *art* to pass over H8085
12:28 Observe and **h** all these words which I H8085
13:11 And all Israel shall **h**, and fear, and H8085
12 If thou shalt **h** *say* in one of thy cities, H8085
17:13 And all the people shall **h**, and fear, and H8085
18:16 saying, Let me not **h** again the voice of. H8085
19:20 And those which remain shall **h**, and H8085
20: 3 And shall say unto them, **H**, O Israel, ye H8085
21:21 you; and all Israel shall **h**, and fear. H8085
29: 4 eyes to see, and ears to **h**, unto this day. H8085
30:12 it unto us, that we may **h** it, and do it? H8085
13 it unto us, that we may **h** it, and do it? H8085
17 that thou wilt not **h**, but shalt be drawn H8085
31:12 that they may **h**, and that they may H8085
13 *any thing*, may **h**, and learn to fear the H8085
32: 1 and **h**, O earth, the words of my mouth. H8085
33: 7 and he said, **H**, LORD, the voice of H8085
Jos 3: 9 and **h** the words of the LORD your God. H8085
6: 5 horn, *and* when ye **h** the sound of the H8085
7: 9 of the land shall **h** *of it*, and shall H8085
Jdg 5: 3 **H**, O ye kings; give ear, O ye princes; I, H8085
16 the sheepfolds, to **h** the bleatings of the H8085
7:11 And thou shalt **h** what they say; and H8085
14:13 Put forth thy riddle, that we may **h** it. H8085
1Sa 2:23 ye such things? for I **h** of your evil H8085
24 no good report that I **h**: ye make the H8085
8:18 the LORD will not **h** you in that day. H6030
13: 3 all the land, saying, Let the Hebrews **h**. H8085
15:14 and the lowing of the oxen which I **h**? H8085
16: 2 can I go? if Saul **h** *it*, he will kill me. H8085
22: 7 that stood about him, **H** now, ye H8085
12 And Saul said, **H** now, thou son of H8085
25:24 and **h** the words of thine handmaid. H8085
26:19 let my lord the king **h** the words of his H8085
2Sa 14:16 For the king will **h**, to deliver his H8085
15: 3 no man *deputed* of the king to **h** thee. H8085
10 As soon as ye **h** the sound of the H8085
35 soever thou shalt **h** out of the king's H8085
36 send unto me every thing that ye can **h**. H8085
16:21 and all Israel shall **h** that thou art H8085
17: 5 and let us **h** likewise what he saith. H8085
19:35 I drink? can I **h** any more the voice H8085
20:16 out of the city, **H**, hear; say, I pray you, H8085
16 of the city, Hear, **h**; say, I pray you, unto H8085
17 she said unto him, **H** the words of thine H8085
17 handmaid. And he answered, I do **h**. H8085
22: 7 God: and he did **h** my voice out of his H8085
45 they **h**, they shall be obedient unto me. H8085
1Ki 4:34 And there came of all people to **h** the H8085
8:30 this place: and **h** thou in heaven thy H8085
32 Then **h** thou in heaven, and do, and H8085
34 Then **h** thou in heaven, and forgive the H8085
36 Then **h** thou in heaven, and forgive the H8085
39 Then **h** thou in heaven thy dwelling H8085
42 (For they shall **h** of thy great name, H8085
43 **H** thou in heaven thy dwelling place, H8085
45 Then **h** thou in heaven their prayer and H8085
49 Then **h** thou their prayer and their H8085
10: 8 before thee, *and* that **h** thy wisdom. H8085
24 to Solomon, to **h** his wisdom, which H8085
18:26 saying, O Baal, **h** us. But *there was* no H6030
37 **H** me, O LORD, hear me, that this H6030
37 Hear me, O LORD, **h** me, that this H6030
22:19 And he said, **H** thou therefore the word H8085
2Ki 7: 1 Then Elisha said, **H** ye the word of the H8085
6 of the Syrians to **h** a noise of chariots, H8085
14:11 But Amaziah would not **h**. Therefore H8085
17:14 Notwithstanding they would not **h**, but H8085
18:12 and would not **h** *them*, nor do *them*. H8085
28 spake, saying, **H** the word of the great H8085
19: 4 It may be the LORD thy God will **h** all H8085
7 him, and he shall **h** a rumour, and H8085
16 LORD, bow down thine ear, and **h**: H8085
16 thine eyes, and see: and **h** the words of H8085
20:16 And Isaiah said unto Hezekiah, **H** the H8085
1Ch 14:15 And it shall be, when thou shalt **h** a H8085
28: 2 his feet, and said, **H** me, my brethren, H8085
2Ch 6:21 toward this place: **h** thou from thy H8085
23 Then **h** thou from heaven, and do, and H8085
25 Then **h** thou from the heavens, and H8085
27 Then **h** thou from heaven, and forgive H8085
30 Then **h** thou from heaven thy dwelling H8085
33 Then **h** thou from the heavens, *even* H8085
35 Then **h** thou from the heavens their H8085
39 Then **h** thou from the heavens, *even* H8085
7:14 ways; then will I **h** from heaven, and H8085

2Ch 9: 7 before thee, and **h** thy wisdom. H8085
23 of Solomon, to **h** his wisdom, that God H8085
13: 4 **H** me, thou Jeroboam, and all Israel; H8085
15: 2 said unto him, **H** ye me, Asa, and all H8085
18:18 Again he said, Therefore **h** the word of H8085
20: 9 affliction, then thou wilt **h** and help. H8085
20 stood and said, **H** me, O Judah, and ye H8085
25:20 But Amaziah would not **h**; for it *came* of H8085
28:11 Now **h** me therefore, and deliver the H8085
29: 5 And said unto them, **H** me, ye Levites, H8085
Neh 1: 6 that thou mayest **h** the prayer of thy H8085
4: 4 **H**, O our God; for we are despised: and H8085
20 In what place *therefore* ye **h** the sound H8085
8: 2 women, and all that could **h** with H8085
9:29 hardened their neck, and would not **h**. H8085
Job 3:18 they **h** not the voice of the oppressor. H8085
5:27 Lo this, we have searched it, so it *is*; **h** H8085
13: 6 **H** now my reasoning, and hearken to H8085
17 **H** diligently my speech, and my H8085
15:17 I will shew thee, **h** me; and that *which* I H8085
21: 2 **H** diligently my speech, and let this be H8085
22:27 **h** thee, and thou shalt pay thy vows. H8085
27: 9 Will God **h** his cry when trouble H8085
30:20 I cry unto thee, and thou dost not **h** me: H6030
31:35 Oh that one would **h** me! behold, my H8085
33: 1 Wherefore, Job, I pray thee, **h** my H8085
34: 2 **H** my words, O ye wise *men*; and give H8085
16 If now *thou hast* understanding, **h** this: H8085
35:13 Surely God will not **h** vanity, neither H8085
37: 2 **H** attentively the noise of his voice, and H8085
42: 4 **H**, I beseech thee, and I will speak: I will H8085
Ps 4: 1 **H** me when I call, O God of my H6030
1 have mercy upon me, and **h** my prayer. H8085
3 the LORD will **h** when I call unto him. H8085
5: 3 My voice shalt thou **h** in the morning, H8085
10:17 heart, thou wilt cause thine ear to **h**: H7181
13: 3 Consider *and* **h** me, O LORD my God: H6030
17: 1 **H** the right, O LORD, attend unto my H8085
6 I have called upon thee, for thou wilt **h** H6030
6 thine ear unto me, *and* **h** my speech. H8085
18:44 As soon as they **h** of me, they shall H8085
20: 1 The LORD **h** thee in the day of trouble; H6030
6 anointed; he will **h** him from his holy H6030
9 Save, LORD: let the king **h** us when we H6030
27: 7 **H**, O LORD, *when* I cry with my voice: H8085
28: 2 **H** the voice of my supplications, when I H8085
30:10 **H**, O LORD, and have mercy upon me: H8085
34: 2 humble shall **h** *thereof*, and be glad. H8085
38:15 do I hope: thou wilt **h**, O Lord my God. H6030
16 For I said, *H me*, lest *otherwise* they
39:12 **H** my prayer, O LORD, and give ear H8085
49: 1 **H** this, all *ye* people; give ear, all *ye* H8085
50: 7 **H**, O my people, and I will speak; O H8085
51: 8 Make me to **h** joy and gladness; *that* H8085
54: 2 **H** my prayer, O God; give ear to the H8085
55: 2 Attend unto me, and **h** me: I mourn in H6030
17 and cry aloud: and he shall **h** my voice. H8085
19 God shall **h**, and afflict them, even he H8085
59: 7 in their lips: for who, *say they*, doth **h**? H8085
60: 5 save *with* thy right hand, and **h** me. H6030
61: 1 **H** my cry, O God; attend unto my H8085
64: 1 **H** my voice, O God, in my prayer: H8085
66:16 Come *and* **h**, all ye that fear God, and I H8085
18 in my heart, the Lord will not **h** *me*: H8085
69:13 **h** me, in the truth of thy salvation. H6030
16 **H** me, O LORD; for thy lovingkindness H6030
17 for I am in trouble: **h** me speedily. H6030
81: 8 **H**, O my people, and I will testify unto H8085
84: 8 O LORD God of hosts, **h** my prayer: H8085
85: 8 I will **h** what God the LORD will speak: H8085
86: 1 Bow down thine ear, O LORD, **h** me: H6030
92:11 *and* mine ears shall **h** *my desire* of the H8085
94: 9 He that planted the ear, shall he not **h**? H8085
95: 7 his hand. To day if ye will **h** his voice, H8085
102: 1 **H** my prayer, O LORD, and let my cry H8085
20 To **h** the groaning of the prisoner; to H8085
115: 6 They have ears, but they **h** not: noses H8085
119:145 I cried with *my* whole heart; **h** me, O H6030
149 **H** my voice according unto thy H8085
130: 2 Lord, **h** my voice: let thine ears be H8085
135:17 They have ears, but they **h** not; neither is H238
138: 4 when they **h** the words of thy mouth. H8085
140: 6 Thou *art* my God: **h** the voice of my H238
141: 6 shall **h** my words; for they are sweet. H8085
143: 1 **H** my prayer, O LORD, give ear to my H8085
7 **H** me speedily, O LORD: my spirit H6030
8 Cause me to **h** thy lovingkindness in H8085
145:19 will **h** their cry, and will save them. H8085
Prv 1: 5 A wise *man* will **h**, and will increase H8085
Prv 1: 8 My son, **h** the instruction of thy father, H8085
4: 1 **H**, ye children, the instruction of a H8085
10 **H**, O my son, and receive my sayings; H8085
5: 7 **H** me now therefore, O ye children, and H8085
8: 6 **H**; for I will speak of excellent things; H8085
33 **H** instruction, and be wise, and refuse H8085
19:20 **H** counsel, and receive instruction, that H8085
27 Cease, my son, to **h** the instruction *that* H8085
22:17 Bow down thine ear, and **h** the words H8085
23:19 **H** thou, my son, and be wise, and guide H8085
Ecc 5: 1 and be more ready to **h**, than to give the H8085
7: 5 *It is* better to **h** the rebuke of the wise, H8085
5 than for a man to **h** the song of fools. H8085
21 lest thou **h** thy servant curse thee: H8085
12:13 Let us **h** the conclusion of the whole H8085
Song 2:14 let me **h** thy voice; for sweet H8085
8:13 hearken to thy voice: cause me to **h** *it*. H8085
Isa 1: 2 **H**, O heavens, and give ear, O earth: for H8085
10 **H** the word of the LORD, ye rulers of H8085
15 will not **h**: your hands are full of blood. H8085
6: 9 And he said, Go, and tell this people, **H** H8085
10 their eyes, and **h** with their ears, and H8085
7:13 And he said, **H** ye now, O house of H8085
18: 3 and when he bloweth a trumpet, **h** ye. H8085
28:12 *is* the refreshing: yet they would not **h**. H8085
14 Wherefore **h** the word of the LORD, ye H8085
23 Give ye ear, and **h** my voice; hearken, H8085
23 my voice; hearken, and **h** my speech. H8085
29:18 And in that day shall the deaf **h** the H8085
30: 9 *that* will not **h** the law of the LORD: H8085
19 when he shall **h** it, he will answer thee. H8085
21 And thine ears shall **h** a word behind H8085
32: 3 the ears of them that **h** shall hearken. H8085
9 Rise up, ye women that are at ease; **h** H8085
33:13 **H**, ye *that are* far off, what I have done; H8085
34: 1 Come near, ye nations, to **h**; and H8085
1 let the earth **h**, and all that is therein; H8085
36:13 and said, **H** ye the words of the H8085
37: 4 It may be the LORD thy God will **h** the H8085
7 him, and he shall **h** a rumour, and H8085
17 Incline thine ear, O LORD, and **h**; open H8085
17 LORD, and see: and **h** all the words of H8085
39: 5 Then said Isaiah to Hezekiah, **H** the H8085
41:17 I the LORD will **h** them, I the God of H6030
42:18 **H**, ye deaf; and look, ye blind, that ye H8085
23 hearken and **h** for the time to come? H8085
43: 9 or let them **h**, and say, *It is* truth. H8085
44: 1 Yet now **h**, O Jacob my servant; and H8085
47: 8 Therefore **h** now this, *thou that art* H8085
48: 1 **H** ye this, O house of Jacob, which are H8085
14 All ye, assemble yourselves, and **h**; H8085
16 Come ye near unto me, **h** ye this; I have H8085
50: 4 wakeneth mine ear to **h** as the learned. H8085
51:21 Therefore **h** now this, thou afflicted, H8085
55: 3 Incline your ear, and come unto me: **h**, H8085
59: 1 neither his ear heavy, that it cannot **h**: H8085
2 hid *his* face from you, that he will not **h**. H8085
65:12 I spake, ye did not **h**; but did evil before H8085
24 and while they are yet speaking, I will **h**. H8085
66: 4 they did not **h**: but they did evil before H8085
5 **H** the word of the LORD, ye that H8085
Jer 2: 4 **H** ye the word of the LORD, O house of H8085
4:21 *and* **h** the sound of the trumpet? H8085
5:21 **H** now this, O foolish people, and H8085
21 see not; which have ears, and **h** not: H8085
6:10 that they may **h**? behold, their ear *is* H8085
18 Therefore **h**, ye nations, and know, O H8085
19 **H**, O earth: behold, I will bring evil H8085
7: 2 this word, and say, **H** the word of the H8085
16 intercession to me: for I will not **h** thee. H8085
9:10 neither can *men* **h** the voice of the H8085
20 Yet **h** the word of the LORD, O ye H8085
10: 1 **H** ye the word which the LORD H8085
11: 2 **H** ye the words of this covenant, and H8085
6 saying, **H** ye the words of this H8085
10 which refused to **h** my words; and they H8085
14 for I will not **h** *them* in the time that H8085
13:10 This evil people, which refuse to **h** my H8085
11 and for a glory: but they would not **h**. H8085
15 **H** ye, and give ear; be not proud: for H8085
17 But if ye will not **h** it, my soul shall H8085
14:12 When they fast, I will not **h** their cry; H8085
17:20 And say unto them, **H** ye the word of H8085
23 might not **h**, nor receive instruction. H8085
18: 2 there I will cause thee to **h** my words. H8085
19: 3 And say, **H** ye the word of the LORD, O H8085
15 necks, that they might not **h** my words. H8085
20:16 not: and let him **h** the cry in the H8085
21:11 Judah, *say*, **H** ye the word of the LORD; H8085
Jer 22: 2 And say, **H** the word of the LORD, O H8085
5 But if ye will not **h** these words, I swear H8085
21 saidst, I will not **h**. This *hath been* thy H8085
29 O earth, earth, earth, **h** the word of the H8085
23:22 my people to **h** my words, then they H8085
25: 4 hearkened, nor inclined your ear to **h**. H8085
28: 7 Nevertheless **h** thou now this word that H8085
15 the prophet, **H** now, Hananiah; The H8085
29:19 but ye would not **h**, saith the LORD. H8085
20 **H** ye therefore the word of the LORD, H8085
31:10 **H** the word of the LORD, O ye nations, H8085
33: 9 earth, which shall **h** all the good that I H8085
34: 4 Yet **h** the word of the LORD, O H8085
36: 3 It may be that the house of Judah will **h** H8085
25 burn the roll: but he would not **h** them. H8085
37:20 Therefore **h** now, I pray thee, O my lord H8085
38:25 But if the princes **h** that I have talked H8085
42:14 shall see no war, nor **h** the sound of the H8085
15 And now therefore **h** the word of the H8085
44:24 to all the women, **H** the word of the H8085
26 Therefore **h** ye the word of the LORD, H8085
49:20 Therefore **h** the counsel of the LORD, H8085
50:45 Therefore **h** ye the counsel of the H8085
Lam 1:18 his commandment: **h**, I pray you, all H8085
Ezk 2: 5 And they, whether they will **h**, or H8085
7 whether they will **h**, or whether they will H8085
8 But thou, son of man, **h** what I say H8085
3:10 in thine heart, and **h** with thine ears. H8085
11 they will **h**, or whether they will forbear. H8085
17 of Israel: therefore **h** the word at my H8085
27 that heareth, let him **h**; and he that H8085
6: 3 And say, Ye mountains of Israel, **h** the H8085
8:18 with a loud voice, *yet* will I not **h** them. H8085
12: 2 they have ears to **h**, and hear not: for H8085
2 **h** not: for they *are* a rebellious house. H8085
13: 2 hearts, **H** ye the word of the LORD; H8085
19 lying to my people that **h** *your* lies? H8085
16:35 Wherefore, O harlot, **h** the word of the H8085
18:25 Lord is not equal. **H** now, O house of H8085
20:47 And say to the forest of the south, **H** H8085
24:26 to cause *thee* to **h** *it* with *thine* ears? H2045
25: 3 And say unto the Ammonites, **H** the H8085
33: 7 thou shalt **h** the word at my mouth, H8085
30 I pray you, and **h** what is the word that H8085
31 people, and they **h** thy words, but they H8085
32 they **h** thy words, but they do them not. H8085
34: 7 Therefore, ye shepherds, **h** the word of H8085
9 Therefore, O ye shepherds, **h** the word H8085
36: 1 of Israel, **h** the word of the LORD: H8085
4 Therefore, ye mountains of Israel, **h** H8085
15 Neither will I cause *men* to **h** in thee H8085
37: 4 ye dry bones, **h** the word of the LORD. H8085
40: 4 thine eyes, and **h** with thine ears, and H8085
44: 5 thine eyes, and **h** with thine ears all H8085
Dan 3: 5 *That* at what time ye **h** the sound of the H8086
10 every man that shall **h** the sound of the H8086
15 that at what time ye **h** the sound of the H8086
5:23 which see not, nor **h**, nor know: and the H8086
9:17 Now therefore, O our God, **h** the prayer H8085
18 O my God, incline thine ear, and **h**; H8085
19 O Lord, **h**; O Lord, forgive; O Lord, H8085
Hos 2:21 in that day, I will **h**, saith the LORD, I H6030
21 the LORD, I will **h** the heavens, and H6030
21 the heavens, and they shall **h** the earth; H6030
22 And the earth shall **h** the corn, and the H6030
22 and the oil; and they shall **h** Jezreel. H6030
4: 1 **H** the word of the LORD, ye children of H8085
5: 1 **H** ye this, O priests; and hearken, ye H8085
Joel 1: 2 **H** this, ye old men, and give ear, all ye H8085
Am 3: 1 **H** this word that the LORD hath H8085
13 **H** ye, and testify in the house of Jacob, H8085
4: 1 **H** this word, ye kine of Bashan, that H8085
5: 1 **H** ye this word which I take up against H8085
23 for I will not **h** the melody of thy viols. H8085
7:16 Now therefore **h** thou the word of the H8085
8: 4 **H** this, O ye that swallow up the needy, H8085
Mic 1: 2 **H**, all ye people; hearken, O earth, and H8085
3: 1 And I said, **H**, I pray you, O heads of H8085
4 but he will not **h** them: he will even H6030
9 **H** this, I pray you, ye heads of the H8085
6: 1 **H** ye now what the LORD saith; Arise, H8085
1 mountains, and let the hills **h** thy voice. H8085
2 **H** ye, O mountains, the LORD'S H8085
9 see thy name: **h** ye the rod, and who H8085
7: 7 God of my salvation: my God will **h** me. H8085
Nah 3:19 is grievous: all that **h** the bruit of thee H8085
Hab 1: 2 and thou wilt not **h**! *even* cry out unto H8085
Zec 1: 4 but they did not **h**, nor hearken unto H8085
3: 8 **H** now, O Joshua the high priest, thou, H8085

Zec 7: 7 *Should ye* not **h** the words which the
11 their ears, that they should not **h**. H8085
12 lest they should **h** the law, and the H8085
13 they would not **h**; so they cried, and I H8085
13 I would not **h**, saith the LORD of hosts: H8085
8: 9 be strong, ye that **h** in these days these H8085
10: 6 the LORD their God, and will **h** them. H6030
13: 9 name, and I will **h** them: I will say, It *is* H6030
Mal 2: 2 If ye will not **h**, and if ye will not lay *it* to H8085
Mt 10:14 receive you, nor **h** your words, when ye G191
27 in light: and what ye **h** in the ear, *that* G191
11: 4 those things which ye do **h** and see: G191
5 and the deaf **h**, the dead are raised up, G191
15 He that hath ears to **h**, let him hear. G191
15 He that hath ears to hear, let him **h**. G191
12:19 shall any man **h** his voice in the streets. G191
42 of the earth to **h** the wisdom of Solomon; G191
13: 9 Who hath ears to **h**, let him hear. G191
9 Who hath ears to hear, let him **h**. G191
13 they **h** not, neither do they understand. G191
14 saith, By hearing ye shall **h**, and shall not G191
15 *their* eyes, and **h** with *their* ears, and G191
16 for they see: and your ears, for they **h**. G191
17 seen *them*; and to **h** *those things* which G191
17 which ye **h**, and have not heard *them*. G191
18 **H** ye therefore the parable of the sower. G191
43 Father. Who hath ears to **h**, let him hear. G191
43 Father. Who hath ears to hear, let him **h**. G191
15:10 and said unto them, **H**, and understand: G191
17: 5 in whom I am well pleased; **h** ye him. G191
18:15 **h** thee, thou hast gained thy brother. G191
16 But if he will not **h** *thee, then* take with G191
17 And if he shall neglect to **h** them, tell *it* G3878
17 but if he neglect to **h** the church, let G3878
21:33 **H** another parable: There was a certain G191
24: 6 And ye shall **h** of wars and rumours of G191
Mk 4: 9 He that hath ears to **h**, let him hear. G191
9 He that hath ears to hear, let him **h**. G191
12 hearing they may **h**, and not understand; G191
18 sown among thorns; such as **h** the word, G191
20 ground; such as **h** the word, and receive G191
23 If any man have ears to **h**, let him hear. G191
23 If any man have ears to hear, let him **h**. G191
24 Take heed what ye **h**: with what measure G191
24 and unto you that **h** shall more be given. G191
33 unto them, as they were able to **h** *it*. G191
6:11 receive you, nor **h** you, when ye depart G191
7:16 If any man have ears to **h**, let him hear. G191
16 If any man have ears to hear, let him **h**. G191
37 the deaf to **h**, and the dumb to speak. G191
8:18 ears, **h** ye not? and do ye not remember? G191
9: 7 saying, This is my beloved Son: **h** him. G191
12:29 *is*, **H**, O Israel; The Lord our G191
13: 7 And when ye shall **h** of wars and G191
Lk 5: 1 upon him to **h** the word of God, he G191
15 came together to **h**, and to be healed by G191
6:17 **h** him, and to be healed of their diseases; G191
27 But I say unto you which **h**, Love your G191
7:22 cleansed, the deaf **h**, the dead are raised, G191
8: 8 He that hath ears to **h**, let him hear. G191
8 He that hath ears to hear, let him **h**. G191
12 Those by the way side are they that **h**; G191
13 which, when they **h**, receive the word G191
18 Take heed therefore how ye **h**: for G191
21 these which **h** the word of God, and do it. G191
9: 9 is this, of whom I **h** such things? And he G191
35 saying, This is my beloved Son: **h** him. G191
10:24 seen *them*; and to **h** those things which G191
24 which ye **h**, and have not heard *them*. G191
11:28 they that **h** the word of God, and keep it. G191
31 of the earth to **h** the wisdom of Solomon; G191
14:35 out. He that hath ears to **h**, let him hear. G191
35 out. He that hath ears to hear, let him **h**. G191
15: 1 the publicans and sinners for to **h** him. G191
16: 2 How is it that I **h** this of thee? give an G191
29 and the prophets; let them **h** them. G191
31 And he said unto him, If they **h** not G191
18: 6 And the Lord said, **H** what the unjust G191
19:48 the people were very attentive to **h** him. G191
21: 9 But when ye shall **h** of wars and G191
38 to him in the temple, for to **h** him. G191
Jn 5:25 the dead shall **h** the voice of the Son G191
25 Son of God: and they that **h** shall live. G191
28 that are in the graves shall **h** his voice, G191
30 I can of mine own self do nothing: as I **h**, G191
6:60 This is an hard saying; who can **h** it? G191
7:51 Doth our law judge *any* man, before it **h** G191
8:43 *even* because ye cannot **h** my word. G191
47 **h** *them* not, because ye are not of God. G191
Jn 9:27 and ye did not **h**: wherefore would ye G191
27 **h** *it* again? will ye also be his disciples? G191
10: 3 and the sheep **h** his voice: and he calleth G191
8 robbers: but the sheep did not **h** them. G191
16 and they shall **h** my voice; and there G191
20 hath a devil, and is mad; why **h** ye him? G191
27 My sheep **h** my voice, and I know them, G191
12:47 And if any man **h** my words, and believe G191
14:24 the word which ye **h** is not mine, but the G191
16:13 he shall **h**, *that* shall he speak: G191
Act 2: 8 And how **h** we every man in our own G191
11 Cretes and Arabians, we do **h** them G191
22 Ye men of Israel, **h** these words; Jesus of G191
33 shed forth this, which ye now see and **h**. G191
3:22 unto me; him shall ye **h** in all things G191
23 which will not **h** that prophet, shall be G191
7:37 brethren, like unto me; him shall ye **h**. G191
10:22 into his house, and to **h** words of thee. G191
33 before God, to **h** all things that are G191
13: 7 Saul, and desired to **h** the word of God. G191
44 whole city together to **h** the word of God. G191
15: 7 **h** the word of the gospel, and believe. G191
17:21 either to tell, or to **h** some new thing.) G191
32 said, We will **h** thee again of this *matter*. G191
19:26 Moreover ye see and **h**, that not alone at G191
21:22 for they will **h** that thou art come. G191
22: 1 Men, brethren, and fathers, **h** ye my G191
14 and shouldest **h** the voice of his mouth. G191
23:35 I will **h** thee, said he, when thine G1251
24: 4 **h** us of thy clemency a few words. G191
25:22 I would also **h** the man myself. To G191
22 To morrow, said he, thou shalt **h** him. G191
26: 3 I beseech thee to **h** me patiently. G191
29 but also all that **h** me this day, were both G191
28:22 But we desire to **h** of thee what thou G191
26 say, Hearing ye shall **h**, and shall not G191
27 *their* eyes, and **h** with *their* ears, and G191
28 unto the Gentiles, and *that* they will **h** it. G191
Ro 10:14 how shall they **h** without a preacher? G191
11: 8 that they should not **h**;) unto this day. G191
1Co 11:18 in the church, I **h** that there be divisions G191
14:21 that will they not **h** me, saith the Lord. G1522
Gal 4:21 to be under the law, do ye not **h** the law? G191
Php 1:27 be absent, I may **h** of your affairs, that G191
30 ye saw in me, and now **h** *to be* in me. G191
2Th 3:11 For we **h** that there are some which walk G191
1Ti 4:16 both save thyself, and them that **h** thee. G191
2Ti 4:17 the Gentiles might **h**: and I was delivered G191
Heb 3: 7 Ghost saith, To day if ye will **h** his voice, G191
15 While it is said, To day if ye will **h** his G191
4: 7 will **h** his voice, harden not your hearts. G191
Jas 1:19 swift to **h**, slow to speak, slow to wrath: G191
1Jn 5:15 And if we know that he **h** us, whatsoever G191
3Jn 4 I have no greater joy than to **h** that my G191
Rev 1: 3 and they that **h** the words of this G191
2: 7 He that hath an ear, let him **h** what the G191
11 He that hath an ear, let him **h** what the G191
17 He that hath an ear, let him **h** what the G191
29 He that hath an ear, let him **h** what the G191
3: 6 He that hath an ear, let him **h** what the G191
13 He that hath an ear, let him **h** what the G191
20 knock: if any man **h** my voice, and open G191
22 He that hath an ear, let him **h** what the G191
9:20 which neither can see, nor **h**, nor walk: G191
13: 9 If any man have an ear, let him **h**. G191

HEARD

Gen 3: 8 And they **h** the voice of the LORD God H8085
10 And he said, I **h** thy voice in the H8085
14:14 And when Abram **h** that his brother H8085
16:11 because the LORD hath **h** thy affliction. H8085
17:20 And as for Ishmael, I have **h** thee: H8085
18:10 a son. And Sarah **h** *it* in the tent door, H8085
21:17 And God **h** the voice of the lad; and the H8085
17 hath **h** the voice of the lad where he *is*. H8085
26 tell me, neither yet **h** I *of it*, but to day. H8085
24:30 and when he **h** the words of Rebekah H8085
52 servant **h** their words, he worshipped H8085
27: 5 And Rebekah **h** when Isaac spake to H8085
6 saying, Behold, I **h** thy father speak H8085
34 And when Esau **h** the words of his H8085
29:13 And it came to pass, when Laban **h** the H8085
33 the LORD hath **h** that I *was* hated, he H8085
30: 6 me, and hath also **h** my voice, and hath H8085
31: 1 And he **h** the words of Laban's sons, H8085
34: 5 And Jacob **h** that he had defiled Dinah H8085
7 field when they **h** *it*: and the men were H8085
35:22 **h** *it*. Now the sons of Jacob were twelve: H8085
37:17 hence; for I **h** them say, Let us go H8085
Gen 37:21 And Reuben **h** *it*, and he delivered him H8085
39:15 And it came to pass, when he **h** that I H8085
19 And it came to pass, when his master **h** H8085
41:15 it: and I have **h** say of thee, *that* thou H8085
42: 2 And he said, Behold, I have **h** that H8085
43:25 they **h** that they should eat bread there. H8085
45: 2 Egyptians and the house of Pharaoh **h**. H8085
16 And the fame thereof was **h** in H8085
Ex 2:15 Now when Pharaoh **h** this thing, he H8085
24 And God **h** their groaning, and God H8085
3: 7 Egypt, and have **h** their cry by reason H8085
4:31 and when they **h** that the LORD had H8085
6: 5 And I have also **h** the groaning of the H8085
16: 9 LORD: for he hath **h** your murmurings. H8085
12 I have **h** the murmurings of the H8085
18: 1 father in law, **h** of all that God had H8085
23:13 neither let it be **h** out of thy mouth. H8085
28:35 his sound shall be **h** when he goeth in H8085
32:17 And when Joshua **h** the noise of the H8085
33: 4 And when the people **h** these evil H8085
Lev 10:20 And when Moses **h** *that*, he was H8085
24:14 and let all that **h** *him* lay their hands H8085
Nu 7:89 with him, then he **h** the voice of one H8085
11: 1 and the LORD **h** *it*; and his anger was H8085
10 Then Moses **h** the people weep H8085
12: 2 spoken also by us? And the LORD **h** *it*. H8085
14:14 *for* they have **h** that thou LORD *art* H8085
15 **h** the fame of thee will speak, saying, H8085
27 me? I have **h** the murmurings of H8085
16: 4 And when Moses **h** *it*, he fell upon his H8085
20:16 unto the LORD, he **h** our voice, and H8085
21: 1 dwelt in the south, **h** tell that Israel H8085
22:36 And when Balak **h** that Balaam was H8085
24: 4 He hath said, which **h** the words of H8085
16 He hath said, which **h** the words of H8085
30: 7 And her husband **h** *it*, and held his H8085
7 in the day that he **h** *it*: then her vows H8085
8 on the day that he **h** *it*; then he shall H8085
11 And her husband **h** *it*, and held his H8085
12 them void on the day he **h** *them; then* H8085
14 peace at her in the day that he **h** *them*. H8085
15 **h** *them;* then he shall bear her iniquity. H8085
33:40 land of Canaan, **h** of the coming of the H8085
Dt 1:34 And the LORD **h** the voice of your H8085
4:12 of the fire: ye **h** the voice of the words, H8085
12 but saw no similitude; only *ye* **h** a voice.
32 great thing *is*, or hath been **h** like it? H8085
33 of the fire, as thou hast **h**, and live? H8085
5:23 And it came to pass, when ye **h** the H8085
24 and we have **h** his voice out of the H8085
26 For who *is there of* all flesh, that hath **h** H8085
28 And the LORD **h** the voice of your H8085
28 said unto me, I have **h** the voice of the H8085
9: 2 *whom* thou hast **h** *say*, Who can stand H8085
17: 4 And it be told thee, and thou hast **h** *of* H8085
26: 7 our fathers, the LORD **h** our voice, and H8085
Jos 2:10 For we have **h** how the LORD dried up H8085
11 And as soon as we had **h** *these things*, H8085
5: 1 *were* by the sea, **h** that the LORD had H8085
6:20 when the people **h** the sound of the H8085
9: 1 the Hivite, and the Jebusite, **h** *thereof*; H8085
3 And when the inhabitants of Gibeon **h** H8085
9 thy God: for we have **h** the fame of him, H8085
16 them, that they **h** that they *were* their H8085
10: 1 of Jerusalem had **h** how Joshua had H8085
11: 1 king of Hazor had **h** *those things*, that H8085
22:11 And the children of Israel **h** say, H8085
12 And when the children of Israel **h** *of it*, H8085
30 *were* with him, **h** the words that the H8085
24:27 us; for it hath **h** all the words of the H8085
Jdg 7:15 And it was *so*, when Gideon **h** the H8085
9:30 And when Zebul the ruler of the city **h** H8085
46 tower of Shechem **h** *that*, they entered H8085
18:25 not thy voice be **h** among us, lest angry H8085
20: 3 (Now the children of Benjamin **h** that H8085
Ru 1: 6 Moab: for she had **h** in the country of H8085
1Sa 1:13 but her voice was not **h**: therefore Eli H8085
2:22 Now Eli was very old, and **h** all that his H8085
4: 6 And when the Philistines **h** the noise of H8085
14 And when Eli **h** the noise of the crying, H8085
19 and when she **h** the tidings that the H8085
7: 7 And when the Philistines **h** that the H8085
7 **h** *it*, they were afraid of the Philistines. H8085
9 LORD for Israel; and the LORD **h** him. H6030
8:21 And Samuel **h** all the words of the H8085
11: 6 Saul when he **h** those tidings, and his H8085
13: 3 the Philistines **h** *of it*. And Saul blew H8085
4 And all Israel **h** say *that* Saul had H8085
14:22 *when* they **h** that the Philistines H8085

H

1Sa 14:27 But Jonathan **h** not when his father H8085
17:11 When Saul and all Israel **h** those words H8085
23 to the same words: and David **h** *them.* H8085
28 And Eliab his eldest brother **h** when he H8085
31 And when the words were **h** which H8085
22: 1 **h** *it,* they went down thither to him. H8085
6 When Saul **h** that David was H8085
23:10 hath certainly **h** that Saul seeketh to H8085
11 as thy servant hath **h**? O LORD God of H8085
25 And when Saul **h** *that,* he pursued after H8085
25: 4 And David **h** in the wilderness that H8085
7 And now I have **h** that thou hast H8085
39 And when David **h** that Nabal was H8085
31:11 of Jabesh-gilead **h** of that which the H8085
2Sa 3:28 And afterward when David **h** *it,* he H8085
4: 1 And when Saul's son **h** that Abner was H8085
5:17 But when the Philistines **h** that they H8085
17 **h** *of it,* and went down to the hold. H8085
7:22 to all that we have **h** with our ears. H8085
8: 9 When Toi king of Hamath **h** that David H8085
10: 7 And when David **h** of *it,* he sent Joab, H8085
11:26 And when the wife of Uriah **h** that H8085
13:21 But when king David **h** of all these H8085
18: 5 And all the people **h** when the king H8085
19: 2 for the people **h** say that day how the H8085
1Ki 1:11 Hast thou not **h** that Adonijah the son H8085
41 *were* with him **h** *it* as they had made H8085
41 And when Joab **h** the sound of the H8085
45 again. This *is* the noise that ye have **h**. H8085
2:42 me, The word *that* I have **h** *is* good. H8085
3:28 And all Israel **h** of the judgment which H8085
4:34 the earth, which had **h** of his wisdom. H8085
5: 1 for he had **h** that they had anointed H8085
7 And it came to pass, when Hiram **h** the H8085
6: 7 **h** in the house, while it was in building. H8085
9: 3 And the LORD said unto him, I have **h** H8085
10: 1 And when the queen of Sheba **h** of the H8085
6 true report that I **h** in mine own land of H8085
7 exceedeth the fame which I **h**. H8085
11:21 And when Hadad **h** in Egypt that H8085
12: 2 was yet in Egypt, **h** *of it,* (for he was H8085
20 And it came to pass, when all Israel **h** H8085
13: 4 king Jeroboam **h** the saying of the man H8085
26 from the way **h** *thereof,* he said, It *is* H8085
14: 6 And it was *so,* when Ahijah **h** the H8085
15:21 And it came to pass, when Baasha **h** H8085
16:16 And the people *that were* encamped **h** H8085
17:22 And the LORD **h** the voice of Elijah; H8085
19:13 And it was *so,* when Elijah **h** *it,* that he H8085
20:12 when *Ben-hadad* **h** this message, as he H8085
31 now, we have **h** that the kings of the H8085
21:15 And it came to pass, when Jezebel **h** H8085
16 And it came to pass, when Ahab **h** that H8085
27 And it came to pass, when Ahab **h** H8085
2Ki 3:21 And when all the Moabites **h** that the H8085
5: 8 the man of God had **h** that the king of H8085
6:30 And it came to pass, when the king **h** H8085
9:30 come to Jezreel, Jezebel **h** *of it;* and she H8085
11:13 And when Athaliah **h** the noise of the H8085
19: 1 king Hezekiah **h** *it,* that he rent his H8085
4 thy God hath **h**: wherefore lift up *thy* H8085
6 which thou hast **h**, with which the H8085
8 **h** that he was departed from Lachish. H8085
9 And when he **h** say of Tirhakah king of H8085
11 Behold, thou hast **h** what the kings of H8085
20 Sennacherib king of Assyria I have **h**. H8085
25 Hast thou not **h** long ago *how* I have H8085
20: 5 thy father, I have **h** thy prayer, I have H8085
12 he had **h** that Hezekiah had been sick. H8085
22:11 when the king had **h** the words of the H8085
18 *touching* the words which thou hast **h**; H8085
19 me; I also have **h** *thee,* saith the LORD. H8085
25:23 they and their men, **h** that the king of H8085
1Ch 10:11 And when all Jabesh-gilead **h** all that H8085
14: 8 And when the Philistines **h** that David H8085
8 **h** *of it,* and went out against them. H8085
17:20 to all that we have **h** with our ears. H8085
18: 9 Now when Tou king of Hamath **h** how H8085
19: 8 And when David **h** *of it,* he sent Joab, H8085
2Ch 5:13 one sound to be **h** in praising and H8085
7:12 said unto him, I have **h** thy prayer, and H8085
9: 1 And when the queen of Sheba **h** of the H8085
5 report which I **h** in mine own land of H8085
6 *for* thou exceedest the fame that I **h**. H8085
10: 2 Solomon the king, **h** *it,* that Jeroboam H8085
15: 8 And when Asa **h** these words, and the H8085
16: 5 And it came to pass, when Baasha **h** *it,* H8085
20:29 when they had **h** that the LORD fought H8085
23:12 Now when Athaliah **h** the noise of the H8085
2Ch 30:27 and their voice was **h**, and their prayer H8085
33:13 of him, and **h** his supplication, and H8085
34:19 when the king had **h** the words of the H8085
26 the words which thou hast **h**; H8085
27 have even **h** *thee* also, saith the LORD. H8085
Ezr 3:13 shout, and the noise was **h** afar off. H8085
4: 1 and Benjamin **h** that the children of H8085
9: 3 And when I **h** this thing, I rent my H8085
Neh 1: 4 And it came to pass, when I **h** these H8085
2:10 the Ammonite, **h** *of it,* it grieved them H8085
19 the Arabian, **h** *it,* they laughed us to H8085
4: 1 when Sanballat **h** that we builded the H8085
7 and the Ashdodites, **h** that the walls of H8085
15 when our enemies **h** that it was known H8085
5: 6 And I was very angry when I **h** their cry H8085
6: 1 of our enemies, **h** that I had builded the H8085
16 all our enemies **h** *thereof,* and all the H8085
8: 9 wept, when they **h** the words of the law. H8085
12:43 joy of Jerusalem was **h** even afar off. H8085
13: 3 Now it came to pass, when they had **h** H8085
Est 1:18 which have **h** of the deed of the queen. H8085
2: 8 and his decree was **h**, and when many H8085
Job 2:11 Now when Job's three friends **h** of all H8085
4:16 *was* silence, and I **h** a voice, *saying,* H8085
13: 1 mine ear hath **h** and understood it. H8085
15: 8 Hast thou **h** the secret of God? and dost H8085
16: 2 I have **h** many such things: miserable H8085
19: 7 **h**: I cry aloud, but *there is* no judgment. H6030
20: 3 I have **h** the check of my reproach, and H8085
26:14 little a portion is **h** of him? but the H8085
28:22 Destruction and death say, We have **h** H8085
29:11 When the ear **h** *me,* then it blessed me; H8085
33: 8 I have **h** the voice of *thy* words, *saying,* H8085
37: 4 will not stay them when his voice is **h**. H8085
42: 5 I have **h** of thee by the hearing of the H8085
Ps 3: 4 and he **h** me out of his holy hill. Selah. H6030
6: 8 LORD hath **h** the voice of my weeping. H8085
9 The LORD hath **h** my supplication; the H8085
10:17 LORD, thou hast **h** the desire of the H8085
18: 6 unto my God: he **h** my voice out of his H8085
19: 3 nor language, *where* their voice is not **h**. H8085
22:21 **h** me from the horns of the unicorns. H6030
24 him; but when he cried unto him, he **h**. H8085
28: 6 hath **h** the voice of my supplications. H8085
31:13 For I have **h** the slander of many: fear H8085
34: 4 I sought the LORD, and he **h** me, and H6030
6 This poor man cried, and the LORD **h** H8085
38:13 But I, as a deaf *man,* **h** not; and *I was* H8085
40: 1 and he inclined unto me, and **h** my cry. H8085
44: 1 We have **h** with our ears, O God, our H8085
48: 8 As we have **h**, so have we seen in the H8085
61: 5 For thou, O God, hast **h** my vows: thou H8085
62:11 God hath spoken once; twice have I **h**. H8085
66: 8 and make the voice of his praise to be **h**: H8085
19 *But* verily God hath **h** *me;* he hath H8085
76: 8 Thou didst cause judgment to be **h** H8085
78: 3 Which we have **h** and known, and our H8085
21 Therefore the LORD **h** *this,* and was H8085
59 When God **h** *this,* he was wroth, and H8085
81: 5 I **h** a language *that* I understood not. H8085
97: 8 Zion **h**, and was glad; and the H8085
106:44 their affliction, when he **h** their cry: H8085
116: 1 I love the LORD, because he hath **h** my H8085
118:21 I will praise thee: for thou hast **h** me, H6030
120: 1 I cried unto the LORD, and he **h** me. H6030
132: 6 Lo, we **h** of it at Ephratah: we found it H8085
Prv 21:13 also shall cry himself, but shall not be **h**. H6030
Ecc 9:16 *is* despised, and his words are not **h**. H8085
17 The words of wise *men are* **h** in quiet H8085
Song 2:12 the voice of the turtle is **h** in our land; H8085
Isa 6: 8 Also I **h** the voice of the Lord, saying, H8085
10:30 it to be **h** unto Laish, O poor Anathoth. H7181
15: 4 their voice shall be **h** *even* unto Jahaz: H8085
16: 6 We have **h** of the pride of Moab; *he is* H8085
21:10 that which I have **h** of the LORD of H8085
24:16 the earth have we **h** songs, *even* glory H8085
28:22 strong: for I have **h** from the Lord GOD H8085
30:30 voice to be **h**, and shall shew the H8085
37: 1 king Hezekiah **h** *it,* that he rent his H8085
4 thy God hath **h**: wherefore lift up *thy* H8085
6 words that thou hast **h**, wherewith the H8085
8 **h** that he was departed from Lachish. H8085
9 And he **h** say concerning Tirhakah H8085
9 with thee. And when he **h** *it,* he sent H8085
11 Behold, thou hast **h** what the kings of H8085
26 Hast thou not **h** long ago, *how* I have H8085
38: 5 thy father, I have **h** thy prayer, I have H8085
39: 1 for he had **h** that he had been sick, H8085
40:21 Have ye not known? have ye not **h**? hath H8085
Isa 40:28 Hast thou not known? hast thou not **h**, H8085
42: 2 nor cause his voice to be **h** in the street. H8085
48: 6 Thou hast **h**, see all this; and will not ye H8085
49: 8 time have I **h** thee, and in a day of H6030
52:15 they had not **h** shall they consider. H8085
58: 4 to make your voice to be **h** on high. H8085
60:18 Violence shall no more be **h** in thy H8085
64: 4 *men* have not **h**, nor perceived by the H8085
65:19 more **h** in her, nor the voice of crying. H8085
66: 8 Who hath **h** such a thing? who hath H8085
19 off, that have not **h** my fame, neither H8085
Jer 3:21 A voice was **h** upon the high places, H8085
4:19 because thou hast **h**, O my soul, the H8085
31 For I have **h** a voice as of a woman in H8085
6: 7 and spoil is **h** in her; before me H8085
24 We have **h** the fame thereof: our hands H8085
7:13 and speaking, but ye **h** not; and I called H8085
8: 6 I hearkened and **h**, *but* they spake not H8085
16 The snorting of his horses was **h** from H8085
9:19 For a voice of wailing is **h** out of Zion, H8085
18:13 who hath **h** such things: the virgin H8085
22 Let a cry be **h** from their houses, when H8085
20: 1 house of the LORD, **h** that Jeremiah H8085
10 For I **h** the defaming of many, fear on H8085
23:18 perceived and **h** his word? who hath H8085
18 who hath marked his word, and **h** *it?* H8085
25 I have **h** what the prophets said, that H8085
25: 8 hosts; Because ye have not **h** my words, H8085
36 of the flock, *shall be h*: for the LORD hath
26: 7 and all the people **h** Jeremiah speaking H8085
10 When the princes of Judah **h** these H8085
11 this city, as ye have **h** with your ears. H8085
12 this city all the words that ye have **h**. H8085
21 all the princes, **h** his words, the king H8085
21 but when Urijah **h** it, he was afraid, H8085
30: 5 For thus saith the LORD; We have **h** a H8085
31:15 Thus saith the LORD; A voice was **h** in H8085
18 I have surely **h** Ephraim bemoaning H8085
33:10 there shall be **h** in this place, which H8085
34:10 into the covenant, **h** that every one H8085
35:17 but they have not **h**; and I have called H8085
36:11 of Shaphan, had **h** out of the book all H8085
13 words that he had **h**, when Baruch read H8085
16 Now it came to pass, when they had **h** H8085
24 of his servants that **h** all these words. H8085
37: 5 Jerusalem **h** tidings of them, they H8085
38: 1 the son of Malchiah, **h** the words that H8085
7 in the king's house, **h** that they had put H8085
40: 7 they and their men, **h** that the king of H8085
11 in all the countries, **h** that the king of H8085
41:11 that *were* with him, **h** of all the evil that H8085
42: 4 unto them, I have **h** *you;* behold, I will H8085
46:12 The nations have **h** of thy shame, and H8085
48: 4 her little ones have caused a cry to be **h**. H8085
5 enemies have **h** a cry of destruction. H8085
29 We have **h** the pride of Moab, (he is H8085
49: 2 alarm of war to be **h** in Rabbah of the H8085
14 I have **h** a rumour from the LORD, and H8085
21 the noise thereof was **h** in the Red sea. H8085
23 for they have **h** evil tidings: they are H8085
50:43 The king of Babylon hath **h** the report H8085
46 and the cry is **h** among the nations. H8085
51:46 that shall be **h** in the land; a rumour H8085
51 We are confounded, because we have **h** H8085
Lam 1:21 They have **h** that I sigh: *there is* none to H8085
21 enemies have **h** of my trouble; they H8085
3:56 Thou hast **h** my voice: hide not thine H8085
61 Thou hast **h** their reproach, O LORD, H8085
Ezk 1:24 And when they went, I **h** the noise of H8085
28 face, and I **h** a voice of one that spake. H8085
2: 2 feet, that I **h** him that spake unto me. H8085
3:12 Then the spirit took me up, and I **h** H8085
13 *I h* also the noise of the wings of the
10: 5 wings was **h** *even* to the outer court, H8085
19: 4 The nations also **h** of him; he was H8085
9 be **h** upon the mountains of Israel. H8085
26:13 sound of thy harps shall be no more **h**. H8085
27:30 And shall cause their voice to be **h** H8085
33: 5 He **h** the sound of the trumpet, and H8085
35:12 *and that* I have **h** all thy blasphemies H8085
13 your words against me: I have **h** *them.* H8085
43: 6 And I **h** *him* speaking unto me out of H8085
Dan 3: 7 all the people **h** the sound of the cornet, H8086
5:14 I have even **h** of thee, that the spirit of H8086
16 And I have **h** of thee, that thou canst H8086
6:14 Then the king, when he **h** *these* words, H8086
8:13 Then I **h** one saint speaking, and H8085
16 And I **h** a man's voice between *the* H8085
10: 9 Yet **h** I the voice of his words: and H8085

Dan 10: 9 his words: and when I **h** the voice of his H8085
12 were **h**, and I am come for thy words. H8085
12: 7 And I **h** the man clothed in linen, H8085
8 And I **h**, but I understood not: then said H8085
Hos 7:12 them, as their congregation hath **h**. H8088
14: 8 with idols? I have **h** *him*, and observed H6030
Oba 1 Edom; We have **h** a rumour from the H8085
Jna 2: 2 the LORD, and he **h** me; out of the belly H6030
Mic 5:15 the heathen, such as they have not **h**. H8085
Nah 2:13 of thy messengers shall no more be **h**. H8085
Hab 3: 2 O LORD, I have **h** thy speech, *and* was H8085
16 When I **h**, my belly trembled; my lips H8085
Zep 2: 8 I have **h** the reproach of Moab, and the H8085
Zec 8:23 you: for we have **h** *that* God *is* with you. H8085
Mal 3:16 hearkened, and **h** *it*, and a book of H8085
Mt 2: 3 When Herod the king had **h** *these things*, G191
9 When they had **h** the king, they G191
18 In Rama was there a voice **h**, G191
22 But when he **h** that Archelaus did reign G191
4:12 Now when Jesus had **h** that John was G191
5:21 Ye have **h** that it was said by them of old G191
27 Ye have **h** that it was said by them of old G191
33 Again, ye have **h** that it hath been said G191
38 Ye have **h** that it hath been said, An eye G191
43 Ye have **h** that it hath been said, Thou G191
6: 7 they shall be **h** for their much speaking. G1522
8:10 When Jesus **h** *it*, he marvelled, and said G191
9:12 But when Jesus **h** *that*, he said unto G191
11: 2 Now when John had **h** in the prison the G191
12:24 But when the Pharisees **h** *it*, they said, G191
13:17 which ye hear, and have not **h** *them*. G191
14: 1 At that time Herod the tetrarch **h** of the G191
13 When Jesus **h** *of it*, he departed thence G191
13 the people had **h** *thereof*, they followed G191
15:12 were offended, after they **h** this saying? G191
17: 6 And when the disciples **h** *it*, they fell on G191
19:22 But when the young man **h** that saying, G191
25 When his disciples **h** *it*, they were G191
20:24 And when the ten **h** *it*, they were moved G191
30 side, when they **h** that Jesus passed by, G191
21:45 and Pharisees had **h** his parables, they G191
22: 7 But when the king **h** *thereof*, he was G191
22 When they had **h** *these words*, they G191
33 And when the multitude **h** *this*, they G191
34 But when the Pharisees had **h** that he G191
26:65 behold, now ye have **h** his blasphemy. G191
27:47 **h** *that*, said, This *man* calleth for Elias. G191
Mk 2:17 When Jesus **h** *it*, he saith unto them, G191
3: 8 when they had **h** what great things he G191
21 And when his friends **h** *of it*, they went G191
4:15 but when they have **h**, Satan cometh G191
16 when they have **h** the word, immediately G191
5:27 When she had **h** of Jesus, came in the G191
36 As soon as Jesus **h** the word that was G191
6:14 And king Herod **h** *of him*; (for his name G191
16 But when Herod **h** *thereof*, he said, It is G191
20 him; and when he **h** him, he did many G191
20 he did many things, and **h** him gladly. G191
29 And when his disciples **h** *of it*, they came G191
55 that were sick, where they **h** he was. G191
7:25 **h** of him, and came and fell at his feet: G191
10:41 And when the ten **h** *it*, they began to be G191
47 And when he **h** that it was Jesus of G191
11:14 hereafter for ever. And his disciples **h** *it*. G191
18 And the scribes and chief priests **h** *it*, G191
12:28 came, and having **h** them reasoning G191
37 And the common people **h** him gladly. G191
14:11 And when they **h** *it*, they were glad, and G191
58 We **h** him say, I will destroy this temple G191
64 Ye have **h** the blasphemy: what think ye? G191
15:35 they **h** *it*, said, Behold, he calleth Elias. G191
16:11 And they, when they had **h** that he was G191
Lk 1:13 for thy prayer is **h**; and thy wife G1522
41 when Elisabeth **h** the salutation of Mary, G191
58 And her neighbours and her cousins **h** G191
66 And all they that **h** *them* laid *them* up in G191
2:18 And all they that **h** *it* wondered at those G191
20 **h** and seen, as it was told unto them. G191
47 And all that **h** him were astonished at G191
4:23 we have **h** done in Capernaum, G191
28 **h** these things, were filled with wrath, G191
7: 3 And when he **h** of Jesus, he sent unto G191
9 When Jesus **h** these things, he marvelled G191
22 ye have seen and **h**; how that the blind G191
29 And all the people that **h** *him*, and the G191
8:14 when they have **h**, go forth, and are G191
15 good heart, having **h** the word, keep *it*, G191
50 But when Jesus **h** *it*, he answered him, G191
9: 7 Now Herod the tetrarch **h** of all that was G191

Lk 10:24 which ye hear, and have not **h** *them*. G191
39 also sat at Jesus' feet, and **h** his word. G191
12: 3 darkness shall be **h** in the light; and that G191
14:15 at meat with him **h** these things, he said G191
15:25 to the house, he **h** musick and dancing. G191
16:14 **h** all these things: and they derided him. G191
18:22 Now when Jesus **h** these things, he said G191
23 And when he **h** this, he was very G191
26 And they that **h** *it* said, Who then can be G191
19:11 And as they **h** these things, he added G191
20:16 when they **h** *it*, they said, God forbid. G191
22:71 we ourselves have **h** of his own mouth. G191
23: 6 When Pilate **h** of Galilee, he asked G191
8 because he had **h** many things of him; G191
Jn 1:37 And the two disciples **h** him speak, and G191
40 One of the two which **h** John *speak*, and G191
3:32 And what he hath seen and **h**, that he G191
4: 1 the Pharisees had **h** that Jesus made and G191
42 saying: for we have **h** *him* ourselves, and G191
47 When he **h** that Jesus was come out of G191
5:37 Ye have neither **h** his voice at any time, G191
6:45 therefore that hath **h**, and hath learned G191
60 when they had **h** *this*, said, This is an G191
7:32 The Pharisees **h** that the people G191
40 when they **h** this saying, said, Of G191
8: 6 on the ground, *as though he* **h** *them not*.
9 And they which **h** *it*, being convicted by G191
26 those things which I have **h** of him. G191
40 I have **h** of God: this did not Abraham. G191
9:32 Since the world began was it not **h** that G191
35 Jesus **h** that they had cast him out; and G191
40 were with him **h** these words, and said G191
11: 4 When Jesus **h** *that*, he said, This G191
6 When he had **h** therefore that he was G191
20 Then Martha, as soon as she **h** that Jesus G191
29 As soon as she **h** *that*, she arose quickly, G191
41 Father, I thank thee that thou hast **h** me. G191
12:12 **h** that Jesus was coming to Jerusalem, G191
18 they **h** that he had done this miracle. G191
29 that stood by, and **h** *it*, said that it G191
34 The people answered him, We have **h** G191
14:28 Ye have **h** how I said unto you, I go G191
15:15 things that I have **h** of my Father I have G191
18:21 Why askest thou me? ask them which **h** G191
19: 8 When Pilate therefore **h** that saying, he G191
13 When Pilate therefore **h** that saying, he G191
21: 7 when Simon Peter **h** that it was the Lord, G191
Act 1: 4 Father, which, *saith he*, ye have **h** of me. G191
2: 6 man **h** them speak in his own language. G191
37 Now when they **h** *this*, they were pricked G191
4: 4 Howbeit many of them which **h** the word G191
20 the things which we have seen and **h**. G191
24 And when they **h** that, they lifted up G191
5: 5 came on all them that **h** these things. G191
11 and upon as many as **h** these things. G191
21 And when they **h** *that*, they entered into G191
24 and the chief priests **h** these things, they G191
33 When they **h** *that*, they were cut *to the* G191
6:11 said, We have **h** him speak blasphemous G191
14 For we have **h** him say, that this Jesus of G191
7:12 But when Jacob **h** that there was corn in G191
34 Egypt, and I have **h** their groaning, and G191
54 When they **h** these things, they were cut G191
8:14 were at Jerusalem **h** that Samaria had G191
30 And Philip ran thither to *him*, and **h** him G191
9: 4 And he fell to the earth, and **h** a voice G191
13 Then Ananias answered, Lord, I have **h** G191
21 But all that **h** *him* were amazed, and G191
38 the disciples had **h** that Peter was there, G191
10:31 And said, Cornelius, thy prayer is **h**, G1522
44 Ghost fell on all them which **h** the word. G191
46 For they **h** them speak with tongues, and G191
11: 1 were in Judaea **h** that the Gentiles had G191
7 And I **h** a voice saying unto me, Arise, G191
18 When they **h** these things, they held their G191
13:48 And when the Gentiles **h** this, they were G191
14: 9 The same **h** Paul speak: who stedfastly G191
14 and Paul, **h** *of*, they rent their clothes, G191
15:24 Forasmuch as we have **h**, that certain G191
16:14 worshipped God, **h** *us*: whose heart the G191
25 unto God: and the prisoners **h** them. G1874
38 when they **h** that they were Romans. G191
17: 8 of the city, when they **h** these things. G191
32 And when they **h** of the resurrection of G191
18:26 and Priscilla had **h**, they took him unto G191
19: 2 as **h** whether there be any Holy Ghost. G191
5 When they **h** *this*, they were baptized in G191
10 dwelt in Asia **h** the word of the Lord G191
28 And when they **h** *these sayings*, they G191

Act 21:12 And when we **h** these things, both we, G191
20 And when they **h** *it*, they glorified the G191
22: 2 (And when they **h** that he spake in the G191
7 And I fell unto the ground, and **h** a voice G191
9 **h** not the voice of him that spake to me. G191
15 all men of what thou hast seen and **h**. G191
26 When the centurion **h** *that*, he went and G191
23:16 And when Paul's sister's son **h** of their G191
24:22 And when Felix **h** these things, having G191
24 and **h** him concerning the faith in Christ. G191
26:14 to the earth, I **h** a voice speaking unto G191
28:15 And from thence, when the brethren **h** of G191
Ro 10:14 they have not **h**? and how shall they hear G191
18 But I say, Have they not **h**? Yes verily, G191
15:21 they that have not **h** shall understand. G191
1Co 2: 9 not seen, nor ear **h**, neither have entered G191
2Co 6: 2 (For he saith, I have **h** thee in a time G1873
12: 4 into paradise, and **h** unspeakable words, G191
Gal 1:13 For ye have **h** of my conversation in time G191
23 But they had **h** only, That he which G191
Eph 1:13 In whom ye also *trusted*, after that ye **h** G191
15 Wherefore I also, after I **h** of your faith G191
3: 2 If ye have **h** of the dispensation of the G191
4:21 If so be that ye have **h** him, and have G191
Php 2:26 that ye had **h** that he had been sick. G191
4: 9 and received, and **h**, and seen in me, do: G191
Col 1: 4 Since we **h** of your faith in Christ Jesus, G191
5 whereof ye **h** before in the word of G4257
6 since the day ye **h** *of it*, and knew the G191
9 since the day we **h** *it*, do not cease to G191
23 gospel, which ye have **h**, *and* which was G191
1Th 2:13 of God which ye **h** of us, ye received *it* G189
2Ti 1:13 which thou hast **h** of me, in faith and G191
2: 2 And the things that thou hast **h** of me G191
Heb 2: 1 which we have **h**, lest at any time we G191
3 confirmed unto us by them that **h** *him*; G191
3:16 For some, when they had **h**, did provoke: G191
4: 2 being mixed with faith in them that **h** *it*. G191
5: 7 death, and was **h** in that he feared; G1522
12:19 *voice* they that **h** entreated that the word G191
Jas 5:11 endure. Ye have **h** of the patience of Job, G191
2Pt 1:18 from heaven we **h**, when we were with G191
1Jn 1: 1 which we have **h**, which we have seen G191
3 That which we have seen and **h** declare G191
5 which we have **h** of him, and declare G191
2: 7 which ye have **h** from the beginning. G191
18 and as ye have **h** that antichrist shall G191
24 in you, which ye have **h** from the G191
24 that which ye have **h** from the beginning G191
3:11 For this is the message that ye **h** from G191
4: 3 whereof ye have **h** that it should come; G191
2Jn 6 That, as ye have **h** from the beginning, G191
Rev 1:10 the Lord's day, and **h** behind me a great G191
3: 3 hast received and **h**, and hold fast, and G191
4: 1 first voice which I **h** *was* as it were of a G191
5:11 And I beheld, and I **h** the voice of many G191
13 all that are in them, **h** I saying, Blessing, G191
6: 1 of the seals, and I **h**, as it were the noise G191
3 I **h** the second beast say, Come and see. G191
5 the third seal, I **h** the third beast say, G191
6 And I **h** a voice in the midst of the four G191
7 the fourth seal, I **h** the voice of the fourth G191
7: 4 And I **h** the number of them which were G191
8:13 And I beheld, and **h** an angel flying G191
9:13 And the sixth angel sounded, and I **h** a G191
16 thousand: and I **h** the number of them. G191
10: 4 to write: and I **h** a voice from heaven G191
8 And the voice which I **h** from heaven G191
11:12 And they **h** a great voice from heaven G191
12:10 And I **h** a loud voice saying in heaven, G191
14: 2 And I **h** a voice from heaven, as the G191
2 thunder: and I **h** the voice of harpers G191
13 And I **h** a voice from heaven saying unto G191
16: 1 And I **h** a great voice out of the temple G191
5 And I **h** the angel of the waters say, Thou G191
7 And I **h** another out of the altar say, G191
18: 4 And I **h** another voice from heaven, G191
22 shall be **h** no more at all in thee; G191
22 shall be **h** no more at all in thee; G191
23 of the bride shall be **h** no more at all in G191
19: 1 And after these things I **h** a great voice G191
6 And I **h** as it were the voice of a great G191
21: 3 And I **h** a great voice out of heaven G191
22: 8 And I John saw these things, and **h** G191
8 And when I had **h** and seen, I fell down G191

HEARDEST
Dt 4:36 **h** his words out of the midst of the fire. H8085
Jos 14:12 that day; for thou **h** in that day how the H8085

H

2Ki 22:19 the LORD, when thou **h** what I spake H8085
2Ch 34:27 God, when thou **h** his words against H8085
Neh 9: 9 Egypt, and **h** their cry by the Red sea; H8085
27 unto thee, thou **h** *them* from heaven; H8085
28 unto thee, thou **h** *them* from heaven; H8085
Ps 31:22 nevertheless thou **h** the voice of my H8085
119:26 I have declared my ways, and thou **h** H6030
Isa 48: 7 the day when thou **h** them not; lest H8085
8 Yea, thou **h** not; yea, thou knewest not; H8085
Jna 2: 2 of hell cried I, *and* thou **h** my voice. H8085

HEARER
Jas 1:23 For if any be a **h** of the word, and not a *G202*
25 not a forgetful **h**, but a doer of the work, *G202*

HEARERS
Ro 2:13 (For not the **h** of the law *are* just before *G202*
Eph 4:29 that it may minister grace unto the **h**. *G191*
2Ti 2:14 no profit, *but* to the subverting of the **h**. *G191*
Jas 1:22 But be ye doers of the word, and not **h** *G202*

HEAREST
Ru 2: 8 Then said Boaz unto Ruth, **H** thou not, H8085
1Sa 24: 9 And David said to Saul, Wherefore **h** H8085
2Sa 5:24 And let it be, when thou **h** the sound of H8085
1Ki 8:30 place: and when thou **h**, forgive. H8085
2Ch 6:21 from heaven; and when thou **h**, forgive. H8085
Ps 22: 2 the daytime, but thou **h** not; and in the H6030
65: 2 O thou that **h** prayer, unto thee shall all H8085
Mt 21:16 And said unto him, **H** thou what these *G191*
27:13 Then said Pilate unto him, **H** thou not *G191*
Jn 3: 8 it listeth, and thou **h** the sound thereof, *G191*
11:42 And I knew that thou **h** me always: but *G191*

HEARETH
Ex 16: 7 LORD; for that he **h** your murmurings H8085
8 for that the LORD **h** your murmurings H8085
Nu 30: 5 her in the day that he **h**; not any of her H8085
Dt 29:19 And it come to pass, when he **h** the H8085
1Sa 3: 9 for thy servant **h**. So Samuel went and H8085
10 answered, Speak; for thy servant **h**. H8085
11 ears of every one that **h** it shall tingle. H8085
2Sa 17: 9 that whosoever **h** it will say, There is H8085
2Ki 21:12 **h** of it, both his ears shall tingle. H8085
Job 34:28 him, and he **h** the cry of the afflicted. H8085
Ps 34:17 *The righteous* cry, and the LORD **h**, and H8085
38:14 Thus I was as a man that **h** not, and in H8085
69:33 For the LORD **h** the poor, and H8085
Prv 8:34 Blessed *is* the man that **h** me, watching H8085
13: 1 A wise son *h* his father's instruction: but
1 instruction: but a scorner **h** not rebuke. H8085
8 his riches: but the poor **h** not rebuke. H8085
15:29 but he **h** the prayer of the righteous. H8085
31 The ear that **h** the reproof of life H8085
32 that **h** reproof getteth understanding. H8085
18:13 He that answereth a matter before he **h** H8085
21:28 the man that **h** speaketh constantly. H8085
25:10 Lest he that **h** *it* put thee to shame, and H8085
29:24 he **h** cursing, and bewrayeth *it* not. H8085
Isa 41:26 yea, *there is* none that **h** your words. H8085
42:20 not; opening the ears, but he **h** not. H8085
Jer 19: 3 whosoever **h**, his ears shall tingle. H8085
Ezk 3:27 GOD; He that **h**, let him hear; and he H8085
33: 4 Then whosoever **h** the sound of the H8085
Mt 7:24 Therefore whosoever **h** these sayings of *G191*
26 And every one that **h** these sayings of *G191*
13:19 When any one **h** the word of the *G191*
20 the same is he that **h** the word, and anon *G191*
22 the thorns is he that **h** the word; and the *G191*
23 good ground is he that **h** the word, and *G191*
Lk 6:47 Whosoever cometh to me, and **h** my *G191*
49 But he that **h**, and doeth not, is like a *G191*
10:16 He that **h** you heareth me; and he that *G191*
16 He that heareth you **h** me; and he that *G191*
Jn 3:29 standeth and **h** him, rejoiceth greatly *G191*
5:24 Verily, verily, I say unto you, He that **h** *G191*
8:47 He that is of God **h** God's words: ye *G191*
9:31 Now we know that God **h** not sinners: *G191*
31 of God, and doeth his will, him he **h**. *G191*
18:37 Every one that is of the truth **h** my voice. *G191*
2Co 12: 6 he seeth me *to be*, or *that* he **h** of me. *G191*
1Jn 4: 5 they of the world, and the world **h** them. *G191*
6 We are of God: he that knoweth God **h** *G191*
6 that is not of God **h** not us. Hereby know *G191*
5:14 any thing according to his will, he **h** us: *G191*
Rev 22:17 And let him that **h** say, Come. And let *G191*
18 For I testify unto every man that **h** the *G191*

HEARING
Dt 31:11 read this law before all Israel in their **h**. H241
2Sa 18:12 son: for in our **h** the king charged thee H241
2Ki 4:31 neither voice, nor **h**. Wherefore he went H7182
Job 33: 8 Surely thou hast spoken in mine **h**, and I H241
42: 5 I have heard of thee by the **h** of the ear: H8088
Prv 20:12 The **h** ear, and the seeing eye, the H8085
28: 9 He that turneth away his ear from **h** H8085
Ecc 1: 8 with seeing, nor the ear filled with **h**. H8085
Isa 11: 3 neither reprove after the **h** of his ears: H4926
21: 3 down at the **h** *of it*; I was dismayed H8085
33:15 his ears from **h** of blood, and shutteth H8085
Ezk 9: 5 And to the others he said in mine **h**, Go H241
10:13 it was cried unto them in my **h**, O wheel. H241
Am 8:11 water, but of **h** the words of the LORD: H8085
Mt 13:13 they seeing see not; and **h** they hear not, *G191*
14 which saith, By **h** ye shall hear, and shall *G189*
15 ears are dull of **h**, and their eyes they *G191*
Mk 4:12 not perceive; and **h** they may hear, and *G191*
6: 2 and many **h** *him* were astonished, *G191*
Lk 2:46 **h** them, and asking them questions. *G191*
8:10 see, and **h** they might not understand. *G191*
18:36 And **h** the multitude pass by, he asked *G191*
Act 5: 5 And Ananias **h** these words fell down, *G191*
8: 6 **h** and seeing the miracles which he did. *G191*
9: 7 speechless, **h** a voice, but seeing no man. *G191*
18: 8 **h** believed, and were baptized. *G191*
25:21 be reserved unto the **h** of Augustus, I *G1233*
23 entered into the place of **h**, with the chief *G201*
28:26 Saying, Go unto this people, and say, **H** *G189*
27 ears are dull of **h**, and their eyes have *G191*
Ro 10:17 So then faith *cometh* by **h**, and hearing *G189*
17 So then faith *cometh* by hearing, and **h** *G189*
1Co 12:17 eye, where *were* the **h**? If the whole *were* *G189*
17 whole *were* **h**, where *were* the smelling? *G189*
Gal 3: 2 the works of the law, or by the **h** of faith? *G189*
5 the works of the law, or by the **h** of faith? *G189*
Phlm 5 **H** of thy love and faith, which thou hast *G191*
Heb 5:11 hard to be uttered, seeing ye are dull of **h**. *G189*
2Pt 2: 8 in seeing and **h**, vexed *his* righteous *G189*

HEARKEN
Gen 4:23 wives of Lamech, **h** unto my speech: for H238
21:12 said unto thee, **h** unto her voice; for in H8085
23:15 My lord, **h** unto me: the land *is worth* H8085
34:17 But if ye will not **h** unto us, to be H8085
49: 2 of Jacob; and **h** unto Israel your father. H8085
Ex 3:18 And they shall **h** to thy voice: and thou H8085
4: 1 believe me, nor **h** unto my voice: for H8085
8 thee, neither **h** to the voice of the first H8085
9 two signs, neither **h** unto thy voice, that H8085
6:30 lips, and how shall Pharaoh **h** unto me? H8085
7: 4 But Pharaoh shall not **h** unto you, that H8085
22 he **h** unto them; as the LORD had said. H8085
11: 9 Pharaoh shall not **h** unto you; that my H8085
15:26 And said, If thou wilt diligently **h** to the H8085
18:19 **H** now unto my voice, I will give thee H8085
Lev 26:14 But if ye will not **h** unto me, and will H8085
18 And if ye will not yet for all this **h** unto H8085
21 me, and will not **h** unto me; I will bring H8085
27 And if ye will not for all this **h** unto me, H8085
Nu 23:18 and hear; **h** unto me, thou son of Zippor: H238
Dt 1:45 **h** to your voice, nor give ear unto you. H8085
4: 1 Now therefore **h**, O Israel, unto the H8085
7:12 Wherefore it shall come to pass, if ye **h** H8085
11:13 And it shall come to pass, if ye shall **h** H8085
13: 3 Thou shalt not **h** unto the words of that H8085
8 Thou shalt not consent unto him, nor **h** H8085
18 When thou shalt **h** to the voice of the H8085
15: 5 Only if thou carefully **h** unto the voice H8085
17:12 and will not **h** unto the priest that H8085
18:15 like unto me; unto him ye shall **h**; H8085
19 will not **h** unto my words which H8085
21:18 chastened him, will not **h** unto them: H8085
23: 5 thy God would not **h** unto Balaam; but H8085
26:17 his judgments, and to **h** unto his voice: H8085
27: 9 Take heed, and **h**, O Israel; this day H8085
28: 1 pass, if thou shalt **h** diligently unto the H8085
2 **h** unto the voice of the LORD thy God. H8085
13 if that thou **h** unto the commandments H8085
15 if thou wilt not **h** unto the voice of the H8085
30:10 If thou shalt **h** unto the voice of the H8085
Jos 1:17 things, so will we **h** unto thee: only the H8085
18 and will not **h** unto thy words in all H8085
24:10 But I would not **h** unto Balaam; H8085
Jdg 2:17 And yet they would not **h** unto their H8085
3: 4 they would **h** unto the commandments H8085
9: 7 said unto them, **H** unto me, ye men of H8085
7 of Shechem, that God may **h** unto you. H8085
Jdg 11:17 Edom would not **h** *thereto*. And in like H8085
19:25 But the men would not **h** to him: so the H8085
20:13 would not **h** to the voice of their H8085
1Sa 8: 7 And the LORD said unto Samuel, **H** H8085
9 Now therefore **h** unto their voice: H8085
22 And the LORD said to Samuel, **H** unto H8085
15: 1 now therefore **h** thou unto the voice H8085
22 sacrifice, *and* to **h** than the fat of rams. H7181
28:22 Now therefore, I pray thee, **h** thou also H8085
30:24 For who will **h** unto you in this matter? H8085
2Sa 12:18 and he would not **h** unto our voice: H8085
13:14 Howbeit he would not **h** unto her voice: H8085
16 unto me. But he would not **h** unto her. H8085
1Ki 8:28 LORD my God, to **h** unto the cry and to H8085
29 that thou mayest **h** unto the prayer H8085
30 And **h** thou to the supplication of thy H8085
52 people Israel, to **h** unto them in all that H8085
11:38 And it shall be, if thou wilt **h** unto all H8085
20: 8 unto him, **H** not *unto him*, nor consent. H8085
22:28 he said, **H**, O people, every one of you. H8085
2Ki 10: 6 and *if* ye will **h** unto my voice, take H8085
17:40 Howbeit they did not **h**, but they did H8085
18:31 **H** not to Hezekiah: for thus saith the H8085
32 and not die: and **h** not unto Hezekiah, H8085
2Ch 6:19 O LORD my God, to **h** unto the cry and H8085
20 thy name there; to **h** unto the prayer H8085
21 **H** therefore unto the supplications of H8085
10:16 king would not **h** unto them, the people H8085
18:27 by me. And he said, **H**, all ye people. H8085
20:15 And he said, **H** ye, all Judah, and ye H7181
33:10 and to his people: but they would not **h**. H7181
Neh 13:27 Shall we then **h** unto you to do all this H8085
Job 13: 6 Hear now my reasoning, and **h** to the H7181
32:10 Therefore I said, **H** to me; I also will H8085
33: 1 my speeches, and **h** to all my words. H238
31 Mark well, O Job, **h** unto me: hold thy H8085
33 If not, **h** unto me: hold thy peace, and I H8085
34:10 Therefore **h** unto me, ye men of H8085
16 hear this: **h** to the voice of my words. H238
34 tell me, and let a wise man **h** unto me. H8085
37:14 **H** unto this, O Job: stand still, and H238
Ps 5: 2 **H** unto the voice of my cry, my King, H7181
34:11 Come, ye children, **h** unto me: I will H8085
45:10 **H**, O daughter, and consider, and H8085
58: 5 Which will not **h** to the voice of H8085
81: 8 thee: O Israel, if thou wilt **h** unto me; H8085
11 But my people would not **h** to my voice; H8085
Prv 7:24 **H** unto me now therefore, O ye H8085
8:32 Now therefore **h** unto me, O ye H8085
23:22 **H** unto thy father that begat thee, and H8085
29:12 If a ruler **h** to lies, all his servants *are* H7181
Song 8:13 **h** to thy voice: cause me to hear *it*. H7181
Isa 28:23 Give ye ear, and hear my voice; **h**, and H7181
32: 3 and the ears of them that hear shall **h**. H7181
34: 1 Come near, ye nations, to hear; and **h**, H7181
36:16 **H** not to Hezekiah: for thus saith the H8085
42:23 will **h** and hear for the time to come? H7181
46: 3 **H** unto me, O house of Jacob, and all H8085
12 **H** unto me, ye stouthearted, that *are* H8085
48:12 **H** unto me, O Jacob and Israel, my H8085
49: 1 Listen, O isles, unto me; and **h**, ye H7181
51: 1 **H** to me, ye that follow after H8085
4 **H** unto me, my people; and give ear H7181
7 **H** unto me, ye that know H8085
55: 2 satisfieth not? **h** diligently unto me, H8085
Jer 6:10 and they cannot **h**: behold, the word of H7181
17 over you, *saying*, **H** to the sound of the H7181
17 trumpet. But they said, We will not **h**. H7181
7:27 but they will not **h** to thee: thou shalt H8085
11:11 cry unto me, I will not **h** unto them. H8085
16:12 heart, that they may not **h** unto me: H8085
17:24 if ye diligently **h** unto me, saith the H8085
27 But if ye will not **h** unto me to hallow H8085
18:19 Give heed to me, O LORD, and **h** to the H8085
23:16 Thus saith the LORD of hosts, **H** not H8085
26: 3 If so be they will **h**, and turn every man H8085
4 If ye will not **h** to me, to walk in my H8085
5 To **h** to the words of my servants the H8085
27: 9 Therefore **h** not ye to your prophets, H8085
14 Therefore **h** not unto the words of the H8085
16 saith the LORD; **H** not to the words of H8085
17 **H** not unto them; serve the king of H8085
29: 8 you, neither **h** to your dreams which H8085
12 pray unto me, and I will **h** unto you. H8085
35:13 to **h** to my words? saith the LORD. H8085
37: 2 of the land, did **h** unto the words of the H8085
38:15 thee counsel, wilt thou not **h** unto me? H8085
44:16 of the LORD, we will not **h** unto thee. H8085
Ezk 3: 7 But the house of Israel will not **h** unto H8085

Ezk 3: 7 for they will not **h** unto me: for all the H8085
20: 8 and would not **h** unto me: they did not H8085
39 *also*, if ye will not **h** unto me: but H8085
Dan 9:19 O Lord, hear; O Lord, forgive; O Lord, **h** H7181
Hos 5: 1 Hear ye this, O priests; and **h**, ye house H7181
9:17 they did not **h** unto him: and they H8085
Mic 1: 2 Hear, all ye people; **h**, O earth, and all H7181
Zec 1: 4 hear, nor **h** unto me, saith the LORD. H7181
7:11 But they refused to **h**, and pulled away H7181
Mk 4: 3 **H**; Behold, there went out a sower to sow: *G191*
7:14 he said unto them, **H** unto me every one *G191*
Act 2:14 known unto you, and **h** to my words: *G1801*
4:19 the sight of God to **h** unto you more than *G191*
7: 2 and fathers, **h**; The God of glory *G191*
12:13 a damsel came to **h**, named Rhoda. *G5219*
15:13 saying, Men *and* brethren, **h** unto me: *G191*
Jas 2: 5 **H**, my beloved brethren, Hath not God *G191*

HEARKENED
Gen 3:17 Because thou hast **h** unto the voice of H8085
16: 2 her. And Abram **h** to the voice of Sarai. H8085
23:16 And Abraham **h** unto Ephron; and H8085
30:17 And God **h** unto Leah, and she H8085
22 God **h** to her, and opened her womb. H8085
34:24 Shechem his son **h** all that went out of H8085
39:10 by day, that he **h** not unto her, to lie by H8085
Ex 6: 9 of Israel: but they **h** not unto Moses for H8085
12 of Israel have not **h** unto me; how then H8085
7:13 heart, that he **h** not unto them; as the H8085
8:15 his heart, and **h** not unto them; as the H8085
19 hardened, and he **h** not unto them; as H8085
9:12 of Pharaoh, and he **h** not unto them; as H8085
16:20 Notwithstanding they **h** not unto H8085
18:24 So Moses **h** to the voice of his father in H8085
Nu 14:22 ten times, and have not **h** to my voice; H8085
21: 3 And the LORD **h** to the voice of Israel, H8085
Dt 9:19 the LORD **h** unto me at that time also. H8085
23 ye believed him not, nor **h** to his voice. H8085
10:10 and the LORD **h** unto me at that time H8085
18:14 thou shalt possess, **h** unto observers of H8085
26:14 dead: *but* I have **h** to the voice of the H8085
34: 9 children of Israel **h** unto him, and did H8085
Jos 1:17 According as we **h** unto Moses in all H8085
10:14 it, that the LORD **h** unto the voice of a H8085
Jdg 2:20 fathers, and have not **h** unto my voice; H8085
11:28 of Ammon **h** not unto the words H8085
13: 9 And God **h** to the voice of Manoah; and H8085
1Sa 2:25 they **h** not unto the voice of H8085
12: 1 Behold, I have **h** unto your voice in all H8085
19: 6 And Saul **h** unto the voice of Jonathan: H8085
25:35 house; see, I have **h** to thy voice, and H8085
28:21 my hand, and have **h** unto thy words H8085
23 him; and he **h** unto their voice. So H8085
1Ki 12:15 Wherefore the king **h** not unto the H8085
16 So when all Israel saw that the king **h** H8085
24 is from me. They **h** therefore to the H8085
15:20 So Ben-hadad **h** unto king Asa, and H8085
20:25 And he **h** unto their voice, and did so. H8085
2Ki 13: 4 and the LORD **h** unto him: for he saw H8085
16: 9 And the king of Assyria **h** unto him: for H8085
20:13 And Hezekiah **h** unto them, and H8085
21: 9 But they **h** not: and Manasseh seduced H8085
22:13 fathers have not **h** unto the words of H8085
2Ch 10:15 So the king **h** not unto the people: for H8085
16: 4 And Ben-hadad **h** unto king Asa, and H8085
24:17 to the king. Then the king **h** unto them. H8085
25:16 this, and hast not **h** unto my counsel. H8085
30:20 And the LORD **h** to Hezekiah, and H8085
35:22 with him, and **h** not unto the words H8085
Neh 9:16 and **h** not to thy commandments, H8085
29 they dealt proudly, and **h** not unto thy H8085
34 fathers, kept thy law, nor **h** unto thy H7181
Est 3: 4 unto him, and he **h** not unto them, that H8085
Job 9:16 not believe that he had **h** unto my voice. H238
Ps 81:13 Oh that my people had **h** unto me, *and* H8085
106:25 But murmured in their tents, *and* **h** not H8085
Isa 21: 7 and he **h** diligently with much heed: H7181
48:18 O that thou hadst **h** to my H7181
Jer 6:19 they have not **h** unto my words, nor H7181
7:24 But they **h** not, nor inclined their ear, H8085
26 Yet they **h** not unto me, nor inclined H8085
8: 6 I **h** and heard, *but* they spake not H7181
25: 3 early and speaking; but ye have not **h**. H8085
4 not **h**, nor inclined your ear to hear. H8085
7 Yet ye have not **h** unto me, saith the H8085
26: 5 and sending *them*, but ye have not **h**; H8085
29:19 Because they have not **h** to my words, H8085
32:33 they have not **h** to receive instruction. H8085
34:14 but your fathers **h** not unto me, neither H8085
Jer 34:17 Ye have not **h** unto me, in proclaiming H8085
35:14 and speaking; but ye **h** not unto me. H8085
15 not inclined your ear, nor **h** unto me. H8085
16 but this people hath not **h** unto me: H8085
36:31 against them; but they **h** not. H8085
37:14 the Chaldeans. But he **h** not to him: so H8085
44: 5 But they **h** not, nor inclined their ear to H8085
Ezk 3: 6 to them, they would have **h** unto thee. H8085
Dan 9: 6 Neither have we **h** unto thy servants H8085
Mal 3:16 and the LORD **h**, and heard *it*, and a H7181
Act 27:21 Sirs, ye should have **h** unto me, and not *G3980*

HEARKENEDST
Dt 28:45 because thou **h** not unto the voice of H8085

HEARKENETH
Prv 1:33 But whoso **h** unto me shall dwell safely, H8085
12:15 eyes: but he that **h** unto counsel *is* wise. H8085

HEARKENING
Ps 103:20 **h** unto the voice of his word. H8085

HEART
Gen 6: 5 of his **h** *was* only evil continually. H3820
6 on the earth, and it grieved him at his **h**. H3820
8:21 the LORD said in his **h**, I will not again H3820
21 of man's **h** *is* evil from his youth; H3820
17:17 and said in his **h**, Shall *a child* be born H3820
20: 5 the integrity of my **h** and innocency of H3824
6 the integrity of thy **h**; for I also withheld H3824
24:45 speaking in mine **h**, behold, Rebekah H3820
27:41 and Esau said in his **h**, The days of H3820
42:28 my sack: and their **h** failed *them*, and H3820
45:26 **h** fainted, for he believed them not. H3820
Ex 4:14 he seeth thee, he will be glad in his **h**. H3820
21 his **h**, that he shall not let the people go. H3820
7: 3 And I will harden Pharaoh's **h**, and H3820
13 And he hardened Pharaoh's **h**, that he H3820
14 Moses, Pharaoh's **h** *is* hardened, he H3820
22 and Pharaoh's **h** was hardened, neither H3820
23 neither did he set his **h** to this also. H3820
8:15 he hardened his **h**, and hearkened not H3820
19 and Pharaoh's **h** was hardened, and H3820
32 And Pharaoh hardened his **h** at this H3820
9: 7 dead. And the **h** of Pharaoh was H3820
12 And the LORD hardened the **h** of H3820
14 upon thine **h**, and upon thy servants, H3820
34 hardened his **h**, he and his servants. H3820
35 And the **h** of Pharaoh was hardened, H3820
10: 1 I have hardened his **h**, and the heart of H3820
1 his heart, and the **h** of his servants, H3820
20 But the LORD hardened Pharaoh's **h**, so H3820
27 But the LORD hardened Pharaoh's **h**, H3820
11:10 Pharaoh's **h**, so that he would not H3820
14: 4 And I will harden Pharaoh's **h**, that he H3820
5 fled: and the **h** of Pharaoh and of his H3824
8 And the LORD hardened the **h** of H3820
15: 8 were congealed in the **h** of the sea. H3820
23: 9 for ye know the **h** of a stranger, seeing H5315
25: 2 with his **h** ye shall take my offering. H3820
28:29 upon his **h**, when he goeth in unto H3820
30 be upon Aaron's **h**, when he goeth in H3820
30 his **h** before the LORD continually. H3820
35: 5 *is* of a willing **h**, let him bring it, an H3820
21 And they came, every one whose **h** H3820
26 And all the women whose **h** stirred H3820
29 woman, whose **h** made them willing H3820
34 And he hath put in his **h** that he may H3820
35 Them hath he filled with wisdom of **h**, H3820
36: 2 man, in whose **h** the LORD had put H3820
2 every one whose **h** stirred him up to H3820
Lev 19:17 thy brother in thine **h**: thou shalt in any H3824
26:16 and cause sorrow of **h**: and ye shall sow H5315
Nu 15:39 after your own **h** and your own eyes, H3824
32: 7 And wherefore discourage ye the **h** of H3820
9 discouraged the **h** of the children of H3820
Dt 1:28 discouraged our **h**, saying, The people H3824
2:30 and made his **h** obstinate, that he H3824
4: 9 depart from thy **h** all the days of thy H3824
29 him with all thy **h** and with all thy soul. H3824
39 *it* in thine **h**, that the LORD he *is* H3824
5:29 O that there were such an **h** in them, H3824
6: 5 God with all thine **h**, and with all thy H3824
6 thee this day, shall be in thine **h**: H3824
7:17 If thou shalt say in thine **h**, These H3824
8: 2 know what *was* in thine **h**, whether thou H3824
5 Thou shalt also consider in thine **h**, H3824
14 Then thine **h** be lifted up, and thou H3824
17 And thou say in thine **h**, My power and H3824
Dt 9: 4 Speak not thou in thine **h**, after that the H3824
5 of thine **h**, dost thou go to possess H3824
10:12 God with all thy **h** and with all thy soul, H3824
16 of your **h**, and be no more stiffnecked. H3824
11:13 with all your **h** and with all your soul, H3824
16 Take heed to yourselves, that your **h** be H3824
18 my words in your **h** and in your soul, H3824
13: 3 with all your **h** and with all your soul. H3824
15: 7 not harden thine **h**, nor shut thine hand H3824
9 in thy wicked **h**, saying, The seventh H3824
10 Thou shalt surely give him, and thine **h** H3824
17:17 to himself, that his **h** turn not away: H3824
20 That his **h** be not lifted up above his H3824
18:21 And if thou say in thine **h**, How shall we H3824
19: 6 slayer, while his **h** is hot, and overtake H3824
20: 8 brethren's **h** faint as well as his heart. H3824
8 brethren's heart faint as well as his **h**. H3824
24:15 and setteth his **h** upon it: lest he cry H5315
26:16 with all thine **h**, and with all thy soul. H3824
28:28 and blindness, and astonishment of **h**: H3824
47 of **h**, for the abundance of all *things;* H3824
65 there a trembling **h**, and failing of eyes, H3820
67 the fear of thine **h** wherewith thou shalt H3824
29: 4 Yet the LORD hath not given you an **h** H3820
18 or tribe, whose **h** turneth away this day H3824
19 himself in his **h**, saying, I shall have H3824
19 of mine **h**, to add drunkenness to thirst: H3820
30: 2 with all thine **h**, and with all thy soul; H3824
6 circumcise thine **h**, and the heart of thy H3824
6 heart, and the **h** of thy seed, to love the H3824
6 God with all thine **h**, and with all thy H3824
10 with all thine **h**, and with all thy soul. H3824
14 and in thy **h**, that thou mayest do it. H3824
17 But if thine **h** turn away, so that thou H3824
Jos 5: 1 over, that their **h** melted, neither was H3824
14: 7 him word again as *it was* in mine **h**. H3824
8 with me made the **h** of the people melt: H3820
22: 5 with all your **h** and with all your soul. H3824
24:23 your **h** unto the LORD God of Israel. H3824
Jdg 5: 9 My **h** *is* toward the governors of Israel, H3820
15 Reuben *there were* great thoughts of **h**. H3820
16 *there were* great searchings of **h**. H3820
16:15 thee, when thine **h** *is* not with me? thou H3820
17 That he told her all his **h**, and said unto H3820
18 told her all his **h**, she sent and called H3820
18 shewed me all his **h**. Then the lords of H3820
18:20 And the priest's **h** was glad, and he H3820
19: 5 law, Comfort thine **h** with a morsel of H3820
6 all night, and let thine **h** be merry. H3820
8 Comfort thine **h**, I pray thee. And they H3824
9 here, that thine **h** may be merry; and H3824
Ru 3: 7 drunk, and his **h** was merry, he went H3820
1Sa 1: 8 not? and why is thy **h** grieved? *am* not I H3824
13 Now Hannah, she spake in her **h**; only H3820
2: 1 And Hannah prayed, and said, My **h** H3820
33 to grieve thine **h**: and all the increase H5315
35 which *is* in mine **h** and in my mind: H3824
4:13 watching: for his **h** trembled for the ark H3820
9:19 and will tell thee all that *is* in thine **h**. H3824
10: 9 gave him another **h**: and all those signs H3820
12:20 but serve the LORD with all your **h**; H3824
24 truth with all your **h**: for consider how H3824
13:14 a man after his own **h**, and the LORD H3824
14: 7 all that *is* in thine **h**: turn thee; behold, I H3824
7 I *am* with thee according to thy **h**. H3824
16: 7 but the LORD looketh on the **h**. H3824
17:28 of thine **h**; for thou art come down H3824
32 And David said to Saul, Let no man's **h** H3820
21:12 And David laid up these words in his **h**, H3824
24: 5 that David's **h** smote him, because H3820
25:31 nor offence of **h** unto my lord, either H3820
36 a king; and Nabal's **h** *was* merry within H3820
37 things, that his **h** died within him, and H3820
27: 1 And David said in his **h**, I shall now H3820
28: 5 was afraid, and his **h** greatly trembled. H3820
2Sa 3:21 reign over all that thine **h** desireth. And H5315
6:16 LORD; and she despised him in her **h**. H3820
7: 3 *is* in thine **h**; for the LORD *is* with thee. H3824
21 to thine own **h**, hast thou done all these H3820
27 in his **h** to pray this prayer unto thee. H3820
13:28 when Amnon's **h** is merry with wine, H3820
33 the thing to his **h**, to think that all the H3820
14: 1 that the king's **h** *was* toward Absalom. H3820
17:10 And he also *that is* valiant, whose **h** *is* H3820
10 heart *is* as the **h** of a lion, shall utterly H3820
18:14 them through the **h** of Absalom, while H3820
19:14 And he bowed the **h** of all the men of H3824
14 Judah, even as *the* **h** *of* one man; so that
19 that the king should take it to his **h**. H3820

2Sa 24:10 And David's **h** smote him after that he H3820
1Ki 2: 4 truth with all their **h** and with all their H3824
44 which thine **h** is privy to, that thou H3824
3: 6 in uprightness of **h** with thee; and thou H3824
9 an understanding **h** to judge thy people, H3820
12 an understanding **h**; so that there was H3820
4:29 and largeness of **h**, even as the sand H3820
8:17 And it was in the **h** of David my father H3824
18 it was in thine **h** to build an house unto H3824
18 thou didst well that it was in thine **h**. H3824
23 that walk before thee with all their **h**: H3820
38 plague of his own **h**, and spread forth H3824
39 to his ways, whose **h** thou knowest; (for H3824
48 And *so* return unto thee with all their **h**, H3824
61 Let your **h** therefore be perfect with the H3824
66 joyful and glad of **h** for all the goodness H3820
9: 3 and mine **h** shall be there perpetually. H3820
4 in integrity of **h**, and in uprightness, H3824
10: 2 with him of all that was in her **h**. H3824
24 wisdom, which God had put in his **h**. H3820
11: 2 will turn away your **h** after their gods: H3824
3 and his wives turned away his **h**. H3820
4 turned away his **h** after other gods: and H3824
4 gods: and his **h** was not perfect with H3824
4 God, as *was* the **h** of David his father. H3824
9 because his **h** was turned from the H3824
12:26 And Jeroboam said in his **h**, Now shall H3820
27 then shall the **h** of this people turn H3820
33 devised of his own **h**; and ordained a H3820
14: 8 me with all his **h**, to do *that* only *which* H3824
15: 3 him: and his **h** was not perfect with H3824
3 his God, as the **h** of David his father. H3824
14 nevertheless Asa's **h** was perfect with H3824
18:37 thou hast turned their **h** back again. H3820
21: 7 and let thine **h** be merry: I will give H3820
2Ki 5:26 Went not mine **h** *with thee*, when the H3820
6:11 Therefore the **h** of the king of Syria was H3820
9:24 his **h**, and he sunk down in his chariot. H3820
10:15 to him, Is thine **h** right, as my heart *is* H3824
15 heart right, as my **h** *is* with thy heart? H3824
15 my heart *is* with thy **h**? And Jehonadab H3824
30 that *was* in mine **h**, thy children of the H3824
31 Israel with all his **h**: for he departed not H3824
12: 4 **h** to bring into the house of the LORD, H3820
14:10 Edom, and thine **h** hath lifted thee up: H3820
20: 3 and with a perfect **h**, and have done H3824
22:19 Because thine **h** was tender, and thou H3824
23: 3 with all *their* **h** and all *their* soul, to H3820
25 the LORD with all his **h**, and with all his H3824
1Ch 12:17 to help me, mine **h** shall be knit unto H3824
33 keep rank: *they were* not of double **h**. H3820
38 with a perfect **h** to Hebron, to make H3824
38 *were* of one **h** to make David king. H3820
15:29 playing: and she despised him in her **h**. H3820
16:10 Glory ye in his holy name: let the **h** of H3820
17: 2 that *is* in thine **h**; for God *is* with thee. H3824
19 to thine own **h**, hast thou done all this H3820
25 hath found *in his* **h** to pray before thee.
22:19 Now set your **h** and your soul to seek H3824
28: 2 *me*, I *had* in mine **h** to build an house H3824
9 him with a perfect **h** and with a willing H3820
29: 9 with perfect **h** they offered willingly H3820
17 thou triest the **h**, and hast pleasure in H3824
17 of mine **h** I have willingly offered H3824
18 the thoughts of the **h** of thy people, and H3824
18 people, and prepare their **h** unto thee: H3824
19 Solomon my son a perfect **h**, to keep thy H3824
2Ch 1:11 this was in thine **h**, and thou hast not H3824
6: 7 Now it was in the **h** of David my father H3824
8 as it was in thine **h** to build an house H3824
8 thou didst well in that it was in thine **h**: H3824
30 his ways, whose **h** thou knowest; (for H3824
38 If they return to thee with all their **h** H3820
7:10 glad and merry in **h** for the goodness H3820
11 into Solomon's **h** to make in the house H3820
16 and mine **h** shall be there perpetually. H3820
9: 1 with him of all that was in her **h**. H3824
23 his wisdom, that God had put in his **h**. H3820
12:14 prepared not his **h** to seek the LORD. H3820
15:12 with all their **h** and with all their soul; H3824
15 with all their **h**, and sought him with H3824
17 the **h** of Asa was perfect all his days. H3824
16: 9 of *them* whose **h** *is* perfect toward him. H3824
17: 6 And his **h** was lifted up in the ways of H3820
19: 3 and hast prepared thine **h** to seek God. H3824
9 LORD, faithfully, and with a perfect **h**. H3824
22: 9 the LORD with all his **h**. So the house of H3824
25: 2 of the LORD, but not with a perfect **h**. H3824
19 and thine **h** lifteth thee up to boast: H3820

2Ch 26:16 But when he was strong, his **h** was H3820
29:10 Now *it is* in mine **h** to make a covenant H3824
31 as were of a free **h** burnt offerings. H3820
34 *were* more upright in **h** to sanctify H3824
30:12 was to give them one **h** to do the H3820
19 *That* prepareth his **h** to seek God, the H3824
31:21 he did *it* with all his **h**, and prospered. H3824
32:25 *done* unto him; for his **h** was lifted up: H3820
26 for the pride of his **h**, *both* he and the H3820
31 that he might know all *that was* in his **h**. H3824
34:27 Because thine **h** was tender, and thou H3824
31 with all his **h**, and with all his soul, H3824
36:13 and hardened his **h** from turning unto H3824
Ezr 6:22 and turned the **h** of the king of Assyria H3820
7:10 For Ezra had prepared his **h** to seek the H3824
27 as this in the king's **h**, to beautify the H3820
Neh 2: 2 of **h**. Then I was very sore afraid, H3820
12 had put in my **h** to do at Jerusalem: H3820
6: 8 thou feignest them out of thine own **h**. H3820
7: 5 And my God put into mine **h** to gather H3820
9: 8 And foundest his **h** faithful before thee, H3824
Est 1:10 On the seventh day, when the **h** of the H3820
5: 9 and with a glad **h**: but when Haman H3820
6: 6 thought in his **h**, To whom would the H3820
7: 5 that durst presume in his **h** to do so? H3820
Job 7:17 thou shouldest set thine **h** upon him? H3820
8:10 tell thee, and utter words out of their **h**? H3820
9: 4 *He is* wise in **h**, and mighty in strength: H3824
10:13 in thine **h**: I know that this *is* with thee. H3824
11:13 If thou prepare thine **h**, and stretch out H3820
12:24 He taketh away the **h** of the chief of the H3820
15:12 Why doth thine **h** carry thee away? and H3820
17: 4 For thou hast hid their **h** from H3820
11 broken off, *even* the thoughts of my **h**. H3824
22:22 mouth, and lay up his words in thine **h**. H3824
23:16 For God maketh my **h** soft, and the H3820
27: 6 not let it go: my **h** shall not reproach H3824
29:13 I caused the widow's **h** to sing for joy. H3820
31: 7 the way, and mine **h** walked after mine H3820
9 If mine **h** have been deceived by a H3820
27 And my **h** hath been secretly enticed, H3820
33: 3 uprightness of my **h**: and my lips shall H3820
34:14 If he set his **h** upon man, *if* he gather H3820
36:13 But the hypocrites in **h** heap up wrath: H3820
37: 1 At this also my **h** trembleth, and is H3820
24 he respecteth not any *that are* wise of **h**. H3820
38:36 who hath given understanding to the **h**? H7907
41:24 His **h** is as firm as a stone; yea, as hard H3820
Ps 4: 4 **h** upon your bed, and be still. Selah. H3824
7 Thou hast put gladness in my **h**, more H3820
7:10 *is* of God, which saveth the upright in **h**. H3820
9: 1 with my whole **h**; I will shew forth all H3820
10: 6 He hath said in his **h**, I shall not be H3820
11 He hath said in his **h**, God hath H3820
13 said in his **h**, Thou wilt not require *it*. H3820
17 **h**, thou wilt cause thine ear to hear: H3820
11: 2 may privily shoot at the upright in **h**. H3820
12: 2 lips *and* with a double **h** do they speak. H3820
13: 2 sorrow in my **h** daily? how long shall H3824
5 But I have trusted in thy mercy; my **h** H3820
14: 1 The fool hath said in his **h**, *There is* no H3820
15: 2 and speaketh the truth in his **h**. H3824
16: 9 Therefore my **h** is glad, and my glory H3820
17: 3 Thou hast proved mine **h**; thou hast H3820
19: 8 *are* right, rejoicing the **h**: the H3820
14 meditation of my **h**, be acceptable in H3820
20: 4 Grant thee according to thine own **h**, H3824
22:14 are out of joint: my **h** is like wax; it is H3820
26 that seek him: your **h** shall live for ever. H3824
24: 4 He that hath clean hands, and a pure **h**; H3824
25:17 The troubles of my **h** are enlarged: *O* H3824
26: 2 and prove me; try my reins and my **h**. H3820
27: 3 against me, my **h** shall not fear: though H3820
8 ye my face; my **h** said unto thee, Thy H3820
14 thine **h**: wait, I say, on the LORD. H3820
28: 7 and my shield; my **h** trusted in him, H3820
7 therefore my **h** greatly rejoiceth; and H3820
31:24 your **h**, all ye that hope in the LORD. H3824
32:11 for joy, all *ye that are* upright in **h**. H3820
33:11 the thoughts of his **h** to all generations. H3820
21 For our **h** shall rejoice in him, because H3820
34:18 are of a broken **h**; and saveth such as H3820
36: 1 saith within my **h**, *that there is* no fear H3820
10 thy righteousness to the upright in **h**. H3820
37: 4 he shall give thee the desires of thine **h**. H3820
15 own **h**, and their bows shall be broken. H3820
31 The law of his God *is* in his **h**; none of H3820
38: 8 by reason of the disquietness of my **h**. H3820
10 My **h** panteth, my strength faileth me: H3820

Ps 39: 3 My **h** was hot within me, while I was H3820
40: 8 O my God: yea, thy law *is* within my **h**. H4578
10 within my **h**; I have declared thy H3820
12 mine head: therefore my **h** faileth me. H3820
41: 6 vanity: his **h** gathereth iniquity to H3820
44:18 Our **h** is not turned back, neither have H3820
21 out? for he knoweth the secrets of the **h**. H3820
45: 1 My **h** is inditing a good matter: I speak H3820
5 Thine arrows *are* sharp in the **h** of the H3820
49: 3 of my **h** *shall be* of understanding. H3820
51:10 Create in me a clean **h**, O God; and H3820
17 contrite **h**, O God, thou wilt not despise. H3820
53: 1 The fool hath said in his **h**, *There is* no H3820
55: 4 My **h** is sore pained within me: and the H3820
21 but war *was* in his **h**: his words were H3820
57: 7 My **h** is fixed, O God, my heart is fixed: H3820
7 My heart is fixed, O God, my **h** is fixed: H3820
58: 2 Yea, in **h** ye work wickedness; ye weigh H3820
61: 2 thee, when my **h** is overwhelmed: lead H3820
62: 8 pour out your **h** before him: God *is* a H3824
10 increase, set not your **h** *upon them*. H3820
64: 6 of every one *of them*, and the **h**, *is* deep. H3820
10 and all the upright in **h** shall glory. H3820
66:18 If I regard iniquity in my **h**, the Lord H3820
69:20 Reproach hath broken my **h**; and I am H3820
32 and your **h** shall live that seek God. H3824
73: 1 Israel, *even* to such as are of a clean **h**. H3824
7 they have more than **h** could wish. H3824
13 Verily I have cleansed my **h** *in* vain, H3824
21 Thus my **h** was grieved, and I was H3824
26 My flesh and my **h** faileth: *but* God *is* H3824
26 of my **h**, and my portion for ever. H3824
77: 6 **h**: and my spirit made diligent search. H3824
78: 8 *that* set not their **h** aright, and whose H3820
18 And they tempted God in their **h** by H3824
37 For their **h** was not right with him, H3820
72 the integrity of his **h**; and guided them H3824
84: 2 of the LORD: my **h** and my flesh crieth H3820
5 thee; in whose **h** *are* the ways *of them*. H3824
86:11 thy truth: unite my **h** to fear thy name. H3824
12 God, with all my **h**: and I will glorify thy H3824
94:15 and all the upright in **h** shall follow it. H3820
95: 8 Harden not your **h**, as in the H3824
10 **h**, and they have not known my ways: H3824
97:11 and gladness for the upright in **h**. H3820
101: 2 walk within my house with a perfect **h**. H3824
4 A froward **h** shall depart from me: I H3824
5 look and a proud **h** will not I suffer. H3824
102: 4 My **h** is smitten, and withered like H3820
104:15 And wine *that* maketh glad the **h** of H3824
15 bread *which* strengtheneth man's **h**. H3824
105: 3 Glory ye in his holy name: let the **h** of H3820
25 He turned their **h** to hate his people, to H3820
107:12 Therefore he brought down their **h** H3820
108: 1 O God, my **h** is fixed; I will sing and H3820
109:16 that he might even slay the broken in **h**. H3824
22 For I *am* poor and needy, and my **h** is H3820
111: 1 with *my* whole **h**, in the assembly of the H3824
112: 7 his **h** is fixed, trusting in the LORD. H3820
8 His **h** *is* established, he shall not be H3820
119: 2 *and that* seek him with the whole **h**. H3820
7 I will praise thee with uprightness of **h**, H3824
10 With my whole **h** have I sought thee: O H3820
11 Thy word have I hid in mine **h**, that I H3820
32 when thou shalt enlarge my **h**. H3820
34 yea, I shall observe it with *my* whole **h**. H3820
36 Incline my **h** unto thy testimonies, and H3820
58 I entreated thy favour with *my* whole **h**: H3820
69 will keep thy precepts with *my* whole **h**. H3820
70 Their **h** is as fat as grease; *but* I delight H3820
80 Let my **h** be sound in thy statutes; that H3820
111 ever: for they *are* the rejoicing of my **h**. H3820
112 I have inclined mine **h** to perform thy H3820
145 I cried with *my* whole **h**; hear me, O H3820
161 but my **h** standeth in awe of thy word. H3820
131: 1 LORD, my **h** is not haughty, nor mine H3820
138: 1 I will praise thee with my whole **h**: H3820
139:23 Search me, O God, and know my **h**: try H3824
140: 2 Which imagine mischiefs in *their* **h**; H3820
141: 4 Incline not my **h** to *any* evil thing, to H3820
143: 4 within me; my **h** within me is desolate. H3820
147: 3 He healeth the broken in **h**, and bindeth H3820
Prv 2: 2 *and* apply thine **h** to understanding; H3820
10 When wisdom entereth into thine **h**, H3820
3: 1 let thine **h** keep my commandments: H3820
3 write them upon the table of thine **h**: H3820
5 Trust in the LORD with all thine **h**; and H3820
4: 4 unto me, Let thine **h** retain my words: H3820
21 eyes; keep them in the midst of thine **h**. H3824

Prv 4:23 Keep thy **h** with all diligence; for out of H3820
5:12 and my **h** despised reproof; H3820
6:14 Frowardness *is* in his **h**, he deviseth H3820
18 An **h** that deviseth wicked H3820
21 Bind them continually upon thine **h**, H3820
25 Lust not after her beauty in thine **h**; H3824
7: 3 write them upon the table of thine **h**. H3820
10 the attire of an harlot, and subtil of **h**. H3820
25 Let not thine **h** decline to her ways, go H3820
8: 5 ye fools, be ye of an understanding **h**. H3820
10: 8 The wise in **h** will receive H3820
20 the **h** of the wicked *is* little worth. H3820
11:20 They that are of a froward **h** *are* H3820
29 the fool *shall be* servant to the wise of **h**. H3820
12: 8 is of a perverse **h** shall be despised. H3820
20 Deceit *is* in the **h** of them that imagine H3820
23 the **h** of fools proclaimeth foolishness. H3820
25 Heaviness in the **h** of man maketh it H3820
13:12 Hope deferred maketh the **h** sick: but H3820
14:10 The **h** knoweth his own bitterness; and H3820
13 Even in laughter the **h** is sorrowful; and H3820
14 The backslider in **h** shall be filled with H3820
30 A sound **h** *is* the life of the flesh: but H3820
33 Wisdom resteth in the **h** of him that H3820
15: 7 but the **h** of the foolish *doeth* not so. H3820
13 A merry **h** maketh a cheerful H3820
13 by sorrow of the **h** the spirit is broken. H3820
14 The **h** of him that hath understanding H3820
15 is of a merry **h** *hath* a continual feast. H3820
28 The **h** of the righteous studieth to H3820
30 The light of the eyes rejoiceth the **h**: *and* H3820
16: 1 The preparations of the **h** in man, and H3820
5 Every one *that is* proud in **h** *is* an H3820
9 A man's **h** deviseth his way: but the H3820
21 The wise in **h** shall be called prudent: H3820
23 The **h** of the wise teacheth his mouth, H3820
17:16 get wisdom, seeing *he hath* no **h** *to it?* H3820
20 He that hath a froward **h** findeth no H3820
22 A merry **h** doeth good *like* a medicine: H3820
18: 2 but that his **h** may discover itself. H3820
12 Before destruction the **h** of man is H3820
15 The **h** of the prudent getteth H3820
19: 3 and his **h** fretteth against the LORD. H3820
21 *There are* many devices in a man's **h**; H3820
20: 5 Counsel in the **h** of man *is like* deep H3820
9 Who can say, I have made my **h** clean, H3820
21: 1 The king's **h** *is* in the hand of the H3820
4 An high look, and a proud **h**, *and* the H3820
22:11 He that loveth pureness of **h**, *for* the H3820
15 Foolishness *is* bound in the **h** of a child; H3820
17 and apply thine **h** unto my knowledge. H3820
23: 7 For as he thinketh in his **h**, so *is* he: Eat H5315
7 he to thee; but his **h** *is* not with thee. H3820
12 Apply thine **h** unto instruction, and H3820
15 My son, if thine **h** be wise, my heart H3820
15 My son, if thine heart be wise, my **h** H3820
17 Let not thine **h** envy sinners: but *be* H3820
19 be wise, and guide thine **h** in the way. H3820
26 My son, give me thine **h**, and let thine H3820
33 and thine **h** shall utter perverse things. H3820
24: 2 For their **h** studieth destruction, and H3820
12 pondereth the **h** consider *it?* and he H3826
17 not thine **h** be glad when he stumbleth: H3820
25: 3 and the **h** of kings *is* unsearchable. H3820
20 *is* he that singeth songs to an heavy **h**. H3820
26:23 Burning lips and a wicked **h** *are like* a H3820
25 *there are* seven abominations in his **h**. H3820
27: 9 Ointment and perfume rejoice the **h**: so H3820
11 My son, be wise, and make my **h** glad, H3820
19 to face, so the **h** of man to man. H3820
28:14 hardeneth his **h** shall fall into mischief. H3820
25 He that is of a proud **h** stirreth up H5315
26 He that trusteth in his own **h** is a fool: H3820
31:11 The **h** of her husband doth safely trust H3820
Ecc 1:13 And I gave my **h** to seek and search out H3820
16 I communed with mine own **h**, saying, H3820
16 yea, my **h** had great experience H3820
17 And I gave my **h** to know wisdom, and H3820
2: 1 I said in mine **h**, Go to now, I will prove H3820
3 I sought in mine **h** to give myself unto H3820
3 acquainting mine **h** with wisdom; and H3820
10 I withheld not my **h** from any joy; for H3820
10 any joy; for my **h** rejoiced in all my H3820
15 Then said I in my **h**, As it happeneth to H3820
15 I said in my **h**, that this also *is* vanity. H3820
20 Therefore I went about to cause my **h** H3820
22 of the vexation of his **h**, wherein he hath H3820
23 grief; yea, his **h** taketh not rest in the H3820
3:11 the world in their **h**, so that no man can H3820

Ecc 3:17 I said in mine **h**, God shall judge the H3820
18 I said in mine **h** concerning the estate H3820
5: 2 and let not thine **h** be hasty to utter *any* H3820
20 God answereth *him* in the joy of his **h**. H3820
7: 2 men; and the living will lay *it* to his **h**. H3820
3 the countenance the **h** is made better. H3820
4 The **h** of the wise *is* in the house of H3820
4 the **h** of fools *is* in the house of mirth. H3820
7 man mad; and a gift destroyeth the **h**. H3820
22 For oftentimes also thine own **h** H3820
25 I applied mine **h** to know, and to H3820
26 woman, whose **h** *is* snares and nets, H3820
8: 5 **h** discerneth both time and judgment. H3820
9 All this have I seen, and applied my **h** H3820
11 therefore the **h** of the sons of men is H3820
16 When I applied mine **h** to know H3820
9: 1 For all this I considered in my **h** even to H3820
3 all: yea, also the **h** of the sons of men is H3820
3 *is* in their **h** while they live, and H3824
7 **h**; for God now accepteth thy works. H3820
10: 2 A wise man's **h** *is* at his right hand; but H3820
2 his right hand; but a fool's **h** at his left. H3820
11: 9 youth; and let thy **h** cheer thee in the H3820
9 the ways of thine **h**, and in the sight of H3820
10 Therefore remove sorrow from thy **h**, H3820
Song 3:11 and in the day of the gladness of his **h**. H3820
4: 9 Thou hast ravished my **h**, my sister, *my* H3823
9 hast ravished my **h** with one of thine H3823
5: 2 I sleep, but my **h** waketh: *it is* the voice H3820
8: 6 Set me as a seal upon thine **h**, as a seal H3820
Isa 1: 5 head is sick, and the whole **h** faint. H3824
6:10 Make the **h** of this people fat, and H3820
10 their **h**, and convert, and be healed. H3824
7: 2 Ephraim. And his **h** was moved, and H3824
2 moved, and the **h** of his people, as the H3824
9: 9 that say in the pride and stoutness of **h**, H3824
10: 7 neither doth his **h** think so; but *it is* in H3824
7 so; but *it is* in his **h** to destroy and cut H3824
12 the fruit of the stout **h** of the king of H3824
13: 7 be faint, and every man's **h** shall melt: H3824
14:13 For thou hast said in thine **h**, I will H3824
15: 5 My **h** shall cry out for Moab; his H3820
19: 1 **h** of Egypt shall melt in the midst of it. H3824
21: 4 My **h** panted, fearfulness affrighted H3824
29:13 removed their **h** far from me, and their H3820
30:29 and gladness of **h**, as when one goeth H3824
32: 4 The **h** also of the rash shall understand H3824
6 villany, and his **h** will work iniquity, to H3820
33:18 Thine **h** shall meditate terror. Where *is* H3820
35: 4 Say to them *that are* of a fearful **h**, Be H3820
38: 3 and with a perfect **h**, and have done H3820
42:25 it burned him, yet he laid *it* not to **h**. H3820
44:19 And none considereth in his **h**, neither H3820
20 He feedeth on ashes: a deceived **h** hath H3820
47: 7 lay these *things* to thy **h**, neither didst H3820
8 sayest in thine **h**, I *am*, and none else H3824
10 thine **h**, I *am*, and none else beside me. H3820
49:21 Then shalt thou say in thine **h**, Who H3824
51: 7 the people in whose **h** *is* my law; fear ye H3820
57: 1 no man layeth *it* to **h**: and merciful men H3820
11 nor laid *it* to thy **h**? have not I held my H3820
15 and to revive the **h** of the contrite ones. H3820
17 went on frowardly in the way of his **h**. H3820
59:13 uttering from the **h** words of falsehood. H3820
60: 5 and thine **h** shall fear, and be enlarged; H3824
63: 4 For the day of vengeance *is* in mine **h**, H3820
17 *and* hardened our **h** from thy fear? H3820
65:14 sing for joy of **h**, but ye shall cry for H3820
14 **h**, and shall howl for vexation of spirit. H3820
66:14 And when ye see *this*, your **h** shall H3820
Jer 3:10 whole **h**, but feignedly, saith the LORD. H3820
15 according to mine **h**, which shall feed H3820
17 after the imagination of their evil **h**. H3820
4: 4 the foreskins of your **h**, ye men of Judah H3824
9 the LORD, *that* the **h** of the king shall H3820
9 perish, and the **h** of the princes; and H3820
14 O Jerusalem, wash thine **h** from H3820
18 bitter, because it reacheth unto thine **h**. H3820
19 pained at my very **h**; my heart maketh a H3820
19 my very heart; my **h** maketh a noise in H3820
5:23 rebellious **h**; they are revolted and gone. H3820
24 Neither say they in their **h**, Let us now H3824
7:24 of their evil **h**, and went backward, H3820
31 *them* not, neither came it into my **h**. H3820
8:18 against sorrow, my **h** *is* faint in me. H3820
9: 8 his mouth, but in **h** he layeth his wait. H7130
14 of their own **h**, and after Baalim, which H3820
26 of Israel *are* uncircumcised in the **h**. H3820
11: 8 of their evil **h**: therefore I will bring H3820

Jer 11:20 triest the reins and the **h**, let me see thy H3820
12: 3 me, and tried mine **h** toward thee: pull H3820
11 desolate, because no man layeth *it* to **h**. H3820
13:10 of their **h**, and walk after other H3820
22 And if thou say in thine **h**, Wherefore H3824
14:14 of nought, and the deceit of their **h**. H3820
15:16 rejoicing of mine **h**: for I am called by H3824
16:12 **h**, that they may not hearken unto me: H3820
17: 1 **h**, and upon the horns of your altars; H3820
5 and whose **h** departeth from the LORD. H3820
9 The **h** *is* deceitful above all *things*, and H3820
10 I the LORD search the **h**, *I* try the reins, H3820
18:12 one do the imagination of his evil **h**. H3820
20: 9 *word* was in mine **h** as a burning fire H3820
12 seest the reins and the **h**, let me see thy H3820
22:17 But thine eyes and thine **h** *are* not but H3820
23: 9 Mine **h** within me is broken because of H3820
16 of their own **h**, *and* not out of the mouth H3820
17 his own **h**, No evil shall come upon you. H3820
20 the thoughts of his **h**: in the latter days H3820
26 How long shall *this* be in the **h** of the H3820
26 prophets of the deceit of their own **h**; H3820
24: 7 And I will give them an **h** to know me, H3820
7 shall return unto me with their whole **h**. H3820
29:13 ye shall search for me with all your **h**. H3824
30:21 that engaged his **h** to approach unto H3820
24 **h**: in the latter days ye shall consider it. H3820
31:21 heaps: set thine **h** toward the highway, H3820
32:39 And I will give them one **h**, and one H3820
41 my whole **h** and with my whole soul. H3820
48:29 his pride, and the haughtiness of his **h**. H3820
31 *h* shall mourn for the men of Kir-heres.
36 Therefore mine **h** shall sound for Moab H3820
36 like pipes, and mine **h** shall sound like H3820
41 be as the **h** of a woman in her pangs. H3820
49:16 *and* the pride of thine **h**, O thou that H3820
22 that day shall the **h** of the mighty men H3820
22 be as the **h** of a woman in her pangs. H3820
51:46 And lest your **h** faint, and ye fear for H3824
Lam 1:20 troubled; mine **h** is turned within me; H3820
22 my sighs *are* many, and my **h** *is* faint. H3820
2:18 Their **h** cried unto the Lord, O wall of H3820
19 pour out thine **h** like water before the H3820
3:41 Let us lift up our **h** with *our* hands unto H3824
51 Mine eye affecteth mine **h** because of H5315
65 Give them sorrow of **h**, thy curse unto H3820
5:15 The joy of our **h** is ceased; our dance is H3820
17 For this our **h** is faint; for these *things* H3820
Ezk 3:10 in thine **h**, and hear with thine ears. H3824
6: 9 with their whorish **h**, which hath H3820
11:19 And I will give them one **h**, and I will H3820
19 I will take the stony **h** out of their flesh, H3820
19 flesh, and will give them an **h** of flesh: H3820
21 But *as for them* whose **h** walketh after H3820
21 walketh after the **h** of their detestable H3820
13:17 **h**; and prophesy thou against them, H3820
22 Because with lies ye have made the **h** of H3820
14: 3 up their idols in their **h**, and put the H3820
4 up his idols in his **h**, and putteth the H3820
5 Israel in their own **h**, because they are H3820
7 up his idols in his **h**, and putteth the H3820
16:30 How weak is thine **h**, saith the Lord H3826
18:31 make you a new **h** and a new spirit: for H3820
20:16 for their **h** went after their idols. H3820
21: 7 cometh: and every **h** shall melt, and all H3820
15 gates, that *their* **h** may faint, and *their* H3820
22:14 Can thine **h** endure, or can thine hands H3820
25: 6 and rejoiced in **h** with all thy despite H5315
15 **h**, to destroy *it* for the old hatred; H5315
27:31 with bitterness of **h** *and* bitter wailing. H5315
28: 2 Because thine **h** *is* lifted up, and thou H3820
2 thou set thine **h** as the heart of God: H3820
2 thou set thine heart as the **h** of God: H3820
5 **h** is lifted up because of thy riches: H3824
6 hast set thine **h** as the heart of God; H3824
6 hast set thine heart as the **h** of God; H3820
17 Thine **h** was lifted up because of thy H3820
31:10 and his **h** is lifted up in his height; H3824
33:31 their **h** goeth after their covetousness. H3820
36: 5 the joy of all *their* **h**, with despiteful H3824
26 A new **h** also will I give you, and a new H3820
26 away the stony **h** out of your flesh, and H3820
26 flesh, and I will give you an **h** of flesh. H3820
40: 4 ears, and set thine **h** upon all that I H3820
44: 7 uncircumcised in **h**, and uncircumcised H3820
9 uncircumcised in **h**, nor uncircumcised H3820
Dan 1: 8 But Daniel purposed in his **h** that he H3820
2:30 mightest know the thoughts of thy **h**. H3825
4:16 Let his **h** be changed from man's, and H3825

Dan 4:16 and let a beast's **h** be given unto him; H3825
5:20 But when his **h** was lifted up, and his H3825
21 of men; and his **h** was made like the H3825
22 thine **h**, though thou knewest all this; H3825
6:14 and set *his* **h** on Daniel to deliver H1079
7: 4 a man, and a man's **h** was given to it. H3825
28 in me: but I kept the matter in my **h**. H3821
8:25 *himself* in his **h**, and by peace shall H3824
10:12 didst set thine **h** to understand, and H3820
11:12 the multitude, his **h** shall be lifted up; H3824
28 riches; and his **h** *shall be* against the H3824
Hos 4: 8 and they set their **h** on their iniquity. H5315
11 wine and new wine take away the **h**. H3820
7: 6 For they have made ready their **h** like H3820
11 **h**: they call to Egypt, they go to Assyria. H3820
14 unto me with their **h**, when they howled H3820
10: 2 Their **h** is divided; now shall they be H3820
11: 8 as Zeboim? mine **h** is turned within H3820
13: 6 were filled, and their **h** was exalted; H3820
8 rend the caul of their **h**, and there will I H3820
Joel 2:12 to me with all your **h**, and with fasting, H3824
13 And rend your **h**, and not your H3824
Oba 3 The pride of thine **h** hath deceived H3820
3 that saith in his **h**, Who shall bring me H3820
Nah 2:10 waste: and the **h** melteth, and the knees H3820
Zep 1:12 that say in their **h**, The LORD will not H3824
2:15 that said in her **h**, I *am*, and *there is* H3824
3:14 with all the **h**, O daughter of Jerusalem. H3820
Zec 7:10 evil against his brother in your **h**. H3824
10: 7 *man*, and their **h** shall rejoice as H3820
7 glad; their **h** shall rejoice in the LORD. H3820
12: 5 shall say in their **h**, The inhabitants of H3820
Mal 2: 2 ye will not lay *it* to **h**, to give glory unto H3820
2 already, because ye do not lay *it* to **h**. H3820
4: 6 And he shall turn the **h** of the fathers to H3820
6 children, and the **h** of the children to H3820
Mt 5: 8 Blessed *are* the pure in **h**: for they shall G2588
28 adultery with her already in his **h**. G2588
6:21 treasure is, there will your **h** be also. G2588
11:29 **h**: and ye shall find rest unto your souls. G2588
12:34 of the **h** the mouth speaketh. G2588
35 treasure of the **h** bringeth forth good G2588
40 and three nights in the **h** of the earth. G2588
13:15 For this people's **h** is waxed gross, and G2588
15 with *their* **h**, and should be converted, G2588
19 was sown in his **h**. This is he which G2588
15: 8 *their* lips; but their **h** is far from me. G2588
18 from the **h**; and they defile the man. G2588
19 For out of the **h** proceed evil thoughts, G2588
22:37 God with all thy **h**, and with all thy soul, G2588
24:48 in his **h**, My lord delayeth his coming; G2588
Mk 6:52 of the loaves: for their **h** was hardened. G2588
7: 6 *their* lips, but their **h** is far from me. G2588
19 Because it entereth not into his **h**, but G2588
21 For from within, out of the **h** of men, G2588
8:17 have ye your **h** yet hardened? G2588
10: 5 of your **h** he wrote you this precept. G4641
11:23 not doubt in his **h**, but shall believe that G2588
12:30 God with all thy **h**, and with all thy soul, G2588
33 And to love him with all the **h**, and with G2588
16:14 and hardness of **h**, because they G4641
Lk 2:19 things, and pondered *them* in her **h**. G2588
51 mother kept all these sayings in her **h**. G2588
6:45 treasure of his **h** bringeth forth that G2588
45 evil treasure of his **h** bringeth forth that G2588
45 of the **h** his mouth speaketh. G2588
8:15 an honest and good **h**, having heard the G2588
9:47 **h**, took a child, and set him by him, G2588
10:27 God with all thy **h**, and with all thy soul, G2588
12:34 treasure is, there will your **h** be also. G2588
45 But and if that servant say in his **h**, My G2588
24:25 O fools, and slow of **h** to believe all that G2588
32 Did not our **h** burn within us, while G2588
Jn 12:40 hardened their **h**; that they should not G2588
40 with *their* **h**, and be converted, and G2588
13: 2 now put into the **h** of Judas Iscariot, G2588
14: 1 Let not your **h** be troubled: ye believe in G2588
27 **h** be troubled, neither let it be afraid. G2588
16: 6 unto you, sorrow hath filled your **h**. G2588
22 again, and your **h** shall rejoice, and G2588
Act 2:26 Therefore did my **h** rejoice, and my G2588
37 pricked in their **h**, and said unto Peter G2588
46 meat with gladness and singleness of **h**, G2588
4:32 were of one **h** and of one soul: neither G2588
5: 3 Satan filled thine **h** to lie to the Holy G2588
4 this thing in thine **h**? thou hast not lied G2588
33 *to the* **h**, and took counsel to slay them.
7:23 it came into his **h** to visit his brethren G2588
51 Ye stiffnecked and uncircumcised in **h** G2588

Act 7:54 were cut to the **h**, and they gnashed on G2588
8:21 for thy **h** is not right in the sight of God. G2588
22 of thine **h** may be forgiven thee. G2588
37 with all thine **h**, thou mayest. And he G2588
11:23 of **h** they would cleave unto the Lord. G2588
13:22 own **h**, which shall fulfil all my will. G2588
16:14 heard *us*: whose **h** the Lord opened, G2588
21:13 and to break mine **h**? for I am ready not G2588
28:27 For the **h** of this people is waxed gross, G2588
27 with *their* **h**, and should be converted, G2588
Ro 1:21 and their foolish **h** was darkened. G2588
2: 5 and impenitent **h** treasurest up unto G2588
29 *is that* of the **h**, in the spirit, *and* not G2588
6:17 have obeyed from the **h** that form of G2588
9: 2 and continual sorrow in my **h**. G2588
10: 6 Say not in thine **h**, Who shall ascend G2588
8 mouth, and in thy **h**: that is, the word of G2588
9 believe in thine **h** that God hath raised G2588
10 For with the **h** man believeth unto G2588
1Co 2: 9 entered into the **h** of man, the things G2588
7:37 stedfast in his **h**, having no necessity, G2588
37 so decreed in his **h** that he will keep his G2588
14:25 And thus are the secrets of his **h** made G2588
2Co 2: 4 and anguish of **h** I wrote unto you with G2588
3: 3 of stone, but in fleshy tables of the **h**. G2588
15 Moses is read, the veil is upon their **h**. G2588
5:12 glory in appearance, and not in **h**. G2588
6:11 is open unto you, our **h** is enlarged. G2588
8:16 earnest care into the **h** of Titus for you. G2588
9: 7 purposeth in his **h**, *so let him give*; not G2588
Eph 4:18 because of the blindness of their **h**: G2588
5:19 making melody in your **h** to the Lord; G2588
6: 5 in singleness of your **h**, as unto Christ; G2588
6 Christ, doing the will of God from the **h**; G5590
Php 1: 7 I have you in my **h**; inasmuch as both in G2588
Col 3:22 but in singleness of **h**, fearing God: G2588
1Th 2:17 in presence, not in **h**, endeavoured the G2588
1Ti 1: 5 charity out of a pure **h**, and *of* a good G2588
2Ti 2:22 that call on the Lord out of a pure **h**. G2588
Heb 3:10 **h**; and they have not known my ways. G2588
12 in any of you an evil **h** of unbelief, in G2588
4:12 of the thoughts and intents of the **h**. G2588
10:22 Let us draw near with a true **h** in full G2588
13: 9 thing that the **h** be established with G2588
Jas 1:26 his own **h**, this man's religion *is* vain. G2588
1Pt 1:22 one another with a pure **h** fervently: G2588
3: 4 But *let it be* the hidden man of the **h**, in G2588
2Pt 2:14 unstable souls: an **h** they have G2588
1Jn 3:20 For if our **h** condemn us, God is greater G2588
20 than our **h**, and knoweth all things. G2588
21 Beloved, if our **h** condemn us not, *then* G2588
Rev 18: 7 she saith in her **h**, I sit a queen, and am G2588

HEARTED

Ex 28: 3 all *that are* wise **h**, whom I have filled H3820
31: 6 hearts of all that are wise **h** I have put H3820
35:10 And every wise **h** among you shall H3820
22 many as were willing **h**, *and* brought H3820
25 And all the women that were wise **h** did H3820
36: 1 and every wise **h** man, in whom the H3820
2 and every wise **h** man, in whose heart H3820
8 And every wise **h** man among them H3820

HEARTH

Gen 18: 6 knead *it*, and make cakes upon the **h**.
Ps 102: 3 and my bones are burned as an **h**. H4168
Isa 30:14 **h**, or to take water *withal* out of the pit. H3344
Jer 36:22 *was a fire* on the **h** burning before him. H254
23 the fire that *was* on the **h**, until all the roll H254
23 consumed in the fire that *was* on the **h**. H254
Zec 12: 6 of Judah like an **h** of fire among the H3595

HEARTILY

Col 3:23 And whatsoever ye do, do *it* **h**, as to the G1537

HEARTS

Gen 18: 5 comfort ye your **h**; after that ye shall H3820
Ex 14:17 And I, behold, I will harden the **h** of the H3820
31: 6 of Dan: and in the **h** of all that are wise H3820
Lev 26:36 into their **h** in the lands of their H3824
41 uncircumcised **h** be humbled, and they H3824
Dt 20: 3 let not your **h** faint, fear not, and H3824
32:46 And he said unto them, Set your **h** unto H3824
Jos 2:11 *these things*, our **h** did melt, neither H3824
7: 5 wherefore the **h** of the people melted, H3824
11:20 to harden their **h**, that they should H3820
23:14 ye know in all your **h** and in all your H3824
Jdg 9: 3 words: and their **h** inclined to follow H3820
16:25 And it came to pass, when their **h** were H3820

Jdg 19:22 *Now* as they were making their **h** H3820
1Sa 6: 6 Wherefore then do ye harden your **h**, as H3824
6 hardened their **h**? when he had wrought H3820
7: 3 with all your **h**, *then* put away the H3824
3 and prepare your **h** unto the LORD, H3824
10:26 of men, whose **h** God had touched. H3820
2Sa 15: 6 stole the **h** of the men of Israel. H3820
13 saying, The **h** of the men of Israel H3820
1Ki 8:39 the **h** of all the children of men;) H3824
58 That he may incline our **h** unto him, to H3824
1Ch 28: 9 searcheth all **h**, and understandeth H3824
2Ch 6:14 that walk before thee with all their **h**: H3820
30 knowest the **h** of the children of men:) H3824
11:16 such as set their **h** to seek the LORD H3824
20:33 their **h** unto the God of their fathers. H3824
Job 1: 5 in their **h**. Thus did Job continually. H3824
Ps 7: 9 righteous God trieth the **h** and reins. H3826
28: 3 neighbours, but mischief *is* in their **h**. H3824
33:15 He fashioneth their **h** alike; he H3820
35:25 Let them not say in their **h**, Ah, so H3820
74: 8 They said in their **h**, Let us destroy H3820
90:12 that we may apply *our* **h** unto wisdom. H3824
125: 4 and *to them that are* upright in their **h**. H3826
Prv 15:11 more then the **h** of the children of men? H3826
17: 3 for gold: but the LORD trieth the **h**. H3826
21: 2 eyes: but the LORD pondereth the **h**. H3826
31: 6 and wine unto those that be of heavy **h**. H5315
Isa 44:18 their **h**, that they cannot understand. H3826
Jer 31:33 write it in their **h**; and will be their God, H3820
32:40 **h**, that they shall not depart from me. H3824
42:20 For ye dissembled in your **h**, when ye H5315
48:41 the mighty men's **h** in Moab at that day H3820
Ezk 13: 2 own **h**, Hear ye the word of the LORD; H3820
32: 9 I will also vex the **h** of many people, H3820
Dan 11:27 And both these kings' **h** *shall be* to do H3824
Hos 7: 2 And they consider not in their **h** *that* I H3824
Zec 7:12 Yea, they made their **h** *as* an adamant H3820
8:17 evil in your **h** against his neighbour; H3824
Mt 9: 4 said, Wherefore think ye evil in your **h**? G2588
18:35 if ye from your **h** forgive not every one G2588
19: 8 hardness of your **h** suffered you to put G4641
Mk 2: 6 sitting there, and reasoning in their **h**, G2588
8 Why reason ye these things in your **h**? G2588
3: 5 hardness of their **h**, he saith unto the G2588
4:15 away the word that was sown in their **h**. G2588
Lk 1:17 Elias, to turn the **h** of the fathers to the G2588
51 the proud in the imagination of their **h**. G2588
66 laid *them* up in their **h**, saying, What G2588
2:35 thoughts of many **h** may be revealed. G2588
3:15 mused in their **h** of John, whether he G2588
5:22 unto them, What reason ye in your **h**? G2588
8:12 **h**, lest they should believe and be saved. G2588
16:15 God knoweth your **h**: for that which is G2588
21:14 Settle *it* therefore in your **h**, not to G2588
26 Men's **h** failing them for fear, and for G674
34 at any time your **h** be overcharged with G2588
24:38 and why do thoughts arise in your **h**? G2588
Act 1:24 knowest the **h** of all *men*, shew whether G2589
7:39 in their **h** turned back again into Egypt, G2588
14:17 filling our **h** with food and gladness. G2588
15: 8 And God, which knoweth the **h**, bare G2589
9 us and them, purifying their **h** by faith. G2588
Ro 1:24 lusts of their own **h**, to dishonour their G2588
2:15 written in their **h**, their conscience also G2588
5: 5 shed abroad in our **h** by the Holy Ghost G2588
8:27 And he that searcheth the **h** knoweth G2588
16:18 speeches deceive the **h** of the simple. G2588
1Co 4: 5 the counsels of the **h**: and then shall G2588
2Co 1:22 given the earnest of the Spirit in our **h**. G2588
3: 2 Ye are our epistle written in our **h**, G2588
4: 6 hath shined in our **h**, to *give* the light of G2588
7: 3 ye are in our **h** to die and live with *you*. G2588
Gal 4: 6 Son into your **h**, crying, Abba, Father. G2588
Eph 3:17 That Christ may dwell in your **h** by G2588
6:22 and *that* he might comfort your **h**. G2588
Php 4: 7 your **h** and minds through Christ Jesus. G2588
Col 2: 2 That their **h** might be comforted, being G2588
3:15 And let the peace of God rule in your **h**, G2588
16 with grace in your **h** to the Lord. G2588
4: 8 know your estate, and comfort your **h**; G2588
1Th 2: 4 men, but God, which trieth our **h**. G2588
3:13 To the end he may stablish your **h** G2588
2Th 2:17 Comfort your **h**, and stablish you in G2588
3: 5 And the Lord direct your **h** into the G2588
Heb 3: 8 Harden not your **h**, as in the G2588
15 not your **h**, as in the provocation. G2588
4: 7 will hear his voice, harden not your **h**. G2588
8:10 them in their **h**: and I will be to them G2588
10:16 **h**, and in their minds will I write them; G2588

Heb 10:22 faith, having our **h** sprinkled from an G2588
Jas 3:14 and strife in your **h**, glory not, and lie G2588
4: 8 and purify *your* **h**, *ye* double minded. G2588
5: 5 your **h**, as in a day of slaughter. G2588
8 Be ye also patient; stablish your **h**: for G2588
1Pt 3:15 But sanctify the Lord God in your **h**: G2588
2Pt 1:19 dawn, and the day star arise in your **h**: G2588
1Jn 3:19 and shall assure our **h** before him. G2588
Rev 2:23 the reins and **h**: and I will give unto G2588
17:17 For God hath put in their **h** to fulfil his G2588

HEART'S
Ps 10: 3 For the wicked boasteth of his **h** desire, H5315
21: 2 Thou hast given him his **h** desire, and H3820
Ro 10: 1 Brethren, my **h** desire and prayer to G2588

HEARTS'
Ps 81:12 So I gave them up unto their own **h** H3820

HEARTY
Prv 27: 9 of a man's friend by **h** counsel. H5315

HE-ASSES See ASSES.

HEAT
Gen 8:22 and cold and **h**, and summer and H2527
18: 1 sat in the tent door in the **h** of the day; H2527
Dt 29:24 what *meaneth* the **h** of this great anger? H2750
32:24 with burning **h**, and with bitter H7565
1Sa 11:11 until the **h** of the day: and it came H2527
2Sa 4: 5 and came about the **h** of the day to the H2527
1Ki 1: 1 him with clothes, but he gat no **h**. H3179
2 bosom, that my lord the king may get **h**. H2552
Job 24:19 Drought and **h** consume the snow H2527
30:30 me, and my bones are burned with **h**. H2721
Ps 19: 6 there is nothing hid from the **h** thereof. H2535
Ecc 4:11 **h**: but how can one be warm *alone*? H2552
Isa 4: 6 daytime from the **h**, and for a place of H2721
18: 4 place like a clear **h** upon herbs, *and* H2527
4 like a cloud of dew in the **h** of harvest. H2527
25: 4 a shadow from the **h**, when the blast of H2721
5 strangers, as the **h** in a dry place; *even* H2721
5 place; *even* the **h** with the shadow of H2721
49:10 neither shall the **h** nor sun smite them: H8273
Jer 17: 8 shall not see when **h** cometh, but her H2527
36:30 to the **h**, and in the night to the frost. H2721
51:39 In their **h** I will make their feasts, and I H2527
Ezk 3:14 bitterness, in the **h** of my spirit; but the H2534
Dan 3:19 that they should **h** the furnace one seven H228
Mt 20:12 borne the burden and **h** of the day. G2742
Lk 12:55 There will be **h**; and it cometh to pass. G2742
Act 28: 3 out of the **h**, and fastened on his hand. G2329
Jas 1:11 with a burning **h**, but it withereth the G2742
2Pt 3:10 melt with fervent **h**, the earth also and G2741
12 the elements shall melt with fervent **h**? G2741
Rev 7:16 shall the sun light on them, nor any **h**. G2738
16: 9 And men were scorched with great **h**, G2738

HEATED
Dan 3:19 times more than it was wont to be **h**. H228
Hos 7: 4 They *are* all adulterers, as an oven **h** by H1197

HEATH
Jer 17: 6 For he shall be like the **h** in the desert, H6176
48: 6 Flee, save your lives, and be like the **h** H6176

HEATHEN
Lev 25:44 *shall be* of the **h** that are round about H1471
26:33 And I will scatter you among the **h**, and H1471
38 And ye shall perish among the **h**, and H1471
45 in the sight of the **h**, that I might be H1471
Dt 4:27 the **h**, whither the LORD shall lead you. H1471
2Sa 22:44 me *to be* head of the **h**: a people *which* I H1471
50 **h**, and I will sing praises unto thy name. H1471
2Ki 16: 3 of the **h**, whom the LORD cast H1471
17: 8 And walked in the statutes of the **h**, H1471
11 places, as *did* the **h** whom the LORD H1471
15 and went after the **h** that *were* round H1471
21: 2 of the **h**, whom the LORD cast H1471
1Ch 16:24 Declare his glory among the **h**; his H1471
35 us from the **h**, that we may give thanks H1471
2Ch 20: 6 kingdoms of the **h**? and in thine hand *is* H1471
28: 3 of the **h** whom the LORD had H1471
33: 2 of the **h**, whom the LORD had H1471
9 to do worse than the **h**, whom the LORD H1471
36:14 of the **h**; and polluted the house H1471
Ezr 6:21 filthiness of the **h** of the land, to seek H1471
Neh 5: 8 were sold unto the **h**; and will ye even H1471
9 of the reproach of the **h** our enemies? H1471
Neh 5:17 us from among the **h** that *are* about us. H1471
6: 6 among the **h**, and Gashmu saith *it*, H1471
16 and all the **h** that *were* about us H1471
Ps 2: 1 Why do the **h** rage, and the people H1471
8 Ask of me, and I shall give *thee* the **h** H1471
9: 5 Thou hast rebuked the **h**, thou hast H1471
15 The **h** are sunk down in the pit *that* H1471
19 prevail: let the **h** be judged in thy sight. H1471
10:16 ever: the **h** are perished out of his land. H1471
18:43 me the head of the **h**: a people *whom* I H1471
49 the **h**, and sing praises unto thy name. H1471
33:10 The LORD bringeth the counsel of the **h** H1471
44: 2 *How* thou didst drive out the **h** with thy H1471
11 and hast scattered us among the **h**. H1471
14 Thou makest us a byword among the **h**, H1471
46: 6 The **h** raged, the kingdoms were H1471
10 the **h**, I will be exalted in the earth. H1471
47: 8 God reigneth over the **h**: God sitteth H1471
59: 5 to visit all the **h**: be not merciful to any H1471
8 thou shalt have all the **h** in derision. H1471
78:55 He cast out the **h** also before them, and H1471
79: 1 O God, the **h** are come into thine H1471
6 Pour out thy wrath upon the **h** that H1471
10 Wherefore should the **h** say, Where *is* H1471
10 known among the **h** in our sight *by* the H1471
80: 8 thou hast cast out the **h**, and planted it. H1471
94:10 He that chastiseth the **h**, shall not he H1471
96: 3 Declare his glory among the **h**, his H1471
10 Say among the **h** *that* the LORD H1471
98: 2 he openly shewed in the sight of the **h**. H1471
102:15 So the **h** shall fear the name of the H1471
105:44 And gave them the lands of the **h**: and H1471
106:35 But were mingled among the **h**, and H1471
41 the hand of the **h**; and they that hated H1471
47 from among the **h**, to give thanks unto H1471
110: 6 He shall judge among the **h**, he shall fill H1471
111: 6 he may give them the heritage of the **h**. H1471
115: 2 Wherefore should the **h** say, Where *is* H1471
126: 2 they among the **h**, The LORD hath done H1471
135:15 The idols of the **h** *are* silver and gold, H1471
149: 7 To execute vengeance upon the **h**, *and* H1471
Isa 16: 8 the lords of the **h** have broken down H1471
Jer 9:16 I will scatter them also among the **h**, H1471
10: 2 Learn not the way of the **h**, and be not H1471
2 for the **h** are dismayed at them. H1471
25 Pour out thy fury upon the **h** that know H1471
18:13 ye now among the **h**, who hath heard H1471
49:14 is sent unto the **h**, *saying*, Gather ye H1471
15 among the **h**, *and* despised among men. H1471
Lam 1: 3 among the **h**, she findeth no rest: H1471
10 hath seen *that* the **h** entered into her H1471
4:15 the **h**, They shall no more sojourn *there*. H1471
20 his shadow we shall live among the **h**. H1471
Ezk 7:24 bring the worst of the **h**, and they shall H1471
11:12 of the **h** that *are* round about you. H1471
16 far off among the **h**, and although I H1471
12:16 among the **h** whither they come; H1471
16:14 forth among the **h** for thy beauty: for it H1471
20: 9 before the **h**, among whom they H1471
14 **h**, in whose sight I brought them out. H1471
22 **h**, in whose sight I brought them forth. H1471
23 them among the **h**, and disperse them H1471
32 We will be as the **h**, as the families of H1471
41 I will be sanctified in you before the **h**. H1471
22: 4 the **h**, and a mocking to all countries. H1471
15 And I will scatter thee among the **h**, and H1471
16 in the sight of the **h**, and thou shalt H1471
23:30 a whoring after the **h**, *and* because thou H1471
25: 7 for a spoil to the **h**; and I will cut thee H1471
8 the house of Judah *is* like unto all the **h**; H1471
28:25 in the sight of the **h**, then shall they H1471
30: 3 cloudy day; it shall be the time of the **h**. H1471
31:11 mighty one of the **h**; he shall surely deal H1471
17 under his shadow in the midst of the **h**. H1471
34:28 be a prey to the **h**, neither shall the H1471
29 bear the shame of the **h** any more. H1471
36: 3 the residue of the **h**, and ye are taken up H1471
4 residue of the **h** that *are* round about; H1471
5 the residue of the **h**, and against all H1471
6 ye have borne the shame of the **h**: H1471
7 hand, Surely the **h** that *are* about you, H1471
15 the shame of the **h** any more, neither H1471
19 And I scattered them among the **h**, and H1471
20 And when they entered unto the **h**, H1471
21 among the **h**, whither they went. H1471
22 profaned among the **h**, whither ye went. H1471
23 among the **h**, which ye have profaned H1471
23 of them; and the **h** shall know that I *am* H1471
24 For I will take you from among the **h**, H1471
Ezk 36:30 more reproach of famine among the **h**. H1471
36 Then the **h** that are left round about H1471
37:21 from among the **h**, whither they be H1471
28 And the **h** shall know that I the LORD H1471
38:16 my land, that the **h** may know me, H1471
39: 7 any more: and the **h** shall know that I H1471
21 And I will set my glory among the **h**, H1471
21 and all the **h** shall see my judgment H1471
23 And the **h** shall know that the house of H1471
28 among the **h**: but I have gathered H1471
Joel 2:17 to reproach, that the **h** should rule over H1471
19 make you a reproach among the **h**: H1471
3:11 and come, all ye **h**, and gather H1471
12 Let the **h** be wakened, and come up to H1471
12 will I sit to judge all the **h** round about. H1471
Am 9:12 and of all the **h**, which are called by H1471
Oba 1 is sent among the **h**, Arise ye, and let us H1471
2 among the **h**: thou art greatly despised. H1471
15 near upon all the **h**: as thou hast done, H1471
16 *so* shall all the **h** drink continually, yea, H1471
Mic 5:15 the **h**, such as they have not heard. H1471
Hab 1: 5 Behold ye among the **h**, and regard, and H1471
3:12 thou didst thresh the **h** in anger. H1471
Zep 2:11 his place, *even* all the isles of the **h**. H1471
Hag 2:22 kingdoms of the **h**; and I will overthrow H1471
Zec 1:15 with the **h** *that are* at ease: for H1471
8:13 a curse among the **h**, O house of Judah, H1471
9:10 peace unto the **h**: and his dominion H1471
14:14 wealth of all the **h** round about shall be H1471
18 will smite the **h** that come not up to H1471
Mal 1:11 among the **h**, saith the LORD of hosts. H1471
14 and my name *is* dreadful among the **h**. H1471
Mt 6: 7 repetitions, as the **h** *do*: for they think G1482
18:17 unto thee as an **h** man and a publican. G1482
Act 4:25 hast said, Why did the **h** rage, and the G1484
2Co 11:26 *in* perils by the **h**, *in* perils in the city, G1484
Gal 1:16 preach him among the **h**; immediately I G1484
2: 9 the **h**, and they unto the circumcision. G1484
3: 8 God would justify the **h** through faith, G1484

HEAVE
Ex 29:27 the shoulder of the **h** offering, which is H8641
28 of Israel: for it *is* an **h** offering: and it H8641
28 and it shall be an **h** offering from the H8641
28 *even* their **h** offering unto the LORD. H8641
Lev 7:14 oblation *for* an **h** offering unto the H8641
32 unto the priest *for* an **h** offering of the H8641
34 For the wave breast and the **h** shoulder H8641
10:14 And the wave breast and **h** shoulder H8641
15 The **h** shoulder and the wave breast H8641
Nu 6:20 wave breast and **h** shoulder: and after H8641
15:19 offer up an **h** offering unto the LORD. H8641
20 your dough *for* an **h** offering: as *ye do* H8641
20 offering: as *ye do* the **h** offering of the H8641
20 of the threshingfloor, so shall ye **h** it. H7311
21 an **h** offering in your generations. H8641
18: 8 the charge of mine **h** offerings of all the H8641
11 And this *is* thine; the **h** offering of their H8641
19 All the **h** offerings of the holy things, H8641
24 they offer *as* an **h** offering unto the H8641
26 shall offer up an **h** offering of it for the H8641
27 And *this* your **h** offering shall be H8641
28 Thus ye also shall offer an **h** offering H8641
28 LORD'S **h** offering to Aaron the priest. H8641
29 ye shall offer every **h** offering of the H8641
31:29 priest, *for* an **h** offering of the LORD. H8641
41 *which was* the LORD'S **h** offering, unto H8641
Dt 12: 6 and your tithes, and **h** offerings of your H8641
11 tithes, and the **h** offering of your hand, H8641
17 offerings, or **h** offering of thine hand: H8641

HEAVED
Ex 29:27 and which is **h** up, of the ram of the H8641
Nu 18:30 When ye have **h** the best thereof from H7311
32 of it, when ye have **h** from it the best of H7311

HEAVEN
Gen 1: 1 In the beginning God created the **h** and H8064
8 And God called the firmament **H**. And H8064
9 the waters under the **h** be gathered H8064
14 firmament of the **h** to divide the day H8064
15 firmament of the **h** to give light upon H8064
17 of the **h** to give light upon the earth, H8064
20 the earth in the open firmament of **h**. H8064
6:17 of life, from under **h**; *and* every thing H8064
7:11 up, and the windows of **h** were opened. H8064
19 *were* under the whole **h**, were covered. H8064
23 and the fowl of the **h**; and they were H8064
8: 2 the windows of **h** were stopped, and H8064

Gen 8: 2 and the rain from **h** was restrained; H8064
11: 4 *may reach* unto **h**; and let us make us H8064
14:19 high God, possessor of **h** and earth: H8064
22 high God, the possessor of **h** and earth, H8064
15: 5 Look now toward **h**, and tell the stars, if H8064
19:24 and fire from the LORD out of **h**; H8064
21:17 to Hagar out of **h**, and said unto her, H8064
22:11 unto him out of **h**, and said, Abraham, H8064
15 Abraham out of **h** the second time, H8064
17 as the stars of the **h**, and as the sand H8064
24: 3 LORD, the God of **h**, and the God of the H8064
7 The LORD God of **h**, which took me H8064
26: 4 as the stars of **h**, and will give unto thy H8064
27:28 Therefore God give thee of the dew of **h**, H8064
39 earth, and of the dew of **h** from above; H8064
28:12 of it reached to **h**: and behold the angels H8064
17 house of God, and this *is* the gate of **h**. H8064
49:25 with blessings of **h** above, blessings of H8064
Ex 9: 8 it toward the **h** in the sight of Pharaoh. H8064
10 it up toward **h**; and it became a boil H8064
22 hand toward **h**, that there may be hail H8064
23 his rod toward **h**: and the LORD sent H8064
10:21 thine hand toward **h**, that there may be H8064
22 his hand toward **h**; and there was a H8064
16: 4 will rain bread from **h** for you; and the H8064
17:14 remembrance of Amalek from under **h**. H8064
20: 4 *thing* that *is* in **h** above, or that *is* in H8064
11 For *in* six days the LORD made **h** and H8064
22 seen that I have talked with you from **h**. H8064
24:10 it were the body of **h** in *his* clearness. H8064
31:17 the LORD made **h** and earth, and on H8064
32:13 as the stars of **h**, and all this land that H8064
Lev 26:19 your **h** as iron, and your earth as brass: H8064
Dt 1:10 this day as the stars of **h** for multitude. H8064
28 and walled up to **h**; and moreover we H8064
2:25 *are* under the whole **h**, who shall hear H8064
3:24 God *is there* in **h** or in earth, that can H8064
4:11 fire unto the midst of **h**, with darkness, H8064
19 And lest thou lift up thine eyes unto **h**, H8064
19 all the host of **h**, shouldest be driven H8064
19 unto all nations under the whole **h**. H8064
26 I call **h** and earth to witness against H8064
32 from the one side of **h** unto the other, H8064
36 Out of **h** he made thee to hear his voice, H8064
39 LORD he *is* God in **h** above, and upon H8064
5: 8 *thing* that *is* in **h** above, or that *is* in H8064
7:24 name from under **h**: there shall no man H8064
9: 1 thyself, cities great and fenced up to **h**, H8064
14 name from under **h**: and I will make of H8064
10:14 Behold, the **h** and the heaven of H8064
14 Behold, the heaven and the **h** of H8064
22 thee as the stars of **h** for multitude. H8064
11:11 *and* drinketh water of the rain of **h**: H8064
17 he shut up the **h**, that there be no rain, H8064
21 them, as the days of **h** upon the earth. H8064
17: 3 of **h**, which I have not commanded; H8064
25:19 from under **h**; thou shalt not forget *it*. H8064
26:15 habitation, from **h**, and bless thy people H8064
28:12 his good treasure, the **h** to give the rain H8064
23 And thy **h** that *is* over thy head shall be H8064
24 and dust: from **h** shall it come down H8064
62 as the stars of **h** for multitude; because H8064
29:20 shall blot out his name from under **h**. H8064
30: 4 outmost *parts* of **h**, from thence will the H8064
12 It *is* not in **h**, that thou shouldest say, H8064
12 go up for us to **h**, and bring it unto us, H8064
19 I call **h** and earth to record this day H8064
31:28 **h** and earth to record against them. H8064
32:40 For I lift up my hand to **h**, and say, I H8064
33:13 precious things of **h**, for the dew, and H8064
26 rideth upon the **h** in thy help, and in H8064
Jos 2:11 God in **h** above, and in earth beneath. H8064
8:20 city ascended up to **h**, and they had no H8064
10:11 great stones from **h** upon them unto H8064
13 in the midst of **h**, and hasted not to go H8064
Jdg 5:20 They fought from **h**; the stars in their H8064
13:20 went up toward **h** from off the altar, H8064
20:40 the flame of the city ascended up to **h**. H8064
1Sa 2:10 to pieces; out of **h** shall he thunder H8064
5:12 and the cry of the city went up to **h**. H8064
2Sa 18: 9 up between the **h** and the earth; and H8064
21:10 upon them out of **h**, and suffered H8064
22: 8 the foundations of **h** moved and shook, H8064
14 The LORD thundered from **h**, and the H8064
1Ki 8:22 and spread forth his hands toward **h**: H8064
23 God like thee, in **h** above, or on earth H8064
27 the earth? behold, the **h** and heaven of H8064
27 the heaven and **h** of heavens cannot H8064
30 and hear thou in **h** thy dwelling place: H8064
1Ki 8:32 Then hear thou in **h**, and do, and judge H8064
34 Then hear thou in **h**, and forgive the sin H8064
35 When **h** is shut up, and there is no rain, H8064
36 Then hear thou in **h**, and forgive the sin H8064
39 Then hear thou in **h** thy dwelling place, H8064
43 Hear thou in **h** thy dwelling place, and H8064
45 Then hear thou in **h** their prayer and H8064
49 supplication in **h** thy dwelling place, H8064
54 his knees with his hands spread up to **h**. H8064
18:45 while, that the **h** was black with clouds H8064
22:19 and all the host of **h** standing by him H8064
2Ki 1:10 come down from **h**, and consume thee H8064
10 **h**, and consumed him and his fifty. H8064
12 come down from **h**, and consume thee H8064
12 **h**, and consumed him and his fifty. H8064
14 Behold, there came fire down from **h**, H8064
2: 1 take up Elijah into **h** by a whirlwind, H8064
11 Elijah went up by a whirlwind into **h**. H8064
7: 2 make windows in **h**, might this thing H8064
19 make windows in **h**, might such a thing H8064
14:27 Israel from under **h**: but he saved them H8064
17:16 all the host of **h**, and served Baal. H8064
19:15 the earth; thou hast made **h** and earth. H8064
21: 3 all the host of **h**, and served them. H8064
5 And he built altars for all the host of **h** H8064
23: 4 and for all the host of **h**: and he burned H8064
5 to the planets, and to all the host of **h**. H8064
1Ch 21:16 the earth and the **h**, having a drawn H8064
26 him from **h** by fire upon the altar H8064
29:11 for all *that is* in the **h** and in the earth *is* H8064
2Ch 2: 6 an house, seeing the **h** and heaven of H8064
6 the heaven and **h** of heavens cannot H8064
12 of Israel, that made **h** and earth, who H8064
6:13 and spread forth his hands toward **h**, H8064
14 God like thee in the **h**, nor in the earth; H8064
18 the earth? behold, **h** and the heaven of H8064
18 heaven and the **h** of heavens cannot H8064
21 from **h**; and when thou hearest, forgive. H8064
23 Then hear thou from **h**, and do, and H8064
26 When the **h** is shut up, and there is no H8064
27 Then hear thou from **h**, and forgive the H8064
30 Then hear thou from **h** thy dwelling H8064
7: 1 came down from **h**, and consumed the H8064
13 If I shut up **h** that there be no rain, or if H8064
14 will I hear from **h**, and will forgive their H8064
18:18 and all the host of **h** standing on his H8064
20: 6 not thou God in **h**? and rulest *not* thou H8064
28: 9 them in a rage *that* reacheth up unto **h**. H8064
30:27 to his holy dwelling place, *even* unto **h**. H8064
32:20 the son of Amoz, prayed and cried to **h**. H8064
33: 3 all the host of **h**, and served them. H8064
5 And he built altars for all the host of **h** H8064
36:23 the LORD God of **h** given me; and he H8064
Ezr 1: 2 The LORD God of **h** hath given me all H8064
5:11 of the God of **h** and earth, and build H8065
12 the God of **h** unto wrath, he gave H8065
6: 9 of the God of **h**, wheat, salt, wine, and H8065
10 unto the God of **h**, and pray for the life H8065
7:12 of **h**, perfect *peace*, and at such a time. H8065
21 law of the God of **h**, shall require of you, H8065
23 by the God of **h**, let it be diligently done H8065
23 of the God of **h**: for why should there H8065
Neh 1: 4 fasted, and prayed before the God of **h**, H8064
5 O LORD God of **h**, the great and terrible H8064
9 part of the **h**, *yet* will I gather them H8064
2: 4 request? So I prayed to the God of **h**. H8064
20 them, The God of **h**, he will prosper us; H8064
9: 6 alone; thou hast made **h**, the heaven of H8064
6 made heaven, the **h** of heavens, with all H8064
6 all; and the host of **h** worshippeth thee. H8064
13 with them from **h**, and gavest them H8064
15 And gavest them bread from **h** for their H8064
23 as the stars of **h**, and broughtest them H8064
27 *them* from **h**; and according to thy H8064
28 *them* from **h**; and many times didst H8064
Job 1:16 God is fallen from **h**, and hath burned H8064
2:12 dust upon their heads toward **h**. H8064
11: 8 *It is* as high as **h**; what canst thou do? H8064
16:19 Also now, behold, my witness *is* in **h**, H8064
20:27 The **h** shall reveal his iniquity; and the H8064
22:12 *Is* not God in the height of **h**? and H8064
14 not; and he walketh in the circuit of **h**. H8064
26:11 The pillars of **h** tremble and are H8064
28:24 the earth, *and* seeth under the whole **h**; H8064
35:11 maketh us wiser than the fowls of **h**? H8064
37: 3 He directeth it under the whole **h**, and H8064
38:29 hoary frost of **h**, who hath gendered it? H8064
33 Knowest thou the ordinances of **h**? H8064
37 or who can stay the bottles of **h**, H8064
Job 41:11 *is* under the whole **h** is mine. H8064
Ps 11: 4 throne *is* in **h**: his eyes behold, his H8064
14: 2 The LORD looked down from **h** upon H8064
19: 6 His going forth *is* from the end of the **h**, H8064
20: 6 him from his holy **h** with the saving H8064
33:13 The LORD looketh from **h**; he beholdeth H8064
53: 2 God looked down from **h** upon the H8064
57: 3 He shall send from **h**, and save me *from* H8064
69:34 Let the **h** and earth praise him, the H8064
73:25 Whom have I in **h** *but thee*? and *there* H8064
76: 8 from **h**; the earth feared, and was still, H8064
77:18 The voice of thy thunder *was* in the **h**: H1534
78:23 from above, and opened the doors of **h**, H8064
24 and had given them of the corn of **h**. H8064
26 to blow in the **h**: and by his power he H8064
79: 2 the fowls of the **h**, the flesh of thy saints H8064
80:14 from **h**, and behold, and visit this vine; H8064
85:11 righteousness shall look down from **h**. H8064
89: 6 For who in the **h** can be compared unto H7834
29 for ever, and his throne as the days of **h**. H8064
37 and *as* a faithful witness in **h**. Selah. H7834
102:19 from **h** did the LORD behold the earth; H8064
103:11 For as the **h** is high above the earth, *so* H8064
104:12 By them shall the fowls of the **h** have H8064
105:40 and satisfied them with the bread of **h**. H8064
107:26 They mount up to the **h**, they go down H8064
113: 6 *things that are* in **h**, and in the earth! H8064
115:15 of the LORD which made **h** and earth. H8064
16 The **h**, *even* the heavens, *are* the H8064
119:89 ever, O LORD, thy word is settled in **h**. H8064
121: 2 the LORD, which made **h** and earth. H8064
124: 8 of the LORD, who made **h** and earth. H8064
134: 3 The LORD that made **h** and earth bless H8064
135: 6 *that* did he in **h**, and in earth, in the H8064
136:26 O give thanks unto the God of **h**: for his H8064
139: 8 If I ascend up into **h**, thou *art* there: if I H8064
146: 6 Which made **h**, and earth, the sea, and H8064
147: 8 Who covereth the **h** with clouds, who H8064
148:13 his glory *is* above the earth and **h**. H8064
Prv 23: 5 they fly away as an eagle toward **h**. H8064
25: 3 The **h** for height, and the earth for H8064
30: 4 Who hath ascended up into **h**, or H8064
Ecc 1:13 are done under **h**: this sore travail hath H8064
2: 3 do under the **h** all the days of their life. H8064
3: 1 a time to every purpose under the **h**: H8064
5: 2 God: for God *is* in **h**, and thou upon H8064
Isa 13: 5 from the end of **h**, *even* the LORD, and H8064
10 For the stars of **h** and the H8064
14:12 How art thou fallen from **h**, O Lucifer, H8064
13 I will ascend into **h**, I will exalt my H8064
34: 4 And all the host of **h** shall be dissolved, H8064
5 For my sword shall be bathed in **h**: H8064
37:16 the earth: thou hast made **h** and earth. H8064
40:12 and meted out **h** with the span, and H8064
55:10 and the snow from **h**, and returneth not H8064
63:15 Look down from **h**, and behold from the H8064
66: 1 Thus saith the LORD, The **h** *is* my H8064
Jer 7:18 to the queen of **h**, and to pour out drink H8064
33 the fowls of the **h**, and for the beasts of H8064
8: 2 and all the host of **h**, whom they have H8064
7 Yea, the stork in the **h** knoweth her H8064
10: 2 at the signs of **h**; for the heathen are H8064
15: 3 the fowls of the **h**, and the beasts of the H8064
16: 4 of **h**, and for the beasts of the earth. H8064
19: 7 of the **h**, and for the beasts of the earth. H8064
13 all the host of **h**, and have poured out H8064
23:24 not I fill **h** and earth? saith the LORD. H8064
31:37 Thus saith the LORD; If **h** above can be H8064
32:17 hast made the **h** and the earth by thy H8064
33:22 As the host of **h** cannot be numbered, H8064
25 the ordinances of **h** and earth; H8064
34:20 of the **h**, and to the beasts of the earth. H8064
44:17 unto the queen of **h**, and to pour out H8064
18 to the queen of **h**, and to pour out drink H8064
19 to the queen of **h**, and poured out drink H8064
25 to the queen of **h**, and to pour out drink H8064
49:36 four quarters of **h**, and will scatter them H8064
51: 9 **h**, and is lifted up *even* to the skies. H8064
15 out the **h** by his understanding. H8064
48 Then the **h** and the earth, and all that H8064
53 Though Babylon should mount up to **h**, H8064
Lam 2: 1 cast down from **h** unto the earth the H8064
3:50 LORD look down, and behold from **h**. H8064
4:19 the eagles of the **h**: they pursued us H8064
Ezk 8: 3 the earth and the **h**, and brought me in H8064
29: 5 of the field and to the fowls of the **h**. H8064
31: 6 All the fowls of **h** made their nests in H8064
13 all the fowls of the **h** remain, and all H8064
32: 4 all the fowls of the **h** to remain upon H8064

Ezk 32: 7 I will cover the **h**, and make the stars H8064
8 All the bright lights of **h** will I make H8064
38:20 the fowls of the **h**, and the beasts of the H8064
Dan 2:18 of the God of **h** concerning this secret; H8065
19 Then Daniel blessed the God of **h**. H8065
28 But there is a God in **h** that revealeth H8065
37 for the God of **h** hath given thee a H8065
38 the fowls of the **h** hath he given into H8065
44 shall the God of **h** set up a kingdom, H8065
4:11 reached unto **h**, and the sight thereof H8065
12 the fowls of the **h** dwelt in the boughs H8065
13 and an holy one came down from **h**; H8065
15 with the dew of **h**, and *let* his portion *be* H8065
20 **h**, and the sight thereof to all the earth; H8065
21 the fowls of the **h** had their habitation: H8065
22 and reacheth unto **h**, and thy dominion H8065
23 down from **h**, and saying, Hew the H8065
23 with the dew of **h**, and *let* his portion *be* H8065
25 with the dew of **h**, and seven times shall H8065
31 there fell a voice from **h**, *saying*, O king H8065
33 wet with the dew of **h**, till his hairs were H8065
34 lifted up mine eyes unto **h**, and mine H8065
35 his will in the army of **h**, and *among* the H8065
37 the King of **h**, all whose works *are* H8065
5:21 with the dew of **h**; till he knew that the H8065
23 the Lord of **h**; and they have brought H8065
6:27 and wonders in **h** and in earth, who H8065
7: 2 of the **h** strove upon the great sea. H8065
13 with the clouds of **h**, and came to the H8065
27 under the whole **h**, shall be given to the H8065
8: 8 ones toward the four winds of **h**. H8064
10 *even* to the host of **h**; and it cast down H8064
9:12 under the whole **h** hath not been done H8064
11: 4 the four winds of **h**; and not to his H8064
12: 7 his left hand unto **h**, and sware by him H8064
Hos 2:18 and with the fowls of **h**, and *with* the H8064
4: 3 with the fowls of **h**; yea, the fishes of the H8064
7:12 as the fowls of the **h**; I will chastise H8064
Am 9: 2 up to **h**, thence will I bring them down: H8064
6 *It is* he that buildeth his stories in the **h**, H8064
Jna 1: 9 LORD, the God of **h**, which hath made H8064
Nah 3:16 above the stars of **h**: the cankerworm H8064
Zep 1: 3 the fowls of the **h**, and the fishes of the H8064
5 And them that worship the host of **h** H8064
Hag 1:10 Therefore the **h** over you is stayed from H8064
Zec 2: 6 the four winds of the **h**, saith the LORD. H8064
5: 9 the ephah between the earth and the **h**. H8064
Mal 3:10 the windows of **h**, and pour you out a H8064
Mt 3: 2 ye: for the kingdom of **h** is at hand. G3772
17 And lo a voice from **h**, saying, This is G3772
4:17 for the kingdom of **h** is at hand. G3772
5: 3 in spirit: for theirs is the kingdom of **h**. G3772
10 sake: for theirs is the kingdom of **h**. G3772
12 *is* your reward in **h**: for so persecuted G3772
16 and glorify your Father which is in **h**. G3772
18 For verily I say unto you, Till **h** and G3772
19 in the kingdom of **h**: but whosoever G3772
19 be called great in the kingdom of **h**. G3772
20 in no case enter into the kingdom of **h**. G3772
34 all; neither by **h**; for it is God's throne: G3772
45 Father which is in **h**: for he maketh his G3772
48 as your Father which is in **h** is perfect. G3772
6: 1 no reward of your Father which is in **h**. G3772
9 which art in **h**, Hallowed be thy name. G3772
10 Thy will be done in earth, as *it is* in **h**. G3772
20 But lay up for yourselves treasures in **h**, G3772
7:11 Father which is in **h** give good things to G3772
21 the kingdom of **h**; but he that doeth the G3772
21 the will of my Father which is in **h**. G3772
8:11 Isaac, and Jacob, in the kingdom of **h**. G3772
10: 7 saying, The kingdom of **h** is at hand. G3772
32 also before my Father which is in **h**. G3772
33 deny before my Father which is in **h**. G3772
11:11 in the kingdom of **h** is greater than he. G3772
12 the kingdom of **h** suffereth violence, G3772
23 art exalted unto **h**, shalt be brought G3772
25 O Father, Lord of **h** and earth, because G3772
12:50 my Father which is in **h**, the same is my G3772
13:11 of **h**, but to them it is not given. G3772
24 The kingdom of **h** is likened unto a G3772
31 The kingdom of **h** is like to a grain of G3772
33 The kingdom of **h** is like unto leaven, G3772
44 Again, the kingdom of **h** is like unto G3772
45 Again, the kingdom of **h** is like unto a G3772
47 Again, the kingdom of **h** is like unto a G3772
52 the kingdom of **h** is like unto a man G3772
14:19 and looking up to **h**, he blessed, and G3772
16: 1 that he would shew them a sign from **h**. G3772
17 unto thee, but my Father which is in **h**. G3772

Mt 16:19 of the kingdom of **h**: and whatsoever G3772
19 shall be bound in **h**: and whatsoever G3772
19 shalt loose on earth shall be loosed in **h**. G3772
18: 1 Who is the greatest in the kingdom of **h**? G3772
3 ye shall not enter into the kingdom of **h**. G3772
4 same is greatest in the kingdom of **h**. G3772
10 say unto you, That in **h** their angels do G3772
10 the face of my Father which is in **h**. G3772
14 Father which is in **h**, that one of these G3772
18 shall be bound in **h**: and whatsoever ye G3772
18 shall loose on earth shall be loosed in **h**. G3772
19 for them of my Father which is in **h**. G3772
23 Therefore is the kingdom of **h** likened G3772
19:14 me: for of such is the kingdom of **h**. G3772
21 treasure in **h**: and come *and* follow me. G3772
23 hardly enter into the kingdom of **h**. G3772
20: 1 For the kingdom of **h** is like unto a G3772
21:25 was it? from **h**, or of men? And they G3772
25 shall say, From **h**; he will say unto us, G3772
22: 2 The kingdom of **h** is like unto a certain G3772
30 but are as the angels of God in **h**. G3772
23: 9 for one is your Father, which is in **h**. G3772
13 up the kingdom of **h** against men: for G3772
22 And he that shall swear by **h**, sweareth G3772
24:29 shall fall from **h**, and the powers of the G3772
30 the Son of man in **h**: and then shall all G3772
30 clouds of **h** with power and great glory. G3772
31 winds, from one end of **h** to the other. G3772
35 **H** and earth shall pass away, but my G3772
36 not the angels of **h**, but my Father only. G3772
25: 1 Then shall the kingdom of **h** be likened G3772
14 For *the kingdom of* **h** *is* as a man
26:64 of power, and coming in the clouds of **h**. G3772
28: 2 descended from **h**, and came and rolled G3772
18 is given unto me in **h** and in earth. G3772
Mk 1:11 And there came a voice from **h**, *saying*, G3772
6:41 he looked up to **h**, and blessed, and G3772
7:34 And looking up to **h**, he sighed, and G3772
8:11 of him a sign from **h**, tempting him. G3772
10:21 have treasure in **h**: and come, take up G3772
11:25 is in **h** may forgive you your trespasses. G3772
26 which is in **h** forgive your trespasses. G3772
30 The baptism of John, was *it* from **h**, or G3772
31 shall say, From **h**; he will say, Why then G3772
12:25 but are as the angels which are in **h**. G3772
13:25 And the stars of **h** shall fall, and the G3772
25 powers that are in **h** shall be shaken. G3772
27 of the earth to the uttermost part of **h**. G3772
31 **H** and earth shall pass away: but my G3772
32 are in **h**, neither the Son, but the Father. G3772
14:62 of power, and coming in the clouds of **h**. G3772
16:19 into **h**, and sat on the right hand of God. G3772
Lk 2:15 from them into **h**, the shepherds said G3772
3:21 and praying, the **h** was opened, G3772
22 a voice came from **h**, which said, Thou G3772
4:25 of Elias, when the **h** was shut up three G3772
6:23 your reward *is* great in **h**: for in the like G3772
9:16 and looking up to **h**, he blessed them, G3772
54 come down from **h**, and consume them, G3772
10:15 to **h**, shalt be thrust down to hell. G3772
18 I beheld Satan as lightning fall from **h**. G3772
20 because your names are written in **h**. G3772
21 O Father, Lord of **h** and earth, that G3772
11: 2 which art in **h**, Hallowed be thy name. G3772
2 Thy will be done, as in **h**, so in earth. G3772
16 *him*, sought of him a sign from **h**. G3772
15: 7 joy shall be in **h** over one sinner that G3772
18 have sinned against **h**, and before thee, G3772
21 sinned against **h**, and in thy sight, and G3772
16:17 And it is easier for **h** and earth to pass, G3772
17:24 the one *part* under **h**, shineth unto the G3772
24 other *part* under **h**; so shall also the Son G3772
29 from **h**, and destroyed *them* all. G3772
18:13 as *his* eyes unto **h**, but smote upon his G3772
22 treasure in **h**: and come, follow me. G3772
19:38 peace in **h**, and glory in the highest. G3772
20: 4 The baptism of John, was it from **h**, or G3772
5 shall say, From **h**; he will say, Why then G3772
21:11 and great signs shall there be from **h**. G3772
26 for the powers of **h** shall be shaken. G3772
33 **H** and earth shall pass away: but my G3772
22:43 unto him from **h**, strengthening him. G3772
24:51 from them, and carried up into **h**. G3772
Jn 1:32 **h** like a dove, and it abode upon him. G3772
51 ye shall see **h** open, and the angels G3772
3:13 And no man hath ascended up to **h**, but G3772
13 that came down from **h**, *even* the Son of G3772
13 *even* the Son of man which is in **h**. G3772
27 nothing, except it be given him from **h**. G3772

Jn 3:31 he that cometh from **h** is above all. G3772
6:31 He gave them bread from **h** to eat. G3772
32 that bread from **h**; but my Father giveth G3772
32 giveth you the true bread from **h**. G3772
33 from **h**, and giveth life unto the world. G3772
38 For I came down from **h**, not to do mine G3772
41 am the bread which came down from **h**. G3772
42 then that he saith, I came down from **h**? G3772
50 down from **h**, that a man may eat G3772
51 came down from **h**: if any man eat of G3772
58 came down from **h**: not as your fathers G3772
12:28 there a voice from **h**, *saying*, I have both G3772
17: 1 up his eyes to **h**, and said, Father, the G3772
Act 1:10 stedfastly toward **h** as he went up, G3772
11 ye gazing up into **h**? this same Jesus, G3772
11 up from you into **h**, shall so come in like G3772
11 manner as ye have seen him go into **h**. G3772
2: 2 a sound from **h** as of a rushing mighty G3772
5 men, out of every nation under **h**. G3772
19 And I will shew wonders in **h** above, G3772
3:21 Whom the **h** must receive until the G3772
4:12 other name under **h** given among men, G3772
24 which hast made **h**, and earth, and the G3772
7:42 the host of **h**; as it is written in the G3772
49 **H** *is* my throne, and earth *is* my G3772
55 up stedfastly into **h**, and saw the glory G3772
9: 3 shined round about him a light from **h**: G3772
10:11 And saw **h** opened, and a certain vessel G3772
16 the vessel was received up again into **h**. G3772
11: 5 let down from **h** by four corners; and G3772
9 me again from **h**, What God hath G3772
10 and all were drawn up again into **h**. G3772
14:15 God, which made **h**, and earth, and the G3772
17 and gave us rain from **h**, and fruitful G3771
17:24 that he is Lord of **h** and earth, dwelleth G3772
22: 6 from **h** a great light round about me. G3772
26:13 way a light from **h**, above the brightness G3771
Ro 1:18 For the wrath of God is revealed from **h** G3772
10: 6 shall ascend into **h**? (that is, to bring G3772
1Co 8: 5 gods, whether in **h** or in earth, (as G3772
15:47 the second man *is* the Lord from **h**. G3772
2Co 5: 2 upon with our house which is from **h**: G3772
12: 2 such an one caught up to the third **h**. G3772
Gal 1: 8 But though we, or an angel from **h**, G3772
Eph 1:10 **h**, and which are on earth; *even* in him: G3772
3:15 Of whom the whole family in **h** and G3772
6: 9 your Master also is in **h**; neither is there G3772
Php 2:10 bow, of *things* in **h**, and *things* in earth, G2032
3:20 For our conversation is in **h**; from G3772
Col 1: 5 is laid up for you in **h**, whereof ye heard G3772
16 that are in **h**, and that are in earth, G3772
20 *they be* things in earth, or things in **h**. G3772
23 **h**; whereof I Paul am made a minister; G3772
4: 1 that ye also have a Master in **h**. G3772
1Th 1:10 And to wait for his Son from **h**, whom G3772
4:16 descend from **h** with a shout, with the G3772
2Th 1: 7 from **h** with his mighty angels, G3772
Heb 9:24 of the true; but into **h** itself, now to G3772
10:34 **h** a better and an enduring substance. G3772
12:23 are written in **h**, and to God the Judge G3772
25 away from him that *speaketh* from **h**: G3772
26 I shake not the earth only, but also **h**. G3772
Jas 5:12 not, neither by **h**, neither by the earth, G3772
18 And he prayed again, and the **h** gave G3772
1Pt 1: 4 fadeth not away, reserved in **h** for you, G3772
12 sent down from **h**; which things the G3772
3:22 Who is gone into **h**, and is on the right G3772
2Pt 1:18 And this voice which came from **h** we G3772
1Jn 5: 7 bear record in **h**, the Father, the Word, G3772
Rev 3:12 down out of **h** from my God: and *I* G3772
4: 1 *was* opened in **h**: and the first voice G3772
2 was set in **h**, and *one* sat on the throne. G3772
5: 3 And no man in **h**, nor in earth, neither G3772
13 And every creature which is in **h**, and G3772
6:13 And the stars of **h** fell unto the earth, G3772
14 And the **h** departed as a scroll when it G3772
8: 1 in **h** about the space of half an hour. G3772
10 a great star from **h**, burning as it were a G3772
13 the midst of **h**, saying with a loud voice, G3321
9: 1 a star fall from **h** unto the earth: and G3772
10: 1 angel come down from **h**, clothed with a G3772
4 a voice from **h** saying unto me, Seal G3772
5 upon the earth lifted up his hand to **h**, G3772
6 ever, who created **h**, and the things that G3772
8 And the voice which I heard from **h** G3772
11: 6 These have power to shut **h**, that it rain G3772
12 And they heard a great voice from **h** G3772
12 ascended up to **h** in a cloud; and their G3772
13 and gave glory to the God of **h**. G3772

Rev 11:15 great voices in **h**, saying, The kingdoms *G3772*
19 And the temple of God was opened in **h**, *G3772*
12: 1 a great wonder in **h**; a woman clothed *G3772*
3 wonder in **h**; and behold a great *G3772*
4 part of the stars of **h**, and did cast them *G3772*
7 And there was war in **h**: Michael and *G3772*
8 was their place found any more in **h**. *G3772*
10 And I heard a loud voice saying in **h**, *G3772*
13: 6 tabernacle, and them that dwell in **h**. *G3772*
13 from **h** on the earth in the sight of men, *G3772*
14: 2 And I heard a voice from **h**, as the voice *G3772*
6 angel fly in the midst of **h**, having the *G3321*
7 him that made **h**, and earth, and the *G3772*
13 And I heard a voice from **h** saying unto *G3772*
17 is in **h**, he also having a sharp sickle. *G3772*
15: 1 And I saw another sign in **h**, great and *G3772*
5 of the testimony in **h** was opened: *G3772*
16:11 And blasphemed the God of **h** because *G3772*
17 of **h**, from the throne, saying, It is done. *G3772*
21 a great hail out of **h**, *every stone* about *G3772*
18: 1 come down from **h**, having great power; *G3772*
4 And I heard another voice from **h**, *G3772*
5 For her sins have reached unto **h**, and *G3772*
20 Rejoice over her, *thou* **h**, and *ye* holy *G3772*
19: 1 of much people in **h**, saying, Alleluia; *G3772*
11 And I saw **h** opened, and behold a *G3772*
14 And the armies *which were* in **h** *G3772*
17 fly in the midst of **h**, Come and gather *G3321*
20: 1 And I saw an angel come down from **h**, *G3772*
9 from God out of **h**, and devoured them. *G3772*
11 face the earth and the **h** fled away; and *G3772*
21: 1 And I saw a new **h** and a new earth: for *G3772*
1 earth: for the first **h** and the first earth *G3772*
2 from God out of **h**, prepared as a bride *G3772*
3 And I heard a great voice out of **h** *G3772*
10 descending out of **h** from God, *G3772*

HEAVENLY
Mt 6:14 your **h** Father will also forgive you: *G3770*
26 barns; yet your **h** Father feedeth them. *G3770*
32 seek:) for your **h** Father knoweth that *G3770*
15:13 plant, which my **h** Father hath not *G3770*
18:35 So likewise shall my **h** Father do also *G2032*
Lk 2:13 of the **h** host praising God, and saying, *G3770*
11:13 more shall *your* **h** Father give the Holy *G1537*
Jn 3:12 shall ye believe, if I tell you *of* **h** things? *G2032*
Act 26:19 I was not disobedient unto the **h** vision: *G3770*
1Co 15:48 **h**, such *are* they also that are heavenly. *G2032*
48 heavenly, such *are* they also that are **h**. *G2032*
49 we shall also bear the image of the **h**. *G2032*
Eph 1: 3 spiritual blessings in **h** *places* in Christ: *G2032*
20 at his own right hand in the **h** *places*, *G2032*
2: 6 sit together in **h** *places* in Christ Jesus: *G2032*
3:10 and powers in **h** *places* might be *G2032*
2Ti 4:18 *me* unto his **h** kingdom: to whom *G2032*
Heb 3: 1 partakers of the **h** calling, consider the *G2032*
6: 4 and have tasted of the **h** gift, and were *G2032*
8: 5 and shadow of **h** things, as Moses was *G2032*
9:23 with these; but the **h** things themselves *G2032*
11:16 that is, an **h**: wherefore God is not *G2032*
12:22 the living God, the **h** Jerusalem, and to *G2032*

HEAVENS
Gen 2: 1 Thus the **h** and the earth were finished, H8064
4 These *are* the generations of the **h** and H8064
4 LORD God made the earth and the **h**, H8064
Dt 10:14 Behold, the heaven and the heaven of **h** H8064
32: 1 Give ear, O ye **h**, and I will speak; and H8064
33:28 wine; also his **h** shall drop down dew. H8064
Jdg 5: 4 earth trembled, and the **h** dropped, the H8064
2Sa 22:10 He bowed the **h** also, and came down; H8064
1Ki 8:27 and heaven of **h** cannot contain thee; H8064
1Ch 16:26 *are* idols: but the LORD made the **h**. H8064
31 Let the **h** be glad, and let the earth H8064
27:23 increase Israel like to the stars of the **h**. H8064
2Ch 2: 6 and heaven of **h** cannot contain him? H8064
6:18 and the heaven of **h** cannot contain H8064
25 Then hear thou from the **h**, and forgive H8064
33 Then hear thou from the **h**, *even* from H8064
35 Then hear thou from the **h** their prayer H8064
39 Then hear thou from the **h**, *even* from H8064
Ezr 9: 6 our trespass is grown up unto the **h**. H8064
Neh 9: 6 the heaven of **h**, with all their host, the H8064
Job 9: 8 Which alone spreadeth out the **h**, and H8064
14:12 riseth not: till the **h** *be* no more, they H8064
15:15 yea, the **h** are not clean in his sight. H8064
20: 6 **h**, and his head reach unto the clouds; H8064
26:13 By his spirit he hath garnished the **h**; H8064
35: 5 Look unto the **h**, and see; and behold H8064
Ps 2: 4 He that sitteth in the **h** shall laugh: the H8064
8: 1 who hast set thy glory above the **h**. H8064
3 When I consider thy **h**, the work of thy H8064
18: 9 He bowed the **h** also, and came down: H8064
13 The LORD also thundered in the **h**, and H8064
19: 1 The **h** declare the glory of God; and the H8064
33: 6 By the word of the LORD were the **h** H8064
36: 5 Thy mercy, O LORD, *is* in the **h**; *and* thy H8064
50: 4 He shall call to the **h** from above, and H8064
6 And the **h** shall declare his H8064
57: 5 Be thou exalted, O God, above the **h**; *let* H8064
10 For thy mercy *is* great unto the **h**, and H8064
11 Be thou exalted, O God, above the **h**: *let* H8064
68: 4 rideth upon the **h** by his name JAH, H6160
8 The earth shook, the **h** also dropped at H8064
33 To him that rideth upon the **h** of H8064
33 the heavens of **h**, *which were* of old; lo, H8064
73: 9 They set their mouth against the **h**, and H8064
89: 2 shalt thou establish in the very **h**. H8064
5 And the **h** shall praise thy wonders, O H8064
11 The **h** *are* thine, the earth also *is* thine: H8064
96: 5 *are* idols: but the LORD made the **h**. H8064
11 Let the **h** rejoice, and let the earth be H8064
97: 6 The **h** declare his righteousness, and all H8064
102:25 and the **h** *are* the work of thy hands. H8064
103:19 the **h**; and his kingdom ruleth over all. H8064
104: 2 who stretchest out the **h** like a curtain: H8064
108: 4 For thy mercy *is* great above the **h**: and H8064
5 Be thou exalted, O God, above the **h**: H8064
113: 4 all nations, *and* his glory above the **h**. H8064
115: 3 But our God *is* in the **h**: he hath done H8064
16 The heaven, *even* the **h**, *are* the LORD'S: H8064
123: 1 mine eyes, O thou that dwellest in the **h**. H8064
136: 5 To him that by wisdom made the **h**: for H8064
144: 5 Bow thy **h**, O LORD, and come down: H8064
148: 1 from the **h**: praise him in the heights. H8064
4 Praise him, ye **h** of heavens, and ye H8064
4 Praise him, ye heavens of **h**, and ye H8064
4 and ye waters that *be* above the **h**. H8064
Prv 3:19 hath he established the **h**. H8064
8:27 When he prepared the **h**, I *was* there: H8064
Isa 1: 2 Hear, O **h**, and give ear, O earth: for the H8064
5:30 the light is darkened in the **h** thereof. H6183
13:13 Therefore I will shake the **h**, and the H8064
34: 4 be dissolved, and the **h** shall be rolled H8064
40:22 stretcheth out the **h** as a curtain, and H8064
42: 5 that created the **h**, and stretched them H8064
44:23 Sing, O ye **h**; for the LORD hath done *it*: H8064
24 forth the **h** alone; that spreadeth H8064
45: 8 Drop down, ye **h**, from above, and let H8064
12 **h**, and all their host have I commanded. H8064
18 that created the **h**; God himself that H8064
48:13 hath spanned the **h**: *when* I call unto H8064
49:13 Sing, O **h**; and be joyful, O earth; and H8064
50: 3 I clothe the **h** with blackness, and I H8064
51: 6 Lift up your eyes to the **h**, and look H8064
6 beneath: for the **h** shall vanish away H8064
13 hath stretched forth the **h**, and laid the H8064
16 that I may plant the **h**, and lay the H8064
55: 9 For *as* the **h** are higher than the earth, H8064
64: 1 Oh that thou wouldest rend the **h**, that H8064
65:17 For, behold, I create new **h** and a new H8064
66:22 For as the new **h** and the new earth, H8064
Jer 2:12 Be astonished, O ye **h**, at this, and be H8064
4:23 void; and the **h**, and they *had* no light. H8064
25 and all the birds of the **h** were fled. H8064
28 earth mourn, and the **h** above be black: H8064
9:10 **h** and the beast are fled; they are gone. H8064
10:11 have not made the **h** and the earth, H8065
11 from the earth, and from under these **h**. H8065
12 stretched out the **h** by his discretion. H8064
13 of waters in the **h**, and he causeth the H8064
14:22 rain? or can the **h** give showers? *art* not H8064
51:16 of waters in the **h**; and he causeth the H8064
Lam 3:41 heart with *our* hands unto God in the **h**. H8064
66 in anger from under the **h** of the LORD. H8064
Ezk 1: 1 Chebar, *that* the **h** were opened, and I H8064
Dan 4:26 shalt have known that the **h** do rule. H8065
Hos 2:21 the **h**, and they shall hear the earth; H8064
Joel 2:10 before them; the **h** shall tremble: the H8064
30 And I will shew wonders in the **h** and H8064
3:16 and the **h** and the earth shall H8064
Hab 3: 3 **h**, and the earth was full of his praise. H8064
Hag 2: 6 I will shake the **h**, and the earth, and H8064
21 saying, I will shake the **h** and the earth; H8064
Zec 6: 5 the four spirits of the **h**, which go forth H8064
8:12 increase, and the **h** shall give their dew; H8064
12: 1 forth the **h**, and layeth the foundation H8064
Mt 3:16 water: and, lo, the **h** were opened unto *G3772*
24:29 the powers of the **h** shall be shaken: *G3772*
Mk 1:10 the water, he saw the **h** opened, and the *G3772*
Lk 12:33 old, a treasure in the **h** that faileth not, *G3772*
Act 2:34 For David is not ascended into the **h**: *G3772*
7:56 And said, Behold, I see the **h** opened, *G3772*
2Co 5: 1 not made with hands, eternal in the **h**. *G3772*
Eph 4:10 above all **h**, that he might fill all things.) *G3772*
Heb 1:10 and the **h** are the works of thine hands: *G3772*
4:14 is passed into the **h**, Jesus the Son of *G3772*
7:26 sinners, and made higher than the **h**; *G3772*
8: 1 of the throne of the Majesty in the **h**; *G3772*
9:23 of things in the **h** should be purified *G3772*
2Pt 3: 5 word of God the **h** were of old, and the *G3772*
7 But the **h** and the earth, which are now, *G3772*
10 in the which the **h** shall pass away with *G3772*
12 God, wherein the **h** being on fire shall *G3772*
13 look for new **h** and a new earth, *G3772*
Rev 12:12 Therefore rejoice, *ye* **h**, and ye that *G3772*

HEAVEN'S
Mt 19:12 the kingdom of **h** sake. He that is able *G3772*

HEAVE-OFFERING See HEAVE and OFFERING.

HEAVE-SHOULDER See HEAVE and SHOULDER.

HEAVIER
Job 6: 3 For now it would be **h** than the sand of H3513
23: 2 my stroke is **h** than my groaning. H3513
Prv 27: 3 but a fool's wrath *is* **h** than them both. H3515

HEAVILY
Ex 14:25 that they drave them **h**: so that the H3517
Ps 35:14 **h**, as one that mourneth *for his* mother. H6937
Isa 47: 6 ancient hast thou very **h** laid thy yoke. H3513

HEAVINESS
Ezr 9: 5 I arose up from my **h**; and having rent H8589
Job 9:27 will leave off my **h**, and comfort *myself*: H6440
Ps 69:20 and I am full of **h**: and I looked *for* H5136
119:28 My soul melteth for **h**: strengthen thou H8424
Prv 10: 1 but a foolish son *is* the **h** of his mother. H8424
12:25 **H** in the heart of man maketh it stoop: H1674
14:13 and the end of that mirth *is* **h**. H8424
Isa 29: 2 and there shall be **h** and sorrow: and it H8386
61: 3 for the spirit of **h**; that they might be H3544
Ro 9: 2 That I have great **h** and continual *G3077*
2Co 2: 1 that I would not come again to you in **h**. *G3077*
Php 2:26 all, and was full of **h**, because that ye had *G85*
Jas 4: 9 turned to mourning, and *your* joy to **h**. *G2726*
1Pt 1: 6 are in **h** through manifold temptations: *G3076*

HEAVY
Ex 17:12 But Moses' hands *were* **h**; and they took H3515
18:18 this thing *is* too **h** for thee; thou art not H3515
Nu 11:14 people alone, because *it is* too **h** for me. H3515
1Sa 4:18 **h**. And he had judged Israel forty years. H3513
5: 6 But the hand of the LORD was **h** upon H3513
11 city; the hand of God was very **h** there. H3513
2Sa 14:26 *the hair* was **h** on him, therefore he H3513
1Ki 12: 4 thy father, and his **h** yoke which he put H3515
10 made our yoke **h**, but make thou *it* H3513
11 did lade you with a **h** yoke, I will add to H3515
14 made your yoke **h**, and I will add to H3513
14: 6 for I *am* sent to thee *with* **h** *tidings*. H7186
20:43 went to his house **h** and displeased, H5620
21: 4 And Ahab came into his house **h** and H5620
2Ch 10: 4 of thy father, and his **h** yoke that he put H3515
10 made our yoke **h**, but make thou *it* H3513
11 For whereas my father put a **h** yoke H3515
14 father made your yoke **h**, but I will add H3513
Neh 5:18 the bondage was **h** upon this people. H3513
Job 33: 7 neither shall my hand be **h** upon thee. H3513
Ps 32: 4 For day and night thy hand was **h** upon H3513
38: 4 an **h** burden they are too heavy for me. H3515
4 an heavy burden they are too **h** for me. H3513
Prv 25:20 *is* he that singeth songs to an **h** heart. H7451
27: 3 A stone *is* **h**, and the sand weighty; but H3514
31: 6 wine unto those that be of **h** hearts. H4751
Isa 6:10 make their ears **h**, and shut their eyes; H3513
24:20 thereof shall be **h** upon it; and it shall H3513
30:27 burden *thereof is* **h**: his lips are full of H3514
46: 1 your carriages *were* **h** loaden; *they are* a
58: 6 to undo the **h** burdens, and to let H4133
59: 1 neither his ear **h**, that it cannot hear: H3513
Lam 3: 7 get out: he hath made my chain **h**. H3513
Mt 11:28 and are **h** laden, and I will give you rest.
23: 4 For they bind **h** burdens and grievous to *G926*
26:37 and began to be sorrowful and very **h**. *G85*

Mt 26:43 them asleep again: for their eyes were **h**. *G916*
Mk 14:33 to be sore amazed, and to be very **h**; *G85*
40 **h**,) neither wist they what to answer him. *G916*
Lk 9:32 with him were **h** with sleep: and when *G916*

HEBER
Gen 46:17 the sons of Beriah; **H**, and Malchiel. H2268
Nu 26:45 Of the sons of Beriah: of **H**, the family of H2268
Jdg 4:11 Now **H** the Kenite, *which was* of the H2268
17 tent of Jael the wife of **H** the Kenite: for H2268
17 of Hazor and the house of **H** the Kenite. H2268
5:24 Jael the wife of **H** the Kenite be, blessed H2268
1Ch 4:18 of Gedor, and **H** the father of Socho, H2268
5:13 and Jachan, and Zia, and **H**, seven. H5677
7:31 And the sons of Beriah; **H**, and H2268
32 And **H** begat Japhlet, and Shomer, and H2268
8:17 and Meshullam, and Hezeki, and **H**, H2268
22 And Ishpan, and **H**, and Eliel, H5677
Lk 3:35 *the son* of **H**, which was *the son* of Sala, *G1443*

HEBERITES
Nu 26:45 the family of the **H**: of Malchiel, the H2277

HEBER'S
Jdg 4:21 Then Jael **H** wife took a nail of the tent, H2268

HEBREW
Gen 14:13 told Abram the **H**; for he dwelt in the H5680
39:14 brought in an **H** unto us to mock us; H5680
17 saying, The **H** servant, which thou H5680
41:12 us a young man, an **H**, servant to the H5680
Ex 1:15 And the king of Egypt spake to the **H** H5680
16 of a midwife to the **H** women, and see H5680
19 Because the **H** women *are* not as the H5680
2: 7 a nurse of the **H** women, that she may H5680
11 smiting an **H**, one of his brethren. H5680
21: 2 If thou buy an **H** servant, six years he H5680
Dt 15:12 *And* if thy brother, an **H** man, or an H5680
12 man, or an **H** woman, be sold unto H5680
Jer 34: 9 *being* an **H** or an Hebrewess, go H5680
14 his brother an **H**, which hath been sold H5680
Jna 1: 9 And he said unto them, I *am* an **H**; and H5680
Lk 23:38 **H**, THIS IS THE KING OF THE JEWS. *G1444*
Jn 5: 2 is called in the **H** tongue Bethesda, *G1447*
19:13 the Pavement, but in the **H**, Gabbatha. *G1447*
17 skull, which is called in the **H** Golgotha: *G1447*
20 was written in **H**, *and* Greek, *and* Latin. *G1447*
Act 21:40 unto *them* in the **H** tongue, saying, *G1446*
22: 2 he spake in the **H** tongue to them, they *G1446*
26:14 and saying in the **H** tongue, Saul, Saul, *G1446*
Php 3: 5 of Benjamin, an **H** of the Hebrews; as *G1445*
Rev 9:11 name in the **H** tongue *is* Abaddon, *G1447*
16:16 called in the **H** tongue Armageddon. *G1447*

HEBREWESS
Jer 34: 9 an Hebrew or an **H**, go free; that none H5680

HEBREWS
Gen 40:15 of the land of the **H**: and here also have H5680
43:32 not eat bread with the **H**; for that *is* an H5680
Ex 2:13 two men of the **H** strove together: and H5680
3:18 LORD God of the **H** hath met with us: H5680
5: 3 And they said, The God of the **H** hath H5680
7:16 LORD God of the **H** hath sent me unto H5680
9: 1 LORD God of the **H**, Let my people go, H5680
13 LORD God of the **H**, Let my people go, H5680
10: 3 LORD God of the **H**, How long wilt thou H5680
1Sa 4: 6 shout in the camp of the **H**? And they H5680
9 servants unto the **H**, as they have been H5680
13: 3 all the land, saying, Let the **H** hear. H5680
7 And *some of* the **H** went over Jordan to H5680
19 the **H** make *them* swords or spears: H5680
14:11 said, Behold, the **H** come forth out of H5680
21 Moreover the **H** *that* were with the H5680
29: 3 What *do* these **H** *here*? And Achish said H5680
Act 6: 1 against the **H**, because their widows *G1445*
2Co 11:22 Are they **H**? so *am* I. Are they Israelites? *G1445*
Php 3: 5 the **H**; as touching the law, a Pharisee; *G1445*

HEBREWS'
Ex 2: 6 and said, This *is one* of the **H** children. H5680

HEBRON
Gen 13:18 which *is* in **H**, and built there an altar H2275
23: 2 the same *is* **H** in the land of Canaan: H2275
19 the same *is* **H** in the land of Canaan. H2275
35:27 of Arbah, which *is* **H**, where Abraham H2275
37:14 the vale of **H**, and he came to Shechem. H2275
Ex 6:18 and Izhar, and **H**, and Uzziel: and the H2275
Nu 3:19 Amram, and Izehar, **H**, and Uzziel. H2275
13:22 and came unto **H**; where Ahiman, H2275
22 of Anak, *were*. (Now **H** was built seven H2275
Jos 10: 3 Hoham king of **H**, and unto Piram king H2275
5 the king of **H**, the king of Jarmuth, H2275
23 the king of **H**, the king of Jarmuth, H2275
36 him, unto **H**; and they fought against it: H2275
39 as he had done to **H**, so he did to Debir, H2275
11:21 mountains, from **H**, from Debir, from H2275
12:10 of Jerusalem, one; the king of **H**, one; H2275
14:13 son of Jephunneh **H** for an inheritance. H2275
14 **H** therefore became the inheritance of H2275
15 And the name of **H** before *was* H2275
15:13 the father of Anak, which *city is* **H**. H2275
54 which *is* **H**, and Zior; nine cities H2275
19:28 And **H**, and Rehob, and Hammon, and H5683
20: 7 which *is* **H**, in the mountain of Judah. H2275
21:11 which *city is* **H**, in the hill *country* of H2275
13 Aaron the priest **H** with her suburbs, *to* H2275
Jdg 1:10 that dwelt in **H**: (now the name of H2275
10 (now the name of **H** before *was* H2275
20 And they gave **H** unto Caleb, as Moses H2275
16: 3 up to the top of an hill that *is* before **H**. H2275
1Sa 30:31 And to *them* which *were* in **H**, and to all H2275
2Sa 2: 1 shall I go up? And he said, Unto **H**. H2275
3 and they dwelt in the cities of **H**. H2275
11 And the time that David was king in **H** H2275
32 and they came to **H** at break of day. H2275
3: 2 And unto David were sons born in **H**: H2275
5 wife. These were born to David in **H**. H2275
19 ears of David in **H** all that seemed good H2275
20 So Abner came to David to **H**, and H2275
22 not with David in **H**; for he had sent H2275
27 And when Abner was returned to **H**, H2275
32 And they buried Abner in **H**: and the H2275
4: 1 was dead in **H**, his hands were feeble, H2275
8 unto David to **H**, and said to the king, H2275
12 up over the pool in **H**. But they took the H2275
12 buried *it* in the sepulchre of Abner in **H**. H2275
5: 1 to David unto **H**, and spake, saying, H2275
3 to the king to **H**; and king David made H2275
3 with them in **H** before the LORD: and H2275
5 In **H** he reigned over Judah seven years H2275
13 he was come from **H**: and there were yet H2275
15: 7 I have vowed unto the LORD, in **H**. H2275
9 Go in peace. So he arose, and went to **H**. H2275
10 ye shall say, Absalom reigneth in **H**. H2275
1Ki 2:11 reigned he in **H**, and thirty and three H2275
1Ch 2:42 the sons of Mareshah the father of **H**. H2275
43 And the sons of **H**; Korah, and H2275
3: 1 were born unto him in **H**; the firstborn H2275
4 *These* six were born unto him in **H**; and H2275
6: 2 Amram, Izhar, and **H**, and Uzziel. H2275
18 Amram, and Izhar, and **H**, and Uzziel. H2275
55 And they gave them **H** in the land of H2275
57 of Judah, *namely*, **H**, *the city* of refuge, H2275
11: 1 to David unto **H**, saying, Behold, we H2275
3 to the king to **H**; and David made a H2275
3 with them in **H** before the LORD; and H2275
12:23 *and* came to David to **H**, to turn the H2275
38 a perfect heart to **H**, to make David H2275
15: 9 Of the sons of **H**; Eliel the chief, and his H2275
23:12 The sons of Kohath; Amram, Izhar, **H**, H2275
19 Of the sons of **H**; Jeriah the first, H2275
24:23 And the sons *of* **H**; Jeriah *the first*,
29:27 reigned he in **H**, and thirty and three H2275
2Ch 11:10 And Zorah, and Aijalon, and **H**, which H2275

HEBRONITES
Nu 3:27 the family of the **H**, and the family of H2276
26:58 the family of the **H**, the family of the H2276
1Ch 26:23 the Izharites, the **H**, *and* the Uzzielites: H2276
30 *And* of the **H**, Hashabiah and his H2276
31 Among the **H** *was* Jerijah the chief, H2276
31 *even* among the **H**, according to the H2276

HEDGE
Job 1:10 Hast not thou made an **h** about him, H7753
Prv 15:19 The way of the slothful *man is* as an **h** H4881
Ecc 10: 8 breaketh an **h**, a serpent shall bite him. H1447
Isa 5: 5 I will take away the **h** thereof, and it H4881
Ezk 13: 5 made up the **h** for the house of Israel H1447
22:30 make up the **h**, and stand in the gap H1447
Hos 2: 6 Therefore, behold, I will **h** up thy way H7753
Mic 7: 4 *sharper* than a thorn **h**: the day of thy H4534
Mk 12: 1 and set an **h** about *it*, and digged *G5418*

HEDGED
Job 3:23 way is hid, and whom God hath **h** in? H5526
Lam 3: 7 He hath **h** me about, that I cannot get H1443
Mt 21:33 a vineyard, and **h** it round about, and *G5418*

HEDGES
1Ch 4:23 among plants and **h**: there they dwelt H1448
Ps 80:12 Why hast thou *then* broken down her **h**, H1447
89:40 Thou hast broken down all his **h**; thou H1448
Jer 49: 3 to and fro by the **h**; for their king shall H1448
Nah 3:17 which camp in the **h** in the cold day, H1448
Lk 14:23 the highways and **h**, and compel *them* *G5418*

HEED
Gen 31:24 unto him, Take **h** that thou speak not H8104
29 saying, Take thou **h** that thou speak H8104
Ex 10:28 from me, take **h** to thyself, see my face H8104
19:12 saying, Take **h** to yourselves, *that ye* H8104
34:12 Take **h** to thyself, lest thou make a H8104
Nu 23:12 Must I not take **h** to speak that which H8104
Dt 2: 4 ye good **h** unto yourselves therefore: H8104
4: 9 Only take **h** to thyself, and keep thy H8104
15 Take ye therefore good **h** unto H8104
23 Take **h** unto yourselves, lest ye forget H8104
11:16 Take **h** to yourselves, that your heart H8104
12:13 Take **h** to thyself that thou offer not thy H8104
19 Take **h** to thyself that thou forsake not H8104
30 Take **h** to thyself that thou be not H8104
24: 8 Take **h** in the plague of leprosy, that H8104
27: 9 saying, Take **h**, and hearken, O Israel; H5535
Jos 22: 5 But take diligent **h** to do the H8104
23:11 Take good **h** therefore unto yourselves, H8104
1Sa 19: 2 I pray thee, take **h** to thyself until the H8104
2Sa 20:10 But Amasa took no **h** to the sword that H8104
1Ki 2: 4 If thy children take **h** to their way, to H8104
8:25 thy children take **h** to their way, that H8104
2Ki 10:31 But Jehu took no **h** to walk in the law of H8104
1Ch 22:13 if thou takest **h** to fulfil the statutes H8104
28:10 Take **h** now; for the LORD hath chosen H7200
2Ch 6:16 thy children take **h** to their way to walk H8104
19: 6 And said to the judges, Take **h** what ye H7200
7 be upon you; take **h** and do *it*: for *there* H8104
33: 8 so that they will take **h** to do all that I H8104
Ezr 4:22 Take **h** now that ye fail not to do this: H2095
Job 36:21 Take **h**, regard not iniquity: for this hast H8104
Ps 39: 1 I said, I will take **h** to my ways, that I H8104
119: 9 taking **h** *thereto* according to thy word. H8104
Prv 17: 4 A wicked doer giveth **h** to false lips; H7181
Ecc 7:21 Also take no **h** unto all words that are H3820
12: 9 yea, he gave good **h**, and sought out, *and* H239
Isa 7: 4 And say unto him, Take **h**, and be quiet; H8104
21: 7 he hearkened diligently with much **h**: H7182
Jer 9: 4 Take ye **h** every one of his neighbour, H8104
17:21 Thus saith the LORD; Take **h** to H8104
18:18 let us not give **h** to any of his words. H7181
19 Give **h** to me, O LORD, and hearken to H7181
Hos 4:10 they have left off to take **h** to the LORD. H8104
Mal 2:15 Therefore take **h** to your spirit, and let H8104
16 therefore take **h** to your spirit, that ye H8104
Mt 6: 1 Take **h** that ye do not your alms before *G4337*
16: 6 Then Jesus said unto them, Take **h** and *G3708*
18:10 Take **h** that ye despise not one of these *G3708*
24: 4 them, Take **h** that no man deceive you. *G991*
Mk 4:24 And he said unto them, Take **h** what ye *G991*
8:15 And he charged them, saying, Take **h**, *G3708*
13: 5 to say, Take **h** lest any *man* deceive you: *G991*
9 But take **h** to yourselves: for they shall *G991*
23 But take ye **h**: behold, I have foretold you *G991*
33 Take ye **h**, watch and pray: for ye know *G991*
Lk 8:18 Take **h** therefore how ye hear: for *G991*
11:35 Take **h** therefore that the light which is *G4648*
12:15 And he said unto them, Take **h**, and *G3708*
17: 3 Take **h** to yourselves: If thy brother *G4337*
21: 8 And he said, Take **h** that ye be not *G991*
34 And take **h** to yourselves, lest at any *G4337*
Act 3: 5 And he gave **h** unto them, expecting to *G1907*
5:35 of Israel, take **h** to yourselves what *G4337*
8: 6 And the people with one accord gave **h** *G4337*
10 To whom they all gave **h**, from the least *G4337*
20:28 Take **h** therefore unto yourselves, and *G4337*
22:26 saying, Take **h** what thou doest: for *G3708*
Ro 11:21 *take h* lest he also spare not thee.
1Co 3:10 man take **h** how he buildeth thereupon. *G991*
8: 9 But take **h** lest by any means this liberty *G991*
10:12 thinketh he standeth take **h** lest he fall. *G991*
Gal 5:15 one another, take **h** that ye be not *G991*
Col 4:17 And say to Archippus, Take **h** to the *G991*
1Ti 1: 4 Neither give **h** to fables and endless *G4337*
4: 1 the faith, giving **h** to seducing spirits, *G4337*
16 Take **h** unto thyself, and unto the *G1907*
Tit 1:14 Not giving **h** to Jewish fables, and *G4337*

Heb 2: 1 the more earnest **h** to the things which G4337
3:12 Take **h**, brethren, lest there be in any of G991
2Pt 1:19 well that ye take **h**, as unto a light that G4337

HEEL
Gen 3:15 thy head, and thou shalt bruise his **h**. H6119
25:26 hold on Esau's **h**; and his name was H6119
Job 18: 9 The gin shall take *him* by the **h**, *and* the H6119
Ps 41: 9 bread, hath lifted up *his* **h** against me. H6119
Hos 12: 3 He took his brother by the **h** in the H6117
Jn 13:18 me hath lifted up his **h** against me. G4418

HEELS
Gen 49:17 **h**, so that his rider shall fall backward. H6119
Job 13:27 settest a print upon the **h** of my feet. H8328
Ps 49: 5 of my **h** shall compass me about? H6120
Jer 13:22 skirts discovered, *and* thy **h** made bare. H6119

HEGAI
Est 2: 8 to the custody of **H**, that Esther was H1896
8 the custody of **H**, keeper of the women. H1896
15 required nothing but what **H** the king's H1896

HEGE
Est 2: 3 unto the custody of **H** the king's H1896

HEIFER
Gen 15: 9 And he said unto him, Take me an **h** of H5697
Nu 19: 2 they bring thee a red **h** without spot, H6510
5 And *one* shall burn the **h** in his sight; H6510
6 *it* into the midst of the burning of the **h**. H6510
9 up the ashes of the **h**, and lay *them* up H6510
10 the ashes of the **h** shall wash his H6510
17 ashes of the burnt **h** of purification for
Dt 21: 3 that city shall take an **h**, which hath not H5697
4 bring down the **h** unto a rough valley, H5697
6 the **h** that is beheaded in the valley: H5697
Jdg 14:18 my **h**, ye had not found out my riddle. H5697
1Sa 16: 2 said, Take an **h** with thee, and say, H5697
Isa 15: 5 *flee* unto Zoar, an **h** of three years old: H5697
Jer 46:20 Egypt *is like* a very fair **h**, *but* H5697
48:34 Horonaim, *as* an **h** of three years old: H5697
50:11 as the **h** at grass, and bellow as bulls; H5697
Hos 4:16 as a backsliding **h**: now the LORD will H6510
10:11 And Ephraim *is as* an **h** *that is* taught, H5697
Heb 9:13 and the ashes of an **h** sprinkling the G1151

HEIFER'S
Dt 21: 4 strike off the **h** neck there in the valley: H5697

HEIGHT
Gen 6:15 fifty cubits, and the **h** of it thirty cubits. H6967
Ex 25:10 and a cubit and a half the **h** thereof. H6967
23 and a cubit and a half the **h** thereof. H6967
27: 1 and the **h** thereof *shall be* three cubits. H6967
18 where, and the **h** five cubits *of* fine H6967
30: 2 cubits *shall be* the **h** thereof: the horns H6967
37: 1 of it, and a cubit and a half the **h** of it: H6967
10 and a cubit and a half the **h** thereof: H6967
25 two cubits *was* the **h** of it; the horns H6967
38: 1 and three cubits the **h** thereof. H6967
18 length, and the **h** in the breadth *was* H6967
1Sa 16: 7 or on the **h** of his stature; because H1364
17: 4 whose **h** *was* six cubits and a span. H1363
1Ki 6: 2 *cubits*, and the **h** thereof thirty cubits. H6967
20 cubits in the **h** thereof: and he overlaid H6967
26 The **h** of the one cherub *was* ten cubits, H6967
7: 2 cubits, and the **h** thereof thirty cubits, H6967
16 of the pillars: the **h** of the one chapiter H6967
16 **h** of the other chapiter *was* five cubits: H6967
23 all about, and his **h** *was* five cubits: H6967
27 thereof, and three cubits the **h** of it. H6967
32 to the base: and the **h** of a wheel *was* a H6967
2Ki 19:23 come up to the **h** of the mountains, to H4791
25:17 The **h** of the one pillar *was* eighteen H6967
17 brass: and the **h** of the chapiter three H6967
2Ch 3: 4 cubits, and the **h** *was* an hundred and H1363
4: 1 thereof, and ten cubits the **h** thereof. H6967
2 and five cubits the **h** thereof; and a line H6967
33:14 it up a very great **h**, and put captains of H1361
Ezr 6: 3 strongly laid; the **h** thereof threescore H7314
Job 22:12 *Is* not God in the **h** of heaven? and H1363
12 the **h** of the stars, how high they are! H7218
Ps 102:19 For he hath looked down from the **h** of H4791
Prv 25: 3 The heaven for **h**, and the earth for H7312
Isa 7:11 it either in the depth, or in the **h** above. H1361
37:24 I come up to the **h** of the mountains, to H4791
24 I will enter into the **h** of his border, *and* H4791
Jer 31:12 and sing in the **h** of Zion, and shall H4791
49:16 that holdest the **h** of the hill: though H4791
51:53 should fortify the **h** of her strength, *yet* H4791
52:21 And *concerning* the pillars, the **h** of one H6967
22 upon it; and the **h** of one chapiter *was* H6967
Ezk 17:23 In the mountain of the **h** of Israel will I H4791
19:11 **h** with the multitude of her branches. H1363
20:40 mountain of the **h** of Israel, saith the H4791
31: 5 Therefore his **h** was exalted above all H6967
10 lifted up thyself in **h**, and he hath shot H6967
10 and his heart is lifted up in his **h**; H1363
14 for their **h**, neither shoot up their H6967
14 stand up in their **h**, all that drink water: H1363
32: 5 and fill the valleys with thy **h**. H7419
40: 5 building, one reed; and the **h**, one reed. H6967
41: 8 I saw also the **h** of the house round H1363
Dan 3: 1 of gold, whose **h** *was* threescore cubits, H7314
4:10 the earth, and the **h** thereof *was* great. H7314
11 strong, and the **h** thereof reached unto H7314
20 was strong, whose **h** reached unto the H7314
Am 2: 9 them, whose **h** *was* like the height H1363
9 *was* like the **h** of the cedars, and he H1363
Ro 8:39 Nor **h**, nor depth, nor any other G5313
Eph 3:18 breadth, and length, and depth, and **h**; G5311
Rev 21:16 the breadth and the **h** of it are equal. G5311

HEIGHTS
Ps 148: 1 from the heavens: praise him in the **h**. H4791
Isa 14:14 I will ascend above the **h** of the clouds; H1116

HEINOUS
Job 31:11 For this *is* an **h** crime; yea, it *is* an H2154

HEIR
Gen 15: 3 and, lo, one born in my house is mine **h**. H3423
4 shall not be thine **h**; but he that shall H3423
4 of thine own bowels shall be thine **h**. H3423
21:10 not be **h** with my son, *even* with Isaac. H3423
2Sa 14: 7 we will destroy the **h** also: and so they H3423
Prv 30:23 an handmaid that is **h** to her mistress. H3423
Jer 49: 1 sons? hath he no **h**? why *then* doth their H3423
2 shall Israel be **h** unto them that were H3423
Mic 1:15 Yet will I bring an **h** unto thee, O H3423
Mt 21:38 This is the **h**; come, let us kill him, G2818
Mk 12: 7 This is the **h**; come, let us kill him, G2818
Lk 20:14 saying, This is the **h**: come, let us kill G2818
Ro 4:13 he should be the **h** of the world, *was* G2818
Gal 4: 1 Now I say, *That* the **h**, as long as he is a G2818
7 a son, then an **h** of God through Christ. G2818
30 be **h** with the son of the freewoman. G2816
Heb 1: 2 he hath appointed **h** of all things, by G2818
11: 7 **h** of the righteousness which is by faith. G2818

HEIRS
Jer 49: 2 them that were his **h**, saith the LORD. H3423
Ro 4:14 For if they which are of the law *be* **h**, G2818
8:17 And if children, then **h**; heirs of God, G2818
17 And if children, then heirs; **h** of God, G2818
Gal 3:29 seed, and **h** according to the promise. G2818
Tit 3: 7 **h** according to the hope of eternal life. G2818
Heb 1:14 for them who shall be **h** of salvation? G2816
6:17 to shew unto the **h** of promise the G2818
11: 9 the **h** with him of the same promise: G4789
Jas 2: 5 rich in faith, and **h** of the kingdom G2818
1Pt 3: 7 and as being **h** together of the grace G4789

HELAH
1Ch 4: 5 Tekoa had two wives, **H** and Naarah. H2458
7 And the sons of **H** *were*, Zereth, and H2458

HELAM
2Sa 10:16 and they came to **H**; and Shobach the H2431
17 and came to **H**. And the Syrians set H2431

HELBAH
Jdg 1:31 nor of **H**, nor of Aphik, nor of Rehob: H2462

HELBON
Ezk 27:18 riches; in the wine of **H**, and white wool. H2463

HELD
Gen 24:21 And the man wondering at her **h** his H2790
34: 5 Jacob **h** his peace until they were come. H2790
48:17 him: and he **h** up his father's hand, H8551
Ex 17:11 And it came to pass, when Moses **h** up H7311
36:12 the loops **h** one *curtain* to another. H6901
Lev 10: 3 be glorified. And Aaron **h** his peace. H1826
Nu 30: 7 And her husband heard *it*, and **h** his H2790
11 And her husband heard *it*, and **h** his H2790
14 them, because he **h** his peace at her in H2790
Jdg 7:20 the pitchers, and **h** the lamps in their H2388
16:26 And Samson said unto the lad that **h** H2388
Ru 3:15 it. And when she **h** it, he measured six H270
1Sa 10:27 him no presents. But he **h** his peace. H2790
25:36 and, behold, he **h** a feast in his house,
2Sa 18:16 after Israel: for Joab **h** back the people. H2820
1Ki 8:65 And at that time Solomon **h** a feast, H6213
2Ki 18:36 But the people **h** their peace, and H2790
2Ch 4: 5 it received and **h** three thousand baths. H3557
Neh 4:16 other half of them **h** both the spears, H2388
17 and with the other *hand* **h** a weapon. H2388
21 and half of them **h** the spears from the H2388
5: 8 unto us? Then **h** they their peace, and H2790
Est 5: 2 and the king **h** out to Esther the golden H3447
7: 4 I had **h** my tongue, although H2790
8: 4 Then the king **h** out the golden sceptre H3447
Job 23:11 My foot hath **h** his steps, his way have I H270
29:10 The nobles **h** their peace, and their H2244
Ps 32: 9 mouth must be **h** in with bit and bridle, H1102
39: 2 I was dumb with silence, I **h** my peace, H2814
94:18 slippeth; thy mercy, O LORD, **h** me up. H5528
Song 3: 4 my soul loveth: I **h** him, and would not H270
7: 5 like purple; the king *is* **h** in the galleries. H631
Isa 36:21 But they **h** their peace, and answered H2790
57:11 heart? have not I **h** my peace even of H2814
Jer 50:33 **h** them fast; they refused to let them go. H2388
Dan 12: 7 the river, when he **h** up his right hand H7311
Mt 12:14 Then the Pharisees went out, and **h** a G2983
26:63 But Jesus **h** his peace. And the high G4623
28: 9 **h** him by the feet, and worshipped him. G2902
Mk 3: 4 life, or to kill? But they **h** their peace. G4623
9:34 But they **h** their peace: for by the way G4623
14:61 But he **h** his peace, and answered G4623
15: 1 the chief priests **h** a consultation with G4160
Lk 14: 4 And they **h** their peace. And he took G2270
20:26 at his answer, and **h** their peace. G4601
22:63 And the men that **h** Jesus mocked him, G4912
Act 3:11 which was healed **h** Peter and John, all G2902
11:18 When they heard these things, they **h** G2270
14: 4 divided: and part **h** with the Jews, and G2258
15:13 And after they had **h** their peace, James G4601
Ro 7: 6 dead wherein we were **h**; that we should G2722
Rev 6: 9 and for the testimony which they **h**: G2192

HELDAI
1Ch 27:15 month *was* **H** the Netophathite, of H2469
Zec 6:10 Take of *them of* the captivity, *even* of **H**, H2469

HELDEST See WITHHELDEST.

HELEB
2Sa 23:29 **H** the son of Baanah, a Netophathite, H2460

HELED
1Ch 11:30 Maharai the Netophathite, **H** the son of H2466

HELEK
Nu 26:30 of **H**, the family of the Helekites: H2507
Jos 17: 2 and for the children of **H**, and for the H2507

HELEKITES
Nu 26:30 Jeezerites: of Helek, the family of the **H**: H2516

HELEM
1Ch 7:35 And the sons of his brother **H**; Zophah, H1987
Zec 6:14 And the crowns shall be to **H**, and to H2494

HELEPH
Jos 19:33 And their coast was from **H**, from Allon H2501

HELEZ
2Sa 23:26 **H** the Paltite, Ira the son of Ikkesh the H2503
1Ch 2:39 And Azariah begat **H**, and Helez begat H2503
39 And Azariah begat Helez, and **H** begat H2503
11:27 Shammoth the Harorite, **H** the H2503
27:10 month *was* **H** the Pelonite, of the H2503

HELI
Lk 3:23 son of Joseph, which was *the son* of **H**, G2242

HELKAI
Neh 12:15 Of Harim, Adna; of Meraioth, **H**; H2517

HELKATH
Jos 19:25 And their border was **H**, and Hali, and H2520
21:31 **H** with her suburbs, and Rehob with H2520

HELKATH-HAZZURIM
2Sa 2:16 place was called **H**, which *is* in Gibeon. H2521

HELL

Dt 32:22 unto the lowest **h**, and shall consume H7585
2Sa 22: 6 The sorrows of **h** compassed me about; H7585
Job 11: 8 deeper than **h**; what canst thou know? H7585
26: 6 **H** *is* naked before him, and destruction H7585
Ps 9:17 The wicked shall be turned into **h**, *and* H7585
16:10 For thou wilt not leave my soul in **h**; H7585
18: 5 The sorrows of **h** compassed me about: H7585
55:15 down quick into **h**: for wickedness *is* in H7585
86:13 delivered my soul from the lowest **h**. H7585
116: 3 and the pains of **h** gat hold upon me: I H7585
139: 8 my bed in **h**, behold, thou *art there*. H7585
Prv 5: 5 down to death; her steps take hold on **h**. H7585
7:27 Her house *is* the way to **h**, going down H7585
9:18 *that* her guests *are* in the depths of **h**. H7585
15:11 **H** and destruction *are* before the H7585
24 that he may depart from **h** beneath. H7585
23:14 rod, and shalt deliver his soul from **h**. H7585
27:20 **H** and destruction are never full; so the H7585
Isa 5:14 Therefore **h** hath enlarged herself, and H7585
14: 9 **H** from beneath is moved for thee to H7585
15 Yet thou shalt be brought down to **h**, to H7585
28:15 death, and with **h** are we at agreement; H7585
18 agreement with **h** shall not stand; when H7585
57: 9 and didst debase *thyself even* unto **h**. H7585
Ezk 31:16 I cast him down to **h** with them that H7585
17 They also went down into **h** with him H7585
32:21 out of the midst of **h** with them that H7585
27 are gone down to **h** with their weapons H7585
Am 9: 2 Though they dig into **h**, thence shall H7585
Jna 2: 2 **h** cried I, *and* thou heardest my voice. H7585
Hab 2: 5 his desire as **h**, and *is* as death, and H7585
Mt 5:22 Thou fool, shall be in danger of **h** fire. *G1067*
29 thy whole body should be cast into **h**. *G1067*
30 thy whole body should be cast into **h**. *G1067*
10:28 able to destroy both soul and body in **h**. *G1067*
11:23 be brought down to **h**: for if the mighty *G86*
16:18 the gates of **h** shall not prevail against it. *G86*
18: 9 having two eyes to be cast into **h** fire. *G1067*
23:15 more the child of **h** than yourselves. *G1067*
33 how can ye escape the damnation of **h**? *G1067*
Mk 9:43 two hands to go into **h**, into the fire that *G1067*
45 feet to be cast into **h**, into the fire that *G1067*
47 having two eyes to be cast into **h** fire: *G1067*
Lk 10:15 to heaven, shalt be thrust down to **h**. *G86*
12: 5 into **h**; yea, I say unto you, Fear him. *G1067*
16:23 And in **h** he lift up his eyes, being in *G86*
Act 2:27 Because thou wilt not leave my soul in **h**, *G86*
31 in **h**, neither his flesh did see corruption. *G86*
Jas 3: 6 of nature; and it is set on fire of **h**. *G1067*
2Pt 2: 4 but cast *them* down to **h**, and delivered *G5020*
Rev 1:18 and have the keys of **h** and of death. *G86*
6: 8 was Death, and **H** followed with him. *G86*
20:13 in it; and death and **h** delivered up the *G86*
14 And death and **h** were cast into the lake *G86*

HELL-FIRE See HELL and FIRE.

HELM

Jas 3: 4 **h**, whithersoever the governor listeth. *G4079*

HELMET

1Sa 17: 5 And *he had* an **h** of brass upon his H3553
38 and he put an **h** of brass upon his head; H6959
Isa 59:17 and an **h** of salvation upon his H3553
Ezk 23:24 and shield and **h** round about: and I H6959
27:10 **h** in thee; they set forth thy comeliness. H3553
38: 5 them; all of them with shield and **h**: H3553
Eph 6:17 And take the **h** of salvation, and the *G4030*
1Th 5: 8 and for an **h**, the hope of salvation. *G4030*

HELMETS

2Ch 26:14 and spears, and **h**, and habergeons, H3553
Jer 46: 4 forth with *your* **h**; furbish the spears, H3553

HELON

Nu 1: 9 Of Zebulun; Eliab the son of **H**. H2497
2: 7 Eliab the son of **H** *shall be* captain of H2497
7:24 On the third day Eliab the son of **H**, H2497
29 *was* the offering of Eliab the son of **H**. H2497
10:16 of Zebulun *was* Eliab the son of **H**. H2497

HELP

Gen 2:18 I will make him an **h** meet for him. H5828
20 there was not found an **h** meet for him. H5828
49:25 thy father, who shall **h** thee; and by the H5826
Ex 18: 4 *said he, was* mine **h**, and delivered me H5828
23: 5 **h** him, thou shalt surely help with him. H5800
5 help him, thou shalt surely **h** with him. H5800
Dt 22: 4 shalt surely **h** him to lift *them* up again. H6965
32:38 up and **h** you, *and* be your protection. H5826
33: 7 be thou an **h** *to him* from his enemies. H5828
26 thy **h**, and in his excellency on the sky. H5828
29 the shield of thy **h**, and who *is* the H5828
Jos 1:14 the mighty men of valour, and **h** them; H5826
10: 4 Come up unto me, and **h** me, that we H5826
6 and save us, and **h** us: for all the kings H5826
33 of Gezer came up to **h** Lachish; and H5826
Jdg 5:23 came not to the **h** of the LORD, to the H5833
23 the **h** of the LORD against the mighty. H5833
1Sa 11: 9 be hot, ye shall have **h**. And the H8668
2Sa 10:11 me, then thou shalt **h** me: but if the H3444
11 for thee, then I will come and **h** thee. H3467
19 to **h** the children of Ammon any more. H3467
14: 4 and did obeisance, and said, **H**, O king. H3467
2Ki 6:26 unto him, saying, **H**, my lord, O king. H3467
27 And he said, If the LORD do not **h** thee, H3467
27 thee, whence shall I **h** thee? out of the H3467
1Ch 12:17 unto me to **h** me, mine heart shall H5826
22 came to David to **h** him, until *it was* a H5826
18: 5 came to **h** Hadarezer king of Zobah, H5826
19:12 me, then thou shalt **h** me: but if the H8668
12 too strong for thee, then I will **h** thee. H3467
19 **h** the children of Ammon any more. H3467
22:17 of Israel to **h** Solomon his son, *saying*, H5826
2Ch 14:11 with thee to **h**, whether with many, H5826
11 have no power: **h** us, O LORD our God; H5826
19: 2 Shouldest thou **h** the ungodly, and love H5826
20: 4 together, to ask *h* of the LORD: even out
9 affliction, then thou wilt hear and **h**. H3467
25: 8 God hath power to **h**, and to cast down. H5826
26:13 power, to **h** the king against the enemy. H5826
28:16 unto the kings of Assyria to **h** him. H5826
23 the kings of Syria **h** them, *therefore* will H5826
23 that they may **h** me. But they were the H5826
29:34 the Levites did **h** them, till the work H2388
32: 3 without the city: and they did **h** him. H5826
8 LORD our God to **h** us, and to fight our H5826
Ezr 1: 4 men of his place **h** him with silver, and H5375
8:22 and horsemen to **h** us against the H5826
Job 6:13 *Is* not my **h** in me? and is wisdom H5833
8:20 *man*, neither will he **h** the evil doers: H5833
29:12 and *him that had* none to **h** him. H5826
31:21 fatherless, when I saw my **h** in the gate: H5833
Ps 3: 2 *There is* no **h** for him in God. Selah. H3444
12: 1 **H**, LORD; for the godly man ceaseth; for H3467
20: 2 Send thee **h** from the sanctuary, and H5828
22:11 trouble *is* near; for *there is* none to **h**. H5826
19 O my strength, haste thee to **h** me. H5833
27: 9 thou hast been my **h**; leave me not, H5833
33:20 the LORD: he *is* our **h** and our shield. H5828
35: 2 and buckler, and stand up for mine **h**. H5833
37:40 And the LORD shall **h** them, and H5826
38:22 Make haste to **h** me, O Lord my H5833
40:13 me: O LORD, make haste to **h** me. H5833
17 me: thou *art* my **h** and my deliverer; H5833
42: 5 him *for* the **h** of his countenance. H3444
44:26 Arise for our **h**, and redeem us for thy H5833
46: 1 strength, a very present **h** in trouble. H5833
5 God shall **h** her, *and that* right early. H5826
59: 4 *my* fault: awake to **h** me, and behold. H7125
60:11 Give us **h** from trouble: for vain *is* the H5833
11 from trouble: for vain *is* the **h** of man. H8668
63: 7 Because thou hast been my **h**, therefore H5833
70: 1 me; make haste to **h** me, O LORD. H5833
5 God: thou *art* my **h** and my deliverer; O H5828
71:12 me: O my God, make haste for my **h**. H5833
79: 9 **H** us, O God of our salvation, for the H5826
89:19 saidst, I have laid **h** upon *one that is* H5828
94:17 Unless the LORD *had been* my **h**, my H5833
107:12 they fell down, and *there was* none to **h**. H5826
108:12 Give us **h** from trouble: for vain *is* the H5833
12 from trouble: for vain *is* the **h** of man. H8668
109:26 **H** me, O LORD my God: O save me H5826
115: 9 LORD: he *is* their **h** and their shield. H5828
10 LORD: he *is* their **h** and their shield. H5828
11 LORD: he *is* their **h** and their shield. H5828
118: 7 with them that **h** me: therefore shall H5826
119:86 persecute me wrongfully; **h** thou me. H5826
173 Let thine hand **h** me; for I have chosen H5826
175 thee; and let thy judgments **h** me. H5826
121: 1 the hills, from whence cometh my **h**. H5828
2 My **h** *cometh* from the LORD, which H5828
124: 8 Our **h** *is* in the name of the LORD, who H5828
146: 3 the son of man, in whom *there is* no **h**. H8668
5 **h**, whose hope *is* in the LORD his God: H5828
Ecc 4:10 for *he hath* not another to **h** him up. H6965
Isa 10: 3 **h**? and where will ye leave your glory? H5833
Isa 20: 6 whither we flee for **h** to be delivered H5833
30: 5 them, nor be an **h** nor profit, but a H5828
7 For the Egyptians shall **h** in vain, and H5826
31: 1 go down to Egypt for **h**; and stay on H5833
2 the **h** of them that work iniquity. H5833
41:10 thee; yea, I will **h** thee; yea, I will H5826
13 saying unto thee, Fear not; I will **h** thee. H5826
14 of Israel; I will **h** thee, saith the LORD, H5826
44: 2 womb, *which* will **h** thee; Fear not, O H5826
50: 7 For the Lord GOD will **h** me; therefore H5826
9 Behold, the Lord GOD will **h** me; who *is* H5826
63: 5 And I looked, and *there was* none to **h**; H5826
Jer 37: 7 is come forth to **h** you, shall return to H5833
Lam 1: 7 and none did **h** her: the adversaries H5826
4:17 failed for our vain **h**: in our watching H5833
Ezk 12:14 that *are* about him to **h** him, and all his H5828
32:21 with them that **h** him: they are gone H5826
Dan 10:13 princes, came to **h** me; and I remained H5826
11:34 with a little **h**: but many shall cleave H5828
45 come to his end, and none shall **h** him. H5826
Hos 13: 9 destroyed thyself; but in me *is* thine **h**. H5828
Mt 15:25 worshipped him, saying, Lord, **h** me. *G997*
Mk 9:22 thing, have compassion on us, and **h** us. *G997*
24 Lord, I believe; **h** thou mine unbelief. *G997*
Lk 5: 7 should come and **h** them. And they *G4815*
10:40 alone? bid her therefore that she **h** me. *G4878*
Act 16: 9 Come over into Macedonia, and **h** us. *G997*
21:28 Crying out, Men of Israel, **h**: This is the *G997*
26:22 Having therefore obtained **h** of God, I *G1947*
Php 4: 3 true yokefellow, **h** those women which *G4815*
Heb 4:16 and find grace to **h** in time of need. *G996*

HELPED

Ex 2:17 and **h** them, and watered their flock. H3467
1Sa 7:12 saying, Hitherto hath the LORD **h** us. H5826
1Ki 1: 7 and they following Adonijah **h** *him*. H5826
20:16 the thirty and two kings that **h** him. H5826
1Ch 5:20 And they were **h** against them, and the H5826
12:19 to battle: but they **h** them not: for the H5826
21 And they **h** David against the band *of* H5826
15:26 And it came to pass, when God **h** the H5826
2Ch 18:31 and the LORD **h** him; and God moved H5826
20:23 of Seir, every one **h** to destroy another. H5826
26: 7 And God **h** him against the Philistines, H5826
15 was marvellously **h**, till he was strong. H5826
28:21 the king of Assyria: but he **h** him not. H5833
Ezr 10:15 and Shabbethai the Levite **h** them. H5826
Est 9: 3 of the king, **h** the Jews; because the H5375
Job 26: 2 How hast thou **h** *him that is* without H5826
Ps 28: 7 in him, and I am **h**: therefore my heart H5826
116: 6 I was brought low, and he **h** me. H3467
118:13 that I might fall: but the LORD **h** me. H5826
Isa 41: 6 They **h** every one his neighbour; and H5826
49: 8 of salvation have I **h** thee: and I will H5826
Zec 1:15 and they **h** forward the affliction. H5826
Act 18:27 he was come, **h** them much which had *G4820*
Rev 12:16 And the earth **h** the woman, and the *G997*

HELPER

2Ki 14:26 up, nor any left, nor any **h** for Israel. H5826
Job 30:13 forward my calamity, they have no **h**. H5826
Ps 10:14 thee; thou art the **h** of the fatherless. H5826
30:10 mercy upon me: LORD, be thou my **h**. H5826
54: 4 Behold, God *is* mine **h**: the Lord *is* with H5826
72:12 the poor also, and *him* that hath no **h**. H5826
Jer 47: 4 and Zidon every **h** that remaineth: for H5826
Ro 16: 9 Salute Urbane, our **h** in Christ, and *G4904*
Heb 13: 6 The Lord *is* my **h**, and I will not fear what *G998*

HELPERS

1Ch 12: 1 among the mighty men, **h** of the war. H5826
18 peace *be* to thine **h**; for thy God helpeth H5826
Job 9:13 anger, the proud **h** do stoop under him. H5826
Ezk 30: 8 and *when* all her **h** shall be destroyed. H5826
Nah 3: 9 *was* infinite; Put and Lubim were thy **h**. H5833
Ro 16: 3 Greet Priscilla and Aquila my **h** in *G4904*
2Co 1:24 are **h** of your joy: for by faith ye stand. *G4904*

HELPETH

1Ch 12:18 helpers; for thy God **h** thee. Then David H5826
Isa 31: 3 hand, both he that **h** shall fall, and he H5826
Ro 8:26 Likewise the Spirit also **h** our *G4878*
1Co 16:16 one that **h** with *us*, and laboureth. *G4903*

HELPING

Ezr 5: 2 them *were* the prophets of God **h** them. H5583
Ps 22: 1 *art thou so* far from **h** me, *and from* the H3444
2Co 1:11 Ye also **h** together by prayer for us, that *G4943*

H

HELPS
Act 27:17 up, they used **h**, undergirding the ship; *G996*
1Co 12:28 **h**, governments, diversities of tongues. *G484*

HELVE
Dt 19: 5 slippeth from the **h**, and lighteth upon H6086

HEM
Ex 28:33 And *beneath* upon the **h** of it thou shalt H7757
33 round about the **h** thereof; and bells of H7757
34 upon the **h** of the robe round about. H7757
39:25 upon the **h** of the robe, round about H7757
26 round about the **h** of the robe to H7757
Mt 9:20 *him*, and touched the **h** of his garment: *G2899*
14:36 only touch the **h** of his garment: and *G2899*

HEMAM
Gen 36:22 and **H**; and Lotan's sister *was* Timna. H1967

HEMAN
1Ki 4:31 the Ezrahite, and **H**, and Chalcol, and H1968
1Ch 2: 6 and Ethan, and **H**, and Calcol, and H1968
6:33 of the Kohathites: **H** a singer, the son of H1968
15:17 So the Levites appointed **H** the son of H1968
19 So the singers, **H**, Asaph, and Ethan, H1968
16:41 And with them **H** and Jeduthun, and H1968
42 And with them **H** and Jeduthun with H1968
25: 1 of Asaph, and of **H**, and of Jeduthun, H1968
4 Of **H**: the sons of Heman; Bukkiah, H1968
4 Of Heman: the sons of **H**; Bukkiah, H1968
5 All these *were* the sons of **H** the king's H1968
5 **H** fourteen sons and three daughters. H1968
6 king's order to Asaph, Jeduthun, and **H**. H1968
2Ch 5:12 them of Asaph, of **H**, of Jeduthun, with H1968
29:14 And of the sons of **H**; Jehiel, and H1968
35:15 and Asaph, and **H**, and Jeduthun the H1968
Ps 88:ttl Leannoth, Maschil of **H** the Ezrahite. H1968

HEMATH
1Ch 2:55 of **H**, the father of the house of Rechab. H2574
13: 5 the entering of **H**, to bring the ark of H2574
Am 6:14 in of **H** unto the river of the wilderness. H2574

HEMDAN
Gen 36:26 And these *are* the children of Dishon; **H**, H2533

HEMLOCK
Hos 10: 4 up as **h** in the furrows of the field. H7219
Am 6:12 and the fruit of righteousness into **h**: H3939

HEMS
Ex 39:24 And they made upon the **h** of the robe H7757

HEN
Zec 6:14 and to Jedaiah, and to **H** the son of H2581
Mt 23:37 even as a **h** gathereth her chickens *G3733*
Lk 13:34 together, as a **h** *doth gather* her brood *G3733*

HENA
2Ki 18:34 of Sepharvaim, **H**, and Ivah? have they H2012
19:13 the city of Sepharvaim, of **H**, and Ivah? H2012
Isa 37:13 of the city of Sepharvaim, **H**, and Ivah? H2012

HENADAD
Ezr 3: 9 God: the sons of **H**, *with* their sons and H2582
Neh 3:18 of **H**, the ruler of the half part of Keilah. H2582
24 After him repaired Binnui the son of **H** H2582
10: 9 Binnui of the sons of **H**, Kadmiel; H2582

HENCE
Gen 37:17 And the man said, They are departed **h**; H2088
42:15 ye shall not go forth **h**, except your H2088
50:25 and ye shall carry up my bones from **h**. H2088
Ex 11: 1 he will let you go **h**: when he shall let H2088
1 shall surely thrust you out **h** altogether. H2088
13:19 carry up my bones away **h** with you. H2088
33: 1 Depart, *and* go up **h**, thou and the H2088
15 go not *with me*, carry us not up **h**. H2088
Dt 9:12 quickly from **h**; for thy people which H2088
Jos 4: 3 saying, Take you **h** out of the midst of H2088
Jdg 6:18 Depart not **h**, I pray thee, until I come H2088
Ru 2: 8 **h**, but abide here fast by my maidens: H2088
1Ki 17: 3 Get thee **h**, and turn thee eastward, and H2088
Ps 39:13 strength, before I go **h**, and be no more. H2088
Isa 30:22 cloth; thou shalt say unto it, Get thee **h**. H3318
Jer 38:10 saying, Take from **h** thirty men with H2088
Zec 6: 7 and he said, Get you **h**, walk to and fro H3212
Mt 4:10 Then saith Jesus unto him, Get thee **h**, *G5217*
17:20 Remove **h** to yonder place; and *G1782*
Lk 4: 9 Son of God, cast thyself down from **h**: *G1782*
13:31 and depart **h**: for Herod will kill thee. *G1782*
16:26 would pass from **h** to you cannot; *G1782*
Jn 2:16 Take these things **h**; make not my *G1782*
7: 3 unto him, Depart **h**, and go into Judaea, *G1782*
14:31 even so I do. Arise, let us go **h**. *G1782*
18:36 but now is my kingdom not from **h**. *G1782*
20:15 have borne him **h**, tell me where thou *G941*
Act 1: 5 with the Holy Ghost not many days **h**. *G5025*
22:21 I will send thee far **h** unto the Gentiles. *G3112*
Jas 4: 1 *come they* not **h**, *even* of your lusts that *G1782*

HENCEFORTH
Gen 4:12 it shall not **h** yield unto thee her H3254
Nu 18:22 Neither must the children of Israel **h** H5750
Dt 17:16 Ye shall **h** return no more that way. H3254
19:20 fear, and shall **h** commit no more any H3254
Jdg 2:21 I also will not **h** drive out any from H3254
2Ki 5:17 thy servant will **h** offer neither burnt H5750
2Ch 16: 9 therefore from **h** thou shalt have wars. H6258
Ps 125: 2 about his people from **h** even for ever. H6258
131: 3 Let Israel hope in the LORD from **h** H6258
Isa 9: 7 with justice from **h** even for ever. The H6258
52: 1 the holy city: for **h** there shall no more H5750
59:21 saith the LORD, from **h** and for ever. H6258
Ezk 36:12 shalt no more **h** bereave them *of men*. H5750
Mic 4: 7 in mount Zion from **h**, even for ever. H5750
Mt 23:39 shall not see me **h**, till ye shall say, *G575+G737*
26:29 I will not drink **h** of this fruit of *G575+G737*
Lk 1:48 **h** all generations shall call me blessed. *G3568*
5:10 Fear not; from **h** thou shalt catch men. *G3568*
12:52 For from **h** there shall be five in one *G3568*
Jn 14: 7 from **h** ye know him, and have seen him. *G737*
15:15 **H** I call you not servants; for the *G3765*
Act 4:17 they speak **h** to no man in this name. *G3371*
18: 6 from **h** I will go unto the Gentiles. *G3568*
Ro 6: 6 that **h** we should not serve sin. *G3371*
2Co 5:15 live should not **h** live unto themselves, *G3371*
16 Wherefore **h** know we no man after the *G575*
16 flesh, yet now **h** know we *him* no more. *G3568*
Gal 6:17 From **h** let no man trouble me: for I *G3064*
Eph 4:14 That we *h* be no more children, tossed to
17 in the Lord, that ye **h** walk not as other *G3371*
2Ti 4: 8 **H** there is laid up for me a crown of *G3063*
Heb 10:13 From **h** expecting till his enemies be *G3063*
Rev 14:13 in the Lord from **h**: Yea, saith the Spirit, *G534*

HENCEFORWARD
Nu 15:23 *Moses*, and **h** among your generations; H1973
Mt 21:19 no fruit grow on thee **h** for ever. And *G3371*

HENOCH
1Ch 1: 3 **H**, Methuselah, Lamech, H2585
33 and Epher, and **H**, and Abida, and H2585

HEPHER
Nu 26:32 and *of* **H**, the family of the Hepherites. H2660
33 And Zelophehad the son of **H** had no H2660
27: 1 the son of **H**, the son of Gilead, the H2660
Jos 12:17 of Tappuah, one; the king of **H**, one; H2660
17: 2 and for the children of **H**, and for the H2660
3 But Zelophehad, the son of **H**, the son of H2660
1Ki 4:10 *pertained* Sochoh, and all the land of **H**: H2660
1Ch 4: 6 And Naarah bare him Ahuzam, and **H**, H2660
11:36 **H** the Mecherathite, Ahijah the H2660

HEPHERITES
Nu 26:32 and *of* Hepher, the family of the **H**. H2662

HEPHZI-BAH
2Ki 21: 1 And his mother's name *was* **H**. H2657
Isa 62: 4 shalt be called **H**, and thy land Beulah: H2657

HER See the Appendix.

HERALD
Dan 3: 4 Then an **h** cried aloud, To you it is H3744

HERB
Gen 1:11 forth grass, the **h** yielding seed, *and* the H6212
12 forth grass, *and* **h** yielding seed after H6212
29 given you every **h** bearing seed, which H6212
30 every green **h** for meat: and it was so. H6212
2: 5 earth, and every **h** of the field before it H6212
3:18 and thou shalt eat the **h** of the field; H6212
9: 3 the green **h** have I given you all things. H6212
Ex 9:22 beast, and upon every **h** of the field, H6212
25 the hail smote every **h** of the field, and H6212
10:12 and eat every **h** of the land, *even* all H6212
10:15 they did eat every **h** of the land, and all H6212
Dt 32: 2 **h**, and as the showers upon the grass: H1877
2Ki 19:26 and *as* the green **h**, *as* the grass on the H1877
Job 8:12 down, it withereth before any *other* **h**. H2682
38:27 the bud of the tender **h** to spring forth? H1877
Ps 37: 2 the grass, and wither as the green **h**. H1877
104:14 for the cattle, and **h** for the service of H6212
Isa 37:27 and *as* the green **h**, *as* the grass on the H1877
66:14 flourish like an **h**: and the hand of the H1877

HERBS
Ex 10:15 in the trees, or in the **h** of the field, H6212
12: 8 bread; *and* with bitter *h* they shall eat it.
Nu 9:11 eat it with unleavened bread and bitter *h*.
Dt 11:10 *it* with thy foot, as a garden of **h**: H3419
1Ki 21: 2 it for a garden of **h**, because it *is* near H3419
2Ki 4:39 the field to gather **h**, and found a wild H219
Ps 105:35 And did eat up all the **h** in their land, H6212
Prv 15:17 Better *is* a dinner of **h** where love is, H3419
27:25 and **h** of the mountains are gathered. H6212
Isa 18: 4 a clear heat upon **h**, *and* like a cloud of H216
26:19 **h**, and the earth shall cast out the dead. H219
42:15 dry up all their **h**; and I will make the H6212
Jer 12: 4 mourn, and the **h** of every field wither, H6212
Mt 13:32 greatest among **h**, and becometh a tree, *G3001*
Mk 4:32 greater than all **h**, and shooteth out *G3001*
Lk 11:42 rue and all manner of **h**, and pass over *G3001*
Ro 14: 2 things: another, who is weak, eateth **h**. *G3001*
Heb 6: 7 and bringeth forth **h** meet for them by *G1008*

HERD
Gen 18: 7 And Abraham ran unto the **h**, and H1241
Lev 1: 2 cattle, *even* of the **h**, and of the flock. H1241
3 sacrifice of the **h**, let him offer a male H1241
3: 1 if he offer *it* of the **h**; whether *it be* a H1241
27:32 And concerning the tithe of the **h**, or of H1241
Nu 15: 3 unto the LORD, of the **h**, or of the flock: H1241
Dt 12:21 thou shalt kill of thy **h** and of thy flock, H1241
15:19 that come of thy **h** and of thy flock thou H1241
16: 2 the flock and the **h**, in the place which H1241
1Sa 11: 5 And, behold, Saul came after the **h** out H1241
2Sa 12: 4 flock and of his own **h**, to dress for the H1241
Jer 31:12 flock and of the **h**: and their soul shall H1241
Jna 3: 7 man nor beast, **h** nor flock, taste any H1241
Hab 3:17 and *there shall be* no **h** in the stalls: H1241
Mt 8:30 from them an **h** of many swine feeding. *G34*
31 suffer us to go away into the **h** of swine. *G34*
32 out, they went into the **h** of swine: and, *G34*
32 and, behold, the whole **h** of swine ran *G34*
Mk 5:11 mountains a great **h** of swine feeding. *G34*
13 the swine: and the **h** ran violently down *G34*
Lk 8:32 And there was there an **h** of many swine *G34*
33 the swine: and the **h** ran violently down *G34*

HERDMAN
Am 7:14 an **h**, and a gatherer of sycomore fruit: H951

HERDMEN
Gen 13: 7 And there was a strife between the **h** of H7462
7 cattle and the **h** of Lot's cattle: and the H7462
8 **h** and thy herdmen; for we *be* brethren. H7462
8 herdmen and thy **h**; for we *be* brethren. H7462
26:20 And the **h** of Gerar did strive with H7462
20 strive with Isaac's **h**, saying, The water H7462
1Sa 21: 7 chiefest of the **h** that *belonged* to Saul. H7462
Am 1: 1 was among the **h** of Tekoa, which he H5349

HERDS
Gen 13: 5 Abram, had flocks, and **h**, and tents. H1241
24:35 him flocks, and **h**, and silver, and gold, H1241
26:14 and possession of **h**, and great store of H1241
32: 7 and **h**, and the camels, into two bands; H1241
33:13 and the flocks and **h** with young *are* H1241
45:10 flocks, and thy **h**, and all that thou hast: H1241
46:32 and their **h**, and all that they have. H1241
47: 1 flocks, and their **h**, and all that they H1241
17 for the cattle of the **h**, and for the asses: H1241
18 lord also hath our **h** of cattle; there is H4735
50: 8 their **h**, they left in the land of Goshen. H1241
Ex 10: 9 and with our **h** will we go; for we *must* H1241
24 flocks and your **h** be stayed: let your H1241
12:32 Also take your flocks and your **h**, as ye H1241
38 flocks, and **h**, *even* very much cattle. H1241
34: 3 flocks nor **h** feed before that mount. H1241
Nu 11:22 Shall the flocks and the **h** be slain for H1241
Dt 8:13 And *when* thy **h** and thy flocks H1241
12: 6 firstlings of your **h** and of your flocks: H1241
17 firstlings of thy **h** or of thy flock, nor H1241
14:23 firstlings of thy **h** and of thy flocks; that H1241

1Sa 30:20 And David took all the flocks and the **h**, H1241
2Sa 12: 2 *man* had exceeding many flocks and **h**: H1241
1Ch 27:29 And over the **h** that fed in Sharon *was* H1241
29 and over the **h** *that were* in the valleys H1241
2Ch 32:29 of flocks and **h** in abundance: for God H1241
Neh 10:36 firstlings of our **h** and of our flocks, to H1241
Prv 27:23 of thy flocks, *and* look well to thy **h**. H5739
Isa 65:10 a place for the **h** to lie down in, for my H1241
Jer 3:24 their **h**, their sons and their daughters. H1241
5:17 flocks and thine **h**: they shall eat up thy H1241
Hos 5: 6 and with their **h** to seek the LORD; but H1241
Joel 1:18 How do the beasts groan! the **h** of cattle H5739

HERE
Gen 16:13 I also **h** looked after him that seeth me? H1988
19:12 Lot, Hast thou **h** any besides? son in H6311
15 which are **h**; lest thou be consumed H4672
21:23 Now therefore swear unto me **h** by God H2008
22: 1 Abraham: and he said, Behold, ***h*** I *am*.
5 men, Abide ye **h** with the ass; and I and H6311
7 and he said, **H** *am* I, my son. And H2009
11 Abraham: and he said, **H** *am* I. H2009
24:13 Behold, I stand ***h*** by the well of water;
27: 1 and he said unto him, Behold, ***h*** *am* I.
18 he said, **H** *am* I; who *art* thou, my son? H2009
31:11 *saying*, Jacob: And I said, **H** *am* I. H2009
37 stuff? set *it* **h** before my brethren H3541
37:13 unto them. And he said to him, **H** *am I*. H2009
40:15 of the Hebrews: and **h** also have I done H6311
42:33 of your brethren ***h*** with me, and take
46: 2 Jacob, Jacob. And he said, **H** *am* I. H2009
47:23 for Pharaoh: lo, ***h*** *is* seed for you, and
Ex 3: 4 Moses, Moses. And he said, **H** *am* I. H2009
24:14 And he said unto the elders, Tarry ye **h** H2088
33:16 For wherein shall it be known **h** that I H645
Nu 14:40 saying, Lo, we *be* ***h***, and will go up unto
22: 8 And he said unto them, Lodge **h** this H6311
19 you, tarry ye also **h** this night, that I H2088
23: 1 Balak, Build me **h** seven altars, and H2088
1 me **h** seven oxen and seven rams. H2088
15 And he said unto Balak, Stand **h** by thy H3541
29 Balak, Build me **h** seven altars, and H2088
29 me **h** seven bullocks and seven rams. H2088
32: 6 brethren go to war, and shall ye sit **h**? H6311
16 build sheepfolds **h** for our cattle, and H6311
Dt 5: 3 us, who *are* all of us **h** alive this day. H6311
31 But as for thee, stand thou **h** by me, H6311
12: 8 *things* that we do **h** this day, every man H6311
29:15 But with *him* that standeth **h** with us H6311
15 with *him* that *is* not **h** with us this day: H6311
Jos 18: 6 for you **h** before the LORD our God. H6311
8 to me, that I may **h** cast lots for you H6311
21: 9 cities which are ***h*** mentioned by name,
Jdg 4:20 any man **h**? that thou shalt say, No. H6311
18: 3 in this *place*? and what hast thou **h**? H6311
19: 9 to an end, lodge **h**, that thine heart may H6311
24 Behold, ***h*** *is* my daughter a maiden, and
20: 7 Israel; give **h** your advice and counsel. H1988
Ru 2: 8 hence, but abide **h** fast by my maidens: H3541
4: 1 **h**. And he turned aside, and sat down. H6311
2 said, Sit ye down **h**. And they sat down. H6311
1Sa 1:26 by thee **h**, praying unto the LORD. H2088
3: 4 Samuel: and he answered, **H** *am* I. H2009
5 And he ran unto Eli, and said, **H** *am* I; H2005
6 to Eli, and said, **H** *am* I; for thou didst H2005
8 to Eli, and said, **H** *am* I; for thou didst H2009
16 my son. And he answered, **H** *am* I. H2009
9: 8 Behold, I have ***h*** at hand the fourth part
11 and said unto them, Is the seer **h**? H2088
12: 3 Behold, ***h*** I *am*: witness against me
14:34 and slay *them* **h**, and eat; and sin not H2088
16:11 And Samuel said unto Jesse, Are **h** all H8552
21: 8 And is there not **h** under thine hand H6311
9 Elah, behold, it *is* ***h*** wrapped in a cloth
9 *is* no other save that **h**. And David said, H2088
22:12 And he answered, **H** I *am*, my lord. H2005
23: 3 we be afraid **h** in Judah: how much H6311
29: 3 *do* these Hebrews ***h***? And Achish said
2Sa 1: 7 unto me. And I answered, **H** *am* I. H2009
11:12 And David said to Uriah, Tarry **h** to H2088
15:26 in thee; behold, ***h*** *am* I, let him do to me
18:30 **h**. And he turned aside, and stood still. H3541
20: 4 three days, and be thou **h** present. H6311
24:22 unto him: behold, ***h*** *be* oxen for burnt
1Ki 2:30 said, Nay; but I will die **h**. And Benaiah H6311
18: 8 I *am*: go, tell thy lord, Behold, Elijah *is* ***h***.
11 Go, tell thy lord, Behold, Elijah *is* ***h***.
14 Behold, Elijah *is* ***h***: and he shall slay me.
19: 9 unto him, What doest thou **h**, Elijah? H6311
1Ki 19:13 and said, What doest thou **h**, Elijah? H6311
20:40 And as thy servant was busy **h** and H2008
22: 7 And Jehoshaphat said, *Is there* not **h** a H6311
2Ki 2: 2 And Elijah said unto Elisha, Tarry **h**, I H6311
4 him, Elisha, tarry **h**, I pray thee; for the H6311
6 Tarry, I pray thee, **h**; for the LORD hath H6311
3:11 But Jehoshaphat said, *Is there* not **h** a H6311
11 and said, **H** *is* Elisha the son of H6311
7: 3 to another, Why sit we **h** until we die? H6311
4 and if we sit still **h**, we die also. Now H6311
10:23 look that there be **h** with you none of H6311
1Ch 29:17 present **h**, to offer willingly unto thee. H6311
2Ch 18: 6 But Jehoshaphat said, *Is there* not **h** a H6311
Job 38:11 and **h** shall thy proud waves be stayed? H6311
35 may go, and say unto thee, **H** we *are*? H2009
Ps 132:14 This *is* my rest for ever: **h** will I dwell; H6311
Isa 6: 8 for us? Then said I, **H** *am* I; send me. H2005
21: 9 And, behold, **h** cometh a chariot of H2008
22:16 What hast thou **h**? and whom hast thou H6311
16 and whom hast thou **h**, that thou hast H6311
16 out a sepulchre **h**, *as* he that heweth H6311
28:10 upon line; **h** a little, *and* there a little: H8033
13 line upon line; **h** a little, *and* there a H8033
52: 5 Now therefore, what have I **h**, saith the H6311
58: 9 and he shall say, **H** I *am*. If thou take H2009
Ezk 8: 6 Israel committeth **h**, that I should go far H6311
9 wicked abominations that they do **h**. H6311
17 they commit **h**? for they have filled H6311
Hos 7: 9 yea, gray hairs are **h** and there upon H2236
Mt 12:41 and, behold, a greater than Jonas *is* **h**. G5602
42 behold, a greater than Solomon *is* **h**. G5602
14: 8 me **h** John Baptist's head in a charger. G5602
17 And they say unto him, We have **h** but G5602
16:28 be some standing **h**, which shall not G5602
17: 4 is good for us to be **h**: if thou wilt, let us G5602
4 wilt, let us make **h** three tabernacles; G5602
20: 6 them, Why stand ye **h** all the day idle? G5602
24: 2 There shall not be left **h** one stone upon G5602
23 Lo, **h** *is* Christ, or there; believe *it* not. G5602
26:36 Sit ye **h**, while I go and pray yonder. G847
38 death: tarry ye **h**, and watch with me. G5602
28: 6 He is not **h**: for he is risen, as he said. G5602
Mk 6: 3 are not his sisters **h** with us? And they G5602
8: 4 *men* with bread **h** in the wilderness? G5602
9: 1 of them that stand **h**, which shall not G5602
5 is good for us to be **h**: and let us make G5602
13: 1 of stones and what buildings *are* ***h***!
21 say to you, Lo, **h** *is* Christ; or, lo, *he is* G5602
14:32 his disciples, Sit ye **h**, while I shall pray. G5602
34 unto death: tarry ye **h**, and watch. G5602
16: 6 **h**: behold the place where they laid him. G5602
Lk 4:23 Capernaum, do also **h** in thy country. G5602
9:12 victuals: for we are **h** in a desert place. G5602
27 be some standing **h**, which shall not G5602
33 is good for us to be **h**: and let us make G5602
11:31 behold, a greater than Solomon *is* **h**. G5602
32 and, behold, a greater than Jonas *is* **h**. G5602
17:21 Neither shall they say, Lo **h**! or, lo there! G5602
23 And they shall say to you, See **h**; or, see G5602
19:20 Lord, behold, ***h*** *is* thy pound, which
22:38 And they said, Lord, behold, **h** *are* two G5602
24: 6 He is not **h**, but is risen: remember how G5602
41 said unto them, Have ye **h** any meat? G1759
Jn 6: 9 There is a lad **h**, which hath five barley G5602
11:21 hadst been **h**, my brother had not died. G5602
32 hadst been **h**, my brother had not died. G5602
Act 4:10 this man stand **h** before you whole. G3936
8:36 eunuch said, See, ***h*** *is* water; what doth
9:10 And he said, Behold, I *am* ***h***, Lord.
14 And **h** he hath authority from the chief G5602
10:33 are we all **h** present before God, G3918
16:28 Do thyself no harm: for we are all **h**. G1759
24:19 Who ought to have been **h** before thee, G3918
20 Or else let these same ***h*** say, if they have
25:24 all men which are **h** present with us, ye G4840
24 and *also* **h**, crying that he ought G1759
Col 4: 9 unto you all things which *are done* **h**. G5602
Heb 7: 8 And **h** men that die receive tithes; but G5602
13:14 For **h** have we no continuing city, but G5602
Jas 2: 3 unto him, Sit thou **h** in a good place; G5602
3 thou there, or sit **h** under my footstool: G5602
1Pt 1:17 the time of your sojourning ***h*** in fear:
Rev 13:10 with the sword. **H** is the patience and G5602
18 **H** is wisdom. Let him that hath G5602
14:12 **H** is the patience of the saints: here *are* G5602
12 Here is the patience of the saints: **h** *are* G5602
17: 9 And **h** *is* the mind which hath wisdom. G5602

HEREAFTER
Isa 41:23 Shew the things that are to come **h**, that H268
Ezk 20:39 one his idols, and **h** *also*, if ye will not H310
Dan 2:29 come to pass **h**: and he that H311+H1836
45 come to pass **h**: and the dream *is* H311+H1836
Mt 26:64 I say unto you, **H** shall ye see the G575+G737
Mk 11:14 **h** for ever. And his disciples heard *it*. G3371
Lk 22:69 **H** shall the Son of man sit on the G575+G3568
Jn 1:51 I say unto you, **H** ye shall see G575+G737
13: 7 now; but thou shalt know **h**. G3326+G5023
14:30 **H** I will not talk much with you: for the G2089
1Ti 1:16 **h** believe on him to life everlasting. G3195
Rev 1:19 and the things which shall be **h**; G3326+G5023
4: 1 thee things which must be **h**. G3326+G5023
9:12 there come two woes more **h**. G3326+G5023

HEREBY
Gen 42:15 **H** ye shall be proved: By the life of H2063
33 said unto us, **H** shall I know that ye H2063
Nu 16:28 And Moses said, **H** ye shall know that H2063
Jos 3:10 And Joshua said, **H** ye shall know that H2063
1Co 4: 4 yet am I not **h** justified: but he G1722+G5129
1Jn 2: 3 And **h** we do know that we G1722+G5129
5 **h** know we that we are in him. G1722+G5129
3:16 **H** perceive we the love *of God*, G1722+G5129
19 And **h** we know that we are of G1722+G5129
24 in him. And **h** we know that he G1722+G5129
4: 2 **H** know ye the Spirit of God: G1722+G5129
6 not us. **H** know we the spirit G1537+G5127
13 **H** know we that we dwell in G1722+G5129

HEREIN
Gen 34:22 Only **h** will the men consent unto us for H2063
2Ch 16: 9 toward him. **H** thou hast done H5921+H2063
Jn 4:37 And **h** is that saying true, One G1722+G5129
9:30 them, Why **h** is a marvellous G1722+G5129
15: 8 **H** is my Father glorified, that G1722+G5129
Act 24:16 And **h** do I exercise myself, to G1722+G5129
2Co 8:10 And **h** I give *my* advice: for G1722+G5129
1Jn 4:10 **H** is love, not that we loved G1722+G5129
17 **H** is our love made perfect, G1722+G5129

HEREOF
Mt 9:26 And the fame **h** went abroad into all G3778
Heb 5: 3 And by reason **h** he ought, as for the G5026

HERES
Jdg 1:35 dwell in mount **H** in Aijalon, and in H2776

HERESH
1Ch 9:15 And Bakbakkar, **H**, and Galal, and H2792

HERESIES
1Co 11:19 For there must be also **h** among you, G139
Gal 5:20 emulations, wrath, strife, seditions, **h**, G139
2Pt 2: 1 bring in damnable **h**, even denying the G139

HERESY
Act 24:14 which they call **h**, so worship I the God G139

HERETICK
Tit 3:10 A man that is an **h** after the first and G141

HERETOFORE
Ex 4:10 neither **h**, nor since thou hast H8543+H8032
5: 7 brick, as **h**: let them go and H8543+H8032
8 they did make **h**, ye shall lay H8543+H8032
14 yesterday and to day, as **h**? H8543+H8032
Jos 3: 4 ye have not passed *this* way **h**. H8543+H8032
Ru 2:11 which thou knewest not **h**. H8543+H8032
1Sa 4: 7 hath not been such a thing **h**. H865+H8032
2Co 13: 2 to them which **h** have sinned, and to G4258

HEREUNTO
Ecc 2:25 or who else can hasten ***h***, more than I?
1Pt 2:21 For even **h** were ye called: G1519+G5124

HEREWITH
Ezk 16:29 and yet thou wast not satisfied **h**. H2063
Mal 3:10 and prove me now **h**, saith the LORD of H2063

HERITAGE
Ex 6: 8 will give it you for an **h**: I *am* the LORD. H4181
Job 20:29 and the **h** appointed unto him by God. H5159
27:13 man with God, and the **h** of oppressors, H5159
Ps 16: 6 pleasant *places*; yea, I have a goodly **h**. H5159
61: 5 *me* the **h** of those that fear thy name. H3425
94: 5 thy people, O LORD, and afflict thine **h**. H5159
111: 6 he may give them the **h** of the heathen. H5159

Ps119:111 Thy testimonies have I taken as an **h** H5157
127: 3 Lo, children *are* an **h** of the LORD: *and* H5159
135:12 And gave their land *for* an **h**, an H5159
12 heritage, an **h** unto Israel his people. H5159
136:21 And gave their land for an **h**: for his H5159
22 *Even* an **h** unto Israel his servant: for H5159
Isa 54:17 This *is* the **h** of the servants of the H5159
58:14 feed thee with the **h** of Jacob thy father: H5159
Jer 2: 7 and made mine **h** an abomination. H5159
3:19 land, a goodly **h** of the hosts of nations? H5159
12: 7 I have left mine **h**; I have given the H5159
8 Mine **h** is unto me as a lion in the H5159
9 Mine **h** *is* unto me *as* a speckled bird, H5159
15 to his **h**, and every man to his land. H5159
17: 4 from thine **h** that I gave thee; and H5159
50:11 of mine **h**, because ye are grown H5159
Joel 2:17 and give not thine **h** to reproach, that H5159
3: 2 people and *for* my **h** Israel, whom they H5159
Mic 2: 2 and his house, even a man and his **h**. H5159
7:14 rod, the flock of thine **h**, which dwell H5159
18 of the remnant of his **h**? he retaineth not H5159
Mal 1: 3 and his **h** waste for the dragons H5159
1Pt 5: 3 Neither as being lords over *God's* **h**, but *G2819*

HERITAGES
Isa 49: 8 earth, to cause to inherit the desolate **h**; H5159

HERMAS
Ro 16:14 Salute Asyncritus, Phlegon, **H**, *G2057*

HERMES
Ro 16:14 Patrobas, **H**, and the brethren which *G2060*

HERMOGENES
2Ti 1:15 from me; of whom are Phygellus and **H**. *G2061*

HERMON
Dt 3: 8 from the river of Arnon unto mount **H**; H2768
9 (*Which* **H** the Sidonians call Sirion; H2768
4:48 even unto mount Sion, which *is* **H**, H2768
Jos 11: 3 Hivite under **H** in the land of Mizpeh. H2768
17 under mount **H**: and all their kings he H2768
12: 1 mount **H**, and all the plain on the east: H2768
5 And reigned in mount **H**, and in Salcah, H2768
13: 5 **H** unto the entering into Hamath. H2768
11 mount **H**, and all Bashan unto Salcah; H2768
1Ch 5:23 and Senir, and unto mount **H**. H2768
Ps 89:12 Tabor and **H** shall rejoice in thy name. H2768
133: 3 As the dew of **H**, *and as the dew* that H2768
Song 4: 8 the top of Shenir and **H**, from the lions' H2768

HERMONITES
Ps 42: 6 and of the **H**, from the hill Mizar. H2769

HEROD
Mt 2: 1 in the days of **H** the king, behold, there *G2264*
3 When **H** the king had heard *these* *G2264*
7 Then **H**, when he had privily called the *G2264*
12 not return to **H**, they departed into *G2264*
13 thee word: for **H** will seek the young *G2264*
15 And was there until the death of **H**: that *G2264*
16 Then **H**, when he saw that he was *G2264*
19 But when **H** was dead, behold, an angel *G2264*
22 room of his father **H**, he was afraid to *G2264*
14: 1 At that time **H** the tetrarch heard of the *G2264*
3 For **H** had laid hold on John, and *G2264*
6 danced before them, and pleased **H**. *G2264*
Mk 6:14 And king **H** heard *of him*; (for his *G2264*
16 But when **H** heard *thereof*, he said, It is *G2264*
17 For **H** himself had sent forth and laid *G2264*
18 For John had said unto **H**, It is not *G2264*
20 For **H** feared John, knowing that he *G2264*
21 was come, that **H** on his birthday made *G2264*
22 and pleased **H** and them that sat with *G2264*
8:15 of the Pharisees, and *of* the leaven of **H**. *G2264*
Lk 1: 5 There was in the days of **H**, the king of *G2264*
3: 1 of Judaea, and **H** being tetrarch of *G2264*
19 But **H** the tetrarch, being reproved by *G2264*
19 and for all the evils which **H** had done, *G2264*
9: 7 Now **H** the tetrarch heard of all that *G2264*
9 And **H** said, John have I beheaded: but *G2264*
13:31 and depart hence: for **H** will kill thee. *G2264*
23: 7 he sent him to **H**, who himself also was *G2264*
8 And when **H** saw Jesus, he was *G2264*
11 And **H** with his men of war set him at *G2264*
12 And the same day Pilate and **H** were *G2264*
15 No, nor yet **H**: for I sent you to him; *G2264*
Act 4:27 anointed, both **H**, and Pontius Pilate, *G2264*
12: 1 Now about that time **H** the king *G2264*
6 And when **H** would have brought him *G2264*
11 out of the hand of **H**, and *from* all the *G2264*
19 And when **H** had sought for him, and *G2264*
20 And **H** was highly displeased with *G2264*
21 And upon a set day **H**, arrayed in royal *G2264*
13: 1 up with **H** the tetrarch, and Saul. *G2264*

HERODIANS
Mt 22:16 disciples with the **H**, saying, Master, we *G2265*
Mk 3: 6 counsel with the **H** against him, how *G2265*
12:13 and of the **H**, to catch him in *his* words. *G2265*

HERODIAS
Mt 14: 6 the daughter of **H** danced before them, *G2266*
Mk 6:19 Therefore **H** had a quarrel against him, *G2266*
22 And when the daughter of the said **H** *G2266*
Lk 3:19 by him for **H** his brother Philip's *G2266*

HERODIAS'
Mt 14: 3 for **H** sake, his brother Philip's wife. *G2266*
Mk 6:17 him in prison for **H** sake, his brother *G2266*

HERODION
Ro 16:11 Salute **H** my kinsman. Greet them that *G2267*

HEROD'S
Mt 14: 6 But when **H** birthday was kept, the *G2264*
Lk 8: 3 And Joanna the wife of Chuza **H** *G2264*
23: 7 he belonged unto **H** jurisdiction, he *G2264*
Act 23:35 him to be kept in **H** judgment hall. *G2264*

HERON
Lev 11:19 And the stork, the **h** after her kind, and H601
Dt 14:18 And the stork, and the **h** after her kind, H601

HERS See the Appendix.

HERSELF See the Appendix.

HESED
1Ki 4:10 The son of **H**, in Aruboth; to him H2618

HESHBON
Nu 21:25 in **H**, and in all the villages thereof. H2809
26 For **H** *was* the city of Sihon the king of H2809
27 say, Come into **H**, let the city of Sihon H2809
28 For there is a fire gone out of **H**, a flame H2809
30 We have shot at them; **H** is perished H2809
34 king of the Amorites, which dwelt at **H**. H2809
32: 3 and Nimrah, and **H**, and Elealeh, and H2809
37 And the children of Reuben built **H**, and H2809
Dt 1: 4 which dwelt in **H**, and Og the king of H2809
2:24 Amorite, king of **H**, and his land: begin H2809
26 king of **H** with words of peace, saying, H2809
30 But Sihon king of **H** would not let us H2809
3: 2 king of the Amorites, which dwelt at **H**. H2809
6 Sihon king of **H**, utterly destroying the H2809
4:46 who dwelt at **H**, whom Moses and the H2809
29: 7 Sihon the king of **H**, and Og the king of H2809
Jos 9:10 to Sihon king of **H**, and to Og king of H2809
12: 2 who dwelt in **H**, *and* ruled from Aroer, H2809
5 Gilead, the border of Sihon king of **H**. H2809
13:10 which reigned in **H**, unto the border of H2809
17 **H**, and all her cities that *are* in the H2809
21 which reigned in **H**, whom Moses smote H2809
26 And from **H** unto Ramath-mizpeh, and H2809
27 of Sihon king of **H**, Jordan and *his* H2809
21:39 **H** with her suburbs, Jazer with her H2809
Jdg 11:19 the king of **H**; and Israel said unto H2809
26 While Israel dwelt in **H** and her towns, H2809
1Ch 6:81 And **H** with her suburbs, and Jazer H2809
Neh 9:22 of **H**, and the land of Og king of Bashan. H2809
Song 7: 4 *like* the fishpools in **H**, by the gate of H2809
Isa 15: 4 And **H** shall cry, and Elealeh: their H2809
16: 8 For the fields of **H** languish, *and* the H2809
9 with my tears, O **H**, and Elealeh: for the H2809
Jer 48: 2 praise of Moab: in **H** they have devised H2809
34 From the cry of **H** *even* unto Elealeh, H2809
45 the shadow of **H** because of the force: H2809
45 come forth out of **H**, and a flame from H2809
49: 3 Howl, O **H**, for Ai is spoiled: cry, ye H2809

HESHMON
Jos 15:27 And Hazar-gaddah, and **H**, and H2829

HETH
Gen 10:15 begat Sidon his firstborn, and **H**, H2845
23: 3 and spake unto the sons of **H**, saying, H2845
5 And the children of **H** answered H2845
7 of the land, *even* to the children of **H**. H2845
10 the children of **H**: and Ephron the H2845
10 of the children of **H**, *even* of all that H2845
16 of the sons of **H**, four hundred shekels H2845
18 of the children of **H**, before all that went H2845
20 of a burying-place by the sons of **H**. H2845
25:10 of the sons of **H**: there was Abraham H2845
27:46 the daughters of **H**: if Jacob take a wife H2845
46 the daughters of **H**, such as these *which* H2845
49:32 *is* therein *was* from the children of **H**. H2845
1Ch 1:13 begat Zidon his firstborn, and **H**, H2845

HETHLON
Ezk 47:15 sea, the way of **H**, as men go to Zedad; H2855
48: 1 coast of the way of **H**, as one goeth to H2855

HEW
Ex 34: 1 And the LORD said unto Moses, **H** thee H6458
Dt 10: 1 At that time the LORD said unto me, **H** H6458
12: 3 fire; and ye shall **h** down the graven H1438
19: 5 his neighbour to **h** wood, and his hand H2404
1Ki 5: 6 thou that they **h** me cedar trees out of H3772
6 to **h** timber like unto the Sidonians. H3772
18 Hiram's builders did **h** *them*, and the H6458
1Ch 22: 2 he set masons to **h** wrought stones to H2672
2Ch 2: 2 thousand to **h** in the mountain, and H2672
Jer 6: 6 of hosts said, **H** ye down trees, and H3772
Dan 4:14 He cried aloud, and said thus, **H** down H1414
23 and saying, **H** the tree down, and H1414

HEWED
Ex 34: 4 And he **h** two tables of stone like unto H6458
Dt 10: 3 shittim wood, and **h** two tables of stone H6458
1Sa 11: 7 And he took a yoke of oxen, and **h** H5408
15:33 And Samuel **h** Agag in pieces before H8158
1Ki 5:17 costly stones, *and* **h** stones, to lay the H1496
6:36 of **h** stone, and a row of cedar beams. H1496
7: 9 to the measures of **h** stones, sawed H1496
11 the measures of **h** stones, and cedars. H1496
12 with three rows of **h** stones, and a row H1496
2Ki 12:12 to buy timber and **h** stone to repair the H4274
Isa 22:16 that thou hast **h** thee out a sepulchre H2672
Jer 2:13 living waters, *and* **h** them out cisterns, H2672
Hos 6: 5 Therefore have I **h** *them* by the H2672

HEWER
Dt 29:11 camp, from the **h** of thy wood unto the H2404

HEWERS
Jos 9:21 but let them be **h** of wood and drawers H2404
23 bondmen, and **h** of wood and drawers H2404
27 And Joshua made them that day **h** of H2404
1Ki 5:15 thousand **h** in the mountains; H2672
2Ki 12:12 And to masons, and **h** of stone, and to H2672
1Ch 22:15 in abundance, **h** and workers of stone H2672
2Ch 2:10 to thy servants, the **h** that cut timber, H2404
18 thousand *to be* **h** in the mountain, and H2672
Jer 46:22 against her with axes, as **h** of wood. H2404

HEWETH
Isa 10:15 against him that **h** therewith? *or* shall H2672
22:16 here, *as* he that **h** him out a sepulchre H2672
44:14 He **h** him down cedars, and taketh the H3772

HEWN
Ex 20:25 not build it of **h** stone: for if thou lift H1496
2Ki 22: 6 timber and **h** stone to repair the house. H4274
2Ch 34:11 they *it*, to buy **h** stone, and timber for H4274
Prv 9: 1 house, she hath **h** out her seven pillars: H2672
Isa 9:10 but we will build with **h** stones: the H1496
10:33 of stature *shall be* **h** down, and the H1438
33: 9 is ashamed *and* **h** down: Sharon is like H7060
51: 1 *whence* ye are **h**, and to the hole of the H2672
Lam 3: 9 He hath inclosed my ways with **h** H1496
Ezk 40:42 And the four tables *were* of **h** stone for H1496
Am 5:11 built houses of **h** stone, but ye shall not H1496
Mt 3:10 fruit is **h** down, and cast into the fire. *G1581*
7:19 fruit is **h** down, and cast into the fire. *G1581*
27:60 which he had **h** out in the rock: and *G2998*
Mk 15:46 which was **h** out of a rock, and rolled *G2998*
Lk 3: 9 fruit is **h** down, and cast into the fire. *G1581*
23:53 that was **h** in stone, wherein never *G2991*

HEZEKI
1Ch 8:17 And Zebadiah, and Meshullam, and **H**, H2395

HEZEKIAH
2Ki 16:20 and **H** his son reigned in his stead. H2396
18: 1 of Israel, *that* **H** the son of Ahaz king H2396

2Ki 18: 9 year of king **H**, which *was* the seventh H2396
10 in the sixth year of **H**, that *is* the ninth H2396
13 Now in the fourteenth year of king **H** H2396
14 And **H** king of Judah sent to the king of H2396
14 appointed unto **H** king of Judah three H2396
15 And **H** gave *him* all the silver that was H2396
16 At that time did **H** cut off *the gold from* H2396
16 the pillars which **H** king of Judah had H2396
17 Lachish to king **H** with a great host H2396
19 Speak ye now to **H**, Thus saith the great H2396
22 and whose altars **H** hath taken away, H2396
29 Thus saith the king, Let not **H** deceive H2396
30 Neither let **H** make you trust in the H2396
31 Hearken not to **H**: for thus saith the H2396
32 and hearken not unto **H**, when he H2396
37 the recorder, to **H** with *their* clothes H2396
19: 1 And it came to pass, when king **H** H2396
3 And they said unto him, Thus saith **H**, H2396
5 So the servants of king **H** came to H2396
9 sent messengers again unto **H**, saying, H2396
10 Thus shall ye speak to **H** king of Judah, H2396
14 And **H** received the letter of the hand of H2396
14 and read it: and **H** went up into the H2396
15 And **H** prayed before the LORD, and H2396
20 Then Isaiah the son of Amoz sent to **H**, H2396
20: 1 In those days was **H** sick unto death. H2396
3 *is* good in thy sight. And **H** wept sore. H2396
5 Turn again, and tell **H** the captain of H2396
8 And **H** said unto Isaiah, What *shall be* H2396
10 And **H** answered, It is a light thing for H2396
12 a present unto **H**: for he had heard that H2396
12 for he had heard that **H** had been sick. H2396
13 And **H** hearkened unto them, and H2396
13 his dominion, that **H** shewed them not. H2396
14 the prophet unto king **H**, and said unto H2396
14 unto thee? And **H** said, They are come H2396
15 thine house? And **H** answered, All *the* H2396
16 And Isaiah said unto **H**, Hear the word H2396
19 Then said **H** unto Isaiah, Good *is* the H2396
20 And the rest of the acts of **H**, and all his H2396
21 And **H** slept with his fathers: and H2396
21: 3 the high places which **H** his father had H2396
1Ch 3:13 Ahaz his son, **H** his son, Manasseh his H2396
23 Elioenai, and **H**, and Azrikam, three. H2396
4:41 in the days of **H** king of Judah, and H2396
2Ch 28:27 and **H** his son reigned in his stead. H2396
29: 1 **H** began to reign *when he was* five and H2396
18 Then they went in to **H** the king, and H2396
20 Then **H** the king rose early, and H2396
27 And **H** commanded to offer the burnt H2396
30 Moreover **H** the king and the princes H2396
31 Then **H** answered and said, Now ye H2396
36 And **H** rejoiced, and all the people, that H2396
30: 1 And **H** sent to all Israel and Judah, and H2396
18 it was written. But **H** prayed for them, H2396
20 And the LORD hearkened to **H**, and H2396
22 And **H** spake comfortably unto all the H2396
24 For **H** king of Judah did give to the H2396
31: 2 And **H** appointed the courses of the H2396
8 And when **H** and the princes came and H2396
9 Then **H** questioned with the priests and H2396
11 Then **H** commanded to prepare H2396
13 the commandment of **H** the king, and H2396
20 And thus did **H** throughout all Judah, H2396
32: 2 And when **H** saw that Sennacherib was H2396
8 upon the words of **H** king of Judah. H2396
9 with him,) unto **H** king of Judah, and H2396
11 Doth not **H** persuade you to give over H2396
12 Hath not the same **H** taken away his H2396
15 Now therefore let not **H** deceive you, H2396
16 LORD God, and against his servant **H**. H2396
17 **H** deliver his people out of mine hand. H2396
20 And for this *cause* **H** the king, and the H2396
22 Thus the LORD saved **H** and the H2396
23 and presents to **H** king of Judah: so H2396
24 In those days **H** was sick to the death, H2396
25 But **H** rendered not again according to H2396
26 Notwithstanding **H** humbled himself H2396
26 came not upon them in the days of **H**. H2396
27 And **H** had exceeding much riches and H2396
30 This same **H** also stopped the upper H2396
30 And **H** prospered in all his works. H2396
32 Now the rest of the acts of **H**, and his H2396
33 And **H** slept with his fathers, and they H2396
33: 3 the high places which **H** his father had H2396
Ezr 2:16 The children of Ater of **H**, ninety and H2396
Neh 7:21 The children of Ater of **H**, ninety and H2396
Prv 25: 1 the men of **H** king of Judah copied out. H2396
Isa 1: 1 Jotham, Ahaz, *and* **H**, kings of Judah. H2396
Isa 36: 1 year of king **H**, *that* Sennacherib king H2396
2 unto king **H** with a great army. H2396
4 Say ye now to **H**, Thus saith the great H2396
7 and whose altars **H** hath taken away, H2396
14 Thus saith the king, Let not **H** deceive H2396
15 Neither let **H** make you trust in the H2396
16 Hearken not to **H**: for thus saith the H2396
18 *Beware* lest **H** persuade you, saying, H2396
22 the recorder, to **H** with *their* clothes H2396
37: 1 And it came to pass, when king **H** H2396
3 And they said unto him, Thus saith **H**, H2396
5 So the servants of king **H** came to H2396
9 *it*, he sent messengers to **H**, saying, H2396
10 Thus shall ye speak to **H** king of Judah, H2396
14 And **H** received the letter from the H2396
14 and read it: and **H** went up unto the H2396
15 And **H** prayed unto the LORD, saying, H2396
21 of Amoz sent unto **H**, saying, Thus saith H2396
38: 1 In those days was **H** sick unto death. H2396
2 Then **H** turned his face toward the H2396
3 *is* good in thy sight. And **H** wept sore. H2396
5 Go, and say to **H**, Thus saith the LORD, H2396
9 The writing of **H** king of Judah, when H2396
22 **H** also had said, What *is* the sign that I H2396
39: 1 and a present to **H**: for he had heard H2396
2 And **H** was glad of them, and shewed H2396
2 his dominion, that **H** shewed them not. H2396
3 the prophet unto king **H**, and said unto H2396
3 unto thee? And **H** said, They are come H2396
4 thine house? And **H** answered, All that H2396
5 Then said Isaiah to **H**, Hear the word of H2396
8 Then said **H** to Isaiah, Good *is* the H2396
Jer 15: 4 the son of **H** king of Judah, for *that* H2396
26:18 in the days of **H** king of Judah, and H2396
19 Did **H** king of Judah and all Judah put H2396
Hos 1: 1 Ahaz, *and* **H**, kings of Judah, and H2396
Mic 1: 1 Ahaz, *and* **H**, kings of Judah, which H2396

HEZION

1Ki 15:18 the son of **H**, king of Syria, that dwelt H2383

HEZIR

1Ch 24:15 The seventeenth to **H**, the eighteenth to H2387
Neh 10:20 Magpiash, Meshullam, **H**, H2387

HEZRAI

2Sa 23:35 **H** the Carmelite, Paarai the Arbite, H2695

HEZRO

1Ch 11:37 **H** the Carmelite, Naarai the son of H2695

HEZRON

Gen 46: 9 Hanoch, and Phallu, and **H**, and Carmi. H2696
12 the sons of Pharez were **H** and Hamul. H2696
Ex 6:14 and Pallu, **H**, and Carmi: these *be* H2696
Nu 26: 6 Of **H**, the family of the Hezronites: of H2696
21 And the sons of Pharez were; of **H**, the H2696
Jos 15: 3 and passed along to **H**, and went up to H2696
25 and Kerioth, *and* **H**, which is Hazor, H2696
Ru 4:18 generations of Pharez: Pharez begat **H**, H2696
19 And **H** begat Ram, and Ram begat H2696
1Ch 2: 5 The sons of Pharez; **H**, and Hamul. H2696
9 The sons also of **H**, that were born unto H2696
18 And Caleb the son of **H** begat *children* H2696
21 And afterward **H** went in to the H2696
24 And after that **H** was dead in H2696
25 the firstborn of **H** were, Ram the H2696
4: 1 The sons of Judah; Pharez, **H**, and H2696
5: 3 *were*, Hanoch, and Pallu, **H**, and Carmi. H2696

HEZRONITES

Nu 26: 6 Of Hezron, the family of the **H**: of H2697
21 the family of the **H**: of Hamul, the H2697

HEZRON'S

1Ch 2:24 then Abiah **H** wife bare him Ashur H2696

HID

Gen 3: 8 and his wife **h** themselves from the H2244
10 because I *was* naked; and I **h** myself. H2244
4:14 thy face shall I be **h**; and I shall be a H5641
35: 4 ears; and Jacob **h** them under the oak H2934
Ex 2: 2 *a* goodly *child*, she **h** him three months. H6845
12 the Egyptian, and **h** him in the sand. H2934
3: 6 Jacob. And Moses **h** his face; for he was H5641
Lev 4:13 and the thing be **h** from the eyes of the H5956
5: 3 withal, and it be **h** from him; when he H5956
4 an oath, and it be **h** from him; when he H5956
Nu 5:13 carnally, and it be **h** from the eyes of H5956
Dt 33:19 the seas, and *of* treasures **h** in the sand. H2934
Jos 2: 4 the two men, and **h** them, and said H6845
6 roof of the house, and **h** them with the H2934
6:17 she **h** the messengers that we sent. H2244
25 this day; because she **h** the messengers, H2244
7:21 behold, they *are* **h** in the earth in the H2934
22 **h** in his tent, and the silver under it. H2934
10:16 But these five kings fled, and **h** H2244
17 are found **h** in a cave at Makkedah. H2244
27 they had been **h**, and laid great stones H2244
Jdg 9: 5 of Jerubbaal was left; for he **h** himself. H2244
1Sa 3:18 And Samuel told him every whit, and **h** H3582
10:22 he hath **h** himself among the stuff. H2244
14:11 the holes where they had **h** themselves. H2244
22 of Israel which had **h** themselves in H2244
20:24 So David **h** himself in the field: and H5641
2Sa 17: 9 Behold, he is **h** now in some pit, or in H2244
18:13 there is no matter **h** from the king, and H3582
1Ki 10: 3 **h** from the king, which he told her not. H5956
18: 4 prophets, and **h** them by fifty in a cave, H2244
13 the LORD, how I **h** an hundred men of H2244
2Ki 4:27 **h** *it* from me, and hath not told me. H5956
6:29 may eat him: and she hath **h** her son. H2244
7: 8 and went and **h** *it*; and came again, H2934
8 carried thence *also*, and went and **h** *it*. H2934
11: 2 slain; and they **h** him, *even* him and H5641
3 And he was with her **h** in the house of H2244
1Ch 21:20 four sons with him **h** themselves. Now H2244
2Ch 9: 2 **h** from Solomon which he told her not. H5956
22: 9 him, (for he was **h** in Samaria,) and H2244
11 the sister of Ahaziah,) **h** him from H5641
12 And he was with them **h** in the house of H2244
Job 3:10 womb, nor **h** sorrow from mine eyes. H5641
21 dig for it more than for **h** treasures; H4301
23 is **h**, and whom God hath hedged in? H5641
5:21 Thou shalt be **h** from the scourge of the H2244
6:16 of the ice, *and* wherein the snow is **h**: H5956
10:13 And these *things* hast thou **h** in thine H6845
15:18 from their fathers, and have not **h** *it*: H3582
17: 4 For thou hast **h** their heart from H6845
20:26 All darkness *shall be* **h** in his secret H2934
28:11 *that is* **h** bringeth he forth to light. H8587
21 Seeing it is **h** from the eyes of all living, H5956
29: 8 The young men saw me, and **h** H2244
38:30 The waters are **h** as *with* a stone, and H2244
Ps 9:15 which they **h** is their own foot taken. H2934
17:14 fillest with thy **h** *treasure*: they are full H6845
19: 6 is nothing **h** from the heat thereof. H5641
22:24 neither hath he **h** his face from him; H5641
32: 5 mine iniquity have I not **h**. I said, I will H3680
35: 7 For without cause have they **h** for me H2934
8 net that he hath **h** catch himself: into H2934
38: 9 and my groaning is not **h** from thee. H5641
40:10 I have not **h** thy righteousness within H3680
55:12 then I would have **h** myself from him: H5641
69: 5 and my sins are not **h** from thee. H3582
119:11 Thy word have I **h** in mine heart, that I H6845
139:15 My substance was not **h** from thee, H3582
140: 5 The proud have **h** a snare for me, and H2934
Prv 2: 4 searchest for her as *for* **h** treasures; H4301
Isa 28:15 under falsehood have we **h** ourselves: H5641
29:14 of their prudent *men* shall be **h**. H5641
40:27 O Israel, My way is **h** from the LORD, H5641
42:22 and they are **h** in prison houses: they H2244
49: 2 his hand hath he **h** me, and made me a H2244
2 shaft; in his quiver hath he **h** me; H5641
50: 6 **h** not my face from shame and spitting. H5641
53: 3 with grief: and we **h** as it were *our* faces H4564
54: 8 In a little wrath I **h** my face from thee H5641
57:17 and smote him: I **h** me, and was wroth, H5641
59: 2 your sins have **h** *his* face from you, that H5641
64: 7 thee: for thou hast **h** thy face from us, H5641
65:16 and because they are **h** from mine eyes. H5641
Jer 13: 5 So I went, and **h** it by Euphrates, as the H2934
7 place where I had **h** it: and, behold, the H2934
16:17 ways: they are not **h** from my face, H5641
17 is their iniquity **h** from mine eyes. H6845
18:22 to take me, and **h** snares for my feet. H2934
33: 5 I have **h** my face from this city. H5641
36:26 the prophet: but the LORD **h** them. H5641
43:10 these stones that I have **h**; and he shall H2934
Ezk 22:26 clean, and have **h** their eyes from my H5956
39:23 me, therefore **h** I my face from them, H5641
24 unto them, and **h** my face from them. H5641
Hos 5: 3 I know Ephraim, and Israel is not **h** H3582
13:12 of Ephraim *is* bound up; his sin *is* **h**. H6845
14 repentance shall be **h** from mine eyes. H5641
Am 9: 3 though they be **h** from my sight in the H5641
Nah 3:11 thou shalt be **h**, thou also shalt seek H5956

Zep 2: 3 be **h** in the day of the LORD'S anger. H5641
Mt 5:14 A city that is set on an hill cannot be **h**. G2928
10:26 and **h**, that shall not be known. G2927
11:25 because thou hast **h** these things from G613
13:33 woman took, and **h** in three measures G1470
44 is like unto treasure **h** in a field; the G2928
25:18 in the earth, and **h** his lord's money. G613
25 And I was afraid, and went and **h** thy G2928
Mk 4:22 For there is nothing **h**, which shall not G2927
7:24 no man know *it*: but he could not be **h**. G2990
Lk 1:24 and **h** herself five months, saying, G4032
8:17 neither *any thing* **h**, that shall not be G614
47 that she was not **h**, she came trembling, G2990
9:45 saying, and it was **h** from them, that G3871
10:21 that thou hast **h** these things from the G613
12: 2 neither **h**, that shall not be known. G2927
13:21 a woman took and **h** in three measures G1470
18:34 this saying was **h** from them, neither G2928
19:42 but now they are **h** from thine eyes. G2928
Jn 8:59 at him: but Jesus **h** himself, and went G2928
2Co 4: 3 But if our gospel be **h**, it is hid to them G2572
3 But if our gospel be hid, it is **h** to them G2572
Eph 3: 9 world hath been **h** in God, who created G613
Col 1:26 *Even* the mystery which hath been **h** G613
2: 3 In whom are **h** all the treasures of G614
3: 3 For ye are dead, and your life is **h** with G2928
1Ti 5:25 they that are otherwise cannot be **h**. G2928
Heb 11:23 he was born, was **h** three months of his G2928
Rev 6:15 every free man, **h** themselves in the G2928

HIDDAI
2Sa 23:30 Benaiah the Pirathonite, **H** of the H1914

HIDDEKEL
Gen 2:14 And the name of the third river *is* **H**: H2313
Dan 10: 4 the side of the great river, which *is* **H**; H2313

HIDDEN
Lev 5: 2 things, and *if* it be **h** from him; he also H5956
Dt 30:11 it *is* not **h** from thee, neither *is* it far off. H6381
Job 3:16 Or as an **h** untimely birth I had not H2934
15:20 number of years is **h** to the oppressor. H6845
24: 1 Why, seeing times are not **h** from the H6845
Ps 51: 6 parts: and in the **h** *part* thou shalt H5640
83: 3 and consulted against thy **h** ones. H6845
Prv 28:12 but when the wicked rise, a man is **h**. H2664
Isa 45: 3 of darkness, and **h** riches of secret H4301
48: 6 this time, even **h** things, and thou didst H5341
Oba 6 out! *how* are his **h** things sought up! H4710
Act 26:26 of these things are **h** from him; for this G2990
1Co 2: 7 mystery, *even* the **h** *wisdom*, which God G613
4: 5 bring to light the **h** things of darkness, G2927
2Co 4: 2 But have renounced the **h** things of G2927
1Pt 3: 4 But *let it be* the **h** man of the heart, in G2927
Rev 2:17 I give to eat of the **h** manna, and will G2928

HIDE
Gen 18:17 And the LORD said, Shall I **h** from H3680
47:18 him, We will not **h** *it* from my lord, H3582
Ex 2: 3 And when she could not longer **h** him, H6845
Lev 8:17 But the bullock, and his **h**, his flesh, and H5785
9:11 And the flesh and the **h** he burnt with H5785
20: 4 land do any ways **h** their eyes from the H5956
Dt 7:20 **h** themselves from thee, be destroyed. H5641
22: 1 go astray, and **h** thyself from them: H5956
3 do likewise: thou mayest not **h** thyself. H5956
4 by the way, and **h** thyself from them: H5956
31:17 them, and I will **h** my face from them, H5641
18 And I will surely **h** my face in that day H5641
32:20 And he said, I will **h** my face from H5641
Jos 2:16 meet you; and **h** yourselves there three H2247
7:19 what thou hast done; **h** *it* not from me. H3582
Jdg 6:11 winepress, to **h** *it* from the Midianites. H5127
1Sa 3:17 thee? I pray thee **h** *it* not from me: God H3582
17 more also, if thou **h** *any* thing from me H3582
13: 6 the people did **h** themselves in caves, H2244
19: 2 abide in a secret *place*, and **h** thyself: H2244
20: 2 father **h** this thing from me? it *is* not *so*. H5641
5 me go, that I may **h** myself in the field H5641
19 where thou didst **h** thyself when the H5641
23:19 Doth not David **h** himself with us in H5641
26: 1 Doth not David **h** himself in the hill of H5641
2Sa 14:18 unto the woman, **H** not from me, I pray H3582
1Ki 17: 3 eastward, and **h** thyself by the brook H5641
22:25 go into an inner chamber to **h** thyself. H2247
2Ki 7:12 out of the camp to **h** themselves in the H2247
2Ch 18:24 go into an inner chamber to **h** thyself. H2244
Job 13:20 me: then will I not **h** myself from thee. H5641
14:13 O that thou wouldest **h** me in the grave, H6845
Job 20:12 *though* he **h** it under his tongue; H3582
24: 4 of the earth **h** themselves together. H2244
33:17 *his* purpose, and **h** pride from man. H3680
34:22 workers of iniquity may **h** themselves. H5641
40:13 **H** them in the dust together; *and* bind H2934
Ps 13: 1 how long wilt thou **h** thy face from me? H5641
17: 8 Keep me as the apple of the eye, **h** me H5641
27: 5 For in the time of trouble he shall **h** me H6845
5 **h** me; he shall set me up upon a rock. H5641
9 **H** not thy face *far* from me; put not thy H5641
30: 7 didst **h** thy face, *and* I was troubled. H5641
31:20 Thou shalt **h** them in the secret of thy H5641
51: 9 **H** thy face from my sins, and blot out H5641
54:ttl Saul, Doth not David **h** himself with us? H5641
55: 1 Give ear to my prayer, O God; and **h** H5956
56: 6 together, they **h** themselves, they mark H6845
64: 2 **H** me from the secret counsel of the H5641
69:17 And **h** not thy face from thy servant; H5641
78: 4 We will not **h** *them* from their children, H3582
89:46 How long, LORD? wilt thou **h** thyself H5641
102: 2 **H** not thy face from me in the day H5641
119:19 I *am* a stranger in the earth: **h** not thy H5641
143: 7 my spirit faileth: **h** not thy face from H5641
9 mine enemies: I flee unto thee to **h** me. H3680
Prv 2: 1 and **h** my commandments with thee; H6845
28:28 When the wicked rise, men **h** H5641
Isa 1:15 your hands, I will **h** mine eyes from H5956
2:10 Enter into the rock, and **h** thee in the H2934
3: 9 as Sodom, they **h** *it* not. Woe unto their H3582
16: 3 of the noonday; **h** the outcasts; bewray H5641
26:20 doors about thee: **h** thyself as it were H2247
29:15 Woe unto them that seek deep to **h** H5641
58: 7 **h** not thyself from thine own flesh? H5956
Jer 13: 4 and **h** it there in a hole of the rock. H2934
6 which I commanded thee to **h** there. H2934
23:24 Can any **h** himself in secret places that H5641
36:19 unto Baruch, Go, **h** thee, thou and H5641
38:14 ask thee a thing; **h** nothing from me. H3582
25 unto the king, **h** it not from us, and H3582
43: 9 Take great stones in thine hand, and **h** H2934
49:10 not be able to **h** himself: his seed is H2247
Lam 3:56 Thou hast heard my voice: **h** not thine H5956
Ezk 28: 3 is no secret that they can **h** from thee: H6004
31: 8 of God could not **h** him: the fir trees H6004
39:29 Neither will I **h** my face any more from H5641
Dan 10: 7 them, so that they fled to **h** themselves. H2244
Am 9: 3 And though they **h** themselves in the H2244
Mic 3: 4 them: he will even **h** his face from them H5641
Jn 12:36 and did **h** himself from them. G2928
Jas 5:20 death, and shall **h** a multitude of sins. G2572
Rev 6:16 Fall on us, and **h** us from the face of G2928

HIDEST
Job 13:24 Wherefore **h** thou thy face, and holdest H5641
Ps 10: 1 *why* **h** thou *thyself* in times of trouble? H5956
44:24 Wherefore **h** thou thy face, *and* H5641
88:14 my soul? *why* **h** thou thy face from me? H5641
104:29 Thou **h** thy face, they are troubled: H5641
Isa 45:15 Verily thou *art* a God that **h** thyself, O H5641

HIDETH
1Sa 23:23 places where he **h** himself, and come ye H2244
Job 23: 9 behold *him*: he **h** himself on the right H5848
34:29 and when he **h** *his* face, who then can H5641
42: 3 Who *is* he that **h** counsel without H5956
Ps 10:11 he **h** his face; he will never see *it*. H5641
139:12 Yea, the darkness **h** not from thee; but H2821
Prv 10:18 He that **h** hatred *with* lying lips, and he H3680
19:24 A slothful *man* **h** his hand in *his* H2934
22: 3 the evil, and **h** himself: but the simple H5641
26:15 The slothful **h** his hand in *his* bosom; it H2934
27:12 the evil, *and* **h** himself; *but* the simple H5641
16 Whosoever **h** her hideth the wind, and H6845
16 Whosoever hideth her **h** the wind, and H6845
28:27 that **h** his eyes shall have many a curse. H5956
Isa 8:17 And I will wait upon the LORD, that **h** H5641
Mt 13:44 hath found, he **h**, and for joy thereof G2928

HIDING
Job 31:33 by **h** mine iniquity in my bosom: H2934
Ps 32: 7 Thou *art* my **h** place; thou shalt H5643
119:114 Thou *art* my **h** place and my shield: I H5643
Isa 28:17 the waters shall overflow the **h** place. H5643
32: 2 And a man shall be as an **h** place from H4224
Hab 3: 4 hand: and there *was* the **h** of his power. H2253

HIDING-PLACE See HIDING and PLACE.

HIEL
1Ki 16:34 In his days did **H** the Beth-elite build H2419

HIERAPOLIS
Col 4:13 *that are* in Laodicea, and them in **H**. G2404

HIGGAION
Ps 9:16 in the work of his own hands. **H**. Selah. H1902

HIGH
Gen 7:19 the earth; and all the **h** hills, that *were* H1364
14:18 he *was* the priest of the most **h** God. H5945
19 **h** God, possessor of heaven and earth: H5945
20 And blessed be the most **h** God, which H5945
22 LORD, the most **h** God, the possessor H5945
29: 7 And he said, Lo, *it is* yet **h** day, neither H1419
Ex 14: 8 of Israel went out with an **h** hand. H7311
25:20 *their* wings on **h**, covering the mercy H4605
37: 9 out *their* wings on **h**, *and* covered with H4605
39:31 to fasten *it* on **h** upon the mitre; as the H4605
Lev 21:10 And *he that is* the **h** priest among his H1419
26:22 and your *h* ways shall be desolate.
30 And I will destroy your **h** places, and H1116
Nu 11:31 two cubits *h* upon the face of the earth.
20:17 go by the king's *h* way, we will not turn
19 We will go by the **h** way: and if I and H4546
21:22 *h* way, until we be past thy borders.
28 *and* the lords of the **h** places of Arnon. H1116
22:41 him up into the **h** places of Baal, that H1116
23: 3 tell thee. And he went to an **h** place. H8205
24:16 of the most **H**, *which* saw the vision H5945
33: 3 **h** hand in the sight of all the Egyptians. H7311
52 and quite pluck down all their **h** places: H1116
35:25 the death of the **h** priest, which was H1419
28 the death of the **h** priest: but after the H1419
28 the death of the **h** priest the slayer shall H1419
Dt 2:27 go along by the **h** way, I will neither H1870
3: 5 All these cities *were* fenced with **h** H1364
12: 2 gods, upon the **h** mountains, and upon H7311
26:19 And to make thee **h** above all nations H5945
28: 1 thee on **h** above all nations of the earth: H5945
43 **h**; and thou shalt come down very low. H4605
52 thy gates, until thy **h** and fenced walls H1364
32: 8 When the most **H** divided to the H5945
13 He made him ride on the **h** places of H1116
27 **h**, and the LORD hath not done all this. H7311
33:29 thou shalt tread upon their **h** places. H1116
Jos 20: 6 the death of the **h** priest that shall be in H1419
Jdg 5:18 the death in the **h** places of the field. H4791
1Sa 9:12 of the people to day in the **h** place: H1116
13 he go up to the **h** place to eat: for the H1116
14 them, for to go up to the **h** place. H1116
19 me unto the **h** place; for ye shall eat H1116
25 down from the **h** place into the city, H1116
10: 5 down from the **h** place with a psaltery, H1116
13 of prophesying, he came to the **h** place. H1116
13: 6 in rocks, and in **h** places, and in pits. H6877
2Sa 1:19 The beauty of Israel is slain upon thy **h** H1116
25 *thou wast* slain in thine **h** places. H1116
22: 3 of my salvation, my **h** tower, and my H4869
14 and the most **H** uttered his voice. H5945
34 *feet:* and setteth me upon my **h** places. H1116
49 lifted me up on **h** above them that rose H7311
23: 1 *was* raised up on **h**, the anointed of the H5920
1Ki 3: 2 Only the people sacrificed in **h** places, H1116
3 and burnt incense in **h** places. H1116
4 that *was* the great **h** place: a thousand H1116
6:10 house, five cubits **h**: and they rested on H6967
23 *of* olive tree, *each* ten cubits **h**. H6967
7:15 of eighteen cubits **h** apiece: and a line H6967
35 of half a cubit **h**: and on the top of the H6967
9: 8 And at this house, *which* is **h**, every one H5945
11: 7 Then did Solomon build an **h** place for H1116
12:31 And he made an house of **h** places, and H1116
32 of the **h** places which he had made. H1116
13: 2 the priests of the **h** places that burn H1116
32 the houses of the **h** places which *are* in H1116
33 priests of the **h** places: whosoever H1116
33 *one* of the priests of the **h** places. H1116
14:23 For they also built them **h** places, and H1364
23 **h** hill, and under every green tree. H1364
15:14 But the **h** places were not removed: H1116
21: 9 and set Naboth on **h** among the people: H7218
12 and set Naboth on **h** among the people. H7218
22:43 nevertheless the **h** places were not H1116
43 and burnt incense yet in the **h** places. H1116
2Ki 12: 3 But the **h** places were not taken away: H1116
3 and burnt incense in the **h** places. H1116
10 scribe and the **h** priest came up, and H1419

2Ki 14: 4 Howbeit the **h** places were not taken H1116
4 and burnt incense on the **h** places. H1116
15: 4 Save that the **h** places were not H1116
4 and burnt incense still on the **h** places. H1116
35 Howbeit the **h** places were not H1116
35 incense still in the **h** places. He built H1116
16: 4 incense in the **h** places, and on the H1116
17: 9 and they built them **h** places in all their H1116
10 **h** hill, and under every green tree: H1364
11 incense in all the **h** places, as *did* the H1116
29 in the houses of the **h** places which the H1116
32 priests of the **h** places, which sacrificed H1116
32 for them in the houses of the **h** places. H1116
18: 4 He removed the **h** places, and brake H1116
22 not that he, whose **h** places and whose H1116
19:22 **h**? *even* against the Holy *One* of Israel. H4791
21: 3 For he built up again the **h** places H1116
22: 4 Go up to Hilkiah the **h** priest, that he H1419
8 And Hilkiah the **h** priest said unto H1419
23: 4 Hilkiah the **h** priest, and the priests H1419
5 incense in the **h** places in the cities of H1116
8 and defiled the **h** places where the H1116
8 brake down the **h** places of the gates H1116
9 Nevertheless the priests of the **h** places H1116
13 And the **h** places that *were* before H1116
15 *was* at Beth-el, *and* the **h** place which H1116
15 that altar and the **h** place he brake H1116
15 and burned the **h** place, *and* stamped H1116
19 And all the houses also of the **h** places H1116
20 And he slew all the priests of the **h** H1116
1Ch 11:23 *great* stature, five cubits **h**; and in the H1116
14: 2 up on **h**, because of his people Israel. H4605
16:39 in the **h** place that *was* at Gibeon, H1116
17:17 of a man of **h** degree, O LORD God. H4608
21:29 at that season in the **h** place at Gibeon. H1116
2Ch 1: 3 him, went to the **h** place that *was* at H1116
13 *his journey* to the **h** place that *was* at H1116
3:15 and five cubits **h**, and the chapiter that H753
6:13 and three cubits **h**, and had set it in the H6967
7:21 And this house, which is **h**, shall be an H5945
11:15 And he ordained him priests for the **h** H1116
14: 3 *gods*, and the **h** places, and brake H1116
5 the cities of Judah the **h** places and the H1116
15:17 But the **h** places were not taken away H1116
17: 6 the **h** places and groves out of Judah. H1116
20:19 God of Israel with a loud voice on **h**. H4605
33 Howbeit the **h** places were not taken H1116
21:11 Moreover he made **h** places in the H1116
23:20 came through the **h** gate into the king's H5945
24:11 scribe and the **h** priest's officer came H7218
27: 3 He built the **h** gate of the house of the H5945
28: 4 incense in the **h** places, and on the H1116
25 city of Judah he made **h** places to burn H1116
31: 1 threw down the **h** places and the altars H1116
32:12 taken away his **h** places and his altars, H1116
33: 3 For he built again the **h** places which H1116
17 still in the **h** places, *yet* unto the H1116
19 wherein he built **h** places, and set up H1116
34: 3 from the **h** places, and the groves, H1116
4 that *were* on **h** above them, he cut H4605
9 And when they came to Hilkiah the **h** H1419
Neh 3: 1 Then Eliashib the **h** priest rose up with H1419
20 of the house of Eliashib the **h** priest. H1419
25 from the king's **h** house, that *was* by H5945
13:28 son of Eliashib the **h** priest, *was* son in H1419
Est 5:14 of fifty cubits **h**, and to morrow speak H1364
7: 9 fifty cubits **h**, which Haman had H1364
Job 5:11 To set up on **h** those that be low; that H4791
11: 8 *It is* as **h** as heaven; what canst thou H1363
16:19 *is* in heaven, and my record *is* on **h**. H4791
21:22 seeing he judgeth those that are **h**. H7311
22:12 the height of the stars, how **h** they are! H7311
25: 2 him, he maketh peace in his **h** places. H4791
31: 2 inheritance of the Almighty from on **h**? H4791
38:15 and the **h** arm shall be broken. H7311
39:18 What time she lifteth up herself on **h**, H4791
27 thy command, and make her nest on **h**? H7311
41:34 He beholdeth all **h** *things*: he *is* a king H1364
Ps 7: 7 their sakes therefore return thou on **h**. H4791
17 praise to the name of the LORD most **h**. H5945
9: 2 sing praise to thy name, O thou most **H**. H5945
18: 2 horn of my salvation, *and* my **h** tower. H4869
27 people; but wilt bring down **h** looks. H7311
33 *feet*, and setteth me upon my **h** places. H1116
21: 7 of the most **H** he shall not be moved. H5945
46: 4 *place* of the tabernacles of the most **H**. H5945
47: 2 For the LORD most **h** *is* terrible; *he is* a H5945
49: 2 Both low and **h**, rich and poor, together. H376
50:14 and pay thy vows unto the most **H**: H5945
Ps 56: 2 that fight against me, O thou most **H**. H4791
57: 2 I will cry unto God most **h**; unto God H5945
62: 9 vanity, *and* men of **h** degree *are* a lie: to H376
68:15 Bashan; an **h** hill *as* the hill of Bashan. H1386
16 Why leap ye, ye **h** hills? *this is* the hill H1386
18 Thou hast ascended on **h**, thou hast led H4791
69:29 let thy salvation, O God, set me up on **h**. H7682
71:19 O God, *is* very **h**, who hast done great H4791
73:11 and is there knowledge in the most **H**? H5945
75: 5 Lift not up your horn on **h**: speak *not* H4791
77:10 years of the right hand of the most **H**. H5945
78:17 the most **H** in the wilderness. H5945
35 rock, and the **h** God their redeemer. H5945
56 **h** God, and kept not his testimonies: H5945
58 him to anger with their **h** places, and H1116
69 And he built his sanctuary like **h** H7311
82: 6 all of you *are* children of the most **H**. H5945
83:18 *art* the most **h** over all the earth. H5945
89:13 is thy hand, *and* **h** is thy right hand. H7311
91: 1 place of the most **H** shall abide under H5945
9 refuge, *even* the most **H**, thy habitation; H5945
14 on **h**, because he hath known my name. H7682
92: 1 sing praises unto thy name, O most **H**: H5945
8 But thou, LORD, *art most* **h** for H4791
93: 4 The LORD on **h** *is* mightier than the H4791
97: 9 For thou, LORD, *art* **h** above all the H5945
99: 2 The LORD *is* great in Zion; and he *is* **h** H7311
101: 5 him that hath an **h** look and a proud H1362
103:11 For as the heaven is **h** above the earth, H1361
104:18 The **h** hills *are* a refuge for the wild H1364
107:11 contemned the counsel of the most **H**: H5945
41 Yet setteth he the poor on **h** from H7682
113: 4 The LORD *is* **h** above all nations, *and* H7311
5 the LORD our God, who dwelleth on **h**, H1361
131: 1 great matters, or in things too **h** for me. H6381
138: 6 Though the LORD *be* **h**, yet hath he H7311
139: 6 for me; it is **h**, I cannot *attain* unto it. H7682
144: 2 My goodness, and my fortress; my **h** H4869
149: 6 *Let* the **h** *praises* of God *be* in their H7319
150: 5 him upon the **h** sounding cymbals. H8643
Prv 8: 2 She standeth in the top of **h** places, by H4791
9:14 on a seat in the **h** places of the city, H4791
18:11 and as an **h** wall in his own conceit. H7682
21: 4 An **h** look, and a proud heart, *and* the H7312
24: 7 Wisdom *is* too **h** for a fool: he openeth H7311
Ecc 12: 5 of *that which is* **h**, and fears *shall be* in H1364
Isa 2:13 Lebanon, *that are* **h** and lifted up, and H7311
14 And upon all the **h** mountains, and H7311
15 And upon every **h** tower, and upon H1364
6: 1 upon a throne, **h** and lifted up, and his H7311
10:12 of Assyria, and the glory of his **h** looks. H7311
33 terror: and the **h** ones of stature *shall* H7311
13: 2 Lift ye up a banner upon the **h** H8192
14:14 of the clouds; I will be like the most **H**. H5945
15: 2 and to Dibon, the **h** places, to weep: H1116
16:12 is weary on the **h** place, that he shall H1116
22:16 out a sepulchre on **h**, *and* that graveth H4791
24:18 windows from on **h** are open, and the H4791
21 the host of the **h** ones *that are* on high, H4791
21 ones *that are* on **h**, and the kings of the H4791
25:12 And the fortress of the **h** fort of thy H4869
26: 5 that dwell on **h**; the lofty city, he layeth H4791
30:13 fall, swelling out in a **h** wall, whose H7682
25 And there shall be upon every **h** H1364
25 and upon every **h** hill, rivers *and* H5375
32:15 upon us from on **h**, and the wilderness H4791
33: 5 for he dwelleth on **h**: he hath filled Zion H4791
16 He shall dwell on **h**: his place of defence H4791
36: 7 *is it* not he, whose **h** places and whose H1111
37:23 **h**? *even* against the Holy One of Israel. H4791
40: 9 get thee up into the **h** mountain; O H1364
26 Lift up your eyes on **h**, and behold who H4791
41:18 I will open rivers in **h** places, and H8203
49: 9 their pastures *shall be* in all **h** places. H8203
52:13 be exalted and extolled, and be very **h**. H1361
57: 7 Upon a lofty and **h** mountain hast thou H5375
15 For thus saith the **h** and lofty One that H7311
15 I dwell in the **h** and holy *place*, with H4791
58: 4 to make your voice to be heard on **h**. H4791
14 to ride upon the **h** places of the earth, H1116
Jer 2:20 when upon every **h** hill and under H1364
3: 2 Lift up thine eyes unto the **h** places, H8205
6 up upon every **h** mountain and under H1364
21 A voice was heard upon the **h** places, H8205
4:11 A dry wind of the **h** places in the H8205
7:29 up a lamentation on **h** places; for the H8205
31 And they have built the **h** places of H8564
12:12 The spoilers are come upon all **h** places H1116
14: 6 And the wild asses did stand in the **h** H1116
Jer 17: 2 by the green trees upon the **h** hills. H1364
3 to the spoil, *and* thy **h** places for sin, H1116
12 A glorious **h** throne from the beginning H4791
19: 5 They have built also the **h** places of H1116
20: 2 that *were* in the **h** gate of Benjamin, H5945
25:30 shall roar from on **h**, and utter his voice H4791
26:18 of the house as the **h** places of a forest. H1116
31:21 Set thee up waymarks, make thee **h** H8564
32:35 And they built the **h** places of Baal, H1116
48:35 offereth in the **h** places, and him that H1116
49:16 make thy nest as **h** as the eagle, I will H1361
51:58 utterly broken, and her **h** gates shall be H1364
Lam 3:35 of a man before the face of the most **H**, H5945
38 Out of the mouth of the most **H** H5945
Ezk 1:18 As for their rings, they were so **h** that H1363
6: 3 you, and I will destroy your **h** places. H1116
6 laid waste, and the **h** places shall be H1116
13 altars, upon every **h** hill, in all the tops H7311
16:16 and deckedst thy **h** places with divers H1116
24 made thee an **h** place in every street. H7413
25 Thou hast built thy **h** place at every H7413
31 way, and makest thine **h** place in every H7413
39 break down thy **h** places: they shall H7413
17:22 branch of the **h** cedar, and will set *it*; H7311
22 *it* upon an **h** mountain and eminent: H1364
24 brought down the **h** tree, have exalted H1364
20:28 they saw every **h** hill, and all the thick H7311
29 Then I said unto them, What *is* the **h** H1116
21:26 *that is* low, and abase *him that is* **h**. H1364
31: 3 shroud, and of an **h** stature; and his H1362
4 set him up on **h** with her rivers running H7311
34: 6 and upon every **h** hill: yea, my flock H7311
14 and upon the **h** mountains of Israel H4791
36: 2 ancient **h** places are ours in possession: H1116
40: 2 me upon a very **h** mountain, by which H1364
42 and one cubit **h**: whereupon also they H1363
41:22 The altar of wood *was* three cubits **h**, H1364
43: 7 carcases of their kings in their **h** places. H1116
Dan 3:26 of the most **h** God, come forth, and H5943
4: 2 the **h** God hath wrought toward me. H5943
17 that the most **H** ruleth in the kingdom H5943
24 the decree of the most **H**, which is come H5943
25 that the most **H** ruleth in the kingdom H5943
32 that the most **H** ruleth in the kingdom H5943
34 I blessed the most **H**, and I praised and H5943
5:18 O thou king, the most **h** God gave H5943
21 knew that the most **h** God ruled in the H5943
7:18 But the saints of the most **H** shall take H5946
22 saints of the most **H**; and the time came H5946
25 against the most **H**, and shall wear out H5943
25 the saints of the most **H**, and think to H5946
27 saints of the most **H**, whose kingdom *is* H5946
8: 3 *two* horns *were* **h**; but one *was* higher H1364
Hos 7:16 They return, *but* not to the most **H**: they H5920
10: 8 The **h** places also of Aven, the sin of H1116
11: 7 the most **H**, none at all would exalt *him*. H5920
Am 4:13 treadeth upon the **h** places of the earth, H1116
7: 9 And the **h** places of Isaac shall be H1116
Oba 3 habitation *is* **h**; that saith in his heart, H4791
Mic 1: 3 tread upon the **h** places of the earth. H1116
5 and what *are* the **h** places of Judah? *are* H1116
3:12 the house as the **h** places of the forest. H1116
6: 6 myself before the **h** God? shall I come H4791
Hab 2: 9 may set his nest on **h**, that he may be H4791
3:10 his voice, *and* lifted up his hands on **h**. H7315
19 walk upon mine **h** places. To the chief H1116
Zep 1:16 fenced cities, and against the **h** towers. H1364
Hag 1: 1 son of Josedech, the **h** priest, saying, H1419
12 of Josedech, the **h** priest, with all the H1419
14 of Josedech, the **h** priest, and the spirit H1419
2: 2 son of Josedech, the **h** priest, and to the H1419
4 of Josedech, the **h** priest; and be strong, H1419
Zec 3: 1 And he shewed me Joshua the **h** priest H1419
8 Hear now, O Joshua the **h** priest, thou, H1419
6:11 the son of Josedech, the **h** priest; H1419
Mt 4: 8 up into an exceeding **h** mountain, and *G5308*
17: 1 them up into an **h** mountain apart, *G5308*
26: 3 of the **h** priest, who was called Caiaphas, *G749*
51 of the **h** priest's, and smote off his ear. *G749*
57 away to Caiaphas the **h** priest, where the *G749*
58 afar off unto the **h** priest's palace, and *G749*
62 And the **h** priest arose, and said unto *G749*
63 But Jesus held his peace. And the **h** *G749*
65 Then the **h** priest rent his clothes, *G749*
Mk 2:26 of Abiathar the **h** priest, and did eat the *G749*
5: 7 Son of the most **h** God? I adjure thee by *G5310*
6:21 **h** captains, and chief *estates* of Galilee;
9: 2 them up into an **h** mountain apart by *G5308*
14:47 of the **h** priest, and cut off his ear. *G749*

Mk 14:53 And they led Jesus away to the **h** priest: G749
54 into the palace of the **h** priest: and he sat G749
60 And the **h** priest stood up in the midst, G749
61 nothing. Again the **h** priest asked him, G749
63 Then the **h** priest rent his clothes, and G749
66 cometh one of the maids of the **h** priest: G749
Lk 1:78 dayspring from on **h** hath visited us, G5311
3: 2 Annas and Caiaphas being the **h** priests, G749
4: 5 And the devil, taking him up into an **h** G5308
8:28 most **h**? I beseech thee, torment me not. G5310
22:50 of the **h** priest, and cut off his right ear. G749
54 him into the **h** priest's house. And Peter G749
24:49 ye be endued with power from on **h**. G5311
Jn 11:49 being the **h** priest that same year, G749
51 himself: but being **h** priest that year, he G749
18:10 it, and smote the **h** priest's servant, and G749
13 which was the **h** priest that same year. G749
15 known unto the **h** priest, and went in G749
15 with Jesus into the palace of the **h** priest. G749
16 known unto the **h** priest, and spake unto G749
19 The **h** priest then asked Jesus of his G749
22 saying, Answerest thou the **h** priest so? G749
24 him bound unto Caiaphas the **h** priest. G749
26 One of the servants of the **h** priest, being G749
19:31 day was an **h** day,) besought Pilate G3173
Act 4: 6 And Annas the **h** priest, and Caiaphas, G749
6 of the kindred of the **h** priest, were G749
5:17 Then the **h** priest rose up, and all they G749
21 taught. But the **h** priest came, and they G749
24 Now when the **h** priest and the captain G2409
27 the council: and the **h** priest asked them, G749
7: 1 Then said the **h** priest, Are these things G749
48 Howbeit the most **H** dwelleth not in G5310
9: 1 of the Lord, went unto the **h** priest, G749
13:17 an **h** arm brought he them out of it. G5308
16:17 of the most **h** God, which shew unto G5310
22: 5 As also the **h** priest doth bear me G749
23: 2 And the **h** priest Ananias commanded G749
4 by said, Revilest thou God's **h** priest? G749
5 that he was the **h** priest: for it is written, G749
24: 1 And after five days Ananias the **h** priest G749
25: 2 Then the **h** priest and the chief of the G749
Ro 12:16 toward another. Mind not **h** things, but G5308
13:11 time, that now *it is* **h** time to awake out
2Co 10: 5 and every **h** thing that exalteth itself G5313
Eph 4: 8 he ascended up on **h**, he led captivity G5311
6:12 spiritual wickedness in **h** *places*. G2032
Php 3:14 of the **h** calling of God in Christ Jesus. G507
Heb 1: 3 on the right hand of the Majesty on **h**; G5308
2:17 and faithful **h** priest in things *pertaining* G749
3: 1 **H** Priest of our profession, Christ Jesus; G749
4:14 Seeing then that we have a great **h** G749
15 For we have not an **h** priest which G749
5: 1 For every **h** priest taken from among G749
5 to be made an **h** priest; but he that said G749
10 Called of God an **h** priest after the order G749
6:20 Jesus, made an **h** priest for ever after the G749
7: 1 priest of the most **h** God, who met G5310
26 For such an **h** priest became us, *who is* G749
27 Who needeth not daily, as those **h** G749
28 For the law maketh men **h** priests which G749
8: 1 We have such an **h** priest, who is set on G749
3 For every **h** priest is ordained to offer G749
9: 7 But into the second *went* the **h** priest G749
11 But Christ being come an **h** priest of G749
25 often, as the **h** priest entereth into the G749
10:21 And *having* an **h** priest over the house G3173
13:11 the sanctuary by the **h** priest for sin, are G749
Rev 21:10 to a great and **h** mountain, and shewed G5308
12 And had a wall great and **h**, *and* had G5308

HIGHER
Nu 24: 7 his king shall be **h** than Agag, and his H7311
1Sa 9: 2 *he was* **h** than any of the people. H1364
10:23 the people, he was **h** than any of the H1361
2Ki 15:35 the **h** gate of the house of the LORD. H5945
Neh 4:13 wall, *and* on the **h** places, I even set the H6706
Job 35: 5 the clouds *which* are **h** than thou. H1361
Ps 61: 2 lead me to the rock *that* is **h** than I. H7311
89:27 Also I will make him *my* firstborn, **h** H5945
Ecc 5: 8 matter: for *he that is* **h** than the highest H1364
8 regardeth; and *there be* **h** than they. H1364
Isa 55: 9 For *as* the heavens are **h** than the H1361
9 so are my ways **h** than your ways, and H1361
Jer 36:10 the scribe, in the **h** court, at the entry of H5945
Ezk 9: 2 from the way of the **h** gate, which lieth H5945
42: 5 the galleries were **h** than these, than the H398
43:13 this *shall be* the **h** place of the altar. H1354
Dan 8: 3 high; but one *was* **h** than the other, and H1364
Dan 8: 3 than the other, and the **h** came up last. H1364
Lk 14:10 thee, Friend, go up **h**: then shalt thou G511
Ro 13: 1 Let every soul be subject unto the **h** G5242
Heb 7:26 sinners, and made **h** than the heavens; G5308

HIGHEST
Ps 18:13 heavens, and the **H** gave his voice; hail H5945
87: 5 and the **h** himself shall establish her. H5945
Prv 8:26 nor the **h** part of the dust of the world. H7218
9: 3 she crieth upon the **h** places of the city, H4791
Ecc 5: 8 *that is* higher than the **h** regardeth; and H1364
Ezk 17: 3 and took the **h** branch of the cedar: H6788
22 also take of the **h** branch of the high H6788
41: 7 lowest *chamber* to the **h** by the midst. H5945
Mt 21: 9 the name of the Lord; Hosanna in the **h**. G5310
Mk 11:10 the name of the Lord: Hosanna in the **h**. G5310
Lk 1:32 the Son of the **H**: and the Lord God shall G5310
35 the power of the **H** shall overshadow G5310
76 the prophet of the **H**: for thou shalt go G5310
2:14 Glory to God in the **h**, and on earth G5310
6:35 the children of the **H**: for he is kind unto G5310
14: 8 sit not down in the **h** room; lest a more G4411
19:38 peace in heaven, and glory in the **h**. G5310
20:46 the markets, and the **h** seats in the G4410

HIGHLY
Lk 1:28 Hail, *thou that art* **h** favoured, the Lord G5308
16:15 for that which is **h** esteemed among G5308
Act 12:20 And Herod was **h** displeased with them G2371
Ro 12: 3 *of himself* more **h** than he ought to G5252
Php 2: 9 Wherefore God also hath **h** exalted G5251
1Th 5:13 And to esteem them very **h** in G1537+G4053

HIGHMINDED
Ro 11:20 standest by faith. Be not **h**, but fear: G5309
1Ti 6:17 world, that they be not **h**, nor trust in G5309
2Ti 3: 4 Traitors, heady, **h**, lovers of pleasures G5187

HIGHNESS
Job 31:23 by reason of his **h** I could not endure. H7613
Isa 13: 3 anger, *even* them that rejoice in my **h**. H1346

HIGH-PRIEST See HIGH and PRIEST.

HIGHWAY
Jdg 21:19 on the east side of the **h** that goeth up H4546
1Sa 6:12 went along the **h**, lowing as they went, H4546
2Sa 20:12 in the midst of the **h**. And when the H4546
12 Amasa out of the **h** into the field, and H4546
13 When he was removed out of the **h**, all H4546
2Ki 18:17 which *is* in the **h** of the fuller's field. H4546
Prv 16:17 The **h** of the upright *is* to depart from H4546
Isa 7: 3 upper pool in the **h** of the fuller's field; H4546
11:16 And there shall be an **h** for the remnant H4546
19:23 In that day shall there be a **h** out of H4546
35: 8 And an **h** shall be there, and a way, H4547
36: 2 upper pool in the **h** of the fuller's field. H4546
40: 3 straight in the desert a **h** for our God. H4546
62:10 up, cast up the **h**; gather out the stones; H4546
Jer 31:21 heart toward the **h**, *even* the way *which* H4546
Mk 10:46 of Timaeus, sat by the **h** side begging. G3598

HIGHWAYS
Jdg 5: 6 days of Jael, the **h** were unoccupied, and H734
20:31 other times, in the **h**, of which one goeth H4546
32 and draw them from the city unto the **h**. H4546
45 of them in the **h** five thousand men; H4546
Isa 33: 8 The **h** lie waste, the wayfaring man H4546
49:11 a way, and my **h** shall be exalted. H4546
Am 5:16 shall say in all the **h**, Alas! alas! and H2351
Mt 22: 9 Go ye therefore into the **h**, and as many G1327
10 So those servants went out into the **h**, G3598
Lk 14:23 Go out into the **h** and hedges, and G3598

HILEN
1Ch 6:58 And **H** with her suburbs, Debir with H2432

HILKIAH
2Ki 18:18 Eliakim the son of **H**, which *was* over H2518
26 Then said Eliakim the son of **H**, and H2518
37 Then came Eliakim the son of **H**, which H2518
22: 4 Go up to **H** the high priest, that he may H2518
8 And **H** the high priest said unto H2518
8 of the LORD. And **H** gave the book to H2518
10 the king, saying, **H** the priest hath H2518
12 And the king commanded **H** the priest, H2518
14 So **H** the priest, and Ahikam, and H2518
23: 4 And the king commanded **H** the high H2518
24 in the book that **H** the priest found in H2518
1Ch 6:13 And Shallum begat **H**, and Hilkiah H2518
13 And Shallum begat Hilkiah, and **H** H2518
45 the son of Amaziah, the son of **H**, H2518
9:11 And Azariah the son of **H**, the son of H2518
26:11 **H** the second, Tebaliah the third, H2518
2Ch 34: 9 And when they came to **H** the high H2518
14 of the LORD, **H** the priest found a book H2518
15 And **H** answered and said to Shaphan H2518
15 And **H** delivered the book to Shaphan. H2518
18 told the king, saying, **H** the priest hath H2518
20 And the king commanded **H**, and H2518
22 And **H**, and *they* that the king *had* H2518
35: 8 and to the Levites: **H** and Zechariah H2518
Ezr 7: 1 the son of Azariah, the son of **H**, H2518
Neh 8: 4 and Urijah, and **H**, and Maaseiah, on H2518
11:11 Seraiah the son of **H**, the son of H2518
12: 7 Sallu, Amok, **H**, Jedaiah. These *were* the H2518
21 Of **H**, Hashabiah; of Jedaiah, Nethaneel. H2518
Isa 22:20 call my servant Eliakim the son of **H**: H2518
36:22 Then came Eliakim, the son of **H**, that H2518
Jer 1: 1 The words of Jeremiah the son of **H**, of H2518
29: 3 the son of **H**, (whom Zedekiah king H2518

HILKIAH'S
Isa 36: 3 Then came forth unto him Eliakim, **H** H2518

HILL
Ex 17: 9 the **h** with the rod of God in mine hand. H1389
10 and Hur went up to the top of the **h**. H1389
24: 4 an altar under the **h**, and twelve pillars, H2022
Nu 14:44 But they presumed to go up unto the **h** H2022
45 dwelt in that **h**, and smote them, and H2022
Dt 1:41 war, ye were ready to go up into the **h**. H2022
43 and went presumptuously up into the **h**. H2022
Jos 5: 3 of Israel at the **h** of the foreskins. H1389
13: 6 All the inhabitants of the **h** country H2022
15: 9 the top of the **h** unto the fountain of H2022
17:16 And the children of Joseph said, The **h** H2022
18:13 near the **h** that *lieth* on the south H2022
14 from the **h** that *lieth* before Beth-horon H2022
21:11 *is* Hebron, in the **h** *country* of Judah, H2022
24:30 on the north side of the **h** of Gaash. H2022
33 buried him in a **h** *that pertained to* H1389
Jdg 2: 9 on the north side of the **h** Gaash. H2022
7: 1 them, by the **h** of Moreh, in the valley. H1389
16: 3 to the top of an **h** that *is* before Hebron. H2022
1Sa 7: 1 of Abinadab in the **h**, and sanctified H1389
9:11 *And* as they went up the **h** to the city, H4608
10: 5 After that thou shalt come to the **h** of H1389
10 And when they came thither to the **h**, H1389
23:19 the wood, in the **h** of Hachilah, which H1389
25:20 the covert of the **h**, and, behold, David H2022
26: 1 himself in the **h** of Hachilah, *which* H1389
3 And Saul pitched in the **h** of Hachilah, H1389
13 on the top of an **h** afar off; a great H2022
2Sa 2:24 were come to the **h** of Ammah, that H1389
25 one troop, and stood on the top of an **h**. H1389
13:34 by the way of the **h** side behind him. H2022
16: 1 past the top *of the* **h**, behold, Ziba the
21: 9 them in the **h** before the LORD: and H2022
1Ki 11: 7 of Moab, in the **h** that *is* before H2022
14:23 high **h**, and under every green tree. H1389
16:24 And he bought the **h** Samaria of H2022
24 and built on the **h**, and called the name H2022
24 of Shemer, owner of the **h**, Samaria. H2022
2Ki 1: 9 on the top of an **h**. And he spake unto H2022
4:27 man of God to the **h**, she caught him by H2022
17:10 high **h**, and under every green tree: H1389
Ps 2: 6 Yet have I set my king upon my holy **h** H2022
3: 4 he heard me out of his holy **h**. Selah. H2022
15: 1 who shall dwell in thy holy **h**? H2022
24: 3 Who shall ascend into the **h** of the H2022
42: 6 of the Hermonites, from the **h** Mizar. H2022
43: 3 unto thy holy **h**, and to thy tabernacles. H2022
68:15 The **h** of God *is as* the hill of Bashan; H2022
15 The hill of God *is as* the **h** of Bashan; H2022
15 an high **h** *as* the hill of Bashan. H2022
15 an high hill *as* the **h** of Bashan. H2022
16 Why leap ye, ye high hills? *this is* the **h** H2022
99: 9 holy **h**; for the LORD our God *is* holy. H2022
Song 4: 6 of myrrh, and to the **h** of frankincense. H1389
Isa 5: 1 hath a vineyard in a very fruitful **h**: H7161
10:32 daughter of Zion, the **h** of Jerusalem. H1389
30:17 a mountain, and as an ensign on an **h**. H1389
25 upon every high **h**, rivers *and* streams H1389
31: 4 for mount Zion, and for the **h** thereof. H1389
40: 4 mountain and **h** shall be made low: H1389
Jer 2:20 upon every high **h** and under every H1389
16:16 **h**, and out of the holes of the rocks. H1389

Jer 31:39 it upon the **h** Gareb, and shall compass H1389
49:16 holdest the height of the **h**: though thou H1389
50: 6 gone from mountain to **h**, they have H1389
Ezk 6:13 upon every high **h**, in all the tops of the H1389
20:28 saw every high **h**, and all the thick trees, H1389
34: 6 upon every high **h**: yea, my flock was H1389
26 round about my **h** a blessing; and I will H1389
Mt 5:14 A city that is set on an **h** cannot be hid. *G3735*
Lk 1:39 and went into the **h** country with haste, *G3714*
65 throughout all the **h** country of Judaea. *G3714*
3: 5 mountain and **h** shall be brought low; *G1015*
4:29 the brow of the **h** whereon their city *G3735*
9:37 from the **h**, much people met him. *G3735*
Act 17:22 Then Paul stood in the midst of Mars' **h**, *G697*

HILLEL
Jdg 12:13 And after him Abdon the son of **H**, a H1985
15 And Abdon the son of **H** the H1985

HILLS
Gen 7:19 and all the high **h**, that *were* under the H2022
49:26 of the everlasting **h**: they shall be on the H1389
Nu 23: 9 him, and from the **h** I behold him: lo, H1389
Dt 1: 7 in the plain, in the **h**, and in the vale, H2022
8: 7 depths that spring out of valleys and **h**; H2022
9 out of whose **h** thou mayest dig brass. H2042
11:11 it, *is* a land of **h** and valleys, *and* H2022
12: 2 upon the **h**, and under every green tree: H1389
33:15 for the precious things of the lasting **h**, H1389
Jos 9: 1 side Jordan, in the **h**, and in the valleys, H2022
10:40 the country of the **h**, and of the south, H2022
11:16 So Joshua took all that land, the **h**, and H2022
1Ki 20:23 *are* gods of the **h**; therefore they were H2022
28 *is* God of the **h**, but he *is* not God of H2022
22:17 upon the **h**, as sheep that have not H2022
2Ki 16: 4 on the **h**, and under every green tree. H1389
2Ch 28: 4 on the **h**, and under every green tree. H1389
Job 15: 7 born? or wast thou made before the **h**? H1389
Ps 18: 7 also of the **h** moved and were shaken, H2022
50:10 mine, *and* the cattle upon a thousand **h**. H2042
65:12 and the little **h** rejoice on every side. H1389
68:16 Why leap ye, ye high **h**? *this is* the hill H2022
72: 3 and the little **h**, by righteousness. H1389
80:10 The **h** were covered with the shadow of H2022
95: 4 earth: the strength of the **h** *is* his also. H2022
97: 5 The **h** melted like wax at the presence H2022
98: 8 Let the floods clap *their* hands: let the **h** H2022
104:10 into the valleys, *which* run among the **h**. H2022
13 He watereth the **h** from his chambers: H2022
18 The high **h** *are* a refuge for the wild H2022
32 he toucheth the **h**, and they smoke. H2022
114: 4 like rams, *and* the little **h** like lambs. H1389
6 like rams; *and* ye little **h**, like lambs? H1389
121: 1 I will lift up mine eyes unto the **h**, from H2022
148: 9 Mountains, and all **h**; fruitful trees, and H1389
Prv 8:25 before the **h** was I brought forth: H1389
Song 2: 8 the mountains, skipping upon the **h**. H1389
Isa 2: 2 the **h**; and all nations shall flow unto it. H1389
14 and upon all the **h** *that are* lifted up, H1389
5:25 them: and the **h** did tremble, and their H2022
7:25 And *on* all **h** that shall be digged with H2022
40:12 in scales, and the **h** in a balance? H1389
41:15 small, and shalt make the **h** as chaff. H1389
42:15 I will make waste mountains and **h**, H1389
54:10 depart, and the **h** be removed; but my H1389
55:12 and the **h** shall break forth before H1389
65: 7 me upon the **h**: therefore will I measure H1389
Jer 3:23 *for* from the **h**, *and from* the multitude H1389
4:24 trembled, and all the **h** moved lightly. H1389
13:27 on the **h** in the fields. Woe unto H1389
17: 2 by the green trees upon the high **h**. H1389
Ezk 6: 3 and to the **h**, to the rivers, and to H1389
35: 8 slain *men*: in thy **h**, and in thy valleys, H1389
36: 4 and to the **h**, to the rivers, and to H1389
6 and to the **h**, to the rivers, and to H1389
Hos 4:13 incense upon the **h**, under oaks and H1389
10: 8 Cover us; and to the **h**, Fall on us. H1389
Joel 3:18 new wine, and the **h** shall flow with H1389
Am 9:13 sweet wine, and all the **h** shall melt. H1389
Mic 4: 1 the **h**; and people shall flow unto it. H1389
6: 1 and let the **h** hear thy voice. H1389
Nah 1: 5 at him, and the **h** melt, and the earth H1389
Hab 3: 6 **h** did bow: his ways *are* everlasting. H1389
Zep 1:10 and a great crashing from the **h**. H1389
Lk 23:30 Fall on us; and to the **h**, Cover us. *G1015*

HILL'S
2Sa 16:13 went along on the **h** side over against H2022

HILL-TOP See HILL and TOP.

HIM See the Appendix.

HIMSELF See the Appendix.

HIMTHAT
Mk 13:15 And let **h** is on the housetop not go *G3588*

HIN
Ex 29:40 fourth part of an **h** of beaten oil; and H1969
40 of an **h** of wine *for* a drink offering. H1969
30:24 of the sanctuary, and of oil olive an **h**: H1969
Lev 19:36 ephah, and a just **h**, shall ye have: I *am* H1969
23:13 *shall be* of wine, the fourth *part* of an **h**. H1969
Nu 15: 4 with the fourth *part* of an **h** of oil. H1969
5 And the fourth *part* of an **h** of wine for H1969
6 with the third *part* of an **h** of oil. H1969
7 third *part* of an **h** of wine, *for* a sweet H1969
9 of flour mingled with half an **h** of oil. H1969
10 drink offering half an **h** of wine, *for* an H1969
28: 5 the fourth *part* of an **h** of beaten oil. H1969
7 fourth *part* of an **h** for the one lamb: in H1969
14 shall be half an **h** of wine unto a H1969
14 the third *part* of an **h** unto a ram, and a H1969
14 a fourth *part* of an **h** unto a lamb: this H1969
Ezk 4:11 **h**: from time to time shalt thou drink. H1969
45:24 for a ram, and an **h** of oil for an ephah. H1969
46: 5 to give, and an **h** of oil to an ephah. H1969
7 unto, and an **h** of oil to an ephah. H1969
11 to give, and an **h** of oil to an ephah. H1969
14 third part of an **h** of oil, to temper with H1969

HIND
Gen 49:21 Naphtali *is* a **h** let loose: he giveth goodly H355
Prv 5:19 *Let her be as* the loving **h** and pleasant H365
Jer 14: 5 Yea, the **h** also calved in the field, and H365

HINDER
Gen 24:56 And he said unto them, **H** me not, seeing H309
Nu 22:16 thee, **h** thee from coming unto me: H4513
2Sa 2:23 Abner with the **h** end of the spear smote H310
1Ki 7:25 them, and all their **h** parts *were* inward. H268
2Ch 4: 4 them, and all their **h** parts *were* inward. H268
Neh 4: 8 against Jerusalem, and to **h** it. H6213+H8442
Job 9:12 Behold, he taketh away, who can **h** H7725
11:10 gather together, then who can **h** him? H7725
Ps 78:66 And he smote his enemies in the **h** parts: H268
Joel 2:20 the east sea, and his **h** part toward the H5490
Zec 14: 8 of them toward the **h** sea: in summer H314
Mk 4:38 And he was in the **h** part of the ship, *G4403*
Act 8:36 water; what doth **h** me to be baptized? *G2967*
27:41 but the **h** part was broken with *G4403*
1Co 9:12 lest we should **h** the gospel of Christ. *G1464*
Gal 5: 7 Ye did run well; who did **h** you that ye *G348*

HINDERED
Ezr 6: 8 given unto these men, that they be not **h**. H989
Lk 11:52 and them that were entering in ye **h**. *G2967*
Ro 15:22 have been much **h** from coming to you. *G1465*
1Th 2:18 I Paul, once and again; but Satan **h** us. *G1465*
1Pt 3: 7 grace of life; that your prayers be not **h**. *G1581*

HINDERETH
Isa 14: 6 in anger, is persecuted, *and* none **h**. H2820

HINDERMOST
Gen 33: 2 children after, and Rachel and Joseph **h**. H314
Jer 50:12 behold, the **h** of the nations *shall be* H319

HINDMOST
Nu 2:31 They shall go **h** with their standards. H314
Dt 25:18 and smote the **h** of thee, *even* all *that* H2179
Jos 10:19 and smite the **h** of them; suffer them H2179

HINDS
Job 39: 1 *or* canst thou mark when the **h** do calve? H355
Ps 29: 9 The voice of the LORD maketh the **h** to H355
Song 2: 7 roes, and by the **h** of the field, that ye stir H355
3: 5 roes, and by the **h** of the field, that ye stir H355

HINDS'
2Sa 22:34 He maketh my feet like **h** *feet*: and H355
Ps 18:33 He maketh my feet like **h** *feet*, and H355
Hab 3:19 will make my feet like **h** *feet*, and he will H355

HINGES
1Ki 7:50 *of* pure gold; and the **h** *of* gold, *both* for H6596
Prv 26:14 *As* the door turneth upon his **h**, so *doth* H6735

HINNOM
Jos 15: 8 of the son of **H** unto the south side H2011
8 the valley of **H** westward, which *is* H2011
18:16 of the son of **H**, *and* which *is* in the H2011
16 to the valley of **H**, to the side of Jebusi H2011
2Ki 23:10 of the children of **H**, that no man might H2011
2Ch 28: 3 of the son of **H**, and burnt his children H2011
33: 6 of the son of **H**: also he observed times, H2011
Neh 11:30 from Beer-sheba unto the valley of **H**. H2011
Jer 7:31 of the son of **H**, to burn their sons and H2011
32 valley of the son of **H**, but the valley of H2011
19: 2 of the son of **H**, which *is* by the entry H2011
6 son of **H**, but The valley of slaughter. H2011
32:35 of the son of **H**, to cause their sons H2011

HIP
Jdg 15: 8 And he smote them **h** and thigh with a H7785

HIRAH
Gen 38: 1 certain Adullamite, whose name *was* **H**. H2437
12 he and his friend **H** the Adullamite. H2437

HIRAM
2Sa 5:11 And **H** king of Tyre sent messengers to H2438
1Ki 5: 1 And **H** king of Tyre sent his servants H2438
1 father: for **H** was ever a lover of David. H2438
2 And Solomon sent to **H**, saying, H2438
7 And it came to pass, when **H** heard the H2438
8 And **H** sent to Solomon, saying, I have H2438
10 So **H** gave Solomon cedar trees and fir H2438
11 And Solomon gave **H** twenty thousand H2438
11 thus gave Solomon to **H** year by year. H2438
12 peace between **H** and Solomon; and H2438
7:13 And king Solomon sent and fetched **H** H2438
40 And **H** made the lavers, and the H2438
40 the basons. So **H** made an end of doing H2438
45 these vessels, which **H** made to king H2438
9:11 (*Now* **H** the king of Tyre had furnished H2438
11 **H** twenty cities in the land of Galilee. H2438
12 And **H** came out from Tyre to see the H2438
14 And **H** sent to the king sixscore talents H2438
27 And **H** sent in the navy his servants, H2438
10:11 And the navy also of **H**, that brought H2438
22 with the navy of **H**: once in three years H2438
1Ch 14: 1 Now **H** king of Tyre sent messengers to H2438

HIRAM'S
1Ki 5:18 And Solomon's builders and **H** builders H2438

HIRE
Gen 30:18 hath given me my **h**, because I have H7939
32 the goats: and *of such* shall be my **h**. H7939
33 it shall come for my **h** before thy face: H7939
31: 8 **h**; then bare all the cattle ringstraked. H7939
Ex 22:15 if it *be* an hired *thing*, it came for his **h**. H7939
Dt 23:18 Thou shalt not bring the **h** of a whore, or H868
24:15 At his day thou shalt give *him* his **h**, H7939
1Ki 5: 6 unto thee will I give **h** for thy servants H7939
1Ch 19: 6 talents of silver to **h** them chariots and H7936
Isa 23:17 she shall turn to her **h**, and shall commit H868
18 And her merchandise and her **h** shall be H868
46: 6 the balance, *and* **h** a goldsmith; and he H7936
Ezk 16:31 as an harlot, in that thou scornest **h**; H868
41 and thou also shalt give no **h** any more. H868
Mic 1: 7 she gathered *it* of the **h** of an harlot, and H868
7 they shall return to the **h** of an harlot. H868
3:11 thereof teach for **h**, and the prophets H4242
Zec 8:10 For before these days there was no **h** H7939
10 for man, nor any **h** for beast; neither H7939
Mt 20: 1 to **h** labourers into his vineyard. *G3409*
8 **h**, beginning from the last unto the first. *G3408*
Lk 10: 7 of his **h**. Go not from house to house. *G3408*
Jas 5: 4 Behold, the **h** of the labourers who *G3408*

HIRED
Gen 30:16 for surely I have **h** thee with my son's H7936
Ex 12:45 A foreigner and an **h** servant shall not H7916
22:15 if it *be* an **h** *thing*, it came for his hire. H7916
Lev 19:13 of him that is **h** shall not abide with H7916
22:10 of the priest, or an **h** servant, shall not H7916
25: 6 maid, and for thy **h** servant, and for H7916
40 *But* as an **h** servant, *and* as a H7916
50 of an **h** servant shall it be with him. H7916
53 *And* as a yearly **h** servant shall he be H7916
Dt 15:18 worth a double **h** servant *to thee*, in H7916
23: 4 Egypt; and because they **h** against thee H7936
24:14 Thou shalt not oppress an **h** servant H7916
Jdg 9: 4 Abimelech **h** vain and light persons, H7936
18: 4 me, and hath **h** me, and I am his priest. H7936

1Sa 2: 5 *They that were* full have **h** out H7936
2Sa 10: 6 of Ammon sent and **h** the Syrians of H7936
2Ki 7: 6 the king of Israel hath **h** against us the H7936
1Ch 19: 7 So they **h** thirty and two thousand H7936
2Ch 24:12 house of the LORD, and **h** masons and H7936
25: 6 He **h** also an hundred thousand mighty H7936
Ezr 4: 5 And **h** counsellors against them, to H7936
Neh 6:12 for Tobiah and Sanballat had **h** him. H7936
13 Therefore *was* he **h**, that I should be H7936
13: 2 and with water, but **h** Balaam against H7936
Isa 7:20 with a razor that is **h**, *namely*, by them H7917
Jer 46:21 Also her **h** men *are* in the midst of her H7916
Hos 8: 9 by himself: Ephraim hath **h** lovers. H8566
10 Yea, though they have **h** among the H8566
Mt 20: 7 no man hath **h** us. He saith unto them, *G3409*
9 And when they came that *were* **h** about
Mk 1:20 the **h** servants, and went after him. *G3411*
Lk 15:17 he said, How many **h** servants of my *G3407*
19 son: make me as one of thy **h** servants. *G3407*
Act 28:30 years in his own **h** house, and received *G3410*

HIRELING
Job 7: 1 *not* his days also like the days of an **h**? H7916
2 **h** looketh for *the reward of* his work: H7916
14: 6 he shall accomplish, as an **h**, his day. H7916
Isa 16:14 as the years of an **h**, and the glory of H7916
21:16 **h**, and all the glory of Kedar shall fail: H7916
Mal 3: 5 that oppress the **h** in *his* wages, the H7916
Jn 10:12 But he that is an **h**, and not the *G3411*
13 The **h** fleeth, because he is an hireling, *G3411*
13 The hireling fleeth, because he is an **h**, *G3411*

HIRES
Mic 1: 7 to pieces, and all the **h** thereof shall be H868

HIREST
Ezk 16:33 to all thy lovers, and **h** them, that they H7809

HIS See the Appendix.

HISS
1Ki 9: 8 and shall **h**; and they shall say, Why H8319
Job 27:23 him, and shall **h** him out of his place. H8319
Isa 5:26 from far, and will **h** unto them from the H8319
7:18 the LORD shall **h** for the fly that *is* in H8319
Jer 19: 8 **h** because of all the plagues thereof. H8319
49:17 and shall **h** at all the plagues thereof. H8319
50:13 be astonished, and **h** at all her plagues. H8319
Lam 2:15 at thee; they **h** and wag their head H8319
16 against thee: they **h** and gnash the H8319
Ezk 27:36 the people shall **h** at thee; thou shalt be H8319
Zep 2:15 by her shall **h**, *and* wag his hand. H8319
Zec 10: 8 I will **h** for them, and gather them; for I H8319

HISSING
2Ch 29: 8 and to **h**, as ye see with your eyes. H8322
Jer 18:16 *and* a perpetual **h**; every one that H8322
19: 8 city desolate, and an **h**; every one that H8322
25: 9 and an **h**, and perpetual desolations. H8322
18 an **h**, and a curse; as *it is* this day; H8322
29:18 and an **h**, and a reproach, among H8322
51:37 and an **h**, without an inhabitant. H8322
Mic 6:16 thereof an **h**: therefore ye shall bear H8322

HIT
1Sa 31: 3 and the archers **h** him; and he was sore H4672
1Ch 10: 3 and the archers **h** him, and he was H4672

HITHER
Gen 15:16 they shall come **h** again: for the H2008
42:15 except your youngest brother come **h**. H2008
45: 5 that ye sold me **h**: for God did send me H2008
8 So now *it was* not you *that* sent me **h**, H2008
13 shall haste and bring down my father **h**. H2008
Ex 3: 5 And he said, Draw not nigh **h**: put off H1988
Jos 2: 2 came men in **h** to night of the children H2008
3: 9 of Israel, Come **h**, and hear the words H5066
18: 6 *the description* **h** to me, that I may cast H2008
Jdg 16: 2 Samson is come **h**. And they compassed H2008
18: 3 Who brought thee **h**? and what makest H1988
19:12 will not turn aside **h** into the city of a H2008
Ru 2:14 come thou **h**, and eat of the bread, H1988
1Sa 13: 9 And Saul said, Bring **h** a burnt offering H5066
14:18 And Saul said unto Ahiah, Bring **h** the H5066
34 them, Bring me **h** every man his ox, H5066
36 priest, Let us draw near **h** unto God. H1988
38 And Saul said, Draw ye near **h**, all the H1988
15:32 Then said Samuel, Bring ye **h** to me H5066
16:11 for we will not sit down till he come **h**. H6311
17:28 camest thou down **h**? and with whom
23: 9 Abiathar the priest, Bring **h** the ephod. H5066
30: 7 pray thee, bring me **h** the ephod. And H5066
2Sa 1:10 have brought them **h** unto my lord. H2008
5: 6 shalt not come in **h**: thinking, David H2008
6 thinking, David cannot come in **h**. H2008
14:32 saying, Come **h**, that I may send thee H2008
20:16 **h**, that I may speak with thee. H5704+H2008
1Ki 22: 9 said, Hasten ***h*** Micaiah the son of Imlah.
2Ki 2: 8 they were divided **h** and thither, so that H2008
14 **h** and thither: and Elisha went over. H2008
8: 7 The man of God is come **h**. H5704+H2008
1Ch 11: 5 shalt not come **h**. Nevertheless David H2008
2Ch 28:13 in the captives **h**: for whereas we have
Ezr 4: 2 king of Assur, which brought us up **h**. H6311
Ps 73:10 Therefore his people return **h**: and H1988
81: 2 Take a psalm, and bring **h** the timbrel,
Prv 9: 4 Whoso *is* simple, let him turn in **h**: *as* H2008
16 Whoso *is* simple, let him turn in **h**: and H2008
25: 7 unto thee, Come up **h**; than that thou H2008
Isa 57: 3 But draw near **h**, ye sons of the H2008
Ezk 40: 4 *art* thou brought **h**: declare all that thou H2008
Dan 3:26 come forth, and come ***h***. Then Shadrach,
Mt 8:29 come **h** to torment us before the time? *G5602*
14:18 He said, Bring them **h** to me. *G5602*
17:17 shall I suffer you? bring him **h** to me. *G5602*
22:12 camest thou in **h** not having a wedding *G5602*
Mk 11: 3 and straightway he will send him **h**. *G5602*
Lk 9:41 you, and suffer you? Bring thy son **h**. *G5602*
14:21 city, and bring in **h** the poor, and the *G5602*
15:23 And bring **h** the fatted calf, and kill *it*; *G5342*
19:27 them, bring **h**, and slay *them* before me. *G5602*
30 man sat: loose him, and bring *him* **h**.
Jn 4:15 I thirst not, neither come **h** to draw. *G1759*
16 her, Go, call thy husband, and come **h**. *G1759*
6:25 unto him, Rabbi, when camest thou **h**? *G5602*
20:27 Then saith he to Thomas, Reach **h** thy *G5342*
27 my hands; and reach **h** thy hand, and *G5342*
Act 9:21 and came **h** for that intent, that *G5602*
10:32 Send therefore to Joppa, and call **h** *G3333*
17: 6 world upside down are come **h** also; *G1759*
19:37 For ye have brought **h** these men, which
25:17 Therefore, when they were come **h**, *G1759*
Rev 4: 1 said, Come up **h**, and I will shew thee *G5602*
11:12 them, Come up **h**. And they ascended *G5602*
17: 1 unto me, Come **h**; I will shew unto thee *G1204*
21: 9 me, saying, Come **h**, I will shew thee the *G1204*

HITHERTO
Ex 7:16 **h** thou wouldest not hear. H5704+H3541
Jos 17:14 the LORD hath blessed me **h**? H5704+H3541
Jdg 16:13 said unto Samson, **H** thou hast H5704+H2008
1Sa 1:16 and grief have I spoken **h**. H5704+H2008
7:12 **H** hath the LORD helped us. H5704+H2008
2Sa 7:18 that thou hast brought me **h**? H5704+H1988
15:34 father's servant **h**, so *will* I now also *be* H227
1Ch 9:18 Who **h** *waited* in the king's H5704+H2008
12:29 thousand: for **h** the greatest H5704+H2008
17:16 that thou hast brought me **h**? H5704+H1988
Job 38:11 And said, **H** shalt thou come, H5704+H6311
Ps 71:17 youth: and **h** have I declared H5704+H2008
Isa 18: 2 their beginning **h**; a nation meted out H1973
7 their beginning **h**; a nation meted out H1973
Dan 7:28 **H** *is* the end of the matter. As H5705+H3542
Jn 5:17 Father worketh **h**, and I work. *G2193+G737*
16:24 **H** have ye asked nothing in my *G2193+G737*
Ro 1:13 (but was let **h**,) that I might have *G891+G1204*
1Co 3: 2 not with meat: for **h** ye were not able *to* *G3768*

HITTITE
Gen 23:10 and Ephron the **H** answered Abraham H2850
25: 9 of Zohar the **H**, which *is* before Mamre; H2850
26:34 of Beeri the **H**, and Bashemath the H2850
34 Bashemath the daughter of Elon the **H**: H2850
36: 2 of Elon the **H**, and Aholibamah the H2850
49:29 cave that *is* in the field of Ephron the **H**, H2850
30 **H** for a possession of a buryingplace. H2850
50:13 of Ephron the **H**, before Mamre. H2850
Ex 23:28 Canaanite, and the **H**, from before thee. H2850
33: 2 Amorite, and the **H**, and the Perizzite, H2850
34:11 and the **H**, and the Perizzite, and H2850
Jos 9: 1 Lebanon, the **H**, and the Amorite, the H2850
11: 3 Amorite, and the **H**, and the Perizzite, H2850
1Sa 26: 6 to Ahimelech the **H**, and to Abishai the H2850
2Sa 11: 3 of Eliam, the wife of Uriah the **H**? H2850
6 the **H**. And Joab sent Uriah to David. H2850
17 of David; and Uriah the **H** died also. H2850
21 Thy servant Uriah the **H** is dead also. H2850
24 thy servant Uriah the **H** is dead also. H2850
2Sa 12: 9 killed Uriah the **H** with the sword, and H2850
10 the wife of Uriah the **H** to be thy wife. H2850
23:39 Uriah the **H**: thirty and seven in all. H2850
1Ki 15: 5 save only in the matter of Uriah the **H**. H2850
1Ch 11:41 Uriah the **H**, Zabad the son of Ahlai, H2850
Ezk 16: 3 *was* an Amorite, and thy mother an **H**. H2850
45 *was* an **H**, and your father an Amorite. H2850

HITTITES
Gen 15:20 And the **H**, and the Perizzites, and the H2850
Ex 3: 8 and the **H**, and the Amorites, and H2850
17 and the **H**, and the Amorites, and H2850
13: 5 and the **H**, and the Amorites, and H2850
23:23 Amorites, and the **H**, and the Perizzites, H2850
Nu 13:29 the south: and the **H**, and the Jebusites, H2850
Dt 7: 1 before thee, the **H**, and the Girgashites, H2850
20:17 them; *namely*, the **H**, and the Amorites, H2850
Jos 1: 4 all the land of the **H**, and unto the great H2850
3:10 and the **H**, and the Hivites, and H2850
12: 8 south country; the **H**, the Amorites, and H2850
24:11 and the **H**, and the Girgashites, H2850
Jdg 1:26 the land of the **H**, and built a city, and H2850
3: 5 the Canaanites, **H**, and Amorites, and H2850
1Ki 9:20 of the Amorites, **H**, Perizzites, Hivites, H2850
10:29 all the kings of the **H**, and for the kings H2850
11: 1 Edomites, Zidonians, *and* **H**; H2850
2Ki 7: 6 us the kings of the **H**, and the kings of H2850
2Ch 1:17 all the kings of the **H**, and for the kings H2850
8: 7 *were* left of the **H**, and the Amorites, H2850
Ezr 9: 1 Canaanites, the **H**, the Perizzites, the H2850
Neh 9: 8 Canaanites, the **H**, the Amorites, and H2850

HIVITE
Gen 10:17 And the **H**, and the Arkite, and the H2340
34: 2 the son of Hamor the **H**, prince of the H2340
36: 2 of Anah the daughter of Zibeon the **H**; H2340
Ex 23:28 shall drive out the **H**, the Canaanite, H2340
33: 2 the Perizzite, the **H**, and the Jebusite: H2340
34:11 Perizzite, and the **H**, and the Jebusite. H2340
Jos 9: 1 the **H**, and the Jebusite, heard *thereof*; H2340
11: 3 and *to* the **H** under Hermon in the H2340
1Ch 1:15 And the **H**, and the Arkite, and the H2340

HIVITES
Ex 3: 8 Perizzites, and the **H**, and the Jebusites. H2340
17 and the **H**, and the Jebusites, unto H2340
13: 5 Amorites, and the **H**, and the Jebusites, H2340
23:23 Canaanites, the **H**, and the Jebusites: H2340
Dt 7: 1 and the **H**, and the Jebusites, seven H2340
20:17 the Perizzites, the **H**, and the Jebusites; H2340
Jos 3:10 Hittites, and the **H**, and the Perizzites, H2340
9: 7 And the men of Israel said unto the **H**, H2340
11:19 of Israel, save the **H** the inhabitants of H2340
12: 8 the Perizzites, the **H**, and the Jebusites: H2340
24:11 Girgashites, the **H**, and the Jebusites; H2340
Jdg 3: 3 and the **H** that dwelt in mount H2340
5 and Perizzites, and **H**, and Jebusites: H2340
2Sa 24: 7 to all the cities of the **H**, and of the H2340
1Ki 9:20 Perizzites, **H**, and Jebusites, which H2340
2Ch 8: 7 and the **H**, and the Jebusites, which H2340

HIZKIAH
Zep 1: 1 the son of **H**, in the days of Josiah H2396

HIZKIJAH
Neh 10:17 Ater, **H**, Azzur, H2396

HO
Ru 4: 1 unto whom he said, **H**, such a one! turn H1945
Isa 55: 1 **H**, every one that thirsteth, come ye to H1945
Zec 2: 6 **H**, ho, *come forth*, and flee from the H1945
6 Ho, **h**, *come forth*, and flee from the H1945

HOAR
Ex 16:14 *as* small as the **h** frost on the ground. H3713
1Ki 2: 6 **h** head go down to the grave in peace. H7872
9 do unto him; but his **h** head bring thou H7872
Isa 46: 4 he; and *even* to **h** hairs will I carry *you*: H7872

HOARFROST
Ps 147:16 like wool: he scattereth the **h** like ashes. H3713

HOARY
Lev 19:32 Thou shalt rise up before the **h** head, H7872
Job 38:29 the ice? and the **h** frost of heaven, who H3713
41:32 him; *one* would think the deep *to be* **h**. H7872
Prv 16:31 The **h** head *is* a crown of glory, *if* it be H7872

HOBAB

Nu 10:29 And Moses said unto **H**, the son of H2246
Jdg 4:11 of the children of **H** the father in law of H2246

HOBAH

Gen 14:15 them unto **H**, which *is* on the left H2327

HOD

1Ch 7:37 Bezer, and **H**, and Shamma, and H1936

HODAIAH

1Ch 3:24 And the sons of Elioenai *were*, **H**, and H1939

HODAVIAH

1Ch 5:24 Jeremiah, and **H**, and Jahdiel, mighty H1938
9: 7 the son of **H**, the son of Hasenuah, H1938
Ezr 2:40 of the children of **H**, seventy and four. H1938

HODESH

1Ch 8: 9 And he begat of **H** his wife, Jobab, and H2321

HODEVAH

Neh 7:43 of the children of **H**, seventy and four. H1937

HODIAH

1Ch 4:19 And the sons of *his* wife **H** the sister of H1940

HODIJAH

Neh 8: 7 Shabbethai, **H**, Maaseiah, Kelita, H1941
9: 5 Sherebiah, **H**, Shebaniah, *and* H1941
10:10 And their brethren, Shebaniah, **H**, H1941
13 **H**, Bani, Beninu. H1941
18 **H**, Hashum, Bezai, H1941

HOGLAH

Nu 26:33 and Noah, **H**, Milcah, and Tirzah. H2295
27: 1 Noah, and **H**, and Milcah, and Tirzah. H2295
36:11 For Mahlah, Tirzah, and **H**, and H2295
Jos 17: 3 and Noah, **H**, Milcah, and Tirzah. H2295

HOHAM

Jos 10: 3 sent unto **H** king of Hebron, and H1944

HOISED

Act 27:40 bands, and **h** up the mainsail to the *G1869*

HOLD

Gen 19:16 And while he lingered, the men laid **h** H2388
21:18 Arise, lift up the lad, and **h** him in thine H2388
25:26 and his hand took **h** on Esau's heel; and H270
Ex 5: 1 may **h** a feast unto me in the wilderness.
9: 2 to let *them* go, and wilt **h** them still, H2388
10: 9 go; for we *must* **h** a feast unto the LORD.
14:14 fight for you, and ye shall **h** your peace. H2790
15:14 take **h** on the inhabitants of Palestina. H270
15 trembling shall take **h** upon them; all the H270
20: 7 the LORD will not **h** him guiltless that
26: 5 the loops may take **h** one of another. H6901
Nu 30: 4 her father shall **h** his peace at her: then H2790
14 But if her husband altogether **h** his H2790
Dt 5:11 the LORD will not **h** *him* guiltless that
21:19 his mother lay **h** on him, and bring him H8610
22:28 not betrothed, and lay **h** on her, and lie H8610
32:41 mine hand take **h** on judgment; I will H270
Jdg 9:46 into an **h** of the house of the god Berith. H6877
49 put *them* to the **h**, and set the hold on H6877
49 hold, and set the **h** on fire upon them; H6877
16:29 And Samson took **h** of the two middle H3943
18:19 And they said unto him, **H** thy peace, H2790
19:29 a knife, and laid **h** on his concubine, H2388
Ru 3:15 upon thee, and **h** it. And when she held H270
1Sa 15:27 go away, he laid **h** upon the skirt of his H2388
22: 4 all the while that David was in the **h**. H4686
5 Abide not in the **h**; depart, and get thee H4686
24:22 and his men gat them up unto the **h**. H4686
2Sa 1:11 Then David took **h** on his clothes, and H2388
2:21 left, and lay thee **h** on one of the young H270
22 I **h** up my face to Joab thy brother? H5375
4:10 tidings, I took **h** of him, and slew him H270
5: 7 Nevertheless David took the strong **h** of H4686
17 heard *of it*, and went down to the **h**. H4686
6: 6 and took **h** of it; for the oxen shook *it*. H270
13:11 to eat, he took **h** of her, and said unto H2388
20 with thee? but **h** now thy peace, my H2790
18: 9 his head caught **h** of the oak, and he H2388
23:14 And David *was* then in an **h**, and the H4686
24: 7 And came to the strong **h** of Tyre, and H4013
1Ki 1:50 and caught **h** on the horns of the altar. H2388
51 lo, he hath caught **h** on the horns of the H270
2: 9 Now therefore **h** him not guiltless: for
28 and caught **h** on the horns of the altar. H2388
9: 9 and have taken **h** upon other gods, and H2388
13: 4 the altar, saying, Lay **h** on him. And his H8610
2Ki 2: 3 he said, Yea, I know *it*; **h** ye your peace. H2814
5 Yea, I know *it*; **h** ye your peace. H2814
12 more: and he took **h** of his own clothes, H2388
6:32 shut the door, and **h** him fast at the H3905
7: 9 tidings, and we **h** our peace: if we tarry H2814
1Ch 11:16 And David *was* then in the **h**, and the H4686
12: 8 David into the **h** to the wilderness men H4679
16 and Judah to the **h** unto David. H4679
13: 9 hand to **h** the ark; for the oxen stumbled. H270
2Ch 7:22 of Egypt, and laid **h** on other gods, and H2388
Neh 8:11 people, saying, **H** your peace, for the H2013
Est 4:11 the king shall **h** out the golden sceptre, H3447
Job 6:24 Teach me, and I will **h** my tongue: and H2790
8:15 shall **h** it fast, but it shall not endure. H2388
9:28 I know that thou wilt not **h** me innocent.
11: 3 Should thy lies make men **h** their H2790
13: 5 O that ye would altogether **h** your H2790
13 **H** your peace, let me alone, that I may H2790
19 I **h** my tongue, I shall give up the ghost. H2790
17: 9 The righteous also shall **h** on his way, H270
21: 6 and trembling taketh **h** on my flesh. H270
27: 6 My righteousness I **h** fast, and will not H2388
20 Terrors take **h** on him as waters, a H5381
30:16 days of affliction have taken **h** upon me. H270
33:31 Mark well, O Job, hearken unto me: **h** H2790
33 If not, hearken unto me: **h** thy peace, H2790
36:17 judgment and justice take **h** *on thee*. H8551
38:13 That it might take **h** of the ends of the H270
41:26 at him cannot **h**: the spear, the dart, H6965
Ps 17: 5 **H** up my goings in thy paths, *that* my H8557
35: 2 Take **h** of shield and buckler, and H2388
39:12 ear unto my cry; **h** not thy peace at my H2790
40:12 have taken **h** upon me, so that I am H5381
48: 6 Fear took **h** upon them there, *and* pain, H270
69:24 let thy wrathful anger take **h** of them. H5381
83: 1 Keep not thou silence, O God: **h** not thy H2790
109: 1 **H** not thy peace, O God of my praise; H2790
116: 3 the pains of hell gat **h** upon me: I found H4672
119:53 Horror hath taken **h** upon me because of H270
117 **H** thou me up, and I shall be safe: and I H5582
143 Trouble and anguish have taken **h** on H4672
139:10 lead me, and thy right hand shall **h** me. H270
Prv 2:19 neither take they **h** of the paths of life. H5381
3:18 She *is* a tree of life to them that lay **h** H2388
4:13 Take fast **h** of instruction; let *her* not H2388
5: 5 down to death; her steps take **h** on hell. H8551
30:28 The spider taketh **h** with her hands, H8610
31:19 spindle, and her hands **h** the distaff. H8551
Ecc 2: 3 wisdom; and to lay **h** on folly, till I might H270
7:18 *It is* good that thou shouldest take **h** of H270
Song 3: 8 They all **h** swords, *being* expert in war: H270
7: 8 tree, I will take **h** of the boughs thereof: H270
Isa 3: 6 When a man shall take **h** of his brother H8610
4: 1 seven women shall take **h** of one man, H2388
5:29 shall roar, and lay **h** of the prey, and H270
13: 8 sorrows shall take **h** of them; they shall H270
21: 3 pangs have taken **h** upon me, as the H270
27: 5 Or let him take **h** of my strength, *that* H2388
31: 9 And he shall pass over to his strong **h** H5553
41:13 For I the LORD thy God will **h** thy right H2388
42: 6 and will **h** thine hand, and will H2388
56: 2 of man *that* layeth **h** on it; that keepeth H2388
4 please me, and take **h** of my covenant; H2388
6 it, and taketh **h** of my covenant; H2388
62: 1 For Zion's sake will I not **h** my peace, H2814
6 *which* shall never **h** their peace day nor H2814
64: 7 up himself to take **h** of thee: for thou H2388
12 **h** thy peace, and afflict us very sore? H2814
Jer 2:13 broken cisterns, that can **h** no water. H3557
4:19 in me; I cannot **h** my peace, because H2790
6:23 They shall lay **h** on bow and spear; they H2388
24 hath taken **h** of us, *and* pain, as of H2388
8: 5 they **h** fast deceit, they refuse to return. H2388
21 astonishment hath taken **h** on me. H2388
50:42 They shall **h** the bow and the lance: H2388
43 anguish took **h** of him, *and* pangs as H2388
Ezk 29: 7 When they took **h** of thee by thy hand, H8610
30:21 it, to make it strong to **h** the sword. H8610
41: 6 they might have **h**, but they had not hold H270
6 they had not **h** in the wall of the house. H270
Am 6:10 Then shall he say, **H** thy tongue: for we H2013
Mic 4: 8 flock, the strong **h** of the daughter of H6076
6:14 thou shalt take **h**, but shalt not deliver; H5253
Nah 1: 7 The LORD *is* good, a strong **h** in the H4581
Hab 1:10 **h**; for they shall heap dust, and take it. H4013
Zep 1: 7 **H** thy peace at the presence of the Lord H4581
Zec 1: 6 did they not take **h** of your fathers? and H5381
8:23 that ten men shall take **h** out of all H2388
23 even shall take **h** of the skirt of him H2388
9: 3 And Tyrus did build herself a strong **h**, H4692
12 Turn you to the strong **h**, ye prisoners H1225
11: 5 Whose possessors slay them, and **h**
14:13 and they shall lay **h** every one on the H2388
Mt 6:24 or else he will **h** to the one, and despise *G472*
12:11 will he not lay **h** on it, and lift *it* out? *G2902*
14: 3 For Herod had laid **h** on John, and *G2902*
20:31 they should **h** their peace: but they *G4623*
21:26 the people; for all **h** John as a prophet. *G2192*
26:48 I shall kiss, that same is he: **h** him fast. *G2902*
55 in the temple, and ye laid no **h** on me. *G2902*
57 And they that had laid **h** on Jesus led *G2902*
Mk 1:25 And Jesus rebuked him, saying, **H** thy *G5392*
3:21 went out to lay **h** on him: for they said, *G2902*
6:17 sent forth and laid **h** upon John, and *G2902*
7: 4 have received to **h**, *as* the washing of *G2902*
8 of God, ye **h** the tradition of men, *G2902*
10:48 that he should **h** his peace: but he cried *G4623*
12:12 And they sought to lay **h** on him, but *G2902*
14:51 and the young men laid **h** on him: *G2902*
Lk 4:35 And Jesus rebuked him, saying, **H** thy *G5392*
16:13 or else he will **h** to the one, and despise *G472*
18:39 that he should **h** his peace: but he cried *G4623*
19:40 if these should **h** their peace, the stones *G4623*
20:20 they might take **h** of his words, that so *G1949*
26 And they could not take **h** of his words *G1949*
23:26 And as they led him away, they laid **h** *G1949*
Act 4: 3 and put *them* in **h** unto the next day: *G5084*
12:17 them with the hand to **h** their peace, *G4601*
18: 9 afraid, but speak, and **h** not thy peace: *G4623*
Ro 1:18 who **h** the truth in unrighteousness; *G2722*
1Co 14:30 that sitteth by, let the first **h** his peace. *G4601*
Php 2:29 all gladness; and **h** such in reputation: *G2192*
1Th 5:21 Prove all things; **h** fast that which is *G2722*
2Th 2:15 Therefore, brethren, stand fast, and **h** *G2902*
1Ti 6:12 Fight the good fight of faith, lay **h** on *G1949*
19 that they may lay **h** on eternal life. *G1949*
2Ti 1:13 **H** fast the form of sound words, which *G2192*
Heb 3: 6 are we, if we **h** fast the confidence *G2722*
14 of Christ, if we **h** the beginning of our *G2722*
4:14 Son of God, let us **h** fast *our* profession. *G2722*
6:18 to lay **h** upon the hope set before us: *G2902*
10:23 Let us **h** fast the profession of *our* faith *G2722*
Rev 2:14 hast there them that **h** the doctrine of *G2902*
15 So hast thou also them that **h** the *G2902*
25 But that which ye have *already* **h** fast *G2902*
3: 3 and heard, and **h** fast, and repent. If *G5083*
11 Behold, I come quickly: **h** that fast *G2902*
18: 2 of devils, and the **h** of every foul spirit, *G5438*
20: 2 And he laid **h** on the dragon, that old *G2902*

HOLDEN

2Ki 23:22 Surely there was not **h** such a passover H6213
23 was **h** to the LORD in Jerusalem. H6213
Job 36: 8 fetters, *and* be **h** in cords of affliction; H3920
Ps 18:35 thy right hand hath **h** me up, and thy H5582
71: 6 By thee have I been **h** up from the H5564
73:23 thee: thou hast **h** *me* by my right hand. H270
Prv 5:22 he shall be **h** with the cords of his sins. H8551
Isa 42:14 I have long time **h** my peace; I have H2814
45: 1 right hand I have **h**, to subdue nations H2388
Lk 24:16 But their eyes were **h** that they should *G2902*
Act 2:24 not possible that he should be **h** of it. *G2902*
Ro 14: 4 Yea, he shall be **h** up: for God is able to *G2476*

HOLDEST

Est 4:14 For if thou altogether **h** thy peace at H2790
Job 13:24 Wherefore hidest thou thy face, and **h** H2803
Ps 77: 4 Thou **h** mine eyes waking: I am so H270
Jer 49:16 of the rock, that **h** the height of the hill: H8610
Hab 1:13 *and* **h** thy tongue when the H2790
Rev 2:13 seat *is*: and thou **h** fast my name, and *G2902*

HOLDETH

Job 2: 3 evil? and still he **h** fast his integrity, H2388
26: 9 He **h** back the face of his throne, *and* H270
Ps 66: 9 Which **h** our soul in life, and suffereth H7760
Prv 11:12 a man of understanding **h** his peace. H2790
17:28 Even a fool, when he **h** his peace, is H2790
Dan 10:21 *there is* none that **h** with me in these H2388
Am 1: 5 and him that **h** the sceptre from the H8551
8 and him that **h** the sceptre from H8551
Rev 2: 1 saith he that **h** the seven stars in his *G2902*

HOLDING
Isa 33:15 his hands from **h** of bribes, that H8551
Jer 6:11 I am weary with **h** in: I will pour it out H3557
Mk 7: 3 eat not, **h** the tradition of the elders. *G2902*
Php 2:16 **H** forth the word of life; that I may *G1907*
Col 2:19 And not **h** the Head, from which all the *G2902*
1Ti 1:19 **H** faith, and a good conscience; which *G2192*
3: 9 **H** the mystery of the faith in a pure *G2192*
Tit 1: 9 **H** fast the faithful word as he hath been *G472*
Rev 7: 1 of the earth, **h** the four winds of the *G2902*

HOLDS
Nu 13:19 in, whether in tents, or in strong **h**; H4013
Jdg 6: 2 mountains, and caves, and strong **h**. H4679
1Sa 23:14 in strong **h**, and remained in a H4679
19 with us in strong **h** in the wood, in the H4679
29 and dwelt in strong **h** at En-gedi. H4679
2Ki 8:12 of Israel: their strong **h** wilt thou set on H4013
2Ch 11:11 And he fortified the strong **h**, and put H4694
Ps 89:40 thou hast brought his strong **h** to ruin. H4013
Isa 23:11 *city*, to destroy the strong **h** thereof. H4581
Jer 48:18 thee, *and* he shall destroy thy strong **h**. H4013
41 Kerioth is taken, and the strong **h** are H4679
51:30 remained in *their* **h**: their might hath H4679
Lam 2: 2 wrath the strong **h** of the daughter of H4013
5 his strong **h**, and hath increased H4013
Ezk 19: 9 they brought him into **h**, that his voice H4685
Dan 11:24 against the strong **h**, even for a time. H4013
39 Thus shall he do in the most strong **h** H4013
Mic 5:11 land, and throw down all thy strong **h**: H4013
Nah 3:12 All thy strong **h** *shall be like* fig trees H4013
14 fortify thy strong **h**: go into clay, and H4013
2Co 10: 4 God to the pulling down of strong **h**;) *G3794*

HOLE
Ex 28:32 And there shall be an **h** in the top of it, H6310
32 round about the **h** of it, as it were the H6310
32 **h** of an habergeon, that it be not rent. H6310
39:23 And *there was* an **h** in the midst of the H6310
23 of the robe, as the **h** of an habergeon, H6310
23 about the **h**, that it should not rend. H6310
2Ki 12: 9 chest, and bored a **h** in the lid of it, and H2356
Song 5: 4 My beloved put in his hand by the **h** *of* H2356
Isa 11: 8 shall play on the **h** of the asp, and the H2352
51: 1 to the **h** of the pit *whence* ye are digged. H4718
Jer 13: 4 and hide it there in a **h** of the rock. H5357
Ezk 8: 7 when I looked, behold a **h** in the wall. H2356

HOLES
1Sa 14:11 of the **h** where they had hid themselves. H2356
Isa 2:19 And they shall go into the **h** of the H4631
7:19 valleys, and in the **h** of the rocks, and H5357
42:22 of them snared in **h**, and they are hid in H2356
Jer 16:16 every hill, and out of the **h** of the rocks. H5357
Mic 7:17 move out of their **h** like worms of the H4526
Nah 2:12 **h** with prey, and his dens with ravin. H2356
Hag 1: 6 wages *to put it* into a bag with **h**. H5344
Zec 14:12 away in their **h**, and their tongue shall H2356
Mt 8:20 The foxes have **h**, and the birds of the *G5454*
Lk 9:58 And Jesus said unto him, Foxes have **h**, *G5454*

HOLE'S
Jer 48:28 her nest in the sides of the **h** mouth. H6354

HOLIDAY See HOLYDAY.

HOLIER
Isa 65: 5 to me; for I am **h** than thou. These *are* H6942

HOLIEST
Heb 9: 3 tabernacle which is called the **H** of all; *G39*
8 that the way into the **h** of all was not yet *G39*
10:19 to enter into the **h** by the blood of Jesus, *G39*

HOLILY
1Th 2:10 Ye *are* witnesses, and God *also*, how **h** *G3743*

HOLINESS
Ex 15:11 in **h**, fearful *in* praises, doing wonders? H6944
28:36 of a signet, **H** TO THE LORD. H6944
39:30 of a signet, **H** TO THE LORD. H6944
1Ch 16:29 worship the LORD in the beauty of **h**. H6944
2Ch 20:21 the beauty of **h**, as they went out before H6944
31:18 office they sanctified themselves in **h**: H6944
Ps 29: 2 worship the LORD in the beauty of **h**. H6944
30: 4 thanks at the remembrance of his **h**. H6944
47: 8 God sitteth upon the throne of his **h**. H6944
48: 1 of our God, *in* the mountain of his **h**. H6944
60: 6 God hath spoken in his **h**; I will rejoice, H6944
Ps 89:35 Once have I sworn by my **h** that I will H6944
93: 5 Thy testimonies are very sure: **h** H6944
96: 9 O worship the LORD in the beauty of **h**: H6944
97:12 thanks at the remembrance of his **h**. H6944
108: 7 God hath spoken in his **h**; I will rejoice, H6944
110: 3 in the beauties of **h** from the womb of H6944
Isa 23:18 her hire shall be **h** to the LORD: it shall H6944
35: 8 called The way of **h**; the unclean shall H6944
62: 9 shall drink it in the courts of my **h**. H6944
63:15 the habitation of thy **h** and of thy glory: H6944
18 The people of thy **h** have possessed *it* H6944
Jer 2: 3 Israel *was* **h** unto the LORD, *and* the H6944
23: 9 and because of the words of his **h**. H6944
31:23 of justice, *and* mountain of **h**. H6944
Am 4: 2 The Lord GOD hath sworn by his **h**, H6944
Oba 17 and there shall be **h**; and the house of H6944
Zec 14:20 of the horses, **H** UNTO THE LORD; H6944
21 in Judah shall be **h** unto the LORD of H6944
Mal 2:11 hath profaned the **h** of the LORD which H6944
Lk 1:75 In **h** and righteousness before him, all *G3742*
Act 3:12 or **h** we had made this man to walk? *G2150*
Ro 1: 4 of **h**, by the resurrection from the dead: *G42*
6:19 servants to righteousness unto **h**. *G38*
22 fruit unto **h**, and the end everlasting life. *G38*
2Co 7: 1 spirit, perfecting **h** in the fear of God. *G42*
Eph 4:24 is created in righteousness and true **h**. *G3742*
1Th 3:13 unblameable in **h** before God, even our *G42*
4: 7 called us unto uncleanness, but unto **h**. *G38*
1Ti 2:15 in faith and charity and **h** with sobriety. *G38*
Tit 2: 3 as becometh **h**, not false accusers, not *G2412*
Heb 12:10 that *we* might be partakers of his **h**. *G41*
14 Follow peace with all *men*, and **h**, *G38*

HOLLOW
Gen 32:25 he touched the **h** of his thigh; and the H3709
25 of his thigh; and the **h** of Jacob's thigh H3709
32 which *is* upon the **h** of the thigh, unto H3709
32 he touched the **h** of Jacob's thigh in the H3709
Ex 27: 8 **H** with boards shalt thou make it: as it H5014
38: 7 he made the altar **h** with boards. H5014
Lev 14:37 of the house with **h** strakes, greenish or H8258
Jdg 15:19 But God clave an **h** place that *was* in H4388
Isa 40:12 Who hath measured the waters in the **h** H8168
Jer 52:21 thereof *was* four fingers: *it was* **h**. H5014

HOLON
Jos 15:51 And Goshen, and **H**, and Giloh; eleven H2473
21:15 And **H** with her suburbs, and Debir H2473
Jer 48:21 country; upon **H**, and upon Jahazah, H2473

HOLPEN
Ps 83: 8 they have **h** the children of Lot. Selah. H2220
86:17 LORD, hast **h** me, and comforted me. H5826
Isa 31: 3 fall, and he that is **h** shall fall down, H5826
Dan 11:34 fall, they shall be **h** with a little help: H5826
Lk 1:54 He hath **h** his servant Israel, in *G482*

HOLY
Ex 3: 5 whereon thou standest *is* **h** ground. H6944
12:16 And in the first day *there shall be* an **h** H6944
16 there shall be an **h** convocation to you; H6944
15:13 in thy strength unto thy **h** habitation. H6944
16:23 *is* the rest of the **h** sabbath unto the H6944
19: 6 of priests, and an **h** nation. These *are* H6918
20: 8 the sabbath day, to keep it **h**. H6942
22:31 And ye shall be **h** men unto me: neither H6944
26:33 between the **h** *place* and the most holy. H6944
33 between the holy *place* and the most **h**. H6944
34 of the testimony in the most **h** *place*. H6944
28: 2 And thou shalt make **h** garments for H6944
4 they shall make **h** garments for Aaron H6944
29 he goeth in unto the **h** *place*, for a H6944
35 he goeth in unto the **h** *place* before the H6944
38 the iniquity of the **h** things, which the H6944
38 hallow in all their **h** gifts; and it shall be H6944
43 to minister in the **h** *place;* that they H6944
29: 6 and put the **h** crown upon the mitre. H6944
29 And the **h** garments of Aaron shall be H6944
30 congregation to minister in the **h** *place*. H6944
31 and seethe his flesh in the **h** place. H6918
33 not eat *thereof*, because they *are* **h**. H6944
34 fire: it shall not be eaten, because it *is* **h**. H6944
37 shall be an altar most **h**: whatsoever H6944
37 toucheth the altar shall be **h**. H6942
30:10 it *is* most **h** unto the LORD. H6944
25 And thou shalt make it an oil of **h** H6944
25 it shall be an **h** anointing oil. H6944
29 that they may be most **h**: whatsoever H6944
29 whatsoever toucheth them shall be **h**. H6942
Ex 30:31 This shall be an **h** anointing oil unto H6944
32 it: it *is* **h**, *and* it shall be holy unto you. H6944
32 it: it *is* holy, *and* it shall be **h** unto you. H6944
35 tempered together, pure *and* **h**: H6944
36 with thee: it shall be unto you most **h**. H6944
37 it shall be unto thee **h** for the LORD. H6944
31:10 And the cloths of service, and the **h** H6944
11 incense for the **h** *place:* according to H6944
14 therefore; for it *is* **h** unto you: every one H6944
15 the sabbath of rest, **h** to the LORD: H6944
35: 2 shall be to you an **h** day, a sabbath of H6944
19 to do service in the **h** *place*, the holy H6944
19 in the holy *place*, the **h** garments for H6944
21 all his service, and for the **h** garments. H6944
37:29 And he made the **h** anointing oil, and H6944
38:24 in all the work of the **h** *place*, even the H6944
39: 1 do service in the **h** *place*, and made the H6944
1 and made the **h** garments for Aaron; H6944
30 And they made the plate of the **h** crown H6944
41 do service in the **h** *place*, and the holy H6944
41 *place*, and the **h** garments for Aaron H6944
40: 9 all the vessels thereof: and it shall be **h**. H6944
10 altar: and it shall be an altar most **h**. H6944
13 And thou shalt put upon Aaron the **h** H6944
Lev 2: 3 *it is* a thing most **h** of the offerings of H6944
10 *it is* a thing most **h** of the offerings of H6944
5:15 ignorance, in the **h** things of the LORD; H6944
16 hath done in the **h** thing, and shall add H6944
6:16 it be eaten in the **h** place; in the court of H6918
17 made by fire; it *is* most **h**, as *is* the sin H6944
18 every one that toucheth them shall be **h**. H6942
25 be killed before the LORD: it *is* most **h**. H6944
26 sin shall eat it: in the **h** place shall it be H6918
27 thereof shall be **h**: and when there is H6942
27 it was sprinkled in the **h** place. H6918
29 the priests shall eat thereof: it *is* most **h**. H6944
30 *withal* in the **h** *place*, shall be eaten: H6944
7: 1 law of the trespass offering: it *is* most **h**. H6944
6 be eaten in the **h** place: it *is* most holy. H6918
6 be eaten in the holy place: it *is* most **h**. H6944
8: 9 golden plate, the **h** crown; as the LORD H6944
10:10 between **h** and unholy, and between H6944
12 leaven beside the altar: for it *is* most **h**: H6944
13 And ye shall eat it in the **h** place, H6918
17 sin offering in the **h** place, seeing it *is* H6944
17 seeing it *is* most **h**, and *God* hath given H6944
18 in within the **h** *place*: ye should indeed H6944
18 it in the **h** *place*, as I commanded. H6944
11:44 and ye shall be **h**; for I *am* holy: neither H6918
44 shall be holy; for I *am* **h**: neither shall ye H6918
45 ye shall therefore be **h**, for I *am* holy. H6918
45 ye shall therefore be holy, for I *am* **h**. H6918
14:13 offering, in the **h** place: for as the sin H6944
13 *so is* the trespass offering: it *is* most **h**: H6944
16: 2 all times into the **h** *place* within the vail H6944
3 Thus shall Aaron come into the **h** H6944
4 He shall put on the **h** linen coat, and he H6944
4 attired: these *are* **h** garments; therefore H6944
16 atonement for the **h** *place*, because of H6944
17 an atonement in the **h** *place*, until he H6944
20 end of reconciling the **h** *place*, and the H6944
23 the **h** *place*, and shall leave them there: H6944
24 with water in the **h** place, and put on H6918
27 atonement in the **h** *place*, shall *one* H6944
32 the linen clothes, *even* the **h** garments: H6944
33 atonement for the **h** sanctuary, and he H6944
19: 2 be **h**: for I the LORD your God *am* holy. H6918
2 be holy: for I the LORD your God *am* **h**. H6918
24 shall be **h** to praise the LORD *withal*. H6944
20: 3 sanctuary, and to profane my **h** name. H6944
7 be ye **h**: for I *am* the LORD your God. H6918
26 And ye shall be **h** unto me: for I the H6918
26 for I the LORD *am* **h**, and have severed H6918
21: 6 They shall be **h** unto their God, and not H6944
6 they do offer: therefore they shall be **h**. H6918
7 her husband: for he *is* **h** unto his God. H6918
8 God: he shall be **h** unto thee: for I the H6918
8 I the LORD, which sanctify you, *am* **h**. H6918
22 *both* of the most **h**, and of the holy. H6944
22 *both* of the most holy, and of the **h**. H6944
22: 2 from the **h** things of the children H6944
2 profane not my **h** name *in those things* H6944
3 that goeth unto the **h** things, which the H6944
4 shall not eat of the **h** things, until he be H6944
6 shall not eat of the **h** things, unless he H6944
7 of the **h** things; because it *is* his food. H6944
10 There shall no stranger eat *of* the **h** H6944
10 servant, shall not eat *of* the **h** thing. H6944
12 not eat of an offering of the **h** things. H6944

Lev 22:14 And if a man eat *of* the **h** thing H6944
14 give *it* unto the priest with the **h** thing. H6944
15 And they shall not profane the **h** things H6944
16 they eat their **h** things: for I the LORD H6944
32 Neither shall ye profane my **h** name; H6944
23: 2 proclaim *to be* **h** convocations, *even* H6944
3 of rest, an **h** convocation; ye shall H6944
4 of the LORD, *even* **h** convocations, H6944
7 In the first day ye shall have an **h** H6944
8 the seventh day *is* an **h** convocation: ye H6944
20 shall be **h** to the LORD for the priest. H6944
21 *that* it may be an **h** convocation unto H6944
24 blowing of trumpets, an **h** convocation. H6944
27 it shall be an **h** convocation unto you; H6944
35 On the first day *shall be* an **h** H6944
36 day shall be an **h** convocation unto H6944
37 proclaim *to be* **h** convocations, to offer H6944
24: 9 shall eat it in the **h** place: for it *is* most H6918
9 place: for it *is* most **h** unto him of the H6944
25:12 For it *is* the jubile; it shall be **h** unto H6944
27: 9 giveth of such unto the LORD shall be **h**. H6944
10 it and the exchange thereof shall be **h**. H6944
14 his house *to be* **h** unto the LORD, then H6944
21 the jubile, shall be **h** unto the LORD, as H6944
23 that day, *as* a **h** thing unto the LORD. H6944
28 thing *is* most **h** unto the LORD. H6944
30 *is* the LORD'S: *it is* **h** unto the LORD. H6944
32 the tenth shall be **h** unto the LORD. H6944
33 shall be **h**; it shall not be redeemed. H6944
Nu 4: 4 congregation, *about* the most **h** things: H6944
15 not touch *any* **h** thing, lest they die. H6944
19 unto the most **h** things: Aaron and his H6944
20 the **h** things are covered, lest they die. H6944
5: 9 And every offering of all the **h** things of H6944
17 And the priest shall take **h** water in an H6918
6: 5 LORD, he shall be **h**, *and* shall let the H6918
8 All the days of his separation he *is* **h** H6918
20 the LORD: this *is* **h** for the priest, with H6944
15:40 and be **h** unto your God. H6918
16: 3 congregation *are* **h**, every one of them, H6918
5 his, and *who is* **h**; and will cause *him* H6918
7 he *shall be* **h**: *ye take* too much upon H6918
18: 9 This shall be thine of the most **h** things, H6944
9 *be* most **h** for thee and for thy sons. H6944
10 In the most **h** *place* shalt thou eat it; H6944
10 male shall eat it: it shall be **h** unto thee. H6944
17 redeem; they *are* **h**: thou shalt sprinkle H6944
19 All the heave offerings of the **h** things, H6944
32 ye pollute the **h** things of the children H6944
28: 7 the one lamb: in the **h** *place* shalt thou H6944
18 In the first day *shall be* an **h** H6944
25 ye shall have an **h** convocation; ye shall H6944
26 ye shall have an **h** convocation; ye shall H6944
29: 1 ye shall have an **h** convocation; ye shall H6944
7 seventh month an **h** convocation; and H6944
12 ye shall have an **h** convocation; ye shall H6944
31: 6 to the war, with the **h** instruments, and H6944
35:25 which was anointed with the **h** oil. H6944
Dt 7: 6 For thou *art* an **h** people unto the H6918
12:26 Only thy **h** things which thou hast, and H6944
14: 2 For thou *art* an **h** people unto the H6918
21 for thou *art* an **h** people unto the LORD H6918
23:14 shall thy camp be **h**: that he see no H6918
26:15 Look down from thy **h** habitation, from H6944
19 thou mayest be an **h** people unto the H6918
28: 9 The LORD shall establish thee an **h** H6918
33: 8 thy Urim *be* with thy **h** one, whom thou H2623
Jos 5:15 thou standest *is* **h**. And Joshua did so. H6944
24:19 the LORD: for he *is* an **h** God; he *is* a H6918
1Sa 2: 2 *There is* none **h** as the LORD: for *there* H6918
6:20 stand before this **h** LORD God? and to H6918
21: 5 young men are **h**, and *the bread is* in H6944
1Ki 6:16 the oracle, *even* for the most **h** *place*. H6944
7:50 house, the most **h** *place*, *and* for the H6944
8: 4 and all the **h** vessels that *were* in H6944
6 house, to the most **h** *place*, *even* under H6944
8 were seen out in the **h** *place* before the H6944
10 come out of the **h** *place*, that the cloud H6944
2Ki 4: 9 that this *is* an **h** man of God, which H6918
19:22 high? *even* against the **H** *One* of Israel. H6918
1Ch 6:49 of the *place* most **h**, and to make an H6944
16:10 Glory ye in his **h** name: let the heart of H6944
35 to thy **h** name, *and* glory in thy praise. H6944
22:19 of the LORD, and the **h** vessels of God, H6944
23:13 sanctify the most **h** things, he and his H6944
28 in the purifying of all **h** things, and the H6944
32 and the charge of the **h** *place*, and the H6944
29: 3 that I have prepared for the **h** house, H6944
16 an house for thine **h** name *cometh* of H6944
2Ch 3: 8 And he made the most **h** house, the H6944
10 And in the most **h** house he made two H6944
4:22 for the most **h** *place*, and the doors H6944
5: 5 and all the **h** vessels that *were* in H6944
7 into the most **h** *place*, *even* under the H6944
11 come out of the **h** *place*: (for all the H6944
8:11 *the places are* **h**, whereunto the ark of H6944
23: 6 go in, for they *are* **h**: but all the people H6944
29: 5 forth the filthiness out of the **h** *place*. H6944
7 in the **h** *place* unto the God of Israel. H6944
30:27 his **h** dwelling place, *even* unto heaven. H6944
31: 6 and the tithe of **h** things which were H6944
14 of the LORD, and the most **h** things. H6944
35: 3 all Israel, which were **h** unto the LORD, H6918
3 the LORD, Put the **h** ark in the house H6944
5 And stand in the **h** *place* according to H6944
13 but the *other* **h** *offerings* sod they in H6944
Ezr 2:63 eat of the most **h** things, till there stood H6944
8:28 And I said unto them, Ye *are* **h** unto the H6944
28 the vessels *are* **h** also; and the silver H6944
9: 2 sons: so that the **h** seed have mingled H6944
8 us a nail in his **h** place, that our God H6944
Neh 7:65 eat of the most **h** things, till there stood H6944
8: 9 This day *is* **h** unto the LORD your H6918
10 for *this* day *is* **h** unto our Lord: neither H6918
11 for the day *is* **h**; neither be ye grieved. H6918
9:14 And madest known unto them thy **h** H6944
10:31 sabbath, or on the **h** day: and *that* we H6944
33 feasts, and for the **h** *things*, and for the H6944
11: 1 in Jerusalem the **h** city, and nine parts H6944
18 All the Levites in the **h** city *were* two H6944
12:47 and they sanctified *h things* unto the
Job 6:10 not concealed the words of the **H** One. H6918
Ps 2: 6 Yet have I set my king upon my **h** hill H6944
3: 4 he heard me out of his **h** hill. Selah. H6944
5: 7 will I worship toward thy **h** temple. H6944
11: 4 The LORD *is* in his **h** temple, the H6944
15: 1 who shall dwell in thy **h** hill? H6944
16:10 suffer thine **H** One to see corruption. H2623
20: 6 hear him from his **h** heaven with the H6944
22: 3 But thou *art* **h**, *O thou* that inhabitest H6918
24: 3 or who shall stand in his **h** place? H6944
28: 2 I lift up my hands toward thy **h** oracle. H6944
33:21 because we have trusted in his **h** name. H6944
43: 3 unto thy **h** hill, and to thy tabernacles. H6944
46: 4 the city of God, the **h** *place* of the H6918
51:11 and take not thy **h** spirit from me. H6944
65: 4 of thy house, *even* of thy **h** temple. H6918
68: 5 the widows, *is* God in his **h** habitation. H6944
17 among them, *as in* Sinai, in the **h** *place*. H6944
35 O God, *thou art* terrible out of thy **h** H4720
71:22 with the harp, O thou **H** One of Israel. H6918
78:41 God, and limited the **H** One of Israel. H6918
79: 1 inheritance; thy **h** temple have they H6944
86: 2 Preserve my soul; for I *am* **h**: O thou my H2623
87: 1 His foundation *is* in the **h** mountains. H6944
89:18 For the LORD *is* our defence; and the **H** H6918
19 Then thou spakest in vision to thy **h** H2623
20 with my **h** oil have I anointed him: H6944
98: 1 his **h** arm, hath gotten him the victory. H6944
99: 3 thy great and terrible name; *for it is* **h**. H6918
5 and worship at his footstool; *for he is* **h**. H6918
9 his **h** hill; for the LORD our God *is* holy. H6944
9 his holy hill; for the LORD our God *is* **h**. H6918
103: 1 all that is within me, *bless* his **h** name. H6944
105: 3 Glory ye in his **h** name: let the heart of H6944
42 For he remembered his **h** promise, *and* H6944
106:47 **h** name, *and* to triumph in thy praise. H6944
111: 9 for ever: **h** and reverend *is* his name. H6918
138: 2 I will worship toward thy **h** temple, and H6944
145:17 in all his ways, and **h** in all his works. H2623
21 bless his **h** name for ever and ever. H6944
Prv 9:10 knowledge of the **h** *is* understanding. H6918
20:25 *is* **h**, and after vows to make inquiry. H6944
30: 3 nor have the knowledge of the **h**. H6918
Ecc 8:10 from the place of the **h**, and they were H6918
Isa 1: 4 have provoked the **H** One of Israel unto H6918
4: 3 shall be called **h**, *even* every one that H6918
5:16 **h** shall be sanctified in righteousness. H6918
19 the counsel of the **H** One of Israel draw H6918
24 the word of the **H** One of Israel. H6918
6: 3 another, and said, **H**, holy, holy, *is* the H6918
3 and said, Holy, **h**, holy, *is* the LORD of H6918
3 and said, Holy, holy, **h**, *is* the LORD of H6918
13 **h** seed *shall be* the substance thereof. H6944
10:17 be for a fire, and his **H** One for a flame: H6918
20 the LORD, the **H** One of Israel, in truth. H6918
11: 9 destroy in all my **h** mountain: for the H6944
12: 6 the **H** One of Israel in the midst of thee. H6918
Isa 17: 7 have respect to the **H** One of Israel. H6918
27:13 the LORD in the **h** mount at Jerusalem. H6944
29:19 men shall rejoice in the **H** One of Israel. H6918
23 and sanctify the **H** One of Jacob, and H6918
30:11 **H** One of Israel to cease from before us. H6918
12 Wherefore thus saith the **H** One of H6918
15 For thus saith the Lord GOD, the **H** One H6918
29 in the night *when* a **h** solemnity is kept; H6942
31: 1 **H** One of Israel, neither seek the LORD! H6918
37:23 high? *even* against the **H** One of Israel. H6918
40:25 or shall I be equal? saith the **H** One. H6918
41:14 and thy redeemer, the **H** One of Israel. H6918
16 *and* shalt glory in the **H** One of Israel. H6918
20 and the **H** One of Israel hath created it. H6918
43: 3 For I *am* the LORD thy God, the **H** One H6918
14 redeemer, the **H** One of Israel; For your H6918
15 I *am* the LORD, your **H** One, the H6918
45:11 Thus saith the LORD, the **H** One of H6918
47: 4 hosts *is* his name, the **H** One of Israel. H6918
48: 2 For they call themselves of the **h** city, H6944
17 thy Redeemer, the **H** One of Israel; I H6918
49: 7 of Israel, *and* his **H** One, to him whom H6918
7 is faithful, *and* the **H** One of Israel, and H6918
52: 1 O Jerusalem, the **h** city: for henceforth H6944
10 The LORD hath made bare his **h** arm H6944
54: 5 thy Redeemer the **H** One of Israel; The H6918
55: 5 God, and for the **H** One of Israel; for he H6918
56: 7 Even them will I bring to my **h** H6944
57:13 land, and shall inherit my **h** mountain; H6944
15 whose name *is* **H**; I dwell in the high H6918
15 in the high and **h** *place*, with him also H6918
58:13 thy pleasure on my **h** day; and call the H6944
13 sabbath a delight, the **h** of the LORD, H6918
60: 9 thy God, and to the **H** One of Israel, H6918
14 LORD, The Zion of the **H** One of Israel. H6918
62:12 And they shall call them, The **h** people, H6944
63:10 But they rebelled, and vexed his **h** H6944
11 *is* he that put his **h** Spirit within him? H6944
64:10 Thy **h** cities are a wilderness, Zion is a H6944
11 Our **h** and our beautiful house, where H6944
65:11 LORD, that forget my **h** mountain, that H6944
25 in all my **h** mountain, saith the LORD. H6944
66:20 beasts, to my **h** mountain Jerusalem, H6944
Jer 11:15 many, and the **h** flesh is passed from H6944
25:30 his voice from his **h** habitation; he shall H6944
31:40 the east, *shall be* **h** unto the LORD; it H6944
50:29 the LORD, against the **H** One of Israel. H6918
51: 5 with sin against the **H** One of Israel. H6918
Ezk 7:24 and their **h** places shall be defiled. H6924
20:39 but pollute ye my **h** name no more with H6944
40 For in mine **h** mountain, in the H6944
40 of your oblations, with all your **h** things.
21: 2 *thy word* toward the **h** places, and H4720
22: 8 Thou hast despised mine **h** things, and H6944
26 profaned mine **h** things: they have put H6944
26 between the **h** and profane, neither H6944
28:14 wast upon the **h** mountain of God; thou H6944
36:20 they profaned my **h** name, when they H6944
21 But I had pity for mine **h** name, which H6944
22 but for mine **h** name's sake, which H6944
38 As the **h** flock, as the flock of Jerusalem H6944
39: 7 So will I make my **h** name known in the H6944
7 *let them* pollute my **h** name any more: H6944
7 I *am* the LORD, the **H** One in Israel. H6918
25 and will be jealous for my **h** name; H6944
41: 4 said unto me, This *is* the most **h** *place*. H6944
42:13 place, they *be* **h** chambers, where the H6944
13 shall eat the most **h** things: there shall H6944
13 they lay the most **h** things, and the H6944
13 the trespass offering; for the place *is* **h**. H6918
14 not go out of the **h** *place* into the utter H6944
14 for they *are* **h**; and shall put on other H6944
43: 7 for ever, and my **h** name, shall the H6944
8 have even defiled my **h** name by their H6944
12 **h**. Behold, this *is* the law of the house. H6944
44: 8 charge of mine **h** things: but ye have H6944
13 near to any of my **h** things, in the most H6944
13 in the most **h** *place*: but they shall H6944
19 lay them in the **h** chambers, and they H6944
23 between the **h** and profane, and cause H6944
45: 1 the LORD, an **h** portion of the land: H6944
1 This *shall be* **h** in all the borders H6944
3 be the sanctuary *and* the most **h** *place*. H6944
4 The **h** *portion* of the land shall be for H6944
4 and an **h** place for the sanctuary. H4720
6 the oblation of the **h** *portion*: it shall be H6944
7 the oblation of the **h** *portion*, and of the H6944
7 the oblation of the **h** *portion*, and H6944
46:19 of the gate, into the **h** chambers of the H6944

Ezk 48:10 shall be *this* **h** oblation; toward the H6944
12 most **h** by the border of the Levites. H6944
14 of the land: for *it is* **h** unto the LORD. H6944
18 the oblation of the **h** *portion shall be* H6944
18 the oblation of the **h** *portion*; and the H6944
20 ye shall offer the **h** oblation foursquare, H6944
21 on the other of the **h** oblation, and of H6944
21 and it shall be the **h** oblation; and the H6944
Dan 4: 8 *is* the spirit of the **h** gods: and before H6922
9 the spirit of the **h** gods *is* in thee, and H6922
13 and an **h** one came down from heaven; H6922
17 by the word of the **h** ones: to the intent H6922
18 for the spirit of the **h** gods *is* in thee. H6922
23 a watcher and an **h** one coming down H6922
5:11 *is* the spirit of the **h** gods; and in the H6922
8:24 destroy the mighty and the **h** people. H6918
9:16 Jerusalem, thy **h** mountain: because H6944
20 my God for the **h** mountain of my God; H6944
24 and upon thy **h** city, to finish the H6944
24 prophecy, and to anoint the most **H.** H6944
11:28 *be* against the **h** covenant; and he shall H6944
30 against the **h** covenant: so shall he H6944
30 with them that forsake the **h** covenant. H6944
45 in the glorious **h** mountain; yet he shall H6944
12: 7 the power of the **h** people, all these H6944
Hos 11: 9 and not man; the **H** One in the midst of H6918
Joel 2: 1 an alarm in my **h** mountain: let all the H6944
3:17 in Zion, my **h** mountain: then shall H6944
17 shall Jerusalem be **h**, and there shall no H6944
Am 2: 7 the *same* maid, to profane my **h** name: H6944
Oba 16 For as ye have drunk upon my **h** H6944
Jna 2: 4 I will look again toward thy **h** temple. H6944
7 came in unto thee, into thine **h** temple. H6944
Mic 1: 2 you, the Lord from his **h** temple. H6944
Hab 1:12 my God, mine **H** One? we shall not die. H6918
2:20 But the LORD *is* in his **h** temple: let all H6944
3: 3 God came from Teman, and the **H** One H6918
Zep 3:11 be haughty because of my **h** mountain. H6944
Hag 2:12 If one bear **h** flesh in the skirt of his H6944
12 any meat, shall it be **h**? And the priests H6942
Zec 2:12 his portion in the **h** land, and shall H6944
13 he is raised up out of his **h** habitation. H6944
8: 3 of the LORD of hosts the **h** mountain. H6944
Mt 1:18 she was found with child of the **H** Ghost. *G40*
20 is conceived in her is of the **H** Ghost. *G40*
3:11 you with the **H** Ghost, and *with* fire: *G40*
4: 5 Then the devil taketh him up into the **h** *G40*
7: 6 Give not that which is **h** unto the dogs, *G40*
12:31 *H* Ghost shall not be forgiven unto men.
32 against the **H** Ghost, it shall not be *G40*
24:15 stand in the **h** place, (whoso readeth, *G40*
25:31 glory, and all the **h** angels with him, then *G40*
27:53 the **h** city, and appeared unto many. *G40*
28:19 and of the Son, and of the **H** Ghost: *G40*
Mk 1: 8 he shall baptize you with the **H** Ghost. *G40*
24 thee who thou art, the **H** One of God. *G40*
3:29 against the **H** Ghost hath never *G40*
6:20 a just man and an **h**, and observed him; *G40*
8:38 the glory of his Father with the **h** angels. *G40*
12:36 For David himself said by the **H** Ghost, *G40*
13:11 it is not ye that speak, but the **H** Ghost. *G40*
Lk 1:15 **H** Ghost, even from his mother's womb. *G40*
35 said unto her, The **H** Ghost shall come *G40*
35 therefore also that **h** thing which shall be *G40*
41 Elisabeth was filled with the **H** Ghost: *G40*
49 to me great things; and **h** *is* his name. *G40*
67 the **H** Ghost, and prophesied, saying, *G40*
70 As he spake by the mouth of his **h** *G40*
72 and to remember his **h** covenant; *G40*
2:23 the womb shall be called **h** to the Lord;) *G40*
25 Israel: and the **H** Ghost was upon him. *G40*
26 And it was revealed unto him by the **H** *G40*
3:16 you with the **H** Ghost and with fire: *G40*
22 And the **H** Ghost descended in a bodily *G40*
4: 1 And Jesus being full of the **H** Ghost *G40*
34 thee who thou art; the **H** One of God. *G40*
9:26 and *in his* Father's, and of the **h** angels. *G40*
11:13 give the **H** Spirit to them that ask him? *G40*
12:10 the **H** Ghost it shall not be forgiven. *G40*
12 For the **H** Ghost shall teach you in the *G40*
Jn 1:33 is he which baptizeth with the **H** Ghost. *G40*
7:39 receive: for the **H** Ghost was not yet *G40*
14:26 But the Comforter, *which is* the **H** Ghost, *G40*
17:11 I come to thee. **H** Father, keep through *G40*
20:22 saith unto them, Receive ye the **H** Ghost: *G40*
Act 1: 2 that he through the **H** Ghost had given *G40*
5 with the **H** Ghost not many days hence. *G40*
8 after that the **H** Ghost is come upon *G40*
16 been fulfilled, which the **H** Ghost by the *G40*

Act 2: 4 And they were all filled with the **H** *G40*
27 suffer thine **H** One to see corruption. *G3741*
33 the promise of the **H** Ghost, he hath shed *G40*
38 ye shall receive the gift of the **H** Ghost. *G40*
3:14 But ye denied the **H** One and the Just, *G40*
21 all his **h** prophets since the world began. *G40*
4: 8 Then Peter, filled with the **H** Ghost, said *G40*
27 For of a truth against thy **h** child Jesus, *G40*
30 be done by the name of thy **h** child Jesus. *G40*
31 were all filled with the **H** Ghost, and they *G40*
5: 3 heart to lie to the **H** Ghost, and to keep *G40*
32 and *so is* also the **H** Ghost, whom God *G40*
6: 3 report, full of the **H** Ghost and wisdom, *G40*
5 of faith and of the **H** Ghost, and Philip, *G40*
13 words against this **h** place, and the law: *G40*
7:33 place where thou standest is **h** ground. *G40*
51 **H** Ghost: as your fathers *did*, so *do* ye. *G40*
55 But he, being full of the **H** Ghost, looked *G40*
8:15 that they might receive the **H** Ghost: *G40*
17 on them, and they received the **H** Ghost. *G40*
18 hands the **H** Ghost was given, he *G40*
19 I lay hands, he may receive the **H** Ghost. *G40*
9:17 thy sight, and be filled with the **H** Ghost. *G40*
31 comfort of the **H** Ghost, were multiplied. *G40*
10:22 from God by an **h** angel to send for thee *G40*
38 of Nazareth with the **H** Ghost and with *G40*
44 While Peter yet spake these words, the **H** *G40*
45 was poured out the gift of the **H** Ghost. *G40*
47 have received the **H** Ghost as well as we? *G40*
11:15 And as I began to speak, the **H** Ghost fell *G40*
16 ye shall be baptized with the **H** Ghost. *G40*
24 For he was a good man, and full of the **H** *G40*
13: 2 and fasted, the **H** Ghost said, Separate *G40*
4 So they, being sent forth by the **H** Ghost, *G40*
9 with the **H** Ghost, set his eyes on him, *G40*
35 suffer thine **H** One to see corruption. *G3741*
52 filled with joy, and with the **H** Ghost. *G40*
15: 8 the **H** Ghost, even as *he did* unto us; *G40*
28 For it seemed good to the **H** Ghost, and *G40*
16: 6 the **H** Ghost to preach the word in Asia, *G40*
19: 2 Have ye received the **H** Ghost since ye *G40*
2 as heard whether there be any **H** Ghost. *G40*
6 upon them, the **H** Ghost came on them; *G40*
20:23 Save that the **H** Ghost witnesseth in *G40*
28 over the which the **H** Ghost hath made *G40*
21:11 Thus saith the **H** Ghost, So shall the Jews *G40*
28 temple, and hath polluted this **h** place. *G40*
28:25 Well spake the **H** Ghost by Esaias the *G40*
Ro 1: 2 by his prophets in the **h** scriptures,) *G40*
5: 5 by the **H** Ghost which is given unto us. *G40*
7:12 Wherefore the law *is* **h**, and the *G40*
12 the commandment **h**, and just, and good. *G40*
9: 1 also bearing me witness in the **H** Ghost, *G40*
11:16 For if the firstfruit *be* **h**, the lump *is* also *G40*
16 the lump *is also* **h**: and if the root *be* holy, *G40*
16 and if the root *be* **h**, so *are* the branches. *G40*
12: 1 a living sacrifice, **h**, acceptable unto God, *G40*
14:17 and peace, and joy in the **H** Ghost. *G40*
15:13 hope, through the power of the **H** Ghost. *G40*
16 being sanctified by the **H** Ghost. *G40*
16:16 Salute one another with an **h** kiss. The *G40*
1Co 2:13 but which the **H** Ghost teacheth; *G40*
3:17 temple of God is **h**, which *temple* ye are. *G40*
6:19 is the temple of the **H** Ghost *which is* in *G40*
7:14 children unclean; but now are they **h**. *G40*
34 that she may be **h** both in body and in *G40*
9:13 minister about **h** things live *of the* *G2413*
12: 3 Jesus is the Lord, but by the **H** Ghost. *G40*
16:20 you. Greet ye one another with an **h** kiss. *G40*
2Co 6: 6 by the **H** Ghost, by love unfeigned, *G40*
13:12 Greet one another with an **h** kiss. *G40*
14 of the **H** Ghost, *be* with you all. Amen. *G40*
Eph 1: 4 **h** and without blame before him in love: *G40*
13 sealed with that **h** Spirit of promise, *G40*
2:21 groweth unto an **h** temple in the Lord: *G40*
3: 5 his **h** apostles and prophets by the Spirit; *G40*
4:30 And grieve not the **h** Spirit of God, *G40*
5:27 that it should be **h** and without blemish. *G40*
Col 1:22 to present you **h** and unblameable and *G40*
3:12 Put on therefore, as the elect of God, **h** *G40*
1Th 1: 5 power, and in the **H** Ghost, and in much *G40*
6 much affliction, with joy of the **H** Ghost: *G40*
4: 8 who hath also given unto us his **h** Spirit. *G40*
5:26 Greet all the brethren with an **h** kiss. *G40*
27 epistle be read unto all the **h** brethren. *G40*
1Ti 2: 8 **h** hands, without wrath and doubting. *G3741*
2Ti 1: 9 and called *us* with an **h** calling, not *G40*
14 by the **H** Ghost which dwelleth in us. *G40*
3:15 hast known the **h** scriptures, which are *G2413*

Tit 1: 8 of good men, sober, just, **h**, temperate; *G3741*
3: 5 and renewing of the **H** Ghost; *G40*
Heb 2: 4 the **H** Ghost, according to his own will? *G40*
3: 1 Wherefore, **h** brethren, partakers of the *G40*
7 Wherefore (as the **H** Ghost saith, To day *G40*
6: 4 were made partakers of the **H** Ghost, *G40*
7:26 priest became us, *who is* **h**, harmless, *G3741*
9: 8 The **H** Ghost this signifying, that the way *G40*
12 in once into the **h** place, having obtained *G39*
24 For Christ is not entered into the **h** *G39*
25 **h** place every year with blood of others; *G39*
10:15 *Whereof* the **H** Ghost also is a witness to *G40*
1Pt 1:12 unto you with the **H** Ghost sent down *G40*
15 But as he which hath called you is **h**, so *G40*
15 so be ye **h** in all manner of conversation; *G40*
16 Because it is written, Be ye **h**; for I am *G40*
16 it is written, Be ye holy; for I am **h.** *G40*
2: 5 spiritual house, an **h** priesthood, to offer *G40*
9 royal priesthood, an **h** nation, a peculiar *G40*
3: 5 in the old time the **h** women also, who *G40*
2Pt 1:18 when we were with him in the **h** mount. *G40*
21 will of man: but **h** men of God spake *as* *G40*
21 *as they were* moved by the **H** Ghost. *G40*
2:21 **h** commandment delivered unto them. *G40*
3: 2 before by the **h** prophets, and of the *G40*
11 to be in *all* **h** conversation and godliness, *G40*
1Jn 2:20 But ye have an unction from the **H** One, *G40*
5: 7 the **H** Ghost: and these three are one. *G40*
Jude 20 most **h** faith, praying in the Holy Ghost, *G40*
20 most holy faith, praying in the **H** Ghost, *G40*
Rev 3: 7 saith he that is **h**, he that is true, he that *G40*
4: 8 day and night, saying, **H**, holy, holy, Lord *G40*
8 saying, Holy, **h**, holy, Lord God Almighty, *G40*
8 saying, Holy, holy, **h**, Lord God Almighty, *G40*
6:10 How long, O Lord, **h** and true, dost thou *G40*
11: 2 Gentiles: and the **h** city shall they tread *G40*
14:10 the presence of the **h** angels, and in the *G40*
15: 4 for *thou* only *art* **h**: for all nations shall *G3741*
18:20 Rejoice over her, *thou* heaven, and *ye* **h** *G40*
20: 6 Blessed and **h** *is* he that hath part in the *G40*
21: 2 And I John saw the **h** city, new *G40*
10 me that great city, the **h** Jerusalem, *G40*
22: 6 the Lord God of the **h** prophets sent his *G40*
11 still: and he that is **h**, let him be holy still. *G40*
11 and he that is holy, let him be **h** still. *G37*
19 of life, and out of the **h** city, and *from* the *G40*

HOLYDAY

Ps 42: 4 praise, with a multitude that kept **h**. H2287
Col 2:16 or in respect of an **h**, or of the new *G1859*

HOMAM

1Ch 1:39 And the sons of Lotan; Hori, and **H**: and H1950

HOME

Gen 39:16 garment by her, until his lord came **h**. H1004
43:16 Bring *these* men **h**, and slay, and make H1004
26 And when Joseph came **h**, they brought H1004
Ex 9:19 not be brought **h**, the hail shall come H1004
Lev 18: 9 *she be* born at **h**, or born abroad, *even* H1004
Dt 21:12 Then thou shalt bring her **h** to thine H8432
24: 5 he shall be free at **h** one year, and shall H1004
Jos 2:18 all thy father's household, **h** unto thee. H1004
Jdg 11: 9 If ye bring me **h** again to fight against
19: 9 early on your way, that thou mayest go **h**. H168
Ru 1:21 hath brought me **h** again empty: why
1Sa 2:20 LORD. And they went unto their own **h**. H4725
6: 7 and bring their calves **h** from them: H1004
10 the cart, and shut up their calves at **h**: H1004
10:26 And Saul also went **h** to Gibeah; and H1004
18: 2 him go no more **h** to his father's house. H7725
24:22 And Saul went **h**; but David and his H1004
2Sa 13: 7 Then David sent **h** to Tamar, saying, H1004
14:13 king doth not fetch **h** again his banished.
17:23 arose, and gat him **h** to his house, to his
1Ki 5:14 at **h**: and Adoniram *was* over the levy. H1004
13: 7 of God, Come **h** with me, and refresh H1004
15 Then he said unto him, Come **h** with H1004
2Ki 14:10 *of this*, and tarry at **h**: for why shouldest H1004
1Ch 13:12 shall I bring the ark of God **h** to me?
13 So David brought not the ark **h** to
2Ch 25:10 of Ephraim, to go **h** again: wherefore H4725
10 and they returned **h** in great anger. H4725
19 abide now at **h**; why shouldest thou H1004
Est 5:10 when he came **h**, he sent and called for H1004
Job 39:12 **h** thy seed, and gather *it into* thy barn? H7725
Ps 68:12 she that tarried at **h** divided the spoil. H1004
Prv 7:19 For the goodman *is* not at **h**, he is gone H1004
20 *and* will come **h** at the day appointed. H1004

Ecc 12: 5 goeth to his long **h**, and the mourners H1004
Jer 39:14 him **h**: so he dwelt among the people. H1004
Lam 1:20 sword bereaveth, at **h** *there is* as death. H1004
Hab 2: 5 neither keepeth at **h**, who enlargeth his H5115
Hag 1: 9 when ye brought *it* **h**, I did blow upon it. H1004
Mt 8: 6 And saying, Lord, my servant lieth at **h** *G3614*
Mk 5:19 unto him, Go **h** to thy friends, and tell *G1519*
Lk 9:61 farewell, which are at **h** at my house.
15: 6 And when he cometh **h**, he calleth *G3624*
Jn 19:27 that disciple took her unto his own ***h***.
20:10 went away again unto their own **h**. *G1438*
Act 21: 6 took ship; and they returned **h** again. *G1519*
1Co 11:34 And if any man hunger, let him eat at **h**; *G3624*
14:35 their husbands at **h**: for it is a shame for *G3624*
2Co 5: 6 whilst we are at **h** in the body, we are *G1736*
1Ti 5: 4 to shew piety at **h**, and to requite their *G3624*
Tit 2: 5 *To be* discreet, chaste, keepers at **h**, *G3626*

HOMEBORN

Ex 12:49 One law shall be to him that is **h**, and H249
Jer 2:14 *Is* Israel a servant? *is* he a **h** *slave*? why H1004

HOMER

Lev 27:16 seed thereof: an **h** of barley seed *shall* H2563
Isa 5:10 the seed of an **h** shall yield an ephah. H2563
Ezk 45:11 tenth part of an **h**, and the ephah the H2563
11 tenth part of an **h**: the measure thereof H2563
11 the measure thereof shall be after the **h**. H2563
13 of an ephah of an **h** of wheat, and ye H2563
13 sixth part of an ephah of an **h** of barley: H2563
14 cor, *which is* an **h** of ten baths; for ten H2563
14 of ten baths; for ten baths *are* an **h**: H2563
Hos 3: 2 of silver, and *for* an **h** of barley, and an H2563
2 of barley, and an half **h** of barley: H3963

HOMERS

Nu 11:32 least gathered ten **h**: and they spread H2563

HONEST

Lk 8:15 are they, which in an **h** and good heart, *G2570*
Act 6: 3 you seven men of **h** report, full of the
Ro 12:17 Provide things **h** in the sight of all men. *G2570*
2Co 8:21 Providing for **h** things, not only in the *G2570*
13: 7 which is **h**, though we be as reprobates. *G2570*
Php 4: 8 things *are* **h**, whatsoever things *are* *G4586*
1Pt 2:12 Having your conversation **h** among the *G2570*

HONESTLY

Ro 13:13 Let us walk **h**, as in the day; not in *G2156*
1Th 4:12 That ye may walk **h** toward them that *G2156*
Heb 13:18 in all things willing to live **h**. *G2573*

HONESTY

1Ti 2: 2 peaceable life in all godliness and **h**. *G4587*

HONEY

Gen 43:11 balm, and a little **h**, spices, and myrrh, H1706
Ex 3: 8 with milk and **h**; unto the place of the H1706
17 unto a land flowing with milk and **h**. H1706
13: 5 with milk and **h**, that thou shalt keep H1706
16:31 taste of it *was* like wafers *made* with **h**. H1706
33: 3 Unto a land flowing with milk and **h**: H1706
Lev 2:11 no leaven, nor any **h**, in any offering of H1706
20:24 with milk and **h**: I *am* the LORD your H1706
Nu 13:27 milk and **h**; and this *is* the fruit of it. H1706
14: 8 a land which floweth with milk and **h**. H1706
16:13 floweth with milk and **h**, to kill us in the H1706
14 with milk and **h**, or given us inheritance H1706
Dt 6: 3 the land that floweth with milk and **h**. H1706
8: 8 a land of oil olive, and **h**; H1706
11: 9 a land that floweth with milk and **h**. H1706
26: 9 a land that floweth with milk and **h**. H1706
15 a land that floweth with milk and **h**. H1706
27: 3 with milk and **h**; as the LORD God of H1706
31:20 with milk and **h**; and they shall have H1706
32:13 he made him to suck **h** out of the rock, H1706
Jos 5: 6 us, a land that floweth with milk and **h**. H1706
Jdg 14: 8 of bees and **h** in the carcase of the lion. H1706
9 the **h** out of the carcase of the lion. H1706
18 *is* sweeter than **h**? and what *is* stronger H1706
1Sa 14:25 and there was **h** upon the ground. H1706
26 wood, behold, the **h** dropped; but no H1706
29 because I tasted a little of this **h**. H1706
43 but taste a little **h** with the end of the H1706
2Sa 17:29 And **h**, and butter, and sheep, and H1706
1Ki 14: 3 and a cruse of **h**, and go to him: he shall H1706
2Ki 18:32 of oil olive and of **h**, that ye may live, H1706
2Ch 31: 5 corn, wine, and oil, and **h**, and of all the H1706
Job 20:17 the floods, the brooks of **h** and butter. H1706
Ps 19:10 also than **h** and the honeycomb. H1706
81:16 the wheat: and with **h** out of the rock H1706
119:103 taste! *yea, sweeter* than **h** to my mouth! H1706
Prv 24:13 My son, eat thou **h**, because *it is* good; H1706
25:16 Hast thou found **h**? eat so much as is H1706
27 *It is* not good to eat much **h**: so *for men* H1706
Song 4:11 the honeycomb: **h** and milk *are* under H1706
5: 1 with my **h**; I have drunk my wine H1706
Isa 7:15 Butter and **h** shall he eat, that he may H1706
22 for butter and **h** shall every one eat that H1706
Jer 11: 5 with milk and **h**, as *it is* this day. Then H1706
32:22 them, a land flowing with milk and **h**; H1706
41: 8 and of oil, and of **h**. So he forbare, and H1706
Ezk 3: 3 it was in my mouth as **h** for sweetness. H1706
16:13 eat fine flour, and **h**, and oil: and thou H1706
19 flour, and oil, and **h**, *wherewith* I fed H1706
20: 6 and **h**, which *is* the glory of all lands: H1706
15 and **h**, which *is* the glory of all lands; H1706
27:17 and Pannag, and **h**, and oil, and balm. H1706
Mt 3: 4 and his meat was locusts and wild **h**. *G3192*
Mk 1: 6 loins; and he did eat locusts and wild **h**; *G3192*
Rev 10: 9 but it shall be in thy mouth sweet as **h**. *G3192*
10 mouth sweet as **h**: and as soon as I had *G3192*

HONEYCOMB

1Sa 14:27 it in an **h**, and put his hand H3295+H1706
Ps 19:10 also than honey and the **h**. H5317+H6688
Prv 5: 3 **h**, and her mouth *is* smoother than oil: H5317
16:24 Pleasant words *are as* an **h**, H6688+H1706
24:13 and the **h**, *which is* sweet to thy taste: H5317
27: 7 The full soul loatheth an **h**; but to the H5317
Song 4:11 Thy lips, O *my* spouse, drop *as* the **h**: H5317
5: 1 I have eaten my **h** with my honey; I H3293
Lk 24:42 of a broiled fish, and of an **h**. *G3193+G2781*

HONOUR

Gen 49: 6 assembly, mine **h**, be not thou united: H3519
Ex 14:17 and I will get me **h** upon Pharaoh, and H3513
18 I have gotten me **h** upon Pharaoh, H3513
20:12 **H** thy father and thy mother: that thy H3513
Lev 19:15 of the poor, nor **h** the person of the H1921
32 hoary head, and **h** the face of the old H1921
Nu 22:17 thee unto very great **h**, and I will do H3513
37 I not able indeed to promote thee to **h**? H3513
24:11 thee unto great **h**; but, lo, the LORD H3513
11 the LORD hath kept thee back from **h**. H3519
27:20 And thou shalt put *some* of thine **h** H1935
Dt 5:16 **H** thy father and thy mother, as the H3513
26:19 and in name, and in **h**; and that thou H8597
Jdg 4: 9 not be for thine **h**; for the LORD shall H8597
9: 9 by me they **h** God and man, and H3513
13:17 sayings come to pass we may do thee **h**? H3513
1Sa 2:30 me; for them that **h** me I will honour, H3513
30 that honour me I will **h**, and they that H3513
15:30 Then he said, I have sinned: *yet* **h** me H3513
2Sa 6:22 spoken of, of them shall I be had in **h**. H3513
10: 3 that David doth **h** thy father, that he H3513
1Ki 3:13 both riches, and **h**: so that there shall H3519
1Ch 16:27 Glory and **h** *are* in his presence; H1926
17:18 to thee for the **h** of thy servant? for thou H3519
19: 3 that David doth **h** thy father, that he H3513
29:12 Both riches and **h** *come* of thee, and H3519
28 of days, riches, and **h**: and Solomon his H3519
2Ch 1:11 riches, wealth, or **h**, nor the life of thine H3519
12 and wealth, and **h**, such as none of the H3519
17: 5 and he had riches and **h** in abundance. H3519
18: 1 Now Jehoshaphat had riches and **h** in H3519
26:18 *it be* for thine **h** from the LORD God. H3519
32:27 much riches and **h**: and he made H3519
33 Jerusalem did him **h** at his death. And H3519
Est 1: 4 kingdom and the **h** of his excellent H3366
20 husbands **h**, both to great and small. H3366
6: 3 And the king said, What **h** and dignity H3366
6 the king delighteth to **h**? Now Haman H3366
6 delight to do **h** more than to myself? H3366
7 the man whom the king delighteth to **h**, H3366
9 king delighteth to **h**, and bring him on H3366
9 the man whom the king delighteth to **h**. H3366
11 the man whom the king delighteth to **h**. H3366
8:16 had light, and gladness, and joy, and **h**. H3366
Job 14:21 His sons come to **h**, and he knoweth *it* H3513
Ps 7: 5 and lay mine **h** in the dust. Selah. H3519
8: 5 and hast crowned him with glory and **h**. H1926
21: 5 His glory *is* great in thy salvation: **h** H1935
26: 8 and the place where thine **h** dwelleth. H3519
49:12 Nevertheless man *being* in **h** abideth H3366
20 Man *that is* in **h**, and understandeth H3366
66: 2 Sing forth the **h** of his name: make his H3519
71: 8 thy praise *and with* thy **h** all the day. H8597
Ps 91:15 trouble; I will deliver him, and **h** him. H3513
96: 6 **H** and majesty *are* before him: strength H1935
104: 1 thou art clothed with **h** and majesty. H1935
112: 9 ever; his horn shall be exalted with **h**. H3519
145: 5 I will speak of the glorious **h** of thy H1926
149: 9 written: this **h** have all his saints. H1926
Prv 3: 9 **H** the LORD with thy substance, and H3513
16 hand; *and* in her left hand riches and **h**. H3519
4: 8 thee to **h**, when thou dost embrace her. H3513
5: 9 Lest thou give thine **h** unto others, and H1935
8:18 Riches and **h** *are* with me; *yea*, durable H3519
11:16 A gracious woman retaineth **h**: and H3519
14:28 *is* the king's **h**: but in the want of people H1927
15:33 of wisdom; and before **h** *is* humility. H3519
18:12 is haughty, and before **h** *is* humility. H3519
20: 3 *It is* an **h** for a man to cease from strife: H3519
21:21 findeth life, righteousness, and **h**. H3519
22: 4 of the LORD *are* riches, and **h**, and life. H3519
25: 2 the **h** of kings *is* to search out a matter. H3519
26: 1 in harvest, so **h** is not seemly for a fool. H3519
8 a sling, so *is* he that giveth **h** to a fool. H3519
29:23 but **h** shall uphold the humble in spirit. H3519
31:25 Strength and **h** *are* her clothing; and H1926
Ecc 6: 2 wealth, and **h**, so that he wanteth H3519
10: 1 that is in reputation for wisdom *and* **h**. H3519
Isa 29:13 and with their lips do **h** me, but have H3513
43:20 The beast of the field shall **h** me, the H3513
58:13 and shalt **h** him, not doing thine H3513
Jer 33: 9 a praise and an **h** before all the nations H8597
Dan 2: 6 rewards and great **h**: therefore shew me H3367
4:30 my power, and for the **h** of my majesty? H3367
36 my kingdom, mine **h** and brightness H1923
37 and extol and **h** the King of heaven, H1922
5:18 and majesty, and glory, and **h**: H1923
11:21 shall not give the **h** of the kingdom: but H1935
38 But in his estate shall he **h** the God of H3513
38 knew not shall he **h** with gold, and H3513
Mal 1: 6 where *is* mine **h**? and if I *be* a master, H3519
Mt 13:57 is not without **h**, save in his own country, *G820*
15: 4 For God commanded, saying, **H** thy *G5091*
6 And **h** not his father or his mother, *he* *G5091*
19:19 **H** thy father and *thy* mother: and, *G5091*
Mk 6: 4 is not without **h**, but in his own country, *G820*
7:10 For Moses said, **H** thy father and thy *G5091*
10:19 Defraud not, **H** thy father and mother. *G5091*
Lk 18:20 witness, **H** thy father and thy mother. *G5091*
Jn 4:44 prophet hath no **h** in his own country. *G5092*
5:23 That all *men* should **h** the Son, even as *G5091*
23 Son, even as they **h** the Father. He that *G5091*
41 I receive not **h** from men. *G1391*
44 How can ye believe, which receive **h** *G1391*
44 not the **h** that *cometh* from God only? *G1391*
8:49 **h** my Father, and ye do dishonour me. *G5091*
54 Jesus answered, If I **h** myself, my *G1392*
54 myself, my **h** is nothing: it is my Father *G1391*
12:26 man serve me, him will *my* Father **h**. *G5091*
Ro 2: 7 and **h** and immortality, eternal life: *G5092*
10 But glory, **h**, and peace, to every man *G5092*
9:21 unto **h**, and another unto dishonour? *G5092*
12:10 love; in **h** preferring one another; *G5092*
13: 7 fear to whom fear; **h** to whom honour. *G5092*
7 fear to whom fear; honour to whom **h**. *G5092*
1Co 12:23 more abundant **h**; and our uncomely *G5092*
24 abundant **h** to that *part* which lacked: *G5092*
2Co 6: 8 By **h** and dishonour, by evil report and *G1391*
Eph 6: 2 **H** thy father and mother; which is the *G5091*
Col 2:23 in any **h** to the satisfying of the flesh. *G5092*
1Th 4: 4 his vessel in sanctification and **h**; *G5092*
1Ti 1:17 *be* **h** and glory for ever and ever. Amen. *G5092*
5: 3 **H** widows that are widows indeed. *G5091*
17 worthy of double **h**, especially they who *G5092*
6: 1 worthy of all **h**, that the name of God *G5092*
16 *be* **h** and power everlasting. Amen. *G5092*
2Ti 2:20 and some to **h**, and some to dishonour. *G5092*
21 be a vessel unto **h**, sanctified, and meet *G5092*
Heb 2: 7 with glory and **h**, and didst set him over *G5092*
9 with glory and **h**; that he by the grace *G5092*
3: 3 the house hath more **h** than the house. *G5092*
5: 4 And no man taketh this **h** unto himself, *G5092*
1Pt 1: 7 unto praise and **h** and glory at the *G5092*
2:17 **H** all *men*. Love the brotherhood. Fear *G5091*
17 the brotherhood. Fear God. **H** the king. *G5091*
3: 7 to knowledge, giving **h** unto the wife, as *G5092*
2Pt 1:17 For he received from God the Father **h** *G5092*
Rev 4: 9 And when those beasts give glory and **h** *G5092*
11 receive glory and **h** and power: for thou *G5092*
5:12 and **h**, and glory, and blessing. *G5092*
13 Blessing, and **h**, and glory, and power, *G5092*
7:12 thanksgiving, and **h**, and power, and *G5092*

H

Rev 19: 1 **h**, and power, unto the Lord our God: *G5092*
7 Let us be glad and rejoice, and give **h** to *G1391*
21:24 earth do bring their glory and **h** into it. *G5092*
26 And they shall bring the glory and **h** of *G5092*

HONOURABLE
Gen 34:19 more **h** than all the house of his father. H3513
Nu 22:15 princes, more, and more **h** than they. H3513
1Sa 9: 6 of God, and *he is* an **h** man; all that he H3513
22:14 at thy bidding, and is **h** in thine house? H3513
2Sa 23:19 Was he not most **h** of three? therefore H3513
23 He was more **h** than the thirty, but he H3513
2Ki 5: 1 master, and **h**, because by him H5375+H6440
1Ch 4: 9 And Jabez was more **h** than his H3513
11:21 Of the three, he was more **h** than the H3513
25 Behold, he was **h** among the thirty, but H3513
Job 22: 8 and the **h** man dwelt in it. H5375+H6440
Ps 45: 9 Kings' daughters *were* among thy **h** H3368
111: 3 His work *is* **h** and glorious: and his H1935
Isa 3: 3 The captain of fifty, and the **h** H5375+H6440
5 the ancient, and the base against the **h**. H3513
5:13 and their **h** men *are* famished, H3519
9:15 The ancient and **h**, he *is* the H5375+H6440
23: 8 whose traffickers *are* the **h** of the earth? H3513
9 into contempt all the **h** of the earth. H3513
42:21 he will magnify the law, and make *it* **h**. H142
43: 4 thou hast been **h**, and I have loved thee: H3513
58:13 holy of the LORD, **h**; and shalt honour H3513
Nah 3:10 they cast lots for her **h** men, and all her H3513
Mk 15:43 Joseph of Arimathaea, an **h** counsellor, *G2158*
Lk 14: 8 **h** man than thou be bidden of him; *G1484*
Act 13:50 up the devout and **h** women, and the *G2158*
17:12 believed; also of **h** women which were *G2158*
1Co 4:10 strong; ye *are* **h**, but we *are* despised. *G1741*
12:23 we think to be less **h**, upon these we *G820*
Heb 13: 4 Marriage *is* **h** in all, and the bed *G5093*

HONOURED
Ex 14: 4 and I will be **h** upon Pharaoh, and H3513
Prv 13:18 but he that regardeth reproof shall be **h**. H3513
27:18 he that waiteth on his master shall be **h**. H3513
Isa 43:23 neither hast thou **h** me with thy H3513
Lam 1: 8 is removed: all that **h** her despise her, H3513
5:12 hand: the faces of elders were not **h**. H1921
Dan 4:34 and I praised and **h** him that liveth for H1922
Act 28:10 Who also **h** us with many honours; and *G5092*
1Co 12:26 be **h**, all the members rejoice with it. *G1392*

HONOUREST
1Sa 2:29 habitation; and **h** thy sons above me, H3513

HONOURETH
Ps 15: 4 but he **h** them that fear the LORD. H3513
Prv 12: 9 he that **h** himself, and lacketh bread. H3513
14:31 he that **h** him hath mercy on the poor. H3513
Mal 1: 6 A son **h** *his* father, and a servant his H3513
Mt 15: 8 their mouth, and **h** me with *their* lips; *G5091*
Mk 7: 6 This people **h** me with *their* lips, but *G5091*
Jn 5:23 the Father. He that **h** not the Son *G5091*
23 **h** not the Father which hath sent him. *G5091*
8:54 it is my Father that **h** me; of whom ye *G1392*

HONOURS
Act 28:10 Who also honoured us with many **h**; *G5091*

HOODS
Isa 3:23 the fine linen, and the **h**, and the vails. H6797

HOOF
Ex 10:26 there shall not an **h** be left behind; for H6541
Lev 11: 3 Whatsoever parteth the **h**, and is H6541
4 that divide the **h**: *as* the camel, because H6541
4 not the **h**; he *is* unclean unto you. H6541
5 not the **h**; he *is* unclean unto you. H6541
6 not the **h**; he *is* unclean unto you. H6541
7 And the swine, though he divide the **h**, H6541
26 divideth the **h**, and *is* not clovenfooted, H6541
Dt 14: 6 And every beast that parteth the **h**, and H6541
7 divide the cloven **h**; *as* the camel, and H6541
7 **h**; *therefore* they *are* unclean unto you. H6541
8 it divideth the **h**, yet cheweth not the H6541

HOOFS
Ps 69:31 an ox *or* bullock that hath horns and **h**. H6536
Isa 5:28 bent, their horses' **h** shall be counted H6541
Jer 47: 3 At the noise of the stamping of the **h** of H6541
Ezk 26:11 With the **h** of his horses shall he tread H6541
32:13 more, nor the **h** of beasts trouble them. H6541
Mic 4:13 I will make thy **h** brass: and thou shalt H6541

HOOK
2Ki 19:28 I will put my **h** in thy nose, and my H2397
Job 41: 1 leviathan with an **h**? or his tongue with H2443
2 Canst thou put an **h** into his nose? or H100
Isa 37:29 will I put my **h** in thy nose, and my H2397
Mt 17:27 sea, and cast an **h**, and take up the fish *G44*

HOOKS
Ex 26:32 with gold: their **h** *shall be of* gold, upon H2053
37 gold, *and* their **h** *shall be of* gold: and H2053
27:10 *be of* brass; the **h** of the pillars and H2053
11 **h** of the pillars and their fillets *of* silver. H2053
17 with silver; their **h** *shall be of* silver, H2053
36:36 with gold: their **h** *were of* gold; and he H2053
38 And the five pillars of it with their **h**: H2053
38:10 twenty; the **h** of the pillars and their H2053
11 **h** of the pillars and their fillets *of* silver. H2053
12 **h** of the pillars and their fillets *of* silver. H2053
17 *were of* brass; the **h** of the pillars and H2053
19 *of* brass four; their **h** *of* silver, and the H2053
28 shekels he made **h** for the pillars, and H2053
Isa 18: 5 with pruning **h**, and take away *and* H4211
Ezk 29: 4 But I will put **h** in thy jaws, and I will H2397
38: 4 And I will turn thee back, and put **h** H2397
40:43 And within *were* **h**, an hand broad, H8240
Am 4: 2 **h**, and your posterity with fishhooks. H6793

HOPE
Ru 1:12 should say, I have **h**, *if* I should have an H8615
Ezr 10: 2 is **h** in Israel concerning this thing. H4723
Job 4: 6 thy **h**, and the uprightness of thy ways? H8615
5:16 So the poor hath **h**, and iniquity H8615
6:11 What *is* my strength, that I should **h**? H3176
7: 6 shuttle, and are spent without **h**. H8615
8:13 and the hypocrite's **h** shall perish: H8615
14 Whose **h** shall be cut off, and whose H3689
11:18 because there is **h**; yea, thou shalt dig H8615
20 **h** *shall be as* the giving up of the ghost. H8615
14: 7 For there is **h** of a tree, if it be cut H8615
19 and thou destroyest the **h** of man. H8615
17:15 And where *is* now my **h**? as for my hope, H8615
15 my hope? as for my **h**, who shall see it? H8615
19:10 mine **h** hath he removed like a tree. H8615
27: 8 For what *is* the **h** of the hypocrite, H8615
31:24 If I have made gold my **h**, or have said H3689
41: 9 Behold, the **h** of him is in vain: shall H8431
Ps 16: 9 rejoiceth: my flesh also shall rest in **h**. H983
22: 9 **h** *when I was* upon my mother's breasts. H982
31:24 your heart, all ye that **h** in the LORD. H3176
33:18 him, upon them that **h** in his mercy; H3176
22 be upon us, according as we **h** in thee. H3176
38:15 For in thee, O LORD, do I **h**: thou wilt H3176
39: 7 And now, Lord, what wait I for? my **h** *is* H8431
42: 5 disquieted in me? **h** thou in God: for I H3176
11 within me? **h** thou in God: for I shall H3176
43: 5 within me? **h** in God: for I shall yet H3176
71: 5 For thou *art* my **h**, O Lord GOD: *thou* H8615
14 But I will **h** continually, and will yet H3176
78: 7 That they might set their **h** in God, and H3689
119:49 upon which thou hast caused me to **h**. H3176
81 for thy salvation: *but* I **h** in thy word. H3176
114 place and my shield: I **h** in thy word. H3176
116 and let me not be ashamed of my **h**. H7664
130: 5 soul doth wait, and in his word do I **h**. H3176
7 Let Israel **h** in the LORD: for with the H3176
131: 3 Let Israel **h** in the LORD from H3176
146: 5 help, whose **h** *is* in the LORD his God: H7664
147:11 fear him, in those that **h** in his mercy. H3176
Prv 10:28 The **h** of the righteous *shall be* H8431
11: 7 and the **h** of unjust *men* perisheth. H8431
13:12 **H** deferred maketh the heart sick: but H8431
14:32 but the righteous hath **h** in his death. H2620
19:18 Chasten thy son while there is **h**, and let H8615
26:12 *there is* more **h** of a fool than of him. H8615
29:20 *there is* more **h** of a fool than of him. H8615
Ecc 9: 4 all the living there is **h**: for a living dog is H986
Isa 38:18 into the pit cannot **h** for thy truth. H7663
57:10 not, There is no **h**: thou hast found the H2976
Jer 2:25 thou saidst, There is no **h**: no; for I have H2976
14: 8 O the **h** of Israel, the saviour thereof in H4723
17: 7 in the LORD, and whose **h** the LORD is. H4009
13 O LORD, the **h** of Israel, all that forsake H4723
17 Be not a terror unto me: thou *art* my **h** H4268
18:12 And they said, There is no **h**: but we will H2976
31:17 And there is **h** in thine end, saith the H8615
50: 7 even the LORD, the **h** of their fathers. H4723
Lam 3:18 And I said, My strength and my **h** is H8431
21 I recall to my mind, therefore have I **h**. H3176
24 saith my soul; therefore will I **h** in him. H3176
Lam 3:26 *It is* good that *a man* should both **h** H2342
29 in the dust; if so be there may be **h**. H8615
Ezk 13: 6 to **h** that they would confirm the word. H3176
19: 5 waited, *and* her **h** was lost, then she H8615
37:11 **h** is lost: we are cut off for our parts. H8615
Hos 2:15 for a door of **h**: and she shall sing there, H8615
Joel 3:16 LORD *will be* the **h** of his people, and H4268
Zec 9:12 hold, ye prisoners of **h**: even to day do I H8615
Lk 6:34 And if ye lend *to them* of whom ye **h** to *G1679*
Act 2:26 moreover also my flesh shall rest in **h**: *G1680*
16:19 And when her masters saw that the **h** *G1680*
23: 6 a Pharisee: of the **h** and resurrection of *G1680*
24:15 And have **h** toward God, which they *G1680*
26: 6 and am judged for the **h** of the promise *G1680*
7 day and night, **h** to come. For which *G1679*
27:20 lay on *us*, all **h** that we should be saved *G1680*
28:20 **h** of Israel I am bound with this chain. *G1680*
Ro 4:18 Who against **h** believed in hope, that *G1680*
18 Who against hope believed in **h**, that he *G1680*
5: 2 and rejoice in **h** of the glory of God. *G1680*
4 patience, experience; and experience, **h**: *G1680*
5 And **h** maketh not ashamed; because *G1680*
8:20 him who hath subjected *the same* in **h**, *G1680*
24 For we are saved by **h**: but hope that is *G1680*
24 For we are saved by hope: but **h** that is *G1680*
24 that is seen is not **h**: for what a man *G1680*
24 a man seeth, why doth he yet **h** for? *G1679*
25 But if we **h** for that we see not, *then* do *G1679*
12:12 Rejoicing in **h**; patient in tribulation; *G1680*
15: 4 comfort of the scriptures might have **h**. *G1680*
13 Now the God of **h** fill you with all joy *G1680*
13 **h**, through the power of the Holy Ghost. *G1680*
1Co 9:10 should plow in **h**; and that he that *G1680*
10 in **h** should be partaker of his hope. *G1680*
10 in hope should be partaker of his **h**. *G1680*
13:13 And now abideth faith, **h**, charity, these *G1680*
15:19 If in this life only we have **h** in Christ, *G1679*
2Co 1: 7 And our **h** of you *is* stedfast, knowing, *G1680*
3:12 Seeing then that we have such **h**, we use *G1680*
10:15 but having **h**, when your faith is *G1680*
Gal 5: 5 For we through the Spirit wait for the **h** *G1680*
Eph 1:18 know what is the **h** of his calling, and *G1680*
2:12 no **h**, and without God in the world: *G1680*
4: 4 as ye are called in one **h** of your calling; *G1680*
Php 1:20 and *my* **h**, that in nothing I shall *G1680*
2:23 Him therefore I **h** to send presently, so *G1679*
Col 1: 5 For the **h** which is laid up for you in *G1680*
23 away from the **h** of the gospel, which *G1680*
27 which is Christ in you, the **h** of glory: *G1680*
1Th 1: 3 and patience of **h** in our Lord Jesus *G1680*
2:19 For what *is* our **h**, or joy, or crown of *G1680*
4:13 not, even as others which have no **h**. *G1680*
5: 8 and for an helmet, the **h** of salvation. *G1680*
2Th 2:16 consolation and good **h** through grace, *G1680*
1Ti 1: 1 and Lord Jesus Christ, *which is* our **h**; *G1680*
Tit 1: 2 In **h** of eternal life, which God, that *G1680*
2:13 Looking for that blessed **h**, and the *G1680*
3: 7 heirs according to the **h** of eternal life. *G1680*
Heb 3: 6 the rejoicing of the **h** firm unto the end. *G1680*
6:11 to the full assurance of **h** unto the end: *G1680*
18 to lay hold upon the **h** set before us: *G1680*
19 Which *h* we have as an anchor of the
7:19 in of a better **h** *did*; by the which we *G1680*
1Pt 1: 3 us again unto a lively **h** by the *G1680*
13 be sober, and **h** to the end for the grace *G1679*
21 that your faith and **h** might be in God. *G1680*
3:15 you a reason of the **h** that is in you with *G1680*
1Jn 3: 3 And every man that hath this **h** in him *G1680*

HOPED
Est 9: 1 of the Jews **h** to have power over H7663
Job 6:20 **h**; they came thither, and were ashamed. H982
Ps 119:43 mouth; for I have **h** in thy judgments. H3176
74 see me; because I have **h** in thy word. H3176
147 morning, and cried: I **h** in thy word. H3176
166 LORD, I have **h** for thy salvation, and H7663
Jer 3:23 Truly in vain *is salvation **h** for* from the
Lk 23: 8 of him; and he **h** to have seen some *G1679*
Act 24:26 He **h** also that money should have been *G1679*
2Co 8: 5 And *this they did*, not as we **h**, but first *G1679*
Heb 11: 1 Now faith is the substance of things **h** *G1679*

HOPE'S
Act 26: 7 come. For which **h** sake, king Agrippa, *G1679*

HOPETH
1Co 13: 7 things, **h** all things, endureth all things. *G1679*

HOPHNI
1Sa 1: 3 two sons of Eli, H and Phinehas, the H2652
2:34 thy two sons, on H and Phinehas; in H2652
4: 4 two sons of Eli, H and Phinehas, *were* H2652
11 sons of Eli, H and Phinehas, were slain. H2652
17 thy two sons also, H and Phinehas, are H2652

HOPHRA See PHARAOH-HOPHRA.

HOPING
Lk 6:35 do good, and lend, h for nothing again; *G560*
1Ti 3:14 These things write I unto thee, h to *G1679*

HOR
Nu 20:22 from Kadesh, and came unto mount H. H2023
23 Aaron in mount H, by the coast of the H2023
25 son, and bring them up unto mount H: H2023
27 H in the sight of all the congregation. H2023
21: 4 And they journeyed from mount H by H2023
33:37 H, in the edge of the land of Edom. H2023
38 up into mount H at the commandment H2023
39 years old when he died in mount H. H2023
41 And they departed from mount H, and H2023
34: 7 sea ye shall point out for you mount H: H2023
8 From mount H ye shall point out *your* H2023
Dt 32:50 H, and was gathered unto his people: H2023

HORAM
Jos 10:33 Then H king of Gezer came up to help H2036

HOREB
Ex 3: 1 to the mountain of God, *even* to H. H2722
17: 6 there upon the rock in H; and thou shalt H2722
33: 6 of their ornaments by the mount H. H2722
Dt 1: 2 (*There are* eleven days' *journey* from H H2722
6 The LORD our God spake unto us in H, H2722
19 And when we departed from H, we H2722
4:10 the LORD thy God in H, when the LORD H2722
15 you in H out of the midst of the fire: H2722
5: 2 our God made a covenant with us in H. H2722
9: 8 Also in H ye provoked the LORD to H2722
18:16 LORD thy God in H in the day of the H2722
29: 1 which he made with them in H. H2722
1Ki 8: 9 put there at H, when the LORD made H2722
19: 8 forty nights unto H the mount of God. H2722
2Ch 5:10 put *therein* at H, when the LORD made H2722
Ps 106:19 They made a calf in H, and worshipped H2722
Mal 4: 4 unto him in H for all Israel, *with* the H2722

HOREM
Jos 19:38 And Iron, and Migdal-el, H, and H2765

HOR-HAGIDGAD
Nu 33:32 from Bene-jaakan, and encamped at H. H2735
33 And they went from H, and pitched in H2735

HORI
Gen 36:22 And the children of Lotan were H and H2753
30 *that came* of H, among their dukes H2753
Nu 13: 5 tribe of Simeon, Shaphat the son of H. H2753
1Ch 1:39 And the sons of Lotan; H, and Homam: H2753

HORIMS
Dt 2:12 The H also dwelt in Seir beforetime; H2752
22 he destroyed the H from before them; H2752

HORITE
Gen 36:20 These *are* the sons of Seir the H, who H2752

HORITES
Gen 14: 6 And the H in their mount Seir, unto H2752
36:21 the dukes of the H, the children of Seir H2752
29 These *are* the dukes *that came* of the H; H2752

HORMAH
Nu 14:45 and discomfited them, *even* unto H. H2767
21: 3 and he called the name of the place H. H2767
Dt 1:44 and destroyed you in Seir, *even* unto H. H2767
Jos 12:14 The king of H, one; the king of Arad, H2767
15:30 And Eltolad, and Chesil, and H, H2767
19: 4 And Eltolad, and Bethul, and H, H2767
Jdg 1:17 And the name of the city was called H. H2767
1Sa 30:30 And to *them* which *were* in H, and to H2767
1Ch 4:30 And at Bethuel, and at H, and at Ziklag, H2767

HORN
Ex 21:29 to push with his h in time past, and it
Jos 6: 5 with the ram's h, *and* when ye hear the H7161
1Sa 2: 1 in the LORD, mine h is exalted in the H7161
2:10 king, and exalt the h of his anointed. H7161
16: 1 Israel? fill thine h with oil, and go, I will H7161
13 Then Samuel took the h of oil, and H7161
2Sa 22: 3 *is* my shield, and the h of my salvation, H7161
1Ki 1:39 And Zadok the priest took an h of oil H7161
1Ch 25: 5 of God, to lift up the h. And God gave to H7161
Job 16:15 my skin, and defiled my h in the dust. H7161
Ps 18: 2 h of my salvation, *and* my high tower. H7161
75: 4 and to the wicked, Lift not up the h: H7161
5 Lift not up your h on high: speak *not* H7161
89:17 in thy favour our h shall be exalted. H7161
24 and in my name shall his h be exalted. H7161
92:10 But my h shalt thou exalt like *the horn* H7161
10 But my horn shalt thou exalt like *the h of*
112: 9 his h shall be exalted with honour. H7161
132:17 There will I make the h of David to H7161
148:14 He also exalteth the h of his people, the H7161
Jer 48:25 The h of Moab is cut off, and his arm is H7161
Lam 2: 3 fierce anger all the h of Israel: he hath H7161
17 hath set up the h of thine adversaries. H7161
Ezk 29:21 In that day will I cause the h of the H7161
Dan 7: 8 another little h, before whom there H7162
8 behold, in this h *were* eyes like the eyes H7162
11 words which the h spake: I beheld *even* H7162
20 fell; even *of* that h that had eyes, and a H7162
21 I beheld, and the same h made war H7162
8: 5 goat *had* a notable h between his eyes. H7161
8 strong, the great h was broken; and for H7161
9 them came forth a little h, which waxed H7161
21 and the great h that *is* between his H7161
Mic 4:13 for I will make thine h iron, and I will H7161
Zec 1:21 h over the land of Judah to scatter it. H7161
Lk 1:69 And hath raised up an h of salvation *G2768*

HORNET
Dt 7:20 God will send the h among them, until H6880
Jos 24:12 And I sent the h before you, which H6880

HORNETS
Ex 23:28 And I will send h before thee, which H6880

HORNS
Gen 22:13 in a thicket by his h: and Abraham H7161
Ex 27: 2 And thou shalt make the h of it upon H7161
2 thereof: his h shall be of the same: H7161
29:12 put *it* upon the h of the altar with thy H7161
30: 2 the h thereof *shall be* of the same. H7161
3 about, and the h thereof; and thou H7161
10 upon the h of it once in a year with H7161
37:25 of it; the h thereof were of the same. H7161
26 about, and the h of it: also he made H7161
38: 2 And he made the h thereof on the four H7161
2 corners of it; the h thereof were of the H7161
Lev 4: 7 blood upon the h of the altar of sweet H7161
18 blood upon the h of the altar which *is* H7161
25 put *it* upon the h of the altar of burnt H7161
30 put *it* upon the h of the altar of burnt H7161
34 put *it* upon the h of the altar of burnt H7161
8:15 and put *it* upon the h of the altar round H7161
9: 9 and put *it* upon the h of the altar, and H7161
16:18 *it* upon the h of the altar round about. H7161
Dt 33:17 bullock, and his h *are like* the horns of H7161
17 horns *are like* the h of unicorns: with H7161
Jos 6: 4 trumpets of rams' h: and the seventh H3104
6 of rams' h before the ark of the LORD. H3104
8 trumpets of rams' h passed on before H3104
13 trumpets of rams' h before the ark of H3104
1Ki 1:50 and caught hold on the h of the altar. H7161
51 hold on the h of the altar, saying, H7161
2:28 and caught hold on the h of the altar. H7161
22:11 made him h of iron: and he said, H7161
2Ch 18:10 had made him h of iron, and said, H7161
Ps 22:21 heard me from the h of the unicorns. H7161
69:31 an ox *or* bullock that hath h and hoofs. H7160
75:10 All the h of the wicked also will I cut H7161
10 the h of the righteous shall be exalted. H7161
118:27 with cords, *even* unto the h of the altar. H7161
Jer 17: 1 heart, and upon the h of your altars; H7161
Ezk 27:15 thee *for* a present h of ivory and ebony. H7161
34:21 h, till ye have scattered them abroad; H7161
43:15 the altar and upward *shall be* four h. H7161
20 and put *it* on the four h of it, and on the H7161
Dan 7: 7 that *were* before it; and it had ten h. H7162
8 I considered the h, and, behold, there H7162
8 three of the first h plucked up by the H7162
20 And of the ten h that *were* in his head, H7162
24 And the ten h out of this kingdom *are* H7162
8: 3 which had *two* h: and the *two* horns H7161
3 and the *two* h *were* high; but one *was* H7161
8: 6 And he came to the ram that had *two* h, H7161
7 and brake his two h: and there was no H7161
20 h *are* the kings of Media and Persia. H7161
Am 3:14 of Beth-el: and the h of the altar shall H7161
6:13 not taken to us h by our own strength? H7161
Hab 3: 4 as the light; he had h *coming* out of his H7161
Zec 1:18 mine eyes, and saw, and behold four h. H7161
19 me, These *are* the h which have H7161
21 These *are* the h which have scattered H7161
21 to cast out the h of the Gentiles, which H7161
Rev 5: 6 having seven h and seven eyes, which *G2768*
9:13 from the four h of the golden altar *G2768*
12: 3 h, and seven crowns upon his heads. *G2768*
13: 1 heads and ten h, and upon his horns *G2768*
1 and upon his h ten crowns, and upon *G2768*
11 and he had two h like a lamb, and he *G2768*
17: 3 having seven heads and ten h. *G2768*
7 which hath the seven heads and ten h. *G2768*
12 And the ten h which thou sawest are *G2768*
16 And the ten h which thou sawest upon *G2768*

HORON See BETH-HORON and HORONITE.

HORONAIM
Isa 15: 5 for in the way of H they shall raise up a H2773
Jer 48: 3 A voice of crying *shall be* from H, H2773
5 the going down of H the enemies have H2773
34 Zoar *even* unto H, *as* an heifer of three H2773

HORONITE
Neh 2:10 When Sanballat the H, and Tobiah the H2772
19 But when Sanballat the H, and Tobiah H2772
13:28 the H: therefore I chased him from me. H2772

HORRIBLE
Ps 11: 6 brimstone, and an h tempest: *this shall* H2152
40: 2 He brought me up also out of an h pit, H7588
Jer 5:30 A wonderful and h thing is committed H8186
18:13 of Israel hath done a very h thing. H8186
23:14 of Jerusalem an h thing: they commit H8186
Hos 6:10 I have seen an h thing in the house of H8186

HORRIBLY
Jer 2:12 at this, and be h afraid, be ye very H8175
Ezk 32:10 kings shall be h afraid for thee, when H8178

HORROR
Gen 15:12 lo, an h of great darkness fell upon him. H367
Ps 55: 5 upon me, and h hath overwhelmed me. H6427
119:53 H hath taken hold upon me because of H2152
Ezk 7:18 sackcloth, and h shall cover them; and H6427

HORSE
Gen 49:17 that biteth the h heels, so that his rider H5483
Ex 15: 1 gloriously: the h and his rider hath he H5483
19 For the h of Pharaoh went in with his H5483
21 gloriously; the h and his rider hath he H5483
1Ki 10:29 of silver, and an h for an hundred and H5483
20:20 escaped on an h with the horsemen. H5483
25 thou hast lost, h for horse, and chariot H5483
25 hast lost, horse for h, and chariot for H5483
2Ch 1:17 of silver, and an h for an hundred and H5483
23:15 the entering of the h gate by the king's H5483
Neh 3:28 From above the h gate repaired the H5483
Est 6: 8 to wear, and the h that the king rideth H5483
9 And let this apparel and h be delivered H5483
10 the apparel and the h, as thou hast said, H5483
11 the apparel and the h, and arrayed H5483
Job 39:18 high, she scorneth the h and his rider. H5483
19 Hast thou given the h strength? hast H5483
Ps 32: 9 Be ye not as the h, *or* as the mule, *which* H5483
33:17 An h *is* a vain thing for safety: neither H5483
76: 6 and h are cast into a dead sleep. H5483
147:10 in the strength of the h: he taketh not H5483
Prv 21:31 The h *is* prepared against the day of H5483
26: 3 A whip for the h, a bridle for the ass, H5483
Isa 43:17 Which bringeth forth the chariot and h, H5483
63:13 the deep, as an h in the wilderness, *that* H5483
Jer 8: 6 course, as the h rusheth into the battle. H5483
31:40 the corner of the h gate toward the H5483
51:21 in pieces the h and his rider; and with H5483
Am 2:15 he that rideth the h deliver himself. H5483
Zec 1: 8 man riding upon a red h, and he stood H5483
9:10 Ephraim, and the h from Jerusalem, H5483
10: 3 them as his goodly h in the battle. H5483
12: 4 I will smite every h with astonishment, H5483
4 every h of the people with blindness. H5483
14:15 And so shall be the plague of the h, of H5483
Rev 6: 2 And I saw, and behold a white h: and *G2462*

Rev 6: 4 And there went out another **h** *that was* G2462
5 and lo a black **h**; and he that sat on him G2462
8 And I looked, and behold a pale **h**: and G2462
14:20 even unto the **h** bridles, by the space G2462
19:11 behold a white **h**; and he that sat upon G2462
19 that sat on the **h**, and against his army. G2462
21 him that sat upon the **h**, which *sword* G2462

HORSEBACK
2Ki 9:18 So there went one on **h** to meet H7392+H5483
19 Then he sent out a second on **h**, H7392+H5483
Est 6: 9 bring him on **h** through the H7392+H5483
11 brought him on **h** through the street of H7392
8:10 sent letters by posts on **h**, *and* riders on H5483

HORSE-GATE See HORSE and GATE.

HORSE-HEELS See HORSE and HEELS.

HORSEHOOFS
Jdg 5:22 Then were the **h** broken by the H6119+H5483

HORSELEACH
Prv 30:15 The **h** hath two daughters, *crying*, Give, H5936

HORSEMAN
2Ki 9:17 said, Take an **h**, and send to meet them, H7395
Nah 3: 3 The **h** lifteth up both the bright sword H6571

HORSEMEN
Gen 50: 9 and **h**: and it was a very great company. H6571
Ex 14: 9 Pharaoh, and his **h**, and his army, and H6571
17 host, upon his chariots, and upon his **h**. H6571
18 upon his chariots, and upon his **h**. H6571
23 horses, his chariots, and his **h**. H6571
26 upon their chariots, and upon their **h**. H6571
28 chariots, and the **h**, *and* all the host of H6571
15:19 and with his **h** into the sea, and the H6571
Jos 24: 6 with chariots and **h** unto the Red sea. H6571
1Sa 8:11 and *to be* his **h**; and *some* shall run H6571
13: 5 and six thousand **h**, and people as the H6571
2Sa 1: 6 and **h** followed hard after him. H1167+H6571
8: 4 seven hundred **h**, and twenty thousand H6571
10:18 forty thousand **h**, and smote Shobach H6571
1Ki 1: 5 and **h**, and fifty men to run before him. H6571
4:26 for his chariots, and twelve thousand **h**. H6571
9:19 and cities for his **h**, and that which H6571
22 and rulers of his chariots, and his **h**. H6571
10:26 chariots and **h**: and he had a thousand H6571
26 twelve thousand **h**, whom he bestowed H6571
20:20 of Syria escaped on an horse with the **h**. H6571
2Ki 2:12 of Israel, and the **h** thereof. And he saw H6571
13: 7 Jehoahaz but fifty **h**, and ten chariots, H6571
14 the chariot of Israel, and the **h** thereof. H6571
18:24 trust on Egypt for chariots and for **h**? H6571
1Ch 18: 4 seven thousand **h**, and twenty thousand H6571
19: 6 hire them chariots and **h** out of H6571
2Ch 1:14 And Solomon gathered chariots and **h**: H6571
14 twelve thousand **h**, which he placed in H6571
8: 6 the cities of the **h**, and all that Solomon H6571
9 and captains of his chariots and **h**. H6571
9:25 twelve thousand **h**; whom he bestowed H6571
12: 3 thousand **h**: and the people *were* H6571
16: 8 chariots and **h**? yet, because thou didst H6571
Ezr 8:22 of soldiers and **h** to help us against the H6571
Neh 2: 9 captains of the army and **h** with me. H6571
Isa 21: 7 And he saw a chariot *with* a couple of **h**, H6571
9 *with* a couple of **h**. And he answered H6571
22: 6 *and* **h**, and Kir uncovered the shield. H6571
7 chariots, and the **h** shall set themselves H6571
28:28 of his cart, nor bruise it *with* his **h**. H6571
31: 1 *are* many; and in **h**, because they are H6571
36: 9 trust on Egypt for chariots and for **h**? H6571
Jer 4:29 the noise of the **h** and bowmen; they H6571
46: 4 Harness the horses; and get up, ye **h**, H6571
Ezk 23: 6 young men, **h** riding upon horses. H6571
12 most gorgeously, **h** riding upon horses, H6571
26: 7 **h**, and companies, and much people. H6571
10 at the noise of the **h**, and of the wheels, H6571
27:14 thy fairs with horses and **h** and mules. H6571
38: 4 army, horses and **h**, all of them clothed H6571
Dan 11:40 chariots, and with **h**, and with many H6571
Hos 1: 7 nor by battle, by horses, nor by **h**. H6571
Joel 2: 4 of horses; and as **h**, so shall they run. H6571
Hab 1: 8 wolves: and their **h** shall spread H6571
8 and their **h** shall come from far; H6571
Act 23:23 to Caesarea, and **h** threescore and ten, G2460
32 On the morrow they left the **h** to go G2460
Rev 9:16 And the number of the army of the **h** G2461

HORSES
Gen 47:17 *in exchange* for **h**, and for the flocks, H5483
Ex 9: 3 in the field, upon the **h**, upon the asses, H5483
14: 9 after them, all the **h** *and* chariots of H5483
23 **h**, his chariots, and his horsemen. H5483
Dt 11: 4 of Egypt, unto their **h**, and to their H5483
17:16 But he shall not multiply **h** to himself, H5483
16 he should multiply **h**: forasmuch as the H5483
20: 1 and seest **h**, and chariots, *and* a H5483
Jos 11: 4 with **h** and chariots very many. H5483
6 **h**, and burn their chariots with fire. H5483
9 **h**, and burnt their chariots with fire. H5483
2Sa 8: 4 all the chariot *h*, but reserved of them H5483
15: 1 and **h**, and fifty men to run before him. H5483
1Ki 4:26 thousand stalls of **h** for his chariots, H5483
28 Barley also and straw for the **h** and H5483
10:25 **h**, and mules, a rate year by year. H5483
28 And Solomon had **h** brought out of H5483
18: 5 grass to save the **h** and mules alive, H5483
20: 1 with him, and **h**, and chariots: and he H5483
21 and smote the **h** and chariots, and slew H5483
22: 4 as thy people, my **h** as thy horses. H5483
4 as thy people, my horses as thy **h**. H5483
2Ki 2:11 of fire, and **h** of fire, and parted them H5483
3: 7 as thy people, *and* my **h** as thy horses. H5483
7 as thy people, *and* my horses as thy **h**. H5483
5: 9 So Naaman came with his **h** and with H5483
6:14 Therefore sent he thither **h**, and H5483
15 the city both with **h** and chariots. And H5483
17 *was* full of **h** and chariots of fire H5483
7: 6 and a noise of **h**, *even* the noise of a H5483
7 tents, and their **h**, and their asses, even H5483
10 voice of man, but **h** tied, and asses tied, H5483
13 thee, five of the **h** that remain, which H5483
14 They took therefore two chariot **h**; and H5483
9:33 on the **h**: and he trode her under foot. H5483
10: 2 and **h**, a fenced city also, and armour; H5483
11:16 by the which the **h** came into the king's H5483
14:20 And they brought him on **h**: and he was H5483
18:23 thee two thousand **h**, if thou be able on H5483
23:11 And he took away the **h** that the kings H5483
1Ch 18: 4 all the chariot *h*, but reserved of them
2Ch 1:16 And Solomon had **h** brought out of H5483
17 brought they out *h* for all the kings of the
9:24 **h**, and mules, a rate year by year. H5483
25 stalls for **h** and chariots, and twelve H5483
28 And they brought unto Solomon **h** out H5483
25:28 And they brought him upon **h**, and H5483
Ezr 2:66 Their **h** *were* seven hundred thirty and H5483
Neh 7:68 Their **h**, seven hundred thirty and six: H5483
Ps 20: 7 Some *trust* in chariots, and some in **h**: H5483
Ecc 10: 7 I have seen servants upon **h**, and H5483
Song 1: 9 a company of **h** in Pharaoh's chariots. H5484
Isa 2: 7 land is also full of **h**, neither *is there any* H5483
30:16 But ye said, No; for we will flee upon **h**; H5483
31: 1 for help; and stay on **h**, and trust in H5483
3 and not God; and their **h** flesh, and not H5483
36: 8 thee two thousand **h**, if thou be able on H5483
66:20 all nations upon **h**, and in chariots, and H5483
Jer 4:13 as a whirlwind: his **h** are swifter than H5483
5: 8 They were *as* fed **h** in the morning: H5483
6:23 they ride upon **h**, set in array as men H5483
8:16 The snorting of his **h** was heard from H5483
12: 5 thou contend with **h**? and *if* in the land H5483
17:25 in chariots and on **h**, they, and their H5483
22: 4 **h**, he, and his servants, and his people. H5483
46: 4 Harness the **h**; and get up, ye horsemen, H5483
9 Come up, ye **h**; and rage, ye chariots; H5483
47: 3 hoofs of his strong *h*, at the rushing of his
50:37 A sword *is* upon their **h**, and upon their H5483
42 they shall ride upon **h**, *every one* put in H5483
51:27 **h** to come up as the rough caterpillers. H5483
Ezk 17:15 might give him **h** and much people. H5483
23: 6 young men, horsemen riding upon **h**. H5483
12 **h**, all of them desirable young men. H5483
20 and whose issue *is like* the issue of **h**. H5483
23 renowned, all of them riding upon **h**. H5483
26: 7 the north, with **h**, and with chariots, H5483
10 By reason of the abundance of his **h** H5483
11 With the hoofs of his **h** shall he tread H5483
27:14 fairs with **h** and horsemen and mules. H5483
38: 4 all thine army, **h** and horsemen, all of H5483
15 them riding upon **h**, a great company, H5483
39:20 at my table with **h** and chariots, with H5483
Hos 1: 7 nor by battle, by **h**, nor by horsemen. H5483
14: 3 will not ride upon **h**: neither will we say H5483
Joel 2: 4 **h**; and as horsemen, so shall they run. H5483
Am 4:10 taken away your **h**; and I have made H5483
6:12 Shall **h** run upon the rock? will *one* H5483
Mic 5:10 I will cut off thy **h** out of the midst of H5483
Nah 3: 2 **h**, and of the jumping chariots. H5483
Hab 1: 8 Their **h** also are swifter than the H5483
3: 8 thine **h** *and* thy chariots of salvation? H5483
15 **h**, *through* the heap of great waters. H5483
Hag 2:22 ride in them; and the **h** and their riders H5483
Zec 1: 8 *were there* red **h**, speckled, and white. H5483
6: 2 In the first chariot *were* red **h**; and in H5483
2 and in the second chariot black **h**; H5483
3 And in the third chariot white **h**; and in H5483
3 in the fourth chariot grisled and bay **h**. H5483
6 The black **h** which *are* therein go forth H5483
10: 5 the riders on **h** shall be confounded. H5483
14:20 the bells of the **h**, HOLINESS UNTO H5483
Rev 9: 7 *were* like unto **h** prepared unto battle; G2462
9 of chariots of many **h** running to battle. G2462
17 And thus I saw the **h** in the vision, and G2462
17 the heads of the **h** *were* as the heads of G2462
18:13 and sheep, and **h**, and chariots, and G2462
19:14 **h**, clothed in fine linen, white and clean. G2462
18 and the flesh of **h**, and of them that sit G2462

HORSES'
Isa 5:28 their bows bent, their **h** hoofs shall be H5483
Jas 3: 3 Behold, we put bits in the **h** mouths, G2462

HOSAH
Jos 19:29 coast turneth to **H**; and the outgoings H2621
1Ch 16:38 son of Jeduthun and **H** *to be* porters: H2621
26:10 Also **H**, of the children of Merari, had H2621
11 sons and brethren of **H** *were* thirteen. H2621
16 To Shuppim and **H** *the lot came forth* H2621

HOSANNA
Mt 21: 9 cried, saying, **H** to the son of David: G5614
9 the name of the Lord; **H** in the highest. G5614
15 and saying, **H** to the son of David; G5614
Mk 11: 9 cried, saying, **H**; Blessed *is* he that G5614
10 the name of the Lord: **H** in the highest. G5614
Jn 12:13 him, and cried, **H**: Blessed *is* the King G5614

HOSEA
Hos 1: 1 that came unto **H**, the son of Beeri, in H1954
2 of the LORD by **H**. And the LORD said H1954
2 the LORD said to **H**, Go, take unto thee H1954

HOSEN
Dan 3:21 their coats, their **h**, and their hats, and H6361

HOSHAIAH
Neh 12:32 And after them went **H**, and half of the H1955
Jer 42: 1 the son of **H**, and all the people from H1955
43: 2 Then spake Azariah the son of **H**, and H1955

HOSHAMA
1Ch 3:18 Shenazar, Jecamiah, **H**, and Nedabiah. H1953

HOSHEA
Dt 32:44 of the people, he, and **H** the son of Nun. H1954
2Ki 15:30 And **H** the son of Elah made a H1954
17: 1 of Judah began **H** the son of Elah to H1954
3 of Assyria; and **H** became his servant, H1954
4 found conspiracy in **H**: for he had sent H1954
6 In the ninth year of **H** the king of H1954
18: 1 the third year of **H** son of Elah king of H1954
9 seventh year of **H** son of Elah king of H1954
10 of **H** king of Israel, Samaria was taken. H1954
1Ch 27:20 Of the children of Ephraim, **H** the son H1954
Neh 10:23 **H**, Hananiah, Hashub, H1954

HOSPITALITY
Ro 12:13 to the necessity of saints; given to **h**. G5381
1Ti 3: 2 behaviour, given to **h**, apt to teach; G5382
Tit 1: 8 But a lover of **h**, a lover of good men, G5382
1Pt 4: 9 Use **h** one to another without grudging. G5382

HOST
Gen 2: 1 were finished, and all the **h** of them. H6635
21:22 captain of his **h** spake unto Abraham, H6635
32 captain of his **h**, and they returned into H6635
32: 2 said, This *is* God's **h**: and he called the H4264
Ex 14: 4 and upon all his **h**; that the Egyptians H2428
17 and upon all his **h**, upon his chariots, H2428
24 looked unto the **h** of the Egyptians H4264
24 and troubled the **h** of the Egyptians, H4264
28 *and* all the **h** of Pharaoh that came H2428
15: 4 Pharaoh's chariots and his **h** hath he H2428
16:13 morning the dew lay round about the **h**. H4264
Nu 2: 4 And his **h**, and those that were H6635

Nu 2: 6 And his **h**, and those that were H6635
8 And his **h**, and those that were H6635
11 And his **h**, and those that were H6635
13 And his **h**, and those that were H6635
15 And his **h**, and those that were H6635
19 And his **h**, and those that were H6635
21 And his **h**, and those that were H6635
23 And his **h**, and those that were H6635
26 And his **h**, and those that were H6635
28 And his **h**, and those that were H6635
30 And his **h**, and those that were H6635
4: 3 that enter into the **h**, to do the work in H6635
10:14 and over his **h** *was* Nahshon the son H6635
15 And over the **h** of the tribe of the H6635
16 And over the **h** of the tribe of the H6635
18 his **h** *was* Elizur the son of Shedeur. H6635
19 And over the **h** of the tribe of the H6635
20 And over the **h** of the tribe of the H6635
22 **h** *was* Elishama the son of Ammihud. H6635
23 And over the **h** of the tribe of the H6635
24 And over the **h** of the tribe of the H6635
25 and over his **h** *was* Ahiezer the son H6635
26 And over the **h** of the tribe of the H6635
27 And over the **h** of the tribe of the H6635
31:14 the officers of the **h**, *with* the captains H2428
48 over thousands of the **h**, the captains of H6635
Dt 2:14 the **h**, as the LORD sware unto them. H4264
15 among the **h**, until they were consumed. H4264
4:19 the stars, *even* all the **h** of heaven, H6635
17: 3 or any of the **h** of heaven, which I have H6635
23: 9 When the **h** goeth forth against thine H4264
Jos 1:11 Pass through the **h**, and command the H4264
3: 2 that the officers went through the **h**; H4264
5:14 *as* captain of the **h** of the LORD am I H6635
15 And the captain of the LORD'S **h** said H6635
8:13 *even* all the **h** that *was* on the north H4264
18: 9 *again* to Joshua to the **h** at Shiloh. H4264
Jdg 4: 2 captain of whose **h** *was* Sisera, which H6635
15 and all *his* **h**, with the edge of the H4264
16 and after the **h**, unto Harosheth of the H4264
16 and all the **h** of Sisera fell upon the H4264
7: 1 Harod: so that the **h** of the Midianites H4264
8 men: and the **h** of Midian was beneath H4264
9 down unto the **h**; for I have delivered H4264
10 with Phurah thy servant down to the **h**: H4264
11 go down unto the **h**. Then went he down H4264
11 of the armed men that *were* in the **h**. H4264
13 tumbled into the **h** of Midian, and H4264
14 God delivered Midian, and all the **h**. H4264
15 returned into the **h** of Israel, and said, H4264
15 into your hand the **h** of Midian. H4264
21 and all the **h** ran, and cried, and fled. H4264
22 throughout all the **h**: and the host fled H4264
22 the host: and the **h** fled to Beth-shittah H4264
8:11 smote the **h**: for the host was secure. H4264
11 smote the host: for the **h** was secure. H4264
12 Zalmunna, and discomfited all the **h**. H4264
1Sa 11:11 into the midst of the **h** in the morning H4264
12: 9 captain of the **h** of Hazor, and into the H6635
14:15 And there was trembling in the **h**, in the H4264
19 that *was* in the **h** of the Philistines went H4264
48 And he gathered an **h**, and smote the H2428
50 the captain of his **h** *was* Abner, the son H6635
17:20 the trench, as the **h** was going forth to H2428
46 the carcases of the **h** of the Philistines H4264
55 the captain of the **h**, Abner, whose son H6635
26: 5 the captain of his **h**: and Saul lay in the H6635
28: 5 And when Saul saw the **h** of the H4264
19 also shall deliver the **h** of Israel into the H4264
29: 6 in with me in the **h** *is* good in my sight: H4264
2Sa 2: 8 captain of Saul's **h**, took Ish-bosheth H6635
3:23 When Joab and all the **h** that *was* with H6635
5:24 thee, to smite the **h** of the Philistines. H4264
8: 9 had smitten all the **h** of Hadadezer, H2428
16 *was* over the **h**; and Jehoshaphat the H6635
10: 7 Joab, and all the **h** of the mighty men. H6635
16 the **h** of Hadarezer *went* before them. H6635
18 the captain of their **h**, who died there. H6635
17:25 captain of the **h** instead of Joab: which H6635
19:13 be not captain of the **h** before me H6635
20:23 Now Joab *was* over all the **h** of Israel: H6635
23:16 brake through the **h** of the Philistines, H4264
24: 2 the captain of the **h**, which *was* with H2428
4 the captains of the **h**. And Joab and the H2428
4 the captains of the **h** went out from the H2428
1Ki 1:19 the captain of the **h**: but Solomon thy H6635
25 the captains of the **h**, and Abiathar the H6635
2:32 captain of the **h** of Israel, and Amasa H6635
32 son of Jether, captain of the **h** of Judah. H6635

1Ki 2:35 in his room over the **h**: and Zadok the H6635
4: 4 *was* over the **h**: and Zadok and H6635
11:15 the captain of the **h** was gone up to H6635
21 the captain of the **h** was dead, Hadad H6635
16:16 **h**, king over Israel that day in the camp. H6635
20: 1 gathered all his **h** together: and *there* H2428
22:19 his throne, and all the **h** of heaven H6635
34 me out of the **h**; for I am wounded. H4264
36 throughout the **h** about the going down H4264
2Ki 3: 9 **h**, and for the cattle that followed them. H4264
4:13 the captain of the **h**? And she answered, H6635
5: 1 Now Naaman, captain of the **h** of the H6635
6:14 and a great **h**: and they came by night, H2428
15 forth, behold, an **h** compassed the city H2428
24 **h**, and went up, and besieged Samaria. H4264
7: 4 let us fall unto the **h** of the Syrians: if H4264
6 For the Lord had made the **h** of the H4264
6 noise of a great **h**: and they said one to H2428
14 **h** of the Syrians, saying, Go and see. H4264
9: 5 the captains of the **h** *were* sitting; and H2428
11:15 the officers of the **h**, and said unto H2428
17:16 all the **h** of heaven, and served Baal. H6635
18:17 with a great **h** against Jerusalem. H2426
21: 3 all the **h** of heaven, and served them. H6635
5 And he built altars for all the **h** of H6635
23: 4 and for all the **h** of heaven: and he H6635
5 the planets, and to all the **h** of heaven. H6635
25: 1 he, and all his **h**, against Jerusalem, H2428
19 scribe of the **h**, which mustered the H6635
1Ch 9:19 *being* over the **h** of the LORD, *were* H4264
11:15 of Adullam; and the **h** of the Philistines H4264
18 And the three brake through the **h** of H4264
12:14 captains of the **h**: one of the least *was* H6635
21 of valour, and were captains in the **h**. H6635
22 *it was* a great **h**, like the host of God. H4264
22 *it was* a great host, like the **h** of God. H4264
14:15 thee to smite the **h** of the Philistines. H4264
16 they smote the **h** of the Philistines from H4264
18: 9 all the **h** of Hadarezer king of Zobah; H2428
15 *was* over the **h**; and Jehoshaphat the H6635
19: 8 Joab, and all the **h** of the mighty men. H6635
16 the **h** of Hadarezer *went* before them. H6635
18 killed Shophach the captain of the **h**. H6635
25: 1 the captains of the **h** separated to the H6635
26:26 the captains of the **h**, had dedicated. H6635
27: 3 captains of the **h** for the first month. H6635
5 The third captain of the **h** for the third H6635
2Ch 14: 9 the Ethiopian with an **h** of a thousand H2428
13 and before his **h**; and they carried away H4264
16: 7 therefore is the **h** of the king of Syria H2428
8 the Lubims a huge **h**, with very many H2428
18:18 his throne, and all the **h** of heaven H6635
33 me out of the **h**; for I am wounded. H4264
23:14 were set over the **h**, and said unto them, H2428
24:23 of the year, *that* the **h** of Syria came up H2428
24 a very great **h** into their hand, because H2428
26:11 Moreover Uzziah had an **h** of fighting H2428
14 them throughout all the **h** shields, and H6635
28: 9 out before the **h** that came to Samaria, H6635
33: 3 all the **h** of heaven, and served them. H6635
5 And he built altars for all the **h** of H6635
11 the captains of the **h** of the king of H6635
Neh 9: 6 with all their **h**, the earth, and all *things* H6635
6 and the **h** of heaven worshippeth thee. H6635
Ps 27: 3 Though an **h** should encamp against H4264
33: 6 **h** of them by the breath of his mouth. H6635
16 multitude of an **h**: a mighty man is not H2428
136:15 But overthrew Pharaoh and his **h** in the H2428
Isa 13: 4 of hosts mustereth the **h** of the battle. H6635
24:21 shall punish the **h** of the high ones *that* H6635
34: 4 And all the **h** of heaven shall be H6635
4 and all their **h** shall fall down, as the H6635
40:26 that bringeth out their **h** by number: he H6635
45:12 and all their **h** have I commanded. H6635
Jer 8: 2 moon, and all the **h** of heaven, whom H6635
19:13 unto all the **h** of heaven, and have H6635
33:22 As the **h** of heaven cannot be H6635
51: 3 young men; destroy ye utterly all her **h**. H6635
52:25 scribe of the **h**, who mustered the H6635
Ezk 1:24 as the noise of an **h**: when they stood, H4264
Dan 8:10 And it waxed great, *even* to the **h** of H6635
10 down *some* of the **h** and of the stars to H6635
11 the prince of the **h**, and by him the daily H6635
12 And an **h** was given *him* against the H6635
13 and the **h** to be trodden under foot? H6635
Oba 20 And the captivity of this **h** of the H2426
Zep 1: 5 And them that worship the **h** of heaven H6635
Lk 2:13 heavenly **h** praising God, and saying, *G4756*
10:35 gave *them* to the **h**, and said unto him, *G3830*

Act 7:42 up to worship the **h** of heaven; as it is *G4756*
Ro 16:23 Gaius mine **h**, and of the whole church, *G3581*

HOSTAGES

2Ki 14:14 **h**, and returned to Samaria. H1121+H8594
2Ch 25:24 house, the **h** also, and returned H1121+H8594

HOSTS

Ex 12:41 to pass, that all the **h** of the LORD went H6635
Nu 1:52 his own standard, throughout their **h**. H6635
2:32 throughout their **h** *were* six hundred H6635
10:25 throughout their **h**: and over his host H6635
Jos 10: 5 up, they and all their **h**, and encamped H4264
11: 4 And they went out, they and all their **h** H4264
Jdg 8:10 Karkor, and their **h** with them, about H4264
10 were left of all the **h** of the children of H4264
1Sa 1: 3 unto the LORD of **h** in Shiloh. And the H6635
11 said, O LORD of **h**, if thou wilt indeed H6635
4: 4 of the LORD of **h**, which dwelleth H6635
15: 2 Thus saith the LORD of **h**, I remember H6635
17:45 of the LORD of **h**, the God of the armies H6635
2Sa 5:10 and the LORD God of **h** *was* with him. H6635
6: 2 **h** that dwelleth *between* the cherubims. H6635
18 people in the name of the LORD of **h**. H6635
7: 8 saith the LORD of **h**, I took thee from H6635
26 The LORD of **h** *is* the God over Israel: H6635
27 For thou, O LORD of **h**, God of Israel, H6635
1Ki 2: 5 captains of the **h** of Israel, unto Abner H6635
15:20 sent the captains of the **h** which he had H2428
18:15 And Elijah said, *As* the LORD of **h** H6635
19:10 the LORD God of **h**: for the children of H6635
14 for the LORD God of **h**: because the H6635
2Ki 3:14 And Elisha said, *As* the LORD of **h** H6635
19:31 the zeal of the LORD *of* **h** shall do this.
1Ch 11: 9 for the LORD of **h** *was* with him. H6635
17: 7 saith the LORD of **h**, I took thee from H6635
24 The LORD of **h** *is* the God of Israel, H6635
Ps 24:10 of **h**, he *is* the King of glory. Selah. H6635
46: 7 The LORD of **h** *is* with us; the God of H6635
11 The LORD of **h** *is* with us; the God of H6635
48: 8 of the LORD of **h**, in the city of our God: H6635
59: 5 Thou therefore, O LORD God of **h**, the H6635
69: 6 O Lord GOD of **h**, be ashamed for my H6635
80: 4 O LORD God of **h**, how long wilt thou be H6635
7 Turn us again, O God of **h**, and cause H6635
14 Return, we beseech thee, O God of **h**: H6635
19 Turn us again, O LORD God of **h**, cause H6635
84: 1 *are* thy tabernacles, O LORD of **h**! H6635
3 O LORD of **h**, my King, and my God. H6635
8 O LORD God of **h**, hear my prayer: give H6635
12 O LORD of **h**, blessed *is* the man that H6635
89: 8 O LORD God of **h**, who *is* a strong H6635
103:21 Bless ye the LORD, all *ye* his **h**; *ye* H6635
108:11 not thou, O God, go forth with our **h**? H6635
148: 2 all his angels: praise ye him, all his **h**. H6635
Isa 1: 9 Except the LORD of **h** had left unto us a H6635
24 Lord, the LORD of **h**, the mighty One of H6635
2:12 For the day of the LORD of **h** *shall be* H6635
3: 1 For, behold, the Lord, the LORD of **h**, H6635
15 of the poor? saith the Lord GOD of **h**. H6635
5: 7 For the vineyard of the LORD of **h** *is* H6635
9 In mine ears *said* the LORD of **h**, Of a H6635
16 But the LORD of **h** shall be exalted in H6635
24 law of the LORD of **h**, and despised the H6635
6: 3 of **h**: the whole earth *is* full of his glory. H6635
5 eyes have seen the King, the LORD of **h**. H6635
8:13 Sanctify the LORD of **h** himself; and *let* H6635
18 of **h**, which dwelleth in mount Zion. H6635
9: 7 zeal of the LORD of **h** will perform this. H6635
13 neither do they seek the LORD of **h**. H6635
19 Through the wrath of the LORD of **h** is H6635
10:16 Therefore shall the Lord, the Lord of **h**, H6635
23 For the Lord GOD of **h** shall make a H6635
24 Therefore thus saith the Lord GOD of **h**, H6635
26 And the LORD of **h** shall stir up a H6635
33 Behold, the Lord, the LORD of **h**, shall H6635
13: 4 of **h** mustereth the host of the battle. H6635
13 of **h**, and in the day of his fierce anger. H6635
14:22 saith the LORD of **h**, and cut off from H6635
23 of destruction, saith the LORD of **h**. H6635
24 The LORD of **h** hath sworn, saying, H6635
27 For the LORD of **h** hath purposed, and H6635
17: 3 children of Israel, saith the LORD of **h**. H6635
18: 7 brought unto the LORD of **h** of a people H6635
7 of the LORD of **h**, the mount Zion. H6635
19: 4 them, saith the Lord, the LORD of **h**. H6635
12 LORD of **h** hath purposed upon Egypt. H6635
16 LORD of **h**, which he shaketh over it. H6635
17 **h**, which he hath determined against it. H6635

Isa 19:18 to the LORD of **h**; one shall be called, H6635
20 unto the LORD of **h** in the land of H6635
25 Whom the LORD of **h** shall bless, H6635
21:10 of the LORD of **h**, the God of Israel, H6635
22: 5 by the Lord GOD of **h** in the valley of H6635
12 And in that day did the Lord GOD of **h** H6635
14 by the LORD of **h**, Surely this iniquity H6635
14 you till ye die, saith the Lord GOD of **h**. H6635
15 Thus saith the Lord GOD of **h**, Go, get H6635
25 In that day, saith the LORD of **h**, shall H6635
23: 9 The LORD of **h** hath purposed it, to H6635
24:23 when the LORD of **h** shall reign in H6635
25: 6 shall the LORD of **h** make unto all H6635
28: 5 In that day shall the LORD of **h** be for a H6635
22 the Lord GOD of **h** a consumption, H6635
29 from the LORD of **h**, *which* is wonderful H6635
29: 6 Thou shalt be visited of the LORD of **h** H6635
31: 4 shall the LORD of **h** come down to fight H6635
5 As birds flying, so will the LORD of **h** H6635
37:16 O LORD of **h**, God of Israel, that H6635
32 the zeal of the LORD of **h** shall do this. H6635
39: 5 Hear the word of the LORD of **h**: H6635
44: 6 the LORD of **h**; I *am* the first, and I H6635
45:13 price nor reward, saith the LORD of **h**. H6635
47: 4 *As for* our redeemer, the LORD of **h** *is* H6635
48: 2 of Israel; The LORD of **h** *is* his name. H6635
51:15 roared: The LORD of **h** *is* his name. H6635
54: 5 the LORD of **h** *is* his name; and thy H6635
Jer 2:19 *is* not in thee, saith the Lord GOD of **h**. H6635
3:19 heritage of the **h** of nations? and I said, H6635
5:14 the LORD God of **h**, Because ye speak H6635
6: 6 For thus hath the LORD of **h** said, Hew H6635
9 Thus saith the LORD of **h**, They shall H6635
7: 3 Thus saith the LORD of **h**, the God of H6635
21 Thus saith the LORD of **h**, the God of H6635
8: 3 have driven them, saith the LORD of **h**. H6635
9: 7 Therefore thus saith the LORD of **h**, H6635
15 Therefore thus saith the LORD of **h**, the H6635
17 Thus saith the LORD of **h**, Consider ye, H6635
10:16 The LORD of **h** *is* his name. H6635
11:17 For the LORD of **h**, that planted thee, H6635
20 But, O LORD of **h**, that judgest H6635
22 Therefore thus saith the LORD of **h**, H6635
15:16 called by thy name, O LORD God of **h**. H6635
16: 9 For thus saith the LORD of **h**, the God of H6635
19: 3 saith the LORD of **h**, the God of Israel; H6635
11 Thus saith the LORD of **h**; Even so will I H6635
15 Thus saith the LORD of **h**, the God of H6635
20:12 But, O LORD of **h**, that triest the H6635
23:15 Therefore thus saith the LORD of **h** H6635
16 Thus saith the LORD of **h**, Hearken not H6635
36 living God, of the LORD of **h** our God. H6635
25: 8 Therefore thus saith the LORD of **h**; H6635
27 saith the LORD of **h**, the God of Israel; H6635
28 the LORD of **h**; Ye shall certainly drink. H6635
29 of the earth, saith the LORD of **h**. H6635
32 Thus saith the LORD of **h**, Behold, evil H6635
26:18 Thus saith the LORD of **h**; Zion shall be H6635
27: 4 saith the LORD of **h**, the God of Israel; H6635
18 to the LORD of **h**, that the vessels which H6635
19 For thus saith the LORD of **h** H6635
21 Yea, thus saith the LORD of **h**, the God H6635
28: 2 Thus speaketh the LORD of **h**, the God H6635
14 For thus saith the LORD of **h**, the God of H6635
29: 4 Thus saith the LORD of **h**, the God of H6635
8 For thus saith the LORD of **h**, the God of H6635
17 Thus saith the LORD of **h**; Behold, I will H6635
21 Thus saith the LORD of **h**, the God of H6635
25 Thus speaketh the LORD of **h**, the God H6635
30: 8 saith the LORD of **h**, *that* I will break H6635
31:23 Thus saith the LORD of **h**, the God of H6635
35 roar; The LORD of **h** *is* his name: H6635
32:14 Thus saith the LORD of **h**, the God of H6635
15 For thus saith the LORD of **h**, the God of H6635
18 God, the LORD of **h**, *is* his name, H6635
33:11 the LORD of **h**: for the LORD *is* good; H6635
12 Thus saith the LORD of **h**; Again in this H6635
35:13 Thus saith the LORD of **h**, the God of H6635
17 the LORD God of **h**, the God of Israel; H6635
18 saith the LORD of **h**, the God of Israel; H6635
19 Therefore thus saith the LORD of **h**, the H6635
38:17 LORD, the God of **h**, the God of Israel; If H6635
39:16 saith the LORD of **h**, the God of Israel; H6635
42:15 saith the LORD of **h**, the God of Israel; If H6635
18 For thus saith the LORD of **h**, the God of H6635
43:10 saith the LORD of **h**, the God of Israel; H6635
44: 2 Thus saith the LORD of **h**, the God of H6635
7 LORD, the God of **h**, the God of Israel; H6635
11 Therefore thus saith the LORD of **h**, the H6635
Jer 44:25 Thus saith the LORD of **h**, the God of H6635
46:10 For this *is* the day of the Lord GOD of **h**, H6635
10 the Lord GOD of **h** hath a sacrifice in H6635
18 *is* the LORD of **h**, Surely as Tabor *is* H6635
25 The LORD of **h**, the God of Israel, saith; H6635
48: 1 Against Moab thus saith the LORD of **h**, H6635
15 the King, whose name *is* the LORD of **h**. H6635
49: 5 the Lord GOD of **h**, from all those that H6635
7 saith the LORD of **h**; *Is* wisdom no more H6635
26 cut off in that day, saith the LORD of **h**. H6635
35 Thus saith the LORD of **h**; Behold, I will H6635
50:18 Therefore thus saith the LORD of **h**, the H6635
25 GOD of **h** in the land of the Chaldeans. H6635
31 the Lord GOD of **h**: for thy day is come, H6635
33 Thus saith the LORD of **h**; The children H6635
34 the LORD of **h** *is* his name: he shall H6635
51: 5 of the LORD of **h**; though their land was H6635
14 The LORD of **h** hath sworn by himself, H6635
19 inheritance: the LORD of **h** *is* his name. H6635
33 For thus saith the LORD of **h**, the God of H6635
57 the King, whose name *is* the LORD of **h**. H6635
58 Thus saith the LORD of **h**; The broad H6635
Hos 12: 5 Even the LORD God of **h**; the LORD *is* H6635
Am 3:13 Jacob, saith the Lord GOD, the God of **h**, H6635
4:13 The LORD, The God of **h**, *is* his name. H6635
5:14 **h**, shall be with you, as ye have spoken. H6635
15 the LORD God of **h** will be gracious H6635
16 Therefore the LORD, the God of **h**, the H6635
27 the LORD, whose name *is* The God of **h**. H6635
6: 8 the LORD the God of **h**, I abhor the H6635
14 the LORD the God of **h**; and they shall H6635
9: 5 And the Lord GOD of **h** *is* he that H6635
Mic 4: 4 mouth of the LORD of **h** hath spoken *it*. H6635
Nah 2:13 saith the LORD of **h**, and I will burn her H6635
3: 5 saith the LORD of **h**; and I will discover H6635
Hab 2:13 Behold, *is it* not of the LORD of **h** that H6635
Zep 2: 9 Therefore *as* I live, saith the LORD of **h**, H6635
10 against the people of the LORD of **h**. H6635
Hag 1: 2 Thus speaketh the LORD of **h**, saying, H6635
5 Now therefore thus saith the LORD of **h**; H6635
7 Thus saith the LORD of **h**; Consider H6635
9 saith the LORD of **h**. Because of mine H6635
14 the house of the LORD of **h**, their God, H6635
2: 4 for I *am* with you, saith the LORD of **h**: H6635
6 For thus saith the LORD of **h**; Yet once, H6635
7 house with glory, saith the LORD of **h**. H6635
8 the gold *is* mine, saith the LORD of **h**. H6635
9 saith the LORD of **h**: and in this place H6635
9 will I give peace, saith the LORD of **h**. H6635
11 Thus saith the LORD of **h**; Ask now the H6635
23 In that day, saith the LORD of **h**, will I H6635
23 I have chosen thee, saith the LORD of **h**. H6635
Zec 1: 3 saith the LORD of **h**; Turn ye unto me, H6635
3 me, saith the LORD of **h**, and I will turn H6635
3 will turn unto you, saith the LORD of **h**. H6635
4 saith the LORD of **h**; Turn ye now from H6635
6 as the LORD of **h** thought to do unto H6635
12 said, O LORD of **h**, how long wilt thou H6635
14 saith the LORD of **h**; I am jealous for H6635
16 saith the LORD of **h**, and a line shall be H6635
17 saith the LORD of **h**; My cities through H6635
2: 8 For thus saith the LORD of **h**; After the H6635
9 know that the LORD of **h** hath sent me. H6635
11 the LORD of **h** hath sent me unto thee. H6635
3: 7 Thus saith the LORD of **h**; If thou wilt H6635
9 saith the LORD of **h**, and I will remove H6635
10 In that day, saith the LORD of **h**, shall H6635
4: 6 but by my spirit, saith the LORD of **h**. H6635
9 the LORD of **h** hath sent me unto you. H6635
5: 4 I will bring it forth, saith the LORD of **h**, H6635
6:12 the LORD of **h**, saying, Behold the man H6635
15 that the LORD of **h** hath sent me unto H6635
7: 3 of the LORD of **h**, and to the prophets, H6635
4 Then came the word of the LORD of **h** H6635
9 Thus speaketh the LORD of **h**, saying, H6635
12 the LORD of **h** hath sent in his spirit H6635
12 came a great wrath from the LORD of **h**. H6635
13 I would not hear, saith the LORD of **h**: H6635
8: 1 Again the word of the LORD of **h** came H6635
2 Thus saith the LORD of **h**; I was jealous H6635
3 of the LORD of **h** the holy mountain. H6635
4 Thus saith the LORD of **h**; There shall H6635
6 Thus saith the LORD of **h**; If it be H6635
6 in mine eyes? saith the LORD of **h**. H6635
7 Thus saith the LORD of **h**; Behold, I will H6635
9 Thus saith the LORD of **h**; Let your H6635
9 of the LORD of **h** was laid, that the H6635
11 in the former days, saith the LORD of **h**. H6635
14 For thus saith the LORD of **h**; As I H6635
Zec 8:14 saith the LORD of **h**, and I repented not: H6635
18 And the word of the LORD of **h** came H6635
19 Thus saith the LORD of **h**; The fast of H6635
20 Thus saith the LORD of **h**; *It shall* yet H6635
21 to seek the LORD of **h**: I will go also. H6635
22 seek the LORD of **h** in Jerusalem, and H6635
23 Thus saith the LORD of **h**; In those days H6635
9:15 The LORD of **h** shall defend them; and H6635
10: 3 for the LORD of **h** hath visited his flock H6635
12: 5 strength in the LORD of **h** their God. H6635
13: 2 saith the LORD of **h**, *that* I will cut off H6635
7 fellow, saith the LORD of **h**: smite the H6635
14:16 **h**, and to keep the feast of tabernacles. H6635
17 of **h**, even upon them shall be no rain. H6635
21 unto the LORD of **h**: and all they that H6635
21 in the house of the LORD of **h**. H6635
Mal 1: 4 saith the LORD of **h**, They shall build, H6635
6 fear? saith the LORD of **h** unto you, O H6635
8 accept thy person? saith the LORD of **h**. H6635
9 your persons? saith the LORD of **h**. H6635
10 you, saith the LORD of **h**, neither will I H6635
11 the heathen, saith the LORD of **h**. H6635
13 it, saith the LORD of **h**; and ye brought H6635
14 saith the LORD of **h**, and my name *is* H6635
2: 2 saith the LORD of **h**, I will even send a H6635
4 might be with Levi, saith the LORD of **h**. H6635
7 he *is* the messenger of the LORD of **h**. H6635
8 covenant of Levi, saith the LORD of **h**. H6635
12 offereth an offering unto the LORD of **h**. H6635
16 saith the LORD of **h**: therefore take H6635
3: 1 he shall come, saith the LORD of **h**. H6635
5 and fear not me, saith the LORD of **h**. H6635
7 **h**. But ye said, Wherein shall we return? H6635
10 saith the LORD of **h**, if I will not open H6635
11 time in the field, saith the LORD of **h**. H6635
12 delightsome land, saith the LORD of **h**. H6635
14 mournfully before the LORD of **h**? H6635
17 saith the LORD of **h**, in that day when I H6635
4: 1 saith the LORD of **h**, that it shall leave H6635
3 that I shall do *this*, saith the LORD of **h**. H6635

HOT
Ex 16:21 and when the sun waxed **h**, it melted. H2552
22:24 And my wrath shall wax **h**, and I will H2734
32:10 wrath may wax **h** against them, and H2734
11 thy wrath wax **h** against thy people, H2734
19 anger waxed **h**, and he cast the tables H2734
22 of my lord wax **h**: thou knowest the H2734
Lev 13:24 whereof *there is* a **h** burning, and the H784
Dt 9:19 For I was afraid of the anger and **h** H2534
19: 6 while his heart is **h**, and overtake him, H3179
Jos 9:12 This our bread we took **h** *for* our H2525
Jdg 2:14 And the anger of the LORD was **h** H2734
20 And the anger of the LORD was **h** H2734
3: 8 Therefore the anger of the LORD was **h** H2734
6:39 not thine anger be **h** against me, and I H2734
10: 7 And the anger of the LORD was **h** H2734
1Sa 11: 9 *time* the sun be **h**, ye shall have help. H2527
21: 6 the LORD, to put **h** bread in the day H2527
Neh 7: 3 until the sun be **h**; and while they stand H2527
Job 6:17 **h**, they are consumed out of their place. H2527
Ps 6: 1 chasten me in thy **h** displeasure. H2534
38: 1 chasten me in thy **h** displeasure. H2534
39: 3 My heart was **h** within me, while I was H2552
78:48 hail, and their flocks to **h** thunderbolts. H7565
Prv 6:28 Can one go upon **h** coals, and his feet
Ezk 24:11 brass of it may be **h**, and may burn, and H3179
Dan 3:22 furnace exceeding **h**, the flame of the fire H228
Hos 7: 7 They are all **h** as an oven, and have H2552
1Ti 4: 2 their conscience seared with a **h** iron; *G2743*
Rev 3:15 nor **h**: I would thou wert cold or hot. *G2200*
15 nor hot: I would thou wert cold or **h**. *G2200*
16 nor **h**, I will spue thee out of my mouth. *G2200*

HOTHAM
1Ch 7:32 Shomer, and **H**, and Shua their sister. H2369

HOTHAN
1Ch 11:44 and Jehiel the sons of **H** the Aroerite, H2369

HOTHIR
1Ch 25: 4 Mallothi, **H**, *and* Mahazioth: H1956
28 The one and twentieth to **H**, *he*, his H1956

HOTLY
Gen 31:36 that thou hast so **h** pursued after me? H1814

HOTTEST
2Sa 11:15 forefront of the **h** battle, and retire ye H2389

HOUGH
Jos 11: 6 Israel: thou shalt **h** their horses, and H6131

HOUGHED
Jos 11: 9 bade him: he **h** their horses, and burnt H6131
2Sa 8: 4 and David **h** all the chariot *horses,* H6131
1Ch 18: 4 David also **h** all the chariot *horses,* H6131

HOUND
See GREYHOUND.

HOUR
Dan 3: 6 shall the same **h** be cast into the midst H8160
15 be cast the same **h** into the midst of a H8160
4:19 astonied for one **h**, and his thoughts H8160
33 The same **h** was the thing fulfilled upon H8160
5: 5 In the same **h** came forth fingers of a H8160
Mt 8:13 servant was healed in the selfsame **h**. G5610
9:22 woman was made whole from that **h**. G5610
10:19 you in that same **h** what ye shall speak. G5610
15:28 was made whole from that very **h**. G5610
17:18 the child was cured from that very **h**. G5610
20: 3 And he went out about the third **h**, and G5610
5 the sixth and ninth **h**, and did likewise. G5610
6 And about the eleventh **h** he went out, G5610
9 **h**, they received every man a penny. G5610
12 wrought *but* one **h**, and thou hast made G5610
24:36 But of that day and **h** knoweth no *man,* G5610
42 know not what **h** your Lord doth come. G5610
44 for in such an **h** as ye think not the Son G5610
50 and in an **h** that he is not aware of, G5610
25:13 the **h** wherein the Son of man cometh. G5610
26:40 could ye not watch with me one **h**? G5610
45 rest: behold, the **h** is at hand, and the G5610
55 In that same **h** said Jesus to the G5610
27:45 Now from the sixth **h** there was G5610
45 over all the land unto the ninth **h**. G5610
46 And about the ninth **h** Jesus cried with G5610
Mk 13:11 given you in that **h**, that speak ye: for it G5610
32 But of that day and *that* **h** knoweth no G5610
14:35 possible, the **h** might pass from him. G5610
37 thou? couldest not thou watch one **h**? G5610
41 it is enough, the **h** is come; behold, the G5610
15:25 And it was the third **h**, and they G5610
33 And when the sixth **h** was come, there G5610
33 over the whole land until the ninth **h**. G5610
34 And at the ninth **h** Jesus cried with a G5610
Lk 7:21 And in that same **h** he cured many of G5610
10:21 In that **h** Jesus rejoiced in spirit, and G5610
12:12 you in the same **h** what ye ought to say. G5610
39 had known what **h** the thief would G5610
40 man cometh at an **h** when ye think not. G5610
46 not for *him,* and at an **h** when he is not G5610
20:19 scribes the same **h** sought to lay hands G5610
22:14 And when the **h** was come, he sat G5610
53 is your **h**, and the power of darkness. G5610
59 And about the space of one **h** after G5610
23:44 And it was about the sixth **h**, and there G5610
44 over all the earth until the ninth **h**. G5610
24:33 And they rose up the same **h**, and G5610
Jn 1:39 that day: for it was about the tenth **h**. G5610
2: 4 to do with thee? mine **h** is not yet come. G5610
4: 6 the well: *and* it was about the sixth **h**. G5610
21 believe me, the **h** cometh, when ye shall G5610
23 But the **h** cometh, and now is, when the G5610
52 Then inquired he of them the **h** when G5610
52 at the seventh **h** the fever left him. G5610
53 *it was* at the same **h**, in the which Jesus G5610
5:25 Verily, verily, I say unto you, The **h** is G5610
28 Marvel not at this: for the **h** is coming, G5610
7:30 him, because his **h** was not yet come. G5610
8:20 on him; for his **h** was not yet come. G5610
12:23 them, saying, The **h** is come, that the G5610
27 save me from this **h**: but for this cause G5610
27 but for this cause came I unto this **h**. G5610
13: 1 Jesus knew that his **h** was come that he G5610
16:21 because her **h** is come: but as soon G5610
32 Behold, the **h** cometh, yea, is now G5610
17: 1 said, Father, the **h** is come; glorify thy G5610
19:14 about the sixth **h**: and he saith unto the G5610
27 And from that **h** that disciple took her G5610
Act 2:15 seeing it is *but* the third **h** of the day. G5610
3: 1 at the **h** of prayer, *being* the ninth *hour.* G5610
1 at the hour of prayer, *being* the ninth **h**.
10: 3 about the ninth **h** of the day an angel G5610
9 the housetop to pray about the sixth **h**: G5610
30 was fasting until this **h**; and at the ninth G5610
30 hour; and at the ninth **h** I prayed in my G5610
16:18 out of her. And he came out the same **h**. G5610
33 And he took them the same **h** of the G5610
Act 22:13 And the same **h** I looked up upon him. G5610
23:23 hundred, at the third **h** of the night; G5610
1Co 4:11 Even unto this present **h** we both G5610
8: 7 of the idol unto this **h** eat *it* as a thing G737
15:30 And why stand we in jeopardy every **h**? G5610
Gal 2: 5 no, not for an **h**; that the truth of the G5610
Rev 3: 3 not know what **h** I will come upon thee. G5610
10 thee from the **h** of temptation, which G5610
8: 1 in heaven about the space of half an **h**. G2256
9:15 prepared for an **h**, and a day, and a G5610
11:13 And the same **h** was there a great G5610
14: 7 to him; for the **h** of his judgment is G5610
17:12 power as kings one **h** with the beast. G5610
18:10 city! for in one **h** is thy judgment come. G5610
17 For in one **h** so great riches is come to G5610
19 for in one **h** is she made desolate. G5610

HOURS
Jn 11: 9 Jesus answered, Are there not twelve **h** G5610
Act 5: 7 And it was about the space of three **h** G5610
19:34 the space of two **h** cried out, Great *is* G5610

HOUSE
Gen 7: 1 thou and all thy **h** into the ark; for thee H1004
12: 1 **h**, unto a land that I will shew thee: H1004
15 the woman was taken into Pharaoh's **h**. H1004
17 Pharaoh and his **h** with great plagues H1004
14:14 born in his own **h**, three hundred and H1004
15: 2 of my **h** *is* this Eliezer of Damascus? H1004
3 and, lo, one born in my **h** is mine heir. H1004
17:12 he that is born in the **h**, or bought with H1004
13 He that is born in thy **h**, and he that is H1004
23 were born in his **h**, and all that were H1004
23 of Abraham's **h**; and circumcised the H1004
27 And all the men of his **h**, born in the H1004
27 house, born in the **h**, and bought with H1004
19: 2 your servant's **h**, and tarry all night, H1004
3 entered into his **h**; and he made them H1004
4 compassed the **h** round, both old and H1004
10 the **h** to them, and shut to the door. H1004
11 at the door of the **h** with blindness, H1004
20:13 from my father's **h**, that I said unto her, H1004
18 all the wombs of the **h** of Abimelech, H1004
24: 2 servant of his **h**, that ruled over all that H1004
7 from my father's **h**, and from the land H1004
23 *in* thy father's **h** for us to lodge in? H1004
27 me to the **h** of my master's brethren. H1004
28 *them of* her mother's **h** these things. H1004
31 the **h**, and room for the camels. H1004
32 And the man came into the **h**: and he H1004
38 But thou shalt go unto my father's **h**, H1004
40 son of my kindred, and of my father's **h**: H1004
27:15 with her in the **h**, and put them upon H1004
28: 2 Arise, go to Padan-aram, to the **h** of H1004
17 **h** of God, and this *is* the gate of heaven. H1004
21 So that I come again to my father's **h** in H1004
22 shall be God's **h**: and of all that thou H1004
29:13 **h**. And he told Laban all these things. H1004
30:30 shall I provide for mine own **h** also? H1004
31:14 or inheritance for us in our father's **h**? H1004
30 after thy father's **h**, *yet* wherefore hast H1004
41 Thus have I been twenty years in thy **h**; H1004
33:17 and built him an **h**, and made booths H1004
34:19 honourable than all the **h** of his father. H1004
26 out of Shechem's **h**, and went out. H1004
29 and spoiled even all that *was* in the **h**. H1004
30 and I shall be destroyed, I and my **h**. H1004
36: 6 the persons of his **h**, and his cattle, and H1004
38:11 at thy father's **h**, till Shelah my son be H1004
11 Tamar went and dwelt in her father's **h**. H1004
39: 2 was in the **h** of his master the Egyptian. H1004
4 overseer over his **h**, and all *that* he had H1004
5 overseer in his **h**, and over all that he H1004
5 the Egyptian's **h** for Joseph's sake; and H1004
5 all that he had in the **h**, and in the field. H1004
8 what *is* with me in the **h**, and he hath H1004
9 *There is* none greater in this **h** than I; H1004
11 went into the **h** to do his business; and H1004
11 none of the men of the **h** there within. H1004
14 That she called unto the men of her **h**, H1004
40: 3 And he put them in ward in the **h** of the H1004
7 ward of his lord's **h**, saying, Wherefore H1004
14 Pharaoh, and bring me out of this **h**: H1004
41:10 guard's **h**, *both* me and the chief baker: H1004
40 Thou shalt be over my **h**, and according H1004
51 forget all my toil, and all my father's **h**. H1004
42:19 be bound in the **h** of your prison: go ye, H1004
43:16 to the ruler of his **h**, Bring *these* men H1004
17 man brought the men into Joseph's **h**. H1004
Gen 43:18 into Joseph's **h**; and they said, Because H1004
19 of Joseph's **h**, and they communed H1004
19 with him at the door of the **h**, H1004
24 the men into Joseph's **h**, and gave *them* H1004
26 hand into the **h**, and bowed themselves H1004
44: 1 the steward of his **h**, saying, Fill the H1004
8 steal out of thy lord's **h** silver or gold? H1004
14 came to Joseph's **h**; for he *was* yet there: H1004
45: 2 Egyptians and the **h** of Pharaoh heard. H1004
8 and lord of all his **h**, and a ruler H1004
16 heard in Pharaoh's **h**, saying, Joseph's H1004
46:27 all the souls of the **h** of Jacob, which H1004
31 and unto his father's **h**, I will go up, and H1004
31 and my father's **h**, which *were* in the H1004
47:14 brought the money into Pharaoh's **h**. H1004
50: 4 spake unto the **h** of Pharaoh, saying, H1004
7 the elders of his **h**, and all the elders of H1004
8 And all the **h** of Joseph, and his H1004
8 and his father's **h**: only their little ones, H1004
22 and his father's **h**: and Joseph lived an H1004
Ex 2: 1 And there went a man of the **h** of Levi, H1004
3:22 sojourneth in her **h**, jewels of silver, and H1004
7:23 and went into his **h**, neither did he set H1004
8: 3 and come into thine **h**, and into thy H1004
3 bed, and into the **h** of thy servants, and H1004
24 *of flies* into the **h** of Pharaoh, and *into* H1004
12: 3 **h** of *their* fathers, a lamb for an house: H1004
3 house of *their* fathers, a lamb for an **h**: H1004
4 next unto his **h** take *it* according to H1004
22 at the door of his **h** until the morning. H1004
30 not a **h** where *there was* not one dead. H1004
46 In one **h** shall it be eaten; thou shalt H1004
46 **h**; neither shall ye break a bone thereof. H1004
13: 3 Egypt, out of the **h** of bondage; for by H1004
14 out from Egypt, from the **h** of bondage: H1004
16:31 And the **h** of Israel called the name H1004
19: 3 thou say to the **h** of Jacob, and tell the H1004
20: 2 land of Egypt, out of the **h** of bondage. H1004
17 Thou shalt not covet thy neighbour's **h**, H1004
22: 7 out of the man's **h**; if the thief be found, H1004
8 the master of the **h** shall be brought H1004
23:19 bring into the **h** of the LORD thy God. H1004
34:26 bring unto the **h** of the LORD thy God. H1004
40:38 in the sight of all the **h** of Israel, H1004
Lev 10: 6 the whole **h** of Israel, bewail the H1004
14:34 in a **h** of the land of your possession; H1004
35 And he that owneth the **h** shall come H1004
35 me *there is* as it were a plague in the **h**: H1004
36 they empty the **h**, before the priest go H1004
36 all that *is* in the **h** be not made unclean: H1004
36 the priest shall go in to see the **h**: H1004
37 *be* in the walls of the **h** with hollow H1004
38 Then the priest shall go out of the **h** to H1004
38 **h**, and shut up the house seven days: H1004
38 house, and shut up the **h** seven days: H1004
39 plague be spread in the walls of the **h**; H1004
41 And he shall cause the **h** to be scraped H1004
42 other morter, and shall plaister the **h**. H1004
43 break out in the **h**, after that he hath H1004
43 scraped the **h**, and after it is plaistered; H1004
44 plague be spread in the **h**, it *is* a fretting H1004
44 a fretting leprosy in the **h**: it *is* unclean. H1004
45 And he shall break down the **h**, the H1004
45 the morter of the **h**; and he shall carry H1004
46 Moreover he that goeth into the **h** all H1004
47 And he that lieth in the **h** shall wash his H1004
47 eateth in the **h** shall wash his clothes. H1004
48 not spread in the **h**, after the house was H1004
48 house, after the **h** was plaistered: then H1004
48 **h** clean, because the plague is healed. H1004
49 And he shall take to cleanse the **h** two H1004
51 water, and sprinkle the **h** seven times: H1004
52 And he shall cleanse the **h** with the H1004
53 for the **h**: and it shall be clean. H1004
55 for the leprosy of a garment, and of a **h**, H1004
16: 6 an atonement for himself, and for his **h**. H1004
11 and for his **h**, and shall kill the bullock H1004
17: 3 What man soever *there be* of the **h** of H1004
8 man *there be* of the **h** of Israel, or of the H1004
10 And whatsoever man *there be* of the **h** H1004
22:11 born in his **h**: they shall eat of his meat. H1004
13 unto her father's **h**, as in her youth, she H1004
18 *he be* of the **h** of Israel, or of the H1004
25:29 And if a man sell a dwelling **h** in a H1004
30 a full year, then the **h** that *is* in the H1004
33 Levites, then the **h** that was sold, and H1004
27:14 And when a man shall sanctify his **h** *to* H1004
15 it will redeem his **h**, then he shall add H1004
Nu 1: 2 families, by the **h** of their fathers, with H1004

Nu 1: 4 every one head of the **h** of his fathers. H1004
18 their families, by the **h** of their fathers, H1004
20 their families, by the **h** of their fathers, H1004
22 families, by the **h** of their fathers, those H1004
24 their families, by the **h** of their fathers, H1004
26 their families, by the **h** of their fathers, H1004
28 their families, by the **h** of their fathers, H1004
30 their families, by the **h** of their fathers, H1004
32 their families, by the **h** of their fathers, H1004
34 their families, by the **h** of their fathers, H1004
36 their families, by the **h** of their fathers, H1004
38 their families, by the **h** of their fathers, H1004
40 their families, by the **h** of their fathers, H1004
42 their families, by the **h** of their fathers, H1004
44 each one was for the **h** of his fathers. H1004
45 of Israel, by the **h** of their fathers, from H1004
2: 2 of their father's **h**: far off about the H1004
32 of Israel by the **h** of their fathers: all H1004
34 according to the **h** of their fathers. H1004
3:15 Number the children of Levi after the **h** H1004
20 according to the **h** of their fathers. H1004
24 And the chief of the **h** of the father of H1004
30 And the chief of the **h** of the father of H1004
35 And the chief of the **h** of the father of H1004
4: 2 their families, by the **h** of their fathers, H1004
29 their families, by the **h** of their fathers; H1004
34 and after the **h** of their fathers, H1004
38 families, and by the **h** of their fathers, H1004
40 families, by the **h** of their fathers, were H1004
42 their families, by the **h** of their fathers, H1004
46 and after the **h** of their fathers, H1004
7: 2 heads of the **h** of their fathers, who H1004
12: 7 *is* not so, who *is* faithful in all mine **h**. H1004
17: 2 according to the **h** of *their* fathers, of H1004
2 according to the **h** of their fathers H1004
3 *be* for the head of the **h** of their fathers. H1004
8 of Aaron for the **h** of Levi was budded, H1004
18: 1 and thy father's **h** with thee shall bear H1004
11 one that is clean in thy **h** shall eat of it. H1004
13 that is clean in thine **h** shall eat *of* it. H1004
20:29 thirty days, *even* all the **h** of Israel. H1004
22:18 would give me his **h** full of silver and H1004
24:13 If Balak would give me his **h** full of H1004
25:14 of a chief **h** among the Simeonites. H1004
15 a people, *and* of a chief **h** in Midian. H1004
26: 2 **h**, all that are able to go to war in Israel. H1004
30: 3 *being* in her father's **h** in her youth; H1004
10 And if she vowed in her husband's **h**, or H1004
16 *being yet* in her youth in her father's **h**. H1004
34:14 according to the **h** of their fathers, and H1004
14 according to the **h** of their fathers, have H1004
Dt 5: 6 land of Egypt, from the **h** of bondage. H1004
21 covet thy neighbour's **h**, his field, or his H1004
6: 7 thou sittest in thine **h**, and when thou H1004
9 the posts of thy **h**, and on thy gates. H1004
12 land of Egypt, from the **h** of bondage. H1004
7: 8 you out of the **h** of bondmen, from the H1004
26 into thine **h**, lest thou be a cursed H1004
8:14 land of Egypt, from the **h** of bondage; H1004
11:19 thou sittest in thine **h**, and when thou H1004
20 posts of thine **h**, and upon thy gates: H1004
13: 5 you out of the **h** of bondage, to thrust H1004
10 land of Egypt, from the **h** of bondage. H1004
15:16 thine **h**, because he is well with thee; H1004
20: 5 that hath built a new **h**, and hath not H1004
5 go and return to his **h**, lest he die in the H1004
6 and return unto his **h**, lest he die in the H1004
7 and return unto his **h**, lest he die in the H1004
8 return unto his **h**, lest his brethren's H1004
21:12 bring her home to thine **h**; and she shall H1004
13 remain in thine **h**, and bewail her father H1004
22: 2 it unto thine own **h**, and it shall be with H1004
8 When thou buildest a new **h**, then thou H1004
8 thine **h**, if any man fall from thence. H1004
21 of her father's **h**, and the men of her H1004
21 in her father's **h**: so shalt thou put evil H1004
23:18 of a dog, into the **h** of the LORD thy H1004
24: 1 *it* in her hand, and send her out of his **h**. H1004
2 And when she is departed out of his **h**, H1004
3 her out of his **h**; or if the latter husband H1004
10 not go into his **h** to fetch his pledge. H1004
25: 9 that will not build up his brother's **h**. H1004
10 The **h** of him that hath his shoe loosed. H1004
14 Thou shalt not have in thine **h** divers H1004
26:11 and unto thine **h**, thou, and the Levite, H1004
13 things out of *mine* **h**, and also have H1004
28:30 shalt build an **h**, and thou shalt not H1004
Jos 2: 1 **h**, named Rahab, and lodged there. H1004
3 entered into thine **h**: for they be come to H1004
Jos 2: 6 up to the roof of the **h**, and hid them with
12 my father's **h**, and give me a true token: H1004
15 window: for her **h** *was* upon the town H1004
19 of the doors of thy **h** into the street, his H1004
19 be with thee in the **h**, his blood *shall be* H1004
6:17 *are* with her in the **h**, because she hid H1004
22 into the harlot's **h**, and bring out thence H1004
24 into the treasury of the **h** of the LORD. H1004
9:23 drawers of water for the **h** of my God. H1004
17:17 And Joshua spake unto the **h** of Joseph, H1004
18: 5 on the south, and the **h** of Joseph shall H1004
20: 6 **h**, unto the city from whence he fled. H1004
21:45 unto the **h** of Israel; all came to pass. H1004
22:14 of each chief **h** a prince throughout H1004
14 an head of the **h** of their fathers among H1004
24:15 me and my **h**, we will serve the LORD. H1004
17 of Egypt, from the **h** of bondage, and H1004
Jdg 1:22 And the **h** of Joseph, they also went up H1004
23 And the **h** of Joseph sent to descry H1004
35 the hand of the **h** of Joseph prevailed, H1004
4:17 of Hazor and the **h** of Heber the Kenite. H1004
6: 8 you forth out of the **h** of bondage; H1004
15 and I *am* the least in my father's **h**. H1004
8:27 a snare unto Gideon, and to his **h**. H1004
29 of Joash went and dwelt in his own **h**. H1004
35 Neither shewed they kindness to the **h** H1004
9: 1 of the **h** of his mother's father, saying, H1004
4 of silver out of the **h** of Baal-berith, H1004
5 And he went unto his father's **h** at H1004
6 and all the **h** of Millo, and went, H1004
16 Jerubbaal and his **h**, and have done H1004
18 my father's **h** this day, and have slain H1004
19 and with his **h** this day, *then* rejoice H1004
20 of Shechem, and the **h** of Millo; and let H1004
20 the **h** of Millo, and devour Abimelech. H1004
27 and went into the **h** of their god, and H1004
46 into an hold of the **h** of the god Berith. H1004
10: 9 and against the **h** of Ephraim; so that H1004
11: 2 in our father's **h**; for thou *art* the son H1004
7 me out of my father's **h**? and why are ye H1004
31 of the doors of my **h** to meet me, when H1004
34 to Mizpeh unto his **h**, and, behold, his H1004
12: 1 will burn thine **h** upon thee with fire. H1004
14:15 and thy father's **h** with fire: have ye H1004
19 and he went up to his father's **h**. H1004
16:21 brass; and he did grind in the prison **h**. H1004
25 out of the prison **h**; and he made them H1004
26 **h** standeth, that I may lean upon them. H1004
27 Now the **h** was full of men and women; H1004
29 upon which the **h** stood, and on which H1004
30 *his* might; and the **h** fell upon the lords, H1004
31 Then his brethren and all the **h** of his H1004
17: 4 image: and they were in the **h** of Micah. H1004
5 And the man Micah had an **h** of gods, H1004
8 to the **h** of Micah, as he journeyed. H1004
12 his priest, and was in the **h** of Micah. H1004
18: 2 to the **h** of Micah, they lodged there. H1004
3 When they *were* by the **h** of Micah, they H1004
13 and came unto the **h** of Micah. H1004
15 and came to the **h** of the young man H1004
15 unto the **h** of Micah, and saluted him. H1004
18 And these went into Micah's **h**, and H1004
19 a priest unto the **h** of one man, or that H1004
22 way from the **h** of Micah, the men that H1004
22 near to Micah's **h** were gathered H1004
26 he turned and went back unto his **h**. H1004
31 time that the **h** of God was in Shiloh. H1004
19: 2 him unto her father's **h** to H1004
3 into her father's **h**: and when the father H1004
15 that took them into his **h** to lodging. H1004
18 *now* going to the **h** of the LORD; and H1004
18 there *is* no man that receiveth me to **h**. H1004
21 So he brought him into his **h**, and gave H1004
22 of Belial, beset the **h** round about, *and* H1004
22 to the master of the **h**, the old man, H1004
22 into thine **h**, that we may know him. H1004
23 And the man, the master of the **h**, went H1004
23 is come into mine **h**, do not this folly. H1004
26 **h** where her lord *was*, till it was light. H1004
27 the doors of the **h**, and went out to go H1004
27 *at* the door of the **h**, and her hands *were* H1004
29 And when he was come into his **h**, he H1004
20: 5 me, and beset the **h** round about upon H1004
8 neither will we any *of us* turn into his **h**. H1004
18 and went up to the **h** of God, and asked H1008
26 came unto the **h** of God, and wept, and H1008
31 goeth up to the **h** of God, and the other H1008
21: 2 And the people came to the **h** of God, H1008
Ru 1: 8 to her mother's **h**: the LORD deal kindly H1004
Ru 1: 9 each *of you* in the **h** of her husband. H1004
2: 7 now, that she tarried a little in the **h**. H1004
4:11 is come into thine **h** like Rachel and H1004
11 two did build the **h** of Israel: and do H1004
12 And let thy **h** be like the house of H1004
12 And let thy house be like the **h** of H1004
1Sa 1: 7 she went up to the **h** of the LORD, so H1004
19 and came to their **h** to Ramah: and H1004
21 And the man Elkanah, and all his **h**, H1004
24 him unto the **h** of the LORD in Shiloh: H1004
2:11 And Elkanah went to Ramah to his **h**. H1004
27 appear unto the **h** of thy father, when H1004
27 when they were in Egypt in Pharaoh's **h**? H1004
28 did I give unto the **h** of thy father all H1004
30 indeed *that* thy **h**, and the house of thy H1004
30 *that* thy house, and the **h** of thy father, H1004
31 arm of thy father's **h**, that there shall H1004
31 there shall not be an old man in thine **h**. H1004
32 not be an old man in thine **h** for ever. H1004
33 **h** shall die in the flower of their age. H1004
35 build him a sure **h**; and he shall walk H1004
36 that is left in thine **h** shall come *and* H1004
3:12 concerning his **h**: when I begin, I will H1004
13 that I will judge his **h** for ever for the H1004
14 And therefore I have sworn unto the **h** H1004
14 iniquity of Eli's **h** shall not be purged H1004
15 the doors of the **h** of the LORD. And H1004
5: 2 the **h** of Dagon, and set it by Dagon. H1004
5 into Dagon's **h**, tread on the threshold H1004
7: 1 brought it into the **h** of Abinadab in the H1004
2 **h** of Israel lamented after the LORD. H1004
3 And Samuel spake unto all the **h** of H1004
17 for there *was* his **h**; and there he judged H1004
9:18 me, I pray thee, where the seer's **h** *is*. H1004
20 *it* not on thee, and on all thy father's **h**? H1004
25 with Saul upon the top of the **h**.
26 to the top of the **h**, saying, Up, that I may
10:25 all the people away, every man to his **h**. H1004
15:34 Saul went up to his **h** to Gibeah of Saul. H1004
17:25 and make his father's **h** free in Israel. H1004
18: 2 him go no more home to his father's **h**. H1004
10 in the midst of the **h**: and David played H1004
19: 9 as he sat in his **h** with his javelin in his H1004
11 unto David's **h**, to watch him, and to H1004
20:15 kindness from my **h** for ever: no, not H1004
16 *a covenant* with the **h** of David, *saying*, H1004
21:15 shall this *fellow* come into my **h**? H1004
22: 1 and all his father's **h** heard *it*, they H1004
11 and all his father's **h**, the priests that H1004
14 bidding, and is honourable in thine **h**? H1004
15 *nor* to all the **h** of my father: for thy H1004
16 Ahimelech, thou, and all thy father's **h**. H1004
22 *death* of all the persons of thy father's **h**. H1004
23:18 the wood, and Jonathan went to his **h**. H1004
24:21 destroy my name out of my father's **h**. H1004
25: 1 and buried him in his **h** at Ramah. And H1004
3 his doings; and he *was* of the **h** of Caleb.
6 **h**, and peace *be* unto all that thou hast. H1004
28 make my lord a sure **h**; because my lord H1004
35 up in peace to thine **h**; see, I have H1004
36 held a feast in his **h**, like the feast of a H1004
28:24 And the woman had a fat calf in the **h**; H1004
31: 9 **h** of their idols, and among the people. H1004
10 And they put his armour in the **h** of H1004
2Sa 1:12 LORD, and for the **h** of Israel; because H1004
2: 4 king over the **h** of Judah. And they H1004
7 is dead, and also the **h** of Judah have H1004
10 But the **h** of Judah followed David. H1004
11 Hebron over the **h** of Judah was seven H1004
3: 1 Now there was long war between the **h** H1004
1 of Saul and the **h** of David: but David H1004
1 **h** of Saul waxed weaker and weaker. H1004
6 was war between the **h** of Saul and the H1004
6 of Saul and the **h** of David, that Abner H1004
6 made himself strong for the **h** of Saul. H1004
8 this day unto the **h** of Saul thy father, H1004
10 To translate the kingdom from the **h** of H1004
19 good to the whole **h** of Benjamin. H1004
29 on all his father's **h**; and let there not H1004
29 not fail from the **h** of Joab one that H1004
4: 5 of the day to the **h** of Ish-bosheth, who H1004
6 the midst of the **h**, *as though* they would H1004
7 For when they came into the **h**, he lay H1004
11 person in his own **h** upon his bed? shall H1004
5: 8 and the lame shall not come into the **h**. H1004
11 and masons: and they built David an **h**. H1004
6: 3 it out of the **h** of Abinadab that *was* H1004
4 And they brought it out of the **h** of H1004
5 And David and all the **h** of Israel H1004

2Sa 6:10 into the **h** of Obed-edom the Gittite. H1004
11 continued in the **h** of Obed-edom the H1004
12 hath blessed the **h** of Obed-edom, and H1004
12 of God from the **h** of Obed-edom into H1004
15 So David and all the **h** of Israel brought H1004
19 the people departed every one to his **h**. H1004
21 and before all his **h**, to appoint me ruler H1004
7: 1 the king sat in his **h**, and the LORD had H1004
2 now, I dwell in an **h** of cedar, but the H1004
5 thou build me an **h** for me to dwell in? H1004
6 Whereas I have not dwelt in *any* **h** H1004
7 Why build ye not me an **h** of cedar? H1004
11 telleth thee that he will make thee an **h**. H1004
13 He shall build an **h** for my name, and I H1004
16 And thine **h** and thy kingdom shall be H1004
18 **h**, that thou hast brought me hitherto? H1004
19 of thy servant's **h** for a great while to H1004
25 concerning his **h**, establish *it* for ever, H1004
26 over Israel: and let the **h** of thy servant H1004
27 I will build thee an **h**: therefore hath thy H1004
29 thee to bless the **h** of thy servant, that H1004
29 the **h** of thy servant be blessed for ever. H1004
9: 1 that is left of the **h** of Saul, that I may H1004
2 And *there was* of the **h** of Saul a H1004
3 not yet any of the **h** of Saul, that I may H1004
4 he *is* in the **h** of Machir, the son of H1004
5 him out of the **h** of Machir, the son of H1004
9 that pertained to Saul and to all his **h**. H1004
12 all that dwelt in the **h** of Ziba *were* H1004
11: 2 roof of the king's **h**: and from the roof H1004
4 and she returned unto her **h**. H1004
8 Go down to thy **h**, and wash thy feet. H1004
8 out of the king's **h**, and there followed H1004
9 the door of the king's **h** with all the H1004
9 of his lord, and went not down to his **h**. H1004
10 not down unto his **h**, David said unto H1004
10 didst thou not go down unto thine **h**? H1004
11 then go into mine **h**, to eat and to drink, H1004
13 of his lord, but went not down to his **h**. H1004
27 fetched her to his **h**, and she became his H1004
12: 8 And I gave thee thy master's **h**, and thy H1004
8 and gave thee the **h** of Israel and of H1004
10 depart from thine **h**; because thou hast H1004
11 out of thine own **h**, and I will take thy H1004
15 And Nathan departed unto his **h**. And H1004
17 And the elders of his **h** arose, *and went* H1004
20 and came into the **h** of the LORD, and H1004
20 he came to his own **h**; and when he H1004
13: 7 Amnon's **h**, and dress him meat. H1004
8 her brother Amnon's **h**; and he was laid H1004
20 desolate in her brother Absalom's **h**. H1004
14: 8 Go to thine **h**, and I will give charge H1004
9 on my father's **h**: and the king and his H1004
24 turn to his own **h**, and let him not see H1004
24 his own **h**, and saw not the king's face. H1004
31 Absalom unto *his* **h**, and said unto him, H1004
15:16 *which were* concubines, to keep the **h**. H1004
35 out of the king's **h**, thou shalt tell *it* to H1004
16: 3 To day shall the **h** of Israel restore me H1004
5 the family of the **h** of Saul, whose name H1004
8 all the blood of the **h** of Saul, in whose H1004
21 left to keep the **h**; and all Israel shall H1004
22 upon the top of the **h**; and Absalom went
17:18 came to a man's **h** in Bahurim, which H1004
20 the woman to the **h**, they said, Where *is* H1004
23 him home to his **h**, to his city, and put H1004
19: 5 And Joab came into the **h** to the king, H1004
11 king back to his **h**? seeing the speech of H1004
11 Israel is come to the king, *even* to his **h**. H1004
17 the servant of the **h** of Saul, and his H1004
20 first this day of all the **h** of Joseph to go H1004
28 For all *of* my father's **h** were but dead H1004
30 is come again in peace unto his own **h**. H1004
20: 3 And David came to his **h** at Jerusalem; H1004
3 left to keep the **h**, and put them in ward, H1004
21: 1 **h**, because he slew the Gibeonites. H1004
4 of Saul, nor of his **h**; neither for us shalt H1004
23: 5 Although my **h** *be* not so with God; yet H1004
24:17 against me, and against my father's **h**. H1004
1Ki 1:53 Solomon said unto him, Go to thine **h**. H1004
2:24 hath made me an **h**, as he promised, H1004
27 spake concerning the **h** of Eli in Shiloh. H1004
31 from me, and from the **h** of my father. H1004
33 and upon his **h**, and upon his throne, H1004
34 buried in his own **h** in the wilderness. H1004
36 him, Build thee an **h** in Jerusalem, and H1004
3: 1 building his own **h**, and the house of the H1004
1 house, and the **h** of the LORD, and the H1004
2 there was no **h** built unto the name H1004

1Ki 3:17 dwell in one **h**; and I was delivered H1004
17 delivered of a child with her in the **h**. H1004
18 us in the **h**, save we two in the house. H1004
18 us in the house, save we two in the **h**. H1004
5: 3 could not build an **h** unto the name of H1004
5 And, behold, I purpose to build an **h** H1004
5 he shall build an **h** unto my name. H1004
17 stones, to lay the foundation of the **h**. H1004
18 timber and stones to build the **h**. H1004
6: 1 he began to build the **h** of the LORD. H1004
2 And the **h** which king Solomon built for H1004
3 the temple of the **h**, twenty cubits *was* H1004
3 the breadth of the **h**; *and* ten cubits *was* H1004
3 *was* the breadth thereof before the **h**. H1004
4 And for the **h** he made windows of H1004
5 And against the wall of the **h** he built H1004
5 the walls of the **h** round about, *both* of H1004
6 *in the wall* of the **h** he made narrowed H1004
6 not be fastened in the walls of the **h**. H1004
7 And the **h**, when it was in building, was H1004
7 heard in the **h**, while it was in building. H1004
8 the right side of the **h**: and they went up H1004
9 So he built the **h**, and finished it; and H1004
9 the **h** with beams and boards of cedar. H1004
10 against all the **h**, five cubits high: and H1004
10 rested on the **h** *with* timber of cedar. H1004
12 *Concerning* this **h** which thou art in H1004
14 So Solomon built the **h**, and finished it. H1004
15 And he built the walls of the **h** within H1004
15 the floor of the **h**, and the walls of the H1004
15 the floor of the **h** with planks of fir. H1004
16 on the sides of the **h**, both the floor and H1004
17 And the **h**, that *is*, the temple before it, H1004
18 And the cedar of the **h** within *was* H1004
19 And the oracle he prepared in the **h** H1004
21 So Solomon overlaid the **h** within with H1004
22 And the whole **h** he overlaid with gold, H1004
22 finished all the **h**: also the whole altar H1004
27 within the inner **h**: and they stretched H1004
27 one another in the midst of the **h**. H1004
29 And he carved all the walls of the **h** H1004
30 And the floor of the **h** he overlaid with H1004
37 **h** of the LORD laid, in the month Zif: H1004
38 month, was the **h** finished throughout H1004
7: 1 But Solomon was building his own **h** H1004
1 thirteen years, and he finished all his **h**. H1004
2 He built also the **h** of the forest of H1004
8 And his **h** where he dwelt *had* another H1004
8 Solomon made also an **h** for Pharaoh's H1004
12 inner court of the **h** of the LORD, and H1004
12 of the LORD, and for the porch of the **h**. H1004
39 right side of the **h**, and five on the left H1004
39 the left side of the **h**: and he set the sea H1004
39 the **h** eastward over against the south. H1004
40 king Solomon for the **h** of the LORD: H1004
45 the **h** of the LORD, *were of* bright brass. H1004
48 unto the **h** of the LORD: the altar H1004
50 the doors of the inner **h**, the most holy H1004
50 the doors of the **h**, *to wit*, of the temple. H1004
51 made for the **h** of the LORD. And H1004
51 the treasures of the **h** of the LORD. H1004
8: 6 into the oracle of the **h**, to the most holy H1004
10 that the cloud filled the **h** of the LORD, H1004
11 the LORD had filled the **h** of the LORD. H1004
13 I have surely built thee an **h** to dwell in, H1004
16 of Israel to build an **h**, that my name H1004
17 father to build an **h** for the name of the H1004
18 heart to build an **h** unto my name, H1004
19 Nevertheless thou shalt not build the **h**; H1004
19 he shall build the **h** unto my name. H1004
20 and have built an **h** for the name of the H1004
27 much less this **h** that I have builded? H1004
29 open toward this **h** night and day, *even* H1004
31 oath come before thine altar in this **h**: H1004
33 make supplication unto thee in this **h**: H1004
38 spread forth his hands toward this **h**: H1004
42 he shall come and pray toward this **h**; H1004
43 know that this **h**, which I have builded, H1004
44 the **h** that I have built for thy name: H1004
48 the **h** which I have built for thy name: H1004
63 of Israel dedicated the **h** of the LORD. H1004
64 *was* before the **h** of the LORD: for there H1004
9: 1 the building of the **h** of the LORD, and H1004
1 and the king's **h**, and all Solomon's H1004
3 hallowed this **h**, which thou hast built, H1004
7 them; and this **h**, which I have hallowed H1004
8 And at this **h**, *which* is high, every one H1004
8 done thus unto this land, and to this **h**? H1004
10 **h** of the LORD, and the king's house, H1004

1Ki 9:10 the house of the LORD, and the king's **h**, H1004
15 for to build the **h** of the LORD, and his H1004
15 and his own **h**, and Millo, and the wall H1004
24 of David unto her **h** which *Solomon* H1004
25 before the LORD. So he finished the **h**. H1004
10: 4 wisdom, and the **h** that he had built, H1004
5 went up unto the **h** of the LORD; there H1004
12 pillars for the **h** of the LORD, and for H1004
12 and for the king's **h**, harps also and H1004
17 them in the **h** of the forest of Lebanon. H1004
21 all the vessels of the **h** of the forest of H1004
11:18 gave him an **h**, and appointed him H1004
20 in Pharaoh's **h**: and Genubath was H1004
28 over all the charge of the **h** of Joseph. H1004
38 build thee a sure **h**, as I built for David, H1004
12:16 now see to thine own **h**, David. So Israel H1004
19 So Israel rebelled against the **h** of H1004
20 **h** of David, but the tribe of Judah only. H1004
21 assembled all the **h** of Judah, with the H1004
21 to fight against the **h** of Israel, to bring H1004
23 Judah, and unto all the **h** of Judah and H1004
24 every man to his **h**; for this thing is H1004
26 the kingdom return to the **h** of David: H1004
27 to do sacrifice in the **h** of the LORD at H1004
31 And he made an **h** of high places, and H1004
13: 2 be born unto the **h** of David, Josiah by H1004
8 wilt give me half thine **h**, I will not go in H1004
18 thee into thine **h**, that he may eat bread H1004
19 did eat bread in his **h**, and drank water. H1004
34 And this thing became sin unto the **h** of H1004
14: 4 and came to the **h** of Ahijah. But H1004
8 And rent the kingdom away from the **h** H1004
10 evil upon the **h** of Jeroboam, and will H1004
10 the remnant of the **h** of Jeroboam, as a H1004
12 thee to thine own **h**: *and* when thy feet H1004
13 God of Israel in the **h** of Jeroboam. H1004
14 who shall cut off the **h** of Jeroboam that H1004
26 treasures of the **h** of the LORD, and the H1004
26 of the king's **h**; he even took away all: H1004
27 which kept the door of the king's **h**. H1004
28 king went into the **h** of the LORD, that H1004
15:15 into the **h** of the LORD, silver, H1004
18 treasures of the **h** of the LORD, and the H1004
18 of the king's **h**, and delivered them H1004
27 And Baasha the son of Ahijah, of the **h** H1004
29 he smote all the **h** of Jeroboam; he left H1004
16: 3 the posterity of his **h**; and will make thy H1004
3 and will make thy **h** like the house of H1004
3 the **h** of Jeroboam the son of Nebat. H1004
7 and against his **h**, even for all the evil H1004
7 in being like the **h** of Jeroboam; and H1004
9 drunk in the **h** of Arza steward of *his* H1004
9 of Arza steward of *his* **h** in Tirzah. H1004
11 he slew all the **h** of Baasha: he left him H1004
12 Thus did Zimri destroy all the **h** of H1004
18 of the king's **h**, and burnt the king's H1004
18 king's **h** over him with fire, and died, H1004
32 for Baal in the **h** of Baal, which he had H1004
17:15 and he, and her **h**, did eat *many* days. H1004
17 the mistress of the **h**, fell sick; and his H1004
23 chamber into the **h**, and delivered him H1004
18: 3 governor of *his* **h**. (Now Obadiah feared H1004
18 thou, and thy father's **h**, in that ye have H1004
20: 6 shall search thine **h**, and the houses of H1004
31 the kings of the **h** of Israel *are* merciful H1004
43 And the king of Israel went to his **h** H1004
21: 2 it *is* near unto my **h**: and I will give thee H1004
4 And Ahab came into his **h** heavy and H1004
22 And will make thine **h** like the house of H1004
22 And will make thine house like the **h** of H1004
22 and like the **h** of Baasha the son of H1004
29 days will I bring the evil upon his **h**. H1004
22:17 return every man to his **h** in peace. H1004
39 he did, and the ivory **h** which he made, H1004
2Ki 4: 2 hast thou in the **h**? And she said, Thine H1004
2 not any thing in the **h**, save a pot of oil. H1004
32 And when Elisha was come into the **h**, H1004
35 Then he returned, and walked in the **h** H1004
5: 9 and stood at the door of the **h** of Elisha. H1004
18 goeth into the **h** of Rimmon to worship H1004
18 bow myself in the **h** of Rimmon: when I H1004
18 myself in the **h** of Rimmon, the LORD H1004
24 *them* in the **h**: and he let the men go, H1004
6:32 But Elisha sat in his **h**, and the elders H1004
7:11 and they told *it* to the king's **h** within. H1004
8: 3 the king for her **h** and for her land. H1004
5 to the king for her **h** and for her land. H1004
18 of Israel, as did the **h** of Ahab: for the H1004
27 And he walked in the way of the **h** of H1004

2Ki 8:27 LORD, as *did* the **h** of Ahab: for he *was* H1004
27 he *was* the son in law of the **h** of Ahab. H1004
9: 6 And he arose, and went into the **h**; and H1004
7 And thou shalt smite the **h** of Ahab thy H1004
8 For the whole **h** of Ahab shall perish: H1004
9 And I will make the **h** of Ahab like the H1004
9 of Ahab like the **h** of Jeroboam the son H1004
9 like the **h** of Baasha the son of Ahijah: H1004
27 way of the garden **h**. And Jehu followed H1004
10: 3 throne, and fight for your master's **h**. H1004
5 And he that *was* over the **h**, and he that H1004
10 spake concerning the **h** of Ahab: for the H1004
11 So Jehu slew all that remained of the **h** H1004
12 as he *was* at the shearing **h** in the way, H1004
14 pit of the shearing **h**, *even* two and forty H1004
21 they came into the **h** of Baal; and the H1004
21 of Baal; and the **h** of Baal was full from H1004
23 of Rechab, into the **h** of Baal, and said H1004
25 and went to the city of the **h** of Baal. H1004
26 out of the **h** of Baal, and burned them. H1004
27 brake down the **h** of Baal, and made it H1004
27 and made it a draught **h** unto this day.
30 done unto the **h** of Ahab according to H1004
11: 3 And he was with her hid in the **h** of the H1004
4 to him into the **h** of the LORD, and H1004
4 oath of them in the **h** of the LORD, and H1004
5 be keepers of the watch of the king's **h**; H1004
6 of the **h**, that it be not broken down. H1004
7 of the **h** of the LORD about the king. H1004
15 her not be slain in the **h** of the LORD. H1004
16 the king's **h**: and there was she slain. H1004
18 land went into the **h** of Baal, and brake H1004
18 officers over the **h** of the LORD. H1004
19 the king from the **h** of the LORD, and H1004
19 **h**. And he sat on the throne of the kings. H1004
20 with the sword *beside* the king's **h**. H1004
12: 4 is brought into the **h** of the LORD, *even* H1004
4 heart to bring into the **h** of the LORD, H1004
5 the breaches of the **h**, wheresoever any H1004
6 had not repaired the breaches of the **h**. H1004
7 breaches of the **h**? now therefore receive H1004
7 but deliver it for the breaches of the **h**. H1004
8 neither to repair the breaches of the **h**. H1004
9 cometh into the **h** of the LORD: and the H1004
9 *was* brought into the **h** of the LORD. H1004
10 that was found in the **h** of the LORD. H1004
11 the oversight of the **h** of the LORD: and H1004
11 that wrought upon the **h** of the LORD, H1004
12 breaches of the **h** of the LORD, and for H1004
12 that was laid out for the **h** to repair *it*. H1004
13 Howbeit there were not made for the **h** H1004
13 *was* brought into the **h** of the LORD: H1004
14 repaired therewith the **h** of the LORD. H1004
16 the **h** of the LORD: it was the priests'. H1004
18 treasures of the **h** of the LORD, and in H1004
18 LORD, and in the king's **h**, and sent *it* to H1004
20 **h** of Millo, which goeth down to Silla. H1004
13: 6 from the sins of the **h** of Jeroboam, who H1004
14:14 were found in the **h** of the LORD, and H1004
14 of the king's **h**, and hostages, and H1004
15: 5 dwelt in a several **h**. And Jotham the H1004
5 the **h**, judging the people of the land. H1004
25 of the king's **h**, with Argob and Arieh, H1004
35 the higher gate of the **h** of the LORD. H1004
16: 8 was found in the **h** of the LORD, and in H1004
8 of the king's **h**, and sent *it for* a present H1004
14 the forefront of the **h**, from between the H1004
14 the altar and the **h** of the LORD, and H1004
18 had built in the **h**, and the king's entry H1004
18 **h** of the LORD for the king of Assyria. H1004
17:21 For he rent Israel from the **h** of David; H1004
18:15 was found in the **h** of the LORD, and in H1004
15 and in the treasures of the king's **h**. H1004
19: 1 and went into the **h** of the LORD. H1004
14 went up into the **h** of the LORD, and H1004
30 is escaped of the **h** of Judah shall yet H1004
37 in the **h** of Nisroch his god, H1004
20: 1 the LORD, Set thine **h** in order; for thou H1004
5 shalt go up unto the **h** of the LORD. H1004
8 into the **h** of the LORD the third day? H1004
13 them all the **h** of his precious things, H1004
13 and *all* the **h** of his armour, and H1004
13 there was nothing in his **h**, nor in all his H1004
15 have they seen in thine **h**? And Hezekiah H1004
15 that *are* in mine **h** have they seen: there H1004
17 all that *is* in thine **h**, and that which thy H1004
21: 4 And he built altars in the **h** of the H1004
5 in the two courts of the **h** of the LORD. H1004
7 had made in the **h**, of which the LORD H1004
2Ki 21: 7 his son, In this **h**, and in Jerusalem, H1004
13 plummet of the **h** of Ahab: and I will H1004
18 garden of his own **h**, in the garden of H1004
23 him, and slew the king in his own **h**. H1004
22: 3 scribe, to the **h** of the LORD, saying, H1004
4 is brought into the **h** of the LORD, H1004
5 oversight of the **h** of the LORD: and let H1004
5 which *is* in the **h** of the LORD, to repair H1004
5 LORD, to repair the breaches of the **h**, H1004
6 timber and hewn stone to repair the **h**. H1004
8 of the law in the **h** of the LORD. And H1004
9 was found in the **h**, and have delivered H1004
9 the oversight of the **h** of the LORD. H1004
23: 2 And the king went up into the **h** of the H1004
2 which was found in the **h** of the LORD. H1004
6 out the grove from the **h** of the LORD, H1004
7 that *were* by the **h** of the LORD, where H1004
11 entering in of the **h** of the LORD, by the H1004
12 two courts of the **h** of the LORD, did H1004
24 the priest found in the **h** of the LORD. H1004
27 chosen, and the **h** of which I said, My H1004
24:13 treasures of the **h** of the LORD, and the H1004
13 of the king's **h**, and cut in pieces all H1004
25: 9 And he burnt the **h** of the LORD, and H1004
9 and the king's **h**, and all the houses of H1004
9 every great *man's* **h** burnt he with fire. H1004
13 that *were* in the **h** of the LORD, and the H1004
13 that *was* in the **h** of the LORD, did the H1004
16 had made for the **h** of the LORD; the H1004
1Ch 2:54 Ataroth, the **h** of Joab, and half of H5854
55 Hemath, the father of the **h** of Rechab. H1004
4:21 and the families of the **h** of them that H1004
21 wrought fine linen, of the **h** of Ashbea, H1004
38 the **h** of their fathers increased greatly. H1004
5:13 And their brethren of the **h** of their H1004
15 of Guni, chief of the **h** of their fathers. H1004
24 And these *were* the heads of the **h** of H1004
24 *and* heads of the **h** of their fathers. H1004
6:31 of song in the **h** of the LORD, after that H1004
32 Solomon had built the **h** of the LORD in H1004
48 of the tabernacle of the **h** of God. H1004
7: 2 of their father's **h**, *to wit*, of Tola: *they* H1004
4 after the **h** of their fathers, *were* H1004
7 Iri, five; heads of the **h** of *their* fathers, H1004
9 heads of the **h** of their fathers, mighty H1004
23 Beriah, because it went evil with his **h**. H1004
40 of *their* father's **h**, choice *and* mighty H1004
9: 9 of the fathers in the **h** of their fathers. H1004
11 son of Ahitub, the ruler of the **h** of God; H1004
13 And their brethren, heads of the **h** of H1004
13 the work of the service of the **h** of God. H1004
19 his brethren, of the **h** of his father, the H1004
23 of the gates of the **h** of the LORD, H1004
23 the **h** of the tabernacle, by wards. H1004
26 and treasuries of the **h** of God. H1004
27 And they lodged round about the **h** of H1004
10: 6 three sons, and all his **h** died together. H1004
10 And they put his armour in the **h** of H1004
12:28 his father's **h** twenty and two captains. H1004
29 had kept the ward of the **h** of Saul. H1004
30 throughout the **h** of their fathers. H1004
13: 7 cart out of the **h** of Abinadab: and Uzza H1004
13 into the **h** of Obed-edom the Gittite. H1004
14 Obed-edom in his **h** three months. And H1004
14 **h** of Obed-edom, and all that he had. H1004
14: 1 and carpenters, to build him an **h**. H1004
15:25 out of the **h** of Obed-edom with joy. H1004
16:43 every man to his **h**: and David returned H1004
43 and David returned to bless his **h**. H1004
17: 1 as David sat in his **h**, that David said to H1004
1 Lo, I dwell in an **h** of cedars, but the H1004
4 shalt not build me an **h** to dwell in: H1004
5 For I have not dwelt in an **h** since the H1004
6 have ye not built me an **h** of cedars? H1004
10 thee that the LORD will build thee an **h**. H1004
12 He shall build me an **h**, and I will H1004
14 But I will settle him in mine **h** and in H1004
16 **h**, that thou hast brought me hitherto? H1004
17 of thy servant's **h** for a great while to H1004
23 and concerning his **h** be established for H1004
24 to Israel: and *let* the **h** of David thy H1004
25 thou wilt build him an **h**: therefore thy H1004
27 thee to bless the **h** of thy servant, that H1004
21:17 on my father's **h**; but not on thy people, H1004
22: 1 Then David said, This *is* the **h** of the H1004
2 wrought stones to build the **h** of God. H1004
5 tender, and the **h** *that is* to be builded H1004
6 build an **h** for the LORD God of Israel. H1004
7 **h** unto the name of the LORD my God: H1004
1Ch 22: 8 shalt not build an **h** unto my name, H1004
10 He shall build an **h** for my name; and H1004
11 and build the **h** of the LORD thy God, H1004
14 have prepared for the **h** of the LORD an H1004
19 of God, into the **h** that is to be built to H1004
23: 4 the work of the **h** of the LORD; and six H1004
11 reckoning, according to *their* father's **h**. H1004
24 These *were* the sons of Levi after the **h** H1004
24 the service of the **h** of the LORD, from H1004
28 the service of the **h** of the LORD, in the H1004
28 the work of the service of the **h** of God; H1004
32 in the service of the **h** of the LORD. H1004
24: 4 chief men of the **h** of *their* fathers, and H1004
4 according to the **h** of their fathers. H1004
5 governors *of the* **h** of God, were of the
19 service to come into the **h** of the LORD, H1004
30 the Levites after the **h** of their fathers. H1004
25: 6 for song *in* the **h** of the LORD, with H1004
6 the service of the **h** of God, according to H1004
26: 6 throughout the **h** of their father: for H1004
12 to minister in the **h** of the LORD. H1004
13 to the **h** of their fathers, for every gate. H1004
15 and to his sons the **h** of Asuppim. H1004
20 treasures of the **h** of God, and over the H1004
22 over the treasures of the **h** of the LORD. H1004
27 to maintain the **h** of the LORD. H1004
28: 2 heart to build an **h** of rest for the ark of H1004
3 Thou shalt not build an **h** for my name, H1004
4 me before all the **h** of my father to be H1004
4 ruler; and of the **h** of Judah, the house H1004
4 house of Judah, the **h** of my father; and H1004
6 he shall build my **h** and my courts: for I H1004
10 thee to build an **h** for the sanctuary: be H1004
12 the courts of the **h** of the LORD, and of H1004
12 treasuries of the **h** of God, and of the H1004
13 of the service of the **h** of the LORD, and H1004
13 vessels of service in the **h** of the LORD. H1004
20 for the service of the **h** of the LORD. H1004
21 the service of the **h** of God: and *there* H1004
29: 2 my might for the **h** of my God the gold H1004
3 affection to the **h** of my God, I have of H1004
3 I have given to the **h** of my God, over H1004
3 all that I have prepared for the holy **h**, H1004
7 And gave for the service of the **h** of God H1004
8 to the treasure of the **h** of the LORD, by H1004
16 to build thee an **h** for thine holy name H1004
2Ch 2: 1 And Solomon determined to build an **h** H1004
1 of the LORD, and an **h** for his kingdom. H1004
3 to build him an **h** to dwell therein, *even* H1004
4 Behold, I build an **h** to the name of the H1004
5 And the **h** which I build *is* great: for H1004
6 But who is able to build him an **h**, H1004
6 build him an **h**, save only to burn H1004
9 for the **h** which I am about to H1004
12 might build an **h** for the LORD, and an H1004
12 the LORD, and an **h** for his kingdom. H1004
3: 1 Then Solomon began to build the **h** of H1004
3 the building of the **h** of God. The length H1004
4 in the front *of the* **h**, the length *of it was*
4 the breadth of the **h**, twenty cubits, and H1004
5 And the greater **h** he cieled with fir H1004
6 And he garnished the **h** with precious H1004
7 He overlaid also the **h**, the beams, the H1004
8 And he made the most holy **h**, the H1004
8 the breadth of the **h**, twenty cubits, and H1004
10 And in the most holy **h** he made two H1004
11 to the wall of the **h**: and the other wing H1004
12 to the wall of the **h**: and the other wing H1004
15 Also he made before the **h** two pillars H1004
4:11 for king Solomon for the **h** of God; H1004
16 for the **h** of the LORD of bright brass. H1004
19 that *were for* the **h** of God, the golden H1004
22 and the entry of the **h**, the inner doors H1004
22 of the **h** of the temple, *were of* gold. H1004
5: 1 made for the **h** of the LORD was H1004
1 he among the treasures of the **h** of God. H1004
7 to the oracle of the **h**, into the most holy H1004
13 ever: that *then* the **h** was filled with a H1004
13 with a cloud, *even* the **h** of the LORD; H1004
14 of the LORD had filled the **h** of God. H1004
6: 2 But I have built an **h** of habitation for H1004
5 of Israel to build an **h** in, that my name H1004
7 father to build an **h** for the name of the H1004
8 heart to build an **h** for my name, thou H1004
9 shalt not build the **h**; but thy son which H1004
9 loins, he shall build the **h** for my name. H1004
10 and have built the **h** for the name of the H1004
18 much less this **h** which I have built! H1004
20 be open upon this **h** day and night, H1004

2Ch 6:22 oath come before thine altar in this **h**; H1004
24 make supplication before thee in this **h**; H1004
29 shall spread forth his hands in this **h**: H1004
32 arm; if they come and pray in this **h**; H1004
33 know that this **h** which I have built is H1004
34 the **h** which I have built for thy name; H1004
38 the **h** which I have built for thy name: H1004
7: 1 and the glory of the LORD filled the **h**. H1004
2 could not enter into the **h** of the LORD, H1004
2 of the LORD had filled the LORD'S **h**. H1004
3 the LORD upon the **h**, they bowed H1004
5 all the people dedicated the **h** of God. H1004
7 *was* before the **h** of the LORD: for there H1004
11 Thus Solomon finished the **h** of the H1004
11 and the king's **h**: and all that came into H1004
11 to make in the **h** of the LORD, and in H1004
11 in his own **h**, he prosperously effected. H1004
12 place to myself for an **h** of sacrifice. H1004
16 sanctified this **h**, that my name may H1004
20 given them; and this **h**, which I have H1004
21 And this **h**, which is high, shall be an H1004
21 thus unto this land, and unto this **h**? H1004
8: 1 the **h** of the LORD, and his own house, H1004
1 the house of the LORD, and his own **h**, H1004
11 of David unto the **h** that he had built H1004
11 shall not dwell in the **h** of David king of H1004
16 foundation of the **h** of the LORD, and H1004
16 *So* the **h** of the LORD was perfected. H1004
9: 3 Solomon, and the **h** that he had built, H1004
4 went up into the **h** of the LORD; there H1004
11 terraces to the **h** of the LORD, and to H1004
16 them in the **h** of the forest of Lebanon. H1004
20 all the vessels of the **h** of the forest of H1004
10:16 own **h**. So all Israel went to their tents. H1004
19 And Israel rebelled against the **h** of H1004
11: 1 he gathered of the **h** of Judah and H1004
4 every man to his **h**: for this thing is H1004
12: 9 treasures of the **h** of the LORD, and the H1004
9 of the king's **h**; he took all: he carried H1004
10 that kept the entrance of the king's **h**. H1004
11 And when the king entered into the **h** H1004
15:18 And he brought into the **h** of God the H1004
16: 2 treasures of the **h** of the LORD and of H1004
2 LORD and of the king's **h**, and sent to H1004
10 him in a prison **h**; for *he was* in a rage H1004
17:14 according to the **h** of their fathers: Of H1004
18:16 *therefore* every man to his **h** in peace. H1004
19: 1 returned to his **h** in peace to Jerusalem. H1004
11 the ruler of the **h** of Judah, for all the H1004
20: 5 **h** of the LORD, before the new court, H1004
9 stand before this **h**, and in thy presence, H1004
9 thy name *is* in this **h**,) and cry unto thee H1004
28 and trumpets unto the **h** of the LORD. H1004
21: 6 like as did the **h** of Ahab: for he had H1004
7 not destroy the **h** of David, because of H1004
13 whoredoms of the **h** of Ahab, and also H1004
13 **h**, *which were* better than thyself: H1004
17 in the king's **h**, and his sons also, and H1004
22: 3 He also walked in the ways of the **h** of H1004
4 of the LORD like the **h** of Ahab: for they H1004
7 had anointed to cut off the **h** of Ahab. H1004
8 upon the **h** of Ahab, and found H1004
9 his heart. So the **h** of Ahaziah had no H1004
10 all the seed royal of the **h** of Judah. H1004
12 And he was with them hid in the **h** of H1004
23: 3 the king in the **h** of God. And he said H1004
5 And a third part *shall be* at the king's **h**; H1004
5 *be* in the courts of the **h** of the LORD. H1004
6 But let none come into the **h** of the H1004
7 *else* cometh into the **h**, he shall be put to H1004
9 David's, which *were* in the **h** of God. H1004
12 to the people into the **h** of the LORD: H1004
14 said, Slay her not in the **h** of the LORD. H1004
15 gate by the king's **h**, they slew her there. H1004
17 Then all the people went to the **h** of H1004
18 the offices of the **h** of the LORD by the H1004
18 distributed in the **h** of the LORD, to H1004
19 at the gates of the **h** of the LORD, that H1004
20 the king from the **h** of the LORD: and H1004
20 into the king's **h**, and set the king upon H1004
24: 4 minded to repair the **h** of the LORD. H1004
5 to repair the **h** of your God from year H1004
7 had broken up the **h** of God; and also H1004
7 things of the **h** of the LORD did they H1004
8 at the gate of the **h** of the LORD. H1004
12 of the service of the **h** of the LORD, and H1004
12 to repair the **h** of the LORD, and also H1004
12 and brass to mend the **h** of the LORD. H1004
13 and they set the **h** of God in his state, H1004

2Ch 24:14 vessels for the **h** of the LORD, *even* H1004
14 burnt offerings in the **h** of the LORD H1004
16 both toward God, and toward his **h**. H1004
18 And they left the **h** of the LORD God of H1004
21 king in the court of the **h** of the LORD. H1004
27 repairing of the **h** of God, behold, they H1004
25:24 that were found in the **h** of God with H1004
24 of the king's **h**, the hostages also, and H1004
26:19 the priests in the **h** of the LORD, from H1004
21 dwelt in a several **h**, *being* a leper; for H1004
21 cut off from the **h** of the LORD: and H1004
21 king's **h**, judging the people of the land. H1004
27: 3 He built the high gate of the **h** of the H1004
28: 7 the governor of the **h**, and Elkanah *that* H1004
21 a portion *out* of the **h** of the LORD, and H1004
21 and *out* of the **h** of the king, and of the H1004
24 the vessels of the **h** of God, and cut in H1004
24 the vessels of the **h** of God, and shut up H1004
24 the doors of the **h** of the LORD, and he H1004
29: 3 the **h** of the LORD, and repaired them. H1004
5 and sanctify the **h** of the LORD God of H1004
15 LORD, to cleanse the **h** of the LORD. H1004
16 the inner part of the **h** of the LORD, to H1004
16 the court of the **h** of the LORD. And the H1004
17 so they sanctified the **h** of the LORD in H1004
18 cleansed all the **h** of the LORD, and the H1004
20 city, and went up to the **h** of the LORD. H1004
25 And he set the Levites in the **h** of the H1004
31 offerings into the **h** of the LORD. And H1004
35 of the **h** of the LORD was set in order. H1004
30: 1 should come to the **h** of the LORD at H1004
15 burnt offerings into the **h** of the LORD. H1004
31:10 And Azariah the chief priest of the **h** of H1004
10 the offerings into the **h** of the LORD, we H1004
11 chambers in the **h** of the LORD; and H1004
13 and Azariah the ruler of the **h** of God. H1004
16 entereth into the **h** of the LORD, his H1004
17 the priests by the **h** of their fathers, and H1004
21 the service of the **h** of God, and in the H1004
32:21 he was come into the **h** of his god, they H1004
33: 4 Also he built altars in the **h** of the H1004
5 in the two courts of the **h** of the LORD. H1004
7 he had made, in the **h** of God, of which H1004
7 his son, In this **h**, and in Jerusalem, H1004
15 the idol out of the **h** of the LORD, and H1004
15 the mount of the **h** of the LORD, and in H1004
20 him in his own **h**: and Amon his son H1004
24 against him, and slew him in his own **h**. H1004
34: 8 the land, and the **h**, he sent Shaphan H1004
8 to repair the **h** of the LORD his God. H1004
9 brought into the **h** of God, which the H1004
10 the oversight of the **h** of the LORD, and H1004
10 wrought in the **h** of the LORD, to repair H1004
10 the LORD, to repair and amend the **h**: H1004
14 was brought into the **h** of the LORD, H1004
15 of the law in the **h** of the LORD. And H1004
17 was found in the **h** of the LORD, and H1004
30 And the king went up into the **h** of the H1004
30 that was found in the **h** of the LORD. H1004
35: 2 to the service of the **h** of the LORD, H1004
3 the holy ark in the **h** which Solomon H1004
8 rulers of the **h** of God, gave unto the H1004
21 day, but against the **h** wherewith I have H1004
36: 7 of the vessels of the **h** of the LORD to H1004
10 vessels of the **h** of the LORD, and made H1004
14 and polluted the **h** of the LORD which H1004
17 the sword in the **h** of their sanctuary, H1004
18 And all the vessels of the **h** of God, H1004
18 treasures of the **h** of the LORD, and the H1004
19 And they burnt the **h** of God, and brake H1004
23 to build him an **h** in Jerusalem, which H1004
Ezr 1: 2 an **h** at Jerusalem, which *is* in Judah. H1004
3 and build the **h** of the LORD God of H1004
4 for the **h** of God that *is* in Jerusalem. H1004
5 **h** of the LORD which *is* in Jerusalem. H1004
7 the vessels of the **h** of the LORD, which H1004
7 and had put them in the **h** of his gods; H1004
2:36 of Jedaiah, of the **h** of Jeshua, nine H1004
59 not shew their father's **h**, and their seed, H1004
68 they came to the **h** of the LORD which H1004
68 for the **h** of God to set it up in his place: H1004
3: 8 coming unto the **h** of God at Jerusalem, H1004
8 forward the work of the **h** of the LORD. H1004
9 workmen in the **h** of God: the sons of H1004
11 of the **h** of the LORD was laid. H1004
12 that had seen the first **h**, when the H1004
12 the foundation of this **h** was laid before H1004
4: 3 us to build an **h** unto our God; but we H1004
24 Then ceased the work of the **h** of God H1005

Ezr 5: 2 began to build the **h** of God which *is* at H1005
3 build this **h**, and to make up this wall? H1005
8 of Judea, to the **h** of the great God, H1005
9 this **h**, and to make up these walls? H1005
11 and build the **h** that was builded these H1005
12 destroyed this **h**, and carried the people H1005
13 made a decree to build this **h** of God. H1005
14 gold and silver of the **h** of God, which H1005
15 let the **h** of God be builded in his place. H1005
16 foundation of the **h** of God which *is* in H1005
17 the king's treasure **h**, which *is* there at H1005
17 the king to build this **h** of God at H1005
6: 1 was made in the **h** of the rolls, where H1005
3 *concerning* the **h** of God at Jerusalem, H1005
3 at Jerusalem, Let the **h** be builded, the H1005
4 expenses be given out of the king's **h**: H1005
5 silver vessels of the **h** of God, which H1005
5 place, and place *them* in the **h** of God. H1005
7 Let the work of this **h** of God alone; let H1005
7 Jews build this **h** of God in his place. H1005
8 the building of this **h** of God: that of the H1005
11 down from his **h**, and being set up, let H1005
11 let his **h** be made a dunghill for this. H1005
12 *and* to destroy this **h** of God which *is* at H1005
15 And this **h** was finished on the third H1005
16 the dedication of this **h** of God with joy, H1005
17 And offered at the dedication of this **h** H1005
22 work of the **h** of God, the God of Israel. H1004
7:16 **h** of their God which *is* in Jerusalem: H1005
17 **h** of your God which *is* in Jerusalem. H1005
19 the service of the **h** of thy God, *those* H1005
20 be needful for the **h** of thy God, which H1005
20 bestow *it* out of the king's treasure **h**. H1005
23 done for the **h** of the God of heaven: H1005
24 ministers of this **h** of God, it shall not H1005
27 **h** of the LORD which *is* in Jerusalem: H1004
8:17 unto us ministers for the **h** of our God. H1004
25 the offering of the **h** of our God, which H1004
29 in the chambers of the **h** of the LORD. H1004
30 to Jerusalem unto the **h** of our God. H1004
33 weighed in the **h** of our God by the H1004
36 furthered the people, and the **h** of God. H1004
9: 9 to set up the **h** of our God, and to repair H1004
10: 1 himself down before the **h** of God, there H1004
6 Then Ezra rose up from before the **h** of H1004
9 in the street of the **h** of God, trembling H1004
16 fathers, after the **h** of their fathers, and H1004
Neh 1: 6 both I and my father's **h** have sinned. H1004
2: 8 *appertained* to the **h**, and for the wall of H1004
8 the city, and for the **h** that I shall enter H1004
3:10 over against his **h**. And next unto him H1004
16 made, and unto the **h** of the mighty. H1004
20 of the **h** of Eliashib the high priest. H1004
21 the door of the **h** of Eliashib even to the H1004
21 even to the end of the **h** of Eliashib. H1004
23 over against their **h**. After him repaired H1004
23 Maaseiah the son of Ananiah by his **h**. H1004
24 piece, from the **h** of Azariah unto the H1004
25 the king's high **h**, that *was* by the court H1004
28 the priests, every one over against his **h**. H1004
29 over against his **h**. After him repaired H1004
4:16 rulers *were* behind all the **h** of Judah. H1004
5:13 man from his **h**, and from his labour, H1004
6:10 Afterward I came unto the **h** of H1004
10 together in the **h** of God, within the H1004
7: 3 and every one *to be* over against his **h**. H1004
39 of Jedaiah, of the **h** of Jeshua, nine H1004
61 not shew their father's **h**, nor their seed, H1004
8:16 the roof of his **h**, and in their courts, and
16 in the courts of the **h** of God, and in the H1004
10:32 for the service of the **h** of our God; H1004
33 and *for* all the work of the **h** of our God. H1004
34 to bring *it* into the **h** of our God, after H1004
35 year by year, unto the **h** of the LORD: H1004
36 to bring to the **h** of our God, unto the H1004
36 that minister in the **h** of our God: H1004
37 chambers of the **h** of our God; and the H1004
38 the tithes unto the **h** of our God, to the H1004
38 to the chambers, into the treasure **h**. H1004
39 we will not forsake the **h** of our God. H1004
11:11 of Ahitub, *was* the ruler of the **h** of God. H1004
12 the work of the **h** *were* eight hundred H1004
16 the outward business of the **h** of God. H1004
22 *were* over the business of the **h** of God. H1004
12:29 Also from the **h** of Gilgal, and out of the H1004
37 wall, above the **h** of David, even unto H1004
40 *gave* thanks in the **h** of God, and I, and H1004
13: 4 **h** of our God, *was* allied unto Tobiah: H1004
7 chamber in the courts of the **h** of God. H1004

Neh 13: 9 the vessels of the **h** of God, with the H1004
11 said, Why is the **h** of God forsaken? H1004
14 have done for the **h** of my God, and for H1004
Est 1: 8 the officers of his **h**, that they should do H1004
9 **h** which *belonged* to king Ahasuerus. H1004
22 rule in his own **h**, and that *it* should be H1004
2: 3 the palace, to the **h** of the women, unto H1004
8 also unto the king's **h**, to the custody of H1004
9 out of the king's **h**: and he preferred her H1004
9 the best *place* of the **h** of the women. H1004
11 of the women's **h**, to know how Esther H1004
13 **h** of the women unto the king's house. H1004
13 house of the women unto the king's **h**. H1004
14 into the second **h** of the women, to the H1004
16 into his **h** royal in the tenth month, H1004
4:13 in the king's **h**, more than all the Jews. H1004
14 and thy father's **h** shall be destroyed: H1004
5: 1 court of the king's **h**, over against the H1004
1 against the king's **h**: and the king sat H1004
1 **h**, over against the gate of the house. H1004
1 house, over against the gate of the **h**. H1004
6: 4 court of the king's **h**, to speak unto the H1004
12 hasted to his **h** mourning, and having H1004
7: 8 before me in the **h**? As the word went H1004
9 standeth in the **h** of Haman. Then the H1004
8: 1 give the **h** of Haman the Jews' H1004
2 set Mordecai over the **h** of Haman. H1004
7 given Esther the **h** of Haman, and him H1004
9: 4 For Mordecai *was* great in the king's **h**, H1004
Job 1:10 and about his **h**, and about all that he H1004
13 wine in their eldest brother's **h**: H1004
18 wine in their eldest brother's **h**: H1004
19 four corners of the **h**, and it fell upon H1004
7:10 He shall return no more to his **h**, H1004
8:15 He shall lean upon his **h**, but it shall not H1004
17:13 If I wait, the grave *is* mine **h**: I have H1004
19:15 They that dwell in mine **h**, and my H1004
20:19 taken away an **h** which he builded not; H1004
28 The increase of his **h** shall depart, *and* H1004
21:21 For what pleasure *hath* he in his **h** after H1004
28 For ye say, Where *is* the **h** of the H1004
27:18 He buildeth his **h** as a moth, and as a H1004
30:23 and *to* the **h** appointed for all living. H1004
38:20 know the paths *to* the **h** thereof? H1004
39: 6 Whose **h** I have made the wilderness, H1004
42:11 with him in his **h**: and they bemoaned H1004
Ps 5: 7 But as for me, I will come *into* thy **h** in H1004
23: 6 will dwell in the **h** of the LORD for ever. H1004
26: 8 habitation of thy **h**, and the place where H1004
27: 4 I may dwell in the **h** of the LORD all the H1004
30:ttl *at* the dedication of the **h** of David. H1004
31: 2 rock, for an **h** of defence to save me. H1004
36: 8 with the fatness of thy **h**; and thou shalt H1004
42: 4 with them to the **h** of God, with the H1004
45:10 thine own people, and thy father's **h**; H1004
49:16 when the glory of his **h** is increased; H1004
50: 9 I will take no bullock out of thy **h**, *nor* H1004
52: 8 But I *am* like a green olive tree in the **h** H1004
ttl David is come to the **h** of Ahimelech. H1004
55:14 walked unto the **h** of God in company. H1004
59:ttl and they watched the **h** to kill him. H1004
65: 4 of thy **h**, *even* of thy holy temple. H1004
66:13 I will go into thy **h** with burnt offerings: H1004
69: 9 For the zeal of thine **h** hath eaten me H1004
84: 3 Yea, the sparrow hath found an **h**, and H1004
4 Blessed *are* they that dwell in thy **h**: H1004
10 doorkeeper in the **h** of my God, than to H1004
92:13 Those that be planted in the **h** of the H1004
93: 5 becometh thine **h**, O LORD, for ever. H1004
98: 3 his truth toward the **h** of Israel: all the H1004
101: 2 walk within my **h** with a perfect heart. H1004
7 dwell within my **h**: he that telleth lies H1004
102: 7 am as a sparrow alone upon the **h** top.
104:17 *as for* the stork, the fir trees *are* her **h**. H1004
105:21 He made him lord of his **h**, and ruler of H1004
112: 3 Wealth and riches *shall be* in his **h**: and H1004
113: 9 woman to keep **h**, *and to be* a joyful H1004
114: 1 When Israel went out of Egypt, the **h** of H1004
115:10 O **h** of Aaron, trust in the LORD: he *is* H1004
12 he will bless the **h** of Israel; he will bless H1004
12 of Israel; he will bless the **h** of Aaron. H1004
116:19 In the courts of the LORD'S **h**, in the H1004
118: 3 Let the **h** of Aaron now say, that his H1004
26 blessed you out of the **h** of the LORD. H1004
119:54 my songs in the **h** of my pilgrimage. H1004
122: 1 me, Let us go into the **h** of the LORD. H1004
5 the thrones of the **h** of David. H1004
9 Because of the **h** of the LORD our God I H1004
127: 1 Except the LORD build the **h**, they H1004
Ps 128: 3 by the sides of thine **h**: thy children like H1004
132: 3 of my **h**, nor go up into my bed; H1004
134: 1 by night stand in the **h** of the LORD. H1004
135: 2 Ye that stand in the **h** of the LORD, in H1004
2 in the courts of the **h** of our God, H1004
19 Bless the LORD, O **h** of Israel: bless the H1004
19 of Israel: bless the LORD, O **h** of Aaron: H1004
20 Bless the LORD, O **h** of Levi: ye that H1004
Prv 2:18 For her **h** inclineth unto death, and her H1004
3:33 The curse of the LORD *is* in the **h** of the H1004
5: 8 and come not nigh the door of her **h**: H1004
10 thy labours *be* in the **h** of a stranger; H1004
6:31 he shall give all the substance of his **h**. H1004
7: 6 For at the window of my **h** I looked H1004
8 corner; and he went the way to her **h**, H1004
11 stubborn; her feet abide not in her **h**: H1004
27 Her **h** *is* the way to hell, going down to H1004
9: 1 Wisdom hath builded her **h**, she hath H1004
14 For she sitteth at the door of her **h**, on a H1004
11:29 He that troubleth his own **h** shall H1004
12: 7 but the **h** of the righteous shall stand. H1004
14: 1 Every wise woman buildeth her **h**: but H1004
11 The **h** of the wicked shall be H1004
15: 6 In the **h** of the righteous *is* much H1004
25 The LORD will destroy the **h** of the H1004
27 own **h**; but he that hateth gifts shall live. H1004
17: 1 than an **h** full of sacrifices *with* strife. H1004
13 good, evil shall not depart from his **h**. H1004
19:14 **H** and riches *are* the inheritance of H1004
21: 9 with a brawling woman in a wide **h**. H1004
12 considereth the **h** of the wicked: *but* H1004
24: 3 Through wisdom is an **h** builded; and H1004
27 the field; and afterwards build thine **h**. H1004
25:17 thy neighbour's **h**; lest he be weary of H1004
24 a brawling woman and in a wide **h**. H1004
27:10 go into thy brother's **h** in the day of thy H1004
Ecc 2: 7 servants born in my **h**; also I had great H1004
5: 1 Keep thy foot when thou goest to the **h** H1004
7: 2 *It is* better to go to the **h** of mourning, H1004
2 than to go to the **h** of feasting: for that H1004
4 The heart of the wise *is* in the **h** of H1004
4 the heart of fools *is* in the **h** of mirth. H1004
10:18 of the hands the **h** droppeth through. H1004
12: 3 In the day when the keepers of the **h** H1004
Song 1:17 The beams of our **h** *are* cedar, *and* our H1004
2: 4 He brought me to the banqueting **h**, H1004
3: 4 him into my mother's **h**, and into the H1004
8: 2 into my mother's **h**, *who* would instruct H1004
7 the substance of his **h** for love, it would H1004
Isa 2: 2 of the LORD'S **h** shall be established H1004
3 the LORD, to the **h** of the God of Jacob; H1004
5 O **h** of Jacob, come ye, and let us walk H1004
6 thy people the **h** of Jacob, because they H1004
3: 6 of his brother of the **h** of his father, H1004
7 healer; for in my **h** *is* neither bread nor H1004
5: 7 of hosts *is* the **h** of Israel, and the men H1004
8 Woe unto them that join **h** to house, H1004
8 Woe unto them that join house to **h**, H1004
6: 4 cried, and the **h** was filled with smoke. H1004
7: 2 And it was told the **h** of David, saying, H1004
13 And he said, Hear ye now, O **h** of H1004
17 upon thy father's **h**, days that have not H1004
8:17 the **h** of Jacob, and I will look for him. H1004
10:20 are escaped of the **h** of Jacob, shall no H1004
14: 1 and they shall cleave to the **h** of Jacob. H1004
2 place: and the **h** of Israel shall possess H1004
17 *that* opened not the **h** of his prisoners? H1004
18 lie in glory, every one in his own **h**. H1004
22: 8 day to the armour of the **h** of the forest. H1004
15 Shebna, which *is* over the **h**, *and say*, H1004
18 glory *shall be* the shame of thy lord's **h**. H1004
21 of Jerusalem, and to the **h** of Judah. H1004
22 And the key of the **h** of David will I lay H1004
23 be for a glorious throne to his father's **h**. H1004
24 of his father's **h**, the offspring and the H1004
23: 1 so that there is no **h**, no entering in: H1004
24:10 **h** is shut up, that no man may come in. H1004
29:22 concerning the **h** of Jacob, Jacob shall H1004
31: 2 arise against the **h** of the evildoers, and H1004
36: 3 was over the **h**, and Shebna the scribe, H1004
37: 1 and went into the **h** of the LORD. H1004
14 went up unto the **h** of the LORD, and H1004
31 is escaped of the **h** of Judah shall again H1004
38 in the **h** of Nisroch his god, H1004
38: 1 the LORD, Set thine **h** in order: for thou H1004
20 days of our life in the **h** of the LORD. H1004
22 that I shall go up to the **h** of the LORD? H1004
39: 2 and shewed them the **h** of his precious H1004
2 and all the **h** of his armour, and H1004
Isa 39: 2 there was nothing in his **h**, nor in all his H1004
4 have they seen in thine **h**? And Hezekiah H1004
4 All that *is* in mine **h** have they seen: H1004
6 all that *is* in thine **h**, and *that* which thy H1004
42: 7 that sit in darkness out of the prison **h**. H1004
44:13 of a man; that it may remain in the **h**. H1004
46: 3 Hearken unto me, O **h** of Jacob, and all H1004
3 remnant of the **h** of Israel, which are H1004
48: 1 Hear ye this, O **h** of Jacob, which are H1004
56: 5 Even unto them will I give in mine **h** H1004
7 them joyful in my **h** of prayer: their H1004
7 altar; for mine **h** shall be called an H1004
7 be called an **h** of prayer for all people. H1004
58: 1 and the **h** of Jacob their sins. H1004
7 are cast out to thy **h**? when thou seest H1004
60: 7 and I will glorify the **h** of my glory. H1004
63: 7 toward the **h** of Israel, which he hath H1004
64:11 Our holy and our beautiful **h**, where our H1004
66: 1 where *is* the **h** that ye build unto me? H1004
20 a clean vessel into the **h** of the LORD. H1004
Jer 2: 4 Hear ye the word of the LORD, O **h** of H1004
4 and all the families of the **h** of Israel: H1004
26 is found, so is the **h** of Israel ashamed; H1004
3:18 In those days the **h** of Judah shall walk H1004
18 walk with the **h** of Israel, and they shall H1004
20 with me, O **h** of Israel, saith the LORD. H1004
5:11 For the **h** of Israel and the house of H1004
11 For the house of Israel and the **h** of H1004
15 you from far, O **h** of Israel, saith the H1004
20 Declare this in the **h** of Jacob, and H1004
7: 2 Stand in the gate of the LORD'S **h**, and H1004
10 before me in this **h**, which is called by H1004
11 Is this **h**, which is called by my name, H1004
14 Therefore will I do unto *this* **h**, which is H1004
30 in the **h** which is called by my H1004
9:26 and all the **h** of Israel *are* H1004
10: 1 LORD speaketh unto you, O **h** of Israel: H1004
11:10 to serve them: the **h** of Israel and the H1004
10 house of Israel and the **h** of Judah have H1004
15 What hath my beloved to do in mine **h**, H1004
17 for the evil of the **h** of Israel and of the H1004
17 Israel and of the **h** of Judah, which they H1004
12: 6 For even thy brethren, and the **h** of thy H1004
7 I have forsaken mine **h**, I have left mine H1004
14 out the **h** of Judah from among them. H1004
13:11 unto me the whole **h** of Israel and the H1004
11 and the whole **h** of Judah, saith the H1004
16: 5 Enter not into the **h** of mourning, H1004
8 Thou shalt not also go into the **h** of H1004
17:26 of praise, unto the **h** of the LORD. H1004
18: 2 Arise, and go down to the potter's **h**, H1004
3 Then I went down to the potter's **h**, and, H1004
6 O **h** of Israel, cannot I do with you as H1004
6 so *are* ye in mine hand, O **h** of Israel. H1004
19:14 LORD'S **h**; and said to all the people, H1004
20: 1 governor in the **h** of the LORD, heard H1004
2 which *was* by the **h** of the LORD. H1004
6 all that dwell in thine **h** shall go into H1004
21:11 And touching the **h** of the king of H1004
12 O **h** of David, thus saith the LORD; H1004
22: 1 Thus saith the LORD; Go down to the **h** H1004
4 by the gates of this **h** kings sitting upon H1004
5 that this **h** shall become a desolation. H1004
6 unto the king's **h** of Judah; Thou *art* H1004
13 Woe unto him that buildeth his **h** by H1004
14 That saith, I will build me a wide **h** and H1004
23: 8 led the seed of the **h** of Israel out of the H1004
11 yea, in my **h** have I found their H1004
34 I will even punish that man and his **h**. H1004
26: 2 of the LORD'S **h**, and speak unto all the H1004
2 in the LORD'S **h**, all the words that I H1004
6 Then will I make this **h** like Shiloh, and H1004
7 these words in the **h** of the LORD. H1004
9 saying, This **h** shall be like Shiloh, H1004
9 against Jeremiah in the **h** of the LORD. H1004
10 up from the king's **h** unto the house of H1004
10 house unto the **h** of the LORD, and sat H1004
10 entry of the new gate of the LORD'S **h**.
12 against this **h** and against this city H1004
18 of the **h** as the high places of a forest. H1004
27:16 of the LORD'S **h** shall now shortly be H1004
18 are left in the **h** of the LORD, and *in* H1004
18 the LORD, and *in* the **h** of the king of H1004
21 that remain *in* the **h** of the LORD, and H1004
21 LORD, and *in* the **h** of the king of Judah H1004
28: 1 unto me in the **h** of the LORD, in the H1004
3 of the LORD'S **h**, that Nebuchadnezzar H1004
5 people that stood in the **h** of the LORD, H1004
6 of the LORD'S **h**, and all that is carried H1004

Jer 29:26 be officers in the **h** of the LORD, for H1004
31:27 that I will sow the **h** of Israel and the H1004
27 of Israel and the **h** of Judah with the H1004
31 covenant with the **h** of Israel, and with H1004
31 of Israel, and with the **h** of Judah: H1004
33 I will make with the **h** of Israel; After H1004
32: 2 which *was* in the king of Judah's **h**. H1004
34 in the **h**, which is called by my H1004
33:11 of praise into the **h** of the LORD. For I H1004
14 **h** of Israel and to the house of Judah. H1004
14 house of Israel and to the **h** of Judah. H1004
17 to sit upon the throne of the **h** of Israel; H1004
34:13 Egypt, out of the **h** of bondmen, saying, H1004
15 in the **h** which is called by my name: H1004
35: 2 Go unto the **h** of the Rechabites, and H1004
2 them into the **h** of the LORD, into one H1004
3 and the whole **h** of the Rechabites; H1004
4 And I brought them into the **h** of the H1004
5 And I set before the sons of the **h** of the H1004
7 Neither shall ye build **h**, nor sow seed, H1004
18 And Jeremiah said unto the **h** of the H1004
36: 3 It may be that the **h** of Judah will hear H1004
5 up; I cannot go into the **h** of the LORD: H1004
6 in the LORD'S **h** upon the fasting day: H1004
8 the words of the LORD in the LORD'S **h**. H1004
10 of Jeremiah in the **h** of the LORD, in the H1004
10 LORD'S **h**, in the ears of all the people. H1004
12 Then he went down into the king's **h**, H1004
37:15 him in prison in the **h** of Jonathan the H1004
17 him secretly in his **h**, and said, Is there H1004
20 not to return to the **h** of Jonathan the H1004
38: 7 was in the king's **h**, heard that they had H1004
8 king's **h**, and spake to the king, saying, H1004
11 and went into the **h** of the king under H1004
14 entry that *is* in the **h** of the LORD: and H1004
17 fire; and thou shalt live, and thine **h**: H1004
22 king of Judah's **h** *shall be* brought forth H1004
26 to return to Jonathan's **h**, to die there. H1004
39: 8 And the Chaldeans burned the king's **h**, H1004
41: 5 to bring *them* to the **h** of the LORD. H1004
43: 9 entry of Pharaoh's **h** in Tahpanhes, in H1004
48:13 of Chemosh, as the **h** of Israel was H1004
51:51 into the sanctuaries of the LORD'S **h**. H1004
52:13 And burned the **h** of the LORD, and the H1004
13 and the king's **h**; and all the houses of H1004
17 that *were* in the **h** of the LORD, and the H1004
17 sea that *was* in the **h** of the LORD, the H1004
20 had made in the **h** of the LORD: the H1004
Lam 2: 7 a noise in the **h** of the LORD, as in the H1004
Ezk 2: 5 *are* a rebellious **h**,) yet shall know that H1004
6 looks, though they *be* a rebellious **h**. H1004
8 that rebellious **h**: open thy mouth, and H1004
3: 1 roll, and go speak unto the **h** of Israel. H1004
4 get thee unto the **h** of Israel, and speak H1004
5 hard language, *but* to the **h** of Israel; H1004
7 But the **h** of Israel will not hearken H1004
7 me: for all the **h** of Israel *are* impudent H1004
9 looks, though they *be* a rebellious **h**. H1004
17 unto the **h** of Israel: therefore hear H1004
24 me, Go, shut thyself within thine **h**. H1004
26 a reprover: for they *are* a rebellious **h**. H1004
27 him forbear: for they *are* a rebellious **h**. H1004
4: 3 it. This *shall be* a sign to the **h** of Israel. H1004
4 the iniquity of the **h** of Israel upon it: H1004
5 thou bear the iniquity of the **h** of Israel. H1004
6 bear the iniquity of the **h** of Judah forty H1004
5: 4 a fire come forth into all the **h** of Israel. H1004
6:11 of the **h** of Israel! for they shall H1004
8: 1 *as* I sat in mine **h**, and the elders of H1004
6 that the **h** of Israel committeth H1004
10 and all the idols of the **h** of Israel, H1004
11 of the ancients of the **h** of Israel, and in H1004
12 the ancients of the **h** of Israel do in the H1004
14 of the LORD'S **h** which *was* toward the H1004
16 of the LORD'S **h**, and, behold, at the H1004
17 a light thing to the **h** of Judah that they H1004
9: 3 threshold of the **h**. And he called to the H1004
6 ancient men which *were* before the **h**. H1004
7 And he said unto them, Defile the **h**, H1004
9 me, The iniquity of the **h** of Israel and H1004
10: 3 right side of the **h**, when the man went H1004
4 threshold of the **h**; and the house was H1004
4 the house; and the **h** was filled with the H1004
18 of the **h**, and stood over the cherubims. H1004
19 of the LORD'S **h**; and the glory of the H1004
11: 1 gate of the LORD'S **h**, which looketh H1004
5 have ye said, O **h** of Israel: for I know H1004
15 and all the **h** of Israel wholly, *are* H1004
12: 2 of a rebellious **h**, which have eyes to H1004

Ezk 12: 2 and hear not: for they *are* a rebellious **h**. H1004
3 consider, though they *be* a rebellious **h**. H1004
6 set thee *for* a sign unto the **h** of Israel. H1004
9 Son of man, hath not the **h** of Israel, H1004
9 **h**, said unto thee, What doest thou? H1004
10 all the **h** of Israel that *are* among them. H1004
24 divination within the **h** of Israel. H1004
25 days, O rebellious **h**, will I say the word, H1004
27 Son of man, behold, *they of* the **h** of H1004
13: 5 the hedge for the **h** of Israel to stand in H1004
9 in the writing of the **h** of Israel, neither H1004
14: 4 Every man of the **h** of Israel that setteth H1004
5 That I may take the **h** of Israel in their H1004
6 Therefore say unto the **h** of Israel, Thus H1004
7 For every one of the **h** of Israel, or of H1004
11 That the **h** of Israel may go no more H1004
17: 2 speak a parable unto the **h** of Israel; H1004
12 Say now to the rebellious **h**, Know ye H1004
18: 6 to the idols of the **h** of Israel, neither H1004
15 to the idols of the **h** of Israel, hath not H1004
25 Hear now, O **h** of Israel; Is not my H1004
29 Yet saith the **h** of Israel, The way of the H1004
29 is not equal. O **h** of Israel, are not my H1004
30 Therefore I will judge you, O **h** of H1004
31 spirit: for why will ye die, O **h** of Israel? H1004
20: 5 the seed of the **h** of Jacob, and made H1004
13 But the **h** of Israel rebelled against me H1004
27 speak unto the **h** of Israel, and say unto H1004
30 Wherefore say unto the **h** of Israel, H1004
31 of by you, O **h** of Israel? *As* I live, saith H1004
39 As for you, O **h** of Israel, thus saith the H1004
40 there shall all the **h** of Israel, all of H1004
44 O ye **h** of Israel, saith the Lord GOD. H1004
22:18 Son of man, the **h** of Israel is to me H1004
23:39 have they done in the midst of mine **h**. H1004
24: 3 the rebellious **h**, and say unto them, H1004
21 Speak unto the **h** of Israel, Thus saith H1004
25: 3 and against the **h** of Judah, when they H1004
8 **h** of Judah *is* like unto all the heathen; H1004
12 dealt against the **h** of Judah by taking H1004
27:14 They of the **h** of Togarmah traded in H1004
28:24 brier unto the **h** of Israel, nor *any* H1004
25 have gathered the **h** of Israel from the H1004
29: 6 been a staff of reed to the **h** of Israel. H1004
16 the confidence of the **h** of Israel, which H1004
21 the horn of the **h** of Israel to bud forth, H1004
33: 7 unto the **h** of Israel; therefore thou H1004
10 speak unto the **h** of Israel; Thus ye H1004
11 ways; for why will ye die, O **h** of Israel? H1004
20 Lord is not equal. O ye **h** of Israel, I will H1004
34:30 *that* they, *even* the **h** of Israel, *are* my H1004
35:15 inheritance of the **h** of Israel, because it H1004
36:10 upon you, all the **h** of Israel, *even* all of H1004
17 Son of man, when the **h** of Israel dwelt H1004
21 holy name, which the **h** of Israel had H1004
22 Therefore say unto the **h** of Israel, Thus H1004
22 for your sakes, O **h** of Israel, but for H1004
32 for your own ways, O **h** of Israel. H1004
37 be inquired of by the **h** of Israel, to do *it* H1004
37:11 are the whole **h** of Israel: behold, they H1004
16 *for* all the **h** of Israel his companions: H1004
38: 6 Gomer, and all his bands; the **h** of H1004
39:12 And seven months shall the **h** of Israel H1004
22 So the **h** of Israel shall know that I *am* H1004
23 And the heathen shall know that the **h** H1004
25 upon the whole **h** of Israel, and will be H1004
29 the **h** of Israel, saith the Lord GOD. H1004
40: 4 all that thou seest to the **h** of Israel. H1004
5 the outside of the **h** round about, and H1004
45 the keepers of the charge of the **h**. H1004
47 and the altar *that was* before the **h**. H1004
48 me to the porch of the **h**, and measured H1004
41: 5 After he measured the wall of the **h**, six H1004
5 round about the **h** on every side. H1004
6 wall which *was* of the **h** for the side H1004
6 they had not hold in the wall of the **h**. H1004
7 about of the **h** went still upward round H1004
7 round about the **h**: therefore the H1004
7 the breadth of the **h** *was still* upward, H1004
8 I saw also the height of the **h** round H1004
10 cubits round about the **h** on every side. H1004
13 So he measured the **h**, an hundred H1004
14 Also the breadth of the face of the **h**, H1004
17 unto the inner **h**, and without, and by H1004
19 made through all the **h** round about. H1004
26 chambers of the **h**, and thick planks. H1004
42:15 the inner **h**, he brought me forth H1004
43: 4 came into the **h** by the way of the gate H1004
5 the glory of the LORD filled the **h**. H1004

Ezk 43: 6 out of the **h**; and the man stood by me. H1004
7 name, shall the **h** of Israel no more H1004
10 Thou son of man, shew the **h** to the H1004
10 the house to the **h** of Israel, that they H1004
11 them the form of the **h**, and the fashion H1004
12 This *is* the law of the **h**; Upon the top of H1004
12 holy. Behold, this *is* the law of the **h**. H1004
21 place of the **h**, without the sanctuary. H1004
44: 4 gate before the **h**: and I looked, and, H1004
4 **h** of the LORD: and I fell upon my face. H1004
5 ordinances of the **h** of the LORD, and H1004
5 entering in of the **h**, with every going H1004
6 *even* to the **h** of Israel, Thus saith H1004
6 Lord GOD; O ye **h** of Israel, let it suffice H1004
7 pollute it, *even* my **h**, when ye offer my H1004
11 at the gates of the **h**, and ministering to H1004
11 ministering to the **h**: they shall slay the H1004
12 and caused the **h** of Israel to fall into H1004
14 of the charge of the **h**, for all the service H1004
22 of the seed of the **h** of Israel, or a H1004
30 cause the blessing to rest in thine **h**. H1004
45: 5 ministers of the **h**, have for themselves, H1004
6 it shall be for the whole **h** of Israel. H1004
8 the **h** of Israel according to their tribes. H1004
17 solemnities of the **h** of Israel: he shall H1004
17 make reconciliation for the **h** of Israel. H1004
19 the posts of the **h**, and upon the four H1004
20 *is* simple: so shall ye reconcile the **h**. H1004
46:24 **h** shall boil the sacrifice of the people. H1004
47: 1 the door of the **h**; and, behold, waters H1004
1 the threshold of the **h** eastward: for the H1004
1 the forefront of the **h** *stood toward* the H1004
1 of the **h**, at the south *side* of the altar. H1004
48:21 of the **h** *shall be* in the midst thereof. H1004
Dan 1: 2 of the vessels of the **h** of God: which he H1004
2 of Shinar to the **h** of his god; and he H1004
2 vessels into the treasure **h** of his god. H1004
2:17 Then Daniel went to his **h**, and made H1005
4: 4 in mine **h**, and flourishing in my palace: H1005
30 I have built for the **h** of the kingdom by H1005
5: 3 the temple of the **h** of God which *was* at H1005
10 came into the banquet **h**: *and* the queen H1005
23 the vessels of his **h** before thee, and H1005
6:10 he went into his **h**; and his windows H1005
Hos 1: 4 of Jezreel upon the **h** of Jehu, and will H1004
4 to cease the kingdom of the **h** of Israel. H1004
6 mercy upon the **h** of Israel; but I will H1004
7 But I will have mercy upon the **h** of H1004
5: 1 and hearken, ye **h** of Israel; and give ye H1004
1 and give ye ear, O **h** of the king; for H1004
12 and to the **h** of Judah as rottenness. H1004
14 a young lion to the **h** of Judah: I, *even* I, H1004
6:10 I have seen an horrible thing in the **h** of H1004
8: 1 an eagle against the **h** of the LORD, H1004
9: 4 shall not come into the **h** of the LORD. H1004
8 ways, *and* hatred in the **h** of his God. H1004
15 them out of mine **h**, I will love them no H1004
11:12 about with lies, and the **h** of Israel with H1004
Joel 1: 9 is cut off from the **h** of the LORD; the H1004
13 is withholden from the **h** of your God. H1004
14 of the land *into* the **h** of the LORD your H1004
16 and gladness from the **h** of our God? H1004
3:18 come forth of the **h** of the LORD, and H1004
Am 1: 4 But I will send a fire into the **h** of H1004
5 the sceptre from the **h** of Eden: and the H1004
2: 8 of the condemned *in* the **h** of their god. H1004
3:13 Hear ye, and testify in the **h** of Jacob, H1004
15 And I will smite the winter **h** with the H1004
15 with the summer **h**; and the houses of H1004
5: 1 you, *even* a lamentation, O **h** of Israel. H1004
3 shall leave ten, to the **h** of Israel. H1004
4 For thus saith the LORD unto the **h** of H1004
6 out like fire in the **h** of Joseph, and H1004
19 or went into the **h**, and leaned his hand H1004
25 wilderness forty years, O **h** of Israel? H1004
6: 1 nations, to whom the **h** of Israel came! H1004
9 ten men in one **h**, that they shall die. H1004
10 bones out of the **h**, and shall say unto H1004
10 *is* by the sides of the **h**, *Is there* yet *any* H1004
11 smite the great **h** with breaches, and H1004
11 breaches, and the little **h** with clefts. H1004
14 you a nation, O **h** of Israel, saith the H1004
7: 9 the **h** of Jeroboam with the sword. H1004
10 in the midst of the **h** of Israel: the land H1004
16 not *thy word* against the **h** of Isaac. H1004
9: 8 destroy the **h** of Jacob, saith the LORD. H1004
9 and I will sift the **h** of Israel among all H1004
Oba 17 be holiness; and the **h** of Jacob shall H1004
18 And the **h** of Jacob shall be a fire, and H1004

Oba 18 be a fire, and the **h** of Joseph a flame, H1004
18 a flame, and the **h** of Esau for stubble, H1004
18 **h** of Esau; for the LORD hath spoken *it*. H1004
Mic 1: 5 for the sins of the **h** of Israel. What *is* H1004
10 the **h** of Aphrah roll thyself in the dust. H1036
2: 2 and his **h**, even a man and his heritage. H1004
7 O *thou that art* named the **h** of Jacob, is H1004
3: 1 ye princes of the **h** of Israel; *Is it* not for H1004
9 Hear this, I pray you, ye heads of the **h** H1004
9 and princes of the **h** of Israel, that H1004
12 of the **h** as the high places of the forest. H1004
4: 1 mountain of the **h** of the LORD shall be H1004
2 LORD, and to the **h** of the God of Jacob; H1004
6: 4 thee out of the **h** of servants; and I sent H1004
10 wickedness in the **h** of the wicked, and H1004
16 the works of the **h** of Ahab, and ye walk H1004
7: 6 enemies *are* the men of his own **h**. H1004
Nah 1:14 sown: out of the **h** of thy gods will I cut H1004
Hab 2: 9 to his **h**, that he may set his H1004
10 Thou hast consulted shame to thy **h** by H1004
3:13 the head out of the **h** of the wicked, by H1004
Zep 2: 7 remnant of the **h** of Judah; they shall H1004
Hag 1: 2 time that the LORD'S **h** should be built. H1004
4 cieled houses, and this **h** *lie* waste? H1004
8 and build the **h**; and I will take pleasure H1004
9 Because of mine **h** that *is* waste, and ye H1004
9 and ye run every man unto his own **h**. H1004
14 the **h** of the LORD of hosts, their God, H1004
2: 3 Who *is* left among you that saw this **h** H1004
7 **h** with glory, saith the LORD of hosts. H1004
9 The glory of this latter **h** shall be H1004
Zec 1:16 with mercies: my **h** shall be built in it, H1004
3: 7 also judge my **h**, and shalt also keep H1004
4: 9 the foundation of this **h**; his hands shall H1004
5: 4 enter into the **h** of the thief, and into H1004
4 the thief, and into the **h** of him that H1004
4 in the midst of his **h**, and shall consume H1004
11 And he said unto me, To build it an **h** H1004
6:10 the **h** of Josiah the son of Zephaniah; H1004
7: 2 When they had sent unto the **h** of God H1004
3 which *were* in the **h** of the LORD of H1004
8: 9 the foundation of the **h** of the LORD of H1004
13 the heathen, O **h** of Judah, and house H1004
13 of Judah, and **h** of Israel; so will I save H1004
15 and to the **h** of Judah: fear ye not. H1004
19 tenth, shall be to the **h** of Judah joy and H1004
9: 8 And I will encamp about mine **h** H1004
10: 3 his flock the **h** of Judah, and hath H1004
6 And I will strengthen the **h** of Judah, H1004
6 and I will save the **h** of Joseph, and I H1004
11:13 to the potter in the **h** of the LORD. H1004
12: 4 mine eyes upon the **h** of Judah, and will H1004
7 that the glory of the **h** of David and the H1004
8 as David; and the **h** of David *shall be* as H1004
10 And I will pour upon the **h** of David, H1004
12 the family of the **h** of David apart, and H1004
12 the family of the **h** of Nathan apart, H1004
13 The family of the **h** of Levi apart, and H1004
13: 1 opened to the **h** of David and to the H1004
6 I was wounded *in* the **h** of my friends. H1004
14:20 in the LORD'S **h** shall be like the bowls H1004
21 in the **h** of the LORD of hosts. H1004
Mal 3:10 be meat in mine **h**, and prove me now H1004
Mt 2:11 And when they were come into the **h**, *G3614*
5:15 it giveth light unto all that are in the **h**. *G3614*
7:24 man, which built his **h** upon a rock: *G3614*
25 beat upon that **h**; and it fell not: for it *G3614*
26 man, which built his **h** upon the sand: *G3614*
27 **h**; and it fell: and great was the fall of it. *G3614*
8:14 come into Peter's **h**, he saw his wife's *G3614*
9: 6 take up thy bed, and go unto thine **h**. *G3624*
7 And he arose, and departed to his **h**. *G3624*
10 Jesus sat at meat in the **h**, behold, many *G3614*
23 And when Jesus came into the ruler's **h**, *G3614*
28 And when he was come into the **h**, the *G3614*
10: 6 But go rather to the lost sheep of the **h** *G3624*
12 And when ye come into an **h**, salute it. *G3614*
13 And if the **h** be worthy, let your peace *G3614*
14 **h** or city, shake off the dust of your feet. *G3614*
25 the master of the **h** Beelzebub, how *G3617*
12: 4 How he entered into the **h** of God, and *G3624*
25 **h** divided against itself shall not stand: *G3614*
29 a strong man's **h**, and spoil his goods, *G3614*
29 man? and then he will spoil his **h**. *G3614*
44 Then he saith, I will return into my **h** *G3624*
13: 1 The same day went Jesus out of the **h**, *G3614*
36 and went into the **h**: and his disciples *G3614*
57 in his own country, and in his own **h**. *G3614*
15:24 unto the lost sheep of the **h** of Israel. *G3624*

Mt 17:25 he was come into the **h**, Jesus prevented *G3614*
20:11 against the goodman of the **h**, *G3617*
21:13 And said unto them, It is written, My **h** *G3624*
13 shall be called the **h** of prayer; but ye *G3624*
23:38 Behold, your **h** is left unto you desolate. *G3624*
24:17 down to take any thing out of his **h**: *G3614*
43 goodman of the **h** had known in what *G3617*
43 have suffered his **h** to be broken up. *G3614*
26: 6 in Bethany, in the **h** of Simon the leper, *G3614*
18 the passover at thy **h** with my disciples. *G4571*
Mk 1:29 they entered into the **h** of Simon and *G3614*
2: 1 and it was noised that he was in the **h**. *G3624*
11 up thy bed, and go thy way into thine **h**. *G3624*
15 sat at meat in his **h**, many publicans *G3614*
26 How he went into the **h** of God in the *G3624*
3:19 betrayed him: and they went into an **h**. *G3624*
25 And if a **h** be divided against itself, that *G3614*
25 against itself, that **h** cannot stand. *G3614*
27 a strong man's **h**, and spoil his goods, *G3614*
27 strong man; and then he will spoil his **h**. *G3614*
5:35 of the synagogue's **h** *certain* which said,
38 And he cometh to the **h** of the ruler of *G3624*
6: 4 among his own kin, and in his own **h**. *G3614*
10 ye enter into an **h**, there abide till ye *G3614*
7:17 And when he was entered into the **h** *G3624*
24 entered into an **h**, and would have no *G3614*
30 And when she was come to her **h**, she *G3624*
8:26 And he sent him away to his **h**, saying, *G3624*
9:28 And when he was come into the **h**, his *G3624*
33 and being in the **h** he asked them, *G3614*
10:10 And in the **h** his disciples asked him *G3614*
29 no man that hath left **h**, or brethren, or *G3614*
11:17 Is it not written, My **h** shall be called of *G3624*
17 of all nations the **h** of prayer? but ye *G3624*
13:15 not go down into the **h**, neither enter *G3614*
15 *therein*, to take any thing out of his **h**: *G3614*
34 who left his **h**, and gave authority *G3614*
35 the master of the **h** cometh, at even, or *G3614*
14: 3 And being in Bethany in the **h** of Simon *G3614*
14 the goodman of the **h**, The Master saith, *G3617*
Lk 1:23 he departed to his own **h**. *G3624*
27 was Joseph, of the **h** of David; and the *G3624*
33 And he shall reign over the **h** of Jacob *G3624*
40 And entered into the **h** of Zacharias, *G3624*
56 months, and returned to her own **h**. *G3624*
69 for us in the **h** of his servant David; *G3624*
2: 4 he was of the **h** and lineage of David:) *G3624*
4:38 into Simon's **h**. And Simon's wife's *G3614*
5:24 take up thy couch, and go into thine **h**. *G3624*
25 departed to his own **h**, glorifying God. *G3624*
29 feast in his own **h**: and there was a *G3614*
6: 4 How he went into the **h** of God, and did *G3624*
48 He is like a man which built an **h**, and *G3614*
48 upon that **h**, and could not shake *G3614*
49 built an **h** upon the earth; against *G3614*
49 it fell; and the ruin of that **h** was great. *G3614*
7: 6 not far from the **h**, the centurion sent *G3614*
10 returning to the **h**, found the servant *G3624*
36 the Pharisee's **h**, and sat down to meat. *G3614*
37 meat in the Pharisee's **h**, brought an *G3614*
44 entered into thine **h**, thou gavest me no *G3614*
8:27 abode in *any* **h**, but in the tombs. *G3614*
39 Return to thine own **h**, and shew how *G3624*
41 him that he would come into his **h**: *G3624*
49 of the synagogue's *h*, saying to him, Thy
51 And when he came into the **h**, he *G3614*
9: 4 And whatsoever **h** ye enter into, there *G3614*
61 farewell, which are at home at my **h**. *G3624*
10: 5 And into whatsoever **h** ye enter, first *G3614*
5 ye enter, first say, Peace *be* to this **h**. *G3624*
7 And in the same **h** remain, eating and *G3614*
7 of his hire. Go not from **h** to house. *G3614*
7 of his hire. Go not from house to **h**. *G3614*
38 named Martha received him into her **h**. *G3624*
11:17 and a **h** *divided* against a house falleth. *G3624*
17 and a house *divided* against a **h** falleth. *G3624*
24 return unto my **h** whence I came out. *G3624*
12:39 the goodman of the **h** had known what *G3617*
39 suffered his **h** to be broken through. *G3624*
52 be five in one **h** divided, three against *G3624*
13:25 When once the master of the **h** is risen *G3617*
35 Behold, your **h** is left unto you desolate: *G3624*
14: 1 as he went into the **h** of one of the chief *G3624*
21 the master of the **h** being angry said to *G3617*
23 to come in, that my **h** may be filled. *G3624*
15: 8 the **h**, and seek diligently till she find *it*? *G3614*
25 to the **h**, he heard musick and dancing. *G3614*
16:27 wouldest send him to my father's **h**: *G3624*
17:31 and his stuff in the **h**, let him not come *G3614*

Lk 18:14 I tell you, this man went down to his **h** *G3624*
29 no man that hath left **h**, or parents, or *G3614*
19: 5 down; for to day I must abide at thy **h**. *G3624*
9 come to this **h**, forsomuch as he also *G3624*
46 Saying unto them, It is written, My **h** is *G3624*
46 My house is the **h** of prayer: but ye *G3624*
22:10 him into the **h** where he entereth in. *G3614*
11 the goodman of the **h**, The Master saith *G3614*
54 priest's **h**. And Peter followed afar off. *G3624*
Jn 2:16 Father's **h** an house of merchandise. *G3624*
16 Father's house an **h** of merchandise. *G3624*
17 The zeal of thine **h** hath eaten me up. *G3624*
4:53 and himself believed, and his whole **h**. *G3614*
7:53 And every man went unto his own **h**. *G3624*
8:35 And the servant abideth not in the **h** *G3614*
11:20 and met him: but Mary sat *still* in the **h**. *G3624*
31 with her in the **h**, and comforted her, *G3614*
12: 3 her hair: and the **h** was filled with the *G3614*
14: 2 In my Father's **h** are many mansions: if *G3614*
Act 2: 2 filled all the **h** where they were sitting. *G3624*
36 Therefore let all the **h** of Israel know *G3624*
46 bread from **h** to house, did eat their *G3624*
46 from house to **h**, did eat their meat with *G2596*
5:42 And daily in the temple, and in every **h**, *G2596*
7:10 him governor over Egypt and all his **h**. *G3624*
20 up in his father's **h** three months: *G3624*
42 the prophets, O ye **h** of Israel, have ye *G3624*
47 But Solomon built him an **h**. *G3624*
49 footstool: what **h** will ye build me? saith *G3624*
8: 3 into every **h**, and haling men and *G2596*
9:11 and inquire in the **h** of Judas for *one* *G3614*
17 and entered into the **h**; and putting his *G3614*
10: 2 God with all his **h**, which gave much *G3624*
6 a tanner, whose **h** is by the sea side: he *G3614*
17 Simon's **h**, and stood before the gate, *G3614*
22 into his **h**, and to hear words of thee. *G3624*
30 I prayed in my **h**, and, behold, a man *G3624*
32 he is lodged in the **h** of *one* Simon a *G3614*
11:11 come unto the **h** where I was, sent from *G3614*
12 me, and we entered into the man's **h**: *G3624*
13 an angel in his **h**, which stood and said *G3624*
14 thou and all thy **h** shall be saved. *G3624*
12:12 he came to the **h** of Mary the mother *G3614*
16:15 come into my **h**, and abide *there*. And *G3624*
31 and thou shalt be saved, and thy **h**. *G3624*
32 of the Lord, and to all that were in his **h**. *G3614*
34 them into his **h**, he set meat before *G3624*
34 rejoiced, believing in God with all his **h**. *G3832*
40 entered into *the* **h** *of* Lydia: and when
17: 5 and assaulted the **h** of Jason, and *G3614*
18: 7 a certain *man's* **h**, named Justus, *one* *G3614*
7 whose **h** joined hard to the synagogue. *G3614*
8 the Lord with all his **h**; and many of the *G3624*
19:16 fled out of that **h** naked and wounded. *G3624*
20:20 you publickly, and from **h** to house, *G3624*
20 you publickly, and from house to **h**, *G2596*
21: 8 we entered into the **h** of Philip the *G3624*
28:30 in his own hired **h**, and received all that *G3410*
Ro 16: 5 that is in their **h**. Salute my well beloved *G3624*
1Co 1:11 *which are of the* **h** of Chloe, that there
16:15 I beseech you, brethren, (ye know the **h** *G3614*
19 Lord, with the church that is in their **h**. *G3624*
2Co 5: 1 For we know that if our earthly **h** of *G3614*
1 of God, an **h** not made with hands, *G3614*
2 upon with our **h** which is from heaven: *G3613*
Col 4:15 and the church which is in his **h**. *G3624*
1Ti 3: 4 One that ruleth well his own **h**, having *G3624*
5 to rule his own **h**, how shall he take care *G3624*
15 thyself in the **h** of God, which is the *G3624*
5: 8 those of his own **h**, he hath denied the *G3609*
13 about from **h** to house; and not only *G3614*
13 from house to **h**; and not only idle, but *G3614*
14 guide the **h**, give none occasion *G3616*
2Ti 1:16 The Lord give mercy unto the **h** of *G3624*
2:20 But in a great **h** there are not only *G3614*
Phlm 2 and to the church in thy **h**: *G3624*
Heb 3: 2 as also Moses *was faithful* in all his **h**. *G3624*
3 the **h** hath more honour than the house. *G846*
3 the house hath more honour than the **h**. *G3624*
4 For every **h** is builded by some *man*; *G3624*
5 faithful in all his **h**, as a servant, for a *G3624*
6 But Christ as a son over his own **h**; *G3624*
6 own house; whose **h** are we, if we hold *G3624*
8: 8 **h** of Israel and with the house of Judah: *G3624*
8 house of Israel and with the **h** of Judah: *G3624*
10 I will make with the **h** of Israel after *G3624*
10:21 And *having* an high priest over the **h** of *G3624*
11: 7 to the saving of his **h**; by the which he *G3624*
1Pt 2: 5 up a spiritual **h**, an holy priesthood, *G3624*

1Pt 4:17 must begin at the h of God: and if *it* G3624
2Jn 10 into *your* h, neither bid him God speed: G3614

HOUSEHOLD
Gen 18:19 children and his h after him, and they H1004
31:37 thou found of all thy h stuff? set *it* here H1004
35: 2 Then Jacob said unto his h, and to all H1004
45:11 lest thou, and thy h, and all that thou H1004
47:12 and all his father's h, with bread, H1004
Ex 1: 1 every man and his h came with Jacob. H1004
12: 4 And if the h be too little for the lamb, H1004
Lev 16:17 h, and for all the congregation of Israel. H1004
Dt 6:22 and upon all his h, before our eyes: H1004
14:26 thou shalt rejoice, thou, and thine h, H1004
15:20 the LORD shall choose, thou and thy h. H1004
Jos 2:18 and all thy father's h, home unto thee. H1004
6:25 and her father's h, and all that she had; H1004
7:14 and the h which the LORD shall H1004
18 And he brought his h man by man; and H1004
Jdg 6:27 feared his father's h, and the men of the H1004
18:25 thou lose thy life, with the lives of thy h. H1004
1Sa 25:17 and against all his h: for he *is such* a H1004
27: 3 man with his h, *even* David with his H1004
2Sa 2: 3 man with his h: and they dwelt in the H1004
6:11 blessed Obed-edom, and all his h. H1004
20 Then David returned to bless his h. And H1004
15:16 And the king went forth, and all his h H1004
16: 2 *be* for the king's h to ride on; and the H1004
17:23 his city, and put his h in order, and H1004
19:18 over the king's h, and to do what he H1004
41 the king, and his h, and all David's men H1004
1Ki 4: 6 And Ahishar *was* over the h: and H1004
7 the king and his h: each man his month H1004
5: 9 my desire, in giving food for my h. H1004
11 *for* food to his h, and twenty measures H1004
11:20 h among the sons of Pharaoh. H1004
2Ki 7: 9 that we may go and tell the king's h. H1004
8: 1 and go thou and thine h, and sojourn H1004
2 she went with her h, and sojourned in H1004
18:18 *was* over the h, and Shebna the scribe, H1004
37 *was* over the h, and Shebna the scribe, H1004
19: 2 *was* over the h, and Shebna the scribe, H1004
1Ch 24: 6 Levites: one principal h being taken for H1004
Neh 13: 8 h stuff of Tobiah out of the chamber. H1004
Job 1: 3 and a very great h; so that this man was H5657
Prv 27:27 food, for the food of thy h, and *for* the H1004
31:15 to her h, and a portion to her maidens. H1004
21 She is not afraid of the snow for her h: H1004
21 for all her h *are* clothed with scarlet. H1004
27 She looketh well to the ways of her h, H1004
Isa 36:22 that *was* over the h, and Shebna the H1004
37: 2 who *was* over the h, and Shebna the H1004
Mt 10:25 much more *shall they call* them of his h? G3615
36 a man's foes *shall be* they of his own h. G3615
24:45 his h, to give them meat in due season? G2322
Lk 12:42 make ruler over his h, to give *them their* G2322
Act 10: 7 he called two of his h servants, and a G3610
16:15 And when she was baptized, and her h, G3624
Ro 16:10 Salute them which are of Aristobulus' *h*.
11 *h* of Narcissus, which are in the Lord.
1Co 1:16 And I baptized also the h of Stephanas: G3624
Gal 6:10 unto them who are of the h of faith. G3609
Eph 2:19 with the saints, and of the h of God; G3609
Php 4:22 you, chiefly they that are of Caesar's h. G3614
2Ti 4:19 Salute Prisca and Aquila, and the h of G3624

HOUSEHOLDER
Mt 13:27 So the servants of the h came and said G3617
52 a man *that is* an h, which bringeth forth G3617
20: 1 unto a man *that is* an h, which went out G3617
21:33 There was a certain h, which planted a G3617

HOUSEHOLDS
Gen 42:33 *for* the famine of your h, and be gone: H1004
45:18 And take your father and your h, and H1004
47:24 your h, and for food for your little ones. H1004
Nu 18:31 every place, ye and your h: for it *is* your H1004
Dt 11: 6 up, and their h, and their tents, and H1004
12: 7 unto, ye and your h, wherein the LORD H1004
Jos 7:14 take shall come by h; and the household H1004

HOUSES
Gen 42:19 ye, carry corn for the famine of your h: H1004
Ex 1:21 feared God, that he made them h. H1004
6:14 These *be* the heads of their fathers' h: H1004
8: 9 from thee and thy h, *that* they may H1004
11 from thee, and from thy h, and from thy H1004
13 died out of the h, out of the villages, and H1004
21 and into thy h: and the houses of the H1004
Ex 8:21 thy houses: and the h of the Egyptians H1004
24 and *into* his servants' h, and into all the H1004
9:20 servants and his cattle flee into the h: H1004
10: 6 And they shall fill thy h, and the houses H1004
6 And they shall fill thy houses, and the h H1004
6 servants, and the h of all the Egyptians; H1004
12: 7 post of the h, wherein they shall eat it. H1004
13 a token upon the h where ye *are*: and H1004
15 leaven out of your h: for whosoever H1004
19 found in your h: for whosoever eateth H1004
23 to come in unto your h to smite *you*. H1004
27 passed over the h of the children of H1004
27 and delivered our h. And the people H1004
Lev 25:31 But the h of the villages which have no H1004
32 Levites, *and* the h of the cities of their H1004
33 *of* jubile: for the h of the cities of the H1004
Nu 4:22 the h of their fathers, by their families; H1004
16:32 up, and their h, and all the men that H1004
17: 6 to their fathers' h, *even* twelve rods: and H1004
32:18 We will not return unto our h, until the H1004
Dt 6:11 And h full of all good *things*, which H1004
8:12 hast built goodly h, and dwelt *therein*; H1004
19: 1 dwellest in their cities, and in their h; H1004
Jos 9:12 out of our h on the day we came H1004
Jdg 18:14 that there is in these h an ephod, and H1004
22 men that *were* in the h near to Micah's H1004
1Ki 9:10 had built the two h, the house of the H1004
13:32 and against all the h of the high places H1004
20: 6 house, and the h of thy servants; and H1004
2Ki 17:29 put *them* in the h of the high places H1004
32 for them in the h of the high places. H1004
23: 7 And he brake down the h of the H1004
19 And all the h also of the high places H1004
25: 9 house, and all the h of Jerusalem, and H1004
1Ch 15: 1 And *David* made him h in the city of H1004
28:11 porch, and of the h thereof, and of the H1004
29: 4 to overlay the walls of the h *withal*: H1004
2Ch 25: 5 according to the h of *their* fathers, H1004
34:11 and to floor the h which the kings of H1004
35: 4 And prepare *yourselves* by the h of H1004
Neh 4:14 your daughters, your wives, and your h. H1004
5: 3 vineyards, and h, that we might buy H1004
11 and their h, also the hundredth H1004
7: 4 therein, and the h *were* not builded. H1004
9:25 and possessed h full of all goods, wells H1004
10:34 of our God, after the h of our fathers, at H1004
Job 1: 4 feasted *in their* h, every one his day; H1004
3:15 had gold, who filled their h with silver: H1004
4:19 How much less *in* them that dwell in h H1004
15:28 desolate cities, *and* in h which no man H1004
21: 9 Their h *are* safe from fear, neither *is* H1004
22:18 Yet he filled their h with good *things*: H1004
24:16 In the dark they dig through h, *which* H1004
Ps 49:11 Their inward thought *is*, *that* their h H1004
83:12 to ourselves the h of God in possession. H4999
Prv 1:13 substance, we shall fill our h with spoil: H1004
30:26 folk, yet make they their h in the rocks; H1004
Ecc 2: 4 I made me great works; I builded me h; H1004
Isa 3:14 the spoil of the poor *is* in your h. H1004
5: 9 Of a truth many h shall be desolate, H1004
6:11 and the h without man, and the H1004
8:14 to both the h of Israel, for a gin and H1004
13:16 their eyes; their h shall be spoiled, and H1004
21 lie there; and their h shall be full of H1004
22 in their desolate h, and dragons in *their* H490
15: 3 on the tops of their h, and in their streets,
22:10 And ye have numbered the h of H1004
10 and the h have ye broken down H1004
32:13 upon all the h of joy *in* the joyous city: H1004
42:22 are hid in prison h: they are for a prey, H1004
65:21 And they shall build h, and inhabit H1004
Jer 5: 7 themselves by troops in the harlots' h. H1004
27 As a cage is full of birds, so *are* their h H1004
6:12 And their h shall be turned unto H1004
17:22 out of your h on the sabbath day, H1004
18:22 Let a cry be heard from their h, when H1004
19:13 And the h of Jerusalem, and the houses H1004
13 And the houses of Jerusalem, and the h H1004
13 because of all the h upon whose roofs H1004
29: 5 Build ye h, and dwell *in them*; and plant H1004
28 *is* long: build ye h, and dwell *in them*; H1004
32:15 the God of Israel; H and fields and H1004
29 burn it with the h, upon whose roofs H1004
33: 4 concerning the h of this city, and H1004
4 concerning the h of the kings of Judah, H1004
35: 9 Nor to build h for us to dwell in: H1004
39: 8 house, and the h of the people, with H1004
43:12 And I will kindle a fire in the h of the H1004
13 of Egypt; and the h of the gods of the H1004
Jer 52:13 house; and all the h of Jerusalem, and H1004
13 h of the great *men*, burned he with fire: H1004
Lam 5: 2 is turned to strangers, our h to aliens. H1004
Ezk 7:24 shall possess their h: I will also make H1004
11: 3 Which say, *It is* not near; let us build h: H1004
16:41 And they shall burn thine h with fire, H1004
23:47 and burn up their h with fire. H1004
26:12 thy pleasant h: and they shall lay thy H1004
28:26 and shall build h, and plant vineyards; H1004
33:30 in the doors of the h, and speak one to H1004
45: 4 h, and an holy place for the sanctuary. H1004
Dan 2: 5 and your h shall be made a dunghill. H1005
3:29 in pieces, and their h shall be made a H1005
Hos 11:11 place them in their h, saith the LORD. H1004
Joel 2: 9 climb up upon the h; they shall enter in H1004
Am 3:15 house; and the h of ivory shall perish, H1004
15 h shall have an end, saith the LORD. H1004
5:11 ye have built h of hewn stone, but ye H1004
Mic 1:14 the h of Achzib *shall be* a H1004
2: 2 *them* by violence; and h, and take *them* H1004
9 their pleasant h; from their children H1004
Zep 1: 9 masters' h with violence and deceit. H1004
13 a booty, and their h a desolation: they H1004
13 shall also build h, but not inhabit *them*; H1004
2: 7 thereupon: in the h of Ashkelon shall H1004
Hag 1: 4 your cieled h, and this house *lie* waste? H1004
Zec 14: 2 shall be taken, and the h rifled, and the H1004
Mt 11: 8 that wear soft *clothing* are in kings' h. G3624
19:29 And every one that hath forsaken h, or G3614
23:14 ye devour widows' h, and for a pretence G3614
Mk 8: 3 to their own h, they will faint by the G3624
10:30 now in this time, h, and brethren, and G3614
12:40 Which devour widows' h, and for a G3614
Lk 16: 4 they may receive me into their h. G3624
20:47 Which devour widows' h, and for a G3614
Act 4:34 of lands or h sold them, and brought G3614
1Co 11:22 What? have ye not h to eat and to drink G3614
1Ti 3:12 their children and their own h well. G3624
2Ti 3: 6 which creep into h, and lead captive G3614
Tit 1:11 subvert whole h, teaching things which G3624

HOUSETOP
Prv 21: 9 *It is* better to dwell in a corner of the h, H1406
25:24 in the corner of the h, than with a H1406
Mt 24:17 Let him which is on the h not come G1430
Mk 13:15 And let himthat is on the h not go G1430
Lk 5:19 they went upon the h, and let him down G1430
17:31 shall be upon the h, and his stuff in the G1430
Act 10: 9 the h to pray about the sixth hour: G1430

HOUSETOPS
2Ki 19:26 herb, *as* the grass on the h, and *as corn* H1406
Ps 129: 6 Let them be as the grass *upon* the h, H1406
Isa 22: 1 that thou art wholly gone up to the h? H1406
37:27 herb, *as* the grass on the h, and *as corn* H1406
Jer 48:38 upon all the h of Moab, and in the H1406
Zep 1: 5 of heaven upon the h; and them that H1406
Mt 10:27 in the ear, *that* preach ye upon the h. G1430
Lk 12: 3 closets shall be proclaimed upon the h. G1430

HOW
Gen 26: 9 she *is* thy wife: and h saidst thou, She *is* H349
27:20 And Isaac said unto his son, H *is it* that H4100
28:17 And he was afraid, and said, H H4100
30:29 Thou knowest h I have served H854+H834
29 and h thy cattle was with me. H854+H834
38:29 out: and she said, H hast thou broken H4100
39: 9 thou *art* his wife: h then can I do this H349
44: 8 land of Canaan: h then should we steal H349
16 what shall we speak? or h shall we clear H4100
34 For h shall I go up to my father, and the H349
47: 8 And Pharaoh said unto Jacob, H old H4100
18 from my lord, h that our money H3588+H518
Ex 2:18 H *is it that* ye are come so soon to day? H4069
6:12 unto me; h then shall Pharaoh hear H349
30 and h shall Pharaoh hearken unto me?
9:29 know h that the earth *is* the LORD'S.
10: 2 that ye may know h that I *am* the LORD.
3 of the Hebrews, H long wilt thou refuse H5704
7 said unto him, H long shall this man H5704
11: 7 that ye may know h that the LORD H5704
16:28 And the LORD said unto Moses, H long H5704
18: 8 way, and *h* the LORD delivered them.
19: 4 unto the Egyptians, and *h* I bare you on
36: 1 to know h to work all manner of
Nu 10:31 as thou knowest h we are to encamp in
14:11 And the LORD said unto Moses, H long H5704
11 provoke me? and h long will it be ere H5704
27 H long *shall I bear with* this evil H5704

H

Nu 20:15 **H** our fathers went down into Egypt, and
23: 8 **H** shall I curse, whom God hath not H4100
8 not cursed? or **h** shall I defy, *whom* the H4100
24: 5 **H** goodly are thy tents, O Jacob, *and* H4100
Dt 1:12 **H** can I myself alone bear your H349
31 thou hast seen **h** that the LORD thy God
7:17 more than I; **h** can I dispossess them? H349
9: 7 Remember, *and* forget not, **h** H854+H834
11: 4 to their chariots; **h** he made the water of H834
4 pursued after you, and *h* the LORD hath
6 the son of Reuben: **h** the earth opened H834
12:30 their gods, saying, **H** did these nations H349
18:21 And if thou say in thine heart, **H** shall we H349
25:18 **H** he met thee by the way, and smote the H834
29:16 (For ye know **h** we have dwelt in the H834
16 land of Egypt; and **h** we came through H834
31:27 and **h** much more after my death? H637
32:30 **H** should one chase a thousand, and two H349
Jos 2:10 For we have heard **h** the LORD H854+H834
9: 7 and **h** shall we make a league with you? H349
24 thy servants, **h** that the LORD thy H854+H834
10: 1 had heard **h** Joshua had taken Ai, H3588
1 and her king; and **h** the inhabitants of H3588
14:12 in that day **h** the Anakims *were* there, H3588
18: 3 children of Israel, **H** long *are* ye slack H5704
Jdg 13:12 come to pass. **H** shall we order the H4100
12 the child, and *h* shall we do unto him?
16:15 And she said unto him, **H** canst thou H349
18: 7 that *were* therein, **h** they dwelt careless,
20: 3 of Israel, Tell *us*, **h** was this wickedness? H349
21: 7 **H** shall we do for wives for them that H4100
16 said, **H** shall we do for wives H4100
Ru 1: 6 country of Moab **h** that the LORD had
2:11 husband: and *h* thou hast left thy father
3:18 until thou know **h** the matter will fall: for H349
1Sa 1:14 And Eli said unto her, **H** long wilt thou H5704
2:22 all Israel; and **h** they lay with the H854+H834
10:27 But the children of Belial said, **H** shall H4100
12:24 for consider **h** great *things* he H854+H834
14:29 see, I pray you, **h** mine eyes have been H3588
30 **H** much more, if haply the people had H637
15: 2 did to Israel, **h** he laid *wait* for him H834
16: 1 And the LORD said unto Samuel, **H** H5704
2 And Samuel said, **H** can I go? if Saul H349
17:18 and look **h** thy brethren fare, and H854
23: 3 here in Judah: **h** much more then if we H637
24:10 Behold, this day thine eyes have seen **h** H854
18 And thou hast shewed this day **h** that H854
28: 9 Saul hath done, **h** he hath cut off those H834
2Sa 1: 4 And David said unto him, **H** went the H4100
5 man that told him, **H** knowest thou that H349
14 And David said unto him, **H** wast thou H349
19 thy high places: **h** are the mighty fallen! H349
25 **H** are the mighty fallen in the midst of H349
27 **H** are the mighty fallen, and the H349
2:22 thee to the ground? **h** then should I hold H349
26 in the latter end? **h** long shall it be then, H5704
4:11 **H** much more, when wicked men have H637
6: 9 **H** shall the ark of the LORD come to me?
20 David, and said, **H** glorious was the H4100
11: 7 demanded *of him* **h** Joab did, and how
7 how Joab did, and **h** the people did, and
7 the people did, and **h** the war prospered.
12:18 unto our voice: **h** will he then vex H349
16:11 seeketh my life: **h** much more now *may* H637
18:19 the king tidings, **h** that the LORD hath
19: 2 day **h** the king was grieved for his son.
34 And Barzillai said unto the king, **H** H4100
24: 3 unto the people, **h** many soever they be,
1Ki 3: 7 child: I know not *h* to go out or come in.
5: 3 Thou knowest **h** that David my father
8:27 contain thee; **h** much less this house H637
12: 6 yet lived, and said, **H** do ye advise that I H349
14:19 And the rest of the acts of Jeroboam, **h** H834
19 he warred, and **h** he reigned, behold,
18:13 of the LORD, **h** I hid an hundred men
21 the people, and said, **H** long halt ye H5704
19: 1 done, and withal **h** he had slain all the H834
20: 7 I pray you, and see **h** this *man* seeketh H3588
21:29 Seest thou **h** Ahab humbleth himself H3588
22:16 And the king said unto him, **H** many H5704
45 he shewed, and **h** he warred, *are* they H834
2Ki 5: 7 see **h** he seeketh a quarrel against me. H3588
13 not have done *it*? **h** much rather then, H637
6:15 him, Alas, my master! **h** shall we do? H349
32 to the elders, See ye **h** this son of a H3588
8: 5 telling the king **h** he had restored H854+H834
9:25 for remember **h** that, when I and thou
10: 4 not before him: **h** then shall we stand? H349
2Ki 14:15 did, and his might, and **h** he fought with H834
28 he did, and his might, **h** he warred, and H834
28 how he warred, and **h** he recovered H834
17:28 them **h** they should fear the LORD. H349
18:24 **H** then wilt thou turn away the face of H349
19:25 Hast thou not heard long ago **h** I have
20: 3 remember now **h** I have walked H854+H834
20 all his might, and **h** he made a pool, and H834
1Ch 13:12 that day, saying, **H** shall I bring the ark H1963
18: 9 of Hamath heard **h** David had smitten H3588
19: 5 and told David **h** the men were served.
2Ch 6:18 contain thee; **h** much less this house H637
7: 3 And when all the children of Israel saw **h**
18:15 And the king said to him, **H** many H5704
20:11 Behold, *I say*, **h** they reward us, to come
32:15 of my fathers: **h** much less shall your H637
33:19 His prayer also, and *h God* was entreated
Ezr 7:22 oil, and salt without prescribing *h much*.
Neh 2: 6 by him,) For **h** long shall thy journey H5704
17 that we *are* in, **h** Jerusalem *lieth* waste, H834
Est 2:11 house, to know **h** Esther did, and what
5:11 him, and **h** he had advanced him H834
8: 6 For **h** can I endure to see the evil that H349
6 unto my people? or **h** can I endure to see H349
Job 4:19 **H** much less *in* them that dwell in H637
6:25 **H** forcible are right words! but what H4100
7:19 **H** long wilt thou not depart from me, H4100
8: 2 **H** long wilt thou speak these *things*? and H575
2 these *things*? and *h long shall* the words
9: 2 I know *it is* so of a truth: but **h** should H4100
14 **H** much less shall I answer him, *and* H637
13:23 **H** many *are* mine iniquities and sins? H4100
15:16 **H** much more abominable and filthy *is* H637
18: 2 **H** long *will it be ere* ye make an end of H5704
19: 2 **H** long will ye vex my soul, and break H5704
21:17 **H** oft is the candle of the wicked put H4100
17 wicked put out! and *h oft* cometh their
34 **H** then comfort ye me in vain, seeing in H349
22:12 the height of the stars, **h** high they are! H3588
13 And thou sayest, **H** doth God know? H4100
25: 4 **H** then can man be justified with God? H4100
4 with God? or **h** can he be clean *that* H4100
6 **H** much less man, *that is* a worm? and H637
26: 2 **H** hast thou helped *him that is* without H4100
2 *is* without power? *h* savest thou the arm
3 **H** hast thou counselled *him that hath* H4100
3 no wisdom? and *h* hast thou plentifully
14 Lo, these *are* parts of his ways: but **h** H4100
34:19 *H much less to him* that accepteth not H834
37:17 **H** thy garments *are* warm, when he H834
Ps 3: 1 LORD, **h** are they increased that H4100
4: 2 O ye sons of men, **h** long *will ye turn* H5704
2 my glory into shame? *h long* will ye love
6: 3 sore vexed: but thou, O LORD, **h** long? H5704
8: 1 O LORD our Lord, **h** excellent *is* thy H4100
9 O LORD our Lord, **h** excellent *is* thy H4100
11: 1 In the LORD put I my trust: **h** say ye to H349
13: 1 **H** long wilt thou forget me, O LORD? H5704
1 **h** long wilt thou hide thy face from me? H5704
2 **H** long shall I take counsel in my soul, H5704
2 in my heart daily? **h** long shall mine H5704
21: 1 thy salvation **h** greatly shall he rejoice! H4100
31:19 *Oh* **h** great *is* thy goodness, which thou H4100
35:17 Lord, **h** long wilt thou look on? rescue H4100
36: 7 **H** excellent *is* thy lovingkindness, O H4100
39: 4 what it *is; that* I may know **h** frail I *am*. H4100
44: 2 *H* thou didst drive out the heathen with
2 plantedst them; *h* thou didst afflict the
62: 3 **H** long will ye imagine mischief against H5704
66: 3 Say unto God, **H** terrible *art thou in* thy H4100
73:11 And they say, **H** doth God know? and is H349
19 **H** are they *brought* into desolation, as in H349
74: 9 among us any that knoweth **h** long. H5407
10 O God, **h** long shall the adversary H5407
22 own cause: remember **h** the foolish man
78:40 **H** oft did they provoke him in the H4100
43 **H** he had wrought his signs in Egypt, H834
79: 5 **H** long, LORD? wilt thou be angry for H5704
80: 4 O LORD God of hosts, **h** long wilt thou H5704
82: 2 **H** long will ye judge unjustly, and H5704
84: 1 **H** amiable *are* thy tabernacles, O H4100
89:46 **H** long, LORD? wilt thou hide thyself H5704
47 Remember **h** short my time is: H4100
50 of thy servants; *h* I do bear in my bosom
90:13 Return, O LORD, **h** long? and let it H5704
92: 5 O LORD, **h** great are thy works! *and* thy H4100
94: 3 LORD, **h** long shall the wicked, how H5704
3 LORD, how long shall the wicked, **h** H5704
4 *H long* shall they utter *and* speak hard
Ps 104:24 O LORD, **h** manifold are thy works! in H4100
119:84 **H** many *are* the days of thy servant? H4100
97 O **h** love I thy law! it *is* my meditation H4100
103 **H** sweet are thy words unto my taste! H4100
159 Consider **h** I love thy precepts: quicken H3588
132: 2 **H** he sware unto the LORD, *and* vowed H834
133: 1 Behold, **h** good and how pleasant *it is* H4100
1 Behold, how good and **h** pleasant *it is* H4100
137: 4 **H** shall we sing the LORD'S song in a H349
139:17 **H** precious also are thy thoughts unto H4100
17 me, O God! **h** great is the sum of them! H4100
Prv 1:22 **H** long, ye simple ones, will ye love H5704
5:12 And say, **H** have I hated instruction, and H349
6: 9 **H** long wilt thou sleep, O sluggard? H5704
15:11 before the LORD: **h** much more then the H637
23 *spoken* in due season, **h** good *is it*! H4100
16:16 **H** much better *is it* to get wisdom than H4100
19: 7 poor do hate him: **h** much more do his H637
20:24 Man's goings *are* of the LORD; **h** can a H4100
21:27 *is* abomination: **h** much more, *when* he H637
30:13 *There is* a generation, O **h** lofty are H4100
Ecc 2:16 And **h** dieth the wise *man*? as the fool. H349
4:11 have heat: but **h** can one be warm *alone*? H349
10:15 he knoweth not **h** to go to the city.
11: 5 of the spirit, *nor* **h** the bones *do grow* in
Song 4:10 **H** fair is thy love, my sister, *my* spouse! H4100
10 sister, *my* spouse! **h** much better is thy H4100
5: 3 I have put off my coat; **h** shall I put it on? H349
3 washed my feet; **h** shall I defile them? H349
7: 1 **H** beautiful are thy feet with shoes, O H4100
6 **H** fair and how pleasant art thou, O H4100
6 How fair and **h** pleasant art thou, O H4100
Isa 1:21 **H** is the faithful city become an harlot! it H349
6:11 Then said I, Lord, **h** long? And he H5704
14: 4 Babylon, and say, **H** hath the oppressor H349
12 **H** art thou fallen from heaven, O Lucifer, H349
12 of the morning! *h* art thou cut down to H349
19:11 is become brutish: **h** say ye unto H349
20: 6 king of Assyria: and **h** shall we escape? H349
36: 9 **H** then wilt thou turn away the face of H349
37:26 Hast thou not heard long ago, *h* I have H349
38: 3 I beseech thee, **h** I have walked H854+H834
48:11 will I do *it*: for **h** should *my name* be H349
50: 4 that I should know **h** to speak a word in
52: 7 **H** beautiful upon the mountains are H4100
Jer 2:21 a right seed: **h** then art thou turned H349
23 **H** canst thou say, I am not polluted, I H349
3:19 But I said, **H** shall I put thee among the H349
4:14 mayest be saved. **H** long shall thy vain H5704
21 **H** long shall I see the standard, *and* H5704
5: 7 **H** shall I pardon thee for this? thy H335
8: 8 **H** do ye say, We *are* wise, and the law of H349
9: 7 and try them; for **h** shall I do for the H349
19 heard out of Zion, **H** are we spoiled! we H349
12: 4 **H** long shall the land mourn, and the H5704
5 wearied thee, then **h** canst thou contend H349
5 **h** wilt thou do in the swelling of Jordan? H349
15: 5 who shall go aside to ask **h** thou doest?
22:23 thy nest in the cedars, **h** gracious shalt H4100
23:26 **H** long shall *this* be in the heart of the H5704
31:22 **H** long wilt thou go about, O thou H5704
36:17 Tell us now, **H** didst thou write all these H349
46:13 the prophet, **h** Nebuchadrezzar king
47: 5 their valley: **h** long wilt thou cut thyself?
6 O thou sword of the LORD, **h** long *will* H5704
7 **H** can it be quiet, seeing the LORD hath H349
48:14 **H** say ye, We *are* mighty and strong men H349
17 know his name, say, **H** is the strong staff H349
39 They shall howl, *saying*, **H** is it broken H349
39 is it broken down! **h** hath Moab turned H349
49:25 **H** is the city of praise not left, the city of H349
50:23 **H** is the hammer of the whole earth cut H349
23 and broken! **h** is Babylon become a H349
51:41 **H** is Sheshach taken! and how is the H349
41 How is Sheshach taken! and **h** is the
41 earth surprised! **h** is Babylon become an H349
Lam 1: 1 **H** doth the city sit solitary, *that was* full H349
1 *was* full of people! **h** is she become as a
1 the provinces, **h** is she become tributary!
2: 1 **H** hath the Lord covered the daughter of H349
4: 1 **H** is the gold become dim! *how* is the H349
1 How is the gold become dim! **h** is the
2 to fine gold, **h** are they esteemed as
Ezk 14:21 For thus saith the Lord GOD; **H** much H637
15: 5 meet for no work: **h** much less shall it be H637
16:30 **H** weak is thine heart, saith the Lord H4100
26:17 and say to thee, **H** art thou destroyed, H349
33:10 away in them, **h** should we then live? H349
Dan 4: 3 **H** great *are* his signs! and how mighty H4101

Dan 4: 3 How great *are* his signs! and **h** mighty H4101
8:13 which spake, **H** long *shall be* the vision H5704
10:17 For **h** can the servant of this my lord H1963
12: 6 of the river, **H** long *shall it be to* the H5704
Hos 8: 5 against them: **h** long *will it be* ere they H349
11: 8 **H** shall I give thee up, Ephraim? *how* H349
8 How shall I give thee up, Ephraim? *h*
8 thee, Israel? **h** shall I make thee as H349
8 thee as Admah? *h* shall I set thee as
Joel 1:18 **H** do the beasts groan! the herds of H4100
Oba 5 if robbers by night, (**h** art thou cut off!) H349
6 **H** are *the things* of Esau searched out! H349
6 out! *h* are his hidden things sought up!
Mic 2: 4 of my people: **h** hath he removed *it* from H349
Hab 1: 2 O LORD, **h** long shall I cry, and thou H5704
2: 6 *which is* not his! **h** long? and to him H5704
Zep 2:15 *is* none beside me: **h** is she become a H349
Hag 2: 3 first glory? and **h** do ye see it now? *is* H4100
Zec 1:12 O LORD of hosts, **h** long wilt thou not H5704
9:17 For **h** great *is* his goodness, and how H4100
17 For how great *is* his goodness, and **h** H4100
Mt 6:23 be darkness, **h** great *is* that darkness! G4214
28 lilies of the field, **h** they grow; they toil G4459
7: 4 Or **h** wilt thou say to thy brother, Let G4459
11 If ye then, being evil, know **h** to give
11 your children, **h** much more shall your G4214
10:19 up, take no thought **h** or what ye shall G4459
25 house Beelzebub, **h** much more *shall* G4214
12: 4 **H** he entered into the house of God, G4459
5 Or have ye not read in the law, **h** that on
12 **H** much then is a man better than a G4214
14 against him, **h** they might destroy him. G3704
26 **h** shall then his kingdom stand? G4459
29 Or else **h** can one enter into a strong G4459
34 O generation of vipers, **h** can ye, being G4459
15:34 And Jesus saith unto them, **H** many G4214
16: 9 and **h** many baskets ye took up? G4214
10 and **h** many baskets ye took up? G4214
11 **H** is it that ye do not understand that I G4459
12 Then understood they **h** that he bade
21 unto his disciples, **h** that he must go
17:17 generation, **h** long shall I be with G2193
17 I be with you? **h** long shall I suffer you? G4219
18:12 **H** think ye? if a man have an hundred G5101
21 and said, Lord, **h** oft shall my brother G4212
21:20 **H** soon is the fig tree withered away! G4459
22:12 And he saith unto him, Friend, **h** G4459
15 **h** they might entangle him in *his* talk. G3704
43 He saith unto them, **H** then doth David G4459
45 If David then call him Lord, **h** is he his G4459
23:33 *Ye* serpents, *ye* generation of vipers, **h** G4459
37 are sent unto thee, **h** often would I have
26:54 But **h** then shall the scriptures be G4459
27:13 Hearest thou not **h** many things they G4214
Mk 2:16 unto his disciples, **H** is it that he eateth G5101
26 **H** he went into the house of God in the G4459
3: 6 against him, **h** they might destroy him. G3704
23 parables, **H** can Satan cast out Satan? G4459
4:13 and **h** then will ye know all parables? G4459
27 spring and grow up, he knoweth not **h**. G5613
40 so fearful? **h** is it that ye have no faith? G4459
5:16 And they that saw *it* told them **h** it G4459
19 and tell them **h** great things the Lord G3745
20 in Decapolis **h** great things Jesus had G3745
6:38 He saith unto them, **H** many loaves G4214
8: 5 And he asked them, **H** many loaves G4214
19 five thousand, **h** many baskets full of G4214
20 four thousand, **h** many baskets full of G4214
21 And he said unto them, **H** is it that ye G4459
9:12 all things; and **h** it is written of the Son G4459
19 generation, **h** long shall I be with G2193
19 I be with you? **h** long shall I suffer you? G2193
21 And he asked his father, **H** long is it G4214
10:23 unto his disciples, **H** hardly shall they G4459
24 them, Children, **h** hard is it for them G4459
11:18 *it*, and sought **h** they might destroy G4459
12:26 the book of Moses, **h** in the bush God G5613
35 in the temple, **H** say the scribes that G4459
41 and beheld **h** the people cast money G4459
14: 1 the scribes sought **h** they might take G4459
11 **h** he might conveniently betray him. G4459
15: 4 nothing? behold **h** many things they G4214
Lk 1:34 Then said Mary unto the angel, **H** shall G4459
58 and her cousins heard **h** the Lord had G3754
62 And they made signs to his father, **h** he G5101
2:49 And he said unto them, **H** is it that ye G5101
6: 4 **H** he went into the house of God, and G5613
42 Either **h** canst thou say to thy brother, G4459
7:22 seen and heard; **h** that the blind see, G3754

Lk 8:18 Take heed therefore **h** ye hear: for G4459
39 Return to thine own house, and shew **h** G3754
39 the whole city **h** great things Jesus had G3754
47 and **h** she was healed immediately. G5613
9:41 generation, **h** long shall I be with G2193
10:26 is written in the law? **h** readest thou? G4459
11:13 If ye then, being evil, know **h** to give
13 your children: **h** much more shall *your* G4214
18 against himself, **h** shall his kingdom G4459
12:11 ye no thought **h** or what thing ye shall G4459
24 God feedeth them: **h** much more are ye G4214
27 Consider the lilies **h** they grow: they toil G4459
28 cast into the oven; **h** much more *will he* G4214
50 with; and **h** am I straitened till G4459
56 **h** is it that ye do not discern this time? G4459
13:34 are sent unto thee; **h** often would I have G4214
14: 7 when he marked **h** they chose out the G4459
15:17 to himself, he said, **H** many hired G4214
16: 2 said unto him, **H** is it that I hear this G5101
5 first, **H** much owest thou unto my lord? G4214
7 Then said he to another, And **h** much G4214
18:24 he said, **H** hardly shall they that G4459
19:15 he might know **h** much every man had G5101
20:41 And he said unto them, **H** say they that G4459
44 David therefore calleth him Lord, **h** is G4459
21: 5 And as some spake of the temple, **h** it G3754
22: 2 scribes sought **h** they might kill him; G4459
4 **h** he might betray him unto them. G4459
61 word of the Lord, **h** he had said unto G5613
23:55 the sepulchre, and **h** his body was laid. G5613
24: 6 is risen: remember **h** he spake unto you G5613
20 And **h** the chief priests and our rulers G3704
35 in the way, and **h** he was known of G5613
Jn 3: 4 Nicodemus saith unto him, **H** can a G4459
9 said unto him, **H** can these things be? G4459
12 ye believe not, **h** shall ye believe, if I G4459
4: 1 When therefore the Lord knew **h** the G3754
9 unto him, **H** is it that thou, being G4459
5:44 **H** can ye believe, which receive honour G4459
47 But if ye believe not his writings, **h** G4459
6:42 mother we know? **h** is it then that he G4459
52 **H** can this man give us *his* flesh to eat? G4459
7:15 And the Jews marvelled, saying, **H** G4459
8:33 **h** sayest thou, Ye shall be made free? G4459
9:10 Therefore said they unto him, **H** were G4459
15 also asked him **h** he had received his G4459
16 day. Others said, **H** can a man that is a G4459
19 born blind? **h** then doth he now see? G4459
26 did he to thee? **h** opened he thine eyes? G4459
10:24 said unto him, **H** long dost thou make G2193
11:36 Then said the Jews, Behold **h** he loved G4459
12:19 Perceive ye **h** ye prevail nothing? G3754
34 for ever: and **h** sayest thou, The Son G4459
14: 5 goest; and **h** can we know the way? G4459
9 **h** sayest thou *then*, Shew us the Father? G4459
22 not Iscariot, Lord, **h** is it that thou wilt G5101
28 Ye have heard **h** I said unto you, I go G3754
Act 2: 8 And **h** hear we every man in our own G4459
4:21 finding nothing **h** they might punish G4459
5: 9 Then Peter said unto her, **H** is it that ye G5101
7:25 have understood **h** that God by his hand
8:31 And he said, **H** can I, except some man G4459
9:13 many of this man, **h** much evil he hath G3745
16 For I will shew him **h** great things he G3745
27 unto them **h** he had seen the Lord G4459
27 to him, and **h** he had preached boldly G4459
10:28 And he said unto them, Ye know **h** that G5613
38 **H** God anointed Jesus of Nazareth with G5613
11:13 And he shewed us **h** he had seen an G4459
16 word of the Lord, **h** that he said, John G5613
12:14 and told **h** Peter stood before the gate. G518
17 unto them **h** the Lord had brought G4459
13:32 And we declare unto you glad tidings, **h**
14:27 with them, and **h** he had opened the G3754
15: 7 brethren, ye know **h** that a good while
14 Simeon hath declared **h** God at the first G2531
36 the word of the Lord, *and see* **h** they do. G4459
19:35 that knoweth not **h** that the city of the
20:20 *And* **h** I kept back nothing that was G5613
35 I have shewed you all things, **h** that so
35 of the Lord Jesus, **h** he said, It is more G3754
21:20 seest, brother, **h** many thousands of G4214
23:30 And when it was told me **h** that the Jews
Ro 3: 6 God forbid: for then **h** shall God judge G4459
4:10 **H** was it then reckoned? when he was G4459
6: 2 God forbid. **H** shall we, that are dead to G4459
7: 1 that know the law,) **h** that the law hath
18 with me; but *h* to perform that which
8:32 him up for us all, **h** shall he not with G4459

Ro 10:14 **H** then shall they call on him in whom G4459
14 not believed? and **h** shall they believe in G4459
14 **h** shall they hear without a preacher? G4459
15 And **h** shall they preach, except they be G4459
15 as it is written, **H** beautiful are the feet G5613
11: 2 saith of Elias? **h** he maketh intercession G5613
12 Gentiles; **h** much more their fulness? G4214
24 a good olive tree: **h** much more shall G4214
33 of God! **h** unsearchable *are* his G5613
1Co 1:26 For ye see your calling, brethren, **h** that
3:10 take heed **h** he buildeth thereupon. G4459
6: 3 judge angels? **h** much more things that G3386
7:16 *thy* husband? or **h** knowest thou, O G5101
32 to the Lord, **h** he may please the Lord: G4459
33 of the world, **h** he may please *his* wife. G4459
34 world, **h** she may please *her* husband. G4459
10: 1 be ignorant, **h** that all our fathers were
14: 7 in the sounds, **h** shall it be known what G4459
9 to be understood, **h** shall it be known G4459
16 bless with the spirit, **h** shall he that G4459
26 **H** is it then, brethren? when ye come G5101
15: 3 I also received, **h** that Christ died for our
12 from the dead, **h** say some among you G4459
35 But some *man* will say, **H** are the dead G4459
2Co 3: 8 **H** shall not the ministration of the G4459
7:15 of you all, **h** with fear and trembling G5613
8: 2 **H** that in a great trial of affliction the
12: 4 **H** that he was caught up into paradise,
13: 5 your own selves, **h** that Jesus Christ is in
Gal 1:13 in the Jews' religion, **h** that beyond
4: 9 are known of God, **h** turn ye again to G4459
13 Ye know **h** through infirmity of the G3754
6:11 Ye see **h** large a letter I have written G4080
Eph 3: 3 **H** that by revelation he made known
6:21 my affairs, *and* **h** I do, Tychicus, a G5101
Php 1: 8 For God is my record, **h** greatly I long G5613
2:23 soon as I shall see **h** it will go with me. G4012
4:12 I know both **h** to be abased, and I know
12 and I know **h** to abound: every where
Col 4: 6 know **h** ye ought to answer every man. G4459
1Th 1: 9 had unto you, and **h** ye turned to God G4459
2:10 Ye *are* witnesses, and God *also*, **h** holily G5613
11 As ye know **h** we exhorted and G5613
4: 1 received of us **h** ye ought to walk and G4459
4 That every one of you should know **h** to
2Th 3: 7 For yourselves know **h** ye ought to G4459
1Ti 3: 5 (For if a man know not **h** to rule his G1492
5 his own house, **h** shall he take care of G4459
15 thou mayest know **h** thou oughtest to G4459
2Ti 1:18 in that day: and in **h** many things he G3745
Phlm 16 to me, but **h** much more unto thee, G4214
19 I do not say to thee **h** thou owest unto G3754
Heb 2: 3 **H** shall we escape, if we neglect so G4459
7: 4 Now consider **h** great this man *was*, G4080
8: 6 ministry, by **h** much also he is the G3745
9:14 **H** much more shall the blood of Christ, G4214
10:29 Of **h** much sorer punishment, suppose G4214
12:17 For ye know **h** that afterward, when he G3754
Jas 2:22 Seest thou **h** faith wrought with his G3754
24 Ye see then **h** that by works a man is
3: 5 **h** great a matter a little fire kindleth! G2245
2Pt 2: 9 The Lord knoweth **h** to deliver the godly
1Jn 3:17 him, **h** dwelleth the love of God in him? G4459
4:20 he hath seen, **h** can he love God whom G4459
Jude 5 ye once knew this, **h** that the Lord,
18 **H** that they told you there should be
Rev 2: 2 thy patience, and **h** thou canst not bear G3754
3: 3 Remember therefore **h** thou hast G4459
6:10 voice, saying, **H** long, O Lord, holy and G2193
18: 7 **H** much she hath glorified herself, and G3745

HOWBEIT

Jdg 4:17 **H** Sisera fled away on his feet to the tent
11:28 **H** the king of the children of Ammon
16:22 **H** the hair of his head began to grow
18:29 born unto Israel: **h** the name of the city H199
21:18 **H** we may not give them wives of our
Ru 3:12 **h** there is a kinsman nearer than I.
1Sa 8: 9 unto their voice: **h** yet protest solemnly H389
2Sa 2:23 **H** he refused to turn aside: wherefore
12:14 **H**, because by this deed thou hast given H657
13:14 **H** he would not hearken unto her voice:
25 him: **h** he would not go, but blessed him.
23:19 **h** he attained not unto the *first* three.
1Ki 2:15 me, that I should reign: **h** the kingdom is
10: 7 **H** I believed not the words, until I came,
11:13 **H** I will not rend away all the kingdom; H7535
22 Nothing: **h** let me go in any wise. H3588
34 **H** I will not take the whole kingdom out

2Ki 3:25 the stones thereof; **h** the slingers went
8:10 certainly recover: **h** the LORD hath
10:29 **H** *from* the sins of Jeroboam the son of H7535
12:13 **H** there were not made for the house of H389
14: 4 **H** the high places were not taken away: H7535
15:35 **H** the high places were not removed: H7535
17:29 **H** every nation made gods of their own,
40 **H** they did not hearken, but they did
22: 7 **H** there was no reckoning made with H389
1Ch 11:21 **h** he attained not to the *first* three.
28: 4 **H** the LORD God of Israel chose me
2Ch 9: 6 **H** I believed not their words, until I
18:34 And the battle increased that day: **h** the
20:33 **H** the high places were not taken away: H389
21: 7 **H** the LORD would not destroy the house
20 being desired. **H** they buried him in the
24: 5 the matter. **H** the Levites hastened *it* not.
27: 2 father Uzziah did: **h** he entered not into H7535
32:31 **H** in *the business of* the ambassadors H3651
Neh 9:33 **H** thou *art* just in all that is brought
13: 2 should curse them: **h** our God turned the
Job 30:24 **H** he will not stretch out *his* hand to the H389
Isa 10: 7 **H** he meaneth not so, neither doth his
Jer 44: 4 **H** I sent unto you all my servants the
Mt 17:21 **H** this kind goeth not out but by prayer *G1161*
Mk 5:19 **H** Jesus suffered him not, but saith *G1161*
7: 7 **H** in vain do they worship me, teaching *G1161*
Jn 6:23 (**H** there came other boats from *G1161*
7:13 **H** no man spake openly of him for fear *G3305*
27 **H** we know this man whence he is: but *G235*
11:13 **H** Jesus spake of his death: but they *G1161*
16:13 **H** when he, the Spirit of truth, is come, *G1161*
Act 4: 4 **H** many of them which heard the word *G1161*
7:48 **H** the most High dwelleth not in temples *G235*
14:20 **H**, as the disciples stood round about *G1161*
17:34 **H** certain men clave unto him, and *G1161*
27:26 **H** we must be cast upon a certain *G1161*
28: 6 **H** they looked when he should have *G1161*
1Co 2: 6 **H** we speak wisdom among them that *G1161*
8: 7 **H** *there is* not in every man that *G235*
14: 2 **h** in the spirit he speaketh mysteries. *G1161*
20 in understanding: **h** in malice be ye *G235*
15:46 **H** that *was* not first which is spiritual, *G235*
2Co 11:21 had been weak. **H** whereinsoever any *G1161*
Gal 4: 8 **H** then, when ye knew not God, ye did *G235*
1Ti 1:16 **H** for this cause I obtained mercy, that *G235*
Heb 3:16 did provoke: **h** not all that came out *G235*

HOWL

Isa 13: 6 **H** ye; for the day of the LORD *is* at H3213
14:31 **H**, O gate; cry, O city; thou, whole H3213
15: 2 to weep: Moab shall **h** over Nebo, and H3213
3 every one shall **h**, weeping abundantly. H3213
16: 7 Therefore shall Moab **h** for Moab, H3213
7 every one shall **h**: for the foundations H3213
23: 1 The burden of Tyre. **H**, ye ships of H3213
6 Pass ye over to Tarshish; **h**, ye H3213
14 **H**, ye ships of Tarshish: for your H3213
52: 5 make them to **h**, saith the LORD; and H3213
65:14 heart, and shall **h** for vexation of spirit. H3213
Jer 4: 8 lament and **h**: for the fierce anger H3213
25:34 **H**, ye shepherds, and cry; and wallow H3213
47: 2 all the inhabitants of the land shall **h**. H3213
48:20 it is broken down: **h** and cry; tell ye it in H3213
31 Therefore will I **h** for Moab, and I will H3213
39 They shall **h**, *saying*, How is it broken H3213
49: 3 **H**, O Heshbon, for Ai is spoiled: cry, ye H3213
51: 8 and destroyed: **h** for her; take balm for H3213
Ezk 21:12 Cry and **h**, son of man: for it shall be H3213
30: 2 Lord GOD; **H** ye, Woe worth the day! H3213
Joel 1: 5 Awake, ye drunkards, and weep; and **h**, H3213
11 Be ye ashamed, O ye husbandmen; **h**, O H3213
13 lament, ye priests: **h**, ye ministers of the H3213
Mic 1: 8 Therefore I will wail and **h**, I will go H3213
Zep 1:11 **H**, ye inhabitants of Maktesh, for all the H3213
Zec 11: 2 **H**, fir tree; for the cedar is fallen; H3213
2 are spoiled: **h**, O ye oaks of Bashan; H3213
Jas 5: 1 Go to now, *ye* rich men, weep and **h** for *G3649*

HOWLED

Hos 7:14 heart, when they **h** upon their beds: H3213

HOWLING

Dt 32:10 and in the waste **h** wilderness; he led H3214
Isa 15: 8 of Moab; the **h** thereof unto Eglaim, H3215
8 and the **h** thereof unto Beer-elim. H3215
Jer 25:36 shepherds, and an **h** of the principal of H3215
Zep 1:10 the fish gate, and an **h** from the second, H3215
Zec 11: 3 *There is* a voice of the **h** of the H3215

HOWLINGS

Am 8: 3 And the songs of the temple shall be **h** H3213

HOWSOEVER

Jdg 19:20 *be* with thee; **h** *let* all thy wants *lie* H7535
2Sa 18:22 again to Joab, But **h**, let me, I pray thee, H4100
23 But **h**, *said he*, let me run. And he said H4100
Zep 3: 7 not be cut off, **h** I punished H834+H3605

HOZEH See COL-HOZEH.

HUGE

2Ch 16: 8 and the Lubims a **h** host, with very H7230

HUKKOK

Jos 19:34 out from thence to **H**, and reacheth to H2712

HUKOK

1Ch 6:75 And **H** with her suburbs, and Rehob H2712

HUL

Gen 10:23 And the children of Aram; Uz, and **H**, H2343
1Ch 1:17 Uz, and **H**, and Gether, and Meshech. H2343

HULDAH

2Ki 22:14 went unto **H** the prophetess, the H2468
2Ch 34:22 went to **H** the prophetess, the H2468

HUMBLE

Ex 10: 3 wilt thou refuse to **h** thyself before me? H6031
Dt 8: 2 the wilderness, to **h** thee, *and* to prove H6031
16 not, that he might **h** thee, and that he H6031
Jdg 19:24 out now, and **h** ye them, and do with H6031
2Ch 7:14 by my name, shall **h** themselves, and H3665
34:27 and thou didst **h** thyself before God, H3665
Job 22:29 and he shall save the **h** person. H7807+H5869
Ps 9:12 them: he forgetteth not the cry of the **h**. H6041
10:12 God, lift up thine hand: forget not the **h**. H6041
17 the desire of the **h**: thou wilt prepare H6035
34: 2 the **h** shall hear *thereof*, and be glad. H6035
69:32 The **h** shall see *this, and* be glad: and H6035
Prv 6: 3 go, **h** thyself, and make sure thy friend. H7511
16:19 Better *it is to be* of an **h** spirit with the H8217
29:23 but honour shall uphold the **h** in spirit. H8217
Isa 57:15 of a contrite and **h** spirit, to revive the H8217
15 the spirit of the **h**, and to revive the H8217
Jer 13:18 Say unto the king and to the queen, **H** H8213
Mt 18: 4 Whosoever therefore shall **h** himself as *G5013*
23:12 he that shall **h** himself shall be exalted. *G5013*
2Co 12:21 my God will **h** me among you, and *G5013*
Jas 4: 6 the proud, but giveth grace unto the **h**. *G5011*
10 **H** yourselves in the sight of the Lord, *G5013*
1Pt 5: 5 the proud, and giveth grace to the **h**. *G5011*
6 **H** yourselves therefore under the *G5013*

HUMBLED

Lev 26:41 hearts be **h**, and they then accept H3665
Dt 8: 3 And he **h** thee, and suffered thee to H6031
21:14 of her, because thou hast **h** her. H6031
22:24 because he hath **h** his neighbour's wife: H6031
29 because he hath **h** her, he may not put H6031
2Ki 22:19 and thou hast **h** thyself before the H3665
2Ch 12: 6 and the king **h** themselves; and they H3665
7 And when the LORD saw that they **h** H3665
7 saying, They have **h** themselves; H3665
12 And when he **h** himself, the wrath of H3665
30:11 **h** themselves, and came to Jerusalem. H3665
32:26 Notwithstanding Hezekiah **h** himself H3665
33:12 his God, and **h** himself greatly before H3665
19 before he was **h**: behold, they *are* H3665
23 And **h** not himself before the LORD, as H3665
23 his father had **h** himself; but Amon H3665
36:12 his God, *and* **h** not himself before H3665
Ps 35:13 *was* sackcloth: I **h** my soul with fasting; H6031
Isa 2:11 The lofty looks of man shall be **h**, and H8213
5:15 man shall be **h**, and the eyes of the H8213
15 and the eyes of the lofty shall be **h**: H8213
10:33 hewn down, and the haughty shall be **h**. H8213
Jer 44:10 They are not **h** *even* unto this day, H1792
Lam 3:20 still in remembrance, and is **h** in me. H7743
Ezk 22:10 **h** her that was set apart for pollution. H6031
11 hath **h** his sister, his father's daughter. H6031
Dan 5:22 hast not **h** thine heart, though H8214
Php 2: 8 as a man, he **h** himself, and became *G5013*

HUMBLEDST

2Ch 34:27 thereof, and **h** thyself before me, and H3665

HUMBLENESS

Col 3:12 **h** of mind, meekness, longsuffering; *G5012*

HUMBLETH

1Ki 21:29 Seest thou how Ahab **h** himself before H3665
29 me? because he **h** himself before me, H3665
Ps 10:10 He croucheth, *and* **h** himself, that the H7817
113: 6 Who **h** *himself* to behold *the things* H8213
Isa 2: 9 **h** himself: therefore forgive them not. H8213
Lk 14:11 and he that **h** himself shall be exalted. *G5013*
18:14 and he that **h** himself shall be exalted. *G5013*

HUMBLY

2Sa 16: 4 And Ziba said, I **h** beseech thee *that* I H7812
Mic 6: 8 mercy, and to walk **h** with thy God? H6800

HUMILIATION

Act 8:33 In his **h** his judgment was taken away: *G5014*

HUMILITY

Prv 15:33 of wisdom; and before honour *is* **h**. H6038
18:12 man is haughty, and before honour *is* **h**. H6038
22: 4 By **h** *and* the fear of the LORD *are* H6038
Act 20:19 Serving the Lord with all **h** of mind, *G5012*
Col 2:18 in a voluntary **h** and worshipping of *G5012*
23 in will worship, and **h**, and neglecting of *G5012*
1Pt 5: 5 be clothed with **h**: for God resisteth the *G5012*

HUMTAH

Jos 15:54 And **H**, and Kirjath-arba, which *is* H2547

HUNDRED

Gen 5: 3 And Adam lived an **h** and thirty years, H3967
4 Seth were eight **h** years: and he begat H3967
5 nine **h** and thirty years: and he died. H3967
6 And Seth lived an **h** and five years, and H3967
7 he begat Enos eight **h** and seven years, H3967
8 And all the days of Seth were nine **h** H3967
10 Cainan eight **h** and fifteen years, and H3967
11 And all the days of Enos were nine **h** H3967
13 Mahalaleel eight **h** and forty years, and H3967
14 And all the days of Cainan were nine **h** H3967
16 he begat Jared eight **h** and thirty years, H3967
17 **h** ninety and five years: and he died. H3967
18 And Jared lived an **h** sixty and two H3967
19 **h** years, and begat sons and daughters: H3967
20 And all the days of Jared were nine **h** H3967
22 **h** years, and begat sons and daughters: H3967
23 And all the days of Enoch were three **h** H3967
25 And Methuselah lived an **h** eighty and H3967
26 Lamech seven **h** eighty and two years, H3967
27 **h** sixty and nine years: and he died. H3967
28 And Lamech lived an **h** eighty and two H3967
30 he begat Noah five **h** ninety and five H3967
31 **h** seventy and seven years: and he died. H3967
32 And Noah was five **h** years old: and H3967
6: 3 days shall be an **h** and twenty years. H3967
15 ark *shall be* three **h** cubits, the breadth H3967
7: 6 And Noah *was* six **h** years old when the H3967
24 upon the earth an **h** and fifty days. H3967
8: 3 after the end of the **h** and fifty days the H3967
9:28 And Noah lived after the flood three **h** H3967
29 And all the days of Noah were nine **h** H3967
11:10 Shem *was* an **h** years old, and begat H3967
11 **h** years, and begat sons and daughters. H3967
13 begat Salah four **h** and three years, and H3967
15 he begat Eber four **h** and three years, H3967
17 begat Peleg four **h** and thirty years, and H3967
19 he begat Reu two **h** and nine years, and H3967
21 begat Serug two **h** and seven years, and H3967
23 **h** years, and begat sons and daughters. H3967
25 after he begat Terah an **h** and nineteen H3967
32 And the days of Terah were two **h** and H3967
14:14 own house, three **h** and eighteen, and H3967
15:13 and they shall afflict them four **h** years; H3967
17:17 him that is an **h** years old? and shall H3967
21: 5 And Abraham was an **h** years old, H3967
23: 1 And Sarah was an **h** and seven and H3967
15 land *is worth* four **h** shekels of silver; H3967
16 sons of Heth, four **h** shekels of silver, H3967
25: 7 lived, an **h** threescore and fifteen years. H3967
17 the life of Ishmael, an **h** and thirty and H3967
32: 6 to meet thee, and four **h** men with him. H3967
14 Two **h** she goats, and twenty he goats, H3967
14 he goats, two **h** ewes, and twenty rams, H3967
33: 1 and with him four **h** men. And he H3967
19 father, for an **h** pieces of money. H3967
35:28 And the days of Isaac were an **h** and H3967
45:22 he gave three **h** *pieces* of silver, and H3967

Gen 47: 9 pilgrimage *are* an **h** and thirty years: H3967
28 Jacob was an **h** forty and seven years. H3967
50:22 and Joseph lived an **h** and ten years. H3967
26 So Joseph died, *being* an **h** and ten H3967
Ex 6:16 Levi *were* an **h** thirty and seven years. H3967
18 *were* an **h** thirty and three years. H3967
20 *were* an **h** and thirty and seven years. H3967
12:37 Succoth, about six **h** thousand on foot H3967
40 in Egypt, *was* four **h** and thirty years. H3967
41 the end of the four **h** and thirty years, H3967
14: 7 And he took six **h** chosen chariots, and H3967
27: 9 linen of an **h** cubits long for one side: H3967
11 *be* hangings of an **h** *cubits* long, and H3967
18 The length of the court *shall be* an **h** H3967
30:23 of pure myrrh five **h** *shekels,* and of H3967
23 so much, *even* two **h** and fifty *shekels,* H3967
23 sweet calamus two **h** and fifty *shekels,* H3967
24 And of cassia five **h** *shekels,* after the H3967
38: 9 *were of* fine twined linen, an **h** cubits: H3967
11 *hangings were* an **h** cubits, their pillars H3967
24 talents, and seven **h** and thirty shekels, H3967
25 *was* an **h** talents, and a thousand H3967
25 a thousand seven **h** and threescore and H3967
26 upward, for six **h** thousand and three H3967
26 thousand and five **h** and fifty *men.* H3967
27 And of the **h** talents of silver were cast H3967
27 of the vail; an **h** sockets of the hundred H3967
27 of the **h** talents, a talent for a socket. H3967
28 And of the thousand seven **h** seventy H3967
29 and two thousand and four **h** shekels. H3967
Lev 26: 8 And five of you shall chase an **h**, and an H3967
8 hundred, and an **h** of you shall put ten H3967
Nu 1:21 *were* forty and six thousand and five **h**. H3967
23 fifty and nine thousand and three **h**. H3967
25 forty and five thousand six **h** and fifty. H3967
27 and fourteen thousand and six **h**. H3967
29 fifty and four thousand and four **h**. H3967
31 fifty and seven thousand and four **h**. H3967
33 *were* forty thousand and five **h**. H3967
35 thirty and two thousand and two **h**. H3967
37 thirty and five thousand and four **h**. H3967
39 and two thousand and seven **h**. H3967
41 *were* forty and one thousand and five **h**. H3967
43 fifty and three thousand and four **h**. H3967
46 were six **h** thousand and three H3967
46 three thousand and five **h** and fifty. H3967
2: 4 and fourteen thousand and six **h**. H3967
6 fifty and four thousand and four **h**. H3967
8 fifty and seven thousand and four **h**. H3967
9 camp of Judah *were* an **h** thousand and H3967
9 and four **h**, throughout their armies. H3967
11 *were* forty and six thousand and five **h**. H3967
13 fifty and nine thousand and three **h**. H3967
15 and five thousand and six **h** and fifty. H3967
16 Reuben *were* an **h** thousand and fifty H3967
16 and four **h** and fifty, throughout H3967
19 of them, *were* forty thousand and five **h**. H3967
21 thirty and two thousand and two **h**. H3967
23 thirty and five thousand and four **h**. H3967
24 Ephraim *were* an **h** thousand and eight H3967
24 thousand and an **h**, throughout their H3967
26 and two thousand and seven **h**. H3967
28 *were* forty and one thousand and five **h**. H3967
30 fifty and three thousand and four **h**. H3967
31 of Dan *were* an **h** thousand and fifty H3967
31 seven thousand and six **h**. They shall go H3967
32 hosts *were* six **h** thousand and three H3967
32 three thousand and five **h** and fifty. H3967
3:22 them *were* seven thousand and five **h**. H3967
28 **h**, keeping the charge of the sanctuary. H3967
34 upward, *were* six thousand and two **h**. H3967
43 two **h** and threescore and thirteen. H3967
46 of the two **h** and threescore and H3967
50 a thousand three **h** and threescore and H3967
4:36 were two thousand seven **h** and fifty. H3967
40 two thousand and six **h** and thirty. H3967
44 were three thousand and two **h**. H3967
48 thousand and five **h** and fourscore. H3967
7:13 thereof *was* an **h** and thirty *shekels,* H3967
19 whereof *was* an **h** and thirty *shekels,* H3967
25 whereof *was* an **h** and thirty *shekels,* H3967
31 of the weight of an **h** and thirty *shekels,* H3967
37 whereof *was* an **h** and thirty *shekels,* H3967
43 of the weight of an **h** and thirty *shekels,* H3967
49 whereof *was* an **h** and thirty *shekels,* H3967
55 of the weight of an **h** and thirty *shekels,* H3967
61 whereof *was* an **h** and thirty *shekels,* H3967
67 whereof *was* an **h** and thirty *shekels,* H3967
73 whereof *was* an **h** and thirty *shekels,* H3967

Nu 7:79 whereof *was* an **h** and thirty *shekels,* H3967
85 Each charger of silver *weighing* an **h** H3967
85 and four **h** *shekels,* after the shekel H3967
86 spoons *was* an **h** and twenty *shekels.* H3967
11:21 I *am, are* six **h** thousand footmen; H3967
16: 2 of Israel, two **h** and fifty princes of H3967
17 his censer, two **h** and fifty censers; thou H3967
35 **h** and fifty men that offered incense. H3967
49 and seven **h**, beside them that died H3967
26: 7 three thousand and seven **h** and thirty. H3967
10 fire devoured two **h** and fifty men: and H3967
14 twenty and two thousand and two **h**. H3967
18 of them, forty thousand and five **h**. H3967
22 and sixteen thousand and five **h**. H3967
25 and four thousand and three **h**. H3967
27 them, threescore thousand and five **h**. H3967
34 fifty and two thousand and seven **h**. H3967
37 thousand and five **h**. These *are* the sons H3967
41 *were* forty and five thousand and six **h**. H3967
43 and four thousand and four **h**. H3967
47 fifty and three thousand and four **h**. H3967
50 forty and five thousand and four **h**. H3967
51 children of Israel, six **h** thousand and a H3967
51 and a thousand seven **h** and thirty. H3967
31:28 one soul of five **h**, *both* of the persons, H3967
32 had caught, was six **h** thousand and H3967
36 in number three **h** thousand and seven H3967
36 and thirty thousand and five **h** sheep: H3967
37 was six **h** and threescore and fifteen. H3967
39 thirty thousand and five **h**; of which the H3967
43 was three **h** thousand and thirty H3967
43 *and* seven thousand and five **h** sheep, H3967
45 And thirty thousand asses and five **h**, H3967
52 thousand seven **h** and fifty shekels. H3967
33:39 And Aaron *was* an **h** and twenty and H3967
Dt 22:19 And they shall amerce him in an **h** H3967
31: 2 And he said unto them, I *am* an **h** and H3967
34: 7 And Moses *was* an **h** and twenty years H3967
Jos 7:21 garment, and two **h** shekels of silver, H3967
24:29 died, *being* an **h** and ten years old. H3967
32 of Shechem for an **h** pieces of silver: H3967
Jdg 2: 8 died, *being* an **h** and ten years old. H3967
3:31 of the Philistines six **h** men with an ox H3967
4: 3 for he had nine **h** chariots of iron; and H3967
13 *even* nine **h** chariots of iron, and H3967
7: 6 mouth, were three **h** men: but all the H3967
7 By the three **h** men that lapped will H3967
8 those three **h** men: and the host of H3967
16 And he divided the three **h** men *into* H3967
19 So Gideon, and the **h** men that *were* H3967
22 And the three **h** blew the trumpets, and H3967
8: 4 he, and the three **h** men that *were* with H3967
10 for there fell an **h** and twenty thousand H3967
26 and seven **h** *shekels* of gold; beside H3967
11:26 of Arnon, three **h** years? why therefore H3967
15: 4 And Samson went and caught three **h** H3967
16: 5 every one of us eleven **h** *pieces* of silver. H3967
17: 2 The eleven **h** *shekels* of silver that H3967
3 And when he had restored the eleven **h** H3967
4 his mother took two **h** *shekels* of silver, H3967
18:11 **h** men appointed with weapons of war. H3967
16 And the six **h** men appointed with their H3967
17 the gate with the six **h** men *that were* H3967
20: 2 **h** thousand footmen that drew sword. H3967
10 And we will take ten men of an **h** H3967
10 of Israel, and an **h** of a thousand, and H3967
15 were numbered seven **h** chosen men. H3967
16 people *there were* seven **h** chosen men H3967
17 numbered four **h** thousand men that H3967
35 an **h** men: all these drew the sword. H3967
47 But six **h** men turned and fled to the H3967
21:12 Jabesh-gilead four **h** young virgins, that H3967
1Sa 11: 8 Israel were three **h** thousand, and the H3967
13:15 present with him, about six **h** men. H3967
14: 2 *were* with him *were* about six **h** men; H3967
15: 4 in Telaim, two **h** thousand footmen, H3967
17: 7 head *weighed* six **h** shekels of iron: and H3967
18:25 any dowry, but an **h** foreskins of the H3967
27 of the Philistines two **h** men; and David H3967
22: 2 there were with him about four **h** men. H3967
23:13 *were* about six **h**, arose and departed H3967
25:13 after David about four **h** men; and two H3967
13 men; and two **h** abode by the stuff. H3967
18 and took two **h** loaves, and two bottles H3967
18 *corn,* and an **h** clusters of raisins, and H3967
18 **h** cakes of figs, and laid *them* on asses. H3967
27: 2 over with the six **h** men that *were* with H3967
30: 9 So David went, he and the six **h** men H3967
10 But David pursued, he and four **h** men: H3967

1Sa 30:10 men: for two **h** abode behind, which H3967
17 of them, save four **h** young men, which H3967
21 And David came to the two **h** men, H3967
2Sa 2:31 *that* three **h** and threescore men died. H3967
3:14 me for an **h** foreskins of the Philistines. H3967
8: 4 and seven **h** horsemen, and twenty H3967
4 but reserved of them *for* an **h** chariots. H3967
10:18 slew *the men of* seven **h** chariots of the H3967
14:26 at two **h** shekels after the king's weight. H3967
15:11 And with Absalom went two **h** men out H3967
18 all the Gittites, six **h** men which came H3967
16: 1 upon them two **h** *loaves* of bread, and H3967
1 of bread, and an **h** bunches of raisins, H3967
1 of raisins, and an **h** of summer fruits, H3967
21:16 *weighed* three **h** *shekels* of brass in H3967
23: 8 eight **h**, whom he slew at one time. H3967
18 against three **h**, *and* slew *them,* and H3967
24: 9 in Israel eight **h** thousand valiant men H3967
9 of Judah *were* five **h** thousand men. H3967
1Ki 4:23 pastures, and an **h** sheep, beside harts, H3967
5:16 and three **h**, which ruled over the H3967
6: 1 And it came to pass in the four **h** and H3967
7: 2 length thereof *was* an **h** cubits, and the H3967
20 *were* two **h** in rows round about H3967
42 And four **h** pomegranates for the two H3967
8:63 oxen, and an **h** and twenty thousand H3967
9:23 work, five **h** and fifty, which bare H3967
28 thence gold, four **h** and twenty talents, H3967
10:10 And she gave the king an **h** and twenty H3967
14 six **h** threescore and six talents of gold, H3967
16 And king Solomon made two **h** targets H3967
16 six **h** *shekels* of gold went to one target. H3967
17 And *he made* three **h** shields *of* beaten H3967
26 and four **h** chariots, and twelve H3967
29 of Egypt for six **h** *shekels* of silver, and H3967
29 an horse for an **h** and fifty: and so for H3967
11: 3 And he had seven **h** wives, princesses, H3967
3 and three **h** concubines: and his H3967
12:21 tribe of Benjamin, an **h** and fourscore H3967
18: 4 Obadiah took an **h** prophets, and hid H3967
13 how I hid an **h** men of the LORD'S H3967
19 of Baal four **h** and fifty, and the H3967
19 four **h**, which eat at Jezebel's table. H3967
22 prophets *are* four **h** and fifty men. H3967
20:15 and they were two **h** and thirty two: H3967
29 an **h** thousand footmen in one day. H3967
22: 6 about four **h** men, and said unto H3967
2Ki 3: 4 the king of Israel an **h** thousand lambs, H3967
4 an **h** thousand rams, with the wool. H3967
26 took with him seven **h** men that drew H3967
4:43 I set this before an **h** men? He said H3967
14:13 unto the corner gate, four **h** cubits. H3967
18:14 of Judah three **h** talents of silver and H3967
19:35 the Assyrians an **h** fourscore and five H3967
23:33 **h** talents of silver, and a talent of gold. H3967
1Ch 4:42 of Simeon, five **h** men, went to mount H3967
5:18 thousand seven **h** and threescore, that H3967
21 and of sheep two **h** and fifty thousand, H3967
21 thousand, and of men an **h** thousand. H3967
7: 2 two and twenty thousand and six **h**. H3967
9 valour, *was* twenty thousand and two **h**. H3967
11 thousand and two **h** *soldiers,* fit to go H3967
8:40 and sons' sons, an **h** and fifty. All these H3967
9: 6 and their brethren, six **h** and ninety. H3967
9 generations, nine **h** and fifty and six. H3967
13 and seven **h** and threescore; very H3967
22 the gates *were* two **h** and twelve. These H3967
11:11 three **h** slain *by him* at one time. H3967
20 against three **h**, he slew *them,* and had H3967
12:14 an **h**, and the greatest over a thousand. H3967
24 and eight **h**, ready armed to the war. H3967
25 for the war, seven thousand and one **h**. H3967
26 of Levi four thousand and six **h**. H3967
27 him *were* three thousand and seven **h**; H3967
30 and eight **h**, mighty men of valour, H3967
32 heads of them *were* two **h**; and all their H3967
35 twenty and eight thousand and six **h**. H3967
37 the battle, an **h** and twenty thousand. H3967
15: 5 and his brethren an **h** and twenty: H3967
6 and his brethren two **h** and twenty: H3967
7 chief, and his brethren an **h** and thirty: H3967
8 the chief, and his brethren two **h**: H3967
10 and his brethren an **h** and twelve. H3967
18: 4 but reserved of them an **h** chariots. H3967
21: 3 his people an **h** times so many more H3967
5 thousand and an **h** thousand men that H3967
5 Judah *was* four **h** threescore and ten H3967
25 place six **h** shekels of gold by weight. H3967
22:14 of the LORD an **h** thousand talents of H3967

1Ch 25: 7 was two **h** fourscore and eight. H3967
26:30 and seven **h**, *were* officers among H3967
32 and seven **h** chief fathers, whom H3967
29: 7 and one **h** thousand talents of iron. H3967
2Ch 1:14 and four **h** chariots, and twelve H3967
17 a chariot for six **h** *shekels* of silver, and H3967
17 and an horse for an **h** and fifty: and so H3967
2: 2 thousand and six **h** to oversee them. H3967
17 were found an **h** and fifty thousand H3967
17 thousand and three thousand and six **h**. H3967
18 six **h** overseers to set the people a work. H3967
3: 4 the height *was* an **h** and twenty: and he H3967
8 fine gold, *amounting* to six **h** talents. H3967
16 and made an **h** pomegranates, and H3967
4: 8 left. And he made an **h** basons of gold. H3967
13 And four **h** pomegranates on the two H3967
5:12 and with them an **h** and twenty priests H3967
7: 5 oxen, and an **h** and twenty thousand H3967
8:10 officers, *even* two **h** and fifty, that bare H3967
18 took thence four **h** and fifty talents of H3967
9: 9 And she gave the king an **h** and twenty H3967
13 one year was six **h** and threescore and H3967
15 And king Solomon made two **h** targets H3967
15 *of* beaten gold: six **h** *shekels* of beaten H3967
16 And three **h** shields *made he of* beaten H3967
16 *of* beaten gold: three **h** *shekels* of gold H3967
11: 1 and Benjamin an **h** and fourscore H3967
12: 3 With twelve **h** chariots, and threescore H3967
13: 3 of war, *even* four **h** thousand chosen H3967
3 him with eight **h** thousand chosen H3967
17 of Israel five **h** thousand chosen men. H3967
14: 8 out of Judah three **h** thousand; and out H3967
8 and drew bows, two **h** and fourscore H3967
9 **h** chariots; and came unto Mareshah. H3967
15:11 **h** oxen and seven thousand sheep. H3967
17:11 and seven **h** rams, and seven thousand H3967
11 seven thousand and seven **h** he goats. H3967
14 men of valour three **h** thousand. H3967
15 him two **h** and fourscore thousand. H3967
16 two **h** thousand mighty men of valour. H3967
17 with bow and shield two **h** thousand. H3967
18 and with him an **h** and fourscore H3967
18: 5 of prophets four **h** men, and said unto H3967
24:15 when he died; an **h** and thirty years old H3967
25: 5 found them three **h** thousand choice H3967
6 He hired also an **h** thousand mighty H3967
6 out of Israel for an **h** talents of silver. H3967
9 shall we do for the **h** talents which I H3967
23 to the corner gate, four **h** cubits. H3967
26:12 of valour *were* two thousand and six **h**. H3967
13 an army, three **h** thousand and seven H3967
13 thousand and five **h**, that made war H3967
27: 5 the same year an **h** talents of silver, H3967
28: 6 slew in Judah an **h** and twenty H3967
8 their brethren two **h** thousand, women, H3967
29:32 and ten bullocks, an **h** rams, *and* two H3967
32 rams, *and* two **h** lambs: all these *were* H3967
33 And the consecrated things *were* six **h** H3967
35: 8 **h** *small cattle,* and three hundred oxen. H3967
8 hundred *small cattle,* and three **h** oxen. H3967
9 thousand *small cattle,* and five **h** oxen. H3967
36: 3 **h** talents of silver and a talent of gold. H3967
Ezr 1:10 a second *sort* four **h** and ten, *and* other H3967
11 and four **h**. All *these* did Sheshbazzar H3967
2: 3 two thousand an **h** seventy and two. H3967
4 The children of Shephatiah, three **h** H3967
5 The children of Arah, seven **h** seventy H3967
6 Joab, two thousand eight **h** and twelve. H3967
7 Elam, a thousand two **h** fifty and four. H3967
8 The children of Zattu, nine **h** forty and H3967
9 The children of Zaccai, seven **h** and H3967
10 The children of Bani, six **h** forty and H3967
11 The children of Bebai, six **h** twenty and H3967
12 a thousand two **h** twenty and two. H3967
13 The children of Adonikam, six **h** sixty H3967
15 The children of Adin, four **h** fifty and H3967
17 The children of Bezai, three **h** twenty H3967
18 The children of Jorah, an **h** and twelve. H3967
19 The children of Hashum, two **h** twenty H3967
21 The children of Beth-lehem, an **h** H3967
23 The men of Anathoth, an **h** twenty and H3967
25 Beeroth, seven **h** and forty and three. H3967
26 The children of Ramah and Gaba, six **h** H3967
27 The men of Michmas, an **h** twenty and H3967
28 The men of Beth-el and Ai, two **h** H3967
30 The children of Magbish, an **h** fifty and H3967
31 Elam, a thousand two **h** fifty and four. H3967
32 The children of Harim, three **h** and H3967
33 and Ono, seven **h** twenty and five. H3967

Ezr 2:34 The children of Jericho, three **h** forty H3967
35 three thousand and six **h** and thirty. H3967
36 of Jeshua, nine **h** seventy and three. H3967
38 a thousand two **h** forty and seven. H3967
41 of Asaph, an **h** twenty and eight. H3967
42 of Shobai, *in* all an **h** thirty and nine. H3967
58 servants, *were* three **h** ninety and two. H3967
60 children of Nekoda, six **h** fifty and two. H3967
64 two thousand three **h** *and* threescore, H3967
65 thousand three **h** thirty and seven: and H3967
65 two **h** singing men and singing women. H3967
66 Their horses *were* seven **h** thirty and H3967
66 six; their mules, two **h** forty and five; H3967
67 Their camels, four **h** thirty and five; H3967
67 six thousand seven **h** and twenty. H3967
69 of silver, and one **h** priests' garments. H3967
6:17 this house of God an **h** bullocks, two H3969
17 bullocks, two **h** rams, four hundred H3969
17 rams, four **h** lambs; and for a sin H3969
7:22 Unto an **h** talents of silver, and to an H3969
22 silver, and to an **h** measures of wheat, H3969
22 wheat, and to an **h** baths of wine, and H3969
22 of wine, and to an **h** baths of oil, and H3969
8: 3 genealogy of the males an **h** and fifty. H3967
4 of Zerahiah, and with him two **h** males. H3967
5 Jahaziel, and with him three **h** males. H3967
9 with him two **h** and eighteen males. H3967
10 with him an **h** and threescore males. H3967
12 and with him an **h** and ten males. H3967
20 service of the Levites, two **h** and twenty H3967
26 I even weighed unto their hand six **h** H3967
26 silver vessels an **h** talents, *and* of gold H3967
26 talents, *and* of gold an **h** talents; H3967
Neh 5:17 Moreover *there were* at my table an **h** H3967
7: 8 two thousand an **h** seventy and two. H3967
9 The children of Shephatiah, three **h** H3967
10 The children of Arah, six **h** fifty and H3967
11 thousand and eight **h** *and* eighteen. H3967
12 Elam, a thousand two **h** fifty and four. H3967
13 The children of Zattu, eight **h** forty and H3967
14 The children of Zaccai, seven **h** and H3967
15 The children of Binnui, six **h** forty and H3967
16 The children of Bebai, six **h** twenty and H3967
17 two thousand three **h** twenty and two. H3967
18 The children of Adonikam, six **h**. H3967
20 The children of Adin, six **h** fifty and H3967
22 The children of Hashum, three **h** H3967
23 The children of Bezai, three **h** twenty H3967
24 The children of Hariph, an **h** and H3967
26 Netophah, an **h** fourscore and eight. H3967
27 The men of Anathoth, an **h** twenty and H3967
29 and Beeroth, seven **h** forty and three. H3967
30 The men of Ramah and Geba, six **h** H3967
31 The men of Michmas, an **h** and twenty H3967
32 The men of Beth-el and Ai, an **h** twenty H3967
34 Elam, a thousand two **h** fifty and four. H3967
35 The children of Harim, three **h** and H3967
36 The children of Jericho, three **h** forty H3967
37 and Ono, seven **h** twenty and one. H3967
38 three thousand nine **h** and thirty. H3967
39 of Jeshua, nine **h** seventy and three. H3967
41 a thousand two **h** forty and seven. H3967
44 children of Asaph, an **h** forty and eight. H3967
45 of Shobai, an **h** thirty and eight. H3967
60 servants, *were* three **h** ninety and two. H3967
62 of Nekoda, six **h** forty and two. H3967
66 two thousand three **h** and threescore, H3967
67 thousand three **h** thirty and seven: and H3967
67 and they had two **h** forty and five H3967
68 Their horses, seven **h** thirty and six: H3967
68 six: their mules, two **h** forty and five: H3967
69 *Their* camels, four **h** thirty and five: six H3967
69 six thousand seven **h** and twenty asses. H3967
70 five **h** and thirty priests' garments. H3967
71 thousand and two **h** pound of silver. H3967
11: 6 **h** threescore and eight valiant men. H3967
8 And after him Gabbai, Sallai, nine **h** H3967
12 the house *were* eight **h** twenty and two: H3967
13 of the fathers, two **h** forty and two: and H3967
14 men of valour, an **h** twenty and eight: H3967
18 city *were* two **h** fourscore and four. H3967
19 the gates, *were* an **h** seventy and two. H3967
Est 1: 1 an **h** and seven and twenty provinces:) H3967
4 days, *even* an **h** and fourscore days. H3967
8: 9 unto Ethiopia, an **h** twenty and seven H3967
9: 6 Jews slew and destroyed five **h** men. H3967
12 and destroyed five **h** men in Shushan H3967
15 and slew three **h** men at Shushan; but H3967
30 all the Jews, to the **h** twenty and seven H3967

Job 1: 3 camels, and five **h** yoke of oxen, and H3967
3 of oxen, and five **h** she asses, and a H3967
42:16 After this lived Job an **h** and forty H3967
Prv 17:10 wise man than an **h** stripes into a fool. H3967
Ecc 6: 3 If a man beget an **h** *children*, and live H3967
8:12 Though a sinner do evil an **h** times, H3967
Song 8:12 those that keep the fruit thereof two **h**. H3967
Isa 37:36 of the Assyrians a **h** and fourscore and H3967
65:20 child shall die an **h** years old; but the H3967
20 *being* an **h** years old shall be accursed. H3967
Jer 52:23 the network *were* an **h** round about. H3967
29 eight **h** thirty and two persons: H3967
30 of the Jews seven **h** forty and five H3967
30 persons *were* four thousand and six **h**. H3967
Ezk 4: 5 of the days, three **h** and ninety days: so H3967
9 thy side, three **h** and ninety days shalt H3967
40:19 an **h** cubits eastward and northward. H3967
23 from gate to gate an **h** cubits. H3967
27 to gate toward the south an **h** cubits. H3967
47 So he measured the court, an **h** cubits H3967
47 cubits long, and an **h** cubits broad, H3967
41:13 So he measured the house, an **h** cubits H3967
13 with the walls thereof, an **h** cubits long; H3967
14 place toward the east, an **h** cubits. H3967
15 on the other side, an **h** cubits, with the H3967
42: 2 Before the length of an **h** cubits *was* the H3967
8 lo, before the temple *were* an **h** cubits. H3967
16 reed, five **h** reeds, with the measuring H520
17 He measured the north side, five **h** H3967
18 He measured the south side, five **h** H3967
19 five **h** reeds with the measuring reed. H3967
20 round about, five **h** *reeds* long, and five H3967
20 *reeds* long, and five **h** broad, to make a H3967
45: 2 the sanctuary five **h** *in length*, with five H3967
2 *in length*, with five **h** *in breadth*, square H3967
15 the flock, out of two **h**, out of the fat H3967
48:16 thousand and five **h**, and the south side H3967
16 thousand and five **h**, and on the east H3967
16 thousand and five **h**, and the west side H3967
16 the west side four thousand and five **h**. H3967
17 the north two **h** and fifty, and toward H3967
17 the south two **h** and fifty, and toward H3967
17 the east two **h** and fifty, and toward H3967
17 and toward the west two **h** and fifty. H3967
30 four thousand and five **h** measures. H3967
32 thousand and five **h**: and three gates; H3967
33 thousand and five **h** measures: and H3967
34 thousand and five **h**, *with* their three H3967
Dan 6: 1 the kingdom an **h** and twenty princes, H3969
8:14 and three **h** days; then shall the H3967
12:11 *be* a thousand two **h** and ninety days. H3967
12 three **h** and five and thirty days. H3967
Am 5: 3 shall leave an **h**, and that which went H3967
3 **h** shall leave ten, to the house of Israel. H3967
Mt 18:12 How think ye? if a man have an **h** *G1540*
28 owed him an **h** pence: and he laid *G1540*
Mk 4: 8 thirty, and some sixty, and some an **h**. *G1540*
20 thirtyfold, some sixty, and some an **h**. *G1540*
6:37 go and buy two **h** pennyworth of bread, *G1250*
14: 5 for more than three **h** pence, and have *G5145*
Lk 7:41 owed five **h** pence, and the other fifty. *G4001*
15: 4 What man of you, having an **h** sheep, if *G1540*
16: 6 And he said, An **h** measures of oil. And *G1540*
7 And he said, An **h** measures of wheat. *G1540*
Jn 6: 7 Philip answered him, Two **h** *G1250*
12: 5 three **h** pence, and given to the poor? *G5145*
19:39 and aloes, about an **h** pound *weight*. *G1540*
21: 8 **h** cubits,) dragging the net with fishes. *G1250*
11 of great fishes, an **h** and fifty and three: *G1540*
Act 1:15 together were about an **h** and twenty,) *G1540*
5:36 men, about four **h**, joined themselves: *G5071*
7: 6 and entreat *them* evil four **h** years. *G5071*
13:20 the space of four **h** and fifty years, until *G5071*
23:23 Make ready two **h** soldiers to go to *G1250*
23 two **h**, at the third hour of the night; *G1250*
27:37 And we were in all in the ship two **h** *G1250*
Ro 4:19 he was about an **h** years old, neither *G1541*
1Co 15: 6 After that, he was seen of above five **h** *G4001*
Gal 3:17 which was four **h** and thirty years after, *G5071*
Rev 7: 4 *were* sealed an **h** *and* forty *and* four *G1540*
9:16 *were* two **h** thousand thousand: *G3461*
11: 3 a thousand two **h** *and* threescore days, *G1250*
12: 6 a thousand two **h** *and* threescore days. *G1250*
13:18 his number *is* Six **h** threescore *and* six. *G1812*
14: 1 Sion, and with him an **h** forty *and* four *G1540*
3 that song but the **h** *and* forty *and* four *G1540*
20 space of a thousand *and* six **h** furlongs. *G1812*
21:17 And he measured the wall thereof, an **h** *G1540*

HUNDREDFOLD
Gen 26:12 **h**: and the LORD blessed him. H3967+H8180
2Sa 24: 3 they be, an **h**, and that the eyes H3967+H6471
Mt 13: 8 an **h**, some sixtyfold, some thirtyfold. *G1540*
23 some an **h**, some sixty, some thirty. *G1540*
19:29 an **h**, and shall inherit everlasting life. *G1542*
Mk 10:30 But he shall receive an **h** now in this *G1542*
Lk 8: 8 and bare fruit an **h**. And when he had *G1542*

HUNDREDS
Ex 18:21 of **h**, rulers of fifties, and rulers of tens: H3967
25 of **h**, rulers of fifties, and rulers of tens. H3967
Nu 31:14 over **h**, which came from the battle. H3967
48 captains of **h**, came near unto Moses: H3967
52 and of the captains of **h**, was sixteen H3967
54 thousands and of **h**, and brought it into H3967
Dt 1:15 and captains over **h**, and captains over H3967
1Sa 22: 7 of thousands, and captains of **h**; H3967
29: 2 passed on by **h**, and by thousands: but H3967
2Sa 18: 1 and captains of **h** over them. H3967
4 came out by **h** and by thousands. H3967
2Ki 11: 4 the rulers over **h**, with the captains and H3967
9 And the captains over the **h** did H3967
10 And to the captains over **h** did the H3967
15 the captains of the **h**, the officers of the H3967
19 And he took the rulers over **h**, and the H3967
1Ch 13: 1 and **h**, *and* with every leader. H3967
26:26 thousands and **h**, and the captains of H3967
27: 1 of thousands and **h**, and their officers H3967
28: 1 captains over the **h**, and the stewards H3967
29: 6 of thousands and of **h**, with the rulers of H3967
2Ch 1: 2 thousands and of **h**, and to the judges, H3967
23: 1 the captains of **h**, Azariah the son of H3967
9 to the captains of **h** spears, and H3967
14 the captains of **h** that were set over the H3967
20 And he took the captains of **h**, and the H3967
25: 5 and captains over **h**, according to the H3967
Mk 6:40 And they sat down in ranks, by **h**, and *G1540*

HUNDREDTH
Gen 7:11 In the six **h** year of Noah's life, in the H3967
8:13 And it came to pass in the six **h** and H3967
Neh 5:11 houses, also the **h** *part* of the money, H3967

HUNG See HANGED.

HUNGER
Ex 16: 3 to kill this whole assembly with **h**. H7458
Dt 8: 3 suffered thee to **h**, and fed thee with H7456
28:48 against thee, in **h**, and in thirst, and in H7458
32:24 *They shall be* burnt with **h**, and H7458
Neh 9:15 heaven for their **h**, and broughtest forth H7458
Ps 34:10 The young lions do lack, and suffer **h**: H7456
Prv 19:15 sleep; and an idle soul shall suffer **h**. H7456
Isa 49:10 They shall not **h** nor thirst; neither H7456
Jer 38: 9 he is like to die for **h** in the place where H7458
42:14 **h** of bread; and there will we dwell: H7456
Lam 2:19 faint for **h** in the top of every street. H7458
4: 9 *they that be* slain with **h**: for these pine H7458
Ezk 34:29 consumed with **h** in the land, neither H7458
Mt 5: 6 Blessed *are* they which do **h** and thirst *G3983*
Lk 6:21 Blessed *are ye* that **h** now: for ye shall *G3983*
25 full! for ye shall **h**. Woe unto you that *G3983*
15:17 and to spare, and I perish with **h**! *G3042*
Jn 6:35 cometh to me shall never **h**; and he that *G3983*
Ro 12:20 Therefore if thine enemy **h**, feed him; if *G3983*
1Co 4:11 Even unto this present hour we both **h**, *G3983*
11:34 And if any man **h**, let him eat at home; *G3983*
2Co 11:27 often, in **h** and thirst, in fastings *G3042*
Rev 6: 8 sword, and with **h**, and with death, and *G3042*
7:16 They shall **h** no more, neither thirst *G3983*

HUNGER-BITTEN
Job 18:12 His strength shall be **h**, and destruction H7457

HUNGERED
Mt 21:18 as he returned into the city, he **h**. *G3983*
Lk 4: 2 when they were ended, he afterward **h**. *G3983*

HUNGRED
Mt 4: 2 and forty nights, he was afterward an **h**. *G3983*
12: 1 disciples were an **h**, and began to pluck *G3983*
3 was an **h**, and they that were with him; *G3983*
25:35 For I was an **h**, and ye gave me meat: I *G3983*
37 when saw we thee an **h**, and fed *thee*? or *G3983*
42 For I was an **h**, and ye gave me no *G3983*
44 when saw we thee an **h**, or athirst, or a *G3983*
Mk 2:25 an **h**, he, and they that were with him? *G3983*
Lk 6: 3 an **h**, and they which were with him; *G3983*

HUNGRY
1Sa 2: 5 and *they that were* **h** ceased: so that the H7457
2Sa 17:29 said, The people *is* **h**, and weary, and H7457
2Ki 7:12 know that we *be* **h**; therefore are they H7457
Job 5: 5 Whose harvest the **h** eateth up, and H7457
22: 7 thou hast withholden bread from the **h**. H7457
24:10 they take away the sheaf *from* the **h**; H7457
Ps 50:12 If I were **h**, I would not tell thee: for the H7456
107: 5 **H** and thirsty, their soul fainted in H7457
9 and filleth the **h** soul with goodness. H7457
36 And there he maketh the **h** to dwell, H7457
146: 7 the **h**. The LORD looseth the prisoners: H7457
Prv 6:30 he steal to satisfy his soul when he is **h**; H7456
25:21 If thine enemy be **h**, give him bread to H7457
27: 7 to the **h** soul every bitter thing is sweet. H7457
Isa 8:21 bestead and **h**: and it shall come to H7457
21 that when they shall be **h**, they shall fret H7456
9:20 right hand, and be **h**; and he shall eat H7457
29: 8 It shall even be as when an **h** *man* H7457
32: 6 the soul of the **h**, and he will cause the H7457
44:12 his arms: yea, he is **h**, and his strength H7457
58: 7 *Is it* not to deal thy bread to the **h**, and H7457
10 And *if* thou draw out thy soul to the **h**, H7457
65:13 shall eat, but ye shall be **h**: behold, my H7456
Ezk 18: 7 his bread to the **h**, and hath covered the H7457
16 his bread to the **h**, and hath covered the H7457
Mk 11:12 were come from Bethany, he was **h**: *G3983*
Lk 1:53 He hath filled the **h** with good things; *G3983*
Act 10:10 And he became very **h**, and would have *G4361*
1Co 11:21 and one is **h**, and another is drunken. *G3983*
Php 4:12 be **h**, both to abound and to suffer need. *G3983*

HUNT
Gen 27: 5 field to **h** *for* venison, *and* to bring *it*. H6679
1Sa 26:20 doth **h** a partridge in the mountains. H7291
Job 38:39 Wilt thou **h** the prey for the lion? or fill H6679
Ps 140:11 **h** the violent man to overthrow *him*. H6679
Prv 6:26 adulteress will **h** for the precious life. H6679
Jer 16:16 and they shall **h** them from every H6679
Lam 4:18 They **h** our steps, that we cannot go in H6679
Ezk 13:18 of every stature to **h** souls! Will ye hunt H6679
18 souls! Will ye **h** the souls of my people, H6679
20 ye there **h** the souls to make *them* H6679
20 the souls that ye **h** to make *them* fly. H6679
Mic 7: 2 **h** every man his brother with a net. H6679

HUNTED
Ezk 13:21 in your hand to be **h**; and ye shall know H4686

HUNTER
Gen 10: 9 He was a mighty **h** before the LORD: H6718
9 Nimrod the mighty **h** before the LORD. H6718
25:27 was a cunning **h**, a man of the field; and H6718
Prv 6: 5 the hand *of the* **h**, and as a bird from H6718

HUNTERS
Jer 16:16 I send for many **h**, and they shall hunt H6719

HUNTEST
1Sa 24:11 thee; yet thou **h** my soul to take it. H6658
Job 10:16 For it increaseth. Thou **h** me as a fierce H6679

HUNTETH
Lev 17:13 among you, which **h** and catcheth any H6679

HUNTING
Gen 27:30 Esau his brother came in from his **h**. H6718
Prv 12:27 which he took in **h**: but the substance of H6718

HUPHAM
Nu 26:39 of **H**, the family of the Huphamites. H2349

HUPHAMITES
Nu 26:39 of Hupham, the family of the **H**. H2350

HUPPAH
1Ch 24:13 The thirteenth to **H**, the fourteenth to H2647

HUPPIM
Gen 46:21 and Rosh, Muppim, and **H**, and Ard. H2650
1Ch 7:12 Shuppim also, and **H**, the children of Ir, H2650
15 And Machir took to wife *the sister* of **H** H2650

HUR
Ex 17:10 and **H** went up to the top of the hill. H2354
12 and Aaron and **H** stayed up his hands, H2354
24:14 Aaron and **H** *are* with you: if any H2354
31: 2 Uri, the son of **H**, of the tribe of Judah: H2354
35:30 Uri, the son of **H**, of the tribe of Judah; H2354
38:22 son of Uri, the son of **H**, of the tribe of H2354
Nu 31: 8 and Zur, and **H**, and Reba, five kings H2354
Jos 13:21 and Zur, and **H**, and Reba, *which were* H2354
1Ki 4: 8 The son of **H**, in mount Ephraim: H2354
1Ch 2:19 unto him Ephrath, which bare him **H**. H2354
20 And **H** begat Uri, and Uri begat H2354
50 of Caleb the son of **H**, the firstborn of H2354
4: 1 Hezron, and Carmi, and **H**, and Shobal. H2354
4 These *are* the sons of **H**, the firstborn of H2354
2Ch 1: 5 of Uri, the son of **H**, had made, he put H2354
Neh 3: 9 the son of **H**, the ruler of the half H2354

HURAI
1Ch 11:32 **H** of the brooks of Gaash, Abiel the H2360

HURAM
1Ch 8: 5 And Gera, and Shephuphan, and **H**. H2361
2Ch 2: 3 And Solomon sent to **H** the king of H2361
11 Then **H** the king of Tyre answered in H2361
12 **H** said moreover, Blessed *be* the LORD H2361
13 with understanding, of **H** my father's, H2361
4:11 And **H** made the pots, and the shovels, H2361
11 the basons. And **H** finished the work H2361
16 instruments, did **H** his father make to H2361
8: 2 That the cities which **H** had restored to H2361
18 And **H** sent him by the hands of his H2361
9:10 And the servants also of **H**, and the H2361
21 with the servants of **H**: every three years H2361

HURI
1Ch 5:14 Abihail the son of **H**, the son of Jaroah, H2359

HURL
Nu 35:20 But if he thrust him of hatred, or **h** at H7993

HURLETH
Job 27:21 and as a storm **h** him out of his place. H8175

HURLING
1Ch 12: 2 and the left in ***h*** stones and *shooting*

HURT
Gen 4:23 wounding, and a young man to my **h**. H2250
26:29 That thou wilt do us no **h**, as we have H7451
31: 7 but God suffered him not to **h** me. H7489
29 hand to do you **h**: but the God of your H7451
Ex 21:22 If men strive, and **h** a woman with H5062
35 And if one man's ox **h** another's, that H5062
22:10 be **h**, or driven away, no man seeing *it*: H7665
14 and it be **h**, or die, the owner thereof H7665
Nu 16:15 them, neither have I **h** one of them. H7489
Jos 24:20 turn and do you **h**, and consume you, H7489
1Sa 20:21 to thee, and no **h**; *as* the LORD liveth. H1697
24: 9 saying, Behold, David seeketh thy **h**? H7451
25: 7 were with us, we **h** them not, neither H3637
15 and we were not **h**, neither missed we H3637
2Sa 18:32 to do *thee* **h**, be as *that* young man *is*. H7451
2Ki 14:10 meddle to *thy* **h**, that thou shouldest H7451
2Ch 25:19 meddle to *thine* **h**, that thou shouldest H7451
Ezr 4:22 damage grow to the **h** of the kings? H5142
Est 9: 2 as sought their **h**: and no man could H7451
Job 35: 8 Thy wickedness *may* **h** a man as thou
Ps 15: 4 to *his own* **h**, and changeth not. H7489
35: 4 brought to confusion that devise my **h**. H7451
26 rejoice at mine **h**: let them be clothed H7451
38:12 they that seek my **h** speak mischievous H7451
41: 7 me: against me do they devise my **h**. H7451
70: 2 and put to confusion, that desire my **h**. H7451
71:13 and dishonour that seek my **h**. H7451
24 brought unto shame, that seek my **h**. H7451
105:18 Whose feet they **h** with fetters: he was H6031
Ecc 5:13 kept for the owners thereof to their **h**. H7451
8: 9 man ruleth over another to his own **h**. H7451
10: 9 Whoso removeth stones shall be **h** H6087
Isa 11: 9 They shall not **h** nor destroy in all my H7489
27: 3 *any* **h** it, I will keep it night and day. H6485
65:25 They shall not **h** nor destroy in all my H7489
Jer 6:14 They have healed also the **h** *of the* H7667
7: 6 neither walk after other gods to your **h**: H7451
8:11 For they have healed the **h** of the H7667
21 For the **h** of the daughter of my people H7667
21 of my people am I **h**; I am black; H7665
10:19 Woe is me for my **h**! my wound is H7667
24: 9 of the earth for *their* **h**, *to be* a reproach H7451
25: 6 of your hands; and I will do you no **h**. H7489
7 the works of your hands to your own **h**. H7451
38: 4 not the welfare of this people, but the **h**. H7451
Dan 3:25 and they have no **h**; and the form of the H2257
6:22 that they have not **h** me: forasmuch as H2255

Dan 6:22 before thee, O king, have I done no **h**. H2248
23 and no manner of **h** was found upon H2257
Mk 16:18 thing, it shall not **h** them; they shall lay *G984*
Lk 4:35 he came out of him, and **h** him not. *G984*
10:19 and nothing shall by any means **h** you. *G91*
Act 18:10 shall set on thee to **h** thee: for I have *G2559*
27:10 will be with **h** and much damage, *G5196*
Rev 2:11 shall not be **h** of the second death. *G91*
6: 6 and *see* thou **h** not the oil and the wine. *G91*
7: 2 it was given to **h** the earth and the sea, *G91*
3 Saying, **H** not the earth, neither the sea, *G91*
9: 4 they should not **h** the grass of the earth, *G91*
10 their power *was* to **h** men five months. *G91*
19 and had heads, and with them they do **h**. *G91*
11: 5 And if any man will **h** them, fire *G91*
5 if any man will **h** them, he must in this *G91*

HURTFUL
Ezr 4:15 city, and **h** unto kings and provinces, H5142
Ps 144:10 David his servant from the **h** sword. H7451
1Ti 6: 9 many foolish and **h** lusts, which drown *G983*

HURTING
1Sa 25:34 me back from **h** thee, except thou hadst H7489

HUSBAND
Gen 3: 6 also unto her **h** with her; and he did eat. H376
16 *be* to thy **h**, and he shall rule over thee. H376
16: 3 gave her to her **h** Abram to be his wife. H376
29:32 now therefore my **h** will love me. H376
34 this time will my **h** be joined unto me, H376
30:15 hast taken my **h**? and wouldest thou take H376
18 my **h**: and she called his name Issachar. H376
20 now will my **h** dwell with me, because H376
Ex 4:25 said, Surely a bloody **h** *art* thou to me. H2860
26 she said, A bloody **h** *thou art*, because H2860
21:22 as the woman's **h** will lay upon him; H1167
Lev 19:20 betrothed to an **h**, and not at all H376
21: 3 hath had no **h**; for her may he be defiled. H376
7 from her **h**: for he *is* holy unto his God. H376
Nu 5:13 the eyes of her **h**, and be kept close, and H376
19 instead of thy **h**, be thou free from this H376
20 instead of thy **h**, and if thou be defiled, H376
20 man have lain with thee beside thine **h**: H376
27 against her **h**, that the water that causeth H376
29 *another* instead of her **h**, and is defiled; H376
30: 6 And if she had at all an **h**, when she H376
7 And her **h** heard *it*, and held his peace at H376
8 But if her **h** disallowed her on the day H376
11 And her **h** heard *it*, and held his peace at H376
12 But if her **h** hath utterly made them void H376
12 not stand: her **h** hath made them void; H376
13 afflict the soul, her **h** may establish it, or H376
13 establish it, or her **h** may make it void. H376
14 But if her **h** altogether hold his peace at H376
Dt 21:13 and be her **h**, and she shall be thy wife. H1166
22:22 married to an **h**, then they shall both H1167
23 betrothed unto an **h**, and a man find her H376
24: 3 And *if* the latter **h** hate her, and write H376
3 **h** die, which took her *to be* his wife; H376
4 Her former **h**, which sent her away, H1167
25:11 for to deliver her **h** out of the hand of H376
28:56 be evil toward the **h** of her bosom, and H376
Jdg 13: 6 Then the woman came and told her **h**, H376
9 but Manoah her **h** *was* not with her. H376
10 and shewed her **h**, and said unto him, H376
14:15 wife, Entice thy **h**, that he may declare H376
19: 3 And her **h** arose, and went after her, to H376
20: 4 And the Levite, the **h** of the woman that H376
Ru 1: 3 And Elimelech Naomi's **h** died; and she H376
5 was left of her two sons and her **h**. H376
9 in the house of her **h**. Then she kissed H376
12 am too old to have an **h**. If I should say, I H376
12 *if* I should have an **h** also to night, and H376
2:11 the death of thine **h**: and *how* thou hast H376
1Sa 1: 8 Then said Elkanah her **h** to her, H376
22 she said unto her **h**, *I will not go up* until H376
23 And Elkanah her **h** said unto her, Do H376
2:19 with her **h** to offer the yearly sacrifice. H376
4:19 in law and her **h** were dead, she bowed H376
21 because of her father in law and her **h**. H376
25:19 after you. But she told not her **h** Nabal. H376
2Sa 3:15 **h**, *even* from Phaltiel the son of Laish. H376
16 And her **h** went with her along weeping H376
11:26 that Uriah her **h** was dead, she mourned H376
26 was dead, she mourned for her **h**. H1167
14: 5 a widow woman, and mine **h** is dead. H376
7 shall not leave to my **h** *neither* name nor H376
2Ki 4: 1 Thy servant my **h** is dead; and thou H376
2Ki 4: 9 And she said unto her **h**, Behold now, I H376
14 she hath no child, and her **h** is old. H376
22 And she called unto her **h**, and said, Send H376
26 *is it* well with thy **h**? *is it* well with the H376
Prv 12: 4 A virtuous woman *is* a crown to her **h**: H1167
31:11 The heart of her **h** doth safely trust in H1167
23 Her **h** is known in the gates, when he H1167
28 her **h** *also*, and he praiseth her. H1167
Isa 54: 5 For thy Maker *is* thine **h**; the LORD of H1166
Jer 3:20 departeth from her **h**, so have ye dealt H7453
6:11 for even the **h** with the wife shall be H376
31:32 I was an **h** unto them, saith the LORD: H1166
Ezk 16:32 *which* taketh strangers instead of her **h**! H376
45 that lotheth her **h** and her children; and H376
44:25 had no **h**, they may defile themselves. H376
Hos 2: 2 neither *am* I her **h**: let her therefore put H376
7 return to my first **h**; for then *was it* better H376
Joel 1: 8 with sackcloth for the **h** of her youth. H1167
Mt 1:16 And Jacob begat Joseph the **h** of Mary, of *G435*
19 Then Joseph her **h**, being a just *man*, and *G435*
Mk 10:12 And if a woman shall put away her **h**, *G435*
Lk 2:36 with an **h** seven years from her virginity; *G435*
16:18 away from *her* **h** committeth adultery. *G435*
Jn 4:16 Jesus saith unto her, Go, call thy **h**, and *G435*
17 and said, I have no **h**. Jesus said unto *G435*
17 her, Thou hast well said, I have no **h**: *G435*
18 hast is not thy **h**: in that saidst thou truly. *G435*
Act 5: 9 have buried thy **h** *are* at the door, and *G435*
10 carrying *her* forth, buried *her* by her **h**. *G435*
Ro 7: 2 For the woman which hath an **h** is *G5220*
2 by the law to *her* **h** so long as he liveth; *G435*
2 as he liveth; but if the **h** be dead, she is *G435*
2 dead, she is loosed from the law of *her* **h**. *G435*
3 So then if, while *her* **h** liveth, she be *G435*
3 but if her **h** be dead, she is free from *G435*
1Co 7: 2 and let every woman have her own **h**. *G435*
3 Let the **h** render unto the wife due *G435*
3 and likewise also the wife unto the **h**. *G435*
4 own body, but the **h**: and likewise also *G435*
4 likewise also the **h** hath not power of his *G435*
10 Lord, Let not the wife depart from *her* **h**: *G435*
11 be reconciled to *her* **h**: and let not the *G435*
11 and let not the **h** put away *his* wife. *G435*
13 And the woman which hath an **h** that *G435*
14 For the unbelieving **h** is sanctified by the *G435*
14 wife is sanctified by the **h**: else were your *G435*
16 thou shalt save *thy* **h**? or how knowest *G435*
34 of the world, how she may please *her* **h**. *G435*
39 the law as long as her **h** liveth; but if her *G435*
39 liveth; but if her **h** be dead, she is at *G435*
2Co 11: 2 you to one **h**, that I may present *you* *G435*
Gal 4:27 more children than she which hath an **h**. *G435*
Eph 5:23 For the **h** is the head of the wife, even as *G435*
33 and the wife *see* that she reverence *her* **h**. *G435*
1Ti 3: 2 A bishop then must be blameless, the **h** *G435*
Tit 1: 6 If any be blameless, the **h** of one wife, *G435*
Rev 21: 2 prepared as a bride adorned for her **h**. *G435*

HUSBANDMAN
Gen 9:20 And Noah began *to be* an **h**, and H376+H127
Jer 51:23 I break in pieces the **h** and his yoke of H406
Am 5:16 they shall call the **h** to mourning, and H406
Zec 13: 5 I *am* an **h**; for man taught H376+H5647+H127
Jn 15: 1 the true vine, and my Father is the **h**. *G1092*
2Ti 2: 6 The **h** that laboureth must be first *G1092*
Jas 5: 7 the Lord. Behold, the **h** waiteth for the *G1092*

HUSBANDMEN
2Ki 25:12 of the land *to be* vinedressers and **h**. H1461
2Ch 26:10 and in the plains: **h** *also*, and vine H406
Jer 31:24 **h**, and they *that* go forth with flocks. H406
52:16 of the land for vinedressers and for **h**. H3009
Joel 1:11 Be ye ashamed, O ye **h**; howl, O ye H406
Mt 21:33 it out to **h**, and went into a far country: *G1092*
34 his servants to the **h**, that they might *G1092*
35 And the **h** took his servants, and beat *G1092*
38 But when the **h** saw the son, they said *G1092*
40 cometh, what will he do unto those **h**? *G1092*
41 unto other **h**, which shall render *G1092*
Mk 12: 1 it out to **h**, and went into a far country. *G1092*
2 And at the season he sent to the **h** a *G1092*
2 from the **h** of the fruit of the vineyard. *G1092*
7 But those **h** said among themselves, *G1092*
9 and destroy the **h**, and will give the *G1092*
Lk 20: 9 and let it forth to **h**, and went into a far *G1092*
10 a servant to the **h**, that they should give *G1092*
10 **h** beat him, and sent *him* away empty. *G1092*
14 But when the **h** saw him, they reasoned *G1092*
16 He shall come and destroy these **h**, and *G1092*

HUSBANDRY
2Ch 26:10 and in Carmel: for he loved **h**. H127
1Co 3: 9 ye are God's **h**, *ye are* God's building. *G1091*

HUSBANDS
Ru 1:11 in my womb, that they may be your **h**? H582
13 them from having **h**? nay, my daughters; H376
Est 1:17 shall despise their **h** in their eyes, when H1167
20 **h** honour, both to great and small. H1167
Jer 29: 6 your daughters to **h**, that they may bear H582
Ezk 16:45 which lothed their **h** and their children: H582
Jn 4:18 For thou hast had five **h**; and he whom *G435*
1Co 14:35 let them ask their **h** at home: for it is a *G435*
Eph 5:22 unto your own **h**, as unto the Lord. *G435*
24 wives *be* to their own **h** in every thing. *G435*
25 **H**, love your wives, even as Christ also *G435*
Col 3:18 unto your own **h**, as it is fit in the Lord. *G435*
19 **H**, love *your* wives, and be not bitter *G435*
1Ti 3:12 Let the deacons be the **h** of one wife, *G435*
Tit 2: 4 to love their **h**, to love their children, *G5362*
5 to their own **h**, that the word of God *G435*
1Pt 3: 1 to your own **h**; that, if any obey not *G435*
5 being in subjection unto their own **h**: *G435*
7 Likewise, ye **h**, dwell with *them* *G435*

HUSBAND'S
Nu 30:10 And if she vowed in her **h** house, or H376
Dt 25: 5 a stranger: her **h** brother shall go in H2993
5 the duty of an **h** brother unto her. H2992
7 and say, My **h** brother refuseth to H2993
7 not perform the duty of my **h** brother. H2992
Ru 2: 1 And Naomi had a kinsman of her **h**, a H376

HUSHAH
1Ch 4: 4 Ezer the father of **H**. These *are* the sons H2364

HUSHAI
2Sa 15:32 God, behold, **H** the Archite came to H2365
37 So **H** David's friend came into the city, H2365
16:16 And it came to pass, when **H** the H2365
16 Absalom, that **H** said unto Absalom, H2365
17 And Absalom said to **H**, *Is* this thy H2365
18 And **H** said unto Absalom, Nay; but H2365
17: 5 Then said Absalom, Call now **H** the H2365
6 And when **H** was come to Absalom, H2365
7 And **H** said unto Absalom, The counsel H2365
8 For, said **H**, thou knowest thy father H2365
14 The counsel of **H** the Archite *is* better H2365
15 Then said **H** unto Zadok and to H2365
1Ki 4:16 Baanah the son of **H** *was* in Asher and H2365
1Ch 27:33 counsellor: and **H** the Archite *was* the H2365

HUSHAM
Gen 36:34 And Jobab died, and **H** of the land of H2367
35 And **H** died, and Hadad the son of H2367
1Ch 1:45 And when Jobab was dead, **H** of the H2367
46 And when **H** was dead, Hadad the son H2367

HUSHATHITE
2Sa 21:18 Sibbechai the **H** slew Saph, which *was* H2843
23:27 the Anethothite, Mebunnai the **H**, H2843
1Ch 11:29 Sibbecai the **H**, Ilai the Ahohite, H2843
20: 4 Sibbechai the **H** slew Sippai, *that was* H2843
27:11 *was* Sibbecai the **H**, of the Zarhites: and H2843

HUSHIM
Gen 46:23 And the sons of Dan; **H**. H2366
1Ch 7:12 children of Ir, *and* **H**, the sons of Aher. H2366
8: 8 away; **H** and Baara *were* his wives. H2366
11 And of **H** he begat Abitub, and Elpaal. H2366

HUSK
Nu 6: 4 vine tree, from the kernels even to the **h**. H2085
2Ki 4:42 ears of corn in the **h** thereof. And he H6861

HUSKS
Lk 15:16 his belly with the **h** that the swine did *G2769*

HUZ
Gen 22:21 **H** his firstborn, and Buz his brother, H5780

HUZOTH See KIRJATH-HUZOTH.

HUZZAB
Nah 2: 7 And **H** shall be led away captive, she H5324

HYACINTH See JACINTH.

HYMENAEUS
1Ti 1:20 Of whom is H and Alexander; whom I G5211
2Ti 2:17 a canker: of whom is H and Philetus; G5211

HYMN
Mt 26:30 And when they had sung an h, they G5214
Mk 14:26 And when they had sung an h, they G5214

HYMNS
Eph 5:19 Speaking to yourselves in psalms and h G5215
Col 3:16 in psalms and h and spiritual songs, G5215

HYPOCRISIES
1Pt 2: 1 h, and envies, and all evil speakings, G5272

HYPOCRISY
Isa 32: 6 to practise h, and to utter error against H2612
Mt 23:28 but within ye are full of h and iniquity. G5272
Mk 12:15 he, knowing their h, said unto them, G5272
Lk 12: 1 the leaven of the Pharisees, which is h. G5272
1Ti 4: 2 Speaking lies in h; having their G5272
Jas 3:17 fruits, without partiality, and without h. G505

HYPOCRITE
Job 13:16 He also *shall be* my salvation: for an h H2611
Job 17: 8 shall stir up himself against the h. H2611
20: 5 and the joy of the h *but* for a moment? H2611
27: 8 For what *is* the hope of the h, though he H2611
34:30 That the h reign not, lest the H120+H2611
Prv 11: 9 An h with *his* mouth destroyeth his H2611
Isa 9:17 for every one *is* an h and an evildoer, H2611
Mt 7: 5 Thou h, first cast out the beam out of G5273
Lk 6:42 thine own eye? Thou h, cast out first the G5273
13:15 and said, *Thou* h, doth not each one of G5273

HYPOCRITES
Job 15:34 For the congregation of h *shall be* H2611
36:13 But the h in heart heap up wrath: they H2611
Isa 33:14 hath surprised the h. Who among us H2611
Mt 6: 2 trumpet before thee, as the h do in the G5273
5 shalt not be as the h *are*: for they love G5273
16 Moreover when ye fast, be not, as the h, G5273
15: 7 *Ye* h, well did Esaias prophesy of you, G5273
16: 3 and lowring. O *ye* h, ye can discern the G5273
22:18 and said, Why tempt ye me, *ye* h? G5273
23:13 and Pharisees, h! for ye shut up the G5273
14 Woe unto you, scribes and Pharisees, h! G5273
15 Woe unto you, scribes and Pharisees, h! G5273
23 Woe unto you, scribes and Pharisees, h! G5273
25 Woe unto you, scribes and Pharisees, h! G5273
27 Woe unto you, scribes and Pharisees, h! G5273
Mt 23:29 Woe unto you, scribes and Pharisees, h! G5273
24:51 his portion with the h: there shall be G5273
Mk 7: 6 prophesied of you h, as it is written, G5273
Lk 11:44 Woe unto you, scribes and Pharisees, h! G5273
12:56 *Ye* h, ye can discern the face of the sky G5273

HYPOCRITE'S
Job 8:13 forget God; and the h hope shall perish: H2611

HYPOCRITICAL
Ps 35:16 With h mockers in feasts, they gnashed H2611
Isa 10: 6 I will send him against an h nation, H2611

HYSSOP
Ex 12:22 And ye shall take a bunch of h, and dip *it* H231
Lev 14: 4 and cedar wood, and scarlet, and h: H231
6 the scarlet, and the h, and shall dip them H231
49 and cedar wood, and scarlet, and h: H231
51 wood, and the h, and the scarlet, and H231
52 and with the h, and with the scarlet: H231
Nu 19: 6 cedar wood, and h, and scarlet, and cast H231
18 And a clean person shall take h, and dip H231
1Ki 4:33 even unto the h that springeth out of H231
Ps 51: 7 Purge me with h, and I shall be clean: H231
Jn 19:29 put *it* upon h, and put *it* to his mouth. G5301
Heb 9:19 scarlet wool, and h, and sprinkled both G5301

I

I See the Appendix.

IBHAR
2Sa 5:15 I also, and Elishua, and Nepheg, and H2984
1Ch 3: 6 I also, and Elishama, and Eliphelet, H2984
14: 5 And I, and Elishua, and Elpalet, H2984

IBLEAM
Jos 17:11 her towns, and I and her towns, and H2991
Jdg 1:27 the inhabitants of I and her towns, nor H2991
2Ki 9:27 up to Gur, which *is* by I. And he fled to H2991

IBNEIAH
1Ch 9: 8 And I the son of Jeroham, and Elah the H2997

IBNIJAH
1Ch 9: 8 the son of Reuel, the son of I; H2998

IBRI
1Ch 24:27 Beno, and Shoham, and Zaccur, and I. H5681

IBZAN
Jdg 12: 8 And after him I of Beth-lehem judged H78
10 Then died I, and was buried at H78

ICE
Job 6:16 Which are blackish by reason of the i, H7140
38:29 Out of whose womb came the i? and the H7140
Ps 147:17 He casteth forth his i like morsels: who H7140

ICHABOD
1Sa 4:21 And she named the child I, saying, The H350

ICHABOD'S
1Sa 14: 3 And Ahiah, the son of Ahitub, I brother, H350

ICONIUM
Act 13:51 feet against them, and came unto I. G2430
14: 1 And it came to pass in I, that they went G2430
19 from Antioch and I, who persuaded the G2430
21 again to Lystra, and *to* I, and Antioch, G2430
16: 2 the brethren that were at Lystra and I. G2430
2Ti 3:11 me at Antioch, at I, at Lystra; what G2430

IDALAH
Jos 19:15 and Shimron, and I, and Beth-lehem: H3030

IDBASH
1Ch 4: 3 and Ishma, and I: and the name of their H3031

IDDO
1Ki 4:14 Ahinadab the son of I *had* Mahanaim: H5714
1Ch 6:21 Joah his son, I his son, Zerah his son, H5714
27:21 in Gilead, I the son of Zechariah: H3035
2Ch 9:29 and in the visions of I the seer against H3260
2Ch 12:15 prophet, and of I the seer concerning H5714
13:22 *are* written in the story of the prophet I. H5714
Ezr 5: 1 the son of I, prophesied unto the H5714
6:14 the son of I. And they builded, and H5714
8:17 unto I the chief at the place H112
17 should say unto I, *and* to his brethren the H112
Neh 12: 4 I, Ginnetho, Abijah, H5714
16 Of I, Zechariah; of Ginnethon, H5714
Zec 1: 1 the son of I the prophet, saying, H5714
7 the son of I the prophet, saying, H5714

IDLE
Ex 5: 8 for they *be* i; therefore they cry, saying, H7503
17 But he said, Ye *are* i, *ye are* idle: H7503
17 But he said, Ye *are* idle, *ye are* i: H7503
Prv 19:15 sleep; and an i soul shall suffer hunger. H7423
Mt 12:36 But I say unto you, That every i word G692
20: 3 others standing i in the marketplace, G692
6 others standing i, and saith unto them, G692
6 them, Why stand ye here all the day i? G692
Lk 24:11 And their words seemed to them as i G3029
1Ti 5:13 And withal they learn *to be* i, wandering G692
13 and not only i, but tattlers also and G692

IDLENESS
Prv 31:27 and eateth not the bread of i. H6104
Ecc 10:18 and through i of the hands the house H8220
Ezk 16:49 and abundance of i was in her and in H8252

IDOL
1Ki 15:13 she had made an i in a grove; and Asa H4656
13 her i, and burnt *it* by the brook Kidron. H4656
2Ch 15:16 she had made an i in a grove: and Asa H4656
16 Asa cut down her i, and stamped *it*, and H4656
33: 7 And he set a carved image, the i which H5566
15 gods, and the i out of the house of the H5566
Isa 48: 5 say, Mine i hath done them, and H6090
66: 3 *as if* he blessed an i. Yea, they have H205
Jer 22:28 *Is* this man Coniah a despised broken i? H6089
Zec 11:17 Woe to the i shepherd that leaveth the H457
Act 7:41 sacrifice unto the i, and rejoiced in the G1497
1Co 8: 4 we know that an i *is* nothing in the G1497
7 conscience of the i unto this hour eat *it* G1497
7 offered unto an i; and their conscience G1494
10:19 What say I then? that the i is any thing, G1497

IDOLATER
1Co 5:11 or covetous, or an i, or a railer, or a G1496
Eph 5: 5 man, who is an i, hath any inheritance G1496

IDOLATERS
1Co 5:10 or with i; for then must ye needs G1496
6: 9 fornicators, nor i, nor adulterers, nor G1496
10: 7 Neither be ye i, as *were* some of them; G1496
Rev 21: 8 and sorcerers, and i, and all liars, shall G1496
22:15 murderers, and i, and whosoever loveth G1496

IDOLATRIES
1Pt 4: 3 banquetings, and abominable i: G1495

IDOLATROUS
2Ki 23: 5 And he put down the i priests, whom H3649

IDOLATRY
1Sa 15:23 *is as* iniquity and i. Because thou hast H8655
Act 17:16 when he saw the city wholly given to i. G2712
1Co 10:14 my dearly beloved, flee from i. G1495
Gal 5:20 I, witchcraft, hatred, variance, G1495
Col 3: 5 and covetousness, which is i: G1495

IDOLS
Lev 19: 4 Turn ye not unto i, nor make to H457
26: 1 Ye shall make you no i nor graven H457
30 of your i, and my soul shall abhor you. H1544
Dt 29:17 and their i, wood and stone, silver H1544
1Sa 31: 9 house of their i, and among the people. H6091
1Ki 15:12 all the i that his fathers had made. H1544
21:26 in following i, according to all *things* H1544
2Ki 17:12 For they served i, whereof the LORD H1544
21:11 hath made Judah also to sin with his i: H1544
21 in, and served the i that his father H1544
23:24 the images, and the i, and all the H1544
1Ch 10: 9 tidings unto their i, and to the people. H6091
16:26 For all the gods of the people *are* i: but H457
2Ch 15: 8 the abominable i out of all the land of H8251
24:18 served groves and i: and wrath came H6091
34: 7 cut down all the i throughout all the H2553
Ps 96: 5 For all the gods of the nations *are* i: but H457
97: 7 themselves of i: worship him, all *ye* gods. H457
106:36 And they served their i: which were a H6091
38 sacrificed unto the i of Canaan: and the H6091
115: 4 Their i *are* silver and gold, the work of H6091
135:15 The i of the heathen *are* silver and H6091
Isa 2: 8 Their land also is full of i; they worship H457
18 And the i he shall utterly abolish. H457
20 In that day a man shall cast his i of H457
20 of silver, and his i of gold, which they H457
10:10 the kingdoms of the i, and whose graven H457
11 her i, so do to Jerusalem and her idols? H457
11 her idols, so do to Jerusalem and her i? H6091
19: 1 into Egypt: and the i of Egypt shall be H457
3 shall seek to the i, and to the charmers, H457
31: 7 shall cast away his i of silver, and his H457
7 of silver, and his i of gold, which your H457
45:16 confusion together *that are* makers of i. H6736
46: 1 stoopeth, their i were upon the beasts, H6091
57: 5 Enflaming yourselves with i under every H410
Jer 50: 2 in pieces; her i are confounded, her H6091
38 images, and they are mad upon *their* i. H367
Ezk 6: 4 cast down your slain *men* before your i. H1544
5 of Israel before their i; and I will scatter H1544
6 desolate, and your i may be broken H1544
9 after their i: and they shall lothe H1544

Ezk 6:13 be among their i round about their H1544
13 they did offer sweet savour to all their i. H1544
8:10 beasts, and all the i of the house of H1544
14: 3 have set up their i in their heart, and H1544
4 that setteth up his i in his heart, and H1544
4 according to the multitude of his i; H1544
5 all estranged from me through their i. H1544
6 from your i; and turn away your H1544
7 and setteth up his i in his heart, and H1544
16:36 and with all the i of thy abominations, H1544
18: 6 lifted up his eyes to the i of the house of H1544
12 to the i, hath committed abomination, H1544
15 lifted up his eyes to the i of the house of H1544
20: 7 i of Egypt: I *am* the LORD your God. H1544
8 they forsake the i of Egypt: then I said, H1544
16 for their heart went after their i. H1544
18 nor defile yourselves with their i: H1544
24 and their eyes were after their fathers' i. H1544
31 with all your i, even unto this day: H1544
39 ye every one his i, and hereafter *also*, if H1544
39 more with your gifts, and with your i. H1544
22: 3 i against herself to defile herself. H1544
4 thyself in thine i which thou hast H1544
23: 7 with all their i she defiled herself. H1544
30 because thou art polluted with their i. H1544
37 and with their i have they committed H1544
39 children to their i, then they came the H1544
49 the sins of your i: and ye shall know H1544
30:13 also destroy the i, and I will cause *their* H1544
33:25 eyes toward your i, and shed blood: and H1544
36:18 their i *wherewith* they had polluted it: H1544
25 and from all your i, will I cleanse you. H1544
37:23 any more with their i, nor with their H1544
44:10 i; they shall even bear their iniquity. H1544
12 unto them before their i, and caused the H1544
Hos 4:17 Ephraim *is* joined to i: let him alone. H6091
8: 4 made them i, that they may be cut off. H6091
13: 2 of their silver, *and* i according to their H6091
14: 8 do any more with i? I have heard *him*, H6091
Mic 1: 7 the fire, and all the i thereof will I lay H6091
Hab 2:18 work trusteth therein, to make dumb i? H457
Zec 10: 2 For the i have spoken vanity, and the H8655
13: 2 the names of the i out of the land, and H6091
Act 15:20 abstain from pollutions of i, and *from* G1497
29 That ye abstain from meats offered to i, G1494
21:25 *things* offered to i, and from blood, and G1494
Ro 2:22 i, dost thou commit sacrilege? G1497
1Co 8: 1 Now as touching things offered unto i, G1494
4 in sacrifice unto i, we know that an idol G1494
10 eat those things which are offered to i; G1494
10:19 is offered in sacrifice to i is any thing? G1494
28 in sacrifice unto i, eat not for his sake G1494
12: 2 unto these dumb i, even as ye were led. G1497
2Co 6:16 of God with i? for ye are the temple G1497
1Th 1: 9 from i to serve the living and true God; G1497
1Jn 5:21 Little children, keep yourselves from i. G1497
Rev 2:14 unto i, and to commit fornication. G1494
20 and to eat things sacrificed unto i. G1494
9:20 devils, and i of gold, and silver, and G1497

IDOL'S
1Co 8:10 sit at meat in the i temple, shall not the G1493

IDUMAEA
Mk 3: 8 And from Jerusalem, and from I, and G2401

IDUMEA
Isa 34: 5 come down upon I, and upon the people H123
6 and a great slaughter in the land of I. H123
Ezk 35:15 O mount Seir, and all I, *even* all of it: and H123
36: 5 and against all I, which have appointed H123

IF See the Appendix.

IGAL
Nu 13: 7 Of the tribe of Issachar, I the son of H3008
2Sa 23:36 I the son of Nathan of Zobah, Bani the H3008

IGDALIAH
Jer 35: 4 of Hanan, the son of I, a man of God, H3012

IGEAL
1Ch 3:22 Hattush, and I, and Bariah, and H3008

IGNOMINY
Prv 18: 3 also contempt, and with i reproach. H7036

IGNORANCE
Lev 4: 2 shall sin through i against any of the H7684
Lev 4:13 of Israel sin through i, and the thing be H7686
22 *somewhat* through i *against* any of the H7684
27 people sin through i, while he doeth H7684
5:15 and sin through i, in the holy things of H7684
18 concerning his i wherein he erred and H7684
Nu 15:24 *ought* be committed by i without the H7684
25 them; for it *is* i: and they shall bring H7684
25 sin offering before the LORD, for their i: H7684
26 them; seeing all the people *were* in i. H7684
27 And if any soul sin through i, then he H7684
28 he sinneth by i before the LORD, to H7684
29 sinneth through i, *both for* him that is H7684
Act 3:17 And now, brethren, I wot that through i G52
17:30 And the times of this i God winked at; G52
Eph 4:18 life of God through the i that is in them, G52
1Pt 1:14 according to the former lusts in your i: G52
2:15 may put to silence the i of foolish men: G56

IGNORANT
Ps 73:22 So foolish *was* I, and i: I was *as* H3808+H3045
Isa 56:10 they are all i, they *are* all dumb H3808+H3045
63:16 Abraham be i of us, and Israel H3808+H3045
Act 4:13 unlearned and i men, they marvelled; G2399
Ro 1:13 Now I would not have you i, brethren, G50
10: 3 For they being i of God's righteousness, G50
11:25 that ye should be i of this mystery, lest G50
1Co 10: 1 not that ye should be i, how that all our G50
12: 1 *gifts*, brethren, I would not have you i. G50
14:38 But if any man be i, let him be ignorant. G50
38 But if any man be ignorant, let him be i. G50
2Co 1: 8 For we would not, brethren, have you i G50
2:11 of us: for we are not i of his devices. G50
1Th 4:13 But I would not have you to be i, G50
Heb 5: 2 Who can have compassion on the i, and G50
2Pt 3: 5 For this they willingly are i of, that by G2990
8 But, beloved, be not i of this one thing, G2990

IGNORANTLY
Nu 15:28 soul that sinneth i, when he sinneth by H7683
Dt 19: 4 his neighbour i, whom he hated H1097+H1847
Act 17:23 ye i worship, him declare I unto you. G50
1Ti 1:13 mercy, because I did *it* i in unbelief. G50

IIM
Nu 33:45 And they departed from I, and pitched H5864
Jos 15:29 Baalah, and I, and Azem, H5864

IJEABARIM
Nu 21:11 and pitched at I, in the wilderness H5863
33:44 and pitched in I, in the border of Moab. H5863

IJON
1Ki 15:20 of Israel, and smote I, and Dan, and H5859
2Ki 15:29 of Assyria, and took I, and H5859
2Ch 16: 4 Israel; and they smote I, and Dan, and H5859

IKKESH
2Sa 23:26 Helez the Paltite, Ira the son of I the H6142
1Ch 11:28 Ira the son of I the Tekoite, Abi-ezer H6142
27: 9 *was* Ira the son of I the Tekoite: and in H6142

ILAI
1Ch 11:29 Sibbecai the Hushathite, I the Ahohite, H5866

ILL
Gen 41: 3 them out of the river, i favoured and H7451
4 And the i favoured and leanfleshed H7451
19 them, poor and very i favoured and H7451
20 And the lean and the i favoured kine H7451
21 but they *were* still i favoured, as at the H7451
27 And the seven thin and i favoured kine H7451
43: 6 And Israel said, Wherefore dealt ye *so* i H7489
Dt 15:21 blind, *or have* any i blemish, thou shalt H7451
Job 20:26 i with him that is left in his tabernacle. H3415
Ps 106:32 it went i with Moses for their sakes: H3415
Isa 3:11 Woe unto the wicked! *it shall be* i *with* H7451
Jer 40: 4 thee: but if it seem i unto thee to come H7489
Joel 2:20 come up, and his i savour shall come H6709
Mic 3: 4 behaved themselves i in their doings. H7489
Ro 13:10 Love worketh no i to his neighbour: G2556

ILL-FAVOURED See ILL and FAVOURED.

ILLUMINATED
Heb 10:32 i, ye endured a great fight of afflictions; G5461

ILLYRICUM
Ro 15:19 and round about unto I, I have fully G2437

IMAGE
Gen 1:26 make man in our i, after our likeness: H6754
27 So God created man in his *own* i, in the H6754
27 *own* image, in the i of God created he H6754
5: 3 after his i; and called his name Seth: H6754
9: 6 shed: for in the i of God made he man. H6754
Ex 20: 4 thee any graven i, or any likeness *of any* H6459
Lev 26: 1 Ye shall make you no idols nor graven i, H6459
1 you up a standing i, neither shall ye set H4676
1 shall ye set up *any* i of stone in your H4906
Dt 4:16 you a graven i, the similitude of any H6459
23 you a graven i, *or* the likeness of any H6459
25 make a graven i, *or* the likeness of any H6459
5: 8 Thou shalt not make thee *any* graven i, H6459
9:12 them; they have made them a molten i. H4541
16:22 Neither shalt thou set thee up *any* i; H4676
27:15 *any* graven or molten i, an abomination H4541
Jdg 17: 3 son, to make a graven i and a molten H6459
3 and a molten i: now therefore I will H4541
4 thereof a graven i and a molten image: H6459
4 i: and they were in the house of Micah. H4541
18:14 and a graven i, and a molten image? H6459
14 and a molten i? now therefore consider H4541
17 took the graven i, and the ephod, and H6459
17 and the molten i: and the priest stood H4541
18 fetched the carved i, the ephod, and the H6459
18 and the molten i. Then said the priest H4541
20 i, and went in the midst of the people. H6459
30 set up the graven i: and Jonathan, the H6459
31 And they set them up Micah's graven i, H6459
1Sa 19:13 And Michal took an i, and laid *it* in the H8655
16 *there was* an i in the bed, with a pillow H8655
2Ki 3: 2 the i of Baal that his father had made. H4676
10:27 And they brake down the i of Baal, and H4676
21: 7 And he set a graven i of the grove that H6459
2Ch 3:10 of i work, and overlaid them with gold. H6816
33: 7 And he set a carved i, the idol which he H6459
Job 4:16 the form thereof: an i *was* before mine H8544
Ps 73:20 thou awakest, thou shalt despise their i. H6754
106:19 in Horeb, and worshipped the molten i.
Isa 40:19 The workman melteth a graven i, and H6459
20 a graven i, *that* shall not be moved. H6459
44: 9 They that make a graven i *are* all of H6459
10 graven i *that* is profitable for nothing? H6459
15 it a graven i, and falleth down thereto. H6459
17 *even* his graven i: he falleth down unto H6459
45:20 i, and pray unto a god *that* cannot save. H6459
48: 5 and my graven i, and my molten image, H6459
5 my molten i, hath commanded them. H5262
Jer 10:14 by the graven i: for his molten image H6459
14 for his molten i *is* falsehood, and *there* H5262
51:17 by the graven i: for his molten image H6459
17 for his molten i *is* falsehood, and *there* H5262
Ezk 8: 3 *was* the seat of the i of jealousy, which H5566
5 the altar this i of jealousy in the entry. H5566
Dan 2:31 and behold a great i. This great image, H6755
31 image. This great i, whose brightness H6755
34 which smote the i upon his feet *that* H6755
35 stone that smote the i became a great H6755
3: 1 Nebuchadnezzar the king made an i of H6755
2 the dedication of the i which H6755
3 the dedication of the i that H6755
3 the i that Nebuchadnezzar had set up. H6755
5 the golden i that Nebuchadnezzar H6755
7 the golden i that Nebuchadnezzar H6755
10 fall down and worship the golden i: H6755
12 the golden i which thou hast set up. H6755
14 the golden i which I have set up? H6755
15 and worship the i which I have made; H6755
18 the golden i which thou hast set up. H6755
Hos 3: 4 and without an i, and without an H4676
Nah 1:14 I cut off the graven i and the molten H6459
14 i: I will make thy grave; for thou art vile. H4541
Hab 2:18 What profiteth the graven i that the H6459
18 it; the molten i, and a teacher of lies, H4541
Mt 22:20 And he saith unto them, Whose *is* this i G1504
Mk 12:16 Whose *is* this i and superscription? G1504
Lk 20:24 Shew me a penny. Whose i and G1504
Act 19:35 of the *i* which fell down from Jupiter?
Ro 1:23 God into an i made like to corruptible G1504
8:29 conformed to the i of his Son, that he G1504
11: 4 have not bowed the knee to *the i of* Baal.
1Co 11: 7 as he is the i and glory of God: but G1504
15:49 And as we have borne the i of the G1504
49 we shall also bear the i of the heavenly. G1504
2Co 3:18 into the same i from glory to glory, G1504
4: 4 is the i of God, should shine unto them. G1504
Col 1:15 Who is the i of the invisible God, the G1504
3:10 after the i of him that created him: G1504

Heb 1: 3 and the express **i** of his person, and G5481
10: 1 *and* not the very **i** of the things, can G1504
Rev 13:14 should make an **i** to the beast, which G1504
15 And he had power to give life unto the **i** G1504
15 the beast, that the **i** of the beast should G1504
15 the **i** of the beast should be killed. G1504
14: 9 the beast and his **i**, and receive *his* G1504
11 the beast and his **i**, and whosoever G1504
15: 2 the beast, and over his **i**, and over his G1504
16: 2 and *upon* them which worshipped his **i**. G1504
19:20 worshipped his **i**. These both were cast G1504
20: 4 beast, neither his **i**, neither had received G1504

IMAGERY
Ezk 8:12 the chambers of his **i**? for they say, The H4906

IMAGES
Gen 31:19 had stolen the **i** that *were* her father's. H8655
34 Now Rachel had taken the **i**, and put H8655
35 And he searched, but found not the **i**. H8655
Ex 23:24 them, and quite break down their **i**. H4676
34:13 break their **i**, and cut down their groves: H4676
Lev 26:30 and cut down your **i**, and cast your H2553
Nu 33:52 all their molten **i**, and quite pluck down H6754
Dt 7: 5 break down their **i**, and cut down their H4676
5 and burn their graven **i** with fire. H6456
25 The graven **i** of their gods shall ye burn H6456
12: 3 down the graven **i** of their gods, and H6456
1Sa 6: 5 Wherefore ye shall make **i** of your H6754
5 emerods, and **i** of your mice that mar H6754
11 mice of gold and the **i** of their emerods. H6754
2Sa 5:21 And there they left their **i**, and David H6091
1Ki 14: 9 gods, and molten **i**, to provoke me to H4541
23 high places, and **i**, and groves, on every H4676
2Ki 10:26 And they brought forth the **i** out of the H4676
11:18 his altars and his **i** brake they in pieces H6754
17:10 And they set them up **i** and groves in H4676
16 them molten **i**, *even* two calves, and H4541
41 their graven **i**, both their children, H6456
18: 4 and brake the **i**, and cut down the H4676
23:14 And he brake in pieces the **i**, and cut H4676
24 wizards, and the **i**, and the idols, and all H8655
2Ch 14: 3 down the **i**, and cut down the groves: H4676
5 places and the **i**: and the kingdom was H2553
23:17 his altars and his **i** in pieces, and slew H6754
28: 2 and made also molten **i** for Baalim. H4541
31: 1 and brake the **i** in pieces, and cut down H4676
33:19 up groves and graven **i**, before he was H6456
22 unto all the carved **i** which Manasseh H6456
34: 3 the carved **i**, and the molten images. H6456
3 the carved images, and the molten **i**. H4541
4 presence; and the **i**, that *were* on high H2553
4 and the carved **i**, and the molten H6456
4 and the molten **i**, he brake in pieces, H4541
7 beaten the graven **i** into powder, and H6456
Ps 78:58 him to jealousy with their graven **i**. H6456
97: 7 they that serve graven **i**, that boast H6459
Isa 10:10 and whose graven **i** did excel them of H6456
17: 8 have made, either the groves, or the **i**. H2553
21: 9 and all the graven **i** of her gods he hath H6456
27: 9 the groves and **i** shall not stand up. H2553
30:22 of thy graven **i** of silver, and the H6456
22 of thy molten **i** of gold: thou shalt cast H4541
41:29 their molten **i** *are* wind and confusion.
42: 8 another, neither my praise to graven **i**. H6456
17 trust in graven **i**, that say to the molten H6459
17 say to the molten **i**, Ye *are* our gods. H4541
Jer 8:19 graven **i**, *and* with strange vanities? H6456
43:13 He shall break also the **i** of H4676
50: 2 confounded, her **i** are broken in pieces. H1544
38 **i**, and they are mad upon *their* idols. H6456
51:47 upon the graven **i** of Babylon: and her H6456
52 upon her graven **i**: and through all her H6456
Ezk 6: 4 be desolate, and your **i** shall be broken: H2553
6 cease, and your **i** may be cut down, H2553
7:20 majesty: but they made the **i** of their H6754
16:17 madest to thyself **i** of men, and didst H6754
21:21 consulted with **i**, he looked in the liver. H8655
23:14 upon the wall, the **i** of the Chaldeans H6754
30:13 I will cause *their* **i** to cease out of Noph; H457
Hos 10: 1 of his land they have made goodly **i**. H4676
2 down their altars, he shall spoil their **i**. H4676
11: 2 Baalim, and burned incense to graven **i**. H6456
13: 2 them molten **i** of their silver, *and* idols H4541
Am 5:26 and Chiun your **i**, the star of your god, H6754
Mic 1: 7 And all the graven **i** thereof shall be H6456
5:13 Thy graven **i** also will I cut off, and thy H6456
13 and thy standing **i** out of the midst of H4676

IMAGE'S
Dan 2:32 This **i** head *was* of fine gold, his breast H6755

IMAGE-WORK See IMAGE and WORK.

IMAGINATION
Gen 6: 5 and *that* every **i** of the thoughts of his H3336
8:21 sake; for the **i** of man's heart *is* evil H3336
Dt 29:19 I walk in the **i** of mine heart, to add H8307
31:21 for I know their **i** which they go about, H3336
1Ch 29:18 this for ever in the **i** of the thoughts of H3336
Jer 3:17 any more after the **i** of their evil heart. H8307
7:24 *and* in the **i** of their evil heart, and H8307
9:14 But have walked after the **i** of their own H8307
11: 8 every one in the **i** of their evil heart: H8307
13:10 which walk in the **i** of their heart, and H8307
16:12 every one after the **i** of his evil heart, H8307
18:12 will every one do the **i** of his evil heart. H8307
23:17 walketh after the **i** of his own heart, No H8307
Lk 1:51 the proud in the **i** of their hearts. G1271

IMAGINATIONS
1Ch 28: 9 all the **i** of the thoughts: if thou H3336
Prv 6:18 An heart that deviseth wicked **i**, feet H4284
Lam 3:60 vengeance *and* all their **i** against me. H4284
61 O LORD, *and* all their **i** against me; H4284
Ro 1:21 **i**, and their foolish heart was darkened. G1261
2Co 10: 5 Casting down **i**, and every high thing G3053

IMAGINE
Job 6:26 Do ye **i** to reprove words, and the H2803
21:27 *which* ye wrongfully **i** against me. H2554
Ps 2: 1 rage, and the people **i** a vain thing? H1897
38:12 things, and **i** deceits all the day long. H1897
62: 3 How long will ye **i** mischief against a H2050
140: 2 Which **i** mischiefs in *their* heart; H2803
Prv 12:20 Deceit *is* in the heart of them that **i** evil: H2790
Hos 7:15 yet do they **i** mischief against me. H2803
Nah 1: 9 What do ye **i** against the LORD? he will H2803
Zec 7:10 **i** evil against his brother in your heart. H2803
8:17 And let none of you **i** evil in your hearts H2803
Act 4:25 rage, and the people **i** vain things? G3191

IMAGINED
Gen 11: 6 from them, which they have **i** to do. H2161
Ps 10: 2 be taken in the devices that they have **i**. H2803
21:11 evil against thee: they **i** a mischievous H2803

IMAGINETH
Nah 1:11 There is *one* come out of thee, that **i** H2803

IMLA
2Ch 18: 7 Micaiah the son of **I**. And Jehoshaphat H3229
8 said, Fetch quickly Micaiah the son of **I**. H3229

IMLAH
1Ki 22: 8 Micaiah the son of **I**, by whom we may H3229
9 Hasten *hither* Micaiah the son of **I**. H3229

IMMANUEL
Isa 7:14 bear a son, and shall call his name **I**. H6005
8: 8 shall fill the breadth of thy land, O **I**. H6005

IMMEDIATELY
Mt 4:22 And they **i** left the ship and their father, G2112
8: 3 clean. And **i** his leprosy was cleansed. G2112
14:31 And **i** Jesus stretched forth *his* hand, G2112
20:34 their eyes: and **i** their eyes received G2112
24:29 **I** after the tribulation of those days G2112
26:74 not the man. And **i** the cock crew. G2112
Mk 1:12 And **i** the Spirit driveth him into the G2117
28 And **i** his fame spread abroad G2117
31 lifted her up; and **i** the fever left her, G2112
42 And as soon as he had spoken, **i** the G2112
2: 8 And **i** when Jesus perceived in his spirit G2112
12 And **i** he arose, took up the bed, and G2112
4: 5 not much earth; and **i** it sprang up, G2112
15 Satan cometh **i**, and taketh away the G2112
16 the word, **i** receive it with gladness; G2112
17 for the word's sake, **i** they are offended. G2112
29 But when the fruit is brought forth, **i** he G2112
5: 2 out of the ship, **i** there met him out of G2112
30 And Jesus, **i** knowing in himself that G2112
6:27 And **i** the king sent an executioner, and G2112
50 troubled. And **i** he talked with them, G2112
10:52 thee whole. And **i** he received his sight, G2112
14:43 And **i**, while he yet spake, cometh G2112
Lk 1:64 And his mouth was opened **i**, and his G3916
4:39 **i** she arose and ministered unto them. G3916
5:13 And **i** the leprosy departed from him. G2112
25 And **i** he rose up before them, and took G3916
6:49 vehemently, and **i** it fell; and the ruin of G2112
8:44 and **i** her issue of blood stanched. G3916
47 touched him, and how she was healed **i**. G3916
12:36 knocketh, they may open unto him **i**. G2112
13:13 And he laid *his* hands on her: and **i** she G3916
18:43 And **i** he received his sight, and G3916
19:11 the kingdom of God should **i** appear. G3916
40 their peace, the stones would **i** cry out.
22:60 And **i**, while he yet spake, the cock crew. G3916
Jn 5: 9 And **i** the man was made whole, and G2112
6:21 into the ship: and **i** the ship was at the G2112
13:30 He then having received the sop went **i** G2112
18:27 Peter then denied again: and **i** the cock G2112
21: 3 **i**; and that night they caught nothing. G2117
Act 3: 7 lifted *him* up: and **i** his feet and ankle G3916
9:18 And **i** there fell from his eyes as it had G2112
34 and make thy bed. And he arose **i**. G2112
10:33 I therefore **I** sent to thee; and thou hast G1824
11:11 And, behold, **i** there were three men G1824
12:23 And **i** the angel of the Lord smote him, G3916
13:11 for a season. And **i** there fell on him a G3916
16:10 And after he had seen the vision, **i** we G2112
26 were shaken: and **i** all the doors were G3916
17:10 And the brethren **i** sent away Paul and G2112
14 And then **i** the brethren sent away Paul G2112
21:32 Who **i** took soldiers and centurions, G1824
Gal 1:16 **i** I conferred not with flesh and blood: G2112
Rev 4: 2 And **i** I was in the spirit: and, behold, a G2112

IMMER
1Ch 9:12 the son of Meshillemith, the son of **I**; H564
24:14 The fifteenth to Bilgah, the sixteenth to **I**, H564
Ezr 2:37 The children of **I**, a thousand fifty and H564
59 Addan, *and* **I**: but they could not shew H564
10:20 And of the sons of **I**; Hanani, and H564
Neh 3:29 After them repaired Zadok the son of **I** H564
7:40 The children of **I**, a thousand fifty and H564
61 Addon, and **I**: but they could not shew H564
11:13 the son of Meshillemoth, the son of **I**, H564
Jer 20: 1 Now Pashur the son of **I** the priest, who H564

IMMORTAL
1Ti 1:17 Now unto the King eternal, **i**, invisible, G862

IMMORTALITY
Ro 2: 7 for glory and honour and **i**, eternal life: G861
1Co 15:53 and this mortal *must* put on **i**. G110
54 shall have put on **i**, then shall be brought G110
1Ti 6:16 Who only hath **i**, dwelling in the light G110
2Ti 1:10 life and **i** to light through the gospel: G861

IMMOVABLE See UNMOVEABLE.

IMMUTABILITY
Heb 6:17 **i** of his counsel, confirmed *it* by an oath: G276

IMMUTABLE
Heb 6:18 That by two **i** things, in which *it was* G276

IMNA
1Ch 7:35 Zophah, and **I**, and Shelesh, and Amal. H3234

IMNAH
1Ch 7:30 The sons of Asher; **I**, and Isuah, and H3232
2Ch 31:14 And Kore the son of **I** the Levite, the H3232

IMPART
Lk 3:11 two coats, let him **i** to him that hath G3330
Ro 1:11 For I long to see you, that I may **i** unto G3330

IMPARTED
Job 39:17 neither hath he **i** to her understanding. H2505
1Th 2: 8 were willing to have **i** unto you, not the G3330

IMPEDIMENT
Mk 7:32 deaf, and had an **i** in his speech; and G3424

IMPENITENT
Ro 2: 5 But after thy hardness and **i** heart G279

IMPERFECT See UNPERFECT.

IMPERIOUS
Ezk 16:30 the work of an **i** whorish woman; H7986

IMPLACABLE
Ro 1:31 without natural affection, **i**, unmerciful: G786

IMPLEAD
Act 19:38 are deputies: let them **i** one another. *G1458*

IMPORTUNITY
Lk 11: 8 yet because of his **i** he will rise and give *G335*

IMPOSE
Ezr 7:24 to **i** toll, tribute, or custom, upon them. H7412

IMPOSED
Heb 9:10 **i** *on them* until the time of reformation. *G1945*

IMPOSSIBLE
Mt 17:20 remove; and nothing shall be **i** unto you. *G101*
19:26 is **i**; but with God all things are possible. *G102*
Mk 10:27 With men *it is* **i**, but not with God: for *G102*
Lk 1:37 For with God nothing shall be **i**. *G101*
17: 1 Then said he unto the disciples, It is **i** *G418*
18:27 And he said, The things which are **i** with *G102*
Heb 6: 4 For *it is* **i** for those who were once *G102*
18 in which *it was* **i** for God to lie, we might *G102*
11: 6 But without faith *it is* **i** to please *him*: for *G102*

IMPOTENT
Jn 5: 3 In these lay a great multitude of **i** folk, of *G770*
7 The **i** man answered him, Sir, I have no *G770*
Act 4: 9 **i** man, by what means he is made whole; *G772*
14: 8 And there sat a certain man at Lystra, **i** *G102*

IMPOVERISH
Jer 5:17 fig trees: they shall **i** thy fenced cities, H7567

IMPOVERISHED
Jdg 6: 6 And Israel was greatly **i** because of the H1809
Isa 40:20 He that *is* so **i** that he hath no oblation H5533
Mal 1: 4 Whereas Edom saith, We are **i**, but we H7567

IMPRISONED
Act 22:19 And I said, Lord, they know that I **i** and *G2252*

IMPRISONMENT
Ezr 7:26 or to confiscation of goods, or to **i**. H613
Heb 11:36 yea, moreover of bonds and **i**: *G5438*

IMPRISONMENTS
2Co 6: 5 In stripes, in **i**, in tumults, in labours, in *G5438*

IMPUDENT
Prv 7:13 him, *and* with an **i** face said unto him, H5810
Ezk 2: 4 For *they are* **i** children and H7186+H6440
3: 7 Israel *are* **i** and hardhearted. H2389+H4696

IMPUTE
1Sa 22:15 me: let not the king **i** *any* thing unto his H7760
2Sa 19:19 Let not my lord **i** iniquity unto me, H2803
Ro 4: 8 man to whom the Lord will not **i** sin. *G3049*

IMPUTED
Lev 7:18 neither shall it be **i** unto him that H2803
17: 4 blood shall be **i** unto that man; he hath H2803
Ro 4:11 might be **i** unto them also: *G3049*
22 And therefore it was **i** to him for *G3049*
23 for his sake alone, that it was **i** to him; *G3049*
24 But for us also, to whom it shall be **i**, if *G3049*
5:13 but sin is not **i** when there is no law. *G1677*
Jas 2:23 believed God, and it was **i** unto him for *G3049*

IMPUTETH
Ps 32: 2 whom the LORD **i** not iniquity, and in H2803
Ro 4: 6 God **i** righteousness without works, *G3049*

IMPUTING
Hab 1:11 and offend, *i* this his power unto his god. H2803
2Co 5:19 unto himself, not **i** their trespasses *G3049*

IMRAH
1Ch 7:36 Harnepher, and Shual, and Beri, and I, H3236

IMRI
1Ch 9: 4 of Omri, the son of I, the son of Bani, of H566
Neh 3: 2 next to them builded Zaccur the son of I. H566

IN See the Appendix.

INASMUCH
Dt 19: 6 **i** as he hated him not in time past. H3588
Ru 3:10 at the beginning, **i** as thou followedst H1115
Mt 25:40 I say unto you, I as ye have *G1909+G3745*
45 say unto you, I as ye did *it* not *G1909+G3745*
Ro 11:13 For I speak to you Gentiles, **i** *G1909+G3745*
Php 1: 7 in my heart; **i** as both in my *G1909+G3745*
Heb 3: 3 than Moses, **i** as he who hath *G2596+G3745*
7:20 And **i** as not without an oath *G2596+G3745*
1Pt 4:13 But rejoice, **i** as ye are partakers of *G2526*

INCENSE
Ex 25: 6 spices for anointing oil, and for sweet **i**, H7004
30: 1 And thou shalt make an altar to burn **i** H7004
7 And Aaron shall burn thereon sweet **i** H7004
7 the lamps, he shall burn **i** upon it. H6999
8 he shall burn **i** upon it, a perpetual H6999
8 upon it, a perpetual **i** before the LORD H7004
9 Ye shall offer no strange **i** thereon, nor H7004
27 and his vessels, and the altar of **i**, H7004
31: 8 with all his furniture, and the altar of **i**, H7004
11 And the anointing oil, and sweet **i** for H7004
35: 8 for anointing oil, and for the sweet **i**, H7004
15 And the **i** altar, and his staves, and the H7004
15 oil, and the sweet **i**, and the hanging for H7004
28 for the anointing oil, and for the sweet **i**. H7004
37:25 And he made the **i** altar *of* shittim H7004
29 oil, and the pure **i** of sweet spices, H7004
39:38 oil, and the sweet **i**, and the hanging for H7004
40: 5 of gold for the **i** before the ark of the H7004
27 And he burnt sweet **i** thereon; as the H7004
Lev 4: 7 of the altar of sweet **i** before the LORD, H7004
10: 1 therein, and put **i** thereon, and offered H7004
16:12 hands full of sweet **i** beaten small, and H7004
13 And he shall put the **i** upon the fire H7004
13 the cloud of the **i** may cover the mercy H7004
Nu 4:16 and the sweet **i**, and the daily meat H7004
7:14 spoon of ten *shekels* of gold, full of **i**: H7004
20 spoon of gold of ten *shekels*, full of **i**: H7004
26 golden spoon of ten *shekels*, full of **i**: H7004
32 golden spoon of ten *shekels*, full of **i**: H7004
38 golden spoon of ten *shekels*, full of **i**: H7004
44 golden spoon of ten *shekels*, full of **i**: H7004
50 golden spoon of ten *shekels*, full of **i**: H7004
56 golden spoon of ten *shekels*, full of **i**: H7004
62 golden spoon of ten *shekels*, full of **i**: H7004
68 golden spoon of ten *shekels*, full of **i**: H7004
74 golden spoon of ten *shekels*, full of **i**: H7004
80 golden spoon of ten *shekels*, full of **i**: H7004
86 The golden spoons *were* twelve, full of **i**, H7004
16: 7 And put fire therein, and put **i** in them H7004
17 censer, and put **i** in them, and bring ye H7004
18 in them, and laid **i** thereon, and stood H7004
35 hundred and fifty men that offered **i**. H7004
40 come near to offer **i** before the LORD; H7004
46 altar, and put on **i**, and go quickly unto H7004
47 people: and he put on **i**, and made an H7004
Dt 33:10 law: they shall put **i** before thee, and H6988
1Sa 2:28 altar, to burn **i**, to wear an ephod before H7004
1Ki 3: 3 he sacrificed and burnt **i** in high places. H6999
9:25 and he burnt **i** upon the altar that *was* H6999
11: 8 burnt **i** and sacrificed unto their gods. H6999
12:33 he offered upon the altar, and burnt **i**. H6999
13: 1 Jeroboam stood by the altar to burn **i**. H6999
2 high places that burn **i** upon thee, and H6999
22:43 and burnt **i** yet in the high places. H6999
2Ki 12: 3 and burnt **i** in the high places. H6999
14: 4 sacrifice and burnt **i** on the high places. H6999
15: 4 and burnt **i** still on the high places. H6999
35 and burned **i** still in the high places. H6999
16: 4 And he sacrificed and burnt **i** in the H6999
17:11 And there they burnt **i** in all the high H6999
18: 4 burn **i** to it: and he called it Nehushtan. H6999
22:17 me, and have burned **i** unto other gods, H6999
23: 5 ordained to burn **i** in the high places in H6999
5 also that burned **i** unto Baal, to the H6999
8 had burned **i**, from Geba to Beer-sheba, H6999
1Ch 6:49 offering, and on the altar of **i**, *and were* H7004
23:13 for ever, to burn **i** before the LORD, to H6999
28:18 And for the altar of **i** refined gold by H7004
2Ch 2: 4 burn before him sweet **i**, and for the H7004
13:11 and sweet **i**: the shewbread also H7004
25:14 before them, and burned **i** unto them. H6999
26:16 to burn **i** upon the altar of incense. H6999
16 to burn incense upon the altar of **i**. H7004
18 Uzziah, to burn **i** unto the LORD, but H6999
18 to burn **i**: go out of the sanctuary; H6999
19 in his hand to burn **i**: and while he was H6999
19 of the LORD, from beside the **i** altar. H7004
28: 3 Moreover he burnt **i** in the valley of the H6999
4 He sacrificed also and burnt **i** in the H6999
25 places to burn **i** unto other gods, and H6999
29: 7 have not burned **i** nor offered burnt H7004
11 should minister unto him, and burn **i**. H6999
2Ch 30:14 all the altars for **i** took they away, and H6999
32:12 before one altar, and burn **i** upon it? H6999
34:25 me, and have burned **i** unto other gods, H6999
Ps 66:15 fatlings, with the **i** of rams; I will offer H7004
141: 2 before thee *as* **i**; *and* the lifting up of H7004
Isa 1:13 Bring no more vain oblations; **i** is an H7004
43:23 an offering, nor wearied thee with **i**. H3828
60: 6 bring gold and **i**; and they shall shew H3828
65: 3 and burneth **i** upon altars of brick; H6999
7 have burned **i** upon the mountains, H6999
66: 3 he that burneth **i**, *as if* he blessed an H3828
Jer 1:16 me, and have burned **i** unto other gods, H6999
6:20 To what purpose cometh there to me **i** H3828
7: 9 falsely, and burn **i** unto Baal, and walk H6999
11:12 whom they offer **i**: but they shall not H6999
13 thing, *even* altars to burn **i** unto Baal. H6999
17 me to anger in offering **i** unto Baal. H6999
17:26 offerings, and **i**, and bringing sacrifices H3828
18:15 they have burned **i** to vanity, and they H6999
19: 4 and have burned **i** in it unto other H6999
13 they have burned **i** unto all the host of H6999
32:29 roofs they have offered **i** unto Baal, and H6999
41: 5 with offerings and **i** in their hand, to H3828
44: 3 they went to burn **i**, *and* to serve other H6999
5 to burn no **i** unto other gods. H6999
8 hands, burning **i** unto other gods in the H6999
15 wives had burned **i** unto other gods, H6999
17 own mouth, to burn **i** unto the queen of H6999
18 But since we left off to burn **i** to the H6999
19 And when we burned **i** to the queen of H6999
21 The **i** that ye burned in the cities of H7002
23 Because ye have burned **i**, and because H6999
25 have vowed, to burn **i** to the queen of H6999
48:35 and him that burneth **i** to his gods. H6999
Ezk 8:11 hand; and a thick cloud of **i** went up. H7004
16:18 set mine oil and mine **i** before them. H7004
23:41 thou hast set mine **i** and mine oil. H7004
Hos 2:13 she burned **i** to them, and she decked H6999
4:13 and burn **i** upon the hills, under H6999
11: 2 and burned **i** to graven images. H6999
Hab 1:16 their net, and burn **i** unto their drag; H6999
Mal 1:11 and in every place **i** *shall be* offered H6999
Lk 1: 9 his lot was to burn **i** when he went into *G2370*
10 were praying without at the time of **i**. *G2368*
11 on the right side of the altar of **i**. *G2368*
Rev 8: 3 unto him much **i**, that he should offer *G2368*
4 And the smoke of the **i**, *which came* *G2368*

INCENSED
Isa 41:11 Behold, all they that were **i** against thee H2734
45:24 are **i** against him shall be ashamed. H2734

INCLINE
Jos 24:23 among you, and **i** your heart unto the H5186
1Ki 8:58 That he may **i** our hearts unto him, to H5186
Ps 17: 6 hear me, O God: **i** thine ear unto me, H5186
45:10 and consider, and **i** thine ear; forget H5186
49: 4 I will **i** mine ear to a parable: I will H5186
71: 2 **i** thine ear unto me, and save me. H5186
78: 1 Give ear, O my people, *to* my law: **i** H5186
88: 2 Let my prayer come before thee: **i** thine H5186
102: 2 I am in trouble; **i** thine ear unto me: in H5186
119:36 I my heart unto thy testimonies, and H5186
141: 4 I not my heart to *any* evil thing, to H5186
Prv 2: 2 So that thou **i** thine ear unto wisdom, H7181
4:20 My son, attend to my words; **i** thine ear H5186
Isa 37:17 I thine ear, O LORD, and hear; open H5186
55: 3 I your ear, and come unto me: hear, H5186
Dan 9:18 O my God, **i** thine ear, and hear; open H5186

INCLINED
Jdg 9: 3 and their hearts **i** to follow Abimelech; H5186
Ps 40: 1 and he **i** unto me, and heard my cry. H5186
116: 2 Because he hath **i** his ear unto me, H5186
119:112 I have **i** mine heart to perform thy H5186
Prv 5:13 **i** mine ear to them that instructed me! H5186
Jer 7:24 But they hearkened not, nor **i** their ear, H5186
26 Yet they hearkened not unto me, nor **i** H5186
11: 8 Yet they obeyed not, nor **i** their ear, but H5186
17:23 But they obeyed not, neither **i** their ear, H5186
25: 4 not hearkened, nor **i** your ear to hear. H5186
34:14 not unto me, neither **i** their ear. H5186
35:15 not **i** your ear, nor hearkened unto me. H5186
44: 5 But they hearkened not, nor **i** their ear H5186

INCLINETH
Prv 2:18 For her house **i** unto death, and her H7743

INCLOSE
Song 8: 9 we will **i** her with boards of cedar. H6696

INCLOSED
Ex 39: 6 And they wrought onyx stones **i** in H4142
13 **i** in ouches of gold in their inclosings. H4142
Jdg 20:43 *Thus* they **i** the Benjamites round H3803
Ps 17:10 They are **i** in their own fat: with their H5462
22:16 of the wicked have **i** me: they pierced H5362
Song 4:12 A garden **i** *is* my sister, *my* spouse; a H5274
Lam 3: 9 He hath **i** my ways with hewn stone, he H1443
Lk 5: 6 And when they had this done, they **i** a *G4788*

INCLOSINGS
Ex 28:20 they shall be set in gold in their **i**. H4396
39:13 inclosed in ouches of gold in their **i**. H4396

INCONTINENCY
1Co 7: 5 that Satan tempt you not for your **i**. *G192*

INCONTINENT
2Ti 3: 3 **i**, fierce, despisers of those that are good, *G193*

INCORRUPTIBLE
1Co 9:25 obtain a corruptible crown; but we an **i**. *G862*
15:52 be raised **i**, and we shall be changed. *G862*
1Pt 1: 4 To an inheritance **i**, and undefiled, and *G862*
23 seed, but of **i**, by the word of God, *G862*

INCORRUPTION
1Co 15:42 It is sown in corruption; it is raised in **i**: *G861*
50 of God; neither doth corruption inherit **i**. *G861*
53 For this corruptible must put on **i**, and *G861*
54 shall have put on **i**, and this mortal shall *G861*

INCREASE
Gen 47:24 And it shall come to pass in the **i**, that H8393
Lev 19:25 the **i** thereof: I *am* the LORD your God. H8393
25: 7 thy land, shall all the **i** thereof be meat. H8393
12 ye shall eat the **i** thereof out of the field. H8393
16 of years thou shalt **i** the price thereof, H7235
20 we shall not sow, nor gather in our **i**: H8393
36 Take thou no usury of him, or **i**: but fear H8636
37 usury, nor lend him thy victuals for **i**. H4768
26: 4 shall yield her **i**, and the trees of the H2981
20 shall not yield her **i**, neither shall the H2981
Nu 18:30 unto the Levites as the **i** of the H8393
30 and as the **i** of the winepress. H8393
32:14 fathers' stead, an **i** of sinful men, to H8635
Dt 6: 3 thee, and that ye may **i** mightily, as the H7235
7:13 and thine oil, the **i** of thy kine, and the H7698
22 lest the beasts of the field **i** upon thee. H7235
14:22 Thou shalt truly tithe all the **i** of thy H8393
28 the tithe of thine **i** the same year, and H8393
16:15 thee in all thine **i**, and in all the works H8393
26:12 all the tithes of thine **i** the third year, H8393
28: 4 of thy cattle, the **i** of thy kine, and the H7698
18 of thy land, the **i** of thy kine, and the H7698
51 wine, or oil, *or* the **i** of thy kine, or H7698
32:13 he might eat the **i** of the fields; and he H8570
22 the earth with her **i**, and set on fire the H2981
Jdg 6: 4 and destroyed the **i** of the earth, till H2981
9:29 **I** thine army, and come out. H7235
1Sa 2:33 heart: and all the **i** of thine house shall H4768
1Ch 27:23 **i** Israel like to the stars of the heavens. H7235
27 over the **i** of the vineyards for the
2Ch 31: 5 and of all the **i** of the field; and the H8393
32:28 Storehouses also for the **i** of corn, and H8393
Ezr 10:10 wives, to **i** the trespass of Israel. H3254
Neh 9:37 And it yieldeth much **i** unto the kings H8393
Job 8: 7 yet thy latter end should greatly **i**. H7685
20:28 The **i** of his house shall depart, *and his* H2981
31:12 and would root out all mine **i**. H8393
Ps 44:12 and dost not **i** *thy wealth* by their price. H7235
62:10 riches **i**, set not your heart *upon them*. H5107
67: 6 *Then* shall the earth yield her **i**; *and* H2981
71:21 Thou shalt **i** my greatness, and comfort H7325
73:12 prosper in the world; they **i** *in* riches. H7685
78:46 He gave also their **i** unto the caterpiller, H2981
85:12 *is* good; and our land shall yield her **i**. H2981
107:37 vineyards, which may yield fruits of **i**. H8393
115:14 The LORD shall **i** you more and more, H3254
Prv 1: 5 A wise *man* will hear, and will **i** H3254
3: 9 and with the firstfruits of all thine **i**: H8393
9: 9 a just *man*, and he will **i** in learning. H3254
13:11 but he that gathereth by labour shall **i**. H7235
14: 4 but much **i** *is* by the strength of the ox. H8393
18:20 with the **i** of his lips shall he be filled. H8393
22:16 He that oppresseth the poor to **i** his H7235
Prv 28:28 but when they perish, the righteous **i**. H7235
Ecc 5:10 abundance with **i**: this *is* also vanity. H8393
11 When goods **i**, they are increased that H7235
6:11 Seeing there be many things that **i** H7235
Isa 9: 7 Of the **i** of *his* government and peace H4766
29:19 The meek also shall **i** *their* joy in the H3254
30:23 and bread of the **i** of the earth, and it H8393
57: 9 and didst **i** thy perfumes, and didst H7235
Jer 2: 3 firstfruits of his **i**: all that devour him H8393
23: 3 folds; and they shall be fruitful and **i**. H7235
Ezk 5:16 you: and I will **i** the famine upon you, H3254
18: 8 hath taken any **i**, *that* hath withdrawn H8636
13 and hath taken **i**: shall he then live? he H8636
17 received usury nor **i**, hath executed my H8636
22:12 hast taken usury and **i**, and thou hast H8636
34:27 shall yield her **i**, and they shall be safe H2981
36:11 and they shall **i** and bring fruit: and H7235
29 will **i** it, and lay no famine upon you. H7235
30 of the tree, and the **i** of the field, that ye H8570
37 I will **i** them with men like a flock. H7235
48:18 *portion*; and the **i** thereof shall be for H8393
Dan 11:39 acknowledge *and* **i** with glory: and he H7235
Hos 4:10 and shall not **i**: because they have left H6555
Zec 8:12 shall give her **i**, and the heavens shall H2981
10: 8 and they shall **i** as they have increased. H7235
Lk 17: 5 And the apostles said unto the Lord, I *G4369*
Jn 3:30 He must **i**, but I *must* decrease. *G837*
1Co 3: 6 Apollos watered; but God gave the **i**. *G837*
7 that watereth; but God that giveth the **i**. *G837*
2Co 9:10 and **i** the fruits of your righteousness;) *G837*
Eph 4:16 every part, maketh **i** of the body unto the *G838*
Col 2:19 together, increaseth with the **i** of God. *G838*
1Th 3:12 And the Lord make you to **i** and *G4121*
4:10 you, brethren, that ye **i** more and more; *G4052*
2Ti 2:16 for they will **i** unto more ungodliness. *G4298*

INCREASED
Gen 7:17 and the waters **i**, and bare up the ark, H7235
18 And the waters prevailed, and were **i** H7235
30:30 and it is *now* **i** unto a multitude; and H6555
43 And the man **i** exceedingly, and had H6555
Ex 1: 7 were fruitful, and **i** abundantly, and H8317
23:30 until thou be **i**, and inherit the land. H6509
1Sa 14:19 went on and **i**: and Saul said unto the H7227
2Sa 15:12 the people **i** continually with Absalom. H7227
1Ki 22:35 And the battle **i** that day: and the king H5927
1Ch 4:38 and the house of their fathers **i** greatly. H6555
5:23 in the land: they **i** from Bashan unto H7235
2Ch 18:34 And the battle **i** that day: howbeit the H5927
Ezr 9: 6 our iniquities are **i** over *our* head, and H7235
Job 1:10 and his substance is **i** in the land. H6555
Ps 3: 1 LORD, how are they **i** that trouble me! H7231
4: 7 the time *that* their corn and their wine **i**. H7231
49:16 rich, when the glory of his house is **i**; H7325
105:24 And he **i** his people greatly; and made H6509
Prv 9:11 and the years of thy life shall be **i**. H3254
Ecc 2: 9 So I was great, and **i** more than all that H3254
5:11 When goods increase, they are **i** that H7231
Isa 9: 3 the nation, *and* not **i** the joy: they joy H1431
26:15 Thou hast **i** the nation, O LORD, thou H3254
15 O LORD, thou hast **i** the nation: thou H3254
51: 2 him alone, and blessed him, and **i** him. H7235
Jer 3:16 be multiplied and **i** in the land, in those H6509
5: 6 are many, *and* their backslidings are **i**. H6105
15: 8 Their widows are **i** to me above the H6105
29: 6 ye may be **i** there, and not diminished. H7235
30:14 thine iniquity; *because* thy sins were **i**. H6105
15 **i**, I have done these things unto thee. H6105
Lam 2: 5 holds, and hath **i** in the daughter of H7235
Ezk 16: 7 and thou hast **i** and waxen great, and H7235
26 of flesh; and hast **i** thy whoredoms, to H7235
23:14 And *that* she **i** her whoredoms: for H3254
28: 5 thy traffick hast thou **i** thy riches, and H7235
41: 7 *still* upward, and so **i** *from* the lowest H5927
Dan 12: 4 to and fro, and knowledge shall be **i**. H7235
Hos 4: 7 As they were **i**, so they sinned against H7230
10: 1 of his fruit he hath **i** the altars; H7235
Am 4: 9 and your olive trees **i**, the palmerworm H7235
Zec 10: 8 and they shall increase as they have **i**. H7235
Mk 4: 8 that sprang up and **i**; and brought forth, *G837*
Lk 2:52 And Jesus **i** in wisdom and stature, and *G4298*
Act 6: 7 And the word of God **i**; and the number *G837*
9:22 But Saul **i** the more in strength, and *G1743*
16: 5 in the faith, and **i** in number daily. *G4052*
2Co 10:15 when your faith is **i**, that we shall be *G837*
Rev 3:17 Because thou sayest, I am rich, and **i** *G4147*

INCREASEST
Job 10:17 against me, and **i** thine indignation H7235

INCREASETH
Job 10:16 For it **i**. Thou huntest me as a fierce H1342
12:23 He **i** the nations, and destroyeth them: H7679
Ps 74:23 that rise up against thee **i** continually. H5927
Prv 11:24 There is that scattereth, and yet **i**; and H3254
16:21 and the sweetness of the lips **i** learning. H3254
23:28 and **i** the transgressors among men. H3254
24: 5 yea, a man of knowledge **i** strength. H553
28: 8 He that by usury and unjust gain **i** his H7235
29:16 **i**: but the righteous shall see their fall. H7235
Ecc 1:18 he that **i** knowledge increaseth sorrow. H3254
18 he that increaseth knowledge **i** sorrow. H3254
Isa 40:29 *them that have* no might he **i** strength. H7235
Hos 12: 1 the east wind: he daily **i** lies and H7235
Hab 2: 6 Woe to him that **i** *that which is* not his! H7235
Col 2:19 knit together, **i** with the increase of God. *G837*

INCREASING
Col 1:10 work, and **i** in the knowledge of God; *G837*

INCREDIBLE
Act 26: 8 Why should it be thought a thing **i** with *G571*

INCURABLE
2Ch 21:18 in his bowels with an **i** disease. H369+H4832
Job 34: 6 my wound *is* **i** without transgression. H605
Jer 15:18 and my wound **i**, *which* refuseth to be H605
30:12 For thus saith the LORD, Thy bruise *is* **i**, H605
15 thy sorrow *is* **i** for the multitude of thine H605
Mic 1: 9 For her wound *is* **i**; for it is come unto H605

INDEBTED
Lk 11: 4 every one that is **i** to us. And lead us *G3784*

INDEED
Gen 17:19 bear thee a son **i**; and thou shalt call his H61
20:12 And yet **i** *she is* my sister; she *is* the H546
37: 8 to him, Shalt thou **i** reign over us? or H4427
8 us? or shalt thou **i** have dominion over H4910
10 and thy brethren **i** come to bow down H935
40:15 For **i** I was stolen away out of the land H1589
43:20 And said, O sir, we came **i** down at the H3381
44: 5 and whereby **i** he divineth? ye have H5172
Ex 19: 5 ye will obey my voice **i**, and keep my H8085
23:22 But if thou shalt **i** obey his voice, and H8085
Lev 10:18 *place*: ye should **i** have eaten it in the H398
Nu 12: 2 And they said, Hath the LORD **i** spoken
21: 2 said, If thou wilt **i** deliver this people H5414
22:37 I not able **i** to promote thee to honour? H552
Dt 2:15 For **i** the hand of the LORD was against H1571
21:16 son of the hated, *which is* **i** the firstborn:
Jos 7:20 And Achan answered Joshua, and said, I H546
1Sa 1:11 of hosts, if thou wilt **i** look on the H7200
2:30 Israel saith, I said **i** *that* thy house, and H559
2Sa 14: 5 she answered, I *am* **i** a widow woman, H61
15: 8 bring me again **i** to Jerusalem, then I
1Ki 8:27 But will God **i** dwell on the earth? behold, H552
2Ki 14:10 Thou hast **i** smitten Edom, and thine H5221
1Ch 4:10 wouldest bless me **i**, and enlarge my H1288
21:17 and done evil **i**; but *as for* these sheep, H7489
Job 19: 4 And be it **i** *that* I have erred, mine error H551
5 If **i** ye will magnify *yourselves* against H551
Ps 58: 1 Do ye **i** speak righteousness, O H552
Isa 6: 9 people, Hear ye **i**, but understand not; H8085
9 not; and see ye **i**, but perceive not. H7200
Jer 22: 4 For if ye do this thing **i**, then shall there H6213
Mt 3:11 I **i** baptize you with water unto *G3303*
13:32 Which **i** is the least of all seeds: but *G3303*
20:23 Ye shall drink **i** of my cup, and be *G3303*
23:27 sepulchres, which **i** appear beautiful *G3303*
26:41 spirit **i** *is* willing, but the flesh *is* weak. *G3303*
Mk 1: 8 I **i** have baptized you with water: but he *G3303*
9:13 But I say unto you, That Elias is **i** *G2532*
10:39 them, Ye shall **i** drink of the cup that *G3303*
11:32 counted John, that he was a prophet **i**. *G3689*
14:21 The Son of man **i** goeth, as it is written *G3303*
Lk 3:16 unto *them* all, I **i** baptize you with *G3303*
11:48 fathers: for they **i** killed them, and ye *G3303*
23:41 And we **i** justly; for we receive the due *G3303*
24:34 Saying, The Lord is risen **i**, and hath *G3689*
Jn 1:47 Behold an Israelite **i**, in whom is no guile! *G230*
4:42 is **i** the Christ, the Saviour of the world. *G230*
6:55 For my flesh is meat **i**, and my blood is *G230*
55 is meat indeed, and my blood is drink **i**. *G230*
7:26 rulers know **i** that this is the very Christ? *G230*
8:31 in my word, *then* are ye my disciples **i**; *G230*
36 shall make you free, ye shall be free **i**. *G3689*
Act 4:16 men? for that **i** a notable miracle hath *G3303*
11:16 how that he said, John **i** baptized with *G3303*

Act 22: 9 And they that were with me saw i the G3303
Ro 6:11 to be dead i unto sin, but alive unto G3303
8: 7 to the law of God, neither i can be. G1063
14:20 of God. All things i *are* pure; but *it is* G3303
1Co 11: 7 For a man i ought not to cover *his* G3303
2Co 8:17 For i he accepted the exhortation; but G3303
11: 1 a little in *my* folly: and i bear with me. G2532
Php 1:15 Some i preach Christ even of envy and G3303
2:27 For i he was sick nigh unto death: but G2532
3: 1 i *is* not grievous, but for you *it is* safe. G3303
Col 2:23 Which things have i a shew of wisdom G3303
1Th 4:10 And i ye do it toward all the brethren G2532
1Ti 5: 3 Honour widows that are widows i. G3689
5 Now she that is a widow i, and desolate, G3689
16 it may relieve them that are widows i. G3689
1Pt 2: 4 stone, disallowed i of men, but chosen G3303

INDIA
Est 1: 1 reigned, from I even unto Ethiopia, H1912
8: 9 which *are* from I unto Ethiopia, an H1912

INDIGNATION
Dt 29:28 and in great i, and cast them into H7110
2Ki 3:27 there was great i against Israel: and H7110
Neh 4: 1 and took great i, and mocked the Jews. H3707
Est 5: 9 him, he was full of i against Mordecai. H2534
Job 10:17 increasest thine i upon me; changes H3708
Ps 69:24 Pour out thine i upon them, and let thy H2195
78:49 his anger, wrath, and i, and trouble, by H2195
102:10 Because of thine i and thy wrath: for H2195
Isa 10: 5 and the staff in their hand is mine i. H2195
25 For yet a very little while, and the i H2195
13: 5 of his i, to destroy the whole land. H2195
26:20 a little moment, until the i be overpast. H2195
30:27 of i, and his tongue as a devouring fire: H2195
30 of his arm, with the i of *his* anger, and H2197
34: 2 For the i of the LORD *is* upon all H7110
66:14 servants, and *his* i toward his enemies. H2194
Jer 10:10 nations shall not be able to abide his i. H2195
15:17 thy hand: for thou hast filled me with i. H2195
50:25 the weapons of his i: for this *is* the work H2195
Lam 2: 6 i of his anger the king and the priest. H2195
Ezk 21:31 And I will pour out mine i upon thee, I H2195
22:24 nor rained upon in the day of i. H2195
31 Therefore have I poured out mine i H2195
Dan 8:19 in the last end of the i: for at the time H2195
11:30 and return, and have i against the holy H2194
36 prosper till the i be accomplished: for H2195
Mic 7: 9 I will bear the i of the LORD, because I H2197
Nah 1: 6 Who can stand before his i? and who H2195
Hab 3:12 Thou didst march through the land in i, H2195
Zep 3: 8 upon them mine i, *even* all my fierce H2195
Zec 1:12 had i these threescore and ten years? H2194
Mal 1: 4 whom the LORD hath i for ever. H2194
Mt 20:24 moved with i against the two brethren. G23
26: 8 But when his disciples saw *it*, they had i, G23
Mk 14: 4 And there were some that had i within G23
Lk 13:14 answered with i, because that Jesus had G23
Act 5:17 the Sadducees,) and were filled with i, G2205
Ro 2: 8 but obey unrighteousness, i and wrath, G2372
2Co 7:11 yea, *what* i, yea, *what* fear, yea, *what* G24
Heb 10:27 i, which shall devour the adversaries. G2205
Rev 14:10 into the cup of his i; and he shall be G3709

INDITING
Ps 45: 1 My heart is i a good matter: I speak of H7370

INDUSTRIOUS
1Ki 11:28 that he was i, he made him H6213+H4399

INEXCUSABLE
Ro 2: 1 Therefore thou art i, O man, whosoever G379

INFALLIBLE
Act 1: 3 passion by many i proofs, being seen of

INFAMOUS
Ezk 22: 5 *which art* i *and* much vexed. H2931+H8034

INFAMY
Prv 25:10 to shame, and thine i turn not away. H1681
Ezk 36: 3 of talkers, and *are* an i of the people: H1681

INFANT
1Sa 15: 3 man and woman, i and suckling, ox H5768
Isa 65:20 There shall be no more thence an i of H5764

INFANTS
Job 3:16 not been; as i *which* never saw light. H5768
Hos 13:16 by the sword: their i shall be dashed in H5768
Lk 18:15 And they brought unto him also i, that G1025

INFERIOR
Job 12: 3 well as you; I *am* not i to you: yea, who H5307
13: 2 do I know also: I *am* not i unto you. H5307
Dan 2:39 another kingdom i to thee, and another H772
2Co 12:13 For what is it wherein ye were i to other G2274

INFIDEL
2Co 6:15 part hath he that believeth with an i? G571
1Ti 5: 8 denied the faith, and is worse than an i. G571

INFINITE
Job 22: 5 great? and thine iniquities i? H369+H7093
Ps 147: 5 power: his understanding *is* i. H369+H4557
Nah 3: 9 and *it was* i; Put and Lubim were H369+H7097

INFIRMITIES
Mt 8:17 took our i, and bare *our* sicknesses. G769
Lk 5:15 hear, and to be healed by him of their i. G769
7:21 many of *their* i and plagues, and of G3554
8: 2 healed of evil spirits and i, Mary called G769
Ro 8:26 Likewise the Spirit also helpeth our i: for G769
15: 1 ought to bear the i of the weak, and not G771
2Co 11:30 glory of the things which concern mine i. G769
12: 5 of myself I will not glory, but in mine i. G769
9 I rather glory in my i, that the power of G769
10 Therefore I take pleasure in i, in G769
1Ti 5:23 for thy stomach's sake and thine often i. G769
Heb 4:15 the feeling of our i; but was in all points G769

INFIRMITY
Lev 12: 2 for her i shall she be unclean. H1738
Ps 77:10 And I said, This *is* my i: *but I will* H2470
Prv 18:14 The spirit of a man will sustain his i; H4245
Lk 13:11 had a spirit of i eighteen years, and was G769
12 Woman, thou art loosed from thine i. G769
Jn 5: 5 which had an i thirty and eight years. G769
Ro 6:19 men because of the i of your flesh: for as G769
Gal 4:13 Ye know how through i of the flesh I G769
Heb 5: 2 that he himself also is compassed with i. G769
7:28 priests which have i; but the word of the G769

INFLAME
Isa 5:11 continue until night, *till* wine i them! H1814

INFLAMMATION
Lev 13:28 him clean: for it *is* an i of the burning. H6867
Dt 28:22 a fever, and with an i, and with an H1816

INFLICTED
2Co 2: 6 this punishment, which *was* i of many.

INFLUENCES
Job 38:31 Canst thou bind the sweet i of Pleiades, H4575

INFOLDING
Ezk 1: 4 great cloud, and a fire i itself, and a H3947

INFORM
Dt 17:10 to do according to all that they i thee: H3384

INFORMED
Dan 9:22 And he i *me*, and talked with me, and H995
Act 21:21 And they are i of thee, that thou G2727
24 whereof they were i concerning thee, G2727
24: 1 who i the governor against Paul. G1718
25: 2 i him against Paul, and besought him, G1718
15 elders of the Jews i *me*, desiring *to have* G1718

INGATHERING
Ex 23:16 and the feast of i, *which is* in the end of H614
34:22 and the feast of i at the year's end. H614

INHABIT
Nu 35:34 which ye shall i, wherein I dwell: for H3427
Prv 10:30 but the wicked shall not i the earth. H7931
Isa 42:11 *that* Kedar doth i: let the inhabitants of H3427
65:21 And they shall build houses, and i H3427
22 They shall not build, and another i; they H3427
Jer 17: 6 cometh; but shall i the parched places H7931
48:18 Thou daughter that dost i Dibon, come H3427
Ezk 33:24 Son of man, they that i those wastes of H3427
Am 9:14 waste cities, and i *them*; and they shall H3427
Zep 1:13 houses, but not i *them*; and they shall H3427

INHABITANT
Job 28: 4 The flood breaketh out from the i; *even* H1481
Isa 5: 9 desolate, *even* great and fair, without i. H3427
6:11 be wasted without i, and the houses H3427
9: 9 Ephraim and the i of Samaria, that say H3427
12: 6 Cry out and shout, thou i of Zion: for H3427
20: 6 And the i of this isle shall say in that H3427
24:17 snare, *are* upon thee, O i of the earth. H3427
33:24 And the i shall not say, I am sick: the H7934
Jer 2:15 waste: his cities are burned without i. H3427
4: 7 cities shall be laid waste, without an i. H3427
9:11 cities of Judah desolate, without an i. H3427
10:17 Gather up thy wares out of the land, O i H3427
21:13 Behold, I *am* against thee, O i of the H3427
22:23 O i of Lebanon, that makest thy nest in H3427
26: 9 without an i? And all the people were H3427
33:10 man, and without i, and without beast, H3427
34:22 of Judah a desolation without an i. H3427
44:22 and a curse, without an i, as at this day. H3427
46:19 be waste and desolate without an i. H3427
48:19 O i of Aroer, stand by the way, and H3427
43 thee, O i of Moab, saith the LORD. H3427
51:29 of Babylon a desolation without an i. H3427
35 Babylon, shall the i of Zion say; and my H3427
37 and an hissing, without an i. H3427
Am 1: 5 and cut off the i from the plain of Aven, H3427
8 And I will cut off the i from Ashdod, H3427
Mic 1:11 Pass ye away, thou i of Saphir, having H3427
11 thy shame naked: the i of Zaanan came H3427
12 For the i of Maroth waited carefully for H3427
13 O thou i of Lachish, bind the chariot to H3427
15 Yet will I bring an heir unto thee, O i of H3427
Zep 2: 5 destroy thee, that there shall be no i. H3427
3: 6 there is no man, that there is none i. H3427

INHABITANTS
Gen 19:25 the plain, and all the i of the cities, and H3427
34:30 to stink among the i of the land, among H3427
50:11 And when the i of the land, the H3427
Ex 15:14 shall take hold on the i of Palestina. H3427
15 all the i of Canaan shall melt away. H3427
23:31 I will deliver the i of the land into your H3427
34:12 covenant with the i of the land whither H3427
15 Lest thou make a covenant with the i of H3427
Lev 18:25 it, and the land itself vomiteth out her i. H3427
25:10 land unto all the i thereof: it shall be a H3427
Nu 13:32 that eateth up the i thereof; and all the H3427
14:14 And they will tell *it* to the i of this land: H3427
32:17 cities because of the i of the land. H3427
33:52 Then ye shall drive out all the i of the H3427
53 And ye shall dispossess *the* i of the land,
55 But if ye will not drive out the i of the H3427
Dt 13:13 withdrawn the i of their city, saying, H3427
15 Thou shalt surely smite the i of that H3427
Jos 2: 9 the i of the land faint because of you. H3427
24 i of the country do faint because of us. H3427
7: 9 For the Canaanites and all the i of the H3427
8:24 of slaying all the i of Ai in the field, in H3427
26 he had utterly destroyed all the i of Ai. H3427
9: 3 And when the i of Gibeon heard what H3427
11 Wherefore our elders and all the i of H3427
24 and to destroy all the i of the land from H3427
10: 1 her king; and how the i of Gibeon had H3427
11:19 the Hivites the i of Gibeon: all *other* H3427
13: 6 All the i of the hill country from H3427
15:15 And he went up thence to the i of H3427
63 As for the Jebusites the i of Jerusalem, H3427
17: 7 right hand unto the i of En-tap-puah. H3427
11 and her towns, and the i of Dor and her H3427
11 her towns, and the i of Endor and her H3427
11 her towns, and the i of Taanach and H3427
11 her towns, and the i of Megiddo and H3427
12 not drive out *the* i *of* those cities; but the
Jdg 1:11 And from thence he went against the i H3427
19 he drave out *the* i *of* the mountain; but
19 could not drive out the i of the valley, H3427
27 Neither did Manasseh drive out *the* i *of*
27 and her towns, nor the i of Dor and her H3427
27 her towns, nor the i of Ibleam and her H3427
27 her towns, nor the i of Megiddo and H3427
30 Neither did Zebulun drive out the i of H3427
30 of Kitron, nor the i of Nahalol; but the H3427
31 Neither did Asher drive out the i of H3427
31 of Accho, nor the i of Zidon, nor of H3427
32 Canaanites, the i of the land: for they H3427
33 Neither did Naphtali drive out the i of H3427
33 nor the i of Beth-anath; but he H3427
33 the Canaanites, the i of the land: H3427
33 nevertheless the i of Beth-shemesh and H3427
2: 2 And ye shall make no league with the i H3427
5: 7 *The* i *of* the villages ceased, they ceased

Jdg 5:11 acts *toward the* **i** of his villages in Israel:
23 ye bitterly the **i** thereof; because they H3427
10:18 he shall be head over all the **i** of Gilead. H3427
11: 8 and be our head over all the **i** of Gilead. H3427
21 of the Amorites, the **i** of that country. H3427
20:15 sword, beside the **i** of Gibeah, which H3427
21: 9 none of the **i** of Jabesh-gilead there. H3427
10 Go and smite the **i** of Jabesh-gilead H3427
12 And they found among the **i** of H3427
Ru 4: 4 Buy *it* before the **i**, and before the elders H3427
1Sa 6:21 And they sent messengers to the **i** of H3427
23: 5 So David saved the **i** of Keilah. H3427
27: 8 *were* of old the **i** of the land, as thou H3427
31:11 And when the **i** of Jabesh-gilead heard H3427
2Sa 5: 6 the Jebusites, the **i** of the land: which H3427
1Ki 17: 1 *who was* of the **i** of Gilead, said unto H8453
21:11 who were the **i** in his city, did as Jezebel H3427
2Ki 19:26 Therefore their **i** were of small power, H3427
22:16 and upon the **i** thereof, *even* all the H3427
19 and against the **i** thereof, that they H3427
23: 2 of Judah and all the **i** of Jerusalem with H3427
1Ch 8: 6 of the fathers of the **i** of Geba, and they H3427
13 of the fathers of the **i** of Aijalon, who H3427
13 Aijalon, who drove away the **i** of Gath: H3427
9: 2 Now the first **i** that *dwelt* in their H3427
11: 4 the Jebusites *were*, the **i** of the land. H3427
5 And the **i** of Jebus said to David, Thou H3427
22:18 for he hath given the **i** of the land into H3427
2Ch 15: 5 *were* upon all the **i** of the countries. H3427
20: 7 didst drive out the **i** of this land before H3427
15 all Judah, and ye **i** of Jerusalem, and H3427
18 all Judah and the **i** of Jerusalem fell H3427
20 O Judah, and ye **i** of Jerusalem; Believe H3427
23 up against the **i** of mount Seir, utterly H3427
23 an end of the **i** of Seir, every one helped H3427
21:11 Judah, and caused the **i** of Jerusalem to H3427
13 Judah and the **i** of Jerusalem to go a H3427
22: 1 And the **i** of Jerusalem made Ahaziah H3427
32:22 Hezekiah and the **i** of Jerusalem from H3427
26 *both* he and the **i** of Jerusalem, so that H3427
33 all Judah and the **i** of Jerusalem did H3427
33: 9 So Manasseh made Judah and the **i** of H3427
34:24 and upon the **i** thereof, *even* all the H3427
27 place, and against the **i** thereof, and H3427
28 and upon the **i** of the same. So they H3427
30 of Judah, and the **i** of Jerusalem, and H3427
32 stand *to it*. And the **i** of Jerusalem did H3427
35:18 were present, and the **i** of Jerusalem. H3427
Ezr 4: 6 against the **i** of Judah and Jerusalem. H3427
Neh 3:13 Hanun, and the **i** of Zanoah; they built H3427
7: 3 watches of the **i** of Jerusalem, every H3427
9:24 before them the **i** of the land, the H3427
Job 26: 5 under the waters, and the **i** thereof. H7931
Ps 33: 8 the **i** of the world stand in awe of him. H3427
14 he looketh upon all the **i** of the earth. H3427
49: 1 Hear this, all *ye* people; give ear, all *ye* **i** H3427
75: 3 The earth and all the **i** thereof are H3427
83: 7 the Philistines with the **i** of Tyre; H3427
Isa 5: 3 And now, O **i** of Jerusalem, and men of H3427
8:14 and for a snare to the **i** of Jerusalem. H3427
10:13 have put down the **i** like a valiant *man*: H3427
31 Madmenah is removed; the **i** of Gebim H3427
18: 3 All ye **i** of the world, and dwellers on H3427
21:14 The **i** of the land of Tema brought H3427
22:21 be a father to the **i** of Jerusalem, and to H3427
23: 2 Be still, ye **i** of the isle; thou whom the H3427
6 Pass ye over to Tarshish; howl, ye **i** of H3427
24: 1 and scattereth abroad the **i** thereof. H3427
5 The earth also is defiled under the **i** H3427
6 therefore the **i** of the earth are burned, H3427
26: 9 **i** of the world will learn righteousness. H3427
18 neither have the **i** of the world fallen. H3427
21 to punish the **i** of the earth for their H3427
37:27 Therefore their **i** *were* of small power, H3427
38:11 man no more with the **i** of the world. H3427
40:22 of the earth, and the **i** thereof *are* as H3427
42:10 is therein; the isles, and the **i** thereof. H3427
11 inhabit: let the **i** of the rock sing, let H3427
49:19 narrow by reason of the **i**, and they that H3427
Jer 1:14 break forth upon all the **i** of the land. H3427
4: 4 men of Judah and **i** of Jerusalem: lest H3427
6:12 upon the **i** of the land, saith the LORD. H3427
8: 1 the **i** of Jerusalem, out of their graves: H3427
10:18 I will sling out the **i** of the land at this H3427
11: 2 of Judah, and to the **i** of Jerusalem; H3427
9 Judah, and among the **i** of Jerusalem. H3427
12 Then shall the cities of Judah and **i** of H3427
13:13 I will fill all the **i** of this land, even the H3427
13 the **i** of Jerusalem, with drunkenness. H3427

Jer 17:20 Judah, and all the **i** of Jerusalem, that H3427
25 of Judah, and the **i** of Jerusalem: and H3427
18:11 of Judah, and to the **i** of Jerusalem, H3427
19: 3 of Judah, and **i** of Jerusalem; Thus H3427
12 LORD, and to the **i** thereof, and *even* H3427
21: 6 And I will smite the **i** of this city, both H3427
23:14 Sodom, and the **i** thereof as Gomorrah. H3427
25: 2 and to all the **i** of Jerusalem, saying, H3427
9 and against the **i** thereof, and against H3427
29 **i** of the earth, saith the LORD of hosts. H3427
30 *the grapes*, against all the **i** of the earth. H3427
26:15 city, and upon the **i** thereof: for of a H3427
32:32 men of Judah, and the **i** of Jerusalem. H3427
35:13 of Judah and the **i** of Jerusalem, Will ye H3427
17 and upon all the **i** of Jerusalem all the H3427
36:31 and upon the **i** of Jerusalem, and upon H3427
42:18 forth upon the **i** of Jerusalem; so shall H3427
46: 8 I will destroy the city and the **i** thereof. H3427
47: 2 cry, and all the **i** of the land shall howl. H3427
49: 8 Flee ye, turn back, dwell deep, O **i** of H3427
20 against the **i** of Teman: Surely the H3427
30 Flee, get you far off, dwell deep, O ye **i** H3427
50:21 it, and against the **i** of Pekod: waste H3427
34 the land, and disquiet the **i** of Babylon. H3427
35 and upon the **i** of Babylon, and upon H3427
51:12 he spake against the **i** of Babylon. H3427
24 and to all the **i** of Chaldea all their H3427
35 the **i** of Chaldea, shall Jerusalem say. H3427
Lam 4:12 The kings of the earth, and all the **i** of H3427
Ezk 11:15 unto whom the **i** of Jerusalem have H3427
12:19 Lord GOD of the **i** of Jerusalem, *and* of H3427
15: 6 for fuel, so will I give the **i** of Jerusalem. H3427
26:17 the sea, she and her **i**, which cause their H3427
27: 8 The **i** of Zidon and Arvad were thy H3427
35 All the **i** of the isles shall be astonished H3427
29: 6 And all the **i** of Egypt shall know that I H3427
Dan 4:35 And all the **i** of the earth *are* reputed as H1753
35 and *among* the **i** of the earth: and none H1753
9: 7 of Judah, and to the **i** of Jerusalem, and H3427
Hos 4: 1 with the **i** of the land, because H3427
10: 5 The **i** of Samaria shall fear because of H7934
Joel 1: 2 and give ear, all ye **i** of the land. Hath H3427
14 elders *and* all the **i** of the land *into* the H3427
2: 1 let all the **i** of the land tremble: H3427
Mic 6:12 violence, and the **i** thereof have spoken H3427
16 and the **i** thereof an hissing: therefore H3427
Zep 1: 4 and upon all the **i** of Jerusalem; and I H3427
11 Howl, ye **i** of Maktesh, for all the H3427
2: 5 Woe unto the **i** of the sea coast, the H3427
Zec 8:20 come people, and the **i** of many cities: H3427
21 And the **i** of one *city* shall go to H3427
11: 6 For I will no more pity the **i** of the land, H3427
12: 5 in their heart, The **i** of Jerusalem *shall* H3427
7 the glory of the **i** of Jerusalem do not H3427
8 In that day shall the LORD defend the **i** H3427
10 and upon the **i** of Jerusalem, the spirit H3427
13: 1 David and to the **i** of Jerusalem for sin H3427
Rev 17: 2 and the **i** of the earth have been *G2730*

INHABITED
Gen 36:20 the Horite, who **i** the land; Lotan, and H3427
Ex 16:35 came to a land **i**; they did eat manna, H3427
Lev 16:22 unto a land not **i**: and he shall let go the H1509
Jdg 1:17 Canaanites that **i** Zephath, and utterly H3427
21 the Jebusites that **i** Jerusalem; but the H3427
1Ch 5: 9 And eastward he **i** unto the entering in H3427
Isa 13:20 It shall never be **i**, neither shall it be H3427
44:26 Thou shalt be **i**; and to the cities of H3427
45:18 he formed it to be **i**: I *am* the LORD; and H3427
54: 3 and make the desolate cities to be **i**. H3427
Jer 6: 8 lest I make thee desolate, a land not **i**. H3427
17: 6 the wilderness, *in* a salt land and not **i**. H3427
22: 6 a wilderness, *and* cities *which* are not **i**. H3427
46:26 **i**, as in the days of old, saith the LORD. H7931
50:13 it shall not be **i**, but it shall be wholly H3427
39 it shall be no more **i** for ever; neither H3427
Ezk 12:20 And the cities that are **i** shall be laid H3427
26:17 *that wast* **i** of seafaring men, the H3427
19 cities that are not **i**; when I shall bring H3427
20 that thou be not **i**; and I shall set glory H3427
29:11 it, neither shall it be **i** forty years. H3427
34:13 and in all the **i** places of the country. H4186
36:10 be **i**, and the wastes shall be builded: H3427
35 cities *are become* fenced, *and* are **i**. H3427
38:12 *that are now* **i**, and upon the people H3427
Zec 2: 4 Jerusalem shall be **i** *as* towns without H3427
7: 7 Jerusalem was **i** and in prosperity, and H3427
7 when *men* **i** the south and the plain? H3427
9: 5 from Gaza, and Ashkelon shall not be **i**. H3427

Zec 12: 6 Jerusalem shall be **i** again in her own H3427
14:10 be lifted up, and **i** in her place, from H3427
11 but Jerusalem shall be safely **i**. H3427

INHABITERS
Rev 8:13 Woe, woe, woe, to the **i** of the earth by *G2730*
12:12 them. Woe to the **i** of the earth and of *G2730*

INHABITEST
Ps 22: 3 But thou *art* holy, *O thou* that **i** the H3427

INHABITETH
Job 15:28 **i**, which are ready to become heaps. H3427
Isa 57:15 and lofty One that **i** eternity, whose H7931

INHABITING
Ps 74:14 *to be* meat to the people **i** the wilderness.

INHERIT
Gen 15: 7 Chaldees, to give thee this land to **i** it. H3423
8 whereby shall I know that I shall **i** it? H3423
28: 4 that thou mayest **i** the land wherein H3423
Ex 23:30 until thou be increased, and **i** the land. H5157
32:13 your seed, and they shall **i** *it* for ever. H5157
Lev 20:24 But I have said unto you, Ye shall **i** H3423
25:46 after you, to **i** *them for* a possession; H3423
Nu 18:24 to the Levites to **i**: therefore I have said H5159
26:55 of the tribes of their fathers they shall **i**. H5157
32:19 For we will not **i** with them on yonder H5157
33:54 to the tribes of your fathers ye shall **i**. H5157
34:13 which ye shall **i** by lot, which the LORD H5157
Dt 1:38 him: for he shall cause Israel to **i** it. H5157
2:31 to possess, that thou mayest **i** his land. H3423
3:28 them to **i** the land which thou shalt see. H5157
12:10 God giveth you to **i**, and *when* he giveth H5157
16:20 mayest live, and **i** the land which the H3423
19: 3 God giveth thee to **i**, into three parts, H5157
14 which thou shalt **i** in the land that the H5157
21:16 he maketh his sons to **i** *that* which he H5157
31: 7 them; and thou shalt cause them to **i** it. H5157
Jos 17:14 and one portion to **i**, seeing I *am* a great H5159
Jdg 11: 2 Thou shalt not **i** in our father's house; H5157
1Sa 2: 8 and to make them **i** the throne of glory: H5157
2Ch 20:11 which thou hast given us to **i**. H3423
Ps 25:13 at ease; and his seed shall **i** the earth. H3423
37: 9 upon the LORD, they shall **i** the earth. H3423
11 But the meek shall **i** the earth; and H3423
22 For *such as be* blessed of him shall **i** the H3423
29 The righteous shall **i** the land, and H3423
34 shall exalt thee to **i** the land: when the H3423
69:36 The seed also of his servants shall **i** it: H5157
82: 8 the earth: for thou shalt **i** all nations. H5157
Prv 3:35 The wise shall **i** glory: but shame shall H5157
8:21 that love me to **i** substance; and I will H5157
11:29 He that troubleth his own house shall **i** H5157
14:18 The simple **i** folly: but the prudent are H5157
Isa 49: 8 to cause to **i** the desolate heritages; H5157
54: 3 and thy seed shall **i** the Gentiles, and H3423
57:13 the land, and shall **i** my holy mountain; H3423
60:21 they shall **i** the land for ever, the H3423
65: 9 **i** it, and my servants shall dwell there. H3423
Jer 8:10 to them that shall **i** *them*: for every one H3423
12:14 people Israel to **i**; Behold, I will pluck H5157
49: 1 doth their king **i** Gad, and his people H3423
Ezk 47:13 whereby ye shall **i** the land according H5157
14 And ye shall **i** it, one as well as another: H5157
Zec 2:12 And the LORD shall **i** Judah his portion H5157
Mt 5: 5 Blessed *are* the meek: for they shall **i** *G2816*
19:29 and shall **i** everlasting life. *G2816*
25:34 of my Father, **i** the kingdom prepared *G2816*
Mk 10:17 what shall I do that I may **i** eternal life? *G2816*
Lk 10:25 Master, what shall I do to **i** eternal life? *G2816*
18:18 Master, what shall I do to **i** eternal life? *G2816*
1Co 6: 9 shall not **i** the kingdom of God? *G2816*
10 shall **i** the kingdom of God. *G2816*
15:50 and blood cannot **i** the kingdom of *G2816*
50 neither doth corruption **i** incorruption. *G2816*
Gal 5:21 things shall not **i** the kingdom of God. *G2816*
Heb 6:12 faith and patience **i** the promises. *G2816*
1Pt 3: 9 called, that ye should **i** a blessing. *G2816*
Rev 21: 7 He that overcometh shall **i** all things; *G2816*

INHERITANCE
Gen 31:14 or **i** for us in our father's house? H5159
48: 6 the name of their brethren in their **i**. H5159
Ex 15:17 the mountain of thine **i**, *in* the place, O H5159
34: 9 and our sin, and take us for thine **i**. H5157
Lev 25:46 And ye shall take them as an **i** for your H5157
Nu 16:14 and honey, or given us **i** of fields and H5159

Nu 18:20 shalt have no **i** in their land, neither H5157
20 thine **i** among the children of Israel. H5159
21 in Israel for an **i**, for their service which H5159
23 the children of Israel they have no **i**. H5159
24 children of Israel they shall have no **i**. H5159
26 them for your **i**, then ye shall offer up H5159
26:53 an **i** according to the number of names. H5159
54 To many thou shalt give the more **i**, and H5159
54 shalt give the less **i**: to every one shall H5159
54 every one shall his **i** be given according H5159
62 there was no **i** given them among the H5159
27: 7 them a possession of an **i** among their H5159
7 the **i** of their father to pass unto them. H5159
8 cause his **i** to pass unto his daughter. H5159
9 ye shall give his **i** unto his brethren. H5159
10 give his **i** unto his father's brethren. H5159
11 ye shall give his **i** unto his kinsman H5159
32:18 of Israel have inherited every man his **i**. H5159
19 because our **i** is fallen to us on this H5159
32 our **i** on this side Jordan *may be* ours. H5159
33:54 the land by lot for an **i** among your H5157
54 shall give the more **i**, and to the fewer H5159
54 ye shall give the less **i**: every man's H5159
54 every man's *i* shall be in the place
34: 2 fall unto you for an **i**, *even* the land of H5159
14 have received *their i*; and half the tribe of
14 tribe of Manasseh have received their **i**: H5159
15 received their **i** on this side Jordan *near* H5159
18 of every tribe, to divide the land by **i**. H5157
29 to divide the **i** unto the children of H5157
35: 2 the Levites of the **i** of their possession H5159
8 according to his **i** which he inheriteth. H5159
36: 2 the land for an **i** by lot to the children H5159
2 LORD to give the **i** of Zelophehad our H5159
3 then shall their **i** be taken from the H5159
3 be taken from the **i** of our fathers, and H5159
3 and shall be put to the **i** of the tribe H5159
3 so shall it be taken from the lot of our **i**. H5159
4 be, then shall their **i** be put unto the H5159
4 be put unto the **i** of the tribe whereunto H5159
4 so shall their **i** be taken away from H5159
4 from the **i** of the tribe of our fathers. H5159
7 So shall not the **i** of the children of H5159
7 to the **i** of the tribe of his fathers. H5159
8 that possesseth an **i** in any tribe of the H5159
8 enjoy every man the **i** of his fathers. H5159
9 Neither shall the **i** remove from *one* H5159
9 of Israel shall keep himself to his own **i**. H5159
12 of Joseph, and their **i** remained in the H5159
Dt 4:20 him a people of **i**, as *ye are* this day. H5159
21 the LORD thy God giveth thee *for* an **i**: H5159
38 thee their land *for* an **i**, as *it is* this day. H5159
9:26 thy people and thine **i**, which thou hast H5159
29 Yet they *are* thy people and thine **i**, H5159
10: 9 Wherefore Levi hath no part nor **i** with H5159
9 the LORD *is* his **i**, according as the H5159
12: 9 **i**, which the LORD your God giveth you. H5159
12 as he hath no part nor **i** with you. H5159
14:27 for he hath no part nor **i** with thee. H5159
29 hath no part nor **i** with thee,) and the H5159
15: 4 God giveth thee *for* an **i** to possess it: H5159
18: 1 have no part nor **i** with Israel: they H5159
1 of the LORD made by fire, and his **i**. H5159
2 Therefore shall they have no **i** among H5159
2 *is* their **i**, as he hath said unto them. H5159
19:10 thee *for* an **i**, and *so* blood be upon thee. H5159
14 have set in thine **i**, which thou shalt H5159
20:16 give thee *for* an **i**, thou shalt save alive H5159
21:23 the LORD thy God giveth thee *for* an **i**. H5159
24: 4 the LORD thy God giveth thee *for* an **i**. H5159
25:19 giveth thee *for* an **i** to possess it, *that* H5159
26: 1 giveth thee *for* an **i**, and possessest it, H5159
29: 8 land, and gave it for an **i** unto the H5159
32: 8 the nations their **i**, when he separated H5157
9 *is* his people; Jacob *is* the lot of his **i**. H5159
33: 4 Moses commanded us a law, *even* the **i** H4181
Jos 1: 6 thou divide for an **i** the land, which I H5157
11:23 gave it for an **i** unto Israel according H5159
13: 6 for an **i**, as I have commanded thee. H5159
7 Now therefore divide this land for an **i** H5159
8 have received their **i**, which Moses gave H5159
14 Levi he gave none **i**; the sacrifices of the H5159
14 by fire *are* their **i**, as he said unto them. H5159
15 of Reuben *i* according to their families.
23 This *was* the **i** of the children of Reuben H5159
24 And Moses gave *i* unto the tribe of Gad,
28 This *is* the **i** of the children of Gad after H5159
29 And Moses gave *i* unto the half tribe of
32 did distribute for **i** in the plains of H5157

Jos 13:33 gave not *any* **i**: the LORD God of Israel H5159
33 Israel *was* their **i**, as he said unto them. H5159
14: 1 of Israel, distributed for **i** to them. H5157
2 By lot *was* their **i**, as the LORD H5159
3 For Moses had given the **i** of two tribes H5159
3 the Levites he gave none **i** among them. H5159
9 shall be thine **i**, and thy children's for H5159
13 the son of Jephunneh Hebron for an **i**. H5159
14 Hebron therefore became the **i** of Caleb H5159
15:20 This *is* the **i** of the tribe of the children H5159
16: 4 Manasseh and Ephraim, took their **i**. H5157
5 the border of their **i** on the east side H5159
8 the sea. This *is* the **i** of the tribe of the H5159
9 *were* among the **i** of the children of H5159
17: 4 to give us an **i** among our brethren. H5159
4 an **i** among the brethren of their father. H5159
6 of Manasseh had an **i** among his sons: H5159
18: 2 which had not yet received their **i**. H5159
4 it according to the **i** of them; and they H5159
7 of the LORD *is* their **i**: and Gad, and H5159
7 received their **i** beyond Jordan on the H5159
20 side. This *was* the **i** of the children of H5159
28 This *is* the **i** of the children of Benjamin H5159
19: 1 families: and their **i** was within the H5159
1 within the **i** of the children of Judah. H5159
2 And they had in their **i** Beer-sheba, or H5159
8 south. This *is* the **i** of the tribe of the H5159
9 of Judah *was* the **i** of the children of H5159
9 their **i** within the inheritance of them. H5157
9 their inheritance within the **i** of them. H5159
10 the border of their **i** was unto Sarid: H5159
16 This *is* the **i** of the children of Zebulun H5159
23 This *is* the **i** of the tribe of the children H5159
31 This *is* the **i** of the tribe of the children H5159
39 This *is* the **i** of the tribe of the children H5159
41 And the coast of their **i** was Zorah, and H5159
48 This *is* the **i** of the tribe of the children H5159
49 the land for **i** by their coasts, the H5157
49 of Israel gave an **i** to Joshua the son of H5159
51 divided for an **i** by lot in Shiloh before H5157
21: 3 the Levites out of their **i**, at the H5159
23: 4 remain, to be an **i** for your tribes, from H5159
24:28 the people depart, every man unto his **i**. H5159
30 in the border of his **i** in Timnath-serah, H5159
32 became the **i** of the children of Joseph. H5159
Jdg 2: 6 man unto his **i** to possess the land. H5159
9 the border of his **i** in Timnath-heres, in H5159
18: 1 sought them an **i** to dwell in; for unto H5159
1 that day *all their* **i** had not fallen unto H5159
20: 6 all the country of the **i** of Israel: for they H5159
21:17 And they said, *There must be* an **i** for H3425
23 unto their **i**, and repaired the cities, H5159
24 out from thence every man to his **i**. H5159
Ru 4: 5 up the name of the dead upon his **i**. H5159
6 lest I mar mine own **i**: redeem thou my H5159
10 of the dead upon his **i**, that the name of H5159
1Sa 10: 1 anointed thee *to be* captain over his **i**? H5159
26:19 abiding in the **i** of the LORD, saying, H5159
2Sa 14:16 my son together out of the **i** of God. H5159
20: 1 neither have we **i** in the son of Jesse: H5159
19 wilt thou swallow up the **i** of the LORD? H5159
21: 3 that ye may bless the **i** of the LORD? H5159
1Ki 8:36 thou hast given to thy people for an **i**. H5159
51 For they *be* thy people, and thine **i**, H5159
53 earth, *to be* thine **i**, as thou spakest by H5159
12:16 neither *have we* **i** in the son of Jesse: to H5159
21: 3 give the **i** of my fathers unto thee. H5159
4 not give thee the **i** of my fathers. And H5159
2Ki 21:14 the remnant of mine **i**, and deliver them H5159
1Ch 16:18 the land of Canaan, the lot of your **i**; H5159
28: 8 **i** for your children after you for ever. H5157
2Ch 6:27 thou hast given unto thy people for an **i**. H5159
10:16 and *we have* none **i** in the son of Jesse: H5159
Ezr 9:12 *it* for an **i** to your children for ever. H3423
Neh 11:20 all the cities of Judah, every one in his **i**. H5159
Job 31: 2 *what* **i** of the Almighty from on high? H5159
42:15 gave them **i** among their brethren. H5159
Ps 2: 8 heathen *for* thine **i**, and the uttermost H5159
16: 5 The LORD *is* the portion of mine **i** and H2506
28: 9 Save thy people, and bless thine **i**: feed H5159
33:12 *whom* he hath chosen for his own **i**. H5159
37:18 upright: and their **i** shall be for ever. H5159
47: 4 He shall choose our **i** for us, the H5159
68: 9 confirm thine **i**, when it was weary. H5159
74: 2 old; the rod of thine **i**, *which* thou hast H5159
78:55 divided them an **i** by line, and made H5159
62 the sword; and was wroth with his **i**. H5159
71 feed Jacob his people, and Israel his **i**. H5159
79: 1 come into thine **i**; thy holy temple have H5159

Ps 94:14 his people, neither will he forsake his **i**. H5159
105:11 the land of Canaan, the lot of your **i**: H5159
106: 5 thy nation, that I may glory with thine **i**. H5159
40 insomuch that he abhorred his own **i**. H5159
Prv 13:22 A good *man* leaveth an **i** to his H5157
17: 2 have part of the **i** among the brethren. H5159
19:14 House and riches *are* the **i** of fathers: H5159
20:21 An **i** *may be* gotten hastily at the H5159
Ecc 7:11 Wisdom *is* good with an **i**: and *by it* H5159
Isa 19:25 work of my hands, and Israel mine **i**. H5159
47: 6 polluted mine **i**, and given them into H5159
63:17 thy servants' sake, the tribes of thine **i**. H5159
Jer 3:18 I have given for an **i** unto your fathers. H5157
10:16 of his **i**: The LORD of hosts *is* his name. H5159
12:14 that touch the **i** which I have caused H5159
16:18 have filled mine **i** with the carcases of H5159
32: 8 for the right of **i** *is* thine, and the H3425
51:19 of his **i**: the LORD of hosts *is* his name. H5159
Lam 5: 2 Our **i** is turned to strangers, our houses H5159
Ezk 22:16 And thou shalt take thine **i** in thyself in H2490
33:24 we *are* many; the land is given us for **i**. H4181
35:15 As thou didst rejoice at the **i** of the H5159
36:12 thou shalt be their **i**, and thou shalt no H5159
44:28 And it shall be unto them for an **i**: I *am* H5159
28 I *am* their **i**: and ye shall give them H5159
45: 1 by lot the land for **i**, ye shall offer an H5159
46:16 of his sons, the **i** thereof shall be his H5159
16 sons'; it *shall be* their possession by **i**. H5159
17 But if he give a gift of his **i** to one of his H5159
17 but his **i** shall be his sons' for them. H5159
18 take of the people's **i** by oppression, to H5159
18 he shall give his sons **i** out of his own H5157
47:14 and this land shall fall unto you for **i**. H5159
22 it by lot for an **i** unto you, and to the H5159
22 **i** with you among the tribes of Israel. H5159
23 ye give *him* his **i**, saith the Lord GOD. H5159
48:29 tribes of Israel for **i**, and these *are* their H5159
Mt 21:38 let us kill him, and let us seize on his **i**. *G2817*
Mk 12: 7 let us kill him, and the **i** shall be ours. *G2817*
Lk 12:13 brother, that he divide the **i** with me. *G2817*
20:14 let us kill him, that the **i** may be ours. *G2817*
Act 7: 5 And he gave him none **i** in it, no, not *so* *G2817*
20:32 **i** among all them which are sanctified. *G2817*
26:18 of sins, and **i** among them which *G2819*
Gal 3:18 For if the **i** *be* of the law, *it is* no more *G2817*
Eph 1:11 In whom also we have obtained an **i**, *G2820*
14 Which is the earnest of our **i** until the *G2817*
18 riches of the glory of his **i** in the saints, *G2817*
5: 5 **i** in the kingdom of Christ and of God. *G2817*
Col 1:12 partakers of the **i** of the saints in light: *G2819*
3:24 of the **i**: for ye serve the Lord Christ. *G2817*
Heb 1: 4 angels, as he hath by **i** obtained a more *G2820*
9:15 might receive the promise of eternal **i**. *G2817*
11: 8 after receive for an **i**, obeyed; and he *G2817*
1Pt 1: 4 To an **i** incorruptible, and undefiled, *G2817*

INHERITANCES
Jos 19:51 These *are* the **i**, which Eleazar the H5159

INHERITED
Nu 32:18 Israel have **i** every man his inheritance. H5157
Jos 14: 1 the children of Israel **i** in the land of H5157
Ps 105:44 and they **i** the labour of the people; H3423
Jer 16:19 our fathers have **i** lies, vanity, and H5157
Ezk 33:24 was one, and he **i** the land: but we *are* H3423
Heb 12:17 he would have **i** the blessing, he was *G2816*

INHERITETH
Nu 35: 8 according to his inheritance which he **i**. H5157

INHERITOR
Isa 65: 9 out of Judah an **i** of my mountains: and H3423

INIQUITIES
Lev 16:21 over him all the **i** of the children of H5771
22 upon him all their **i** unto a land not H5771
26:39 and also in the **i** of their fathers shall H5771
Nu 14:34 shall ye bear your **i**, *even* forty years, H5771
Ezr 9: 6 my God: for our **i** are increased over H5771
7 day; and for our **i** have we, our kings, H5771
13 us less than our **i** *deserve*, and hast H5771
Neh 9: 2 their sins, and the **i** of their fathers. H5771
Job 13:23 How many *are* mine **i** and sins? make H5771
26 me to possess the **i** of my youth. H5771
22: 5 *Is* not thy wickedness great? and thine **i** H5771
Ps 38: 4 For mine **i** are gone over mine head: as H5771
40:12 me about: mine **i** have taken hold upon H5771
51: 9 from my sins, and blot out all mine **i**. H5771
64: 6 They search out **i**; they accomplish a H5766

Ps 65: 3 I prevail against me: *as for* our H1697+H5771
79: 8 O remember not against us former i: let H5771
90: 8 Thou hast set our i before thee, our H5771
103: 3 Who forgiveth all thine i; who healeth H5771
10 nor rewarded us according to our i. H5771
107:17 and because of their i, are afflicted. H5771
130: 3 If thou, LORD, shouldest mark i, O H5771
8 he shall redeem Israel from all his i. H5771
Prv 5:22 His own i shall take the wicked himself, H5771
Isa 43:24 sins, thou hast wearied me with thine i. H5771
50: 1 you? Behold, for your i have ye sold H5771
53: 5 bruised for our i: the chastisement of H5771
11 justify many; for he shall bear their i. H5771
59: 2 But your i have separated between you H5771
12 with us; and *as for* our i, we know them; H5771
64: 6 i, like the wind, have taken us away. H5771
7 and hast consumed us, because of our i. H5771
65: 7 Your i, and the iniquities of your H5771
7 Your iniquities, and the i of your H5771
Jer 5:25 Your i have turned away these *things*, H5771
11:10 They are turned back to the i of their H5771
14: 7 O LORD, though our i testify against H5771
33: 8 pardon all their i, whereby they have H5771
Lam 4:13 For the sins of her prophets, *and* the i H5771
5: 7 *and are* not; and we have borne their i. H5771
Ezk 24:23 your i, and mourn one toward another. H5771
28:18 multitude of thine i, by the iniquity of H5771
32:27 heads, but their i shall be upon their H5771
36:31 for your i and for your abominations. H5771
33 you from all your i I will also cause *you* H5771
43:10 i: and let them measure the pattern. H5771
Dan 4:27 and thine i by shewing mercy to H5758
9:13 from our i, and understand thy truth. H5771
16 our sins, and for the i of our fathers, H5771
Am 3: 2 therefore I will punish you for all your i. H5771
Mic 7:19 he will subdue our i; and thou wilt cast H5771
Act 3:26 away every one of you from his i. *G4189*
Ro 4: 7 *Saying*, Blessed *are* they whose i are *G458*
Heb 8:12 and their i will I remember no more. *G458*
10:17 And their sins and i will I remember no *G458*
Rev 18: 5 heaven, and God hath remembered her i. *G92*

INIQUITY

Gen 15:16 for the i of the Amorites *is* not yet full. H5771
19:15 thou be consumed in the i of the city. H5771
44:16 hath found out the i of thy servants: H5771
Ex 20: 5 God, visiting the i of the fathers upon H5771
28:38 may bear the i of the holy things, which H5771
43 that they bear not i, and die: *it shall be* H5771
34: 7 forgiving i and transgression and H5771
7 *guilty;* visiting the i of the fathers upon H5771
9 and pardon our i and our sin, and take H5771
Lev 5: 1 do not utter *it*, then he shall bear his i. H5771
17 not, yet is he guilty, and shall bear his i. H5771
7:18 the soul that eateth of it shall bear his i. H5771
10:17 it you to bear the i of the congregation, H5771
17:16 bathe his flesh; then he shall bear his i. H5771
18:25 I do visit the i thereof upon it, and H5771
19: 8 it shall bear his i, because he hath H5771
20:17 sister's nakedness; he shall bear his i. H5771
19 his near kin: they shall bear their i. H5771
22:16 Or suffer them to bear the i of trespass, H5771
26:39 pine away in their i in your enemies' H5771
40 If they shall confess their i, and the H5771
40 iniquity, and the i of their fathers, with H5771
41 then accept of the punishment of their i: H5771
43 of their i: because, even because H5771
Nu 5:15 memorial, bringing i to remembrance. H5771
31 Then shall the man be guiltless from i, H5771
31 and this woman shall bear her i. H5771
14:18 mercy, forgiving i and transgression, H5771
18 *guilty,* visiting the i of the fathers upon H5771
19 Pardon, I beseech thee, the i of this H5771
15:31 be cut off; his i *shall be* upon him. H5771
18: 1 thee shall bear the i of the sanctuary: H5771
1 thee shall bear the i of your priesthood. H5771
23 shall bear their i: *it shall be* a statute for H5771
23:21 He hath not beheld i in Jacob, neither H205
30:15 heard *them;* then he shall bear her i. H5771
Dt 5: 9 God, visiting the i of the fathers upon H5771
19:15 a man for any i, or for any sin, in any H5771
32: 4 truth and without i, just and right *is* he. H5766
Jos 22:17 *Is* the i of Peor too little for us, from H5771
20 that man perished not alone in his i. H5771
1Sa 3:13 for ever for the i which he knoweth; H5771
14 of Eli, that the i of Eli's house shall not H5771
15:23 and stubbornness *is as* i and idolatry. H205
20: 1 what *is* mine i? and what *is* my sin H5771
8 if there be in me i, slay me thyself; for H5771
1Sa 25:24 lord, *upon* me *let this* i *be:* and let thine H5771
2Sa 7:14 son. If he commit i, I will chasten him H5753
14: 9 lord, O king, the i *be* on me, and on my H5771
32 if there be *any* i in me, let him kill me. H5771
19:19 my lord impute i unto me, neither do H5771
22:24 him, and have kept myself from mine i. H5771
24:10 take away the i of thy servant; for I H5771
1Ch 21: 8 thee, do away the i of thy servant; for I H5771
2Ch 19: 7 *it:* for *there is* no i with the LORD our H5766
Neh 4: 5 And cover not their i, and let not their H5771
Job 4: 8 Even as I have seen, they that plow i, and H205
5:16 So the poor hath hope, and i stoppeth H5766
6:29 Return, I pray you, let it not be i; yea, H5766
30 Is there i in my tongue? cannot my H5766
7:21 take away mine i? for now shall I sleep H5771
10: 6 That thou inquirest after mine i, and H5771
14 thou wilt not acquit me from mine i. H5771
11: 6 of thee *less* than thine i *deserveth*. H5771
14 If i *be* in thine hand, put it far away, and H205
14:17 up in a bag, and thou sewest up mine i. H5771
15: 5 For thy mouth uttereth thine i, and thou H5771
16 *is* man, which drinketh i like water? H5766
20:27 The heaven shall reveal his i; and the H5771
21:19 God layeth up his i for his children: he H205
22:23 put away i far from thy tabernacles. H5766
31: 3 a strange *punishment* to the workers of i? H205
11 it *is* an i *to be punished by* the judges. H5771
28 This also *were* an i *to be punished by* H5771
33 Adam, by hiding mine i in my bosom: H5771
33: 9 I *am* innocent; neither *is there* i in me. H5771
34: 8 of i, and walketh with wicked men. H205
10 the Almighty, *that he should commit* i. H5766
22 the workers of i may hide themselves. H205
32 me: if I have done i, I will do no more. H5766
36:10 and commandeth that they return from i. H205
21 Take heed, regard not i: for this hast thou H205
23 or who can say, Thou hast wrought i? H5766
Ps 5: 5 in thy sight: thou hatest all workers of i. H205
6: 8 Depart from me, all ye workers of i; for H205
7: 3 done this; if there be i in my hands; H5766
14 Behold, he travaileth with i, and hath H205
14: 4 Have all the workers of i no knowledge? H205
18:23 him, and I kept myself from mine i. H5771
25:11 O LORD, pardon mine i; for it *is* great. H5771
28: 3 with the workers of i, which speak peace H205
31:10 of mine i, and my bones are consumed. H5771
32: 2 i, and in whose spirit *there is* no guile. H5771
5 thee, and mine i have I not hid. I said, H5771
5 thou forgavest the i of my sin. Selah. H5771
36: 2 eyes, until his i be found to be hateful. H5771
3 The words of his mouth *are* i and deceit: H205
12 There are the workers of i fallen: they H205
37: 1 thou envious against the workers of i. H5766
38:18 For I will declare mine i; I will be sorry H5771
39:11 dost correct man for i, thou makest his H5771
41: 6 his heart gathereth i to itself; *when* he H205
49: 5 i of my heels shall compass me about? H5771
51: 2 Wash me throughly from mine i, and H5771
5 Behold, I was shapen in i; and in sin did H5771
53: 1 i: *there is* none that doeth good. H5766
4 Have the workers of i no knowledge? H205
55: 3 i upon me, and in wrath they hate me. H205
56: 7 Shall they escape by i? in *thine* anger cast H205
59: 2 Deliver me from the workers of i, and H205
64: 2 from the insurrection of the workers of i: H205
66:18 If I regard i in my heart, the Lord will H205
69:27 Add i unto their iniquity: and let them H5771
27 Add iniquity unto their i: and let them H5771
78:38 forgave *their* i, and destroyed *them* H5771
85: 2 Thou hast forgiven the i of thy people, H5771
89:32 with the rod, and their i with stripes. H5771
92: 7 all the workers of i do flourish; *it is* that H205
9 all the workers of i shall be scattered. H205
94: 4 all the workers of i boast themselves? H205
16 stand up for me against the workers of i? H205
20 Shall the throne of i have fellowship H1942
23 them their own i, and shall cut them off H205
106: 6 committed i, we have done wickedly. H5753
43 and were brought low for their i. H5771
107:42 rejoice: and all i shall stop her mouth. H5766
109:14 Let the i of his fathers be remembered H5771
119: 3 They also do no i: they walk in his ways. H5766
133 let not any i have dominion over me. H205
125: 3 righteous put forth their hands unto i. H5766
5 of i: *but* peace *shall be* upon Israel. H205
141: 4 i: and let me not eat of their dainties. H205
9 for me, and the gins of the workers of i. H205
Prv 10:29 destruction *shall be* to the workers of i. H205
16: 6 By mercy and truth i is purged: and by H5771
Prv 19:28 and the mouth of the wicked devoureth i. H205
21:15 destruction *shall be* to the workers of i. H205
22: 8 He that soweth i shall reap vanity: and H5766
Ecc 3:16 place of righteousness, *that* i *was* there. H7562
Isa 1: 4 Ah sinful nation, a people laden with i, H5771
13 with; *it is* i, even the solemn meeting. H205
5:18 Woe unto them that draw i with cords H5771
6: 7 i is taken away, and thy sin purged. H5771
13:11 wicked for their i; and I will cause the H5771
14:21 children for the i of their fathers; that H5771
22:14 hosts, Surely this i shall not be purged H5771
26:21 the earth for their i: the earth also shall H5771
27: 9 By this therefore shall the i of Jacob be H5771
29:20 and all that watch for i are cut off: H205
30:13 Therefore this i shall be to you as a H5771
31: 2 and against the help of them that work i. H205
32: 6 and his heart will work i, to practise H205
33:24 dwell therein *shall be* forgiven *their* i. H5771
40: 2 that her i is pardoned: for she H5771
53: 6 LORD hath laid on him the i of us all. H5771
57:17 For the i of his covetousness was I H5771
59: 3 and your fingers with i; your lips have H5771
4 they conceive mischief, and bring forth i. H205
6 their works *are* works of i, and the act of H205
7 thoughts *are* thoughts of i; wasting and H205
64: 9 neither remember i for ever: behold, H5771
Jer 2: 5 Thus saith the LORD, What i have your H5766
22 soap, *yet* thine i is marked before me, H5771
3:13 Only acknowledge thine i, that thou H5771
9: 5 lies, *and* weary themselves to commit i. H5753
13:22 the greatness of thine i are thy skirts H5771
14:10 remember their i, and visit their sins. H5771
20 *and* the i of our fathers: for we H5771
16:10 us? or what *is* our i? or what *is* our sin H5771
17 neither is their i hid from mine eyes. H5771
18 And first I will recompense their i and H5771
18:23 forgive not their i, neither blot out their H5771
25:12 LORD, for their i, and the land of the H5771
30:14 thine i; *because* thy sins were increased. H5771
15 multitude of thine i: *because* thy sins H5771
31:30 But every one shall die for his own i: H5771
34 for I will forgive their i, and I will H5771
32:18 recompensest the i of the fathers into H5771
33: 8 And I will cleanse them from all their i, H5771
36: 3 that I may forgive their i and their sin. H5771
31 his servants for their i; and I will bring H5771
50:20 saith the LORD, the i of Israel shall be H5771
51: 6 not cut off in her i; for this *is* the time of H5771
Lam 2:14 not discovered thine i, to turn away thy H5771
4: 6 For the punishment of the i of the H5771
22 The punishment of thine i is H5771
22 he will visit thine i, O daughter of H5771
Ezk 3:18 shall die in his i; but his blood will I H5771
19 in his i; but thou hast delivered thy soul. H5771
20 and commit i, and I lay a H5766
4: 4 side, and lay the i of the house of Israel H5771
4 shalt lie upon it thou shalt bear their i. H5771
5 the years of their i, according to the H5771
5 thou bear the i of the house of Israel. H5771
6 thou shalt bear the i of the house of H5771
17 another, and consume away for their i. H5771
7:13 strengthen himself in the i of his life. H5771
16 of them mourning, every one for his i. H5771
19 it is the stumblingblock of their i. H5771
9: 9 Then said he unto me, The i of the H5771
14: 3 of their i before their face: should H5771
4 of his i before his face, and H5771
7 of his i before his face, and H5771
10 of their i: the punishment of the H5771
16:49 Behold, this was the i of thy sister H5771
18: 8 his hand from i, hath executed true H5766
17 the i of his father, he shall surely live. H5771
18 his people, lo, even he shall die in his i. H5771
19 the son bear the i of the father? When H5771
20 son shall not bear the i of the father, H5771
20 the father bear the i of the son: the H5771
24 and committeth i, *and* doeth according H5766
26 and committeth i, and dieth in them; H5766
26 for his i that he hath done shall he die. H5766
30 so i shall not be your ruin. H5771
21:23 the i, that they may be taken. H5771
24 have made your i to be remembered, H5771
25 day is come, when i *shall have* an end, H5771
29 is come, when their i *shall have* an end. H5771
28:15 wast created, till i was found in thee. H5766
18 thine iniquities, by the i of thy traffick; H5766
29:16 bringeth *their* i to remembrance, when H5771
33: 6 taken away in his i; but his blood will I H5771
8 shall die in his i; but his blood will I H5771

Ezk 33: 9 in his i; but thou hast delivered thy soul. H5771
13 and commit i, all his righteousnesses H5766
13 but for his i that he hath committed, H5766
15 i; he shall surely live, he shall not die. H5766
18 committeth i, he shall even die thereby. H5766
35: 5 in the time *that their* i *had* an end: H5771
39:23 into captivity for their i: because they H5771
44:10 their idols; they shall even bear their i. H5771
12 of Israel to fall into i; therefore have I H5771
12 Lord GOD, and they shall bear their i. H5771
Dan 9: 5 We have sinned, and have committed i, H5753
24 reconciliation for i, and to bring in H5771
Hos 4: 8 and they set their heart on their i. H5771
5: 5 their i; Judah also shall fall with them. H5771
6: 8 Gilead *is* a city of them that work i, *and* H205
7: 1 Israel, then the i of Ephraim was H5771
8:13 will he remember their i, and visit their H5771
9: 7 of thine i, and the great hatred. H5771
9 remember their i, he will visit their sins. H5771
10: 9 the children of i did not overtake them. H5932
13 ye have reaped i; ye have eaten the fruit H5766
12: 8 shall find none i in me that *were* sin. H5771
11 *Is there* i *in* Gilead? surely they are H205
13:12 The i of Ephraim *is* bound up; his sin *is* H5771
14: 1 thy God; for thou hast fallen by thine i. H5771
2 him, Take away all i, and receive *us* H5771
Mic 2: 1 Woe to them that devise i, and work evil H205
3:10 Zion with blood, and Jerusalem with i. H5766
7:18 that pardoneth i, and passeth by the H5771
Hab 1: 3 Why dost thou shew me i, and cause *me* H205
13 canst not look on i: wherefore lookest H5999
2:12 with blood, and stablisheth a city by i! H5766
Zep 3: 5 he will not do i: every morning doth H5766
13 The remnant of Israel shall not do i, nor H5766
Zec 3: 4 I have caused thine i to pass from thee, H5771
9 remove the i of that land in one day. H5771
Mal 2: 6 in his mouth, and i was not found in H5766
6 equity, and did turn many away from i. H5771
Mt 7:23 you: depart from me, ye that work i. *G458*
13:41 things that offend, and them which do i; *G458*
23:28 but within ye are full of hypocrisy and i. *G458*
24:12 And because i shall abound, the love of *G458*
Lk 13:27 are; depart from me, all *ye* workers of i. *G93*
Act 1:18 field with the reward of i; and falling *G93*
8:23 gall of bitterness, and *in* the bond of i. *G93*
Ro 6:19 uncleanness and to iniquity unto i; even *G458*
19 to iniquity unto i; even so now yield your *G458*
1Co 13: 6 Rejoiceth not in i, but rejoiceth in the *G93*
2Th 2: 7 For the mystery of i doth already work: *G458*
2Ti 2:19 nameth the name of Christ depart from i. *G93*
Tit 2:14 redeem us from all i, and purify unto *G458*
Heb 1: 9 and hated i; therefore God, *even* *G458*
Jas 3: 6 And the tongue *is* a fire, a world of i: so is *G93*
2Pt 2:16 But was rebuked for his i: the dumb ass *G3892*

INJOIN See ENJOIN.

INJURED
Gal 4:12 for I *am* as ye *are*: ye have not i me at all. *G91*

INJURIOUS
1Ti 1:13 and a persecutor, and i: but I obtained *G5197*

INJUSTICE
Job 16:17 Not for *any* i in mine hands: also my H2555

INK
Jer 36:18 and I wrote *them* with i in the book. H1773
2Co 3: 3 written not with i, but with the Spirit of *G3188*
2Jn 12 with paper and i: but I trust to come *G3188*
3Jn 13 will not with i and pen write unto thee: *G3188*

INKHORN
Ezk 9: 2 with a writer's i by his side: and they H7083
3 which *had* the writer's i by his side; H7083
11 which *had* the i by his side, reported H7083

INN
Gen 42:27 provender in the i, he espied his money; H4411
43:21 we came to the i, that we opened our H4411
Ex 4:24 And it came to pass by the way in the i, H4411
Lk 2: 7 there was no room for them in the i. *G2646*
10:34 him to an i, and took care of him. *G3829*

INNER
1Ki 6:27 And he set the cherubims within the i H6442
36 And he built the i court with three rows H6442
7:12 both for the i court of the house of H6442
50 the doors of the i house, the most holy H6442
1Ki 20:30 came into the city, into an i chamber. H2315
22:25 go into an i chamber to hide thyself. H2315
2Ki 9: 2 and carry him to an i chamber; H2315
1Ch 28:11 thereof, and of the i parlours thereof, H6442
2Ch 4:22 of the house, the i doors thereof for the H6442
18:24 go into an i chamber to hide thyself. H2315
29:16 And the priests went into the i part of H6411
Est 4:11 the king into the i court, who is not H6442
5: 1 and stood in the i court of the king's H6442
Ezk 8: 3 to the door of the i gate that looketh H6442
16 And he brought me into the i court of H6442
10: 3 went in; and the cloud filled the i court. H6442
40:15 the porch of the i gate *were* fifty cubits. H6442
19 the forefront of the i court without, an H6442
23 And the gate of the i court *was* over H6442
27 And *there was* a gate in the i court H6442
28 And he brought me to the i court by the H6442
32 And he brought me into the i court H6442
44 And without the i gate *were* the H6442
44 the singers in the i court, which *was* at H6442
41:15 i temple, and the porches of the court; H6442
17 To that above the door, even unto the i H6442
42: 3 which *were* for the i court, and over H6442
15 of measuring the i house, he brought H6442
43: 5 me into the i court; and, behold, H6442
44:17 at the gates of the i court, they shall be H6442
17 in the gates of the i court, and within. H6442
21 wine, when they enter into the i court. H6442
27 unto the i court, to minister in H6442
45:19 the posts of the gate of the i court. H6442
46: 1 The gate of the i court that looketh H6442
Act 16:24 them into the i prison, and made their *G2082*
Eph 3:16 with might by his Spirit in the i man; *G2080*

INNERMOST
Prv 18: 8 go down into the i parts of the belly. H2315
26:22 go down into the i parts of the belly. H2315

INNOCENCY
Gen 20: 5 and i of my hands have I done this. H5356
Ps 26: 6 I will wash mine hands in i: so will I H5356
73:13 *in* vain, and washed my hands in i. H5356
Dan 6:22 as before him i was found in me; and H2136
Hos 8: 5 how long *will it be* ere they attain to i? H5356

INNOCENT
Ex 23: 7 matter; and the i and righteous slay H5355
Dt 19:10 That i blood be not shed in thy land, H5355
13 away *the guilt of* i blood from Israel, H5355
21: 8 and lay not i blood unto thy people H5355
9 So shalt thou put away the *guilt of* i H5355
27:25 reward to slay an i person. And all the H5355
1Sa 19: 5 i blood, to slay David without a cause? H5355
1Ki 2:31 take away the i blood, which Joab shed, H2600
2Ki 21:16 Moreover Manasseh shed i blood very H5355
24: 4 And also for the i blood that he shed: H5355
4 filled Jerusalem with i blood; which the H5355
Job 4: 7 i? or where were the righteous cut off? H5355
9:23 he will laugh at the trial of the i. H5355
28 I know that thou wilt not hold me i. H5352
17: 8 at this, and the i shall stir up himself H5355
22:19 are glad: and the i laugh them to scorn. H5355
30 He shall deliver the island of the i: and H5355
27:17 *it* on, and the i shall divide the silver. H5355
33: 9 I *am* i; neither *is there* iniquity in me. H2643
Ps 10: 8 he murder the i: his eyes are privily set H5355
15: 5 reward against the i. He that doeth H5355
19:13 shall be i from the great transgression. H5352
94:21 righteous, and condemn the i blood. H5355
106:38 And shed i blood, *even* the blood of H5355
Prv 1:11 us lurk privily for the i without cause: H5355
6:17 tongue, and hands that shed i blood, H5355
29 whosoever toucheth her shall not be i. H5352
28:20 maketh haste to be rich shall not be i. H5352
Isa 59: 7 haste to shed i blood: their thoughts H5355
Jer 2:35 Yet thou sayest, Because I am i, surely H5352
7: 6 and shed not i blood in this place, H5355
22: 3 neither shed i blood in this place. H5355
17 and for to shed i blood, and for H5355
26:15 ye shall surely bring i blood upon H5355
Joel 3:19 they have shed i blood in their land. H5355
Jna 1:14 and lay not upon us i blood: for thou, O H5355
Mt 27: 4 I have betrayed the i blood. And they *G121*
24 saying, I am i of the blood of this just *G121*

INNOCENTS
Jer 2:34 souls of the poor i: I have not found it H5355
19: 4 have filled this place with the blood of i; H5355

INNUMERABLE
Job 21:33 him, as *there are* i before him. H369+H4557
Ps 40:12 For i evils have compassed me H369+H4557
104:25 i, both small and great beasts. H369+H4557
Jer 46:23 than the grasshoppers, and *are* i. H369+H4557
Lk 12: 1 together an i multitude of people, *G3461*
Heb 11:12 as the sand which is by the sea shore i. *G382*
12:22 and to an i company of angels, *G3461*

INORDINATE
Ezk 23:11 corrupt in her i love than she, and in H5691
Col 3: 5 uncleanness, i affection, evil *G3806*

INQUIRE
Gen 24:57 call the damsel, and i at her mouth. H7592
25:22 I thus? And she went to i of the LORD. H1875
Ex 18:15 the people come unto me to i of God: H1875
Dt 12:30 and that thou i not after their gods, H1875
13:14 Then shalt thou i, and make search, H1875
17: 9 be in those days, and i; and they shall H1875
Jdg 4:20 doth come and i of thee, and say, Is H7592
1Sa 9: 9 a man went to i of God, thus he spake, H1875
17:56 And the king said, I thou whose son the H7592
22:15 Did I then begin to i of God for him? be H7592
28: 7 I may go to her, and i of her. And his H1875
1Ki 22: 5 the king of Israel, I, I pray thee, at the H1875
7 LORD besides, that we might i of him? H1875
8 by whom we may i of the LORD: but I H1875
2Ki 1: 2 unto them, Go, i of Baal-zebub the god H1875
3 go to i of Baal-zebub the god of Ekron? H1875
6 thou sendest to i of Baal-zebub the god H1875
16 messengers to i of Baalzebub the god H1875
16 *is* no God in Israel to i of his word? H1875
3:11 that we may i of the LORD by him? H1875
8: 8 man of God, and i of the LORD by him, H1875
16:15 the brasen altar shall be for me to i *by*. H1239
22:13 Go ye, i of the LORD for me, and for the H1875
18 which sent you to i of the LORD, thus H1875
1Ch 10:13 *one that had* a familiar spirit, to i *of it*; H1875
18:10 to king David, to i of his welfare, and to H7592
21:30 But David could not go before it to i of H1875
2Ch 18: 4 the king of Israel, I, I pray thee, at the H1875
6 LORD besides, that we might i of him? H1875
7 by whom we may i of the LORD: but I H1875
32:31 sent unto him to i of the wonder that H1875
34:21 Go, i of the LORD for me, and for them H1875
26 who sent you to i of the LORD, so shall H1875
Ezr 7:14 counsellors, to i concerning Judah and H1240
Job 8: 8 For i, I pray thee, of the former age, and H7592
Ps 27: 4 of the LORD, and to i in his temple. H1239
Ecc 7:10 thou dost not i wisely concerning this. H7592
Isa 21:12 if ye will i, inquire ye: return, come. H1158
12 if ye will inquire, i ye: return, come. H1158
Jer 21: 2 I, I pray thee, of the LORD for us; for H1875
37: 7 sent you unto me to i of me; Behold, H1875
Ezk 14: 7 to a prophet to i of him concerning me; H1875
20: 1 to i of the LORD, and sat before me. H1875
3 Are ye come to i of me? *As* I live, saith H1875
Mt 10:11 ye shall enter, i who in it is worthy; *G1833*
Lk 22:23 And they began to i among themselves, *G4802*
Jn 16:19 unto them, Do ye i among yourselves *G2212*
Act 9:11 Straight, and i in the house of Judas *G2212*
19:39 But if ye i any thing concerning other *G1934*
23:15 as though ye would i something more *G1231*
20 i somewhat of him more perfectly. *G4441*
2Co 8:23 Whether *any do* i *of Titus, he is my*

INQUIRED
Dt 17: 4 hast heard *of it*, and i diligently, and, H1875
Jdg 6:29 And when they i and asked, they said, H1875
8:14 men of Succoth, and i of him: and he H7592
20:27 And the children of Israel i of the H7592
1Sa 10:22 Therefore they i of the LORD further, if H7592
22:10 And he i of the LORD for him, and gave H7592
13 a sword, and hast i of God for him, that H7592
23: 2 Therefore David i of the LORD, saying, H7592
4 Then David i of the LORD yet again. H7592
28: 6 And when Saul i of the LORD, the H7592
30: 8 And David i at the LORD, saying, Shall H7592
2Sa 2: 1 this, that David i of the LORD, saying, H7592
5:19 And David i of the LORD, saying, Shall H7592
23 And when David i of the LORD, he H7592
11: 3 And David sent and i after the woman. H1875
16:23 as if a man had i at the oracle of God: H7592
21: 1 year; and David i of the LORD. And the H1245
1Ch 10:14 And i not of the LORD: therefore he H1875
13: 3 us: for we i not at it in the days of Saul. H1875
14:10 And David i of God, saying, Shall I go H7592
14 Therefore David i again of God; and H7592

Ps 78:34 they returned and **i** early after God. H7836
Ezk 14: 3 face: should I be **i** of at all by them? H1875
20: 3 the Lord GOD, I will not be **i** of by you. H1875
31 day: and shall I be **i** of by you, O house H1875
31 the Lord GOD, I will not be **i** of by you. H1875
36:37 I will yet *for* this be **i** of by the house of H1875
Dan 1:20 that the king **i** of them, he found them H1245
Zep 1: 6 not sought the LORD, nor **i** for him. H1875
Mt 2: 7 the wise men, **i** of them diligently what *G198*
16 he had diligently **i** of the wise men. *G198*
Jn 4:52 Then **i** he of them the hour when he *G4441*
2Co 8:23 you: or our brethren *be i of, they are* the
1Pt 1:10 Of which salvation the prophets have **i** *G1567*

INQUIREST
Job 10: 6 That thou **i** after mine iniquity, and H1245

INQUIRY
Prv 20:25 *which is* holy, and after vows to make **i**. H1239
Act 10:17 had made **i** for Simon's house, and *G1331*

INQUISITION
Dt 19:18 And the judges shall make diligent **i**: H1875
Est 2:23 And when **i** was made of the matter, it H1245
Ps 9:12 When he maketh **i** for blood, he H1875

INSCRIPTION
Act 17:23 found an altar with this **i**, TO THE *G1924*

INSIDE
1Ki 6:15 *them* on the **i** with wood, and covered H1004

INSOMUCH
Ps 106:40 **i** that he abhorred his own inheritance.
Mal 2:13 with crying out, **i** that he regardeth not
Mt 8:24 tempest in the sea, **i** that the ship was *G5628*
12:22 and he healed him, **i** that the blind and *G5628*
13:54 in their synagogue, **i** that they were *G5628*
15:31 **I** that the multitude wondered, when *G5628*
24:24 and wonders; **i** that, if *it were* possible, *G5628*
27:14 **i** that the governor marvelled greatly. *G5620*
Mk 1:27 And they were all amazed, **i** that they *G5628*
45 the matter, **i** that Jesus could no *G5628*
2: 2 gathered together, **i** that there was no *G5628*
12 before them all; **i** that they were all *G5628*
3:10 For he had healed many; **i** that they *G5628*
9:26 one dead; **i** that many said, He is dead. *G5628*
Lk 12: 1 of people, **i** that they trode one *G5628*
Act 1:19 at Jerusalem; **i** as that field is called *G5628*
5:15 **I** that they brought forth the sick into *G5628*
2Co 1: 8 **i** that we despaired even of life: *G5628*
8: 6 **I** that we desired Titus, that as he had *G1519*
Gal 2:13 likewise with him; **i** that Barnabas also *G5628*

INSPIRATION
Job 32: 8 But *there is* a spirit in man: and the **i** of H5397
2Ti 3:16 All scripture *is* given by **i** of God, and *is* *G2315*

INSTANT
Isa 29: 5 away: yea, it shall be at an **i** suddenly. H6621
30:13 breaking cometh suddenly at an **i**. H6621
Jer 18: 7 *At what* **i** I shall speak concerning a H7281
9 And *at what* **i** I shall speak concerning H7281
Lk 2:38 And she coming in that **i** gave thanks *G846*
23:23 And they were **i** with loud voices, *G1945*
Ro 12:12 in tribulation; continuing **i** in prayer; *G4342*
2Ti 4: 2 Preach the word; be **i** in season, out of *G2186*

INSTANTLY
Lk 7: 4 they besought him **i**, saying, That he *G4709*
Act 26: 7 Unto which *promise* our twelve tribes, **i** *G1722*

INSTEAD
Gen 2:21 ribs, and closed up the flesh **i** thereof; H8478
4:25 seed **i** of Abel, whom Cain slew. H8478
44:33 let thy servant abide **i** of the lad a H8478
Ex 4:16 he shall be to thee **i** of a mouth, and thou
16 and thou shalt be to him **i** of God.
5:12 of Egypt to gather stubble **i** of straw.
Nu 3:12 children of Israel **i** of all the firstborn H8478
41 (I *am* the LORD) **i** of all the firstborn H8478
41 cattle of the Levites **i** of all the firstlings H8478
45 Take the Levites **i** of all the firstborn H8478
45 of the Levites **i** of their cattle; and the H8478
5:19 *with another* **i** of thy husband, be thou H8478
20 But if thou hast gone aside *to another* **i** H8478
29 **i** of her husband, and is defiled; H8478
8:16 the children of Israel; **i** of such as open H8478
16 every womb, *even* **i** *of* the firstborn of all
Nu 10:31 and thou mayest be to us **i** of eyes. H8478
Jdg 15: 2 than she? take her, I pray thee, **i** of her. H8478
2Sa 17:25 captain of the host **i** of Joab: which H8478
1Ki 3: 7 thy servant king **i** of David my father: H8478
2Ki 14:21 made him king **i** of his father Amaziah. H8478
17:24 the cities of Samaria **i** of the children of H8478
1Ch 29:23 the LORD as king **i** of David his father, H8478
2Ch 12:10 **I** of which king Rehoboam made H8478
Est 2: 4 the king be queen **i** of Vashti. And the H8478
17 head, and made her queen **i** of Vashti. H8478
Job 31:40 Let thistles grow **i** of wheat, and cockle H8478
40 **i** of barley. The words of Job are ended. H8478
Ps 45:16 **I** of thy fathers shall be thy children, H8478
Isa 3:24 And it shall come to pass, *that* **i** of H8478
24 shall be stink; and **i** of a girdle a rent; H8478
24 a girdle a rent; and **i** of well set hair H8478
24 hair baldness; and **i** of a stomacher a H8478
24 of sackcloth; *and* burning **i** of beauty. H8478
55:13 **I** of the thorn shall come up the fir tree, H8478
13 up the fir tree, and **i** of the brier shall H8478
Jer 22:11 which reigned **i** of Josiah his father, H8478
37: 1 of Josiah reigned **i** of Coniah the son of H8478
Ezk 16:32 taketh strangers **i** of her husband! H8478

INSTRUCT
Dt 4:36 that he might **i** thee: and upon earth H3256
Neh 9:20 Thou gavest also thy good spirit to **i** H7919
Job 40: 2 with the Almighty **i** *him*? he that H3250
Ps 16: 7 my reins also **i** me in the night seasons. H3256
32: 8 I will **i** thee and teach thee in the way H7919
Song 8: 2 house, *who* would **i** me: I would cause H3925
Isa 28:26 For his God doth **i** him to discretion, H3256
Dan 11:33 the people shall **i** many: yet they shall H995
1Co 2:16 **i** him? But we have the mind of Christ. *G4822*

INSTRUCTED
Dt 32:10 led him about, he **i** him, he kept him as H995
2Ki 12: 2 days wherein Jehoiada the priest **i** him. H3384
1Ch 15:22 *was* for song: he **i** about the song, H3256
25: 7 brethren that were **i** in the songs of the H3925
2Ch 3: 3 Solomon was **i** for the building of the H3245
Job 4: 3 Behold, thou hast **i** many, and thou H3256
Ps 2:10 Be wise now therefore, O ye kings: be **i**, H3256
Prv 5:13 inclined mine ear to them that **i** me! H3925
21:11 the wise is **i**, he receiveth knowledge. H7919
Isa 8:11 strong hand, and **i** me that I should not H3256
40:14 With whom took he counsel, and *who* **i** H995
Jer 6: 8 Be thou **i**, O Jerusalem, lest my soul H3256
31:19 and after that I was **i**, I smote upon *my* H3045
Mt 13:52 scribe *which is* **i** unto the kingdom of *G3100*
14: 8 And she, being before **i** of her mother, *G4264*
Lk 1: 4 those things, wherein thou hast been **i**. *G2727*
Act 18:25 This man was **i** in the way of the Lord; *G2727*
Ro 2:18 more excellent, being **i** out of the law; *G2727*
Php 4:12 in all things I am **i** both to be full and *G3453*

INSTRUCTING
2Ti 2:25 In meekness **i** those that oppose *G3811*

INSTRUCTION
Job 33:16 the ears of men, and sealeth their **i**, H4561
Ps 50:17 Seeing thou hatest **i**, and castest my H4148
Prv 1: 2 To know wisdom and **i**; to perceive the H4148
3 To receive the **i** of wisdom, justice, and H4148
7 *but* fools despise wisdom and **i**. H4148
8 My son, hear the **i** of thy father, and H4148
4: 1 Hear, ye children, the **i** of a father, and H4148
13 Take fast hold of **i**; let *her* not go: keep H4148
5:12 And say, How have I hated **i**, and my H4148
23 He shall die without **i**; and in the H4148
6:23 and reproofs of **i** *are* the way of life: H4148
8:10 Receive my **i**, and not silver; and H4148
33 Hear **i**, and be wise, and refuse it not. H4148
9: 9 Give *i* to a wise *man*, and he will be yet
10:17 He *is in* the way of life that keepeth **i**: H4148
12: 1 Whoso loveth **i** loveth knowledge: but H4148
13: 1 A wise son *heareth* his father's **i**: but a H4148
18 *to* him that refuseth **i**: but he that H4148
15: 5 A fool despiseth his father's **i**: but he H4148
32 He that refuseth **i** despiseth his own H4148
33 The fear of the LORD *is* the **i** of H4148
16:22 that hath it: but the **i** of fools *is* folly. H4148
19:20 Hear counsel, and receive **i**, that thou H4148
27 Cease, my son, to hear the **i** *that* H4148
23:12 Apply thine heart unto **i**, and thine ears H4148
23 *also* wisdom, and **i**, and understanding. H4148
24:32 *it* well: I looked upon *it, and* received **i**. H4148
Jer 17:23 that they might not hear, nor receive **i**. H4148
32:33 yet they have not hearkened to receive **i**. H4148
Jer 35:13 Will ye not receive **i** to hearken to my H4148
Ezk 5:15 and a taunt, an **i** and an astonishment H4148
Zep 3: 7 me, thou wilt receive **i**; so their dwelling H4148
2Ti 3:16 for correction, for **i** in righteousness: *G3809*

INSTRUCTOR
Gen 4:22 Tubal-cain, an **i** of every artificer in H3913
Ro 2:20 An **i** of the foolish, a teacher of babes, *G3810*

INSTRUCTORS
1Co 4:15 For though ye have ten thousand **i** in *G3807*

INSTRUMENT
Nu 35:16 And if he smite him with an **i** of iron, H3627
Ps 33: 2 with the psaltery *and* an **i** of ten strings.
92: 3 Upon an **i** of ten strings, and upon the
144: 9 a psaltery *and* an **i** of ten strings will I
Isa 28:27 with a threshing **i**, neither is a cart H2742
41:15 sharp threshing **i** having teeth: thou H4173
54:16 bringeth forth an **i** for his work; and I H3627
Ezk 33:32 can play well on an **i**: for they hear thy

INSTRUMENTS
Gen 49: 5 Simeon and Levi *are* brethren; **i** of H3627
Ex 25: 9 the **i** thereof, even so shall ye make *it*. H3627
Nu 3: 8 And they shall keep all the **i** of the H3627
4:12 And they shall take all the **i** of ministry, H3627
26 cords, and all the **i** of their service, and H3627
32 cords, with all their **i**, and with all their H3627
32 the **i** of the charge of their burden. H3627
7: 1 it, and all the **i** thereof, both the altar H3627
31: 6 **i**, and the trumpets to blow in his hand. H3627
1Sa 8:12 harvest, and to make his **i** of war, and H3627
12 of war, and **i** of his chariots. H3627
18: 6 tabrets, with joy, and with **i** of musick. H7991
2Sa 6: 5 on all manner of *i made of* fir wood,
24:22 and threshing **i** and *other* instruments H4173
22 and *other* **i** of the oxen for wood. H3627
1Ki 19:21 their flesh with the **i** of the oxen, and H3627
1Ch 9:29 vessels, and all the **i** of the sanctuary, H3627
12:33 in war, with all **i** of war, fifty thousand, H3627
37 with all manner of **i** of war for the H3627
15:16 *to be* the singers with **i** of musick, H3627
16:42 and with musical **i** of God. And the H3627
21:23 and the threshing **i** for wood, and the H4173
23: 5 the LORD with the **i** which I made, *said* H3627
28:14 *things* of gold, for all **i** of all manner of H3627
14 *silver also* for all **i** of silver by weight, H3627
14 weight, for all **i** of every kind of service: H3627
2Ch 4:16 and all their **i**, did Huram his father H3627
5: 1 the gold, and all the **i**, put he among the H3627
13 and cymbals and **i** of musick, and H3627
7: 6 the Levites also with **i** of musick of the H3627
23:13 the singers with **i** of musick, and such H3627
29:26 And the Levites stood with the **i** of H3627
27 the **i** *ordained* by David king of Israel. H3627
30:21 *singing* with loud **i** unto the LORD. H3627
34:12 all that could skill of **i** of musick. H3627
Neh 12:36 with the musical **i** of David the man of H3627
Ps 7:13 He hath also prepared for him the **i** of H3627
68:25 the players on *i followed* after; among H5059
87: 7 As well the singers as the players on **i**
150: 4 praise him with stringed **i** and organs. H4482
Ecc 2: 8 men, *as* musical **i**, and that of all sorts. H7705
Isa 32: 7 The **i** also of the churl *are* evil: he H3627
38:20 to the stringed **i** all the days of our life H5059
Ezk 40:42 also they laid the **i** wherewith they slew H3627
Dan 6:18 neither were **i** of musick brought before H1761
Am 1: 3 threshed Gilead with threshing **i** of iron:
6: 5 to themselves **i** of musick, like David; H3627
Hab 3:19 To the chief singer on my stringed **i**. H5058
Zec 11:15 thee yet the **i** of a foolish shepherd. H3627
Ro 6:13 Neither yield ye your members *as* **i** of *G3696*
13 *as* **i** of righteousness unto God. *G3696*

INSURRECTION
Ezr 4:19 time hath made **i** against kings, and H5376
Ps 64: 2 from the **i** of the workers of iniquity: H7285
Mk 15: 7 that had made **i** with him, who had *G4955*
7 who had committed murder in the **i**. *G4714*
Act 18:12 the Jews made **i** with one accord *G2721*

INTANGLE See ENTANGLE.

INTEGRITY
Gen 20: 5 *is* my brother: in the **i** of my heart and H8537
6 didst this in the **i** of thy heart; for I also H8537
1Ki 9: 4 thy father walked, in **i** of heart, and in H8537
Job 2: 3 still he holdeth fast his **i**, although thou H8538

Job 2: 9 still retain thine **i**? curse God, and die. H8538
27: 5 I die I will not remove mine **i** from me. H8538
31: 6 balance, that God may know mine **i**. H8538
Ps 7: 8 and according to mine **i** *that is* in me. H8537
25:21 Let **i** and uprightness preserve me; for I H8537
26: 1 walked in mine **i**: I have trusted also in H8537
11 But as for me, I will walk in mine **i**: H8537
41:12 me in mine **i**, and settest me before H8537
78:72 So he fed them according to the **i** of his H8537
Prv 11: 3 The **i** of the upright shall guide them: H8538
19: 1 Better *is* the poor that walketh in his **i**, H8537
20: 7 The just *man* walketh in his **i**: his H8537

INTELLIGENCE
Dan 11:30 even return, and have **i** with them that H995

INTEND
Jos 22:33 God, and did not **i** to go up against them H559
2Ch 28:13 LORD *already*, ye **i** to add *more* to our H559
Act 5:28 **i** to bring this man's blood upon us. *G1014*
35 what ye **i** to do as touching these men. *G3195*

INTENDED
Ps 21:11 For they **i** evil against thee: they H5186

INTENDEST
Ex 2:14 a judge over us? **i** thou to kill me, as thou H559

INTENDING
Lk 14:28 For which of you, **i** to build a tower, *G2309*
Act 12: 4 to keep him; **i** after Easter to bring *G1014*
20:13 unto Assos, there **i** to take in Paul: for *G3195*

INTENT
2Sa 17:14 of Ahithophel, to the **i** that the LORD H5668
2Ki 10:19 *it* in subtilty, to the **i** that he might H4616
2Ch 16: 1 Ramah, to the **i** that he might let none H1115
Ezk 40: 4 thee; for to the **i** that I might shew *them* H4616
Dan 4:17 holy ones: to the **i** that the living may H1701
Jn 11:15 was not there, to the **i** ye may believe; *G2443*
13:28 knew for what **i** he spake this unto him. *G5101*
Act 9:21 hither for that **i**, that he might bring *G5124*
10:29 for what **i** ye have sent for me? *G3056*
1Co 10: 6 examples, to the **i** we should not lust *G1519*
Eph 3:10 To the **i** that now unto the *G2443*

INTENTS
Jer 30:24 performed the **i** of his heart: in the H4209
Heb 4:12 of the thoughts and **i** of the heart. *G1771*

INTERCESSION
Isa 53:12 and made **i** for the transgressors. H6293
Jer 7:16 make **i** to me: for I will not hear thee. H6293
27:18 them now make **i** to the LORD of hosts, H6293
36:25 had made **i** to the king that he would H6293
Ro 8:26 itself maketh **i** for us with groanings *G5241*
27 he maketh **i** for the saints according *G1793*
34 hand of God, who also maketh **i** for us. *G1793*
11: 2 maketh **i** to God against Israel, saying, *G1793*
Heb 7:25 he ever liveth to make **i** for them. *G1793*

INTERCESSIONS
1Ti 2: 1 prayers, **i**, *and* giving of thanks, *G1783*

INTERCESSOR
Isa 59:16 that *there was* no **i**: therefore his arm H6293

INTERMEDDLE
Prv 14:10 and a stranger doth not **i** with his joy. H6148

INTERMEDDLETH
Prv 18: 1 himself, seeketh *and* **i** with all wisdom. H1566

INTERMISSION
Lam 3:49 down, and ceaseth not, without any **i**, H2014

INTERPRET
Gen 41: 8 none that could **i** them unto Pharaoh. H6622
12 man according to his dream he did **i**. H6622
15 *is* none that can **i** it: and I have heard H6622
15 thou canst understand a dream to **i** it. H6622
1Co 12:30 do all speak with tongues? do all **i**? *G1329*
14: 5 **i**, that the church may receive edifying. *G1329*
13 an *unknown* tongue pray that he may **i**. *G1329*
27 three, and *that* by course; and let one **i**. *G1329*

INTERPRETATION
Gen 40: 5 according to the **i** of his dream, the H6623
12 And Joseph said unto him, This *is* the **i** H6623
40:16 When the chief baker saw that the **i** H6622
18 said, This *is* the **i** thereof: The three H6623
41:11 man according to the **i** of his dream. H6623
Jdg 7:15 the dream, and the **i** thereof, that he H7667
Prv 1: 6 To understand a proverb, and the **i**; the H4426
Ecc 8: 1 who knoweth the **i** of a thing? a man's H6592
Dan 2: 4 the dream, and we will shew the **i**. H6591
5 dream, with the **i** thereof, ye shall be H6591
6 But if ye shew the dream, and the **i** H6591
6 shew me the dream, and the **i** thereof. H6591
7 the dream, and we will shew the **i** of it. H6591
9 know that ye can shew me the **i** thereof. H6591
16 and that he would shew the king the **i**. H6591
24 king, and I will shew unto the king the **i**. H6591
25 will make known unto the king the **i**. H6591
26 which I have seen, and the **i** thereof? H6591
30 make known the **i** to the king, and that H6591
36 This *is* the dream; and we will tell the **i** H6591
45 dream *is* certain, and the **i** thereof sure. H6591
4: 6 known unto me the **i** of the dream. H6591
7 not make known unto me the **i** thereof. H6591
9 that I have seen, and the **i** thereof. H6591
18 declare the **i** thereof, forasmuch H6591
18 unto me the **i**: but thou *art* able; for H6591
19 not the dream, or the **i** thereof, trouble H6591
19 thee, and the **i** thereof to thine enemies. H6591
24 This *is* the **i**, O king, and this *is* the H6591
5: 7 and shew me the **i** thereof, shall be H6591
8 make known to the king the **i** thereof. H6591
12 Daniel be called, and he will shew the **i**. H6591
15 unto me the **i** thereof: but they could H6591
15 they could not shew the **i** of the thing: H6591
16 known to me the **i** thereof, thou shalt H6591
17 the king, and make known to him the **i**. H6591
26 This *is* the **i** of the thing: MENE; God H6591
7:16 and made me know the **i** of the things. H6591
Jn 1:42 be called Cephas, which is by **i**, A stone. *G2059*
9: 7 (which is by **i**, Sent.) He went his way *G2059*
Act 9:36 Tabitha, which by **i** is called Dorcas: *G1329*
13: 8 so is his name by **i**) withstood them, *G3177*
1Co 12:10 of tongues; to another the **i** of tongues: *G2058*
14:26 **i**. Let all things be done unto edifying. *G2058*
Heb 7: 2 of all; first being by **i** King of *G2059*
2Pt 1:20 of the scripture is of any private **i**. *G1955*

INTERPRETATIONS
Gen 40: 8 unto them, *Do* not **i** *belong* to God? tell H6623
Dan 5:16 thou canst make **i**, and dissolve doubts: H6591

INTERPRETED
Gen 40:22 chief baker: as Joseph had **i** to them. H6622
41:12 told him, and he **i** to us our dreams; to H6622
13 And it came to pass, as he **i** to us, so it H6622
Ezr 4: 7 tongue, and **i** in the Syrian tongue. H8638
Mt 1:23 which being **i** is, God with us. *G3177*
Mk 5:41 being **i**, Damsel, I say unto thee, arise. *G3177*
15:22 which is, being **i**, The place of a skull. *G3177*
34 which is, being **i**, My God, my God, why *G3177*
Jn 1:38 being **i**, Master,) where dwellest thou? *G2059*
41 Messias, which is, being **i**, the Christ. *G3177*
Act 4:36 Barnabas, (which is, being **i**, The son of *G3177*

INTERPRETER
Gen 40: 8 and *there is* no **i** of it. And Joseph said H6622
42:23 *them;* for he spake unto them by an **i**. H3887
Job 33:23 If there be a messenger with him, an **i**, H3887
1Co 14:28 But if there be no **i**, let him keep silence *G1328*

INTERPRETING
Dan 5:12 and understanding, **i** of dreams, and H6590

INTO See the Appendix.

INTREAT See ENTREAT.

INTREATED See ENTREATED.

INTREATETH See ENTREATETH.

INTREATIES See ENTREATIES.

INTREATY See ENTREATY.

INTRUDING
Col 2:18 of angels, **i** into those things which *G1687*

INVADE
2Ch 20:10 not let Israel **i**, when they came out H935
Hab 3:16 people, he will **i** them with his troops. H1464

INVADED
1Sa 23:27 for the Philistines have **i** the land. H6584
27: 8 And David and his men went up, and **i** H6584
30: 1 Amalekites had **i** the south, and Ziklag, H6584
2Ki 13:20 **i** the land at the coming in of the year. H935
2Ch 28:18 The Philistines also had **i** the cities of H6584

INVASION
1Sa 30:14 We made an **i** *upon* the south of the H6584

INVENT
Am 6: 5 sound of the viol, *and* **i** to themselves H2803

INVENTED
2Ch 26:15 And he made in Jerusalem engines, **i** H4284

INVENTIONS
Ps 99: 8 thou tookest vengeance of their **i**. H5949
106:29 **i**: and the plague brake in upon them. H4611
39 and went a whoring with their own **i**. H4611
Prv 8:12 and find out knowledge of witty **i**. H4209
Ecc 7:29 but they have sought out many **i**. H2810

INVENTORS
Ro 1:30 **i** of evil things, disobedient to parents, *G2182*

INVISIBLE
Ro 1:20 For the **i** things of him from the creation *G517*
Col 1:15 Who is the image of the **i** God, the *G517*
16 in earth, visible and **i**, whether *they be* *G517*
1Ti 1:17 Now unto the King eternal, immortal, **i**, *G517*
Heb 11:27 for he endured, as seeing him who is **i**. *G517*

INVITED
1Sa 9:24 since I said, I have **i** the people. So Saul H7121
2Sa 13:23 and Absalom **i** all the king's sons. H7121
Est 5:12 am I **i** unto her also with the king. H7121

INWARD
Ex 28:26 which *is* in the side of the ephod **i**. H1004
39:19 it, which *was* on the side of the ephod **i**. H1004
Lev 13:55 **i**, *whether it be* bare within or without.
2Sa 5: 9 built round about from Millo and **i**. H1004
1Ki 7:25 them, and all their hinder parts *were* **i**. H1004
2Ch 3:13 on their feet, and their faces *were* **i**. H1004
4: 4 them, and all their hinder parts *were* **i**. H1004
Job 19:19 All my **i** friends abhorred me: and they H5475
38:36 Who hath put wisdom in the **i** parts? or H2910
Ps 5: 9 in their mouth; their **i** part *is* very H7130
49:11 Their **i** thought *is, that* their houses H7130
51: 6 Behold, thou desirest truth in the **i** H2910
64: 6 search: both the **i** *thought* of every one H7130
Prv 20:27 searching all the **i** parts of the belly. H2315
30 so *do* stripes the **i** parts of the belly. H2315
Isa 16:11 Moab, and mine **i** parts for Kir-haresh. H7130
Jer 31:33 my law in their **i** parts, and write it in H7130
Ezk 40: 9 cubits; and the porch of the gate *was* **i**. H1004
16 **i**: and upon *each* post *were* palm trees. H6441
41: 3 Then went he **i**, and measured the post H6441
42: 4 ten cubits breadth **i**, a way of one cubit; H6442
Lk 11:39 the platter; but your **i** part is full of *G2081*
Ro 7:22 in the law of God after the **i** man: *G2080*
2Co 4:16 yet the **i** *man* is renewed day by day. *G2081*
7:15 And his **i** affection is more abundant *G4698*

INWARDLY
Ps 62: 4 their mouth, but they curse **i**. Selah. H7130
Mt 7:15 but **i** they are ravening wolves. *G2081*
Ro 2:29 But he *is* a Jew, which is one **i**; and *G1722*

INWARDS
Ex 29:13 that covereth the **i**, and the caul *that is* H7130
17 and wash the **i** of him, and his legs, H7130
22 that covereth the **i**, and the caul *above* H7130
Lev 1: 9 But his **i** and his legs shall he wash in H7130
13 But he shall wash the **i** and the legs H7130
3: 3 that covereth the **i**, and all the fat that *is* H7130
3 and all the fat that *is* upon the **i**, H7130
9 that covereth the **i**, and all the fat that *is* H7130
9 and all the fat that *is* upon the **i**, H7130
14 that covereth the **i**, and all the fat that *is* H7130
14 and all the fat that *is* upon the **i**, H7130
4: 8 that covereth the **i**, and all the fat that *is* H7130
8 and all the fat that *is* upon the **i**, H7130
11 with his legs, and his **i**, and his dung, H7130
7: 3 rump, and the fat that covereth the **i**, H7130
8:16 that *was* upon the **i**, and the caul *above* H7130
21 And he washed the **i** and the legs in H7130
25 that *was* upon the **i**, and the caul *above* H7130

Lev 9:14 And he did wash the i and the legs, and H7130
19 which covereth *the i*, and the kidneys,

IPHEDEIAH
1Ch 8:25 And I, and Penuel, the sons of Shashak; H3301

IR
1Ch 7:12 of I, *and* Hushim, the sons of Aher. H5893

IRA
2Sa 20:26 And I also the Jairite was a chief ruler H5896
23:26 Helez the Paltite, I the son of Ikkesh the H5896
38 I an Ithrite, Gareb an Ithrite, H5896
1Ch 11:28 I the son of Ikkesh the Tekoite, H5896
40 I the Ithrite, Gareb the Ithrite, H5896
27: 9 sixth month *was* I the son of Ikkesh the H5896

IRAD
Gen 4:18 And unto Enoch was born I: and Irad H5897
18 And unto Enoch was born Irad: and I H5897

IRAM
Gen 36:43 Duke Magdiel, duke I: these *be* the H5902
1Ch 1:54 Duke Magdiel, duke I. These *are* the H5902

IRI
1Ch 7: 7 and Jerimoth, and I, five; heads of the H5901

IRIJAH
Jer 37:13 there, whose name *was* I, the son of H3376
14 not to him: so I took Jeremiah, and H3376

IRNAHASH
1Ch 4:12 of I. These *are* the men of Rechah. H5904

IRON
Gen 4:22 artificer in brass and i: and the sister of H1270
Lev 26:19 heaven as i, and your earth as brass: H1270
Nu 31:22 the brass, the i, the tin, and the lead, H1270
35:16 an instrument of i, so that he die, he *is* H1270
Dt 3:11 *was* a bedstead of i; *is* it not in Rabbath H1270
4:20 forth out of the i furnace, *even* out of H1270
8: 9 whose stones *are* i, and out of whose H1270
27: 5 shalt not lift up *any* i *tool* upon them. H1270
28:23 the earth that is under thee *shall be* i. H1270
48 he shall put a yoke of i upon thy neck, H1270
33:25 Thy shoes *shall be* i and brass; and as H1270
Jos 6:19 of brass and i, *are* consecrated unto H1270
24 of brass and of i, they put into the H1270
8:31 man hath lift up *any* i: and they offered H1270
17:16 have chariots of i, *both they* who *are* of H1270
18 i chariots, *and* though they *be* strong. H1270
19:38 And I, and Migdal-el, Horem, and H3375
22: 8 brass, and with i, and with very much H1270
Jdg 1:19 valley, because they had chariots of i. H1270
4: 3 chariots of i; and twenty years he H1270
13 chariots of i, and all the people that H1270
1Sa 17: 7 shekels of i: and one bearing a shield H1270
2Sa 12:31 under harrows of i, and under axes of H1270
31 and under axes of i, and made them H1270
23: 7 must be fenced with i and the staff of a H1270
1Ki 6: 7 nor axe *nor* any tool of i heard in the H1270
8:51 from the midst of the furnace of i: H1270
22:11 him horns of i: and he said, Thus saith H1270
2Ki 6: 6 cast *it* in thither; and the i did swim. H1270
1Ch 20: 3 with harrows of i, and with axes. Even H1270
22: 3 And David prepared i in abundance H1270
14 and of brass and i without weight; for H1270
16 the brass, and the i, *there is* no number. H1270
29: 2 of brass, the i for *things* of iron, and H1270
2 iron for *things* of i, and wood for *things* H1270
7 and one hundred thousand talents of i. H1270
2Ch 2: 7 in brass, and in i, and in purple, and H1270
14 in silver, in brass, in i, in stone, and in H1270
18:10 him horns of i, and said, Thus saith H1270
24:12 such as wrought i and brass to mend H1270
Job 19:24 That they were graven with an i pen H1270
20:24 He shall flee from the i weapon, *and* H1270
28: 2 I is taken out of the earth, and brass *is* H1270
40:18 of brass; his bones *are* like bars of i. H1270
41:27 He esteemeth i as straw, *and* brass as H1270
Ps 2: 9 Thou shalt break them with a rod of i; H1270
105:18 they hurt with fetters: he was laid in i: H1270
107:10 death, *being* bound in affliction and i; H1270
16 brass, and cut the bars of i in sunder. H1270
149: 8 and their nobles with fetters of i; H1270
Prv 27:17 I sharpeneth iron; so a man H1270
17 Iron sharpeneth i; so a man sharpeneth H1270
Ecc 10:10 If the i be blunt, and he do not whet the H1270
Isa 10:34 of the forest with i, and Lebanon shall H1270
45: 2 of brass, and cut in sunder the bars of i: H1270
48: 4 neck *is* an i sinew, and thy brow brass; H1270
60:17 For brass I will bring gold, and for i I H1270
17 and for stones i: I will also make thy H1270
Jer 1:18 city, and an i pillar, and brasen walls H1270
6:28 *are* brass and i; they *are* all corrupters. H1270
11: 4 of Egypt, from the i furnace, saying, H1270
15:12 Shall i break the northern iron and the H1270
12 Shall iron break the northern i and the H1270
17: 1 with a pen of i, *and* with the point of H1270
28:13 but thou shalt make for them yokes of i. H1270
14 I have put a yoke of i upon the neck of H1270
Ezk 4: 3 Moreover take thou unto thee an i pan, H1270
3 set it *for* a wall of i between thee and H1270
22:18 brass, and tin, and i, and lead, in the H1270
20 *As* they gather silver, and brass, and i, H1270
27:12 i, tin, and lead, they traded in thy fairs. H1270
19 in thy fairs: bright i, cassia, and H1270
Dan 2:33 His legs of i, his feet part of iron and H6523
33 His legs of iron, his feet part of i and H6523
34 of i and clay, and brake them to pieces. H6523
35 Then was the i, the clay, the brass, the H6523
40 shall be strong as i: forasmuch as iron H6523
40 forasmuch as i breaketh in pieces and H6523
40 all *things*: and as i that breaketh all H6523
41 clay, and part of i, the kingdom shall be H6523
41 the strength of the i, forasmuch as thou H6523
41 thou sawest the i mixed with miry clay. H6523
42 And *as* the toes of the feet *were* part of i, H6523
43 And whereas thou sawest i mixed with H6523
43 even as i is not mixed with clay. H6523
45 brake in pieces the i, the brass, the clay, H6523
4:15 even with a band of i and brass, in the H6523
23 even with a band of i and brass, in the H6523
5: 4 of brass, of i, of wood, and of stone. H6523
23 and gold, of brass, i, wood, and stone, H6523
7: 7 and it had great i teeth: it devoured H6523
19 teeth *were of* i, and his nails *of* brass; H6523
Am 1: 3 Gilead with threshing instruments of i: H1270
Mic 4:13 make thine horn i, and I will make thy H1270
Act 12:10 came unto the i gate that leadeth unto *G4603*
1Ti 4: 2 their conscience seared with a hot i; *G2743*
Rev 2:27 And he shall rule them with a rod of i; *G4603*
9: 9 breastplates of i; and the sound of their *G4603*
12: 5 with a rod of i: and her child was *G4603*
18:12 wood, and of brass, and i, and marble, *G4604*
19:15 them with a rod of i: and he treadeth *G4603*

IRONS
Job 41: 7 Canst thou fill his skin with barbed i? or H7905

IRPEEL
Jos 18:27 And Rekem, and I, and Taralah, H3416

IR-SHEMESH
Jos 19:41 was Zorah, and Eshtaol, and I, H5905

IRU
1Ch 4:15 son of Jephunneh; I, Elah, and Naam: H5900

IS See the Appendix.

ISAAC
Gen 17:19 thou shalt call his name I: and I will H3327
21 But my covenant will I establish with I, H3327
21: 3 unto him, whom Sarah bare to him, I. H3327
4 And Abraham circumcised his son I H3327
5 old, when his son I was born unto him. H3327
8 feast the *same* day that I was weaned. H3327
10 not be heir with my son, *even* with I. H3327
12 voice; for in I shall thy seed be called. H3327
22: 2 thine only *son* I, whom thou lovest, and H3327
3 with him, and I his son, and clave the H3327
6 and laid *it* upon I his son; and he took H3327
7 And I spake unto Abraham his father, H3327
9 in order, and bound I his son, and laid H3327
24: 4 kindred, and take a wife unto my son I. H3327
14 for thy servant I; and thereby shall I H3327
62 And I came from the way of the well H3327
63 And I went out to meditate in the field H3327
64 she saw I, she lighted off the camel. H3327
66 And the servant told I all things that he H3327
67 And I brought her into his mother H3327
67 he loved her: and I was comforted after H3327
25: 5 Abraham gave all that he had unto I. H3327
6 them away from I his son, while he yet H3327
9 And his sons I and Ishmael buried him H3327
11 I; and Isaac dwelt by the well Lahai-roi. H3327
Gen 25:11 and I dwelt by the well Lahai-roi. H3327
19 And these *are* the generations of I, H3327
19 Abraham's son: Abraham begat I: H3327
20 And I was forty years old when he took H3327
21 And I entreated the LORD for his wife, H3327
26 was called Jacob: and I *was* threescore H3327
28 And I loved Esau, because he did eat of H3327
26: 1 days of Abraham. And I went unto H3327
6 And I dwelt in Gerar: H3327
8 I *was* sporting with Rebekah his wife. H3327
9 And Abimelech called I, and said, H3327
9 She *is* my sister? And I said unto him, H3327
12 Then I sowed in that land, and H3327
16 And Abimelech said unto I, Go from us; H3327
17 And I departed thence, and pitched his H3327
18 And I digged again the wells of water, H3327
27 And I said unto them, Wherefore come H3327
31 to another: and I sent them away, and H3327
35 Which were a grief of mind unto I and H3327
27: 1 And it came to pass, that when I was H3327
5 And Rebekah heard when I spake to H3327
20 And I said unto his son, How *is it* that H3327
21 And I said unto Jacob, Come near, I H3327
22 And Jacob went near unto I his father; H3327
26 And his father I said unto him, Come H3327
30 And it came to pass, as soon as I had H3327
30 the presence of I his father, that Esau H3327
32 And I his father said unto him, Who H3327
33 And I trembled very exceedingly, and H3327
37 And I answered and said unto Esau, H3327
39 And I his father answered and said H3327
46 And Rebekah said to I, I am weary of H3327
28: 1 And I called Jacob, and blessed him, H3327
5 And I sent away Jacob: and he went to H3327
6 When Esau saw that I had blessed H3327
8 of Canaan pleased not I his father; H3327
13 and the God of I: the land whereon thou H3327
31:18 go to I his father in the land of Canaan. H3327
42 and the fear of I, had been with me, H3327
53 Jacob sware by the fear of his father I. H3327
32: 9 God of my father I, the LORD which H3327
35:12 Abraham and I, to thee I will give it, H3327
27 And Jacob came unto I his father unto H3327
27 where Abraham and I sojourned. H3327
28 And the days of I were an hundred and H3327
29 And I gave up the ghost, and died, and H3327
46: 1 sacrifices unto the God of his father I. H3327
48:15 Abraham and I did walk, the God H3327
16 Abraham and I; and let them grow into H3327
49:31 there they buried I and Rebekah his H3327
50:24 sware to Abraham, to I, and to Jacob. H3327
Ex 2:24 with Abraham, with I, and with Jacob. H3327
3: 6 the God of I, and the God of Jacob. H3327
15 the God of I, and the God of Jacob, H3327
16 God of Abraham, of I, and of Jacob, H3327
4: 5 the God of I, and the God of Jacob, H3327
6: 3 And I appeared unto Abraham, unto I, H3327
8 it to Abraham, to I, and to Jacob; and I H3327
32:13 Remember Abraham, I, and Israel, thy H3327
33: 1 unto Abraham, to I, and to Jacob, H3327
Lev 26:42 also my covenant with I, and also my H3327
Nu 32:11 unto Abraham, unto I, and unto Jacob; H3327
Dt 1: 8 fathers, Abraham, I, and Jacob, to give H3327
6:10 to Abraham, to I, and to Jacob, to give H3327
9: 5 thy fathers, Abraham, I, and Jacob. H3327
27 Remember thy servants, Abraham, I, H3327
29:13 fathers, to Abraham, to I, and to Jacob. H3327
30:20 to I, and to Jacob, to give them. H3327
34: 4 unto Abraham, unto I, and unto Jacob, H3327
Jos 24: 3 multiplied his seed, and gave him I. H3327
4 And I gave unto I Jacob and Esau: and H3327
1Ki 18:36 God of Abraham, I, and of Israel, let it H3327
2Ki 13:23 with Abraham, I, and Jacob, and would H3327
1Ch 1:28 The sons of Abraham; I, and Ishmael. H3327
34 And Abraham begat I. The sons of H3327
34 Isaac. The sons of I; Esau and Israel. H3327
16:16 with Abraham, and of his oath unto I; H3327
29:18 O LORD God of Abraham, I, and of H3327
2Ch 30: 6 God of Abraham, I, and Israel, and he H3327
Ps 105: 9 with Abraham, and his oath unto I; H3446
Jer 33:26 seed of Abraham, I, and Jacob: for I will H3446
Am 7: 9 And the high places of I shall be H3446
16 not *thy word* against the house of I. H3446
Mt 1: 2 Abraham begat I; and Isaac begat *G2464*
2 Abraham begat Isaac; and I begat *G2464*
8:11 I, and Jacob, in the kingdom of heaven. *G2464*
22:32 and the God of I, and the God of Jacob? *G2464*
Mk 12:26 and the God of I, and the God of Jacob? *G2464*
Lk 3:34 was *the son* of I, which was *the son* of *G2464*

Lk 13:28 see Abraham, and I, and Jacob, and all G2464
20:37 and the God of I, and the God of Jacob. G2464
Act 3:13 The God of Abraham, and of I, and of G2464
7: 8 so *Abraham* begat I, and circumcised G2464
8 the eighth day; and I *begat* Jacob; and G2464
32 and the God of I, and the God of Jacob. G2464
Ro 9: 7 but, In I shall thy seed be called. G2464
10 conceived by one, *even* by our father I; G2464
Gal 4:28 Now we, brethren, as I was, are the G2464
Heb 11: 9 tabernacles with I and Jacob, the heirs G2464
17 was tried, offered up I: and he that had G2464
18 Of whom it was said, That in I shall thy G2464
20 By faith I blessed Jacob and Esau G2464
Jas 2:21 he had offered I his son upon the altar? G2464

ISAAC'S
Gen 26:19 And I servants digged in the valley, H3327
20 did strive with I herdmen, saying, The H3327
25 and there I servants digged a well. H3327
32 the same day, that I servants came, H3327

ISAIAH
2Ki 19: 2 to I the prophet the son of Amoz. H3470
5 the servants of king Hezekiah came to I. H3470
6 And I said unto them, Thus shall ye say H3470
20 Then I the son of Amoz sent to H3470
20: 1 And the prophet I the son of Amoz H3470
4 And it came to pass, afore I was gone H3470
7 And I said, Take a lump of figs. And H3470
8 And Hezekiah said unto I, What *shall* H3470
9 And I said, This sign shalt thou have of H3470
11 And I the prophet cried unto the H3470
14 Then came I the prophet unto king H3470
16 And I said unto Hezekiah, Hear the H3470
19 Then said Hezekiah unto I, Good *is* the H3470
2Ch 26:22 I the prophet, the son of Amoz, write. H3470
32:20 and the prophet I the son of Amoz, H3470
32 in the vision of I the prophet, the son H3470
Isa 1: 1 The vision of I the son of Amoz, which H3470
2: 1 The word that I the son of Amoz saw H3470
7: 3 Then said the LORD unto I, Go forth H3470
13: 1 The burden of Babylon, which I the son H3470
20: 2 At the same time spake the LORD by I H3470
3 as my servant I hath walked naked H3470
37: 2 unto I the prophet the son of Amoz. H3470
5 the servants of king Hezekiah came to I. H3470
6 And I said unto them, Thus shall ye say H3470
21 Then I the son of Amoz sent unto H3470
38: 1 unto death. And I the prophet the son H3470
4 Then came the word of the LORD to I, H3470
21 For I had said, Let them take a lump of H3470
39: 3 Then came I the prophet unto king H3470
5 Then said I to Hezekiah, Hear the word H3470
8 Then said Hezekiah to I, Good *is* the H3470

ISCAH
Gen 11:29 the father of Milcah, and the father of I. H3252

ISCARIOT
Mt 10: 4 Simon the Canaanite, and Judas I, who G2469
26:14 Then one of the twelve, called Judas I, G2469
Mk 3:19 And Judas I, which also betrayed him: G2469
14:10 And Judas I, one of the twelve, went G2469
Lk 6:16 and Judas I, which also was the traitor. G2469
22: 3 I, being of the number of the twelve. G2469
Jn 6:71 He spake of Judas I *the son* of Simon: G2469
12: 4 Then saith one of his disciples, Judas I, G2469
13: 2 of Judas I, Simon's *son*, to betray him; G2469
26 he gave *it* to Judas I, *the son* of Simon. G2469
14:22 Judas saith unto him, not I, Lord, how G2469

ISHBAH
1Ch 4:17 and I the father of Eshtemoa. H3431

ISHBAK
Gen 25: 2 Medan, and Midian, and I, and Shuah. H3435
1Ch 1:32 and Midian, and I, and Shuah. And the H3435

ISHBI-BENOB
2Sa 21:16 And I, which *was* of the sons of the H3430

ISH-BOSHETH
2Sa 2: 8 of Saul's host, took I the son of Saul, and H378
10 I Saul's son *was* forty years old when he H378
12 and the servants of I the son of Saul, H378
15 which *pertained* to I the son of Saul, and H378
3: 7 of Aiah: and *I* said to Abner, Wherefore
8 for the words of I, and said, *Am* I a dog's H378
14 And David sent messengers to I Saul's H378
2Sa 3:15 And I sent, and took her from *her* H378
4: 5 the house of I, who lay on a bed at noon. H378
8 And they brought the head of I unto H378
8 king, Behold the head of I the son of Saul H378
12 took the head of I, and buried *it* in the H378

ISHI
1Ch 2:31 And the sons of Appaim; I. And the H3469
31 And the sons of I; Sheshan. And the H3469
4:20 of I *were*, Zoheth, and Ben-zoheth. H3469
42 and Rephaiah, and Uzziel, the sons of I. H3469
5:24 even Epher, and I, and Eliel, and Azriel, H3469
Hos 2:16 me I; and shalt call me no more Baali. H376

ISHIAH
1Ch 7: 3 and Joel, I, five: all of them chief men. H3449

ISHIJAH
Ezr 10:31 And *of* the sons of Harim; Eliezer, I, H3449

ISHMA
1Ch 4: 3 of Etam; Jezreel, and I, and Idbash: and H3457

ISHMAEL
Gen 16:11 shalt call his name I; because the LORD H3458
15 his son's name, which Hagar bare, I. H3458
16 old, when Hagar bare I to Abram. H3458
17:18 And Abraham said unto God, O that I H3458
20 And as for I, I have heard thee: Behold, H3458
23 And Abraham took I his son, and all H3458
25 And I his son *was* thirteen years old, H3458
26 Abraham circumcised, and I his son. H3458
25: 9 And his sons Isaac and I buried him in H3458
12 Now these *are* the generations of I, H3458
13 names of the sons of I, by their names, H3458
13 the firstborn of I, Nebajoth; and Kedar, H3458
16 These *are* the sons of I, and these *are* H3458
17 And these *are* the years of the life of I, H3458
28: 9 Then went Esau unto I, and took unto H3458
9 the daughter of I Abraham's son, the H3458
2Ki 25:23 to Mizpah, even I the son of Nethaniah, H3458
25 month, that I the son of Nethaniah, H3458
1Ch 1:28 The sons of Abraham; Isaac, and I. H3458
29 The firstborn of I, Nebaioth; then H3458
31 and Kedemah. These are the sons of I. H3458
8:38 Bocheru, and I, and Sheariah, and H3458
9:44 Bocheru, and I, and Sheariah, and H3458
2Ch 19:11 the son of I, the ruler of the house H3458
23: 1 son of Jeroham, and I the son of H3458
Ezr 10:22 I, Nethaneel, Jozabad, and Elasah. H3458
Jer 40: 8 to Mizpah, even I the son of Nethaniah, H3458
14 hath sent I the son of Nethaniah H3458
15 and I will slay I the son of Nethaniah, H3458
16 this thing: for thou speakest falsely of I. H3458
41: 1 month, *that* I the son of Nethaniah H3458
2 Then arose I the son of Nethaniah, and H3458
3 I also slew all the Jews that were with H3458
6 And I the son of Nethaniah went forth H3458
7 of the city, that I the son of Nethaniah H3458
8 that said unto I, Slay us not: for we H3458
9 Now the pit wherein I had cast all the H3458
9 Baasha king of Israel: *and* I the son of H3458
10 Then I carried away captive all the H3458
10 of Ahikam: and I the son of Nethaniah H3458
11 that I the son of Nethaniah had done, H3458
12 and went to fight with I the son of H3458
13 which *were* with I saw Johanan the son H3458
14 So all the people that I had carried H3458
15 But I the son of Nethaniah escaped H3458
16 recovered from I the son of Nethaniah, H3458
18 afraid of them, because I the son of H3458

ISHMAELITE
1Ch 27:30 Over the camels also *was* Obil the I: and H3459

ISHMAELITES
Jdg 8:24 golden earrings, because they *were* I.) H3459
Ps 83: 6 The tabernacles of Edom, and the I; of H3459

ISHMAEL'S
Gen 36: 3 And Bashemath I daughter, sister of H3458

ISHMAIAH
1Ch 27:19 Of Zebulun, I the son of Obadiah: of H3460

ISHMEELITE
1Ch 2:17 the father of Amasa *was* Jether the I. H3459

ISHMEELITES
Gen 37:25 a company of I came from Gilead with H3459
27 Come, and let us sell him to the I, and H3459
28 sold Joseph to the I for twenty *pieces* of H3459
39: 1 I, which had brought him down thither. H3459

ISHMERAI
1Ch 8:18 I also, and Jezliah, and Jobab, the sons H3461

ISHOD
1Ch 7:18 And his sister Hammoleketh bare I, and H379

ISHPAN
1Ch 8:22 And I, and Heber, and Eliel, H3473

ISH-TOB
2Sa 10: 6 men, and of I twelve thousand men. H382
8 and of Rehob, and I, and Maacah, *were* H382

ISHUAH
Gen 46:17 And the sons of Asher; Jimnah, and I, H3438

ISHUAI
1Ch 7:30 I, and Beriah, and Serah their sister. H3438

ISHUI
1Sa 14:49 Jonathan, and I, and Melchishua: and H3440

ISLAND
Job 22:30 He shall deliver the **i** of the innocent: H336
Isa 34:14 wild beasts of the **i**, and the satyr shall H338
Act 27:16 And running under a certain **i** which is G3519
26 we must be cast upon a certain **i**. G3520
28: 1 they knew that the **i** was called Melita. G3520
7 the chief man of the **i**, whose name was G3520
9 in the **i**, came, and were healed: G3520
Rev 6:14 and **i** were moved out of their places. G3520
16:20 And every **i** fled away, and the G3520

ISLANDS
Isa 11:11 from Hamath, and from the **i** of the sea. H339
13:22 And the wild beasts of the **i** shall cry in H338
41: 1 Keep silence before me, O **i**; and let the H339
42:12 the LORD, and declare his praise in the **i**. H339
15 the rivers **i**, and I will dry up the pools. H339
59:18 to the **i** he will repay recompence. H339
Jer 50:39 wild beasts of the **i** shall dwell *there*, and H339

ISLE
Isa 20: 6 And the inhabitant of this **i** shall say in H339
23: 2 Be still, ye inhabitants of the **i**; thou H339
6 to Tarshish; howl, ye inhabitants of the **i**. H339
Act 13: 6 And when they had gone through the **i** G3520
28:11 the **i**, whose sign was Castor and Pollux. G3520
Rev 1: 9 Jesus Christ, was in the **i** that is called G3520

ISLES
Gen 10: 5 By these were the **i** of the Gentiles H339
Est 10: 1 upon the land, and *upon* the **i** of the sea. H339
Ps 72:10 The kings of Tarshish and of the **i** shall H339
97: 1 let the multitude of **i** be glad *thereof*. H339
Isa 24:15 LORD God of Israel in the **i** of the sea. H339
40:15 he taketh up the **i** as a very little thing. H339
41: 5 The **i** saw *it*, and feared; the ends of the H339
42: 4 the earth: and the **i** shall wait for his law. H339
10 the **i**, and the inhabitants thereof. H339
49: 1 Listen, O **i**, unto me; and hearken, ye H339
51: 5 the people; the **i** shall wait upon me, H339
60: 9 Surely the **i** shall wait for me, and the H339
66:19 and Javan, *to* the **i** afar off, that have not H339
Jer 2:10 For pass over the **i** of Chittim, and see; H339
25:22 kings of the **i** which *are* beyond the sea, H339
31:10 declare *it* in the **i** afar off, and say, He H339
Ezk 26:15 Tyrus; Shall not the **i** shake at the sound H339
18 Now shall the **i** tremble in the day of thy H339
18 of thy fall; yea, the **i** that *are* in the sea H339
27: 3 people for many **i**, Thus saith the Lord H339
6 *of* ivory, *brought* out of the **i** of Chittim. H339
7 **i** of Elishah was that which covered thee. H339
15 thy merchants; many **i** *were* the H339
35 All the inhabitants of the **i** shall be H339
39: 6 carelessly in the **i**: and they shall know H339
Dan 11:18 After this shall he turn his face unto the **i**, H339
Zep 2:11 his place, *even* all the **i** of the heathen. H339

ISMACHIAH
2Ch 31:13 and Eliel, and I, and Mahath, and H3253

ISMAIAH
1Ch 12: 4 And I the Gibeonite, a mighty man H3460

ISPAH
1Ch 8:16 And Michael, and I, and Joha, the sons H3472

ISRAEL
Gen 32:28 more Jacob, but I: for as a prince hast H3478
32 Therefore the children of I eat not *of* H3478
34: 7 wrought folly in I in lying with Jacob's H3478
35:10 more Jacob, but I shall be thy name: H3478
10 be thy name: and he called his name I. H3478
21 And I journeyed, and spread his tent H3478
22 And it came to pass, when I dwelt in H3478
22 concubine: and I heard *it*. Now the H3478
36:31 reigned any king over the children of I. H3478
37: 3 Now I loved Joseph more than all his H3478
13 And I said unto Joseph, Do not thy H3478
42: 5 And the sons of I came to buy *corn* H3478
43: 6 And I said, Wherefore dealt ye *so* ill H3478
8 And Judah said unto I his father, Send H3478
11 And their father I said unto them, If *it* H3478
45:21 And the children of I did so: and H3478
28 And I said, *It is* enough; Joseph my son H3478
46: 1 And I took his journey with all that he H3478
2 And God spake unto I in the visions of H3478
5 and the sons of I carried Jacob their H3478
8 of the children of I, which came into H3478
29 went up to meet I his father, to Goshen, H3478
30 And I said unto Joseph, Now let me die, H3478
47:27 And I dwelt in the land of Egypt, in the H3478
29 And the time drew nigh that I must die: H3478
31 I bowed himself upon the bed's head. H3478
48: 2 unto thee: and I strengthened himself, H3478
8 And I beheld Joseph's sons, and said, H3478
10 Now the eyes of I were dim for age, *so* H3478
11 And I said unto Joseph, I had not H3478
14 And I stretched out his right hand, and H3478
20 In thee shall I bless, saying, God make H3478
21 And I said unto Joseph, Behold, I die: H3478
49: 2 Jacob; and hearken unto I your father. H3478
7 them in Jacob, and scatter them in I. H3478
16 his people, as one of the tribes of I. H3478
24 thence *is* the shepherd, the stone of I:) H3478
28 All these *are* the twelve tribes of I: and H3478
50: 2 father: and the physicians embalmed I. H3478
25 of the children of I, saying, God will H3478
Ex 1: 1 of the children of I, which came into H3478
7 And the children of I were fruitful, and H3478
9 of I *are* more and mightier than we: H3478
12 grieved because of the children of I. H3478
13 the children of I to serve with rigour: H3478
2:23 the children of I sighed by reason of H3478
25 And God looked upon the children of I, H3478
3: 9 of the children of I is come unto me: H3478
10 people the children of I out of Egypt. H3478
11 forth the children of I out of Egypt? H3478
13 the children of I, and shall say unto H3478
14 of I, I AM hath sent me unto you. H3478
15 the children of I, The LORD God of your H3478
16 Go, and gather the elders of I together, H3478
18 and the elders of I, unto the king of H3478
4:22 LORD, I *is* my son, *even* my firstborn: H3478
29 all the elders of the children of I: H3478
31 visited the children of I, and that he had H3478
5: 1 the LORD God of I, Let my people go, H3478
2 his voice to let I go? I know not the H3478
2 not the LORD, neither will I let I go. H3478
14 And the officers of the children of I, H3478
15 Then the officers of the children of I H3478
19 And the officers of the children of I did H3478
6: 5 of the children of I, whom the Egyptians H3478
6 Wherefore say unto the children of I, I H3478
9 the children of I: but they hearkened H3478
11 let the children of I go out of his land. H3478
12 the children of I have not hearkened H3478
13 the children of I, and unto Pharaoh H3478
13 children of I out of the land of Egypt. H3478
14 the firstborn of I; Hanoch, and Pallu, H3478
26 out the children of I from the land of H3478
27 out the children of I from Egypt: these H3478
7: 2 send the children of I out of his land. H3478
4 the children of I, out of the land of H3478
5 out the children of I from among them. H3478
9: 4 the cattle of I and the cattle of Egypt: H3478
4 die of all *that is* the children's of I. H3478
6 cattle of the children of I died not one. H3478
26 children of I *were*, was there no hail. H3478
35 he let the children of I go; as the LORD H3478
Ex 10:20 he would not let the children of I go. H3478
23 of I had light in their dwellings. H3478
11: 7 But against any of the children of I H3478
7 difference between the Egyptians and I. H3478
10 let the children of I go out of his land. H3478
12: 3 Speak ye unto all the congregation of I, H3478
6 of I shall kill it in the evening. H3478
15 day, that soul shall be cut off from I. H3478
19 the congregation of I, whether he be a H3478
21 Then Moses called for all the elders of I, H3478
27 of the children of I in Egypt, when he H3478
28 And the children of I went away, and H3478
31 and the children of I; and go, serve the H3478
35 And the children of I did according to H3478
37 And the children of I journeyed from H3478
40 Now the sojourning of the children of I, H3478
42 the children of I in their generations. H3478
47 All the congregation of I shall keep it. H3478
50 Thus did all the children of I; as the H3478
51 bring the children of I out of the land of H3478
13: 2 I, *both* of man and of beast: it *is* mine. H3478
18 the children of I went up harnessed H3478
19 the children of I, saying, God will surely H3478
14: 2 Speak unto the children of I, that they H3478
3 of the children of I, They *are* entangled H3478
5 that we have let I go from serving us? H3478
8 the children of I: and the children of H3478
8 of I went out with an high hand. H3478
10 the children of I lifted up their eyes, H3478
10 children of I cried out unto the LORD. H3478
15 the children of I, that they go forward: H3478
16 the children of I shall go on dry *ground* H3478
19 before the camp of I, removed and went H3478
20 and the camp of I; and it was a cloud H3478
22 And the children of I went into the H3478
25 from the face of I; for the LORD fighteth H3478
29 But the children of I walked upon dry H3478
30 Thus the LORD saved I that day out of H3478
30 the Egyptians; and I saw the Egyptians H3478
31 And I saw that great work which the H3478
15: 1 Then sang Moses and the children of I H3478
19 but the children of I went on dry *land* H3478
22 So Moses brought I from the Red sea, H3478
16: 1 of the children of I came unto the H3478
2 of the children of I murmured against H3478
3 And the children of I said unto them, H3478
6 all the children of I, At even, then ye H3478
9 of the children of I, Come near before H3478
10 of the children of I, that they looked H3478
12 of the children of I: speak unto them, H3478
15 And when the children of I saw *it*, they H3478
17 And the children of I did so, and H3478
31 And the house of I called the name H3478
35 And the children of I did eat manna H3478
17: 1 of the children of I journeyed from the H3478
5 thee of the elders of I; and thy rod, H3478
6 did so in the sight of the elders of I. H3478
7 of the children of I, and because they H3478
8 Then came Amalek, and fought with I H3478
11 up his hand, that I prevailed: and when H3478
18: 1 for Moses, and for I his people, *and* H3478
1 the LORD had brought I out of Egypt; H3478
9 the LORD had done to I, whom he had H3478
12 and all the elders of I, to eat bread with H3478
25 And Moses chose able men out of all I, H3478
19: 1 the children of I were gone forth out H3478
2 and there I camped before the mount. H3478
3 of Jacob, and tell the children of I; H3478
6 thou shalt speak unto the children of I. H3478
20:22 the children of I, Ye have seen that I H3478
24: 1 the elders of I; and worship ye afar off. H3478
4 according to the twelve tribes of I. H3478
5 of the children of I, which offered burnt H3478
9 Abihu, and seventy of the elders of I: H3478
10 And they saw the God of I: and *there* H3478
11 of the children of I he laid not his hand: H3478
17 mount in the eyes of the children of I. H3478
25: 2 Speak unto the children of I, that they H3478
22 commandment unto the children of I. H3478
27:20 the children of I, that they bring thee H3478
21 on the behalf of the children of I. H3478
28: 1 the children of I, that he may minister H3478
9 on them the names of the children of I: H3478
11 of the children of I: thou shalt make H3478
12 the children of I: and Aaron shall bear H3478
21 of the children of I, twelve, according to H3478
29 of the children of I in the breastplate of H3478
30 of the children of I upon his heart H3478
38 the children of I shall hallow in all their H3478
Ex 29:28 from the children of I: for it *is* an heave H3478
28 the children of I of the sacrifice of their H3478
43 the children of I, and *the tabernacle* H3478
45 the children of I, and will be their God. H3478
30:12 of the children of I after their number, H3478
16 of the children of I, and shalt appoint it H3478
16 the children of I before the LORD, to H3478
31 the children of I, saying, This shall be H3478
31:13 Speak thou also unto the children of I, H3478
16 Wherefore the children of I shall keep H3478
17 the children of I for ever: for *in* six days H3478
32: 4 *be* thy gods, O I, which brought thee H3478
8 *be* thy gods, O I, which have brought H3478
13 Remember Abraham, Isaac, and I, thy H3478
20 and made the children of I drink *of it*. H3478
27 the LORD God of I, Put every man his H3478
33: 5 the children of I, Ye *are* a stiffnecked H3478
6 And the children of I stripped H3478
34:23 before the Lord GOD, the God of I. H3478
27 made a covenant with thee and with I. H3478
30 all the children of I saw Moses, behold, H3478
32 And afterward all the children of I H3478
34 of I *that* which he was commanded. H3478
35 And the children of I saw the face of H3478
35: 1 of the children of I together, and said H3478
4 of the children of I, saying, This *is* the H3478
20 I departed from the presence of Moses. H3478
29 The children of I brought a willing H3478
30 And Moses said unto the children of I, H3478
36: 3 the children of I had brought for the H3478
39: 6 with the names of the children of I. H3478
7 of I; as the LORD commanded Moses. H3478
14 of the children of I, twelve, according to H3478
32 the children of I did according to all H3478
42 so the children of I made all the work. H3478
40:36 of I went onward in all their journeys: H3478
38 of I, throughout all their journeys. H3478
Lev 1: 2 Speak unto the children of I, and say H3478
4: 2 Speak unto the children of I, saying, If a H3478
13 And if the whole congregation of I sin H3478
7:23 Speak unto the children of I, saying, Ye H3478
29 Speak unto the children of I, saying, He H3478
34 taken of the children of I from off the H3478
34 for ever from among the children of I. H3478
36 of the children of I, in the day that he H3478
38 the children of I to offer their oblations H3478
9: 1 Aaron and his sons, and the elders of I; H3478
3 And unto the children of I thou shalt H3478
10: 6 the whole house of I, bewail the burning H3478
11 And that ye may teach the children of I H3478
14 of peace offerings of the children of I. H3478
11: 2 Speak unto the children of I, saying, H3478
12: 2 Speak unto the children of I, saying, If a H3478
15: 2 Speak unto the children of I, and say H3478
31 Thus shall ye separate the children of I H3478
16: 5 of the children of I two kids of the goats H3478
16 of the children of I, and because of their H3478
17 and for all the congregation of I. H3478
19 the uncleanness of the children of I. H3478
21 of the children of I, and all their H3478
34 for the children of I for all their sins H3478
17: 2 all the children of I, and say unto them; H3478
3 *be* of the house of I, that killeth an ox, H3478
5 To the end that the children of I may H3478
8 *be* of the house of I, or of the strangers H3478
10 *be* of the house of I, or of the strangers H3478
12 Therefore I said unto the children of I, H3478
13 of the children of I, or of the strangers H3478
14 the children of I, Ye shall eat the blood H3478
18: 2 Speak unto the children of I, and say H3478
19: 2 of the children of I, and say unto them, H3478
20: 2 to the children of I, Whosoever *he be* of H3478
2 of the children of I, or of the strangers H3478
2 that sojourn in I, that giveth *any* of his H3478
21:24 his sons, and unto all the children of I. H3478
22: 2 things of the children of I, and that they H3478
3 the children of I hallow unto the LORD, H3478
15 of I, which they offer unto the LORD; H3478
18 all the children of I, and say unto them, H3478
18 *be* of the house of I, or of the strangers H3478
18 of the strangers in I, that will offer his H3478
32 of I: I *am* the LORD which hallow you, H3478
23: 2 Speak unto the children of I, and say H3478
10 Speak unto the children of I, and say H3478
24 Speak unto the children of I, saying, In H3478
34 Speak unto the children of I, saying, H3478
43 the children of I to dwell in booths, H3478
44 the children of I the feasts of the LORD. H3478
24: 2 Command the children of I, that they H3478

Lev 24: 8 of I by an everlasting covenant. H3478
10 the children of I: and this son of the H3478
10 a man of I strove together in the camp; H3481
15 the children of I, saying, Whosoever H3478
23 And Moses spake to the children of I, H3478
23 I did as the LORD commanded Moses. H3478
25: 2 Speak unto the children of I, and say H3478
33 possession among the children of I. H3478
46 the children of I, ye shall not rule one H3478
55 For unto me the children of I *are* H3478
26:46 I in mount Sinai by the hand of Moses. H3478
27: 2 Speak unto the children of I, and say H3478
34 for the children of I in mount Sinai. H3478
Nu 1: 2 of the children of I, after their families, H3478
3 to go forth to war in I: thou and Aaron H3478
16 of their fathers, heads of thousands in I. H3478
44 and the princes of I, *being* twelve men: H3478
45 of the children of I, by the house of their H3478
45 all that were able to go forth to war in I; H3478
49 sum of them among the children of I: H3478
52 And the children of I shall pitch their H3478
53 of the children of I: and the Levites shall H3478
54 And the children of I did according to H3478
2: 2 Every man of the children of I shall H3478
32 of the children of I by the house of their H3478
33 of I; as the LORD commanded Moses. H3478
34 And the children of I did according to H3478
3: 8 of I, to do the service of the tabernacle. H3478
9 given unto him out of the children of I. H3478
12 the children of I instead of all the H3478
12 of I: therefore the Levites shall be mine; H3478
13 me all the firstborn in I, both man and H3478
38 of the children of I; and the stranger H3478
40 of the children of I from a month old H3478
41 the children of I; and the cattle of the H3478
41 among the cattle of the children of I. H3478
42 the firstborn among the children of I. H3478
45 the children of I, and the cattle of the H3478
46 of I, which are more than the Levites; H3478
50 Of the firstborn of the children of I took H3478
4:46 and the chief of I numbered, after their H3478
5: 2 Command the children of I, that they H3478
4 And the children of I did so, and put H3478
4 unto Moses, so did the children of I. H3478
6 Speak unto the children of I, When a H3478
9 of the children of I, which they bring H3478
12 Speak unto the children of I, and say H3478
6: 2 Speak unto the children of I, and say H3478
23 the children of I, saying unto them, H3478
27 the children of I; and I will bless them. H3478
7: 2 That the princes of I, heads of the house H3478
84 by the princes of I: twelve chargers of H3478
8: 6 the children of I, and cleanse them. H3478
9 assembly of the children of I together: H3478
10 the children of I shall put their hands H3478
11 of the children of I, that they may H3478
14 of I: and the Levites shall be mine. H3478
16 the children of I; instead of such as H3478
16 of I, have I taken them unto me. H3478
17 For all the firstborn of the children of I H3478
18 for all the firstborn of the children of I. H3478
19 the children of I, to do the service of the H3478
19 of the children of I in the tabernacle of H3478
19 for the children of I: that there be no H3478
19 the children of I, when the children of H3478
19 of I come nigh unto the sanctuary. H3478
20 of the children of I, did to the Levites H3478
20 so did the children of I unto them. H3478
9: 2 Let the children of I also keep the H3478
4 And Moses spake unto the children of I, H3478
5 Moses, so did the children of I. H3478
7 season among the children of I? H3478
10 Speak unto the children of I, saying, If H3478
17 the children of I journeyed: and in the H3478
17 the children of I pitched their tents. H3478
18 the children of I journeyed, and at the H3478
19 the children of I kept the charge of the H3478
22 the children of I abode in their tents, H3478
10: 4 of I, shall gather themselves unto thee. H3478
12 And the children of I took their H3478
28 of the children of I according to their H3478
29 LORD hath spoken good concerning I. H3478
36 O LORD, unto the many thousands of I. H3478
11: 4 the children of I also wept again, and H3478
16 of the elders of I, whom thou knowest H3478
30 into the camp, he and the elders of I. H3478
13: 2 the children of I: of every tribe of their H3478
3 men *were* heads of the children of I. H3478
24 the children of I cut down from thence. H3478
Nu 13:26 of the children of I, unto the wilderness H3478
32 unto the children of I, saying, The land, H3478
14: 2 And all the children of I murmured H3478
5 of the congregation of the children of I. H3478
7 of the children of I, saying, The land, H3478
10 before all the children of I. H3478
27 of I, which they murmur against me. H3478
39 of I: and the people mourned greatly. H3478
15: 2 Speak unto the children of I, and say H3478
18 Speak unto the children of I, and say H3478
25 of the children of I, and it shall be H3478
26 of the children of I, and the stranger H3478
29 the children of I, and for the stranger H3478
32 And while the children of I were in the H3478
38 Speak unto the children of I, and bid H3478
16: 2 of the children of I, two hundred and H3478
9 that the God of I hath separated you H3478
9 congregation of I, to bring you near to H3478
25 and the elders of I followed him. H3478
34 And all I that *were* round about them H3478
38 shall be a sign unto the children of I. H3478
40 *To be* a memorial unto the children of I, H3478
41 of the children of I murmured against H3478
17: 2 Speak unto the children of I, and take of H3478
5 of I, whereby they murmur against you. H3478
6 And Moses spake unto the children of I, H3478
9 all the children of I: and they looked, H3478
12 And the children of I spake unto H3478
18: 5 wrath any more upon the children of I. H3478
6 the children of I: to you *they are* given H3478
8 of the children of I; unto thee have I H3478
11 of the children of I: I have given them H3478
14 Every thing devoted in I shall be thine. H3478
19 the children of I offer unto the LORD, H3478
20 inheritance among the children of I. H3478
21 all the tenth in I for an inheritance, for H3478
22 Neither must the children of I H3478
23 children of I they have no inheritance. H3478
24 But the tithes of the children of I, which H3478
24 of I they shall have no inheritance. H3478
26 of the children of I the tithes which I H3478
28 of the children of I; and ye shall give H3478
32 things of the children of I, lest ye die. H3478
19: 2 the children of I, that they bring thee H3478
9 of the children of I for a water of H3478
10 the children of I, and unto the stranger H3478
13 be cut off from I: because the water of H3478
20: 1 Then came the children of I, *even* the H3478
12 of the children of I, therefore ye shall H3478
13 the children of I strove with the LORD, H3478
14 saith thy brother I, Thou knowest all H3478
19 And the children of I said unto him, H3478
21 Thus Edom refused to give I passage H3478
21 wherefore I turned away from him. H3478
22 And the children of I, *even* the whole H3478
24 the children of I, because ye rebelled H3478
29 thirty days, *even* all the house of I. H3478
21: 1 heard tell that I came by the way of H3478
1 I, and took *some* of them prisoners. H3478
2 And I vowed a vow unto the LORD, H3478
3 to the voice of I, and delivered up the H3478
6 the people; and much people of I died. H3478
10 And the children of I set forward, and H3478
17 Then I sang this song, Spring up, O H3478
21 And I sent messengers unto Sihon king H3478
23 And Sihon would not suffer I to pass H3478
23 went out against I into the wilderness: H3478
23 he came to Jahaz, and fought against I. H3478
24 And I smote him with the edge of the H3478
25 And I took all these cities: and Israel H3478
25 And Israel took all these cities: and I H3478
31 Thus I dwelt in the land of the H3478
22: 1 And the children of I set forward, and H3478
2 saw all that I had done to the Amorites. H3478
3 distressed because of the children of I. H3478
23: 7 curse me Jacob, and come, defy I. H3478
10 the fourth *part* of I? Let me die the death H3478
21 perverseness in I: the LORD his God *is* H3478
23 divination against I: according to this H3478
23 Jacob and of I, What hath God wrought! H3478
24: 1 the LORD to bless I, he went not, as at H3478
2 eyes, and he saw I abiding *in his tents* H3478
5 tents, O Jacob, *and* thy tabernacles, O I! H3478
17 shall rise out of I, and shall smite the H3478
18 his enemies; and I shall do valiantly. H3478
25: 1 And I abode in Shittim, and the people H3478
3 And I joined himself unto Baal-peor: H3478
3 of the LORD was kindled against I. H3478
4 the LORD may be turned away from I. H3478
Nu 25: 5 And Moses said unto the judges of I, H3478
6 And, behold, one of the children of I H3478
6 of the children of I, who *were* weeping H3478
8 And he went after the man of I into the H3478
8 the man of I, and the woman through H3478
8 was stayed from the children of I. H3478
11 the children of I, while he was zealous H3478
11 not the children of I in my jealousy. H3478
13 an atonement for the children of I. H3478
26: 2 of the children of I, from twenty years H3478
2 house, all that are able to go to war in I. H3478
4 the children of I, which went forth out H3478
5 Reuben, the eldest son of I: the children H3478
51 of the children of I, six hundred H3478
62 the children of I, because there was no H3478
62 given them among the children of I. H3478
63 the children of I in the plains of Moab H3478
64 children of I in the wilderness of Sinai. H3478
27: 8 the children of I, saying, If a man die, H3478
11 the children of I a statute of judgment, H3478
12 I have given unto the children of I. H3478
20 of the children of I may be obedient. H3478
21 I with him, even all the congregation. H3478
28: 2 Command the children of I, and say H3478
29:40 And Moses told the children of I H3478
30: 1 the children of I, saying, This *is* the H3478
31: 2 Avenge the children of I of the H3478
4 the tribes of I, shall ye send to the war. H3478
5 the thousands of I, a thousand of *every* H3478
9 And the children of I took *all* the H3478
12 of the children of I, unto the camp at H3478
16 Behold, these caused the children of I, H3478
54 for the children of I before the LORD. H3478
32: 4 congregation of I, *is* a land for cattle, H3478
7 of the children of I from going over into H3478
9 of the children of I, that they should not H3478
13 kindled against I, and he made them H3478
14 the fierce anger of the LORD toward I. H3478
17 the children of I, until we have brought H3478
18 the children of I have inherited every H3478
22 LORD, and before I; and this land shall H3478
28 fathers of the tribes of the children of I: H3478
33: 1 of the children of I, which went forth H3478
3 the children of I went out with an high H3478
5 And the children of I removed from H3478
38 the children of I were come out of the H3478
40 heard of the coming of the children of I. H3478
51 Speak unto the children of I, and say H3478
34: 2 Command the children of I, and say H3478
13 the children of I, saying, This *is* the land H3478
29 the children of I in the land of Canaan. H3478
35: 2 Command the children of I, that they H3478
8 of the children of I: from *them that* H3478
10 Speak unto the children of I, and say H3478
15 *both* for the children of I, and for the H3478
34 LORD dwell among the children of I. H3478
36: 1 the chief fathers of the children of I: H3478
2 lot to the children of I: and my lord was H3478
3 of the children of I, then shall their H3478
4 And when the jubile of the children of I H3478
5 the children of I according to the word H3478
7 of the children of I remove from tribe H3478
7 of the children of I shall keep himself to H3478
8 of the children of I, shall be wife unto H3478
8 the children of I may enjoy every man H3478
9 of the children of I shall keep himself to H3478
13 the children of I in the plains of Moab H3478
Dt 1: 1 spake unto all I on this side Jordan H3478
3 the children of I, according unto all that H3478
38 him: for he shall cause I to inherit it. H3478
2:12 in their stead; as I did unto the land of H3478
3:18 of I, all *that are* meet for the war. H3478
4: 1 Now therefore hearken, O I, unto the H3478
44 Moses set before the children of I: H3478
45 of I, after they came forth out of Egypt, H3478
46 the children of I smote, after they were H3478
5: 1 And Moses called all I, and said unto H3478
1 unto them, Hear, O I, the statutes and H3478
6: 3 Hear therefore, O I, and observe to do H3478
4 Hear, O I: The LORD our God *is* one H3478
9: 1 Hear, O I: Thou *art* to pass over Jordan H3478
10: 6 And the children of I took their journey H3478
12 And now, I, what doth the LORD thy H3478
11: 6 in their possession, in the midst of all I: H3478
13:11 And all I shall hear, and fear, and shall H3478
17: 4 *that* such abomination is wrought in I: H3478
12 and thou shalt put away the evil from I. H3478
20 he, and his children, in the midst of I. H3478
18: 1 nor inheritance with I: they shall eat the H3478

Dt 18: 6 of thy gates out of all I, where he H3478
19:13 from I, that it may go well with thee. H3478
20: 3 And shall say unto them, Hear, O I, ye H3478
21: 8 Be merciful, O LORD, unto thy people I, H3478
21 you; and all I shall hear, and fear. H3478
22:19 upon a virgin of I: and she shall be his H3478
21 wrought folly in I, to play the whore in H3478
22 so shalt thou put away evil from I. H3478
23:17 I, nor a sodomite of the sons of Israel. H3478
17 Israel, nor a sodomite of the sons of I. H3478
24: 7 of the children of I, and maketh H3478
25: 6 dead, that his name be not put out of I. H3478
7 brother a name in I, he will not perform H3478
10 And his name shall be called in I, The H3478
26:15 bless thy people I, and the land which H3478
27: 1 And Moses with the elders of I H3478
9 spake unto all I, saying, Take heed, and H3478
9 and hearken, O I; this day thou art H3478
14 unto all the men of I with a loud voice, H3478
29: 1 the children of I in the land of Moab, H3478
2 And Moses called unto all I, and said H3478
10 and your officers, *with* all the men of I, H3478
21 of all the tribes of I, according to all the H3478
31: 1 went and spake these words unto all I. H3478
7 in the sight of all I, Be strong and of a H3478
9 the LORD, and unto all the elders of I. H3478
11 When all I is come to appear before the H3478
11 this law before all I in their hearing. H3478
19 teach it the children of I: put it in their H3478
19 witness for me against the children of I. H3478
22 day, and taught it the children of I. H3478
23 the children of I into the land which H3478
30 the congregation of I the words of this H3478
32: 8 to the number of the children of I. H3478
45 end of speaking all these words to all I: H3478
49 unto the children of I for a possession: H3478
51 among the children of I at the waters of H3478
51 me not in the midst of the children of I. H3478
52 the land which I give the children of I. H3478
33: 1 the children of I before his death. H3478
5 the tribes of I were gathered together. H3478
10 thy judgments, and I thy law: they shall H3478
21 of the LORD, and his judgments with I. H3478
28 I then shall dwell in safety alone: the H3478
29 Happy *art* thou, O I: who *is* like unto H3478
34: 8 And the children of I wept for Moses in H3478
9 the children of I hearkened unto him, H3478
10 a prophet since in I like unto Moses, H3478
12 Moses shewed in the sight of all I. H3478
Jos 1: 2 give to them, *even* to the children of I. H3478
2: 2 children of I to search out the country. H3478
3: 1 all the children of I, and lodged there H3478
7 in the sight of all I, that they may know H3478
9 And Joshua said unto the children of I, H3478
12 the tribes of I, out of every tribe a man. H3478
4: 4 children of I, out of every tribe a man: H3478
5 number of the tribes of the children of I: H3478
7 unto the children of I for ever. H3478
8 And the children of I did so as Joshua H3478
8 of the children of I, and carried them H3478
12 of I, as Moses spake unto them: H3478
14 in the sight of all I; and they feared him, H3478
21 And he spake unto the children of I, H3478
22 I came over this Jordan on dry land. H3478
5: 1 the children of I, until we were passed H3478
1 any more, because of the children of I. H3478
2 again the children of I the second time. H3478
3 children of I at the hill of the foreskins. H3478
6 For the children of I walked forty years H3478
10 And the children of I encamped in H3478
12 the children of I manna any more; but H3478
6: 1 of I: none went out, and none came in. H3478
18 the camp of I a curse, and trouble it. H3478
23 and left them without the camp of I. H3478
25 she dwelleth in I *even* unto this day; H3478
7: 1 But the children of I committed a H3478
1 was kindled against the children of I. H3478
6 of I, and put dust upon their heads. H3478
8 O Lord, what shall I say, when I H3478
11 I hath sinned, and they have also H3478
12 Therefore the children of I could not H3478
13 saith the LORD God of I, *There is* an H3478
13 midst of thee, O I: thou canst not stand H3478
15 and because he hath wrought folly in I. H3478
16 and brought I by their tribes; and H3478
19 to the LORD God of I, and make H3478
20 God of I, and thus and thus have I done: H3478
23 I, and laid them out before the LORD. H3478
24 And Joshua, and all I with him, took H3478

Jos 7:25 thee this day. And all I stoned him with H3478
8:10 the elders of I, before the people to Ai. H3478
14 went out against I to battle, he and all H3478
15 And Joshua and all I made as if they H3478
17 went not out after I: and they left the H3478
17 left the city open, and pursued after I. H3478
21 And when Joshua and all I saw that the H3478
22 in the midst of I, some on this side, and H3478
24 And it came to pass, when I had made H3478
27 spoil of that city I took for a prey unto H3478
30 unto the LORD God of I in mount Ebal, H3478
31 the children of I, as it is written in the H3478
32 in the presence of the children of I. H3478
33 And all I, and their elders, and officers, H3478
33 that they should bless the people of I. H3478
35 congregation of I, with the women, and H3478
9: 2 Joshua and with I, with one accord. H3478
6 and to the men of I, We be come from a H3478
7 And the men of I said unto the Hivites, H3478
17 And the children of I journeyed, and H3478
18 And the children of I smote them not, H3478
18 by the LORD God of I. And all the H3478
19 by the LORD God of I: now therefore we H3478
26 children of I, that they slew them not. H3478
10: 1 peace with I, and were among them; H3478
4 with Joshua and with the children of I. H3478
10 them before I, and slew them with H3478
11 they fled from before I, *and* were in the H3478
11 the children of I slew with the sword. H3478
12 the children of I, and he said in the H3478
12 he said in the sight of I, Sun, stand thou H3478
14 of a man: for the LORD fought for I. H3478
15 And Joshua returned, and all I with H3478
20 the children of I had made an end of H3478
21 tongue against any of the children of I. H3478
24 for all the men of I, and said unto the H3478
29 and all I with him, unto Libnah, H3478
30 into the hand of I; and he smote it with H3478
31 from Libnah, and all I with him, unto H3478
32 into the hand of I, which took it on the H3478
34 Eglon, and all I with him; and they H3478
36 Eglon, and all I with him, unto Hebron; H3478
38 And Joshua returned, and all I with H3478
40 as the LORD God of I commanded. H3478
42 the LORD God of I fought for Israel. H3478
42 the LORD God of Israel fought for I. H3478
43 And Joshua returned, and all I with H3478
11: 5 the waters of Merom, to fight against I. H3478
6 up all slain before I: thou shalt hough H3478
8 into the hand of I, who smote them, H3478
13 still in their strength, I burned none of H3478
14 the children of I took for a prey unto H3478
16 of I, and the valley of the same; H3478
19 the children of I, save the Hivites the H3478
20 come against I in battle, that he might H3478
21 all the mountains of I: Joshua destroyed H3478
22 of the children of I: only in Gaza, in H3478
23 inheritance unto I according to their H3478
12: 1 the children of I smote, and possessed H3478
6 the children of I smite: and Moses the H3478
7 and the children of I smote on this side H3478
7 unto the tribes of I *for* a possession H3478
13: 6 the children of I: only divide thou it by H3478
13 Nevertheless the children of I expelled H3478
14 of the LORD God of I made by fire *are* H3478
22 did the children of I slay with the H3478
33 the LORD God of I *was* their H3478
14: 1 the children of I inherited in the land H3478
1 of I, distributed for inheritance to them. H3478
5 of I did, and they divided the land. H3478
10 while *the children of* I wandered in the H3478
14 he wholly followed the LORD God of I. H3478
17:13 the children of I were waxen strong, H3478
18: 1 of the children of I assembled together H3478
2 the children of I seven tribes, which H3478
3 And Joshua said unto the children of I, H3478
10 of I according to their divisions. H3478
19:49 the children of I gave an inheritance H3478
51 tribes of the children of I, divided for an H3478
20: 2 Speak to the children of I, saying, H3478
9 all the children of I, and for the stranger H3478
21: 1 fathers of the tribes of the children of I; H3478
3 And the children of I gave unto the H3478
8 And the children of I gave by lot unto H3478
41 of the children of I *were* forty and eight H3478
43 And the LORD gave unto I all the land H3478
45 unto the house of I; all came to pass. H3478
22: 9 the children of I out of Shiloh, which H3478
11 And the children of I heard say, H3478

Jos 22:11 at the passage of the children of I. H3478
12 And when the children of I heard *of it,* H3478
12 of the children of I gathered themselves H3478
13 And the children of I sent unto the H3478
14 all the tribes of I; and each one *was* an H3478
14 their fathers among the thousands of I. H3478
16 against the God of I, to turn away this H3478
18 wroth with the whole congregation of I. H3478
20 the congregation of I? and that man H3478
21 unto the heads of the thousands of I, H3478
22 he knoweth, and I he shall know; if *it* H3478
24 have ye to do with the LORD God of I? H3478
30 of the thousands of I which *were* with H3478
31 of I out of the hand of the LORD. H3478
32 of I, and brought them word again. H3478
33 And the thing pleased the children of I; H3478
33 the children of I blessed God, and did H3478
23: 1 given rest unto I from all their enemies H3478
2 And Joshua called for all I, *and* for their H3478
24: 1 And Joshua gathered all the tribes of I H3478
1 for the elders of I, and for their heads, H3478
2 the LORD God of I, Your fathers dwelt H3478
9 warred against I, and sent and called H3478
23 your heart unto the LORD God of I. H3478
31 And I served the LORD all the days of H3478
31 of the LORD, that he had done for I. H3478
32 the children of I brought up out of H3478
Jdg 1: 1 that the children of I asked the LORD, H3478
28 And it came to pass, when I was H3478
2: 4 all the children of I, that the people H3478
6 go, the children of I went every man H3478
7 works of the LORD, that he did for I. H3478
10 yet the works which he had done for I. H3478
11 And the children of I did evil in the H3478
14 was hot against I, and he delivered H3478
20 was hot against I; and he said, Because H3478
22 That through them I may prove I, H3478
3: 1 left, to prove I by them, *even* as many H3478
1 *even* as many *of I* as had not known all
2 of the children of I might know, to H3478
4 And they were to prove I by them, to H3478
5 And the children of I dwelt among the H3478
7 And the children of I did evil in the H3478
8 was hot against I, and he sold them into H3478
8 and the children of I served H3478
9 And when the children of I cried unto H3478
9 to the children of I, who delivered them, H3478
10 and he judged I, and went out to war: H3478
12 And the children of I did evil again in H3478
12 of Moab against I, because they had H3478
13 I, and possessed the city of palm trees. H3478
14 So the children of I served Eglon the H3478
15 But when the children of I cried unto H3478
15 the children of I sent a present unto H3478
27 the children of I went down with him H3478
30 under the hand of I. And the land had H3478
31 an ox goad: and he also delivered I. H3478
4: 1 And the children of I again did evil in H3478
3 And the children of I cried unto the H3478
3 he mightily oppressed the children of I. H3478
4 of Lapidoth, she judged I at that time. H3478
5 of I came up to her for judgment. H3478
6 not the LORD God of I commanded, H3478
23 king of Canaan before the children of I. H3478
24 And the hand of the children of I H3478
5: 2 for the avenging of I, when the people H3478
3 I will sing *praise* to the LORD God of I. H3478
5 Sinai from before the LORD God of I. H3478
7 they ceased in I, until that I Deborah H3478
7 arose, that I arose a mother in I. H3478
8 spear seen among forty thousand in I? H3478
9 My heart *is* toward the governors of I, H3478
11 of his villages in I: then shall the people H3478
6: 1 And the children of I did evil in the H3478
2 prevailed against I: *and* because of the H3478
2 the children of I made them the dens H3478
3 And *so* it was, when I had sown, that H3478
4 for I, neither sheep, nor ox, nor ass. H3478
6 And I was greatly impoverished H3478
6 the children of I cried unto the LORD. H3478
7 the children of I cried unto the LORD H3478
8 the children of I, which said unto them, H3478
8 the LORD God of I, I brought you up H3478
14 thou shalt save I from the hand of the H3478
15 shall I save I? behold, my family *is* H3478
36 save I by mine hand, as thou hast said, H3478
37 save I by mine hand, as thou hast said. H3478
7: 2 their hands, lest I vaunt themselves H3478
8 sent all *the rest of* I every man unto his H3478

Jdg 7:14 of Joash, a man of I: *for* into his hand H3478
15 into the host of I, and said, Arise; for H3478
23 And the men of I gathered themselves H3478
8:22 Then the men of I said unto Gideon, H3478
27 *even* in Ophrah: and all I went thither a H3478
28 the children of I, so that they lifted up H3478
33 that the children of I turned again, and H3478
34 And the children of I remembered not H3478
35 goodness which he had shewed unto I. H3478
9:22 had reigned three years over I, H3478
55 And when the men of I saw that H3478
10: 1 arose to defend I Tola the son of Puah, H3478
2 And he judged I twenty and three H3478
3 and judged I twenty and two years. H3478
6 And the children of I did evil again in H3478
7 was hot against I, and he sold them into H3478
8 the children of I: eighteen years, all the H3478
8 all the children of I that *were* on the H3478
9 Ephraim; so that I was sore distressed. H3478
10 And the children of I cried unto the H3478
11 the children of I, *Did* not *I deliver you* H3478
15 And the children of I said unto the H3478
16 his soul was grieved for the misery of I. H3478
17 the children of I assembled themselves H3478
11: 4 of Ammon made war against I. H3478
5 made war against I, the elders of Gilead H3478
13 of Jephthah, Because I took away my H3478
15 saith Jephthah, I took not away the H3478
16 But when I came up from Egypt, and H3478
17 Then I sent messengers unto the king H3478
17 not *consent*: and I abode in Kadesh. H3478
19 And I sent messengers unto Sihon king H3478
19 of Heshbon; and I said unto him, Let H3478
20 But Sihon trusted not I to pass through H3478
20 pitched in Jahaz, and fought against I. H3478
21 And the LORD God of I delivered Sihon H3478
21 into the hand of I, and they smote H3478
21 smote them: so I possessed all the land H3478
23 So now the LORD God of I hath H3478
23 people I, and shouldest thou possess it? H3478
25 I, or did he ever fight against them, H3478
26 While I dwelt in Heshbon and her H3478
27 of I and the children of Ammon. H3478
33 were subdued before the children of I. H3478
39 knew no man. And it was a custom in I, H3478
40 *That* the daughters of I went yearly to H3478
12: 7 And Jephthah judged I six years. Then H3478
8 after him Ibzan of Beth-lehem judged I. H3478
9 his sons. And he judged I seven years. H3478
11 judged I; and he judged Israel ten years. H3478
11 Israel; and he judged I ten years. H3478
13 the son of Hillel, a Pirathonite, judged I. H3478
14 ass colts: and he judged I eight years. H3478
13: 1 And the children of I did evil again in H3478
5 I out of the hand of the Philistines. H3478
14: 4 the Philistines had dominion over I. H3478
15:20 And he judged I in the days of the H3478
16:31 father. And he judged I twenty years. H3478
17: 6 In those days *there was* no king in I, *but* H3478
18: 1 In those days *there was* no king in I: H3478
1 fallen unto them among the tribes of I. H3478
19 a priest unto a tribe and a family in I? H3478
29 was born unto I: howbeit the name of H3478
19: 1 *there was* no king in I, that there was a H3478
12 of I; we will pass over to Gibeah. H3478
29 and sent her into all the coasts of I. H3478
30 the children of I came up out of the H3478
20: 1 Then all the children of I went out, and H3478
2 *even* of all the tribes of I, presented H3478
3 that the children of I were gone up to H3478
3 of I, Tell *us*, how was this wickedness? H3478
6 of the inheritance of I: for they have H3478
6 have committed lewdness and folly in I. H3478
7 Behold, ye *are* all children of I; give here H3478
10 all the tribes of I, and an hundred of a H3478
10 all the folly that they have wrought in I. H3478
11 So all the men of I were gathered H3478
12 And the tribes of I sent men through all H3478
13 put away evil from I. But the children of H3478
13 voice of their brethren the children of I: H3478
14 go out to battle against the children of I. H3478
17 And the men of I, beside Benjamin, H3478
18 And the children of I arose, and went H3478
19 And the children of I rose up in the H3478
20 And the men of I went out to battle H3478
20 and the men of I put themselves in H3478
22 And the people the men of I H3478
23 (And the children of I went up and H3478
24 And the children of I came near H3478
Jdg 20:25 of the children of I again eighteen H3478
26 Then all the children of I, and all the H3478
27 And the children of I inquired of the H3478
29 And I set liers in wait round about H3478
30 And the children of I went up against H3478
31 in the field, about thirty men of I. H3478
32 But the children of I said, Let us flee, H3478
33 And all the men of I rose up out of their H3478
33 the liers in wait of I came forth out of H3478
34 men out of all I, and the battle was sore: H3478
35 Benjamin before I: and the children of H3478
35 and the children of I destroyed of the H3478
36 for the men of I gave place to the H3478
38 the men of I and the liers in wait, H3478
39 And when the men of I retired in the H3478
39 *and* kill of the men of I about thirty H3478
41 And when the men of I turned again, H3478
42 before the men of I unto the way of the H3478
48 And the men of I turned again upon H3478
21: 1 Now the men of I had sworn in H3478
3 And said, O LORD God of I, why is this H3478
3 come to pass in I, that there should be H3478
3 should be to day one tribe lacking in I? H3478
5 And the children of I said, Who *is there* H3478
5 all the tribes of I that came not up with H3478
6 And the children of I repented them for H3478
6 is one tribe cut off from I this day. H3478
8 of the tribes of I that came not up to H3478
15 had made a breach in the tribes of I. H3478
17 that a tribe be not destroyed out of I. H3478
18 for the children of I have sworn, H3478
24 And the children of I departed thence H3478
25 In those days *there was* no king in I: H3478
Ru 2:12 the LORD God of I, under whose wings H3478
4: 7 *manner* in former time in I concerning H3478
7 and this *was* a testimony in I. H3478
11 did build the house of I: and do thou H3478
14 that his name may be famous in I. H3478
1Sa 1:17 and the God of I grant *thee* thy petition H3478
2:22 his sons did unto all I; and how they lay H3478
28 of all the tribes of I *to be* my priest, to H3478
28 made by fire of the children of I? H3478
29 of all the offerings of I my people? H3478
30 Wherefore the LORD God of I saith, I H3478
32 *God* shall give I: and there shall not be H3478
3:11 I will do a thing in I, at which both the H3478
20 And all I from Dan even to Beer-sheba H3478
4: 1 And the word of Samuel came to all I. H3478
1 to all Israel. Now I went out against the H3478
2 in array against I: and when they joined H3478
2 they joined battle, I was smitten before H3478
3 the elders of I said, Wherefore hath H3478
5 into the camp, all I shouted with a H3478
10 And the Philistines fought, and I was H3478
10 there fell of I thirty thousand footmen. H3478
17 and said, I is fled before the Philistines, H3478
18 heavy. And he had judged I forty years. H3478
21 is departed from I: because the ark of H3478
22 from I: for the ark of God is taken. H3478
5: 7 ark of the God of I shall not abide with H3478
8 ark of the God of I? And they answered, H3478
8 the ark of the God of I be carried about H3478
8 the ark of the God of I about *thither.* H3478
10 of I to us, to slay us and our people. H3478
11 ark of the God of I, and let it go again to H3478
6: 3 ark of the God of I, send it not empty; H3478
5 unto the God of I: peradventure he will H3478
7: 2 house of I lamented after the LORD. H3478
3 all the house of I, saying, If ye do return H3478
4 Then the children of I did put away H3478
5 And Samuel said, Gather all I to H3478
6 judged the children of I in Mizpeh. H3478
7 the children of I were gathered together H3478
7 went up against I. And when the H3478
7 the children of I heard *it*, they were H3478
8 And the children of I said to Samuel, H3478
9 LORD for I; and the LORD heard him. H3478
10 near to battle against I: but the LORD H3478
10 them; and they were smitten before I. H3478
11 And the men of I went out of Mizpeh, H3478
13 into the coast of I: and the hand of the H3478
14 had taken from I were restored to H3478
14 were restored to I, from Ekron even H3478
14 coasts thereof did I deliver out of the H3478
14 was peace between I and the Amorites. H3478
15 And Samuel judged I all the days of his H3478
16 and judged I in all those places. H3478
17 there he judged I; and there he built an H3478
8: 1 old, that he made his sons judges over I. H3478
1Sa 8: 4 Then all the elders of I gathered H3478
22 men of I, Go ye every man unto his city. H3478
9: 2 the children of I a goodlier person than H3478
9 (Beforetime in I, when a man went to H3478
16 over my people I, that he may save my H3478
20 *is* all the desire of I? *Is it* not on thee, H3478
21 of the tribes of I? and my family the H3478
10:18 And said unto the children of I, Thus H3478
18 the LORD God of I, I brought up Israel H3478
18 Israel, I brought up I out of Egypt, and H3478
20 all the tribes of I to come near, the tribe H3478
11: 2 and lay it *for* a reproach upon all I. H3478
3 all the coasts of I: and then, if *there be* H3478
7 all the coasts of I by the hands of H3478
8 the children of I were three hundred H3478
13 the LORD hath wrought salvation in I. H3478
15 and all the men of I rejoiced greatly. H3478
12: 1 And Samuel said unto all I, Behold, I H3478
13: 1 when he had reigned two years over I, H3478
2 three thousand *men* of I; *whereof* two H3478
4 And all I heard say *that* Saul had H3478
4 Philistines, and *that* I also was had in H3478
5 to fight with I, thirty thousand chariots, H3478
6 When the men of I saw that they were H3478
13 thy kingdom upon I for ever. H3478
19 all the land of I: for the Philistines said, H3478
14:12 hath delivered them into the hand of I. H3478
18 was at that time with the children of I. H3478
22 Likewise all the men of I which had hid H3478
23 So the LORD saved I that day: and the H3478
24 And the men of I were distressed that H3478
37 of I? But he answered him not that day. H3478
39 For, *as* the LORD liveth, which saveth I, H3478
40 Then said he unto all I, Be ye on one H3478
41 the LORD God of I, Give a perfect *lot.* H3478
45 great salvation in I? God forbid: *as* the H3478
47 So Saul took the kingdom over I, and H3478
48 and delivered I out of the hands of H3478
15: 1 over his people, over I: now therefore H3478
2 Amalek did to I, how he laid *wait* for H3478
6 all the children of I, when they came up H3478
17 head of the tribes of I, and the LORD H3478
17 the LORD anointed thee king over I? H3478
26 rejected thee from being king over I. H3478
28 the kingdom of I from thee this day, H3478
29 And also the Strength of I will not lie H3478
30 my people, and before I, and turn again H3478
35 that he had made Saul king over I. H3478
16: 1 from reigning over I? fill thine horn with H3478
17: 2 And Saul and the men of I were H3478
3 on the one side, and I stood on a H3478
8 unto the armies of I, and said unto H3478
10 defy the armies of I this day; give me a H3478
11 When Saul and all I heard those words H3478
19 and all the men of I, *were* in the valley H3478
21 For I and the Philistines had put the H3478
24 And all the men of I, when they saw the H3478
25 And the men of I said, Have ye seen H3478
25 up? surely to defy I is he come up: and H3478
25 and make his father's house free in I. H3478
26 the reproach from I? for who *is* this H3478
45 the armies of I, whom thou hast defied. H3478
46 earth may know that there is a God in I. H3478
52 And the men of I and of Judah arose, H3478
53 And the children of I returned from H3478
18: 6 came out of all cities of I, singing and H3478
16 But all I and Judah loved David, H3478
18 father's family in I, that I should be son H3478
19: 5 salvation for all I: thou sawest *it*, and H3478
20:12 O LORD God of I, when I have sounded H3478
23:10 Then said David, O LORD God of I, thy H3478
11 O LORD God of I, I beseech thee, tell thy H3478
17 shalt be king over I, and I shall be next H3478
24: 2 men out of all I, and went to seek David H3478
14 After whom is the king of I come out? H3478
20 of I shall be established in thine hand. H3478
25:30 shall have appointed thee ruler over I; H3478
32 I, which sent thee this day to meet me: H3478
34 For in very deed, *as* the LORD God of I H3478
26: 2 chosen men of I with him, to seek H3478
15 *is* like to thee in I? wherefore then hast H3478
20 for the king of I is come out to seek H3478
27: 1 of I: so shall I escape out of his hand. H3478
12 made his people I utterly to abhor him; H3478
28: 1 to fight with I. And Achish said unto H3478
3 Now Samuel was dead, and all I had H3478
4 I together, and they pitched in Gilboa. H3478
19 Moreover the LORD will also deliver I H3478
19 of I into the hand of the Philistines. H3478

1Sa 29: 3 of Saul the king of I, which hath been H3478
30:25 and an ordinance for I unto this day. H3478
31: 1 Now the Philistines fought against I: H3478
1 and the men of I fled from before the H3478
7 And when the men of I that *were* on the H3478
7 that the men of I fled, and that Saul H3478
2Sa 1: 3 him, Out of the camp of I am I escaped. H3478
12 for the house of I; because they were H3478
19 The beauty of I is slain upon thy high H3478
24 Ye daughters of I, weep over Saul, who H3478
2: 9 and over Benjamin, and over all I. H3478
10 to reign over I, and reigned two years. H3478
17 men of I, before the servants of David. H3478
28 and pursued after I no more, neither H3478
3:10 of David over I and over Judah, from H3478
12 thee, to bring about all I unto thee. H3478
17 with the elders of I, saying, Ye sought H3478
18 save my people I out of the hand of the H3478
19 that seemed good to I, and that seemed H3478
21 and will gather all I unto my lord the H3478
37 For all the people and all I understood H3478
38 and a great man fallen this day in I? H3478
5: 1 Then came all the tribes of I to David H3478
2 and broughtest in I: and the LORD said H3478
2 feed my people I, and thou shalt be a H3478
2 and thou shalt be a captain over I. H3478
3 So all the elders of I came to the king to H3478
3 and they anointed David king over I. H3478
5 and three years over all I and Judah. H3478
12 him king over I, and that he had exalted H3478
17 David king over I, all the Philistines H3478
6: 1 all *the* chosen *men* of I, thirty thousand. H3478
5 And David and all the house of I H3478
15 So David and all the house of I brought H3478
19 multitude of I, as well to the women H3478
20 glorious was the king of I to day, who H3478
21 I: therefore will I play before the LORD. H3478
7: 6 up the children of I out of Egypt, even H3478
7 all the children of I spake I a word with H3478
7 with any of the tribes of I, whom I H3478
7 to feed my people I, saying, Why build H3478
8 to be ruler over my people, over I: H3478
10 for my people I, and will plant them, H3478
11 *to be* over my people I, and have caused H3478
23 people, *even* like I, whom God went to H3478
24 thyself thy people I *to be* a people unto H3478
26 *is* the God over I: and let the house of H3478
27 For thou, O LORD of hosts, God of I, H3478
8:15 And David reigned over all I; and David H3478
10: 9 all the choice *men* of I, and put *them* in H3478
15 I, they gathered themselves together. H3478
17 he gathered all I together, and passed H3478
18 And the Syrians fled before I; and H3478
19 smitten before I, they made peace with H3478
19 made peace with I, and served them. So H3478
11: 1 with him, and all I; and they destroyed H3478
11 The ark, and I, and Judah, abide in H3478
12: 7 the LORD God of I, I anointed thee king H3478
7 thee king over I, and I delivered thee H3478
8 thee the house of I and of Judah; and if H3478
12 thing before all I, and before the sun. H3478
13:12 to be done in I: do not thou this folly. H3478
13 as one of the fools in I. Now therefore, I H3478
14:25 But in all I there was none to be so H3478
15: 2 Thy servant *is* of one of the tribes of I. H3478
6 did Absalom to all I that came to the H3478
6 stole the hearts of the men of I. H3478
10 all the tribes of I, saying, As soon as ye H3478
13 of the men of I are after Absalom. H3478
16: 3 I restore me the kingdom of my father. H3478
15 people the men of I, came to Jerusalem, H3478
18 and all the men of I, choose, his will I H3478
21 the house; and all I shall hear that thou H3478
22 father's concubines in the sight of all I. H3478
17: 4 Absalom well, and all the elders of I. H3478
10 utterly melt: for all I knoweth that thy H3478
11 Therefore I counsel that all I be H3478
13 city, then shall all I bring ropes to that H3478
14 And Absalom and all the men of I said, H3478
15 I; and thus and thus have I counselled. H3478
24 he and all the men of I with him. H3478
26 So I and Absalom pitched in the land H3478
18: 6 the field against I: and the battle was in H3478
7 Where the people of I were slain before H3478
16 after I: for Joab held back the people. H3478
17 him: and all I fled every one to his tent. H3478
19: 8 for I had fled every man to his tent. H3478
9 all the tribes of I, saying, The king H3478
11 I is come to the king, *even* to his house. H3478

2Sa 19:22 to death this day in I? for do not I know H3478
22 I know that I *am* this day king over I? H3478
40 the king, and also half the people of I. H3478
41 And, behold, all the men of I came to H3478
42 the men of I, Because the king *is* H3478
43 And the men of I answered the men of H3478
43 fiercer than the words of the men of I. H3478
20: 1 son of Jesse: every man to his tents, O I. H3478
2 So every man of I went up from after H3478
14 And he went through all the tribes of I H3478
19 *and* faithful in I: thou seekest to destroy H3478
19 city and a mother in I: why wilt thou H3478
23 Now Joab *was* over all the host of I: and H3478
21: 2 of the children of I, but of the remnant H3478
2 the children of I had sworn unto them: H3478
2 his zeal to the children of I and Judah.) H3478
4 kill any man in I. And he said, What ye H3478
5 remaining in any of the coasts of I, H3478
15 yet war again with I; and David went H3478
17 that thou quench not the light of I. H3478
21 And when he defied I, Jonathan the son H3478
23: 1 Jacob, and the sweet psalmist of I, said, H3478
3 The God of I said, the Rock of Israel H3478
3 The God of Israel said, the Rock of I H3478
9 and the men of I were gone away: H3478
24: 1 kindled against I, and he moved David H3478
1 them to say, Go, number I and Judah. H3478
2 all the tribes of I, from Dan even to H3478
4 of the king, to number the people of I. H3478
9 king: and there were in I eight hundred H3478
15 So the LORD sent a pestilence upon I H3478
25 land, and the plague was stayed from I. H3478
1Ki 1: 3 all the coasts of I, and found Abishag H3478
20 the eyes of all I *are* upon thee, that H3478
30 the LORD God of I, saying, Assuredly H3478
34 there king over I: and blow ye with the H3478
35 him to be ruler over I and over Judah. H3478
48 *be* the LORD God of I, which hath given H3478
2: 4 thee (said he) a man on the throne of I. H3478
5 of the hosts of I, unto Abner the son H3478
11 And the days that David reigned over I H3478
15 mine, and *that* all I set their faces on H3478
32 of the host of I, and Amasa the son H3478
3:28 And all I heard of the judgment which H3478
4: 1 So king Solomon was king over all I. H3478
7 officers over all I, which provided H3478
20 Judah and I *were* many, as the sand H3478
25 And Judah and I dwelt safely, every H3478
5:13 a levy out of all I; and the levy was H3478
6: 1 the children of I were come out of the H3478
1 reign over I, in the month Zif, which H3478
13 I, and will not forsake my people Israel. H3478
13 Israel, and will not forsake my people I. H3478
8: 1 the elders of I, and all the heads of H3478
1 of the children of I, unto king Solomon H3478
2 And all the men of I assembled H3478
3 And all the elders of I came, and the H3478
5 congregation of I, that were assembled H3478
9 the children of I, when they came out H3478
14 the congregation of I: (and all the H3478
14 (and all the congregation of I stood;) H3478
15 *be* the LORD God of I, which spake with H3478
16 forth my people I out of Egypt, I chose H3478
16 of all the tribes of I to build an house, H3478
16 I chose David to be over my people I. H3478
17 for the name of the LORD God of I. H3478
20 sit on the throne of I, as the LORD H3478
20 for the name of the LORD God of I. H3478
22 congregation of I, and spread forth his H3478
23 And he said, LORD God of I, *there is* no H3478
25 Therefore now, LORD God of I, keep H3478
25 on the throne of I; so that thy children H3478
26 And now, O God of I, let thy word, I H3478
30 and of thy people I, when they shall H3478
33 When thy people I be smitten down H3478
34 the sin of thy people I, and bring them H3478
36 and of thy people I, that thou teach H3478
38 *or* by all thy people I, which shall know H3478
41 not of thy people I, but cometh out of a H3478
43 as *do* thy people I; and that they may H3478
52 of thy people I, to hearken unto them H3478
55 of I with a loud voice, saying, H3478
56 unto his people I, according to all that H3478
59 cause of his people I at all times, as the H3478
62 And the king, and all I with him, H3478
63 of I dedicated the house of the LORD. H3478
65 held a feast, and all I with him, a great H3478
66 David his servant, and for I his people. H3478
9: 5 of thy kingdom upon I for ever, as I H3478

1Ki 9: 5 not fail thee a man upon the throne of I. H3478
7 Then will I cut off I out of the land H3478
7 of my sight; and I shall be a proverb H3478
20 which *were* not of the children of I, H3478
21 the children of I also were not able H3478
22 But of the children of I did Solomon H3478
10: 9 on the throne of I: because the LORD H3478
9 the LORD loved I for ever, therefore H3478
11: 2 the children of I, Ye shall not go in to H3478
9 I, which had appeared unto him twice, H3478
16 there with all I, until he had cut off H3478
25 And he was an adversary to I all the H3478
25 he abhorred I, and reigned over Syria. H3478
31 LORD, the God of I, Behold, I will rend H3478
32 I have chosen out of all the tribes of I:) H3478
37 soul desireth, and shalt be king over I. H3478
38 for David, and will give I unto thee. H3478
42 in Jerusalem over all I *was* forty years. H3478
12: 1 went to Shechem: for all I were come to H3478
3 the congregation of I came, and spake H3478
16 So when all I saw that the king H3478
16 to your tents, O I: now see to thine own H3478
16 David. So I departed unto their tents. H3478
17 But *as for* the children of I which dwelt H3478
18 the tribute; and all I stoned him with H3478
19 So I rebelled against the house of H3478
20 And it came to pass, when all I heard H3478
20 him king over all I: there was none that H3478
21 the house of I, to bring the kingdom H3478
24 the children of I: return every man to H3478
28 behold thy gods, O I, which brought H3478
33 the children of I: and he offered upon H3478
14: 7 the LORD God of I, Forasmuch as I H3478
7 and made thee prince over my people I, H3478
10 shut up and left in I, and will take away H3478
13 And all I shall mourn for him, and H3478
13 God of I in the house of Jeroboam. H3478
14 up a king over I, who shall cut off the H3478
15 For the LORD shall smite I, as a reed is H3478
15 he shall root up I out of this good land, H3478
16 And he shall give I up because of the H3478
16 who did sin, and who made I to sin. H3478
18 And they buried him; and all I H3478
19 book of the chronicles of the kings of I. H3478
21 out of all the tribes of I, to put his name H3478
24 LORD cast out before the children of I. H3478
15: 9 king of I reigned Asa over Judah. H3478
16 Asa and Baasha king of I all their days. H3478
17 And Baasha king of I went up against H3478
19 king of I, that he may depart from me. H3478
20 the cities of I, and smote Ijon, and H3478
25 to reign over I in the second year of H3478
25 of Judah, and reigned over I two years. H3478
26 in his sin wherewith he made I to sin. H3478
27 and all I laid siege to Gibbethon. H3478
30 and which he made I sin, by his H3478
30 provoked the LORD God of I to anger. H3478
31 book of the chronicles of the kings of I? H3478
32 Asa and Baasha king of I all their days. H3478
33 all I in Tirzah, twenty and four years. H3478
34 in his sin wherewith he made I to sin. H3478
16: 2 over my people I; and thou hast walked H3478
2 made my people I to sin, to provoke H3478
5 book of the chronicles of the kings of I? H3478
8 to reign over I in Tirzah, two years. H3478
13 which they made I to sin, in provoking H3478
13 God of I to anger with their vanities. H3478
14 book of the chronicles of the kings of I? H3478
16 king: wherefore all I made Omri, the H3478
16 host, king over I that day in the camp. H3478
17 I with him, and they besieged Tirzah. H3478
19 his sin which he did, to make I to sin. H3478
20 book of the chronicles of the kings of I? H3478
21 Then were the people of I divided into H3478
23 Omri to reign over I, twelve years: six H3478
26 he made I to sin, to provoke the H3478
26 God of I to anger with their vanities. H3478
27 book of the chronicles of the kings of I? H3478
29 Omri to reign over I: and Ahab the son H3478
29 I in Samaria twenty and two years. H3478
33 the LORD God of I to anger than all the H3478
33 all the kings of I that were before him. H3478
17: 1 the LORD God of I liveth, before whom H3478
14 For thus saith the LORD God of I, The H3478
18:17 unto him, *Art* thou he that troubleth I? H3478
18 And he answered, I have not troubled I; H3478
19 gather to me all I unto mount Carmel, H3478
20 So Ahab sent unto all the children of I, H3478
31 came, saying, I shall be thy name: H3478

1Ki 18:36 Isaac, and of I, let it be known this H3478
36 that thou *art* God in I, and *that* I *am* thy H3478
19:10 for the children of I have forsaken thy H3478
14 the children of I have forsaken thy H3478
16 *to be* king over I: and Elisha the son of H3478
18 Yet I have left *me* seven thousand in I, H3478
20: 2 to Ahab king of I into the city, and said H3478
4 And the king of I answered and said, H3478
7 Then the king of I called all the elders H3478
11 And the king of I answered and said, H3478
13 unto Ahab king of I, saying, Thus saith H3478
15 the children of I, *being* seven thousand. H3478
20 Syrians fled; and I pursued them: and H3478
21 And the king of I went out, and smote H3478
22 And the prophet came to the king of I, H3478
26 went up to Aphek, to fight against I. H3478
27 And the children of I were numbered, H3478
27 the children of I pitched before them H3478
28 unto the king of I, and said, Thus saith H3478
29 the children of I slew of the Syrians an H3478
31 of the house of I *are* merciful kings: let H3478
31 of I: peradventure he will save thy life. H3478
32 to the king of I, and said, Thy servant H3478
40 And the king of I said unto him, So H3478
41 and the king of I discerned him that H3478
43 And the king of I went to his house H3478
21: 7 the kingdom of I? arise, *and* eat bread, H3478
18 Arise, go down to meet Ahab king of I, H3478
21 and him that is shut up and left in I, H3478
22 *me* to anger, and made I to sin. H3478
26 LORD cast out before the children of I. H3478
22: 1 years without war between Syria and I. H3478
2 of Judah came down to the king of I. H3478
3 And the king of I said unto his H3478
4 said to the king of I, I *am* as thou *art*, H3478
5 unto the king of I, Inquire, I pray thee, H3478
6 Then the king of I gathered the H3478
8 And the king of I said unto H3478
9 Then the king of I called an officer, and H3478
10 And the king of I and Jehoshaphat the H3478
17 And he said, I saw all I scattered upon H3478
18 And the king of I said unto H3478
26 And the king of I said, Take Micaiah, H3478
29 So the king of I and Jehoshaphat the H3478
30 And the king of I said unto H3478
30 And the king of I disguised himself, H3478
31 nor great, save only with the king of I. H3478
32 it *is* the king of I. And they turned aside H3478
33 not the king of I, that they turned back H3478
34 smote the king of I between the joints H3478
39 book of the chronicles of the kings of I? H3478
41 in the fourth year of Ahab king of I. H3478
44 made peace with the king of I. H3478
51 began to reign over I in Samaria the H3478
51 of Judah, and reigned two years over I. H3478
52 the son of Nebat, who made I to sin: H3478
53 the LORD God of I, according to all that H3478
2Ki 1: 1 Then Moab rebelled against I after the H3478
3 *is* not a God in I, *that* ye go to inquire H3478
6 *is* not a God in I, *that* thou sendest to H3478
16 *there is* no God in I to inquire of his H3478
18 book of the chronicles of the kings of I? H3478
2:12 the chariot of I, and the horsemen H3478
3: 1 began to reign over I in Samaria the H3478
3 I to sin; he departed not therefrom. H3478
4 rendered unto the king of I an hundred H3478
5 of Moab rebelled against the king of I. H3478
6 the same time, and numbered all I. H3478
9 So the king of I went, and the king of H3478
10 And the king of I said, Alas! that the H3478
12 him. So the king of I and Jehoshaphat H3478
13 And Elisha said unto the king of I, H3478
13 And the king of I said unto him, Nay: H3478
24 And when they came to the camp of I, H3478
27 against I: and they departed from H3478
5: 2 out of the land of I a little maid; and H3478
4 said the maid that *is* of the land of I. H3478
5 unto the king of I. And he departed, and H3478
6 to the king of I, saying, Now when this H3478
7 And it came to pass, when the king of I H3478
8 that the king of I had rent his clothes, H3478
8 shall know that there is a prophet in I. H3478
12 all the waters of I? may I not wash in H3478
15 the earth, but in I: now therefore, I pray H3478
6: 8 Then the king of Syria warred against I, H3478
9 unto the king of I, saying, Beware that H3478
10 And the king of I sent to the place H3478
11 shew me which of us *is* for the king of I? H3478
12 prophet that *is* in I, telleth the king of H3478

2Ki 6:12 telleth the king of I the words that thou H3478
21 And the king of I said unto Elisha, H3478
23 Syria came no more into the land of I. H3478
26 And as the king of I was passing by H3478
7: 6 Lo, the king of I hath hired against us H3478
13 all the multitude of I that are left in it: H3478
8:12 the children of I: their strong holds wilt H3478
16 of Ahab king of I, Jehoshaphat *being* H3478
18 way of the kings of I, as did the house of H3478
25 of Ahab king of I did Ahaziah the son H3478
26 the daughter of Omri king of I. H3478
9: 3 thee king over I. Then open the door, H3478
6 the LORD God of I, I have anointed thee H3478
6 the people of the LORD, *even* over I. H3478
8 and him that is shut up and left in I: H3478
12 LORD, I have anointed thee king over I. H3478
14 all I, because of Hazael king of Syria. H3478
21 And Joram king of I and Ahaziah king H3478
10:21 And Jehu sent through all I: and all the H3478
28 Thus Jehu destroyed Baal out of I. H3478
29 of Nebat, who made I to sin, Jehu H3478
30 *generation* shall sit on the throne of I. H3478
31 of the LORD God of I with all his heart: H3478
31 sins of Jeroboam, which made I to sin. H3478
32 In those days the LORD began to cut I H3478
32 Hazael smote them in all the coasts of I; H3478
34 book of the chronicles of the kings of I? H3478
36 And the time that Jehu reigned over I H3478
13: 1 to reign over I in Samaria, *and reigned* H3478
2 I to sin; he departed not therefrom. H3478
3 was kindled against I, and he delivered H3478
4 the oppression of I, because the king of H3478
5 (And the LORD gave I a saviour, so H3478
5 of I dwelt in their tents, as beforetime. H3478
6 who made I sin, *but* walked therein: H3478
8 book of the chronicles of the kings of I? H3478
10 to reign over I in Samaria, *and reigned* H3478
11 who made I sin: *but* he walked therein. H3478
12 book of the chronicles of the kings of I? H3478
13 buried in Samaria with the kings of I. H3478
14 Joash the king of I came down unto H3478
14 chariot of I, and the horsemen thereof. H3478
16 And he said to the king of I, Put thine H3478
18 said unto the king of I, Smite upon the H3478
22 But Hazael king of Syria oppressed I all H3478
25 beat him, and recovered the cities of I. H3478
14: 1 of Jehoahaz king of I reigned Amaziah H3478
8 of Jehu, king of I, saying, Come, let us H3478
9 And Jehoash the king of I sent to H3478
11 Jehoash king of I went up; and he and H3478
12 I; and they fled every man to their tents. H3478
13 And Jehoash king of I took Amaziah H3478
15 book of the chronicles of the kings of I? H3478
16 with the kings of I; and Jeroboam his H3478
17 son of Jehoahaz king of I fifteen years. H3478
23 son of Joash king of I began to reign in H3478
24 the son of Nebat, who made I to sin. H3478
25 He restored the coast of I from the H3478
25 the LORD God of I, which he spake by H3478
26 For the LORD saw the affliction of I, H3478
26 up, nor any left, nor any helper for I. H3478
27 out the name of I from under heaven: H3478
28 to Judah, for I, are they not written H3478
28 book of the chronicles of the kings of I? H3478
29 with the kings of I; and Zachariah his H3478
15: 1 Jeroboam king of I began Azariah son H3478
8 reign over I in Samaria six months. H3478
9 the son of Nebat, who made I to sin. H3478
11 book of the chronicles of the kings of I. H3478
12 sit on the throne of I unto the fourth H3478
15 book of the chronicles of the kings of I. H3478
17 I, *and reigned* ten years in Samaria. H3478
18 the son of Nebat, who made I to sin. H3478
20 And Menahem exacted the money of I, H3478
21 book of the chronicles of the kings of I? H3478
23 I in Samaria, *and reigned* two years. H3478
24 the son of Nebat, who made I to sin. H3478
26 book of the chronicles of the kings of I. H3478
27 I in Samaria, *and reigned* twenty years. H3478
28 the son of Nebat, who made I to sin. H3478
29 In the days of Pekah king of I came H3478
31 book of the chronicles of the kings of I. H3478
32 of Remaliah king of I began Jotham the H3478
16: 3 way of the kings of I, yea, and made his H3478
3 cast out from before the children of I. H3478
5 of Remaliah king of I came up to H3478
7 the king of I, which rise up against me. H3478
17: 1 to reign in Samaria over I nine years. H3478
2 as the kings of I that were before him. H3478

2Ki 17: 6 and carried I away into Assyria, and H3478
7 For *so* it was, that the children of I had H3478
8 the children of I, and of the kings of H3478
8 of the kings of I, which they had made. H3478
9 And the children of I did secretly *those* H3478
13 Yet the LORD testified against I, and H3478
18 very angry with I, and removed them H3478
19 in the statutes of I which they made. H3478
20 And the LORD rejected all the seed of I, H3478
21 For he rent I from the house of David; H3478
21 Jeroboam drave I from following the H3478
22 For the children of I walked in all the H3478
23 Until the LORD removed I out of his H3478
23 prophets. So was I carried away out of H3478
24 of the children of I: and they possessed H3478
34 children of Jacob, whom he named I; H3478
18: 1 son of Elah king of I, *that* Hezekiah the H3478
4 the children of I did burn incense to H3478
5 He trusted in the LORD God of I; so that H3478
9 son of Elah king of I, *that* Shalmaneser H3478
10 of Hoshea king of I, Samaria was taken. H3478
11 did carry away I unto Assyria, and put H3478
19:15 said, O LORD God of I, which dwellest H3478
20 the LORD God of I, *That* which thou H3478
22 on high? *even* against the Holy *One* of I. H3478
21: 2 LORD cast out before the children of I. H3478
3 did Ahab king of I; and worshipped all H3478
7 tribes of I, will I put my name for ever: H3478
8 Neither will I make the feet of I move H3478
9 destroyed before the children of I. H3478
12 Therefore thus saith the LORD God of I, H3478
22:15 of I, Tell the man that sent you to me, H3478
18 the LORD God of I, *As touching* the H3478
23:13 the king of I had builded for Ashtoreth H3478
15 of Nebat, who made I to sin, had made, H3478
19 which the kings of I had made to H3478
22 judges that judged I, nor in all the days H3478
22 the kings of I, nor of the kings of Judah; H3478
27 as I have removed I, and will cast off H3478
24:13 Solomon king of I had made in the H3478
1Ch 1:34 Isaac. The sons of Isaac; Esau and I. H3478
43 the children of I; Bela the son of Beor: H3478
2: 1 These *are* the sons of I; Reuben, H3478
7 the troubler of I, who transgressed in H3478
4:10 And Jabez called on the God of I, H3478
5: 1 the firstborn of I, (for he *was* the H3478
1 Joseph the son of I: and the genealogy is H3478
3 the firstborn of I *were*, Hanoch, and H3478
17 and in the days of Jeroboam king of I. H3478
26 And the God of I stirred up the spirit of H3478
6:38 of Kohath, the son of Levi, the son of I. H3478
49 an atonement for I, according to all H3478
64 And the children of I gave to the H3478
7:29 dwelt the children of Joseph the son of I. H3478
9: 1 So all I were reckoned by genealogies; H3478
1 of the kings of I and Judah, *who* were H3478
10: 1 Now the Philistines fought against I; H3478
1 and the men of I fled from before the H3478
7 And when all the men of I that *were* in H3478
11: 1 Then all I gathered themselves to H3478
2 and broughtest in I: and the LORD thy H3478
2 feed my people I, and thou shalt be H3478
2 thou shalt be ruler over my people I. H3478
3 Therefore came all the elders of I to the H3478
3 David king over I, according to the H3478
4 And David and all I went to Jerusalem, H3478
10 *and* with all I, to make him king, H3478
10 to the word of the LORD concerning I. H3478
12:32 to know what I ought to do; the heads H3478
38 king over all I: and all the rest also H3478
38 I *were* of one heart to make David king. H3478
40 abundantly: for *there was* joy in I. H3478
13: 2 congregation of I, If *it seem* good unto H3478
2 in all the land of I, and with them *also* H3478
5 So David gathered all I together, from H3478
6 And David went up, and all I, to H3478
8 And David and all I played before God H3478
14: 2 him king over I, for his kingdom was H3478
2 up on high, because of his people I. H3478
8 king over all I, all the Philistines went H3478
15: 3 And David gathered all I together to H3478
12 the LORD God of I unto *the place that* I H3478
14 bring up the ark of the LORD God of I. H3478
25 So David, and the elders of I, and the H3478
28 Thus all I brought up the ark of the H3478
16: 3 And he dealt to every one of I, both H3478
4 to thank and praise the LORD God of I: H3478
13 O ye seed of I his servant, ye children of H3478
17 *and* to I *for* an everlasting covenant, H3478

1Ch 16:36 Blessed *be* the LORD God of I for ever H3478
40 of the LORD, which he commanded I; H3478
17: 5 that I brought up I unto this day; but H3478
6 Wheresoever I have walked with all I, H3478
6 of the judges of I, whom I commanded H3478
7 shouldest be ruler over my people I: H3478
9 for my people I, and will plant them, H3478
10 *to be* over my people I. Moreover I will H3478
21 *is* like thy people I, whom God went to H3478
22 For thy people I didst thou make thine H3478
24 of hosts *is* the God of I, *even* a God to H3478
24 *even* a God to I: and *let* the house of H3478
18:14 So David reigned over all I, and H3478
19:10 of all the choice of I, and put *them* in H3478
16 to the worse before I, they sent H3478
17 and he gathered all I, and passed over H3478
18 But the Syrians fled before I; and David H3478
19 to the worse before I, they made peace H3478
20: 7 But when he defied I, Jonathan the son H3478
21: 1 And Satan stood up against I, and H3478
1 and provoked David to number I. H3478
2 Go, number I from Beer-sheba even H3478
3 why will he be a cause of trespass to I? H3478
4 all I, and came to Jerusalem. H3478
5 And all *they of* I were a thousand H3478
7 with this thing; therefore he smote I. H3478
12 all the coasts of I. Now therefore advise H3478
14 So the LORD sent pestilence upon I: H3478
14 there fell of I seventy thousand men. H3478
16 and the elders *of I, who were* clothed in
22: 1 *is* the altar of the burnt offering for I. H3478
2 *were* in the land of I; and he set masons H3478
6 build an house for the LORD God of I. H3478
9 peace and quietness unto I in his days. H3478
10 throne of his kingdom over I for ever. H3478
12 charge concerning I, that thou mayest H3478
13 with concerning I: be strong, and of H3478
17 of I to help Solomon his son, *saying,* H3478
23: 1 he made Solomon his son king over I. H3478
2 of I, with the priests and the Levites. H3478
25 For David said, The LORD God of I H3478
24:19 LORD God of I had commanded him. H3478
26:29 business over I, for officers and judges. H3478
30 among them of I on this side Jordan H3478
27: 1 Now the children of I after their H3478
16 Furthermore over the tribes of I: the H3478
22 These *were* the princes of the tribes of I. H3478
23 I like to the stars of the heavens. H3478
24 for it against I; neither was the number H3478
28: 1 all the princes of I, the princes of the H3478
4 Howbeit the LORD God of I chose me H3478
4 to be king over I for ever: for he hath H3478
4 he liked me to make *me* king over all I: H3478
5 of the kingdom of the LORD over I. H3478
8 Now therefore in the sight of all I the H3478
29: 6 of the tribes of I, and the captains of H3478
10 God of I our father, for ever and ever. H3478
18 Isaac, and of I, our fathers, keep this H3478
21 and sacrifices in abundance for all I: H3478
23 and prospered; and all I obeyed him. H3478
25 in the sight of all I, and bestowed upon H3478
25 not been on any king before him in I. H3478
26 David the son of Jesse reigned over all I. H3478
27 And the time that he reigned over I *was* H3478
30 over him, and over I, and over all the H3478
2Ch 1: 2 Then Solomon spake unto all I, to the H3478
2 governor in all I, the chief of the fathers. H3478
13 of the congregation, and reigned over I. H3478
2: 4 God. This *is an ordinance* for ever to I. H3478
12 the LORD God of I, that made heaven H3478
17 that *were* in the land of I, after the H3478
5: 2 the elders of I, and all the heads of H3478
2 of the children of I, unto Jerusalem, to H3478
3 Wherefore all the men of I assembled H3478
4 And all the elders of I came; and the H3478
6 congregation of I that were assembled H3478
10 of I, when they came out of Egypt. H3478
6: 3 whole congregation of I: and all the H3478
3 and all the congregation of I stood. H3478
4 the LORD God of I, who hath with his H3478
5 all the tribes of I to build an house in, H3478
5 any man to be a ruler over my people I: H3478
6 chosen David to be over my people I. H3478
7 for the name of the LORD God of I. H3478
10 set on the throne of I, as the LORD H3478
10 for the name of the LORD God of I. H3478
11 that he made with the children of I. H3478
12 of I, and spread forth his hands: H3478
13 congregation of I, and spread forth his H3478
2Ch 6:14 And said, O LORD God of I, *there is* no H3478
16 Now therefore, O LORD God of I, keep H3478
16 sit upon the throne of I; yet so that thy H3478
17 Now then, O LORD God of I, let thy H3478
21 and of thy people I, which they shall H3478
24 And if thy people I be put to the worse H3478
25 the sin of thy people I, and bring them H3478
27 and of thy people I, when thou hast H3478
29 or of all thy people I, when every one H3478
32 not of thy people I, but is come from a H3478
33 as *doth* thy people I, and may know H3478
7: 3 And when all the children of I saw how H3478
6 trumpets before them, and all I stood. H3478
8 days, and all I with him, a very great H3478
10 and to Solomon, and to I his people. H3478
18 shall not fail thee a man *to be* ruler in I. H3478
8: 2 caused the children of I to dwell there. H3478
7 and the Jebusites, which *were* not of I, H3478
8 the children of I consumed not, them H3478
9 But of the children of I did Solomon H3478
11 of David king of I, because *the places* H3478
9: 8 thy God loved I, to establish them for H3478
30 in Jerusalem over all I forty years. H3478
10: 1 were all I come to make him king. H3478
3 Jeroboam and all I came and spake to H3478
16 And when all I *saw* that the king would H3478
16 to your tents, O I: *and* now, David, see H3478
16 own house. So all I went to their tents. H3478
17 But *as for* the children of I that dwelt in H3478
18 and the children of I stoned him with H3478
19 And I rebelled against the house of H3478
11: 1 to fight against I, that he might bring H3478
3 to all I in Judah and Benjamin, saying, H3478
13 I resorted to him out of all their coasts. H3478
16 And after them out of all the tribes of I H3478
16 the LORD God of I came to Jerusalem, H3478
12: 1 law of the LORD, and all I with him. H3478
6 Whereupon the princes of I and the H3478
13 out of all the tribes of I, to put his name H3478
13: 4 Hear me, thou Jeroboam, and all I; H3478
5 the LORD God of I gave the kingdom H3478
5 the kingdom over I to David for ever, H3478
12 you. O children of I, fight ye not against H3478
15 and all I before Abijah and Judah. H3478
16 And the children of I fled before Judah: H3478
17 I five hundred thousand chosen men. H3478
18 Thus the children of I were brought H3478
15: 3 Now for a long season I *hath been* H3478
4 the LORD God of I, and sought him, he H3478
9 fell to him out of I in abundance, when H3478
13 the LORD God of I should be put to H3478
17 taken away out of I: nevertheless the H3478
16: 1 Asa Baasha king of I came up against H3478
3 king of I, that he may depart from me. H3478
4 the cities of I; and they smote Ijon, H3478
11 in the book of the kings of Judah and I. H3478
17: 1 and strengthened himself against I. H3478
4 and not after the doings of I. H3478
18: 3 And Ahab king of I said unto H3478
4 unto the king of I, Inquire, I pray thee, H3478
5 Therefore the king of I gathered H3478
7 And the king of I said unto H3478
8 And the king of I called for one *of his* H3478
9 And the king of I and Jehoshaphat king H3478
16 Then he said, I did see all I scattered H3478
17 And the king of I said to Jehoshaphat, H3478
19 Ahab king of I, that he may go up and H3478
25 Then the king of I said, Take ye H3478
28 So the king of I and Jehoshaphat the H3478
29 And the king of I said unto H3478
29 So the king of I disguised himself; and H3478
30 or great, save only with the king of I. H3478
31 said, It *is* the king of I. Therefore they H3478
32 was not the king of I, they turned back H3478
33 smote the king of I between the joints H3478
34 the king of I stayed *himself* up in H3478
19: 8 of the fathers of I, for the judgment of H3478
20: 7 before thy people I, and gavest it to the H3478
10 wouldest not let I invade, when they H3478
19 God of I with a loud voice on high. H3478
29 LORD fought against the enemies of I. H3478
34 mentioned in the book of the kings of I. H3478
35 king of I, who did very wickedly: H3478
21: 2 *were* the sons of Jehoshaphat king of I. H3478
4 and *divers* also of the princes of I. H3478
6 the way of the kings of I, like as did the H3478
13 the way of the kings of I, and hast made H3478
22: 5 of Ahab king of I to war against Hazael H3478
23: 2 of I, and they came to Jerusalem. H3478
2Ch 24: 5 and gather of all I money to repair the H3478
6 of I, for the tabernacle of witness? H3478
9 of God *laid* upon I in the wilderness. H3478
16 had done good in I, both toward God, H3478
25: 6 out of I for an hundred talents of silver. H3478
7 let not the army of I go with thee; for H3478
7 LORD *is* not with I, *to wit, with* all the H3478
9 to the army of I? And the man of God H3478
17 of Jehu, king of I, saying, Come, let us H3478
18 And Joash king of I sent to Amaziah H3478
21 So Joash the king of I went up; and H3478
22 I, and they fled every man to his tent. H3478
23 And Joash the king of I took Amaziah H3478
25 son of Jehoahaz king of I fifteen years. H3478
26 in the book of the kings of Judah and I? H3478
27: 7 in the book of the kings of I and Judah. H3478
28: 2 of the kings of I, and made also molten H3478
3 had cast out before the children of I. H3478
5 of the king of I, who smote him with H3478
8 And the children of I carried away H3478
13 and *there is* fierce wrath against I. H3478
19 of Ahaz king of I; for he made Judah H3478
23 they were the ruin of him, and of all I. H3478
26 in the book of the kings of Judah and I. H3478
27 of the kings of I: and Hezekiah his son H3478
29: 7 in the holy *place* unto the God of I. H3478
10 the LORD God of I, that his fierce wrath H3478
24 an atonement for all I: for the king H3478
24 the sin offering *should be made* for all I. H3478
27 *ordained* by David king of I. H3478
30: 1 And Hezekiah sent to all I and Judah, H3478
1 the passover unto the LORD God of I. H3478
5 throughout all I, from Beer-sheba even H3478
5 the LORD God of I at Jerusalem: for H3478
6 throughout all I and Judah, and H3478
6 Ye children of I, turn again unto the H3478
6 Isaac, and I, and he will return to H3478
21 And the children of I that were present H3478
25 that came out of I, and the strangers H3478
25 of I, and that dwelt in Judah, rejoiced. H3478
26 of I *there was* not the like in Jerusalem. H3478
31: 1 Now when all this was finished, all I H3478
1 all the children of I returned, every H3478
5 the children of I brought in abundance H3478
6 And *concerning* the children of I and H3478
8 blessed the LORD, and his people I. H3478
32:17 on the LORD God of I, and to speak H3478
32 in the book of the kings of Judah and I. H3478
33: 2 had cast out before the children of I. H3478
7 tribes of I, will I put my name for ever: H3478
8 remove the foot of I from out of the H3478
9 had destroyed before the children of I. H3478
16 Judah to serve the LORD God of I. H3478
18 of the LORD God of I, behold, they *are* H3478
18 *are written* in the book of the kings of I. H3478
34: 7 the land of I, he returned to Jerusalem. H3478
9 of all the remnant of I, and of all Judah H3478
21 them that are left in I and in Judah, H3478
23 I, Tell ye the man that sent you to me, H3478
26 saith the LORD God of I *concerning* the H3478
33 to the children of I, and made all that H3478
33 were present in I to serve, *even* to serve H3478
35: 3 that taught all I, which were holy unto H3478
3 of David king of I did build; *it shall* not H3478
3 the LORD your God, and his people I, H3478
4 of David king of I, and according to the H3478
17 And the children of I that were present H3478
18 like to that kept in I from the days of H3478
18 did all the kings of I keep such a H3478
18 and all Judah and I that were present, H3478
25 an ordinance in I: and, behold, they *are* H3478
27 in the book of the kings of I and Judah. H3478
36: 8 book of the kings of I and Judah: and H3478
13 from turning unto the LORD God of I. H3478
Ezr 1: 3 I, (he *is* the God,) which *is* in Jerusalem. H3478
2: 2 number of the men of the people of I: H3478
59 and their seed, whether they *were* of I: H3478
70 in their cities, and all I in their cities. H3478
3: 1 the children of I *were* in the cities, the H3478
2 the altar of the God of I, to offer burnt H3478
10 after the ordinance of David king of I. H3478
11 for ever toward I. And all the people H3478
4: 1 the temple unto the LORD God of I; H3478
3 of the fathers of I, said unto them, Ye H3478
3 the LORD God of I, as king Cyrus the H3478
5: 1 name of the God of I, *even* unto them. H3479
11 a great king of I builded and set up. H3479
6:14 of the God of I, and according to the H3479
16 And the children of I, the priests, and H3479

Ezr 6:17 a sin offering for all I, twelve he goats, H3479
17 to the number of the tribes of I. H3479
21 And the children of I, which were come H3478
21 to seek the LORD God of I, did eat, H3478
22 work of the house of God, the God of I. H3478
7: 6 the LORD God of I had given: and the H3478
7 of the children of I, and of the priests, H3478
10 to teach in I statutes and judgments. H3478
11 of the LORD, and of his statutes to I. H3478
13 of the people of I, and *of* his priests and H3479
15 of I, whose habitation *is* in Jerusalem, H3479
28 out of I chief men to go up with me. H3478
8:18 son of Levi, the son of I; and Sherebiah, H3478
25 and all I *there* present, had offered: H3478
29 of the fathers of I, at Jerusalem, in the H3478
35 unto the God of I, twelve bullocks for all H3478
35 bullocks for all I, ninety and six rams, H3478
9: 1 The people of I, and the priests, and H3478
4 words of the God of I, because of the H3478
15 O LORD God of I, thou *art* righteous: for H3478
10: 1 unto him out of I a very great H3478
2 there is hope in I concerning this thing. H3478
5 the Levites, and all I, to swear that they H3478
10 wives, to increase the trespass of I. H3478
25 Moreover of I: of the sons of Parosh; H3478
Neh 1: 6 for the children of I thy servants, and H3478
6 sins of the children of I, which we have H3478
2:10 to seek the welfare of the children of I. H3478
7: 7 of the men of the people of I *was this*; H3478
61 nor their seed, whether they *were* of I. H3478
73 the Nethinims, and all I, dwelt in their H3478
73 the children of I *were* in their cities. H3478
8: 1 which the LORD had commanded to I. H3478
14 the children of I should dwell in booths H3478
17 not the children of I done so. And there H3478
9: 1 the children of I were assembled with H3478
2 And the seed of I separated themselves H3478
10:33 an atonement for I, and *for* all the work H3478
39 For the children of I and the children of H3478
11: 3 their cities, *to wit*, I, the priests, and the H3478
20 And the residue of I, of the priests, *and* H3478
12:47 And all I in the days of Zerubbabel, H3478
13: 2 Because they met not the children of I H3478
3 from I all the mixed multitude. H3478
18 wrath upon I by profaning the sabbath. H3478
26 Did not Solomon king of I sin by these H3478
26 him king over all I: nevertheless even H3478
Ps 14: 7 Oh that the salvation of I *were come* H3478
7 Jacob shall rejoice, *and* I shall be glad. H3478
22: 3 *O thou* that inhabitest the praises of I. H3478
23 him; and fear him, all ye the seed of I. H3478
25:22 Redeem I, O God, out of all his troubles. H3478
41:13 Blessed *be* the LORD God of I from H3478
50: 7 and I will speak; O I, and I will testify H3478
53: 6 Oh that the salvation of I *were come* H3478
6 Jacob shall rejoice, *and* I shall be glad. H3478
59: 5 hosts, the God of I, awake to visit all the H3478
68: 8 at the presence of God, the God of I. H3478
26 *even* the Lord, from the fountain of I. H3478
34 over I, and his strength *is* in the clouds. H3478
35 places: the God of I *is* he that giveth H3478
69: 6 be confounded for my sake, O God of I. H3478
71:22 with the harp, O thou Holy One of I. H3478
72:18 Blessed *be* the LORD God, the God of I, H3478
73: 1 Truly God *is* good to I, *even* to such as H3478
76: 1 *is* God known: his name *is* great in I. H3478
78: 5 and appointed a law in I, which he H3478
21 and anger also came up against I; H3478
31 and smote down the chosen *men* of I. H3478
41 God, and limited the Holy One of I. H3478
55 the tribes of I to dwell in their tents. H3478
59 he was wroth, and greatly abhorred I: H3478
71 Jacob his people, and I his inheritance. H3478
80: 1 Give ear, O Shepherd of I, thou that H3478
81: 4 For this *was* a statute for I, *and* a law of H3478
8 thee: O I, if thou wilt hearken unto me; H3478
11 to my voice; and I would none of me. H3478
13 unto me, *and* I had walked in my ways! H3478
83: 4 of I may be no more in remembrance. H3478
89:18 and the Holy One of I *is* our king. H3478
98: 3 the house of I: all the ends of the earth H3478
103: 7 Moses, his acts unto the children of I. H3478
105:10 *and* to I *for* an everlasting covenant: H3478
23 I also came into Egypt; and Jacob H3478
106:48 Blessed *be* the LORD God of I from H3478
114: 1 When I went out of Egypt, the house of H3478
2 Judah was his sanctuary, *and* I his H3478
115: 9 O I, trust thou in the LORD: he *is* their H3478
12 of I; he will bless the house of Aaron. H3478

Ps 118: 2 Let I now say, that his mercy *endureth* H3478
121: 4 Behold, he that keepeth I shall neither H3478
122: 4 the testimony of I, to give thanks unto H3478
124: 1 who was on our side, now may I say; H3478
125: 5 of iniquity: *but* peace *shall be* upon I. H3478
128: 6 children's children, *and* peace upon I. H3478
129: 1 me from my youth, may I now say: H3478
130: 7 Let I hope in the LORD: for with the H3478
8 And he shall redeem I from all his H3478
131: 3 Let I hope in the LORD from H3478
135: 4 himself, *and* I for his peculiar treasure. H3478
12 heritage, an heritage unto I his people. H3478
19 Bless the LORD, O house of I: bless the H3478
136:11 And brought out I from among them: H3478
14 And made I to pass through the midst H3478
22 *Even* an heritage unto I his servant: for H3478
147: 2 he gathereth together the outcasts of I. H3478
19 his statutes and his judgments unto I. H3478
148:14 of the children of I, a people near unto H3478
149: 2 Let I rejoice in him that made him: let H3478
Prv 1: 1 of Solomon the son of David, king of I; H3478
Ecc 1:12 I the Preacher was king over I in H3478
Song 3: 7 men *are* about it, of the valiant of I. H3478
Isa 1: 3 master's crib: *but* I doth not know, my H3478
4 the Holy One of I unto anger, they are H3478
24 the mighty One of I, Ah, I will ease me H3478
4: 2 comely for them that are escaped of I. H3478
5: 7 *is* the house of I, and the men of Judah H3478
19 of the Holy One of I draw nigh and H3478
24 despised the word of the Holy One of I. H3478
7: 1 of Remaliah, king of I, went up toward H3478
8:14 both the houses of I, for a gin and for a H3478
18 and for wonders in I from the LORD of H3478
9: 8 into Jacob, and it hath lighted upon I. H3478
12 they shall devour I with open mouth. H3478
14 Therefore the LORD will cut off from I H3478
10:17 And the light of I shall be for a fire, and H3478
20 *that* the remnant of I, and such as are H3478
20 the LORD, the Holy One of I, in truth. H3478
22 For though thy people I be as the sand H3478
11:12 the outcasts of I, and gather together H3478
16 like as it was to I in the day that he H3478
12: 6 *is* the Holy One of I in the midst of thee. H3478
14: 1 will yet choose I, and set them in their H3478
2 and the house of I shall possess them H3478
17: 3 children of I, saith the LORD of hosts. H3478
6 thereof, saith the LORD God of I. H3478
7 shall have respect to the Holy One of I. H3478
9 of I: and there shall be desolation. H3478
19:24 In that day shall I be the third with H3478
25 of my hands, and I mine inheritance. H3478
21:10 the God of I, have I declared unto you. H3478
17 for the LORD God of I hath spoken *it*. H3478
24:15 LORD God of I in the isles of the sea. H3478
27: 6 Jacob to take root: I shall blossom and H3478
12 gathered one by one, O ye children of I. H3478
29:19 men shall rejoice in the Holy One of I. H3478
23 of Jacob, and shall fear the God of I. H3478
30:11 Holy One of I to cease from before us. H3478
12 Wherefore thus saith the Holy One of I, H3478
15 the Holy One of I; In returning and rest H3478
29 of the LORD, to the mighty One of I. H3478
31: 1 Holy One of I, neither seek the LORD! H3478
6 the children of I have deeply revolted. H3478
37:16 O LORD of hosts, God of I, that dwellest H3478
21 the LORD God of I, Whereas thou hast H3478
23 on high? *even* against the Holy One of I. H3478
40:27 and speakest, O I, My way is hid from H3478
41: 8 But thou, I, *art* my servant, Jacob whom H3478
14 *and* ye men of I; I will help thee, saith H3478
14 and thy redeemer, the Holy One of I. H3478
16 *and* shalt glory in the Holy One of I. H3478
17 I the God of I will not forsake them. H3478
20 and the Holy One of I hath created it. H3478
42:24 Who gave Jacob for a spoil, and I to the H3478
43: 1 formed thee, O I, Fear not: for I have H3478
3 the Holy One of I, thy Saviour: I gave H3478
14 the Holy One of I; For your sake I have H3478
15 Holy One, the creator of I, your King. H3478
22 but thou hast been weary of me, O I. H3478
28 Jacob to the curse, and I to reproaches. H3478
44: 1 my servant; and I, whom I have chosen: H3478
5 and surname *himself* by the name of I. H3478
6 Thus saith the LORD the King of I, and H3478
21 Remember these, O Jacob and I; for H3478
21 O I, thou shalt not be forgotten of me. H3478
23 Jacob, and glorified himself in I. H3478
45: 3 call *thee* by thy name, *am* the God of I. H3478
4 For Jacob my servant's sake, and I H3478

Isa 45:11 Thus saith the LORD, the Holy One of I, H3478
15 hidest thyself, O God of I, the Saviour. H3478
17 *But* I shall be saved in the LORD with H3478
25 In the LORD shall all the seed of I be H3478
46: 3 of the house of I, which are borne *by* H3478
13 place salvation in Zion for I my glory. H3478
47: 4 of hosts *is* his name, the Holy One of I. H3478
48: 1 by the name of I, and are come forth H3478
1 I, *but* not in truth, nor in righteousness. H3478
2 of I; The LORD of hosts *is* his name. H3478
12 Hearken unto me, O Jacob and I, my H3478
17 the Holy One of I; I *am* the LORD thy H3478
49: 3 servant, O I, in whom I will be glorified. H3478
5 to him, Though I be not gathered, yet H3478
6 the preserved of I: I will also give thee H3478
7 the Redeemer of I, *and* his Holy One, to H3478
7 Holy One of I, and he shall choose thee. H3478
52:12 and the God of I *will be* your rearward. H3478
54: 5 the Holy One of I; The God of the whole H3478
55: 5 Holy One of I; for he hath glorified thee. H3478
56: 8 the outcasts of I saith, Yet will I gather H3478
60: 9 One of I, because he hath glorified thee. H3478
14 LORD, The Zion of the Holy One of I. H3478
63: 7 the house of I, which he hath bestowed H3478
16 of us, and I acknowledge us not: H3478
66:20 as the children of I bring an offering in H3478
Jer 2: 3 I *was* holiness unto the LORD, *and the* H3478
4 and all the families of the house of I: H3478
14 *Is* I a servant? *is* he a homeborn *slave*? H3478
26 so is the house of I ashamed; they, H3478
31 a wilderness unto I? a land of darkness? H3478
3: 6 which backsliding I hath done? she is H3478
8 backsliding I committed adultery H3478
11 The backsliding I hath justified herself H3478
12 thou backsliding I, saith the LORD; *and* H3478
18 with the house of I, and they shall come H3478
20 with me, O house of I, saith the LORD. H3478
21 of the children of I: for they have H3478
23 the LORD our God *is* the salvation of I. H3478
4: 1 If thou wilt return, O I, saith the LORD, H3478
5:11 For the house of I and the house of H3478
15 far, O house of I, saith the LORD: it *is* H3478
6: 9 the remnant of I as a vine: turn back H3478
7: 3 of hosts, the God of I, Amend your ways H3478
12 to it for the wickedness of my people I. H3478
21 of hosts, the God of I; Put your burnt H3478
9:15 of hosts, the God of I; Behold, I will feed H3478
26 of I *are* uncircumcised in the heart. H3478
10: 1 LORD speaketh unto you, O house of I: H3478
16 of all *things*; and I *is* the rod of his H3478
11: 3 the LORD God of I; Cursed *be* the man H3478
10 them: the house of I and the house of H3478
17 evil of the house of I and of the house H3478
12:14 caused my people I to inherit; Behold, I H3478
13:11 me the whole house of I and the whole H3478
12 the LORD God of I, Every bottle shall be H3478
14: 8 O the hope of I, the saviour thereof in H3478
16: 9 hosts, the God of I; Behold, I will cause H3478
14 children of I out of the land of Egypt; H3478
15 up the children of I from the land of the H3478
17:13 O LORD, the hope of I, all that forsake H3478
18: 6 O house of I, cannot I do with you as H3478
6 so *are* ye in mine hand, O house of I. H3478
13 of I hath done a very horrible thing. H3478
19: 3 hosts, the God of I; Behold, I will bring H3478
15 hosts, the God of I; Behold, I will bring H3478
21: 4 Thus saith the LORD God of I; Behold, I H3478
23: 2 Therefore thus saith the LORD God of I H3478
6 In his days Judah shall be saved, and I H3478
7 children of I out of the land of Egypt; H3478
8 seed of the house of I out of the north H3478
13 in Baal, and caused my people I to err. H3478
24: 5 Thus saith the LORD, the God of I; Like H3478
25:15 For thus saith the LORD God of I unto H3478
27 of hosts, the God of I; Drink ye, and be H3478
27: 4 I; Thus shall ye say unto your masters; H3478
21 of hosts, the God of I, concerning the H3478
28: 2 of hosts, the God of I, saying, I have H3478
14 hosts, the God of I; I have put a yoke of H3478
29: 4 of hosts, the God of I, unto all that are H3478
8 of hosts, the God of I; Let not your H3478
21 of hosts, the God of I, of Ahab the son of H3478
23 villany in I, and have committed H3478
25 of hosts, the God of I, saying, Because H3478
30: 2 Thus speaketh the LORD God of I, H3478
3 of my people I and Judah, saith the H3478
4 concerning I and concerning Judah. H3478
10 be dismayed, O I: for, lo, I will save thee H3478
31: 1 of I, and they shall be my people. H3478

Jer 31: 2 *even* I, when I went to cause him to rest. H3478
4 built, O virgin of I: thou shalt again be H3478
7 save thy people, the remnant of I. H3478
9 to I, and Ephraim *is* my firstborn. H3478
10 He that scattered I will gather him, and H3478
21 virgin of I, turn again to these thy cities. H3478
23 hosts, the God of I; As yet they shall use H3478
27 will sow the house of I and the house of H3478
31 house of I, and with the house of Judah: H3478
33 with the house of I; After those days, H3478
36 *then* the seed of I also shall cease from H3478
37 off all the seed of I for all that they have H3478
32:14 of hosts, the God of I; Take these H3478
15 of hosts, the God of I; Houses and fields H3478
20 this day, and in I, and among *other* H3478
21 And hast brought forth thy people I out H3478
30 For the children of I and the children of H3478
30 youth: for the children of I have only H3478
32 of the children of I and of the children H3478
36 the LORD, the God of I, concerning this H3478
33: 4 For thus saith the LORD, the God of I, H3478
7 and the captivity of I to return, and will H3478
14 house of I and to the house of Judah. H3478
17 to sit upon the throne of the house of I; H3478
34: 2 Thus saith the LORD, the God of I; Go H3478
13 Thus saith the LORD, the God of I; I H3478
35:13 hosts, the God of I; Go and tell the men H3478
17 hosts, the God of I; Behold, I will bring H3478
18 of hosts, the God of I; Because ye have H3478
19 hosts, the God of I; Jonadab the son of H3478
36: 2 unto thee against I, and against Judah, H3478
37: 7 Thus saith the LORD, the God of I; Thus H3478
38:17 of hosts, the God of I; If thou wilt H3478
39:16 hosts, the God of I; Behold, I will bring H3478
41: 9 of Baasha king of I: *and* Ishmael the H3478
42: 9 LORD, the God of I, unto whom ye sent H3478
15 hosts, the God of I; If ye wholly set your H3478
18 hosts, the God of I; As mine anger and H3478
43:10 hosts, the God of I; Behold, I will send H3478
44: 2 hosts, the God of I; Ye have seen all the H3478
7 hosts, the God of I; Wherefore commit H3478
11 hosts, the God of I; Behold, I will set my H3478
25 hosts, the God of I, saying; Ye and your H3478
45: 2 Thus saith the LORD, the God of I, unto H3478
46:25 The LORD of hosts, the God of I, saith; H3478
27 be not dismayed, O I: for, behold, I will H3478
48: 1 hosts, the God of I; Woe unto Nebo! for H3478
13 as the house of I was ashamed of H3478
27 For was not I a derision unto thee? was H3478
49: 1 the LORD; Hath I no sons? hath he no H3478
2 fire: then shall I be heir unto them that H3478
50: 4 the children of I shall come, they and H3478
17 I *is* a scattered sheep; the lions have H3478
18 hosts, the God of I; Behold, I will punish H3478
19 And I will bring I again to his H3478
20 the iniquity of I shall be sought for, H3478
29 the LORD, against the Holy One of I. H3478
33 The children of I and the children of H3478
51: 5 For I *hath* not *been* forsaken, nor H3478
5 filled with sin against the Holy One of I. H3478
19 of all things: and I *is* the rod of his H3478
33 of hosts, the God of I; The daughter of H3478
49 As Babylon *hath caused* the slain of I H3478
Lam 2: 1 the beauty of I, and remembered not H3478
3 all the horn of I: he hath drawn back H3478
5 swallowed up I, he hath swallowed up H3478
Ezk 2: 3 thee to the children of I, to a rebellious H3478
3: 1 roll, and go speak unto the house of I. H3478
4 I, and speak with my words unto them. H3478
5 an hard language, *but* to the house of I; H3478
7 But the house of I will not hearken H3478
7 of I *are* impudent and hardhearted. H3478
17 unto the house of I: therefore hear the H3478
4: 3 it. This *shall be* a sign to the house of I. H3478
4 of the house of I upon it: *according* to H3478
5 thou bear the iniquity of the house of I. H3478
13 the children of I eat their defiled bread H3478
5: 4 a fire come forth into all the house of I. H3478
6: 2 of I, and prophesy against them, H3478
3 And say, Ye mountains of I, hear the H3478
5 of the children of I before their idols; H3478
11 of the house of I! for they shall fall by H3478
7: 2 unto the land of I; An end, the end is H3478
8: 4 And, behold, the glory of the God of I H3478
6 that the house of I committeth here, H3478
10 of the house of I, pourtrayed upon the H3478
11 of the house of I, and in the midst of H3478
12 of the house of I do in the dark, every H3478
9: 3 And the glory of the God of I was gone H3478

Ezk 9: 8 all the residue of I in thy pouring out of H3478
9 iniquity of the house of I and Judah *is* H3478
10:19 of the God of I *was* over them above. H3478
20 saw under the God of I by the river of H3478
11: 5 ye said, O house of I: for I know the H3478
10 in the border of I; and ye shall know H3478
11 *but* I will judge you in the border of I: H3478
13 make a full end of the remnant of I? H3478
15 all the house of I wholly, *are* they unto H3478
17 and I will give you the land of I. H3478
22 of the God of I *was* over them above. H3478
12: 6 set thee *for* a sign unto the house of I. H3478
9 Son of man, hath not the house of I, the H3478
10 all the house of I that *are* among them. H3478
19 *and* of the land of I; They shall eat their H3478
22 have in the land of I, saying, The days H3478
23 it as a proverb in I; but say unto them, H3478
24 divination within the house of I. H3478
27 *of* the house of I say, The vision that H3478
13: 2 the prophets of I that prophesy, and H3478
4 O I, thy prophets are like the foxes in H3478
5 for the house of I to stand in the battle H3478
9 of the house of I, neither shall they H3478
9 into the land of I; and ye shall know H3478
16 *To wit*, the prophets of I which H3478
14: 1 Then came certain of the elders of I H3478
4 of the house of I that setteth up his H3478
5 That I may take the house of I in their H3478
6 Therefore say unto the house of I, Thus H3478
7 For every one of the house of I, or of the H3478
7 that sojourneth in I, which separateth H3478
9 him from the midst of my people I. H3478
11 That the house of I may go no more H3478
17: 2 and speak a parable unto the house of I; H3478
23 In the mountain of the height of I will I H3478
18: 2 the land of I, saying, The fathers H3478
3 any more to use this proverb in I. H3478
6 of the house of I, neither hath defiled H3478
15 I, hath not defiled his neighbour's wife, H3478
25 now, O house of I; Is not my way equal? H3478
29 Yet saith the house of I, The way of the H3478
29 not equal. O house of I, are not my ways H3478
30 Therefore I will judge you, O house of I, H3478
31 spirit: for why will ye die, O house of I? H3478
19: 1 up a lamentation for the princes of I, H3478
9 more be heard upon the mountains of I. H3478
20: 1 of the elders of I came to inquire of the H3478
3 Son of man, speak unto the elders of I, H3478
5 day when I chose I, and lifted up mine H3478
13 But the house of I rebelled against me H3478
27 unto the house of I, and say unto them, H3478
30 Wherefore say unto the house of I, Thus H3478
31 by you, O house of I? *As* I live, saith the H3478
38 into the land of I: and ye shall know H3478
39 As for you, O house of I, thus saith the H3478
40 of the height of I, saith the Lord GOD, H3478
40 shall all the house of I, all of them in the H3478
42 into the land of I, into the country *for* H3478
44 O ye house of I, saith the Lord GOD. H3478
21: 2 and prophesy against the land of I, H3478
3 And say to the land of I, Thus saith the H3478
12 all the princes of I: terrors by reason of H3478
25 And thou, profane wicked prince of I, H3478
22: 6 Behold, the princes of I, every one were H3478
18 Son of man, the house of I is to me H3478
24:21 Speak unto the house of I, Thus saith H3478
25: 3 and against the land of I, when it was H3478
6 all thy despite against the land of I; H3478
14 hand of my people I: and they shall do H3478
27:17 Judah, and the land of I, they *were* thy H3478
28:24 unto the house of I, nor *any* grieving H3478
25 the house of I from the people among H3478
29: 6 been a staff of reed to the house of I. H3478
16 of the house of I, which bringeth *their* H3478
21 of the house of I to bud forth, and I will H3478
33: 7 unto the house of I; therefore thou shalt H3478
10 unto the house of I; Thus ye speak, H3478
11 ways; for why will ye die, O house of I? H3478
20 O ye house of I, I will judge you every H3478
24 of the land of I speak, saying, Abraham H3478
28 the mountains of I shall be desolate, H3478
34: 2 the shepherds of I, prophesy, and say H3478
2 to the shepherds of I that do feed H3478
13 the mountains of I by the rivers, and in H3478
14 high mountains of I shall their fold be: H3478
14 shall they feed upon the mountains of I. H3478
30 of I, *are* my people, saith the Lord GOD. H3478
35: 5 *of* the children of I by the force of the H3478
12 the mountains of I, saying, They are H3478

Ezk 35:15 of the house of I, because it was H3478
36: 1 unto the mountains of I, and say, Ye H3478
1 of I, hear the word of the LORD: H3478
4 Therefore, ye mountains of I, hear the H3478
6 the land of I, and say unto the H3478
8 But ye, O mountains of I, ye shall shoot H3478
8 of I; for they are at hand to come. H3478
10 all the house of I, *even* all of it: and the H3478
12 you, *even* my people I; and they shall H3478
17 Son of man, when the house of I dwelt H3478
21 which the house of I had profaned H3478
22 Therefore say unto the house of I, Thus H3478
22 sakes, O house of I, but for mine holy H3478
32 for your own ways, O house of I. H3478
37 of by the house of I, to do *it* for them; I H3478
37:11 the whole house of I: behold, they say, H3478
12 graves, and bring you into the land of I. H3478
16 for the children of I his companions: H3478
16 *for* all the house of I his companions: H3478
19 and the tribes of I his fellows, and will H3478
21 take the children of I from among the H3478
22 the mountains of I; and one king shall H3478
28 LORD do sanctify I, when my sanctuary H3478
38: 8 the mountains of I, which have been H3478
14 my people of I dwelleth safely, shalt H3478
16 my people of I, as a cloud to cover the H3478
17 the prophets of I, which prophesied in H3478
18 against the land of I, saith the Lord H3478
19 shall be a great shaking in the land of I; H3478
39: 2 will bring thee upon the mountains of I: H3478
4 Thou shalt fall upon the mountains of I, H3478
7 of my people I; and I will not *let them* H3478
7 that I *am* the LORD, the Holy One in I. H3478
9 And they that dwell in the cities of I H3478
11 there of graves in I, the valley of the H3478
12 And seven months shall the house of I H3478
17 the mountains of I, that ye may eat H3478
22 So the house of I shall know that I *am* H3478
23 that the house of I went into captivity H3478
25 I, and will be jealous for my holy name; H3478
29 the house of I, saith the Lord GOD. H3478
40: 2 me into the land of I, and set me upon a H3478
4 all that thou seest to the house of I. H3478
43: 2 And, behold, the glory of the God of I H3478
7 of the children of I for ever, and my H3478
7 shall the house of I no more defile, H3478
10 to the house of I, that they may be H3478
44: 2 LORD, the God of I, hath entered in by H3478
6 to the house of I, Thus saith the Lord H3478
6 O ye house of I, let it suffice you of all H3478
9 stranger that *is* among the children of I. H3478
10 far from me, when I went astray, which H3478
12 the house of I to fall into iniquity; H3478
15 the children of I went astray from me, H3478
22 of I, or a widow that had a priest before. H3478
28 possession in I: I *am* their possession. H3478
29 dedicated thing in I shall be theirs. H3478
45: 6 it shall be for the whole house of I. H3478
8 In the land shall be his possession in I: H3478
8 the house of I according to their tribes. H3478
9 you, O princes of I: remove violence and H3478
15 the fat pastures of I; for a meat offering, H3478
16 give this oblation for the prince in I. H3478
17 of the house of I: he shall prepare the H3478
17 make reconciliation for the house of I. H3478
47:13 of I: Joseph *shall have two* portions. H3478
18 from the land of I *by* Jordan, from the H3478
21 unto you according to the tribes of I. H3478
22 among the children of I; they shall have H3478
22 with you among the tribes of I. H3478
48:11 the children of I went astray, as the H3478
19 shall serve it out of all the tribes of I. H3478
29 unto the tribes of I for inheritance, and H3478
31 of the tribes of I: three gates northward; H3478
Dan 1: 3 of the children of I, and of the king's H3478
9: 7 and unto all I, *that are* near, and *that* H3478
11 Yea, all I have transgressed thy law, H3478
20 sin of my people I, and presenting my H3478
Hos 1: 1 of Jeroboam the son of Joash, king of I. H3478
4 to cease the kingdom of the house of I. H3478
5 the bow of I in the valley of Jezreel. H3478
6 of I; but I will utterly take them away. H3478
10 Yet the number of the children of I H3478
11 the children of I be gathered together, H3478
3: 1 the children of I, who look to other H3478
4 For the children of I shall abide many H3478
5 Afterward shall the children of I H3478
4: 1 ye children of I: for the LORD hath a H3478
15 Though thou, I, play the harlot, *yet* let H3478

Hos 4:16 For I slideth back as a backsliding H3478
5: 1 ye house of I; and give ye ear, O house H3478
3 I know Ephraim, and I is not hid from H3478
3 committest whoredom, *and* I is defiled. H3478
5 And the pride of I doth testify to his H3478
5 therefore shall I and Ephraim fall in H3478
9 the tribes of I have I made known H3478
6:10 in the house of I: there *is* the whoredom H3478
10 the whoredom of Ephraim, I is defiled. H3478
7: 1 When I would have healed I, then the H3478
10 And the pride of I testifieth to his face: H3478
8: 2 I shall cry unto me, My God, we know H3478
3 I hath cast off *the thing that is* good: H3478
6 For from I *was* it also: the workman H3478
8 I is swallowed up: now shall they be H3478
14 For I hath forgotten his Maker, and H3478
9: 1 Rejoice not, O I, for joy, as *other* people: H3478
7 are come; I shall know *it*: the prophet H3478
10 I found I like grapes in the wilderness; H3478
10: 1 I *is* an empty vine, he bringeth forth H3478
6 I shall be ashamed of his own counsel. H3478
8 of Aven, the sin of I, shall be destroyed: H3478
9 O I, thou hast sinned from the days of H3478
15 shall the king of I utterly be cut off. H3478
11: 1 When I *was* a child, then I loved him, H3478
8 I deliver thee, I? how shall I make thee H3478
12 lies, and the house of I with deceit: but H3478
12:12 of Syria, and I served for a wife, and H3478
13 And by a prophet the LORD brought I H3478
13: 1 he exalted himself in I; but when he H3478
9 O I, thou hast destroyed thyself; but in H3478
14: 1 O I, return unto the LORD thy God; for H3478
5 I will be as the dew unto I: he shall grow H3478
Joel 2:27 I *am* in the midst of I, and *that* I *am* the H3478
3: 2 and *for* my heritage I, whom they have H3478
16 and the strength of the children of I. H3478
Am 1: 1 he saw concerning I in the days of H3478
1 of I, two years before the earthquake. H3478
2: 6 transgressions of I, and for four, I will H3478
11 thus, O ye children of I? saith the LORD. H3478
3: 1 you, O children of I, against the whole H3478
12 the children of I be taken out that dwell H3478
14 transgressions of I upon him I will also H3478
4: 5 O ye children of I, saith the Lord GOD. H3478
12 Therefore thus will I do unto thee, O I: H3478
12 unto thee, prepare to meet thy God, O I. H3478
5: 1 you, *even* a lamentation, O house of I. H3478
2 The virgin of I is fallen; she shall no H3478
3 shall leave ten, to the house of I. H3478
4 house of I, Seek ye me, and ye shall live: H3478
25 the wilderness forty years, O house of I? H3478
6: 1 nations, to whom the house of I came! H3478
14 nation, O house of I, saith the LORD the H3478
7: 8 of my people I: I will not again pass H3478
9 the sanctuaries of I shall be laid waste; H3478
10 Jeroboam king of I, saying, Amos hath H3478
10 of the house of I: the land is not able H3478
11 by the sword, and I shall surely be led H3478
15 me, Go, prophesy unto my people I. H3478
16 not against I, and drop not *thy word* H3478
17 polluted land: and I shall surely go into H3478
8: 2 upon my people of I; I will not again H3478
9: 7 me, O children of I? saith the LORD. H3478
7 not I brought up I out of the land of H3478
9 sift the house of I among all nations, H3478
14 of my people of I, and they shall build H3478
Oba 20 of the children of I *shall possess* that of H3478
Mic 1: 5 sins of the house of I. What *is* the H3478
13 transgressions of I were found in thee. H3478
14 of Achzib *shall be* a lie to the kings of I. H3478
15 shall come unto Adullam the glory of I. H3478
2:12 gather the remnant of I; I will put them H3478
3: 1 of I; *Is it* not for you to know judgment? H3478
8 his transgression, and to I his sin. H3478
9 of the house of I, that abhor judgment, H3478
5: 1 judge of I with a rod upon the cheek. H3478
2 *is* to be ruler in I; whose goings forth H3478
3 shall return unto the children of I. H3478
6: 2 his people, and he will plead with I. H3478
Nah 2: 2 as the excellency of I: for the emptiers H3478
Zep 2: 9 of hosts, the God of I, Surely Moab shall H3478
3:13 The remnant of I shall not do iniquity, H3478
14 Sing, O daughter of Zion; shout, O I; be H3478
15 enemy: the king of I, *even* the LORD, *is* H3478
Zec 1:19 have scattered Judah, I, and Jerusalem. H3478
8:13 and house of I; so will I save you, and H3478
9: 1 tribes of I, *shall be* toward the LORD. H3478
11:14 the brotherhood between Judah and I. H3478
12: 1 word of the LORD for I, saith the LORD, H3478
Mal 1: 1 the word of the LORD to I by Malachi. H3478
5 will be magnified from the border of I. H3478
2:11 is committed in I and in Jerusalem; for H3478
16 For the LORD, the God of I, saith that H3478
4: 4 all I, *with* the statutes and judgments. H3478
Mt 2: 6 a Governor, that shall rule my people I. G2474
20 go into the land of I: for they are dead G2474
21 his mother, and came into the land of I. G2474
8:10 not found so great faith, no, not in I. G2474
9:33 saying, It was never so seen in I. G2474
10: 6 rather to the lost sheep of the house of I. G2474
23 cities of I, till the Son of man be come. G2474
15:24 but unto the lost sheep of the house of I. G2474
31 to see: and they glorified the God of I. G2474
19:28 thrones, judging the twelve tribes of I. G2474
27: 9 they of the children of I did value; G2474
42 If he be the King of I, let him now come G2474
Mk 12:29 O I; The Lord our God is one Lord: G2474
15:32 Let Christ the King of I descend now G2474
Lk 1:16 And many of the children of I shall he G2474
54 He hath holpen his servant I, in G2474
68 Blessed *be* the Lord God of I; for he hath G2474
80 till the day of his shewing unto I. G2474
2:25 of I: and the Holy Ghost was upon him. G2474
32 Gentiles, and the glory of thy people I. G2474
34 again of many in I; and for a sign which G2474
4:25 widows were in I in the days of Elias, G2474
27 And many lepers were in I in the time G2474
7: 9 not found so great faith, no, not in I. G2474
22:30 thrones judging the twelve tribes of I. G2474
24:21 have redeemed I: and beside all this, to G2474
Jn 1:31 be made manifest to I, therefore am I G2474
49 the Son of God; thou art the King of I. G2474
3:10 of I, and knowest not these things? G2474
12:13 I that cometh in the name of the Lord. G2474
Act 1: 6 time restore again the kingdom to I? G2474
2:22 Ye men of I, hear these words; Jesus of G2475
36 Therefore let all the house of I know G2474
3:12 people, Ye men of I, why marvel ye at G2475
4: 8 Ye rulers of the people, and elders of I, G2474
10 to all the people of I, that by the name G2474
27 the people of I, were gathered together, G2474
5:21 of the children of I, and sent to the G2474
31 repentance to I, and forgiveness of sins. G2474
35 And said unto them, Ye men of I, take G2475
7:23 to visit his brethren the children of I. G2474
37 the children of I, A prophet shall the G2474
42 O ye house of I, have ye offered to me G2474
9:15 and kings, and the children of I: G2474
10:36 the children of I, preaching peace by G2474
13:16 I, and ye that fear God, give audience. G2475
17 The God of this people of I chose our G2474
23 promise raised unto I a Saviour, Jesus: G2474
24 of repentance to all the people of I. G2474
21:28 Crying out, Men of I, help: This is the G2475
28:20 hope of I I am bound with this chain. G2474
Ro 9: 6 they *are* not all I, which are of Israel: G2474
6 they *are* not all Israel, which are of I: G2474
27 Esaias also crieth concerning I, Though G2474
27 of the children of I be as the sand of the G2474
31 But I, which followed after the law of G2474
10: 1 God for I is, that they might be saved. G2474
19 But I say, Did not I know? First Moses G2474
21 But to I he saith, All day long I have G2474
11: 2 intercession to God against I, saying, G2474
7 What then? I hath not obtained that G2474
25 is happened to I, until the fulness of the G2474
26 And so all I shall be saved: as it is G2474
1Co 10:18 Behold I after the flesh: are not they G2474
2Co 3: 7 the children of I could not stedfastly G2474
13 the children of I could not stedfastly G2474
Gal 6:16 and mercy, and upon the I of God. G2474
Eph 2:12 commonwealth of I, and strangers from G2474
Php 3: 5 day, of the stock of I, *of* the tribe of G2474
Heb 8: 8 house of I and with the house of Judah: G2474
10 with the house of I after those days, G2474
11:22 departing of the children of I; and gave G2474
Rev 2:14 the children of I, to eat things sacrificed G2474
7: 4 of all the tribes of the children of I. G2474
21:12 of the twelve tribes of the children of I: G2474

ISRAELITE

Nu 25:14 Now the name of the I that was slain, H3478
2Sa 17:25 *was* Ithra an I, that went in to Abigail H3481
Jn 1:47 an I indeed, in whom is no guile! G2475
Ro 11: 1 forbid. For I also am an I, of the seed of G2475

ISRAELITES

Ex 9: 7 one of the cattle of the I dead. And the H3478
Lev 23:42 all that are I born shall dwell in booths: H3478
Jos 3:17 Jordan, and all the I passed over on dry H3478
8:24 that all the I returned unto Ai, and H3478
13: 6 it by lot unto the I for an inheritance, H3478
13 dwell among the I until this day. H3478
Jdg 20:21 the ground of the I that day twenty and H3478
1Sa 2:14 Shiloh unto all the I that came thither. H3478
13:20 But all the I went down to the H3478
14:21 the I that *were* with Saul and Jonathan. H3478
25: 1 And Samuel died; and all the I were H3478
29: 1 armies to Aphek: and the I pitched by a H3478
2Sa 4: 1 were feeble, and all the I were troubled. H3478
2Ki 3:24 camp of Israel, the I rose up and smote H3478
7:13 multitude of the I that are consumed:) H3478
1Ch 9: 2 cities *were*, the I, the priests, Levites, H3478
Ro 9: 4 Who are I; to whom *pertaineth* the G2475
2Co 11:22 Are they Hebrews? so *am* I. Are they I? G2475

ISRAELITISH

Lev 24:10 And the son of an I woman, whose H3482
10 and this son of the I *woman* and a man H3482
11 And the I woman's son blasphemed the H3482

ISRAEL'S

Gen 48:13 his right hand toward I left hand, and H3478
13 his left hand toward I right hand, and H3478
Ex 18: 8 to the Egyptians for I sake, *and* all the H3478
Nu 1:20 And the children of Reuben, I eldest H3478
31:30 And of the children of I half, thou shalt H3478
42 And of the children of I half, which H3478
47 Even of the children of I half, Moses H3478
Dt 21: 8 unto thy people of I charge. And the H3478
2Sa 5:12 his kingdom for his people I sake. H3478
2Ki 3:11 one of the king of I servants answered H3478

ISSACHAR

Gen 30:18 my husband: and she called his name I. H3485
35:23 Levi, and Judah, and I, and Zebulun: H3485
46:13 And the sons of I; Tola, and Phuvah, H3485
49:14 I *is* a strong ass couching down H3485
Ex 1: 3 I, Zebulun, and Benjamin, H3485
Nu 1: 8 Of I; Nethaneel the son of Zuar. H3485
28 Of the children of I, by their H3485
29 *even* of the tribe of I, *were* fifty and four H3485
2: 5 *be* the tribe of I: and Nethaneel the son H3485
5 *shall be* captain of the children of I. H3485
7:18 the son of Zuar, prince of I, did offer: H3485
10:15 of I *was* Nethaneel the son of Zuar. H3485
13: 7 Of the tribe of I, Igal the son of Joseph. H3485
26:23 *Of* the sons of I after their families: *of* H3485
25 These *are* the families of I according to H3485
34:26 children of I, Paltiel the son of Azzan. H3485
Dt 27:12 and I, and Joseph, and Benjamin: H3485
33:18 in thy going out; and, I, in thy tents. H3485
Jos 17:10 on the north, and in I on the east. H3485
11 And Manasseh had in I and in Asher H3485
19:17 *And* the fourth lot came out to I, for the H3485
17 of I according to their families. H3485
23 of the children of I according to their H3485
21: 6 of the tribe of I, and out of the tribe H3485
28 And out of the tribe of I, Kishon with H3485
Jdg 5:15 And the princes of I *were* with H3485
15 Deborah; even I, and also Barak: he H3485
10: 1 son of Dodo, a man of I; and he dwelt in H3485
1Ki 4:17 Jehoshaphat the son of Paruah, in I: H3485
15:27 of the house of I, conspired against H3485
1Ch 2: 1 Levi, and Judah, I, and Zebulun, H3485
6:62 out of the tribe of I, and out of the tribe H3485
72 And out of the tribe of I; Kedesh with H3485
7: 1 Now the sons of I *were*, Tola, and H3485
5 all the families of I *were* valiant men of H3485
12:32 And of the children of I, *which were* H3485
40 them, *even* unto I and Zebulun and H3485
26: 5 Ammiel the sixth, I the seventh, H3485
27:18 of David: of I, Omri the son of Michael: H3485
2Ch 30:18 and Manasseh, I, and Zebulun, had not H3485
Ezk 48:25 side unto the west side, I a *portion*. H3485
26 And by the border of I, from the east H3485
33 one gate of I, one gate of Zebulun. H3485
Rev 7: 7 tribe of I *were* sealed twelve thousand. G2466

ISSHIAH

1Ch 24:21 of the sons of Rehabiah, the first *was* I. H3449
25 The brother of Michah *was* I: of the H3449
25 *was* Isshiah: of the sons of I; Zechariah. H3449

ISSUE

Gen 48: 6 And thy i, which thou begettest after H4138
Lev 12: 7 cleansed from the i of her blood. This *is* H4726

Lev 15: 2 man hath a running **i** out of his flesh, H2100
2 his flesh, *because of* his **i** he *is* unclean. H2101
3 uncleanness in his **i**: whether his flesh H2101
3 his flesh run with his **i**, or his flesh be H2101
3 stopped from his **i**, it *is* his uncleanness. H2101
4 he lieth that hath the **i**, is unclean: and H2100
6 he sat that hath the **i** shall wash his H2100
7 of him that hath the **i** shall wash his H2100
8 And if he that hath the **i** spit upon him H2100
9 upon that hath the **i** shall be unclean. H2100
11 that hath the **i**, and hath not rinsed H2100
12 which hath the **i**, shall be broken: and H2100
13 And when he that hath an **i** is cleansed H2100
13 issue is cleansed of his **i**; then he shall H2101
15 for him before the LORD for his **i**. H2101
19 And if a woman have an **i**, *and* her H2100
19 have an issue, *and* her **i** in her flesh be H2101
25 And if a woman have an **i** of her blood H2101
25 all the days of the **i** of her uncleanness H2101
26 all the days of her **i** shall be unto her as H2101
28 But if she be cleansed of her **i**, then she H2101
30 the LORD for the **i** of her uncleanness. H2101
32 This *is* the law of him that hath an **i**, H2100
33 of him that hath an **i**, of the man, and of H2101
22: 4 or hath a running **i**; he shall not eat of H2100
Nu 5: 2 **i**, and whosoever is defiled by the dead: H2100
2Sa 3:29 one that hath an **i**, or that is a leper, or H2100
2Ki 20:18 And of thy sons that shall **i** from thee, H3318
Isa 22:24 offspring and the **i**, all vessels of small H6849
39: 7 And of thy sons that shall **i** from thee, H3318
Ezk 23:20 and whose **i** *is like* the issue of horses. H2231
20 and whose issue *is like* the **i** of horses. H2231
47: 8 Then said he unto me, These waters **i** H3318
Mt 9:20 diseased with an **i** of blood twelve years, *G131*
22:25 no **i**, left his wife unto his brother: *G4690*
Mk 5:25 And a certain woman, which had an **i** *G4511*
Lk 8:43 And a woman having an **i** of blood *G4511*
44 immediately her **i** of blood stanched. *G4511*

ISSUED
Jos 8:22 And the other **i** out of the city against H3318
Job 38: 8 forth, *as if* it had **i** out of the womb? H3318
Ezk 47: 1 behold, waters **i** out from under the H3318
12 their waters they **i** out of the sanctuary: H3318
Dan 7:10 A fiery stream **i** and came forth from H5047
Rev 9:17 **i** fire and smoke and brimstone. *G1607*
18 brimstone, which **i** out of their mouths. *G1607*

ISSUES
Ps 68:20 GOD the Lord *belong* the **i** from death. H8444
Prv 4:23 diligence; for out of it *are* the **i** of life. H8444

ISUAH
1Ch 7:30 The sons of Asher; Imnah, and **I**, and H3440

ISUI
Gen 46:17 and Ishuah, and **I**, and Beriah, and H3440

IT See the Appendix.

ITALIAN
Act 10: 1 of the band called the **I** *band*, *G2483*

ITALY
Act 18: 2 lately come from **I**, with his wife *G2482*
27: 1 that we should sail into **I**, they delivered *G2482*
6 sailing into **I**; and he put us therein. *G2482*
Heb 13:24 and all the saints. They of **I** salute you. *G2482*

ITCH
Dt 28:27 the **i**, whereof thou canst not be healed. H2775

ITCHING
2Ti 4: 3 to themselves teachers, having **i** ears; *G2833*

ITHAI
1Ch 11:31 **I** the son of Ribai of Gibeah, *that* H863

ITHAMAR
Ex 6:23 him Nadab, and Abihu, Eleazar, and **I**. H385
28: 1 and Abihu, Eleazar and **I**, Aaron's sons. H385
38:21 by the hand of **I**, son to Aaron the priest. H385
Lev 10: 6 Eleazar and unto **I**, his sons, Uncover not H385
12 Eleazar and unto **I**, his sons that were H385
16 with Eleazar and **I**, the sons of Aaron H385
Nu 3: 2 the firstborn, and Abihu, Eleazar, and **I**. H385
4 and Eleazar and **I** ministered in the H385
4:28 the hand of **I** the son of Aaron the priest. H385
33 the hand of **I** the son of Aaron the priest. H385
7: 8 the hand of **I** the son of Aaron the priest. H385
26:60 born Nadab, and Abihu, Eleazar, and **I**. H385
1Ch 6: 3 Nadab, and Abihu, Eleazar, and **I**. H385
24: 1 Nadab, and Abihu, Eleazar, and **I**. H385
2 Eleazar and **I** executed the priest's office. H385
3 of the sons of **I**, according to their offices H385
4 than of the sons of **I**; and *thus* were they H385
4 **I** according to the house of their fathers. H385
5 the sons of Eleazar, and of the sons of **I**. H385
6 taken for Eleazar, and *one* taken for **I**. H385
Ezr 8: 2 **I**; Daniel: of the sons of David; Hattush. H385

ITHIEL
Neh 11: 7 the son of **I**, the son of Jesaiah. H384
Prv 30: 1 spake unto **I**, even unto Ithiel and Ucal, H384
1 spake unto Ithiel, even unto **I** and Ucal, H384

ITHMAH
1Ch 11:46 the sons of Elnaam, and **I** the Moabite, H3495

ITHNAN
Jos 15:23 And Kedesh, and Hazor, and **I**, H3497

ITHRA
2Sa 17:25 whose name *was* **I** an Israelite, that H3501

ITHRAN
Gen 36:26 and Eshban, and **I**, and Cheran. H3506
1Ch 1:41 and Eshban, and **I**, and Cheran. H3506
7:37 and Shilshah, and **I**, and Beera. H3506

ITHREAM
2Sa 3: 5 And the sixth, **I**, by Eglah David's wife. H3507
1Ch 3: 3 of Abital: the sixth, **I** by Eglah his wife. H3507

ITHRITE
2Sa 23:38 Ira an **I**, Gareb an Ithrite, H3505
38 Ira an Ithrite, Gareb an **I**, H3505
1Ch 11:40 Ira the **I**, Gareb the Ithrite, H3505
40 Ira the Ithrite, Gareb the **I**, H3505

ITHRITES
1Ch 2:53 the **I**, and the Puhites, and H3505

ITS
Lev 25: 5 That which groweth of **i** own accord of

ITSELF See the Appendix.

ITTAH-KAZIN
Jos 19:13 to Gittah-hepher, to **I**, and goeth out to H6278

ITTAI
2Sa 15:19 Then said the king to **I** the Gittite, H863
21 And **I** answered the king, and said, *As* H863
22 And David said to **I**, Go and pass over. H863
22 and pass over. And **I** the Gittite passed H863
18: 2 under the hand of **I** the Gittite. And the H863
5 and Abishai and **I**, saying, *Deal* gently H863
12 and Abishai and **I**, saying, Beware that H863
23:29 a Netophathite, **I** the son of Ribai out H863

ITURAEA
Lk 3: 1 Philip tetrarch of **I** and of the region of *G2484*

IVAH
2Ki 18:34 Hena, and **I**? have they delivered H5755
19:13 the city of Sepharvaim, of Hena, and **I**? H5755
Isa 37:13 of the city of Sepharvaim, Hena, and **I**? H5755

IVORY
1Ki 10:18 of **i**, and overlaid it with the best gold. H8127
22 and silver, **i**, and apes, and peacocks. H8143
22:39 he did, and the **i** house which he made, H8127
2Ch 9:17 of **i**, and overlaid it with pure gold. H8127
21 and silver, **i**, and apes, and peacocks. H8143
Ps 45: 8 cassia, out of the **i** palaces, whereby H8127
Song 5:14 *is as* bright **i** overlaid *with* sapphires. H8127
7: 4 Thy neck *is* as a tower of **i**; thine eyes H8127
Ezk 27: 6 *of* **i**, *brought* out of the isles of Chittim. H8127
15 thee *for* a present horns of **i** and ebony. H8127
Am 3:15 and the houses of **i** shall perish, and H8127
6: 4 That lie upon beds of **i**, and stretch H8127
Rev 18:12 all manner vessels of **i**, and all manner *G1661*

IZEHAR
Nu 3:19 Amram, and **I**, Hebron, and Uzziel. H3324

IZEHARITES
Nu 3:27 the family of the **I**, and the family of the H3325

IZHAR
Ex 6:18 And the sons of Kohath; Amram, and **I**, H3324
21 And the sons of **I**; Korah, and Nepheg, H3324
Nu 16: 1 Now Korah, the son of **I**, the son of H3324
1Ch 6: 2 And the sons of Kohath; Amram, **I**, and H3324
18 Amram, and **I**, and Hebron, and Uzziel. H3324
38 The son of **I**, the son of Kohath, the son H3324
23:12 The sons of Kohath; Amram, **I**, Hebron, H3324
18 Of the sons of **I**; Shelomith the chief. H3324

IZHARITES
1Ch 24:22 Of the **I**; Shelomoth: of the sons of H3325
26:23 Of the Amramites, *and* the **I**, the H3325
29 Of the **I**, Chenaniah and his sons *were* H3325

IZRAHIAH
1Ch 7: 3 And the sons of Uzzi; **I**: and the sons of H3156
3 and the sons of **I**; Michael, and H3156

IZRAHITE
1Ch 27: 8 *was* Shamhuth the **I**: and in his course H3155

IZRI
1Ch 25:11 The fourth to **I**, *he*, his sons, and his H3339

J

JAAKAN
Dt 10: 6 of the children of **J** to Mosera: there H885

JAAKOBAH
1Ch 4:36 And Elioenai, and **J**, and Jeshohaiah, H3291

JAALA
Neh 7:58 The children of **J**, the children of H3279

JAALAH
Ezr 2:56 The children of **J**, the children of H3279

JAALAM
Gen 36: 5 And Aholibamah bare Jeush, and **J**, and H3281
14 bare to Esau Jeush, and **J**, and Korah. H3281
18 duke Jeush, duke **J**, duke Korah: these H3281
1Ch 1:35 Reuel, and Jeush, and **J**, and Korah. H3281

JAAN See DAN-JAAN.

JAANAI
1Ch 5:12 the next, and **J**, and Shaphat in Bashan. H3285

JAARE-OREGIM
2Sa 21:19 Elhanan the son of **J**, a Beth-lehemite, H3296

JAASAU
Ezr 10:37 Mattaniah, Mattenai, and **J**, H3299

JAASIEL
1Ch 27:21 of Benjamin, **J** the son of Abner: H3300

JAAZANIAH
2Ki 25:23 the Netophathite, and **J** the son of a H2970
Jer 35: 3 Then I took **J** the son of Jeremiah, the H2970
Ezk 8:11 of them stood **J** the son of Shaphan, H2970
11: 1 whom I saw **J** the son of Azur, and H2970

JAAZER
Nu 21:32 And Moses sent to spy out **J**, and they H3270

Nu 32:35 And Atroth, Shophan, and J, and H3270

JAAZIAH
1Ch 24:26 Mahli and Mushi: the sons of J; Beno. H3269
27 The sons of Merari by J; Beno, and H3269

JAAZIEL
1Ch 15:18 Ben, and J, and Shemiramoth, H3268

JABAL
Gen 4:20 And Adah bare J: he was the father of H2989

JABBOK
Gen 32:22 eleven sons, and passed over the ford J. H2999
Nu 21:24 land from Arnon unto J, even unto the H2999
Dt 2:37 place of the river J, nor unto the cities in H2999
3:16 unto the river J, *which is* the border H2999
Jos 12: 2 unto the river J, *which is* the border H2999
Jdg 11:13 Arnon even unto J, and unto Jordan: H2999
22 from Arnon even unto J, and from the H2999

JABESH
1Sa 11: 1 and all the men of J said unto Nahash, H3003
3 And the elders of J said unto him, Give H3003
5 told him the tidings of the men of J. H3003
9 *it* to the men of J; and they were glad. H3003
10 Therefore the men of J said, To H3003
31:12 and came to J, and burnt them there. H3003
13 under a tree at J, and fasted seven days. H3003
2Ki 15:10 And Shallum the son of J conspired H3003
13 Shallum the son of J began to reign in H3003
14 Shallum the son of J in Samaria, and H3003
1Ch 10:12 and brought them to J, and buried their H3003
12 the oak in J, and fasted seven days. H3003

JABESH-GILEAD
Jdg 21: 8 camp from J to the assembly. H3003+H1568
9 of the inhabitants of J there. H3003+H1568
10 inhabitants of J with the edge H3003+H1568
12 inhabitants of J four hundred H3003+H1568
14 the women of J: and yet so they H3003+H1568
1Sa 11: 1 against J: and all the men H3003+H1568
9 the men of J, To morrow, by H3003+H1568
31:11 And when the inhabitants of J H3003+H1568
2Sa 2: 4 of J *were they* that buried Saul. H3003+H1568
5 the men of J, and said unto H3003+H1568
21:12 the men of J, which had stolen H3003+H1568
1Ch 10:11 And when all J heard all that H3003+H1568

JABEZ
1Ch 2:55 which dwelt at J; the Tirathites, the H3258
4: 9 And J was more honourable than his H3258
9 called his name J, saying, Because I H3258
10 And J called on the God of Israel, H3258

JABIN
Jos 11: 1 And it came to pass, when J king of H2985
Jdg 4: 2 into the hand of J king of Canaan, that H2985
17 peace between J the king of Hazor and H2985
23 So God subdued on that day J the king H2985
24 prevailed against J the king of Canaan, H2985
24 they had destroyed J king of Canaan. H2985
Ps 83: 9 *to* Sisera, as *to* J, at the brook of Kison: H2985

JABIN'S
Jdg 4: 7 the captain of J army, with his chariots H2985

JABNEEL
Jos 15:11 and went out unto J; and the goings out H2995
19:33 Nekeb, and J, unto Lakum; and the H2995

JABNEH
2Ch 26: 6 Gath, and the wall of J, and the wall of H2996

JACHAN
1Ch 5:13 Jorai, and J, and Zia, and Heber, seven. H3275

JACHIN
Gen 46:10 and Ohad, and J, and Zohar, and Shaul H3199
Ex 6:15 and Ohad, and J, and Zohar, and Shaul H3199
Nu 26:12 of J, the family of the Jachinites: H3199
1Ki 7:21 the name thereof J: and he set up the H3199
1Ch 9:10 priests; Jedaiah, and Jehoiarib, and J, H3199
24:17 The one and twentieth to J, the two and H3199
2Ch 3:17 J, and the name of that on the left Boaz. H3199
Neh 11:10 the priests: Jedaiah the son of Joiarib, J. H3199

JACHINITES
Nu 26:12 Jaminites: of Jachin, the family of the J: H3200

JACINTH
Rev 9:17 of fire, and of j, and brimstone: and *G5191*
21:20 eleventh, a j; the twelfth, an amethyst. *G5192*

JACOB
Gen 25:26 his name was called J: and Isaac *was* H3290
27 J *was* a plain man, dwelling in tents. H3290
28 eat of *his* venison: but Rebekah loved J. H3290
29 And J sod pottage: and Esau came H3290
30 And Esau said to J, Feed me, I pray H3290
31 And J said, Sell me this day thy H3290
33 And J said, Swear to me this day; and H3290
33 him: and he sold his birthright unto J. H3290
34 Then J gave Esau bread and pottage of H3290
27: 6 And Rebekah spake unto J her son, H3290
11 And J said to Rebekah his mother, H3290
15 and put them upon J her younger son: H3290
17 prepared, into the hand of her son J. H3290
19 And J said unto his father, I *am* Esau H3290
21 And Isaac said unto J, Come near, I H3290
22 And J went near unto Isaac his father; H3290
30 an end of blessing J, and Jacob was yet H3290
30 Jacob, and J was yet scarce gone H3290
36 And he said, Is not he rightly named J? H3290
41 And Esau hated J because of the H3290
41 at hand; then will I slay my brother J. H3290
42 sent and called J her younger son, and H3290
46 of Heth: if J take a wife of the daughters H3290
28: 1 And Isaac called J, and blessed him, H3290
5 And Isaac sent away J: and he went to H3290
6 Isaac had blessed J, and sent him away H3290
7 And that J obeyed his father and his H3290
10 And J went out from Beer-sheba, and H3290
16 And J awaked out of his sleep, and he H3290
18 And J rose up early in the morning, H3290
20 And J vowed a vow, saying, If God will H3290
29: 1 Then J went on his journey, and came H3290
4 And J said unto them, My brethren, H3290
10 And it came to pass, when J saw Rachel H3290
10 brother, that J went near, and rolled H3290
11 And J kissed Rachel, and lifted up his H3290
12 And J told Rachel that he *was* her H3290
13 the tidings of J his sister's son, that H3290
15 And Laban said unto J, Because thou H3290
18 And J loved Rachel; and said, I will H3290
20 And J served seven years for Rachel; H3290
21 And J said unto Laban, Give *me* my H3290
28 And J did so, and fulfilled her week: H3290
30: 1 And when Rachel saw that she bare J H3290
1 unto J, Give me children, or else I die. H3290
4 to wife: and J went in unto her. H3290
5 And Bilhah conceived, and bare J a H3290
7 again, and bare J a second son. H3290
9 Zilpah her maid, and gave her J to wife. H3290
10 And Zilpah Leah's maid bare J a son. H3290
12 And Zilpah Leah's maid bare J a H3290
16 And J came out of the field in the H3290
17 she conceived, and bare J the fifth son. H3290
19 And Leah conceived again, and bare J H3290
25 born Joseph, that J said unto Laban, H3290
31 I give thee? And J said, Thou shalt not H3290
36 himself and J: and Jacob fed the rest H3290
36 and J fed the rest of Laban's flocks. H3290
37 And J took him rods of green poplar, H3290
40 And J did separate the lambs, and set H3290
41 did conceive, that J laid the rods before H3290
31: 1 sons, saying, J hath taken away all H3290
2 And J beheld the countenance of H3290
3 And the LORD said unto J, Return unto H3290
4 And J sent and called Rachel and Leah H3290
11 dream, *saying*, J: And I said, Here *am* I. H3290
17 Then J rose up, and set his sons and his H3290
20 And J stole away unawares to Laban H3290
22 Laban on the third day that J was fled. H3290
24 thou speak not to J either good or bad. H3290
25 Then Laban overtook J. Now Jacob had H3290
25 Then Laban overtook Jacob. Now J had H3290
26 And Laban said to J, What hast thou H3290
29 thou speak not to J either good or bad. H3290
31 And J answered and said to Laban, H3290
32 and take *it* to thee. For J knew not that H3290
36 And J was wroth, and chode with H3290
36 with Laban: and J answered and said H3290
43 And Laban answered and said unto J, H3290
45 And J took a stone, and set it up *for* a H3290
46 And J said unto his brethren, Gather H3290
47 Jegar-sahadutha: but J called it Galeed. H3290
51 And Laban said to J, Behold this heap, H3290
53 J sware by the fear of his father Isaac. H3290
Gen 31:54 Then J offered sacrifice upon the H3290
32: 1 And J went on his way, and the angels H3290
2 And when J saw them, he said, This *is* H3290
3 And J sent messengers before him to H3290
4 Esau; Thy servant J saith thus, I have H3290
6 And the messengers returned to J, H3290
7 Then J was greatly afraid and H3290
9 And J said, O God of my father H3290
20 thy servant J *is* behind us. For he H3290
24 And J was left alone; and there H3290
27 him, What *is* thy name? And he said, J. H3290
28 be called no more J, but Israel: for as a H3290
29 And J asked *him*, and said, Tell *me*, I H3290
30 And J called the name of the place H3290
33: 1 And J lifted up his eyes, and looked, H3290
10 And J said, Nay, I pray thee, if now I H3290
17 And J journeyed to Succoth, and built H3290
18 And J came to Shalem, a city of H3290
34: 1 she bare unto J, went out to see the H3290
3 the daughter of J, and he loved the H3290
5 And J heard that he had defiled Dinah H3290
5 J held his peace until they were come. H3290
6 went out unto J to commune with him. H3290
7 And the sons of J came out of the field H3290
13 And the sons of J answered Shechem H3290
25 two of the sons of J, Simeon and Levi, H3290
27 The sons of J came upon the slain, and H3290
30 And J said to Simeon and Levi, Ye have H3290
35: 1 And God said unto J, Arise, go up to H3290
2 Then J said unto his household, and to H3290
4 And they gave unto J all the strange H3290
4 in their ears; and J hid them under the H3290
5 they did not pursue after the sons of J. H3290
6 So J came to Luz, which *is* in the land H3290
9 And God appeared unto J again, when H3290
10 And God said unto him, Thy name *is* J: H3290
10 called any more J, but Israel shall be thy H3290
14 And J set up a pillar in the place where H3290
15 And J called the name of the place H3290
20 And J set a pillar upon her grave: that H3290
22 heard *it*. Now the sons of J were twelve: H3290
26 *are* the sons of J, which were born to H3290
27 And J came unto Isaac his father unto H3290
29 and his sons Esau and J buried him. H3290
36: 6 country from the face of his brother J. H3290
37: 1 And J dwelt in the land wherein his H3290
2 These *are* the generations of J. Joseph, H3290
34 And J rent his clothes, and put H3290
42: 1 Now when J saw that there was corn in H3290
1 was corn in Egypt, J said unto his sons, H3290
4 But Benjamin, Joseph's brother, J sent H3290
29 And they came unto J their father unto H3290
36 And J their father said unto them, Me H3290
45:25 the land of Canaan unto J their father, H3290
27 him, the spirit of J their father revived: H3290
46: 2 said, J, Jacob. And he said, Here *am* I. H3290
2 said, Jacob, J. And he said, Here *am* I. H3290
5 And J rose up from Beer-sheba: and H3290
5 sons of Israel carried J their father, and H3290
6 into Egypt, J, and all his seed with him: H3290
8 which came into Egypt, J and his sons: H3290
15 she bare unto J in Padan-aram, with H3290
18 she bare unto J, *even* sixteen souls. H3290
22 born to J: all the souls *were* fourteen. H3290
25 these unto J: all the souls *were* seven. H3290
26 All the souls that came with J into H3290
27 souls of the house of J, which came into H3290
47: 7 And Joseph brought in J his father, and H3290
7 Pharaoh: and J blessed Pharaoh. H3290
8 And Pharaoh said unto J, How old *art* H3290
9 And J said unto Pharaoh, The days of H3290
10 And J blessed Pharaoh, and went out H3290
28 And J lived in the land of Egypt H3290
28 so the whole age of J was an hundred H3290
48: 2 And *one* told J, and said, Behold, thy H3290
3 And J said unto Joseph, God Almighty H3290
49: 1 And J called unto his sons, and said, H3290
2 J; and hearken unto Israel your father. H3290
7 them in J, and scatter them in Israel. H3290
24 the mighty *God* of J; (from thence *is* the H3290
33 And when J had made an end of H3290
50:24 he sware to Abraham, to Isaac, and to J. H3290
Ex 1: 1 man and his household came with J. H3290
5 out of the loins of J were seventy souls: H3290
2:24 with Abraham, with Isaac, and with J. H3290
3: 6 and the God of J. And Moses hid his H3290
15 and the God of J, hath sent me unto H3290
16 of Isaac, and of J, appeared unto me, H3290
4: 5 the God of J, hath appeared unto thee. H3290

Ex 6: 3 Isaac, and unto J, by *the name of* God H3290
8 to Isaac, and to J; and I will give it you H3290
19: 3 of J, and tell the children of Israel; H3290
33: 1 to J, saying, Unto thy seed will I give it: H3290
Lev 26:42 my covenant with J, and also my H3290
Nu 23: 7 curse me J, and come, defy Israel. H3290
10 Who can count the dust of J, and the H3290
21 He hath not beheld iniquity in J, neither H3290
23 against J, neither *is there* any H3290
23 it shall be said of J and of Israel, What H3290
24: 5 How goodly are thy tents, O J, *and* thy H3290
17 come a Star out of J, and a Sceptre shall H3290
19 Out of J shall come he that shall have H3290
32:11 Isaac, and unto J; because they have H3290
Dt 1: 8 Isaac, and J, to give unto them and H3290
6:10 to Isaac, and to J, to give thee great and H3290
9: 5 thy fathers, Abraham, Isaac, and J. H3290
27 Isaac, and J; look not unto the H3290
29:13 fathers, to Abraham, to Isaac, and to J. H3290
30:20 to Isaac, and to J, to give them. H3290
32: 9 For the LORD'S portion *is* his people; J H3290
33: 4 the inheritance of the congregation of J. H3290
10 They shall teach J thy judgments, and H3290
28 the fountain of J *shall be* upon a land H3290
34: 4 Isaac, and unto J, saying, I will give it H3290
Jos 24: 4 And I gave unto Isaac J and Esau: and H3290
4 to possess it; but J and his children H3290
32 of ground which J bought of the sons of H3290
1Sa 12: 8 When J was come into Egypt, and your H3290
2Sa 23: 1 J, and the sweet psalmist of Israel, said, H3290
1Ki 18:31 of the sons of J, unto whom the word H3290
2Ki 13:23 Isaac, and J, and would not destroy H3290
17:34 children of J, whom he named Israel; H3290
1Ch 16:13 ye children of J, his chosen ones. H3290
17 And hath confirmed the same to J for a H3290
Ps 14: 7 J shall rejoice, *and* Israel shall be glad. H3290
20: 1 the name of the God of J defend thee; H3290
22:23 all ye the seed of J, glorify him; and fear H3290
24: 6 seek him, that seek thy face, O J. Selah. H3290
44: 4 O God: command deliverances for J. H3290
46: 7 us; the God of J *is* our refuge. Selah. H3290
11 us; the God of J *is* our refuge. Selah. H3290
47: 4 excellency of J whom he loved. Selah. H3290
53: 6 J shall rejoice, *and* Israel shall be glad. H3290
59:13 in J unto the ends of the earth. Selah. H3290
75: 9 ever; I will sing praises to the God of J. H3290
76: 6 At thy rebuke, O God of J, both the H3290
77:15 people, the sons of J and Joseph. Selah. H3290
78: 5 For he established a testimony in J, and H3290
21 kindled against J, and anger also came H3290
71 J his people, and Israel his inheritance. H3290
79: 7 For they have devoured J, and laid H3290
81: 1 make a joyful noise unto the God of J. H3290
4 for Israel, *and* a law of the God of J. H3290
84: 8 my prayer: give ear, O God of J. Selah. H3290
85: 1 hast brought back the captivity of J. H3290
87: 2 of Zion more than all the dwellings of J. H3290
94: 7 see, neither shall the God of J regard *it*. H3290
99: 4 judgment and righteousness in J. H3290
105: 6 his servant, ye children of J his chosen. H3290
10 And confirmed the same unto J for a H3290
23 Israel also came into Egypt; and J H3290
114: 1 of J from a people of strange language; H3290
7 the Lord, at the presence of the God of J; H3290
132: 2 *and* vowed unto the mighty *God* of J; H3290
5 an habitation for the mighty *God* of J. H3290
135: 4 For the LORD hath chosen J unto H3290
146: 5 Happy *is he* that *hath* the God of J for H3290
147:19 He sheweth his word unto J, his statutes H3290
Isa 2: 3 of the God of J; and he will teach us H3290
5 O house of J, come ye, and let us walk in H3290
6 people the house of J, because they be H3290
8:17 the house of J, and I will look for him. H3290
9: 8 The Lord sent a word into J, and it hath H3290
10:20 of the house of J, shall no more again H3290
21 the remnant of J, unto the mighty God. H3290
14: 1 For the LORD will have mercy on J, and H3290
1 and they shall cleave to the house of J. H3290
17: 4 *that* the glory of J shall be made thin, H3290
27: 6 He shall cause them that come of J to H3290
9 By this therefore shall the iniquity of J H3290
29:22 the house of J, Jacob shall not now H3290
22 the house of Jacob, J shall not now be H3290
23 of J, and shall fear the God of Israel. H3290
40:27 Why sayest thou, O J, and speakest, O H3290
41: 8 But thou, Israel, *art* my servant, J H3290
14 Fear not, thou worm J, *and* ye men of H3290
21 your strong *reasons*, saith the King of J. H3290
42:24 Who gave J for a spoil, and Israel to the H3290

Isa 43: 1 created thee, O J, and he that formed H3290
22 But thou hast not called upon me, O J; H3290
28 J to the curse, and Israel to reproaches. H3290
44: 1 Yet now hear, O J my servant; and H3290
2 thee; Fear not, O J, my servant; and H3290
5 by the name of J; and another shall H3290
21 Remember these, O J and Israel; for H3290
23 J, and glorified himself in Israel. H3290
45: 4 For J my servant's sake, and Israel H3290
19 unto the seed of J, Seek ye me in vain: H3290
46: 3 Hearken unto me, O house of J, and all H3290
48: 1 Hear ye this, O house of J, which are H3290
12 Hearken unto me, O J and Israel, my H3290
20 The LORD hath redeemed his servant J. H3290
49: 5 his servant, to bring J again to him, H3290
6 up the tribes of J, and to restore the H3290
26 and thy Redeemer, the mighty One of J. H3290
58: 1 and the house of J their sins. H3290
14 with the heritage of J thy father: for the H3290
59:20 transgression in J, saith the LORD. H3290
60:16 and thy Redeemer, the mighty One of J. H3290
65: 9 And I will bring forth a seed out of J, H3290
Jer 2: 4 LORD, O house of J, and all the families H3290
5:20 Declare this in the house of J, and H3290
10:16 The portion of J *is* not like them: for he H3290
25 for they have eaten up J, and devoured H3290
30:10 Therefore fear thou not, O my servant J, H3290
10 captivity; and J shall return, and shall H3290
31: 7 with gladness for J, and shout among H3290
11 For the LORD hath redeemed J, and H3290
33:26 Then will I cast away the seed of J, and H3290
26 Isaac, and J: for I will cause their H3290
46:27 But fear not thou, O my servant J, and H3290
27 captivity; and J shall return, and be H3290
28 Fear thou not, O J my servant, saith the H3290
51:19 The portion of J *is* not like them; for he H3290
Lam 1:17 concerning J, *that* his adversaries H3290
2: 2 all the habitations of J, and hath not H3290
3 he burned against J like a flaming fire, H3290
Ezk 20: 5 seed of the house of J, and made myself H3290
28:25 land that I have given to my servant J. H3290
37:25 that I have given unto J my servant, H3290
39:25 the captivity of J, and have mercy upon H3290
Hos 10:11 shall plow, *and* J shall break his clods. H3290
12: 2 and will punish J according to his H3290
12 And J fled into the country of Syria, H3290
Am 3:13 Hear ye, and testify in the house of J, H3290
6: 8 the excellency of J, and hate his palaces: H3290
7: 2 by whom shall J arise? for he *is* small. H3290
5 by whom shall J arise? for he *is* small. H3290
8: 7 by the excellency of J, Surely I will never H3290
9: 8 destroy the house of J, saith the LORD. H3290
Oba 10 For *thy* violence against thy brother J H3290
17 of J shall possess their possessions. H3290
18 And the house of J shall be a fire, and H3290
Mic 1: 5 For the transgression of J *is* all this, H3290
5 the transgression of J? *is it* not Samaria? H3290
2: 7 O *thou that art* named the house of J, is H3290
12 I will surely assemble, O J, all of thee; I H3290
3: 1 you, O heads of J, and ye princes of the H3290
8 to declare unto J his transgression, and H3290
9 of the house of J, and princes of the H3290
4: 2 of the God of J; and he will teach us H3290
5: 7 And the remnant of J shall be in the H3290
8 And the remnant of J shall be among H3290
7:20 Thou wilt perform the truth to J, *and* H3290
Nah 2: 2 the excellency of J, as the excellency of H3290
Mal 1: 2 brother? saith the LORD: yet I loved J, H3290
2:12 of the tabernacles of J, and him that H3290
3: 6 ye sons of J are not consumed. H3290
Mt 1: 2 and Isaac begat J; and Jacob begat *G2384*
2 and J begat Judas and his brethren; *G2384*
15 begat Matthan; and Matthan begat J; *G2384*
16 And J begat Joseph the husband of *G2384*
8:11 Isaac, and J, in the kingdom of heaven. *G2384*
22:32 and the God of J? God is not the God of *G2384*
Mk 12:26 and the God of Isaac, and the God of J? *G2384*
Lk 1:33 And he shall reign over the house of J *G2384*
3:34 Which was *the son* of J, which was *the* *G2384*
13:28 and Isaac, and J, and all the prophets, *G2384*
20:37 and the God of Isaac, and the God of J. *G2384*
Jn 4: 5 of ground that J gave to his son Joseph. *G2384*
12 Art thou greater than our father J, *G2384*
Act 3:13 and of Isaac, and of J, the God of our *G2384*
7: 8 and Isaac *begat* J; and Jacob *begat* the *G2384*
8 and J *begat* the twelve patriarchs. *G2384*
12 But when J heard that there was corn *G2384*
14 called his father J to *him*, and all his *G2384*
15 So J went down into Egypt, and died, *G2384*

Act 7:32 and the God of J. Then Moses trembled, *G2384*
46 to find a tabernacle for the God of J. *G2384*
Ro 9:13 As it is written, J have I loved, but Esau *G2384*
11:26 and shall turn away ungodliness from J: *G2384*
Heb 11: 9 with Isaac and J, the heirs with him of *G2384*
20 By faith Isaac blessed J and Esau *G2384*
21 By faith J, when he was a dying, blessed *G2384*

JACOB'S

Gen 27:22 said, The voice *is* J voice, but the hands H3290
28: 5 of Rebekah, J and Esau's mother. H3290
30: 2 And J anger was kindled against H3290
42 were Laban's, and the stronger J. H3290
31:33 And Laban went into J tent, and into H3290
32:18 *be* thy servant J; it *is* a present sent unto H3290
25 and the hollow of J thigh was out of H3290
32 of J thigh in the sinew that shrank. H3290
34: 7 in Israel in lying with J daughter; which H3290
19 he had delight in J daughter: and he H3290
35:23 The sons of Leah; Reuben, J firstborn, H3290
45:26 J heart fainted, for he believed them not.
46: 8 Jacob and his sons: Reuben, J firstborn. H3290
19 The sons of Rachel J wife; Joseph, and H3290
26 his loins, besides J sons' wives, all the H3290
Jer 30: 7 J trouble; but he shall be saved out of it. H3290
18 the captivity of J tents, and have mercy H3290
Mal 1: 2 us? *Was* not Esau J brother? saith the H3290
Jn 4: 6 Now J well was there. Jesus therefore, *G2384*

JADA

1Ch 2:28 were, Shammai, and J. And the sons of H3047
32 And the sons of J the brother of H3047

JADAU

Ezr 10:43 Zabad, Zebina, J, and Joel, Benaiah. H3035

JADDUA

Neh 10:21 Meshezabeel, Zadok, J, H3037
12:11 begat Jonathan, and Jonathan begat J. H3037
22 and Johanan, and J, *were* recorded H3037

JADON

Neh 3: 7 the Gibeonite, and J the Meronothite, H3036

JAEL

Jdg 4:17 feet to the tent of J the wife of Heber the H3278
18 And J went out to meet Sisera, and said H3278
21 Then J Heber's wife took a nail of the H3278
22 pursued Sisera, J came out to meet H3278
5: 6 in the days of J, the highways were H3278
24 Blessed above women shall J the wife H3278

JAGUR

Jos 15:21 were Kabzeel, and Eder, and J, H3017

JAH

Ps 68: 4 by his name J, and rejoice before him. H3050

JAHATH

1Ch 4: 2 And Reaiah the son of Shobal begat J; H3189
2 begat Jahath; and J begat Ahumai, and H3189
6:20 Of Gershom; Libni his son, J his son, H3189
43 The son of J, the son of Gershom, the H3189
23:10 And the sons of Shimei *were*, J, Zina, H3189
11 And J was the chief, and Zizah the H3189
24:22 Shelomoth: of the sons of Shelomoth; J. H3189
2Ch 34:12 of them *were* J and Obadiah, the H3189

JAHAZ

Nu 21:23 he came to J, and fought against Israel. H3096
Dt 2:32 us, he and all his people, to fight at J. H3096
Jdg 11:20 pitched in J, and fought against Israel. H3096
Isa 15: 4 heard *even* unto J: therefore the armed H3096
Jer 48:34 *and even* unto J, have they uttered their H3096

JAHAZAH

Jos 13:18 And J, and Kedemoth, and Mephaath, H3096
21:36 her suburbs, and J with her suburbs, H3096
Jer 48:21 and upon J, and upon Mephaath, H3096

JAHAZIAH

Ezr 10:15 Only Jonathan the son of Asahel and J H3167

JAHAZIEL

1Ch 12: 4 and Jeremiah, and J, and Johanan, and H3166
16: 6 Benaiah also and J the priests with H3166
23:19 J the third, and Jekameam the fourth. H3166
24:23 J the third, Jekameam the fourth. H3166
2Ch 20:14 Then upon J the son of Zechariah, the H3166

J

Ezr 8: 5 Of the sons of Shechaniah; the son of J, H3166

JAHDAI
1Ch 2:47 And the sons of J; Regem, and Jotham, H3056

JAHDIEL
1Ch 5:24 Hodaviah, and J, mighty men of valour, H3164

JAHDO
1Ch 5:14 of Jeshishai, the son of J, the son of Buz; H3163

JAHLEEL
Gen 46:14 sons of Zebulun; Sered, and Elon, and J. H3177
Nu 26:26 of J, the family of the Jahleelites. H3177

JAHLEELITES
Nu 26:26 Elonites: of Jahleel, the family of the J. H3178

JAHMAI
1Ch 7: 2 and Jeriel, and J, and Jibsam, and H3181

JAHZAH
1Ch 6:78 her suburbs, and J with her suburbs, H3096

JAHZEEL
Gen 46:24 And the sons of Naphtali; J, and Guni, H3183
Nu 26:48 their families: of J, the family of the H3183

JAHZEELITES
Nu 26:48 the J: of Guni, the family of the Gunites: H3184

JAHZERAH
1Ch 9:12 son of Adiel, the son of J, the son of H3170

JAHZIEL
1Ch 7:13 The sons of Naphtali; J, and Guni, and H3185

JAILOR
Act 16:23 charging the j to keep them safely: *G1200*

JAIR
Nu 32:41 And J the son of Manasseh went and H2971
Dt 3:14 J the son of Manasseh took all the H2971
Jos 13:30 all the towns of J, which *are* in Bashan, H2971
Jdg 10: 3 And after him arose J, a Gileadite, and H2971
5 And J died, and was buried in Camon. H2971
1Ki 4:13 the towns of J the son of Manasseh, H2971
1Ch 2:22 And Segub begat J, who had three and H2971
23 with the towns of J, from them, with H2971
20: 5 Elhanan the son of J slew Lahmi the H3265
Est 2: 5 the son of J, the son of Shimei, the H2971

JAIRITE
2Sa 20:26 And Ira also the J was a chief ruler H2972

JAIRUS
Mk 5:22 of the synagogue, J by name; and when *G2383*
Lk 8:41 a man named J, and he was a ruler of *G2383*

JAKAN
1Ch 1:42 J. The sons of Dishan; Uz, and Aran. H3292

JAKEH
Prv 30: 1 The words of Agur the son of J, *even* the H3348

JAKIM
1Ch 8:19 And J, and Zichri, and Zabdi, H3356
24:12 eleventh to Eliashib, the twelfth to J, H3356

JALON
1Ch 4:17 and Epher, and J: and she bare Miriam, H3210

JAMBRES
2Ti 3: 8 Now as Jannes and J withstood Moses, *G2387*

JAMES
Mt 4:21 two brethren, J *the son* of Zebedee, *G2385*
10: 2 his brother; J *the son* of Zebedee, *G2385*
3 the publican; J *the son* of Alphaeus, *G2385*
13:55 J, and Joses, and Simon, and Judas? *G2385*
17: 1 And after six days Jesus taketh Peter, J, *G2385*
27:56 the mother of J and Joses, and the *G2385*
Mk 1:19 thence, he saw J the *son* of Zebedee, *G2385*
29 of Simon and Andrew, with J and John. *G2385*
3:17 And J the *son* of Zebedee, and John the *G2385*
17 the brother of J; and he surnamed them *G2385*
18 Matthew, and Thomas, and J the *son* of *G2385*
5:37 and J, and John the brother of James. *G2385*
37 and James, and John the brother of J. *G2385*
Mk 6: 3 the brother of J, and Joses, and of Juda, *G2385*
9: 2 *him* Peter, and J, and John, and leadeth *G2385*
10:35 And J and John, the sons of Zebedee, *G2385*
41 to be much displeased with J and John. *G2385*
13: 3 the temple, Peter and J and John and *G2385*
14:33 And he taketh with him Peter and J *G2385*
15:40 of J the less and of Joses, and Salome; *G2385*
16: 1 Mary the *mother* of J, and Salome, had *G2385*
Lk 5:10 And so *was* also J, and John, the sons of *G2385*
6:14 J and John, Philip and Bartholomew, *G2385*
15 Matthew and Thomas, J the *son* of *G2385*
16 And Judas *the brother* of J, and Judas *G2385*
8:51 in, save Peter, and J, and John, and the *G2385*
9:28 J, and went up into a mountain to pray. *G2385*
54 And when his disciples J and John saw *G2385*
24:10 *the mother* of J, and other *women that* *G2385*
Act 1:13 abode both Peter, and J, and John, and *G2385*
13 and Matthew, J *the son* of Alphaeus, *G2385*
13 Zelotes, and Judas *the brother* of J. *G2385*
12: 2 And he killed J the brother of John with *G2385*
17 these things unto J, and to the brethren. *G2385*
15:13 And after they had held their peace, J *G2385*
21:18 unto J; and all the elders were present. *G2385*
1Co 15: 7 After that, he was seen of J; then of all *G2385*
Gal 1:19 saw I none, save J the Lord's brother. *G2385*
2: 9 And when J, Cephas, and John, who *G2385*
12 For before that certain came from J, he *G2385*
Jas 1: 1 J, a servant of God and of the Lord Jesus *G2385*
Jude 1 and brother of J, to them that are *G2385*

JAMIN
Gen 46:10 And the sons of Simeon; Jemuel, and J, H3226
Ex 6:15 And the sons of Simeon; Jemuel, and J, H3226
Nu 26:12 of the Nemuelites: of J, the family of the H3226
1Ch 2:27 Jerahmeel were, Maaz, and J, and Eker. H3226
4:24 Nemuel, and J, Jarib, Zerah, *and* Shaul: H3226
Neh 8: 7 and Sherebiah, J, Akkub, Shabbethai, H3226

JAMINITES
Nu 26:12 J: of Jachin, the family of the Jachinites: H3228

JAMLECH
1Ch 4:34 And Meshobab, and J, and Joshah the H3230

JANGLING
1Ti 1: 6 swerved have turned aside unto vain j; *G3150*

JANNA
Lk 3:24 *son* of J, which was *the son* of Joseph, *G2388*

JANNES
2Ti 3: 8 Now as J and Jambres withstood *G2389*

JANOAH
2Ki 15:29 and J, and Kedesh, and Hazor, H3239

JANOHAH
Jos 16: 6 and passed by it on the east to J; H3239
7 And it went down from J to Ataroth, H3239

JANUM
Jos 15:53 And J, and Beth-tappuah, and H3241

JAPHETH
Gen 5:32 old: and Noah begat Shem, Ham, and J. H3315
6:10 begat three sons, Shem, Ham, and J. H3315
7:13 and Ham, and J, the sons of Noah, and H3315
9:18 and J: and Ham *is* the father of Canaan. H3315
23 And Shem and J took a garment, and H3315
27 God shall enlarge J, and he shall dwell H3315
10: 1 Shem, Ham, and J: and unto them were H3315
2 The sons of J; Gomer, and Magog, and H3315
21 the brother of J the elder, even to him H3315
1Ch 1: 4 Noah, Shem, Ham, and J. H3315
5 The sons of J; Gomer, and Magog, and H3315

JAPHIA
Jos 10: 3 of Jarmuth, and unto J king of Lachish, H3309
19:12 out to Daberath, and goeth up to J, H3309
2Sa 5:15 also, and Elishua, and Nepheg, and J, H3309
1Ch 3: 7 And Nogah, and Nepheg, and J, H3309
14: 6 And Nogah, and Nepheg, and J, H3309

JAPHLET
1Ch 7:32 And Heber begat J, and Shomer, and H3310
33 And the sons of J; Pasach, and Bimhal, H3310
33 Ashvath. These *are* the children of J. H3310

JAPHLETI
Jos 16: 3 to the coast of J, unto the coast of H3311

JAPHO
Jos 19:46 and Rakkon, with the border before J. H3305

JARAH
1Ch 9:42 And Ahaz begat J; and Jarah begat H3294
42 And Ahaz begat Jarah; and J begat H3294

JAREB
Hos 5:13 and sent to king J: yet could he not heal H3377
10: 6 *for* a present to king J: Ephraim shall H3377

JARED
Gen 5:15 lived sixty and five years, and begat J: H3382
16 And Mahalaleel lived after he begat J H3382
18 And J lived an hundred sixty and two H3382
19 And J lived after he begat Enoch eight H3382
20 And all the days of J were nine hundred H3382
Lk 3:37 was *the son* of J, which was *the son* of *G2391*

JARESIAH
1Ch 8:27 And J, and Eliah, and Zichri, the sons of H3298

JARHA
1Ch 2:34 an Egyptian, whose name *was* J. H3398
35 And Sheshan gave his daughter to J his H3398

JARIB
1Ch 4:24 and Jamin, J, Zerah, *and* Shaul: H3402
Ezr 8:16 Elnathan, and for J, and for Elnathan, H3402
10:18 and Eliezer, and J, and Gedaliah. H3402

JARKON See ME-JARKON.

JARMUTH
Jos 10: 3 Piram king of J, and unto Japhia king H3412
5 the king of J, the king of Lachish, H3412
23 the king of J, the king of Lachish, H3412
12:11 The king of J, one; the king of Lachish, H3412
15:35 J, and Adullam, Socoh, and Azekah, H3412
21:29 J with her suburbs, En-gannim with H3412
Neh 11:29 at En-rimmon, and at Zareah, and at J, H3412

JAROAH
1Ch 5:14 of Huri, the son of J, the son of Gilead, H3386

JASHEN
2Sa 23:32 Shaalbonite, of the sons of J, Jonathan, H3464

JASHER
Jos 10:13 in the book of J? So the sun stood still H3477
2Sa 1:18 behold, *it is* written in the book of J.) H3477

JASHOBEAM
1Ch 11:11 whom David had; J, an Hachmonite, H3434
12: 6 Azareel, and Joezer, and J, the Korhites, H3434
27: 2 first month *was* J the son of Zabdiel: H3434

JASHUB
Nu 26:24 Of J, the family of the Jashubites: of H3437
1Ch 7: 1 Tola, and Puah, J, and Shimron, four. H3437
Ezr 10:29 and Adaiah, J, and Sheal, and Ramoth. H3437

JASHUBILEHEM
1Ch 4:22 and J. And *these are* ancient things. H3433

JASHUBITES
Nu 26:24 Of Jashub, the family of the J: of H3432

JASIEL
1Ch 11:47 Eliel, and Obed, and J the Mesobaite. H3300

JASON
Act 17: 5 the house of J, and sought to bring *G2394*
6 not, they drew J and certain brethren *G2394*
7 Whom J hath received: and these all do *G2394*
9 And when they had taken security of J, *G2394*
Ro 16:21 and Lucius, and J, and Sosipater, my *G2394*

JASPER
Ex 28:20 and an onyx, and a j: they shall be set in H3471
39:13 an onyx, and a j: *they were* inclosed in H3471
Ezk 28:13 the onyx, and the j, the sapphire, the H3471
Rev 4: 3 was to look upon like a j and a sardine *G2393*
21:11 even like a j stone, clear as crystal; *G2393*
18 wall of it was *of* j: and the city *was* pure *G2393*
19 foundation *was* j; the second, sapphire; *G2393*

JATHNIEL
1Ch 26: 2 Zebadiah the third, J the fourth, H3496

JATTIR
Jos 15:48 And in the mountains, Shamir, and J, H3492
21:14 And J with her suburbs, and Eshtemoa H3492
1Sa 30:27 Ramoth, and to *them* which *were* in J, H3492
1Ch 6:57 J, and Eshtemoa, with their suburbs, H3492

JAVAN
Gen 10: 2 J, and Tubal, and Meshech, and Tiras. H3120
4 And the sons of J; Elishah, and H3120
1Ch 1: 5 J, and Tubal, and Meshech, and Tiras. H3120
7 And the sons of J; Elishah, and H3120
Isa 66:19 *to* Tubal, and J, *to* the isles afar off, H3120
Ezk 27:13 J, Tubal, and Meshech, they *were* thy H3120
19 Dan also and J going to and fro H3120

JAVELIN
Nu 25: 7 congregation, and took a j in his hand; H7420
1Sa 18:10 times: and *there was* a j in Saul's hand. H2595
11 And Saul cast the j; for he said, I will H2595
19: 9 in his house with his j in his hand: and H2595
10 the wall with the j; but he slipped away H2595
10 and he smote the j into the wall: and H2595
20:33 And Saul cast a j at him to smite him: H2595

JAW
Jdg 15:16 j of an ass have I slain a thousand men. H3895
19 that *was* in the j, and there came water H3895
Job 41: 2 or bore his j through with a thorn? H3895
Prv 30:14 swords, and their j teeth *as* knives, to H4973

JAWBONE
Jdg 15:15 And he found a new j of an ass, and H3895
16 And Samson said, With the j of an ass, H3895
17 he cast away the j out of his hand, and H3895

JAWS
Job 29:17 And I brake the j of the wicked, and H4973
Ps 22:15 cleaveth to my j; and thou hast brought H4455
Isa 30:28 the j of the people, causing *them* to err. H3895
Ezk 29: 4 But I will put hooks in thy j, and I will H3895
38: 4 put hooks into thy j, and I will bring H3895
Hos 11: 4 on their j, and I laid meat unto them. H3895

JAZER
Nu 32: 1 they saw the land of J, and the land of H3270
3 Ataroth, and Dibon, and J, and H3270
Jos 13:25 And their coast was J, and all the cities H3270
21:39 Heshbon with her suburbs, J with her H3270
2Sa 24: 5 midst of the river of Gad, and toward J: H3270
1Ch 6:81 And Heshbon with her suburbs, and J H3270
26:31 mighty men of valour at J of Gilead. H3270
Isa 16: 8 are come *even* unto J, they wandered H3270
9 the weeping of J the vine of Sibmah: H3270
Jer 48:32 the weeping of J: thy plants are gone H3270
32 *even* to the sea of J: the spoiler is fallen H3270

JAZIZ
1Ch 27:31 And over the flocks *was* J the Hagerite. H3151

JEALOUS
Ex 20: 5 LORD thy God *am* a j God, visiting the H7067
34:14 whose name *is* J, *is* a jealous God: H7067
14 whose name *is* Jealous, *is* a j God: H7067
Nu 5:14 him, and he be j of his wife, and she H7065
14 be j of his wife, and she be not defiled: H7065
30 him, and he be j over his wife, and H7065
Dt 4:24 God *is* a consuming fire, *even* a j God. H7067
5: 9 LORD thy God *am* a j God, visiting the H7067
6:15 (For the LORD thy God *is* a j God H7067
Jos 24:19 an holy God; he *is* a j God; he will not H7072
1Ki 19:10 And he said, I have been very j for the H7065
14 And he said, I have been very j for the H7065
Ezk 39:25 Israel, and will be j for my holy name; H7065
Joel 2:18 Then will the LORD be j for his land, H7065
Nah 1: 2 God *is* j, and the LORD revengeth; the H7072
Zec 1:14 of hosts; I am j for Jerusalem and for H7065
8: 2 Thus saith the LORD of hosts; I was j H7065
2 and I was j for her with great fury. H7065
2Co 11: 2 For I am j over you with godly jealousy: *G2206*

JEALOUSIES
Nu 5:29 This *is* the law of j, when a wife goeth H7068

JEALOUSY
Nu 5:14 And the spirit of j come upon him, and H7068
14 or if the spirit of j come upon him, and H7068
Nu 5:15 for it *is* an offering of j, an offering of H7068
18 which *is* the j offering: and the priest H7068
25 Then the priest shall take the j offering H7068
30 Or when the spirit of j cometh upon H7068
25:11 not the children of Israel in my j. H7068
Dt 29:20 the LORD and his j shall smoke against H7068
32:16 They provoked him to j with strange H7065
21 They have moved me to j with *that* H7065
21 I will move them to j with *those which* H7065
1Ki 14:22 provoked him to j with their sins which H7065
Ps 78:58 him to j with their graven images. H7065
79: 5 angry for ever? shall thy j burn like fire? H7068
Prv 6:34 For j *is* the rage of a man: therefore he H7068
Song 8: 6 love *is* strong as death; j *is* cruel as the H7068
Isa 42:13 he shall stir up j like a man of war: he H7068
Ezk 8: 3 image of j, which provoketh to jealousy. H7068
3 image of jealousy, which provoketh to j. H7069
5 of the altar this image of j in the entry. H7068
16:38 and I will give thee blood in fury and j. H7068
42 thee to rest, and my j shall depart from H7068
23:25 And I will set my j against thee, and H7068
36: 5 in the fire of my j have I spoken against H7068
6 I have spoken in my j and in my fury, H7068
38:19 For in my j *and* in the fire of my wrath H7068
Zep 1:18 by the fire of his j: for he shall make H7068
3: 8 shall be devoured with the fire of my j. H7068
Zec 1:14 Jerusalem and for Zion with a great j. H7068
8: 2 for Zion with great j, and I was jealous H7068
Ro 10:19 provoke you to j by *them that are* no *G3863*
11:11 the Gentiles, for to provoke them to j. *G3863*
1Co 10:22 Do we provoke the Lord to j? are we *G3863*
2Co 11: 2 For I am jealous over you with godly j: *G2205*

JEARIM
Jos 15:10 the side of mount J, which *is* Chesalon, H3297

JEATERAI
1Ch 6:21 Iddo his son, Zerah his son, J his son. H2979

JEBERECHIAH
Isa 8: 2 the priest, and Zechariah the son of J. H3000

JEBUS
Jdg 19:10 and came over against J, which *is* H2982
11 *And* when they *were* by J, the day was H2982
1Ch 11: 4 which *is* J; where the Jebusites H2982
5 And the inhabitants of J said to David, H2982

JEBUSI
Jos 18:16 to the side of J on the south, and H2983
28 And Zelah, Eleph, and J, which *is* H2983

JEBUSITE
Gen 10:16 And the J, and the Amorite, and the H2983
Ex 33: 2 and the Perizzite, the Hivite, and the J: H2983
34:11 the Perizzite, and the Hivite, and the J. H2983
Jos 9: 1 the Hivite, and the J, heard *thereof*; H2983
11: 3 Perizzite, and the J in the mountains, H2983
15: 8 the south side of the J; the same *is* H2983
2Sa 24:16 by the threshingplace of Araunah the J. H2983
18 in the threshingfloor of Araunah the J. H2983
1Ch 1:14 The J also, and the Amorite, and the H2983
21:15 by the threshingfloor of Ornan the J. H2983
18 in the threshingfloor of Ornan the J. H2983
28 of Ornan the J, then he sacrificed there. H2983
2Ch 3: 1 in the threshingfloor of Ornan the J. H2983
Zec 9: 7 a governor in Judah, and Ekron as a J. H2983

JEBUSITES
Gen 15:21 and the Girgashites, and the J. H2983
Ex 3: 8 Perizzites, and the Hivites, and the J. H2983
17 Hivites, and the J, unto a land flowing H2983
13: 5 Hivites, and the J, which he sware unto H2983
23:23 and the J: and I will cut them off. H2983
Nu 13:29 Hittites, and the J, and the Amorites, H2983
Dt 7: 1 Hivites, and the J, seven nations greater H2983
20:17 Hivites, and the J; as the LORD thy God H2983
Jos 3:10 and the Amorites, and the J. H2983
12: 8 the Perizzites, the Hivites, and the J: H2983
15:63 As for the J the inhabitants of H2983
63 drive them out: but the J dwell with the H2983
24:11 J; and I delivered them into your hand. H2983
Jdg 1:21 did not drive out the J that inhabited H2983
21 Jerusalem; but the J dwell with the H2983
3: 5 and Perizzites, and Hivites, and J: H2983
19:11 in into this city of the J, and lodge in it. H2983
2Sa 5: 6 unto the J, the inhabitants of the H2983
8 and smiteth the J, and the lame and the H2983
1Ki 9:20 Hivites, and J, which *were* not of the H2983
1Ch 11: 4 the J *were*, the inhabitants of the land. H2983
6 smiteth the J first shall be chief and H2983
2Ch 8: 7 and the J, which *were* not of Israel, H2983
Ezr 9: 1 the Perizzites, the J, the Ammonites, the H2983
Neh 9: 8 the Perizzites, and the J, and the H2983

JECAMIAH
1Ch 3:18 Shenazar, J, Hoshama, and Nedabiah. H3359

JECHOLIAH
2Ki 15: 2 his mother's name *was* J of Jerusalem. H3203

JECHONIAS
Mt 1:11 And Josias begat J and his brethren, *G2423*
12 to Babylon, J begat Salathiel; and *G2423*

JECOLIAH
2Ch 26: 3 mother's name also *was* J of Jerusalem. H3203

JECONIAH
1Ch 3:16 And the sons of Jehoiakim: J his son, H3204
17 And the sons of J; Assir, Salathiel his H3204
Est 2: 6 been carried away with J king of Judah, H3204
Jer 24: 1 away captive J the son of Jehoiakim H3204
27:20 away captive J the son of Jehoiakim H3204
28: 4 And I will bring again to this place J H3204
29: 2 (After that J the king, and the queen, H3204

JEDAIAH
1Ch 4:37 of Allon, the son of J, the son of Shimri, H3042
9:10 And of the priests; J, and Jehoiarib, and H3048
24: 7 came forth to Jehoiarib, the second to J, H3048
Ezr 2:36 The priests: the children of J, of the H3048
Neh 3:10 And next unto them repaired J the son H3042
7:39 The priests: the children of J, of the H3048
11:10 Of the priests: J the son of Joiarib, H3048
12: 6 Shemaiah, and Joiarib, J, H3048
7 Sallu, Amok, Hilkiah, J. These *were* the H3048
19 And of Joiarib, Mattenai; of J, Uzzi; H3048
21 Of Hilkiah, Hashabiah; of J, Nethaneel. H3048
Zec 6:10 of Tobijah, and of J, which are come H3048
14 to Tobijah, and to J, and to Hen the son H3048

JEDIAEL
1Ch 7: 6 Bela, and Becher, and J, three. H3043
10 The sons also of J; Bilhan: and the sons H3043
11 All these the sons of J, by the heads of H3043
11:45 J the son of Shimri, and Joha his H3043
12:20 and Jozabad, and J, and Michael, and H3043
26: 2 the firstborn, J the second, Zebadiah H3043

JEDIDAH
2Ki 22: 1 J, the daughter of Adaiah of Boscath. H3040

JEDIDIAH
2Sa 12:25 called his name J, because of the LORD. H3041

JEDUTHUN
1Ch 9:16 of Galal, the son of J, and Berechiah the H3038
16:38 the son of J and Hosah *to be* porters: H3038
41 And with them Heman and J, and the H3038
42 And with them Heman and J with H3038
42 of God. And the sons of J *were* porters. H3038
25: 1 and of Heman, and of J, who should H3038
3 Of J: the sons of Jeduthun; Gedaliah, H3038
3 Of Jeduthun: the sons of J; Gedaliah, H3038
3 of their father J, who prophesied with H3038
6 king's order to Asaph, J, and Heman. H3038
2Ch 5:12 of Heman, of J, with their sons and H3038
29:14 of the sons of J; Shemaiah, and Uzziel. H3038
35:15 and Heman, and J the king's seer; and H3038
Neh 11:17 Shammua, the son of Galal, the son of J. H3038
Ps 39:ttl To the chief Musician, *even* to J, A H3038
62:ttl To the chief Musician, to J, A Psalm of H3038
77:ttl To the chief Musician, to J, A Psalm of H3038

JEEZER
Nu 26:30 These *are* the sons of Gilead: *of* J, the H372

JEEZERITES
Nu 26:30 J: of Helek, the family of the Helekites: H373

JEGAR-SAHADUTHA
Gen 31:47 And Laban called it J: but Jacob called H3026

JEHALELEEL
1Ch 4:16 And the sons of J; Ziph, and Ziphah, H3094

JEHALELEL
2Ch 29:12 and Azariah the son of J: and of the H3094

JEHDEIAH
1Ch 24:20 Shubael: of the sons of Shubael; J. H3165
27:30 over the asses *was* J the Meronothite: H3165

JEHEZEKEL
1Ch 24:16 to Pethahiah, the twentieth to J, H3168

JEHIAH
1Ch 15:24 and J *were* doorkeepers for the ark. H3174

JEHIEL
1Ch 9:35 J, whose wife's name *was* Maachah: H3273
11:44 Uzzia the Ashterathite, Shama and J H3273
15:18 and J, and Unni, Eliab, and H3171
20 and J, and Unni, and Eliab, H3171
16: 5 and J, and Mattithiah, and H3171
23: 8 The sons of Laadan; the chief *was* J, H3171
27:32 man, and a scribe: and J the son of H3171
29: 8 LORD, by the hand of J the Gershonite. H3171
2Ch 21: 2 Azariah, and J, and Zechariah, and H3171
29:14 And of the sons of Heman; J, and H3171
31:13 And J, and Azaziah, and Nahath, and H3171
35: 8 Zechariah and J, rulers of the house of H3171
Ezr 8: 9 the son of J, and with him two hundred H3171
10: 2 And Shechaniah the son of J, *one* of the H3171
21 and Shemaiah, and J, and Uzziah. H3171
26 J, and Abdi, and Jeremoth, and Eliah. H3171

JEHIELI
1Ch 26:21 *even* of Laadan the Gershonite, *were* J. H3172
22 The sons of J; Zetham, and Joel his H3172

JEHIZKIAH
2Ch 28:12 and J the son of Shallum, H3169

JEHOADAH
1Ch 8:36 And Ahaz begat J; and Jehoadah begat H3085
36 And Ahaz begat Jehoadah; and J begat H3085

JEHOADDAN
2Ki 14: 2 his mother's name *was* J of Jerusalem. H3086
2Ch 25: 1 his mother's name *was* J of Jerusalem. H3086

JEHOAHAZ
2Ki 10:35 And J his son reigned in his stead. H3059
13: 1 king of Judah J the son of Jehu began H3059
4 And J besought the LORD, and the H3059
7 Neither did he leave of the people to J H3059
8 Now the rest of the acts of J, and all that H3059
9 And J slept with his fathers; and they H3059
10 Jehoash the son of J to reign over Israel H3059
22 Syria oppressed Israel all the days of J. H3059
25 And Jehoash the son of J took again out H3059
25 out of the hand of J his father by war. H3059
14: 1 In the second year of Joash son of J H3099
8 the son of J son of Jehu, king of H3059
17 son of J king of Israel fifteen years. H3059
23:30 of the land took J the son of Josiah, and H3059
31 J *was* twenty and three years old when H3059
34 and took J away: and he came H3059
2Ch 21:17 him, save J, the youngest of his sons. H3059
25:17 Joash, the son of J, the son of Jehu, king H3059
23 of Joash, the son of J, at Beth-shemesh, H3059
25 son of J king of Israel fifteen years. H3059
36: 1 Then the people of the land took J the H3059
2 J *was* twenty and three years old when H3099
4 J his brother, and carried him to Egypt. H3099

JEHOASH
2Ki 11:21 Seven years old *was* J when he began to H3060
12: 1 In the seventh year of Jehu J began to H3060
2 And J did *that which was* right in the H3060
4 And J said to the priests, All the money H3060
6 year of king J the priests had not H3060
7 Then king J called for Jehoiada the H3060
18 And J king of Judah took all the H3060
13:10 of Judah began J the son of Jehoahaz H3060
25 And J the son of Jehoahaz took again H3060
14: 8 Then Amaziah sent messengers to J, the H3060
9 And J the king of Israel sent to H3060
11 hear. Therefore J king of Israel went H3060
13 And J king of Israel took Amaziah king H3060
13 Judah, the son of J the son of Ahaziah, H3060
15 Now the rest of the acts of J which he H3060
16 And J slept with his fathers, and was H3060
17 after the death of J son of Jehoahaz H3060

JEHOHANAN
1Ch 26: 3 Elam the fifth, J the sixth, Elioenai the H3076
2Ch 17:15 And next to him *was* J the captain, and H3076
23: 1 Ishmael the son of J, and Azariah the H3076
Ezr 10:28 Of the sons also of Bebai; J, Hananiah, H3076
Neh 12:13 Of Ezra, Meshullam; of Amariah, J; H3076
42 and Uzzi, and J, and Malchijah, and H3076

JEHOIACHIN
2Ki 24: 6 and J his son reigned in his stead. H3078
8 J *was* eighteen years old when he began H3078
12 And J the king of Judah went out to the H3078
15 And he carried away J to Babylon, and H3078
25:27 of the captivity of J king of Judah, in H3078
27 head of J king of Judah out of prison; H3078
2Ch 36: 8 and J his son reigned in his stead. H3078
9 J *was* eight years old when he began to H3078
Jer 52:31 of the captivity of J king of Judah, in H3078
31 up the head of J king of Judah, and H3078

JEHOIACHIN'S
Ezk 1: 2 *was* the fifth year of king J captivity, H3112

JEHOIADA
2Sa 8:18 And Benaiah the son of J *was over* both H3077
20:23 and Benaiah the son of J *was* over the H3077
23:20 And Benaiah the son of J, the son of a H3077
22 These *things* did Benaiah the son of J, H3077
1Ki 1: 8 Benaiah the son of J, and Nathan the H3077
26 Benaiah the son of J, and thy servant H3077
32 son of J. And they came before the king. H3077
36 And Benaiah the son of J answered the H3077
38 and Benaiah the son of J, and the H3077
44 and Benaiah the son of J, and the H3077
2:25 of J; and he fell upon him that he died. H3077
29 the son of J, saying, Go, fall upon him. H3077
34 So Benaiah the son of J went up, and H3077
35 And the king put Benaiah the son of J H3077
46 Benaiah the son of J; which went out, H3077
4: 4 And Benaiah the son of J *was* over the H3077
2Ki 11: 4 And the seventh year J sent and fetched H3077
9 according to all *things* that J the priest H3077
9 the sabbath, and came to J the priest. H3077
15 But J the priest commanded the H3077
17 And J made a covenant between the H3077
12: 2 wherein J the priest instructed him. H3077
7 Then king Jehoash called for J the H3077
9 But J the priest took a chest, and bored H3077
1Ch 11:22 Benaiah the son of J, the son of a H3077
24 These *things* did Benaiah the son of J, H3077
12:27 And J *was* the leader of the Aaronites, H3077
18:17 And Benaiah the son of J *was* over the H3077
27: 5 Benaiah the son of J, a chief priest: and H3077
34 And after Ahithophel *was* J the son of H3077
2Ch 22:11 the wife of J the priest, (for she was H3077
23: 1 And in the seventh year J strengthened H3077
8 to all things that J the priest had H3077
8 J the priest dismissed not the courses. H3077
9 Moreover J the priest delivered to the H3077
11 him king. And J and his sons anointed H3077
14 Then J the priest brought out the H3077
16 And J made a covenant between him, H3077
18 Also J appointed the offices of the H3077
24: 2 of the LORD all the days of J the priest. H3077
3 And J took for him two wives; and he H3077
6 And the king called for J the chief, and H3077
12 And the king and J gave it to such as H3077
14 the king and J, whereof were made H3077
14 the LORD continually all the days of J. H3077
15 But J waxed old, and was full of days H3077
17 Now after the death of J came the H3077
20 the son of J the priest, which stood H3077
22 kindness which J his father had done H3077
25 of the sons of J the priest, and slew H3077
Neh 3: 6 Moreover the old gate repaired J the H3111
Jer 29:26 in the stead of J the priest, that ye H3077

JEHOIAKIM
2Ki 23:34 his name to J, and took Jehoahaz away: H3079
35 And J gave the silver and the gold to H3079
36 J *was* twenty and five years old when H3079
24: 1 came up, and J became his servant H3079
5 Now the rest of the acts of J, and all that H3079
6 So J slept with his fathers: and H3079
19 LORD, according to all that J had done. H3079
1Ch 3:15 the second J, the third Zedekiah, H3079
16 And the sons of J: Jeconiah his son, H3079
2Ch 36: 4 turned his name to J. And Necho took H3079
5 J *was* twenty and five years old when H3079
2Ch 36: 8 Now the rest of the acts of J, and his H3079
Jer 1: 3 It came also in the days of J the son of H3079
22:18 LORD concerning J the son of Josiah H3079
24 Coniah the son of J king of Judah were H3079
24: 1 the son of J king of Judah, and the H3079
25: 1 in the fourth year of J the son of Josiah H3079
26: 1 In the beginning of the reign of J the H3079
21 And when J the king, with all his H3079
22 And J the king sent men into Egypt, H3079
23 brought him unto J the king; who slew H3079
27: 1 In the beginning of the reign of J the H3079
20 the son of J king of Judah from H3079
28: 4 the son of J king of Judah, with H3079
35: 1 in the days of J the son of Josiah king H3079
36: 1 in the fourth year of J the son of Josiah H3079
9 And it came to pass in the fifth year of J H3079
28 which J the king of Judah hath burned. H3079
29 And thou shalt say to J king of Judah, H3079
30 Therefore thus saith the LORD of J king H3079
32 of the book which J king of Judah had H3079
37: 1 of Coniah the son of J, whom H3079
45: 1 in the fourth year of J the son of Josiah H3079
46: 2 of J the son of Josiah king of Judah. H3079
52: 2 LORD, according to all that J had done. H3079
Dan 1: 1 In the third year of the reign of J king H3079
2 And the Lord gave J king of Judah into H3079

JEHOIARIB
1Ch 9:10 And of the priests; Jedaiah, and J, and H3080
24: 7 Now the first lot came forth to J, the H3080

JEHONADAB
2Ki 10:15 he lighted on J the son of Rechab H3082
15 thy heart? And J answered, It is. If it H3082
23 And Jehu went, and J the son of H3082

JEHONATHAN
1Ch 27:25 in the castles, *was* J the son of Uzziah: H3083
2Ch 17: 8 and J, and Adonijah, and H3083
Neh 12:18 Of Bilgah, Shammua; of Shemaiah, J; H3083

JEHORAM
1Ki 22:50 and J his son reigned in his stead. H3088
2Ki 1:17 had spoken. And J reigned in his stead H3088
17 in the second year of J the son of H3088
3: 1 Now J the son of Ahab began to reign H3088
6 And king J went out of Samaria the H3088
8:16 king of Judah, J the son of Jehoshaphat H3088
25 son of J king of Judah begin to reign. H3088
29 Ahaziah the son of J king of Judah went H3088
9:24 and smote J between his arms, and H3088
12:18 Jehoshaphat, and J, and Ahaziah, his H3088
2Ch 17: 8 and with them Elishama and J, priests. H3088
21: 1 And J his son reigned in his stead. H3088
3 he to J; because he *was* the firstborn. H3088
4 Now when J was risen up to the H3088
5 J *was* thirty and two years old when he H3088
9 Then J went forth with his princes, and H3088
16 stirred up against J the spirit of the H3088
22: 1 the son of J king of Judah reigned. H3088
5 and went with J the son of Ahab king H3088
6 Azariah the son of J king of Judah went H3088
6 went down to see J the son of Ahab at H3088
7 he went out with J against Jehu the son H3088
11 daughter of king J, the wife of Jehoiada H3088

JEHOSHABEATH
2Ch 22:11 But J, the daughter of the king, took H3090
11 in a bedchamber. So J, the daughter of H3090

JEHOSHAPHAT
2Sa 8:16 and J the son of Ahilud *was* recorder; H3092
20:24 and J the son of Ahilud *was* recorder: H3092
1Ki 4: 3 J the son of Ahilud, the recorder. H3092
17 J the son of Paruah, in Issachar: H3092
15:24 and J his son reigned in his stead. H3092
22: 2 the third year, that J the king of Judah H3092
4 And he said unto J, Wilt thou go with H3092
4 And J said to the king of Israel, H3092
5 And J said unto the king of Israel, H3092
7 And J said, *Is there* not here a prophet H3092
8 And the king of Israel said unto J, *There* H3092
8 evil. And J said, Let not the king say so. H3092
10 And the king of Israel and J the king of H3092
18 And the king of Israel said unto J, Did I H3092
29 So the king of Israel and J the king of H3092
30 And the king of Israel said unto J, I will H3092
32 the chariots saw J, that they said, Surely H3092
32 to fight against him: and J cried out. H3092

1Ki 22:41 And J the son of Asa began to reign H3092
42 J *was* thirty and five years old when he H3092
44 And J made peace with the king of H3092
45 Now the rest of the acts of J, and his H3092
48 J made ships of Tharshish to go to H3092
49 son of Ahab unto J, Let my servants go H3092
49 servants in the ships. But J would not. H3092
50 And J slept with his fathers, and was H3092
51 year of J king of Judah, and reigned H3092
2Ki 1:17 J king of Judah; because he had no son. H3092
3: 1 eighteenth year of J king of Judah, and H3092
7 And he went and sent to J the king of H3092
11 But J said, *Is there* not here a prophet H3092
12 And J said, The word of the LORD is H3092
12 the king of Israel and J and the king of H3092
14 the presence of J the king of Judah, I H3092
8:16 king of Israel, J *being* then king of H3092
16 son of J king of Judah began to reign. H3092
9: 2 Jehu the son of J the son of Nimshi, and H3092
14 So Jehu the son of J the son of Nimshi H3092
12:18 things that J, and Jehoram, and H3092
1Ch 3:10 Abia his son, Asa his son, J his son, H3092
15:24 And Shebaniah, and J, and Nethaneel, H3046
18:15 host; and J the son of Ahilud, recorder. H3092
2Ch 17: 1 And J his son reigned in his stead, and H3092
3 And the LORD was with J, because he H3092
5 all Judah brought to J presents; and he H3092
10 so that they made no war against J. H3092
11 Also *some* of the Philistines brought J H3092
12 And J waxed great exceedingly; and he H3092
18: 1 Now J had riches and honour in H3092
3 And Ahab king of Israel said unto J H3092
4 And J said unto the king of Israel, H3092
6 But J said, *Is there* not here a prophet H3092
7 And the king of Israel said unto J, *There* H3092
7 And J said, Let not the king say so. H3092
9 And the king of Israel and J king of H3092
17 And the king of Israel said to J, Did I H3092
28 So the king of Israel and J the king of H3092
29 And the king of Israel said unto J, I will H3092
31 of the chariots saw J, that they said, It *is* H3092
31 him to fight: but J cried out, and the H3092
19: 1 And J the king of Judah returned to his H3092
2 and said to king J, Shouldest thou help H3092
4 And J dwelt at Jerusalem: and he went H3092
8 Moreover in Jerusalem did J set of the H3092
20: 1 Ammonites, came against J to battle. H3092
2 Then there came some that told J, H3092
3 And J feared, and set himself to seek H3092
5 And J stood in the congregation of H3092
15 and thou king J, Thus saith the LORD H3092
18 And J bowed his head with *his* face to H3092
20 as they went forth, J stood and said, H3092
25 And when J and his people came to H3092
27 and Jerusalem, and J in the forefront of H3092
30 So the realm of J was quiet: for his God H3092
31 And J reigned over Judah: *he was* thirty H3092
34 Now the rest of the acts of J, first and H3092
35 And after this did J king of Judah join H3092
37 against J, saying, Because thou H3092
21: 1 Now J slept with his fathers, and was H3092
2 And he had brethren the sons of J, H3092
2 these *were* the sons of J king of Israel. H3092
12 in the ways of J thy father, nor in the H3092
22: 9 he *is* the son of J, who sought the LORD H3092
Joel 3: 2 into the valley of J, and will plead with H3092
12 up to the valley of J: for there will I sit to H3092

JEHOSHEBA
2Ki 11: 2 But J, the daughter of king Joram, sister H3089

JEHOSHUA
Nu 13:16 Moses called Oshea the son of Nun J. H3091
1Ch 7:27 Non his son, J his son. H3091

JEHOVAH
Ex 6: 3 my name J was I not known to them. H3068
Ps 83:18 *is* J, *art* the most high over all the earth. H3068
Isa 12: 2 for the LORD J *is* my strength and *my* H3068
26: 4 in the LORD J *is* everlasting strength: H3068

JEHOVAH-JIREH
Gen 22:14 name of that place J: as it is said *to* this H3070

JEHOVAH-NISSI
Ex 17:15 an altar, and called the name of it J: H3068

JEHOVAH-SHALOM
Jdg 6:24 and called it J: unto this day it *is* yet H3073

JEHOZABAD
2Ki 12:21 of Shimeath, and J the son of Shomer, H3075
1Ch 26: 4 the firstborn, J the second, Joah the H3075
2Ch 17:18 And next him *was* J, and with him an H3075
24:26 and J the son of Shimrith a Moabitess. H3075

JEHOZADAK
1Ch 6:14 begat Seraiah, and Seraiah begat J, H3087
15 And J went *into captivity*, when the H3087

JEHU
1Ki 16: 1 Then the word of the LORD came to J H3058
7 And also by the hand of the prophet J H3058
12 spake against Baasha by J the prophet, H3058
19:16 And J the son of Nimshi shalt thou H3058
17 of Hazael shall J slay: and him that H3058
17 from the sword of J shall Elisha slay. H3058
2Ki 9: 2 look out there J the son of Jehoshaphat H3058
5 O captain. And J said, Unto which of H3058
11 Then J came forth to the servants of his H3058
13 blew with trumpets, saying, J is king. H3058
14 So J the son of Jehoshaphat the son of H3058
15 king of Syria.) And J said, If it be your H3058
16 So J rode in a chariot, and went to H3058
17 the company of J as he came, and said, H3058
18 *Is it* peace? And J said, What hast thou H3058
19 *Is it* peace? And J answered, What hast H3058
20 like the driving of J the son of Nimshi; H3058
21 went out against J, and met him in the H3058
22 And it came to pass, when Joram saw J, H3058
22 he said, *Is it* peace, J? And he answered, H3058
24 And J drew a bow with his full strength, H3058
25 Then said *J* to Bidkar his captain, Take
27 house. And J followed after him, H3058
30 And when J was come to Jezreel, H3058
31 And as J entered in at the gate, she H3058
10: 1 in Samaria. And J wrote letters, and H3058
5 *children*, sent to J, saying, We *are* thy H3058
11 So J slew all that remained of the house H3058
13 J met with the brethren of Ahaziah H3058
18 And J gathered all the people together, H3058
18 a little; *but* J shall serve him much. H3058
19 shall not live. But J did *it* in subtilty, to H3058
20 And J said, Proclaim a solemn H3058
21 And J sent through all Israel: and all H3058
23 And J went, and Jehonadab the son of H3058
24 burnt offerings, J appointed fourscore H3058
25 offering, that J said to the guard and H3058
28 Thus J destroyed Baal out of Israel. H3058
29 made Israel to sin, J departed not from H3058
30 And the LORD said unto J, Because H3058
31 But J took no heed to walk in the law of H3058
34 Now the rest of the acts of J, and all that H3058
35 And J slept with his fathers: and they H3058
36 And the time that J reigned over Israel H3058
12: 1 In the seventh year of J Jehoash began H3058
13: 1 the son of J began to reign over H3058
14: 8 son of Jehoahaz son of J, king of Israel, H3058
15:12 he spake unto J, saying, Thy sons shall H3058
1Ch 2:38 And Obed begat J, and Jehu begat H3058
38 And Obed begat Jehu, and J begat H3058
4:35 And Joel, and J the son of Josibiah, the H3058
12: 3 and Berachah, and J the Antothite, H3058
2Ch 19: 2 And J the son of Hanani the seer went H3058
20:34 in the book of J the son of Hanani, who H3058
22: 7 Jehoram against J the son of Nimshi, H3058
8 And it came to pass, that, when J was H3058
9 brought him to J: and when they had H3058
25:17 the son of J, king of Israel, saying, H3058
Hos 1: 4 upon the house of J, and will cause to H3058

JEHUBBAH
1Ch 7:34 Shamer; Ahi, and Rohgah, J, and Aram. H3160

JEHUCAL
Jer 37: 3 And Zedekiah the king sent J the son of H3081

JEHUD
Jos 19:45 And J, and Bene-berak, and H3055

JEHUDI
Jer 36:14 Therefore all the princes sent J the son H3065
21 So the king sent J to fetch the roll: and H3065
21 chamber. And J read it in the ears of H3065
23 And it came to pass, *that* when J had H3065

JEHUDIJAH
1Ch 4:18 And his wife J bare Jered the father of H3057

JEHUSH
1Ch 8:39 J the second, and Eliphelet the third. H3266

JEIEL
1Ch 5: 7 *were* the chief, J, and Zechariah, H3273
15:18 and Obed-edom, and J, the porters. H3273
21 Obed-edom, and J, and Azaziah, with H3273
16: 5 to him Zechariah, J, and Shemiramoth, H3273
5 Obed-edom: and J with psalteries and H3273
2Ch 20:14 the son of J, the son of Mattaniah, H3273
26:11 account by the hand of J the scribe and H3273
29:13 Shimri, and J: and of the sons of Asaph; H3273
35: 9 Hashabiah and J and Jozabad, chief of H3273
Ezr 8:13 these, Eliphelet, J, and Shemaiah, and H3273
10:43 Of the sons of Nebo; J, Mattithiah, H3273

JEKABZEEL
Neh 11:25 and at J, and *in* the villages thereof, H3343

JEKAMEAM
1Ch 23:19 Jahaziel the third, and J the fourth. H3360
24:23 second, Jahaziel the third, J the fourth. H3360

JEKAMIAH
1Ch 2:41 And Shallum begat J, and Jekamiah H3359
41 And Shallum begat Jekamiah, and J H3359

JEKUTHIEL
1Ch 4:18 of Socho, and J the father of Zanoah. H3354

JEMIMA
Job 42:14 And he called the name of the first, J; H3224

JEMUEL
Gen 46:10 And the sons of Simeon; J, and Jamin, H3223
Ex 6:15 And the sons of Simeon; J, and Jamin, H3223

JEOPARDED
Jdg 5:18 *were* a people *that* j their lives unto the H2778

JEOPARDY
2Sa 23:17 the men that went in j of their lives?
1Ch 11:19 put their lives in j? for with *the jeopardy* H5315
19 for with *the j of* their lives they brought
12:19 to his master Saul to *the j of* our heads.
Lk 8:23 were filled *with water*, and were in j. *G2793*
1Co 15:30 And why stand we in j every hour? *G2793*

JEPHTHAE
Heb 11:32 *of* Samson, and *of* J; *of* David also, and *G2422*

JEPHTHAH
Jdg 11: 1 Now J the Gileadite was a mighty man H3316
1 the son of an harlot: and Gilead begat J. H3316
2 they thrust out J, and said unto him, H3316
3 Then J fled from his brethren, and H3316
3 vain men to J, and went out with him. H3316
5 went to fetch J out of the land of Tob: H3316
6 And they said unto J, Come, and be our H3316
7 And J said unto the elders of Gilead, H3316
8 And the elders of Gilead said unto J, H3316
9 And J said unto the elders of Gilead, If H3316
10 And the elders of Gilead said unto J, H3316
11 Then J went with the elders of Gilead, H3316
11 over them: and J uttered all his words H3316
12 And J sent messengers unto the king of H3316
13 the messengers of J, Because Israel took H3316
14 And J sent messengers again unto the H3316
15 And said unto him, Thus saith J, Israel H3316
28 unto the words of J which he sent him. H3316
29 LORD came upon J, and he passed over H3316
30 And J vowed a vow unto the LORD, H3316
32 So J passed over unto the children of H3316
34 And J came to Mizpeh unto his house, H3316
40 of J the Gileadite four days in a year. H3316
12: 1 and said unto J, Wherefore passedst H3316
2 And J said unto them, I and my people H3316
4 Then J gathered together all the men of H3316
7 And J judged Israel six years. Then H3316
7 years. Then died J the Gileadite, and H3316
1Sa 12:11 and Bedan, and J, and Samuel, and H3316

JEPHUNNEH
Nu 13: 6 Of the tribe of Judah, Caleb the son of J. H3312
14: 6 Caleb the son of J, *which were* of them H3312
30 the son of J, and Joshua the son of Nun. H3312
38 Caleb the son of J, *which were* of the H3312
26:65 the son of J, and Joshua the son of Nun. H3312
32:12 Save Caleb the son of J the Kenezite, H3312

Nu 34:19 Of the tribe of Judah, Caleb the son of J. H3312
Dt 1:36 Save Caleb the son of J; he shall see it, H3312
Jos 14: 6 and Caleb the son of J the Kenezite said H3312
13 the son of J Hebron for an inheritance. H3312
14 of Caleb the son of J the Kenezite unto H3312
15:13 And unto Caleb the son of J he gave a H3312
21:12 to Caleb the son of J for his possession. H3312
1Ch 4:15 And the sons of Caleb the son of J; Iru, H3312
6:56 thereof, they gave to Caleb the son of J. H3312
7:38 And the sons of Jether; J, and Pispah, H3312

JERAH
Gen 10:26 and Sheleph, and Hazarmaveth, and J, H3392
1Ch 1:20 and Sheleph, and Hazarmaveth, and J, H3392

JERAHMEEL
1Ch 2: 9 unto him; J, and Ram, and Chelubai. H3396
25 And the sons of J the firstborn of H3396
26 J had also another wife, whose name H3396
27 And the sons of Ram the firstborn of J H3396
33 and Zaza. These were the sons of J. H3396
42 Now the sons of Caleb the brother of J H3396
24:29 Concerning Kish: the son of Kish *was* J. H3396
Jer 36:26 But the king commanded J the son of H3396

JERAHMEELITES
1Sa 27:10 J, and against the south of the Kenites. H3397
30:29 in the cities of the J, and to *them* which H3397

JERED
1Ch 1: 2 Kenan, Mahalaleel, J, H3382
4:18 And his wife Jehudijah bare J the father H3382

JEREMAI
Ezr 10:33 Eliphelet, J, Manasseh, *and* Shimei. H3413

JEREMIAH
2Ki 23:31 Hamutal, the daughter of J of Libnah. H3414
24:18 Hamutal, the daughter of J of Libnah. H3414
1Ch 5:24 and Azriel, and J, and Hodaviah, and H3414
12: 4 over the thirty; and J, and Jahaziel, and H3414
10 Mishmannah the fourth, J the fifth, H3414
13 J the tenth, Machbanai the eleventh. H3414
2Ch 35:25 And J lamented for Josiah: and all the H3414
36:12 not himself before J the prophet H3414
21 by the mouth of J, until the land had H3414
22 *spoken* by the mouth of J might be H3414
Ezr 1: 1 by the mouth of J might be fulfilled, the H3414
Neh 10: 2 Seraiah, Azariah, J, H3414
12: 1 Shealtiel, and Jeshua: Seraiah, J, Ezra, H3414
12 of Seraiah, Meraiah; of J, Hananiah; H3414
34 and Benjamin, and Shemaiah, and J, H3414
Jer 1: 1 The words of J the son of Hilkiah, of H3414
11 unto me, saying, J, what seest thou? H3414
7: 1 The word that came to J from the H3414
11: 1 The word that came to J from the H3414
14: 1 The word of the LORD that came to J H3414
18: 1 The word which came to J from the H3414
18 devices against J; for the law shall not H3414
19:14 Then came J from Tophet, whither the H3414
20: 1 heard that J prophesied these things. H3414
2 Then Pashur smote J the prophet, and H3414
3 brought forth J out of the stocks. Then H3414
3 the stocks. Then said J unto him, The H3414
21: 1 The word which came unto J from the H3414
3 Then said J unto them, Thus shall ye H3414
24: 3 What seest thou, J? And I said, Figs; the H3414
25: 1 The word that came to J concerning all H3414
2 The which J the prophet spake unto all H3414
13 in this book, which J hath prophesied H3414
26: 7 all the people heard J speaking these H3414
8 Now it came to pass, when J had made H3414
9 against J in the house of the LORD. H3414
12 Then spake J unto all the princes and H3414
20 this land according to all the words of J: H3414
24 of Shaphan was with J, that they should H3414
27: 1 word unto J from the LORD, saying, H3414
28: 5 Then the prophet J said unto the H3414
6 Even the prophet J said, Amen: the H3414
11 years. And the prophet J went his way. H3414
12 LORD came unto J *the prophet,* after H3414
12 off the neck of the prophet J, saying, H3414
15 Then said the prophet J unto Hananiah H3414
29: 1 of the letter that J the prophet sent H3414
27 thou not reproved J of Anathoth, which H3414
29 this letter in the ears of J the prophet. H3414
30 the word of the LORD unto J, saying, H3414
30: 1 The word that came to J from the H3414
32: 1 The word that came to J from the H3414
Jer 32: 2 Jerusalem: and J the prophet was shut H3414
6 And J said, The word of the LORD H3414
26 the word of the LORD unto J, saying, H3414
33: 1 the LORD came unto J the second time, H3414
19 And the word of the LORD came unto J, H3414
23 the word of the LORD came to J, saying, H3414
34: 1 The word which came unto J from the H3414
6 Then J the prophet spake all these H3414
8 *This is* the word that came unto J from H3414
12 came to J from the LORD, saying, H3414
35: 1 The word which came unto J from the H3414
3 Then I took Jaazaniah the son of J, the H3414
12 the word of the LORD unto J, saying, H3414
18 And J said unto the house of the H3414
36: 1 came unto J from the LORD, saying, H3414
4 Then J called Baruch the son of Neriah: H3414
4 from the mouth of J all the words of the H3414
5 And J commanded Baruch, saying, I H3414
8 to all that J the prophet commanded H3414
10 book the words of J in the house of the H3414
19 J; and let no man know where ye be. H3414
26 J the prophet: but the LORD hid them. H3414
27 Then the word of the LORD came to J, H3414
27 Baruch wrote at the mouth of J, saying, H3414
32 Then took J another roll, and gave it to H3414
32 from the mouth of J all the words of the H3414
37: 2 LORD, which he spake by the prophet J. H3414
3 to the prophet J, saying, Pray now unto H3414
4 Now J came in and went out among the H3414
6 of the LORD unto the prophet J, saying, H3414
12 Then J went forth out of Jerusalem to H3414
13 and he took J the prophet, saying, H3414
14 Then said J, *It is* false; I fall not away to H3414
14 took J, and brought him to the princes. H3414
15 were wroth with J, and smote him, and H3414
16 When J was entered into the dungeon, H3414
16 and J had remained there many days; H3414
17 the LORD? And J said, There is: for, H3414
18 Moreover J said unto king Zedekiah, H3414
21 should commit J into the court of the H3414
21 J remained in the court of the prison. H3414
38: 1 the words that J had spoken unto all H3414
6 Then took they J, and cast him into the H3414
6 and they let down J with cords. And in H3414
6 water, but mire: so J sunk in the mire. H3414
7 that they had put J in the dungeon; the H3414
9 they have done to J the prophet, whom H3414
10 thee, and take up J the prophet out of H3414
11 down by cords into the dungeon to J. H3414
12 said unto J, Put now *these* old cast H3414
12 under the cords. And J did so. H3414
13 So they drew up J with cords, and took H3414
13 J remained in the court of the prison. H3414
14 sent, and took J the prophet unto him H3414
14 the king said unto J, I will ask thee a H3414
15 Then J said unto Zedekiah, If I declare H3414
16 secretly unto J, saying, *As* the LORD H3414
17 Then said J unto Zedekiah, Thus saith H3414
19 And Zedekiah the king said unto J, I am H3414
20 But J said, They shall not deliver *thee*. H3414
24 Then said Zedekiah unto J, Let no man H3414
27 Then came all the princes unto J, and H3414
28 So J abode in the court of the prison H3414
39:11 charge concerning J to Nebuzar-adan H3414
14 Even they sent, and took J out of the H3414
15 Now the word of the LORD came unto J, H3414
40: 1 The word that came to J from the H3414
2 And the captain of the guard took J, H3414
6 Then went J unto Gedaliah the son of H3414
42: 2 And said unto J the prophet, Let, we H3414
4 Then J the prophet said unto them, I H3414
5 Then they said to J, The LORD be a true H3414
7 that the word of the LORD came unto J. H3414
43: 1 And it came to pass, *that* when J had H3414
2 men, saying unto J, Thou speakest H3414
6 son of Shaphan, and J the prophet, and H3414
8 the LORD unto J in Tahpanhes, saying, H3414
44: 1 The word that came to J concerning all H3414
15 Egypt, in Pathros, answered J, saying, H3414
20 Then J said unto all the people, to the H3414
24 Moreover J said unto all the people, H3414
45: 1 The word that J the prophet spake unto H3414
1 at the mouth of J, in the fourth year of H3414
46: 1 The word of the LORD which came to J H3414
13 The word that the LORD spake to J the H3414
47: 1 The word of the LORD that came to J H3414
49:34 The word of the LORD that came to J H3414
50: 1 land of the Chaldeans by J the prophet. H3414
51:59 The word which J the prophet H3414
Jer 51:60 So J wrote in a book all the evil that H3414
61 And J said to Seraiah, When thou H3414
64 be weary. Thus far *are* the words of J. H3414
52: 1 Hamutal the daughter of J of Libnah. H3414
Dan 9: 2 the LORD came to J the prophet, that H3414

JEREMIAH'S
Jer 28:10 off the prophet J neck, and brake it. H3414

JEREMIAS
Mt 16:14 and others, J, or one of the prophets. *G2408*

JEREMOTH
1Ch 8:14 And Ahio, Shashak, and J, H3406
23:23 of Mushi; Mahli, and Eder, and J, three. H3406
25:22 The fifteenth to J, *he,* his sons, and his H3406
Ezr 10:26 and Jehiel, and Abdi, and J, and Eliah. H3406
27 and J, and Zabad, and Aziza. H3406

JEREMY
Mt 2:17 was spoken by J the prophet, saying, *G2408*
27: 9 was spoken by J the prophet, saying, *G2408*

JERIAH
1Ch 23:19 Of the sons of Hebron; J the first, H3404
24:23 And the sons *of Hebron; J the first,* H3404

JERIBAI
1Ch 11:46 Eliel the Mahavite, and J, and H3403

JERICHO
Nu 22: 1 plains of Moab on this side Jordan *by* J. H3405
26: 3 of Moab by Jordan *near* J, saying, H3405
63 in the plains of Moab by Jordan *near* J. H3405
31:12 of Moab, which *are* by Jordan *near* J. H3405
33:48 in the plains of Moab by Jordan *near* J. H3405
50 of Moab by Jordan *near* J, saying, H3405
34:15 *near* J eastward, toward the sunrising. H3405
35: 1 of Moab by Jordan *near* J, saying, H3405
36:13 in the plains of Moab by Jordan *near* J. H3405
Dt 32:49 *is* over against J; and behold the land H3405
34: 1 *is* over against J. And the LORD shewed H3405
3 of J, the city of palm trees, unto Zoar. H3405
Jos 2: 1 the land, even J. And they went, and H3405
2 And it was told the king of J, saying, H3405
3 And the king of J sent unto Rahab, H3405
3:16 the people passed over right against J. H3405
4:13 the LORD unto battle, to the plains of J. H3405
19 in Gilgal, in the east border of J. H3405
5:10 of the month at even in the plains of J. H3405
13 Joshua was by J, that he lifted up his H3405
6: 1 Now J was straitly shut up because of H3405
2 into thine hand J, and the king thereof, H3405
25 which Joshua sent to spy out J. H3405
26 and buildeth this city J: he shall lay the H3405
7: 2 And Joshua sent men from J to Ai, H3405
8: 2 as thou didst unto J and her king: only H3405
9: 3 what Joshua had done unto J and to Ai, H3405
10: 1 as he had done to J and her king, so he H3405
28 Makkedah as he did unto the king of J. H3405
30 king thereof as he did unto the king of J. H3405
12: 9 The king of J, one; the king of Ai, which H3405
13:32 on the other side Jordan, by J, eastward. H3405
16: 1 fell from Jordan by J, unto the water of H3405
1 unto the water of J on the east, to the H3405
1 up from J throughout mount Beth-el, H3405
7 and came to J, and went out at Jordan. H3405
18:12 up to the side of J on the north side, H3405
21 their families were J, and Beth-hoglah, H3405
20: 8 And on the other side Jordan by J H3405
24:11 and came unto J: and the men of H3405
11 and the men of J fought against you, H3405
2Sa 10: 5 king said, Tarry at J until your beards H3405
1Ki 16:34 Hiel the Beth-elite build J: he laid the H3405
2Ki 2: 4 hath sent me to J. And he said, *As* the H3405
4 I will not leave thee. So they came to J. H3405
5 that *were* at J came to Elisha, and H3405
15 *were* to view at J saw him, they said, H3405
18 (for he tarried at J,) he said unto them, H3405
25: 5 in the plains of J: and all his army were H3405
1Ch 6:78 And on the other side Jordan by J, on H3405
19: 5 king said, Tarry at J until your beards H3405
2Ch 28:15 and brought them to J, the city of palm H3405
Ezr 2:34 The children of J, three hundred forty H3405
Neh 3: 2 builded the men of J. And next to them H3405
7:36 The children of J, three hundred forty H3405
Jer 39: 5 in the plains of J: and when they had H3405
52: 8 in the plains of J; and all his army was H3405
Mt 20:29 And as they departed from J, a great *G2410*

Mk 10:46 And they came to J: and as he went out G2410
46 as he went out of J with his disciples G2410
Lk 10:30 from Jerusalem to J, and fell among G2410
18:35 come nigh unto J, a certain blind man G2410
19: 1 *Jesus* entered and passed through J. G2410
Heb 11:30 By faith the walls of J fell down, after G2410

JERIEL
1Ch 7: 2 and Rephaiah, and J, and Jahmai, and H3400

JERIJAH
1Ch 26:31 Among the Hebronites *was* J the chief, H3404

JERIMOTH
1Ch 7: 7 and Uzziel, and J, and Iri, five; heads of H3406
8 and Omri, and J, and Abiah, and H3406
12: 5 Eluzai, and J, and Bealiah, and H3406
24:30 and Eder, and J. These *were* the sons H3406
25: 4 Shebuel, and J, Hananiah, Hanani, H3406
27:19 of Naphtali, J the son of Azriel: H3406
2Ch 11:18 the daughter of J the son of David to H3406
31:13 and Asahel, and J, and Jozabad, and H3406

JERIOTH
1Ch 2:18 *his* wife, and of J: her sons *are* these; H3408

JEROBOAM
1Ki 11:26 And J the son of Nebat, an Ephrathite H3379
28 And the man J *was* a mighty man of H3379
29 And it came to pass at that time when J H3379
31 And he said to J, Take thee ten pieces: H3379
40 Solomon sought therefore to kill J. And H3379
40 Jeroboam. And J arose, and fled into H3379
12: 2 And it came to pass, when J the son of H3379
2 of king Solomon, and J dwelt in Egypt;) H3379
3 That they sent and called him. And J H3379
12 So J and all the people came to H3379
15 the Shilonite unto J the son of Nebat. H3379
20 all Israel heard that J was come again, H3379
25 Then J built Shechem in mount H3379
26 And J said in his heart, Now shall the H3379
32 And J ordained a feast in the eighth H3379
13: 1 J stood by the altar to burn incense. H3379
4 And it came to pass, when king J heard H3379
33 After this thing J returned not from his H3379
34 sin unto the house of J, even to cut *it* off, H3379
14: 1 At that time Abijah the son of J fell H3379
2 And J said to his wife, Arise, I pray H3379
2 to be the wife of J; and get thee to H3379
5 Behold, the wife of J cometh to ask a H3379
6 in, thou wife of J; why feignest thou H3379
7 Go, tell J, Thus saith the LORD God of H3379
10 evil upon the house of J, and will cut off H3379
10 and will cut off from J him that pisseth H3379
10 of the house of J, as a man taketh away H3379
11 Him that dieth of J in the city shall the H3379
13 him: for he only of J shall come to the H3379
13 LORD God of Israel in the house of J. H3379
14 of J that day: but what? even now. H3379
16 of the sins of J, who did sin, and who H3379
19 And the rest of the acts of J, how he H3379
20 And the days which J reigned *were* two H3379
30 Rehoboam and J all *their* days. H3379
15: 1 Now in the eighteenth year of king J the H3379
6 Rehoboam and J all the days of his life. H3379
7 there was war between Abijam and J. H3379
9 And in the twentieth year of J king of H3379
25 And Nadab the son of J began to reign H3379
29 smote all the house of J; he left not to H3379
29 he left not to J any that breathed, until H3379
30 Because of the sins of J which he H3379
34 in the way of J, and in his sin wherewith H3379
16: 2 in the way of J, and hast made my H3379
3 like the house of J the son of Nebat. H3379
7 house of J; and because he killed him. H3379
19 in the way of J, and in his sin which H3379
26 For he walked in all the way of J the H3379
31 to walk in the sins of J the son of Nebat, H3379
21:22 like the house of J the son of Nebat, H3379
22:52 and in the way of J the son of Nebat, H3379
2Ki 3: 3 unto the sins of J the son of Nebat, H3379
9: 9 like the house of J the son of Nebat, H3379
10:29 Howbeit *from* the sins of J the son of H3379
31 the sins of J, which made Israel to sin. H3379
13: 2 the sins of J the son of Nebat, which H3379
6 of the house of J, who made Israel sin, H3379
11 from all the sins of J the son of Nebat, H3379
13 And Joash slept with his fathers; and J H3379
14:16 and J his son reigned in his stead. H3379
2Ki 14:23 king of Judah J the son of Joash king H3379
24 from all the sins of J the son of Nebat, H3379
27 them by the hand of J the son of Joash. H3379
28 Now the rest of the acts of J, and all that H3379
29 And J slept with his fathers, *even* with H3379
15: 1 In the twenty and seventh year of J H3379
8 the son of J reign over Israel in H3379
9 from the sins of J the son of Nebat, who H3379
18 from the sins of J the son of Nebat, who H3379
24 from the sins of J the son of Nebat, who H3379
28 from the sins of J the son of Nebat, who H3379
17:21 and they made J the son of Nebat king: H3379
21 of Nebat king: and J drave Israel from H3379
22 in all the sins of J which he did; they H3379
23:15 the high place which J the son of Nebat, H3379
1Ch 5:17 and in the days of J king of Israel. H3379
2Ch 9:29 the seer against J the son of Nebat? H3379
10: 2 And it came to pass, when J the son of H3379
2 heard *it*, that J returned out of Egypt. H3379
3 And they sent and called him. So J and H3379
12 So J and all the people came to H3379
15 the Shilonite to J the son of Nebat. H3379
11: 4 and returned from going against J. H3379
14 and Jerusalem: for J and his sons had H3379
12:15 between Rehoboam and J continually. H3379
13: 1 Now in the eighteenth year of king J H3379
2 there was war between Abijah and J. H3379
3 chosen men: J also set the battle in H3379
4 said, Hear me, thou J, and all Israel; H3379
6 Yet J the son of Nebat, the servant of H3379
8 calves, which J made you for gods. H3379
13 But J caused an ambushment to come H3379
15 that God smote J and all Israel before H3379
19 And Abijah pursued after J, and took H3379
20 Neither did J recover strength again in H3379
Hos 1: 1 of J the son of Joash, king of Israel. H3379
Am 1: 1 and in the days of J the son of Joash H3379
7: 9 against the house of J with the sword. H3379
10 priest of Beth-el sent to J king of Israel, H3379
11 For thus Amos saith, J shall die by the H3379

JEROBOAM'S
1Ki 14: 4 And J wife did so, and arose, and went H3379
17 And J wife arose, and departed, and H3379

JEROHAM
1Sa 1: 1 the son of J, the son of Elihu, the H3395
1Ch 6:27 Eliab his son, J his son, Elkanah his H3395
34 The son of Elkanah, the son of J, the son H3395
8:27 and Eliah, and Zichri, the sons of J. H3395
9: 8 And Ibneiah the son of J, and Elah the H3395
12 And Adaiah the son of J, the son of H3395
12: 7 And Joelah, and Zebadiah, the sons of J H3395
27:22 Of Dan, Azareel the son of J. These *were* H3395
2Ch 23: 1 Azariah the son of J, and Ishmael the H3395
Neh 11:12 Adaiah the son of J, the son of Pelaliah, H3395

JERUBBAAL
Jdg 6:32 Therefore on that day he called him J, H3378
7: 1 Then J, who *is* Gideon, and all the H3378
8:29 And J the son of Joash went and dwelt H3378
35 to the house of J, *namely*, Gideon, H3378
9: 1 And Abimelech the son of J went to H3378
2 either that all the sons of J, *which are* H3378
5 the sons of J, *being* threescore and H3378
5 son of J was left; for he hid himself. H3378
16 dealt well with J and his house, and H3378
19 and sincerely with J and with his house H3378
24 and ten sons of J might come, and their H3378
28 *is* not *he* the son of J? and Zebul his H3378
57 came the curse of Jotham the son of J. H3378
1Sa 12:11 And the LORD sent J, and Bedan, and H3378

JERUBBESHETH
2Sa 11:21 Who smote Abimelech the son of J? did H3380

JERUEL
2Ch 20:16 of the brook, before the wilderness of J. H3385

JERUSALEM
Jos 10: 1 king of J had heard how Joshua H3389
3 Wherefore Adoni-zedek king of J sent H3389
5 the king of J, the king of Hebron, H3389
23 cave, the king of J, the king of Hebron, H3389
12:10 The king of J, one; the king of Hebron, H3389
15: 8 the same *is* J: and the border went H3389
63 As for the Jebusites the inhabitants of J, H3389
63 the children of Judah at J unto this day. H3389
18:28 Jebusi, which *is* J, Gibeath, *and* Kirjath; H3389
Jdg 1: 7 brought him to J, and there he died. H3389
8 fought against J, and had taken it, and H3389
21 that inhabited J; but the Jebusites dwell H3389
21 children of Benjamin in J unto this day. H3389
19:10 Jebus, which *is* J; and *there were* with H3389
1Sa 17:54 it to J; but he put his armour in his tent. H3389
2Sa 5: 5 six months: and in J he reigned thirty H3389
6 And the king and his men went to J H3389
13 and wives out of J, after he was come H3389
14 born unto him in J; Shammua, and H3389
8: 7 of Hadadezer, and brought them to J. H3389
9:13 So Mephibosheth dwelt in J: for he did H3389
10:14 the children of Ammon, and came to J. H3389
11: 1 Rabbah. But David tarried still at J. H3389
12 abode in J that day, and the morrow. H3389
12:31 and all the people returned unto J. H3389
14:23 to Geshur, and brought Absalom to J. H3389
28 So Absalom dwelt two full years in J, H3389
15: 8 indeed to J, then I will serve the LORD. H3389
11 men out of J, *that were* called; and H3389
14 that *were* with him at J, Arise, and let us H3389
29 God again to J: and they tarried there. H3389
37 into the city, and Absalom came into J. H3389
16: 3 he abideth at J: for he said, To day shall H3389
15 came to J, and Ahithophel with him. H3389
17:20 could not find *them*, they returned to J. H3389
19:19 king went out of J, that the king should H3389
25 he was come to J to meet the king, that H3389
33 me, and I will feed thee with me in J. H3389
34 that I should go up with the king unto J? H3389
20: 2 unto their king, from Jordan even to J. H3389
3 And David came to his house at J; and H3389
7 they went out of J, to pursue after Sheba H3389
22 And Joab returned to J unto the king. H3389
24: 8 land, they came to J at the end of nine H3389
16 out his hand upon J to destroy it, the H3389
1Ki 2:11 thirty and three years reigned he in J. H3389
36 thee an house in J, and dwell there, and H3389
38 do. And Shimei dwelt in J many days. H3389
41 from J to Gath, and was come again. H3389
3: 1 LORD, and the wall of J round about. H3389
15 And he came to J, and stood before the H3389
8: 1 unto king Solomon in J, that they might H3389
9:15 J, and Hazor, and Megiddo, and Gezer. H3389
19 desired to build in J, and in Lebanon, H3389
10: 2 And she came to J with a very great H3389
26 for chariots, and with the king at J. H3389
27 And the king made silver *to be* in J as H3389
11: 7 hill that *is* before J, and for Molech, the H3389
29 went out of J, that the prophet Ahijah H3389
36 before me in J, the city which I have H3389
42 And the time that Solomon reigned in J H3389
12:18 to get him up to his chariot, to flee to J. H3389
21 And when Rehoboam was come to J, he H3389
27 of the LORD at J, then shall the heart H3389
28 for you to go up to J: behold thy gods, O H3389
14:21 seventeen years in J, the city which the H3389
25 king of Egypt came up against J: H3389
15: 2 Three years reigned he in J. And his H3389
4 give him a lamp in J, to set up his son H3389
4 up his son after him, and to establish J: H3389
10 And forty and one years reigned he in J. H3389
22:42 and five years in J. And his mother's H3389
2Ki 8:17 to reign; and he reigned eight years in J. H3389
26 one year in J. And his mother's name H3389
9:28 him in a chariot to J, and buried him in H3389
12: 1 reigned he in J. And his mother's name H3389
17 it: and Hazael set his face to go up to J. H3389
18 king of Syria: and he went away from J. H3389
14: 2 and nine years in J. And his mother's H3389
2 his mother's name *was* Jehoaddan of J. H3389
13 and came to J, and brake down the H3389
13 down the wall of J from the gate of H3389
19 against him in J: and he fled to Lachish; H3389
20 at J with his fathers in the city of David. H3389
15: 2 and fifty years in J. And his mother's H3389
2 his mother's name *was* Jecholiah of J. H3389
33 sixteen years in J. And his mother's H3389
16: 2 sixteen years in J, and did not *that* H3389
5 of Israel came up to J to war: and they H3389
18: 2 and nine years in J. His mother's name H3389
17 a great host against J. And they went up H3389
17 up and came to J. And when they were H3389
22 said to Judah and J, Ye shall worship H3389
22 Ye shall worship before this altar in J? H3389
35 should deliver J out of mine hand? H3389
19:10 thee, saying, J shall not be delivered H3389
21 of J hath shaken her head at thee. H3389
31 For out of J shall go forth a remnant, H3389

2Ki 21: 1 and five years in J. And his mother's H3389
4 the LORD said, In J will I put my name. H3389
7 In this house, and in J, which I have H3389
12 *such* evil upon J and Judah, that H3389
13 And I will stretch over J the line of H3389
13 and I will wipe J as *a man* wipeth a H3389
16 till he had filled J from one end to H3389
19 two years in J. And his mother's name H3389
22: 1 and one years in J. And his mother's H3389
14 (now she dwelt in J in the college;) and H3389
23: 1 him all the elders of Judah and of J. H3389
2 the inhabitants of J with him, and the H3389
4 them without J in the fields of Kidron, H3389
5 round about J; them also that burned H3389
6 of the LORD, without J, unto the brook H3389
9 of the LORD in J, but they did eat of the H3389
13 And the high places that *were* before J, H3389
20 bones upon them, and returned to J. H3389
23 passover was holden to the LORD in J. H3389
24 of Judah and in J, did Josiah put away, H3389
27 cast off this city J which I have chosen, H3389
30 brought him to J, and buried him in his H3389
31 three months in J. And his mother's H3389
33 might not reign in J; and put the land to H3389
36 eleven years in J. And his mother's H3389
24: 4 he shed: for he filled J with innocent H3389
8 and he reigned in J three months. And H3389
8 the daughter of Elnathan of J. H3389
10 up against J, and the city was besieged. H3389
14 And he carried away all J, and all the H3389
15 he into captivity from J to Babylon. H3389
18 eleven years in J. And his mother's H3389
20 it came to pass in J and Judah, until he H3389
25: 1 his host, against J, and pitched against H3389
8 a servant of the king of Babylon, unto J: H3389
9 and all the houses of J, and every great H3389
10 brake down the walls of J round about. H3389
1Ch 3: 4 in J he reigned thirty and three years. H3389
5 And these were born unto him in J; H3389
6:10 in the temple that Solomon built in J:) H3389
15 and J by the hand of Nebuchadnezzar. H3389
32 of the LORD in J: and *then* they waited H3389
8:28 chief *men*. These dwelt in J. H3389
32 their brethren in J, over against them. H3389
9: 3 And in J dwelt of the children of Judah, H3389
34 their generations; these dwelt at J. H3389
38 at J, over against their brethren. H3389
11: 4 And David and all Israel went to J, H3389
14: 3 And David took more wives at J: and H3389
4 which he had in J; Shammua, and H3389
15: 3 Israel together to J, to bring up the ark H3389
18: 7 of Hadarezer, and brought them to J. H3389
19:15 into the city. Then Joab came to J. H3389
20: 1 But David tarried at J. And Joab smote H3389
3 David and all the people returned to J. H3389
21: 4 throughout all Israel, and came to J. H3389
15 And God sent an angel unto J to H3389
16 stretched out over J. Then David and H3389
23:25 that they may dwell in J for ever: H3389
28: 1 and with all the valiant men, unto J. H3389
29:27 thirty and three *years* reigned he in J. H3389
2Ch 1: 4 it: for he had pitched a tent for it at J. H3389
13 that *was* at Gibeon to J, from before the H3389
14 the chariot cities, and with the king at J. H3389
15 And the king made silver and gold at J H3389
2: 7 J, whom David my father did provide. H3389
16 to Joppa; and thou shalt carry it up to J. H3389
3: 1 of the LORD at J in mount Moriah, H3389
5: 2 of Israel, unto J, to bring up the ark of H3389
6: 6 But I have chosen J, that my name H3389
8: 6 desired to build in J, and in Lebanon, H3389
9: 1 hard questions at J, with a very great H3389
25 the chariot cities, and with the king at J. H3389
27 And the king made silver in J as stones, H3389
30 And Solomon reigned in J over all H3389
10:18 to get him up to *his* chariot, to flee to J. H3389
11: 1 And when Rehoboam was come to J, he H3389
5 And Rehoboam dwelt in J, and built H3389
14 to Judah and J: for Jeroboam and his H3389
16 of Israel came to J, to sacrifice unto the H3389
12: 2 came up against J, because they had H3389
4 *pertained* to Judah, and came to J. H3389
5 together to J because of Shishak, H3389
7 out upon J by the hand of Shishak. H3389
9 came up against J, and took away the H3389
13 himself in J, and reigned: for Rehoboam H3389
13 seventeen years in J, the city which the H3389
13: 2 He reigned three years in J. His H3389
14:15 in abundance, and returned to J. H3389
2Ch 15:10 together at J in the third month, H3389
17:13 of war, mighty men of valour, *were* in J. H3389
19: 1 returned to his house in peace to J. H3389
4 And Jehoshaphat dwelt at J: and he H3389
8 Moreover in J did Jehoshaphat set of H3389
8 controversies, when they returned to J. H3389
20: 5 of Judah and J, in the house of the H3389
15 and ye inhabitants of J, and thou king H3389
17 you, O Judah and J: fear not, nor be H3389
18 and the inhabitants of J fell before the H3389
20 ye inhabitants of J; Believe in the LORD H3389
27 man of Judah and J, and Jehoshaphat H3389
27 to go again to J with joy; for the LORD H3389
28 And they came to J with psalteries and H3389
31 and five years in J. And his mother's H3389
21: 5 to reign, and he reigned eight years in J. H3389
11 caused the inhabitants of J to commit H3389
13 the inhabitants of J to go a whoring, H3389
20 and he reigned in J eight years, and H3389
22: 1 And the inhabitants of J made Ahaziah H3389
2 one year in J. His mother's name H3389
23: 2 the fathers of Israel, and they came to J. H3389
24: 1 forty years in J. His mother's name H3389
6 of Judah and out of J the collection, H3389
9 Judah and J, to bring in to the LORD H3389
18 Judah and J for this their trespass. H3389
23 to Judah and J, and destroyed all the H3389
25: 1 and nine years in J. And his mother's H3389
1 his mother's name *was* Jehoaddan of J. H3389
23 brought him to J, and brake down the H3389
23 down the wall of J from the gate of H3389
27 against him in J; and he fled to Lachish: H3389
26: 3 and two years in J. His mother's name H3389
3 mother's name also *was* Jecoliah of J. H3389
9 Moreover Uzziah built towers in J at H3389
15 And he made in J engines, invented by H3389
27: 1 sixteen years in J. His mother's name H3389
8 to reign, and reigned sixteen years in J. H3389
28: 1 sixteen years in J: but he did not *that* H3389
10 of Judah and J for bondmen and H3389
24 he made him altars in every corner of J. H3389
27 in the city, *even* in J: but they brought H3389
29: 1 and twenty years in J. And his mother's H3389
8 was upon Judah and J, and he hath H3389
30: 1 of the LORD at J, to keep the passover H3389
2 congregation in J, to keep the passover H3389
3 gathered themselves together to J. H3389
5 God of Israel at J: for they had not done H3389
11 humbled themselves, and came to J. H3389
13 And there assembled at J much people H3389
14 altars that *were* in J, and all the altars H3389
21 that were present at J kept the feast of H3389
26 So there was great joy in J: for since the H3389
26 king of Israel *there was* not the like in J. H3389
31: 4 that dwelt in J to give the portion of H3389
32: 2 that he was purposed to fight against J, H3389
9 his servants to J, (but he *himself laid* H3389
9 unto all Judah that *were* at J, saying, H3389
10 ye trust, that ye abide in the siege in J? H3389
12 Judah and J, saying, Ye shall worship H3389
18 unto the people of J that *were* on the H3389
19 And they spake against the God of J, as H3389
22 the inhabitants of J from the hand of H3389
23 unto the LORD to J, and presents to H3389
25 wrath upon him, and upon Judah and J. H3389
26 the inhabitants of J, so that the wrath of H3389
33 the inhabitants of J did him honour at H3389
33: 1 and he reigned fifty and five years in J: H3389
4 said, In J shall my name be for ever. H3389
7 In this house, and in J, which I have H3389
9 the inhabitants of J to err, *and* to do H3389
13 him again to J into his kingdom. Then H3389
15 and in J, and cast *them* out of the city. H3389
21 to reign, and reigned two years in J. H3389
34: 1 he reigned in J one and thirty years. H3389
3 to purge Judah and J from the high H3389
5 their altars, and cleansed Judah and J. H3389
7 all the land of Israel, he returned to J. H3389
9 and Benjamin; and they returned to J. H3389
22 (now she dwelt in J in the college:) and H3389
29 together all the elders of Judah and J. H3389
30 the inhabitants of J, and the priests, H3389
32 that were present in J and Benjamin to H3389
32 the inhabitants of J did according to H3389
35: 1 unto the LORD in J: and they killed the H3389
18 were present, and the inhabitants of J. H3389
24 brought him to J, and he died, and was H3389
24 all Judah and J mourned for Josiah. H3389
36: 1 made him king in his father's stead in J. H3389
2Ch 36: 2 reign, and he reigned three months in J. H3389
3 put him down at J, and condemned the H3389
4 over Judah and J, and turned his name H3389
5 eleven years in J: and he did *that which* H3389
9 and ten days in J: and he did *that which* H3389
10 his brother king over Judah and J. H3389
11 to reign, and reigned eleven years in J. H3389
14 the LORD which he had hallowed in J. H3389
19 down the wall of J, and burnt all the H3389
23 him an house in J, which *is* in Judah. H3389
Ezr 1: 2 him an house at J, which *is* in Judah. H3389
3 let him go up to J, which *is* in Judah, H3389
3 of Israel, (he *is* the God,) which *is* in J. H3389
4 offering for the house of God that *is* in J. H3389
5 the house of the LORD which *is* in J. H3389
7 forth out of J, and had put them in H3389
11 were brought up from Babylon unto J. H3389
2: 1 J and Judah, every one unto his city; H3389
68 LORD which *is* at J, offered freely for H3389
3: 1 themselves together as one man to J. H3389
8 house of God at J, in the second month, H3389
8 the captivity unto J; and appointed the H3389
4: 6 against the inhabitants of Judah and J. H3389
8 J to Artaxerxes the king in this sort: H3390
12 to us are come unto J, building the H3390
20 kings also over J, which have ruled over H3390
23 went up in haste to J unto the Jews, and H3390
24 of God which *is* at J. So it ceased unto H3390
5: 1 *were* in Judah and J in the name of the H3390
2 of God which *is* at J: and with them H3390
14 temple that *was* in J, and brought them H3390
15 temple that *is* in J, and let the house of H3390
16 of God which *is* in J: and since that time H3390
17 house of God at J, and let the king send H3390
6: 3 the house of God at J, Let the house be H3390
5 temple which *is* at J, and brought unto H3390
5 the temple which *is* at J, *every one* to his H3390
9 which *are* at J, let it be given them H3390
12 of God which *is* at J. I Darius have made H3390
18 J; as it is written in the book of Moses. H3390
7: 7 Nethinims, unto J, in the seventh year H3389
8 And he came to J in the fifth month, H3389
9 month came he to J, according to the H3389
13 own freewill to go up to J, go with thee. H3390
14 Judah and J, according to the law H3390
15 God of Israel, whose habitation *is* in J, H3390
16 for the house of their God which *is* in J: H3390
17 of the house of your God which *is* in J. H3390
19 *those* deliver thou before the God of J. H3390
27 the house of the LORD which *is* in J: H3389
8:29 of Israel, at J, in the chambers of the H3389
30 *them* to J unto the house of our God. H3389
31 month, to go unto J: and the hand of H3389
32 And we came to J, and abode there H3389
9: 9 and to give us a wall in Judah and in J. H3389
10: 7 Judah and J unto all the children H3389
7 gather themselves together unto J; H3389
9 together unto J within three days. It H3389
Neh 1: 2 left of the captivity, and concerning J. H3389
3 the wall of J also *is* broken down, H3389
2:11 So I came to J, and was there three H3389
12 in my heart to do at J: neither *was there* H3389
13 the walls of J, which were broken H3389
17 we *are* in, how J *lieth* waste, and the H3389
17 of J, that we be no more a reproach. H3389
20 portion, nor right, nor memorial, in J. H3389
3: 8 they fortified J unto the broad wall. H3389
9 of Hur, the ruler of the half part of J. H3389
12 the half part of J, he and his daughters. H3389
4: 7 that the walls of J were made up, *and* H3389
8 *and* to fight against J, and to hinder it. H3389
22 lodge within J, that in the night they H3389
6: 7 to preach of thee at J, saying, *There is* a H3389
7: 2 charge over J: for he *was* a faithful H3389
3 not the gates of J be opened until the H3389
3 of the inhabitants of J, every one in his H3389
6 J and to Judah, every one unto his city; H3389
8:15 all their cities, and in J, saying, Go forth H3389
11: 1 And the rulers of the people dwelt at J: H3389
1 of ten to dwell in J the holy city, and H3389
2 offered themselves to dwell at J. H3389
3 that dwelt in J: but in the cities of Judah H3389
4 And at J dwelt *certain* of the children of H3389
6 All the sons of Perez that dwelt at J H3389
22 The overseer also of the Levites at J H3389
12:27 And at the dedication of the wall of J H3389
27 places, to bring them to J, to keep the H3389
28 J, and from the villages of Netophathi; H3389
29 builded them villages round about J. H3389

Neh 12:43 the joy of J was heard even afar off. H3389
13: 6 But in all this *time* was not I at J: for in H3389
7 And I came to J, and understood of the H3389
15 they brought into J on the sabbath day: H3389
16 unto the children of Judah, and in J. H3389
19 when the gates of J began to be dark H3389
20 of ware lodged without J once or twice. H3389
Est 2: 6 Who had been carried away from J H3389
Ps 51:18 unto Zion: build thou the walls of J. H3389
68:29 Because of thy temple at J shall kings H3389
79: 1 they defiled; they have laid J on heaps. H3389
3 J; and *there was* none to bury *them*. H3389
102:21 of the LORD in Zion, and his praise in J; H3389
116:19 midst of thee, O J. Praise ye the LORD. H3389
122: 2 feet shall stand within thy gates, O J. H3389
3 J is builded as a city that is compact H3389
6 Pray for the peace of J: they shall H3389
125: 2 As the mountains *are* round about J, so H3389
128: 5 see the good of J all the days of thy life. H3389
135:21 which dwelleth at J. Praise ye the LORD. H3389
137: 5 If I forget thee, O J, let my right hand H3389
6 if I prefer not J above my chief joy. H3389
7 in the day of J; who said, Rase *it*, rase H3389
147: 2 The LORD doth build up J: he gathereth H3389
12 Praise the LORD, O J; praise thy God, O H3389
Ecc 1: 1 Preacher, the son of David, king in J. H3389
12 I the Preacher was king over Israel in J. H3389
16 been before me in J: yea, my heart had H3389
2: 7 above all that were in J before me: H3389
9 J: also my wisdom remained with me. H3389
Song 1: 5 O ye daughters of J, as the tents of H3389
2: 7 I charge you, O ye daughters of J, by the H3389
3: 5 I charge you, O ye daughters of J, by the H3389
10 paved *with* love, for the daughters of J. H3389
5: 8 I charge you, O daughters of J, if ye find H3389
16 and this *is* my friend, O daughters of J. H3389
6: 4 as J, terrible as *an army* with banners. H3389
8: 4 I charge you, O daughters of J, that ye H3389
Isa 1: 1 Judah and J in the days of Uzziah, H3389
2: 1 of Amoz saw concerning Judah and J. H3389
3 law, and the word of the LORD from J. H3389
3: 1 take away from J and from Judah the H3389
8 For J is ruined, and Judah is fallen: H3389
4: 3 *that* remaineth in J, shall be called holy, H3389
3 that is written among the living in J: H3389
4 the blood of J from the midst thereof H3389
5: 3 And now, O inhabitants of J, and men H3389
7: 1 went up toward J to war against it, but H3389
8:14 and for a snare to the inhabitants of J. H3389
10:10 did excel them of J and of Samaria; H3389
11 and her idols, so do to J and her idols? H3389
12 Zion and on J, I will punish the fruit H3389
32 of the daughter of Zion, the hill of J. H3389
22:10 And ye have numbered the houses of J, H3389
21 of J, and to the house of Judah. H3389
24:23 in J, and before his ancients gloriously. H3389
27:13 the LORD in the holy mount at J. H3389
28:14 men, that rule this people which *is* in J. H3389
30:19 For the people shall dwell in Zion at J: H3389
31: 5 of hosts defend J; defending also he will H3389
9 fire *is* in Zion, and his furnace in J. H3389
33:20 eyes shall see J a quiet habitation, a H3389
36: 2 from Lachish to J unto king Hezekiah H3389
7 to J, Ye shall worship before this altar? H3389
20 LORD should deliver J out of my hand? H3389
37:10 thee, saying, J shall not be given into H3389
22 of J hath shaken her head at thee. H3389
32 For out of J shall go forth a remnant, H3389
40: 2 Speak ye comfortably to J, and cry unto H3389
9 high mountain; O J, that bringest good H3389
41:27 give to J one that bringeth good tidings. H3389
44:26 that saith to J, Thou shalt be inhabited; H3389
28 even saying to J, Thou shalt be built; H3389
51:17 Awake, awake, stand up, O J, which H3389
52: 1 garments, O J, the holy city: for H3389
2 *and* sit down, O J: loose thyself from the H3389
9 ye waste places of J: for the LORD hath H3389
9 his people, he hath redeemed J. H3389
62: 6 upon thy walls, O J, *which* shall never H3389
7 and till he make J a praise in the earth. H3389
64:10 Zion is a wilderness, J a desolation. H3389
65:18 J a rejoicing, and her people a joy. H3389
19 And I will rejoice in J, and joy in my H3389
66:10 Rejoice ye with J, and be glad with her, H3389
13 you; and ye shall be comforted in J. H3389
20 my holy mountain J, saith the LORD, as H3389
Jer 1: 3 away of J captive in the fifth month. H3389
15 of the gates of J, and against all the H3389
2: 2 Go and cry in the ears of J, saying, Thus H3389

Jer 3:17 At that time they shall call J the throne H3389
17 of the LORD, to J: neither shall they H3389
4: 3 the men of Judah and J, Break up your H3389
4 and inhabitants of J: lest my fury come H3389
5 Declare ye in Judah, and publish in J; H3389
10 this people and J, saying, Ye shall have H3389
11 this people and to J, A dry wind of the H3389
14 O J, wash thine heart from wickedness, H3389
16 publish against J, *that* watchers come H3389
5: 1 the streets of J, and see now, and know, H3389
6: 1 flee out of the midst of J, and blow the H3389
6 a mount against J: this *is* the city to be H3389
8 Be thou instructed, O J, lest my soul H3389
7:17 cities of Judah and in the streets of J? H3389
29 Cut off thine hair, *O J*, and cast *it* away,
34 from the streets of J, the voice of mirth, H3389
8: 1 the inhabitants of J, out of their graves: H3389
5 Why *then* is this people of J slidden H3389
9:11 And I will make J heaps, *and* a den of H3389
11: 2 of Judah, and to the inhabitants of J; H3389
6 in the streets of J, saying, Hear ye the H3389
9 Judah, and among the inhabitants of J. H3389
12 and inhabitants of J go, and cry unto H3389
13 of the streets of J have ye set up altars H3389
13: 9 pride of Judah, and the great pride of J. H3389
13 the inhabitants of J, with drunkenness. H3389
27 Woe unto thee, O J! wilt thou not be H3389
14: 2 the ground; and the cry of J is gone up. H3389
16 in the streets of J because of the famine H3389
15: 4 king of Judah, for *that* which he did in J. H3389
5 For who shall have pity upon thee, O J? H3389
17:19 they go out, and in all the gates of J; H3389
20 of J, that enter in by these gates: H3389
21 day, nor bring *it* in by the gates of J; H3389
25 of J: and this city shall remain for ever. H3389
26 the places about J, and from the land of H3389
27 in at the gates of J on the sabbath day; H3389
27 of J, and it shall not be quenched. H3389
18:11 the inhabitants of J, saying, Thus saith H3389
19: 3 and inhabitants of J; Thus saith the H3389
7 of Judah and J in this place; and I will H3389
13 And the houses of J, and the houses of H3389
22:19 and cast forth beyond the gates of J. H3389
23:14 I have seen also in the prophets of J an H3389
15 the prophets of J is profaneness gone H3389
24: 1 J, and had brought them to Babylon. H3389
8 and the residue of J, that remain in this H3389
25: 2 and to all the inhabitants of J, saying, H3389
18 *To wit*, J, and the cities of Judah, and H3389
26:18 *like* a field, and J shall become heaps, H3389
27: 3 come to J unto Zedekiah king of Judah; H3389
18 of Judah, and at J, go not to Babylon. H3389
20 of Judah from J to Babylon, and all H3389
20 and all the nobles of Judah and J; H3389
21 the house of the king of Judah and of J; H3389
29: 1 prophet sent from J unto the residue of H3389
1 away captive from J to Babylon; H3389
2 of Judah and J, and the carpenters, H3389
2 and the smiths, were departed from J;) H3389
4 be carried away from J unto Babylon; H3389
20 whom I have sent from J to Babylon: H3389
25 people that *are* at J, and to Zephaniah H3389
32: 2 army besieged J: and Jeremiah the H3389
32 men of Judah, and the inhabitants of J. H3389
44 in the places about J, and in the cities of H3389
33:10 and in the streets of J, that are desolate, H3389
13 in the places about J, and in the cities of H3389
16 be saved, and J shall dwell safely: and H3389
34: 1 fought against J, and against all the H3389
6 words unto Zedekiah king of Judah in J, H3389
7 fought against J, and against all the H3389
8 *were* at J, to proclaim liberty unto them; H3389
19 and the princes of J, the eunuchs, and H3389
35:11 and let us go to J for fear of the army H3389
11 army of the Syrians: so we dwell at J. H3389
13 the inhabitants of J, Will ye not receive H3389
17 all the inhabitants of J all the evil that I H3389
36: 9 to all the people in J, and to all the H3389
9 came from the cities of Judah unto J. H3389
31 the inhabitants of J, and upon the men H3389
37: 5 that besieged J heard tidings of them, H3389
5 tidings of them, they departed from J. H3389
11 up from J for fear of Pharaoh's army, H3389
12 Then Jeremiah went forth out of J to go H3389
38:28 until the day that J was taken: and he H3389
28 and he was *there* when J was taken. H3389
39: 1 his army against J, and they besieged it. H3389
8 with fire, and brake down the walls of J. H3389
40: 1 away captive of J and Judah, which H3389

Jer 42:18 the inhabitants of J; so shall my fury be H3389
44: 2 brought upon J, and upon all the cities H3389
6 in the streets of J; and they are wasted H3389
9 the land of Judah, and in the streets of J? H3389
13 as I have punished J, by the sword, by H3389
17 and in the streets of J: for *then* had we H3389
21 in the streets of J, ye, and your fathers, H3389
51:35 the inhabitants of Chaldea, shall J say. H3389
50 afar off, and let J come into your mind. H3389
52: 1 eleven years in J. And his mother's H3389
3 it came to pass in J and Judah, till he H3389
4 his army, against J, and pitched against H3389
12 served the king of Babylon, into J, H3389
13 all the houses of J, and all the houses of H3389
14 down all the walls of J round about. H3389
29 J eight hundred thirty and two persons: H3389
Lam 1: 7 J remembered in the days of her H3389
8 J hath grievously sinned; therefore she H3389
17 round about him: J is as a menstruous H3389
2:10 J hang down their heads to the ground. H3389
13 O daughter of J? what shall I equal to H3389
15 at the daughter of J, *saying*, *Is* this the H3389
4:12 should have entered into the gates of J. H3389
Ezk 4: 1 and pourtray upon it the city, *even* J: H3389
7 the siege of J, and thine arm *shall* H3389
16 the staff of bread in J: and they shall eat H3389
5: 5 Thus saith the Lord GOD; This *is* J: I H3389
8: 3 the visions of God to J, to the door of the H3389
9: 4 the midst of J, and set a mark upon H3389
8 in thy pouring out of thy fury upon J? H3389
11:15 the inhabitants of J have said, Get you H3389
12:10 the prince in J, and all the house of H3389
19 the inhabitants of J, *and* of the land of H3389
13:16 concerning J, and which see visions H3389
14:21 judgments upon J, the sword, and the H3389
22 brought upon J, *even* concerning all H3389
15: 6 fuel, so will I give the inhabitants of J. H3389
16: 2 Son of man, cause J to know her H3389
3 the Lord GOD unto J; Thy birth and thy H3389
17:12 is come to J, and hath taken the H3389
21: 2 Son of man, set thy face toward J, and H3389
20 and to Judah in J the defenced. H3389
22 was the divination for J, to appoint H3389
22:19 I will gather you into the midst of J. H3389
23: 4 Samaria *is* Aholah, and J Aholibah. H3389
24: 2 set himself against J this same day. H3389
26: 2 hath said against J, Aha, she is broken H3389
33:21 escaped out of J came unto me, saying, H3389
36:38 As the holy flock, as the flock of J in her H3389
Dan 1: 1 king of Babylon unto J, and besieged it. H3389
5: 2 which *was* in J; that the king, and his H3390
3 God which *was* at J; and the king, and H3390
6:10 chamber toward J, he kneeled upon his H3390
9: 2 seventy years in the desolations of J. H3389
7 the inhabitants of J, and unto all Israel, H3389
12 been done as hath been done upon J. H3389
16 turned away from thy city J, thy holy H3389
16 of our fathers, J and thy people *are* H3389
25 and to build J unto the Messiah the H3389
Joel 2:32 Zion and in J shall be deliverance, H3389
3: 1 bring again the captivity of Judah and J, H3389
6 the children of J have ye sold unto the H3389
16 his voice from J; and the heavens and H3389
17 then shall J be holy, and there shall H3389
20 But Judah shall dwell for ever, and J H3389
Am 1: 2 his voice from J; and the habitations H3389
2: 5 and it shall devour the palaces of J. H3389
Oba 11 upon J, even thou *wast* as one of them. H3389
20 the captivity of J, which *is* in Sepharad, H3389
Mic 1: 1 he saw concerning Samaria and J. H3389
5 the high places of Judah? *are they* not J? H3389
9 unto the gate of my people, *even* to J. H3389
12 down from the LORD unto the gate of J. H3389
3:10 They build up Zion with blood, and J H3389
12 *as* a field, and J shall become heaps, H3389
4: 2 Zion, and the word of the LORD from J. H3389
8 shall come to the daughter of J. H3389
Zep 1: 4 all the inhabitants of J; and I will cut off H3389
12 *that* I will search J with candles, and H3389
3:14 with all the heart, O daughter of J. H3389
16 In that day it shall be said to J, Fear H3389
Zec 1:12 not have mercy on J and on the cities of H3389
14 for J and for Zion with a great jealousy. H3389
16 I am returned to J with mercies: my H3389
16 a line shall be stretched forth upon J. H3389
17 yet comfort Zion, and shall yet choose J. H3389
19 have scattered Judah, Israel, and J. H3389
2: 2 me, To measure J, to see what *is* the H3389
4 man, saying, J shall be inhabited *as* H3389

J

Zec 2:12 the holy land, and shall choose J again. H3389
3: 2 that hath chosen J rebuke thee: *is* not H3389
7: 7 prophets, when J was inhabited and in H3389
8: 3 in the midst of J: and Jerusalem shall H3389
3 of Jerusalem: and J shall be called a H3389
4 in the streets of J, and every man with H3389
8 in the midst of J: and they shall be my H3389
15 J and to the house of Judah: fear ye not. H3389
22 hosts in J, and to pray before the LORD. H3389
9: 9 shout, O daughter of J: behold, thy King H3389
10 the horse from J, and the battle bow H3389
12: 2 Behold, I will make J a cup of H3389
2 siege both against Judah *and* against J. H3389
3 And in that day will I make J a H3389
5 heart, The inhabitants of J *shall be* my H3389
6 and on the left: and J shall be inhabited H3389
6 again in her own place, *even* in J. H3389
7 of the inhabitants of J do not magnify H3389
8 the inhabitants of J; and he that is H3389
9 all the nations that come against J. H3389
10 the inhabitants of J, the spirit of grace H3389
11 great mourning in J, as the mourning of H3389
13: 1 of J for sin and for uncleanness. H3389
14: 2 For I will gather all nations against J to H3389
4 which *is* before J on the east, and the H3389
8 shall go out from J; half of them toward H3389
10 Rimmon south of J: and it shall be lifted H3389
11 but J shall be safely inhabited. H3389
12 have fought against J; Their flesh shall H3389
14 And Judah also shall fight at J; and the H3389
16 came against J shall even go up from H3389
17 of the earth unto J to worship the King, H3389
21 Yea, every pot in J and in Judah shall H3389
Mal 2:11 in Israel and in J; for Judah hath H3389
3: 4 Then shall the offering of Judah and J H3389
Mt 2: 1 there came wise men from the east to J, G2414
3 he was troubled, and all J with him. G2414
3: 5 Then went out to him J, and all Judaea, G2414
4:25 and *from* J, and *from* Judaea, and G2414
5:35 by J; for it is the city of the great King. G2414
15: 1 and Pharisees, which were of J, saying, G2414
16:21 that he must go unto J, and suffer many G2414
20:17 And Jesus going up to J took the twelve G2414
18 Behold, we go up to J; and the Son of G2414
21: 1 And when they drew nigh unto J, and G2414
10 And when he was come into J, all the G2414
23:37 O J, Jerusalem, *thou* that killest the G2419
37 O Jerusalem, J, *thou* that killest the G2419
Mk 1: 5 and they of J, and were all baptized G2415
3: 8 And from J, and from Idumaea, and G2414
22 which came down from J said, He hath G2414
7: 1 of the scribes, which came from J. G2414
10:32 And they were in the way going up to J; G2414
33 *Saying*, Behold, we go up to J; and the G2414
11: 1 And when they came nigh to J, unto G2419
11 And Jesus entered into J, and into the G2414
15 And they come to J: and Jesus went into G2414
27 And they come again to J: and as he G2414
15:41 women which came up with him unto J. G2414
Lk 2:22 him to J, to present *him* to the Lord; G2414
25 And, behold, there was a man in J, G2419
38 them that looked for redemption in J. G2419
41 Now his parents went to J every year at G2419
42 up to J after the custom of the feast. G2414
43 tarried behind in J; and Joseph and his G2419
45 turned back again to J, seeking him. G2419
4: 9 And he brought him to J, and set him G2419
5:17 and Judaea, and J: and the power of the G2419
6:17 of all Judaea and J, and from the sea G2419
9:31 which he should accomplish at J. G2419
51 up, he stedfastly set his face to go to J, G2419
53 his face was as though he would go to J. G2419
10:30 went down from J to Jericho, and fell G2419
13: 4 sinners above all men that dwelt in J? G2419
22 teaching, and journeying toward J. G2419
33 cannot be that a prophet perish out of J. G2419
34 O J, Jerusalem, which killest the G2419
34 O Jerusalem, J, which killest the G2419
17:11 And it came to pass, as he went to J, G2419
18:31 we go up to J, and all things that are G2414
19:11 he was nigh to J, and because they G2419
28 he went before, ascending up to J. G2414
21:20 And when ye shall see J compassed G2419
24 into all nations: and J shall be trodden G2419
23: 7 who himself also was at J at that time. G2414
28 said, Daughters of J, weep not for me, G2419
24:13 was from J *about* threescore furlongs. G2419
18 thou only a stranger in J, and hast not G2419
33 and returned to J, and found the eleven G2419
Lk 24:47 among all nations, beginning at J. G2419
49 ye in the city of J, until ye be endued G2419
52 him, and returned to J with great joy: G2419
Jn 1:19 from J to ask him, Who art thou? G2414
2:13 was at hand, and Jesus went up to J, G2414
23 Now when he was in J at the passover, G2414
4:20 and ye say, that in J is the place where G2414
21 nor yet at J, worship the Father. G2414
45 that he did at J at the feast: for they G2414
5: 1 feast of the Jews; and Jesus went up to J. G2414
2 Now there is at J by the sheep *market* a G2414
7:25 Then said some of them of J, Is not this G2415
10:22 And it was at J the feast of the G2414
11:18 Now Bethany was nigh unto J, about G2414
55 the country up to J before the passover, G2414
12:12 they heard that Jesus was coming to J, G2414
Act 1: 4 not depart from J, but wait for the G2414
8 unto me both in J, and in all Judaea, G2419
12 Then returned they unto J from the G2419
12 is from J a sabbath day's journey. G2419
19 all the dwellers at J; insomuch as that G2419
2: 5 And there were dwelling at J Jews, G2419
14 all *ye* that dwell at J, be this known unto G2419
4: 6 high priest, were gathered together at J. G2419
16 that dwell in J; and we cannot deny *it*. G2419
5:16 round about unto J, bringing sick folks, G2419
28 ye have filled J with your doctrine, G2419
6: 7 multiplied in J greatly; and a great G2419
8: 1 church which was at J; and they were all G2414
14 Now when the apostles which were at J G2414
25 Lord, returned to J, and preached the G2419
26 from J unto Gaza, which is desert. G2419
27 and had come to J for to worship, G2419
9: 2 he might bring them bound unto J. G2419
13 evil he hath done to thy saints at J: G2419
21 on this name in J, and came hither for G2419
26 And when Saul was come to J, he G2419
28 with them coming in and going out at J. G2419
10:39 of the Jews, and in J; whom they slew G2419
11: 2 And when Peter was come up to J, they G2414
22 which was in J: and they sent forth G2414
27 came prophets from J unto Antioch. G2414
12:25 returned from J, when they had fulfilled G2419
13:13 John departing from them returned to J. G2414
27 For they that dwell at J, and their rulers, G2419
31 from Galilee to J, who are his witnesses G2419
15: 2 should go up to J unto the apostles and G2419
4 And when they were come to J, they G2419
16: 4 the apostles and elders which were at J. G2419
18:21 that cometh in J: but I will return again G2414
19:21 Achaia, to go to J, saying, After I have G2419
20:16 for him, to be at J the day of Pentecost. G2414
22 in the spirit unto J, not knowing the G2419
21: 4 the Spirit, that he should not go up to J. G2419
11 So shall the Jews at J bind the man that G2419
12 place, besought him not to go up to J. G2419
13 die at J for the name of the Lord Jesus. G2419
15 took up our carriages, and went up to J. G2419
17 And when we were come to J, the G2414
31 of the band, that all J was in an uproar. G2419
22: 5 there bound unto J, for to be punished. G2419
17 I was come again to J, even while I G2419
18 thee quickly out of J: for they will not G2419
23:11 testified of me in J, so must thou bear G2419
24:11 days since I went up to J for to worship. G2419
25: 1 days he ascended from Caesarea to J. G2414
3 to J, laying wait in the way to kill him. G2419
7 came down from J stood round about, G2414
9 said, Wilt thou go up to J, and there be G2414
15 About whom, when I was at J, the chief G2414
20 J, and there be judged of these matters. G2419
24 with me, both at J, and *also* here, crying G2414
26: 4 mine own nation at J, know all the Jews; G2414
10 Which thing I also did in J: and many of G2414
20 Damascus, and at J, and throughout all G2414
28:17 from J into the hands of the Romans. G2414
Ro 15:19 of God; so that from J, and round about G2419
25 But now I go unto J to minister unto G2419
26 for the poor saints which are at J. G2419
31 for J may be accepted of the saints; G2419
1Co 16: 3 I send to bring your liberality unto J. G2419
Gal 1:17 Neither went I up to J to them which G2414
18 Then after three years I went up to J to G2414
2: 1 I went up again to J with Barnabas, G2414
4:25 and answereth to J which now is, and G2419
26 But J which is above is free, which is G2419
Heb 12:22 living God, the heavenly J, and to an G2419
Rev 3:12 my God, *which is* new J, which cometh G2419
21: 2 And I John saw the holy city, new J, G2419
Rev 21:10 J, descending out of heaven from God, G2419

JERUSALEM'S

1Ki 11:13 and for J sake which I have chosen. H3389
32 sake, and for J sake, the city which H3389
Isa 62: 1 my peace, and for J sake I will not rest, H3389

JERUSHA

2Ki 15:33 name *was* J, the daughter of Zadok. H3388

JERUSHAH

2Ch 27: 1 name also *was* J, the daughter of Zadok. H3388

JESAIAH

1Ch 3:21 Pelatiah, and J: the sons of Rephaiah, H3470
Neh 11: 7 Maaseiah, the son of Ithiel, the son of J. H3470

JESHAIAH

1Ch 25: 3 and Zeri, and J, Hashabiah, and H3470
15 The eighth to J, *he*, his sons, and his H3470
26:25 his son, and J his son, and Joram H3470
Ezr 8: 7 And of the sons of Elam; J the son of H3470
19 And Hashabiah, and with him J of the H3470

JESHANAH

2Ch 13:19 the towns thereof, and J with the towns H3466

JESHARELAH

1Ch 25:14 The seventh to J, *he*, his sons, and his H3480

JESHEBEAB

1Ch 24:13 to Huppah, the fourteenth to J, H3428

JESHER

1Ch 2:18 *are* these; J, and Shobab, and Ardon. H3475

JESHIMON

Nu 21:20 top of Pisgah, which looketh toward J. H3452
23:28 the top of Peor, that looketh toward J. H3452
1Sa 23:19 of Hachilah, which *is* on the south of J? H3452
24 of Maon, in the plain on the south of J. H3452
26: 1 in the hill of Hachilah, *which is* before J? H3452
3 which *is* before J, by the way. But David H3452

JESHIMOTH

See BETH-JESHIMOTH.

JESHISHAI

1Ch 5:14 of J, the son of Jahdo, the son of Buz; H3454

JESHOHAIAH

1Ch 4:36 And Elioenai, and Jaakobah, and J, and H3439

JESHUA

1Ch 24:11 The ninth to J, the tenth to Shecaniah, H3442
2Ch 31:15 and Miniamin, and J, and Shemaiah, H3442
Ezr 2: 2 Which came with Zerubbabel: J, H3442
6 of the children of J *and* Joab, two H3442
36 of J, nine hundred seventy and three. H3442
40 The Levites: the children of J and H3442
3: 2 Then stood up J the son of Jozadak, H3442
8 of Shealtiel, and J the son of Jozadak, H3442
9 Then stood J *with* his sons and his H3442
4: 3 But Zerubbabel, and J, and the rest of H3442
5: 2 of Shealtiel, and J the son of Jozadak, H3443
8:33 Jozabad the son of J, and Noadiah the H3443
10:18 of the sons of J the son of Jozadak, H3442
Neh 3:19 Ezer the son of J, the ruler of Mizpah, H3442
7: 7 Who came with Zerubbabel, J, H3442
11 of the children of J and Joab, two H3442
39 of J, nine hundred seventy and three. H3442
43 The Levites: the children of J, of H3442
8: 7 Also J, and Bani, and Sherebiah, Jamin, H3442
17 since the days of J the son of Nun unto H3442
9: 4 of the Levites, J, and Bani, Kadmiel, H3442
5 Then the Levites, J, and Kadmiel, Bani, H3442
10: 9 And the Levites: both J the son of H3442
11:26 And at J, and at Moladah, and at H3442
12: 1 and J: Seraiah, Jeremiah, Ezra, H3442
7 and of their brethren in the days of J. H3442
8 Moreover the Levites: J, Binnui, H3442
10 And J begat Joiakim, Joiakim also H3442
24 Sherebiah, and J the son of Kadmiel, H3442
26 Joiakim the son of J, the son of Jozadak, H3442

JESHURUN

Dt 32:15 But J waxed fat, and kicked: thou art H3484
33: 5 And he was king in J, when the heads of H3484
26 *There is* none like unto the God of J, H3484

JESIAH
1Ch 12: 6 Elkanah, and J, and Azareel, and H3449
23:20 Michah the first, and J the second. H3449

JESIMIEL
1Ch 4:36 Asaiah, and Adiel, and J, and Benaiah, H3450

JESIMOTH See BETH-JESIMOTH.

JESSE
Ru 4:17 he *is* the father of J, the father of David. H3448
22 And Obed begat J, and Jesse begat H3448
22 And Obed begat Jesse, and J begat H3448
1Sa 16: 1 I will send thee to J the Beth-lehemite: H3448
3 And call J to the sacrifice, and I will H3448
5 And he sanctified J and his sons, and H3448
8 Then J called Abinadab, and made him H3448
9 Then J made Shammah to pass by. H3448
10 Again, J made seven of his sons to pass H3448
10 J, The LORD hath not chosen these. H3448
11 And Samuel said unto J, Are here all *thy* H3448
11 Samuel said unto J, Send and fetch him: H3448
18 have seen a son of J the Beth-lehemite, H3448
19 Wherefore Saul sent messengers unto J, H3448
20 And J took an ass *laden* with bread, H3448
22 And Saul sent to J, saying, Let David, I H3448
17:12 whose name *was* J; and he had eight H3448
13 And the three eldest sons of J went *and* H3448
17 And J said unto David his son, Take H3448
20 took, and went, as J had commanded H3448
58 son of thy servant J the Beth-lehemite. H3448
20:27 not the son of J to meat, neither H3448
30 hast chosen the son of J to thine own H3448
31 For as long as the son of J liveth upon H3448
22: 7 will the son of J give every one of you H3448
8 with the son of J, and *there is* none of H3448
9 I saw the son of J coming to Nob, to H3448
13 and the son of J, in that thou hast given H3448
25:10 and who *is* the son of J? there be many H3448
2Sa 20: 1 of J: every man to his tents, O Israel. H3448
23: 1 David the son of J said, and the man H3448
1Ki 12:16 in the son of J: to your tents, O Israel: H3448
1Ch 2:12 Boaz begat Obed, and Obed begat J, H3448
13 And J begat his firstborn Eliab, and H3448
10:14 the kingdom unto David the son of J. H3448
12:18 side, thou son of J: peace, peace *be* unto H3448
29:26 Thus David the son of J reigned over all H3448
2Ch 10:16 in the son of J: every man to your tents, H3448
11:18 the daughter of Eliab the son of J; H3448
Ps 72:20 The prayers of David the son of J are H3448
Isa 11: 1 out of the stem of J, and a Branch shall H3448
10 shall be a root of J, which shall stand for H3448
Mt 1: 5 begat Obed of Ruth; and Obed begat J; *G2421*
6 And J begat David the king; and David *G2421*
Lk 3:32 Which was *the son* of J, which was *the* *G2421*
Act 13:22 David the *son* of J, a man after mine *G2421*
Ro 15:12 shall be a root of J, and he that shall rise *G2421*

JESTING
Eph 5: 4 talking, nor j, which are not convenient: *G2160*

JESUI
Nu 26:44 of the Jimnites: of J, the family of the H3440

JESUITES
Nu 26:44 J: of Beriah, the family of the Beriites. H3441

JESURUN
Isa 44: 2 and thou, J, whom I have chosen. H3484

JESUS
Mt 1: 1 The book of the generation of J Christ, *G2424*
16 whom was born J, who is called Christ. *G2424*
18 Now the birth of J Christ was on this *G2424*
21 shalt call his name J: for he shall save *G2424*
25 firstborn son: and he called his name J. *G2424*
2: 1 Now when J was born in Bethlehem of *G2424*
3:13 Then cometh J from Galilee to Jordan *G2424*
15 And J answering said unto him, Suffer *G2424*
16 And J, when he was baptized, went up *G2424*
4: 1 Then was J led up of the Spirit into the *G2424*
7 J said unto him, It is written again, *G2424*
10 Then saith J unto him, Get thee hence, *G2424*
12 Now when J had heard that John was *G2424*
17 From that time J began to preach, and *G2424*
18 And J, walking by the sea of Galilee, *G2424*
23 And J went about all Galilee, teaching *G2424*
7:28 And it came to pass, when J had ended *G2424*
8: 3 And J put forth *his* hand, and touched *G2424*
Mt 8: 4 And J saith unto him, See thou tell no *G2424*
5 And when J was entered into *G2424*
7 And J saith unto him, I will come and *G2424*
10 When J heard *it*, he marvelled, and *G2424*
13 And J said unto the centurion, Go thy *G2424*
14 And when J was come into Peter's *G2424*
18 Now when J saw great multitudes *G2424*
20 And J saith unto him, The foxes have *G2424*
22 But J said unto him, Follow me; and let *G2424*
29 we to do with thee, J, thou Son of God? *G2424*
34 came out to meet J: and when they saw *G2424*
9: 2 on a bed: and J seeing their faith said *G2424*
4 And J knowing their thoughts said, *G2424*
9 And as J passed forth from thence, he *G2424*
10 And it came to pass, as J sat at meat in *G846*
12 But when J heard *that*, he said unto *G2424*
15 And J said unto them, Can the children *G2424*
19 And J arose, and followed him, and *so* *G2424*
22 But J turned him about, and when he *G2424*
23 And when J came into the ruler's *G2424*
27 And when J departed thence, two blind *G2424*
28 came to him: and J saith unto them, *G2424*
30 And their eyes were opened; and J *G2424*
35 And J went about all the cities and *G2424*
10: 5 These twelve J sent forth, and *G2424*
11: 1 And it came to pass, when J had made *G2424*
4 J answered and said unto them, Go *G2424*
7 And as they departed, J began to say *G2424*
25 At that time J answered and said, I *G2424*
12: 1 At that time J went on the sabbath day *G2424*
15 But when J knew *it*, he withdrew *G2424*
25 And J knew their thoughts, and said *G2424*
13: 1 The same day went J out of the house, *G2424*
34 All these things spake J unto the *G2424*
36 Then J sent the multitude away, and *G2424*
51 J saith unto them, Have ye understood *G2424*
53 And it came to pass, *that* when J had *G2424*
57 And they were offended in him. But J *G2424*
14: 1 the tetrarch heard of the fame of J, *G2424*
12 and buried it, and went and told J. *G2424*
13 When J heard *of it*, he departed thence *G2424*
14 And J went forth, and saw a great *G2424*
16 But J said unto them, They need not *G2424*
22 And straightway J constrained his *G2424*
25 And in the fourth watch of the night J *G2424*
27 But straightway J spake unto them, *G2424*
29 ship, he walked on the water, to go to J. *G2424*
31 And immediately J stretched forth *his* *G2424*
15: 1 Then came to J scribes and Pharisees, *G2424*
16 And J said, Are ye also yet without *G2424*
21 Then J went thence, and departed into *G2424*
28 Then J answered and said unto her, O *G2424*
29 And J departed from thence, and came *G2424*
32 Then J called his disciples *unto him*, *G2424*
34 And J saith unto them, How many *G2424*
16: 6 Then J said unto them, Take heed and *G2424*
8 *Which* when J perceived, he said unto *G2424*
13 When J came into the coasts of *G2424*
17 And J answered and said unto him, *G2424*
20 tell no man that he was J the Christ. *G2424*
21 From that time forth began J to shew *G2424*
24 Then said J unto his disciples, If any *G2424*
17: 1 And after six days J taketh Peter, *G2424*
4 Then answered Peter, and said unto J, *G2424*
7 And J came and touched them, and *G2424*
8 eyes, they saw no man, save J only. *G2424*
9 the mountain, J charged them, saying, *G2424*
11 And J answered and said unto them, *G2424*
17 Then J answered and said, O faithless *G2424*
18 And J rebuked the devil; and he *G2424*
19 Then came the disciples to J apart, and *G2424*
20 And J said unto them, Because of your *G2424*
22 And while they abode in Galilee, J said *G2424*
25 come into the house, J prevented him, *G2424*
26 Peter saith unto him, Of strangers. J *G2424*
18: 1 the disciples unto J, saying, Who is the *G2424*
2 And J called a little child unto him, and *G2424*
22 J saith unto him, I say not unto thee, *G2424*
19: 1 And it came to pass, *that* when J had *G2424*
14 But J said, Suffer little children, and *G2424*
18 He saith unto him, Which? J said, Thou *G2424*
21 J said unto him, If thou wilt be perfect, *G2424*
23 Then said J unto his disciples, Verily I *G2424*
26 But J beheld *them*, and said unto them, *G2424*
28 And J said unto them, Verily I say unto *G2424*
20:17 And J going up to Jerusalem took the *G2424*
22 But J answered and said, Ye know not *G2424*
25 But J called them *unto him*, and said, *G2424*
30 they heard that J passed by, cried out, *G2424*
Mt 20:32 And J stood still, and called them, and *G2424*
34 So J had compassion *on them*, and *G2424*
21: 1 of Olives, then sent J two disciples, *G2424*
6 And the disciples went, and did as J *G2424*
11 And the multitude said, This is J the *G2424*
12 And J went into the temple of God, and *G2424*
16 these say? And J saith unto them, Yea; *G2424*
21 J answered and said unto them, Verily *G2424*
24 And J answered and said unto them, I *G2424*
27 And they answered J, and said, We *G2424*
31 him, The first. J saith unto them, Verily *G2424*
42 J saith unto them, Did ye never read in *G2424*
22: 1 And J answered and spake unto them *G2424*
18 But J perceived their wickedness, and *G2424*
29 J answered and said unto them, Ye do *G2424*
37 J said unto him, Thou shalt love the *G2424*
41 were gathered together, J asked them, *G2424*
23: 1 Then spake J to the multitude, and to *G2424*
24: 1 And J went out, and departed from the *G2424*
2 And J said unto them, See ye not all *G2424*
4 And J answered and said unto them, *G2424*
26: 1 And it came to pass, when J had *G2424*
4 And consulted that they might take J *G2424*
6 Now when J was in Bethany, in the *G2424*
10 When J understood *it*, he said unto *G2424*
17 disciples came to J, saying unto him, *G2424*
19 And the disciples did as J had *G2424*
26 And as they were eating, J took bread, *G2424*
31 Then saith J unto them, All ye shall be *G2424*
34 J said unto him, Verily I say unto thee, *G2424*
36 Then cometh J with them unto a place *G2424*
49 And forthwith he came to J, and said, *G2424*
50 And J said unto him, Friend, wherefore *G2424*
50 and laid hands on J, and took him. *G2424*
51 which were with J stretched out *his* *G2424*
52 Then said J unto him, Put up again thy *G2424*
55 In that same hour said J to the *G2424*
57 And they that had laid hold on J led *G2424*
59 witness against J, to put him to death; *G2424*
63 But J held his peace. And the high *G2424*
64 J saith unto him, Thou hast said: *G2424*
69 Thou also wast with J of Galilee. *G2424*
71 This *fellow* was also with J of Nazareth. *G2424*
75 And Peter remembered the word of J, *G2424*
27: 1 counsel against J to put him to death: *G2424*
11 And J stood before the governor: and *G2424*
11 And J said unto him, Thou sayest. *G2424*
17 Barabbas, or J which is called Christ? *G2424*
20 should ask Barabbas, and destroy J. *G2424*
22 I do then with J which is called Christ? *G2424*
26 J, he delivered *him* to be crucified. *G2424*
27 Then the soldiers of the governor took J *G2424*
37 THIS IS J THE KING OF THE JEWS. *G2424*
46 And about the ninth hour J cried with a *G2424*
50 J, when he had cried again with a loud *G2424*
54 him, watching J, saw the earthquake, *G2424*
55 J from Galilee, ministering unto him: *G2424*
58 and begged the body of J. Then Pilate *G2424*
28: 5 that ye seek J, which was crucified. *G2424*
9 disciples, behold, J met them, saying, *G2424*
10 Then said J unto them, Be not afraid: *G2424*
16 where J had appointed them. *G2424*
18 And J came and spake unto them, *G2424*
Mk 1: 1 The beginning of the gospel of J Christ, *G2424*
9 pass in those days, that J came from *G2424*
14 was put in prison, J came into Galilee, *G2424*
17 And J said unto them, Come ye after *G2424*
24 to do with thee, thou J of Nazareth? art *G2424*
25 And J rebuked him, saying, Hold thy *G2424*
41 And J, moved with compassion, put *G2424*
45 insomuch that J could no more openly *G846*
2: 5 When J saw their faith, he said unto *G2424*
8 And immediately when J perceived in *G2424*
15 And it came to pass, that, as J sat at *G846*
15 also together with J and his disciples: *G2424*
17 When J heard *it*, he saith unto them, *G2424*
19 And J said unto them, Can the children *G2424*
3: 7 But J withdrew himself with his *G2424*
5: 6 But when he saw J afar off, he ran and *G2424*
7 I to do with thee, J, *thou* Son of the most *G2424*
13 And forthwith J gave them leave. And *G2424*
15 And they come to J, and see him that *G2424*
19 Howbeit J suffered him not, but saith *G2424*
20 how great things J had done for him: *G2424*
21 And when J was passed over again by *G2424*
24 And *J* went with him; and much people
27 When she had heard of J, came in the *G2424*
30 And J, immediately knowing in himself *G2424*
36 As soon as J heard the word that was *G2424*

Mk 6: 4 But J said unto them, A prophet is not G2424
30 together unto J, and told him all things, G2424
34 And J, when he came out, saw much G2424
7:27 But J said unto her, Let the children G2424
8: 1 nothing to eat, J called his disciples G2424
17 And when J knew *it*, he saith unto G2424
27 And J went out, and his disciples, into G2424
9: 2 And after six days J taketh *with him* G2424
4 Moses: and they were talking with J. G2424
5 And Peter answered and said to J, G2424
8 any more, save J only with themselves. G2424
23 J said unto him, If thou canst believe, G2424
25 When J saw that the people came G2424
27 But J took him by the hand, and lifted G2424
39 But J said, Forbid him not: for there is G2424
10: 5 And J answered and said unto them, G2424
14 But when J saw *it*, he was much G2424
18 And J said unto him, Why callest thou G2424
21 Then J beholding him loved him, and G2424
23 And J looked round about, and saith G2424
24 at his words. But J answereth again, G2424
27 And J looking upon them saith, With G2424
29 And J answered and said, Verily I say G2424
32 to Jerusalem; and J went before them: G2424
38 But J said unto them, Ye know not G2424
39 And they said unto him, We can. And J G2424
42 But J called them *to him*, and saith G2424
47 And when he heard that it was J of G2424
47 J, *thou* son of David, have mercy on me. G2424
49 And J stood still, and commanded him G2424
50 away his garment, rose, and came to J. G2424
51 And J answered and said unto him, G2424
52 And J said unto him, Go thy way; thy G2424
52 his sight, and followed J in the way. G2424
11: 6 And they said unto them even as J had G2424
7 And they brought the colt to J, and cast G2424
11 And J entered into Jerusalem, and into G2424
14 And J answered and said unto it, No G2424
15 And they come to Jerusalem: and J G2424
22 And J answering saith unto them, Have G2424
29 And J answered and said unto them, I G2424
33 And they answered and said unto J, We G2424
33 cannot tell. And J answering saith unto G2424
12:17 And J answering said unto them, G2424
24 And J answering said unto them, Do ye G2424
29 And J answered him, The first of all the G2424
34 And when J saw that he answered G2424
35 And J answered and said, while he G2424
41 And J sat over against the treasury, G2424
13: 2 And J answering said unto him, Seest G2424
5 And J answering them began to say, G2424
14: 6 And J said, Let her alone; why trouble G2424
18 And as they sat and did eat, J said, G2424
22 And as they did eat, J took bread, and G2424
27 And J saith unto them, All ye shall be G2424
30 And J saith unto him, Verily I say unto G2424
48 And J answered and said unto them, G2424
53 And they led J away to the high priest: G2424
55 J to put him to death; and found none. G2424
60 midst, and asked J, saying, Answerest G2424
62 And J said, I am: and ye shall see the G2424
67 And thou also wast with J of Nazareth. G2424
72 the word that J said unto him, Before G2424
15: 1 and bound J, and carried *him* away, G2424
5 But J yet answered nothing; so that G2424
15 and delivered J, when he had scourged G2424
34 And at the ninth hour J cried with a G2424
37 And J cried with a loud voice, and gave G2424
43 unto Pilate, and craved the body of J. G2424
16: 6 affrighted: Ye seek J of Nazareth, which G2424
9 Now when *J* was risen early the first *day*
Lk 1:31 forth a son, and shalt call his name J. G2424
2:21 name was called J, which was so named G2424
27 in the child J, to do for him after the G2424
43 returned, the child J tarried behind in G2424
52 And J increased in wisdom and G2424
3:21 it came to pass, that J also being G2424
23 And J himself began to be about thirty G2424
4: 1 And J being full of the Holy Ghost G2424
4 And J answered him, saying, It is G2424
8 And J answered and said unto him, Get G2424
12 And J answering said unto him, It is G2424
14 And J returned in the power of the G2424
34 to do with thee, *thou* J of Nazareth? art G2424
35 And J rebuked him, saying, Hold thy G2424
5:10 with Simon. And J said unto Simon, G2424
12 who seeing J fell on *his* face, and G2424
19 with *his* couch into the midst before J. G2424
22 But when J perceived their thoughts, he G2424
Lk 5:31 And J answering said unto them, They G2424
6: 3 And J answering them said, Have ye G2424
9 Then said J unto them, I will ask you G2424
11 with another what they might do to J. G2424
7: 3 And when he heard of J, he sent unto G2424
4 And when they came to J, they besought G2424
6 Then J went with them. And when he G2424
9 When J heard these things, he G2424
19 sent *them* to J, saying, Art thou he G2424
22 Then J answering said unto them, Go G2424
37 when she knew that *J* sat at meat in the
40 And J answering said unto him, Simon, G2424
8:28 When he saw J, he cried out, and fell G2424
28 I to do with thee, J, *thou* Son of God G2424
30 And J asked him, saying, What is thy G2424
35 was done; and came to J, and found the G2424
35 at the feet of J, clothed, and in his right G2424
38 with him: but J sent him away, saying, G2424
39 how great things J had done unto him. G2424
40 And it came to pass, that, when J was G2424
45 And J said, Who touched me? When all G2424
46 And J said, Somebody hath touched G2424
50 But when J heard *it*, he answered him, G2424
9:33 Peter said unto J, Master, it is good for G2424
36 And when the voice was past, J was G2424
41 And J answering said, O faithless and G2424
42 down, and tare *him*. And J rebuked the G2424
43 which J did, he said unto his disciples, G2424
47 And J, perceiving the thought of their G2424
50 And J said unto him, Forbid *him* not: G2424
58 And J said unto him, Foxes have holes, G2424
60 J said unto him, Let the dead bury their G2424
62 And J said unto him, No man, having G2424
10:21 In that hour J rejoiced in spirit, and G2424
29 said unto J, And who is my neighbour? G2424
30 And J answering said, A certain *man* G2424
37 J unto him, Go, and do thou likewise. G2424
41 And J answered and said unto her, G2424
13: 2 And J answering said unto them, G2424
12 And when J saw her, he called *her to* G2424
14 because that J had healed on the G2424
14: 3 And J answering spake unto the G2424
17:13 and said, J, Master, have mercy on us. G2424
17 And J answering said, Were there not G2424
18:16 But J called them *unto him*, and said, G2424
19 And J said unto him, Why callest thou G2424
22 Now when J heard these things, he said G2424
24 And when J saw that he was very G2424
37 And they told him, that J of Nazareth G2424
38 And he cried, saying, J, *thou* son of G2424
40 And J stood, and commanded him to G2424
42 And J said unto him, Receive thy sight: G2424
19: 1 And *J* entered and passed through
3 And he sought to see J who he was; and G2424
5 And when J came to the place, he G2424
9 And J said unto him, This day is G2424
35 And they brought him to J: and they G2424
35 upon the colt, and they set J thereon. G2424
20: 8 And J said unto them, Neither tell I you G2424
34 And J answering said unto them, The G2424
22:47 and drew near unto J to kiss him. G2424
48 But J said unto him, Judas, betrayest G2424
51 And J answered and said, Suffer ye G2424
52 Then J said unto the chief priests, and G2424
63 And the men that held J mocked him, G2424
23: 8 And when Herod saw J, he was G2424
20 Pilate therefore, willing to release J, G2424
25 desired; but he delivered J to their will. G2424
26 the cross, that he might bear *it* after J. G2424
28 But J turning unto them said, G2424
34 Then said J, Father, forgive them; for G2424
42 And he said unto J, Lord, remember me G2424
43 And J said unto him, Verily I say unto G2424
46 And when J had cried with a loud G2424
52 unto Pilate, and begged the body of J. G2424
24: 3 and found not the body of the Lord J. G2424
15 and reasoned, J himself drew near, and G2424
19 him, Concerning J of Nazareth, which G2424
36 And as they thus spake, J himself stood G2424
Jn 1:17 *but* grace and truth came by J Christ. G2424
29 The next day John seeth J coming unto G2424
36 And looking upon J as he walked, he G2424
37 heard him speak, and they followed J. G2424
38 Then J turned, and saw them G2424
42 And he brought him to J. And when G2424
42 Jesus. And when J beheld him, he said, G2424
43 The day following J would go forth into G2424
45 write, J of Nazareth, the son of Joseph. G2424
47 J saw Nathanael coming to him, and G2424
Jn 1:48 knowest thou me? J answered and said G2424
50 J answered and said unto him, Because G2424
2: 1 Galilee; and the mother of J was there: G2424
2 And both J was called, and his G2424
3 of J saith unto him, They have no wine. G2424
4 J saith unto her, Woman, what have I G2424
7 J saith unto them, Fill the waterpots G2424
11 This beginning of miracles did J in G2424
13 at hand, and J went up to Jerusalem, G2424
19 J answered and said unto them, G2424
22 and the word which J had said. G2424
24 But J did not commit himself unto G2424
3: 2 The same came to J by night, and said G2424
3 J answered and said unto him, Verily, G2424
5 J answered, Verily, verily, I say unto G2424
10 J answered and said unto him, Art G2424
22 After these things came J and his G2424
4: 1 had heard that J made and baptized G2424
2 (Though J himself baptized not, but his G2424
6 Now Jacob's well was there. J therefore, G2424
7 J saith unto her, Give me to drink. G2424
10 J answered and said unto her, If thou G2424
13 J answered and said unto her, G2424
16 J saith unto her, Go, call thy husband, G2424
17 have no husband. J said unto her, Thou G2424
21 J saith unto her, Woman, believe me, G2424
26 J saith unto her, I that speak unto thee G2424
34 J saith unto them, My meat is to do the G2424
44 For J himself testified, that a prophet G2424
46 So J came again into Cana of Galilee, G2424
47 When he heard that J was come out of G2424
48 Then said J unto him, Except ye see G2424
50 J saith unto him, Go thy way; thy son G2424
50 the word that J had spoken unto him, G2424
53 hour, in the which J said unto him, Thy G2424
54 This *is* again the second miracle *that* J G2424
5: 1 the Jews; and J went up to Jerusalem. G2424
6 When J saw him lie, and knew that he G2424
8 J saith unto him, Rise, take up thy bed, G2424
13 wist not who it was: for J had conveyed G2424
14 Afterward J findeth him in the temple, G2424
15 it was J, which had made him whole. G2424
16 And therefore did the Jews persecute J, G2424
17 But J answered them, My Father G2424
19 Then answered J and said unto them, G2424
6: 1 After these things J went over the sea of G2424
3 And J went up into a mountain, and G2424
5 When J then lifted up *his* eyes, and saw G2424
10 And J said, Make the men sit down. G2424
11 And J took the loaves; and when he had G2424
14 the miracle that J did, said, This is of G2424
15 When J therefore perceived that they G2424
17 now dark, and J was not come to them. G2424
19 furlongs, they see J walking on the sea, G2424
22 entered, and that J went not with his G2424
24 When the people therefore saw that J G2424
24 and came to Capernaum, seeking for J. G2424
26 J answered them and said, Verily, G2424
29 J answered and said unto them, This is G2424
32 Then J said unto them, Verily, verily, I G2424
35 And J said unto them, I am the bread G2424
42 And they said, Is not this J, the son of G2424
43 J therefore answered and said unto G2424
53 Then J said unto them, Verily, verily, I G2424
61 When J knew in himself that his G2424
64 that believe not. For J knew from the G2424
67 Then said J unto the twelve, Will ye G2424
70 J answered them, Have not I chosen G2424
7: 1 After these things J walked in Galilee: G2424
6 Then J said unto them, My time is not G2424
14 Now about the midst of the feast J went G2424
16 J answered them, and said, My G2424
21 J answered and said unto them, I have G2424
28 Then cried J in the temple as he taught, G2424
33 Then said J unto them, Yet a little while G2424
37 *day* of the feast, J stood and cried, G2424
39 because that J was not yet glorified.) G2424
50 came to J by night, being one of them,) G846
8: 1 J went unto the mount of Olives. G2424
6 to accuse him. But J stooped down, G2424
9 unto the last: and J was left alone, and G2424
10 When J had lifted up himself, and saw G2424
11 She said, No man, Lord. And J said G2424
12 Then spake J again unto them, saying, G2424
14 J answered and said unto them, G2424
19 is thy Father? J answered, Ye neither G2424
20 These words spake J in the treasury, as G2424
21 Then said J again unto them, I go my G2424
25 art thou? And J saith unto them, Even G2424

Jn 8:28 Then said J unto them, When ye have G2424
31 Then said J to those Jews which G2424
34 J answered them, Verily, verily, I say G2424
39 is our father. J saith unto them, If ye G2424
42 J said unto them, If God were your G2424
49 J answered, I have not a devil; but I G2424
54 J answered, If I honour myself, my G2424
58 J said unto them, Verily, verily, I say G2424
59 to cast at him: but J hid himself, and G2424
9: 1 And as J passed by, he saw a man which
3 J answered, Neither hath this man G2424
11 A man that is called J made clay, and G2424
14 And it was the sabbath day when J G2424
35 J heard that they had cast him out; and G2424
37 And J said unto him, Thou hast both G2424
39 And J said, For judgment I am come G2424
41 J said unto them, If ye were blind, ye G2424
10: 6 This parable spake J unto them: but G2424
7 Then said J unto them again, Verily, G2424
23 And J walked in the temple in G2424
25 J answered them, I told you, and ye G2424
32 J answered them, Many good works G2424
34 J answered them, Is it not written in G2424
11: 4 When J heard that, he said, This G2424
5 Now J loved Martha, and her sister, G2424
9 J answered, Are there not twelve hours G2424
13 Howbeit J spake of his death: but they G2424
14 Then said J unto them plainly, Lazarus G2424
17 Then when J came, he found that he G2424
20 as she heard that J was coming, went G2424
21 Then said Martha unto J, Lord, if thou G2424
23 J saith unto her, Thy brother shall rise G2424
25 J said unto her, I am the resurrection, G2424
30 Now J was not yet come into the town, G2424
32 Then when Mary was come where J G2424
33 When J therefore saw her weeping, and G2424
35 J wept. G2424
38 J therefore again groaning in himself G2424
39 J said, Take ye away the stone. Martha, G2424
40 J saith unto her, Said I not unto thee, G2424
41 was laid. And J lifted up *his* eyes, and G2424
44 with a napkin. J saith unto them, Loose G2424
45 the things which J did, believed on him. G2424
46 and told them what things J had done. G2424
51 that J should die for that nation; G2424
54 J therefore walked no more openly G2424
56 Then sought they for J, and spake G2424
12: 1 Then J six days before the passover G2424
3 the feet of J, and wiped his feet with G2424
7 Then said J, Let her alone: against the G2424
11 the Jews went away, and believed on J. G2424
12 heard that J was coming to Jerusalem, G2424
14 And J, when he had found a young ass, G2424
16 the first: but when J was glorified, then G2424
21 desired him, saying, Sir, we would see J. G2424
22 and again Andrew and Philip tell J. G2424
23 And J answered them, saying, The G2424
30 J answered and said, This voice came G2424
35 Then J said unto them, Yet a little while G2424
36 things spake J, and departed, and did G2424
44 J cried and said, He that believeth on G2424
13: 1 passover, when J knew that his hour G2424
3 J knowing that the Father had given all G2424
7 J answered and said unto him, What I G2424
8 wash my feet. J answered him, If I G2424
10 J saith to him, He that is washed G2424
21 When J had thus said, he was troubled G2424
23 one of his disciples, whom J loved. G2424
26 J answered, He it is, to whom I shall G2424
27 him. Then said J unto him, That thou G2424
29 had the bag, that J had said unto him, G2424
31 Therefore, when he was gone out, J G2424
36 goest thou? J answered him, Whither G2424
38 J answered him, Wilt thou lay down G2424
14: 6 J saith unto him, I am the way, the G2424
9 J saith unto him, Have I been so long G2424
23 J answered and said unto him, If a G2424
16:19 Now J knew that they were desirous to G2424
31 J answered them, Do ye now believe? G2424
17: 1 These words spake J, and lifted up his G2424
3 and J Christ, whom thou hast sent. G2424
18: 1 When J had spoken these words, he G2424
2 the place: for J ofttimes resorted thither G2424
4 J therefore, knowing all things that G2424
5 They answered him, J of Nazareth. G2424
5 Jesus of Nazareth. J saith unto them, I G2424
7 seek ye? And they said, J of Nazareth. G2424
8 J answered, I have told you that I am G2424
11 Then said J unto Peter, Put up thy G2424

Jn 18:12 of the Jews took J, and bound him, G2424
15 And Simon Peter followed J, and *so did* G2424
15 with J into the palace of the high priest. G2424
19 The high priest then asked J of his G2424
20 J answered him, I spake openly to the G2424
22 stood by struck J with the palm of his G2424
23 J answered him, If I have spoken evil, G2424
28 Then led they J from Caiaphas unto the G2424
32 That the saying of J might be fulfilled, G2424
33 again, and called J, and said unto him, G2424
34 J answered him, Sayest thou this thing G2424
36 J answered, My kingdom is not of this G2424
37 Art thou a king then? J answered, Thou G2424
19: 1 Then Pilate therefore took J, and G2424
5 Then came J forth, wearing the crown G2424
9 and saith unto J, Whence art thou? But G2424
9 art thou? But J gave him no answer. G2424
11 J answered, Thou couldest have no G2424
13 that saying, he brought J forth, and sat G2424
16 And they took J, and led *him* away. G2424
18 on either side one, and J in the midst. G2424
19 the writing was, J OF NAZARETH THE G2424
20 for the place where J was crucified was G2424
23 they had crucified J, took his garments, G2424
25 Now there stood by the cross of J his G2424
26 When J therefore saw his mother, and G2424
28 After this, J knowing that all things G2424
30 When J therefore had received the G2424
33 But when they came to J, and saw that G2424
38 being a disciple of J, but secretly for fear G2424
38 away the body of J: and Pilate gave *him* G2424
38 came therefore, and took the body of J. G2424
39 at the first came to J by night, and G2424
40 Then took they the body of J, and G2424
42 There laid they J therefore because of G2424
20: 2 disciple, whom J loved, and saith unto G2424
12 the feet, where the body of J had lain. G2424
14 back, and saw J standing, and knew G2424
14 standing, and knew not that it was J. G2424
15 J saith unto her, Woman, why weepest G2424
16 J saith unto her, Mary. She turned G2424
17 J saith unto her, Touch me not; for I G2424
19 of the Jews, came J and stood in the G2424
21 Then said J to them again, Peace be G2424
24 was not with them when J came. G2424
26 with them: *then* came J, the doors being G2424
29 J saith unto him, Thomas, because G2424
30 And many other signs truly did J in the G2424
31 ye might believe that J is the Christ, the G2424
21: 1 After these things J shewed himself G2424
4 was now come, J stood on the shore: G2424
4 but the disciples knew not that it was J. G2424
5 Then J saith unto them, Children, have G2424
7 Therefore that disciple whom J loved G2424
10 J saith unto them, Bring of the fish G2424
12 J saith unto them, Come *and* dine. And G2424
13 J then cometh, and taketh bread, and G2424
14 This is now the third time that J G2424
15 So when they had dined, J saith to G2424
17 thee. J saith unto him, Feed my sheep. G2424
20 the disciple whom J loved following; G2424
21 Peter seeing him saith to J, Lord, and G2424
22 J saith unto him, If I will that he tarry G2424
23 should not die: yet J said not unto him, G2424
25 other things which J did, the which, if G2424
Act 1: 1 of all that J began both to do and teach, G2424
11 heaven? this same J, which is taken up G2424
14 the mother of J, and with his brethren. G2424
16 which was guide to them that took J. G2424
21 the Lord J went in and out among us, G2424
2:22 Ye men of Israel, hear these words; J of G2424
32 This J hath God raised up, whereof we G2424
36 hath made that same J, whom ye have G2424
38 of you in the name of J Christ for the G2424
3: 6 J Christ of Nazareth rise up and walk. G2424
13 glorified his Son J; whom ye delivered G2424
20 And he shall send J Christ, which G2424
26 raised up his Son J, sent him to bless G2424
4: 2 J the resurrection from the dead. G2424
10 by the name of J Christ of Nazareth, G2424
13 of them, that they had been with J. G2424
18 speak at all nor teach in the name of J. G2424
27 For of a truth against thy holy child J, G2424
30 be done by the name of thy holy child J. G2424
33 J: and great grace was upon them all. G2424
5:30 The God of our fathers raised up J, G2424
40 speak in the name of J, and let them go. G2424
42 not to teach and preach J Christ. G2424
6:14 For we have heard him say, that this J G2424

Act 7:45 brought in with J into the possession G2424
55 J standing on the right hand of God, G2424
59 and saying, Lord J, receive my spirit. G2424
8:12 and the name of J Christ, they were G2424
16 were baptized in the name of the Lord J.) G2424
35 scripture, and preached unto him J. G2424
37 I believe that J Christ is the Son of God. G2424
9: 5 the Lord said, I am J whom thou G2424
17 the Lord, *even* J, that appeared unto G2424
27 boldly at Damascus in the name of J. G2424
29 the name of the Lord J, and disputed G2424
34 And Peter said unto him, Aeneas, J G2424
10:36 peace by J Christ: (he is Lord of all:) G2424
38 How God anointed J of Nazareth with G2424
11:17 on the Lord J Christ; what was I, that G2424
20 unto the Grecians, preaching the Lord J. G2424
13:23 promise raised unto Israel a Saviour, J: G2424
33 he hath raised up J again; as it is also G2424
15:11 J Christ we shall be saved, even as they. G2424
26 lives for the name of our Lord J Christ. G2424
16:18 in the name of J Christ to come out of G2424
31 And they said, Believe on the Lord J G2424
17: 3 J, whom I preach unto you, is Christ. G2424
7 saying that there is another king, *one* J. G2424
18 unto them J, and the resurrection. G2424
18: 5 testified to the Jews *that* J *was* Christ. G2424
28 by the scriptures that J was Christ. G2424
19: 4 come after him, that is, on Christ J. G2424
5 were baptized in the name of the Lord J. G2424
10 of the Lord J, both Jews and Greeks. G2424
13 name of the Lord J, saying, We adjure G2424
13 adjure you by J whom Paul preacheth. G2424
15 And the evil spirit answered and said, J G2424
17 the name of the Lord J was magnified. G2424
20:21 and faith toward our Lord J Christ. G2424
24 of the Lord J, to testify the gospel G2424
35 words of the Lord J, how he said, It is G2424
21:13 at Jerusalem for the name of the Lord J. G2424
22: 8 J of Nazareth, whom thou persecutest. G2424
25:19 and of one J, which was dead, whom G2424
26: 9 contrary to the name of J of Nazareth. G2424
15 he said, I am J whom thou persecutest. G2424
28:23 them concerning J, both out of the law G2424
31 concern the Lord J Christ, with all G2424
Ro 1: 1 Paul, a servant of J Christ, called *to be* G2424
3 Concerning his Son J Christ our Lord, G2424
6 Among whom are ye also the called of J G2424
7 God our Father, and the Lord J Christ. G2424
8 First, I thank my God through J Christ G2424
2:16 by J Christ according to my gospel. G2424
3:22 *is* by faith of J Christ unto all and upon G2424
24 the redemption that is in Christ J: G2424
26 the justifier of him which believeth in J. G2424
4:24 raised up J our Lord from the dead; G2424
5: 1 with God through our Lord J Christ: G2424
11 through our Lord J Christ, by whom we G2424
15 J Christ, hath abounded unto many. G2424
17 shall reign in life by one, J Christ.) G2424
21 unto eternal life by J Christ our Lord. G2424
6: 3 J Christ were baptized into his death? G2424
11 unto God through J Christ our Lord. G2424
23 *is* eternal life through J Christ our Lord. G2424
7:25 I thank God through J Christ our Lord. G2424
8: 1 are in Christ J, who walk not after the G2424
2 of life in Christ J hath made me free G2424
11 But if the Spirit of him that raised up J G2424
39 of God, which is in Christ J our Lord. G2424
10: 9 mouth the Lord J, and shalt believe in G2424
13:14 But put ye on the Lord J Christ, and G2424
14:14 by the Lord J, that *there is* nothing G2424
15: 5 toward another according to Christ J: G2424
6 even the Father of our Lord J Christ. G2424
8 Now I say that J Christ was a minister G2424
16 That I should be the minister of J G2424
17 I may glory through J Christ in those G2424
30 for the Lord J Christ's sake, and for G2424
16: 3 and Aquila my helpers in Christ J: G2424
18 serve not our Lord J Christ, but their G2424
20 of our Lord J Christ *be* with you. Amen. G2424
24 The grace of our Lord J Christ *be* with G2424
25 the preaching of J Christ, according to G2424
27 To God only wise, *be* glory through J G2424
1Co 1: 1 Paul, called *to be* an apostle of J Christ G2424
2 in Christ J, called *to be* saints, with G2424
2 J Christ our Lord, both theirs and ours: G2424
3 our Father, and *from* the Lord J Christ. G2424
4 of God which is given you by J Christ; G2424
7 for the coming of our Lord J Christ: G2424
8 in the day of our Lord J Christ. G2424

1Co 1: 9 fellowship of his Son J Christ our Lord. G2424
10 name of our Lord J Christ, that ye all G2424
30 But of him are ye in Christ J, who of G2424
2: 2 you, save J Christ, and him crucified. G2424
3:11 lay than that is laid, which is J Christ. G2424
4:15 for in Christ J I have begotten you G2424
5: 4 In the name of our Lord J Christ, when G2424
4 with the power of our Lord J Christ, G2424
5 may be saved in the day of the Lord J. G2424
6:11 the Lord J, and by the Spirit of our God. G2424
8: 6 him; and one Lord J Christ, by whom G2424
9: 1 have I not seen J Christ our Lord? are G2424
11:23 you, That the Lord J the *same* night in G2424
12: 3 of God calleth J accursed: and *that* no G2424
3 J is the Lord, but by the Holy Ghost. G2424
15:31 I have in Christ J our Lord, I die daily. G2424
57 the victory through our Lord J Christ. G2424
16:22 If any man love not the Lord J Christ, G2424
23 The grace of our Lord J Christ *be* with G2424
24 My love *be* with you all in Christ J. G2424
2Co 1: 1 Paul, an apostle of J Christ by the will G2424
2 our Father, and *from* the Lord J Christ. G2424
3 Father of our Lord J Christ, the Father G2424
14 ye also *are* ours in the day of the Lord J. G2424
19 For the Son of God, J Christ, who was G2424
4: 5 but Christ J the Lord; and ourselves G2424
6 the glory of God in the face of J Christ. G2424
10 dying of the Lord J, that the life also of G2424
10 J might be made manifest in our body. G2424
11 that the life also of J might be made G2424
14 raised up the Lord J shall raise up us G2424
14 also by J, and shall present *us* with you. G2424
5:18 us to himself by J Christ, and hath G2424
8: 9 For ye know the grace of our Lord J G2424
11: 4 preacheth another J, whom we have not G2424
31 The God and Father of our Lord J G2424
13: 5 own selves, how that J Christ is in you, G2424
14 The grace of the Lord J Christ, and the G2424
Gal 1: 1 by man, but by J Christ, and God the G2424
3 the Father, and *from* our Lord J Christ, G2424
12 *it*, but by the revelation of J Christ. G2424
2: 4 we have in Christ J, that they might G2424
16 but by the faith of J Christ, even we G2424
16 have believed in J Christ, that we might G2424
3: 1 before whose eyes J Christ hath been G2424
14 the Gentiles through J Christ; that we G2424
22 by faith of J Christ might be given G2424
26 the children of God by faith in Christ J. G2424
28 nor female: for ye are all one in Christ J. G2424
4:14 me as an angel of God, *even* as Christ J. G2424
5: 6 For in J Christ neither circumcision G2424
6:14 cross of our Lord J Christ, by whom the G2424
15 For in Christ J neither circumcision G2424
17 in my body the marks of the Lord J. G2424
18 Brethren, the grace of our Lord J Christ G2424
Eph 1: 1 Paul, an apostle of J Christ by the will G2424
1 Ephesus, and to the faithful in Christ J: G2424
2 our Father, and *from* the Lord J Christ. G2424
3 Father of our Lord J Christ, who hath G2424
5 of children by J Christ to himself, G2424
15 the Lord J, and love unto all the saints, G2424
17 That the God of our Lord J Christ, the G2424
2: 6 together in heavenly *places* in Christ J: G2424
7 kindness toward us through Christ J. G2424
10 created in Christ J unto good works, G2424
13 But now in Christ J ye who sometimes G2424
20 and prophets, J Christ himself being G2424
3: 1 For this cause I Paul, the prisoner of J G2424
9 God, who created all things by J Christ: G2424
11 he purposed in Christ J our Lord: G2424
14 unto the Father of our Lord J Christ, G2424
21 church by Christ J throughout all ages, G2424
4:21 been taught by him, as the truth is in J: G2424
5:20 in the name of our Lord J Christ; G2424
6:23 God the Father and the Lord J Christ. G2424
24 our Lord J Christ in sincerity. Amen. G2424
Php 1: 1 Paul and Timotheus, the servants of J G2424
1 saints in Christ J which are at Philippi, G2424
2 our Father, and *from* the Lord J Christ. G2424
6 will perform *it* until the day of J Christ: G2424
8 after you all in the bowels of J Christ. G2424
11 which are by J Christ, unto the glory G2424
19 and the supply of the Spirit of J Christ, G2424
26 be more abundant in J Christ for me by G2424
2: 5 be in you, which was also in Christ J: G2424
10 That at the name of J every knee G2424
11 confess that J Christ *is* Lord, to the G2424
19 But I trust in the Lord J to send G2424
21 not the things which are J Christ's. G2424
Php 3: 3 J, and have no confidence in the flesh. G2424
8 of Christ J my Lord: for whom G2424
12 also I am apprehended of Christ J. G2424
14 of the high calling of God in Christ J. G2424
20 look for the Saviour, the Lord J Christ: G2424
4: 7 your hearts and minds through Christ J. G2424
19 to his riches in glory by Christ J. G2424
21 Salute every saint in Christ J. The G2424
23 The grace of our Lord J Christ *be* with G2424
Col 1: 1 Paul, an apostle of J Christ by the will G2424
2 God our Father and the Lord J Christ. G2424
3 Lord J Christ, praying always for you, G2424
4 Since we heard of your faith in Christ J, G2424
28 present every man perfect in Christ J: G2424
2: 6 As ye have therefore received Christ J G2424
3:17 the name of the Lord J, giving thanks to G2424
4:11 And J, which is called Justus, who are of G2424
1Th 1: 1 and *in* the Lord J Christ: Grace *be* unto G2424
1 God our Father, and the Lord J Christ. G2424
3 hope in our Lord J Christ, in the sight G2424
10 the dead, *even* J, which delivered us G2424
2:14 are in Christ J: for ye also have suffered G2424
15 Who both killed the Lord J, and their G2424
19 of our Lord J Christ at his coming? G2424
3:11 Lord J Christ, direct our way unto you. G2424
13 of our Lord J Christ with all his saints. G2424
4: 1 *you* by the Lord J, that as ye have G2424
2 we gave you by the Lord J. G2424
14 For if we believe that J died and rose G2424
14 sleep in J will God bring with him. G2424
5: 9 obtain salvation by our Lord J Christ, G2424
18 will of God in Christ J concerning you. G2424
23 unto the coming of our Lord J Christ. G2424
28 The grace of our Lord J Christ *be* with G2424
2Th 1: 1 God our Father and the Lord J Christ: G2424
2 God our Father and the Lord J Christ. G2424
7 us, when the Lord J shall be revealed G2424
8 not the gospel of our Lord J Christ: G2424
12 That the name of our Lord J Christ may G2424
12 grace of our God and the Lord J Christ. G2424
2: 1 coming of our Lord J Christ, and *by* our G2424
14 of the glory of our Lord J Christ. G2424
16 Now our Lord J Christ himself, and G2424
3: 6 the name of our Lord J Christ, that ye G2424
12 exhort by our Lord J Christ, that with G2424
18 The grace of our Lord J Christ *be* with G2424
1Ti 1: 1 Paul, an apostle of J Christ by the G2424
1 and Lord J Christ, *which is* our hope; G2424
2 God our Father and J Christ our Lord. G2424
12 And I thank Christ J our Lord, who G2424
14 with faith and love which is in Christ J. G2424
15 that Christ J came into the world G2424
16 that in me first J Christ might shew G2424
2: 5 God and men, the man Christ J; G2424
3:13 in the faith which is in Christ J. G2424
4: 6 a good minister of J Christ, nourished G2424
5:21 God, and the Lord J Christ, and the G2424
6: 3 words of our Lord J Christ, and to the G2424
13 and *before* Christ J, who before Pontius G2424
14 the appearing of our Lord J Christ: G2424
2Ti 1: 1 Paul, an apostle of J Christ by the will G2424
1 the promise of life which is in Christ J, G2424
2 God the Father and Christ J our Lord. G2424
9 us in Christ J before the world began, G2424
10 of our Saviour J Christ, who hath G2424
13 in faith and love which is in Christ J. G2424
2: 1 be strong in the grace that is in Christ J. G2424
3 hardness, as a good soldier of J Christ. G2424
8 Remember that J Christ of the seed of G2424
10 which is in Christ J with eternal glory. G2424
3:12 in Christ J shall suffer persecution. G2424
15 through faith which is in Christ J. G2424
4: 1 God, and the Lord J Christ, who shall G2424
22 The Lord J Christ *be* with thy spirit. G2424
Tit 1: 1 and an apostle of J Christ, according to G2424
4 and the Lord J Christ our Saviour. G2424
2:13 the great God and our Saviour J Christ; G2424
3: 6 through J Christ our Saviour; G2424
Phlm 1 Paul, a prisoner of J Christ, and G2424
3 God our Father and the Lord J Christ. G2424
5 the Lord J, and toward all saints; G2424
6 good thing which is in you in Christ J. G2424
9 and now also a prisoner of J Christ. G2424
23 my fellowprisoner in Christ J; G2424
25 The grace of our Lord J Christ *be* with G2424
Heb 2: 9 But we see J, who was made a little G2424
3: 1 High Priest of our profession, Christ J; G2424
4: 8 For if J had given them rest, then would G2424
14 into the heavens, J the Son of God, let G2424
Heb 6:20 us entered, *even* J, made an high priest G2424
7:22 By so much was J made a surety of a G2424
10:10 of the body of J Christ once *for all*. G2424
19 enter into the holiest by the blood of J, G2424
12: 2 Looking unto J the author and finisher G2424
24 And to J the mediator of the new G2424
13: 8 J Christ the same yesterday, and to G2424
12 Wherefore J also, that he might G2424
20 from the dead our Lord J, that great G2424
21 his sight, through J Christ; to whom *be* G2424
Jas 1: 1 and of the Lord J Christ, to the twelve G2424
2: 1 faith of our Lord J Christ, *the Lord* of G2424
1Pt 1: 1 Peter, an apostle of J Christ, to the G2424
2 of the blood of J Christ: Grace unto you, G2424
3 and Father of our Lord J Christ, which G2424
3 resurrection of J Christ from the dead, G2424
7 and glory at the appearing of J Christ: G2424
13 unto you at the revelation of J Christ; G2424
2: 5 acceptable to God by J Christ. G2424
3:21 God,) by the resurrection of J Christ: G2424
4:11 glorified through J Christ, to whom be G2424
5:10 glory by Christ J, after that ye have G2424
14 with you all that are in Christ J. Amen. G2424
2Pt 1: 1 and an apostle of J Christ, to them that G2424
1 of God and our Saviour J Christ: G2424
2 knowledge of God, and of J our Lord, G2424
8 in the knowledge of our Lord J Christ. G2424
11 of our Lord and Saviour J Christ. G2424
14 as our Lord J Christ hath shewed me. G2424
16 coming of our Lord J Christ, but were G2424
2:20 the Lord and Saviour J Christ, they are G2424
3:18 Lord and Saviour J Christ. To him *be* G2424
1Jn 1: 3 the Father, and with his Son J Christ. G2424
7 and the blood of J Christ his Son G2424
2: 1 with the Father, J Christ the righteous: G2424
22 Who is a liar but he that denieth that J G2424
3:23 name of his Son J Christ, and love one G2424
4: 2 J Christ is come in the flesh is of God: G2424
3 not that J Christ is come in the G2424
15 Whosoever shall confess that J is the G2424
5: 1 Whosoever believeth that J is the Christ G2424
5 that believeth that J is the Son of God? G2424
6 and blood, *even* J Christ; not by water G2424
20 *even* in his Son J Christ. This is the true G2424
2Jn 3 and from the Lord J Christ, the Son of G2424
7 confess not that J Christ is come in the G2424
Jude 1 Jude, the servant of J Christ, and G2424
1 and preserved in J Christ, *and* called: G2424
4 only Lord God, and our Lord J Christ. G2424
17 of the apostles of our Lord J Christ; G2424
21 of our Lord J Christ unto eternal life. G2424
Rev 1: 1 The Revelation of J Christ, which God G2424
2 J Christ, and of all things that he saw. G2424
5 And from J Christ, *who is* the faithful G2424
9 and patience of J Christ, was in the isle G2424
9 God, and for the testimony of J Christ. G2424
12:17 and have the testimony of J Christ. G2424
14:12 of God, and the faith of J. G2424
17: 6 of the martyrs of J: and when I saw her, G2424
19:10 the testimony of J: worship God: for the G2424
10 testimony of J is the spirit of prophecy. G2424
20: 4 for the witness of J, and for the word of G2424
22:16 I J have sent mine angel to testify unto G2424
20 quickly. Amen. Even so, come, Lord J. G2424
21 The grace of our Lord J Christ *be* with G2424

JESUS'

Mt 15:30 down at J feet; and he healed them: G2424
27:57 Joseph, who also himself was J disciple: G2424
Lk 5: 8 saw *it*, he fell down at J knees, saying, G2424
8:41 he fell down at J feet, and besought him G2424
10:39 also sat at J feet, and heard his word. G2424
Jn 12: 9 they came not for J sake only, but that G2424
13:23 Now there was leaning on J bosom one G2424
25 He then lying on J breast saith unto G2424
2Co 4: 5 and ourselves your servants for J sake. G2424
11 unto death for J sake, that the life also G2424

JESUS CHRIST See JESUS and CHRIST.

JETHER

Jdg 8:20 And he said unto J his firstborn, Up, H3500
1Ki 2: 5 Amasa the son of J, whom he slew, and H3500
32 son of J, captain of the host of Judah. H3500
1Ch 2:17 father of Amasa *was* J the Ishmeelite. H3500
32 of Shammai; J, and Jonathan: and H3500
32 Jonathan: and J died without children. H3500
4:17 And the sons of Ezra *were*, J, and H3500
7:38 And the sons of J; Jephunneh, and H3500

JETHETH
Gen 36:40 duke Timnah, duke Alvah, duke J, H3509
1Ch 1:51 were; duke Timnah, duke Aliah, duke J, H3509

JETHLAH
Jos 19:42 And Shaalabbin, and Ajalon, and J, H3494

JETHRO
Ex 3: 1 Now Moses kept the flock of J his H3503
4:18 And Moses went and returned to J his H3500
18 alive. And J said to Moses, Go in peace. H3503
18: 1 When J, the priest of Midian, Moses' H3503
2 Then J, Moses' father in law, took H3503
5 And J, Moses' father in law, came with H3503
6 I thy father in law J am come unto thee, H3503
9 And J rejoiced for all the goodness H3503
10 And J said, Blessed *be* the LORD, who H3503
12 And J, Moses' father in law, took a H3503

JETUR
Gen 25:15 Hadar, and Tema, J, Naphish, and H3195
1Ch 1:31 J, Naphish, and Kedemah. These are H3195
5:19 with J, and Nephish, and Nodab. H3195

JEUEL
1Ch 9: 6 And of the sons of Zerah; J, and their H3262

JEUSH
Gen 36: 5 And Aholibamah bare J, and Jaalam, H3274
14 bare to Esau J, and Jaalam, and Korah. H3274
18 Esau's wife; duke J, duke Jaalam, duke H3266
1Ch 1:35 The sons of Esau; Eliphaz, Reuel, and J, H3266
7:10 the sons of Bilhan; J, and Benjamin, H3274
23:10 Jahath, Zina, and J, and Beriah. These H3266
11 the second: but J and Beriah had not H3266
2Ch 11:19 Which bare him children; J, and H3266

JEUZ
1Ch 8:10 And J, and Shachia, and Mirma. These H3263

JEW
Est 2: 5 there was a certain J, whose name *was* H3064
3: 4 for he had told them that he *was* a J. H3064
5:13 the J sitting at the king's gate. H3064
6:10 so to Mordecai the J, that sitteth at the H3064
8: 7 to Mordecai the J, Behold, I have given H3064
9:29 and Mordecai the J, wrote with all H3064
31 as Mordecai the J and Esther the queen H3064
10: 3 For Mordecai the J *was* next unto king H3064
Jer 34: 9 of them, *to wit*, of a J his brother. H3064
Zec 8:23 of him that is a J, saying, We will go H3064
Jn 4: 9 that thou, being a J, askest drink of me, *G2453*
18:35 Pilate answered, Am I a J? Thine own *G2453*
Act 10:28 for a man that is a J to keep company, *G2453*
13: 6 prophet, a J, whose name *was* Barjesus: *G2453*
18: 2 And found a certain J named Aquila, *G2453*
24 And a certain J named Apollos, born at *G2453*
19:14 J, *and* chief of the priests, which did so. *G2453*
34 But when they knew that he was a J, all *G2453*
21:39 a man *which am* a J of Tarsus, *a city* in *G2453*
22: 3 I am verily a man *which am* a J, born in *G2453*
Ro 1:16 to the J first, and also to the Greek. *G2453*
2: 9 of the J first, and also of the Gentile; *G2453*
10 to the J first, and also to the Gentile: *G2453*
17 Behold, thou art called a J, and restest *G2453*
28 For he is not a J, which is one *G2453*
29 But he *is* a J, which is one inwardly; and *G2453*
3: 1 What advantage then hath the J? or *G2453*
10:12 For there is no difference between the J *G2453*
1Co 9:20 And unto the Jews I became as a J, that *G2453*
Gal 2:14 all, If thou, being a J, livest after the *G2453*
3:28 There is neither J nor Greek, there is *G2453*
Col 3:11 Where there is neither Greek nor J, *G2453*

JEWEL
Prv 11:22 *As* a j of gold in a swine's snout, *so is* a H5141
20:15 the lips of knowledge *are* a precious j. H3627
Ezk 16:12 And I put a j on thy forehead, and H5141

JEWELS
Gen 24:53 And the servant brought forth j of H3627
53 of silver, and j of gold, and raiment, H3627
Ex 3:22 in her house, j of silver, and jewels H3627
22 of silver, and j of gold, and raiment: H3627
11: 2 j of silver, and jewels of gold. H3627
2 jewels of silver, and j of gold. H3627
12:35 of the Egyptians j of silver, and jewels H3627
35 of silver, and j of gold, and raiment: H3627
35:22 and tablets, all j of gold: and every man H3627
Nu 31:50 hath gotten, of j of gold, chains, and H3627
51 the gold of them, *even* all wrought j. H3627
1Sa 6: 8 the cart; and put the j of gold, which ye H3627
15 it, wherein the j of gold *were*, and put H3627
2Ch 20:25 and precious j, which they stripped H3627
32:27 and for all manner of pleasant j; H3627
Job 28:17 of it *shall not be for* j of fine gold. H3627
Song 1:10 Thy cheeks are comely with rows *of* j, thy
7: 1 of thy thighs *are* like j, the work of the H2481
Isa 3:21 The rings, and nose j, H5141
61:10 as a bride adorneth *herself* with her j. H3627
Ezk 16:17 Thou hast also taken thy fair j of my H3627
39 fair j, and leave thee naked and bare. H3627
23:26 of thy clothes, and take away thy fair j. H3627
Hos 2:13 earrings and her j, and she went after H2484
Mal 3:17 I make up my j; and I will spare them, H5459

JEWESS
Act 16: 1 which was a J, and believed; but his *G2453*
24:24 which was a J, he sent for Paul, and *G2453*

JEWISH
Tit 1:14 Not giving heed to J fables, and *G2451*

JEWRY
Dan 5:13 the king my father brought out of J? H3061
Lk 23: 5 J, beginning from Galilee to this place. *G2449*
Jn 7: 1 in J, because the Jews sought to kill him. *G2449*

JEWS
2Ki 16: 6 and drave the J from Elath: and the H3064
25:25 he died, and the J and the Chaldees H3064
Ezr 4:12 Be it known unto the king, that the J H3062
23 unto the J, and made them to cease H3062
5: 1 unto the J that *were* in Judah and H3062
5 the elders of the J, that they could not H3062
6: 7 governor of the J and the elders of the H3062
7 J build this house of God in his place. H3062
8 the elders of these J for the building of H3062
14 And the elders of the J builded, and H3062
Neh 1: 2 concerning the J that had escaped, H3064
2:16 I as yet told *it* to the J, nor to the priests, H3064
4: 1 great indignation, and mocked the J. H3064
2 What do these feeble J? will they fortify H3064
12 And it came to pass, that when the J H3064
5: 1 their wives against their brethren the J. H3064
8 our brethren the J, which were sold H3064
17 and fifty of the J and rulers, beside H3064
6: 6 *it, that* thou and the J think to rebel: for H3064
13:23 In those days also saw I J *that* had H3064
Est 3: 6 sought to destroy all the J that *were* H3064
13 to cause to perish, all J, both young and H3064
4: 3 among the J, and fasting, and weeping, H3064
7 treasuries for the J, to destroy them. H3064
13 in the king's house, more than all the J. H3064
14 arise to the J from another place; H3064
16 Go, gather together all the J that are H3064
6:13 of the seed of the J, before whom thou H3064
8: 3 device that he had devised against the J. H3064
5 J which *are* in all the king's provinces: H3064
7 because he laid his hand upon the J. H3064
8 Write ye also for the J, as it liketh you, H3064
9 unto the J, and to the lieutenants, H3064
9 and to the J according to their writing, H3064
11 Wherein the king granted the J which H3064
13 and that the J should be ready against H3064
16 The J had light, and gladness, and joy, H3064
17 his decree came, the J had joy and H3064
17 J; for the fear of the Jews fell upon them. H3054
17 for the fear of the J fell upon them. H3064
9: 1 that the enemies of the J hoped to have H3064
1 J had rule over them that hated them;) H3064
2 The J gathered themselves together in H3064
3 king, helped the J; because the fear of H3064
5 Thus the J smote all their enemies with H3064
6 And in Shushan the palace the J slew H3064
10 the enemy of the J, slew they; but on the H3064
12 Esther the queen, The J have slain and H3064
13 it be granted to the J which *are* in H3064
15 For the J that *were* in Shushan H3064
16 But the other J that *were* in the king's H3064
18 But the J that *were* at Shushan H3064
19 Therefore the J of the villages, that H3064
20 letters unto all the J that *were* in all the H3064
22 As the days wherein the J rested from H3064
23 And the J undertook to do as they had H3064
24 enemy of all the J, had devised against H3064
24 against the J to destroy them, and H3064
25 against the J, should return upon H3064
Est 9:27 The J ordained, and took upon them, H3064
28 from among the J, nor the memorial of H3064
30 And he sent the letters unto all the J, to H3064
10: 3 great among the J, and accepted of the H3064
Jer 32:12 the J that sat in the court of the prison. H3064
38:19 I am afraid of the J that are fallen to H3064
40:11 Likewise when all the J that *were* in H3064
12 Even all the J returned out of all places H3064
15 thee, that all the J which are gathered H3064
41: 3 Ishmael also slew all the J that were H3064
44: 1 concerning all the J which dwell in the H3064
52:28 three thousand J and three and twenty: H3064
30 captive of the J seven hundred forty H3064
Dan 3: 8 came near, and accused the J. H3062
12 There are certain J whom thou hast set H3062
Mt 2: 2 is born King of the J? for we have seen *G2453*
27:11 the King of the J? And Jesus said unto *G2453*
29 mocked him, saying, Hail, King of the J! *G2453*
37 THIS IS JESUS THE KING OF THE J. *G2453*
28:15 reported among the J until this day. *G2453*
Mk 7: 3 For the Pharisees, and all the J, except *G2453*
15: 2 the King of the J? And he answering said *G2453*
9 that I release unto you the King of the J? *G2453*
12 *unto him* whom ye call the King of the J? *G2453*
18 began to salute him, Hail, King of the J! *G2453*
26 was written over, THE KING OF THE J. *G2453*
Lk 7: 3 the elders of the J, beseeching him that *G2453*
23: 3 the King of the J? And he answered him *G2453*
37 And saying, If thou be the king of the J, *G2453*
38 Hebrew, THIS IS THE KING OF THE J. *G2453*
51 a city of the J: who also himself waited *G2453*
Jn 1:19 of John, when the J sent priests and *G2453*
2: 6 the purifying of the J, containing two or *G2453*
18 Then answered the J and said unto *G2453*
20 Then said the J, Forty and six years was *G2453*
3: 1 named Nicodemus, a ruler of the J: *G2453*
25 disciples and the J about purifying. *G2453*
4: 9 of Samaria? for the J have no dealings *G2453*
22 we worship: for salvation is of the J. *G2453*
5: 1 After this there was a feast of the J; and *G2453*
10 The J therefore said unto him that was *G2453*
15 The man departed, and told the J that *G2453*
16 And therefore did the J persecute Jesus, *G2453*
18 Therefore the J sought the more to kill *G2453*
6: 4 And the passover, a feast of the J, was *G2453*
41 The J then murmured at him, because *G2453*
52 The J therefore strove among *G2453*
7: 1 Jewry, because the J sought to kill him. *G2453*
11 Then the J sought him at the feast, and *G2453*
13 spake openly of him for fear of the J. *G2453*
15 And the J marvelled, saying, How *G2453*
35 Then said the J among themselves, *G2453*
8:22 Then said the J, Will he kill himself? *G2453*
31 Then said Jesus to those J which *G2453*
48 Then answered the J, and said unto *G2453*
52 Then said the J unto him, Now we *G2453*
57 Then said the J unto him, Thou art not *G2453*
9:18 But the J did not believe concerning *G2453*
22 they feared the J: for the Jews had *G2453*
22 the Jews: for the J had agreed already, *G2453*
10:19 again among the J for these sayings. *G2453*
24 Then came the J round about him, and *G2453*
31 Then the J took up stones again to *G2453*
33 The J answered him, saying, For a good *G2453*
11: 8 him, Master, the J of late sought to *G2453*
19 And many of the J came to Martha and *G2453*
31 The J then which were with her in the *G2453*
33 weeping, and the J also weeping which *G2453*
36 Then said the J, Behold how he loved *G2453*
45 Then many of the J which came to *G2453*
54 openly among the J; but went thence *G2453*
12: 9 Much people of the J therefore knew *G2453*
11 the J went away, and believed on Jesus. *G2453*
13:33 as I said unto the J, Whither I go, ye *G2453*
18:12 of the J took Jesus, and bound him, *G2453*
14 counsel to the J, that it was expedient *G2453*
20 whither the J always resort; and in *G2453*
31 to your law. The J therefore said unto *G2453*
33 unto him, Art thou the King of the J? *G2453*
36 not be delivered to the J: but now is my *G2453*
38 out again unto the J, and saith unto *G2453*
39 that I release unto you the King of the J? *G2453*
19: 3 And said, Hail, King of the J! and they *G2453*
7 The J answered him, We have a law, *G2453*
12 him: but the J cried out, saying, If *G2453*
14 he saith unto the J, Behold your King! *G2453*
19 OF NAZARETH THE KING OF THE J. *G2453*
20 This title then read many of the J: for *G2453*
21 Then said the chief priests of the J to *G2453*

Jn 19:21 The King of the J; but that he said, I am G2453
21 but that he said, I am King of the J. G2453
31 The J therefore, because it was the G2453
38 for fear of the J, besought Pilate that G2453
40 as the manner of the J is to bury. G2453
20:19 for fear of the J, came Jesus and stood G2453
Act 2: 5 And there were dwelling at Jerusalem J, G2453
10 strangers of Rome, J and proselytes, G2453
9:22 and confounded the J which dwelt at G2453
23 fulfilled, the J took counsel to kill him: G2453
10:22 all the nation of the J, was warned from G2453
39 in the land of the J, and in Jerusalem; G2453
11:19 the word to none but unto the J only. G2453
12: 3 And because he saw it pleased the J, he G2453
11 all the expectation of the people of the J. G2453
13: 5 synagogues of the J: and they had also G2453
42 And when the J were gone out of the G2453
43 broken up, many of the J and religious G2453
45 But when the J saw the multitudes, G2453
50 But the J stirred up the devout and G2453
14: 1 synagogue of the J, and so spake, that a G2453
1 of the J and also of the Greeks believed. G2453
2 But the unbelieving J stirred up the G2453
4 with the J, and part with the apostles. G2453
5 and also of the J with their rulers, to G2453
19 And there came thither *certain* J from G2453
16: 3 him because of the J which were in G2453
20 being J, do exceedingly trouble our city, G2453
17: 1 where was a synagogue of the J: G2453
5 But the J which believed not, moved G2453
10 *thither* went into the synagogue of the J. G2453
13 But when the J of Thessalonica had G2453
17 with the J, and with the devout G2453
18: 2 had commanded all J to depart from G2453
4 and persuaded the J and the Greeks. G2453
5 testified to the J *that* Jesus *was* Christ. G2453
12 of Achaia, the J made insurrection with G2453
14 said unto the J, If it were a matter of G2453
14 lewdness, O *ye* J, reason would that I G2453
19 the synagogue, and reasoned with the J. G2453
28 For he mightily convinced the J, *and* G2453
19:10 of the Lord Jesus, both J and Greeks. G2453
13 Then certain of the vagabond J, G2453
17 And this was known to all the J and G2453
33 of the multitude, the J putting him G2453
20: 3 And when the J laid wait for him, as G5259
19 befell me by the lying in wait of the J: G2453
21 Testifying both to the J, and also to the G2453
21:11 Ghost, So shall the J at Jerusalem bind G2453
20 thousands of J there are which believe; G2453
21 teachest all the J which are among the G2453
27 almost ended, the J which were of Asia, G2453
22:12 report of all the J which dwelt *there*, G2453
30 he was accused of the J, he loosed him G2453
23:12 And when it was day, certain of the J G2453
20 And he said, The J have agreed to G2453
27 This man was taken of the J, and G2453
30 And when it was told me how that the J G2453
24: 5 among all the J throughout the world, G2453
9 And the J also assented, saying that G2453
18 Whereupon certain J from Asia found G2453
27 shew the J a pleasure, left Paul bound. G2453
25: 2 the chief of the J informed him against G2453
7 And when he was come, the J which G2453
8 the law of the J, neither against the G2453
9 But Festus, willing to do the J a G2453
10 to be judged: to the J have I done no G2453
15 and the elders of the J informed *me*, G2453
24 multitude of the J have dealt with me, G2453
26: 2 things whereof I am accused of the J: G2453
3 are among the J: wherefore I beseech G2453
4 own nation at Jerusalem, know all the J; G2453
7 king Agrippa, I am accused of the J. G2453
21 For these causes the J caught me in the G2453
28:17 the chief of the J together: and when G2453
19 But when the J spake against *it*, I was G2453
29 these words, the J departed, and had G2453
Ro 3: 9 proved both J and Gentiles, that they G2453
29 *Is he* the God of the J only? *is he* not G2453
9:24 of the J only, but also of the Gentiles? G2453
1Co 1:22 For the J require a sign, and the Greeks G2453
23 crucified, unto the J a stumblingblock, G2453
24 But unto them which are called, both J G2453
9:20 And unto the J I became as a Jew, that I G2453
20 that I might gain the J; to them that are G2453
10:32 Give none offence, neither to the J, nor G2453
12:13 whether *we be* J or Gentiles, whether G2453
2Co 11:24 Of the J five times received I forty G2453
Gal 2:13 And the other J dissembled likewise G2453
Gal 2:14 and not as do the J, why compellest G2452
14 thou the Gentiles to live as do the J? G2450
15 We *who are* J by nature, and not G2453
1Th 2:14 countrymen, even as they *have* of the J: G2453
Rev 2: 9 which say they are J, and are not, but G2453
3: 9 which say they are J, and are not, but G2453

JEWS'
2Ki 18:26 not with us in the J language in the ears H3066
28 with a loud voice in the J language, and H3066
2Ch 32:18 a loud voice in the J speech unto the H3066
Neh 13:24 could not speak in the J language, but H3066
Est 3:10 Hammedatha the Agagite, the J enemy. H3064
8: 1 of Haman the J enemy unto Esther H3064
Isa 36:11 not to us in the J language, in the ears H3064
13 with a loud voice in the J language, and H3064
Jn 2:13 And the J passover was at hand, and G2453
7: 2 Now the J feast of tabernacles was at G2453
11:55 And the J passover was nigh at hand: G2453
19:42 because of the J preparation *day*; for G2453
Gal 1:13 in time past in the J religion, how that G2454
14 And profited in the J religion above G2454

JEZANIAH
Jer 40: 8 the Netophathite, and J the son of a H3153
42: 1 of Kareah, and J the son of Hoshaiah, H3153

JEZEBEL
1Ki 16:31 that he took to wife J the daughter of H348
18: 4 For it was *so*, when J cut off the prophets H348
13 what I did when J slew the prophets of H348
19: 1 And Ahab told J all that Elijah had done, H348
2 Then J sent a messenger unto Elijah, H348
21: 5 But J his wife came to him, and said H348
7 And J his wife said unto him, Dost thou H348
11 in his city, did as J had sent unto them, H348
14 Then they sent to J, saying, Naboth is H348
15 And it came to pass, when J heard that H348
15 and was dead, that J said to Ahab, Arise, H348
23 And of J also spake the LORD, saying, H348
23 dogs shall eat J by the wall of Jezreel. H348
25 of the LORD, whom J his wife stirred up. H348
2Ki 9: 7 servants of the LORD, at the hand of J. H348
10 And the dogs shall eat J in the portion of H348
22 J and her witchcrafts *are so* many? H348
30 And when Jehu was come to Jezreel, J H348
36 of Jezreel shall dogs eat the flesh of J: H348
37 And the carcase of J shall be as dung H348
37 *so* that they shall not say, This *is* J. H348
Rev 2:20 that woman J, which calleth herself G2403

JEZEBEL'S
1Ki 18:19 four hundred, which eat at J table. H348

JEZER
Gen 46:24 Jahzeel, and Guni, and J, and Shillem. H3337
Nu 26:49 Of J, the family of the Jezerites: of H3337
1Ch 7:13 and J, and Shallum, the sons of Bilhah. H3337

JEZERITES
Nu 26:49 Of Jezer, the family of the J: of Shillem, H3340

JEZIAH
Ezr 10:25 Ramiah, and J, and Malchiah, and H3150

JEZIEL
1Ch 12: 3 Gibeathite; and J, and Pelet, the sons of H3149

JEZLIAH
1Ch 8:18 Ishmerai also, and J, and Jobab, the H3152

JEZOAR
1Ch 4: 7 Helah *were*, Zereth, and J, and Ethnan. H3328

JEZRAHIAH
Neh 12:42 singers sang loud, with J *their* overseer. H3156

JEZREEL
Jos 15:56 And J, and Jokdeam, and Zanoah, H3157
17:16 and *they* who *are* of the valley of J. H3157
19:18 And their border was toward J, and H3157
Jdg 6:33 went over, and pitched in the valley of J. H3157
1Sa 25:43 David also took Ahinoam of J; and they H3157
29: 1 pitched by a fountain which *is* in J. H3157
11 And the Philistines went up to J. H3157
2Sa 2: 9 and over J, and over Ephraim, H3157
4: 4 Jonathan out of J, and his nurse took H3157
1Ki 4:12 Zartanah beneath J, from Beth-shean to H3157
18:45 rain. And Ahab rode, and went to J. H3157
1Ki 18:46 ran before Ahab to the entrance of J. H3157
21: 1 which *was* in J, hard by the palace of H3157
23 dogs shall eat Jezebel by the wall of J. H3157
2Ki 8:29 to be healed in J of the wounds which H3157
29 son of Ahab in J, because he was sick. H3157
9:10 in the portion of J, and *there shall be* H3157
15 to be healed in J of the wounds which H3157
15 escape out of the city to go to tell *it* in J. H3157
16 So Jehu rode in a chariot, and went to J; H3157
17 on the tower in J, and he spied the H3157
30 And when Jehu was come to J, Jezebel H3157
36 of J shall dogs eat the flesh of Jezebel: H3157
37 in the portion of J; *so* that they shall not H3157
10: 1 unto the rulers of J, to the elders, and to H3157
6 and come to me to J by to morrow this H3157
7 in baskets, and sent him *them* to J. H3157
11 the house of Ahab in J, and all his great H3157
1Ch 4: 3 And these *were of* the father of Etam; J, H3157
2Ch 22: 6 And he returned to be healed in J H3157
6 son of Ahab at J, because he was sick. H3157
Hos 1: 4 Call his name J; for yet a little *while*, H3157
4 the blood of J upon the house of Jehu, H3157
5 break the bow of Israel in the valley of J. H3157
11 the land: for great *shall be* the day of J. H3157
2:22 wine, and the oil; and they shall hear J. H3157

JEZREELITE
1Ki 21: 1 *that* Naboth the J had a vineyard, H3158
4 which Naboth the J had spoken to him: H3158
6 unto Naboth the J, and said unto him, H3158
7 give thee the vineyard of Naboth the J. H3158
15 of Naboth the J, which he refused to H3158
16 of Naboth the J, to take possession of it. H3158
2Ki 9:21 met him in the portion of Naboth the J. H3158
25 field of Naboth the J: for remember how H3158

JEZREELITESS
1Sa 27: 3 wives, Ahinoam the J, and Abigail the H3159
30: 5 Ahinoam the J, and Abigail the wife H3159
2Sa 2: 2 wives also, Ahinoam the J, and Abigail H3159
3: 2 was Amnon, of Ahinoam the J; H3159
1Ch 3: 1 of Ahinoam the J; the second Daniel, of H3159

JIBSAM
1Ch 7: 2 and Jahmai, and J, and Shemuel, heads H3005

JIDLAPH
Gen 22:22 Hazo, and Pildash, and J, and Bethuel. H3044

JIMNA
Nu 26:44 their families: of J, the family of the H3232

JIMNAH
Gen 46:17 And the sons of Asher; J, and Ishuah, H3232

JIMNITES
Nu 26:44 the family of the J: of Jesui, the family of H3232

JIPHTAH
Jos 15:43 And J, and Ashnah, and Nezib, H3316

JIPHTHAH-EL
Jos 19:14 outgoings thereof are in the valley of J: H3317
27 to the valley of J toward the north side H3317

JOAB
1Sa 26: 6 brother to J, saying, Who will go H3097
2Sa 2:13 And J the son of Zeruiah, and the H3097
14 And Abner said to J, Let the young men H3097
14 before us. And J said, Let them arise. H3097
18 of Zeruiah there, J, and Abishai, and H3097
22 I hold up my face to J thy brother? H3097
24 J also and Abishai pursued after H3097
26 Then Abner called to J, and said, Shall H3097
27 And J said, *As* God liveth, unless thou H3097
28 So J blew a trumpet, and all the people H3097
30 And J returned from following Abner: H3097
32 *in* Beth-lehem. And J and his men went H3097
3:22 of David and J came from *pursuing* H3097
23 When J and all the host that *was* with H3097
23 come, they told J, saying, Abner the son H3097
24 Then J came to the king, and said, H3097
26 And when J was come out from David, H3097
27 to Hebron, J took him aside in the H3097
29 Let it rest on the head of J, and on all H3097
29 from the house of J one that hath an H3097
30 So J and Abishai his brother slew H3097
31 And David said to J, and to all the H3097
8:16 And J the son of Zeruiah *was* over the H3097

2Sa 10: 7 And when David heard of *it*, he sent J, H3097
9 When J saw that the front of the battle H3097
13 And J drew nigh, and the people that H3097
14 into the city. So J returned from the H3097
11: 1 that David sent J, and his servants with H3097
6 And David sent to J, *saying*, Send me H3097
6 the Hittite. And J sent Uriah to David. H3097
7 *of him* how J did, and how the people H3097
11 tents; and my lord J, and the servants of H3097
14 to J, and sent *it* by the hand of Uriah. H3097
16 And it came to pass, when J observed H3097
17 and fought with J: and there fell *some* H3097
18 Then J sent and told David all the H3097
22 David all that J had sent him for. H3097
25 shalt thou say unto J, Let not this thing H3097
12:26 And J fought against Rabbah of the H3097
27 And J sent messengers to David, and H3097
14: 1 Now J the son of Zeruiah perceived H3097
2 And J sent to Tekoah, and fetched H3097
3 him. So J put the words in her mouth. H3097
19 And the king said, *Is not* the hand of J H3097
19 for thy servant J, he bade me, and he H3097
20 hath thy servant J done this thing: and H3097
21 And the king said unto J, Behold now, I H3097
22 And J fell to the ground on his face, H3097
22 the king: and J said, To day thy servant H3097
23 So J arose and went to Geshur, and H3097
29 Therefore Absalom sent for J, to have H3097
31 Then J arose, and came to Absalom H3097
32 And Absalom answered J, Behold, I H3097
33 So J came to the king, and told him: H3097
17:25 the host instead of J: which Amasa *was* H3097
18: 2 under the hand of J, and a third part H3097
5 And the king commanded J and H3097
10 And a certain man saw *it*, and told J, H3097
11 And J said unto the man that told him, H3097
12 And the man said unto J, Though I H3097
14 Then said J, I may not tarry thus with H3097
16 And J blew the trumpet, and the people H3097
16 after Israel: for J held back the people. H3097
20 And J said unto him, Thou shalt not H3097
21 Then said J to Cushi, Go tell the king H3097
21 Cushi bowed himself unto J, and ran. H3097
22 Zadok yet again to J, But howsoever, let H3097
22 after Cushi. And J said, Wherefore wilt H3097
29 answered, When J sent the king's H3097
19: 1 And it was told J, Behold, the king H3097
5 And J came into the house to the king, H3097
13 before me continually in the room of J. H3097
20: 9 And J said to Amasa, *Art* thou in H3097
9 my brother? And J took Amasa by the H3097
10 and he died. So J and Abishai his H3097
11 He that favoureth J, and he that *is* for H3097
11 he that *is* for David, *let him go* after J. H3097
13 went on after J, to pursue after Sheba H3097
15 J battered the wall, to throw it down. H3097
16 I pray you, unto J, Come near hither, H3097
17 said, *Art* thou J? And he answered, I H3097
20 And J answered and said, Far be it, far H3097
21 woman said unto J, Behold, his head H3097
22 and cast *it* out to J. And he blew a H3097
22 J returned to Jerusalem unto the king. H3097
23 Now J *was* over all the host of Israel: H3097
23:18 And Abishai, the brother of J, the son of H3097
24 Asahel the brother of J *was* one of the H3097
37 armourbearer to J the son of Zeruiah, H3097
24: 2 For the king said to J the captain of the H3097
3 And J said unto the king, Now the H3097
4 prevailed against J, and against the H3097
4 of the host. And J and the captains of H3097
9 And J gave up the sum of the number H3097
1Ki 1: 7 And he conferred with J the son of H3097
19 the priest, and J the captain of the host: H3097
41 eating. And when J heard the sound of H3097
2: 5 Moreover thou knowest also what J the H3097
22 the priest, and for J the son of Zeruiah. H3097
28 Then tidings came to J: for Joab had H3097
28 Then tidings came to Joab: for J had H3097
28 after Absalom. And J fled unto the H3097
29 And it was told king Solomon that J H3097
30 Thus said J, and thus he answered me. H3097
31 blood, which J shed, from me, and H3097
33 upon the head of J, and upon the head H3097
11:15 was in Edom, and J the captain of the H3097
16 (For six months did J remain there H3097
21 fathers, and that J the captain of the H3097
1Ch 2:16 Abishai, and J, and Asahel, three. H3097
54 Ataroth, the house of J, and half of the H5854
4:14 and Seraiah begat J, the father of the H3097
1Ch 11: 6 and captain. So J the son of Zeruiah H3097
8 and J repaired the rest of the city. H3097
20 And Abishai the brother of J, he was H3097
26 the brother of J, Elhanan the son of H3097
39 armourbearer of J the son of Zeruiah, H3097
18:15 And J the son of Zeruiah *was* over the H3097
19: 8 And when David heard of *it*, he sent J, H3097
10 Now when J saw that the battle was set H3097
14 So J and the people that *were* with him H3097
15 into the city. Then J came to Jerusalem. H3097
20: 1 go out *to battle*, J led forth the power H3097
1 And J smote Rabbah, and destroyed it. H3097
21: 2 And David said to J and to the rulers of H3097
3 And J answered, The LORD make his H3097
4 prevailed against J. Wherefore Joab H3097
4 Joab. Wherefore J departed, and went H3097
5 And J gave the sum of the number of H3097
6 the king's word was abominable to J. H3097
26:28 son of Ner, and J the son of Zeruiah, H3097
27: 7 the brother of J, and Zebadiah his son H3097
24 J the son of Zeruiah began to number, H3097
34 the general of the king's army *was* J. H3097
Ezr 2: 6 of Jeshua *and* J, two thousand eight H3097
8: 9 Of the sons of J; Obadiah the son of H3097
Neh 7:11 of Jeshua and J, two thousand and eight H3097
Ps 60:ttl when J returned, and smote H3097

JOAB'S

2Sa 14:30 his servants, See, J field is near mine, H3097
17:25 of Nahash, sister to Zeruiah J mother. H3097
18: 2 son of Zeruiah, J brother, and a third H3097
15 And ten young men that bare J armour H3097
20: 7 And there went out after him J men, H3097
8 before them. And J garment that he H3097
10 sword that *was* in J hand: so he smote H3097
11 And one of J men stood by him, and H3097

JOAH

2Ki 18:18 and J the son of Asaph the recorder. H3098
26 and Shebna, and J, unto Rab-shakeh, H3098
37 the scribe, and J the son of Asaph the H3098
1Ch 6:21 J his son, Iddo his son, Zerah his son, H3098
26: 4 the second, J the third, and Sacar H3098
2Ch 29:12 and of the Gershonites; J the son of H3098
12 son of Zimmah, and Eden the son of J: H3098
34: 8 of the city, and J the son of Joahaz the H3098
Isa 36: 3 scribe, and J, Asaph's son, the recorder. H3098
11 Then said Eliakim and Shebna and J H3098
22 the scribe, and J, the son of Asaph, the H3098

JOAHAZ

2Ch 34: 8 Joah the son of J the recorder, to repair H3099

JOANNA

Lk 3:27 Which was *the son* of J, which was *the* G2490
8: 3 And J the wife of Chuza Herod's G2489
24:10 It was Mary Magdalene, and J, and G2489

JOASH

Jdg 6:11 *pertained* unto J the Abi-ezrite: and his H3101
29 the son of J hath done this thing. H3101
30 Then the men of the city said unto J, H3101
31 And J said unto all that stood against H3101
7:14 Gideon the son of J, a man of Israel: *for* H3101
8:13 And Gideon the son of J returned from H3101
29 And Jerubbaal the son of J went and H3101
32 And Gideon the son of J died in a good H3101
32 in the sepulchre of J his father, in H3101
1Ki 22:26 of the city, and to J the king's son; H3101
2Ki 11: 2 of Ahaziah, took J the son of Ahaziah, H3101
12:19 And the rest of the acts of J, and all that H3101
20 and slew J in the house of Millo, H3101
13: 1 In the three and twentieth year of J the H3101
9 and J his son reigned in his stead. H3101
10 In the thirty and seventh year of J king H3101
12 And the rest of the acts of J, and all that H3101
13 And J slept with his fathers; and H3101
13 upon his throne: and J was buried in H3101
14 he died. And J the king of Israel came H3101
25 war. Three times did J beat him, and H3101
14: 1 In the second year of J son of Jehoahaz H3101
1 Amaziah the son of J king of Judah. H3101
3 to all things as J his father did. H3101
17 And Amaziah the son of J king of H3101
23 the son of J king of Judah Jeroboam H3101
23 the son of J king of Israel began H3101
27 by the hand of Jeroboam the son of J. H3101
1Ch 3:11 Joram his son, Ahaziah his son, J his H3101
4:22 of Chozeba, and J, and Saraph, who had H3101
1Ch 7: 8 And the sons of Becher; Zemira, and J, H3135
12: 3 The chief *was* Ahiezer, then J, the sons H3101
27:28 and over the cellars of oil *was* J: H3135
2Ch 18:25 of the city, and to J the king's son; H3101
22:11 of the king, took J the son of Ahaziah, H3101
24: 1 J *was* seven years old when he began to H3101
2 And J did *that which was* right in the H3101
4 And it came to pass after this, *that* J H3101
22 Thus J the king remembered not the H3101
24 So they executed judgment against J. H3101
25:17 took advice, and sent to J, the son of H3101
18 And J king of Israel sent to Amaziah H3101
21 So J the king of Israel went up; and H3101
23 And J the king of Israel took Amaziah H3101
23 Judah, the son of J, the son of Jehoahaz, H3101
25 And Amaziah the son of J king of H3101
25 after the death of J son of Jehoahaz H3101
Hos 1: 1 of Jeroboam the son of J, king of Israel. H3101
Am 1: 1 the son of J king of Israel, two years H3101

JOATHAM

Mt 1: 9 And Ozias begat J; and Joatham begat G2488
9 And Ozias begat Joatham; and J begat G2488

JOB

Gen 46:13 Tola, and Phuvah, and J, and Shimron. H3102
Job 1: 1 Uz, whose name *was* J; and that man was H347
5 gone about, that J sent and sanctified H347
5 of them all: for J said, It may be that my H347
5 in their hearts. Thus did J continually. H347
8 my servant J, that *there is* none like H347
9 and said, Doth J fear God for nought? H347
14 And there came a messenger unto J, and H347
20 Then J arose, and rent his mantle, and H347
22 In all this J sinned not, nor charged God H347
2: 3 my servant J, that *there is* none like H347
7 LORD, and smote J with sore boils from H347
10 evil? In all this did not J sin with his lips. H347
3: 1 After this opened J his mouth, and H347
2 And J spake, and said, H347
6: 1 But J answered and said, H347
9: 1 Then J answered and said, H347
12: 1 And J answered and said, H347
16: 1 Then J answered and said, H347
19: 1 Then J answered and said, H347
21: 1 But J answered and said, H347
23: 1 Then J answered and said, H347
26: 1 But J answered and said, H347
27: 1 Moreover J continued his parable, and H347
29: 1 Moreover J continued his parable, and H347
31:40 of barley. The words of J are ended. H347
32: 1 So these three men ceased to answer J, H347
2 of Ram: against J was his wrath kindled, H347
3 no answer, and *yet* had condemned J. H347
4 Now Elihu had waited till J had spoken, H347
12 convinced J, *or* that answered his words: H347
33: 1 Wherefore, J, I pray thee, hear my H347
31 Mark well, O J, hearken unto me: hold H347
34: 5 For J hath said, I am righteous: and God H347
7 What man *is* like J, *who* drinketh up H347
35 J hath spoken without knowledge, and H347
36 My desire *is that* J may be tried unto the H347
35:16 Therefore doth J open his mouth in vain; H347
37:14 Hearken unto this, O J: stand still, and H347
38: 1 Then the LORD answered J out of the H347
40: 1 Moreover the LORD answered J, and said, H347
3 Then J answered the LORD, and said, H347
6 Then answered the LORD unto J out of H347
42: 1 Then J answered the LORD, and said, H347
7 these words unto J, the LORD said to H347
7 *thing that is* right, as my servant J *hath*. H347
8 and go to my servant J, and offer up for H347
8 and my servant J shall pray for you: for H347
8 *thing which is* right, like my servant J. H347
9 them: the LORD also accepted J. H347
10 And the LORD turned the captivity of J, H347
10 gave J twice as much as he had before. H347
12 So the LORD blessed the latter end of J H347
15 fair as the daughters of J: and their father H347
16 After this lived J an hundred and forty H347
17 So J died, *being* old and full of days. H347
Ezk 14:14 men, Noah, Daniel, and J, were in it, they H347
20 Though Noah, Daniel, and J, *were* in it, H347
Jas 5:11 of the patience of J, and have seen the G2492

JOBAB

Gen 10:29 And Ophir, and Havilah, and J: all these H3103
36:33 And Bela died, and J the son of Zerah H3103
34 And J died, and Husham of the land of H3103

Jos 11: 1 that he sent to J king of Madon, and H3103
1Ch 1:23 And Ophir, and Havilah, and J. All H3103
44 And when Bela was dead, J the son of H3103
45 And when J was dead, Husham of the H3103
8: 9 And he begat of Hodesh his wife, J, and H3103
18 Ishmerai also, and Jezliah, and J, the H3103

JOB'S
Job 2:11 Now when J three friends heard of all H347

JOCHEBED
Ex 6:20 And Amram took him J his father's H3115
Nu 26:59 And the name of Amram's wife *was* J, H3115

JOED
Neh 11: 7 the son of J, the son of Pedaiah, H3133

JOEL
1Sa 8: 2 Now the name of his firstborn was J; H3100
1Ch 4:35 And J, and Jehu the son of Josibiah, the H3100
5: 4 The sons of J; Shemaiah his son, Gog H3100
8 Shema, the son of J, who dwelt in Aroer, H3100
12 J the chief, and Shapham the next, and H3100
6:33 singer, the son of J, the son of Shemuel, H3100
36 The son of Elkanah, the son of J, the son H3100
7: 3 J, Ishiah, five: all of them chief men. H3100
11:38 J the brother of Nathan, Mibhar the H3100
15: 7 Of the sons of Gershom; J the chief, and H3100
11 for Uriel, Asaiah, and J, Shemaiah, and H3100
17 Heman the son of J; and of his brethren, H3100
23: 8 *was* Jehiel, and Zetham, and J, three. H3100
26:22 The sons of Jehieli; Zetham, and J his H3100
27:20 of Manasseh, J the son of Pedaiah: H3100
2Ch 29:12 of Amasai, and J the son of Azariah, H3100
Ezr 10:43 Zabad, Zebina, Jadau, and J, Benaiah. H3100
Neh 11: 9 And J the son of Zichri *was* their H3100
Joel 1: 1 The word of the LORD that came to J H3100
Act 2:16 that which was spoken by the prophet J; *G2493*

JOELAH
1Ch 12: 7 And J, and Zebadiah, the sons of H3132

JOEZER
1Ch 12: 6 and J, and Jashobeam, the Korhites, H3134

JOGBEHAH
Nu 32:35 Atroth, Shophan, and Jaazer, and J, H3011
Jdg 8:11 the east of Nobah and J, and smote the H3011

JOGLI
Nu 34:22 the children of Dan, Bukki the son of J. H3020

JOHA
1Ch 8:16 And Michael, and Ispah, and J, the sons H3109
11:45 Jediael the son of Shimri, and J his H3109

JOHANAN
2Ki 25:23 of Nethaniah, and J the son of Careah, H3110
1Ch 3:15 Josiah *were*, the firstborn J, the second H3110
24 and J, and Dalaiah, and Anani, seven. H3110
6: 9 begat Azariah, and Azariah begat J, H3110
10 And J begat Azariah, (he *it is* that H3110
12: 4 and J, and Josabad the Gederathite, H3110
12 J the eighth, Elzabad the ninth, H3110
2Ch 28:12 Azariah the son of J, Berechiah the son H3076
Ezr 8:12 And of the sons of Azgad; J the son of H3110
10: 6 the chamber of J the son of Eliashib: H3076
Neh 6:18 of Arah; and his son J had taken the H3076
12:22 Joiada, and J, and Jaddua, *were* H3110
23 until the days of J the son of Eliashib. H3110
Jer 40: 8 of Nethaniah, and J and Jonathan the H3110
13 Moreover J the son of Kareah, and all H3110
15 Then J the son of Kareah spake to H3110
16 Ahikam said unto J the son of Kareah, H3110
41:11 But when J the son of Kareah, and all H3110
13 with Ishmael saw J the son of Kareah, H3110
14 and went unto J the son of Kareah. H3110
15 escaped from J with eight men, and H3110
16 Then took J the son of Kareah, and all H3110
42: 1 of the forces, and J the son of Kareah, H3110
8 Then called he J the son of Kareah, and H3110
43: 2 of Hoshaiah, and J the son of Kareah, H3110
4 So J the son of Kareah, and all the H3110
5 But J the son of Kareah, and all the H3110

JOHN
Mt 3: 1 In those days came J the Baptist, *G2491*
4 And the same J had his raiment of *G2491*
13 to Jordan unto J, to be baptized of him. *G2491*
Mt 3:14 But J forbad him, saying, I have need *G2491*
4:12 Now when Jesus had heard that J was *G2491*
21 of Zebedee, and J his brother, in a ship *G2491*
9:14 Then came to him the disciples of J, *G2491*
10: 2 *the son* of Zebedee, and J his brother; *G2491*
11: 2 Now when J had heard in the prison *G2491*
4 them, Go and shew J again those things *G2491*
7 concerning J, What went ye out into *G2491*
11 risen a greater than J the Baptist: *G2491*
12 And from the days of J the Baptist until *G2491*
13 and the law prophesied until J. *G2491*
18 For J came neither eating nor drinking, *G2491*
14: 2 And said unto his servants, This is J *G2491*
3 For Herod had laid hold on J, and *G2491*
4 For J said unto him, It is not lawful for *G2491*
8 me here J Baptist's head in a charger. *G2491*
10 And he sent, and beheaded J in the *G2491*
16:14 And they said, Some *say that thou art* J *G2491*
17: 1 Peter, James, and J his brother, and *G2491*
13 he spake unto them of J the Baptist. *G2491*
21:25 The baptism of J, whence was it? from *G2491*
26 the people; for all hold J as a prophet. *G2491*
32 For J came unto you in the way of *G2491*
Mk 1: 4 J did baptize in the wilderness, and *G2491*
6 And J was clothed with camel's hair, *G2491*
9 and was baptized of J in Jordan. *G2491*
14 Now after that J was put in prison, *G2491*
19 of Zebedee, and J his brother, who also *G2491*
29 Simon and Andrew, with James and J. *G2491*
2:18 And the disciples of J and of the *G2491*
18 Why do the disciples of J and of the *G2491*
3:17 And James the *son* of Zebedee, and J *G2491*
5:37 and James, and J the brother of James. *G2491*
6:14 and he said, That J the Baptist was *G2491*
16 he said, It is J, whom I beheaded: he *G2491*
17 and laid hold upon J, and bound him in *G2491*
18 For J had said unto Herod, It is not *G2491*
20 For Herod feared J, knowing that he *G2491*
24 And she said, The head of J the Baptist. *G2491*
25 in a charger the head of J the Baptist. *G2491*
8:28 And they answered, J the Baptist: but *G2491*
9: 2 and James, and J, and leadeth them up *G2491*
38 And J answered him, saying, Master, *G2491*
10:35 And James and J, the sons of Zebedee, *G2491*
41 be much displeased with James and J. *G2491*
11:30 The baptism of J, was *it* from heaven, or *G2491*
32 J, that he was a prophet indeed. *G2491*
13: 3 and J and Andrew asked him privately, *G2491*
14:33 and James and J, and began to be sore *G2491*
Lk 1:13 a son, and thou shalt call his name J. *G2491*
60 said, Not *so*; but he shall be called J. *G2491*
63 His name is J. And they marvelled all. *G2491*
3: 2 word of God came unto J the son of *G2491*
15 of J, whether he were the Christ, or not; *G2491*
16 J answered, saying unto *them* all, I *G2491*
20 above all, that he shut up J in prison. *G2491*
5:10 And so *was* also James, and J, the sons *G2491*
33 do the disciples of J fast often, and *G2491*
6:14 James and J, Philip and Bartholomew, *G2491*
7:18 And the disciples of J shewed him of all *G2491*
19 And J calling *unto him* two of his *G2491*
20 him, they said, J Baptist hath sent us *G2491*
22 Go your way, and tell J what things ye *G2491*
24 And when the messengers of J were *G2491*
24 people concerning J, What went ye out *G2491*
28 prophet than J the Baptist: but he that *G2491*
29 being baptized with the baptism of J. *G2491*
33 For J the Baptist came neither eating *G2491*
8:51 and James, and J, and the father and *G2491*
9: 7 some, that J was risen from the dead; *G2491*
9 And Herod said, J have I beheaded: but *G2491*
19 They answering said, J the Baptist; but *G2491*
28 he took Peter and J and James, and *G2491*
49 And J answered and said, Master, we *G2491*
54 And when his disciples James and J *G2491*
11: 1 to pray, as J also taught his disciples. *G2491*
16:16 The law and the prophets *were* until J: *G2491*
20: 4 The baptism of J, was it from heaven, or *G2491*
6 be persuaded that J was a prophet. *G2491*
22: 8 And he sent Peter and J, saying, Go and *G2491*
Jn 1: 6 man sent from God, whose name *was* J. *G2491*
15 J bare witness of him, and cried, *G2491*
19 And this is the record of J, when the *G2491*
26 J answered them, saying, I baptize with *G2491*
28 beyond Jordan, where J was baptizing. *G2491*
29 The next day J seeth Jesus coming unto *G2491*
32 And J bare record, saying, I saw the *G2491*
35 Again the next day after J stood, and *G2491*
40 One of the two which heard J *speak*, *G2491*
Jn 3:23 And J also was baptizing in Aenon *G2491*
24 For J was not yet cast into prison. *G2491*
26 And they came unto J, and said unto *G2491*
27 J answered and said, A man can *G2491*
4: 1 and baptized more disciples than J, *G2491*
5:33 Ye sent unto J, and he bare witness unto *G2491*
36 than *that* of J: for the works which *G2491*
10:40 J at first baptized; and there he abode. *G2491*
41 him, and said, J did no miracle: but *G2491*
41 that J spake of this man were true. *G2491*
Act 1: 5 For J truly baptized with water; but ye *G2491*
13 and James, and J, and Andrew, Philip, *G2491*
22 Beginning from the baptism of J, unto *G2491*
3: 1 Now Peter and J went up together into *G2491*
3 Who seeing Peter and J about to go *G2491*
4 eyes upon him with J, said, Look on us. *G2491*
11 held Peter and J, all the people ran *G2491*
4: 6 Caiaphas, and J, and Alexander, and *G2491*
13 of Peter and J, and perceived that they *G2491*
19 But Peter and J answered and said *G2491*
8:14 of God, they sent unto them Peter and J: *G2491*
10:37 after the baptism which J preached; *G2491*
11:16 how that he said, J indeed baptized *G2491*
12: 2 And he killed James the brother of J *G2491*
12 the mother of J, whose surname was *G2491*
25 with them J, whose surname was Mark. *G2491*
13: 5 and they had also J to *their* minister. *G2491*
13 in Pamphylia: and J departing from *G2491*
24 When J had first preached before his *G2491*
25 And as J fulfilled his course, he said, *G2491*
15:37 with them J, whose surname was Mark. *G2491*
18:25 Lord, knowing only the baptism of J. *G2491*
19: 4 Then said Paul, J verily baptized with *G2491*
Gal 2: 9 And when James, Cephas, and J, who *G2491*
Rev 1: 1 *it* by his angel unto his servant J: *G2491*
4 J to the seven churches which are in *G2491*
9 I J, who also am your brother, and *G2491*
21: 2 And I J saw the holy city, new *G2491*
22: 8 And I J saw these things, and heard *G2491*

JOHN'S
Jn 3:25 between *some* of J disciples and the *G2491*
Act 19: 3 And they said, Unto J baptism. *G2491*

JOIADA
Neh 12:10 begat Eliashib, and Eliashib begat J, H3111
11 And J begat Jonathan, and Jonathan H3111
22 The Levites in the days of Eliashib, J, H3111
13:28 And *one* of the sons of J, the son of H3111

JOIAKIM
Neh 12:10 And Jeshua begat J, Joiakim also begat H3113
10 And Jeshua begat Joiakim, J also begat H3113
12 And in the days of J were priests, the H3113
26 These *were* in the days of J the son of H3113

JOIARIB
Ezr 8:16 chief men; also for J, and for Elnathan, H3114
Neh 11: 5 of Adaiah, the son of J, the son of H3114
10 Of the priests: Jedaiah the son of J, H3114
12: 6 Shemaiah, and J, Jedaiah, H3114
19 And of J, Mattenai; of Jedaiah, Uzzi; H3114

JOIN
Ex 1:10 falleth out any war, they j also unto our H3254
2Ch 20:35 king of Judah j himself with Ahaziah H2266
Ezr 9:14 and j in affinity with the people H2859
Prv 11:21 *Though* hand *j* in hand, the wicked shall
16: 5 *j* in hand, he shall not be unpunished.
Isa 5: 8 Woe unto them that j house to house, H5060
9:11 him, and j his enemies together; H5526
56: 6 Also the sons of the stranger, that j H3867
Jer 50: 5 Come, and let us j ourselves to the H3867
Ezk 37:17 And j them one to another into one H7126
Dan 11: 6 And in the end of years they shall j H2266
Act 5:13 And of the rest durst no man j himself *G2853*
8:29 Go near, and j thyself to this chariot. *G2853*
9:26 he assayed to j himself to the disciples: *G2853*

JOINED
Gen 14: 3 All these were j together in the vale of H2266
8 j battle with them in the vale of Siddim; H6186
29:34 my husband be j unto me, because I H3867
Ex 28: 7 thereof j at the two edges thereof; H2266
7 thereof; and *so* it shall be j together. H2266
Nu 18: 2 thee, that they may be j unto thee, and H3867
4 And they shall be j unto thee, and keep H3867
25: 3 And Israel j himself unto Baal-peor: H6775
5 his men that were j unto Baal-peor. H6775

1Sa 4: 2 and when they j battle, Israel was H5203
1Ki 7:32 of the wheels *were* j to the base: and the
20:29 day the battle was j: and the children of H7126
2Ch 18: 1 in abundance, and j affinity with Ahab. H2859
20:36 And he j himself with him to make H2266
37 saying, Because thou hast j thyself with H2266
Ezr 4:12 walls *thereof*, and j the foundations. H2338
Neh 4: 6 all the wall was j together unto the half H7194
Est 9:27 and upon all such as j themselves unto H3867
Job 3: 6 it; let it not be j unto the days of the H2302
41:17 They are j one to another, they stick H1692
23 The flakes of his flesh are j together: H1692
Ps 83: 8 Assur also is j with them: they have H3867
106:28 They j themselves also unto Baal-peor, H6775
Ecc 9: 4 For to him that is j to all the living there H977
Isa 13:15 is j *unto them* shall fall by the sword. H5595
14: 1 strangers shall be j with them, and they H3867
20 Thou shalt not be j with them in burial, H3161
56: 3 the stranger, that hath j himself to the H3867
Ezk 1: 9 Their wings *were* j one to another; they H2266
11 of every one *were* j one to another, and H2266
46:22 *there were* courts j of forty *cubits* long H7000
Hos 4:17 Ephraim *is* j to idols: let him alone. H2266
Zec 2:11 And many nations shall be j to the H3867
Mt 19: 6 j together, let not man put asunder. *G4801*
Mk 10: 9 What therefore God hath j together, let *G4801*
Lk 15:15 And he went and j himself to a citizen *G2853*
Act 5:36 four hundred, j themselves: who was *G4347*
18: 7 whose house j hard to the synagogue. *G4927*
1Co 1:10 ye be perfectly j together in the same *G2675*
6:16 What? know ye not that he which is j to *G2853*
17 But he that is j unto the Lord is one *G2853*
Eph 4:16 From whom the whole body fitly j *G4883*
5:31 and shall be j unto his wife, and they *G4347*

JOINING
2Ch 3:12 *also*, j to the wing of the other cherub. H1695

JOININGS
1Ch 22: 3 the gates, and for the j; and brass in H4226

JOINT
Gen 32:25 was out of j, as he wrestled with him. H3363
Ps 22:14 bones are out of j: my heart is like wax; H6504
Prv 25:19 *like* a broken tooth, and a foot out of j. H4154
Eph 4:16 by that which every j supplieth, *G860*

JOINT-HEIRS
Ro 8:17 heirs of God, and j with Christ; if so be *G4789*

JOINTS
1Ki 22:34 of Israel between the j of the harness: H1694
2Ch 18:33 of Israel between the j of the harness: H1694
Song 7: 1 daughter! the j of thy thighs *are* like H2542
Dan 5: 6 him, so that the j of his loins were H7001
Col 2:19 all the body by j and bands having *G860*
Heb 4:12 spirit, and of the j and marrow, and *is* *G719*

JOKDEAM
Jos 15:56 And Jezreel, and J, and Zanoah, H3347

JOKIM
1Ch 4:22 And J, and the men of Chozeba, and H3137

JOKMEAM
1Ch 6:68 And J with her suburbs, and H3361

JOKNEAM
Jos 12:22 The king of Kedesh, one; the king of J H3362
19:11 and reached to the river that *is* before J; H3362
21:34 tribe of Zebulun, J with her suburbs, H3362
1Ki 4:12 *even* unto *the place that is* beyond J: H3361

JOKSHAN
Gen 25: 2 And she bare him Zimran, and J, and H3370
3 And J begat Sheba, and Dedan. And H3370
1Ch 1:32 bare Zimran, and J, and Medan, and H3370
32 And the sons of J; Sheba, and Dedan. H3370

JOKTAN
Gen 10:25 divided; and his brother's name *was* J. H3355
26 And J begat Almodad, and Sheleph, H3355
29 and Jobab: all these *were* the sons of J. H3355
1Ch 1:19 divided: and his brother's name *was* J. H3355
20 And J begat Almodad, and Sheleph, H3355
23 and Jobab. All these *were* the sons of J. H3355

JOKTHEEL
Jos 15:38 And Dilean, and Mizpeh, and J, H3371
2Ki 14: 7 called the name of it J unto this day. H3371

JONA
Jn 1:42 Simon the son of J: thou shalt be called *G2495*

JONADAB
2Sa 13: 3 whose name *was* J, the son of Shimeah H3122
3 brother: and J *was* a very subtil man. H3122
5 And J said unto him, Lay thee down on H3082
32 And J, the son of Shimeah David's H3122
35 And J said unto the king, Behold, the H3122
Jer 35: 6 drink no wine: for J the son of Rechab H3122
8 Thus have we obeyed the voice of J the H3082
10 to all that J our father commanded us. H3122
14 The words of J the son of Rechab, that H3082
16 Because the sons of J the son of Rechab H3082
18 commandment of J your father, and H3082
19 the God of Israel; J the son of Rechab H3122

JONAH
2Ki 14:25 of his servant J, the son of Amittai, the H3124
Jna 1: 1 Now the word of the LORD came unto J H3124
3 But J rose up to flee unto Tarshish from H3124
5 *it* of them. But J was gone down into H3124
7 So they cast lots, and the lot fell upon J. H3124
15 So they took up J, and cast him forth H3124
17 fish to swallow up J. And Jonah was in H3124
17 up Jonah. And J was in the belly of the H3124
2: 1 Then J prayed unto the LORD his God H3124
10 and it vomited out J upon the dry *land*. H3124
3: 1 And the word of the LORD came unto J H3124
3 So J arose, and went unto Nineveh, H3124
4 And J began to enter into the city a H3124
4: 1 But it displeased J exceedingly, and he H3124
5 So J went out of the city, and sat on the H3124
6 *it* to come up over J, that it might be a H3124
6 So J was exceeding glad of the gourd. H3124
8 upon the head of J, that he fainted, and H3124
9 And God said to J, Doest thou well to be H3124

JONAN
Lk 3:30 *son* of J, which was *the son* of Eliakim, *G2494*

JONAS
Mt 12:39 given to it, but the sign of the prophet J: *G2495*
40 For as J was three days and three *G2495*
41 at the preaching of J; and, behold, a *G2495*
41 and, behold, a greater than J *is* here. *G2495*
16: 4 J. And he left them, and departed. *G2495*
Lk 11:29 given it, but the sign of J the prophet. *G2495*
30 For as J was a sign unto the Ninevites, *G2495*
32 at the preaching of J; and, behold, a *G2495*
32 and, behold, a greater than J *is* here. *G2495*
Jn 21:15 Simon, *son* of J, lovest thou me more *G2495*
16 Simon, *son* of J, lovest thou me? He *G2495*
17 Simon, *son* of J, lovest thou me? Peter *G2495*

JONATHAN
Jdg 18:30 the graven image: and J, the son of H3083
1Sa 13: 2 were with J in Gibeah of Benjamin: H3129
3 And J smote the garrison of the H3129
16 And Saul, and J his son, and the people H3129
22 with Saul and J: but with Saul and with H3129
22 and with J his son was there found. H3129
14: 1 Now it came to pass upon a day, that J H3129
3 the people knew not that J was gone. H3129
4 And between the passages, by which J H3129
6 And J said to the young man that bare H3083
8 Then said J, Behold, we will pass over H3083
12 the garrison answered J and his H3129
12 shew you a thing. And J said unto his H3129
13 And J climbed up upon his hands and H3129
13 J; and his armourbearer slew after him. H3129
14 And that first slaughter, which J and H3129
17 J and his armourbearer *were* not *there*. H3129
21 the Israelites that *were* with Saul and J. H3129
27 But J heard not when his father H3129
29 Then said J, My father hath troubled H3129
39 though it be in J my son, he shall surely H3129
40 side, and I and J my son will be on the H3129
41 J were taken: but the people escaped. H3129
42 J my son. And Jonathan was taken. H3129
42 Jonathan my son. And J was taken. H3129
43 Then Saul said to J, Tell me what thou H3129
43 hast done. And J told him, and said, H3129
44 more also: for thou shalt surely die, J. H3129
45 And the people said unto Saul, Shall J H3129
45 the people rescued J, that he died not. H3129
49 Now the sons of Saul were J, and Ishui, H3129
1Sa 18: 1 that the soul of J was knit with the soul H3083
1 David, and J loved him as his own soul. H3083
3 Then J and David made a covenant, H3083
4 And J stripped himself of the robe that H3083
19: 1 And Saul spake to J his son, and to all H3129
2 But J Saul's son delighted much in H3083
2 in David: and J told David, saying, H3083
4 And J spake good of David unto Saul H3083
6 And Saul hearkened unto the voice of J: H3083
7 And J called David, and Jonathan H3083
7 And Jonathan called David, and J H3083
7 those things. And J brought David to H3083
20: 1 and said before J, What have I done? H3083
3 he saith, Let not J know this, lest he be H3083
4 Then said J unto David, Whatsoever H3083
5 And David said unto J, Behold, to H3083
9 And J said, Far be it from thee: for if I H3083
10 Then said David to J, Who shall tell me? H3083
11 And J said unto David, Come, and let H3083
12 And J said unto David, O LORD God of H3083
13 The LORD do so and much more to J: H3083
16 So J made *a covenant* with the house of H3083
17 And J caused David to swear again, H3083
18 Then J said to David, To morrow *is* the H3083
25 by the wall: and J arose, and Abner sat H3083
27 empty: and Saul said unto J his son, H3083
28 And J answered Saul, David earnestly H3083
30 kindled against J, and he said unto him, H3083
32 And J answered Saul his father, and H3083
33 smite him: whereby J knew that it was H3083
34 So J arose from the table in fierce H3083
35 in the morning, that J went out into the H3083
37 place of the arrow which J had shot, H3083
37 had shot, J cried after the lad, and H3083
38 And J cried after the lad, Make speed, H3083
39 But the lad knew not any thing: only J H3083
40 And J gave his artillery unto his lad, H3083
42 And J said to David, Go in peace, H3083
42 and departed: and J went into the city. H3083
23:16 And J Saul's son arose, and went to H3083
18 in the wood, and J went to his house. H3083
31: 2 Philistines slew J, and Abinadab, and H3083
2Sa 1: 4 and Saul and J his son are dead also. H3083
5 thou that Saul and J his son be dead? H3083
12 for Saul, and for J his son, and for the H3083
17 over Saul and over J his son: H3083
22 mighty, the bow of J turned not back, H3083
23 Saul and J *were* lovely and pleasant in H3083
25 O J, *thou wast* slain in thine high places. H3083
26 I am distressed for thee, my brother J: H3083
4: 4 And J, Saul's son, had a son *that was* H3083
4 came of Saul and J out of Jezreel, and H3083
9: 3 said unto the king, J hath yet a son, H3083
6 Now when Mephibosheth, the son of J, H3083
7 thee kindness for J thy father's sake, H3083
15:27 thy son, and J the son of Abiathar. H3083
36 Zadok's *son*, and J Abiathar's *son*; and H3083
17:17 Now J and Ahimaaz stayed by H3083
20 *is* Ahimaaz and J? And the woman said H3083
21: 7 the son of J the son of Saul, because H3083
7 between David and J the son of Saul. H3083
12 and the bones of J his son from the H3083
13 and the bones of J his son; and they H3083
14 And the bones of Saul and J his son H3083
21 And when he defied Israel, J the son of H3083
23:32 the Shaalbonite, of the sons of Jashen, J, H3083
1Ki 1:42 And while he yet spake, behold, J the H3129
43 And J answered and said to Adonijah, H3129
1Ch 2:32 and J: and Jether died without children. H3129
33 And the sons of J; Peleth, and Zaza. H3129
8:33 and Saul begat J, and Malchishua, and H3083
34 And the son of J *was* Merib-baal; and H3083
9:39 and Saul begat J, and Malchishua, and H3083
40 And the son of J *was* Merib-baal: and H3083
10: 2 Philistines slew J, and Abinadab, and H3129
11:34 The sons of Hashem the Gizonite, J the H3129
20: 7 But when he defied Israel, J the son of H3083
27:32 Also J David's uncle was a counsellor, a H3083
Ezr 8: 6 the son of J, and with him fifty males. H3083
10:15 Only J the son of Asahel and Jahaziah H3083
Neh 12:11 And Joiada begat J, and Jonathan begat H3083
11 And Joiada begat Jonathan, and J H3083
14 Of Melicu, J; of Shebaniah, Joseph; H3083
35 the son of J, the son of Shemaiah, H3083
Jer 37:15 in the house of J the scribe: for they H3083
20 house of J the scribe, lest I die there. H3083
40: 8 and Johanan and J the sons of Kareah, H3129

J

JONATHAN'S
1Sa 20:38 stay not. And J lad gathered up the H3083
Jer 38:26 me to return to J house, to die there. H3083

JON-ATHAN'S
2Sa 9: 1 I may shew him kindness for J sake? H3083

JONATH-ELEM-RECHOKIM
Ps 56:ttl To the chief Musician upon J, Michtam

JOPPA
2Ch 2:16 thee in floats by sea to J; and thou shalt H3305
Ezr 3: 7 to the sea of J, according to the grant H3305
Jna 1: 3 and went down to J; and he found a H3305
Act 9:36 Now there was at J a certain disciple *G2445*
38 And forasmuch as Lydda was nigh to J, *G2445*
42 And it was known throughout all J; and *G2445*
43 days in J with one Simon a tanner. *G2445*
10: 5 And now send men to J, and call for *one* *G2445*
8 things unto them, he sent them to J. *G2445*
23 brethren from J accompanied him. *G2445*
32 Send therefore to J, and call hither *G2445*
11: 5 I was in the city of J praying: and in a *G2445*
13 him, Send men to J, and call for Simon, *G2445*

JORAH
Ezr 2:18 The children of J, an hundred and H3139

JORAI
1Ch 5:13 and Sheba, and J, and Jachan, and Zia, H3140

JORAM
2Sa 8:10 Then Toi sent J his son unto king H3141
10 wars with Toi. And *J* brought with him
2Ki 8:16 And in the fifth year of J the son of H3141
21 So J went over to Zair, and all the H3141
23 And the rest of the acts of J, and all that H3141
24 And J slept with his fathers, and was H3141
25 In the twelfth year of J the son of Ahab H3141
28 And he went with J the son of Ahab to H3141
28 and the Syrians wounded J. H3141
29 And king J went back to be healed in H3141
29 went down to see J the son of Ahab in H3141
9:14 conspired against J. (Now Joram had H3141
14 Joram. (Now J had kept Ramothgilead, H3141
15 But king J was returned to be healed in H3088
16 and went to Jezreel; for J lay there. And H3141
16 king of Judah was come down to see J. H3141
17 see a company. And J said, Take an H3088
21 And J said, Make ready. And his H3088
21 made ready. And J king of Israel and H3088
22 And it came to pass, when J saw Jehu, H3088
23 And J turned his hands, and fled, and H3088
29 And in the eleventh year of J the son of H3141
11: 2 But Jehosheba, the daughter of king J, H3141
1Ch 3:11 J his son, Ahaziah his son, Joash his H3141
26:25 his son, and J his son, and Zichri his H3141
2Ch 22: 5 and the Syrians smote J. H3141
7 of God by coming to J: for when he was H3141
Mt 1: 8 begat J; and Joram begat Ozias; *G2496*
8 begat Joram; and J begat Ozias; *G2496*

JORDAN
Gen 13:10 beheld all the plain of J, that it *was* well H3383
11 Then Lot chose him all the plain of J; H3383
32:10 this J; and now I am become two bands. H3383
50:10 Atad, which *is* beyond J, and there they H3383
11 called Abel-mizraim, which *is* beyond J. H3383
Nu 13:29 dwell by the sea, and by the coast of J. H3383
22: 1 of Moab on this side J *by* Jericho. H3383
26: 3 of Moab by J *near* Jericho, saying, H3383
63 in the plains of Moab by J *near* Jericho. H3383
31:12 of Moab, which *are* by J *near* Jericho. H3383
32: 5 a possession, *and* bring us not over J. H3383
19 on yonder side J, or forward; because H3383
19 is fallen to us on this side J eastward. H3383
21 And will go all of you armed over J H3383
29 pass with you over J, every man armed H3383
32 inheritance on this side J *may be* ours. H3383
33:48 in the plains of Moab by J *near* Jericho. H3383
49 And they pitched by J, from H3383
50 of Moab by J *near* Jericho, saying, H3383
51 passed over J into the land of Canaan; H3383
34:12 And the border shall go down to J, and H3383
15 on this side J *near* Jericho eastward, H3383
35: 1 of Moab by J *near* Jericho, saying, H3383
10 be come over J into the land of Canaan; H3383
14 Ye shall give three cities on this side J, H3383
36:13 in the plains of Moab by J *near* Jericho. H3383
Dt 1: 1 Israel on this side J in the wilderness, H3383
5 On this side J, in the land of Moab, H3383
2:29 I shall pass over J into the land which H3383
3: 8 that *was* on this side J, from the river of H3383
17 The plain also, and J, and the coast H3383
20 them beyond J: and *then* shall ye return H3383
25 J, that goodly mountain, and Lebanon. H3383
27 eyes: for thou shalt not go over this J. H3383
4:21 I should not go over J, and that I should H3383
22 I must not go over J: but ye shall go H3383
26 ye go over J to possess it; ye shall H3383
41 on this side J toward the sunrising; H3383
46 On this side J, in the valley over against H3383
47 on this side J toward the sunrising; H3383
49 And all the plain on this side J H3383
9: 1 Hear, O Israel: Thou *art* to pass over J H3383
11:30 *Are* they not on the other side J, by the H3383
31 For ye shall pass over J to go in to H3383
12:10 But *when* ye go over J, and dwell in the H3383
27: 2 ye shall pass over J unto the land which H3383
4 ye be gone over J, *that* ye shall set up H3383
12 ye are come over J; Simeon, and Levi, H3383
30:18 thou passest over J to go to possess it. H3383
31: 2 unto me, Thou shalt not go over this J. H3383
13 land whither ye go over J to possess it. H3383
32:47 land, whither ye go over J to possess it. H3383
Jos 1: 2 arise, go over this J, thou, and all this H3383
11 pass over this J, to go in to possess the H3383
14 gave you on this side J; but ye shall pass H3383
15 you on this side J toward the sunrising. H3383
2: 7 them the way to J unto the fords: and H3383
10 *were* on the other side J, Sihon and Og, H3383
3: 1 and came to J, he and all the children H3383
8 water of J, ye shall stand still in Jordan. H3383
8 water of Jordan, ye shall stand still in J. H3383
11 the earth passeth over before you into J. H3383
13 rest in the waters of J, *that* the waters of H3383
13 *that* the waters of J shall be cut off *from* H3383
14 tents, to pass over J, and the priests H3383
15 were come unto J, and the feet of the H3383
15 of the water, (for J overfloweth all his H3383
17 in the midst of J, and all the Israelites H3383
17 all the people were passed clean over J. H3383
4: 1 were clean passed over J, that the LORD H3383
3 out of the midst of J, out of the place H3383
5 into the midst of J, and take ye up every H3383
7 That the waters of J were cut off before H3383
7 it passed over J, the waters of Jordan H3383
7 the waters of J were cut off: and these H3383
8 out of the midst of J, as the LORD spake H3383
9 in the midst of J, in the place where the H3383
10 in the midst of J, until every thing was H3383
16 testimony, that they come up out of J. H3383
17 the priests, saying, Come ye up out of J. H3383
18 out of the midst of J, *and* the soles of the H3383
18 that the waters of J returned unto their H3383
19 And the people came up out of J on the H3383
20 took out of J, did Joshua pitch in Gilgal. H3383
22 Israel came over this J on dry land. H3383
23 up the waters of J from before you, H3383
5: 1 *were* on the side of J westward, and all H3383
1 dried up the waters of J from before the H3383
7: 7 this people over J, to deliver us into the H3383
7 content, and dwelt on the other side J! H3383
9: 1 *were* on this side J, in the hills, and in H3383
10 that *were* beyond J, to Sihon king of H3383
12: 1 on the other side J toward the rising of H3383
7 smote on this side J on the west, from H3383
13: 8 gave them, beyond J eastward, *even* as H3383
23 of Reuben was J, and the border H3383
27 king of Heshbon, J and *his* border, *even* H3383
27 on the other side J eastward. H3383
32 the other side J, by Jericho, eastward. H3383
14: 3 on the other side J: but unto the Levites H3383
15: 5 unto the end of J. And *their* border in H3383
5 bay of the sea at the uttermost part of J: H3383
16: 1 of Joseph fell from J by Jericho, unto H3383
7 and came to Jericho, and went out at J. H3383
17: 5 Bashan, which *were* on the other side J; H3383
18: 7 beyond J on the east, which Moses H3383
12 side was from J; and the border went H3383
19 south end of J: this *was* the south coast. H3383
20 And J was the border of it on the east H3383
19:22 at J: sixteen cities with their villages. H3383
33 and the outgoings thereof were at J: H3383
34 to Judah upon J toward the sunrising. H3383
20: 8 And on the other side J by Jericho H3383
22: 4 the LORD gave you on the other side J. H3383
7 on this side J westward. And when H3383
Jos 22:10 the borders of J, that *are* in the land H3383
10 an altar by J, a great altar to see to. H3383
11 in the borders of J, at the passage of the H3383
25 For the LORD hath made J a border H3383
23: 4 your tribes, from J, with all the nations H3383
24: 8 on the other side J; and they fought with H3383
11 And ye went over J, and came unto H3383
Jdg 3:28 took the fords of J toward Moab, and H3383
5:17 Gilead abode beyond J: and why did H3383
7:24 Beth-barah and J. Then all the men of H3383
24 took the waters unto Beth-barah and J. H3383
25 and Zeeb to Gideon on the other side J. H3383
8: 4 And Gideon came to J, *and* passed over, H3383
10: 8 on the other side J in the land of the H3383
9 passed over J to fight also against H3383
11:13 unto Jabbok, and unto J: now therefore H3383
22 and from the wilderness even unto J. H3383
12: 5 took the passages of J before the H3383
6 at the passages of J: and there fell at H3383
1Sa 13: 7 And *some of* the Hebrews went over J H3383
31: 7 on the other side J, saw that the men of H3383
2Sa 2:29 and passed over J, and went through all H3383
10:17 and passed over J, and came to Helam. H3383
17:22 they passed over J: by the morning light H3383
22 one of them that was not gone over J. H3383
24 J, he and all the men of Israel with him. H3383
19:15 So the king returned, and came to J. H3383
15 the king, to conduct the king over J. H3383
17 and they went over J before the king. H3383
18 before the king, as he was come over J; H3383
31 and went over J with the king, to H3383
31 with the king, to conduct him over J. H3383
36 Thy servant will go a little way over J H3383
39 And all the people went over J. And H3383
41 and all David's men with him, over J? H3383
20: 2 their king, from J even to Jerusalem. H3383
24: 5 And they passed over J, and pitched in H3383
1Ki 2: 8 to meet me at J, and I sware to him H3383
7:46 In the plain of J did the king cast them, H3383
17: 3 by the brook Cherith, that *is* before J. H3383
5 by the brook Cherith, that *is* before J. H3383
2Ki 2: 6 hath sent me to J. And he said, *As* the H3383
7 view afar off: and they two stood by J. H3383
13 went back, and stood by the bank of J; H3383
5:10 Go and wash in J seven times, and thy H3383
14 seven times in J, according to the saying H3383
6: 2 Let us go, we pray thee, unto J, and take H3383
4 they came to J, they cut down wood. H3383
7:15 And they went after them unto J: and, H3383
10:33 From J eastward, all the land of Gilead, H3383
1Ch 6:78 And on the other side J by Jericho, on H3383
78 on the east side of J, *were given them* H3383
12:15 These *are* they that went over J in the H3383
37 And on the other side of J, of the H3383
19:17 and passed over J, and came upon H3383
26:30 Israel on this side J westward in all the H3383
2Ch 4:17 In the plain of J did the king cast them, H3383
Job 40:23 that he can draw up J into his mouth. H3383
Ps 42: 6 thee from the land of J, and of the H3383
114: 3 The sea saw *it*, and fled: J was driven H3383
5 thou J, *that* thou wast driven back? H3383
Isa 9: 1 sea, beyond J, in Galilee of the nations. H3383
Jer 12: 5 how wilt thou do in the swelling of J? H3383
49:19 the swelling of J against the habitation H3383
50:44 the swelling of J unto the habitation H3383
Ezk 47:18 land of Israel *by* J, from the border unto H3383
Zec 11: 3 lions; for the pride of J is spoiled. H3383
Mt 3: 5 and all the region round about J, *G2446*
6 And were baptized of him in J, *G2446*
13 Then cometh Jesus from Galilee to J *G2446*
4:15 sea, beyond J, Galilee of the Gentiles; *G2446*
25 and *from* Judaea, and *from* beyond J. *G2446*
19: 1 into the coasts of Judaea beyond J; *G2446*
Mk 1: 5 in the river of J, confessing their sins. *G2446*
9 Galilee, and was baptized of John in J. *G2446*
3: 8 and *from* beyond J; and they about Tyre *G2446*
10: 1 by the farther side of J: and the people *G2446*
Lk 3: 3 all the country about J, preaching the *G2446*
4: 1 returned from J, and was led by the *G2446*
Jn 1:28 beyond J, where John was baptizing. *G2446*
3:26 was with thee beyond J, to whom thou *G2446*
10:40 And went away again beyond J into the *G2446*

JORIM
Lk 3:29 was *the son* of J, which was *the son* of *G2497*

JORKOAM
1Ch 2:44 father of J: and Rekem begat Shammai. H3421

JOSABAD
1Ch 12: 4 and Johanan, and J the Gederathite, H3107

JOSAPHAT
Mt 1: 8 And Asa begat J; and Josaphat begat *G2498*
8 And Asa begat Josaphat; and J begat *G2498*

JOSE
Lk 3:29 Which was *the son* of J, which was *the* *G2499*

JOSEDECH
Hag 1: 1 the son of J, the high priest, saying, H3087
12 Joshua the son of J, the high priest, with H3087
14 Joshua the son of J, the high priest, and H3087
2: 2 Joshua the son of J, the high priest, and H3087
4 O Joshua, son of J, the high priest; and H3087
Zec 6:11 of Joshua the son of J, the high priest; H3087

JOSEPH
Gen 30:24 And she called his name J; and said, H3130
25 Rachel had born J, that Jacob said unto H3130
33: 2 after, and Rachel and J hindermost. H3130
7 and after came J near and Rachel, and H3130
35:24 The sons of Rachel; J, and Benjamin: H3130
37: 2 These *are* the generations of Jacob. J, H3130
2 father's wives: and J brought unto his H3130
3 Now Israel loved J more than all his H3130
5 And J dreamed a dream, and he told *it* H3130
13 And Israel said unto J, Do not thy H3130
17 us go to Dothan. And J went after his H3130
23 And it came to pass, when J was come H3130
23 that they stript J out of his coat, *his* H3130
28 drew and lifted up J out of the pit, and H3130
28 of the pit, and sold J to the Ishmeelites H3130
28 of silver: and they brought J into Egypt. H3130
29 pit; and, behold, J *was* not in the pit; H3130
33 him; J is without doubt rent in pieces. H3130
39: 1 And J was brought down to Egypt; and H3130
2 And the LORD was with J, and he was a H3130
4 And J found grace in his sight, and he H3130
6 he did eat. And J was *a* goodly *person,* H3130
7 eyes upon J; and she said, Lie with me. H3130
10 And it came to pass, as she spake to J H3130
11 this time, that J went into the house
21 But the LORD was with J, and shewed H3130
40: 3 prison, the place where J *was* bound. H3130
4 And the captain of the guard charged J H3130
6 And J came in unto them in the H3130
8 of it. And J said unto them, *Do* H3130
9 And the chief butler told his dream to J, H3130
12 And J said unto him, This *is* the H3130
16 good, he said unto J, I also *was* in my H3130
18 And J answered and said, This *is* the H3130
22 But he hanged the chief baker: as J had H3130
23 Yet did not the chief butler remember J, H3130
41:14 Then Pharaoh sent and called J, and H3130
15 And Pharaoh said unto J, I have H3130
16 And J answered Pharaoh, saying, *It is* H3130
17 And Pharaoh said unto J, In my dream, H3130
25 And J said unto Pharaoh, The dream of H3130
39 And Pharaoh said unto J, Forasmuch as H3130
41 And Pharaoh said unto J, See, I have set H3130
44 And Pharaoh said unto J, I *am* H3130
45 J went out over *all* the land of Egypt. H3130
46 And J *was* thirty years old when he H3130
46 king of Egypt. And J went out from the H3130
49 And J gathered corn as the sand of the H3130
50 And unto J were born two sons before H3130
51 And J called the name of the firstborn H3130
54 according as J had said: and the dearth H3130
55 Go unto J; what he saith to you, do. H3130
56 face of the earth: And J opened all the H3130
57 And all countries came into Egypt to J H3130
42: 6 And J *was* the governor over the land, H3130
7 And J saw his brethren, and he knew H3130
8 And J knew his brethren, but they knew H3130
9 And J remembered the dreams which H3130
14 And J said unto them, That *is it* that I H3130
18 And J said unto them the third day, H3130
23 And they knew not that J understood H3130
25 Then J commanded to fill their sacks H3130
36 *of my children:* J *is* not, and Simeon *is* H3130
43:15 went down to Egypt, and stood before J. H3130
16 And when J saw Benjamin with them, H3130
17 And the man did as J bade; and the H3130
25 the present against J came at noon: for H3130
26 And when J came home, they brought H3130
30 And J made haste; for his bowels did H3130
44: 2 to the word that J had spoken. H3130
Gen 44: 4 city, *and* not *yet* far off, J said unto his H3130
15 And J said unto them, What deed *is* H3130
45: 1 Then J could not refrain himself before H3130
1 with him, while J made himself known H3130
3 And J said unto his brethren, I *am* H3130
3 his brethren, I *am* J; doth my father yet H3130
4 And J said unto his brethren, Come H3130
4 near. And he said, I *am* J your brother, H3130
9 Thus saith thy son J, God hath made me H3130
17 And Pharaoh said unto J, Say unto thy H3130
21 And the children of Israel did so: and J H3130
26 And told him, saying, J *is* yet alive, and H3130
27 And they told him all the words of J, H3130
27 the wagons which J had sent to carry H3130
28 And Israel said, *It is* enough; J my son H3130
46: 4 J shall put his hand upon thine eyes. H3130
19 The sons of Rachel Jacob's wife; J, and H3130
20 And unto J in the land of Egypt were H3130
27 And the sons of J, which were born him H3130
28 And he sent Judah before him unto J, to H3130
29 And J made ready his chariot, and H3130
30 And Israel said unto J, Now let me die, H3130
31 And J said unto his brethren, and unto H3130
47: 1 Then J came and told Pharaoh, and H3130
5 And Pharaoh spake unto J, saying, Thy H3130
7 And J brought in Jacob his father, and H3130
11 And J placed his father and his H3130
12 And J nourished his father, and his H3130
14 And J gathered up all the money that H3130
14 they bought: and J brought the money H3130
15 came unto J, and said, Give us bread: H3130
16 And J said, Give your cattle; and I will H3130
17 And they brought their cattle unto J: H3130
17 unto Joseph: and J gave them bread *in* H3130
20 And J bought all the land of Egypt for H3130
23 Then J said unto the people, Behold, I H3130
26 And J made it a law over the land of H3130
29 he called his son J, and said unto him, H3130
48: 1 that *one* told J, Behold, thy father *is* H3130
2 Behold, thy son J cometh unto thee: H3130
3 And Jacob said unto J, God Almighty H3130
9 And J said unto his father, They *are* my H3130
11 And Israel said unto J, I had not H3130
12 And J brought them out from between H3130
13 And J took them both, Ephraim in his H3130
15 And he blessed J, and said, God, before H3130
17 And when J saw that his father laid his H3130
18 And J said unto his father, Not so, my H3130
21 And Israel said unto J, Behold, I die: but H3130
49:22 J *is* a fruitful bough, *even* a fruitful H3130
26 be on the head of J, and on the crown of H3130
50: 1 And J fell upon his father's face, and H3130
2 And J commanded his servants the H3130
4 were past, J spake unto the house H3130
7 And J went up to bury his father: and H3130
8 And all the house of J, and his brethren, H3130
14 And J returned into Egypt, he, and his H3130
15 dead, they said, J will peradventure H3130
16 And they sent a messenger unto J, H3130
17 So shall ye say unto J, Forgive, I pray H3130
17 And J wept when they spake unto him. H3130
19 And J said unto them, Fear not: for *am* H3130
22 And J dwelt in Egypt, he, and his H3130
22 and J lived an hundred and ten years. H3130
23 And J saw Ephraim's children of the H3130
24 And J said unto his brethren, I die: and H3130
25 And J took an oath of the children of H3130
26 So J died, *being* an hundred and ten H3130
Ex 1: 5 souls: for J was in Egypt *already.* H3130
6 And J died, and all his brethren, and all H3130
8 new king over Egypt, which knew not J. H3130
13:19 And Moses took the bones of J with H3130
Nu 1:10 Of the children of J: of Ephraim; H3130
32 Of the children of J, *namely,* of the H3130
13: 7 the tribe of Issachar, Igal the son of J. H3130
11 Of the tribe of J, *namely,* of the tribe of H3130
26:28 The sons of J after their families *were* H3130
37 *are* the sons of J after their families. H3130
27: 1 the son of J: and these *are* the names H3130
32:33 the son of J, the kingdom of Sihon H3130
34:23 The prince of the children of J, for the H3130
36: 1 of the sons of J, came near, and spake H3130
5 The tribe of the sons of J hath said well. H3130
12 the son of J, and their inheritance H3130
Dt 27:12 and Issachar, and J, and Benjamin: H3130
33:13 And of J he said, Blessed of the LORD H3130
16 upon the head of J, and upon the top of H3130
Jos 14: 4 For the children of J were two tribes, H3130
16: 1 And the lot of the children of J fell from H3130
Jos 16: 4 So the children of J, Manasseh and H3130
17: 1 the firstborn of J; *to wit,* for Machir the H3130
2 Manasseh the son of J by their families. H3130
14 And the children of J spake unto H3130
16 And the children of J said, The hill is H3130
17 And Joshua spake unto the house of J, H3130
18: 5 and the house of J shall abide in their H3130
11 children of Judah and the children of J. H3130
24:32 And the bones of J, which the children H3130
32 the inheritance of the children of J. H3130
Jdg 1:22 And the house of J, they also went up H3130
23 And the house of J sent to descry H3130
35 of the house of J prevailed, so that they H3130
2Sa 19:20 J to go down to meet my lord the king. H3130
1Ki 11:28 over all the charge of the house of J. H3130
1Ch 2: 2 Dan, J, and Benjamin, Naphtali, Gad, H3130
5: 1 unto the sons of J the son of Israel: and H3130
7:29 dwelt the children of J the son of Israel. H3130
25: 2 Of the sons of Asaph; Zaccur, and J, and H3130
9 came forth for Asaph to J: the second to H3130
Ezr 10:42 Shallum, Amariah, *and* J. H3130
Neh 12:14 Of Melicu, Jonathan; of Shebaniah, J; H3130
Ps 77:15 people, the sons of Jacob and J. Selah. H3130
78:67 Moreover he refused the tabernacle of J, H3130
80: 1 thou that leadest J like a flock; thou H3130
81: 5 This he ordained in J *for* a testimony, H3084
105:17 He sent a man before them, *even* J, *who* H3130
Ezk 37:16 and write upon it, For J, the stick of H3130
19 take the stick of J, which *is* in the hand H3130
47:13 of Israel: J *shall have two* portions. H3130
48:32 and one gate of J, one gate of Benjamin, H3130
Am 5: 6 fire in the house of J, and devour *it,* and H3130
15 will be gracious unto the remnant of J. H3130
6: 6 are not grieved for the affliction of J. H3130
Oba 18 fire, and the house of J a flame, and the H3130
Zec 10: 6 will save the house of J, and I will bring H3130
Mt 1:16 And Jacob begat J the husband of *G2501*
18 was espoused to J, before they came *G2501*
19 Then J her husband, being a just *man,* *G2501*
20 a dream, saying, J, thou son of David, *G2501*
24 Then J being raised from sleep did as *G2501*
2:13 Lord appeareth to J in a dream, saying, *G2501*
19 appeareth in a dream to J in Egypt, *G2501*
27:57 J, who also himself was Jesus' disciple: *G2501*
59 And when J had taken the body, he *G2501*
Mk 15:43 J of Arimathaea, an honourable *G2501*
45 of the centurion, he gave the body to J. *G2501*
Lk 1:27 man whose name was J, of the house of *G2501*
2: 4 And J also went up from Galilee, out of *G2501*
16 and J, and the babe lying in a manger. *G2501*
33 And J and his mother marvelled at *G2501*
43 and J and his mother knew not *of it.* *G2501*
3:23 the son of J, which was *the son* of Heli, *G2501*
24 *son* of Janna, which was *the son* of J, *G2501*
26 *the son* of J, which was *the son* of Juda, *G2501*
30 was *the son* of J, which was *the son* of *G2501*
23:50 And, behold, *there was* a man named J, *G2501*
Jn 1:45 write, Jesus of Nazareth, the son of J. *G2501*
4: 5 of ground that Jacob gave to his son J. *G2501*
6:42 Jesus, the son of J, whose father and *G2501*
19:38 And after this J of Arimathaea, being a *G2501*
Act 1:23 And they appointed two, J called *G2501*
7: 9 J into Egypt: but God was with him, *G2501*
13 And at the second *time* J was made *G2501*
14 Then sent J, and called his father Jacob *G2501*
18 another king arose, which knew not J. *G2501*
Heb 11:21 both the sons of J; and worshipped, *G2501*
22 By faith J, when he died, made mention *G2501*
Rev 7: 8 Of the tribe of J *were* sealed twelve *G2501*

JOSEPH'S
Gen 37:31 And they took J coat, and killed a kid of H3130
39: 5 house for J sake; and the blessing H3130
6 And he left all that he had in J hand; H3130
20 And J master took him, and put him H3130
22 committed to J hand all the prisoners H3130
41:42 and put it upon J hand, and arrayed H3130
45 And Pharaoh called J name H3130
42: 3 And J ten brethren went down to buy H3130
4 But Benjamin, J brother, Jacob sent not H3130
6 of the land: and J brethren came, and H3130
43:17 the man brought the men into J house. H3130
18 were brought into J house; and they H3130
19 And they came near to the steward of J H3130
24 And the man brought the men into J H3130
44:14 And Judah and his brethren came to J H3130
45:16 house, saying, J brethren are come: H3130
48: 8 And Israel beheld J sons, and said, H3130
50:15 And when J brethren saw that their H3130

Gen 50:23 were brought up upon J knees. H3130
1Ch 5: 2 the chief ruler; but the birthright *was* J:) H3130
Lk 4:22 mouth. And they said, Is not this J son? *G2501*
Act 7:13 his brethren; and J kindred was made *G2501*

JOSES
Mt 13:55 James, and J, and Simon, and Judas? *G2500*
27:56 J, and the mother of Zebedee's children. *G2500*
Mk 6: 3 of James, and J, and of Juda, and *G2500*
15:40 of James the less and of J, and Salome; *G2500*
47 *mother* of J beheld where he was laid. *G2500*
Act 4:36 And J, who by the apostles was *G2500*

JOSHAH
1Ch 4:34 And Meshobab, and Jamlech, and J the H3144

JOSHAPHAT
1Ch 11:43 Hanan the son of Maachah, and J the H3146

JOSHAVIAH
1Ch 11:46 Eliel the Mahavite, and Jeribai, and J, H3145

JOSHBEKASHAH
1Ch 25: 4 J, Mallothi, Hothir, *and* Mahazioth: H3436
24 The seventeenth to J, *he,* his sons, and H3436

JOSHUA
Ex 17: 9 And Moses said unto J, Choose us out H3091
10 So J did as Moses had said to him, and H3091
13 And J discomfited Amalek and his H3091
14 *it* in the ears of J: for I will utterly put H3091
24:13 And Moses rose up, and his minister J: H3091
32:17 And when J heard the noise of the H3091
33:11 but his servant J, the son of Nun, a H3091
Nu 11:28 And J the son of Nun, the servant of H3091
14: 6 And J the son of Nun, and Caleb the H3091
30 of Jephunneh, and J the son of Nun. H3091
38 But J the son of Nun, and Caleb the son H3091
26:65 of Jephunneh, and J the son of Nun. H3091
27:18 Moses, Take thee J the son of Nun, a H3091
22 him: and he took J, and set him before H3091
32:12 the Kenezite, and J the son of Nun: for H3091
28 the priest, and J the son of Nun, and H3091
34:17 the priest, and J the son of Nun. H3091
Dt 1:38 *But* J the son of Nun, which standeth H3091
3:21 And I commanded J at that time, H3091
28 But charge J, and encourage him, and H3091
31: 3 possess them: *and* J, he shall go over H3091
7 And Moses called unto J, and said unto H3091
14 that thou must die: call J, and present H3091
14 And Moses and J went, and presented H3091
23 And he gave J the son of Nun a charge, H3091
34: 9 And J the son of Nun was full of the H3091
Jos 1: 1 the LORD spake unto J the son of Nun, H3091
10 Then J commanded the officers of the H3091
12 the tribe of Manasseh, spake J, saying, H3091
16 And they answered J, saying, All that H3091
2: 1 And J the son of Nun sent out of H3091
23 over, and came to J the son of Nun, and H3091
24 And they said unto J, Truly the LORD H3091
3: 1 And J rose early in the morning; and H3091
5 And J said unto the people, Sanctify H3091
6 And J spake unto the priests, saying, H3091
7 And the LORD said unto J, This day will H3091
9 And J said unto the children of Israel, H3091
10 And J said, Hereby ye shall know that H3091
4: 1 that the LORD spake unto J, saying, H3091
4 Then J called the twelve men, whom he H3091
5 And J said unto them, Pass over before H3091
8 And the children of Israel did so as J H3091
8 LORD spake unto J, according to the H3091
9 And J set up twelve stones in the midst H3091
10 LORD commanded J to speak unto the H3091
10 commanded J: and the people hasted H3091
14 On that day the LORD magnified J in H3091
15 And the LORD spake unto J, saying, H3091
17 J therefore commanded the priests, H3091
20 took out of Jordan, did J pitch in Gilgal. H3091
5: 2 At that time the LORD said unto J, H3091
3 And J made him sharp knives, and H3091
4 And this *is* the cause why J did H3091
7 in their stead, them J circumcised: for H3091
9 And the LORD said unto J, This day H3091
13 And it came to pass, when J was by H3091
13 in his hand: and J went unto him, and H3091
14 I now come. And J fell on his face to the H3091
15 host said unto J, Loose thy shoe from H3091
15 thou standest *is* holy. And J did so. H3091
6: 2 And the LORD said unto J, See, I have H3091
Jos 6: 6 And J the son of Nun called the priests, H3091
8 And it came to pass, when J had H3091
10 And J had commanded the people, H3091
12 And J rose early in the morning, and H3091
16 blew with the trumpets, J said unto the H3091
22 But J had said unto the two men that H3091
25 And J saved Rahab the harlot alive, H3091
25 which J sent to spy out Jericho. H3091
26 And J adjured *them* at that time, H3091
27 So the LORD was with J; and his fame H3091
7: 2 And J sent men from Jericho to Ai, H3091
3 And they returned to J, and said unto H3091
6 And J rent his clothes, and fell to the H3091
7 And J said, Alas, O Lord GOD, H3091
10 And the LORD said unto J, Get thee up; H3091
16 So J rose up early in the morning, and H3091
19 And J said unto Achan, My son, give, I H3091
20 And Achan answered J, and said, H3091
22 So J sent messengers, and they ran H3091
23 them unto J, and unto all the children H3091
24 And J, and all Israel with him, took H3091
25 And J said, Why hast thou troubled us? H3091
8: 1 And the LORD said unto J, Fear not, H3091
3 So J arose, and all the people of war, to H3091
3 go up against Ai: and J chose out thirty H3091
9 J therefore sent them forth: and they H3091
9 J lodged that night among the people. H3091
10 And J rose up early in the morning, H3091
13 west of the city, J went that night into H3091
15 And J and all Israel made as if they H3091
16 J, and were drawn away from the city. H3091
18 And the LORD said unto J, Stretch out H3091
18 thine hand. And J stretched out the H3091
21 And when J and all Israel saw that the H3091
23 Ai they took alive, and brought him to J. H3091
26 For J drew not his hand back, H3091
27 of the LORD which he commanded J. H3091
28 And J burnt Ai, and made it an heap H3091
29 the sun was down, J commanded that H3091
30 Then J built an altar unto the LORD H3091
35 which J read not before all the H3091
9: 2 with J and with Israel, with one accord. H3091
3 what J had done unto Jericho and to Ai, H3091
6 And they went to J unto the camp at H3091
8 And they said unto J, We *are* thy H3091
8 *are* thy servants. And J said unto them, H3091
15 And J made peace with them, and H3091
22 And J called for them, and he spake H3091
24 And they answered J, and said, Because H3091
27 And J made them that day hewers of H3091
10: 1 had heard how J had taken Ai, and had H3091
4 with J and with the children of Israel. H3091
6 And the men of Gibeon sent unto J to H3091
7 So J ascended from Gilgal, he, and all H3091
8 And the LORD said unto J, Fear them H3091
9 J therefore came unto them suddenly, H3091
12 Then spake J to the LORD in the day H3091
15 And J returned, and all Israel with him, H3091
17 And it was told J, saying, The five kings H3091
18 And J said, Roll great stones upon the H3091
20 And it came to pass, when J and the H3091
21 to the camp to J at Makkedah in peace: H3091
22 Then said J, Open the mouth of the H3091
24 those kings unto J, that Joshua called H3091
24 unto Joshua, that J called for all the H3091
25 And J said unto them, Fear not, nor be H3091
26 And afterward J smote them, and slew H3091
27 of the sun, *that* J commanded, and they H3091
28 And that day J took Makkedah, and H3091
29 Then J passed from Makkedah, and all H3091
31 And J passed from Libnah, and all H3091
33 help Lachish; and J smote him and his H3091
34 And from Lachish J passed unto Eglon, H3091
36 And J went up from Eglon, and all H3091
38 And J returned, and all Israel with him, H3091
40 So J smote all the country of the hills, H3091
41 And J smote them from H3091
42 And all these kings and their land did J H3091
43 And J returned, and all Israel with him, H3091
11: 6 And the LORD said unto J, Be not H3091
7 So J came, and all the people of war H3091
9 And J did unto them as the LORD bade H3091
10 And J at that time turned back, and H3091
12 kings of them, did J take, and smote H3091
13 them, save Hazor only; *that* did J burn. H3091
15 Moses command J, and so did Joshua; H3091
15 Joshua, and so did J; he left nothing H3091
16 So J took all that land, the hills, and all H3091
18 J made war a long time with all those H3091
Jos 11:21 And at that time came J, and cut off the H3091
21 of Israel: J destroyed them utterly H3091
23 So J took the whole land, according to H3091
23 said unto Moses; and J gave it for an H3091
12: 7 the country which J and the children of H3091
7 up to Seir; which J gave unto the tribes H3091
13: 1 Now J was old *and* stricken in years; H3091
14: 1 the priest, and J the son of Nun, and H3091
6 Then the children of Judah came unto J H3091
13 And J blessed him, and gave unto H3091
15:13 of the LORD to J, *even* the city of Arba H3091
17: 4 priest, and before J the son of Nun, and H3091
14 Joseph spake unto J, saying, Why hast H3091
15 And J answered them, If thou *be* a H3091
17 And J spake unto the house of Joseph, H3091
18: 3 And J said unto the children of Israel, H3091
8 went away: and J charged them that H3091
9 came *again* to J to the host at Shiloh. H3091
10 And J cast lots for them in Shiloh H3091
10 the LORD: and there J divided the land H3091
19:49 to J the son of Nun among them: H3091
51 the priest, and J the son of Nun, and H3091
20: 1 The LORD also spake unto J, saying, H3091
21: 1 priest, and unto J the son of Nun, and H3091
22: 1 Then J called the Reubenites, and the H3091
6 So J blessed them, and sent them away: H3091
7 *other* half thereof gave J among their H3091
7 And when J sent them away also H3091
23: 1 that J waxed old *and* stricken in age. H3091
2 And J called for all Israel, *and* for their H3091
24: 1 And J gathered all the tribes of Israel to H3091
2 And J said unto all the people, Thus H3091
19 And J said unto the people, Ye cannot H3091
21 And the people said unto J, Nay; but we H3091
22 And J said unto the people, Ye *are* H3091
24 And the people said unto J, The LORD H3091
25 So J made a covenant with the people H3091
26 And J wrote these words in the book of H3091
27 And J said unto all the people, Behold, H3091
28 So J let the people depart, every man H3091
29 these things, that J the son of Nun, the H3091
31 all the days of J, and all the days of the H3091
31 that overlived J, and which had known H3091
Jdg 1: 1 Now after the death of J it came to H3091
2: 6 And when J had let the people go, the H3091
7 all the days of J, and all the days of the H3091
7 that outlived J, who had seen all the H3091
8 And J the son of Nun, the servant of the H3091
21 the nations which J left when he died: H3091
23 delivered he them into the hand of J. H3091
1Sa 6:14 And the cart came into the field of J, a H3091
18 day in the field of J, the Beth-shemite. H3091
1Ki 16:34 which he spake by J the son of Nun. H3091
2Ki 23: 8 in of the gate of J the governor of the H3091
Hag 1: 1 of Judah, and to J the son of Josedech, H3091
12 of Shealtiel, and J the son of Josedech, H3091
14 and the spirit of J the son of Josedech, H3091
2: 2 of Judah, and to J the son of Josedech, H3091
4 and be strong, O J, son of Josedech, the H3091
Zec 3: 1 And he shewed me J the high priest H3091
3 Now J was clothed with filthy H3091
6 of the LORD protested unto J, saying, H3091
8 Hear now, O J the high priest, thou, H3091
9 that I have laid before J; upon one stone H3091
6:11 of J the son of Josedech, the high priest; H3091

JOSIAH
1Ki 13: 2 house of David, J by name; and upon H2977
2Ki 21:24 land made J his son king in his stead. H2977
26 and J his son reigned in his stead. H2977
22: 1 J *was* eight years old when he began to H2977
3 year of king J, *that* the king sent H2977
23:16 And as J turned himself, he spied the H2977
19 *LORD* to anger, J took away, and did H2977
23 But in the eighteenth year of king J, H2977
24 in Jerusalem, did J put away, that he H2977
28 Now the rest of the acts of J, and all that H2977
29 and king J went against him; and H2977
30 the son of J, and anointed him, and H2977
34 Eliakim the son of J king in the room of H2977
34 in the room of J his father, and turned H2977
1Ch 3:14 Amon his son, J his son. H2977
15 And the sons of J *were,* the firstborn H2977
2Ch 33:25 land made J his son king in his stead. H2977
34: 1 J *was* eight years old when he began to H2977
33 And J took away all the abominations H2977
35: 1 Moreover J kept a passover unto the H2977
7 And J gave to the people, of the flock, H2977
16 to the commandment of king J. H2977

2Ch 35:18 keep such a passover as J kept, and the H2977
19 In the eighteenth year of the reign of J H2977
20 After all this, when J had prepared the H2977
20 Euphrates: and J went out against him. H2977
22 Nevertheless J would not turn his face H2977
23 And the archers shot at king J; and the H2977
24 all Judah and Jerusalem mourned for J. H2977
25 And Jeremiah lamented for J: and all H2977
25 women spake of J in their lamentations H2977
26 Now the rest of the acts of J, and his H2977
36: 1 the son of J, and made him king H2977
Jer 1: 2 in the days of J the son of Amon king H2977
3 the son of J king of Judah, unto H2977
3 the son of J king of Judah, unto H2977
3: 6 me in the days of J the king, Hast thou H2977
22:11 Shallum the son of J king of Judah, H2977
11 reigned instead of J his father, which H2977
18 the son of J king of Judah; They H2977
25: 1 the son of J king of Judah, that *was* H2977
3 From the thirteenth year of J the son of H2977
26: 1 the son of J king of Judah came H2977
27: 1 the son of J king of Judah came H2977
35: 1 the son of J king of Judah, saying, H2977
36: 1 the son of J king of Judah, *that* this H2977
2 from the days of J, even unto this day. H2977
9 the son of J king of Judah, in the H2977
37: 1 And king Zedekiah the son of J reigned H2977
45: 1 the son of J king of Judah, saying, H2977
46: 2 of Jehoiakim the son of J king of Judah. H2977
Zep 1: 1 of J the son of Amon, king of Judah. H2977
Zec 6:10 the house of J the son of Zephaniah; H2977

JOSIAS
Mt 1:10 begat Amon; and Amon begat J; *G2502*
11 And J begat Jechonias and his *G2502*

JOSIBIAH
1Ch 4:35 And Joel, and Jehu the son of J, the son H3143

JOSIPHIAH
Ezr 8:10 the son of J, and with him an hundred H3131

JOT
Mt 5:18 earth pass, one j or one tittle shall in *G2503*

JOTBAH
2Ki 21:19 the daughter of Haruz of J. H3192

JOTBATH
Dt 10: 7 to J, a land of rivers of waters. H3193

JOTBATHAH
Nu 33:33 from Hor-hagidgad, and pitched in J. H3193
34 And they removed from J, and H3193

JOTHAM
Jdg 9: 5 yet J the youngest son of H3147
7 And when they told *it* to J, he went and H3147
21 And J ran away, and fled, and went to H3147
57 the curse of J the son of Jerubbaal. H3147
2Ki 15: 5 house. And J the king's son *was* over H3147
7 and J his son reigned in his stead. H3147
30 twentieth year of J the son of Uzziah. H3147
32 of Israel began J the son of Uzziah king H3147
36 Now the rest of the acts of J, and all that H3147
38 And J slept with his fathers, and was H3147
16: 1 son of J king of Judah began to reign. H3147
1Ch 2:47 And the sons of Jahdai; Regem, and J, H3147
3:12 Amaziah his son, Azariah his son, J his H3147
5:17 in the days of J king of Judah, and in H3147
2Ch 26:21 of the LORD: and J his son *was* over the H3147
23 and J his son reigned in his stead. H3147
27: 1 J *was* twenty and five years old when H3147
6 So J became mighty, because he H3147
7 Now the rest of the acts of J, and all his H3147
9 And J slept with his fathers, and they H3147
Isa 1: 1 J, Ahaz, *and* Hezekiah, kings of Judah. H3147
7: 1 of Ahaz the son of J, the son of Uzziah, H3147
Hos 1: 1 days of Uzziah, J, Ahaz, *and* Hezekiah, H3147
Mic 1: 1 in the days of J, Ahaz, *and* Hezekiah, H3147

JOURNEY
Gen 24:21 had made his j prosperous or not. H1870
29: 1 Then Jacob went on his j, and came into H7272
30:36 And he set three days' j betwixt himself H1870
31:23 him seven days' j; and they overtook H1870
33:12 And he said, Let us take our j, and let us H5265
46: 1 And Israel took his j with all that he H5265
Ex 3:18 thee, three days' j into the wilderness, H1870
5: 3 thee, three days' j into the desert, and H1870
8:27 We will go three days' j into the H1870
13:20 And they took their j from Succoth, H5265
16: 1 And they took their j from Elim, and all H5265
Nu 9:10 body, or *be* in a j afar off, yet he shall H1870
13 and is not in a j, and forbeareth to keep H1870
10: 6 side shall take their j: they shall blow an H5265
13 And they first took their j according to H5265
33 LORD three days' j: and the ark of the H1870
33 j, to search out a resting place for them. H1870
11:31 as it were a day's j on this side, and as H1870
31 as it were a day's j on the other side, H1870
33: 8 went three days' j in the wilderness of H1870
12 And they took their j out of the H5265
Dt 1: 2 (*There are* eleven days' j from Horeb by H1870
7 Turn you, and take your j, and go to the H5265
40 you, and take your j into the wilderness H5265
2: 1 Then we turned, and took our j into the H5265
24 Rise ye up, take your j, and pass over H5265
10: 6 And the children of Israel took their j H5265
11 me, Arise, take *thy* j before the people, H4550
Jos 9:11 with you for the j, and go to meet them, H1870
13 become old by reason of the very long j. H1870
Jdg 4: 9 the j that thou takest shall H1870
1Sa 15:18 And the LORD sent thee on a j, and H1870
2Sa 11:10 thou not from *thy* j? why *then* didst thou H1870
1Ki 18:27 or he is in a j, *or* peradventure he H1870
19: 4 But he himself went a day's j into the H1870
7 eat; because the j *is* too great for thee. H1870
2Ki 3: 9 of seven days' j: and there was no water H1870
2Ch 1:13 Then Solomon came *from his* j to the
Neh 2: 6 how long shall thy j be? and when wilt H4109
Prv 7:19 *is* not at home, he is gone a long j: H1870
Jna 3: 3 an exceeding great city of three days' j. H4109
4 the city a day's j, and he cried, and said, H4109
Mt 10:10 Nor scrip for *your* j, neither two coats, *G3598*
25:15 ability; and straightway took his j. *G589*
Mk 6: 8 nothing for *their* j, save a staff only; no *G3598*
13:34 a man taking a far j, who left his house, *G590*
Lk 2:44 went a day's j; and they sought him *G3598*
9: 3 nothing for *your* j, neither staves, nor *G3598*
11: 6 For a friend of mine in his j is come to *G3598*
15:13 and took his j into a far country, and *G589*
Jn 4: 6 wearied with *his* j, sat thus on the well: *G3597*
Act 1:12 is from Jerusalem a sabbath day's j. *G3598*
10: 9 On the morrow, as they went on their j, *G3596*
22: 6 that, as I made my j, and was come *G4198*
Ro 1:10 j by the will of God to come unto you. *G2137*
15:24 Whensoever I take my j into Spain, I *G4198*
24 to see you in my j, and to be brought on *G1279*
1Co 16: 6 bring me on my j whithersoever I go. *G4311*
Tit 3:13 and Apollos on their j diligently, that *G4311*
3Jn 6 j after a godly sort, thou shalt do well: *G4311*

JOURNEYED
Gen 11: 2 And it came to pass, as they j from the H5265
12: 9 And Abram j, going on still toward the H5265
13:11 of Jordan; and Lot j east: and they H5265
20: 1 And Abraham j from thence toward H5265
33:17 And Jacob j to Succoth, and built him H5265
35: 5 And they j: and the terror of God was H5265
16 And they j from Beth-el; and there was H5265
21 And Israel j, and spread his tent beyond H5265
Ex 12:37 And the children of Israel j from H5265
17: 1 children of Israel j from the wilderness H5265
40:37 j not till the day that it was taken up. H5265
Nu 9:17 the children of Israel j: and in the place H5265
18 the children of Israel j, and at the H5265
19 kept the charge of the LORD, and j not. H5265
20 the commandment of the LORD they j. H5265
21 then they j: whether *it was* by day H5265
21 that the cloud was taken up, they j. H5265
22 in their tents, and j not: but when it H5265
22 not: but when it was taken up, they j. H5265
23 of the LORD they j: they kept the charge H5265
11:35 *And* the people j from H5265
12:15 j not till Miriam was brought in *again*. H5265
20:22 congregation, j from Kadesh, and H5265
21: 4 And they j from mount Hor by the way H5265
11 And they j from Oboth, and pitched at H5265
33:22 And they j from Rissah, and pitched in H5265
Dt 10: 7 From thence they j unto Gudgodah; H5265
Jos 9:17 And the children of Israel j, and came H5265
Jdg 17: 8 to the house of Micah, as he j. H6213+H1870
Lk 10:33 But a certain Samaritan, as he j, came *G3593*
Act 9: 3 And as he j, he came near Damascus: *G4198*
7 And the men which j with him stood *G4922*
26:13 about me and them which j with me. *G4198*

JOURNEYING
Nu 10: 2 assembly, and for the j of the camps. H4550
29 in law, We are j unto the place of which H5265
Lk 13:22 teaching, and j toward Jerusalem. *G4160*

JOURNEYINGS
Nu 10:28 Thus *were* the j of the children of Israel H4550
2Co 11:26 *In* j often, *in* perils of waters, *in* perils *G3597*

JOURNEYS
Gen 13: 3 And he went on his j from the south H4550
Ex 17: 1 of Sin, after their j, according to the H4550
40:36 of Israel went onward in all their j: H4550
38 house of Israel, throughout all their j. H4550
Nu 10: 6 they shall blow an alarm for their j. H4550
12 And the children of Israel took their j H4550
33: 1 These *are* the j of the children of Israel, H4550
2 out according to their j by the H4550
2 their j according to their goings out. H4550

JOY
1Sa 18: 6 with j, and with instruments of musick. H8057
1Ki 1:40 rejoiced with great j, so that the earth H8057
1Ch 12:40 abundantly: for *there was* j in Israel. H8057
15:16 sounding, by lifting up the voice with j. H8057
25 out of the house of Obed-edom with j. H8057
29: 9 the king also rejoiced with great j. H8057
17 have I seen with j thy people, which are H8057
2Ch 20:27 to Jerusalem with j; for the LORD had H8057
30:26 So there was great j in Jerusalem: for H8057
Ezr 3:12 voice; and many shouted aloud for j: H8057
13 of the shout of j from the noise of the H8057
6:16 dedication of this house of God with j, H2305
22 seven days with j: for the LORD had H8057
Neh 8:10 for the j of the LORD is your strength. H2304
12:43 rejoice with great j: the wives also and H8057
43 j of Jerusalem was heard even afar off. H8057
Est 8:16 The Jews had light, and gladness, and j, H8342
17 the Jews had j and gladness, a feast H8057
9:22 from sorrow to j, and from mourning H8057
22 days of feasting and j, and of sending H8057
Job 8:19 Behold, this *is* the j of his way, and out H4885
20: 5 j of the hypocrite *but* for a moment? H8057
29:13 I caused the widow's heart to sing for j. H7442
33:26 see his face with j: for he will render H8643
38: 7 and all the sons of God shouted for j?
41:22 and sorrow is turned into j before him. H1750
Ps 5:11 ever shout for j, because thou defendest H7442
16:11 *is* fulness of j; at thy right hand *there* H8057
21: 1 The king shall j in thy strength, O H8055
27: 6 sacrifices of j; I will sing, yea, I will H8643
30: 5 a night, but j *cometh* in the morning. H7440
32:11 for j, all *ye that are* upright in heart. H7442
35:27 Let them shout for j, and be glad, that H7442
42: 4 with the voice of j and praise, with a H7440
43: 4 God my exceeding j: yea, upon the harp H1524
48: 2 Beautiful for situation, the j of the H4885
51: 8 Make me to hear j and gladness; *that* H8342
12 Restore unto me the j of thy salvation; H8342
65:13 corn; they shout for j, they also sing. H7321
67: 4 O let the nations be glad and sing for j: H7442
105:43 And he brought forth his people with j, H8342
126: 5 They that sow in tears shall reap in j. H7440
132: 9 and let thy saints shout for j. H7442
16 and her saints shall shout aloud for j.
137: 6 I prefer not Jerusalem above my chief j. H8057
Prv 12:20 evil: but to the counsellors of peace *is* j. H8057
14:10 doth not intermeddle with his j. H8057
15:21 Folly *is* j to *him that is* destitute of H8057
23 A man hath j by the answer of his H8057
17:21 and the father of a fool hath no j. H8055
21:15 *It is* j to the just to do judgment: but H8057
23:24 a wise *child* shall have j of him. H8055
Ecc 2:10 not my heart from any j; for my heart H8057
26 knowledge, and j: but to the sinner he H8057
5:20 answereth *him* in the j of his heart. H8057
9: 7 Go thy way, eat thy bread with j, and H8057
Isa 9: 3 not increased the j: they joy before thee H8057
3 the joy: they j before thee according H8055
3 according to the j in harvest, *and* as H8057
17 Therefore the Lord shall have no j in H8055
12: 3 Therefore with j shall ye draw water H8342
16:10 And gladness is taken away, and j out H1524
22:13 And behold j and gladness, slaying H8342
24: 8 endeth, the j of the harp ceaseth. H4885
11 wine in the streets; all j is darkened, the H8057
29:19 The meek also shall increase *their* j in H8057
32:13 all the houses of j *in* the joyous city: H4885
14 a j of wild asses, a pasture of flocks; H4885

J

Isa 35: 2 and rejoice even with **j** and singing: the H1525
10 and everlasting **j** upon their heads: H8057
10 they shall obtain **j** and gladness, and H8342
51: 3 of the LORD; **j** and gladness shall be H8342
11 and everlasting **j** *shall be* upon their H8057
11 obtain gladness and **j**; *and* sorrow and H8057
52: 9 Break forth into **j**, sing together, ye H6476
55:12 For ye shall go out with **j**, and be led H8057
60:15 excellency, a **j** of many generations. H4885
61: 3 for ashes, the oil of **j** for mourning, the H8342
7 everlasting **j** shall be unto them. H8057
65:14 Behold, my servants shall sing for **j** of H2898
18 a rejoicing, and her people a **j**. H4885
19 And I will rejoice in Jerusalem, and **j** in H7797
66: 5 to your **j**, and they shall be ashamed. H8057
10 for **j** with her, all ye that mourn for her: H4885
Jer 15:16 was unto me the **j** and rejoicing of H8342
31:13 mourning into **j**, and will comfort them, H8342
33: 9 And it shall be to me a name of **j**, a H8342
11 The voice of **j**, and the voice of gladness, H8342
48:27 thou spakest of him, thou skippedst for **j**.
33 And **j** and gladness is taken from the H8057
49:25 city of praise not left, the city of my **j**! H4885
Lam 2:15 of beauty, The **j** of the whole earth? H4885
5:15 The **j** of our heart is ceased; our dance H4885
Ezk 24:25 their strength, the **j** of their glory, the H4885
36: 5 with the **j** of all *their* heart, with H8057
Hos 9: 1 Rejoice not, O Israel, for **j**, as *other* H1524
Joel 1:12 withered: because **j** is withered away H8342
16 our eyes, *yea*, **j** and gladness from the H8057
Hab 3:18 Yet I will rejoice in the LORD, I will **j** in H1523
Zep 3:17 over thee with **j**; he will rest in his love, H8057
17 love, he will **j** over thee with singing. H1523
Zec 8:19 the house of Judah **j** and gladness, and H8342
Mt 2:10 they rejoiced with exceeding great **j**. *G5479*
13:20 the word, and anon with **j** receiveth it; *G5479*
44 he hideth, and for **j** thereof goeth and *G5479*
25:21 things: enter thou into the **j** of thy lord. *G5479*
23 things: enter thou into the **j** of thy lord. *G5479*
28: 8 fear and great **j**; and did run to bring *G5479*
Lk 1:14 And thou shalt have **j** and gladness; *G5479*
44 ears, the babe leaped in my womb for **j**. *G20*
2:10 of great **j**, which shall be to all people. *G5479*
6:23 Rejoice ye in that day, and leap for **j**: *G4640*
8:13 the word with **j**; and these have no root, *G5479*
10:17 And the seventy returned again with **j**, *G5479*
15: 7 I say unto you, that likewise **j** shall be *G5479*
10 Likewise, I say unto you, there is **j** in *G5479*
24:41 And while they yet believed not for **j**, *G5479*
52 and returned to Jerusalem with great **j**: *G5479*
Jn 3:29 voice: this my **j** therefore is fulfilled. *G5479*
15:11 unto you, that my **j** might remain in *G5479*
11 in you, and *that* your **j** might be full. *G5479*
16:20 but your sorrow shall be turned into **j**. *G5479*
21 for **j** that a man is born into the world. *G5479*
22 and your **j** no man taketh from you. *G5479*
24 ye shall receive, that your **j** may be full. *G5479*
17:13 might have my **j** fulfilled in themselves. *G5479*
Act 2:28 make me full of **j** with thy countenance. *G2167*
8: 8 And there was great **j** in that city. *G5479*
13:52 And the disciples were filled with **j**, and *G5479*
15: 3 caused great **j** unto all the brethren. *G5479*
20:24 my course with **j**, and the ministry, *G5479*
Ro 5:11 And not only *so*, but we also **j** in God *G2744*
14:17 and peace, and **j** in the Holy Ghost. *G5479*
15:13 Now the God of hope fill you with all **j** *G5479*
32 That I may come unto you with **j** by the *G5479*
2Co 1:24 helpers of your **j**: for by faith ye stand. *G5479*
2: 3 in you all, that my **j** is *the joy* of you all. *G5479*
3 in you all, that my joy is *the* **j** of you all. *G5479*
7:13 joyed we for the **j** of Titus, because his *G5479*
8: 2 of their **j** and their deep poverty *G5479*
Gal 5:22 But the fruit of the Spirit is love, **j**, *G5479*
Php 1: 4 mine for you all making request with **j**, *G5479*
25 all for your furtherance and **j** of faith; *G5479*
2: 2 Fulfil ye my **j**, that ye be likeminded, *G5479*
17 your faith, I **j**, and rejoice with you all. *G5463*
18 For the same cause also do ye **j**, and *G5463*
4: 1 longed for, my **j** and crown, so stand *G5479*
1Th 1: 6 affliction, with **j** of the Holy Ghost: *G5479*
2:19 For what *is* our hope, or **j**, or crown of *G5479*
20 For ye are our glory and **j**. *G5479*
3: 9 for you, for all the **j** wherewith we joy *G5479*
9 we **j** for your sakes before our God; *G5463*
2Ti 1: 4 of thy tears, that I may be filled with **j**; *G5479*
Phlm 7 For we have great **j** and consolation in *G5485*
20 Yea, brother, let me have **j** of thee in *G3685*
Heb 12: 2 faith; who for the **j** that was set before *G5479*
13:17 may do it with **j**, and not with grief: for *G5479*
Jas 1: 2 My brethren, count it all **j** when ye fall *G5479*
4: 9 to mourning, and *your* **j** to heaviness. *G5479*
1Pt 1: 8 with **j** unspeakable and full of glory: *G5479*
4:13 ye may be glad also with exceeding **j**. *G21*
1Jn 1: 4 we unto you, that your **j** may be full. *G5479*
2Jn 12 face to face, that our **j** may be full. *G5479*
3Jn 4 I have no greater **j** than to hear that my *G5479*
Jude 24 the presence of his glory with exceeding **j**, *G20*

JOYED
2Co 7:13 the more **j** we for the joy of Titus, *G5463*

JOYFUL
1Ki 8:66 unto their tents **j** and glad of heart for H8056
Ezr 6:22 had made them **j**, and turned the heart H8055
Est 5: 9 Then went Haman forth that day **j** and H8056
Job 3: 7 Lo, let that night be solitary, let no **j** H7445
Ps 5:11 also that love thy name be **j** in thee. H5970
35: 9 And my soul shall be **j** in the LORD: it H1523
63: 5 my mouth shall praise *thee* with **j** lips: H7445
66: 1 Make a **j** noise unto God, all ye lands:
81: 1 make a **j** noise unto the God of Jacob.
89:15 Blessed *is* the people that know the **j**
95: 1 a **j** noise to the rock of our salvation.
2 make a **j** noise unto him with psalms.
96:12 Let the field be **j**, and all that *is* therein: H5937
98: 4 Make a **j** noise unto the LORD, all the
6 a **j** noise before the LORD, the King.
8 *their* hands: let the hills be **j** together H7442
100: 1 Make a **j** noise unto the LORD, all ye
113: 9 house, *and to be* a **j** mother of children. H8056
149: 2 the children of Zion be **j** in their King. H1523
5 Let the saints be **j** in glory: let them H5937
Ecc 7:14 In the day of prosperity be **j**, but in the H2896
Isa 49:13 Sing, O heavens; and be **j**, O earth; and H1523
56: 7 and make them **j** in my house of H8055
61:10 my soul shall be **j** in my God; for he H1523
2Co 7: 4 I am exceeding **j** in all our tribulation. *G5479*

JOYFULLY
Ecc 9: 9 Live **j** with the wife whom thou lovest H7200
Lk 19: 6 and came down, and received him **j**. *G5463*
Heb 10:34 bonds, and took **j** the spoiling of your *G3326*

JOYFULNESS
Dt 28:47 thy God with **j**, and with gladness of H8057
Col 1:11 all patience and longsuffering with **j**; *G5479*

JOYING
Col 2: 5 you in the spirit, **j** and beholding your *G5463*

JOYOUS
Isa 22: 2 tumultuous city, a **j** city: thy slain *men* H5947
23: 7 *Is* this your **j** *city*, whose antiquity *is* of H5947
32:13 upon all the houses of joy *in* the **j** city: H5947
Heb 12:11 present seemeth to be **j**, but grievous: *G5479*

JOZABAD
1Ch 12:20 Adnah, and **J**, and Jediael, and Michael, H3107
20 and Michael, and **J**, and Elihu, and H3107
2Ch 31:13 and Jerimoth, and **J**, and Eliel, and H3107
35: 9 and Jeiel and **J**, chief of the Levites, H3107
Ezr 8:33 with them *was* **J** the son of Jeshua, and H3107
10:22 Ishmael, Nethaneel, **J**, and Elasah. H3107
23 Also of the Levites; **J**, and Shimei, and H3107
Neh 8: 7 Kelita, Azariah, **J**, Hanan, Pelaiah, and H3107
11:16 And Shabbethai and **J**, of the chief of H3107

JOZACHAR
2Ki 12:21 For **J** the son of Shimeath, and H3108

JOZADAK
Ezr 3: 2 Then stood up Jeshua the son of **J**, and H3136
8 Jeshua the son of **J**, and the remnant of H3136
5: 2 Jeshua the son of **J**, and began to build H3136
10:18 of Jeshua the son of **J**, and his brethren; H3136
Neh 12:26 Jeshua, the son of **J**, and in the days of H3136

JUBAL
Gen 4:21 And his brother's name *was* **J**: he was H3106

JUBILE
Lev 25: 9 the trumpet of the **j** to sound on the H8643
10 it shall be a **j** unto you; and ye shall H3104
11 A **j** shall that fiftieth year be unto you: H3104
12 For it *is* the **j**; it shall be holy unto you: H3104
13 In the year of this **j** ye shall return H3104
15 of years after the **j** thou shalt buy of thy H3104
28 it until the year of **j**: and in the jubile it H3104
Lev 25:28 jubile: and in the **j** it shall go out, and H3104
30 generations: it shall not go out in the **j**. H3104
31 redeemed, and they shall go out in the **j**. H3104
33 out in *the year of* **j**: for the houses of the H3104
40 *and* shall serve thee unto the year of **j**: H3104
50 unto the year of **j**: and the price of his H3104
52 unto the year of **j**, then he shall count H3104
54 of **j**, *both* he, and his children with him. H3104
27:17 If he sanctify his field from the year of **j**, H3104
18 But if he sanctify his field after the **j**, H3104
18 the year of the **j**, and it shall be abated H3104
21 But the field, when it goeth out in the **j**, H3104
23 the year of the **j**: and he shall give thine H3104
24 In the year of the **j** the field shall return H3104
Nu 36: 4 And when the **j** of the children of Israel H3104

JUBILEE See JUBILE.

JUCAL
Jer 38: 1 the son of Pashur, and **J** the son of H3116

JUDA
Mt 2: 6 And thou Bethlehem, *in* the land of **J**, *G2448*
6 the princes of **J**: for out of thee shall *G2448*
Mk 6: 3 and Joses, and of **J**, and Simon? and are *G2455*
Lk 1:39 hill country with haste, into a city of **J**; *G2448*
3:26 *son* of Joseph, which was *the son* of **J**, *G2455*
30 was *the son* of **J**, which was *the son* of *G2455*
33 *son* of Phares, which was *the son* of **J**, *G2455*
Heb 7:14 our Lord sprang out of **J**; of which tribe *G2455*
Rev 5: 5 Lion of the tribe of **J**, the Root of David, *G2455*
7: 5 Of the tribe of **J** *were* sealed twelve *G2455*

JUDAEA
Mt 2: 1 in Bethlehem of **J** in the days of Herod *G2449*
5 of **J**: for thus it is written by the prophet, *G2449*
22 did reign in **J** in the room of his father *G2449*
3: 1 preaching in the wilderness of **J**, *G2449*
5 Jerusalem, and all **J**, and all the region *G2449*
4:25 and *from* **J**, and *from* beyond Jordan. *G2449*
19: 1 into the coasts of **J** beyond Jordan; *G2449*
24:16 Then let them which be in **J** flee into *G2449*
Mk 1: 5 unto him all the land of **J**, and they of *G2449*
3: 7 from Galilee followed him, and from **J**, *G2449*
10: 1 into the coasts of **J** by the farther side *G2449*
13:14 them that be in **J** flee to the mountains: *G2449*
Lk 1: 5 of Herod, the king of **J**, a certain priest *G2449*
65 throughout all the hill country of **J**. *G2449*
2: 4 city of Nazareth, into **J**, unto the city of *G2449*
3: 1 being governor of **J**, and Herod being *G2449*
5:17 of Galilee, and **J**, and Jerusalem: and *G2449*
6:17 of people out of all **J** and Jerusalem, *G2449*
7:17 throughout all **J**, and throughout all *G2449*
21:21 Then let them which are in **J** flee to the *G2449*
Jn 3:22 into the land of **J**; and there he tarried *G2453*
4: 3 He left **J**, and departed again into *G2449*
47 was come out of **J** into Galilee, he went *G2449*
54 when he was come out of **J** into Galilee. *G2449*
7: 3 hence, and go into **J**, that thy disciples *G2449*
11: 7 to *his* disciples, Let us go into **J** again. *G2449*
Act 1: 8 and in all **J**, and in Samaria, and *G2449*
2: 9 **J**, and Cappadocia, in Pontus, and Asia, *G2449*
14 them, Ye men of **J**, and all *ye* that dwell *G2453*
8: 1 of **J** and Samaria, except the apostles. *G2449*
9:31 rest throughout all **J** and Galilee and *G2449*
10:37 throughout all **J**, and began from *G2449*
11: 1 that were in **J** heard that the Gentiles *G2449*
29 unto the brethren which dwelt in **J**: *G2449*
12:19 from **J** to Caesarea, and *there* abode. *G2449*
15: 1 came down from **J** taught the brethren, *G2449*
21:10 **J** a certain prophet, named Agabus. *G2449*
26:20 all the coasts of **J**, and *then* to the *G2449*
28:21 letters out of **J** concerning thee, neither *G2449*
Ro 15:31 do not believe in **J**; and that my service *G2449*
2Co 1:16 you to be brought on my way toward **J**. *G2449*
Gal 1:22 the churches of **J** which were in Christ: *G2449*
1Th 2:14 of God which in **J** are in Christ Jesus: *G2449*

JUDAH
Gen 29:35 she called his name **J**; and left bearing. H3063
35:23 Levi, and **J**, and Issachar, and Zebulun: H3063
37:26 And **J** said unto his brethren, What H3063
38: 1 And it came to pass at that time, that **J** H3063
2 And **J** saw there a daughter of a certain H3063
6 And **J** took a wife for Er his firstborn, H3063
8 And **J** said unto Onan, Go in unto thy H3063
11 Then said **J** to Tamar his daughter in H3063
12 wife died; and **J** was comforted, and H3063
15 When **J** saw her, he thought her *to be* H3063

Gen 38:20 And J sent the kid by the hand of his H3063
22 And he returned to J, and said, I cannot H3063
23 And J said, Let her take *it* to her, lest H3063
24 that it was told J, saying, Tamar thy H3063
24 whoredom. And J said, Bring her forth, H3063
26 And J acknowledged *them,* and said, H3063
43: 3 And J spake unto him, saying, The H3063
8 And J said unto Israel his father, Send H3063
44:14 And J and his brethren came to H3063
16 And J said, What shall we say unto my H3063
18 Then J came near unto him, and said, H3063
46:12 And the sons of J; Er, and Onan, and H3063
28 And he sent J before him unto Joseph, H3063
49: 8 J, thou *art he* whom thy brethren shall H3063
9 J *is* a lion's whelp: from the prey, my H3063
10 The sceptre shall not depart from J, nor H3063
Ex 1: 2 Reuben, Simeon, Levi, and J, H3063
31: 2 of Uri, the son of Hur, of the tribe of J: H3063
35:30 of Uri, the son of Hur, of the tribe of J; H3063
38:22 Hur, of the tribe of J, made all that the H3063
Nu 1: 7 Of J; Nahshon the son of Amminadab. H3063
26 Of the children of J, by their H3063
27 *even* of the tribe of J, *were* threescore H3063
2: 3 of the camp of J pitch throughout their H3063
3 *shall be* captain of the children of J. H3063
9 in the camp of J *were* an hundred H3063
7:12 the son of Amminadab, of the tribe of J: H3063
10:14 of the children of J according to their H3063
13: 6 Of the tribe of J, Caleb the son of H3063
26:19 The sons of J *were* Er and Onan: and Er H3063
20 And the sons of J after their families H3063
22 These *are* the families of J according to H3063
34:19 tribe of J, Caleb the son of Jephunneh. H3063
Dt 27:12 and Levi, and J, and Issachar, and H3063
33: 7 And this *is the blessing* of J: and he H3063
7 LORD, the voice of J, and bring him H3063
34: 2 all the land of J, unto the utmost sea, H3063
Jos 7: 1 of the tribe of J, took of the accursed H3063
16 tribes; and the tribe of J was taken: H3063
17 And he brought the family of J; and he H3063
18 of Zerah, of the tribe of J, was taken. H3063
11:21 all the mountains of J, and from all the H3063
14: 6 Then the children of J came unto H3063
15: 1 of the children of J by their families; H3063
12 coast of the children of J round about H3063
13 the children of J, according to the H3063
20 of J according to their families. H3063
21 of the children of J toward the coast of H3063
63 the children of J could not drive them H3063
63 of J at Jerusalem unto this day. H3063
18: 5 it into seven parts: J shall abide in their H3063
11 of J and the children of Joseph. H3063
14 children of J: this *was* the west quarter. H3063
19: 1 the inheritance of the children of J. H3063
9 Out of the portion of the children of J H3063
9 of the children of J was too much for H3063
34 to J upon Jordan toward the sunrising. H3063
20: 7 which *is* Hebron, in the mountain of J. H3063
21: 4 out of the tribe of J, and out of the tribe H3063
9 of the children of J, and out of the tribe H3063
11 in the hill *country* of J, with the suburbs H3063
Jdg 1: 2 And the LORD said, J shall go up: H3063
3 And J said unto Simeon his brother, H3063
4 And J went up; and the LORD delivered H3063
8 Now the children of J had fought H3063
9 And afterward the children of J went H3063
10 And J went against the Canaanites that H3063
16 the children of J into the wilderness H3063
16 the wilderness of J, which *lieth* in the H3063
17 And J went with Simeon his brother, H3063
18 Also J took Gaza with the coast thereof, H3063
19 And the LORD was with J; and he drave H3063
10: 9 to fight also against J, and against H3063
15: 9 in J, and spread themselves in Lehi. H3063
10 And the men of J said, Why are ye H3063
11 Then three thousand men of J went to H3063
17: 7 of the family of J, who *was* a Levite, and H3063
18:12 in Kirjath-jearim, in J: wherefore they H3063
20:18 And the LORD said, J *shall go up* first. H3063
Ru 1: 7 on the way to return unto the land of J. H3063
4:12 Tamar bare unto J, of the seed which H3063
1Sa 11: 8 and the men of J thirty thousand. H3063
15: 4 footmen, and ten thousand men of J. H3063
17: 1 *belongeth* to J, and pitched between H3063
52 And the men of Israel and of J arose, H3063
18:16 But all Israel and J loved David, H3063
22: 5 into the land of J. Then David departed, H3063
23: 3 we be afraid here in J: how much more H3063
23 out throughout all the thousands of J. H3063

1Sa 27: 6 unto the kings of J unto this day. H3063
10 the south of J, and against the south H3063
30:14 *belongeth* to J, and upon the south H3063
16 the Philistines, and out of the land of J. H3063
26 unto the elders of J, *even* to his friends, H3063
2Sa 1:18 the children of J *the use of* the bow: H3063
2: 1 any of the cities of J? And the LORD said H3063
4 And the men of J came, and there they H3063
4 king over the house of J. And they told H3063
7 of J have anointed me king over them. H3063
10 But the house of J followed David. H3063
11 of J was seven years and six months. H3063
3: 8 which against J do shew kindness this H3063
10 over J, from Dan even to Beer-sheba. H3063
5: 5 In Hebron he reigned over J seven H3063
5 and three years over all Israel and J. H3063
6: 2 him from Baale of J, to bring up from H3063
11:11 and Israel, and J, abide in tents; and my H3063
12: 8 of Israel and of J; and if *that had been* H3063
19:11 unto the elders of J, saying, Why are ye H3063
14 of all the men of J, even as *the heart of* H3063
15 to Jordan. And J came to Gilgal, to go H3063
16 with the men of J to meet king David. H3063
40 all the people of J conducted the king, H3063
41 the men of J stolen thee away, and H3063
42 And all the men of J answered the men H3063
43 the men of J, and said, We have ten H3063
43 of the men of J were fiercer than the H3063
20: 2 but the men of J clave unto their king, H3063
4 me the men of J within three days, and H3063
5 *the men of* J: but he tarried longer H3063
21: 2 his zeal to the children of Israel and J.) H3063
24: 1 them to say, Go, number Israel and J. H3063
7 to the south of J, *even* to Beer-sheba. H3063
9 of J *were* five hundred thousand men. H3063
1Ki 1: 9 and all the men of J the king's servants: H3063
35 him to be ruler over Israel and over J. H3063
2:32 son of Jether, captain of the host of J. H3063
4:20 J and Israel *were* many, as the sand H3063
25 And J and Israel dwelt safely, every H3063
12:17 of J, Rehoboam reigned over them. H3063
20 house of David, but the tribe of J only. H3063
21 all the house of J, with the tribe of H3063
23 of Solomon, king of J, and unto all the H3063
23 all the house of J and Benjamin, and H3063
27 Rehoboam king of J, and they shall kill H3063
27 and go again to Rehoboam king of J. H3063
32 unto the feast that *is* in J, and he offered H3063
13: 1 man of God out of J by the word of the H3063
12 man of God went, which came from J. H3063
14 that camest from J? And he said, I *am.* H3063
21 that came from J, saying, Thus saith the H3063
14:21 reigned in J. Rehoboam *was* forty H3063
22 And J did evil in the sight of the LORD, H3063
29 book of the chronicles of the kings of J? H3063
15: 1 the son of Nebat reigned Abijam over J. H3063
7 of the kings of J? And there was war H3063
9 king of Israel reigned Asa over J. H3063
17 went up against J, and built Ramah, H3063
17 to go out or come in to Asa king of J. H3063
22 throughout all J; none *was* exempted: H3063
23 of the kings of J? Nevertheless in the H3063
25 of J, and reigned over Israel two years. H3063
28 Even in the third year of Asa king of J H3063
33 In the third year of Asa king of J began H3063
16: 8 year of Asa king of J began Elah the H3063
10 Asa king of J, and reigned in his stead. H3063
15 year of Asa king of J did Zimri reign H3063
23 year of Asa king of J began Omri to H3063
29 year of Asa king of J began Ahab the H3063
19: 3 to J, and left his servant there. H3063
22: 2 of J came down to the king of Israel. H3063
10 the king of J sat each on his throne, H3063
29 the king of J went up to Ramoth-gilead. H3063
41 to reign over J in the fourth year of H3063
45 book of the chronicles of the kings of J? H3063
51 of J, and reigned two years over Israel. H3063
2Ki 1:17 king of J; because he had no son. H3063
3: 1 king of J, and reigned twelve years. H3063
7 the king of J, saying, The king of H3063
9 and the king of J, and the king of Edom: H3063
14 the king of J, I would not look toward H3063
8:16 *being* then king of J, Jehoram the son of H3063
16 of Jehoshaphat king of J began to reign. H3063
19 Yet the LORD would not destroy J for H3063
20 of J, and made a king over themselves. H3063
22 under the hand of J unto this day. Then H3063
23 book of the chronicles of the kings of J? H3063
25 son of Jehoram king of J begin to reign. H3063

2Ki 8:29 of Jehoram king of J went down to see H3063
9:16 king of J was come down to see Joram. H3063
21 Ahaziah king of J went out, each in his H3063
27 But when Ahaziah the king of J saw H3063
29 of Ahab began Ahaziah to reign over J. H3063
10:13 of Ahaziah king of J, and said, Who *are* H3063
12:18 And Jehoash king of J took all the H3063
18 fathers, kings of J, had dedicated, and H3063
19 book of the chronicles of the kings of J? H3063
13: 1 of Ahaziah king of J Jehoahaz the son H3063
10 of Joash king of J began Jehoash the H3063
12 Amaziah king of J, *are* they not written H3063
14: 1 Amaziah the son of Joash king of J. H3063
9 to Amaziah king of J, saying, The thistle H3063
10 fall, *even* thou, and J with thee? H3063
11 Amaziah king of J looked one another H3063
11 at Beth-shemesh, which *belongeth* to J. H3063
12 And J was put to the worse before H3063
13 Amaziah king of J, the son of Jehoash H3063
15 Amaziah king of J, *are* they not written H3063
17 And Amaziah the son of Joash king of J H3063
18 book of the chronicles of the kings of J? H3063
21 And all the people of J took Azariah, H3063
22 He built Elath, and restored it to J, after H3063
23 of Joash king of J Jeroboam the son of H3063
28 *which belonged* to J, for Israel, are they H3063
15: 1 son of Amaziah king of J to reign. H3063
6 book of the chronicles of the kings of J? H3063
8 of Azariah king of J did Zachariah the H3063
13 of Uzziah king of J; and he reigned a full H3063
17 of Azariah king of J began Menahem H3063
23 In the fiftieth year of Azariah king of J H3063
27 of Azariah king of J Pekah the son of H3063
32 the son of Uzziah king of J to reign. H3063
36 book of the chronicles of the kings of J? H3063
37 to send against J Rezin the king of H3063
16: 1 son of Jotham king of J began to reign. H3063
19 book of the chronicles of the kings of J? H3063
17: 1 In the twelfth year of Ahaz king of J H3063
13 against Israel, and against J, by all the H3063
18 was none left but the tribe of J only. H3063
19 Also J kept not the commandments of H3063
18: 1 son of Ahaz king of J began to reign. H3063
5 of J, nor *any* that were before him. H3063
13 all the fenced cities of J, and took them. H3063
14 And Hezekiah king of J sent to the king H3063
14 unto Hezekiah king of J three hundred H3063
16 Hezekiah king of J had overlaid, and H3063
22 and hath said to J and Jerusalem, Ye H3063
19:10 Hezekiah king of J, saying, Let not thy H3063
30 of the house of J shall yet again take H3063
20:20 book of the chronicles of the kings of J? H3063
21:11 Because Manasseh king of J hath done H3063
11 hath made J also to sin with his idols: H3063
12 upon Jerusalem and J, that whosoever H3063
16 he made J to sin, in doing *that* H3063
17 book of the chronicles of the kings of J? H3063
25 book of the chronicles of the kings of J? H3063
22:13 the people, and for all J, concerning the H3063
16 the book which the king of J hath read: H3063
18 But to the king of J which sent you to H3063
23: 1 him all the elders of J and of Jerusalem. H3063
2 LORD, and all the men of J and all the H3063
5 whom the kings of J had ordained to H3063
5 in the cities of J, and in the places round H3063
8 out of the cities of J, and defiled the H3063
11 that the kings of J had given to the sun, H3063
12 which the kings of J had made, and the H3063
17 which came from J, and proclaimed H3063
22 the kings of Israel, nor of the kings of J; H3063
24 in the land of J and in Jerusalem, did H3063
26 was kindled against J, because of all the H3063
27 And the LORD said, I will remove J H3063
28 book of the chronicles of the kings of J? H3063
24: 2 and sent them against J to destroy it, H3063
3 came *this* upon J, to remove *them* out H3063
5 book of the chronicles of the kings of J? H3063
12 And Jehoiachin the king of J went out H3063
20 in Jerusalem and J, until he had cast H3063
25:21 So J was carried away out of their land. H3063
22 in the land of J, whom Nebuchadnezzar H3063
27 of Jehoiachin king of J, in the twelfth H3063
27 of Jehoiachin king of J out of prison; H3063
1Ch 2: 1 Levi, and J, Issachar, and Zebulun, H3063
3 The sons of J; Er, and Onan, and H3063
3 And Er, the firstborn of J, was evil in the H3063
4 and Zerah. All the sons of J *were* five. H3063
10 Nahshon, prince of the children of J; H3063
4: 1 The sons of J; Pharez, Hezron, and H3063

1Ch 4:21 The sons of Shelah the son of J *were*, Er H3063
27 family multiply, like to the children of J. H3063
41 of Hezekiah king of J, and smote their H3063
5: 2 For J prevailed above his brethren, and H3063
17 of Jotham king of J, and in the days of H3063
6:15 carried away J and Jerusalem by the H3063
55 in the land of J, and the suburbs thereof H3063
57 gave the cities of J, *namely*, Hebron, *the* H3063
65 of the children of J, and out of the tribe H3063
9: 1 kings of Israel and J, *who* were carried H3063
3 of the children of J, and of the children H3063
4 of the children of Pharez the son of J. H3063
12:16 Benjamin and J to the hold unto David. H3063
24 The children of J that bare shield and H3063
13: 6 which *belonged* to J, to bring up thence H3063
21: 5 drew sword: and J *was* four hundred H3063
27:18 Of J, Elihu, *one* of the brethren of David: H3063
28: 4 for he hath chosen J *to be* the ruler; and H3063
4 and of the house of J, the house of my H3063
2Ch 2: 7 that *are* with me in J and in Jerusalem, H3063
9:11 none such seen before in the land of J. H3063
10:17 of J, Rehoboam reigned over them. H3063
11: 1 of the house of J and Benjamin an H3063
3 Solomon, king of J, and to all Israel in H3063
3 to all Israel in J and Benjamin, saying, H3063
5 and built cities for defence in J. H3063
10 *are* in J and in Benjamin fenced cities. H3063
12 having J and Benjamin on his side. H3063
14 and came to J and Jerusalem: for H3063
17 So they strengthened the kingdom of J, H3063
23 all the countries of J and Benjamin, H3063
12: 4 *pertained* to J, and came to Jerusalem. H3063
5 *to* the princes of J, that were gathered H3063
12 and also in J things went well. H3063
13: 1 Jeroboam began Abijah to reign over J. H3063
13 so they were before J, and the H3063
14 And when J looked back, behold, the H3063
15 Then the men of J gave a shout: and as H3063
15 and as the men of J shouted, it came to H3063
15 and all Israel before Abijah and J. H3063
16 And the children of Israel fled before J: H3063
18 and the children of J prevailed, because H3063
14: 4 And commanded J to seek the LORD H3063
5 of all the cities of J the high places and H3063
6 And he built fenced cities in J: for the H3063
7 Therefore he said unto J, Let us build H3063
8 and spears, out of J three hundred H3063
12 and before J; and the Ethiopians fled. H3063
15: 2 me, Asa, and all J and Benjamin; The H3063
8 of all the land of J and Benjamin, and H3063
9 And he gathered all J and Benjamin, H3063
15 And all J rejoiced at the oath: for they H3063
16: 1 came up against J, and built Ramah, to H3063
1 none go out or come in to Asa king of J. H3063
6 Then Asa the king took all J; and they H3063
7 to Asa king of J, and said unto him, H3063
11 in the book of the kings of J and Israel. H3063
17: 2 the fenced cities of J, and set garrisons H3063
2 in the land of J, and in the cities of H3063
5 in his hand; and all J brought to H3063
6 the high places and groves out of J. H3063
7 to Michaiah, to teach in the cities of J. H3063
9 And they taught in J, and *had* the book H3063
9 all the cities of J, and taught the people. H3063
10 *were* round about J, so that they made H3063
12 he built in J castles, and cities of store. H3063
13 in the cities of J: and the men of war, H3063
14 of their fathers: Of J, the captains of H3063
19 put in the fenced cities throughout all J. H3063
18: 3 king of J, Wilt thou go with me H3063
9 king of J sat either of them on H3063
28 the king of J went up to Ramoth-gilead. H3063
19: 1 And Jehoshaphat the king of J returned H3063
5 all the fenced cities of J, city by city, H3063
11 ruler of the house of J, for all the king's H3063
20: 3 and proclaimed a fast throughout all J. H3063
4 And J gathered themselves together, to H3063
4 cities of J they came to seek the LORD. H3063
5 congregation of J and Jerusalem, in the H3063
13 And all J stood before the LORD, with H3063
15 And he said, Hearken ye, all J, and ye H3063
17 the LORD with you, O J and Jerusalem: H3063
18 ground: and all J and the inhabitants H3063
20 said, Hear me, O J, and ye inhabitants H3063
22 come against J; and they were smitten. H3063
24 And when J came toward the watch H3063
27 Then they returned, every man of J and H3063
31 And Jehoshaphat reigned over J: *he was* H3063
35 king of J join himself with Ahaziah H3063

2Ch 21: 3 fenced cities in J: but the kingdom gave H3063
8 of J, and made themselves a king. H3063
10 under the hand of J unto this day. The H3063
11 in the mountains of J, and caused the H3063
11 fornication, and compelled J *thereto*. H3063
12 father, nor in the ways of Asa king of J, H3063
13 and hast made J and the inhabitants H3063
17 And they came up into J, and brake into H3063
22: 1 the son of Jehoram king of J reigned. H3063
6 of Jehoram king of J went down to see H3063
8 the princes of J, and the sons of the H3063
10 all the seed royal of the house of J. H3063
23: 2 And they went about in J, and gathered H3063
2 of all the cities of J, and the chief of the H3063
8 So the Levites and all J did according to H3063
24: 5 out unto the cities of J, and gather of all H3063
6 Levites to bring in out of J and out of H3063
9 through J and Jerusalem, to bring H3063
17 the princes of J, and made obeisance H3063
18 J and Jerusalem for this their trespass. H3063
23 and they came to J and Jerusalem, and H3063
25: 5 Moreover Amaziah gathered J H3063
5 throughout all J and Benjamin: and H3063
10 kindled against J, and they returned H3063
12 alive did the children of J carry away H3063
13 upon the cities of J, from Samaria even H3063
17 Then Amaziah king of J took advice, H3063
18 to Amaziah king of J, saying, The thistle H3063
19 fall, *even* thou, and J with thee? H3063
21 Amaziah king of J, at Beth-shemesh, H3063
21 at Beth-shemesh, which *belongeth* to J. H3063
22 And J was put to the worse before H3063
23 Amaziah king of J, the son of Joash, the H3063
25 And Amaziah the son of Joash king of J H3063
26 in the book of the kings of J and Israel? H3063
28 him with his fathers in the city of J. H3063
26: 1 Then all the people of J took Uzziah, H3063
2 He built Eloth, and restored it to J, after H3063
27: 4 the mountains of J, and in the forests he H3063
7 in the book of the kings of Israel and J. H3063
28: 6 of Remaliah slew in J an hundred and H3063
9 was wroth with J, he hath delivered H3063
10 the children of J and Jerusalem for H3063
17 smitten J, and carried away captives. H3063
18 and of the south of J, and had taken H3063
19 For the LORD brought J low because of H3063
19 for he made J naked, and transgressed H3063
25 And in every several city of J he made H3063
26 in the book of the kings of J and Israel. H3063
29: 8 LORD was upon J and Jerusalem, and H3063
21 the sanctuary, and for J. And he H3063
30: 1 And Hezekiah sent to all Israel and J, H3063
6 all Israel and J, and according to the H3063
12 Also in J the hand of God was to give H3063
24 For Hezekiah king of J did give to the H3063
25 And all the congregation of J, with the H3063
25 of Israel, and that dwelt in J, rejoiced. H3063
31: 1 went out to the cities of J, and brake the H3063
1 the altars out of all J and Benjamin, in H3063
6 of Israel and J, that dwelt in the cities H3063
6 in the cities of J, they also brought in H3063
20 And thus did Hezekiah throughout all J, H3063
32: 1 and entered into J, and encamped H3063
8 upon the words of Hezekiah king of J. H3063
9 Hezekiah king of J, and unto all Judah H3063
9 all J that *were* at Jerusalem, saying, H3063
12 and commanded J and Jerusalem, H3063
23 to Hezekiah king of J: so that he was H3063
25 upon him, and upon J and Jerusalem. H3063
32 in the book of the kings of J and Israel. H3063
33 of David: and all J and the inhabitants H3063
33: 9 So Manasseh made J and the H3063
14 of war in all the fenced cities of J. H3063
16 J to serve the LORD God of Israel. H3063
34: 3 year he began to purge J and Jerusalem H3063
5 altars, and cleansed J and Jerusalem. H3063
9 of Israel, and of all J and Benjamin; H3063
11 which the kings of J had destroyed. H3063
21 in Israel and in J, concerning the words H3063
24 they have read before the king of J: H3063
26 And as for the king of J, who sent you to H3063
29 all the elders of J and Jerusalem. H3063
30 LORD, and all the men of J, and the H3063
35:18 Levites, and all J and Israel that were H3063
21 thee, thou king of J? *I come* not against H3063
24 J and Jerusalem mourned for Josiah. H3063
27 in the book of the kings of Israel and J. H3063
36: 4 brother king over J and Jerusalem, and H3063
8 kings of Israel and J: and Jehoiachin his H3063

2Ch 36:10 his brother king over J and Jerusalem. H3063
23 which *is* in J. Who *is there* among H3063
Ezr 1: 2 an house at Jerusalem, which *is* in J. H3063
3 which *is* in J, and build the house H3063
5 of the fathers of J and Benjamin, and H3063
8 them unto Sheshbazzar, the prince of J. H3063
2: 1 Jerusalem and J, every one unto his city; H3063
3: 9 his sons, the sons of J, together, to set H3063
4: 1 Now when the adversaries of J and H3063
4 of J, and troubled them in building, H3063
6 the inhabitants of J and Jerusalem. H3063
5: 1 Jews that *were* in J and Jerusalem in H3061
7:14 concerning J and Jerusalem, according H3061
9: 9 to give us a wall in J and in Jerusalem. H3063
10: 7 throughout J and Jerusalem unto H3063
9 Then all the men of J and Benjamin H3063
23 *is* Kelita,) Pethahiah, J, and Eliezer. H3063
Neh 1: 2 and *certain* men of J; and I asked them H3063
2: 5 send me unto J, unto the city of my H3063
7 may convey me over till I come into J; H3063
4:10 And J said, The strength of the bearers H3063
16 the rulers *were* behind all the house of J. H3063
5:14 in the land of J, from the twentieth year H3063
6: 7 *There is* a king in J: and now shall it be H3063
17 Moreover in those days the nobles of J H3063
18 For *there were* many in J sworn unto H3063
7: 6 and to J, every one unto his city; H3063
11: 3 but in the cities of J dwelt every one in H3063
4 of the children of J, and of the children H3063
4 Of the children of J; Athaiah the son of H3063
9 their overseer: and J the son of Senuah H3063
20 cities of J, every one in his inheritance. H3063
24 of Zerah the son of J, *was* at the king's H3063
25 *some* of the children of J dwelt at H3063
36 And of the Levites *were* divisions *in* J, H3063
12: 8 Sherebiah, J, *and* Mattaniah, *which* H3063
31 Then I brought up the princes of J upon H3063
32 Hoshaiah, and half of the princes of J, H3063
34 J, and Benjamin, and Shemaiah, and H3063
36 Nethaneel, and J, Hanani, with the H3063
44 and Levites: for J rejoiced for the H3063
13:12 Then brought all J the tithe of the corn H3063
15 In those days saw I in J *some* treading H3063
16 unto the children of J, and in Jerusalem. H3063
17 Then I contended with the nobles of J, H3063
Est 2: 6 with Jeconiah king of J, whom H3063
Ps 48:11 of J be glad, because of thy judgments. H3063
60: 7 of mine head; J *is* my lawgiver; H3063
63:ttl when he was in the wilderness of J. H3063
68:27 the princes of J *and* their council, the H3063
69:35 build the cities of J: that they may dwell H3063
76: 1 In J *is* God known: his name *is* great in H3063
78:68 But chose the tribe of J, the mount Zion H3063
97: 8 the daughters of J rejoiced because of H3063
108: 8 of mine head; J *is* my lawgiver; H3063
114: 2 J was his sanctuary, *and* Israel his H3063
Prv 25: 1 men of Hezekiah king of J copied out. H3063
Isa 1: 1 he saw concerning J and Jerusalem in H3063
1 Jotham, Ahaz, *and* Hezekiah, kings of J. H3063
2: 1 Amoz saw concerning J and Jerusalem. H3063
3: 1 and from J the stay and the staff, H3063
8 For Jerusalem is ruined, and J is fallen: H3063
5: 3 and men of J, judge, I pray you, betwixt H3063
7 and the men of J his pleasant plant: H3063
7: 1 of Uzziah, king of J, *that* Rezin the king H3063
6 Let us go up against J, and vex it, and H3063
17 from J; *even* the king of Assyria. H3063
8: 8 And he shall pass through J; he shall H3063
9:21 *shall be* against J. For all this his anger H3063
11:12 of J from the four corners of the earth. H3063
13 and the adversaries of J shall be cut off: H3063
13 J, and Judah shall not vex Ephraim. H3063
13 Judah, and J shall not vex Ephraim. H3063
19:17 And the land of J shall be a terror unto H3063
22: 8 And he discovered the covering of J, H3063
21 of Jerusalem, and to the house of J. H3063
26: 1 sung in the land of J; We have a strong H3063
36: 1 the defenced cities of J, and took them. H3063
7 away, and said to J and to Jerusalem, H3063
37:10 Hezekiah king of J, saying, Let not thy H3063
31 of the house of J shall again take root H3063
38: 9 The writing of Hezekiah king of J, when H3063
40: 9 unto the cities of J, Behold your God! H3063
44:26 and to the cities of J, Ye shall be built, H3063
48: 1 of the waters of J, which swear by the H3063
65: 9 Jacob, and out of J an inheritor of my H3063
Jer 1: 2 of J, in the thirteenth year of his reign. H3063
3 of Josiah king of J, unto the end of the H3063
3 of Josiah king of J, unto the carrying H3063

Jer 1:15 about, and against all the cities of J. H3063
18 the kings of J, against the princes H3063
2:28 number of thy cities are thy gods, O J. H3063
3: 7 not. And her treacherous sister J saw *it*. H3063
8 her treacherous sister J feared not, but H3063
10 her treacherous sister J hath not turned H3063
11 herself more than treacherous J. H3063
18 In those days the house of J shall walk H3063
4: 3 For thus saith the LORD to the men of J H3063
4 heart, ye men of J and inhabitants of H3063
5 Declare ye in J, and publish in H3063
16 out their voice against the cities of J. H3063
5:11 and the house of J have dealt very H3063
20 of Jacob, and publish it in J, saying, H3063
7: 2 of the LORD, all *ye of* J, that enter in at H3063
17 of J and in the streets of Jerusalem? H3063
30 For the children of J have done evil in H3063
34 from the cities of J, and from the streets H3063
8: 1 of the kings of J, and the bones of his H3063
9:11 of J desolate, without an inhabitant. H3063
26 Egypt, and J, and Edom, and the H3063
10:22 of J desolate, *and* a den of dragons. H3063
11: 2 J, and to the inhabitants of Jerusalem; H3063
6 in the cities of J, and in the streets of H3063
9 among the men of J, and among the H3063
10 and the house of J have broken my H3063
12 Then shall the cities of J and H3063
13 were thy gods, O J; and *according to* the H3063
17 of the house of J, which they have done H3063
12:14 out the house of J from among them. H3063
13: 9 of J, and the great pride of Jerusalem. H3063
11 the whole house of J, saith the LORD; H3063
19 none shall open *them*: J shall be carried H3063
14: 2 J mourneth, and the gates thereof H3063
19 Hast thou utterly rejected J? hath thy H3063
15: 4 of J, for *that* which he did in Jerusalem. H3063
17: 1 The sin of J *is* written with a pen of H3063
19 the kings of J come in, and by the H3063
20 LORD, ye kings of J, and all Judah, and H3063
20 kings of Judah, and all J, and all the H3063
25 the men of J, and the inhabitants H3063
26 And they shall come from the cities of J, H3063
18:11 to the men of J, and to the inhabitants H3063
19: 3 LORD, O kings of J, and inhabitants of H3063
4 nor the kings of J, and have filled this H3063
7 And I will make void the counsel of J H3063
13 of the kings of J, shall be defiled as the H3063
20: 4 and I will give all J into the hand of the H3063
5 of the kings of J will I give into the H3063
21: 7 Zedekiah king of J, and his servants, H3063
11 And touching the house of the king of J, H3063
22: 1 the king of J, and speak there this word, H3063
2 LORD, O king of J, that sittest upon the H3063
6 the king's house of J; Thou *art* Gilead H3063
11 son of Josiah king of J, which reigned H3063
18 son of Josiah king of J; They shall not H3063
24 of Jehoiakim king of J were the signet H3063
30 of David, and ruling any more in J. H3063
23: 6 In his days J shall be saved, and Israel H3063
24: 1 Jehoiakim king of J, and the princes of H3063
1 and the princes of J, with the carpenters H3063
5 away captive of J, whom I have sent out H3063
8 the king of J, and his princes, and H3063
25: 1 all the people of J in the fourth year of H3063
1 son of Josiah king of J, that *was* the first H3063
2 unto all the people of J, and to all the H3063
3 of Amon king of J, even unto this day, H3063
18 *To wit*, Jerusalem, and the cities of J, H3063
26: 1 of Josiah king of J came this word from H3063
2 unto all the cities of J, which come to H3063
10 When the princes of J heard these H3063
18 Hezekiah king of J, and spake to all the H3063
18 to all the people of J, saying, Thus saith H3063
19 Did Hezekiah king of J and all Judah H3063
19 Did Hezekiah king of Judah and all J H3063
27: 1 of Josiah king of J came this word unto H3063
3 to Jerusalem unto Zedekiah king of J; H3063
12 I spake also to Zedekiah king of J H3063
18 J, and at Jerusalem, go not to Babylon. H3063
20 Jehoiakim king of J from Jerusalem to H3063
20 and all the nobles of J and Jerusalem; H3063
21 house of the king of J and of Jerusalem; H3063
28: 1 of Zedekiah king of J, in the fourth year, H3063
4 of Jehoiakim king of J, with all the H3063
4 with all the captives of J, that went into H3063
29: 2 the princes of J and Jerusalem, and H3063
3 Zedekiah king of J sent unto Babylon to H3063
22 by all the captivity of J which *are* in H3063
30: 3 my people Israel and J, saith the LORD: H3063

Jer 30: 4 concerning Israel and concerning J. H3063
31:23 in the land of J and in the cities thereof, H3063
24 And there shall dwell in J itself, and in H3063
27 and the house of J with the seed of H3063
31 house of Israel, and with the house of J: H3063
32: 1 of Zedekiah king of J, which *was* the H3063
3 For Zedekiah king of J had shut him H3063
4 And Zedekiah king of J shall not escape H3063
30 the children of J have only done evil H3063
32 of the children of J, which they have H3063
32 of J, and the inhabitants of Jerusalem. H3063
35 do this abomination, to cause J to sin. H3063
44 and in the cities of J, and in the cities of H3063
33: 4 of the kings of J, which are thrown H3063
7 And I will cause the captivity of J and H3063
10 in the cities of J, and in the streets of H3063
13 and in the cities of J, shall the flocks H3063
14 the house of Israel and to the house of J. H3063
16 In those days shall J be saved, and H3063
34: 2 to Zedekiah king of J, and tell him, Thus H3063
4 O Zedekiah king of J; Thus saith the H3063
6 unto Zedekiah king of J in Jerusalem, H3063
7 all the cities of J that were left, against H3063
7 cities remained of the cities of J. H3063
19 The princes of J, and the princes of H3063
21 And Zedekiah king of J and his princes H3063
22 of J a desolation without an inhabitant. H3063
35: 1 the son of Josiah king of J, saying, H3063
13 Go and tell the men of J and the H3063
17 I will bring upon J and upon all the H3063
36: 1 of Josiah king of J, *that* this word came H3063
2 Israel, and against J, and against all the H3063
3 It may be that the house of J will hear H3063
6 of all J that come out of their cities. H3063
9 of Josiah king of J, in the ninth month, H3063
9 from the cities of J unto Jerusalem. H3063
28 Jehoiakim the king of J hath burned. H3063
29 to Jehoiakim king of J, Thus saith the H3063
30 Jehoiakim king of J; He shall have none H3063
31 and upon the men of J, all the evil that I H3063
32 Jehoiakim king of J had burned in the H3063
37: 1 of Babylon made king in the land of J. H3063
7 say to the king of J, that sent you unto H3063
39: 1 In the ninth year of Zedekiah king of J, H3063
4 the king of J saw them, and all the H3063
6 king of Babylon slew all the nobles of J. H3063
10 nothing, in the land of J, and gave them H3063
40: 1 of Jerusalem and J, which were carried H3063
5 over the cities of J, and dwell with him H3063
11 left a remnant of J, and that he had set H3063
12 came to the land of J, to Gedaliah, unto H3063
15 scattered, and the remnant in J perish? H3063
42:15 ye remnant of J; Thus saith the LORD H3063
19 O ye remnant of J; Go ye not into Egypt: H3063
43: 4 of the LORD, to dwell in the land of J. H3063
5 all the remnant of J, that were returned H3063
5 been driven, to dwell in the land of J; H3063
9 Tahpanhes, in the sight of the men of J; H3064
44: 2 all the cities of J; and, behold, this day H3063
6 in the cities of J and in the streets of H3063
7 out of J, to leave you none to remain; H3063
9 of the kings of J, and the wickedness H3063
9 of J, and in the streets of Jerusalem? H3063
11 against you for evil, and to cut off all J. H3063
12 And I will take the remnant of J, that H3063
14 So that none of the remnant of J, which H3063
14 into the land of J, to the which they H3063
17 in the cities of J, and in the streets of H3063
21 in the cities of J, and in the streets of H3063
24 all J that *are* in the land of Egypt: H3063
26 of the LORD, all J that dwell in the land H3063
26 of any man of J in all the land of Egypt, H3063
27 and all the men of J that *are* in the land H3063
28 into the land of J, and all the remnant H3063
28 all the remnant of J, that are gone into H3063
30 Zedekiah king of J into the hand of H3063
45: 1 the son of Josiah king of J, saying, H3063
46: 2 of Jehoiakim the son of Josiah king of J. H3063
49:34 the reign of Zedekiah king of J, saying, H3063
50: 4 the children of J together, going and H3063
20 and the sins of J, and they shall not be H3063
33 and the children of J *were* oppressed H3063
51: 5 For Israel *hath* not *been* forsaken, nor J H3063
59 the king of J into Babylon in the H3063
52: 3 in Jerusalem and J, till he had cast them H3063
10 slew also all the princes of J in Riblah. H3063
27 of Hamath. Thus J was carried away H3063
31 of Jehoiachin king of J, in the twelfth H3063
31 J, and brought him forth out of prison, H3063

Lam 1: 3 J is gone into captivity because of H3063
15 the daughter of J, *as* in a winepress. H3063
2: 2 of the daughter of J; he hath brought H3063
5 of J mourning and lamentation. H3063
5:11 in Zion, *and* the maids in the cities of J. H3063
Ezk 4: 6 of the house of J forty days: I have H3063
8: 1 and the elders of J sat before me, that H3063
17 to the house of J that they commit the H3063
9: 9 of Israel and J *is* exceeding great, and H3063
21:20 and to J in Jerusalem the defenced. H3063
25: 3 of J, when they went into captivity; H3063
8 house of J *is* like unto all the heathen; H3063
12 the house of J by taking vengeance, H3063
27:17 J, and the land of Israel, they *were* thy H3063
37:16 write upon it, For J, and for the children H3063
19 with the stick of J, and make them one H3063
48: 7 side unto the west side, a *portion for* J. H3063
8 And by the border of J, from the east H3063
22 the border of J and the border of H3063
31 Reuben, one gate of J, one gate of Levi. H3063
Dan 1: 1 of Jehoiakim king of J came H3063
2 And the Lord gave Jehoiakim king of J H3063
6 of the children of J, Daniel, Hananiah, H3063
2:25 man of the captives of J, that will make H3061
5:13 of the captivity of J, whom the king my H3061
6:13 of the captivity of J, regardeth not thee, H3061
9: 7 this day; to the men of J, and to the H3063
Hos 1: 1 Hezekiah, kings of J, and in the days of H3063
7 upon the house of J, and will save them H3063
11 Then shall the children of J and the H3063
4:15 harlot, *yet* let not J offend; and come H3063
5: 5 iniquity; J also shall fall with them. H3063
10 The princes of J were like them that H3063
12 and to the house of J as rottenness. H3063
13 When Ephraim saw his sickness, and J H3063
14 to the house of J: I, *even* I, will tear and H3063
6: 4 I do unto thee? O J, what shall I do unto H3063
11 Also, O J, he hath set an harvest for H3063
8:14 temples; and J hath multiplied fenced H3063
10:11 Ephraim to ride; J shall plow, *and* H3063
11:12 with deceit: but J yet ruleth with God, H3063
12: 2 a controversy with J, and will punish H3063
Joel 3: 1 again the captivity of J and Jerusalem, H3063
6 The children also of J and the children H3063
8 of the children of J, and they shall sell H3063
18 all the rivers of J shall flow with waters, H3063
19 the children of J, because they have H3063
20 But J shall dwell for ever, and H3063
Am 1: 1 of Uzziah king of J, and in the days of H3063
2: 4 transgressions of J, and for four, I will H3063
5 But I will send a fire upon J, and it shall H3063
7:12 into the land of J, and there eat bread, H3063
Oba 12 over the children of J in the day of their H3063
Mic 1: 1 *and* Hezekiah, kings of J, which he saw H3063
5 high places of J? *are they* not Jerusalem? H3063
9 for it is come unto J; he is come unto the H3063
5: 2 the thousands of J, *yet* out of thee shall H3063
Nah 1:15 peace! O J, keep thy solemn feasts, H3063
Zep 1: 1 of Josiah the son of Amon, king of J. H3063
4 I will also stretch out mine hand upon J, H3063
2: 7 of the house of J; they shall feed H3063
Hag 1: 1 governor of J, and to Joshua the son H3063
14 governor of J, and the spirit of Joshua H3063
2: 2 governor of J, and to Joshua the son H3063
21 Speak to Zerubbabel, governor of J, H3063
Zec 1:12 on the cities of J, against which thou H3063
19 have scattered J, Israel, and Jerusalem. H3063
21 have scattered J, so that no man did H3063
21 horn over the land of J to scatter it. H3063
2:12 And the LORD shall inherit J his H3063
8:13 O house of J, and house of Israel; H3063
15 and to the house of J: fear ye not. H3063
19 be to the house of J joy and gladness, H3063
9: 7 governor in J, and Ekron as a Jebusite. H3063
13 When I have bent J for me, filled the H3063
10: 3 his flock the house of J, and hath made H3063
6 And I will strengthen the house of J, H3063
11:14 the brotherhood between J and Israel. H3063
12: 2 both against J *and* against Jerusalem. H3063
4 eyes upon the house of J, and will smite H3063
5 And the governors of J shall say in their H3063
6 the governors of J like an hearth of fire H3063
7 The LORD also shall save the tents of J H3063
7 do not magnify *themselves* against J. H3063
14: 5 of Uzziah king of J: and the LORD my H3063
14 And J also shall fight at Jerusalem; and H3063
21 Yea, every pot in Jerusalem and in J H3063
Mal 2:11 J hath dealt treacherously, and an H3063
11 in Jerusalem; for J hath profaned the H3063

Mal 3: 4 Then shall the offering of J and H3063
Heb 8: 8 house of Israel and with the house of J: G2455

JUDAH'S
Gen 38: 7 And Er, J firstborn, was wicked in the H3063
12 the daughter of Shuah J wife died; and H3063
Jer 32: 2 which *was* in the king of J house. H3063
38:22 are left in the king of J house *shall be* H3063

JUDAS
Mt 1: 2 and Jacob begat J and his brethren; G2455
3 And J begat Phares and Zara of G2455
10: 4 Simon the Canaanite, and J Iscariot, G2455
13:55 James, and Joses, and Simon, and J? G2455
26:14 Then one of the twelve, called J G2455
25 Then J, which betrayed him, answered G2455
47 And while he yet spake, lo, J, one of the G2455
27: 3 Then J, which had betrayed him, when G2455
Mk 3:19 And J Iscariot, which also betrayed G2455
14:10 And J Iscariot, one of the twelve, went G2455
43 yet spake, cometh J, one of the twelve, G2455
Lk 6:16 And J *the brother* of James, and Judas G2455
16 And Judas *the brother* of James, and J G2455
22: 3 Then entered Satan into J surnamed G2455
47 he that was called J, one of the twelve, G2455
48 But Jesus said unto him, J, betrayest G2455
Jn 6:71 He spake of J Iscariot *the son* of Simon: G2455
12: 4 Then saith one of his disciples, J G2455
13: 2 J Iscariot, Simon's *son*, to betray him; G2455
26 gave *it* to J Iscariot, *the son* of Simon. G2455
29 For some of *them* thought, because J G2455
14:22 J saith unto him, not Iscariot, Lord, G2455
18: 2 And J also, which betrayed him, knew G2455
3 J then, having received a band of *men* G2455
5 I am *he*. And J also, which betrayed G2455
Act 1:13 Zelotes, and J *the brother* of James. G2455
16 before concerning J, which was guide to G2455
25 from which J by transgression fell, G2455
5:37 After this man rose up J of Galilee in G2455
9:11 in the house of J for *one* called Saul, G2455
15:22 *namely*, J surnamed Barsabas, G2455
27 We have sent therefore J and Silas, who G2455
32 And J and Silas, being prophets also G2455

JUDE
Jude 1 J, the servant of Jesus Christ, and G2455

JUDEA
Ezr 5: 8 the province of J, to the house of the H3061

JUDGE
Gen 15:14 shall serve, will I j: and afterward shall H1777
16: 5 eyes: the LORD j between me and thee. H8199
18:25 Shall not the J of all the earth do right? H8199
19: 9 he will needs be a j: now will we deal H8199
31:37 that they may j betwixt us both. H3198
53 of their father, j betwixt us. And Jacob H8199
49:16 Dan shall j his people, as one of the H1777
Ex 2:14 a prince and a j over us? intendest thou H8199
5:21 upon you, and j; because ye have made H8199
18:13 that Moses sat to j the people: and the H8199
16 come unto me; and I j between one and H8199
22 And let them j the people at all H8199
22 matter they shall j: so shall it be easier H8199
Lev 19:15 shalt thou j thy neighbour. H8199
Nu 35:24 Then the congregation shall j between H8199
Dt 1:16 brethren, and j righteously between H8199
16:18 shall j the people with just judgment. H8199
17: 9 and unto the j that shall be in those H8199
12 God, or unto the j, even that man shall H8199
25: 1 *the judges* may j them; then they shall H8199
2 be beaten, that the j shall cause him to H8199
32:36 For the LORD shall j his people, and H1777
Jdg 2:18 was with the j, and delivered them H8199
18 all the days of the j: for it repented the H8199
19 And it came to pass, when the j was H8199
11:27 me: the LORD the J be judge this day H8199
27 the Judge be j this day between the H8199
1Sa 2:10 the LORD shall j the ends of the earth; H1777
25 If one man sin against another, the j H430
25 the judge shall j him: but if a man sin H6419
3:13 For I have told him that I will j his H8199
8: 5 us a king to j us like all the nations. H8199
6 said, Give us a king to j us. And Samuel H8199
20 and that our king may j us, and go out H8199
24:12 The LORD j between me and thee, and H8199
15 The LORD therefore be j, and judge H1781
15 The LORD therefore be judge, and j H8199
2Sa 15: 4 Oh that I were made j in the land, that H8199
1Ki 3: 9 heart to j thy people, that I H8199
9 is able to j this thy so great a people? H8199
7: 7 where he might j, *even* the porch of H8199
8:32 heaven, and do, and j thy servants, H8199
1Ch 16:33 because he cometh to j the earth. H8199
2Ch 1:10 can j this thy people, *that is so* great? H8199
11 that thou mayest j my people, over H8199
6:23 and do, and j thy servants, by requiting H8199
19: 6 what ye do: for ye j not for man, but for H8199
20:12 O our God, wilt thou not j them? for we H8199
Ezr 7:25 which may j all the people that H1934+H1778
Job 9:15 *but* I would make supplication to my j. H8199
22:13 know? can he j through the dark cloud? H8199
23: 7 should I be delivered for ever from my j. H8199
31:28 *be punished by* the j: for I should have H6416
Ps 7: 8 The LORD shall j the people: judge me, H1777
8 The LORD shall judge the people: j me, H8199
9: 8 And he shall j the world in H8199
10:18 To j the fatherless and the oppressed, H8199
26: 1 J me, O LORD; for I have walked in H8199
35:24 J me, O LORD my God, according to H8199
43: 1 J me, O God, and plead my cause H8199
50: 4 to the earth, that he may j his people. H1777
6 for God *is* j himself. Selah. H8199
54: 1 Save me, O God, by thy name, and j me H1777
58: 1 do ye j uprightly, O ye sons of men? H8199
67: 4 for joy: for thou shalt j the people H8199
68: 5 A father of the fatherless, and a j of the H1781
72: 2 He shall j thy people with H1777
4 He shall j the poor of the people, he H8199
75: 2 the congregation I will j uprightly. H8199
7 But God *is* the j: he putteth down one, H8199
82: 2 How long will ye j unjustly, and accept H8199
8 Arise, O God, j the earth: for thou shalt H8199
94: 2 Lift up thyself, thou j of the earth: H8199
96:10 he shall j the people righteously. H1777
13 for he cometh to j the earth: he shall H8199
13 the earth: he shall j the world with H8199
98: 9 Before the LORD; for he cometh to j the H8199
9 j the world, and the people with equity. H8199
110: 6 He shall j among the heathen, he shall H1777
135:14 For the LORD will j his people, and he H1777
Prv 31: 9 Open thy mouth, j righteously, and H8199
Ecc 3:17 I said in mine heart, God shall j the H8199
Isa 1:17 j the fatherless, plead for the widow. H8199
23 after rewards: they j not the fatherless, H8199
2: 4 And he shall j among the nations, and H8199
3: 2 man of war, the j, and the prophet, and H8199
13 to plead, and standeth to j the people. H1777
5: 3 and men of Judah, j, I pray you, betwixt H8199
11: 3 and he shall not j after the sight of his H8199
4 But with righteousness shall he j the H8199
33:22 For the LORD *is* our j, the LORD *is* our H8199
51: 5 mine arms shall j the people; the isles H8199
Jer 5:28 of the wicked: they j not the cause, the H1777
28 and the right of the needy do they not j. H8199
Lam 3:59 O LORD, thou hast seen my wrong: j H8199
Ezk 7: 3 thee, and will j thee according to thy H8199
8 thee: and I will j thee according to thy H8199
27 to their deserts will I j them; and they H8199
11:10 Ye shall fall by the sword; I will j you in H8199
11 *but* I will j you in the border of Israel: H8199
16:38 And I will j thee, as women that break H8199
18:30 Therefore I will j you, O house of Israel, H8199
20: 4 Wilt thou j them, son of man, wilt thou H8199
4 of man, wilt thou j *them*? cause them to H8199
21:30 into his sheath? I will j thee in the place H8199
22: 2 Now, thou son of man, wilt thou j, wilt H8199
2 judge, wilt thou j the bloody city? yea, H8199
23:24 j thee according to their judgments. H8199
36 Son of man, wilt thou j Aholah and H8199
45 And the righteous men, they shall j H8199
24:14 shall they j thee, saith the Lord GOD. H8199
33:20 I will j you every one after his ways. H8199
34:17 GOD; Behold, I j between cattle and H8199
20 I, *even* I, will j between the fat cattle H8199
22 and I will j between cattle and cattle. H8199
44:24 *and* they shall j it according to my H8199
Joel 3:12 I sit to j all the heathen round about. H8199
Am 2: 3 And I will cut off the j from the midst H8199
Oba 21 on mount Zion to j the mount of Esau; H8199
Mic 3:11 The heads thereof j for reward, and the H8199
4: 3 And he shall j among many people, H8199
5: 1 j of Israel with a rod upon the cheek. H8199
7: 3 asketh, and the j *asketh* for a reward; H8199
Zec 3: 7 thou shalt also j my house, and shalt H1777
Mt 5:25 deliver thee to the j, and the judge G2923
25 the judge, and the j deliver thee to the G2923
7: 1 J not, that ye be not judged. G2919
Mt 7: 2 For with what judgment ye j, ye shall be G2919
Lk 6:37 J not, and ye shall not be judged: G2919
12:14 who made me a j or a divider over you? G1348
57 Yea, and why even of yourselves j ye G2919
58 lest he hale thee to the j, and the judge G2923
58 the judge, and the j deliver thee to the G2923
18: 2 Saying, There was in a city a j, which G2923
6 Lord said, Hear what the unjust j saith. G2923
19:22 own mouth will I j thee, *thou* wicked G2919
Jn 5:30 as I hear, I j: and my judgment is G2919
7:24 J not according to the appearance, but G2919
24 appearance, but j righteous judgment. G2919
51 Doth our law j *any* man, before it hear G2919
8:15 Ye j after the flesh; I judge no man. G2919
15 Ye judge after the flesh; I j no man. G2919
16 And yet if I j, my judgment is true: for I G2919
26 I have many things to say and to j of G2919
12:47 and believe not, I j him not: for I came G2919
47 to j the world, but to save the world. G2919
48 the same shall j him in the last day. G2919
18:31 Take ye him, and j him according to G2919
Act 4:19 unto you more than unto God, j ye. G2919
7: 7 in bondage will I j, said God: and after G2919
27 Who made thee a ruler and a j over us? G1348
35 thee a ruler and a j? the same did God G1348
10:42 of God *to be* the J of quick and dead. G2923
13:46 it from you, and j yourselves unworthy G2919
17:31 in the which he will j the world in G2919
18:15 *to it*; for I will be no j of such *matters*. G2923
23: 3 for sittest thou to j me after the law, G2919
24:10 of many years a j unto this nation, I do G2923
Ro 2:16 In the day when God shall j the secrets G2919
27 if it fulfil the law, j thee, who by the G2919
3: 6 God forbid: for then how shall God j the G2919
14: 3 which eateth not j him that eateth: for G2919
10 But why dost thou j thy brother? or why G2919
13 Let us not therefore j one another any G2919
13 any more: but j this rather, that no G2919
1Co 4: 3 judgment: yea, I j not mine own self. G350
5 Therefore j nothing before the time, G2919
5:12 For what have I to do to j them also G2919
12 do not ye j them that are within? G2919
6: 2 Do ye not know that the saints shall j G2919
2 ye unworthy to j the smallest matters? G2922
3 Know ye not that we shall j angels? how G2919
4 j who are least esteemed in the church.
5 shall be able to j between his brethren? G1252
10:15 I speak as to wise men; j ye what I say. G2919
11:13 J in yourselves: is it comely that a G2919
31 For if we would j ourselves, we should G1252
14:29 speak two or three, and let the other j. G1252
2Co 5:14 because we thus j, that if one died for G2919
Col 2:16 Let no man therefore j you in meat, or G2919
2Ti 4: 1 Christ, who shall j the quick and the G2919
8 the righteous j, shall give me at that G2923
Heb 10:30 And again, The Lord shall j his people. G2919
12:23 and to God the J of all, and to the G2923
13: 4 and adulterers God will j. G2919
Jas 4:11 the law: but if thou j the law, thou art G2919
11 thou art not a doer of the law, but a j. G2923
5: 9 behold, the j standeth before the door. G2923
1Pt 4: 5 is ready to j the quick and the dead. G2919
Rev 6:10 true, dost thou not j and avenge our G2919
19:11 righteousness he doth j and make war. G2919

JUDGED
Gen 30: 6 And Rachel said, God hath j me, and H1777
Ex 18:26 And they j the people at all seasons: the H8199
26 every small matter they j themselves. H8199
Jdg 3:10 upon him, and he j Israel, and went out H8199
4: 4 of Lapidoth, she j Israel at that time. H8199
10: 2 And he j Israel twenty and three years, H8199
3 and j Israel twenty and two years. H8199
12: 7 And Jephthah j Israel six years. Then H8199
8 And after him Ibzan of Beth-lehem j H8199
9 his sons. And he j Israel seven years. H8199
11 And after him Elon, a Zebulonite, j H8199
11 judged Israel; and he j Israel ten years. H8199
13 the son of Hillel, a Pirathonite, j Israel. H8199
14 ten ass colts: and he j Israel eight years. H8199
15:20 And he j Israel in the days of the H8199
16:31 his father. And he had j Israel twenty years. H8199
1Sa 4:18 heavy. And he had j Israel forty years. H8199
7: 6 j the children of Israel in Mizpeh. H8199
15 And Samuel j Israel all the days of his H8199
16 Mizpeh, and j Israel in all those places. H8199
17 and there he j Israel; and there he H8199
1Ki 3:28 the king had j; and they feared the H8199
2Ki 23:22 of the judges that j Israel, nor in all the H8199

Ps 9:19 prevail: let the heathen be j in thy sight. H8199
37:33 hand, nor condemn him when he is j. H8199
109: 7 When he shall be j, let him be H8199
Jer 22:16 He j the cause of the poor and needy; H1777
Ezk 16:38 shed blood are j; and I will give thee H4941
52 Thou also, which hast j thy sisters, bear H6419
28:23 wounded shall be j in the midst of her H5307
35:11 among them, when I have j thee. H8199
36:19 and according to their doings I j them. H8199
Dan 9:12 our judges that j us, by bringing upon H8199
Mt 7: 1 Judge not, that ye be not j. G2919
2 ye judge, ye shall be j: and with what G2919
Lk 6:37 Judge not, and ye shall not be j: G2919
7:43 he said unto him, Thou hast rightly j. G2919
Jn 16:11 because the prince of this world is j. G2919
Act 16:15 saying, If ye have j me to be faithful to G2919
24: 6 and would have j according to our law. G2919
25: 9 there be j of these things before me? G2919
10 I ought to be j: to the Jews have I done G2919
20 and there be j of these matters. G2919
26: 6 And now I stand and am j for the hope G2919
Ro 2:12 sinned in the law shall be j by the law; G2919
3: 4 and mightest overcome when thou art j. G2919
7 glory; why yet am I also j as a sinner? G2919
1Co 2:15 all things, yet he himself is j of no man. G350
4: 3 that I should be j of you, or of man's G350
5: 3 in spirit, have j already, as though I G2919
6: 2 if the world shall be j by you, are ye G2919
10:29 liberty j of another *man's* conscience? G2919
11:31 judge ourselves, we should not be j. G2919
32 But when we are j, we are chastened of G2919
14:24 he is convinced of all, he is j of all: G350
Heb 11:11 she j him faithful who had promised. G2233
Jas 2:12 they that shall be j by the law of liberty. G2919
1Pt 4: 6 that they might be j according to men G2919
Rev 11:18 that they should be j, and that thou G2919
16: 5 and shalt be, because thou hast j thus. G2919
19: 2 for he hath j the great whore, which G2919
20:12 and the dead were j out of those things G2919
13 j every man according to their works. G2919

JUDGES

Ex 21: 6 bring him unto the j; he shall also bring H430
22 and he shall pay as the j *determine*. H6414
22: 8 be brought unto the j, *to see* whether he H430
9 come before the j; *and* whom the judges H430
9 *and* whom the j shall condemn, he shall H430
Nu 25: 5 And Moses said unto the j of Israel, H8199
Dt 1:16 And I charged your j at that time, H8199
16:18 J and officers shalt thou make thee in H8199
19:17 and the j, which shall be in those days; H8199
18 And the j shall make diligent H8199
21: 2 Then thy elders and thy j shall come H8199
25: 1 judgment, that *the j* may judge them; H8199
32:31 even our enemies themselves *being* j. H6414
Jos 8:33 officers, and their j, stood on this side H8199
23: 2 and for their j, and for their officers, H8199
24: 1 and for their j, and for their officers; H8199
Jdg 2:16 Nevertheless the LORD raised up j, H8199
17 hearken unto their j, but they went a H8199
18 And when the LORD raised them up j, H8199
Ru 1: 1 in the days when the j ruled, that there H8199
1Sa 8: 1 old, that he made his sons j over Israel. H8199
2 Abiah: *they were* j in Beer-sheba. H8199
2Sa 7:11 time that I commanded j *to be* over my H8199
2Ki 23:22 the days of the j that judged Israel, nor H8199
1Ch 17: 6 a word to any of the j of Israel, whom I H8199
10 And since the time that I commanded j H8199
23: 4 and six thousand *were* officers and j: H8199
26:29 business over Israel, for officers and j. H8199
2Ch 1: 2 and to the j, and to every governor H8199
19: 5 And he set j in the land throughout all H8199
6 And said to the j, Take heed what ye do: H8199
Ezr 7:25 magistrates and j, which may judge all H1782
10:14 of every city, and the j thereof, until the H8199
Job 9:24 j thereof; if not, where, *and* who *is* he? H8199
12:17 away spoiled, and maketh the j fools. H8199
31:11 it *is* an iniquity *to be punished by* the j. H6414
Ps 2:10 kings: be instructed, ye j of the earth. H8199
141: 6 When their j are overthrown in stony H8199
148:11 people; princes, and all j of the earth: H8199
Prv 8:16 and nobles, *even* all the j of the earth. H8199
Isa 1:26 And I will restore thy j as at the first, H8199
40:23 he maketh the j of the earth as vanity. H8199
Dan 3: 2 the captains, the j, the treasurers, the H148
3 and captains, the j, the treasurers, the H148
9:12 us, and against our j that judged us, by H8199
Hos 7: 7 have devoured their j; all their kings are H8199
13:10 all thy cities? and thy j of whom thou H8199

Zep 3: 3 roaring lions; her j *are* evening wolves; H8199
Mt 12:27 *them* out? therefore they shall be your j. G2923
Lk 11:19 *them* out? therefore shall they be your j. G2923
Act 13:20 And after that he gave *unto them* j G2923
Jas 2: 4 and are become j of evil thoughts? G2923

JUDGEST

Ps 51: 4 speakest, *and* be clear when thou j. H8199
Jer 11:20 But, O LORD of hosts, that j H8199
Ro 2: 1 thou art that j: for wherein thou judgest G2919
1 for wherein thou j another, thou G2919
1 for thou that j doest the same things. G2919
3 And thinkest thou this, O man, that j G2919
14: 4 Who art thou that j another man's G2919
Jas 4:12 to destroy: who art thou that j another? G2919

JUDGETH

Job 21:22 seeing he j those that are high. H8199
36:31 For by them j he the people; he giveth H1777
Ps 7:11 God j the righteous, and God is angry H8199
58:11 verily he is a God that j in the earth. H8199
82: 1 of the mighty; he j among the gods. H8199
Prv 29:14 The king that faithfully j the poor, his H8199
Jn 5:22 For the Father j no man, but hath G2919
8:50 glory: there is one that seeketh and j. G2919
12:48 hath one that j him: the word that I G2919
1Co 2:15 But he that is spiritual j all things, yet he G350
4: 4 justified: but he that j me is the Lord. G350
5:13 But them that are without God j. G2919
Jas 4:11 evil of *his* brother, and j his brother, G2919
11 evil of the law, and j the law: but if thou G2919
1Pt 1:17 respect of persons j according to every G2919
2:23 *himself* to him that j righteously: G2919
Rev 18: 8 for strong *is* the Lord God who j her. G2919

JUDGING

2Ki 15: 5 over the house, j the people of the land. H8199
2Ch 26:21 king's house, j the people of the land. H8199
Ps 9: 4 cause; thou satest in the throne j right. H8199
Isa 16: 5 of David, j, and seeking judgment, H8199
Mt 19:28 thrones, j the twelve tribes of Israel. G2919
Lk 22:30 on thrones j the twelve tribes of Israel. G2919

JUDGMENT

Gen 18:19 to do justice and j; that the LORD may H4941
Ex 12:12 of Egypt I will execute j: I *am* the LORD. H8201
21:31 to this j shall it be done unto him. H4941
23: 2 a cause to decline after many to wrest *j*:
6 Thou shalt not wrest the j of thy poor H4941
28:15 the breastplate of j with cunning work; H4941
29 in the breastplate of j upon his heart, H4941
30 in the breastplate of j the Urim and the H4941
30 shall bear the j of the children of Israel H4941
Lev 19:15 Ye shall do no unrighteousness in j: H4941
35 Ye shall do no unrighteousness in j, in H4941
Nu 27:11 of j, as the LORD commanded Moses. H4941
21 for him after the j of Urim before the H4941
35:12 he stand before the congregation in j. H4941
29 So these *things* shall be for a statute of j H4941
Dt 1:17 Ye shall not respect persons in j; *but* ye H4941
17 of man; for the j *is* God's: and the cause H4941
10:18 He doth execute the j of the fatherless H4941
16:18 they shall judge the people with just j. H4941
19 Thou shalt not wrest j; thou shalt not H4941
17: 8 hard for thee in j, between blood and H4941
9 they shall shew thee the sentence of j: H4941
11 according to the j which they shall tell H4941
24:17 Thou shalt not pervert the j of the H4941
25: 1 they come unto j, that *the judges* may H4941
27:19 Cursed *be* he that perverteth the j of the H4941
32: 4 for all his ways *are* j: a God of truth and H4941
41 mine hand take hold on j; I will render H4941
Jos 20: 6 congregation for j, *and* until the death H4941
Jdg 4: 5 children of Israel came up to her for j. H4941
5:10 ye that sit in j, and walk by the way. H4055
1Sa 8: 3 lucre, and took bribes, and perverted j. H4941
2Sa 8:15 j and justice unto all his people. H4941
15: 2 to the king for j, then Absalom called H4941
6 to the king for j: so Absalom stole the H4941
1Ki 3:11 for thyself understanding to discern j; H4941
28 And all Israel heard of the j which the H4941
28 the wisdom of God *was* in him, to do j. H4941
7: 7 *even* the porch of j: and *it was* covered H4941
10: 9 made he thee king, to do j and justice. H4941
20:40 So *shall* thy j *be*; thyself hast decided *it*. H4941
2Ki 25: 6 to Riblah; and they gave j upon him. H4941
1Ch 18:14 j and justice among all his people. H4941
2Ch 9: 8 thee king over them, to do j and justice. H4941
19: 6 LORD, who *is* with you in the j. H1697+H4941

2Ch 19: 8 of Israel, for the j of the LORD, and for H4941
20: 9 us, *as* the sword, j, or pestilence, or H8196
22: 8 Jehu was executing j upon the house of H8199
24:24 So they executed j against Joash. H8201
Ezr 7:26 the law of the king, let j be executed H1780
Est 1:13 manner toward all that knew law and j: H1779
Job 8: 3 Doth God pervert j? or doth the H4941
9:19 if of j, who shall set me a time *to plead*? H4941
32 him, *and* we should come together in j. H4941
14: 3 one, and bringest me into j with thee? H4941
19: 7 not heard: I cry aloud, but *there is* no j. H4941
29 sword, that ye may know *there is* a j. H1179
22: 4 of thee? will he enter with thee into j? H4941
27: 2 taken away my j; and the Almighty, H4941
29:14 me: my j *was* as a robe and a diadem. H4941
32: 9 wise: neither do the aged understand j. H4941
34: 4 Let us choose to us j: let us know among H4941
5 and God hath taken away my j. H4941
12 neither will the Almighty pervert j. H4941
23 that he should enter into j with God. H4941
35:14 shalt not see him, *yet* j *is* before him; H1779
36:17 But thou hast fulfilled the j of the H1779
17 wicked: j and justice take hold *on thee*. H1779
37:23 in power, and in j, and in plenty of H4941
40: 8 Wilt thou also disannul my j? wilt thou H4941
Ps 1: 5 not stand in the j, nor sinners in the H4941
7: 6 me *to* the j *that* thou hast commanded. H4941
9: 7 ever: he hath prepared his throne for j. H4941
8 minister j to the people in uprightness. H1777
16 The LORD is known *by* the j *which* he H4941
25: 9 The meek will he guide in j: and the H4941
33: 5 He loveth righteousness and j: the earth H4941
35:23 Stir up thyself, and awake to my j, *even* H4941
37: 6 as the light, and thy j as the noonday. H4941
28 For the LORD loveth j, and forsaketh H4941
30 wisdom, and his tongue talketh of j. H4941
72: 2 with righteousness, and thy poor with j. H4941
76: 8 Thou didst cause j to be heard from H1779
9 When God arose to j, to save all the H4941
89:14 Justice and j *are* the habitation of thy H4941
94:15 But j shall return unto righteousness: H4941
97: 2 and j *are* the habitation of his throne. H4941
99: 4 The king's strength also loveth j; thou H4941
4 executest j and righteousness in Jacob. H4941
101: 1 I will sing of mercy and j: unto thee, O H4941
103: 6 and j for all that are oppressed. H4941
106: 3 Blessed *are* they that keep j, *and* he that H4941
30 j: and *so* the plague was stayed. H6419
111: 7 The works of his hands *are* verity and j; H4941
119:66 Teach me good j and knowledge: for I H2940
84 execute j on them that persecute me? H4941
121 I have done j and justice: leave me not H4941
149 O LORD, quicken me according to thy j. H4941
122: 5 For there are set thrones of j, the H4941
143: 2 And enter not into j with thy servant: H4941
146: 7 Which executeth j for the oppressed: H4941
149: 9 To execute upon them the j written: H4941
Prv 1: 3 of wisdom, justice, and j, and equity; H4941
2: 8 He keepeth the paths of j, and H4941
9 and j, and equity; *yea*, every good path. H4941
8:20 in the midst of the paths of j: H4941
13:23 there is *that is* destroyed for want of j. H4941
16:10 king: his mouth transgresseth not in j. H4941
17:23 of the bosom to pervert the ways of j. H4941
18: 5 wicked, to overthrow the righteous in j. H4941
19:28 An ungodly witness scorneth j: and the H4941
20: 8 A king that sitteth in the throne of j H1779
21: 3 To do justice and j *is* more acceptable H4941
7 them; because they refuse to do j. H4941
15 *It is* joy to the just to do j: but H4941
24:23 not good to have respect of persons in j. H4941
28: 5 Evil men understand not j: but they that H4941
29: 4 The king by j establisheth the land: but H4941
26 *every* man's j *cometh* from the LORD. H4941
31: 5 and pervert the j of any of the afflicted. H1779
Ecc 3:16 sun the place of j, *that* wickedness *was* H4941
5: 8 violent perverting of j and justice in a H4941
8: 5 man's heart discerneth both time and j. H4941
6 there is time and j, therefore the misery H4941
11: 9 these *things* God will bring thee into j. H4941
12:14 For God shall bring every work into j, H4941
Isa 1:17 Learn to do well; seek j, relieve the H4941
21 it was full of j; righteousness lodged H4941
27 Zion shall be redeemed with j, and her H4941
3:14 The LORD will enter into j with the H4941
4: 4 spirit of j, and by the spirit of burning. H4941
5: 7 plant: and he looked for j, but behold H4941
16 shall be exalted in j, and God that is H4941
9: 7 to establish it with j and with justice H4941

J

Isa 10: 2 To turn aside the needy from **j**, and to H1779
16: 3 Take counsel, execute **j**; make thy H6415
5 seeking **j**, and hasting righteousness. H4941
28: 6 And for a spirit of **j** to him that sitteth H4941
6 him that sitteth in **j**, and for strength to H4941
7 they err in vision, they stumble *in* **j**. H6417
17 **J** also will I lay to the line, and H4941
30:18 **j**: blessed *are* all they that wait for him. H4941
32: 1 and princes shall rule in **j**. H4941
16 Then **j** shall dwell in the wilderness, H4941
33: 5 filled Zion with **j** and righteousness. H4941
34: 5 and upon the people of my curse, to **j**. H4941
40:14 him in the path of **j**, and taught him H4941
27 and my **j** is passed over from my God? H4941
41: 1 speak: let us come near together to **j**. H4941
42: 1 he shall bring forth **j** to the Gentiles. H4941
3 he shall bring forth **j** unto truth. H4941
4 till he have set **j** in the earth: and the H4941
49: 4 vain: *yet* surely my **j** *is* with the LORD, H4941
51: 4 my **j** to rest for a light of the people. H4941
53: 8 He was taken from prison and from **j**: H4941
54:17 against thee in **j** thou shalt condemn. H4941
56: 1 Thus saith the LORD, Keep ye **j**, and do H4941
59: 8 and *there is* no **j** in their goings: they H4941
9 Therefore is **j** far from us, neither doth H4941
11 doves: we look for **j**, but *there is* none; H4941
14 And **j** is turned away backward, and H4941
15 it displeased him that *there was* no **j**. H4941
61: 8 For I the LORD love **j**, I hate robbery for H4941
Jer 4: 2 LORD liveth, in truth, in **j**, and in H4941
5: 1 be *any* that executeth **j**, that seeketh the H4941
4 way of the LORD, *nor* the **j** of their God. H4941
5 of the LORD, *and* the **j** of their God: but H4941
7: 5 **j** between a man and his neighbour; H4941
8: 7 my people know not the **j** of the LORD. H4941
9:24 lovingkindness, **j**, and righteousness, H4941
10:24 O LORD, correct me, but with **j**; not in H4941
21:12 the LORD; Execute **j** in the morning, H4941
22: 3 Thus saith the LORD; Execute ye **j** and H4941
15 eat and drink, and do **j** and justice, *and* H4941
23: 5 shall execute **j** and justice in the earth. H4941
33:15 execute **j** and righteousness in the land. H4941
39: 5 of Hamath, where he gave **j** upon him. H4941
48:21 And **j** is come upon the plain country; H4941
47 the LORD. Thus far *is* the **j** of Moab. H4941
49:12 they whose **j** *was* not to drink of the H4941
51: 9 own country: for her **j** reacheth unto H4941
47 that I will do **j** upon the graven images H6485
52 that I will do **j** upon her graven images: H6485
52: 9 of Hamath; where he gave **j** upon him. H4941
Ezk 18: 8 executed true **j** between man and man, H4941
23:10 for they had executed **j** upon her. H8196
24 and I will set **j** before them, and they H4941
34:16 and the strong; I will feed them with **j**. H4941
39:21 shall see my **j** that I have executed, H4941
44:24 And in controversy they shall stand in **j**; H8199
45: 9 spoil, and execute **j** and justice, take H4941
Dan 4:37 and his ways **j**: and those that walk H1780
7:10 **j** was set, and the books were opened. H1780
22 Until the Ancient of days came, and **j** H1780
26 But the **j** shall sit, and they shall take H1780
Hos 2:19 and in **j**, and in lovingkindness, H4941
5: 1 of the king; for **j** *is* toward you, because H4941
11 Ephraim *is* oppressed *and* broken in **j**, H4941
10: 4 a covenant: thus **j** springeth up as H4941
12: 6 and **j**, and wait on thy God continually. H4941
Am 5: 7 Ye who turn **j** to wormwood, and leave H4941
15 and establish **j** in the gate: it may be H4941
24 But let **j** run down as waters, and H4941
6:12 for ye have turned **j** into gall, and the H4941
Mic 3: 1 of Israel; *Is it* not for you to know **j**? H4941
8 of the LORD, and of **j**, and of might, to H4941
9 that abhor **j**, and pervert all equity. H4941
7: 9 my cause, and execute **j** for me: he will H4941
Hab 1: 4 Therefore the law is slacked, and **j** doth H4941
4 therefore wrong **j** proceedeth. H4941
7 They *are* terrible and dreadful: their **j** H4941
12 hast ordained them for **j**; and, O mighty H4941
Zep 2: 3 have wrought his **j**; seek righteousness, H4941
3: 5 doth he bring his **j** to light, he faileth H4941
Zec 7: 9 Execute true **j**, and shew mercy and H4941
8:16 the **j** of truth and peace in your gates: H4941
Mal 2:17 in them; or, Where *is* the God of **j**? H4941
3: 5 And I will come near to you to **j**; and I H4941
Mt 5:21 shall kill shall be in danger of the **j**: *G2920*
22 be in danger of the **j**: and whosoever *G2920*
7: 2 For with what **j** ye judge, ye shall be *G2917*
10:15 in the day of **j**, than for that city. *G2920*
11:22 and Sidon at the day of **j**, than for you. *G2920*
Mt 11:24 of Sodom in the day of **j**, than for thee. *G2920*
12:18 and he shall shew **j** to the Gentiles. *G2920*
20 quench, till he send forth **j** unto victory. *G2920*
36 give account thereof in the day of **j**. *G2920*
41 The men of Nineveh shall rise in **j** with *G2920*
42 south shall rise up in the **j** with this *G2920*
23:23 *matters* of the law, **j**, mercy, and faith: *G2920*
27:19 When he was set down on the **j** seat, his
Mk 6:11 in the day of **j**, than for that city. *G2920*
Lk 10:14 Tyre and Sidon at the **j**, than for you. *G2920*
11:31 shall rise up in the **j** with the men of *G2920*
32 The men of Nineve shall rise up in the **j** *G2920*
42 and pass over **j** and the love of God: *G2920*
Jn 5:22 but hath committed all **j** unto the Son: *G2920*
27 **j** also, because he is the Son of man. *G2920*
30 I judge: and my **j** is just; because I seek *G2920*
7:24 the appearance, but judge righteous **j**. *G2920*
8:16 And yet if I judge, my **j** is true: for I am *G2920*
9:39 And Jesus said, For **j** I am come into *G2917*
12:31 Now is the **j** of this world: now shall the *G2920*
16: 8 of sin, and of righteousness, and of **j**: *G2920*
11 Of **j**, because the prince of this world is *G2920*
18:28 unto the hall of **j**: and it was early; and *G4232*
28 went not into the **j** hall, lest they should *G4232*
33 Then Pilate entered into the **j** hall *G4232*
19: 9 And went again into the **j** hall, and *G4232*
13 sat down in the **j** seat in a place that is
Act 8:33 In his humiliation his **j** was taken *G2920*
18:12 Paul, and brought him to the **j** seat,
16 And he drave them from the **j** seat.
17 beat *him* before the **j** seat. And Gallio
23:35 him to be kept in Herod's **j** hall. *G4232*
24:25 temperance, and **j** to come, Felix *G2917*
25: 6 **j** seat commanded Paul to be brought.
10 Then said Paul, I stand at Caesar's **j**
15 *me*, desiring *to have* **j** against him. *G1349*
17 I sat on the **j** seat, and commanded
Ro 1:32 Who knowing the **j** of God, that they *G1345*
2: 2 But we are sure that the **j** of God is *G2917*
3 that thou shalt escape the **j** of God? *G2917*
5 revelation of the righteous **j** of God; *G1341*
5:16 *so is* the gift: for the **j** *was* by one to *G2917*
18 Therefore as by the offence of one *j came*
14:10 shall all stand before the **j** seat of Christ.
1Co 1:10 in the same mind and in the same **j**. *G1106*
4: 3 man's **j**: yea, I judge not mine own self. *G2250*
7:25 Lord: yet I give my **j**, as one that hath *G1106*
40 she so abide, after my **j**: and I think also *G1106*
2Co 5:10 For we must all appear before the **j** seat
Gal 5:10 you shall bear his **j**, whosoever he be. *G2917*
Php 1: 9 more and more in knowledge and *in* all **j**; *G144*
2Th 1: 5 of the righteous **j** of God, that ye may *G2920*
1Ti 5:24 to **j**; and some *men* they follow after. *G2920*
Heb 6: 2 of the dead, and of eternal **j**. *G2917*
9:27 men once to die, but after this the **j**: *G2920*
10:27 But a certain fearful looking for of **j** *G2920*
Jas 2: 6 you, and draw you before the **j** seats? *G2922*
13 For he shall have **j** without mercy, that *G2920*
13 mercy; and mercy rejoiceth against **j**. *G2920*
1Pt 4:17 For the time *is come* that **j** must begin *G2917*
2Pt 2: 3 of you: whose **j** now of a long time *G2917*
4 of darkness, to be reserved unto **j**; *G2920*
9 unjust unto the day of **j** to be punished: *G2920*
3: 7 day of **j** and perdition of ungodly men. *G2920*
1Jn 4:17 in the day of **j**: because as he is, so *G2920*
Jude 6 darkness unto the **j** of the great day. *G2920*
15 To execute **j** upon all, and to convince *G2920*
Rev 14: 7 him; for the hour of his **j** is come: and *G2920*
17: 1 shew unto thee the **j** of the great whore *G2917*
18:10 city! for in one hour is thy **j** come. *G2920*
20: 4 upon them, and **j** was given unto them: *G2917*

JUDGMENT-HALL See JUDGMENT and HALL.

JUDGMENTS

Ex 6: 6 a stretched out arm, and with great **j**: H8201
7: 4 out of the land of Egypt by great **j**. H8201
21: 1 Now these *are* the **j** which thou shalt H4941
24: 3 LORD, and all the **j**: and all the people H4941
Lev 18: 4 Ye shall do my **j**, and keep mine H4941
5 statutes, and my **j**: which if a man do, H4941
26 statutes and my **j**, and shall not commit H4941
19:37 all my **j**, and do them: I *am* the LORD. H4941
20:22 and all my **j**, and do them: that the H4941
25:18 and keep my **j**, and do them; and ye H4941
26:15 soul abhor my **j**, so that ye will not do H4941
43 they despised my **j**, and because their H4941
46 These *are* the statutes and **j** and laws, H4941
Nu 33: 4 their gods also the LORD executed **j**. H8201
Nu 35:24 revenger of blood according to these **j**: H4941
36:13 and the **j**, which the LORD commanded H4941
Dt 4: 1 and unto the **j**, which I teach you, for H4941
5 you statutes and **j**, even as the LORD H4941
8 hath statutes and **j** *so* righteous as all H4941
14 you statutes and **j**, that ye might do H4941
45 statutes, and the **j**, which Moses spake H4941
5: 1 the statutes and **j** which I speak in your H4941
31 the statutes, and the **j**, which thou shalt H4941
6: 1 the statutes, and the **j**, which the LORD H4941
20 statutes, and the **j**, which the LORD our H4941
7:11 statutes, and the **j**, which I command H4941
12 ye hearken to these **j**, and keep, and do H4941
8:11 and his **j**, and his statutes, which H4941
11: 1 his **j**, and his commandments, alway. H4941
32 and **j** which I set before you this day. H4941
12: 1 These *are* the statutes and **j**, which ye H4941
26:16 do these statutes and **j**: thou shalt H4941
17 and his **j**, and to hearken unto his voice: H4941
30:16 statutes and his **j**, that thou mayest live H4941
33:10 They shall teach Jacob thy **j**, and Israel H4941
21 of the LORD, and his **j** with Israel. H4941
2Sa 22:23 For all his **j** *were* before me: and *as for* H4941
1Ki 2: 3 and his **j**, and his testimonies, H4941
6:12 and execute my **j**, and keep all my H4941
8:58 his **j**, which he commanded our fathers. H4941
9: 4 *and* wilt keep my statutes and my **j**: H4941
11:33 and my **j**, as *did* David his father. H4941
1Ch 16:12 his wonders, and the **j** of his mouth; H4941
14 He *is* the LORD our God; his **j** *are* in all H4941
22:13 fulfil the statutes and **j** which the LORD H4941
28: 7 and my **j**, as at this day. H4941
2Ch 7:17 and shalt observe my statutes and my **j**; H4941
19:10 statutes and **j**, ye shall even warn them H4941
Ezr 7:10 *it*, and to teach in Israel statutes and **j**. H4941
Neh 1: 7 the statutes, nor the **j**, which thou H4941
9:13 gavest them right **j**, and true laws, good H4941
29 sinned against thy **j**, (which if a man H4941
10:29 our Lord, and his **j** and his statutes; H4941
Ps 10: 5 His ways are always grievous; thy **j** *are* H4941
18:22 For all his **j** *were* before me, and I did H4941
19: 9 for ever: the **j** of the LORD *are* true H4941
36: 6 mountains; thy **j** *are* a great deep: O H4941
48:11 of Judah be glad, because of thy **j**. H4941
72: 1 Give the king thy **j**, O God, and thy H4941
89:30 forsake my law, and walk not in my **j**; H4941
97: 8 rejoiced because of thy **j**, O LORD. H4941
105: 5 his wonders, and the **j** of his mouth; H4941
7 He *is* the LORD our God: his **j** *are* in all H4941
119: 7 I shall have learned thy righteous **j**. H4941
13 With my lips have I declared all the **j** of H4941
20 *that it hath* unto thy **j** at all times. H4941
30 I have chosen the way of truth: thy **j** H4941
39 which I fear: for thy **j** *are* good. H4941
43 of my mouth; for I have hoped in thy **j**. H4941
52 I remembered thy **j** of old, O LORD; H4941
62 unto thee because of thy righteous **j**. H4941
75 I know, O LORD, that thy **j** *are* right, H4941
102 I have not departed from thy **j**: for thou H4941
106 *it*, that I will keep thy righteous **j**. H4941
108 my mouth, O LORD, and teach me thy **j**. H4941
120 for fear of thee; and I am afraid of thy **j**. H4941
137 *art* thou, O LORD, and upright *are* thy **j**. H4941
156 O LORD: quicken me according to thy **j**. H4941
160 of thy righteous **j** *endureth* for ever. H4941
164 I praise thee because of thy righteous **j**. H4941
175 shall praise thee; and let thy **j** help me. H4941
147:19 Jacob, his statutes and his **j** unto Israel. H4941
20 and *as for his* **j**, they have not known H4941
Prv 19:29 **J** are prepared for scorners, and stripes H8201
Isa 26: 8 Yea, in the way of thy **j**, O LORD, have H4941
9 early: for when thy **j** *are* in the earth, H4941
Jer 1:16 And I will utter my **j** against them H4941
12: 1 with thee of *thy* **j**: Wherefore doth the H4941
Ezk 5: 6 And she hath changed my **j** into H4941
6 have refused my **j** and my statutes, H4941
7 have kept my **j**, neither have done H4941
7 according to the **j** of the nations that H4941
8 and will execute **j** in the midst of thee H4941
10 and I will execute **j** in thee, and the H8201
15 I shall execute **j** in thee in anger and H8201
11: 9 and will execute **j** among you. H8201
12 executed my **j**, but have done after H4941
14:21 I send my four sore **j** upon Jerusalem, H8201
16:41 with fire, and execute **j** upon thee in the H8201
18: 9 and hath kept my **j**, to deal truly; he *is* H4941
17 hath executed my **j**, hath walked in my H4941
20:11 shewed them my **j**, which *if* a man do, H4941
13 they despised my **j**, which *if* a man do, H4941

Ezk 20:16 Because they despised my j, and walked H4941
18 j, nor defile yourselves with their idols: H4941
19 statutes, and keep my j, and do them; H4941
21 neither kept my j to do them, which *if* H4941
24 Because they had not executed my j, but H4941
25 and j whereby they should not live; H4941
23:24 shall judge thee according to their j. H4941
25:11 And I will execute j upon Moab; and H8201
28:22 j in her, and shall be sanctified in her. H8201
26 I have executed j upon all those that H8201
30:14 fire in Zoan, and will execute j in No. H8201
19 Thus will I execute j in Egypt: and they H8201
36:27 and ye shall keep my j, and do *them*. H4941
37:24 shall also walk in my j, and observe my H4941
44:24 it according to my j: and they shall keep H4941
Dan 9: 5 from thy precepts and from thy j: H4941
Hos 6: 5 thy j *are as* the light *that* goeth forth. H4941
Zep 3:15 The LORD hath taken away thy j, he H4941
Mal 4: 4 for all Israel, *with* the statutes and j. H4941
Ro 11:33 *are* his j, and his ways past finding out! G2917
1Co 6: 4 If then ye have j of things pertaining to G2922
Rev 15: 4 thee; for thy j are made manifest. G1345
16: 7 Almighty, true and righteous *are* thy j. G2920
19: 2 For true and righteous *are* his j: for he G2920

JUDGMENT-SEAT See JUDGMENT and SEAT.

JUDITH
Gen 26:34 he took to wife J the daughter of Beeri H3067

JUICE
Song 8: 2 wine of the j of my pomegranate. H6071

JULIA
Ro 16:15 Salute Philologus, and J, Nereus, and G2456

JULIUS
Act 27: 1 J, a centurion of Augustus' band. G2457
3 at Sidon. And J courteously entreated G2457

JUMPING
Nah 3: 2 pransing horses, and of the j chariots. H7540

JUNIA
Ro 16: 7 Salute Andronicus and J, my kinsmen, G2458

JUNIPER
1Ki 19: 4 and sat down under a j tree: and he H7574
5 And as he lay and slept under a j tree, H7574
Job 30: 4 the bushes, and j roots *for* their meat. H7574
Ps 120: 4 arrows of the mighty, with coals of j. H7574

JUPITER
Act 14:12 And they called Barnabas, J; and Paul, G2203
13 Then the priest of J, which was before G2203
19:35 of the *image* which fell down from J? G1356

JURISDICTION
Lk 23: 7 unto Herod's j, he sent him to Herod, G1849

JUSHABHESED
1Ch 3:20 and Berechiah, and Hasadiah, J, five. H3142

JUST
Gen 6: 9 Noah: Noah was a j man *and* perfect in H6662
Lev 19:36 J balances, just weights, a just ephah, H6664
36 Just balances, j weights, a just ephah, H6664
36 Just balances, just weights, a j ephah, H6664
36 just ephah, and a j hin, shall ye have: I H6664
Dt 16:18 shall judge the people with j judgment. H6664
20 That which is altogether j shalt thou H6664
25:15 *But* thou shalt have a perfect and j H6664
15 a perfect and j measure shalt thou H6664
32: 4 and without iniquity, j and right *is* he. H6662
2Sa 23: 3 men *must be* j, ruling in the fear of God. H6662
Neh 9:33 Howbeit thou *art* j in all that is brought H6662
Job 4:17 Shall mortal man be more j than God? H6663
9: 2 but how should man be j with God? H6663
12: 4 the j upright *man is* laughed to scorn. H6662
27:17 He may prepare *it*, but the j shall put *it* H6662
33:12 Behold, *in* this thou art not j: I will H6663
34:17 wilt thou condemn him that is most j? H6662
Ps 7: 9 but establish the j: for the righteous God H6662
37:12 The wicked plotteth against the j, and H6662
Prv 3:33 but he blesseth the habitation of the j. H6662
4:18 But the path of the j *is* as the shining H6662
9: 9 j *man*, and he will increase in learning. H6662
10: 6 Blessings *are* upon the head of the j: but H6662
7 The memory of the j *is* blessed: but the H6662
Prv 10:20 The tongue of the j *is as* choice silver: H6662
31 The mouth of the j bringeth forth H6662
11: 1 the LORD: but a j weight *is* his delight. H8003
9 knowledge shall the j be delivered. H6662
12:13 lips: but the j shall come out of trouble. H6662
21 There shall no evil happen to the j: but H6662
13:22 wealth of the sinner *is* laid up for the j. H6662
16:11 A j weight and balance *are* the LORD'S: H4941
17:15 condemneth the j, even they both *are* H6662
26 Also to punish the j *is* not good, *nor* to H6662
18:17 own cause *seemeth* j; but his neighbour H6662
20: 7 The j *man* walketh in his integrity: his H6662
21:15 *It is* joy to the j to do judgment: but H6662
24:16 For a j *man* falleth seven times, and H6662
29:10 hate the upright: but the j seek his soul. H3477
27 to the j: and *he that is* upright H6662
Ecc 7:15 vanity: there is a j *man* that perisheth H6662
20 For *there is* not a j man upon earth, H6662
8:14 that there be j *men*, unto whom it H6662
Isa 26: 7 The way of the j *is* uprightness: thou, H6662
7 upright, dost weigh the path of the j. H6662
29:21 turn aside the j for a thing of nought. H6662
45:21 else beside me; a j God and a Saviour; H6662
Lam 4:13 the blood of the j in the midst of her, H6662
Ezk 18: 5 But if a man be j, and do that which is H6662
9 to deal truly; he *is* j, he shall surely live, H6662
45:10 Ye shall have j balances, and a just H6664
10 Ye shall have just balances, and a j H6664
10 and a just ephah, and a j bath. H6664
Hos 14: 9 *are* right, and the j shall walk in them: H6662
Am 5:12 they afflict the j, they take a bribe, and H6662
Hab 2: 4 in him: but the j shall live by his faith. H6662
Zep 3: 5 The j LORD *is* in the midst thereof; he H6662
Zec 9: 9 unto thee: he *is* j, and having salvation; H6662
Mt 1:19 Then Joseph her husband, being a j G1342
5:45 sendeth rain on the j and on the unjust. G1342
13:49 and sever the wicked from among the j, G1342
27:19 to do with that j man: for I have G1342
24 of the blood of this j person: see ye *to it*. G1342
Mk 6:20 that he was a j man and an holy, and G1342
Lk 1:17 to the wisdom of the j; to make ready a G1342
2:25 and the same man *was* j and devout, G1342
14:14 at the resurrection of the j. G1342
15: 7 j persons, which need no repentance. G1342
20:20 feign themselves j men, that they might G1342
23:50 *and he was* a good man, and a j: G1342
Jn 5:30 my judgment is j; because I seek not G1342
Act 3:14 But ye denied the Holy One and the J, G1342
7:52 of the coming of the J One; of whom ye G1342
10:22 the centurion, a j man, and one that G1342
22:14 will, and see that J One, and shouldest G1342
24:15 of the dead, both of the j and unjust. G1342
Ro 1:17 as it is written, The j shall live by faith. G1342
2:13 (For not the hearers of the law *are* j G1342
3: 8 good may come? whose damnation is j. G1738
26 that he might be j, and the justifier of G1342
7:12 commandment holy, and j, and good. G1342
Gal 3:11 *is* evident: for, The j shall live by faith. G1342
Php 4: 8 things *are* j, whatsoever things *are* G1342
Col 4: 1 that which is j and equal; knowing G1342
Tit 1: 8 of good men, sober, j, holy, temperate; G1342
Heb 2: 2 received a j recompence of reward; G1738
10:38 Now the j shall live by faith: but if *any* G1342
12:23 to the spirits of j men made perfect, G1342
Jas 5: 6 Ye have condemned *and* killed the j; G1342
1Pt 3:18 for sins, the j for the unjust, that he G1342
2Pt 2: 7 And delivered j Lot, vexed with the G1342
1Jn 1: 9 he is faithful and j to forgive us *our* G1342
Rev 15: 3 God Almighty; j and true *are* thy ways, G1342

JUSTICE
Gen 18:19 of the LORD, to do j and judgment; H6666
Dt 33:21 he executed the j of the LORD, and his H6666
2Sa 8:15 judgment and j unto all his people. H6666
15: 4 come unto me, and I would do him j! H6663
1Ki 10: 9 he thee king, to do judgment and j. H6666
1Ch 18:14 judgment and j among all his people. H6666
2Ch 9: 8 king over them, to do judgment and j. H6666
Job 8: 3 or doth the Almighty pervert j? H6664
36:17 judgment and j take hold *on thee*. H4941
37:23 and in plenty of j: he will not afflict. H6666
Ps 82: 3 Defend the poor and fatherless: do j to H6663
89:14 J and judgment *are* the habitation of H6664
119:121 I have done judgment and j: leave me H6664
Prv 1: 3 To receive the instruction of wisdom, j, H6664
8:15 By me kings reign, and princes decree j. H6664
21: 3 To do j and judgment *is* more H6666
Ecc 5: 8 of judgment and j in a province, H6664
Isa 9: 7 and with j from henceforth even H6666
Isa 56: 1 judgment, and do j: for my salvation *is* H6666
58: 2 the ordinances of j; they take delight in H6664
59: 4 None calleth for j, nor *any* pleadeth for H6664
9 us, neither doth j overtake us: we wait H6666
14 backward, and j standeth afar off: for H6666
Jer 22:15 and j, *and* then *it was* well with him? H6666
23: 5 execute judgment and j in the earth. H6666
31:23 of j, *and* mountain of holiness. H6664
50: 7 the habitation of j, even the LORD, the H6664
Ezk 45: 9 execute judgment and j, take away your H6666

JUSTIFICATION
Ro 4:25 offences, and was raised again for our j. G1347
5:16 the free gift *is* of many offences unto j. G1345
18 *gift came* upon all men unto j of life. G1347

JUSTIFIED
Job 11: 2 and should a man full of talk be j? H6663
13:18 *my* cause; I know that I shall be j. H6663
25: 4 How then can man be j with God? or H6663
32: 2 because he j himself rather than God. H6663
Ps 51: 4 thou mightest be j when thou speakest, H6663
143: 2 for in thy sight shall no man living be j. H6663
Isa 43: 9 j: or let them hear, and say, *It is* truth. H6663
26 declare thou, that thou mayest be j. H6663
45:25 the seed of Israel be j, and shall glory. H6663
Jer 3:11 j herself more than treacherous Judah. H6663
Ezk 16:51 they, and hast j thy sisters in all thine H6663
52 shame, in that thou hast j thy sisters. H6663
Mt 11:19 But wisdom is j of her children. G1344
12:37 For by thy words thou shalt be j, and by G1344
Lk 7:29 *him*, and the publicans, j God, being G1344
35 But wisdom is j of all her children. G1344
18:14 down to his house j *rather* than the G1344
Act 13:39 And by him all that believe are j from G1344
39 ye could not be j by the law of Moses. G1344
Ro 2:13 God, but the doers of the law shall be j. G1344
3: 4 thou mightest be j in thy sayings, and G1344
20 shall no flesh be j in his sight: for by the G1344
24 Being j freely by his grace through the G1344
28 Therefore we conclude that a man is j G1344
4: 2 For if Abraham were j by works, he G1344
5: 1 Therefore being j by faith, we have G1344
9 Much more then, being now j by his G1344
8:30 them he also j: and whom he justified, G1344
30 and whom he j, them he also glorified. G1344
1Co 4: 4 j: but he that judgeth me is the Lord. G1344
6:11 but ye are j in the name of the Lord G1344
Gal 2:16 Knowing that a man is not j by the G1344
16 that we might be j by the faith of G1344
16 the works of the law shall no flesh be j. G1344
17 But if, while we seek to be j by Christ, G1344
3:11 But that no man is j by the law in the G1344
24 unto Christ, that we might be j by faith. G1344
5: 4 j by the law; ye are fallen from grace. G1344
1Ti 3:16 in the flesh, j in the Spirit, seen of G1344
Tit 3: 7 That being j by his grace, we should be G1344
Jas 2:21 Was not Abraham our father j by G1344
24 works a man is j, and not by faith only. G1344
25 Rahab the harlot j by works, when she G1344

JUSTIFIER
Ro 3:26 the j of him which believeth in Jesus. G1344

JUSTIFIETH
Prv 17:15 He that j the wicked, and he that H6663
Isa 50: 8 *He is* near that j me; who will contend H6663
Ro 4: 5 on him that j the ungodly, his faith G1344
8:33 charge of God's elect? *It is* God that j. G1344

JUSTIFY
Ex 23: 7 thou not: for I will not j the wicked. H6663
Dt 25: 1 then they shall j the righteous, and H6663
Job 9:20 If I j myself, mine own mouth shall H6663
27: 5 God forbid that I should j you: till I die H6663
33:32 answer me: speak, for I desire to j thee. H6663
Isa 5:23 Which j the wicked for reward, and H6663
53:11 righteous servant j many; for he shall H6663
Lk 10:29 But he, willing to j himself, said unto G1344
16:15 Ye are they which j yourselves before G1344
Ro 3:30 Seeing *it is* one God, which shall j the G1344
Gal 3: 8 that God would j the heathen through G1344

JUSTIFYING
1Ki 8:32 his head; and j the righteous, to give H6663
2Ch 6:23 own head; and by j the righteous, by H6663

JUSTLE
Nah 2: 4 streets, they shall j one against another H8264

JUSTLY
Mic 6: 8 of thee, but to do j, and to love mercy, H4941
Lk 23:41 And we indeed j; for we receive the due G1346
1Th 2:10 how holily and j and unblameably we G1346

JUSTUS
Act 1:23 who was surnamed J, and Matthias. G2459
18: 7 house, named J, *one* that worshipped G2459
Col 4:11 And Jesus, which is called J, who are of G2459

JUTTAH
Jos 15:55 Maon, Carmel, and Ziph, and J, H3194
21:16 And Ain with her suburbs, and J with H3194

K

KABZEEL
Jos 15:21 were K, and Eder, and Jagur, H6909
2Sa 23:20 of a valiant man, of K, who had done H6909
1Ch 11:22 of a valiant man of K, who had done H6909

KADESH
Gen 14: 7 which *is* K, and smote all the country H6946
16:14 behold, *it is* between K and Bered. H6946
20: 1 K and Shur, and sojourned in Gerar. H6946
Nu 13:26 of Paran, to K; and brought back word H6946
20: 1 the people abode in K; and Miriam died H6946
14 And Moses sent messengers from K H6946
16 K, a city in the uttermost of thy border: H6946
22 from K, and came unto mount Hor. H6946
27:14 Meribah in K in the wilderness of Zin. H6946
33:36 in the wilderness of Zin, which *is* K. H6946
37 And they removed from K, and pitched H6946
Dt 1:46 So ye abode in K many days, according H6946
Jdg 11:16 unto the Red sea, and came to K; H6946
17 not *consent*: and Israel abode in K. H6946
Ps 29: 8 the LORD shaketh the wilderness of K. H6946
Ezk 47:19 the waters of strife *in* K, the river to the H6946
48:28 K, *and* to the river toward the great sea. H6946

KADESH-BARNEA
Nu 32: 8 I sent them from K to see the land. H6947
34: 4 from the south to K, and shall go on to H6947
Dt 1: 2 Horeb by the way of mount Seir unto K.) H6947
19 God commanded us; and we came to K. H6947
2:14 we came from K, until we were come H6947
9:23 sent you from K, saying, Go up and H6947
Jos 10:41 And Joshua smote them from K even H6947
14: 6 of God concerning me and thee in K. H6947
7 sent me from K to espy out the land; H6947
15: 3 south side unto K, and passed along to H6947

KADMIEL
Ezr 2:40 of Jeshua and K, of the children of H6934
3: 9 and his brethren, K and his sons, the H6934
Neh 7:43 of Jeshua, of K, *and* of the children H6934
9: 4 Jeshua, and Bani, K, Shebaniah, Bunni, H6934
5 Then the Levites, Jeshua, and K, Bani, H6934
10: 9 Binnui of the sons of Henadad, K; H6934
12: 8 Jeshua, Binnui, K, Sherebiah, Judah, H6934
24 Jeshua the son of K, with their brethren H6934

KADMONITES
Gen 15:19 Kenites, and the Kenizzites, and the K, H6935

KALLAI
Neh 12:20 Of Sallai, K; of Amok, Eber; H7040

KANAH
Jos 16: 8 unto the river K; and the goings out H7071
17: 9 unto the river K, southward of the river: H7071
19:28 and K, *even* unto great Zidon; H7071

KAREAH
Jer 40: 8 the sons of K, and Seraiah the son H7143
13 Moreover Johanan the son of K, and all H7143
15 Then Johanan the son of K spake to H7143
16 the son of K, Thou shalt not do this H7143
41:11 But when Johanan the son of K, and all H7143
13 the son of K, and all the captains H7143
14 and went unto Johanan the son of K. H7143
16 Then took Johanan the son of K, and all H7143
42: 1 the son of K, and Jezaniah the son H7143
8 Then called he Johanan the son of K, H7143
43: 2 the son of K, and all the proud men, H7143
4 So Johanan the son of K, and all the H7143
5 But Johanan the son of K, and all the H7143

KARKAA
Jos 15: 3 up to Adar, and fetched a compass to K: H7173

KARKOR
Jdg 8:10 Now Zebah and Zalmunna *were* in K, H7174

KARNAIM
Gen 14: 5 in Ashteroth K, and the Zuzims in Ham, H6255

KARTAH
Jos 21:34 her suburbs, and K with her suburbs, H7177

KARTAN
Jos 21:32 and K with her suburbs; three cities. H7178

KATTATH
Jos 19:15 And K, and Nahallal, and Shimron, and H7005

KEDAR
Gen 25:13 and K, and Adbeel, and Mibsam, H6938
1Ch 1:29 then K, and Adbeel, and Mibsam, H6938
Ps 120: 5 in Mesech, *that* I dwell in the tents of K! H6938
Song 1: 5 tents of K, as the curtains of Solomon. H6938
Isa 21:16 and all the glory of K shall fail: H6938
17 men of the children of K, shall be H6938
42:11 the villages *that* K doth inhabit: let the H6938
60: 7 All the flocks of K shall be gathered H6938
Jer 2:10 see; and send unto K, and consider H6938
49:28 Concerning K, and concerning the H6938
28 up to K, and spoil the men of the east. H6938
Ezk 27:21 Arabia, and all the princes of K, they H6938

KEDEMAH
Gen 25:15 and Tema, Jetur, Naphish, and K: H6929
1Ch 1:31 Jetur, Naphish, and K. These are the H6929

KEDEMOTH
Dt 2:26 the wilderness of K unto Sihon king of H6932
Jos 13:18 And Jahazah, and K, and Mephaath, H6932
21:37 K with her suburbs, and Mephaath H6932
1Ch 6:79 K also with her suburbs, and H6932

KEDESH
Jos 12:22 The king of K, one; the king of Jokneam H6943
15:23 And K, and Hazor, and Ithnan, H6943
19:37 And K, and Edrei, and En-hazor, H6943
20: 7 And they appointed K in Galilee in H6943
21:32 And out of the tribe of Naphtali, K in H6943
Jdg 4: 9 arose, and went with Barak to K. H6943
10 and Naphtali to K; and he went up with H6943
11 the plain of Zaanaim, which *is* by K. H6943
2Ki 15:29 and Janoah, and K, and Hazor, and H6943
1Ch 6:72 And out of the tribe of Issachar; K with H6943
76 And out of the tribe of Naphtali; K in H6943

KEDESH-NAPHTALI
Jdg 4: 6 out of K, and said unto him, H6943+H5321

KEEP
Gen 2:15 garden of Eden to dress it and to k it. H8104
3:24 way, to k the way of the tree of life. H8104
6:19 into the ark, to k *them* alive with thee;
20 shall come unto thee, to k *them* alive.
7: 3 and the female; to k seed alive upon H2421
17: 9 Thou shalt k my covenant therefore, H8104
10 This *is* my covenant, which ye shall k, H8104
18:19 and they shall k the way of the LORD, H8104
28:15 And, behold, I *am* with thee, and will k H8104
20 with me, and will k me in this way that H8104
30:31 me, I will again feed *and* k thy flock: H8104
33: 9 brother; k that thou hast unto thyself. H1961
41:35 and let them k food in the cities. H8104
Ex 6: 5 the Egyptians k in bondage; and I have
12: 6 And ye shall k it up until the fourteenth H4931
14 and ye shall k it a feast to the LORD H2287
14 k it a feast by an ordinance for ever. H2287
25 promised, that ye shall k this service. H8104
47 All the congregation of Israel shall k it. H6213
48 with thee, and will k the passover to H6213
48 come near and k it; and he shall be as H6213
Ex 13: 5 thou shalt k this service in this month. H5647
10 Thou shalt therefore k this ordinance H8104
15:26 and k all his statutes, I will H8104
16:28 to k my commandments and my laws? H8104
19: 5 voice indeed, and k my covenant, then H8104
20: 6 love me, and k my commandments. H8104
8 Remember the sabbath day, to k it holy.
22: 7 money or stuff to k, and it be stolen out H8104
10 or any beast, to k; and it die, or be hurt, H8104
23: 7 K thee far from a false matter; and the H7368
14 Three times thou shalt k a feast unto H2287
15 Thou shalt k the feast of unleavened H8104
20 before thee, to k thee in the way, and H8104
31:13 my sabbaths ye shall k: for it *is* a sign H8104
14 Ye shall k the sabbath therefore; for it H8104
16 Wherefore the children of Israel shall k H8104
34:18 bread shalt thou k. Seven days thou H8104
Lev 6: 2 delivered him to k, or in fellowship, or H6485
4 to k, or the lost thing which he found, H6485
8:35 seven days, and k the charge of the H8104
18: 4 Ye shall do my judgments, and k mine H8104
5 Ye shall therefore k my statutes, and H8104
26 Ye shall therefore k my statutes and H8104
30 Therefore shall ye k mine ordinance, H8104
19: 3 his father, and k my sabbaths: I *am* H8104
19 Ye shall k my statutes. Thou shalt not H8104
30 Ye shall k my sabbaths, and reverence H8104
20: 8 And ye shall k my statutes, and do H8104
22 Ye shall therefore k all my statutes, and H8104
22: 9 They shall therefore k mine ordinance, H8104
31 Therefore shall ye k my H8104
23:39 of the land, ye shall k a feast unto the H2287
41 And ye shall k it a feast unto the LORD H2287
25: 2 the land k a sabbath unto the LORD. H7673
18 my statutes, and k my judgments, and H8104
26: 2 Ye shall k my sabbaths, and reverence H8104
3 If ye walk in my statutes, and k my H8104
Nu 1:53 and the Levites shall k the charge of the H8104
3: 7 And they shall k his charge, and the H8104
8 And they shall k all the instruments of H8104
32 that k the charge of the sanctuary. H8104
6:24 The LORD bless thee, and k thee: H8104
8:26 congregation, to k the charge, and shall H8104
9: 2 Let the children of Israel also k the H6213
3 at even, ye shall k it in his appointed H6213
3 all the ceremonies thereof, shall ye k it. H6213
4 Israel, that they should k the passover. H6213
6 they could not k the passover on that H6213
10 he shall k the passover unto the LORD. H6213
11 at even they shall k it, *and* eat it with H6213
12 of the passover they shall k it. H6213
13 and forbeareth to k the passover, even H6213
14 you, and will k the passover unto the H6213
18: 3 And they shall k thy charge, and the H8104
4 unto thee, and k the charge of the H8104
5 And ye shall k the charge of the H8104
7 with thee shall k your priest's office for H8104
29:12 k a feast unto the LORD seven days: H2287
31:18 by lying with him, k alive for yourselves.
30 the Levites, which k the charge of the H8104
36: 7 children of Israel shall k himself to the H1692
9 shall k himself to his own inheritance. H1692
Dt 4: 2 it, that ye may k the commandments H8104
6 K therefore and do *them;* for this *is* H8104
9 Only take heed to thyself, and k thy H8104
40 Thou shalt k therefore his statutes, and H8104
5: 1 ye may learn them, and k, and do them. H8104
10 love me and k my commandments. H8104
12 K the sabbath day to sanctify it, as the H8104
15 commanded thee to k the sabbath day. H6213
29 fear me, and k all my commandments H8104
6: 2 LORD thy God, to k all his statutes and H8104
17 Ye shall diligently k the H8104
7: 8 because he would k the oath which he H8104
9 them that love him and k his H8104
11 Thou shalt therefore k the H8104
12 judgments, and k, and do them, that H8104

Dt 7:12 thy God shall **k** unto thee the covenant H8104
8: 2 wouldest **k** his commandments, or no. H8104
6 Therefore thou shalt **k** the H8104
10:13 To **k** the commandments of the LORD, H8104
11: 1 thy God, and **k** his charge, and his H8104
8 Therefore shall ye **k** all the H8104
22 For if ye shall diligently **k** all these H8104
13: 4 God, and fear him, and **k** his H8104
18 the LORD thy God, to **k** all his H8104
16: 1 Observe the month of Abib, and **k** the H6213
10 And thou shalt **k** the feast of weeks H6213
15 Seven days shalt thou **k** a solemn feast H2287
17:19 LORD his God, to **k** all the words of this H8104
19: 9 If thou shalt **k** all these H8104
23: 9 then **k** thee from every wicked thing. H8104
23 thy lips thou shalt **k** and perform; *even* H8104
26:16 shalt therefore **k** and do them with all H8104
17 his ways, and to **k** his statutes, and his H8104
18 shouldest **k** all his commandments; H8104
27: 1 the people, saying, **K** all the H8104
28: 9 unto thee, if thou shalt **k** the H8104
45 the LORD thy God, to **k** his H8104
29: 9 **K** therefore the words of this covenant, H8104
30:10 the LORD thy God, to **k** his H8104
16 his ways, and to **k** his commandments H8104
Jos 6:18 And ye, in any wise **k** *yourselves* from H8104
10:18 cave, and set men by it for to **k** them: H8104
22: 5 his ways, and to **k** his commandments, H8104
23: 6 Be ye therefore very courageous to **k** H8104
Jdg 2:22 whether they will **k** the way of the H8104
22 therein, as their fathers did **k** *it*, or not. H8104
3:19 O king: who said, **K** silence. And all H2013
Ru 2:21 me also, Thou shalt **k** fast by my young
1Sa 2: 9 He will **k** the feet of his saints, and the H8104
7: 1 his son to **k** the ark of the LORD. H8104
2Sa 8: 2 with one full line to **k** alive. And *so* the
15:16 *which were* concubines, to **k** the house. H8104
16:21 he hath left to **k** the house; and all H8104
18:18 said, I have no son to **k** my name in
20: 3 he had left to **k** the house, and put H8104
1Ki 2: 3 And **k** the charge of the LORD thy God, H8104
3 in his ways, to **k** his statutes, and his H8104
3:14 And if thou wilt walk in my ways, to **k** H8104
6:12 my judgments, and **k** all my H8104
8:25 Therefore now, LORD God of Israel, **k** H8104
58 his ways, and to **k** his commandments, H8104
61 to **k** his commandments, as at this day. H8104
9: 4 wilt **k** my statutes and my judgments: H8104
6 and will not **k** my commandments H8104
11:33 mine eyes, and *to* **k** my statutes and my
38 in my sight, to **k** my statutes and my H8104
20:39 me, and said, **K** this man: if by any H8104
2Ki 11: 6 the guard: so shall ye **k** the watch of the H8104
7 even they shall **k** the watch of the house H8104
17:13 evil ways, and **k** my commandments H8104
23: 3 after the LORD, and to **k** his H8104
21 people, saying, **K** the passover unto the H6213
1Ch 4:10 thou wouldest **k** *me* from evil, that it H6213
12:33 **k** rank: *they were* not of double heart. H5737
38 All these men of war, that could **k** rank, H5737
22:12 mayest **k** the law of the LORD thy God. H8104
23:32 And that they should **k** the charge of H8104
28: 8 of our God, **k** and seek for all the H8104
29:18 Israel, our fathers, **k** this for ever in the H8104
19 son a perfect heart, to **k** thy H8104
2Ch 6:16 Now therefore, O LORD God of Israel, **k** H8104
13:11 evening: for we **k** the charge of the H8104
22: 9 had no power to **k** still the kingdom. H6113
23: 6 people shall **k** the watch of the LORD. H8104
28:10 And now ye purpose to **k** under the H3533
30: 1 at Jerusalem, to **k** the passover unto H6213
2 to **k** the passover in the second month. H6213
3 For they could not **k** it at that time, H6213
5 should come to **k** the passover unto the H6213
13 Jerusalem much people to **k** the feast of H6213
23 took counsel to **k** other seven days: and H6213
34:31 after the LORD, and to **k** his H8104
35:16 the same day, to **k** the passover, and to H6213
18 the kings of Israel **k** such a passover as H6213
Ezr 8:29 Watch ye, and **k** *them*, until ye weigh H8104
Neh 1: 9 But *if* ye turn unto me, and **k** my H8104
12:27 to Jerusalem, to **k** the dedication with H6213
13:22 they should come *and* **k** the gates, to H8104
Est 3: 8 all people; neither **k** they the king's H6213
9:21 that they should **k** the fourteenth day H6213
27 fail, that they would **k** these two days H6213
Job 14:13 that thou wouldest **k** me secret, until thy
20:13 it not; but **k** it still within his mouth: H4513
Ps 12: 7 Thou shalt **k** them, O LORD, thou shalt H8104
Ps 17: 8 **K** me as the apple of the eye, hide me H8104
19:13 **K** back thy servant also from H2820
22:29 him: and none can **k** alive his own soul.
25:10 as **k** his covenant and his testimonies. H5341
20 O **k** my soul, and deliver me: let me not H8104
31:20 of man: thou shalt **k** them secretly in a
33:19 death, and to **k** them alive in famine.
34:13 **K** thy tongue from evil, and thy lips H5341
35:22 *This* thou hast seen, O LORD: **k** not
37:34 Wait on the LORD, and **k** his way, and H8104
39: 1 my tongue: I will **k** my mouth with a H8104
41: 2 The LORD will preserve him, and **k** him
50: 3 Our God shall come, and shall not **k**
78: 7 of God, but **k** his commandments: H5341
83: 1 **K** not thou silence, O God: hold not thy
89:28 My mercy will I **k** for him for evermore, H8104
31 If they break my statutes, and **k** not my H8104
91:11 over thee, to **k** thee in all thy ways. H8104
103: 9 neither will he **k** *his anger* for ever. H5201
18 To such as **k** his covenant, and to those H8104
105:45 and **k** his laws. Praise ye the LORD. H5341
106: 3 Blessed *are* they that **k** judgment, *and* H8104
113: 9 He maketh the barren woman to **k** H3427
119: 2 Blessed *are* they that **k** his testimonies, H5341
4 Thou hast commanded *us* to **k** thy H8104
5 O that my ways were directed to **k** thy H8104
8 I will **k** thy statutes: O forsake me not H8104
17 *that* I may live, and **k** thy word. H8104
33 statutes; and I shall **k** it *unto* the end. H5341
34 Give me understanding, and I shall **k** H5341
44 So shall I **k** thy law continually for ever H8104
57 I have said that I would **k** thy words. H8104
60 I made haste, and delayed not to **k** thy H8104
63 thee, and of them that **k** thy precepts. H8104
69 **k** thy precepts with *my* whole heart. H5341
88 so shall I **k** the testimony of thy mouth. H8104
100 the ancients, because I **k** thy precepts. H5341
101 every evil way, that I might **k** thy word. H8104
106 that I will **k** thy righteous judgments. H8104
115 I will **k** the commandments of my God. H5341
129 therefore doth my soul **k** them. H5341
134 of man: so will I **k** thy precepts. H8104
136 mine eyes, because they **k** not thy law. H8104
145 hear me, O LORD: I will **k** thy statutes. H5341
146 I cried unto thee; save me, and I shall **k** H8104
127: 1 it: except the LORD **k** the city, the H8104
132:12 If thy children will **k** my covenant and H8104
140: 4 **K** me, O LORD, from the hands of the H8104
141: 3 my mouth; **k** the door of my lips. H5341
9 **K** me from the snares *which* they have H8104
Prv 2:11 thee, understanding shall **k** thee: H5341
20 *men*, and **k** the paths of the righteous. H8104
3: 1 let thine heart **k** my commandments: H5341
21 eyes: **k** sound wisdom and discretion: H5341
26 and shall **k** thy foot from being taken. H8104
4: 4 words: **k** my commandments, and live. H8104
6 thee: love her, and she shall **k** thee. H5341
13 let *her* not go: **k** her; for she *is* thy life. H5341
21 Let them not depart from thine eyes; **k** H8104
23 **K** thy heart with all diligence; for out of H5341
5: 2 and *that* thy lips may **k** knowledge. H5341
6:20 My son, **k** thy father's commandment, H5341
22 sleepest, it shall **k** thee; and *when* thou H8104
24 To **k** thee from the evil woman, from H8104
7: 1 My son, **k** my words, and lay up my H8104
2 **K** my commandments, and live; and H8104
5 That they may **k** thee from the strange H8104
8:32 for blessed *are they that* **k** my ways. H8104
22: 5 doth **k** his soul shall be far from them. H8104
18 For *it is* a pleasant thing if thou **k** them H8104
28: 4 such as **k** the law contend with them. H8104
Ecc 3: 6 a time to **k**, and a time to cast away; H8104
7 a time to **k** silence, and a time to speak;
5: 1 **K** thy foot when thou goest to the house H8104
8: 2 I *counsel thee* to **k** the king's H8104
12:13 Fear God, and **k** his commandments: H8104
Song 8:12 that **k** the fruit thereof two hundred. H5201
Isa 26: 3 Thou wilt **k** *him* in perfect peace, H5341
27: 3 I the LORD do **k** it; I will water it every H5341
3 lest *any* hurt it, I will **k** it night and day. H5341
41: 1 **K** silence before me, O islands; and let
42: 6 hand, and will **k** thee, and give thee H5341
43: 6 and to the south, **K** not back: bring my H3607
56: 1 Thus saith the LORD, **K** ye judgment, H8104
4 the eunuchs that **k** my sabbaths, and H8104
62: 6 mention of the LORD, **k** not silence,
65: 6 before me: I will not **k** silence, but will
Jer 3: 5 for ever? will he **k** *it* to the end? Behold, H8104
12 LORD, *and* I will not **k** *anger* for ever. H5201
Jer 31:10 **k** him, as a shepherd *doth* his flock. H8104
42: 4 you; I will **k** nothing back from you. H4513
Lam 2:10 the ground, *and* **k** silence: they have cast
Ezk 11:20 in my statutes, and **k** mine ordinances, H8104
18:21 committed, and **k** all my statutes, and H8104
20:19 and **k** my judgments, and do them; H8104
36:27 ye shall **k** my judgments, and do *them*. H8104
43:11 sight, that they may **k** the whole form H8104
44:16 unto me, and they shall **k** my charge. H8104
24 and they shall **k** my laws and my H8104
Dan 9: 4 to them that **k** his commandments; H8104
Hos 12: 6 Therefore turn thou to thy God: **k** H8104
Am 5:13 Therefore the prudent shall **k** silence in
Mic 7: 5 in a guide: **k** the doors of thy mouth H8104
Nah 1:15 peace! O Judah, **k** thy solemn feasts, H2287
2: 1 up before thy face: **k** the munition, H5341
Hab 2:20 let all the earth **k** silence before him.
Zec 3: 7 and if thou wilt **k** my charge, then thou H8104
7 and shalt also **k** my courts, and I will H8104
13: 5 taught me to **k** cattle from my youth. H7069
14:16 hosts, and to **k** the feast of tabernacles. H2287
18 not up to **k** the feast of tabernacles. H2287
19 not up to **k** the feast of tabernacles. H2287
Mal 2: 7 For the priest's lips should **k** H8104
Mt 19:17 enter into life, **k** the commandments. *G5083*
26:18 is at hand; I will **k** the passover at thy *G4160*
Mk 7: 9 God, that ye may **k** your own tradition. *G5083*
Lk 4:10 his angels charge over thee, to **k** thee: *G1314*
8:15 **k** *it*, and bring forth fruit with patience. *G2722*
11:28 that hear the word of God, and **k** it. *G5442*
19:43 thee round, and **k** thee in on every side, *G4912*
Jn 8:51 **k** my saying, he shall never see death. *G5083*
52 sayest, If a man **k** my saying, he shall *G5083*
55 you: but I know him, and **k** his saying. *G5083*
12:25 in this world shall **k** it unto life eternal. *G5442*
14:15 If ye love me, **k** my commandments. *G5083*
23 love me, he will **k** my words: and my *G5083*
15:10 If ye **k** my commandments, ye shall *G5083*
20 kept my saying, they will **k** yours also. *G5083*
17:11 thee. Holy Father, **k** through thine own *G5083*
15 thou shouldest **k** them from the evil. *G5083*
Act 5: 3 to **k** back *part* of the price of the land? *G3557*
10:28 that is a Jew to **k** company, or come *G2853*
12: 4 of soldiers to **k** him; intending after *G5442*
15: 5 command *them* to **k** the law of Moses. *G5083*
24 circumcised, and **k** the law: to whom *G5083*
29 from which if ye **k** yourselves, ye shall *G1301*
16: 4 the decrees for to **k**, that were ordained *G5442*
23 charging the jailor to **k** them safely: *G5083*
18:21 I must by all means **k** this feast that *G4160*
21:25 only that they **k** themselves from *things* *G5442*
24:23 And he commanded a centurion to **k** *G5083*
Ro 2:25 profiteth, if thou **k** the law: but if thou *G4238*
26 Therefore if the uncircumcision **k** the *G5442*
1Co 5: 8 Therefore let us **k** the feast, not with *G1858*
11 unto you not to **k** company, if any man *G4874*
7:37 that he will **k** his virgin, doeth well. *G5083*
9:27 But I **k** under my body, and bring *it* *G5299*
11: 2 in all things, and **k** the ordinances, as I *G2722*
14:28 But if there be no interpreter, let him **k** *G4601*
34 Let your women **k** silence in the *G4601*
15: 2 By which also ye are saved, if ye **k** in *G2722*
2Co 11: 9 unto you, and *so* will I **k** *myself*. *G5083*
Gal 6:13 are circumcised **k** the law; but desire to *G5442*
Eph 4: 3 Endeavouring to **k** the unity of the *G5083*
Php 4: 7 shall **k** your hearts and minds *G5432*
2Th 3: 3 shall stablish you, and **k** *you* from evil. *G5442*
1Ti 5:22 of other men's sins: **k** thyself pure. *G5083*
6:14 That thou **k** *this* commandment *G5083*
20 O Timothy, **k** that which is committed *G5442*
2Ti 1:12 that he is able to **k** that which I have *G5442*
14 unto thee **k** by the Holy Ghost which *G5442*
Jas 1:27 to **k** himself unspotted from the world. *G5083*
2:10 For whosoever shall **k** the whole law, *G5083*
1Jn 2: 3 know him, if we **k** his commandments. *G5083*
3:22 him, because we **k** his commandments, *G5083*
5: 2 love God, and **k** his commandments. *G5083*
3 For this is the love of God, that we **k** his *G5083*
21 Little children, **k** yourselves from idols. *G5442*
Jude 21 **K** yourselves in the love of God, looking *G5083*
24 Now unto him that is able to **k** you *G5442*
Rev 1: 3 prophecy, and **k** those things which *G5083*
3:10 I also will **k** thee from the hour *G5083*
12:17 remnant of her seed, which **k** the *G5083*
14:12 saints: here *are* they that **k** the *G5083*
22: 9 and of them which **k** the sayings of this *G5083*

KEEPER

Gen 4: 2 And Abel was a **k** of sheep, but Cain H7462

K

Gen 4: 9 said, I know not: *Am* I my brother's **k**? H8104
39:21 in the sight of the **k** of the prison. H8269
22 And the **k** of the prison committed to H8269
23 The **k** of the prison looked not to any H8269
1Sa 17:20 the sheep with a **k**, and took, and went, H8104
22 in the hand of the **k** of the carriage, and H8104
28: 2 I make thee **k** of mine head for ever. H8104
2Ki 22:14 the son of Harhas, **k** of the wardrobe; H8104
2Ch 34:22 the son of Hasrah, **k** of the wardrobe; H8104
Neh 2: 8 And a letter unto Asaph the **k** of the H8104
3:29 of Shechaniah, the **k** of the east gate. H8104
Est 2: 3 chamberlain, **k** of the women; and H8104
8 the custody of Hegai, **k** of the women. H8104
15 chamberlain, the **k** of the women, H8104
Job 27:18 and as a booth *that* the **k** maketh. H5341
Ps 121: 5 The LORD *is* thy **k**: the LORD *is* thy H8104
Song 1: 6 they made me the **k** of the vineyards; H5201
Jer 35: 4 the son of Shallum, the **k** of the door: H8104
Act 16:27 And the **k** of the prison awaking out of *G1200*
36 And the **k** of the prison told this saying *G1200*

KEEPERS
2Ki 11: 5 be **k** of the watch of the king's house; H8104
22: 4 the LORD, which the **k** of the door have H8104
23: 4 order, and the **k** of the door, to bring H8104
25:18 priest, and the three **k** of the door: H8104
1Ch 9:19 work of the service, **k** of the gates of the H8104
19 host of the LORD, *were* **k** of the entry. H8104
Est 6: 2 chamberlains, the **k** of the door, who H8104
Ecc 12: 3 In the day when the **k** of the house shall H8104
Song 5: 7 wounded me; the **k** of the walls took H8104
8:11 the vineyard unto **k**; every one for the H5201
Jer 4:17 As **k** of a field, are they against her H8104
52:24 priest, and the three **k** of the door: H8104
Ezk 40:45 the **k** of the charge of the house. H8104
46 *is* for the priests, the **k** of the charge of H8104
44: 8 but ye have set **k** of my charge in my H8104
14 But I will make them **k** of the charge of H8104
Mt 28: 4 And for fear of him the **k** did shake, *G5083*
Act 5:23 all safety, and the **k** standing without *G5441*
12: 6 the **k** before the door kept the prison. *G5441*
19 he examined the **k**, and commanded *G5441*
Tit 2: 5 *To be* discreet, chaste, **k** at home, good, *G3626*

KEEPEST
1Ki 8:23 beneath, who **k** covenant and mercy H8104
2Ch 6:14 in the earth; which **k** covenant, and H8104
Neh 9:32 the terrible God, who **k** covenant and H8104
Act 21:24 also walkest orderly, and **k** the law. *G5442*

KEEPETH
Ex 21:18 *his* fist, and he die not, but **k** *his* bed: H5307
Dt 7: 9 God, which **k** covenant and mercy H8104
1Sa 16:11 and, behold, he **k** the sheep. And H7462
Neh 1: 5 and terrible God, that **k** covenant and H8104
Job 33:18 He **k** back his soul from the pit, and his H2820
Ps 34:20 He **k** all his bones: not one of them is H8104
121: 3 moved: he that **k** thee will not slumber. H8104
4 Behold, he that **k** Israel shall neither H8104
146: 6 that therein *is*: which **k** truth for ever: H8104
Prv 2: 8 He **k** the paths of judgment, and H5341
10:17 He *is in* the way of life that **k** H8104
13: 3 He that **k** his mouth keepeth his life: H5341
3 He that keepeth his mouth **k** his life: H8104
6 Righteousness **k** *him that is* upright in H5341
16:17 he that **k** his way preserveth his soul. H5341
19: 8 that **k** understanding shall find good. H8104
16 He that **k** the commandment keepeth H8104
16 He that keepeth the commandment **k** H8104
21:23 Whoso **k** his mouth and his tongue H8104
23 his tongue **k** his soul from troubles. H8104
24:12 *it*? and he that **k** thy soul, doth *not* he H5341
27:18 Whoso **k** the fig tree shall eat the fruit H5341
28: 7 Whoso **k** the law *is* a wise son: but he H5341
29: 3 his father: but he that **k** company with
11 but a wise *man* **k** it in till afterwards. H7623
18 but he that **k** the law, happy *is* he. H8104
Ecc 8: 5 Whoso **k** the commandment shall feel H8104
Isa 26: 2 nation which **k** the truth may enter in. H8104
56: 2 hold on it; that **k** the sabbath from H8104
2 it, and **k** his hand from doing any evil. H8104
6 every one that **k** the sabbath from H8104
Jer 48:10 he that **k** back his sword from blood. H4513
Lam 3:28 He sitteth alone and **k** silence, because
Hab 2: 5 man, neither **k** at home, who enlargeth
Lk 11:21 When a strong man armed **k** his *G5442*
Jn 7:19 **k** the law? Why go ye about to kill me? *G4160*
9:16 God, because he **k** not the sabbath day. *G5083*
14:21 and **k** them, he it is that loveth *G5083*
Jn 14:24 He that loveth me not **k** not my *G5083*
1Jn 2: 4 He that saith, I know him, and **k** not *G5083*
5 But whoso **k** his word, in him verily is *G5083*
3:24 And he that **k** his commandments *G5083*
5:18 is begotten of God **k** himself, and that *G5083*
Rev 2:26 And he that overcometh, and **k** my *G5083*
16:15 watcheth, and **k** his garments, lest he *G5083*
22: 7 blessed *is* he that **k** the sayings of the *G5083*

KEEPING
Ex 34: 7 **K** mercy for thousands, forgiving H5341
Nu 3:28 hundred, **k** the charge of the sanctuary. H8104
38 Aaron and his sons, **k** the charge of the H8104
Dt 8:11 thy God, in not **k** his commandments, H8104
1Sa 25:16 while we were with them **k** the sheep. H7462
Neh 12:25 Akkub, *were* porters **k** the ward at the H8104
Ps 19:11 *and* in **k** of them *there is* great reward. H8104
Ezk 17:14 by **k** of his covenant it might stand. H8104
Dan 9: 4 and dreadful God, **k** the covenant and H8104
Lk 2: 8 field, **k** watch over their flock by night. *G5442*
1Co 7:19 the **k** of the commandments of God. *G5084*
1Pt 4:19 will of God commit the **k** of their souls *to*

KEHELATHAH
Nu 33:22 from Rissah, and pitched in **K**. H6954
23 And they went from **K**, and pitched in H6954

KEILAH
Jos 15:44 And **K**, and Achzib, and Mareshah; H7084
1Sa 23: 1 **K**, and they rob the threshingfloors. H7084
2 and smite the Philistines, and save **K**. H7084
3 **K** against the armies of the Philistines? H7084
4 Arise, go down to **K**; for I will deliver H7084
5 So David and his men went to **K**, and H7084
5 So David saved the inhabitants of **K**. H7084
6 fled to David to **K**, *that* he came down H7084
7 was come to **K**. And Saul said, God H7084
8 to **K**, to besiege David and his men. H7084
10 to **K**, to destroy the city for my sake. H7084
11 Will the men of **K** deliver me up into H7084
12 Then said David, Will the men of **K** H7084
13 and departed out of **K**, and went H7084
13 from **K**; and he forbare to go forth. H7084
1Ch 4:19 the father of **K** the Garmite, and H7084
Neh 3:17 ruler of the half part of **K**, in his part. H7084
18 Henadad, the ruler of the half part of **K**. H7084

KELAIAH
Ezr 10:23 and Shimei, and **K**, (the same *is* Kelita,) H7041

KELITA
Ezr 10:23 *is* **K**,) Pethahiah, Judah, and Eliezer. H7042
Neh 8: 7 Maaseiah, **K**, Azariah, Jozabad, Hanan, H7042
10:10 Hodijah, **K**, Pelaiah, Hanan, H7042

KEMUEL
Gen 22:21 his brother, and **K** the father of Aram, H7055
Nu 34:24 of Ephraim, **K** the son of Shiphtan. H7055
1Ch 27:17 Of the Levites, Hashabiah the son of **K**: H7055

KENAN
1Ch 1: 2 **K**, Mahalaleel, Jered, H7018

KENATH
Nu 32:42 And Nobah went and took **K**, and the H7079
1Ch 2:23 Jair, from them, with **K**, and the towns H7079

KENAZ
Gen 36:11 Omar, Zepho, and Gatam, and **K**. H7073
15 duke Omar, duke Zepho, duke **K**, H7073
42 Duke **K**, duke Teman, duke Mibzar, H7073
Jos 15:17 And Othniel the son of **K**, the brother of H7073
Jdg 1:13 And Othniel the son of **K**, Caleb's H7073
3: 9 the son of **K**, Caleb's younger brother. H7073
11 years. And Othniel the son of **K** died. H7073
1Ch 1:36 Gatam, **K**, and Timna, and Amalek. H7073
53 Duke **K**, duke Teman, duke Mibzar, H7073
4:13 And the sons of **K**; Othniel, and Seraiah: H7073
15 Naam: and the sons of Elah, even **K**. H7073

KENEZITE
Nu 32:12 Save Caleb the son of Jephunneh the **K**, H7074
Jos 14: 6 son of Jephunneh the **K** said unto him, H7074
14 son of Jephunneh the **K** unto this day, H7074

KENITE
Nu 24:22 Nevertheless the **K** shall be wasted, H7014
Jdg 1:16 And the children of the **K**, Moses' father H7017
4:11 Now Heber the **K**, *which was* of the H7017
Jdg 4:17 wife of Heber the **K**: for *there was* peace H7017
17 of Hazor and the house of Heber the **K**. H7017
5:24 wife of Heber the **K** be, blessed shall H7017

KENITES
Gen 15:19 The **K**, and the Kenizzites, and the H7017
Nu 24:21 And he looked on the **K**, and took up his H7017
Jdg 4:11 himself from the **K**, and pitched his tent H7014
1Sa 15: 6 And Saul said unto the **K**, Go, depart, H7017
6 out of Egypt. So the **K** departed from H7017
27:10 and against the south of the **K**. H7017
30:29 *them* which *were* in the cities of the **K**, H7017
1Ch 2:55 These *are* the **K** that came of Hemath, H7017

KENIZZITES
Gen 15:19 The Kenites, and the **K**, and the H7074

KEPT
Gen 26: 5 obeyed my voice, and **k** my charge, my H8104
29: 9 with her father's sheep: for she **k** them. H7462
39: 9 I; neither hath he **k** back any thing H2820
42:16 and ye shall be **k** in prison, that your H631
Ex 3: 1 Now Moses **k** the flock of Jethro his H7462
16:23 up for you to be **k** until the morning. H4931
32 Fill an omer of it to be **k** for your H4931
33 the LORD, to be **k** for your generations. H4931
34 laid it up before the Testimony, to be **k**. H4931
21:29 and he hath not **k** him in, but that he H8104
36 his owner hath not **k** him in; he shall H8104
Nu 5:13 husband, and be **k** close, and she be H5641
9: 5 And they **k** the passover on the H6213
7 wherefore are we **k** back, that we may H1639
19 children of Israel **k** the charge of the H8104
23 they journeyed: they **k** the charge of the H8104
17:10 testimony, to be **k** for a token against H4931
19: 9 and it shall be **k** for the congregation H4931
24:11 LORD hath **k** thee back from honour. H4513
31:47 the Levites, which **k** the charge of the H8104
Dt 32:10 him, he **k** him as the apple of his eye. H5341
33: 9 observed thy word, and **k** thy covenant. H5341
Jos 5:10 in Gilgal, and **k** the passover on the H6213
14:10 And now, behold, the LORD hath **k** me
22: 2 And said unto them, Ye have **k** all that H8104
3 this day, but have **k** the charge of the H8104
Ru 2:23 So she **k** fast by the maidens of Boaz to
1Sa 9:24 time hath it been **k** for thee since I said, H8104
13:13 thou hast not **k** the commandment H8104
14 thou hast not **k** *that* which the LORD H8104
17:34 Saul, Thy servant **k** his father's sheep, H7462
21: 4 **k** themselves at least from women. H8104
5 women *have been* **k** from us about H6113
25:21 in vain have I **k** all that this *fellow* hath H8104
33 *be* thou, which hast **k** me this day from H3607
34 liveth, which hath **k** me back from H4513
39 of Nabal, and hath **k** his servant from H2820
26:15 then hast thou not **k** thy lord the king? H8104
16 ye have not **k** your master, the LORD'S H8104
2Sa 13:34 young man that **k** the watch lifted up his
22:22 For I have **k** the ways of the LORD, and H8104
24 and have **k** myself from mine iniquity. H8104
44 people, thou hast **k** me *to be* head of H8104
1Ki 2:43 Why then hast thou not **k** the oath of H8104
3: 6 thee; and thou hast **k** for him this great H8104
8:24 Who hast **k** with thy servant David my H8104
11:10 other gods: but he **k** not that which the H8104
11 and thou hast not **k** my covenant and H8104
34 **k** my commandments and my statutes: H8104
13:21 and hast not **k** the commandment H8104
14: 8 David, who **k** my commandments, H8104
27 which **k** the door of the king's house. H8104
2Ki 9:14 (Now Joram had **k** Ramothgilead, he H8104
12: 9 the priests that **k** the door put therein H8104
17:19 Also Judah **k** not the commandments H8104
18: 6 from following him, but **k** his H8104
1Ch 10:13 the LORD, which he **k** not, and also for H8104
12: 1 while he yet **k** himself close because H6113
29 had **k** the ward of the house of Saul. H8104
2Ch 6:15 Thou which hast **k** with thy servant H8104
7: 8 Also at the same time Solomon **k** the H6213
9 assembly: for they **k** the dedication of H6213
12:10 that **k** the entrance of the king's house. H8104
30:21 at Jerusalem **k** the feast of unleavened H6213
23 they **k** *other* seven days with gladness. H6213
34: 9 which the Levites that **k** the doors had H8104
21 our fathers have not **k** the word of the H8104
35: 1 Moreover Josiah **k** a passover unto the H6213
17 that were present **k** the passover at that H6213
18 like to that **k** in Israel from the days H6213
18 a passover as Josiah **k**, and the priests, H6213

2Ch 35:19 the reign of Josiah was this passover **k**. H6213
36:21 she lay desolate she **k** sabbath, to fulfil H7673
Ezr 3: 4 They **k** also the feast of tabernacles, as H6213
6:16 of the captivity, **k** the dedication of this H5648
19 And the children of the captivity **k** the H6213
22 And **k** the feast of unleavened bread H6213
Neh 1: 7 against thee, and have not **k** the H8104
8:18 law of God. And they **k** the feast seven H6213
9:34 priests, nor our fathers, **k** thy law, nor H6213
11:19 their brethren that **k** the gates, *were* an H8104
12:45 And both the singers and the porters **k** H8104
Est 2:14 which **k** the concubines: she H8104
21 of those which **k** the door, were wroth, H8104
9:28 remembered and **k** throughout every H6213
Job 23:11 his way have I **k**, and not declined. H8104
28:21 and **k** close from the fowls of the air. H5641
29:21 and waited, and **k** silence at my counsel.
31:34 I **k** silence, *and* went not out of the door?
Ps 17: 4 **k** *me from* the paths of the destroyer. H8104
18:21 For I have **k** the ways of the LORD, and H8104
23 I was also upright before him, and I **k** H8104
30: 3 grave: thou hast **k** me alive, that I should
32: 3 When I **k** silence, my bones waxed old H2790
42: 4 praise, with a multitude that **k** holyday.
50:21 These *things* hast thou done, and I **k** H2790
78:10 They **k** not the covenant of God, and H8104
56 high God, and **k** not his testimonies: H8104
99: 7 cloudy pillar: they **k** his testimonies, H8104
119:22 contempt; for I have **k** thy testimonies. H5341
55 LORD, in the night, and have **k** thy law. H8104
56 This I had, because I **k** thy precepts. H5341
67 astray: but now have I **k** thy word. H8104
158 grieved; because they **k** not thy word. H8104
167 My soul hath **k** thy testimonies; and I H8104
168 I have **k** thy precepts and thy H8104
Ecc 2:10 And whatsoever mine eyes desired I **k** H680
5:13 **k** for the owners thereof to their hurt. H8104
Song 1: 6 *but* mine own vineyard have I not **k**. H5201
Isa 30:29 a holy solemnity is **k**; and gladness of H6942
Jer 16:11 forsaken me, and have not **k** my law; H8104
35:18 your father, and **k** all his precepts, and H8104
Ezk 5: 7 neither have **k** my judgments, neither H6213
18: 9 Hath walked in my statutes, and hath **k** H8104
19 right, *and* hath **k** all my statutes, and H8104
20:21 statutes, neither **k** my judgments to do H8104
44: 8 And ye have not **k** the charge of mine H8104
15 sons of Zadok, that **k** the charge of my H8104
48:11 which have **k** my charge, which went H8104
Dan 5:19 whom he would he **k** alive; and whom he
7:28 in me: but I **k** the matter in my heart. H5202
Hos 12:12 for a wife, and for a wife he **k** *sheep*. H8104
Am 1:11 and he **k** his wrath for ever: H8104
2: 4 and have not **k** his commandments, H8104
Mic 6:16 For the statutes of Omri are **k**, and all H8104
Mal 2: 9 as ye have not **k** my ways, but have H8104
3: 7 and have not **k** *them*. Return unto me, H8104
14 *is it* that we have **k** his ordinance, and H8104
Mt 8:33 And they that **k** them fled, and went *G1006*
13:35 things which have been **k** secret from the
14: 6 But when Herod's birthday was **k**, the *G71*
19:20 I **k** from my youth up: what lack I yet? *G5442*
Mk 4:22 was any thing **k** secret, but that it *G1096*
9:10 And they **k** that saying with *G2902*
Lk 2:19 But Mary **k** all these things, and *G4933*
51 mother **k** all these sayings in her heart. *G1301*
8:29 him: and he was **k** bound with chains *G5442*
9:36 alone. And they **k** *it* close, and told no *G4601*
18:21 And he said, All these have I **k** from my *G5442*
19:20 which I have **k** laid up in a napkin: *G2192*
Jn 2:10 thou hast **k** the good wine until now. *G5083*
12: 7 the day of my burying hath she **k** this. *G5083*
15:10 love; even as I have **k** my Father's *G5083*
20 **k** my saying, they will keep yours also. *G5083*
17: 6 them me; and they have **k** thy word. *G5083*
12 While I was with them in the world, I **k** *G5083*
12 gavest me I have **k**, and none of them is *G5442*
18:16 that **k** the door, and brought in Peter. *G2377*
17 Then saith the damsel that **k** the door *G2377*
Act 5: 2 And **k** back *part* of the price, his wife *G3557*
7:53 disposition of angels, and have not **k** *it*. *G5442*
9:33 which had **k** his bed eight years, *G2621*
12: 5 Peter therefore was **k** in prison: but *G5083*
6 keepers before the door **k** the prison. *G5083*
15:12 Then all the multitude **k** silence, and *G4601*
20:20 *And* how I **k** back nothing that was *G5288*
22: 2 they **k** the more silence: and he saith,) *G3930*
20 **k** the raiment of them that slew him. *G5442*
23:35 him to be **k** in Herod's judgment hall. *G5442*
25: 4 Paul should be **k** at Caesarea, and that *G5083*
Act 25:21 to be **k** till I might send him to Caesar. *G5083*
27:43 willing to save Paul, **k** them from *their* *G2967*
28:16 by himself with a soldier that **k** him. *G5442*
Ro 16:25 was **k** secret since the world began,
2Co 11: 9 in all *things* I have **k** myself from being *G5083*
32 under Aretas the king **k** the city of the *G5432*
Gal 3:23 But before faith came, we were **k** under *G5432*
2Ti 4: 7 finished *my* course, I have **k** the faith: *G5083*
Heb 11:28 Through faith he **k** the passover, and *G4160*
Jas 5: 4 which is of you **k** back by fraud, crieth: *G650*
1Pt 1: 5 Who are **k** by the power of God *G5432*
2Pt 3: 7 the same word are **k** in store, reserved *G2343*
Jude 6 And the angels which **k** not their first *G5083*
Rev 3: 8 strength, and hast **k** my word, and hast *G5083*
10 Because thou hast **k** the word of my *G5083*

KERCHIEFS
Ezk 13:18 and make **k** upon the head of every H4555
21 Your **k** also will I tear, and deliver my H4555

KEREN-HAPPUCH
Job 42:14 Kezia; and the name of the third, **K**. H7163

KERIOTH
Jos 15:25 And Hazor, Hadattah, and **K**, *and* H7152
Jer 48:24 And upon **K**, and upon Bozrah, and H7152
41 **K** is taken, and the strong holds are H7152
Am 2: 2 the palaces of **K**: and Moab shall die H7152

KERNELS
Nu 6: 4 vine tree, from the **k** even to the husk. H2785

KEROS
Ezr 2:44 The children of **K**, the children of Siaha, H7026
Neh 7:47 The children of **K**, the children of Sia, H7026

KETTLE
1Sa 2:14 And he struck *it* into the pan, or **k**, or H1731

KETURAH
Gen 25: 1 took a wife, and her name *was* **K**. H6989
4 Eldaah. All these *were* the children of **K**. H6989
1Ch 1:32 Now the sons of **K**, Abraham's H6989
33 and Eldaah. All these *are* the sons of **K**. H6989

KEY
Jdg 3:25 they took a **k**, and opened *them*: and, H4668
Isa 22:22 And the **k** of the house of David will I H4668
Lk 11:52 have taken away the **k** of knowledge: ye *G2807*
Rev 3: 7 he that hath the **k** of David, he that *G2807*
9: 1 was given the **k** of the bottomless pit. *G2807*
20: 1 having the **k** of the bottomless pit *G2807*

KEYS
Mt 16:19 And I will give unto thee the **k** of the *G2807*
Rev 1:18 and have the **k** of hell and of death. *G2807*

KEZIA
Job 42:14 of the second, **K**; and the name of the H7103

KEZIZ
Jos 18:21 and Beth-hoglah, and the valley of **K**, H7104

KIBROTH-HATTAAVAH
Nu 11:35 *And* the people journeyed from **K** unto H6914
33:16 the desert of Sinai, and pitched at **K**. H6914
17 And they departed from **K**, and H6914

KIBROTH-HAT-TAAVAH
Nu 11:34 And he called the name of that place **K**: H6914
Dt 9:22 at **K**, ye provoked the LORD to wrath. H6914

KIBZAIM
Jos 21:22 And **K** with her suburbs, and H6911

KICK
1Sa 2:29 Wherefore **k** ye at my sacrifice and at H1163
Act 9: 5 *is* hard for thee to **k** against the pricks. *G2979*
26:14 *is* hard for thee to **k** against the pricks. *G2979*

KICKED
Dt 32:15 But Jeshurun waxed fat, and **k**: thou art H1163

KID
Gen 37:31 coat, and killed a **k** of the goats, and H8163
38:17 send *thee* a **k** from the flock. H1423+H5795
20 And Judah sent the **k** by the H1423+H5795
23 sent this **k**, and thou hast not found her. H1423
Ex 23:19 not seethe a **k** in his mother's milk. H1423
Ex 34:26 not seethe a **k** in his mother's milk. H1423
Lev 4:23 **k** of the goats, a male without blemish: H8163
28 his offering, a **k** of the goats, a female H8166
5: 6 flock, a lamb or a **k** of the goats, for a H8166
9: 3 saying, Take ye a **k** of the goats for a H8163
23:19 Then ye shall sacrifice one **k** of the H8163
Nu 7:16 One **k** of the goats for a sin offering: H8163
22 One **k** of the goats for a sin offering: H8163
28 One **k** of the goats for a sin offering: H8163
34 One **k** of the goats for a sin offering: H8163
40 One **k** of the goats for a sin offering: H8163
46 One **k** of the goats for a sin offering: H8163
52 One **k** of the goats for a sin offering: H8163
58 One **k** of the goats for a sin offering: H8163
64 One **k** of the goats for a sin offering: H8163
70 One **k** of the goats for a sin offering: H8163
76 One **k** of the goats for a sin offering: H8163
82 One **k** of the goats for a sin offering: H8163
15:11 or for one ram, or for a lamb, or a **k**. H5795
24 one **k** of the goats for a sin offering. H8163
28:15 And one **k** of the goats for a sin offering H8163
30 *And* one **k** of the goats, to make an H8163
29: 5 And one **k** of the goats *for* a sin H8163
11 One **k** of the goats *for* a sin offering; H8163
16 And one **k** of the goats *for* a sin H8163
19 And one **k** of the goats *for* a sin H8163
25 And one **k** of the goats *for* a sin H8163
Dt 14:21 not seethe a **k** in his mother's milk. H1423
Jdg 6:19 and made ready a **k**, and H1423+H5795
13:15 have made ready a **k** for thee. H1423+H5795
19 So Manoah took a **k** with a H1423+H5795
14: 6 he would have rent a **k**, and *he had* H1423
15: 1 wife with a **k**; and he said, I will H1423+H5795
1Sa 16:20 of wine, and a **k**, and sent *them* H1423+H5795
Isa 11: 6 lie down with the **k**; and the calf and the H1423
Ezk 43:22 thou shalt offer a **k** of the goats without H8163
45:23 a **k** of the goats daily *for* a sin offering. H8163
Lk 15:29 never gavest me a **k**, that I might make *G2056*

KIDNEYS
Ex 29:13 liver, and the two **k**, and the fat that *is* H3629
22 liver, and the two **k**, and the fat that *is* H3629
Lev 3: 4 And the two **k**, and the fat that *is* on H3629
4 liver, with the **k**, it shall he take away. H3629
10 And the two **k**, and the fat that *is* upon H3629
10 liver, with the **k**, it shall he take away. H3629
15 And the two **k**, and the fat that *is* upon H3629
15 liver, with the **k**, it shall he take away. H3629
4: 9 And the two **k**, and the fat that *is* upon H3629
9 liver, with the **k**, it shall he take away, H3629
7: 4 And the two **k**, and the fat that *is* on H3629
4 liver, with the **k**, it shall he take away: H3629
8:16 liver, and the two **k**, and their fat, and H3629
25 **k**, and their fat, and the right shoulder: H3629
9:10 But the fat, and the **k**, and the caul H3629
19 and the **k**, and the caul *above* the liver: H3629
Dt 32:14 with the fat of **k** of wheat; and thou H3629
Isa 34: 6 with the fat of the **k** of rams: for the H3629

KIDRON
2Sa 15:23 over the brook **K**, and all the people H6939
1Ki 2:37 over the brook **K**, thou shalt know for H6939
15:13 her idol, and burnt *it* by the brook **K**. H6939
2Ki 23: 4 in the fields of **K**, and carried the ashes H6939
6 unto the brook **K**, and burned it at the H6939
6 it at the brook **K**, and stamped *it* small H6939
12 cast the dust of them into the brook **K**. H6939
2Ch 15:16 stamped *it*, and burnt *it* at the brook **K**. H6939
29:16 to carry *it* out abroad into the brook **K**. H6939
30:14 away, and cast *them* into the brook **K**. H6939
Jer 31:40 unto the brook of **K**, unto the corner of H6939

KIDS
Gen 27: 9 thence two good **k** of the goats; and I H1423
16 And she put the skins of the **k** of the H1423
Lev 16: 5 of Israel two **k** of the goats for a sin H8163
Nu 7:87 **k** of the goats for sin offering twelve. H8163
1Sa 10: 3 one carrying three **k**, and another H1423
1Ki 20:27 of **k**; but the Syrians filled the country. H5795
2Ch 35: 7 flock, lambs and **k**, all for the H1121+H5795
Song 1: 8 feed thy **k** beside the shepherds' tents. H1429

KILL
Gen 4:15 lest any finding him should **k** him. H5221
12:12 will **k** me, but they will save thee alive. H2026
26: 7 of the place should **k** me for Rebekah; H2026
27:42 comfort himself, *purposing* to **k** thee. H2026
37:21 their hands; and said, Let us not **k** him. H5221
Ex 1:16 a son, then ye shall **k** him: but if it *be* a H4191

K

Ex 2:14 intendest thou to **k** me, as thou killedst H2026
4:24 LORD met him, and sought to **k** him. H4191
12: 6 of Israel shall **k** it in the evening. H7819
21 to your families, and **k** the passover. H7819
16: 3 to **k** this whole assembly with hunger. H4191
17: 3 us up out of Egypt, to **k** us and our H4191
20:13 Thou shalt not **k**. H7523
22: 1 or a sheep, and **k** it, or sell it; he shall H2873
24 shall wax hot, and I will **k** you with the H2026
29:11 And thou shalt **k** the bullock before the H7819
20 Then shalt thou **k** the ram, and take of H7819
Lev 1: 5 And he shall **k** the bullock before the H7819
11 And he shall **k** it on the side of the altar H7819
3: 2 his offering, and **k** it *at* the door of the H7819
8 of his offering, and **k** it before the H7819
13 upon the head of it, and **k** it before the H7819
4: 4 and **k** the bullock before the LORD. H7819
24 of the goat, and **k** it in the place where H7819
24 place where they **k** the burnt offering H7819
33 place where they **k** the burnt offering. H7819
7: 2 In the place where they **k** the burnt H7819
2 burnt offering shall they **k** the trespass H7819
14:13 where he shall **k** the sin offering and H7819
19 afterward he shall **k** the burnt offering: H7819
25 And he shall **k** the lamb of the trespass H7819
50 And he shall **k** the one of the birds in H7819
16:11 house, and shall **k** the bullock of the sin H7819
15 Then shall he **k** the goat of the sin H7819
20: 4 his seed unto Molech, and **k** him not: H4191
16 thereto, thou shalt **k** the woman, and H2026
22:28 not **k** it and her young both in one day. H7819
Nu 11:15 And if thou deal thus with me, **k** me, I H2026
14:15 Now *if* thou shalt **k** *all* this people as H4191
16:13 and honey, to **k** us in the wilderness, H4191
22:29 in mine hand, for now would I **k** thee. H2026
31:17 Now therefore **k** every male among the H2026
17 the little ones, and **k** every woman that H2026
35:27 revenger of blood **k** the slayer; he shall H7523
Dt 4:42 thither, which should **k** his neighbour H7523
5:17 Thou shalt not **k**. H7523
12:15 Notwithstanding thou mayest **k** and H2076
21 then thou shalt **k** of thy herd and of thy H2076
13: 9 But thou shalt surely **k** him; thine hand H2026
32:39 no god with me: I **k**, and I make alive; I H4191
Jdg 13:23 were pleased to **k** us, he would not H4191
15:13 but surely we will not **k** thee. And they H4191
16: 2 when it is day, we shall **k** him. H2026
20:31 of the people, *and* **k**, as at other times, H2491
39 to smite *and* **k** of the men of Israel H2491
1Sa 16: 2 hear *it*, he will **k** me. And the LORD H2026
17: 9 If he be able to fight with me, and to **k** H5221
9 against him, and **k** him, then shall ye H5221
19: 1 his servants, that they should **k** David. H4191
2 father seeketh to **k** thee: now therefore, H4191
17 me, Let me go; why should I **k** thee? H4191
24:10 and *some* bade *me* **k** thee: but *mine eye* H2026
30:15 thou wilt neither **k** me, nor deliver me H4191
2Sa 13:28 Amnon; then **k** him, fear not: have H4191
14: 7 that we may **k** him, for the life of his H4191
32 be *any* iniquity in me, let him **k** me. H4191
21: 4 for us shalt thou **k** any man in Israel. H4191
1Ki 11:40 Solomon sought therefore to **k** H4191
12:27 and they shall **k** me, and go again to H2026
2Ki 5: 7 said, *Am* I God, to **k** and to make alive, H4191
7: 4 live; and if they **k** us, we shall but die. H4191
11:15 that followeth her **k** with the sword. H4191
2Ch 35: 6 So **k** the passover, and sanctify H7819
Est 3:13 to destroy, to **k**, and to cause to perish, H2026
Ps 59: ttl and they watched the house to **k** him. H4191
Ecc 3: 3 A time to **k**, and a time to heal; a time H2026
Isa 14:30 in safety: and I will **k** thy root with H4191
29: 1 ye year to year; let them **k** sacrifices. H5362
Ezk 34: 3 with the wool, ye **k** them that are fed: H2076
Mt 5:21 Thou shalt not **k**; and whosoever shall *G5407*
21 **k** shall be in danger of the judgment: *G5407*
10:28 And fear not them which **k** the body, but *G615*
28 but are not able to **k** the soul: but rather *G615*
17:23 And they shall **k** him, and the third day *G615*
21:38 heir; come, let us **k** him, and let us seize *G615*
23:34 of them ye shall **k** and crucify; and *some* *G615*
24: 9 afflicted, and shall **k** you: and ye shall be *G615*
26: 4 might take Jesus by subtilty, and **k** *him*. *G615*
Mk 3: 4 life, or to **k**? But they held their peace. *G615*
9:31 and they shall **k** him; and after that he *G615*
10:19 adultery, Do not **k**, Do not steal, Do not *G5407*
34 him, and shall **k** him: and the third day *G615*
12: 7 **k** him, and the inheritance shall be ours. *G615*
Lk 12: 4 afraid of them that **k** the body, and after *G615*
13:31 and depart hence: for Herod will **k** thee. *G615*
Lk 15:23 And bring hither the fatted calf, and **k** *G2380*
18:20 adultery, Do not **k**, Do not steal, Do not *G5407*
20:14 **k** him, that the inheritance may be ours. *G615*
22: 2 might **k** him; for they feared the people. *G337*
Jn 5:18 Therefore the Jews sought the more to **k** *G615*
7: 1 Jewry, because the Jews sought to **k** him. *G615*
19 the law? Why go ye about to **k** me? *G615*
20 hast a devil: who goeth about to **k** thee? *G615*
25 Is not this he, whom they seek to **k**? *G615*
8:22 Then said the Jews, Will he **k** himself? *G615*
37 seed; but ye seek to **k** me, because my *G615*
40 But now ye seek to **k** me, a man that *G615*
10:10 for to steal, and to **k**, and to destroy: I *G2380*
Act 7:28 Wilt thou **k** me, as thou diddest the *G337*
9:23 fulfilled, the Jews took counsel to **k** him: *G337*
24 the gates day and night to **k** him. *G337*
10:13 a voice to him, Rise, Peter; **k**, and eat. *G2380*
21:31 And as they went about to **k** him, tidings *G615*
23:15 ever he come near, are ready to **k** him. *G337*
25: 3 laying wait in the way to **k** him. *G337*
26:21 in the temple, and went about to **k** *me*. *G1315*
27:42 And the soldiers' counsel was to **k** the *G615*
Ro 13: 9 Thou shalt not **k**, Thou shalt not steal, *G5407*
Jas 2:11 said also, Do not **k**. Now if thou commit *G5407*
11 yet if thou **k**, thou art become a *G5407*
4: 2 Ye lust, and have not: ye **k**, and desire *G5407*
Rev 2:23 And I will **k** her children with death; and *G615*
6: 4 that they should **k** one another: and *G4969*
8 of the earth, to **k** with sword, and with *G615*
9: 5 they should not **k** them, but that they *G615*
11: 7 and shall overcome them, and **k** them. *G615*

KILLED
Gen 37:31 And they took Joseph's coat, and **k** a H7819
Ex 21:29 but that he hath **k** a man or a woman; H4191
Lev 4:15 the bullock shall be **k** before the LORD. H7819
6:25 burnt offering is **k** shall the sin offering H7819
25 be **k** before the LORD: it *is* most holy. H7819
8:19 And he **k** *it*; and Moses sprinkled the H7819
14: 5 that one of the birds be **k** in an earthen H7819
6 bird *that was* **k** over the running water: H7819
Nu 16:41 Ye have **k** the people of the LORD. H4191
31:19 whosoever hath **k** any person, and H2026
1Sa 24:11 of thy robe, and **k** thee not, know thou H2026
25:11 flesh that I have **k** for my shearers, and H2873
28:24 she hasted, and **k** it, and took flour, H2076
2Sa 12: 9 his sight? thou hast **k** Uriah the Hittite H5221
21:17 the Philistine, and **k** him. Then the H4191
1Ki 16: 7 of Jeroboam; and because he **k** him. H5221
10 smote him, and **k** him, in the twenty H4191
21:19 the LORD, Hast thou **k**, and also taken H7523
2Ki 15:25 and he **k** him, and reigned in his room. H4191
1Ch 19:18 **k** Shophach the captain of the host. H4191
2Ch 18: 2 And Ahab **k** sheep and oxen for H2076
25: 3 servants that had **k** the king his father. H5221
29:22 So they **k** the bullocks, and the priests H7819
22 when they had **k** the rams, they H7819
22 the altar: they **k** also the lambs, and H7819
24 And the priests **k** them, and they made H7819
30:15 Then they **k** the passover on the H7819
35: 1 and they **k** the passover on the H7819
11 And they **k** the passover, and the H7819
Ezr 6:20 *were* pure, and **k** the passover for all H7819
Ps 44:22 Yea, for thy sake are we **k** all the day H2026
Prv 9: 2 She hath **k** her beasts; she hath H2873
Lam 2:21 thine anger; thou hast **k**, *and* not pitied. H2873
Mt 16:21 be **k**, and be raised again the third day. *G615*
21:35 one, and **k** another, and stoned another. *G615*
22: 4 and *my* fatlings *are* **k**, and all things *are* *G2380*
23:31 children of them which **k** the prophets. *G5407*
Mk 6:19 would have **k** him; but she could not: *G615*
8:31 and be **k**, and after three days rise again. *G615*
9:31 that he is **k**, he shall rise the third day. *G615*
12: 5 and him they **k**, and many others; *G615*
8 And they took him, and **k** *him*, and cast *G615*
14:12 bread, when they **k** the passover, his *G2380*
Lk 11:47 the prophets, and your fathers **k** them. *G615*
48 **k** them, and ye build their sepulchres. *G615*
12: 5 after he hath **k** hath power to cast into *G615*
15:27 and thy father hath **k** the fatted calf, *G2380*
30 thou hast **k** for him the fatted calf. *G2380*
20:15 the vineyard, and **k** *him*. What therefore *G615*
22: 7 bread, when the passover must be **k**. *G2380*
Act 3:15 And **k** the Prince of life, whom God hath *G615*
12: 2 And he **k** James the brother of John with *G337*
16:27 and would have **k** himself, supposing *G337*
23:12 neither eat nor drink till they had **k** Paul. *G615*
21 drink till they have **k** him: and now are *G337*
27 should have been **k** of them: then came I *G337*
Ro 8:36 As it is written, For thy sake we are **k** *G2289*
11: 3 Lord, they have **k** thy prophets, and *G615*
2Co 6: 9 we live; as chastened, and not **k**; *G2289*
1Th 2:15 Who both **k** the Lord Jesus, and their *G615*
Jas 5: 6 Ye have condemned *and* **k** the just; *and* *G5407*
Rev 6:11 be **k** as they *were*, should be fulfilled. *G615*
9:18 third part of men **k**, by the fire, and by *G615*
20 which were not **k** by these plagues yet *G615*
11: 5 hurt them, he must in this manner be **k**. *G615*
13:10 the sword must be **k** with the sword. *G615*
15 the image of the beast should be **k**. *G2443*

KILLEDST
Ex 2:14 to kill me, as thou **k** the Egyptian? And H2026
1Sa 24:18 me into thine hand, thou **k** me not. H2026

KILLEST
Mt 23:37 O Jerusalem, Jerusalem, *thou* that **k** the *G615*
Lk 13:34 O Jerusalem, Jerusalem, which **k** the *G615*

KILLETH
Lev 17: 3 of Israel, that **k** an ox, or lamb, or goat, H7819
3 the camp, or that **k** *it* out of the camp, H7819
24:17 And he that **k** any man shall surely be H5221
18 And he that **k** a beast shall make it H5221
21 And he that **k** a beast, he shall restore H5221
21 that **k** a man, he shall be put to death. H5221
Nu 35:11 which **k** any person at unawares. H5221
15 every one that **k** any person unawares H5221
30 Whoso **k** any person, the murderer H5221
Dt 19: 4 he may live: Whoso **k** his neighbour H5221
Jos 20: 3 That the slayer that **k** *any* person H5221
9 them, that whosoever **k** *any* person at H5221
1Sa 2: 6 The LORD **k**, and maketh alive: he H4191
17:25 *that* the man who **k** him, the king will H5221
26 to the man that **k** this Philistine, and H5221
27 shall it be done to the man that **k** him. H5221
Job 5: 2 For wrath **k** the foolish man, and envy H2026
24:14 The murderer rising with the light **k** the H6991
Prv 21:25 The desire of the slothful **k** him; for his H4191
Isa 66: 3 He that **k** an ox *is as if* he slew a man; H7819
Jn 16: 2 that whosoever **k** you will think that he *G615*
2Co 3: 6 for the letter **k**, but the spirit giveth life. *G615*
Rev 13:10 captivity: he that **k** with the sword must *G615*

KILLING
Jdg 9:24 aided him in the **k** of his brethren. H2026
2Ch 30:17 the charge of the **k** of the passovers for H7821
Isa 22:13 slaying oxen, and **k** sheep, eating flesh, H7819
Hos 4: 2 By swearing, and lying, and **k**, and H7523
Mk 12: 5 many others; beating some, and **k** some. *G615*

KIN
Lev 18: 6 any that is near of **k** to him, to uncover H7607
20:19 his near **k**: they shall bear their iniquity. H7607
21: 2 But for his **k**, that is near unto him, *that* H7607
25:25 and if any of his **k** come to redeem it, H7138
49 or *any* that is nigh of **k** unto him of his H7607
Ru 2:20 of **k** unto us, one of our next kinsmen. H7138
2Sa 19:42 the king *is* near of **k** to us: wherefore H7138
Mk 6: 4 his own **k**, and in his own house. *G4773*

KINAH
Jos 15:22 And **K**, and Dimonah, and Adadah, H7016

KIND
Gen 1:11 fruit after his **k**, whose seed *is* in itself, H4327
12 seed after his **k**, and the tree yielding H4327
12 his **k**: and God saw that *it was* good. H4327
21 after their **k**, and every winged fowl H4327
21 his **k**: and God saw that *it was* good. H4327
24 creature after his **k**, cattle, and creeping H4327
24 of the earth after his **k**: and it was so. H4327
25 of the earth after his **k**, and cattle after H4327
25 cattle after their **k**, and every thing that H4327
25 his **k**: and God saw that *it was* good. H4327
6:20 Of fowls after their **k**, and of cattle after H4327
20 of cattle after their **k**, of every creeping H4327
20 of the earth after his **k**, two of every *sort* H4327
7:14 They, and every beast after his **k**, and H4327
14 cattle after their **k**, and every creeping H4327
14 the earth after his **k**, and every fowl H4327
14 fowl after his **k**, every bird of every sort. H4327
Lev 11:14 And the vulture, and the kite after his **k**; H4327
15 Every raven after his **k**; H4327
16 the cuckow, and the hawk after his **k**, H4327
19 And the stork, the heron after her **k**, H4327
22 eat; the locust after his **k**, and the bald H4327
22 locust after his **k**, and the beetle after H4327

Lev 11:22 **k**, and the grasshopper after his kind. H4327
22 kind, and the grasshopper after his **k**. H4327
29 the mouse, and the tortoise after his **k**, H4327
19:19 with a diverse **k**: thou shalt not sow thy H3610
Dt 14:13 and the kite, and the vulture after his **k**, H4327
14 And every raven after his **k**, H4327
15 the cuckow, and the hawk after his **k**, H4327
18 her **k**, and the lapwing, and the bat. H4327
1Ch 28:14 for all instruments of every **k** of service:
2Ch 10: 7 saying, If thou be **k** to this people, and H2896
Neh 13:20 So the merchants and sellers of all **k** of
Ecc 2: 5 I planted trees in them of all **k** *of* fruits:
Ezk 27:12 of the multitude of all **k** *of* riches; with
Mt 13:47 into the sea, and gathered of every **k**: G1085
17:21 Howbeit this **k** goeth not out but by G1085
Mk 9:29 And he said unto them, This **k** can G1085
Lk 6:35 is **k** unto the unthankful and *to* the evil. G5543
1Co 13: 4 Charity suffereth long, *and* is **k**; charity G5541
15:39 flesh: but *there is* one **k** of flesh of men,
Eph 4:32 And be ye **k** one to another, G5543
Jas 1:18 be a **k** of firstfruits of his creatures. G5100
3: 7 For every **k** of beasts, and of birds, and G5449

KINDLE

Ex 35: 3 Ye shall **k** no fire throughout your H1197
Prv 26:21 fire; so *is* a contentious man to **k** strife. H2787
Isa 9:18 thorns, and shall **k** in the thickets of H3341
10:16 **k** a burning like the burning of a fire. H3344
30:33 like a stream of brimstone, doth **k** it. H1197
43: 2 neither shall the flame **k** upon thee. H1197
50:11 Behold, all ye that **k** a fire, that H6919
Jer 7:18 and the fathers **k** the fire, and the H1197
17:27 day; then will I **k** a fire in the gates H3341
21:14 LORD: and I will **k** a fire in the forest H3341
33:18 offerings, and to **k** meat offerings, and H6999
43:12 And I will **k** a fire in the houses of the H3341
49:27 And I will **k** a fire in the wall of H3341
50:32 him up: and I will **k** a fire in his cities, H3341
Ezk 20:47 Behold, I will **k** a fire in thee, and it H3341
24:10 Heap on wood, **k** the fire, consume the H1814
Am 1:14 But I will **k** a fire in the wall of Rabbah, H3341
Oba 18 and they shall **k** in them, and devour H1814
Mal 1:10 neither do ye **k** *fire* on mine altar for H215

KINDLED

Gen 30: 2 And Jacob's anger was **k** against H2734
39:19 thy servant to me; that his wrath was **k**. H2734
Ex 4:14 And the anger of the LORD was **k** H2734
22: 6 **k** the fire shall surely make restitution. H1197
Lev 10: 6 the burning which the LORD hath **k**. H8313
Nu 11: 1 and his anger was **k**; and the fire of the H2734
10 **k** greatly; Moses also was displeased. H2734
33 of the LORD was **k** against the people, H2734
12: 9 And the anger of the LORD was **k** H2734
22:22 And God's anger was **k** because he H2734
27 was **k**, and he smote the ass with a staff. H2734
24:10 And Balak's anger was **k** against H2734
25: 3 of the LORD was **k** against Israel. H2734
32:10 And the LORD'S anger was **k** the same H2734
13 And the LORD'S anger was **k** against H2734
Dt 6:15 LORD thy God be **k** against thee, and H2734
7: 4 of the LORD be **k** against you, and H2734
11:17 And *then* the LORD'S wrath be **k** H2734
29:27 And the anger of the LORD was **k** H2734
31:17 Then my anger shall be **k** against them H2734
32:22 For a fire is **k** in mine anger, and shall H6919
Jos 7: 1 was **k** against the children of Israel. H2734
23:16 of the LORD be **k** against you, and ye H2734
Jdg 9:30 Gaal the son of Ebed, his anger was **k**. H2734
14:19 **k**, and he went up to his father's house. H2734
1Sa 11: 6 tidings, and his anger was **k** greatly. H2734
17:28 Eliab's anger was **k** against David, and H2734
20:30 Then Saul's anger was **k** against H2734
2Sa 6: 7 And the anger of the LORD was **k** H2734
12: 5 And David's anger was greatly **k** H2734
22: 9 his mouth devoured: coals were **k** by it. H1197
13 before him were coals of fire **k**. H1197
24: 1 And again the anger of the LORD was **k** H2734
2Ki 13: 3 And the anger of the LORD was **k** H2734
22:13 the LORD that is **k** against us, because H3341
17 my wrath shall be **k** against this place, H3341
23:26 his anger was **k** against Judah, because H2734
1Ch 13:10 And the anger of the LORD was **k** H2734
2Ch 25:10 anger was greatly **k** against Judah, and H2734
15 of the LORD was **k** against Amaziah, H2734
Job 19:11 He hath also **k** his wrath against me, H2734
32: 2 Then was **k** the wrath of Elihu the son H2734
2 against Job was his wrath **k**, because he H2734
3 was his wrath **k**, because they had H2734
Job 32: 5 *these* three men, then his wrath was **k**. H2734
42: 7 My wrath is **k** against thee, and against H2734
Ps 2:12 when his wrath is **k** but a little. Blessed H1197
18: 8 his mouth devoured: coals were **k** by it. H1197
78:21 so a fire was **k** against Jacob, and H5400
106:18 And a fire was **k** in their company; the H1197
40 Therefore was the wrath of the LORD **k** H2734
124: 3 when their wrath was **k** against us: H2734
Isa 5:25 Therefore is the anger of the LORD **k** H2734
50:11 *that* ye have **k**. This shall ye have of H1197
Jer 11:16 tumult he hath **k** fire upon it, and the H3341
15:14 not: for a fire is **k** in mine anger, *which* H6919
17: 4 not: for ye have **k** a fire in mine anger, H6919
44: 6 forth, and was **k** in the cities of Judah H1197
Lam 4:11 anger, and hath **k** a fire in Zion, and it H3341
Ezk 20:48 have **k** it: it shall not be quenched. H1197
Hos 8: 5 off; mine anger is **k** against them: how H2734
11: 8 me, my repentings are **k** together. H3648
Zec 10: 3 Mine anger was **k** against the H2734
Lk 12:49 earth; and what will I, if it be already **k**? G381
22:55 And when they had **k** a fire in the midst G681
Act 28: 2 kindness: for they **k** a fire, and received G381

KINDLETH

Job 41:21 His breath **k** coals, and a flame goeth H3857
Isa 44:15 himself; yea, he **k** *it*, and baketh bread; H5400
Jas 3: 5 Behold, how great a matter a little fire **k**! G381

KINDLY

Gen 24:49 And now if ye will deal **k** and truly with H2617
34: 3 damsel, and spake **k** unto the damsel. H3820
47:29 thigh, and deal **k** and truly with me; H2617
50:21 them, and spake **k** unto them. H3820
Jos 2:14 that we will deal **k** and truly with thee. H2617
Ru 1: 8 the LORD deal **k** with you, as ye have H2617
1Sa 20: 8 Therefore thou shalt deal **k** with thy H2617
2Ki 25:28 And he spake **k** to him, and set his H2896
Jer 52:32 And spake **k** unto him, and set his H2896
Ro 12:10 *Be* **k** affectioned one to another with G5387

KINDLY-AFFECTIONED See KINDLY and AFFECTIONED.

KINDNESS

Gen 20:13 her, This *is* thy **k** which thou shalt shew H2617
21:23 *but* according to the **k** that I have done H2617
24:12 and shew **k** unto my master Abraham. H2617
14 thou hast shewed **k** unto my master. H2617
40:14 thee, and shew **k**, I pray thee, unto me, H2617
Jos 2:12 I have shewed you **k**, that ye will also H2617
12 ye will also shew **k** unto my father's H2617
Jdg 8:35 Neither shewed they **k** to the house of H2617
Ru 2:20 not left off his **k** to the living and to H2617
3:10 hast shewed more **k** in the latter end H2617
1Sa 15: 6 for ye shewed **k** to all the children of H2617
20:14 me the **k** of the LORD, that I die not: H2617
15 But *also* thou shalt not cut off thy **k** H2617
2Sa 2: 5 ye have shewed this **k** unto your lord, H2617
6 And now the LORD shew **k** and truth H2617
6 this **k**, because ye have done this thing. H2896
3: 8 Judah do shew **k** this day unto the H2617
9: 1 I may shew him **k** for Jonathan's sake? H2617
3 I may shew the **k** of God unto him? And H2617
7 will surely shew thee **k** for Jonathan thy H2617
10: 2 Then said David, I will shew **k** unto H2617
2 as his father shewed **k** unto me. And H2617
16:17 Hushai, *Is* this thy **k** to thy friend? why H2617
1Ki 2: 7 But shew **k** unto the sons of Barzillai H2617
3: 6 kept for him this great **k**, that thou hast H2617
1Ch 19: 2 And David said, I will shew **k** unto H2617
2 his father shewed **k** to me. And David H2617
2Ch 24:22 not the **k** which Jehoiada his H2617
Neh 9:17 and of great **k**, and forsookest them not. H2617
Est 2: 9 him, and she obtained **k** of him; and he H2617
Ps 31:21 me his marvellous **k** in a strong city. H2617
117: 2 For his merciful **k** is great toward us: H2617
119:76 Let, I pray thee, thy merciful **k** be for H2617
141: 5 me; *it shall be* a **k**: and let him reprove H2617
Prv 19:22 The desire of a man *is* his **k**: and a poor H2617
31:26 and in her tongue *is* the law of **k**. H2617
Isa 54: 8 with everlasting **k** will I have mercy on H2617
10 be removed; but my **k** shall not depart H2617
Jer 2: 2 thee, the **k** of thy youth, the love H2617
Joel 2:13 of great **k**, and repenteth him of the evil. H2617
Jna 4: 2 of great **k**, and repentest thee of the evil. H2617
Act 28: 2 shewed us no little **k**: for they kindled a G5363
2Co 6: 6 **k**, by the Holy Ghost, by love unfeigned, G5544
Eph 2: 7 in *his* **k** toward us through Christ Jesus. G5544
Col 3:12 bowels of mercies, **k**, humbleness of G5544
Tit 3: 4 But after that the **k** and love of God our G5544
2Pt 1: 7 And to godliness brotherly **k**; and to G5360
7 kindness; and to brotherly **k** charity. G5360

KINDRED

Gen 12: 1 and from thy **k**, and from thy father's H4138
24: 4 **k**, and take a wife unto my son Isaac. H4138
7 the land of my **k**, and which spake unto H4138
38 to my **k**, and take a wife unto my son. H4940
40 son of my **k**, and of my father's house: H4940
41 thou comest to my **k**; and if they give H4940
31: 3 and to thy **k**; and I will be with thee. H4138
13 land, and return unto the land of thy **k**. H4138
32: 9 to thy **k**, and I will deal well with thee: H4138
43: 7 our state, and of our **k**, saying, *Is* your H4138
Nu 10:30 depart to mine own land, and to my **k**. H4138
Jos 6:23 out all her **k**, and left them without H4940
Ru 2: 3 Boaz, who *was* of the **k** of Elimelech. H4940
3: 2 And now *is* not Boaz of our **k**, with H4130
1Ch 12:29 And of the children of Benjamin, the **k** of H251
Est 2:10 her people nor her **k**: for Mordecai had H4138
20 Esther had not *yet* shewed her **k** nor H4138
8: 6 I endure to see the destruction of my **k**? H4138
Job 32: 2 the Buzite, of the **k** of Ram: against Job H4940
Ezk 11:15 the men of thy **k**, and all the house of H1353
Lk 1:61 of thy **k** that is called by this name. G4772
Act 4: 6 as were of the **k** of the high priest, were G1085
7: 3 and from thy **k**, and come into the land G4772
13 **k** was made known unto Pharaoh. G1085
14 all his **k**, threescore and fifteen souls. G4772
19 The same dealt subtilly with our **k**, and G1085
Rev 5: 9 **k**, and tongue, and people, and nation; G5443
14: 6 nation, and **k**, and tongue, and people, G5443

KINDREDS

1Ch 16:28 Give unto the LORD, ye **k** of the people, H4940
Ps 22:27 LORD: and all the **k** of the nations shall H4940
96: 7 Give unto the LORD, O ye **k** of the H4940
Act 3:25 shall all the **k** of the earth be blessed. G3965
Rev 1: 7 him: and all **k** of the earth shall wail G5443
7: 9 of all nations, and **k**, and people, and G5443
11: 9 And they of the people and **k** and G5443
13: 7 over all **k**, and tongues, and nations. G5443

KINDS

Gen 8:19 after their **k**, went forth out of the ark. H4940
2Ch 16:14 odours and divers **k** *of spices* prepared H2177
Jer 15: 3 And I will appoint over them four **k**, H4940
Ezk 47:10 be according to their **k**, as the fish of the H4327
Dan 3: 5 dulcimer, and all **k** of musick, ye fall H2178
7 psaltery, and all **k** of musick, all the H2178
10 dulcimer, and all **k** of musick, shall fall H2178
15 dulcimer, and all **k** of musick, ye fall H2178
1Co 12:10 to another *divers* **k** of tongues; to G1085
14:10 There are, it may be, so many **k** of G1085

KINE

Gen 32:15 their colts, forty **k**, and ten bulls, twenty H6510
41: 2 well favoured **k** and fatfleshed; and H6510
3 And, behold, seven other **k** came up H6510
3 the *other* **k** upon the brink of the river. H6510
4 And the ill favoured and leanfleshed **k** H6510
4 favoured and fat **k**. So Pharaoh awoke. H6510
18 of the river seven **k**, fatfleshed and well H6510
19 And, behold, seven other **k** came up H6510
20 And the lean and the ill favoured **k** did H6510
20 kine did eat up the first seven fat **k**: H6510
26 The seven good **k** *are* seven years; and H6510
27 And the seven thin and ill favoured **k** H6510
Dt 7:13 the increase of thy **k**, and the flocks of thy H504
28: 4 of thy **k**, and the flocks of thy sheep. H504
18 of thy **k**, and the flocks of thy sheep. H504
51 *or* the increase of thy **k**, or flocks of thy H504
32:14 Butter of **k**, and milk of sheep, with fat H1241
1Sa 6: 7 take two milch **k**, on which there hath H6510
7 no yoke, and tie the **k** to the cart, and H6510
10 took two milch **k**, and tied them to the H6510
12 And the **k** took the straight way to the H6510
14 the **k** a burnt offering unto the LORD. H6510
2Sa 17:29 and cheese of **k**, for David, and for the H1241
Am 4: 1 Hear this word, ye **k** of Bashan, that H6510

KING

Gen 14: 1 days of Amraphel **k** of Shinar, Arioch H4428
1 king of Shinar, Arioch **k** of Ellasar, H4428
1 **k** of Elam, and Tidal king of nations; H4428
1 king of Elam, and Tidal **k** of nations; H4428
2 *That these* made war with Bera **k** of H4428
2 and with Birsha **k** of Gomorrah, H4428

2 Shinab **k** of Admah, and Shemeber H4428
Gen 14: 2 and Shemeber **k** of Zeboiim, and the H4428
2 and the **k** of Bela, which is Zoar. H4428
8 And there went out the **k** of Sodom, H4428
8 of Sodom, and the **k** of Gomorrah, and H4428
8 and the **k** of Admah, and the H4428
8 Admah, and the **k** of Zeboiim, and the H4428
8 Zeboiim, and the **k** of Bela (the same *is* H4428
9 With Chedorlaomer the **k** of Elam, and H4428
9 Elam, and with Tidal **k** of nations, and H4428
9 and Amraphel **k** of Shinar, and Arioch H4428
9 **k** of Ellasar; four kings with five. H4428
17 And the **k** of Sodom went out to meet H4428
18 And Melchizedek **k** of Salem brought H4428
21 And the **k** of Sodom said unto Abram, H4428
22 And Abram said to the **k** of Sodom, I H4428
20: 2 **k** of Gerar sent, and took Sarah. H4428
26: 1 **k** of the Philistines unto Gerar. H4428
8 that Abimelech **k** of the Philistines H4428
36:31 any **k** over the children of Israel. H4428
40: 1 *that* the butler of the **k** of Egypt and *his* H4428
1 had offended their lord the **k** of Egypt. H4428
5 the baker of the **k** of Egypt, which *were* H4428
41:46 before Pharaoh **k** of Egypt. And Joseph H4428
Ex 1: 8 Now there arose up a new **k** over Egypt, H4428
15 And the **k** of Egypt spake to the Hebrew H4428
17 God, and did not as the **k** of Egypt H4428
18 And the **k** of Egypt called for the H4428
2:23 of time, that the **k** of Egypt died: and H4428
3:18 of Israel, unto the **k** of Egypt, and ye H4428
19 And I am sure that the **k** of Egypt will H4428
5: 4 And the **k** of Egypt said unto them, H4428
6:11 Go in, speak unto Pharaoh **k** of Egypt, H4428
13 and unto Pharaoh **k** of Egypt, to bring H4428
27 spake to Pharaoh **k** of Egypt, to bring H4428
29 **k** of Egypt all that I say unto thee. H4428
14: 5 And it was told the **k** of Egypt that the H4428
8 the heart of Pharaoh **k** of Egypt, and he H4428
Nu 20:14 Kadesh unto the **k** of Edom, Thus saith H4428
21: 1 And *when* **k** Arad the Canaanite, which H4428
21 unto Sihon **k** of the Amorites, saying, H4428
26 city of Sihon the **k** of the Amorites, who H4428
26 against the former **k** of Moab, and H4428
29 captivity unto Sihon **k** of the Amorites. H4428
33 and Og the **k** of Bashan went out H4428
34 didst unto Sihon **k** of the Amorites, H4428
22: 4 *was* **k** of the Moabites at that time. H4428
10 **k** of Moab, hath sent unto me, *saying*, H4428
23: 7 said, Balak the **k** of Moab hath brought H4428
21 and the shout of a **k** *is* among them. H4428
24: 7 waters, and his **k** shall be higher than H4428
32:33 kingdom of Sihon **k** of the Amorites, H4428
33 the kingdom of Og **k** of Bashan, the H4428
33:40 And **k** Arad the Canaanite, which dwelt H4428
Dt 1: 4 After he had slain Sihon the **k** of the H4428
4 and Og the **k** of Bashan, which dwelt H4428
2:24 the Amorite, **k** of Heshbon, and his H4428
26 unto Sihon **k** of Heshbon with words H4428
30 But Sihon **k** of Heshbon would not let H4428
3: 1 and Og the **k** of Bashan came out H4428
2 didst unto Sihon **k** of the Amorites, H4428
3 hands Og also, the **k** of Bashan, and all H4428
6 as we did unto Sihon **k** of Heshbon, H4428
11 For only Og **k** of Bashan remained of H4428
4:46 in the land of Sihon **k** of the Amorites, H4428
47 and the land of Og **k** of Bashan, two H4428
7: 8 from the hand of Pharaoh **k** of Egypt. H4428
11: 3 the **k** of Egypt, and unto all his land; H4428
17:14 say, I will set a **k** over me, like as all the H4428
15 Thou shalt in any wise set *him* **k** over H4428
15 shalt thou set **k** over thee: thou mayest H4428
28:36 The LORD shall bring thee, and thy **k** H4428
29: 7 place, Sihon the **k** of Heshbon, and Og H4428
7 and Og the **k** of Bashan, came out H4428
33: 5 And he was **k** in Jeshurun, when the H4428
Jos 2: 2 And it was told the **k** of Jericho, saying, H4428
3 And the **k** of Jericho sent unto Rahab, H4428
6: 2 Jericho, and the **k** thereof, *and* the H4428
8: 1 given into thy hand the **k** of Ai, and his H4428
2 And thou shalt do to Ai and her **k** as H4428
2 Jericho and her **k**: only the spoil thereof, H4428
14 And it came to pass, when the **k** of Ai H4428
23 And the **k** of Ai they took alive, and H4428
29 And the **k** of Ai he hanged on a tree H4428
9:10 Jordan, to Sihon **k** of Heshbon, and to H4428
10 **k** of Bashan, which *was* at Ashtaroth. H4428
10: 1 Adoni-zedek **k** of Jerusalem had heard H4428
1 to Jericho and her **k**, so he had done to H4428
1 had done to Ai and her **k**; and how the H4428

3 Wherefore Adoni-zedek **k** of Jerusalem H4428
Jos 10: 3 sent unto Hoham **k** of Hebron, and H4428
3 and unto Piram **k** of Jarmuth, and unto H4428
3 and unto Japhia **k** of Lachish, and unto H4428
3 and unto Debir **k** of Eglon, saying, H4428
5 of the Amorites, the **k** of Jerusalem, the H4428
5 of Jerusalem, the **k** of Hebron, the king H4428
5 of Hebron, the **k** of Jarmuth, the king H4428
5 of Jarmuth, the **k** of Lachish, the king H4428
5 of Lachish, the **k** of Eglon, gathered H4428
23 of the cave, the **k** of Jerusalem, the king H4428
23 of Jerusalem, the **k** of Hebron, the king H4428
23 of Hebron, the **k** of Jarmuth, the king H4428
23 the **k** of Lachish, *and* the king of Eglon. H4428
23 the king of Lachish, *and* the **k** of Eglon. H4428
28 the sword, and the **k** thereof he utterly H4428
28 and he did to the **k** of Makkedah as he H4428
28 as he did unto the **k** of Jericho. H4428
30 it also, and the **k** thereof, into the hand H4428
30 it; but did unto the **k** thereof as he did H4428
30 thereof as he did unto the **k** of Jericho. H4428
33 Then Horam **k** of Gezer came up to H4428
37 of the sword, and the **k** thereof, and all H4428
39 And he took it, and the **k** thereof, and H4428
39 Debir, and to the **k** thereof; as he had H4428
39 had done also to Libnah, and to her **k**. H4428
11: 1 And it came to pass, when Jabin **k** of H4428
1 he sent to Jobab **k** of Madon, and to the H4428
1 Madon, and to the **k** of Shimron, and H4428
1 of Shimron, and to the **k** of Achshaph, H4428
10 and smote the **k** thereof with the H4428
12: 2 Sihon **k** of the Amorites, who dwelt in H4428
4 And the coast of Og **k** of Bashan, *which* H4428
5 the border of Sihon **k** of Heshbon. H4428
9 The **k** of Jericho, one; the king of Ai, H4428
9 The king of Jericho, one; the **k** of Ai, H4428
10 The **k** of Jerusalem, one; the king of H4428
10 The king of Jerusalem, one; the **k** of H4428
11 The **k** of Jarmuth, one; the king of H4428
11 The king of Jarmuth, one; the **k** of H4428
12 The **k** of Eglon, one; the king of Gezer, H4428
12 The king of Eglon, one; the **k** of Gezer, H4428
13 The **k** of Debir, one; the king of Geder, H4428
13 The king of Debir, one; the **k** of Geder, H4428
14 The **k** of Hormah, one; the king of H4428
14 The king of Hormah, one; the **k** of H4428
15 The **k** of Libnah, one; the king of H4428
15 The king of Libnah, one; the **k** of H4428
16 The **k** of Makkedah, one; the king of H4428
16 The king of Makkedah, one; the **k** of H4428
17 The **k** of Tappuah, one; the king of H4428
17 The king of Tappuah, one; the **k** of H4428
18 The **k** of Aphek, one; the king of H4428
18 The king of Aphek, one; the **k** of H4428
19 The **k** of Madon, one; the king of H4428
19 The king of Madon, one; the **k** of H4428
20 The **k** of Shimron-meron, one; the king H4428
20 The king of Shimron-meron, one; the **k** H4428
21 The **k** of Taanach, one; the king of H4428
21 The king of Taanach, one; the **k** of H4428
22 The **k** of Kedesh, one; the king of H4428
22 The king of Kedesh, one; the **k** of H4428
23 The **k** of Dor in the coast of Dor, one; H4428
23 one; the **k** of the nations of Gilgal, one; H4428
24 The **k** of Tirzah, one: all the kings thirty H4428
13:10 And all the cities of Sihon **k** of the H4428
21 kingdom of Sihon **k** of the Amorites, H4428
27 the kingdom of Sihon **k** of Heshbon, H4428
30 the kingdom of Og **k** of Bashan, and all H4428
24: 9 Then Balak the son of Zippor, **k** of H4428
Jdg 3: 8 **k** of Mesopotamia: and H4428
10 **k** of Mesopotamia into H4428
12 Eglon the **k** of Moab against Israel, H4428
14 Eglon the **k** of Moab eighteen years. H4428
15 a present unto Eglon the **k** of Moab. H4428
17 unto Eglon **k** of Moab: and Eglon H4428
19 unto thee, O **k**: who said, Keep silence. H4428
4: 2 the hand of Jabin **k** of Canaan, that H4428
17 between Jabin the **k** of Hazor and the H4428
23 that day Jabin the **k** of Canaan before H4428
24 against Jabin the **k** of Canaan, until H4428
24 they had destroyed Jabin **k** of Canaan. H4428
8:18 each one resembled the children of a **k**. H4428
9: 6 made Abimelech **k**, by the plain of the H4428
8 *on a time* to anoint a **k** over them; and H4428
15 ye anoint me **k** over you, *then* come H4428
16 made Abimelech **k**, and if ye have dealt H4427
18 of his maidservant, **k** over the men of H4427
11:12 unto the **k** of the children of Ammon, H4428

13 And the **k** of the children of Ammon H4428
Jdg 11:14 unto the **k** of the children of Ammon: H4428
17 Then Israel sent messengers unto the **k** H4428
17 thy land: but the **k** of Edom would not H4428
17 they sent unto the **k** of Moab: but he H4428
19 unto Sihon **k** of the Amorites, the H4428
19 of the Amorites, the **k** of Heshbon; and H4428
25 the son of Zippor, **k** of Moab? did he H4428
28 Howbeit the **k** of the children of H4428
17: 6 In those days *there was* no **k** in Israel, H4428
18: 1 In those days *there was* no **k** in Israel: H4428
19: 1 *there was* no **k** in Israel, that there H4428
21:25 In those days *there was* no **k** in Israel: H4428
1Sa 2:10 **k**, and exalt the horn of his anointed. H4428
8: 5 us a **k** to judge us like all the nations. H4428
6 they said, Give us a **k** to judge us. And H4428
9 of the **k** that shall reign over them. H4428
10 unto the people that asked of him a **k**. H4428
11 be the manner of the **k** that shall reign H4428
18 because of your **k** which ye shall have H4428
19 said, Nay; but we will have a **k** over us; H4428
20 and that our **k** may judge us, and go H4428
22 and make them a **k**. And Samuel said H4428
10:19 *Nay*, but set a **k** over us. Now therefore H4428
24 shouted, and said, God save the **k**. H4428
11:15 they made Saul **k** before the LORD in H4427
12: 1 unto me, and have made a **k** over you. H4428
2 And now, behold, the **k** walketh before H4428
9 the hand of the **k** of Moab, and they H4428
12 And when ye saw that Nahash the **k** of H4428
12 me, Nay; but a **k** shall reign over us: H4428
12 when the LORD your God *was* your **k**. H4428
13 Now therefore behold the **k** whom ye H4428
13 the LORD hath set a **k** over you. H4428
14 ye and also the **k** that reigneth over you H4428
17 sight of the LORD, in asking you a **k**. H4428
19 unto all our sins *this* evil, to ask us a **k**. H4428
25 shall be consumed, both ye and your **k**. H4428
15: 1 to anoint thee *to be* **k** over his people, H4428
8 And he took Agag the **k** of the H4428
11 set up Saul *to be* **k**: for he is turned back H4428
17 the LORD anointed thee **k** over Israel? H4428
20 brought Agag the **k** of Amalek, and H4428
23 he hath also rejected thee from *being* **k**. H4428
26 rejected thee from being **k** over Israel. H4428
32 to me Agag the **k** of the Amalekites. H4428
35 that he had made Saul **k** over Israel. H4427
16: 1 have provided me a **k** among his sons. H4428
17:25 killeth him, the **k** will enrich him with H4428
55 *As* thy soul liveth, O **k**, I cannot tell. H4428
56 And the **k** said, Inquire thou whose son H4428
18: 6 dancing, to meet **k** Saul, with tabrets, H4428
18 that I should be son in law to the **k**? H4428
22 say, Behold, the **k** hath delight in thee, H4428
25 ye say to David, The **k** desireth not any H4428
27 in full tale to the **k**, that he might be the H4428
19: 4 unto him, Let not the **k** sin against his H4428
20: 5 fail to sit with the **k** at meat: but let me H4428
24 come, the **k** sat him down to eat meat. H4428
25 And the **k** sat upon his seat, as at other H4428
21: 2 the priest, The **k** hath commanded me H4428
10 Saul, and went to Achish the **k** of Gath. H4428
11 *Is* not this David the **k** of the land? did H4428
12 was sore afraid of Achish the **k** of Gath. H4428
22: 3 and he said unto the **k** of Moab, Let my H4428
4 And he brought them before the **k** of H4428
11 Then the **k** sent to call Ahimelech the H4428
11 Nob: and they came all of them to the **k**. H4428
14 Then Ahimelech answered the **k**, and H4428
15 me: let not the **k** impute *any* thing unto H4428
16 And the **k** said, Thou shalt surely die, H4428
17 And the **k** said unto the footmen that H4428
17 But the servants of the **k** would not put H4428
18 And the **k** said to Doeg, Turn thou, and H4428
23:17 and thou shalt be **k** over Israel, and I H4427
20 Now therefore, O **k**, come down H4428
24: 8 My lord the **k**. And when Saul looked H4428
14 After whom is the **k** of Israel come out? H4428
20 shalt surely be **k**, and that the kingdom H4427
25:36 like the feast of a **k**; and Nabal's heart H4428
26:14 said, Who *art* thou *that* criest to the **k**? H4428
15 kept thy lord the **k**? for there came one H4428
15 the people in to destroy the **k** thy lord. H4428
17 David said, *It is* my voice, my lord, O **k**. H4428
19 let my lord the **k** hear the words of his H4428
20 of the LORD: for the **k** of Israel is come H4428
27: 2 Achish, the son of Maoch, **k** of Gath. H4428
28:13 And the **k** said unto her, Be not afraid: H4428
29: 3 servant of Saul the **k** of Israel, which H4428

8 against the enemies of my lord the **k**? H4428
2Sa 2: 4 anointed David **k** over the house of H4428
7 Judah have anointed me **k** over them. H4428
9 And made him **k** over Gilead, and over H4427
11 And the time that David was **k** in H4428
3: 3 the daughter of Talmai **k** of Geshur; H4428
17 David in times past *to be* **k** over you: H4428
21 unto my lord the **k**, that they may make H4428
23 of Ner came to the **k**, and he hath sent H4428
24 Then Joab came to the **k**, and said, H4428
31 And **k** David *himself* followed the bier. H4428
32 in Hebron: and the **k** lifted up his voice, H4428
33 And the **k** lamented over Abner, and H4428
36 the **k** did pleased all the people. H4428
37 of the **k** to slay Abner the son of Ner. H4428
38 And the **k** said unto his servants, Know H4428
39 though anointed **k**; and these men the H4428
4: 8 and said to the **k**, Behold the head of H4428
8 the **k** this day of Saul, and of his seed. H4428
5: 2 Also in time past, when Saul was **k** H4428
3 So all the elders of Israel came to the **k** H4428
3 to Hebron; and **k** David made a league H4428
3 and they anointed David **k** over Israel. H4428
6 And the **k** and his men went to H4428
11 And Hiram **k** of Tyre sent messengers H4428
12 established him **k** over Israel, and that H4428
17 anointed David **k** over Israel, all the H4428
6:12 And it was told **k** David, saying, The H4428
16 window, and saw **k** David leaping and H4428
20 glorious was the **k** of Israel to day, who H4428
7: 1 And it came to pass, when the **k** sat in H4428
2 That the **k** said unto Nathan the H4428
3 And Nathan said to the **k**, Go, do all H4428
18 Then went **k** David in, and sat before H4428
8: 3 the son of Rehob, **k** of Zobah, as he H4428
5 Hadadezer **k** of Zobah, David slew H4428
8 **k** David took exceeding much brass. H4428
9 When Toi **k** of Hamath heard that H4428
10 Then Toi sent Joram his son unto **k** H4428
11 Which also **k** David did dedicate unto H4428
12 Hadadezer, son of Rehob, **k** of Zobah. H4428
9: 2 unto David, the **k** said unto him, *Art* H4428
3 And the **k** said, *Is* there not yet any of H4428
3 Ziba said unto the **k**, Jonathan hath yet H4428
4 And the **k** said unto him, Where *is* he? H4428
4 Ziba said unto the **k**, Behold, he *is* in the H4428
5 Then **k** David sent, and fetched him H4428
9 Then the **k** called to Ziba, Saul's H4428
11 Then said Ziba unto the **k**, According to H4428
11 all that my lord the **k** hath commanded H4428
11 *said the* **k**, he shall eat at my table, H4428
10: 1 after this, that the **k** of the children of H4428
5 ashamed: and the **k** said, Tarry at H4428
6 footmen, and of **k** Maacah a thousand H4428
11: 8 him a mess *of meat* from the **k**. H4428
19 the matters of the war unto the **k**, H4428
12: 7 I anointed thee **k** over Israel, and I H4428
13: 6 and when the **k** was come to see him, H4428
6 said unto the **k**, I pray thee, let Tamar H4428
13 thee, speak unto the **k**; for he will not H4428
21 But when **k** David heard of all these H4428
24 And Absalom came to the **k**, and said, H4428
24 let the **k**, I beseech thee, and H4428
25 And the **k** said to Absalom, Nay, my H4428
26 with us. And the **k** said unto him, Why H4428
31 Then the **k** arose, and tare his H4428
33 Now therefore let not my lord the **k** H4428
35 And Jonadab said unto the **k**, Behold, H4428
36 and wept: and the **k** also and all his H4428
37 the son of Ammihud, **k** of Geshur. And H4428
39 And *the soul of* **k** David longed to go H4428
14: 3 And come to the **k**, and speak on this H4428
4 spake to the **k**, she fell on her face to H4428
4 and did obeisance, and said, Help, O **k**. H4428
5 And the **k** said unto her, What aileth H4428
8 And the **k** said unto the woman, Go to H4428
9 said unto the **k**, My lord, O king, the H4428
9 king, My lord, O **k**, the iniquity *be* on H4428
9 and the **k** and his throne *be* guiltless. H4428
10 And the **k** said, Whosoever saith *ought* H4428
11 Then said she, I pray thee, let the **k** H4428
12 unto my lord the **k**. And he said, Say on. H4428
13 of God? for the **k** doth speak this thing H4428
13 is faulty, in that the **k** doth not fetch H4428
15 unto my lord the **k**, *it is* because the H4428
15 now speak unto the **k**; it may be that the H4428
15 it may be that the **k** will perform the H4428
16 For the **k** will hear, to deliver his H4428
17 word of my lord the **k** shall now be H4428
17 so *is* my lord the **k** to discern good and H4428
2Sa 14:18 Then the **k** answered and said unto the H4428
18 said, Let my lord the **k** now speak. H4428
19 And the **k** said, *Is not* the hand of Joab H4428
19 liveth, my lord the **k**, none can turn to H4428
19 that my lord the **k** hath spoken: for thy H4428
21 And the **k** said unto Joab, Behold now, H4428
22 and thanked the **k**: and Joab said, To H4428
22 sight, my lord, O **k**, in that the king hath H4428
22 O king, in that the **k** hath fulfilled the H4428
24 And the **k** said, Let him turn to his own H4428
29 have sent him to the **k**; but he would not H4428
32 send thee to the **k**, to say, Wherefore am H4428
33 So Joab came to the **k**, and told him: H4428
33 he came to the **k**, and bowed himself H4428
33 the **k**: and the king kissed Absalom. H4428
33 the king: and the **k** kissed Absalom. H4428
15: 2 came to the **k** for judgment, then H4428
3 no man *deputed* of the **k** to hear thee. H4428
6 that came to the **k** for judgment: so H4428
7 said unto the **k**, I pray thee, let me go H4428
9 And the **k** said unto him, Go in peace. H4428
15 And the king's servants said unto the **k**, H4428
15 my lord the **k** shall appoint. H4428
16 And the **k** went forth, and all his H4428
16 after him. And the **k** left ten women, H4428
17 And the **k** went forth, and all the H4428
18 him from Gath, passed on before the **k**. H4428
19 Then said the **k** to Ittai the Gittite, H4428
19 abide with the **k**: for thou *art* a stranger, H4428
21 And Ittai answered the **k**, and said, *As* H4428
21 *as* my lord the **k** liveth, surely in what H4428
21 place my lord the **k** shall be, whether in H4428
23 passed over: the **k** also himself passed H4428
25 And the **k** said unto Zadok, Carry back H4428
27 The **k** said also unto Zadok the priest, H4428
34 be thy servant, O **k**; *as* I *have been* thy H4428
16: 2 And the **k** said unto Ziba, What H4428
3 And the **k** said, And where *is* thy H4428
3 Ziba said unto the **k**, Behold, he abideth H4428
4 Then said the **k** to Ziba, Behold, thine H4428
4 find grace in thy sight, my lord, O **k**. H4428
5 And when **k** David came to Bahurim, H4428
6 all the servants of **k** David: and all the H4428
9 of Zeruiah unto the **k**, Why should this H4428
9 curse my lord the **k**? let me go over, I H4428
10 And the **k** said, What have I to do with H4428
14 And the **k**, and all the people that *were* H4428
16 God save the **k**, God save the king. H4428
16 God save the king, God save the **k**. H4428
17: 2 shall flee; and I will smite the **k** only: H4428
16 pass over; lest the **k** be swallowed up, H4428
17 them; and they went and told **k** David. H4428
21 and went and told **k** David, and said H4428
18: 2 Gittite. And the **k** said unto the people, H4428
4 And the **k** said unto them, What H4428
4 I will do. And the **k** stood by the gate H4428
5 And the **k** commanded Joab and H4428
5 heard when the **k** gave all the captains H4428
12 in our hearing the **k** charged thee and H4428
13 matter hid from the **k**, and thou thyself H4428
19 run, and bear the **k** tidings, how that H4428
21 Then said Joab to Cushi, Go tell the **k** H4428
25 cried, and told the **k**. And the king said, H4428
25 the king. And the **k** said, If he *be* alone, H4428
26 the **k** said, He also bringeth tidings. H4428
27 of Zadok. And the **k** said, He *is* a good H4428
28 and said unto the **k**, All is well. And he H4428
28 his face before the **k**, and said, Blessed H4428
28 up their hand against my lord the **k**. H4428
29 And the **k** said, Is the young man H4428
30 And the **k** said *unto him*, Turn aside, H4428
31 my lord the **k**: for the LORD hath H4428
32 And the **k** said unto Cushi, Is the young H4428
32 of my lord the **k**, and all that rise H4428
33 And the **k** was much moved, and went H4428
19: 1 And it was told Joab, Behold, the **k** H4428
2 day how the **k** was grieved for his son. H4428
4 But the **k** covered his face, and the king H4428
4 But the king covered his face, and the **k** H4428
5 And Joab came into the house to the **k**, H4428
8 Then the **k** arose, and sat in the gate. H4428
8 Behold, the **k** doth sit in the gate. H4428
8 came before the **k**: for Israel had fled H4428
9 Israel, saying, The **k** saved us out of the H4428
10 ye not a word of bringing the **k** back? H4428
11 And **k** David sent to Zadok and to H4428
11 last to bring the **k** back to his house? H4428
11 is come to the **k**, *even* to his house. H4428
12 then are ye the last to bring back the **k**? H4428
2Sa 19:14 the **k**, Return thou, and all thy servants. H4428
15 So the **k** returned, and came to Jordan. H4428
15 the **k**, to conduct the king over Jordan. H4428
15 the king, to conduct the **k** over Jordan. H4428
16 with the men of Judah to meet **k** David. H4428
17 and they went over Jordan before the **k**. H4428
18 the **k**, as he was come over Jordan; H4428
19 And said unto the **k**, Let not my lord H4428
19 day that my lord the **k** went out of H4428
19 that the **k** should take it to his heart. H4428
20 to go down to meet my lord the **k**. H4428
22 I know that I *am* this day **k** over Israel? H4428
23 Therefore the **k** said unto Shimei, Thou H4428
23 not die. And the **k** sware unto him. H4428
24 down to meet the **k**, and had neither H4428
24 from the day the **k** departed until the H4428
25 to meet the **k**, that the king said unto H4428
25 meet the king, that the **k** said unto him, H4428
26 And he answered, My lord, O **k**, my H4428
26 go to the **k**; because thy servant *is* lame. H4428
27 unto my lord the **k**; but my lord the king H4428
27 but my lord the **k** *is* as an angel of God: H4428
28 before my lord the **k**: yet didst thou set H4428
28 have I yet to cry any more unto the **k**? H4428
29 And the **k** said unto him, Why speakest H4428
30 And Mephibosheth said unto the **k**, H4428
30 as my lord the **k** is come again in peace H4428
31 with the **k**, to conduct him over Jordan. H4428
32 had provided the **k** of sustenance while H4428
33 And the **k** said unto Barzillai, Come H4428
34 And Barzillai said unto the **k**, How long H4428
34 go up with the **k** unto Jerusalem? H4428
35 be yet a burden unto my lord the **k**? H4428
36 Jordan with the **k**: and why should the H4428
36 why should the **k** recompense it me H4428
37 with my lord the **k**; and do to him what H4428
38 And the **k** answered, Chimham shall go H4428
39 And when the **k** was come over, the H4428
39 come over, the **k** kissed Barzillai, and H4428
40 Then the **k** went on to Gilgal, and H4428
40 the **k**, and also half the people of Israel. H4428
41 Israel came to the **k**, and said unto the H4428
41 king, and said unto the **k**, Why have our H4428
41 have brought the **k**, and his household, H4428
42 Because the **k** *is* near of kin to us: H4428
43 ten parts in the **k**, and we have also H4428
43 bringing back our **k**? And the words of H4428
20: 2 their **k**, from Jordan even to Jerusalem. H4428
3 and the **k** took the ten women H4428
4 Then said the **k** to Amasa, Assemble H4428
21 hand against the **k**, *even* against David: H4428
22 Joab returned to Jerusalem unto the **k**. H4428
21: 2 And the **k** called the Gibeonites, and H4428
5 And they answered the **k**, The man that H4428
6 And the **k** said, I will give *them*. H4428
7 But the **k** spared Mephibosheth, the H4428
8 But the **k** took the two sons of Rizpah H4428
14 all that the **k** commanded. And after H4428
22:51 *He is* the tower of salvation for his **k**: H4428
24: 2 For the **k** said to Joab the captain of the H4428
3 And Joab said unto the **k**, Now the H4428
3 of my lord the **k** may see *it*: but why H4428
3 doth my lord the **k** delight in this thing? H4428
4 of the **k**, to number the people of Israel. H4428
9 the people unto the **k**: and there were in H4428
20 And Araunah looked, and saw the **k** H4428
20 the **k** on his face upon the ground. H4428
21 is my lord the **k** come to his servant? H4428
22 Let my lord the **k** take and offer up H4428
23 All these *things* did Araunah, *as* a **k**, H4428
23 king, give unto the **k**. And Araunah said H4428
23 the **k**, The LORD thy God accept thee. H4428
24 And the **k** said unto Araunah, Nay; but H4428
1Ki 1: 1 Now **k** David was old *and* stricken in H4428
2 for my lord the **k** a young virgin: and H4428
2 stand before the **k**, and let her cherish H4428
2 that my lord the **k** may get heat. H4428
3 Shunammite, and brought her to the **k**. H4428
4 and cherished the **k**, and ministered to H4428
4 to him: but the **k** knew her not. H4428
5 saying, I will be **k**: and he prepared him H4427
13 Go and get thee in unto **k** David, and H4428
13 not thou, my lord, O **k**, swear unto thine H4428
14 there with the **k**, I also will come in after H4428
15 And Bath-sheba went in unto the **k** H4428
15 chamber: and the **k** was very old; and H4428
15 the Shunammite ministered unto the **k**. H4428
16 unto the **k**. And the king said, What H4428

K

16 And the **k** said, What wouldest thou? H4428
1Ki 1:18 now, my lord the **k**, thou knowest *it* not: H4428
19 all the sons of the **k**, and Abiathar the H4428
20 And thou, my lord, O **k**, the eyes of all H4428
20 the throne of my lord the **k** after him. H4428
21 when my lord the **k** shall sleep with his H4428
22 And, lo, while she yet talked with the **k**, H4428
23 And they told the **k**, saying, Behold H4428
23 come in before the **k**, he bowed himself H4428
23 the **k** with his face to the ground. H4428
24 And Nathan said, My lord, O **k**, hast H4428
25 him, and say, God save **k** Adonijah. H4428
27 Is this thing done by my lord the **k**, and H4428
27 the throne of my lord the **k** after him? H4428
28 Then **k** David answered and said, Call H4428
28 king's presence, and stood before the **k**. H4428
29 And the **k** sware, and said, *As* the H4428
31 did reverence to the **k**, and said, Let my H4428
31 said, Let my lord **k** David live for ever. H4428
32 And **k** David said, Call me Zadok the H4428
32 Jehoiada. And they came before the **k**. H4428
33 The **k** also said unto them, Take with H4428
34 anoint him there **k** over Israel: and H4428
34 trumpet, and say, God save **k** Solomon. H4428
35 for he shall be **k** in my stead: and I H4427
36 answered the **k**, and said, Amen: the H4428
36 LORD God of my lord the **k** say so *too*. H4428
37 with my lord the **k**, even so be he with H4428
37 than the throne of my lord **k** David. H4428
38 to ride upon **k** David's mule, and H4428
39 the people said, God save **k** Solomon. H4428
43 lord **k** David hath made Solomon king. H4428
43 lord king David hath made Solomon **k**. H4427
44 And the **k** hath sent with him Zadok H4428
45 anointed him **k** in Gihon: and they are H4428
47 to bless our lord **k** David, saying, God H4428
47 And the **k** bowed himself upon the bed. H4428
48 And also thus said the **k**, Blessed *be* the H4428
51 Adonijah feareth **k** Solomon: for, lo, he H4428
51 the altar, saying, Let **k** Solomon swear H4428
53 So **k** Solomon sent, and they brought H4428
53 and bowed himself to **k** Solomon: and H4428
2:17 unto Solomon the **k**, (for he will not say H4428
18 Well; I will speak for thee unto the **k**. H4428
19 Bath-sheba therefore went unto **k** H4428
19 Adonijah. And the **k** rose up to meet H4428
20 not nay. And the **k** said unto her, Ask H4428
22 And **k** Solomon answered and said H4428
23 Then **k** Solomon sware by the LORD, H4428
25 And **k** Solomon sent by the hand of H4428
26 And unto Abiathar the priest said the **k**, H4428
29 And it was told **k** Solomon that Joab H4428
30 Thus saith the **k**, Come forth. And he H4428
30 brought the **k** word again, saying, H4428
31 And the **k** said unto him, Do as he hath H4428
35 And the **k** put Benaiah the son of H4428
35 did the **k** put in the room of Abiathar. H4428
36 And the **k** sent and called for Shimei, H4428
38 And Shimei said unto the **k**, The saying H4428
38 as my lord the **k** hath said, so will thy H4428
39 son of Maachah **k** of Gath. And they H4428
42 And the **k** sent and called for Shimei, H4428
44 The **k** said moreover to Shimei, Thou H4428
45 And **k** Solomon *shall be* blessed, and H4428
46 So the **k** commanded Benaiah the son H4428
3: 1 with Pharaoh **k** of Egypt, and took H4428
4 And the **k** went to Gibeon to sacrifice H4428
7 made thy servant **k** instead of David H4427
16 unto the **k**, and stood before him. H4428
22 *is* my son. Thus they spake before the **k**. H4428
23 Then said the **k**, The one saith, This *is* H4428
24 And the **k** said, Bring me a sword. And H4428
24 And they brought a sword before the **k**. H4428
25 And the **k** said, Divide the living child H4428
26 child *was* unto the **k**, for her bowels H4428
27 Then the **k** answered and said, Give her H4428
28 which the **k** had judged; and they H4428
28 they feared the **k**: for they saw that the H4428
4: 1 So **k** Solomon was king over all Israel. H4428
1 So king Solomon was **k** over all Israel. H4428
7 victuals for the **k** and his household: H4428
19 country of Sihon **k** of the Amorites, and H4428
19 and of Og **k** of Bashan; and *he was* H4428
27 victual for **k** Solomon, and for all H4428
27 all that came unto **k** Solomon's table, H4428
5: 1 And Hiram **k** of Tyre sent his servants H4428
1 had anointed him **k** in the room of his H4428
13 And **k** Solomon raised a levy out of all H4428
17 And the **k** commanded, and they H4428
6: 2 And the house which **k** Solomon built H4428
1Ki 7:13 And **k** Solomon sent and fetched H4428
14 **k** Solomon, and wrought all his work. H4428
40 **k** Solomon for the house of the LORD: H4428
45 Hiram made to **k** Solomon for the H4428
46 In the plain of Jordan did the **k** cast H4428
51 So was ended all the work that **k** H4428
8: 1 of Israel, unto **k** Solomon in Jerusalem, H4428
2 themselves unto **k** Solomon at the feast H4428
5 And **k** Solomon, and all the H4428
14 And the **k** turned his face about, and H4428
62 And the **k**, and all Israel with him, H4428
63 sheep. So the **k** and all the children H4428
64 The same day did the **k** hallow the H4428
66 they blessed the **k**, and went unto their H4428
9:11 (*Now* Hiram the **k** of Tyre had H4428
11 his desire,) that then **k** Solomon gave H4428
14 And Hiram sent to the **k** sixscore H4428
15 of the levy which **k** Solomon raised; for H4428
16 *For* Pharaoh **k** of Egypt had gone up, H4428
26 And **k** Solomon made a navy of ships H4428
28 talents, and brought *it* to **k** Solomon. H4428
10: 3 hid from the **k**, which he told her not. H4428
6 And she said to the **k**, It was a true H4428
9 he thee **k**, to do judgment and justice. H4428
10 And she gave the **k** an hundred and H4428
10 the queen of Sheba gave to **k** Solomon. H4428
12 And the **k** made of the almug trees H4428
13 And **k** Solomon gave unto the queen of H4428
16 And **k** Solomon made two hundred H4428
17 shield: and the **k** put them in the house H4428
18 Moreover the **k** made a great throne of H4428
21 And all **k** Solomon's drinking vessels H4428
22 For the **k** had at sea a navy of H4428
23 So **k** Solomon exceeded all the kings of H4428
26 chariots, and with the **k** at Jerusalem. H4428
27 And the **k** made silver *to be* in H4428
11: 1 But **k** Solomon loved many strange H4428
18 unto Pharaoh **k** of Egypt; which gave H4428
23 from his lord Hadadezer **k** of Zobah: H4428
26 even he lifted up *his* hand against the **k**. H4428
27 *his* hand against the **k**: Solomon built H4428
37 desireth, and shalt be **k** over Israel. H4428
40 unto Shishak **k** of Egypt, and was in H4428
12: 1 were come to Shechem to make him **k**. H4427
2 from the presence of **k** Solomon, and H4428
6 And **k** Rehoboam consulted with the H4428
12 the third day, as the **k** had appointed, H4428
13 And the **k** answered the people H4428
15 Wherefore the **k** hearkened not unto H4428
16 So when all Israel saw that the **k** H4428
16 answered the **k**, saying, What portion H4428
18 Then **k** Rehoboam sent Adoram, who H4428
18 he died. Therefore **k** Rehoboam made H4428
20 and made him **k** over all Israel: there H4427
23 son of Solomon, **k** of Judah, and unto H4428
27 unto Rehoboam **k** of Judah, and they H4428
27 and go again to Rehoboam **k** of Judah. H4428
28 Whereupon the **k** took counsel, and H4428
13: 4 And it came to pass, when **k** Jeroboam H4428
6 And the **k** answered and said unto the H4428
7 And the **k** said unto the man of God, H4428
8 And the man of God said unto the **k**, If H4428
11 **k**, them they told also to their father. H4428
14: 2 me that *I should be* **k** over this people. H4428
14 raise him up a **k** over Israel, who shall H4428
25 in the fifth year of **k** Rehoboam, *that* H4428
25 **k** of Egypt came up against Jerusalem: H4428
27 And **k** Rehoboam made in their stead H4428
28 And it was *so*, when the **k** went into the H4428
15: 1 Now in the eighteenth year of **k** H4428
9 **k** of Israel reigned Asa over Judah. H4428
16 and Baasha **k** of Israel all their days. H4428
17 And Baasha **k** of Israel went up against H4428
17 to go out or come in to Asa **k** of Judah. H4428
18 of his servants: and **k** Asa sent them to H4428
18 the son of Hezion, **k** of Syria, that dwelt H4428
19 with Baasha **k** of Israel, that he may H4428
20 So Ben-hadad hearkened unto **k** Asa, H4428
22 Then **k** Asa made a proclamation H4428
22 had builded; and **k** Asa built with them H4428
25 year of Asa **k** of Judah, and reigned H4428
28 Even in the third year of Asa **k** of Judah H4428
32 and Baasha **k** of Israel all their days. H4428
33 In the third year of Asa **k** of Judah H4428
16: 8 In the twenty and sixth year of Asa **k** of H4428
10 **k** of Judah, and reigned in his stead. H4428
15 In the twenty and seventh year of Asa **k** H4428
16 and hath also slain the **k**: wherefore all H4428
16 **k** over Israel that day in the camp. H4427
1Ki 16:21 to make him **k**; and half followed Omri. H4427
23 In the thirty and first year of Asa **k** of H4428
29 eighth year of Asa **k** of Judah began H4428
31 of Ethbaal **k** of the Zidonians, and H4428
19:15 anoint Hazael *to be* **k** over Syria: H4428
16 thou anoint *to be* **k** over Israel: and H4428
20: 1 And Ben-hadad the **k** of Syria gathered H4428
2 And he sent messengers to Ahab **k** of H4428
4 And the **k** of Israel answered and said, H4428
4 and said, My lord, O **k**, according to thy H4428
7 Then the **k** of Israel called all the elders H4428
9 Tell my lord the **k**, All that thou didst H4428
11 And the **k** of Israel answered and said, H4428
13 unto Ahab **k** of Israel, saying, Thus H4428
20 Ben-hadad the **k** of Syria escaped on H4428
21 And the **k** of Israel went out, and smote H4428
22 And the prophet came to the **k** of H4428
22 **k** of Syria will come up against thee. H4428
23 And the servants of the **k** of Syria said H4428
28 spake unto the **k** of Israel, and said, H4428
31 heads, and go out to the **k** of Israel: H4428
32 and came to the **k** of Israel, and said, H4428
38 and waited for the **k** by the way, and H4428
39 And as the **k** passed by, he cried unto H4428
39 by, he cried unto the **k**: and he said, Thy H4428
40 was gone. And the **k** of Israel said unto H4428
41 his face; and the **k** of Israel discerned H4428
43 And the **k** of Israel went to his house H4428
21: 1 by the palace of Ahab **k** of Samaria. H4428
10 God and the **k**. And *then* carry him H4428
13 God and the **k**. Then they carried him H4428
18 Arise, go down to meet Ahab **k** of H4428
22: 2 Jehoshaphat the **k** of Judah came down H4428
2 of Judah came down to the **k** of Israel. H4428
3 And the **k** of Israel said unto his H4428
3 it not out of the hand of the **k** of Syria? H4428
4 said to the **k** of Israel, I *am* as thou H4428
5 And Jehoshaphat said unto the **k** of H4428
6 Then the **k** of Israel gathered the H4428
6 shall deliver *it* into the hand of the **k**. H4428
8 And the **k** of Israel said unto H4428
8 Jehoshaphat said, Let not the **k** say so. H4428
9 Then the **k** of Israel called an officer, H4428
10 And the **k** of Israel and Jehoshaphat H4428
10 Jehoshaphat the **k** of Judah sat each on H4428
13 good unto the **k** with one mouth: let H4428
15 So he came to the **k**. And the king said H4428
15 So he came to the king. And the **k** said H4428
15 shall deliver *it* into the hand of the **k**. H4428
16 And the **k** said unto him, How many H4428
18 And the **k** of Israel said unto H4428
26 And the **k** of Israel said, Take Micaiah, H4428
27 And say, Thus saith the **k**, Put this H4428
29 So the **k** of Israel and Jehoshaphat the H4428
29 **k** of Judah went up to Ramoth-gilead. H4428
30 And the **k** of Israel said unto H4428
30 thy robes. And the **k** of Israel disguised H4428
31 But the **k** of Syria commanded his H4428
31 nor great, save only with the **k** of Israel. H4428
32 Surely it *is* the **k** of Israel. And they H4428
33 that it *was* not the **k** of Israel, that they H4428
34 and smote the **k** of Israel between the H4428
35 that day: and the **k** was stayed up in H4428
37 So the **k** died, and was brought to H4428
37 and they buried the **k** in Samaria. H4428
41 in the fourth year of Ahab **k** of Israel. H4428
44 made peace with the **k** of Israel. H4428
47 *There was* then no **k** in Edom: a deputy H4428
47 then no king in Edom: a deputy *was* **k**. H4428
51 of Jehoshaphat **k** of Judah, and reigned H4428
2Ki 1: 3 messengers of the **k** of Samaria, and H4428
6 again unto the **k** that sent you, and say H4428
9 Then the **k** sent unto him a captain of H4428
9 of God, the **k** hath said, Come down. H4428
11 hath the **k** said, Come down quickly. H4428
15 and went down with him unto the **k**. H4428
17 **k** of Judah; because he had no son. H4428
3: 1 **k** of Judah, and reigned twelve years. H4428
4 And Mesha **k** of Moab was a H4428
4 and rendered unto the **k** of Israel an H4428
5 was dead, that the **k** of Moab rebelled H4428
5 Moab rebelled against the **k** of Israel. H4428
6 And **k** Jehoram went out of Samaria H4428
7 to Jehoshaphat the **k** of Judah, saying, H4428
7 saying, The **k** of Moab hath rebelled H4428
9 So the **k** of Israel went, and the king of H4428
9 So the king of Israel went, and the **k** of H4428
9 of Judah, and the **k** of Edom: and they H4428

10 And the **k** of Israel said, Alas! that the H4428
2Ki 3:11 And one of the **k** of Israel's servants H4428
12 is with him. So the **k** of Israel and H4428
12 and the **k** of Edom went down to him. H4428
13 And Elisha said unto the **k** of Israel, H4428
13 mother. And the **k** of Israel said unto H4428
14 of Jehoshaphat the **k** of Judah, I would H4428
26 And when the **k** of Moab saw that the H4428
26 unto the **k** of Edom: but they could not. H4428
4:13 spoken for to the **k**, or to the captain of H4428
5: 1 of the host of the **k** of Syria, was a great H4428
5 And the **k** of Syria said, Go to, go, and I H4428
5 a letter unto the **k** of Israel. And he H4428
6 And he brought the letter to the **k** of H4428
7 And it came to pass, when the **k** of H4428
8 had heard that the **k** of Israel had rent H4428
8 that he sent to the **k**, saying, Wherefore H4428
6: 8 Then the **k** of Syria warred against H4428
9 And the man of God sent unto the **k** of H4428
10 And the **k** of Israel sent to the place H4428
11 Therefore the heart of the **k** of Syria H4428
11 me which of us *is* for the **k** of Israel? H4428
12 said, None, my lord, O **k**: but Elisha, the H4428
12 Israel, telleth the **k** of Israel the words H4428
21 And the **k** of Israel said unto Elisha, H4428
24 that Ben-hadad **k** of Syria gathered all H4428
26 And as the **k** of Israel was passing by H4428
26 unto him, saying, Help, my lord, O **k**. H4428
28 And the **k** said unto her, What aileth H4428
30 And it came to pass, when the **k** heard H4428
32 with him; and *the* **k** sent a man from H4428
7: 2 Then a lord on whose hand the **k** H4428
6 one to another, Lo, the **k** of Israel hath H4428
12 And the **k** arose in the night, and said H4428
14 horses; and the **k** sent after the host of H4428
15 messengers returned, and told the **k**. H4428
17 And the **k** appointed the lord on whose H4428
17 spake when the **k** came down to him. H4428
18 God had spoken to the **k**, saying, Two H4428
8: 3 the **k** for her house and for her land. H4428
4 And the **k** talked with Gehazi the H4428
5 as he was telling the **k** how he had H4428
5 to life, cried to the **k** for her house and H4428
5 said, My lord, O **k**, this *is* the woman, H4428
6 And when the **k** asked the woman, she H4428
6 told him. So the **k** appointed unto her H4428
7 Ben-hadad the **k** of Syria was sick; and H4428
8 And the **k** said unto Hazael, Take a H4428
9 son Ben-hadad **k** of Syria hath sent me H4428
13 me that thou *shalt be* **k** over Syria. H4428
16 Joram the son of Ahab **k** of Israel, H4428
16 *being* then **k** of Judah, Jehoram the H4428
16 Jehoshaphat **k** of Judah began to reign. H4428
20 Judah, and made a **k** over themselves. H4428
25 the son of Ahab **k** of Israel did Ahaziah H4428
25 of Jehoram **k** of Judah begin to reign. H4428
26 the daughter of Omri **k** of Israel. H4428
28 war against Hazael **k** of Syria in H4428
29 And **k** Joram went back to be healed in H4428
29 against Hazael **k** of Syria. And Ahaziah H4428
29 son of Jehoram **k** of Judah went down H4428
9: 3 anointed thee **k** over Israel. Then open H4428
6 anointed thee **k** over the people of the H4428
12 I have anointed thee **k** over Israel. H4428
13 blew with trumpets, saying, Jehu is **k**. H4427
14 all Israel, because of Hazael **k** of Syria. H4428
15 But **k** Joram was returned to be healed H4428
15 with Hazael **k** of Syria.) And Jehu H4428
16 And Ahaziah **k** of Judah was come H4428
18 Thus saith the **k**, *Is it* peace? And Jehu H4428
19 Thus saith the **k**, *Is it* peace? And Jehu H4428
21 made ready. And Joram **k** of Israel and H4428
21 and Ahaziah **k** of Judah went out, each H4428
27 But when Ahaziah the **k** of Judah saw H4428
10: 5 will not make any **k**: do thou *that which* H4427
13 of Ahaziah **k** of Judah, and said, H4428
13 of the **k** and the children of the queen. H4428
11: 2 But Jehosheba, the daughter of **k** H4428
7 of the house of the LORD about the **k**. H4428
8 And ye shall compass the **k** round H4428
8 **k** as he goeth out and as he cometh in. H4428
10 did the priest give **k** David's spears and H4428
11 hand, round about the **k**, from the right H4428
12 they made him **k**, and anointed him; H4427
12 their hands, and said, God save the **k**. H4428
14 And when she looked, behold, the **k** H4428
14 trumpeters by the **k**, and all the people H4428
17 the LORD and the **k** and the people, H4428
17 between the **k** also and the people. H4428

19 brought down the **k** from the house of H4428
2Ki 12: 6 twentieth year of **k** Jehoash the priests H4428
7 Then **k** Jehoash called for Jehoiada the H4428
17 Then Hazael **k** of Syria went up, and H4428
18 And Jehoash **k** of Judah took all the H4428
18 and sent *it* to Hazael **k** of Syria: and he H4428
13: 1 son of Ahaziah **k** of Judah Jehoahaz the H4428
3 hand of Hazael **k** of Syria, and into the H4428
4 because the **k** of Syria oppressed them. H4428
7 footmen; for the **k** of Syria had H4428
10 year of Joash **k** of Judah began Jehoash H4428
12 against Amaziah **k** of Judah, *are* they H4428
14 And Joash the **k** of Israel came down H4428
16 And he said to the **k** of Israel, Put thine H4428
18 he said unto the **k** of Israel, Smite upon H4428
22 But Hazael **k** of Syria oppressed Israel H4428
24 So Hazael **k** of Syria died; and H4428
14: 1 son of Jehoahaz **k** of Israel reigned H4428
1 Amaziah the son of Joash **k** of Judah. H4428
5 which had slain the **k** his father. H4428
8 son of Jehu, **k** of Israel, saying, Come, H4428
9 And Jehoash the **k** of Israel sent to H4428
9 sent to Amaziah **k** of Judah, saying, H4428
11 Therefore Jehoash **k** of Israel went up; H4428
11 he and Amaziah **k** of Judah looked one H4428
13 And Jehoash **k** of Israel took Amaziah H4428
13 took Amaziah **k** of Judah, the son of H4428
15 with Amaziah **k** of Judah, *are* they not H4428
17 And Amaziah the son of Joash **k** of H4428
17 of Jehoahaz **k** of Israel fifteen years. H4428
21 him **k** instead of his father Amaziah. H4427
22 after that the **k** slept with his fathers. H4428
23 the son of Joash **k** of Judah Jeroboam H4428
23 the son of Joash **k** of Israel began to H4428
15: 1 year of Jeroboam **k** of Israel began H4428
1 son of Amaziah **k** of Judah to reign. H4428
5 And the LORD smote the **k**, so that he H4428
8 eighth year of Azariah **k** of Judah did H4428
13 year of Uzziah **k** of Judah; and he H4428
17 year of Azariah **k** of Judah began H4428
19 *And* Pul the **k** of Assyria came against H4428
20 to give to the **k** of Assyria. So the king H4428
20 of Assyria. So the **k** of Assyria turned H4428
23 In the fiftieth year of Azariah **k** of H4428
27 year of Azariah **k** of Judah Pekah the H4428
29 In the days of Pekah **k** of Israel came H4428
29 Tiglath-pileser **k** of Assyria, and took H4428
32 the son of Remaliah **k** of Israel began H4428
32 the son of Uzziah **k** of Judah to reign. H4428
37 Judah Rezin the **k** of Syria, and Pekah H4428
16: 1 of Jotham **k** of Judah began to reign. H4428
5 Then Rezin **k** of Syria and Pekah son of H4428
5 son of Remaliah **k** of Israel came up to H4428
6 At that time Rezin **k** of Syria recovered H4428
7 to Tiglath-pileser **k** of Assyria, saying, I H4428
7 of the hand of the **k** of Syria, and out of H4428
7 **k** of Israel, which rise up against me. H4428
8 sent *it for* a present to the **k** of Assyria. H4428
9 And the **k** of Assyria hearkened unto H4428
9 unto him: for the **k** of Assyria went up H4428
10 And **k** Ahaz went to Damascus to meet H4428
10 Tiglath-pileser **k** of Assyria, and saw H4428
10 *was* at Damascus: and **k** Ahaz sent to H4428
11 to all that **k** Ahaz had sent from H4428
11 against **k** Ahaz came from Damascus. H4428
12 And when the **k** was come from H4428
12 Damascus, the **k** saw the altar: and the H4428
12 the altar: and the **k** approached to the H4428
15 And **k** Ahaz commanded Urijah the H4428
16 to all that **k** Ahaz commanded. H4428
17 And **k** Ahaz cut off the borders of the H4428
18 house of the LORD for the **k** of Assyria. H4428
17: 1 In the twelfth year of Ahaz **k** of Judah H4428
3 Against him came up Shalmaneser **k** of H4428
4 And the **k** of Assyria found conspiracy H4428
4 sent messengers to So **k** of Egypt, and H4428
4 no present to the **k** of Assyria, as *he* H4428
4 by year: therefore the **k** of Assyria shut H4428
5 Then the **k** of Assyria came up H4428
6 In the ninth year of Hoshea the **k** of H4428
7 **k** of Egypt, and had feared other gods, H4428
21 the son of Nebat **k**: and Jeroboam drave H4427
24 And the **k** of Assyria brought *men* from H4428
26 Wherefore they spake to the **k** of H4428
27 Then the **k** of Assyria commanded, H4428
18: 1 son of Elah **k** of Israel, *that* Hezekiah H4428
1 son of Ahaz **k** of Judah began to reign. H4428
7 the **k** of Assyria, and served him not. H4428
9 in the fourth year of **k** Hezekiah, which H4428

9 Hoshea son of Elah **k** of Israel, *that* H4428
2Ki 18: 9 *that* Shalmaneser **k** of Assyria came up H4428
10 Hoshea **k** of Israel, Samaria was taken. H4428
11 And the **k** of Assyria did carry away H4428
13 Now in the fourteenth year of **k** H4428
13 did Sennacherib **k** of Assyria come up H4428
14 And Hezekiah **k** of Judah sent to the H4428
14 of Judah sent to the **k** of Assyria to H4428
14 I bear. And the **k** of Assyria appointed H4428
14 unto Hezekiah **k** of Judah three H4428
16 pillars which Hezekiah **k** of Judah had H4428
16 and gave it to the **k** of Assyria. H4428
17 And the **k** of Assyria sent Tartan and H4428
17 from Lachish to **k** Hezekiah with a H4428
18 And when they had called to the **k**, H4428
19 saith the great **k**, the king of Assyria, H4428
19 the great king, the **k** of Assyria, What H4428
21 **k** of Egypt unto all that trust on him. H4428
23 to my lord the **k** of Assyria, and I will H4428
28 word of the great **k**, the king of Assyria: H4428
28 word of the great king, the **k** of Assyria: H4428
29 Thus saith the **k**, Let not Hezekiah H4428
30 into the hand of the **k** of Assyria. H4428
31 for thus saith the **k** of Assyria, Make *an* H4428
33 out of the hand of the **k** of Assyria? H4428
19: 1 And it came to pass, when **k** Hezekiah H4428
4 whom the **k** of Assyria his master H4428
5 So the servants of **k** Hezekiah came to H4428
6 the **k** of Assyria have blasphemed me. H4428
8 and found the **k** of Assyria warring H4428
9 And when he heard say of Tirhakah **k** H4428
10 Thus shall ye speak to Hezekiah **k** of H4428
10 into the hand of the **k** of Assyria. H4428
13 Where *is* the **k** of Hamath, and the king H4428
13 Where *is* the king of Hamath, and the **k** H4428
13 king of Arpad, and the **k** of the city of H4428
20 Sennacherib **k** of Assyria I have heard. H4428
32 concerning the **k** of Assyria, He shall H4428
36 So Sennacherib **k** of Assyria departed, H4428
20: 6 of the hand of the **k** of Assyria; and I H4428
12 the son of Baladan, **k** of Babylon, sent H4428
14 Then came Isaiah the prophet unto **k** H4428
18 in the palace of the **k** of Babylon. H4428
21: 3 grove, as did Ahab **k** of Israel; and H4428
11 Because Manasseh **k** of Judah hath H4428
23 him, and slew the **k** in his own house. H4428
24 conspired against **k** Amon; and the H4428
24 made Josiah his son **k** in his stead. H4427
22: 3 the eighteenth year of **k** Josiah, *that* the H4428
3 Josiah, *that* the **k** sent Shaphan the son H4428
9 And Shaphan the scribe came to the **k**, H4428
9 and brought the **k** word again, and H4428
10 And Shaphan the scribe shewed the **k**, H4428
10 book. And Shaphan read it before the **k**. H4428
11 And it came to pass, when the **k** had H4428
12 And the **k** commanded Hilkiah the H4428
16 book which the **k** of Judah hath read: H4428
18 But to the **k** of Judah which sent you to H4428
20 And they brought the **k** word again. H4428
23: 1 And the **k** sent, and they gathered unto H4428
2 And the **k** went up into the house of the H4428
3 And the **k** stood by a pillar, and made a H4428
4 And the **k** commanded Hilkiah the H4428
12 of the LORD, did the **k** beat down, and H4428
13 Solomon the **k** of Israel had builded H4428
13 children of Ammon, did the **k** defile. H4428
21 And the **k** commanded all the people, H4428
23 But in the eighteenth year of **k** Josiah, H4428
25 And like unto him was there no **k** H4428
29 In his days Pharaoh-nechoh **k** of Egypt H4428
29 up against the **k** of Assyria to the river H4428
29 Euphrates: and **k** Josiah went against H4428
30 and made him **k** in his father's stead. H4427
34 the son of Josiah **k** in the room of H4427
24: 1 In his days Nebuchadnezzar **k** of H4428
7 And the **k** of Egypt came not again any H4428
7 of his land: for the **k** of Babylon had H4428
7 all that pertained to the **k** of Egypt. H4428
10 Nebuchadnezzar **k** of Babylon came up H4428
11 And Nebuchadnezzar **k** of Babylon H4428
12 And Jehoiachin the **k** of Judah went out H4428
12 went out to the **k** of Babylon, he, and H4428
12 officers: and the **k** of Babylon took him H4428
13 which Solomon **k** of Israel had made H4428
16 even them the **k** of Babylon brought H4428
17 And the **k** of Babylon made Mattaniah H4428
17 his father's brother **k** in his stead, and H4427
20 rebelled against the **k** of Babylon. H4428
25: 1 Nebuchadnezzar **k** of Babylon came, H4428

2 unto the eleventh year of **k** Zedekiah. H4428
2Ki 25: 4 and *the k* went the way toward the plain.
5 pursued after the **k**, and overtook him H4428
6 So they took the **k**, and brought him up H4428
6 him up to the **k** of Babylon to Riblah; H4428
8 nineteenth year of **k** Nebuchadnezzar H4428
8 Nebuchadnezzar **k** of Babylon, came H4428
8 of the **k** of Babylon, unto Jerusalem: H4428
11 fell away to the **k** of Babylon, with the H4428
20 them to the **k** of Babylon to Riblah: H4428
21 And the **k** of Babylon smote them, and H4428
22 Nebuchadnezzar **k** of Babylon had left, H4428
23 heard that the **k** of Babylon had made H4428
24 and serve the **k** of Babylon; and it shall H4428
27 of Jehoiachin **k** of Judah, in the twelfth H4428
27 Evil-merodach **k** of Babylon in the year H4428
27 of Jehoiachin **k** of Judah out of prison; H4428
30 given him of the **k**, a daily rate for every H4428
1Ch 1:43 of Edom before *any* **k** reigned over the H4428
3: 2 of Talmai **k** of Geshur: the fourth, H4428
4:23 they dwelt with the **k** for his work. H4428
41 the days of Hezekiah **k** of Judah, and H4428
5: 6 Tilgath-pilneser **k** of Assyria carried H4428
17 days of Jotham **k** of Judah, and in the H4428
17 and in the days of Jeroboam **k** of Israel. H4428
26 up the spirit of Pul **k** of Assyria, and H4428
26 of Tilgath-pilneser **k** of Assyria, and he H4428
11: 2 when Saul was **k**, thou *wast* he that H4428
3 of Israel to the **k** to Hebron; and David H4428
3 they anointed David **k** over Israel, H4428
10 to make him **k**, according to the word H4427
12:31 by name, to come and make David **k**. H4427
38 to make David **k** over all Israel: and H4427
38 *were* of one heart to make David **k**. H4427
14: 1 Now Hiram **k** of Tyre sent messengers H4428
2 confirmed him **k** over Israel, for his H4428
8 was anointed **k** over all Israel, all the H4428
15:29 at a window saw **k** David dancing and H4428
17:16 And David the **k** came and sat before H4428
18: 3 And David smote Hadarezer **k** of H4428
5 to help Hadarezer **k** of Zobah, David H4428
9 Now when Tou **k** of Hamath heard how H4428
9 all the host of Hadarezer **k** of Zobah; H4428
10 He sent Hadoram his son to **k** David, to H4428
11 Them also **k** David dedicated unto the H4428
17 sons of David *were* chief about the **k**. H4428
19: 1 that Nahash the **k** of the children of H4428
5 ashamed. And the **k** said, Tarry at H4428
7 chariots, and the **k** of Maachah and his H4428
20: 2 And David took the crown of their **k** H4428
21: 3 but, my lord the **k**, *are* they not all my H4428
23 let my lord the **k** do *that which is* good H4428
24 And **k** David said to Ornan, Nay; but I H4428
23: 1 he made Solomon his son **k** over Israel. H4427
24: 6 them before the **k**, and the princes, and H4428
31 of David the **k**, and Zadok, and H4428
25: 2 according to the order of the **k**. H4428
26:26 things, which David the **k**, and the chief H4428
30 of the LORD, and in the service of the **k**. H4428
32 fathers, whom **k** David made rulers H4428
32 pertaining to God, and affairs of the **k**. H4428
27: 1 that served the **k** in any matter of the H4428
24 account of the chronicles of **k** David. H4428
31 of the substance which *was* **k** David's. H4428
28: 1 ministered to the **k** by course, and the H4428
1 and possession of the **k**, and of his sons, H4428
2 Then David the **k** stood up upon his H4428
4 of my father to be **k** over Israel for ever: H4428
4 liked me to make *me* **k** over all Israel: H4427
29: 1 Furthermore David the **k** said unto all H4428
9 David the **k** also rejoiced with great joy. H4428
20 and worshipped the LORD, and the **k**. H4428
22 the son of David **k** the second time, and H4427
23 of the LORD as **k** instead of David his H4428
24 the sons likewise of **k** David, submitted H4428
24 themselves unto Solomon the **k**. H4428
25 not been on any **k** before him in Israel. H4428
29 Now the acts of David the **k**, first and H4428
2Ch 1: 9 hast made me **k** over a people like the H4427
11 people, over whom I have made thee **k**: H4427
14 cities, and with the **k** at Jerusalem. H4428
15 And the **k** made silver and gold at H4428
2: 3 And Solomon sent to Huram the **k** of H4428
11 Then Huram the **k** of Tyre answered in H4428
11 people, he hath made thee **k** over them. H4428
12 given to David the **k** a wise son, endued H4428
4:11 for **k** Solomon for the house of God; H4428
16 his father make to **k** Solomon for the H4428
17 In the plain of Jordan did the **k** cast H4428
5: 3 unto the **k** in the feast which *was* H4428
2Ch 5: 6 Also **k** Solomon, and all the H4428
6: 3 And the **k** turned his face, and blessed H4428
7: 4 Then the **k** and all the people offered H4428
5 And **k** Solomon offered a sacrifice of H4428
5 sheep: so the **k** and all the people H4428
6 which David the **k** had made to praise H4428
8:10 And these *were* the chief of **k** H4428
11 house of David **k** of Israel, because *the* H4428
15 of the **k** unto the priests and H4428
18 gold, and brought *them* to **k** Solomon. H4428
9: 5 And she said to the **k**, *It was* a true H4428
8 on his throne, *to be* **k** for the LORD thy H4428
8 made he thee **k** over them, to do H4428
9 And she gave the **k** an hundred and H4428
9 as the queen of Sheba gave **k** Solomon. H4428
11 And the **k** made *of* the algum trees H4428
12 And **k** Solomon gave to the queen of H4428
12 brought unto the **k**. So she turned, and H4428
15 And **k** Solomon made two hundred H4428
16 shield. And the **k** put them in the house H4428
17 Moreover the **k** made a great throne of H4428
20 And all the drinking vessels of **k** H4428
22 And **k** Solomon passed all the kings of H4428
25 cities, and with the **k** at Jerusalem. H4428
27 And the **k** made silver in Jerusalem as H4428
10: 1 were all Israel come to make him **k**. H4427
2 of Solomon the **k**, heard *it*, that H4428
6 And **k** Rehoboam took counsel with the H4428
12 third day, as the **k** bade, saying, Come H4428
13 And the **k** answered them roughly; and H4428
13 them roughly; and **k** Rehoboam H4428
15 So the **k** hearkened not unto the H4428
16 And when all Israel *saw* that the **k** H4428
16 answered the **k**, saying, What portion H4428
18 Then **k** Rehoboam sent Hadoram that H4428
18 that he died. But **k** Rehoboam made H4428
11: 3 son of Solomon, **k** of Judah, and to all H4428
22 brethren: for *he thought* to make him **k**. H4427
12: 2 *that* in the fifth year of **k** Rehoboam H4428
2 Shishak **k** of Egypt came up against H4428
6 princes of Israel and the **k** humbled H4428
9 So Shishak **k** of Egypt came up against H4428
10 Instead of which **k** Rehoboam made H4428
11 And when the **k** entered into the house H4428
13 So **k** Rehoboam strengthened himself H4428
13: 1 Now in the eighteenth year of **k** H4428
15:16 the mother of Asa the **k**, he removed her H4428
16: 1 of Asa Baasha **k** of Israel came up H4428
1 go out or come in to Asa **k** of Judah. H4428
2 and sent to Ben-hadad **k** of Syria, that H4428
3 with Baasha **k** of Israel, that he may H4428
4 And Ben-hadad hearkened unto **k** Asa, H4428
6 Then Asa the **k** took all Judah; and they H4428
7 seer came to Asa **k** of Judah, and said H4428
7 hast relied on the **k** of Syria, and not H4428
7 **k** of Syria escaped out of thine hand. H4428
17:19 These waited on the **k**, beside *those* H4428
19 *those* whom the **k** put in the fenced H4428
18: 3 And Ahab **k** of Israel said unto H4428
3 unto Jehoshaphat **k** of Judah, Wilt thou H4428
4 And Jehoshaphat said unto the **k** of H4428
5 Therefore the **k** of Israel gathered H4428
7 And the **k** of Israel said unto H4428
7 Jehoshaphat said, Let not the **k** say so. H4428
8 And the **k** of Israel called for one *of his* H4428
9 And the **k** of Israel and Jehoshaphat H4428
9 and Jehoshaphat **k** of Judah sat either H4428
11 shall deliver *it* into the hand of the **k**. H4428
12 good to the **k** with one assent; let H4428
14 And when he was come to the **k**, the H4428
14 come to the king, the **k** said unto him, H4428
15 And the **k** said to him, How many H4428
17 And the **k** of Israel said to Jehoshaphat, H4428
19 shall entice Ahab **k** of Israel, that he H4428
25 Then the **k** of Israel said, Take ye H4428
26 And say, Thus saith the **k**, Put this H4428
28 So the **k** of Israel and Jehoshaphat the H4428
28 **k** of Judah went up to Ramoth-gilead. H4428
29 And the **k** of Israel said unto H4428
29 thy robes. So the **k** of Israel disguised H4428
30 Now the **k** of Syria had commanded H4428
30 or great, save only with the **k** of Israel. H4428
31 they said, It *is* the **k** of Israel. Therefore H4428
32 that it was not the **k** of Israel, they H4428
33 and smote the **k** of Israel between the H4428
34 that day: howbeit the **k** of Israel stayed H4428
19: 1 And Jehoshaphat the **k** of Judah H4428
2 meet him, and said to **k** Jehoshaphat, H4428
20:15 and thou **k** Jehoshaphat, Thus H4428
2Ch 20:35 And after this did Jehoshaphat **k** of H4428
35 **k** of Israel, who did very wickedly: H4428
21: 2 the sons of Jehoshaphat **k** of Israel. H4428
8 of Judah, and made themselves a **k**. H4428
12 nor in the ways of Asa **k** of Judah, H4428
22: 1 his youngest son **k** in his stead: for the H4427
1 the son of Jehoram **k** of Judah reigned. H4428
5 the son of Ahab **k** of Israel to war H4428
5 war against Hazael **k** of Syria at H4428
6 with Hazael **k** of Syria. And Azariah H4428
6 son of Jehoram **k** of Judah went down H4428
11 daughter of the **k**, took Joash the son of H4428
11 the daughter of **k** Jehoram, the wife of H4428
23: 3 a covenant with the **k** in the house of H4428
7 And the Levites shall compass the **k** H4428
7 but be ye with the **k** when he cometh in, H4428
9 that *had been* **k** David's, which *were* H4428
10 and the temple, by the **k** round about. H4428
11 and made him **k**. And Jehoiada and his H4427
11 anointed him, and said, God save the **k**. H4428
12 and praising the **k**, she came to the H4428
13 And she looked, and, behold, the **k** H4428
13 trumpets by the **k**: and all the people of H4428
16 and between the **k**, that they should be H4428
20 brought down the **k** from the house of H4428
20 the **k** upon the throne of the kingdom. H4428
24: 6 And the **k** called for Jehoiada the chief, H4428
12 And the **k** and Jehoiada gave it to such H4428
14 the money before the **k** and Jehoiada, H4428
17 **k**. Then the king hearkened unto them. H4428
17 king. Then the **k** hearkened unto them. H4428
21 **k** in the court of the house of the LORD. H4428
22 Thus Joash the **k** remembered not the H4428
23 spoil of them unto the **k** of Damascus. H4428
25: 3 that had killed the **k** his father. H4428
7 to him, saying, O **k**, let not the army of H4428
16 with him, that *the k* said unto him, Art
17 Then Amaziah **k** of Judah took advice, H4428
17 the son of Jehu, **k** of Israel, saying, H4428
18 And Joash **k** of Israel sent to Amaziah H4428
18 sent to Amaziah **k** of Judah, saying, H4428
21 So Joash the **k** of Israel went up; and H4428
21 *both* he and Amaziah **k** of Judah, at H4428
23 And Joash the **k** of Israel took Amaziah H4428
23 took Amaziah **k** of Judah, the son of H4428
25 And Amaziah the son of Joash **k** of H4428
25 of Jehoahaz **k** of Israel fifteen years. H4428
26: 1 **k** in the room of his father Amaziah. H4427
2 after that the **k** slept with his fathers. H4428
13 power, to help the **k** against the enemy. H4428
18 And they withstood Uzziah the **k**, and H4428
21 And Uzziah the **k** was a leper unto the H4428
27: 5 He fought also with the **k** of the H4428
28: 5 into the hand of the **k** of Syria; and they H4428
5 the hand of the **k** of Israel, who smote H4428
7 and Elkanah *that was* next to the **k**. H4428
16 At that time did **k** Ahaz send unto the H4428
19 low because of Ahaz **k** of Israel; for he H4428
20 And Tilgath-pilneser **k** of Assyria came H4428
21 of the house of the **k**, and of the princes, H4428
21 the **k** of Assyria: but he helped him not. H4428
22 against the LORD: this *is that* **k** Ahaz. H4428
29:15 of the **k**, by the words of the H4428
18 Then they went in to Hezekiah the **k**, H4428
19 Moreover all the vessels, which **k** Ahaz H4428
20 Then Hezekiah the **k** rose early, and H4428
23 sin offering before the **k** and the H4428
24 for all Israel: for the **k** commanded *that* H4428
27 *ordained* by David **k** of Israel. H4428
29 end of offering, the **k** and all that were H4428
30 Moreover Hezekiah the **k** and the H4428
30: 2 For the **k** had taken counsel, and his H4428
4 And the thing pleased the **k** and all the H4428
6 the letters from the **k** and his princes H4428
6 of the **k**, saying, Ye children H4428
12 of the **k** and of the princes, H4428
24 For Hezekiah **k** of Judah did give to the H4428
26 the son of David **k** of Israel *there was* H4428
31:13 of Hezekiah the **k**, and Azariah the ruler H4428
32: 1 Sennacherib **k** of Assyria came, and H4428
7 dismayed for the **k** of Assyria, nor for H4428
8 upon the words of Hezekiah **k** of Judah. H4428
9 After this did Sennacherib **k** of Assyria H4428
9 unto Hezekiah **k** of Judah, and unto H4428
10 Thus saith Sennacherib **k** of Assyria, H4428
11 us out of the hand of the **k** of Assyria? H4428
20 And for this *cause* Hezekiah the **k**, and H4428
21 in the camp of the **k** of Assyria. So he H4428

22 Sennacherib the **k** of Assyria, and from H4428
2Ch 32:23 to Hezekiah **k** of Judah: so that he H4428
33:11 of the host of the **k** of Assyria, which H4428
25 conspired against **k** Amon; and the H4428
25 made Josiah his son **k** in his stead. H4427
34:16 And Shaphan carried the book to the **k**, H4428
16 and brought the **k** word back again, H4428
18 Then Shaphan the scribe told the **k**, H4428
18 book. And Shaphan read it before the **k**. H4428
19 And it came to pass, when the **k** had H4428
20 And the **k** commanded Hilkiah, and H4428
22 And Hilkiah, and *they* that the **k** *had* H4428
24 they have read before the **k** of Judah: H4428
26 And as for the **k** of Judah, who sent you H4428
28 So they brought the **k** word again. H4428
29 Then the **k** sent and gathered together H4428
30 And the **k** went up into the house of the H4428
31 And the **k** stood in his place, and made H4428
35: 3 the son of David **k** of Israel did build; *it* H4428
4 the writing of David **k** of Israel, and H4428
16 to the commandment of **k** Josiah. H4428
20 the temple, Necho **k** of Egypt came up H4428
21 do with thee, thou **k** of Judah? *I come* H4428
23 And the archers shot at **k** Josiah; and H4428
23 Josiah; and the **k** said to his servants, H4428
36: 1 **k** in his father's stead in Jerusalem. H4427
3 And the **k** of Egypt put him down at H4428
4 And the **k** of Egypt made Eliakim his H4428
4 Eliakim his brother **k** over Judah and H4427
6 up Nebuchadnezzar **k** of Babylon, and H4428
10 And when the year was expired, **k** H4428
10 brother **k** over Judah and Jerusalem. H4427
13 And he also rebelled against **k** H4428
17 Therefore he brought upon them the **k** H4428
18 treasures of the **k**, and of his princes; all H4428
22 Now in the first year of Cyrus **k** of H4428
22 the spirit of Cyrus **k** of Persia, that he H4428
23 Thus saith Cyrus **k** of Persia, All the H4428
Ezr 1: 1 Now in the first year of Cyrus **k** of H4428
1 the spirit of Cyrus **k** of Persia, that he H4428
2 Thus saith Cyrus **k** of Persia, The H4428
7 Also Cyrus the **k** brought forth the H4428
8 Even those did Cyrus **k** of Persia bring H4428
2: 1 the **k** of Babylon had carried H4428
3: 7 that they had of Cyrus **k** of Persia. H4428
10 after the ordinance of David **k** of Israel. H4428
4: 2 **k** of Assur, which brought us up hither. H4428
3 God of Israel, as **k** Cyrus the king of H4428
3 the **k** of Persia hath commanded us. H4428
5 the days of Cyrus **k** of Persia, even until H4428
5 until the reign of Darius **k** of Persia. H4428
7 unto Artaxerxes **k** of Persia; and the H4428
8 to Artaxerxes the **k** in this sort: H4430
11 Artaxerxes the **k**; Thy servants the men H4430
12 Be it known unto the **k**, that the Jews H4430
13 Be it known now unto the **k**, that, if this H4430
14 have we sent and certified the **k**; H4430
16 We certify the **k** that, if this city be H4430
17 *Then* sent the **k** an answer unto Rehum H4430
23 Now when the copy of **k** Artaxerxes' H4430
24 year of the reign of Darius **k** of Persia. H4430
5: 6 side the river, sent unto Darius the **k**: H4430
7 thus; Unto Darius the **k**, all peace. H4430
8 Be it known unto the **k**, that we went H4430
11 a great **k** of Israel builded and set up. H4430
12 the **k** of Babylon, the Chaldean, H4430
13 But in the first year of Cyrus the **k** of H4430
13 of Babylon *the same* **k** Cyrus made a H4430
14 did Cyrus the **k** take out of the temple H4430
17 Now therefore, if *it seem* good to the **k**, H4430
17 made of Cyrus the **k** to build this house H4430
17 and let the **k** send his pleasure to H4430
6: 1 Then Darius the **k** made a decree, and H4430
3 In the first year of Cyrus the **k** *the same* H4430
3 *the same* Cyrus the **k** made a decree H4430
10 pray for the life of the **k**, and of his sons. H4430
13 the **k** had sent, so they did speedily. H4430
14 Darius, and Artaxerxes **k** of Persia. H4430
15 sixth year of the reign of Darius the **k**. H4430
22 the heart of the **k** of Assyria unto them, H4428
7: 1 of Artaxerxes **k** of Persia, Ezra the son H4428
6 had given: and the **k** granted him all H4428
7 in the seventh year of Artaxerxes the **k**. H4428
8 which *was* in the seventh year of the **k**. H4428
11 of the letter that the **k** Artaxerxes gave H4428
12 Artaxerxes, **k** of kings, unto Ezra the H4430
14 Forasmuch as thou art sent of the **k**, H4430
15 gold, which the **k** and his counsellors H4430
21 And I, *even* I Artaxerxes the **k**, do make H4430
23 against the realm of the **k** and his sons? H4430
Ezr 7:26 and the law of the **k**, let judgment be H4430
28 me before the **k**, and his counsellors, H4428
8: 1 in the reign of Artaxerxes the **k**. H4428
22 For I was ashamed to require of the **k** a H4428
22 spoken unto the **k**, saying, The hand of H4428
25 God, which the **k**, and his counsellors, H4428
Neh 2: 1 year of Artaxerxes the **k**, *that* wine *was* H4428
1 gave *it* unto the **k**. Now I had not been H4428
2 Wherefore the **k** said unto me, Why *is* H4428
3 And said unto the **k**, Let the king live H4428
3 And said unto the king, Let the **k** live H4428
4 Then the **k** said unto me, For what dost H4428
5 And I said unto the **k**, If it please the H4428
5 If it please the **k**, and if thy servant have H4428
6 And the **k** said unto me, (the queen H4428
6 the **k** to send me; and I set him a time. H4428
7 Moreover I said unto the **k**, If it please H4428
7 If it please the **k**, let letters be given me H4428
8 into. And the **k** granted me, according H4428
9 letters. Now the **k** had sent captains of H4428
19 that ye do? will ye rebel against the **k**? H4428
5:14 year of Artaxerxes the **k**, *that is*, twelve H4428
6: 6 be their **k**, according to these words. H4428
7 saying, *There is* a **k** in Judah: and now H4428
7 be reported to the **k** according to these H4428
7: 6 the **k** of Babylon had carried H4428
9:22 the land of the **k** of Heshbon, and the H4428
22 and the land of Og **k** of Bashan. H4428
13: 6 year of Artaxerxes **k** of Babylon came I H4428
6 came I unto the **k**, and after certain H4428
6 certain days obtained I leave of the **k**: H4428
26 Did not Solomon **k** of Israel sin by H4428
26 was there no **k** like him, who was H4428
26 and God made him **k** over all Israel: H4428
Est 1: 2 *That* in those days, when the **k** H4428
5 were expired, the **k** made a feast unto H4428
7 according to the state of the **k**. H4428
8 compel: for so the **k** had appointed to H4428
9 house which *belonged* to **k** Ahasuerus. H4428
10 the heart of the **k** was merry with wine, H4428
10 in the presence of Ahasuerus the **k**, H4428
11 To bring Vashti the queen before the **k** H4428
12 therefore was the **k** very wroth, and his H4428
13 Then the **k** said to the wise men, which H4428
15 the **k** Ahasuerus by the chamberlains? H4428
16 And Memucan answered before the **k** H4428
16 done wrong to the **k** only, but also to all H4428
16 in all the provinces of the **k** Ahasuerus. H4428
17 shall be reported, The **k** Ahasuerus H4428
19 If it please the **k**, let there go a royal H4428
19 no more before **k** Ahasuerus; and let H4428
19 and let the **k** give her royal estate H4428
21 And the saying pleased the **k** and the H4428
21 princes; and the **k** did according to the H4428
2: 1 After these things, when the wrath of **k** H4428
2 be fair young virgins sought for the **k**: H4428
3 And let the **k** appoint officers in all the H4428
4 pleaseth the **k** be queen instead of H4428
4 the thing pleased the **k**; and he did so. H4428
6 away with Jeconiah **k** of Judah, whom H4428
6 the **k** of Babylon had carried away. H4428
12 was come to go in to **k** Ahasuerus, after H4428
13 maiden unto the **k**; whatsoever she H4428
14 came in unto the **k** no more, except the H4428
14 no more, except the **k** delighted in her, H4428
15 come to go in unto the **k**, she required H4428
16 So Esther was taken unto **k** Ahasuerus H4428
17 And the **k** loved Esther above all the H4428
18 Then the **k** made a great feast unto all H4428
18 gifts, according to the state of the **k**. H4428
21 sought to lay hand on the **k** Ahasuerus. H4428
22 the **k** *thereof* in Mordecai's name. H4428
23 the book of the chronicles before the **k**. H4428
3: 1 After these things did **k** Ahasuerus H4428
2 Haman: for the **k** had so commanded H4428
7 in the twelfth year of **k** Ahasuerus, they H4428
8 And Haman said unto **k** Ahasuerus, H4428
9 If it please the **k**, let it be written that H4428
10 And the **k** took his ring from his hand, H4428
11 And the **k** said unto Haman, The silver H4428
12 in the name of **k** Ahasuerus was it H4428
15 the palace. And the **k** and Haman sat H4428
4: 8 go in unto the **k**, to make supplication H4428
11 come unto the **k** into the inner court, H4428
11 such to whom the **k** shall hold out the H4428
11 to come in unto the **k** these thirty days. H4428
16 will I go in unto the **k**, which *is* not H4428
5: 1 house: and the **k** sat upon his royal H4428
2 And it was so, when the **k** saw Esther H4428
Est 5: 2 his sight: and the **k** held out to Esther H4428
3 Then said the **k** unto her, What wilt H4428
4 *seem* good unto the **k**, let the king and H4428
4 the king, let the **k** and Haman come H4428
5 Then the **k** said, Cause Haman to make H4428
5 hath said. So the **k** and Haman came to H4428
6 And the **k** said unto Esther at the H4428
8 in the sight of the **k**, and if it please the H4428
8 king, and if it please the **k** to grant my H4428
8 my request, let the **k** and Haman come H4428
8 I will do to morrow as the **k** hath said. H4428
11 *the things* wherein the **k** had promoted H4428
11 above the princes and servants of the **k**. H4428
12 come in with the **k** unto the banquet H4428
12 am I invited unto her also with the **k**. H4428
14 thou unto the **k** that Mordecai may H4428
14 in merrily with the **k** unto the banquet. H4428
6: 1 On that night could not the **k** sleep, and H4428
1 and they were read before the **k**. H4428
2 sought to lay hand on the **k** Ahasuerus. H4428
3 And the **k** said, What honour and H4428
4 And the **k** said, Who *is* in the court? H4428
4 to speak unto the **k** to hang Mordecai H4428
5 court. And the **k** said, Let him come in. H4428
6 So Haman came in. And the **k** said H4428
6 man whom the **k** delighteth to honour? H4428
6 whom would the **k** delight to do honour H4428
7 And Haman answered the **k**, For the H4428
7 man whom the **k** delighteth to honour, H4428
8 brought which the **k** *useth* to wear, and H4428
8 the horse that the **k** rideth upon, and H4428
9 man *withal* whom the **k** delighteth to H4428
9 man whom the **k** delighteth to honour. H4428
10 Then the **k** said to Haman, Make haste, H4428
11 man whom the **k** delighteth to honour. H4428
7: 1 So the **k** and Haman came to banquet H4428
2 And the **k** said again unto Esther on H4428
3 in thy sight, O **k**, and if it please the H4428
3 and if it please the **k**, let my life be given H4428
5 Then the **k** Ahasuerus answered and H4428
6 was afraid before the **k** and the queen. H4428
7 And the **k** arising from the banquet of H4428
7 evil determined against him by the **k**. H4428
8 Then the **k** returned out of the palace H4428
8 Then said the **k**, Will he force the queen H4428
9 said before the **k**, Behold also, the H4428
9 good for the **k**, standeth in the house H4428
9 Then the **k** said, Hang him thereon. H4428
8: 1 On that day did the **k** Ahasuerus give H4428
1 came before the **k**; for Esther had told H4428
2 And the **k** took off his ring, which he H4428
3 again before the **k**, and fell down at his H4428
4 Then the **k** held out the golden sceptre H4428
4 So Esther arose, and stood before the **k**, H4428
5 And said, If it please the **k**, and if I have H4428
5 right before the **k**, and I *be* pleasing in H4428
7 Then the **k** Ahasuerus said unto Esther H4428
10 And he wrote in the **k** Ahasuerus' H4428
11 Wherein the **k** granted the Jews which H4428
12 Upon one day in all the provinces of **k** H4428
15 the presence of the **k** in royal apparel of H4428
9: 2 the provinces of the **k** Ahasuerus, to lay H4428
3 and officers of the **k**, helped the Jews; H4428
11 the palace was brought before the **k**. H4428
12 And the **k** said unto Esther the queen, H4428
13 Then said Esther, If it please the **k**, let it H4428
14 And the **k** commanded it so to be done: H4428
20 of the **k** Ahasuerus, *both* nigh and far, H4428
25 But when *Esther* came before the **k**, he H4428
10: 1 And the **k** Ahasuerus laid a tribute H4428
2 whereunto the **k** advanced him, *are* H4428
3 For Mordecai the Jew *was* next unto **k** H4428
Job 15:24 against him, as a **k** ready to the battle. H4428
18:14 it shall bring him to the **k** of terrors. H4428
29:25 and dwelt as a **k** in the army, as one H4428
34:18 *Is it fit* to say to a **k**, *Thou art* wicked? H4428
41:34 He beholdeth all high *things*: he *is* a **k** H4428
Ps 2: 6 Yet have I set my **k** upon my holy hill of H4428
5: 2 of my cry, my **K**, and my God: for unto H4428
10:16 The LORD *is* **K** for ever and ever: the H4428
18:50 Great deliverance giveth he to his **k**; H4428
20: 9 Save, LORD: let the **k** hear us when we H4428
21: 1 The **k** shall joy in thy strength, O H4428
7 For the **k** trusteth in the LORD, and H4428
24: 7 doors; and the **K** of glory shall come in. H4428
8 Who *is* this **K** of glory? The LORD H4428
9 doors; and the **K** of glory shall come in. H4428
10 Who is this **K** of glory? The LORD of H4428

10 of hosts, he *is* the **K** of glory. Selah. H4428
Ps 29:10 flood; yea, the LORD sitteth **K** for ever. H4428
33:16 There is no **k** saved by the multitude of H4428
44: 4 Thou art my **K**, O God: command H4428
45: 1 touching the **k**: my tongue *is* the pen H4428
11 So shall the **k** greatly desire thy beauty: H4428
14 She shall be brought unto the **k** in H4428
47: 2 *he is* a great **K** over all the earth. H4428
6 sing praises unto our **K**, sing praises. H4428
7 For God *is* the **K** of all the earth: sing ye H4428
48: 2 of the north, the city of the great **K**. H4428
63:11 But the **k** shall rejoice in God; every one H4428
68:24 of my God, my **K**, in the sanctuary. H4428
72: 1 Give the **k** thy judgments, O God, and H4428
74:12 For God *is* my **K** of old, working H4428
84: 3 O LORD of hosts, my **K**, and my God. H4428
89:18 and the Holy One of Israel *is* our **k**. H4428
95: 3 God, and a great **K** above all gods. H4428
98: 6 a joyful noise before the LORD, the **K**. H4428
105:20 The **k** sent and loosed him; *even* the H4428
135:11 Sihon **k** of the Amorites, and Og king of H4428
11 Sihon king of the Amorites, and Og **k** of H4428
136:19 Sihon **k** of the Amorites: for his mercy H4428
20 And Og the **k** of Bashan: for his mercy H4428
145: 1 I will extol thee, my God, O **k**; and I will H4428
149: 2 the children of Zion be joyful in their **K**. H4428
Prv 1: 1 Solomon the son of David, **k** of Israel; H4428
16:10 A divine sentence *is* in the lips of the **k**: H4428
14 The wrath of a **k** *is as* messengers of H4428
20: 2 The fear of a **k** *is* as the roaring of a H4428
8 A **k** that sitteth in the throne of H4428
26 A wise **k** scattereth the wicked, and H4428
28 Mercy and truth preserve the **k**: and his H4428
22:11 of his lips the **k** *shall be* his friend. H4428
24:21 My son, fear thou the LORD and the **k**: H4428
25: 1 men of Hezekiah **k** of Judah copied out. H4428
5 *from* before the **k**, and his throne shall H4428
6 presence of the **k**, and stand not in the H4428
29: 4 The **k** by judgment establisheth the H4428
14 The **k** that faithfully judgeth the poor, H4428
30:27 The locusts have no **k**, yet go they forth H4428
31 A greyhound; an he goat also; and a **k**, H4428
31: 1 The words of **k** Lemuel, the prophecy H4428
Ecc 1: 1 the son of David, **k** in Jerusalem. H4428
12 I the Preacher was **k** over Israel in H4428
2:12 that cometh after the **k**? *even* that which H4428
4:13 **k**, who will no more be admonished. H4428
5: 9 all: the **k** *himself* is served by the field. H4428
8: 4 Where the word of a **k** *is, there is* H4428
9:14 there came a great **k** against it, and H4428
10:16 Woe to thee, O land, when thy **k** *is* a H4428
17 Blessed *art* thou, O land, when thy **k** *is* H4428
20 Curse not the **k**, no not in thy thought; H4428
Song 1: 4 Draw me, we will run after thee: the **k** H4428
12 While the **k** *sitteth* at his table, my H4428
3: 9 **K** Solomon made himself a chariot of H4428
11 of Zion, and behold **k** Solomon with the H4428
7: 5 purple; the **k** *is* held in the galleries. H4428
Isa 6: 1 In the year that **k** Uzziah died I saw H4428
5 have seen the **K**, the LORD of hosts. H4428
7: 1 the son of Uzziah, **k** of Judah, *that* H4428
1 *that* Rezin the **k** of Syria, and Pekah H4428
1 son of Remaliah, **k** of Israel, went up H4428
6 for us, and set a **k** in the midst of it, H4428
17 from Judah; *even* the **k** of Assyria. H4428
20 the river, by the **k** of Assyria, the head, H4428
8: 4 be taken away before the **k** of Assyria. H4428
7 many, *even* the **k** of Assyria, and all his H4428
21 **k** and their God, and look upward. H4428
10:12 stout heart of the **k** of Assyria, and the H4428
14: 4 against the **k** of Babylon, and say, H4428
28 In the year that **k** Ahaz died was this H4428
19: 4 cruel lord; and a fierce **k** shall rule over H4428
20: 1 (when Sargon the **k** of Assyria sent H4428
4 So shall the **k** of Assyria lead away the H4428
6 **k** of Assyria: and how shall we escape? H4428
23:15 to the days of one **k**: after the end of H4428
30:33 of old; yea, for the **k** it is prepared; he H4428
32: 1 Behold, a **k** shall reign in H4428
33:17 Thine eyes shall see the **k** in his beauty: H4428
22 the LORD *is* our **k**; he will save us. H4428
36: 1 the fourteenth year of **k** Hezekiah, *that* H4428
1 *that* Sennacherib **k** of Assyria came up H4428
2 And the **k** of Assyria sent Rabshakeh H4428
2 to Jerusalem unto **k** Hezekiah with a H4428
4 saith the great **k**, the king of Assyria, H4428
4 the great king, the **k** of Assyria, What H4428
6 **k** of Egypt to all that trust in him. H4428
8 to my master the **k** of Assyria, and I H4428
13 of the great **k**, the king of Assyria. H4428
Isa 36:13 of the great king, the **k** of Assyria. H4428
14 Thus saith the **k**, Let not Hezekiah H4428
15 into the hand of the **k** of Assyria. H4428
16 for thus saith the **k** of Assyria, Make *an* H4428
18 out of the hand of the **k** of Assyria? H4428
37: 1 And it came to pass, when **k** Hezekiah H4428
4 whom the **k** of Assyria his master H4428
5 So the servants of **k** Hezekiah came to H4428
6 the **k** of Assyria have blasphemed me. H4428
8 and found the **k** of Assyria warring H4428
9 Tirhakah **k** of Ethiopia, He is come H4428
10 Thus shall ye speak to Hezekiah **k** of H4428
10 given into the hand of the **k** of Assyria. H4428
13 Where *is* the **k** of Hamath, and the king H4428
13 Where *is* the king of Hamath, and the **k** H4428
13 of Arphad, and the **k** of the city of H4428
21 me against Sennacherib **k** of Assyria: H4428
33 concerning the **k** of Assyria, He shall H4428
37 So Sennacherib **k** of Assyria departed, H4428
38: 6 **k** of Assyria: and I will defend this city. H4428
9 The writing of Hezekiah **k** of Judah, H4428
39: 1 the son of Baladan, **k** of Babylon, sent H4428
3 Then came Isaiah the prophet unto **k** H4428
7 in the palace of the **k** of Babylon. H4428
41:21 strong *reasons*, saith the **K** of Jacob. H4428
43:15 Holy One, the creator of Israel, your **K**. H4428
44: 6 Thus saith the LORD the **K** of Israel, H4428
57: 9 And thou wentest to the **k** with H4428
Jer 1: 2 the son of Amon **k** of Judah, in the H4428
3 the son of Josiah **k** of Judah, unto the H4428
3 the son of Josiah **k** of Judah, unto the H4428
3: 6 the days of Josiah the **k**, Hast thou seen H4428
4: 9 the heart of the **k** shall perish, and the H4428
8:19 in Zion? *is* not her **k** in her? Why have H4428
10: 7 Who would not fear thee, O **K** of H4428
10 and an everlasting **k**: at his wrath the H4428
13:18 Say unto the **k** and to the queen, H4428
15: 4 the son of Hezekiah **k** of Judah, for *that* H4428
20: 4 the hand of the **k** of Babylon, and he H4428
21: 1 the LORD, when **k** Zedekiah sent unto H4428
2 Nebuchadrezzar **k** of Babylon maketh H4428
4 ye fight against the **k** of Babylon, and H4428
7 deliver Zedekiah **k** of Judah, and his H4428
7 Nebuchadrezzar **k** of Babylon, and into H4428
10 the hand of the **k** of Babylon, and he H4428
11 And touching the house of the **k** of H4428
22: 1 **k** of Judah, and speak there this word, H4428
2 of the LORD, O **k** of Judah, that sittest H4428
11 the son of Josiah **k** of Judah, which H4428
18 the son of Josiah **k** of Judah; They shall H4428
24 son of Jehoiakim **k** of Judah were the H4428
25 Nebuchadrezzar **k** of Babylon, and into H4428
23: 5 Branch, and a **K** shall reign and H4428
24: 1 that Nebuchadrezzar **k** of Babylon had H4428
1 son of Jehoiakim **k** of Judah, and the H4428
8 I give Zedekiah the **k** of Judah, and his H4428
25: 1 the son of Josiah **k** of Judah, that *was* H4428
1 year of Nebuchadrezzar **k** of Babylon; H4428
3 the son of Amon **k** of Judah, even unto H4428
9 the **k** of Babylon, my servant, H4428
11 serve the **k** of Babylon seventy years. H4428
12 I will punish the **k** of Babylon, and that H4428
19 Pharaoh **k** of Egypt, and his servants, H4428
26 **k** of Sheshach shall drink after them. H4428
26: 1 the son of Josiah **k** of Judah came this H4428
18 days of Hezekiah **k** of Judah, and spake H4428
19 Did Hezekiah **k** of Judah and all Judah H4428
21 And when Jehoiakim the **k**, with all his H4428
21 his words, the **k** sought to put him to H4428
22 And Jehoiakim the **k** sent men into H4428
23 Jehoiakim the **k**; who slew him with H4428
27: 1 the son of Josiah **k** of Judah came this H4428
3 And send them to the **k** of Edom, and H4428
3 Edom, and to the **k** of Moab, and to the H4428
3 Moab, and to the **k** of the Ammonites, H4428
3 and to the **k** of Tyrus, and to the H4428
3 of Tyrus, and to the **k** of Zidon, by the H4428
3 to Jerusalem unto Zedekiah **k** of Judah; H4428
6 the **k** of Babylon, my servant; H4428
8 the **k** of Babylon, and that H4428
8 under the yoke of the **k** of Babylon, that H4428
9 Ye shall not serve the **k** of Babylon: H4428
11 the yoke of the **k** of Babylon, and serve H4428
12 I spake also to Zedekiah **k** of Judah H4428
12 the yoke of the **k** of Babylon, and serve H4428
13 that will not serve the **k** of Babylon? H4428
14 Ye shall not serve the **k** of Babylon: for H4428
17 Hearken not unto them; serve the **k** of H4428
18 *in* the house of the **k** of Judah, and at H4428
Jer 27:20 Which Nebuchadnezzar **k** of Babylon H4428
20 the son of Jehoiakim **k** of Judah from H4428
21 of the **k** of Judah and of Jerusalem; H4428
28: 1 the reign of Zedekiah **k** of Judah, in the H4428
2 broken the yoke of the **k** of Babylon. H4428
3 Nebuchadnezzar **k** of Babylon took H4428
4 son of Jehoiakim **k** of Judah, with all H4428
4 will break the yoke of the **k** of Babylon. H4428
11 Nebuchadnezzar **k** of Babylon from the H4428
14 Nebuchadnezzar **k** of Babylon; and H4428
29: 2 (After that Jeconiah the **k**, and the H4428
3 (whom Zedekiah **k** of Judah sent unto H4428
3 Nebuchadnezzar **k** of Babylon) saying, H4428
16 *Know* that thus saith the LORD of the **k** H4428
21 Nebuchadrezzar **k** of Babylon; and he H4428
22 the **k** of Babylon roasted in the fire; H4428
30: 9 their **k**, whom I will raise up unto them. H4428
32: 1 year of Zedekiah **k** of Judah, which *was* H4428
2 For then the **k** of Babylon's army H4428
2 which *was* in the **k** of Judah's house. H4428
3 For Zedekiah **k** of Judah had shut him H4428
3 of the **k** of Babylon, and he shall take it; H4428
4 And Zedekiah **k** of Judah shall not H4428
4 the hand of the **k** of Babylon, and shall H4428
28 **k** of Babylon, and he shall take it: H4428
36 into the hand of the **k** of Babylon by the H4428
34: 1 Nebuchadnezzar **k** of Babylon, and all H4428
2 speak to Zedekiah **k** of Judah, and tell H4428
2 the hand of the **k** of Babylon, and he H4428
3 the eyes of the **k** of Babylon, and he H4428
4 O Zedekiah **k** of Judah; Thus saith H4428
6 unto Zedekiah **k** of Judah in Jerusalem, H4428
7 When the **k** of Babylon's army fought H4428
8 after that the **k** Zedekiah had made H4428
21 And Zedekiah **k** of Judah and his H4428
21 the hand of the **k** of Babylon's army, H4428
35: 1 the son of Josiah **k** of Judah, saying, H4428
11 Nebuchadrezzar **k** of Babylon came up H4428
36: 1 the son of Josiah **k** of Judah, *that* this H4428
9 the son of Josiah **k** of Judah, in the H4428
16 will surely tell the **k** of all these words. H4428
20 And they went in to the **k** into the H4428
20 told all the words in the ears of the **k**. H4428
21 So the **k** sent Jehudi to fetch the roll: H4428
21 in the ears of the **k**, and in the ears of all H4428
21 all the princes which stood beside the **k**. H4428
22 Now the **k** sat in the winterhouse in the H4428
24 *neither* the **k**, nor any of his servants H4428
25 intercession to the **k** that he would not H4428
26 But the **k** commanded Jerahmeel the H4428
27 after that the **k** had burned the roll, H4428
28 Jehoiakim the **k** of Judah hath burned. H4428
29 And thou shalt say to Jehoiakim **k** of H4428
29 saying, The **k** of Babylon shall certainly H4428
30 of Jehoiakim **k** of Judah; He shall have H4428
32 book which Jehoiakim **k** of Judah had H4428
37: 1 And **k** Zedekiah the son of Josiah H4428
1 Nebuchadrezzar **k** of Babylon made H4428
1 Babylon made **k** in the land of Judah. H4427
3 And Zedekiah the **k** sent Jehucal the H4428
7 shall ye say to the **k** of Judah, that sent H4428
17 Then Zedekiah the **k** sent, and took H4428
17 him out: and the **k** asked him secretly H4428
17 into the hand of the **k** of Babylon. H4428
18 Moreover Jeremiah said unto **k** H4428
19 you, saying, The **k** of Babylon shall not H4428
20 O my lord the **k**: let my supplication, H4428
21 Then Zedekiah the **k** commanded that H4428
38: 3 the hand of the **k** of Babylon's army, H4428
4 Therefore the princes said unto the **k**, H4428
5 Then Zedekiah the **k** said, Behold, he *is* H4428
5 your hand: for the **k** *is* not *he that* can H4428
7 **k** then sitting in the gate of Benjamin; H4428
8 king's house, and spake to the **k**, saying, H4428
9 My lord the **k**, these men have done evil H4428
10 Then the **k** commanded Ebed-melech H4428
11 the house of the **k** under the treasury, H4428
14 Then Zedekiah the **k** sent, and took H4428
14 of the LORD: and the **k** said unto H4428
16 So Zedekiah the **k** sware secretly unto H4428
17 go forth unto the **k** of Babylon's H4428
18 But if thou wilt not go forth to the **k** of H4428
19 And Zedekiah the **k** said unto H4428
22 that are left in the **k** of Judah's house H4428
22 forth to the **k** of Babylon's princes, H4428
23 by the hand of the **k** of Babylon: and H4428
25 hast said unto the **k**, hide it not from us, H4428
25 death; also what the **k** said unto thee: H4428

26 before the **k**, that he would not cause H4428
Jer 38:27 words that the **k** had commanded. So H4428
39: 1 In the ninth year of Zedekiah **k** of H4428
1 Nebuchadrezzar **k** of Babylon and all H4428
3 And all the princes of the **k** of Babylon H4428
3 of the princes of the **k** of Babylon. H4428
4 Zedekiah the **k** of Judah saw them, H4428
5 to Nebuchadnezzar **k** of Babylon to H4428
6 Then the **k** of Babylon slew the sons of H4428
6 his eyes: also the **k** of Babylon slew all H4428
11 Now Nebuchadrezzar **k** of Babylon H4428
13 and all the **k** of Babylon's princes; H4428
40: 5 whom the **k** of Babylon hath made H4428
7 heard that the **k** of Babylon had made H4428
9 and serve the **k** of Babylon, and it shall H4428
11 heard that the **k** of Babylon had left H4428
14 that Baalis the **k** of the Ammonites H4428
41: 1 the princes of the **k**, even ten men with H4428
2 him, whom the **k** of Babylon had made H4428
9 it which Asa the **k** had made for fear of H4428
9 for fear of Baasha **k** of Israel: *and* H4428
18 whom the **k** of Babylon made governor H4428
42:11 Be not afraid of the **k** of Babylon, of H4428
43:10 the **k** of Babylon, my servant, H4428
44:30 give Pharaoh-hophra **k** of Egypt into the H4428
30 as I gave Zedekiah **k** of Judah into the H4428
30 of Nebuchadrezzar **k** of Babylon, his H4428
45: 1 the son of Josiah **k** of Judah, saying, H4428
46: 2 of Pharaoh-necho **k** of Egypt, which H4428
2 Nebuchadrezzar **k** of Babylon smote in H4428
2 Jehoiakim the son of Josiah **k** of Judah. H4428
13 Nebuchadrezzar **k** of Babylon should H4428
17 They did cry there, Pharaoh **k** of Egypt H4428
18 *As* I live, saith the **K**, whose name *is* the H4428
26 Nebuchadrezzar **k** of Babylon, and into H4428
48:15 **K**, whose name *is* the LORD of hosts. H4428
49: 1 *then* doth their **k** inherit Gad, and his H4428
3 the hedges; for their **k** shall go into H4428
28 Nebuchadrezzar **k** of Babylon shall H4428
30 for Nebuchadrezzar **k** of Babylon hath H4428
34 reign of Zedekiah **k** of Judah, saying, H4428
38 the **k** and the princes, saith the LORD. H4428
50:17 *him* away: first the **k** of Assyria hath H4428
17 **k** of Babylon hath broken his bones. H4428
18 I will punish the **k** of Babylon and his H4428
18 as I have punished the **k** of Assyria. H4428
43 The **k** of Babylon hath heard the report H4428
51:31 to shew the **k** of Babylon that his H4428
34 Nebuchadrezzar the **k** of Babylon hath H4428
57 **K**, whose name *is* the LORD of hosts. H4428
59 went with Zedekiah the **k** of Judah into H4428
52: 3 rebelled against the **k** of Babylon. H4428
4 Nebuchadrezzar **k** of Babylon came, he H4428
5 unto the eleventh year of **k** Zedekiah. H4428
8 pursued after the **k**, and overtook H4428
9 Then they took the **k**, and carried him H4428
9 him up unto the **k** of Babylon to Riblah H4428
10 And the **k** of Babylon slew the sons of H4428
11 Zedekiah; and the **k** of Babylon bound H4428
12 of Nebuchadrezzar **k** of Babylon, came H4428
12 the **k** of Babylon, into Jerusalem, H4428
15 that fell to the **k** of Babylon, and the H4428
20 the bases, which **k** Solomon had made H4428
26 them to the **k** of Babylon to Riblah. H4428
27 And the **k** of Babylon smote them, and H4428
31 of Jehoiachin **k** of Judah, in the twelfth H4428
31 Evil-merodach **k** of Babylon in the *first* H4428
31 of Jehoiachin **k** of Judah, and brought H4428
34 given him of the **k** of Babylon, every H4428
Lam 2: 6 of his anger the **k** and the priest. H4428
9 her bars: her **k** and her princes *are* H4428
Ezk 1: 2 fifth year of **k** Jehoiachin's captivity, H4428
7:27 The **k** shall mourn, and the prince shall H4428
17:12 *them*, Behold, the **k** of Babylon is come H4428
12 and hath taken the **k** thereof, and the H4428
16 place *where* the **k** *dwelleth* that made H4428
16 that made him **k**, whose oath he H4427
19: 9 him to the **k** of Babylon: they brought H4428
21:19 that the sword of the **k** of Babylon may H4428
21 For the **k** of Babylon stood at the H4428
24: 2 of this same day: the **k** of Babylon set H4428
26: 7 Nebuchadrezzar **k** of Babylon, a king H4428
7 king of Babylon, a **k** of kings, from the H4428
28:12 upon the **k** of Tyrus, and say unto H4428
29: 2 face against Pharaoh **k** of Egypt, and H4428
3 thee, Pharaoh **k** of Egypt, the great H4428
18 Son of man, Nebuchadrezzar **k** of H4428
19 Nebuchadrezzar **k** of Babylon; and he H4428
30:10 hand of Nebuchadrezzar **k** of Babylon. H4428
21 arm of Pharaoh **k** of Egypt; and, lo, it H4428
Ezk 30:22 against Pharaoh **k** of Egypt, and will H4428
24 And I will strengthen the arms of the **k** H4428
25 But I will strengthen the arms of the **k** H4428
25 the hand of the **k** of Babylon, and he H4428
31: 2 Son of man, speak unto Pharaoh **k** of H4428
32: 2 for Pharaoh **k** of Egypt, and say unto H4428
11 the **k** of Babylon shall come upon thee. H4428
37:22 of Israel; and one **k** shall be king to H4428
22 and one king shall be **k** to them all: and H4428
24 And David my servant *shall be* **k** over H4428
Dan 1: 1 the reign of Jehoiakim **k** of Judah came H4428
1 Nebuchadnezzar **k** of Babylon unto H4428
2 And the Lord gave Jehoiakim **k** of H4428
3 And the **k** spake unto Ashpenaz the H4428
5 And the **k** appointed them a daily H4428
5 thereof they might stand before the **k**. H4428
10 Daniel, I fear my lord the **k**, who hath H4428
10 ye make *me* endanger my head to the **k**. H4428
18 Now at the end of the days that the **k** H4428
19 And the **k** communed with them; and H4428
19 therefore stood they before the **k**. H4428
20 that the **k** inquired of them, he H4428
21 *even* unto the first year of **k** Cyrus. H4428
2: 2 Then the **k** commanded to call the H4428
2 for to shew the **k** his dreams. So they H4428
2 So they came and stood before the **k**. H4428
3 And the **k** said unto them, I have H4428
4 Then spake the Chaldeans to the **k** in H4428
4 king in Syriack, O **k**, live for ever: tell H4430
5 The **k** answered and said to the H4430
7 and said, Let the **k** tell his servants the H4430
8 The **k** answered and said, I know of H4430
10 The Chaldeans answered before the **k**, H4430
10 *there is* no **k**, lord, nor ruler, *that* H4430
11 And *it is* a rare thing that the **k** H4430
11 shew it before the **k**, except the gods, H4430
12 For this cause the **k** was angry and very H4430
15 *so* hasty from the **k**? Then Arioch made H4430
16 and desired of the **k** that he would give H4430
16 he would shew the **k** the interpretation. H4430
24 Arioch, whom the **k** had ordained to H4430
24 me in before the **k**, and I will shew unto H4430
24 will shew unto the **k** the interpretation. H4430
25 Daniel before the **k** in haste, and said H4430
25 known unto the **k** the interpretation. H4430
26 The **k** answered and said to Daniel, H4430
27 presence of the **k**, and said, The secret H4430
27 The secret which the **k** hath demanded H4430
27 the soothsayers, shew unto the **k**; H4430
28 known to the **k** Nebuchadnezzar what H4430
29 As for thee, O **k**, thy thoughts came *into* H4430
30 to the **k**, and that thou mightest H4430
31 Thou, O **k**, sawest, and behold a great H4430
36 the interpretation thereof before the **k**. H4430
37 Thou, O **k**, *art* a king of kings: for the H4430
37 Thou, O king, *art* a **k** of kings: for the H4430
45 known to the **k** what shall come to H4430
46 Then the **k** Nebuchadnezzar fell upon H4430
47 The **k** answered unto Daniel, and said, H4430
48 Then the **k** made Daniel a great man, H4430
49 Then Daniel requested of the **k**, and he H4430
49 but Daniel *sat* in the gate of the **k**. H4430
3: 1 Nebuchadnezzar the **k** made an image H4430
2 Then Nebuchadnezzar the **k** sent to H4430
2 Nebuchadnezzar the **k** had set up. H4430
3 the **k** had set up; and they H4430
5 that Nebuchadnezzar the **k** hath set up: H4430
7 that Nebuchadnezzar the **k** had set up. H4430
9 They spake and said to the **k** H4430
9 king Nebuchadnezzar, O **k**, live for ever. H4430
10 Thou, O **k**, hast made a decree, that H4430
12 these men, O **k**, have not regarded thee: H4430
13 they brought these men before the **k**. H4430
16 and said to the **k**, O Nebuchadnezzar, H4430
17 he will deliver *us* out of thine hand, O **k**. H4430
18 But if not, be it known unto thee, O **k**, H4430
24 Then Nebuchadnezzar the **k** was H4430
24 and said unto the **k**, True, O king. H4430
24 and said unto the king, True, O **k**. H4430
30 Then the **k** promoted Shadrach, H4430
4: 1 Nebuchadnezzar the **k**, unto all people, H4430
18 This dream I **k** Nebuchadnezzar have H4430
19 troubled him. The **k** spake, and said, H4430
22 It *is* thou, O **k**, that art grown and H4430
23 And whereas the **k** saw a watcher and H4430
24 This *is* the interpretation, O **k**, and this H4430
24 which is come upon my lord the **k**: H4430
27 Wherefore, O **k**, let my counsel be H4430
28 All this came upon the **k** H4430
Dan 4:30 The **k** spake, and said, Is not this great H4430
31 heaven, *saying*, O **k** Nebuchadnezzar, H4430
37 and honour the **K** of heaven, all whose H4430
5: 1 Belshazzar the **k** made a great feast to H4430
2 that the **k**, and his princes, his H4430
3 and the **k**, and his princes, his H4430
5 **k** saw the part of the hand that wrote. H4430
7 The **k** cried aloud to bring in the H4430
7 *And* the **k** spake, and said to the H4430
8 to the **k** the interpretation thereof. H4430
9 Then was **k** Belshazzar greatly H4430
10 of the words of the **k** and his lords, H4430
10 spake and said, O **k**, live for ever: let not H4430
11 in him; whom the **k** Nebuchadnezzar H4430
11 thy father, the **k**, *I say*, thy father, made H4430
12 same Daniel, whom the **k** named H4430
13 in before the **k**. *And* the king spake H4430
13 the king. *And* the **k** spake and said H4430
13 the **k** my father brought out of Jewry? H4430
17 and said before the **k**, Let thy gifts be to H4430
17 writing unto the **k**, and make known to H4430
18 O thou **k**, the most high God gave H4430
30 In that night was Belshazzar the **k** of H4430
6: 2 and the **k** should have no damage. H4430
3 in him; and the **k** thought to set him H4430
6 together to the **k**, and said thus unto H4430
6 thus unto him, **K** Darius, live for ever. H4430
7 **k**, he shall be cast into the den of lions. H4430
8 Now, O **k**, establish the decree, and sign H4430
9 Wherefore **k** Darius signed the writing H4430
12 and spake before the **k** concerning the H4430
12 save of thee, O **k**, shall be cast into the H4430
12 den of lions? The **k** answered and said, H4430
13 said before the **k**, That Daniel, which H4430
13 not thee, O **k**, nor the decree that H4430
14 Then the **k**, when he heard *these* words, H4430
15 Then these men assembled unto the **k**, H4430
15 and said unto the **k**, Know, O king, that H4430
15 the king, Know, O **k**, that the law of the H4430
15 the **k** establisheth may be changed. H4430
16 Then the **k** commanded, and they H4430
16 of lions. *Now* the **k** spake and said unto H4430
17 of the den; and the **k** sealed it with his H4430
18 Then the **k** went to his palace, and H4430
19 Then the **k** arose very early in the H4430
20 Daniel: *and* the **k** spake and said to H4430
21 Then said Daniel unto the **k**, O king, live H4430
21 Then said Daniel unto the king, O **k**, live H4430
22 before thee, O **k**, have I done no hurt. H4430
23 Then was the **k** exceeding glad for him, H4430
24 And the **k** commanded, and they H4430
25 Then **k** Darius wrote unto all people, H4430
7: 1 In the first year of Belshazzar **k** of H4430
8: 1 In the third year of the reign of **k** H4428
21 And the rough goat *is* the **k** of Grecia: H4428
21 that *is* between his eyes *is* the first **k**. H4428
23 are come to the full, a **k** of fierce H4428
9: 1 **k** over the realm of the Chaldeans; H4427
10: 1 In the third year of Cyrus **k** of Persia a H4428
11: 3 And a mighty **k** shall stand up, that H4428
5 And the **k** of the south shall be strong, H4428
6 shall come to the **k** of the north to H4428
7 the fortress of the **k** of the north, and H4428
8 *more* years than the **k** of the north. H4428
9 So the **k** of the south shall come into H4428
11 And the **k** of the south shall be moved H4428
11 him, *even* with the **k** of the north: and H4428
13 For the **k** of the north shall return, and H4428
14 up against the **k** of the south: also the H4428
15 So the **k** of the north shall come, and H4428
25 against the **k** of the south with a great H4428
25 army; and the **k** of the south shall be H4428
36 And the **k** shall do according to his will; H4428
40 And at the time of the end shall the **k** of H4428
40 at him: and the **k** of the north shall H4428
Hos 1: 1 Jeroboam the son of Joash, **k** of Israel. H4428
3: 4 days without a **k**, and without a prince, H4428
5 and David their **k**; and shall fear the H4428
5: 1 ear, O house of the **k**; for judgment *is* H4428
13 and sent to **k** Jareb: yet could he not H4428
7: 3 They make the **k** glad with their H4428
5 In the day of our **k** the princes have H4428
8:10 little for the burden of the **k** of princes. H4428
10: 3 For now they shall say, We have no **k**, H4428
3 LORD; what then should a **k** do to us? H4428
6 *for* a present to **k** Jareb: Ephraim shall H4428
7 *As for* Samaria, her **k** is cut off as the H4428
15 shall the **k** of Israel utterly be cut off. H4428

11: 5 be his **k**, because they refused to return. H4428
Hos 13:10 I will be thy **k**: where *is any other* that H4428
10 thou saidst, Give me a **k** and princes? H4428
11 I gave thee a **k** in mine anger, and took H4428
Am 1: 1 in the days of Uzziah **k** of Judah, and in H4428
1 the son of Joash **k** of Israel, two years H4428
15 And their **k** shall go into captivity, he H4428
2: 1 the bones of the **k** of Edom into lime: H4428
7:10 sent to Jeroboam **k** of Israel, saying, H4428
Jna 3: 6 For word came unto the **k** of Nineveh, H4428
7 by the decree of the **k** and his nobles, H4428
Mic 2:13 out by it: and their **k** shall pass before H4428
4: 9 out aloud? *is there* no **k** in thee? is thy H4428
6: 5 now what Balak **k** of Moab consulted, H4428
Nah 3:18 Thy shepherds slumber, O **k** of Assyria: H4428
Zep 1: 1 of Josiah the son of Amon, **k** of Judah. H4428
3:15 thine enemy: the **k** of Israel, *even* the H4428
Hag 1: 1 In the second year of Darius the **k**, in H4428
15 in the second year of Darius the **k**. H4428
Zec 7: 1 in the fourth year of **k** Darius, *that* the H4428
9: 5 ashamed; and the **k** shall perish from H4428
9 behold, thy **K** cometh unto thee: he H4428
11: 6 the hand of his **k**: and they shall smite H4428
14: 5 the days of Uzziah **k** of Judah: and the H4428
9 And the LORD shall be **k** over all the H4428
16 to worship the **K**, the LORD of hosts, H4428
17 to worship the **K**, the LORD of hosts, H4428
Mal 1:14 for I *am* a great **K**, saith the LORD of H4428
Mt 1: 6 And Jesse begat David the **k**; and David *G935*
6 and David the **k** begat Solomon of her *G935*
2: 1 days of Herod the **k**, behold, there came *G935*
2 Saying, Where is he that is born **K** of the *G935*
3 When Herod the **k** had heard *these* *G935*
9 When they had heard the **k**, they *G935*
5:35 Jerusalem; for it is the city of the great **K**. *G935*
14: 9 And the **k** was sorry: nevertheless for the *G935*
18:23 unto a certain **k**, which would take *G935*
21: 5 of Sion, Behold, thy **K** cometh unto thee, *G935*
22: 2 **k**, which made a marriage for his son, *G935*
7 But when the **k** heard *thereof*, he was *G935*
11 And when the **k** came in to see the *G935*
13 Then said the **k** to the servants, Bind *G935*
25:34 Then shall the **K** say unto them on his *G935*
40 And the **K** shall answer and say unto *G935*
27:11 Art thou the **K** of the Jews? And Jesus *G935*
29 mocked him, saying, Hail, **K** of the Jews! *G935*
37 THIS IS JESUS THE **K** OF THE JEWS. *G935*
42 save. If he be the **K** of Israel, let him now *G935*
Mk 6:14 And **k** Herod heard *of him*; (for his *G935*
22 sat with him, the **k** said unto the damsel, *G935*
25 with haste unto the **k**, and asked, saying, *G935*
26 And the **k** was exceeding sorry; *yet* for *G935*
27 And immediately the **k** sent an *G935*
15: 2 And Pilate asked him, Art thou the **K** of *G935*
9 that I release unto you the **K** of the Jews? *G935*
12 *unto him* whom ye call the **K** of the Jews? *G935*
18 And began to salute him, Hail, **K** of the *G935*
26 was written over, THE **K** OF THE JEWS. *G935*
32 Let Christ the **K** of Israel descend now *G935*
Lk 1: 5 There was in the days of Herod, the **k** of *G935*
14:31 Or what **k**, going to make war against *G935*
31 against another **k**, sitteth not down first, *G935*
19:38 Saying, Blessed *be* the **K** that cometh in *G935*
23: 2 saying that he himself is Christ a **K**. *G935*
3 Art thou the **K** of the Jews? And he *G935*
37 And saying, If thou be the **k** of the Jews, *G935*
38 Hebrew, THIS IS THE **K** OF THE JEWS. *G935*
Jn 1:49 the Son of God; thou art the **K** of Israel. *G935*
6:15 to make him a **k**, he departed again into *G935*
12:13 Blessed *is* the **K** of Israel that cometh *G935*
15 Fear not, daughter of Sion: behold, thy **K** *G935*
18:33 unto him, Art thou the **K** of the Jews? *G935*
37 him, Art thou a **k** then? Jesus answered, *G935*
37 sayest that I am a **k**. To this end was I *G935*
39 that I release unto you the **K** of the Jews? *G935*
19: 3 And said, Hail, **K** of the Jews! and they *G935*
12 himself a **k** speaketh against Caesar. *G935*
14 he saith unto the Jews, Behold your **K**! *G935*
15 Shall I crucify your **K**? The chief priests *G935*
15 answered, We have no **k** but Caesar. *G935*
19 OF NAZARETH THE **K** OF THE JEWS. *G935*
21 Write not, The **K** of the Jews; but that *G935*
21 but that he said, I am **K** of the Jews. *G935*
Act 7:10 the sight of Pharaoh **k** of Egypt; and he *G935*
18 Till another **k** arose, which knew not *G935*
12: 1 Now about that time Herod the **k** *G935*
13:21 And afterward they desired a **k**: and God *G935*
22 David to be their **k**; to whom also he *G1519*
17: 7 saying that there is another **k**, *one* Jesus. *G935*
25:13 And after certain days **k** Agrippa and *G935*
Act 25:14 cause unto the **k**, saying, There is a *G935*
24 And Festus said, **K** Agrippa, and all men *G935*
26 before thee, O **k** Agrippa, that, after *G935*
26: 2 I think myself happy, **k** Agrippa, *G935*
7 **k** Agrippa, I am accused of the Jews. *G935*
13 At midday, O **k**, I saw in the way a light *G935*
19 Whereupon, O **k** Agrippa, I was not *G935*
26 For the **k** knoweth of these things, before *G935*
27 **K** Agrippa, believest thou the prophets? I *G935*
30 And when he had thus spoken, the **k** *G935*
2Co 11:32 under Aretas the **k** kept the city of the *G935*
1Ti 1:17 Now unto the **K** eternal, immortal, *G935*
6:15 the **K** of kings, and Lord of lords; *G935*
Heb 7: 1 For this Melchisedec, **k** of Salem, priest *G935*
2 by interpretation **K** of righteousness, *G935*
2 also **K** of Salem, which is, King of peace; *G935*
2 also King of Salem, which is, **K** of peace; *G935*
11:27 the wrath of the **k**: for he endured, as *G935*
1Pt 2:13 sake: whether it be to the **k**, as supreme; *G935*
17 brotherhood. Fear God. Honour the **k**. *G935*
Rev 9:11 And they had a **k** over them, *which is* the *G935*
15: 3 and true *are* thy ways, thou **K** of saints. *G935*
17:14 is Lord of lords, and **K** of kings: and they *G935*
19:16 **K** OF KINGS, AND LORD OF LORDS. *G935*

KINGDOM

Gen 10:10 And the beginning of his **k** was Babel, H4467
20: 9 on me and on my **k** a great sin? thou H4467
Ex 19: 6 And ye shall be unto me a **k** of priests, H4467
Nu 24: 7 than Agag, and his **k** shall be exalted. H4438
32:33 son of Joseph, the **k** of Sihon king of the H4467
33 the Amorites, and the **k** of Og king of H4467
Dt 3: 4 region of Argob, the **k** of Og in Bashan. H4467
10 Edrei, cities of the **k** of Og in Bashan. H4467
13 Bashan, *being* the **k** of Og, gave I unto H4467
17:18 the throne of his **k**, that he shall write H4467
20 *his* days in his **k**, he, and his children, H4467
Jos 13:12 All the **k** of Og in Bashan, which H4468
21 plain, and all the **k** of Sihon king of the H4468
27 the rest of the **k** of Sihon king of H4468
30 all Bashan, all the **k** of Og king of H4468
31 Edrei, cities of the **k** of Og in Bashan, H4468
1Sa 10:16 of the matter of the **k**, whereof Samuel H4410
25 the manner of the **k**, and wrote *it* in a H4410
11:14 us go to Gilgal, and renew the **k** there. H4410
13:13 established thy **k** upon Israel for ever. H4467
14 But now thy **k** shall not continue: the H4467
14:47 So Saul took the **k** over Israel, and H4410
15:28 hath rent the **k** of Israel from thee this H4468
18: 8 and *what* can he have more but the **k**? H4410
20:31 nor thy **k**. Wherefore now send H4438
24:20 be king, and that the **k** of Israel shall be H4467
28:17 hath rent the **k** out of thine hand, and H4467
2Sa 3:10 To translate the **k** from the house of H4467
28 he said, I and my **k** *are* guiltless before H4467
5:12 his **k** for his people Israel's sake. H4467
7:12 of thy bowels, and I will establish his **k**. H4467
13 will stablish the throne of his **k** for ever. H4467
16 And thine house and thy **k** shall be H4467
16: 3 of Israel restore me the **k** of my father. H4468
8 hath delivered the **k** into the hand of H4410
1Ki 1:46 Solomon sitteth on the throne of the **k**. H4410
2:12 and his **k** was established greatly. H4438
15 And he said, Thou knowest that the **k** H4410
15 reign: howbeit the **k** is turned about, H4410
22 ask for him the **k** also; for he *is* mine H4410
46 he died. And the **k** was established in H4467
9: 5 Then I will establish the throne of thy **k** H4467
10:20 there was not the like made in any **k**. H4467
11:11 surely rend the **k** from thee, and will H4467
13 Howbeit I will not rend away all the **k**; H4467
31 I will rend the **k** out of the hand of H4467
34 Howbeit I will not take the whole **k** out H4467
35 But I will take the **k** out of his son's H4410
12:21 of Israel, to bring the **k** again to H4410
26 the **k** return to the house of David: H4467
14: 8 And rent the **k** away from the house of H4467
18:10 is no nation or **k**, whither my lord hath H4467
10 **k** and nation, that they found thee not. H4467
21: 7 now govern the **k** of Israel? arise, *and* H4410
2Ki 14: 5 And it came to pass, as soon as the **k** H4467
15:19 with him to confirm the **k** in his hand. H4467
1Ch 10:14 the **k** unto David the son of Jesse. H4410
11:10 with him in his **k**, *and* with all Israel, H4438
12:23 to turn the **k** of Saul to him, according H4438
14: 2 over Israel, for his **k** was lifted up on H4438
16:20 and from *one* **k** to another people; H4467
17:11 be of thy sons; and I will establish his **k**. H4438
14 house and in my **k** for ever: and his H4438
1Ch 22:10 the throne of his **k** over Israel for ever. H4438
28: 5 throne of the **k** of the LORD over Israel. H4438
7 Moreover I will establish his **k** for ever, H4438
29:11 *thine;* thine *is* the **k**, O LORD, and thou H4467
2Ch 1: 1 in his **k**, and the LORD his God H4438
2: 1 of the LORD, and an house for his **k**. H4438
12 for the LORD, and an house for his **k**. H4438
7:18 Then will I stablish the throne of thy **k**, H4438
9:19 There was not the like made in any **k**. H4467
11: 1 might bring the **k** again to Rehoboam. H4467
17 So they strengthened the **k** of Judah, H4438
12: 1 established the **k**, and had strengthened H4438
13: 5 of Israel gave the **k** over Israel to David H4467
8 And now ye think to withstand the **k** of H4467
14: 5 and the **k** was quiet before him. H4467
17: 5 Therefore the LORD stablished the **k** in H4467
21: 3 in Judah: but the **k** gave he to Jehoram; H4467
4 was risen up to the **k** of his father, he H4467
22: 9 had no power to keep still the **k**. H4467
23:20 set the king upon the throne of the **k**. H4467
25: 3 Now it came to pass, when the **k** was H4467
29:21 a sin offering for the **k**, and for the H4467
32:15 of any nation or **k** was able to deliver H4467
33:13 to Jerusalem into his **k**. Then Manasseh H4438
36:20 sons until the reign of the **k** of Persia: H4438
22 his **k**, and *put it* also in writing, saying, H4438
Ezr 1: 1 his **k**, and *put it* also in writing, saying, H4438
Neh 9:35 For they have not served thee in their **k**, H4438
Est 1: 2 his **k**, which *was* in Shushan the palace, H4438
4 of his glorious **k** and the honour of his H4438
14 face, *and* which sat the first in the **k**;) H4438
2: 3 provinces of his **k**, that they may gather H4438
3: 6 the whole **k** of Ahasuerus, *even* H4438
8 provinces of thy **k**; and their laws *are* H4438
4:14 come to the **k** for *such* a time as this? H4438
5: 3 be even given thee to the half of the **k**. H4438
6 the half of the **k** it shall be performed. H4438
7: 2 be performed, *even* to the half of the **k**. H4438
9:30 provinces of the **k** of Ahasuerus, *with* H4438
Ps 22:28 For the **k** *is* the LORD'S: and he *is* the H4410
45: 6 the sceptre of thy **k** *is* a right sceptre. H4438
103:19 the heavens; and his **k** ruleth over all. H4438
105:13 another, from *one* **k** to another people; H4467
145:11 They shall speak of the glory of thy **k**, H4438
12 acts, and the glorious majesty of his **k**. H4438
13 Thy **k** *is* an everlasting kingdom, and H4438
13 Thy kingdom *is* an everlasting **k**, and H4438
Ecc 4:14 *he that is* born in his **k** becometh poor. H4438
Isa 9: 7 and upon his **k**, to order it, and to H4467
17: 3 Ephraim, and the **k** from Damascus, H4467
19: 2 against city, *and* **k** against kingdom. H4467
2 against city, *and* kingdom against **k**. H4467
34:12 thereof to the **k**, but none *shall be* there, H4410
60:12 For the nation and **k** that will not serve H4467
Jer 18: 7 and concerning a **k**, to pluck up, and to H4467
9 concerning a **k**, to build and to plant *it*; H4467
27: 8 the nation and **k** which will not serve H4467
Lam 2: 2 polluted the **k** and the princes thereof. H4467
Ezk 16:13 and thou didst prosper into a **k**. H4410
17:14 That the **k** might be base, that it might H4467
29:14 and they shall be there a base **k**. H4467
Dan 2:37 a **k**, power, and strength, and glory. H4437
39 And after thee shall arise another **k** H4437
39 and another third **k** of brass, which H4437
40 And the fourth **k** shall be strong as H4437
41 part of iron, the **k** shall be divided; but H4437
42 and part of clay, *so* the **k** shall be partly H4437
44 of heaven set up a **k**, which shall never H4437
44 destroyed: and the **k** shall not be left to H4437
4: 3 *are* his wonders! his **k** *is* an everlasting H4437
3 *is* an everlasting **k**, and his dominion *is* H4437
17 High ruleth in the **k** of men, and giveth H4437
18 wise *men* of my **k** are not able to make H4437
25 High ruleth in the **k** of men, and giveth H4437
26 the tree roots; thy **k** shall be sure unto H4437
29 in the palace of the **k** of Babylon. H4437
30 the house of the **k** by the might of my H4437
31 is spoken; The **k** is departed from thee. H4437
32 High ruleth in the **k** of men, and giveth H4437
34 his **k** *is* from generation to generation: H4437
36 for the glory of my **k**, mine honour and H4437
36 was established in my **k**, and excellent H4437
5: 7 and shall be the third ruler in the **k**. H4437
11 There is a man in thy **k**, in whom *is* the H4437
16 and shalt be the third ruler in the **k**. H4437
18 **k**, and majesty, and glory, and honour: H4437
21 God ruled in the **k** of men, and *that* he H4437
26 hath numbered thy **k**, and finished it. H4437

28 PERES; Thy **k** is divided, and given to H4437
Dan 5:29 he should be the third ruler in the **k**. H4437
31 And Darius the Median took the **k**, H4437
6: 1 It pleased Darius to set over the **k** an H4437
1 which should be over the whole **k**; H4437
4 concerning the **k**; but they could find H4437
7 All the presidents of the **k**, the H4437
26 dominion of my **k** men tremble and H4437
26 for ever, and his **k** *that* which shall not H4437
7:14 and glory, and a **k**, that all people, H4437
14 his **k** *that* which shall not be destroyed. H4437
18 High shall take the **k**, and possess the H4437
18 the **k** for ever, even for ever and ever. H4437
22 came that the saints possessed the **k**. H4437
23 shall be the fourth **k** upon earth, which H4437
24 And the ten horns out of this **k** *are* ten H4437
27 And the **k** and dominion, and the H4437
27 the greatness of the **k** under the whole H4437
27 most High, whose **k** *is* an everlasting H4437
27 *is* an everlasting **k**, and all dominions H4437
8:23 And in the latter time of their **k**, when H4438
10:13 But the prince of the **k** of Persia H4438
11: 4 And when he shall stand up, his **k** shall H4438
4 he ruled: for his **k** shall be plucked up, H4438
9 **k**, and shall return into his own land. H4438
17 of his whole **k**, and upright ones with H4438
20 *in* the glory of the **k**: but within few days H4438
21 the honour of the **k**: but he shall come H4438
21 and obtain the **k** by flatteries. H4438
Hos 1: 4 to cease the **k** of the house of Israel. H4468
Am 9: 8 upon the sinful **k**, and I will destroy it H4467
Oba 21 of Esau; and the **k** shall be the LORD'S. H4410
Mic 4: 8 first dominion; the **k** shall come to the H4467
Mt 3: 2 And saying, Repent ye: for the **k** of *G932*
4:17 Repent: for the **k** of heaven is at hand. *G932*
23 the gospel of the **k**, and healing all *G932*
5: 3 in spirit: for theirs is the **k** of heaven. *G932*
10 sake: for theirs is the **k** of heaven. *G932*
19 called the least in the **k** of heaven: but *G932*
19 shall be called great in the **k** of heaven. *G932*
20 in no case enter into the **k** of heaven. *G932*
6:10 Thy **k** come. Thy will be done in earth, *G932*
13 For thine is the **k**, and the power, and *G932*
33 But seek ye first the **k** of God, and his *G932*
7:21 shall enter into the **k** of heaven; but he *G932*
8:11 and Isaac, and Jacob, in the **k** of heaven. *G932*
12 But the children of the **k** shall be cast out *G932*
9:35 the gospel of the **k**, and healing every *G932*
10: 7 And as ye go, preach, saying, The **k** of *G932*
11:11 in the **k** of heaven is greater than he. *G932*
12 until now the **k** of heaven suffereth *G932*
12:25 unto them, Every **k** divided against itself *G932*
26 himself; how shall then his **k** stand? *G932*
28 God, then the **k** of God is come unto you. *G932*
13:11 **k** of heaven, but to them it is not given. *G932*
19 When any one heareth the word of the **k**, *G932*
24 them, saying, The **k** of heaven is likened *G932*
31 them, saying, The **k** of heaven is like to a *G932*
33 he unto them; The **k** of heaven is like *G932*
38 the children of the **k**; but the tares are the *G932*
41 gather out of his **k** all things that offend, *G932*
43 as the sun in the **k** of their Father. Who *G932*
44 Again, the **k** of heaven is like unto *G932*
45 Again, the **k** of heaven is like unto a *G932*
47 Again, the **k** of heaven is like unto a net, *G932*
52 *is* instructed unto the **k** of heaven is like *G932*
16:19 thee the keys of the **k** of heaven: and *G932*
28 they see the Son of man coming in his **k**. *G932*
18: 1 Who is the greatest in the **k** of heaven? *G932*
3 ye shall not enter into the **k** of heaven. *G932*
4 the same is greatest in the **k** of heaven. *G932*
23 Therefore is the **k** of heaven likened unto *G932*
19:12 eunuchs for the **k** of heaven's sake. He *G932*
14 unto me: for of such is the **k** of heaven. *G932*
23 shall hardly enter into the **k** of heaven. *G932*
24 for a rich man to enter into the **k** of God. *G932*
20: 1 For the **k** of heaven is like unto a man *G932*
21 hand, and the other on the left, in thy **k**. *G932*
21:31 harlots go into the **k** of God before you. *G932*
43 Therefore say I unto you, The **k** of God *G932*
22: 2 The **k** of heaven is like unto a certain *G932*
23:13 for ye shut up the **k** of heaven against *G932*
24: 7 nation, and **k** against kingdom: and *G932*
7 kingdom against **k**: and there shall be *G932*
14 And this gospel of the **k** shall be *G932*
25: 1 Then shall the **k** of heaven be likened *G932*
14 For *the k of heaven is* as a man *G932*
34 Father, inherit the **k** prepared for you *G932*
26:29 I drink it new with you in my Father's **k**. *G932*
Mk 1:14 preaching the gospel of the **k** of God, *G932*
Mk 1:15 is fulfilled, and the **k** of God is at hand: *G932*
3:24 And if a **k** be divided against itself, that *G932*
24 against itself, that **k** cannot stand. *G932*
4:11 the mystery of the **k** of God: but unto *G932*
26 And he said, So is the **k** of God, as if a *G932*
30 shall we liken the **k** of God? or with what *G932*
6:23 I will give *it* thee, unto the half of my **k**. *G932*
9: 1 have seen the **k** of God come with power. *G932*
47 to enter into the **k** of God with one eye, *G932*
10:14 them not: for of such is the **k** of God. *G932*
15 not receive the **k** of God as a little child, *G932*
23 that have riches enter into the **k** of God! *G932*
24 trust in riches to enter into the **k** of God! *G932*
25 for a rich man to enter into the **k** of God. *G932*
11:10 Blessed *be* the **k** of our father David, that *G932*
12:34 not far from the **k** of God. And no man *G932*
13: 8 nation, and **k** against kingdom: and *G932*
8 kingdom against **k**: and there shall be *G932*
14:25 day that I drink it new in the **k** of God. *G932*
15:43 also waited for the **k** of God, came, and *G932*
Lk 1:33 ever; and of his **k** there shall be no end. *G932*
4:43 I must preach the **k** of God to other cities *G932*
6:20 *be ye* poor: for yours is the **k** of God. *G932*
7:28 is least in the **k** of God is greater than he. *G932*
8: 1 **k** of God: and the twelve *were* with him, *G932*
10 mysteries of the **k** of God: but to others *G932*
9: 2 And he sent them to preach the **k** of God, *G932*
11 unto them of the **k** of God, and healed *G932*
27 taste of death, till they see the **k** of God. *G932*
60 but go thou and preach the **k** of God. *G932*
62 and looking back, is fit for the **k** of God. *G932*
10: 9 The **k** of God is come nigh unto you. *G932*
11 that the **k** of God is come nigh unto you. *G932*
11: 2 be thy name. Thy **k** come. Thy will be *G932*
17 unto them, Every **k** divided against itself *G932*
18 how shall his **k** stand? because ye say *G932*
20 no doubt the **k** of God is come upon you. *G932*
12:31 But rather seek ye the **k** of God; and all *G932*
32 Father's good pleasure to give you the **k**. *G932*
13:18 Then said he, Unto what is the **k** of God *G932*
20 Whereunto shall I liken the **k** of God? *G932*
28 **k** of God, and you *yourselves* thrust out. *G932*
29 south, and shall sit down in the **k** of God. *G932*
14:15 *is* he that shall eat bread in the **k** of God. *G932*
16:16 since that time the **k** of God is preached, *G932*
17:20 when the **k** of God should come, *G932*
20 **k** of God cometh not with observation: *G932*
21 for, behold, the **k** of God is within you. *G932*
18:16 them not: for of such is the **k** of God. *G932*
17 not receive the **k** of God as a little child *G932*
24 that have riches enter into the **k** of God! *G932*
25 for a rich man to enter into the **k** of God. *G932*
29 wife, or children, for the **k** of God's sake, *G932*
19:11 the **k** of God should immediately appear. *G932*
12 to receive for himself a **k**, and to return. *G932*
15 received the **k**, then he commanded *G932*
21:10 against nation, and **k** against kingdom: *G932*
10 against nation, and kingdom against **k**: *G932*
31 ye that the **k** of God is nigh at hand. *G932*
22:16 until it be fulfilled in the **k** of God. *G932*
18 of the vine, until the **k** of God shall come. *G932*
29 And I appoint unto you a **k**, as my Father *G932*
30 at my table in my **k**, and sit on thrones *G932*
23:42 me when thou comest into thy **k**. *G932*
51 who also himself waited for the **k** of God. *G932*
Jn 3: 3 born again, he cannot see the **k** of God. *G932*
5 Spirit, he cannot enter into the **k** of God. *G932*
18:36 Jesus answered, My **k** is not of this *G932*
36 of this world: if my **k** were of this world, *G932*
36 Jews: but now is my **k** not from hence. *G932*
Act 1: 3 of the things pertaining to the **k** of God: *G932*
6 at this time restore again the **k** to Israel? *G932*
8:12 concerning the **k** of God, and the name *G932*
14:22 much tribulation enter into the **k** of God. *G932*
19: 8 the things concerning the **k** of God. *G932*
20:25 the **k** of God, shall see my face no more. *G932*
28:23 and testified the **k** of God, persuading *G932*
31 Preaching the **k** of God, and teaching *G932*
Ro 14:17 For the **k** of God is not meat and drink; *G932*
1Co 4:20 For the **k** of God *is* not in word, but in *G932*
6: 9 shall not inherit the **k** of God? Be not *G932*
10 extortioners, shall inherit the **k** of God. *G932*
15:24 have delivered up the **k** to God, even the *G932*
50 cannot inherit the **k** of God; neither doth *G932*
Gal 5:21 things shall not inherit the **k** of God. *G932*
Eph 5: 5 inheritance in the **k** of Christ and of God. *G932*
Col 1:13 translated *us* into the **k** of his dear Son: *G932*
4:11 unto the **k** of God, which have been *G932*
1Th 2:12 hath called you unto his **k** and glory. *G932*
2Th 1: 5 of the **k** of God, for which ye also suffer: *G932*
2Ti 4: 1 and the dead at his appearing and his **k**; *G932*
18 unto his heavenly **k**: to whom *be* glory for *G932*
Heb 1: 8 of righteousness *is* the sceptre of thy **k**. *G932*
12:28 Wherefore we receiving a **k** which *G932*
Jas 2: 5 faith, and heirs of the **k** which he hath *G932*
2Pt 1:11 **k** of our Lord and Saviour Jesus Christ. *G932*
Rev 1: 9 and in the **k** and patience of Jesus *G932*
12:10 strength, and the **k** of our God, and the *G932*
16:10 the beast; and his **k** was full of darkness; *G932*
17:12 have received no **k** as yet; but receive *G932*
17 and give their **k** unto the beast, until *G932*

KINGDOMS

Dt 3:21 do unto all the **k** whither thou passest. H4467
28:25 be removed into all the **k** of the earth. H4467
Jos 11:10 beforetime was the head of all those **k**. H4467
1Sa 10:18 all **k**, *and* of them that oppressed you: H4467
1Ki 4:21 And Solomon reigned over all **k** from H4467
2Ki 19:15 alone, of all the **k** of the earth; thou H4467
19 his hand, that all the **k** of the earth may H4467
1Ch 29:30 and over all the **k** of the countries. H4467
2Ch 12: 8 the service of the **k** of the countries. H4467
17:10 fell upon all the **k** of the lands that *were* H4467
20: 6 thou over all the **k** of the heathen? and H4467
29 And the fear of God was on all the **k** of H4467
36:23 of Persia, All the **k** of the earth hath the H4467
Ezr 1: 2 given me all the **k** of the earth; and he H4467
Neh 9:22 Moreover thou gavest them **k** and H4467
Ps 46: 6 The heathen raged, the **k** were moved: H4467
68:32 Sing unto God, ye **k** of the earth; O sing H4467
79: 6 **k** that have not called upon thy name. H4467
102:22 together, and the **k**, to serve the LORD. H4467
135:11 of Bashan, and all the **k** of Canaan: H4467
Isa 10:10 As my hand hath found the **k** of the H4467
13: 4 noise of the **k** of nations gathered H4467
19 And Babylon, the glory of **k**, the beauty H4467
14:16 the earth to tremble, that did shake **k**; H4467
23:11 the sea, he shook the **k**: the LORD hath H4467
17 with all the **k** of the world upon the H4467
37:16 alone, of all the **k** of the earth: thou H4467
20 his hand, that all the **k** of the earth may H4467
47: 5 shalt no more be called, The lady of **k**. H4467
Jer 1:10 and over the **k**, to root out, and to pull H4467
15 the families of the **k** of the north, saith H4467
10: 7 all their **k**, *there is* none like unto thee. H4438
15: 4 removed into all **k** of the earth, because H4467
24: 9 into all the **k** of the earth for *their* H4467
25:26 and all the **k** of the world, which H4467
28: 8 **k**, of war, and of evil, and of pestilence. H4467
29:18 removed to all the **k** of the earth, to be H4467
34: 1 army, and all the **k** of the earth of his H4467
17 be removed into all the **k** of the earth. H4467
49:28 and concerning the **k** of Hazor, which H4467
51:20 nations, and with thee will I destroy **k**; H4467
27 against her the **k** of Ararat, Minni, and H4467
Ezk 29:15 It shall be the basest of the **k**; neither H4467
37:22 be divided into two **k** any more at all: H4467
Dan 2:44 all these **k**, and it shall stand for ever. H4437
7:23 be diverse from all **k**, and shall devour H4437
8:22 up for it, four **k** shall stand up out of H4438
Am 6: 2 *they* better than these **k**? or their border H4467
Nah 3: 5 thy nakedness, and the **k** thy shame. H4467
Zep 3: 8 may assemble the **k**, to pour upon them H4467
Hag 2:22 And I will overthrow the throne of **k**, H4467
22 the strength of the **k** of the heathen; H4467
Mt 4: 8 the **k** of the world, and the glory of them; *G932*
Lk 4: 5 the **k** of the world in a moment of time. *G932*
Heb 11:33 Who through faith subdued **k**, wrought *G932*
Rev 11:15 saying, The **k** of this world are become *G932*
15 are become *the k* of our Lord, and of his *G932*

KINGLY

Dan 5:20 deposed from his **k** throne, and they H4437

KINGS

Gen 14: 5 and the **k** that *were* with him, H4428
9 Arioch king of Ellasar; four **k** with five. H4428
10 *of* slimepits; and the **k** of Sodom and H4428
17 and of the **k** that *were* with him, H4428
17: 6 of thee, and **k** shall come out of thee. H4428
16 of nations; **k** of people shall be of her. H4428
35:11 thee, and **k** shall come out of thy loins; H4428
36:31 And these *are* the **k** that reigned in the H4428
Nu 31: 8 And they slew the **k** of Midian, beside H4428
8 and Reba, five **k** of Midian: Balaam H4428
Dt 3: 8 hand of the two **k** of the Amorites the H4428
21 unto these two **k**: so shall the LORD do H4428

4:47 king of Bashan, two **k** of the Amorites, H4428
Dt 7:24 And he shall deliver their **k** into thine H4428
31: 4 Sihon and to Og, **k** of the Amorites, and H4428
Jos 2:10 did unto the two **k** of the Amorites, that H4428
5: 1 And it came to pass, when all the **k** of H4428
1 and all the **k** of the Canaanites, which H4428
9: 1 And it came to pass, when all the **k** H4428
10 And all that he did to the two **k** of the H4428
10: 5 Therefore the five **k** of the Amorites, H4428
6 help us: for all the **k** of the Amorites H4428
16 But these five **k** fled, and hid H4428
17 **k** are found hid in a cave at Makkedah. H4428
22 those five **k** unto me out of the cave. H4428
23 forth those five **k** unto him out of the H4428
24 brought out those **k** unto Joshua, that H4428
24 the necks of these **k**. And they came H4428
40 and all their **k**: he left none remaining, H4428
42 And all these **k** and their land did H4428
11: 2 And to the **k** that *were* on the north of H4428
5 And when all these **k** were met H4428
12 And all the cities of those **k**, and all the H4428
12 kings, and all the **k** of them, did Joshua H4428
17 and all their **k** he took, and smote H4428
18 made war a long time with all those **k**. H4428
12: 1 Now these *are* the **k** of the land, which H4428
7 And these *are* the **k** of the country H4428
24 The king of Tirzah, one: all the **k** thirty H4428
24:12 you, *even* the two **k** of the Amorites; H4428
Jdg 1: 7 and ten **k**, having their thumbs H4428
5: 3 Hear, O ye **k**; give ear, O ye princes; I, H4428
19 The **k** came *and* fought, then fought the H4428
19 fought, then fought the **k** of Canaan in H4428
8: 5 Zebah and Zalmunna, **k** of Midian. H4428
12 and took the two **k** of Midian, Zebah H4428
26 that *was* on the **k** of Midian, and beside H4428
1Sa 14:47 Edom, and against the **k** of Zobah, and H4428
27: 6 unto the **k** of Judah unto this day. H4428
2Sa 10:19 And when all the **k** *that were* servants H4428
11: 1 at the time when **k** go forth *to battle,* H4428
1Ki 3:13 among the **k** like unto thee all thy days. H4428
4:24 to Azzah, over all the **k** on this side the H4428
34 Solomon, from all **k** of the earth, which H4428
10:15 and of all the **k** of Arabia, and of the H4428
23 So king Solomon exceeded all the **k** of H4428
29 and so for all the **k** of the Hittites, and H4428
29 and for the **k** of Syria, did they bring H4428
14:19 book of the chronicles of the **k** of Israel. H4428
29 of the chronicles of the **k** of Judah? H4428
15: 7 chronicles of the **k** of Judah? And there H4428
23 the chronicles of the **k** of Judah? H4428
31 of the chronicles of the **k** of Israel? H4428
16: 5 of the chronicles of the **k** of Israel? H4428
14 of the chronicles of the **k** of Israel? H4428
20 of the chronicles of the **k** of Israel? H4428
27 of the chronicles of the **k** of Israel? H4428
33 all the **k** of Israel that were before him. H4428
20: 1 thirty and two **k** with him, and horses, H4428
12 he and the **k** in the pavilions, that H4428
16 he and the **k**, the thirty and two kings H4428
16 the thirty and two **k** that helped him. H4428
24 And do this thing, Take the **k** away, H4428
31 heard that the **k** of the house of Israel H4428
31 Israel *are* merciful **k**: let us, I pray thee, H4428
22:39 of the chronicles of the **k** of Israel? H4428
45 of the chronicles of the **k** of Judah? H4428
2Ki 1:18 of the chronicles of the **k** of Israel? H4428
3:10 called these three **k** together, to deliver H4428
13 called these three **k** together, to deliver H4428
21 heard that the **k** were come up to fight H4428
23 And they said, This *is* blood: the **k** are H4428
7: 6 against us the **k** of the Hittites, and H4428
6 **k** of the Egyptians, to come upon us. H4428
8:18 And he walked in the way of the **k** of H4428
23 of the chronicles of the **k** of Judah? H4428
10: 4 said, Behold, two **k** stood not before H4428
34 of the chronicles of the **k** of Israel? H4428
11:19 And he sat on the throne of the **k**. H4428
12:18 his fathers, **k** of Judah, had dedicated, H4428
19 of the chronicles of the **k** of Judah? H4428
13: 8 of the chronicles of the **k** of Israel? H4428
12 of the chronicles of the **k** of Israel? H4428
13 buried in Samaria with the **k** of Israel. H4428
14:15 of the chronicles of the **k** of Israel? H4428
16 in Samaria with the **k** of Israel; and H4428
18 of the chronicles of the **k** of Judah? H4428
28 of the chronicles of the **k** of Israel? H4428
29 fathers, *even* with the **k** of Israel; and H4428
15: 6 of the chronicles of the **k** of Judah? H4428
11 book of the chronicles of the **k** of Israel. H4428
15 book of the chronicles of the **k** of Israel. H4428
2Ki 15:21 of the chronicles of the **k** of Israel? H4428
26 book of the chronicles of the **k** of Israel. H4428
31 book of the chronicles of the **k** of Israel. H4428
36 of the chronicles of the **k** of Judah? H4428
16: 3 But he walked in the way of the **k** of H4428
19 of the chronicles of the **k** of Judah? H4428
17: 2 as the **k** of Israel that were before him. H4428
8 of the **k** of Israel, which they had made. H4428
18: 5 him among all the **k** of Judah, nor *any* H4428
19:11 Behold, thou hast heard what the **k** of H4428
17 Of a truth, LORD, the **k** of Assyria have H4428
20:20 of the chronicles of the **k** of Judah? H4428
21:17 of the chronicles of the **k** of Judah? H4428
25 of the chronicles of the **k** of Judah? H4428
23: 5 priests, whom the **k** of Judah had H4428
11 And he took away the horses that the **k** H4428
12 of Ahaz, which the **k** of Judah had H4428
19 which the **k** of Israel had made H4428
22 **k** of Israel, nor of the kings of Judah; H4428
22 kings of Israel, nor of the **k** of Judah; H4428
28 of the chronicles of the **k** of Judah? H4428
24: 5 of the chronicles of the **k** of Judah? H4428
25:28 of the **k** that *were* with him in Babylon; H4428
1Ch 1:43 Now these *are* the **k** that reigned in the H4428
9: 1 in the book of the **k** of Israel and H4428
16:21 yea, he reproved **k** for their sakes, H4428
19: 9 of the city: and the **k** that were come H4428
20: 1 at the time that **k** go out *to battle,* Joab H4428
2Ch 1:12 as none of the **k** have had that *have* H4428
17 *horses* for all the **k** of the Hittites, and H4428
17 and for the **k** of Syria, by their means. H4428
9:14 And all the **k** of Arabia and governors H4428
22 And king Solomon passed all the **k** of H4428
23 And all the **k** of the earth sought the H4428
26 And he reigned over all the **k** from the H4428
16:11 the book of the **k** of Judah and Israel. H4428
20:34 in the book of the **k** of Israel. H4428
21: 6 And he walked in the way of the **k** of H4428
13 But hast walked in the way of the **k** of H4428
20 but not in the sepulchres of the **k**. H4428
24:16 of David among the **k**, because he had H4428
25 him not in the sepulchres of the **k**. H4428
27 of the book of the **k**. And Amaziah his H4428
25:26 the book of the **k** of Judah and Israel? H4428
26:23 *belonged* to the **k**; for they said, He *is* H4428
27: 7 the book of the **k** of Israel and Judah. H4428
28: 2 For he walked in the ways of the **k** of H4428
16 send unto the **k** of Assyria to help him. H4428
23 the gods of the **k** of Syria help them, H4428
26 the book of the **k** of Judah and Israel. H4428
27 the sepulchres of the **k** of Israel: and H4428
30: 6 out of the hand of the **k** of Assyria. H4428
32: 4 Why should the **k** of Assyria come, and H4428
32 the book of the **k** of Judah and Israel. H4428
33:18 *written* in the book of the **k** of Israel. H4428
34:11 which the **k** of Judah had destroyed. H4428
35:18 neither did all the **k** of Israel keep such H4428
27 the book of the **k** of Israel and Judah. H4428
36: 8 in the book of the **k** of Israel and H4428
Ezr 4:13 shalt endamage the revenue of the **k**. H4430
15 and hurtful unto **k** and provinces, and H4430
19 against **k**, and *that* rebellion and H4430
20 There have been mighty **k** also over H4430
22 damage grow to the hurt of the **k**? H4430
6:12 there destroy all **k** and people, that H4430
7:12 Artaxerxes, king of **k**, unto Ezra the H4430
9: 7 have we, our **k**, *and* our priests, been H4428
7 the hand of the **k** of the lands, to the H4428
9 in the sight of the **k** of Persia, to give us H4428
Neh 9:24 hands, with their **k**, and the people of H4428
32 upon us, on our **k**, on our princes, and H4428
32 time of the **k** of Assyria unto this day. H4428
34 Neither have our **k**, our princes, our H4428
37 increase unto the **k** whom thou hast set H4428
Est 10: 2 of the **k** of Media and Persia? H4428
Job 3:14 With **k** and counsellors of the earth, H4428
12:18 He looseth the bond of **k**, and girdeth H4428
36: 7 but with **k** *are they* on the throne; H4428
Ps 2: 2 The **k** of the earth set themselves, and H4428
10 Be wise now therefore, O ye **k**: be H4428
48: 4 For, lo, the **k** were assembled, they H4428
68:12 **K** of armies did flee apace: and she that H4428
14 When the Almighty scattered **k** in it, it H4428
29 shall **k** bring presents unto thee. H4428
72:10 The **k** of Tarshish and of the isles shall H4428
10 **k** of Sheba and Seba shall offer gifts. H4428
11 Yea, all **k** shall fall down before him: all H4428
76:12 *he is* terrible to the **k** of the earth. H4428
89:27 higher than the **k** of the earth. H4428
Ps 102:15 and all the **k** of the earth thy glory. H4428
105:14 yea, he reproved **k** for their sakes; H4428
30 abundance, in the chambers of their **k**. H4428
110: 5 through **k** in the day of his wrath. H4428
119:46 also before **k**, and will not be ashamed. H4428
135:10 smote great nations, and slew mighty **k**; H4428
136:17 To him which smote great **k**: for his H4428
18 And slew famous **k**: for his mercy H4428
138: 4 All the **k** of the earth shall praise thee, H4428
144:10 *It is he* that giveth salvation unto **k**: H4428
148:11 **K** of the earth, and all people; princes, H4428
149: 8 To bind their **k** with chains, and their H4428
Prv 8:15 By me **k** reign, and princes decree H4428
16:12 *It is* an abomination to **k** to commit H4428
13 Righteous lips *are* the delight of **k**; and H4428
22:29 **k**; he shall not stand before mean *men*. H4428
25: 2 honour of **k** *is* to search out a matter. H4428
3 and the heart of **k** *is* unsearchable. H4428
31: 3 nor thy ways to that which destroyeth **k**. H4428
4 *It is* not for **k**, O Lemuel, *it is* not for H4428
4 *it is* not for **k** to drink wine; nor for H4428
Ecc 2: 8 treasure of **k** and of the provinces: H4428
Isa 1: 1 Ahaz, *and* Hezekiah, **k** of Judah. H4428
7:16 shall be forsaken of both her **k**. H4428
10: 8 saith, *Are* not my princes altogether **k**? H4428
14: 9 their thrones all the **k** of the nations. H4428
18 All the **k** of the nations, *even* all of H4428
19:11 the son of the wise, the son of ancient **k**? H4428
24:21 and the **k** of the earth upon the earth. H4428
37:11 Behold, thou hast heard what the **k** of H4428
18 Of a truth, LORD, the **k** of Assyria have H4428
41: 2 *him* rule over **k**? he gave *them* as the H4428
45: 1 loose the loins of **k**, to open before him H4428
49: 7 servant of rulers, **K** shall see and arise, H4428
23 And **k** shall be thy nursing fathers, and H4428
52:15 many nations; the **k** shall shut their H4428
60: 3 and **k** to the brightness of thy rising. H4428
10 walls, and their **k** shall minister unto H4428
11 and *that* their **k** *may be* brought. H4428
16 suck the breast of **k**: and thou shalt H4428
62: 2 and all **k** thy glory: and thou H4428
Jer 1:18 land, against the **k** of Judah, against H4428
2:26 they, their **k**, their princes, and their H4428
8: 1 out the bones of the **k** of Judah, and the H4428
13:13 of this land, even the **k** that sit upon H4428
17:19 whereby the **k** of Judah come in, and H4428
20 of the LORD, ye **k** of Judah, and all H4428
25 gates of this city **k** and princes sitting H4428
19: 3 word of the LORD, O **k** of Judah, and H4428
4 known, nor the **k** of Judah, and have H4428
13 the houses of the **k** of Judah, shall be H4428
20: 5 treasures of the **k** of Judah will I give H4428
22: 4 gates of this house **k** sitting upon the H4428
25:14 For many nations and great **k** shall H4428
18 of Judah, and the **k** thereof, and the H4428
20 people, and all the **k** of the land of Uz, H4428
20 of Uz, and all the **k** of the land of the H4428
22 And all the **k** of Tyrus, and all the kings H4428
22 And all the kings of Tyrus, and all the **k** H4428
22 **k** of the isles which *are* beyond the sea, H4428
24 And all the **k** of Arabia, and all the H4428
24 and all the **k** of the mingled people H4428
25 And all the **k** of Zimri, and all the kings H4428
25 And all the kings of Zimri, and all the **k** H4428
25 of Elam, and all the **k** of the Medes, H4428
26 And all the **k** of the north, far and near, H4428
27: 7 great **k** shall serve themselves of him. H4428
32:32 anger, they, their **k**, their princes, their H4428
33: 4 the houses of the **k** of Judah, which are H4428
34: 5 the former **k** which were before thee, H4428
44: 9 wickedness of the **k** of Judah, and the H4428
17 our fathers, our **k**, and our princes, in H4428
21 your fathers, your **k**, and your princes, H4428
46:25 gods, and their **k**; even Pharaoh, and H4428
50:41 nation, and many **k** shall be raised up H4428
51:11 up the spirit of the **k** of the Medes: for H4428
28 the nations with the **k** of the Medes, the H4428
52:32 of the **k** that *were* with him in Babylon, H4428
Lam 4:12 The **k** of the earth, and all the H4428
Ezk 26: 7 of Babylon, a king of **k**, from the north, H4428
27:33 didst enrich the **k** of the earth with the H4428
35 at thee, and their **k** shall be sore afraid, H4428
28:17 before **k**, that they may behold thee. H4428
32:10 at thee, and their **k** shall be horribly H4428
29 There *is* Edom, her **k**, and all her H4428
43: 7 they, nor their **k**, by their whoredom, H4428
7 carcases of their **k** in their high places. H4428
9 carcases of their **k**, far from me, and I H4428

Dan 2:21 he removeth **k**, and setteth up kings: H4430
Dan 2:21 and setteth up **k**: he giveth wisdom unto H4430
37 Thou, O king, *art* a king of **k**: for the H4430
44 And in the days of these **k** shall the God H4430
47 gods, and a Lord of **k**, and a revealer of H4430
7:17 **k**, *which* shall arise out of the earth. H4430
24 kingdom *are* ten **k** *that* shall arise: and H4430
24 the first, and he shall subdue three **k**. H4430
8:20 horns *are* the **k** of Media and Persia. H4428
9: 6 in thy name to our **k**, our princes, and H4428
8 of face, to our **k**, to our princes, and H4428
10:13 I remained there with the **k** of Persia. H4428
11: 2 stand up yet three **k** in Persia; and the H4428
Hos 1: 1 *and* Hezekiah, **k** of Judah, and in the H4428
7: 7 judges; all their **k** are fallen: *there is* H4428
8: 4 They have set up **k**, but not by me: they H4427
Mic 1: 1 *and* Hezekiah, **k** of Judah, which he H4428
14 Achzib *shall be* a lie to the **k** of Israel. H4428
Hab 1:10 And they shall scoff at the **k**, and the H4428
Mt 10:18 governors and **k** for my sake, for a *G935*
17:25 of whom do the **k** of the earth take *G935*
Mk 13: 9 before rulers and **k** for my sake, for a *G935*
Lk 10:24 For I tell you, that many prophets and **k** *G935*
21:12 before **k** and rulers for my name's sake. *G935*
22:25 And he said unto them, The **k** of the *G935*
Act 4:26 The **k** of the earth stood up, and the *G935*
9:15 and **k**, and the children of Israel: *G935*
1Co 4: 8 ye have reigned as **k** without us: and I *G936*
1Ti 2: 2 For **k**, and *for* all that are in authority; *G935*
6:15 the King of **k**, and Lord of lords; *G936*
Heb 7: 1 the slaughter of the **k**, and blessed him; *G935*
Rev 1: 5 the prince of the **k** of the earth. Unto him *G935*
6 And hath made us **k** and priests unto *G935*
5:10 And hast made us unto our God **k** and *G935*
6:15 And the **k** of the earth, and the great *G935*
10:11 and nations, and tongues, and **k**. *G935*
16:12 of the **k** of the east might be prepared. *G935*
14 go forth unto the **k** of the earth and of *G935*
17: 2 With whom the **k** of the earth have *G935*
10 And there are seven **k**: five are fallen, and *G935*
12 sawest are ten **k**, which have received *G935*
12 power as **k** one hour with the beast. *G935*
14 of lords, and King of **k**: and they that are *G935*
18 which reigneth over the **k** of the earth. *G935*
18: 3 and the **k** of the earth have committed *G935*
9 And the **k** of the earth, who have *G935*
19:16 KING OF **K**, AND LORD OF LORDS. *G935*
18 That ye may eat the flesh of **k**, and the *G935*
19 And I saw the beast, and the **k** of the *G935*
21:24 light of it: and the **k** of the earth do bring *G935*

KING'S

Gen 14:17 valley of Shaveh, which *is* the **k** dale. H4428
39:20 a place where the **k** prisoners *were* H4428
Nu 20:17 we will go by the **k** *high* way, we will H4428
21:22 go along by the **k** *high* way, until we be H4428
1Sa 18:22 thee: now therefore be the **k** son in law. H4428
23 *a* light *thing* to be a **k** son in law, seeing H4428
25 be avenged of the **k** enemies. But Saul H4428
26 well to be the **k** son in law: and the H4428
27 he might be the **k** son in law. And Saul H4428
20:29 he cometh not unto the **k** table. H4428
21: 8 because the **k** business required haste. H4428
22:14 which is the **k** son in law, and goeth H4428
23:20 *shall be* to deliver him into the **k** hand. H4428
26:16 now see where the **k** spear *is*, and the H4428
22 said, Behold the **k** spear! and let one of H4428
2Sa 9:11 eat at my table, as one of the **k** sons. H4428
13 **k** table; and was lame on both his feet. H4428
11: 2 the roof of the **k** house: and from the H4428
8 out of the **k** house, and there followed H4428
9 But Uriah slept at the door of the **k** H4428
20 And if so be that the **k** wrath arise, and H4428
24 and *some* of the **k** servants be dead, H4428
12:30 And he took their **k** crown from off his H4428
13: 4 *art* thou, *being* the **k** son, lean from day H4428
18 robes were the **k** daughters *that were* H4428
23 and Absalom invited all the **k** sons. H4428
27 Amnon and all the **k** sons go with him. H4428
29 Then all the **k** sons arose, and every H4428
30 hath slain all the **k** sons, and there is H4428
32 the young men the **k** sons; for Amnon H4428
33 to think that all the **k** sons are dead: for H4428
35 king, Behold, the **k** sons come: as thy H4428
36 that, behold, the **k** sons came, and H4428
14: 1 that the **k** heart *was* toward Absalom. H4428
24 his own house, and saw not the **k** face. H4428
26 two hundred shekels after the **k** weight. H4428
28 in Jerusalem, and saw not the **k** face. H4428
32 let me see the **k** face; and if there be H4428
2Sa 15:15 And the **k** servants said unto the king, H4428
35 hear out of the **k** house, thou shalt tell H4428
16: 2 asses *be* for the **k** household to ride on; H4428
18:12 mine hand against the **k** son: for in our H4428
18 which *is* in the **k** dale: for he said, I H4428
20 no tidings, because the **k** son is dead. H4428
29 Joab sent the **k** servant, and *me* thy H4428
19:18 to carry over the **k** household, and to H4428
42 the **k** *cost?* or hath he given us any gift? H4428
24: 4 Notwithstanding the **k** word prevailed H4428
1Ki 1: 9 his brethren the **k** sons, and all the men H4428
9 all the men of Judah the **k** servants: H4428
25 and hath called all the **k** sons, and the H4428
28 **k** presence, and stood before the king. H4428
44 caused him to ride upon the **k** mule: H4428
47 And moreover the **k** servants came to H4428
2:19 to be set for the **k** mother; and she sat H4428
4: 5 *was* principal officer, *and* the **k** friend: H4428
9: 1 of the LORD, and the **k** house, and all H4428
10 house of the LORD, and the **k** house, H4428
10:12 LORD, and for the **k** house, harps also H4428
28 linen yarn: the **k** merchants received H4428
11:14 Edomite: he *was* of the **k** seed in Edom. H4428
13: 6 the LORD, and the **k** hand was restored H4428
14:26 treasures of the **k** house; he even took H4428
27 which kept the door of the **k** house. H4428
15:18 treasures of the **k** house, and delivered H4428
16:18 the palace of the **k** house, and burnt H4428
18 **k** house over him with fire, and died, H4428
22:12 LORD shall deliver *it* into the **k** hand. H4428
26 of the city, and to Joash the **k** son; H4428
2Ki 7: 9 we may go and tell the **k** household. H4428
11 and they told *it* to the **k** house within. H4428
9:34 and bury her: for she *is* a **k** daughter. H4428
10: 6 this time. Now the **k** sons, *being* H4428
7 that they took the **k** sons, and slew H4428
8 the heads of the **k** sons. And he said, H4428
11: 2 him from among the **k** sons *which were* H4428
4 the LORD, and shewed them the **k** son. H4428
5 be keepers of the watch of the **k** house; H4428
12 And he brought forth the **k** son, and H4428
16 the **k** house: and there was she slain. H4428
19 of the guard to the **k** house. And he sat H4428
20 with the sword *beside* the **k** house. H4428
12:10 the chest, that the **k** scribe and the high H4428
18 LORD, and in the **k** house, and sent *it* H4428
13:16 Elisha put his hands upon the **k** hands. H4428
14:14 treasures of the **k** house, and hostages, H4428
15: 5 And Jotham the **k** son *was* over the H4428
25 the palace of the **k** house, with Argob H4428
16: 8 treasures of the **k** house, and sent *it for* H4428
15 offering, and the **k** burnt sacrifice, and H4428
18 in the house, and the **k** entry without, H4428
18:15 and in the treasures of the **k** house. H4428
36 not a word: for the **k** commandment H4428
22:12 and Asahiah a servant of the **k**, saying, H4428
24:13 the treasures of the **k** house, and cut in H4428
15 to Babylon, and the **k** mother, and the H4428
15 king's mother, and the **k** wives, and his H4428
25: 4 which *is* by the **k** garden: (now the H4428
9 the LORD, and the **k** house, and all the H4428
19 that were in the **k** presence, which were H4428
1Ch 9:18 Who hitherto *waited* in the **k** gate H4428
21: 4 Nevertheless the **k** word prevailed H4428
6 for the **k** word was abominable to Joab. H4428
25: 5 All these *were* the sons of Heman the **k** H4428
6 God, according to the **k** order to Asaph, H4428
27:25 And over the **k** treasures *was* H4428
32 son of Hachmoni *was* with the **k** sons: H4428
33 And Ahithophel *was* the **k** counsellor: H4428
33 the Archite *was* the **k** companion: H4428
34 the general of the **k** army *was* Joab. H4428
29: 6 rulers of the **k** work, offered willingly, H4428
2Ch 1:16 linen yarn: the **k** merchants received H4428
7:11 the LORD, and the **k** house: and all that H4428
9:11 LORD, and to the **k** palace, and harps H4428
21 For the **k** ships went to Tarshish with H4428
12: 9 treasures of the **k** house; he took all: he H4428
10 that kept the entrance of the **k** house. H4428
16: 2 LORD and of the **k** house, and sent to H4428
18: 5 for God will deliver *it* into the **k** hand. H4428
25 of the city, and to Joash the **k** son; H4428
19:11 of Judah, for all the **k** matters: also the H4428
21:17 was found in the **k** house, and his sons H4428
22:11 from among the **k** sons that were slain, H4428
23: 3 them, Behold, the **k** son shall reign, as H4428
5 And a third part *shall be* at the **k** H4428
11 Then they brought out the **k** son, and H4428
15 by the **k** house, they slew her there. H4428
2Ch 23:20 high gate into the **k** house, and set the H4428
24: 8 And at the **k** commandment they made H4428
11 brought unto the **k** office by the hand H4428
11 much money, the **k** scribe and the high H4428
25:16 thou made of the **k** counsel? forbear; H4428
24 treasures of the **k** house, the hostages H4428
26:11 of Hananiah, *one* of the **k** captains. H4428
21 **k** house, judging the people of the land. H4428
28: 7 slew Maaseiah the **k** son, and Azrikam H4428
29:25 and of Gad the **k** seer, and Nathan the H4428
31: 3 *He appointed* also the **k** portion of his H4428
34:20 and Asaiah a servant of the **k**, saying, H4428
35: 7 bullocks: these *were* of the **k** substance. H4428
10 according to the **k** commandment. H4428
15 and Jeduthun the **k** seer; and the H4428
Ezr 4:14 from *the* **k** palace, and it was not
14 for us to see the **k** dishonour, therefore H4430
5:17 made in the **k** treasure house, which H4430
6: 4 expenses be given out of the **k** house: H4430
8 of God: that of the **k** goods, *even* of the H4430
7:20 bestow *it* out of the **k** treasure house. H4430
27 *thing* as this in the **k** heart, to beautify H4428
28 and before all the **k** mighty princes. H4428
8:36 And they delivered the **k** commissions H4428
36 unto the **k** lieutenants, and to H4428
Neh 1:11 of this man. For I was the **k** cupbearer. H4428
2: 8 the keeper of the **k** forest, that he may H4428
9 and gave them the **k** letters. Now the H4428
14 and to the **k** pool: but *there was* H4428
18 me; as also the **k** words that he had H4428
3:15 of Siloah by the **k** garden, and unto the H4428
25 lieth out from the **k** high house, that H4428
5: 4 money for the **k** tribute, *and that upon* H4428
11:23 For *it was* the **k** commandment H4428
24 Judah, *was* at the **k** hand in all matters H4428
Est 1: 5 the court of the garden of the **k** palace; H4428
12 to come at the **k** commandment by *his* H4428
13 (for so *was* the **k** manner toward all H4428
14 which saw the **k** face, *and* which sat H4428
18 day unto all the **k** princes, which have H4428
20 And when the **k** decree which he shall H4428
22 For he sent letters into all the **k** H4428
2: 2 Then said the **k** servants that H4428
3 of Hege the **k** chamberlain, keeper H4428
8 So it came to pass, when the **k** H4428
8 also unto the **k** house, to the custody H4428
9 given her, out of the **k** house: and he H4428
13 house of the women unto the **k** house. H4428
14 of Shaashgaz, the **k** chamberlain, H4428
15 but what Hegai the **k** chamberlain, the H4428
19 time, then Mordecai sat in the **k** gate. H4428
21 sat in the **k** gate, two of the king's H4428
21 king's gate, two of the **k** chamberlains, H4428
3: 2 And all the **k** servants, that *were* in the H4428
2 that *were* in the **k** gate, bowed, and H4428
3 Then the **k** servants, which *were* in the H4428
3 which *were* in the **k** gate, said unto H4428
3 thou the **k** commandment? H4428
8 keep they the **k** laws: therefore it *is* H4428
8 it *is* not for the **k** profit to suffer them. H4428
9 to bring *it* into the **k** treasuries. H4428
12 Then were the **k** scribes called on the H4428
12 unto the **k** lieutenants, and to H4428
12 it written, and sealed with the **k** ring. H4428
13 by posts into all the **k** provinces, to H4428
15 hastened by the **k** commandment, and H4428
4: 2 And came even before the **k** gate: for H4428
2 into the **k** gate clothed with sackcloth. H4428
3 whithersoever the **k** commandment H4428
5 for Hatach, *one* of the **k** chamberlains, H4428
6 of the city, which *was* before the **k** gate. H4428
7 to pay to the **k** treasuries for the Jews, H4428
11 All the **k** servants, and the people of the H4428
11 the people of the **k** provinces, do know, H4428
13 in the **k** house, more than all the Jews. H4428
5: 1 inner court of the **k** house, over against H4428
1 over against the **k** house: and the king H4428
9 Mordecai in the **k** gate, that he stood H4428
13 Mordecai the Jew sitting at the **k** gate. H4428
6: 2 Teresh, two of the **k** chamberlains, the H4428
3 this? Then said the **k** servants that H4428
4 court of the **k** house, to speak unto H4428
5 And the **k** servants said unto him, H4428
9 the hand of one of the **k** most noble H4428
10 that sitteth at the **k** gate: let nothing fail H4428
12 And Mordecai came again to the **k** H4428
14 him, came the **k** chamberlains, and H4428
7: 4 could not countervail the **k** damage. H4428

8 **k** mouth, they covered Haman's face. H4428
Est 7:10 Then was the **k** wrath pacified. H4428
8: 5 Jews which *are* in all the **k** provinces: H4428
8 it liketh you, in the **k** name, and seal *it* H4428
8 seal *it* with the **k** ring: for the writing H4428
8 is written in the **k** name, and sealed H4428
8 with the **k** ring, may no man reverse. H4428
9 Then were the **k** scribes called at that H4428
10 and sealed *it* with the **k** ring, and sent H4428
14 pressed on by the **k** commandment. H4428
17 whithersoever the **k** commandment H4428
9: 1 same, when the **k** commandment and H4428
4 For Mordecai *was* great in the **k** house, H4428
12 in the rest of the **k** provinces? now what H4428
16 But the other Jews that *were* in the **k** H4428
Ps 45: 5 in the heart of the **k** enemies; *whereby* H4428
13 The **k** daughter *is* all glorious within: H4428
15 they shall enter into the **k** palace. H4428
61: 6 Thou wilt prolong the **k** life: *and* his H4428
72: 1 and thy righteousness unto the **k** son. H4428
99: 4 The **k** strength also loveth judgment; H4428
Prv 14:28 In the multitude of people *is* the **k** H4428
35 The **k** favour *is* toward a wise servant: H4428
16:15 In the light of the **k** countenance *is* life; H4428
19:12 The **k** wrath *is* as the roaring of a lion; H4428
21: 1 The **k** heart *is* in the hand of the LORD, H4428
Ecc 8: 2 I *counsel thee* to keep the **k** H4428
Isa 36:21 not a word: for the **k** commandment H4428
Jer 22: 6 For thus saith the LORD unto the **k** H4428
26:10 came up from the **k** house unto the H4428
36:12 Then he went down into the **k** house, H4428
38: 7 which was in the **k** house, heard that H4428
8 Ebed-melech went forth out of the **k** H4428
39: 4 by the way of the **k** garden, by the gate H4428
8 And the Chaldeans burned the **k** house, H4428
41:10 Mizpah, *even* the **k** daughters, and all H4428
43: 6 and children, and the **k** daughters, and H4428
52: 7 which *was* by the **k** garden; (now the H4428
13 the LORD, and the **k** house; and all the H4428
25 that were near the **k** person, which H4428
Ezk 17:13 And hath taken of the **k** seed, and H4410
Dan 1: 3 and of the **k** seed, and of the princes; H4410
4 to stand in the **k** palace, and whom H4428
5 provision of the **k** meat, and of the H4428
8 the portion of the **k** meat, nor with the H4428
13 the portion of the **k** meat: and as thou H4428
15 which did eat the portion of the **k** meat. H4428
2:10 that can shew the **k** matter: therefore H4430
14 the captain of the **k** guard, which was H4430
15 He answered and said to Arioch the **k** H4430
23 *now* made known unto us the **k** matter. H4430
3:22 Therefore because the **k** H4430
27 captains, and the **k** counsellors, being H4430
28 have changed the **k** word, and yielded H4430
4:31 While the word *was* in the **k** mouth, H4430
5: 5 of the wall of the **k** palace: and the king H4430
6 Then the **k** countenance was changed, H4430
8 Then came in all the **k** wise *men*: but H4430
6:12 concerning the **k** decree; Hast thou not H4430
8:27 up, and did the **k** business; and I was H4428
11: 6 together; for the **k** daughter of the H4428
Am 7: 1 the latter growth after the **k** mowings. H4428
13 the **k** chapel, and it *is* the king's court. H4428
13 the king's chapel, and it *is* the **k** court. H4467
Zep 1: 8 the princes, and the **k** children, and all H4428
Zec 14:10 of Hananeel unto the **k** winepresses. H4428
Act 12:20 made Blastus the **k** chamberlain their *G935*
20 country was nourished by the **k** *country*. *G937*
Heb 11:23 were not afraid of the **k** commandment. *G935*

KINGS'

Ps 45: 9 **K** daughters *were* among thy H4428
Prv 30:28 with her hands, and is in **k** palaces. H4428
Dan 11:27 And both these **k** hearts *shall be* to do H4428
Mt 11: 8 that wear soft *clothing* are in **k** houses. *G935*
Lk 7:25 and live delicately, are in **k** courts. *G933*

KINSFOLK

Job 19:14 My **k** have failed, and my familiar H7138
Lk 2:44 him among *their* **k** and acquaintance. *G4773*

KINSFOLKS

1Ki 16:11 wall, neither of his **k**, nor of his friends. H1350
2Ki 10:11 men, and his **k**, and his priests, until H3045
Lk 21:16 and brethren, and **k**, and friends; and *G4773*

KINSMAN

Nu 5: 8 But if the man have no **k** to H1350
27:11 unto his **k** that is next to him of H7607
Ru 2: 1 And Naomi had a **k** of her husband's, a H3045
Ru 3: 9 thine handmaid; for thou *art* a near **k**. H1350
12 And now it is true that I *am thy* near **k**: H1350
12 howbeit there is a **k** nearer than I. H1350
13 thee the part of a **k**, well; let him do the H1350
13 do the part of a **k** to thee, then will I do H1350
13 I do the part of a **k** to thee, *as* the LORD H1350
4: 1 and, behold, the **k** of whom Boaz spake H1350
3 And he said unto the **k**, Naomi, that is H1350
6 And the **k** said, I cannot redeem *it* for H1350
8 Therefore the **k** said unto Boaz, Buy *it* H1350
14 this day without a **k**, that his name may H1350
Jn 18:26 priest, being *his* **k** whose ear Peter cut *G4773*
Ro 16:11 Salute Herodion my **k**. Greet them that *G4773*

KINSMAN'S

Ru 3:13 let him do the **k** part: but if he will not H1350

KINSMEN

Ru 2:20 *is* near of kin unto us, one of our next **k**. H1350
Ps 38:11 from my sore; and my **k** stand afar off. H7138
Lk 14:12 neither thy **k**, nor *thy* rich neighbours; *G4773*
Act 10:24 called together his **k** and near friends. *G4773*
Ro 9: 3 brethren, my **k** according to the flesh: *G4773*
16: 7 Salute Andronicus and Junia, my **k**, and *G4773*
21 Jason, and Sosipater, my **k**, salute you. *G4773*

KINSWOMAN

Lev 18:12 father's sister: she *is* thy father's near **k**. H7607
13 sister: for she *is* thy mother's near **k**. H7607
Prv 7: 4 my sister; and call understanding *thy* **k**: H4129

KINSWOMEN

Lev 18:17 *for* they *are* her near **k**: it *is* wickedness. H7608

KIR

2Ki 16: 9 *of* it captive to **K**, and slew Rezin. H7024
Isa 15: 1 in the night **K** of Moab is laid waste, H7024
22: 6 horsemen, and **K** uncovered the shield. H7024
Am 1: 5 into captivity unto **K**, saith the LORD. H7024
9: 7 from Caphtor, and the Syrians from **K**? H7024

KIR-HARASETH

2Ki 3:25 the good trees: only in **K** left they the H7025

KIR-HARESETH

Isa 16: 7 the foundations of **K** shall ye mourn; H7025

KIR-HARESH

Isa 16:11 for Moab, and mine inward parts for **K**. H7025

KIR-HERES

Jer 48:31 *heart* shall mourn for the men of **K**. H7025
36 for the men of **K**: because the riches H7025

KIRIATHAIM

Gen 14: 5 in Ham, and the Emims in Shaveh **K**, H7741
Jer 48: 1 for it is spoiled: **K** is confounded *and* H7156
23 And upon **K**, and upon Beth-gamul, H7156
Ezk 25: 9 Beth-jeshimoth, Baal-meon, and **K**, H7156

KIRJATH

Jos 18:28 Gibeath, *and* **K**; fourteen cities with H7157

KIRJATHAIM

Nu 32:37 built Heshbon, and Elealeh, and **K**, H7156
Jos 13:19 And **K**, and Sibmah, and Zareth-shahar H7156
1Ch 6:76 her suburbs, and **K** with her suburbs. H7156

KIRJATHARBA

Jos 20: 7 Ephraim, and **K**, which *is* Hebron, in H7153
Jdg 1:10 before *was* **K**:) and they slew Sheshai, H7153

KIRJATH-ARBA

Gen 23: 2 And Sarah died in **K**; the same *is* H7153
Jos 14:15 And the name of Hebron before *was* **K**; H7153
15:54 And Humtah, and **K**, which *is* Hebron, H7153
Neh 11:25 of Judah dwelt at **K**, and *in* the villages H7153

KIRJATH-ARIM

Ezr 2:25 The children of **K**, Chephirah, and H7157

KIRJATH-BAAL

Jos 15:60 **K**, which *is* Kirjath-jearim, and H7154
18:14 out thereof were at **K**, which *is* H7154

KIRJATH-HUZOTH

Nu 22:39 went with Balak, and they came unto **K**. H7155

KIRJATHJEARIM

Jos 18:15 from the end of **K**, and the border went H7157
1Sa 7: 2 the ark abode in **K**, that the time was H7157
Jer 26:20 son of Shemaiah of **K**, who prophesied H7157

KIRJATH-JEARIM

Jos 9:17 and Chephirah, and Beeroth, and **K**. H7157
15: 9 was drawn to Baalah, which *is* **K**: H7157
60 Kirjath-baal, which *is* **K**, and Rabbah; H7157
18:14 which *is* **K**, a city of the children H7157
Jdg 18:12 And they went up, and pitched in **K**, in H7157
12 unto this day: behold, *it is* behind **K**. H7157
1Sa 7: 1 And the men of **K** came, and fetched H7157
1Ch 2:50 of Ephratah; Shobal the father of **K**, H7157
52 And Shobal the father of **K** had sons; H7157
53 And the families of **K**; the Ithrites, and H7157
13: 5 to bring the ark of God from **K**. H7157
6 Baalah, *that is*, to **K**, which *belonged* to H7157
Neh 7:29 The men of **K**, Chephirah, and Beeroth, H7157

KIR-JATH-JEARIM

1Sa 6:21 to the inhabitants of **K**, saying, The H7157
2Ch 1: 4 brought up from **K** to *the place which* H7157

KIRJATH-SANNAH

Jos 15:49 And Dannah, and **K**, which *is* Debir, H7158

KIRJATH-SEPHER

Jos 15:15 and the name of Debir before *was* **K**. H7158
16 And Caleb said, He that smiteth **K**, and H7158
Jdg 1:11 and the name of Debir before *was* **K**: H7158
12 And Caleb said, He that smiteth **K**, and H7158

KISH

1Sa 9: 1 whose name *was* **K**, the son of Abiel, the H7027
3 And the asses of **K** Saul's father were H7027
3 were lost. And **K** said to Saul his son, H7027
10:11 of **K**? *Is* Saul also among the prophets? H7027
21 Saul the son of **K** was taken: and when H7027
14:51 And **K** *was* the father of Saul; and Ner H7027
2Sa 21:14 the sepulchre of **K** his father: and they H7027
1Ch 8:30 and Zur, and **K**, and Baal, and Nadab, H7027
33 And Ner begat **K**, and Kish begat Saul, H7027
33 And Ner begat Kish, and **K** begat Saul, H7027
9:36 and **K**, and Baal, and Ner, and Nadab, H7027
39 And Ner begat **K**; and Kish begat Saul; H7027
39 And Ner begat Kish; and **K** begat Saul; H7027
12: 1 of Saul the son of **K**: and they *were* H7027
23:21 The sons of Mahli; Eleazar, and **K**. H7027
22 their brethren the sons of **K** took them. H7027
24:29 Concerning **K**: the son of Kish *was* H7027
29 Concerning Kish: the son of **K** *was* H7027
26:28 Saul the son of **K**, and Abner the son H7027
2Ch 29:12 sons of Merari, **K** the son of Abdi, and H7027
Est 2: 5 of Shimei, the son of **K**, a Benjamite; H7027

KISHI

1Ch 6:44 **K**, the son of Abdi, the son of Malluch, H7029

KISHION

Jos 19:20 And Rabbith, and **K**, and Abez, H7191

KISHON

Jos 21:28 And out of the tribe of Issachar, **K** with H7191
Jdg 4: 7 And I will draw unto thee to the river **K** H7028
13 of the Gentiles unto the river of **K**. H7028
5:21 The river of **K** swept them away, that H7028
21 river, the river **K**. O my soul, thou hast H7028
1Ki 18:40 to the brook **K**, and slew them there. H7028

KISON

Ps 83: 9 *to* Sisera, as *to* Jabin, at the brook of **K**: H7028

KISS

Gen 27:26 Come near now, and **k** me, my son. H5401
31:28 And hast not suffered me to **k** my sons H5401
2Sa 20: 9 the beard with the right hand to **k** him. H5401
1Ki 19:20 me, I pray thee, **k** my father and my H5401
Ps 2:12 **K** the Son, lest he be angry, and ye H5401
Prv 24:26 *Every man* shall **k** *his* lips that giveth a H5401
Song 1: 2 Let him **k** me with the kisses of his H5401
8: 1 **k** thee; yea, I should not be despised. H5401
Hos 13: 2 Let the men that sacrifice **k** the calves. H5401
Mt 26:48 I shall **k**, that same is he: hold him fast. *G5368*
Mk 14:44 I shall **k**, that same is he; take *G5368*
Lk 7:45 Thou gavest me no **k**: but this woman *G5370*
45 I came in hath not ceased to **k** my feet. *G2705*
22:47 and drew near unto Jesus to **k** him. *G5368*
48 betrayest thou the Son of man with a **k**? *G5370*

Ro 16:16 Salute one another with an holy **k**. The *G5370*
1Co 16:20 Greet ye one another with an holy **k**. *G5370*
2Co 13:12 Greet one another with an holy **k**. *G5370*
1Th 5:26 Greet all the brethren with an holy **k**. *G5370*
1Pt 5:14 Greet ye one another with a **k** of *G5370*

KISSED
Gen 27:27 And he came near, and **k** him: and he H5401
29:11 And Jacob **k** Rachel, and lifted up his H5401
13 him, and **k** him, and brought him H5401
31:55 Laban rose up, and **k** his sons and his H5401
33: 4 on his neck, and **k** him: and they wept. H5401
45:15 Moreover he **k** all his brethren, and H5401
48:10 and he **k** them, and embraced them. H5401
50: 1 face, and wept upon him, and **k** him. H5401
Ex 4:27 him in the mount of God, and **k** him. H5401
18: 7 obeisance, and **k** him; and they asked H5401
Ru 1: 9 Then she **k** them; and they lifted H5401
14 again: and Orpah **k** her mother in law; H5401
1Sa 10: 1 his head, and **k** him, and said, *Is it* H5401
20:41 times: and they **k** one another, and H5401
2Sa 14:33 the king: and the king **k** Absalom. H5401
15: 5 his hand, and took him, and **k** him. H5401
19:39 over, the king **k** Barzillai, and blessed H5401
1Ki 19:18 every mouth which hath not **k** him. H5401
Job 31:27 enticed, or my mouth hath **k** my hand: H5401
Ps 85:10 and peace have **k** *each other*. H5401
Prv 7:13 So she caught him, and **k** him, *and* H5401
Mt 26:49 and said, Hail, master; and **k** him. *G2705*
Mk 14:45 and saith, Master, master; and **k** him. *G2705*
Lk 7:38 hairs of her head, and **k** his feet, and *G2705*
15:20 ran, and fell on his neck, and **k** him. *G2705*
Act 20:37 and fell on Paul's neck, and **k** him, *G2705*

KISSES
Prv 27: 6 but the **k** of an enemy *are* deceitful. H5390
Song 1: 2 Let him kiss me with the **k** of his H5390

KITE
Lev 11:14 And the vulture, and the **k** after his kind; H344
Dt 14:13 And the glede, and the **k**, and the vulture H344

KITHLISH
Jos 15:40 And Cabbon, and Lahmam, and **K**, H3798

KITRON
Jdg 1:30 out the inhabitants of **K**, nor the H7003

KITTIM
Gen 10: 4 and Tarshish, **K**, and Dodanim. H3794
1Ch 1: 7 and Tarshish, **K**, and Dodanim. H3794

KNEAD
Gen 18: 6 **k** *it*, and make cakes upon the hearth. H3888
Jer 7:18 and the women **k** *their* dough, to make H3888

KNEADED
1Sa 28:24 and took flour, and **k** *it*, and did bake H3888
2Sa 13: 8 took flour, and **k** *it*, and made cakes H3888
Hos 7: 4 hath **k** the dough, until it be leavened. H3888

KNEADINGTROUGHS
Ex 8: 3 and into thine ovens, and into thy **k**: H4863
12:34 leavened, their **k** being bound up in H4863

KNEE
Gen 41:43 him, Bow the **k**: and he made him *ruler* H86
Isa 45:23 **k** shall bow, every tongue shall swear. H1290
Mt 27:29 and they bowed the **k** before him, and *G1120*
Ro 11: 4 not bowed the **k** to *the image of* Baal. *G1119*
14:11 the Lord, every **k** shall bow to me, and *G1119*
Php 2:10 That at the name of Jesus every **k** *G1119*

KNEEL
Gen 24:11 And he made his camels to **k** down H1288
Ps 95: 6 let us **k** before the LORD our maker. H1288

KNEELED
2Ch 6:13 it he stood, and **k** down upon his knees H1288
Dan 6:10 Jerusalem, he **k** upon his knees three H1289
Mk 10:17 one running, and **k** to him, and asked *G1120*
Lk 22:41 a stone's cast, and **k** down, and prayed, *G1119*
Act 7:60 And he **k** down, and cried with a loud *G1119*
9:40 But Peter put them all forth, and **k** *G1119*
20:36 And when he had thus spoken, he **k** *G1119*
21: 5 we **k** down on the shore, and prayed. *G1119*

KNEELING
1Ki 8:54 of the LORD, from **k** on his knees with H3766

Mt 17:14 man, **k** down to him, and saying, *G1120*
Mk 1:40 him, and **k** down to him, and saying *G1120*

KNEES
Gen 30: 3 **k**, that I may also have children by her. H1290
48:12 out from between his **k**, and he bowed H1290
50:23 were brought up upon Joseph's **k**. H1290
Dt 28:35 The LORD shall smite thee in the **k**, and H1290
Jdg 7: 5 that boweth down upon his **k** to drink. H1290
6 down upon their **k** to drink water. H1290
16:19 And she made him sleep upon her **k**; H1290
1Ki 8:54 **k** with his hands spread up to heaven. H1290
18:42 earth, and put his face between his **k**, H1290
19:18 in Israel, all the **k** which have not H1290
2Ki 1:13 and fell on his **k** before Elijah, and H1290
4:20 he sat on her **k** till noon, and *then* died. H1290
2Ch 6:13 kneeled down upon his **k** before all the H1290
Ezr 9: 5 I fell upon my **k**, and spread out my H1290
Job 3:12 Why did the **k** prevent me? or why the H1290
4: 4 and thou hast strengthened the feeble **k**. H1290
Ps 109:24 My **k** are weak through fasting; and my H1290
Isa 35: 3 weak hands, and confirm the feeble **k**. H1290
66:12 *her* sides, and be dandled upon *her* **k**. H1290
Ezk 7:17 All hands shall be feeble, and all **k** shall H1290
21: 7 shall faint, and all **k** shall be weak *as* H1290
47: 4 the waters *were* to the **k**. Again he H1290
Dan 5: 6 and his **k** smote one against another. H755
6:10 kneeled upon his **k** three times a day, H1291
10:10 my **k** and *upon* the palms of my hands. H1290
Nah 2:10 melteth, and the **k** smite together, and H1290
Mk 15:19 and bowing *their* **k** worshipped him. *G1119*
Lk 5: 8 he fell down at Jesus' **k**, saying, Depart *G1119*
Eph 3:14 For this cause I bow my **k** unto the *G1119*
Heb 12:12 which hang down, and the feeble **k**; *G1119*

KNEW
Gen 3: 7 were opened, and they **k** that they *were* H3045
4: 1 And Adam **k** Eve his wife; and she H3045
17 And Cain **k** his wife; and she H3045
25 And Adam **k** his wife again; and she H3045
8:11 off: so Noah **k** that the waters were H3045
9:24 And Noah awoke from his wine, and **k** H3045
28:16 the LORD is in this place; and I **k** *it* not. H3045
31:32 **k** not that Rachel had stolen them. H3045
37:33 And he **k** it, and said, *It is* my son's H5234
38: 9 And Onan **k** that the seed should not be H3045
16 unto thee; (for he **k** not that she *was* his H3045
26 my son. And he **k** her again no more. H3045
39: 6 hand; and he **k** not ought he had, save H3045
42: 7 And Joseph saw his brethren, and he **k** H5234
8 And Joseph **k** his brethren, but they H5234
8 knew his brethren, but they **k** not him. H5234
23 And they **k** not that Joseph understood H3045
Ex 1: 8 king over Egypt, which **k** not Joseph. H3045
Nu 22:34 I have sinned; for I **k** not that thou H3045
24:16 words of God, and **k** the knowledge of H3045
Dt 8:16 which thy fathers **k** not, that he might H3045
9:24 the LORD from the day that I **k** you. H3045
29:26 gods whom they **k** not, and *whom* he H3045
32:17 to gods whom they **k** not, to new *gods* H3045
33: 9 his brethren, nor **k** his own children: H3045
34:10 Moses, whom the LORD **k** face to face, H3045
Jdg 2:10 after them, which **k** not the LORD, nor H3045
3: 2 least such as before **k** nothing thereof; H3045
11:39 vowed: and she **k** no man. And it was H3045
13:16 For Manoah **k** not that he *was* an angel H3045
21 **k** that he *was* an angel of the LORD. H3045
14: 4 But his father and his mother **k** not H3045
18: 3 of Micah, they **k** the voice of the young H5234
19:25 them; and they **k** her, and abused her H3045
20:34 but they **k** not that evil *was* near them. H3045
1Sa 1:19 and Elkanah **k** Hannah his wife; and H3045
2:12 sons of Belial; they **k** not the LORD. H3045
3:20 even to Beer-sheba **k** that Samuel *was* H3045
10:11 And it came to pass, when all that **k** H3045
14: 3 people **k** not that Jonathan was gone. H3045
18:28 And Saul saw and **k** that the LORD *was* H3045
20: 9 it from thee: for if I **k** certainly that evil H3045
33 him: whereby Jonathan **k** that it was H3045
39 But the lad **k** not any thing: only H3045
39 only Jonathan and David **k** the matter. H3045
22:15 **k** nothing of all this, less or more. H3045
17 and because they **k** when he fled, and H3045
22 And David said unto Abiathar, I **k** *it* H3045
23: 9 And David **k** that Saul secretly H3045
26:12 man saw *it*, nor **k** *it*, neither awaked: H3045
17 And Saul **k** David's voice, and said, *Is* H5234
2Sa 3:26 the well of Sirah: but David **k** *it* not. H3045
11:16 where he **k** that valiant men *were*. H3045
2Sa 11:20 when ye did fight? **k** ye not that they H3045
15:11 simplicity, and they **k** not any thing. H3045
18:29 a great tumult, but I **k** not what *it was*. H3045
22:44 a people *which* I **k** not shall serve me. H3045
1Ki 1: 4 to him: but the king **k** her not. H3045
18: 7 met him: and he **k** him, and fell on his H5234
2Ki 4:39 the pot of pottage: for they **k** *them* not. H3045
2Ch 33:13 **k** that the LORD he *was* God. H3045
Neh 2:16 And the rulers **k** not whither I went, or H3045
Est 1:13 wise men, which **k** the times, (for so H3045
13 toward all that **k** law and judgment: H3045
Job 2:12 eyes afar off, and **k** him not, they lifted H5234
23: 3 Oh that I **k** where I might find him! H3045
29:16 the cause *which* I **k** not I searched out. H3045
42: 3 too wonderful for me, which I **k** not. H3045
Ps 35:11 laid to my charge *things* that I **k** not. H3045
15 against me, and I **k** *it* not; they did tear H3045
Prv 24:12 If thou sayest, Behold, we **k** it not; doth H3045
Isa 42:16 by a way *that* they **k** not; I will lead H3045
25 about, yet he **k** not; and it burned him, H3045
48: 4 Because I **k** that thou *art* obstinate, H1847
7 thou shouldest say, Behold, I **k** them. H3045
8 not opened: for I **k** that thou wouldest H3045
55: 5 and nations *that* **k** not thee shall run H3045
Jer 1: 5 Before I formed thee in the belly I **k** H3045
2: 8 handle the law **k** me not: the pastors H3045
11:19 the slaughter; and I **k** not that they had H3045
32: 8 I **k** that this *was* the word of the LORD. H3045
41: 4 he had slain Gedaliah, and no man **k** *it*, H3045
44: 3 gods, whom they **k** not, *neither* they, H3045
15 Then all the men which **k** that their H3045
Ezk 10:20 and I **k** that they *were* the cherubims. H3045
19: 7 And he **k** their desolate palaces, and he H3045
Dan 5:21 of heaven; till he **k** that the most high H3046
6:10 Now when Daniel **k** that the writing H3046
11:38 whom his fathers **k** not shall he honour H3045
Hos 8: 4 princes, and I **k** *it* not: of their silver H3045
11: 3 but they **k** not that I healed them. H3045
Jna 1:10 this? For the men **k** that he fled from H3045
4: 2 unto Tarshish: for I **k** that thou *art* a H3045
Zec 7:14 whom they **k** not. Thus the land was H3045
11:11 me **k** that it *was* the word of the LORD. H3045
Mt 1:25 And **k** her not till she had brought forth *G1097*
7:23 unto them, I never **k** you: depart from *G1097*
12:15 But when Jesus **k** *it*, he withdrew *G1097*
25 And Jesus **k** their thoughts, and said *G1492*
17:12 already, and they **k** him not, but have *G1921*
24:39 And **k** not until the flood came, and *G1097*
25:24 and said, Lord, I **k** thee that thou art an *G1097*
27:18 For he **k** that for envy they had *G1492*
Mk 1:34 the devils to speak, because they **k** him. *G1492*
6:33 and many **k** him, and ran afoot *G1921*
38 they **k**, they say, Five, and two fishes. *G1097*
54 out of the ship, straightway they **k** him, *G1921*
8:17 And when Jesus **k** *it*, he saith unto *G1097*
12:12 people: for they **k** that he had spoken *G1097*
15:10 For he **k** that the chief priests had *G1097*
45 And when he **k** *it* of the centurion, he *G1097*
Lk 2:43 and Joseph and his mother **k** not *of it*. *G1097*
4:41 to speak: for they **k** that he was Christ. *G1492*
6: 8 But he **k** their thoughts, and said to the *G1492*
7:37 a sinner, when she **k** that *Jesus* sat at *G1921*
9:11 And the people, when they **k** *it*, *G1097*
12:47 And that servant, which **k** his lord's *G1097*
48 But he that **k** not, and did commit *G1097*
18:34 **k** they the things which were spoken. *G1097*
23: 7 And as soon as he **k** that he belonged *G1921*
24:31 And their eyes were opened, and they **k** *G1921*
Jn 1:10 made by him, and the world **k** him not. *G1097*
31 And I **k** him not: but that he should be *G1492*
33 And I **k** him not: but he that sent me to *G1492*
2: 9 made wine, and **k** not whence it was: *G1492*
9 drew the water **k**;) the governor of the *G1492*
24 unto them, because he **k** all *men*, *G1097*
25 of man: for he **k** what was in man. *G1097*
4: 1 When therefore the Lord **k** how the *G1097*
53 So the father **k** that *it was* at the same *G1097*
5: 6 When Jesus saw him lie, and **k** that he *G1097*
6: 6 for he himself **k** what he would do. *G1492*
61 When Jesus **k** in himself that his *G1492*
64 not. For Jesus **k** from the beginning *G1492*
11:42 And I **k** that thou hearest me always: *G1492*
57 that, if any man **k** where he were, he *G1097*
12: 9 Much people of the Jews therefore **k** *G1097*
13: 1 when Jesus **k** that his hour was come *G1492*
11 For he **k** who should betray him; *G1492*
28 Now no man at the table **k** for what *G1097*
16:19 Now Jesus **k** that they were desirous to *G1097*
18: 2 And Judas also, which betrayed him, **k** *G1492*

K

Jn 20: 9 For as yet they **k** not the scripture, that G1492
14 standing, and **k** not that it was Jesus. G1492
21: 4 but the disciples **k** not that it was Jesus. G1492
Act 3:10 And they **k** that it was he which sat for G1921
7:18 Till another king arose, which **k** not G1492
9:30 *Which* when the brethren **k**, they G1921
12:14 And when she **k** Peter's voice, she G1921
13:27 because they **k** him not, nor yet the G50
16: 3 they **k** all that his father was a Greek. G1492
19:32 and the more part **k** not wherefore they G1492
34 But when they **k** that he was a Jew, all G1921
22:29 afraid, after he **k** that he was a Roman, G1921
26: 5 Which **k** me from the beginning, if they G4267
27:39 And when it was day, they **k** not the G1921
28: 1 **k** that the island was called Melita. G1921
Ro 1:21 Because that, when they **k** God, they G1097
1Co 1:21 world by wisdom **k** not God, it pleased G1097
2: 8 of this world **k**: for had they known G1097
2Co 5:21 *to be* sin for us, who **k** no sin; that we G1097
12: 2 I **k** a man in Christ above fourteen G1492
3 And I **k** such a man, (whether in the G1492
Gal 4: 8 Howbeit then, when ye **k** not God, ye G1492
Col 1: 6 *of it*, and **k** the grace of God in truth: G1921
2: 1 For I would that ye **k** what great G1492
1Jn 3: 1 knoweth us not, because it **k** him not. G1097
Jude 5 though ye once **k** this, how that the G1492
Rev 19:12 written, that no man **k**, but he himself. G1492

KNEWEST

Dt 8: 3 which thou **k** not, neither did thy H3045
Ru 2:11 a people which thou **k** not heretofore. H3045
Neh 9:10 of his land: for thou **k** that they dealt H3045
Ps 142: 3 me, then thou **k** my path. In the way H3045
Isa 48: 8 Yea, thou heardest not; yea, thou **k** not; H3045
Dan 5:22 thine heart, though thou **k** all this; H3046
Mt 25:26 servant, thou **k** that I reap where I G1492
Lk 19:22 servant. Thou **k** that I was an austere G1492
44 thou **k** not the time of thy visitation. G1097
Jn 4:10 unto her, If thou **k** the gift of God, and G1492

KNIFE

Gen 22: 6 **k**; and they went both of them together. H3979
10 hand, and took the **k** to slay his son. H3979
Jdg 19:29 house, he took a **k**, and laid hold on his H3979
Prv 23: 2 And put a **k** to thy throat, if thou *be* a H7915
Ezk 5: 1 take thee a sharp **k**, take thee a barber's H2719
2 about it with a **k**: and a third part thou H2719

KNIT

Jdg 20:11 against the city, **k** together as one man. H2270
1Sa 18: 1 soul of Jonathan was **k** with the soul of H7194
1Ch 12:17 heart shall be **k** unto you: but if *ye be* H3162
Act 10:11 been a great sheet **k** at the four corners, G1210
Col 2: 2 be comforted, being **k** together in love, G4822
19 ministered, and **k** together, increaseth G4822

KNIVES

Jos 5: 2 Make thee sharp **k**, and circumcise H2719
3 And Joshua made him sharp **k**, and H2719
1Ki 18:28 their manner with **k** and lancets, till H2719
Ezr 1: 9 chargers of silver, nine and twenty **k**, H4252
Prv 30:14 their jaw teeth *as* **k**, to devour the poor H3979

KNOCK

Mt 7: 7 find; **k**, and it shall be opened unto you: G2925
Lk 11: 9 find; **k**, and it shall be opened unto you. G2925
13:25 without, and to **k** at the door, saying, G2925
Rev 3:20 Behold, I stand at the door, and **k**: if G2925

KNOCKED

Act 12:13 And as Peter **k** at the door of the gate, a G2925

KNOCKETH

Song 5: 2 my beloved that **k**, *saying*, Open to me, H1849
Mt 7: 8 and to him that **k** it shall be opened. G2925
Lk 11:10 and to him that **k** it shall be opened. G2925
12:36 he cometh and **k**, they may open unto G2925

KNOCKING

Act 12:16 But Peter continued **k**: and when they G2925

KNOP

Ex 25:33 almonds, *with* a **k** and a flower in one H3730
33 branch, *with* a **k** and a flower: so in the H3730
35 And *there shall be* a **k** under two H3730
35 of the same, and a **k** under two H3730
35 of the same, and a **k** under two H3730
37:19 in one branch, a **k** and a flower; and H3730
19 in another branch, a **k** and a flower: so H3730
Ex 37:21 And a **k** under two branches of the H3730
21 of the same, and a **k** under two H3730
21 of the same, and a **k** under two H3730

KNOPS

Ex 25:31 **k**, and his flowers, shall be of the same. H3730
34 *with* their **k** and their flowers. H3730
36 Their **k** and their branches shall be of H3730
37:17 his **k**, and his flowers, were of the same: H3730
20 like almonds, his **k**, and his flowers: H3730
22 Their **k** and their branches were of the H3730
1Ki 6:18 *was* carved with **k** and open flowers: all H6497
7:24 about *there were* **k** compassing it, ten H6497
24 sea round about: the **k** *were* cast in two H6497

KNOW

Gen 3: 5 For God doth **k** that in the day ye eat H3045
22 as one of us, to **k** good and evil: and H3045
4: 9 said, I **k** not: *Am* I my brother's keeper? H3045
12:11 Behold now, I **k** that thou *art* a fair H3045
15: 8 whereby shall I **k** that I shall inherit it? H3045
13 And he said unto Abram, **K** of a surety H3045
18:19 For I **k** him, that he will command his H3045
21 is come unto me; and if not, I will **k**. H3045
19: 5 them out unto us, that we may **k** them. H3045
20: 6 in a dream, Yea, I **k** that thou didst this H3045
7 restore *her* not, **k** thou that thou shalt H3045
22:12 him: for now I **k** that thou fearest God, H3045
24:14 thereby shall I **k** that thou hast shewed H3045
27: 2 And he said, Behold now, I am old, I **k** H3045
29: 5 And he said unto them, **K** ye Laban the H3045
5 of Nahor? And they said, We **k** *him*. H3045
31: 6 And ye **k** that with all my power I have H3045
37:32 have we found: **k** now whether it *be* thy H5234
42:33 us, Hereby shall I **k** that ye *are* true H3045
34 me: then shall I **k** that ye *are* no spies, H3045
43: 7 could we certainly **k** that he would say, H3045
44:27 us, Ye **k** that my wife bare me two *sons:* H3045
48:19 And his father refused, and said, I **k** *it*, H3045
19 I know *it*, my son, I **k** *it:* he also shall H3045
Ex 3: 7 their taskmasters; for I **k** their sorrows; H3045
4:14 thy brother? I **k** that he can speak well. H3045
5: 2 voice to let Israel go? I **k** not the LORD, H3045
6: 7 God: and ye shall **k** that I *am* the LORD H3045
7: 5 And the Egyptians shall **k** that I *am* the H3045
17 In this thou shalt **k** that I *am* the H3045
8:10 that thou mayest **k** that *there is* none H3045
22 end thou mayest **k** that I *am* the LORD H3045
9:14 that thou mayest **k** that *there is* none H3045
29 **k** how that the earth *is* the LORD'S. H3045
30 But as for thee and thy servants, I **k** H3045
10: 2 that ye may **k** how that I *am* the LORD. H3045
26 our God; and we **k** not with what we H3045
11: 7 or beast: that ye may **k** how that the H3045
14: 4 **k** that I *am* the LORD. And they did so. H3045
18 And the Egyptians shall **k** that I *am* the H3045
16: 6 At even, then ye shall **k** that the LORD H3045
12 shall **k** that I *am* the LORD your God. H3045
18:11 Now I **k** that the LORD *is* greater than H3045
16 **k** the statutes of God, and his laws. H3045
23: 9 a stranger: for ye **k** the heart of a H3045
29:46 And they shall **k** that I *am* the LORD H3045
31:13 that *ye* may **k** that I *am* the LORD H3045
33: 5 thee, that I may **k** what to do unto thee. H3045
12 hast not let me **k** whom thou wilt send H3045
12 thou hast said, I **k** thee by name, and H3045
13 way, that I may **k** thee, that I may find H3045
17 in my sight, and I **k** thee by name. H3045
36: 1 understanding to **k** how to work all H3045
Lev 23:43 That your generations may **k** that I H3045
Nu 14:31 **k** the land which ye have despised. H3045
34 and ye shall **k** my breach of promise. H3045
16:28 And Moses said, Hereby ye shall **k** that H3045
22:19 night, that I may **k** what the LORD will H3045
Dt 3:19 your cattle, (*for* I **k** that ye have much H3045
4:35 that thou mightest **k** that the LORD he H3045
39 **K** therefore this day, and consider *it* in H3045
7: 9 **K** therefore that the LORD thy God, he H3045
8: 2 to prove thee, to **k** what *was* in thine H3045
3 did thy fathers **k**; that he might make H3045
3 might make thee **k** that man doth not H3045
11: 2 And **k** ye this day: for *I speak* not with H3045
13: 3 proveth you, to **k** whether ye love the H3045
18:21 How shall we **k** the word which the H3045
22: 2 thee, or if thou **k** him not, then thou H3045
29: 6 might **k** that I *am* the LORD your God. H3045
16 (For ye **k** how we have dwelt in the H3045
31:21 of their seed: for I **k** their imagination H3045
27 For I **k** thy rebellion, and thy stiff neck: H3045
Dt 31:29 For I **k** that after my death ye will H3045
Jos 2: 9 And she said unto the men, I **k** that the H3045
3: 4 it, that ye may **k** the way by which ye H3045
7 that they may **k** that, as I was with H3045
10 And Joshua said, Hereby ye shall **k** that H3045
4:22 Then ye shall let your children **k**, H3045
24 That all the people of the earth might **k** H3045
22:22 and Israel he shall **k**; if it *be* in rebellion, H3045
23:13 **K** for a certainty that the LORD your H3045
14 all the earth: and ye **k** in all your hearts H3045
Jdg 3: 2 of Israel might **k**, to teach them war, H3045
4 prove Israel by them, to **k** whether they H3045
6:37 then shall I **k** that thou wilt save Israel H3045
17:13 Then said Micah, Now **k** I that the H3045
18: 5 of God, that we may **k** whether our way H3045
14 brethren, Do ye **k** that there is in these H3045
19:22 into thine house, that we may **k** him. H3045
Ru 3:11 doth **k** that thou *art* a virtuous woman. H3045
14 up before one could **k** another. And he H5234
18 until thou **k** how the matter will H3045
4: 4 tell me, that I may **k**: for *there is* none to H3045
1Sa 3: 7 Now Samuel did not yet **k** the LORD, H3045
6: 9 if not, then we shall **k** that *it is* not his H3045
14:38 of the people: and **k** and see wherein H3045
17:28 in the wilderness? I **k** thy pride, and the H3045
46 may **k** that there is a God in Israel. H3045
47 And all this assembly shall **k** that the H3045
20: 3 saith, Let not Jonathan **k** this, lest he be H3045
30 *woman*, do not I **k** that thou hast H3045
21: 2 unto me, Let no man **k** any thing of the H3045
22: 3 you, till I **k** what God will do for me. H3045
23:22 Go, I pray you, prepare yet, and **k** and H3045
24:11 and killed thee not, **k** thou and see that H3045
20 And now, behold, I **k** well that thou H3045
25:11 men, whom I **k** not whence they *be?* H3045
17 Now therefore **k** and consider what H3045
28: 1 said unto David, **K** thou assuredly, that H3045
2 Surely thou shalt **k** what thy servant H3045
29: 9 said to David, I **k** that thou *art* good in H3045
2Sa 3:25 thee, and to **k** thy going out and thy H3045
25 coming in, and to **k** all that thou doest. H3045
38 And the king said unto his servants, **K** H3045
7:21 things, to make thy servant **k** *them*. H3045
14:20 to **k** all *things* that *are* in the earth. H3045
19:20 For thy servant doth **k** that I have H3045
22 I **k** that I *am* this day king over Israel? H3045
24: 2 that I may **k** the number of the people. H3045
1Ki 2:37 Kidron, thou shalt **k** for certain that H3045
42 unto thee, saying, **K** for a certain, on H3045
3: 7 child: I **k** not *how* to go out or come in. H3045
8:38 Israel, which shall **k** every man the H3045
43 of the earth may **k** thy name, to fear H3045
43 and that they may **k** that this house, H3045
60 That all the people of the earth may **k** H3045
17:24 Now by this I **k** that thou *art* a man H3045
18:12 thee whither I **k** not; and *so* when I H3045
37 that this people may **k** that thou *art* the H3045
20:13 and thou shalt **k** that I *am* the LORD. H3045
28 and ye shall **k** that I *am* the LORD. H3045
22: 3 unto his servants, **K** ye that Ramoth in H3045
2Ki 2: 3 he said, Yea, I **k** *it;* hold ye your peace. H3045
5 Yea, I **k** *it;* hold ye your peace. H3045
5: 8 shall **k** that there is a prophet in Israel. H3045
15 Behold, now I **k** that *there is* no God H3045
7:12 done to us. They **k** that we *be* hungry; H3045
8:12 Because I **k** the evil that thou wilt H3045
9:11 Ye **k** the man, and his communication. H3045
10:10 **K** now that there shall fall unto the H3045
17:26 cities of Samaria, **k** not the manner of H3045
26 because they **k** not the manner of the H3045
19:19 of the earth may **k** that thou *art* the H3045
27 But I **k** thy abode, and thy going out, H3045
1Ch 12:32 of the times, to **k** what Israel ought to H3045
21: 2 number of them to me, that I may **k** *it*. H3045
28: 9 And thou, Solomon my son, **k** thou the H3045
29:17 I **k** also, my God, that thou triest the H3045
2Ch 2: 8 of Lebanon: for I **k** that thy servants H3045
6:29 every one shall **k** his own sore and his H3045
33 of the earth may **k** thy name, and fear H3045
33 Israel, and may **k** that this house which H3045
12: 8 that they may **k** my service, and the H3045
13: 5 Ought ye not to **k** that the LORD God of H3045
20:12 against us; neither **k** we what to do: but H3045
25:16 and said, I **k** that God hath determined H3045
32:13 **K** ye not what I and my fathers have H3045
31 he might **k** all *that was* in his heart. H3045
Ezr 4:15 of the records, and **k** that this city *is* a H3046
7:25 river, all such as **k** the laws of thy God; H3046
25 and teach ye them that **k** *them* not. H3046

Neh 4:11 They shall not **k**, neither see, till we H3045
Est 2:11 women's house, to **k** how Esther did, H3045
4: 5 to **k** what it *was*, and why it *was*. H3045
11 king's provinces, do **k**, that whosoever, H3045
Job 5:24 And thou shalt **k** that thy tabernacle H3045
25 Thou shalt **k** also that thy seed *shall be* H3045
27 it *is*; hear it, and **k** thou *it* for thy good. H3045
7:10 neither shall his place **k** him any more. H5234
8: 9 (For we *are but of* yesterday, and **k** H3045
9: 2 I **k** *it is* so of a truth: but how should H3045
5 and they **k** not: which overturneth H3045
21 not **k** my soul: I would despise my life. H3045
28 I am afraid of all my sorrows, I **k** that H3045
10:13 in thine heart: I **k** that this *is* with thee. H3045
11: 6 to that which is! **K** therefore that God H3045
8 do? deeper than hell; what canst thou **k**? H3045
13: 2 What ye **k**, *the same* do I know also: I H1847
2 What ye know, *the same* do I **k** also: I H3045
18 *my* cause; I **k** that I shall be justified. H3045
23 me to **k** my transgression and my sin. H3045
15: 9 What knowest thou, that we **k** not? H3045
19: 6 **K** now that God hath overthrown me, H3045
25 For I **k** *that* my redeemer liveth, and H3045
29 that ye may **k** *there is* a judgment. H3045
21:19 he rewardeth him, and he shall **k** *it*. H3045
27 Behold, I **k** your thoughts, and the H3045
29 the way? and do ye not **k** their tokens, H5234
22:13 And thou sayest, How doth God **k**? can H3045
23: 5 I would **k** the words *which* he would H3045
24: 1 do they that **k** him not see his days? H3045
13 the light; they **k** not the ways thereof, H5234
16 in the daytime: they **k** not the light. H3045
17 of death: if *one* **k** *them, they are in* the H5234
30:23 For I **k** *that* thou wilt bring me *to* H3045
31: 6 that God may **k** mine integrity. H3045
32:22 For I **k** not to give flattering titles; *in so* H3045
34: 4 Let us choose to us judgment: let us **k** H3045
36:26 Behold, God *is* great, and we **k** *him* not, H3045
37: 7 man; that all men may **k** his work. H3045
15 Dost thou **k** when God disposed them, H3045
16 Dost thou **k** the balancings of the H3045
38:12 caused the dayspring to **k** his place; H3045
20 **k** the paths *to* the house thereof? H995
42: 2 I **k** that thou canst do every *thing*, and H3045
Ps 4: 3 But **k** that the LORD hath set apart him H3045
9:10 And they that **k** thy name will put their H3045
20 may **k** themselves *to be but* men. Selah. H3045
20: 6 Now **k** I that the LORD saveth his H3045
36:10 unto them that **k** thee; and thy H3045
39: 4 LORD, make me to **k** mine end, and the H3045
4 what it *is*; *that* I may **k** how frail I *am*. H3045
41:11 By this I **k** that thou favourest me, H3045
46:10 Be still, and **k** that I *am* God: I will be H3045
50:11 I **k** all the fowls of the mountains: and H3045
51: 6 *part* thou shalt make me to **k** wisdom. H3045
56: 9 turn back: this I **k**; for God *is* for me. H3045
59:13 *be*: and let them **k** that God ruleth in H3045
71:15 day; for I **k** not the numbers *thereof*. H3045
73:11 And they say, How doth God **k**? and is H3045
16 When I thought to **k** this, it *was* too H3045
78: 6 That the generation to come might **k** H3045
82: 5 They **k** not, neither will they H3045
83:18 That *men* may **k** that thou, whose H3045
87: 4 to them that **k** me: behold Philistia, H3045
89:15 Blessed *is* the people that **k** the joyful H3045
94:10 teacheth man knowledge, *shall not he* **k**?
100: 3 **K** ye that the LORD he *is* God: *it is* he H3045
101: 4 from me: I will not **k** a wicked *person*. H3045
103:16 the place thereof shall **k** it no more. H5234
109:27 That they may **k** that this *is* thy hand; H3045
119:75 I **k**, O LORD, that thy judgments *are* H3045
125 that I may **k** thy testimonies. H3045
135: 5 For I **k** that the LORD *is* great, and *that* H3045
139:23 Search me, O God, and **k** my heart: try H3045
23 my heart: try me, and **k** my thoughts: H3045
140:12 I **k** that the LORD will maintain the H3045
142: 4 man that would **k** me: refuge failed me; H5234
143: 8 I trust: cause me to **k** the way wherein I H3045
Prv 1: 2 To **k** wisdom and instruction; to H3045
4: 1 father, and attend to **k** understanding. H3045
19 they **k** not at what they stumble. H3045
5: 6 moveable, *that* thou canst not **k** *them*. H3045
10:32 The lips of the righteous **k** what is H3045
22:21 That I might make thee **k** the certainty H3045
24:12 soul, doth *not* he **k** *it*? and shall *not* he H3045
25: 8 Go not forth hastily to strive, lest *thou* **k**
27:23 Be thou diligent to **k** the state of thy H3045
29: 7 *but* the wicked regardeth not to **k** *it*. H1847
30:18 for me, yea, four which I **k** not: H3045

Ecc 1:17 And I gave my heart to **k** wisdom, and H3045
17 wisdom, and to **k** madness and folly: H3045
3:12 I **k** that *there is* no good in them, but H3045
14 I **k** that, whatsoever God doeth, it shall H3045
7:25 I applied mine heart to **k**, and to search, H3045
25 *of things*, and to **k** the wickedness of H3045
8:12 yet surely I **k** that it shall be well H3045
16 When I applied mine heart to **k** H3045
17 to **k** *it*, yet shall he not be able to find *it*. H3045
9: 5 For the living **k** that they shall die: but H3045
5 shall die: but the dead **k** not any thing, H3045
11: 9 of thine eyes: but **k** thou, that for all H3045
Song 1: 8 If thou **k** not, O thou fairest among H3045
Isa 1: 3 not **k**, my people doth not consider. H3045
5:19 draw nigh and come, that we may **k** *it*! H3045
7:15 he eat, that he may **k** to refuse the evil, H3045
16 For before the child shall **k** to refuse the H3045
9: 9 And all the people shall **k**, *even* H3045
19:12 now, and let them **k** what the LORD of H3045
21 Egyptians shall **k** the LORD in that day, H3045
37:20 of the earth may **k** that thou *art* the H3045
28 But I **k** thy abode, and thy going out, H3045
41:20 That they may see, and **k**, and consider, H3045
22 them, and **k** the latter end of them; H3045
23 that we may **k** that ye *are* gods: yea, H3045
26 that we may **k**? and beforetime, that H3045
43:10 that ye may **k** and believe me, and H3045
19 forth; shall ye not **k** it? I will even make H3045
44: 8 me? yea, *there is* no God; I **k** not *any*. H3045
9 not, nor **k**; that they may be ashamed. H3045
45: 3 that thou mayest **k** that I, the LORD, H3045
6 That they may **k** from the rising of the H3045
47: 8 neither shall I **k** the loss of children: H3045
11 thou shalt not **k** from whence it riseth: H3045
11 thee suddenly, *which* thou shalt not **k**. H3045
48: 6 things, and thou didst not **k** them. H3045
49:23 and thou shalt **k** that I *am* the LORD: H3045
26 and all flesh shall **k** that I the LORD *am* H3045
50: 4 that I should **k** how to speak a word H3045
7 and I **k** that I shall not be ashamed. H3045
51: 7 Hearken unto me, ye that **k** H3045
52: 6 Therefore my people shall **k** my name: H3045
6 *they shall* **k** in that day that I *am* H3045
58: 2 Yet they seek me daily, and delight to **k** H1847
59: 8 The way of peace they **k** not; and *there* H3045
8 goeth therein shall not **k** peace. H3045
12 and *as for* our iniquities, we **k** them; H3045
60:16 and thou shalt **k** that I the LORD *am* H3045
66:18 For I *k* their works and their thoughts: it
Jer 2:19 shall reprove thee: **k** therefore and see H3045
23 thy way in the valley, **k** what thou hast H3045
5: 1 and see now, and **k**, and seek in the H3045
4 foolish: for they **k** not the way of the H3045
6:18 Therefore hear, ye nations, and **k**, O H3045
27 that thou mayest **k** and try their way. H3045
7: 9 walk after other gods whom ye **k** not; H3045
8: 7 **k** not the judgment of the LORD. H3045
9: 3 and they **k** not me, saith the LORD. H3045
6 they refuse to **k** me, saith the LORD. H3045
10:23 O LORD, I **k** that the way of man *is* not H3045
25 the heathen that **k** thee not, and upon H3045
11:18 *of it*, and I **k** *it*: then thou shewedst H3045
13:12 Do we not certainly **k** that every bottle H3045
14:18 go about into a land that they **k** not. H3045
15:15 thy longsuffering: **k** that for thy sake I H3045
16:13 into a land that ye **k** not, *neither* ye nor H3045
21 cause them to **k**, I will cause them to H3045
21 will cause them to **k** mine hand and my H3045
21 shall **k** that my name *is* The LORD. H3045
17: 9 and desperately wicked: who can **k** it? H3045
22:16 *was* not this to **k** me? saith the LORD. H1847
28 are cast into a land which they **k** not? H3045
24: 7 And I will give them an heart to **k** me, H3045
26:15 But **k** ye for certain, that if ye put me to H3045
29:11 For I **k** the thoughts that I think toward H3045
16 *K* that thus saith the LORD of the king
23 I **k**, and *am* a witness, saith the LORD. H3045
31:34 brother, saying, **K** the LORD: for they H3045
34 for they shall all **k** me, from the least of H3045
36:19 and let no man **k** where ye be. H3045
38:24 Let no man **k** of these words, and H3045
40:14 thou certainly **k** that Baalis the king H3045
15 and no man shall **k** *it*: wherefore H3045
42:19 Go ye not into Egypt: **k** certainly that I H3045
22 Now therefore **k** certainly that ye shall H3045
44:28 there, shall **k** whose words shall stand, H3045
29 this place, that ye may **k** that my words H3045
48:17 and all ye that **k** his name, say, How H3045
30 I **k** his wrath, saith the LORD; but *it* H3045

Ezk 2: 5 house,) yet shall **k** that there hath been H3045
5:13 and they shall **k** that I the LORD have H3045
6: 7 you, and ye shall **k** that I *am* the LORD. H3045
10 And they shall **k** that I *am* the LORD, H3045
13 Then shall ye **k** that I *am* the LORD, H3045
14 and they shall **k** that I *am* the LORD. H3045
7: 4 and ye shall **k** that I *am* the LORD. H3045
9 **k** that I *am* the LORD that smiteth. H3045
27 and they shall **k** that I *am* the LORD. H3045
11: 5 of Israel: for I **k** the things that come H3045
10 and ye shall **k** that I *am* the LORD. H3045
12 And ye shall **k** that I *am* the LORD: for H3045
12:15 And they shall **k** that I *am* the LORD, H3045
16 and they shall **k** that I *am* the LORD. H3045
20 and ye shall **k** that I *am* the LORD. H3045
13: 9 and ye shall **k** that I *am* the Lord GOD. H3045
14 and ye shall **k** that I *am* the LORD. H3045
21 and ye shall **k** that I *am* the LORD. H3045
23 and ye shall **k** that I *am* the LORD. H3045
14: 8 and ye shall **k** that I *am* the LORD. H3045
23 and ye shall **k** that I have not done H3045
15: 7 them; and ye shall **k** that I *am* the H3045
16: 2 Son of man, cause Jerusalem to **k** her H3045
62 and thou shalt **k** that I *am* the LORD: H3045
17:12 Say now to the rebellious house, **K** ye H3045
21 shall **k** that I the LORD have spoken *it*. H3045
24 And all the trees of the field shall **k** that H3045
20: 4 to **k** the abominations of their fathers: H3045
12 that they might **k** that I *am* the LORD H3045
20 ye may **k** that I *am* the LORD your God. H3045
26 that they might **k** that I *am* the LORD. H3045
38 and ye shall **k** that I *am* the LORD. H3045
42 And ye shall **k** that I *am* the LORD, H3045
44 And ye shall **k** that I *am* the LORD, H3045
21: 5 That all flesh may **k** that I the LORD H3045
22:16 and thou shalt **k** that I *am* the LORD. H3045
22 and ye shall **k** that I the LORD have H3045
23:49 and ye shall **k** that I *am* the Lord GOD. H3045
24:24 ye shall **k** that I *am* the Lord GOD. H3045
27 and they shall **k** that I *am* the LORD. H3045
25: 5 and ye shall **k** that I *am* the LORD. H3045
7 and thou shalt **k** that I *am* the LORD. H3045
11 and they shall **k** that I *am* the LORD. H3045
14 **k** my vengeance, saith the Lord GOD. H3045
17 and they shall **k** that I *am* the LORD, H3045
26: 6 and they shall **k** that I *am* the LORD. H3045
28:19 All they that **k** thee among the people H3045
22 and they shall **k** that I *am* the LORD, H3045
23 and they shall **k** that I *am* the LORD. H3045
24 they shall **k** that I *am* the Lord GOD. H3045
26 shall **k** that I *am* the LORD their God. H3045
29: 6 And all the inhabitants of Egypt shall **k** H3045
9 and they shall **k** that I *am* the LORD: H3045
16 they shall **k** that I *am* the Lord GOD. H3045
21 and they shall **k** that I *am* the LORD. H3045
30: 8 And they shall **k** that I *am* the LORD, H3045
19 and they shall **k** that I *am* the LORD. H3045
25 and they shall **k** that I *am* the LORD, H3045
26 and they shall **k** that I *am* the LORD. H3045
32:15 then shall they **k** that I *am* the LORD. H3045
33:29 Then shall they **k** that I *am* the LORD, H3045
33 then shall they **k** that a prophet hath H3045
34:27 land, and shall **k** that I *am* the LORD, H3045
30 Thus shall they **k** that I the LORD their H3045
35: 4 and thou shalt **k** that I *am* the LORD. H3045
9 and ye shall **k** that I *am* the LORD. H3045
12 And thou shalt **k** that I *am* the LORD, H3045
15 it: and they shall **k** that I *am* the LORD. H3045
36:11 and ye shall **k** that I *am* the LORD. H3045
23 and the heathen shall **k** that I *am* the H3045
36 about you shall **k** that I the LORD build H3045
38 and they shall **k** that I *am* the LORD. H3045
37: 6 live; and ye shall **k** that I *am* the LORD. H3045
13 And ye shall **k** that I *am* the LORD, H3045
14 land: then shall ye **k** that I the LORD H3045
28 And the heathen shall **k** that I the H3045
38:14 dwelleth safely, shalt thou not **k** *it*? H3045
16 the heathen may **k** me, when I shall be H3045
23 and they shall **k** that I *am* the LORD. H3045
39: 6 and they shall **k** that I *am* the LORD. H3045
7 and the heathen shall **k** that I *am* the H3045
22 So the house of Israel shall **k** that I *am* H3045
23 And the heathen shall **k** that the house H3045
28 Then shall they **k** that I *am* the LORD H3045
Dan 2: 3 my spirit was troubled to **k** the dream. H3045
8 The king answered and said, I **k** of H3046
9 dream, and I shall **k** that ye can shew H3046
21 to them that **k** understanding: H3046
30 mightest **k** the thoughts of thy heart. H3046

Dan 4: 9 because I **k** that the spirit of the H3046
17 the living may **k** that the most High H3046
25 over thee, till thou **k** that the most High H3046
32 thee, until thou **k** that the most High H3046
5:23 see not, nor hear, nor **k**: and the God in H3046
6:15 unto the king, **K**, O king, that the law H3046
7:16 me **k** the interpretation of the things. H3046
19 Then I would **k** the truth of the fourth H3046
8:19 And he said, Behold, I will make thee **k** H3045
9:25 **K** therefore and understand, *that* from H3045
11:32 the people that do **k** their God shall be H3045
Hos 2: 8 For she did not **k** that I gave her corn, H3045
20 and thou shalt **k** the LORD. H3045
5: 3 I **k** Ephraim, and Israel is not hid from H3045
6: 3 Then shall we **k**, *if* we follow on to know H3045
3 *if* we follow on to **k** the LORD: his going H3045
8: 2 Israel shall cry unto me, My God, we **k** H3045
9: 7 come; Israel shall **k** *it*: the prophet *is* a H3045
13: 4 and thou shalt **k** no god but me: for H3045
5 I did **k** thee in the wilderness, in the H3045
14: 9 and he shall **k** them? for the ways H3045
Joel 2:27 And ye shall **k** that I *am* in the midst of H3045
3:17 So shall ye **k** that I *am* the LORD your H3045
Am 3:10 For they **k** not to do right, saith the H3045
5:12 For I **k** your manifold transgressions H3045
Jna 1: 7 lots, that we may **k** for whose cause H3045
12 unto you: for I **k** that for my sake this H3045
Mic 3: 1 Israel; *Is it* not for you to **k** judgment? H3045
4:12 But they **k** not the thoughts of the H3045
6: 5 may **k** the righteousness of the LORD. H3045
Zec 2: 9 **k** that the LORD of hosts hath sent me. H3045
11 thee, and thou shalt **k** that the LORD of H3045
4: 9 it; and thou shalt **k** that the LORD of H3045
6:15 and ye shall **k** that the LORD of hosts H3045
Mal 2: 4 And ye shall **k** that I have sent this H3045
Mt 6: 3 left hand **k** what thy right hand doeth: G1097
7:11 If ye then, being evil, **k** how to give G1492
16 Ye shall **k** them by their fruits. Do men G1921
20 Wherefore by their fruits ye shall **k** G1921
9: 6 But that ye may **k** that the Son of man G1492
30 them, saying, See *that* no man **k** *it*. G1097
13:11 given unto you to **k** the mysteries of the G1097
20:22 But Jesus answered and said, Ye **k** not G1492
25 *him*, and said, Ye **k** that the princes of G1492
22:16 Master, we **k** that thou art true, and G1492
24:32 forth leaves, ye **k** that summer *is* nigh: G1097
33 **k** that it is near, *even* at the doors. G1097
42 Watch therefore: for ye **k** not what G1492
43 But **k** this, that if the goodman of the G1097
25:12 said, Verily I say unto you, I **k** you not. G1492
13 Watch therefore, for ye **k** neither the G1492
26: 2 Ye **k** that after two days is *the feast of* G1492
70 all, saying, I **k** not what thou sayest. G1492
72 with an oath, I do not **k** the man. G1492
74 to swear, *saying*, I **k** not the man. And G1492
28: 5 Fear not ye: for I **k** that ye seek Jesus, G1492
Mk 1:24 to destroy us? I **k** thee who thou art, the G1492
2:10 But that ye may **k** that the Son of man G1492
4:11 you it is given to **k** the mystery of the G1097
13 And he said unto them, **K** ye not this G1492
13 and how then will ye **k** all parables? G1097
5:43 no man should **k** it; and commanded G1097
7:24 no man **k** *it*: but he could not be hid. G1097
9:30 he would not that any man should **k** *it*. G1097
10:38 But Jesus said unto them, Ye **k** not G1492
42 unto them, Ye **k** that they which are G1492
12:14 him, Master, we **k** that thou art true, G1492
24 err, because ye **k** not the scriptures, G1492
13:28 forth leaves, ye **k** that summer is near: G1097
29 **k** that it is nigh, *even* at the doors. G1097
33 Take ye heed, watch and pray: for ye **k** G1492
35 Watch ye therefore: for ye **k** not when G1492
14:68 But he denied, saying, I **k** not, neither G1492
71 I **k** not this man of whom ye speak. G1492
Lk 1: 4 That thou mightest **k** the certainty of G1921
18 Whereby shall I **k** this? for I am an old G1097
34 How shall this be, seeing I **k** not a man? G1097
4:34 to destroy us? I **k** thee who thou art; the G1492
5:24 But that ye may **k** that the Son of man G1492
8:10 And he said, Unto you it is given to **k** G1097
9:55 **k** not what manner of spirit ye are of. G1492
11:13 If ye then, being evil, **k** how to give G1492
12:39 And this **k**, that if the goodman of the G1097
13:25 unto you, I **k** you not whence ye are: G1492
27 But he shall say, I tell you, I **k** you not G1492
19:15 that he might **k** how much every man G1097
20:21 Master, we **k** that thou sayest and G1492
21:20 **k** that the desolation thereof is nigh. G1097
30 forth, ye see and **k** of your own selves G1097
Lk 21:31 come to pass, **k** ye that the kingdom G1097
22:57 him, saying, Woman, I **k** him not. G1492
60 And Peter said, Man, I **k** not what thou G1492
23:34 them; for they **k** not what they do. And G1492
24:16 holden that they should not **k** him. G1921
Jn 1:26 one among you, whom ye **k** not; G1492
3: 2 unto him, Rabbi, we **k** that thou art a G1492
11 speak that we do **k**, and testify that we G1492
4:22 Ye worship ye **k** not what: we know G1492
22 Ye worship ye know not what: we **k** G1492
25 The woman saith unto him, I **k** that G1492
32 I have meat to eat that ye **k** not of. G1492
42 ourselves, and **k** that this is indeed the G1492
5:32 of me; and I **k** that the witness which G1492
42 But I **k** you, that ye have not the love of G1097
6:42 and mother we **k**? how is it then that he G1492
7:17 If any man will do his will, he shall **k** of G1097
26 **k** indeed that this is the very Christ? G1097
27 Howbeit we **k** this man whence he is: G1492
28 saying, Ye both **k** me, and ye know G1492
28 know me, and ye **k** whence I am: and I G1492
28 he that sent me is true, whom ye **k** not. G1492
29 But I **k** him: for I am from him, and he G1492
51 it hear him, and **k** what he doeth? G1097
8:14 is true: for I **k** whence I came, and G1492
19 Ye neither **k** me, nor my Father: G1492
28 man, then shall ye **k** that I am *he*, and G1097
32 And ye shall **k** the truth, and the truth G1097
37 I **k** that ye are Abraham's seed; but ye G1492
52 Then said the Jews unto him, Now we **k** G1097
55 Yet ye have not known him; but I **k** G1492
55 if I should say, I **k** him not, I shall be a G1492
55 you: but I **k** him, and keep his saying. G1492
9:12 unto him, Where is he? He said, I **k** not. G1492
20 and said, We **k** that this is our son, G1492
21 But by what means he now seeth, we **k** G1492
21 his eyes, we **k** not: he is of age; ask G1492
24 praise: we **k** that this man is a sinner. G1492
25 be a sinner *or no*, I **k** not: one thing I G1492
25 I **k**, that, whereas I was blind, now I see. G1492
29 We **k** that God spake unto Moses: *as* G1492
29 this *fellow*, we **k** not from whence he is. G1492
30 thing, that ye **k** not from whence he G1492
31 Now we **k** that God heareth not G1492
10: 4 sheep follow him: for they **k** his voice. G1492
5 for they **k** not the voice of strangers. G1492
14 I am the good shepherd, and **k** my G1097
15 As the Father knoweth me, even so **k** I G1097
27 My sheep hear my voice, and I **k** them, G1097
38 that ye may **k**, and believe, that the G1097
11:22 But I **k**, that even now, whatsoever thou G1492
24 Martha saith unto him, I **k** that he shall G1492
49 said unto them, Ye **k** nothing at all, G1492
12:50 And I **k** that his commandment is life G1492
13: 7 not now; but thou shalt **k** hereafter. G1097
12 them, **K** ye what I have done to you? G1097
17 If ye **k** these things, happy are ye if ye G1492
18 I speak not of you all: I **k** whom I have G1492
35 By this shall all *men* **k** that ye are my G1097
14: 4 And whither I go ye **k**, and the way ye G1492
4 whither I go ye know, and the way ye **k**. G1492
5 Thomas saith unto him, Lord, we **k** not G1492
5 thou goest; and how can we **k** the way? G1492
7 ye **k** him, and have seen him. G1097
17 him: but ye **k** him; for he dwelleth G1097
20 At that day ye shall **k** that I *am* in my G1097
31 But that the world may **k** that I love the G1097
15:18 If the world hate you, ye **k** that it hated G1097
21 because they **k** not him that sent me. G1492
17: 3 that they might **k** thee the only true G1097
23 the world may **k** that thou hast sent G1097
18:21 unto them: behold, they **k** what I said. G1492
19: 4 ye may **k** that I find no fault in him. G1097
20: 2 and we **k** not where they have laid him. G1492
13 and I **k** not where they have laid him. G1492
21:24 and we **k** that his testimony is true. G1492
Act 1: 7 It is not for you to **k** the times or the G1097
2:22 midst of you, as ye yourselves also **k**: G1492
36 Therefore let all the house of Israel **k** G1097
3:16 whom ye see and **k**: yea, the faith which G1492
10:28 And he said unto them, Ye **k** how that G1987
37 That word, *I say*, ye **k**, which was G1492
12:11 he said, Now I **k** of a surety, that the G1492
15: 7 *and* brethren, ye **k** how that a good G1987
17:19 saying, May we **k** what this new G1097
20 **k** therefore what these things mean. G1097
19:15 I **k**, and Paul I know; but who are ye? G1097
15 I know, and Paul I **k**; but who are ye? G1987
25 **k** that by this craft we have our wealth. G1987
Act 20:18 unto them, Ye **k**, from the first day that G1987
25 And now, behold, I **k** that ye all, among G1492
29 For I **k** this, that after my departing G1492
34 Yea, ye yourselves **k**, that these hands G1097
21:24 heads: and all may **k** that those things, G1097
34 when he could not **k** the certainty for G1097
22:14 thou shouldest **k** his will, and see that G1097
19 And I said, Lord, they **k** that I G1987
24 **k** wherefore they cried so against him. G1921
24:10 Forasmuch as I **k** that thou hast been G1987
22 I will **k** the uttermost of your matter. G1231
26: 3 Especially *because I* **k** thee to be expert
4 own nation at Jerusalem, **k** all the Jews; G2467
27 the prophets? I **k** that thou believest. G1492
28:22 **k** that every where it is spoken against. G2076
Ro 3:19 Now we **k** that what things soever the G1492
6: 3 **K** ye not, that so many of us as were G50
16 **K** ye not, that to whom ye yield G1492
7: 1 **K** ye not, brethren, (for I speak to them G50
1 to them that **k** the law,) how that the G1097
14 For we **k** that the law is spiritual: but I G1492
18 For I **k** that in me (that is, in my flesh,) G1492
8:22 For we **k** that the whole creation G1492
26 our infirmities: for we **k** not what we G1492
28 And we **k** that all things work together G1492
10:19 But I say, Did not Israel **k**? First Moses G1097
14:14 I **k**, and am persuaded by the Lord G1492
1Co 1:16 I **k** not whether I baptized any other. G1492
2: 2 For I determined not to **k** any thing G1492
12 that we might **k** the things that are G1492
14 neither can he **k** *them*, because they G1097
3:16 **K** ye not that ye are the temple of God, G1492
4: 4 For I **k** nothing by myself; yet am I not G4894
19 Lord will, and will **k**, not the speech of G1097
5: 6 Your glorying *is* not good. **K** ye not that G1492
6: 2 Do ye not **k** that the saints shall judge G1492
3 **K** ye not that we shall judge angels? G1492
9 **K** ye not that the unrighteous shall not G1492
15 **K** ye not that your bodies are the G1492
16 What? **k** ye not that he which is joined G1492
19 What? **k** ye not that your body is the G1492
8: 1 unto idols, we **k** that we all have G1492
2 knoweth nothing yet as he ought to **k**. G1097
4 unto idols, we **k** that an idol *is* nothing G1492
9:13 Do ye not **k** that they which minister G1492
24 **K** ye not that they which run in a race G1492
11: 3 But I would have you **k**, that the head of G1492
12: 2 Ye **k** that ye were Gentiles, carried G1492
13: 9 For we **k** in part, and we prophesy in G1097
12 face to face: now I **k** in part; but then G1097
12 then shall I **k** even as also I am known. G1921
14:11 Therefore if I **k** not the meaning of the G1492
15:58 forasmuch as ye **k** that your labour is G1492
16:15 I beseech you, brethren, (ye **k** the G1492
2Co 2: 4 but that ye might **k** the love which I G1097
9 I write, that I might **k** the proof of you, G1097
5: 1 For we **k** that if our earthly house of G1492
16 Wherefore henceforth **k** we no man G1492
16 yet now henceforth **k** we *him* no more. G1492
8: 9 For ye **k** the grace of our Lord Jesus G1097
9: 2 For I **k** the forwardness of your mind, G1492
13: 5 your own selves. **K** ye not your own G1921
6 But I trust that ye shall **k** that we are G1097
Gal 3: 7 **K** ye therefore that they which are of G1097
4:13 Ye **k** how through infirmity of the flesh G1492
Eph 1:18 that ye may **k** what is the hope of G1492
3:19 And to **k** the love of Christ, which G1097
5: 5 For this ye **k**, that no whoremonger, nor G2075
6:21 But that ye also may **k** my affairs, *and* G1492
22 that ye might **k** our affairs, and *that* G1097
Php 1:19 For I **k** that this shall turn to my G1492
25 And having this confidence, I **k** that I G1492
2:19 of good comfort, when I **k** your state. G1097
22 But ye **k** the proof of him, that, as a son G1097
3:10 That I may **k** him, and the power of his G1097
4:12 I **k** both how to be abased, and I know G1492
12 I know both how to be abased, and I **k** G1492
15 Now ye Philippians **k** also, that in the G1492
Col 4: 6 **k** how ye ought to answer every man. G1492
8 **k** your estate, and comfort your hearts; G1097
1Th 1: 5 assurance; as ye **k** what manner of G1492
2: 1 For yourselves, brethren, **k** our G1492
2 entreated, as ye **k**, at Philippi, we were G1492
5 flattering words, as ye **k**, nor a cloak of G1492
11 As ye **k** how we exhorted and G1492
3: 3 **k** that we are appointed thereunto. G1492
4 even as it came to pass, and ye **k**. G1492
5 forbear, I sent to **k** your faith, lest by G1097
4: 2 For ye **k** what commandments we gave G1492

1Th 4: 4 That every one of you should **k** how to *G1492*
5 even as the Gentiles which **k** not God: *G1492*
5: 2 For yourselves **k** perfectly that the day *G1492*
12 And we beseech you, brethren, to **k** *G1492*
2Th 1: 8 on them that **k** not God, and that obey *G1492*
2: 6 And now ye **k** what withholdeth that he *G1492*
3: 7 For yourselves **k** how ye ought to follow *G1492*
1Ti 1: 8 But we **k** that the law *is* good, if a man *G1492*
3: 5 (For if a man **k** not how to rule his own *G1492*
15 But if I tarry long, that thou mayest **k** *G1492*
4: 3 of them which believe and **k** the truth. *G1921*
2Ti 1:12 am not ashamed: for I **k** whom I have *G1492*
3: 1 This **k** also, that in the last days *G1097*
Tit 1:16 They profess that they **k** God; but in *G1492*
Heb 8:11 brother, saying, **K** the Lord: for all shall *G1097*
11 **k** me, from the least to the greatest. *G1492*
10:30 For we **k** him that hath said, *G1492*
12:17 For ye **k** how that afterward, when he *G2467*
13:23 **K** ye that *our* brother Timothy is set at *G1097*
Jas 2:20 But wilt thou **k**, O vain man, that faith *G1097*
4: 4 Ye adulterers and adulteresses, **k** ye *G1492*
14 Whereas ye **k** not what *shall be* on the *G1987*
5:20 Let him **k**, that he which converteth the *G1097*
1Pt 1:18 Forasmuch as ye **k** that ye were not *G1492*
2Pt 1:12 these things, though ye **k** *them*, and be *G1492*
3:17 Ye therefore, beloved, seeing ye **k** *these* *G4267*
1Jn 2: 3 And hereby we do **k** that we know him, *G1097*
3 And hereby we do know that we **k** him, *G1097*
4 He that saith, I **k** him, and keepeth not *G1097*
5 hereby **k** we that we are in him. *G1097*
18 whereby we **k** that it is the last time. *G1097*
20 from the Holy One, and ye **k** all things. *G1492*
21 you because ye **k** not the truth, but *G1492*
21 ye **k** it, and that no lie is of the truth. *G1492*
29 If ye **k** that he is righteous, ye know *G1492*
29 If ye know that he is righteous, ye **k** *G1097*
3: 2 shall be: but we **k** that, when he shall *G1492*
5 And ye **k** that he was manifested to *G1492*
14 We **k** that we have passed from death *G1492*
15 a murderer: and ye **k** that no murderer *G1492*
19 And hereby we **k** that we are of the *G1097*
24 And hereby we **k** that he abideth in us, *G1097*
4: 2 Hereby **k** ye the Spirit of God: Every *G1097*
6 not us. Hereby **k** we the spirit of truth, *G1097*
13 Hereby **k** we that we dwell in him, and *G1097*
5: 2 By this we **k** that we love the children of *G1097*
13 God; that ye may **k** that ye have eternal *G1492*
15 And if we **k** that he hear us, whatsoever *G1492*
15 we ask, we **k** that we have the petitions *G1492*
18 We **k** that whosoever is born of God *G1492*
19 *And* we **k** that we are of God, and the *G1492*
20 And we **k** that the Son of God is come, *G1492*
20 that we may **k** him that is true, and *G1097*
3Jn 12 record; and ye **k** that our record is true. *G1492*
Jude 10 things which they **k** not: but what they *G1492*
10 not: but what they **k** naturally, as brute *G1987*
Rev 2: 2 I **k** thy works, and thy labour, and thy *G1492*
9 I **k** thy works, and tribulation, and *G1492*
9 art rich) and *I* **k** the blasphemy of them
13 I **k** thy works, and where thou dwellest, *G1492*
19 I **k** thy works, and charity, and service, *G1492*
23 the churches shall **k** that I am he which *G1097*
3: 1 the seven stars; I **k** thy works, that thou *G1492*
3 not **k** what hour I will come upon thee. *G1097*
8 I **k** thy works: behold, I have set before *G1492*
9 thy feet, and to **k** that I have loved thee. *G1097*
15 I **k** thy works, that thou art neither cold *G1492*

KNOWEST
Gen 30:26 **k** my service which I have done thee. H3045
29 And he said unto him, Thou **k** how I H3045
47: 6 dwell: and if thou **k** *any* men of activity H3045
Ex 10: 7 **k** thou not yet that Egypt is destroyed? H3045
32:22 lord wax hot: thou **k** the people, that H3045
Nu 10:31 as thou **k** how we are to encamp H3045
11:16 Israel, whom thou **k** to be the elders of H3045
20:14 **k** all the travail that hath befallen us: H3045
Dt 7:15 Egypt, which thou **k**, upon thee; but will H3045
9: 2 whom thou **k**, and *of whom* thou hast H3045
20:20 Only the trees which thou **k** that they H3045
28:33 a nation which thou **k** not eat up; and H3045
Jos 14: 6 unto him, Thou **k** the thing that the H3045
Jdg 15:11 said to Samson, **K** thou not that the H3045
1Sa 28: 9 him, Behold, thou **k** what Saul hath H3045
2Sa 1: 5 told him, How **k** thou that Saul and H3045
2:26 devour for ever? **k** thou not that it will H3045
3:25 Thou **k** Abner the son of Ner, that he H3045
7:20 for thou, Lord GOD, **k** thy servant. H3045
17: 8 For, said Hushai, thou **k** thy father and H3045
1Ki 1:18 now, my lord the king, thou **k** *it* not: H3045
2: 5 Moreover thou **k** also what Joab the H3045
9 a wise man, and **k** what thou oughtest H3045
15 And he said, Thou **k** that the kingdom H3045
44 to Shimei, Thou **k** all the wickedness H3045
5: 3 Thou **k** how that David my father could H3045
6 appoint: for thou **k** that *there is* not H3045
8:39 whose heart thou **k**; (for thou, *even* H3045
39 **k** the hearts of all the children of men;) H3045
2Ki 2: 3 said unto him, **K** thou that the LORD H3045
5 said unto him, **K** thou that the LORD H3045
4: 1 is dead; and thou **k** that thy servant did H3045
1Ch 17:18 of thy servant? for thou **k** thy servant. H3045
2Ch 6:30 whose heart thou **k**; (for thou only H3045
30 **k** the hearts of the children of men:) H3045
Job 10: 7 Thou **k** that I am not wicked; and *there* H1847
15: 9 What **k** thou, that we know not? *what* H3045
20: 4 **K** thou *not* this of old, since man was H3045
34:33 and not I: therefore speak what thou **k**. H3045
38: 5 thereof, if thou **k**? or who hath stretched H3045
18 of the earth? declare if thou **k** it all. H3045
21 **K** thou *it*, because thou wast then H3045
33 **K** thou the ordinances of heaven? canst H3045
39: 1 **K** thou the time when the wild goats of H3045
2 **k** thou the time when they bring forth? H3045
Ps 40: 9 not refrained my lips, O LORD, thou **k**. H3045
69: 5 O God, thou **k** my foolishness; and my H3045
139: 2 Thou **k** my downsitting and mine H3045
4 *but*, lo, O LORD, thou **k** it altogether. H3045
Prv 27: 1 thou **k** not what a day may bring forth. H3045
Ecc 11: 2 **k** not what evil shall be upon the earth. H3045
5 As thou **k** not what *is* the way of the H3045
5 **k** not the works of God who maketh all. H3045
6 hand: for thou **k** not whether shall H3045
Isa 55: 5 a nation *that* thou **k** not, and nations H3045
Jer 5:15 whose language thou **k** not, neither H3045
12: 3 But thou, O LORD, **k** me: thou hast H3045
15:14 a land *which* thou **k** not: for a fire is H3045
15 O LORD, thou **k**: remember me, and H3045
17: 4 the land which thou **k** not: for ye have H3045
16 woeful day; thou **k**: that which came out H3045
18:23 Yet, LORD, thou **k** all their counsel H3045
33: 3 and mighty things, which thou **k** not. H3045
Ezk 37: 3 And I answered, O Lord GOD, thou **k**. H3045
Dan 10:20 Then said he, **K** thou wherefore I come H3045
Zec 4: 5 and said unto me, **K** thou not what H3045
13 And he answered me and said, **K** thou H3045
Mt 15:12 and said unto him, **K** thou that the *G1492*
Mk 10:19 Thou **k** the commandments, Do not *G1492*
Lk 18:20 Thou **k** the commandments, Do not *G1492*
22:34 thou shalt thrice deny that thou **k** me. *G1492*
Jn 1:48 Nathanael saith unto him, Whence **k** *G1097*
3:10 of Israel, and **k** not these things? *G1097*
13: 7 What I do thou **k** not now; but thou *G1492*
16:30 Now are we sure that thou **k** all things, *G1492*
19:10 thou not unto me? **k** thou not that I *G1492*
21:15 Yea, Lord; thou **k** that I love thee. He *G1492*
16 Yea, Lord; thou **k** that I love thee. He *G1492*
17 unto him, Lord, thou **k** all things; thou *G1492*
17 all things; thou **k** that I love thee. Jesus *G1097*
Act 1:24 Thou, Lord, which **k** the hearts of all *G2589*
25:10 I done no wrong, as thou very well **k**. *G1921*
Ro 2:18 And **k** *his* will, and approvest the *G1097*
1Co 7:16 For what **k** thou, O wife, whether thou *G1492*
16 *thy* husband? or how **k** thou, O man, *G1492*
2Ti 1:15 This thou **k**, that all they which are in *G1492*
18 unto me at Ephesus, thou **k** very well. *G1097*
Rev 3:17 of nothing; and **k** not that thou art *G1492*
7:14 And I said unto him, Sir, thou **k**. And he *G1492*

KNOWETH
Gen 33:13 And he said unto him, My lord **k** that H3045
Lev 5: 3 when he **k** *of it*, then he shall be guilty. H3045
4 him; when he **k** *of it*, then he shall be H3045
Dt 2: 7 of thy hand: he **k** thy walking through H3045
34: 6 man **k** of his sepulchre unto this day. H3045
Jos 22:22 God of gods, he **k**, and Israel he shall H3045
1Sa 3:13 iniquity which he **k**; because his sons H3045
20: 3 Thy father certainly **k** that I have found H3045
23:17 thee; and that also Saul my father **k**. H3045
2Sa 14:22 To day thy servant **k** that I have found H3045
17:10 melt: for all Israel **k** that thy father *is* a H3045
1Ki 1:11 doth reign, and David our lord **k** *it* not? H3045
Est 4:14 and who **k** whether thou art come H3045
Job 11:11 For he **k** vain men: he seeth wickedness H3045
12: 3 you: yea, who **k** not such things as these? H854
9 Who **k** not in all these that the hand of H3045
14:21 His sons come to honour, and he **k** *it* H3045
15:23 *saying*, Where *is it*? he **k** that the day of H3045
Job 18:21 this *is* the place *of him that* **k** not God. H3045
23:10 But he **k** the way that I take: *when* he H3045
28: 7 *There is* a path which no fowl **k**, and H3045
13 Man **k** not the price thereof; neither is H3045
23 way thereof, and he **k** the place thereof. H3045
34:25 Therefore he **k** their works, and he H5234
35:15 anger; yet he **k** *it* not in great extremity: H3045
Ps 1: 6 For the LORD **k** the way of the H3045
37:18 The LORD **k** the days of the upright: H3045
39: 6 and **k** not who shall gather them. H3045
44:21 Shall not God search this out? for he **k** H3045
74: 9 *is there* among us any that **k** how long. H3045
90:11 Who **k** the power of thine anger? even H3045
92: 6 A brutish man **k** not; neither doth a H3045
94:11 The LORD **k** the thoughts of man, that H3045
103:14 For he **k** our frame; he remembereth H3045
104:19 for seasons: the sun **k** his going down. H3045
138: 6 the lowly: but the proud he **k** afar off. H3045
139:14 works; and *that* my soul **k** right well. H3045
Prv 7:23 snare, and **k** not that it *is* for his life. H3045
9:13 *she is* simple, and **k** nothing. H3045
18 But he **k** not that the dead *are* there; H3045
14:10 The heart **k** his own bitterness; and a H3045
24:22 and who **k** the ruin of them both? H3045
Ecc 2:19 And who **k** whether he shall be a wise H3045
3:21 Who **k** the spirit of man that goeth H3045
6: 8 poor, that **k** to walk before the living? H3045
12 For who **k** what *is* good for man in *this* H3045
7:22 For oftentimes also thine own heart **k** H3045
8: 1 Who *is* as the wise *man*? and who **k** the H3045
7 For he **k** not that which shall be: for H3045
9: 1 of God: no man **k** either love or hatred H3045
12 For man also **k** not his time: as the H3045
10:15 because he **k** not how to go to the city. H3045
Isa 1: 3 The ox **k** his owner, and the ass his H3045
29:15 they say, Who seeth us? and who **k** us? H3045
Jer 8: 7 Yea, the stork in the heaven **k** her H3045
9:24 and **k** me, that I *am* the LORD H3045
Dan 2:22 and secret things: he **k** what *is* in the H3046
Hos 7: 9 his strength, and he **k** *it* not: yea, gray H3045
9 here and there upon him, yet he **k** not. H3045
Joel 2:14 Who **k** *if* he will return and repent, and H3045
Nah 1: 7 and he **k** them that trust in him. H3045
Zep 3: 5 faileth not; but the unjust **k** no shame. H3045
Mt 6: 8 for your Father **k** what things ye have *G1492*
32 **k** that ye have need of all these things. *G1492*
11:27 and no man **k** the Son, but the Father; *G1921*
27 Father; neither **k** any man the Father, *G1921*
24:36 But of that day and hour **k** no *man*, no, *G1492*
Mk 4:27 spring and grow up, he **k** not how. *G1492*
13:32 But of that day and *that* hour **k** no *G1492*
Lk 10:22 and no man **k** who the Son is, but *G1097*
12:30 **k** that ye have need of these things. *G1492*
16:15 men; but God **k** your hearts: for that *G1097*
Jn 7:15 And the Jews marvelled, saying, How **k** *G1492*
27 Christ cometh, no man **k** whence he is. *G1097*
49 But this people who **k** not the law are *G1097*
10:15 As the Father **k** me, even so know I the *G1097*
12:35 in darkness **k** not whither he goeth. *G1492*
14:17 him not, neither **k** him: but ye know *G1097*
15:15 for the servant **k** not what his lord *G1492*
19:35 is true: and he **k** that he saith true, that *G1492*
Act 15: 8 And God, which **k** the hearts, bare *G2589*
19:35 man is there that **k** not how that the *G1097*
26:26 For the king **k** of these things, before *G1987*
Ro 8:27 And he that searcheth the hearts **k** *G1492*
1Co 2:11 For what man **k** the things of a man, *G1492*
11 of God **k** no man, but the Spirit of God. *G1492*
3:20 And again, The Lord **k** the thoughts of *G1097*
8: 2 And if any man think that he **k** any *G1492*
2 he **k** nothing yet as he ought to know. *G1097*
2Co 11:11 because I love you not? God **k**. *G1492*
31 is blessed for evermore, **k** that I lie not. *G1492*
12: 2 I cannot tell: God **k**;) such an one caught *G1492*
3 or out of the body, I cannot tell: God **k**;) *G1492*
2Ti 2:19 this seal, The Lord **k** them that are his. *G1097*
Jas 4:17 Therefore to him that **k** to do good, and *G1492*
2Pt 2: 9 The Lord **k** how to deliver the godly out *G1492*
1Jn 2:11 in darkness, and **k** not whither he *G1492*
3: 1 **k** us not, because it knew him not. *G1097*
20 greater than our heart, and **k** all things. *G1097*
4: 6 We are of God: he that **k** God heareth *G1097*
7 that loveth is born of God, and **k** God. *G1097*
8 He that loveth not **k** not God; for God is *G1097*
Rev 2:17 no man **k** saving he that receiveth *it*. *G1097*
12:12 he **k** that he hath but a short time. *G1492*

KNOWING
Gen 3: 5 ye shall be as gods, **k** good and evil. H3045

1Ki 2:32 my father David not **k** *thereof, to wit,* H3045
Mt 9: 4 And Jesus **k** their thoughts said, G1492
22:29 **k** the scriptures, nor the power of God. G1492
Mk 5:30 And Jesus, immediately **k** in himself G1921
33 and trembling, **k** what was done in her, G1492
6:20 For Herod feared John, **k** that he was a G1492
12:15 not give? But he, **k** their hypocrisy, said G1492
Lk 8:53 And they laughed him to scorn, **k** that G1492
9:33 and one for Elias: not **k** what he said. G1492
11:17 But he, **k** their thoughts, said unto G1492
Jn 13: 3 Jesus **k** that the Father had given all G1492
18: 4 Jesus therefore, **k** all things that should G1492
19:28 After this, Jesus **k** that all things were G1492
21:12 Who art thou? **k** that it was the Lord. G1492
Act 2:30 Therefore being a prophet, and **k** that G1492
5: 7 his wife, not **k** what was done, came in. G1492
18:25 of the Lord, **k** only the baptism of John. G1987
20:22 **k** the things that shall befall me there: G1492
Ro 1:32 Who **k** the judgment of God, that they G1921
2: 4 longsuffering; not **k** that the goodness of G50
5: 3 **k** that tribulation worketh patience; G1492
6: 6 **K** this, that our old man is crucified G1097
9 **K** that Christ being raised from the G1492
13:11 And that, **k** the time, that now *it is* high G1492
2Co 1: 7 And our hope of you *is* stedfast, **k**, that G1492
4:14 **K** that he which raised up the Lord G1492
5: 6 Therefore *we are* always confident, **k** G1492
11 **K** therefore the terror of the Lord, we G1492
Gal 2:16 **K** that a man is not justified by the G1492
Eph 6: 8 **K** that whatsoever good thing any man G1492
9 threatening: **k** that your Master also G1492
Php 1:17 But the other of love, **k** that I am set for G1492
Col 3:24 **K** that of the Lord ye shall receive the G1492
4: 1 **k** that ye also have a Master in heaven. G1492
1Th 1: 4 **K**, brethren beloved, your election of G1492
1Ti 1: 9 **K** this, that the law is not made for a G1492
6: 4 He is proud, **k** nothing, but doting G1987
2Ti 2:23 avoid, **k** that they do gender strifes. G1492
3:14 of, **k** of whom thou hast learned *them*; G1492
Tit 3:11 **K** that he that is such is subverted, and G1492
Phlm 21 I wrote unto thee, **k** that thou wilt also G1492
Heb 10:34 of your goods, **k** in yourselves that ye G1097
11: 8 he went out, not **k** whither he went. G1987
Jas 1: 3 **K** *this*, that the trying of your faith G1097
3: 1 My brethren, be not many masters, **k** G1492
1Pt 3: 9 blessing; **k** that ye are thereunto G1492
5: 9 Whom resist stedfast in the faith, **k** G1492
2Pt 1:14 **K** that shortly I must put off *this* my G1492
20 **K** this first, that no prophecy of the G1097
3: 3 **K** this first, that there shall come in the G1097

KNOWLEDGE

Gen 2: 9 and the tree of **k** of good and evil. H1847
17 But of the tree of the **k** of good and evil, H1847
Ex 31: 3 **k**, and in all manner of workmanship, H1847
35:31 **k**, and in all manner of workmanship; H1847
Lev 4:23 sinned, come to his **k**; he shall bring his H3045
28 come to his **k**: then he shall bring H3045
Nu 15:24 without the **k** of the congregation, H5869
24:16 God, and knew the **k** of the most High, H1847
Dt 1:39 in that day had no **k** between good and H3045
Ru 2:10 take **k** of me, seeing I *am* a stranger? H5234
19 be he that did take **k** of thee. And she H5234
1Sa 2: 3 of **k**, and by him actions are weighed. H1844
23:23 See therefore, and take **k** of all the H3045
1Ki 9:27 shipmen that had **k** of the sea, with the H3045
2Ch 1:10 Give me now wisdom and **k**, that I may H4093
11 wisdom and **k** for thyself, that thou H4093
12 Wisdom and **k** *is* granted unto thee; H4093
8:18 servants that had **k** of the sea; and they H3045
30:22 taught the good **k** of the LORD: and H7922
Neh 10:28 having **k**, and having understanding; H3045
Job 15: 2 Should a wise man utter vain **k**, and fill H1847
21:14 us; for we desire not the **k** of thy ways. H1847
22 Shall *any* teach God **k**? seeing he H1847
33: 3 heart: and my lips shall utter **k** clearly. H1847
34: 2 and give ear unto me, ye that have **k**. H3045
35 Job hath spoken without **k**, and his H1847
35:16 in vain; he multiplieth words without **k**. H1847
36: 3 I will fetch my **k** from afar, and will H1843
4 false: he that is perfect in **k** *is* with thee. H1844
12 the sword, and they shall die without **k**. H1847
37:16 works of him which is perfect in **k**? H1843
38: 2 darkeneth counsel by words without **k**? H1847
42: 3 counsel without **k**? therefore have I H1847
Ps 14: 4 Have all the workers of iniquity no **k**? H3045
19: 2 speech, and night unto night sheweth **k**. H1847
53: 4 Have the workers of iniquity no **k**? who H3045
73:11 know? and is there **k** in the most High? H1844
94:10 that teacheth man **k**, *shall not he know*? H1847
119:66 Teach me good judgment and **k**: for I H1847
139: 6 *Such* **k** *is* too wonderful for me; it is H1847
144: 3 LORD, what *is* man, that thou takest **k** H3045
Prv 1: 4 to the young man **k** and discretion. H1847
7 *is* the beginning of **k**: *but* fools despise H1847
22 in their scorning, and fools hate **k**? H1847
29 For that they hated **k**, and did not H1847
2: 3 Yea, if thou criest after **k**, *and* liftest up H998
5 of the LORD, and find the **k** of God. H1847
6 mouth *cometh* **k** and understanding. H1847
10 heart, and **k** is pleasant unto thy soul; H1847
3:20 By his **k** the depths are broken up, and H1847
5: 2 and *that* thy lips may keep **k**. H1847
8: 9 and right to them that find **k**. H1847
10 silver; and **k** rather than choice gold. H1847
12 and find out **k** of witty inventions. H1847
9:10 and the **k** of the holy *is* understanding. H1847
10:14 Wise *men* lay up **k**: but the mouth of the H1847
11: 9 through **k** shall the just be delivered. H1847
12: 1 Whoso loveth instruction loveth **k**: but H1847
23 A prudent man concealeth **k**: but the H1847
13:16 Every prudent *man* dealeth with **k**: but H1847
14: 6 **k** *is* easy unto him that understandeth. H1847
7 thou perceivest not *in him* the lips of **k**. H1847
18 but the prudent are crowned with **k**. H1847
15: 2 The tongue of the wise useth **k** aright: H1847
7 The lips of the wise disperse **k**: but the H1847
14 seeketh **k**: but the mouth of fools H1847
17:27 He that hath **k** spareth his words: *and* H1847
18:15 The heart of the prudent getteth **k**; and H1847
15 and the ear of the wise seeketh **k**. H1847
19: 2 Also, *that* the soul *be* without **k**, *it is* not H1847
25 *and* he will understand **k**. H1847
27 *that causeth* to err from the words of **k**. H1847
20:15 but the lips of **k** *are* a precious jewel. H1847
21:11 the wise is instructed, he receiveth **k**. H1847
22:12 The eyes of the LORD preserve **k**, and H1847
17 wise, and apply thine heart unto my **k**. H1847
20 thee excellent things in counsels and **k**, H1847
23:12 and thine ears to the words of **k**. H1847
24: 4 And by **k** shall the chambers be filled H1847
5 A wise man *is* strong; yea, a man of **k** H1847
14 So *shall* the **k** of wisdom *be* unto thy H3045
28: 2 **k** the state *thereof* shall be prolonged. H3045
30: 3 wisdom, nor have the **k** of the holy. H1847
Ecc 1:16 had great experience of wisdom and **k**. H1847
18 he that increaseth **k** increaseth sorrow. H1847
2:21 in wisdom, and in **k**, and in equity; yet H1847
26 sight wisdom, and **k**, and joy: but to the H1847
7:12 but the excellency of **k** *is, that* wisdom H1847
9:10 nor device, nor **k**, nor wisdom, in the H1847
12: 9 taught the people **k**; yea, he gave good H1847
Isa 5:13 *they have* no **k**: and their honourable H1847
8: 4 For before the child shall have **k** to cry, H3045
11: 2 spirit of **k** and of the fear of the LORD; H1847
9 shall be full of the **k** of the LORD, as the H1844
28: 9 Whom shall he teach **k**? and whom shall H1844
32: 4 shall understand **k**, and the tongue of H1847
33: 6 And wisdom and **k** shall be the H1847
40:14 and taught him **k**, and shewed to him H1847
44:19 neither *is there* **k** nor understanding H1847
25 backward, and maketh their **k** foolish; H1847
45:20 they have no **k** that set up the wood H3045
47:10 wisdom and thy **k**, it hath perverted H1847
53:11 be satisfied: by his **k** shall my righteous H1847
58: 3 thou takest no **k**? Behold, in the day of H3045
Jer 3:15 feed you with **k** and understanding. H1844
4:22 do evil, but to do good they have no **k**. H3045
10:14 Every man is brutish in *his* **k**: every H1847
11:18 And the LORD hath given me **k** *of it*, H3045
51:17 Every man is brutish by *his* **k**; every H1847
Dan 1: 4 and cunning in **k**, and understanding H1847
17 God gave them **k** and skill in all H4093
2:21 **k** to them that know understanding: H4486
5:12 Forasmuch as an excellent spirit, and **k**, H4486
12: 4 to and fro, and **k** shall be increased. H1847
Hos 4: 1 nor mercy, nor **k** of God in the land. H1847
6 My people are destroyed for lack of **k**: H1847
6 thou hast rejected **k**, I will also reject H1847
6: 6 the **k** of God more than burnt offerings. H1847
Hab 2:14 For the earth shall be filled with the **k** H3045
Mal 2: 7 For the priest's lips should keep **k**, and H1847
Mt 14:35 And when the men of that place had **k** G1921
Lk 1:77 To give **k** of salvation unto his people G1108
11:52 away the key of **k**: ye entered not in G1108
Act 4:13 and they took **k** of them, that they had G1921
17:13 of Thessalonica had **k** that the word of G1097
24: 8 mayest take **k** of all these things, G1921
Act 24:22 more perfect **k** of *that* way, he deferred G1492
Ro 1:28 to retain God in *their* **k**, God gave them G1922
2:20 form of **k** and of the truth in the law. G1108
3:20 his sight: for by the law *is* the **k** of sin. G1922
10: 2 a zeal of God, but not according to **k**. G1922
11:33 both of the wisdom and **k** of God! how G1108
15:14 **k**, able also to admonish one another. G1108
1Co 1: 5 by him, in all utterance, and *in* all **k**; G1108
8: 1 that we all have **k**. Knowledge puffeth G1108
1 **K** puffeth up, but charity edifieth. G1108
7 not in every man that **k**: for some with G1108
10 For if any man see thee which hast **k** sit G1108
11 And through thy **k** shall the weak G1108
12: 8 the word of **k** by the same Spirit; G1108
13: 2 mysteries, and all **k**; and though I have G1108
8 whether *there be* **k**, it shall vanish away. G1108
14: 6 by **k**, or by prophesying, or by doctrine? G1108
15:34 **k** of God: I speak *this* to your shame. G2192
2Co 2:14 the savour of his **k** by us in every place. G1108
4: 6 the light of the **k** of the glory of God in G1108
6: 6 By pureness, by **k**, by longsuffering, by G1108
8: 7 utterance, and **k**, and *in* all diligence, G1108
10: 5 exalteth itself against the **k** of God, and G1108
11: 6 speech, yet not in **k**; but we have been G1108
Eph 1:17 wisdom and revelation in the **k** of him: G1922
3: 4 my **k** in the mystery of Christ) G4907
19 which passeth **k**, that ye might be filled G1108
4:13 faith, and of the **k** of the Son of God, G1922
Php 1: 9 and more in **k** and *in* all judgment; G1922
3: 8 excellency of the **k** of Christ Jesus my G1108
Col 1: 9 be filled with the **k** of his will in all G1922
10 work, and increasing in the **k** of God; G1922
2: 3 hid all the treasures of wisdom and **k**. G1108
3:10 is renewed in **k** after the image of him G1922
1Ti 2: 4 and to come unto the **k** of the truth. G1922
2Ti 3: 7 never able to come to the **k** of the truth. G1922
Heb 10:26 have received the **k** of the truth, there G1922
Jas 3:13 Who *is* a wise man and endued with **k** G1990
1Pt 3: 7 *them* according to **k**, giving honour G1108
2Pt 1: 2 the **k** of God, and of Jesus our Lord, G1922
3 through the **k** of him that hath called G1922
5 add to your faith virtue; and to virtue **k**; G1108
6 And to **k** temperance; and to G1108
8 in the **k** of our Lord Jesus Christ. G1922
2:20 the world through the **k** of the Lord and G1922
3:18 But grow in grace, and *in* the **k** of our G1108

KNOWN

Gen 19: 8 which have not **k** man; let me, I pray H3045
24:16 had any man **k** her: and she went down H3045
41:21 them up, it could not be **k** that they had H3045
31 And the plenty shall not be **k** in the H3045
45: 1 made himself **k** unto his brethren. H3045
Ex 2:14 feared, and said, Surely this thing is **k**. H3045
6: 3 name JEHOVAH was I not **k** to them. H3045
21:36 Or if it be **k** that the ox hath used to H3045
33:16 For wherein shall it be **k** here that I and H3045
Lev 4:14 against it, is **k**, then the congregation H3045
5: 1 he hath seen or **k** *of it*; if he do not utter H3045
Nu 12: 6 LORD will make myself **k** unto him in a H3045
31:17 that hath **k** man by lying with him. H3045
18 that have not **k** a man by lying with H3045
35 that had not **k** man by lying with him. H3045
Dt 1:13 and **k** among your tribes, H3045
15 wise men, and **k**, and made them heads H3045
11: 2 which have not **k**, and which have not H3045
28 after other gods, which ye have not **k**. H3045
13: 2 thou hast not **k**, and let us serve them; H3045
6 thou hast not **k**, thou, nor thy fathers; H3045
13 serve other gods, which ye have not **k**; H3045
21: 1 *and* it be not **k** who hath slain him: H3045
28:36 thy fathers have **k**; and there shalt thou H3045
64 fathers have **k**, *even* wood and stone. H3045
31:13 which have not **k** *any thing*, may hear, H3045
Jos 24:31 and which had **k** all the works of the H3045
Jdg 3: 1 as had not **k** all the wars of Canaan; H3045
16: 9 the fire. So his strength was not **k**. H3045
21:12 virgins, that had **k** no man by lying H3045
Ru 3: 3 make not thyself **k** unto the man, until H3045
14 be **k** that a woman came into the floor. H3045
1Sa 6: 3 and it shall be **k** to you why his hand H3045
28:15 make **k** unto me what I shall do. H3045
2Sa 17:19 corn thereon; and the thing was not **k**. H3045
1Ki 14: 2 that thou be not **k** to be the wife of H3045
18:36 of Israel, let it be **k** this day that thou H3045
1Ch 16: 8 make **k** his deeds among the people. H3045
17:19 in making **k** all *these* great things. H3045
Ezr 4:12 Be it **k** unto the king, that the Jews H3046
13 Be it **k** now unto the king, that, if this H3046

Ezr 5: 8 Be it **k** unto the king, that we went into H3046
Neh 4:15 heard that it was **k** unto us, and God H3045
9:14 And madest **k** unto them thy holy H3045
Est 2:22 And the thing was **k** to Mordecai, who H3045
Ps 9:16 The LORD is **k** *by* the judgment *which* H3045
18:43 *whom* I have not **k** shall serve me. H3045
31: 7 thou hast **k** my soul in adversities; H3045
48: 3 God is **k** in her palaces for a refuge. H3045
67: 2 That thy way may be **k** upon earth, thy H3045
69:19 Thou hast **k** my reproach, and my H3045
76: 1 In Judah *is* God **k**: his name *is* great in H3045
77:19 waters, and thy footsteps are not **k**. H3045
78: 3 Which we have heard and **k**, and our H3045
5 should make them **k** to their children: H3045
79: 6 that have not **k** thee, and upon the H3045
10 God? let him be **k** among the heathen H3045
88:12 Shall thy wonders be **k** in the dark? and H3045
89: 1 **k** thy faithfulness to all generations. H3045
91:14 on high, because he hath **k** my name. H3045
95:10 heart, and they have not **k** my ways: H3045
98: 2 The LORD hath made **k** his salvation: H3045
103: 7 He made **k** his ways unto Moses, his H3045
105: 1 make **k** his deeds among the people. H3045
106: 8 might make his mighty power to be **k**. H3045
119:79 and those that have **k** thy testimonies. H3045
152 Concerning thy testimonies, I have **k** of H3045
139: 1 O LORD, thou hast searched me, and **k** H3045
145:12 To make **k** to the sons of men his H3045
147:20 have not **k** them. Praise ye the LORD. H3045
Prv 1:23 you, I will make **k** my words unto you. H3045
10: 9 he that perverteth his ways shall be **k**. H3045
12:16 A fool's wrath is presently **k**: but a H3045
14:33 *which is* in the midst of fools is made **k**. H3045
20:11 Even a child is **k** by his doings, whether H5234
22:19 made **k** to thee this day, even to thee. H3045
31:23 Her husband is **k** in the gates, when he H3045
Ecc 5: 3 a fool's voice *is* **k** by multitude of words.
6: 5 seen the sun, nor **k** *any thing*: this hath H3045
10 already, and it is **k** that it *is* man: H3045
Isa 12: 5 things: this *is* **k** in all the earth. H3045
19:21 And the LORD shall be **k** to Egypt, and H3045
38:19 to the children shall make **k** thy truth. H3045
40:21 Have ye not **k**? have ye not heard? hath H3045
28 Hast thou not **k**? hast thou not heard, H3045
42:16 paths *that* they have not **k**: I will make H3045
44:18 They have not **k** nor understood: for he H3045
45: 4 thee, though thou hast not **k** me. H3045
5 girded thee, though thou hast not **k** me: H3045
61: 9 And their seed shall be **k** among the H3045
64: 2 boil, to make thy name **k** to thine H3045
66:14 of the LORD shall be **k** toward his H3045
Jer 4:22 they have not **k** me; they *are* sottish H3045
5: 5 for they have **k** the way of the LORD, H3045
9:16 their fathers have **k**: and I will send a H3045
19: 4 their fathers have **k**, nor the kings of H3045
28: 9 be **k**, that the LORD hath truly sent him. H3045
Lam 4: 8 coal; they are not **k** in the streets: their H5234
Ezk 20: 5 and made myself **k** unto them in the H3045
9 I made myself **k** unto them, in bringing H3045
32: 9 the countries which thou hast not **k**. H3045
35:11 and I will make myself **k** among them, H3045
36:32 the Lord GOD, be it **k** unto you: be H3045
38:23 and I will be **k** in the eyes of many H3045
39: 7 So will I make my holy name **k** in the H3045
Dan 2: 5 me: if ye will not make **k** unto me the H3046
9 But if ye will not make **k** unto me the H3046
15 Arioch made the thing **k** to Daniel. H3046
17 and made the thing **k** to Hananiah, H3046
23 and hast made **k** unto me now what H3046
23 *now* made **k** unto us the king's matter. H3046
25 **k** unto the king the interpretation. H3046
26 thou able to make **k** unto me the dream H3046
28 secrets, and maketh **k** to the king H3046
29 **k** to thee what shall come to pass. H3046
30 that shall make **k** the interpretation to H3046
45 God hath made **k** to the king what shall H3046
3:18 But if not, be it **k** unto thee, O king, that H3046
4: 6 that they might make **k** unto me the H3046
7 **k** unto me the interpretation thereof. H3046
18 are not able to make **k** unto me the H3046
26 shalt have **k** that the heavens do rule. H3046
5: 8 **k** to the king the interpretation thereof. H3046
15 this writing, and make **k** unto me the H3046
16 the writing, and make **k** to me the H3046
17 and make **k** to him the interpretation. H3046
Hos 5: 4 of them, and they have not **k** the LORD. H3045
9 I made **k** that which shall surely be. H3045
Am 3: 2 You only have I **k** of all the families of H3045
Nah 3:17 and their place is not **k** where they *are*. H3045

Hab 3: 2 make **k**; in wrath remember mercy. H3045
Zec 14: 7 But it shall be one day which shall be **k** H3045
Mt 10:26 be revealed; and hid, that shall not be **k**. G1097
12: 7 But if ye had **k** what *this* meaneth, I G1097
16 them that they should not make him **k**: G5318
33 corrupt: for the tree is **k** by *his* fruit. G1097
24:43 of the house had **k** in what watch the G1492
Mk 3:12 them that they should not make him **k**. G5318
Lk 2:15 which the Lord hath made **k** unto us. G1107
17 seen *it*, they made **k** abroad the saying G1232
6:44 For every tree is **k** by his own fruit. For G1097
7:39 would have **k** who and what manner G1097
8:17 that shall not be **k** and come abroad. G1097
12: 2 neither hid, that shall not be **k**. G1097
39 of the house had **k** what hour the thief G1492
19:42 Saying, If thou hadst **k**, even thou, at G1097
24:18 and hast not **k** the things which are G1097
35 he was **k** of them in breaking of bread. G1097
Jn 7: 4 seeketh to be **k** openly. If thou do these
8:19 Father: if ye had **k** me, ye should have G1492
19 me, ye should have **k** my Father also. G1492
55 Yet ye have not **k** him; but I know him: G1097
10:14 and know my *sheep*, and am **k** of mine. G1097
14: 7 If ye had **k** me, ye should have known G1097
7 If ye had known me, ye should have **k** G1097
9 yet hast thou not **k** me, Philip? he that G1097
15:15 of my Father I have made **k** unto you. G1107
16: 3 they have not **k** the Father, nor me. G1097
17: 7 Now they have **k** that all things G1097
8 *them*, and have **k** surely that I came G1097
25 the world hath not **k** thee: but I have G1097
25 thee: but I have **k** thee, and these have G1097
25 these have **k** that thou hast sent me. G1097
18:15 that disciple was **k** unto the high priest, G1110
16 which was **k** unto the high priest, G1110
Act 1:19 And it was **k** unto all the dwellers at G1110
2:14 **k** unto you, and hearken to my words: G1110
28 Thou hast made **k** to me the ways of G1107
4:10 Be it **k** unto you all, and to all the G1110
7:13 Joseph was made **k** to his brethren; and G319
13 kindred was made **k** unto Pharaoh. G5318
9:24 But their laying await was **k** of Saul. G1097
42 And it was **k** throughout all Joppa; and G1110
13:38 Be it **k** unto you therefore, men *and* G1110
15:18 **K** unto God are all his works from the G1110
19:17 And this was **k** to all the Jews and G1110
22:30 because he would have **k** the certainty G1097
23:28 And when I would have **k** the cause G1097
28:28 Be it **k** therefore unto you, that the G1110
Ro 1:19 Because that which may be **k** of God is G1110
3:17 And the way of peace have they not **k**: G1097
7: 7 Nay, I had not **k** sin, but by the law: G1097
7 law: for I had not **k** lust, except the law G1492
9:22 and to make his power **k**, endured with G1107
23 And that he might make **k** the riches of G1107
11:34 For who hath **k** the mind of the Lord? G1097
16:26 God, made **k** to all nations for the G1107
1Co 2: 8 for had they **k** *it*, they would not have G1097
16 For who hath **k** the mind of the Lord, G1097
8: 3 But if any man love God, the same is **k** G1097
13:12 then shall I know even as also I am **k**. G1921
14: 7 shall it be **k** what is piped or harped? G1097
9 how shall it be **k** what is spoken? for G1097
2Co 3: 2 in our hearts, **k** and read of all men: G1097
5:16 though we have **k** Christ after the flesh, G1097
6: 9 As unknown, and *yet* well **k**; as dying, G1921
Gal 4: 9 But now, after that ye have **k** God, or G1097
9 God, or rather are **k** of God, how turn G1097
Eph 1: 9 Having made **k** unto us the mystery of G1107
3: 3 How that by revelation he made **k** unto G1107
5 Which in other ages was not made **k** G1107
10 *places* might be **k** by the church the G1107
6:19 to make **k** the mystery of the gospel, G1107
21 Lord, shall make **k** to you all things: G1107
Php 4: 5 Let your moderation be **k** unto all men. G1097
6 let your requests be made **k** unto God. G1107
Col 1:27 To whom God would make **k** what *is* G1107
4: 9 They shall make **k** unto you all things G1107
2Ti 3:10 But thou hast fully **k** my doctrine, G3877
15 And that from a child thou hast **k** the G1492
4:17 might be fully **k**, and *that* all the G4135
Heb 3:10 heart; and they have not **k** my ways. G1097
2Pt 1:16 when we made **k** unto you the power G1107
2:21 for them not to have **k** the way of G1921
21 after they have **k** *it*, to turn from the G1921
1Jn 2:13 because ye have **k** him *that is* from the G1097
13 children, because ye have **k** the Father. G1097
14 because ye have **k** him *that is* from the G1097
3: 6 hath not seen him, neither **k** him. G1097

1Jn 4:16 And we have **k** and believed the love G1097
2Jn 1 but also all they that have **k** the truth; G1097
Rev 2:24 which have not **k** the depths of Satan, G1097

KOA
Ezk 23:23 and Shoa, and K, *and* all the Assyrians H6970

KOHATH
Gen 46:11 And the sons of Levi; Gershon, K, and H6955
Ex 6:16 Gershon, and K, and Merari: and the H6955
18 And the sons of K; Amram, and Izhar, H6955
18 years of the life of K *were* an hundred H6955
Nu 3:17 names; Gershon, and K, and Merari. H6955
19 And the sons of K by their families; H6955
27 And of K *was* the family of the H6955
29 The families of the sons of K shall pitch H6955
4: 2 Take the sum of the sons of K from H6955
4 of the sons of K in the tabernacle of H6955
15 that, the sons of K shall come to bear H6955
15 of the sons of K in the tabernacle of H6955
7: 9 But unto the sons of K he gave none: H6955
16: 1 Izhar, the son of K, the son of Levi, and H6955
26:57 the Gershonites: of K, the family of the H6955
58 of the Korathites. And K begat Amram. H6955
Jos 21: 5 And the rest of the children of K *had* by H6955
20 And the families of the children of K, H6955
20 of the children of K, even they had the H6955
26 of the children of K that remained. H6955
1Ch 6: 1 The sons of Levi; Gershon, K, and H6955
2 And the sons of K; Amram, Izhar, and H6955
16 The sons of Levi; Gershom, K, and H6955
18 And the sons of K *were*, Amram, and H6955
22 The sons of K; Amminadab his son, H6955
38 The son of Izhar, the son of K, the son H6955
61 And unto the sons of K, *which were* left H6955
66 of the sons of K had cities of their H6955
70 family of the remnant of the sons of K. H6955
15: 5 Of the sons of K; Uriel the chief, and his H6955
23: 6 Levi, *namely*, Gershon, K, and Merari. H6955
12 The sons of K; Amram, Izhar, Hebron, H6955

KOHATHITES
Nu 3:27 these *are* the families of the K. H6956
30 K *shall be* Elizaphan the son of Uzziel. H6956
4:18 of the K from among the Levites: H6956
34 the sons of the K after their families, H6956
37 the families of the K, all that might do H6956
10:21 And the K set forward, bearing the H6956
26:57 the family of the K: of Merari, the H6956
Jos 21: 4 the families of the K: and the children H6956
10 of the families of the K, *who were* of the H6956
1Ch 6:33 Of the sons of the K: Heman a singer, H6956
54 families of the K: for theirs was the lot. H6956
9:32 of the sons of the K, *were* over the H6956
2Ch 20:19 of the children of the K, and of the H6956
29:12 of the sons of the K: and of the sons of H6956
34:12 of the sons of the K, to set *it* forward; H6956

KOLAIAH
Neh 11: 7 the son of K, the son of Maaseiah, H6964
Jer 29:21 of Ahab the son of K, and of Zedekiah H6964

KORAH
Gen 36: 5 and Jaalam, and K: these *are* the sons H7141
14 bare to Esau Jeush, and Jaalam, and K. H7141
16 Duke K, duke Gatam, *and* duke H7141
18 Jaalam, duke K: these *were* the dukes H7141
Ex 6:21 And the sons of Izhar; K, and Nepheg, H7141
24 And the sons of K; Assir, and Elkanah, H7141
Nu 16: 1 Now K, the son of Izhar, the son of H7141
5 And he spake unto K and unto all his H7141
6 This do; Take you censers, K, and all H7141
8 And Moses said unto K, Hear, I pray H7141
16 And Moses said unto K, Be thou and all H7141
19 And K gathered all the congregation H7141
24 tabernacle of K, Dathan, and Abiram. H7141
27 So they gat up from the tabernacle of K, H7141
32 *appertained* unto K, and all *their* goods. H7141
40 LORD; that he be not as K, and as his H7141
49 them that died about the matter of K. H7141
26: 9 K, when they strove against the LORD: H7141
10 up together with K, when that company H7141
11 Notwithstanding the children of K died H7141
27: 3 in the company of K; but died in his H7141
1Ch 1:35 Reuel, and Jeush, and Jaalam, and K. H7141
2:43 And the sons of Hebron; K, and H7141
6:22 his son, K his son, Assir his son, H7141
37 Assir, the son of Ebiasaph, the son of K, H7141
9:19 the son of K, and his brethren, of H7141

Ps 42:ttl Musician, Maschil, for the sons of **K**. H7141
44:ttl To the chief Musician for the sons of **K**, H7141
45:ttl the sons of **K**, Maschil, A Song of loves. H7141
46:ttl To the chief Musician for the sons of **K**, H7141
47:ttl Musician, A Psalm for the sons of **K**. H7141
48:ttl A Song *and* Psalm for the sons of **K**. H7141
49:ttl Musician, A Psalm for the sons of **K**. H7141
84:ttl upon Gittith, A Psalm for the sons of **K**. H7141
85:ttl Musician, A Psalm for the sons of **K**. H7141
87:ttl A Psalm *or* Song for the sons of **K**. H7141
88:ttl A Song or Psalm for the sons of **K**, to H7141

KORAHITE
1Ch 9:31 of Shallum the **K**, had the set office over H7145

KORAHITES
1Ch 9:19 of his father, the **K**, *were* over the work H7145

KORATHITES
Nu 26:58 of the **K**. And Kohath begat Amram. H7145

KORE
1Ch 9:19 And Shallum the son of **K**, the son of H6981
26: 1 the son of **K**, of the sons of Asaph. H6981
19 of **K**, and among the sons of Merari. H7145
2Ch 31:14 And **K** the son of Imnah the Levite, the H6981

KORHITES
Ex 6:24 these *are* the families of the **K**. H7145
1Ch 12: 6 and Joezer, and Jashobeam, the **K**, H7145
26: 1 the porters: Of the **K** *was* Meshelemiah H7145
2Ch 20:19 the children of the **K**, stood up to praise H7145

KOZ
Ezr 2:61 the children of **K**, the children of H6976
Neh 3: 4 of Urijah, the son of **K**. And next unto H6976
21 Urijah the son of **K** another piece, from H6976
7:63 the children of **K**, the children of H6976

KUSHAIAH
1Ch 15:17 their brethren, Ethan the son of **K**; H6984

L

LAADAH
1Ch 4:21 father of Lecah, and **L** the father of H3935

LAADAN
1Ch 7:26 **L** his son, Ammihud his son, Elishama H3936
23: 7 Of the Gershonites *were*, **L**, and Shimei. H3936
8 The sons of **L**; the chief *was* Jehiel, and H3936
9 These *were* the chief of the fathers of **L**. H3936
26:21 *As concerning* the sons of **L**; the sons of H3936
21 of the Gershonite **L**, chief fathers, *even* H3936
21 *even* of **L** the Gershonite, *were* Jehieli. H3936

LABAN
Gen 24:29 and his name *was* **L**: and Laban ran out H3837
29 **L** ran out unto the man, unto the well. H3837
50 Then **L** and Bethuel answered and H3837
25:20 Padan-aram, the sister to **L** the Syrian. H3837
27:43 flee thou to **L** my brother to Haran; H3837
28: 2 daughters of **L** thy mother's brother. H3837
5 Padan-aram unto **L**, son of Bethuel the H3837
29: 5 And he said unto them, Know ye **L** the H3837
10 the daughter of **L** his mother's brother, H3837
10 and the sheep of **L** his mother's H3837
10 the flock of **L** his mother's brother. H3837
13 And it came to pass, when **L** heard the H3837
13 house. And he told **L** all these things. H3837
14 And **L** said to him, Surely thou *art* my H3837
15 And **L** said unto Jacob, Because thou H3837
16 And **L** had two daughters: the name of H3837
19 And **L** said, *It is* better that I give her to H3837
21 And Jacob said unto **L**, Give *me* my H3837
22 And **L** gathered together all the men of H3837
24 And **L** gave unto his daughter Leah H3837
25 and he said to **L**, What *is* this thou hast H3837
26 And **L** said, It must not be so done in H3837
29 And **L** gave to Rachel his daughter H3837
30:25 Jacob said unto **L**, Send me away, that H3837
27 And **L** said unto him, I pray thee, if I H3837
34 And **L** said, Behold, I would it might be H3837
40 in the flock of **L**; and he put his own H3837
31: 2 And Jacob beheld the countenance of **L**, H3837
12 I have seen all that **L** doeth unto thee. H3837
19 And **L** went to shear his sheep: and H3837
20 And Jacob stole away unawares to **L** H3837
22 And it was told **L** on the third day that H3837
24 And God came to **L** the Syrian in a H3837
25 Then **L** overtook Jacob. Now Jacob had H3837
25 in the mount: and **L** with his brethren H3837
26 And **L** said to Jacob, What hast thou H3837
31 And Jacob answered and said to **L**, H3837
33 And **L** went into Jacob's tent, and into H3837
34 sat upon them. And **L** searched all the H3837
36 and chode with **L**: and Jacob answered H3837
36 and said to **L**, What *is* my trespass? H3837
43 And **L** answered and said unto Jacob, H3837
47 And **L** called it Jegar-sahadutha: but H3837
48 And **L** said, This heap *is* a witness H3837
51 And **L** said to Jacob, Behold this heap, H3837
55 And early in the morning **L** rose up, H3837
55 and blessed them: and **L** departed, and H3837
32: 4 with **L**, and stayed there until now: H3837
46:18 These *are* the sons of Zilpah, whom **L** H3837
25 These *are* the sons of Bilhah, which **L** H3837
Dt 1: 1 and **L**, and Hazeroth, and Dizahab. H3837

LABAN'S
Gen 30:36 and Jacob fed the rest of **L** flocks. H3837
30:40 and put them not unto **L** cattle. H3837
42 feebler were **L**, and the stronger Jacob's. H3837
31: 1 And he heard the words of **L** sons, H3837

LABOUR
Gen 31:42 affliction and the **l** of my hands, and H3018
35:16 Rachel travailed, and she had hard **l**. H3205
17 she was in hard **l**, that the midwife said H3205
Ex 5: 9 that they may **l** therein; and let them H6213
20: 9 Six days shalt thou **l**, and do all thy H5647
Dt 5:13 Six days thou shalt **l**, and do all thy H5647
26: 7 and our **l**, and our oppression: H5999
Jos 7: 3 people to **l** thither; for they *are but* few. H3021
24:13 which ye did not **l**, and cities which ye H3021
Neh 4:22 may be a guard to us, and **l** on the day. H4399
5:13 and from his **l**, that performeth not H3018
Job 9:29 *If* I be wicked, why then **l** I in vain? H3021
39:11 *is* great? or wilt thou leave thy **l** to him? H3018
16 not hers: her **l** is in vain without fear; H3018
Ps 78:46 caterpiller, and their **l** unto the locust. H3018
90:10 *is* their strength **l** and sorrow; for it is H5999
104:23 his work and to his **l** until the evening. H5656
105:44 and they inherited the **l** of the people; H5999
107:12 their heart with **l**; they fell down, and H5999
109:11 he hath; and let the strangers spoil his **l**. H3018
127: 1 the house, they **l** in vain that build it: H5998
128: 2 For thou shalt eat the **l** of thine hands: H3018
144:14 *That* our oxen *may be* strong to **l**; *that* H5445
Prv 10:16 The **l** of the righteous *tendeth* to life: H6468
13:11 he that gathereth by **l** shall increase. H3027
14:23 In all **l** there is profit: but the talk of the H6089
21:25 killeth him; for his hands refuse to **l**. H6213
23: 4 **L** not to be rich: cease from thine own H3021
Ecc 1: 3 What profit hath a man of all his **l** H5999
8 All things *are* full of **l**; man cannot utter H3023
2:10 rejoiced in all my **l**: and this was my H5999
10 and this was my portion of all my **l**. H5999
11 and on the **l** that I had laboured H5999
18 Yea, I hated all my **l** which I had taken H5999
19 have rule over all my **l** wherein I have H5999
20 of all the **l** which I took under the sun. H5999
21 For there is a man whose **l** *is* in H5999
22 For what hath man of all his **l**, and of H5999
24 enjoy good in his **l**. This also I saw, that H5999
3:13 the good of all his **l**, it *is* the gift of God. H5999
4: 8 no end of all his **l**; neither is his eye H5999
8 *he*, For whom do I **l**, and bereave my H6001
9 they have a good reward for their **l**. H5999
5:15 **l**, which he may carry away in his hand. H5999
18 enjoy the good of all his **l** that he taketh H5999
19 to rejoice in his **l**; this *is* the gift of God. H5999
6: 7 All the **l** of man *is* for his mouth, and H5999
8:15 with him of his **l** the days of his life, H5999
17 though a man **l** to seek *it* out, yet he H5998
9: 9 thy **l** which thou takest under the sun. H5999
10:15 The **l** of the foolish wearieth every one H5999
Isa 22: 4 I will weep bitterly, **l** not to comfort me, H213
45:14 Thus saith the LORD, The **l** of Egypt, H3018
55: 2 not bread? and your **l** for *that which* H3018
65:23 They shall not **l** in vain, nor bring forth H3021
Jer 3:24 For shame hath devoured the **l** of our H3018
20:18 of the womb to see **l** and sorrow, that H5999
51:58 the people shall **l** in vain, and the folk H3021
Lam 5: 5 Our necks *are* under persecution: we **l**, H3021
Ezk 23:29 take away all thy **l**, and shall leave thee H3018
29:20 of Egypt *for* his **l** wherewith he served H6468
Mic 4:10 Be in pain, and **l** to bring forth, O H1518
Hab 2:13 the people shall **l** in the very fire, and H3021
Hab 3:17 *be* in the vines; the **l** of the olive shall H4639
Hag 1:11 cattle, and upon all the **l** of the hands. H3018
Mt 11:28 Come unto me, all *ye* that **l** and are *G2872*
Jn 4:38 ye bestowed no **l**: other men laboured, *G2872*
6:27 **L** not for the meat which perisheth, but *G2038*
Ro 16: 6 Greet Mary, who bestowed much **l** on *G2872*
12 Salute Tryphena and Tryphosa, who **l** *G2872*
1Co 3: 8 his own reward according to his own **l**. *G2873*
4:12 And **l**, working with our own hands: *G2872*
15:58 that your **l** is not in vain in the Lord. *G2873*
2Co 5: 9 Wherefore we **l**, that, whether present *G5389*
Gal 4:11 lest I have bestowed upon you **l** in vain. *G2872*
Eph 4:28 but rather let him **l**, working with *his* *G2872*
Php 1:22 my **l**: yet what I shall choose I wot not. *G2041*
2:25 and companion in **l**, and fellowsoldier, *G4904*
Col 1:29 Whereunto I also **l**, striving according *G2872*
1Th 1: 3 your work of faith, and **l** of love, and *G2873*
2: 9 For ye remember, brethren, our **l** and *G2873*
3: 5 have tempted you, and our **l** be in vain. *G2873*
5:12 to know them which **l** among you, and *G2872*
2Th 3: 8 but wrought with **l** and travail night *G2873*
1Ti 4:10 For therefore we both **l** and suffer *G2872*
5:17 they who **l** in the word and doctrine. *G2872*
Heb 4:11 Let us **l** therefore to enter into that rest, *G4704*
6:10 your work and **l** of love, which ye have *G2873*
Rev 2: 2 I know thy works, and thy **l**, and thy *G2873*

LABOURED
Neh 4:21 So we **l** in the work: and half of them H6213
Job 20:18 That which he **l** for shall he restore, H3022
Ecc 2:11 labour that I had **l** to do: and, behold, H5998
19 wherein I have **l**, and wherein I have H5998
21 a man that hath not **l** therein shall he H5998
22 heart, wherein he hath **l** under the sun? H6001
5:16 profit hath he that hath **l** for the wind? H5998
Isa 47:12 wherein thou hast **l** from thy youth; if H3021
15 whom thou hast **l**, *even* thy merchants, H3021
49: 4 Then I said, I have **l** in vain, I have H3021
62: 8 thy wine, for the which thou hast **l**: H3021
Dan 6:14 him: and he **l** till the going down of H7712
Jna 4:10 thou hast not **l**, neither madest it grow; H5998
Jn 4:38 **l**, and ye are entered into their labours. *G2872*
Ro 16:12 Persis, which **l** much in the Lord. *G2872*
1Co 15:10 not in vain; but I **l** more abundantly *G2872*
Php 2:16 I have not run in vain, neither **l** in vain. *G2872*
4: 3 women which **l** with me in the gospel, *G4866*
Rev 2: 3 sake hast **l**, and hast not fainted. *G2872*

LABOURER
Lk 10: 7 they give: for the **l** is worthy of his hire. *G2040*
1Ti 5:18 And, The **l** *is* worthy of his reward. *G2040*

LABOURERS
Mt 9:37 truly *is* plenteous, but the **l** *are* few; *G2040*
38 he will send forth **l** into his harvest. *G2040*
20: 1 the morning to hire **l** into his vineyard. *G2040*
2 And when he had agreed with the **l** for *G2040*
8 steward, Call the **l**, and give them *their* *G2040*
Lk 10: 2 truly *is* great, but the **l** *are* few: pray ye *G2040*
2 he would send forth **l** into his harvest. *G2040*
1Co 3: 9 For we are **l** together with God: ye are *G4904*
Jas 5: 4 Behold, the hire of the **l** who have *G2040*

LABOURETH
Prv 16:26 He that **l** laboureth for himself; for his H6001
26 He that laboureth **l** for himself; for his H5998
Ecc 3: 9 he that worketh in that wherein he **l**? H6001
1Co 16:16 to every one that helpeth with *us*, and **l**. *G2872*

2Ti 2: 6 The husbandman that l must be first G2872

LABOURING
Ecc 5:12 The sleep of a l man *is* sweet, whether H5647
Act 20:35 how that so l ye ought to support G2872
Col 4:12 you, always l fervently for you in G75
1Th 2: 9 labour and travail: for l night and day, G2873

LABOURS
Ex 23:16 firstfruits of thy l, which thou hast sown H4639
16 hast gathered in thy l out of the field. H4639
Dt 28:33 The fruit of thy land, and all thy l, shall H3018
Prv 5:10 and thy l *be* in the house of a stranger; H6089
Isa 58: 3 ye find pleasure, and exact all your l. H6092
Jer 20: 5 city, and all the l thereof, and all the H3018
Hos 12: 8 *in* all my l they shall find none H3018
Hag 2:17 with hail in all the l of your hands; yet H4639
Jn 4:38 and ye are entered into their l. G2873
2Co 6: 5 tumults, in l, in watchings, in fastings; G2873
10:15 *is*, of other men's l; but having hope, G2873
11:23 fool) I *am* more; in l more abundant, in G2873
Rev 14:13 their l; and their works do follow them. G2873

LACE
Ex 28:28 the ephod with a l of blue, that *it* may H6616
37 And thou shalt put it on a blue l, that it H6616
39:21 the ephod with a l of blue, that it might H6616
31 And they tied unto it a l of blue, to H6616

LACHISH
Jos 10: 3 L, and unto Debir king of Eglon, saying, H3923
5 the king of L, the king of Eglon, H3923
23 the king of L, *and* the king of Eglon. H3923
31 Israel with him, unto L, and encamped H3923
32 And the LORD delivered L into the H3923
33 came up to help L; and Joshua smote H3923
34 And from L Joshua passed unto Eglon, H3923
35 according to all that he had done to L. H3923
12:11 The king of Jarmuth, one; the king of L, H3923
15:39 L, and Bozkath, and Eglon, H3923
2Ki 14:19 and he fled to L; but they sent after him H3923
19 sent after him to L, and slew him there. H3923
18:14 the king of Assyria to L, saying, I have H3923
17 Rab-shakeh from L to king Hezekiah H3923
19: 8 had heard that he was departed from L. H3923
2Ch 11: 9 And Adoraim, and L, and Azekah, H3923
25:27 and he fled to L: but they sent to H3923
27 sent to L after him, and slew him there. H3923
32: 9 *laid siege* against L, and all his power H3923
Neh 11:30 and *in* their villages, at L, and the fields H3923
Isa 36: 2 Rabshakeh from L to Jerusalem unto H3923
37: 8 had heard that he was departed from L. H3923
Jer 34: 7 that were left, against L, and against H3923
Mic 1:13 O thou inhabitant of L, bind the chariot H3923

LACK
Gen 18:28 Peradventure there shall l five of the H2637
28 all the city for *l of* five? And he said,
Ex 16:18 little had no l; they gathered every H2637
Dt 8: 9 thou shalt not l any *thing* in it; a land H2637
Job 4:11 The old lion perisheth for l of prey, and H1097
38:41 unto God, they wander for l of meat. H1097
Ps 34:10 The young lions do l, and suffer hunger: H7326
Prv 28:27 He that giveth unto the poor shall not l: H4270
Ecc 9: 8 white; and let thy head l no ointment. H2637
Hos 4: 6 My people are destroyed for l of H1097
Mt 19:20 I kept from my youth up: what l I yet? G5302
2Co 8:15 and he that *had gathered* little had no l. G1641
Php 2:30 to supply your l of service toward me. G5303
1Th 4:12 and *that* ye may have l of nothing. G5532
Jas 1: 5 If any of you l wisdom, let him ask of G3007

LACKED
Dt 2: 7 *been* with thee; thou hast l nothing. H2637
2Sa 2:30 together, there l of David's servants H6485
17:22 light there l not one of them that H5737
1Ki 4:27 every man in his month: they l nothing. H5737
11:22 what hast thou l with me, that, behold, H2638
Neh 9:21 *so that* they l nothing; their clothes H2637
Lk 8: 6 it withered away, because it l moisture. G3361
22:35 l ye any thing? And they said, Nothing. G5302
Act 4:34 among them that l: for as many as were G1729
1Co 12:24 abundant honour to that *part* which l: G5302
Php 4:10 were also careful, but ye l opportunity. G170

LACKEST
Mk 10:21 him, One thing thou l: go thy way, sell G5302
Lk 18:22 said unto him, Yet l thou one thing: sell G3007

LACKETH
Nu 31:49 charge, and there l not one man of us. H6485
2Sa 3:29 falleth on the sword, or that l bread. H2638
Prv 6:32 with a woman l understanding: he *that* H2638
12: 9 he that honoureth himself, and l bread. H2638
2Pt 1: 9 But he that l these things is blind, and G3361

LACKING
Lev 2:13 of thy God to be l from thy meat H7673
22:23 thing superfluous or l in his parts, that H7038
Jdg 21: 3 should be to day one tribe l in Israel? H6485
1Sa 30:19 And there was nothing l to them, H5737
Jer 23: 4 neither shall they be l, saith the LORD. H6485
1Co 16:17 was l on your part they have supplied. G5303
2Co 11: 9 for that which was l to me the brethren G5303
1Th 3:10 perfect that which is l in your faith? G5303

LAD
Gen 21:12 because of the l, and because of thy H5288
17 And God heard the voice of the l; and H5288
17 heard the voice of the l where he *is*. H5288
18 Arise, lift up the l, and hold him in thine H5288
19 bottle with water, and gave the l drink. H5288
20 And God was with the l; and he grew, H5288
22: 5 ass; and I and the l will go yonder and H5288
12 hand upon the l, neither do thou any H5288
37: 2 brethren; and the l *was* with the sons of H5288
43: 8 father, Send the l with me, and we will H5288
44:22 And we said unto my lord, The l H5288
30 my father, and the l *be* not with us; H5288
31 he seeth that the l *is* not *with us*, that H5288
32 For thy servant became surety for the l H5288
33 instead of the l a bondman to my lord; H5288
33 and let the l go up with his brethren. H5288
34 to my father, and the l *be* not with me? H5288
Jdg 16:26 And Samson said unto the l that held H5288
1Sa 20:21 And, behold, I will send a l, *saying*, Go, H5288
21 say unto the l, Behold, the arrows *are* H5288
35 with David, and a little l with him. H5288
36 And he said unto his l, Run, find out H5288
36 the l ran, he shot an arrow beyond him. H5288
37 And when the l was come to the place H5288
37 cried after the l, and said, *Is* not the H5288
38 And Jonathan cried after the l, Make H5288
38 not. And Jonathan's l gathered up the H5288
39 But the l knew not any thing: only H5288
40 artillery unto his l, and said unto him, H5288
41 *And* as soon as the l was gone, David H5288
2Sa 17:18 Nevertheless a l saw them, and told H5288
2Ki 4:19 he said to a l, Carry him to his mother. H5288
Jn 6: 9 There is a l here, which hath five barley G3808

LADDER
Gen 28:12 And he dreamed, and behold a l set up H5551

LADE
Gen 45:17 This do ye; l your beasts, and go, H2943
1Ki 12:11 And now whereas my father did l you H6006
Lk 11:46 *ye* lawyers! for ye l men with burdens G5412

LADED
Gen 42:26 And they l their asses with the corn, H5375
44:13 Then they rent their clothes, and l H6006
Neh 4:17 with those that l, *every one* with one of H6006
Act 28:10 l *us* with such things as were necessary. G2007

LADEN
Gen 45:23 this *manner*; ten asses l with the good H5375
23 and ten she asses l with corn and bread H5375
1Sa 16:20 And Jesse took an ass *l* with bread, and
Isa 1: 4 Ah sinful nation, a people l with H3515
Mt 11:28 and are heavy l, and I will give you rest. G5412
2Ti 3: 6 l with sins, led away with divers lusts, G4987

LADETH
Hab 2: 6 to him that l himself with thick clay! H3513

LADIES
Jdg 5:29 Her wise l answered her, yea, she H8282
Est 1:18 *Likewise* shall the l of Persia and H8282

LADING
Neh 13:15 in sheaves, and l asses; as also wine, H6006
Act 27:10 of the l and ship, but also of our lives. G5414

LADS
Gen 48:16 all evil, bless the l; and let my name be H5288

LAD'S
Gen 44:30 that his life is bound up in the l life;

LADY
Isa 47: 5 no more be called, The l of kingdoms. H1404
7 And thou saidst, I shall be a l for ever: H1404
2Jn 1 The elder unto the elect l and her G2959
5 And now I beseech thee, l, not as G2959

LAEL
Nu 3:24 *shall be* Eliasaph the son of L. H3815

LAHAD
1Ch 4: 2 Ahumai, and L. These *are* the families H3855

LAHAI-ROI
Gen 24:62 well L; for he dwelt in the south country. H883
25:11 son Isaac; and Isaac dwelt by the well L. H883

LAHMAM
Jos 15:40 And Cabbon, and L, and Kithlish, H3903

LAHMI
1Ch 20: 5 son of Jair slew L the brother of Goliath H3902

LAID
Gen 9:23 a garment, and l *it* upon both their H7760
15:10 them in the midst, and l each piece one H5414
19:16 And while he lingered, the men l hold
22: 6 offering, and l *it* upon Isaac his son; H7760
9 an altar there, and l the wood in order, H6186
9 and l him on the altar upon the wood. H7760
30:41 that Jacob l the rods before the eyes H7760
38:19 And she arose, and went away, and l H5493
39:16 And she l up his garment by her, until H3241
41:48 land of Egypt, and l up the food in the H5414
48 about every city, l he up in the same. H5414
48:14 his right hand, and l *it* upon Ephraim's H7896
17 And when Joseph saw that his father l H7896
Ex 2: 3 she l *it* in the flags by the river's brink. H7760
5: 9 Let there more work be l upon the men, H3513
16:24 And they l it up till the morning, as H3241
34 l it up before the Testimony, to be kept. H3241
19: 7 of the people, and l before their faces H7760
21:30 If there be l on him a sum of money, H7896
30 of his life whatsoever is l upon him. H7896
24:11 of Israel he l not his hand: also they H7971
Lev 8:14 and his sons l their hands upon the H5564
18 l their hands upon the head of the ram. H5564
22 l their hands upon the head of the ram. H5564
Nu 16:18 fire in them, and l incense thereon, and H7760
17: 7 And Moses l up the rods before the H3241
21:30 and we have l them waste even unto
27:23 And he l his hands upon him, and gave H5564
Dt 26: 6 us, and l upon us hard bondage: H5414
29:22 which the LORD hath l upon it; H2470
32:34 *Is* not this l up in store with me, *and* H3617
34: 9 for Moses had l his hands upon him: H5564
Jos 2: 6 which she had l in order upon the roof.
8 And before they were l down, she came H7901
4: 8 they lodged, and l them down there. H3241
7:23 Israel, and l them out before the LORD. H3332
10:27 had been hid, and l great stones in the H7760
Jdg 9:24 and their blood be l upon Abimelech H7760
34 him, by night, and they l wait against
43 companies, and l wait in the field, and
48 and took it, and l *it* on his shoulder, H7760
16: 2 *him* in, and l wait for him all night
19:29 he took a knife, and l hold on his
Ru 3: 7 and uncovered his feet, and l her down. H7901
15 l *it* on her: and she went into the city. H7896
4:16 And Naomi took the child, and l it in H7896
1Sa 3: 2 time, when Eli *was* l down in his place, H7901
3 *was*, and Samuel was l down *to sleep*; H7901
6:11 And they l the ark of the LORD upon H7760
10:25 wrote *it* in a book, and l *it* up before the H3241
15: 2 to Israel, how he l *wait* for him in the H7760
5 And Saul came to a city of Amalek, and l
27 to go away, he l hold upon the skirt of
19:13 And Michal took an image, and l *it* in H7760
21:12 And David l up these words in his H7760
25:18 cakes of figs, and l *them* on asses. H7760
2Sa 13: 8 house; and he was l down. And she H7901
19 that *was* on her, and l her hand on her H7760
18:17 in the wood, and l a very great heap of H5324
1Ki 3:20 slept, and l it in her bosom, and H7901
20 and l her dead child in my bosom. H7901
6:37 house of the LORD l, in the month Zif: H3245
8:31 and an oath be l upon him to cause H5375

1Ki 13:29 man of God, and l it upon the ass, and H3241
30 And he l his carcase in his own grave; H3241
15:27 and all Israel l siege to Gibbethon.
16:34 build Jericho: he l the foundation thereof
17:19 he abode, and l him upon his own bed. H7901
18:33 in pieces, and l *him* on the wood, and H7760
19: 6 eat and drink, and l him down again. H7901
21: 4 fathers. And he l him down upon his H7901
2Ki 4:21 And she went up, and l him on the bed H7901
31 on before them, and l the staff upon the H7760
32 the child was dead, *and* l upon his bed. H7901
5:23 of garments, and l *them* upon two of H5414
9:25 the LORD l this burden upon him; H5375
11:16 And they l hands on her; and she went H7760
12:11 the LORD: and they l it out to the H3318
12 that was l out for the house to repair *it*. H3318
20: 7 and l *it* on the boil, and he recovered. H7760
17 thy fathers have l up in store unto this
2Ch 6:22 and an oath be l upon him to make H5375
7:22 land of Egypt, and l hold on other gods,
16:14 the city of David, and l him in the bed H7901
23:15 So they l hands on her; and when she H7760
24: 9 of God *l* upon Israel in the wilderness.
27 of the burdens *l* upon him, and the
29:23 and they l their hands upon them: H5564
31: 6 LORD their God, and l *them* by heaps. H5414
32: 9 (but he *himself l* siege against Lachish,
Ezr 3: 6 of the temple of the LORD was not *yet* l. H3245
10 And when the builders l the foundation
11 of the house of the LORD was l. H3245
12 of this house was l before their eyes, H3245
5: 8 and timber is l in the walls, and this H7761
16 Sheshbazzar, *and* l the foundation of H3052
6: 1 the treasures were l up in Babylon. H5182
3 thereof be strongly l; the height thereof H5446
Neh 3: 3 build, who *also* l the beams thereof, and
6 of Besodeiah; they l the beams thereof,
13: 5 aforetime they l the meat offerings, the H5414
Est 8: 7 because he l his hand upon the Jews. H7971
9:10 but on the spoil l they not their hand. H7971
15 but on the prey they l not their hand. H7971
16 but they l not their hands on the prey, H7971
10: 1 And the king Ahasuerus l a tribute H7760
Job 6: 2 my calamity l in the balances together! H5375
18:10 The snare *is* l for him in the ground, H2934
29: 9 The princes refrained talking, and l H7760
31: 9 *if* I have l wait at my neighbour's door;
38: 4 Where wast thou when I l the
5 Who hath l the measures thereof, if H7760
6 or who l the corner stone thereof; H3384
Ps 3: 5 I l me down and slept; I awaked; for H7901
21: 5 and majesty hast thou l upon him. H7737
31: 4 Pull me out of the net that they have l H2934
19 which thou hast l up for them that fear H6845
35:11 False witnesses did rise up; they l to my
49:14 Like sheep they are l in the grave; H8371
62: 9 *are* a lie: to be l in the balance, they H5927
79: 1 they have l Jerusalem on heaps. H7760
7 For they have devoured Jacob, and l
88: 6 Thou hast l me in the lowest pit, in H7896
89:19 and saidst, I have l help upon *one that* H7737
102:25 Of old hast thou l the foundation of the
104: 5 *Who* l the foundations of the earth, H3245
105:18 they hurt with fetters: he was l in iron: H935
119:30 thy judgments have I l *before me*. H7737
110 The wicked have l a snare for me: yet I H5414
139: 5 and before, and l thine hand upon me. H7896
141: 9 *which* they have l for me, and the gins H3369
142: 3 have they privily l a snare for me. H2934
Prv 13:22 wealth of the sinner *is* l up for the just. H6845
Song 7:13 I have l up for thee, O my beloved. H6845
Isa 6: 7 And he l *it* upon my mouth, and said, H5060
10:28 Michmash he hath l up his carriages: H6485
14: 8 l down, no feller is come up against us. H7901
15: 1 night Ar of Moab is l waste, *and* brought
1 Moab is l waste, *and* brought to silence;
7 which they have l up, shall they carry H6486
23: 1 of Tarshish; for it is l waste, so that there
14 of Tarshish: for your strength is l waste.
18 not be treasured nor l up; for her H2630
37:18 of Assyria have l waste all the nations,
39: 6 thy fathers have l up in store until this
42:25 it burned him, yet he l *it* not to heart. H7760
44:28 to the temple, Thy foundation shall be l. H3245
47: 6 hast thou very heavily l thy yoke. H3513
48:13 Mine hand also hath l the foundation of
51:13 the heavens, and l the foundations of the
23 and thou hast l thy body as the ground, H7760
53: 6 hath l on him the iniquity of us all. H6293

Isa 57:11 me, nor l *it* to thy heart? have H7760
64:11 and all our pleasant things are l waste.
Jer 4: 7 shall be l waste, without an inhabitant.
27:17 wherefore should this city be l waste?
36:20 the court, but they l up the roll in the H6485
50:24 I have l a snare for thee, and thou art
Lam 4:19 they l wait for us in the wilderness.
Ezk 4: 5 For I have l upon thee the years of their H5414
6: 6 the cities shall be l waste, and the high
6 your altars may be l waste and made
11: 7 whom ye have l in the midst of it, they H7760
12:20 inhabited shall be l waste, and the land
19: 7 palaces, and he l waste their cities; and
26: 2 I shall be replenished, *now* she is l waste:
29:12 among the cities *that are* l waste shall be
32:19 and be thou l with the uncircumcised. H7901
27 and they have l their swords under H5414
29 their might are l by *them that were* H5414
32 and he shall be l in the midst of the H7901
33:29 when I have l the land most desolate H5414
35:12 l desolate, they are given us to consume.
39:21 and my hand that I have l upon them. H7760
40:42 also they l the instruments wherewith H3240
Dan 6:17 And a stone was brought, and l upon H7761
Hos 11: 4 on their jaws, and I l meat unto them. H5186
Joel 1: 7 He hath l my vine waste, and barked H7760
17 the garners are l desolate, the barns are
Am 2: 8 down upon clothes l to pledge by every
7: 9 of Israel shall be l waste; and I will rise
Oba 7 *eat* thy bread have l a wound under H7760
13 calamity, nor have l *hands* on their H7971
Jna 3: 6 his throne, and he l his robe from him, H5674
Mic 5: 1 of troops: he hath l siege against us: H7760
Nah 3: 7 and say, Nineveh is l waste: who will
Hab 2:19 teach! Behold, it *is* l over with gold and H8610
Hag 2:15 before a stone was l upon a stone in the H7760
18 of the LORD'S temple was l, consider *it*. H3245
Zec 3: 9 For behold the stone that I have l H5414
4: 9 The hands of Zerubbabel have l the
7:14 for they l the pleasant land desolate. H7760
8: 9 was l, that the temple might be built. H3245
Mal 1: 3 And I hated Esau, and l his mountains H7760
Mt 3:10 And now also the axe is l unto the root G2749
8:14 his wife's mother l, and sick of a fever. G906
14: 3 For Herod had l hold on John, and took
18:28 pence: and he l hands on him, and took
19:15 And he l *his* hands on them, and G2007
26:50 and l hands on Jesus, and took him. G1911
55 in the temple, and ye l no hold on me. G2902
57 And they that had l hold on Jesus led
27:60 And l it in his own new tomb, which he G5087
Mk 6: 5 work, save that he l his hands upon a G2007
17 For Herod himself had sent forth and l
29 took up his corpse, and l it in a tomb. G5087
56 or country, they l the sick in the streets, G5087
7:30 out, and her daughter l upon the bed. G906
14:46 And they l their hands on him, and G1911
51 *body*; and the young men l hold on him:
15:46 in the linen, and l him in a sepulchre G2698
47 *mother* of Joses beheld where he was l. G5087
16: 6 behold the place where they l him. G5087
Lk 1:66 And all they that heard *them* l *them* up G5087
2: 7 clothes, and l him in a manger; because G347
3: 9 And now also the axe is l unto the root G2749
4:40 unto him; and he l his hands on every G2007
6:48 digged deep, and l the foundation on a G5087
12:19 hast much goods l up for many years; G2749
13:13 And he l *his* hands on her: and G2007
14:29 Lest haply, after he hath l the G5087
16:20 which was l at his gate, full of sores, G906
19:20 which I have kept l up in a napkin: G606
22 man, taking up that I l not down, and G5087
23:26 And as they led him away, they l hold
26 and on him they l the cross, that he G2007
53 it in linen, and l it in a sepulchre that G5087
53 stone, wherein never man before was l. G2749
55 the sepulchre, and how his body was l. G5087
24:12 the linen clothes l by themselves, and G2749
Jn 7:30 take him: but no man l hands on him, G1911
44 taken him; but no man l hands on him. G1911
8:20 and no man l hands on him; for his
11:34 And said, Where have ye l him? They G5087
41 the dead was l. And Jesus lifted up *his* G2749
13: 4 He riseth from supper, and l aside his G5087
19:41 sepulchre, wherein was never man yet l. G5087
42 There l they Jesus therefore because of G5087
20: 2 we know not where they have l him. G5087
13 and I know not where they have l him. G5087
15 hast l him, and I will take him away. G5087

Jn 21: 9 there, and fish l thereon, and bread. G1945
Act 3: 2 whom they l daily at the gate of the G5087
4: 3 And they l hands on them, and put G1911
35 And l *them* down at the apostles' feet: G5087
37 the money, and l *it* at the apostles' feet. G5087
5: 2 part, and l *it* at the apostles' feet. G5087
15 into the streets, and l *them* on beds and G5087
18 And l their hands on the apostles, and G1911
6: 6 had prayed, they l *their* hands on them. G2007
7:16 into Sychem, and l in the sepulchre G5087
58 and the witnesses l down their clothes at G659
8:17 Then l they *their* hands on them, and G2007
9:37 they l *her* in an upper chamber. G5087
13: 3 and prayed, and l *their* hands on them, G2007
29 from the tree, and l *him* in a sepulchre. G5087
36 l unto his fathers, and saw corruption: G4369
16:23 And when they had l many stripes G2007
19: 6 And when Paul had l *his* hands upon G2007
20: 3 when the Jews l wait for him, as he was G1096
21:27 up all the people, and l hands on him, G1911
23:29 to have nothing l to his charge worthy G1462
30 how that the Jews l wait for the man, I G2071
25: 7 round about, and l many and grievous G5342
16 concerning the crime l against him. G1462
27 to signify the crimes *l* against him.
28: 3 of sticks, and l *them* on the fire, there G2007
8 l his hands on him, and healed him. G2007
Ro 16: 4 Who have for my life l down their own G5294
1Co 3:10 I have l the foundation, and G5087
11 lay than that is l, which is Jesus Christ. G2749
9:16 of: for necessity is l upon me; yea, woe G1945
Col 1: 5 For the hope which is l up for you in G606
2Ti 4: 8 Henceforth there is l up for me a crown G606
16 *God* that it may not be l to their charge. G3049
Heb 1:10 And, Thou, Lord, in the beginning hast l
1Jn 3:16 *of God*, because he l down his life for G5087
Rev 1:17 as dead. And he l his right hand upon G2007
20: 2 And he l hold on the dragon, that old

LAIDST

Ps 66:11 Thou broughtest us into the net; thou l H7760

LAIN

Nu 5:19 If no man have l with thee, and if thou H7901
20 man have l with thee beside H5414+H7903
Jdg 21:11 woman that hath l by man. H3045+H4904
Job 3:13 For now should I have l still and been H7901
Jn 11:17 he had *l* in the grave four days already.
20:12 the feet, where the body of Jesus had l. G2749

LAISH

Jdg 18: 7 and came to L, and saw the people H3919
14 out the country of L, and said unto their H3919
27 and came unto L, unto a people *that* H3919
29 the name of the city *was* L at the first. H3919
1Sa 25:44 the son of L, which *was* of Gallim. H3919
2Sa 3:15 *even* from Phaltiel the son of L. H3919
Isa 10:30 it to be heard unto L, O poor Anathoth. H3919

LAKE

Lk 5: 1 of God, he stood by the l of Gennesaret, G3041
2 And saw two ships standing by the l: G3041
8:22 side of the l. And they launched forth. G3041
23 of wind on the l; and they were filled G3041
33 steep place into the l, and were choked. G3041
Rev 19:20 into a l of fire burning with brimstone. G3041
20:10 them was cast into the l of fire and G3041
14 And death and hell were cast into the l G3041
15 book of life was cast into the l of fire. G3041
21: 8 their part in the l which burneth with G3041

LAKUM

Jos 19:33 and Jabneel, unto L; and the outgoings H3946

LAMA

Mt 27:46 saying, Eli, Eli, l sabachthani? that is G2982
Mk 15:34 saying, Eloi, Eloi, l sabachthani? which G2982

LAMB

Gen 22: 7 but where *is* the l for a burnt offering? H7716
8 provide himself a l for a burnt offering: H7716
Ex 12: 3 to them every man a l, according to the H7716
3 house of *their* fathers, a l for an house: H7716
4 be too little for the l, let him and his H7716
4 eating shall make your count for the l. H7716
5 Your l shall be without blemish, a male H7716
21 out and take you a l according to your H6629
13:13 redeem with a l; and if thou wilt not H7716
29:39 The one l thou shalt offer in the H3532

Ex 29:39 and the other l thou shalt offer at even: H3532
40 And with the one l a tenth deal of flour H3532
41 And the other l thou shalt offer at even, H3532
34:20 redeem with a l: and if thou redeem H7716
Lev 3: 7 If he offer a l for his offering, then shall H3775
4:32 And if he bring a l for a sin offering, he H3532
35 as the fat of the l is taken away from H3775
5: 6 from the flock, a l or a kid of the goats, H3776
7 And if he be not able to bring a l, then H7716
9: 3 and a calf and a l, *both* of the first year, H3532
12: 6 she shall bring a l of the first year for a H3532
8 And if she be not able to bring a l, then H7716
14:10 and one ewe l of the first year without H3535
12 And the priest shall take one he l, and H3532
13 And he shall slay the l in the place H3532
21 then he shall take one l *for* a trespass H3532
24 And the priest shall take the l of the H3532
25 And he shall kill the l of the trespass H3532
17: 3 killeth an ox, or l, or goat, in the camp, H3775
22:23 Either a bullock or a l that hath any H7716
23:12 the sheaf an he l without blemish of the H3532
Nu 6:12 and shall bring a l of the first year for a H3532
14 the LORD, one he l of the first year H3532
14 and one ewe l of the first year without H3535
7:15 One young bullock, one ram, one l of H3532
21 One young bullock, one ram, one l of H3532
27 One young bullock, one ram, one l of H3532
33 One young bullock, one ram, one l of H3532
39 One young bullock, one ram, one l of H3532
45 One young bullock, one ram, one l of H3532
51 One young bullock, one ram, one l of H3532
57 One young bullock, one ram, one l of H3532
63 One young bullock, one ram, one l of H3532
69 One young bullock, one ram, one l of H3532
75 One young bullock, one ram, one l of H3532
81 One young bullock, one ram, one l of H3532
15: 5 the burnt offering or sacrifice, for one l. H3532
11 or for one ram, or for a l, or a kid. H7716
28: 4 The one l shalt thou offer in the H3532
4 and the other l shalt thou offer at even; H3532
7 of an hin for the one l: in the holy *place* H3532
8 And the other l shalt thou offer at even: H3532
13 offering unto one l; *for* a burnt offering H3532
14 *part* of an hin unto a l: this *is* the burnt H3532
21 for every l, throughout the seven lambs: H3532
29 A several tenth deal unto one l, H3532
29: 4 And one tenth deal for one l, H3532
10 A several tenth deal for one l, H3532
15 And a several tenth deal to each l of the H3532
1Sa 7: 9 And Samuel took a sucking l, and H2924
17:34 a bear, and took a l out of the flock: H7716
2Sa 12: 3 save one little ewe l, which he had H3535
4 the poor man's l, and dressed it for the H3535
6 And he shall restore the l fourfold, H3535
Isa 11: 6 The wolf also shall dwell with the l, and H3532
16: 1 Send ye the l to the ruler of the land H3733
53: 7 he is brought as a l to the slaughter, H7716
65:25 The wolf and the l shall feed together, H2924
66: 3 he that sacrificeth a l, *as if* he cut off a H7716
Jer 11:19 But I *was* like a l *or* an ox *that* is H3532
Ezk 45:15 And one l out of the flock, out of two H7716
46:13 the LORD *of* a l of the first year without H3532
15 Thus shall they prepare the l, and the H3532
Hos 4:16 will feed them as a l in a large place. H3532
Jn 1:29 saith, Behold the L of God, which taketh *G286*
36 he walked, he saith, Behold the L of God! *G286*
Act 8:32 and like a l dumb before his shearer, *G286*
1Pt 1:19 of a l without blemish and without spot: *G286*
Rev 5: 6 the elders, stood a L as it had been slain, *G721*
8 down before the L, having every one of *G721*
12 Saying with a loud voice, Worthy is the L *G721*
13 throne, and unto the L for ever and ever. *G721*
6: 1 And I saw when the L opened one of the *G721*
16 the throne, and from the wrath of the L: *G721*
7: 9 and before the L, clothed with white *G721*
10 sitteth upon the throne, and unto the L. *G721*
14 made them white in the blood of the L. *G721*
17 For the L which is in the midst of the *G721*
12:11 by the blood of the L, and by the word of *G721*
13: 8 L slain from the foundation of the world. *G721*
11 horns like a l, and he spake as a dragon. *G721*
14: 1 And I looked, and, lo, a L stood on the *G721*
4 they which follow the L whithersoever he *G721*
4 the firstfruits unto God and to the L. *G721*
10 holy angels, and in the presence of the L: *G721*
15: 3 and the song of the L, saying, Great and *G721*
17:14 These shall make war with the L, and the *G721*
14 with the Lamb, and the L shall overcome *G721*
19: 7 the marriage of the L is come, and his *G721*
Rev 19: 9 supper of the L. And he saith unto me, *G721*
21:14 the names of the twelve apostles of the L. *G721*
22 Almighty and the L are the temple of it. *G721*
23 lighten it, and the L *is* the light thereof. *G721*
22: 1 out of the throne of God and of the L. *G721*
3 of God and of the L shall be in it; and his *G721*

LAMBS

Gen 21:28 And Abraham set seven ewe l of the H3535
29 l which thou hast set by themselves? H3535
30 And he said, For *these* seven ewe l shalt H3535
30:40 And Jacob did separate the l, and set H3775
Ex 29:38 the altar; two l of the first year day H3532
Lev 14:10 he shall take two he l without blemish, H3532
23:18 the bread seven l without blemish of H3532
19 offering, and two l of the first year for a H3532
20 with the two l: they shall be holy to H3532
Nu 7:17 five he goats, five l of the first year: this H3532
23 five he goats, five l of the first year: this H3532
29 five he goats, five l of the first year: this H3532
35 five he goats, five l of the first year: this H3532
41 five he goats, five l of the first year: this H3532
47 five he goats, five l of the first year: this H3532
53 five he goats, five l of the first year: this H3532
59 five he goats, five l of the first year: this H3532
65 five he goats, five l of the first year: this H3532
71 five he goats, five l of the first year: this H3532
77 five he goats, five l of the first year: this H3532
83 five he goats, five l of the first year: this H3532
87 the rams twelve, the l of the first year H3532
88 the he goats sixty, the l of the first year H3532
28: 3 unto the LORD; two l of the first year H3532
9 And on the sabbath day two l of the H3532
11 seven l of the first year without spot; H3532
19 ram, and seven l of the first year: they H3532
21 for every lamb, throughout the seven l: H3532
27 one ram, seven l of the first year; H3532
29 unto one lamb, throughout the seven l; H3532
29: 2 l of the first year without blemish: H3532
4 for one lamb, throughout the seven l: H3532
8 ram, *and* seven l of the first year; they H3532
10 for one lamb, throughout the seven l: H3532
13 *and* fourteen l of the first year; they H3532
15 deal to each lamb of the fourteen l: H3532
17 fourteen l of the first year without spot: H3532
18 rams, and for the l, *shall be* according H3532
20 l of the first year without blemish; H3532
21 rams, and for the l, *shall be* according H3532
23 l of the first year without blemish: H3532
24 rams, and for the l, *shall be* according H3532
26 fourteen l of the first year without spot: H3532
27 rams, and for the l, *shall be* according H3532
29 l of the first year without blemish: H3532
30 rams, and for the l, *shall be* according H3532
32 l of the first year without blemish: H3532
33 rams, and for the l, *shall be* according H3532
36 l of the first year without blemish: H3532
37 ram, and for the l, *shall be* according to H3532
Dt 32:14 of sheep, with fat of l, and rams of the H3733
1Sa 15: 9 the fatlings, and the l, and all *that was* H3733
2Ki 3: 4 hundred thousand l, and an hundred H3733
1Ch 29:21 *and* a thousand l, with their drink H3532
2Ch 29:21 rams, and seven l, and seven he goats, H3532
22 they killed also the l, and they sprinkled H3532
32 *and* two hundred l: all these *were* for a H3532
35: 7 of the flock, l and kids, all for the H3532
Ezr 6: 9 and rams, and l, for the burnt offerings H563
17 four hundred l; and for a sin offering H563
7:17 money bullocks, rams, l, with their meat H563
8:35 seventy and seven l, twelve he goats *for* H3532
Ps 37:20 *be* as the fat of l: they shall consume; H3733
114: 4 rams, *and* the little hills like l. H1121+H6629
6 rams; *and* ye little hills, like l? H1121+H6629
Prv 27:26 The l *are* for thy clothing, and the goats H3532
Isa 1:11 blood of bullocks, or of l, or of he goats. H3532
5:17 Then shall the l feed after their H3532
34: 6 with the blood of l and goats, with the H3733
40:11 he shall gather the l with his arm, and H2922
Jer 51:40 I will bring them down like l to the H3733
Ezk 27:21 with thee in l, and rams, and goats: H3733
39:18 the earth, of rams, of l, and of goats, of H3733
46: 4 day *shall be* six l without blemish, and H3532
5 offering for the l as he shall be able to H3532
6 blemish, and six l, and a ram: they shall H3532
7 a ram, and for the l according as his H3532
11 a ram, and to the l as he is able to give, H3532
Am 6: 4 and eat the l out of the flock, and H3733
Lk 10: 3 I send you forth as l among wolves. *G704*
Jn 21:15 I love thee. He saith unto him, Feed my l. *G721*

LAMB'S

Rev 21: 9 I will shew thee the bride, the L wife. *G721*
27 which are written in the L book of life. *G721*

LAME

Lev 21:18 a blind man, or a l, or he that hath a flat H6455
Dt 15:21 therein, *as if it be* l, or blind, *or have* H6455
2Sa 4: 4 had a son *that was* l of *his* feet. He was H5223
4 l. And his name *was* Mephibosheth. H6452
5: 6 the blind and the l, thou shalt not come H6455
8 Jebusites, and the l and the blind, *that* H6455
8 and the l shall not come into the house. H6455
9: 3 hath yet a son, *which is* l on *his* feet. H5223
13 king's table; and was l on both his feet. H6455
19:26 go to the king; because thy servant *is* l. H6455
Job 29:15 eyes to the blind, and feet *was* I to the l. H6455
Prv 26: 7 The legs of the l are not equal: so *is* a H6455
Isa 33:23 great spoil divided; the l take the prey. H6455
35: 6 Then shall the l *man* leap as an hart, H6455
Jer 31: 8 the blind and the l, the woman with H6455
Mal 1: 8 and if ye offer the l and sick, *is it* not H6455
13 *was* torn, and the l, and the sick; thus ye H6455
Mt 11: 5 The blind receive their sight, and the l *G5560*
15:30 them *those that were* l, blind, dumb, *G5560*
31 to be whole, the l to walk, and the blind *G5560*
21:14 And the blind and the l came to him in *G5560*
Lk 7:22 the blind see, the l walk, the lepers are *G5560*
14:13 the poor, the maimed, the l, the blind: *G5560*
Act 3: 2 And a certain man l from his mother's *G5560*
11 And as the l man which was healed *G5560*
8: 7 palsies, and that were l, were healed. *G5560*
Heb 12:13 lest that which is l be turned out of the *G5560*

LAMECH

Gen 4:18 Methusael: and Methusael begat L. H3929
19 And L took unto him two wives: the H3929
23 And L said unto his wives, Adah and H3929
23 voice; ye wives of L, hearken unto my H3929
24 truly L seventy and sevenfold. H3929
5:25 eighty and seven years, and begat L: H3929
26 And Methuselah lived after he begat L H3929
28 And L lived an hundred eighty and two H3929
30 And L lived after he begat Noah five H3929
31 And all the days of L were seven H3929
1Ch 1: 3 Henoch, Methuselah, L, H3929
Lk 3:36 *the son* of Noe, which was *the son* of L, *G2984*

LAMENT

Jdg 11:40 Israel went yearly to l the daughter of H8567
Isa 3:26 And her gates shall l and mourn; and H578
19: 8 the brooks shall l, and they that spread H56
32:12 They shall l for the teats, for the H5594
Jer 4: 8 For this gird you with sackcloth, l and H5594
16: 5 neither go to l nor bemoan them: for H5594
6 neither shall *men* l for them, nor cut H5594
22:18 They shall not l for him, *saying*, Ah H5594
18 they shall not l for him, *saying*, Ah H5594
34: 5 for thee; and they will l thee, *saying*, Ah H5594
49: 3 with sackcloth; l, and run to and fro by H5594
Lam 2: 8 the wall to l; they languished together. H56
Ezk 27:32 for thee, and l over thee, *saying*, What H6969
32:16 they shall l her: the daughters of H6969
16 of the nations shall l her: they shall H6969
16 her: they shall l for her, *even* for Egypt, H6969
Joel 1: 8 L like a virgin girded with sackcloth for H421
13 Gird yourselves, and l, ye priests: howl, H5594
Mic 2: 4 against you, and l with a doleful H5091
Jn 16:20 ye shall weep and l, but the world shall *G2354*
Rev 18: 9 bewail her, and l for her, when they *G2875*

LAMENTABLE

Dan 6:20 he cried with a l voice unto Daniel: *and* H6088

LAMENTATION

Gen 50:10 great and very sore l: and he made a H4553
2Sa 1:17 And David lamented with this l over H7015
Ps 78:64 the sword; and their widows made no l. H1058
Jer 6:26 son, most bitter l: for the spoiler shall H4553
7:29 and take up a l on high places; for the H7015
9:10 of the wilderness a l, because they are H7015
20 wailing, and every one her neighbour l. H7015
31:15 heard in Ramah, l, *and* bitter weeping; H5092
48:38 *There shall be* l generally upon all the H4553
Lam 2: 5 in the daughter of Judah mourning and l. H592
Ezk 19: 1 Moreover take thou up a l for the H7015
14 *is* a l, and shall be for a lamentation. H7015
14 *is* a lamentation, and shall be for a l. H7015
26:17 And they shall take up a l for thee, and H7015
27: 2 Now, thou son of man, take up a l for H7015

Ezk 27:32 shall take up a l for thee, and lament H7015
28:12 Son of man, take up a l upon the king H7015
32: 2 Son of man, take up a l for Pharaoh H7015
16 This *is* the l wherewith they shall H7015
Am 5: 1 against you, *even* a l, O house of Israel. H7015
16 and such as are skilful of l to wailing. H5092
8:10 all your songs into l; and I will bring up H7015
Mic 2: 4 with a doleful l, *and* say, We be utterly H5092
Mt 2:18 In Rama was there a voice heard, l, and *G2355*
Act 8: 2 *his burial,* and made great l over him. *G2870*

LAMENTATIONS
2Ch 35:25 of Josiah in their l to this day, and H7015
25 and, behold, they *are* written in the l. H7015
Ezk 2:10 therein l, and mourning, and woe. H7015

LAMENTED
1Sa 6:19 and the people l, because the LORD had H56
7: 2 all the house of Israel l after the LORD. H5091
25: 1 together, and l him, and buried him H5594
28: 3 and all Israel had l him, and buried H5594
2Sa 1:17 And David l with this lamentation over H6969
3:33 And the king l over Abner, and said, H6969
2Ch 35:25 And Jeremiah l for Josiah: and all the H6969
Jer 16: 4 they shall not be l; neither shall they be H5594
25:33 they shall not be l, neither gathered, nor H5594
Mt 11:17 mourned unto you, and ye have not l. *G2875*
Lk 23:27 women, which also bewailed and l him. *G2354*

LAMP
Gen 15:17 l that passed between those pieces. H3940
Ex 27:20 the light, to cause the l to burn always. H5216
1Sa 3: 3 And ere the l of God went out in the H5216
2Sa 22:29 For thou *art* my l, O LORD: and the H5216
1Ki 15: 4 his God give him a l in Jerusalem, to set H5216
Job 12: 5 with *his* feet *is as* a l despised in the H3940
Ps119:105 Thy word *is* a l unto my feet, and a H5216
132:17 I have ordained a l for mine anointed. H5216
Prv 6:23 For the commandment *is* a l; and the H5216
13: 9 but the l of the wicked shall be put out. H5216
20:20 l shall be put out in obscure darkness. H5216
Isa 62: 1 salvation thereof as a l *that* burneth. H3940
Rev 8:10 as it were a l, and it fell upon the third *G2985*

LAMPS
Ex 25:37 And thou shalt make the seven l H5216
37 they shall light the l thereof, that they H5216
30: 7 the l, he shall burn incense upon it. H5216
8 And when Aaron lighteth the l at even, H5216
35:14 and his l, with the oil for the light, H5216
37:23 And he made his seven l, and his H5216
39:37 The pure candlestick, *with* the l H5216
37 *even with* the l to be set in order, and H5216
40: 4 the candlestick, and light the l thereof. H5216
25 And he lighted the l before the LORD; H5216
Lev 24: 2 light, to cause the l to burn continually. H5216
4 He shall order the l upon the pure H5216
Nu 4: 9 of the light, and his l, and his tongs, and H5216
8: 2 thou lightest the seven l, the seven lamps shall H5216
2 lamps, the seven l shall give light over H5216
3 And Aaron did so; he lighted the l H5216
Jdg 7:16 pitchers, and l within the pitchers. H3940
20 and held the l in their left hands, and H3940
1Ki 7:49 flowers, and the l, and the tongs *of* gold, H5216
1Ch 28:15 gold, and for their l of gold, by weight H5216
15 and for the l thereof: and for the H5216
15 and *also* for the l thereof, according to H5216
2Ch 4:20 Moreover the candlesticks with their l, H5216
21 And the flowers, and the l, and the H5216
13:11 of gold with the l thereof, to burn every H5216
29: 7 and put out the l, and have not burned H5216
Job 41:19 Out of his mouth go burning l, *and* H3940
Ezk 1:13 like the appearance of l: it went up and H3940
Dan 10: 6 and his eyes as l of fire, and his arms H3940
Zec 4: 2 of it, and his seven l thereon, and seven H5216
2 seven l, which *are* upon the top thereof: H5216
Mt 25: 1 which took their l, and went forth to *G2985*
3 They that *were* foolish took their l, and *G2985*
4 wise took oil in their vessels with their l. *G2985*
7 virgins arose, and trimmed their l. *G2985*
8 us of your oil; for our l are gone out. *G2985*
Rev 4: 5 and *there were* seven l of fire burning *G2985*

LANCE
Jer 50:42 They shall hold the bow and the l: they H3591

LANCETS
1Ki 18:28 l, till the blood gushed out upon them. H7420

LAND
Gen 1: 9 and let the dry *l* appear: and it was so. H3004
10 And God called the dry *l* Earth; and the H776
2:11 whole l of Havilah, where *there is* gold; H776
12 And the gold of that l *is* good: there *is* H776
13 that compasseth the whole l of Ethiopia. H776
4:16 in the l of Nod, on the east of Eden. H776
7:22 of life, of all that *was* in the dry *l*, died. H2724
10:10 Accad, and Calneh, in the l of Shinar. H776
11 Out of that l went forth Asshur, and H776
11: 2 in the l of Shinar; and they dwelt there. H776
28 l of his nativity, in Ur of the Chaldees. H776
31 to go into the l of Canaan; and they H776
12: 1 house, unto a l that I will shew thee: H776
5 forth to go into the l of Canaan; and into H776
5 and into the l of Canaan they came. H776
6 And Abram passed through the l unto H776
6 And the Canaanite *was* then in the l. H776
7 seed will I give this l: and there builded H776
10 And there was a famine in the l: and H776
10 for the famine *was* grievous in the l. H776
13: 6 And the l was not able to bear them, that H776
7 and the Perizzite dwelled then in the l. H776
9 *Is* not the whole l before thee? separate H776
10 the l of Egypt, as thou comest unto Zoar. H776
12 Abram dwelled in the l of Canaan, and H776
15 For all the l which thou seest, to thee will H776
17 Arise, walk through the l in the length of H776
15: 7 Chaldees, to give thee this l to inherit it. H776
13 be a stranger in a l *that is* not theirs, and H776
18 have I given this l, from the river of Egypt H776
16: 3 ten years in the l of Canaan, and gave H776
17: 8 seed after thee, the l wherein thou art a H776
8 art a stranger, all the l of Canaan, for an H776
19:28 and toward all the l of the plain, and H776
20:15 And Abimelech said, Behold, my l *is* H776
21:21 took him a wife out of the l of Egypt. H776
23 to the l wherein thou hast sojourned. H776
32 they returned into the l of the Philistines. H776
34 in the Philistines' l many days. H776
22: 2 get thee into the l of Moriah; and offer H776
23: 2 same *is* Hebron in the l of Canaan: and H776
7 of the l, *even* to the children of Heth. H776
12 down himself before the people of the l. H776
13 of the people of the l, saying, But if thou H776
15 My lord, hearken unto me: the l *is worth* H776
19 the same *is* Hebron in the l of Canaan. H776
24: 5 follow me unto this l: must I needs bring H776
5 unto the l from whence thou camest? H776
7 and from the l of my kindred, and which H776
7 thy seed will I give this l; he shall send his H776
37 of the Canaanites, in whose l I dwell: H776
26: 1 And there was a famine in the l, beside H776
2 dwell in the l which I shall tell thee of: H776
3 Sojourn in this l, and I will be with thee, H776
12 Then Isaac sowed in that l, and received H776
22 for us, and we shall be fruitful in the l. H776
27:46 of the l, what good shall my life do me? H776
28: 4 mayest inherit the l wherein thou art a H776
13 God of Isaac: the l whereon thou liest, to H776
15 thee again into this l; for I will not leave H127
29: 1 came into the l of the people of the east. H776
31: 3 Return unto the l of thy fathers, and to H776
13 thee out from this l, and return unto the H776
13 and return unto the l of thy kindred. H776
18 go to Isaac his father in the l of Canaan. H776
32: 3 unto the l of Seir, the country of Edom. H776
33:18 which *is* in the l of Canaan, when he H776
34: 1 went out to see the daughters of the l. H776
10 And ye shall dwell with us: and the l H776
21 them dwell in the l, and trade therein; for H776
21 trade therein; for the l, behold, *it is* large H776
30 the inhabitants of the l, among the H776
35: 6 So Jacob came to Luz, which *is* in the l of H776
12 And the l which I gave Abraham and H776
12 and to thy seed after thee will I give the l. H776
22 Israel dwelt in that l, that Reuben went H776
36: 5 were born unto him in the l of Canaan. H776
6 he had got in the l of Canaan; and went H776
7 together; and the l wherein they were H776
16 l of Edom; these *were* the sons of Adah. H776
17 of Reuel in the l of Edom; these *are* the H776
20 who inhabited the l; Lotan, and Shobal, H776
21 the children of Seir in the l of Edom. H776
30 Hori, among their dukes in the l of Seir. H776
31 that reigned in the l of Edom, before H776
34 And Jobab died, and Husham of the l of H776
43 habitations in the l of their possession: H776
37: 1 And Jacob dwelt in the l wherein his H776
Gen 37: 1 father was a stranger, in the l of Canaan. H776
40:15 For indeed I was stolen away out of the l H776
41:19 saw in all the l of Egypt for badness: H776
29 plenty throughout all the l of Egypt: H776
30 be forgotten in the l of Egypt; and the H776
30 and the famine shall consume the l; H776
31 not be known in the l by reason of that H776
33 wise, and set him over the l of Egypt. H776
34 officers over the l, and take up the fifth H776
34 l of Egypt in the seven plenteous years. H776
36 And that food shall be for store to the l H776
36 shall be in the l of Egypt; that the land H776
36 that the l perish not through the famine. H776
41 I have set thee over all the l of Egypt. H776
43 he made him *ruler* over all the l of Egypt. H776
44 up his hand or foot in all the l of Egypt. H776
45 Joseph went out over *all* the l of Egypt. H776
46 and went throughout all the l of Egypt. H776
48 which were in the l of Egypt, and laid up H776
52 me to be fruitful in the l of my affliction. H776
53 that was in the l of Egypt, were ended. H776
54 but in all the l of Egypt there was bread. H776
55 And when all the l of Egypt was H776
56 the famine waxed sore in the l of Egypt. H776
42: 5 for the famine was in the l of Canaan. H776
6 And Joseph *was* the governor over the l, H776
6 to all the people of the l: and Joseph's H776
7 said, From the l of Canaan to buy food. H776
9 to see the nakedness of the l ye are come. H776
12 to see the nakedness of the l ye are come. H776
13 sons of one man in the l of Canaan; and, H776
29 father unto the l of Canaan, and told H776
30 The man, *who is* the lord of the l, spake H776
32 day with our father in the l of Canaan. H776
34 brother, and ye shall traffick in the l. H776
43: 1 And the famine *was* sore in the l. H776
11 best fruits in the l in your vessels, and H776
44: 8 unto thee out of the l of Canaan: how H776
45: 6 the famine *been* in the l: and yet *there are* H776
8 and a ruler throughout all the l of Egypt. H776
10 And thou shalt dwell in the l of Goshen, H776
17 and go, get you unto the l of Canaan; H776
18 you the good of the l of Egypt, and ye H776
18 of Egypt, and ye shall eat the fat of the l. H776
19 you wagons out of the l of Egypt for your H776
20 for the good of all the l of Egypt *is* yours. H776
25 the l of Canaan unto Jacob their father, H776
26 over all the l of Egypt. And Jacob's H776
46: 6 had gotten in the l of Canaan, and came H776
12 Onan died in the l of Canaan. And the H776
20 And unto Joseph in the l of Egypt were H776
28 and they came into the l of Goshen. H776
31 in the l of Canaan, are come unto me; H776
34 that ye may dwell in the l of Goshen; for H776
47: 1 are come out of the l of Canaan; and, H776
1 and, behold, they *are* in the l of Goshen. H776
4 to sojourn in the l are we come; for thy H776
4 *is* sore in the l of Canaan: now therefore, H776
4 let thy servants dwell in the l of Goshen. H776
6 The l of Egypt *is* before thee; in the best H776
6 in the best of the l make thy father and H776
6 to dwell; in the l of Goshen let them H776
11 a possession in the l of Egypt, in the best H776
11 Egypt, in the best of the l, in the land of H776
11 best of the land, in the l of Rameses, as H776
13 And *there was* no bread in all the l; for H776
13 sore, so that the l of Egypt and *all* the H776
13 of Egypt and *all* the l of Canaan fainted H776
14 was found in the l of Egypt, and in the H776
14 of Egypt, and in the l of Canaan, for the H776
15 And when money failed in the l of Egypt, H776
15 of Egypt, and in the l of Canaan, all the H776
19 both we and our l? buy us and our land H127
19 buy us and our l for bread, and we and H127
19 and we and our l will be servants unto H127
19 and not die, that the l be not desolate. H127
20 And Joseph bought all the l of Egypt for H127
20 over them: so the l became Pharaoh's. H776
22 Only the l of the priests bought he not; H127
23 this day and your l for Pharaoh: lo, *here* H127
23 *is* seed for you, and ye shall sow the l. H127
26 And Joseph made it a law over the l of H127
26 fifth *part;* except the l of the priests only, H127
27 And Israel dwelt in the l of Egypt, in the H776
28 And Jacob lived in the l of Egypt H776
48: 3 Luz in the l of Canaan, and blessed me, H776
4 and will give this l to thy seed after thee H776
5 unto thee in the l of Egypt before I came H776
7 died by me in the l of Canaan in the way, H776

Gen 48:21 you again unto the l of your fathers. H776
49:15 And he saw that rest *was* good, and the l H776
30 before Mamre, in the l of Canaan, which H776
50: 5 for me in the l of Canaan, there shalt H776
7 and all the elders of the l of Egypt, H776
8 their herds, they left in the l of Goshen. H776
11 And when the inhabitants of the l, the H776
13 For his sons carried him into the l of H776
24 you out of this l unto the land which H776
24 of this land unto the l which he sware to H776
Ex 1: 7 mighty; and the l was filled with them. H776
10 us, and *so* get them up out of the l. H776
2:15 l of Midian: and he sat down by a well. H776
22 I have been a stranger in a strange l. H776
3: 8 them up out of that l unto a good land H776
8 land unto a good l and a large, unto a H776
8 and a large, unto a l flowing with milk H776
17 of Egypt unto the l of the Canaanites, H776
17 unto a l flowing with milk and honey. H776
4: 9 *it* upon the dry *l*: and the water which
9 river shall become blood upon the dry *l*.
20 he returned to the l of Egypt: and Moses H776
5: 5 the people of the l now *are* many, and ye H776
12 throughout all the l of Egypt to gather H776
6: 1 hand shall he drive them out of his l. H776
4 to give them the l of Canaan, the land H776
4 land of Canaan, the l of their pilgrimage, H776
8 And I will bring you in unto the l, H776
11 he let the children of Israel go out of his l. H776
13 children of Israel out of the l of Egypt. H776
26 the l of Egypt according to their armies. H776
28 spake unto Moses in the l of Egypt, H776
7: 2 he send the children of Israel out of his l. H776
3 signs and my wonders in the l of Egypt. H776
4 out of the l of Egypt by great judgments. H776
19 throughout all the l of Egypt, both in H776
21 was blood throughout all the l of Egypt. H776
8: 5 frogs to come up upon the l of Egypt. H776
6 came up, and covered the l of Egypt. H776
7 brought up frogs upon the l of Egypt. H776
14 together upon heaps: and the l stank. H776
16 the dust of the l, that it may become lice H776
16 become lice throughout all the l of Egypt. H776
17 beast; all the dust of the l became lice H776
17 became lice throughout all the l of Egypt. H776
22 And I will sever in that day the l of H776
24 and into all the l of Egypt: the land was H776
24 the land of Egypt: the l was corrupted by H776
25 said, Go ye, sacrifice to your God in the l. H776
9: 5 the LORD shall do this thing in the l. H776
9 dust in all the l of Egypt, and shall be H776
9 upon beast, throughout all the l of Egypt. H776
22 be hail in all the l of Egypt, upon man, H776
22 of the field, throughout the l of Egypt. H776
23 LORD rained hail upon the l of Egypt. H776
24 the l of Egypt since it became a nation. H776
25 And the hail smote throughout all the l H776
26 Only in the l of Goshen, where the H776
10:12 out thine hand over the l of Egypt for the H776
12 come up upon the l of Egypt, and eat H776
12 of the l, *even* all that the hail hath left. H776
13 forth his rod over the l of Egypt, and the H776
13 east wind upon the l all that day, and all H776
14 And the locusts went up over all the l of H776
15 earth, so that the l was darkened; and H776
15 every herb of the l, and all the fruit of the H776
15 of the field, through all the l of Egypt. H776
21 be darkness over the l of Egypt, even H776
22 darkness in all the l of Egypt three days: H776
11: 3 very great in the l of Egypt, in the sight H776
5 And all the firstborn in the l of Egypt H776
6 cry throughout all the l of Egypt, such as H776
9 may be multiplied in the l of Egypt. H776
10 let the children of Israel go out of his l. H776
12: 1 and Aaron in the l of Egypt, saying, H776
12 For I will pass through the l of Egypt this H776
12 the firstborn in the l of Egypt, both man H776
13 destroy *you*, when I smite the l of Egypt. H776
17 armies out of the l of Egypt: therefore H776
19 whether he be a stranger, or born in the l. H776
25 ye be come to the l which the LORD will H776
29 the firstborn in the l of Egypt, from the H776
33 them out of the l in haste; for they said, H776
41 the LORD went out from the l of Egypt. H776
42 them out from the l of Egypt: this *is* that H776
48 one that is born in the l: for no H776
51 out of the l of Egypt by their armies. H776
13: 5 bring thee into the l of the Canaanites, H776
5 to give thee, a l flowing with milk and H776

Ex 13:11 bring thee into the l of the Canaanites, H776
15 the firstborn in the l of Egypt, both the H776
17 the way of the l of the Philistines, H776
18 went up harnessed out of the l of Egypt. H776
14: 3 in the l, the wilderness hath shut them in. H776
21 sea dry *l*, and the waters were divided.
29 walked upon dry *l* in the midst of the
15:19 went on dry *l* in the midst of the sea.
16: 1 their departing out of the l of Egypt. H776
3 of the LORD in the l of Egypt, when we H776
6 brought you out from the l of Egypt: H776
32 I brought you forth from the l of Egypt. H776
35 they came to a l inhabited; they did eat H776
35 unto the borders of the l of Canaan. H776
18: 3 said, I have been an alien in a strange l: H776
27 and he went his way into his own l. H776
19: 1 forth out of the l of Egypt, the same day H776
20: 2 l of Egypt, out of the house of bondage. H776
12 l which the LORD thy God giveth thee. H127
22:21 for ye were strangers in the l of Egypt. H776
23: 9 ye were strangers in the l of Egypt. H776
10 And six years thou shalt sow thy l, and H776
19 The first of the firstfruits of thy l thou H127
26 thy l: the number of thy days I will fulfil. H776
29 in one year; lest the l become desolate, H776
30 until thou be increased, and inherit the l. H776
31 inhabitants of the l into your hand; and H776
33 They shall not dwell in thy l, lest they H776
29:46 forth out of the l of Egypt, that I may H776
32: 1 us up out of the l of Egypt, we wot not H776
4 brought thee up out of the l of Egypt. H776
7 l of Egypt, have corrupted *themselves:* H776
8 brought thee up out of the l of Egypt. H776
11 forth out of the l of Egypt with great H776
13 heaven, and all this l that I have spoken H776
23 us up out of the l of Egypt, we wot not H776
33: 1 up out of the l of Egypt, unto the land H776
1 of Egypt, unto the l which I sware unto H776
3 Unto a l flowing with milk and honey: H776
34:12 inhabitants of the l whither thou goest, H776
15 the inhabitants of the l, and they go a H776
24 any man desire thy l, when thou shalt go H776
26 The first of the firstfruits of thy l thou H127
Lev 11:45 you up out of the l of Egypt, to be your H776
14:34 When ye be come into the l of Canaan, H776
34 in a house of the l of your possession; H776
16:22 iniquities unto a l not inhabited: and he H776
18: 3 After the doings of the l of Egypt, H776
3 the doings of the l of Canaan, whither I H776
25 And the l is defiled: therefore I do visit H776
25 the l itself vomiteth out her inhabitants. H776
27 the men of the l done, which *were* before H776
27 *were* before you, and the l is defiled;) H776
28 That the l spue not you out also, when ye H776
19: 9 And when ye reap the harvest of your l, H776
23 And when ye shall come into the l, and H776
29 be a whore; lest the l fall to whoredom, H776
29 and the l become full of wickedness. H776
33 with thee in your l, ye shall not vex him. H776
34 the l of Egypt: I *am* the LORD your God. H776
36 which brought you out of the l of Egypt. H776
20: 2 of the l shall stone him with stones. H776
4 And if the people of the l do any ways H776
22 do them: that the l, whither I bring you to H776
24 shall inherit their l, and I will give it unto H127
24 you to possess it, a l that floweth with H776
22:24 ye make *any offering thereof* in your l. H776
33 That brought you out of the l of Egypt, to H776
23:10 ye be come into the l which I give unto H776
22 And when ye reap the harvest of your l, H776
39 in the fruit of the l, ye shall keep a feast H776
43 the l of Egypt: I *am* the LORD your God. H776
24:16 he that is born in the l, when he H249
25: 2 ye come into the l which I give you, then H776
2 the l keep a sabbath unto the LORD. H776
4 of rest unto the l, a sabbath for the H776
5 *for* it is a year of rest unto the l. H776
6 And the sabbath of the l shall be meat H776
7 l, shall all the increase thereof be meat. H776
9 the trumpet sound throughout all your l. H776
10 liberty throughout *all* the l unto all the H776
18 and ye shall dwell in the l in safety. H776
19 And the l shall yield her fruit, and ye H776
23 The l shall not be sold for ever: for the H776
23 sold for ever: for the l *is* mine; for ye *are* H776
24 And in all the l of your possession ye H776
24 ye shall grant a redemption for the l. H776
38 you forth out of the l of Egypt, to give H776
38 you the l of Canaan, *and* to be your God. H776

Lev 25:42 forth out of the l of Egypt: they shall not H776
45 your l: and they shall be your possession. H776
55 the l of Egypt: I *am* the LORD your God. H776
26: 1 of stone in your l, to bow down unto it: H776
4 season, and the l shall yield her increase, H776
5 to the full, and dwell in your l safely. H776
6 And I will give peace in the l, and ye shall H776
6 evil beasts out of the l, neither shall the H776
6 neither shall the sword go through your l. H776
13 you forth out of the l of Egypt, that ye H776
20 in vain: for your l shall not yield her H776
20 shall the trees of the l yield their fruits. H776
32 And I will bring the l into desolation: H776
33 l shall be desolate, and your cities waste. H776
34 Then shall the l enjoy her sabbaths, as H776
34 *be* in your enemies' l; *even* then shall the H776
34 shall the l rest, and enjoy her sabbaths. H776
38 the l of your enemies shall eat you up. H776
41 them into the l of their enemies; if then H776
42 I remember; and I will remember the l. H776
43 The l also shall be left of them, and shall H776
44 And yet for all that, when they be in the l H776
45 forth out of the l of Egypt in the sight H776
27:24 whom the possession of the l *did belong*. H776
30 And all the tithe of the l, *whether* of the H776
30 of the seed of the l, *or* of the fruit of the H776
Nu 1: 1 were come out of the l of Egypt, saying, H776
3:13 the firstborn in the l of Egypt I hallowed H776
8:17 l of Egypt I sanctified them for myself. H776
9: 1 were come out of the l of Egypt, saying, H776
14 and for him that was born in the l. H776
10: 9 And if ye go to war in your l against the H776
30 depart to mine own l, and to my kindred. H776
11:12 l which thou swarest unto their fathers? H127
13: 2 may search the l of Canaan, which I give H776
16 sent to spy out the l. And Moses called H776
17 And Moses sent them to spy out the l of H776
18 And see the l, what it *is*; and the people H776
19 And what the l *is* that they dwell in, H776
20 And what the l *is*, whether it *be* fat or H776
20 of the fruit of the l. Now the time *was* the H776
21 So they went up, and searched the l from H776
25 from searching of the l after forty days. H776
26 and shewed them the fruit of the l. H776
27 We came unto the l whither thou sentest H776
28 that dwell in the l, and the cities *are* H776
29 The Amalekites dwell in the l of the H776
32 up an evil report of the l which they had H776
32 of Israel, saying, The l, through which we H776
32 gone to search it, *is* a l that eateth up the H776
14: 2 we had died in the l of Egypt! or would H776
3 us unto this l, to fall by the sword, H776
6 that searched the l, rent their clothes: H776
7 of Israel, saying, The l, which we passed H776
7 to search it, *is* an exceeding good l. H776
8 bring us into this l, and give it us; a land H776
8 a l which floweth with milk and honey. H776
9 ye the people of the l; for they *are* bread H776
14 inhabitants of this l: *for* they have heard H776
16 this people into the l which he sware H776
23 Surely they shall not see the l which I H776
24 will I bring into the l whereinto he went; H776
30 Doubtless ye shall not come into the l, H776
31 shall know the l which ye have despised. H776
34 ye searched the l, *even* forty days, each H776
36 sent to search the l, who returned, and H776
36 him, by bringing up a slander upon the l, H776
37 l, died by the plague before the LORD. H776
38 men that went to search the l, lived *still*. H776
15: 2 ye be come into the l of your habitations, H776
18 ye come into the l whither I bring you, H776
19 of the bread of the l, ye shall offer up an H776
30 *he be* born in the l, or a stranger, the H249
41 you out of the l of Egypt, to be your God: H776
16:13 us up out of a l that floweth with milk H776
14 not brought us into a l that floweth with H776
18:13 *And* whatsoever is first ripe in the l, H776
20 inheritance in their l, neither shalt thou H776
20:12 into the l which I have given them. H776
23 by the coast of the l of Edom, saying, H776
24 not enter into the l which I have given H776
21: 4 sea, to compass the l of Edom: and the H776
22 Let me pass through thy l: we will not H776
24 and possessed his l from Arnon unto H776
26 his l out of his hand, even unto Arnon. H776
31 Thus Israel dwelt in the l of the H776
34 his people, and his l; and thou shalt do to H776
35 left him alive: and they possessed his l. H776
22: 5 by the river of the l of the children of his H776

Nu 22: 6 them out of the l: for I wot that he whom H776
13 Balak, Get you into your l: for the LORD H776
26: 4 which went forth out of the l of Egypt. H776
19 Er and Onan died in the l of Canaan. H776
53 Unto these the l shall be divided for an H776
55 Notwithstanding the l shall be divided H776
27:12 and see the l which I have given unto H776
32: 1 and when they saw the l of Jazer, and the H776
1 of Jazer, and the l of Gilead, that, behold, H776
4 l for cattle, and thy servants have cattle: H776
5 in thy sight, let this l be given unto thy H776
7 the l which the LORD hath given them? H776
8 them from Kadesh-barnea to see the l. H776
9 and saw the l, they discouraged the H776
9 the l which the LORD had given them. H776
11 shall see the l which I sware unto H127
17 cities because of the inhabitants of the l. H776
22 And the l be subdued before the LORD: H776
22 before Israel; and this l shall be your H776
29 the LORD, and the l shall be subdued H776
29 them the l of Gilead for a possession: H776
30 among you in the l of Canaan. H776
32 the LORD into the l of Canaan, that the H776
33 Og king of Bashan, the l, with the cities H776
33: 1 went forth out of the l of Egypt with their H776
37 mount Hor, in the edge of the l of Edom. H776
38 come out of the l of Egypt, in the first H776
40 in the south in the l of Canaan, heard of H776
51 passed over Jordan into the l of Canaan; H776
52 inhabitants of the l from before you, and H776
53 *inhabitants* of the l, and dwell therein: H776
53 for I have given you the l to possess it. H776
54 And ye shall divide the l by lot for an H776
55 the inhabitants of the l from before you; H776
55 shall vex you in the l wherein ye dwell. H776
34: 2 ye come into the l of Canaan; (this *is* the H776
2 Canaan; (this *is* the l that shall fall unto H776
2 the l of Canaan with the coasts thereof:) H776
12 l with the coasts thereof round about. H776
13 Israel, saying, This *is* the l which ye shall H776
17 shall divide the l unto you: Eleazar the H776
18 tribe, to divide the l by inheritance. H776
29 the children of Israel in the l of Canaan. H776
35:10 come over Jordan into the l of Canaan; H776
14 shall ye give in the l of Canaan, *which* H776
28 shall return into the l of his possession. H776
32 in the l, until the death of the priest. H776
33 So ye shall not pollute the l wherein ye H776
33 for blood it defileth the l: and the land H776
33 the land: and the l cannot be cleansed of H776
34 Defile not therefore the l which ye shall H776
36: 2 my lord to give the l for an inheritance H776
Dt 1: 5 On this side Jordan, in the l of Moab, H776
7 the sea side, to the l of the Canaanites, H776
8 Behold, I have set the l before you: go in H776
8 go in and possess the l which the LORD H776
21 Behold, the LORD thy God hath set the l H776
22 search us out the l, and bring us word H776
25 And they took of the fruit of the l in their H776
25 l which the LORD our God doth give us. H776
27 us forth out of the l of Egypt, to deliver H776
35 l, which I sware to give unto your fathers, H776
36 him will I give the l that he hath trodden H776
2: 5 give you of their l, no, not so much as a H776
9 not give thee of their l *for* a possession; H776
12 as Israel did unto the l of his possession, H776
19 not give thee of the l of the children of H776
20 (That also was accounted a l of giants: H776
24 of Heshbon, and his l: begin to possess *it*, H776
27 Let me pass through thy l: I will go along H776
29 the l which the LORD our God giveth us. H776
31 give Sihon and his l before thee: begin to H776
31 to possess, that thou mayest inherit his l. H776
37 Only unto the l of the children of H776
3: 2 his people, and his l, into thy hand; and H776
8 of the Amorites the l that *was* on this H776
12 And this l, *which* we possessed at that H776
13 Bashan, which was called the l of giants. H776
18 God hath given you this l to possess it: ye H776
20 also possess the l which the LORD your H776
25 and see the good l that *is* beyond Jordan, H776
28 to inherit the l which thou shalt see. H776
4: 1 go in and possess the l which the LORD H776
5 do so in the l whither ye go to possess it. H776
14 in the l whither ye go over to possess it. H776
21 in unto that good l, which the LORD thy H776
22 But I must die in this l, I must not go over H776
22 ye shall go over, and possess that good l. H776
25 remained long in the l, and shall corrupt H776

Dt 4:26 perish from off the l whereunto ye go H776
38 l *for* an inheritance, as *it is* this day. H776
46 Beth-peor, in the l of Sihon king of the H776
47 And they possessed his l, and the land of H776
47 And they possessed his land, and the l of H776
5: 6 l of Egypt, from the house of bondage. H776
15 a servant in the l of Egypt, and *that* the H776
16 l which the LORD thy God giveth thee. H127
31 in the l which I give them to possess it. H776
33 *your* days in the l which ye shall possess. H776
6: 1 *them* in the l whither ye go to possess it: H776
3 the l that floweth with milk and honey. H776
10 thee into the l which he sware unto H776
12 l of Egypt, from the house of bondage. H776
18 and possess the good l which the LORD H776
23 us the l which he sware unto our fathers. H776
7: 1 bring thee into the l whither thou goest H776
13 and the fruit of thy l, thy corn, and thy H127
13 of thy sheep, in the l which he sware H127
8: 1 go in and possess the l which the LORD H776
7 thee into a good l, a land of brooks of H776
7 into a good land, a l of brooks of water, H776
8 A l of wheat, and barley, and vines, and H776
8 a l of oil olive, and honey; H776
9 A l wherein thou shalt eat bread without H776
9 any *thing* in it; a l whose stones *are* iron, H776
10 for the good l which he hath given thee. H776
14 l of Egypt, from the house of bondage; H776
9: 4 me in to possess this l: but for the H776
5 thou go to possess their l: but for the H776
6 thee not this good l to possess it for thy H776
7 didst depart out of the l of Egypt, until ye H776
23 up and possess the l which I have given H776
28 Lest the l whence thou broughtest us out H776
28 bring them into the l which he promised H776
10: 7 to Jotbath, a l of rivers of waters. H776
11 in and possess the l, which I sware unto H776
19 for ye were strangers in the l of Egypt. H776
11: 3 the king of Egypt, and unto all his l; H776
8 possess the l, whither ye go to possess it; H776
9 *your* days in the l, which the LORD sware H127
9 a l that floweth with milk and honey. H776
10 For the l, whither thou goest in to possess H776
10 it, *is* not as the l of Egypt, from whence H776
11 But the l, whither ye go to possess it, *is* a H776
11 go to possess it, *is* a l of hills and valleys, H776
12 A l which the LORD thy God careth for: H776
14 That I will give *you* the rain of your l in H776
17 no rain, and that the l yield not her fruit; H127
17 the good l which the LORD giveth you. H776
21 children, in the l which the LORD sware H127
25 of you upon all the l that ye shall tread H776
29 thee in unto the l whither thou goest to H776
30 goeth down, in the l of the Canaanites, H776
31 to go in to possess the l which the LORD H776
12: 1 observe to do in the l, which the LORD H776
10 and dwell in the l which the LORD your H776
29 succeedest them, and dwellest in their l; H776
13: 5 you out of the l of Egypt, and redeemed H776
10 l of Egypt, from the house of bondage. H776
15: 4 bless thee in the l which the LORD thy H776
7 of thy gates in thy l which the LORD thy H776
11 cease out of the l: therefore I command H776
11 to thy poor, and to thy needy, in thy l. H776
15 a bondman in the l of Egypt, and the H776
16: 3 forth out of the l of Egypt in haste: that H776
3 of the l of Egypt all the days of thy life. H776
20 l which the LORD thy God giveth thee. H776
17:14 When thou art come unto the l which the H776
18: 9 When thou art come into the l which the H776
19: 1 the nations, whose l the LORD thy God H776
2 in the midst of thy l, which the LORD thy H776
3 the coasts of thy l, which the LORD thy H776
8 give thee all the l which he promised to H776
10 That innocent blood be not shed in thy l, H776
14 shalt inherit in the l that the LORD thy H776
20: 1 brought thee up out of the l of Egypt. H776
21: 1 If *one* be found slain in the l which the H127
23 of God;) that thy l be not defiled, which H127
23: 7 because thou wast a stranger in his l. H776
20 in the l whither thou goest to possess it. H776
24: 4 shalt not cause the l to sin, which the H776
14 that *are* in thy l within thy gates: H776
22 a bondman in the l of Egypt: therefore I H776
25:15 l which the LORD thy God giveth thee. H127
19 round about, in the l which the LORD H776
26: 1 come in unto the l which the LORD thy H776
2 shalt bring of thy l that the LORD thy H776
9 and hath given us this l, *even* a land that H776

Dt 26: 9 a l that floweth with milk and honey. H776
10 the firstfruits of the l, which thou, O H127
15 Israel, and the l which thou hast given H127
15 a l that floweth with milk and honey. H776
27: 2 Jordan unto the l which the LORD thy H776
3 go in unto the l which the LORD thy H776
3 thy God giveth thee, a l that floweth with H776
28: 8 l which the LORD thy God giveth thee. H776
11 of thy ground, in the l which the LORD H127
12 the rain unto thy l in his season, and to H776
18 and the fruit of thy l, the increase of thy H127
21 off the l, whither thou goest to possess it. H127
24 The LORD shall make the rain of thy l H776
33 The fruit of thy l, and all thy labours, H127
42 All thy trees and fruit of thy l shall the H127
51 cattle, and the fruit of thy l, until thou be H127
52 throughout all thy l: and he shall besiege H776
52 throughout all thy l, which the LORD thy H776
63 off the l whither thou goest to possess it. H127
29: 1 of Israel in the l of Moab, beside the H776
2 your eyes in the l of Egypt unto Pharaoh, H776
2 unto all his servants, and unto all his l; H776
8 And we took their l, and gave it for an H776
16 (For ye know how we have dwelt in the l H776
22 come from a far l, shall say, when they H776
22 the plagues of that l, and the sicknesses H776
23 *And that* the whole l thereof *is* H776
24 done thus unto this l? what *meaneth* the H776
25 brought them forth out of the l of Egypt: H776
27 against this l, to bring upon it all the H776
28 And the LORD rooted them out of their l H127
28 cast them into another l, as *it is* this day. H776
30: 5 bring thee into the l which thy fathers H776
9 and in the fruit of thy l, for good: for the H127
16 in the l whither thou goest to possess it. H776
18 *your* days upon the l, whither thou H127
20 mayest dwell in the l which the LORD H127
31: 4 unto the l of them, whom he destroyed. H776
7 people unto the l which the LORD hath H776
13 l whither ye go over Jordan to possess it. H127
16 the strangers of the l, whither they go *to* H776
20 them into the l which I sware unto their H127
21 brought them into the l which I sware. H776
23 of Israel into the l which I sware unto H776
32:10 He found him in a desert l, and in the H776
43 be merciful unto his l, *and* to his people. H127
47 l, whither ye go over Jordan to possess it. H127
49 which *is* in the l of Moab, that *is* over H776
49 and behold the l of Canaan, which I give H776
52 Yet thou shalt see the l before *thee;* but H776
52 the l which I give the children of Israel. H776
33:13 of the LORD *be* his l, for the precious H776
28 *shall be* upon a l of corn and wine; also H776
34: 1 shewed him all the l of Gilead, unto Dan, H776
2 And all Naphtali, and the l of Ephraim, H776
2 all the l of Judah, unto the utmost sea, H776
4 him, This *is* the l which I sware unto H776
5 died there in the l of Moab, according to H776
6 And he buried him in a valley in the l of H776
11 him to do in the l of Egypt to Pharaoh, H776
11 and to all his servants, and to all his l, H776
Jos 1: 2 this people, unto the l which I do give to H776
4 Euphrates, all the l of the Hittites, and H776
6 an inheritance the l, which I sware unto H776
11 to go in to possess the l, which the LORD H776
13 given you rest, and hath given you this l. H776
14 shall remain in the l which Moses gave H776
15 have possessed the l which the LORD H776
15 return unto the l of your possession, and H776
2: 1 saying, Go view the l, even Jericho. And H776
9 hath given you the l, and that your terror H776
9 inhabitants of the l faint because of you. H776
14 hath given us the l, that we will deal H776
18 Behold, *when* we come into the l, thou H776
24 into our hands all the l; for even all the H776
4:18 up unto the dry l, that the waters of H2724
22 Israel came over this Jordan on dry l. H3004
5: 6 not shew them the l, which the LORD H776
6 us, a l that floweth with milk and honey. H776
11 And they did eat of the old corn of the l H776
12 of the old corn of the l; neither had the H776
12 of the fruit of the l of Canaan that year. H776
7: 9 inhabitants of the l shall hear of *it*, and H776
8: 1 Ai, and his people, and his city, and his l: H776
9:24 to give you all the l, and to destroy all the H776
24 the inhabitants of the l from before you, H776
10:42 And all these kings and their l did H776
11: 3 Hivite under Hermon in the l of Mizpeh. H776
16 So Joshua took all that l, the hills, and all H776

Jos 11:16 country, and all the l of Goshen, and the H776
22 Anakims left in the l of the children of H776
23 So Joshua took the whole l, according to H776
23 their tribes. And the l rested from war. H776
12: 1 Now these *are* the kings of the l, which H776
1 and possessed their l on the other side H776
13: 1 yet very much l to be possessed. H776
2 This *is* the l that yet remaineth: all the H776
4 From the south, all the l of the H776
5 And the l of the Giblites, and all H776
7 Now therefore divide this l for an H776
25 and half the l of the children of Ammon, H776
14: 1 Israel inherited in the l of Canaan, which H776
4 the Levites in the l, save cities to dwell *in,* H776
5 of Israel did, and they divided the l. H776
7 to espy out the l; and I brought him word H776
9 day, saying, Surely the l whereon thy feet H776
15 Anakims. And the l had rest from war. H776
15:19 given me a south l; give me also springs H776
17: 5 beside the l of Gilead and Bashan, H776
6 of Manasseh's sons had the l of Gilead. H776
8 *Now* Manasseh had the l of Tappuah: H776
12 but the Canaanites would dwell in that l. H776
15 thyself there in the l of the Perizzites and H776
16 that dwell in the l of the valley have H776
18: 1 And the l was subdued before them. H776
3 to go to possess the l, which the LORD H776
4 rise, and go through the l, and describe it H776
6 Ye shall therefore describe the l *into* H776
8 to describe the l, saying, Go and walk H776
8 walk through the l, and describe it, and H776
9 passed through the l, and described it by H776
10 Joshua divided the l unto the children of H776
19:49 end of dividing the l for inheritance by H776
21: 2 at Shiloh in the l of Canaan, saying, The H776
43 And the LORD gave unto Israel all the l H776
22: 4 tents, *and* unto the l of your possession, H776
9 which *is* in the l of Canaan, to go unto H776
9 of Gilead, to the l of their possession, H776
10 that *are* in the l of Canaan, the children H776
11 altar over against the l of Canaan, in the H776
13 Manasseh, into the l of Gilead, Phinehas H776
15 unto the l of Gilead, and they spake H776
19 Notwithstanding, if the l of your H776
19 ye over unto the l of the possession of H776
32 of Gad, out of the l of Gilead, unto the H776
32 of Gilead, unto the l of Canaan, to the H776
33 to destroy the l wherein the children H776
23: 5 ye shall possess their l, as the LORD your H776
13 from off this good l which the LORD H127
15 you from off this good l which the LORD H127
16 the good l which he hath given unto you. H776
24: 3 him throughout all the l of Canaan, and H776
8 And I brought you into the l of the H776
8 l; and I destroyed them from before you. H776
13 And I have given you a l for which ye did H776
15 Amorites, in whose l ye dwell: but as for H776
17 our fathers out of the l of Egypt, from the H776
18 which dwelt in the l: *therefore* will we H776
Jdg 1: 2 I have delivered the l into his hand. H776
15 given me a south l; give me also springs H776
26 And the man went into the l of the H776
27 but the Canaanites would dwell in that l. H776
32 of the l: for they did not drive them out. H776
33 the inhabitants of the l: nevertheless the H776
2: 1 you unto the l which I sware unto your H776
2 inhabitants of this l; ye shall throw down H776
6 man unto his inheritance to possess the l. H776
12 them out of the l of Egypt, and followed H776
3:11 And the l had rest forty years. And H776
30 And the l had rest fourscore years. H776
5:31 his might. And the l had rest forty years. H776
6: 5 and they entered into the l to destroy it. H776
9 out from before you, and gave you their l; H776
10 the Amorites, in whose l ye dwell: but ye H776
9:37 the middle of the l, and another company H776
10: 4 this day, which *are* in the l of Gilead. H776
8 the l of the Amorites, which *is* in Gilead. H776
11: 3 and dwelt in the l of Tob: and there were H776
5 to fetch Jephthah out of the l of Tob: H776
12 thou art come against me to fight in my l? H776
13 took away my l, when they came up out H776
15 took not away the l of Moab, nor the H776
15 nor the l of the children of Ammon: H776
17 pass through thy l: but the king of Edom H776
18 and compassed the l of Edom, and the H776
18 of Edom, and the l of Moab, and came H776
18 by the east side of the l of Moab, and H776
19 pray thee, through thy l into my place. H776

Jdg 11:21 possessed all the l of the Amorites, the H776
12:15 in Pirathon in the l of Ephraim, in the H776
18: 2 to spy out the l, and to search it; and H776
2 Go, search the l: who when they came H776
7 magistrate in the l, that might put *them* H776
9 we have seen the l, and, behold, it *is* very H776
9 to go, *and* to enter to possess the l. H776
10 and to a large l: for God hath given it H776
17 went to spy out the l went up, *and* came H776
30 Dan until the day of the captivity of the l. H776
19:30 came up out of the l of Egypt unto this H776
20: 1 l of Gilead, unto the LORD in Mizpeh. H776
21:12 to Shiloh, which *is* in the l of Canaan. H776
21 of Shiloh, and go to the l of Benjamin. H776
Ru 1: 1 was a famine in the l. And a certain man H776
7 on the way to return unto the l of Judah. H776
2:11 mother, and the l of thy nativity, and art H776
4: 3 of l, which *was* our brother Elimelech's: H7704
1Sa 6: 5 mice that mar the l; and ye shall give H776
5 from off your gods, and from off your l. H776
9: 4 and passed through the l of Shalisha, but H776
4 they passed through the l of Shalim, and H776
4 passed through the l of the Benjamites, H776
5 *And* when they were come to the l of H776
16 a man out of the l of Benjamin, and thou H776
12: 6 your fathers up out of the l of Egypt. H776
13: 3 all the l, saying, Let the Hebrews hear. H776
7 over Jordan to the l of Gad and Gilead. H776
17 *leadeth to* Ophrah, unto the l of Shual: H776
19 throughout all the l of Israel: for the H776
14:14 of l, *which* a yoke *of oxen might plow.* H7704
25 And all *they of* the l came to a wood; and H776
29 hath troubled the l: see, I pray you, how H776
21:11 the king of the l? did they not sing one H776
22: 5 get thee into the l of Judah. Then David H776
23:23 to pass, if he be in the l, that I will search H776
27 for the Philistines have invaded the l. H776
27: 1 escape into the l of the Philistines; and H776
8 the inhabitants of the l, as thou goest to H776
8 goest to Shur, even unto the l of Egypt. H776
9 And David smote the l, and left neither H776
28: 3 spirits, and the wizards, out of the l. H776
9 the wizards, out of the l: wherefore then H776
29:11 to return into the l of the Philistines. H776
30:16 taken out of the l of the Philistines, and H776
16 the Philistines, and out of the l of Judah. H776
31: 9 and sent into the l of the Philistines H776
2Sa 3:12 Whose *is* the l? saying *also,* Make thy H776
5: 6 the inhabitants of the l: which spake unto H776
7:23 and terrible, for thy l, before thy people, H776
9: 7 restore thee all the l of Saul thy father; H7704
10 shall till the l for him, and thou shalt H127
10: 2 into the l of the children of Ammon. H776
15: 4 were made judge in the l, that every man H776
17:26 So Israel and Absalom pitched in the l of H776
19: 9 now he is fled out of the l for Absalom. H776
29 I have said, Thou and Ziba divide the l. H7704
21:14 after that God was entreated for the l. H776
24: 6 Then they came to Gilead, and to the l of H776
8 So when they had gone through all the l, H776
13 unto thee in thy l? or wilt thou flee three H776
13 pestilence in thy l? now advise, and see H776
25 l, and the plague was stayed from Israel. H776
1Ki 4:10 Sochoh, and all the l of Hepher: H776
19 *he was* the only officer which *was* in the l. H776
21 the river unto the l of the Philistines, and H776
6: 1 come out of the l of Egypt, in the fourth H776
8: 9 when they came out of the l of Egypt. H776
21 he brought them out of the l of Egypt. H776
34 l which thou gavest unto their fathers. H127
36 and give rain upon thy l, which thou hast H776
37 If there be in the l famine, if there be H776
37 besiege them in the l of their cities; H776
40 the l which thou gavest unto our fathers. H127
46 unto the l of the enemy, far or near; H776
47 themselves in the l whither they were H776
47 unto thee in the l of them that carried H776
48 all their soul, in the l of their enemies, H776
48 thee toward their l, which thou gavest H776
9: 7 Then will I cut off Israel out of the l H127
8 done thus unto this l, and to this house? H776
9 fathers out of the l of Egypt, and have H776
11 Hiram twenty cities in the l of Galilee. H776
13 called them the l of Cabul unto this day. H776
18 and Tadmor in the wilderness, in the l, H776
19 and in all the l of his dominion. H776
21 after them in the l, whom the children of H776
26 shore of the Red sea, in the l of Edom. H776
10: 6 own l of thy acts and of thy wisdom. H776

1Ki 11:18 appointed him victuals, and gave him l. H776
12:28 brought thee up out of the l of Egypt. H776
14:15 out of this good l, which he gave to their H127
24 And there were also sodomites in the l: H776
15:12 out of the l, and removed all the H776
20 all Cinneroth, with all the l of Naphtali. H776
17: 7 because there had been no rain in the l. H776
18: 5 Go into the l, unto all fountains of H776
6 So they divided the l between them to H776
20: 7 all the elders of the l, and said, Mark, I H776
22:46 of his father Asa, he took out of the l. H776
2Ki 2:21 from thence any more death or barren *l.*
3:19 mar every good piece of l with stones.
25 every good piece of l cast every man his
27 from him, and returned to *their own* l. H776
4:38 *was* a dearth in the l; and the sons of the H776
5: 2 captive out of the l of Israel a little maid; H776
4 said the maid that *is* of the l of Israel. H776
6:23 Syria came no more into the l of Israel. H776
8: 1 it shall also come upon the l seven years. H776
2 in the l of the Philistines seven years. H776
3 returned out of the l of the Philistines: H776
3 the king for her house and for her l. H7704
5 house and for her l. And Gehazi said, H7704
6 the day that she left the l, even until now. H776
10:33 From Jordan eastward, all the l of H776
11: 3 years. And Athaliah did reign over the l. H776
14 all the people of the l rejoiced, and blew H776
18 And all the people of the l went into the H776
19 all the people of the l; and they brought H776
20 And all the people of the l rejoiced, and H776
13:20 the l at the coming in of the year. H776
15: 5 the house, judging the people of the l. H776
19 came against the l: and Menahem gave H776
20 back, and stayed not there in the l. H776
29 and Galilee, all the l of Naphtali, and H776
16:15 of all the people of the l, and their meat H776
17: 5 up throughout all the l, and went up to H776
7 them up out of the l of Egypt, from H776
23 of their own l to Assyria unto this day. H127
26 of the God of the l: therefore he hath sent H776
26 know not the manner of the God of the l. H776
27 them the manner of the God of the l. H776
36 you up out of the l of Egypt with great H776
18:25 me, Go up against this l, and destroy it. H776
32 Until I come and take you away to a l H776
32 a land like your own l, a land of corn and H776
32 your own land, a l of corn and wine, a H776
32 land of corn and wine, a l of bread and H776
32 and vineyards, a l of oil olive and of H776
33 l out of the hand of the king of Assyria? H776
19: 7 return to his own l; and I will cause him H776
7 him to fall by the sword in his own l. H776
37 they escaped into the l of Armenia. And H776
21: 8 any more out of the l which I gave their H127
24 And the people of the l slew all them that H776
24 l made Josiah his son king in his stead. H776
23:24 that were spied in the l of Judah and in H776
30 the people of the l took Jehoahaz the son H776
33 at Riblah in the l of Hamath, that he H776
33 and put the l to a tribute of an hundred H776
35 but he taxed the l to give the money H776
35 gold of the people of the l, of every one H776
24: 7 any more out of his l: for the king of H776
14 the poorest sort of the people of the l. H776
15 the mighty of the l, *those* carried he into H776
25: 3 there was no bread for the people of the l. H776
12 l *to be* vinedressers and husbandmen. H776
19 the people of the l, and threescore men H776
19 of the l *that were* found in the city: H776
21 at Riblah in the l of Hamath. So Judah H776
21 So Judah was carried away out of their l. H127
22 that remained in the l of Judah, whom H776
24 dwell in the l, and serve the king of H776
1Ch 1:43 that reigned in the l of Edom before *any* H776
45 l of the Temanites reigned in his stead. H776
2:22 three and twenty cities in the l of Gilead. H776
4:40 and good, and the l *was* wide, and quiet, H776
5: 9 cattle were multiplied in the l of Gilead. H776
10 tents throughout all the east *l* of Gilead.
11 them, in the l of Bashan unto Salchah: H776
23 dwelt in the l: they increased from H776
25 the l, whom God destroyed before them. H776
6:55 And they gave them Hebron in the l of H776
7:21 *were* born in *that* l slew, because they H776
10: 9 and sent into the l of the Philistines H776
11: 4 Jebusites *were,* the inhabitants of the l. H776
13: 2 *that are* left in all the l of Israel, and with H776
16:18 Saying, Unto thee will I give the l of H776

1Ch 19: 2 David came into the l of the children of H776
3 and to overthrow, and to spy out the l? H776
21:12 pestilence, in the l, and the angel of the H776
22: 2 that *were* in the l of Israel; and he set H776
18 inhabitants of the l into mine hand; and H776
18 hand; and the l is subdued before the H776
28: 8 possess this good l, and leave *it* for an H776
2Ch 2:17 that *were* in the l of Israel, after the H776
6: 5 people out of the l of Egypt I chose no H776
25 again unto the l which thou gavest to H127
27 send rain upon thy l, which thou hast H776
28 If there be dearth in the l, if there be H776
28 in the cities of their l; whatsoever sore or H776
31 the l which thou gavest unto our fathers. H127
36 away captives unto a l far off or near; H776
37 Yet *if* they bethink themselves in the l H776
37 pray unto thee in the l of their captivity, H776
38 all their soul in the l of their captivity, H776
38 pray toward their l, which thou gavest H776
7:13 to devour the l, or if I send pestilence H776
14 will forgive their sin, and will heal their l. H776
20 the roots out of my l which I have given H127
21 thus unto this l, and unto this house? H776
22 forth out of the l of Egypt, and laid hold H776
8: 6 and throughout all the l of his dominion. H776
8 after them in the l, whom the children of H776
17 to Eloth, at the sea side in the l of Edom. H776
9: 5 own l of thine acts, and of thy wisdom: H776
11 none such seen before in the l of Judah. H776
12 away to her own l, she and her servants. H776
26 river even unto the l of the Philistines, H776
14: 1 In his days the l was quiet ten years. H776
6 in Judah: for the l had rest, and he had H776
7 and bars, *while* the l *is* yet before us; H776
15: 8 idols out of all the l of Judah and H776
17: 2 set garrisons in the l of Judah, and in the H776
19: 3 the groves out of the l, and hast prepared H776
5 And he set judges in the l throughout all H776
20: 7 inhabitants of this l before thy people H776
10 they came out of the l of Egypt, but they H776
22:12 years: and Athaliah reigned over the l. H776
23:13 and all the people of the l rejoiced, and H776
20 all the people of the l, and brought down H776
21 And all the people of the l rejoiced: and H776
26:21 king's house, judging the people of the l. H776
30: 9 again into this l: for the LORD your God H776
25 that came out of the l of Israel, and that H776
32: 4 the midst of the l, saying, Why should H776
21 of face to his own l. And when he was H776
31 that was *done* in the l, God left him, to try H776
33: 8 from out of the l which I have appointed H127
25 But the people of the l slew all them that H776
25 I made Josiah his son king in his stead. H776
34: 7 the l of Israel, he returned to Jerusalem. H776
8 he had purged the l, and the house, he H776
36: 1 Then the people of the l took Jehoahaz H776
3 condemned the l in an hundred talents H776
21 of Jeremiah, until the l had enjoyed her H776
Ezr 4: 4 Then the people of the l weakened the H776
6:21 l, to seek the LORD God of Israel, did eat, H776
9:11 saying, The l, unto which ye go to possess H776
11 it, is an unclean l with the filthiness of H776
12 eat the good of the l, and leave *it* for an H776
10: 2 of the people of the l: yet now there is H776
11 of the l, and from the strange wives. H776
Neh 4: 4 give them for a prey in the l of captivity: H776
5:14 their governor in the l of Judah, from the H776
16 bought we any l: and all my servants H7704
9: 8 him to give the l of the Canaanites, the H776
10 all the people of his l: for thou knewest H776
11 of the sea on the dry l; and their H3004
15 l which thou hadst sworn to give them. H776
22 so they possessed the l of Sihon, and the H776
22 land of Sihon, and the l of the king of H776
22 Heshbon, and the l of Og king of Bashan. H776
23 them into the l, concerning which thou H776
24 and possessed the l, and thou subduedst H776
24 inhabitants of the l, the Canaanites, and H776
24 the people of the l, that they might do H776
25 And they took strong cities, and a fat l, H127
35 in the large and fat l which thou gavest H776
36 day, and *for* the l that thou gavest unto H776
10:30 l, nor take their daughters for our sons: H776
31 And *if* the people of the l bring ware or H776
Est 8:17 of the people of the l became Jews; for H776
10: 1 upon the l, and *upon* the isles of the sea. H776
Job 1: 1 There was a man in the l of Uz, whose H776
10 and his substance is increased in the l. H776
10:21 l of darkness and the shadow of death; H776
Job 10:22 A l of darkness, as darkness *itself*; *and* of H776
28:13 neither is it found in the l of the living. H776
31:38 If my l cry against me, or that the H127
37:13 for correction, or for his l, or for mercy. H776
39: 6 and the barren l his dwellings.
42:15 And in all the l were no women found *so* H776
Ps 10:16 the heathen are perished out of his l. H776
27:13 of the LORD in the l of the living. H776
35:20 against *them that are* quiet in the l. H776
37: 3 in the l, and verily thou shalt be fed. H776
29 The righteous shall inherit the l, and H776
34 thee to inherit the l: when the wicked are H776
42: 6 thee from the l of Jordan, and of the H776
44: 3 For they got not the l in possession by H776
52: 5 root thee out of the l of the living. Selah. H776
63: 1 in a dry and thirsty l, where no water is; H776
66: 6 He turned the sea into dry *l*: they went H776
68: 6 chains: but the rebellious dwell in a dry *l*.
74: 8 up all the synagogues of God in the l. H776
78:12 in the l of Egypt, *in* the field of Zoan. H776
80: 9 it to take deep root, and it filled the l. H776
81: 5 out through the l of Egypt: *where* I heard H776
10 thee out of the l of Egypt: open thy H776
85: 1 unto thy l: thou hast brought back H776
9 fear him; that glory may dwell in our l. H776
12 good; and our l shall yield her increase. H776
88:12 righteousness in the l of forgetfulness? H776
95: 5 made it: and his hands formed the dry *l*.
101: 6 the faithful of the l, that they may dwell H776
8 I will early destroy all the wicked of the l; H776
105:11 Saying, Unto thee will I give the l of H776
16 the l: he brake the whole staff of bread. H776
23 and Jacob sojourned in the l of Ham. H776
27 them, and wonders in the l of Ham. H776
30 Their l brought forth frogs in H776
32 hail for rain, *and* flaming fire in their l. H776
35 And did eat up all the herbs in their l, H776
36 He smote also all the firstborn in their l, H776
106:22 Wondrous works in the l of Ham, *and* H776
24 Yea, they despised the pleasant l, they H776
38 and the l was polluted with blood. H776
107:34 A fruitful l into barrenness, for the H776
116: 9 I will walk before the LORD in the l of H776
135:12 And gave their l *for* an heritage, an H776
136:21 And gave their l for an heritage: for his H776
137: 4 we sing the LORD'S song in a strange l? H127
142: 5 *and* my portion in the l of the living. H776
143: 6 *thirsteth* after thee, as a thirsty l. Selah. H776
10 good; lead me into the l of uprightness. H776
Prv 2:21 For the upright shall dwell in the l, and H776
12:11 He that tilleth his l shall be satisfied with H127
28: 2 For the transgression of a l many *are* the H776
19 He that tilleth his l shall have plenty of H127
29: 4 The king by judgment establisheth the l: H776
31:23 when he sitteth among the elders of the l. H776
Ecc 10:16 Woe to thee, O l, when thy king *is* a child, H776
17 Blessed *art* thou, O l, when thy king *is* the H776
Song 2:12 the voice of the turtle is heard in our l; H776
Isa 1: 7 with fire: your l, strangers devour it in H127
19 obedient, ye shall eat the good of the l: H776
2: 7 Their l also is full of silver and gold, H776
7 treasures; their l is also full of horses, H776
8 Their l also is full of idols; they worship H776
5:30 if *one* look unto the l, behold darkness H776
6:11 man, and the l be utterly desolate, H127
12 *be* a great forsaking in the midst of the l. H776
7:16 the good, the l that thou abhorrest shall H127
18 and for the bee that *is* in the l of Assyria. H776
22 shall every one eat that is left in the l. H776
24 all the l shall become briers and thorns. H776
8: 8 fill the breadth of thy l, O Immanuel. H776
9: 1 lightly afflicted the l of Zebulun and the H776
1 of Zebulun and the l of Naphtali, and H776
2 they that dwell in the l of the shadow of H776
19 of hosts is the l darkened, and the people H776
10:23 even determined, in the midst of all the l. H776
11:16 that he came up out of the l of Egypt. H776
13: 5 of his indignation, to destroy the whole l. H776
9 anger, to lay the l desolate: and he shall H776
14 people, and flee every one into his own l. H776
14: 1 set them in their own l: and the strangers H127
2 possess them in the l of the LORD for H127
20 thou hast destroyed thy l, *and* slain thy H776
21 l, nor fill the face of the world with cities. H776
25 That I will break the Assyrian in my l, H776
15: 9 of Moab, and upon the remnant of the l. H127
16: 1 Send ye the lamb to the ruler of the l H776
4 the oppressors are consumed out of the l. H776
18: 1 Woe to the l shadowing with wings, H776
Isa 18: 2 down, whose l the rivers have spoiled! H776
7 under foot, whose l the rivers have H776
19:17 And the l of Judah shall be a terror unto H127
18 In that day shall five cities in the l of H776
19 in the midst of the l of Egypt, and a pillar H776
20 of hosts in the l of Egypt: for they shall H776
24 *even* a blessing in the midst of the l: H776
21: 1 cometh from the desert, from a terrible l. H776
14 The inhabitants of the l of Tema brought H776
23: 1 the l of Chittim it is revealed to them. H776
10 Pass through thy l as a river, O daughter H776
13 Behold the l of the Chaldeans; this H776
24: 3 The l shall be utterly emptied, and H776
11 is darkened, the mirth of the l is gone. H776
13 in the midst of the l among the people, H776
26: 1 song be sung in the l of Judah; We have H776
10 in the l of uprightness will he H776
27:13 to perish in the l of Assyria, and the H776
13 the outcasts in the l of Egypt, and shall H776
30: 6 of the south: into the l of trouble and H776
32: 2 the shadow of a great rock in a weary l. H776
13 Upon the l of my people shall come up H127
33:17 they shall behold the l that is very far off. H776
34: 6 and a great slaughter in the l of Idumea. H776
7 the bulls; and their l shall be soaked with H776
9 the l thereof shall become burning pitch. H776
35: 7 and the thirsty l springs of water: in H6774
36:10 the LORD against this l to destroy it? the H776
10 me, Go up against this l, and destroy it. H776
17 Until I come and take you away to a l H776
17 a land like your own l, a land of corn and H776
17 your own land, a l of corn and wine, a H776
17 and wine, a l of bread and vineyards. H776
18 l out of the hand of the king of Assyria? H776
20 delivered their l out of my hand, that H776
37: 7 return to his own l; and I will cause him H776
7 him to fall by the sword in his own l. H776
38 they escaped into the l of Armenia: and H776
38:11 the LORD, in the l of the living: I shall H776
41:18 of water, and the dry l springs of water. H776
49:12 the west; and these from the l of Sinim. H776
19 places, and the l of thy destruction, shall H776
53: 8 cut off out of the l of the living: for the H776
57:13 l, and shall inherit my holy mountain; H776
60:18 Violence shall no more be heard in thy l, H776
21 shall inherit the l for ever, the branch H776
61: 7 therefore in their l they shall possess the H776
62: 4 neither shall thy l any more be termed H776
4 and thy l Beulah: for the LORD H776
4 in thee, and thy l shall be married. H776
Jer 1: 1 *were* in Anathoth in the l of Benjamin: H776
14 forth upon all the inhabitants of the l. H776
18 against the whole l, against the kings of H776
18 thereof, and against the people of the l. H776
2: 2 the wilderness, in a l *that was* not sown. H776
6 us up out of the l of Egypt, that led us H776
6 through a l of deserts and of pits, H776
6 of pits, through a l of drought, and of the H776
6 of death, through a l that no man passed H776
7 ye defiled my l, and made mine heritage H776
15 and they made his l waste: his cities are H776
31 unto Israel? a l of darkness? wherefore H776
3: 1 shall not that l be greatly polluted? but H776
2 hast polluted the l with thy whoredoms H776
9 that she defiled the l, and committed H776
16 increased in the l, in those days, saith the H776
18 together out of the l of the north to the H776
18 of the north to the l that I have given for H776
19 thee a pleasant l, a goodly heritage of H776
4: 5 the trumpet in the l: cry, gather together, H776
7 his place to make thy l desolate; *and* thy H776
20 cried; for the whole l is spoiled: suddenly H776
27 said, The whole l shall be desolate; yet H776
5:19 gods in your l, so shall ye serve strangers H776
19 ye serve strangers in a l *that is* not yours. H776
30 and horrible thing is committed in the l; H776
6: 8 I make thee desolate, a l not inhabited. H776
12 the inhabitants of the l, saith the LORD. H776
7: 7 in this place, in the l that I gave to your H776
22 them out of the l of Egypt, concerning H776
25 forth out of the l of Egypt unto this day H776
34 of the bride: for the l shall be desolate. H776
8:16 Dan: the whole l trembled at the sound H776
16 have devoured the l, and all that is in it; H776
9:12 it, for what the l perisheth *and* is burned H776
19 l, because our dwellings have cast *us* out. H776
10:17 Gather up thy wares out of the l, O H776
18 inhabitants of the l at this once, and will H776
11: 4 forth out of the l of Egypt, from the iron H776

Jer 11: 5 to give them a l flowing with milk and H776
7 them up out of the l of Egypt, *even* unto H776
19 him off from the l of the living, that his H776
12: 4 How long shall the l mourn, and the H776
5 and *if* in the l of peace, *wherein* thou H776
11 unto me; the whole l is made desolate, H776
12 the *one* end of the l even to the *other* end H776
12 end of the l: no flesh shall have peace. H776
14 them out of their l, and pluck out the H127
15 to his heritage, and every man to his l. H776
13:13 inhabitants of this l, even the kings that H776
14: 8 as a stranger in the l, and as a wayfaring H776
15 shall not be in this l; By sword and H776
18 go about into a l that they know not. H776
15: 7 in the gates of the l; I will bereave *them* of H776
14 enemies into a l *which* thou knowest H776
16: 3 their fathers that begat them in this l; H776
6 small shall die in this l: they shall not be H776
13 Therefore will I cast you out of this l into H776
13 out of this land into a l that ye know not, H776
14 children of Israel out of the l of Egypt; H776
15 of Israel from the l of the north, and H776
15 into their l that I gave unto their fathers. H127
18 have defiled my l, they have filled mine H776
17: 4 enemies in the l which thou knowest H776
6 wilderness, *in* a salt l and not inhabited. H776
26 and from the l of Benjamin, and from H776
18:16 To make their l desolate, *and* a H776
22:12 him captive, and shall see this l no more. H776
27 But to the l whereunto they desire to H776
28 are cast into a l which they know not? H776
23: 7 children of Israel out of the l of Egypt; H776
8 them; and they shall dwell in their own l. H127
10 For the l is full of adulterers; for because H776
10 of swearing the l mourneth; the pleasant H776
15 is profaneness gone forth into all the l. H776
24: 5 the l of the Chaldeans for *their* good. H776
6 them again to this l: and I will build H776
8 that remain in this l, and them that dwell H776
8 and them that dwell in the l of Egypt: H776
10 from off the l that I gave unto them H127
25: 5 and dwell in the l that the LORD hath H127
9 bring them against this l, and against the H776
11 And this whole l shall be a desolation, H776
12 iniquity, and the l of the Chaldeans, and H776
13 And I will bring upon that l all my words H776
20 all the kings of the l of Uz, and all the H776
20 all the kings of the l of the Philistines, H776
38 the lion: for their l is desolate because of H776
26:17 Then rose up certain of the elders of the l, H776
20 l according to all the words of Jeremiah: H776
27: 7 the very time of his l come: and then H776
10 you far from your l; and that I should H127
11 still in their own l, saith the LORD; and H127
30: 3 to return to the l that I gave to their H776
10 thy seed from the l of their captivity; and H776
31:16 come again from the l of the enemy. H776
23 this speech in the l of Judah and in the H776
32 them out of the l of Egypt; which my H776
32:15 shall be possessed again in this l. H776
20 and wonders in the l of Egypt, *even* unto H776
21 Israel out of the l of Egypt with signs, H776
22 And hast given them this l, which thou H776
22 them, a l flowing with milk and honey; H776
41 plant them in this l assuredly with my H776
43 And fields shall be bought in this l, H776
44 witnesses in the l of Benjamin, and in H776
33:11 of the l, as at the first, saith the LORD. H776
13 south, and in the l of Benjamin, and in H776
15 judgment and righteousness in the l. H776
34:13 forth out of the l of Egypt, out of the H776
19 and all the people of the l, which passed H776
35: 7 days in the l where ye *be* strangers. H127
11 came up into the l, that we said, Come, H776
15 shall dwell in the l which I have given to H127
36:29 and destroy this l, and shall cause to H776
37: 1 of Babylon made king in the l of Judah. H776
2 the people of the l, did hearken unto the H776
7 shall return to Egypt into their own l. H776
12 to go into the l of Benjamin, to separate H776
19 not come against you, nor against this l? H776
39: 5 to Riblah in the l of Hamath, where he H776
10 had nothing, in the l of Judah, and gave H776
40: 4 behold, all the l *is* before thee: whither H776
6 among the people that were left in the l. H776
7 governor in the l, and had committed H776
7 of the poor of the l, of them that were not H776
9 dwell in the l, and serve the king of H776
12 and came to the l of Judah, to Gedaliah, H776

Jer 41: 2 of Babylon had made governor over the l. H776
18 king of Babylon made governor in the l. H776
42:10 If ye will still abide in this l, then will I H776
12 and cause you to return to your own l. H127
13 But if ye say, We will not dwell in this l, H776
14 Saying, No; but we will go into the l of H776
16 you there in the l of Egypt, and the H776
43: 4 of the LORD, to dwell in the l of Judah. H776
5 been driven, to dwell in the l of Judah; H776
7 So they came into the l of Egypt: for they H776
11 And when he cometh, he shall smite the l H776
12 array himself with the l of Egypt, as a H776
13 that *is* in the l of Egypt; and the houses H776
44: 1 Jews which dwell in the l of Egypt, which H776
8 other gods in the l of Egypt, whither ye H776
9 committed in the l of Judah, and in the H776
12 faces to go into the l of Egypt to sojourn H776
12 *and* fall in the l of Egypt; they shall *even* H776
13 For I will punish them that dwell in the l H776
14 are gone into the l of Egypt to sojourn H776
14 return into the l of Judah, to the which H776
15 that dwelt in the l of Egypt, in Pathros, H776
21 and the people of the l, did not the LORD H776
22 therefore is your l a desolation, and an H776
24 all Judah that *are* in the l of Egypt: H776
26 that dwell in the l of Egypt; Behold, I H776
26 l of Egypt, saying, The Lord GOD liveth. H776
27 Judah that *are* in the l of Egypt shall be H776
28 return out of the l of Egypt into the land H776
28 of Egypt into the l of Judah, and all the H776
28 are gone into the l of Egypt to sojourn H776
45: 4 planted I will pluck up, even this whole l. H776
46:12 cry hath filled the l: for the mighty man H776
13 should come *and* smite the l of Egypt. H776
16 people, and to the l of our nativity, from H776
27 thy seed from the l of their captivity; and H776
47: 2 and shall overflow the l, and all that is H776
2 all the inhabitants of the l shall howl. H776
48:24 all the cities of the l of Moab, far or near. H776
33 field, and from the l of Moab; and I have H776
50: 1 *and* against the l of the Chaldeans by H776
3 shall make her l desolate, and none shall H776
8 go forth out of the l of the Chaldeans, H776
12 *be* a wilderness, a dry l, and a desert.
16 and they shall flee every one to his own l. H776
18 l, as I have punished the king of Assyria. H776
21 Go up against the l of Merathaim, *even* H776
22 A sound of battle *is* in the l, and of great H776
25 GOD of hosts in the l of the Chaldeans. H776
28 escape out of the l of Babylon, to declare H776
34 he may give rest to the l, and disquiet the H776
38 up: for it *is* the l of graven images, and H776
45 against the l of the Chaldeans: Surely H776
51: 2 shall empty her l: for in the day of trouble H776
4 Thus the slain shall fall in the l of the H776
5 hosts; though their l was filled with sin H776
27 Set ye up a standard in the l, blow the H776
28 thereof, and all the l of his dominion. H776
29 And the l shall tremble and sorrow: for H776
29 to make the l of Babylon a desolation H776
43 Her cities are a desolation, a dry l, and a H776
43 and a wilderness, a l wherein no man H776
46 be heard in the l; a rumour shall both H776
46 and violence in the l, ruler against ruler. H776
47 and her whole l shall be confounded, H776
52 all her l the wounded shall groan. H776
54 destruction from the l of the Chaldeans: H776
52: 6 there was no bread for the people of the l. H776
9 to Riblah in the l of Hamath; where he H776
16 l for vinedressers and for husbandmen. H776
25 the people of the l; and threescore men H776
25 l, that were found in the midst of the city. H776
27 in Riblah in the l of Hamath. Thus Judah H776
27 carried away captive out of his own l. H127
Lam 4:21 that dwellest in the l of Uz; the cup also H776
Ezk 1: 3 son of Buzi, in the l of the Chaldeans by H776
6:14 and make the l desolate, yea, more H776
7: 2 Lord GOD unto the l of Israel; An end, H127
2 is come upon the four corners of the l. H776
7 that dwellest in the l: the time is come, H776
23 Make a chain: for the l is full of bloody H776
27 of the people of the l shall be troubled: I H776
8:17 they have filled the l with violence, and H776
9: 9 great, and the l is full of blood, and the H776
11:15 unto us is this l given in possession. H776
17 and I will give you the l of Israel. H127
12:13 to Babylon *to* the l of the Chaldeans; yet H776
19 And say unto the people of the l, Thus H776
19 *and* of the l of Israel; They shall H127

Ezk 12:19 that her l may be desolate from H776
20 be laid waste, and the l shall be desolate; H776
22 *that* ye have in the l of Israel, saying, H127
13: 9 they enter into the l of Israel; and ye H127
14:13 Son of man, when the l sinneth against H776
15 to pass through the l, and they spoil it, so H776
16 be delivered, but the l shall be desolate. H776
17 Or *if* I bring a sword upon that l, and say, H776
17 l; so that I cut off man and beast from it: H776
19 Or *if* I send a pestilence into that l, and H776
15: 8 And I will make the l desolate, because H776
16: 3 nativity *is* of the l of Canaan; thy father H776
29 thy fornication in the l of Canaan unto H776
17: 4 carried it into a l of traffick; he set it in H776
5 He took also of the seed of the l, and H776
13 he hath also taken the mighty of the l: H776
18: 2 concerning the l of Israel, saying, The H127
19: 4 him with chains unto the l of Egypt. H776
7 their cities; and the l was desolate, and H776
20: 5 unto them in the l of Egypt, when I lifted H776
6 them forth of the l of Egypt into a land H776
6 of Egypt into a l that I had espied for H776
8 them in the midst of the l of Egypt. H776
9 bringing them forth out of the l of Egypt. H776
10 to go forth out of the l of Egypt, and H776
15 bring them into the l which I had given H776
28 *For* when I had brought them into the l, H776
36 the wilderness of the l of Egypt, so will I H776
38 not enter into the l of Israel: and ye shall H127
40 all of them in the l, serve me: there will I H776
42 bring you into the l of Israel, into the H127
21: 2 and prophesy against the l of Israel, H127
3 And say to the l of Israel, Thus saith the H127
19 forth out of one l: and choose thou a H776
30 wast created, in the l of thy nativity. H776
32 be in the midst of the l; thou shalt be no H776
22:24 Son of man, say unto her, Thou *art* the l H776
29 The people of the l have used H776
30 gap before me for the l, that I should not H776
23:15 of Chaldea, the l of their nativity: H776
19 had played the harlot in the l of Egypt. H776
27 *brought* from the l of Egypt: so that thou H776
48 to cease out of the l, that all women may H776
25: 3 and against the l of Israel, when it was H127
6 all thy despite against the l of Israel; H127
26:20 and I shall set glory in the l of the living; H776
27:17 Judah, and the l of Israel, they *were* thy H776
29 their ships, they shall stand upon the l; H776
28:25 l that I have given to my servant Jacob. H127
29: 9 And the l of Egypt shall be desolate and H776
10 and I will make the l of Egypt utterly H776
12 And I will make the l of Egypt desolate H776
14 to return *into* the l of Pathros, into the H776
14 of Pathros, into the l of their habitation; H776
19 Behold, I will give the l of Egypt unto H776
20 I have given him the l of Egypt *for* his H776
30: 5 and the men of the l that is in league, H776
11 to destroy the l: and they shall draw H776
11 Egypt, and fill the l with the slain. H776
12 dry, and sell the l into the hand of the H776
12 and I will make the l waste, and all that H776
13 a prince of the l of Egypt: and I will put H776
13 and I will put a fear in the l of Egypt. H776
25 shall stretch it out upon the l of Egypt. H776
31:12 all the rivers of the l; and all the people of H776
32: 4 Then will I leave thee upon the l, I will H776
6 I will also water with thy blood the l H776
8 darkness upon thy l, saith the Lord GOD. H776
15 When I shall make the l of Egypt H776
23 which caused terror in the l of the living. H776
24 their terror in the l of the living; yet have H776
25 was caused in the l of the living, yet have H776
26 caused their terror in the l of the living. H776
27 terror of the mighty in the l of the living. H776
32 For I have caused my terror in the l of H776
33: 2 the sword upon a l, if the people of the H776
2 if the people of the l take a man of their H776
3 come upon the l, he blow the trumpet, H776
24 those wastes of the l of Israel speak, H127
24 he inherited the l: but we *are* many; the H776
24 many; the l is given us for inheritance. H776
25 shed blood: and shall ye possess the l? H776
26 wife: and shall ye possess the l? H776
28 For I will lay the l most desolate, and the H776
29 I have laid the l most desolate because H776
34:13 them to their own l, and feed them upon H127
25 to cease out of the l: and they shall dwell H776
27 be safe in their l, and shall know that H127
28 the beast of the l devour them; but they H776

Ezk 34:29 with hunger in the l, neither bear the H776
36: 5 which have appointed my l into their H776
6 Prophesy therefore concerning the l of H127
13 say unto you, Thou *l* devourest up men,
17 dwelt in their own l, they defiled it by H127
18 had shed upon the l, and for their idols H776
20 the LORD, and are gone forth out of his l. H776
24 and will bring you into your own l. H127
28 And ye shall dwell in the l that I gave to H776
34 And the desolate l shall be tilled, H776
35 And they shall say, This l that was H776
37:12 graves, and bring you into the l of Israel. H127
14 you in your own l: then shall ye know H127
21 side, and bring them into their own l: H127
22 And I will make them one nation in the l H776
25 And they shall dwell in the l that I have H776
38: 2 against Gog, the l of Magog, the chief H776
8 thou shalt come into the l *that is* brought H776
9 a cloud to cover the l, thou, and all thy H776
11 And thou shalt say, I will go up to the l of H776
12 goods, that dwell in the midst of the l. H776
16 as a cloud to cover the l; it shall be in the H776
16 thee against my l, that the heathen may H776
18 come against the l of Israel, saith the H127
19 shall be a great shaking in the l of Israel; H127
39:12 of them, that they may cleanse the l. H776
13 Yea, all the people of the l shall bury H776
14 passing through the l to bury with the H776
15 *that* pass through the l, when *any* seeth a H776
16 Hamonah. Thus shall they cleanse the l. H776
26 in their l, and none made *them* afraid. H127
28 unto their own l, and have left none of H127
40: 2 he me into the l of Israel, and set me H776
45: 1 divide by lot the l for inheritance, ye H776
1 holy portion of the l: the length *shall be* H776
4 The holy *portion* of the l shall be for the H776
8 In the l shall be his possession in Israel: H776
8 and *the rest of* the l shall they give to the H776
16 All the people of the l shall give this H776
22 of the l a bullock *for* a sin offering. H776
46: 3 Likewise the people of the l shall H776
9 But when the people of the l shall come H776
47:13 ye shall inherit the l according to the H776
14 this l shall fall unto you for inheritance. H776
15 And this *shall be* the border of the l H776
18 and from the l of Israel *by* Jordan, from H776
21 So shall ye divide this l unto you H776
48:12 And *this* oblation of the l that is offered H776
14 of the l: for *it is* holy unto the LORD. H776
29 This *is* the l which ye shall divide by lot H776
Dan 1: 2 he carried into the l of Shinar to the H776
8: 9 the east, and toward the pleasant *l*.
9: 6 our fathers, and to all the people of the l. H776
15 forth out of the l of Egypt with a mighty H776
11: 9 kingdom, and shall return into his own l. H127
16 l, which by his hand shall be consumed. H776
19 the fort of his own l: but he shall stumble H776
28 Then shall he return into his l with great H776
28 shall do *exploits*, and return to his own l. H776
39 many, and shall divide the l for gain. H127
41 He shall enter also into the glorious l, H776
42 and the l of Egypt shall not escape. H776
Hos 1: 2 of whoredoms: for the l hath committed H776
11 the l: for great *shall be* the day of Jezreel. H776
2: 3 her like a dry l, and slay her with thirst. H776
15 when she came up out of the l of Egypt. H776
4: 1 inhabitants of the l, because *there is* no H776
1 nor mercy, nor knowledge of God in the l. H776
3 Therefore shall the l mourn, and every H776
7:16 *shall be* their derision in the l of Egypt. H776
9: 3 They shall not dwell in the LORD'S l; but H776
10: 1 of his l they have made goodly images. H776
11: 5 He shall not return into the l of Egypt, H776
11 as a dove out of the l of Assyria: and I H776
12: 9 thy God from the l of Egypt will yet make H776
13: 4 Yet I *am* the LORD thy God from the l of H776
5 the wilderness, in the l of great drought. H776
Joel 1: 2 ye inhabitants of the l. Hath this been in H776
6 For a nation is come up upon my l, H776
10 The field is wasted, the l mourneth; for H127
14 inhabitants of the l *into* the house of the H776
2: 1 inhabitants of the l tremble: for the day H776
3 a flame burneth: the l *is* as the garden of H776
18 Then will the LORD be jealous for his l, H776
20 drive him into a l barren and desolate, H776
21 Fear not, O l; be glad and rejoice: for the H127
3: 2 among the nations, and parted my l. H776
19 they have shed innocent blood in their l. H776
Am 2:10 Also I brought you up from the l of H776
Am 2:10 to possess the l of the Amorite. H776
3: 1 I brought up from the l of Egypt, saying, H776
9 in the palaces in the l of Egypt, and say, H776
11 round about the l; and he shall bring H776
5: 2 upon her l; *there is* none to raise her up. H127
7: 2 the grass of the l, then I said, O Lord H776
10 the l is not able to bear all his words. H776
11 be led away captive out of their own l. H127
12 thee away into the l of Judah, and there H776
17 the sword, and thy l shall be divided by H127
17 die in a polluted l: and Israel shall surely H127
17 shall surely go into captivity forth of his l. H127
8: 4 even to make the poor of the l to fail, H776
8 Shall not the l tremble for this, and every H776
11 a famine in the l, not a famine of bread, H776
9: 5 that toucheth the l, and it shall melt, and H776
7 up Israel out of the l of Egypt? and the H776
15 And I will plant them upon their l, and H127
15 up out of their l which I have given H127
Jna 1: 9 which hath made the sea and the dry *l*.
13 to bring *it* to the l; but they could not: H3004
2:10 and it vomited out Jonah upon the dry *l*.
Mic 5: 5 shall come into our l: and when he shall H776
6 And they shall waste the l of Assyria H776
6 the sword, and the l of Nimrod in the H776
6 when he cometh into our l, and when he H776
11 And I will cut off the cities of thy l, and H776
6: 4 For I brought thee up out of the l of H776
7:13 Notwithstanding the l shall be desolate H776
15 coming out of the l of Egypt will I shew H776
Nah 3:13 the gates of thy l shall be set wide open H776
Hab 1: 6 the breadth of the l, to possess the H776
2: 8 l, of the city, and of all that dwell therein. H776
17 l, of the city, and of all that dwell therein. H776
3: 7 curtains of the l of Midian did tremble. H776
12 Thou didst march through the l in H776
Zep 1: 2 all *things* from off the l, saith the LORD. H127
3 off man from off the l, saith the LORD. H127
18 but the whole l shall be devoured by H776
18 riddance of all them that dwell in the l. H776
2: 5 you; O Canaan, the l of the Philistines, I H776
3:19 l where they have been put to shame. H776
Hag 1:11 And I called for a drought upon the l, and H776
2: 4 all ye people of the l, saith the LORD, and H776
6 and the earth, and the sea, and the dry *l*;
Zec 1:21 horn over the l of Judah to scatter it. H776
2: 6 Ho, ho, *come forth*, and flee from the l of H776
12 holy l, and shall choose Jerusalem again. H127
3: 9 remove the iniquity of that l in one day. H776
5:11 it an house in the l of Shinar: and it shall H776
7: 5 Speak unto all the people of the l, and to H776
14 knew not. Thus the l was desolate after H776
14 for they laid the pleasant l desolate. H776
9: 1 of the LORD in the l of Hadrach, and H776
16 crown, lifted up as an ensign upon his l. H127
10:10 I will bring them again also out of the l H776
10 will bring them into the l of Gilead and H776
11: 6 inhabitants of the l, saith the LORD: but, H776
6 they shall smite the l, and out of their H776
16 For, lo, I will raise up a shepherd in the l, H776
12:12 And the l shall mourn, every family H776
13: 2 of the idols out of the l, and they shall no H776
2 and the unclean spirit to pass out of the l. H776
8 And it shall come to pass, *that* in all the l, H776
14:10 All the l shall be turned as a plain from H776
Mal 3:12 a delightsome l, saith the LORD of hosts. H776
Mt 2: 6 And thou Bethlehem, *in* the l of Juda, G1093
20 and go into the l of Israel: for they are G1093
21 mother, and came into the l of Israel. G1093
4:15 The l of Zabulon, and the land of G1093
15 The land of Zabulon, and the l of G1093
9:26 fame hereof went abroad into all that l. G1093
10:15 more tolerable for the l of Sodom and G1093
11:24 tolerable for the l of Sodom in the day G1093
14:34 they came into the l of Gennesaret. G1093
23:15 ye compass sea and l to make one G3584
27:45 over all the l unto the ninth hour. G1093
Mk 1: 5 And there went out unto him all the l of G5561
4: 1 whole multitude was by the sea on the l. G1093
6:47 midst of the sea, and he alone on the l. G1093
53 l of Gennesaret, and drew to the shore. G1093
15:33 over the whole l until the ninth hour. G1093
Lk 4:25 great famine was throughout all the l; G1093
5: 3 a little from the l. And he sat down, and G1093
11 to l, they forsook all, and followed him. G1093
8:27 And when he went forth to l, there met G1093
14:35 It is neither fit for the l, nor yet for the G1093
15:14 in that l; and he began to be in want. G5561
21:23 in the l, and wrath upon this people. G1093
Jn 3:22 disciples into the l of Judaea; and there G1093
6:21 the ship was at the l whither they went. G1093
21: 8 were not far from l, but as it were two G1093
9 As soon then as they were come to l, G1093
11 drew the net to l full of great fishes, an G1093
Act 4:37 Having l, sold *it*, and brought the money, G68
5: 3 to keep back *part* of the price of the l? G5564
8 ye sold the l for so much? And she G5564
7: 3 come into the l which I shall shew thee. G1093
4 Then came he out of the l of the G1093
4 him into this l, wherein ye now dwell. G1093
6 in a strange l; and that they should G1093
11 Now there came a dearth over all the l G1093
29 l of Madian, where he begat two sons. G1093
36 and signs in the l of Egypt, and in the G1093
40 us out of the l of Egypt, we wot not G1093
10:39 he did both in the l of the Jews, and in G5561
13:17 as strangers in the l of Egypt, and with G1093
19 nations in the l of Chanaan, he divided G1093
19 he divided their l to them by lot. G1093
27:39 they knew not the l: but they discovered G1093
43 first *into the sea*, and get to l: G1093
44 to pass, that they escaped all safe to l. G1093
Heb 8: 9 them out of the l of Egypt; because they G1093
11: 9 By faith he sojourned in the l of G1093
29 Red sea as by dry *l*: which the Egyptians
Jude 5 people out of the l of Egypt, afterward G1093

LANDED
Act 18:22 And when he had l at Caesarea, and G2718
21: 3 into Syria, and l at Tyre: for there the G2609

LANDING
Act 28:12 And l at Syracuse, we tarried *there* G2609

LANDMARK
Dt 19:14 thy neighbour's l, which they of old time H1366
27:17 l. And all the people shall say, Amen. H1366
Prv 22:28 Remove not the ancient l, which thy H1366
23:10 Remove not the old l; and enter not into H1366

LANDMARKS
Job 24: 2 *Some* remove the l; they violently take H1367

LANDS
Gen 10: 5 divided in their l; every one after his H776
31 tongues, in their l, after their nations. H776
41:54 dearth was in all l; but in all the land of H776
57 that the famine was *so* sore in all l. H776
47:18 of my lord, but our bodies, and our l: H127
22 them: wherefore they sold not their l. H127
Lev 26:36 their hearts in the l of their enemies; and H776
39 in your enemies' l; and also in the H776
Jdg 11:13 restore those *l* again peaceably.
2Ki 19:11 have done to all l, by destroying them H776
17 have destroyed the nations and their l, H776
1Ch 14:17 And the fame of David went out into all l; H776
2Ch 9:28 horses out of Egypt, and out of all l. H776
13: 9 the nations of *other* l? so that whosoever H776
17:10 kingdoms of the l that *were* round about H776
32:13 the people of *other* l? were the gods of the H776
13 the nations of those l any ways able to H776
13 able to deliver their l out of mine hand? H776
17 the nations of *other* l have not delivered H776
Ezr 9: 1 the people of the l, *doing* according to H776
2 the people of *those* l: yea, the hand of the H776
7 hand of the kings of the l, to the sword, to H776
11 filthiness of the people of the l, with their H776
Neh 5: 3 have mortgaged our l, vineyards, and H7704
4 *and that upon* our l and vineyards. H7704
5 other men have our l and vineyards. H7704
11 this day, their l, their vineyards, their H7704
9:30 them into the hand of the people of the l. H776
10:28 the people of the l unto the law of God, H776
Ps 49:11 they call *their* l after their own names. H127
66: 1 Make a joyful noise unto God, all ye l: H776
100: 1 a joyful noise unto the LORD, all ye l. H776
105:44 And gave them the l of the heathen: and H776
106:27 the nations, and to scatter them in the l. H776
107: 3 And gathered them out of the l, from the H776
Isa 36:20 all the gods of these l, that have delivered H776
37:11 have done to all l by destroying them H776
Jer 16:15 and from all the l whither he had driven H776
27: 6 And now have I given all these l into the H776
Ezk 20: 6 and honey, which *is* the glory of all l: H776
15 and honey, which *is* the glory of all l; H776
39:27 of their enemies' l, and am sanctified in H776
Mt 19:29 or children, or l, for my name's sake, G68
Mk 10:29 or l, for my sake, and the gospel's, G68

Mk 10:30 and children, and l, with persecutions; G68
Act 4:34 as were possessors of l or houses sold G5564

LANES
Lk 14:21 the streets and l of the city, and bring G4505

LANGUAGE
Gen 11: 1 And the whole earth was of one l, and of H8193
6 they have all one l; and this they begin H8193
7 confound their l, that they may not H8193
9 confound the l of all the earth: and H8193
2Ki 18:26 in the Syrian l; for we understand *it:*
26 with us in the Jews' l in the ears of the H3066
28 voice in the Jews' l, and spake, saying, H3066
Neh 13:24 speak in the Jews' l, but according to H3066
24 but according to the l of each people. H3956
Est 1:22 people after their l, that every man H3956
22 according to the l of every people. H3956
3:12 people after their l; in the name of king H3956
8: 9 people after their l, and to the Jews H3956
9 their writing, and according to their l. H3956
Ps 19: 3 *There is* no speech nor l, *where* their H1697
81: 5 *where* I heard a l *that* I understood not. H8193
114: 1 of Jacob from a people of strange l; H3937
Isa 19:18 of Egypt speak the l of Canaan, and H8193
36:11 in the Syrian l; for we understand *it*:
11 not to us in the Jews' l, in the ears of the H3066
13 voice in the Jews' l, and said, Hear ye H3066
Jer 5:15 a nation whose l thou knowest not, H3956
Ezk 3: 5 of an hard l, *but* to the house of Israel; H3956
6 and of an hard l, whose words thou H3956
Dan 3:29 nation, and l, which speak any thing H3961
Zep 3: 9 to the people a pure l, that they may all H8193
Act 2: 6 man heard them speak in his own l. G1258

LANGUAGES
Dan 3: 4 commanded, O people, nations, and l, H3961
7 the nations, and the l, fell down *and* H3961
4: 1 nations, and l, that dwell in all the H3961
5:19 nations, and l, trembled and feared H3961
6:25 nations, and l, that dwell in all the H3961
7:14 nations, and l, should serve him: his H3961
Zec 8:23 take hold out of all l of the nations, H3956

LANGUISH
Isa 16: 8 For the fields of Heshbon l, *and* the vine H535
19: 8 that spread nets upon the waters shall l. H535
24: 4 the haughty people of the earth do l. H535
Jer 14: 2 Judah mourneth, and the gates thereof l; H535
Hos 4: 3 therein shall l, with the beasts of the H535

LANGUISHED
Lam 2: 8 and the wall to lament; they l together. H535

LANGUISHETH
Isa 24: 4 away, the world l *and* fadeth away, the H535
7 The new wine mourneth, the vine l, all H535
33: 9 The earth mourneth *and* l: Lebanon is H535
Jer 15: 9 She that hath borne seven l: she hath H535
Joel 1:10 the new wine is dried up, the oil l. H535
12 The vine is dried up, and the fig tree l; the H535
Nah 1: 4 the rivers: Bashan l, and Carmel, and the H535
4 and Carmel, and the flower of Lebanon l. H535

LANGUISHING
Ps 41: 3 upon the bed of l: thou wilt make all his H1741

LANTERNS
Jn 18: 3 with l and torches and weapons. G5322

LAODICEA
Col 2: 1 and *for* them at L, and *for* as many as G2993
4:13 *that are* in L, and them in Hierapolis. G2993
15 Salute the brethren which are in L, and G2993
16 that ye likewise read the *epistle* from L. G2993
Rev 1:11 and unto Philadelphia, and unto L. G2993

LAODICEANS
Col 4:16 the church of the L; and that ye likewise G2994
Rev 3:14 the church of the L write; These things G2994

LAP
2Ki 4:39 wild gourds his l full, and came and H899
Neh 5:13 Also I shook my l, and said, So God H2684
Prv 16:33 The lot is cast into the l; but the whole H2436

LAPIDOTH
Jdg 4: 4 wife of L, she judged Israel at that time. H3941

LAPPED
Jdg 7: 6 And the number of them that l, *putting* H3952
7 hundred men that l will I save you, and H3952

LAPPETH
Jdg 7: 5 Every one that l of the water with his H3952
5 tongue, as a dog l, him shalt thou set by H3952

LAPWING
Lev 11:19 after her kind, and the l, and the bat. H1744
Dt 14:18 after her kind, and the l, and the bat. H1744

LARGE
Gen 34:21 land, behold, *it is* l enough for them; let H7342
Ex 3: 8 a good land and a l, unto a land flowing H7342
Jdg 18:10 and to a l land: for God hath H7342+H3027
2Sa 22:20 He brought me forth also into a l place: H4800
Neh 4:19 The work *is* great and l, and we are H7342
7: 4 Now the city *was* l and great: H7342+H3027
9:35 them, and in the l and fat land which H7342
Ps 18:19 He brought me forth also into a l place; H4800
31: 8 thou hast set my feet in a l room. H4800
118: 5 answered me, *and set me* in a l place. H4800
Isa 22:18 a ball into a l country: there H7342+H3027
30:23 day shall thy cattle feed in l pastures. H7337
33 made *it* deep *and* l: the pile thereof *is* H7337
Jer 22:14 me a wide house and l chambers, and H7304
Ezk 23:32 cup deep and l: thou shalt be laughed H7342
Hos 4:16 will feed them as a lamb in a l place. H4800
Mt 28:12 they gave l money unto the soldiers, G2425
Mk 14:15 And he will shew you a l upper room G3173
Lk 22:12 And he shall shew you a l upper room G3173
Gal 6:11 Ye see how l a letter I have written unto G4080
Rev 21:16 the length is as l as the breadth: and G5118

LARGENESS
1Ki 4:29 much, and l of heart, even as the H7341

LASAEA See LASEA.

LASCIVIOUSNESS
Mk 7:22 wickedness, deceit, l, an evil eye, G766
2Co 12:21 and l which they have committed. G766
Gal 5:19 Adultery, fornication, uncleanness, l, G766
Eph 4:19 over unto l, to work all uncleanness G766
1Pt 4: 3 when we walked in l, lusts, excess of G766
Jude 4 of our God into l, and denying the only G766

LASEA
Act 27: 8 nigh whereunto was the city *of* L. G2996

LASHA
Gen 10:19 and Admah, and Zeboim, even unto L. H3962

LASHARON
Jos 12:18 The king of Aphek, one; the king of L, H8289

LAST
Gen 49: 1 *that* which shall befall you in the l days. H319
19 him: but he shall overcome at the l. H6119
Nu 23:10 righteous, and let my l end be like his! H319
2Sa 19:11 Why are ye the l to bring the king back H314
12 then are ye the l to bring back the king? H314
23: 1 Now these *be* the l words of David. H314
1Ch 23:27 For by the l words of David the Levites H314
29:29 the king, first and l, behold, they *are* H314
2Ch 9:29 Solomon, first and l, *are* they not written H314
12:15 Now the acts of Rehoboam, first and l, H314
16:11 And, behold, the acts of Asa, first and l, H314
20:34 first and l, behold, they *are* written H314
25:26 Amaziah, first and l, behold, *are* they not H314
26:22 acts of Uzziah, first and l, did Isaiah the H314
28:26 all his ways, first and l, behold, they *are* H314
35:27 And his deeds, first and l, behold, they H314
Ezr 8:13 And of the l sons of Adonikam, whose H314
Neh 8:18 first day unto the l day, he read in the H314
Prv 5:11 And thou mourn at the l, when thy flesh H319
23:32 At the l it biteth like a serpent, and H319
Isa 2: 2 And it shall come to pass in the l days, H319
41: 4 LORD, the first, and with the l; I *am* he. H314
44: 6 I *am* the l; and beside me *there is* no God. H314
48:12 I *am* he; I *am* the first, I also *am* the l. H314
Jer 12: 4 they said, He shall not see our l end. H319
50:17 hath devoured him; and l this H314
Lam 1: 9 not her l end; therefore she came H319
Dan 4: 8 But at the l Daniel came in before me, H318
8: 3 than the other, and the higher came up l. H314
19 know what shall be in the l end of the H319
Am 9: 1 and I will slay the l of them with the H319
Mic 4: 1 But in the l days it shall come to pass, H319
Mt 12:45 there: and the l *state* of that man is G2078
19:30 But many *that are* first shall be l; and G2078
30 shall be last; and the l *shall be* first. G2078
20: 8 beginning from the l unto the first. G2078
12 Saying, These l have wrought *but* one G2078
14 I will give unto this l, even as unto thee. G2078
16 So the l shall be first, and the first last: G2078
16 So the last shall be first, and the first l: G2078
21:37 But l of all he sent unto them his son, G5305
22:27 And l of all the woman died also. G5305
26:60 none. At the l came two false witnesses, G5305
27:64 the l error shall be worse than the first. G2078
Mk 9:35 *same* shall be l of all, and servant of all. G2078
10:31 But many *that are* first shall be l; and G2078
31 *are* first shall be last; and the l first. G2078
12: 6 he sent him also l unto them, saying, G2078
22 no seed: l of all the woman died also. G2078
Lk 11:26 there: and the l *state* of that man is G2078
12:59 till thou hast paid the very l mite. G2078
13:30 And, behold, there are l which shall be G2078
30 first, and there are first which shall be l. G2078
20:32 L of all the woman died also. G5305
Jn 6:39 should raise it up again at the l day. G2078
40 life: and I will raise him up at the l day. G2078
44 and I will raise him up at the l day. G2078
54 life; and I will raise him up at the l day. G2078
7:37 In the l day, that great *day* of the feast, G2078
8: 9 *even* unto the l: and Jesus was left G2078
11:24 again in the resurrection at the l day. G2078
12:48 the same shall judge him in the l day. G2078
Act 2:17 And it shall come to pass in the l days, G2078
1Co 4: 9 us the apostles l, as it were appointed G2078
15: 8 And l of all he was seen of me also, as G2078
26 The l enemy *that* shall be destroyed *is* G2078
45 l Adam *was made* a quickening spirit. G2078
52 of an eye, at the l trump: for the G2078
Php 4:10 that now at the l your care of me hath G4218
2Ti 3: 1 This know also, that in the l days G2078
Heb 1: 2 Hath in these l days spoken unto us by G2078
Jas 5: 3 heaped treasure together for the l days. G2078
1Pt 1: 5 ready to be revealed in the l time. G2078
20 was manifest in these l times for you, G2078
2Pt 3: 3 there shall come in the l days scoffers, G2078
1Jn 2:18 Little children, it is the l time: and as ye G2078
18 whereby we know that it is the l time. G2078
Jude 18 be mockers in the l time, who should G2078
Rev 1:11 the first and the l: and, What thou seest, G2078
17 me, Fear not; I am the first and the l: G2078
2: 8 and the l, which was dead, and is alive; G2078
19 and the l *to be* more than the first. G2078
15: 1 having the seven l plagues; for in them G2078
21: 9 full of the seven l plagues, and talked G2078
22:13 and the end, the first and the l. G2078

LASTED
Jdg 14:17 while their feast l: and it came to pass H1961

LASTING
Dt 33:15 for the precious things of the l hills, H5769

LATCHET
Isa 5:27 nor the l of their shoes be broken: H8288
Mk 1: 7 I after me, the l of whose shoes I am G2438
Lk 3:16 than I cometh, the l of whose shoes I G2438
Jn 1:27 shoe's l I am not worthy to unloose. G2438

LATE
Ps 127: 2 up early, to sit up l, to eat the bread of H309
Mic 2: 8 Even of l my people is risen up as an H865
Jn 11: 8 the Jews of l sought to stone thee; G3568

LATELY
Act 18: 2 born in Pontus, l come from Italy, with G4373

LATIN
Lk 23:38 of Greek, and L, and Hebrew, THIS G4513
Jn 19:20 written in Hebrew, *and* Greek, *and* L. G4515

LATTER
Ex 4: 8 they will believe the voice of the l sign. H314
Nu 24:14 shall do to thy people in the l days. H319
20 his l end *shall be* that he perish for ever. H319
Dt 4:30 thee, *even* in the l days, if thou turn to H319
8:16 prove thee, to do thee good at thy l end; H319
11:14 the first rain and the l rain, that thou H4456
24: 3 And *if* the l husband hate her, and write H314
3 his house; or if the l husband die, which H314
31:29 befall you in the l days; because ye will H319

Dt 32:29 *that* they would consider their l end! H319
Ru 3:10 more kindness in the l end than at the H314
2Sa 2:26 be bitterness in the l end? how long shall H314
Job 8: 7 yet thy l end should greatly increase. H319
19:25 shall stand at the l *day* upon the earth: H314
29:23 their mouth wide *as* for the l rain. H4456
42:12 So the LORD blessed the l end of Job H319
Prv 16:15 his favour *is* as a cloud of the l rain. H4456
19:20 that thou mayest be wise in thy l end. H319
Isa 41:22 and know the l end of them; or declare H319
47: 7 neither didst remember the l end of it. H319
Jer 3: 3 and there hath been no l rain; and thou H4456
5:24 the former and the l, in his season: he H4456
23:20 the l days ye shall consider it perfectly. H319
30:24 heart: in the l days ye shall consider it. H319
48:47 of Moab in the l days, saith the LORD. H319
49:39 But it shall come to pass in the l days, H319
Ezk 38: 8 be visited: in the l years thou shalt come H319
16 it shall be in the l days, and I will bring H319
Dan 2:28 what shall be in the l days. Thy dream, H320
8:23 And in the l time of their kingdom, when H319
10:14 thy people in the l days: for yet the vision H319
11:29 it shall not be as the former, or as the l. H314
Hos 3: 5 the LORD and his goodness in the l days. H319
6: 3 as the l *and* former rain unto the earth. H4456
Joel 2:23 rain, and the l rain in the first *month*. H4456
Am 7: 1 shooting up of the l growth; and, lo, *it* H3954
1 the l growth after the king's mowings. H3954
Hag 2: 9 The glory of this l house shall be greater H314
Zec 10: 1 in the time of the l rain; *so* the LORD H4456
1Ti 4: 1 that in the l times some shall depart G5306
Jas 5: 7 it, until he receive the early and l rain. G3797
2Pt 2:20 and overcome, the l end is worse with G2078

LATTICE
Jdg 5:28 cried through the l, Why is his chariot *so* H822
2Ki 1: 2 And Ahaziah fell down through a l in H7639
Song 2: 9 shewing himself through the l. H2762

LAUD
Ro 15:11 all ye Gentiles; and l him, all ye people. G1867

LAUGH
Gen 18:13 did Sarah l, saying, Shall I of a surety H6711
15 And he said, Nay; but thou didst l. H6711
21: 6 And Sarah said, God hath made me to l, H6712
6 *so that* all that hear will l with me. H6711
Job 5:22 At destruction and famine thou shalt l: H7832
9:23 If the scourge slay suddenly, he will l at H3932
22:19 glad: and the innocent l them to scorn. H3932
Ps 2: 4 He that sitteth in the heavens shall l: the H7832
22: 7 All they that see me l me to scorn: they H3923
37:13 The Lord shall l at him: for he seeth H7832
52: 6 shall see, and fear, and shall l at him: H7832
59: 8 But thou, O LORD, shalt l at them; thou H7832
80: 6 and our enemies l among themselves. H3932
Prv 1:26 I also will l at your calamity; I will H7832
29: 9 whether he rage or l, *there is* no rest. H7832
Ecc 3: 4 A time to weep, and a time to l; a time H7832
Lk 6:21 *are ye* that weep now: for ye shall l. G1070
25 l now! for ye shall mourn and weep. G1070

LAUGHED
Gen 17:17 Then Abraham fell upon his face, and l, H6711
18:12 Therefore Sarah l within herself, H6711
15 Then Sarah denied, saying, I l not; for H6711
2Ki 19:21 despised thee, *and* l thee to scorn; the H3932
2Ch 30:10 l them to scorn, and mocked them. H7881
Neh 2:19 heard *it*, they l us to scorn, and H3932
Job 12: 4 him: the just upright *man is* l to scorn. H7831
29:24 *If* I l on them, they believed *it* not; and H7832
Isa 37:22 despised thee, *and* l thee to scorn; the H3392
Ezk 23:32 thou shalt be l to scorn and had in H6712
Mt 9:24 but sleepeth. And they l him to scorn. G2606
Mk 5:40 And they l him to scorn. But when he G2606
Lk 8:53 And they l him to scorn, knowing that G2606

LAUGHETH
Job 41:29 Darts are counted as stubble: he l at H7832

LAUGHING
Job 8:21 Till he fill thy mouth with l, and thy lips H7814

LAUGHTER
Ps 126: 2 Then was our mouth filled with l, and H7814
Prv 14:13 Even in l the heart is sorrowful; and the H7814
Ecc 2: 2 I said of l, *It is* mad: and of mirth, What H7814
7: 3 Sorrow *is* better than l: for by the H7814
6 so *is* the l of the fool: this also *is* vanity. H7814
10:19 A feast is made for l, and wine maketh H7814
Jas 4: 9 and weep: let your l be turned to G1071

LAUNCH
Lk 5: 4 said unto Simon, L out into the deep, G1877

LAUNCHED
Lk 8:22 other side of the lake. And they l forth. G321
Act 21: 1 them, and had l, we came with a straight G321
27: 2 of Adramyttium, we l, meaning to sail by G321
4 And when we had l from thence, we G321

LAVER
Ex 30:18 Thou shalt also make a l *of* brass, and H3595
28 all his vessels, and the l and his foot. H3595
31: 9 all his furniture, and the l and his foot, H3595
35:16 and all his vessels, the l and his foot, H3595
38: 8 And he made the l *of* brass, and the H3595
39:39 and all his vessels, the l and his foot, H3595
40: 7 And thou shalt set the l between the H3595
11 And thou shalt anoint the l and his H3595
30 And he set the l between the tent of the H3595
Lev 8:11 the l and his foot, to sanctify them. H3595
1Ki 7:30 under the l *were* undersetters molten, H3595
38 Then made he ten lavers of brass: one l H3595
38 baths: *and* every l was four cubits: *and* H3595
38 upon every one of the ten bases one l. H3595
2Ki 16:17 and removed the l from off them; and H3595

LAVERS
1Ki 7:38 Then made he ten l of brass: one laver H3595
40 And Hiram made the l, and the shovels, H3595
43 And the ten bases, and ten l on the H3595
2Ch 4: 6 He made also ten l, and put five on the H3595
14 He made also bases, and l made he H3595

LAVISH
Isa 46: 6 They l gold out of the bag, and weigh H2107

LAW
Gen 11:31 his daughter in l, his son Abram's wife; H3618
19:12 besides? son in l, and thy sons, and thy H2860
14 unto his sons in l, which married his H2860
14 as one that mocked unto his sons in l. H2860
38:11 his daughter in l, Remain a widow at H3618
13 thy father in l goeth up to Timnath H2524
16 his daughter in l.) And she said, What H3618
24 thy daughter in l hath played the H3618
25 to her father in l, saying, By the man, H2524
47:26 And Joseph made it a l over the land of H2706
Ex 3: 1 of Jethro his father in l, the priest of H2859
4:18 to Jethro his father in l, and said unto H2859
12:49 One l shall be to him that is homeborn, H8451
13: 9 that the LORD'S l may be in thy mouth: H8451
16: 4 whether they will walk in my l, or no. H8451
18: 1 Moses' father in l, heard of all that God H2859
2 Then Jethro, Moses' father in l, took H2859
5 And Jethro, Moses' father in l, came H2859
6 I thy father in l Jethro am come unto H2859
7 meet his father in l, and did obeisance, H2859
8 And Moses told his father in l all that H2859
12 And Jethro, Moses' father in l, took a H2859
12 with Moses' father in l before God. H2859
14 And when Moses' father in l saw all H2859
15 And Moses said unto his father in l, H2859
17 And Moses' father in l said unto him, H2859
24 father in l, and did all that he had said. H2859
27 And Moses let his father in l depart; H2859
24:12 of stone, and a l, and commandments H8451
Lev 6: 9 sons, saying, This *is* the l of the burnt H8451
14 And this *is* the l of the meat offering: H8451
25 saying, This *is* the l of the sin offering: H8451
7: 1 Likewise this *is* the l of the trespass H8451
7 *there is* one l for them: the priest H8451
11 And this *is* the l of the sacrifice of peace H8451
37 This *is* the l of the burnt offering, of the H8451
11:46 This *is* the l of the beasts, and of the H8451
12: 7 her blood. This *is* the l for her that hath H8451
13:59 This *is* the l of the plague of leprosy in H8451
14: 2 This shall be the l of the leper in the H8451
32 This *is* the l *of him* in whom *is* the H8451
54 This *is* the l for all manner of plague of H8451
57 when *it is* clean: this *is* the l of leprosy. H8451
15:32 This *is* the l of him that hath an issue, H8451
18:15 of thy daughter in l: she *is* thy son's H3618
20:12 And if a man lie with his daughter in l, H3618
24:22 Ye shall have one manner of l, as well H4941
Nu 5:29 This *is* the l of jealousies, when a wife H8451
30 priest shall execute upon her all this l. H8451
6:13 And this *is* the l of the Nazarite, when H8451
21 This *is* the l of the Nazarite who hath H8451
21 he must do after the l of his separation. H8451
10:29 Moses' father in l, We are journeying H2859
15:16 One l and one manner shall be for you, H8451
29 Ye shall have one l for him that sinneth H8451
19: 2 This *is* the ordinance of the l which the H8451
14 This *is* the l, when a man dieth in a tent: H8451
31:21 l which the LORD commanded Moses; H8451
Dt 1: 5 began Moses to declare this l, saying, H8451
4: 8 this l, which I set before you this day? H8451
44 And this *is* the l which Moses set before H8451
17:11 According to the sentence of the l H8451
18 him a copy of this l in a book out of H8451
19 of this l and these statutes, to do them: H8451
27: 3 all the words of this l, when thou art H8451
8 all the words of this l very plainly. H8451
23 in l. And all the people shall say, Amen. H2859
26 the words of this l to do them. And all H8451
28:58 the words of this l that are written in H8451
61 in the book of this l, them will the LORD H8451
29:21 that are written in this book of the l: H8451
29 that *we* may do all the words of this l. H8451
30:10 in this book of the l, *and* if thou turn H8451
31: 9 And Moses wrote this l, and delivered it H8451
11 this l before all Israel in their hearing. H8451
12 and observe to do all the words of this l: H8451
24 l in a book, until they were finished, H8451
26 Take this book of the l, and put it in the H8451
32:46 to observe to do, all the words of this l. H8451
33: 2 his right hand *went* a fiery l for them. H1881
4 Moses commanded us a l, *even* the H8451
10 and Israel thy l: they shall put incense H8451
Jos 1: 7 to all the l, which Moses my servant H8451
8 This book of the l shall not depart out H8451
8:31 in the book of the l of Moses, an altar H8451
32 a copy of the l of Moses, which he H8451
34 all the words of the l, the blessings and H8451
34 to all that is written in the book of the l. H8451
22: 5 and the l, which Moses the servant H8451
23: 6 in the book of the l of Moses, that ye H8451
24:26 in the book of the l of God, and took a H8451
Jdg 1:16 Moses' father in l, went up out of the H2859
4:11 the father in l of Moses, had severed H2859
15: 6 the son in l of the Timnite, because H2860
19: 4 And his father in l, the damsel's father, H2859
5 unto his son in l, Comfort thine heart H2860
7 his father in l urged him: therefore H2859
9 his father in l, the damsel's father, H2859
Ru 1: 6 Then she arose with her daughters in l, H3618
7 two daughters in l with her; and they H3618
8 two daughters in l, Go, return each to H3618
14 mother in l; but Ruth clave unto her. H2545
15 And she said, Behold, thy sister in l is H2994
15 gods: return thou after thy sister in l. H2994
22 her daughter in l, with her, which H3618
2:11 unto thy mother in l since the death of H2545
18 and her mother in l saw what she had H2545
19 And her mother in l said unto her, H2545
19 her mother in l with whom she had H2545
20 And Naomi said unto her daughter in l, H3618
22 Ruth her daughter in l, *It is* good, my H3618
23 harvest; and dwelt with her mother in l. H2545
3: 1 Then Naomi her mother in l said unto H2545
6 to all that her mother in l bade her. H2545
16 And when she came to her mother in l, H2545
17 me, Go not empty unto thy mother in l. H2545
4:15 for thy daughter in l, which loveth thee, H3618
1Sa 4:19 And his daughter in l, Phinehas' wife, H3618
19 that her father in l and her husband H2524
21 of her father in l and her husband. H2524
18:18 that I should be son in l to the king? H2860
21 be my son in l in *the one of* the twain. H2859
22 now therefore be the king's son in l. H2859
23 to be a king's son in l, seeing that I *am* a H2859
26 son in l: and the days were not expired. H2859
27 the king's son in l. And Saul gave him H2859
22:14 is the king's son in l, and goeth at thy H2860
1Ki 2: 3 it is written in the l of Moses, that thou H8451
2Ki 8:27 *was* the son in l of the house of Ahab. H2860
10:31 But Jehu took no heed to walk in the l H8451
14: 6 in the book of the l of Moses, wherein H8451
17:13 to all the l which I commanded H8451
34 or after the l and commandment H8451
37 and the l, and the commandment, H8451
21: 8 to all the l that my servant Moses H8451
22: 8 the book of the l in the house of the H8451
11 book of the l, that he rent his clothes. H8451
23:24 the words of the l which were written H8451

2Ki 23:25 to all the l of Moses; neither after H8451
1Ch 2: 4 And Tamar his daughter in l bare him H3618
16:17 to Jacob for a l, *and* to Israel *for* an H2706
40 is written in the l of the LORD, which H8451
22:12 mayest keep the l of the LORD thy God. H8451
2Ch 6:16 in my l, as thou hast walked before me. H8451
12: 1 l of the LORD, and all Israel with him. H8451
14: 4 and to do the l and the commandment. H8451
15: 3 without a teaching priest, and without l. H8451
17: 9 *had* the book of the l of the LORD with H8451
19:10 blood, between l and commandment, H8451
23:18 as *it is* written in the l of Moses, with H8451
25: 4 as *it is* written in the l in the book of H8451
30:16 according to the l of Moses the man of H8451
31: 3 as *it is* written in the l of the LORD. H8451
4 be encouraged in the l of the LORD. H8451
21 house of God, and in the l, and in the H8451
33: 8 to the whole l and the statutes and H8451
34:14 of the l of the LORD *given* by Moses. H8451
15 the book of the l in the house of the H8451
19 words of the l, that he rent his clothes. H8451
35:26 *which was* written in the l of the LORD, H8451
Ezr 3: 2 in the l of Moses the man of God. H8451
7: 6 a ready scribe in the l of Moses, which H8451
10 heart to seek the l of the LORD, and to H8451
12 a scribe of the l of the God of heaven, H1882
14 the l of thy God which *is* in thine hand; H1882
21 the scribe of the l of the God of heaven, H1882
26 And whosoever will not do the l of thy H1882
26 of thy God, and the l of the king, let H1882
10: 3 and let it be done according to the l. H8451
Neh 6:18 he *was* the son in l of Shechaniah the H2860
8: 1 the book of the l of Moses, which the H8451
2 And Ezra the priest brought the l H8451
3 *were attentive* unto the book of the l. H8451
7 l: and the people *stood* in their place. H8451
8 So they read in the book in the l of God H8451
9 when they heard the words of the l. H8451
13 even to understand the words of the l. H8451
14 And they found written in the l which H8451
18 in the book of the l of God. And they H8451
9: 3 in the book of the l of the LORD their H8451
26 thee, and cast thy l behind their backs, H8451
29 again unto thy l: yet they dealt proudly, H8451
34 fathers, kept thy l, nor hearkened unto H8451
10:28 the lands unto the l of God, their wives, H8451
29 to walk in God's l, which was given by H8451
34 LORD our God, as *it is* written in the l: H8451
36 *it is* written in the l, and the firstlings of H8451
12:44 the portions of the l for the priests and H8451
13: 3 when they had heard the l, that they H8451
28 priest, *was* son in l to Sanballat the H2860
Est 1: 8 according to the l; none did compel: for H1881
13 toward all that knew l and judgment: H1881
15 according to l, because she hath not H1881
4:11 called, *there is* one l of his to put *him* to H1881
16 to the l: and if I perish, I perish. H1881
Job 22:22 Receive, I pray thee, the l from his H8451
Ps 1: 2 But his delight *is* in the l of the LORD; H8451
2 in his l doth he meditate day and night. H8451
19: 7 The l of the LORD *is* perfect, converting H8451
37:31 The l of his God *is* in his heart; none of H8451
40: 8 O my God: yea, thy l *is* within my heart. H8451
78: 1 Give ear, O my people, *to* my l: incline H8451
5 and appointed a l in Israel, which he H8451
10 of God, and refused to walk in his l; H8451
81: 4 For this *was* a statute for Israel, *and* a l H4941
89:30 If his children forsake my l, and walk H8451
94:12 O LORD, and teachest him out of thy l; H8451
20 thee, which frameth mischief by a l? H2706
105:10 unto Jacob for a l, *and* to Israel *for* an H2706
119: 1 the way, who walk in the l of the LORD. H8451
18 behold wondrous things out of thy l. H8451
29 of lying: and grant me thy l graciously. H8451
34 I shall keep thy l; yea, I shall observe H8451
44 So shall I keep thy l continually for ever H8451
51 *yet* have I not declined from thy l. H8451
53 because of the wicked that forsake thy l. H8451
55 LORD, in the night, and have kept thy l. H8451
61 me: *but* I have not forgotten thy l. H8451
70 is as fat as grease; *but* I delight in thy l. H8451
72 The l of thy mouth *is* better unto me H8451
77 that I may live: for thy l *is* my delight. H8451
85 pits for me, which *are* not after thy l. H8451
92 Unless thy l *had been* my delights, I H8451
97 O how love I thy l! it *is* my meditation H8451
109 in my hand: yet do I not forget thy l. H8451
113 I hate *vain* thoughts: but thy l do I love. H8451
126 to work: *for* they have made void thy l. H8451

Ps119:136 mine eyes, because they keep not thy l. H8451
142 righteousness, and thy l *is* the truth. H8451
150 after mischief: they are far from thy l. H8451
153 and deliver me: for I do not forget thy l. H8451
163 I hate and abhor lying: *but* thy l do I H8451
165 Great peace have they which love thy l: H8451
174 O LORD; and thy l *is* my delight. H8451
Prv 1: 8 and forsake not the l of thy mother: H8451
3: 1 My son, forget not my l; but let thine H8451
4: 2 you good doctrine, forsake ye not my l. H8451
6:20 and forsake not the l of thy mother: H8451
23 *is* a lamp; and the l *is* light; and H8451
7: 2 live; and my l as the apple of thine eye. H8451
13:14 The l of the wise *is* a fountain of life, to H8451
28: 4 They that forsake the l praise the H8451
4 such as keep the l contend with them. H8451
7 Whoso keepeth the l *is* a wise son: but H8451
9 l, even his prayer *shall be* abomination. H8451
29:18 but he that keepeth the l, happy *is* he. H8451
31: 5 Lest they drink, and forget the l, and H2710
26 and in her tongue *is* the l of kindness. H8451
Isa 1:10 l of our God, ye people of Gomorrah. H8451
2: 3 shall go forth the l, and the word of the H8451
5:24 have cast away the l of the LORD of H8451
8:16 Bind up the testimony, seal the l H8451
20 To the l and to the testimony: if they H8451
30: 9 *that* will not hear the l of the LORD: H8451
42: 4 earth: and the isles shall wait for his l. H8451
21 magnify the l, and make *it* honourable. H8451
24 neither were they obedient unto his l. H8451
51: 4 O my nation: for a l shall proceed from H8451
7 in whose heart *is* my l; fear ye not the H8451
Jer 2: 8 they that handle the l knew me not: the H8451
6:19 my words, nor to my l, but rejected it. H8451
8: 8 How do ye say, We *are* wise, and the l H8451
9:13 have forsaken my l which I set before H8451
16:11 forsaken me, and have not kept my l; H8451
18:18 Jeremiah; for the l shall not perish H8451
26: 4 in my l, which I have set before you, H8451
31:33 I will put my l in their inward parts, H8451
32:11 *according* to the l and custom, and that H4687
23 walked in thy l; they have done nothing H8451
44:10 nor walked in my l, nor in my statutes, H8451
23 nor walked in his l, nor in his statutes, H8451
Lam 2: 9 the Gentiles: the l is no *more*; her H8451
Ezk 7:26 prophet; but the l shall perish from the H8451
22:11 his daughter in l; and another in thee H3618
26 Her priests have violated my l, and H8451
43:12 This *is* the l of the house; Upon the top H8451
12 holy. Behold, this *is* the l of the house. H8451
Dan 6: 5 him concerning the l of his God. H1882
8 according to the l of the Medes and H1882
12 according to the l of the Medes and H1882
15 O king, that the l of the Medes and H1882
9:11 Yea, all Israel have transgressed thy l, H8451
11 *is* written in the l of Moses the servant H8451
13 As *it is* written in the l of Moses, all this H8451
Hos 4: 6 hast forgotten the l of thy God, I will H8451
8: 1 covenant, and trespassed against my l. H8451
12 the great things of my l, *but* they were H8451
Am 2: 4 have despised the l of the LORD, and H8451
Mic 4: 2 in his paths: for the l shall go forth of H8451
7: 6 the daughter in l against her mother H3618
6 her mother in l; a man's enemies *are* H2545
Hab 1: 4 Therefore the l is slacked, and H8451
Zep 3: 4 they have done violence to the l. H8451
Hag 2:11 the priests *concerning* the l, saying, H8451
Zec 7:12 should hear the l, and the words which H8451
Mal 2: 6 The l of truth was in his mouth, and H8451
7 should seek the l at his mouth: for he H8451
8 to stumble at the l; ye have corrupted H8451
9 my ways, but have been partial in the l. H8451
4: 4 Remember ye the l of Moses my H8451
Mt 5:17 to destroy the l, or the prophets: I am G3551
18 wise pass from the l, till all be fulfilled. G3551
40 And if any man will sue thee at the l, G2919
7:12 them: for this is the l and the prophets. G3551
10:35 in l against her mother in law. G3565
35 daughter in law against her mother in l. G3994
11:13 For all the prophets and the l G3551
12: 5 Or have ye not read in the l, how that on G3551
22:36 *is* the great commandment in the l? G3551
40 hang all the l and the prophets. G3551
23:23 *matters* of the l, judgment, mercy, and G3551
Lk 2:22 according to the l of Moses were G3551
23 (As it is written in the l of the Lord, G3551
24 is said in the l of the Lord, A pair of G3551
27 to do for him after the custom of the l, G3551
39 according to the l of the Lord, they G3551

Lk 5:17 and doctors of the l sitting by, which G3547
10:26 is written in the l? how readest thou? G3551
12:53 the mother in l against her daughter G3994
53 her daughter in l, and the daughter in G3565
53 in l against her mother in law. G3565
53 daughter in law against her mother in l. G3994
16:16 The l and the prophets *were* until John: G3551
17 to pass, than one tittle of the l to fail. G3551
24:44 were written in the l of Moses, and *in* G3551
Jn 1:17 For the l was given by Moses, *but* grace G3551
45 Moses in the l, and the prophets, did G3551
7:19 Did not Moses give you the l, and *yet* G3551
19 the l? Why go ye about to kill me? G3551
23 that the l of Moses should not G3551
49 But this people who knoweth not the l G3551
51 Doth our l judge *any* man, before it G3551
8: 5 Now Moses in the l commanded us, G3551
17 It is also written in your l, that the G3551
10:34 written in your l, I said, Ye are gods? G3551
12:34 heard out of the l that Christ abideth G3551
15:25 their l, They hated me without a cause. G3551
18:13 he was father in l to Caiaphas, which G3995
31 according to your l. The Jews therefore G3551
19: 7 The Jews answered him, We have a l, G3551
7 a law, and by our l he ought to die, G3551
Act 5:34 a doctor of the l, had in reputation G3547
6:13 words against this holy place, and the l: G3551
7:53 Who have received the l by the G3551
13:15 And after the reading of the l and the G3551
39 could not be justified by the l of Moses. G3551
15: 5 command *them* to keep the l of Moses. G3551
24 and keep the l: to whom we gave no G3551
18:13 men to worship God contrary to the l. G3551
15 and *of* your l, look ye *to it*; for I will G3551
19:38 any man, the l is open, and there are G60
21:20 believe; and they are all zealous of the l: G3551
24 also walkest orderly, and keepest the l. G3551
28 people, and the l, and this place: and G3551
22: 3 manner of the l of the fathers, and was G3551
12 according to the l, having a good report G3551
23: 3 judge me after the l, and commandest G3551
3 me to be smitten contrary to the l? G3891
29 questions of their l, but to have nothing G3551
24: 6 would have judged according to our l. G3551
14 are written in the l and in the prophets: G3551
25: 8 against the l of the Jews, neither G3551
28:23 both out of the l of Moses, and *out of* G3551
Ro 2:12 For as many as have sinned without l G460
12 also perish without l: and as many as G460
12 in the l shall be judged by the law; G3551
12 in the law shall be judged by the l; G3551
13 (For not the hearers of the l *are* just G3551
13 but the doers of the l shall be justified. G3551
14 have not the l, do by nature the things G3551
14 contained in the l, these, having not the G3551
14 not the l, are a law unto themselves: G3551
14 not the law, are a l unto themselves: G3551
15 Which shew the work of the l written in G3551
17 in the l, and makest thy boast of God, G3551
18 excellent, being instructed out of the l; G3551
20 of knowledge and of the truth in the l. G3551
23 Thou that makest thy boast of the l, G3551
23 breaking the l dishonourest thou God? G3551
25 if thou keep the l: but if thou be a G3551
25 be a breaker of the l, thy circumcision is G3551
26 of the l, shall not his uncircumcision G3551
27 if it fulfil the l, judge thee, who by the G3551
27 and circumcision dost transgress the l? G3551
3:19 things soever the l saith, it saith to G3551
19 who are under the l: that every mouth G3551
20 Therefore by the deeds of the l there G3551
20 for by the l *is* the knowledge of sin. G3551
21 of God without the l is manifested, G3551
21 witnessed by the l and the prophets; G3551
27 l? of works? Nay: but by the law of faith. G3551
27 of works? Nay: but by the l of faith. G3551
28 by faith without the deeds of the l. G3551
31 Do we then make void the l through G3551
31 God forbid: yea, we establish the l. G3551
4:13 his seed, through the l, but through the G3551
14 For if they which are of the l *be* heirs, G3551
15 Because the l worketh wrath: for where G3551
15 where no l is, *there is* no transgression. G3551
16 which is of the l, but to that also which G3551
5:13 (For until the l sin was in the world: G3551
13 sin is not imputed when there is no l. G3551
20 Moreover the l entered, that the offence G3551
6:14 ye are not under the l, but under grace. G3551
15 the l, but under grace? God forbid. G3551

Ro 7: 1 that know the l,) how that the law hath G3551
1 the law,) how that the l hath dominion G3551
2 is bound by the l to *her* husband so G3551
2 she is loosed from the l of *her* husband. G3551
3 she is free from that l; so that she is no G3551
4 dead to the l by the body of Christ; G3551
5 which were by the l, did work in our G3551
6 But now we are delivered from the l, G3551
7 What shall we say then? *Is* the l sin? G3551
7 sin, but by the l: for I had not known G3551
7 the l had said, Thou shalt not covet. G3551
8 For without the l sin *was* dead. G3551
9 For I was alive without the l once: but G3551
12 Wherefore the l *is* holy, and the G3551
14 For we know that the l is spiritual: but I G3551
16 not, I consent unto the l that *it is* good. G3551
21 I find then a l, that, when I would do G3551
22 For I delight in the l of God after the G3551
23 But I see another l in my members, G3551
23 against the l of my mind, and bringing G3551
23 to the l of sin which is in my members. G3551
25 I myself serve the l of God; but with the G3551
25 of God; but with the flesh the l of sin. G3551
8: 2 For the l of the Spirit of life in Christ G3551
2 me free from the l of sin and death. G3551
3 For what the l could not do, in that it G3551
4 That the righteousness of the l might G3551
7 to the l of God, neither indeed can be. G3551
9: 4 the giving of the l, and the service *of* G3548
31 But Israel, which followed after the l of G3551
31 not attained to the l of righteousness. G3551
32 by the works of the l. For they stumbled G3551
10: 4 For Christ *is* the end of the l for G3551
5 which is of the l, That the man which G3551
13: 8 that loveth another hath fulfilled the l. G3551
10 therefore love *is* the fulfilling of the l. G3551
1Co 6: 1 another, go to l before the unjust, and G2919
6 But brother goeth to l with brother, and G2919
7 because ye go to l one with another. G2192
7:39 The wife is bound by the l as long as G3551
9: 8 a man? or saith not the l the same also? G3551
9 For it is written in the l of Moses, Thou G3551
20 that are under the l, as under the law, G3551
20 the law, as under the l, that I might gain G3551
20 I might gain them that are under the l; G3551
21 To them that are without l, as without G459
21 law, as without l, (being not without law G459
21 (being not without l to God, but under G459
21 to God, but under the l to Christ,) that I G1772
21 that I might gain them that are without l. G459
14:21 In the l it is written, With *men of* other G3551
34 be under obedience, as also saith the l. G3551
15:56 *is* sin; and the strength of sin *is* the l. G3551
Gal 2:16 by the works of the l, but by the faith of G3551
16 by the works of the l: for by the works of G3551
16 works of the l shall no flesh be justified. G3551
19 For I through the l am dead to the law, G3551
19 For I through the law am dead to the l, G3551
21 by the l, then Christ is dead in vain. G3551
3: 2 of the l, or by the hearing of faith? G3551
5 of the l, or by the hearing of faith? G3551
10 For as many as are of the works of the l G3551
10 written in the book of the l to do them. G3551
11 But that no man is justified by the l in G3551
12 And the l is not of faith: but, The man G3551
13 the curse of the l, being made a curse G3551
17 of God in Christ, the l, which was four G3551
18 For if the inheritance *be* of the l, *it is* no G3551
19 Wherefore then *serveth* the l? It was G3551
21 *Is* the l then against the promises of G3551
21 if there had been a l given which could G3551
21 should have been by the l. G3551
23 kept under the l, shut up unto the faith G3551
24 Wherefore the l was our schoolmaster G3551
4: 4 made of a woman, made under the l, G3551
5 To redeem them that were under the l, G3551
21 Tell me, ye that desire to be under the l, G3551
21 to be under the law, do ye not hear the l? G3551
5: 3 that he is a debtor to do the whole l. G3551
4 by the l; ye are fallen from grace. G3551
14 For all the l is fulfilled in one word, G3551
18 led of the Spirit, ye are not under the l. G3551
23 temperance: against such there is no l. G3551
6: 2 burdens, and so fulfil the l of Christ. G3551
13 keep the l; but desire to have you G3551
Eph 2:15 enmity, *even* the l of commandments G3551
Php 3: 5 Hebrews; as touching the l, a Pharisee; G3551
6 which is in the l, blameless. G3551
9 which is of the l, but that which is G3551
1Ti 1: 7 Desiring to be teachers of the l; G3547
8 But we know that the l *is* good, if a man G3551
9 Knowing this, that the l is not made for G3551
Tit 3: 9 the l; for they are unprofitable and vain. G3544
Heb 7: 5 according to the l, that is, of their G3551
11 received the l,) what further need *was* G3549
12 made of necessity a change also of the l. G3551
16 Who is made, not after the l of a carnal G3551
19 For the l made nothing perfect, but the G3551
28 For the l maketh men high priests G3551
28 was since the l, *maketh* the Son, who G3551
8: 4 priests that offer gifts according to the l: G3551
9:19 according to the l, he took the blood of G3551
22 And almost all things are by the l G3551
10: 1 For the l having a shadow of good G3551
8 *therein*; which are offered by the l; G3551
28 He that despised Moses' l died without G3551
Jas 1:25 But whoso looketh into the perfect l of G3551
2: 8 If ye fulfil the royal l according to the G3551
9 are convinced of the l as transgressors. G3551
10 For whosoever shall keep the whole l, G3551
11 thou art become a transgressor of the l. G3551
12 that shall be judged by the l of liberty. G3551
4:11 evil of the l, and judgeth the law: G3551
11 and judgeth the l: but if thou judge the G3551
11 if thou judge the l, thou art not a doer of G3551
11 thou art not a doer of the l, but a judge. G3551
1Jn 3: 4 l: for sin is the transgression of the law. G458
4 law: for sin is the transgression of the l. G458

LAWFUL

Ezr 7:24 of God, it shall not be l to impose toll, H7990
Isa 49:24 the mighty, or the l captive delivered? H6662
Ezk 18: 5 just, and do that which is l and right, H4941
19 done that which is l and right, *and* H4941
21 do that which is l and right, he shall H4941
27 l and right, he shall save his soul alive. H4941
33:14 sin, and do that which is l and right; H4941
16 which is l and right; he shall surely live. H4941
19 is l and right, he shall live thereby. H4941
Mt 12: 2 is not l to do upon the sabbath day. G1832
4 which was not l for him to eat, neither G1832
10 asked him, saying, Is it l to heal on the G1832
12 it is l to do well on the sabbath days. G1832
14: 4 For John said unto him, It is not l for G1832
19: 3 unto him, Is it l for a man to put away G1832
20:15 Is it not l for me to do what I will with G1832
22:17 it l to give tribute unto Caesar, or not? G1832
27: 6 and said, It is not l for to put them into G1832
Mk 2:24 on the sabbath day that which is not l? G1832
26 which is not l to eat but for the priests, G1832
3: 4 And he saith unto them, Is it l to do G1832
6:18 not l for thee to have thy brother's wife. G1832
10: 2 asked him, Is it l for a man to put away G1832
12:14 Is it l to give tribute to Caesar, or not? G1832
Lk 6: 2 is not l to do on the sabbath days? G1832
4 is not l to eat but for the priests alone? G1832
9 ask you one thing; Is it l on the sabbath G1832
14: 3 Is it l to heal on the sabbath day? G1832
20:22 Is it l for us to give tribute unto Caesar, G1832
Jn 5:10 day: it is not l for thee to carry *thy* bed. G1832
18:31 is not l for us to put any man to death: G1832
Act 16:21 And teach customs, which are not l for G1832
19:39 it shall be determined in a l assembly. G1772
22:25 that stood by, Is it l for you to scourge a G1832
1Co 6:12 All things are l unto me, but all things G1832
12 all things are l for me, but I will not G1832
10:23 All things are l for me, but all things G1832
23 are l for me, but all things edify not. G1832
2Co 12: 4 which it is not l for a man to utter. G1832

LAWFULLY

1Ti 1: 8 that the law *is* good, if a man use it l; G3545
2Ti 2: 5 *yet* is he not crowned, except he strive l. G3545

LAWGIVER

Gen 49:10 from Judah, nor a l from between his H2710
Nu 21:18 *direction of* the l, with their staves. And H2710
Dt 33:21 *in* a portion of the l, *was he* seated; and H2710
Ps 60: 7 strength of mine head; Judah *is* my l; H2710
108: 8 strength of mine head; Judah *is* my l; H2710
Isa 33:22 l, the LORD *is* our king; he will save us. H2710
Jas 4:12 There is one l, who is able to save and G3550

LAWLESS

1Ti 1: 9 man, but for the l and disobedient, for G459

LAWS

Gen 26: 5 commandments, my statutes, and my l. H8451
Ex 16:28 to keep my commandments and my l? H8451
18:16 know the statutes of God, and his l. H8451
20 ordinances and l, and shalt shew them H8451
Lev 26:46 judgments and l, which the LORD made H8451
Ezr 7:25 all such as know the l of thy God; and H1882
Neh 9:13 l, good statutes and commandments: H8451
14 and l, by the hand of Moses thy servant: H8451
Est 1:19 written among the l of the Persians and H1881
3: 8 and their l *are* diverse from all H1881
8 they the king's l: therefore it *is* not for H1881
Ps 105:45 and keep his l. Praise ye the LORD. H8451
Isa 24: 5 have transgressed the l, changed the H8451
Ezk 43:11 thereof, and all the l thereof: and write H8451
44: 5 LORD, and all the l thereof; and mark H8451
24 they shall keep my l and my statutes in H8451
Dan 7:25 to change times and l: and they shall be H1882
9:10 our God, to walk in his l, which he set H8451
Heb 8:10 Lord; I will put my l into their mind, G3551
10:16 Lord, I will put my l into their hearts, G3551

LAWYER

Mt 22:35 Then one of them, *which was* a l, asked G3544
Lk 10:25 And, behold, a certain l stood up, and G3544
Tit 3:13 Bring Zenas the l and Apollos on their G3544

LAWYERS

Lk 7:30 But the Pharisees and l rejected the G3544
11:45 Then answered one of the l, and said G3544
46 And he said, Woe unto you also, *ye* l! G3544
52 Woe unto you, l! for ye have taken away G3544
14: 3 And Jesus answering spake unto the l G3544

LAY

Gen 19: 4 But before they l down, the men of the H7901
33 went in, and l with her father; and H7901
33 when she l down, nor when she arose. H7901
34 younger, Behold, I l yesternight with H7901
35 arose, and l with him; and he perceived H7901
35 when she l down, nor when she arose. H7901
22:12 And he said, L not thine hand upon the H7971
28:11 and l down in that place to sleep. H7901
30:16 And he l with her that night. H7901
34: 2 her, and l with her, and defiled her. H7901
35:22 that Reuben went and l with Bilhah his H7901
37:22 wilderness, and l no hand upon him; H7971
41:35 that come, and l up corn under the H6651
Ex 5: 8 ye shall l upon them; ye shall H7760
7: 4 you, that I may l my hand upon Egypt, H5414
16:13 the dew l round about the host. H7902
14 And when the dew that l was gone up, H7902
14 wilderness *there l* a small round thing,
23 remaineth over l up for you to be kept H3240
33 therein, and l it up before the LORD, H3240
21:22 husband will l upon him; and he shall H7896
22:25 neither shalt thou l upon him usury. H7760
Lev 1: 7 and l the wood in order upon the fire:
8 And the priests, Aaron's sons, shall l the
12 and the priest shall l them in order on
2:15 And thou shalt put oil upon it, and l H7760
3: 2 And he shall l his hand upon the head H5564
8 And he shall l his hand upon the head H5564
13 And he shall l his hand upon the head H5564
4: 4 LORD; and shall l his hand upon the H5564
15 congregation shall l their hands upon H5564
24 And he shall l his hand upon the head H5564
29 And he shall l his hand upon the head H5564
33 And he shall l his hand upon the head H5564
6:12 morning, and l the burnt offering in
16:21 And Aaron shall l both his hands upon H5564
24:14 all that heard *him* l their hands upon H5564
Nu 8:12 And the Levites shall l their hands H5564
12:11 I beseech thee, l not the sin upon us, H7896
17: 4 And thou shalt l them up in the H3240
19: 9 of the heifer, and l *them* up without the H3240
24: 9 He couched, he l down as a lion, and as H7901
27:18 the spirit, and l thine hand upon him; H5564
Dt 7:15 l them upon all *them* that hate thee. H5414
11:18 Therefore shall ye l up these my words H7760
25 your God shall l the fear of you and the H5414
14:28 year, and shalt l *it* up within thy gates: H3240
21: 8 redeemed, and l not innocent blood H5414
19 Then shall his father and his mother l
22:22 *both* the man that l with the woman, H7901
25 the man only that l with her shall die: H7901
28 not betrothed, and l hold on her, and lie
29 Then the man that l with her shall give H7901
Jos 6:26 Jericho: he shall l the foundation thereof
8: 2 l thee an ambush for the city behind it. H7760
15:46 From Ekron even unto the sea, all that *l*

Jdg 4:22 l dead, and the nail *was* in his temples. H5307
5:27 At her feet he bowed, he fell, he l down: H7901
6:20 cakes, and l *them* upon this rock, H3240
7:12 of the east l along in the valley like H5307
13 and overturned it, that the tent l along. H5307
14:17 her, because she l sore upon him: and
16: 3 And Samson l till midnight, and arose H7901
18:19 Hold thy peace, l thine hand upon thy H7760
Ru 3: 4 his feet, and l thee down; and he will H7901
8 and, behold, a woman l at his feet. H7901
14 And she l at his feet until the morning: H7901
1Sa 2:22 and how they l with the women that H7901
3: 5 down again. And he went and l down. H7901
9 Samuel went and l down in his place. H7901
15 And Samuel l until the morning, and H7901
6: 8 And take the ark of the LORD, and l it H5414
11: 2 and l it *for* a reproach upon all Israel. H7760
19:24 like manner, and l down naked all that H5307
26: 5 place where Saul l, and Abner the son of H7901
5 his host: and Saul l in the trench, and H7901
7 and, behold, Saul l sleeping within the H7901
7 and the people l round about him. H7901
2Sa 2:21 or to thy left, and l thee hold on one of
4: 5 of Ish-bosheth, who l on a bed at noon. H7901
7 into the house, he l on his bed in his H7901
11: 4 in unto him, and he l with her; for she H7901
12: 3 of his own cup, and l in his bosom, and H7901
16 went in, and l all night upon the earth. H7901
24 in unto her, and l with her: and she H7901
13: 5 And Jonadab said unto him, L thee H7901
6 So Amnon l down, and made himself H7901
14 than she, forced her, and l with her. H7901
31 his garments, and l on the earth; and H7901
19:32 while he l at Mahanaim; for he H7871
1Ki 5:17 stones, to l the foundation of the house.
7: 3 *l* on forty five pillars, fifteen *in* a row.
13: 4 the altar, saying, L hold on him. And his
31 *is* buried; l my bones beside his bones: H3240
18:23 it in pieces, and l *it* on wood, and put H7760
23 and l *it* on wood, and put no fire *under:* H5414
19: 5 And as he l and slept under a juniper H7901
21:27 and l in sackcloth, and went softly. H7901
2Ki 4:11 turned into the chamber, and l there. H7901
29 l my staff upon the face of the child. H7760
34 And he went up, and l upon the child, H7901
9:16 Jezreel; for Joram l there. And Ahaziah H7901
10: 8 sons. And he said, L ye them in two H7760
19:25 l waste fenced cities *into* ruinous heaps.
2Ch 31: 7 In the third month they began to l the
36:21 *for* as long as she l desolate she kept
Ezr 8:31 and of such as l in wait by the way.
Neh 13:21 ye do *so* again, I will l hands on you. H7971
Est 2:21 to l hand on the king Ahasuerus. H7971
3: 6 And he thought scorn to l hands on H7971
4: 3 and many l in sackcloth and ashes. H3331
6: 2 to l hand on the king Ahasuerus. H7971
9: 2 king Ahasuerus, to l hand on such as H7971
Job 9:33 us, *that* might l his hand upon us both. H7896
17: 3 L down now, put me in a surety with H7760
21: 5 Mark me, and be astonished, and l H7760
22:22 and l up his words in thine heart. H7760
24 Then shalt thou l up gold as dust, and H7896
29:19 the dew l all night upon my branch. H3885
34:23 For he will not l upon man more *than* H7760
40: 4 I will l mine hand upon my mouth. H7760
41: 8 L thine hand upon him, remember the H7760
Ps 4: 8 I will both l me down in peace, and H7901
7: 5 and l mine honour in the dust. Selah. H7931
38:12 They also that seek after my life l snares
71:10 l wait for my soul take counsel together,
84: 3 where she may l her young, *even* thine H7896
104:22 and l them down in their dens. H7257
Prv 1:11 If they say, Come with us, let us l wait
18 And they l wait for their *own* blood; they
3:18 She *is* a tree of life to them that l hold
7: 1 My son, keep my words, and l up my H6845
10:14 Wise *men* l up knowledge: but the H6845
24:15 L not wait, O wicked *man*, against the
30:32 evil, *l* thine hand upon thy mouth.
Ecc 2: 3 with wisdom; and to l hold on folly, till I
7: 2 men; and the living will l *it* to his heart. H5414
Isa 5: 6 And I will l it waste: it shall not be H7896
8 to house, *that* l field to field, till *there* H7126
29 they shall roar, and l hold of the prey,
11:14 they shall l their hand upon Edom H4916
13: 9 fierce anger, to l the land desolate: and H7760
11 will l low the haughtiness of the terrible.
22:22 of David will I l upon his shoulder; so H5414
25:12 he bring down, l low, *and* bring to the

Isa 28:16 Lord GOD, Behold, I l in Zion for a H3245
17 Judgment also will I l to the line, and H7760
29: 3 about, and will l siege against thee with
21 for a word, and l a snare for him that
30:32 the LORD shall l upon him, *it* shall be H5117
34:15 her nest, and l, and hatch, and gather H4422
35: 7 l, *shall be* grass with reeds and rushes. H7258
37:26 shouldest be to l waste defenced cities
38:21 a lump of figs, and l *it* for a plaister upon
47: 7 that thou didst not l these *things* to thy H7760
51:16 the heavens, and l the foundations of the
54:11 behold, I will l thy stones with fair H7257
11 and l thy foundations with sapphires.
Jer 5:26 wicked *men*: they l wait, as he that
6:21 Behold, I will l stumblingblocks before H5414
23 They shall l hold on bow and spear; they
Ezk 3:20 iniquity, and I l a stumblingblock H5414
4: 1 take thee a tile, and l it before thee, and H5414
2 And l siege against it, and build a fort H5414
3 and thou shalt l siege against it. This
4 Lie thou also upon thy left side, and l H7760
8 And, behold, I will l bands upon thee, H5414
6: 5 And I will l the dead carcases of the H5414
19: 2 A lioness: she l down among lions, H7257
23: 8 in her youth they l with her, and they H7901
25:14 And I will l my vengeance upon Edom H5414
17 I shall l my vengeance upon them. H5414
26:12 and they shall l thy stones and thy H7760
16 their thrones, and l away their robes, H5493
28:17 to the ground, I will l thee before kings, H5414
32: 5 And I will l thy flesh upon the H5414
33:28 For I will l the land most desolate, and H5414
35: 4 I will l thy cities waste, and thou shalt H7760
36:29 increase it, and l no famine upon you. H5414
34 be tilled, whereas it l desolate in the
37: 6 And I will l sinews upon you, and will H5414
42:13 there shall they l the most holy things, H3240
14 but there they shall l their garments H3240
44:19 they ministered, and l them in the holy H3240
Am 2: 8 And they l *themselves* down upon H5186
Jna 1: 5 the ship; and he l, and was fast asleep. H7901
14 man's life, and l not upon us innocent H5414
Mic 1: 7 idols thereof will I l desolate: for she H7760
7:16 might: they shall l *their* hand upon H7760
Zec 14:13 and they shall l hold every one on the
Mal 2: 2 If ye will not hear, and if ye will not l *it* H7760
2 already, because ye do not l *it* to heart. H7760
Mt 6:19 L not up for yourselves treasures upon
20 But l up for yourselves treasures in
8:20 of man hath not where to l *his* head. G2827
9:18 l thy hand upon her, and she shall live. G2007
12:11 will he not l hold on it, and lift *it* out?
21:46 But when they sought to l hands on him,
23: 4 to be borne, and l *them* on men's G2007
28: 6 Come, see the place where the Lord l. G2749
Mk 1:30 But Simon's wife's mother l sick of a G2621
2: 4 the bed wherein the sick of the palsy l. G2621
3:21 *of it*, they went out to l hold on him: for
5:23 *thee*, come and l thy hands on her, that G2007
12:12 And they sought to l hold on him, but
15: 7 Barabbas, *which l* bound with them that
16:18 them; they shall l hands on the sick, G2007
Lk 5:18 bring him in, and to l *him* before him. G5087
25 that whereon he l, and departed to his G2621
8:42 of age, and she l a dying. But as he went
9:58 of man hath not where to l *his* head. G2827
19:44 And shall l thee even with the ground, G1474
20:19 hour sought to l hands on him; and G1911
21:12 But before all these, they shall l their G1911
Jn 5: 3 In these l a great multitude of impotent G2621
10:15 and I l down my life for the sheep. G5087
17 love me, because I l down my life, that G5087
18 No man taketh it from me, but I l it G5087
18 I have power to l it down, and I have G5087
11:38 It was a cave, and a stone l upon it. G1945
13:37 now? I will l down my life for thy sake. G5087
38 Jesus answered him, Wilt thou l down G5087
15:13 a man l down his life for his friends. G5087
Act 7:60 a loud voice, Lord, l not this sin to their G2476
8:19 l hands, he may receive the Holy Ghost. G2007
15:28 and to us, to l upon you no greater G2007
27:20 no small tempest l on *us*, all hope that G1945
28: 8 father of Publius l sick of a fever and of G2621
Ro 8:33 Who shall l any thing to the charge of G1458
9:33 As it is written, Behold, I l in Sion a G5087
1Co 3:11 For other foundation can no man l G5087
16: 2 let every one of you l by him in store, as G5087
2Co 12:14 ought not to l up for the parents, but G2343
1Ti 5:22 L hands suddenly on no man, neither G2007

1Ti 6:12 Fight the good fight of faith, l hold on G1949
19 that they may l hold on eternal life. G1949
Heb 6:18 to l hold upon the hope set before us:
12: 1 of witnesses, let us l aside every weight, G659
Jas 1:21 Wherefore l apart all filthiness and G659
1Pt 2: 6 Behold, I l in Sion a chief corner G5087
1Jn 3:16 to l down *our* lives for the brethren. G5087

LAYEDST
Lk 19:21 up that thou l not down, and reapest G5087

LAYEST
Nu 11:11 l the burden of all this people upon me? H7760
1Sa 28: 9 wherefore then l thou a snare for my

LAYETH
Job 21:19 God l up his iniquity for his children: H6845
24:12 crieth out: yet God l not folly *to them*. H7760
41:26 The sword of him that l at him cannot H5381
Ps 33: 7 heap: he l up the depth in storehouses. H5414
104: 3 Who l the beams of his chambers in H7760
Prv 2: 7 He l up sound wisdom for the H6845
13:16 knowledge: but a fool l open *his* folly.
26:24 his lips, and l up deceit within him; H7896
31:19 She l her hands to the spindle, and her H7971
Isa 26: 5 the lofty city, he l it low; he layeth it low,
5 he layeth it low; he l it low, *even* to the
56: 2 and the son of man *that* l hold on it; that
57: 1 The righteous perisheth, and no man l H7760
Jer 9: 8 his mouth, but in heart he l his wait. H7760
12:11 desolate, because no man l *it* to heart. H7760
Zec 12: 1 the heavens, and l the foundation of the
Lk 12:21 So *is* he that l up treasure for himself,
15: 5 And when he hath found *it*, he l *it* on G2007

LAYING
Nu 35:20 or hurl at him by l of wait, that he die;
22 upon him any thing without l of wait,
Ps 64: 5 they commune of l snares privily; they H2934
Mk 7: 8 For l aside the commandment of God, ye G863
Lk 11:54 L wait for him, and seeking to catch G1748
Act 8:18 And when Simon saw that through l on G1936
9:24 But their l await was known of Saul. G1914
25: 3 Jerusalem, l wait in the way to kill him. G4160
1Ti 4:14 the l on of the hands of the presbytery. G1936
6:19 L up in store for themselves a good G597
Heb 6: 1 perfection; not l again the foundation G2598
2 Of the doctrine of baptisms, and of l on G1936
1Pt 2: 1 Wherefore l aside all malice, and all G659

LAZARUS
Lk 16:20 beggar named L, which was laid at his G2976
23 Abraham afar off, and L in his bosom. G2976
24 on me, and send L, that he may dip the G2976
25 and likewise L evil things: but now G2976
Jn 11: 1 Now a certain *man* was sick, *named* L, G2976
2 her hair, whose brother L was sick.) G2976
5 loved Martha, and her sister, and L. G2976
11 them, Our friend L sleepeth; but I go, G2976
14 Then said Jesus unto them plainly, L is G2976
43 cried with a loud voice, L, come forth. G2976
12: 1 to Bethany, where L was which had G2976
2 served: but L was one of them that G2976
9 they might see L also, whom he had G2976
10 that they might put L also to death; G2976
17 when he called L out of his grave, and G2976

LEACH See HORSELEACH.

LEAD
Gen 33:14 his servant: and I will l on softly, H5095
Ex 13:21 pillar of a cloud, to l them the way; and H5148
15:10 they sank as l in the mighty waters. H5777
32:34 Therefore now go, l the people unto *the* H5148
Nu 27:17 and which may l them out, and which H3318
31:22 the brass, the iron, the tin, and the l, H5777
Dt 4:27 heathen, whither the LORD shall l you. H5090
20: 9 captains of the armies to l the people. H7218
28:37 nations whither the LORD shall l thee. H5090
32:12 *So* the LORD alone did l him, and *there* H5148
Jdg 5:12 arise, Barak, and l thy captivity captive,
1Sa 30:22 that they may l *them* away, and depart. H5090
2Ch 30: 9 before them that l them captive, so that
Neh 9:19 from them by day, to l them in the way; H5148
Job 19:24 an iron pen and l in the rock for ever! H5777
Ps 5: 8 L me, O LORD, in thy righteousness H5148
25: 5 L me in thy truth, and teach me: for H1869
27:11 Teach me thy way, O LORD, and l me H5148
31: 3 thy name's sake l me, and guide me. H5148

L

Ps 43: 3 thy truth: let them l me; let them bring H5148
60: 9 strong city? who will l me into Edom? H5148
61: 2 l me to the rock *that* is higher than I. H5148
108:10 strong city? who will l me into Edom? H5148
125: 5 the LORD shall l them forth with the H3212
139:10 Even there shall thy hand l me, and thy H5148
24 in me, and l me in the way everlasting. H5148
143:10 good; l me into the land of uprightness. H5148
Prv 6:22 When thou goest, it shall l thee; when H5148
8:20 I l in the way of righteousness, in the H1980
Song 8: 2 I would l thee, *and* bring thee into my H5090
Isa 3:12 people, they which l thee cause *thee* to H833
11: 6 together; and a little child shall l them. H5090
20: 4 So shall the king of Assyria l away the H5090
40:11 shall gently l those that are with young. H5095
42:16 knew not; I will l them in paths *that* H1869
49:10 on them shall l them, even by the H5090
57:18 heal him: I will l him also, and restore H5148
63:14 rest: so didst thou l thy people, to make H5090
Jer 6:29 The bellows are burned, the l is H5777
31: 9 will I l them: I will cause them H2986
32: 5 And he shall l Zedekiah to Babylon, H3212
Ezk 22:18 tin, and iron, and l, in the midst of the H5777
20 and iron, and l, and tin, into the midst H5777
27:12 iron, tin, and l, they traded in thy fairs. H5777
Nah 2: 7 her maids shall l *her* as with the voice H5090
Zec 5: 7 up a talent of l: and this *is* a woman H5777
8 the weight of l upon the mouth thereof. H5777
Mt 6:13 And l us not into temptation, but G1533
15:14 l the blind, both shall fall into the ditch. G3594
Mk 13:11 But when they shall l *you*, and deliver G71
14:44 is he; take him, and l *him* away safely. G520
Lk 6:39 Can the blind l the blind? shall they G3594
11: 4 to us. And l us not into temptation; G1533
13:15 the stall, and l *him* away to watering? G520
Act 13:11 seeking some to l him by the hand. G5497
1Co 9: 5 Have we not power to l about a sister, a G4013
1Ti 2: 2 that we may l a quiet and peaceable G1236
2Ti 3: 6 into houses, and l captive silly women G162
Heb 8: 9 by the hand to l them out of the land G1806
Rev 7:17 feed them, and shall l them unto living G3594

LEADER
1Ch 12:27 And Jehoiada *was* the l of the H5057
13: 1 and hundreds, *and* with every l. H5057
Isa 55: 4 a l and commander to the people. H5057

LEADERS
2Ch 32:21 of valour, and the l and captains in the H5057
Isa 9:16 For the l of this people cause *them* to err; H833
Mt 15:14 Let them alone: they be blind l of the G3595

LEADEST
Ps 80: 1 of Israel, thou that l Joseph like a flock; H5090

LEADETH
1Sa 13:17 *that* l *to* Ophrah, unto the land of Shual:
Job 12:17 He l counsellors away spoiled, and H3212
19 He l princes away spoiled, and H3212
Ps 23: 2 he l me beside the still waters. H5095
3 He restoreth my soul: he l me in the H5148
Prv 16:29 and l him into the way *that is* not good. H3212
Isa 48:17 to profit, which l thee by the way *that* H1869
Mt 7:13 is the way, that l to destruction, and G520
14 l unto life, and few there be that find it. G520
Mk 9: 2 and John, and l them up into an high G399
Jn 10: 3 own sheep by name, and l them out. G1806
Act 12:10 the iron gate that l unto the city; which G5342
Ro 2: 4 goodness of God l thee to repentance? G71
Rev 13:10 He that l into captivity shall go into G4863

LEAF
Gen 8:11 *was* an olive l pluckt off: so Noah H5929
Lev 26:36 sound of a shaken l shall chase them; H5929
Job 13:25 Wilt thou break a l driven to and fro? H5929
Ps 1: 3 fruit in his season; his l also shall not H5929
Isa 1:30 For ye shall be as an oak whose l H5929
34: 4 fall down, as the l falleth off from the H5929
64: 6 we all do fade as a l; and our iniquities, H5929
Jer 8:13 the fig tree, and the l shall fade; and *the* H5929
17: 8 cometh, but her l shall be green; and H5929
Ezk 47:12 trees for meat, whose l shall not fade, H5929
12 meat, and the l thereof for medicine. H5929

LEAGUE
Jos 9: 6 now therefore make ye a l with us. H1285
7 and how shall we make a l with you? H1285
11 therefore now make ye a l with us. H1285
15 them, and made a l with them, to let H1285
16 they had made a l with them, that they H1285
Jdg 2: 2 And ye shall make no l with the H1285
1Sa 22: 8 son hath made a l with the son of Jesse, H3772
2Sa 3:12 *also,* Make thy l with me, and, behold, H1285
13 And he said, Well; I will make a l with H1285
21 they may make a l with thee, and that H1285
5: 3 David made a l with them in Hebron H1285
1Ki 5:12 and they two made a l together. H1285
15:19 *There is* a l between me and thee, *and* H1285
19 and break thy l with Baasha king of H1285
2Ch 16: 3 *There is* a l between me and thee, as H1285
3 gold; go, break thy l with Baasha king H1285
Job 5:23 For thou shalt be in l with the stones of H1285
Ezk 30: 5 is in l, shall fall with them by the sword. H1285
Dan 11:23 And after the l *made* with him he shall H2266

LEAH
Gen 29:16 of the elder *was* L, and the name of the H3812
17 L *was* tender eyed; but Rachel was H3812
23 that he took L his daughter, and H3812
24 And Laban gave unto his daughter L H3812
25 behold, it *was* L: and he said to Laban, H3812
30 Rachel more than L, and served with H3812
31 And when the LORD saw that L *was* H3812
32 And L conceived, and bare a son, and H3812
30: 9 When L saw that she had left bearing, H3812
11 And L said, A troop cometh: and she H3812
13 And L said, Happy am I, for the H3812
14 unto his mother L. Then Rachel said to H3812
14 Rachel said to L, Give me, I pray thee, H3812
16 in the evening, and L went out to meet H3812
17 And God hearkened unto L, and she H3812
18 And L said, God hath given me my H3812
19 And L conceived again, and bare Jacob H3812
20 And L said, God hath endued me *with* H3812
31: 4 Rachel and L to the field unto his flock, H3812
14 And Rachel and L answered and said H3812
33: 1 the children unto L, and unto Rachel, H3812
2 foremost, and L and her children after, H3812
7 And L also with her children came H3812
34: 1 And Dinah the daughter of L, which she H3812
35:23 The sons of L; Reuben, Jacob's H3812
46:15 These *be* the sons of L, which she bare H3812
18 Laban gave to L his daughter, and H3812
49:31 Rebekah his wife; and there I buried L. H3812
Ru 4:11 Rachel and like L, which two did build H3812

LEAH'S
Gen 30:10 And Zilpah L maid bare Jacob a son. H3812
12 And Zilpah L maid bare Jacob a H3812
31:33 tent, and into L tent, and into the two H3812
33 L tent, and entered into Rachel's tent. H3812
35:26 And the sons of Zilpah, L handmaid; H3812

LEAN
Gen 41:20 And the l and the ill favoured kine did H7534
Nu 13:20 it *be* fat or l, whether there be wood H7330
Jdg 16:26 standeth, that I may l upon them. H8172
2Sa 13: 4 the king's son, l from day to day? wilt H1800
2Ki 18:21 on which if a man l, it will go into his H5564
Job 8:15 He shall l upon his house, but it shall H8172
Prv 3: 5 l not unto thine own understanding. H8172
Isa 17: 4 and the fatness of his flesh shall wax l. H7329
36: 6 whereon if a man l, it will go into his H5564
Ezk 34:20 the fat cattle and between the l cattle. H7330
Mic 3:11 yet will they l upon the LORD, and H8172

LEANED
2Sa 1: 6 behold, Saul l upon his spear; and, H8172
2Ki 7: 2 Then a lord on whose hand the king l H8172
17 on whose hand he l to have the charge H8172
Ezk 29: 7 and when they l upon thee, thou H8172
Am 5:19 the house, and l his hand on the wall, H5564
Jn 21:20 which also l on his breast at supper, G377

LEANETH
2Sa 3:29 is a leper, or that l on a staff, or that H2388
2Ki 5:18 there, and he l on my hand, and I bow H8172

LEANFLESHED
Gen 41: 3 ill favoured and l; and stood by H1851+H1320
4 And the ill favoured and l kine H1851+H1320
19 favoured and l, such as I never H7534+H1320

LEANING
Song 8: 5 the wilderness, l upon her beloved? I H7514
Jn 13:23 Now there was l on Jesus' bosom one of G345
Heb 11:21 worshipped, *l* upon the top of his staff.

LEANNESS
Job 16: 8 *me*: and my l rising up in me beareth H3585
Ps 106:15 their request; but sent l into their soul. H7332
Isa 10:16 his fat ones l; and under his glory H7332
24:16 But I said, My l, my leanness, woe unto H7334
16 My leanness, my l, woe unto me! the H7334

LEANNOTH
Ps 88: ttl L, Maschil of Heman the Ezrahite. H6030

LEAP
Gen 31:12 all the rams which l upon the cattle *are* H5927
Lev 11:21 their feet, to l withal upon the earth; H5425
Dt 33:22 a lion's whelp: he shall l from Bashan. H2187
Job 41:19 burning lamps, *and* sparks of fire l out. H4422
Ps 68:16 Why l ye, ye high hills? *this is* the hill H7520
Isa 35: 6 Then shall the lame *man* l as an hart, H1801
Joel 2: 5 shall they l, like the noise of a flame H7540
Zep 1: 9 all those that l on the threshold, which H1801
Lk 6:23 Rejoice ye in that day, and l for joy: for, G4640

LEAPED
Gen 31:10 the rams which l upon the cattle *were* H5927
2Sa 22:30 a troop: by my God have I l over a wall. H1801
1Ki 18:26 they l upon the altar which was made. H6452
Ps 18:29 and by my God have I l over a wall. H1801
Lk 1:41 of Mary, the babe l in her womb; and G4640
44 ears, the babe l in my womb for joy. G4640
Act 14:10 upright on thy feet. And he l and walked. G242
19:16 whom the evil spirit was l on them, and G2177

LEAPING
2Sa 6:16 saw king David l and dancing before H6339
Song 2: 8 beloved! behold, he cometh l upon the H1801
Act 3: 8 And he l up stood, and walked, and G1814
8 temple, walking, and l, and praising God. G242

LEARN
Dt 4:10 that they may l to fear me all the days H3925
5: 1 ye may l them, and keep, and do them. H3925
14:23 l to fear the LORD thy God always. H3925
17:19 life: that he may l to fear the LORD his H3925
18: 9 thee, thou shalt not l to do after the H3925
31:12 and that they may l, and fear the LORD H3925
13 may hear, and l to fear the LORD your H3925
Ps 119:71 afflicted; that I might l thy statutes. H3925
73 that I may l thy commandments. H3925
Prv 22:25 Lest thou l his ways, and get a snare to H502
Isa 1:17 L to do well; seek judgment, relieve the H3925
2: 4 neither shall they l war any more. H3925
26: 9 of the world will l righteousness. H3925
10 *yet* will he not l righteousness: in the H3925
29:24 they that murmured shall l doctrine. H3925
Jer 10: 2 Thus saith the LORD, L not the way of H3925
12:16 if they will diligently l the ways of my H3925
Mic 4: 3 neither shall they l war any more. H3925
Mt 9:13 But go ye and l what *that* meaneth, I G3129
11:29 Take my yoke upon you, and l of me; G3129
24:32 Now l a parable of the fig tree; When G3129
Mk 13:28 Now l a parable of the fig tree; When G3129
1Co 4: 6 that ye might l in us not to think *of* G3129
14:31 all may l, and all may be comforted. G3129
35 And if they will l any thing, let them G3129
Gal 3: 2 This only would I l of you, Received ye G3129
1Ti 1:20 that they may l not to blaspheme. G3811
2:11 Let the woman l in silence with all G3129
5: 4 nephews, let them l first to shew piety G3129
13 And withal they l *to be* idle, wandering G3129
Tit 3:14 And let ours also l to maintain good G3129
Rev 14: 3 and no man could l that song but the G3129

LEARNED
Gen 30:27 *tarry: for* I have l by experience that the H5172
Ps 106:35 among the heathen, and l their works. H3925
119: 7 I shall have l thy righteous judgments. H3925
Prv 30: 3 I neither l wisdom, nor have the H3925
Isa 29:11 to one that is l, saying, Read H3045+H5612
12 that is not l, saying, Read this, H3045+H5612
12 thee: and he saith, I am not l. H3045+H5612
50: 4 the tongue of the l, that I should know H3928
4 he wakeneth mine ear to hear as the l. H3928
Ezk 19: 3 it l to catch the prey; it devoured men. H3925
6 l to catch the prey, *and* devoured men. H3925
Jn 6:45 hath l of the Father, cometh unto me. G3129
7:15 this man letters, having never l? G3129
Act 7:22 And Moses was l in all the wisdom of G3811
Ro 16:17 which ye have l; and avoid them. G3129
Eph 4:20 But ye have not so l Christ; G3129
Php 4: 9 Those things, which ye have both l, and G3129

Php 4:11 of want: for I have l, in whatsoever state G3129
Col 1: 7 As ye also l of Epaphras our dear G3129
2Ti 3:14 things which thou hast l and hast been G3129
14 of, knowing of whom thou hast l *them*; G3129
Heb 5: 8 Though he were a Son, yet l he G3129

LEARNING

Prv 1: 5 hear, and will increase l; and a man of H3948
9: 9 a just *man*, and he will increase in l. H3948
16:21 the sweetness of the lips increaseth l. H3948
23 his mouth, and addeth l to his lips. H3948
Dan 1: 4 the l and the tongue of the Chaldeans. H5612
17 and skill in all l and wisdom: and H5612
Act 26:24 thyself; much l doth make thee mad. G1121
Ro 15: 4 were written for our l, that we through G1319
2Ti 3: 7 Ever l, and never able to come to the G3129

LEASING

Ps 4: 2 ye love vanity, *and* seek after l? Selah. H3577
5: 6 Thou shalt destroy them that speak l: H3577

LEAST

Gen 24:55 days, at the l ten; after that she shall go. H176
32:10 I am not worthy of the l of all the H6996
Nu 11:32 he that gathered l gathered ten homers: H4591
Jdg 3: 2 l such as before knew nothing thereof; H7535
6:15 and I *am* the l in my father's house. H6810
1Sa 9:21 and my family the l of all the families H6810
21: 4 have kept themselves at l from women. H389
2Ki 18:24 of one captain of the l of my master's H6996
1Ch 12:14 host: one of the l *was* over an hundred, H6996
Isa 36: 9 of one captain of the l of my master's H6996
Jer 6:13 For from the l of them even unto the H6996
8:10 for every one from the l even unto the H6996
31:34 know me, from the l of them unto the H6996
42: 1 the l even unto the greatest, came near, H6996
8 people from the l even to the greatest, H6996
44:12 they shall die, from the l even unto the H6996
49:20 of Teman: Surely the l of the flock shall H6810
50:45 Surely the l of the flock shall draw H6810
Am 9: 9 shall not the l grain fall upon the earth.
Jna 3: 5 greatest of them even to the l of them. H6996
Mt 2: 6 of Juda, art not the l among the princes G1646
5:19 break one of these l commandments, G1646
19 shall be called the l in the kingdom of G1646
11:11 he that is l in the kingdom of heaven G3398
13:32 Which indeed is the l of all seeds: but G3398
25:40 done *it* unto one of the l of these my G1646
45 one of the l of these, ye did *it* not to me. G1646
Lk 7:28 but he that is l in the kingdom of God G3398
9:48 me: for he that is l among you all, the G3398
12:26 is l, why take ye thought for the rest? G1646
16:10 He that is faithful in that which is l is G1646
10 is unjust in the l is unjust also in much. G1646
19:42 even thou, at l in this thy day, the G2532
Act 5:15 that at the l the shadow of Peter G2579
8:10 To whom they all gave heed, from the l G3398
1Co 6: 4 who are l esteemed in the church. G1848
15: 9 For I am the l of the apostles, that am G1646
Eph 3: 8 Unto me, who am less than the l of all G1647
Heb 8:11 know me, from the l to the greatest. G3398

LEATHER

2Ki 1: 8 with a girdle of l about his loins. And H5785

LEATHERN

Mt 3: 4 hair, and a l girdle about his loins; G1193

LEAVE

Gen 2:24 Therefore shall a man l his father and H5800
28:15 land; for I will not l thee, until I have H5800
33:15 And Esau said, Let me now l with thee H3322
42:33 ye *are* true *men*; l one of your brethren H3240
44:22 The lad cannot l his father: for *if* he H5800
22 l his father, *his father* would die. H5800
Ex 16:19 And Moses said, Let no man l of it till H3498
23:11 eat: and what they l the beasts of the H3499
Lev 7:15 shall not l any of it until the morning. H3240
16:23 the holy *place*, and shall l them there: H3240
19:10 thou shalt l them for the poor and H5800
22:30 eaten up; ye shall l none of it until the H3498
23:22 thy harvest: thou shalt l them unto the H5800
Nu 9:12 They shall l none of it unto the H7604
10:31 And he said, L us not, I pray thee; H5800
22:13 refuseth to give me l to go with you. H5414
32:15 him, he will yet again l them in the H3240
Dt 28:51 *also* shall not l thee *either* corn, wine, H7604
54 of his children which he shall l: H3498
Jos 4: 3 them over with you, and l them in the H3240
Jdg 9: 9 them, Should I l my fatness, wherewith H2308
13 And the vine said unto them, Should I l H2308
Ru 1:16 And Ruth said, Entreat me not to l thee, H5800
2:16 for her, and l *them*, that she may H5800
1Sa 9: 5 lest my father l *caring* for the asses, H2308
14:36 and let us not l a man of them. And H7604
20: 6 earnestly asked *l* of me that he might
28 asked *l* of me *to go* to Beth-lehem:
25:22 of David, if I l of all that *pertain* to H7604
2Sa 14: 7 is left, and shall not l to my husband H7760
1Ki 8:57 fathers: let him not l us, nor forsake us: H5800
2Ki 2: 2 l thee. So they went down to Beth-el. H5800
4 will not l thee. So they came to Jericho. H5800
6 I will not l thee. And they two went on. H5800
4:30 l thee. And he arose, and followed her. H5800
43 They shall eat, and shall l *thereof*. H3498
13: 7 Neither did he l of the people to H7604
1Ch 28: 8 good land, and l *it* for an inheritance H5157
Ezr 9: 8 the LORD our God, to l us a remnant to H7604
12 of the land, and l *it* for an inheritance
Neh 5:10 corn: I pray you, let us l off this usury. H5800
6: 3 whilst I l it, and come down to you? H7503
10:31 and *that* we would l the seventh year, H5203
13: 6 certain days obtained I l of the king: H7592
Job 9:27 l off my heaviness, and comfort *myself*: H5800
10: 1 My soul is weary of my life; I will l my H5800
39:11 great? or wilt thou l thy labour to him? H5800
Ps 16:10 For thou wilt not l my soul in hell; H5800
17:14 full of children, and l the rest of their H3240
27: 9 hast been my help; l me not, neither H5203
37:33 The LORD will not l him in his hand, H5800
49:10 perish, and l their wealth to others. H5800
119:121 I have done judgment and justice: l me H3240
141: 8 thee is my trust; l not my soul destitute. H6168
Prv 2:13 Who l the paths of uprightness, to walk H5800
17:14 water: therefore l off contention, before H5203
Ecc 2:18 l it unto the man that shall be after me. H3240
21 therein shall he l it *for* his portion. This H5414
10: 4 rise up against thee, l not thy place; for H3240
Isa 10: 3 for help? and where will ye l your glory? H5800
65:15 And ye shall l your name for a curse H3240
Jer 9: 2 men; that I might l my people, and go H5800
14: 9 and we are called by thy name; l us not. H3240
17:11 not by right, shall l them in the midst H5800
18:14 Will *a man* l the snow of Lebanon H5800
30:11 will not l thee altogether unpunished.
44: 7 out of Judah, to l you none to remain; H3498
46:28 yet will I not l thee wholly unpunished.
48:28 O ye that dwell in Moab, l the cities, H5800
49: 9 would they not l *some* gleaning grapes? H7604
11 L thy fatherless children, I will preserve H5800
Ezk 6: 8 Yet will I l a remnant, that ye may have H3498
12:16 But I will l a few men of them from the H3498
16:39 fair jewels, and l thee naked and bare. H3240
22:20 and I will l *you there*, and melt you. H3240
23:29 thy labour, and shall l thee naked and H5800
29: 5 And I will l thee *thrown* into the H5203
32: 4 Then will I l thee upon the land, I will H5203
39: 2 And I will turn thee back, and l but the H8338
Dan 4:15 Nevertheless l the stump of his roots in H7662
23 and destroy it; yet l the stump of the H7662
26 And whereas they commanded to l the H7662
Hos 12:14 therefore shall he l his blood upon him, H5203
Joel 2:14 and repent, and l a blessing behind H7604
Am 5: 3 *by* a thousand shall l an hundred, and H7604
3 shall l ten, to the house of Israel. H7604
7 and l off righteousness in the earth, H3240
Oba 5 to thee, would they not l *some* grapes? H7604
Zep 3:12 I will also l in the midst of thee an H7604
Mal 4: 1 it shall l them neither root nor branch. H5800
Mt 5:24 L there thy gift before the altar, and go G863
18:12 astray, doth he not l the ninety and nine, G863
19: 5 And said, For this cause shall a man l G2641
23:23 done, and not to l the other undone. G863
Mk 5:13 And forthwith Jesus gave them l. And G2010
10: 7 For this cause shall a man l his father G2641
12:19 brother die, and l *his* wife *behind him*, G2641
19 *behind him*, and l no children, that his G863
Lk 11:42 done, and not to l the other undone. G863
15: 4 of them, doth not l the ninety and nine G2641
19:44 and they shall not l in thee one stone G863
Jn 14:18 I will not l you comfortless: I will come G863
27 Peace I l with you, my peace I give unto G863
16:28 again, I l the world, and go to the Father. G863
32 his own, and shall l me alone: and yet I G863
19:38 Pilate gave *him* l. He came therefore, G2010
Act 2:27 Because thou wilt not l my soul in hell, G1459
6: 2 l the word of God, and serve tables. G2641
18:18 and then took his l of the brethren, and G657
21: 6 And when we had taken our l one of G782
1Co 7:13 to dwell with her, let her not l him. G863
2Co 2:13 but taking my l of them, I went from G657
Eph 5:31 For this cause shall a man l his father G2641
Heb 13: 5 said, I will never l thee, nor forsake thee. G447
Rev 11: 2 without the temple l out, and measure G1544

LEAVED

Isa 45: 1 l gates; and the gates shall not be shut; H1817

LEAVEN

Ex 12:15 ye shall put away l out of your houses: H7603
19 Seven days shall there be no l found in H7603
13: 7 be l seen with thee in all thy quarters. H7603
34:25 of my sacrifice with l; neither shall the H2557
Lev 2:11 shall be made with l: for ye shall burn H2557
11 for ye shall burn no l, nor any honey, in H7603
6:17 It shall not be baken with l. I have given H2557
10:12 l beside the altar: for it *is* most holy: H4682
23:17 l; *they are* the firstfruits unto the LORD. H2557
Am 4: 5 thanksgiving with l, and proclaim *and* H2557
Mt 13:33 of heaven is like unto l, which a woman G2219
16: 6 l of the Pharisees and of the Sadducees. G2219
11 beware of the l of the Pharisees and G2219
12 not beware of the l of bread, but of the G2219
Mk 8:15 beware of the l of the Pharisees, and G2219
15 of the Pharisees, and *of* the l of Herod. G2219
Lk 12: 1 l of the Pharisees, which is hypocrisy. G2219
13:21 It is like l, which a woman took and hid G2219
1Co 5: 6 that a little l leaveneth the whole lump? G2219
7 Purge out therefore the old l, that ye G2219
8 the feast, not with old l, neither with the G2219
8 leaven, neither with the l of malice and G2219
Gal 5: 9 A little l leaveneth the whole lump. G2219

LEAVENED

Ex 12:15 whosoever eateth l bread from the first H2557
19 that which is l, even that soul shall H2557
20 Ye shall eat nothing l; in all your H2557
34 before it was l, their kneadingtroughs H2557
39 for it was not l; because they were H2557
13: 3 *place*: there shall no l bread be eaten. H2557
7 and there shall no l bread be seen with H2557
23:18 my sacrifice with l bread; neither shall H2557
Lev 7:13 offer *for* his offering l bread with the H2557
Dt 16: 3 Thou shalt eat no l bread with it; seven H2557
4 And there shall be no l bread seen with H7603
Hos 7: 4 he hath kneaded the dough, until it be l. H2556
Mt 13:33 measures of meal, till the whole was l. G2220
Lk 13:21 measures of meal, till the whole was l. G2220

LEAVENETH

1Co 5: 6 that a little leaven l the whole lump? G2220
Gal 5: 9 A little leaven l the whole lump. G2220

LEAVES

Gen 3: 7 and they sewed fig l together, and H5929
1Ki 6:34 *of* fir tree: the two l of the one door H6763
34 the two l of the other door *were* folding. H7050
Isa 6:13 they cast *their l*: *so* the holy seed *shall*
Jer 36:23 read three or four l, he cut it with the H1817
Ezk 17: 9 wither in all the l of her spring, even H2964
41:24 And the doors had two l *apiece*, two H1817
24 two turning l; two *leaves* for the one H1817
24 turning leaves; two *l* for the one door,
24 one door, and two l for the other *door*. H1817
Dan 4:12 The l thereof *were* fair, and the fruit H6074
14 shake off his l, and scatter his fruit: H6074
21 Whose l *were* fair, and the fruit thereof H6074
Mt 21:19 thereon, but l only, and said unto G5444
24:32 forth l, ye know that summer *is* nigh: G5444
Mk 11:13 And seeing a fig tree afar off having l, G5444
13 but l; for the time of figs was not *yet*. G5444
13:28 forth l, ye know that summer is near: G5444
Rev 22: 2 month: and the l of the tree *were* for G5444

LEAVETH

Job 39:14 Which l her eggs in the earth, and H5800
Prv 13:22 A good *man* l an inheritance to his
28: 3 *is like* a sweeping rain which l no food.
Zec 11:17 Woe to the idol shepherd that l the H5800
Mt 4:11 Then the devil l him, and, behold, angels G863
Jn 10:12 wolf coming, and l the sheep, and fleeth: G863

LEAVING

Mt 4:13 And l Nazareth, he came and dwelt in G2641
Lk 10:30 *him*, and departed, l *him* half dead. G863
Ro 1:27 And likewise also the men, l the natural G863
Heb 6: 1 Therefore l the principles of the doctrine G863

1Pt 2:21 suffered for us, l us an example, that G5277

LEBANA
Neh 7:48 The children of L, the children of H3838

LEBANAH
Ezr 2:45 The children of L, the children of H3838

LEBANON
Dt 1: 7 and unto L, unto the great river, H3844
3:25 Jordan, that goodly mountain, and L. H3844
11:24 the wilderness and L, from the river, the H3844
Jos 1: 4 From the wilderness and this L even H3844
9: 1 sea over against L, the Hittite, and the H3844
11:17 in the valley of L under mount H3844
12: 7 in the valley of L even unto the mount H3844
13: 5 And the land of the Giblites, and all L, H3844
6 the hill country from L unto H3844
Jdg 3: 3 that dwelt in mount L, from mount H3844
9:15 bramble, and devour the cedars of L. H3844
1Ki 4:33 tree that *is* in L even unto the hyssop H3844
5: 6 cedar trees out of L; and my servants H3844
9 *them* down from L unto the sea: and I H3844
14 And he sent them to L, ten thousand a H3844
14 they were in L, *and* two months at H3844
7: 2 of the forest of L; the length thereof *was* H3844
9:19 L, and in all the land of his dominion. H3844
10:17 put them in the house of the forest of L. H3844
21 of the forest of L *were of* pure gold; H3844
2Ki 14: 9 thistle that *was* in L sent to the cedar H3844
9 the cedar that *was* in L, saying, Give thy H3844
9 *was* in L, and trode down the thistle. H3844
19:23 to the sides of L, and will cut down the H3844
2Ch 2: 8 trees, out of L: for I know that thy H3844
8 skill to cut timber in L; and, behold, my H3844
16 And we will cut wood out of L, as much H3844
8: 6 Jerusalem, and in L, and throughout all H3844
9:16 put them in the house of the forest of L. H3844
20 of the forest of L *were of* pure gold: H3844
25:18 thistle that *was* in L sent to the cedar H3844
18 the cedar that *was* in L, saying, Give thy H3844
18 *was* in L, and trode down the thistle. H3844
Ezr 3: 7 cedar trees from L to the sea of Joppa, H3844
Ps 29: 5 yea, the LORD breaketh the cedars of L. H3844
6 calf; L and Sirion like a young unicorn. H3844
72:16 shall shake like L: and *they* of the city H3844
92:12 tree: he shall grow like a cedar in L. H3844
104:16 the cedars of L, which he hath planted; H3844
Song 3: 9 himself a chariot of the wood of L. H3844
4: 8 Come with me from L, *my* spouse, with H3844
8 with me from L: look from the top of H3844
11 of thy garments *is* like the smell of L. H3844
15 of living waters, and streams from L. H3844
5:15 *is* as L, excellent as the cedars. H3844
7: 4 of L which looketh toward Damascus. H3844
Isa 2:13 And upon all the cedars of L, *that are* H3844
10:34 iron, and L shall fall by a mighty one. H3844
14: 8 *and* the cedars of L, *saying*, Since thou H3844
29:17 *Is* it not yet a very little while, and L H3844
33: 9 *and* languisheth: L is ashamed *and* H3844
35: 2 the glory of L shall be given unto H3844
37:24 to the sides of L; and I will cut down H3844
40:16 And L *is* not sufficient to burn, nor the H3844
60:13 The glory of L shall come unto thee, the H3844
Jer 18:14 Will *a man* leave the snow of L *which* H3844
22: 6 *and* the head of L: *yet* surely I will make H3844
20 Go up to L, and cry; and lift up thy voice H3844
23 O inhabitant of L, that makest thy nest H3844
Ezk 17: 3 came unto L, and took the highest H3844
27: 5 cedars from L to make masts for thee. H3844
31: 3 Behold, the Assyrian *was* a cedar in L H3844
15 and I caused L to mourn for him, and H3844
16 the choice and best of L, all that drink H3844
Hos 14: 5 as the lily, and cast forth his roots as L. H3844
6 be as the olive tree, and his smell as L. H3844
7 scent thereof *shall be* as the wine of L. H3844
Nah 1: 4 and the flower of L languisheth. H3844
Hab 2:17 For the violence of L shall cover thee, H3844
Zec 10:10 land of Gilead and L; and *place* shall H3844
11: 1 Open thy doors, O L, that the fire may H3844

LEBAOTH
Jos 15:32 And L, and Shilhim, and Ain, and H3822

LEBBAEUS
Mt 10: 3 and L, whose surname was Thaddaeus; G3002

LEBONAH
Jdg 21:19 to Shechem, and on the south of L. H3829

LECAH
1Ch 4:21 *were*, Er the father of L, and Laadah the H3922

LED
Gen 24:27 the way, the LORD l me to the house of H5148
48 which had l me in the right way H5148
Ex 3: 1 of Midian: and he l the flock to the H5090
13:17 go, that God l them not *through* the H5148
18 But God l the people about, *through* the H5437
15:13 Thou in thy mercy hast l forth the H5148
Dt 8: 2 the LORD thy God l thee these forty H3212
15 Who l thee through that great and H3212
29: 5 And I have l you forty years in the H3212
32:10 howling wilderness; he l him about, he H5437
Jos 24: 3 of the flood, and l him throughout all H3212
1Ki 8:48 enemies, which l them away captive,
2Ki 6:19 ye seek. But he l them to Samaria. H3212
1Ch 20: 1 out *to battle*, Joab l forth the power of H5090
2Ch 25:11 himself, and l forth his people, and H5090
Ps 68:18 Thou hast ascended on high, thou hast l
78:14 In the daytime also he l them with a H5148
53 And he l them on safely, so that they H5148
106: 9 was dried up: so he l them through the H3212
107: 7 And he l them forth by the right way, H1869
136:16 To him which l his people through the H3212
Prv 4:11 of wisdom; I have l thee in right paths. H1869
Isa 9:16 *they that are* l of them *are* destroyed. H833
48:21 And they thirsted not *when* he l them H3212
55:12 For ye shall go out with joy, and be l H2986
63:12 That l *them* by the right hand of Moses H3212
13 That l them through the deep, as an H3212
Jer 2: 6 the land of Egypt, that l us through the H3212
17 thy God, when he l thee by the way? H3212
22:12 whither they have l him captive, and
23: 8 up and which l the seed of the house H935
Lam 3: 2 He hath l me, and brought *me into* H5090
Ezk 17:12 thereof, and l them with him to Babylon; H935
39:28 caused them to be l into captivity among
47: 2 northward, and l me about the way H5437
Am 2:10 the land of Egypt, and l you forty years H5437
7:11 be l away captive out of their own land.
Nah 2: 7 And Huzzab shall be l away captive, she
Mt 4: 1 Then was Jesus l up of the Spirit into the G321
26:57 And they that had laid hold on Jesus l G520
27: 2 And when they had bound him, they l G520
31 on him, and l him away to crucify *him*. G520
Mk 8:23 by the hand, and l him out of the town; G1806
14:53 And they l Jesus away to the high priest: G520
15:16 And the soldiers l him away into the G520
20 on him, and l him out to crucify him. G1806
Lk 4: 1 was l by the Spirit into the wilderness, G71
29 out of the city, and l him unto the brow G71
21:24 sword, and shall be l away captive into G163
22:54 Then took they him, and l *him*, and G71
66 and l him into their council, saying, G321
23: 1 of them arose, and l him unto Pilate. G71
26 And as they l him away, they laid hold G520
32 l with him to be put to death. G71
24:50 And he l them out as far as to Bethany, G1806
Jn 18:13 And l him away to Annas first; for he G520
28 Then l they Jesus from Caiaphas unto G71
19:16 And they took Jesus, and l *him* away. G520
Act 8:32 read was this, He was l as a sheep to the G71
9: 8 no man: but they l him by the hand, G5496
21:37 And as Paul was to be l into the castle, G1521
22:11 of that light, being l by the hand of G5496
Ro 8:14 For as many as are l by the Spirit of God, G71
1Co 12: 2 unto these dumb idols, even as ye were l. G71
Gal 5:18 But if ye be l of the Spirit, ye are not G71
Eph 4: 8 up on high, he l captivity captive, and G162
2Ti 3: 6 laden with sins, l away with divers lusts, G71
2Pt 3:17 lest ye also, being l away with the error G4879

LEDDEST
2Sa 5: 2 thou wast he that l out and broughtest H3318
1Ch 11: 2 thou *wast* he that l out and broughtest H3318
Neh 9:12 Moreover thou l them in the day by a H5148
Ps 77:20 Thou l thy people like a flock by the H5148
Act 21:38 madest an uproar, and l out into the G1806

LEDGES
1Ki 7:28 and the borders *were* between the l: H7948
29 *were* between the l *were* lions, oxen, H7948
29 and upon the l *there was* a base above: H7948
35 the top of the base the l thereof and the H3027
36 For on the plates of the l thereof, and H3027

LEEKS
Nu 11: 5 the l, and the onions, and the garlick: H2682

LEES
Isa 25: 6 of wines on the l, of fat things full of H8105
6 marrow, of wines on the l well refined. H8105
Jer 48:11 hath settled on his l, and hath not been H8105
Zep 1:12 are settled on their l: that say in their H8105

LEFT
Gen 11: 8 earth: and they l off to build the city. H2308
13: 9 *thou wilt take* the l hand, then I will go H8040
9 to the right hand, then I will go to the l. H8041
14:15 which *is* on the l hand of Damascus. H8040
17:22 And he l off talking with him, and God H3615
18:33 as soon as he had l communing with H3615
24:27 who hath not l destitute my master H5800
49 I may turn to the right hand, or to the l. H8040
29:35 called his name Judah; and l bearing. H5975
30: 9 When Leah saw that she had l bearing, H5975
32: 8 other company which is l shall escape. H7604
24 And Jacob was l alone; and there H3498
39: 6 And he l all that he had in Joseph's H5800
12 with me: and he l his garment in her H5800
13 saw that he had l his garment in her H5800
15 and cried, that he l his garment with H5800
18 he l his garment with me, and fled out. H5800
41:49 much, until he l numbering; for *it was* H2308
42:38 is dead, and he is l alone: if mischief H7604
44:12 at the eldest, and l at the youngest: and H3615
20 and he alone is l of his mother, and his H3498
47:18 there is not ought l in the sight of my H7604
48:13 toward Israel's l hand, and Manasseh H8040
13 Manasseh in his l hand toward Israel's H8040
14 the younger, and his l hand upon H8040
50: 8 herds, they l in the land of Goshen. H5800
Ex 2:20 *is* it *that* ye have l the man? call him, H5800
9:21 l his servants and his cattle in the field. H5800
10:12 of the land, *even* all that the hail hath l. H7604
15 trees which the hail had l: and there H3498
26 not an hoof be l behind; for thereof H7604
14:22 them on their right hand, and on their l. H8040
29 them on their right hand, and on their l. H8040
16:20 but some of them l of it until the H3498
34:25 of the passover be l unto the morning. H3885
Lev 2:10 And that which is l of the meat offering H3498
10:12 his sons that were l, Take the meat H3498
16 of Aaron *which were* l *alive*, saying, H3498
14:15 pour *it* into the palm of his own l hand: H8042
16 the oil that *is* in his l hand, and shall H8042
26 the oil into the palm of his own l hand: H8042
27 l hand seven times before the LORD: H8042
26:36 And upon them that are l *alive* of you I H7604
39 And they that are l of you shall pine H7604
43 The land also shall be l of them, and H5800
Nu 20:17 the l, until we have passed thy borders. H8040
21:35 there was none l him alive: and they H7604
22:26 turn either to the right hand or to the l. H8040
26:65 And there was not l a man of them, H3498
Dt 2:27 turn unto the right hand nor to the l. H8040
34 ones, of every city, we l none to remain: H7604
3: 3 him until none was l to him remaining. H7604
4:27 and ye shall be l few in number among H7604
5:32 turn aside to the right hand or to the l. H8040
7:20 them, until they that are l, and hide H7604
17:11 thee, *to* the right hand, nor *to* the l. H8040
20 hand, or *to* the l: to the end that he may H8040
28:14 l, to go after other gods to serve them. H8040
55 he hath nothing l him in the siege, and H7604
62 And ye shall be l few in number, H7604
32:36 is gone, and *there is* none shut up, or l. H5800
Jos 1: 7 right hand or *to* the l, that thou mayest H8040
6:23 and l them without the camp of Israel. H3240
8:17 And there was not a man l in Ai or H7604
17 Israel: and they l the city open, and H5800
10:33 until he had l him none remaining. H7604
37 that *were* therein; he l none remaining, H7604
39 *were* therein; he l none remaining: as H7604
40 all their kings: he l none remaining, but H7604
11: 8 until they l them none remaining. H7604
11 there was not any l to breathe: and he H3498
14 them, neither l they any to breathe. H7604
15 so did Joshua; he l nothing undone of H5493
22 There was none of the Anakims l in the H3498
19:27 and goeth out to Cabul on the l hand, H8040
22: 3 Ye have not l your brethren these many H5800
23: 6 therefrom *to* the right hand or *to* the l; H8040
Jdg 2:21 nations which Joshua l when he died: H5800
23 Therefore the LORD l those nations, H3240
3: 1 which the LORD l, to prove Israel by H3240
21 And Ehud put forth his l hand, and H8040
4:16 of the sword; *and* there was not a man l. H7604

Jdg 6: 4 unto Gaza, and l no sustenance for H7604
7:20 held the lamps in their l hands, and the H8040
8:10 *men,* all that were l of all the hosts of H3498
9: 5 of Jerubbaal was l; for he hid himself. H3498
16:29 right hand, and of the other with his l. H8040
Ru 1: 3 died; and she was l, and her two sons. H7604
5 was l of her two sons and her husband. H7604
18 with her, then she l speaking unto her. H2308
2:11 and *how* thou hast l thy father and thy H5800
14 and she did eat, and was sufficed, and l. H3498
20 who hath not l off his kindness to the H5800
4:14 which hath not l thee this day without H7673
1Sa 2:36 every one that is l in thine house shall H3498
5: 4 only *the stump of* Dagon was l to him. H7604
6:12 hand or *to* the l; and the lords of the H8040
9:24 that which is l! set *it* before thee, *and* H7604
10: 2 and, lo, thy father hath l the care of the H5203
11:11 so that two of them were not l together. H7604
17:20 in the morning, and l the sheep with a H5203
22 And David l his carriage in the hand of H5203
28 whom hast thou l those few sheep in H5203
25:34 there had not been l unto Nabal by the H3498
27: 9 And David smote the land, and l neither
30: 9 where those that were l behind stayed. H3498
13 and my master l me, because three H5800
2Sa 2:19 hand nor to the l from following Abner. H8040
21 hand or to thy l, and lay thee hold on H8040
5:21 And there they l their images, and H5800
9: 1 yet any that is l of the house of Saul, H3498
13:30 sons, and there is not one of them l. H3498
14: 7 my coal which is l, and shall not leave H7604
19 hand or to the l from ought that my H8041
15:16 him. And the king l ten women, *which* H5800
16: 6 *were* on his right hand and on his l. H8040
21 which he hath l to keep the house; and H3240
17:12 there shall not be l so much as one. H3498
20: 3 whom he had l to keep the house, and H3240
1Ki 7:21 and he set up the l pillar, and called the H8042
39 and five on the l side of the house: and H8040
47 And Solomon l all the vessels H3240
49 and five on the l, before the oracle, with H8040
9:20 *And* all the people *that were* l of the H3498
21 Their children that were l after them in H3498
14:10 that is shut up and l in Israel, and will H5800
15:18 the gold *that were* l in the treasures of H3498
21 heard *thereof,* that he l off building of H2308
29 of Jeroboam; he l not to Jeroboam any H7604
16:11 house of Baasha: he l him not one that H7604
17:17 sore, that there was no breath l in him. H3498
19: 3 to Judah, and l his servant there. H3240
10 l; and they seek my life, to take it away. H3498
14 l; and they seek my life, to take it away. H3498
18 Yet I have l *me* seven thousand in H7604
20 And he l the oxen, and ran after Elijah, H5800
20:30 of the men *that were* l. And Ben-hadad H3498
21:21 and him that is shut up and l in Israel, H5800
22:19 by him on his right hand and on his l. H8040
2Ki 3:25 only in Kir-haraseth l they the stones H7604
4:44 they did eat, and l *thereof,* according to H3498
7: 7 the twilight, and l their tents, and their H5800
13 remain, which are l in the city, (behold, H7604
13 of Israel that are l in it: behold, *I say,* H7604
8: 6 day that she l the land, even until now. H5800
9: 8 and him that is shut up and l in Israel: H5800
10:11 priests, until he l him none remaining. H7604
14 forty men; neither l he any of them. H7604
21 was not a man l that came not. And H7604
11:11 the temple to the l corner of the temple, H8042
14:26 up, nor any l, nor any helper for Israel. H5800
17:16 And they l all the commandments of H5800
18 was none l but the tribe of Judah only. H7604
19: 4 up *thy* prayer for the remnant that are l. H4672
20:17 nothing shall be l, saith the LORD. H3498
22: 2 not aside to the right hand or to the l. H8040
23: 8 a man's l hand at the gate of the city. H8040
25:11 Now the rest of the people *that were* l H7604
12 But the captain of the guard l of the H7604
22 of Babylon had l, even over them he H7604
1Ch 6:44 *stood* on the l hand: Ethan the son H8040
61 *which were* l of the family of that H3498
12: 2 right hand and the l in *hurling* stones H8041
13: 2 every where, *that are* l in all the land of H7604
14:12 And when they had l their gods there, H5800
16:37 So he l there before the ark of the H5800
2Ch 3:17 the other on the l; and called the name H8040
17 and the name of that on the l Boaz. H8042
4: 6 and five on the l, to wash in them: such H8040
7 five on the right hand, and five on the l. H8040
8 side, and five on the l. And he made an H8040

2Ch 8: 7 *As for* all the people *that were* l of the H3498
8 *But* of their children, who were l after H3498
11:14 For the Levites l their suburbs and H5800
12: 5 I also l you in the hand of Shishak. H5800
16: 5 heard *it,* that he l off building of H2308
18:18 standing on his right hand and *on* his l. H8040
21:17 was never a son l him, save Jehoahaz, H7604
23:10 of the temple to the l side of the temple, H8042
24:18 And they l the house of the LORD God H5800
25 him, (for they l him in great diseases,) H5800
25:12 And *other* ten thousand *l* alive did the
28:14 So the armed men l the captives and H5800
31:10 to eat, and have l plenty: for the LORD H3498
10 and that which is l *is* this great store. H3498
32:31 in the land, God l him, to try him, that H5800
34: 2 *neither* to the right hand, nor to the l. H8040
21 and for them that are l in Israel and in H7604
Neh 1: 2 which were l of the captivity, and H7604
3 remnant that are l of the captivity there H7604
6: 1 was no breach l therein; (though at H3498
8: 4 hand; and on his l hand, Pedaiah, and H8040
Job 20:21 There shall none of his meat be l; H8300
26 ill with him that is l in his tabernacle. H8300
23: 9 On the l hand, where he doth work, but H8040
32:15 answered no more: they l off speaking. H6275
Ps 36: 3 he hath l off to be wise, *and* to do good. H2308
106:11 enemies: there was not one of them l. H3498
Prv 3:16 *and* in her l hand riches and honour. H8040
4:27 Turn not to the right hand nor to the l: H8040
29:15 but a child l *to himself* bringeth H7971
Ecc 10: 2 his right hand; but a fool's heart at his l. H8040
Song 2: 6 His l hand *is* under my head, and his H8040
8: 3 His l hand *should be* under my head, H8040
Isa 1: 8 And the daughter of Zion is l as a H3498
9 Except the LORD of hosts had l unto us H3498
4: 3 *that he that is* l in Zion, and *he that* H7604
7:22 shall every one eat that is l in the land. H3498
9:20 and he shall eat on the l hand, and they H8040
10:14 eggs *that are* l, have I gathered all the H5800
11:11 which shall be l, from Assyria, and from H7604
16 which shall be l, from Assyria; like as H7604
17: 6 Yet gleaning grapes shall be l in it, as H7604
9 which they l because of the children H5800
18: 6 They shall be l together unto the fowls H5800
24: 6 of the earth are burned, and few men l. H7604
12 In the city is l desolation, and the gate H7604
27:10 forsaken, and l like a wilderness: there H5800
30:17 ye flee: till ye be l as a beacon upon the H3498
21 right hand, and when ye turn to the l. H8041
32:14 of the city shall be l; the forts and H5800
37: 4 up *thy* prayer for the remnant that is l. H4672
39: 6 nothing shall be l, saith the LORD. H3498
49:21 l alone; these, where *had* they *been?* H7604
54: 3 hand and on the l; and thy seed shall H8040
Jer 12: 7 I have forsaken mine house, I have l H5203
21: 7 and such as are l in this city from the H7604
27:18 vessels which are l in the house of the H3498
31: 2 people *which were* l of the sword found H8300
34: 7 of Judah that were l, against Lachish, H3498
38:22 And, behold, all the women that are l H7604
27 So they l off speaking with him; H2790
39:10 of the guard l of the poor of the people, H7604
40: 6 the people that were l in the land. H7604
11 of Babylon had l a remnant of Judah, H5414
42: 2 (for we are l *but* a few of many, as H7604
43: 6 of the guard had l with Gedaliah the H3240
44:18 But since we l off to burn incense to the H2308
49:25 How is the city of praise not l, the city of H5800
50:26 her utterly: let nothing of her be l. H7611
52:16 of the guard l *certain* of the poor of H7604
Ezk 1:10 of an ox on the l side; they four also H8040
4: 4 Lie thou also upon thy l side, and lay H8042
9: 8 them, and I was l, that I fell upon my H7604
14:22 Yet, behold, therein shall be l a H3498
16:46 that dwell at thy l hand: and thy H8040
21:16 *or* on the l, whithersoever thy face *is* set. H8041
23: 8 Neither l she her whoredoms *brought* H5800
24:21 whom ye have l shall fall by the sword. H5800
31:12 cut him off, and have l him: upon the H5203
12 from his shadow, and have l him. H5203
36:36 Then the heathen that are l round H7604
39: 3 And I will smite thy bow out of thy l H8040
28 have l none of them any more there. H3498
41: 9 *that* which *was* l *was* the place of the H3240
11 *the place that was* l, one door toward H3240
11 that was l *was* five cubits round about. H3240
48:15 And the five thousand, that are l in the H3498
Dan 2:44 shall not be l to other people, *but* H7662
10: 8 Therefore I was l alone, and saw this H7604

Dan 10:17 in me, neither is there breath l in me. H7604
12: 7 right hand and his l hand unto heaven, H8040
Hos 4:10 have l off to take heed to the LORD. H5800
9:12 *shall* not *be* a man *l*: yea, woe also to
Joel 1: 4 That which the palmerworm hath l H3499
4 the locust hath l hath the cankerworm H3499
4 hath l hath the caterpiller eaten. H3499
Jna 4:11 and their l hand; and *also* much cattle? H8040
Hag 2: 3 Who *is* l among you that saw this H7604
Zec 4: 3 and the other upon the l *side* thereof. H8040
11 candlestick and upon the l *side* thereof? H8040
12: 6 hand and on the l: and Jerusalem shall H8040
13: 8 *and* die; but the third shall be l therein. H3498
14:16 *that* every one that is l of all the nations H3498
Mt 4:20 And they straightway l *their* nets, and *G863*
22 And they immediately l the ship and *G863*
6: 3 But when thou doest alms, let not thy l *G710*
8:15 And he touched her hand, and the fever l *G863*
15:37 *meat* that was l seven baskets full. *G4052*
16: 4 Jonas. And he l them, and departed. *G2641*
20:21 and the other on the l, in thy kingdom. *G2176*
23 hand, and on my l, is not mine to give, *G2176*
21:17 And he l them, and went out of the city *G2641*
22:22 and l him, and went their way. *G863*
25 no issue, l his wife unto his brother: *G863*
23:38 Behold, your house is l unto you *G863*
24: 2 There shall not be l here one stone upon *G863*
40 the one shall be taken, and the other l. *G863*
41 the one shall be taken, and the other l. *G863*
25:33 on his right hand, but the goats on the l. *G2176*
41 unto them on the l hand, Depart from *G2176*
26:44 And he l them, and went away again, *G863*
27:38 on the right hand, and another on the l. *G2176*
Mk 1:20 them: and they l their father Zebedee *G863*
31 l her, and she ministered unto them. *G863*
8: 8 broken *meat* that was l seven baskets. *G4051*
13 And he l them, and entering into the *G863*
10:28 Lo, we have l all, and have followed thee. *G863*
29 is no man that hath l house, or brethren, *G863*
37 the other on thy l hand, in thy glory. *G2176*
40 But to sit on my right hand and on my l *G2176*
12:12 and they l him, and went their way. *G863*
20 the first took a wife, and dying l no seed. *G863*
21 l he any seed: and the third likewise. *G863*
22 And the seven had her, and l no seed: *G863*
13: 2 there shall not be l one stone upon *G863*
34 a far journey, who l his house, and gave *G863*
14:52 And he l the linen cloth, and fled from *G2641*
15:27 his right hand, and the other on his l. *G2176*
Lk 4:39 the fever; and it l her: and immediately *G863*
5: 4 Now when he had l speaking, he said *G3973*
28 And he l all, rose up, and followed him. *G2641*
10:40 that my sister hath l me to serve alone? *G2641*
13:35 Behold, your house is l unto you *G863*
17:34 shall be taken, and the other shall be l. *G863*
35 the one shall be taken, and the other l. *G863*
36 the one shall be taken, and the other l. *G863*
18:28 Then Peter said, Lo, we have l all, and *G863*
29 no man that hath l house, or parents, or *G863*
20:31 also: and they l no children, and died. *G2641*
21: 6 which there shall not be l one stone upon *G863*
23:33 on the right hand, and the other on the l. *G710*
Jn 4: 3 He l Judaea, and departed again into *G863*
28 The woman then l her waterpot, and *G863*
52 at the seventh hour the fever l him. *G863*
8: 9 the last: and Jesus was l alone, and the *G2641*
29 the Father hath not l me alone; for I do *G863*
Act 2:31 his soul was not l in hell, neither his *G2641*
14:17 Nevertheless he l not himself without *G863*
18:19 And he came to Ephesus, and l them *G2641*
21: 3 Cyprus, we l it on the left hand, and *G2641*
3 we left it on the l hand, and sailed into *G2176*
32 and the soldiers, they l beating of Paul. *G3973*
23:32 On the morrow they l the horsemen to *G1439*
24:27 shew the Jews a pleasure, l Paul bound. *G2641*
25:14 is a certain man l in bonds by Felix: *G2641*
Ro 9:29 of Sabaoth had l us a seed, we had *G1459*
11: 3 and I am l alone, and they seek my life. *G5275*
2Co 6: 7 on the right hand and on the l, *G710*
1Th 3: 1 thought it good to be l at Athens alone; *G2641*
2Ti 4:13 The cloak that I l at Troas with Carpus, *G620*
20 but Trophimus have I l at Miletum sick. *G620*
Tit 1: 5 For this cause l I thee in Crete, that *G2641*
Heb 2: 8 under him, he l nothing *that is* not put *G863*
4: 1 a promise being l *us* of entering into *G2641*
Jude 6 first estate, but l their own habitation, *G620*
Rev 2: 4 thee, because thou hast l thy first love. *G863*
10: 2 the sea, and *his* l *foot* on the earth, *G2176*

LEFTEST
Neh 9:28 thee: therefore l thou them in the hand H5800

LEFTHANDED
Jdg 3:15 a man l: and by him H334+H3027+H3225
20:16 men l; every one could H334+H3027+H3225

LEG
Isa 47: 2 make bare the l, uncover the thigh, pass H7640

LEGION
Mk 5: 9 saying, My name *is* L: for we are many. G3003
15 the devil, and had the l, sitting, and G3003
Lk 8:30 And he said, L: because many devils G3003

LEGIONS
Mt 26:53 give me more than twelve l of angels? G3003

LEGS
Ex 12: 9 his l, and with the purtenance thereof. H3767
29:17 of him, and his l, and put *them* unto his H3767
Lev 1: 9 But his inwards and his l shall he wash H3767
13 But he shall wash the inwards and the l H3767
4:11 his l, and his inwards, and his dung, H3767
8:21 And he washed the inwards and the l H3767
9:14 And he did wash the inwards and the l, H3767
11:21 four, which have l above their feet, to H3767
Dt 28:35 knees, and in the l, with a sore botch H7785
1Sa 17: 6 And *he had* greaves of brass upon his l, H7272
Ps 147:10 taketh not pleasure in the l of a man. H7785
Prv 26: 7 The l of the lame are not equal: so *is* a H7785
Song 5:15 His l *are as* pillars of marble, set upon H7785
Isa 3:20 ornaments of the l, and the headbands, H6807
Dan 2:33 His l of iron, his feet part of iron and H8243
Am 3:12 of the lion two l, or a piece of an ear; H3767
Jn 19:31 Pilate that their l might be broken, and G4628
32 Then came the soldiers, and brake the l G4628
33 was dead already, they brake not his l: G4628

LEHABIM
Gen 10:13 and Anamim, and L, and Naphtuhim, H3853
1Ch 1:11 and Anamim, and L, and Naphtuhim, H3853

LEHI
Jdg 15: 9 in Judah, and spread themselves in L. H3896
14 *And* when he came unto L, the H3896
19 which *is* in L unto this day. H3896

LEISURE
Mk 6:31 and they had no l so much as to eat. G2119

LEMUEL
Prv 31: 1 The words of king L, the prophecy that H3927
4 *It is* not for kings, O L, *it is* not for kings H3927

LEND
Ex 22:25 If thou l money to *any of* my people H3867
Lev 25:37 nor l him thy victuals for increase. H5414
Dt 15: 6 and thou shalt l unto many nations, H5670
8 and shalt surely l him sufficient for his H5670
23:19 Thou shalt not l upon usury to thy H5391
20 Unto a stranger thou mayest l upon H5391
20 thou shalt not l upon usury: that the H5391
24:10 When thou dost l thy brother any H5383
11 to whom thou dost l shall bring out the H5383
28:12 and thou shalt l unto many nations, H3867
44 He shall l to thee, and thou shalt not H3867
44 and thou shalt not l to him: he shall be H3867
Lk 6:34 And if ye l *to them* of whom ye hope to G1155
34 l to sinners, to receive as much again. G1155
35 and do good, and l, hoping for nothing G1155
11: 5 say unto him, Friend, l me three loaves; G5531

LENDER
Prv 22: 7 and the borrower *is* servant to the l. H3867
Isa 24: 2 the seller; as with the l, so with the H3867

LENDETH
Dt 15: 2 Every creditor that l *ought* unto his H5383
Ps 37:26 *He is* ever merciful, and l; and his seed H3867
112: 5 A good man sheweth favour, and l: he H3867
Prv 19:17 He that hath pity upon the poor l unto H3867

LENGTH
Gen 6:15 make it *of*: The l of the ark *shall be* three H753
13:17 Arise, walk through the land in the l of it H753
Ex 25:10 a half *shall be* the l thereof, and a cubit H753
17 a half *shall be* the l thereof, and a cubit H753
23 cubits *shall be* the l thereof, and a cubit H753
Ex 26: 2 The l of one curtain *shall be* eight and H753
8 The l of one curtain *shall be* thirty H753
13 remaineth in the l of the curtains of the H753
16 Ten cubits *shall be* the l of a board, and H753
27:11 And likewise for the north side in l *there* H753
18 The l of the court *shall be* an hundred H753
28:16 a span *shall be* the l thereof, and a span H753
30: 2 A cubit *shall be* the l thereof, and a cubit H753
36: 9 The l of one curtain *was* twenty and H753
15 The l of one curtain *was* thirty cubits, H753
21 The l of a board *was* ten cubits, and the H753
37: 1 and a half *was* the l of it, and a cubit and H753
6 and a half *was* the l thereof, and one H753
10 two cubits *was* the l thereof, and a cubit H753
25 shittim wood: the l of it *was* a cubit, and H753
38: 1 five cubits *was* the l thereof, and five H753
18 cubits *was* the l, and the height in the H753
39: 9 a span *was* the l thereof, and a span the H753
Dt 3:11 nine cubits *was* the l thereof, and four H753
30:20 *is* thy life, and the l of thy days: that thou H753
Jdg 3:16 two edges, of a cubit l; and he did gird it H753
1Ki 6: 2 built for the LORD, the l thereof *was* H753
3 cubits *was* the l thereof, according to H753
20 twenty cubits in l, and twenty cubits in H753
7: 2 forest of Lebanon; the l thereof *was* an H753
6 And he made a porch of pillars; the l H753
27 four cubits *was* the l of one base, and H753
2Ch 3: 3 house of God. The l by cubits after the H753
4 *of the house*, the l *of it was* according to H753
8 And he made the most holy house, the l H753
4: 1 twenty cubits the l thereof, and twenty H753
Job 12:12 With the ancient *is* wisdom; and in l of H753
Ps 21: 4 *it* him, *even* l of days for ever and ever. H753
Prv 3: 2 For l of days, and long life, and peace, H753
16 L of days *is* in her right hand; *and* in her H753
29:21 shall have him become *his* son at the l. H319
Ezk 31: 7 Thus was he fair in his greatness, in the l H753
40:11 *and* the l of the gate, thirteen cubits. H753
18 l of the gates *was* the lower pavement. H753
20 the l thereof, and the breadth thereof. H753
21 of the first gate: the l thereof *was* fifty H753
25 like those windows: the l *was* fifty cubits, H753
36 it round about: the l *was* fifty cubits, and H753
49 The l of the porch *was* twenty cubits, H753
41: 2 he measured the l thereof, forty cubits: H753
4 So he measured the l thereof, twenty H753
12 about, and the l thereof ninety cubits. H753
15 And he measured the l of the building H753
22 high, and the l thereof two cubits; and H753
22 thereof, and the l thereof, and the walls H753
42: 2 Before the l of an hundred cubits *was* the H753
7 chambers, the l thereof *was* fifty cubits. H753
8 For the l of the chambers that *were* in H753
45: 1 of the land: the l *shall be* the length of H753
1 length *shall be* the l of five and twenty H753
2 five hundred *in* l, with five hundred *in*
3 thou measure the l of five and twenty H753
5 And the five and twenty thousand of l, H753
7 eastward: and the l *shall be* over against H753
48: 8 *in* breadth, and *in* l as one of the *other* H753
9 in l, and of ten thousand in breadth. H753
10 and twenty thousand *in* l, and toward the H753
10 twenty thousand in l: and the sanctuary H753
13 twenty thousand in l, and ten thousand H753
13 in breadth: all the l *shall be* five and H753
18 And the residue in l over against the H753
Zec 2: 2 thereof, and what *is* the l thereof. H753
5: 2 I see a flying roll; the l thereof *is* twenty H753
Ro 1:10 by any means now at l I might have a G4218
Eph 3:18 breadth, and l, and depth, and height; G3372
Rev 21:16 And the city lieth foursquare, and the l G3372
16 furlongs. The l and the breadth and G3372

LENGTHEN
1Ki 3:14 David did walk, then I will l thy days. H748
Isa 54: 2 l thy cords, and strengthen thy stakes; H748

LENGTHENED
Dt 25:15 thy days may be l in the land which the H748

LENGTHENING
Dan 4:27 poor; if it may be a l of thy tranquillity. H754

LENT
Ex 12:36 so that they l unto them *such things* H7592
Dt 23:19 usury of any thing that is l upon usury: H5391
1Sa 1:28 Therefore also I have l him to the H7592
28 liveth he shall be l to the LORD. And he H7592
2:20 the loan which is l to the LORD. And H7592
Jer 15:10 I have neither l on usury, nor men have H5383
10 nor men have l to me on usury; *yet* H5383

LENTILES
Gen 25:34 and pottage of l; and he did eat and H5742
2Sa 17:28 and beans, and l, and parched *pulse*, H5742
23:11 of ground full of l: and the people fled H5742
Ezk 4: 9 and beans, and l, and millet, and H5742

LEOPARD
Isa 11: 6 the lamb, and the l shall lie down with H5246
Jer 5: 6 shall spoil them, a l shall watch over H5246
13:23 his skin, or the l his spots? *then* may H5246
Dan 7: 6 lo another, like a l, which had upon the H5245
Hos 13: 7 as a l by the way will I observe *them*: H5246
Rev 13: 2 was like unto a l, and his feet were as G3917

LEOPARDS
Song 4: 8 lions' dens, from the mountains of the l. H5246
Hab 1: 8 Their horses also are swifter than the l, H5246

LEPER
Lev 13:45 And the l in whom the plague *is*, his H6879
14: 2 This shall be the law of the l in the day H6879
3 the plague of leprosy be healed in the l; H6879
22: 4 seed of Aaron *is* a l, or hath a running H6879
Nu 5: 2 of the camp every l, and every one that H6879
2Sa 3:29 issue, or that is a l, or that leaneth on a H6879
2Ki 5: 1 a mighty man in valour, *but he was* a l. H6879
11 hand over the place, and recover the l. H6879
27 from his presence a l *as white* as snow. H6879
15: 5 so that he was a l unto the day of his H6879
2Ch 26:21 And Uzziah the king was a l unto the H6879
21 house, *being* a l; for he was cut off from H6879
23 they said, He *is* a l: and Jotham his son H6879
Mt 8: 2 And, behold, there came a l and G3015
26: 6 in Bethany, in the house of Simon the l, G3015
Mk 1:40 And there came a l to him, beseeching G3015
14: 3 of Simon the l, as he sat at meat, there G3015

LEPERS
2Ki 7: 8 And when these l came to the H6879
Mt 10: 8 Heal the sick, cleanse the l, raise the G3015
11: 5 the lame walk, the l are cleansed, and G3015
Lk 4:27 And many l were in Israel in the time G3015
7:22 the lame walk, the l are cleansed, the G3015
17:12 men that were l, which stood afar off: G3015

LEPROSY
Lev 13: 2 *like* the plague of l; then he shall be H6883
3 it *is* a plague of l: and the priest shall H6883
8 shall pronounce him unclean: it *is* a l. H6883
9 When the plague of l is in a man, then H6883
11 It *is* an old l in the skin of his flesh, and H6883
12 And if a l break out abroad in the skin, H6883
12 the skin, and the l cover all the skin of H6883
13 and, behold, *if* the l have covered all his H6883
15 *for* the raw flesh *is* unclean: it *is* a l. H6883
20 it *is* a plague of l broken out of the boil. H6883
25 than the skin; it *is* a l broken out of the H6883
25 him unclean: it *is* the plague of l. H6883
27 him unclean: it *is* the plague of l. H6883
30 scall, *even* a l upon the head or beard. H6883
42 sore; it *is* a l sprung up in his bald H6883
43 the l appeareth in the skin of the flesh; H6883
47 The garment also that the plague of l is H6883
49 l, and shall be shewed unto the priest: H6883
51 the plague *is* a fretting l; it *is* unclean. H6883
52 a fretting l; it shall be burnt in the fire. H6883
59 This *is* the law of the plague of l in a H6883
14: 3 *if* the plague of l be healed in the leper; H6883
7 be cleansed from the l seven times, and H6883
32 *is* the plague of l, whose hand is not H6883
34 I put the plague of l in a house of the H6883
44 *is* a fretting l in the house: it *is* unclean. H6883
54 for all manner of plague of l, and scall, H6883
55 And for the l of a garment, and of a H6883
57 and when *it is* clean: this *is* the law of l. H6883
Dt 24: 8 Take heed in the plague of l, that thou H6883
2Ki 5: 3 for he would recover him of his l. H6883
6 that thou mayest recover him of his l. H6883
7 a man of his l? wherefore consider, H6883
27 The l therefore of Naaman shall cleave H6883
2Ch 26:19 the priests, the l even rose up in his H6883
Mt 8: 3 And immediately his l was cleansed. G3014
Mk 1:42 immediately the l departed from him, G3014
Lk 5:12 a man full of l: who seeing Jesus fell G3014
13 immediately the l departed from him. G3014

LEPROUS

Ex 4: 6 it out, behold, his hand *was* l as snow. H6879
Lev 13:44 He is a l man, he *is* unclean: the priest H6879
Nu 12:10 Miriam *became* l, *white* as snow: and H6879
10 upon Miriam, and, behold, *she was* l. H6879
2Ki 7: 3 And there were four l men at the H6879
2Ch 26:20 behold, he *was* l in his forehead, and H6879

LESHEM

Jos 19:47 up to fight against L, and took it, and H3959
47 and called L, Dan, after the name H3959

LESS

Ex 16:17 so, and gathered, some more, some l. H4591
30:15 poor shall not give l than half a shekel, H4591
Nu 22:18 of the LORD my God, to do l or more. H6996
26:54 few thou shalt give the l inheritance: to H4591
33:54 ye shall give the l inheritance: every H4591
1Sa 22:15 knew nothing of all this, l or more. H6996
25:36 l or more, until the morning light. H6996
1Ki 8:27 much l this house that I have builded? H637
2Ch 6:18 much l this house which I have built!
32:15 my fathers: how much l shall your God
Ezr 9:13 hast punished us l than our iniquities H4295
Job 4:19 How much l *in* them that dwell in houses H637
9:14 How much l shall I answer him, *and*
11: 6 of thee *l* than thine iniquity *deserveth*.
25: 6 How much l man, *that is* a worm? and
34:19 *How much l to him* that accepteth not
Prv 17: 7 not a fool: much l do lying lips a prince.
19:10 Delight is not seemly for a fool; much l
Isa 40:17 to him l than nothing, and vanity. H657
Ezk 15: 5 work: how much l shall it be meet yet H3398
Mk 4:31 l than all the seeds that be in the earth: *G3398*
15:40 James the l and of Joses, and Salome; *G3398*
1Co 12:23 we think to be l honourable, upon these *G820*
2Co 12:15 abundantly I love you, the l I be loved. *G2276*
Eph 3: 8 Unto me, who am l than the least of all *G1647*
Php 2:28 and that I may be the l sorrowful. *G253*
Heb 7: 7 And without all contradiction the l is *G1640*

LESSER

Gen 1:16 the day, and the l light to rule the night: H6996
Isa 7:25 of oxen, and for the treading of l cattle. H7716
Ezk 43:14 and from the l settle *even* to the greater H6996

LEST

Gen 3: 3 of it, neither shall ye touch it, l ye die. H6435
22 and evil: and now, l he put forth his H6435
4:15 Cain, l any finding him should kill him. H1115
11: 4 us make us a name, l we be scattered H6435
14:23 thing that *is* thine, l thou shouldest say, H3808
19:15 which are here; l thou be consumed in H6435
17 to the mountain, l thou be consumed. H6435
19 l some evil take me, and I die: H6435
26: 7 *She is* my wife; l, *said he*, the men of H6435
9 him, Because I said, L I die for her. H6435
32:11 for I fear him, l he will come and smite H6435
38: 9 *it* on the ground, l that he should give H1115
11 for he said, L peradventure he die H6435
23 And Judah said, Let her take *it* to her, l H6435
42: 4 L peradventure mischief befall him. H6435
44:34 *be* not with me? l peradventure I see H6435
45:11 five years of famine; l thou, and thy H6435
Ex 1:10 Come on, let us deal wisely with them; l H6435
5: 3 LORD our God; l he fall upon us with H6435
13:17 near; for God said, L peradventure the H6435
19:21 charge the people, l they break through H6435
22 l the LORD break forth upon them. H6435
24 the LORD, l he break forth upon them. H6435
20:19 but let not God speak with us, l we die. H6435
23:29 thee in one year; l the land become H6435
33 They shall not dwell in thy land, l they H6435
33: 3 people: l I consume thee in the way. H6435
34:12 Take heed to thyself, l thou make a H6435
12 l it be for a snare in the midst of thee: H6435
15 L thou make a covenant with the H6435
Lev 10: 6 rend your clothes; l ye die, and lest H3308
6 lest ye die, and l wrath come upon all
7 of the congregation, l ye die: for the H6435
9 the congregation, l ye die: *it shall be* a H3808
19:29 her to be a whore; l the land fall to H3808
22: 9 mine ordinance, l they bear sin for it, H3808
Nu 4:15 *any* holy thing, l they die. These *things*
20 the holy things are covered, l they die.
16:26 l ye be consumed in all their sins. H6435
34 said, L the earth swallow us up *also*. H6435
18:22 congregation, l they bear sin, and die.
32 things of the children of Israel, l ye die. H3808

Nu 20:18 l I come out against thee with the sword.
Dt 1:42 you; l ye be smitten before your enemies.
4: 9 thy soul diligently, l thou forget the H6435
9 have seen, and l they depart from thy H6435
16 L ye corrupt *yourselves*, and make you H6435
19 And l thou lift up thine eyes unto H6435
23 Take heed unto yourselves, l ye forget H6435
6:12 *Then* beware l thou forget the LORD, H6435
15 God among you) l the anger of the H6435
7:22 them at once, l the beasts of the field H6435
25 nor take *it* unto thee, l thou be snared H6435
26 into thine house, l thou be a cursed thing
8:12 L *when* thou hast eaten and art full, H6435
9:28 L the land whence thou broughtest us H6435
11:17 not her fruit; and *l* ye perish quickly
19: 6 L the avenger of the blood pursue the H6435
20: 5 to his house, l he die in the battle, H6435
6 unto his house, l he die in the battle, H6435
7 unto his house, l he die in the battle, H6435
8 unto his house, l his brethren's heart H3808
22: 9 with divers seeds: l the fruit of thy seed H6435
24:15 his heart upon it: l he cry against thee H3808
25: 3 *and* not exceed: l, *if* he should exceed, H6435
29:18 L there should be among you man, or H6435
18 gods of these nations; l there should be H6435
32:27 of the enemy, l their adversaries should H6435
27 strangely, *and* l they should say, Our H6435
Jos 2:16 to the mountain, l the pursuers meet H6435
6:18 accursed thing, l ye make *yourselves* H6435
9:20 even let them live, l wrath be upon us, H3808
24:27 a witness unto you, l ye deny your God. H6435
Jdg 7: 2 into their hands, l Israel vaunt H6435
14:15 unto us the riddle, l we burn thee and H6435
18:25 be heard among us, l angry fellows run H6435
Ru 4: 6 redeem *it* for myself, l I mar mine own H6435
1Sa 9: 5 and let us return; l my father leave H6435
13:19 Philistines said, L the Hebrews make H6435
15: 6 the Amalekites, l I destroy you with H6435
20: 3 know this, l he be grieved: but truly H6435
27:11 to Gath, saying, L they should tell on H6435
29: 4 with us to battle, l in the battle he be an H3808
31: 4 me through therewith; l these H6435
2Sa 1:20 streets of Askelon; l the daughters of H6435
20 Philistines rejoice, l the daughters of H6435
12:28 city, and take it: l I take the city, and it H6435
13:25 let us not all now go, l we be chargeable H3808
14:11 destroy any more, l they destroy my son.
15:14 make speed to depart, l he overtake us H6435
17:16 but speedily pass over; l the king be H6435
20: 6 pursue after him, l he get him fenced H6435
2Ki 2:16 seek thy master: l peradventure the H6435
1Ch 10: 4 me through therewith; l these H6435
Job 32:13 L ye should say, We have found out H6435
34:30 That the hypocrite reign not, l the people
36:18 Because *there is* wrath, *beware* l he H6435
42: 8 him will I accept: l I deal with you *after* H1115
Ps 2:12 Kiss the Son, l he be angry, and ye H6435
7: 2 L he tear my soul like a lion, rending *it* H6435
13: 3 mine eyes, l I sleep the *sleep of* death; H6435
4 L mine enemy say, I have prevailed H6435
28: 1 be not silent to me: l, *if* thou be silent to H6435
32: 9 and bridle, l they come near unto thee. H1077
38:16 For I said, *Hear me*, l *otherwise* they H6435
50:22 Now consider this, ye that forget God, l H6435
59:11 Slay them not, l my people forget: H6435
91:12 They shall bear thee up in *their* hands, l
106:23 his wrath, l he should destroy *them*.
125: 3 the righteous; l the righteous H4616+H3808
140: 8 device; *l* they exalt themselves. Selah.
143: 7 thy face from me, l I be like unto them
Prv 5: 6 L thou shouldest ponder the path of H6435
9 L thou give thine honour unto others, H6435
10 L strangers be filled with thy wealth; H6435
9: 8 Reprove not a scorner, l he hate thee: H6435
20:13 Love not sleep, l thou come to poverty; H6435
22:25 L thou learn his ways, and get a snare H6435
24:18 L the LORD see *it*, and it displease him, H6435
25: 8 Go not forth hastily to strive, l *thou* H6435
10 L he that heareth *it* put thee to shame, H6435
16 l thou be filled therewith, and vomit it. H6435
17 l he be weary of thee, and *so* hate thee. H6435
26: 4 to his folly, l thou also be like unto him. H6435
5 Answer a fool according to his folly, l H6435
30: 6 Add thou not unto his words, l he H6435
9 L I be full, and deny *thee*, and say, H6435
9 *is* the LORD? or l I be poor, and steal, H6435
10 Accuse not a servant unto his master, l H6435
31: 5 L they drink, and forget the law, and H6435
Ecc 7:21 that are spoken; l thou hear thy H634+H3808

Isa 6:10 and shut their eyes; l they see with their H6435
27: 3 it every moment: l *any* hurt it, I will H6435
28:22 Now therefore be ye not mockers, l H6435
36:18 *Beware* l Hezekiah persuade you, H6435
48: 5 I shewed *it* thee: l thou shouldest say, H6435
7 them not; l thou shouldest say, H6435
Jer 1:17 faces, l I confound thee before them. H6435
4: 4 of Jerusalem: l my fury come forth H6435
6: 8 Be thou instructed, O Jerusalem, l my H6435
8 soul depart from thee; l I make thee H6435
10:24 thine anger, l thou bring me to nothing. H6435
21:12 of the oppressor, l my fury go out like H6435
37:20 of Jonathan the scribe, l I die there. H3808
38:19 to the Chaldeans, l they deliver me into H6435
51:46 And l your heart faint, and ye fear for H6435
Hos 2: 3 L I strip her naked, and set her as in H6435
Am 5: 6 Seek the LORD, and ye shall live; l he H6435
Zec 7:12 *as* an adamant stone, l they should hear
Mal 4: 6 to their fathers, l I come and smite the H6435
Mt 4: 6 shall bear thee up, l at any time thou *G3379*
5:25 in the way with him; l at any time the *G3379*
7: 6 before swine, l they trample them *G3379*
13:15 they have closed; l at any time they *G3379*
29 But he said, Nay; l while ye gather up *G3379*
15:32 away fasting, l they faint in the way. *G3379*
17:27 Notwithstanding, l we should *G2443+G3361*
25: 9 But the wise answered, saying, *Not so*; l *G3379*
26: 5 on the feast *day*, l there be an *G2443+G3361*
27:64 until the third day, l his disciples come *G3379*
Mk 3: 9 l they should throng him. *G2443+G3361*
4:12 and not understand; l at any time they *G3379*
13: 5 say, Take heed l any *man* deceive you: *G3361*
36 L coming suddenly he find you *G3361*
14: 2 But they said, Not on the feast *day*, l *G3379*
38 Watch ye and pray, l ye enter into *G3363*
Lk 4:11 shall bear thee up, l at any time thou *G3379*
8:12 of their hearts, l they should *G2443+G3361*
12:58 from him; l he hale thee to the judge, *G3379*
14: 8 the highest room; l a more honourable *G3379*
12 *thy* rich neighbours; l they also bid thee *G3379*
29 L haply, after he hath laid the *G2443+G3361*
16:28 unto them, l they also come *G2443+G3361*
18: 5 avenge her, l by her continual *G2443+G3361*
21:34 And take heed to yourselves, l at any *G3379*
22:46 l ye enter into temptation. *G2443+G3361*
Jn 3:20 l his deeds should be reproved. *G2443+G3361*
5:14 sin no more, l a worse thing *G2443+G3361*
12:35 have the light, l darkness come *G2443+G3361*
42 confess *him*, l they should be *G2443+G3361*
18:28 judgment hall, l they should be *G2443+G3361*
Act 5:26 the people, l they should have *G2443+G3361*
39 overthrow it; l haply ye be found even *G3379*
13:40 Beware therefore, l that come upon *G3361*
23:10 captain, fearing l Paul should have *G3361*
27:17 ship; and, fearing l they should fall into *G3361*
29 Then fearing l we should have fallen *G3381*
42 kill the prisoners, l any of them should *G3361*
28:27 have they closed; l they should see with *G3379*
Ro 11:21 *take heed* l he also spare not thee. *G3381*
25 of this mystery, l ye should be *G2443+G3361*
15:20 was named, l I should build *G2443+G3361*
1Co 1:15 L any should say that I had *G2443+G3361*
17 of words, l the cross of Christ *G2443+G3361*
8: 9 But take heed l by any means this *G3381*
13 l I make my brother to offend. *G2443+G3361*
9:12 all things, l we should hinder *G2443+G3361*
27 *it* into subjection: l that by any means, *G3381*
10:12 thinketh he standeth take heed l he fall. *G3361*
2Co 2: 3 And I wrote this same unto you, l, when *G3363*
7 and comfort *him*, l perhaps such a one *G3381*
11 L Satan should get an *G2443+G3361*
4: 4 which believe not, l the light of the *G3361*
9: 3 Yet have I sent the brethren, l our *G3363*
4 L haply if they of Macedonia come *G3381*
11: 3 But I fear, l by any means, as the *G3381*
12: 6 but *now* I forbear, l any man should *G3361*
7 And l I should be exalted *G2443+G3361*
7 to buffet me, l I should be *G2443+G3361*
20 For I fear, l, when I come, I shall not *G3381*
20 as ye would not: l *there be* debates, *G3381*
21 *And* l, when I come again, my God will *G3361*
13:10 being absent, l being present I *G2443+G3361*
Gal 2: 2 of reputation, l by any means I should *G3381*
4:11 I am afraid of you, l I have bestowed *G3381*
6: 1 thyself, l thou also be tempted. *G3361*
12 only l they should suffer *G2443+G3361*
Eph 2: 9 Not of works, l any man *G2443+G3361*
Php 2:27 but on me also, l I should have *G2443+G3361*
Col 2: 4 And this I say, l any man *G2443+G3361*

Col 2: 8 Beware l any man spoil you through G3361
3:21 *anger,* l they be discouraged. G2443+G3361
1Th 3: 5 know your faith, l by some means the G3381
1Ti 3: 6 Not a novice, l being lifted up G2443+G3361
7 are without; l he fall into G2443+G3361
Heb 2: 1 l at any time we should let *them* slip. G3379
3:12 Take heed, brethren, l there be in any G3379
13 called To day; l any of you be G2443+G3361
4: 1 Let us therefore fear, l, a promise being G3379
11 into that rest, l any man fall G2443+G3361
11:28 of blood, l he that destroyed G2443+G3361
12: 3 himself, l ye be wearied and G2443+G3361
13 for your feet, l that which is G2443+G3361
15 Looking diligently l any man fail of the G3361
15 of the grace of God; l any root of G3361
16 L there *be* any fornicator, or profane G3361
Jas 5: 9 brethren, l ye be condemned: G2443+G3361
12 l ye fall into condemnation. G2443+G3361
2Pt 3:17 beware l ye also, being led G2443+G3361
Rev 16:15 his garments, l he walk naked, G2443+G3361

LET See the Appendix.

LETTER
2Sa 11:14 that David wrote a l to Joab, and sent *it* H5612
15 And he wrote in the l, saying, Set ye H5612
2Ki 5: 5 go, and I will send a l unto the king of H5612
6 And he brought the l to the king of H5612
6 Now when this l is come unto thee, H5612
7 of Israel had read the l, that he rent his H5612
10: 2 Now as soon as this l cometh to you, H5612
6 Then he wrote a l the second time to H5612
7 And it came to pass, when the l came H5612
19:14 And Hezekiah received the l of the H5612
Ezr 4: 7 the writing of the l *was* written in the H5406
8 the scribe wrote a l against Jerusalem to H104
11 This *is* the copy of the l that they sent H104
18 The l which ye sent unto us hath been H5407
23 of king Artaxerxes' l *was* read before H5407
5: 5 answer by l concerning this *matter.* H5407
6 The copy of the l that Tatnai, governor H104
7 They sent a l unto him, wherein was H6600
7:11 Now this *is* the copy of the l that the H5406
Neh 2: 8 And a l unto Asaph the keeper of the H107
6: 5 the fifth time with an open l in his hand; H107
Est 9:26 the words of this l, and *of that* which they H107
29 to confirm this second l of Purim. H107
Isa 37:14 And Hezekiah received the l from the H5612
Jer 29: 1 Now these *are* the words of the l that H5612
29 And Zephaniah the priest read this l in H5612
Act 23:25 And he wrote a l after this manner: G1992
34 And when the governor had read *the l,* he
Ro 2:27 thee, who by the l and circumcision G1121
29 *and* not in the l; whose praise *is* not G1121
7: 6 of spirit, and not *in* the oldness of the l. G1121
2Co 3: 6 not of the l, but of the spirit: for G1121
6 the l killeth, but the spirit giveth life. G1121
7: 8 For though I made you sorry with a l, I G1992
Gal 6:11 Ye see how large a l I have written unto G1121
2Th 2: 2 by word, nor by l as from us, as that G1992
Heb 13:22 have written a l unto you in few words. G1989

LETTERS
1Ki 21: 8 So she wrote l in Ahab's name, and H5612
8 seal, and sent the l unto the elders and H5612
9 And she wrote in the l, saying, Proclaim H5612
11 in the l which she had sent unto them. H5612
2Ki 10: 1 And Jehu wrote l, and sent to Samaria, H5612
20:12 of Babylon, sent l and a present unto H5612
2Ch 30: 1 Judah, and wrote l also to Ephraim and H107
6 So the posts went with the l from the H107
32:17 He wrote also l to rail on the LORD God H5612
Neh 2: 7 it please the king, let l be given me to the H107
9 them the king's l. Now the king had sent H107
6:17 of Judah sent many l unto Tobiah, and H107
17 and *the l* of Tobiah came unto them.
19 him. *And* Tobiah sent l to put me in fear. H107
Est 1:22 For he sent l into all the king's H5612
3:13 And the l were sent by posts into all the H5612
8: 5 to reverse the l devised by Haman the H5612
10 ring, and sent l by posts on horseback, H5612
9:20 things, and sent l unto all the Jews that H5612
25 he commanded by l that his wicked H5612
30 And he sent the l unto all the Jews, to H5612
Isa 39: 1 king of Babylon, sent l and a present to H5612
Jer 29:25 thou hast sent l in thy name unto all H5612
Lk 23:38 over him in l of Greek, and Latin, G1121
Jn 7:15 this man l, having never learned? G1121
Act 9: 2 And desired of him l to Damascus to G1992
Act 15:23 And they wrote *l* by them after this
22: 5 also I received l unto the brethren, and G1992
28:21 We neither received l out of Judaea G1121
1Co 16: 3 approve by *your* l, them will I send to G1992
2Co 3: 1 to you, or *l* of commendation from you?
10: 9 not seem as if I would terrify you by l. G1992
10 For *his* l, say they, *are* weighty and G1992
11 as we are in word by l when we are G1992

LETTEST
Job 15:13 and l *such* words go out of thy mouth?
41: 1 tongue with a cord *which* thou l down? H8257
Lk 2:29 Lord, now l thou thy servant depart in G630

LETTETH
2Ki 10:24 escape, *he that l him go,* his life *shall*
Prv 17:14 The beginning of strife *is as* when one l H6362
2Th 2: 7 only he who now l *will let,* until he be G2722

LETTING
Ex 8:29 l the people go to sacrifice to the LORD.

LETUSHIM
Gen 25: 3 were Asshurim, and L, and Leummim. H3912

LEUMMIM
Gen 25: 3 were Asshurim, and Letushim, and L. H3817

LEVI
Gen 29:34 sons: therefore was his name called L. H3878
34:25 Simeon and L, Dinah's brethren, took H3878
30 And Jacob said to Simeon and L, Ye H3878
35:23 and Simeon, and L, and Judah, and H3878
46:11 And the sons of L; Gershon, Kohath, H3878
49: 5 Simeon and L *are* brethren; H3878
Ex 1: 2 Reuben, Simeon, L, and Judah, H3878
2: 1 And there went a man of the house of L, H3878
1 Levi, and took *to wife* a daughter of L. H3878
6:16 of the sons of L according to their H3878
16 years of the life of L *were* an hundred H3878
19 of L according to their generations. H3878
32:26 me. And all the sons of L gathered H3878
28 And the children of L did according to H3878
Nu 1:49 the tribe of L, neither take the sum H3878
3: 6 Bring the tribe of L near, and present H3878
15 Number the children of L after the H3878
17 And these were the sons of L by their H3878
4: 2 from among the sons of L, after their H3878
16: 1 Kohath, the son of L, and Dathan and H3878
7 *take* too much upon you, ye sons of L. H3878
8 Korah, Hear, I pray you, ye sons of L: H3878
10 the sons of L with thee: and seek H3878
17: 3 upon the rod of L: for one rod *shall be* H3878
8 for the house of L was budded, and H3878
18: 2 And thy brethren also of the tribe of L, H3878
21 the children of L all the tenth in Israel H3878
26:59 the daughter of L, whom *her mother* H3878
59 *her mother* bare to L in Egypt: and she H3878
Dt 10: 8 the tribe of L, to bear the ark of the H3878
9 Wherefore L hath no part nor H3878
18: 1 *and* all the tribe of L, shall have no part H3878
21: 5 And the priests the sons of L shall H3878
27:12 Jordan; Simeon, and L, and Judah, and H3878
31: 9 priests the sons of L, which bare the ark H3878
33: 8 And of L he said, *Let* thy Thummim H3878
Jos 13:14 Only unto the tribe of L he gave none H3878
33 But unto the tribe of L Moses gave not H3878
21:10 of L, had: for theirs was the first lot. H3878
1Ki 12:31 people, which were not of the sons of L. H3878
1Ch 2: 1 L, and Judah, Issachar, and Zebulun, H3878
6: 1 The sons of L; Gershon, Kohath, and H3878
16 The sons of L; Gershom, Kohath, and H3878
38 Kohath, the son of L, the son of Israel. H3878
43 the son of Gershom, the son of L. H3878
47 Mushi, the son of Merari, the son of L. H3878
9:18 in the companies of the children of L. H3878
12:26 Of the children of L four thousand and H3878
21: 6 But L and Benjamin counted he not H3878
23: 6 among the sons of L, *namely,* Gershon, H3878
14 his sons were named of the tribe of L. H3878
24 These *were* the sons of L after the H3878
24:20 And the rest of the sons of L *were* H3878
Ezr 8:15 and found there none of the sons of L. H3878
18 of Mahli, the son of L, the son of Israel; H3878
Neh 10:39 and the children of L shall bring the H3878
12:23 The sons of L, the chief of the fathers, H3878
Ps 135:20 Bless the LORD, O house of L: ye that H3878
Ezk 40:46 among the sons of L, which come near H3878
48:31 one gate of Judah, one gate of L. H3878
Zec 12:13 The family of the house of L apart, and H3878
Mal 2: 4 be with L, saith the LORD of hosts. H3878
8 covenant of L, saith the LORD of hosts. H3878
3: 3 purify the sons of L, and purge them as H3878
Mk 2:14 And as he passed by, he saw L the *son* G3018
Lk 3:24 was *the son* of L, which was *the son* of G3017
29 *son* of Matthat, which was *the son* of L, G3017
5:27 publican, named L, sitting at the receipt G3018
29 And L made him a great feast in his G3018
Heb 7: 5 And verily they that are of the sons of L, G3017
9 And as I may so say, L also, who G3017
Rev 7: 7 Of the tribe of L *were* sealed twelve G3017

LEVIATHAN
Job 41: 1 Canst thou draw out l with an hook? or H3882
Ps 74:14 Thou brakest the heads of l in pieces, H3882
104:26 There go the ships: *there is* that l, *whom* H3882
Isa 27: 1 shall punish l the piercing serpent, H3882
1 serpent, even l that crooked serpent; H3882

LEVITE
Ex 4:14 *Is* not Aaron the L thy brother? I know H3881
Dt 12:12 and the L that *is* within your gates; H3881
18 and the L that *is* within thy gates: H3881
19 L as long as thou livest upon the earth. H3881
14:27 And the L that *is* within thy gates; thou H3881
29 And the L, (because he hath no part nor H3881
16:11 and the L that *is* within thy gates, H3881
14 and the L, the stranger, and the H3881
18: 6 And if a L come from any of thy gates H3881
26:11 L, and the stranger that *is* among you. H3881
12 given *it* unto the L, the stranger, the H3881
13 them unto the L, and unto the stranger, H3881
Jdg 17: 7 who *was* a L, and he sojourned there. H3881
9 said unto him, I *am* a L of H3881
10 and thy victuals. So the L went in. H3881
11 And the L was content to dwell with the H3881
12 And Micah consecrated the L; and the H3881
13 good, seeing I have a L to *my* priest. H3881
18: 3 young man the L: and they turned in H3881
15 young man the L, *even* unto the house H3881
19: 1 was a certain L sojourning on the side H3881
20: 4 And the L, the husband of the woman H3881
2Ch 20:14 of Mattaniah, a L of the sons of Asaph, H3881
31:12 Cononiah the L *was* ruler, and Shimei H3881
14 And Kore the son of Imnah the L, the H3881
Ezr 10:15 and Shabbethai the L helped them. H3881
Lk 10:32 And likewise a L, when he was at the G3019
Act 4:36 a L, *and* of the country of Cyprus, G3019

LEVITES
Ex 6:25 of the L according to their families. H3881
38:21 *for* the service of the L, by the hand of H3881
Lev 25:32 Notwithstanding the cities of the L, *and* H3881
32 may the L redeem at any time. H3881
33 And if a man purchase of the L, then H3881
33 houses of the cities of the L *are* their H3881
Nu 1:47 But the L after the tribe of their fathers H3881
50 But thou shalt appoint the L over the H3881
51 forward, the L shall take it down: and H3881
51 to be pitched, the L shall set it up: and H3881
53 But the L shall pitch round about the H3881
53 of Israel: and the L shall keep the H3881
2:17 the camp of the L in the midst of the H3881
33 But the L were not numbered among H3881
3: 9 And thou shalt give the L unto Aaron H3881
12 And I, behold, I have taken the L from H3881
12 of Israel: therefore the L shall be mine; H3881
20 the families of the L according to the H3881
32 over the chief of the L, *and have* the H3881
39 All that were numbered of the L, which H3881
41 And thou shalt take the L for me (I *am* H3881
41 and the cattle of the L instead of all the H3881
45 Take the L instead of all the firstborn H3881
45 and the cattle of the L instead of their H3881
45 the L shall be mine: I *am* the LORD. H3881
46 of Israel, which are more than the L; H3881
49 them that were redeemed by the L: H3881
4:18 of the Kohathites from among the L: H3881
46 All those that were numbered of the L, H3881
7: 5 give them unto the L, to every man H3881
6 the oxen, and gave them unto the L. H3881
8: 6 Take the L from among the children of H3881
9 And thou shalt bring the L before the H3881
10 And thou shalt bring the L before the H3881
10 Israel shall put their hands upon the L: H3881
11 And Aaron shall offer the L before the H3881
12 And the L shall lay their hands upon H3881
12 LORD, to make an atonement for the L. H3881

Nu 8:13 And thou shalt set the L before Aaron, H3881
14 Thus shalt thou separate the L from H3881
14 of Israel: and the L shall be mine. H3881
15 And after that shall the L go in to do H3881
18 And I have taken the L for all the H3881
19 And I have given the L *as* a gift to H3881
20 Israel, did to the L according unto all H3881
20 concerning the L, so did the children H3881
21 And the L were purified, and they H3881
22 And after that went the L in to do their H3881
22 the L, so did they unto them. H3881
24 This *is it* that *belongeth* unto the L: H3881
26 do unto the L touching their charge. H3881
18: 6 your brethren the L from among the H3881
23 But the L shall do the service of the H3881
24 LORD, I have given to the L to inherit: H3881
26 Thus speak unto the L, and say unto H3881
30 counted unto the L as the increase of H3881
26:57 numbered of the L after their families: H3881
58 These *are* the families of the L: the H3881
31:30 them unto the L, which keep the charge H3881
47 them unto the L, which kept the charge H3881
35: 2 they give unto the L of the inheritance H3881
2 give *also* unto the L suburbs for the H3881
4 shall give unto the L, *shall reach* from H3881
6 shall give unto the L *there shall be* six H3881
7 ye shall give to the L *shall be* forty and H3881
8 of his cities unto the L according to his H3881
Dt 17: 9 the priests the L, and unto the judge H3881
18 of *that which is* before the priests the L: H3881
18: 1 The priests the L, *and* all the tribe of H3881
7 all his brethren the L *do,* which stand H3881
24: 8 the priests the L shall teach you: as I H3881
27: 9 And Moses and the priests the L spake H3881
14 And the L shall speak, and say unto all H3881
31:25 That Moses commanded the L, which H3881
Jos 3: 3 and the priests the L bearing it, then ye H3881
8:33 the priests the L, which bare the ark H3881
14: 3 Jordan: but unto the L he gave none H3881
4 no part unto the L in the land, save H3881
18: 7 But the L have no part among you; for H3881
21: 1 of the fathers of the L unto Eleazar the H3881
3 Israel gave unto the L out of their H3881
4 *which were* of the L, had by lot out of H3881
8 by lot unto the L these cities with their H3881
20 of Kohath, the L which remained of H3881
27 of the families of the L, out of the *other* H3881
34 the rest of the L, out of the tribe of H3881
40 of the L, were *by* their lot twelve cities. H3881
41 All the cities of the L within the H3881
1Sa 6:15 And the L took down the ark of the H3881
2Sa 15:24 And lo Zadok also, and all the L *were* H3881
1Ki 8: 4 did the priests and the L bring up. H3881
1Ch 6:19 of the L according to their fathers. H3881
48 Their brethren also the L *were* H3881
64 And the children of Israel gave to the L H3881
9: 2 the priests, L, and the Nethinims. H3881
14 And of the L; Shemaiah the son of H3881
26 For these L, the four chief porters, were H3881
31 And Mattithiah, *one* of the L, who *was* H3881
33 the fathers of the L, *who remaining* in H3881
34 These chief fathers of the L *were* chief H3881
13: 2 to the priests and L *which are* in their H3881
15: 2 ark of God but the L: for them hath the H3881
4 the children of Aaron, and the L: H3881
11 and for the L, for Uriel, Asaiah, and H3881
12 the fathers of the L: sanctify yourselves, H3881
14 So the priests and the L sanctified H3881
15 And the children of the L bare the ark H3881
16 And David spake to the chief of the L to H3881
17 So the L appointed Heman the son of H3881
22 And Chenaniah, chief of the L, *was* for H3881
26 God helped the L that bare the ark of H3881
27 linen, and all the L that bare the ark, H3881
16: 4 And he appointed *certain* of the L to H3881
23: 2 of Israel, with the priests and the L. H3881
3 Now the L were numbered from the H3881
26 And also unto the L; they shall no *more* H3881
27 For by the last words of David the L H3881
24: 6 scribe, *one* of the L, wrote them before H3881
6 of the priests and L: one principal H3881
30 of the L after the house of their fathers. H3881
31 of the priests and L, even the principal H3881
26:17 Eastward *were* six L, northward four a H3881
20 And of the L, Ahijah *was* over the H3881
27:17 Of the L, Hashabiah the son of Kemuel: H3881
28:13 of the priests and the L, and for all the H3881
21 the priests and the L, *even they shall be* H3881
2Ch 5: 4 Israel came; and the L took up the ark. H3881
2Ch 5: 5 did the priests *and* the L bring up. H3881
12 Also the L *which were* the singers, all of H3881
7: 6 on their offices: the L also with H3881
8:14 service, and the L to their charges, to H3881
15 unto the priests and L concerning any H3881
11:13 And the priests and the L that *were* in H3881
14 For the L left their suburbs and their H3881
13: 9 of Aaron, and the L, and have made H3881
10 and the L *wait* upon *their* business: H3881
17: 8 And with them *he sent* L, *even* H3881
8 and Tob-adonijah, L; and with them H3881
19: 8 set of the L, and *of* the priests, and H3881
11 matters: also the L *shall be* officers H3881
20:19 And the L, of the children of the H3881
23: 2 and gathered the L out of all the cities H3881
4 of the L, *shall be* porters of the doors; H3881
6 minister of the L; they shall go in, for H3881
7 And the L shall compass the king H3881
8 So the L and all Judah did according to H3881
18 of the priests the L, whom David had H3881
24: 5 the priests and the L, and said to them, H3881
5 matter. Howbeit the L hastened *it* not. H3881
6 not required of the L to bring in out of H3881
11 by the hand of the L, and when they H3881
29: 4 And he brought in the priests and the L, H3881
5 And said unto them, Hear me, ye L, H3881
12 Then the L arose, Mahath the son of H3881
16 LORD. And the L took *it,* to carry *it* out H3881
25 And he set the L in the house of the H3881
26 And the L stood with the instruments H3881
30 commanded the L to sing praise unto H3881
34 their brethren the L did help them, till H3881
34 for the L *were* more upright H3881
30:15 the priests and the L were ashamed, H3881
16 *they received* of the hand of the L. H3881
17 therefore the L had the charge of the H3881
21 gladness: and the L and the priests H3881
22 unto all the L that taught the good H3881
25 with the priests and the L, and all the H3881
27 Then the priests the L arose and H3881
31: 2 of the priests and the L after their H3881
2 the priests and L for burnt offerings H3881
4 the priests and the L, that they might be H3881
9 priests and the L concerning the heaps. H3881
17 fathers, and the L from twenty years H3881
19 reckoned by genealogies among the L. H3881
34: 9 of God, which the L that kept the doors H3881
12 and Obadiah, the L, of the sons of H3881
12 and *other of* the L, all that could skill of H3881
13 service: and of the L *there were* scribes, H3881
30 priests, and the L, and all the people, H3881
35: 3 And said unto the L that taught all H3881
5 the division of the families of the L. H3881
8 the priests, and to the L: Hilkiah and H3881
9 chief of the L, gave unto the Levites H3881
9 gave unto the L for passover offerings H3881
10 their place, and the L in their courses, H3881
11 their hands, and the L flayed *them.* H3881
14 night; therefore the L prepared for H3881
15 their brethren the L prepared for them. H3881
18 the priests, and the L, and all Judah and H3881
Ezr 1: 5 priests, and the L, with all *them* whose H3881
2:40 The L: the children of Jeshua and H3881
70 So the priests, and the L, and *some* of H3881
3: 8 the priests and the L, and all they that H3881
8 and appointed the L, from twenty years H3881
9 *with* their sons and their brethren the L. H3881
10 trumpets, and the L the sons of Asaph H3881
12 But many of the priests and L and chief H3881
6:16 priests, and the L, and the rest of the H3879
18 divisions, and the L in their courses, H3879
20 For the priests and the L were purified H3881
7: 7 priests, and the L, and the singers, and H3881
13 *of* his priests and L, in my realm, which H3879
24 of the priests and L, singers, porters, H3879
8:20 the service of the L, two hundred and H3881
29 of the priests and the L, and chief of the H3881
30 So took the priests and the L the weight H3881
33 and Noadiah the son of Binnui, L; H3881
9: 1 priests, and the L, have not separated H3881
10: 5 the chief priests, the L, and all Israel, to H3881
23 Also of the L; Jozabad, and Shimei, and H3881
Neh 3:17 After him repaired the L, Rehum the H3881
7: 1 the singers and the L were appointed, H3881
43 The L: the children of Jeshua, of H3881
73 So the priests, and the L, and the H3881
8: 7 Pelaiah, and the L, caused the people to H3881
9 the scribe, and the L that taught the H3881
11 So the L stilled all the people, saying, H3881
Neh 8:13 priests, and the L, unto Ezra the scribe, H3881
9: 4 Then stood up upon the stairs, of the L, H3881
5 Then the L, Jeshua, and Kadmiel, Bani, H3881
38 our princes, L, *and* priests, seal *unto it.* H3881
10: 9 And the L: both Jeshua the son of H3881
28 the priests, the L, the porters, the H3881
34 the priests, the L, and the people, for H3881
37 our ground unto the L, that the same H3881
37 that the same L might have the tithes H3881
38 shall be with the L, when the Levites H3881
38 Levites, when the L take tithes: and the H3881
38 tithes: and the L shall bring up the tithe H3881
11: 3 priests, and the L, and the Nethinims, H3881
15 Also of the L: Shemaiah the son of H3881
16 of the chief of the L, *had* the oversight of H3881
18 All the L in the holy city *were* two H3881
20 priests, *and* the L, *were* in all the cities H3881
22 The overseer also of the L at Jerusalem H3881
36 And of the L *were* divisions *in* Judah, H3881
12: 1 Now these *are* the priests and the L H3881
8 Moreover the L: Jeshua, Binnui, H3881
22 The L in the days of Eliashib, Joiada, H3881
24 And the chief of the L: Hashabiah, H3881
27 they sought the L out of all their places, H3881
30 And the priests and the L purified H3881
44 for the priests and L: for Judah rejoiced H3881
44 the priests and for the L that waited. H3881
47 *holy things* unto the L; and the Levites H3881
47 Levites; and the L sanctified *them* unto H3881
13: 5 *to be given* to the L, and the singers, H3881
10 that the portions of the L had not been H3881
10 *them*: for the L and the singers, that H3881
13 scribe, and of the L, Pedaiah: and next H3881
22 And I commanded the L that they H3881
29 of the priesthood, and of the L. H3881
30 and the L, every one in his business; H3881
Isa 66:21 for priests *and* for L, saith the LORD. H3881
Jer 33:18 Neither shall the priests the L want a H3881
21 with the L the priests, my ministers. H3881
22 and the L that minister unto me. H3881
Ezk 43:19 And thou shalt give to the priests the L H3881
44:10 And the L that are gone away far from H3881
15 But the priests the L, the sons of Zadok, H3881
45: 5 shall also the L, the ministers of the H3881
48:11 went astray, as the L went astray. H3881
12 a thing most holy by the border of the L. H3881
13 of the priests the L *shall have* five and H3881
22 Moreover from the possession of the L, H3881
Jn 1:19 sent priests and L from Jerusalem to *G3019*

LEVITICAL

Heb 7:11 If therefore perfection were by the L *G3020*

LEVY

Nu 31:28 And l a tribute unto the LORD of the H7311
1Ki 5:13 And king Solomon raised a l out of all H4522
13 and the l was thirty thousand men. H4522
14 at home: and Adoniram *was* over the l. H4522
9:15 And this *is* the reason of the l which H4522
21 l a tribute of bondservice unto this day. H5927

LEWD

Ezk 16:27 which are ashamed of thy l way. H2154
23:44 and unto Aholibah, the l women. H2154
Act 17: 5 unto them certain l fellows of the baser *G4190*

LEWDLY

Ezk 22:11 and another hath l defiled his daughter H2154

LEWDNESS

Jdg 20: 6 have committed l and folly in Israel. H2154
Jer 11:15 she hath wrought l with many, and the H4209
13:27 thy neighings, the l of thy whoredom, H2154
Ezk 16:43 this l above all thine abominations. H2154
58 Thou hast borne thy l and thine H2154
22: 9 in the midst of thee they commit l. H2154
23:21 to remembrance the l of thy youth, in H2154
27 Thus will I make thy l to cease from H2154
29 both thy l and thy whoredoms. H2154
35 thou also thy l and thy whoredoms. H2154
48 Thus will I cause l to cease out of the H2154
48 may be taught not to do after your l. H2154
49 And they shall recompense your l upon H2154
24:13 In thy filthiness *is* l: because I have H2154
Hos 2:10 And now will I discover her l in the H5040
6: 9 the way by consent: for they commit l. H2154
Act 18:14 of wrong or wicked l, O *ye* Jews, reason *G4467*

LIAR
Job 24:25 l, and make my speech nothing worth? H3576
Prv 17: 4 *and* a l giveth ear to a naughty tongue. H8267
19:22 and a poor man *is* better than a l. H3577
30: 6 he reprove thee, and thou be found a l. H3576
Jer 15:18 unto me as a l, *and as* waters *that* fail? H391
Jn 8:44 own: for he is a l, and the father of it. G5583
55 not, I shall be a l like unto you: but I G5583
Ro 3: 4 but every man a l; as it is written, That G5583
1Jn 1:10 make him a l, and his word is not in us. G5583
2: 4 is a l, and the truth is not in him. G5583
22 Who is a l but he that denieth that G5583
4:20 his brother, he is a l: for he that loveth G5583
5:10 hath made him a l; because he believeth G5583

LIARS
Dt 33:29 shall be found l unto thee; and thou H3584
Ps 116:11 I said in my haste, All men *are* l. H3576
Isa 44:25 That frustrateth the tokens of the l, and H907
Jer 50:36 A sword *is* upon the l; and they shall H907
1Ti 1:10 menstealers, for l, for perjured persons, G5583
Tit 1:12 *are* alway l, evil beasts, slow bellies. G5583
Rev 2: 2 and are not, and hast found them l: G5571
21: 8 idolaters, and all l, shall have their part G5571

LIBERAL
Prv 11:25 The l soul shall be made fat: and he H1293
Isa 32: 5 l, nor the churl said *to be* bountiful. H5081
8 But the l deviseth liberal things; and by H5081
8 But the liberal deviseth l things; and by H5081
8 things; and by l things shall he stand. H5081
2Co 9:13 and for *your* l distribution unto them, G572

LIBERALITY
1Co 16: 3 I send to bring your l unto Jerusalem. G5485
2Co 8: 2 abounded unto the riches of their l. G572

LIBERALLY
Dt 15:14 Thou shalt furnish him l out of thy H6059
Jas 1: 5 giveth to all *men* l, and upbraideth not; G574

LIBERTINES
Act 6: 9 *synagogue* of the L, and Cyrenians, and G3032

LIBERTY
Lev 25:10 and proclaim l throughout *all* the land H1865
Ps 119:45 And I will walk at l: for I seek thy H7342
Isa 61: 1 to proclaim l to the captives, and H1865
Jer 34: 8 at Jerusalem, to proclaim l unto them; H1865
15 sight, in proclaiming l every man to his H1865
16 ye had set at l at their pleasure, to H2670
17 me, in proclaiming l, every one to his H1865
17 I proclaim a l for you, saith the LORD, H1865
Ezk 46:17 his to the year of l; after it shall return H1865
Lk 4:18 blind, to set at l them that are bruised, G859
Act 24:23 and to let *him* have l, and that he should G425
26:32 at l, if he had not appealed unto Caesar. G630
27: 3 and gave *him* l to go unto his friends G2010
Ro 8:21 the glorious l of the children of God. G1657
1Co 7:39 be dead, she is at l to be married to G1658
8: 9 But take heed lest by any means this l G1849
10:29 l judged of another *man's* conscience? G1657
2Co 3:17 where the Spirit of the Lord *is*, there *is* l. G1657
Gal 2: 4 to spy out our l which we have in Christ G1657
5: 1 Stand fast therefore in the l wherewith G1657
13 been called unto l; only *use* not liberty G1657
13 only *use* not l for an occasion to the G1657
Heb 13:23 Timothy is set at l; with whom, if he G630
Jas 1:25 into the perfect law of l, and continueth G1657
2:12 they that shall be judged by the law of l. G1657
1Pt 2:16 As free, and not using *your* l for a cloak G1657
2Pt 2:19 While they promise them l, they G1657

LIBNAH
Nu 33:20 from Rimmon-parez, and pitched in L. H3841
21 And they removed from L, and pitched H3841
Jos 10:29 unto L, and fought against Libnah: H3841
29 unto Libnah, and fought against L: H3841
31 And Joshua passed from L, and all H3841
32 according to all that he had done to L. H3841
39 he had done also to L, and to her king. H3841
12:15 The king of L, one; the king of Adullam, H3841
15:42 L, and Ether, and Ashan, H3841
21:13 for the slayer; and L with her suburbs, H3841
2Ki 8:22 day. Then L revolted at the same time. H3841
19: 8 warring against L: for he had heard H3841
23:31 the daughter of Jeremiah of L. H3841
24:18 the daughter of Jeremiah of L. H3841
1Ch 6:57 *city* of refuge, and L with her suburbs, H3841
2Ch 21:10 time *also* did L revolt from under his H3841
Isa 37: 8 warring against L: for he had heard H3841
Jer 52: 1 Hamutal the daughter of Jeremiah of L. H3841

LIBNATH See SHIHOR-LIBNATH.

LIBNI
Ex 6:17 The sons of Gershon; L, and Shimi, H3845
Nu 3:18 by their families; L, and Shimei. H3845
1Ch 6:17 of the sons of Gershom; L, and Shimei. H3845
20 Of Gershom; L his son, Jahath his son, H3845
29 The sons of Merari; Mahli, L his son, H3845

LIBNITES
Nu 3:21 Of Gershon *was* the family of the L, and H3846
26:58 the family of the L, the family of the H3846

LIBYA
Ezk 30: 5 Ethiopia, and L, and Lydia, and all the H6316
38: 5 Persia, Ethiopia, and L with them; all H6316
Act 2:10 and in the parts of L about Cyrene, and G3033

LIBYANS
Jer 46: 9 and the L, that handle the shield; H6316
Dan 11:43 of Egypt: and the L and the Ethiopians H3864

LICE
Ex 8:16 l throughout all the land of Egypt. H3654
17 and it became l in man, and in beast; H3654
17 l throughout all the land of Egypt. H3654
18 to bring forth l, but they could not: so H3654
18 were l upon man, and upon beast. H3654
Ps 105:31 sorts of flies, *and* l in all their coasts. H3654

LICENCE
Act 21:40 And when he had given him l, Paul G2010
25:16 face to face, and have l to answer for G5117

LICK
Nu 22: 4 this company l up all *that are* round H3897
1Ki 21:19 shall dogs l thy blood, even thine. H3952
Ps 72: 9 him; and his enemies shall l the dust. H3897
Isa 49:23 the earth, and l up the dust of thy feet; H3897
Mic 7:17 They shall l the dust like a serpent, they H3897

LICKED
1Ki 18:38 l up the water that *was* in the trench. H3897
21:19 place where dogs l the blood of Naboth H3952
22:38 and the dogs l up his blood; and they H3952
Lk 16:21 moreover the dogs came and l his sores. G621

LICKETH
Nu 22: 4 about us, as the ox l up the grass of the H3897

LID
2Ki 12: 9 and bored a hole in the l of it, and set it H1817

LIE
Gen 19:32 wine, and we will l with him, that we H7901
34 go thou in, *and* l with him, that we may H7901
30:15 Therefore he shall l with thee to night H7901
39: 7 upon Joseph; and she said, L with me. H7901
10 unto her, to l by her, *or* to be with her. H7901
12 garment, saying, L with me: and he left H7901
14 l with me, and I cried with a loud voice: H7901
47:30 But I will l with my fathers, and thou H7901
Ex 21:13 And if a man l not in wait, but God H6658
22:16 not betrothed, and l with her, he shall H7901
23:11 shalt let it rest and l still; that the poor H5203
Lev 6: 2 the LORD, and l unto his neighbour H3584
15:18 with whom man shall l *with* seed of H7901
24 And if any man l with her at all, and H7901
18:20 Moreover thou shalt not l H5414+H7903
22 Thou shalt not l with mankind, as with H7901
23 Neither shalt thou l with any H5414+H7903
23 beast to l down thereto: it *is* confusion. H7250
19:11 deal falsely, neither l one to another. H8266
20:12 And if a man l with his daughter in H7901
13 If a man also l with mankind, as he H7901
15 And if a man l with a beast, he H5414+H7903
16 any beast, and l down thereto, thou H7250
18 And if a man shall l with a woman H7901
20 And if a man shall l with his uncle's H7901
26: 6 the land, and ye shall l down, and none H7901
Nu 5:13 And a man l with her carnally, and it H7901
10: 5 l on the east parts shall go forward. H2583
6 the camps that l on the south side shall H2583
23:19 God *is* not a man, that he should l; H3576
24 lion: he shall not l down until he eat *of* H7901
Dt 19:11 But if any man hate his neighbour, and l H693
22:23 man find her in the city, and l with her; H7901
25 force her, and l with her: then the man H7901
28 her, and l with her, and they be found; H7901
25: 2 shall cause him to l down, and to be H5307
28:30 and another man shall l with her: thou H7693
29:20 in this book shall l upon him, and the H7257
Jos 8: 4 Behold, ye shall l in wait against the city, H693
9 and they went to l in ambush, and abode
12 and set them to l in ambush between
Jdg 9:32 *is* with thee, and l in wait in the field:
19:20 *l* upon me; only lodge not in the street.
21:20 saying, Go and l in wait in the vineyards;
Ru 3: 4 where he shall l, and thou shalt go in, H7901
7 merry, he went to l down at the end of H7901
13 LORD liveth: l down until the morning. H7901
1Sa 3: 5 said, I called not; l down again. And he H7901
6 I called not, my son; l down again. H7901
9 Therefore Eli said unto Samuel, Go, l H7901
15:29 of Israel will not l nor repent: for he *is* H8266
22: 8 against me, to l in wait, as at this day?
13 against me, to l in wait, as at this day? H7901
2Sa 11:11 to drink, and to l with my wife? *as* thou H7901
13 he went out to l on his bed with the H7901
12:11 l with thy wives in the sight of this sun. H7901
13:11 unto her, Come l with me, my sister. H7901
1Ki 1: 2 him, and let her l in thy bosom, that H7901
2Ki 4:16 of God, do not l unto thine handmaid. H3576
Job 6:28 upon me; for *it is* evident unto you if I l. H3576
7: 4 When I l down, I say, When shall I H7901
11:19 Also thou shalt l down, and none shall H7257
20:11 shall l down with him in the dust. H7901
21:26 They shall l down alike in the dust, and H7901
27:19 The rich man shall l down, but he shall H7901
34: 6 Should I l against my right? my wound H3576
38:40 dens, *and* abide in the covert to l in wait?
Ps 23: 2 He maketh me to l down in green H7257
57: 4 My soul *is* among lions: *and* I l *even* H7901
59: 3 For, lo, they l in wait for my soul: the
62: 9 of high degree *are* a l: to be laid in the H3577
88: 5 like the slain that l in the grave, whom H7901
89:35 holiness that I will not l unto David. H3576
119:69 The proud have forged a l against me: H8267
Prv 3:24 l down, and thy sleep shall be sweet. H7901
12: 6 The words of the wicked *are* to l in wait
14: 5 A faithful witness will not l: but a false H3576
Ecc 4:11 Again, if two l together, then they have H7901
Song 1:13 he shall l all night betwixt my breasts. H3885
Isa 11: 6 the leopard shall l down with the kid; H7257
7 young ones shall l down together: and H7257
13:21 But wild beasts of the desert shall l H7257
14:18 l in glory, every one in his own house. H7901
30 the needy shall l down in safety: and H7257
17: 2 flocks, which shall l down, and none H7257
27:10 feed, and there shall he l down, and H7257
33: 8 The highways l waste, the wayfaring
34:10 to generation it shall l waste; none shall
43:17 power; they shall l down together, they H7901
44:20 say, *Is there* not a l in my right hand? H8267
50:11 mine hand; ye shall l down in sorrow. H7901
51:20 Thy sons have fainted, they l at the H7901
63: 8 *that* will not l: so he was their Saviour. H8266
65:10 place for the herds to l down in, for my H7258
Jer 3:25 We l down in our shame, and our H7901
27:10 For they prophesy a l unto you, to H8267
14 for they prophesy a l unto you. H8267
15 they prophesy a l in my name; that I H8267
16 for they prophesy a l unto you. H8267
28:15 thou makest this people to trust in a l. H8267
29:21 which prophesy a l unto you in my H8267
31 not, and he caused you to trust in a l: H8267
33:12 causing *their* flocks to l down. H7257
Lam 2:21 The young and the old l on the ground H7901
Ezk 4: 4 L thou also upon thy left side, and lay H7901
4 l upon it thou shalt bear their iniquity. H7901
6 them, l again on thy right side, H7901
9 that thou shalt l upon thy side, three H7901
21:29 they divine a l unto thee, to bring thee H3577
31:18 earth: thou shalt l in the midst of the H7901
32:21 l uncircumcised, slain by the sword. H7901
27 And they shall not l with the mighty H7901
28 and shalt l with *them that are* slain H7901
29 the sword: they shall l with the H7901
30 might; and they l uncircumcised with H7901
34:14 be: there shall they l in a good fold, and H7257
15 them to l down, saith the Lord GOD. H7257
Hos 2:18 and will make them to l down safely. H7901
7: 6 oven, whiles they l in wait: their baker
Joel 1:13 of the altar: come, l all night in H3885

Am 6: 4 That l upon beds of ivory, and stretch H7901
Mic 1:14 Achzib *shall be* a l to the kings of Israel. H391
2:11 spirit and falsehood do l, *saying*, I will H3576
7: 2 men: they all l in wait for blood; they
Hab 2: 3 speak, and not l: though it tarry, wait H3576
Zep 2: 7 shall they l down in the evening: H7257
14 And flocks shall l down in the midst of H7257
15 place for beasts to l down in! every one H4769
3:13 they shall feed and l down, and none H7257
Hag 1: 4 cieled houses, and this house *l* waste?
Zec 10: 2 have seen a l, and have told false H8267
Jn 5: 6 When Jesus saw him l, and knew that *G2621*
8:44 he speaketh a l, he speaketh of his own: *G5579*
20: 6 sepulchre, and seeth the linen clothes l, *G2749*
Act 5: 3 thine heart to l to the Holy Ghost, and *G5574*
23:21 them: for there l in wait for him of them
Ro 1:25 Who changed the truth of God into a l, *G5579*
3: 7 through my l unto his glory; why *G5582*
9: 1 I say the truth in Christ, I l not, my *G5574*
2Co 11:31 for evermore, knoweth that I l not. *G5574*
Gal 1:20 unto you, behold, before God, I l not. *G5574*
Eph 4:14 whereby they l in wait to deceive; *G3180*
Col 3: 9 L not one to another, seeing that ye *G5574*
2Th 2:11 delusion, that they should believe a l: *G5579*
1Ti 2: 7 in Christ, *and* I not;) a teacher of the *G5574*
Tit 1: 2 l, promised before the world began; *G893*
Heb 6:18 for God to l, we might have a strong *G5574*
Jas 3:14 glory not, and l not against the truth. *G5574*
1Jn 1: 6 in darkness, we l, and do not the truth: *G5574*
2:21 ye know it, and that no l is of the truth. *G5579*
27 is truth, and is no l, and even as it hath *G5579*
Rev 3: 9 are not, but do l; behold, I will make *G5574*
11: 8 And their dead bodies *shall l* in the
21:27 or *maketh* a l: but they which are *G5579*
22:15 and whosoever loveth and maketh a l. *G5579*

LIED
1Ki 13:18 and drink water. *But* he l unto him. H3584
Ps 78:36 and they l unto him with their tongues. H3576
Isa 57:11 feared, that thou hast l, and hast not H3576
Act 5: 4 hast not l unto men, but unto God. *G5574*

LIEN
Gen 26:10 might lightly have l with thy wife, and H7901
Ps 68:13 Though ye have l among the pots, *yet* H7901
Jer 3: 2 thou hast not been l with. In the ways H7901

LIERS
Jos 8:13 the city, and their l in wait on the west of
14 l in ambush against him behind the city.
Jdg 9:25 And the men of Shechem set l in wait for
16:12 And *there were* l in wait abiding in the
20:29 And Israel set l in wait round about
33 and the l in wait of Israel came
36 trusted unto the l in wait which they had
37 And the l in wait hasted, and rushed
37 upon Gibeah; and the l in wait drew
38 men of Israel and the l in wait, that they

LIES
Jdg 16:10 me, and told me l: now tell me, I pray H3577
13 me, and told me l: tell me wherewith H3577
Job 11: 3 Should thy l make men hold their peace? H907
13: 4 But ye *are* forgers of l, ye *are* all H8267
Ps 40: 4 the proud, nor such as turn aside to l. H3577
58: 3 as soon as they be born, speaking l. H3577
62: 4 they delight in l: they bless with their H3577
63:11 of them that speak l shall be stopped. H8267
101: 7 that telleth l shall not tarry in my sight. H8267
Prv 6:19 A false witness *that* speaketh l, and he H3577
14: 5 not lie: but a false witness will utter l. H3577
25 souls: but a deceitful *witness* speaketh l. H3577
19: 5 and *he that* speaketh l shall not escape. H3577
9 and *he that* speaketh l shall perish. H3577
29:12 If a ruler hearken to l, all his H1697+H8267
30: 8 from me vanity and l: give me H1697+H3577
Isa 9:15 prophet that teacheth l, he *is* the tail. H8267
16: 6 and his wrath: *but* his l *shall* not *be* so. H907
28:15 us: for we have made l our refuge, and H3577
17 away the refuge of l, and the waters H3577
59: 3 lips have spoken l, your tongue hath H8267
4 in vanity, and speak l; they conceive H7723
Jer 9: 3 *like* their bow *for* l: but they are not H8267
5 their tongue to speak l, *and* weary H8267
14:14 prophets prophesy l in my name: I sent H8267
16:19 have inherited l, vanity, and *things* H8267
20: 6 to whom thou hast prophesied l. H8267
23:14 and walk in l: they strengthen also H8267
25 that prophesy l in my name, saying, H8267
Jer 23:26 that prophesy l? yea, *they are* prophets H8267
32 to err by their l, and by their lightness; H8267
48:30 *shall* not *be* so; his l shall not so effect *it*. H907
Ezk 13: 8 vanity, and seen l, therefore, behold, I H3577
9 and that divine l: they shall not be in H3577
19 lying to my people that hear *your* l? H3577
22 Because with l ye have made the heart H8267
22:28 and divining l unto them, saying, Thus H3577
24:12 She hath wearied *herself* with l, and her H8383
Dan 11:27 they shall speak l at one table; but it H3577
Hos 7: 3 and the princes with their l. H3585
13 yet they have spoken l against me. H3577
10:13 eaten the fruit of l: because thou didst H3585
11:12 Ephraim compasseth me about with l, H3585
12: 1 he daily increaseth l and desolation; H3577
Am 2: 4 and their l caused them to err, H3577
Mic 6:12 have spoken l, and their tongue *is* H8267
Nah 3: 1 Woe to the bloody city! it *is* all full of l H3585
Hab 2:18 and a teacher of l, that the maker of his H8267
Zep 3:13 nor speak l; neither shall a deceitful H3577
Zec 13: 3 for thou speakest l in the name of the H8267
1Ti 4: 2 Speaking l in hypocrisy; having their *G5573*

LIEST
Gen 28:13 l, to thee will I give it, and to thy seed; H7901
Dt 6: 7 thou l down, and when thou risest up. H7901
11:19 thou l down, and when thou risest up. H7901
Jos 7:10 wherefore l thou thus upon thy face? H5307
Prv 3:24 When thou l down, thou shalt not be H7901

LIETH
Gen 4: 7 doest not well, sin l at the door. And H7257
49:25 of the deep that l under, blessings of H7257
Ex 22:19 Whosoever l with a beast shall surely H7901
Lev 6: 3 was lost, and l concerning it, and H3584
14:47 And he that l in the house shall wash H7901
15: 4 Every bed, whereon he l that hath the H7901
20 And every thing that she l upon in her H7901
24 the bed whereon he l shall be unclean. H7901
26 Every bed whereon she l all the days of H7901
33 of him that l with her that is unclean. H7901
19:20 And whosoever l carnally with a H7901
20:11 And the man that l with his father's H7901
13 If a man also lie with mankind, as he l H4904
26:34 as long as it l desolate, and ye *be* in
35 As long as it l desolate it shall rest;
43 sabbaths, while she l desolate without
Nu 21:15 of Ar, and l upon the border of Moab. H8172
Dt 27:20 Cursed *be* he that l with his father's H7901
21 Cursed *be* he that l with any manner of H7901
22 Cursed *be* he that l with his sister, the H7901
23 Cursed *be* he that l with his mother in H7901
Jos 15: 8 the mountain that *l* before the valley of
17: 7 Michmethah, that *l* before Shechem; and
18:13 near the hill that *l* on the south side of
14 from the hill that *l* before Beth-horon
16 the mountain that *l* before the valley of
Jdg 1:16 of Judah, which *l* in the south of Arad;
16: 5 his great strength *l*, and by what *means*
6 thy great strength *l*, and wherewith thou
15 not told me wherein thy great strength *l*.
18:28 in the valley that *l* by Beth-rehob. And
Ru 3: 4 And it shall be, when he l down, that H7901
2Sa 2:24 of Ammah, that *l* before Giah by the way
24: 5 side of the city that *l* in the midst of the
Neh 2: 3 my fathers' sepulchres, *l* waste, and the
17 in, how Jerusalem *l* waste, and the gates
3:25 the tower which l out from the king's H3318
26 the east, and the tower that l out. H3318
27 that l out, even unto the wall of Ophel. H3318
Job 14:12 So man l down, and riseth not: till the H7901
40:21 He l under the shady trees, in the H7901
Ps 10: 9 He l in wait secretly as a lion in his den:
9 a lion in his den: he l in wait to catch the
41: 8 *now* that he l he shall rise up no more. H7901
88: 7 Thy wrath l hard upon me, and thou H5564
Prv 7:12 streets, and l in wait at every corner.)
23:28 She also l in wait as *for* a prey, and
34 Yea, thou shalt be as he that l down in H7901
34 or as he that l upon the top of a mast. H7901
Ezk 9: 2 higher gate, which l toward the north, H6437
29: 3 great dragon that l in the midst of his H7257
Mic 7: 5 mouth from her that l in thy bosom. H7901
Mt 8: 6 And saying, Lord, my servant l at home *G906*
Mk 5:23 My little daughter l at the point of *G2192*
Act 14: 6 and unto the region that l round about:
27:12 l toward the south west and north west. *G991*
Ro 12:18 If it be possible, as much as l in you, live
1Jn 5:19 and the whole world l in wickedness. *G2749*
Rev 21:16 And the city l foursquare, and the *G2749*

LIEUTENANTS
Ezr 8:36 unto the king's l, and to the governors H323
Est 3:12 unto the king's l, and to the governors H323
8: 9 the Jews, and to the l, and the deputies H323
9: 3 provinces, and the l, and the deputies, H323

LIFE
Gen 1:20 creature that hath l, and fowl *that* may H2416
30 wherein *there is* l, *I have given* every H2416
2: 7 of l; and man became a living soul. H2416
9 food; the tree of l also in the midst of H2416
3:14 dust shalt thou eat all the days of thy l: H2416
17 shalt thou eat *of* it all the days of thy l; H2416
22 the tree of l, and eat, and live for ever: H2416
24 way, to keep the way of the tree of l. H2416
6:17 *is* the breath of l, from under heaven; H2416
7:11 In the six hundredth year of Noah's l, in H2416
15 of all flesh, wherein *is* the breath of l. H2416
22 All in whose nostrils *was* the breath of l, H2416
9: 4 But flesh with the l thereof, *which is* the H5315
5 brother will I require the l of man. H5315
18:10 to the time of l; and, lo, Sarah thy wife H2416
14 time of l, and Sarah shall have a son. H2416
19:17 Escape for thy l; look not behind thee, H5315
19 me in saving my l; and I cannot escape H5315
23: 1 *these were* the years of the l of Sarah. H2416
25: 7 years of Abraham's l which he lived, an H2416
17 And these *are* the years of the l of H2416
27:46 I am weary of my l because of the H2416
46 the land, what good shall my l do me? H2416
32:30 God face to face, and my l is preserved. H5315
42:15 Hereby ye shall be proved: By the l of H2416
16 by the l of Pharaoh surely ye *are* spies. H2416
44:30 that his l is bound up in the lad's life; H5315
30 that his life is bound up in the lad's l; H5315
45: 5 did send me before you to preserve l. H4241
47: 9 of the years of my l been, and have not H2416
9 of the years of the l of my fathers in the H2416
48:15 fed me all my l long unto this day, H5750
Ex 4:19 all the men are dead which sought thy l. H5315
6:16 and the years of the l of Levi *were* an H2416
18 the years of the l of Kohath *were* an H2416
20 the years of the l of Amram *were* an H2416
21:23 follow, then thou shalt give l for life, H5315
23 follow, then thou shalt give life for l, H5315
30 of his l whatsoever is laid upon him. H5315
Lev 17:11 For the l of the flesh *is* in the blood: and H5315
14 For *it is* the l of all flesh; the blood of it H5315
14 of it *is* for the l thereof: therefore I said H5315
14 of flesh: for the l of all flesh *is* the blood H5315
18:18 beside the other in her l *time*. H2416
Nu 35:31 no satisfaction for the l of a murderer, H5315
Dt 4: 9 all the days of thy l: but teach them thy H2416
6: 2 l; and that thy days may be prolonged. H2416
12:23 for the blood *is* the l; and thou mayest H5315
23 thou mayest not eat the l with the flesh. H5315
16: 3 of the land of Egypt all the days of thy l. H2416
17:19 all the days of his l: that he may learn to H2416
19:21 And thine eye shall not pity; *but* l *shall* H5315
21 *but* life *shall go* for l, eye for eye, tooth H5315
20:19 *is* man's *l*) to employ *them* in the siege:
24: 6 for he taketh *a man's* l to pledge. H5315
28:66 And thy l shall hang in doubt before H2416
66 and shalt have none assurance of thy l: H2416
30:15 See, I have set before thee this day l H2416
19 set before you l and death, blessing H2416
19 l, that both thou and thy seed may live: H2416
20 him: for he *is* thy l, and the length of thy H2416
32:47 because it *is* your l: and through this H2416
Jos 1: 5 thee all the days of thy l: as I was with H2416
2:14 And the men answered her, Our l for H5315
4:14 they feared Moses, all the days of his l. H2416
Jdg 9:17 adventured his l far, and delivered you H5315
12: 3 *me* not, I put my l in my hands, and H5315
16:30 more than *they* which he slew in his l. H2416
18:25 thy l, with the lives of thy household. H5315
Ru 4:15 a restorer of *thy* l, and a nourisher of H5315
1Sa 1:11 all the days of his l, and there shall no H2416
7:15 judged Israel all the days of his l. H2416
18:18 *am* I? and what *is* my l, *or* my father's H2416
19: 5 For he did put his l in his hand, and H5315
11 thou save not thy l to night, to morrow H5315
20: 1 before thy father, that he seeketh my l? H5315
22:23 for he that seeketh my l seeketh thy life: H5315
23 my life seeketh thy l: but with me thou H5315
23:15 out to seek his l: and David *was* in the H5315
25:29 in the bundle of l with the LORD thy H2416

1Sa 26:24 And, behold, as thy **l** was much set by H5315
24 eyes, so let my **l** be much set by in the H5315
28: 9 a snare for my **l**, to cause me to die? H5315
21 and I have put my **l** in my hand, and H5315
2Sa 1: 9 me, because my **l** *is* yet whole in me. H5315
4: 8 which sought thy **l**; and the LORD hath H5315
14: 7 kill him, for the **l** of his brother whom H5315
15:21 or **l**, even there also will thy servant be. H2416
16:11 seeketh my **l**: how much more now H5315
18:13 against mine own **l**: for there is no H5315
19: 5 have saved thy **l**, and the lives of thy H5315
1Ki 1:12 own **l**, and the life of thy son Solomon. H5315
12 own life, and the **l** of thy son Solomon. H5315
2:23 not spoken this word against his own **l**. H5315
3:11 for thyself long **l**; neither hast asked H3117
11 nor hast asked the **l** of thine enemies; H5315
4:21 served Solomon all the days of his **l**. H2416
11:34 prince all the days of his **l** for David my H2416
15: 5 him all the days of his **l**, save only in the H2416
6 and Jeroboam all the days of his **l**. H2416
19: 2 if I make not thy **l** as the life of one of H5315
2 not thy life as the **l** of one of them by to H5315
3 arose, and went for his **l**, and came to H5315
4 **l**; for I *am* not better than my fathers. H5315
10 left; and they seek my **l**, to take it away. H5315
14 left; and they seek my **l**, to take it away. H5315
20:31 Israel: peradventure he will save thy **l**. H5315
39 then shall thy **l** be for his life, or else H5315
39 thy life be for his **l**, or else thou shalt H5315
42 therefore thy **l** shall go for his life, and H5315
42 for his **l**, and thy people for his people. H5315
2Ki 1:13 I pray thee, let my **l**, and the life of these H5315
13 let my life, and the **l** of these fifty thy H5315
14 let my **l** now be precious in thy sight. H5315
4:16 to the time of **l**, thou shalt embrace H2416
17 said unto her, according to the time of **l**. H2416
7: 7 the camp as it *was*, and fled for their **l**. H5315
8: 1 he had restored to **l**, saying, Arise, and H2421
5 a dead body to **l**, that, behold, the H2421
5 he had restored to **l**, cried to the king for H2421
5 *is* her son, whom Elisha restored to **l**. H2421
10:24 *him go*, his **l** *shall be* for the life of him. H5315
24 *him go*, his life *shall be* for the **l** of him. H5315
25:29 before him all the days of his **l**. H2416
30 rate for every day, all the days of his **l**. H2416
2Ch 1:11 or honour, nor the **l** of thine enemies, H5315
11 yet hast asked long **l**; but hast asked H3117
Ezr 6:10 for the **l** of the king, and of his sons. H2417
Neh 6:11 the temple to save his **l**? I will not go in. H2425
Est 7: 3 the king, let my **l** be given me at my H5315
7 request for his **l** to Esther the queen; H5315
8:11 to stand for their **l**, to destroy, to slay, H5315
Job 2: 4 all that a man hath will he give for his **l**. H5315
6 he *is* in thine hand; but save his **l**. H5315
3:20 in misery, and **l** unto the bitter *in* soul; H2416
6:11 *is* mine end, that I should prolong my **l**? H5315
7: 7 O remember that my **l** *is* wind: mine H2416
15 strangling, *and* death rather than my **l**. H6106
9:21 not know my soul: I would despise my **l**. H2416
10: 1 My soul is weary of my **l**; I will leave my H2416
12 Thou hast granted me **l** and favour, H2416
13:14 my teeth, and put my **l** in mine hand? H5315
24:22 he riseth up, and no *man* is sure of **l**. H2416
31:39 the owners thereof to lose their **l**: H5315
33: 4 breath of the Almighty hath given me **l**. H2421
18 and his **l** from perishing by the sword. H2416
20 So that his **l** abhorreth bread, and his H2416
22 the grave, and his **l** to the destroyers. H2416
28 into the pit, and his **l** shall see the light. H2416
36: 6 He preserveth not the **l** of the wicked: H2421
14 They die in youth, and their **l** *is* among H2416
Ps 7: 5 tread down my **l** upon the earth, and H2416
16:11 Thou wilt shew me the path of **l**: in thy H2416
17:14 portion in *this* **l**, and whose belly thou H2416
21: 4 He asked **l** of thee, *and* thou gavest *it* H2416
23: 6 all the days of my **l**: and I will dwell in H2416
26: 9 sinners, nor my **l** with bloody men: H2416
27: 1 of my **l**; of whom shall I be afraid? H2416
4 LORD all the days of my **l**, to behold the H2416
30: 5 in his favour *is* **l**: weeping may endure H2416
31:10 For my **l** is spent with grief, and my H2416
13 me, they devised to take away my **l**. H5315
34:12 What man *is he that* desireth **l**, *and* H2416
36: 9 For with thee *is* the fountain of **l**: in thy H2416
38:12 They also that seek after my **l** lay H5315
42: 8 *and* my prayer unto the God of my **l**. H2416
61: 6 Thou wilt prolong the king's **l**: *and* his H3117
63: 3 better than **l**, my lips shall praise thee. H2416
64: 1 preserve my **l** from fear of the enemy. H2416
Ps 66: 9 Which holdeth our soul in **l**, and H2416
78:50 but gave their **l** over to the pestilence; H2416
88: 3 For my soul is full of troubles: and my **l** H2416
91:16 With long **l** will I satisfy him, and shew H3117
103: 4 Who redeemeth thy **l** from destruction; H2416
128: 5 good of Jerusalem all the days of thy **l**. H2416
133: 3 the blessing, *even* **l** for evermore. H2416
143: 3 hath smitten my **l** down to the ground; H2416
Prv 1:19 taketh away the **l** of the owners thereof. H5315
2:19 neither take they hold of the paths of **l**. H2416
3: 2 For length of days, and long **l**, and H2416
18 She *is* a tree of **l** to them that lay hold H2416
22 So shall they be **l** unto thy soul, and H2416
4:10 and the years of thy **l** shall be many. H2416
13 let *her* not go: keep her; for she *is* thy **l**. H2416
22 For they *are* **l** unto those that find H2416
23 diligence; for out of it *are* the issues of **l**. H2416
5: 6 ponder the path of **l**, her ways are H2416
6:23 reproofs of instruction *are* the way of **l**: H2416
26 adulteress will hunt for the precious **l**. H5315
7:23 and knoweth not that it *is* for his **l**. H5315
8:35 For whoso findeth me findeth **l**, and H2416
9:11 the years of thy **l** shall be increased. H2416
10:11 *man is* a well of **l**: but violence covereth H2416
16 The labour of the righteous *tendeth* to **l**: H2416
17 He *is in* the way of **l** that keepeth H2416
11:19 As righteousness *tendeth* to **l**: so he that H2416
30 The fruit of the righteous *is* a tree of **l**; H2416
12:10 A righteous *man* regardeth the **l** of his H5315
28 In the way of righteousness *is* **l**; and *in* H2416
13: 3 his mouth keepeth his **l**: *but* he that H5315
8 The ransom of a man's **l** *are* his riches: H5315
12 *when* the desire cometh, *it is* a tree of **l**. H2416
14 The law of the wise *is* a fountain of **l**, to H2416
14:27 The fear of the LORD *is* a fountain of **l**, H2416
30 A sound heart *is* the **l** of the flesh: but H2416
15: 4 A wholesome tongue *is* a tree of **l**: but H2416
24 The way of **l** *is* above to the wise, that H2416
31 The ear that heareth the reproof of **l** H2416
16:15 countenance *is* **l**; and his favour *is* as H2416
22 Understanding *is* a wellspring of **l** unto H2416
18:21 Death and **l** *are* in the power of the H2416
19:23 The fear of the LORD *tendeth* to **l**: and H2416
21:21 findeth **l**, righteousness, and honour. H2416
22: 4 the LORD *are* riches, and honour, and **l**. H2416
31:12 good and not evil all the days of her **l**. H2416
Ecc 2: 3 under the heaven all the days of their **l**. H2416
17 Therefore I hated **l**; because the work H2416
3:12 *a man* to rejoice, and to do good in his **l**. H2416
5:18 all the days of his **l**, which God giveth H2416
20 the days of his **l**; because God H2416
6:12 for man in *this* **l**, all the days of his vain H2416
12 days of his vain **l** which he spendeth as H2416
7:12 wisdom giveth **l** to them that have it. H2421
15 that prolongeth *his l* in his wickedness.
8:15 **l**, which God giveth him under the sun. H2416
9: 9 all the days of the **l** of thy vanity, which H2416
9 *is* thy portion in *this* **l**, and in thy labour H2416
Isa 15: 4 out; his **l** shall be grievous unto him. H5315
38:12 off like a weaver my **l**: he will cut me off H2416
16 these *things is* the **l** of my spirit: so wilt H2416
20 days of our **l** in the house of the LORD. H2416
43: 4 I give men for thee, and people for thy **l**. H5315
57:10 thou hast found the **l** of thine hand; H2416
Jer 4:30 will despise thee, they will seek thy **l**. H5315
8: 3 And death shall be chosen rather than **l** H2416
11:21 that seek thy **l**, saying, Prophesy not H5315
21: 7 that seek their **l**: and he shall smite H5315
8 you the way of **l**, and the way of death. H2416
9 and his **l** shall be unto him for a prey. H5315
22:25 them that seek thy **l**, and into the hand H5315
34:20 that seek their **l**: and their dead bodies H5315
21 that seek their **l**, and into the hand of H5315
38: 2 have his **l** for a prey, and shall live. H5315
16 the hand of these men that seek thy **l**. H5315
39:18 the sword, but thy **l** shall be for a prey H5315
44:30 them that seek his **l**; as I gave Zedekiah H5315
30 his enemy, and that sought his **l**. H5315
45: 5 the LORD: but thy **l** will I give unto thee H5315
49:37 that seek their **l**: and I will bring evil H5315
52:33 bread before him all the days of his **l**. H2416
34 the day of his death, all the days of his **l**. H2416
Lam 2:19 toward him for the **l** of thy young H5315
3:53 They have cut off my **l** in the dungeon, H2416
58 of my soul; thou hast redeemed my **l**. H2416
Ezk 3:18 way, to save his **l**; the same wicked *man* H2421
7:13 himself in the iniquity of his **l**. H2416
13:22 his wicked way, by promising him **l**: H2421
32:10 man for his own **l**, in the day of thy fall. H5315
Ezk 33:15 in the statutes of **l**, without committing H2416
Dan 12: 2 to everlasting **l**, and some to shame H2416
Jna 1:14 for this man's **l**, and lay not upon us H5315
2: 6 **l** from corruption, O LORD my God. H2416
4: 3 I beseech thee, my **l** from me; for *it is* H5315
Mal 2: 5 My covenant was with him of **l** and H2416
Mt 2:20 dead which sought the young child's **l**. *G5590*
6:25 thought for your **l**, what ye shall eat, or *G5590*
25 put on. Is not the **l** more than meat, *G5590*
7:14 unto **l**, and few there be that find it. *G2222*
10:39 He that findeth his **l** shall lose it: and *G5590*
39 loseth his **l** for my sake shall find it. *G5590*
16:25 For whosoever will save his **l** shall lose *G5590*
25 will lose his **l** for my sake shall find it. *G5590*
18: 8 for thee to enter into **l** halt or maimed, *G2222*
9 thee to enter into **l** with one eye, rather *G2222*
19:16 shall I do, that I may have eternal **l**? *G2222*
17 enter into **l**, keep the commandments. *G2222*
29 and shall inherit everlasting **l**. *G2222*
20:28 and to give his **l** a ransom for many. *G5590*
25:46 but the righteous into **l** eternal. *G2222*
Mk 3: 4 **l**, or to kill? But they held their peace. *G5590*
8:35 For whosoever will save his **l** shall lose *G5590*
35 shall lose his **l** for my sake and the *G5590*
9:43 for thee to enter into **l** maimed, than *G2222*
45 to enter halt into **l**, than having two feet *G2222*
10:17 shall I do that I may inherit eternal **l**? *G2222*
30 and in the world to come eternal **l**. *G2222*
45 and to give his **l** a ransom for many. *G5590*
Lk 1:75 before him, all the days of our **l**. *G2222*
6: 9 or to do evil? to save **l**, or to destroy *it*? *G5590*
8:14 of *this* **l**, and bring no fruit to perfection. *G979*
9:24 For whosoever will save his **l** shall lose *G5590*
24 his **l** for my sake, the same shall save it. *G5590*
10:25 what shall I do to inherit eternal **l**? *G2222*
12:15 for a man's **l** consisteth not in the *G2222*
22 no thought for your **l**, what ye shall eat; *G5590*
23 The **l** is more than meat, and the body *G5590*
14:26 own **l** also, he cannot be my disciple. *G5590*
17:33 Whosoever shall seek to save his **l** shall *G5590*
33 shall lose his **l** shall preserve it. *G846*
18:18 what shall I do to inherit eternal **l**? *G2222*
30 and in the world to come **l** everlasting. *G2222*
21:34 and cares of this **l**, and *so* that day come *G982*
Jn 1: 4 In him was **l**; and the life was the light *G2222*
4 In him was life; and the **l** was the light *G2222*
3:15 should not perish, but have eternal **l**. *G2222*
16 not perish, but have everlasting **l**. *G2222*
36 hath everlasting **l**: and he that believeth *G2222*
36 **l**; but the wrath of God abideth on him. *G2222*
4:14 of water springing up into everlasting **l**. *G2222*
36 fruit unto **l** eternal: that both he *G2222*
5:24 hath everlasting **l**, and shall not come *G2222*
24 but is passed from death unto **l**. *G2222*
26 For as the Father hath **l** in himself; so *G2222*
26 he given to the Son to have **l** in himself; *G2222*
29 the resurrection of **l**; and they that have *G2222*
39 **l**: and they are they which testify of me. *G2222*
40 not come to me, that ye might have **l**. *G2222*
6:27 unto everlasting **l**, which the Son of *G2222*
33 heaven, and giveth **l** unto the world. *G2222*
35 I am the bread of **l**: he that cometh to *G2222*
40 **l**: and I will raise him up at the last day. *G2222*
47 that believeth on me hath everlasting **l**. *G2222*
48 I am that bread of **l**. *G2222*
51 which I will give for the **l** of the world. *G2222*
53 drink his blood, ye have no **l** in you. *G2222*
54 **l**; and I will raise him up at the last day. *G2222*
63 unto you, *they* are spirit, and *they* are **l**. *G2222*
68 we go? thou hast the words of eternal **l**. *G2222*
8:12 in darkness, but shall have the light of **l**. *G2222*
10:10 they might have **l**, and that they might *G2222*
11 shepherd giveth his **l** for the sheep. *G5590*
15 and I lay down my **l** for the sheep. *G5590*
17 down my **l**, that I might take it again. *G5590*
28 And I give unto them eternal **l**; and they *G2222*
11:25 and the **l**: he that believeth in *G2222*
12:25 He that loveth his **l** shall lose it; and he *G5590*
25 he that hateth his **l** in this world shall *G5590*
25 this world shall keep it unto **l** eternal. *G2222*
50 And I know that his commandment is **l** *G2222*
13:37 now? I will lay down my **l** for thy sake. *G5590*
38 thou lay down thy **l** for my sake? Verily, *G5590*
14: 6 the truth, and the **l**: no man cometh *G2222*
15:13 a man lay down his **l** for his friends. *G5590*
17: 2 **l** to as many as thou hast given him. *G2222*
3 And this is **l** eternal, that they might *G2222*
20:31 ye might have **l** through his name. *G2222*
Act 2:28 to me the ways of **l**; thou shalt make me *G2222*

Act 3:15 And killed the Prince of l, whom God G2222
5:20 to the people all the words of this l. G2222
8:33 for his l is taken from the earth. G2222
11:18 the Gentiles granted repentance unto l. G2222
13:46 everlasting l, lo, we turn to the Gentiles. G2222
48 as were ordained to eternal l believed. G2222
17:25 to all l, and breath, and all things; G2222
20:10 not yourselves; for his l is in him. G5590
24 neither count I my l dear unto myself, G5590
26: 4 My manner of l from my youth, which G981
27:22 *any man's* l among you, but of the ship. G5590
Ro 2: 7 and honour and immortality, eternal l: G2222
5:10 reconciled, we shall be saved by his l. G2222
17 shall reign in l by one, Jesus Christ.) G2222
18 upon all men unto justification of l. G2222
21 unto eternal l by Jesus Christ our Lord. G2222
6: 4 so we also should walk in newness of l. G2222
22 unto holiness, and the end everlasting l. G2222
23 eternal l through Jesus Christ our Lord. G2222
7:10 *ordained* to l, I found *to be* unto death. G2222
8: 2 For the law of the Spirit of l in Christ G2222
6 to be spiritually minded *is* l and peace. G2222
10 the Spirit *is* l because of righteousness. G2222
38 neither death, nor l, nor angels, nor G2222
11: 3 and I am left alone, and they seek my l. G5590
15 *of them be*, but l from the dead? G2222
16: 4 Who have for my l laid down their own G5590
1Co 3:22 or the world, or l, or death, or things G2222
6: 3 much more things that pertain to this l? G982
4 pertaining to this l, set them to judge G982
14: 7 And even things without l giving sound, G895
15:19 If in this l only we have hope in Christ, G2222
2Co 1: 8 insomuch that we despaired even of l: G2198
2:16 other the savour of l unto life. And who G2222
16 l. And who *is* sufficient for these things? G2222
3: 6 the letter killeth, but the spirit giveth l. G2227
4:10 Jesus, that the l also of Jesus might be G2222
11 sake, that the l also of Jesus might be G2222
12 So then death worketh in us, but l in G2222
5: 4 mortality might be swallowed up of l. G2222
Gal 2:20 in me: and the l which I now live in the
3:21 could have given l, verily righteousness G2227
6: 8 shall of the Spirit reap l everlasting. G2222
Eph 4:18 alienated from the l of God through the G2222
Php 1:20 my body, whether *it be* by l, or by death. G2222
2:16 Holding forth the word of l; that I may G2222
30 not regarding his l, to supply your lack G5590
4: 3 whose names *are* in the book of l. G2222
Col 3: 3 For ye are dead, and your l is hid with G2222
4 When Christ, *who is* our l, shall appear, G2222
1Ti 1:16 believe on him to l everlasting. G2222
2: 2 peaceable l in all godliness and honesty. G979
4: 8 promise of the l that now is, and of that G2222
6:12 lay hold on eternal l, whereunto thou G2222
19 that they may lay hold on eternal l. G2222
2Ti 1: 1 promise of l which is in Christ Jesus, G2222
10 and hath brought l and immortality to G2222
2: 4 the affairs of *this* l; that he may please G979
3:10 doctrine, manner of l, purpose, faith, G72
Tit 1: 2 In hope of eternal l, which God, that G2222
3: 7 heirs according to the hope of eternal l. G2222
Heb 7: 3 of days, nor end of l; but made like unto G2222
16 but after the power of an endless l. G2222
11:35 Women received their dead raised to l
Jas 1:12 the crown of l, which the Lord hath G2222
4:14 For what *is* your l? It is even a vapour, G2222
1Pt 3: 7 of l; that your prayers be not hindered. G2222
10 For he that will love l, and see good G2222
4: 3 For the time past of *our* l may suffice us G979
2Pt 1: 3 that *pertain* unto l and godliness, G2222
1Jn 1: 1 hands have handled, of the Word of l; G2222
2 (For the l was manifested, and we have G2222
2 you that eternal l, which was with the G2222
2:16 l, is not of the Father, but is of the world. G979
25 he hath promised us, *even* eternal l. G2222
3:14 from death unto l, because we love the G2222
15 murderer hath eternal l abiding in him. G2222
16 he laid down his l for us: and we ought G5590
5:11 to us eternal l, and this life is in his Son. G2222
11 us eternal life, and this l is in his Son. G2222
12 He that hath the Son hath l; *and* he that G2222
12 that hath not the Son of God hath not l. G2222
13 that ye may have eternal l, and that ye may G2222
16 he shall give him l for them that sin not G2222
20 This is the true God, and eternal l. G2222
Jude 21 of our Lord Jesus Christ unto eternal l. G2222
Rev 2: 7 give to eat of the tree of l, which is in the G2222
10 death, and I will give thee a crown of l. G2222
3: 5 out of the book of l, but I will confess G2222
8: 9 in the sea, and had l, died; and the third G5590
11:11 an half the Spirit of l from God entered G2222
13: 8 in the book of l of the Lamb slain from G2222
15 And he had power to give l unto the G4151
17: 8 in the book of l from the foundation G2222
20:12 is *the book* of l: and the dead were G2222
15 book of l was cast into the lake of fire. G2222
21: 6 of the fountain of the water of l freely. G2222
27 are written in the Lamb's book of l. G2222
22: 1 pure river of water of l, clear as crystal, G2222
2 *there* the tree of l, which bare twelve G2222
14 right to the tree of l, and may enter in G2222
17 will, let him take the water of l freely. G2222
19 out of the book of l, and out of the holy G2222

LIFETIME

2Sa 18:18 Now Absalom in his l had taken and H2416
Lk 16:25 that thou in thy l receivedst thy good G2222
Heb 2:15 were all their l subject to bondage. G2198

LIFT

Gen 7:17 ark, and it was l up above the earth. H7311
13:14 from him, L up now thine eyes, H5375
14:22 of Sodom, I have l up mine hand unto H7311
18: 2 And he l up his eyes and looked, and, H5375
21:16 *him*, and l up her voice, and wept. H5375
18 Arise, l up the lad, and hold him in H6965
31:12 And he said, L up now thine eyes, and H5375
40:13 Yet within three days shall Pharaoh l H5375
19 Yet within three days shall Pharaoh l H5375
41:44 thee shall no man l up his hand or foot H7311
Ex 14:16 But l thou up thy rod, and stretch out H7311
20:25 stone: for if thou l up thy tool upon it, H5130
Nu 6:26 The LORD l up his countenance upon H5375
16: 3 wherefore then l ye up yourselves H5375
23:24 as a great lion, and l up himself as a H5375
Dt 3:27 Get thee up into the top of Pisgah, and l H5375
4:19 And lest thou l up thine eyes unto H5375
22: 4 surely help him to l *them* up again. H6965
27: 5 shalt not l up *any* iron *tool* upon them. H5130
32:40 For I l up my hand to heaven, and say, H5375
Jos 8:31 no man hath l up *any* iron: and they H5130
2Sa 23: 8 the Eznite: *he l up his spear* against
2Ki 19: 4 heard: wherefore l up *thy* prayer for the H5375
25:27 he began to reign did l up the head of H5375
1Ch 25: 5 the words of God, to l up the horn. And H7311
Ezr 9: 6 and blush to l up my face to thee, my H7311
Job 10:15 *yet* will I not l up my head. *I am* full H5375
11:15 For then shalt thou l up thy face H5375
22:26 and shalt l up thy face unto God. H5375
38:34 Canst thou l up thy voice to the clouds, H7311
Ps 4: 6 *any* good? LORD, l thou up the light of H5375
7: 6 Arise, O LORD, in thine anger, l up H5375
10:12 Arise, O LORD; O God, l up thine hand: H5375
24: 7 L up your heads, O ye gates; and be ye H5375
7 ye gates; and be ye l up, ye everlasting H5375
9 L up your heads, O ye gates; even lift H5375
9 Lift up your heads, O ye gates; even l H5375
25: 1 Unto thee, O LORD, do I l up my soul. H5375
28: 2 I l up my hands toward thy holy oracle. H5375
9 feed them also, and l them up for ever. H5375
63: 4 Thus will I bless thee while I live: I will l H5375
74: 3 L up thy feet unto the perpetual H7311
75: 4 and to the wicked, L not up the horn: H7311
5 L not up your horn on high: speak *not* H7311
86: 4 for unto thee, O Lord, do I l up my soul. H5375
93: 3 their voice; the floods l up their waves. H5375
94: 2 L up thyself, thou judge of the earth: H5375
110: 7 way: therefore shall he l up the head. H7311
119:48 My hands also will I l up unto thy H5375
121: 1 I will l up mine eyes unto the hills, H5375
123: 1 Unto thee l I up mine eyes, O thou that H5375
134: 2 L up your hands *in* the sanctuary, and H5375
143: 8 walk; for I l up my soul unto thee. H5375
Ecc 4:10 For if they fall, the one will l up his H6965
Isa 2: 4 nation shall not l up sword against H5375
5:26 And he will l up an ensign to the H5375
10:15 against them that l it up, *or* as if the H7311
15 should l up *itself, as if it were* no wood. H7311
24 a rod, and shall l up his staff against H5375
26 he l it up after the manner of Egypt. H5375
30 L up thy voice, O daughter of Gallim: H6670
13: 2 L ye up a banner upon the high H5375
24:14 They shall l up their voice, they shall H5375
33:10 will I be exalted; now will I l up myself. H5375
37: 4 heard: wherefore l up *thy* prayer for the H5375
40: 9 good tidings, l up thy voice with H7311
9 with strength; l *it* up, be not afraid; H7311
26 L up your eyes on high, and behold H5375
42: 2 He shall not cry, nor l up, nor cause his H5375
11 the cities thereof l up *their voice*, the H5375
49:18 L up thine eyes round about, and H5375
22 Behold, I will l up mine hand to the H5375
51: 6 L up your eyes to the heavens, and look H5375
52: 8 Thy watchmen shall l up the voice; H5375
58: 1 Cry aloud, spare not, l up thy voice like H7311
59:19 shall l up a standard against him. H5127
60: 4 L up thine eyes round about, and see: H5375
62:10 stones; l up a standard for the people. H7311
Jer 3: 2 L up thine eyes unto the high places, H5375
7:16 people, neither l up cry nor prayer for H5375
11:14 people, neither l up a cry or prayer for H5375
13:20 L up your eyes, and behold them that H5375
22:20 Go up to Lebanon, and cry; and l up H5414
51:14 they shall l up a shout against thee. H6030
Lam 2:19 face of the Lord: l up thy hands toward H5375
3:41 Let us l up our heart with *our* hands H5375
Ezk 8: 5 Then said he unto me, Son of man, l up H5375
11:22 Then did the cherubims l up their H5375
17:14 that it might not l itself up, *but* that by H5375
21:22 in the slaughter, to l up the voice with H7311
23:27 that thou shalt not l up thine eyes unto H5375
26: 8 thee, and l up the buckler against thee. H6965
33:25 the blood, and l up your eyes toward H5375
Mic 4: 3 nation shall not l up a sword against H5375
Zec 1:21 so that no man did l up his head: but H5375
5: 5 and said unto me, L up now thine eyes, H5375
Mt 12:11 will he not lay hold on it, and l *it* out? G1453
Lk 13:11 and could in no wise l up *herself*. G352
16:23 And in hell he l up his eyes, being in G1869
18:13 afar off, would not l up so much as *his* G1869
21:28 then look up, and l up your heads; for G1869
Jn 4:35 I say unto you, L up your eyes, and G1869
Heb 12:12 Wherefore l up the hands which hang G461
Jas 4:10 sight of the Lord, and he shall l you up. G5312

LIFTED

Gen 13:10 And Lot l up his eyes, and beheld all H5375
22: 4 Then on the third day Abraham l up H5375
13 And Abraham l up his eyes, and H5375
24:63 eventide: and he l up his eyes, and saw, H5375
64 And Rebekah l up her eyes, and when H5375
27:38 And Esau l up his voice, and wept. H5375
29:11 And Jacob kissed Rachel, and l up his H5375
31:10 conceived, that I l up mine eyes, and H5375
33: 1 And Jacob l up his eyes, and looked, H5375
5 And he l up his eyes, and saw the H5375
37:25 eat bread: and they l up their eyes and H5375
28 and they drew and l up Joseph out of H5927
39:15 he heard that I l up my voice and cried, H7311
18 And it came to pass, as I l up my voice H7311
40:20 servants: and he l up the head of the H5375
43:29 And he l up his eyes, and saw his H5375
Ex 7:20 and he l up the rod, and smote H7311
14:10 children of Israel l up their eyes, and, H5375
Lev 9:22 And Aaron l up his hand toward the H5375
Nu 14: 1 And all the congregation l up their H5375
20:11 And Moses l up his hand, and with his H7311
24: 2 And Balaam l up his eyes, and he saw H5375
Dt 8:14 Then thine heart be l up, and thou H7311
17:20 That his heart be not l up above his H7311
Jos 4:18 priests' feet were l up unto the dry land, H5423
5:13 by Jericho, that he l up his eyes and H5375
Jdg 2: 4 the people l up their voice, and wept. H5375
8:28 Israel, so that they l up their heads no H5375
9: 7 Gerizim, and l up his voice, and cried, H5375
19:17 And when he had l up his eyes, he saw H5375
21: 2 and l up their voices, and wept sore; H5375
Ru 1: 9 and they l up their voice, and wept. H5375
14 And they l up their voice, and wept H5375
1Sa 6:13 the valley: and they l up their eyes, and H5375
11: 4 the people l up their voices, and wept. H5375
24:16 And Saul l up his voice, and wept. H5375
30: 4 that *were* with him l up their voice and H5375
2Sa 3:32 and the king l up his voice, and wept H5375
13:34 that kept the watch l up his eyes, and H5375
36 sons came, and l up their voice and H5375
18:24 unto the wall, and l up his eyes, and H5375
28 up the men that l up their hand against H5375
20:21 by name, hath l up his hand against H5375
22:49 thou also hast l me up on high above H7311
23:18 three. And he l up his spear against H5782
1Ki 11:26 even he l up *his* hand against the king. H7311
27 And this *was* the cause that he l up *his* H7311
2Ki 9:32 And he l up his face to the window, and H5375
14:10 thine heart hath l thee up: glory *of this*, H5375
19:22 *thy* voice, and l up thine eyes on high? H5375
1Ch 11:11 chief of the captains: he l up his spear H5782

1Ch 14: 2 his kingdom was l up on high, because H5375
21:16 And David l up his eyes, and saw the H5375
2Ch 5:13 and when they l up *their* voice with the H7311
17: 6 And his heart was l up in the ways of H1361
26:16 But when he was strong, his heart was l H1361
32:25 for his heart was l up: therefore there H1361
Job 2:12 And when they l up their eyes afar off, H5375
12 him not, they l up their voice, and H5375
31:21 If I have l up my hand against the H5130
29 or l up myself when evil found him: H5782
Ps 24: 4 who hath not l up his soul unto vanity, H5375
27: 6 And now shall mine head be l up above H7311
30: 1 for thou hast l me up, and hast not H1802
41: 9 bread, hath l up *his* heel against me. H1431
74: 5 as he had l up axes upon the thick trees. H935
83: 2 they that hate thee have l up the head. H5375
93: 3 The floods have l up, O LORD, the H5375
3 the floods have l up their voice; the H5375
102:10 thou hast l me up, and cast me down. H5375
106:26 Therefore he l up his hand against H5375
Prv 30:13 their eyes! and their eyelids are l up. H5375
Isa 2:12 *is* l up; and he shall be brought low: H5375
13 l up, and upon all the oaks of Bashan, H5375
14 and upon all the hills *that are* l up, H5375
6: 1 l up, and his train filled the temple. H5375
26:11 LORD, *when* thy hand is l up, they will H7311
37:23 *thy* voice, and l up thine eyes on high? H5375
Jer 51: 9 heaven, and is l up *even* to the skies. H5375
52:31 *first* year of his reign l up the head of H5375
Ezk 1:19 creatures were l up from the earth, the H5375
19 up from the earth, the wheels were l up. H5375
20 the wheels were l up over against them: H5375
21 when those were l up from the earth, H5375
21 the wheels were l up over against them: H5375
3:14 So the spirit l me up, and took me H5375
8: 3 and the spirit l me up between the H5375
5 the north. So I l up mine eyes the way H5375
10:15 And the cherubims were l up. This *is* H7426
16 when the cherubims l up their wings to H5375
17 when they were l up, *these* lifted up H7311
17 lifted up, *these* l up themselves *also*: H7426
19 And the cherubims l up their wings, H5375
11: 1 Moreover the spirit l me up, and H5375
18: 6 neither hath l up his eyes to the idols H5375
12 the pledge, and hath l up his eyes to the H5375
15 neither hath l up his eyes to the idols H5375
20: 5 I chose Israel, and l up mine hand unto H5375
5 of Egypt, when I l up mine hand unto H5375
6 In the day *that* I l up mine hand unto H5375
15 Yet also I l up my hand unto them in H5375
23 I l up mine hand unto them also in the H5375
28 *for* the which I l up mine hand to give H5375
42 *for* the which I l up mine hand to give H5375
28: 2 thine heart *is* l up, and thou hast said, H1361
5 heart is l up because of thy riches: H1361
17 Thine heart was l up because of thy H1361
31:10 GOD; Because thou hast l up thyself in H1361
10 and his heart is l up in his height; H7311
36: 7 the Lord GOD; I have l up mine hand, H5375
44:12 therefore have I l up mine hand against H5375
47:14 the which I l up mine hand to give H5375
Dan 4:34 I Nebuchadnezzar l up mine eyes unto H5191
5:20 But when his heart was l up, and his H7313
23 But hast l up thyself against the Lord of H7313
7: 4 and it was l up from the earth, and H5191
8: 3 Then I l up mine eyes, and saw, and, H5375
10: 5 Then I l up mine eyes, and looked, and H5375
11:12 his heart shall be l up; and he shall cast H7311
Mic 5: 9 Thine hand shall be l up upon thine H7311
Hab 2: 4 Behold, his soul *which* is l up is not H6075
3:10 his voice, *and* l up his hands on high. H5375
Zec 1:18 Then l I up mine eyes, and saw, and H5375
21 Gentiles, which l up *their* horn over the H5375
2: 1 I l up mine eyes again, and looked, and H5375
5: 1 Then I turned, and l up mine eyes, and H5375
7 And, behold, there was l up a talent of H5375
9 Then l I up mine eyes, and looked, and, H5375
9 of a stork: and they l up the ephah H5375
6: 1 And I turned, and l up mine eyes, and H5375
9:16 crown, l up as an ensign upon his land. H5264
14:10 and it shall be l up, and inhabited in H7213
Mt 17: 8 And when they had l up their eyes, they *G1869*
Mk 1:31 her by the hand, and l her up; and *G1453*
9:27 But Jesus took him by the hand, and l *G1453*
Lk 6:20 And he l up his eyes on his disciples, *G1869*
11:27 of the company l up her voice, and said *G1869*
17:13 And they l up *their* voices, and said, *G142*
24:50 he l up his hands, and blessed them. *G1869*
Jn 3:14 And as Moses l up the serpent in the *G5312*
Jn 3:14 even so must the Son of man be l up: *G5312*
6: 5 When Jesus then l up *his* eyes, and saw *G1869*
8: 7 So when they continued asking him, he l *G352*
10 When Jesus had l up himself, and saw *G352*
28 When ye have l up the Son of man, *G5312*
11:41 was laid. And Jesus l up *his* eyes, and *G142*
12:32 And I, if I be l up from the earth, will *G5312*
34 must be l up? who is this Son of man? *G5312*
13:18 with me hath l up his heel against me. *G1869*
17: 1 These words spake Jesus, and l up his *G1869*
Act 2:14 up with the eleven, l up his voice, and *G1869*
3: 7 the right hand, and l *him* up: and *G1453*
4:24 And when they heard that, they l up *G142*
9:41 And he gave her *his* hand, and l her up, *G450*
14:11 had done, they l up their voices, saying *G1869*
22:22 word, and *then* l up their voices, and *G1869*
1Ti 3: 6 Not a novice, lest being l up with pride *G5188*
Rev 10: 5 upon the earth l up his hand to heaven, *G142*

LIFTER
Ps 3: 3 my glory, and the l up of mine head. H7311

LIFTEST
Job 30:22 Thou l me up to the wind; thou causest H5375
Ps 9:13 that l me up from the gates of death: H7311
18:48 enemies: yea, thou l me up above those H7311
Prv 2: 3 *and* l up thy voice for understanding; H5414

LIFTETH
1Sa 2: 7 maketh rich: he bringeth low, and l up. H7311
8 of the dust, *and* l up the beggar from H7311
2Ch 25:19 and thine heart l thee up to boast: H5375
Job 39:18 What time she l up herself on high, she H4754
Ps 107:25 wind, which l up the waves thereof. H7311
113: 7 *and* l the needy out of the dunghill; H7311
147: 6 The LORD l up the meek: he casteth the H5749
Isa 18: 3 see ye, when he l up an ensign on the H5375
Jer 51: 3 and against *him that* l himself up in his H5927
Nah 3: 3 The horseman l up both the bright H5927

LIFTING
1Ch 11:20 of the three: for l up his spear against H5782
15:16 sounding, by l up the voice with joy. H7311
Neh 8: 6 Amen, Amen, with l up their hands: H4607
Job 22:29 shalt say, *There is* l up; and he shall H1466
Ps 141: 2 *as* incense; *and* the l up of my hands *as* H4864
Prv 30:32 If thou hast done foolishly in l up H5375
Isa 9:18 shall mount up *like* the l up of smoke. H1348
33: 3 the people fled; at the l up of thyself the H7427
1Ti 2: 8 men pray every where, l up holy hands, *G1859*

LIGHT
Gen 1: 3 And God said, Let there be l: and there H216
3 said, Let there be light: and there was l. H216
4 And God saw the l, that *it was* good: and H216
4 and God divided the l from the darkness. H216
5 And God called the l Day, and the H216
15 to give l upon the earth: and it was so. H215
16 lights; the greater l to rule the day, and H3974
16 day, and the lesser l to rule the night: H3974
17 of the heaven to give l upon the earth, H215
18 and to divide the l from the darkness: H216
44: 3 As soon as the morning was l, the men H215
Ex 10:23 of Israel had l in their dwellings. H216
13:21 to give them l; to go by day and night: H215
14:20 *to them,* but it gave l by night *to these:* H215
25: 6 Oil for the l, spices for anointing oil, H3974
37 and they shall l the lamps thereof, that H5927
37 that they may give l over against it. H215
27:20 the l, to cause the lamp to burn always. H3974
35: 8 And oil for the l, and spices for H3974
14 The candlestick also for the l, and his H3974
14 and his lamps, with the oil for the l, H3974
28 And spice, and oil for the l, and for the H3974
39:37 all the vessels thereof, and the oil for l, H3974
40: 4 candlestick, and l the lamps thereof. H5927
Lev 24: 2 beaten for the l, to cause the lamps to H3974
Nu 4: 9 candlestick of the l, and his lamps, and H3974
16 the oil for the l, and the sweet incense, H3974
8: 2 shall give l over against the candlestick. H215
21: 5 and our soul loatheth this l bread. H7052
Dt 27:16 Cursed *be* he that setteth l by his father H7034
Jdg 9: 4 and l persons, which followed him. H6348
19:26 house where her lord *was,* till it was l. H216
Ru 2: 3 her hap was to l on a part of the field H7136
1Sa 14:36 until the morning l, and let us not leave a H216
18:23 it to you *a* l *thing* to be a king's son H7043
25:22 l any that pisseth against the wall. H216
34 l any that pisseth against the wall. H216
1Sa 25:36 less or more, until the morning l. H216
29:10 early in the morning, and have l, depart. H215
2Sa 2:18 Asahel *was as* l of foot as a wild roe. H7031
17:12 be found, and we will l upon him as the H5117
22 by the morning l there lacked not one H216
21:17 that thou quench not the l of Israel. H5216
23: 4 And *he shall be* as the l of the morning, H216
1Ki 7: 4 and l *was* against light *in* three ranks. H4237
4 and light *was* against l *in* three ranks. H4237
5 and l *was* against light *in* three ranks. H4237
5 and light *was* against l *in* three ranks. H4237
11:36 may have a l alway before me in H5216
16:31 as if it had been a l thing for him to H7043
2Ki 3:18 And this is *but* a l thing in the sight of H7043
7: 9 till the morning l, some mischief will H216
8:19 give him alway a l, *and* to his children. H5216
20:10 And Hezekiah answered, It is a l thing H7043
2Ch 21: 7 give a l to him and to his sons for ever. H5216
Neh 9:12 l in the way wherein they should go. H215
19 l, and the way wherein they should go. H215
Est 8:16 The Jews had l, and gladness, and joy, H219
Job 3: 4 above, neither let the l shine upon it. H5105
9 be dark; let it look for l, but *have* none; H216
16 not been; as infants *which* never saw l. H216
20 Wherefore is l given to him that is in H216
23 *Why is l given* to a man whose way is
10:22 order, and *where* the l *is* as darkness. H3313
12:22 bringeth out to l the shadow of death. H216
25 They grope in the dark without l, and he H216
17:12 They change the night into day: the l *is* H216
18: 5 Yea, the l of the wicked shall be put out, H216
6 The l shall be dark in his tabernacle, and H216
18 He shall be driven from l into darkness, H216
22:28 and the l shall shine upon thy ways. H216
24:13 They are of those that rebel against the l; H216
14 The murderer rising with the l killeth the H216
16 in the daytime: they know not the l. H216
25: 3 and upon whom doth not his l arise? H216
28:11 *the thing that is* hid bringeth he forth to l. H216
29: 3 by his l I walked *through* darkness; H216
24 l of my countenance they cast not down. H216
30:26 when I waited for l, there came darkness. H216
33:28 into the pit, and his life shall see the l. H216
30 to be enlightened with the l of the living. H216
36:30 Behold, he spreadeth his l upon it, and H216
32 With clouds he covereth the l; and H216
37:15 and caused the l of his cloud to shine? H216
21 And now *men* see not the bright l which H216
38:15 And from the wicked their l is H216
19 Where *is* the way *where* l dwelleth? and H216
24 By what way is the l parted, *which* H216
41:18 By his neesings a l doth shine, and his H216
Ps 4: 6 up the l of thy countenance upon us. H216
18:28 For thou wilt l my candle: the LORD my H215
27: 1 The LORD *is* my l and my salvation; H216
36: 9 fountain of life: in thy l shall we see light. H216
9 fountain of life: in thy light shall we see l. H216
37: 6 the l, and thy judgment as the noonday. H216
38:10 l of mine eyes, it also is gone from me. H216
43: 3 O send out thy l and thy truth: let them H216
44: 3 thine arm, and the l of thy countenance, H216
49:19 of his fathers; they shall never see l. H216
56:13 walk before God in the l of the living? H216
74:16 thou hast prepared the l and the sun. H3974
78:14 a cloud, and all the night with a l of fire. H216
89:15 O LORD, in the l of thy countenance. H216
90: 8 secret *sins* in the l of thy countenance. H3974
97:11 L is sown for the righteous, and gladness H216
104: 2 Who coverest *thyself* with l as *with* a H216
105:39 a covering; and fire to give l in the night. H215
112: 4 Unto the upright there ariseth l in the H216
118:27 hath shewed us l: bind the sacrifice with H215
119:105 Thy word *is* a lamp unto my feet, and a l H216
130 The entrance of thy words giveth l; it H215
139:11 me; even the night shall be l about me. H216
12 darkness and the l *are* both alike *to thee.* H219
148: 3 and moon: praise him, all ye stars of l. H216
Prv 4:18 But the path of the just *is* as the shining l, H216
6:23 lamp; and the law *is* l; and reproofs of H216
13: 9 The l of the righteous rejoiceth: but the H216
15:30 The l of the eyes rejoiceth the heart: H3974
16:15 In the l of the king's countenance *is* life; H216
Ecc 2:13 folly, as far as l excelleth darkness. H216
11: 7 Truly the l *is* sweet, and a pleasant *thing* H216
12: 2 While the sun, or the l, or the moon, or H216
Isa 2: 5 ye, and let us walk in the l of the LORD. H216
5:20 put darkness for l, and light for darkness; H216
20 for light, and l for darkness; that put H216
30 the l is darkened in the heavens thereof. H216

Isa 8:20 *it is* because *there is* no l in them. H7837
9: 2 have seen a great l: they that dwell in the H216
2 of death, upon them hath the l shined. H216
10:17 And the l of Israel shall be for a fire, and H216
13:10 shall not give their l: the sun shall be H216
10 the moon shall not cause her l to shine. H216
30:26 Moreover the l of the moon shall be as H216
26 shall be as the l of the sun, and the light H216
26 of the sun, and the l of the sun shall be H216
26 be sevenfold, as the l of seven days, in H216
42: 6 of the people, for a l of the Gentiles; H216
16 I will make darkness l before them, and H216
45: 7 I form the l, and create darkness: I make H216
49: 6 And he said, It is a l thing that thou H7043
6 also give thee for a l to the Gentiles, that H216
50:10 and hath no l? let him trust in the name H5051
11 sparks: walk in the l of your fire, and in H217
51: 4 my judgment to rest for a l of the people. H216
58: 8 Then shall thy l break forth as the H216
10 soul; then shall thy l rise in obscurity, H216
59: 9 us: we wait for l, but behold obscurity; H216
60: 1 Arise, shine; for thy l is come, and the H216
3 And the Gentiles shall come to thy l, and H216
19 The sun shall be no more thy l by day; H216
19 shall the moon give l unto thee: but the H215
19 an everlasting l, and thy God thy glory. H216
20 be thine everlasting l, and the days of thy H216
Jer 4:23 void; and the heavens, and they *had* no l. H216
13:16 and, while ye look for l, he turn it into the H216
25:10 of the millstones, and the l of the candle. H216
31:35 giveth the sun for a l by day, *and* the H216
35 and of the stars for a l by night, which H216
Lam 3: 2 brought *me into* darkness, but not *into* l. H216
Ezk 8:17 son of man? Is it a l thing to the house H7043
22: 7 In thee have they set l by father and H7043
32: 7 cloud, and the moon shall not give her l. H216
Dan 2:22 darkness, and the l dwelleth with him. H5094
5:11 days of thy father l and understanding H5094
14 gods *is* in thee, and *that* l and H5094
Hos 6: 5 judgments *are as* the l *that* goeth forth. H216
Am 5:18 day of the LORD *is* darkness, and not l. H216
20 l? even very dark, and no brightness in it? H216
Mic 2: 1 the morning is l, they practise it, because H216
7: 8 darkness, the LORD *shall be* a l unto me. H216
9 l, *and* I shall behold his righteousness. H216
Hab 3: 4 And *his* brightness was as the l; he had H216
11 habitation: at the l of thine arrows they H216
Zep 3: 4 Her prophets *are* l *and* treacherous H6348
5 his judgment to l, he faileth not; but the H216
Zec 14: 6 *that* the l shall not be clear, *nor* dark: H216
7 to pass, *that* at evening time it shall be l. H216
Mt 4:16 saw great l; and to them which sat G5457
16 and shadow of death l is sprung up. G5457
5:14 Ye are the l of the world. A city that is G5457
15 Neither do men l a candle, and put it G2545
15 it giveth l unto all that are in the house. G2989
16 Let your l so shine before men, that G5457
6:22 The l of the body is the eye: if therefore G3088
22 single, thy whole body shall be full of l. G5460
23 If therefore the l that is in thee be G5457
10:27 *that* speak ye in l: and what ye hear in G5457
11:30 For my yoke *is* easy, and my burden is l. G1645
17: 2 sun, and his raiment was white as the l. G5457
22: 5 But they made l of *it*, and went their G272
24:29 shall not give her l, and the stars shall G5338
Mk 13:24 and the moon shall not give her l, G5338
Lk 1:79 To give l to them that sit in darkness G2014
2:32 A l to lighten the Gentiles, and the glory G5457
8:16 that they which enter in may see the l. G5457
11:33 that they which come in may see the l. G5338
34 The l of the body is the eye: therefore G3088
34 body also is full of l; but when *thine eye* G5460
35 Take heed therefore that the l which is G5457
36 If thy whole body therefore *be* full of l, G5460
36 shall be full of l, as when the bright G5460
36 shining of a candle doth give thee l. G5461
12: 3 be heard in the l; and that which ye G5457
15: 8 one piece, doth not l a candle, and sweep G681
16: 8 generation wiser than the children of l. G5457
Jn 1: 4 In him was life; and the life was the l of G5457
5 And the l shineth in darkness; and the G5457
7 witness of the L, that all *men* through G5457
8 He was not that L, but *was sent* to bear G5457
8 but *was sent* to bear witness of that L. G5457
9 *That* was the true L, which lighteth G5457
3:19 And this is the condemnation, that l is G5457
19 than l, because their deeds were evil. G5457
20 evil hateth the l, neither cometh to the G5457
20 the l, lest his deeds should be reproved. G5457
Jn 3:21 But he that doeth truth cometh to the l, G5457
5:35 He was a burning and a shining l: and G3088
35 willing for a season to rejoice in his l. G5457
8:12 saying, I am the l of the world: he that G5457
12 in darkness, but shall have the l of life. G5457
9: 5 As long as I am in the world, I am the l G5457
11: 9 because he seeth the l of this world. G5457
10 stumbleth, because there is no l in him. G5457
12:35 Yet a little while is the l with you. Walk G5457
35 while ye have the l, lest darkness come G5457
36 While ye have l, believe in the light, that G5457
36 While ye have light, believe in the l, that G5457
36 be the children of l. These things spake G5457
46 I am come a l into the world, that G5457
Act 9: 3 round about him a l from heaven: G5457
12: 7 upon *him*, and a l shined in the prison: G5457
13:47 set thee to be a l of the Gentiles, that G5457
16:29 Then he called for a l, and sprang in, G5457
22: 6 from heaven a great l round about me. G5457
9 me saw indeed the l, and were afraid; G5457
11 the glory of that l, being led by the hand G5457
26:13 At midday, O king, I saw in the way a l G5457
18 from darkness to l, and *from* the power G5457
23 l unto the people, and to the Gentiles. G5457
Ro 2:19 a l of them which are in darkness, G5457
13:12 and let us put on the armour of l. G5457
1Co 4: 5 both will bring to l the hidden things of G5461
2Co 4: 4 not, lest the l of the glorious gospel G5462
6 For God, who commanded the l to G5457
6 hearts, to *give* the l of the knowledge of G5462
17 For our l affliction, which is but for a G1645
6:14 communion hath l with darkness? G5457
11:14 is transformed into an angel of l. G5457
Eph 5: 8 l in the Lord: walk as children of light: G5457
8 light in the Lord: walk as children of l: G5457
13 manifest by the l: for whatsoever doth G5457
13 for whatsoever doth make manifest is l. G5457
14 the dead, and Christ shall give thee l. G2017
Col 1:12 of the inheritance of the saints in l: G5457
1Th 5: 5 Ye are all the children of l, and the G5457
1Ti 6:16 dwelling in the l which no man can G5457
2Ti 1:10 immortality to l through the gospel: G5461
1Pt 2: 9 out of darkness into his marvellous l: G5457
2Pt 1:19 heed, as unto a l that shineth in a dark G3088
1Jn 1: 5 is l, and in him is no darkness at all. G5457
7 But if we walk in the l, as he is in the G5457
7 as he is in the l, we have fellowship one G5457
2: 8 is past, and the true l now shineth. G5457
9 He that saith he is in the l, and hateth G5457
10 abideth in the l, and there is none G5457
Rev 7:16 shall the sun l on them, nor any heat. G4098
18:23 And the l of a candle shall shine no G5457
21:11 Having the glory of God: and her l *was* G5458
23 lighten it, and the Lamb *is* the l thereof. G3088
24 shall walk in the l of it: and the kings of G5457
22: 5 no candle, neither l of the sun; for the G5457
5 l: and they shall reign for ever and ever. G5461

LIGHTED
Gen 24:64 when she saw Isaac, she l off the camel. H5307
28:11 And he l upon a certain place, and H6293
Ex 40:25 And he l the lamps before the LORD; as H5927
Nu 8: 3 And Aaron did so; he l the lamps H5927
Jos 15:18 a field: and she l off *her* ass; and Caleb H6795
Jdg 1:14 a field: and she l from off *her* ass; and H6795
4:15 so that Sisera l down off *his* chariot, H3381
1Sa 25:23 she hasted, and l off the ass, and fell H3381
2Ki 5:21 after him, he l down from the chariot H5307
10:15 And when he was departed thence, he l H4672
Isa 9: 8 into Jacob, and it hath l upon Israel. H5307
Lk 8:16 No man, when he hath l a candle, G681
11:33 No man, when he hath l a candle, G681

LIGHTEN
1Sa 6: 5 he will l his hand from off you, H7043
2Sa 22:29 and the LORD will l my darkness. H5050
Ezr 9: 8 that our God may l our eyes, and give us H215
Ps 13: 3 O LORD my God: l mine eyes, lest I sleep H215
Jna 1: 5 into the sea, to l *it* of them. But Jonah H7043
Lk 2:32 A light to l the Gentiles, and the glory of G602
Rev 21:23 l it, and the Lamb *is* the light thereof. G5461

LIGHTENED
Ps 34: 5 They looked unto him, and were l: and H5102
77:18 the lightnings l the world: the earth H215
Act 27:18 the next *day* they l the ship; G1546+G4160
38 enough, they l the ship, and cast out G2893
Rev 18: 1 and the earth was l with his glory. G5461

LIGHTENETH
Prv 29:13 together: the LORD l both their eyes. H215
Lk 17:24 For as the lightning, that l out of the one G797

LIGHTER
1Ki 12: 4 put upon us, l, and we will serve thee. H7043
9 yoke which thy father did put upon us l? H7043
10 but make thou *it* l unto us; thus shalt H7043
2Ch 10:10 thou *it* somewhat l for us; thus shalt H7043
Ps 62: 9 they *are* altogether *l* than vanity.

LIGHTEST
Nu 8: 2 him, When thou l the lamps, the seven H5927

LIGHTETH
Ex 30: 8 And when Aaron l the lamps at even, H5927
Dt 19: 5 the helve, and l upon his neighbour, H4672
Jn 1: 9 *That* was the true Light, which l every G5461

LIGHTING
Isa 30:30 and shall shew the l down of his arm, H5183
Mt 3:16 like a dove, and l upon him: G2064

LIGHTLY
Gen 26:10 of the people might l have lien with thy H4592
Dt 32:15 l esteemed the Rock of his salvation. H5034
1Sa 2:30 that despise me shall be l esteemed. H7043
18:23 that I *am* a poor man, and l esteemed? H7034
Isa 9: 1 at the first he l afflicted the land of H7043
Jer 4:24 they trembled, and all the hills moved l. H7043
Mk 9:39 my name, that can l speak evil of me. G5035

LIGHTNESS
Jer 3: 9 And it came to pass through the l of her H6963
23:32 lies, and by their l; yet I sent them not, H6350
2Co 1:17 minded, did I use l? or the things that I G1644

LIGHTNING
2Sa 22:15 them; l, and discomfited them. H1300
Job 28:26 rain, and a way for the l of the thunder: H2385
37: 3 and his l unto the ends of the earth. H216
38:25 of waters, or a way for the l of thunder; H2385
Ps 144: 6 Cast forth l, and scatter them: shoot out H1300
Ezk 1:13 bright, and out of the fire went forth l. H1300
14 returned as the appearance of a flash of l. H965
Dan 10: 6 as the appearance of l, and his eyes as H1300
Zec 9:14 go forth as the l: and the Lord GOD H1300
Mt 24:27 For as the l cometh out of the east, and G796
28: 3 His countenance was like l, and his G796
Lk 10:18 I beheld Satan as l fall from heaven. G796
17:24 For as the l, that lighteneth out of the one G796

LIGHTNINGS
Ex 19:16 were thunders and l, and a thick cloud H1300
20:18 and the l, and the noise of the H3940
Job 38:35 Canst thou send l, that they may go, H1300
Ps 18:14 he shot out l, and discomfited them. H1300
77:18 in the heaven: the l lightened the world: H1300
97: 4 His l enlightened the world: the earth H1300
135: 7 the earth; he maketh l for the rain; he H1300
Jer 10:13 the earth; he maketh l with rain, and H1300
51:16 the earth: he maketh l with rain, and H1300
Nah 2: 4 like torches, they shall run like the l. H1300
Rev 4: 5 And out of the throne proceeded l and G796
8: 5 thunderings, and l, and an earthquake. G796
11:19 and there were l, and voices, and G796
16:18 and thunders, and l; and there was a G796

LIGHTS
Gen 1:14 And God said, Let there be l in the H3974
15 And let them be for l in the firmament H3974
16 And God made two great l; the greater H3974
1Ki 6: 4 house he made windows of narrow l. H8261
Ps 136: 7 To him that made great l: for his mercy H216
Ezk 32: 8 All the bright l of heaven will I make H216
Lk 12:35 be girded about, and *your* l burning; G3088
Act 20: 8 And there were many l in the upper G2985
Php 2:15 whom ye shine as l in the world; G5458
Jas 1:17 from the Father of l, with whom is no G5457

LIGN
Nu 24: 6 side, as the trees of l aloes which the

LIGN-ALOES See LIGN and ALOES.

LIGURE
Ex 28:19 And the third row a l, an agate, and an H3958
39:12 And the third row, a l, an agate, and an H3958

LIKE
Gen 13:10 of the LORD, l the land of Egypt, as
25:25 And the first came out red, all over l an
Ex 7:11 in l manner with their enchantments. H3651
8:10 *there is* none l unto the LORD our God. H3644
9:14 that *there is* none l me in all the earth. H3644
24 as there was none l it in all the land of H3644
11: 6 none l it, nor shall be like it any more. H3644
6 none like it, nor shall be l it any more. H3644
15:11 Who *is* l unto thee, O LORD, among the H3644
11 the gods? who *is* l thee, glorious in H3644
16:31 Manna: and it *was* l coriander seed,
31 taste of it *was* l wafers *made* with honey.
23:11 field shall eat. In l manner thou shalt H3651
24:17 of the LORD *was* l devouring fire on the
25:33 Three bowls made l unto almonds, *with*
33 three bowls made l almonds in the other
34 four bowls made l unto almonds, *with*
28:11 With the work of an engraver in stone, *l*
21 to their names, *l* the engravings of a
36 and grave upon it, *l* the engravings of a
30:32 shall ye make *any other* l it, after the H3644
33 Whosoever compoundeth *any* l it, or H3644
34 of each shall there be a l *weight:* H905
38 Whosoever shall make l unto that, to H3644
34: 1 two tables of stone l unto the first: and I
4 And he hewed two tables of stone l unto
37:19 three bowls made l almonds in another
20 l almonds, his knops, and his flowers:
39: 8 *of* cunning work, l the work of the
14 to their names, *l* the engravings of a
30 upon it a writing, *l to* the engravings of
Lev 13: 2 in the skin of his flesh *l* the plague of
Nu 23:10 righteous, and let my last end be l his! H3644
Dt 4:32 great thing *is*, or hath been heard l it? H3644
7:26 be a cursed thing l it: *but* thou shalt H3644
10: 1 two tables of stone l unto the first, and
3 two tables of stone l unto the first, and
17:14 l as all the nations that *are* about me;
18: 8 They shall have l portions to eat, beside
15 l unto me; unto him ye shall hearken; H3644
18 their brethren, l unto thee, and will put H3644
22: 3 In l manner shalt thou do with his ass; H3651
25: 7 And if the man l not to take his H2654
8 stand *to it*, and say, I l not to take her; H2654
29:23 grass groweth therein, l the overthrow of
33:17 His glory *is l* the firstling of his bullock,
17 bullock, and his horns *are l* the horns of
26 *There is* none l unto the God of
29 Happy *art* thou, O Israel: who *is* l unto H3644
34:10 since in Israel l unto Moses, whom the
Jos 10:14 And there was no day l that before it or
Jdg 7:12 lay along in the valley l grasshoppers for
11:17 *thereto*. And in l manner they sent H1571
13: 6 countenance *was* l the countenance of
16:12 brake them from off his arms l a thread.
17 become weak, and be l any *other* man.
Ru 2:13 be not l unto one of thine handmaidens.
4:11 into thine house l Rachel and like Leah, H7354
11 like Rachel and l Leah, which two did
12 And let thy house be l the house of
1Sa 2: 2 thee: neither *is there* any rock l our God.
4: 9 Be strong, and quit yourselves l men, O
9 to you: quit yourselves l men, and fight.
8: 5 us a king to judge us l all the nations.
20 That we also may be l all the nations;
10:24 that *there is* none l him among all the H3644
17: 7 And the staff of his spear *was* l a
19:24 before Samuel in l manner, and lay H1571
21: 9 said, *There is* none l that; give it me.
25:36 a feast in his house, l the feast of a king;
26:15 man? and who *is* l to thee in Israel? H3644
2Sa 7: 9 thee a great name, l unto the name of
22 for *there is* none l thee, neither *is there* H3644
23 And what one nation in the earth *is* l thy
23 like thy people, *even* l Israel, whom God
18:27 of the foremost is l the running of
21:19 of whose spear *was* l a weaver's beam.
22:34 He maketh my feet l hinds' *feet:* and H7737
1Ki 3:12 that there was none l thee before thee, H3644
12 after thee shall any arise l unto thee. H3644
13 the kings l unto thee all thy days. H3644
5: 6 skill to hew timber l unto the Sidonians.
7: 8 *which* was of the l work. Solomon made
8 he had taken *to wife*, l unto this porch.
26 was wrought l the brim of a cup, with
33 And the work of the wheels *was* l the
8:23 *there is* no God l thee, in heaven above, H3644
10:20 was not the l made in any kingdom. H3651
1Ki 12:32 day of the month, l unto the feast that *is*
16: 3 make thy house l the house of Jeroboam
7 of his hands, in being l the house of
18:44 out of the sea, l a man's hand. And he
20:25 And number thee an army, l the army
27 before them l two little flocks of kids;
21:22 And will make thine house l the house of
22 son of Nebat, and l the house of Baasha
25 But there was none l unto Ahab, which
22:13 I pray thee, be l the word of one of them,
2Ki 3: 2 the LORD; but not l his father, and like
2 like his father, and l his mother: for he
5:14 his flesh came again l unto the flesh of a
9: 9 And I will make the house of Ahab l the
9 l the house of Baasha the son of Ahijah:
20 and the driving *is* l the driving of Jehu
13: 7 had made them l the dust by threshing.
14: 3 the LORD, yet not l David his father: he
16: 2 of the LORD his God, l David his father.
17:14 their necks, l to the neck of their fathers,
15 them, that they should not do l them.
18: 5 after him was none l him among all the H3644
32 you away to a land l your own land, a
23:25 And l unto him was there no king H3644
25 neither after him arose there *any* l him. H3644
25:17 all of brass: and l unto these had the
1Ch 4:27 multiply, l to the children of Judah.
11:23 hand *was* a spear l a weaver's beam; and
12: 8 whose faces *were l* the faces of lions, and
22 *it was* a great host, l the host of God.
14:11 by mine hand l the breaking forth of
17: 8 made thee a name l the name of the
20 O LORD, *there is* none l thee, neither *is* H3644
21 And what one nation in the earth *is* l thy
20: 5 whose spear staff *was* l a weaver's beam.
27:23 Israel l to the stars of the heavens.
2Ch 1: 9 l the dust of the earth in multitude.
12 shall there any after thee have the l. H3651
4: 5 and the brim of it l the work of the H3651
6:14 *there is* no God l thee in the heaven, nor
9:19 was not the l made in any kingdom.
18:12 be l one of theirs, and speak thou good.
21: 6 the kings of Israel, l as did the house of
13 to go a whoring, l to the whoredoms of
19 for him, l the burning of his fathers.
22: 4 sight of the LORD l the house of Ahab:
28: 1 the sight of the LORD, l David his father:
30: 7 And be not ye l your fathers, and like
7 And be not ye like your fathers, and l
26 of Israel *there was* not the l in Jerusalem.
33: 2 the sight of the LORD, l unto the
35:18 And there was no passover l to that H3644
Neh 6: 5 servant unto me in l manner the fifth H2088
13:26 was there no king l him, who was H3644
Est 2:20 l as when she was brought up with him.
Job 1: 8 that *there is* none l him in the earth, a H3644
2: 3 that *there is* none l him in the earth, a H3644
3:24 my roarings are poured out l the waters.
5:26 grave in a full age, l as a shock of corn
7: 1 his days also l the days of an hireling?
8: 2 words of thy mouth *be l* a strong wind?
10:10 me out as milk, and curdled me l cheese?
11:12 though man be born *l* a wild ass's colt.
12:25 them to stagger l a drunken *man*.
13:12 Your remembrances *are* l unto ashes, H4912
14: 2 He cometh forth l a flower, and is cut
9 bud, and bring forth boughs l a plant. H3644
15:16 *is* man, which drinketh iniquity l water?
16:14 breach, he runneth upon me l a giant.
19:10 and mine hope hath he removed l a tree.
20: 7 *Yet* he shall perish for ever l his own
21:11 They send forth their little ones l a flock,
30:19 and I am become l dust and ashes. H4911
32:19 no vent; it is ready to burst l new bottles.
34: 7 What man *is* l Job, *who* drinketh up
7 Job, *who* drinketh up scorning l water?
36:22 by his power: who teacheth l him? H3644
38: 3 Gird up now thy loins l a man; for I will
40: 7 Gird up thy loins now l a man: I will
9 Hast thou an arm l God? or canst thou
9 canst thou thunder with a voice l him? H3644
17 He moveth his tail l a cedar: the sinews H3644
18 of brass; his bones *are* l bars of iron.
41:18 his eyes *are* l the eyelids of the morning.
31 He maketh the deep to boil l a pot: he
31 he maketh the sea l a pot of ointment.
33 Upon earth there is not his l, who is H4915
42: 8 *thing which is* right, l my servant Job.
Ps 1: 3 And he shall be l a tree planted by the
Ps 1: 4 The ungodly *are* not so: but *are* l the
2: 9 dash them in pieces l a potter's vessel.
7: 2 Lest he tear my soul l a lion, rending *it* in
17:12 L as a lion *that* is greedy of his prey, H1825
18:33 He maketh my feet l hinds' *feet*, and
22:14 I am poured out l water, and all my
14 of joint: my heart is l wax; it is melted in
15 My strength is dried up l a potsherd; and
28: 1 l them that go down into the pit. H5973
29: 6 He maketh them also to skip l a calf; H3644
6 Lebanon and Sirion l a young unicorn. H3644
31:12 man out of mind: I am l a broken vessel.
35:10 All my bones shall say, LORD, who *is* l
36: 6 Thy righteousness *is* l the great
37: 2 For they shall soon be cut down l the
35 and spreading himself l a green bay tree.
39:11 to consume away l a moth: surely every
44:11 Thou hast given us l sheep *appointed* for
49:12 not: he is l the beasts *that* perish. H4911
14 L sheep they are laid in the grave; death
20 not, is l the beasts *that* perish. H4911
52: 2 Thy tongue deviseth mischiefs; l a sharp
8 But I *am* l a green olive tree in the house
55: 6 And I said, Oh that I had wings l a dove!
58: 4 Their poison *is* l the poison of a H1823
4 l the deaf adder *that* stoppeth her ear; H3644
8 *of them* pass away: *l* the untimely birth
59: 6 l a dog, and go round about the city.
14 l a dog, and go round about the city.
64: 3 Who whet their tongue l a sword, *and*
71:19 great things: O God, who *is* l unto thee! H3644
72: 6 He shall come down l rain upon the
16 thereof shall shake l Lebanon: and *they*
16 the city shall flourish l grass of the earth.
73: 5 neither are they plagued l *other* men. H5973
77:20 Thou leddest thy people l a flock by the
78:16 and caused waters to run down l rivers.
27 feathered fowls l as the sand of the sea:
52 But made his own people to go forth l
52 guided them in the wilderness l a flock.
57 But turned back, and dealt unfaithfully l
57 they were turned aside l a deceitful bow.
65 out of sleep, *and* l a mighty man that
69 And he built his sanctuary l high
69 like high *palaces*, l the earth which he
79: 3 Their blood have they shed l water
5 for ever? shall thy jealousy burn l fire?
80: 1 that leadest Joseph l a flock; thou that
10 boughs thereof *were l* the goodly cedars.
82: 7 But ye shall die l men, and fall like one
7 But ye shall die like men, and fall l one
83:11 Make their nobles l Oreb, and like Zeeb:
11 Make their nobles like Oreb, and l Zeeb:
13 O my God, make them l a wheel; as the
86: 8 Among the gods *there is* none l unto
8 *are there any works* l unto thy works.
88: 5 Free among the dead, l the slain that lie H3644
17 They came round about me daily l
89: 8 *is* a strong LORD l unto thee? or to thy H3644
46 for ever? shall thy wrath burn l fire? H3644
90: 5 *they are* l grass *which* groweth up.
92:10 But my horn shalt thou exalt l *the horn*
12 The righteous shall flourish l the palm
12 tree: he shall grow l a cedar in Lebanon.
97: 5 The hills melted l wax at the presence of
102: 3 For my days are consumed l smoke, and
4 My heart is smitten, and withered l
6 I am l a pelican of the wilderness: I am H1819
6 wilderness: I am l an owl of the desert.
9 For I have eaten ashes l bread, and
11 My days *are* l a shadow that declineth;
11 declineth; and I am withered l grass.
26 of them shall wax old l a garment; as a
103: 5 *so that* thy youth is renewed l the eagle's.
13 L as a father pitieth *his* children, *so* the
104: 2 stretchest out the heavens l a curtain:
105:41 out; they ran in the dry places *l* a river.
107:27 They reel to and fro, and stagger l a
41 and maketh *him* families l a flock.
109:18 As he clothed himself with cursing l as
18 l water, and like oil into his bones.
18 like water, and l oil into his bones.
23 I am gone l the shadow when it
113: 5 Who *is* l unto the LORD our God, who
114: 4 The mountains skipped l rams, *and* the
4 like rams, *and* the little hills l lambs.
6 Ye mountains, *that* ye skipped l rams;
6 like rams; *and* ye little hills, l lambs?
115: 8 They that make them are l unto them; H3644

Ps 118:12 They compassed me about l bees; they
119:83 For I am become l a bottle in the smoke;
119 *l* dross: therefore I love thy testimonies.
176 I have gone astray l a lost sheep; seek
126: 1 of Zion, we were l them that dream.
128: 3 l olive plants round about thy table.
133: 2 *It is* l the precious ointment upon the
135:18 They that make them are l unto them: H3644
140: 3 They have sharpened their tongues l a H3644
143: 7 l unto them that go down into the pit. H4911
144: 4 Man is l to vanity: his days *are* as a H1819
147:16 He giveth snow l wool: he scattereth the
16 wool: he scattereth the hoarfrost l ashes.
17 He casteth forth his ice l morsels: who
Prv 12:18 There is that speaketh l the piercings of
17:22 A merry heart doeth good *l* a medicine:
18:19 contentions *are* l the bars of a castle.
20: 5 Counsel in the heart of man *is l* deep
23:32 At the last it biteth l a serpent, and
32 like a serpent, and stingeth l an adder.
25:11 A word fitly spoken *is l* apples of gold in
14 Whoso boasteth himself of a false gift *is l*
19 *l* a broken tooth, and a foot out of joint.
28 his own spirit *is* l a city *that is* broken
26: 4 to his folly, lest thou also be l unto him. H7737
17 *is* l one that taketh a dog by the ears.
23 Burning lips and a wicked heart *are l* a
28: 3 A poor man that oppresseth the poor *is l*
31:14 She is l the merchants' ships; she
Song 2: 9 My beloved is l a roe or a young hart: H1819
17 and be thou l a roe or a young hart H1819
3: 6 out of the wilderness l pillars of smoke,
4: 2 Thy teeth *are* l a flock *of sheep that are*
3 Thy lips *are* l a thread of scarlet, and thy
3 comely: thy temples *are* l a piece of a
4 Thy neck *is* l the tower of David builded
5 Thy two breasts *are* l two young roes
11 thy garments *is* l the smell of Lebanon.
5:13 *l* lilies, dropping sweet smelling myrrh.
6:12 Or ever I was aware, my soul made me *l*
7: 1 of thy thighs *are* l jewels, the work of H3644
2 Thy navel *is l* a round goblet, *which*
2 *l* an heap of wheat set about with lilies.
3 Thy two breasts *are* l two young roes
4 of ivory; thine eyes *l* the fishpools in
5 Thine head upon thee *is* l Carmel, and
5 l purple; the king *is* held in the galleries.
7 This thy stature is l to a palm tree, and H1819
8 vine, and the smell of thy nose l apples;
9 And the roof of thy mouth l the best wine
8:10 I *am* a wall, and my breasts l towers:
14 Make haste, my beloved, and be thou l H1819
Isa 1: 9 we should have been l unto Gomorrah. H1819
18 be red l crimson, they shall be as wool. H1819
2: 6 *are* soothsayers l the Philistines, and
3:18 cauls, and *their* round tires l the moon,
5:28 l flint, and their wheels like a whirlwind:
28 like flint, and their wheels l a whirlwind:
29 Their roaring *shall be* l a lion, they shall
29 a lion, they shall roar l young lions: yea,
30 roar against them l the roaring of the
9:18 shall mount up *l* the lifting up of smoke.
10: 6 them down l the mire of the streets.
13 down the inhabitants l a valiant *man*:
16 kindle a burning l the burning of a fire.
11: 7 and the lion shall eat straw l the ox.
16 left, from Assyria; l as it was to Israel in
13: 4 in the mountains, l as of a great people; H1823
14:10 weak as we? art thou become l unto us? H4911
14 of the clouds; I will be l the most High. H1819
19 But thou art cast out of thy grave l an
16:11 Wherefore my bowels shall sound l an
17:12 make a noise l the noise of the seas;
12 a rushing l the rushing of mighty waters!
13 The nations shall rush l the rushing of
13 l a rolling thing before the whirlwind.
18: 4 in my dwelling place l a clear heat upon
4 l a cloud of dew in the heat of harvest.
19:16 In that day shall Egypt be l unto women:
20: 3 And the LORD said, L as my servant
22:18 turn and toss thee *l* a ball into a large
24:20 The earth shall reel to and fro l a
20 shall be removed l a cottage; and the
26:17 L as a woman with child, *that* draweth H3644
27:10 forsaken, and left l a wilderness: there
29: 5 strangers shall be l small dust, and the
30:33 l a stream of brimstone, doth kindle it.
31: 4 spoken unto me, L as the lion and the
33: 4 And your spoil shall be gathered *l* the

Isa 33: 9 down: Sharon is l a wilderness; and
36:17 you away to a land l your own land, a
38:12 tent: I have cut off l a weaver my life: he
14 L a crane *or* a swallow, so did I chatter: I
40:11 He shall feed his flock l a shepherd: he
42:13 stir up jealousy l a man of war: he shall
14 *now* will I cry l a travailing woman;
46: 5 and compare me, that we may be l? H1819
9 else; *I am* God, and *there is* none l me, H3644
48:19 of thy bowels l the gravel thereof; his
49: 2 And he hath made my mouth l a sharp
50: 7 have I set my face l a flint, and I know
51: 3 her wilderness l Eden, and her desert
3 and her desert l the garden of the LORD;
6 shall vanish away l smoke, and the earth
6 earth shall wax old l a garment, and they
6 therein shall die in l manner: but my H3644
8 For the moth shall eat them up l a
8 worm shall eat them l wool: but my
53: 6 All we l sheep have gone astray; we have
57:20 But the wicked *are* l the troubled sea,
58: 1 Cry aloud, spare not, lift up thy voice l a
11 and thou shalt be l a watered garden,
11 garden, and l a spring of water, whose
59:10 We grope for the wall l the blind, and we
11 We roar all l bears, and mourn sore like
11 We roar all like bears, and mourn sore l
19 shall come in l a flood, the Spirit of
63: 2 l him that treadeth in the winefat?
64: 6 l the wind, have taken us away.
65:25 the lion shall eat straw l the bullock: and
66:12 will extend peace to her l a river, and the
12 of the Gentiles l a flowing stream: then
14 shall flourish l an herb: and the hand
15 with his chariots l a whirlwind, to render
Jer 2:30 your prophets, l a destroying lion.
4: 4 my fury come forth l fire, and burn that
5:19 thou answer them, L as ye have forsaken
6:23 their voice roareth l the sea; and they H3644
9: 3 And they bend their tongues *l* their H3644
12 *and* is burned up l a wilderness, that
10: 6 Forasmuch as *there is* none l unto thee,
7 kingdoms, *there is* none l unto thee.
16 The portion of Jacob *is* not l them: for he
11:19 But I *was* l a lamb *or* an ox *that* is
12: 3 thee: pull them out l sheep for the
14: 6 up the wind l dragons; their eyes did
17: 6 For he shall be l the heath in the desert,
21:12 lest my fury go out l fire, and burn that
23: 9 bones shake; I am l a drunken man, and
9 a drunken man, and l a man whom wine
29 *Is* not my word l as a fire? saith the H3541
29 saith the LORD; and l a hammer *that*
24: 2 One basket *had* very good figs, *even* l the
5 the God of Israel; L these good figs, so
25:34 and ye shall fall l a pleasant vessel.
26: 6 Then will I make this house l Shiloh, and
9 This house shall be l Shiloh, and this city
18 shall be plowed *l* a field, and Jerusalem
29:17 will make them l vile figs, that cannot
22 LORD make thee l Zedekiah and like
22 thee like Zedekiah and l Ahab, whom the
30: 7 so that none *is* l it: *it is* even the time H3644
31:28 And it shall come to pass, *that* l as I have
32:42 For thus saith the LORD; L as I have
36:32 added besides unto them many l words.
38: 9 dungeon; and he is l to die for hunger in
46: 8 Egypt riseth up l a flood, and *his* waters
8 *his* waters are moved l the rivers; and he
20 Egypt *is* l a very fair heifer, *but*
21 in the midst of her l fatted bullocks; for
22 The voice thereof shall go l a serpent; for
48: 6 Flee, save your lives, and be l the heath
28 dwell in the rock, and be l the dove *that*
36 sound for Moab l pipes, and mine heart
36 heart shall sound l pipes for the men of
38 I have broken Moab l a vessel wherein *is*
49:19 Behold, he shall come up l a lion from
19 over her? for who *is* l me? and who will H3644
50:42 voice shall roar l the sea, and they shall
42 *one* put in array, l a man to the battle,
44 Behold, he shall come up l a lion from
44 over her? for who *is* l me? and who will H3644
51:19 The portion of Jacob *is* not l them; for he
33 of Babylon *is* l a threshingfloor, *it is*
34 swallowed me up l a dragon, he hath
38 They shall roar together l lions: they
40 I will bring them down l lambs to the
40 to the slaughter, l rams with he goats.

Jer 51:55 her waves do roar l great waters, a noise
52:22 and the pomegranates *were* l unto these.
Lam 1: 6 princes are become l harts *that* find no
12 be any sorrow l unto my sorrow, which
21 hast called, and they shall be l unto me. H3644
2: 3 against Jacob l a flaming fire, *which*
4 He hath bent his bow l an enemy: he
4 of Zion: he poured out his fury l fire.
13 *is* great l the sea: who can heal thee?
18 Zion, let tears run down l a river day and
19 out thine heart l water before the face
3:52 Mine enemies chased me sore, l a bird,
4: 3 cruel, l the ostriches in the wilderness.
8 it is withered, it is become l a stick.
5:10 Our skin was black l an oven because of
Ezk 1: 7 of their feet *was* l the sole of a calf's foot:
7 sparkled l the colour of burnished brass.
13 appearance *was* l burning coals of fire,
13 coals of fire, *and* l the appearance of
16 and their work *was* l unto the colour of a
24 noise of their wings, l the noise of great
2: 8 Be not thou rebellious l that rebellious
5: 9 the l, because of all thine abominations. H3644
7:16 on the mountains l doves of the valleys,
12:11 Say, I *am* your sign: l as I have done, so
13: 4 O Israel, thy prophets are l the foxes in
16:16 thereupon: *the l things* shall not come,
18:10 doeth the l to *any* one of these *things*, H251
14 and considereth, and doeth not such l,
19:10 Thy mother *is* l a vine in thy blood,
20:36 L as I pleaded with your fathers in the
22:25 in the midst thereof, l a roaring lion
27 Her princes in the midst thereof *are* l
23:18 alienated from her, l as my mind was
20 and whose issue *is l* the issue of horses.
25: 8 house of Judah *is* l unto all the heathen;
26: 4 her, and make her l the top of a rock.
14 And I will make thee l the top of a rock:
19 a desolate city, l the cities that are not
27:32 What *city is* l Tyrus, like the destroyed
32 l the destroyed in the midst of the sea?
31: 2 Whom art thou l in thy greatness? H1819
8 fir trees were not l his boughs, and the H1819
8 trees were not l his branches; nor any H1819
8 of God was l unto him in his beauty. H1819
18 To whom art thou thus l in glory and in H1819
32: 2 unto him, Thou art l a young lion of the H1819
14 rivers to run l oil, saith the Lord GOD.
36:35 desolate is become l the garden of Eden;
37 I will increase them with men l a flock.
38: 9 Thou shalt ascend and come l a storm,
9 thou shalt be l a cloud to cover the land,
40: 3 appearance *was* l the appearance of
25 round about, l those windows: the length
41:25 and palm trees, l as *were* made upon the
42:11 And the way before them *was* l the
43: 2 east: and his voice *was* l a noise of many
3 the visions *were* l the vision that I saw
45:25 shall he do the l in the feast of the seven
Dan 1:19 all was found none l Daniel, Hananiah,
2:35 and became l the chaff of the summer
3:25 form of the fourth is l the Son of God. H1821
4:33 hairs were grown l eagles' *feathers*, and
33 *feathers*, and his nails l birds' *claws*.
5:11 and wisdom, l the wisdom of the gods,
21 heart was made l the beasts, and his H5974
21 fed him with grass l oxen, and his body
7: 4 The first *was* l a lion, and had eagle's
5 And behold another beast, a second, l H1821
6 After this I beheld, and lo another, l a
8 in this horn *were* eyes l the eyes of man,
9 the hair of his head l the pure wool: his
9 his throne *was l* the fiery flame, *and* his
13 and, behold, *one* l the Son of man came
10: 6 His body also *was* l the beryl, and his
6 arms and his feet l in colour to polished
6 of his words l the voice of a multitude.
16 And, behold, *one* l the similitude of the
18 touched me *one* l the appearance of a
11:40 come against him l a whirlwind, with
Hos 2: 3 her l a dry land, and slay her with thirst.
4: 9 And there shall be, l people, like priest:
9 And there shall be, like people, l priest:
5:10 The princes of Judah were l them that
10 pour out my wrath upon them l water.
6: 7 But they l men have transgressed the
7: 6 For they have made ready their heart l
11 Ephraim also is l a silly dove without
16 High: they are l a deceitful bow: their

Hos 9:10 I found Israel l grapes in the wilderness;
11 glory shall fly away l a bird, from the
11:10 he shall roar l a lion: when he shall
13: 8 l a lion: the wild beast shall tear them.
14: 8 and observed him: I *am* l a green fir tree.
Joel 1: 8 Lament l a virgin girded with sackcloth
2: 2 not been ever the l, neither shall be any H3644
5 L the noise of chariots on the tops of
5 shall they leap, l the noise of a flame of
7 They shall run l mighty men; they shall
7 shall climb the wall l men of war; and
9 shall enter in at the windows l a thief.
Am 2: 9 whose height *was* l the height of the
5: 6 lest he break out l fire in the house of
6: 5 instruments of musick, l David;
9: 5 it shall rise up wholly l a flood; and shall
9 among all nations, l as *corn* is sifted in a
Jna 1: 4 sea, so that the ship was l to be broken. H2803
Mic 1: 8 l the dragons, and mourning as the owls.
4:10 O daughter of Zion, l a woman in travail:
7:17 They shall lick the dust l a serpent, they
17 out of their holes l worms of the earth:
18 Who *is* a God l unto thee, that H3644
Nah 1: 6 fury is poured out l fire, and the rocks
2: 4 they shall seem l torches, they shall run
4 torches, they shall run l the lightnings.
8 But Nineveh *is* of old l a pool of water:
3:12 All thy strong holds *shall be l* fig trees
15 off, it shall eat thee up l the cankerworm:
Hab 3:19 he will make my feet l hinds' *feet*, and he
Zep 1:17 that they shall walk l blind men, because
2:13 a desolation, *and* dry l a wilderness.
Zec 1: 6 they returned and said, L as the LORD of
5: 9 for they had wings l the wings of a stork:
9:15 l bowls, *and* as the corners of the altar.
10: 7 And *they of* Ephraim shall be l a mighty
12: 6 the governors of Judah l an hearth of fire
6 the wood, and l a torch of fire in a sheaf;
14: 5 yea, ye shall flee, l as ye fled from before
20 shall be l the bowls before the altar.
Mal 3: 2 *is* l a refiner's fire, and like fullers' soap:
2 *is* like a refiner's fire, and l fullers' soap:
Mt 3:16 l a dove, and lighting upon him: G5616
6: 8 Be not ye therefore l unto them: for G3666
29 glory was not arrayed l one of these. G5613
11:16 generation? It is l unto children sitting G3664
12:13 it was restored whole, l as the other. G5613
13:31 of heaven is l to a grain of mustard G3664
33 of heaven is l unto leaven, which G3664
44 Again, the kingdom of heaven is l unto G3664
45 Again, the kingdom of heaven is l unto G3664
47 Again, the kingdom of heaven is l unto G3664
52 of heaven is l unto a man *that is* an G3664
20: 1 For the kingdom of heaven is l unto a G3664
21:24 if ye tell me, I in l wise will tell you by G2504
22: 2 The kingdom of heaven is l unto a G3666
39 And the second *is* l unto it, Thou shalt G3664
23:27 for ye are l unto whited sepulchres, G3945
28: 3 His countenance was l lightning, and G5613
Mk 1:10 Spirit l a dove descending upon him: G5616
4:31 *It is* l a grain of mustard seed, which, G5613
7: 8 and many other such l things ye do. G3946
13 and many such l things do ye. G3946
12:31 And the second *is* l, *namely* this, Thou G3664
13:29 So ye in l manner, when ye shall see G2532
Lk 3:22 in a bodily shape l a dove upon him, G5616
6:23 in heaven: for in the l manner did their G5024
47 them, I will shew you to whom he is l: G3664
48 He is l a man which built an house, and G3664
49 But he that heareth, and doeth not, is l G3664
7:31 this generation? and to what are they l? G3664
32 They are l unto children sitting in the G3664
12:27 glory was not arrayed l one of these. G5613
36 And ye yourselves l unto men that wait G3664
13:18 l? and whereunto shall I resemble it? G3664
19 It is l a grain of mustard seed, which a G3664
21 It is l leaven, which a woman took and G3664
20:31 And the third took her; and in l G5615
Jn 1:32 l a dove, and it abode upon him. G5616
7:46 answered, Never man spake l this man. G5613
8:55 I shall be a liar l unto you: but I know G3664
9: 9 *said*, He is l him: *but* he said, I am *he*. G3664
Act 1:11 shall so come in l manner as ye have G3779
2: 3 cloven tongues l as of fire, and it sat G5616
3:22 of your brethren, l unto me; him shall G3945
7:37 brethren, l unto me; him shall ye hear. G5613
8:32 to the slaughter; and l a lamb dumb G5613
11:17 God gave them the l gift as *he did* unto G2470
14:15 also are men of l passions with you, G3663
17:29 the Godhead is l unto gold, or silver, G3664
19:25 the workmen of l occupation, and said, G5108
Ro 1:23 an image made l to corruptible man, G3667
28 And even as they did not l to retain G1381
6: 4 into death: that l as Christ was raised G5618
9:29 and been made l unto Gomorrha. G3666
1Co 16:13 in the faith, quit you l men, be strong. G407
Gal 5:21 and such l: of the which I tell you G3664
Php 3:21 it may be fashioned l unto his glorious G4832
1Th 2:14 also have suffered l things of your own G5024
1Ti 2: 9 In l manner also, that women adorn G5615
Heb 2:17 him to be made l unto *his* brethren, G3666
4:15 l as *we are, yet* without sin. G2596+G3665
7: 3 of life; but made l unto the Son of God; G871
Jas 1: 6 he that wavereth is l a wave of the sea G1503
23 and not a doer, he is l unto a man G1503
5:17 Elias was a man subject to l passions G3663
1Pt 3:21 The l figure whereunto *even* baptism G499
2Pt 1: 1 that have obtained l precious faith with G2472
1Jn 3: 2 be l him; for we shall see him as he is. G3664
Jude 7 cities about them in l manner, giving G3664
Rev 1:13 candlesticks *one* l unto the Son of man, G3664
14 His head and *his* hairs *were* white l G5616
15 And his feet l unto fine brass, as if they G3664
2:18 who hath his eyes l unto a flame of fire, G5613
18 of fire, and his feet *are* l fine brass; G3664
4: 3 And he that sat was to look upon l a G3664
3 the throne, in sight l unto an emerald. G3664
6 *was* a sea of glass l unto crystal: and in G3664
7 And the first beast *was* l a lion, and the G3664
7 the second beast l a calf, and the third G3664
7 the fourth beast *was* l a flying eagle. G3664
9: 7 And the shapes of the locusts *were* l G3664
7 as it were crowns l gold, and their faces G3664
10 And they had tails l unto scorpions, G3664
19 for their tails *were* l unto serpents, and G3664
11: 1 And there was given me a reed l unto a G3664
13: 2 And the beast which I saw was l unto a G3664
4 saying, Who *is* l unto the beast? who G3664
11 l a lamb, and he spake as a dragon. G3664
14:14 the cloud *one* sat l unto the Son of G3664
16:13 And I saw three unclean spirits l frogs G3664
18:18 What *city is* l unto this great city! G3664
21 And a mighty angel took up a stone l a G5613
21:11 and her light *was* l unto a stone most G3664
11 even l a jasper stone, clear as crystal; G5613
18 city *was* pure gold, l unto clear glass. G3664

LIKED
1Ch 28: 4 he l me to make *me* king over all Israel: H7521

LIKEMINDED
Ro 15: 5 you to be l one toward G3588+G846+5426
Php 2: 2 that ye be l, having the G3588+G846+5426
20 For I have no man l, who will naturally G2473

LIKEN
Isa 40:18 To whom then will ye l God? or what H1819
25 To whom then will ye l me, or shall I be H1819
46: 5 To whom will ye l me, and make *me* H1819
Lam 2:13 what thing shall I l to thee, O daughter H1819
Mt 7:24 doeth them, I will l him unto a wise G3666
11:16 But whereunto shall I l this generation? G3666
Mk 4:30 And he said, Whereunto shall we l the G3666
Lk 7:31 then shall I l the men of this G3666
13:20 And again he said, Whereunto shall I l G3666

LIKENED
Ps 89: 6 of the mighty can be l unto the LORD? H1819
Jer 6: 2 I have l the daughter of Zion to a H1820
Mt 7:26 them not, shall be l unto a foolish man, G3666
13:24 of heaven is l unto a man which sowed G3666
18:23 Therefore is the kingdom of heaven l G3666
25: 1 Then shall the kingdom of heaven be l G3666

LIKENESS
Gen 1:26 image, after our l: and let them have H1823
5: 1 man, in the l of God made he him; H1823
3 *a son* in his own l, after his image; and H1823
Ex 20: 4 image, or any l *of any thing* that *is* in H8544
Dt 4:16 of any figure, the l of male or female, H8403
17 The l of any beast that *is* on the earth, H8403
17 *is* on the earth, the l of any winged fowl H8403
18 The l of any thing that creepeth on the H8403
18 on the ground, the l of any fish that *is* H8403
23 image, *or* the l of any *thing*, which H8544
25 image, *or* the l of any *thing*, and shall H8544
5: 8 image, *or* any l *of any thing* that *is* in H8544
Ps 17:15 be satisfied, when I awake, with thy l. H8544
Isa 40:18 or what l will ye compare unto him? H1823
Ezk 1: 5 Also out of the midst thereof *came* the l H1823
5 appearance; they had the l of a man. H1823
10 As for the l of their faces, they four had H1823
13 As for the l of the living creatures, their H1823
16 and they four had one l: and their H1823
22 And the l of the firmament upon the H1823
26 their heads *was* the l of a throne, as the H1823
26 and upon the l of the throne *was* the H1823
26 the throne *was* the l as the appearance H1823
28 appearance of the l of the glory of the H1823
8: 2 Then I beheld, and lo a l as the H1823
10: 1 as the appearance of the l of a throne. H1823
10 they four had one l, as if a wheel had H1823
21 wings; and the l of the hands of a man H1823
22 And the l of their faces *was* the same H1823
Act 14:11 are come down to us in the l of men. G3666
Ro 6: 5 together in the l of his death, we shall G3667
5 shall be also *in the l of his* resurrection:
8: 3 his own Son in the l of sinful flesh, and G3667
Php 2: 7 servant, and was made in the l of men: G3667

LIKETH
Dt 23:16 l him best: thou shalt not oppress him. H2869
Est 8: 8 Write ye also for the Jews, as it l you, in H2896
Am 4: 5 offerings: for this l you, O ye children of H157

LIKEWISE
Ex 22:30 L shalt thou do with thine oxen, *and* H3651
26: 4 the coupling; and l shalt thou make in H3651
27:11 And l for the north side in length *there* H3651
36:11 in the coupling: l he made in the H3651
Lev 7: 1 L this *is* the law of the trespass H2063
Dt 9:23 L when the LORD sent you from
12:30 serve their gods? even so will I do l. H3651
15:17 unto thy maidservant thou shalt do l. H3651
22: 3 thou do l: thou mayest not hide thyself. H3651
Jdg 1: 3 the Canaanites; and I l will go with thee H1571
7: 5 shalt thou set by himself; l every one that
17 on me, and do l: and, behold, when I H3651
8: 8 and spake unto them l: and the men of H2063
9:49 And all the people l cut down every H1571
1Sa 14:22 L all the men of Israel which had hid
19:21 and they prophesied l. And Saul sent H1571
31: 5 l upon his sword, and died with him. H1571
2Sa 1:11 and l all the men that *were* with him: H1571
17: 5 also, and let us hear l what he saith. H1571
1Ki 11: 8 And l did he for all his strange wives, H3651
1Ch 10: 5 dead, he fell l on the sword, and died. H1571
18: 8 L from Tibhath, and from Chun, cities of
19:15 were fled, they l fled before Abishai H1571
23:30 and praise the LORD, and l at even; H3651
24:31 These l cast lots over against their H1571
27: 4 course l *were* twenty and four thousand.
28:16 table; and *l* silver for the tables of silver:
17 every bason; and *l silver* by weight for
29:24 men, and all the sons l of king David, H1571
2Ch 3:11 the other wing *was l* five cubits, reaching
29:22 *it* on the altar: l, when they had killed
Neh 4:22 L at the same time said I unto the H1571
5:10 I l, *and* my brethren, and my servants, H1571
Est 1:18 *L* shall the ladies of Persia and Media
4:16 maidens will fast l; and so will I go in H3651
Job 31:38 or that the furrows l thereof complain; H3162
37: 6 Be thou *on* the earth; l to the small rain,
Ps 49:10 For he seeth *that* wise men die, l the H3162
52: 5 God shall l destroy thee for ever, he H1571
Ecc 7:22 that thou thyself l hast cursed others. H1571
Isa 30:24 The oxen l and the young asses that ear
Jer 40:11 L when all the Jews that *were* in Moab, H1571
Ezk 13:17 L, thou son of man, set thy face against
40:16 round about, and l to the arches: and H3651
46: 3 L the people of the land shall worship at
Nah 1:12 *they be* quiet, and l many, yet thus H3651
Mt 17:12 they listed. L shall also the Son of G3779
18:35 So l shall my heavenly Father do also G2532
20: 5 the sixth and ninth hour, and did l. G5615
10 and they l received every man a penny. G2532
21:30 And he came to the second, and said l. G5615
36 than the first: and they did unto them l. G5615
22:26 L the second also, and the third, unto G3668
24:33 So l ye, when ye shall see all these G2532
25:17 And l he that *had received* two, he also G5615
26:35 deny thee. L also said all the disciples. G3668
27:41 L also the chief priests mocking *him*, G3668
Mk 4:16 And these are they l which are sown on G3668
12:21 neither left he any seed: and the third l. G5615
14:31 thee in any wise. L also said they all. G5615
15:31 L also the chief priests mocking said G3668

Lk 2:38 gave thanks l unto the Lord, and spake *G437*
3:11 and he that hath meat, let him do l. *G3668*
14 And the soldiers l demanded of him, *G2532*
5:33 make prayers, and l *the disciples* of the *G3668*
6:31 should do to you, do ye also to them l. *G3668*
10:32 And l a Levite, when he was at the *G3668*
37 said Jesus unto him, Go, and do thou l. *G3668*
13: 3 except ye repent, ye shall all l perish. *G5615*
5 except ye repent, ye shall all l perish. *G3668*
14:33 So l, whosoever he be of you that *G3779*
15: 7 I say unto you, that l joy shall be in *G3779*
10 L, I say unto you, there is joy in the *G3779*
16:25 good things, and l Lazarus evil things: *G3668*
17:10 So l ye, when ye shall have done all *G2532*
28 L also as it was in the days of Lot; they *G3668*
31 is in the field, let him l not return back. *G3668*
19:19 And he said l to him, Be thou also over *G2532*
21:31 So l ye, when ye see these things come *G2532*
22:20 L also the cup after supper, saying, *G5615*
36 let him take *it*, and l *his* scrip: and he *G3668*
Jn 5:19 he doeth, these also doeth the Son l. *G3668*
6:11 l of the fishes as much as they would. *G3668*
21:13 bread, and giveth them, and fish l. *G3668*
Act 3:24 spoken, have l foretold of these days. *G2532*
Ro 1:27 And l also the men, leaving the natural *G3668*
6:11 L reckon ye also yourselves to be dead *G3779*
8:26 L the Spirit also helpeth our *G5615*
16: 5 L *greet* the church that is in their *G2532*
1Co 7: 3 and l also the wife unto the husband. *G3668*
4 the husband: and l also the husband *G3668*
22 Lord's freeman: l also he that is called, *G3668*
14: 9 So l ye, except ye utter by the tongue *G2532*
Gal 2:13 And the other Jews dissembled l with *G2532*
Col 4:16 ye l read the *epistle* from Laodicea. *G2532*
1Ti 3: 8 L *must* the deacons *be* grave, not *G5615*
5:25 L also the good works *of some* are *G5615*
Tit 2: 3 The aged women l, that *they be* in *G5615*
6 Young men l exhort to be sober *G5615*
Heb 2:14 he also himself l took part of the same; *G3898*
Jas 2:25 L also was not Rahab the harlot *G3668*
1Pt 3: 1 L, ye wives, *be* in subjection to your *G3668*
7 L, ye husbands, dwell with *them* *G3668*
4: 1 arm yourselves l with the same mind: *G2532*
5: 5 L, ye younger, submit yourselves unto *G3668*
Jude 8 L also these *filthy* dreamers defile the *G3668*
Rev 8:12 not for a third part of it, and the night l. *G3668*

LIKHI
1Ch 7:19 and Shechem, and L, and Aniam. H3949

LIKING
Job 39: 4 Their young ones are in good l, they H2492
Dan 1:10 see your faces worse l than the children H2196

LILIES
1Ki 7:26 of l: it contained two thousand baths. H7799
2Ch 4: 5 with flowers of l; *and* it received and H7799
Song 2:16 and I *am* his: he feedeth among the l. H7799
4: 5 that are twins, which feed among the l. H7799
5:13 *like* l, dropping sweet smelling myrrh. H7799
6: 2 to feed in the gardens, and to gather l. H7799
3 beloved *is* mine: he feedeth among the l. H7799
7: 2 *is like* an heap of wheat set about with l. H7799
Mt 6:28 Consider the l of the field, how they *G2918*
Lk 12:27 Consider the l how they grow: they toil *G2918*

LILY
1Ki 7:19 *were* of l work in the porch, four cubits. H7799
22 And upon the top of the pillars *was* l H7799
Song 2: 1 I *am* the rose of Sharon, *and* the l of the H7799
2 As the l among thorns, so *is* my love H7799
Hos 14: 5 l, and cast forth his roots as Lebanon. H7799

LIME
Isa 33:12 be *as* the burnings of l: *as* thorns cut up H7875
Am 2: 1 the bones of the king of Edom into l: H7875

LIMIT
Ezk 43:12 the whole l thereof round about H1366

LIMITED
Ps 78:41 God, and l the Holy One of Israel. H8428

LIMITETH
Heb 4: 7 Again, he l a certain day, saying in *G3724*

LINE
Jos 2:18 shalt bind this l of scarlet thread in the H8615
21 she bound the scarlet l in the window. H8615
2Sa 8: 2 them with a l, casting them down H2256
2 and with one full l to keep alive. And *so* H2256
1Ki 7:15 high apiece: and a l of twelve cubits did H2339
23 five cubits: and a l of thirty cubits did H6957
2Ki 21:13 And I will stretch over Jerusalem the l H6957
2Ch 4: 2 thereof; and a l of thirty cubits did H6957
Job 38: 5 or who hath stretched the l upon it? H6957
Ps 19: 4 Their l is gone out through all the H6957
78:55 an inheritance by l, and made the tribes H2256
Isa 28:10 upon precept; l upon line, line upon H6957
10 precept; line upon l, line upon line; here H6957
10 line upon line, l upon line; here a little, H6957
10 upon l; here a little, *and* there a little: H6957
13 upon precept; l upon line, line upon H6957
13 precept; line upon l, line upon line; here H6957
13 line upon line, l upon line; here a little, H6957
13 line, line upon l; here a little, *and* there H6957
17 Judgment also will I lay to the l, and H6957
34:11 out upon it the l of confusion, and the H6957
17 it unto them by l: they shall possess it H6957
44:13 it out with a l; he fitteth it with planes, H8279
Jer 31:39 And the measuring l shall yet go forth H6957
Lam 2: 8 hath stretched out a l, he hath not H6957
Ezk 40: 3 of brass, with a l of flax in his hand, H6616
47: 3 And when the man that had the l in his H6957
Am 7:17 shall be divided by l; and thou shalt die H2256
Zec 1:16 of hosts, and a l shall be stretched forth H6957
2: 1 a man with a measuring l in his hand. H2256
2Co 10:16 l of things made ready to our hand. *G2583*

LINEAGE
Lk 2: 4 he was of the house and l of David:) *G3965*

LINEN
Gen 41:42 l, and put a gold chain about his neck; H8336
Ex 25: 4 and scarlet, and fine l, and goats' *hair,* H8336
26: 1 *of* fine twined l, and blue, and purple, H8336
31 and fine twined l of cunning work: with H8336
36 fine twined l, wrought with needlework. H8336
27: 9 *of* fine twined l of an hundred cubits H8336
16 scarlet, and fine twined l, wrought with H8336
18 fine twined l, and their sockets *of* brass. H8336
28: 5 blue, and purple, and scarlet, and fine l. H8336
6 and fine twined l, with cunning work. H8336
8 purple, and scarlet, and fine twined l. H8336
15 and *of* fine twined l, shalt thou make it. H8336
39 the coat of fine l, and thou shalt make H8336
39 the mitre *of* fine l, and thou shalt make H8336
42 And thou shalt make them l breeches to H906
35: 6 and scarlet, and fine l, and goats' *hair,* H8336
23 scarlet, and fine l, and goats' *hair,* and H8336
25 of purple, *and* of scarlet, *and* of fine l. H8336
35 scarlet, and in fine l, and of the weaver, H8336
36: 8 *of* fine twined l, and blue, and purple, H8336
35 and fine twined l: *with* cherubims made H8336
37 and fine twined l, of needlework; H8336
38: 9 *of* fine twined l, an hundred cubits: H8336
16 court round about *were* of fine twined l. H8336
18 and fine twined l: and twenty cubits H8336
23 and in purple, and in scarlet, and fine l. H8336
39: 2 purple, and scarlet, and fine twined l. H8336
3 and in the fine l, *with* cunning work. H8336
5 l; as the LORD commanded Moses. H8336
8 purple, and scarlet, and fine twined l. H8336
24 and purple, and scarlet, *and* twined *l.*
27 And they made coats *of* fine l *of* woven H8336
28 And a mitre *of* fine l, and goodly H8336
28 bonnets *of* fine l, and linen breeches *of* H8336
28 and l breeches *of* fine twined linen, H906
28 and linen breeches *of* fine twined l, H8336
29 And a girdle *of* fine twined l, and blue, H8336
Lev 6:10 And the priest shall put on his l H906
10 garment, and his l breeches shall he put H906
13:47 *it be* a woollen garment, or a l garment; H6593
48 Whether *it be* in the warp, or woof; of l, H6593
52 in woollen or in l, or any thing of skin, H6593
59 of woollen or l, either in the warp, or H6593
16: 4 He shall put on the holy l coat, and he H906
4 and he shall have the l breeches upon his H906
4 be girded with a l girdle, and with the H906
4 girdle, and with the l mitre shall he be H906
23 shall put off the l garments, which he H906
32 on the l clothes, *even* the holy garments: H906
19:19 of l and woollen come upon thee. H8162
Dt 22:11 sorts, *as* of woollen and l together. H6593
1Sa 2:18 *being* a child, girded with a l ephod. H906
22:18 and five persons that did wear a l ephod. H906
2Sa 6:14 and David *was* girded with a l ephod. H906
1Ki 10:28 out of Egypt, and l yarn: the king's H4723
1Ki 10:28 received the l yarn at a price. H4723
1Ch 4:21 wrought fine l, of the house of Ashbea, H948
15:27 with a robe of fine l, and all the Levites H948
27 David also *had* upon him an ephod of l. H906
2Ch 1:16 out of Egypt, and l yarn: the king's H4723
16 received the l yarn at a price. H4723
2:14 in blue, and in fine l, and in crimson; H948
3:14 fine l, and wrought cherubims thereon. H948
5:12 arrayed in white l, having cymbals and H948
Est 1: 6 with cords of fine l and purple to silver H948
8:15 a garment of fine l and purple: and the H948
Prv 7:16 with carved *works,* with fine l of Egypt. H330
31:24 She maketh fine l, and selleth *it;* and H5466
Isa 3:23 The glasses, and the fine l, and the H5466
Jer 13: 1 Go and get thee a l girdle, and put it H6593
Ezk 9: 2 them *was* clothed with l, with a writer's H906
3 the man clothed with l, which *had* the H906
11 And, behold, the man clothed with l, H906
10: 2 the man clothed with l, and said, Go in H906
6 the man clothed with l, saying, Take fire H906
7 clothed with l: who took *it*, and went out. H906
16:10 with fine l, and I covered thee with silk. H8336
13 *was of* fine l, and silk, and broidered H8336
27: 7 Fine l with broidered work from Egypt H8336
16 work, and fine l, and coral, and agate. H948
44:17 be clothed with l garments; and no H6593
18 They shall have l bonnets upon their H6593
18 and shall have l breeches upon their H6593
Dan 10: 5 man clothed in l, whose loins *were* girded H906
12: 6 And *one* said to the man clothed in l, H906
7 And I heard the man clothed in l, which H906
Mt 27:59 body, he wrapped it in a clean l cloth, *G4616*
Mk 14:51 man, having a l cloth cast about *his* *G4616*
52 And he left the l cloth, and fled from *G4616*
15:46 And he bought fine l, and took him *G4616*
46 him in the l, and laid him in a sepulchre *G4616*
Lk 16:19 l, and fared sumptuously every day: *G1040*
23:53 and wrapped it in l, and laid it in a *G4616*
24:12 down, he beheld the l clothes laid by *G3608*
Jn 19:40 and wound it in l clothes with the *G3608*
20: 5 the l clothes lying; yet went he not in. *G3608*
6 sepulchre, and seeth the l clothes lie, *G3608*
7 head, not lying with the l clothes, but *G3608*
Rev 15: 6 in pure and white l, and having their *G3043*
18:12 of pearls, and fine l, and purple, and *G1040*
16 was clothed in fine l, and purple, and *G1039*
19: 8 be arrayed in fine l, clean and white: for *G1039*
8 the fine l is the righteousness of saints. *G1039*
14 clothed in fine l, white and clean. *G1039*

LINES
2Sa 8: 2 even with two l measured he to put H2256
Ps 16: 6 The l are fallen unto me in pleasant H2256

LINGERED
Gen 19:16 And while he l, the men laid hold upon H4102
43:10 For except we had l, surely now we had H4102

LINGERETH
2Pt 2: 3 now of a long time l not, and their *G691*

LINTEL
Ex 12:22 and strike the l and the two side posts H4947
23 the blood upon the l, and on the two H4947
1Ki 6:31 *of* olive tree: the l *and* side posts *were* H352
Am 9: 1 he said, Smite the l of the door, that the H3730

LINTELS
Zep 2:14 lodge in the upper l of it; *their* voice H3730

LINUS
2Ti 4:21 L, and Claudia, and all the brethren. *G3044*

LION
Gen 49: 9 he couched as a l, and as an old lion; who H738
9 and as an old l; who shall rouse him up? H3833
Nu 23:24 rise up as a great l, and lift up himself H3833
24 up himself as a young l: he shall not lie H738
24: 9 He couched, he lay down as a l, and as a H738
9 and as a great l: who shall stir him up? H3833
Dt 33:20 he dwelleth as a l, and teareth the arm H3833
Jdg 14: 5 behold, a young l roared against him. H738
8 the carcase of the l: and, behold, *there* H738
8 of bees and honey in the carcase of the l. H738
9 the honey out of the carcase of the l. H738
18 *is* stronger than a l? And he said unto H738
1Sa 17:34 and there came a l, and a bear, and took H738
36 Thy servant slew both the l and the bear: H738
37 of the paw of the l, and out of the paw of H738

2Sa 17:10 *is* as the heart of a l, shall utterly melt: for H738
23:20 a l in the midst of a pit in time of snow: H738
1Ki 13:24 And when he was gone, a l met him by H738
24 by it, the l also stood by the carcase. H738
25 cast in the way, and the l standing by the H738
26 him unto the l, which hath torn him, H738
28 and the ass and the l standing by the H738
28 by the carcase: the l had not eaten the H738
20:36 from me, a l shall slay thee. And as H738
36 from him, a l found him, and slew him. H738
1Ch 11:22 and slew a l in a pit in a snowy day. H738
Job 4:10 The roaring of the l, and the voice of the H738
10 voice of the fierce l, and the teeth of the H7826
11 The old l perisheth for lack of prey, and H3918
10:16 me as a fierce l: and again thou shewest H7826
28: 8 trodden it, nor the fierce l passed by it. H7826
38:39 Wilt thou hunt the prey for the l? or fill H3833
Ps 7: 2 Lest he tear my soul like a l, rending *it* in H738
10: 9 He lieth in wait secretly as a l in his den: H738
17:12 Like as a l *that* is greedy of his prey, and H738
12 were a young l lurking in secret places. H3715
22:13 mouths, *as* a ravening and a roaring l. H738
91:13 Thou shalt tread upon the l and adder: H7826
13 adder: the young l and the dragon shalt H3715
Prv 19:12 The king's wrath *is* as the roaring of a l; H3715
20: 2 *is* as the roaring of a l: *whoso* provoketh H3715
22:13 The slothful *man* saith, *There is* a l H738
26:13 The slothful *man* saith, *There is* a l in H7826
13 *is* a lion in the way; a l *is* in the streets. H738
28: 1 but the righteous are bold as a l. H3715
15 *As* a roaring l, and a ranging bear; *so is* a H738
30:30 A l *which is* strongest among beasts, H3918
Ecc 9: 4 for a living dog is better than a dead l. H738
Isa 5:29 Their roaring *shall be* like a l, they shall H3833
11: 6 the calf and the young l and the fatling H3715
7 and the l shall eat straw like the ox. H738
21: 8 And he cried, A l: My lord, I stand H738
30: 6 the young and old l, the viper and fiery H3918
31: 4 unto me, Like as the l and the young lion H738
4 the lion and the young l roaring on his H3715
35: 9 No l shall be there, nor *any* ravenous H738
38:13 I reckoned till morning, *that*, as a l, so H738
65:25 together, and the l shall eat straw like H738
Jer 2:30 your prophets, like a destroying l. H738
4: 7 The l is come up from his thicket, and H738
5: 6 Wherefore a l out of the forest shall slay H738
12: 8 Mine heritage is unto me as a l in the H738
25:38 He hath forsaken his covert, as the l: for H3715
49:19 Behold, he shall come up like a l from H738
50:44 Behold, he shall come up like a l from H738
Lam 3:10 lying in wait, *and as* a l in secret places. H738
Ezk 1:10 and the face of a l, on the right side: and H738
10:14 of a l, and the fourth the face of an eagle. H738
19: 3 it became a young l, and it learned to H3715
5 of her whelps, *and* made him a young l. H3715
6 became a young l, and learned to catch H3715
22:25 like a roaring l ravening the prey; they H738
32: 2 art like a young l of the nations, and H3715
41:19 the face of a young l toward the palm H3715
Dan 7: 4 The first *was* like a l, and had eagle's H744
Hos 5:14 For I *will be* unto Ephraim as a l, and as H7826
14 and as a young l to the house of Judah: H3715
11:10 he shall roar like a l: when he shall roar, H738
13: 7 Therefore I will be unto them as a l: as a H7826
8 like a l: the wild beast shall tear them. H3833
Joel 1: 6 *are* the teeth of a l, and he hath the cheek H738
6 and he hath the cheek teeth of a great l. H3833
Am 3: 4 Will a l roar in the forest, when he hath H738
4 prey? will a young l cry out of his den, if H3715
8 The l hath roared, who will not fear? the H738
12 of the mouth of the l two legs, or a piece H738
5:19 As if a man did flee from a l, and a bear H738
Mic 5: 8 many people as a l among the beasts of H738
8 forest, as a young l among the flocks of H3715
Nah 2:11 lions, where the l, *even* the old lion, H738
11 the lion, *even* the old l, walked, *and* the H3833
12 The l did tear in pieces enough for his H738
2Ti 4:17 was delivered out of the mouth of the l. *G3023*
1Pt 5: 8 the devil, as a roaring l, walketh about, *G3023*
Rev 4: 7 And the first beast *was* like a l, and the *G3023*
5: 5 not: behold, the L of the tribe of Juda, *G3023*
10: 3 voice, as *when* a l roareth: and when he *G3023*
13: 2 as the mouth of a l: and the dragon *G3023*

LIONESS

Ezk 19: 2 And say, What *is* thy mother? A l: she H3833

LIONESSES

Nah 2:12 strangled for his l, and filled his holes H3833

LIONLIKE

2Sa 23:20 acts, he slew two l men of Moab: he went H739
1Ch 11:22 acts; he slew two l men of Moab: also he H739

LIONS

2Sa 1:23 than eagles, they were stronger than l. H738
1Ki 7:29 the ledges *were* l, oxen, and cherubims: H738
29 and beneath the l and oxen *were* certain H738
36 he graved cherubims, l, and palm trees, H738
10:19 seat, and two l stood beside the stays. H738
20 And twelve l stood there on the one side H738
2Ki 17:25 l among them, which slew *some* of them. H738
26 he hath sent l among them, and, behold, H738
1Ch 12: 8 *like* the faces of l, and *were* as swift as H738
2Ch 9:18 place, and two l standing by the stays: H738
19 And twelve l stood there on the one side H738
Job 4:10 and the teeth of the young l, are broken. H3715
38:39 lion? or fill the appetite of the young l, H3715
Ps 34:10 The young l do lack, and suffer hunger: H3715
35:17 destructions, my darling from the l. H3715
57: 4 My soul *is* among l: *and* I lie *even* H3833
58: 6 the great teeth of the young l, O LORD. H3715
104:21 The young l roar after their prey, and H3715
Isa 5:29 roar like young l: yea, they shall roar, H3715
15: 9 more upon Dimon, l upon him that H738
Jer 2:15 The young l roared upon him, *and* H3715
50:17 Israel *is* a scattered sheep; the l have H738
51:38 They shall roar together like l: they shall H3715
Ezk 19: 2 she lay down among l, she nourished her H738
2 nourished her whelps among young l. H3715
6 And he went up and down among the l, H738
38:13 with all the young l thereof, shall say H3715
Dan 6: 7 O king, he shall be cast into the den of l. H744
12 cast into the den of l? The king answered H744
16 *him* into the den of l. *Now* the king spake H744
19 and went in haste unto the den of l. H744
20 able to deliver thee from the l? H744
24 into the den of l, them, their children, H744
24 their wives; and the l had the mastery of H744
27 delivered Daniel from the power of the l. H744
Nah 2:11 Where *is* the dwelling of the l, and the H738
11 of the young l, where the lion, *even* H3715
13 devour thy young l: and I will cut off thy H3715
Zep 3: 3 Her princes within her *are* roaring l; her H738
Zec 11: 3 l; for the pride of Jordan is spoiled. H3715
Heb 11:33 promises, stopped the mouths of l, *G3023*
Rev 9: 8 and their teeth were as *the teeth* of l. *G3023*
17 *were* as the heads of l; and out of their *G3023*

LION'S

Gen 49: 9 Judah *is* a l whelp: from the prey, my H738
Dt 33:22 And of Dan he said, Dan *is* a l whelp: he H738
Job 4:11 the stout l whelps are scattered abroad. H3833
28: 8 The l whelps have not trodden it, nor H7830
Ps 22:21 Save me from the l mouth: for thou hast H738
Nah 2:11 the l whelp, and none made *them* afraid? H738

LIONS'

Song 4: 8 and Hermon, from the l dens, from the H738
Jer 51:38 like lions: they shall yell as l whelps. H738
Dan 6:22 and hath shut the l mouths, that they H744

LIP

Lev 13:45 l, and shall cry, Unclean, unclean. H8222
Ps 22: 7 out the l, they shake the head, *saying*, H8193
Prv 12:19 The l of truth shall be established for H8193

LIPS

Ex 6:12 hear me, who *am* of uncircumcised l? H8193
30 *am* of uncircumcised l, and how shall H8193
Lev 5: 4 with *his* l to do evil, or to do good, H8193
Nu 30: 6 of her l, wherewith she bound her soul; H8193
8 uttered with her l, wherewith she bound H8193
12 out of her l concerning her vows, H8193
Dt 23:23 That which is gone out of thy l thou H8193
1Sa 1:13 in her heart; only her l moved, but her H8193
2Ki 19:28 my bridle in thy l, and I will turn thee H8193
Job 2:10 evil? In all this did not Job sin with his l. H8193
8:21 with laughing, and thy l with rejoicing. H8193
11: 5 speak, and open his l against thee; H8193
13: 6 and hearken to the pleadings of my l. H8193
15: 6 l: yea, thine own l testify against thee. H8193
16: 5 of my l should asswage *your grief*. H8193
23:12 of his l; I have esteemed the H8193
27: 4 My l shall not speak wickedness, nor H8193
32:20 refreshed: I will open my l and answer. H8193
33: 3 and my l shall utter knowledge clearly. H8193
Ps 12: 2 *with* flattering l *and* with a double H8193
3 The LORD shall cut off all flattering l, H8193
12: 4 our l *are* our own: who *is* lord over us? H8193
16: 4 offer, nor take up their names into my l. H8193
17: 1 prayer, *that goeth* not out of feigned l. H8193
4 by the word of thy l I have kept *me* H8193
21: 2 withholden the request of his l. Selah. H8193
31:18 Let the lying l be put to silence; which H8193
34:13 Keep thy tongue from evil, and thy l H8193
40: 9 refrained my l, O LORD, thou knowest. H8193
45: 2 is poured into thy l: therefore God hath H8193
51:15 O Lord, open thou my l; and my mouth H8193
59: 7 in their l: for who, *say they*, doth hear? H8193
12 the words of their l let them even be H8193
63: 3 better than life, my l shall praise thee. H8193
5 mouth shall praise *thee* with joyful l: H8193
66:14 Which my l have uttered, and my H8193
71:23 My l shall greatly rejoice when I sing H8193
89:34 alter the thing that is gone out of my l. H8193
106:33 so that he spake unadvisedly with his l. H8193
119:13 With my l have I declared all the H8193
171 My l shall utter praise, when thou hast H8193
120: 2 Deliver my soul, O LORD, from lying l, H8193
140: 3 adders' poison *is* under their l. Selah. H8193
9 the mischief of their own l cover them. H8193
141: 3 before my mouth; keep the door of my l. H8193
Prv 4:24 and perverse l put far from thee. H8193
5: 2 and *that* thy l may keep knowledge. H8193
3 For the l of a strange woman drop *as* H8193
7:21 the flattering of her l she forced him. H8193
8: 6 opening of my l *shall be* right things. H8193
7 wickedness *is* an abomination to my l. H8193
10:13 In the l of him that hath understanding H8193
18 He that hideth hatred *with* lying l, and H8193
19 sin: but he that refraineth his l *is* wise. H8193
21 The l of the righteous feed many: but H8193
32 The l of the righteous know what is H8193
12:13 l: but the just shall come out of trouble. H8193
22 Lying l *are* abomination to the LORD: H8193
13: 3 wide his l shall have destruction. H8193
14: 3 the l of the wise shall preserve them. H8193
7 not *in him* the l of knowledge. H8193
23 the talk of the l *tendeth* only to penury. H8193
15: 7 The l of the wise disperse knowledge: H8193
16:10 A divine sentence *is* in the l of the king: H8193
13 Righteous l *are* the delight of kings; H8193
21 sweetness of the l increaseth learning. H8193
23 mouth, and addeth learning to his l. H8193
27 and in his l *there is* as a burning fire. H8193
30 moving his l he bringeth evil to pass. H8193
17: 4 A wicked doer giveth heed to false l; H8193
7 a fool: much less do lying l a prince. H8193
28 l *is esteemed* a man of understanding. H8193
18: 6 A fool's l enter into contention, and his H8193
7 and his l *are* the snare of his soul. H8193
20 the increase of his l shall he be filled. H8193
19: 1 *he that is* perverse in his l, and is a fool. H8193
20:15 the l of knowledge *are* a precious jewel. H8193
19 not with him that flattereth with his l. H8193
22:11 of his l the king *shall be* his friend. H8193
18 thee; they shall withal be fitted in thy l. H8193
23:16 Yea, my reins shall rejoice, when thy l H8193
24: 2 and their l talk of mischief. H8193
26 *Every man* shall kiss *his* l that giveth a H8193
28 cause; and deceive *not* with thy l. H8193
26:23 Burning l and a wicked heart *are like* a H8193
24 He that hateth dissembleth with his l, H8193
27: 2 mouth; a stranger, and not thine own l. H8193
Ecc 10:12 the l of a fool will swallow up himself. H8193
Song 4: 3 Thy l *are* like a thread of scarlet, and H8193
11 Thy l, O *my* spouse, drop *as* the H8193
5:13 sweet flowers: his l *like* lilies, dropping H8193
7: 9 the l of those that are asleep to speak. H8193
Isa 6: 5 a man of unclean l, and I dwell in the H8193
5 people of unclean l: for mine eyes have H8193
7 hath touched thy l; and thine iniquity is H8193
11: 4 breath of his l shall he slay the wicked. H8193
28:11 For with stammering l and another H8193
29:13 and with their l do honour me, but H8193
30:27 *is* heavy: his l are full of indignation, H8193
37:29 my bridle in thy l, and I will turn thee H8193
57:19 I create the fruit of the l; Peace, peace to H8193
59: 3 with iniquity; your l have spoken lies, H8193
Jer 17:16 came out of my l was *right* before thee. H8193
Lam 3:62 The l of those that rose up against me, H8193
Ezk 24:17 not *thy* l, and eat not the bread of men. H8222
22 cover *your* l, nor eat the bread of men. H8222
36: 3 are taken up in the l of talkers, and *are* H8193
Dan 10:16 of men touched my l: then I opened my H8193
Hos 14: 2 so will we render the calves of our l. H8193
Mic 3: 7 their l; for *there is* no answer of God. H8222

Hab 3:16 When I heard, my belly trembled; my l H8193
Mal 2: 6 not found in his l: he walked with me in H8193
7 For the priest's l should keep H8193
Mt 15: 8 *their* l; but their heart is far from me. G5491
Mk 7: 6 *their* l, but their heart is far from me. G5491
Ro 3:13 the poison of asps *is* under their l: G5491
1Co 14:21 tongues and other l will I speak unto G5491
Heb 13:15 fruit of *our* l giving thanks to his name. G5491
1Pt 3:10 evil, and his l that they speak no guile: G5491

LIQUOR
Nu 6: 3 shall he drink any l of grapes, nor eat H4952
Song 7: 2 *which* wanteth not l: thy belly *is like* an H4197

LIQUORS
Ex 22:29 fruits, and of thy l: the firstborn of thy H1831

LISTED
Mt 17:12 whatsoever they l. Likewise shall also G2309
Mk 9:13 they l, as it is written of him. G2309

LISTEN
Isa 49: 1 L, O isles, unto me; and hearken, ye H8085

LISTETH
Jn 3: 8 The wind bloweth where it l, and thou G2309
Jas 3: 4 helm, whithersoever the governor l. G1014

LITTERS
Isa 66:20 in chariots, and in l, and upon mules, H6632

LITTLE
Gen 18: 4 Let a l water, I pray you, be fetched, H4592
19:20 flee unto, and it *is* a l one: Oh, let me H4705
20 it not a l one?) and my soul shall live. H4705
24:17 thee, drink a l water of thy pitcher. H4592
43 thee, a l water of thy pitcher to drink; H4592
30:30 For *it was* l which thou hadst before I H4592
34:29 And all their wealth, and all their l H2945
35:16 and there was but a l way to come to H3530
43: 2 unto them, Go again, buy us a l food. H4592
8 both we, and thou, *and* also our l ones. H2945
11 the man a present, a l balm, and a little H4592
11 a little balm, and a l honey, spices, and H4592
44:20 of his old age, a l one; and his brother H6996
25 said, Go again, *and* buy us a l food. H4592
45:19 of Egypt for your l ones, and for your H2945
46: 5 their father, and their l ones, and their H2945
47:24 and for food for your l ones. H2945
48: 7 yet *there was* but a l way to come unto H3530
50: 8 house: only their l ones, and their H2945
21 nourish you, and your l ones. And he H2945
Ex 10:10 l ones: look to *it;* for evil *is* before you. H2945
24 stayed: let your l ones also go with you. H2945
12: 4 And if the household be too l for the H4591
16:18 he that gathered l had no lack; they H4591
23:30 By l and little I will drive them out from H4592
30 By little and l I will drive them out from H4592
Lev 11:17 And the l owl, and the cormorant, and H3563
Nu 14:31 But your l ones, which ye said should H2945
16:27 and their sons, and their l children. H2945
31: 9 captives, and their l ones, and took the H2945
17 male among the l ones, and kill every H2945
32:16 for our cattle, and cities for our l ones: H2945
17 place: and our l ones shall dwell in the H2945
24 Build you cities for your l ones, and H2945
26 Our l ones, our wives, our flocks, and H2945
Dt 1:39 Moreover your l ones, which ye said H2945
2:34 women, and the l ones, of every city, H2945
3:19 But your wives, and your l ones, and H2945
7:22 before thee by l and little: thou mayest H4592
22 thee by little and l: thou mayest not H4592
14:16 The l owl, and the great owl, and the H3563
20:14 But the women, and the l ones, and the H2945
28:38 *but* l in; for the locust shall consume it. H4592
29:11 Your l ones, your wives, and thy H2945
Jos 1:14 Your wives, your l ones, and your H2945
8:35 the women, and the l ones, and the H2945
19:47 of Dan went out *too l* for them: therefore
22:17 *Is* the iniquity of Peor too l for us, from H4592
Jdg 4:19 me, I pray thee, a l water to drink; for I H4592
18:21 and put the l ones and the cattle and H2945
Ru 2: 7 now, that she tarried a l in the house. H4592
1Sa 2:19 Moreover his mother made him a l H6996
14:29 because I tasted a l of this honey. H4592
43 I did but taste a l honey with the end H4592
15:17 And Samuel said, When thou *wast* l in H6996
20:35 with David, and a l lad with him. H6996
2Sa 12: 3 nothing, save one l ewe lamb, which he H6996
2Sa 12: 8 if *that had been* too l, I would moreover H4592
15:22 and all the l ones that *were* with him. H2945
16: 1 And when David was a l past the top *of* H4592
19:36 Thy servant will go a l way over Jordan H4592
1Ki 3: 7 and I *am but* a l child: I know not *how* H6996
8:64 the LORD *was* too l to receive the burnt H6996
11:17 into Egypt; Hadad *being* yet a l child. H6996
12:10 say unto them, My l *finger* shall be H6995
17:10 a l water in a vessel, that I may drink. H4592
12 in a barrel, and a l oil in a cruse: and, H4592
13 but make me thereof a l cake first, and H6996
18:44 there ariseth a l cloud out of the sea, H6996
20:27 them like two l flocks of kids; but the H2835
2Ki 2:23 there came forth l children out of the H6996
4:10 Let us make a l chamber, I pray thee, H6996
5: 2 of the land of Israel a l maid; and she H6996
14 the flesh of a l child, and he was clean. H6996
19 So he departed from him a l way. H3530
10:18 Baal a l; *but* Jehu shall serve him much. H4592
2Ch 10:10 say unto them, My l *finger* shall be H6995
20:13 l ones, their wives, and their children. H2945
31:18 And to the genealogy of all their l ones, H2945
Ezr 8:21 our l ones, and for all our substance. H2945
9: 8 And now for a l space grace hath been H4592
8 and give us a l reviving in our bondage. H4592
Neh 9:32 all the trouble seem l before thee, that H4591
Est 3:13 young and old, l children and women, H2945
8:11 assault them, *both* l ones and women, H2945
Job 4:12 me, and mine ear received a l thereof. H8102
10:20 me alone, that I may take comfort a l, H4592
21:11 They send forth their l ones like a flock, H5759
24:24 They are exalted for a l while, but are H4592
26:14 his ways: but how l a portion is heard H8102
36: 2 Suffer me a l, and I will shew thee that *I* H2191
Ps 2:12 is kindled but a l. Blessed *are* all they H4592
8: 5 For thou hast made him a l lower than H4592
37:10 For yet a l while, and the wicked *shall* H4592
16 A l that a righteous man hath *is* better H4592
65:12 and the l hills rejoice on every side.
68:27 There *is* l Benjamin *with* their ruler, the H6810
72: 3 people, and the l hills, by righteousness.
114: 4 like rams, *and* the l hills like lambs.
6 like rams; *and* ye l hills, like lambs?
137: 9 dasheth thy l ones against the stones. H5768
Prv 6:10 *Yet* a l sleep, a little slumber, a little H4592
10 *Yet* a little sleep, a l slumber, a little H4592
10 *Yet* a little sleep, a little slumber, a l H4592
10:20 the heart of the wicked *is* l worth. H4592
15:16 Better *is* l with the fear of the LORD H4592
16: 8 Better *is* a l with righteousness than H4592
24:33 *Yet* a l sleep, a little slumber, a little H4592
33 *Yet* a little sleep, a l slumber, a little H4592
33 *Yet* a little sleep, a little slumber, a l H4592
30:24 There be four *things which are* l upon H6996
Ecc 5:12 whether he eat l or much: but the H4592
9:14 *There was* a l city, and few men within H6996
10: 1 savour: *so doth* a l folly him that is in H4592
Song 2:15 Take us the foxes, the l foxes, that spoil H6996
3: 4 *It was* but a l that I passed from them, H4592
8: 8 We have a l sister, and she hath no H6996
Isa 10:25 For yet a very l while, and the H4592
11: 6 together; and a l child shall lead them. H6996
26:20 as it were for a l moment, until the H4592
28:10 upon line; here a l, *and* there a little: H2191
10 upon line; here a little, *and* there a l: H2191
13 upon line; here a l, *and* there a little; H2191
13 a little, *and* there a l; that they might go, H2191
29:17 *Is* it not yet a very l while, and Lebanon H4592
40:15 he taketh up the isles as a very l thing. H1851
54: 8 In a l wrath I hid my face from thee for H8241
60:22 A l one shall become a thousand, and a H6996
63:18 have possessed *it* but a l while: our H4705
Jer 14: 3 And their nobles have sent their l ones H6810
48: 4 Moab is destroyed; her l ones have H6810
51:33 to thresh her: yet a l while, and the H4592
Ezk 9: 6 young, both maids, and l children, and H2945
11:16 will I be to them as a l sanctuary in the H4592
16:47 as *if that were* a very l *thing*, thou wast H4592
31: 4 her l rivers unto all the trees of the field.
40: 7 And *every* l chamber *was* one reed long,
7 and between the l chambers *were* five
10 And the l chambers of the gate eastward
12 The space also before the l chambers
12 on that side: and the l chambers *were* six
13 the roof of *one* l chamber to the roof
16 And *there were* narrow windows to the l
21 And the l chambers thereof *were* three
29 And the l chambers thereof, and the
33 And the l chambers thereof, and the
Ezk 40:36 The l chambers thereof, the posts
Dan 7: 8 them another l horn, before whom H2192
8: 9 And out of one of them came forth a l H4704
11:34 be holpen with a l help: but many shall H4592
Hos 1: 4 Jezreel; for yet a l *while*, and I will H4592
8:10 a l for the burden of the king of princes. H4592
Am 6:11 breaches, and the l house with clefts. H6996
Mic 5: 2 *though* thou be l among the thousands H6810
Hag 1: 6 Ye have sown much, and bring in l; ye H4592
9 much, and, lo, *it came* to l; and when ye H4592
2: 6 Yet once, *it is* a l while, and I will shake H4592
Zec 1:15 for I was but a l displeased, and they H4592
13: 7 I will turn mine hand upon the l ones. H6819
Mt 6:30 much more *clothe* you, O ye of l faith? G3640
8:26 are ye fearful, O ye of l faith? Then he G3640
10:42 unto one of these l ones a cup of cold G3398
14:31 of l faith, wherefore didst thou doubt? G3640
15:34 they said, Seven, and a few l fishes. G2485
16: 8 unto them, O ye of l faith, why reason G3640
18: 2 And Jesus called a l child unto him, G3813
3 and become as l children, ye shall not G3813
4 himself as this l child, the same is G3813
5 And whoso shall receive one such l G3813
6 But whoso shall offend one of these l G3398
10 not one of these l ones; for I say unto G3398
14 that one of these l ones should perish. G3398
19:13 Then were there brought unto him l G3813
14 But Jesus said, Suffer l children, and G3813
26:39 And he went a l farther, and fell on his G3397
Mk 1:19 And when he had gone a l farther G3641
4:36 there were also with him other l ships. G4143
5:23 And besought him greatly, saying, My l G2365
9:42 offend one of *these* l ones that believe G3393
10:14 them, Suffer the l children to come G3813
15 as a l child, he shall not enter therein. G3813
14:35 And he went forward a l, and fell on the G3397
70 And he denied it again. And a l after, G3397
Lk 5: 3 would thrust out a l from the land. And G3641
7:47 l is forgiven, *the same* loveth little. G3641
47 little is forgiven, *the same* loveth l. G3641
12:28 more *will he clothe* you, O ye of l faith? G3640
32 Fear not, l flock; for it is your Father's G3398
17: 2 he should offend one of these l ones. G3398
18:16 and said, Suffer l children to come unto G3813
17 a l child shall in no wise enter therein. G3813
19: 3 the press, because he was l of stature. G3393
17 l, have thou authority over ten cities. G1646
22:58 And after a l while another saw him, G1024
Jn 6: 7 that every one of them may take a l. G1024
7:33 Then said Jesus unto them, Yet a l G3398
12:35 Then Jesus said unto them, Yet a l G3398
13:33 L children, yet a little while I am with G5040
33 Little children, yet a l while I am with G3397
14:19 Yet a l while, and the world seeth me G3397
16:16 A l while, and ye shall not see me: and G3397
16 me: and again, a l while, and ye shall G3397
17 he saith unto us, A l while, and ye shall G3397
17 me: and again, a l while, and ye shall G3397
18 A l while? we cannot tell what he saith. G3397
19 of that I said, A l while, and ye shall not G3397
19 again, a l while, and ye shall see me? G3397
21: 8 And the other disciples came in a l G4143
Act 5:34 to put the apostles forth a l space; G1024
20:12 man alive, and were not a l comforted. G3357
27:28 they had gone a l further, they sounded G1024
28: 2 shewed us no l kindness: for they G5177
1Co 5: 6 a l leaven leaveneth the whole lump? G3398
2Co 8:15 and he that *had gathered* l had no lack. G3641
11: 1 Would to God ye could bear with me a l G3397
16 receive me, that I may boast myself a l. G3397
Gal 4:19 My l children, of whom I travail in G5040
5: 9 A l leaven leaveneth the whole lump. G3398
1Ti 4: 8 For bodily exercise profiteth l: but G3641
5:23 Drink no longer water, but use a l wine G3641
Heb 2: 7 Thou madest him a l lower than the G1024
9 But we see Jesus, who was made a l G1024
10:37 For yet a l while, and he that shall G3397
Jas 3: 5 Even so the tongue is a l member, and G3398
5 how great a matter a l fire kindleth! G3641
4:14 for a l time, and then vanisheth away. G3641
1Jn 2: 1 My l children, these things write I unto G5040
12 I write unto you, l children, because G5040
13 I write unto you, l children, because ye G3813
18 L children, it is the last time: and as ye G3813
28 And now, l children, abide in him; that, G5040
3: 7 L children, let no man deceive you: he G5040
18 My l children, let us not love in word, G5040
4: 4 Ye are of God, l children, and have G5040
5:21 L children, keep yourselves from idols. G5040

Rev 3: 8 it: for thou hast a l strength, and hast G3398
6:11 rest yet for a l season, until their G3398
10: 2 And he had in his hand a l book open: G974
8 Go *and* take the l book which is open in G974
9 him, Give me the l book. And he said G974
10 And I took the l book out of the angel's G974
20: 3 after that he must be loosed a l season. G3398

LITTLE-OWL See LITTLE and OWL.

LIVE
Gen 3:22 the tree of life, and eat, and l for ever: H2425
12:13 and my soul shall l because of thee. H2421
17:18 O that Ishmael might l before thee! H2421
19:20 it not a little one?) and my soul shall l. H2421
20: 7 and thou shalt l: and if thou restore *her* H2421
27:40 And by thy sword shalt thou l, and shalt H2421
31:32 gods, let him not l: before our brethren H2421
42: 2 from thence; that we may l, and not die. H2421
18 third day, This do, and l; *for* I fear God: H2421
43: 8 go; that we may l, and not die, both we, H2421
45: 3 doth my father yet l? And his brethren H2416
47:19 *us* seed, that we may l, and not die, that H2421
Ex 1:16 but if it *be* a daughter, then she shall l. H2425
19:13 or man, it shall not l: when the trumpet H2421
21:35 they shall sell the l ox, and divide the H2416
22:18 Thou shalt not suffer a witch to l. H2421
33:20 for there shall no man see me, and l. H2425
Lev 16:20 and the altar, he shall bring the l goat: H2416
21 the head of the l goat, and confess over H2416
18: 5 do, he shall l in them: I *am* the LORD. H2425
25:35 or a sojourner; that he may l with thee. H2416
36 God; that thy brother may l with thee. H2416
Nu 4:19 But thus do unto them, that they may l, H2421
14:21 But *as* truly *as* I l, all the earth shall be H2416
28 Say unto them, *As truly as* I l, saith the H2416
21: 8 bitten, when he looketh upon it, shall l. H2425
24:23 Alas, who shall l when God doeth this! H2421
Dt 4: 1 do *them,* that ye may l, and go in and H2421
10 that they shall l upon the earth, and H2416
33 of the fire, as thou hast heard, and l? H2421
42 unto one of these cities he might l: H2425
5:33 you, that ye may l, and *that it may be* H2421
8: 1 to do, that ye may l, and multiply, and H2421
3 that man doth not l by bread only, but H2421
3 of the mouth of the LORD doth man l. H2421
12: 1 it, all the days that ye l upon the earth. H2416
16:20 that thou mayest l, and inherit the land H2421
19: 4 thither, that he may l: Whoso killeth his H2425
5 shall flee unto one of those cities, and l: H2425
30: 6 with all thy soul, that thou mayest l. H2416
16 that thou mayest l and multiply: and H2421
19 life, that both thou and thy seed may l: H2421
31:13 God, as long as ye l in the land whither H2416
32:40 hand to heaven, and say, I l for ever. H2416
33: 6 Let Reuben l, and not die; and let *not* H2421
Jos 6:17 the harlot shall l, she and all that *are* H2421
9:15 them, to let them l: and the princes of H2421
20 will even let them l, lest wrath be upon H2421
21 them, Let them l; but let them be hewers H2421
1Sa 20:14 And thou shalt not only while yet I l H2416
2Sa 1:10 that he could not l after that he was H2421
12:22 be gracious to me, that the child may l? H2416
19:34 How long have I to l, that I should go up H2416
1Ki 1:31 said, Let my lord king David l for ever. H2421
8:40 the days that they l in the land which H2416
20:32 I pray thee, let me l. And he said, *Is* he H2421
2Ki 4: 7 and l thou and thy children of the rest. H2421
7: 4 l; and if they kill us, we shall but die. H2421
10:19 he shall not l. But Jehu did *it* in subtilty, H2421
18:32 that ye may l, and not die: and hearken H2421
20: 1 in order; for thou shalt die, and not l. H2421
2Ch 6:31 so long as they l in the land which thou H2416
Neh 2: 3 And said unto the king, Let the king l H2421
5: 2 corn *for them,* that we may eat, and l. H2421
9:29 if a man do, he shall l in them;) and H2421
Est 4:11 that he may l: but I have not been H2421
Job 7:16 I loathe *it;* I would not l alway: let me H2421
14:14 If a man die, shall he l *again*? all the H2421
21: 7 Wherefore do the wicked l, become old, H2421
27: 6 shall not reproach *me* so long as I l. H3117
Ps 22:26 seek him: your heart shall l for ever. H2421
49: 9 That he should still l for ever, *and* not H2421
55:23 men shall not l out half their days; but
63: 4 Thus will I bless thee while I l: I will lift H2416
69:32 and your heart shall l that seek God. H2421
72:15 And he shall l, and to him shall be given H2421
104:33 I will sing unto the LORD as long as I l: H2416
116: 2 will I call upon *him* as long as I l. H3117

Ps 118:17 I shall not die, but l, and declare the H2421
119:17 *that* I may l, and keep thy word. H2421
77 that I may l: for thy law *is* my delight. H2421
116 thy word, that I may l: and let me not be H2421
144 give me understanding, and I shall l. H2421
175 Let my soul l, and it shall praise thee; H2421
146: 2 While I l will I praise the LORD: I will H2416
Prv 4: 4 words: keep my commandments, and l. H2421
7: 2 Keep my commandments, and l; and H2421
9: 6 Forsake the foolish, and l; and go in the H2421
15:27 house; but he that hateth gifts shall l. H2421
Ecc 6: 3 *children,* and l many years, so that H2421
6 Yea, though he l a thousand years H2421
9: 3 l, and after that *they go* to the dead. H2416
9 L joyfully with the wife whom thou H2416
11: 8 But if a man l many years, *and* rejoice H2421
Isa 6: 6 unto me, having a l coal in his hand, H7531
26:14 *They are* dead, they shall not l; *they are* H2421
19 Thy dead *men* shall l, *together with* my H2421
38: 1 in order: for thou shalt die, and not l. H2421
16 O Lord, by these *things men* l, and in all H2421
16 wilt thou recover me, and make me to l. H2421
49:18 come to thee. *As* I l, saith the LORD, H2416
55: 3 and your soul shall l; and I will make an H2421
Jer 21: 9 you, he shall l, and his life shall be H2421
22:24 *As* I l, saith the LORD, though Coniah H2416
27:12 and serve him and his people, and l. H2421
17 of Babylon, and l: wherefore should this H2421
35: 7 in tents; that ye may l many days in the H2421
38: 2 Chaldeans shall l; for he shall have his H2421
2 shall have his life for a prey, and shall l. H2425
17 then thy soul shall l, and this city shall H2421
17 fire; and thou shalt l, and thine house: H2421
20 be well unto thee, and thy soul shall l. H2421
46:18 *As* I l, saith the King, whose name *is* the H2416
Lam 4:20 shadow we shall l among the heathen. H2421
Ezk 3:21 not sin, he shall surely l, because he is H2421
5:11 Wherefore, *as* I l, saith the Lord GOD; H2416
13:19 that should not l, by your lying to my H2421
14:16 *were* in it, *as* I l, saith the Lord GOD, H2416
18 *were* in it, *as* I l, saith the Lord GOD, H2416
20 and Job, *were* in it, *as* I l, saith the Lord H2416
16: 6 *wast* in thy blood, L; yea, I said unto H2421
6 thee *when thou wast* in thy blood, L. H2421
48 *As* I l, saith the Lord GOD, Sodom thy H2416
17:16 *As* I l, saith the Lord GOD, surely in the H2416
19 Lord GOD; *As* I l, surely mine oath that H2416
18: 3 *As* I l, saith the Lord GOD, ye shall not H2416
9 he shall surely l, saith the Lord GOD. H2421
13 shall he then l? he shall not live: he H2425
13 then live? he shall not l: he hath done all H2421
17 iniquity of his father, he shall surely l. H2421
19 and hath done them, he shall surely l. H2421
21 right, he shall surely l, he shall not die. H2421
22 that he hath done he shall l. H2421
23 he should return from his ways, and l? H2421
24 doeth, shall he l? All his righteousness H2425
28 he shall surely l, he shall not die. H2421
32 wherefore turn *yourselves,* and l ye. H2421
20: 3 to inquire of me? *As* I l, saith the Lord H2416
11 *if* a man do, he shall even l in them. H2425
13 do, he shall even l in them; and my H2425
21 man do, he shall even l in them; they H2425
25 judgments whereby they should not l; H2421
31 of Israel? *As* I l, saith the Lord GOD, H2416
33 *As* I l, saith the Lord GOD, surely with a H2416
33:10 away in them, how should we then l? H2421
11 Say unto them, *As* I l, saith the Lord H2416
11 turn from his way and l: turn ye, turn ye H2421
12 be able to l for his *righteousness* H2421
13 he shall surely l; if he trust to his own H2421
15 he shall surely l, he shall not die. H2421
16 is lawful and right; he shall surely l. H2421
19 is lawful and right, he shall l thereby. H2421
27 Lord GOD; *As* I l, surely they that *are* H2416
34: 8 *As* I l, saith the Lord GOD, surely H2416
35: 6 Therefore, *as* I l, saith the Lord GOD, I H2416
11 Therefore, *as* I l, saith the Lord GOD, I H2416
37: 3 can these bones l? And I answered, O H2421
5 breath to enter into you, and ye shall l: H2421
6 in you, and ye shall l; and ye shall know H2421
9 upon these slain, that they may l. H2421
14 you, and ye shall l, and I shall place you H2421
47: 9 shall come, shall l: and there shall be a H2421
9 thing shall l whither the river cometh. H2425
Dan 2: 4 in Syriack, O king, l for ever: tell thy H2418
3: 9 Nebuchadnezzar, O king, l for ever. H2418
5:10 and said, O king, l for ever: let not thy H2418
6: 6 thus unto him, King Darius, l for ever. H2418

Dan 6:21 Daniel unto the king, O king, l for ever. H2418
Hos 6: 2 raise us up, and we shall l in his sight. H2421
Am 5: 4 of Israel, Seek ye me, and ye shall l: H2421
6 Seek the LORD, and ye shall l; lest he H2421
14 Seek good, and not evil, that ye may l: H2421
Jna 4: 3 for *it is* better for me to die than to l. H2416
8 said, *It is* better for me to die than to l. H2416
Hab 2: 4 in him: but the just shall l by his faith. H2421
Zep 2: 9 Therefore *as* I l, saith the LORD of H2416
Zec 1: 5 and the prophets, do they l for ever? H2421
10: 9 l with their children, and turn again. H2421
13: 3 Thou shalt not l; for thou speakest lies H2421
Mt 4: 4 Man shall not l by bread alone, but G2198
9:18 lay thy hand upon her, and she shall l. G2198
Mk 5:23 that she may be healed; and she shall l. G2198
Lk 4: 4 man shall not l by bread alone, but G2198
7:25 and l delicately, are in kings' courts. G5225
10:28 right: this do, and thou shalt l. G2198
20:38 but of the living: for all l unto him. G2198
Jn 5:25 Son of God: and they that hear shall l. G2198
6:51 bread, he shall l for ever: and the bread G2198
57 sent me, and I l by the Father: so he G2198
57 that eateth me, even he shall l by me. G2198
58 that eateth of this bread shall l for ever. G2198
11:25 me, though he were dead, yet shall he l: G2198
14:19 ye see me: because I l, ye shall live also. G2198
19 ye see me: because I live, ye shall l also. G2198
Act 7:19 children, to the end they might not l. G2225
17:28 For in him we l, and move, and have G2198
22:22 earth: for it is not fit that he should l. G2198
25:24 that he ought not to l any longer. G2198
28: 4 the sea, yet vengeance suffereth not to l. G2198
Ro 1:17 as it is written, The just shall l by faith. G2198
6: 2 are dead to sin, l any longer therein? G2198
8 we believe that we shall also l with him: G4800
8:12 not to the flesh, to l after the flesh. G2198
13 For if ye l after the flesh, ye shall die: G2198
13 mortify the deeds of the body, ye shall l. G2198
10: 5 doeth those things shall l by them. G2198
12:18 lieth in you, l peaceably with all men. G1514
14: 8 For whether we l, we live unto the Lord; G2198
8 For whether we live, we l unto the Lord; G2198
8 we l therefore, or die, we are the Lord's. G2198
11 For it is written, *As* I l, saith the Lord, G2198
1Co 9:13 about holy things l *of the things* of the G2068
14 the gospel should l of the gospel. G2198
2Co 4:11 For we which l are alway delivered G2198
5:15 that they which l should not henceforth G2198
15 not henceforth l unto themselves, but G2198
6: 9 we l; as chastened, and not killed; G2198
7: 3 are in our hearts to die and l with *you.* G4800
13: 4 in him, but we shall l with him by the G2198
11 be of one mind, l in peace; and the God G1514
Gal 2:14 thou the Gentiles to l as do the Jews? G2198
19 to the law, that I might l unto God. G2198
20 nevertheless I l; yet not I, but Christ G2198
20 life which I now l in the flesh I live by G2198
20 live in the flesh I l by the faith of the G2198
3:11 *is* evident: for, The just shall l by faith. G2198
12 man that doeth them shall l in them. G2198
5:25 If we l in the Spirit, let us also walk in G2198
Eph 6: 3 mayest l long on the earth. G2071+G3118
Php 1:21 For to me to l *is* Christ, and to die *is* G2198
22 But if I l in the flesh, this *is* the fruit of G2198
1Th 3: 8 For now we l, if ye stand fast in the G2198
5:10 or sleep, we should l together with him. G2198
2Ti 2:11 with *him,* we shall also l with *him:* G4800
3:12 Yea, and all that will l godly in Christ G2198
Tit 2:12 lusts, we should l soberly, righteously, G2198
Heb 10:38 Now the just shall l by faith: but if *any* G2198
12: 9 unto the Father of spirits, and l? G2198
13:18 in all things willing to l honestly. G390
Jas 4:15 will, we shall l, and do this, or that. G2198
1Pt 2:24 to sins, should l unto righteousness: G2198
4: 2 That he no longer should l the rest of *his* G980
6 but l according to God in the spirit. G2198
2Pt 2: 6 unto those that after should l ungodly; G2198
18 clean escaped from them who l in error. G390
1Jn 4: 9 the world, that we might l through him. G2198
Rev 13:14 had the wound by a sword, and did l. G2198

LIVED
Gen 5: 3 And Adam l an hundred and thirty H2421
5 And all the days that Adam l were nine H2425
6 And Seth l an hundred and five years, H2421
7 And Seth l after he begat Enos eight H2421
9 And Enos l ninety years, and begat H2421
10 And Enos l after he begat Cainan eight H2421
12 And Cainan l seventy years, and begat H2421

Gen 5:13 And Cainan l after he begat Mahalaleel H2421
15 And Mahalaleel l sixty and five years, H2421
16 And Mahalaleel l after he begat Jared H2421
18 And Jared l an hundred sixty and two H2421
19 And Jared l after he begat Enoch eight H2421
21 And Enoch l sixty and five years, and H2421
25 And Methuselah l an hundred eighty H2421
26 And Methuselah l after he begat H2421
28 And Lamech l an hundred eighty and H2421
30 And Lamech l after he begat Noah five H2421
9:28 And Noah l after the flood three H2421
11:11 And Shem l after he begat Arphaxad H2421
12 And Arphaxad l five and thirty years, H2425
13 And Arphaxad l after he begat Salah H2421
14 And Salah l thirty years, and begat H2425
15 And Salah l after he begat Eber four H2421
16 And Eber l four and thirty years, and H2421
17 And Eber l after he begat Peleg four H2421
18 And Peleg l thirty years, and begat Reu: H2421
19 And Peleg l after he begat Reu two H2421
20 And Reu l two and thirty years, and H2421
21 And Reu l after he begat Serug two H2421
22 And Serug l thirty years, and begat H2421
23 And Serug l after he begat Nahor two H2421
24 And Nahor l nine and twenty years, H2421
25 And Nahor l after he begat Terah an H2421
26 And Terah l seventy years, and begat H2421
25: 6 yet l, eastward, unto the east country. H2416
7 life which he l, an hundred threescore H2425
47:28 And Jacob l in the land of Egypt H2421
50:22 and Joseph l an hundred and ten years. H2421
Nu 14:38 men that went to search the land, l *still.* H2421
21: 9 he beheld the serpent of brass, he l. H2425
Dt 5:26 the midst of the fire, as we *have,* and l? H2421
2Sa 19: 6 if Absalom had l, and all we had died H2416
1Ki 12: 6 father while he yet l, and said, How do H2416
2Ki 14:17 Joash king of Judah l after the death of H2421
2Ch 10: 6 his father while he yet l, saying, What H2416
25:25 king of Judah l after the death of Joash H2421
Job 42:16 After this l Job an hundred and forty H2421
Ps 49:18 Though while he l he blessed his soul: H2416
Ezk 37:10 them, and they l, and stood up upon H2421
Lk 2:36 a great age, and had l with an husband *G2198*
Act 23: 1 *and* brethren, I have l in all good *G4176*
26: 5 sect of our religion I l a Pharisee. *G2198*
Col 3: 7 walked some time, when ye l in them. *G2198*
Jas 5: 5 Ye have l in pleasure on the earth, and *G5171*
Rev 18: 7 herself, and l deliciously, so much
9 fornication and l deliciously with her,
20: 4 hands; and they l and reigned with *G2198*
5 But the rest of the dead l not again until *G326*

LIVELY

Ex 1:19 for they *are* l, and are delivered ere H2422
Ps 38:19 But mine enemies *are* l, *and* they are H2416
Act 7:38 received the l oracles to give unto us: *G2198*
1Pt 1: 3 begotten us again unto a l hope by the *G2198*
2: 5 Ye also, as l stones, are built up a *G2198*

LIVER

Ex 29:13 *that is* above the l, and the two kidneys, H3516
22 and the caul *above* the l, and the two H3516
Lev 3: 4 the caul above the l, with the kidneys, it H3516
10 the caul above the l, with the kidneys, it H3516
15 the caul above the l, with the kidneys, it H3516
4: 9 the caul above the l, with the kidneys, it H3516
7: 4 *that is* above the l, with the kidneys, it H3516
8:16 and the caul *above* the l, and the two H3516
25 and the caul *above* the l, and the two H3516
9:10 the caul above the l of the sin offering, H3516
19 the kidneys, and the caul *above* the l: H3516
Prv 7:23 Till a dart strike through his l; as a bird H3516
Lam 2:11 are troubled, my l is poured upon the H3516
Ezk 21:21 with images, he looked in the l. H3516

LIVES

Gen 9: 5 And surely your blood of your l will I H5315
45: 7 to save your l by a great deliverance. H2421
47:25 And they said, Thou hast saved our l: H2421
Ex 1:14 And they made their l bitter with hard H2416
Jos 2:13 have, and deliver our l from death. H5315
9:24 sore afraid of our l because of you, and H5315
Jdg 5:18 jeoparded their l unto the death in the H5315
18:25 thy life, with the l of thy household. H5315
2Sa 1:23 pleasant in their l, and in their death H2416
19: 5 thy life, and the l of thy sons and of thy H5315
5 daughters, and the l of thy wives, and H5315
5 thy wives, and the l of thy concubines; H5315
23:17 jeopardy of their l? therefore he would H5315
1Ch 11:19 that have put their l in jeopardy? for H5315
19 *the jeopardy of* their l they brought it. H5315
Est 9:16 and stood for their l, and had rest from H5315
Prv 1:18 blood; they lurk privily for their *own* l. H5315
Jer 19: 7 that seek their l: and their carcases will H5315
9 that seek their l, shall straiten them. H5315
46:26 that seek their l, and into the hand of H5315
48: 6 Flee, save your l, and be like the heath H5315
Lam 5: 9 We gat our bread with *the peril of* our l H5315
Dan 7:12 l were prolonged for a season and time. H2417
Lk 9:56 to destroy men's l, but to save *them.* *G5590*
Act 15:26 Men that have hazarded their l for the *G5590*
27:10 of the lading and ship, but also of our l. *G5590*
1Jn 3:16 to lay down *our* l for the brethren. *G5590*
Rev 12:11 they loved not their l unto the death. *G5590*

LIVEST

Dt 12:19 Levite as long as thou l upon the earth. H3117
2Sa 11:11 with my wife? *as* thou l, and *as* thy soul H2416
Gal 2:14 thou, being a Jew, l after the manner of *G2198*
Rev 3: 1 hast a name that thou l, and art dead. *G2198*

LIVETH

Gen 9: 3 Every moving thing that l shall be meat H2416
Dt 5:24 that God doth talk with man, and he l. H2425
Jdg 8:19 *as* the LORD l, if ye had saved them H2416
Ru 3:13 the LORD l: lie down until the morning. H2416
1Sa 1:26 And she said, Oh my lord, *as* thy soul l, H2416
28 as long as he l he shall be lent to the H3117
14:39 For, *as* the LORD l, which saveth Israel, H2416
45 *as* the LORD l, there shall not one hair H2416
17:55 said, *As* thy soul l, O king, I cannot tell. H2416
19: 6 *As* the LORD l, he shall not be slain. H2416
20: 3 but truly *as* the LORD l, and *as* thy soul H2416
3 and *as* thy soul l, *there is* but a step H2416
21 to thee, and no hurt; *as* the LORD l. H2416
31 For as long as the son of Jesse l upon H2425
25: 6 And thus shall ye say to him that l *in* H2416
26 Now therefore, my lord, *as* the LORD l, H2416
26 and *as* thy soul l, seeing the LORD hath H2416
34 God of Israel l, which hath kept me H2416
26:10 David said furthermore, *As* the LORD l, H2416
16 *As* the LORD l, ye *are* worthy to die, H2416
28:10 saying, *As* the LORD l, there shall no H2416
29: 6 *as* the LORD l, thou hast been upright, H2416
2Sa 2:27 And Joab said, *As* God l, unless thou H2416
4: 9 *As* the LORD l, who hath redeemed H2416
11:11 and *as* thy soul l, I will not do this thing. H2416
12: 5 *As* the LORD l, the man that hath done H2416
14:11 said, *As* the LORD l, there shall not one H2416
19 said, *As* thy soul l, my lord the king, H2416
15:21 said, *As* the LORD l, and *as* my lord the H2416
21 my lord the king l, surely in what place H2416
22:47 The LORD l; and blessed *be* my rock; H2416
1Ki 1:29 and said, *As* the LORD l, that hath H2416
2:24 Now therefore, *as* the LORD l, which H2416
3:23 *is* my son that l, and thy son *is* the dead: H2416
17: 1 God of Israel l, before whom I stand, H2416
12 And she said, *As* the LORD thy God l, I H2416
23 mother: and Elijah said, See, thy son l. H2416
18:10 *As* the LORD thy God l, there is no H2416
15 And Elijah said, *As* the LORD of hosts l, H2416
22:14 And Micaiah said, *As* the LORD l, what H2416
2Ki 2: 2 *him, As* the LORD l, and *as* thy soul H2416
2 and *as* thy soul l, I will not leave thee. H2416
4 he said, *As* the LORD l, and *as* thy soul H2416
4 and *as* thy soul l, I will not leave thee. H2416
6 he said, *As* the LORD l, and *as* thy soul H2416
6 and *as* thy soul l, I will not leave thee. H2416
3:14 And Elisha said, *As* the LORD of hosts l, H2416
4:30 said, *As* the LORD l, and *as* thy soul H2416
30 and *as* thy soul l, I will not leave thee. H2416
5:16 But he said, *As* the LORD l, before H2416
20 but, *as* the LORD l, I will run after him, H2416
2Ch 18:13 And Micaiah said, *As* the LORD l, even H2416
Job 19:25 For I know *that* my redeemer l, and *that* H2416
27: 2 *As* God l, *who* hath taken away my H2416
Ps 18:46 The LORD l; and blessed *be* my rock; H2416
89:48 What man *is he that* l, and shall not see H2421
Jer 4: 2 And thou shalt swear, The LORD l, in H2416
5: 2 And though they say, The LORD l; H2416
12:16 name, The LORD l; as they taught my H2416
16:14 be said, The LORD l, that brought up H2416
15 But, The LORD l, that brought up the H2416
23: 7 say, The LORD l, which brought up the H2416
8 But, The LORD l, which brought up and H2416
38:16 *As* the LORD l, that made us this soul, H2416
44:26 land of Egypt, saying, The Lord GOD l. H2416
Ezk 47: 9 *that* every thing that l, which moveth, H2416
Dan 4:34 him that l for ever, whose dominion H2417
12: 7 sware by him that l for ever that *it shall* H2416
Hos 4:15 to Beth-aven, nor swear, The LORD l. H2416
Am 8:14 Thy god, O Dan, l; and, The manner of H2416
14 of Beer-sheba l; even they shall fall, H2416
Jn 4:50 Go thy way; thy son l. And the man *G2198*
51 him, and told *him,* saying, Thy son l. *G2198*
53 said unto him, Thy son l: and himself *G2198*
11:26 And whosoever l and believeth in me *G2198*
Ro 6:10 but in that he l, he liveth unto God. *G2198*
10 but in that he liveth, he l unto God. *G2198*
7: 1 dominion over a man as long as he l? *G2198*
2 so long as he l; but if the husband be *G2198*
3 So then if, while *her* husband l, she be *G2198*
14: 7 For none of us l to himself, and no man *G2198*
1Co 7:39 as her husband l; but if her husband be *G2198*
2Co 13: 4 weakness, yet he l by the power of God. *G2198*
Gal 2:20 yet not I, but Christ l in me: and the life *G2198*
1Ti 5: 6 But she that l in pleasure is dead while *G2198*
6 liveth in pleasure is dead while she l. *G2198*
Heb 7: 8 *them,* of whom it is witnessed that he l. *G2198*
25 he ever l to make intercession for them. *G2198*
9:17 of no strength at all while the testator l. *G2198*
1Pt 1:23 of God, which l and abideth for ever. *G2198*
Rev 1:18 I *am* he that l, and was dead; and, *G2198*
4: 9 on the throne, who l for ever and ever, *G2198*
10 worship him that l for ever and ever, *G2198*
5:14 him that l for ever and ever. *G2198*
10: 6 And sware by him that l for ever and *G2198*
15: 7 wrath of God, who l for ever and ever. *G2198*

LIVING

Gen 1:21 great whales, and every l creature that H2416
24 bring forth the l creature after his kind, H2416
28 l thing that moveth upon the earth. H2416
2: 7 breath of life; and man became a l soul. H2416
19 l creature, that *was* the name thereof. H2416
3:20 Eve; because she was the mother of all l. H2416
6:19 And of every l thing of all flesh, two of H2416
7: 4 nights; and every l substance that I H3351
23 And every l substance was destroyed H3351
8: 1 Noah, and every l thing, and all the H2416
17 Bring forth with thee every l thing that H2416
21 any more every thing l, as I have done. H2416
9:10 And with every l creature that *is* with H2416
12 me and you and every l creature that *is* H2416
15 me and you and every l creature of all H2416
16 God and every l creature of all flesh H2416
Lev 11:10 waters, and of any l thing which *is* in H2416
46 the fowl, and of every l creature that H2416
14: 6 As for the l bird, he shall take it, and H2416
6 dip them and the l bird in the blood of H2416
7 let the l bird loose into the open field. H2416
51 scarlet, and the l bird, and dip them in H2416
52 and with the l bird, and with the cedar H2416
53 But he shall let go the l bird out of the H2416
20:25 by any manner of l thing that creepeth
Nu 16:48 and the l; and the plague was stayed. H2416
Dt 5:26 the voice of the l God speaking out of H2416
Jos 3:10 know that the l God *is* among you, and H2416
Ru 2:20 his kindness to the l and to the dead. H2416
1Sa 17:26 he should defy the armies of the l God? H2416
36 he hath defied the armies of the l God. H2416
2Sa 20: 3 the day of their death, l in widowhood. H2424
1Ki 3:22 said, Nay; but the l *is* my son, and the H2416
22 *is* thy son, and the l *is* my son. Thus H2416
23 thy son *is* the dead, and my son *is* the l. H2416
25 And the king said, Divide the l child in H2416
26 Then spake the woman whose the l H2416
26 lord, give her the l child, and in no wise H2416
27 and said, Give her the l child, and in no H2416
2Ki 19: 4 to reproach the l God; and will reprove H2416
16 hath sent him to reproach the l God. H2416
Job 12:10 In whose hand *is* the soul of every l H2416
28:13 neither is it found in the land of the l. H2416
21 Seeing it is hid from the eyes of all l, H2416
30:23 and *to* the house appointed for all l. H2416
33:30 to be enlightened with the light of the l. H2416
Ps 27:13 of the LORD in the land of the l. H2416
42: 2 My soul thirsteth for God, for the l God: H2416
52: 5 root thee out of the land of the l. Selah. H2416
56:13 walk before God in the light of the l? H2416
58: 9 a whirlwind, both l, and in *his* wrath. H2416
69:28 l, and not be written with the righteous. H2416
84: 2 and my flesh crieth out for the l God. H2416
116: 9 before the LORD in the land of the l. H2416
142: 5 *and* my portion in the land of the l. H2416
143: 2 in thy sight shall no man l be justified. H2416
145:16 satisfiest the desire of every l thing. H2416

Ecc 4: 2 more than the l which are yet alive. H2416
15 I considered all the l which walk under H2416
6: 8 poor, that knoweth to walk before the l? H2416
7: 2 all men; and the l will lay it to his heart. H2416
9: 4 For to him that is joined to all the l H2416
4 for a l dog is better than a dead lion. H2416
5 For the l know that they shall die: but H2416
Song 4:15 A fountain of gardens, a well of l H2416
Isa 4: 3 is written among the l in Jerusalem: H2416
8:19 unto their God? for the l to the dead? H2416
37: 4 to reproach the l God, and will reprove H2416
17 which hath sent to reproach the l God. H2416
38:11 in the land of the l: I shall behold man H2416
19 The l, the living, he shall praise thee, as H2416
19 The living, the l, he shall praise thee, as H2416
53: 8 of the land of the l: for the transgression H2416
Jer 2:13 me the fountain of l waters, and hewed H2416
10:10 the true God, he is the l God, and an H2416
11:19 the land of the l, that his name may be H2416
17:13 the LORD, the fountain of l waters. H2416
23:36 l God, of the LORD of hosts our God. H2416
Lam 3:39 Wherefore doth a l man complain, a H2416
Ezk 1: 5 likeness of four l creatures. And this H2416
13 As for the likeness of the l creatures, H2416
13 down among the l creatures; and the H2416
14 And the l creatures ran and returned H2416
15 Now as I beheld the l creatures, behold H2416
15 by the l creatures, with his four faces. H2416
19 And when the l creatures went, the H2416
19 and when the l creatures were lifted H2416
20 of the l creature was in the wheels. H2416
21 of the l creature was in the wheels. H2416
22 the heads of the l creature was as the H2416
3:13 of the wings of the l creatures that H2416
10:15 up. This is the l creature that I saw by H2416
17 the spirit of the l creature was in them. H2416
20 This is the l creature that I saw under H2416
26:20 and I shall set glory in the land of the l; H2416
32:23 which caused terror in the land of the l. H2416
24 in the land of the l; yet have they borne H2416
25 in the land of the l, yet have they borne H2416
26 caused their terror in the land of the l. H2416
27 terror of the mighty in the land of the l. H2416
32 in the land of the l: and he shall be laid H2416
Dan 2:30 more than any l, but for their sakes that H2417
4:17 the intent that the l may know that the H2417
6:20 servant of the l God, is thy God, whom H2417
26 for he is the l God, and stedfast for H2417
Hos 1:10 unto them, Ye are the sons of the l God. H2416
Zec 14: 8 And it shall be in that day, that l waters H2416
Mt 16:16 art the Christ, the Son of the l God. G2198
22:32 is not the God of the dead, but of the l. G2198
26:63 I adjure thee by the l God, that thou tell G2198
Mk 12:27 God of the l: ye therefore do greatly err. G2198
44 did cast in all that she had, even all her l. G979
Lk 8:43 had spent all her l upon physicians, G979
15:12 to me. And he divided unto them his l. G979
13 wasted his substance with riotous l. G2198
30 hath devoured thy l with harlots, thou G979
20:38 dead, but of the l: for all live unto him. G2198
21: 4 penury hath cast in all the l that she had. G979
24: 5 Why seek ye the l among the dead? G2198
Jn 4:10 and he would have given thee l water. G2198
11 whence then hast thou that l water? G2198
6:51 I am the l bread which came down G2198
57 As the l Father hath sent me, and I live G2198
69 art that Christ, the Son of the l God. G2198
7:38 of his belly shall flow rivers of l water. G2198
Act 14:15 vanities unto the l God, which made G2198
Ro 9:26 they be called the children of the l God. G2198
12: 1 present your bodies a l sacrifice, holy, G2198
14: 9 he might be Lord both of the dead and l. G2198
1Co 15:45 man Adam was made a l soul; the last G2198
2Co 3: 3 the Spirit of the l God; not in tables of G2198
6:16 are the temple of the l God; as God hath G2198
Col 2:20 why, as though l in the world, are ye G2198
1Th 1: 9 from idols to serve the l and true God; G2198
1Ti 3:15 is the church of the l God, the pillar and G2198
4:10 we trust in the l God, who is the G2198
6:17 riches, but in the l God, who giveth us G2198
Tit 3: 3 and pleasures, l in malice and envy, G1236
Heb 3:12 unbelief, in departing from the l God. G2198
9:14 from dead works to serve the l God? G2198
10:20 By a new and l way, which he hath G2198
31 thing to fall into the hands of the l God. G2198
12:22 unto the city of the l God, the heavenly G2198
1Pt 2: 4 To whom coming, as unto a l stone, G2198
Rev 7: 2 the seal of the l God: and he cried with G2198
17 lead them unto l fountains of waters: G2198
Rev 16: 3 man: and every l soul died in the sea. G2198

LIZARD

Lev 11:30 and the l, and the snail, and the mole. H3911

LO

Gen 8:11 in the evening; and, l, in her mouth was H2009
15: 3 l, one born in my house is mine heir. H2009
12 upon Abram; and, l, an horror of great H2009
18: 2 and looked, and, l, three men stood by H2009
10 time of life; and, l, Sarah thy wife shall H2009
19:28 and beheld, and, l, the smoke of the H2009
29: 2 well in the field, and, l, there were three H2009
7 And he said, L, it is yet high day, H2005
37: 7 in the field, and, l, my sheaf arose, and H2009
42:28 is restored; and, l, it is even in my sack: H2009
47:23 land for Pharaoh: l, here is seed for you, H1887
48:11 l, God hath shewed me also thy seed. H2009
50: 5 My father made me swear, saying, L, I H2009
Ex 7:15 in the morning; l, he goeth out unto the H2009
8:20 before Pharaoh; l, he cometh forth to H2009
26 LORD our God: l, shall we sacrifice the H2005
19: 9 And the LORD said unto Moses, L, I H2009
Nu 14:40 mountain, saying, L, we be here, and H2009
22:38 And Balaam said unto Balak, L, I am H2009
23: 6 And he returned unto him, and, l, he H2009
9 the hills I behold him: l, the people shall H2005
24:11 great honour; but, l, the LORD hath H2009
Dt 22:17 And, l, he hath given occasions of H2009
Jos 14:10 and now, l, I am this day fourscore H2009
Jdg 7:13 a dream, and, l, a cake of barley bread H2009
13: 5 For, l, thou shalt conceive, and bear a H2009
1Sa 4:13 And when he came, l, Eli sat upon a H2009
10: 2 are found: and, l, thy father hath left the H2009
14:43 was in mine hand, and, l, I must die. H2005
21:14 Then said Achish unto his servants, L, H2009
2Sa 1: 6 upon his spear; and, l, the chariots and H2009
15:24 And l Zadok also, and all the Levites H2009
24:17 people, and said, L, I have sinned, and I H2009
1Ki 1:22 And, l, while she yet talked with the H2009
51 king Solomon: for, l, he hath caught H2009
3:12 to thy words: l, I have given thee a wise H2009
2Ki 7: 6 said one to another, L, the king of Israel H2009
15 unto Jordan: and, l, all the way was full H2009
1Ch 17: 1 the prophet, L, I dwell in an house H2009
21:23 is good in his eyes: l, I give thee the H7200
2Ch 16:11 Asa, first and last, l, they are written in H2009
25:19 Thou sayest, L, thou hast smitten the H2009
27: 7 and his ways, l, they are written in the H2009
29: 9 For, l, our fathers have fallen by the H2009
Neh 5: 5 children: and, l, we bring into bondage H2009
6:12 And, l, I perceived that God had not H2009
Job 3: 7 L, let that night be solitary, let no joyful H2009
5:27 L this, we have searched it, so it is; H2009
9:11 L, he goeth by me, and I see him not: he H2005
19 If I speak of strength, l, he is strong: H2009
13: 1 L, mine eye hath seen all this, mine ear H2005
21:16 L, their good is not in their hand: the H2005
26:14 L, these are parts of his ways: but how H2005
33:29 L, all these things worketh God H2005
40:16 L now, his strength is in his loins, and H2009
Ps 11: 2 For, l, the wicked bend their bow, they H2009
37:36 Yet he passed away, and, l, he was not: H2009
40: 7 Then said I, L, I come: in the volume of H2009
9 congregation: l, I have not refrained H2009
48: 4 For, l, the kings were assembled, they H2009
52: 7 L, this is the man that made not God his H2009
55: 7 L, then would I wander far off, and H2009
59: 3 For, l, they lie in wait for my soul: the H2009
68:33 which were of old; l, he doth send out H2005
73:27 For, l, they that are far from thee shall H2005
83: 2 For, l, thine enemies make a tumult: H2009
92: 9 For, l, thine enemies, O LORD, for, lo, H2009
9 For, lo, thine enemies, O LORD, for, l, H2009
127: 3 L, children are an heritage of the LORD: H2009
132: 6 L, we heard of it at Ephratah: we found H2009
139: 4 l, O LORD, thou knowest it altogether. H2005
Prv 24:31 And, l, it was all grown over with H2009
Ecc 1:16 own heart, saying, L, I am come to H2009
7:29 L, this only have I found, that God hath H7200
Song 2:11 For, l, the winter is past, the rain is over H2009
Isa 6: 7 mouth, and said, L, this hath touched H2009
25: 9 And it shall be said in that day, L, this H2009
36: 6 L, thou trustest in the staff of this H2009
49:12 from far: and, l, these from the north H2009
50: 9 condemn me? l, they all shall wax old H2005
Jer 1:15 For, l, I will call all the families of the H2009
4:23 I beheld the earth, and, l, it was without H2009
24 I beheld the mountains, and, l, they H2009
Jer 4:25 I beheld, and, l, there was no man, and H2009
26 I beheld, and, l, the fruitful place was a H2009
5:15 L, I will bring a nation upon you from H2009
8: 8 the LORD is with us? L, certainly in vain H2009
9 and taken: l, they have rejected the H2009
25:29 For, l, I begin to bring evil on the city H2009
30: 3 For, l, the days come, saith the LORD, H2009
10 O Israel: for, l, I will save thee from H2005
36:12 chamber: and, l, all the princes sat H2009
49:15 For, l, I will make thee small among the H2009
50: 9 For, l, I will raise and cause to come up H2009
Ezk 2: 9 me; and, l, a roll of a book was therein; H2009
4:15 Then he said unto me, L, I have given H7200
8: 2 Then I beheld, and l a likeness as the H2009
17 and, l, they put the branch to their nose. H2009
13:10 up a wall, and, l, others daubed it with H2009
12 L, when the wall is fallen, shall it not be H2009
17:18 the covenant, when, l, he had given his H2009
18:14 Now, l, if he beget a son, that seeth all H2009
18 l, even he shall die in his iniquity. H2009
23:39 to profane it; and, l, thus have they H2009
40 was sent; and, l, they came: for whom H2009
30: 9 as in the day of Egypt: for, l, it cometh. H2009
21 king of Egypt; and, l, it shall not be H2009
33:32 And, l, thou art unto them as a very H2009
33 And when this cometh to pass, (l, it will H2009
37: 2 open valley; and, l, they were very dry. H2009
8 And when I beheld, l, the sinews and H2009
40:17 court, and, l, there were chambers, H2009
42: 8 fifty cubits: and, l, before the temple H2009
Dan 3:25 He answered and said, L, I see four men H1888
7: 6 After this I beheld, and l another, like a H718
10:13 twenty days: but, l, Michael, one of the H2009
20 forth, l, the prince of Grecia shall come. H2009
Hos 9: 6 For, l, they are gone because of H2009
Am 4: 2 his holiness, that, l, the days shall come H2009
13 For, l, he that formeth the mountains, H2009
7: 1 latter growth; and, l, it was the latter H2009
9: 9 For, l, I will command, and I will sift the H2009
Hab 1: 6 For, l, I raise up the Chaldeans, that H2005
Hag 1: 9 Ye looked for much, and, l, it came to H2009
Zec 2:10 of Zion: for, l, I come, and I will dwell H2005
11: 6 the LORD: but, l, I will deliver the men H2009
16 For, l, I will raise up a shepherd in the H2009
Mt 2: 9 departed; and, l, the star, which they G2400
3:16 of the water: and, l, the heavens were G2400
17 And l a voice from heaven, saying, This G2400
24:23 Then if any man shall say unto you, L, G2400
25:25 earth: l, there thou hast that is thine. G2396
26:47 And while he yet spake, l, Judas, one of G2400
28: 7 there shall ye see him: l, I have told you. G2400
20 you: and, l, I am with you alway, G2400
Mk 10:28 Then Peter began to say unto him, L, G2400
13:21 And then if any man shall say to you, L, G2400
21 Christ; or, l, he is there; believe him not: G2400
14:42 Rise up, let us go; l, he that betrayeth G2400
Lk 1:44 For, l, as soon as the voice of thy G2400
2: 9 And, l, the angel of the Lord came upon G2400
9:39 And, l, a spirit taketh him, and he G2400
13:16 Satan hath bound, l, these eighteen G2400
15:29 And he answering said to his father, L, G2400
17:21 Neither shall they say, L here! or, lo G2400
21 Neither shall they say, Lo here! or, l G2400
18:28 Then Peter said, L, we have left all, and G2400
23:15 you to him; and, l, nothing worthy of G2400
Jn 7:26 But, l, he speaketh boldly, and they say G2396
16:29 His disciples said unto him, L, now G2396
Act 13:46 life, l, we turn to the Gentiles. G2400
27:24 Caesar: and, l, God hath given thee G2400
Heb 10: 7 Then said I, L, I come (in the volume of G2400
9 Then said he, L, I come to do thy will, O G2400
Rev 5: 6 And I beheld, and, l, in the midst of the G2400
6: 5 And I beheld, and l a black horse; and G2400
12 the sixth seal, and, l, there was a great G2400
7: 9 After this I beheld, and, l, a great G2400
14: 1 And I looked, and, l, a Lamb stood on G2400

LOADEN

Isa 46: 1 l; they are a burden to the weary beast. H6006

LOADETH

Ps 68:19 Blessed be the Lord, who daily l us with H6006

LOAF

Ex 29:23 And one l of bread, and one cake of H3603
1Ch 16: 3 to every one a l of bread, and a good H3603
Mk 8:14 in the ship with them more than one l. G740

LO-AMMI
Hos 1: 9 Then said *God*, Call his name **L**: for ye H3818

LOAN
1Sa 2:20 this woman for the **l** which is lent to the H7596

LOATHE
Job 7:16 I **l** *it*; I would not live alway: let me H3988

LOATHETH
Nu 21: 5 water; and our soul **l** this light bread. H6973
Prv 27: 7 The full soul **l** an honeycomb; but to the H947

LOATHSOME
Nu 11:20 nostrils, and it be **l** unto you: because H2214
Job 7: 5 dust; my skin is broken, and become **l**. H3988
Ps 38: 7 For my loins are filled with a **l** *disease*: H7033
Prv 13: 5 a wicked *man* is **l**, and cometh to shame. H887

LOAVES
Lev 23:17 two wave **l** of two tenth deals: they H3899
Jdg 8: 5 Give, I pray you, **l** of bread unto the H3603
1Sa 10: 3 carrying three **l** of bread, and another H3603
4 and give thee two *l* of bread; which thou
17:17 **l**, and run to the camp to thy brethren; H3899
21: 3 hand? give *me* five *l of* bread in mine
25:18 took two hundred **l**, and two bottles of H3899
2Sa 16: 1 them two hundred *l* of bread, and an
1Ki 14: 3 And take with thee ten **l**, and cracknels, H3899
2Ki 4:42 firstfruits, twenty **l** of barley, and full H3899
Mt 14:17 We have here but five **l**, and two fishes. G740
19 and took the five **l**, and the two fishes, G740
19 and gave the **l** to *his* disciples, and G740
15:34 And Jesus saith unto them, How many **l** G740
36 And he took the seven **l** and the fishes, G740
16: 9 remember the five **l** of the five thousand, G740
10 Neither the seven **l** of the four thousand, G740
Mk 6:38 He saith unto them, How many **l** have G740
41 And when he had taken the five **l** and the G740
41 and brake the **l**, and gave *them* to his G740
44 And they that did eat of the **l** were about G740
52 of the **l**: for their heart was hardened. G740
8: 5 And he asked them, How many **l** have G740
6 he took the seven **l**, and gave thanks, and G740
19 When I brake the five **l** among five G740
Lk 9:13 no more but five **l** and two fishes; except G740
16 Then he took the five **l** and the two G740
11: 5 say unto him, Friend, lend me three **l**; G740
Jn 6: 9 hath five barley **l**, and two small fishes: G740
11 And Jesus took the **l**; and when he had G740
13 of the five barley **l**, which remained over G740
26 ye did eat of the **l**, and were filled. G740

LOCK
Song 5: 5 myrrh, upon the handles of the **l**. H4514
Ezk 8: 3 and took me by a **l** of mine head; and H6734

LOCKED
Jdg 3:23 of the parlour upon him, and **l** them. H5274
24 the parlour *were* **l**, they said, Surely he H5274

LOCKS
Nu 6: 5 let the **l** of the hair of his head grow. H6545
Jdg 16:13 the seven **l** of my head with the web. H4253
19 to shave off the seven **l** of his head; and H4253
Neh 3: 3 the **l** thereof, and the bars thereof. H4514
6 and the **l** thereof, and the bars thereof. H4514
13 the doors thereof, the **l** thereof, and the H4514
14 the **l** thereof, and the bars thereof. H4514
15 the doors thereof, the **l** thereof, and the H4514
Song 4: 1 eyes within thy **l**: thy hair *is* as a flock H6777
3 a piece of a pomegranate within thy **l**. H6777
5: 2 *and* my **l** with the drops of the night. H6977
11 His head *is as* the most fine gold, his **l** H6977
6: 7 *are* thy temples within thy **l**. H6777
Isa 47: 2 meal: uncover thy **l**, make bare the leg, H6777
Ezk 44:20 nor suffer their **l** to grow long; they H6545

LOCUST
Ex 10:19 not one **l** in all the coasts of Egypt. H697
Lev 11:22 *Even* these of them ye may eat; the **l** H697
22 kind, and the bald **l** after his kind, and H5556
Dt 28:38 *but* little in; for the **l** shall consume it. H697
42 fruit of thy land shall the **l** consume. H6767
1Ki 8:37 blasting, mildew, **l**, *or* if there be H697
Ps 78:46 caterpiller, and their labour unto the **l**. H697
109:23 I am tossed up and down as the **l**. H697
Joel 1: 4 hath left hath the **l** eaten; and that which H697
4 and that which the **l** hath left hath the H697
Joel 2:25 you the years that the **l** hath eaten, the H697

LOCUSTS
Ex 10: 4 morrow will I bring the **l** into thy coast: H697
12 of Egypt for the **l**, that they may come H697
13 morning, the east wind brought the **l**. H697
14 And the **l** went up over all the land of H697
14 there were no such **l** as they, neither H697
19 took away the **l**, and cast them into the H697
2Ch 6:28 or mildew, **l**, or caterpillers; if their H697
7:13 if I command the **l** to devour the land, H2284
Ps 105:34 He spake, and the **l** came, and H697
Prv 30:27 The **l** have no king, yet go they forth all H697
Isa 33: 4 to and fro of **l** shall he run upon them. H1357
Nah 3:15 cankerworm, make thyself many as the **l**. H697
17 Thy crowned *are* as the **l**, and thy H697
Mt 3: 4 and his meat was **l** and wild honey. G200
Mk 1: 6 loins; and he did eat **l** and wild honey; G200
Rev 9: 3 And there came out of the smoke **l** upon G200
7 And the shapes of the **l** *were* like unto G200

LOD
1Ch 8:12 Ono, and **L**, with the towns thereof: H3850
Ezr 2:33 The children of **L**, Hadid, and Ono, H3850
Neh 7:37 The children of **L**, Hadid, and Ono, H3850
11:35 **L**, and Ono, the valley of craftsmen. H3850

LO-DEBAR
2Sa 9: 4 of Machir, the son of Ammiel, in **L**. H3810
5 of Machir, the son of Ammiel, from **L**. H3810
17:27 son of Ammiel of **L**, and Barzillai the H3810

LODGE
Gen 24:23 *in* thy father's house for us to **l** in? H3885
25 provender enough, and room to **l** in. H3885
Nu 22: 8 And he said unto them, **L** here this H3885
Jos 4: 3 place, where ye shall **l** this night. H3885
Jdg 19: 9 groweth to an end, **l** here, that thine H3885
11 this city of the Jebusites, and **l** in it. H3885
13 to **l** all night, in Gibeah, or in Ramah. H3885
15 to go in *and* to **l** in Gibeah: and when H3885
20 *lie* upon me; only **l** not in the street. H3885
20: 4 to Benjamin, I and my concubine, to **l**. H3885
Ru 1:16 thou lodgest, I will **l**: thy people *shall be* H3885
2Sa 17: 8 of war, and will not **l** with the people. H3885
16 tell David, saying, **L** not this night in H3885
Neh 4:22 with his servant **l** within Jerusalem, H3885
13:21 unto them, Why **l** ye about the wall? if H3885
Job 24: 7 They cause the naked to **l** without H3885
31:32 The stranger did not **l** in the street: *but* H3885
Song 7:11 into the field; let us **l** in the villages. H3885
Isa 1: 8 in a vineyard, as a **l** in a garden of H4412
21:13 in Arabia shall ye **l**, O ye travelling H3885
65: 4 Which remain among the graves, and **l** H3885
Jer 4:14 shall thy vain thoughts **l** within thee? H3885
Zep 2:14 the bittern shall **l** in the upper lintels of H3885
Mt 13:32 air come and **l** in the branches thereof. G2681
Mk 4:32 of the air may **l** under the shadow of it. G2681
Lk 9:12 round about, and **l**, and get victuals: for G2647
Act 21:16 an old disciple, with whom we should **l**. G3579

LODGED
Gen 32:13 And he **l** there that same night; and H3885
21 himself **l** that night in the company. H3885
Jos 2: 1 house, named Rahab, and **l** there. H7901
3: 1 and **l** there before they passed over. H3885
4: 8 where they **l**, and laid them down there. H4411
6:11 came into the camp, and **l** in the camp. H3885
8: 9 Joshua **l** that night among the people. H3885
Jdg 18: 2 to the house of Micah, they **l** there. H3885
19: 4 so they did eat and drink, and **l** there. H3885
7 urged him: therefore he **l** there again. H3885
1Ki 19: 9 And he came thither unto a cave, and **l** H3885
1Ch 9:27 And they **l** round about the house of H3885
Neh 13:20 ware **l** without Jerusalem once or twice. H3885
Isa 1:21 **l** in it; but now murderers. H3885
Mt 21:17 of the city into Bethany; and he **l** there. G835
Lk 13:19 fowls of the air **l** in the branches of it. G2681
Act 10:18 was surnamed Peter, were **l** there. G3579
23 Then called he them in, and **l** *them*. G3579
32 is Peter; he is **l** in the house of *one* G3579
28: 7 us, and **l** us three days courteously. G3579
1Ti 5:10 if she have **l** strangers, if she have G3580

LODGEST
Ru 1:16 go; and where thou **l**, I will lodge: thy H3885

LODGETH
Act 10: 6 He **l** with one Simon a tanner, whose G3579

LODGING
Jos 4: 3 **l** place, where ye shall lodge this night. H4411
Jdg 19:15 man that took them into his house to **l**. H3885
Isa 10:29 taken up their **l** at Geba; Ramah is H4411
Jer 9: 2 Oh that I had in the wilderness a **l** place H4411
Act 28:23 many to him into *his* **l**; to whom he G3578
Phlm 22 But withal prepare me also a **l**: for I G3578

LODGINGS
2Ki 19:23 I will enter into the **l** of his borders, *and* H4411

LOFT
1Ki 17:19 him up into a **l**, where he abode, and H5944
Act 20: 9 the third **l**, and was taken up dead. G5152

LOFTILY
Ps 73: 8 *concerning* oppression: they speak **l**. H4791

LOFTINESS
Isa 2:17 And the **l** of man shall be bowed down, H1365
Jer 48:29 proud) his **l**, and his arrogancy, and H1363

LOFTY
Ps 131: 1 nor mine eyes **l**: neither do I exercise H7311
Prv 30:13 *There is* a generation, O how **l** are their H7311
Isa 2:11 The **l** looks of man shall be humbled, H1365
12 *that is* proud and **l**, and upon every *one* H7311
5:15 and the eyes of the **l** shall be humbled: H1364
26: 5 dwell on high; the **l** city, he layeth it H7682
57: 7 Upon a **l** and high mountain hast thou H1364
15 For thus saith the high and **l** One that H5375

LOG
Lev 14:10 mingled with oil, and one **l** of oil. H3849
12 offering, and the **l** of oil, and wave H3849
15 And the priest shall take *some* of the **l** H3849
21 oil for a meat offering, and a **l** of oil; H3849
24 offering, and the **l** of oil, and the priest H3849

LOINS
Gen 35:11 thee, and kings shall come out of thy **l**; H2504
37:34 **l**, and mourned for his son many days. H4975
46:26 came out of his **l**, besides Jacob's sons' H3409
Ex 1: 5 And all the souls that came out of the **l** H3409
12:11 And thus shall ye eat it; *with* your **l** H4975
28:42 **l** even unto the thighs they shall reach: H4975
Dt 33:11 smite through the **l** of them that rise H4975
2Sa 20: 8 sword fastened upon his **l** in the sheath H4975
1Ki 2: 5 **l**, and in his shoes that *were* on his feet. H4975
8:19 forth out of thy **l**, he shall build the H2504
12:10 shall be thicker than my father's **l**. H4975
18:46 he girded up his **l**, and ran before Ahab H4975
20:31 sackcloth on our **l**, and ropes upon our H4975
32 So they girded sackcloth on their **l**, and H4975
2Ki 1: 8 **l**. And he said, It *is* Elijah the Tishbite. H4975
4:29 Then he said to Gehazi, Gird up thy **l**, H4975
9: 1 him, Gird up thy **l**, and take this box of H4975
2Ch 6: 9 **l**, he shall build the house for my name. H2504
10:10 shall be thicker than my father's **l**. H4975
Job 12:18 kings, and girdeth their **l** with a girdle. H4975
31:20 If his **l** have not blessed me, and *if* he H2504
38: 3 Gird up now thy **l** like a man; for I will H2504
40: 7 Gird up thy **l** now like a man: I will H2504
16 Lo now, his strength *is* in his **l**, and his H4975
Ps 38: 7 For my **l** are filled with a loathsome H3689
66:11 the net; thou laidst affliction upon our **l**. H4975
69:23 and make their **l** continually to shake. H4975
Prv 31:17 She girdeth her **l** with strength, and H4975
Isa 5:27 the girdle of their **l** be loosed, nor the H2504
11: 5 be the girdle of his **l**, and faithfulness H4975
20: 2 from off thy **l**, and put off thy shoe H4975
21: 3 Therefore are my **l** filled with pain: H4975
32:11 bare, and gird *sackcloth* upon *your* **l**. H2504
45: 1 and I will loose the **l** of kings, to open H4975
Jer 1:17 Thou therefore gird up thy **l**, and arise, H4975
13: 1 it upon thy **l**, and put it not in water. H4975
2 word of the LORD, and put *it* on my **l**. H4975
4 got, which *is* upon thy **l**, and arise, go to H4975
11 For as the girdle cleaveth to the **l** of a H4975
30: 6 with his hands on his **l**, as a woman in H2504
48:37 *be* cuttings, and upon the **l** sackcloth. H4975
Ezk 1:27 appearance of his **l** even upward, and H4975
27 appearance of his **l** even downward, I H4975
8: 2 appearance of his **l** even downward, H4975
2 fire; and from his **l** even upward, as the H4975
21: 6 with the breaking of *thy* **l**; and with H4975
23:15 Girded with girdles upon their **l**, H4975
29: 7 and madest all their **l** to be at a stand. H4975
44:18 upon their **l**; they shall not gird H4975

Ezk 47: 4 me through; the waters *were* to the l. H4975
Dan 5: 6 the joints of his l were loosed, and his H2783
10: 5 l *were* girded with fine gold of Uphaz: H4975
Am 8:10 sackcloth upon all l, and baldness upon H4975
Nah 2: 1 *thy* l strong, fortify *thy* power mightily. H4975
10 much pain *is* in all l, and the faces of H4975
Mt 3: 4 girdle about his l; and his meat was *G3751*
Mk 1: 6 l; and he did eat locusts and wild honey; *G3751*
Lk 12:35 Let your l be girded about, and *your* *G3751*
Act 2:30 that of the fruit of his l, according to the *G3751*
Eph 6:14 Stand therefore, having your l girt *G3751*
Heb 7: 5 they come out of the l of Abraham: *G3751*
10 For he was yet in the l of his father, *G3751*
1Pt 1:13 Wherefore gird up the l of your mind, *G3751*

LOIS
2Ti 1: 5 in thy grandmother L, and thy mother *G3090*

LONG
Gen 26: 8 when he had been there a l time, that H748
48:15 which fed me all my life l unto this day, H5750
Ex 10: 3 the Hebrews, How l wilt thou refuse to H5704
7 unto him, How l shall this man be a H5704
16:28 And the LORD said unto Moses, How l H5704
19:13 l, they shall come up to the mount. H4900
19 trumpet sounded l, and waxed louder H1980
20:12 thy days may be l upon the land which H748
27: 1 wood, five cubits l, and five cubits broad; H753
9 linen of an hundred cubits l for one side: H753
11 of an hundred *cubits* l, and his twenty H753
Lev 18:19 l as she is put apart for her uncleanness.
26:34 her sabbaths, as l as it lieth desolate, H3117
35 As l as it lieth desolate it shall rest; H3117
Nu 9:18 they pitched: as l as the cloud abode H3117
19 And when the cloud tarried l upon the
14:11 And the LORD said unto Moses, How l H5704
11 me? and how l will it be ere they believe H5704
27 How l *shall I bear with* this evil H5704
20:15 have dwelt in Egypt a l time; and the H7227
Dt 1: 6 Ye have dwelt l enough in this mount: H7227
2: 3 Ye have compassed this mountain l H7227
4:25 have remained l in the land, and shall H3462
12:19 as l as thou livest upon the earth. H3605
14:24 And if the way be too l for thee, so that H7235
19: 6 him, because the way is l, and slay him; H7235
20:19 When thou shalt besiege a city a l time, H7227
28:32 for them all the day l: and *there shall be*
59 plagues, and of l continuance, and sore
59 sore sicknesses, and of l continuance.
31:13 your God, as l as ye live in the land H3117
33:12 cover him all the day l, and he shall dwell
Jos 6: 5 that when they make a l *blast* with the H4900
9:13 old by reason of the very l journey. H7230
11:18 Joshua made war a l time with all those H7227
18: 3 of Israel, How l *are* ye slack to go to H5704
23: 1 And it came to pass a l time after that H7227
24: 7 ye dwelt in the wilderness a l season. H7227
Jdg 5:28 is his chariot *so* l in coming? why tarry H954
1Sa 1:14 And Eli said unto her, How l wilt thou be
28 to the LORD; as l as he liveth he shall H3117
7: 2 that the time was l; for it was twenty H7235
16: 1 unto Samuel, How l wilt thou mourn H5704
20:31 For as l as the son of Jesse liveth upon H3117
25:15 missed we any thing, as l as we were H3117
29: 8 in thy servant so l as I have been with H3117
2Sa 2:26 latter end? how l shall it be then, ere H5704
3: 1 Now there was l war between the house H752
14: 2 that had a l time mourned for the dead: H7227
19:34 And Barzillai said unto the king, How l H3117
1Ki 3:11 not asked for thyself l life; neither hast H7227
6:17 *is*, the temple before it, was forty cubits *l*.
18:21 and said, How l halt ye between two H5704
2Ki 9:22 What peace, so l as the whoredoms of H5704
19:25 Hast thou not heard l ago *how* I have H7350
2Ch 1:11 yet hast asked l life; but hast asked H7227
3:11 *were* twenty cubits l: one wing *of the one* H753
6:13 of five cubits l, and five cubits broad, H753
31 in thy ways, so l as they live in the land H3117
15: 3 Now for a l season Israel *hath been* H7227
26: 5 of God: and as l as he sought the H3117
30: 5 a l *time in such sort* as it was written. H7230
36:21 sabbaths: *for* as l as she lay desolate H3117
Neh 2: 6 by him,) For how l shall thy journey be? H6256
Est 5:13 Yet all this availeth me nothing, so l as H2442
Job 3:21 Which l for death, but it *cometh* not; H2442
6: 8 would grant *me* the thing that I l for! H8615
7:19 How l wilt thou not depart from me, H4100
8: 2 How l wilt thou speak these *things*? and H5704
2 *things*? and *how l shall* the words of thy
Job 18: 2 How l *will it be ere* ye make an end of H5704
19: 2 How l will ye vex my soul, and break H5704
27: 6 shall not reproach *me* so l as I live. H3117
Ps 4: 2 O ye sons of men, how l *will ye turn* my H4100
2 into shame? *how l* will ye love vanity,
6: 3 sore vexed: but thou, O LORD, how l? H5704
13: 1 How l wilt thou forget me, O LORD? for H5704
1 how l wilt thou hide thy face from me? H5704
2 How l shall I take counsel in my soul, H5704
2 l shall mine enemy be exalted over me? H5704
32: 3 old through my roaring all the day l.
35:17 Lord, how l wilt thou look on? rescue H4100
28 *and* of thy praise all the day l.
38: 6 down greatly; I go mourning all the day l.
12 things, and imagine deceits all the day l.
44: 8 In God we boast all the day l, and praise
22 we killed all the day l; we are counted as
62: 3 How l will ye imagine mischief against H5704
71:24 all the day l: for they are confounded,
72: 5 They shall fear thee as l as the sun and H5973
7 of peace so l as the moon endureth. H5704
17 be continued as l as the sun: and *men* H6440
73:14 For all the day l have I been plagued,
74: 9 among us any that knoweth how l. H5704
10 O God, how l shall the adversary H5704
79: 5 How l, LORD? wilt thou be angry for H5704
80: 4 O LORD God of hosts, how l wilt thou H5704
82: 2 How l will ye judge unjustly, and H5704
89:46 How l, LORD? wilt thou hide thyself for H5704
90:13 Return, O LORD, how l? and let it repent H5704
91:16 With l life will I satisfy him, and shew H753
94: 3 LORD, how l shall the wicked, how H5704
3 how l shall the wicked triumph? H5704
4 *How l* shall they utter *and* speak hard H5704
95:10 Forty years l was I grieved with *this*
104:33 I will sing unto the LORD as l as I live: I H5750
116: 2 will I call upon *him* as l as I live. H3117
120: 6 My soul hath l dwelt with him that H7227
129: 3 my back: they made l their furrows. H748
143: 3 as those that have been l dead. H5769
Prv 1:22 How l, ye simple ones, will ye love H5704
3: 2 For length of days, and l life, and H8141
6: 9 How l wilt thou sleep, O sluggard? H5704
7:19 *is* not at home, he is gone a l journey: H7350
21:26 He coveteth greedily all the day l: but the
23:17 *thou* in the fear of the LORD all the day l.
30 They that tarry l at the wine; they that go
25:15 By l forbearing is a prince persuaded, H753
Ecc 12: 5 man goeth to his l home, and the H5769
Isa 6:11 Then said I, Lord, how l? And he H5704
22:11 unto him that fashioned it l ago. H7350
37:26 Hast thou not heard l ago, *how* I have H7350
42:14 I have l time holden my peace; I have H5769
65:22 shall l enjoy the work of their hands.
Jer 4:14 be saved. How l shall thy vain thoughts H5704
21 How l shall I see the standard, *and* H5704
12: 4 How l shall the land mourn, and the H5704
23:26 How l shall *this* be in the heart of the H5704
29:28 This *captivity is* l: build ye houses, and H752
31:22 How l wilt thou go about, O thou H5704
47: 5 their valley: how l wilt thou cut thyself? H5704
6 O thou sword of the LORD, how l *will it* H5704
Lam 2:20 children of a span l? shall the priest and
5:20 us for ever, *and* forsake us so l time? H753
Ezk 31: 5 his branches became l because of the H748
40: 5 reed of six cubits *l* by the cubit and an
7 And *every* little chamber *was* one reed l, H753
29 l, and five and twenty cubits broad. H753
30 twenty cubits l, and five cubits broad. H753
33 l, and five and twenty cubits broad. H753
42 a cubit and an half l, and a cubit and an H753
47 an hundred cubits l, and an hundred H753
41:13 an hundred cubits l; and the separate H753
13 the walls thereof, an hundred cubits l; H753
42:11 the north, as l as they, *and* as broad
20 five hundred *reeds* l, and five hundred H753
43:16 And the altar *shall be* twelve *cubits* l, H753
17 And the settle *shall be* fourteen *cubits* l H753
44:20 to grow l; they shall only poll their heads.
45: 6 and twenty thousand l, over against the H753
46:22 of forty *cubits* l and thirty broad: these H753
Dan 8:13 which spake, How l *shall be* the vision H4100
10: 1 appointed *was* l: and he understood the H1419
12: 6 l *shall it be to* the end of these wonders? H4100
Hos 8: 5 l *will it be* ere they attain to innocency? H4100
13:13 he should not stay l in *the place of* the H6256
Hab 1: 2 O LORD, how l shall I cry, and thou H5704
2: 6 *is* not his! how l? and to him that ladeth H4100
Zec 1:12 of hosts, how l wilt thou not have H4100
Mt 9:15 mourn, as l as the bridegroom is *G1909*
11:21 repented l ago in sackcloth and ashes. *G3819*
17:17 generation, how l shall I be with you? *G2193*
17 l be with you? how l shall I suffer you? *G2193*
23:14 a pretence make l prayer: therefore ye *G3117*
25:19 After a l time the lord of those servants *G4183*
Mk 2:19 is with them? as l as they have the *G5550*
9:19 generation, how l shall I be with you? *G2193*
19 l shall I suffer you? bring him unto me. *G2193*
21 And he asked his father, How l is it ago *G4214*
12:38 which love to go in l clothing, and *love*
40 a pretence make l prayers: these shall *G3117*
16: 5 side, clothed in a l white garment; and *G4749*
Lk 1:21 that he tarried so l in the temple. *G5549*
8:27 which had devils l time, and ware no *G2425*
9:41 generation, how l shall I be with you, *G2193*
18: 7 unto him, though he bear l with them? *G3114*
20: 9 and went into a far country for a l time. *G2425*
46 which desire to walk in l robes, and love
47 for a shew make l prayers: the same *G3117*
23: 8 to see him of a l *season*, because he *G2425*
Jn 5: 6 he had been now a l time *in that case*, *G4183*
9: 5 As l as I am in the world, I am the light *G3752*
10:24 unto him, How l dost thou make us to *G2193*
14: 9 Jesus saith unto him, Have I been so l *G5118*
Act 8:11 because that of l time he had bewitched *G2425*
14: 3 L time therefore abode they speaking *G2425*
28 And there they abode l time *G3756+G3641*
20: 9 as Paul was l preaching, he *G1909+G4119*
11 and talked a l while, even till break *G2425*
27:14 But not l after there arose against it a *G4183*
21 But after l abstinence Paul stood forth *G4183*
Ro 1:11 For I l to see you, that I may impart *G1971*
7: 1 dominion over a man as l as he liveth? *G5550*
2 to *her* husband so l as he liveth; but if
8:36 killed all the day l; we are accounted as
10:21 But to Israel he saith, All day l I have
1Co 7:39 The wife is bound by the law as l as her *G5550*
11:14 have l hair, it is a shame unto him? *G2863*
15 But if a woman have l hair, it is a glory *G2863*
13: 4 Charity suffereth l, *and* is kind; charity *G3114*
2Co 9:14 And by their prayer for you, which l *G1971*
Gal 4: 1 Now I say, *That* the heir, as l as he is a *G5550*
Eph 6: 3 and thou mayest live l on the earth. *G3118*
Php 1: 8 For God is my record, how greatly I l *G1971*
1Ti 3:15 But if I tarry l, that thou mayest know *G1019*
Heb 4: 7 To day, after so l a time; as it is said, *G5118*
Jas 5: 7 earth, and hath l patience for it, until *G3114*
1Pt 3: 6 ye are, as l as ye do well, and are
2Pt 1:13 Yea, I think it meet, as l as I am in this
2: 3 judgment now of a l time lingereth not,
Rev 6:10 voice, saying, How l, O Lord, holy and *G2193*

LONGED
2Sa 13:39 And *the soul of* king David l to go forth H3615
23:15 And David l, and said, Oh that one would H183
1Ch 11:17 And David l, and said, Oh that one would H183
Ps 119:40 Behold, I have l after thy precepts: H8373
131 I opened my mouth, and panted: for I l H2968
174 I have l for thy salvation, O LORD; and H8373
Php 2:26 For he l after you all, and was full of *G1971*
4: 1 beloved and l for, my joy and crown, *G1973*

LONGEDST
Gen 31:30 because thou sore l after thy father's H3700

LONGER
Ex 2: 3 And when she could not l hide him, she H5750
9:28 I will let you go, and ye shall stay no l. H3254
Jdg 2:14 not any l stand before their enemies. H5750
2Sa 20: 5 but he tarried l than the set time which
2Ki 6:33 what should I wait for the LORD any l? H5750
Job 11: 9 The measure thereof *is* l than the earth, H752
Jer 44:22 So that the LORD could no l bear, H5750
Lk 16: 2 for thou mayest be no l steward. *G2089*
Act 18:20 When they desired *him* to tarry l time *G1909*
25:24 crying that he ought not to live any l. *G3371*
Ro 6: 2 that are dead to sin, live any l therein? *G2089*
Gal 3:25 But after that faith is come, we are no l *G3765*
1Th 3: 1 Wherefore when we could no l forbear, *G3371*
5 For this cause, when I could no l *G3371*
1Ti 5:23 Drink no l water, but use a little wine *G3371*
1Pt 4: 2 That he no l should live the rest of *his* *G3371*
Rev 10: 6 therein, that there should be time no l: *G3756*

LONGETH
Gen 34: 8 my son Shechem l for your daughter: I H2836
Dt 12:20 flesh, because thy soul l to eat flesh; thou H183
Ps 63: 1 for thee, my flesh l for thee in a dry and H3642

Ps 84: 2 My soul l, yea, even fainteth for the H3700

LONGING
Dt 28:32 look, and fail *with l* for them all the day
Ps 107: 9 For he satisfieth the l soul, and filleth H8264
119:20 My soul breaketh for the l *that it hath* H8375

LONGSUFFERING
Ex 34: 6 and gracious, l, and abundant in H750+H639
Nu 14:18 The LORD *is* l, and of great mercy, H750+H639
Ps 86:15 and gracious, l, and plenteous in H750+H639
Jer 15:15 not away in thy l: know that for H750+H639
Ro 2: 4 forbearance and l; not knowing that the G3115
9:22 with much l the vessels of wrath G3115
2Co 6: 6 By pureness, by knowledge, by l, by G3115
Gal 5:22 peace, l, gentleness, goodness, faith, G3115
Eph 4: 2 With all lowliness and meekness, with l, G3115
Col 1:11 unto all patience and l with joyfulness; G3115
3:12 humbleness of mind, meekness, l; G3115
1Ti 1:16 shew forth all l, for a pattern to them G3115
2Ti 3:10 life, purpose, faith, l, charity, patience, G3115
4: 2 rebuke, exhort with all l and doctrine. G3115
1Pt 3:20 when once the l of God waited in the G3115
2Pt 3: 9 slackness; but is l to us-ward, not G3114
15 And account *that* the l of our Lord *is* G3115

LONGWINGED
Ezk 17: 3 with great wings, l, full of feathers, H83+H750

LOOK
Gen 9:16 cloud; and I will l upon it, that I may H7200
12:11 that thou *art* a fair woman to l upon: H4758
13:14 thine eyes, and l from the place where H7200
15: 5 forth abroad, and said, L now toward H5027
19:17 Escape for thy life; l not behind thee, H5027
24:16 And the damsel *was* very fair to l upon, H4758
26: 7 because she *was* fair to l upon. H4758
40: 7 saying, Wherefore l ye *so* sadly to day? H6440
41:33 Now therefore let Pharaoh l out a man H7200
42: 1 sons, Why do ye l one upon another? H7200
Ex 3: 6 face; for he was afraid to l upon God. H5027
5:21 And they said unto them, The LORD l H7200
10:10 little ones: l *to it;* for evil *is* before you. H7200
25:20 their faces *shall l* one to another; toward
40 And l that thou make *them* after their H7200
39:43 And Moses did l upon all the work, H7200
Lev 13: 3 And the priest shall l on the plague in H7200
3 l on him, and pronounce him unclean. H7200
5 And the priest shall l on him the H7200
6 And the priest shall l on him again the H7200
21 But if the priest l on it, and, behold, H7200
25 Then the priest shall l upon it: and, H7200
26 But if the priest l on it, and, behold, H7200
27 And the priest shall l upon him the H7200
31 And if the priest l on the plague of the H7200
32 And in the seventh day the priest shall l H7200
34 And in the seventh day the priest shall l H7200
36 Then the priest shall l on him: and, H7200
39 Then the priest shall l: and, behold, *if* H7200
43 Then the priest shall l upon it: and, H7200
50 And the priest shall l upon the plague, H7200
51 And he shall l on the plague on the H7200
53 And if the priest shall l, and, behold, the H7200
55 And the priest shall l on the plague, H7200
56 And if the priest l, and, behold, the H7200
14: 3 and the priest shall l, and, behold, *if* the H7200
37 And he shall l on the plague, and, H7200
39 day, and shall l: and, behold, *if* the H7200
44 Then the priest shall come and l, and, H7200
48 And if the priest shall come in, and l H7200
Nu 15:39 a fringe, that ye may l upon it, and H7200
Dt 9:27 Isaac, and Jacob; l not unto the H6437
26:15 L down from thy holy habitation, from H8259
28:32 thine eyes shall l, and fail *with longing* H7200
Jdg 7:17 And he said unto them, L on me, and H7200
1Sa 1:11 if thou wilt indeed l on the affliction of H7200
16: 7 But the LORD said unto Samuel, L not H5027
12 and goodly to l to. And the LORD said, H7210
17:18 thousand, and l how thy brethren fare, H6485
2Sa 9: 8 l upon such a dead dog as I *am?* H6437
11: 2 woman *was* very beautiful to l upon. H4758
16:12 It may be that the LORD will l on mine H7200
1Ki 18:43 And said to his servant, Go up now, l H5027
2Ki 3:14 I would not l toward thee, nor see thee. H5027
6:32 away mine head? l, when the messenger H7200
9: 2 And when thou comest thither, l out H7200
10: 3 L even out the best and meetest of your H7200
23 of Baal, Search, and l that there be here H7200
14: 8 Come, let us l one another in the face. H7200
1Ch 12:17 of our fathers l *thereon,* and rebuke *it.* H7200
2Ch 24:22 The LORD l upon *it,* and require *it.* H7200
Est 1:11 her beauty: for she *was* fair to l on. H4758
Job 3: 9 be dark; let it l for light, but *have* none; H6960
6:28 Now therefore be content, l upon me; H6437
20:21 therefore shall no man l for his goods. H2342
35: 5 L unto the heavens, and see; and H5027
40:12 L on every one *that is* proud, *and* bring H7200
Ps 5: 3 *my prayer* unto thee, and will l up. H6822
22:17 I may tell all my bones: they l *and* stare H5027
25:18 L upon mine affliction and my pain; H7200
35:17 Lord, how long wilt thou l on? rescue H7200
40:12 I am not able to l up; they are more H7200
80:14 O God of hosts: l down from heaven, H5027
84: 9 Behold, O God our shield, and l upon H5027
85:11 shall l down from heaven. H8259
101: 5 l and a proud heart will not I suffer. H5869
119:132 L thou upon me, and be merciful unto H6437
123: 2 Behold, as the eyes of servants *l* unto the
Prv 4:25 Let thine eyes l right on, and let thine H5027
25 let thine eyelids l straight before thee.
6:17 A proud l, a lying tongue, and hands H5869
21: 4 An high l, and a proud heart, *and* the H5869
23:31 L not thou upon the wine when it is H7200
27:23 of thy flocks, *and* l well to thy herds. H7896
Ecc 12: 3 that l out of the windows be darkened, H7200
Song 1: 6 L not upon me, because I *am* black, H7200
4: 8 me from Lebanon: l from the top of H7789
6:13 that we may l upon thee. What will H2372
Isa 5:30 of the sea: and if *one* l unto the land, H5027
8:17 the house of Jacob, and I will l for him. H6960
21 their king and their God, and l upward. H6437
22 And they shall l unto the earth; and H5027
14:16 They that see thee shall narrowly l H7688
17: 7 At that day shall a man l to his Maker, H8159
8 And he shall not l to the altars, the H8159
22: 4 Therefore said I, L away from me; I H8159
8 and thou didst l in that day to the H5027
31: 1 strong; but they l not unto the Holy H8159
33:20 L upon Zion, the city of our H2372
42:18 Hear, ye deaf; and l, ye blind, that ye H5027
45:22 L unto me, and be ye saved, all the H6437
51: 1 seek the LORD: l unto the rock *whence* H5027
2 L unto Abraham your father, and unto H5027
6 Lift up your eyes to the heavens, and l H5027
56:11 they all l to their own way, every H6437
59:11 sore like doves: we l for judgment, but H6960
63:15 L down from heaven, and behold from H5027
66: 2 to this *man* will I l, *even* to *him that is* H5027
24 And they shall go forth, and l upon the H7200
Jer 13:16 and, while ye l for light, he turn it into H6960
39:12 Take him, and l well to him, and do H7760
40: 4 come; and I will l well unto thee: but if H7760
46: 5 fled apace, and l not back: *for* fear *was* H6437
47: 3 fathers shall not l back to *their* children H6437
Lam 3:50 Till the LORD l down, and behold from H8259
Ezk 23:15 all of them princes to l to, after the H4758
29:16 when they shall l after them: but they H6437
43:17 and his stairs shall l toward the east. H6437
Dan 7:20 l *was* more stout than his fellows. H2376
Hos 3: 1 of Israel, who l to other gods, and love H6437
Jna 2: 4 I will l again toward thy holy temple. H5027
Mic 4:11 be defiled, and let our eye l upon Zion. H2372
7: 7 Therefore I will l unto the LORD; I will H6822
Nah 2: 8 *shall they cry;* but none shall l back. H6437
3: 7 *that* all they that l upon thee shall flee H7200
Hab 1:13 behold evil, and canst not l on iniquity: H5027
2:15 that thou mayest l on their nakedness! H5027
Zec 12:10 and they shall l upon me whom they H5027
Mt 11: 3 should come, or do we l for another? G4328
Mk 8:25 and made him l up: and he was restored, G308
Lk 7:19 that should come? or l we for another? G4328
20 that should come? or l we for another? G4328
9:38 I beseech thee, l upon my son: for he G1914
21:28 come to pass, then l up, and lift up your G352
Jn 4:35 up your eyes, and l on the fields; for G2300
7:52 l: for out of Galilee ariseth no prophet. G1492
19:37 They shall l on him whom they pierced. G3700
Act 3: 4 eyes upon him with John, said, L on us. G991
12 ye at this? or why l ye so earnestly on us, G816
6: 3 Wherefore, brethren, l ye out among G1980
18:15 and *of* your law, l ye *to it;* for I will be G3700
1Co 16:11 me: for I l for him with the brethren. G1551
2Co 3:13 l to the end of that which is abolished: G816
4:18 While we l not at the things which are G4648
10: 7 Do ye l on things after the outward G991
Php 2: 4 L not every man on his own things, but G4648
3:20 l for the Saviour, the Lord Jesus Christ: G553
Heb 9:28 and unto them that l for him shall he G553
1Pt 1:12 which things the angels desire to l into. G3879
2Pt 3:13 to his promise, l for new heavens and G4328
14 Wherefore, beloved, seeing that ye l for G4328
2Jn 8 L to yourselves, that we lose not those G991
Rev 4: 3 And he that sat was to l upon like a G3706
5: 3 to open the book, neither to l thereon. G991
4 to read the book, neither to l thereon. G991

LOOKED
Gen 6:12 And God l upon the earth, and, behold, H7200
8:13 of the ark, and l, and, behold, the face H7200
16:13 I also here l after him that seeth me? H7200
18: 2 And he lift up his eyes and l, and, lo, H7200
16 from thence, and l toward Sodom: and H8259
19:26 But his wife l back from behind him, H5027
28 And he l toward Sodom and H8259
22:13 And Abraham lifted up his eyes, and l, H7200
26: 8 of the Philistines l out at a window, H8259
29: 2 And he l, and behold a well in the field, H7200
32 the LORD hath l upon my affliction; H7200
33: 1 And Jacob lifted up his eyes, and l, and, H7200
37:25 lifted up their eyes and l, and, behold, a H7200
39:23 The keeper of the prison l not to any H7200
40: 6 in the morning, and l upon them, and, H7200
Ex 2:11 his brethren, and l on their burdens: H7200
12 And he l this way and that way, and H6437
25 And God l upon the children of Israel, H7200
3: 2 of a bush: and he l, and, behold, the H7200
4:31 and that he had l upon their affliction, H7200
14:24 watch the LORD l unto the host of the H8259
16:10 of Israel, that they l toward the H6437
33: 8 his tent door, and l after Moses, until H5027
Nu 12:10 snow: and Aaron l upon Miriam, and, H6437
16:42 against Aaron, that they l toward the H6437
17: 9 and they l, and took every man his rod. H7200
24:20 And when he l on Amalek, he took up H7200
21 And he l on the Kenites, and took up H7200
Dt 9:16 And I l, and, behold, ye had sinned H7200
26: 7 our voice, and l on our affliction, and H7200
Jos 5:13 up his eyes and l, and, behold, there H7200
8:20 And when the men of Ai l behind them, H6437
Jdg 5:28 The mother of Sisera l out at a window, H8259
6:14 And the LORD l upon him, and said, H6437
9:43 wait in the field, and l, and, behold, the H7200
13:19 and Manoah and his wife l on. H7200
20 and his wife l on *it,* and fell on their H7200
20:40 the Benjamites l behind them, and, H6437
1Sa 6:19 because they had l into the ark of the H7200
9:16 for I have l upon my people, because H7200
14:16 Gibeah of Benjamin l; and, behold, the H7200
16: 6 were come, that he l on Eliab, and said, H7200
17:42 And when the Philistine l about, and H5027
24: 8 And when Saul l behind him, David H5027
2Sa 1: 7 And when he l behind him, he saw me, H6437
2:20 Then Abner l behind him, and said, *Art* H6437
6:16 Saul's daughter l through a window, H8259
13:34 up his eyes, and l, and, behold, there H7200
18:24 and l, and behold a man running alone. H7200
22:42 They l, but *there was* none to save; *even* H8159
24:20 And Araunah l, and saw the king and H8259
1Ki 18:43 he went up, and l, and said, *There is* H5027
19: 6 And he l, and, behold, *there was* a cake H5027
2Ki 2:24 And he turned back, and l on them, H7200
6:30 and the people l, and, behold, *he had* H7200
9:30 tired her head, and l out at a window. H8259
32 there l out to him two *or* three eunuchs. H8259
11:14 And when she l, behold, the king stood H7200
14:11 king of Judah l one another in the face H7200
1Ch 21:21 And as David came to Ornan, Ornan l H5027
2Ch 13:14 And when Judah l back, behold, the H6437
20:24 wilderness, they l unto the multitude, H6437
23:13 And she l, and, behold, the king stood H7200
26:20 and all the priests, l upon him, and, H6437
Neh 4:14 And I l, and rose up, and said unto the H7200
Est 2:15 in the sight of all them that l upon her. H7200
Job 6:19 The troops of Tema l, the companies of H5027
30:26 When I l for good, then evil came *unto* H6960
Ps 14: 2 The LORD l down from heaven upon H8259
34: 5 They l unto him, and were lightened: H5027
53: 2 God l down from heaven upon the H8259
69:20 of heaviness: and I l *for some* to take H6960
102:19 For he hath l down from the height of H8259
109:25 l upon me they shaked their heads. H7200
142: 4 I l on *my* right hand, and beheld, but H5027
Prv 7: 6 For at the window of my house I l H8259
24:32 Then I saw, *and* considered *it* well: I l H7200
Ecc 2:11 Then I l on all the works that my hands H6437
Song 1: 6 the sun hath l upon me: my mother's H7805
Isa 5: 2 therein: and he l that it should bring H6960

Isa 5: 4 wherefore, when I l that it should bring H6960
7 plant: and he l for judgment, but H6960
22:11 pool: but ye have not l unto the maker H5027
63: 5 And I l, and *there was* none to help; and H5027
64: 3 things *which* we l not for, thou camest H6960
Jer 8:15 We l for peace, but no good *came; and* H6960
14:19 healing for us? we l for peace, and *there* H6960
Lam 2:16 l for; we have found, we have seen *it*. H6960
Ezk 1: 4 And I l, and, behold, a whirlwind came H7200
2: 9 And when I l, behold, an hand *was* sent H7200
8: 7 and when I l, behold a hole in the wall. H7200
10: 1 Then I l, and, behold, in the firmament H7200
9 And when I l, behold the four wheels by H7200
11 whither the head l they followed it; they H6437
16: 8 Now when I passed by thee, and l upon H7200
21:21 consulted with images, he l in the liver. H7200
40:20 court that l toward the north, he H6440
44: 4 the house: and I l, and, behold, the H7200
46:19 of the priests, which l toward the north: H6437
Dan 1:13 Then let our countenances be l upon H7200
10: 5 Then I lifted up mine eyes, and l, and H7200
12: 5 Then I Daniel l, and, behold, there H7200
Oba 12 But thou shouldest not have l on the H7200
13 shouldest not have l on their affliction H7200
Hag 1: 9 Ye l for much, and, lo, *it came* to little; H6437
Zec 2: 1 I lifted up mine eyes again, and l, and H7200
4: 2 thou? And I said, I have l, and behold a H7200
5: 1 eyes, and l, and behold a flying roll. H7200
9 Then lifted I up mine eyes, and l, and, H7200
6: 1 up mine eyes, and l, and, behold, there H7200
Mk 3: 5 And when he had l round about on G4017
34 And he l round about on them which G4017
5:32 And he l round about to see her that G4017
6:41 the two fishes, he l up to heaven, and G308
8:24 And he l up, and said, I see men as trees, G308
33 But when he had turned about and l on G1492
9: 8 And suddenly, when they had l round G4017
10:23 And Jesus l round about, and saith G4017
11:11 and when he had l round about upon G4017
14:67 himself, she l upon him, and said, G1689
16: 4 And when they l, they saw that the stone G308
Lk 1:25 days wherein he l on *me*, to take away G1896
2:38 that l for redemption in Jerusalem. G4327
10:32 place, came and l *on him*, and passed G1492
19: 5 And when Jesus came to the place, he l G308
21: 1 And he l up, and saw the rich men G308
22:56 fire, and earnestly l upon him, and said, G816
61 And the Lord turned, and l upon Peter. G1689
Jn 13:22 Then the disciples l one on another, G991
20:11 stooped down, *and l* into the sepulchre, G3879
Act 1:10 And while they l stedfastly toward G816
7:55 But he, being full of the Holy Ghost, l up G816
10: 4 And when he l on him, he was afraid, G816
22:13 And the same hour I l up upon him. G308
28: 6 Howbeit they l when he should have G4328
6 but after they had l a great while, and G4328
Heb 11:10 For he l for a city which hath G1551
1Jn 1: 1 which we have l upon, and our hands G2300
Rev 4: 1 After this I l, and, behold, a door *was* G1492
6: 8 And I l, and behold a pale horse: and G1492
14: 1 And I l, and, lo, a Lamb stood on the G1492
14 And I l, and behold a white cloud, and G1492
15: 5 And after that I l, and, behold, the G1492

LOOKEST
Job 13:27 in the stocks, and l narrowly unto all H8104
Hab 1:13 wherefore l thou upon them that H5027

LOOKETH
Lev 13:12 foot, wheresoever the priest l; H4758+H5869
Nu 21: 8 is bitten, when he l upon it, shall live. H7200
20 of Pisgah, which l toward Jeshimon. H8259
23:28 the top of Peor, that l toward Jeshimon. H8259
Jos 15: 2 salt sea, from the bay that l southward: H6437
1Sa 13:18 way of the border that l to the valley of H8259
16: 7 man seeth; for man l on the outward H7200
7 but the LORD l on the heart. H7200
Job 7: 2 an hireling l for *the reward of* his work: H6960
28:24 For he l to the ends of the earth, *and* H5027
33:27 He l upon men, and *if any* say, I have H7789
Ps 33:13 The LORD l from heaven; he beholdeth H5027
14 From the place of his habitation he l H7688
104:32 He l on the earth, and it trembleth: he H5027
Prv 14:15 but the prudent *man* l well to his going. H995
31:27 She l well to the ways of her household, H6822
Song 2: 9 our wall, he l forth at the windows, H7688
6:10 Who *is* she *that* l forth as the morning, H8259
7: 4 of Lebanon which l toward Damascus. H6822
Isa 28: 4 *when* he that l upon it seeth, while H7200

Ezk 8: 3 the inner gate that l toward the north; H6437
11: 1 house, which l eastward: and behold H6437
40: 6 Then came he unto the gate which l H6440
22 of the gate that l toward the east; and H6440
43: 1 *even* the gate that l toward the east: H6437
44: 1 l toward the east; and it *was* shut. H6437
46: 1 inner court that l toward the east shall H6437
12 him the gate that l toward the east, and H6437
47: 2 gate by the way that l eastward; and, H6437
Mt 5:28 But I say unto you, That whosoever l on G991
24:50 in a day when he l not for *him*, and in G4328
Lk 12:46 in a day when he l not for *him*, and at G4328
Jas 1:25 But whoso l into the perfect law of G3879

LOOKING
Jos 15: 7 and so northward, l toward Gilgal, that H6437
1Ki 7:25 It stood upon twelve oxen, three l H6437
25 north, and three l toward the west, and H6437
25 west, and three l toward the south, and H6437
25 south, and three l toward the east: and H6437
1Ch 15:29 daughter of Saul l out at a window saw H8259
2Ch 4: 4 It stood upon twelve oxen, three l H6437
4 north, and three l toward the west, and H6437
4 west, and three l toward the south, and H6437
4 south, and three l toward the east: and H6437
Job 37:18 *is* strong, *and* as a molten l glass? H7209
Isa 38:14 mine eyes fail *with l* upward: O LORD, I
Mt 14:19 the two fishes, and l up to heaven, he G308
Mk 7:34 And l up to heaven, he sighed, and saith G308
10:27 And Jesus l upon them saith, With men G1689
15:40 There were also women l on afar off: G2334
Lk 6:10 And l round about upon them all, he G4017
9:16 the two fishes, and l up to heaven, he G308
62 and l back, is fit for the kingdom of God. G991
21:26 for fear, and for l after those things G4329
Jn 1:36 And l upon Jesus as he walked, he G1689
20: 5 And he stooping down, *and l in*, saw the
Act 6:15 And all that sat in the council, l G816
23:21 they ready, l for a promise from thee. G4327
Tit 2:13 L for that blessed hope, and the G4327
Heb 10:27 But a certain fearful l for of judgment G1561
12: 2 L unto Jesus the author and finisher of G872
15 L diligently lest any man fail of the G1983
2Pt 3:12 L for and hasting unto the coming of G4328
Jude 21 Keep yourselves in the love of God, l for G4327

LOOKING-GLASSES
Ex 38: 8 of it *of* brass, of the l of *the women* H4759

LOOKS
Ps 18:27 people; but wilt bring down high l. H5869
Isa 2:11 The lofty l of man shall be humbled, H5869
10:12 of Assyria, and the glory of his high l. H5869
Ezk 2: 6 l, though they *be* a rebellious house. H6440
3: 9 l, though they *be* a rebellious house. H6440

LOOPS
Ex 26: 4 And thou shalt make l of blue upon the H3924
5 Fifty l shalt thou make in the one H3924
5 curtain, and fifty l shalt thou make in H3924
5 that the l may take hold one of another. H3924
10 And thou shalt make fifty l on the edge H3924
10 coupling, and fifty l in the edge of the H3924
11 the taches into the l, and couple the tent H3924
36:11 And he made l of blue on the edge of H3924
12 Fifty l made he in one curtain, and fifty H3924
12 curtain, and fifty l made he in the edge H3924
12 the l held one *curtain* to another. H3924
17 And he made fifty l upon the uttermost H3924
17 coupling, and fifty l made he upon the H3924

LOOSE
Gen 49:21 Naphtali *is* a hind let l: he giveth goodly H7971
Lev 14: 7 let the living bird l into the open field. H7971
Dt 25: 9 of the elders, and l his shoe from off his H2502
Jos 5:15 said unto Joshua, L thy shoe from off H5394
Job 6: 9 he would let l his hand, and cut me off! H5425
30:11 have also let l the bridle before me. H7971
38:31 of Pleiades, or l the bands of Orion? H6605
Ps 102:20 to l those that are appointed to death; H6605
Isa 20: 2 saying, Go and l the sackcloth from off H6605
45: 1 him; and I will l the loins of kings, to H6605
52: 2 O Jerusalem: l thyself from the bands H6605
58: 6 that I have chosen? to l the bands of H6605
Jer 40: 4 And now, behold, I l thee this day from H6605
Dan 3:25 said, Lo, I see four men l, walking in the H8271
Mt 16:19 l on earth shall be loosed in heaven. G3089
18:18 l on earth shall be loosed in heaven. G3089
21: 2 her: l *them*, and bring *them* unto me. G3089

Mk 11: 2 never man sat; l him, and bring *him*. G3089
4 where two ways met; and they l him. G3089
Lk 13:15 on the sabbath l his ox or *his* ass from G3089
19:30 man sat: l him, and bring *him hither*. G3089
31 And if any man ask you, Why do ye l G3089
33 said unto them, Why l ye the colt? G3089
Jn 11:44 saith unto them, L him, and let him go. G3089
Act 13:25 shoes of *his* feet I am not worthy to l. G3089
24:26 that he might l him: wherefore he sent G3089
Rev 5: 2 the book, and to l the seals thereof? G3089
5 book, and to l the seven seals thereof. G3089
9:14 had the trumpet, L the four angels G3089

LOOSED
Ex 28:28 the breastplate be not l from the ephod. H2118
39:21 might not be l from the ephod; as the H2118
Dt 25:10 The house of him that hath his shoe l. H2502
Jdg 15:14 fire, and his bands l from off his hands. H4549
Job 30:11 Because he hath l my cord, and H6605
39: 5 or who hath l the bands of the wild ass? H6605
Ps 105:20 The king sent and l him; *even* the ruler H5425
116:16 thine handmaid: thou hast l my bonds. H6605
Ecc 12: 6 Or ever the silver cord be l, or the H7368
Isa 5:27 of their loins be l, nor the latchet of H6605
33:23 Thy tacklings are l; they could not well H5203
51:14 that he may be l, and that he should not H6605
Dan 5: 6 of his loins were l, and his knees smote H8271
Mt 16:19 loose on earth shall be l in heaven. G3089
18:18 loose on earth shall be l in heaven. G3089
27 and l him, and forgave him the debt. G630
Mk 7:35 of his tongue was l, and he spake plain. G3089
Lk 1:64 tongue *l*, and he spake, and praised God.
13:12 Woman, thou art l from thine infirmity. G630
16 be l from this bond on the sabbath day? G3089
Act 2:24 Whom God hath raised up, having l the G3089
13:13 Now when Paul and his company l from G321
16:26 opened, and every one's bands were l. G447
22:30 of the Jews, he l him from *his* bands, G3089
27:21 me, and not have l from Crete, and to G321
40 unto the sea, and l the rudder bands, G447
Ro 7: 2 she is l from the law of *her* husband. G2673
1Co 7:27 seek not to be l. Art thou loosed from G3080
27 Art thou l from a wife? seek not a wife. G3089
Rev 9:15 And the four angels were l, which were G3089
20: 3 after that he must be l a little season. G3089
7 Satan shall be l out of his prison, G3089

LOOSETH
Job 12:18 He l the bond of kings, and girdeth H6605
Ps 146: 7 the hungry. The LORD l the prisoners: H5425

LOOSING
Mk 11: 5 said unto them, What do ye, l the colt? G3089
Lk 19:33 And as they were l the colt, the owners G3089
Act 16:11 Therefore l from Troas, we came with a G321
27:13 l *thence*, they sailed close by Crete. G142

LOP
Isa 10:33 of hosts, shall l the bough with terror: H5586

LORD
Gen 2: 4 L God made the earth and the heavens, H3068
5 it grew: for the L God had not caused H3068
7 And the L God formed man *of* the dust H3068
8 And the L God planted a garden H3068
9 And out of the ground made the L God H3068
15 And the L God took the man, and put H3068
16 And the L God commanded the man, H3068
18 And the L God said, *It is* not good that H3068
19 And out of the ground the L God H3068
21 And the L God caused a deep sleep to H3068
22 And the rib, which the L God had taken H3068
3: 1 of the field which the L God had made. H3068
8 And they heard the voice of the L God H3068
8 L God amongst the trees of the garden. H3068
9 And the L God called unto Adam, and H3068
13 And the L God said unto the woman, H3068
14 And the L God said unto the serpent, H3068
21 to his wife did the L God make coats of H3068
22 And the L God said, Behold, the man is H3068
23 Therefore the L God sent him forth H3068
4: 1 said, I have gotten a man from the L. H3068
3 of the ground an offering unto the L. H3068
4 fat thereof. And the L had respect unto H3068
6 And the L said unto Cain, Why art thou H3068
9 And the L said unto Cain, Where *is* H3068
13 And Cain said unto the L, My H3068
15 And the L said unto him, Therefore H3068
15 And the L set a mark upon Cain, H3068

Gen 4:16 presence of the L, and dwelt in the land H3068
26 men to call upon the name of the L. H3068
5:29 of the ground which the L hath cursed. H3068
6: 3 And the L said, My spirit shall not H3068
6 And it repented the L that he had made H3068
7 And the L said, I will destroy man H3068
8 Noah found grace in the eyes of the L. H3068
7: 1 And the L said unto Noah, Come thou H3068
5 unto all that the L commanded him. H3068
16 him: and the L shut him in. H3068
8:20 And Noah builded an altar unto the L; H3068
21 And the L smelled a sweet savour; and H3068
21 savour; and the L said in his heart, I H3068
9:26 And he said, Blessed *be* the L God of H3068
10: 9 He was a mighty hunter before the L: H3068
9 Nimrod the mighty hunter before the L. H3068
11: 5 And the L came down to see the city H3068
6 And the L said, Behold, the people *is* H3068
8 So the L scattered them abroad from H3068
9 called Babel; because the L did there H3068
9 thence did the L scatter them abroad H3068
12: 1 Now the L had said unto Abram, Get H3068
4 So Abram departed, as the L had H3068
7 And the L appeared unto Abram, and H3068
7 unto the L, who appeared unto him. H3068
8 an altar unto the L, and called upon the H3068
8 and called upon the name of the L. H3068
17 And the L plagued Pharaoh and his H3068
13: 4 Abram called on the name of the L. H3068
10 where, before the L destroyed Sodom H3068
10 as the garden of the L, like the land of H3068
13 and sinners before the L exceedingly. H3068
14 And the L said unto Abram, after that H3068
18 and built there an altar unto the L. H3068
14:22 hand unto the L, the most high God, H3068
15: 1 After these things the word of the L H3068
2 And Abram said, L GOD, what wilt thou H136
4 And, behold, the word of the L *came* H3068
6 And he believed in the L; and he H3068
7 And he said unto him, I *am* the L that H3068
8 And he said, L GOD, whereby shall I H136
18 In the same day the L made a covenant H3068
16: 2 Behold now, the L hath restrained me H3068
5 eyes: the L judge between me and thee. H3068
7 And the angel of the L found her by a H3068
9 And the angel of the L said unto her, H3068
10 And the angel of the L said unto her, I H3068
11 And the angel of the L said unto her, H3068
11 because the L hath heard thy affliction. H3068
13 And she called the name of the L that H3068
17: 1 years old and nine, the L appeared to H3068
18: 1 And the L appeared unto him in the H3068
3 And said, My L, if now I have found H136
12 I have pleasure, my l being old also? H113
13 And the L said unto Abraham, H3068
14 Is any thing too hard for the L? At the H3068
17 And the L said, Shall I hide from H3068
19 keep the way of the L, to do justice and H3068
19 that the L may bring upon Abraham H3068
20 And the L said, Because the cry of H3068
22 but Abraham stood yet before the L. H3068
26 And the L said, If I find in Sodom fifty H3068
27 unto the L, which *am but* dust and ashes: H136
30 And he said *unto him*, Oh let not the L H136
31 to speak unto the L: Peradventure there H136
32 And he said, Oh let not the L be angry, H136
33 And the L went his way, as soon as he H3068
19:13 the face of the L; and the LORD hath H3068
13 and the L hath sent us to destroy it. H3068
14 of this place; for the L will destroy this H3068
16 daughters; the L being merciful unto H3068
18 Lot said unto them, Oh, not so, my L: H113
24 Then the L rained upon Sodom and H3068
24 and fire from the L out of heaven; H3068
27 the place where he stood before the L: H3068
20: 4 L, wilt thou slay also a righteous nation? H136
18 For the L had fast closed up all the H3068
21: 1 And the L visited Sarah as he had said, H3068
1 the L did unto Sarah as he had spoken. H3068
33 the name of the L, the everlasting God. H3068
22:11 And the angel of the L called unto him H3068
14 In the mount of the L it shall be seen. H3068
15 And the angel of the L called unto H3068
16 I sworn, saith the L, for because thou H3068
23: 6 Hear us, my l: thou *art* a mighty prince H113
11 Nay, my l, hear me: the field give I thee, H113
15 My l, hearken unto me: the land *is worth* H113
24: 1 L had blessed Abraham in all things. H3068
3 And I will make thee swear by the L, the H3068

Gen 24: 7 The L God of heaven, which took me H3068
12 And he said, O L God of my master H3068
18 And she said, Drink, my l: and she H113
21 to wit whether the L had made his H3068
26 down his head, and worshipped the L. H3068
27 And he said, Blessed *be* the L God of H3068
27 in the way, the L led me to the house H3068
31 blessed of the L; wherefore standest H3068
35 And the L hath blessed my master H3068
40 And he said unto me, The L, before H3068
42 well, and said, O L God of my master H3068
44 woman whom the L hath appointed H3068
48 and worshipped the L, and blessed the H3068
48 and blessed the L God of my master H3068
50 from the L: we cannot speak unto H3068
51 son's wife, as the L hath spoken. H3068
52 the L, *bowing himself* to the earth. H3068
56 me not, seeing the L hath prospered H3068
25:21 And Isaac entreated the L for his wife, H3068
21 barren: and the L was entreated of him, H3068
22 I thus? And she went to inquire of the L. H3068
23 And the L said unto her, Two nations H3068
26: 2 And the L appeared unto him, and H3068
12 an hundredfold: and the L blessed him. H3068
22 he said, For now the L hath made room H3068
24 And the L appeared unto him the same H3068
25 the name of the L, and pitched his tent H3068
28 certainly that the L was with thee: and H3068
29 peace: thou *art* now the blessed of the L. H3068
27: 7 thee before the L before my death. H3068
20 Because the L thy God brought *it* to me. H3068
27 of a field which the L hath blessed: H3068
29 down to thee: be l over thy brethren, H1376
37 made him thy l, and all his brethren H1376
28:13 And, behold, the L stood above it, and H3068
13 and said, I *am* the L God of Abraham H3068
16 the L is in this place; and I knew *it* not. H3068
21 in peace; then shall the L be my God: H3068
29:31 And when the L saw that Leah *was* H3068
32 said, Surely the L hath looked upon my H3068
33 said, Because the L hath heard that I H3068
35 will I praise the L: therefore she called H3068
30:24 The L shall add to me another son. H3068
27 that the L hath blessed me for thy sake. H3068
30 and the L hath blessed thee since H3068
31: 3 And the L said unto Jacob, Return unto H3068
35 it not displease my l that I cannot rise up H113
49 And Mizpah; for he said, The L watch H3068
32: 4 ye speak unto my l Esau; Thy servant H113
5 my l, that I may find grace in thy sight. H113
9 father Isaac, the L which saidst unto H3068
18 l Esau: and, behold, also he *is* behind us. H113
33: 8 *are* to find grace in the sight of my l. H113
13 And he said unto him, My l knoweth H113
14 Let my l, I pray thee, pass over before his H113
14 endure, until I come unto my l unto Seir. H113
15 it? let me find grace in the sight of my l. H113
38: 7 sight of the L; and the LORD slew him. H3068
7 sight of the LORD; and the L slew him. H3068
10 the L: wherefore he slew him also. H3068
39: 2 And the L was with Joseph, and he was H3068
3 And his master saw that the L *was* with H3068
3 him, and that the L made all that he H3068
5 that he had, that the L blessed the H3068
5 the blessing of the L was upon all that H3068
16 garment by her, until his l came home. H113
21 But the L was with Joseph, and shewed H3068
23 hand; because the L was with him, and H3068
23 which he did, the L made *it* to prosper. H3068
40: 1 had offended their l the king of Egypt. H113
42:10 And they said unto him, Nay, my l, but to H113
30 The man, *who is* the l of the land, spake H113
33 And the man, the l of the country, said H113
44: 5 *Is* not this *it* in which my l drinketh, and H113
7 saith my l these words? God forbid H113
16 we say unto my l? what shall we speak? H113
18 and said, Oh my l, let thy servant, I pray H113
19 My l asked his servants, saying, Have ye H113
20 And we said unto my l, We have a father, H113
22 And we said unto my l, The lad cannot H113
24 my father, we told him the words of my l. H113
33 l; and let the lad go up with his brethren. H113
45: 8 to Pharaoh, and l of all his house, and H113
9 God hath made me l of all Egypt: come H113
47:18 will not hide *it* from my l, how that our H113
18 money is spent; my l also hath our herds H113
18 of my l, but our bodies, and our lands: H113
25 my l, and we will be Pharaoh's servants. H113
49:18 I have waited for thy salvation, O L. H3068

Ex 3: 2 And the angel of the L appeared unto H3068
4 And when the L saw that he turned H3068
7 And the L said, I have surely seen the H3068
15 of Israel, The L God of your fathers, H3068
16 unto them, The L God of your fathers, H3068
18 shall say unto him, The L God of the H3068
18 that we may sacrifice to the L our God. H3068
4: 1 The L hath not appeared unto thee. H3068
2 And the L said unto him, What *is* that H3068
4 And the L said unto Moses, Put forth H3068
5 That they may believe that the L God of H3068
6 And the L said furthermore unto him, H3068
10 And Moses said unto the L, O my Lord, H3068
10 And Moses said unto the LORD, O my L, H136
11 And the L said unto him, Who hath H3068
11 seeing, or the blind? have not I the L? H3068
13 And he said, O my L, send, I pray thee, H136
14 And the anger of the L was kindled H3068
19 And the L said unto Moses in Midian, H3068
21 And the L said unto Moses, When thou H3068
22 L, Israel *is* my son, *even* my firstborn: H3068
24 the L met him, and sought to kill him. H3068
27 And the L said to Aaron, Go into the H3068
28 the words of the L who had sent him, H3068
30 the words which the L had spoken unto H3068
31 they heard that the L had visited the H3068
5: 1 Thus saith the L God of Israel, Let my H3068
2 And Pharaoh said, Who *is* the L, that I H3068
2 not the L, neither will I let Israel go. H3068
3 sacrifice unto the L our God; lest he fall H3068
17 say, Let us go *and* do sacrifice to the L. H3068
21 And they said unto them, The L look H3068
22 And Moses returned unto the L, and H3068
22 LORD, and said, L, wherefore hast thou H136
6: 1 Then the L said unto Moses, Now shalt H3068
2 Moses, and said unto him, I *am* the L: H3068
6 of Israel, I *am* the L, and I will bring H3068
7 know that I *am* the L your God, which H3068
8 give it you for an heritage: I *am* the L. H3068
10 And the L spake unto Moses, saying, H3068
12 And Moses spake before the L, saying, H3068
13 And the L spake unto Moses and unto H3068
26 to whom the L said, Bring out the H3068
28 the day *when* the L spake unto Moses H3068
29 That the L spake unto Moses, saying, I H3068
29 saying, I *am* the L: speak thou unto H3068
30 And Moses said before the L, Behold, I H3068
7: 1 And the L said unto Moses, See, I have H3068
5 that I *am* the L, when I stretch forth H3068
6 And Moses and Aaron did as the L H3068
8 And the L spake unto Moses and unto H3068
10 they did so as the L had commanded: H3068
13 not unto them; as the L had said. H3068
14 And the L said unto Moses, Pharaoh's H3068
16 And thou shalt say unto him, The L H3068
17 Thus saith the L, In this thou shalt H3068
17 that I *am* the L: behold, I will smite H3068
19 And the L spake unto Moses, Say unto H3068
20 And Moses and Aaron did so, as the L H3068
22 hearken unto them; as the L had said. H3068
25 after that the L had smitten the river. H3068
8: 1 And the L spake unto Moses, Go unto H3068
1 Thus saith the L, Let my people go, that H3068
5 And the L spake unto Moses, Say unto H3068
8 said, Entreat the L, that he may take H3068
8 that they may do sacrifice unto the L. H3068
10 *there is* none like unto the L our God. H3068
12 cried unto the L because of the frogs H3068
13 And the L did according to the word of H3068
15 not unto them; as the L had said. H3068
16 And the L said unto Moses, Say unto H3068
19 not unto them; as the L had said. H3068
20 And the L said unto Moses, Rise up H3068
20 Thus saith the L, Let my people go, that H3068
22 I *am* the L in the midst of the earth. H3068
24 And the L did so; and there came a H3068
26 Egyptians to the L our God: lo, shall we H3068
27 L our God, as he shall command us. H3068
28 may sacrifice to the L your God in the H3068
29 I will entreat the L that the swarms *of* H3068
29 the people go to sacrifice to the L. H3068
30 out from Pharaoh, and entreated the L. H3068
31 And the L did according to the word of H3068
9: 1 Then the L said unto Moses, Go in unto H3068
1 Thus saith the L God of the Hebrews, H3068
3 Behold, the hand of the L is upon thy H3068
4 And the L shall sever between the cattle H3068
5 And the L appointed a set time, saying, H3068
5 the L shall do this thing in the land. H3068

Ex 9: 6 And the L did that thing on the H3068
8 And the L said unto Moses and unto H3068
12 And the L hardened the heart of H3068
12 them; as the L had spoken unto Moses. H3068
13 And the L said unto Moses, Rise up H3068
13 Thus saith the L God of the Hebrews, H3068
20 He that feared the word of the L among H3068
21 the word of the L left his servants and H3068
22 And the L said unto Moses, Stretch H3068
23 heaven: and the L sent thunder and H3068
23 L rained hail upon the land of Egypt. H3068
27 this time: the L *is* righteous, and I and H3068
28 Entreat the L (for *it is* enough) that H3068
29 hands unto the L; *and* the thunder shall H3068
30 that ye will not yet fear the L God. H3068
33 hands unto the L: and the thunders and H3068
35 go; as the L had spoken by Moses. H3068
10: 1 And the L said unto Moses, Go in unto H3068
2 that ye may know how that I *am* the L. H3068
3 Thus saith the L God of the Hebrews, H3068
7 may serve the L their God: knowest H3068
8 Go, serve the L your God: *but* who H3068
9 go; for we *must hold* a feast unto the L. H3068
10 And he said unto them, Let the L be so H3068
11 and serve the L; for that ye did desire. H3068
12 And the L said unto Moses, Stretch out H3068
13 of Egypt, and the L brought an east H3068
16 the L your God, and against you. H3068
17 and entreat the L your God, that he H3068
18 out from Pharaoh, and entreated the L. H3068
19 And the L turned a mighty strong west H3068
20 But the L hardened Pharaoh's heart, so H3068
21 And the L said unto Moses, Stretch out H3068
24 Go ye, serve the L; only let your flocks H3068
25 we may sacrifice unto the L our God. H3068
26 we take to serve the L our God; and we H3068
26 must serve the L, until we come thither. H3068
27 But the L hardened Pharaoh's heart, H3068
11: 1 And the L said unto Moses, Yet will I H3068
3 And the L gave the people favour in the H3068
4 And Moses said, Thus saith the L, H3068
7 how that the L doth put a difference H3068
9 And the L said unto Moses, Pharaoh H3068
10 before Pharaoh: and the L hardened H3068
12: 1 And the L spake unto Moses and H3068
12 I will execute judgment: I *am* the L. H3068
14 keep it a feast to the L throughout your H3068
23 For the L will pass through to smite the H3068
23 two side posts, the L will pass over the H3068
25 to the land which the L will give you, H3068
28 and did as the L had commanded H3068
29 that at midnight the L smote all the H3068
31 and go, serve the L, as ye have said. H3068
36 And the L gave the people favour in the H3068
41 the L went out from the land of Egypt. H3068
42 observed unto the L for bringing them H3068
42 *is* that night of the L to be observed of H3068
43 And the L said unto Moses and Aaron, H3068
48 passover to the L, let all his males be H3068
50 of Israel; as the L commanded Moses H3068
51 day, *that* the L did bring the children H3068
13: 1 And the L spake unto Moses, saying, H3068
3 of hand the L brought you out from H3068
5 And it shall be when the L shall bring H3068
6 the seventh day *shall be* a feast to the L. H3068
8 of that *which* the L did unto me when I H3068
9 hath the L brought thee out of Egypt. H3068
11 And it shall be when the L shall bring H3068
12 That thou shalt set apart unto the L all H3068
14 of hand the L brought us out from H3068
15 hardly let us go, that the L slew all the H3068
15 I sacrifice to the L all that openeth the H3068
16 the L brought us forth out of Egypt. H3068
21 And the L went before them by day in a H3068
14: 1 And the L spake unto Moses, saying, H3068
4 know that I *am* the L. And they did so. H3068
8 And the L hardened the heart of H3068
10 children of Israel cried out unto the L. H3068
13 salvation of the L, which he will shew H3068
14 The L shall fight for you, and ye shall H3068
15 And the L said unto Moses, Wherefore H3068
18 that I *am* the L, when I have gotten H3068
21 the sea; and the L caused the sea to go H3068
24 watch the L looked unto the host H3068
25 of Israel; for the L fighteth for them H3068
26 And the L said unto Moses, Stretch out H3068
27 fled against it; and the L overthrew the H3068
30 Thus the L saved Israel that day out of H3068
31 great work which the L did upon the H3068

Ex 14:31 people feared the L, and believed the H3068
31 believed the L, and his servant Moses. H3068
15: 1 this song unto the L, and spake, saying, H3068
1 I will sing unto the L, for he hath H3068
2 The L *is* my strength and song, and he H3050
3 The L *is* a man of war: the LORD *is* his H3068
3 The LORD *is* a man of war: the L *is* his H3068
6 Thy right hand, O L, is become glorious H3068
6 O L, hath dashed in pieces the enemy. H3068
11 Who *is* like unto thee, O L, among the H3068
16 pass over, O L, till the people pass H3068
17 *in* the place, O L, *which* thou hast made H3068
17 O L, *which* thy hands have established. H136
18 The L shall reign for ever and ever. H3068
19 the sea, and the L brought again the H3068
21 Sing ye to the L, for he hath triumphed H3068
25 And he cried unto the L; and the LORD H3068
25 And he cried unto the LORD; and the L H3068
26 to the voice of the L thy God, and wilt H3068
26 for I *am* the L that healeth thee. H3068
16: 3 died by the hand of the L in the land of H3068
4 Then said the L unto Moses, Behold, I H3068
6 know that the L hath brought you out H3068
7 the glory of the L; for that he heareth H3068
7 against the L: and what *are* we, that H3068
8 *shall be*, when the L shall give you in H3068
8 the full; for that the L heareth your H3068
8 *are* not against us, but against the L. H3068
9 L: for he hath heard your murmurings. H3068
10 glory of the L appeared in the cloud. H3068
11 And the L spake unto Moses, saying, H3068
12 ye shall know that I *am* the L your God. H3068
15 which the L hath given you to eat. H3068
16 This *is* the thing which the L hath H3068
23 This *is that* which the L hath said, To H3068
23 sabbath unto the L: bake *that* which ye H3068
25 L: to day ye shall not find it in the field. H3068
28 And the L said unto Moses, How long H3068
29 See, for that the L hath given you the H3068
32 thing which the L commandeth, Fill an H3068
33 the L, to be kept for your generations. H3068
34 As the L commanded Moses, so Aaron H3068
17: 1 of the L, and pitched in Rephidim: H3068
2 with me? wherefore do ye tempt the L? H3068
4 And Moses cried unto the L, saying, H3068
5 And the L said unto Moses, Go on H3068
7 they tempted the L, saying, Is the LORD H3068
7 saying, Is the L among us, or not? H3068
14 And the L said unto Moses, Write this H3068
16 For he said, Because the L hath sworn H3050
16 sworn *that* the L *will have* war with H3068
18: 1 the L had brought Israel out of Egypt; H3068
8 in law all that the L had done unto H3068
8 the way, and *how* the L delivered them. H3068
9 which the L had done to Israel, H3068
10 And Jethro said, Blessed *be* the L, who H3068
11 Now I know that the L *is* greater than H3068
19: 3 up unto God, and the L called unto him H3068
7 words which the L commanded him. H3068
8 said, All that the L hath spoken we will H3068
8 the words of the people unto the L. H3068
9 And the L said unto Moses, Lo, I come H3068
9 told the words of the people unto the L. H3068
10 And the L said unto Moses, Go unto H3068
11 the third day the L will come down in H3068
18 because the L descended upon it in H3068
20 And the L came down upon mount H3068
20 mount: and the L called Moses *up* to H3068
21 And the L said unto Moses, Go down, H3068
21 L to gaze, and many of them perish. H3068
22 come near to the L, sanctify themselves, H3068
22 lest the L break forth upon them. H3068
23 And Moses said unto the L, The people H3068
24 And the L said unto him, Away, get H3068
24 the L, lest he break forth upon them. H3068
20: 2 I *am* the L thy God, which have H3068
5 them: for I the L thy God *am* a jealous H3068
7 Thou shalt not take the name of the L H3068
7 God in vain; for the L will not hold him H3068
10 the sabbath of the L thy God: *in it* thou H3068
11 For *in* six days the L made heaven and H3068
11 wherefore the L blessed the sabbath H3068
12 land which the L thy God giveth thee. H3068
22 And the L said unto Moses, Thus thou H3068
22:11 *Then* shall an oath of the L be between H3068
20 L only, he shall be utterly destroyed. H3068
23:17 males shall appear before the L GOD. H136
19 the house of the L thy God. Thou shalt H3068
25 And ye shall serve the L your God, and H3068

Ex 24: 1 Come up unto the L, thou, and Aaron, H3068
2 And Moses alone shall come near the L: H3068
3 all the words of the L, and all the H3068
3 words which the L hath said will we do. H3068
4 And Moses wrote all the words of the L, H3068
5 peace offerings of oxen unto the L. H3068
7 said, All that the L hath said will we do, H3068
8 which the L hath made with you H3068
12 And the L said unto Moses, Come up to H3068
16 And the glory of the L abode upon H3068
17 And the sight of the glory of the L *was* H3068
25: 1 And the L spake unto Moses, saying, H3068
27:21 before the L: *it shall be* a statute H3068
28:12 their names before the L upon his two H3068
29 a memorial before the L continually. H3068
30 in before the L: and Aaron shall bear H3068
30 his heart before the L continually. H3068
35 *place* before the L, and when he cometh H3068
36 of a signet, HOLINESS TO THE L. H3068
38 that they may be accepted before the L. H3068
29:11 bullock before the L, *by* the door of the H3068
18 offering unto the L: it *is* a sweet savour, H3068
18 an offering made by fire unto the L. H3068
23 unleavened bread that *is* before the L: H3068
24 them *for* a wave offering before the L. H3068
25 savour before the L: it *is* an offering H3068
25 it *is* an offering made by fire unto the L. H3068
26 before the L: and it shall be thy part. H3068
28 *even* their heave offering unto the L. H3068
41 an offering made by fire unto the L. H3068
42 before the L: where I will meet you, H3068
46 And they shall know that I *am* the L H3068
46 among them: I *am* the L their God. H3068
30: 8 the L throughout your generations. H3068
10 generations: it *is* most holy unto the L. H3068
11 And the L spake unto Moses, saying, H3068
12 for his soul unto the L, when thou H3068
13 half shekel *shall be* the offering of the L. H3068
14 above, shall give an offering unto the L. H3068
15 L, to make an atonement for your souls. H3068
16 L, to make an atonement for your souls. H3068
17 And the L spake unto Moses, saying, H3068
20 burn offering made by fire unto the L: H3068
22 Moreover the L spake unto Moses, H3068
34 And the L said unto Moses, Take unto H3068
37 it shall be unto thee holy for the L. H3068
31: 1 And the L spake unto Moses, saying, H3068
12 And the L spake unto Moses, saying, H3068
13 that I *am* the L that doth sanctify you. H3068
15 of rest, holy to the L: whosoever doeth H3068
17 for *in* six days the L made heaven and H3068
32: 5 and said, To morrow *is* a feast to the L. H3068
7 And the L said unto Moses, Go, get H3068
9 And the L said unto Moses, I have seen H3068
11 And Moses besought the L his God, H3068
11 his God, and said, L, why doth thy H3068
14 And the L repented of the evil which he H3068
22 Let not the anger of my l wax hot: thou H113
27 Thus saith the L God of Israel, Put H3068
29 to day to the L, even every man upon H3068
30 go up unto the L; peradventure I shall H3068
31 And Moses returned unto the L, and H3068
33 And the L said unto Moses, Whosoever H3068
35 And the L plagued the people, because H3068
33: 1 And the L said unto Moses, Depart, H3068
5 For the L had said unto Moses, Say H3068
7 which sought the L went out unto the H3068
9 tabernacle, and *the L* talked with Moses.
11 And the L spake unto Moses face to H3068
12 And Moses said unto the L, See, thou H3068
17 And the L said unto Moses, I will do H3068
19 the name of the L before thee; and will H3068
21 And the L said, Behold, *there is* a place H3068
34: 1 And the L said unto Moses, Hew thee H3068
4 Sinai, as the L had commanded him, H3068
5 And the L descended in the cloud, and H3068
5 and proclaimed the name of the L. H3068
6 And the L passed by before him, and H3068
6 and proclaimed, The L, The LORD God, H3068
6 The LORD, The L God, merciful and H3068
9 in thy sight, O L, let my Lord, I pray thee, H136
9 O Lord, let my L, I pray thee, go among H136
10 see the work of the L: for it *is* a terrible H3068
14 no other god: for the L, whose name *is* H3068
23 before the L GOD, the God of Israel. H113
24 before the L thy God thrice in the year. H3068
26 the house of the L thy God. Thou shalt H3068
27 And the L said unto Moses, Write thou H3068
28 And he was there with the L forty days H3068

Ex 34:32 L had spoken with him in mount Sinai. H3068
34 But when Moses went in before the L to H3068
35: 1 words which the L hath commanded, H3068
2 of rest to the L: whosoever doeth work H3068
4 thing which the L commanded, saying, H3068
5 an offering unto the L: whosoever *is* of a H3068
5 of the L; gold, and silver, and brass, H3068
10 make all that the L hath commanded; H3068
22 *offered* an offering of gold unto the L. H3068
29 offering unto the L, every man and H3068
29 of work, which the L had commanded H3068
30 of Israel, See, the L hath called by H3068
36: 1 man, in whom the L put wisdom and H3068
1 to all that the L had commanded. H3068
2 in whose heart the L had put wisdom, H3068
5 which the L commanded to make. H3068
38:22 all that the L commanded Moses. H3068
39: 1 for Aaron; as the L commanded Moses. H3068
5 linen; as the L commanded Moses. H3068
7 of Israel; as the L commanded Moses. H3068
21 ephod; as the L commanded Moses. H3068
26 *in;* as the L commanded Moses. H3068
29 as the L commanded Moses. H3068
30 of a signet, HOLINESS TO THE L. H3068
31 the mitre; as the L commanded Moses. H3068
32 the L commanded Moses, so did they. H3068
42 According to all that the L commanded H3068
43 had done it as the L had commanded, H3068
40: 1 And the L spake unto Moses, saying, H3068
16 that the L commanded him, so did he. H3068
19 upon it; as the L commanded Moses. H3068
21 as the L commanded Moses. H3068
23 upon it before the L; as the LORD had H3068
23 as the L had commanded Moses. H3068
25 And he lighted the lamps before the L; H3068
25 the LORD; as the L commanded Moses. H3068
27 thereon; as the L commanded Moses. H3068
29 offering; as the L commanded Moses. H3068
32 washed; as the L commanded Moses. H3068
34 the glory of the L filled the tabernacle. H3068
35 the glory of the L filled the tabernacle. H3068
38 For the cloud of the L *was* upon the H3068
Lev 1: 1 And the L called unto Moses, and H3068
2 offering unto the L, ye shall bring your H3068
3 of the congregation before the L. H3068
5 the bullock before the L: and the priests, H3068
9 by fire, of a sweet savour unto the L. H3068
11 before the L: and the priests, Aaron's H3068
13 by fire, of a sweet savour unto the L. H3068
14 his offering to the L *be* of fowls, then he H3068
17 by fire, of a sweet savour unto the L. H3068
2: 1 offering unto the L, his offering shall be H3068
2 by fire, of a sweet savour unto the L: H3068
3 of the offerings of the L made by fire. H3068
8 these things unto the L: and when it is H3068
9 by fire, of a sweet savour unto the L. H3068
10 of the offerings of the L made by fire. H3068
11 bring unto the L, shall be made with H3068
11 in any offering of the L made by fire. H3068
12 them unto the L: but they shall not be H3068
14 firstfruits unto the L, thou shalt offer H3068
16 *it is* an offering made by fire unto the L. H3068
3: 1 offer it without blemish before the L. H3068
3 by fire unto the L; the fat that covereth H3068
5 by fire, of a sweet savour unto the L. H3068
6 offering unto the L *be* of the flock; male H3068
7 then shall he offer it before the L. H3068
9 by fire unto the L; the fat thereof, *and* H3068
11 of the offering made by fire unto the L. H3068
12 goat, then he shall offer it before the L. H3068
14 by fire unto the L; the fat that covereth H3068
4: 1 And the L spake unto Moses, saying, H3068
2 of the L *concerning things* which H3068
3 blemish unto the L for a sin offering. H3068
4 before the L; and shall lay his hand H3068
4 head, and kill the bullock before the L. H3068
6 the L, before the vail of the sanctuary. H3068
7 incense before the L, which *is* in the H3068
13 of the L *concerning things* which H3068
15 bullock before the L: and the bullock H3068
15 the bullock shall be killed before the L. H3068
17 times before the L, *even* before the vail. H3068
18 *is* before the L, that *is* in the tabernacle H3068
22 of the L his God *concerning* H3068
24 offering before the L: it *is* a sin offering. H3068
27 of the L *concerning things* which H3068
31 savour unto the L; and the priest shall H3068
35 by fire unto the L; and the priest shall H3068
5: 6 offering unto the L for his sin which he H3068

Lev 5: 7 young pigeons, unto the L; one for a sin H3068
12 by fire unto the L: it *is* a sin offering. H3068
14 And the L spake unto Moses, saying, H3068
15 holy things of the L; then he shall bring H3068
15 his trespass unto the L a ram without H3068
17 of the L; though he wist *it* not, H3068
19 hath certainly trespassed against the L. H3068
6: 1 And the L spake unto Moses, saying, H3068
2 trespass against the L, and lie unto his H3068
6 offering unto the L, a ram without H3068
7 for him before the L: and it shall be H3068
8 And the L spake unto Moses, saying, H3068
14 offer it before the L, before the altar. H3068
15 *even* the memorial of it, unto the L. H3068
18 offerings of the L made by fire: every H3068
19 And the L spake unto Moses, saying, H3068
20 offer unto the L in the day when he H3068
21 thou offer *for* a sweet savour unto the L. H3068
22 ever unto the L; it shall be wholly burnt. H3068
24 And the L spake unto Moses, saying, H3068
25 be killed before the L: it *is* most holy. H3068
7: 5 fire unto the L: it *is* a trespass offering. H3068
11 which he shall offer unto the L. H3068
14 offering unto the L, *and* it shall be the H3068
20 that *pertain* unto the L, having his H3068
21 *pertain* unto the L, even that soul shall H3068
22 And the L spake unto Moses, saying, H3068
25 by fire unto the L, even the soul that H3068
28 And the L spake unto Moses, saying, H3068
29 offerings unto the L shall bring his H3068
29 L of the sacrifice of his peace offerings. H3068
30 offerings of the L made by fire, the fat H3068
30 waved *for* a wave offering before the L. H3068
35 offerings of the L made by fire, in the H3068
35 unto the L in the priest's office; H3068
36 Which the L commanded to be given H3068
38 Which the L commanded Moses in H3068
38 unto the L, in the wilderness of Sinai. H3068
8: 1 And the L spake unto Moses, saying, H3068
4 And Moses did as the L commanded H3068
5 which the L commanded to be done. H3068
9 crown; as the L commanded Moses. H3068
13 them; as the L commanded Moses. H3068
17 the camp; as the L commanded Moses. H3068
21 the L; as the LORD commanded Moses. H3068
21 the LORD; as the L commanded Moses. H3068
26 that *was* before the L, he took one H3068
27 them *for* a wave offering before the L. H3068
28 it *is* an offering made by fire unto the L. H3068
29 offering before the L: *for* of the ram of H3068
29 part; as the L commanded Moses. H3068
34 As he hath done this day, *so* the L hath H3068
35 the charge of the L, that ye die not: for H3068
36 L commanded by the hand of Moses. H3068
9: 2 blemish, and offer *them* before the L. H3068
4 before the L; and a meat offering H3068
4 for to day the L will appear unto you. H3068
5 drew near and stood before the L. H3068
6 thing which the L commanded that ye H3068
6 glory of the L shall appear unto you. H3068
7 for them; as the L commanded. H3068
10 the altar; as the L commanded Moses. H3068
21 before the L; as Moses commanded. H3068
23 of the L appeared unto all the people. H3068
24 from before the L, and consumed upon H3068
10: 1 the L, which he commanded them not. H3068
2 And there went out fire from the L, and H3068
2 them, and they died before the L. H3068
3 This *is it* that the L spake, saying, I will H3068
6 the burning which the L hath kindled. H3068
7 oil of the L *is* upon you. And they H3068
8 And the L spake unto Aaron, saying, H3068
11 statutes which the L hath spoken unto H3068
12 offerings of the L made by fire, and eat H3068
13 sacrifices of the L made by fire: for so H3068
15 offering before the L; and it shall be H3068
15 for ever; as the L hath commanded. H3068
17 make atonement for them before the L? H3068
19 offering before the L; and such things H3068
19 have been accepted in the sight of the L? H3068
11: 1 And the L spake unto Moses and to H3068
44 For I *am* the L your God: ye shall H3068
45 For I *am* the L that bringeth you up out H3068
12: 1 And the L spake unto Moses, saying, H3068
7 Who shall offer it before the L, and H3068
13: 1 And the L spake unto Moses and H3068
14: 1 And the L spake unto Moses, saying, H3068
11 things, before the L, *at* the door of the H3068
12 them *for* a wave offering before the L: H3068

Lev 14:16 with his finger seven times before the L: H3068
18 an atonement for him before the L. H3068
23 of the congregation, before the L. H3068
24 them *for* a wave offering before the L: H3068
27 his left hand seven times before the L: H3068
29 an atonement for him before the L. H3068
31 him that is to be cleansed before the L. H3068
33 And the L spake unto Moses and unto H3068
15: 1 And the L spake unto Moses and to H3068
14 come before the L unto the door of the H3068
15 for him before the L for his issue. H3068
30 the L for the issue of her uncleanness. H3068
16: 1 And the L spake unto Moses after the H3068
1 they offered before the L, and died; H3068
2 And the L said unto Moses, Speak unto H3068
7 them before the L *at* the door of the H3068
8 L, and the other lot for the scapegoat. H3068
10 presented alive before the L, to make an H3068
12 altar before the L, and his hands full of H3068
13 the fire before the L, that the cloud of H3068
18 altar that *is* before the L, and make an H3068
30 be clean from all your sins before the L. H3068
34 he did as the L commanded Moses. H3068
17: 1 And the L spake unto Moses, saying, H3068
2 which the L hath commanded, saying, H3068
4 an offering unto the L before the H3068
4 the tabernacle of the L; blood shall be H3068
5 them unto the L, unto the door of the H3068
5 them *for* peace offerings unto the L. H3068
6 the altar of the L *at* the door of the H3068
6 the fat for a sweet savour unto the L. H3068
9 to offer it unto the L; even that man H3068
18: 1 And the L spake unto Moses, saying, H3068
2 say unto them, I am the L your God. H3068
4 to walk therein: I *am* the L your God. H3068
5 do, he shall live in them: I *am* the L. H3068
6 to uncover *their* nakedness: I *am* the L. H3068
21 the name of thy God: I *am* the L. H3068
30 therein: I *am* the L your God. H3068
19: 1 And the L spake unto Moses, saying, H3068
2 be holy: for I the L your God *am* holy. H3068
3 my sabbaths: I *am* the L your God. H3068
4 molten gods: I *am* the L your God. H3068
5 the L, ye shall offer it at your own will. H3068
8 thing of the L: and that soul shall be H3068
10 and stranger: I *am* the L your God. H3068
12 the name of thy God: I *am* the L. H3068
14 blind, but shalt fear thy God: I *am* the L. H3068
16 the blood of thy neighbour: I *am* the L. H3068
18 thy neighbour as thyself: I *am* the L. H3068
21 offering unto the L, unto the door of the H3068
22 offering before the L for his sin which H3068
24 shall be holy to praise the L *withal*. H3068
25 increase thereof: I *am* the L your God. H3068
28 print any marks upon you: I *am* the L. H3068
30 reverence my sanctuary: I *am* the L. H3068
31 defiled by them: I *am* the L your God. H3068
32 old man, and fear thy God: I *am* the L. H3068
34 the land of Egypt: I *am* the L your God. H3068
36 ye have: I *am* the L your God, which H3068
37 judgments, and do them: I *am* the L. H3068
20: 1 And the L spake unto Moses, saying, H3068
7 be ye holy: for I *am* the L your God. H3068
8 them: I *am* the L which sanctify you. H3068
24 and honey: I *am* the L your God, which H3068
26 unto me: for I the L *am* holy, and have H3068
21: 1 And the L said unto Moses, Speak unto H3068
6 offerings of the L made by fire, *and* the H3068
8 for I the L, which sanctify you, *am* holy. H3068
12 oil of his God *is* upon him: I *am* the L. H3068
15 his people: for I the L do sanctify him. H3068
16 And the L spake unto Moses, saying, H3068
21 offerings of the L made by fire: he hath H3068
23 for I the L do sanctify them. H3068
22: 1 And the L spake unto Moses, saying, H3068
2 which they hallow unto me: I *am* the L. H3068
3 Israel hallow unto the L, having his H3068
3 be cut off from my presence: I *am* the L. H3068
8 to defile himself therewith: I *am* the L. H3068
9 profane it: I the L do sanctify them. H3068
15 of Israel, which they offer unto the L; H3068
16 things: for I the L do sanctify them. H3068
17 And the L spake unto Moses, saying, H3068
18 offer unto the L for a burnt offering; H3068
21 offerings unto the L to accomplish *his* H3068
22 these unto the L, nor make an offering H3068
22 fire of them upon the altar unto the L. H3068
24 Ye shall not offer unto the L that which H3068
26 And the L spake unto Moses, saying, H3068

Lev 22:27 for an offering made by fire unto the **L**. H3068
29 unto the **L**, offer *it* at your own will. H3068
30 none of it until the morrow: I *am* the **L**. H3068
31 and do them: I *am* the **L**. H3068
32 of Israel: I *am* the **L** which hallow you, H3068
33 of Egypt, to be your God: I *am* the **L**. H3068
23: 1 And the **L** spake unto Moses, saying, H3068
2 the feasts of the **L**, which ye shall H3068
3 sabbath of the **L** in all your dwellings. H3068
4 These *are* the feasts of the **L**, *even* holy H3068
6 bread unto the **L**: seven days ye must H3068
8 by fire unto the **L** seven days: in the H3068
9 And the **L** spake unto Moses, saying, H3068
11 sheaf before the **L**, to be accepted for H3068
12 year for a burnt offering unto the **L**. H3068
13 by fire unto the **L** *for* a sweet savour: H3068
16 offer a new meat offering unto the **L**. H3068
17 *they are* the firstfruits unto the **L**. H3068
18 offering unto the **L**, with their meat H3068
18 by fire, of sweet savour unto the **L**. H3068
20 wave offering before the **L**, with the two H3068
20 they shall be holy to the **L** for the priest. H3068
22 to the stranger: I *am* the **L** your God. H3068
23 And the **L** spake unto Moses, saying, H3068
25 an offering made by fire unto the **L**. H3068
26 And the **L** spake unto Moses, saying, H3068
27 an offering made by fire unto the **L**. H3068
28 for you before the **L** your God. H3068
33 And the **L** spake unto Moses, saying, H3068
34 tabernacles *for* seven days unto the **L**. H3068
36 by fire unto the **L**: on the eighth day H3068
36 made by fire unto the **L**: it *is* a solemn H3068
37 These *are* the feasts of the **L**, which ye H3068
37 by fire unto the **L**, a burnt offering, and H3068
38 Beside the sabbaths of the **L**, and beside H3068
38 offerings, which ye give unto the **L**. H3068
39 a feast unto the **L** seven days: on the H3068
40 before the **L** your God seven days. H3068
41 And ye shall keep it a feast unto the **L** H3068
43 the land of Egypt: I *am* the **L** your God. H3068
44 the children of Israel the feasts of the **L**. H3068
24: 1 And the **L** spake unto Moses, saying, H3068
3 before the **L** continually: *it shall* H3068
4 candlestick before the **L** continually. H3068
6 a row, upon the pure table before the **L**. H3068
7 an offering made by fire unto the **L**. H3068
8 in order before the **L** continually, *being* H3068
9 **L** made by fire by a perpetual statute. H3068
11 the name *of the L*, and cursed. And they
12 mind of the **L** might be shewed them. H3068
13 And the **L** spake unto Moses, saying, H3068
16 the name of the **L**, he shall surely be put H3068
16 the name *of the L*, shall be put to death. H3068
22 own country: for I *am* the **L** your God. H3068
23 Israel did as the **L** commanded Moses. H3068
25: 1 And the **L** spake unto Moses in mount H3068
2 the land keep a sabbath unto the **L**. H3068
4 a sabbath for the **L**: thou shalt neither H3068
17 fear thy God: for I *am* the **L** your God. H3068
38 I *am* the **L** your God, which brought H3068
55 the land of Egypt: I *am* the **L** your God. H3068
26: 1 down unto it: for I *am* the **L** your God. H3068
2 reverence my sanctuary: I *am* the **L**. H3068
13 I *am* the **L** your God, which brought H3068
44 with them: for I *am* the **L** their God. H3068
45 that I might be their God: I *am* the **L**. H3068
46 laws, which the **L** made between him H3068
27: 1 And the **L** spake unto Moses, saying, H3068
2 *shall be* for the **L** by thy estimation. H3068
9 an offering unto the **L**, all that *any man* H3068
9 giveth of such unto the **L** shall be holy. H3068
11 a sacrifice unto the **L**, then he shall H3068
14 *be* holy unto the **L**, then the priest shall H3068
16 And if a man shall sanctify unto the **L** H3068
21 be holy unto the **L**, as a field devoted; H3068
22 And if *a man* sanctify unto the **L** a field H3068
23 in that day, *as* a holy thing unto the **L**. H3068
28 devote unto the **L** of all that he hath, H3068
28 devoted thing *is* most holy unto the **L**. H3068
30 tree, *is* the LORD'S: *it is* holy unto the **L**. H3068
32 rod, the tenth shall be holy unto the **L**. H3068
34 which the **L** commanded Moses H3068
Nu 1: 1 And the **L** spake unto Moses in the H3068
19 As the **L** commanded Moses, so he H3068
48 For the **L** had spoken unto Moses, H3068
54 the **L** commanded Moses, so did they. H3068
2: 1 And the **L** spake unto Moses and unto H3068
33 of Israel; as the **L** commanded Moses. H3068
34 to all that the **L** commanded Moses: H3068

Nu 3: 1 the **L** spake with Moses in mount Sinai. H3068
4 died before the **L**, when they offered H3068
4 fire before the **L**, in the wilderness of H3068
5 And the **L** spake unto Moses, saying, H3068
11 And the **L** spake unto Moses, saying, H3068
13 beast: mine shall they be: I *am* the **L**. H3068
14 And the **L** spake unto Moses in the H3068
16 word of the **L**, as he was commanded. H3068
39 of the **L**, throughout their families, H3068
40 And the **L** said unto Moses, Number all H3068
41 for me (I *am* the **L**) instead of all the H3068
42 And Moses numbered, as the **L** H3068
44 And the **L** spake unto Moses, saying, H3068
45 the Levites shall be mine: I *am* the **L**. H3068
51 the **L**, as the LORD commanded Moses. H3068
51 the LORD, as the **L** commanded Moses. H3068
4: 1 And the **L** spake unto Moses and unto H3068
17 And the **L** spake unto Moses and unto H3068
21 And the **L** spake unto Moses, saying, H3068
37 of the **L** by the hand of Moses. H3068
41 to the commandment of the **L**. H3068
45 the word of the **L** by the hand of Moses. H3068
49 of the **L** they were numbered H3068
49 of him, as the **L** commanded Moses. H3068
5: 1 And the **L** spake unto Moses, saying, H3068
4 the camp: as the **L** spake unto Moses, H3068
5 And the **L** spake unto Moses, saying, H3068
6 against the **L**, and that person be guilty; H3068
8 unto the **L**, *even* to the priest; beside H3068
11 And the **L** spake unto Moses, saying, H3068
16 bring her near, and set her before the **L**: H3068
18 woman before the **L**, and uncover the H3068
21 the woman, The **L** make thee a curse H3068
21 thy people, when the **L** doth make thy H3068
25 before the **L**, and offer it upon the altar: H3068
30 the woman before the **L**, and the priest H3068
6: 1 And the **L** spake unto Moses, saying, H3068
2 to separate *themselves* unto the **L**: H3068
5 *himself* unto the **L**, he shall be holy, *and* H3068
6 the **L** he shall come at no dead body. H3068
8 of his separation he *is* holy unto the **L**. H3068
12 And he shall consecrate unto the **L** the H3068
14 offering unto the **L**, one he lamb of the H3068
16 *them* before the **L**, and shall offer his H3068
17 offerings unto the **L**, with the basket of H3068
20 offering before the **L**: this *is* holy for the H3068
21 offering unto the **L** for his separation, H3068
22 And the **L** spake unto Moses, saying, H3068
24 The **L** bless thee, and keep thee: H3068
25 The **L** make his face shine upon thee, H3068
26 The **L** lift up his countenance upon H3068
7: 3 their offering before the **L**, six covered H3068
4 And the **L** spake unto Moses, saying, H3068
11 And the **L** said unto Moses, They shall H3068
8: 1 And the **L** spake unto Moses, saying, H3068
3 as the **L** commanded Moses. H3068
4 pattern which the **L** had shewed Moses, H3068
5 And the **L** spake unto Moses, saying, H3068
10 Levites before the **L**: and the children of H3068
11 Levites before the **L** *for* an offering of H3068
11 they may execute the service of the **L**. H3068
12 burnt offering, unto the **L**, to make an H3068
13 offer them *for* an offering unto the **L**. H3068
20 unto all that the **L** commanded Moses H3068
21 offering before the **L**; and Aaron made H3068
22 his sons: as the **L** had commanded H3068
23 And the **L** spake unto Moses, saying, H3068
9: 1 And the **L** spake unto Moses in the H3068
5 to all that the **L** commanded Moses, H3068
7 an offering of the **L** in his appointed H3068
8 the **L** will command concerning you. H3068
9 And the **L** spake unto Moses, saying, H3068
10 he shall keep the passover unto the **L**. H3068
13 the offering of the **L** in his appointed H3068
14 passover unto the **L**; according to the H3068
18 At the commandment of the **L** the H3068
18 of the **L** they pitched: as long H3068
19 the charge of the **L**, and journeyed not. H3068
20 of the **L** they abode in their H3068
20 of the **L** they journeyed. H3068
23 At the commandment of the **L** they H3068
23 of the **L** they journeyed: they H3068
23 kept the charge of the **L**, at the H3068
23 of the **L** by the hand of Moses. H3068
10: 1 And the **L** spake unto Moses, saying, H3068
9 before the **L** your God, and ye shall H3068
10 before your God: I *am* the **L** your God. H3068
13 of the **L** by the hand of Moses. H3068
29 place of which the **L** said, I will give it H3068

Nu 10:29 **L** hath spoken good concerning Israel. H3068
32 goodness the **L** shall do unto us, the H3068
33 the mount of the **L** three days' journey: H3068
33 covenant of the **L** went before them in H3068
34 And the cloud of the **L** *was* upon them H3068
35 said, Rise up, **L**, and let thine enemies H3068
36 O **L**, unto the many thousands of Israel. H3068
11: 1 it displeased the **L**: and the LORD heard H3068
1 the LORD: and the **L** heard *it;* and his H3068
1 and the fire of the **L** burnt among H3068
2 unto the **L**, the fire was quenched. H3068
3 the fire of the **L** burnt among them. H3068
10 the anger of the **L** was kindled greatly; H3068
11 And Moses said unto the **L**, Wherefore H3068
16 And the **L** said unto Moses, Gather H3068
18 in the ears of the **L**, saying, Who shall H3068
18 **L** will give you flesh, and ye shall eat. H3068
20 ye have despised the **L** which *is* among H3068
23 And the **L** said unto Moses, Is the H3068
24 the words of the **L**, and gathered the H3068
25 And the **L** came down in a cloud, and H3068
28 and said, My **l** Moses, forbid them. H113
29 the **L** would put his spirit upon them! H3068
31 And there went forth a wind from the **L**, H3068
33 the wrath of the **L** was kindled against H3068
33 the people, and the **L** smote the people H3068
12: 2 And they said, Hath the **L** indeed H3068
2 spoken also by us? And the **L** heard *it*. H3068
4 And the **L** spake suddenly unto Moses, H3068
5 And the **L** came down in the pillar of H3068
6 among you, *I* the **L** will make myself H3068
8 the similitude of the **L** shall he behold: H3068
9 And the anger of the **L** was kindled H3068
11 And Aaron said unto Moses, Alas, my **l**, I H113
13 And Moses cried unto the **L**, saying, H3068
14 And the **L** said unto Moses, If her H3068
13: 1 And the **L** spake unto Moses, saying, H3068
3 of the **L** sent them from the H3068
14: 3 And wherefore hath the **L** brought us H3068
8 If the **L** delight in us, then he will bring H3068
9 Only rebel not ye against the **L**, neither H3068
9 and the **L** *is* with us: fear them not. H3068
10 And the glory of the **L** appeared in the H3068
11 And the **L** said unto Moses, How long H3068
13 And Moses said unto the **L**, Then the H3068
14 have heard that thou **L** *art* among this H3068
14 this people, that thou **L** art seen face to H3068
16 Because the **L** was not able to bring H3068
17 let the power of my **L** be great, according H136
18 The **L** *is* longsuffering, and of great H3068
20 And the **L** said, I have pardoned H3068
21 shall be filled with the glory of the **L**. H3068
26 And the **L** spake unto Moses and unto H3068
28 *as* I live, saith the **L**, as ye have spoken H3068
35 I the **L** have said, I will surely do it unto H3068
37 land, died by the plague before the **L**. H3068
40 **L** hath promised: for we have sinned. H3068
41 of the **L**? but it shall not prosper. H3068
42 Go not up, for the **L** *is* not among you; H3068
43 away from the **L**, therefore the LORD H3068
43 therefore the **L** will not be with you. H3068
44 covenant of the **L**, and Moses, departed H3068
15: 1 And the **L** spake unto Moses, saying, H3068
3 by fire unto the **L**, a burnt offering, or H3068
3 unto the **L**, of the herd, or of the flock: H3068
4 his offering unto the **L** bring a meat H3068
7 of wine, *for* a sweet savour unto the **L**. H3068
8 a vow, or peace offerings unto the **L**: H3068
10 by fire, of a sweet savour unto the **L**. H3068
13 by fire, of a sweet savour unto the **L**. H3068
14 unto the **L**; as ye do, so he shall do. H3068
15 so shall the stranger be before the **L**. H3068
17 And the **L** spake unto Moses, saying, H3068
19 offer up an heave offering unto the **L**. H3068
21 shall give unto the **L** an heave offering H3068
22 which the **L** hath spoken unto Moses, H3068
23 *Even* all that the **L** hath commanded H3068
23 the day that the **L** commanded *Moses*, H3068
24 sweet savour unto the **L**, with his meat H3068
25 by fire unto the **L**, and their sin offering H3068
25 before the **L**, for their ignorance: H3068
28 before the **L**, to make an atonement H3068
30 reproacheth the **L**; and that soul shall H3068
31 the word of the **L**, and hath broken his H3068
35 And the **L** said unto Moses, The man H3068
36 he died; as the **L** commanded Moses. H3068
37 And the **L** spake unto Moses, saying, H3068
39 of the **L**, and do them; and that H3068
41 I *am* the **L** your God, which brought H3068

Nu 15:41 to be your God: I *am* the L your God. H3068
16: 3 one of them, and the L *is* among them: H3068
3 above the congregation of the L? H3068
5 to morrow the L will shew who *are* his, H3068
7 in them before the L to morrow: and it H3068
7 man whom the L doth choose, he *shall* H3068
9 tabernacle of the L, and to stand before H3068
11 against the L: and what *is* Aaron, H3068
15 and said unto the L, Respect not thou H3068
16 before the L, thou, and they, and H3068
17 ye before the L every man his censer, H3068
19 L appeared unto all the congregation. H3068
20 And the L spake unto Moses and unto H3068
23 And the L spake unto Moses, saying, H3068
28 know that the L hath sent me to do H3068
29 of all men; *then* the L hath not sent me. H3068
30 But if the L make a new thing, and the H3068
30 that these men have provoked the L. H3068
35 And there came out a fire from the L, H3068
36 And the L spake unto Moses, saying, H3068
38 them before the L, therefore they are H3068
40 incense before the L; that he be not as H3068
40 the L said to him by the hand of Moses. H3068
41 Ye have killed the people of the L. H3068
42 it, and the glory of the L appeared. H3068
44 And the L spake unto Moses, saying, H3068
46 out from the L; the plague is begun. H3068
17: 1 And the L spake unto Moses, saying, H3068
7 the L in the tabernacle of witness. H3068
9 from before the L unto all the children H3068
10 And the L said unto Moses, Bring H3068
11 And Moses did *so*: as the L H3068
13 tabernacle of the L shall die: shall we H3068
18: 1 And the L said unto Aaron, Thou and H3068
6 *as* a gift for the L, to do the service of H3068
8 And the L spake unto Aaron, Behold, I H3068
12 offer unto the L, them have I given thee. H3068
13 bring unto the L, shall be thine; every H3068
15 bring unto the L, *whether it be* of men H3068
17 by fire, for a sweet savour unto the L. H3068
19 offer unto the L, have I given thee, and H3068
19 L unto thee and to thy seed with thee. H3068
20 And the L spake unto Aaron, Thou H3068
24 offering unto the L, I have given to the H3068
25 And the L spake unto Moses, saying, H3068
26 for the L, *even* a tenth *part* of the tithe. H3068
28 offering unto the L of all your tithes, H3068
29 offering of the L, of all the best thereof, H3068
19: 1 And the L spake unto Moses and unto H3068
2 the law which the L hath commanded, H3068
13 tabernacle of the L; and that soul shall H3068
20 the sanctuary of the L: the water of H3068
20: 3 when our brethren died before the L! H3068
4 of the L into this wilderness, H3068
6 the glory of the L appeared unto them. H3068
7 And the L spake unto Moses, saying, H3068
9 before the L, as he commanded him. H3068
12 And the L spake unto Moses and H3068
13 the L, and he was sanctified in them. H3068
16 And when we cried unto the L, he heard H3068
23 And the L spake unto Moses and H3068
27 And Moses did as the L commanded: H3068
21: 2 And Israel vowed a vow unto the L, and H3068
3 And the L hearkened to the voice of H3068
6 And the L sent fiery serpents among H3068
7 against the L, and against thee; pray H3068
7 pray unto the L, that he take away the H3068
8 And the L said unto Moses, Make thee H3068
14 of the wars of the L, What he did in the H3068
16 well whereof the L spake unto Moses, H3068
34 And the L said unto Moses, Fear him H3068
22: 8 word again, as the L shall speak unto H3068
13 your land: for the L refuseth to give me H3068
18 of the L my God, to do less or more. H3068
19 what the L will say unto me more. H3068
22 the angel of the L stood in the way for H3068
23 And the ass saw the angel of the L H3068
24 But the angel of the L stood in a path of H3068
25 saw the angel of the L, she thrust herself H3068
26 And the angel of the L went further, H3068
27 the angel of the L, she fell down under H3068
28 And the L opened the mouth of the ass, H3068
31 Then the L opened the eyes of Balaam, H3068
31 the angel of the L standing in the way, H3068
32 And the angel of the L said unto him, H3068
34 the angel of the L, I have sinned; for I H3068
35 And the angel of the L said unto H3068
23: 3 peradventure the L will come to meet H3068
5 And the L put a word in Balaam's H3068
Nu 23: 8 I defy, *whom* the L hath not defied? H3068
12 which the L hath put in my mouth? H3068
15 offering, while I meet *the L* yonder. H3068
16 And the L met Balaam, and put a word H3068
17 unto him, What hath the L spoken? H3068
21 in Israel: the L his God *is* with him, H3068
26 All that the L speaketh, that I must do? H3068
24: 1 that it pleased the L to bless Israel, he H3068
6 aloes which the L hath planted, *and* as H3068
11 the L hath kept thee back from honour. H3068
13 of the L, to do *either* good or H3068
13 *but* what the L saith, that will I speak? H3068
25: 3 of the L was kindled against Israel. H3068
4 And the L said unto Moses, Take all H3068
4 up before the L against the sun, that H3068
4 the L may be turned away from Israel. H3068
10 And the L spake unto Moses, saying, H3068
16 And the L spake unto Moses, saying, H3068
26: 1 plague, that the L spake unto Moses H3068
4 upward; as the L commanded Moses H3068
9 Korah, when they strove against the L: H3068
52 And the L spake unto Moses, saying, H3068
61 they offered strange fire before the L. H3068
65 For the L had said of them, They shall H3068
27: 3 against the L in the company of Korah; H3068
5 Moses brought their cause before the L. H3068
6 And the L spake unto Moses, saying, H3068
11 judgment, as the L commanded Moses. H3068
12 And the L said unto Moses, Get thee up H3068
15 And Moses spake unto the L, saying, H3068
16 Let the L, the God of the spirits of all H3068
17 of the L be not as sheep which H3068
18 And the L said unto Moses, Take thee H3068
21 of Urim before the L: at his word shall H3068
22 And Moses did as the L commanded H3068
23 L commanded by the hand of Moses. H3068
28: 1 And the L spake unto Moses, saying, H3068
3 offer unto the L; two lambs of the first H3068
6 a sacrifice made by fire unto the L. H3068
7 poured unto the L *for* a drink offering. H3068
8 by fire, of a sweet savour unto the L. H3068
11 offering unto the L; two young bullocks, H3068
13 a sacrifice made by fire unto the L. H3068
15 sin offering unto the L shall be offered, H3068
16 the first month *is* the passover of the L. H3068
19 offering unto the L; two young bullocks, H3068
24 savour unto the L: it shall be offered H3068
26 offering unto the L, after your weeks *be* H3068
27 savour unto the L; two young bullocks, H3068
29: 2 savour unto the L; one young bullock, H3068
6 a sacrifice made by fire unto the L. H3068
8 offering unto the L *for* a sweet savour; H3068
12 keep a feast unto the L seven days: H3068
13 sweet savour unto the L; thirteen young H3068
36 savour unto the L: one bullock, one H3068
39 These *things* ye shall do unto the L in H3068
40 to all that the L commanded Moses. H3068
30: 1 thing which the L hath commanded. H3068
2 If a man vow a vow unto the L, or swear H3068
3 If a woman also vow a vow unto the L, H3068
5 shall stand: and the L shall forgive her, H3068
8 none effect: and the L shall forgive her. H3068
12 them void; and the L shall forgive her. H3068
16 These *are* the statutes, which the L H3068
31: 1 And the L spake unto Moses, saying, H3068
3 and avenge the L of Midian. H3068
7 the Midianites, as the L commanded H3068
16 against the L in the matter of Peor, H3068
16 among the congregation of the L. H3068
21 law which the L commanded Moses; H3068
25 And the L spake unto Moses, saying, H3068
28 And levy a tribute unto the L of the H3068
29 the priest, *for* an heave offering of the L. H3068
30 the charge of the tabernacle of the L. H3068
31 priest did as the L commanded Moses. H3068
41 the priest, as the L commanded Moses. H3068
47 the L; as the LORD commanded Moses. H3068
47 the LORD; as the L commanded Moses. H3068
50 oblation for the L, what every man hath H3068
50 atonement for our souls before the L. H3068
52 offered up to the L, of the captains of H3068
54 for the children of Israel before the L. H3068
32: 4 *Even* the country which the L smote H3068
7 the land which the L hath given them? H3068
9 the land which the L had given them. H3068
12 for they have wholly followed the L. H3068
13 evil in the sight of the L, was consumed. H3068
14 the fierce anger of the L toward Israel. H3068
20 if ye will go armed before the L to war, H3068
Nu 32:21 over Jordan before the L, until he hath H3068
22 And the land be subdued before the L: H3068
22 before the L, and before Israel; and H3068
22 shall be your possession before the L. H3068
23 sinned against the L: and be sure your H3068
25 servants will do as my l commandeth. H113
27 before the L to battle, as my lord saith. H3068
27 before the LORD to battle, as my l saith. H113
29 battle, before the L, and the land shall H3068
31 saying, As the L hath said unto thy H3068
32 We will pass over armed before the L H3068
33: 2 of the L: and these *are* their H3068
4 which the L had smitten among H3068
4 gods also the L executed judgments. H3068
38 of the L, and died there, in the H3068
50 And the L spake unto Moses in the H3068
34: 1 And the L spake unto Moses, saying, H3068
13 by lot, which the L commanded to give H3068
16 And the L spake unto Moses, saying, H3068
29 These *are they* whom the L H3068
35: 1 And the L spake unto Moses in the H3068
9 And the L spake unto Moses, saying, H3068
34 L dwell among the children of Israel. H3068
36: 2 And they said, The L commanded my H3068
2 commanded my l to give the land for an H113
2 of Israel: and my l was commanded by H113
2 by the L to give the inheritance H3068
5 to the word of the L, saying, The tribe of H3068
6 This *is* the thing which the L doth H3068
10 Even as the L commanded Moses, so H3068
13 which the L commanded by the H3068
Dt 1: 3 unto all that the L had given him in H3068
6 The L our God spake unto us in Horeb, H3068
8 the land which the L sware unto your H3068
10 The L your God hath multiplied you, H3068
11 (The L God of your fathers make you a H3068
19 the Amorites, as the L our God H3068
20 which the L our God doth give unto us. H3068
21 Behold, the L thy God hath set the land H3068
21 possess *it*, as the L God of thy fathers H3068
25 land which the L our God doth give us. H3068
26 the commandment of the L your God: H3068
27 said, Because the L hated us, he hath H3068
30 The L your God which goeth before H3068
31 seen how that the L thy God bare thee, H3068
32 Yet in this thing ye did not believe the L H3068
34 And the L heard the voice of your H3068
36 because he hath wholly followed the L. H3068
37 Also the L was angry with me for your H3068
41 sinned against the L, we will go up and H3068
41 to all that the L our God commanded H3068
42 And the L said unto me, Say unto H3068
43 of the L, and went presumptuously H3068
45 And ye returned and wept before the L; H3068
45 the LORD; but the L would not hearken H3068
2: 1 of the Red sea, as the L spake unto me: H3068
2 And the L spake unto me, saying, H3068
7 For the L thy God hath blessed thee in H3068
7 forty years the L thy God *hath been* H3068
9 And the L said unto me, Distress not H3068
12 which the L gave unto them. H3068
14 the host, as the L sware unto them. H3068
15 For indeed the hand of the L was H3068
17 That the L spake unto me, saying, H3068
21 the Anakims; but the L destroyed them H3068
29 the land which the L our God giveth us. H3068
30 by him: for the L thy God hardened his H3068
31 And the L said unto me, Behold, I have H3068
33 And the L our God delivered him H3068
36 us: the L our God delivered all unto us: H3068
37 whatsoever the L our God forbad us. H3068
3: 2 And the L said unto me, Fear him not: H3068
3 So the L our God delivered into our H3068
18 that time, saying, The L your God hath H3068
20 Until the L have given rest unto your H3068
20 the land which the L your God hath H3068
21 seen all that the L your God hath done H3068
21 two kings: so shall the L do unto all the H3068
22 Ye shall not fear them: for the L your H3068
23 And I besought the L at that time, H3068
24 O L GOD, thou hast begun to shew thy H136
26 But the L was wroth with me for your H3068
26 hear me: and the L said unto me, Let it H3068
4: 1 the L God of your fathers giveth you. H3068
2 the L your God which I command you. H3068
3 Your eyes have seen what the L did H3068
3 followed Baal-peor, the L thy God hath H3068
4 But ye that did cleave unto the L your H3068
5 even as the L my God commanded H3068

Dt 4: 7 unto them, as the L our God *is* in all H3068
10 before the L thy God in Horeb, when H3068
10 in Horeb, when the L said unto me, H3068
12 And the L spake unto you out of the H3068
14 And the L commanded me at that time H3068
15 on the day *that* the L spake unto you in H3068
19 serve them, which the L thy God hath H3068
20 But the L hath taken you, and brought H3068
21 Furthermore the L was angry with me H3068
21 land, which the L thy God giveth thee H3068
23 covenant of the L your God, which he H3068
23 the L thy God hath forbidden thee. H3068
24 For the L thy God *is* a consuming fire, H3068
25 the L thy God, to provoke him to anger: H3068
27 And the L shall scatter you among the H3068
27 heathen, whither the L shall lead you. H3068
29 But if from thence thou shalt seek the L H3068
30 if thou turn to the L thy God, and shalt H3068
31 (For the L thy God *is* a merciful God;) H3068
34 to all that the L your God did for you H3068
35 know that the L he *is* God; *there is* none H3068
39 heart, that the L he *is* God in heaven H3068
40 the L thy God giveth thee, for ever. H3068
5: 2 The L our God made a covenant with H3068
3 The L made not this covenant with our H3068
4 The L talked with you face to face in H3068
5 (I stood between the L and you at that H3068
5 the word of the L: for ye were afraid by H3068
6 I *am* the L thy God, which brought thee H3068
9 them: for I the L thy God *am* a jealous H3068
11 Thou shalt not take the name of the L H3068
11 God in vain: for the L will not hold *him* H3068
12 the L thy God hath commanded thee. H3068
14 the sabbath of the L thy God: *in it* thou H3068
15 and *that* the L thy God brought thee H3068
15 out arm: therefore the L thy God H3068
16 and thy mother, as the L thy God hath H3068
16 land which the L thy God giveth thee. H3068
22 These words the L spake unto all your H3068
24 And ye said, Behold, the L our God H3068
25 L our God any more, then we shall die. H3068
27 Go thou near, and hear all that the L H3068
27 us all that the L our God shall speak H3068
28 And the L heard the voice of your H3068
28 unto me; and the L said unto me, I H3068
32 do therefore as the L your God hath H3068
33 the ways which the L your God hath H3068
6: 1 which the L your God commanded H3068
2 That thou mightest fear the L thy God, H3068
3 mightily, as the L God of thy fathers H3068
4 Hear, O Israel: The L our God *is* one H3068
4 O Israel: The LORD our God *is* one L: H3068
5 And thou shalt love the L thy God with H3068
10 And it shall be, when the L thy God H3068
12 *Then* beware lest thou forget the L, H3068
13 Thou shalt fear the L thy God, and H3068
15 (For the L thy God *is* a jealous God H3068
15 the anger of the L thy God be kindled H3068
16 Ye shall not tempt the L your God, as H3068
17 of the L your God, and his testimonies, H3068
18 in the sight of the L: that it may be well H3068
18 which the L sware unto thy fathers, H3068
19 from before thee, as the L hath spoken. H3068
20 the L our God hath commanded you? H3068
21 in Egypt; and the L brought us out of H3068
22 And the L shewed signs and wonders, H3068
24 And the L commanded us to do all H3068
24 to fear the L our God, for our good H3068
25 L our God, as he hath commanded us. H3068
7: 1 When the L thy God shall bring thee H3068
2 And when the L thy God shall deliver H3068
4 the anger of the L be kindled against H3068
6 For thou *art* an holy people unto the L H3068
6 thy God: the L thy God hath chosen H3068
7 The L did not set his love upon you, H3068
8 But because the L loved you, and H3068
8 fathers, hath the L brought you out H3068
9 Know therefore that the L thy God, he H3068
12 do them, that the L thy God shall keep H3068
15 And the L will take away from thee all H3068
16 the people which the L thy God shall H3068
18 what the L thy God did unto Pharaoh, H3068
19 arm, whereby the L thy God brought H3068
19 out: so shall the L thy God do unto all H3068
20 Moreover the L thy God will send the H3068
21 at them: for the L thy God *is* among H3068
22 And the L thy God will put out those H3068
23 But the L thy God shall deliver them H3068
25 it *is* an abomination to the L thy God. H3068

Dt 8: 1 which the L sware unto your fathers. H3068
2 the way which the L thy God led thee H3068
3 of the mouth of the L doth man live. H3068
5 son, *so* the L thy God chasteneth thee. H3068
6 of the L thy God, to walk in H3068
7 For the L thy God bringeth thee into a H3068
10 shalt bless the L thy God for the good H3068
11 Beware that thou forget not the L thy H3068
14 and thou forget the L thy God, which H3068
18 But thou shalt remember the L thy H3068
19 do at all forget the L thy God, and walk H3068
20 As the nations which the L destroyeth H3068
20 unto the voice of the L your God. H3068
9: 3 this day, that the L thy God *is* he which H3068
3 quickly, as the L hath said unto thee. H3068
4 after that the L thy God hath cast them H3068
4 righteousness the L hath brought me in H3068
4 L doth drive them out from before thee. H3068
5 these nations the L thy God doth drive H3068
5 the word which the L sware unto thy H3068
6 Understand therefore, that the L thy H3068
7 provokedst the L thy God to wrath in H3068
7 ye have been rebellious against the L. H3068
8 Also in Horeb ye provoked the L to H3068
8 wrath, so that the L was angry with you H3068
9 which the L made with you, then H3068
10 And the L delivered unto me two tables H3068
10 words, which the L spake with you in H3068
11 forty nights, *that* the L gave me the two H3068
12 And the L said unto me, Arise, get thee H3068
13 Furthermore the L spake unto me, H3068
16 sinned against the L your God, *and* H3068
16 way which the L had commanded you. H3068
18 And I fell down before the L, as at the H3068
18 sight of the L, to provoke him to anger. H3068
19 wherewith the L was wroth against you H3068
19 L hearkened unto me at that time also. H3068
20 And the L was very angry with Aaron H3068
22 ye provoked the L to wrath. H3068
23 Likewise when the L sent you from H3068
23 of the L your God, and ye believed H3068
24 Ye have been rebellious against the L H3068
25 Thus I fell down before the L forty days H3068
25 the L had said he would destroy you. H3068
26 I prayed therefore unto the L, and said, H3068
26 LORD, and said, O L GOD, destroy not H136
28 out say, Because the L was not able to H3068
10: 1 At that time the L said unto me, Hew H3068
4 which the L spake unto you in the H3068
4 and the L gave them unto me. H3068
5 there they be, as the L commanded me. H3068
8 At that time the L separated the tribe H3068
8 covenant of the L, to stand before the H3068
8 to stand before the L to minister unto H3068
9 his brethren; the L *is* his inheritance, H3068
9 as the L thy God promised him. H3068
10 nights; and the L hearkened unto me H3068
10 also, *and* the L would not destroy thee. H3068
11 And the L said unto me, Arise, take *thy* H3068
12 And now, Israel, what doth the L thy H3068
12 but to fear the L thy God, to walk in H3068
12 and to serve the L thy God with all thy H3068
13 To keep the commandments of the L, H3068
15 Only the L had a delight in thy fathers H3068
17 For the L your God *is* God of gods, and H3068
17 *is* God of gods, and L of lords, a great H113
20 Thou shalt fear the L thy God; him H3068
22 and now the L thy God hath made H3068
11: 1 Therefore thou shalt love the L thy H3068
2 of the L your God, his greatness, H3068
4 L hath destroyed them unto this day; H3068
7 all the great acts of the L which he did. H3068
9 the land, which the L sware unto your H3068
12 A land which the L thy God careth for: H3068
12 careth for: the eyes of the L thy God *are* H3068
13 this day, to love the L your God, and to H3068
17 the good land which the L giveth you. H3068
21 the land which the L sware unto your H3068
22 them, to love the L your God, to walk in H3068
23 Then will the L drive out all these H3068
25 before you: *for* the L your God shall lay H3068
27 of the L your God, which I command H3068
28 of the L your God, but turn H3068
29 And it shall come to pass, when the L H3068
31 the land which the L your God giveth H3068
12: 1 the land, which the L God of thy fathers H3068
4 Ye shall not do so unto the L your God. H3068
5 But unto the place which the L your H3068
7 And there ye shall eat before the L your H3068

Dt 12: 7 the L thy God hath blessed thee. H3068
9 which the L your God giveth you. H3068
10 in the land which the L your God giveth H3068
11 Then there shall be a place which the L H3068
11 choice vows which ye vow unto the L: H3068
12 And ye shall rejoice before the L your H3068
14 But in the place which the L shall H3068
15 the blessing of the L thy God which he H3068
18 But thou must eat them before the L H3068
18 place which the L thy God shall choose, H3068
18 rejoice before the L thy God in all that H3068
20 When the L thy God shall enlarge thy H3068
21 If the place which the L thy God hath H3068
21 flock, which the L hath given thee, as H3068
25 *that which is* right in the sight of the L. H3068
26 the place which the L shall choose: H3068
27 upon the altar of the L thy God: and the H3068
27 L thy God, and thou shalt eat the flesh. H3068
28 and right in the sight of the L thy God. H3068
29 When the L thy God shall cut off the H3068
31 Thou shalt not do so unto the L thy H3068
31 to the L, which he hateth, have H3068
13: 3 of dreams: for the L your God proveth H3068
3 ye love the L your God with all your H3068
4 Ye shall walk after the L your God, and H3068
5 *you* away from the L your God, which H3068
5 of the way which the L thy God H3068
10 thee away from the L thy God, which H3068
12 cities, which the L thy God hath given H3068
16 every whit, for the L thy God: and it H3068
17 hand: that the L may turn from the H3068
18 to the voice of the L thy God, to keep all H3068
18 *is* right in the eyes of the L thy God. H3068
14: 1 Ye *are* the children of the L your God: H3068
2 For thou *art* an holy people unto the L H3068
2 thy God, and the L hath chosen thee to H3068
21 people unto the L thy God. Thou shalt H3068
23 And thou shalt eat before the L thy H3068
23 learn to fear the L thy God always. H3068
24 thee, which the L thy God shall choose H3068
24 when the L thy God hath blessed thee: H3068
25 place which the L thy God shall choose: H3068
26 there before the L thy God, and thou H3068
29 satisfied; that the L thy God may bless H3068
15: 4 you; for the L shall greatly bless thee H3068
4 in the land which the L thy God giveth H3068
5 the voice of the L thy God, to observe H3068
6 For the L thy God blesseth thee, as he H3068
7 in thy land which the L thy God giveth H3068
9 L against thee, and it be sin unto thee. H3068
10 for this thing the L thy God shall bless H3068
14 wherewith the L thy God hath blessed H3068
15 of Egypt, and the L thy God redeemed H3068
18 six years: and the L thy God shall bless H3068
19 sanctify unto the L thy God: thou shalt H3068
20 Thou shalt eat *it* before the L thy God H3068
20 place which the L shall choose, thou H3068
21 shalt not sacrifice it unto the L thy God. H3068
16: 1 passover unto the L thy God: for in the H3068
1 month of Abib the L thy God brought H3068
2 the passover unto the L thy God, of the H3068
2 L shall choose to place his name there. H3068
5 gates, which the L thy God giveth thee: H3068
6 But at the place which the L thy God H3068
7 place which the L thy God shall choose: H3068
8 assembly to the L thy God: thou shalt H3068
10 of weeks unto the L thy God with a H3068
10 shalt give *unto the L thy God,* according
10 as the L thy God hath blessed thee: H3068
11 And thou shalt rejoice before the L thy H3068
11 place which the L thy God hath chosen H3068
15 feast unto the L thy God in the place H3068
15 place which the L shall choose: because H3068
15 because the L thy God shall bless H3068
16 appear before the L thy God in the H3068
16 shall not appear before the L empty: H3068
17 the L thy God which he hath given thee. H3068
18 gates, which the L thy God giveth thee, H3068
20 land which the L thy God giveth thee. H3068
21 L thy God, which thou shalt make thee. H3068
22 *any* image; which the L thy God hateth. H3068
17: 1 Thou shalt not sacrifice unto the L thy H3068
1 *is* an abomination unto the L thy God. H3068
2 gates which the L thy God giveth thee, H3068
2 in the sight of the L thy God, in H3068
8 place which the L thy God shall choose; H3068
10 place which the L shall choose shall H3068
12 there before the L thy God, or unto the H3068
14 the land which the L thy God giveth H3068

Dt 17:15 thee, whom the L thy God shall choose: H3068
16 forasmuch as the L hath said unto you, H3068
19 learn to fear the L his God, to keep all H3068
18: 1 the L made by fire, and his inheritance. H3068
2 among their brethren: the L *is* their H3068
5 For the L thy God hath chosen him out H3068
5 of the L, him and his sons for ever. H3068
6 the place which the L shall choose; H3068
7 in the name of the L his God, as all his H3068
7 *do,* which stand there before the L. H3068
9 the land which the L thy God giveth H3068
12 unto the L: and because of these H3068
12 abominations the L thy God doth drive H3068
13 Thou shalt be perfect with the L thy H3068
14 but as for thee, the L thy God hath not H3068
15 The L thy God will raise up unto thee a H3068
16 desiredst of the L thy God in Horeb in H3068
16 the voice of the L my God, neither let H3068
17 And the L said unto me, They have well H3068
21 the word which the L hath not spoken? H3068
22 in the name of the L, if the thing follow H3068
22 thing which the L hath not spoken, *but* H3068
19: 1 When the L thy God hath cut off the H3068
1 whose land the L thy God giveth thee, H3068
2 the L thy God giveth thee to possess it. H3068
3 land, which the L thy God giveth thee H3068
8 And if the L thy God enlarge thy coast, H3068
9 day, to love the L thy God, and to walk H3068
10 land, which the L thy God giveth thee H3068
14 the L thy God giveth thee to possess it. H3068
17 stand before the L, before the priests H3068
20: 1 of them: for the L thy God *is* with thee, H3068
4 For the L your God *is* he that goeth H3068
13 And when the L thy God hath delivered H3068
14 which the L thy God hath given thee. H3068
16 people, which the L thy God doth give H3068
17 the L thy God hath commanded thee: H3068
18 should ye sin against the L your God. H3068
21: 1 in the land which the L thy God giveth H3068
5 come near; for them the L thy God hath H3068
5 in the name of the L; and by their word H3068
8 Be merciful, O L, unto thy people Israel, H3068
9 *that which is* right in the sight of the L. H3068
10 thine enemies, and the L thy God hath H3068
23 defiled, which the L thy God giveth thee H3068
22: 5 so *are* abomination unto the L thy God. H3068
23: 1 not enter into the congregation of the L. H3068
2 of the L; even to his tenth generation H3068
2 not enter into the congregation of the L. H3068
3 of the L; even to their tenth generation H3068
3 into the congregation of the L for ever: H3068
5 Nevertheless the L thy God would not H3068
5 Balaam; but the L thy God turned the H3068
5 thee, because the L thy God loved thee. H3068
8 of the L in their third generation. H3068
14 For the L thy God walketh in the midst H3068
18 the house of the L thy God for any vow: H3068
18 *are* abomination unto the L thy God. H3068
20 usury: that the L thy God may bless H3068
21 When thou shalt vow a vow unto the L H3068
21 to pay it: for the L thy God will surely H3068
23 vowed unto the L thy God, which thou H3068
24: 4 before the L: and thou shalt not cause H3068
4 to sin, which the L thy God giveth thee H3068
9 Remember what the L thy God did H3068
13 unto thee before the L thy God. H3068
15 thee unto the L, and it be sin unto thee. H3068
18 in Egypt, and the L thy God redeemed H3068
19 widow: that the L thy God may bless H3068
25:15 land which the L thy God giveth thee. H3068
16 an abomination unto the L thy God. H3068
19 Therefore it shall be, when the L thy H3068
19 in the land which the L thy God giveth H3068
26: 1 the land which the L thy God giveth H3068
2 thy land that the L thy God giveth thee, H3068
2 place which the L thy God shall choose H3068
3 this day unto the L thy God, that I am H3068
3 L sware unto our fathers for to give us. H3068
4 down before the altar of the L thy God. H3068
5 and say before the L thy God, A Syrian H3068
7 And when we cried unto the L God of H3068
7 of our fathers, the L heard our voice, H3068
8 And the L brought us forth out of Egypt H3068
10 which thou, O L, hast given me. And H3068
10 set it before the L thy God, and worship H3068
10 God, and worship before the L thy God: H3068
11 *thing* which the L thy God hath given H3068
13 Then thou shalt say before the L thy H3068
14 to the voice of the L my God, *and* have H3068

Dt 26:16 This day the L thy God hath H3068
17 Thou hast avouched the L this day to H3068
18 And the L hath avouched thee this day H3068
19 unto the L thy God, as he hath spoken. H3068
27: 2 the land which the L thy God giveth H3068
3 the land which the L thy God giveth H3068
3 and honey; as the L God of thy fathers H3068
5 an altar unto the L thy God, an altar of H3068
6 Thou shalt build the altar of the L thy H3068
6 offerings thereon unto the L thy God: H3068
7 there, and rejoice before the L thy God. H3068
9 art become the people of the L thy God. H3068
10 the voice of the L thy God, and do his H3068
15 unto the L, the work of the hands H3068
28: 1 the voice of the L thy God, to observe H3068
1 this day, that the L thy God will set thee H3068
2 unto the voice of the L thy God. H3068
7 The L shall cause thine enemies that H3068
8 The L shall command the blessing H3068
8 land which the L thy God giveth thee. H3068
9 The L shall establish thee an holy H3068
9 of the L thy God, and walk in his ways. H3068
10 the L; and they shall be afraid of thee. H3068
11 And the L shall make thee plenteous in H3068
11 L sware unto thy fathers to give thee. H3068
12 The L shall open unto thee his good H3068
13 And the L shall make thee the head, H3068
13 of the L thy God, which I command H3068
15 the voice of the L thy God, to observe H3068
20 The L shall send upon thee cursing, H3068
21 The L shall make the pestilence cleave H3068
22 The L shall smite thee with a H3068
24 The L shall make the rain of thy land H3068
25 The L shall cause thee to be smitten H3068
27 The L will smite thee with the botch of H3068
28 The L shall smite thee with madness, H3068
35 The L shall smite thee in the knees, and H3068
36 The L shall bring thee, and thy king H3068
37 nations whither the L shall lead thee. H3068
45 the voice of the L thy God, to keep his H3068
47 Because thou servedst not the L thy H3068
48 enemies which the L shall send against H3068
49 The L shall bring a nation against thee H3068
52 which the L thy God hath given thee. H3068
53 which the L thy God hath given H3068
58 and fearful name, THE L THY GOD; H3068
59 Then the L will make thy plagues H3068
61 law, them will the L bring upon thee, H3068
62 not obey the voice of the L thy God. H3068
63 And it shall come to pass, *that* as the L H3068
63 you; so the L will rejoice over you H3068
64 And the L shall scatter thee among all H3068
65 have rest: but the L shall give thee there H3068
68 And the L shall bring thee into Egypt H3068
29: 1 which the L commanded Moses H3068
2 seen all that the L did before your eyes H3068
4 Yet the L hath not given you an heart H3068
6 might know that I *am* the L your God. H3068
10 Ye stand this day all of you before the L H3068
12 covenant with the L thy God, and into H3068
12 L thy God maketh with thee this day: H3068
15 this day before the L our God, and also H3068
18 this day from the L our God, to go *and* H3068
20 The L will not spare him, but then the H3068
20 then the anger of the L and his jealousy H3068
20 upon him, and the L shall blot out his H3068
21 And the L shall separate him unto evil H3068
22 which the L hath laid upon it; H3068
23 which the L overthrew in his anger, H3068
24 hath the L done thus unto this H3068
25 covenant of the L God of their fathers, H3068
27 And the anger of the L was kindled H3068
28 And the L rooted them out of their land H3068
29 The secret *things belong* unto the L our H3068
30: 1 whither the L thy God hath driven thee, H3068
2 And shalt return unto the L thy God, H3068
3 That then the L thy God will turn thy H3068
3 the L thy God hath scattered thee. H3068
4 thence will the L thy God gather thee, H3068
5 And the L thy God will bring thee into H3068
6 And the L thy God will circumcise thine H3068
6 thy seed, to love the L thy God with all H3068
7 And the L thy God will put all these H3068
8 obey the voice of the L, and do all his H3068
9 And the L thy God will make thee H3068
9 for good: for the L will again rejoice H3068
10 the voice of the L thy God, to keep his H3068
10 if thou turn unto the L thy God with all H3068
16 day to love the L thy God, to walk in H3068

Dt 30:16 multiply: and the L thy God shall bless H3068
20 That thou mayest love the L thy God, H3068
20 in the land which the L sware unto thy H3068
31: 2 come in: also the L hath said unto me, H3068
3 The L thy God, he will go over before H3068
3 go over before thee, as the L hath said. H3068
4 And the L shall do unto them as he did H3068
5 And the L shall give them up before H3068
6 of them: for the L thy God, he *it is* that H3068
7 the land which the L hath sworn unto H3068
8 And the L, he *it is* that doth go before H3068
9 the L, and unto all the elders of Israel. H3068
11 to appear before the L thy God in the H3068
12 learn, and fear the L your God, and H3068
13 learn to fear the L your God, as long as H3068
14 And the L said unto Moses, Behold, thy H3068
15 And the L appeared in the tabernacle H3068
16 And the L said unto Moses, Behold, H3068
25 the ark of the covenant of the L, saying, H3068
26 covenant of the L your God, that it may H3068
27 L; and how much more after my death? H3068
29 in the sight of the L, to provoke him to H3068
32: 3 L: ascribe ye greatness unto our God. H3068
6 Do ye thus requite the L, O foolish H3068
12 *So* the L alone did lead him, and *there* H3068
19 And when the L saw *it,* he abhorred H3068
27 high, and the L hath not done all this. H3068
30 them, and the L had shut them up? H3068
36 For the L shall judge his people, and H3068
48 And the L spake unto Moses that H3068
33: 2 And he said, The L came from Sinai, H3068
7 and he said, Hear, L, the voice of Judah, H3068
11 Bless, L, his substance, and accept the H3068
12 said, The beloved of the L shall dwell in H3068
12 by him; *and the* L shall cover him all the
13 And of Joseph he said, Blessed of the L H3068
21 of the L, and his judgments with Israel. H3068
23 L: possess thou the west and the south. H3068
29 saved by the L, the shield of thy help, H3068
34: 1 Jericho. And the L shewed him all the H3068
4 And the L said unto him, This *is* the H3068
5 So Moses the servant of the L died H3068
5 Moab, according to the word of the L. H3068
9 and did as the L commanded Moses. H3068
10 Moses, whom the L knew face to face, H3068
11 which the L sent him to do in the H3068
Jos 1: 1 the servant of the L it came to pass, H3068
1 to pass, that the L spake unto Joshua H3068
9 dismayed: for the L thy God *is* with H3068
11 the L your God giveth you to possess it. H3068
13 the servant of the L commanded you, H3068
13 you, saying, The L your God hath given H3068
15 Until the L have given your brethren H3068
15 the land which the L your God giveth H3068
17 thee: only the L thy God be with thee, H3068
2: 9 I know that the L hath given you the H3068
10 For we have heard how the L dried up H3068
11 of you: for the L your God, he *is* God H3068
12 unto me by the L, since I have shewed H3068
14 it shall be, when the L hath given us the H3068
24 And they said unto Joshua, Truly the L H3068
3: 3 the covenant of the L your God, and the H3068
5 the L will do wonders among you. H3068
7 And the L said unto Joshua, This day H3068
9 and hear the words of the L your God. H3068
11 Behold, the ark of the covenant of the L H113
13 bear the ark of the L, the Lord of all the H3068
13 of the LORD, the L of all the earth, shall H113
17 the covenant of the L stood firm on dry H3068
4: 1 that the L spake unto Joshua, saying, H3068
5 the ark of the L your God into the H3068
7 covenant of the L; when it passed over H3068
8 of Jordan, as the L spake unto Joshua, H3068
10 finished that the L commanded Joshua H3068
11 that the ark of the L passed over, and H3068
13 L unto battle, to the plains of Jericho. H3068
14 On that day the L magnified Joshua in H3068
15 And the L spake unto Joshua, saying, H3068
18 covenant of the L were come up out of H3068
23 For the L your God dried up the waters H3068
23 over, as the L your God did to the H3068
24 the hand of the L, that it *is* mighty: that H3068
24 ye might fear the L your God for ever. H3068
5: 1 sea, heard that the L had dried up the H3068
2 At that time the L said unto Joshua, H3068
6 the voice of the L: unto whom the LORD H3068
6 unto whom the L sware that he would H3068
6 the land, which the L sware unto their H3068
9 And the L said unto Joshua, This day H3068

Jos 5:14 of the host of the L am I now come. H3068
14 him, What saith my l unto his servant? H113
6: 2 And the L said unto Joshua, See, I have H3068
6 of rams' horns before the ark of the L. H3068
7 is armed pass on before the ark of the L. H3068
8 on before the L, and blew with the H3068
8 of the covenant of the L followed them. H3068
11 So the ark of the L compassed the city, H3068
12 and the priests took up the ark of the L. H3068
13 the ark of the L went on continually, H3068
13 after the ark of the L, *the priests* going H3068
16 Shout; for the L hath given you the city. H3068
17 *are* therein, to the L: only Rahab the H3068
19 unto the L: they shall come into H3068
19 shall come into the treasury of the L. H3068
24 into the treasury of the house of the L. H3068
26 the man before the L, that riseth up and H3068
27 So the L was with Joshua; and his fame H3068
7: 1 the anger of the L was kindled against H3068
6 the ark of the L until the eventide, he H3068
7 And Joshua said, Alas, O L GOD, H136
8 O L, what shall I say, when Israel turneth H136
10 And the L said unto Joshua, Get thee H3068
13 for thus saith the L God of Israel, *There* H3068
14 the tribe which the L taketh shall come H3068
14 the family which the L shall take shall H3068
14 L shall take shall come man by man. H3068
15 covenant of the L, and because he hath H3068
19 thee, glory to the L God of Israel, and H3068
20 sinned against the L God of Israel, and H3068
23 Israel, and laid them out before the L. H3068
25 troubled us? the L shall trouble thee H3068
26 unto this day. So the L turned from the H3068
8: 1 And the L said unto Joshua, Fear not, H3068
7 the city: for the L your God will deliver H3068
8 of the L shall ye do. See, I have H3068
18 And the L said unto Joshua, Stretch out H3068
27 of the L which he commanded Joshua. H3068
30 Then Joshua built an altar unto the L H3068
31 As Moses the servant of the L H3068
31 the L, and sacrificed peace offerings. H3068
33 covenant of the L, as well the stranger, H3068
33 the servant of the L had commanded H3068
9: 9 of the name of the L thy God: for we H3068
14 asked not *counsel* at the mouth of the L. H3068
18 unto them by the L God of Israel. And H3068
19 unto them by the L God of Israel: now H3068
24 how that the L thy God commanded H3068
27 for the altar of the L, even unto this day, H3068
10: 8 And the L said unto Joshua, Fear them H3068
10 And the L discomfited them before H3068
11 that the L cast down great stones H3068
12 Then spake Joshua to the L in the day H3068
12 in the day when the L delivered up the H3068
14 it or after it, that the L hearkened unto H3068
14 of a man: for the L fought for Israel. H3068
19 their cities: for the L your God hath H3068
25 for thus shall the L do to all your H3068
30 And the L delivered it also, and the H3068
32 And the L delivered Lachish into the H3068
40 as the L God of Israel commanded. H3068
42 the L God of Israel fought for Israel. H3068
11: 6 And the L said unto Joshua, Be not H3068
8 And the L delivered them into the hand H3068
9 And Joshua did unto them as the L H3068
12 the servant of the L commanded. H3068
15 As the L commanded Moses his H3068
15 of all that the L commanded Moses. H3068
20 For it was of the L to harden their H3068
20 them, as the L commanded Moses. H3068
23 to all that the L said unto Moses; and H3068
12: 6 Them did Moses the servant of the L H3068
6 Moses the servant of the L gave it *for* a H3068
13: 1 in years; and the L said unto him, H3068
8 Moses the servant of the L gave them; H3068
14 sacrifices of the L God of Israel made H3068
33 inheritance: the L God of Israel *was* H3068
14: 2 By lot *was* their inheritance, as the L H3068
5 As the L commanded Moses, so the H3068
6 the thing that the L said unto Moses H3068
7 the servant of the L sent me from H3068
8 but I wholly followed the L my God. H3068
9 hast wholly followed the L my God. H3068
10 And now, behold, the L hath kept me H3068
10 even since the L spake this word unto H3068
12 whereof the L spake in that day; for H3068
12 fenced: if so be the L *will be* with me, H3068
12 be able to drive them out, as the L said. H3068
14 he wholly followed the L God of Israel. H3068

Jos 15:13 of the L to Joshua, *even* the H3068
17: 4 saying, The L commanded Moses H3068
4 of the L he gave them an inheritance H3068
14 as the L hath blessed me hitherto? H3068
18: 3 L God of your fathers hath given you? H3068
6 lots for you here before the L our God. H3068
7 priesthood of the L *is* their inheritance: H3068
7 Moses the servant of the L gave them. H3068
8 cast lots for you before the L in Shiloh. H3068
10 in Shiloh before the L: and there Joshua H3068
19:50 According to the word of the L they H3068
51 in Shiloh before the L, at the door of the H3068
20: 1 The L also spake unto Joshua, saying, H3068
21: 2 saying, The L commanded by the H3068
3 of the L, these cities and their suburbs. H3068
8 L commanded by the hand of Moses. H3068
43 And the L gave unto Israel all the land H3068
44 And the L gave them rest round about, H3068
44 before them; the L delivered all their H3068
45 thing which the L had spoken unto the H3068
22: 2 the servant of the L commanded you, H3068
3 the commandment of the L your God. H3068
4 And now the L your God hath given H3068
4 L gave you on the other side Jordan. H3068
5 the servant of the L charged you, to H3068
5 you, to love the L your God, and to H3068
9 the word of the L by the hand of Moses. H3068
16 of the L, What trespass *is* this H3068
16 from following the L, in that ye have H3068
16 ye might rebel this day against the L? H3068
17 a plague in the congregation of the L, H3068
18 day from following the L? and it will be, H3068
18 to day against the L, that to morrow he H3068
19 the possession of the L, wherein the H3068
19 not against the L, nor rebel against us, H3068
19 altar beside the altar of the L our God. H3068
22 The L God of gods, the LORD God of H3068
22 The LORD God of gods, the L God of H3068
22 against the L, (save us not this day,) H3068
23 turn from following the L; or if to offer H3068
23 thereon, let the L himself require *it*; H3068
24 have ye to do with the L God of Israel? H3068
25 For the L hath made Jordan a border H3068
25 no part in the L: so shall your children H3068
25 our children cease from fearing the L. H3068
27 the service of the L before him with our H3068
27 time to come, Ye have no part in the L. H3068
28 of the altar of the L, which our fathers H3068
29 rebel against the L, and turn this day H3068
29 from following the L, to build an altar H3068
29 L our God that *is* before his tabernacle. H3068
31 we perceive that the L *is* among us, H3068
31 against the L: now ye have delivered H3068
31 of Israel out of the hand of the L. H3068
34 a witness between us that the L *is* God. H3068
23: 1 time after that the L had given rest H3068
3 And ye have seen all that the L your H3068
3 of you; for the L your God *is* he that H3068
5 And the L your God, he shall expel H3068
5 L your God hath promised unto you. H3068
8 But cleave unto the L your God, as ye H3068
9 For the L hath driven out from before H3068
10 a thousand: for the L your God, he *it is* H3068
11 yourselves, that ye love the L your God. H3068
13 Know for a certainty that the L your H3068
13 which the L your God hath given you. H3068
14 things which the L your God spake H3068
15 you, which the L your God promised H3068
15 you; so shall the L bring upon you all H3068
15 which the L your God hath given you. H3068
16 covenant of the L your God, which he H3068
16 the anger of the L be kindled against H3068
24: 2 Thus saith the L God of Israel, Your H3068
7 And when they cried unto the L, he put H3068
14 Now therefore fear the L, and serve him H3068
14 flood, and in Egypt; and serve ye the L. H3068
15 you to serve the L, choose you this day H3068
15 me and my house, we will serve the L. H3068
16 forsake the L, to serve other gods; H3068
17 For the L our God, he *it is* that brought H3068
18 And the L drave out from before us all H3068
18 we also serve the L; for he *is* our God. H3068
19 Ye cannot serve the L: for he *is* an holy H3068
20 If ye forsake the L, and serve strange H3068
21 Joshua, Nay; but we will serve the L. H3068
22 chosen you the L, to serve him. And H3068
23 your heart unto the L God of Israel. H3068
24 And the people said unto Joshua, The L H3068
26 oak, that *was* by the sanctuary of the L. H3068

Jos 24:27 the words of the L which he spake unto H3068
29 Nun, the servant of the L, died, *being* an H3068
31 And Israel served the L all the days of H3068
31 of the L, that he had done for Israel. H3068
Jdg 1: 1 of Israel asked the L, saying, Who shall H3068
2 And the L said, Judah shall go up: H3068
4 And Judah went up; and the L H3068
19 And the L was with Judah; and he H3068
22 Beth-el: and the L *was* with them. H3068
2: 1 And an angel of the L came up from H3068
4 the angel of the L spake these words H3068
5 and they sacrificed there unto the L. H3068
7 And the people served the L all the H3068
7 works of the L, that he did for Israel. H3068
8 Nun, the servant of the L, died, *being* an H3068
10 knew not the L, nor yet the works which H3068
11 in the sight of the L, and served Baalim: H3068
12 And they forsook the L God of their H3068
12 them, and provoked the L to anger. H3068
13 And they forsook the L, and served Baal H3068
14 And the anger of the L was hot against H3068
15 the hand of the L was against them for H3068
15 for evil, as the L had said, and as the H3068
15 had said, and as the L had sworn unto H3068
16 Nevertheless the L raised up judges, H3068
17 of the L; *but* they did not so. H3068
18 And when the L raised them up judges, H3068
18 judges, then the L was with the judge, H3068
18 for it repented the L because of their H3068
20 And the anger of the L was hot against H3068
22 the way of the L to walk therein, as H3068
23 Therefore the L left those nations, H3068
3: 1 Now these *are* the nations which the L H3068
4 of the L, which he commanded H3068
7 evil in the sight of the L, and forgat the H3068
7 and forgat the L their God, and served H3068
8 Therefore the anger of the L was hot H3068
9 cried unto the L, the LORD raised up H3068
9 the LORD, the L raised up a deliverer H3068
10 And the spirit of the L came upon him, H3068
10 out to war: and the L delivered H3068
12 in the sight of the L: and the LORD H3068
12 LORD: and the L strengthened Eglon H3068
12 they had done evil in the sight of the L. H3068
15 cried unto the L, the LORD raised them H3068
15 unto the LORD, the L raised them up a H3068
25 l *was* fallen down dead on the earth. H113
28 after me: for the L hath delivered your H3068
4: 1 the sight of the L, when Ehud was dead. H3068
2 And the L sold them into the hand of H3068
3 Israel cried unto the L: for he had nine H3068
6 unto him, Hath not the L God of Israel H3068
9 honour; for the L shall sell Sisera into H3068
14 the day in which the L hath delivered H3068
14 hand: is not the L gone out before thee? H3068
15 And the L discomfited Sisera, and all H3068
18 him, Turn in, my l, turn in to me; fear H113
5: 2 Praise ye the L for the avenging of H3068
3 will sing unto the L; I will sing *praise* to H3068
3 I will sing *praise* to the L God of Israel. H3068
4 L, when thou wentest out of Seir, when H3068
5 from before the L, *even* that Sinai from H3068
5 Sinai from before the L God of Israel. H3068
9 among the people. Bless ye the L. H3068
11 acts of the L, *even* the righteous acts H3068
11 people of the L go down to the gates. H3068
13 among the people: the L made me have H3068
23 Curse ye Meroz, said the angel of the L, H3068
23 to the help of the L, to the help of the H3068
23 to the help of the L against the mighty. H3068
31 So let all thine enemies perish, O L: but H3068
6: 1 evil in the sight of the L: and the LORD H3068
1 LORD: and the L delivered them into H3068
6 the children of Israel cried unto the L. H3068
7 unto the L because of the Midianites, H3068
8 That the L sent a prophet unto the H3068
8 them, Thus saith the L God of Israel, I H3068
10 And I said unto you, I *am* the L your H3068
11 And there came an angel of the L, and H3068
12 And the angel of the L appeared unto H3068
12 said unto him, The L *is* with thee, thou H3068
13 And Gideon said unto him, Oh my L, if H113
13 Oh my Lord, if the L be with us, why H3068
13 Did not the L bring us up from Egypt? H3068
13 but now the L hath forsaken us, and H3068
14 And the L looked upon him, and said, H3068
15 And he said unto him, Oh my L, H136
16 And the L said unto him, Surely I will H3068
21 Then the angel of the L put forth the H3068

Jdg 6:21 angel of the L departed out of his sight. H3068
22 an angel of the L, Gideon said, Alas, O H3068
22 said, Alas, O L GOD! for because I have H136
22 have seen an angel of the L face to face. H3068
23 And the L said unto him, Peace *be* unto H3068
24 altar there unto the L, and called it H3068
25 night, that the L said unto him, Take H3068
26 And build an altar unto the L thy God H3068
27 and did as the L had said unto him: H3068
34 But the spirit of the L came upon H3068
7: 2 And the L said unto Gideon, The H3068
4 And the L said unto Gideon, The H3068
5 the water: and the L said unto Gideon, H3068
7 And the L said unto Gideon, By the H3068
9 night, that the L said unto him, Arise, H3068
15 said, Arise; for the L hath delivered H3068
18 say, *The sword* of the L, and of Gideon. H3068
20 The sword of the L, and of Gideon. H3068
22 the trumpets, and the L set every man's H3068
8: 7 And Gideon said, Therefore when the L H3068
19 of my mother: *as* the L liveth, if ye had H3068
23 rule over you: the L shall rule over you. H3068
34 not the L their God, who had H3068
10: 6 in the sight of the L, and served Baalim, H3068
6 and forsook the L, and served not him. H3068
7 And the anger of the L was hot against H3068
10 Israel cried unto the L, saying, We have H3068
11 And the L said unto the children of H3068
15 said unto the L, We have sinned: do H3068
16 and served the L: and his soul was H3068
11: 9 Ammon, and the L deliver them before H3068
10 Jephthah, The L be witness between H3068
11 all his words before the L in Mizpeh. H3068
21 And the L God of Israel delivered Sihon H3068
23 So now the L God of Israel hath H3068
24 whomsoever the L our God shall drive H3068
27 against me: the L the Judge be judge H3068
29 Then the spirit of the L came upon H3068
30 And Jephthah vowed a vow unto the L, H3068
32 the L delivered them into his hands. H3068
35 unto the L, and I cannot go back. H3068
36 mouth unto the L, do to me according H3068
36 mouth; forasmuch as the L hath taken H3068
12: 3 Ammon, and the L delivered them into H3068
13: 1 in the sight of the L; and the LORD H3068
1 LORD; and the L delivered them into H3068
3 And the angel of the L appeared unto H3068
8 Then Manoah entreated the L, and said, H3068
8 and said, O my L, let the man of God H136
13 And the angel of the L said unto H3068
15 the angel of the L, I pray thee, let us H3068
16 And the angel of the L said unto H3068
16 offer it unto the L. For Manoah knew H3068
16 knew not that he *was* an angel of the L. H3068
17 the angel of the L, What *is* thy name, H3068
18 And the angel of the L said unto him, H3068
19 a rock unto the L: and *the angel* did H3068
20 that the angel of the L ascended in the H3068
21 But the angel of the L did no more H3068
21 knew that he *was* an angel of the L. H3068
23 But his wife said unto him, If the L H3068
24 the child grew, and the L blessed him. H3068
25 And the spirit of the L began to move H3068
14: 4 that it *was* of the L, that he sought an H3068
6 And the spirit of the L came mightily H3068
19 And the spirit of the L came upon him, H3068
15:14 And the spirit of the L came mightily upon H3068
18 and called on the L, and said, Thou H3068
16:20 not that the L was departed from him. H3068
28 And Samson called unto the L, and H3068
28 LORD, and said, O L GOD, remember H136
17: 2 said, Blessed *be thou* of the L, my son. H3068
3 the silver unto the L from my hand for H3068
13 Now know I that the L will do me good, H3068
18: 6 before the L *is* your way wherein ye go. H3068
19:18 to the house of the L; and there *is* no H3068
26 house where her l *was*, till it was light. H113
27 And her l rose up in the morning, and H113
20: 1 land of Gilead, unto the L in Mizpeh. H3068
18 And the L said, Judah *shall go up* first. H3068
23 wept before the L until even, and asked H3068
23 counsel of the L, saying, Shall I go up H3068
23 And the L said, Go up against him.) H3068
26 there before the L, and fasted that day H3068
26 and peace offerings before the L. H3068
27 inquired of the L, (for the ark of the H3068
28 I cease? And the L said, Go up; for to H3068
35 And the L smote Benjamin before H3068
21: 3 And said, O L God of Israel, why is this H3068

Jdg 21: 5 unto the L? For they had made H3068
5 not up to the L to Mizpeh, saying, He H3068
7 we have sworn by the L that we will not H3068
8 to Mizpeh to the L? And, behold, there H3068
15 because that the L had made a breach H3068
19 *is* a feast of the L in Shiloh yearly *in a* H3068
Ru 1: 6 how that the L had visited his people H3068
8 house: the L deal kindly with you, H3068
9 The L grant you that ye may find rest, H3068
13 hand of the L is gone out against me. H3068
17 will I be buried: the L do so to me, and H3068
21 I went out full, and the L hath brought H3068
21 me Naomi, seeing the L hath testified H3068
2: 4 the reapers, The L *be* with you. And H3068
4 they answered him, The L bless thee. H3068
12 The L recompense thy work, and a full H3068
12 given thee of the L God of Israel, under H3068
13 in thy sight, my l; for that thou hast H113
20 *be* he of the L, who hath not left off H3068
3:10 And he said, Blessed *be* thou of the L, H3068
13 L liveth: lie down until the morning. H3068
4:11 *are* witnesses. The L make the woman H3068
12 L shall give thee of this young woman. H3068
13 in unto her, the L gave her conception, H3068
14 Blessed *be* the L, which hath not left H3068
1Sa 1: 3 sacrifice unto the L of hosts in Shiloh. H3068
3 the priests of the L, *were* there. H3068
5 but the L had shut up her womb. H3068
6 because the L had shut up her womb. H3068
7 to the house of the L, so she provoked H3068
9 a seat by a post of the temple of the L. H3068
10 and prayed unto the L, and wept sore. H3068
11 And she vowed a vow, and said, O L of H3068
11 give him unto the L all the days of his H3068
12 the L, that Eli marked her mouth. H3068
15 and said, No, my l, I *am* a woman of a H113
15 have poured out my soul before the L. H3068
19 before the L, and returned, and came H3068
19 his wife; and the L remembered her. H3068
20 Because I have asked him of the L. H3068
21 the L the yearly sacrifice, and his vow. H3068
22 before the L, and there abide for ever. H3068
23 him; only the L establish his word. H3068
24 L in Shiloh: and the child *was* young. H3068
26 And she said, Oh my l, *as* thy soul liveth, H113
26 *as* thy soul liveth, my l, I *am* the woman H113
26 stood by thee here, praying unto the L. H3068
27 For this child I prayed; and the L hath H3068
28 Therefore also I have lent him to the L; H3068
28 L. And he worshipped the LORD there. H3068
28 LORD. And he worshipped the L there. H3068
2: 1 rejoiceth in the L, mine horn is exalted H3068
1 horn is exalted in the L: my mouth is H3068
2 *There is* none holy as the L: for *there is* H3068
3 mouth: for the L *is* a God of knowledge, H3068
6 The L killeth, and maketh alive: he H3068
7 The L maketh poor, and maketh rich: H3068
10 The adversaries of the L shall be H3068
10 upon them: the L shall judge the ends H3068
11 unto the L before Eli the priest. H3068
12 *were* sons of Belial; they knew not the L. H3068
17 great before the L: for men abhorred H3068
17 for men abhorred the offering of the L. H3068
18 But Samuel ministered before the L, H3068
20 and said, The L give thee seed of this H3068
20 L. And they went unto their own home. H3068
21 And the L visited Hannah, so that she H3068
21 And the child Samuel grew before the L. H3068
25 sin against the L, who shall entreat for H3068
25 father, because the L would slay them. H3068
26 both with the L, and also with men. H3068
27 Thus saith the L, Did I plainly appear H3068
30 Wherefore the L God of Israel saith, I H3068
30 ever: but now the L saith, Be it far from H3068
3: 1 unto the L before Eli. And the H3068
1 the word of the L was precious in those H3068
3 in the temple of the L, where the ark of H3068
4 That the L called Samuel: and he H3068
6 And the L called yet again, Samuel. H3068
7 Now Samuel did not yet know the L, H3068
7 word of the L yet revealed unto him. H3068
8 And the L called Samuel again the H3068
8 that the L had called the child. H3068
9 thou shalt say, Speak, L; for thy servant H3068
10 And the L came, and stood, and called H3068
11 And the L said to Samuel, Behold, I will H3068
15 doors of the house of the L. And Samuel H3068
17 And he said, What *is* the thing that *the L*
18 L: let him do what seemeth him good. H3068

1Sa 3:19 And Samuel grew, and the L was with H3068
20 established *to be* a prophet of the L. H3068
21 And the L appeared again in Shiloh: H3068
21 in Shiloh: for the L revealed himself to H3068
21 Samuel in Shiloh by the word of the L. H3068
4: 3 hath the L smitten us to day before H3068
3 covenant of the L out of Shiloh unto us, H3068
4 the covenant of the L of hosts, which H3068
5 covenant of the L came into the camp, H3068
6 ark of the L was come into the camp. H3068
5: 3 the ark of the L. And they took Dagon, H3068
4 the ark of the L; and the head of Dagon H3068
6 But the hand of the L was heavy upon H3068
9 the hand of the L was against the city H3068
6: 1 And the ark of the L was in the country H3068
2 to the ark of the L? tell us wherewith we H3068
8 And take the ark of the L, and lay it H3068
11 And they laid the ark of the L upon the H3068
14 the kine a burnt offering unto the L. H3068
15 the ark of the L, and the coffer that *was* H3068
15 sacrifices the same day unto the L. H3068
17 offering unto the L; for Ashdod one, for H3068
18 the ark of the L: *which stone remaineth* H3068
19 into the ark of the L, even he smote of H3068
19 because the L had smitten *many* of H3068
20 before this holy L God? and to whom H3068
21 L; come ye down, *and* fetch it up to you. H3068
7: 1 up the ark of the L, and brought it into H3068
1 Eleazar his son to keep the ark of the L. H3068
2 the house of Israel lamented after the L. H3068
3 ye do return unto the L with all your H3068
3 hearts unto the L, and serve him only: H3068
4 and Ashtaroth, and served the L only. H3068
5 and I will pray for you unto the L. H3068
6 *it* out before the L, and fasted on that H3068
6 have sinned against the L. And Samuel H3068
8 not to cry unto the L our God for us, H3068
9 wholly unto the L: and Samuel cried H3068
9 L for Israel; and the LORD heard him. H3068
9 LORD for Israel; and the L heard him. H3068
10 Israel: but the L thundered with a great H3068
12 saying, Hitherto hath the L helped us. H3068
13 and the hand of the L was against the H3068
17 and there he built an altar unto the L. H3068
8: 6 us. And Samuel prayed unto the L. H3068
7 And the L said unto Samuel, Hearken H3068
10 And Samuel told all the words of the L H3068
18 and the L will not hear you in that day. H3068
21 he rehearsed them in the ears of the L. H3068
22 And the L said to Samuel, Hearken H3068
9:15 Now the L had told Samuel in his ear a H3068
17 And when Samuel saw Saul, the L said H3068
10: 1 *it* not because the L hath anointed thee H3068
6 And the spirit of the L will come upon H3068
17 people together unto the L to Mizpeh; H3068
18 Israel, Thus saith the L God of Israel, I H3068
19 before the L by your tribes, and H3068
22 Therefore they inquired of the L H3068
22 thither. And the L answered, Behold, H3068
24 ye him whom the L hath chosen, that H3068
25 *it* up before the L. And Samuel sent all H3068
11: 7 the fear of the L fell on the people, and H3068
13 the L hath wrought salvation in Israel. H3068
15 king before the L in Gilgal; and there H3068
15 before the L; and there Saul and H3068
12: 3 against me before the L, and before his H3068
5 And he said unto them, The L *is* H3068
6 people, *It is* the L that advanced Moses H3068
7 you before the L of all the righteous H3068
7 acts of the L, which he did to you H3068
8 cried unto the L, then the LORD sent H3068
8 the LORD, then the L sent Moses and H3068
9 And when they forgat the L their God, H3068
10 And they cried unto the L, and said, We H3068
10 have forsaken the L, and have served H3068
11 And the L sent Jerubbaal, and Bedan, H3068
12 us: when the L your God *was* your king. H3068
13 behold, the L hath set a king over you. H3068
14 If ye will fear the L, and serve him, and H3068
14 of the L, then shall both ye and H3068
14 you continue following the L your God: H3068
15 But if ye will not obey the voice of the L, H3068
15 of the L, then shall the hand H3068
15 the hand of the L be against you, as *it* H3068
16 which the L will do before your eyes. H3068
17 I will call unto the L, and he shall send H3068
17 the sight of the L, in asking you a king. H3068
18 So Samuel called unto the L; and the H3068
18 LORD; and the L sent thunder and rain H3068

1Sa 12:18 greatly feared the **L** and Samuel. H3068
19 servants unto the **L** thy God, that we H3068
20 from following the **L**, but serve the H3068
20 but serve the **L** with all your heart; H3068
22 For the **L** will not forsake his people for H3068
22 pleased the **L** to make you his people. H3068
23 sin against the **L** in ceasing to pray for H3068
24 Only fear the **L**, and serve him in truth H3068
13:12 unto the **L**: I forced myself therefore, H3068
13 of the **L** thy God, which he commanded H3068
13 for now would the **L** have established H3068
14 not continue: the **L** hath sought him a H3068
14 heart, and the **L** hath commanded him H3068
14 *that* which the **L** commanded thee. H3068
14: 6 it may be that the **L** will work for us: H3068
6 to the **L** to save by many or by few. H3068
10 we will go up: for the **L** hath delivered H3068
12 after me: for the **L** hath delivered them H3068
23 So the **L** saved Israel that day: and the H3068
33 sin against the **L**, in that they eat with H3068
34 sin not against the **L** in eating with the H3068
35 And Saul built an altar unto the **L**: the H3068
35 the first altar that he built unto the **L**. H3068
39 For, *as* the **L** liveth, which saveth H3068
41 Therefore Saul said unto the **L** God of H3068
45 God forbid: *as* the **L** liveth, there shall H3068
15: 1 Samuel also said unto Saul, The **L** sent H3068
1 unto the voice of the words of the **L**. H3068
2 Thus saith the **L** of hosts, I remember H3068
10 Then came the word of the **L** unto H3068
11 and he cried unto the **L** all night. H3068
13 *be* thou of the **L**: I have performed the H3068
13 performed the commandment of the **L**. H3068
15 to sacrifice unto the **L** thy God; and the H3068
16 tell thee what the **L** hath said to me this H3068
17 the **L** anointed thee king over Israel? H3068
18 And the **L** sent thee on a journey, and H3068
19 the voice of the **L**, but didst fly upon the H3068
19 spoil, and didst evil in the sight of the **L**? H3068
20 the voice of the **L**, and have gone the H3068
20 the way which the **L** sent me, and have H3068
21 sacrifice unto the **L** thy God in Gilgal. H3068
22 And Samuel said, Hath the **L** *as great* H3068
22 the voice of the **L**? Behold, to obey *is* H3068
23 the word of the **L**, he hath also rejected H3068
24 of the **L**, and thy words: because H3068
25 with me, that I may worship the **L**. H3068
26 the word of the **L**, and the LORD hath H3068
26 the LORD, and the **L** hath rejected thee H3068
28 And Samuel said unto him, The **L** hath H3068
30 me, that I may worship the **L** thy God. H3068
31 after Saul; and Saul worshipped the **L**. H3068
33 Agag in pieces before the **L** in Gilgal. H3068
35 for Saul: and the **L** repented that he H3068
16: 1 And the **L** said unto Samuel, How long H3068
2 kill me. And the **L** said, Take an heifer H3068
2 and say, I am come to sacrifice to the **L**. H3068
4 And Samuel did that which the **L** H3068
5 sacrifice unto the **L**: sanctify yourselves, H3068
7 But the **L** said unto Samuel, Look not H3068
7 him: for *the* **L** *seeth* not as man seeth;
7 but the **L** looketh on the heart. H3068
8 he said, Neither hath the **L** chosen this. H3068
9 he said, Neither hath the **L** chosen this. H3068
10 Jesse, The **L** hath not chosen these. H3068
12 **L** said, Arise, anoint him: for this *is* he. H3068
13 the spirit of the **L** came upon David H3068
14 But the spirit of the **L** departed from H3068
14 an evil spirit from the **L** troubled him. H3068
16 Let our **l** now command thy servants, H113
18 a comely person, and the **L** *is* with him. H3068
17:37 David said moreover, The **L** that H3068
37 unto David, Go, and the **L** be with thee. H3068
45 in the name of the **L** of hosts, the God H3068
46 This day will the **L** deliver thee into H3068
47 know that the **L** saveth not with sword H3068
18:12 because the **L** was with him, and was H3068
14 in all his ways; and the **L** *was* with him. H3068
28 And Saul saw and knew that the **L** *was* H3068
19: 5 Philistine, and the **L** wrought a great H3068
6 *As* the **L** liveth, he shall not be slain. H3068
9 And the evil spirit from the **L** was upon H3068
20: 3 but truly *as* the **L** liveth, and *as* thy soul H3068
8 into a covenant of the **L** with thee: H3068
12 And Jonathan said unto David, O **L** H3068
13 The **L** do so and much more to H3068
13 in peace: and the **L** be with thee, as he H3068
14 me the kindness of the **L**, that I die not: H3068
15 no, not when the **L** hath cut off the H3068

1Sa 20:16 *saying*, Let the **L** even require *it* at the H3068
21 to thee, and no hurt; *as* the **L** liveth. H3068
22 thy way: for the **L** hath sent thee away. H3068
23 the **L** *be* between thee and me for ever. H3068
42 in the name of the **L**, saying, The LORD H3068
42 saying, The **L** be between me and H3068
21: 6 from before the **L**, to put hot bread in H3068
7 before the **L**; and his name *was* Doeg, H3068
22:10 And he inquired of the **L** for him, and H3068
12 And he answered, Here I *am*, my **l**. H113
17 the priests of the **L**; because their hand H3068
17 hand to fall upon the priests of the **L**. H3068
23: 2 Therefore David inquired of the **L**, H3068
2 And the **L** said unto David, Go, H3068
4 Then David inquired of the **L** yet again. H3068
4 yet again. And the **L** answered him and H3068
10 Then said David, O **L** God of Israel, thy H3068
11 servant hath heard? O **L** God of Israel, I H3068
11 And the **L** said, He will come down. H3068
12 the **L** said, They will deliver *thee* up. H3068
18 before the **L**: and David abode in H3068
21 And Saul said, Blessed *be* ye of the **L**; H3068
24: 4 the day of which the **L** said unto thee, H3068
6 And he said unto his men, The **L** forbid H3068
6 him, seeing he *is* the anointed of the **L**. H3068
8 Saul, saying, My **l** the king. And when H113
10 seen how that the **L** had delivered thee H3068
10 my **l**; for he *is* the LORD'S anointed. H113
12 The **L** judge between me and thee, and H3068
12 and thee, and the **L** avenge me of thee: H3068
15 The **L** therefore be judge, and judge H3068
18 as when the **L** had delivered me into H3068
19 wherefore the **L** reward thee good for H3068
21 Swear now therefore unto me by the **L**, H3068
25:24 said, Upon me, my **l**, *upon* me *let this* H113
25 Let not my **l**, I pray thee, regard this man H113
25 men of my **l**, whom thou didst send. H113
26 Now therefore, my **l**, *as* the LORD liveth, H113
26 Now therefore, my lord, *as* the **L** liveth, H3068
26 liveth, seeing the **L** hath withholden H3068
26 they that seek evil to my **l**, be as Nabal. H113
27 brought unto my **l**, let it even be given H113
27 unto the young men that follow my **l**. H113
28 thine handmaid: for the **L** will certainly H3068
28 will certainly make my **l** a sure house; H113
28 house; because my **l** fighteth the battles H113
28 the battles of the **L**, and evil hath not H3068
29 but the soul of my **l** shall be bound in the H113
29 of life with the **L** thy God; and the souls H3068
30 And it shall come to pass, when the **L** H3068
30 have done to my **l** according to all the H113
31 of heart unto my **l**, either that thou hast H113
31 or that my **l** hath avenged himself: H113
31 but when the **L** shall have dealt well H3068
31 my **l**, then remember thine handmaid. H113
32 Blessed *be* the **L** God of Israel, which H3068
34 For in very deed, *as* the **L** God of Israel H3068
38 that the **L** smote Nabal, that he died. H3068
39 Blessed *be* the **L**, that hath pleaded the H3068
39 from evil: for the **L** hath returned the H3068
41 to wash the feet of the servants of my **l**. H113
26:10 David said furthermore, *As* the **L** H3068
10 LORD liveth, the **L** shall smite him; or H3068
11 The **L** forbid that I should stretch forth H3068
12 sleep from the **L** was fallen upon them. H3068
15 thou not kept thy **l** the king? for there H113
15 of the people in to destroy the king thy **l**. H113
16 thou hast done. *As* the **L** liveth, ye *are* H3068
17 David said, *It is* my voice, my **l**, O king. H113
18 And he said, Wherefore doth my **l** thus H113
19 Now therefore, I pray thee, let my **l** the H113
19 of his servant. If the **L** have stirred thee H3068
19 *be* they before the **L**; for they have H3068
19 of the **L**, saying, Go, serve other gods. H3068
20 the face of the **L**: for the king of Israel H3068
23 The **L** render to every man his H3068
23 for the **L** delivered thee into H3068
24 in the eyes of the **L**, and let him deliver H3068
28: 6 And when Saul inquired of the **L**, the H3068
6 of the LORD, the **L** answered him not, H3068
10 And Saul sware to her by the **L**, saying, H3068
10 saying, *As* the **L** liveth, there shall no H3068
16 of me, seeing the **L** is departed from H3068
17 And the **L** hath done to him, as he H3068
17 by me: for the **L** hath rent the kingdom H3068
18 the voice of the **L**, nor executedst his H3068
18 **L** done this thing unto thee this day. H3068
19 Moreover the **L** will also deliver Israel H3068
19 *be* with me: the **L** also shall deliver the H3068

1Sa 29: 6 him, Surely, *as* the **L** liveth, thou hast H3068
8 against the enemies of my **l** the king? H113
30: 6 encouraged himself in the **L** his God. H3068
8 And David inquired at the **L**, saying, H3068
23 that which the **L** hath given us, who H3068
26 you of the spoil of the enemies of the **L**; H3068
2Sa 1:10 and have brought them hither unto my **l**. H113
12 the people of the **L**, and for the house of H3068
2: 1 inquired of the **L**, saying, Shall I go up H3068
1 of Judah? And the **L** said unto him, Go H3068
5 *be* ye of the **L**, that ye have shewed H3068
5 **l**, *even* unto Saul, and have buried him. H113
6 And now the **L** shew kindness and H3068
3: 9 except, as the **L** hath sworn to David, H3068
18 Now then do *it*: for the **L** hath spoken H3068
21 all Israel unto my **l** the king, that they H113
28 before the **L** for ever from the blood H3068
39 too hard for me: the **L** shall reward the H3068
4: 8 thy life; and the **L** hath avenged my H3068
8 hath avenged my **l** the king this day of H113
9 unto them, *As* the **L** liveth, who hath H3068
5: 2 in Israel: and the **L** said to thee, Thou H3068
3 Hebron before the **L**: and they anointed H3068
10 and the **L** God of hosts *was* with him. H3068
12 And David perceived that the **L** had H3068
19 And David inquired of the **L**, saying, H3068
19 hand? And the **L** said unto David, Go H3068
20 and said, The **L** hath broken forth H3068
23 And when David inquired of the **L**, he H3068
24 for then shall the **L** go out before thee, H3068
25 And David did so, as the **L** had H3068
6: 2 by the name of the **L** of hosts that H3068
5 played before the **L** on all manner of H3068
7 And the anger of the **L** was kindled H3068
8 because the **L** had made a breach H3068
9 And David was afraid of the **L** that day, H3068
9 How shall the ark of the **L** come to me? H3068
10 the ark of the **L** unto him into the city H3068
11 And the ark of the **L** continued in the H3068
11 months: and the **L** blessed Obed-edom, H3068
12 saying, The **L** hath blessed the house H3068
13 that bare the ark of the **L** had gone six H3068
14 And David danced before the **L** with all H3068
15 up the ark of the **L** with shouting, and H3068
16 And as the ark of the **L** came into the H3068
16 **L**; and she despised him in her heart. H3068
17 And they brought in the ark of the **L**, H3068
17 and peace offerings before the **L**. H3068
18 people in the name of the **L** of hosts. H3068
21 *It was* before the **L**, which chose me H3068
21 over the people of the **L**, over Israel: H3068
21 Israel: therefore will I play before the **L**. H3068
7: 1 his house, and the **L** had given him rest H3068
3 *is* in thine heart; for the **L** *is* with thee. H3068
4 of the **L** came unto Nathan, saying, H3068
5 Thus saith the **L**, Shalt thou build me H3068
8 Thus saith the **L** of hosts, I took thee H3068
11 enemies. Also the **L** telleth thee that he H3068
18 and sat before the **L**, and he said, Who H3068
18 said, Who *am* I, O **L** GOD? and what *is* H136
19 in thy sight, O **L** GOD; but thou hast H136
19 *is* this the manner of man, O **L** GOD? H136
20 for thou, **L** GOD, knowest thy servant. H136
22 Wherefore thou art great, O **L** God: for H3068
24 ever: and thou, **L**, art become their God. H3068
25 And now, O **L** God, the word that thou H3068
26 ever, saying, The **L** of hosts *is* the God H3068
27 For thou, O **L** of hosts, God of Israel, H3068
28 And now, O **L** GOD, thou *art* that God, H136
29 thee: for thou, O **L** GOD, hast spoken *it*: H136
8: 6 gifts. And the **L** preserved David H3068
11 dedicate unto the **L**, with the silver and H3068
14 servants. And the **L** preserved David H3068
9:11 According to all that my **l** the king hath H113
10: 3 unto Hanun their **l**, Thinkest thou that H113
12 the **L** do that which seemeth him good. H3068
11: 9 of his **l**, and went not down to his house. H113
11 in tents; and my **l** Joab, and the servants H113
11 the servants of my **l**, are encamped in the H113
13 of his **l**, but went not down to his house. H113
27 that David had done displeased the **L**. H3068
12: 1 And the **L** sent Nathan unto David. H3068
5 to Nathan, *As* the **L** liveth, the man H3068
7 man. Thus saith the **L** God of Israel, I H3068
9 of the **L**, to do evil in his sight? H3068
11 Thus saith the **L**, Behold, I will raise up H3068
13 sinned against the **L**. And Nathan said H3068
13 unto David, The **L** also hath put away H3068
14 the enemies of the **L** to blaspheme, the H3068

2Sa 12:15 his house. And the L struck the child H3068
20 the house of the L, and worshipped: H3068
24 name Solomon: and the L loved him. H3068
25 his name Jedidiah, because of the L. H3068
13:32 said, Let not my l suppose *that* they have H113
33 Now therefore let not my l the king take H113
14: 9 unto the king, My l, O king, the iniquity H113
11 remember the L thy God, that thou H3068
11 he said, *As* the L liveth, there shall not H3068
12 unto my l the king. And he said, Say on. H113
15 of this thing unto my l the king, *it is* H113
17 The word of my l the king shall now be H113
17 of God, so *is* my l the king to discern H113
17 the L thy God will be with thee. H3068
18 said, Let my l the king now speak. H113
19 thy soul liveth, my l the king, none can H113
19 left from ought that my l the king hath H113
20 this thing: and my l *is* wise, according to H113
22 in thy sight, my l, O king, in that the king H113
15: 7 I have vowed unto the L, in Hebron. H3068
8 saying, If the L shall bring me again H3068
8 to Jerusalem, then I will serve the L. H3068
15 whatsoever my l the king shall appoint. H113
21 and said, *As* the L liveth, and *as* my H3068
21 liveth, and *as* my l the king liveth, surely H113
21 in what place my l the king shall be, H113
25 in the eyes of the L, he will bring me H3068
31 And David said, O L, I pray thee, turn H3068
16: 4 may find grace in thy sight, my l, O king. H113
8 The L hath returned upon thee all the H3068
8 reigned; and the L hath delivered the H3068
9 dead dog curse my l the king? let me go H113
10 curse, because the L hath said unto H3068
11 him curse; for the L hath bidden him. H3068
12 It may be that the L will look on mine H3068
12 and that the L will requite me good H3068
18 but whom the L, and this people, and H3068
17:14 For the L had appointed to defeat H3068
14 the L might bring evil upon Absalom. H3068
18:19 the L hath avenged him of his enemies. H3068
28 Blessed *be* the L thy God, which hath H3068
28 up their hand against my l the king. H113
31 said, Tidings, my l the king: for the H113
31 the king: for the L hath avenged thee H3068
32 The enemies of my l the king, and all H113
19: 7 for I swear by the L, if thou go not forth, H3068
19 And said unto the king, Let not my l H113
19 the day that my l the king went out of H113
20 Joseph to go down to meet my l the king. H113
26 And he answered, My l, O king, my H113
27 servant unto my l the king; but my lord H113
27 the king; but my l the king *is* as an angel H113
28 men before my l the king: yet didst thou H113
30 all, forasmuch as my l the king is come H113
35 be yet a burden unto my l the king? H113
37 go over with my l the king; and do to H113
20:19 swallow up the inheritance of the L? H3068
21: 1 David inquired of the L. And the LORD H3068
1 the LORD. And the L answered, *It is* for H3068
3 ye may bless the inheritance of the L? H3068
6 them up unto the L in Gibeah of Saul, H3068
6 of Saul, *whom* the L did choose. And H3068
9 in the hill before the L: and they fell *all* H3068
22: 1 And David spake unto the L the words H3068
1 in the day *that* the L had delivered him H3068
2 And he said, The L *is* my rock, and my H3068
4 I will call on the L, *who is* worthy to be H3068
7 In my distress I called upon the L, and H3068
14 The L thundered from heaven, and the H3068
16 the rebuking of the L, at the blast of the H3068
19 of my calamity: but the L was my stay. H3068
21 The L rewarded me according to my H3068
22 For I have kept the ways of the L, and H3068
25 Therefore the L hath recompensed me H3068
29 For thou *art* my lamp, O L: and the H3068
29 and the L will lighten my darkness. H3068
31 the word of the L *is* tried: he *is* a H3068
32 For who *is* God, save the L? and who *is* a H3068
42 unto the L, but he answered them not. H3068
47 The L liveth; and blessed *be* my rock; H3068
50 unto thee, O L, among the heathen, H3068
23: 2 The Spirit of the L spake by me, and his H3068
10 the sword: and the L wrought a great H3068
12 and the L wrought a great victory. H3068
16 thereof, but poured it out unto the L. H3068
17 And he said, Be it far from me, O L, that H3068
24: 1 And again the anger of the L was H3068
3 And Joab said unto the king, Now the L H3068
3 that the eyes of my l the king may see *it*: H113

2Sa 24: 3 doth my l the king delight in this thing? H113
10 said unto the L, I have sinned greatly H3068
10 now, I beseech thee, O L, take away the H3068
11 the word of the L came unto the H3068
12 Thus saith the L, I offer thee three H3068
14 the hand of the L; for his mercies *are* H3068
15 So the L sent a pestilence upon Israel H3068
16 to destroy it, the L repented him of the H3068
16 And the angel of the L was by the H3068
17 And David spake unto the L when he H3068
18 rear an altar unto the L in the H3068
19 of Gad, went up as the L commanded. H3068
21 And Araunah said, Wherefore is my l H113
21 an altar unto the L, that the plague may H3068
22 And Araunah said unto David, Let my l H113
23 the king, The L thy God accept thee. H3068
24 offerings unto the L my God of that H3068
25 an altar unto the L, and offered burnt H3068
25 offerings. So the L was entreated for H3068
1Ki 1: 2 there be sought for my l the king a young H113
2 bosom, that my l the king may get heat. H113
11 reign, and David our l knoweth *it* not? H113
13 Didst not thou, my l, O king, swear unto H113
17 And she said unto him, My l, thou H113
17 swarest by the L thy God unto thine H3068
18 now, my l the king, thou knowest *it* not: H113
20 And thou, my l, O king, the eyes of all H113
20 on the throne of my l the king after him. H113
21 to pass, when my l the king shall sleep H113
24 And Nathan said, My l, O king, hast thou H113
27 Is this thing done by my l the king, and H113
27 on the throne of my l the king after him? H113
29 And the king sware, and said, *As* the L H3068
30 Even as I sware unto thee by the L God H3068
31 said, Let my l king David live for ever. H113
33 servants of your l, and cause Solomon H113
36 L God of my lord the king say so *too*. H3068
36 LORD God of my l the king say so *too*. H113
37 As the L hath been with my lord the H3068
37 As the LORD hath been with my l the H113
37 than the throne of my l king David. H113
43 l king David hath made Solomon king. H113
47 came to bless our l king David, saying, H113
48 Blessed *be* the L God of Israel, which H3068
2: 3 And keep the charge of the L thy God, H3068
4 That the L may continue his word H3068
8 to him by the L, saying, I will not put H3068
15 my brother's: for it was his from the L. H3068
23 Then king Solomon sware by the L, H3068
24 Now therefore, *as* the L liveth, which H3068
26 the ark of the L GOD before David my H136
27 priest unto the L; that he might fulfil H3068
27 fulfil the word of the L, which he spake H3068
28 tabernacle of the L, and caught hold on H3068
29 tabernacle of the L; and, behold, *he is* H3068
30 tabernacle of the L, and said unto him, H3068
32 And the L shall return his blood upon H3068
33 shall there be peace for ever from the L. H3068
38 *is* good: as my l the king hath said, so H113
42 to swear by the L, and protested unto H3068
43 kept the oath of the L, and the H3068
44 father: therefore the L shall return thy H3068
45 be established before the L for ever. H3068
3: 1 and the house of the L, and the wall of H3068
2 the name of the L, until those days. H3068
3 And Solomon loved the L, walking in H3068
5 In Gibeon the L appeared to Solomon H3068
7 And now, O L my God, thou hast made H3068
10 And the speech pleased the L, that H136
15 covenant of the L, and offered up burnt H3068
17 And the one woman said, O my l, I and H113
26 and she said, O my l, give her the living H113
5: 3 the name of the L his God for the wars H3068
3 L put them under the soles of his feet. H3068
4 But now the L my God hath given me H3068
5 unto the name of the L my God, as the H3068
5 my God, as the L spake unto David my H3068
7 Blessed *be* the L this day, which hath H3068
12 And the L gave Solomon wisdom, as he H3068
6: 1 he began to build the house of the L. H3068
2 built for the L, the length thereof *was* H3068
11 And the word of the L came to H3068
19 there the ark of the covenant of the L. H3068
37 house of the L laid, in the month Zif: H3068
7:12 of the L, and for the porch of the house. H3068
40 king Solomon for the house of the L: H3068
45 the house of the L, *were of* bright brass. H3068
48 the house of the L: the altar of gold, and H3068
51 for the house of the L. And Solomon H3068

1Ki 7:51 the treasures of the house of the L. H3068
8: 1 the covenant of the L out of the city of H3068
4 And they brought up the ark of the L, H3068
6 covenant of the L unto his place, into H3068
9 at Horeb, when the L made *a covenant* H3068
10 that the cloud filled the house of the L, H3068
11 the L had filled the house of the LORD. H3068
11 the LORD had filled the house of the L. H3068
12 Then spake Solomon, The L said that H3068
15 And he said, Blessed *be* the L God of H3068
17 for the name of the L God of Israel. H3068
18 And the L said unto David my father, H3068
20 And the L hath performed his word H3068
20 of Israel, as the L promised, and have H3068
20 for the name of the L God of Israel. H3068
21 covenant of the L, which he made with H3068
22 the altar of the L in the presence of all H3068
23 And he said, L God of Israel, *there is* no H3068
25 Therefore now, L God of Israel, keep H3068
28 supplication, O L my God, to hearken H3068
44 pray unto the L toward the city which H3068
53 our fathers out of Egypt, O L GOD. H136
54 unto the L, he arose from before H3068
54 the altar of the L, from kneeling on his H3068
56 Blessed *be* the L, that hath given rest H3068
57 The L our God be with us, as he was H3068
59 before the L, be nigh unto the LORD H3068
59 be nigh unto the L our God day and H3068
60 L *is* God, *and that there is* none else. H3068
61 be perfect with the L our God, to walk H3068
62 with him, offered sacrifice before the L. H3068
63 he offered unto the L, two and twenty H3068
63 of Israel dedicated the house of the L. H3068
64 the house of the L: for there he offered H3068
64 that *was* before the L *was* too little to H3068
65 Egypt, before the L our God, seven days H3068
66 goodness that the L had done for David H3068
9: 1 of the house of the L, and the king's H3068
2 That the L appeared to Solomon the H3068
3 And the L said unto him, I have heard H3068
8 say, Why hath the L done thus unto H3068
9 they forsook the L their God, who H3068
9 the L brought upon them all this evil. H3068
10 the house of the L, and the king's house, H3068
15 the house of the L, and his own house, H3068
25 which he built unto the L, and he burnt H3068
25 before the L. So he finished the house. H3068
10: 1 the name of the L, she came to prove H3068
5 of the L; there was no more spirit in her. H3068
9 Blessed be the L thy God, which H3068
9 because the L loved Israel for ever, H3068
12 for the house of the L, and for the king's H3068
11: 2 Of the nations *concerning* which the L H3068
4 perfect with the L his God, as *was* the H3068
6 in the sight of the L, and went not fully H3068
6 fully after the L, as *did* David his father. H3068
9 And the L was angry with Solomon, H3068
9 turned from the L God of Israel, which H3068
10 kept not that which the L commanded. H3068
11 Wherefore the L said unto Solomon, H3068
14 And the L stirred up an adversary unto H3068
23 fled from his l Hadadezer king of Zobah: H113
31 for thus saith the L, the God of Israel, H3068
12:15 was from the L, that he might perform H3068
15 his saying, which the L spake by Ahijah H3068
24 Thus saith the L, Ye shall not go up, nor H3068
24 to the word of the L, and returned to H3068
24 depart, according to the word of the L. H3068
27 in the house of the L at Jerusalem, then H3068
27 again unto their l, *even* unto Rehoboam H113
13: 1 by the word of the L unto Beth-el: and H3068
2 in the word of the L, and said, O altar, H3068
2 thus saith the L; Behold, a child shall H3068
3 *is* the sign which the L hath spoken; H3068
5 of God had given by the word of the L. H3068
6 the face of the L thy God, and pray for H3068
6 of God besought the L, and the king's H3068
9 me by the word of the L, saying, Eat no H3068
17 by the word of the L, Thou shalt eat no H3068
18 by the word of the L, saying, Bring him H3068
20 that the word of the L came unto the H3068
21 Thus saith the L, Forasmuch as thou H3068
21 the mouth of the L, and hast not kept H3068
21 which the L thy God commanded thee, H3068
22 of the which *the L* did say to thee, Eat no
26 the word of the L: therefore the LORD H3068
26 therefore the L hath delivered him H3068
26 word of the L, which he spake unto him. H3068
32 by the word of the L against the altar in H3068

1Ki 14: 5 And the L said unto Ahijah, Behold, H3068
7 Go, tell Jeroboam, Thus saith the L God H3068
11 of the air eat: for the L hath spoken *it.* H3068
13 thing toward the L God of Israel in the H3068
14 Moreover the L shall raise him up a H3068
15 For the L shall smite Israel, as a reed is H3068
15 their groves, provoking the L to anger. H3068
18 to the word of the L, which he spake by H3068
21 the city which the L did choose out of H3068
22 And Judah did evil in the sight of the L, H3068
24 L cast out before the children of Israel. H3068
26 of the house of the L, and the treasures H3068
28 the house of the L, that the guard bare H3068
15: 3 perfect with the L his God, as the heart H3068
4 Nevertheless for David's sake did the L H3068
5 in the eyes of the L, and turned not H3068
11 eyes of the L, as *did* David his father. H3068
14 was perfect with the L all his days. H3068
15 of the L, silver, and gold, and vessels. H3068
18 of the house of the L, and the treasures H3068
26 And he did evil in the sight of the L, and H3068
29 the saying of the L, which he spake by H3068
30 provoked the L God of Israel to anger. H3068
34 And he did evil in the sight of the L, and H3068
16: 1 Then the word of the L came to Jehu H3068
7 the word of the L against Baasha, and H3068
7 in the sight of the L, in provoking him H3068
12 to the word of the L, which he spake H3068
13 sin, in provoking the L God of Israel to H3068
19 in the sight of the L, in walking in the H3068
25 in the eyes of the L, and did worse than H3068
26 to provoke the L God of Israel to anger H3068
30 of the L above all that *were* before him. H3068
33 to provoke the L God of Israel to anger H3068
34 to the word of the L, which he spake by H3068
17: 1 said unto Ahab, *As* the L God of Israel H3068
2 And the word of the L came unto him, H3068
5 the word of the L: for he went and dwelt H3068
8 And the word of the L came unto him, H3068
12 And she said, *As* the L thy God liveth, I H3068
14 For thus saith the L God of Israel, The H3068
14 *that* the L sendeth rain upon the earth. H3068
16 word of the L, which he spake by Elijah. H3068
20 And he cried unto the L, and said, O H3068
20 and said, O L my God, hast thou also H3068
21 and cried unto the L, and said, O LORD H3068
21 and said, O L my God, I pray thee, H3068
22 And the L heard the voice of Elijah; H3068
24 the word of the L in thy mouth *is* truth. H3068
18: 1 the word of the L came to Elijah in the H3068
3 (Now Obadiah feared the L greatly: H3068
4 prophets of the L, that Obadiah took an H3068
7 face, and said, *Art* thou that my l Elijah? H113
8 And he answered him, I *am:* go, tell thy l, H113
10 *As* the L thy God liveth, there is no H3068
10 whither my l hath not sent to seek H113
11 And now thou sayest, Go, tell thy l, H113
12 that the spirit of the L shall carry thee H3068
12 I thy servant fear the L from my youth. H3068
13 Was it not told my l what I did when H113
13 prophets of the L, how I hid an hundred H3068
14 And now thou sayest, Go, tell thy l, H113
15 And Elijah said, *As* the L of hosts H3068
18 of the L, and thou hast followed Baalim. H3068
21 opinions? if the L *be* God, follow him: H3068
22 a prophet of the L; but Baal's prophets H3068
24 on the name of the L: and the God that H3068
30 altar of the L *that was* broken down. H3068
31 the word of the L came, saying, Israel H3068
32 in the name of the L: and he made a H3068
36 near, and said, L God of Abraham, H3068
37 Hear me, O L, hear me, that this people H3068
37 that thou *art* the L God, and *that* thou H3068
38 Then the fire of the L fell, and H3068
39 and they said, The L, he *is* the God; the H3068
39 he *is* the God; the L, he *is* the God. H3068
46 And the hand of the L was on Elijah; H3068
19: 4 is enough; now, O L, take away my life; H3068
7 And the angel of the L came again the H3068
9 the word of the L *came* to him, and he H3068
10 jealous for the L God of hosts: for the H3068
11 mount before the L. And, behold, the H3068
11 And, behold, the L passed by, and a H3068
11 rocks before the L; *but* the LORD *was* H3068
11 the LORD; *but* the L *was* not in the H3068
11 *but* the L *was* not in the earthquake: H3068
12 a fire; *but* the L *was* not in the fire: H3068
14 jealous for the L God of hosts: because H3068
15 And the L said unto him, Go, return on H3068

1Ki 20: 4 and said, My l, O king, according to H113
9 Tell my l the king, All that thou H113
13 Thus saith the L, Hast thou seen all this H3068
13 and thou shalt know that I *am* the L. H3068
14 Thus saith the L, *Even* by the young H3068
28 Thus saith the L, Because the Syrians H3068
28 have said, The L *is* God of the hills, but H3068
28 and ye shall know that I *am* the L. H3068
35 in the word of the L, Smite me, I pray H3068
36 the voice of the L, behold, as soon as H3068
42 And he said unto him, Thus saith the L, H3068
21: 3 And Naboth said to Ahab, The L forbid H3068
17 And the word of the L came to Elijah H3068
19 Thus saith the L, Hast thou killed, and H3068
19 Thus saith the L, In the place where H3068
20 thyself to work evil in the sight of the L, H3068
23 And of Jezebel also spake the L, saying, H3068
25 the L, whom Jezebel his wife stirred up. H3068
26 L cast out before the children of Israel. H3068
28 And the word of the L came to Elijah H3068
22: 5 I pray thee, at the word of the L to day. H3068
6 said, Go up; for the L shall deliver *it* into H136
7 here a prophet of the L besides, that we H3068
8 may inquire of the L: but I hate him; for H3068
11 Thus saith the L, With these shalt thou H3068
12 L shall deliver *it* into the king's hand. H3068
14 And Micaiah said, *As* the L liveth, what H3068
14 the L saith unto me, that will I speak. H3068
15 prosper: for the L shall deliver *it* into H3068
16 *that which is* true in the name of the L? H3068
17 a shepherd: and the L said, These have H3068
19 the word of the L: I saw the LORD H3068
19 LORD: I saw the L sitting on his throne, H3068
20 And the L said, Who shall persuade H3068
21 the L, and said, I will persuade him. H3068
22 And the L said unto him, Wherewith? H3068
23 Now therefore, behold, the L hath put a H3068
23 the L hath spoken evil concerning thee. H3068
24 of the L from me to speak unto thee? H3068
28 at all in peace, the L hath not spoken H3068
38 unto the word of the L which he spake. H3068
43 in the eyes of the L: nevertheless the H3068
52 And he did evil in the sight of the L, and H3068
53 to anger the L God of Israel, according H3068
2Ki 1: 3 But the angel of the L said to Elijah the H3068
4 Now therefore thus saith the L, Thou H3068
6 Thus saith the L, *Is it* not because *there* H3068
15 And the angel of the L said unto Elijah, H3068
16 And he said unto him, Thus saith the L, H3068
17 to the word of the L which Elijah had H3068
2: 1 And it came to pass, when the L would H3068
2 I pray thee; for the L hath sent me to H3068
2 *unto him, As* the L liveth, and *as* thy H3068
3 thou that the L will take away thy H3068
4 I pray thee; for the L hath sent me to H3068
4 he said, *As* the L liveth, and *as* thy soul H3068
5 thou that the L will take away thy H3068
6 thee, here; for the L hath sent me to H3068
6 he said, *As* the L liveth, and *as* thy soul H3068
14 said, Where *is* the L God of Elijah? and H3068
16 the spirit of the L hath taken him up, H3068
19 *is* pleasant, as my l seeth: but the water H113
21 Thus saith the L, I have healed these H3068
24 in the name of the L. And there came H3068
3: 2 evil in the sight of the L; but not like his H3068
10 Alas! that the L hath called these three H3068
11 a prophet of the L, that we may inquire H3068
11 may inquire of the L by him? And one H3068
12 The word of the L is with him. So the H3068
13 him, Nay: for the L hath called these H3068
14 And Elisha said, *As* the L of hosts H3068
15 that the hand of the L came upon him. H3068
16 And he said, Thus saith the L, Make H3068
17 For thus saith the L, Ye shall not see H3068
18 in the sight of the L: he will deliver the H3068
4: 1 did fear the L: and the creditor is come H3068
16 she said, Nay, my l, *thou* man of God, do H113
27 her: and the L hath hid *it* from me, H3068
28 Then she said, Did I desire a son of my l? H113
30 child said, *As* the L liveth, and *as* thy H3068
33 them twain, and prayed unto the L. H3068
43 for thus saith the L, They shall eat, and H3068
44 *thereof,* according to the word of the L. H3068
5: 1 by him the L had given deliverance H3068
3 Would God my l *were* with the prophet H113
4 And *one* went in, and told his l, saying, H113
11 the name of the L his God, and strike H3068
16 But he said, *As* the L liveth, before H3068
17 unto other gods, but unto the L. H3068

2Ki 5:18 In this thing the L pardon thy servant, H3068
18 the L pardon thy servant in this thing. H3068
20 but, *as* the L liveth, I will run after H3068
6:12 And one of his servants said, None, my l, H113
17 And Elisha prayed, and said, L, I pray H3068
17 may see. And the L opened the eyes of H3068
18 prayed unto the L, and said, Smite this H3068
20 that Elisha said, L, open the eyes of H3068
20 may see. And the L opened their eyes, H3068
26 unto him, saying, Help, my l, O king. H113
27 And he said, If the L do not help thee, H3068
33 this evil *is* of the L; what should I wait H3068
33 should I wait for the L any longer? H3068
7: 1 ye the word of the L; Thus saith the H3068
1 Thus saith the L, To morrow about this H3068
2 Then a l on whose hand the king H7991
2 Behold, *if* the L would make windows H3068
6 For the L had made the host of the H136
16 a shekel, according to the word of the L. H3068
17 And the king appointed the l on whose H7991
19 And that l answered the man of God, H7991
19 behold, *if* the L should make windows H3068
8: 1 sojourn: for the L hath called for a H3068
5 And Gehazi said, My l, O king, this *is* the H113
8 and inquire of the L by him, saying, H3068
10 howbeit the L hath shewed me that H3068
12 And Hazael said, Why weepeth my l? And H113
13 answered, The L hath shewed me that H3068
18 and he did evil in the sight of the L. H3068
19 Yet the L would not destroy Judah for H3068
27 in the sight of the L, as *did* the house of H3068
9: 3 Thus saith the L, I have anointed thee H3068
6 Thus saith the L God of Israel, I have H3068
6 the people of the L, *even* over Israel. H3068
7 servants of the L, at the hand of Jezebel. H3068
11 to the servants of his l: and *one* said unto H113
12 L, I have anointed thee king over Israel. H3068
25 the L laid this burden upon him; H3068
26 his sons, saith the L; and I will requite H3068
26 in this plat, saith the L. Now therefore H3068
26 *ground,* according to the word of the L. H3068
36 *is* the word of the L, which he spake by H3068
10:10 of the word of the L, which the LORD H3068
10 LORD, which the L spake concerning H3068
10 of Ahab: for the L hath done *that* which H3068
16 L. So they made him ride in his chariot. H3068
17 of the L, which he spake to Elijah. H3068
23 the L, but the worshippers of Baal only. H3068
30 And the L said unto Jehu, Because thou H3068
31 in the law of the L God of Israel with all H3068
32 In those days the L began to cut Israel H3068
11: 3 hid in the house of the L six years. And H3068
4 into the house of the L, and made a H3068
4 the L, and shewed them the king's son. H3068
7 of the house of the L about the king. H3068
10 shields, that *were* in the temple of the L. H3068
13 to the people into the temple of the L. H3068
15 her not be slain in the house of the L. H3068
17 between the L and the king and the H3068
18 officers over the house of the L. H3068
19 the house of the L, and came by the way H3068
12: 2 right in the sight of the L all his days H3068
4 the house of the L, *even* the money of H3068
4 heart to bring into the house of the L, H3068
9 the house of the L: and the priests that H3068
9 *was* brought into the house of the L. H3068
10 that was found in the house of the L. H3068
11 of the house of the L: and they laid it H3068
11 that wrought upon the house of the L, H3068
12 of the house of the L, and for all that H3068
13 for the house of the L bowls of silver, H3068
13 *was* brought into the house of the L: H3068
14 repaired therewith the house of the L. H3068
16 the house of the L: it was the priests'. H3068
18 of the house of the L, and in the king's H3068
13: 2 in the sight of the L, and followed the H3068
3 And the anger of the L was kindled H3068
4 And Jehoahaz besought the L, and the H3068
4 LORD, and the L hearkened unto him: H3068
5 (And the L gave Israel a saviour, so H3068
11 in the sight of the L; he departed not H3068
23 And the L was gracious unto them, and H3068
14: 3 in the sight of the L, yet not like David H3068
6 wherein the L commanded, saying, H3068
14 found in the house of the L, and in the H3068
24 in the sight of the L: he departed not H3068
25 to the word of the L God of Israel, H3068
26 For the L saw the affliction of Israel, H3068
27 And the L said not that he would blot H3068

2Ki 15: 3 in the sight of the **L**, according to all H3068
5 And the **L** smote the king, so that he H3068
9 in the sight of the **L**, as his fathers had H3068
12 This *was* the word of the **L** which he H3068
18 in the sight of the **L**: he departed not all H3068
24 in the sight of the **L**: he departed not H3068
28 in the sight of the **L**: he departed not H3068
34 in the sight of the **L**: he did according to H3068
35 the higher gate of the house of the **L**. H3068
37 In those days the **L** began to send H3068
16: 2 of the **L** his God, like David his father. H3068
3 whom the **L** cast out from before H3068
8 found in the house of the **L**, and in the H3068
14 *was* before the **L**, from the forefront of H3068
14 and the house of the **L**, and put it on the H3068
18 house of the **L** for the king of Assyria. H3068
17: 2 in the sight of the **L**, but not as the kings H3068
7 sinned against the **L** their God, which H3068
8 whom the **L** cast out from before H3068
9 right against the **L** their God, and they H3068
11 whom the **L** carried away before H3068
11 things to provoke the **L** to anger: H3068
12 For they served idols, whereof the **L** H3068
13 Yet the **L** testified against Israel, and H3068
14 that did not believe in the **L** their God. H3068
15 whom the **L** had charged them, H3068
16 of the **L** their God, and made H3068
17 sight of the **L**, to provoke him to anger. H3068
18 Therefore the **L** was very angry with H3068
19 of the **L** their God, but walked H3068
20 And the **L** rejected all the seed of Israel, H3068
21 the **L**, and made them sin a great sin. H3068
23 Until the **L** removed Israel out of his H3068
25 feared not the **L**: therefore the LORD H3068
25 therefore the **L** sent lions among them, H3068
28 taught them how they should fear the **L**. H3068
32 So they feared the **L**, and made unto H3068
33 They feared the **L**, and served their own H3068
34 they fear not the **L**, neither do they after H3068
34 which the **L** commanded the children H3068
35 With whom the **L** had made a H3068
36 But the **L**, who brought you up out of H3068
39 But the **L** your God ye shall fear; and he H3068
41 So these nations feared the **L**, and H3068
18: 3 in the sight of the **L**, according to all H3068
5 He trusted in the **L** God of Israel; so H3068
6 For he clave to the **L**, *and* departed not H3068
6 which the **L** commanded Moses. H3068
7 And the **L** was with him; *and* he H3068
12 not the voice of the **L** their God, but H3068
12 the servant of the **L** commanded, and H3068
15 found in the house of the **L**, and in the H3068
16 the temple of the **L**, and *from* the pillars H3068
22 But if ye say unto me, We trust in the **L** H3068
23 give pledges to my **l** the king of Assyria, H113
25 Am I now come up without the **L** H3068
25 to destroy it? The **L** said to me, Go up H3068
30 you trust in the **L**, saying, The LORD H3068
30 saying, The **L** will surely deliver us, H3068
32 you, saying, The **L** will deliver us. H3068
35 mine hand, that the **L** should deliver H3068
19: 1 and went into the house of the **L**. H3068
4 It may be the **L** thy God will hear all the H3068
4 words which the **L** thy God hath heard: H3068
6 Thus saith the **L**, Be not afraid of the H3068
14 of the **L**, and spread it before the LORD. H3068
14 of the LORD, and spread it before the **L**. H3068
15 And Hezekiah prayed before the **L**, and H3068
15 and said, O **L** God of Israel, which H3068
16 **L**, bow down thine ear, and hear: open, H3068
16 and hear: open, **L**, thine eyes, and see: H3068
17 Of a truth, **L**, the kings of Assyria have H3068
19 Now therefore, O **L** our God, I beseech H3068
19 that thou *art* the **L** God, *even* thou only. H3068
20 Thus saith the **L** God of Israel, *That* H3068
21 This *is* the word that the **L** hath spoken H3068
23 reproached the **L**, and hast said, With H136
31 the zeal of the **L** *of hosts* shall do this. H3068
32 Therefore thus saith the **L** concerning H3068
33 shall not come into this city, saith the **L**. H3068
35 the angel of the **L** went out, and smote H3068
20: 1 Thus saith the **L**, Set thine house in H3068
2 the wall, and prayed unto the **L**, saying, H3068
3 I beseech thee, O **L**, remember now how H3068
4 the word of the **L** came to him, saying, H3068
5 Thus saith the **L**, the God of David thy H3068
5 shalt go up unto the house of the **L**. H3068
8 *be* the sign that the **L** will heal me, and H3068
8 into the house of the **L** the third day? H3068

2Ki 20: 9 thou have of the **L**, that the LORD will H3068
9 LORD, that the **L** will do the thing that H3068
11 cried unto the **L**: and he brought the H3068
16 unto Hezekiah, Hear the word of the **L**. H3068
17 nothing shall be left, saith the **L**. H3068
19 *is* the word of the **L** which thou hast H3068
21: 2 evil in the sight of the **L**, after the H3068
2 **L** cast out before the children of Israel. H3068
4 And he built altars in the house of the **L**, H3068
4 of which the **L** said, In Jerusalem will H3068
5 in the two courts of the house of the **L**. H3068
6 sight of the **L**, to provoke *him* to anger. H3068
7 of which the **L** said to David, and to H3068
9 nations whom the **L** destroyed before H3068
10 And the **L** spake by his servants the H3068
12 Therefore thus saith the **L** God of H3068
16 *that which was* evil in the sight of the **L**. H3068
20 of the **L**, as his father Manasseh did. H3068
22 And he forsook the **L** God of his H3068
22 and walked not in the way of the **L**. H3068
22: 2 in the sight of the **L**, and walked in all H3068
3 the scribe, to the house of the **L**, saying, H3068
4 the house of the **L**, which the keepers of H3068
5 of the house of the **L**: and let them give H3068
5 **L**, to repair the breaches of the house, H3068
8 in the house of the **L**. And Hilkiah gave H3068
9 have the oversight of the house of the **L**. H3068
13 Go ye, inquire of the **L** for me, and for H3068
13 *is* the wrath of the **L** that is kindled H3068
15 Thus saith the **L** God of Israel, Tell the H3068
16 Thus saith the **L**, Behold, I will bring H3068
18 to inquire of the **L**, thus shall ye say to H3068
18 him, Thus saith the **L** God of Israel, *As* H3068
19 thyself before the **L**, when thou heardest H3068
19 me; I also have heard *thee*, saith the **L**. H3068
23: 2 the house of the **L**, and all the men of H3068
2 which was found in the house of the **L**. H3068
3 before the **L**, to walk after the LORD, H3068
3 to walk after the **L**, and to keep his H3068
4 the temple of the **L** all the vessels that H3068
6 the house of the **L**, without Jerusalem, H3068
7 by the house of the **L**, where the women H3068
9 to the altar of the **L** in Jerusalem, but H3068
11 of the house of the **L**, by the chamber of H3068
12 of the house of the **L**, did the king beat H3068
16 to the word of the **L** which the man of H3068
19 to provoke *the* **L** to anger, Josiah took H3068
21 passover unto the **L** your God, as *it is* H3068
23 was holden to the **L** in Jerusalem. H3068
24 the priest found in the house of the **L**. H3068
25 that turned to the **L** with all his heart, H3068
26 Notwithstanding the **L** turned not from H3068
27 And the **L** said, I will remove Judah H3068
32 evil in the sight of the **L**, according to all H3068
37 evil in the sight of the **L**, according to all H3068
24: 2 And the **L** sent against him bands of H3068
2 to the word of the **L**, which he spake by H3068
3 Surely at the commandment of the **L** H3068
4 blood; which the **L** would not pardon. H3068
9 evil in the sight of the **L**, according to all H3068
13 of the house of the **L**, and the treasures H3068
13 temple of the **L**, as the LORD had said. H3068
13 temple of the LORD, as the **L** had said. H3068
19 evil in the sight of the **L**, according to all H3068
20 For through the anger of the **L** it came H3068
25: 9 And he burnt the house of the **L**, and H3068
13 in the house of the **L**, and the bases, and H3068
13 in the house of the **L**, did the Chaldees H3068
16 the house of the **L**; the brass of all these H3068
1Ch 2: 3 in the sight of the **L**; and he slew him. H3068
6:15 when the **L** carried away Judah H3068
31 of the **L**, after that the ark had rest. H3068
32 the house of the **L** in Jerusalem: and H3068
9:19 host of the **L**, *were* keepers of the entry. H3068
20 in time past, *and* the **L** *was* with him. H3068
23 of the house of the **L**, *namely*, the house H3068
10:13 against the **L**, *even* against the word H3068
13 the word of the **L**, which he kept not, H3068
14 And inquired not of the **L**: therefore he H3068
11: 2 in Israel: and the **L** thy God said unto H3068
3 Hebron before the **L**; and they anointed H3068
3 to the word of the **L** by Samuel. H3068
9 for the **L** of hosts *was* with him. H3068
10 to the word of the **L** concerning Israel. H3068
14 **L** saved *them* by a great deliverance. H3068
18 drink *of* it, but poured it out to the **L**, H3068
12:23 to him, according to the word of the **L**. H3068
13: 2 *that it be* of the **L** our God, let us send H3068
6 the ark of God the **L**, that dwelleth H3068

1Ch 13:10 And the anger of the **L** was kindled H3068
11 because the **L** had made a breach H3068
14 months. And the **L** blessed the house of H3068
14: 2 And David perceived that the **L** had H3068
10 hand? And the **L** said unto him, Go up; H3068
17 all lands; and the **L** brought the fear of H3068
15: 2 for them hath the **L** chosen to carry the H3068
3 bring up the ark of the **L** unto his place, H3068
12 up the ark of the **L** God of Israel unto H3068
13 *it* not at the first, the **L** our God made a H3068
14 bring up the ark of the **L** God of Israel. H3068
15 according to the word of the **L**. H3068
25 covenant of the **L** out of the house of H3068
26 the covenant of the **L**, that they offered H3068
28 covenant of the **L** with shouting, and H3068
29 covenant of the **L** came to the city of H3068
16: 2 blessed the people in the name of the **L**. H3068
4 the ark of the **L**, and to record, and H3068
4 to thank and praise the **L** God of Israel: H3068
7 to thank the **L** into the hand of Asaph H3068
8 Give thanks unto the **L**, call upon his H3068
10 the heart of them rejoice that seek the **L**. H3068
11 Seek the **L** and his strength, seek his H3068
14 He *is* the **L** our God; his judgments *are* H3068
23 Sing unto the **L**, all the earth; shew forth H3068
25 For great *is* the **L**, and greatly to be H3068
26 *are* idols: but the **L** made the heavens. H3068
28 Give unto the **L**, ye kindreds of the H3068
28 give unto the **L** glory and strength. H3068
29 Give unto the **L** the glory *due* unto his H3068
29 worship the **L** in the beauty of holiness. H3068
31 say among the nations, The **L** reigneth. H3068
33 presence of the **L**, because he cometh H3068
34 O give thanks unto the **L**; for *he is* good; H3068
36 Blessed *be* the **L** God of Israel for ever H3068
36 people said, Amen, and praised the **L**. H3068
37 the covenant of the **L** Asaph and his H3068
39 **L** in the high place that *was* at Gibeon, H3068
40 To offer burnt offerings unto the **L** H3068
40 of the **L**, which he commanded Israel; H3068
41 **L**, because his mercy *endureth* for ever; H3068
17: 1 of the **L** *remaineth* under curtains. H3068
4 Thus saith the **L**, Thou shalt not build H3068
7 Thus saith the **L** of hosts, I took thee H3068
10 thee that the **L** will build thee an house. H3068
16 and sat before the **L**, and said, Who *am* H3068
16 said, Who *am* I, O **L** God, and what *is* H3068
17 of a man of high degree, O **L** God. H3068
19 O **L**, for thy servant's sake, and H3068
20 O **L**, *there is* none like thee, neither *is* H3068
22 ever; and thou, **L**, becamest their God. H3068
23 Therefore now, **L**, let the thing that thou H3068
24 ever, saying, The **L** of hosts *is* the God H3068
26 And now, **L**, thou art God, and hast H3068
27 O **L**, and *it shall be* blessed for ever. H3068
18: 6 gifts. Thus the **L** preserved David H3068
11 unto the **L**, with the silver and the H3068
13 servants. Thus the **L** preserved David H3068
19:13 the **L** do *that which is* good in his sight. H3068
21: 3 And Joab answered, The **L** make his H3068
3 as they *be*: but, my **l** the king, *are* they H113
3 why then doth my **l** require this thing? H113
9 And the **L** spake unto Gad, David's H3068
10 Thus saith the **L**, I offer thee three H3068
11 unto him, Thus saith the **L**, Choose thee H3068
12 the sword of the **L**, even the pestilence, H3068
12 and the angel of the **L** destroying H3068
13 the hand of the **L**; for very great *are* his H3068
14 So the **L** sent pestilence upon Israel: H3068
15 was destroying, the **L** beheld, and he H3068
15 And the angel of the **L** stood by the H3068
16 the angel of the **L** stand between the H3068
17 I pray thee, O **L** my God, be on me, H3068
18 Then the angel of the **L** commanded H3068
18 up an altar unto the **L** in the H3068
19 which he spake in the name of the **L**. H3068
22 therein unto the **L**: thou shalt grant it H3068
23 *it* to thee, and let my **l** the king do *that* H113
24 which *is* thine for the **L**, nor offer burnt H3068
26 an altar unto the **L**, and offered burnt H3068
26 called upon the **L**; and he answered him H3068
27 And the **L** commanded the angel; and H3068
28 At that time when David saw that the **L** H3068
29 For the tabernacle of the **L**, which H3068
30 of the sword of the angel of the **L**. H3068
22: 1 *is* the house of the **L** God, and this *is* H3068
5 be builded for the **L** *must be* exceeding H3068
6 build an house for the **L** God of Israel. H3068
7 house unto the name of the **L** my God: H3068

1Ch 22: 8 But the word of the L came to me, H3068
11 Now, my son, the L be with thee; and H3068
11 the L thy God, as he hath said of thee. H3068
12 Only the L give thee wisdom and H3068
12 mayest keep the law of the L thy God. H3068
13 which the L charged Moses with H3068
14 for the house of the L an hundred H3068
16 and be doing, and the L be with thee. H3068
18 *Is* not the L your God with you? and H3068
18 before the L, and before his people. H3068
19 your soul to seek the L your God; arise H3068
19 sanctuary of the L God, to bring the ark H3068
19 covenant of the L, and the holy vessels H3068
19 that is to be built to the name of the L. H3068
23: 4 of the house of the L; and six thousand H3068
5 praised the L with the instruments H3068
13 incense before the L, to minister unto H3068
24 of the house of the L, from the age of H3068
25 For David said, The L God of Israel H3068
28 of the house of the L, in the courts, and H3068
30 and praise the L, and likewise at even; H3068
31 sacrifices unto the L in the sabbaths, in H3068
31 unto them, continually before the L: H3068
32 in the service of the house of the L. H3068
24:19 the house of the L, according to their H3068
19 L God of Israel had commanded him. H3068
25: 3 harp, to give thanks and to praise the L. H3068
6 *in* the house of the L, with cymbals, H3068
7 in the songs of the L, *even* all that were H3068
26:12 to minister in the house of the L. H3068
22 over the treasures of the house of the L. H3068
27 dedicate to maintain the house of the L. H3068
30 of the L, and in the service of the king. H3068
27:23 because the L had said he would H3068
28: 2 covenant of the L, and for the footstool H3068
4 Howbeit the L God of Israel chose me H3068
5 And of all my sons, (for the L hath H3068
5 of the kingdom of the L over Israel. H3068
8 of the L, and in the audience H3068
8 of the L your God: that ye may H3068
9 mind: for the L searcheth all hearts, H3068
10 Take heed now; for the L hath chosen H3068
12 of the house of the L, and of all the H3068
13 of the house of the L, and for all the H3068
13 vessels of service in the house of the L. H3068
18 covered the ark of the covenant of the L. H3068
19 All *this, said David,* the L made me H3068
20 dismayed: for the L God, *even* my God, H3068
20 for the service of the house of the L. H3068
29: 1 *is* not for man, but for the L God. H3068
5 his service this day unto the L? H3068
8 L, by the hand of Jehiel the Gershonite. H3068
9 willingly to the L: and David the king H3068
10 Wherefore David blessed the L before H3068
10 Blessed *be* thou, L God of Israel our H3068
11 Thine, O L, *is* the greatness, and the H3068
11 thine *is* the kingdom, O L, and thou art H3068
16 O L our God, all this store that we have H3068
18 O L God of Abraham, Isaac, and of H3068
20 Now bless the L your God. And all the H3068
20 blessed the L God of their fathers, H3068
20 and worshipped the L, and the king. H3068
21 sacrifices unto the L, and offered burnt H3068
21 offerings unto the L, on the morrow H3068
22 And did eat and drink before the L on H3068
22 *him* unto the L *to be* the chief governor, H3068
23 the throne of the L as king instead of H3068
25 And the L magnified Solomon H3068
2Ch 1: 1 kingdom, and the L his God *was* with H3068
3 of the L had made in the wilderness. H3068
5 tabernacle of the L: and Solomon and H3068
6 altar before the L, which *was* at the H3068
9 Now, O L God, let thy promise unto H3068
2: 1 of the L, and an house for his kingdom. H3068
4 house to the name of the L my God, to H3068
4 feasts of the L our God. This *is an* H3068
11 Because the L hath loved his people, H3068
12 Huram said moreover, Blessed *be* the L H3068
12 the L, and an house for his kingdom. H3068
14 cunning men of my l David thy father. H113
15 the wine, which my l hath spoken of, let H113
3: 1 build the house of the L at Jerusalem in H3068
1 Moriah, where *the L* appeared unto
4:16 for the house of the L of bright brass. H3068
5: 1 for the house of the L was finished: and H3068
2 the covenant of the L out of the city of H3068
7 covenant of the L unto his place, to the H3068
10 at Horeb, when the L made *a covenant* H3068
13 and thanking the L; and when they H3068

2Ch 5:13 and praised the L, *saying,* For *he is* H3068
13 with a cloud, *even* the house of the L; H3068
14 of the L had filled the house of God. H3068
6: 1 Then said Solomon, The L hath said H3068
4 And he said, Blessed *be* the L God of H3068
7 for the name of the L God of Israel. H3068
8 But the L said to David my father, H3068
10 The L therefore hath performed his H3068
10 of Israel, as the L promised, and have H3068
10 for the name of the L God of Israel. H3068
11 covenant of the L, that he made with H3068
12 And he stood before the altar of the L H3068
14 And said, O L God of Israel, *there is* no H3068
16 Now therefore, O L God of Israel, keep H3068
17 Now then, O L God of Israel, let thy H3068
19 supplication, O L my God, to hearken H3068
41 Now therefore arise, O L God, into thy H3068
41 let thy priests, O L God, be clothed with H3068
42 O L God, turn not away the face of H3068
7: 1 and the glory of the L filled the house. H3068
2 the house of the L, because the glory of H3068
2 of the L had filled the LORD'S house. H3068
3 the glory of the L upon the house, they H3068
3 and praised the L, *saying,* For *he is* H3068
4 people offered sacrifices before the L. H3068
6 of musick of the L, which David the H3068
6 made to praise the L, because his mercy H3068
7 the house of the L: for there he offered H3068
10 goodness that the L had shewed unto H3068
11 the house of the L, and the king's house: H3068
11 in the house of the L, and in his own H3068
12 And the L appeared to Solomon by H3068
21 say, Why hath the L done thus unto H3068
22 they forsook the L God of their fathers, H3068
8: 1 the house of the L, and his own house, H3068
11 whereunto the ark of the L hath come. H3068
12 offerings unto the L on the altar of the H3068
12 L, which he had built before the porch, H3068
16 of the house of the L, and until it was H3068
16 *So* the house of the L was perfected. H3068
9: 4 of the L; there was no more spirit in her. H3068
8 Blessed be the L thy God, which H3068
8 *to be* king for the L thy God: because H3068
11 to the house of the L, and to the king's H3068
10:15 of God, that the L might perform his H3068
11: 2 But the word of the L came to H3068
4 Thus saith the L, Ye shall not go up, nor H3068
4 the words of the L, and returned from H3068
14 executing the priest's office unto the L: H3068
16 hearts to seek the L God of Israel came H3068
16 unto the L God of their fathers. H3068
12: 1 the law of the L, and all Israel with him. H3068
2 they had transgressed against the L, H3068
5 Thus saith the L, Ye have forsaken me, H3068
6 and they said, The L *is* righteous. H3068
7 And when the L saw that they humbled H3068
7 the word of the L came to Shemaiah, H3068
9 of the house of the L, and the treasures H3068
11 the house of the L, the guard came and H3068
12 the wrath of the L turned from him, H3068
13 the city which the L had chosen out of H3068
14 he prepared not his heart to seek the L. H3068
13: 5 Ought ye not to know that the L God of H3068
6 risen up, and hath rebelled against his l. H113
8 the kingdom of the L in the hand of the H3068
9 Have ye not cast out the priests of the L, H3068
10 But as for us, the L *is* our God, and we H3068
10 minister unto the L, *are* the sons of H3068
11 And they burn unto the L every H3068
11 L our God; but ye have forsaken him. H3068
12 fight ye not against the L God of your H3068
14 they cried unto the L, and the priests H3068
18 relied upon the L God of their fathers. H3068
20 and the L struck him, and he died. H3068
14: 2 and right in the eyes of the L his God: H3068
4 And commanded Judah to seek the L H3068
6 because the L had given him rest. H3068
7 we have sought the L our God, we have H3068
11 And Asa cried unto the L his God, and H3068
11 his God, and said, L, *it is* nothing with H3068
11 power: help us, O L our God; for we rest H3068
11 this multitude. O L, thou *art* our God; H3068
12 So the L smote the Ethiopians before H3068
13 before the L, and before his host; H3068
14 for the fear of the L came upon them: H3068
15: 2 Benjamin; The L *is* with you, while ye H3068
4 did turn unto the L God of Israel, and H3068
8 the altar of the L, that *was* before the H3068
8 that *was* before the porch of the L. H3068

2Ch 15: 9 saw that the L his God *was* with him. H3068
11 And they offered unto the L the same H3068
12 to seek the L God of their fathers H3068
13 That whosoever would not seek the L H3068
14 And they sware unto the L with a loud H3068
15 and the L gave them rest round about. H3068
16: 2 of the house of the L and of the king's H3068
7 not relied on the L thy God, therefore is H3068
8 L, he delivered them into thine hand. H3068
9 For the eyes of the L run to and fro H3068
12 not to the L, but to the physicians. H3068
17: 3 And the L was with Jehoshaphat, H3068
4 But sought to the *L* God of his father,
5 Therefore the L stablished the kingdom H3068
6 in the ways of the L: moreover he took H3068
9 of the law of the L with them, and went H3068
10 And the fear of the L fell upon all the H3068
16 himself unto the L; and with him two H3068
18: 4 I pray thee, at the word of the L to day. H3068
6 here a prophet of the L besides, that we H3068
7 may inquire of the L: but I hate him; for H3068
10 Thus saith the L, With these thou shalt H3068
11 prosper: for the L shall deliver *it* into H3068
13 And Micaiah said, *As* the L liveth, even H3068
15 but the truth to me in the name of the L? H3068
16 shepherd: and the L said, These have H3068
18 hear the word of the L; I saw the LORD H3068
18 the LORD; I saw the L sitting upon his H3068
19 And the L said, Who shall entice Ahab H3068
20 and stood before the L, and said, I will H3068
20 And the L said unto him, Wherewith? H3068
21 his prophets. And *the L* said, Thou shalt
22 Now therefore, behold, the L hath put a H3068
22 the L hath spoken evil against thee. H3068
23 of the L from me to speak unto thee? H3068
27 *then* hath not the L spoken by me. And H3068
31 cried out, and the L helped him; and H3068
19: 2 them that hate the L? therefore *is* wrath H3068
2 *is* wrath upon thee from before the L. H3068
4 back unto the L God of their fathers. H3068
6 the L, who *is* with you in the judgment. H3068
7 Wherefore now let the fear of the L be H3068
7 iniquity with the L our God, nor respect H3068
8 the judgment of the L, and for H3068
9 L, faithfully, and with a perfect heart. H3068
10 not against the L, and *so* wrath come H3068
11 all matters of the L; and Zebadiah the H3068
11 and the L shall be with the good. H3068
20: 3 to seek the L, and proclaimed a fast H3068
4 to ask *help* of the L: even out of all the H3068
4 cities of Judah they came to seek the L. H3068
5 the house of the L, before the new court, H3068
6 And said, O L God of our fathers, *art* H3068
13 And all Judah stood before the L, with H3068
14 the L in the midst of the congregation; H3068
15 Thus saith the L unto you, Be not H3068
17 salvation of the L with you, O Judah H3068
17 them: for the L *will be* with you. H3068
18 before the L, worshipping the LORD. H3068
18 before the LORD, worshipping the L. H3068
19 up to praise the L God of Israel with a H3068
20 Believe in the L your God, so shall ye H3068
21 singers unto the L, and that should H3068
21 the L; for his mercy *endureth* for ever. H3068
22 and to praise, the L set ambushments H3068
26 they blessed the L: therefore the name H3068
27 with joy; for the L had made them to H3068
28 and trumpets unto the house of the L. H3068
29 L fought against the enemies of Israel. H3068
32 *which was* right in the sight of the L. H3068
37 with Ahaziah, the L hath broken thy H3068
21: 6 *that which was* evil in the eyes of the L. H3068
7 Howbeit the L would not destroy the H3068
10 had forsaken the L God of his fathers. H3068
12 Thus saith the L God of David thy H3068
14 Behold, with a great plague will the L H3068
16 Moreover the L stirred up against H3068
18 And after all this the L smote him in H3068
22: 4 in the sight of the L like the house of H3068
7 of Nimshi, whom the L had anointed to H3068
9 who sought the L with all his heart. So H3068
23: 3 as the L hath said of the sons of David. H3068
5 *be* in the courts of the house of the L. H3068
6 the house of the L, save the priests, and H3068
6 the people shall keep the watch of the L. H3068
12 to the people into the house of the L: H3068
14 said, Slay her not in the house of the L. H3068
18 of the house of the L by the hand of the H3068
18 in the house of the L, to offer the burnt H3068

2Ch 23:18 offerings of the L, as *it is* written in the H3068
19 of the house of the L, that none *which* H3068
20 from the house of the L: and they came H3068
24: 2 the L all the days of Jehoiada the priest. H3068
4 minded to repair the house of the L. H3068
6 Moses the servant of the L, and of the H3068
7 of the L did they bestow upon Baalim. H3068
8 without at the gate of the house of the L. H3068
9 to bring in to the L the collection *that* H3068
12 of the house of the L, and hired masons H3068
12 the house of the L, and also such as H3068
12 and brass to mend the house of the L. H3068
14 for the house of the L, *even* vessels to H3068
14 L continually all the days of Jehoiada. H3068
18 And they left the house of the L God of H3068
19 again unto the L; and they testified H3068
20 of the L, that ye cannot prosper? H3068
20 the L, he hath also forsaken you. H3068
21 king in the court of the house of the L. H3068
22 said, The L look upon *it*, and require *it*. H3068
24 of men, and the L delivered a very H3068
24 had forsaken the L God of their fathers. H3068
25: 2 of the L, but not with a perfect heart. H3068
4 of Moses, where the L commanded, H3068
7 with thee; for the L *is* not with Israel, *to* H3068
9 answered, The L is able to give thee H3068
15 Wherefore the anger of the L was H3068
27 away from following the L they made a H3068
26: 4 in the sight of the L, according to all H3068
5 sought the L, God made him to prosper. H3068
16 against the L his God, and went into H3068
16 into the temple of the L to burn incense H3068
17 priests of the L, *that were* valiant men: H3068
18 incense unto the L, but to the priests the H3068
18 *it be* for thine honour from the L God. H3068
19 of the L, from beside the incense altar. H3068
20 go out, because the L had smitten him. H3068
21 the house of the L: and Jotham his son H3068
27: 2 in the sight of the L, according to all H3068
2 the L. And the people did yet corruptly. H3068
3 of the house of the L, and on the wall of H3068
6 prepared his ways before the L his God. H3068
28: 1 the sight of the L, like David his father: H3068
3 whom the L had cast out before H3068
5 Wherefore the L his God delivered him H3068
6 had forsaken the L God of their fathers. H3068
9 But a prophet of the L was there, whose H3068
9 because the L God of your fathers H3068
10 with you, sins against the L your God? H3068
11 the fierce wrath of the L *is* upon you. H3068
13 against the L *already*, ye intend to H3068
19 For the L brought Judah low because of H3068
19 and transgressed sore against the L. H3068
21 *out* of the house of the L, and *out* of the H3068
22 against the L: this *is that* king Ahaz. H3068
24 of the house of the L, and he made him H3068
25 to anger the L God of his fathers. H3068
29: 2 in the sight of the L, according to all H3068
3 the house of the L, and repaired them. H3068
5 the house of the L God of your fathers, H3068
6 in the eyes of the L our God, and have H3068
6 of the L, and turned *their* backs. H3068
8 Wherefore the wrath of the L was upon H3068
10 covenant with the L God of Israel, that H3068
11 negligent: for the L hath chosen you to H3068
15 the L, to cleanse the house of the LORD. H3068
15 the LORD, to cleanse the house of the L. H3068
16 of the house of the L, to cleanse *it*, and H3068
16 the temple of the L into the court of the H3068
16 of the house of the L. And the Levites H3068
17 to the porch of the L: so they sanctified H3068
17 the house of the L in eight days; and in H3068
18 all the house of the L, and the altar of H3068
19 they *are* before the altar of the L. H3068
20 city, and went up to the house of the L. H3068
21 to offer *them* on the altar of the L. H3068
25 in the house of the L with cymbals, H3068
25 of the L by his prophets. H3068
27 the song of the L began *also* with the H3068
30 praise unto the L with the words of H3068
31 unto the L, come near and bring H3068
31 into the house of the L. And the H3068
32 these *were* for a burnt offering to the L. H3068
35 of the house of the L was set in order. H3068
30: 1 to the house of the L at Jerusalem, to H3068
1 the passover unto the L God of Israel. H3068
5 the passover unto the L God of Israel at H3068
6 turn again unto the L God of Abraham, H3068
7 against the L God of their fathers, H3068

2Ch 30: 8 unto the L, and enter into his H3068
8 ever: and serve the L your God, that the H3068
9 For if ye turn again unto the L, your H3068
9 into this land: for the L your God *is* H3068
12 and of the princes, by the word of the L. H3068
15 burnt offerings into the house of the L. H3068
17 not clean, to sanctify *them* unto the L. H3068
18 saying, The good L pardon every one H3068
19 to seek God, the L God of his fathers, H3068
20 And the L hearkened to Hezekiah, and H3068
21 the priests praised the L day by day, H3068
21 with loud instruments unto the L. H3068
22 knowledge of the L: and they did eat H3068
22 confession to the L God of their fathers. H3068
31: 2 praise in the gates of the tents of the L. H3068
3 feasts, as *it is* written in the law of the L. H3068
4 might be encouraged in the law of the L. H3068
6 L their God, and laid *them* by heaps. H3068
8 blessed the L, and his people Israel. H3068
10 the house of the L, we have had enough H3068
10 left plenty: for the L hath blessed his H3068
11 house of the L; and they prepared *them*, H3068
14 of the L, and the most holy things. H3068
16 the house of the L, his daily portion for H3068
20 right and truth before the L his God. H3068
32: 8 but with us *is* the L our God to help us, H3068
11 by thirst, saying, The L our God shall H3068
16 *more* against the L God, and against H3068
17 He wrote also letters to rail on the L H3068
21 And the L sent an angel, which cut off H3068
22 Thus the L saved Hezekiah and the H3068
23 And many brought gifts unto the L to H3068
24 prayed unto the L: and he spake unto H3068
26 the wrath of the L came not upon them H3068
33: 2 evil in the sight of the L, like unto the H3068
2 whom the L had cast out before H3068
4 in the house of the L, whereof the LORD H3068
4 whereof the L had said, In Jerusalem H3068
5 in the two courts of the house of the L. H3068
6 sight of the L, to provoke him to anger. H3068
9 whom the L had destroyed before H3068
10 And the L spake to Manasseh, and to H3068
11 Wherefore the L brought upon them H3068
12 he besought the L his God, and H3068
13 Manasseh knew that the L he *was* God. H3068
15 of the house of the L, and all the altars H3068
15 of the house of the L, and in Jerusalem, H3068
16 And he repaired the altar of the L, and H3068
16 Judah to serve the L God of Israel. H3068
17 places, *yet* unto the L their God only. H3068
18 him in the name of the L God of Israel, H3068
22 in the sight of the L, as did Manasseh H3068
23 And humbled not himself before the L, H3068
34: 2 in the sight of the L, and walked in the H3068
8 to repair the house of the L his God. H3068
10 of the house of the L, and they gave it to H3068
10 of the L, to repair and amend the house: H3068
14 the house of the L, Hilkiah the priest H3068
14 of the law of the L *given* by Moses. H3068
15 law in the house of the L. And Hilkiah H3068
17 found in the house of the L, and have H3068
21 Go, inquire of the L for me, and for H3068
21 *is* the wrath of the L that is poured out H3068
21 the word of the L, to do after all that is H3068
23 Thus saith the L God of Israel, Tell ye H3068
24 Thus saith the L, Behold, I will bring H3068
26 to inquire of the L, so shall ye say unto H3068
26 him, Thus saith the L God of Israel H3068
27 I have even heard *thee* also, saith the L. H3068
30 the house of the L, and all the men of H3068
30 that was found in the house of the L. H3068
31 before the L, to walk after the LORD, H3068
31 to walk after the L, and to keep his H3068
33 *even* to serve the L their God. *And* all H3068
33 following the L, the God of their fathers. H3068
35: 1 passover unto the L in Jerusalem: and H3068
2 to the service of the house of the L, H3068
3 were holy unto the L, Put the holy ark in H3068
3 the L your God, and his people Israel, H3068
6 the word of the L by the hand of Moses. H3068
12 to offer unto the L, as *it is* written in the H3068
16 So all the service of the L was prepared H3068
16 upon the altar of the L, according to the H3068
26 *which was* written in the law of the L, H3068
36: 5 *was* evil in the sight of the L his God. H3068
7 of the house of the L to Babylon, and H3068
9 *that which was* evil in the sight of the L. H3068
10 vessels of the house of the L, and made H3068
12 evil in the sight of the L his God, *and* H3068

2Ch 36:12 *speaking* from the mouth of the L. H3068
13 from turning unto the L God of Israel. H3068
14 L which he had hallowed in Jerusalem. H3068
15 And the L God of their fathers sent to H3068
16 the wrath of the L arose against his H3068
18 of the house of the L, and the treasures H3068
21 To fulfil the word of the L by the mouth H3068
22 the word of the L *spoken* by the mouth H3068
22 be accomplished, the L stirred up the H3068
23 of the earth hath the L God of heaven H3068
23 of all his people? The L his God *be* with H3068
Ezr 1: 1 that the word of the L by the mouth of H3068
1 be fulfilled, the L stirred up the spirit H3068
2 Thus saith Cyrus king of Persia, The L H3068
3 the house of the L God of Israel, (he *is* H3068
5 house of the L which *is* in Jerusalem. H3068
7 vessels of the house of the L, which H3068
2:68 came to the house of the L which *is* at H3068
3: 3 thereon unto the L, *even* burnt offerings H3068
5 the set feasts of the L that were H3068
5 offered a freewill offering unto the L. H3068
6 offerings unto the L. But the foundation H3068
6 of the temple of the L was not *yet* laid. H3068
8 forward the work of the house of the L. H3068
10 the temple of the L, they set the priests H3068
10 to praise the L, after the ordinance H3068
11 thanks unto the L; because *he is* good, H3068
11 when they praised the L, because the H3068
11 of the house of the L was laid. H3068
4: 1 the temple unto the L God of Israel; H3068
3 will build unto the L God of Israel, as H3068
6:21 to seek the L God of Israel, did eat, H3068
22 days with joy: for the L had made them H3068
7: 6 of Moses, which the L God of Israel had H3068
6 to the hand of the L his God upon him. H3068
10 seek the law of the L, and to do *it*, and H3068
11 of the L, and of his statutes to Israel. H3068
27 Blessed *be* the L God of our fathers, H3068
27 house of the L which *is* in Jerusalem: H3068
28 as the hand of the L my God *was* upon H3068
8:28 *are* holy unto the L; the vessels *are* holy H3068
28 offering unto the L God of your fathers. H3068
29 in the chambers of the house of the L. H3068
35 all *this was* a burnt offering unto the L. H3068
9: 5 out my hands unto the L my God, H3068
8 *shewed* from the L our God, to leave us H3068
15 O L God of Israel, thou *art* righteous: H3068
10: 3 to the counsel of my l, and of those that H136
11 unto the L God of your fathers, H3068
Neh 1: 5 And said, I beseech thee, O L God of H3068
11 O L, I beseech thee, let now thine ear be H136
3: 5 put not their necks to the work of their L. H113
4:14 remember the L, *which is* great and H136
5:13 and praised the L. And the people did H3068
8: 1 which the L had commanded to Israel. H3068
6 And Ezra blessed the L, the great God. H3068
6 the L with *their* faces to the ground. H3068
9 day *is* holy unto the L your God; mourn H3068
10 *is* holy unto our L: neither be ye sorry; for H113
10 for the joy of the L is your strength. H3068
14 the law which the L had commanded H3068
9: 3 of the law of the L their God *one* fourth H3068
3 and worshipped the L their God. H3068
4 with a loud voice unto the L their God. H3068
5 up *and* bless the L your God for ever H3068
6 Thou, *even* thou, *art* L alone; thou hast H3068
7 Thou *art* the L the God, who didst H3068
10:29 of the L our Lord, and his judgments H3068
29 L, and his judgments and his statutes; H113
34 L our God, as *it is* written in the law: H3068
35 year by year, unto the house of the L: H3068
Job 1: 6 L, and Satan came also among them. H3068
7 And the L said unto Satan, Whence H3068
7 answered the L, and said, From going H3068
8 And the L said unto Satan, Hast thou H3068
9 Then Satan answered the L, and said, H3068
12 And the L said unto Satan, Behold, all H3068
12 went forth from the presence of the L. H3068
21 I return thither: the L gave, and the H3068
21 gave, and the L hath taken away; H3068
21 away; blessed be the name of the L. H3068
2: 1 before the L, and Satan came also H3068
1 them to present himself before the L. H3068
2 And the L said unto Satan, From H3068
2 answered the L, and said, From going H3068
3 And the L said unto Satan, Hast thou H3068
4 And Satan answered the L, and said, H3068
6 And the L said unto Satan, Behold, he H3068
7 presence of the L, and smote Job with H3068

Job 12: 9 the hand of the L hath wrought this? H3068
28:28 the fear of the L, that *is* wisdom; and H136
38: 1 Then the L answered Job out of the H3068
40: 1 Moreover the L answered Job, and H3068
3 Then Job answered the L, and said, H3068
6 Then answered the L unto Job out of H3068
42: 1 Then Job answered the L, and said, H3068
7 And it was *so*, that after the L had H3068
7 unto Job, the L said to Eliphaz the H3068
9 according as the L commanded them: H3068
9 them: the L also accepted Job. H3068
10 And the L turned the captivity of Job, H3068
10 his friends: also the L gave Job twice as H3068
11 all the evil that the L had brought upon H3068
12 So the L blessed the latter end of Job H3068
Ps 1: 2 But his delight *is* in the law of the L; and H3068
6 For the L knoweth the way of the H3068
2: 2 the L, and against his anointed, *saying*, H3068
4 laugh: the L shall have them in derision. H136
7 I will declare the decree: the L hath H3068
11 Serve the L with fear, and rejoice with H3068
3: 1 L, how are they increased that trouble H3068
3 But thou, O L, *art* a shield for me; my H3068
4 I cried unto the L with my voice, and H3068
5 slept; I awaked; for the L sustained me. H3068
7 Arise, O L; save me, O my God: for thou H3068
8 Salvation *belongeth* unto the L: thy H3068
4: 3 But know that the L hath set apart him H3068
3 the L will hear when I call unto him. H3068
5 and put your trust in the L. H3068
6 shew us *any* good? L, lift thou up the H3068
8 thou, L, only makest me dwell in safety. H3068
5: 1 Give ear to my words, O L, consider my H3068
3 in the morning, O L; in the morning will H3068
6 that speak leasing: the L will abhor the H3068
8 Lead me, O L, in thy righteousness H3068
12 For thou, L, wilt bless the righteous; H3068
6: 1 O L, rebuke me not in thine anger, H3068
2 Have mercy upon me, O L; for I *am* H3068
2 O L, heal me; for my bones are vexed. H3068
3 sore vexed: but thou, O L, how long? H3068
4 Return, O L, deliver my soul: oh save H3068
8 L hath heard the voice of my weeping. H3068
9 The L hath heard my supplication; the H3068
9 the L will receive my prayer. H3068
7: 1 O L my God, in thee do I put my trust: H3068
3 O L my God, if I have done this; if there H3068
6 Arise, O L, in thine anger, lift up thyself H3068
8 The L shall judge the people: judge me, H3068
8 people: judge me, O L, according to my H3068
17 I will praise the L according to his H3068
17 praise to the name of the L most high. H3068
ttl he sang unto the L, concerning the H3068
8: 1 O L our Lord, how excellent *is* thy H3068
1 O LORD our L, how excellent *is* thy name H113
9 O L our Lord, how excellent *is* thy H3068
9 O LORD our L, how excellent *is* thy name H113
9: 1 I will praise *thee*, O L, with my whole H3068
7 But the L shall endure for ever: he hath H3068
9 The L also will be a refuge for the H3068
10 in thee: for thou, L, hast not forsaken H3068
11 Sing praises to the L, which dwelleth in H3068
13 Have mercy upon me, O L; consider my H3068
16 The L is known *by* the judgment *which* H3068
19 Arise, O L; let not man prevail: let the H3068
20 Put them in fear, O L: *that* the nations H3068
10: 1 Why standest thou afar off, O L? *why* H3068
3 the covetous, *whom* the L abhorreth. H3068
12 Arise, O L; O God, lift up thine hand: H3068
16 The L *is* King for ever and ever: the H3068
17 L, thou hast heard the desire of the H3068
11: 1 In the L put I my trust: how say ye to H3068
4 The L *is* in his holy temple, the LORD'S H3068
5 The L trieth the righteous: but the H3068
7 For the righteous L loveth H3068
12: 1 Help, L; for the godly man ceaseth; for H3068
3 The L shall cut off all flattering lips, H3068
4 our lips *are* our own: who *is* l over us? H113
5 will I arise, saith the L; I will set *him* in H3068
6 The words of the L *are* pure words: *as* H3068
7 Thou shalt keep them, O L, thou shalt H3068
13: 1 How long wilt thou forget me, O L? for H3068
3 Consider *and* hear me, O L my God: H3068
6 I will sing unto the L, because he hath H3068
14: 2 The L looked down from heaven upon H3068
4 they eat bread, and call not upon the L. H3068
6 of the poor, because the L *is* his refuge. H3068
7 of Zion! when the L bringeth back the H3068
15: 1 L, who shall abide in thy tabernacle? H3068

Ps 15: 4 them that fear the L. *He that* sweareth H3068
16: 2 *O my soul*, thou hast said unto the L, H3068
2 L: my goodness *extendeth* not to thee; H136
5 The L *is* the portion of mine H3068
7 I will bless the L, who hath given me H3068
8 I have set the L always before me: H3068
17: 1 Hear the right, O L, attend unto my cry, H3068
13 Arise, O L, disappoint him, cast him H3068
14 From men *which are* thy hand, O L, H3068
18: 1 I will love thee, O L, my strength. H3068
2 The L *is* my rock, and my fortress, and H3068
3 I will call upon the L, *who is worthy* to H3068
6 In my distress I called upon the L, and H3068
13 The L also thundered in the heavens, H3068
15 at thy rebuke, O L, at the blast of the H3068
18 of my calamity: but the L was my stay. H3068
20 The L rewarded me according to my H3068
21 For I have kept the ways of the L, and H3068
24 Therefore hath the L recompensed me H3068
28 For thou wilt light my candle: the L my H3068
30 the word of the L is tried: he *is* a H3068
31 For who *is* God save the L? or who *is* a H3068
41 unto the L, but he answered them not. H3068
46 The L liveth; and blessed *be* my rock; H3068
49 unto thee, O L, among the heathen, H3068
ttl the servant of the L, who spake unto the H3068
ttl spake unto the L the words of this song H3068
ttl in the day *that* the L delivered him H3068
19: 7 The law of the L *is* perfect, converting H3068
7 the L *is* sure, making wise the simple. H3068
8 The statutes of the L *are* right, rejoicing H3068
8 of the L *is* pure, enlightening the eyes. H3068
9 The fear of the L *is* clean, enduring for H3068
9 the L *are* true *and* righteous altogether. H3068
14 O L, my strength, and my redeemer. H3068
20: 1 The L hear thee in the day of trouble; H3068
5 banners: the L fulfil all thy petitions. H3068
6 Now know I that the L saveth his H3068
7 remember the name of the L our God. H3068
9 Save, L: let the king hear us when we H3068
21: 1 The king shall joy in thy strength, O L; H3068
7 For the king trusteth in the L, and H3068
9 time of thine anger: the L shall swallow H3068
13 Be thou exalted, L, in thine own H3068
22: 8 He trusted on the L *that* he would H3068
19 But be not thou far from me, O L: O my H3068
23 Ye that fear the L, praise him; all ye the H3068
26 shall praise the L that seek him: your H3068
27 and turn unto the L: and all the H3068
30 be accounted to the L for a generation. H136
23: 1 The L *is* my shepherd; I shall not want. H3068
6 will dwell in the house of the L for ever. H3068
24: 3 Who shall ascend into the hill of the L? H3068
5 He shall receive the blessing from the L, H3068
8 Who *is* this King of glory? The L strong H3068
8 and mighty, the L mighty in battle. H3068
10 Who is this King of glory? The L of H3068
25: 1 Unto thee, O L, do I lift up my soul. H3068
4 Shew me thy ways, O L; teach me thy H3068
6 Remember, O L, thy tender mercies and H3068
7 thou me for thy goodness' sake, O L. H3068
8 Good and upright *is* the L: therefore will H3068
10 All the paths of the L *are* mercy and H3068
11 For thy name's sake, O L, pardon mine H3068
12 What man *is* he that feareth the L? him H3068
14 The secret of the L *is* with them that H3068
15 Mine eyes *are* ever toward the L; for he H3068
26: 1 Judge me, O L; for I have walked in H3068
1 also in the L; *therefore* I shall not slide. H3068
2 Examine me, O L, and prove me; try my H3068
6 so will I compass thine altar, O L: H3068
8 L, I have loved the habitation of thy H3068
12 in the congregations will I bless the L. H3068
27: 1 The L *is* my light and my salvation; H3068
1 shall I fear? the L *is* the strength of my H3068
4 One *thing* have I desired of the L, that H3068
4 in the house of the L all the days of my H3068
4 of the L, and to inquire in his temple. H3068
6 sing, yea, I will sing praises unto the L. H3068
7 Hear, O L, *when* I cry with my voice: H3068
8 said unto thee, Thy face, L, will I seek. H3068
10 forsake me, then the L will take me up. H3068
11 Teach me thy way, O L, and lead me in H3068
13 of the L in the land of the living. H3068
14 Wait on the L: be of good courage, and H3068
14 thine heart: wait, I say, on the L. H3068
28: 1 Unto thee will I cry, O L my rock; be H3068
5 the works of the L, nor the operation of H3068
6 Blessed *be* the L, because he hath heard H3068

Ps 28: 7 The L *is* my strength and my shield; my H3068
8 The L *is* their strength, and he *is* the H3068
29: 1 Give unto the L, O ye mighty, give unto H3068
1 give unto the L glory and strength. H3068
2 Give unto the L the glory due unto his H3068
2 worship the L in the beauty of holiness. H3068
3 The voice of the L *is* upon the waters: H3068
3 thundereth: the L *is* upon many waters. H3068
4 The voice of the L *is* powerful; the voice H3068
4 the voice of the L *is* full of majesty. H3068
5 The voice of the L breaketh the cedars; H3068
5 the L breaketh the cedars of Lebanon. H3068
7 The voice of the L divideth the flames H3068
8 The voice of the L shaketh the H3068
8 L shaketh the wilderness of Kadesh. H3068
9 The voice of the L maketh the hinds to H3068
10 The L sitteth upon the flood; yea, the H3068
10 flood; yea, the L sitteth King for ever. H3068
11 The L will give strength unto his H3068
11 the L will bless his people with peace. H3068
30: 1 I will extol thee, O L; for thou hast lifted H3068
2 O L my God, I cried unto thee, and H3068
3 O L, thou hast brought up my soul from H3068
4 Sing unto the L, O ye saints of his, and H3068
7 L, by thy favour thou hast made my H3068
8 I cried to thee, O L; and unto the LORD H3068
8 I cried to thee, O LORD; and unto the L H3068
10 Hear, O L, and have mercy upon me: H3068
10 mercy upon me: L, be thou my helper. H3068
12 not be silent. O L my God, I will give H3068
31: 1 In thee, O L, do I put my trust; let me H3068
5 hast redeemed me, O L God of truth. H3068
6 lying vanities: but I trust in the L. H3068
9 Have mercy upon me, O L, for I am in H3068
14 But I trusted in thee, O L: I said, Thou H3068
17 Let me not be ashamed, O L; for I have H3068
21 Blessed *be* the L: for he hath shewed me H3068
23 O love the L, all ye his saints: *for* the H3068
23 ye his saints: *for* the L preserveth the H3068
24 your heart, all ye that hope in the L. H3068
32: 2 Blessed *is* the man unto whom the L H3068
5 unto the L; and thou forgavest H3068
10 the L, mercy shall compass him about. H3068
11 Be glad in the L, and rejoice, ye H3068
33: 1 Rejoice in the L, O ye righteous: *for* H3068
2 Praise the L with harp: sing unto him H3068
4 For the word of the L *is* right; and all H3068
5 the earth is full of the goodness of the L. H3068
6 By the word of the L were the heavens H3068
8 Let all the earth fear the L: let all the H3068
10 The L bringeth the counsel of the H3068
11 The counsel of the L standeth for ever, H3068
12 whose God *is* the L; *and* the people H3068
13 The L looketh from heaven; he H3068
18 Behold, the eye of the L *is* upon them H3068
20 Our soul waiteth for the L: he *is* our H3068
22 Let thy mercy, O L, be upon us, H3068
34: 1 I will bless the L at all times: his praise H3068
2 My soul shall make her boast in the L: H3068
3 O magnify the L with me, and let us H3068
4 I sought the L, and he heard me, and H3068
6 This poor man cried, and the L heard H3068
7 The angel of the L encampeth round H3068
8 O taste and see that the L *is* good: H3068
9 O fear the L, ye his saints: for *there is* no H3068
10 the L shall not want any good *thing*. H3068
11 me: I will teach you the fear of the L. H3068
15 The eyes of the L *are* upon the H3068
16 The face of the L *is* against them that H3068
17 *The righteous* cry, and the L heareth, H3068
18 The L *is* nigh unto them that are of a H3068
19 the L delivereth him out of them all. H3068
22 The L redeemeth the soul of his H3068
35: 1 Plead *my cause*, O L, with them that H3068
5 and let the angel of the L chase *them*. H3068
6 let the angel of the L persecute them. H3068
9 And my soul shall be joyful in the L: it H3068
10 All my bones shall say, L, who *is* like H3068
17 L, how long wilt thou look on? rescue my H136
22 *This* thou hast seen, O L: keep not H3068
22 keep not silence: O L, be not far from me. H136
23 *even* unto my cause, my God and my L. H136
24 Judge me, O L my God, according to H3068
27 Let the L be magnified, which H3068
36: 5 Thy mercy, O L, *is* in the heavens; *and* H3068
6 O L, thou preservest man and beast. H3068
ttl *A Psalm* of David the servant of the L. H3068
37: 3 Trust in the L, and do good; *so* shalt H3068
4 Delight thyself also in the L; and he H3068

Ps 37: 5 Commit thy way unto the L; trust also H3068
7 Rest in the L, and wait patiently for H3068
9 upon the L, they shall inherit the earth. H3068
13 The L shall laugh at him: for he seeth H136
17 but the L upholdeth the righteous. H3068
18 The L knoweth the days of the upright: H3068
20 the enemies of the L *shall be* as the fat H3068
23 by the L: and he delighteth in his way. H3068
24 for the L upholdeth *him with* his hand. H3068
28 For the L loveth judgment, and H3068
33 The L will not leave him in his hand, H3068
34 Wait on the L, and keep his way, and he H3068
39 righteous *is* of the L: *he is* their strength H3068
40 And the L shall help them, and deliver H3068
38: 1 O L, rebuke me not in thy wrath: H3068
9 L, all my desire *is* before thee; and my H136
15 For in thee, O L, do I hope: thou wilt H3068
15 do I hope: thou wilt hear, O L my God. H136
21 Forsake me not, O L: O my God, be not H3068
22 Make haste to help me, O L my H136
39: 4 L, make me to know mine end, and the H3068
7 And now, L, what wait I for? my hope *is* H136
12 Hear my prayer, O L, and give ear unto H3068
40: 1 I waited patiently for the L; and he H3068
3 see *it*, and fear, and shall trust in the L. H3068
4 Blessed *is* that man that maketh the L H3068
5 Many, O L my God, *are* thy wonderful H3068
9 refrained my lips, O L, thou knowest. H3068
11 from me, O L: let thy lovingkindness H3068
13 Be pleased, O L, to deliver me: O LORD, H3068
13 Be pleased, O LORD, to deliver me: O L, H3068
16 say continually, The L be magnified. H3068
17 But I *am* poor and needy; *yet* the L H136
41: 1 L will deliver him in time of trouble. H3068
2 The L will preserve him, and keep him H3068
3 The L will strengthen him upon the bed H3068
4 I said, L, be merciful unto me: heal my H3068
10 But thou, O L, be merciful unto me, and H3068
13 Blessed *be* the L God of Israel from H3068
42: 8 *Yet* the L will command his H3068
44:23 Awake, why sleepest thou, O L? arise, H136
45:11 for he *is* thy L; and worship thou him. H113
46: 7 The L of hosts *is* with us; the God of H3068
8 Come, behold the works of the L, what H3068
11 The L of hosts *is* with us; the God of H3068
47: 2 For the L most high *is* terrible; *he is* a H3068
5 God is gone up with a shout, the L with H3068
48: 1 Great *is* the L, and greatly to be praised H3068
8 in the city of the L of hosts, in the city H3068
50: 1 The mighty God, *even* the L, hath H3068
51:15 O L, open thou my lips; and my mouth H136
54: 4 Behold, God *is* mine helper: the L *is* with H136
6 will praise thy name, O L; for *it is* good. H3068
55: 9 Destroy, O L, *and* divide their tongues: H136
16 call upon God; and the L shall save me. H3068
22 Cast thy burden upon the L, and he H3068
56:10 In God will I praise *his* word: in the L H3068
57: 9 I will praise thee, O L, among the people: H136
58: 6 the great teeth of the young lions, O L. H3068
59: 3 my transgression, nor *for* my sin, O L. H3068
5 Thou therefore, O L God of hosts, the H3068
8 But thou, O L, shalt laugh at them; thou H3068
11 and bring them down, O L our shield. H136
62:12 Also unto thee, O L, *belongeth* mercy: for H136
64:10 The righteous shall be glad in the L, and H3068
66:18 If I regard iniquity in my heart, the L H136
68:11 The L gave the word: great *was* the H136
16 in; yea, the L will dwell *in it* for ever. H3068
17 of angels: the L *is* among them, *as in* H136
18 the L God might dwell *among them*. H3050
19 Blessed *be* the L, *who* daily loadeth us H136
20 GOD the L *belong* the issues from death. H136
22 The L said, I will bring again from H136
26 *even* the L, from the fountain of Israel. H136
32 earth; O sing praises unto the L; Selah: H136
69: 6 Let not them that wait on thee, O L GOD H136
13 *is* unto thee, O L, *in* an acceptable time: H3068
16 Hear me, O L; for thy lovingkindness *is* H3068
31 *This* also shall please the L better than H3068
33 For the L heareth the poor, and H3068
70: 1 deliver me; make haste to help me, O L. H3068
5 my deliverer; O L, make no tarrying. H3068
71: 1 In thee, O L, do I put my trust: let me H3068
5 For thou *art* my hope, O L GOD: *thou art* H136
16 I will go in the strength of the L GOD: I H136
72:18 Blessed *be* the L God, the God of Israel, H3068
73:20 As a dream when *one* awaketh; *so*, O L, H136
28 L GOD, that I may declare all thy works. H136
74:18 reproached, O L, and *that* the foolish H3068

Ps 75: 8 For in the hand of the L *there is* a cup, H3068
76:11 Vow, and pay unto the L your God: let H3068
77: 2 In the day of my trouble I sought the L: H136
7 Will the L cast off for ever? and will he H136
11 I will remember the works of the L: H3050
78: 4 the praises of the L, and his strength, H3068
21 Therefore the L heard *this*, and was H3068
65 Then the L awaked as one out of sleep, H136
79: 5 How long, L? wilt thou be angry for H3068
12 they have reproached thee, O L. H136
80: 4 O L God of hosts, how long wilt thou be H3068
19 Turn us again, O L God of hosts, cause H3068
81:10 I *am* the L thy God, which brought thee H3068
15 The haters of the L should have H3068
83:16 that they may seek thy name, O L. H3068
84: 1 How amiable *are* thy tabernacles, O L H3068
2 for the courts of the L: my heart and my H3068
3 O L of hosts, my King, and my God. H3068
8 O L God of hosts, hear my prayer: give H3068
11 For the L God *is* a sun and shield: the H3068
11 and shield: the L will give grace and H3068
12 O L of hosts, blessed *is* the man that H3068
85: 1 L, thou hast been favourable unto thy H3068
7 Shew us thy mercy, O L, and grant us H3068
8 I will hear what God the L will speak: H3068
12 Yea, the L shall give *that which is* good; H3068
86: 1 Bow down thine ear, O L, hear me: for I H3068
3 Be merciful unto me, O L: for I cry unto H136
4 for unto thee, O L, do I lift up my soul. H136
5 For thou, L, *art* good, and ready to H136
6 Give ear, O L, unto my prayer; and H3068
8 like unto thee, O L; neither *are there any* H136
9 thee, O L; and shall glorify thy name. H136
11 Teach me thy way, O L; I will walk in H3068
12 I will praise thee, O L my God, with all H136
15 But thou, O L, *art* a God full of H136
17 L, hast holpen me, and comforted me. H3068
87: 2 The L loveth the gates of Zion more H3068
6 The L shall count, when he writeth up H3068
88: 1 O L God of my salvation, I have cried H3068
9 of affliction: L, I have called daily upon H3068
13 But unto thee have I cried, O L; and in H3068
14 L, why castest thou off my soul? *why* H3068
89: 1 I will sing of the mercies of the L for H3068
5 thy wonders, O L: thy faithfulness also H3068
6 unto the L? *who* among the sons H3068
6 of the mighty can be likened unto the L? H3068
8 O L God of hosts, who *is* a strong LORD H3068
8 O LORD God of hosts, who *is* a strong L H3050
15 O L, in the light of thy countenance. H3068
18 For the L *is* our defence; and the Holy H3068
46 How long, L? wilt thou hide thyself for H3068
49 L, where *are* thy former H136
50 Remember, L, the reproach of thy H136
51 reproached, O L; wherewith they have H3068
52 Blessed *be* the L for evermore. Amen, H3068
90: 1 L, thou hast been our dwelling place in H136
13 Return, O L, how long? and let it repent H3068
17 And let the beauty of the L our God be H3068
91: 2 I will say of the L, *He is* my refuge and H3068
9 Because thou hast made the L, *which is* H3068
92: 1 thanks unto the L, and to sing praises H3068
4 For thou, L, hast made me glad through H3068
5 O L, how great are thy works! *and* thy H3068
8 But thou, L, *art most* high for evermore. H3068
9 For, lo, thine enemies, O L, for, lo, thine H3068
13 in the house of the L shall flourish in H3068
15 To shew that the L *is* upright: *he is* my H3068
93: 1 The L reigneth, he is clothed with H3068
1 with majesty; the L is clothed with H3068
3 The floods have lifted up, O L, the H3068
4 The L on high *is* mightier than the H3068
5 becometh thine house, O L, for ever. H3068
94: 1 O L God, to whom vengeance H3068
3 L, how long shall the wicked, how long H3068
5 They break in pieces thy people, O L, H3068
7 Yet they say, The L shall not see, H3050
11 The L knoweth the thoughts of man, H3068
12 O L, and teachest him out of thy law; H3050
14 For the L will not cast off his people, H3068
17 Unless the L *had been* my help, my H3068
18 slippeth; thy mercy, O L, held me up. H3068
22 But the L is my defence; and my God *is* H3068
23 *yea*, the L our God shall cut them off. H3068
95: 1 O come, let us sing unto the L: let us H3068
3 For the L *is* a great God, and a great H3068
6 let us kneel before the L our maker. H3068
96: 1 O sing unto the L a new song: sing unto H3068
1 new song: sing unto the L, all the earth. H3068

Ps 96: 2 Sing unto the L, bless his name; shew H3068
4 For the L *is* great, and greatly to be H3068
5 *are* idols: but the L made the heavens. H3068
7 Give unto the L, O ye kindreds of the H3068
7 give unto the L glory and strength. H3068
8 Give unto the L the glory *due unto* his H3068
9 O worship the L in the beauty of H3068
10 Say among the heathen *that* the L H3068
13 Before the L: for he cometh, for he H3068
97: 1 The L reigneth; let the earth rejoice; let H3068
5 presence of the L, at the presence of the H3068
5 the presence of the L of the whole earth. H113
8 rejoiced because of thy judgments, O L. H3068
9 For thou, L, *art* high above all the earth: H3068
10 Ye that love the L, hate evil: he H3068
12 Rejoice in the L, ye righteous; and give H3068
98: 1 O sing unto the L a new song; for he H3068
2 The L hath made known his salvation: H3068
4 Make a joyful noise unto the L, all the H3068
5 Sing unto the L with the harp; with the H3068
6 a joyful noise before the L, the King. H3068
9 Before the L; for he cometh to judge the H3068
99: 1 The L reigneth; let the people tremble: H3068
2 The L *is* great in Zion; and he *is* high H3068
5 Exalt ye the L our God, and worship at H3068
6 upon the L, and he answered them. H3068
8 Thou answeredst them, O L our God: H3068
9 Exalt the L our God, and worship at his H3068
9 his holy hill; for the L our God *is* holy. H3068
100: 1 Make a joyful noise unto the L, all ye H3068
2 Serve the L with gladness: come before H3068
3 Know ye that the L he *is* God: *it is* he H3068
5 For the L *is* good; his mercy *is* H3068
101: 1 judgment: unto thee, O L, will I sing. H3068
8 all wicked doers from the city of the L. H3068
102: 1 Hear my prayer, O L, and let my cry H3068
12 But thou, O L, shalt endure for ever; H3068
15 the name of the L, and all the kings of H3068
16 When the L shall build up Zion, he H3068
18 shall be created shall praise the L. H3050
19 heaven did the L behold the earth; H3068
21 To declare the name of the L in Zion, H3068
22 and the kingdoms, to serve the L. H3068
ttl poureth out his complaint before the L. H3068
103: 1 Bless the L, O my soul: and all that is H3068
2 Bless the L, O my soul, and forget not H3068
6 The L executeth righteousness and H3068
8 The L *is* merciful and gracious, slow to H3068
13 *so* the L pitieth them that fear him. H3068
17 But the mercy of the L *is* from H3068
19 The L hath prepared his throne in the H3068
20 Bless the L, ye his angels, that excel in H3068
21 Bless ye the L, all *ye* his hosts; *ye* H3068
22 Bless the L, all his works in all places of H3068
22 of his dominion: bless the L, O my soul. H3068
104: 1 Bless the L, O my soul. O LORD my H3068
1 Bless the LORD, O my soul. O L my H3068
16 The trees of the L are full *of sap*; the H3068
24 O L, how manifold are thy works! in H3068
31 The glory of the L shall endure for ever: H3068
31 ever: the L shall rejoice in his works. H3068
33 I will sing unto the L as long as I live: I H3068
34 shall be sweet: I will be glad in the L. H3068
35 the L, O my soul. Praise ye the LORD. H3068
35 the LORD, O my soul. Praise ye the L. H3050
105: 1 O give thanks unto the L; call upon his H3068
3 the heart of them rejoice that seek the L. H3068
4 Seek the L, and his strength: seek his H3068
7 He *is* the L our God: his judgments *are* H3068
19 came: the word of the L tried him. H3068
21 He made him l of his house, and ruler of H113
45 and keep his laws. Praise ye the L. H3050
106: 1 Praise ye the L. O give thanks unto the H3050
1 thanks unto the L; for *he is* good: for his H3068
2 Who can utter the mighty acts of the L? H3068
4 Remember me, O L, with the favour H3068
16 the camp, *and* Aaron the saint of the L. H3068
25 hearkened not unto the voice of the L. H3068
34 whom the L commanded them: H3068
40 Therefore was the wrath of the L H3068
47 Save us, O L our God, and gather us H3068
48 Blessed *be* the L God of Israel from H3068
48 the people say, Amen. Praise ye the L. H3050
107: 1 O give thanks unto the L, for *he is* good: H3068
2 Let the redeemed of the L say *so*, whom H3068
6 Then they cried unto the L in their H3068
8 Oh that *men* would praise the L *for* his H3068
13 Then they cried unto the L in their H3068
15 Oh that *men* would praise the L *for* his H3068

Ps 107:19 Then they cry unto the L in their H3068
21 Oh that *men* would praise the L *for* his H3068
24 These see the works of the L, and his H3068
28 Then they cry unto the L in their H3068
31 Oh that *men* would praise the L *for* his H3068
43 understand the lovingkindness of the L. H3068
108: 3 I will praise thee, O L, among the H3068
109:14 with the L; and let not the sin of H3068
15 Let them be before the L continually, H3068
20 from the L, and of them that speak H3068
21 But do thou for me, O GOD the L, for thy H136
26 Help me, O L my God: O save me H3068
27 *is* thy hand; *that* thou, L, hast done it. H3068
30 I will greatly praise the L with my H3068
110: 1 The L said unto my Lord, Sit thou at H3068
1 The LORD said unto my L, Sit thou at my H113
2 The L shall send the rod of thy strength H3068
4 The L hath sworn, and will not repent, H3068
5 The L at thy right hand shall strike H136
111: 1 Praise ye the L. I will praise the LORD H3050
1 Praise ye the LORD. I will praise the L H3068
2 The works of the L *are* great, sought H3068
4 L *is* gracious and full of compassion. H3068
10 The fear of the L *is* the beginning of H3068
112: 1 Praise ye the L. Blessed *is* the man *that* H3050
1 man *that* feareth the L, *that* delighteth H3068
7 his heart is fixed, trusting in the L. H3068
113: 1 Praise ye the L. Praise, O ye servants of H3050
1 of the L, praise the name of the LORD. H3068
1 of the LORD, praise the name of the L. H3068
2 Blessed be the name of the L from this H3068
4 The L *is* high above all nations, *and* his H3068
5 Who *is* like unto the L our God, who H3068
9 mother of children. Praise ye the L. H3050
114: 7 the L, at the presence of the God of Jacob; H113
115: 1 Not unto us, O L, not unto us, but unto H3068
9 O Israel, trust thou in the L: he *is* their H3068
10 O house of Aaron, trust in the L: he *is* H3068
11 Ye that fear the L, trust in the LORD: he H3068
11 Ye that fear the LORD, trust in the L: he H3068
12 The L hath been mindful of us: he will H3068
13 He will bless them that fear the L, *both* H3068
14 The L shall increase you more and H3068
15 Ye *are* blessed of the L which made H3068
17 The dead praise not the L, neither any H3050
18 But we will bless the L from this time H3050
18 forth and for evermore. Praise the L. H3050
116: 1 I love the L, because he hath heard my H3068
4 Then called I upon the name of the L; O H3068
4 O L, I beseech thee, deliver my soul. H3068
5 Gracious *is* the L, and righteous; yea, H3068
6 The L preserveth the simple: I was H3068
7 the L hath dealt bountifully with thee. H3068
9 I will walk before the L in the land of H3068
12 What shall I render unto the L *for* all H3068
13 and call upon the name of the L. H3068
14 I will pay my vows unto the L now in H3068
15 Precious in the sight of the L *is* the H3068
16 O L, truly I *am* thy servant; I *am* thy H3068
17 and will call upon the name of the L. H3068
18 I will pay my vows unto the L now in H3068
19 of thee, O Jerusalem. Praise ye the L. H3050
117: 1 O praise the L, all ye nations: praise H3068
2 the truth of the L *endureth* for ever. H3068
2 *endureth* for ever. Praise ye the L. H3050
118: 1 O give thanks unto the L; for *he is* good: H3068
4 Let them now that fear the L say, that H3068
5 I called upon the L in distress: the H3050
5 in distress: the L answered me, *and set* H3050
6 The L *is* on my side; I will not fear: H3068
7 The L taketh my part with them that H3068
8 *It is* better to trust in the L than to put H3068
9 *It is* better to trust in the L than to put H3068
10 the name of the L will I destroy them. H3068
11 the name of the L I will destroy them. H3068
12 the name of the L I will destroy them. H3068
13 that I might fall: but the L helped me. H3068
14 The L *is* my strength and song, and is H3050
15 the right hand of the L doeth valiantly. H3068
16 The right hand of the L is exalted: the H3068
16 the right hand of the L doeth valiantly. H3068
17 but live, and declare the works of the L. H3050
18 The L hath chastened me sore: but he H3050
19 go into them, *and* I will praise the L: H3050
20 This gate of the L, into which the H3068
24 This *is* the day *which* the L hath made; H3068
25 Save now, I beseech thee, O L: O LORD, H3068
25 Save now, I beseech thee, O LORD: O L, H3068
26 in the name of the L: we have blessed H3068

Ps 118:26 blessed you out of the house of the L. H3068
27 God *is* the L, which hath shewed us H3068
29 O give thanks unto the L; for *he is* good: H3068
119: 1 in the way, who walk in the law of the L. H3068
12 Blessed *art* thou, O L: teach me thy H3068
31 I have stuck unto thy testimonies: O L, H3068
33 Teach me, O L, the way of thy statutes; H3068
41 Let thy mercies come also unto me, O L, H3068
52 of old, O L; and have comforted myself. H3068
55 I have remembered thy name, O L, in H3068
57 *Thou art* my portion, O L: I have said H3068
64 The earth, O L, is full of thy mercy: H3068
65 servant, O L, according unto thy word. H3068
75 I know, O L, that thy judgments *are* H3068
89 For ever, O L, thy word is settled in H3068
107 me, O L, according unto thy word. H3068
108 O L, and teach me thy judgments. H3068
126 *It is* time for *thee*, L, to work: *for* they H3068
137 Righteous *art* thou, O L, and upright H3068
145 hear me, O L: I will keep thy statutes. H3068
149 thy lovingkindness: O L, quicken me H3068
151 Thou *art* near, O L; and all thy H3068
156 Great *are* thy tender mercies, O L: H3068
159 O L, according to thy lovingkindness. H3068
166 L, I have hoped for thy salvation, and H3068
169 Let my cry come near before thee, O L: H3068
174 I have longed for thy salvation, O L; and H3068
120: 1 In my distress I cried unto the L, and he H3068
2 Deliver my soul, O L, from lying lips, H3068
121: 2 My help *cometh* from the L, which H3068
5 The L *is* thy keeper: the LORD *is* thy H3068
5 The LORD *is* thy keeper: the L *is* thy H3068
7 The L shall preserve thee from all evil: H3068
8 The L shall preserve thy going out and H3068
122: 1 me, Let us go into the house of the L. H3068
4 the tribes of the L, unto the testimony H3050
4 to give thanks unto the name of the L. H3068
9 Because of the house of the L our God I H3068
123: 2 *wait* upon the L our God, until that H3068
3 Have mercy upon us, O L, have mercy H3068
124: 1 If *it had not been* the L who was on our H3068
2 If *it had not been* the L who was on our H3068
6 Blessed *be* the L, who hath not given us H3068
8 Our help *is* in the name of the L, who H3068
125: 1 They that trust in the L *shall be* as H3068
2 Jerusalem, so the L *is* round about his H3068
4 Do good, O L, unto *those that be* good, H3068
5 crooked ways, the L shall lead them H3068
126: 1 When the L turned again the captivity H3068
2 The L hath done great things for them. H3068
3 The L hath done great things for us; H3068
4 Turn again our captivity, O L, as the H3068
127: 1 Except the L build the house, they H3068
1 build it: except the L keep the city, the H3068
3 Lo, children *are* an heritage of the L: H3068
128: 1 Blessed *is* every one that feareth the L; H3068
4 the man be blessed that feareth the L. H3068
5 The L shall bless thee out of Zion: and H3068
129: 4 The L *is* righteous: he hath cut asunder H3068
8 blessing of the L *be* upon you: we bless H3068
8 you: we bless you in the name of the L. H3068
130: 1 the depths have I cried unto thee, O L. H3068
2 L, hear my voice: let thine ears be H136
3 If thou, L, shouldest mark iniquities, O H3050
3 mark iniquities, O L, who shall stand? H136
5 I wait for the L, my soul doth wait, and H3068
6 My soul *waiteth* for the L more than they H136
7 Let Israel hope in the L: for with the H3068
7 for with the L *there is* mercy, and H3068
131: 1 L, my heart is not haughty, nor mine H3068
3 Let Israel hope in the L from H3068
132: 1 L, remember David, *and* all his H3068
2 How he sware unto the L, *and* vowed H3068
5 Until I find out a place for the L, an H3068
8 Arise, O L, into thy rest; thou, and the H3068
11 The L hath sworn *in* truth unto David; H3068
13 For the L hath chosen Zion; he hath H3068
133: 3 of Zion: for there the L commanded the H3068
134: 1 Behold, bless ye the L, all *ye* servants of H3068
1 all *ye* servants of the L, which by night H3068
1 by night stand in the house of the L. H3068
2 hands *in* the sanctuary, and bless the L. H3068
3 The L that made heaven and earth H3068
135: 1 Praise ye the L. Praise ye the name of H3050
1 ye the name of the L; praise *him*, O ye H3068
1 praise *him*, O ye servants of the L. H3068
2 Ye that stand in the house of the L, in H3068
3 Praise the L; for the LORD *is* good: sing H3050
3 Praise the LORD; for the L *is* good: sing H3068

Ps 135: 4 For the L hath chosen Jacob unto H3050
5 For I know that the L *is* great, and *that* H3068
5 *is* great, and *that* our L *is* above all gods. H113
6 Whatsoever the L pleased, *that* did he H3068
13 Thy name, O L, *endureth* for ever; *and* H3068
13 O L, throughout all generations. H3068
14 For the L will judge his people, and he H3068
19 Bless the L, O house of Israel: bless the H3068
19 of Israel: bless the L, O house of Aaron: H3068
20 Bless the L, O house of Levi: ye that fear H3068
20 Levi: ye that fear the L, bless the LORD. H3068
20 Levi: ye that fear the LORD, bless the L. H3068
21 Blessed be the L out of Zion, which H3068
21 dwelleth at Jerusalem. Praise ye the L. H3050
136: 1 O give thanks unto the L; for *he is* good: H3068
3 O give thanks to the L of lords: for his H113
137: 7 Remember, O L, the children of Edom H3068
138: 4 praise thee, O L, when they hear the H3068
5 Yea, they shall sing in the ways of the L: H3068
5 the LORD: for great *is* the glory of the L. H3068
6 Though the L *be* high, yet hath he H3068
8 The L will perfect *that which* H3068
8 me: thy mercy, O L, *endureth* for ever: H3068
139: 1 O L, thou hast searched me, and known H3068
4 *but*, lo, O L, thou knowest it altogether. H3068
21 Do not I hate them, O L, that hate thee? H3068
140: 1 Deliver me, O L, from the evil man: H3068
4 Keep me, O L, from the hands of the H3068
6 I said unto the L, Thou *art* my God: H3068
6 hear the voice of my supplications, O L. H3068
7 O GOD the L, the strength of my H136
8 Grant not, O L, the desires of the H3068
12 I know that the L will maintain the H3068
141: 1 L, I cry unto thee: make haste unto me; H3068
3 Set a watch, O L, before my mouth; H3068
8 thee, O GOD the L: in thee is my trust; H136
142: 1 I cried unto the L with my voice; with H3068
1 unto the L did I make my supplication. H3068
5 I cried unto thee, O L: I said, Thou *art* H3068
143: 1 Hear my prayer, O L, give ear to my H3068
7 Hear me speedily, O L: my spirit faileth: H3068
9 Deliver me, O L, from mine enemies: I H3068
11 Quicken me, O L, for thy name's sake: H3068
144: 1 Blessed *be* the L my strength, which H3068
3 L, what *is* man, that thou takest H3068
5 Bow thy heavens, O L, and come down: H3068
15 *is that* people, whose God *is* the L. H3068
145: 3 Great *is* the L, and greatly to be praised; H3068
8 The L *is* gracious, and full of H3068
9 The L *is* good to all: and his tender H3068
10 All thy works shall praise thee, O L; and H3068
14 The L upholdeth all that fall, and H3068
17 The L *is* righteous in all his ways, and H3068
18 The L *is* nigh unto all them that call H3068
20 The L preserveth all them that love H3068
21 the praise of the L: and let all flesh bless H3068
146: 1 Praise ye the L. Praise the LORD, O my H3050
1 Praise ye the LORD. Praise the L, O my H3068
2 While I live will I praise the L: I will sing H3068
5 help, whose hope *is* in the L his God: H3068
7 hungry. The L looseth the prisoners: H3068
8 The L openeth *the eyes of* the blind: the H3068
8 *of* the blind: the L raiseth them that are H3068
8 down: the L loveth the righteous: H3068
9 The L preserveth the strangers; he H3068
10 The L shall reign for ever, *even* thy H3068
10 unto all generations. Praise ye the L. H3050
147: 1 Praise ye the L: for *it is* good to sing H3050
2 The L doth build up Jerusalem: he H3068
5 Great *is* our L, and of great power: his H113
6 The L lifteth up the meek: he casteth H3068
7 Sing unto the L with thanksgiving; sing H3068
11 The L taketh pleasure in them that fear H3068
12 Praise the L, O Jerusalem; praise thy H3068
20 have not known them. Praise ye the L. H3050
148: 1 Praise ye the L. Praise ye the LORD H3050
1 Praise ye the LORD. Praise ye the L H3068
5 Let them praise the name of the L: for H3068
7 Praise the L from the earth, ye H3068
13 Let them praise the name of the L: for H3068
14 a people near unto him. Praise ye the L. H3050
149: 1 Praise ye the L. Sing unto the LORD a H3050
1 Praise ye the LORD. Sing unto the L a H3068
4 For the L taketh pleasure in his people: H3068
9 have all his saints. Praise ye the L. H3050
150: 1 Praise ye the L. Praise God in his H3050
6 breath praise the L. Praise ye the LORD. H3050
6 breath praise the LORD. Praise ye the L. H3050
Prv 1: 7 The fear of the L *is* the beginning of H3068

Prv 1:29 and did not choose the fear of the L: H3068
2: 5 of the L, and find the knowledge of God. H3068
6 For the L giveth wisdom: out of his H3068
3: 5 Trust in the L with all thine heart; and H3068
7 eyes: fear the L, and depart from evil. H3068
9 Honour the L with thy substance, and H3068
11 L; neither be weary of his correction: H3068
12 For whom the L loveth he correcteth; H3068
19 The L by wisdom hath founded the H3068
26 For the L shall be thy confidence, and H3068
32 L: but his secret *is* with the righteous. H3068
33 The curse of the L *is* in the house of the H3068
5:21 the L, and he pondereth all his goings. H3068
6:16 These six *things* doth the L hate: yea, H3068
8:13 The fear of the L *is* to hate evil: pride, H3068
22 The L possessed me in the beginning of H3068
35 life, and shall obtain favour of the L. H3068
9:10 The fear of the L *is* the beginning of H3068
10: 3 The L will not suffer the soul of the H3068
22 The blessing of the L, it maketh rich, H3068
27 The fear of the L prolongeth days: but H3068
29 The way of the L *is* strength to the H3068
11: 1 A false balance *is* abomination to the L: H3068
20 to the L: but *such as are* upright H3068
12: 2 A good *man* obtaineth favour of the L: H3068
22 Lying lips *are* abomination to the L: but H3068
14: 2 feareth the L: but *he that is* perverse H3068
26 In the fear of the L *is* strong H3068
27 The fear of the L *is* a fountain of life, to H3068
15: 3 The eyes of the L *are* in every place, H3068
8 to the L: but the prayer of the H3068
9 unto the L: but he loveth him that H3068
11 Hell and destruction *are* before the L: H3068
16 Better *is* little with the fear of the L H3068
25 The L will destroy the house of the H3068
26 to the L: but *the words* of the H3068
29 The L *is* far from the wicked: but he H3068
33 The fear of the L *is* the instruction of H3068
16: 1 the answer of the tongue, *is* from the L. H3068
2 eyes; but the L weigheth the spirits. H3068
3 Commit thy works unto the L, and thy H3068
4 The L hath made all *things* for himself: H3068
5 to the L: *though* hand *join* in H3068
6 the fear of the L *men* depart from evil. H3068
7 When a man's ways please the L, he H3068
9 his way: but the L directeth his steps. H3068
20 whoso trusteth in the L, happy *is* he. H3068
33 the whole disposing thereof *is* of the L. H3068
17: 3 for gold: but the L trieth the hearts. H3068
15 they both *are* abomination to the L. H3068
18:10 The name of the L *is* a strong tower: H3068
22 *thing*, and obtaineth favour of the L. H3068
19: 3 and his heart fretteth against the L. H3068
14 and a prudent wife *is* from the L. H3068
17 lendeth unto the L; and that which he H3068
21 the counsel of the L, that shall stand. H3068
23 The fear of the L *tendeth* to life: and *he* H3068
20:10 of them *are* alike abomination to the L. H3068
12 the L hath made even both of them. H3068
22 wait on the L, and he shall save thee. H3068
23 the L; and a false balance *is* not good. H3068
24 Man's goings *are* of the L; how can a H3068
27 The spirit of man *is* the candle of the L, H3068
21: 1 The king's heart *is* in the hand of the L, H3068
2 eyes: but the L pondereth the hearts. H3068
3 more acceptable to the L than sacrifice. H3068
30 nor counsel against the L. H3068
31 the day of battle: but safety *is* of the L. H3068
22: 2 The rich and poor meet together: the L H3068
4 By humility *and* the fear of the L *are* H3068
12 The eyes of the L preserve knowledge, H3068
14 is abhorred of the L shall fall therein. H3068
19 That thy trust may be in the L, I have H3068
23 For the L will plead their cause, and H3068
23:17 in the fear of the L all the day long. H3068
24:18 Lest the L see *it*, and it displease him, H3068
21 My son, fear thou the L and the king: H3068
25:22 his head, and the L shall reward thee. H3068
28: 5 that seek the L understand all *things*. H3068
25 his trust in the L shall be made fat. H3068
29:13 the L lighteneth both their eyes. H3068
25 putteth his trust in the L shall be safe. H3068
26 man's judgment *cometh* from the L. H3068
30: 9 say, Who *is* the L? or lest I be poor, and H3068
31:30 *that* feareth the L, she shall be praised. H3068
Isa 1: 2 O earth: for the L hath spoken, I have H3068
4 they have forsaken the L, they have H3068
9 Except the L of hosts had left unto us a H3068
10 Hear the word of the L, ye rulers of H3068

Isa 1:11 unto me? saith the L: I am full of the H3068
18 together, saith the L: though your sins H3068
20 for the mouth of the L hath spoken *it*. H3068
24 Therefore saith the L, the LORD of hosts, H113
24 Therefore saith the Lord, the L of hosts, H3068
28 that forsake the L shall be consumed. H3068
2: 3 mountain of the L, to the house of the H3068
3 and the word of the L from Jerusalem. H3068
5 ye, and let us walk in the light of the L. H3068
10 the L, and for the glory of his majesty. H3068
11 the L alone shall be exalted in that day. H3068
12 For the day of the L of hosts *shall be* H3068
17 the L alone shall be exalted in that day. H3068
19 for fear of the L, and for the glory of H3068
21 for fear of the L, and for the glory of H3068
3: 1 For, behold, the L, the LORD of hosts, H113
1 For, behold, the Lord, the L of hosts, H3068
8 the L, to provoke the eyes of his glory. H3068
13 The L standeth up to plead, and H3068
14 The L will enter into judgment with the H3068
15 of the poor? saith the L GOD of hosts. H136
16 Moreover the L saith, Because the H3068
17 Therefore the L will smite with a scab H136
17 the L will discover their secret parts. H3068
18 In that day the L will take away the H136
4: 2 In that day shall the branch of the L be H3068
4 When the L shall have washed away the H136
5 And the L will create upon every H3068
5: 7 For the vineyard of the L of hosts *is* the H3068
9 In mine ears *said* the L of hosts, Of a H3068
12 the work of the L, neither consider the H3068
16 But the L of hosts shall be exalted in H3068
24 the law of the L of hosts, and despised H3068
25 Therefore is the anger of the L kindled H3068
6: 1 died I saw also the L sitting upon a H136
3 holy, holy, *is* the L of hosts: the whole H3068
5 eyes have seen the King, the L of hosts. H3068
8 Also I heard the voice of the L, saying, H136
11 Then said I, L, how long? And he H136
12 And the L have removed men far away, H3068
7: 3 Then said the L unto Isaiah, Go forth H3068
7 Thus saith the L GOD, It shall not stand, H136
10 Moreover the L spake again unto Ahaz, H3068
11 Ask thee a sign of the L thy God; ask it H3068
12 I will not ask, neither will I tempt the L. H3068
14 Therefore the L himself shall give you a H136
17 The L shall bring upon thee, and upon H3068
18 that day, *that* the L shall hiss for the fly H3068
20 In the same day shall the L shave with a H136
8: 1 Moreover the L said unto me, Take H3068
3 a son. Then said the L to me, Call his H3068
5 The L spake also unto me again, H3068
7 Now therefore, behold, the L bringeth up H136
11 For the L spake thus to me with a H3068
13 Sanctify the L of hosts himself; and *let* H3068
17 And I will wait upon the L, that hideth H3068
18 Behold, I and the children whom the L H3068
18 in Israel from the L of hosts, which H3068
9: 7 zeal of the L of hosts will perform this. H3068
8 The L sent a word into Jacob, and it hath H136
11 Therefore the L shall set up the H3068
13 neither do they seek the L of hosts. H3068
14 Therefore the L will cut off from Israel H3068
17 Therefore the L shall have no joy in their H136
19 Through the wrath of the L of hosts is H3068
10:12 *that* when the L hath performed his H136
16 Therefore shall the L, the Lord of hosts, H113
16 Therefore shall the Lord, the L of hosts, H3068
20 the L, the Holy One of Israel, in truth. H3068
23 For the L GOD of hosts shall make a H136
24 Therefore thus saith the L GOD of hosts, H136
26 And the L of hosts shall stir up a H3068
33 Behold, the L, the LORD of hosts, shall H113
33 Behold, the Lord, the L of hosts, shall H3068
11: 2 And the spirit of the L shall rest upon H3068
2 of knowledge and of the fear of the L; H3068
3 in the fear of the L: and he shall not H3068
9 of the L, as the waters cover the sea. H3068
11 in that day, *that* the L shall set his hand H136
15 And the L shall utterly destroy the H3068
12: 1 And in that day thou shalt say, O L, I H3068
2 not be afraid: for the L JEHOVAH *is* my H3050
4 ye say, Praise the L, call upon his name, H3068
5 Sing unto the L; for he hath done H3068
13: 4 together: the L of hosts mustereth H3068
5 heaven, *even* the L, and the weapons of H3068
6 Howl ye; for the day of the L *is* at hand; H3068
9 Behold, the day of the L cometh, cruel H3068
13 in the wrath of the L of hosts, and in H3068

Isa 14: 1 For the L will have mercy on Jacob, H3068
2 in the land of the L for servants and H3068
3 in the day that the L shall give thee rest H3068
5 The L hath broken the staff of the H3068
22 them, saith the L of hosts, and cut off H3068
22 and son, and nephew, saith the L. H3068
23 of destruction, saith the L of hosts. H3068
24 The L of hosts hath sworn, saying, H3068
27 For the L of hosts hath purposed, and H3068
32 nation? That the L hath founded Zion, H3068
16:13 This *is* the word that the L hath spoken H3068
14 But now the L hath spoken, saying, H3068
17: 3 children of Israel, saith the L of hosts. H3068
6 thereof, saith the L God of Israel. H3068
18: 4 For so the L said unto me, I will take H3068
7 brought unto the L of hosts of a people H3068
7 name of the L of hosts, the mount Zion. H3068
19: 1 The burden of Egypt. Behold, the L H3068
4 the hand of a cruel l; and a fierce king H113
4 them, saith the L, the LORD of hosts. H113
4 them, saith the Lord, the L of hosts. H3068
12 L of hosts hath purposed upon Egypt. H3068
14 The L hath mingled a perverse spirit in H3068
16 the L of hosts, which he shaketh over it. H3068
17 the counsel of the L of hosts, which he H3068
18 and swear to the L of hosts; one shall H3068
19 be an altar to the L in the midst of the H3068
19 a pillar at the border thereof to the L. H3068
20 for a witness unto the L of hosts in the H3068
20 they shall cry unto the L because of the H3068
21 And the L shall be known to Egypt, and H3068
21 shall know the L in that day, and shall H3068
21 vow a vow unto the L, and perform *it*. H3068
22 And the L shall smite Egypt: he shall H3068
22 return *even* to the L, and he shall be H3068
25 Whom the L of hosts shall bless, H3068
20: 2 At the same time spake the L by Isaiah H3068
3 And the L said, Like as my servant H3068
21: 6 For thus hath the L said unto me, Go, set H136
8 And he cried, A lion: My l, I stand H136
10 have heard of the L of hosts, the God of H3068
16 For thus hath the L said unto me, Within H136
17 for the L God of Israel hath spoken *it*. H3068
22: 5 perplexity by the L GOD of hosts in the H136
12 And in that day did the L GOD of hosts H136
14 mine ears by the L of hosts, Surely this H3068
14 you till ye die, saith the L GOD of hosts. H136
15 Thus saith the L GOD of hosts, Go, get H136
17 Behold, the L will carry thee away with H3068
25 In that day, saith the L of hosts, shall H3068
25 be cut off: for the L hath spoken *it*. H3068
23: 9 The L of hosts hath purposed it, to H3068
11 shook the kingdoms: the L hath given a H3068
17 years, that the L will visit Tyre, and H3068
18 shall be holiness to the L: it shall not be H3068
18 dwell before the L, to eat sufficiently, H3068
24: 1 Behold, the L maketh the earth empty, H3068
3 for the L hath spoken this word. H3068
14 the L, they shall cry aloud from the sea. H3068
15 Wherefore glorify ye the L in the fires, H3068
15 L God of Israel in the isles of the sea. H3068
21 in that day, *that* the L shall punish the H3068
23 when the L of hosts shall reign H3068
25: 1 O L, thou *art* my God; I will exalt thee, I H3068
6 And in this mountain shall the L of H3068
8 in victory; and the L GOD will wipe away H136
8 all the earth: for the L hath spoken *it*. H3068
9 save us: this *is* the L; we have waited for H3068
10 the hand of the L rest, and Moab shall H3068
26: 4 Trust ye in the L for ever: for in the H3068
4 the L JEHOVAH *is* everlasting strength: H3050
8 Yea, in the way of thy judgments, O L, H3068
10 and will not behold the majesty of the L. H3068
11 L, *when* thy hand is lifted up, they will H3068
12 L, thou wilt ordain peace for us: for H3068
13 O L our God, *other* lords beside thee H3068
15 Thou hast increased the nation, O L, H3068
16 L, in trouble have they visited thee, they H3068
17 so have we been in thy sight, O L. H3068
21 For, behold, the L cometh out of his H3068
27: 1 In that day the L with his sore and H3068
3 I the L do keep it; I will water it every H3068
12 that day, *that* the L shall beat off from H3068
13 the L in the holy mount at Jerusalem. H3068
28: 2 Behold, the L hath a mighty and strong H136
5 In that day shall the L of hosts be for a H3068
13 But the word of the L was unto them H3068
14 Wherefore hear the word of the L, ye H3068
16 Therefore thus saith the L GOD, Behold, H136

Isa 28:21 For the L shall rise up as *in* mount H3068
22 have heard from the L GOD of hosts a H136
29 This also cometh forth from the L of H3068
29: 6 Thou shalt be visited of the L of hosts H3068
10 For the L hath poured out upon you the H3068
13 Wherefore the L said, Forasmuch as this H136
15 counsel from the L, and their works are H3068
19 *their* joy in the L, and the poor among H3068
22 Therefore thus saith the L, who H3068
30: 1 children, saith the L, that take counsel, H3068
9 *that* will not hear the law of the L: H3068
15 For thus saith the L GOD, the Holy One H136
18 And therefore will the L wait, that he H3068
18 mercy upon you: for the L *is* a God of H3068
20 And *though* the L give you the bread of H136
26 in the day that the L bindeth up the H3068
27 Behold, the name of the L cometh from H3068
29 of the L, to the mighty One of Israel. H3068
30 And the L shall cause his glorious voice H3068
31 For through the voice of the L shall the H3068
32 pass, which the L shall lay upon him, H3068
33 the breath of the L, like a stream of H3068
31: 1 Holy One of Israel, neither seek the L! H3068
3 spirit. When the L shall stretch out his H3068
4 For thus hath the L spoken unto me, H3068
4 of them: so shall the L of hosts come H3068
5 As birds flying, so will the L of hosts H3068
9 the ensign, saith the L, whose fire *is* in H3068
32: 6 error against the L, to make empty the H3068
33: 2 O L, be gracious unto us; we have H3068
5 The L is exalted; for he dwelleth on H3068
6 the fear of the L *is* his treasure. H3068
10 Now will I rise, saith the L; now will I be H3068
21 But there the glorious L *will be* unto us H3068
22 For the L *is* our judge, the LORD *is* our H3068
22 For the LORD *is* our judge, the L *is* our H3068
22 the L *is* our king; he will save us. H3068
34: 2 For the indignation of the L *is* upon all H3068
6 The sword of the L is filled with blood, H3068
6 of rams: for the L hath a sacrifice in H3068
16 Seek ye out of the book of the L, and H3068
35: 2 of the L, *and* the excellency of our God. H3068
10 And the ransomed of the L shall H3068
36: 7 But if thou say to me, We trust in the L H3068
10 And am I now come up without the L H3068
10 to destroy it? the L said unto me, Go up H3068
15 you trust in the L, saying, The LORD H3068
15 saying, The L will surely deliver us: H3068
18 you, saying, The L will deliver us. Hath H3068
20 of my hand, that the L should deliver H3068
37: 1 and went into the house of the L. H3068
4 It may be the L thy God will hear the H3068
4 words which the L thy God hath heard: H3068
6 Thus saith the L, Be not afraid of the H3068
14 of the L, and spread it before the LORD. H3068
14 of the LORD, and spread it before the L. H3068
15 And Hezekiah prayed unto the L, H3068
16 O L of hosts, God of Israel, that H3068
17 Incline thine ear, O L, and hear; open H3068
17 open thine eyes, O L, and see: and hear H3068
18 Of a truth, L, the kings of Assyria have H3068
20 Now therefore, O L our God, save us H3068
20 that thou *art* the L, *even* thou only. H3068
21 saying, Thus saith the L God of Israel, H3068
22 This *is* the word which the L hath H3068
24 reproached the L, and hast said, By the H136
32 the zeal of the L of hosts shall do this. H3068
33 Therefore thus saith the L concerning H3068
34 shall not come into this city, saith the L. H3068
36 Then the angel of the L went forth, and H3068
38: 1 Thus saith the L, Set thine house in H3068
2 toward the wall, and prayed unto the L, H3068
3 And said, Remember now, O L, I H3068
4 Then came the word of the L to Isaiah, H3068
5 Thus saith the L, the God of David thy H3068
7 thee from the L, that the LORD will H3068
7 LORD, that the L will do this thing that H3068
11 I said, I shall not see the L, *even* the H3050
11 the LORD, *even* the L, in the land of the H3050
14 O L, I am oppressed; undertake for me. H3068
16 O L, by these *things men* live, and in all H136
20 The L *was ready* to save me: therefore H3068
20 the days of our life in the house of the L. H3068
22 that I shall go up to the house of the L? H3068
39: 5 Hear the word of the L of hosts: H3068
6 nothing shall be left, saith the L. H3068
8 *is* the word of the L which thou hast H3068
40: 3 ye the way of the L, make straight in the H3068
5 And the glory of the L shall be revealed, H3068

Isa 40: 5 for the mouth of the L hath spoken *it*. H3068
7 the spirit of the L bloweth upon it: H3068
10 Behold, the L GOD will come with strong H136
13 Who hath directed the spirit of the L, or H3068
27 is hid from the L, and my judgment is H3068
28 God, the L, the Creator of the ends H3068
31 But they that wait upon the L shall H3068
41: 4 L, the first, and with the last; I *am* he. H3068
13 For I the L thy God will hold thy right H3068
14 thee, saith the L, and thy redeemer, the H3068
16 shalt rejoice in the L, *and* shalt glory in H3068
17 for thirst, I the L will hear them, I the H3068
20 the hand of the L hath done this, and H3068
21 Produce your cause, saith the L; bring H3068
42: 5 Thus saith God the L, he that created H3068
6 I the L have called thee in H3068
8 I *am* the L: that *is* my name: and my H3068
10 Sing unto the L a new song, *and* his H3068
12 Let them give glory unto the L, and H3068
13 The L shall go forth as a mighty man, H3068
21 The L is well pleased for his H3068
24 did not the L, he against whom we H3068
43: 1 But now thus saith the L that created H3068
3 For I *am* the L thy God, the Holy One of H3068
10 Ye *are* my witnesses, saith the L, and H3068
11 I, *even* I, *am* the L; and beside me *there* H3068
12 witnesses, saith the L, that I *am* God. H3068
14 Thus saith the L, your redeemer, the H3068
15 I *am* the L, your Holy One, the creator H3068
16 Thus saith the L, which maketh a way H3068
44: 2 Thus saith the L that made thee, and H3068
5 *with* his hand unto the L, and surname H3068
6 Thus saith the L the King of Israel, and H3068
6 his redeemer the L of hosts; I *am* the H3068
23 Sing, O ye heavens; for the L hath done H3068
23 therein: for the L hath redeemed Jacob, H3068
24 Thus saith the L, thy redeemer, and he H3068
24 the womb, I *am* the L that maketh all H3068
45: 1 Thus saith the L to his anointed, to H3068
3 know that I, the L, which call *thee* by H3068
5 I *am* the L, and *there is* none else, *there* H3068
6 me. I *am* the L, and *there is* none else. H3068
7 create evil: I the L do all these *things*. H3068
8 up together; I the L have created it. H3068
11 Thus saith the L, the Holy One of Israel, H3068
13 price nor reward, saith the L of hosts. H3068
14 Thus saith the L, The labour of Egypt, H3068
17 *But* Israel shall be saved in the L with H3068
18 For thus saith the L that created the H3068
18 I *am* the L; and *there is* none else. H3068
19 ye me in vain: I the L speak H3068
21 *have* not I the L? and *there is* no God H3068
24 Surely, shall *one* say, in the L have I H3068
25 In the L shall all the seed of Israel be H3068
47: 4 *As for* our redeemer, the L of hosts *is* H3068
48: 1 swear by the name of the L, and make H3068
2 of Israel; The L of hosts *is* his name. H3068
14 these *things*? The L hath loved him: he H3068
16 the L GOD, and his Spirit, hath sent me. H136
17 Thus saith the L, thy Redeemer, the H3068
17 One of Israel; I *am* the L thy God which H3068
20 L hath redeemed his servant Jacob. H3068
22 *There is* no peace, saith the L, unto the H3068
49: 1 from far; The L hath called me from H3068
4 with the L, and my work with my God. H3068
5 And now, saith the L that formed me H3068
5 the L, and my God shall be my strength. H3068
7 Thus saith the L, the Redeemer of H3068
7 because of the L that is faithful, *and* H3068
8 Thus saith the L, In an acceptable time H3068
13 for the L hath comforted his H3068
14 But Zion said, The L hath forsaken me, H3068
14 me, and my L hath forgotten me. H136
18 *As* I live, saith the L, thou shalt surely H3068
22 Thus saith the L GOD, Behold, I will lift H136
23 that I *am* the L: for they shall not be H3068
25 But thus saith the L, Even the captives H3068
26 know that I the L *am* thy Saviour and H3068
50: 1 Thus saith the L, Where *is* the bill of H3068
4 The L GOD hath given me the tongue of H136
5 The L GOD hath opened mine ear, and I H136
7 For the L GOD will help me; therefore H136
9 Behold, the L GOD will help me; who *is* H136
10 Who *is* among you that feareth the L, H3068
10 name of the L, and stay upon his God. H3068
51: 1 ye that seek the L: look unto the rock H3068
3 For the L shall comfort Zion: he will H3068
3 the garden of the L; joy and gladness H3068
9 O arm of the L; awake, as in the ancient H3068

Isa 51:11 Therefore the redeemed of the L shall H3068
13 And forgettest the L thy maker, that H3068
15 But I *am* the L thy God, that divided H3068
15 roared: The L of hosts *is* his name. H3068
17 at the hand of the L the cup of his fury; H3068
20 the fury of the L, the rebuke of thy God. H3068
22 Thus saith thy L the LORD, and thy God H113
22 Thus saith thy Lord the L, and thy God H3068
52: 3 For thus saith the L, Ye have sold H3068
4 For thus saith the L GOD, My people H136
5 I here, saith the L, that my people is H3068
5 them to howl, saith the L; and my name H3068
8 eye, when the L shall bring again Zion. H3068
9 Jerusalem: for the L hath comforted his H3068
10 The L hath made bare his holy arm in H3068
11 ye clean, that bear the vessels of the L. H3068
12 by flight: for the L will go before you; H3068
53: 1 to whom is the arm of the L revealed? H3068
6 own way; and the L hath laid on him H3068
10 Yet it pleased the L to bruise him; he H3068
10 of the L shall prosper in his hand. H3068
54: 1 of the married wife, saith the L. H3068
5 For thy Maker *is* thine husband; the L H3068
6 For the L hath called thee as a woman H3068
8 on thee, saith the L thy Redeemer. H3068
10 saith the L that hath mercy on thee. H3068
13 *be* taught of the L; and great *shall be* H3068
17 of the servants of the L, and their H3068
17 their righteousness *is* of me, saith the L. H3068
55: 5 because of the L thy God, and for the H3068
6 Seek ye the L while he may be found, H3068
7 him return unto the L, and he will have H3068
8 *are* your ways my ways, saith the L. H3068
13 it shall be to the L for a name, for an H3068
56: 1 Thus saith the L, Keep ye judgment, H3068
3 himself to the L, speak, saying, The H3068
3 speak, saying, The L hath utterly H3068
4 For thus saith the L unto the eunuchs H3068
6 themselves to the L, to serve him, and H3068
6 the name of the L, to be his servants, H3068
8 The L GOD which gathereth the outcasts H136
57:19 *is* near, saith the L; and I will heal him. H3068
58: 5 a fast, and an acceptable day to the L? H3068
8 the glory of the L shall be thy rearward. H3068
9 Then shalt thou call, and the L shall H3068
11 And the L shall guide thee continually, H3068
13 the holy of the L, honourable; and shalt H3068
14 Then shalt thou delight thyself in the L; H3068
14 for the mouth of the L hath spoken *it*. H3068
59:13 lying against the L, and departing away H3068
15 himself a prey: and the L saw *it*, and it H3068
19 So shall they fear the name of the L H3068
19 L shall lift up a standard against him. H3068
20 transgression in Jacob, saith the L. H3068
21 them, saith the L; My spirit that *is* upon H3068
21 the L, from henceforth and for ever. H3068
60: 1 the glory of the L is risen upon thee. H3068
2 the people: but the L shall arise upon H3068
6 shall shew forth the praises of the L. H3068
9 the name of the L thy God, and to the H3068
14 L, The Zion of the Holy One of Israel. H3068
16 know that I the L *am* thy Saviour and H3068
19 unto thee: but the L shall be unto thee H3068
20 withdraw itself: for the L shall be thine H3068
22 nation: I the L will hasten it in his time. H3068
61: 1 The Spirit of the L GOD *is* upon me; H136
1 me; because the L hath anointed me to H3068
2 year of the L, and the day of vengeance H3068
3 of the L, that he might be glorified. H3068
6 the Priests of the L: *men* shall call you H3068
8 For I the L love judgment, I hate H3068
9 *are* the seed *which* the L hath blessed. H3068
10 I will greatly rejoice in the L, my soul H3068
11 to spring forth; so the L GOD will cause H136
62: 2 which the mouth of the L shall name. H3068
3 glory in the hand of the L, and a royal H3068
4 Beulah: for the L delighteth in thee, H3068
6 mention of the L, keep not silence, H3068
8 The L hath sworn by his right hand, H3068
9 it, and praise the L; and they that have H3068
11 Behold, the L hath proclaimed unto the H3068
12 redeemed of the L: and thou shalt be H3068
63: 7 of the L, *and* the praises of the H3068
7 *and* the praises of the L, according to all H3068
7 to all that the L hath bestowed on us, H3068
14 the Spirit of the L caused him to rest: H3068
16 us not: thou, O L, *art* our father, our H3068
17 O L, why hast thou made us to err from H3068
64: 8 But now, O L, thou *art* our father; we H3068

Isa 64: 9 Be not wroth very sore, O L, neither H3068
12 for these *things*, O L? wilt thou hold thy H3068
65: 7 fathers together, saith the L, which have H3068
8 Thus saith the L, As the new wine is H3068
11 But ye *are* they that forsake the L, that H3068
13 Therefore thus saith the L GOD, Behold, H136
15 my chosen: for the L GOD shall slay thee, H136
23 of the L, and their offspring with them. H3068
25 in all my holy mountain, saith the L. H3068
66: 1 Thus saith the L, The heaven *is* my H3068
2 been, saith the L: but to this *man* will H3068
5 Hear the word of the L, ye that tremble H3068
5 sake, said, Let the L be glorified: but he H3068
6 temple, a voice of the L that rendereth H3068
9 forth? saith the L: shall I cause to bring H3068
12 For thus saith the L, Behold, I will H3068
14 and the hand of the L shall be known H3068
15 For, behold, the L will come with fire, H3068
16 For by fire and by his sword will the L H3068
16 and the slain of the L shall be many. H3068
17 shall be consumed together, saith the L. H3068
20 an offering unto the L out of all nations H3068
20 saith the L, as the children of Israel H3068
20 in a clean vessel into the house of the L. H3068
21 for priests *and* for Levites, saith the L. H3068
22 me, saith the L, so shall your seed and H3068
23 come to worship before me, saith the L. H3068
Jer 1: 2 To whom the word of the L came in the H3068
4 Then the word of the L came unto me, H3068
6 Then said I, Ah, L GOD! behold, I cannot H136
7 But the L said unto me, Say not, I *am* a H3068
8 *am* with thee to deliver thee, saith the L. H3068
9 Then the L put forth his hand, and H3068
9 my mouth. And the L said unto me, H3068
11 Moreover the word of the L came unto H3068
12 Then said the L unto me, Thou hast H3068
13 And the word of the L came unto me H3068
14 Then the L said unto me, Out of the H3068
15 north, saith the L; and they shall come, H3068
19 with thee, saith the L, to deliver thee. H3068
2: 1 Moreover the word of the L came to H3068
2 Thus saith the L; I remember thee, the H3068
3 Israel *was* holiness unto the L, *and* the H3068
3 evil shall come upon them, saith the L. H3068
4 Hear ye the word of the L, O house of H3068
5 Thus saith the L, What iniquity have H3068
6 Neither said they, Where *is* the L that H3068
8 The priests said not, Where *is* the L? H3068
9 with you, saith the L, and with your H3068
12 afraid, be ye very desolate, saith the L. H3068
17 hast forsaken the L thy God, when he H3068
19 hast forsaken the L thy God, and that H3068
19 *is* not in thee, saith the L GOD of hosts. H136
22 is marked before me, saith the L GOD. H136
29 transgressed against me, saith the L. H3068
31 O generation, see ye the word of the L. H3068
37 thine head: for the L hath rejected thy H3068
3: 1 yet return again to me, saith the L. H3068
6 The L said also unto me in the days of H3068
10 whole heart, but feignedly, saith the L. H3068
11 And the L said unto me, The H3068
12 Israel, saith the L; *and* I will not cause H3068
12 the L, *and* I will not keep *anger* for ever. H3068
13 against the L thy God, and hast H3068
13 have not obeyed my voice, saith the L. H3068
14 children, saith the L; for I am married H3068
16 those days, saith the L, they shall say no H3068
16 covenant of the L: neither shall it come H3068
17 the throne of the L; and all the nations H3068
17 it, to the name of the L, to Jerusalem: H3068
20 with me, O house of Israel, saith the L. H3068
21 they have forgotten the L their God. H3068
22 unto thee; for thou *art* the L our God. H3068
23 the L our God *is* the salvation of Israel. H3068
25 sinned against the L our God, we and H3068
25 not obeyed the voice of the L our God. H3068
4: 1 If thou wilt return, O Israel, saith the L, H3068
2 And thou shalt swear, The L liveth, in H3068
3 For thus saith the L to the men of H3068
4 Circumcise yourselves to the L, and H3068
8 of the L is not turned back from us. H3068
9 at that day, saith the L, *that* the heart of H3068
10 Then said I, Ah, L GOD! surely thou hast H136
17 been rebellious against me, saith the L. H3068
26 of the L, *and* by his fierce anger. H3068
27 For thus hath the L said, The whole H3068
5: 2 And though they say, The L liveth; H3068
3 O L, *are* not thine eyes upon the truth? H3068
4 of the L, *nor* the judgment of their God. H3068
Jer 5: 5 the way of the L, *and* the judgment of H3068
9 *things*? saith the L: and shall not my H3068
11 treacherously against me, saith the L. H3068
12 They have belied the L, and said, *It is* H3068
14 Wherefore thus saith the L God of H3068
15 of Israel, saith the L: it *is* a mighty H3068
18 Nevertheless in those days, saith the L, I H3068
19 doeth the L our God all these *things* H3068
22 Fear ye not me? saith the L: will ye not H3068
24 us now fear the L our God, that giveth H3068
29 *things*? saith the L: shall not my soul be H3068
6: 6 For thus hath the L of hosts said, Hew H3068
9 Thus saith the L of hosts, They shall H3068
10 the word of the L is unto them a H3068
11 Therefore I am full of the fury of the L; I H3068
12 the inhabitants of the land, saith the L. H3068
15 they shall be cast down, saith the L. H3068
16 Thus saith the L, Stand ye in the ways, H3068
21 Therefore thus saith the L, Behold, I will H3068
22 Thus saith the L, Behold, a people H3068
30 because the L hath rejected them. H3068
7: 1 came to Jeremiah from the L, saying, H3068
2 the word of the L, all *ye of* Judah, that H3068
2 enter in at these gates to worship the L. H3068
3 Thus saith the L of hosts, the God of H3068
4 The temple of the L, The temple of the H3068
4 L, The temple of the LORD, *are* these. H3068
4 LORD, The temple of the L, *are* these. H3068
11 Behold, even I have seen *it*, saith the L. H3068
13 works, saith the L, and I spake unto H3068
19 me to anger? saith the L: *do they* not H3068
20 Therefore thus saith the L GOD; Behold, H136
21 Thus saith the L of hosts, the God of H3068
28 not the voice of the L their God, nor H3068
29 high places; for the L hath rejected and H3068
30 my sight, saith the L: they have set their H3068
32 come, saith the L, that it shall no more H3068
8: 1 At that time, saith the L, they shall H3068
3 have driven them, saith the L of hosts. H3068
4 Thus saith the L; Shall they fall, and H3068
7 people know not the judgment of the L. H3068
8 and the law of the L *is* with us? Lo, H3068
9 of the L; and what wisdom *is* in them? H3068
12 they shall be cast down, saith the L. H3068
13 I will surely consume them, saith the L: H3068
14 there: for the L our God hath put us H3068
14 because we have sinned against the L. H3068
17 and they shall bite you, saith the L. H3068
19 country: *Is* not the L in Zion? *is* not her H3068
9: 3 evil, and they know not me, saith the L. H3068
6 they refuse to know me, saith the L. H3068
7 Therefore thus saith the L of hosts, H3068
9 *things*? saith the L: shall not my soul be H3068
12 the mouth of the L hath spoken, that he H3068
13 And the L saith, Because they have H3068
15 Therefore thus saith the L of hosts, the H3068
17 Thus saith the L of hosts, Consider ye, H3068
20 Yet hear the word of the L, O ye women, H3068
22 Speak, Thus saith the L, Even the H3068
23 Thus saith the L, Let not the wise *man* H3068
24 me, that I *am* the L which exercise H3068
24 for in these *things* I delight, saith the L. H3068
25 Behold, the days come, saith the L, that H3068
10: 1 Hear ye the word which the L speaketh H3068
2 Thus saith the L, Learn not the way of H3068
6 like unto thee, O L; thou *art* great, and H3068
10 But the L *is* the true God, he *is* the H3068
16 inheritance: The L of hosts *is* his name. H3068
18 For thus saith the L, Behold, I will sling H3068
21 not sought the L: therefore they shall H3068
23 O L, I know that the way of man *is* not H3068
24 O L, correct me, but with judgment; not H3068
11: 1 came to Jeremiah from the L, saying, H3068
3 Thus saith the L God of Israel; Cursed H3068
5 answered I, and said, So be it, O L. H3068
6 Then the L said unto me, Proclaim all H3068
9 And the L said unto me, A conspiracy H3068
11 Therefore thus saith the L, Behold, I will H3068
16 The L called thy name, A green olive H3068
17 For the L of hosts, that planted thee, H3068
18 And the L hath given me knowledge *of* H3068
20 But, O L of hosts, that judgest H3068
21 Therefore thus saith the L of the men of H3068
21 of the L, that thou die not by our hand: H3068
22 Therefore thus saith the L of hosts, H3068
12: 1 Righteous *art* thou, O L, when I plead H3068
3 But thou, O L, knowest me: thou hast H3068
12 the sword of the L shall devour from H3068
13 because of the fierce anger of the L. H3068
Jer 12:14 Thus saith the L against all mine evil H3068
16 by my name, The L liveth; as they H3068
17 up and destroy that nation, saith the L. H3068
13: 1 Thus saith the L unto me, Go and get H3068
2 word of the L, and put *it* on my loins. H3068
3 And the word of the L came unto me H3068
5 Euphrates, as the L commanded me. H3068
6 days, that the L said unto me, Arise, H3068
8 Then the word of the L came unto me, H3068
9 Thus saith the L, After this manner will H3068
11 of Judah, saith the L; that they might be H3068
12 Thus saith the L God of Israel, Every H3068
13 Thus saith the L, Behold, I will fill all H3068
14 together, saith the L: I will not pity, nor H3068
15 be not proud: for the L hath spoken. H3068
16 Give glory to the L your God, before he H3068
25 from me, saith the L; because thou hast H3068
14: 1 The word of the L that came to H3068
7 O L, though our iniquities testify H3068
9 save? yet thou, O L, *art* in the midst of H3068
10 Thus saith the L unto this people, Thus H3068
10 feet, therefore the L doth not accept H3068
11 Then said the L unto me, Pray not for H3068
13 Then said I, Ah, L GOD! behold, the H136
14 Then the L said unto me, The prophets H3068
15 Therefore thus saith the L concerning H3068
20 We acknowledge, O L, our wickedness, H3068
22 *art* not thou he, O L our God? therefore H3068
15: 1 Then said the L unto me, Though H3068
2 Thus saith the L; Such as *are* for death, H3068
3 kinds, saith the L: the sword to slay, H3068
6 Thou hast forsaken me, saith the L, H3068
9 sword before their enemies, saith the L. H3068
11 The L said, Verily it shall be well with H3068
15 O L, thou knowest: remember me, and H3068
16 called by thy name, O L God of hosts. H3068
19 Therefore thus saith the L, If thou H3068
20 thee and to deliver thee, saith the L. H3068
16: 1 The word of the L came also unto me, H3068
3 For thus saith the L concerning the H3068
5 For thus saith the L, Enter not into the H3068
5 the L, *even* lovingkindness and mercies. H3068
9 For thus saith the L of hosts, the God of H3068
10 hath the L pronounced all this H3068
10 have committed against the L our God? H3068
11 me, saith the L, and have walked after H3068
14 come, saith the L, that it shall no more H3068
14 no more be said, The L liveth, that H3068
15 But, The L liveth, that brought up the H3068
16 fishers, saith the L, and they shall fish H3068
19 O L, my strength, and my fortress, and H3068
21 they shall know that my name *is* The L. H3068
17: 5 Thus saith the L; Cursed *be* the man H3068
5 and whose heart departeth from the L. H3068
7 in the L, and whose hope the LORD is. H3068
7 in the LORD, and whose hope the L is. H3068
10 I the L search the heart, *I* try the reins, H3068
13 O L, the hope of Israel, all that forsake H3068
13 the L, the fountain of living waters. H3068
14 Heal me, O L, and I shall be healed; H3068
15 *is* the word of the L? let it come now. H3068
19 Thus said the L unto me; Go and stand H3068
20 ye the word of the L, ye kings of Judah, H3068
21 Thus saith the L; Take heed to H3068
24 unto me, saith the L, to bring in no H3068
26 of praise, unto the house of the L. H3068
18: 1 came to Jeremiah from the L, saying, H3068
5 Then the word of the L came to me, H3068
6 potter? saith the L. Behold, as the clay H3068
11 Thus saith the L; Behold, I frame evil H3068
13 Therefore thus saith the L; Ask ye now H3068
19 Give heed to me, O L, and hearken to H3068
23 Yet, L, thou knowest all their counsel H3068
19: 1 Thus saith the L, Go and get a potter's H3068
3 And say, Hear ye the word of the L, O H3068
3 Thus saith the L of hosts, the God of H3068
6 come, saith the L, that this place shall H3068
11 Thus saith the L of hosts; Even so will H3068
12 this place, saith the L, and to the H3068
14 Tophet, whither the L had sent him to H3068
15 Thus saith the L of hosts, the God of H3068
20: 1 in the house of the L, heard that H3068
2 which *was* by the house of the L. H3068
3 unto him, The L hath not called thy H3068
4 For thus saith the L, Behold, I will make H3068
7 O L, thou hast deceived me, and I was H3068
8 the word of the L was made a reproach H3068
11 But the L *is* with me as a mighty H3068
12 But, O L of hosts, that triest the H3068

Jer 20:13 Sing unto the L, praise ye the LORD: for H3068
13 Sing unto the LORD, praise ye the L: for H3068
16 the cities which the L overthrew, and H3068
21: 1 unto Jeremiah from the L, when king H3068
2 Inquire, I pray thee, of the L for us; for H3068
2 us; if so be that the L will deal with us H3068
4 Thus saith the L God of Israel; Behold, H3068
7 And afterward, saith the L, I will deliver H3068
8 Thus saith the L; Behold, I set before H3068
10 for good, saith the L: it shall be given H3068
11 of Judah, *say*, Hear ye the word of the L; H3068
12 O house of David, thus saith the L; H3068
13 plain, saith the L; which say, Who shall H3068
14 doings, saith the L: and I will kindle a H3068
22: 1 Thus saith the L; Go down to the house H3068
2 And say, Hear the word of the L, O king H3068
3 Thus saith the L; Execute ye judgment H3068
5 myself, saith the L, that this house shall H3068
6 For thus saith the L unto the king's H3068
8 the L done unto this great city? H3068
9 the covenant of the L their God, and H3068
11 For thus saith the L touching Shallum H3068
16 *was* not this to know me? saith the L. H3068
18 Therefore thus saith the L concerning H3068
18 for him, *saying*, Ah l! or, Ah his glory! H113
24 *As* I live, saith the L, though Coniah the H3068
29 earth, earth, hear the word of the L. H3068
30 Thus saith the L, Write ye this man H3068
23: 1 the sheep of my pasture! saith the L. H3068
2 Therefore thus saith the L God of Israel H3068
2 you the evil of your doings, saith the L. H3068
4 shall they be lacking, saith the L. H3068
5 Behold, the days come, saith the L, that H3068
6 called, THE L OUR RIGHTEOUSNESS. H3068
7 come, saith the L, that they shall no H3068
7 shall no more say, The L liveth, which H3068
8 But, The L liveth, which brought up H3068
9 because of the L, and because of the H3068
11 I found their wickedness, saith the L. H3068
12 the year of their visitation, saith the L. H3068
15 Therefore thus saith the L of hosts H3068
16 Thus saith the L of hosts, Hearken not H3068
16 *and* not out of the mouth of the L. H3068
17 despise me, The L hath said, Ye shall H3068
18 the counsel of the L, and hath perceived H3068
19 Behold, a whirlwind of the L is gone H3068
20 The anger of the L shall not return, H3068
23 *Am* I a God at hand, saith the L, and H3068
24 see him? saith the L. Do not I fill heaven H3068
24 not I fill heaven and earth? saith the L. H3068
28 *is* the chaff to the wheat? saith the L. H3068
29 as a fire? saith the L; and like a hammer H3068
30 saith the L, that steal my words H3068
31 saith the L, that use their tongues, H3068
32 dreams, saith the L, and do tell them, H3068
32 not profit this people at all, saith the L. H3068
33 the burden of the L? thou shalt then say H3068
33 I will even forsake you, saith the L. H3068
34 The burden of the L, I will even punish H3068
35 What hath the L answered? and, What H3068
35 and, What hath the L spoken? H3068
36 And the burden of the L shall ye H3068
36 living God, of the L of hosts our God. H3068
37 What hath the L answered thee? and, H3068
37 thee? and, What hath the L spoken? H3068
38 But since ye say, The burden of the L; H3068
38 thus saith the L; Because ye say this H3068
38 The burden of the L, and I have sent H3068
38 Ye shall not say, The burden of the L; H3068
24: 1 The L shewed me, and, behold, two H3068
1 before the temple of the L, after that H3068
3 Then said the L unto me, What seest H3068
4 Again the word of the L came unto me, H3068
5 Thus saith the L, the God of Israel; Like H3068
7 me, that I *am* the L: and they shall be H3068
8 thus saith the L, So will I give Zedekiah H3068
25: 3 the word of the L hath come unto me, H3068
4 And the L hath sent unto you all his H3068
5 the land that the L hath given unto you H3068
7 unto me, saith the L; that ye might H3068
8 Therefore thus saith the L of hosts; H3068
9 north, saith the L, and Nebuchadrezzar H3068
12 nation, saith the L, for their iniquity, H3068
15 For thus saith the L God of Israel unto H3068
17 drink, unto whom the L had sent me: H3068
27 Thus saith the L of hosts, the God of H3068
28 the L of hosts; Ye shall certainly drink. H3068
29 of the earth, saith the L of hosts. H3068
30 unto them, The L shall roar from on H3068

Jer 25:31 the earth; for the L hath a controversy H3068
31 *are* wicked to the sword, saith the L. H3068
32 Thus saith the L of hosts, Behold, evil H3068
33 And the slain of the L shall be at that H3068
36 for the L hath spoiled their pasture. H3068
37 because of the fierce anger of the L. H3068
26: 1 came this word from the L, saying, H3068
2 Thus saith the L; Stand in the court of H3068
4 Thus saith the L; If ye will not hearken H3068
7 these words in the house of the L. H3068
8 all that the L had commanded *him* H3068
9 in the name of the L, saying, This house H3068
9 against Jeremiah in the house of the L. H3068
10 the house of the L, and sat down in the H3068
12 saying, The L sent me to prophesy H3068
13 the voice of the L your God; and the H3068
13 your God; and the L will repent him of H3068
15 for of a truth the L hath sent me unto H3068
16 to us in the name of the L our God. H3068
18 Thus saith the L of hosts; Zion shall H3068
19 did he not fear the L, and besought the H3068
19 and besought the L, and the LORD H3068
19 LORD, and the L repented him of the H3068
20 in the name of the L, Urijah the son of H3068
27: 1 word unto Jeremiah from the L, saying, H3068
2 Thus saith the L to me; Make thee H3068
4 Thus saith the L of hosts, the God of H3068
8 I punish, saith the L, with the sword, H3068
11 land, saith the L; and they shall till it, H3068
13 the pestilence, as the L hath spoken H3068
15 For I have not sent them, saith the L, H3068
16 Thus saith the L; Hearken not to the H3068
18 if the word of the L be with them, let H3068
18 intercession to the L of hosts, that the H3068
18 in the house of the L, and *in* the house H3068
19 For thus saith the L of hosts H3068
21 Yea, thus saith the L of hosts, the God H3068
21 *in* the house of the L, and *in* the house H3068
22 them, saith the L; then will I bring them H3068
28: 1 in the house of the L, in the presence of H3068
2 Thus speaketh the L of hosts, the God H3068
4 Babylon, saith the L: for I will break the H3068
5 people that stood in the house of the L, H3068
6 said, Amen: the L do so: the LORD H3068
6 LORD do so: the L perform thy words H3068
9 known, that the L hath truly sent him. H3068
11 Thus saith the L; Even so will I break H3068
12 Then the word of the L came unto H3068
13 Thus saith the L; Thou hast broken the H3068
14 For thus saith the L of hosts, the God of H3068
15 Hananiah; The L hath not sent thee; H3068
16 Therefore thus saith the L; Behold, I will H3068
16 thou hast taught rebellion against the L. H3068
29: 4 Thus saith the L of hosts, the God of H3068
7 and pray unto the L for it: for in the H3068
8 For thus saith the L of hosts, the God of H3068
9 name: I have not sent them, saith the L. H3068
10 For thus saith the L, That after seventy H3068
11 you, saith the L, thoughts of peace, and H3068
14 And I will be found of you, saith the L: H3068
14 you, saith the L; and I will bring you H3068
15 Because ye have said, The L hath H3068
16 *Know* that thus saith the L of the king H3068
17 Thus saith the L of hosts; Behold, I will H3068
19 my words, saith the L, which I sent unto H3068
19 but ye would not hear, saith the L. H3068
20 Hear ye therefore the word of the L, all H3068
21 Thus saith the L of hosts, the God of H3068
22 saying, The L make thee like Zedekiah H3068
23 I know, and *am* a witness, saith the L. H3068
25 Thus speaketh the L of hosts, the God H3068
26 The L hath made thee priest in the H3068
26 in the house of the L, for every man *that* H3068
30 Then came the word of the L unto H3068
31 Thus saith the L concerning Shemaiah H3068
32 Therefore thus saith the L; Behold, I will H3068
32 my people, saith the L; because he hath H3068
32 he hath taught rebellion against the L. H3068
30: 1 came to Jeremiah from the L, saying, H3068
2 Thus speaketh the L God of Israel, H3068
3 For, lo, the days come, saith the L, that H3068
3 and Judah, saith the L: and I will cause H3068
4 And these *are* the words that the L H3068
5 For thus saith the L; We have heard a H3068
8 that day, saith the L of hosts, *that* I will H3068
9 But they shall serve the L their God, H3068
10 Jacob, saith the L; neither be dismayed, H3068
11 For I *am* with thee, saith the L, to save H3068
12 For thus saith the L, Thy bruise *is* H3068

Jer 30:17 wounds, saith the L; because they called H3068
18 Thus saith the L; Behold, I will bring H3068
21 heart to approach unto me? saith the L. H3068
23 Behold, the whirlwind of the L goeth H3068
24 The fierce anger of the L shall not H3068
31: 1 At the same time, saith the L, will I be H3068
2 Thus saith the L, The people *which* H3068
3 The L hath appeared of old unto me, H3068
6 let us go up to Zion unto the L our God. H3068
7 For thus saith the L; Sing with gladness H3068
7 ye, and say, O L, save thy people, the H3068
10 Hear the word of the L, O ye nations, H3068
11 For the L hath redeemed Jacob, and H3068
12 goodness of the L, for wheat, and for H3068
14 satisfied with my goodness, saith the L. H3068
15 Thus saith the L; A voice was heard in H3068
16 Thus saith the L; Refrain thy voice from H3068
16 saith the L; and they shall come H3068
17 end, saith the L, that thy children shall H3068
18 be turned; for thou *art* the L my God. H3068
20 have mercy upon him, saith the L. H3068
22 daughter? for the L hath created a new H3068
23 Thus saith the L of hosts, the God of H3068
23 their captivity; The L bless thee, O H3068
27 Behold, the days come, saith the L, that H3068
28 them, to build, and to plant, saith the L. H3068
31 Behold, the days come, saith the L, that H3068
32 was an husband unto them, saith the L: H3068
33 days, saith the L, I will put my law in H3068
34 saying, Know the L: for they shall all H3068
34 of them, saith the L: for I will forgive H3068
35 Thus saith the L, which giveth the sun H3068
35 roar; The L of hosts *is* his name: H3068
36 me, saith the L, *then* the seed of Israel H3068
37 Thus saith the L; If heaven above can H3068
37 for all that they have done, saith the L. H3068
38 Behold, the days come, saith the L, that H3068
38 shall be built to the L from the tower of H3068
40 *shall be* holy unto the L; it shall not be H3068
32: 1 Jeremiah from the L in the tenth year H3068
3 Thus saith the L, Behold, I will give this H3068
5 him, saith the L: though ye fight with H3068
6 And Jeremiah said, The word of the L H3068
8 to the word of the L, and said unto me, H3068
8 I knew that this *was* the word of the L. H3068
14 Thus saith the L of hosts, the God of H3068
15 For thus saith the L of hosts, the God of H3068
16 of Neriah, I prayed unto the L, saying, H3068
17 Ah L GOD! behold, thou hast made the H136
18 Mighty God, the L of hosts, *is* his name, H3068
25 And thou hast said unto me, O L GOD, H136
26 Then came the word of the L unto H3068
27 Behold, I *am* the L, the God of all flesh: H3068
28 Therefore thus saith the L; Behold, I will H3068
30 the work of their hands, saith the L. H3068
36 And now therefore thus saith the L, the H3068
42 For thus saith the L; Like as I have H3068
44 their captivity to return, saith the L. H3068
33: 1 Moreover the word of the L came unto H3068
2 Thus saith the L the maker thereof, the H3068
2 maker thereof, the L that formed it, to H3068
2 it, to establish it; the L *is* his name; H3068
4 For thus saith the L, the God of Israel, H3068
10 Thus saith the L; Again there shall be H3068
11 say, Praise the L of hosts: for the LORD H3068
11 of hosts: for the L *is* good; for his mercy H3068
11 the house of the L. For I will cause to H3068
11 of the land, as at the first, saith the L. H3068
12 Thus saith the L of hosts; Again in this H3068
13 of him that telleth *them*, saith the L. H3068
14 Behold, the days come, saith the L, that H3068
16 be called, The L our righteousness. H3068
17 For thus saith the L; David shall never H3068
19 And the word of the L came unto H3068
20 Thus saith the L; If ye can break my H3068
23 Moreover the word of the L came to H3068
24 families which the L hath chosen, he H3068
25 Thus saith the L; If my covenant *be* not H3068
34: 1 unto Jeremiah from the L, when H3068
2 Thus saith the L, the God of Israel; Go H3068
2 Thus saith the L; Behold, I will give this H3068
4 Yet hear the word of the L, O Zedekiah H3068
4 Thus saith the L of thee, Thou shalt H3068
5 thee, *saying*, Ah l! for I have pronounced H113
5 have pronounced the word, saith the L. H3068
8 Jeremiah from the L, after that the king H3068
12 Therefore the word of the L came to H3068
12 came to Jeremiah from the L, saying, H3068
13 Thus saith the L, the God of Israel; I H3068

Jer 34:17 Therefore thus saith the L; Ye have not H3068
17 for you, saith the L, to the sword, to the H3068
22 Behold, I will command, saith the L, H3068
35: 1 unto Jeremiah from the L in the days of H3068
2 into the house of the L, into one of the H3068
4 the house of the L, into the chamber of H3068
12 Then came the word of the L unto H3068
13 Thus saith the L of hosts, the God of H3068
13 to hearken to my words? saith the L. H3068
17 Therefore thus saith the L God of hosts, H3068
18 Thus saith the L of hosts, the God of H3068
19 Therefore thus saith the L of hosts, the H3068
36: 1 came unto Jeremiah from the L, saying, H3068
4 all the words of the L, which he had H3068
5 up; I cannot go into the house of the L: H3068
6 the words of the L in the ears of the H3068
7 before the L, and will return every H3068
7 L hath pronounced against this people. H3068
8 words of the L in the LORD'S house. H3068
9 a fast before the L to all the people in H3068
10 in the house of the L, in the chamber of H3068
11 out of the book all the words of the L, H3068
26 the prophet: but the L hid them. H3068
27 Then the word of the L came to H3068
29 Thus saith the L; Thou hast burned this H3068
30 Therefore thus saith the L of Jehoiakim H3068
37: 2 the words of the L, which he spake by H3068
3 Pray now unto the L our God for us. H3068
6 Then came the word of the L unto the H3068
7 Thus saith the L, the God of Israel; Thus H3068
9 Thus saith the L; Deceive not H3068
17 word from the L? And Jeremiah said, H3068
20 Therefore hear now, I pray thee, O my l H113
38: 2 Thus saith the L, He that remaineth in H3068
3 Thus saith the L, This city shall surely H3068
9 My l the king, these men have done evil H113
14 in the house of the L: and the king said H3068
16 saying, *As* the L liveth, that made us H3068
17 Thus saith the L, the God of hosts, the H3068
20 the voice of the L, which I speak unto H3068
21 *is* the word that the L hath shewed me: H3068
39:15 Now the word of the L came unto H3068
16 Thus saith the L of hosts, the God of H3068
17 that day, saith the L: and thou shalt not H3068
18 hast put thy trust in me, saith the L. H3068
40: 1 to Jeremiah from the L, after that H3068
2 said unto him, The L thy God hath H3068
3 Now the L hath brought *it*, and done H3068
3 have sinned against the L, and have not H3068
41: 5 to bring *them* to the house of the L. H3068
42: 2 for us unto the L thy God, *even* for all H3068
3 That the L thy God may shew us the H3068
4 I will pray unto the L your God H3068
4 thing the L shall answer you, I H3068
5 Then they said to Jeremiah, The L be a H3068
5 the L thy God shall send thee to us. H3068
6 the voice of the L our God, to whom we H3068
6 we obey the voice of the L our God. H3068
7 the word of the L came unto Jeremiah. H3068
9 And said unto them, Thus saith the L, H3068
11 of him, saith the L: for I *am* with you to H3068
13 obey the voice of the L your God, H3068
15 the word of the L, ye remnant of Judah; H3068
15 Thus saith the L of hosts, the God of H3068
18 For thus saith the L of hosts, the God of H3068
19 The L hath said concerning you, O ye H3068
20 ye sent me unto the L your God, saying, H3068
20 Pray for us unto the L our God; and H3068
20 unto all that the L our God shall say, so H3068
21 the voice of the L your God, nor any H3068
43: 1 the words of the L their God, for which H3068
1 God, for which the L their God had sent H3068
2 falsely: the L our God hath not sent H3068
4 of the L, to dwell in the land of Judah. H3068
7 L: thus came they *even* to Tahpanhes. H3068
8 Then came the word of the L unto H3068
10 And say unto them, Thus saith the L of H3068
44: 2 Thus saith the L of hosts, the God of H3068
7 Therefore now thus saith the L, the God H3068
11 Therefore thus saith the L of hosts, the H3068
16 of the L, we will not hearken unto thee. H3068
21 the land, did not the L remember them, H3068
22 So that the L could no longer bear, H3068
23 have sinned against the L, and have not H3068
23 the voice of the L, nor walked in his law, H3068
24 the word of the L, all Judah that *are* in H3068
25 Thus saith the L of hosts, the God of H3068
26 Therefore hear ye the word of the L, all H3068
26 name, saith the L, that my name shall H3068

Jer 44:26 land of Egypt, saying, The L GOD liveth. H136
29 you, saith the L, that I will punish you H3068
30 Thus saith the L; Behold, I will give H3068
45: 2 Thus saith the L, the God of Israel, unto H3068
3 is me now! for the L hath added grief to H3068
4 Thus shalt thou say unto him, The L H3068
5 all flesh, saith the L: but thy life will I H3068
46: 1 The word of the L which came to H3068
5 *for* fear *was* round about, saith the L. H3068
10 For this *is* the day of the L GOD of hosts, H136
10 their blood: for the L GOD of hosts hath H136
13 The word that the L spake to Jeremiah H3068
15 not, because the L did drive them. H3068
18 whose name *is* the L of hosts, Surely as H3068
23 forest, saith the L, though it cannot be H3068
25 The L of hosts, the God of Israel, saith; H3068
26 as in the days of old, saith the L. H3068
28 servant, saith the L: for I *am* with thee; H3068
47: 1 The word of the L that came to H3068
2 Thus saith the L; Behold, waters rise up H3068
4 that remaineth: for the L will spoil the H3068
6 O thou sword of the L, how long *will it* H3068
7 How can it be quiet, seeing the L hath H3068
48: 1 Against Moab thus saith the L of hosts, H3068
8 be destroyed, as the L hath spoken. H3068
10 doeth the work of the L deceitfully, and H3068
12 come, saith the L, that I will send unto H3068
15 the King, whose name *is* the L of hosts. H3068
25 off, and his arm is broken, saith the L. H3068
26 against the L: Moab also shall wallow H3068
30 I know his wrath, saith the L; but *it* H3068
35 in Moab, saith the L, him that offereth H3068
38 wherein *is* no pleasure, saith the L. H3068
40 For thus saith the L; Behold, he shall fly H3068
42 hath magnified *himself* against the L. H3068
43 thee, O inhabitant of Moab, saith the L. H3068
44 the year of their visitation, saith the L. H3068
47 L. Thus far *is* the judgment of Moab. H3068
49: 1 thus saith the L; Hath Israel no sons? H3068
2 come, saith the L, that I will cause an H3068
2 them that were his heirs, saith the L. H3068
5 thee, saith the L GOD of hosts, from all H136
6 of the children of Ammon, saith the L. H3068
7 Concerning Edom, thus saith the L of H3068
12 For thus saith the L; Behold, they whose H3068
13 For I have sworn by myself, saith the L, H3068
14 I have heard a rumour from the L, and H3068
16 thee down from thence, saith the L. H3068
18 thereof, saith the L, no man shall abide H3068
20 Therefore hear the counsel of the L, that H3068
26 cut off in that day, saith the L of hosts. H3068
28 thus saith the L; Arise ye, go up to H3068
30 inhabitants of Hazor, saith the L; for H3068
31 care, saith the L, which have neither H3068
32 from all sides thereof, saith the L. H3068
34 The word of the L that came to H3068
35 Thus saith the L of hosts; Behold, I will H3068
37 anger, saith the L; and I will send the H3068
38 the king and the princes, saith the L. H3068
39 again the captivity of Elam, saith the L. H3068
50: 1 The word that the L spake against H3068
4 time, saith the L, the children of Israel H3068
4 they shall go, and seek the L their God. H3068
5 join ourselves to the L in a perpetual H3068
7 sinned against the L, the habitation of H3068
7 even the L, the hope of their fathers. H3068
10 spoil her shall be satisfied, saith the L. H3068
13 Because of the wrath of the L it shall H3068
14 for she hath sinned against the L. H3068
15 the vengeance of the L: take vengeance H3068
18 Therefore thus saith the L of hosts, the H3068
20 time, saith the L, the iniquity of Israel H3068
21 them, saith the L, and do according to H3068
24 because thou hast striven against the L. H3068
25 The L hath opened his armoury, and H3068
25 *is* the work of the L GOD of hosts in the H136
28 L our God, the vengeance of his temple. H3068
29 the L, against the Holy One of Israel. H3068
30 shall be cut off in that day, saith the L. H3068
31 proud, saith the L GOD of hosts: for thy H136
33 Thus saith the L of hosts; The children H3068
34 Their Redeemer *is* strong; the L of H3068
35 saith the L, and upon the inhabitants H3068
40 thereof, saith the L; *so* shall no man H3068
45 Therefore hear ye the counsel of the L, H3068
51: 1 Thus saith the L; Behold, I will raise up H3068
5 of his God, of the L of hosts; though H3068
10 The L hath brought forth our H3068
10 in Zion the work of the L our God. H3068

Jer 51:11 the shields: the L hath raised up the H3068
11 of the L, the vengeance of his temple. H3068
12 ambushes: for the L hath both devised H3068
14 The L of hosts hath sworn by himself, H3068
19 inheritance: the L of hosts *is* his name. H3068
24 done in Zion in your sight, saith the L. H3068
25 saith the L, which destroyest all H3068
26 shalt be desolate for ever, saith the L. H3068
29 purpose of the L shall be performed H3068
33 For thus saith the L of hosts, the God of H3068
36 Therefore thus saith the L; Behold, I will H3068
39 sleep, and not wake, saith the L. H3068
45 his soul from the fierce anger of the L. H3068
48 unto her from the north, saith the L. H3068
50 still: remember the L afar off, and let H3068
52 days come, saith the L, that I will do H3068
53 spoilers come unto her, saith the L. H3068
55 Because the L hath spoiled Babylon, H3068
56 bows is broken: for the L God of H3068
57 the King, whose name *is* the L of hosts. H3068
58 Thus saith the L of hosts; The broad H3068
62 Then shalt thou say, O L, thou hast H3068
52: 2 in the eyes of the L, according to all that H3068
3 For through the anger of the L it came H3068
13 And burned the house of the L, and the H3068
17 in the house of the L, and the bases, and H3068
17 *was* in the house of the L, the Chaldeans H3068
20 in the house of the L: the brass of all H3068
Lam 1: 5 prosper; for the L hath afflicted her for H3068
9 no comforter. O L, behold my affliction: H3068
11 O L, and consider; for I am become vile. H3068
12 me, wherewith the L hath afflicted *me* H3068
14 strength to fall, the L hath delivered me H136
15 The L hath trodden under foot all my H136
15 my young men: the L hath trodden the H136
17 to comfort her: the L hath commanded H3068
18 The L is righteous; for I have rebelled H3068
20 Behold, O L; for I *am* in distress: my H3068
2: 1 How hath the L covered the daughter of H136
2 The L hath swallowed up all the H136
5 The L was as an enemy: he hath H136
6 of the assembly: the L hath caused the H3068
7 The L hath cast off his altar, he hath H136
7 of the L, as in the day of a solemn feast. H3068
8 The L hath purposed to destroy the H3068
9 prophets also find no vision from the L. H3068
17 The L hath done *that* which he had H3068
18 Their heart cried unto the L, O wall of the H136
19 the face of the L: lift up thy hands toward H136
20 Behold, O L, and consider to whom H3068
20 be slain in the sanctuary of the L? H136
3:18 and my hope is perished from the L: H3068
24 The L *is* my portion, saith my soul; H3068
25 The L *is* good unto them that wait for H3068
26 quietly wait for the salvation of the L. H3068
31 For the L will not cast off for ever: H136
36 To subvert a man in his cause, the L H136
37 to pass, *when* the L commandeth *it* not? H136
40 try our ways, and turn again to the L. H3068
50 Till the L look down, and behold from H3068
55 I called upon thy name, O L, out of the H3068
58 O L, thou hast pleaded the causes of my H136
59 O L, thou hast seen my wrong: judge H3068
61 Thou hast heard their reproach, O L, H3068
64 Render unto them a recompence, O L, H3068
66 anger from under the heavens of the L. H3068
4:11 The L hath accomplished his fury; he H3068
16 The anger of the L hath divided them; H3068
20 the anointed of the L, was taken in their H3068
5: 1 Remember, O L, what is come upon us: H3068
19 Thou, O L, remainest for ever; thy H3068
21 Turn thou us unto thee, O L, and we H3068
Ezk 1: 3 The word of the L came expressly unto H3068
3 the hand of the L was there upon him. H3068
28 of the glory of the L. And when I saw *it*, H3068
2: 4 say unto them, Thus saith the L GOD. H136
3:11 Thus saith the L GOD; whether they will H136
12 *be* the glory of the L from his place. H3068
14 the hand of the L was strong upon me. H3068
16 word of the L came unto me, saying, H3068
22 And the hand of the L was there upon H3068
23 the glory of the L stood there, as the H3068
27 Thus saith the L GOD; He that heareth, H136
4:13 And the L said, Even thus shall the H3068
14 Then said I, Ah L GOD! behold, my soul H136
5: 5 Thus saith the L GOD; This *is* Jerusalem: H136
7 Therefore thus saith the L GOD; Because H136
8 Therefore thus saith the L GOD; Behold, H136
11 Wherefore, *as* I live, saith the L GOD; H136

Ezk 5:13 know that I the L have spoken *it* in my H3068
15 furious rebukes. I the L have spoken *it*. H3068
17 upon thee. I the L have spoken *it*. H3068
6: 1 And the word of the L came unto me, H3068
3 the word of the L GOD; Thus saith the H136
3 Thus saith the L GOD to the mountains, H136
7 you, and ye shall know that I *am* the L. H3068
10 And they shall know that I *am* the L, H3068
11 Thus saith the L GOD; Smite with thine H136
13 Then shall ye know that I *am* the L, H3068
14 and they shall know that I *am* the L. H3068
7: 1 Moreover the word of the L came unto H3068
2 Also, thou son of man, thus saith the L H136
4 thee: and ye shall know that I *am* the L. H3068
5 Thus saith the L GOD; An evil, an only H136
9 know that I *am* the L that smiteth. H3068
19 day of the wrath of the L: they shall not H3068
27 and they shall know that I *am* the L. H3068
8: 1 hand of the L GOD fell there upon me. H136
12 for they say, The L seeth us not; the H3068
12 us not; the L hath forsaken the earth. H3068
16 the temple of the L, between the porch H3068
16 the temple of the L, and their faces H3068
9: 4 And the L said unto him, Go through H3068
8 and cried, and said, Ah L GOD! wilt thou H136
9 for they say, The L hath forsaken the H3068
9 forsaken the earth, and the L seeth not. H3068
10: 4 Then the glory of the L went up from H3068
18 Then the glory of the L departed from H3068
11: 5 And the Spirit of the L fell upon me, H3068
5 Thus saith the L; Thus have ye said, O H3068
7 Therefore thus saith the L GOD; Your H136
8 a sword upon you, saith the L GOD. H136
10 and ye shall know that I *am* the L. H3068
12 And ye shall know that I *am* the L: for H3068
13 voice, and said, Ah L GOD! wilt thou H136
14 Again the word of the L came unto me, H3068
15 you far from the L: unto us is this land H3068
16 Therefore say, Thus saith the L GOD; H136
17 Therefore say, Thus saith the L GOD; I H136
21 upon their own heads, saith the L GOD. H136
23 And the glory of the L went up from the H3068
25 the things that the L had shewed me. H3068
12: 1 The word of the L also came unto me, H3068
8 the word of the L unto me, saying, H3068
10 Say thou unto them, Thus saith the L H136
15 And they shall know that I *am* the L, H3068
16 and they shall know that I *am* the L. H3068
17 Moreover the word of the L came to H3068
19 Thus saith the L GOD of the inhabitants H136
20 and ye shall know that I *am* the L. H3068
21 And the word of the L came unto me, H3068
23 Tell them therefore, Thus saith the L H136
25 For I *am* the L: I will speak, and the H3068
25 and will perform it, saith the L GOD. H136
26 Again the word of the L came to me, H3068
28 Thus saith the L GOD; There shall none H136
28 spoken shall be done, saith the L GOD. H136
13: 1 And the word of the L came unto me, H3068
2 own hearts, Hear ye the word of the L; H3068
3 Thus saith the L GOD; Woe unto the H136
5 to stand in the battle in the day of the L. H3068
6 saying, The L saith: and the LORD H3068
6 saith: and the L hath not sent them: H3068
7 The L saith *it*; albeit I have not spoken? H3068
8 Therefore thus saith the L GOD; Because H136
8 I *am* against you, saith the L GOD. H136
9 and ye shall know that I *am* the L GOD. H136
13 Therefore thus saith the L GOD; I will H136
14 and ye shall know that I *am* the L. H3068
16 and *there is* no peace, saith the L GOD. H136
18 And say, Thus saith the L GOD; Woe to H136
20 Wherefore thus saith the L GOD; Behold, H136
21 and ye shall know that I *am* the L. H3068
23 and ye shall know that I *am* the L. H3068
14: 2 And the word of the L came unto me, H3068
4 Thus saith the L GOD; Every man of H136
4 to the prophet; I the L will answer him H3068
6 Thus saith the L GOD; Repent, and turn H136
7 me; I the L will answer him by myself: H3068
8 and ye shall know that I *am* the L. H3068
9 a thing, I the L have deceived that H3068
11 and I may be their God, saith the L GOD. H136
12 The word of the L came again to me, H3068
14 by their righteousness, saith the L GOD. H136
16 it, *as* I live, saith the L GOD, they shall H136
18 it, *as* I live, saith the L GOD, they shall H136
20 it, *as* I live, saith the L GOD, they shall H136
21 For thus saith the L GOD; How much H136

Ezk 14:23 that I have done in it, saith the L GOD. H136
15: 1 And the word of the L came unto me, H3068
6 Therefore thus saith the L GOD; As the H136
7 the L, when I set my face against them. H3068
8 committed a trespass, saith the L GOD. H136
16: 1 Again the word of the L came unto me, H3068
3 And say, Thus saith the L GOD unto H136
8 the L GOD, and thou becamest mine. H136
14 I had put upon thee, saith the L GOD. H136
19 savour: and *thus* it was, saith the L GOD. H136
23 (woe, woe unto thee! saith the L GOD;) H136
30 How weak is thine heart, saith the L H136
35 O harlot, hear the word of the L: H3068
36 Thus saith the L GOD; Because thy H136
43 head, saith the L GOD: and thou shalt H136
48 *As* I live, saith the L GOD, Sodom thy H136
58 and thine abominations, saith the L. H3068
59 For thus saith the L GOD; I will even deal H136
62 and thou shalt know that I *am* the L: H3068
63 all that thou hast done, saith the L GOD. H136
17: 1 And the word of the L came unto me, H3068
3 And say, Thus saith the L GOD; A great H136
9 Say thou, Thus saith the L GOD; Shall it H136
11 Moreover the word of the L came unto H3068
16 *As* I live, saith the L GOD, surely in the H136
19 Therefore thus saith the L GOD; *As* I live, H136
21 shall know that I the L have spoken *it*. H3068
22 Thus saith the L GOD; I will also take of H136
24 know that I the L have brought down H3068
24 I the L have spoken and have done *it*. H3068
18: 1 The word of the L came unto me again, H3068
3 *As* I live, saith the L GOD, ye shall not H136
9 just, he shall surely live, saith the L GOD. H136
23 die? saith the L GOD: *and* not that he H136
25 Yet ye say, The way of the L is not equal. H136
29 The way of the L is not equal. O house H136
30 his ways, saith the L GOD. Repent, and H136
32 dieth, saith the L GOD: wherefore turn H136
20: 1 to inquire of the L, and sat before me. H3068
2 Then came the word of the L unto me, H3068
3 Thus saith the L GOD; Are ye come to H136
3 L GOD, I will not be inquired of by you. H136
5 And say unto them, Thus saith the L H136
5 them, saying, I *am* the L your God; H3068
7 the idols of Egypt: I *am* the L your God. H3068
12 that I *am* the L that sanctify them. H3068
19 I *am* the L your God; walk in my H3068
20 ye may know that I *am* the L your God. H3068
26 that they might know that I *am* the L. H3068
27 Thus saith the L GOD; Yet in this your H136
30 Thus saith the L GOD; Are ye polluted H136
31 L GOD, I will not be inquired of by you. H136
33 *As* I live, saith the L GOD, surely with a H136
36 so will I plead with you, saith the L GOD. H136
38 and ye shall know that I *am* the L. H3068
39 thus saith the L GOD; Go ye, serve ye H136
40 of Israel, saith the L GOD, there shall all H136
42 And ye shall know that I *am* the L, H3068
44 And ye shall know that I *am* the L, H3068
44 O ye house of Israel, saith the L GOD. H136
45 Moreover the word of the L came unto H3068
47 the word of the L; Thus saith the Lord H3068
47 Thus saith the L GOD; Behold, I will H136
48 And all flesh shall see that I the L have H3068
49 Then said I, Ah L GOD! they say of me, H136
21: 1 And the word of the L came unto me, H3068
3 Thus saith the L; Behold, I *am* against H3068
5 That all flesh may know that I the L H3068
7 be brought to pass, saith the L GOD. H136
8 Again the word of the L came unto me, H3068
9 Thus saith the L; Say, A sword, a sword H3068
13 it shall be no *more*, saith the L GOD. H136
17 my fury to rest: I the L have said *it*. H3068
18 The word of the L came unto me again, H3068
24 Therefore thus saith the L GOD; Because H136
26 Thus saith the L GOD; Remove the H136
28 say, Thus saith the L GOD concerning H136
32 remembered: for I the L have spoken *it*. H3068
22: 1 Moreover the word of the L came unto H3068
3 Then say thou, Thus saith the L GOD, H136
12 and hast forgotten me, saith the L GOD. H136
14 I the L have spoken *it*, and will do *it*. H3068
16 and thou shalt know that I *am* the L. H3068
17 And the word of the L came unto me, H3068
19 Therefore thus saith the L GOD; Because H136
22 L have poured out my fury upon you. H3068
23 And the word of the L came unto me, H3068
28 Thus saith the L GOD, when the LORD H136
28 GOD, when the L hath not spoken. H3068

Ezk 22:31 upon their heads, saith the L GOD. H136
23: 1 The word of the L came again unto me, H3068
22 Therefore, O Aholibah, thus saith the L H136
28 For thus saith the L GOD; Behold, I will H136
32 Thus saith the L GOD; Thou shalt drink H136
34 for I have spoken *it*, saith the L GOD. H136
35 Therefore thus saith the L GOD; Because H136
36 The L said moreover unto me; Son of H3068
46 For thus saith the L GOD; I will bring up H136
49 and ye shall know that I *am* the L GOD. H136
24: 1 word of the L came unto me, saying, H3068
3 Thus saith the L GOD; Set on a pot, set H136
6 Wherefore thus saith the L GOD; Woe to H136
9 Therefore thus saith the L GOD; Woe to H136
14 I the L have spoken *it*: it shall come to H3068
14 shall they judge thee, saith the L GOD. H136
15 Also the word of the L came unto me, H3068
20 word of the L came unto me, saying, H3068
21 Thus saith the L GOD; Behold, I will H136
24 ye shall know that I *am* the L GOD. H136
27 and they shall know that I *am* the L. H3068
25: 1 The word of the L came again unto me, H3068
3 the word of the L GOD; Thus saith the H136
3 Thus saith the L GOD; Because thou H136
5 and ye shall know that I *am* the L. H3068
6 For thus saith the L GOD; Because thou H136
7 and thou shalt know that I *am* the L. H3068
8 Thus saith the L GOD; Because that H136
11 and they shall know that I *am* the L. H3068
12 Thus saith the L GOD; Because that H136
13 Therefore thus saith the L GOD; I will H136
14 know my vengeance, saith the L GOD. H136
15 Thus saith the L GOD; Because the H136
16 Therefore thus saith the L GOD; Behold, H136
17 that I *am* the L, when I shall lay my H3068
26: 1 word of the L came unto me, saying, H3068
3 Therefore thus saith the L GOD; Behold, H136
5 spoken *it*, saith the L GOD: and it shall H136
6 and they shall know that I *am* the L. H3068
7 For thus saith the L GOD; Behold, I will H136
14 L have spoken *it*, saith the Lord GOD. H3068
14 LORD have spoken *it*, saith the L GOD. H136
15 Thus saith the L GOD to Tyrus; Shall not H136
19 For thus saith the L GOD; When I shall H136
21 never be found again, saith the L GOD. H136
27: 1 The word of the L came again unto me, H3068
3 Thus saith the L GOD; O Tyrus, thou H136
28: 1 The word of the L came again unto me, H3068
2 Thus saith the L GOD; Because thine H136
6 Therefore thus saith the L GOD; Because H136
10 for I have spoken *it*, saith the L GOD. H136
11 Moreover the word of the L came unto H3068
12 Thus saith the L GOD; Thou sealest up H136
20 Again the word of the L came unto me, H3068
22 And say, Thus saith the L GOD; Behold, H136
22 know that I *am* the L, when I shall have H3068
23 and they shall know that I *am* the L. H3068
24 they shall know that I *am* the L GOD. H136
25 Thus saith the L GOD; When I shall have H136
26 shall know that I *am* the L their God. H3068
29: 1 word of the L came unto me, saying, H3068
3 Speak, and say, Thus saith the L GOD; H136
6 that I *am* the L, because they have been H3068
8 Therefore thus saith the L GOD; Behold, H136
9 that I *am* the L: because he hath said, H3068
13 Yet thus saith the L GOD; At the end of H136
16 but they shall know that I *am* the L GOD. H136
17 word of the L came unto me, saying, H3068
19 Therefore thus saith the L GOD; Behold, H136
20 they wrought for me, saith the L GOD. H136
21 and they shall know that I *am* the L. H3068
30: 1 The word of the L came again unto me, H3068
2 the L GOD; Howl ye, Woe worth the day! H136
3 the day of the L *is* near, a cloudy day; H3068
6 Thus saith the L; They also that uphold H3068
6 fall in it by the sword, saith the L GOD. H136
8 And they shall know that I *am* the L, H3068
10 Thus saith the L GOD; I will also make H136
12 of strangers: I the L have spoken *it*. H3068
13 Thus saith the L GOD; I will also destroy H136
19 and they shall know that I *am* the L. H3068
20 word of the L came unto me, saying, H3068
22 Therefore thus saith the L GOD; Behold, H136
25 that I *am* the L, when I shall put my H3068
26 and they shall know that I *am* the L. H3068
31: 1 word of the L came unto me, saying, H3068
10 Therefore thus saith the L GOD; Because H136
15 Thus saith the L GOD; In the day when H136
18 and all his multitude, saith the L GOD. H136

Ezk 32: 1 word of the L came unto me, saying, H3068
3 Thus saith the L GOD; I will therefore H136
8 upon thy land, saith the L GOD. H136
11 For thus saith the L GOD; The sword of H136
14 rivers to run like oil, saith the L GOD. H136
15 then shall they know that I am the L. H3068
16 for all her multitude, saith the L GOD. H136
17 word of the L came unto me, saying, H3068
31 slain by the sword, saith the L GOD. H136
32 and all his multitude, saith the L GOD. H136
33: 1 Again the word of the L came unto me, H3068
11 Say unto them, As I live, saith the L H136
17 say, The way of the L is not equal: but as H136
20 Yet ye say, The way of the L is not equal. H136
22 Now the hand of the L was upon me in H3068
23 Then the word of the L came unto me, H3068
25 Thus saith the L GOD; Ye eat with the H136
27 Thus saith the L GOD; As I live, surely H136
29 Then shall they know that I am the L, H3068
30 the word that cometh forth from the L. H3068
34: 1 And the word of the L came unto me, H3068
2 them, Thus saith the L GOD unto the H136
7 ye shepherds, hear the word of the L; H3068
8 As I live, saith the L GOD, surely because H136
9 O ye shepherds, hear the word of the L; H3068
10 Thus saith the L GOD; Behold, I am H136
11 For thus saith the L GOD; Behold, I, even H136
15 cause them to lie down, saith the L GOD. H136
17 thus saith the L GOD; Behold, I judge H136
20 Therefore thus saith the L GOD unto H136
24 And I the L will be their God, and my H3068
24 among them; I the L have spoken it. H3068
27 that I am the L, when I have broken H3068
30 Thus shall they know that I the L their H3068
30 Israel, are my people, saith the L GOD. H136
31 and I am your God, saith the L GOD. H136
35: 1 Moreover the word of the L came unto H3068
3 And say unto it, Thus saith the L GOD; H136
4 and thou shalt know that I am the L. H3068
6 Therefore, as I live, saith the L GOD, I H136
9 and ye shall know that I am the L. H3068
10 will possess it; whereas the L was there: H3068
11 Therefore, as I live, saith the L GOD, I H136
12 And thou shalt know that I am the L, H3068
14 Thus saith the L GOD; When the whole H136
15 it: and they shall know that I am the L. H3068
36: 1 of Israel, hear the word of the L: H3068
2 Thus saith the L GOD; Because the H136
3 say, Thus saith the L GOD; Because they H136
4 the word of the L GOD; Thus saith the H136
4 Thus saith the L GOD to the mountains, H136
5 Therefore thus saith the L GOD; Surely H136
6 Thus saith the L GOD; Behold, I have H136
7 Therefore thus saith the L GOD; I have H136
11 and ye shall know that I am the L. H3068
13 Thus saith the L GOD; Because they say H136
14 thy nations any more, saith the L GOD. H136
15 to fall any more, saith the L GOD. H136
16 Moreover the word of the L came unto H3068
20 L, and are gone forth out of his land. H3068
22 Thus saith the L GOD; I do not this for H136
23 that I am the L, saith the Lord GOD, H3068
23 LORD, saith the L GOD, when I shall be H136
32 Not for your sakes do I this, saith the L H136
33 Thus saith the L GOD; In the day that I H136
36 shall know that I the L build the ruined H3068
36 I the L have spoken it, and I will do it. H3068
37 Thus saith the L GOD; I will yet for this H136
38 and they shall know that I am the L. H3068
37: 1 The hand of the L was upon me, and H3068
1 in the spirit of the L, and set me down H3068
3 I answered, O L GOD, thou knowest. H136
4 O ye dry bones, hear the word of the L. H3068
5 Thus saith the L GOD unto these bones; H136
6 live; and ye shall know that I am the L. H3068
9 Thus saith the L GOD; Come from the H136
12 Thus saith the L GOD; Behold, O my H136
13 And ye shall know that I am the L, H3068
14 ye know that I the L have spoken it, H3068
14 spoken it, and performed it, saith the L. H3068
15 The word of the L came again unto me, H3068
19 Say unto them, Thus saith the L GOD; H136
21 And say unto them, Thus saith the L H136
28 And the heathen shall know that I the L H3068
38: 1 And the word of the L came unto me, H3068
3 And say, Thus saith the L GOD; Behold, H136
10 Thus saith the L GOD; It shall also come H136
14 Thus saith the L GOD; In that day when H136
17 Thus saith the L GOD; Art thou he of H136

Ezk 38:18 of Israel, saith the L GOD, that my fury H136
21 saith the L GOD: every man's sword H136
23 and they shall know that I am the L. H3068
39: 1 say, Thus saith the L GOD; Behold, I am H136
5 for I have spoken it, saith the L GOD. H136
6 and they shall know that I am the L. H3068
7 that I am the L, the Holy One in Israel. H3068
8 it is done, saith the L GOD; this is the H136
10 that robbed them, saith the L GOD. H136
13 that I shall be glorified, saith the L GOD. H136
17 And, thou son of man, thus saith the L H136
20 with all men of war, saith the L GOD. H136
22 L their God from that day and forward. H3068
25 Therefore thus saith the L GOD; Now H136
28 Then shall they know that I am the L H3068
29 the house of Israel, saith the L GOD. H136
40: 1 the hand of the L was upon me, and H3068
46 near to the L to minister unto him. H3068
41:22 me, This is the table that is before the L. H3068
42:13 approach unto the L shall eat the most H3068
43: 4 And the glory of the L came into the H3068
5 the glory of the L filled the house. H3068
18 thus saith the L GOD; These are the H136
19 unto me, saith the L GOD, a young H136
24 And thou shalt offer them before the L, H3068
24 them up for a burnt offering unto the L. H3068
27 and I will accept you, saith the L GOD. H136
44: 2 Then said the L unto me; This gate H3068
2 by it; because the L, the God of Israel, H3068
3 bread before the L; he shall enter by the H3068
4 the glory of the L filled the house of the H3068
4 house of the L: and I fell upon my face. H3068
5 And the L said unto me, Son of man, H3068
5 of the house of the L, and all the laws H3068
6 Thus saith the L GOD; O ye house of H136
9 Thus saith the L GOD; No stranger, H136
12 them, saith the L GOD, and they shall H136
15 the fat and the blood, saith the L GOD: H136
27 offer his sin offering, saith the L GOD. H136
45: 1 oblation unto the L, an holy portion of H3068
4 to minister unto the L: and it shall be a H3068
9 Thus saith the L GOD; Let it suffice you, H136
9 from my people, saith the L GOD. H136
15 reconciliation for them, saith the L GOD. H136
18 Thus saith the L GOD; In the first H136
23 offering to the L, seven bullocks and H3068
46: 1 Thus saith the L GOD; The gate of the H136
3 gate before the L in the sabbaths and H3068
4 offer unto the L in the sabbath day H3068
9 come before the L in the solemn feasts, H3068
12 unto the L, one shall then open H3068
13 offering unto the L of a lamb of the first H3068
14 by a perpetual ordinance unto the L. H3068
16 Thus saith the L GOD; If the prince give H136
47:13 Thus saith the L GOD; This shall be the H136
23 him his inheritance, saith the L GOD. H136
48: 9 offer unto the L shall be of five and H3068
10 of the L shall be in the midst thereof. H3068
14 of the land: for it is holy unto the L. H3068
29 are their portions, saith the L GOD. H136
35 from that day shall be, The L is there. H3068
Dan 1: 2 And the L gave Jehoiakim king of Judah H136
10 Daniel, I fear my l the king, who hath H113
2:10 there is no king, l, nor ruler, that asked H7229
47 God of gods, and a L of kings, and a H4756
4:19 and said, My l, the dream be to them H4756
24 which is come upon my l the king: H4756
5:23 But hast lifted up thyself against the L H4756
9: 2 the word of the L came to Jeremiah the H3068
3 And I set my face unto the L God, to seek H136
4 And I prayed unto the L my God, and H3068
4 and said, O L, the great and dreadful H136
7 O L, righteousness belongeth unto thee, H136
8 O L, to us belongeth confusion of face, to H136
9 To the L our God belong mercies and H136
10 the voice of the L our God, to walk in H3068
13 prayer before the L our God, that we H3068
14 Therefore hath the L watched upon the H3068
14 brought it upon us: for the L our God is H3068
15 And now, O L our God, that hast H136
16 O L, according to all thy righteousness, I H136
19 O L, hear; O Lord, forgive; O Lord, H136
19 O Lord, hear; O L, forgive; O Lord, H136
19 O Lord, hear; O Lord, forgive; O L, H136
20 before the L my God for the holy H3068
10:16 stood before me, O my l, by the vision my H113
17 For how can the servant of this my l talk H113
17 lord talk with this my l? for as for me, H113
19 l speak; for thou hast strengthened me. H113

Dan 12: 8 L, what shall be the end of these things? H113
Hos 1: 1 The word of the L that came unto H3068
2 The beginning of the word of the L by H3068
2 by Hosea. And the L said to Hosea, Go, H3068
2 great whoredom, departing from the L. H3068
4 And the L said unto him, Call his name H3068
7 save them by the L their God, and will H3068
2:13 her lovers, and forgat me, saith the L. H3068
16 And it shall be at that day, saith the L, H3068
20 faithfulness: and thou shalt know the L. H3068
21 I will hear, saith the L, I will hear the H3068
3: 1 Then said the L unto me, Go yet, love a H3068
1 to the love of the L toward the children H3068
5 and seek the L their God, and David H3068
5 L and his goodness in the latter days. H3068
4: 1 Hear the word of the L, ye children of H3068
1 of Israel: for the L hath a controversy H3068
10 they have left off to take heed to the L. H3068
15 to Beth-aven, nor swear, The L liveth. H3068
16 heifer: now the L will feed them as a H3068
5: 4 them, and they have not known the L. H3068
6 herds to seek the L; but they shall not H3068
7 against the L: for they have begotten H3068
6: 1 Come, and let us return unto the L: for H3068
3 on to know the L: his going forth is H3068
7:10 L their God, nor seek him for all this. H3068
8: 1 the house of the L, because they have H3068
13 and eat it; but the L accepteth them H3068
9: 4 offerings to the L, neither shall they be H3068
4 shall not come into the house of the L. H3068
5 day, and in the day of the feast of the L? H3068
14 Give them, O L: what wilt thou give? H3068
10: 3 the L; what then should a king do to us? H3068
12 it is time to seek the L, till he come and H3068
11:10 They shall walk after the L: he shall H3068
11 place them in their houses, saith the L. H3068
12: 2 The L hath also a controversy with H3068
5 Even the L God of hosts; the LORD is H3068
5 Even the LORD God of hosts; the L is H3068
9 And I that am the L thy God from the H3068
13 And by a prophet the L brought Israel H3068
14 his reproach shall his L return unto him. H113
13: 4 Yet I am the L thy God from the land of H3068
15 the wind of the L shall come up from H3068
14: 1 O Israel, return unto the L thy God; for H3068
2 Take with you words, and turn to the L: H3068
9 for the ways of the L are right, and the H3068
Joel 1: 1 The word of the L that came to Joel the H3068
9 from the house of the L; the priests, the H3068
14 L your God, and cry unto the LORD, H3068
14 the LORD your God, and cry unto the L, H3068
15 Alas for the day! for the day of the L is H3068
19 O L, to thee will I cry: for the fire hath H3068
2: 1 of the L cometh, for it is nigh at hand; H3068
11 And the L shall utter his voice before H3068
11 for the day of the L is great and very H3068
12 Therefore also now, saith the L, turn ye H3068
13 and turn unto the L your God: for he is H3068
14 a drink offering unto the L your God? H3068
17 Let the priests, the ministers of the L, H3068
17 thy people, O L, and give not thine H3068
18 Then will the L be jealous for his land, H3068
19 Yea, the L will answer and say unto his H3068
21 rejoice: for the L will do great things. H3068
23 and rejoice in the L your God: for he H3068
26 the name of the L your God, that hath H3068
27 and that I am the L your God, and H3068
31 and the terrible day of the L come. H3068
32 the name of the L shall be delivered: for H3068
32 as the L hath said, and in the H3068
32 in the remnant whom the L shall call. H3068
3: 8 people far off: for the L hath spoken it. H3068
11 thy mighty ones to come down, O L. H3068
14 of the L is near in the valley of decision. H3068
16 The L also shall roar out of Zion, and H3068
16 shake: but the L will be the hope of his H3068
17 So shall ye know that I am the L your H3068
18 L, and shall water the valley of Shittim. H3068
21 cleansed: for the L dwelleth in Zion. H3068
Am 1: 2 And he said, The L will roar from Zion, H3068
3 Thus saith the L; For three H3068
5 go into captivity unto Kir, saith the L. H3068
6 Thus saith the L; For three H3068
8 Philistines shall perish, saith the L GOD. H136
9 Thus saith the L; For three H3068
11 Thus saith the L; For three H3068
13 Thus saith the L; For three H3068
15 he and his princes together, saith the L. H3068
2: 1 Thus saith the L; For three H3068

L

Am 2: 3 princes thereof with him, saith the L. H3068
4 Thus saith the L; For three H3068
4 the law of the L, and have not kept his H3068
6 Thus saith the L; For three H3068
11 thus, O ye children of Israel? saith the L. H3068
16 flee away naked in that day, saith the L. H3068
3: 1 Hear this word that the L hath spoken H3068
6 in a city, and the L hath not done *it*? H3068
7 Surely the L GOD will do nothing, but he H136
8 will not fear? the L GOD hath spoken, H136
10 to do right, saith the L, who store up H3068
11 Therefore thus saith the L GOD; An H136
12 Thus saith the L; As the shepherd H3068
13 Jacob, saith the L GOD, the God of hosts, H136
15 houses shall have an end, saith the L. H3068
4: 2 The L GOD hath sworn by his holiness, H136
3 cast *them* into the palace, saith the L. H3068
5 O ye children of Israel, saith the L GOD. H136
6 ye not returned unto me, saith the L. H3068
8 ye not returned unto me, saith the L. H3068
9 ye not returned unto me, saith the L. H3068
10 ye not returned unto me, saith the L. H3068
11 ye not returned unto me, saith the L. H3068
13 The L, The God of hosts, *is* his name. H3068
5: 3 For thus saith the L GOD; The city that H136
4 For thus saith the L unto the house of H3068
6 Seek the L, and ye shall live; lest he H3068
8 the face of the earth: The L *is* his name: H3068
14 live: and so the L, the God of hosts, shall H3068
15 it may be that the L God of hosts will be H3068
16 Therefore the L, the God of hosts, the H3068
16 God of hosts, the L, saith thus; Wailing H136
17 for I will pass through thee, saith the L. H3068
18 the day of the L! to what end *is* it for H3068
18 day of the L *is* darkness, and not light. H3068
20 *Shall* not the day of the L *be* darkness, H3068
27 the L, whose name *is* The God of hosts. H3068
6: 8 The L GOD hath sworn by himself, saith H136
8 himself, saith the L the God of hosts, I H3068
10 not make mention of the name of the L. H3068
11 For, behold, the L commandeth, and H3068
14 of Israel, saith the L the God of hosts; H3068
7: 1 Thus hath the L GOD shewed unto me; H136
2 the land, then I said, O L GOD, forgive, I H136
3 The L repented for this: It shall not be, H3068
3 for this: It shall not be, saith the L. H3068
4 Thus hath the L GOD shewed unto me: H136
4 me: and, behold, the L GOD called to H136
5 Then said I, O L GOD, cease, I beseech H136
6 The L repented for this: This also shall H3068
6 This also shall not be, saith the L GOD. H136
7 Thus he shewed me: and, behold, the L H136
8 And the L said unto me, Amos, what H3068
8 Then said the L, Behold, I will set a H136
15 And the L took me as I followed the H3068
15 the flock, and the L said unto me, Go, H3068
16 thou the word of the L: Thou sayest, H3068
17 Therefore thus saith the L; Thy wife H3068
8: 1 Thus hath the L GOD shewed unto me: H136
2 Then said the L unto me, The end is H3068
3 that day, saith the L GOD: *there shall be* H136
7 The L hath sworn by the excellency of H3068
9 in that day, saith the L GOD, that I will H136
11 Behold, the days come, saith the L GOD, H136
11 water, but of hearing the words of the L: H3068
12 the word of the L, and shall not find *it*. H3068
9: 1 I saw the L standing upon the altar: and H136
5 And the L GOD of hosts *is* he that H136
6 the face of the earth: The L *is* his name. H3068
7 of Israel? saith the L. Have not I H3068
8 Behold, the eyes of the L GOD *are* upon H136
8 destroy the house of Jacob, saith the L. H3068
12 my name, saith the L that doeth this. H3068
13 Behold, the days come, saith the L, that H3068
15 I have given them, saith the L thy God. H3068
Oba 1 The vision of Obadiah. Thus saith the L H136
1 rumour from the L, and an ambassador H3068
4 will I bring thee down, saith the L. H3068
8 Shall I not in that day, saith the L, even H3068
15 For the day of the L *is* near upon all the H3068
18 house of Esau; for the L hath spoken *it*. H3068
Jna 1: 1 Now the word of the L came unto H3068
3 the presence of the L, and went down to H3068
3 Tarshish from the presence of the L. H3068
4 But the L sent out a great wind into the H3068
9 and I fear the L, the God of heaven, H3068
10 of the L, because he had told them. H3068
14 Wherefore they cried unto the L, and H3068
14 beseech thee, O L, we beseech thee, let H3068
Jna 1:14 thou, O L, hast done as it pleased thee. H3068
16 Then the men feared the L exceedingly, H3068
16 a sacrifice unto the L, and made vows. H3068
17 Now the L had prepared a great fish to H3068
2: 1 Then Jonah prayed unto the L his God H3068
2 affliction unto the L, and he heard me; H3068
6 my life from corruption, O L my God. H3068
7 me I remembered the L: and my prayer H3068
9 that I have vowed. Salvation *is* of the L. H3068
10 And the L spake unto the fish, and it H3068
3: 1 And the word of the L came unto Jonah H3068
3 to the word of the L. Now Nineveh was H3068
4: 2 And he prayed unto the L, and said, I H3068
2 I pray thee, O L, *was* not this my saying, H3068
3 Therefore now, O L, take, I beseech H3068
4 Then said the L, Doest thou well to be H3068
6 And the L God prepared a gourd, and H3068
10 Then said the L, Thou hast had pity on H3068
Mic 1: 1 The word of the L that came to Micah H3068
2 is: and let the L GOD be witness against H136
2 against you, the L from his holy temple. H136
3 For, behold, the L cometh forth out of H3068
12 from the L unto the gate of Jerusalem. H3068
2: 3 Therefore thus saith the L; Behold, H3068
5 cord by lot in the congregation of the L. H3068
7 is the spirit of the L straitened? *are* H3068
13 them, and the L on the head of them. H3068
3: 4 Then shall they cry unto the L, but he H3068
5 Thus saith the L concerning the H3068
8 by the spirit of the L, and of judgment, H3068
11 they lean upon the L, and say, *Is* not the H3068
11 and say, *Is* not the L among us? none H3068
4: 1 mountain of the house of the L shall be H3068
2 mountain of the L, and to the house of H3068
2 and the word of the L from Jerusalem. H3068
4 mouth of the L of hosts hath spoken *it*. H3068
5 of the L our God for ever and ever. H3068
6 In that day, saith the L, will I assemble H3068
7 nation: and the L shall reign over them H3068
10 there the L shall redeem thee from H3068
12 But they know not the thoughts of the L, H3068
13 gain unto the L, and their substance H3068
13 substance unto the L of the whole earth. H113
5: 4 the strength of the L, in the majesty of H3068
4 of the name of the L his God; and they H3068
7 as a dew from the L, as the showers H3068
10 that day, saith the L, that I will cut off H3068
6: 1 Hear ye now what the L saith; Arise, H3068
2 the earth: for the L hath a controversy H3068
5 ye may know the righteousness of the L. H3068
6 Wherewith shall I come before the L, H3068
7 Will the L be pleased with thousands of H3068
8 and what doth the L require of thee, H3068
7: 7 Therefore I will look unto the L; I will H3068
8 the L *shall be* a light unto me. H3068
9 I will bear the indignation of the L, H3068
10 me, Where is the L thy God? mine eyes H3068
17 be afraid of the L our God, and shall H3068
Nah 1: 2 God *is* jealous, and the L revengeth; the H3068
2 revengeth; the L revengeth, and *is* H3068
2 and *is* furious; the L will take H3068
3 The L *is* slow to anger, and great in H3068
3 *the wicked*: the L hath his way in the H3068
7 The L *is* good, a strong hold in the day H3068
9 What do ye imagine against the L? he H3068
11 evil against the L, a wicked counsellor. H3068
12 Thus saith the L; Though *they be* quiet, H3068
14 And the L hath given a commandment H3068
2: 2 For the L hath turned away the H3068
13 Behold, I *am* against thee, saith the L H3068
3: 5 Behold, I *am* against thee, saith the L H3068
Hab 1: 2 O L, how long shall I cry, and thou wilt H3068
12 *Art* thou not from everlasting, O L my H3068
12 One? we shall not die. O L, thou hast H3068
2: 2 And the L answered me, and said, H3068
13 Behold, *is it* not of the L of hosts that H3068
14 of the L, as the waters cover the sea. H3068
20 But the L *is* in his holy temple: let all H3068
3: 2 O L, I have heard thy speech, *and* was H3068
2 *and* was afraid: O L, revive thy work in H3068
8 Was the L displeased against the H3068
18 Yet I will rejoice in the L, I will joy in the H3068
19 The L God *is* my strength, and he will H3069
Zep 1: 1 The word of the L which came unto H3068
2 all *things* from off the land, saith the L. H3068
3 off man from off the land, saith the L. H3068
5 by the L, and that swear by Malcham; H3068
6 back from the L; and *those* that have H3068
6 not sought the L, nor inquired for him. H3068
Zep 1: 7 Hold thy peace at the presence of the L H136
7 for the day of the L *is* at hand: for the H3068
7 *is* at hand: for the L hath prepared a H3068
10 that day, saith the L, *that there shall be* H3068
12 in their heart, The L will not do good, H3068
14 The great day of the L *is* near, *it is* H3068
14 of the day of the L: the mighty man H3068
17 sinned against the L: and their blood H3068
2: 2 fierce anger of the L come upon you, H3068
3 Seek ye the L, all ye meek of the earth, H3068
5 the word of the L *is* against you; O H3068
7 evening: for the L their God shall visit H3068
9 Therefore *as* I live, saith the L of hosts, H3068
10 against the people of the L of hosts. H3068
11 The L *will be* terrible unto them: for he H3068
3: 2 in the L; she drew not near to her God. H3068
5 The just L *is* in the midst thereof; he H3068
8 Therefore wait ye upon me, saith the L, H3068
9 of the L, to serve him with one consent. H3068
12 they shall trust in the name of the L. H3068
15 The L hath taken away thy judgments, H3068
15 of Israel, *even* the L, *is* in the midst of H3068
17 The L thy God in the midst of thee *is* H3068
20 captivity before your eyes, saith the L. H3068
Hag 1: 1 came the word of the L by Haggai the H3068
2 Thus speaketh the L of hosts, saying, H3068
3 Then came the word of the L by Haggai H3068
5 Now therefore thus saith the L of hosts; H3068
7 Thus saith the L of hosts; Consider H3068
8 in it, and I will be glorified, saith the L. H3068
9 it. Why? saith the L of hosts. Because of H3068
12 the voice of the L their God, and the H3068
12 prophet, as the L their God had sent H3068
12 and the people did fear before the L. H3068
13 saying, I *am* with you, saith the L. H3068
14 And the L stirred up the spirit of H3068
14 the house of the L of hosts, their God, H3068
2: 1 of the L by the prophet Haggai, saying, H3068
4 saith the L; and be strong, O Joshua, H3068
4 the land, saith the L, and work: for I *am* H3068
4 for I *am* with you, saith the L of hosts: H3068
6 For thus saith the L of hosts; Yet once, H3068
7 house with glory, saith the L of hosts. H3068
8 the gold *is* mine, saith the L of hosts. H3068
9 former, saith the L of hosts: and in this H3068
9 will I give peace, saith the L of hosts. H3068
10 of the L by Haggai the prophet, saying, H3068
11 Thus saith the L of hosts; Ask now the H3068
14 me, saith the L; and so *is* every work H3068
15 laid upon a stone in the temple of the L: H3068
17 yet ye *turned* not to me, saith the L. H3068
20 And again the word of the L came unto H3068
23 In that day, saith the L of hosts, will I H3068
23 of Shealtiel, saith the L, and will make H3068
23 I have chosen thee, saith the L of hosts. H3068
Zec 1: 1 the word of the L unto Zechariah, the H3068
2 The L hath been sore displeased with H3068
3 Thus saith the L of hosts; Turn ye unto H3068
3 unto me, saith the L of hosts, and I will H3068
3 will turn unto you, saith the L of hosts. H3068
4 Thus saith the L of hosts; Turn ye now H3068
4 hear, nor hearken unto me, saith the L. H3068
6 said, Like as the L of hosts thought to H3068
7 the word of the L unto Zechariah, the H3068
9 Then said I, O my l, what *are* these? And H113
10 *they* whom the L hath sent to walk to H3068
11 And they answered the angel of the L H3068
12 Then the angel of the L answered and H3068
12 and said, O L of hosts, how long wilt H3068
13 And the L answered the angel that H3068
14 Thus saith the L of hosts; I am jealous H3068
16 Therefore thus saith the L; I am H3068
16 in it, saith the L of hosts, and a line H3068
17 Cry yet, saying, Thus saith the L of H3068
17 abroad; and the L shall yet comfort H3068
20 And the L shewed me four carpenters. H3068
2: 5 For I, saith the L, will be unto her a wall H3068
6 north, saith the L: for I have spread you H3068
6 four winds of the heaven, saith the L. H3068
8 For thus saith the L of hosts; After the H3068
9 know that the L of hosts hath sent me. H3068
10 dwell in the midst of thee, saith the L. H3068
11 be joined to the L in that day, and shall H3068
11 the L of hosts hath sent me unto thee. H3068
12 And the L shall inherit Judah his H3068
13 Be silent, O all flesh, before the L: for he H3068
3: 1 the angel of the L, and Satan standing H3068
2 And the L said unto Satan, The LORD H3068
2 And the LORD said unto Satan, The L H3068

Zec 3: 2 O Satan; even the L that hath chosen H3068
5 And the angel of the L stood by. H3068
6 And the angel of the L protested unto H3068
7 Thus saith the L of hosts; If thou wilt H3068
9 thereof, saith the L of hosts, and I will H3068
10 In that day, saith the L of hosts, shall H3068
4: 4 with me, saying, What *are* these, my l? H113
5 not what these be? And I said, No, my l. H113
6 *is* the word of the L unto Zerubbabel, H3068
6 but by my spirit, saith the L of hosts. H3068
8 Moreover the word of the L came unto H3068
9 the L of hosts hath sent me unto you. H3068
10 *are* the eyes of the L, which run to and H3068
13 not what these *be*? And I said, No, my l. H113
14 that stand by the L of the whole earth. H113
5: 4 I will bring it forth, saith the L of hosts, H3068
6: 4 talked with me, What *are* these, my l? H113
5 standing before the L of all the earth. H113
9 And the word of the L came unto me, H3068
12 Thus speaketh the L of hosts, saying, H3068
12 and he shall build the temple of the L: H3068
13 Even he shall build the temple of the L; H3068
14 for a memorial in the temple of the L. H3068
15 the temple of the L, and ye shall know H3068
15 know that the L of hosts hath sent me H3068
15 obey the voice of the L your God. H3068
7: 1 the word of the L came unto Zechariah H3068
2 and their men, to pray before the L, H3068
3 in the house of the L of hosts, and to H3068
4 Then came the word of the L of hosts H3068
7 the words which the L hath cried by the H3068
8 And the word of the L came unto H3068
9 Thus speaketh the L of hosts, saying, H3068
12 words which the L of hosts hath sent in H3068
12 came a great wrath from the L of hosts. H3068
13 I would not hear, saith the L of hosts: H3068
8: 1 Again the word of the L of hosts came H3068
2 Thus saith the L of hosts; I was jealous H3068
3 Thus saith the L; I am returned unto H3068
3 of the L of hosts the holy mountain. H3068
4 Thus saith the L of hosts; There shall H3068
6 Thus saith the L of hosts; If it be H3068
6 in mine eyes? saith the L of hosts. H3068
7 Thus saith the L of hosts; Behold, I will H3068
9 Thus saith the L of hosts; Let your H3068
9 of the house of the L of hosts was laid, H3068
11 in the former days, saith the L of hosts. H3068
14 For thus saith the L of hosts; As I H3068
14 saith the L of hosts, and I repented not: H3068
17 these *are things* that I hate, saith the L. H3068
18 And the word of the L of hosts came H3068
19 Thus saith the L of hosts; The fast of H3068
20 Thus saith the L of hosts; *It shall* yet H3068
21 to pray before the L, and to seek the H3068
21 and to seek the L of hosts: I will go also. H3068
22 shall come to seek the L of hosts in H3068
22 in Jerusalem, and to pray before the L. H3068
23 Thus saith the L of hosts; In those days H3068
9: 1 The burden of the word of the L in the H3068
1 tribes of Israel, *shall be* toward the L. H3068
4 Behold, the L will cast her out, and he H136
14 And the L shall be seen over them, and H3068
14 lightning: and the L GOD shall blow the H136
15 The L of hosts shall defend them; and H3068
16 And the L their God shall save them in H3068
10: 1 Ask ye of the L rain in the time of the H3068
1 latter rain; *so* the L shall make bright H3068
3 the goats: for the L of hosts hath visited H3068
5 fight, because the L *is* with them, and H3068
6 *am* the L their God, and will hear them. H3068
7 glad; their heart shall rejoice in the L. H3068
12 And I will strengthen them in the L; and H3068
12 up and down in his name, saith the L. H3068
11: 4 Thus saith the L my God; Feed the flock H3068
5 Blessed *be* the L; for I am rich: and their H3068
6 of the land, saith the L: but, lo, I will H3068
11 me knew that it *was* the word of the L. H3068
13 And the L said unto me, Cast it unto H3068
13 them to the potter in the house of the L. H3068
15 And the L said unto me, Take unto H3068
12: 1 The burden of the word of the L for H3068
1 for Israel, saith the L, which stretcheth H3068
4 In that day, saith the L, I will smite H3068
5 my strength in the L of hosts their God. H3068
7 The L also shall save the tents of Judah H3068
8 In that day shall the L defend the H3068
8 God, as the angel of the L before them. H3068
13: 2 that day, saith the L of hosts, *that* I will H3068
3 in the name of the L: and his father and H3068

Zec 13: 7 fellow, saith the L of hosts: smite the H3068
8 the land, saith the L, two parts therein H3068
9 and they shall say, The L *is* my God. H3068
14: 1 Behold, the day of the L cometh, and H3068
3 Then shall the L go forth, and fight H3068
5 of Judah: and the L my God shall come, H3068
7 be known to the L, not day, nor night: H3068
9 And the L shall be king over all the H3068
9 shall there be one L, and his name one. H3068
12 wherewith the L will smite all the H3068
13 great tumult from the L shall be among H3068
16 the King, the L of hosts, and to keep H3068
17 the King, the L of hosts, even upon H3068
18 wherewith the L will smite the heathen H3068
20 UNTO THE L; and the pots in the H3068
21 be holiness unto the L of hosts: and all H3068
21 in the house of the L of hosts. H3068
Mal 1: 1 The burden of the word of the L to H3068
2 I have loved you, saith the L. Yet ye say, H3068
2 brother? saith the L: yet I loved Jacob, H3068
4 thus saith the L of hosts, They shall H3068
4 whom the L hath indignation for ever. H3068
5 ye shall say, The L will be magnified H3068
6 my fear? saith the L of hosts unto you, H3068
7 say, The table of the L *is* contemptible. H3068
8 accept thy person? saith the L of hosts. H3068
9 your persons? saith the L of hosts. H3068
10 in you, saith the L of hosts, neither will H3068
11 the heathen, saith the L of hosts. H3068
12 The table of the L *is* polluted; and the H3068
13 at it, saith the L of hosts; and ye H3068
13 I accept this of your hand? saith the L. H3068
14 unto the L a corrupt thing: for I H136
14 great King, saith the L of hosts, and my H3068
2: 2 name, saith the L of hosts, I will even H3068
4 might be with Levi, saith the L of hosts. H3068
7 he *is* the messenger of the L of hosts. H3068
8 covenant of Levi, saith the L of hosts. H3068
11 the holiness of the L which he loved, H3068
12 The L will cut off the man that doeth H3068
12 offereth an offering unto the L of hosts. H3068
13 the altar of the L with tears, with H3068
14 Yet ye say, Wherefore? Because the L H3068
16 For the L, the God of Israel, saith that H3068
16 garment, saith the L of hosts: therefore H3068
17 Ye have wearied the L with your words. H3068
17 in the sight of the L, and he delighteth H3068
3: 1 way before me: and the L, whom ye seek, H113
1 he shall come, saith the L of hosts. H3068
3 unto the L an offering in righteousness. H3068
4 be pleasant unto the L, as in the days of H3068
5 and fear not me, saith the L of hosts. H3068
6 For I *am* the L, I change not; therefore H3068
7 you, saith the L of hosts. But ye said, H3068
10 saith the L of hosts, if I will not H3068
11 time in the field, saith the L of hosts. H3068
12 delightsome land, saith the L of hosts. H3068
13 me, saith the L. Yet ye say, What have H3068
14 mournfully before the L of hosts? H3068
16 Then they that feared the L spake often H3068
16 to another: and the L hearkened, and H3068
16 the L, and that thought upon his name. H3068
17 And they shall be mine, saith the L of H3068
4: 1 them up, saith the L of hosts, that it H3068
3 that I shall do *this*, saith the L of hosts. H3068
5 of the great and dreadful day of the L: H3068
Mt 1:20 the angel of the L appeared unto him *G2962*
22 spoken of the L by the prophet, saying, *G2962*
24 as the angel of the L had bidden him, *G2962*
2:13 the angel of the L appeareth to Joseph *G2962*
15 was spoken of the L by the prophet, *G2962*
19 an angel of the L appeareth in a dream *G2962*
3: 3 way of the L, make his paths straight. *G2962*
4: 7 Thou shalt not tempt the L thy God. *G2962*
10 shalt worship the L thy God, and him *G2962*
5:33 shalt perform unto the L thine oaths: *G2962*
7:21 Not every one that saith unto me, L, *G2962*
21 unto me, Lord, L, shall enter into the *G2962*
22 Many will say to me in that day, L, *G2962*
22 me in that day, Lord, L, have we not *G2962*
8: 2 him, saying, L, if thou wilt, thou canst *G2962*
6 And saying, L, my servant lieth at home *G2962*
8 The centurion answered and said, L, I *G2962*
21 said unto him, L, suffer me first to go *G2962*
25 him, saying, L, save us: we perish. *G2962*
9:28 to do this? They said unto him, Yea, L. *G2962*
38 Pray ye therefore the L of the harvest, *G2962*
10:24 *his* master, nor the servant above his l. *G2962*
25 the servant as his l. If they have called *G2962*

Mt 11:25 thee, O Father, L of heaven and earth, *G2962*
12: 8 For the Son of man is L even of the *G2962*
13:51 these things? They say unto him, Yea, L. *G2962*
14:28 And Peter answered him and said, L, if *G2962*
30 to sink, he cried, saying, L, save me. *G2962*
15:22 mercy on me, O L, *thou* son of David; *G2962*
25 worshipped him, saying, L, help me. *G2962*
27 And she said, Truth, L: yet the dogs eat *G2962*
16:22 from thee, L: this shall not be unto thee. *G2962*
17: 4 said unto Jesus, L, it is good for us to be *G2962*
15 L, have mercy on my son: for he is *G2962*
18:21 Then came Peter to him, and said, L, *G2962*
25 had not to pay, his l commanded him *G2962*
26 him, saying, L, have patience with *G2962*
27 Then the l of that servant was moved *G2962*
31 and told unto their l all that was done. *G2962*
32 Then his l, after that he had called him, *G2962*
34 And his l was wroth, and delivered him *G2962*
20: 8 So when even was come, the l of the *G2962*
30 mercy on us, O L, *thou* son of David. *G2962*
31 mercy on us, O L, *thou* son of David. *G2962*
33 They say unto him, L, that our eyes *G2962*
21: 3 ye shall say, The L hath need of them; *G2962*
9 name of the L; Hosanna in the highest. *G2962*
40 When the l therefore of the vineyard *G2962*
22:37 shalt love the L thy God with all thy *G2962*
43 doth David in spirit call him L, saying, *G2962*
44 The L said unto my Lord, Sit thou on *G2962*
44 The LORD said unto my L, *G2962*
45 If David then call him L, how is he his *G2962*
23:39 *is* he that cometh in the name of the L. *G2962*
24:42 know not what hour your L doth come. *G2962*
45 servant, whom his l hath made ruler *G2962*
46 Blessed *is* that servant, whom his l *G2962*
48 in his heart, My l delayeth his coming; *G2962*
50 The l of that servant shall come in a *G2962*
25:11 virgins, saying, L, Lord, open to us. *G2962*
11 virgins, saying, Lord, L, open to us. *G2962*
19 After a long time the l of those servants *G2962*
20 talents, saying, L, thou deliveredst unto *G2962*
21 His l said unto him, Well done, *thou* *G2962*
21 things: enter thou into the joy of thy l. *G2962*
22 came and said, L, thou deliveredst unto *G2962*
23 His l said unto him, Well done, good *G2962*
23 things: enter thou into the joy of thy l. *G2962*
24 came and said, L, I knew thee that thou *G2962*
26 His l answered and said unto him, *G2962*
37 him, saying, L, when saw we thee an *G2962*
44 him, saying, L, when saw we thee an *G2962*
26:22 one of them to say unto him, L, is it I? *G2962*
27:10 potter's field, as the L appointed me. *G2962*
28: 2 for the angel of the L descended from *G2962*
6 Come, see the place where the L lay. *G2962*
Mk 1: 3 way of the L, make his paths straight. *G2962*
2:28 Therefore the Son of man is L also of *G2962*
5:19 great things the L hath done for thee, *G2962*
7:28 unto him, Yes, L: yet the dogs under the *G2962*
9:24 L, I believe; help thou mine unbelief. *G2962*
10:51 him, L, that I might receive my sight. *G4462*
11: 3 say ye that the L hath need of him; and *G2962*
9 *is* he that cometh in the name of the L: *G2962*
10 name of the L: Hosanna in the highest. *G2962*
12: 9 What shall therefore the l of the *G2962*
29 O Israel; The L our God is one Lord: *G2962*
29 O Israel; The Lord our God is one L: *G2962*
30 And thou shalt love the L thy God with *G2962*
36 Holy Ghost, The L said to my Lord, Sit *G2962*
36 said to my L, Sit thou on my right *G2962*
37 David therefore himself calleth him L; *G2962*
13:20 And except that the L had shortened *G2962*
16:19 So then after the L had spoken unto *G2962*
20 every where, the L working with *them*, *G2962*
Lk 1: 6 and ordinances of the L blameless. *G2962*
9 when he went into the temple of the L. *G2962*
11 an angel of the L standing on the right *G2962*
15 in the sight of the L, and shall drink *G2962*
16 Israel shall he turn to the L their God. *G2962*
17 make ready a people prepared for the L. *G2962*
25 Thus hath the L dealt with me in the *G2962*
28 favoured, the L *is* with thee: blessed *G2962*
32 Highest: and the L God shall give unto *G2962*
38 the handmaid of the L; be it unto me *G2962*
43 the mother of my L should come to me? *G2962*
45 things which were told her from the L. *G2962*
46 Mary said, My soul doth magnify the L, *G2962*
58 heard how the L had shewed great *G2962*
66 And the hand of the L was with him. *G2962*
68 Blessed *be* the L God of Israel; for he *G2962*
76 the face of the L to prepare his ways; *G2962*

L

Lk 2: 9 And, lo, the angel of the L came upon G2962
9 the glory of the L shone round about G2962
11 David a Saviour, which is Christ the L. G2962
15 which the L hath made known unto us. G2962
22 to Jerusalem, to present *him* to the L; G2962
23 (As it is written in the law of the L, G2962
23 the womb shall be called holy to the L;) G2962
24 said in the law of the L, A pair of G2962
29 L, now lettest thou thy servant depart in G1203
38 likewise unto the L, and spake of him to G2962
39 to the law of the L, they returned into G2962
3: 4 way of the L, make his paths straight. G2962
4: 8 shalt worship the L thy God, and him G2962
12 Thou shalt not tempt the L thy God. G2962
18 The Spirit of the L *is* upon me, because G2962
19 To preach the acceptable year of the L. G2962
5: 8 from me; for I am a sinful man, O L. G2962
12 him, saying, L, if thou wilt, thou canst G2962
17 of the L was *present* to heal them. G2962
6: 5 the Son of man is L also of the sabbath. G2962
46 And why call ye me, L, Lord, and do not G2962
46 And why call ye me, Lord, L, and do not G2962
7: 6 saying unto him, L, trouble not thyself: G2962
13 And when the L saw her, he had G2962
31 And the L said, Whereunto then shall I G2962
9:54 saw *this*, they said, L, wilt thou that we G2962
57 *man* said unto him, L, I will follow thee G2962
59 me. But he said, L, suffer me first to go G2962
61 And another also said, L, I will follow G2962
10: 1 After these things the L appointed G2962
2 ye therefore the L of the harvest, that G2962
17 with joy, saying, L, even the devils are G2962
21 thee, O Father, L of heaven and earth, G2962
27 shalt love the L thy God with all thy G2962
40 to him, and said, L, dost thou not care G2962
11: 1 said unto him, L, teach us to pray, as G2962
39 And the L said unto him, Now do ye G2962
12:36 that wait for their l, when he will return G2962
37 Blessed *are* those servants, whom the l G2962
41 Then Peter said unto him, L, speakest G2962
42 And the L said, Who then is that G2962
42 whom *his* l shall make ruler over G2962
43 Blessed *is* that servant, whom his l G2962
45 in his heart, My l delayeth his coming; G2962
46 The l of that servant will come in a day G2962
13: 8 And he answering said unto him, L, let G2962
15 The L then answered him, and said, G2962
23 Then said one unto him, L, are there G2962
25 the door, saying, L, Lord, open unto us; G2962
25 saying, Lord, L, open unto us; and he G2962
35 *is* he that cometh in the name of the L. G2962
14:21 So that servant came, and shewed his l G2962
22 And the servant said, L, it is done as G2962
23 And the l said unto the servant, Go out G2962
16: 3 shall I do? for my l taketh away from G2962
5 first, How much owest thou unto my l? G2962
8 And the l commended the unjust G2962
17: 5 And the apostles said unto the L, G2962
6 And the L said, If ye had faith as a G2962
37 unto him, Where, L? And he said unto G2962
18: 6 And the L said, Hear what the unjust G2962
41 he said, L, that I may receive my sight. G2962
19: 8 and said unto the L; Behold, Lord, the G2962
8 unto the Lord; Behold, L, the half of my G2962
16 Then came the first, saying, L, thy G2962
18 And the second came, saying, L, thy G2962
20 And another came, saying, L, behold, G2962
25 (And they said unto him, L, he hath ten G2962
31 him, Because the L hath need of him. G2962
34 And they said, The L hath need of him. G2962
38 in the name of the L: peace in heaven, G2962
20:13 Then said the l of the vineyard, What G2962
15 the l of the vineyard do unto them? G2962
37 he calleth the L the God of Abraham, G2962
42 of Psalms, The L said unto my Lord, G2962
42 unto my L, Sit thou on my right hand, G2962
44 David therefore calleth him L, how is he G2962
22:31 And the L said, Simon, Simon, behold, G2962
33 And he said unto him, L, I am ready to G2962
38 And they said, L, behold, here *are* two G2962
49 him, L, shall we smite with the sword? G2962
61 And the L turned, and looked upon G2962
61 the word of the L, how he had said unto G2962
23:42 And he said unto Jesus, L, remember G2962
24: 3 and found not the body of the L Jesus. G2962
34 Saying, The L is risen indeed, and hath G2962
Jn 1:23 way of the L, as said the prophet Esaias. G2962
4: 1 When therefore the L knew how the G2962
6:23 after that the L had given thanks:) G2962
Jn 6:34 Then said they unto him, L, evermore G2962
68 Then Simon Peter answered him, L, to G2962
8:11 She said, No man, L. And Jesus said G2962
9:36 He answered and said, Who is he, L, G2962
38 And he said, L, I believe. And he G2962
11: 2 (It was *that* Mary which anointed the L G2962
3 L, behold, he whom thou lovest is sick. G2962
12 Then said his disciples, L, if he sleep, he G2962
21 Then said Martha unto Jesus, L, if thou G2962
27 She saith unto him, Yea, L: I believe G2962
32 saying unto him, L, if thou hadst been G2962
34 They said unto him, L, come and see. G2962
39 dead, saith unto him, L, by this time he G2962
12:13 Israel that cometh in the name of the L. G2962
38 which he spake, L, who hath believed G2962
38 hath the arm of the L been revealed? G2962
13: 6 unto him, L, dost thou wash my feet? G2962
9 Simon Peter saith unto him, L, not my G2962
13 Ye call me Master and L: and ye say G2962
14 If I then, *your* L and Master, have G2962
16 greater than his l; neither he that is sent G2962
25 breast saith unto him, L, who is it? G2962
36 Simon Peter said unto him, L, whither G2962
37 Peter said unto him, L, why cannot I G2962
14: 5 Thomas saith unto him, L, we know not G2962
8 Philip saith unto him, L, shew us the G2962
22 Judas saith unto him, not Iscariot, L, G2962
15:15 not what his l doeth: but I have called G2962
20 not greater than his l. If they have G2962
20: 2 taken away the L out of the sepulchre, G2962
13 taken away my L, and I know not where G2962
18 that she had seen the L, and *that* he had G2962
20 the disciples glad, when they saw the L. G2962
25 We have seen the L. But he said unto G2962
28 and said unto him, My L and my God. G2962
21: 7 unto Peter, It is the L. Now when Simon G2962
7 that it was the L, he girt *his* fisher's coat G2962
12 art thou? knowing that it was the L. G2962
15 unto him, Yea, L; thou knowest that I G2962
16 unto him, Yea, L; thou knowest that I G2962
17 he said unto him, L, thou knowest all G2962
20 said, L, which is he that betrayeth thee? G2962
21 Peter seeing him saith to Jesus, L, and G2962
Act 1: 6 of him, saying, L, wilt thou at this time G2962
21 the L Jesus went in and out among us, G2962
24 And they prayed, and said, Thou, L, G2962
2:20 great and notable day of the L come: G2962
21 on the name of the L shall be saved. G2962
25 him, I foresaw the L always before my G2962
34 saith himself, The L said unto my Lord, G2962
34 unto my L, Sit thou on my right hand, G2962
36 ye have crucified, both L and Christ. G2962
39 as many as the L our God shall call. G2962
47 people. And the L added to the church G2962
3:19 shall come from the presence of the L; G2962
22 A prophet shall the L your God raise up G2962
4:24 one accord, and said, L, thou *art* God, G1203
26 against the L, and against his Christ. G2962
29 And now, L, behold their threatenings: G2962
33 resurrection of the L Jesus: and great G2962
5: 9 the Spirit of the L? behold, the feet of G2962
14 L, multitudes both of men and women.) G2962
19 But the angel of the L by night opened G2962
7:30 of the L in a flame of fire in a bush. G2962
31 *it*, the voice of the L came unto him, G2962
33 Then said the L to him, Put off thy G2962
37 A prophet shall the L your God raise up G2962
49 the L: or what *is* the place of my rest? G2962
59 and saying, L Jesus, receive my spirit. G2962
60 with a loud voice, L, lay not this sin to G2962
8:16 baptized in the name of the L Jesus.) G2962
24 Pray ye to the L for me, that none of G2962
25 preached the word of the L, returned to G2962
26 And the angel of the L spake unto G2962
39 the Spirit of the L caught away Philip, G2962
9: 1 of the L, went unto the high priest, G2962
5 And he said, Who art thou, L? And the G2962
5 Lord? And the L said, I am Jesus whom G2962
6 astonished said, L, what wilt thou have G2962
6 me to do? And the L *said* unto him, G2962
10 to him said the L in a vision, Ananias. G2962
10 And he said, Behold, I *am here*, L. G2962
11 And the L *said* unto him, Arise, and go G2962
13 Then Ananias answered, L, I have G2962
15 But the L said unto him, Go thy way: G2962
17 Brother Saul, the L, *even* Jesus, that G2962
27 he had seen the L in the way, and that G2962
29 boldly in the name of the L Jesus, and G2962
31 in the fear of the L, and in the comfort G2962
Act 9:35 Saron saw him, and turned to the L. G2962
42 all Joppa; and many believed in the L. G2962
10: 4 said, What is it, L? And he said unto G2962
14 But Peter said, Not so, L; for I have G2962
36 peace by Jesus Christ: (he is L of all:) G2962
48 in the name of the L. Then prayed they G2962
11: 8 But I said, Not so, L: for nothing G2962
16 Then remembered I the word of the L, G2962
17 believed on the L Jesus Christ; what G2962
20 the Grecians, preaching the L Jesus. G2962
21 And the hand of the L was with them: G2962
21 believed, and turned unto the L. G2962
23 of heart they would cleave unto the L. G2962
24 and much people was added unto the L. G2962
12: 7 And, behold, the angel of the L came G2962
11 a surety, that the L hath sent his angel, G2962
17 them how the L had brought him out G2962
23 And immediately the angel of the L G2962
13: 2 As they ministered to the L, and fasted, G2962
10 cease to pervert the right ways of the L? G2962
11 And now, behold, the hand of the L *is* G2962
12 astonished at the doctrine of the L. G2962
47 For so hath the L commanded us, G2962
48 the word of the L: and as many as were G2962
49 And the word of the L was published G2962
14: 3 boldly in the L, which gave testimony G2962
23 them to the L, on whom they believed. G2962
15:11 the grace of the L Jesus Christ we shall G2962
17 seek after the L, and all the Gentiles, G2962
17 saith the L, who doeth all these things. G2962
26 lives for the name of our L Jesus Christ. G2962
35 word of the L, with many others also. G2962
36 the word of the L, *and see* how they do. G2962
16:10 gathering that the L had called us for to G2962
14 *us*: whose heart the L opened, that she G2962
15 to be faithful to the L, come into my G2962
31 And they said, Believe on the L Jesus G2962
32 the L, and to all that were in his house. G2962
17:24 seeing that he is L of heaven and earth, G2962
27 That they should seek the L, if haply G2962
18: 8 believed on the L with all his house; G2962
9 Then spake the L to Paul in the night G2962
25 in the way of the L; and being fervent in G2962
25 L, knowing only the baptism of John. G2962
19: 5 baptized in the name of the L Jesus. G2962
10 of the L Jesus, both Jews and Greeks. G2962
13 the name of the L Jesus, saying, We G2962
17 the name of the L Jesus was magnified. G2962
20:19 Serving the L with all humility of mind, G2962
21 and faith toward our L Jesus Christ. G2962
24 received of the L Jesus, to testify the G2962
35 the words of the L Jesus, how he said, G2962
21:13 Jerusalem for the name of the L Jesus. G2962
14 saying, The will of the L be done. G2962
20 they glorified the L, and said unto him, G2962
22: 8 And I answered, Who art thou, L? And G2962
10 And I said, What shall I do, L? And the G2962
10 I do, Lord? And the L said unto me, G2962
16 thy sins, calling on the name of the L. G2962
19 And I said, L, they know that I G2962
23:11 And the night following the L stood by G2962
25:26 to write unto my l. Wherefore I have G2962
26:15 And I said, Who art thou, L? And he G2962
28:31 which concern the L Jesus Christ, with G2962
Ro 1: 3 Concerning his Son Jesus Christ our L, G2962
7 God our Father, and the L Jesus Christ. G2962
4: 8 Blessed *is* the man to whom the L will G2962
24 raised up Jesus our L from the dead; G2962
5: 1 with God through our L Jesus Christ: G2962
11 in God through our L Jesus Christ, by G2962
21 unto eternal life by Jesus Christ our L. G2962
6:11 unto God through Jesus Christ our L. G2962
23 eternal life through Jesus Christ our L. G2962
7:25 I thank God through Jesus Christ our L. G2962
8:39 of God, which is in Christ Jesus our L. G2962
9:28 work will the L make upon the earth. G2962
29 And as Esaias said before, Except the L G2962
10: 9 with thy mouth the L Jesus, and shalt G2962
12 for the same L over all is rich unto G2962
13 upon the name of the L shall be saved. G2962
16 saith, L, who hath believed our report? G2962
11: 3 L, they have killed thy prophets, and G2962
34 For who hath known the mind of the L? G2962
12:11 business; fervent in spirit; serving the L; G2962
19 *is* mine; I will repay, saith the L. G2962
13:14 But put ye on the L Jesus Christ, and G2962
14: 6 *it* unto the L; and he that regardeth G2962
6 not the day, to the L he doth not regard G2962
6 eateth, eateth to the L, for he giveth God G2962

Ro 14: 6 L he eateth not, and giveth God thanks. G2962
8 For whether we live, we live unto the L; G2962
8 die, we die unto the L: whether we live G2962
9 might be L both of the dead and living. G2961
11 For it is written, *As* I live, saith the L, G2962
14 I know, and am persuaded by the L G2962
15: 6 even the Father of our L Jesus Christ. G2962
11 And again, Praise the L, all ye Gentiles; G2962
30 Now I beseech you, brethren, for the L G2962
16: 2 That ye receive her in the L, as G2962
8 Greet Amplias my beloved in the L. G2962
11 of Narcissus, which are in the L. G2962
12 who labour in the L. Salute the beloved G2962
12 Persis, which laboured much in the L. G2962
13 Salute Rufus chosen in the L, and his G2962
18 For they that are such serve not our L G2962
20 our L Jesus Christ *be* with you. Amen. G2962
22 wrote *this* epistle, salute you in the L. G2962
24 The grace of our L Jesus Christ *be* with G2962
1Co 1: 2 Jesus Christ our L, both theirs and ours: G2962
3 Father, and *from* the L Jesus Christ. G2962
7 for the coming of our L Jesus Christ: G2962
8 in the day of our L Jesus Christ. G2962
9 fellowship of his Son Jesus Christ our L. G2962
10 the name of our L Jesus Christ, that ye G2962
31 He that glorieth, let him glory in the L. G2962
2: 8 would not have crucified the L of glory. G2962
16 For who hath known the mind of the L, G2962
3: 5 even as the L gave to every man? G2962
20 And again, The L knoweth the G2962
4: 4 but he that judgeth me is the L. G2962
5 the time, until the L come, who both G2962
17 and faithful in the L, who shall bring G2962
19 But I will come to you shortly, if the L G2962
5: 4 In the name of our L Jesus Christ, when G2962
4 with the power of our L Jesus Christ, G2962
5 may be saved in the day of the L Jesus. G2962
6:11 L Jesus, and by the Spirit of our God. G2962
13 but for the L; and the Lord for the body. G2962
13 for the Lord; and the L for the body. G2962
14 And God hath both raised up the L, and G2962
17 But he that is joined unto the L is one G2962
7:10 *yet* not I, but the L, Let not the wife G2962
12 But to the rest speak I, not the L: If any G2962
17 every man, as the L hath called every G2962
22 For he that is called in the L, *being* a G2962
25 of the L: yet I give my judgment, G2962
25 obtained mercy of the L to be faithful. G2962
32 to the L, how he may please the Lord: G2962
32 to the Lord, how he may please the L: G2962
34 the things of the L, that she may be holy G2962
35 attend upon the L without distraction. G2962
39 married to whom she will; only in the L. G2962
8: 6 we in him; and one L Jesus Christ, by G2962
9: 1 our L? are not ye my work in the Lord? G2962
1 our Lord? are not ye my work in the L? G2962
2 seal of mine apostleship are ye in the L. G2962
5 *as* the brethren of the L, and Cephas? G2962
14 Even so hath the L ordained that they G2962
10:21 Ye cannot drink the cup of the L, and G2962
22 Do we provoke the L to jealousy? are G2962
11:11 the woman without the man, in the L. G2962
23 For I have received of the L that which G2962
23 unto you, That the L Jesus the *same* G2962
27 *this* cup of the L, unworthily, shall be G2962
27 be guilty of the body and blood of the L. G2962
32 chastened of the L, that we should not G2962
12: 3 Jesus is the L, but by the Holy Ghost. G2962
5 of administrations, but the same L. G2962
14:21 that will they not hear me, saith the L. G2962
37 you are the commandments of the L. G2962
15:31 I have in Christ Jesus our L, I die daily. G2962
47 the second man *is* the L from heaven. G2962
57 the victory through our L Jesus Christ. G2962
58 in the work of the L, forasmuch as ye G2962
58 that your labour is not in vain in the L. G2962
16: 7 tarry a while with you, if the L permit. G2962
10 worketh the work of the L, as I also *do*. G2962
19 L, with the church that is in their house. G2962
22 If any man love not the L Jesus Christ, G2962
23 The grace of our L Jesus Christ *be* with G2962
2Co 1: 2 Father, and *from* the L Jesus Christ. G2962
3 the Father of our L Jesus Christ, the G2962
14 also *are* ours in the day of the L Jesus. G2962
2:12 a door was opened unto me of the L, G2962
3:16 Nevertheless when it shall turn to the L, G2962
17 Now the L is that Spirit: and where the G2962
17 the Spirit of the L *is*, there *is* liberty. G2962
18 the glory of the L, are changed into the G2962
2Co 3:18 to glory, *even* as by the Spirit of the L. G2962
4: 5 Christ Jesus the L; and ourselves your G2962
10 the dying of the L Jesus, that the life G2962
14 Knowing that he which raised up the L G2962
5: 6 in the body, we are absent from the L: G2962
8 the body, and to be present with the L. G2962
11 Knowing therefore the terror of the L, G2962
6:17 separate, saith the L, and touch not the G2962
18 and daughters, saith the L Almighty. G2962
8: 5 to the L, and unto us by the will of God. G2962
9 For ye know the grace of our L Jesus G2962
19 L, and *declaration of* your ready mind: G2962
21 of the L, but also in the sight of men. G2962
10: 8 which the L hath given us for G2962
17 he that glorieth, let him glory in the L. G2962
18 but whom the L commendeth. G2962
11:17 speak *it* not after the L, but as it were G2962
31 The God and Father of our L Jesus G2962
12: 1 to visions and revelations of the L. G2962
8 For this thing I besought the L thrice, G2962
13:10 the power which the L hath given me to G2962
14 The grace of the L Jesus Christ, and the G2962
Gal 1: 3 Father, and *from* our L Jesus Christ, G2962
4: 1 from a servant, though he be l of all; G2962
5:10 I have confidence in you through the L, G2962
6:14 in the cross of our L Jesus Christ, by G2962
17 in my body the marks of the L Jesus. G2962
18 Brethren, the grace of our L Jesus G2962
Eph 1: 2 Father, and *from* the L Jesus Christ. G2962
3 Blessed *be* the God and Father of our L G2962
15 the L Jesus, and love unto all the saints, G2962
17 That the God of our L Jesus Christ, the G2962
2:21 groweth unto an holy temple in the L: G2962
3:11 he purposed in Christ Jesus our L: G2962
14 unto the Father of our L Jesus Christ, G2962
4: 1 I therefore, the prisoner of the L, G2962
5 One L, one faith, one baptism, G2962
17 This I say therefore, and testify in the L, G2962
5: 8 light in the L: walk as children of light: G2962
10 Proving what is acceptable unto the L. G2962
17 understanding what the will of the L *is*. G2962
19 making melody in your heart to the L; G2962
20 in the name of our L Jesus Christ; G2962
22 unto your own husbands, as unto the L. G2962
29 cherisheth it, even as the L the church: G2962
6: 1 Children, obey your parents in the L: for G2962
4 in the nurture and admonition of the L. G2962
7 service, as to the L, and not to men: G2962
8 of the L, whether *he be* bond or free. G2962
10 Finally, my brethren, be strong in the L, G2962
21 L, shall make known to you all things: G2962
23 God the Father and the L Jesus Christ. G2962
24 Grace *be* with all them that love our L G2962
Php 1: 2 Father, and *from* the L Jesus Christ. G2962
14 And many of the brethren in the L, G2962
2:11 *is* L, to the glory of God the Father. G2962
19 But I trust in the L Jesus to send G2962
24 But I trust in the L that I also myself G2962
29 Receive him therefore in the L with all G2962
3: 1 Finally, my brethren, rejoice in the L. G2962
8 of Christ Jesus my L: for whom I have G2962
20 look for the Saviour, the L Jesus Christ: G2962
4: 1 stand fast in the L, *my* dearly beloved. G2962
2 that they be of the same mind in the L. G2962
4 Rejoice in the L alway: *and* again I say, G2962
5 known unto all men. The L *is* at hand. G2962
10 But I rejoiced in the L greatly, that now G2962
23 The grace of our L Jesus Christ *be* with G2962
Col 1: 2 God our Father and the L Jesus Christ. G2962
3 L Jesus Christ, praying always for you, G2962
10 That ye might walk worthy of the L G2962
2: 6 Christ Jesus the L, *so* walk ye in him: G2962
3:16 with grace in your hearts to the L. G2962
17 all in the name of the L Jesus, giving G2962
18 your own husbands, as it is fit in the L. G2962
20 for this is well pleasing unto the L. G2962
23 heartily, as to the L, and not unto men; G2962
24 Knowing that of the L ye shall receive G2962
24 inheritance: for ye serve the L Christ. G2962
4: 7 minister and fellowservant in the L: G2962
17 hast received in the L, that thou fulfil it. G2962
1Th 1: 1 Father and *in* the L Jesus Christ: Grace G2962
1 God our Father, and the L Jesus Christ. G2962
3 of hope in our L Jesus Christ, in the G2962
6 of us, and of the L, having received the G2962
8 out the word of the L not only in G2962
2:15 Who both killed the L Jesus, and their G2962
19 of our L Jesus Christ at his coming? G2962
3: 8 For now we live, if ye stand fast in the L. G2962
1Th 3:11 L Jesus Christ, direct our way unto you. G2962
12 And the L make you to increase and G2962
13 of our L Jesus Christ with all his saints. G2962
4: 1 exhort *you* by the L Jesus, that as ye G2962
2 we gave you by the L Jesus. G2962
6 because that the L *is* the avenger of all G2962
15 by the word of the L, that we which are G2962
15 the coming of the L shall not prevent G2962
16 For the L himself shall descend from G2962
17 to meet the L in the air: and so shall G2962
17 air: and so shall we ever be with the L. G2962
5: 2 the L so cometh as a thief in the night. G2962
9 obtain salvation by our L Jesus Christ, G2962
12 over you in the L, and admonish you; G2962
23 unto the coming of our L Jesus Christ. G2962
27 I charge you by the L that this epistle G2962
28 The grace of our L Jesus Christ *be* with G2962
2Th 1: 1 God our Father and the L Jesus Christ: G2962
2 God our Father and the L Jesus Christ. G2962
7 rest with us, when the L Jesus shall be G2962
8 not the gospel of our L Jesus Christ: G2962
9 the L, and from the glory of his power; G2962
12 That the name of our L Jesus Christ G2962
12 of our God and the L Jesus Christ. G2962
2: 1 the coming of our L Jesus Christ, and G2962
8 whom the L shall consume with G2962
13 beloved of the L, because God hath G2962
14 of the glory of our L Jesus Christ. G2962
16 Now our L Jesus Christ himself, and G2962
3: 1 the word of the L may have *free* course, G2962
3 But the L is faithful, who shall stablish G2962
4 And we have confidence in the L G2962
5 And the L direct your hearts into the G2962
6 in the name of our L Jesus Christ, that G2962
12 and exhort by our L Jesus Christ, that G2962
16 Now the L of peace himself give you G2962
16 by all means. The L *be* with you all. G2962
18 The grace of our L Jesus Christ *be* with G2962
1Ti 1: 1 and L Jesus Christ, *which is* our hope; G2962
2 God our Father and Jesus Christ our L. G2962
12 And I thank Christ Jesus our L, who G2962
14 And the grace of our L was exceeding G2962
5:21 I charge *thee* before God, and the L G2962
6: 3 the words of our L Jesus Christ, and to G2962
14 the appearing of our L Jesus Christ: G2962
15 the King of kings, and L of lords; G2962
2Ti 1: 2 God the Father and Christ Jesus our L. G2962
8 the testimony of our L, nor of me his G2962
16 The L give mercy unto the house of G2962
18 The L grant unto him that he may find G2962
18 find mercy of the L in that day: and in G2962
2: 7 Consider what I say; and the L give G2962
14 *them* before the L that they strive not G2962
19 this seal, The L knoweth them that G2962
22 that call on the L out of a pure heart. G2962
24 And the servant of the L must not G2962
3:11 but out of *them* all the L delivered me. G2962
4: 1 God, and the L Jesus Christ, who shall G2962
8 which the L, the righteous judge, G2962
14 L reward him according to his works: G2962
17 Notwithstanding the L stood with me, G2962
18 And the L shall deliver me from every G2962
22 The L Jesus Christ *be* with thy spirit. G2962
Tit 1: 4 and the L Jesus Christ our Saviour. G2962
Phlm 3 God our Father and the L Jesus Christ. G2962
5 the L Jesus, and toward all saints; G2962
16 thee, both in the flesh, and in the L? G2962
20 in the L: refresh my bowels in the Lord. G2962
20 in the Lord: refresh my bowels in the L. G2962
25 The grace of our L Jesus Christ *be* with G2962
Heb 1:10 And, Thou, L, in the beginning hast laid G2962
2: 3 be spoken by the L, and was confirmed G2962
7:14 For *it is* evident that our L sprang out G2962
21 unto him, The L sware and will not G2962
8: 2 which the L pitched, and not man. G2962
8 come, saith the L, when I will make a G2962
9 and I regarded them not, saith the L. G2962
10 days, saith the L; I will put my laws into G2962
11 saying, Know the L: for all shall know G2962
10:16 days, saith the L, I will put my laws into G2962
30 saith the L. And again, The Lord G2962
30 again, The L shall judge his people. G2962
12: 5 chastening of the L, nor faint when thou G2962
6 For whom the L loveth he chasteneth, G2962
14 without which no man shall see the L: G2962
13: 6 So that we may boldly say, The L *is* my G2962
20 from the dead our L Jesus, that great G2962
Jas 1: 1 James, a servant of God and of the L G2962
7 that he shall receive any thing of the L. G2962

Jas 1:12 L hath promised to them that love him. *G2962*
2: 1 the faith of our L Jesus Christ, *the Lord* *G2962*
1 *the L* of glory, with respect of persons. *G2962*
4:10 Humble yourselves in the sight of the L, *G2962*
15 For that ye *ought* to say, If the L will, *G2962*
5: 4 into the ears of the L of sabaoth. *G2962*
7 unto the coming of the L. Behold, the *G2962*
8 for the coming of the L draweth nigh. *G2962*
10 in the name of the L, for an example of *G2962*
11 the end of the L; that the Lord is very *G2962*
11 L is very pitiful, and of tender mercy. *G2962*
14 him with oil in the name of the L: *G2962*
15 the sick, and the L shall raise him up; *G2962*
1Pt 1: 3 Blessed *be* the God and Father of our L *G2962*
25 But the word of the L endureth for ever. *G2962*
2: 3 If so be ye have tasted that the L *is* *G2962*
3: 6 calling him l: whose daughters ye *G2962*
12 For the eyes of the L *are* over the *G2962*
12 of the L *is* against them that do evil. *G2962*
15 But sanctify the L God in your hearts: *G2962*
2Pt 1: 2 knowledge of God, and of Jesus our L, *G2962*
8 in the knowledge of our L Jesus Christ. *G2962*
11 of our L and Saviour Jesus Christ. *G2962*
14 as our L Jesus Christ hath shewed me. *G2962*
16 and coming of our L Jesus Christ, but *G2962*
2: 1 even denying the L that bought them, *G1203*
9 The L knoweth how to deliver the godly *G2962*
11 accusation against them before the L. *G2962*
20 knowledge of the L and Saviour Jesus *G2962*
3: 2 of us the apostles of the L and Saviour: *G2962*
8 day *is* with the L as a thousand years, *G2962*
9 The L is not slack concerning his *G2962*
10 But the day of the L will come as a thief *G2962*
15 of our L *is* salvation; even as *G2962*
18 knowledge of our L and Saviour Jesus *G2962*
2Jn 3 and from the L Jesus Christ, the Son *G2962*
Jude 4 only L God, and our Lord Jesus Christ. *G1203*
4 only Lord God, and our L Jesus Christ. *G2962*
5 this, how that the L, having saved the *G2962*
9 but said, The L rebuke thee. *G2962*
14 saying, Behold, the L cometh with ten *G2962*
17 of the apostles of our L Jesus Christ; *G2962*
21 of our L Jesus Christ unto eternal life. *G2962*
Rev 1: 8 ending, saith the L, which is, and which *G2962*
4: 8 Holy, holy, holy, L God Almighty, *G2962*
11 Thou art worthy, O L, to receive glory *G2962*
6:10 How long, O L, holy and true, dost *G1203*
11: 8 Egypt, where also our L was crucified. *G2962*
15 *kingdoms* of our L, and of his Christ; *G2962*
17 Saying, We give thee thanks, O L God *G2962*
14:13 which die in the L from henceforth: *G2962*
15: 3 *are* thy works, L God Almighty; just *G2962*
4 Who shall not fear thee, O L, and glorify *G2962*
16: 5 art righteous, O L, which art, and wast, *G2962*
7 the altar say, Even so, L God Almighty, *G2962*
17:14 them: for he is L of lords, and King of *G2962*
18: 8 strong *is* the L God who judgeth her. *G2962*
19: 1 and power, unto the L our God: *G2962*
6 for the L God omnipotent reigneth. *G2962*
16 KING OF KINGS, AND L OF LORDS. *G2962*
21:22 And I saw no temple therein: for the L *G2962*
22: 5 of the sun; for the L God giveth them *G2962*
6 and true: and the L God of the holy *G2962*
20 quickly. Amen. Even so, come, L Jesus. *G2962*
21 The grace of our L Jesus Christ *be* with *G2962*

LORDLY
Jdg 5:25 milk; she brought forth butter in a l dish. H117

LORDS
Gen 19: 2 And he said, Behold now, my l, turn in, I H113
Nu 21:28 *and* the l of the high places of Arnon. H1167
Dt 10:17 of gods, and Lord of l, a great God, a H113
Jos 13: 3 the Canaanite: five l of the Philistines; H5633
Jdg 3: 3 *Namely,* five l of the Philistines, and all H5633
16: 5 And the l of the Philistines came up H5633
8 Then the l of the Philistines brought up H5633
18 and called for the l of the Philistines, H5633
18 his heart. Then the l of the Philistines H5633
23 Then the l of the Philistines gathered H5633
27 and all the l of the Philistines *were* H5633
30 fell upon the l, and upon all the people H5633
1Sa 5: 8 gathered all the l of the Philistines unto H5633
11 together all the l of the Philistines, and H5633
6: 4 *to* the number of the l of the Philistines: H5633
4 plague *was* on you all, and on your l. H5633
12 or *to* the left; and the l of the Philistines H5633
16 And when the five l of the Philistines H5633
18 to the five l, *both* of fenced cities, H5633
1Sa 7: 7 to Mizpeh, the l of the Philistines went H5633
29: 2 And the l of the Philistines passed on H5633
6 day: nevertheless the l favour thee not. H5633
7 displease not the l of the Philistines. H5633
1Ch 12:19 them not: for the l of the Philistines H5633
Ezr 8:25 and his l, and all Israel *there* present, H8269
Ps 136: 3 O give thanks to the Lord of l: for his H113
Isa 16: 8 of Sibmah: the l of the heathen have H1167
26:13 O LORD our God, *other* l beside thee H113
Jer 2:31 are l; we will come no more unto thee? H7300
Ezk 23:23 and rulers, great l and renowned, all of H7991
Dan 4:36 and my l sought unto me; and H7261
5: 1 l, and drank wine before the thousand. H7261
9 in him, and his l were astonied. H7261
10 of the king and his l, came into the H7261
23 and thou, and thy l, thy wives, and thy H7261
6:17 with the signet of his l; that the purpose H7261
Mk 6:21 a supper to his l, high captains, and *G3175*
1Co 8: 5 (as there be gods many, and l many,) *G2962*
1Ti 6:15 the King of kings, and Lord of l; *G2961*
1Pt 5: 3 Neither as being l over *God's* heritage, *G2634*
Rev 17:14 for he is Lord of l, and King of kings: *G2962*
19:16 KING OF KINGS, AND LORD OF L. *G2962*

LORD'S
Gen 40: 7 him in the ward of his l house, saying, H113
44: 8 we steal out of thy l house silver or gold? H113
9 die, and we also will be my l bondmen. H113
16 behold, we *are* my l servants, both we, H113
18 speak a word in my l ears, and let not H113
Ex 9:29 know how that the earth *is* the L. H3068
12:11 shall eat it in haste: it *is* the L passover. H3068
27 *is* the sacrifice of the L passover, who H3068
13: 9 thine eyes, that the L law may be in thy H3068
12 thou hast; the males *shall be* the L. H3068
32:26 Who *is* on the L side? *let him come* H3068
35:21 they brought the L offering to the work H3068
24 brass brought the L offering: and every H3068
Lev 3:16 for a sweet savour: all the fat *is* the L. H3068
16: 9 upon which the L lot fell, and offer him H3068
23: 5 first month at even *is* the L passover. H3068
27:26 should be the L firstling, no man shall H3068
26 it; whether *it be* ox, or sheep: it *is* the L. H3068
30 tree, *is* the L: *it is* holy unto the LORD. H3068
Nu 11:23 said unto Moses, Is the L hand waxed H3068
29 would God that all the L people were H3068
18:28 L heave offering to Aaron the priest. H3068
31:37 And the L tribute of the sheep was six H3068
38 L tribute *was* threescore and twelve. H3068
39 the L tribute *was* threescore and one. H3068
40 L tribute *was* thirty and two persons. H3068
41 *which was* the L heave offering, unto H3068
32:10 And the L anger was kindled the same H3068
13 And the L anger was kindled against H3068
Dt 10:14 of heavens *is* the L thy God, the earth H3068
11:17 And *then* the L wrath be kindled H3068
15: 2 because it is called the L release. H3068
32: 9 For the L portion *is* his people; Jacob *is* H3068
Jos 1:15 which Moses the L servant gave you on H3068
5:15 And the captain of the L host said unto H3068
22:19 wherein the L tabernacle dwelleth, H3068
Jdg 11:31 shall surely be the L, and I will offer it H3068
1Sa 2: 8 L, and he hath set the world upon them. H3068
24 ye make the L people to transgress. H3068
14: 3 the son of Eli, the L priest in Shiloh, H3068
16: 6 Surely the L anointed *is* before him. H3068
17:47 L, and he will give you into our hands. H3068
18:17 for me, and fight the L battles. For Saul H3068
22:21 David that Saul had slain the L priests. H3068
24: 6 my master, the L anointed, to stretch H3068
10 my lord; for he *is* the L anointed. H3068
26: 9 the L anointed, and be guiltless? H3068
11 hand against the L anointed: but, I H3068
16 your master, the L anointed. And now H3068
23 mine hand against the L anointed. H3068
2Sa 1:14 thine hand to destroy the L anointed? H3068
16 saying, I have slain the L anointed. H3068
19:21 this, because he cursed the L anointed? H3068
20: 6 take thou thy l servants, and pursue H113
21: 7 because of the L oath that *was* between H3068
1Ki 18:13 men of the L prophets by fifty in H3068
2Ki 11:17 they should be the L people; between H3068
13:17 The arrow of the L deliverance, and the H3068
1Ch 21: 3 *are* they not all my l servants? why then H113
2Ch 7: 2 of the LORD had filled the L house. H3068
23:16 king, that they should be the L people. H3068
Ps 11: 4 The LORD *is* in his holy temple, the L H3068
22:28 For the kingdom *is* the L: and he *is* the H3068
24: 1 The earth *is* the L, and the fulness H3068
Ps 113: 3 the same the L name *is* to be praised. H3068
115:16 heavens, *are* the L: but the earth hath H3068
116:19 In the courts of the L house, in the H3068
118:23 This is the L doing; it *is* marvellous in H3068
137: 4 How shall we sing the L song in a H3068
Prv 16:11 A just weight and balance *are* the L: all H3068
Isa 2: 2 the mountain of the L house shall be H3068
22:18 glory *shall be* the shame of thy l house. H113
34: 8 For *it is* the day of the L vengeance, H3068
40: 2 of the L hand double for all her sins. H3068
42:19 *is* perfect, and blind as the L servant? H3068
44: 5 One shall say, I *am* the L; and another H3068
59: 1 Behold, the L hand is not shortened, H3068
Jer 5:10 her battlements; for they *are* not the L. H3068
7: 2 Stand in the gate of the L house, and H3068
13:17 the L flock is carried away captive. H3068
19:14 the L house; and said to all the people, H3068
25:17 Then took I the cup at the L hand, and H3068
26: 2 in the court of the L house, and speak H3068
2 to worship in the L house, all the words H3068
10 entry of the new gate of the L *house.* H3068
27:16 the vessels of the L house shall now H3068
28: 3 all the vessels of the L house, that H3068
6 the vessels of the L house, and all that H3068
36: 6 of the people in the L house upon the H3068
8 the words of the LORD in the L house. H3068
10 L house, in the ears of all the people. H3068
51: 6 *is* the time of the L vengeance; he will H3068
7 golden cup in the L hand, that made all H3068
51 into the sanctuaries of the L house. H3068
Lam 2:22 in the day of the L anger none escaped H3068
3:22 *It is of* the L mercies that we are not H3068
Ezk 8:14 of the gate of the L house which *was* H3068
16 inner court of the L house, and, behold, H3068
10: 4 was full of the brightness of the L glory. H3068
19 east gate of the L house; and the glory H3068
11: 1 east gate of the L house, which looketh H3068
Dan 9:17 that is desolate, for the L sake. H136
Hos 9: 3 They shall not dwell in the L land; but H3068
Joel 1: 9 the priests, the L ministers, mourn. H3068
Oba 21 of Esau; and the kingdom shall be the L. H3068
Mic 6: 2 Hear ye, O mountains, the L H3068
9 The L voice crieth unto the city, and H3068
Hab 2:16 the cup of the L right hand shall be H3068
Zep 1: 8 in the day of the L sacrifice, that I will H3068
18 in the day of the L wrath; but the whole H3068
2: 2 the day of the L anger come upon you. H3068
3 shall be hid in the day of the L anger. H3068
Hag 1: 2 time that the L house should be built. H3068
13 Then spake Haggai the L messenger in H3068
13 messenger in the L message unto the H3068
2:18 of the L temple was laid, consider *it.* H3068
Zec 14:20 the pots in the L house shall be like the H3068
Mt 21:42 the corner: this is the L doing, and it is *G2962*
25:18 in the earth, and hid his l money. *G2962*
Mk 12:11 This was the L doing, and it is *G2962*
Lk 2:26 death, before he had seen the L Christ. *G2962*
12:47 And that servant, which knew his l will, *G2962*
16: 5 So he called every one of his l debtors *G2962*
Ro 14: 8 we live therefore, or die, we are the L. *G2962*
1Co 7:22 a servant, is the L freeman: likewise *G2962*
10:21 of the L table, and of the table of devils. *G2962*
26 For the earth *is* the L, and the fulness *G2962*
28 earth *is* the L, and the fulness thereof: *G2962*
11:20 place, *this* is not to eat the L supper. *G2960*
26 ye do shew the L death till he come. *G2962*
29 to himself, not discerning the L body. *G2962*
Gal 1:19 saw I none, save James the L brother. *G2962*
1Pt 2:13 of man for the L sake: whether it be *G2962*
Rev 1:10 I was in the Spirit on the L day, and *G2960*

LORDSHIP
Mk 10:42 Gentiles exercise l over them; and their *G2634*
Lk 22:25 Gentiles exercise l over them; and they *G2961*

LO-RUHAMAH
Hos 1: 6 Call her name L: for I will no more have H3819
8 Now when she had weaned L, she H3819

LOSE
Jdg 18:25 l thy life, with the lives of thy household. H622
1Ki 18: 5 mules alive, that we l not all the beasts. H3772
Job 31:39 caused the owners thereof to l their life: H5301
Prv 23: 8 thou vomit up, and l thy sweet words. H7843
Ecc 3: 6 A time to get, and a time to l; a time to H6
Mt 10:39 He that findeth his life shall l it: and he *G622*
42 you, he shall in no wise l his reward. *G622*
16:25 For whosoever will save his life shall l it: *G622*
25 will l his life for my sake shall find it. *G622*

Mt 16:26 the whole world, and l his own soul? or G2210
Mk 8:35 For whosoever will save his life shall l it; G622
35 but whosoever shall l his life for my sake G622
36 the whole world, and l his own soul? G2210
9:41 I say unto you, he shall not l his reward. G622
Lk 9:24 For whosoever will save his life shall l it: G622
24 but whosoever will l his life for my sake, G622
25 world, and l himself, or be cast away? G622
15: 4 sheep, if he l one of them, doth not G622
8 of silver, if she l one piece, doth not light G622
17:33 to save his life shall l it; and whosoever G622
33 shall l his life shall preserve it. G622
Jn 6:39 given me I should l nothing, but should G622
12:25 He that loveth his life shall l it; and he G622
2Jn 8 Look to yourselves, that we l not those G622

LOSETH
Mt 10:39 he that l his life for my sake shall find it. G622

LOSS
Gen 31:39 thee; I bare the l of it; of my hand didst H2398
Ex 21:19 shall pay *for* the l of his time, and shall H7674
Isa 47: 8 neither shall I know the l of children: H7921
9 in one day, the l of children, and H7921
Act 27:21 and to have gained this harm and l. G2209
22 for there shall be no l of *any man's* life G580
1Co 3:15 he shall suffer l: but he himself shall G2210
Php 3: 7 gain to me, those I counted l for Christ. G2209
8 all things *but* l for the excellency of G2209
8 I have suffered the l of all things, and G2210

LOST
Ex 22: 9 for any manner of l thing, which *another* H9
Lev 6: 3 Or have found that which was l, and lieth H9
4 to keep, or the l thing which he found, H9
Nu 6:12 be l, because his separation was defiled. H5307
Dt 22: 3 and with all l thing of thy brother's, H9
3 which he hath l, and thou hast found, H6
1Sa 9: 3 And the asses of Kish Saul's father were l. H6
20 And as for thine asses that were l three H6
1Ki 20:25 that thou hast l, horse for horse, and H5307
Ps119:176 I have gone astray like a l sheep; seek H6
Isa 49:20 after thou hast l the other, shall say H7923
21 seeing I have l my children, and am H7908
Jer 50: 6 My people hath been l sheep: their H6
Ezk 19: 5 waited, *and* her hope was l, then she took H6
34: 4 that which was l; but with force and with H6
16 I will seek that which was l, and bring H6
37:11 our hope is l: we are cut off for our parts. H6
Mt 5:13 earth: but if the salt have l his savour, G3471
10: 6 But go rather to the l sheep of the house G622
15:24 unto the l sheep of the house of Israel. G622
18:11 of man is come to save that which was l. G622
Mk 9:50 Salt *is* good: but if the salt have l G358+G1096
Lk 14:34 Salt *is* good: but if the salt have l his G3471
15: 4 go after that which is l, until he find it? G622
6 for I have found my sheep which was l. G622
9 for I have found the piece which I had l. G622
24 is alive again; he was l, and is found. And G622
32 is alive again; and was l, and is found. G622
19:10 to seek and to save that which was l. G622
Jn 6:12 fragments that remain, that nothing be l. G622
17:12 and none of them is l, but the son of G622
18: 9 which thou gavest me have I l none. G622
2Co 4: 3 gospel be hid, it is hid to them that are l: G622

LOT
Gen 11:27 Nahor, and Haran; and Haran begat L. H3876
31 And Terah took Abram his son, and L H3876
12: 4 unto him; and L went with him: and H3876
5 And Abram took Sarai his wife, and L H3876
13: 1 he had, and L with him, into the south. H3876
5 And L also, which went with Abram, H3876
8 And Abram said unto L, Let there be no H3876
10 And L lifted up his eyes, and beheld all H3876
11 Then L chose him all the plain of H3876
11 of Jordan; and L journeyed east: and H3876
12 of Canaan, and L dwelled in the cities H3876
14 Abram, after that L was separated H3876
14:12 And they took L, Abram's brother's son, H3876
16 again his brother L, and his goods, and H3876
19: 1 at even; and L sat in the gate of Sodom: H3876
1 of Sodom: and L seeing *them* rose up H3876
5 And they called unto L, and said unto H3876
6 And L went out at the door unto them, H3876
9 L, and came near to break the door. H3876
10 hand, and pulled L into the house to H3876
12 And the men said unto L, Hast thou H3876
14 And L went out, and spake unto his H3876
Gen 19:15 angels hastened L, saying, Arise, take H3876
18 And L said unto them, Oh, not so, my H3876
23 the earth when L entered into Zoar. H3876
29 and sent L out of the midst of the H3876
29 the cities in the which L dwelt. H3876
30 And L went up out of Zoar, and dwelt H3876
36 Thus were both the daughters of L with H3876
Lev 16: 8 the two goats; one l for the LORD, and H1486
8 and the other l for the scapegoat. H1486
9 l fell, and offer him *for* a sin offering. H1486
10 But the goat, on which the l fell to be H1486
Nu 26:55 shall be divided by l: according to the H1486
56 According to the l shall the possession H1486
33:54 And ye shall divide the land by l for an H1486
54 place where his l falleth; according to H1486
34:13 ye shall inherit by l, which the LORD H1486
36: 2 an inheritance by l to the children of H1486
3 be taken from the l of our inheritance. H1486
Dt 2: 9 unto the children of L *for* a possession. H3876
19 unto the children of L *for* a possession. H3876
32: 9 people; Jacob *is* the l of his inheritance. H2256
Jos 13: 6 divide thou it by l unto the Israelites H5307
14: 2 By l *was* their inheritance, as the LORD H1486
15: 1 *This* then was the l of the tribe of the H1486
16: 1 And the l of the children of Joseph fell H1486
17: 1 There was also a l for the tribe of H1486
2 There was also *a l* for the rest of the
14 given me *but* one l and one portion to H1486
17 power: thou shalt not have one l *only*: H1486
18:11 And the l of the tribe of the children of H1486
11 the coast of their l came forth between H1486
19: 1 And the second l came forth to Simeon, H1486
10 And the third l came up for the H1486
17 *And* the fourth l came out to Issachar, H1486
24 And the fifth l came out for the tribe of H1486
32 The sixth l came out to the children of H1486
40 *And* the seventh l came out for the H1486
51 an inheritance by l in Shiloh before the H1486
21: 4 And the l came out for the families of H1486
4 the Levites, had by l out of the tribe of H1486
5 of Kohath *had* by l out of the families H1486
6 And the children of Gershon *had* by l H1486
8 And the children of Israel gave by l H1486
10 of Levi, had: for theirs was the first l. H1486
20 of their l out of the tribe of Ephraim. H1486
40 the Levites, were *by* their l twelve cities. H1486
23: 4 Behold, I have divided unto you by l H1486
Jdg 1: 3 up with me into my l, that we may fight H1486
3 into thy l. So Simeon went with him. H1486
20: 9 to Gibeah; *we will go up* by l against it; H1486
1Sa 14:41 Give a perfect *l*. And Saul and Jonathan
1Ch 6:54 of the Kohathites: for theirs was the l. H1486
61 half *tribe* of Manasseh, by l, ten cities. H1486
63 Unto the sons of Merari *were given* by l, H1486
65 And they gave by l out of the tribe of H1486
16:18 of Canaan, the l of your inheritance; H2256
24: 5 Thus were they divided by l, one sort H1486
7 Now the first l came forth to Jehoiarib, H1486
25: 9 Now the first l came forth for Asaph to H1486
26:14 And the l eastward fell to Shelemiah. H1486
14 lots; and his l came out northward. H1486
16 To Shuppim and Hosah *the l came forth*
Est 3: 7 Pur, that *is*, the l, before Haman from H1486
9:24 Pur, that *is*, the l, to consume them, and H1486
Ps 16: 5 and of my cup: thou maintainest my l. H1486
83: 8 have holpen the children of L. Selah. H3876
105:11 of Canaan, the l of your inheritance: H2256
125: 3 not rest upon the l of the righteous; lest H1486
Prv 1:14 Cast in thy l among us; let us all have H1486
16:33 The l is cast into the lap; but the whole H1486
18:18 The l causeth contentions to cease, and H1486
Isa 17:14 spoil us, and the l of them that rob us. H1486
34:17 And he hath cast the l for them, and his H1486
57: 6 they, they *are* thy l: even to them hast H1486
Jer 13:25 This *is* thy l, the portion of thy H1486
Ezk 24: 6 out piece by piece; let no l fall upon it. H1486
45: 1 Moreover, when ye shall divide by l the H5307
47:22 ye shall divide it by l for an inheritance H5307
48:29 ye shall divide by l unto the tribes of H5307
Dan 12:13 stand in thy l at the end of the days. H1486
Jna 1: 7 they cast lots, and the l fell upon Jonah. H1486
Mic 2: 5 by l in the congregation of the LORD. H1486
Lk 1: 9 priest's office, his l was to burn incense G2975
17:28 Likewise also as it was in the days of L; G3091
29 But the same day that L went out of G3091
Act 1:26 And they gave forth their lots; and the l G2819
8:21 Thou hast neither part nor l in this G2819
13:19 he divided their land to them by l. G2624
2Pt 2: 7 And delivered just L, vexed with the G3091

LOTAN
Gen 36:20 L, and Shobal, and Zibeon, and Anah, H3877
22 And the children of L were Hori and H3877
29 the Horites; duke L, duke Shobal, duke H3877
1Ch 1:38 And the sons of Seir; L, and Shobal, and H3877
39 And the sons of L; Hori, and Homam: H3877

LOTAN'S
Gen 36:22 and Hemam; and L sister *was* Timna. H3877
1Ch 1:39 and Homam: and Timna *was* L sister. H3877

LOTHE
Ex 7:18 shall l to drink of the water of the river. H3811
Ezk 6: 9 and they shall l themselves for the evils H6962
20:43 and ye shall l yourselves in your own H6962
36:31 not good, and shall l yourselves in your H6962

LOTHED
Jer 14:19 hath thy soul l Zion? why hast thou H1602
Ezk 16:45 thy sisters, which l their husbands and H1602
Zec 11: 8 and my soul l them, and their soul H7114

LOTHETH
Ezk 16:45 Thou *art* thy mother's daughter, that l H1602

LOTHING
Ezk 16: 5 open field, to the l of thy person, in the H1604

LOTS
Lev 16: 8 And Aaron shall cast l upon the two H1486
Jos 18: 6 that I may cast l for you here before H1486
8 l for you before the LORD in Shiloh. H1486
10 And Joshua cast l for them in Shiloh H1486
1Sa 14:42 And Saul said, Cast *l* between me and
1Ch 24:31 These likewise cast l over against their H1486
25: 8 And they cast l, ward against *ward*, as H1486
26:13 And they cast l, as well the small as the H1486
14 cast l; and his lot came out northward. H1486
Neh 10:34 And we cast the l among the priests, H1486
11: 1 people also cast l, to bring one of ten to H1486
Ps 22:18 them, and cast l upon my vesture. H1486
Joel 3: 3 And they have cast l for my people; and H1486
Oba 11 his gates, and cast l upon Jerusalem, H1486
Jna 1: 7 and let us cast l, that we may know for H1486
7 they cast l, and the lot fell upon Jonah. H1486
Nah 3:10 and they cast l for her honourable men, H1486
Mt 27:35 his garments, casting l: that it might be G2819
35 and upon my vesture did they cast l. G2819
Mk 15:24 garments, casting l upon them, what G2819
Lk 23:34 And they parted his raiment, and cast l. G2819
Jn 19:24 rend it, but cast l for it, whose it shall G2975
24 they did cast l. These things therefore G2819
Act 1:26 And they gave forth their l; and the lot G2819

LOT'S
Gen 13: 7 and the herdmen of L cattle: and the H3876
Lk 17:32 Remember L wife. G3091

LOUD
Gen 39:14 lie with me, and I cried with a l voice: H1419
Ex 19:16 the trumpet exceeding l; so that all the H2389
Dt 27:14 unto all the men of Israel with a l voice, H7311
1Sa 28:12 she cried with a l voice: and the woman H1419
2Sa 15:23 And all the country wept with a l voice, H1419
19: 4 the king cried with a l voice, O my son H1419
1Ki 8:55 of Israel with a l voice, saying, H1419
2Ki 18:28 and cried with a l voice in the Jews' H1419
2Ch 15:14 And they sware unto the LORD with a l H1419
20:19 God of Israel with a l voice on high. H1419
30:21 with l instruments unto the LORD. H5797
32:18 Then they cried with a l voice in the H1419
Ezr 3:12 eyes, wept with a l voice; and many H1419
13 shouted with a l shout, and the noise H1419
10:12 and said with a l voice, As thou hast H1419
Neh 9: 4 with a l voice unto the LORD their God. H1419
12:42 sang l, with Jezrahiah *their* overseer. H8085
Est 4: 1 city, and cried with a l and a bitter cry; H1419
Ps 33: 3 a new song; play skilfully with a l noise.
98: 4 a l noise, and rejoice, and sing praise.
150: 5 Praise him upon the l cymbals: praise H8085
Prv 7:11 (She *is* l and stubborn; her feet abide H1993
27:14 He that blesseth his friend with a l H1419
Isa 36:13 and cried with a l voice in the Jews' H1419
Ezk 8:18 with a l voice, *yet* will I not hear them. H1419
9: 1 He cried also in mine ears with a l H1419
11:13 and cried with a l voice, and said, Ah H1419
Mt 27:46 Jesus cried with a l voice, saying, Eli, G3173
50 Jesus, when he had cried again with a l G3173
Mk 1:26 with a l voice, he came out of him. G3173

Mk 5: 7 And cried with a l voice, and said, G3173
15:34 Jesus cried with a l voice, saying, Eloi, G3173
37 And Jesus cried with a l voice, and gave G3173
Lk 1:42 And she spake out with a l voice, and G3173
4:33 devil, and cried out with a l voice, G3173
8:28 him, and with a l voice said, What have G3173
17:15 back, and with a l voice glorified God, G3173
19:37 and praise God with a l voice for all the G3173
23:23 And they were instant with l voices, G3173
46 And when Jesus had cried with a l G3173
Jn 11:43 with a l voice, Lazarus, come forth. G3173
Act 7:57 Then they cried out with a l voice, and G3173
60 and cried with a l voice, Lord, lay not G3173
8: 7 For unclean spirits, crying with l voice, G3173
14:10 Said with a l voice, Stand upright on G3173
16:28 But Paul cried with a l voice, saying, G3173
26:24 Festus said with a l voice, Paul, thou G3173
Rev 5: 2 with a l voice, Who is worthy G3173
12 Saying with a l voice, Worthy is the G3173
6:10 And they cried with a l voice, saying, G3173
7: 2 and he cried with a l voice to the four G3173
10 And cried with a l voice, saying, G3173
8:13 saying with a l voice, Woe, woe, woe, G3173
10: 3 And cried with a l voice, as *when* a lion G3173
12:10 And I heard a l voice saying in heaven, G3173
14: 7 Saying with a l voice, Fear God, and G3173
9 them, saying with a l voice, If any man G3173
15 crying with a l voice to him that sat G3173
18 and cried with a l cry to him that had G3173
19:17 he cried with a l voice, saying to all the G3173

LOUDER
Ex 19:19 long, and waxed l and louder, Moses H2390
19 waxed louder and l, Moses spake, and H3966

LOVE
Gen 27: 4 And make me savoury meat, such as I l, H157
29:20 *but* a few days, for the l he had to her. H160
32 now therefore my husband will l me. H157
Ex 20: 6 that l me, and keep my commandments. H157
21: 5 And if the servant shall plainly say, I l H157
Lev 19:18 but thou shalt l thy neighbour as thyself: H157
34 you, and thou shalt l him as thyself; for H157
Dt 5:10 that l me and keep my commandments. H157
6: 5 And thou shalt l the LORD thy God with H157
7: 7 The LORD did not set his l upon you, H2836
9 mercy with them that l him and keep his H157
13 And he will l thee, and bless thee, and H157
10:12 in all his ways, and to l him, and to serve H157
15 in thy fathers to l them, and he chose H157
19 L ye therefore the stranger: for ye were H157
11: 1 Therefore thou shalt l the LORD thy H157
13 you this day, to l the LORD your God, H157
22 you, to do them, to l the LORD your God, H157
13: 3 to know whether ye l the LORD your God H157
19: 9 thee this day, to l the LORD thy God, and H157
30: 6 of thy seed, to l the LORD thy God with H157
16 In that I command thee this day to l the H157
20 That thou mayest l the LORD thy God, H157
Jos 22: 5 charged you, to l the LORD your God, H157
23:11 yourselves, that ye l the LORD your God. H157
Jdg 5:31 but *let* them that l him *be* as the sun H157
16:15 canst thou say, I l thee, when thine heart H157
1Sa 18:22 and all his servants l thee: now therefore H157
2Sa 1:26 thou been unto me: thy l to me was H160
26 was wonderful, passing the l of women. H160
13: 4 I l Tamar, my brother Absalom's sister. H157
15 *was* greater than the l wherewith he had H160
1Ki 11: 2 their gods: Solomon clave unto these in l. H157
2Ch 19: 2 the ungodly, and l them that hate the H157
Neh 1: 5 l him and observe his commandments: H157
Ps 4: 2 ye l vanity, *and* seek after leasing? Selah. H157
5:11 also that l thy name be joyful in thee. H157
18: 1 I will l thee, O LORD, my strength. H7355
31:23 O l the LORD, all ye his saints: *for* the H157
40:16 in thee: let such as l thy salvation say H157
69:36 they that l his name shall dwell therein. H157
70: 4 thee: and let such as l thy salvation say H157
91:14 Because he hath set his l upon me, H2836
97:10 Ye that l the LORD, hate evil: he H157
109: 4 For my l they are my adversaries: but I H160
5 me evil for good, and hatred for my l. H160
116: 1 I l the LORD, because he hath heard my H157
119:97 O how I l thy law! it *is* my meditation all H157
113 I hate *vain* thoughts: but thy law do I l. H157
119 *like* dross: therefore I l thy testimonies. H157
127 Therefore I l thy commandments above H157
132 usest to do unto those that l thy name. H157
159 Consider how I l thy precepts: quicken H157

Ps119:163 I hate and abhor lying: *but* thy law do I l. H157
165 Great peace have they which l thy law: H157
167 testimonies; and I l them exceedingly. H157
122: 6 Jerusalem: they shall prosper that l thee. H157
145:20 The LORD preserveth all them that l H157
Prv 1:22 How long, ye simple ones, will ye l H157
4: 6 thee: l her, and she shall keep thee. H157
5:19 and be thou ravished always with her l. H160
7:18 Come, let us take our fill of l until the H1730
8:17 I l them that love me; and those that H157
17 I love them that l me; and those that H157
21 That I may cause those that l me to H157
36 own soul: all they that hate me l death. H157
9: 8 rebuke a wise man, and he will l thee. H157
10:12 Hatred stirreth up strifes: but l covereth H160
15:17 Better *is* a dinner of herbs where l is, H160
16:13 and they l him that speaketh right. H157
17: 9 seeketh l; but he that repeateth H160
18:21 they that l it shall eat the fruit thereof. H157
20:13 L not sleep, lest thou come to poverty; H157
27: 5 Open rebuke *is* better than secret l. H160
Ecc 3: 8 A time to l, and a time to hate; a time of H157
9: 1 l or hatred *by* all *that is* before them. H160
6 Also their l, and their hatred, and their H160
Song 1: 2 his mouth: for thy l *is* better than wine. H1730
3 forth, therefore do the virgins l thee. H157
4 l more than wine: the upright love thee. H1730
4 love more than wine: the upright l thee. H157
9 I have compared thee, O my l, to a H7474
15 Behold, thou *art* fair, my l; behold, thou H7474
2: 2 As the lily among thorns, so *is* my l H7474
4 house, and his banner over me *was* l. H160
5 me with apples: for I *am* sick of l. H160
7 stir not up, nor awake *my* l, till he please. H160
10 up, my l, my fair one, and come away. H7474
13 my l, my fair one, and come away. H7474
3: 5 stir not up, nor awake *my* l, till he please. H160
10 *with* l, for the daughters of Jerusalem. H160
4: 1 Behold, thou *art* fair, my l; behold, thou H7474
7 Thou *art* all fair, my l; *there is* no spot H7474
10 How fair is thy l, my sister, *my* spouse! H1730
10 much better is thy l than wine! and the H1730
5: 2 to me, my sister, my l, my dove, my H7474
8 that ye tell him, that I *am* sick of l. H160
6: 4 Thou *art* beautiful, O my l, as Tirzah, H7474
7: 6 How fair and how pleasant art thou, O l, H160
8: 4 not up, nor awake *my* l, until he please. H160
6 upon thine arm: for l *is* strong as death; H160
7 Many waters cannot quench l, neither H160
7 for l, it would utterly be contemned. H160
Isa 38:17 but thou hast in l to my soul *delivered* H2836
56: 6 to serve him, and to l the name of the H157
61: 8 For I the LORD l judgment, I hate H157
63: 9 saved them: in his l and in his pity he H160
66:10 with her, all ye that l her: rejoice for joy H157
Jer 2: 2 of thy youth, the l of thine espousals, H160
33 Why trimmest thou thy way to seek l? H160
5:31 and my people l *to have it* so: and what H157
31: 3 thee with an everlasting l: therefore with H160
Ezk 16: 8 *was* the time of l; and I spread my skirt H1730
23:11 in her inordinate l than she, and in her H5691
17 to her into the bed of l, and they defiled H1730
33:31 they shew much l, *but* their heart goeth H5690
Dan 1: 9 tender l with the prince of the eunuchs. H7356
9: 4 mercy to them that l him, and to them H157
Hos 3: 1 Then said the LORD unto me, Go yet, l a H157
1 according to the l of the LORD toward H160
1 look to other gods, and l flagons of wine. H157
4:18 her rulers *with* shame do l, Give ye. H157
9:15 of mine house, I will l them no more: all H160
11: 4 a man, with bands of l: and I was to them H160
14: 4 I will heal their backsliding, I will l them H157
Am 5:15 Hate the evil, and l the good, and H157
Mic 3: 2 Who hate the good, and l the evil; who H157
6: 8 to do justly, and to l mercy, and to walk H160
Zep 3:17 in his l, he will joy over thee with singing. H160
Zec 8:17 his neighbour; and l no false oath: for all H157
19 feasts; therefore l the truth and peace. H157
Mt 5:43 l thy neighbour, and hate thine enemy. G25
44 But I say unto you, L your enemies, bless G25
46 For if ye l them which love you, what G25
46 For if ye love them which l you, what G25
6: 5 *are*: for they l to pray standing in G5368
24 hate the one, and l the other; or else he G25
19:19 Thou shalt l thy neighbour as thyself. G25
22:37 Jesus said unto him, Thou shalt l the G25
39 it, Thou shalt l thy neighbour as thyself. G25
23: 6 And l the uppermost rooms at feasts, G5368
24:12 And because iniquity shall abound, the l G26

Mk 12:30 And thou shalt l the Lord thy God with G25
31 this, Thou shalt l thy neighbour as G25
33 And to l him with all the heart, and with G25
33 the strength, and to l *his* neighbour as G25
38 of the scribes, which l to go in long G2309
38 and *l* salutations in the marketplaces, G2309
Lk 6:27 But I say unto you which hear, L your G25
32 For if ye l them which love you, what G25
32 For if ye love them which l you, what G25
32 for sinners also l those that love them. G25
32 for sinners also love those that l them. G25
35 But l ye your enemies, and do good, and G25
7:42 therefore, which of them will l him most? G25
10:27 And he answering said, Thou shalt l the G25
11:42 judgment and the l of God: these ought G26
43 Woe unto you, Pharisees! for ye l the G25
16:13 hate the one, and l the other; or else he G25
20:46 in long robes, and l greetings in the G5368
Jn 5:42 But I know you, that ye have not the l of G26
8:42 Father, ye would l me: for I proceeded G25
10:17 Therefore doth my Father l me, because G25
13:34 give unto you, That ye l one another; as I G25
34 loved you, that ye also l one another. G25
35 my disciples, if ye have l one to another. G26
14:15 If ye l me, keep my commandments. G25
21 l him, and will manifest myself to him. G25
23 unto him, If a man l me, he will keep my G25
23 and my Father will l him, and we will G25
31 But that the world may know that I l the G25
15: 9 so have I loved you: continue ye in my l. G26
10 ye shall abide in my l; even as I have kept G26
10 commandments, and abide in his l. G26
12 This is my commandment, That ye l one G25
13 Greater l hath no man than this, that a G26
17 These things I command you, that ye l G25
19 the world would l his own: but because G5368
17:26 declare *it*: that the l wherewith thou hast G26
21:15 knowest that I l thee. He saith unto G5368
16 knowest that I l thee. He saith unto G5368
17 knowest that I l thee. Jesus saith unto G5368
Ro 5: 5 because the l of God is shed abroad G26
8 But God commendeth his l toward us, in G26
8:28 for good to them that l God, to them who G25
35 Who shall separate us from the l of G26
39 us from the l of God, which is in Christ G26
12: 9 *Let* l be without dissimulation. Abhor G26
10 l; in honour preferring one another; G5360
13: 8 Owe no man any thing, but to l one G25
9 Thou shalt l thy neighbour as thyself. G25
10 L worketh no ill to his neighbour: G26
10 therefore l *is* the fulfilling of the law. G26
15:30 sake, and for the l of the Spirit, that ye G26
1Co 2: 9 God hath prepared for them that l him. G25
4:21 rod, or in l, and *in* the spirit of meekness? G26
8: 3 But if any man l God, the same is known G25
16:22 If any man l not the Lord Jesus Christ, G5368
24 My l *be* with you all in Christ Jesus. G26
2Co 2: 4 ye might know the l which I have more G26
8 ye would confirm *your* l toward him. G26
5:14 For the l of Christ constraineth us; G26
6: 6 by the Holy Ghost, by l unfeigned, G26
8: 7 and *in* your l to us, *see* that ye abound G26
8 and to prove the sincerity of your l. G26
24 l, and of our boasting on your behalf. G26
11:11 Wherefore? because I l you not? God G25
12:15 abundantly I l you, the less I be loved. G25
13:11 the God of l and peace shall be with you. G26
14 Jesus Christ, and the l of God, and the G26
Gal 5: 6 but faith which worketh by l. G26
13 to the flesh, but by l serve one another. G26
14 Thou shalt l thy neighbour as thyself. G25
22 But the fruit of the Spirit is l, joy, peace, G26
Eph 1: 4 holy and without blame before him in l: G26
15 the Lord Jesus, and l unto all the saints, G26
2: 4 for his great l wherewith he loved us, G26
3:17 that ye, being rooted and grounded in l, G26
19 And to know the l of Christ, which G26
4: 2 forbearing one another in l; G26
15 But speaking the truth in l, may grow up G26
16 of the body unto the edifying of itself in l. G26
5: 2 And walk in l, as Christ also hath loved G26
25 Husbands, l your wives, even as Christ G25
28 So ought men to l their wives as their G25
33 you in particular so l his wife even as G25
6:23 Peace *be* to the brethren, and l with G26
24 Grace *be* with all them that l our Lord G25
Php 1: 9 And this I pray, that your l may abound G26
17 But the other of l, knowing that I am set G26
2: 1 if any comfort of l, if any fellowship of G26

Php 2: 2 same l, *being* of one accord, of one mind. *G26*
Col 1: 4 of the l *which ye have* to all the saints, *G26*
8 Who also declared unto us your l in the *G26*
2: 2 knit together in l, and unto all riches of *G26*
3:19 Husbands, l *your* wives, and be not *G25*
1Th 1: 3 of faith, and labour of l, and patience of *G26*
3:12 and abound in l one toward another, *G26*
4: 9 But as touching brotherly l ye need not *G5360*
9 are taught of God to l one another. *G25*
5: 8 of faith and l; and for an helmet, the *G26*
13 And to esteem them very highly in l for *G26*
2Th 2:10 l of the truth, that they might be saved. *G26*
3: 5 hearts into the l of God, and into the *G26*
1Ti 1:14 with faith and l which is in Christ Jesus. *G26*
6:10 For the l of money is the root of all evil: *G5365*
11 godliness, faith, l, patience, meekness. *G26*
2Ti 1: 7 of power, and of l, and of a sound mind. *G26*
13 in faith and l which is in Christ Jesus. *G26*
4: 8 unto all them also that l his appearing. *G25*
Tit 2: 4 l their husbands, to love their children, *G5362*
4 love their husbands, to l their children, *G5388*
3: 4 But after that the kindness and l of God *G5363*
15 Greet them that l us in the faith. Grace *G5368*
Phlm 5 Hearing of thy l and faith, which thou *G26*
7 consolation in thy l, because the bowels *G26*
Heb 6:10 your work and labour of l, which ye have *G26*
10:24 to provoke unto l and to good works: *G26*
13: 1 Let brotherly l continue. *G5360*
Jas 1:12 Lord hath promised to them that l him. *G25*
2: 5 he hath promised to them that l him? *G25*
8 l thy neighbour as thyself, ye do well: *G25*
1Pt 1: 8 Whom having not seen, ye l; in whom, *G25*
22 unto unfeigned l of the brethren, *see* *G5360*
22 *see that ye* l one another with a pure *G25*
2:17 Honour all *men*. L the brotherhood. Fear *G25*
3: 8 l as brethren, *be* pitiful, *be* courteous: *G5361*
10 For he that will l life, and see good days, *G25*
1Jn 2: 5 in him verily is the l of God perfected: *G26*
15 L not the world, neither the things *that* *G25*
15 world. If any man l the world, the love of *G25*
15 world, the l of the Father is not in him. *G26*
3: 1 Behold, what manner of l the Father *G26*
11 beginning, that we should l one another. *G25*
14 life, because we l the brethren. He that *G25*
16 Hereby perceive we the l *of God*, because *G26*
17 him, how dwelleth the l of God in him? *G26*
18 My little children, let us not l in word, *G25*
23 Jesus Christ, and l one another, as he *G25*
4: 7 Beloved, let us l one another: for love is *G25*
7 Beloved, let us love one another: for l is *G26*
8 loveth not knoweth not God; for God is l. *G26*
9 In this was manifested the l of God *G26*
10 Herein is l, not that we loved God, but *G26*
11 loved us, we ought also to l one another. *G25*
12 at any time. If we l one another, God *G25*
12 in us, and his l is perfected in us. *G26*
16 And we have known and believed the l *G26*
16 hath to us. God is l; and he that dwelleth *G26*
16 in l dwelleth in God, and God in him. *G26*
17 Herein is our l made perfect, that we *G26*
18 There is no fear in l; but perfect love *G26*
18 There is no fear in love; but perfect l *G26*
18 He that feareth is not made perfect in l. *G26*
19 We l him, because he first loved us. *G25*
20 If a man say, I l God, and hateth his *G25*
20 can he l God whom he hath not seen? *G25*
21 he who loveth God l his brother also. *G25*
5: 2 By this we know that we l the children of *G25*
2 we l God, and keep his commandments. *G25*
3 For this is the l of God, that we keep his *G26*
2Jn 1 children, whom I l in the truth; and not *G25*
3 the Son of the Father, in truth and l. *G26*
5 the beginning, that we l one another. *G25*
6 And this is l, that we walk after his *G26*
3Jn 1 wellbeloved Gaius, whom I l in the truth. *G25*
Jude 2 Mercy unto you, and peace, and l, be *G26*
21 Keep yourselves in the l of God, looking *G26*
Rev 2: 4 thee, because thou hast left thy first l. *G26*
3:19 As many as I l, I rebuke and chasten: be *G5368*

LOVED

Gen 24:67 his wife; and he l her: and Isaac was H157
25:28 And Isaac l Esau, because he did eat of H157
28 eat of *his* venison: but Rebekah l Jacob. H157
27:14 made savoury meat, such as his father l. H157
29:18 And Jacob l Rachel; and said, I will serve H157
30 Rachel, and he l also Rachel more than H157
34: 3 of Jacob, and he l the damsel, and spake H157
37: 3 Now Israel l Joseph more than all his H157
Gen 37: 4 that their father l him more than all his H157
Dt 4:37 And because he l thy fathers, therefore H157
7: 8 But because the LORD l you, and H160
23: 5 thee, because the LORD thy God l thee. H157
33: 3 Yea, he l the people; all his saints *are* in H2245
Jdg 16: 4 And it came to pass afterward, that he l H157
1Sa 1: 5 portion; for he l Hannah: but the LORD H157
16:21 before him: and he l him greatly; and he H157
18: 1 and Jonathan l him as his own soul. H157
3 because he l him as his own soul. H160
16 But all Israel and Judah l David, because H157
20 And Michal Saul's daughter l David: and H157
28 and *that* Michal Saul's daughter l him. H157
20:17 again, because he l him: for he loved H160
17 for he l him as he loved his own soul. H157
17 for he loved him as he l his own soul. H160
2Sa 12:24 his name Solomon: and the LORD l him. H157
13: 1 and Amnon the son of David l her. H157
15 wherewith he had l her. And Amnon H157
1Ki 3: 3 And Solomon l the LORD, walking in the H157
10: 9 because the LORD l Israel for ever, H160
11: 1 But king Solomon l many strange H157
2Ch 2:11 the LORD hath l his people, he hath H160
9: 8 because thy God l Israel, to establish H160
11:21 And Rehoboam l Maachah the daughter H157
26:10 and in Carmel: for he l husbandry. H157
Est 2:17 And the king l Esther above all the H157
Job 19:19 they whom I l are turned against me. H157
Ps 26: 8 LORD, I have l the habitation of thy H157
47: 4 the excellency of Jacob whom he l. Selah. H157
78:68 of Judah, the mount Zion which he l. H157
109:17 As he l cursing, so let it come unto him: H157
119:47 in thy commandments, which I have l. H157
48 have l; and I will meditate in thy statutes. H157
Isa 43: 4 and I have l thee: therefore will I H157
48:14 The LORD hath l him: he will do his H157
Jer 2:25 l strangers, and after them will I go. H157
8: 2 whom they have l, and whom they have H157
14:10 Thus have they l to wander, they have H157
31: 3 me, *saying*, Yea, I have l thee with an H157
Ezk 16:37 that thou hast l, with all *them* that thou H157
Hos 9: 1 hast l a reward upon every cornfloor. H157
10 abominations were according as they l. H157
11: 1 When Israel *was* a child, then I l him, H157
Mal 1: 2 I have l you, saith the LORD. Yet ye say, H157
2 Wherein hast thou l us? *Was* not Esau H157
2 brother? saith the LORD: yet I l Jacob, H157
2:11 the LORD which he l, and hath married H157
Mk 10:21 Then Jesus beholding him l him, and *G25*
Lk 7:47 forgiven; for she l much: but to whom *G25*
Jn 3:16 For God so l the world, that he gave his *G25*
19 the world, and men l darkness rather *G25*
11: 5 Now Jesus l Martha, and her sister, and *G25*
36 Then said the Jews, Behold how he l *G5368*
12:43 For they l the praise of men more than *G25*
13: 1 the Father, having l his own which were *G25*
1 in the world, he l them unto the end. *G25*
23 bosom one of his disciples, whom Jesus l. *G25*
34 have l you, that ye also love one another. *G25*
14:21 loveth me shall be l of my Father, and I *G25*
28 unto you. If ye l me, ye would rejoice, *G25*
15: 9 As the Father hath l me, so have I loved *G25*
9 As the Father loved me, so have I l *G25*
12 That ye love one another, as I have l you. *G25*
16:27 you, because ye have l me, and have *G5368*
17:23 and hast l them, as thou hast loved me. *G25*
23 and hast loved them, as thou hast l me. *G25*
26 hast l me may be in them, and I in them. *G25*
19:26 by, whom he l, he saith unto his mother, *G25*
20: 2 whom Jesus l, and saith unto them, *G5368*
21: 7 Therefore that disciple whom Jesus l *G25*
20 whom Jesus l following; which also *G25*
Ro 8:37 than conquerors through him that l us. *G25*
9:13 As it is written, Jacob have I l, but Esau *G25*
2Co 12:15 abundantly I love you, the less I be l. *G25*
Gal 2:20 God, who l me, and gave himself for me. *G25*
Eph 2: 4 for his great love wherewith he l us, *G25*
5: 2 And walk in love, as Christ also hath l *G25*
25 also l the church, and gave himself for it; *G25*
2Th 2:16 Father, which hath l us, and hath given *G25*
2Ti 4:10 For Demas hath forsaken me, having l *G25*
Heb 1: 9 Thou hast l righteousness, and hated *G25*
2Pt 2:15 who l the wages of unrighteousness; *G25*
1Jn 4:10 Herein is love, not that we l God, but *G25*
10 God, but that he l us, and sent his Son *G25*
11 Beloved, if God so l us, we ought also to *G25*
19 We love him, because he first l us. *G25*
Rev 1: 5 Unto him that l us, and washed us from *G25*
3: 9 thy feet, and to know that I have l thee. *G25*
Rev 12:11 and they l not their lives unto the death. *G25*

LOVEDST

Isa 57: 8 thou l their bed where thou sawest *it*. H157
Jn 17:24 l me before the foundation of the world. *G25*

LOVELY

2Sa 1:23 Saul and Jonathan *were* l and pleasant H157
Song 5:16 he *is* altogether l. This *is* my beloved, H4261
Ezk 33:32 And, lo, thou *art* unto them as a very l H5690
Php 4: 8 things *are* l, whatsoever things *are* *G4375*

LOVER

1Ki 5: 1 father: for Hiram was ever a l of David. H157
Ps 88:18 L and friend hast thou put far from me, H157
Tit 1: 8 But a l of hospitality, a lover of good *G5382*
8 But a lover of hospitality, a l of good *G5358*

LOVERS

Ps 38:11 My l and my friends stand aloof from H157
Jer 3: 1 harlot with many l; yet return again to H7453
4:30 thyself fair; *thy* l will despise thee, they H5689
22:20 the passages: for all thy l are destroyed. H157
22 pastors, and thy l shall go into captivity: H157
30:14 All thy l have forgotten thee; they seek H157
Lam 1: 2 among all her l she hath none to comfort H157
19 I called for my l, *but* they deceived me: H157
Ezk 16:33 thy gifts to all thy l, and hirest them, that H157
36 with thy l, and with all the idols H157
37 Behold, therefore I will gather all thy l, H157
23: 5 her l, on the Assyrians *her* neighbours, H157
9 the hand of her l, into the hand of the H157
22 I will raise up thy l against thee, from H157
Hos 2: 5 said, I will go after my l, that give *me* my H157
7 And she shall follow after her l, but she H157
10 in the sight of her l, and none shall H157
12 rewards that my l have given me: and I H157
13 her l, and forgat me, saith the LORD. H157
8: 9 alone by himself: Ephraim hath hired l. H158
2Ti 3: 2 For men shall be l of their own selves, *G5367*
4 Traitors, heady, highminded, l of *G5369*
4 lovers of pleasures more than l of God; *G5377*

LOVES

Ps 45:ttl the sons of Korah, Maschil, A Song of l. H3039
Prv 7:18 morning: let us solace ourselves with l. H159
Song 7:12 bud forth: there will I give thee my l. H1730

LOVE'S

Phlm 9 Yet for l sake I rather beseech *thee*, *G26*

LOVEST

Gen 22: 2 Isaac, whom thou l, and get thee into the H157
Jdg 14:16 but hate me, and l me not: thou hast put H157
2Sa 19: 6 In that thou l thine enemies, and hatest H157
Ps 45: 7 Thou l righteousness, and hatest H157
52: 3 Thou l evil more than good; *and* lying H157
4 Thou l all devouring words, O *thou* H157
Ecc 9: 9 Live joyfully with the wife whom thou l H157
Jn 11: 3 Lord, behold, he whom thou l is sick. *G5368*
21:15 *son* of Jonas, l thou me more than these? *G25*
16 *son* of Jonas, l thou me? He saith unto *G25*
17 *son* of Jonas, l thou me? Peter was *G5368*
17 the third time, L thou me? And he said *G5368*

LOVETH

Gen 27: 9 savoury meat for thy father, such as he l: H157
44:20 is left of his mother, and his father l him. H157
Dt 10:18 and widow, and l the stranger, in giving H157
15:16 thee; because he l thee and thine house, H157
Ru 4:15 in law, which l thee, which is better H157
Ps 11: 5 and him that l violence his soul hateth. H157
7 For the righteous LORD l righteousness; H157
33: 5 He l righteousness and judgment: the H157
34:12 What man *is he that* desireth life, *and* l H157
37:28 For the LORD l judgment, and forsaketh H157
87: 2 The LORD l the gates of Zion more than H157
99: 4 The king's strength also l judgment; H157
119:140 *is* very pure: therefore thy servant l it. H157
146: 8 bowed down: the LORD l the righteous: H157
Prv 3:12 For whom the LORD l he correcteth; H157
12: 1 Whoso l instruction loveth knowledge: H157
1 Whoso loveth instruction l knowledge: H157
13:24 he that l him chasteneth him betimes. H157
15: 9 l him that followeth after righteousness. H157
12 A scorner l not one that reproveth him: H157
17:17 A friend l at all times, and a brother is H157
19 He l transgression that loveth strife: *and* H157
19 He loveth transgression that l strife: *and* H157

Prv 19: 8 He that getteth wisdom **l** his own soul: H157
21:17 He that **l** pleasure *shall be* a poor man: H157
17 he that **l** wine and oil shall not be rich. H157
22:11 He that **l** pureness of heart, *for* the grace H157
29: 3 Whoso **l** wisdom rejoiceth his father: but H157
Ecc 5:10 He that **l** silver shall not be satisfied with H157
10 with silver; nor he that **l** abundance with H157
Song 1: 7 Tell me, O thou whom my soul **l**, where H157
3: 1 soul **l**: I sought him, but I found him not. H157
2 soul **l**: I sought him, but I found him not. H157
3 *I said*, Saw ye him whom my soul **l**? H157
4 him whom my soul **l**: I held him, and H157
Isa 1:23 thieves: every one **l** gifts, and followeth H157
Hos 10:11 *that is* taught, *and* **l** to tread out *the* H157
12: 7 of deceit *are* in his hand: he **l** to oppress. H157
Mt 10:37 He that **l** father or mother more than G5368
37 of me: and he that **l** son or daughter G5368
Lk 7: 5 For he **l** our nation, and he hath built us G25
47 whom little is forgiven, *the same* **l** little. G25
Jn 3:35 The Father **l** the Son, and hath given all G25
5:20 For the Father **l** the Son, and sheweth G5368
12:25 He that **l** his life shall lose it; and he G5368
14:21 them, he it is that **l** me: and he that G25
21 me: and he that **l** me shall be loved of G25
24 He that **l** me not keepeth not my sayings: G25
16:27 For the Father himself **l** you, because G5368
Ro 13: 8 he that **l** another hath fulfilled the law. G25
2Co 9: 7 or of necessity: for God **l** a cheerful giver. G25
Eph 5:28 bodies. He that **l** his wife loveth himself. G25
28 bodies. He that loveth his wife **l** himself. G25
Heb 12: 6 For whom the Lord **l** he chasteneth, and G25
1Jn 2:10 He that **l** his brother abideth in the light, G25
3:10 of God, neither he that **l** not his brother. G25
14 that **l** not *his* brother abideth in death. G25
4: 7 that **l** is born of God, and knoweth God. G25
8 He that **l** not knoweth not God; for God G25
20 he is a liar: for he that **l** not his brother G25
21 That he who **l** God love his brother also. G25
5: 1 God: and every one that **l** him that begat G25
1 begat **l** him also that is begotten of him. G25
3Jn 9 but Diotrephes, who **l** to have the G5383
Rev 22:15 and whosoever **l** and maketh a lie. G5368

LOVING
Prv 5:19 *Let her be as* the **l** hind and pleasant roe; H158
22: 1 **l** favour rather than silver and gold. H2896
Isa 56:10 bark; sleeping, lying down, **l** to slumber. H157

LOVINGKINDNESS
Ps 17: 7 Shew thy marvellous **l**, O thou that H2617
26: 3 For thy **l** *is* before mine eyes: and I H2617
36: 7 How excellent *is* thy **l**, O God! therefore H2617
10 O continue thy **l** unto them that know H2617
40:10 not concealed thy **l** and thy truth from H2617
11 me, O LORD: let thy **l** and thy truth H2617
42: 8 *Yet* the LORD will command his **l** in H2617
48: 9 We have thought of thy **l**, O God, in the H2617
51: 1 according to thy **l**: according unto the H2617
63: 3 Because thy **l** *is* better than life, my lips H2617
69:16 Hear me, O LORD; for thy **l** *is* good: H2617
88:11 Shall thy **l** be declared in the grave? *or* H2617
89:33 Nevertheless my **l** will I not utterly take H2617
92: 2 To shew forth thy **l** in the morning, and H2617
103: 4 thee with **l** and tender mercies; H2617
107:43 shall understand the **l** of the LORD. H2617
119:88 Quicken me after thy **l**; so shall I keep H2617
149 Hear my voice according unto thy **l**: O H2617
159 me, O LORD, according to thy **l**. H2617
138: 2 thy name for thy **l** and for thy truth: for H2617
143: 8 Cause me to hear thy **l** in the morning; H2617
Jer 9:24 LORD which exercise **l**, judgment, and H2617
16: 5 saith the LORD, *even* **l** and mercies. H2617
31: 3 therefore with **l** have I drawn thee. H2617
32:18 Thou shewest **l** unto thousands, and H2617
Hos 2:19 in judgment, and in **l**, and in mercies. H2617

LOVINGKINDNESSES
Ps 25: 6 and thy **l**; for they *have been* ever of old. H2617
89:49 Lord, where *are* thy former **l**, *which* H2617
Isa 63: 7 I will mention the **l** of the LORD, *and* H2617
7 and according to the multitude of his **l**. H2617

LOW
Dt 28:43 high; and thou shalt come down very **l**. H4295
Jdg 11:35 brought me very **l**, and thou art one of H3766
1Sa 2: 7 rich: he bringeth **l**, and lifteth up. H8213
1Ch 27:28 trees that *were* in the **l** plains *was* H8219
2Ch 9:27 that *are* in the **l** plains in abundance. H8219
26:10 cattle, both in the **l** country, and in the H8219
28:18 the cities of the **l** country, and of the H8219
19 For the LORD brought Judah **l** because H3665
Job 5:11 To set up on high those that be **l**; that H8217
14:21 **l**, but he perceiveth *it* not of them. H6819
24:24 gone and brought **l**; they are taken out H4355
40:12 *and* bring him **l**; and tread down the H3665
Ps 49: 2 Both **l** and high, rich and poor, together. H120
62: 9 Surely men of **l** degree *are* vanity, *and*
79: 8 prevent us: for we are brought very **l**. H1809
106:43 and were brought **l** for their iniquity. H4355
107:39 Again, they are minished and brought **l** H7817
116: 6 I was brought **l**, and he helped me. H1809
136:23 Who remembered us in our **l** estate: for H8213
142: 6 I am brought very **l**: deliver me from my H1809
Prv 29:23 A man's pride shall bring him **l**: but H8213
Ecc 10: 6 great dignity, and the rich sit in **l** place. H8216
12: 4 of the grinding is **l**, and he shall rise up H8217
4 daughters of musick shall be brought **l**; H7817
Isa 2:12 *is* lifted up; and he shall be brought **l**: H8213
17 of men shall be made **l**: and the LORD H8213
13:11 will lay **l** the haughtiness of the terrible. H8213
25: 5 of the terrible ones shall be brought **l**. H6030
12 he bring down, lay **l**, *and* bring to the H8213
26: 5 city, he layeth it **l**; he layeth it low, *even* H8213
5 it low; he layeth it **l**, *even* to the ground; H8213
29: 4 thy speech shall be **l** out of the dust, H7817
32:19 and the city shall be **l** in a low place. H8213
19 and the city shall be low in a **l** place. H8219
40: 4 hill shall be made **l**: and the crooked H8213
Lam 3:55 name, O LORD, out of the **l** dungeon. H8482
Ezk 17: 6 a spreading vine of **l** stature, whose H8217
24 have exalted the **l** tree, have dried up H8217
21:26 *that is* **l**, and abase *him that is* high. H8217
26:20 set thee in the **l** parts of the earth, in H8482
Lk 1:48 For he hath regarded the **l** estate of his G5014
52 seats, and exalted them of **l** degree. G5011
3: 5 shall be brought **l**; and the crooked shall G5013
Ro 12:16 to men of **l** estate. Be not wise in G5011
Jas 1: 9 Let the brother of **l** degree rejoice in G5011
10 But the rich, in that he is made **l**: G5014

LOWER
Gen 6:16 side thereof; *with* **l**, second, and third H8482
Lev 13:20 it *be* in sight **l** than the skin, and the H8217
21 and *if* it *be* not **l** than the skin, but *be* H8217
26 spot, and it *be* no **l** than the *other* skin, H8217
14:37 which in sight *are* **l** than the wall; H8217
Neh 4:13 Therefore set I in the **l** places behind H8482
Ps 8: 5 For thou hast made him a little **l** than H2637
63: 9 *it*, shall go into the **l** parts of the earth. H8482
Prv 25: 7 shouldest be put **l** in the presence of the H8213
Isa 22: 9 together the waters of the **l** pool. H8481
44:23 done *it*: shout, ye **l** parts of the earth: H8482
Ezk 40:18 length of the gates *was* the **l** pavement. H8481
19 from the forefront of the **l** gate unto the H8481
42: 5 than these, than the **l**, and than the H8481
43:14 ground *even* to the **l** settle *shall be* two H8481
Eph 4: 9 first into the **l** parts of the earth? G2737
Heb 2: 7 Thou madest him a little **l** than the G1642
9 was made a little **l** than the angels for G1642

LOWEST
Dt 32:22 burn unto the **l** hell, and shall consume H8482
1Ki 12:31 priests of the **l** of the people, which H7098
13:33 but made again of the **l** of the people H7098
2Ki 17:32 themselves of the **l** of them priests of H7098
Ps 86:13 hast delivered my soul from the **l** hell. H8482
88: 6 Thou hast laid me in the **l** pit, in H8482
139:15 wrought in the **l** parts of the earth. H8482
Ezk 41: 7 **l** *chamber* to the highest by the midst. H8481
42: 6 **l** and the middlemost from the ground. H8481
Lk 14: 9 begin with shame to take the **l** room. G2078
10 sit down in the **l** room; that when he G2078

LOWETH
Job 6: 5 hath grass? or **l** the ox over his fodder? H1600

LOWING
1Sa 6:12 the highway, **l** as they went, and turned H1600
15:14 and the **l** of the oxen which I hear? H6963

LOWLINESS
Eph 4: 2 With all **l** and meekness, with G5012
Php 2: 3 or vainglory; but in **l** of mind let each G5012

LOWLY
Ps 138: 6 the **l**: but the proud he knoweth afar off. H8217
Prv 3:34 scorners: but he giveth grace unto the **l**. H6041
11: 2 shame: but with the **l** *is* wisdom. H6800
16:19 spirit with the **l**, than to divide the spoil H6041
Zec 9: 9 having salvation; **l**, and riding upon an H6041
Mt 11:29 for I am meek and **l** in heart: and ye G5011

LOWRING
Mt 16: 3 the sky is red and **l**. O *ye* hypocrites, ye G4768

LUBIM
Nah 3: 9 infinite; Put and **L** were thy helpers. H3864

LUBIMS
2Ch 12: 3 the **L**, the Sukkiims, and the Ethiopians. H3864
16: 8 Were not the Ethiopians and the **L** a H3864

LUCAS
Phlm 24 Marcus, Aristarchus, Demas, **L**, my G3065

LUCIFER
Isa 14:12 How art thou fallen from heaven, O **L**, H1966

LUCIUS
Act 13: 1 was called Niger, and **L** of Cyrene, and G3066
Ro 16:21 Timotheus my workfellow, and **L**, and G3066

LUCRE
1Sa 8: 3 turned aside after **l**, and took bribes, H1215
1Ti 3: 3 not greedy of filthy **l**; but patient, not a G146
8 given to much wine, not greedy of filthy **l**; G146
Tit 1: 7 to wine, no striker, not given to filthy **l**; G146
1Pt 5: 2 not for filthy **l**, but of a ready mind; G147

LUCRE'S
Tit 1:11 which they ought not, for filthy **l** sake. G2771

LUD
Gen 10:22 and Arphaxad, and **L**, and Aram. H3865
1Ch 1:17 Arphaxad, and **L**, and Aram, and Uz, H3865
Isa 66:19 *to* Tarshish, Pul, and **L**, that draw the H3865
Ezk 27:10 They of Persia and of **L** and of Phut H3865

LUDIM
Gen 10:13 And Mizraim begat **L**, and Anamim, H3866
1Ch 1:11 And Mizraim begat **L**, and Anamim, H3866

LUHITH
Isa 15: 5 mounting up of **L** with weeping shall H3872
Jer 48: 5 For in the going up of **L** continual H3872

LUKE
Col 4:14 **L**, the beloved physician, and Demas, G3065
2Ti 4:11 Only **L** is with me. Take Mark, and G3065

LUKEWARM
Rev 3:16 So then because thou art **l**, and neither G5513

LUMP
2Ki 20: 7 And Isaiah said, Take a **l** of figs. And H1690
Isa 38:21 For Isaiah had said, Let them take a **l** H1690
Ro 9:21 clay, of the same **l** to make one vessel G5445
11:16 For if the firstfruit *be* holy, the **l** *is* also G5445
1Co 5: 6 that a little leaven leaveneth the whole **l**? G5445
7 that ye may be a new **l**, as ye are G5445
Gal 5: 9 A little leaven leaveneth the whole **l**. G5445

LUNATICK
Mt 4:24 those which were **l**, and those that had G4583
17:15 Lord, have mercy on my son: for he is **l**, G4583

LURE See ALLURE.

LURK
Prv 1:11 **l** privily for the innocent without cause: H6845
18 blood; they **l** privily for their *own* lives. H6845

LURKING
1Sa 23:23 of all the **l** places where he hideth H4224
Ps 10: 8 He sitteth in the **l** places of the villages: H3993
17:12 it were a young lion **l** in secret places. H3427

LUST
Ex 15: 9 the spoil; my **l** shall be satisfied upon H5315
Ps 78:18 in their heart by asking meat for their **l**. H5315
30 They were not estranged from their **l**. H8378
81:12 their own hearts' **l**: *and* they walked in H8307
Prv 6:25 **L** not after her beauty in thine heart; H2530
Mt 5:28 looketh on a woman to **l** after her hath G1937
Ro 1:27 burned in their **l** one toward another; G3715
7: 7 I had not known **l**, except the law had G1939
1Co 10: 6 intent we should not **l** after evil G1511+G1938

Gal 5:16 and ye shall not fulfil the l of the flesh. G1939
1Th 4: 5 Not in the l of concupiscence, even as G3806
Jas 1:14 is drawn away of his own l, and enticed. G1939
15 Then when l hath conceived, it G1939
4: 2 Ye l, and have not: ye kill, and desire to G1937
2Pt 1: 4 that is in the world through l. G1939
2:10 the flesh in the l of uncleanness, and G1939
1Jn 2:16 For all that is in the world, the l of the G1939
16 the flesh, and the l of the eyes, and the G1939
17 And the world passeth away, and the l G1939

LUSTED

Nu 11:34 there they buried the people that l. H183
Ps 106:14 But l exceedingly in the wilderness, and H183
1Co 10: 6 not lust after evil things, as they also l. G1937
Rev 18:14 And the fruits that thy soul l after are G1937

LUSTETH

Dt 12:15 thy soul l after, according to the H183
20 eat flesh, whatsoever thy soul l after. H183
21 in thy gates whatsoever thy soul l after. H183
14:26 thy soul l after, for oxen, or for H183
Gal 5:17 For the flesh l against the Spirit, and G1937
Jas 4: 5 The spirit that dwelleth in us l to envy? G1971

LUSTING

Nu 11: 4 among them fell a l: and the children of H183

LUSTS

Mk 4:19 of riches, and the l of other things G1939
Jn 8:44 Ye are of your father the devil, and the l G1939
Ro 1:24 through the l of their own hearts, G1939
6:12 that ye should obey it in the l thereof. G1939
13:14 for the flesh, to fulfil the l thereof. G1939
Gal 5:24 the flesh with the affections and l. G1939
Eph 2: 3 times past in the l of our flesh, fulfilling G1939
4:22 is corrupt according to the deceitful l; G1939
1Ti 6: 9 foolish and hurtful l, which drown men G1939
2Ti 2:22 Flee also youthful l: but follow G1939
3: 6 laden with sins, led away with divers l, G1939
4: 3 but after their own l shall they heap to G1939
Tit 2:12 and worldly l, we should live soberly, G1939
3: 3 serving divers l and pleasures, living G1939
Jas 4: 1 of your l that war in your members? G2237
3 that ye may consume it upon your l. G2237
1Pt 1:14 to the former l in your ignorance: G1939
2:11 fleshly l, which war against the soul; G1939
4: 2 to the l of men, but to the will of God. G1939
3 in lasciviousness, l, excess of wine, G1939
2Pt 2:18 they allure through the l of the flesh, G1939
3: 3 days scoffers, walking after their own l, G1939
Jude 16 after their own l; and their mouth G1939
18 should walk after their own ungodly l. G1939

LUSTY

Jdg 3:29 ten thousand men, all l, and all men of H8082

LUZ

Gen 28:19 of that city was called L at the first. H3870
35: 6 So Jacob came to L, which is in the land H3870
48: 3 unto me at L in the land of Canaan, H3870
Jos 16: 2 And goeth out from Beth-el to L, and H3870
18:13 thence toward L, to the side of Luz, H3870
13 Luz, to the side of L, which is Beth-el, H3870
Jdg 1:23 (Now the name of the city before was L.) H3870
26 the name thereof L: which is the name H3870

LYCAONIA

Act 14: 6 Derbe, cities of L, and unto the region G3071
11 in the speech of L, The gods are come G3072

LYCIA

Act 27: 5 we came to Myra, a city of L. G3073

LYDDA

Act 9:32 also to the saints which dwelt at L. G3069
35 And all that dwelt at L and Saron saw G3069
38 And forasmuch as L was nigh to Joppa, G3069

LYDIA

Ezk 30: 5 Ethiopia, and Libya, and L, and all the H3865
Act 16:14 And a certain woman named L, a seller G3070
40 into the house of L: and when they had G3070

LYDIANS

Jer 46: 9 the L, that handle and bend the bow. H3866

LYING

Gen 29: 2 flocks of sheep l by it; for out of that H7257
34: 7 wrought folly in Israel in l with Jacob's H7901
Ex 23: 5 that hateth thee l under his burden, H7257
Nu 31:17 that hath known man by l with him. H4904
18 by l with him, keep alive for yourselves. H4904
35 that had not known man by l with him. H4904
Dt 21: 1 thee to possess it, l in the field, and it H5307
22:22 If a man be found l with a woman H7901
Jdg 9:35 that were with him, from l in wait.
16: 9 Now there were men l in wait, abiding
21:12 known no man by l with any male: and H4904
1Ki 22:22 and I will be a l spirit in the mouth of H8267
23 LORD hath put a l spirit in the mouth H8267
2Ch 18:21 And he said, I will go out, and be a l H8267
22 LORD hath put a l spirit in the mouth H8267
Ps 31: 6 I have hated them that regard l H7723
18 Let the l lips be put to silence; which H8267
52: 3 Thou lovest evil more than good; and l H8267
59:12 and for cursing and l which they speak. H3585
109: 2 spoken against me with a l tongue. H8267
Ps 119:29 Remove from me the way of l: and H8267
163 I hate and abhor l: but thy law do I love. H8267
120: 2 Deliver my soul, O LORD, from l lips, H8267
139: 3 Thou compassest my path and my l H7252
Prv 6:17 A proud look, a l tongue, and hands H8267
10:18 He that hideth hatred with l lips, and H8267
12:19 but a l tongue is but for a moment. H8267
22 L lips are abomination to the LORD: H8267
13: 5 A righteous man hateth l: but a H1697+H8267
17: 7 not a fool: much less do l lips a prince. H8267
21: 6 The getting of treasures by a l tongue is H8267
26:28 A l tongue hateth those that are H8267
Isa 30: 9 That this is a rebellious people, l H3586
32: 7 the poor with l words, even when the H8267
56:10 sleeping, l down, loving to slumber. H7901
59:13 In transgressing and l against the H3584
Jer 7: 4 Trust ye not in l words, saying, The H8267
8 Behold, ye trust in l words, that cannot H8267
29:23 and have spoken l words in my name, H8267
Lam 3:10 He was unto me as a bear l in wait, and
Ezk 13: 6 They have seen vanity and l divination, H3577
7 ye not spoken a l divination, whereas H3577
19 your l to my people that hear your lies? H3576
Dan 2: 9 ye have prepared l and corrupt words H3538
Hos 4: 2 By swearing, and l, and killing, and H3584
Jna 2: 8 They that observe l vanities forsake H7723
Mt 9: 2 sick of the palsy, l on a bed: and Jesus G906
Mk 5:40 and entereth in where the damsel was l. G345
Lk 2:12 in swaddling clothes, l in a manger. G2749
16 Joseph, and the babe l in a manger. G2749
Jn 13:25 He then l on Jesus' breast saith unto G1968
20: 5 the linen clothes l; yet went he not in. G2749
7 his head, not l with the linen clothes, G2749
Act 20:19 befell me by the l in wait of the Jews:
23:16 son heard of their l in wait, he went and
Eph 4:25 Wherefore putting away l, speak every G5579
2Th 2: 9 all power and signs and l wonders, G5579

LYSANIAS

Lk 3: 1 and L the tetrarch of Abilene, G3078

LYSIAS

Act 23:26 Claudius L unto the most excellent G3079
24: 7 But the chief captain L came upon us, G3079
22 and said, When L the chief captain G3079

LYSTRA

Act 14: 6 They were ware of it, and fled unto L G3082
8 And there sat a certain man at L, G3082
21 to L, and to Iconium, and Antioch, G3082
16: 1 Then came he to Derbe and L: and, G3082
2 brethren that were at L and Iconium. G3082
2Ti 3:11 at Iconium, at L; what persecutions I G3082

M

MAACAH

2Sa 3: 3 the son of M the daughter of Talmai H4601
10: 6 and of king M a thousand men, and H4601
8 and M, were by themselves in the field. H4601

MAACHAH

Gen 22:24 and Gaham, and Thahash, and M. H4601
1Ki 2:39 Achish son of M king of Gath. And they H4601
15: 2 was M, the daughter of Abishalom. H4601
10 was M, the daughter of Abishalom. H4601
13 And also M his mother, even her he H4601
1Ch 2:48 M, Caleb's concubine, bare Sheber, and H4601
3: 2 The third, Absalom the son of M the H4601
7:15 sister's name was M;) and the name of H4601
16 And M the wife of Machir bare a son, H4601
8:29 of Gibeon; whose wife's name was M: H4601
9:35 Jehiel, whose wife's name was M: H4601
11:43 Hanan the son of M, and Joshaphat the H4601
19: 7 and the king of M and his people; who H4601
27:16 Simeonites, Shephatiah the son of M: H4601
2Ch 11:20 And after her he took M the daughter H4601
21 And Rehoboam loved M the daughter H4601
22 Abijah the son of M the chief, to be H4601
15:16 And also concerning M the mother of H4601

MAACHATHI

Dt 3:14 of Geshuri and M; and called them after H4602

MAACHATHITE

2Sa 23:34 the son of the M, Eliam the son of H4602
2Ki 25:23 the son of a M, they and their men. H4602
1Ch 4:19 the Garmite, and Eshtemoa the M. H4602
Jer 40: 8 the son of a M, they and their men. H4602

MAACHATHITES

Jos 12: 5 and the M, and half Gilead, the H4602
13:11 the Geshurites and M, and all mount H4602
13 nor the M: but the Geshurites H4602
13 and the M dwell among the Israelites H4601

MAADAI

Ezr 10:34 Of the sons of Bani; M, Amram, and H4572

MAADIAH

Neh 12: 5 Miamin, M, Bilgah, H4573

MAAI

Neh 12:36 Milalai, Gilalai, M, Nethaneel, and H4597

MAALEHACRABBIM

Jos 15: 3 And it went out to the south side to M, H4610

MAARATH

Jos 15:59 And M, and Beth-anoth, and Eltekon; H4638

MAASEIAH

1Ch 15:18 and Benaiah, and M, and Mattithiah, H4641
20 and Eliab, and M, and Benaiah, with H4641
2Ch 23: 1 son of Obed, and M the son of Adaiah, H4641
26:11 the scribe and M the ruler, under the H4641
28: 7 of Ephraim, slew M the king's son, and H4641
34: 8 of Azaliah, and M the governor of the H4641
Ezr 10:18 and his brethren; M, and Eliezer, and H4641
21 And of the sons of Harim; M, and H4641
22 And of the sons of Pashur; Elioenai, M, H4641
30 and Chelal, Benaiah, M, Mattaniah, H4641
Neh 3:23 of M the son of Ananiah by his house. H4641
8: 4 and Hilkiah, and M, on his right hand; H4641
7 Hodijah, M, Kelita, Azariah, Jozabad, H4641
10:25 Rehum, Hashabnah, M, H4641
11: 5 And M the son of Baruch, the son of H4641
7 M, the son of Ithiel, the son of Jesaiah. H4641
12:41 And the priests; Eliakim, M, Miniamin, H4641
42 And M, and Shemaiah, and Eleazar, H4641
Jer 21: 1 the son of M the priest, saying, H4641
29:21 the son of M, which prophesy a lie H4641
25 the son of M the priest, and to all H4641
32:12 of Neriah, the son of M, in the sight of H4271
35: 4 the chamber of M the son of Shallum, H4641
37: 3 the son of M the priest to the prophet H4641
51:59 of Neriah, the son of M, when he went H4271

MAASIAI
1Ch 9:12 of Malchijah, and **M** the son of Adiel, H4640

MAATH
Lk 3:26 Which was *the son* of **M**, which was *the* G3092

MAAZ
1Ch 2:27 were, **M**, and Jamin, and Eker. H4619

MAAZIAH
1Ch 24:18 to Delaiah, the four and twentieth to **M**. H4590
Neh 10: 8 **M**, Bilgai, Shemaiah: these *were* the H4590

MACEDONIA
Act 16: 9 stood a man of **M**, and prayed him, G3110
9 saying, Come over into **M**, and help us. G3109
10 to go into **M**, assuredly gathering G3109
12 city of that part of **M**, *and* a colony: and G3109
18: 5 were come from **M**, Paul was pressed in G3109
19:21 passed through **M** and Achaia, to go to G3109
22 So he sent into **M** two of them that G3109
29 men of **M**, Paul's companions G3110
20: 1 *them*, and departed for to go into **M**. G3109
3 Syria, he purposed to return through **M**. G3109
Ro 15:26 For it hath pleased them of **M** and G3109
1Co 16: 5 **M**: for I do pass through Macedonia. G3109
5 Macedonia: for I do pass through **M**. G3109
2Co 1:16 And to pass by you into **M**, and to come G3109
16 come again out of **M** unto you, and of G3109
2:13 of them, I went from thence into **M**. G3109
7: 5 For, when we were come into **M**, our G3109
8: 1 of God bestowed on the churches of **M**; G3109
9: 2 of you to them of **M**, that Achaia was G3110
4 Lest haply if they of **M** come with me, G3110
11: 9 which came from **M** supplied: and in G3109
Php 4:15 when I departed from **M**, no church G3109
1Th 1: 7 to all that believe in **M** and Achaia. G3109
8 the Lord not only in **M** and Achaia, but G3109
4:10 which are in all **M**: but we beseech you, G3109
1Ti 1: 3 when I went into **M**, that thou mightest G3109

MACEDONIAN
Act 27: 2 a **M** of Thessalonica, being with us. G3110

MACHBANAI
1Ch 12:13 Jeremiah the tenth, **M** the eleventh. H4344

MACHBENAH
1Ch 2:49 the father of **M**, and the father of Gibea: H4343

MACHI
Nu 13:15 Of the tribe of Gad, Geuel the son of **M**. H4352

MACHIR
Gen 50:23 children also of **M** the son of Manasseh H4353
Nu 26:29 Of the sons of Manasseh: of **M**, the H4353
29 the Machirites: and **M** begat Gilead: of H4353
27: 1 of Gilead, the son of **M**, the son of H4353
32:39 And the children of **M** the son of H4353
40 And Moses gave Gilead unto **M** the son H4353
36: 1 of Gilead, the son of **M**, the son of H4353
Dt 3:15 And I gave Gilead unto **M**. H4353
Jos 13:31 the children of **M** the son of Manasseh, H4353
31 of the children of **M** by their families. H4353
17: 1 of Joseph; *to wit*, for **M** the firstborn of H4353
3 of Gilead, the son of **M**, the son of H4353
Jdg 5:14 thy people; out of **M** came down H4353
2Sa 9: 4 of **M**, the son of Ammiel, in Lo-debar. H4353
5 **M**, the son of Ammiel, from Lo-debar. H4353
17:27 of Ammon, and **M** the son of Ammiel H4353
1Ch 2:21 in to the daughter of **M** the father of H4353
23 *to* the sons of **M** the father of Gilead. H4353
7:14 Aramitess bare **M** the father of Gilead: H4353
15 And **M** took to wife *the sister* of H4353
16 And Maachah the wife of **M** bare a son, H4353
17 the son of **M**, the son of Manasseh. H4353

MACHIRITES
Nu 26:29 the family of the **M**: and Machir begat H4354

MACHNADEBAI
Ezr 10:40 **M**, Shashai, Sharai, H4367

MACHPELAH
Gen 23: 9 That he may give me the cave of **M**, H4375
17 which *was* in **M**, which *was* before H4375
19 cave of the field of **M** before Mamre: H4375
25: 9 him in the cave of **M**, in the field of H4375
49:30 In the cave that *is* in the field of **M**, H4375
50:13 cave of the field of **M**, which Abraham H4375

MAD
Dt 28:34 So that thou shalt be **m** for the sight of H7696
1Sa 21:13 feigned himself **m** in their hands, and H1984
14 Lo, ye see the man is **m**: wherefore *then* H7696
15 Have I need of **m** men, that ye have H7696
15 this *fellow* to play the **m** man in my H7696
2Ki 9:11 came this **m** *fellow* to thee? And H7696
Ps 102: 8 **m** against me are sworn against me. H1984
Prv 26:18 As a **m** *man* who casteth firebrands, H3856
Ecc 2: 2 I said of laughter, *It is* **m**: and of mirth, H1984
7: 7 man **m**; and a gift destroyeth the heart. H1984
Isa 44:25 maketh diviners **m**; that turneth wise H1984
Jer 25:16 and be moved, and be **m**, because of the H1984
29:26 for every man *that is* **m**, and maketh H7696
50:38 and they are **m** upon *their* idols. H1984
51: 7 her wine; therefore the nations are **m**. H1984
Hos 9: 7 spiritual man *is* **m**, for the multitude of H7696
Jn 10:20 hath a devil, and is **m**; why hear ye him? G3105
Act 12:15 And they said unto her, Thou art **m**. But G3105
26:11 being exceedingly **m** against them, I G1693
24 learning doth make thee **m**. G1519+G3130
25 But he said, I am not **m**, most noble G3105
1Co 14:23 will they not say that ye are **m**? G3105

MADAI
Gen 10: 2 and Magog, and **M**, and Javan, and H4074
1Ch 1: 5 and Magog, and **M**, and Javan, and H4074

MADE
Gen 1: 7 And God **m** the firmament, and H6213
16 And God **m** two great lights; the greater H6213
16 to rule the night: *he* **m** the stars also.
25 And God **m** the beast of the earth after H6213
31 thing that he had **m**, and, behold, *it was* H6213
2: 2 which he had **m**; and he rested on the H6213
2 day from all his work which he had **m**. H6213
3 all his work which God created and **m**. H6213
4 God **m** the earth and the heavens, H6213
9 And out of the ground **m** the LORD H6779
22 taken from man, **m** he a woman, and H1129
3: 1 LORD God had **m**. And he said unto the H6213
7 together, and **m** themselves aprons. H6213
5: 1 man, in the likeness of God **m** he him; H6213
6: 6 LORD that he had **m** man on the earth, H6213
7 for it repenteth me that I have **m** them. H6213
7: 4 that I have **m** will I destroy from H6213
8: 1 the ark: and God **m** a wind to pass over H5674
6 the window of the ark which he had **m**: H6213
9: 6 for in the image of God **m** he man. H6213
13: 4 which he had **m** there at the first: and H6213
14: 2 *That these* **m** war with Bera king of H6213
23 shouldest say, I have **m** Abram rich: H6238
15:18 In the same day the LORD **m** a H3772
17: 5 a father of many nations have I **m** thee. H5414
19: 3 his house; and he **m** them a feast, and H6213
33 And they **m** their father drink wine H8248
35 And they **m** their father drink wine H8248
21: 6 And Sarah said, God hath **m** me to H6213
8 and Abraham **m** a great feast the *same* H6213
27 and both of them **m** a covenant. H3772
32 Thus they **m** a covenant at Beer-sheba: H3772
23:17 all the borders round about, were **m** sure
20 *is* therein, were **m** sure unto Abraham
24:11 And he **m** his camels to kneel down H1288
21 had **m** his journey prosperous or not. H6743
37 And my master **m** me swear, saying,
46 And she **m** haste, and let down her
46 and she **m** the camels drink also. H8248
26:22 the LORD hath **m** room for us, and we H7337
30 And he **m** them a feast, and they did H6213
27:14 and his mother **m** savoury meat, such H6213
30 soon as Isaac had **m** an end of blessing
31 And he also had **m** savoury meat, and H6213
37 Behold, I have **m** him thy lord, and all H7760
29:22 all the men of the place, and **m** a feast. H6213
30:37 in them, and **m** the white appear which
31:46 took stones, and **m** an heap: and they H6213
33:17 an house, and **m** booths for his cattle: H6213
37: 3 and he **m** him a coat of *many* colours. H6213
7 about, and **m** obeisance to my sheaf.
9 and the eleven stars **m** obeisance to me.
39: 3 **m** all that he did to prosper in his hand.
4 him: and he **m** him overseer over his
5 time *that* he had **m** him overseer in his
23 which he did, the LORD **m** *it* to prosper.
40:20 birthday, that he **m** a feast unto all his H6213
41:43 And he **m** him to ride in the second
43 **m** him *ruler* over all the land of Egypt. H5414
51 God, *said he*, hath **m** me forget all my
42: 7 he knew them, but **m** himself strange
43:25 And they **m** ready the present against
28 down their heads, and **m** obeisance.
30 And Joseph **m** haste; for his bowels did
45: 1 **m** himself known unto his brethren.
8 but God: and he hath **m** me a father to H7760
9 son Joseph, God hath **m** me lord of all H7760
46:29 And Joseph **m** ready his chariot, and
47:26 And Joseph **m** it a law over the land of H7760
49:24 arms of his hands were **m** strong by the H6339
33 And when Jacob had **m** an end of
50: 5 My father **m** me swear, saying, Lo, I die:
6 father, according as he **m** thee swear.
10 and he **m** a mourning for his H6213
Ex 1:13 And the Egyptians **m** the children of
14 And they **m** their lives bitter with hard H4843
14 they **m** them serve, *was* with rigour.
21 feared God, that he **m** them houses. H6213
2:14 And he said, Who **m** thee a prince and H7760
4:11 him, Who hath **m** man's mouth? or H7760
5:21 because ye have **m** our savour to be
7: 1 unto Moses, See, I have **m** thee a god to H5414
9:20 of Pharaoh **m** his servants and his
14: 6 And he **m** ready his chariot, and took his
21 all that night, and **m** the sea dry *land*, H7760
15:17 *which* thou hast **m** for thee to dwell in, H6466
25 the waters were **m** sweet: there he made
25 sweet: there he **m** for them a statute H7760
16:31 taste of it *was* like wafers **m** with honey.
18:25 of all Israel, and **m** them heads over H5414
20:11 For *in* six days the LORD **m** heaven H6213
24: 8 **m** with you concerning all these words. H3772
25:31 the candlestick be **m**: his shaft, and his H6213
33 Three bowls **m** like unto almonds, *with* a
33 and three bowls **m** like almonds in the
34 *shall be* four bowls **m** like unto almonds,
26:31 work: with cherubims shall it be **m**: H6213
29:18 an offering **m** by fire unto the LORD.
25 it *is* an offering **m** by fire unto the LORD.
33 atonement was **m**, to consecrate *and* to
36 when thou hast **m** an atonement for it,
41 an offering **m** by fire unto the LORD.
30:20 burn offering **m** by fire unto the LORD:
31:17 days the LORD **m** heaven and earth, H6213
18 when he had **m** an end of communing
32: 4 tool, after he had **m** it a molten calf: H6213
5 it; and Aaron **m** proclamation, and said,
8 them: they have **m** them a molten calf, H6213
20 And he took the calf which they had **m**, H6213
20 and **m** the children of Israel drink *of it*.
25 (for Aaron had **m** them naked unto *their*
31 sin, and have **m** them gods of gold. H6213
35 they **m** the calf, which Aaron made. H6213
35 they made the calf, which Aaron **m**. H6213
34: 8 And Moses **m** haste, and bowed his head
27 words I have **m** a covenant with thee H3772
35:21 one whom his spirit **m** willing, *and* they
29 whose heart **m** them willing to bring
29 to be **m** by the hand of Moses. H6213
36: 4 every man from his work which they **m**; H6213
8 of the tabernacle **m** ten curtains *of* fine H6213
8 cherubims of cunning work **m** he them. H6213
11 And he **m** loops of blue on the edge of H6213
11 likewise he **m** in the uttermost side H6213
12 Fifty loops **m** he in one curtain, and H6213
12 and fifty loops **m** he in the edge of the H6213
13 And he **m** fifty taches of gold, and H6213
14 And he **m** curtains *of* goats' *hair* for the H6213
14 tabernacle: eleven curtains he **m** them. H6213
17 And he **m** fifty loops upon the H6213
17 and fifty loops **m** he upon the edge of H6213
18 And he **m** fifty taches *of* brass to couple H6213
19 And he **m** a covering for the tent *of* H6213
20 And he **m** boards for the tabernacle *of* H6213
23 And he **m** boards for the tabernacle; H6213
24 And forty sockets of silver he **m** under H6213
25 the north corner, he **m** twenty boards, H6213
27 tabernacle westward he **m** six boards. H6213
28 And two boards **m** he for the corners of H6213
31 And he **m** bars of shittim wood; five for H6213
33 And he **m** the middle bar to shoot H6213
34 with gold, and **m** their rings *of* gold *to* H6213
35 And he **m** a vail *of* blue, and purple, H6213
35 cherubims **m** he it of cunning work. H6213
36 And he **m** thereunto four pillars *of* H6213
37 And he **m** an hanging for the H6213
37: 1 And Bezaleel **m** the ark *of* shittim H6213

Ex 37: 2 **m** a crown of gold to it round about. H6213
4 And he **m** staves *of* shittim wood, and H6213
6 And he **m** the mercy seat *of* pure gold: H6213
7 And he **m** two cherubims *of* gold, H6213
7 out of one piece **m** he them, on the two H6213
8 of the mercy seat **m** he the cherubims H6213
10 And he **m** the table *of* shittim wood: H6213
11 pure gold, and **m** thereunto a crown H6213
12 Also he **m** thereunto a border of an H6213
12 round about; and **m** a crown of gold H6213
15 And he **m** the staves *of* shittim wood, H6213
16 And he **m** the vessels which *were* upon H6213
17 And he **m** the candlestick *of* pure gold: H6213
17 *of* beaten work **m** he the candlestick; H6213
19 Three bowls **m** after the fashion of
19 and three bowls **m** like almonds in
20 *were* four bowls **m** like almonds, his
23 And he **m** his seven lamps, and his H6213
24 *Of* a talent of pure gold **m** he it, and all H6213
25 And he **m** the incense altar *of* shittim H6213
26 **m** unto it a crown of gold round about. H6213
27 And he **m** two rings of gold for it under H6213
28 And he **m** the staves *of* shittim wood, H6213
29 And he **m** the holy anointing oil, and H6213
38: 1 And he **m** the altar of burnt offering *of* H6213
2 And he **m** the horns thereof on the four H6213
3 And he **m** all the vessels of the altar, H6213
3 all the vessels thereof **m** he *of* brass. H6213
4 And he **m** for the altar a brasen grate H6213
6 And he **m** the staves *of* shittim wood, H6213
7 he **m** the altar hollow with boards. H6213
8 And he **m** the laver *of* brass, and the H6213
9 And he **m** the court: on the south side H6213
22 the tribe of Judah, **m** all that the LORD H6213
28 five shekels he **m** hooks for the pillars, H6213
30 And therewith he **m** the sockets to the H6213
39: 1 and scarlet, they **m** cloths of service, to H6213
1 holy *place*, and **m** the holy garments H6213
2 And he **m** the ephod *of* gold, blue, and H6213
4 They **m** shoulderpieces for it, to couple H6213
8 And he **m** the breastplate *of* cunning H6213
9 It was foursquare; they **m** the H6213
15 And they **m** upon the breastplate H6213
16 And they **m** two ouches *of* gold, and H6213
19 And they **m** two rings of gold, and put H6213
20 And they **m** two *other* golden rings, H6213
22 And he **m** the robe of the ephod *of* H6213
24 And they **m** upon the hems of the robe H6213
25 And they **m** bells *of* pure gold, and put H6213
27 And they **m** coats *of* fine linen *of* woven H6213
30 And they **m** the plate of the holy crown H6213
42 so the children of Israel **m** all the work. H6213
Lev 1: 9 an offering **m** by fire, of a sweet savour H801
13 an offering **m** by fire, of a sweet savour H801
17 an offering **m** by fire, of a sweet savour
2: 2 *to be* an offering **m** by fire, of a sweet
3 of the offerings of the LORD **m** by fire.
7 it shall be **m** *of* fine flour with oil. H6213
8 offering that is **m** of these things unto H6213
9 *it is* an offering **m** by fire, of a sweet
10 of the offerings of the LORD **m** by fire.
11 LORD, shall be **m** with leaven: for ye H6213
11 in any offering of the LORD **m** by fire.
16 *it is* an offering **m** by fire unto the LORD.
3: 3 an offering **m** by fire unto the LORD;
5 fire: *it is* an offering **m** by fire, of a sweet
9 an offering **m** by fire unto the LORD;
11 of the offering **m** by fire unto the LORD.
14 *even* an offering **m** by fire unto the
16 food of the offering **m** by fire for a sweet
4:35 to the offerings **m** by fire unto the LORD;
5:12 to the offerings **m** by fire unto the LORD:
6:17 of my offerings **m** by fire; it *is* most holy,
18 of the LORD **m** by fire: every one that
21 In a pan it shall be **m** with oil; *and* H6213
7: 5 *for* an offering **m** by fire unto the LORD:
25 men offer an offering **m** by fire unto the
30 of the LORD **m** by fire, the fat with
35 of the LORD **m** by fire, in the day *when*
8:21 *and* an offering **m** by fire unto the
28 it *is* an offering **m** by fire unto the LORD.
10:12 of the LORD **m** by fire, and eat it without
13 **m** by fire: for so I am commanded.
15 with the offerings **m** by fire of the fat, to
13:48 in a skin, or in any thing **m** of skin; H4399
51 any work that is **m** of skin; the plague H6213
14:11 the man that is to be **m** clean, and those
36 in the house be not **m** unclean: and
16:17 come out, and have **m** an atonement for

Lev 16:20 And when he hath **m** an end of
21: 6 of the LORD **m** by fire, *and* the bread
21 of the LORD **m** by fire: he hath a
22: 5 he may be **m** unclean, or a man H2930
27 for an offering **m** by fire unto the LORD.
23: 8 But ye shall offer an offering **m** by fire
13 oil, an offering **m** by fire unto the LORD
18 *even* an offering **m** by fire, of sweet
25 an offering **m** by fire unto the LORD.
27 an offering **m** by fire unto the LORD.
36 Seven days ye shall offer an offering **m**
36 shall offer an offering **m** by fire unto the
37 to offer an offering **m** by fire unto the
43 may know that I **m** the children of Israel
24: 7 an offering **m** by fire unto the LORD.
9 LORD **m** by fire by a perpetual statute.
26:13 of your yoke, and **m** you go upright.
46 which the LORD **m** between him and H5414
Nu 4:15 And when Aaron and his sons have **m**
26 that is **m** for them: so shall they serve. H6213
5: 8 an atonement shall be **m** for him.
27 And when he hath **m** her to drink the
6: 4 nothing that is **m** of the vine tree, from H6213
8: 4 shewed Moses, so he **m** the candlestick. H6213
21 LORD; and Aaron **m** an atonement for
11: 8 *it* in pans, and **m** cakes of it: and the H6213
14:36 land, who returned, and **m** all the
15:10 wine, *for* an offering **m** by fire, of a sweet
13 an offering **m** by fire, of a sweet savour
14 will offer an offering **m** by fire, of a sweet
25 a sacrifice **m** by fire unto the LORD,
16:31 And it came to pass, as he had **m** an end
39 and they were **m** broad *plates for* a
47 and **m** an atonement for the people.
18:17 fat *for* an offering **m** by fire, for a sweet
20: 5 And wherefore have ye **m** us to come up
21: 9 And Moses **m** a serpent of brass, and H6213
25:13 for his God, and **m** an atonement for the
28: 2 for my sacrifices **m** by fire, *for* a sweet
3 This *is* the offering **m** by fire which ye
6 a sacrifice **m** by fire unto the LORD.
8 offer *it*, a sacrifice **m** by fire, of a sweet
13 a sacrifice **m** by fire unto the LORD.
19 But ye shall offer a sacrifice **m** by fire *for*
24 meat of the sacrifice **m** by fire, of a sweet
29: 6 a sacrifice **m** by fire unto the LORD.
13 a sacrifice **m** by fire, of a sweet savour
36 a sacrifice **m** by fire, of a sweet savour
30:12 But if her husband hath utterly **m** them
12 her husband hath **m** them void; and the
31:20 and all that is **m** of skins, and all work H3627
20 goats' *hair*, and all things **m** of wood. H3627
32:13 Israel, and he **m** them wander in the
Dt 1:15 and known, and **m** them heads over H5414
2:30 his spirit, and **m** his heart obstinate,
4:23 God, which he **m** with you, and make H3772
36 Out of heaven he **m** thee to hear his
5: 2 The LORD our God **m** a covenant with H3772
3 The LORD **m** not this covenant with H3772
9: 9 which the LORD **m** with you, then I H3772
12 they have **m** them a molten image. H6213
16 God, *and* had **m** you a molten calf: ye H6213
21 calf which ye had **m**, and burnt it with H6213
10: 3 And I **m** an ark *of* shittim wood, and H6213
5 ark which I had **m**; and there they be, H6213
22 thy God hath **m** thee as the stars of H7760
11: 4 chariots; how he **m** the water of the Red
18: 1 the LORD **m** by fire, and his inheritance.
20: 9 And it shall be, when the officers have **m**
26:12 When thou hast **m** an end of tithing all
19 which he hath **m**, in praise, and in H6213
29: 1 which he **m** with them in Horeb. H3772
25 fathers, which he **m** with them when he H3772
31:16 covenant which I have **m** with them. H3772
24 And it came to pass, when Moses had **m**
32: 6 he not **m** thee, and established thee? H6213
13 He **m** him ride on the high places of the
13 the fields; and he **m** him to suck honey
15 forsook God *which* **m** him, and lightly H6213
45 And Moses **m** an end of speaking all
Jos 2:17 thine oath which thou hast **m** us swear.
20 oath which thou hast **m** us to swear.
5: 3 And Joshua **m** him sharp knives, and H6213
8:15 And Joshua and all Israel **m** as if they
24 And it came to pass, when Israel had **m**
28 And Joshua burnt Ai, and **m** it an heap H7760
9: 4 They did work wilily, and went and **m** as
15 And Joshua **m** peace with them, and H6213
15 with them, and **m** a league with them, H3772

Jos 9:16 after they had **m** a league with them, H3772
27 And Joshua **m** them that day hewers of H5414
10: 1 of Gibeon had **m** peace with Israel, and H7999
4 for it hath **m** peace with Joshua and H7999
5 before Gibeon, and **m** war against it.
20 of Israel had **m** an end of slaying them
11:18 Joshua **m** war a long time with all H6213
19 There was not a city that **m** peace with H7999
13:14 LORD God of Israel **m** by fire *are* their
14: 8 that went up with me **m** the heart of the
19:49 When they had **m** an end of dividing the
51 they **m** an end of dividing the country.
22:25 For the LORD hath **m** Jordan a border H5414
28 which our fathers **m**, not for burnt H6213
24:25 So Joshua **m** a covenant with the H3772
Jdg 2: 1 and said, I **m** you to go up out of Egypt,
3:16 But Ehud **m** him a dagger which had H6213
18 And when he had **m** an end to offer the
5:13 Then he **m** him that remaineth have
13 **m** me have dominion over the mighty.
6: 2 the children of Israel **m** them the dens H6213
19 And Gideon went in, and **m** ready a kid,
8:27 And Gideon **m** an ephod thereof, and H6213
33 Baalim, and **m** Baal-berith their god. H7760
9: 6 and went, and **m** Abimelech king, by H4427
16 in that ye have **m** Abimelech king, and
18 stone, and have **m** Abimelech, the son
27 *the grapes*, and **m** merry, and went H6213
11: 4 of Ammon **m** war against Israel.
5 of Ammon **m** war against Israel, the
11 Gilead, and the people **m** him head and H7760
13:10 And the woman **m** haste, and ran, and
15 we shall have **m** ready a kid for thee.
14:10 and Samson **m** there a feast; for so H6213
15:17 And it came to pass, when he had **m** an
16:19 And she **m** him sleep upon her knees;
25 house; and he **m** them sport: and they
27 that beheld while Samson **m** sport.
17: 4 to the founder, who **m** thereof a graven H6213
5 house of gods, and **m** an ephod, and H6213
18:24 my gods which I **m**, and the priest, and H6213
27 which Micah had **m**, and the priest H6213
31 image, which he **m**, all the time that the H6213
21: 5 For they had **m** a great oath concerning
15 had **m** a breach in the tribes of Israel. H6213
1Sa 2:19 Moreover his mother **m** him a little H6213
28 **m** by fire of the children of Israel?
3:13 because his sons **m** themselves vile, and
4:18 And it came to pass, when he **m** mention
8: 1 that he **m** his sons judges over Israel. H7760
9:22 into the parlour, and **m** them sit in the H5414
10:13 And when he had **m** an end of
11:15 and there they **m** Saul king before the
12: 1 unto me, and have **m** a king over you. H4427
8 of Egypt, and **m** them dwell in this place.
13:10 as soon as he had **m** an end of offering
12 and I have not **m** supplication unto the
14:14 his armourbearer **m**, was about twenty H5221
15:17 *wast* thou not *m* the head of the tribes
33 And Samuel said, As thy sword hath **m**
35 that he had **m** Saul king over Israel.
16: 8 Then Jesse called Abinadab, and **m** him
9 Then Jesse **m** Shammah to pass by. And
10 Again, Jesse **m** seven of his sons to pass
18: 1 And it came to pass, when he had **m** an
3 Then Jonathan and David **m** a H3772
13 from him, and **m** him his captain over H7760
20:16 So Jonathan **m** *a covenant* with the H3772
22: 8 me that my son hath **m** a league with the
23:18 And they two **m** a covenant before the H3772
26 and David **m** haste to get away for
24:16 And it came to pass, when David had **m**
25:18 Then Abigail **m** haste, and took two
27:10 And Achish said, Whither have ye **m** a
12 saying, He hath **m** his people Israel
30:11 he did eat; and they **m** him drink water;
14 We **m** an invasion *upon* the south of the
21 whom they had **m** also to abide at the
25 forward, that he **m** it a statute and an H7760
2Sa 2: 9 And **m** him king over Gilead, and over
3: 6 **m** himself strong for the house of Saul.
20 him. And David **m** Abner and the men H6213
4: 4 to pass, as she **m** haste to flee, that he
5: 3 and king David **m** a league with them H3772
6: 5 of *instruments* **m** *of* fir wood, even on
8 the LORD had **m** a breach upon Uzzah: H6555
18 And as soon as David had **m** an end of
7: 9 sight, and have **m** thee a great name, H6213
10:19 before Israel, they **m** peace with Israel,

M

2Sa 11:13 before him; and he **m** him drunk: and at
19 When thou hast **m** an end of telling the
12:31 axes of iron, and **m** them pass through
13: 6 So Amnon lay down, and **m** himself
8 kneaded *it,* and **m** cakes in his sight, and
10 which she had **m**, and brought *them* H6213
36 as soon as he had **m** an end of speaking,
14:15 the people have **m** me afraid: and thy
15: 4 Oh that I were **m** judge in the land, that H7760
17:25 And Absalom **m** Amasa captain of the H7760
22: 5 the floods of ungodly men **m** me afraid;
12 And he **m** darkness pavilions round H7896
36 and thy gentleness hath **m** me great.
23: 5 with God; yet he hath **m** with me an H7760
1Ki 1:41 *it* as they had **m** an end of eating. And
43 lord king David hath **m** Solomon king.
2:24 and who hath **m** me an house, as he H6213
3: 1 And Solomon **m** affinity with Pharaoh
1 until he had **m** an end of building his
7 And now, O LORD my God, thou hast **m**
15 and **m** a feast to all his servants. H6213
4: 7 man his month in a year **m** provision.
5:12 and they two **m** a league together. H3772
6: 4 And for the house he **m** windows of H6213
5 and he **m** chambers round about: H6213
6 *wall* of the house he **m** narrowed rests H5414
7 was built of stone **m** ready before it was
21 pure gold: and he **m** a partition by the
23 And within the oracle he **m** two H6213
31 And for the entering of the oracle he **m** H6213
33 So also **m** he for the door of the temple H6213
7: 6 And he **m** a porch of pillars; the length H6213
7 Then he **m** a porch for the throne H6213
8 work. Solomon **m** also an house for H6213
16 And he **m** two chapiters *of* molten H6213
18 And he **m** the pillars, and two rows H6213
23 And he **m** a molten sea, ten cubits from H6213
27 And he **m** ten bases of brass; four H6213
29 *were* certain additions **m** of thin work.
37 After this *manner* he **m** the ten bases: H6213
38 Then **m** he ten lavers of brass: one H6213
40 And Hiram **m** the lavers, and the H6213
40 basons. So Hiram **m** an end of doing all
40 the work that he **m** king Solomon for H6213
45 which Hiram **m** to king Solomon for H6213
48 And Solomon **m** all the vessels that H6213
51 king Solomon **m** for the house of the H6213
8: 9 when the LORD **m** *a covenant* with the H3772
21 LORD, which he **m** with our fathers, H3772
38 soever be ***m*** by any man, *or* by all
54 Solomon had **m** an end of praying all
59 wherewith I have **m** supplication before
9: 3 that thou hast **m** before me: I have H2603
26 And king Solomon **m** a navy of ships in H6213
10: 9 for ever, therefore **m** he thee king, to do H7760
12 And the king **m** of the almug trees H6213
16 And king Solomon **m** two hundred H6213
17 And *he **m*** three hundred shields *of*
18 Moreover the king **m** a great throne of H6213
20 was not the like **m** in any kingdom. H6213
27 And the king **m** silver *to be* in H5414
27 and cedars **m** he *to be* as the sycomore H5414
11:28 industrious, he **m** him ruler over all the
12: 4 Thy father **m** our yoke grievous: now H7185
10 saying, Thy father **m** our yoke heavy, H3513
14 saying, My father **m** your yoke heavy, H3513
18 king Rehoboam **m** speed to get him up
20 congregation, and **m** him king over all
28 took counsel, and **m** two calves *of* gold, H6213
31 And he **m** an house of high places, and H6213
31 high places, and **m** priests of the lowest H6213
32 calves that he had **m**: and he placed in H6213
32 of the high places which he had **m**. H6213
33 which he had **m** in Beth-el the fifteenth H6213
13:33 his evil way, but **m** again of the lowest H6213
14: 7 **m** thee prince over my people Israel, H5414
9 hast gone and **m** thee other gods, and H6213
15 because they have **m** their groves, H6213
16 who did sin, and who **m** Israel to sin.
26 shields of gold which Solomon had **m**. H6213
27 And king Rehoboam **m** in their stead H6213
15:12 all the idols that his fathers had **m**. H6213
13 because she had **m** an idol in a grove; H6213
22 Then king Asa **m** a proclamation
26 in his sin wherewith he **m** Israel to sin.
30 sinned, and which he **m** Israel sin, by his
34 in his sin wherewith he **m** Israel to sin.
16: 2 of the dust, and **m** thee prince over my H5414
2 and hast **m** my people Israel to

1Ki 16:13 and by which they **m** Israel to sin, in
16 all Israel **m** Omri, the captain of
26 his sin wherewith he **m** Israel to sin, to
33 And Ahab **m** a grove; and Ahab did H6213
18:26 leaped upon the altar which was **m**. H6213
32 the LORD: and he **m** a trench about the H6213
20:34 as my father **m** in Samaria. Then *said* H7760
34 this covenant. So he **m** a covenant with H3772
21:22 *me* to anger, and **m** Israel to sin.
22:11 And Zedekiah the son of Chenaanah **m** H6213
39 house which he **m**, and all the cities that H1129
44 And Jehoshaphat **m** peace with the king
48 Jehoshaphat **m** ships of Tharshish to H6235
52 the son of Nebat, who **m** Israel to sin:
2Ki 3: 2 the image of Baal that his father had **m**. H6213
3 son of Nebat, which **m** Israel to sin; he
7: 6 For the Lord had **m** the host of the
8:20 Judah, and **m** a king over themselves. H4427
9:21 his chariot was **m** ready. And Joram
10:16 LORD. So they **m** him ride in his chariot.
25 as soon as he had **m** an end of offering
27 **m** it a draught house unto this day. H7760
29 son of Nebat, who **m** Israel to sin, Jehu
31 sins of Jeroboam, which **m** Israel to sin.
11: 4 of the LORD, and **m** a covenant with H3772
12 and they **m** him king, and anointed
17 And Jehoiada **m** a covenant between H3772
12:13 Howbeit there were not **m** for the H6213
20 And his servants arose, and **m** a H7194
13: 2 son of Nebat, which **m** Israel to sin; he
6 of Jeroboam, who **m** Israel sin, *but*
7 had **m** them like the dust by threshing. H7760
11 who **m** Israel sin: *but* he walked therein.
14:19 Now they **m** a conspiracy against him H7194
21 years old, and **m** him king instead of
24 the son of Nebat, who **m** Israel to sin.
15: 9 the son of Nebat, who **m** Israel to sin.
15 which he **m**, behold, they *are* written H7194
18 the son of Nebat, who **m** Israel to sin.
24 the son of Nebat, who **m** Israel to sin.
28 the son of Nebat, who **m** Israel to sin.
30 And Hoshea the son of Elah **m** a H7194
16: 3 of Israel, yea, and **m** his son to pass
11 so Urijah the priest **m** *it* against king H6213
17: 8 of the kings of Israel, which they had **m**. H6213
15 covenant that he **m** with their fathers, H3772
16 their God, and **m** them molten images, H6213
16 *even* two calves, and **m** a grove, and H6213
19 in the statutes of Israel which they **m**. H6213
21 of David; and they **m** Jeroboam the son
21 the LORD, and **m** them sin a great sin.
29 Howbeit every nation **m** gods of their H6213
29 the Samaritans had **m**, every nation in H6213
30 And the men of Babylon **m** H6213
30 and the men of Cuth **m** Nergal, and the H6213
30 and the men of Hamath **m** Ashima, H6213
31 And the Avites **m** Nibhaz and Tartak, H6213
32 So they feared the LORD, and **m** unto H6213
35 With whom the LORD had **m** a H3772
38 And the covenant that I have **m** with H3772
18: 4 that Moses had **m**: for unto those days H6213
19:15 earth; thou hast **m** heaven and earth. H6213
20:20 and how he **m** a pool, and a conduit, H6213
21: 3 for Baal, and **m** a grove, as did Ahab H6213
6 And he **m** his son pass through the fire,
7 grove that he had **m** in the house, of H6213
11 hath **m** Judah also to sin with his idols:
16 his sin wherewith he **m** Judah to sin, in
24 land **m** Josiah his son king in his stead.
22: 7 Howbeit there was no reckoning **m** H2803
23: 3 And the king stood by a pillar, and **m** a H3772
4 vessels that were **m** for Baal, and for H6213
12 of Judah had **m**, and the altars which H6213
12 Manasseh had **m** in the two courts of H6213
15 son of Nebat, who **m** Israel to sin, had
15 Israel to sin, had **m**, both that altar and H6213
19 of Israel had **m** to provoke *the LORD* H6213
30 and **m** him king in his father's stead.
34 And Pharaoh-nechoh **m** Eliakim the son
24:13 king of Israel had **m** in the temple of H6213
17 And the king of Babylon **m** Mattaniah
25:16 Solomon had **m** for the house of the H6213
22 even over them he **m** Gedaliah the son of
23 of Babylon had **m** Gedaliah governor,
1Ch 5:10 And in the days of Saul they **m** war H6213
19 And they **m** war with the Hagarites, H6213
9:30 And *some* of the sons of the priests **m** H7543
31 the things that were **m** in the pans. H4639
11: 3 and David **m** a covenant with them H3772

1Ch 12:18 and **m** them captains of the band. H5414
13:11 the LORD had **m** a breach upon Uzza: H6555
15: 1 And *David* **m** him houses in the city of H6213
13 the LORD our God **m** a breach upon us,
16: 2 And when David had **m** an end of
5 but Asaph **m** a sound with cymbals;
16 *Even of the covenant* which he **m** with H3772
26 *are* idols: but the LORD **m** the heavens. H6213
17: 8 thee, and have **m** thee a name like the H6213
18: 8 Solomon **m** the brasen sea, and H6213
19: 6 saw that they had **m** themselves odious
19 before Israel, they **m** peace with David,
21:29 which Moses **m** in the wilderness, and H6213
22: 8 and hast **m** great wars: thou shalt H6213
23: 1 he **m** Solomon his son king over Israel.
5 I **m**, *said David,* to praise *therewith.* H6213
26:10 yet his father **m** him the chief;) H7760
32 whom king David **m** rulers over the
28: 2 God, and had **m** ready for the building:
19 All *this, said David,* the LORD **m** me
29: 2 for *things to be* **m** of gold, and the silver
5 manner of work *to be* **m** by the hands of
19 palace, *for* the which I have **m** provision.
22 And they **m** Solomon the son of
2Ch 1: 3 of the LORD had **m** in the wilderness. H6213
5 the son of Hur, had **m**, he put before the H6213
8 and hast **m** me to reign in his stead.
9 for thou hast **m** me king over a people
11 people, over whom I have **m** thee king:
15 And the king **m** silver and gold at H5414
15 and cedar trees **m** he as the sycomore H5414
2:11 people, he hath **m** thee king over them. H5414
12 God of Israel, that **m** heaven and earth, H6213
3: 8 And he **m** the most holy house, the H6213
10 And in the most holy house he **m** two H6213
14 And he **m** the vail *of* blue, and purple, H6213
15 Also he **m** before the house two pillars H6213
16 And he **m** chains, *as* in the oracle, and H6213
16 heads of the pillars; and **m** an hundred H6213
4: 1 Moreover he **m** an altar of brass, H6213
2 Also he **m** a molten sea of ten cubits H6213
6 He **m** also ten lavers, and put five on H6213
7 And he **m** ten candlesticks of gold H6213
8 He **m** also ten tables, and placed *them* H6213
8 And he **m** an hundred basons of gold. H6213
9 Furthermore he **m** the court of the H6213
11 And Huram **m** the pots, and the H6213
14 He **m** also bases, and lavers made he H6213
14 He made also bases, and lavers **m** he H6213
18 Thus Solomon **m** all these vessels in H6213
19 And Solomon **m** all the vessels that H6213
21 ***m** he of* gold, *and* that perfect gold;
5: 1 Thus all the work that Solomon **m** for H6213
10 when the LORD **m** *a covenant* with the H3772
6:11 that he **m** with the children of Israel. H3772
13 For Solomon had **m** a brasen scaffold, H6213
29 soever shall be **m** of any man, or of all
40 unto the prayer *that is* **m** in this place.
7: 1 Now when Solomon had **m** an end of
6 the king had **m** to praise the LORD, H6213
7 Solomon had **m** was not able to receive H6213
9 And in the eighth day they **m** a solemn H6213
15 unto the prayer *that is* **m** in this place.
9: 8 for ever, therefore **m** he thee king over H5414
11 And the king **m** *of* the algum trees H6213
15 And king Solomon **m** two hundred H6213
16 And three hundred shields ***m** he of*
17 Moreover the king **m** a great throne of H6213
19 was not the like **m** in any kingdom. H6213
27 And the king **m** silver in Jerusalem as H5414
27 and cedar trees **m** he as the sycomore H5414
10: 4 Thy father **m** our yoke grievous: now
10 saying, Thy father **m** our yoke heavy, H3513
14 saying, My father **m** your yoke heavy,
18 king Rehoboam **m** speed to get him up
11:12 and spears, and **m** them exceeding
15 and for the calves which he had **m**. H6213
17 of Judah, and **m** Rehoboam the son of
22 And Rehoboam **m** Abijah the son of H5975
12: 9 shields of gold which Solomon had **m**. H6213
10 Instead of which king Rehoboam **m** H6213
13: 8 which Jeroboam **m** you for gods. H6213
9 Levites, and have **m** you priests after H6213
15:16 because she had **m** an idol in a grove: H6213
16:14 which he had **m** for himself in the city H3738
14 they **m** a very great burning for him. H8313
17:10 that they **m** no war against Jehoshaphat.
18:10 Chenaanah had **m** him horns of iron, H6213
20:23 and when they had **m** an end of the

2Ch 20:27 **m** them to rejoice over their enemies.
36 and they **m** the ships in Ezion-geber. H6213
21: 7 that he had **m** with David, and as H3772
8 of Judah, and **m** themselves a king. H4427
11 Moreover he **m** high places in the H6213
13 of Israel, and hast **m** Judah and the
19 And his people **m** no burning for him, H6213
22: 1 And the inhabitants of Jerusalem **m** H4427
23: 3 And all the congregation **m** a covenant H3772
11 *him* the testimony, and **m** him king. And
16 And Jehoiada **m** a covenant between H3772
24: 8 they **m** a chest, and set it without H6213
9 And they **m** a proclamation through H5414
10 into the chest, until they had **m** an end.
14 whereof were **m** vessels for the house H6213
17 of Judah, and **m** obeisance to the king.
25: 5 together, and **m** them captains over H5975
16 him, Art thou **m** of the king's counsel? H5414
27 the LORD they **m** a conspiracy against H7194
26: 1 years old, and **m** him king in the room
5 the LORD, God **m** him to prosper.
13 five hundred, that **m** war with mighty H6213
15 And he **m** in Jerusalem engines, H6213
28: 2 and **m** also molten images for Baalim. H6213
19 of Israel; for he **m** Judah naked, and H6544
24 of the LORD, and he **m** him altars in H6213
25 And in every several city of Judah he **m** H6213
29:17 day of the first month they **m** an end.
24 And the priests killed them, and they **m**
24 sin offering *should be* **m** for all Israel.
29 And when they had **m** an end of
32: 5 and **m** darts and shields in abundance. H6213
27 honour: and he **m** himself treasuries H6213
33: 3 altars for Baalim, and **m** groves, and H6213
7 the idol which he had **m**, in the house of H6213
9 So Manasseh **m** Judah and the H8582
22 his father had **m**, and served them; H6213
25 land **m** Josiah his son king in his stead. H4427
34: 4 brake in pieces, and **m** dust *of them*, and
31 And the king stood in his place, and **m** H3772
33 of Israel, and **m** all that were present
35:14 And afterward they **m** ready for
25 to this day, and **m** them an ordinance H5414
36: 1 the son of Josiah, and **m** him king in his
4 And the king of Egypt **m** Eliakim his
10 house of the LORD, and **m** Zedekiah his
13 who had **m** him swear by God: but
22 king of Persia, that he **m** a proclamation
Ezr 1: 1 king of Persia, that he **m** a proclamation
4:15 That search may be **m** in the book of the
19 search hath been **m**, and it is found that
19 of old time hath **m** insurrection against
19 and sedition have been **m** therein. H5648
23 **m** them to cease by force and power.
5:13 **m** a decree to build this house of God. H7761
14 whom he had **m** governor; H7761
17 king, let there be search **m** in the king's
17 that a decree was **m** of Cyrus the king H7761
6: 1 Then Darius the king **m** a decree, and H7761
1 and search was **m** in the house of the
3 Cyrus the king **m** a decree *concerning* H7761
11 Also I have **m** a decree, that whosoever H7761
11 let his house be **m** a dunghill for this. H5648
12 **m** a decree; let it be done with speed. H7761
22 for the LORD had **m** them joyful, and
10: 5 Then arose Ezra, and **m** the chief priests,
7 And they **m** proclamation throughout
17 And they **m** an end with all the men that
Neh 3:16 **m**, and unto the house of the mighty. H6213
4: 7 of Jerusalem were **m** up, *and* that the
9 Nevertheless we **m** our prayer unto our
6: 9 For they all **m** us afraid, saying, Their
8: 4 which they had **m** for the purpose; and H6213
16 *them*, and **m** themselves booths, H6213
17 out of the captivity **m** booths, and sat H6213
9: 6 alone; thou hast **m** heaven, the heaven H6213
18 Yea, when they had **m** them a molten H6213
10:32 Also we **m** ordinances for us, to charge H5975
12:43 for God had **m** them rejoice with great
13:13 And I **m** treasurers over the treasuries,
25 off their hair, and **m** them swear by God,
26 his God, and God **m** him king over all H5414
Est 1: 3 In the third year of his reign, he **m** a H6213
5 expired, the king **m** a feast unto all the H6213
9 Also Vashti the queen **m** a feast for the H6213
2:17 and **m** her queen instead of Vashti.
18 Then the king **m** a great feast unto all H6213
18 Esther's feast; and he **m** a release to the H6213
23 And when inquisition was **m** of the
Est 5:14 Let a gallows be **m** of fifty cubits high, H6213
14 and he caused the gallows to be **m**. H6213
7: 9 Haman had **m** for Mordecai, who H6213
9:17 **m** it a day of feasting and gladness. H6213
18 **m** it a day of feasting and gladness. H6213
19 unwalled towns, **m** the fourteenth day H6213
Job 1:10 Hast not thou **m** an hedge about him,
17 The Chaldeans **m** out three bands, and
2:11 for they had **m** an appointment together
4:14 which **m** all my bones to shake.
7: 3 So am I **m** to possess months of vanity,
10: 8 Thine hands have **m** me and fashioned H6087
9 that thou hast **m** me as the clay; and H6213
15: 7 born? or wast thou **m** before the hills? H2342
16: 7 But now he hath **m** me weary: thou hast
7 thou hast **m** desolate all my company.
17: 6 He hath **m** me also a byword of the H3322
13 I have **m** my bed in the darkness. H7502
28:18 No mention shall be **m** of coral, or of
26 When he **m** a decree for the rain, and a H6213
31: 1 I **m** a covenant with mine eyes; why H3772
15 Did not he that **m** me in the womb H6213
24 If I have **m** gold my hope, or have said H7760
33: 4 The Spirit of God hath **m** me, and the H6213
38: 9 When I **m** the cloud the garment H7760
39: 6 Whose house I have **m** the wilderness, H7760
40:15 Behold now behemoth, which I **m** with H6213
19 of God: he that **m** him can make his H6213
41:33 is not his like, who is **m** without fear. H6213
Ps 7:12 he hath bent his bow, and **m** it ready.
15 He **m** a pit, and digged it, and is fallen H3738
15 and is fallen into the ditch *which* he **m**. H6466
8: 5 For thou hast **m** him a little lower than
9:15 in the pit *that* they **m**: in the net which H6213
18: 4 the floods of ungodly men **m** me afraid.
11 He **m** darkness his secret place; his H7896
35 up, and thy gentleness hath **m** me great.
43 *and* thou hast **m** me the head of the H7760
21: 6 For thou hast **m** him most blessed for H7896
6 ever: thou hast **m** him exceeding glad H2302
30: 1 hast not **m** my foes to rejoice over me.
7 LORD, by thy favour thou hast **m** my
8 and unto the LORD I **m** supplication.
33: 6 were the heavens **m**; and all the host of H6213
39: 5 Behold, thou hast **m** my days *as* an H5414
45: 1 which I have **m** touching the king: my H4639
8 palaces, whereby they have **m** thee glad.
46: 8 desolations he hath **m** in the earth. H7760
49:16 Be not thou afraid when one is **m** rich,
50: 5 **m** a covenant with me by sacrifice. H3772
52: 7 Lo, *this is* the man *that* **m** not God his H7760
60: 2 Thou hast **m** the earth to tremble; thou
3 **m** us to drink the wine of astonishment.
69:11 I **m** sackcloth also my garment; and I H5414
72:15 also shall be **m** for him continually; H6419
74:17 thou hast **m** summer and winter. H3335
77: 6 heart: and my spirit **m** diligent search.
78:13 he **m** the waters to stand as an heap.
50 He **m** a way to his anger; he spared not H6424
52 But **m** his own people to go forth like
55 by line, and **m** the tribes of Israel to
64 and their widows **m** no lamentation.
86: 9 All nations whom thou hast **m** shall H6213
88: 8 me; thou hast **m** me an abomination H7896
89: 3 I have **m** a covenant with my chosen, I H3772
39 Thou hast **m** void the covenant of thy
42 thou hast **m** all his enemies to rejoice.
43 hast not **m** him to stand in the battle.
44 Thou hast **m** his glory to cease, and cast
47 wherefore hast thou **m** all men in vain? H1254
91: 9 Because thou hast **m** the LORD, *which* H7760
92: 4 For thou, LORD, hast **m** me glad
95: 5 The sea *is* his, and he **m** it: and his H6213
96: 5 *are* idols: but the LORD **m** the heavens. H6213
98: 2 The LORD hath **m** known his salvation:
100: 3 God: *it is* he *that* hath **m** us, and not we H6213
103: 7 He **m** known his ways unto Moses, his
104:24 wisdom hast thou **m** them all: the earth H6213
26 *whom* thou hast **m** to play therein.
105: 9 Which *covenant* he **m** with Abraham, H3772
21 He **m** him lord of his house, and ruler H7760
24 **m** them stronger than their enemies.
28 He sent darkness, and **m** it dark; and
106:19 They **m** a calf in Horeb, and H6213
46 He **m** them also to be pitied of all those H5414
111: 4 He hath **m** his wonderful works to be H6213
115:15 Ye *are* blessed of the LORD which **m** H6213
118:24 This *is* the day *which* the LORD hath **m**; H6213
119:60 I **m** haste, and delayed not to keep thy
Ps 119:73 Thy hands have **m** me and fashioned H6213
98 hast **m** me wiser than mine
126 to work: *for* they have **m** void thy law.
121: 2 the LORD, which **m** heaven and earth. H6213
124: 8 of the LORD, who **m** heaven and earth. H6213
129: 3 my back: they **m** long their furrows.
134: 3 The LORD that **m** heaven and earth H6213
136: 5 To him that by wisdom **m** the heavens: H6213
7 To him that **m** great lights: for his H6213
14 And **m** Israel to pass through the midst
139:14 *and* wonderfully **m**: marvellous *are* thy H6395
15 from thee, when I was **m** in secret, *and* H6213
143: 3 the ground; he hath **m** me to dwell in
146: 6 Which **m** heaven, and earth, the sea, H6213
148: 6 hath **m** a decree which shall not pass. H5414
149: 2 Let Israel rejoice in him that **m** him: let H6213
Prv 8:26 While as yet he had not **m** the earth, H6213
11:25 The liberal soul shall be **m** fat: and he
13: 4 but the soul of the diligent shall be **m** fat.
14:33 *is* in the midst of fools is **m** known.
15:19 but the way of the righteous *is* **m** plain.
16: 4 The LORD hath **m** all *things* for H6466
20: 9 Who can say, I have **m** my heart clean, I
12 the LORD hath **m** even both of them. H6213
21:11 the simple is **m** wise: and when the
22:19 **m** known to thee this day, even to thee.
28:25 his trust in the LORD shall be **m** fat.
Ecc 1:15 *That which is* crooked cannot be **m**
2: 4 I **m** me great works; I builded me
5 I **m** me gardens and orchards, and I H6213
6 I **m** me pools of water, to water H6213
3:11 He hath **m** every *thing* beautiful in his H6213
7: 3 of the countenance the heart is **m** better.
13 *that* straight, which he hath **m** crooked?
29 that God hath **m** man upright; but they H6213
10:19 A feast is **m** for laughter, and wine H6213
Song 1: 6 with me; they **m** me the keeper of the H7760
3: 9 King Solomon **m** himself a chariot of H6213
10 He **m** the pillars thereof *of* silver, the H6213
6:12 Or ever I was aware, my soul **m** me *like* H7760
Isa 2: 8 that which their own fingers have **m**: H6213
17 of men shall be **m** low: and the LORD
20 of gold, which they **m** *each one* for H6213
5: 2 of it, and also **m** a winepress therein: H2672
14: 3 bondage wherein thou wast **m** to serve,
16 this the man that **m** the earth to tremble,
17 *That* **m** the world as a wilderness, and H7760
16:10 I have **m** *their vintage* shouting to cease.
17: 4 of Jacob shall be **m** thin, and the fatness
8 **m**, either the groves, or the images. H6213
21: 2 all the sighing thereof have I **m** to cease.
22:11 Ye **m** also a ditch between the two H6213
25: 2 For thou hast **m** of a city an heap; *of* a H7760
26:14 them, and **m** all their memory to perish.
27:11 therefore he that **m** them will not have H6213
28:15 Because ye have said, We have **m** a H3772
15 us: for we have **m** lies our refuge, and H7760
22 lest your bands be **m** strong: for I have
25 When he hath **m** plain the face thereof,
29:16 say of him that **m** it, He made me not? H6213
16 that made it, He **m** me not? or shall the H6213
30:33 is prepared; he hath **m** *it* deep *and* large:
31: 7 own hands have **m** unto you *for* a sin. H6213
34: 6 with blood, it is **m** fat with fatness, *and*
7 blood, and their dust **m** fat with fatness.
37:16 earth: thou hast **m** heaven and earth. H6213
40: 4 and hill shall be **m** low: and the crooked
4 **m** straight, and the rough places plain:
41: 2 before him, and **m** *him* rule over kings?
43: 7 I have formed him; yea, I have **m** him. H6213
24 but thou hast **m** me to serve with thy
44: 2 Thus saith the LORD that **m** thee, and H6213
45:12 I have **m** the earth, and created man H6213
18 the earth and **m** it; he hath established H6213
46: 4 I carry *you*: I have **m**, and I will bear; H6213
49: 1 mother hath he **m** mention of my name.
2 And he hath **m** my mouth like a sharp H7760
2 he hid me, and **m** me a polished shaft; H7760
17 that **m** thee waste shall go forth of thee.
51:10 deep; that hath **m** the depths of the sea H7760
12 son of man *which* shall be **m** *as* grass; H5414
52:10 The LORD hath **m** bare his holy arm in
53: 9 And he **m** his grave with the wicked, H5414
12 **m** intercession for the transgressors.
57: 8 thy bed, and **m** thee *a covenant* with H3772
16 me, and the souls *which* I have **m**. H6213
59: 8 their goings: they have **m** them crooked
63:17 O LORD, why hast thou **m** us to err from
66: 2 For all those *things* hath mine hand **m**, H6213

Isa 66: 8 Shall the earth be **m** to bring forth in one
Jer 1:18 For, behold, I have **m** thee this day a H5414
2: 7 and **m** mine heritage an abomination. H7760
15 yelled, and they **m** his land waste: his H7896
28 that thou hast **m** thee? let them arise, H6213
5: 3 they have **m** their faces harder than
8: 8 **m** he *it*; the pen of the scribes *is* in vain. H6213
10:11 that have not **m** the heavens and the H5648
12 He hath **m** the earth by his power, he H6213
25 and have **m** his habitation desolate.
11:10 covenant which I **m** with their fathers. H3772
12:10 foot, they have **m** my pleasant portion H5414
11 They have **m** it desolate, *and being* H7760
11 the whole land is **m** desolate, because no
13:22 skirts discovered, *and* thy heels **m** bare.
27 not be **m** clean? when *shall it* once *be*?
14:22 thee: for thou hast **m** all these *things*. H6213
17:23 their ear, but **m** their neck stiff, that
18: 4 And the vessel that he **m** of clay was H6213
4 of the potter: so he **m** it again another H6213
19:11 that cannot be **m** whole again: and they
20: 8 of the LORD was **m** a reproach unto me,
25:17 LORD'S hand, and **m** all the nations to
26: 8 Jeremiah had **m** an end of speaking
27: 5 I have **m** the earth, the man and the H6213
29:26 The LORD hath **m** thee priest in the H5414
31:32 Not according to the covenant that I **m** H3772
32:17 Ah Lord GOD! behold, thou hast **m** the H6213
20 and hast **m** thee a name, as at this day; H6213
34: 8 Zedekiah had **m** a covenant with all H3772
13 God of Israel; I **m** a covenant with your H3772
15 and ye had **m** a covenant before me H3772
18 which they had **m** before me, when H3772
36:25 and Gemariah had **m** intercession to the
37: 1 of Babylon **m** king in the land of Judah.
15 scribe: for they had **m** that the prison. H6213
38:16 LORD liveth, that **m** us this soul, I will H6213
40: 5 of Babylon hath **m** governor over the
7 of Babylon had **m** Gedaliah the son of
41: 2 Babylon had **m** governor over the land.
9 Asa the king had **m** for fear of Baasha H6213
18 king of Babylon **m** governor in the land.
43: 1 Jeremiah had **m** an end of speaking
46:10 be satiate and **m** drunk with their blood:
16 He **m** many to fall, yea, one fell upon
49:10 But I have **m** Esau bare, I have
51: 7 the LORD'S hand, that **m** all the earth
15 He hath **m** the earth by his power, he H6213
34 me, he hath **m** me an empty vessel, H3322
63 And it shall be, when thou hast **m** an
52:20 Solomon had **m** in the house of the H6213
Lam 1:13 **m** me desolate *and* faint all the day. H5414
14 my neck: he hath **m** my strength to fall,
2: 7 they have **m** a noise in the house H5414
8 therefore he **m** the rampart and the
3: 4 My flesh and my skin hath he **m** old; he
7 get out: he hath **m** my chain heavy.
9 stone, he hath **m** my paths crooked.
11 me in pieces: he hath **m** me desolate. H7760
15 he hath **m** me drunken with wormwood.
45 Thou hast **m** us *as* the offscouring and H7760
Ezk 3: 8 Behold, I have **m** thy face strong H5414
9 than flint have I **m** thy forehead: fear H5414
17 Son of man, I have **m** thee a watchman H5414
6: 6 be laid waste and **m** desolate, and your
7:20 majesty: but they **m** the images of their H6213
13: 5 the gaps, neither **m** up the hedge for the
6 and they have **m** *others* to hope that
22 Because with lies ye have **m** the heart of
22 sad, whom I have not **m** sad; and
16:24 **m** thee an high place in every street. H6213
25 of the way, and hast **m** thy beauty to be
17:13 the king's seed, and **m** a covenant with H3772
16 king *dwelleth* that **m** him king, whose
24 tree, and have **m** the dry tree to flourish:
19: 5 of her whelps, *and* **m** him a young lion. H7760
20: 5 of Jacob, and **m** myself known unto
9 in whose sight I **m** myself known unto
28 there also they **m** their sweet savour, H7760
21:15 ah! *it is* **m** bright, *it is* wrapped H6213
21 use divination: he **m** *his* arrows bright,
24 Because ye have **m** your iniquity to be
22: 4 idols which thou hast **m**; and thou hast H6213
4 therefore have I **m** thee a reproach unto
13 which thou hast **m**, and at thy blood H6213
25 things; they have **m** her many widows in
26:10 enter into a city wherein is **m** a breach.
15 the slaughter is **m** in the midst of thee? H2026
27: 5 They have **m** all thy *ship* boards of fir H1129
Ezk 27: 6 *Of* the oaks of Bashan have they **m** H6213
6 Ashurites have **m** thy benches *of* ivory, H6213
11 about; they have **m** thy beauty perfect. H3634
24 **m** of cedar, among thy merchandise.
25 **m** very glorious in the midst of the seas.
29: 3 mine own, and I have **m** *it* for myself. H6213
9 said, The river *is* mine, and I have **m** *it*. H6213
18 Tyrus: every head *was* **m** bald, and every
31: 4 The waters **m** him great, the deep set
6 All the fowls of heaven **m** their nests in
9 I have **m** him fair by the multitude of H6213
16 I **m** the nations to shake at the sound of
36: 3 Because they have **m** *you* desolate, and
39:26 in their land, and none **m** *them* afraid.
40:14 He **m** also posts of threescore cubits, H6213
17 and a pavement **m** for the court round H6213
41:18 And *it was* **m** with cherubims and H6213
19 **m** through all the house round about. H6213
20 trees **m**, and *on* the wall of the temple. H6213
25 And *there were* **m** on them, on the H6213
25 trees, like as *were* **m** upon the walls; H6213
42:15 Now when he had **m** an end of
43:23 When thou hast **m** an end of cleansing
46:23 four, and *it was* **m** with boiling places H6213
Dan 2: 5 and your houses shall be **m** a dunghill. H7761
15 Arioch **m** the thing known to Daniel.
17 Then Daniel went to his house, and **m**
23 might, and hast **m** known unto me now
23 *now* **m** known unto us the king's matter.
38 hand, and hath **m** thee ruler over them
45 the great God hath **m** known to the king
48 Then the king **m** Daniel a great man, H7236
48 great gifts, and **m** him ruler over the
3: 1 Nebuchadnezzar the king **m** an image H5648
10 Thou, O king, hast **m** a decree, that H7761
15 which I have **m**; *well*: but if ye worship H5648
29 houses shall be **m** a dunghill: because H7739
4: 5 I saw a dream which **m** me afraid, and
6 Therefore **m** I a decree to bring in all H7761
5: 1 Belshazzar the king **m** a great feast to a H5648
11 king, *I say*, thy father, **m** master of the H6966
21 and his heart was **m** like the beasts, H7739
29 about his neck, and **m** a proclamation
7: 4 the earth, and **m** stand upon the feet
16 this. So he told me, and **m** me know the
21 I beheld, and the same horn **m** war H5648
9: 1 **m** king over the realm of the Chaldeans;
4 my God, and **m** my confession, and
13 come upon us: yet **m** we not our prayer
11:23 And after the league *m* with him he shall
12:10 Many shall be purified, and **m** white,
Hos 5: 9 I **m** known that which shall surely be.
7: 5 the princes have **m** *him* sick with bottles
6 For they have **m** ready their heart like an
8: 4 by me: they have **m** princes, and I knew
4 **m** them idols, that they may be cut off. H6213
6 the workman **m** it; therefore it *is* not H6213
11 Because Ephraim hath **m** many altars to
10: 1 of his land they have **m** goodly images.
12: 4 he wept, and **m** supplication unto him:
13: 2 more, and have **m** them molten images H6213
Joel 1: 7 fig tree: he hath **m** it clean bare, and cast
7 away; the branches thereof are **m** white.
18 yea, the flocks of sheep are **m** desolate.
Am 4:10 horses; and I have **m** the stink of your
5:26 of your god, which ye **m** to yourselves. H6213
7: 2 when they had **m** an end of eating the
7 stood upon a wall *m* by a plumbline,
Oba 2 Behold, I have **m** thee small among the H5414
Jna 1: 9 which hath **m** the sea and the dry *land*. H6213
16 sacrifice unto the LORD, and **m** vows. H5087
4: 5 the city, and there **m** him a booth, and H6213
6 a gourd, and **m** *it* to come up over
Nah 2: 3 The shield of his mighty men is **m** red,
11 lion's whelp, and none **m** *them* afraid?
Hab 2:17 of beasts, *which* **m** them afraid, because
3: 9 Thy bow was **m** quite naked, *according*
Zep 3: 6 are desolate; I **m** their streets waste, that
Zec 7:12 Yea, they **m** their hearts *as* an adamant H7760
9:13 **m** thee as the sword of a mighty man. H7760
10: 3 Judah, and hath **m** them as his goodly H7760
11:10 which I had **m** with all the people. H3772
Mal 2: 9 Therefore have I also **m** you H5414
Mt 4: 3 that these stones be **m** bread. G1096
9:16 the garment, and the rent is **m** worse. G1096
22 thy faith hath **m** thee whole. And the G4982
22 woman was **m** whole from that hour. G4982
11: 1 And it came to pass, when Jesus had **m** G5055
14:36 as touched were **m** perfectly whole. G1295
Mt 15: 6 *free.* Thus have ye **m** the commandment G208
28 was **m** whole from that very hour. G2390
18:25 all that he had, and payment to be **m**. G591
19: 4 that he which **m** *them* at the beginning G4160
4 beginning **m** them male and female, G4160
12 which were **m** eunuchs of men: and G2134
12 which have **m** themselves eunuchs G2134
20:12 and thou hast **m** them equal unto us, G4160
21:13 but ye have **m** it a den of thieves. G4160
22: 2 king, which **m** a marriage for his son, G4160
5 But they **m** light of *it*, and went their G272
23:15 and when he is **m**, ye make him twofold G1096
24:45 whom his lord hath **m** ruler over his G2525
25: 6 And at midnight there was a cry **m**, G1096
16 same, and **m** *them* other five talents. G4160
26:19 them; and they **m** ready the passover. G2090
27:24 a tumult was **m**, he took water, and G1096
64 the sepulchre be **m** sure until the third G805
66 So they went, and **m** the sepulchre sure, G805
Mk 2:21 from the old, and the rent is **m** worse. G1096
27 The sabbath was **m** for man, and not G1096
5:34 thy faith hath **m** thee whole; go in G4982
6:21 on his birthday **m** a supper to his lords, G4160
56 as many as touched him were **m** whole. G4982
8:25 his eyes, and **m** him look up: and he G4160
10: 6 creation God **m** them male and female. G4160
52 way; thy faith hath **m** thee whole. And G4982
11:17 but ye have **m** it a den of thieves. G4160
14: 4 Why was this waste of the ointment **m**? G1096
16 them: and they **m** ready the passover. G2090
58 this temple that is **m** with hands, and G5499
58 I will build another **m** without hands. G886
15: 7 them that had **m** insurrection with G4955
Lk 1:62 And they **m** signs to his father, how he G1770
2: 2 (*And* this taxing was first **m** when G1096
15 which the Lord hath **m** known unto us. G1107
17 And when they had seen *it*, they **m** G1232
3: 5 crooked shall be **m** straight, and the G2071
5 and the rough ways *shall be* **m** smooth; G1519
4: 3 this stone that it be **m** bread. G1096
5:29 And Levi **m** him a great feast in his G4160
8:17 that shall not be **m** manifest; neither G1096
48 faith hath **m** thee whole; go in peace. G4982
50 believe only, and she shall be **m** whole. G4982
9:15 And they did so, and **m** them all sit G347
11:40 *Ye* fools, did not he that **m** that which G4160
12:14 And he said unto him, Man, who **m** me G2525
13:13 she was **m** straight, and glorified God. G461
14:12 again, and a recompence be **m** thee. G1096
16 **m** a great supper, and bade many: G4160
17:19 thy way: thy faith hath **m** thee whole. G4982
19: 6 And he **m** haste, and came down, and G4692
46 but ye have **m** it a den of thieves. G4160
22:13 them: and they **m** ready the passover. G2090
23:12 and Herod were **m** friends together: for G1096
19 (Who for a certain sedition **m** in the G1096
24:22 also of our company **m** us astonished, G1839
28 they went: and he **m** as though he G4364
Jn 1: 3 All things were **m** by him; and without G1096
3 was not any thing **m** that was made. G1096
3 was not any thing made that was **m**. G1096
10 the world was **m** by him, and the world G1096
14 And the Word was **m** flesh, and dwelt G1096
31 that he should be **m** manifest to Israel, G1096
2: 9 water that was **m** wine, and knew not G1096
15 And when he had **m** a scourge of small G4160
3:21 his deeds may be **m** manifest, that they G5319
4: 1 heard that Jesus **m** and baptized more G4160
46 of Galilee, where he **m** the water wine. G4160
5: 4 **m** whole of whatsoever disease he had. G1096
6 saith unto him, Wilt thou be **m** whole? G1096
9 And immediately the man was **m** G1096
11 He answered them, He that **m** me G4160
14 Behold, thou art **m** whole: sin no more, G1096
15 it was Jesus, which had **m** him whole. G4160
7:23 me, because I have **m** a man every whit G4160
8:33 how sayest thou, Ye shall be **m** free? G1096
9: 3 of God should be **m** manifest in him.
6 the ground, and **m** clay of the spittle, G4160
11 is called Jesus **m** clay, and anointed G4160
14 Jesus **m** the clay, and opened his eyes. G4160
39 that they which see might be **m** blind. G1096
12: 2 There they **m** him a supper; and G4160
15:15 my Father I have **m** known unto you. G1107
17:23 that they may be **m** perfect in one; and G5048
18:18 there, who had **m** a fire of coals; for it G4160
19: 7 because he **m** himself the Son of God. G4160
23 took his garments, and **m** four parts, to G4160
Act 1: 1 The former treatise have I **m**, O G4160

Act 2:28 Thou hast **m** known to me the ways of G1107
36 that God hath **m** that same Jesus, G4160
3:12 or holiness we had **m** this man to walk? G4160
16 in his name hath **m** this man strong, G4732
25 which God **m** with our fathers, saying G1303
4: 9 man, by what means he is **m** whole; G4982
24 God, which hast **m** heaven, and earth, G4160
35 distribution was **m** unto every man G1239
7:10 of Egypt; and he **m** him governor over G2525
13 And at the second *time* Joseph was **m** G319
13 kindred was **m** known unto Pharaoh. G1096
27 **m** thee a ruler and a judge over us? G2525
35 saying, Who **m** thee a ruler and a G2525
41 And they **m** a calf in those days, and G3447
43 figures which ye **m** to worship them: G4160
48 **m** with hands; as saith the prophet, G5499
50 Hath not my hand **m** all these things? G4160
8: 2 and **m** great lamentation over him. G4160
3 As for Saul, he **m** havock of the church, G4160
9:39 Dorcas **m**, while she was with them. G4160
10:10 they **m** ready, he fell into a trance, G3903
17 Cornelius had **m** inquiry for Simon's G1239
12: 5 but prayer was **m** without ceasing of G1096
20 him, and, having **m** Blastus the king's G3982
21 throne, and **m** an oration unto them. G1215
13:32 promise which was **m** unto the fathers, G1096
14: 2 up the Gentiles, and **m** their minds evil G2559
5 And when there was an assault **m** both G1096
15 living God, which **m** heaven, and earth, G4160
15: 7 while ago God **m** choice among us, that G1586
16:13 was wont to be **m**; and we sat down, G1511
24 and **m** their feet fast in the stocks. G805
17:24 God that **m** the world and all things G4160
24 dwelleth not in temples **m** with hands; G5499
26 And hath **m** of one blood all nations of G4160
18:12 of Achaia, the Jews **m** insurrection with G2721
19:24 which **m** silver shrines for Diana, G4160
26 be no gods, which are **m** with hands: G1096
33 have **m** his defence unto the people. G626
20:28 Holy Ghost hath **m** you overseers, to G5087
21:40 when there was **m** a great silence, he G1096
22: 6 And it came to pass, that, as I **m** my G4198
23:13 forty which had **m** this conspiracy. G4160
26: 6 the promise **m** of God unto our fathers: G1096
27:40 to the wind, and **m** toward shore. G2722
Ro 1: 3 Lord, which was **m** of the seed of David G1096
20 the things that are **m**, *even* his eternal G4161
23 God into an image **m** like to corruptible
2:25 thy circumcision is **m** uncircumcision. G1096
4:14 law *be* heirs, faith is **m** void, and the G2758
14 void, and the promise **m** of none effect: G2673
17 (As it is written, I have **m** thee a father G5087
5:19 many were **m** sinners, so by the G2525
19 of one shall many be **m** righteous. G2525
6:18 Being then **m** free from sin, ye became G1659
22 But now being **m** free from sin, and G1659
7:13 Was then that which is good **m** death G1096
8: 2 in Christ Jesus hath **m** me free from the G1659
20 For the creature was **m** subject to G5293
9:20 formed *it*, Why hast thou **m** me thus? G4160
29 and been **m** like unto Gomorrha. G3666
10:10 mouth confession is **m** unto salvation. G3670
20 me not; I was **m** manifest unto them G1096
11: 9 And David saith, Let their table be **m** a G1096
14:21 stumbleth, or is offended, or is **m** weak. G770
15: 8 the promises *m* unto the fathers:
27 Gentiles have been **m** partakers of their G2841
16:26 But now is **m** manifest, and by the G5319
26 the everlasting God, **m** known to all G1107
1Co 1:17 of Christ should be **m** of none effect. G2758
20 **m** foolish the wisdom of this world? G3471
30 who of God is **m** unto us wisdom, and G1096
3:13 Every man's work shall be **m** manifest: G1096
4: 9 to death: for we are **m** a spectacle unto G1096
13 Being defamed, we entreat: we are **m** G1096
7:21 if thou mayest be **m** free, use *it* rather. G1096
9:19 *men*, yet have I **m** myself servant unto G1402
22 the weak: I am **m** all things to all *men*, G1096
11:19 may be **m** manifest among you. G1096
12:13 been all **m** to drink into one Spirit. G4222
14:25 And thus are the secrets of his heart **m** G1096
15:22 even so in Christ shall all be **m** alive. G2227
45 man Adam was **m** a living soul; the last G1096
45 last Adam *was* **m** a quickening spirit.
2Co 2: 2 but the same which is **m** sorry by me? G3076
3: 6 Who also hath **m** us able ministers of G2427
10 For even that which was **m** glorious G1392
4:10 Jesus might be **m** manifest in our body. G5319
11 be **m** manifest in our mortal flesh. G5319

2Co 5: 1 **m** with hands, eternal in the heavens. G886
11 men; but we are **m** manifest unto God; G5319
11 are **m** manifest in your consciences. G5319
21 For he hath **m** him *to be* sin for us, who G4160
21 be **m** the righteousness of God in him. G1096
7: 8 For though I **m** you sorry with a letter, G3076
8 same epistle hath **m** you sorry, though G3076
9 Now I rejoice, not that ye were **m** sorry, G3076
9 for ye were **m** sorry after a godly G3076
14 which *I* **m** before Titus, is found a truth.
10:16 line of things **m** ready to our hand. G2092
11: 6 **m** manifest among you in all things. G5319
12: 9 thee: for my strength is **m** perfect in G5048
Gal 3: 3 are ye now **m** perfect by the flesh? G2005
13 of the law, being **m** a curse for us: for it G1096
16 the promises **m**. He saith not, And to G4483
19 whom the promise was **m**; *and it was* G1861
4: 4 **m** of a woman, made under the law, G1096
4 made of a woman, **m** under the law, G1096
5: 1 Christ hath **m** us free, and be not G1659
Eph 1: 6 he hath **m** us accepted in the beloved. G5487
9 Having **m** known unto us the mystery G1107
2: 6 And hath raised *us* up together, and **m** G4776
11 Circumcision in the flesh **m** by hands; G5499
13 off are **m** nigh by the blood of Christ. G1096
14 For he is our peace, who hath **m** both G4160
3: 3 How that by revelation he **m** known G1107
5 Which in other ages was not **m** known G1107
7 Whereof I was **m** a minister, according G1096
5:13 But all things that are reproved are **m** G5319
Php 2: 7 But **m** himself of no reputation, and G1096
7 and was **m** in the likeness of men: G1096
3:10 being **m** conformable unto his death; G4832
4: 6 your requests be **m** known unto God. G1107
Col 1:12 which hath **m** us meet to be partakers G2427
20 And, having **m** peace through the G1517
23 whereof I Paul am **m** a minister; G1096
25 Whereof I am **m** a minister, according G1096
26 but now is **m** manifest to his saints: G5319
2:11 the circumcision **m** without hands, in G1096
15 and powers, he **m** a shew of them G1165
1Ti 1: 9 Knowing this, that the law is not **m** for G2749
19 concerning faith have **m** shipwreck: G3489
2: 1 *and* giving of thanks, be **m** for all men; G4160
2Ti 1:10 But is now **m** manifest by the G5319
Tit 3: 7 we should be **m** heirs according to the G1096
Heb 1: 2 things, by whom also he **m** the worlds; G4160
4 Being **m** so much better than the G1096
2: 9 But we see Jesus, who was **m** a little G1642
17 him to be **m** like unto *his* brethren, G3666
3:14 For we are **m** partakers of Christ, if we G1096
5: 5 not himself to be **m** an high priest; but G1096
9 And being **m** perfect, he became the G5048
6: 4 were **m** partakers of the Holy Ghost, G1096
13 For when God **m** promise to Abraham, G1861
20 *even* Jesus, **m** an high priest for ever G1096
7: 3 nor end of life; but **m** like unto the Son of G871
12 **m** of necessity a change also of the law. G1096
16 Who is **m**, not after the law of a carnal G1096
19 For the law **m** nothing perfect, but the G5048
20 as not without an oath *he was m priest*:
21 (For those priests were **m** without an G1096
22 By so much was Jesus **m** a surety of a G1096
26 and **m** higher than the heavens; G1096
8: 9 Not according to the covenant that I **m** G4160
13 *covenant*, he hath **m** the first old. Now G3822
9: 2 For there was a tabernacle **m**; the first, G2680
8 of all was not yet **m** manifest, while as G5319
11 tabernacle, not **m** with hands, that is G5499
24 the holy places **m** with hands, *which* G5499
10: 3 again *m* of sins every year.
13 till his enemies be **m** his footstool. G5087
33 Partly, whilst ye were **m** a gazingstock G2301
11: 3 were not **m** of things which do appear. G1096
22 By faith Joseph, when he died, **m** G3421
34 out of weakness were **m** strong, waxed G1743
40 without us should not be **m** perfect. G5048
12:23 and to the spirits of just men **m** perfect, G5048
27 of things that are **m**, that those things G4160
Jas 1:10 But the rich, in that he is **m** low: G5014
2:22 and by works was faith **m** perfect? G5048
3: 9 are **m** after the similitude of God. G1096
1Pt 2: 7 the same is **m** the head of the corner, G1096
3:22 and powers being **m** subject unto him. G5293
2Pt 1:16 fables, when we **m** known unto you the G1107
2:12 But these, as natural brute beasts, **m** to G1080
1Jn 2:19 **m** manifest that they were not all of us. G5319
4:17 Herein is our love **m** perfect, that we G5048
18 He that feareth is not **m** perfect in love. G5048

1Jn 5:10 not God hath **m** him a liar; because G4160
Rev 1: 6 And hath **m** us kings and priests unto G4160
5:10 And hast **m** us unto our God kings and G4160
7:14 their robes, and **m** them white in the G3021
8:11 the waters, because they were **m** bitter. G4087
14: 7 worship him that **m** heaven, and earth, G4160
8 city, because she **m** all nations drink of G4222
15: 4 for thy judgments are **m** manifest. G5319
17: 2 earth have been **m** drunk with the wine G3182
18:15 which were **m** rich by her, shall stand G4147
19 city, wherein were **m** rich all that had G4147
19 for in one hour is she **m** desolate. G2049
19: 7 and his wife hath **m** herself ready. G2090

MADEST

Neh 9: 8 before thee, and **m** a covenant with H3772
14 And **m** known unto them thy holy H3045
Ps 8: 6 Thou **m** him to have dominion over the
80:15 branch *that* thou **m** strong for thyself.
17 of man *whom* thou **m** strong for thyself.
Ezk 16:17 given thee, and **m** to thyself images of H6213
29: 7 and **m** all their loins to be at a stand.
Jna 4:10 laboured, neither **m** it grow; which came
Act 21:38 before these days **m** an uproar, and G387
Heb 2: 7 Thou **m** him a little lower than the G1642

MADIAN

Act 7:29 the land of **M**, where he begat two sons. G3099

MADMAN

See MAD and MAN.

MADMANNAH

Jos 15:31 And Ziklag, and **M**, and Sansannah, H4089
1Ch 2:49 She bare also Shaaph the father of **M**, H4089

MADMEN

Jer 48: 2 O **M**; the sword shall pursue thee. H4086

MADMENAH

Isa 10:31 **M** is removed; the inhabitants of H4088

MADNESS

Dt 28:28 The LORD shall smite thee with **m**, and H7697
Ecc 1:17 and to know **m** and folly: I perceived H1947
2:12 wisdom, and **m**, and folly: for what H1947
7:25 of folly, even of foolishness *and* **m**: H1947
9: 3 is full of evil, and **m** *is* in their heart H1947
10:13 the end of his talk *is* mischievous **m**. H1948
Zec 12: 4 and his rider with **m**: and I will open H7697
Lk 6:11 And they were filled with **m**; and G454
2Pt 2:16 voice forbad the **m** of the prophet. G3913

MADON

Jos 11: 1 to Jobab king of **M**, and to the king of H4068
12:19 The king of **M**, one; the king of Hazor, H4068

MAG

See RAB-MAG.

MAGBISH

Ezr 2:30 The children of **M**, an hundred fifty and H4019

MAGDALA

Mt 15:39 ship, and came into the coasts of **M**. G3093

MAGDALENE

Mt 27:56 Among which was Mary **M**, and Mary G3094
61 And there was Mary **M**, and the other G3094
28: 1 the week, came Mary **M** and the other G3094
Mk 15:40 whom was Mary **M**, and Mary the G3094
47 And Mary **M** and Mary *the mother* of G3094
16: 1 was past, Mary **M**, and Mary the G3094
9 first to Mary **M**, out of whom he had G3094
Lk 8: 2 **M**, out of whom went seven devils, G3094
24:10 It was Mary **M**, and Joanna, and Mary G3094
Jn 19:25 the *wife* of Cleophas, and Mary **M**. G3094
20: 1 cometh Mary **M** early, when it was yet G3094
18 Mary **M** came and told the disciples G3094

MAGDIEL

Gen 36:43 Duke **M**, duke Iram: these *be* the dukes H4025
1Ch 1:54 Duke **M**, duke Iram. These *are* the H4025

MAGICIAN

Dan 2:10 at any **m**, or astrologer, or Chaldean. H2749

MAGICIANS

Gen 41: 8 called for all the **m** of Egypt, and all the H2748
24 told *this* unto the **m**; but *there was* none H2748
Ex 7:11 now the **m** of Egypt, they also H2748

Ex 7:22 And the **m** of Egypt did so with their H2748
8: 7 And the **m** did so with their H2748
18 And the **m** did so with their H2748
19 Then the **m** said unto Pharaoh, This *is* H2748
9:11 And the **m** could not stand before H2748
11 the **m**, and upon all the Egyptians. H2748
Dan 1:20 better than all the **m** *and* astrologers H2748
2: 2 to call the **m**, and the astrologers, H2748
27 **m**, the soothsayers, shew unto the king; H2749
4: 7 Then came in the **m**, the astrologers, H2749
9 O Belteshazzar, master of the **m**, H2749
5:11 made master of the **m**, astrologers, H2749

MAGISTRATE
Jdg 18: 7 *there was* no **m** in the land, H3423+H6114
Lk 12:58 adversary to the **m**, *as thou art* in the G758

MAGISTRATES
Ezr 7:25 in thine hand, set **m** and judges, which H8200
Lk 12:11 and *unto* **m**, and powers, take ye G746
Act 16:20 And brought them to the **m**, saying, G4755
22 them: and the **m** rent off their clothes, G4755
35 And when it was day, the **m** sent the G4755
36 to Paul, The **m** have sent to let you G4755
38 words unto the **m**: and they feared, G4755
Tit 3: 1 obey **m**, to be ready to every good work, G3980

MAGNIFICAL
1Ch 22: 5 *be* exceeding **m**, of fame and of glory H1431

MAGNIFICENCE
Act 19:27 be despised, and her **m** should be G3168

MAGNIFIED
Gen 19:19 and thou hast **m** thy mercy, which thou H1431
Jos 4:14 On that day the LORD **m** Joshua in the H1431
2Sa 7:26 And let thy name be **m** for ever, saying, H1431
1Ch 17:24 thy name may be **m** for ever, saying, H1431
29:25 And the LORD **m** Solomon exceedingly H1431
2Ch 1: 1 *was* with him, and **m** him exceedingly. H1431
32:23 so that he was **m** in the sight of all H5375
Ps 35:27 Let the LORD be **m**, which hath H1431
40:16 say continually, The LORD be **m**. H1431
70: 4 say continually, Let God be **m**. H1431
138: 2 hast **m** thy word above all thy name. H1431
Jer 48:26 Make ye him drunken: for he **m** H1431
42 he hath **m** *himself* against the LORD. H1431
Lam 1: 9 for the enemy hath **m** *himself*. H1431
Dan 8:11 Yea, he **m** *himself* even to the prince of H1431
Zep 2: 8 and **m** *themselves* against their border. H1431
10 reproached and **m** *themselves* against H1431
Mal 1: 5 will be **m** from the border of Israel. H1431
Act 5:13 to them: but the people **m** them. G3170
19:17 and the name of the Lord Jesus was **m**. G3170
Php 1:20 Christ shall be **m** in my body, whether G3170

MAGNIFY
Jos 3: 7 day will I begin to **m** thee in the sight of H1431
Job 7:17 What *is* man, that thou shouldest **m** H1431
19: 5 If indeed ye will **m** *yourselves* against H1431
36:24 Remember that thou **m** his work, H7679
Ps 34: 3 O **m** the LORD with me, and let us exalt H1431
35:26 that **m** *themselves* against me. H1431
38:16 they **m** *themselves* against me. H1431
55:12 hated me *that* did **m** *himself* against H1431
69:30 and will **m** him with thanksgiving. H1431
Isa 10:15 *or* shall the saw **m** itself against him H1431
42:21 **m** the law, and make *it* honourable. H1431
Ezk 38:23 Thus will I **m** myself, and sanctify H1431
Dan 8:25 and he shall **m** *himself* in his heart, H1431
11:36 exalt himself, and **m** himself above H1431
37 god: for he shall **m** himself above all. H1431
Zec 12: 7 do not **m** *themselves* against Judah. H1431
Lk 1:46 And Mary said, My soul doth **m** the G3170
Act 10:46 and **m** God. Then answered Peter, G3170
Ro 11:13 apostle of the Gentiles, I **m** mine office: G1392

MAGOG
Gen 10: 2 The sons of Japheth; Gomer, and **M**, H4031
1Ch 1: 5 The sons of Japheth; Gomer, and **M**, H4031
Ezk 38: 2 Gog, the land of **M**, the chief prince of H4031
39: 6 And I will send a fire on **M**, and among H4031
Rev 20: 8 the earth, Gog and **M**, to gather them G3098

MAGOR-MISSABIB
Jer 20: 3 not called thy name Pashur, but **M**. H4036

MAGPIASH
Neh 10:20 **M**, Meshullam, Hezir, H4047

MAHALAH
1Ch 7:18 bare Ishod, and Abiezer, and **M**. H4244

MAHALALEEL
Gen 5:12 lived seventy years, and begat **M**: H4111
13 And Cainan lived after he begat **M** H4111
15 And **M** lived sixty and five years, and H4111
16 And **M** lived after he begat Jared eight H4111
17 And all the days of **M** were eight H4111
1Ch 1: 2 Kenan, **M**, Jered, H4111
Neh 11: 4 the son of **M**, of the children of Perez; H4111

MAHALATH
Gen 28: 9 wives which he had **M** the daughter of H4258
2Ch 11:18 And Rehoboam took him **M** the H4258
Ps 53:ttl To the chief Musician upon **M**, Maschil, H4257
88:ttl Musician upon **M** Leannoth, Maschil H4257

MAHALI
Ex 6:19 And the sons of Merari; **M** and Mushi: H4249

MAHANAIM
Gen 32: 2 and he called the name of that place **M**. H4266
Jos 13:26 and from **M** unto the border of Debir; H4266
30 And their coast was from **M**, all H4266
21:38 for the slayer; and **M** with her suburbs, H4266
2Sa 2: 8 son of Saul, and brought him over to **M**; H4266
12 of Saul, went out from **M** to Gibeon. H4266
29 all Bithron, and they came to **M**. H4266
17:24 Then David came to **M**. And Absalom H4266
27 was come to **M**, that Shobi the son of H4266
19:32 lay at **M**; for he *was* a very great man. H4266
1Ki 2: 8 when I went to **M**: but he came down H4266
4:14 Ahinadab the son of Iddo *had* **M**: H4266
1Ch 6:80 her suburbs, and **M** with her suburbs, H4266

MAHANEH-DAN
Jdg 18:12 they called that place **M** unto this day: H4265

MAHARAI
2Sa 23:28 Zalmon the Ahohite, **M** the H4121
1Ch 11:30 **M** the Netophathite, Heled the son of H4121
27:13 tenth month *was* **M** the Netophathite, H4121

MAHATH
1Ch 6:35 the son of **M**, the son of Amasai, H4287
2Ch 29:12 Then the Levites arose, **M** the son of H4287
31:13 Ismachiah, and **M**, and Benaiah, *were* H4287

MAHAVITE
1Ch 11:46 Eliel the **M**, and Jeribai, and Joshaviah, H4233

MAHAZIOTH
1Ch 25: 4 Joshbekashah, Mallothi, Hothir, *and* **M**: H4238
30 The three and twentieth to **M**, *he*, his H4238

MAHER-SHALAL-HASH-BAZ
Isa 8: 1 **M**. H4116+H7998+H2363+H957+H4122
3 **M**. H4116+H7998+H2363+H957+H4122

MAHLAH
Nu 26:33 Zelophehad *were* **M**, and Noah, Hoglah, H4244
27: 1 of his daughters; **M**, Noah, and Hoglah, H4244
36:11 For **M**, Tirzah, and Hoglah, and Milcah, H4244
Jos 17: 3 of his daughters, **M**, and Noah, Hoglah, H4244

MAHLI
Nu 3:20 by their families; **M**, and Mushi. These H4249
1Ch 6:19 The sons of Merari; **M**, and Mushi. And H4249
29 The sons of Merari; **M**, Libni his son, H4249
47 The son of **M**, the son of Mushi, the son H4249
23:21 The sons of Merari; **M**, and Mushi. The H4249
21 The sons of **M**; Eleazar, and Kish. H4249
23 The sons of Mushi; **M**, and Eder, and H4249
24:26 The sons of Merari *were* **M** and Mushi: H4249
28 Of **M** *came* Eleazar, who had no sons. H4249
30 The sons also of Mushi; **M**, and Eder, H4249
Ezr 8:18 of the sons of **M**, the son of Levi, the H4249

MAHLITES
Nu 3:33 Of Merari *was* the family of the **M**, and H4250
26:58 the family of the **M**, the family of the H4250

MAHLON
Ru 1: 2 name of his two sons **M** and Chilion, H4248
5 And **M** and Chilion died also both of H4248
4:10 the wife of **M**, have I purchased to H4248

MAHLON'S
Ru 4: 9 Chilion's and **M**, of the hand of Naomi. H4248

MAHOL
1Ki 4:31 the sons of **M**: and his fame was in H4235

MAID
Gen 16: 2 go in unto my **m**; it may be that I may H8198
3 took Hagar her **m** the Egyptian, after H8198
5 I have given my **m** into thy bosom; and H8198
6 Sarai, Behold, thy **m** *is* in thy hand; do H8198
8 And he said, Hagar, Sarai's **m**, whence H8198
29:24 Leah Zilpah his **m** *for* an handmaid. H8198
29 Bilhah his handmaid to be her **m**. H8198
30: 3 And she said, Behold my **m** Bilhah, go in H519
7 And Bilhah Rachel's **m** conceived H8198
9 her **m**, and gave her Jacob to wife. H8198
10 And Zilpah Leah's **m** bare Jacob a son. H8198
12 And Zilpah Leah's **m** bare Jacob a H8198
Ex 2: 5 the flags, she sent her **m** to fetch it. H519
8 **m** went and called the child's mother. H5959
21:20 And if a man smite his servant, or his **m**, H519
26 or the eye of his **m**, that it perish; he shall H519
22:16 And if a man entice a **m** that is not H1330
Lev 12: 5 But if she bear a **m** child, then she shall H5347
25: 6 and for thy **m**, and for thy hired servant, H519
Dt 22:14 I came to her, I found her not a **m**: H1331
17 thy daughter a **m**; and yet these *are the* H1331
2Ki 5: 2 **m**; and she waited on Naaman's wife. H5291
4 said the **m** that *is* of the land of Israel. H5291
Est 2: 7 nor mother, and the **m** *was* fair and H5291
Job 31: 1 eyes; why then should I think upon a **m**? H1330
Prv 30:19 the sea; and the way of a man with a **m**. H5959
Isa 24: 2 as with the **m**, so with her mistress; H8198
Jer 2:32 Can a **m** forget her ornaments, *or* a H1330
51:22 in pieces the young man and the **m**; H1330
Am 2: 7 the *same* **m**, to profane my holy name: H5291
Mt 9:24 Give place: for the **m** is not dead, but G2877
25 took her by the hand, and the **m** arose. G2877
26:71 the porch, another **m** saw him, and said
Mk 14:69 And a **m** saw him again, and began to G3814
Lk 8:54 the hand, and called, saying, **M**, arise. G3816
22:56 But a certain **m** beheld him as he sat by G3814

MAID-CHILD See MAID and CHILD.

MAIDEN
Gen 30:18 I have given my **m** to my husband: and H8198
Jdg 19:24 Behold, *here is* my daughter a **m**, and H1330
2Ch 36:17 young man or **m**, old man, or him that H1330
Est 2: 4 And let the **m** which pleaseth the king H5291
9 And the **m** pleased him, and she H5291
13 Then thus came *every* **m** unto the king; H5291
Ps 123: 2 as the eyes of a **m** unto the hand of her H8198
Lk 8:51 and the father and the mother of the **m**. G3816

MAIDENS
Ex 2: 5 at the river; and her **m** walked along by H5291
Ru 2: 8 hence, but abide here fast by my **m**: H5291
22 go out with his **m**, that they meet thee H5291
23 So she kept fast by the **m** of Boaz to H5291
3: 2 with whose **m** thou wast? Behold, H5291
1Sa 9:11 they found young **m** going out to draw H5291
Est 2: 8 and when many **m** were gathered H5291
9 to her, and seven **m**, *which were* meet H5291
4:16 I also and my **m** will fast likewise; and H5291
Job 41: 5 a bird? or wilt thou bind him for thy **m**? H5291
Ps 78:63 their **m** were not given to marriage. H1330
148:12 Both young men, and **m**; old men, and H1330
Prv 9: 3 She hath sent forth her **m**: she crieth H5291
27:27 and *for* the maintenance for thy **m**. H5291
31:15 her household, and a portion to her **m**. H5291
Ecc 2: 7 I got *me* servants and **m**, and had H8198
Ezk 44:22 but they shall take **m** of the seed of the H1330
Lk 12:45 the menservants and **m**, and to eat and G3814

MAIDS
Ezr 2:65 Beside their servants and their **m**, of H519
Est 2: 9 her and her **m** unto the best *place* H5291
4: 4 So Esther's **m** and her chamberlains H5291
Job 19:15 mine house, and my **m**, count me for a H519
Lam 5:11 Zion, *and* the **m** in the cities of Judah. H1330
Ezk 9: 6 Slay utterly old *and* young, both **m**, and H1330
Nah 2: 7 up, and her **m** shall lead *her* as with H519
Zec 9:17 men cheerful, and new wine the **m**. H1330
Mk 14:66 cometh one of the **m** of the high priest: G3814

MAID'S
Est 2:12 Now when every **m** turn was come to H5291

MAIDSERVANT
Ex 11: 5 the firstborn of the **m** that *is* behind the H8198
20:10 nor thy **m**, nor thy cattle, nor thy H519
17 nor his **m**, nor his ox, nor his ass, H519
21: 7 And if a man sell his daughter to be a **m**, H519
32 If the ox shall push a manservant or a **m**; H519
Dt 5:14 nor thy **m**, nor thine ox, nor thine H519
14 and thy **m** may rest as well as thou. H519
21 or his **m**, his ox, or his ass, or H519
12:18 and thy **m**, and the Levite that *is* H519
15:17 also unto thy **m** thou shalt do likewise. H519
16:11 and thy **m**, and the Levite that *is* H519
14 and thy **m**, and the Levite, the stranger, H519
Jdg 9:18 the son of his **m**, king over the men of H519
Job 31:13 of my **m**, when they contended with me; H519
Jer 34: 9 every man his **m**, *being* an Hebrew or H8198
10 and every one his **m**, go free, that none H8198

MAIDSERVANTS
Gen 12:16 and **m**, and she asses, and camels. H8198
20:17 wife, and his **m**; and they bare *children*. H519
24:35 and **m**, and camels, and asses. H8198
30:43 much cattle, and **m**, and menservants, H8198
Dt 12:12 and your **m**, and the Levite that *is* H519
1Sa 8:16 and your **m**, and your goodliest H8198
2Sa 6:22 own sight: and of the **m** which thou hast H519
2Ki 5:26 and oxen, and menservants, and **m**? H8198
Neh 7:67 Beside their manservants and their **m**, of H519

MAIDSERVANT'S
Ex 21:27 tooth, or his **m** tooth; he shall let him H519

MAIDSERVANTS'
Gen 31:33 and into the two **m** tents; but he found H519

MAIL
1Sa 17: 5 with a coat of **m**; and the weight of the H7193
38 also he armed him with a coat of **m**. H8302

MAIMED
Lev 22:22 Blind, or broken, or **m**, or having a wen, H2782
Mt 15:30 blind, dumb, **m**, and many others, and G2948
31 to speak, the **m** to be whole, the lame G2948
18: 8 into life halt or **m**, rather than having G2948
Mk 9:43 to enter into life **m**, than having two G2948
Lk 14:13 call the poor, the **m**, the lame, the blind: G376
21 and the **m**, and the halt, and the blind. G376

MAINSAIL
Act 27:40 **m** to the wind, and made toward shore. G736

MAINTAIN
1Ki 8:45 their supplication, and **m** their cause. H6213
49 thy dwelling place, and **m** their cause, H6213
59 and night, that he **m** the cause of his H6213
1Ch 26:27 dedicate to **m** the house of the LORD. H2388
2Ch 6:35 their supplication, and **m** their cause. H6213
39 and **m** their cause, and forgive H6213
Job 13:15 I will **m** mine own ways before him. H3198
Ps 140:12 I know that the LORD will **m** the cause H6213
Tit 3: 8 be careful to **m** good works. These G4291
14 And let ours also learn to **m** good G4291

MAINTAINED
Ps 9: 4 For thou hast **m** my right and my H6213

MAINTAINEST
Ps 16: 5 and of my cup: thou **m** my lot. H8551

MAINTENANCE
Ezr 4:14 Now because we have **m** from *the* H4415
Prv 27:27 and *for* the **m** for thy maidens. H2416

MAJESTY
1Ch 29:11 victory, and the **m**: for all *that is* in the H1935
25 him *such* royal **m** as had not been on H1935
Est 1: 4 of his excellent **m** many days, *even* an H1420
Job 37:22 out of the north: with God *is* terrible **m**. H1935
40:10 Deck thyself now *with* **m** and H1347
Ps 21: 5 and **m** hast thou laid upon him. H1926
29: 4 the voice of the LORD *is* full of **m**. H1926
45: 3 *most* mighty, with thy glory and thy **m**. H1926
4 And in thy **m** ride prosperously H1926
93: 1 he is clothed with **m**; the LORD is H1348
96: 6 Honour and **m** *are* before him: H1926
104: 1 thou art clothed with honour and **m**. H1926
145: 5 of thy **m**, and of thy wondrous works. H1935
12 and the glorious **m** of his kingdom. H1926
Isa 2:10 of the LORD, and for the glory of his **m**. H1347
2:19 the glory of his **m**, when he ariseth to H1347
21 the glory of his **m**, when he ariseth to H1347
24:14 shall sing for the **m** of the LORD, they H1347
26:10 and will not behold the **m** of the LORD. H1348
Ezk 7:20 he set it in **m**: but they made the images H1347
Dan 4:30 my power, and for the honour of my **m**? H1923
36 and excellent **m** was added unto me. H7238
5:18 and **m**, and glory, and honour: H7238
19 And for the **m** that he gave him, all H7238
Mic 5: 4 the LORD, in the **m** of the name of the H1347
Heb 1: 3 on the right hand of the **M** on high; G3172
8: 1 of the throne of the **M** in the heavens; G3172
2Pt 1:16 Christ, but were eyewitnesses of his **m**. G3168
Jude 25 *be* glory and **m**, dominion and power, G3172

MAKAZ
1Ki 4: 9 The son of Dekar, in **M**, and in H4739

MAKE
Gen 1:26 And God said, Let us **m** man in our H6213
2:18 I will **m** him an help meet for him. H6213
3: 6 to be desired to **m** *one* wise, she took of H7919
21 **m** coats of skins, and clothed them. H6213
6:14 **M** thee an ark of gopher wood; rooms H6213
14 rooms shalt thou **m** in the ark, and H6213
15 which thou shalt **m** it *of*: The length of H6213
16 A window shalt thou **m** to the ark, and H6213
16 and third *stories* shalt thou **m** it. H6213
9:12 covenant which I **m** between me and H5414
11: 3 Go to, let us **m** brick, and burn them H3835
4 heaven; and let us **m** us a name, lest we H6213
12: 2 And I will **m** of thee a great nation, and H6213
2 bless thee, and **m** thy name great; and H1431
13:16 And I will **m** thy seed as the dust of the H7760
17: 2 And I will **m** my covenant between me H5414
6 And I will **m** thee exceeding fruitful, H6509
6 fruitful, and I will **m** nations of thee, H5414
20 him, and will **m** him fruitful, and will
20 beget, and I will **m** him a great nation. H5414
18: 6 Sarah, and said, **M** ready quickly three H4116
6 knead *it*, and **m** cakes upon the hearth. H6213
19:32 Come, let us **m** our father drink wine, H8248
34 my father: let us **m** him drink wine this
21:13 I **m** a nation, because he *is* thy seed. H7760
18 hand; for I will **m** him a great nation. H7760
24: 3 And I will **m** thee swear by the LORD,
26: 4 And I will **m** thy seed to multiply as the H7235
28 and let us **m** a covenant with thee; H3772
27: 4 And **m** me savoury meat, such as I H6213
7 Bring me venison, and **m** me savoury H6213
9 goats; and I will **m** them savoury meat H6213
28: 3 And God Almighty bless thee, and **m**
31:44 Now therefore come thou, let us **m** a H3772
32:12 do thee good, and **m** thy seed as the H7760
34: 9 And **m** ye marriages with us, *and* give
30 troubled me to **m** me to stink among the
35: 1 dwell there: and **m** there an altar unto H6213
3 to Beth-el; and I will **m** there an altar H6213
40:14 unto me, and **m** mention of me unto H2142
43:16 and slay, and **m** ready; for *these* men H3559
46: 3 for I will there **m** of thee a great nation: H7760
47: 6 the best of the land **m** thy father and
6 then **m** them rulers over my cattle. H7760
48: 4 And said unto me, Behold, I will **m** thee
4 thee, and I will **m** of thee a multitude H5414
20 bless, saying, God **m** thee as Ephraim H7760
Ex 5: 5 and ye **m** them rest from their burdens.
7 people straw to **m** brick, as heretofore: H3835
8 which they did **m** heretofore, ye shall H6213
16 they say to us, **M** brick: and, behold, H6213
12: 4 eating shall **m** your count for the lamb.
18:16 another, and I do **m** *them* know the H5414
20: 4 Thou shalt not **m** unto thee any graven H6213
23 Ye shall not **m** with me gods of silver, H6213
23 shall ye **m** unto you gods of gold. H6213
24 An altar of earth thou shalt **m** unto me, H6213
25 And if thou wilt **m** me an altar of stone, H6213
21:34 The owner of the pit shall **m** *it* good, *and*
22: 3 him; *for* he should **m** full restitution; if
5 his own vineyard, shall he **m** restitution.
6 the fire shall surely **m** restitution.
11 *thereof*, and he shall not **m** *it* good.
12 And if it be stolen from him, he shall **m**
13 he shall not **m** good that which was torn.
14 not with it, he shall surely **m** *it* good.
15 it, he shall not **m** *it* good: if it *be* an hired
23:13 circumspect: and **m** no mention of the
27 come, and I will **m** all thine enemies H5414
32 Thou shalt **m** no covenant with them, H3772
Ex 23:33 thy land, lest they **m** thee sin against me:
25: 8 And let them **m** me a sanctuary; that I H6213
9 thereof, even so shall ye **m** *it*. H6213
10 And they shall **m** an ark *of* shittim H6213
11 **m** upon it a crown of gold round about. H6213
13 And thou shalt **m** staves *of* shittim H6213
17 And thou shalt **m** a mercy seat *of* pure H6213
18 And thou shalt **m** two cherubims *of* H6213
18 work shalt thou **m** them, in the two H6213
19 And **m** one cherub on the one end, and H6213
19 seat shall ye **m** the cherubims on the H6213
23 Thou shalt also **m** a table *of* shittim H6213
24 **m** thereto a crown of gold round about. H6213
25 And thou shalt **m** unto it a border of an H6213
25 and thou shalt **m** a golden crown to the H6213
26 And thou shalt **m** for it four rings of H6213
28 And thou shalt **m** the staves *of* shittim H6213
29 And thou shalt **m** the dishes thereof, H6213
29 withal: *of* pure gold shalt thou **m** them. H6213
31 And thou shalt **m** a candlestick *of* pure H6213
37 And thou shalt **m** the seven lamps H6213
39 *Of* a talent of pure gold shall he **m** it, H6213
40 And look that thou **m** *them* after their H6213
26: 1 Moreover thou shalt **m** the tabernacle H6213
1 of cunning work shalt thou **m** them. H6213
4 And thou shalt **m** loops of blue upon H6213
4 shalt thou **m** in the uttermost edge H6213
5 Fifty loops shalt thou **m** in the one H6213
5 loops shalt thou **m** in the edge of the H6213
6 And thou shalt **m** fifty taches of gold, H6213
7 And thou shalt **m** curtains *of* goats' H6213
7 eleven curtains shalt thou **m**. H6213
10 And thou shalt **m** fifty loops on the H6213
11 And thou shalt **m** fifty taches of brass, H6213
14 And thou shalt **m** a covering for the H6213
15 And thou shalt **m** boards for the H6213
17 **m** for all the boards of the tabernacle. H6213
18 And thou shalt **m** the boards for the H6213
19 And thou shalt **m** forty sockets of silver H6213
22 westward thou shalt **m** six boards. H6213
23 And two boards shalt thou **m** for the H6213
26 And thou shalt **m** bars *of* shittim wood; H6213
29 with gold, and **m** their rings *of* gold *for* H6213
31 And thou shalt **m** a vail *of* blue, and H6213
36 And thou shalt **m** an hanging for the H6213
37 And thou shalt **m** for the hanging five H6213
27: 1 And thou shalt **m** an altar *of* shittim H6213
2 And thou shalt **m** the horns of it upon H6213
3 And thou shalt **m** his pans to receive H6213
3 vessels thereof thou shalt **m** *of* brass. H6213
4 And thou shalt **m** for it a grate of H6213
4 the net shalt thou **m** four brasen rings H6213
6 And thou shalt **m** staves for the altar, H6213
8 Hollow with boards shalt thou **m** it: as H6213
8 thee in the mount, so shall they **m** *it*. H6213
9 And thou shalt **m** the court of the H6213
28: 2 And thou shalt **m** holy garments for H6213
3 that they may **m** Aaron's garments to H6213
4 which they shall **m**; a breastplate, and H6213
4 and they shall **m** holy garments for H6213
6 And they shall **m** the ephod *of* gold, *of* H6213
11 **m** them to be set in ouches of gold. H6213
13 And thou shalt **m** ouches *of* gold; H6213
14 work shalt thou **m** them, and fasten the H6213
15 And thou shalt **m** the breastplate of H6213
15 ephod thou shalt **m** it; *of* gold, *of* blue, H6213
15 *of* fine twined linen, shalt thou **m** it. H6213
22 And thou shalt **m** upon the breastplate H6213
23 And thou shalt **m** upon the breastplate H6213
26 And thou shalt **m** two rings of gold, H6213
27 rings of gold thou shalt **m**, and shalt put H6213
31 And thou shalt **m** the robe of the ephod H6213
33 of it thou shalt **m** pomegranates *of* H6213
36 And thou shalt **m** a plate *of* pure gold, H6213
39 and thou shalt **m** the mitre *of* fine H6213
39 thou shalt **m** the girdle *of* needlework. H6213
40 And for Aaron's sons thou shalt **m** H6213
40 and thou shalt **m** for them girdles, and H6213
40 **m** for them, for glory and for beauty. H6213
42 And thou shalt **m** them linen breeches H6213
29: 2 *of* wheaten flour shalt thou **m** them. H6213
37 Seven days thou shalt **m** an atonement
30: 1 And thou shalt **m** an altar to burn H6213
1 upon: *of* shittim wood shalt thou **m** it. H6213
3 **m** unto it a crown of gold round about. H6213
4 And two golden rings shalt thou **m** to it H6213
4 of it shalt thou **m** *it*; and they shall be H6213
5 And thou shalt **m** the staves *of* shittim H6213
10 And Aaron shall **m** an atonement upon

Ex 30:10 in the year shall he **m** atonement upon it
15 to **m** an atonement for your souls.
16 to **m** an atonement for your souls.
18 Thou shalt also **m** a laver *of* brass, and H6213
25 And thou shalt **m** it an oil of holy H6213
32 neither shall ye **m** *any other* like it, H6213
35 And thou shalt **m** it a perfume, a H6213
37 which thou shalt **m**, ye shall not make H6213
37 make, ye shall not **m** to yourselves H6213
38 Whosoever shall **m** like unto that, to H6213
31: 6 **m** all that I have commanded thee; H6213
32: 1 unto him, Up, **m** us gods, which shall H6213
10 and I will **m** of thee a great nation. H6213
23 For they said unto me, **M** us gods, H6213
30 I shall **m** an atonement for your sin.
33:19 And he said, I will **m** all my goodness
34:10 And he said, Behold, I **m** a covenant: H3772
12 Take heed to thyself, lest thou **m** a H3772
15 Lest thou **m** a covenant with the H3772
16 after their gods, and **m** thy sons go a H2181
17 Thou shalt **m** thee no molten gods. H6213
35:10 **m** all that the LORD hath commanded; H6213
33 to **m** any manner of cunning work. H6213
36: 3 the sanctuary, to **m** it *withal*. And they H6213
5 which the LORD commanded to **m**. H6213
6 man nor woman **m** any more work for H6213
7 for all the work to **m** it, and too much. H6213
22 **m** for all the boards of the tabernacle. H6213
Lev 1: 4 for him to **m** atonement for him. H3722
4:20 and the priest shall **m** an atonement for
26 the priest shall **m** an atonement for him
31 the priest shall **m** an atonement for him,
35 the priest shall **m** an atonement for his
5: 6 the priest shall **m** an atonement for him
10 the priest shall **m** an atonement for him
13 And the priest shall **m** an atonement for
16 And he shall **m** amends for the harm
16 the priest shall **m** an atonement for him
18 the priest shall **m** an atonement for him
6: 7 And the priest shall **m** an atonement for
8:15 it, to **m** reconciliation upon it. H3722
34 to do, to **m** an atonement for you.
9: 7 burnt offering, and **m** an atonement for
7 of the people, and **m** an atonement for
10:17 the congregation, to **m** atonement for H3722
11:43 Ye shall not **m** yourselves abominable H8262
43 neither shall ye **m** yourselves unclean
47 To **m** a difference between the unclean
12: 7 the LORD, and **m** an atonement for her;
8 the priest shall **m** an atonement for her,
14:18 the priest shall **m** an atonement for him
19 the sin offering, and **m** an atonement for
20 the priest shall **m** an atonement for him,
21 to be waved, to **m** an atonement for him,
29 is to be cleansed, to **m** an atonement for
31 the priest shall **m** an atonement for him
53 open fields, and **m** an atonement for the
15:15 the priest shall **m** an atonement for him
30 the priest shall **m** an atonement for her
16: 6 *is* for himself, and **m** an atonement for
10 the LORD, to **m** an atonement with
11 himself, and shall **m** an atonement for
16 And he shall **m** an atonement for the
17 he goeth in to **m** an atonement in the
18 the LORD, and **m** an atonement for it;
24 of the people, and **m** an atonement for
27 was brought in to **m** atonement in the H3722
30 For on that day shall *the priest* **m** an
32 stead, shall **m** the atonement, and
33 And he shall **m** an atonement for the
33 and he shall **m** an atonement for the
33 altar, and he shall **m** an atonement for
34 unto you, to **m** an atonement for the
17:11 upon the altar to **m** an atonement for
19: 4 Turn ye not unto idols, nor **m** to H6213
22 And the priest shall **m** an atonement for
28 Ye shall not **m** any cuttings in your H5414
20:25 clean: and ye shall not **m** your souls
21: 5 They shall not **m** baldness upon their H7139
5 nor **m** any cuttings in their flesh. H8295
22:22 the LORD, nor **m** an offering by fire of H5414
24 ye **m** *any offering thereof* in your land. H6213
23:22 thou shalt not **m** clean riddance of the
28 of atonement, to **m** an atonement for
24:18 And he that killeth a beast shall **m** it
25: 9 atonement shall ye **m** the trumpet sound
26: 1 Ye shall **m** you no idols nor graven H6213
6 and none shall **m** *you* afraid: and I will
9 For I will have respect unto you, and **m**

Lev 26:19 power; and I will **m** your heaven as H5414
22 your cattle, and **m** you few in number;
31 And I will **m** your cities waste, and H5414
27: 2 When a man shall **m** a singular vow, the
Nu 5:21 The LORD **m** thee a curse and an H5414
21 the LORD doth **m** thy thigh to rot, and H5414
22 into thy bowels, to **m** *thy* belly to swell,
6: 7 He shall not **m** himself unclean for his
11 offering, and **m** an atonement for him,
25 The LORD **m** his face shine upon thee,
8: 7 their clothes, and *so* **m** themselves clean.
12 to **m** an atonement for the Levites.
19 and to **m** an atonement for the
10: 2 **M** thee two trumpets of silver; of a H6213
2 piece shalt thou **m** them: that thou H6213
12: 6 *I* the LORD will **m** myself known unto
14: 4 And they said one to another, Let us **m** H5414
12 them, and will **m** of thee a greater H6213
30 which I sware to **m** you dwell therein,
15: 3 And will **m** an offering by fire unto the H6213
3 solemn feasts, to **m** a sweet savour H6213
25 And the priest shall **m** an atonement for
28 And the priest shall **m** an atonement for
28 the LORD, to **m** an atonement for him;
38 them that they **m** them fringes in the H6213
16:13 **m** thyself altogether a prince over us?
30 But if the LORD **m** a new thing, and the H1254
38 souls, let them **m** them broad plates H6213
46 congregation, and **m** an atonement for
17: 5 and I will **m** to cease from me the
21: 8 And the LORD said unto Moses, **M** H6213
23:19 he spoken, and shall he not **m** it good?
28:22 And one goat *for* a sin offering, to **m** an
30 *And* one kid of the goats, to **m** an
29: 5 sin offering, to **m** an atonement for you:
30: 8 *it*; then he shall **m** her vow which she
13 it, or her husband may **m** it void.
15 But if he shall any ways **m** them void
31:23 the fire, ye shall **m** *it* go through the fire,
23 the fire ye shall **m** go through the water.
50 and tablets, to **m** an atonement for our
Dt 1:11 (The LORD God of your fathers **m** you a
13 and I will **m** them rulers over you. H7760
4:10 together, and I will **m** them hear my
16 Lest ye corrupt *yourselves*, and **m** you H6213
23 with you, and **m** you a graven image, H6213
25 *yourselves*, and **m** a graven image, *or* H6213
5: 8 Thou shalt not **m** thee *any* graven H6213
7: 2 them; thou shalt **m** no covenant with H3772
3 Neither shalt thou **m** marriages with
8: 3 that he might **m** thee know that man
9:14 heaven: and I will **m** of thee a nation H6213
10: 1 the mount, and **m** thee an ark of wood. H6213
13:14 Then shalt thou inquire, and **m** search,
14: 1 cut yourselves, nor **m** any baldness H7760
15: 1 seven years thou shalt **m** a release. H6213
16:18 Judges and officers shalt thou **m** thee H5414
21 thy God, which thou shalt **m** thee. H6213
19:18 And the judges shall **m** diligent
20: 9 that they shall **m** captains of the H6485
11 And it shall be, if it **m** thee answer of
12 And if it will **m** no peace with thee, but
12 with thee, but will **m** war against thee, H6213
21:14 thou shalt not **m** merchandise of her,
16 *that* he may not **m** the son of the beloved
22: 8 then thou shalt **m** a battlement for thy H6213
12 Thou shalt **m** thee fringes upon the H6213
26:19 And to **m** thee high above all nations H5414
28:11 And the LORD shall **m** thee plenteous in
13 And the LORD shall **m** thee the head, H5414
21 The LORD shall **m** the pestilence cleave
24 The LORD shall **m** the rain of thy land H5414
59 Then the LORD will **m** thy plagues H6381
29: 1 Moses to **m** with the children of H3772
14 Neither with you only do I **m** this H3772
30: 9 And the LORD thy God will **m** thee
32:26 corners, I would **m** the remembrance of
35 that shall come upon them **m** haste.
39 me: I kill, and I **m** alive; I wound, and
42 I will **m** mine arrows drunk with blood,
Jos 1: 8 then thou shalt **m** thy way prosperous, H6743
5: 2 said unto Joshua, **M** thee sharp knives, H6213
6: 5 that when they **m** a long *blast* with the
10 not shout, nor **m** any noise with your
18 thing, lest ye **m** *yourselves* accursed,
18 thing, and **m** the camp of Israel a H7760
7: 3 and smite Ai; *and* **m** not all the people to
19 God of Israel, and **m** confession unto H5414
9: 6 now therefore **m** ye a league with us. H3772

Jos 9: 7 and how shall we **m** a league with you? H3772
11 therefore now **m** ye a league with us. H3772
22:25 your children **m** our children cease H7673
23: 7 you; neither **m** mention of the name
12 you, and shall **m** marriages with them,
Jdg 2: 2 And ye shall **m** no league with the H3772
9:48 me do, **m** haste, *and* do as I *have done*.
16:25 that he may **m** us sport. And they called
17: 3 for my son, to **m** a graven image and H6213
20:38 that they should **m** a great flame with
Ru 3: 3 to the floor: *but* **m** not thyself known
4:11 The LORD **m** the woman that is come H5414
1Sa 1: 6 her sore, for to **m** her fret, because the
2: 8 princes, and to **m** them inherit the
24 ye **m** the LORD'S people to transgress.
29 sons above me, to **m** yourselves fat with
3:12 when I begin, I will also **m** an end.
6: 5 Wherefore ye shall **m** images of your H6213
7 Now therefore **m** a new cart, and take H6213
8: 5 in thy ways: now **m** us a king to judge H7760
12 harvest, and to **m** his instruments of H6213
22 their voice, and **m** them a king. And H4427
9:12 *he is* before you: **m** haste now, for he
11: 1 unto Nahash, **M** a covenant with us, H3772
2 *condition* will I **m** *a covenant* with you, H3772
12:22 pleased the LORD to **m** you his people. H6213
13:19 the Hebrews **m** *them* swords or spears: H6213
17:25 and **m** his father's house free in Israel. H6213
18:25 Saul thought to **m** David fall by the hand
20:38 And Jonathan cried after the lad, **M**
22: 7 vineyards, *and* **m** you all captains of H7760
25:28 will certainly **m** my lord a sure house; H6213
28: 2 I **m** thee keeper of mine head for ever. H7760
15 for the Philistines **m** war against me,
15 **m** known unto me what I shall do.
29: 4 said unto him, **M** this fellow return, H7725
2Sa 3:12 land? saying *also*, **M** thy league with H3772
13 And he said, Well; I will **m** a league H3772
21 that they may **m** a league with thee, H3772
7:11 telleth thee that he will **m** thee an house.
21 things, to **m** thy servant know *them*.
23 to himself, and to **m** him a name, and H7760
11:25 as well as another: **m** thy battle more
13: 5 on thy bed, and **m** thyself sick: and when
6 my sister come, and **m** me a couple of H3823
15:14 from Absalom: **m** speed to depart, lest
20 should I this day **m** thee go up and down
17: 2 handed, and will **m** him afraid: and all
21: 3 wherewith shall I **m** the atonement, that
23: 5 *my* desire, although he **m** *it* not to grow.
1Ki 1:37 Solomon, and **m** his throne greater H1431
47 saying, God **m** the name of Solomon
47 thy name, and **m** his throne greater H1431
2:42 him, Did I not **m** thee to swear by the
8:29 thy servant shall **m** toward this place. H6419
33 **m** supplication unto thee in this house:
47 and repent, and **m** supplication unto
9:22 did Solomon **m** no bondmen: but they H5414
11:34 his hand: but I will **m** him prince all the H7896
12: 1 were come to Shechem to **m** him king.
4 now therefore **m** thou the grievous
9 to me, saying, **M** the yoke which thy H7043
10 yoke heavy, but **m** thou *it* lighter unto
16: 3 his house; and will **m** thy house like the H5414
19 his sin which he did, to **m** Israel to sin.
21 to **m** him king; and half followed Omri.
17:13 hast said: but **m** me thereof a little cake H6213
13 and after **m** for thee and for thy son. H6213
19: 2 more also, if I **m** not thy life as the life H7760
20:34 and thou shalt **m** streets for thee in H7760
21:22 And will **m** thine house like the house H5414
2Ki 3:16 And he said, Thus saith the LORD, **M** H6213
4:10 Let us **m** a little chamber, I pray thee, H6213
5: 7 God, to kill and to **m** alive, that this man
6: 2 a beam, and let us **m** us a place there, H6213
7: 2 *if* the LORD would **m** windows in H6213
19 *if* the LORD should **m** windows in H6213
9: 2 and go in, and **m** him arise up from
9 And I will **m** the house of Ahab like the H5414
21 And Joram said, **M** ready. And his
10: 5 bid us; we will not **m** any king: do thou
18:30 Neither let Hezekiah **m** you trust in the
31 king of Assyria, **M** *an agreement* with H6213
21: 8 Neither will I **m** the feet of Israel move
23:10 that no man might **m** his son or his
1Ch 6:49 most holy, and to **m** an atonement for
11:10 with all Israel, to **m** him king, according
12:31 by name, to come and **m** David king.
38 to Hebron, to **m** David king over all

1Ch 12:38 Israel *were* of one heart to **m** David king.
16: 8 **m** known his deeds among the people.
42 those that should **m** a sound, and with
17:21 *be* his own people, to **m** thee a name of H7760
22 For thy people Israel didst thou **m** H5414
21: 3 And Joab answered, The LORD **m** his
22: 5 I will *therefore* now **m** preparation for it.
28: 4 he liked me to **m** *me* king over all Israel:
29:12 to **m** great, and to give strength unto all.
2Ch 4:11 that he was to **m** for king Solomon for H6213
16 Huram his father **m** to king Solomon H6213
5:13 *were* as one, to **m** one sound to be heard
6:21 which they shall **m** toward this place: H6419
22 laid upon him to **m** him swear, and the
24 **m** supplication before thee in this house;
7:11 heart to **m** in the house of the H6213
20 my sight, and will **m** it *to be* a proverb H5414
8: 8 Solomon **m** to pay tribute until this day.
9 did Solomon **m** no servants for his H5414
10: 1 were all Israel come to **m** him king.
10 our yoke heavy, but **m** thou *it* somewhat
11:22 brethren: for *he thought* to **m** him king.
14: 7 these cities, and **m** about *them* walls,
20:36 And he joined himself with him to **m** H6213
25: 8 battle: God shall **m** thee fall before the
29:10 Now *it is* in mine heart to **m** a covenant H3772
24 upon the altar, to **m** an atonement for
30: 5 So they established a decree to **m**
35:21 commanded me to **m** haste: forbear thee
Ezr 5: 3 build this house, and to **m** up this wall?
4 names of the men that **m** this building? H1124
9 this house, and to **m** up these walls?
6: 8 Moreover I **m** a decree what ye shall do H7761
7:13 I **m** a decree, that all they of the people H7761
21 And I, *even* I Artaxerxes the king, do **m** H7761
10: 3 Now therefore let us **m** a covenant with H3772
11 Now therefore **m** confession unto the H5414
Neh 2: 4 what dost thou **m** request? So I prayed
8 give me timber to **m** beams for the gates
4: 2 sacrifice? will they **m** an end in a day?
8:12 send portions, and to **m** great mirth, H6213
15 thick trees, to **m** booths, as *it is* written. H6213
9:38 And because of all this we **m** a sure H3772
10:33 the sin offerings to **m** an atonement for
Est 1:20 which he shall **m** shall be published H6213
4: 8 in unto the king, to **m** supplication unto
8 to **m** request before him for her people.
5: 5 Then the king said, Cause Haman to **m**
6:10 Then the king said to Haman, **M** haste,
7: 7 stood up to **m** request for his life to
9:22 day: that they should **m** them days of H6213
Job 5:18 he woundeth, and his hands **m** whole.
8: 5 and **m** thy supplication to the Almighty;
6 for thee, and **m** the habitation of thy
9:15 *but* I would **m** supplication to my judge.
30 If I wash myself with snow water, and **m**
11: 3 Should thy lies **m** men hold their H2790
3 mockest, shall no man **m** thee ashamed?
19 and none shall **m** *thee* afraid; yea, many
19 afraid; yea, many shall **m** suit unto thee.
13:11 Shall not his excellency **m** you afraid?
21 me: and let not thy dread **m** me afraid.
23 iniquities and sins? **m** me to know my
15:24 Trouble and anguish shall **m** him afraid;
18: 2 How long *will it be ere* ye **m** an end of H7760
11 Terrors shall **m** him afraid on every side,
19: 3 *that* ye **m** yourselves strange to me.
20: 2 me to answer, and for *this* I **m** haste.
22:27 Thou shalt **m** thy prayer unto him, and
24:11 *Which* **m** oil within their walls, *and*
25 And if *it be* not *so* now, who will **m** me a
25 liar, and **m** my speech nothing worth? H7760
28:25 To **m** the weight for the winds; and he H6213
31:15 me in the womb **m** him? and did not H6213
33: 7 Behold, my terror shall not **m** thee
34:29 who then can **m** trouble? and when he
35: 9 oppressions they **m** *the oppressed* to cry:
39:20 Canst thou **m** him afraid as a
27 thy command, and **m** her nest on high? H7311
40:19 can **m** his sword to approach *unto him*. H5066
41: 3 Will he **m** many supplications unto thee?
4 Will he **m** a covenant with thee? wilt H3772
6 Shall the companions **m** a banquet of
28 The arrow cannot **m** him flee:
Ps 5: 8 **m** thy way straight before my face.
6: 6 all the night **m** I my bed to swim; I
11: 2 *their* bow, they **m** ready their arrow
21: 9 Thou shalt **m** them as a fiery oven in H7896
12 Therefore shalt thou **m** them turn their H7896

Ps 21:12 *when* thou shalt **m** ready *thine arrows*
22: 9 the womb: thou didst **m** me hope *when I*
31:16 **M** thy face to shine upon thy servant:
34: 2 My soul shall **m** her boast in the LORD:
36: 8 and thou shalt **m** them drink of the river
38:22 **M** haste to help me, O Lord my
39: 4 LORD, **m** me to know mine end, and the
8 **m** me not the reproach of the foolish. H7760
40:13 deliver me: O LORD, **m** haste to help me.
17 my deliverer; **m** no tarrying, O my God.
41: 3 thou wilt **m** all his bed in his sickness. H2015
45:16 thou mayest **m** princes in all the earth. H7896
17 I will **m** thy name to be remembered in
46: 4 whereof shall **m** glad the city of God,
51: 6 *part* thou shalt **m** me to know wisdom.
8 **M** me to hear joy and gladness; *that* the
55: 2 mourn in my complaint, and **m** a noise;
57: 1 of thy wings will I **m** my refuge, until
59: 6 They return at evening: they **m** a noise
14 *and* let them **m** a noise like a dog, and
64: 8 So they shall **m** their own tongue to fall
66: 1 **M** a joyful noise unto God, all ye lands:
2 Sing forth the honour of his name: **m** H7760
8 O bless our God, ye people, and **m** the
69:23 and **m** their loins continually to shake.
70: 1 *M haste*, O God, to deliver me; make
1 *Make haste*, O God, to deliver me; **m**
5 But I *am* poor and needy: **m** haste unto
5 my deliverer; O LORD, **m** no tarrying.
71:12 O God, be not far from me: O my God, **m**
16 the Lord GOD: I will **m** mention of thy
78: 5 should **m** them known to their children:
81: 1 Sing aloud unto God our strength: **m** a
83: 2 For, lo, thine enemies **m** a tumult: and
11 **M** their nobles like Oreb, and like Zeeb: H7896
13 O my God, **m** them like a wheel; as the H7896
15 and **m** them afraid with thy storm.
84: 6 the valley of Baca **m** it a well; the rain H7896
87: 4 I will **m** mention of Rahab and Babylon
89: 1 with my mouth will I **m** known thy
27 Also I will **m** him *my* firstborn, higher H5414
29 His seed also will I **m** *to endure* for H7760
90:15 **M** us glad according to the days *wherein*
95: 1 the LORD: let us **m** a joyful noise to the
2 **m** a joyful noise unto him with psalms.
98: 4 **M** a joyful noise unto the LORD, all the
4 all the earth: **m** a loud noise, and rejoice,
6 With trumpets and sound of cornet **m** a
100: 1 **M** a joyful noise unto the LORD, all ye
104:15 of man, *and* oil to **m** *his* face to shine,
17 Where the birds **m** their nests: *as for* the
105: 1 **m** known his deeds among the people.
106: 8 might **m** his mighty power to be known.
110: 1 until I **m** thine enemies thy footstool. H7896
115: 8 They that **m** them are like unto them; H6213
119:27 **M** me to understand the way of thy
35 **M** me to go in the path of thy
135 **M** thy face to shine upon thy servant;
132:17 There will I **m** the horn of David to H6779
135:18 They that **m** them are like unto them: H6213
139: 8 **m** my bed in hell, behold, thou *art there*.
141: 1 LORD, I cry unto thee: **m** haste unto me;
142: 1 unto the LORD did I **m** my supplication.
145:12 To **m** known to the sons of men his
Prv 1:16 For their feet run to evil, and **m** haste to
23 you, I will **m** known my words unto you.
6: 3 humble thyself, and **m** sure thy friend.
14: 9 Fools **m** a mock at sin: but among the
20:18 counsel: and with good advice **m** war. H6213
25 *is* holy, and after vows to **m** inquiry.
22:21 That I might **m** thee know the certainty
24 **M** no friendship with an angry man; and
23: 5 *riches* certainly **m** themselves wings; H6213
24: 6 For by wise counsel thou shalt **m** thy H6213
27 Prepare thy work without, and **m** it fit
27:11 My son, be wise, and **m** my heart glad,
30:26 The conies *are but* a feeble folk, yet **m** H7760
Ecc 2:24 and *that* he should **m** his soul enjoy
7:13 God: for who can **m** *that* straight, which
16 Be not righteous over much; neither **m**
Song 1:11 We will **m** thee borders of gold with H6213
8:14 **M** haste, my beloved, and be thou like to
Isa 1:15 you: yea, when ye **m** many prayers, I will
16 Wash you, **m** you clean; put away the
3: 7 **m** me not a ruler of the people. H7760
5:19 That say, Let him **m** speed, *and* hasten
6:10 **M** the heart of this people fat, and make
10 Make the heart of this people fat, and **m**
7: 6 vex it, and let us **m** a breach therein for

Isa 10:23 For the Lord GOD of hosts shall **m** a H6213
11: 3 And shall **m** him of quick understanding
15 streams, and **m** *men* go over dryshod.
12: 4 **m** mention that his name is exalted.
13:12 I will **m** a man more precious than fine
20 shall the shepherds **m** their fold there.
14:23 I will also **m** it a possession for the H7760
16: 3 Take counsel, execute judgment; **m** thy H7896
17: 2 lie down, and none shall **m** *them* afraid.
11 In the day shalt thou **m** thy plant to
11 shalt thou **m** thy seed to flourish:
12 people, *which* **m** a noise like the noise
12 of nations, *that* **m** a rushing like the
19:10 all that **m** sluices *and* ponds for fish. H6213
23:16 been forgotten; **m** sweet melody, sing
25: 6 the LORD of hosts **m** unto all people a H6213
26:13 only will we **m** mention of thy name.
27: 5 *that* he may **m** peace with me; *and* H6213
5 with me; *and* he shall **m** peace with me. H6213
28: 9 and whom shall he **m** to understand
16 he that believeth shall not **m** haste.
29:21 That **m** a man an offender for a word,
32: 6 the LORD, to **m** empty the soul of the
11 strip you, and **m** you bare, and gird
33: 1 *and* when thou shalt **m** an end to deal
34:15 There shall the great owl **m** her nest, and
36:15 Neither let Hezekiah **m** you trust in the
16 king of Assyria, **M** *an agreement* with H6213
37: 9 is come forth to **m** war with thee. And
38:12 *even* to night wilt thou **m** an end of me.
13 *even* to night wilt thou **m** an end of me.
16 wilt thou recover me, and **m** me to live.
19 to the children shall **m** known thy truth.
40: 3 the way of the LORD, **m** straight in the
41:15 Behold, I will **m** thee a new sharp H7760
15 small, and shalt **m** the hills as chaff. H7760
18 of the valleys: I will **m** the wilderness a H7760
42:15 I will **m** waste mountains and hills, and
15 herbs; and I will **m** the rivers islands, H7760
16 have not known: I will **m** darkness light H7760
21 magnify the law, and **m** *it* honourable.
43:19 know it? I will even **m** a way in the H7760
44: 9 They that **m** a graven image *are* all of H3335
19 *it*: and shall I **m** the residue thereof H6213
45: 2 I will go before thee, and **m** the crooked
7 create darkness: I **m** peace, and create H6213
14 thee, they shall **m** supplication unto
46: 5 To whom will ye liken me, and **m** *me*
47: 2 meal: uncover thy locks, **m** bare the leg,
48: 1 of the LORD, and **m** mention of the God
15 him, and he shall **m** his way prosperous.
49:11 And I will **m** all my mountains a way, H7760
17 Thy children shall **m** haste; thy
50: 2 rebuke I dry up the sea, I **m** the rivers a H7760
3 and I **m** sackcloth their covering. H7760
51: 3 and he will **m** her wilderness like H7760
4 me, and I will **m** my judgment to rest
52: 5 rule over them **m** them to howl, saith
53:10 when thou shalt **m** his soul an offering H7760
54: 3 **m** the desolate cities to be inhabited.
12 And I will **m** thy windows of agates, H7760
55: 3 shall live; and I will **m** an everlasting H3772
56: 7 holy mountain, and **m** them joyful in my
57: 4 against whom **m** ye a wide mouth, *and*
58: 4 day, to **m** your voice to be heard on high.
11 in drought, and **m** fat thy bones: and
59: 7 Their feet run to evil, and they **m** haste
60:13 I will **m** the place of my feet glorious.
15 through *thee*, I will **m** thee an eternal H7760
17 iron: I will also **m** thy officers peace, H7760
61: 8 **m** an everlasting covenant with them. H3772
62: 6 day nor night: ye that **m** mention of the
7 he **m** Jerusalem a praise in the earth. H7760
63: 6 in mine anger, and **m** them drunk in my
12 to **m** himself an everlasting name? H6213
14 people, to **m** thyself a glorious name. H6213
64: 2 waters to boil, to **m** thy name known to
66:22 new earth, which I will **m**, shall remain H6213
Jer 4: 7 from his place to **m** thy land desolate; H7760
16 **M** ye mention to the nations; behold,
27 be desolate; yet will I not **m** a full end. H6213
30 in vain shalt thou **m** thyself fair; *thy*
5:10 and destroy; but **m** not a full end: take H6213
14 behold, I will **m** my words in thy mouth H5414
18 LORD, I will not **m** a full end with you. H6213
6: 8 I **m** thee desolate, a land not inhabited. H7760
26 thyself in ashes: **m** thee mourning, *as* H6213
7:16 for them, neither **m** intercession to me:
18 *their* dough, to **m** cakes to the queen H6213

Jer 9:11 And I will **m** Jerusalem heaps, *and* a H5414
11 and I will **m** the cities of Judah H5414
18 And let them **m** haste, and take up a
10:22 north country, to **m** the cities of Judah H7760
13:16 of death, *and* **m** *it* gross darkness. H7896
15:14 And I will **m** *thee* to pass with thine
20 And I will **m** thee unto this people a H5414
16: 6 nor **m** themselves bald for them:
20 Shall a man **m** gods unto himself, and H6213
18: 4 as seemed good to the potter to **m** *it*. H6213
11 and **m** your ways and your doings good.
16 To **m** their land desolate, *and* a H7760
19: 7 And I will **m** void the counsel of Judah
8 And I will **m** this city desolate, and an H7760
12 thereof, and *even* **m** this city as Tophet: H5414
20: 4 Behold, I will **m** thee a terror to thyself, H5414
9 Then I said, I will not **m** mention of him,
22: 6 *yet* surely I will **m** thee a wilderness, H7896
23:15 wormwood, and **m** them drink the water
16 unto you: they **m** you vain: they speak
25: 9 them, and **m** them an astonishment, H7760
12 and will **m** it perpetual desolations. H7760
18 the princes thereof, to **m** them a H5414
26: 6 Then will I **m** this house like Shiloh, H5414
6 Shiloh, and will **m** this city a curse to H5414
27: 2 Thus saith the LORD to me; **M** thee H6213
18 them, let them now **m** intercession to the
28:13 thou shalt **m** for them yokes of iron. H6213
29:17 and will **m** them like vile figs, that H5414
22 The LORD **m** thee like Zedekiah H7760
30:10 be quiet, and none shall **m** *him* afraid.
11 save thee: though I **m** a full end of all H6213
11 thee, yet will I not **m** a full end of thee: H6213
19 voice of them that **m** merry: and I will
31: 4 in the dances of them that **m** merry.
13 and **m** them rejoice from their sorrow.
21 Set thee up waymarks, **m** thee high H7760
31 the LORD, that I will **m** a new covenant H3772
33 that I will **m** with the house of Israel; H3772
32:40 And I will **m** an everlasting covenant H3772
34:17 famine; and I will **m** you to be removed H5414
22 fire: and I will **m** the cities of Judah a H5414
44:19 unto her, did we **m** her cakes to H6213
46:27 at ease, and none shall **m** *him* afraid.
28 thee; for I will **m** a full end of all the H6213
28 thee: but I will not **m** a full end of thee, H6213
48:26 **M** ye him drunken: for he magnified
49:15 For, lo, I will **m** thee small among the H5414
16 thou shouldest **m** thy nest as high as the
19 but I will suddenly **m** him run away
20 **m** their habitations desolate with them.
50: 3 her, which shall **m** her land desolate, H7896
44 strong: but I will **m** them suddenly run H7323
45 **m** *their* habitation desolate with them.
51:11 **M** bright the arrows; gather the shields:
12 walls of Babylon, **m** the watch strong,
25 and will **m** thee a burnt mountain. H5414
29 Babylon, to **m** the land of Babylon H7760
36 dry up her sea, and **m** her springs dry.
39 In their heat I will **m** their feasts, and I H7896
39 feasts, and I will **m** them drunken, that
57 And I will **m** drunk her princes, and her
Lam 4:21 be drunken, and shalt **m** thyself naked.
Ezk 3:26 And I will **m** thy tongue cleave to the
4: 9 them in one vessel, and **m** thee bread H6213
5:14 Moreover I will **m** thee waste, and a H5414
6:14 upon them, and **m** the land desolate, H5414
7:14 They have blown the trumpet, even to **m**
23 **M** a chain: for the land is full of bloody H6213
24 houses: I will also **m** the pomp of the
11:13 **m** a full end of the remnant of Israel? H6213
12:23 Lord GOD; I will **m** this proverb to cease,
13:18 all armholes, and **m** kerchiefs upon the H6213
20 hunt the souls to **m** *them* fly, and I will
20 the souls that ye hunt to **m** *them* fly.
14: 8 that man, and will **m** him a sign and a H8074
15: 8 And I will **m** the land desolate, because H5414
16:42 So will I **m** my fury toward thee to rest,
17:17 great company **m** for him in the war, H6213
18:31 transgressed; and **m** you a new heart H6213
20:17 I **m** an end of them in the wilderness. H6213
26 that I might **m** them desolate, to the
31 For when ye offer your gifts, when ye **m**
21:10 It is sharpened to **m** a sore slaughter; it
10 should we then **m** mirth? it contemneth
22:30 them, that should **m** up the hedge, and
23:27 Thus will I **m** thy lewdness to cease from
24: 5 under it, *and* **m** it boil well, and let them
9 city! I will even **m** the pile for fire great.
Ezk 24:17 Forbear to cry, **m** no mourning for the H6213
25: 4 in thee, and **m** their dwellings in thee: H5414
5 And I will **m** Rabbah a stable for H5414
13 from it; and I will **m** it desolate from H5414
26: 4 her, and **m** her like the top of a rock. H5414
8 the field: and he shall **m** a fort against H5414
12 And they shall **m** a spoil of thy riches,
12 spoil of thy riches, and **m** a prey of thy
14 And I will **m** thee like the top of a rock: H5414
19 When I shall **m** thee a desolate city, H5414
21 I will **m** thee a terror, and thou *shalt be* H5414
27: 5 from Lebanon to **m** masts for thee. H6213
31 And they shall **m** themselves utterly bald
29:10 rivers, and I will **m** the land of Egypt H5414
12 And I will **m** the land of Egypt desolate H5414
30: 9 me in ships to **m** the careless Ethiopians
10 Thus saith the Lord GOD; I will also **m**
12 And I will **m** the rivers dry, and sell the H5414
12 wicked: and I will **m** the land waste, and
14 And I will **m** Pathros desolate, and will
21 bind it, to **m** it strong to hold the sword.
32: 7 the heaven, and **m** the stars thereof H6937
8 All the bright lights of heaven will I **m**
10 Yea, I will **m** many people amazed at
14 Then will I **m** their waters deep, and
15 When I shall **m** the land of Egypt H5414
34:25 And I will **m** with them a covenant of H3772
26 And I will **m** them and the places H5414
28 safely, and none shall **m** *them* afraid.
35: 3 thee, and I will **m** thee most desolate. H5414
7 Thus will I **m** mount Seir most H5414
9 I will **m** thee perpetual desolations, H5414
11 them; and I will **m** myself known among
14 earth rejoiceth, I will **m** thee desolate. H6213
37:19 of Judah, and **m** them one stick, and H6213
22 And I will **m** them one nation in the H6213
26 Moreover I will **m** a covenant of peace H3772
39: 7 So will I **m** my holy name known in the
42:20 five hundred broad, to **m** a separation
43:18 day when they shall **m** it, to offer burnt H6213
27 the priests shall **m** your burnt offerings H6213
44:14 But I will **m** them keepers of the charge H5414
45:15 peace offerings, to **m** reconciliation for
17 **m** reconciliation for the house of Israel.
Dan 1:10 ye **m** *me* endanger my head to the king.
2: 5 me: if ye will not **m** known unto me the
9 But if ye will not **m** known unto me the
25 of Judah, that will **m** known unto the
26 Art thou able to **m** known unto me the
30 *their* sakes that shall **m** known the
3:29 Therefore I **m** a decree, That every H7761
4: 6 that they might **m** known unto me the
7 but they did not **m** known unto me the
18 are not able to **m** known unto me the
25 and they shall **m** thee to eat grass as
32 the field: they shall **m** thee to eat grass as
5: 8 the writing, nor **m** known to the king the
15 this writing, and **m** known unto me the
16 that thou canst **m** interpretations, and H6590
16 the writing, and **m** known to me the
17 and **m** known to him the interpretation.
6: 7 statute, and to **m** a firm decree, that
26 I **m** a decree, That in every dominion H7761
8:16 **m** this *man* to understand the vision.
19 And he said, Behold, I will **m** thee know
9:24 and to **m** an end of sins, and
24 end of sins, and to **m** reconciliation for
27 he shall **m** *it* desolate, even until
10:14 Now I am come to **m** thee understand
11: 6 of the north to **m** an agreement: but H6213
35 to purge, and to **m** *them* white, *even* to
44 to destroy, and utterly to **m** away many.
Hos 2: 3 that she was born, and **m** her as a H7760
6 way with thorns, and **m** a wall, that she H1443
12 me: and I will **m** them a forest, and H7760
18 And in that day will I **m** a covenant for H3772
18 and will **m** them to lie down safely.
5: 2 And the revolters are profound to **m**
7: 3 They **m** the king glad with their
10:11 her fair neck: I will **m** Ephraim to ride;
11: 8 Israel? how shall I **m** thee as Admah? H5414
12: 1 and they do **m** a covenant with the H3772
9 land of Egypt will yet **m** thee to dwell in
Joel 2:19 **m** you a reproach among the heathen: H5414
Am 6:10 not **m** mention of the name of the LORD.
8: 4 even to **m** the poor of the land to fail, H7673
10 head; and I will **m** it as the mourning H7760
9:14 **m** gardens, and eat the fruit of them. H6213
Mic 1: 6 Therefore I will **m** Samaria as an heap H7760
Mic 1: 8 and naked: I will **m** a wailing like the H6213
16 **M** thee bald, and poll thee for thy
2:12 fold: they shall **m** great noise by reason
3: 5 the prophets that **m** my people err, that
4: 4 and none shall **m** *them* afraid: for the
7 And I will **m** her that halted a remnant, H7760
13 of Zion: for I will **m** thine horn iron, H7760
13 iron, and I will **m** thy hoofs brass: and H7760
6:13 Therefore also will I **m** *thee* sick in
16 that I should **m** thee a desolation, and H5414
Nah 1: 8 flood he will **m** an utter end of the H6213
9 the LORD? he will **m** an utter end: H6213
14 I will **m** thy grave; for thou art vile. H7760
2: 1 watch the way, **m** *thy* loins strong,
5 their walk; they shall **m** haste to the wall
3: 6 upon thee, and **m** thee vile, and will set
14 tread the morter, **m** strong the brickkiln.
15 the cankerworm: **m** thyself many as the
15 **m** thyself many as the locusts.
Hab 2: 2 the vision, and **m** *it* plain upon tables,
18 trusteth therein, to **m** dumb idols? H6213
3: 2 **m** known; in wrath remember mercy.
19 and he will **m** my feet like hinds' *feet*, H7760
19 *feet*, and he will **m** me to walk upon
Zep 1:18 for he shall **m** even a speedy riddance H6213
2:13 destroy Assyria; and will **m** Nineveh a H7760
3:13 lie down, and none shall **m** *them* afraid.
20 you: for I will **m** you a name and a H5414
Hag 2:23 LORD, and will **m** thee as a signet: for H7760
Zec 6:11 Then take silver and gold, and **m** H6213
9:15 shall drink, *and* **m** a noise as through
17 his beauty! corn shall **m** the young men
10: 1 *so* the LORD shall **m** bright clouds, and H6213
12: 2 Behold, I will **m** Jerusalem a cup of H7760
3 And in that day will I **m** Jerusalem a H7760
6 In that day will I **m** the governors of H7760
Mal 2:15 And did not he **m** one? Yet had he the H6213
3:17 in that day when I **m** up my jewels; and I
Mt 1:19 and not willing to **m** her a publick *G3856*
3: 3 way of the Lord, **m** his paths straight. *G4160*
4:19 me, and I will **m** you fishers of men. *G4160*
5:36 canst not **m** one hair white or black. *G4160*
8: 2 if thou wilt, thou canst **m** me clean. *G2511*
12:16 that they should not **m** him known: *G4160*
33 Either **m** the tree good, and his fruit *G4160*
33 fruit good; or else **m** the tree corrupt, *G4160*
17: 4 here: if thou wilt, let us **m** here three *G4160*
22:44 till I **m** thine enemies thy footstool? *G5087*
23: 5 be seen of men: they **m** broad their *G4115*
14 for a pretence **m** long prayer: therefore *G4336*
15 sea and land to **m** one proselyte, and *G4160*
15 he is made, ye **m** him twofold more the *G4160*
25 hypocrites! for ye **m** clean the outside *G2511*
24:47 Verily I say unto you, That he shall **m** *G2525*
25:21 a few things, I will **m** thee ruler over *G2525*
23 a few things, I will **m** thee ruler over *G2525*
27:65 go your way, **m** *it* as sure as ye can. *G805*
Mk 1: 3 way of the Lord, **m** his paths straight. *G4160*
17 I will **m** you to become fishers of men. *G4160*
40 If thou wilt, thou canst **m** me clean. *G2511*
3:12 that they should not **m** him known. *G4160*
5:39 unto them, Why **m** ye this ado, and *G2350*
6:39 And he commanded them to **m** all sit *G347*
9: 5 be here: and let us **m** three tabernacles; *G4160*
12:36 till I **m** thine enemies thy footstool. *G5087*
40 for a pretence **m** long prayers: these *G4336*
42 threw in two mites, which **m** a farthing. *G2076*
14:15 *and* prepared: there **m** ready for us. *G2090*
Lk 1:17 wisdom of the just; to **m** ready a people *G2090*
3: 4 way of the Lord, **m** his paths straight. *G4160*
5:12 if thou wilt, thou canst **m** me clean. *G2511*
33 fast often, and **m** prayers, and likewise *G4160*
34 And he said unto them, Can ye **m** the *G4160*
9:14 to his disciples, **M** them sit down by *G2625*
33 be here: and let us **m** three tabernacles; *G4160*
52 of the Samaritans, to **m** ready for him. *G2090*
11:39 do ye Pharisees **m** clean the outside of *G2511*
40 is without **m** that which is within also? *G4160*
12:37 gird himself, and **m** them to sit down to *G347*
42 whom *his* lord shall **m** ruler over his *G2525*
44 Of a truth I say unto you, that he will **m** *G2525*
14:18 *consent* began to **m** excuse. The first *G3868*
31 Or what king, going to **m** war against *G4820*
15:19 son: **m** me as one of thy hired servants. *G4160*
29 that I might **m** merry with my friends: *G2165*
32 It was meet that we should **m** merry, *G2165*
16: 9 And I say unto you, **M** to yourselves *G4160*
17: 8 And will not rather say unto him, **M** *G2090*
19: 5 him, Zacchaeus, **m** haste, and come *G4692*

Lk 20:43 Till I **m** thine enemies thy footstool. G5087
47 and for a shew **m** long prayers: the G4336
22:12 upper room furnished: there **m** ready. G2090
Jn 1:23 in the wilderness, **M** straight the way of G2116
2:16 things hence; **m** not my Father's house G4160
6:10 And Jesus said, **M** the men sit down. G4160
15 take him by force, to **m** him a king, he G4160
8:32 truth, and the truth shall **m** you free. G1659
36 If the Son therefore shall **m** you free, ye G1659
10:24 long dost thou **m** us to doubt? If thou G142
14:23 unto him, and **m** our abode with him. G4160
Act 2:28 **m** me full of joy with thy countenance. G4137
35 Until I **m** thy foes thy footstool. G5087
7:40 Saying unto Aaron, **M** us gods to go G4160
44 that he should **m** it according to the G4160
9:34 **m** thy bed. And he arose immediately. G4766
22: 1 ye my defence *which I* **m** now unto you.
18 And saw him saying unto me, **M** haste, G4692
23:23 saying, **M** ready two hundred G2090
26:16 this purpose, to **m** thee a minister and G4400
24 much learning doth **m** thee mad. G4062
Ro 1: 9 without ceasing I **m** mention of you G4160
3: 3 **m** the faith of God without effect? G2673
31 Do we then **m** void the law through G2673
9:21 of the same lump to **m** one vessel unto G4160
22 *his* wrath, and to **m** his power known, G1107
23 And that he might **m** known the riches G1107
28 work will the Lord **m** upon the earth. G4160
13:14 Jesus Christ, and **m** not provision for G4160
14: 4 up: for God is able to **m** him stand. G2476
19 after the things which **m** for peace, and G3753
15:18 not wrought by me, to **m** the Gentiles G1519
26 and Achaia to **m** a certain contribution G4160
1Co 4: 5 and will **m** manifest the counsels G5319
6:15 of Christ, and **m** *them* the members G4160
8:13 Wherefore, if meat **m** my brother to G4624
13 standeth, lest I **m** my brother to offend. G4624
9:15 any man should **m** my glorying void. G2758
18 the gospel, I may **m** the gospel of Christ G5087
10:13 the temptation also **m** a way to escape, G4160
2Co 2: 2 For if I **m** you sorry, who is he then that G3076
9: 5 unto you, and **m** up beforehand your G4294
8 And God *is* able to **m** all grace abound G4052
10:12 For we dare not **m** ourselves of the G1469
12:17 Did I **m** a gain of you by any of them G4122
18 a brother. Did Titus **m** a gain of you? G4122
Gal 2:18 I destroyed, I **m** myself a transgressor. G4921
3:17 it should **m** the promise of none effect. G2673
6:12 As many as desire to **m** a fair shew in G2146
Eph 2:15 in ordinances; for to **m** in himself of G2936
3: 9 And to **m** all *men* see what *is* the G5461
5:13 for whatsoever doth **m** manifest is light.
6:19 to **m** known the mystery of the gospel, G1107
21 Lord, shall **m** known to you all things: G1107
Col 1:27 To whom God would **m** known what *is* G1107
4: 4 That I may **m** it manifest, as I ought to G5319
9 of you. They shall **m** known unto you G1107
1Th 3:12 And the Lord **m** you to increase and G4121
2Th 3: 9 have not power, but to **m** ourselves an G1325
2Ti 3:15 which are able to **m** thee wise unto G4679
4: 5 evangelist, **m** full proof of thy ministry. G4135
Heb 1:13 until I **m** thine enemies thy footstool? G5087
2:10 unto glory, to **m** the captain of their G5048
17 to God, to **m** reconciliation for the G2433
7:25 ever liveth to **m** intercession for them. G1793
8: 5 he was about to **m** the tabernacle: for, G2005
5 he, *that* thou **m** all things according G4160
8 the Lord, when I will **m** a new covenant G4931
10 For this *is* the covenant that I will **m** G1303
9: 9 that could not **m** him that did the G5048
10: 1 **m** the comers thereunto perfect. G5048
16 This *is* the covenant that I will **m** with G1303
12:13 And **m** straight paths for your feet, lest G4160
13:21 **M** you perfect in every good work to do G2675
Jas 3:18 is sown in peace of them that **m** peace. G4160
1Pt 5:10 have suffered a while, **m** you perfect, G2675
2Pt 1: 8 and abound, they **m** *you that ye shall* G2525
10 give diligence to **m** your calling and G4160
2: 3 feigned words **m** merchandise of you: G1710
1Jn 1:10 **m** him a liar, and his word is not in us. G4160
Rev 3: 9 Behold, I will **m** them of the synagogue G1325
9 lie; behold, I will **m** them to come and G4160
12 Him that overcometh will I **m** a pillar G4160
10: 9 it up; and it shall **m** thy belly bitter, but G4087
11: 7 pit shall **m** war against them, and G4160
10 over them, and **m** merry, and shall G2165
12:17 and went to **m** war with the remnant G4160
13: 4 beast? who is able to **m** war with him? G4170
7 And it was given unto him to **m** war G4160
Rev 13:14 that they should **m** an image to the G4160
17:14 These shall **m** war with the Lamb, and G4170
16 whore, and shall **m** her desolate and G4160
19:11 he doth judge and **m** war. G4170
19 together to **m** war against him that G4160
21: 5 said, Behold, I **m** all things new. And G4160

MAKER

Job 4:17 shall a man be more pure than his **m**? H6213
32:22 *doing* my **m** would soon take me away. H6213
35:10 But none saith, Where *is* God my **m**, H6213
36: 3 and will ascribe righteousness to my **M**. H6466
Ps 95: 6 let us kneel before the LORD our **m**. H6213
Prv 14:31 poor reproacheth his **M**: but he that H6213
17: 5 reproacheth his **M**: *and* he that is glad H6213
22: 2 the LORD *is* the **m** of them all. H6213
Isa 1:31 be as tow, and the **m** of it as a spark, H6467
17: 7 At that day shall a man look to his **M**, H6213
22:11 looked unto the **m** thereof, neither had H6213
45: 9 Woe unto him that striveth with his **M**! H3335
11 of Israel, and his **M**, Ask me of things to H3335
51:13 And forgettest the LORD thy **m**, that H6213
54: 5 For thy **M** *is* thine husband; the LORD H6213
Jer 33: 2 Thus saith the LORD the **m** thereof, the H6213
Hos 8:14 For Israel hath forgotten his **M**, and H6213
Hab 2:18 image that the **m** thereof hath graven H3335
18 of lies, that the **m** of his work trusteth H3335
Heb 11:10 whose builder and **m** *is* God. G1217

MAKERS

Isa 45:16 confusion together *that are* **m** of idols. H2796

MAKEST

Jdg 18: 3 hither? and what **m** thou in this *place*? H6213
Job 13:26 against me, and **m** me to possess the
22: 3 *to him*, that thou **m** thy ways perfect?
Ps 4: 8 thou, LORD, only **m** me dwell in safety.
39:11 man for iniquity, thou **m** his beauty to
44:10 Thou **m** us to turn back from the enemy:
13 Thou **m** us a reproach to our H7760
14 Thou **m** us a byword among the H7760
65: 8 at thy tokens: thou **m** the outgoings of
10 thereof: thou **m** it soft with showers:
80: 6 Thou **m** us a strife unto our H7760
104:20 Thou **m** darkness, and it is night: H7896
144: 3 son of man, that thou **m** account of him!
Song 1: 7 where thou **m** *thy flock* to rest at noon:
Isa 45: 9 it, What **m** thou? or thy work, He H6213
Jer 22:23 O inhabitant of Lebanon, that **m** thy
28:15 but thou **m** this people to trust in a lie.
Ezk 16:31 of every way, and **m** thine high place in H6213
Hab 1:14 And **m** men as the fishes of the sea, as H6213
2:15 bottle to *him*, and **m** *him* drunken also,
Lk 14:12 bade him, When thou **m** a dinner or a G4160
13 But when thou **m** a feast, call the poor, G4160
Jn 8:53 are dead: whom **m** thou thyself? G4160
10:33 that thou, being a man, **m** thyself God. G4160
Ro 2:17 in the law, and **m** thy boast of God, G2744
23 Thou that **m** thy boast of the law, G2744

MAKETH

Ex 4:11 mouth? or who **m** the dumb, or deaf, H7760
Lev 7: 7 **m** atonement therewith shall have *it*.
14:11 And the priest that **m** *him* clean shall
17:11 blood *that* **m** an atonement for the soul.
Dt 18:10 among you *any one* that **m** his son or his
20:20 **m** war with thee, until it be subdued. H6213
21:16 Then it shall be, when he **m** his sons to
24: 7 of Israel, and **m** merchandise of him,
27:15 Cursed *be* the man that **m** *any* graven H6213
18 Cursed *be* he that **m** the blind to wander
29:12 LORD thy God **m** with thee this day: H3772
1Sa 2: 6 The LORD killeth, and **m** alive: he
7 The LORD **m** poor, and maketh rich: he
7 The LORD maketh poor, and **m** rich: he
2Sa 22:33 *and* power: and he **m** my way perfect. H5425
34 He **m** my feet like hinds' *feet*: and H7737
Job 5:18 For he **m** sore, and bindeth up: he
9: 9 Which **m** Arcturus, Orion, and H6213
12:17 away spoiled, and **m** the judges fools.
25 **m** them to stagger like *a* drunken *man*.
15:27 and **m** collops of fat on *his* flanks. H6213
23:16 For God **m** my heart soft, and the
25: 2 Dominion and fear *are* with him, he **m** H6213
27:18 moth, and as a booth *that* the keeper **m**. H6213
35:11 **m** us wiser than the fowls of heaven?
36:27 For he **m** small the drops of water: they
41:31 He **m** the deep to boil like a pot: he
31 he **m** the sea like a pot of ointment. H7760
Job 41:32 He **m** a path to shine after him; *one*
Ps 9:12 When he **m** inquisition for blood, he
18:32 with strength, and **m** my way perfect. H5414
33 He **m** my feet like hinds' *feet*, and H7737
23: 2 He **m** me to lie down in green pastures:
29: 6 He **m** them also to skip like a calf;
9 The voice of the LORD **m** the hinds to
33:10 to nought: he **m** the devices of the H5106
40: 4 Blessed *is* that man that **m** the LORD H7760
46: 9 He **m** wars to cease unto the end of the
104: 3 in the waters: who **m** the clouds his H7760
4 Who **m** his angels spirits; his ministers H6213
15 And wine *that* **m** glad the heart of man,
107:29 He **m** the storm a calm, so that the H6965
36 And there he **m** the hungry to dwell, that
41 and **m** *him* families like a flock. H7760
113: 9 He **m** the barren woman to keep house,
135: 7 of the earth; he **m** lightnings for the H6213
147: 8 **m** grass to grow upon the mountains.
14 He **m** peace *in* thy borders, *and* filleth H7760
Prv 10: 1 The proverbs of Solomon. A wise son **m**
4 but the hand of the diligent **m** rich.
22 The blessing of the LORD, it **m** rich, and
12: 4 but she that **m** ashamed *is* as rottenness
25 Heaviness in the heart of man **m** it
25 it stoop: but a good word **m** it glad.
13: 7 There is that **m** himself rich, yet *hath*
7 **m** himself poor, yet *hath* great riches.
12 Hope deferred **m** the heart sick: but
15:13 A merry heart **m** a cheerful
20 A wise son **m** a glad father: but a foolish
30 *and* a good report **m** the bones fat. H1878
16: 7 the LORD, he **m** even his enemies to
18:16 A man's gift **m** room for him, and
19: 4 Wealth **m** many friends; but the poor is H3254
28:20 **m** haste to be rich shall not be innocent.
31:22 She **m** herself coverings of tapestry; her H6213
24 She **m** fine linen, and selleth *it*; and H6213
Ecc 3:11 God **m** from the beginning to the end. H6213
7: 7 Surely oppression **m** a wise man mad;
8: 1 a man's wisdom **m** his face to shine, and
10:19 A feast is made for laughter, and wine **m**
11: 5 not the works of God who **m** all. H6213
Isa 19:17 every one that **m** mention thereof shall
24: 1 Behold, the LORD **m** the earth empty,
1 the earth empty, and **m** it waste, and
27: 9 his sin; when he **m** all the stones of the H7760
40:23 he **m** the judges of the earth as vanity. H6213
43:16 Thus saith the LORD, which **m** a way H5414
44:13 the compass, and **m** it after the figure H6213
15 baketh bread; yea, he **m** a god, and H6466
15 worshippeth *it*; he **m** it a graven image, H6213
17 And the residue thereof he **m** a god, H6213
24 *am* the LORD that **m** all *things*; that H6213
25 of the liars, and **m** diviners mad; that
25 and **m** their knowledge foolish;
46: 6 goldsmith; and he **m** it a god: they fall H6213
55:10 the earth, and **m** it bring forth and bud,
59:15 from evil **m** himself a prey: and
Jer 4:19 very heart; my heart **m** a noise in me; I
10:13 of the earth; he **m** lightnings with rain, H6213
17: 5 in man, and **m** flesh his arm, and H7760
21: 2 king of Babylon **m** war against us; if so
29:26 *that is* mad, and **m** himself a prophet,
27 which **m** himself a prophet to you?
48:28 like the dove *that* **m** her nest in the sides
51:16 of the earth: he **m** lightnings with rain, H6213
Ezk 22: 3 **m** idols against herself to defile herself. H6213
Dan 2:28 secrets, and **m** known to the king
29 revealeth secrets **m** known to thee what
6:13 but **m** his petition three times a day. H1156
11:31 place the abomination that **m** desolate.
12:11 the abomination that **m** desolate set up,
Am 4:13 *is* his thought, that **m** the morning H6213
5: 8 *Seek him* that **m** the seven stars and H6213
8 the morning, and **m** the day dark with
Nah 1: 4 He rebuketh the sea, and **m** it dry, and
Mt 5:45 in heaven: for he **m** his sun to rise on the G393
Mk 7:37 all things well: he **m** both the deaf to G4160
Lk 5:36 then both the new **m** a rent, and the G4977
Jn 19:12 friend: whosoever **m** himself a king G4160
Act 9:34 Jesus Christ **m** thee whole: arise, and G2390
Ro 5: 5 And hope **m** not ashamed; because the G2617
8:26 the Spirit itself **m** intercession for us G5241
27 Spirit, because he **m** intercession for G1793
34 of God, who also **m** intercession for us. G1793
11: 2 of Elias? how he **m** intercession to God G1793
1Co 4: 7 For who **m** thee to differ *from another*? G1252
2Co 2: 2 is he then that **m** me glad, but the same G2165

2Co 2:14 in Christ, and **m** manifest the savour G5319
Gal 2: 6 they were, it **m** no matter to me: God G1308
Eph 4:16 of every part, **m** increase of the body G4160
Heb 1: 7 And of the angels he saith, Who **m** his G4160
7:28 For the law **m** men high priests which G2525
28 was since the law, *m* the Son, who is
Rev 13:13 so that he **m** fire come down from G4160
21:27 abomination, or *m* a lie: but they which
22:15 and whosoever loveth and **m** a lie. G4160

MAKHELOTH
Nu 33:25 from Haradah, and pitched in **M.** H4722
26 And they removed from **M**, and H4722

MAKING
Ex 5:14 your task in **m** brick both yesterday
Dt 20:19 a city a long time, in **m** war against it to
Jdg 19:22 *Now* as they were **m** their hearts merry,
1Ki 4:20 eating and drinking, and **m** merry.
1Ch 15:28 **m** a noise with psalteries and harps.
17:19 in **m** known all *these* great things.
2Ch 30:22 offerings, and **m** confession to the LORD
Ps 19: 7 of the LORD *is* sure, **m** wise the simple.
Ecc 12:12 admonished: of **m** many books *there is* H6213
Isa 3:16 they go, and **m** a tinkling with their feet:
Jer 20:15 child is born unto thee; **m** him very glad.
Ezk 27:16 the wares of thy **m**: they occupied in thy H4639
18 the wares of thy **m**, for the multitude of H4639
Dan 6:11 and **m** supplication before his God.
Hos 10: 4 falsely in **m** a covenant: thus judgment H3772
Am 8: 5 set forth wheat, **m** the ephah small, and
Mic 6:13 in **m** *thee* desolate because of thy sins.
Mt 9:23 the minstrels and the people **m** a noise, G2350
Mk 7:13 **M** the word of God of none effect G208
Jn 5:18 his Father, **m** himself equal with God. G4160
Ro 1:10 **M** request, if by any means now at G1189
2Co 6:10 as poor, yet **m** many rich; as having G4148
Eph 1:16 Cease not to give thanks for you, **m** G4160
2:15 of twain one new man, *so* **m** peace; G4160
5:19 **m** melody in your heart to the Lord; G5567
Php 1: 4 of mine for you all **m** request with joy, G4160
1Th 1: 2 all, **m** mention of you in our prayers; G4160
Phlm 4 I thank my God, **m** mention of thee G4160
2Pt 2: 6 an overthrow, **m** *them* an ensample G5087
Jude 22 And of some have compassion, **m** a G1252

MAKKEDAH
Jos 10:10 smote them to Azekah, and unto **M.** H4719
16 fled, and hid themselves in a cave at **M.** H4719
17 five kings are found hid in a cave at **M.** H4719
21 the camp to Joshua at **M** in peace: none H4719
28 And that day Joshua took **M**, and smote H4719
28 of **M** as he did unto the king of Jericho. H4719
29 Then Joshua passed from **M**, and all H4719
12:16 The king of **M**, one; the king of Beth-el, H4719
15:41 and **M**; sixteen cities with their villages: H4719

MAKTESH
Zep 1:11 Howl, ye inhabitants of **M**, for all the H4389

MALACHI
Mal 1: 1 of the word of the LORD to Israel by **M.** H4401

MALCHAM
1Ch 8: 9 Jobab, and Zibia, and Mesha, and **M**, H4445
Zep 1: 5 by the LORD, and that swear by **M**; H4445

MALCHIAH
1Ch 6:40 the son of Baaseiah, the son of **M**, H4441
Ezr 10:25 and Jeziah, and **M**, and Miamin, and H4441
31 Eliezer, Ishijah, **M**, Shemaiah, Shimeon, H4441
Neh 3:14 But the dung gate repaired **M** the son H4441
31 After him repaired **M** the goldsmith's H4441
8: 4 and Mishael, and **M**, and Hashum, and H4441
11:12 the son of Pashur, the son of **M**, H4441
Jer 38: 1 Pashur the son of **M**, heard the words H4441
6 into the dungeon of **M** the son of H4441

MALCHIEL
Gen 46:17 and the sons of Beriah; Heber, and **M.** H4439
Nu 26:45 of **M**, the family of the Malchielites. H4439
1Ch 7:31 And the sons of Beriah; Heber, and **M**, H4439

MALCHIELITES
Nu 26:45 of Malchiel, the family of the **M.** H4440

MALCHIJAH
1Ch 9:12 Pashur, the son of **M**, and Maasiai the H4441
24: 9 The fifth to **M**, the sixth to Mijamin, H4441
Ezr 10:25 and Eleazar, and **M**, and Benaiah. H4441
Neh 3:11 **M** the son of Harim, and Hashub the H4441
10: 3 Pashur, Amariah, **M**, H4441
12:42 and Jehohanan, and **M**, and Elam, and H4441

MALCHIRAM
1Ch 3:18 **M** also, and Pedaiah, and Shenazar, H4443

MALCHISHUA
1Sa 31: 2 and Abinadab, and **M**, Saul's sons. H4444
1Ch 8:33 and **M**, and Abinadab, and Eshbaal. H4444
9:39 and **M**, and Abinadab, and Eshbaal. H4444
10: 2 and Abinadab, and **M**, the sons of Saul. H4444

MALCHUS
Jn 18:10 right ear. The servant's name was **M.** G3124

MALE
Gen 1:27 he him; **m** and female created he them. H2145
5: 2 **M** and female created he them; and H2145
6:19 with thee; they shall be **m** and female. H2145
7: 2 to thee by sevens, the **m** and his female: H376
2 not clean by two, the **m** and his female. H376
3 Of fowls also of the air by sevens, the **m** H2145
9 into the ark, the **m** and the female, as H2145
16 And they that went in, went in **m** and H2145
17:23 his money, every **m** among the men of H2145
34:15 *be*, that every **m** of you be circumcised; H2145
22 one people, if every **m** among us be H2145
24 his city; and every **m** was circumcised, H2145
Ex 12: 5 blemish, a **m** of the first year: ye H2145
34:19 cattle, *whether* ox or sheep, *that is* **m.** H2142
Lev 1: 3 let him offer a **m** without blemish: he H2145
10 he shall bring it a **m** without blemish. H2145
3: 1 whether *it be* a **m** or female, he shall H2145
6 *be* of the flock; **m** or female, he shall H2145
4:23 kid of the goats, a **m** without blemish: H2145
7: 6 Every **m** among the priests shall eat H2145
12: 7 for her that hath born a **m** or a female. H2145
22:19 *Ye shall offer* at your own will a **m** H2145
27: 3 And thy estimation shall be of the **m** H2145
5 shall be of the **m** twenty shekels, and H2145
6 shall be of the **m** five shekels of silver, H2145
7 above; if *it be* a **m**, then thy estimation H2145
Nu 1: 2 of *their* names, every **m** by their polls; H2145
20 their polls, every **m** from twenty years H2145
22 their polls, every **m** from twenty years H2145
3:15 families: every **m** from a month old H2145
5: 3 Both **m** and female shall ye put out, H2145
18:10 **m** shall eat it: it shall be holy unto thee. H2145
31:17 Now therefore kill every **m** among the H2145
Dt 4:16 any figure, the likeness of **m** or female, H2145
7:14 there shall not be **m** or female barren H6135
20:13 **m** thereof with the edge of the sword: H2138
Jos 17: 2 these *were* the **m** children of Manasseh H2145
Jdg 21:11 destroy every **m**, and every woman that H2145
12 by lying with any **m**: and they brought H2145
1Ki 11:15 after he had smitten every **m** in Edom; H2145
16 until he had cut off every **m** in Edom:) H2145
Mal 1:14 hath in his flock a **m**, and voweth, and H2145
Mt 19: 4 the beginning made them **m** and female, G730
Mk 10: 6 creation God made them **m** and female. G730
Lk 2:23 of the Lord, Every **m** that openeth the G730
Gal 3:28 there is neither **m** nor female: for ye are G730

MALEFACTOR
Jn 18:30 If he were not a **m**, we would not have G2555

MALEFACTORS
Lk 23:32 And there were also two other, **m**, led G2557
33 him, and the **m**, one on the right hand, G2557
39 And one of the **m** which were hanged G2557

MALELEEL
Lk 3:37 *son* of **M**, which was *the son* of Cainan, G3121

MALES
Gen 34:25 upon the city boldly, and slew all the **m.** H2145
Ex 12:48 LORD, let all his **m** be circumcised, and H2145
13:12 thou hast; the **m** *shall be* the LORD'S. H2145
15 openeth the matrix, being **m**; but all the H2145
23:17 Three times in the year all thy **m** shall H2138
Lev 6:18 All the **m** among the children of Aaron H2145
29 All the **m** among the priests shall eat H2145
Nu 3:22 number of all the **m**, from a month old H2145
28 In the number of all the **m**, from a H2145
34 number of all the **m**, from a month old H2145
39 families, all the **m** from a month old H2145
40 the firstborn of the **m** of the children of H2145
3:43 And all the firstborn **m** by the number H2145
26:62 thousand, all **m** from a month old and H2145
31: 7 Moses; and they slew all the **m.** H2145
Dt 15:19 All the firstling **m** that come of thy herd H2145
16:16 Three times in a year shall all thy **m** H2138
Jos 5: 4 Egypt, *that were* **m**, *even* all the men of H2145
2Ch 31:16 Beside their genealogy of **m**, from three H2145
19 portions to all the **m** among the priests, H2145
Ezr 8: 3 of the **m** an hundred and fifty. H2145
4 and with him two hundred **m.** H2145
5 and with him three hundred **m.** H2145
6 son of Jonathan, and with him fifty **m.** H2145
7 of Athaliah, and with him seventy **m.** H2145
8 of Michael, and with him fourscore **m.** H2145
9 with him two hundred and eighteen **m.** H2145
10 with him an hundred and threescore **m.** H2145
11 and with him twenty and eight **m.** H2145
12 and with him an hundred and ten **m.** H2145
13 Shemaiah, and with them threescore **m.** H2145
14 and Zabbud, and with them seventy **m.** H2145

MALICE
1Co 5: 8 with the leaven of **m** and wickedness; G2549
14:20 howbeit in **m** be ye children, but G2549
Eph 4:31 be put away from you, with all **m**: G2549
Col 3: 8 anger, wrath, **m**, blasphemy, filthy G2549
Tit 3: 3 living in **m** and envy, hateful, *and* G2549
1Pt 2: 1 Wherefore laying aside all **m**, and all G2549

MALICIOUS
3Jn 10 against us with **m** words: and not G4190

MALICIOUSNESS
Ro 1:29 covetousness, **m**; full of envy, murder, G2549
1Pt 2:16 a cloak of **m**, but as the servants of God. G2549

MALIGNITY
Ro 1:29 murder, debate, deceit, **m**; whisperers, G2550

MALLOTHI
1Ch 25: 4 **M**, Hothir, *and* Mahazioth: H4413
26 The nineteenth to **M**, *he*, his sons, and H4413

MALLOWS
Job 30: 4 Who cut up **m** by the bushes, and H4408

MALLUCH
1Ch 6:44 of Kishi, the son of Abdi, the son of **M**, H4409
Ezr 10:29 And of the sons of Bani; Meshullam, **M**, H4409
32 Benjamin, **M**, *and* Shemariah. H4409
Neh 10: 4 Hattush, Shebaniah, **M**, H4409
27 **M**, Harim, Baanah. H4409
12: 2 Amariah, **M**, Hattush, H4409

MAMMON
Mt 6:24 the other. Ye cannot serve God and **m.** G3126
Lk 16: 9 friends of the **m** of unrighteousness; G3126
11 the unrighteous **m**, who will commit to G3126
13 the other. Ye cannot serve God and **m.** G3126

MAMRE
Gen 13:18 in the plain of **M**, which *is* in Hebron, H4471
14:13 in the plain of **M** the Amorite, brother H4471
24 and **M**; let them take their portion. H4471
18: 1 in the plains of **M**: and he sat in the tent H4471
23:17 which *was* before **M**, the field, and the H4471
19 of Machpelah before **M**: the same *is* H4471
25: 9 of Zohar the Hittite, which *is* before **M**; H4471
35:27 Isaac his father unto **M**, unto the city of H4471
49:30 which *is* before **M**, in the land of H4471
50:13 of Ephron the Hittite, before **M.** H4471

MAN
Gen 1:26 And God said, Let us make **m** in our H120
27 So God created **m** in his *own* image, in H120
2: 5 and *there was* not a **m** to till the ground. H120
7 And the LORD God formed **m** *of* the dust H120
7 of life; and **m** became a living soul. H120
8 there he put the **m** whom he had formed. H120
15 And the LORD God took the **m**, and put H120
16 And the LORD God commanded the **m**, H120
18 *is* not good that the **m** should be alone; I H120
22 had taken from **m**, made he a woman, H120
22 a woman, and brought her unto the **m.** H120
23 Woman, because she was taken out of **M.** H376
24 Therefore shall a **m** leave his father and H376
25 And they were both naked, the **m** and H120
3:12 And the **m** said, The woman whom thou H120
22 And the LORD God said, Behold, the **m** H120

Gen 3:24 So he drove out the **m**; and he placed at H120
4: 1 said, I have gotten a **m** from the LORD. H376
23 for I have slain a **m** to my wounding, H376
23 wounding, and a young **m** to my hurt. H3206
5: 1 **m**, in the likeness of God made he him; H120
6: 3 always strive with **m**, for that he also *is* H120
5 And GOD saw that the wickedness of **m** H120
6 that he had made **m** on the earth, and it H120
7 And the LORD said, I will destroy **m** H120
7 of the earth; both **m**, and beast, and the H120
9 Noah was a just **m** *and* perfect in his H376
7:21 creepeth upon the earth, and every **m**: H120
23 the ground, both **m**, and cattle, and the H120
9: 5 it, and at the hand of **m**; at the hand of H120
5 man's brother will I require the life of **m**. H120
6 Whoso sheddeth man's blood, by **m** H120
6 shed: for in the image of God made he **m**. H120
13:16 earth: so that if a **m** can number the dust H376
16:12 And he will be a wild **m**; his hand *will be* H120
12 *will be* against every **m**, and every man's
17:10 after thee; Every **m** child among you H2145
12 among you, every **m** child in your H2145
14 And the uncircumcised **m** child whose H2145
18: 7 a young **m**; and he hasted to dress it. H5288
19: 8 have not known **m**; let me, I pray you, H376
9 sore upon the **m**, *even* Lot, and came H376
31 and *there is* not a **m** in the earth to come H376
20: 3 *art but* a dead **m**, for the woman which H4191
7 Now therefore restore the **m** *his* wife; for H376
24:16 neither had any **m** known her: and she H376
21 And the **m** wondering at her held his H376
22 done drinking, that the **m** took a golden H376
26 And the **m** bowed down his head, and H376
29 Laban ran out unto the **m**, unto the well. H376
30 Thus spake the **m** unto me; that he came H376
30 that he came unto the **m**; and, behold, he H376
32 And the **m** came into the house: and he H376
58 go with this **m**? And she said, I will go. H376
61 and followed the **m**: and the servant took H376
65 the servant, What **m** *is* this that walketh H376
25: 8 old age, an old **m**, and full *of years;* and H2205
27 a cunning hunter, a **m** of the field; and H376
27 Jacob *was* a plain **m**, dwelling in tents. H376
26:11 He that toucheth this **m** or his wife shall H376
13 And the **m** waxed great, and went H376
27:11 *is* a hairy **m**, and I *am* a smooth man: H376
11 *is* a hairy man, and I *am* a smooth **m**: H376
29:19 give her to another **m**: abide with me. H376
30:43 And the **m** increased exceedingly, and H376
31:50 my daughters, no **m** *is* with us; see, God H376
32:24 there wrestled a **m** with him until the H376
34:19 And the young **m** deferred not to do the H5288
25 took each **m** his sword, and came H376
37:15 And a certain **m** found him, and, H376
15 the field: and the **m** asked him, saying, H376
17 And the **m** said, They are departed H376
38:25 in law, saying, By the **m**, whose these *are,* H376
39: 2 was a prosperous **m**; and he was in the H376
40: 5 both of them, each **m** his dream in one H376
5 in one night, each **m** according to the H376
41:11 he; we dreamed each **m** according to the H376
12 And *there was* there with us a young **m**, H5288
12 our dreams; to each **m** according to his H376
33 Now therefore let Pharaoh look out a **m** H376
38 this *is,* a **m** in whom the spirit of God *is?* H376
44 thee shall no **m** lift up his hand or foot H376
42:13 the sons of one **m** in the land of Canaan; H376
30 The **m**, *who is* the lord of the land, spake H376
33 And the **m**, the lord of the country, said H376
43: 3 him, saying, The **m** did solemnly protest H376
5 go down: for the **m** said unto us, Ye shall H376
6 tell the **m** whether ye had yet a brother? H376
7 And they said, The **m** asked us straitly of H376
11 and carry down the **m** a present, a little H376
13 brother, and arise, go again unto the **m**: H376
14 mercy before the **m**, that he may send H376
17 And the **m** did as Joseph bade; and the H376
17 **m** brought the men into Joseph's house. H376
24 And the **m** brought the men into H376
27 **m** of whom ye spake? *Is* he yet alive? H2205
44:11 Then they speedily took down every **m** H376
11 ground, and opened every **m** his sack. H376
13 every **m** his ass, and returned to the city. H376
15 that such a **m** as I can certainly divine? H376
17 do so: *but* the **m** in whose hand the cup H376
20 a father, an old **m**, and a child of his old H2205
45: 1 cried, Cause every **m** to go out from me. H376
1 there stood no **m** with him, while Joseph H376
22 To all of them he gave each **m** changes H376

Gen 47:20 sold every **m** his field, because the H376
49: 6 anger they slew a **m**, and in their selfwill H376
Ex 1: 1 **m** and his household came with Jacob. H376
2: 1 And there went a **m** of the house of Levi, H376
12 saw that *there was* no **m**, he slew the H376
20 the **m**? call him, that he may eat bread. H376
21 to dwell with the **m**: and he gave Moses H376
7:12 For they cast down every **m** his rod, and H376
8:17 it became lice in **m**, and in beast; all the H120
18 there were lice upon **m**, and upon beast. H120
9: 9 *with* blains upon **m**, and upon beast, H120
10 *with* blains upon **m**, and upon beast. H120
19 *for upon* every **m** and beast which shall H120
22 of Egypt, upon **m**, and upon beast, and H120
25 in the field, both **m** and beast; and the H120
10: 7 long shall this **m** be a snare unto us?
11: 2 and let every **m** borrow of his neighbour, H376
3 Moreover the **m** Moses *was* very great H376
7 tongue, against **m** or beast: that ye may H376
12: 3 take to them every **m** a lamb, according H376
4 of the souls; every **m** according to his H376
12 of Egypt, both **m** and beast; and against H120
16 *that* which every **m** must eat, that only H5315
13: 2 Israel, *both* of **m** and of beast: it *is* mine. H120
13 all the firstborn of **m** among thy children H120
15 the firstborn of **m**, and the firstborn of H120
15: 3 The LORD *is* a **m** of war: the LORD *is* his H376
16:16 Gather of it every **m** according to his H376
16 an omer for every **m**, *according to* the H1538
16 every **m** for *them* which *are* in his tents. H376
18 every **m** according to his eating. H376
19 And Moses said, Let no **m** leave of it till H376
21 every morning, every **m** according to his H376
22 two omers for one *m:* and all the rulers of
29 abide ye every **m** in his place, let no man H376
29 **m** go out of his place on the seventh day. H376
19:13 *it be* beast or **m**, it shall not live: when H376
21: 7 And if a **m** sell his daughter to be a H376
12 He that smiteth a **m**, so that he die, shall H376
13 And if a **m** lie not in wait, but God
14 But if a **m** come presumptuously upon H376
16 And he that stealeth a **m**, and selleth H376
20 And if a **m** smite his servant, or his H376
26 And if a **m** smite the eye of his servant, H376
28 If an ox gore a **m** or a woman, that they H376
29 he hath killed a **m** or a woman; the ox H376
33 And if a **m** shall open a pit, or if a man H376
33 And if a man shall open a pit, or if a **m** H376
22: 1 If a **m** shall steal an ox, or a sheep, and H376
5 If a **m** shall cause a field or vineyard to H376
7 If a **m** shall deliver unto his neighbour H376
10 If a **m** deliver unto his neighbour an ass, H376
10 be hurt, or driven away, no **m** seeing *it*:
14 And if a **m** borrow *ought* of his H376
16 And if a **m** entice a maid that is not H376
23: 3 thou countenance a poor **m** in his cause.
24:14 with you: if any **m** have any matters to H1167
25: 2 an offering: of every **m** that giveth it H376
30:12 they give every **m** a ransom for his soul H376
32: 1 *for* this Moses, the **m** that brought us up H376
23 *for* this Moses, the **m** that brought us up H376
27 of Israel, Put every **m** his sword by his H376
27 and slay every **m** his brother, and every H376
27 his brother, and every **m** his companion, H376
27 companion, and every **m** his neighbour. H376
29 LORD, even every **m** upon his son, and H376
33: 4 and no **m** did put on him his ornaments. H376
8 and stood every **m** *at* his tent door, and H376
10 worshipped, every **m** *in* his tent door. H376
11 face to face, as a **m** speaketh unto his H376
11 **m**, departed not out of the tabernacle. H5288
20 for there shall no **m** see me, and live. H120
34: 3 And no **m** shall come up with thee, H376
3 neither let any **m** be seen throughout H376
24 neither shall any **m** desire thy land, H376
35:22 of gold: and every **m** that offered *offered* H376
23 And every **m**, with whom was found H376
24 offering: and every **m**, with whom was H376
29 the LORD, every **m** and woman, whose H376
36: 1 every wise hearted **m**, in whom the LORD H376
2 every wise hearted **m**, in whose heart the H376
4 every **m** from his work which they made; H376
6 saying, Let neither **m** nor woman make H376
8 And every wise hearted **m** among them
38:26 A bekah for every **m**, *that is,* half a H1538
Lev 1: 2 say unto them, If any **m** of you bring an H120
5: 3 Or if he touch the uncleanness of **m**, H120
3 *it be* that a **m** shall be defiled withal, H120
4 *it be* that a **m** shall pronounce with H120

Lev 6: 3 all these that a **m** doeth, sinning therein: H120
7:21 *as* the uncleanness of **m**, or *any* unclean H120
12: 2 seed, and born a **m** child: then she H2145
13: 2 When a **m** shall have in the skin of his H120
9 When the plague of leprosy is in a **m**, H120
29 If a **m** or woman have a plague upon the H376
38 If a **m** also or a woman have in the skin H376
40 And the **m** whose hair is fallen off his H376
44 He is a leprous **m**, he *is* unclean: the H376
14:11 shall present the **m** that is to be made H376
15: 2 them, When any **m** hath a running issue H376
18 The woman also with whom **m** shall lie H376
24 And if any **m** lie with her at all, and her H376
33 an issue, of the **m**, and of the woman, H2145
16:17 And there shall be no **m** in the H120
21 the hand of a fit **m** into the wilderness: H376
17: 3 What **m** soever *there be* of the house of H376
4 be imputed unto that **m**; he hath shed H376
4 blood; and that **m** shall be cut off from H376
8 them, Whatsoever **m** *there be* of the H376
9 LORD; even that **m** shall be cut off from H376
10 And whatsoever **m** *there be* of the house H376
13 And whatsoever **m** *there be* of the H376
18: 5 which if a **m** do, he shall live in them: H120
19: 3 Ye shall fear every **m** his mother, and his H376
32 old **m**, and fear thy God: I *am* the LORD.
20: 3 And I will set my face against that **m**, H376
4 their eyes from the **m**, when he giveth of H376
5 Then I will set my face against that **m**, H376
10 And the **m** that committeth adultery H376
11 And the **m** that lieth with his father's H376
12 And if a **m** lie with his daughter in law, H376
13 If a **m** also lie with mankind, as he lieth H376
14 And if a **m** take a wife and her mother, it H376
15 And if a **m** lie with a beast, he shall H376
17 And if a **m** shall take his sister, his H376
18 And if a **m** shall lie with a woman H376
20 And if a **m** shall lie with his uncle's wife, H376
21 And if a **m** shall take his brother's wife, H376
27 A **m** also or woman that hath a familiar H376
21: 4 *being* a chief **m** among his people, H1167
18 For whatsoever **m** *he be* that hath a H376
18 not approach: a blind **m**, or a lame, or he H376
19 Or a **m** that is brokenfooted, or H376
21 No **m** that hath a blemish of the seed of H376
22: 4 What **m** soever of the seed of Aaron *is* a H376
4 or a **m** whose seed goeth from him; H376
5 unclean, or a **m** of whom he may take H120
14 And if a **m** eat *of* the holy thing H376
24:10 **m** of Israel strove together in the camp; H376
17 And he that killeth any **m** shall surely be H120
19 And if a **m** cause a blemish in his H376
20 in a **m**, so shall it be done to him *again*. H120
21 that killeth a **m**, he shall be put to death. H120
25:10 shall return every **m** unto his possession, H376
10 ye shall return every **m** unto his family. H376
13 shall return every **m** unto his possession. H376
26 And if the **m** have none to redeem it, and H376
27 overplus unto the **m** to whom he sold it; H376
29 And if a **m** sell a dwelling house in a H376
33 And if a **m** purchase of the Levites, then
27: 2 them, When a **m** shall make a singular H376
9 LORD, all that *any m* giveth of such unto
14 And when a **m** shall sanctify his house *to* H376
16 And if a **m** shall sanctify unto the LORD H376
20 **m**, it shall not be redeemed any more. H376
22 And if *a m* sanctify unto the LORD a
26 firstling, no **m** shall sanctify it; whether H376
28 thing, that a **m** shall devote unto the H376
28 he hath, *both* of **m** and beast, and of the H120
31 And if a **m** will at all redeem *ought* of his H376
Nu 1: 4 And with you there shall be a **m** of every H376
52 their tents, every **m** by his own camp, H376
52 camp, and every **m** by his own standard, H376
2: 2 Every **m** of the children of Israel shall H376
17 every **m** in his place by their standards. H376
3:13 in Israel, both **m** and beast: mine shall H120
5: 6 of Israel, When a **m** or woman shall H376
8 But if the **m** have no kinsman to H376
10 any **m** giveth the priest, it shall be his. H376
13 And a **m** lie with her carnally, and it be H376
15 Then shall the **m** bring his wife unto the H376
19 the woman, If no **m** have lain with thee, H376
20 defiled, and some **m** have lain with thee H376
31 Then shall the **m** be guiltless from H376
6: 2 them, When either **m** or woman shall H376
9 And if any **m** die very suddenly by him, H4191
7: 5 to every **m** according to his service. H376
8:17 *are* mine, *both* **m** and beast: on the day H120

Nu 9: 6 the dead body of a **m**, that they could not H120
7 the dead body of a **m**: wherefore are we H120
10 Israel, saying, If any **m** of you or of your H376
13 But the **m** that *is* clean, and is not in a H376
13 season, that **m** shall bear his sin. H376
11:10 families, every **m** in the door of his tent: H376
27 And there ran a young **m**, and told H5288
12: 3 (Now the **m** Moses *was* very meek, H376
13: 2 send a **m**, every one a ruler among them. H376
14:15 *all* this people as one **m**, then the nations H376
15:32 they found a **m** that gathered sticks H376
35 And the LORD said unto Moses, The **m** H376
16: 7 it shall be *that* the **m** whom the LORD H376
17 And take every **m** his censer, and put H376
17 before the LORD every **m** his censer, two H376
18 And they took every **m** his censer, and H376
22 all flesh, shall one **m** sin, and wilt thou H376
17: 9 they looked, and took every **m** his rod. H376
18:15 the firstborn of **m** shalt thou surely H120
19: 9 And a **m** *that is* clean shall gather up the H376
11 He that toucheth the dead body of any **m** H120
13 the dead body of any **m** that is dead, and H120
14 This *is* the law, when a **m** dieth in a tent: H120
16 or a bone of a **m**, or a grave, shall be H120
20 But the **m** that shall be unclean, and H376
21: 9 had bitten any **m**, when he beheld the H376
23:19 God *is* not a **m**, that he should lie; neither H376
19 lie; neither the son of **m**, that he should H120
24: 3 the **m** whose eyes are open hath said: H1397
15 the **m** whose eyes are open hath said: H1397
25: 8 And he went after the **m** of Israel into H376
8 of them through, the **m** of Israel, and the H376
26:64 But among these there was not a **m** of H376
65 was not left a **m** of them, save Caleb H376
27: 8 of Israel, saying, If a **m** die, and have no H376
16 all flesh, set a **m** over the congregation, H376
18 the son of Nun, a **m** in whom *is* the H376
30: 2 If a **m** vow a vow unto the LORD, or H376
16 Moses, between a **m** and his wife, H376
31:17 that hath known **m** by lying with him. H376
18 have not known a **m** by lying with him, H2145
26 was taken, *both* of **m** and of beast, thou, H120
35 had not known **m** by lying with him. H2145
47 of fifty, *both* of **m** and of beast, and gave H120
49 and there lacketh not one **m** of us. H376
50 the LORD, what every **m** hath gotten, of H376
53 had taken spoil, every **m** for himself.) H376
32:18 have inherited every **m** his inheritance. H376
27 But thy servants will pass over, every **m**
29 over Jordan, every **m** armed to battle,
35:23 Or with any stone, wherewith a **m** may
36: 8 every **m** the inheritance of his fathers. H376
Dt 1:16 between *every* **m** and his brother, and H376
17 of the face of **m**; for the judgment *is* H376
31 bare thee, as a **m** doth bear his son, in H376
41 girded on every **m** his weapons of war, H376
3:11 the breadth of it, after the cubit of a **m**. H376
20 ye return every **m** unto his possession, H376
4:32 that God created **m** upon the earth, and H120
5:24 that God doth talk with **m**, and he liveth. H120
7:24 there shall no **m** be able to stand before H376
8: 3 thee know that **m** doth not live by bread H120
3 of the mouth of the LORD doth **m** live. H120
5 heart, that, as a **m** chasteneth his son, H376
11:25 There shall no **m** be able to stand before H376
12: 8 **m** whatsoever *is* right in his own eyes. H376
15: 7 If there be among you a poor **m** of one of H34
12 *And* if thy brother, an Hebrew **m**, or an H5680
16:17 Every **m** *shall give* as he is able, H376
17: 2 God giveth thee, **m** or woman, that hath H376
5 Then shalt thou bring forth that **m** or H376
5 gates, *even* that **m** or that woman, and H376
12 And the **m** that will do presumptuously, H376
12 judge, even that **m** shall die: and thou H376
19: 5 As when a **m** goeth into the wood with H935
11 But if any **m** hate his neighbour, and lie H376
15 rise up against a **m** for any iniquity, or H376
16 If a false witness rise up against any **m** H376
20: 5 saying, What **m** *is there* that hath built H376
5 in the battle, and another **m** dedicate it. H376
6 And what **m** *is he* that hath planted a H376
6 die in the battle, and another **m** eat of it. H376
7 And what **m** *is there* that hath betrothed H376
7 in the battle, and another **m** take her. H376
8 shall say, What **m** *is there that is* fearful H376
21: 3 unto the slain **m**, even the elders of that H2491
6 next unto the slain *m*, shall wash their
15 If a **m** have two wives, one beloved, and H376
18 If a **m** have a stubborn and rebellious H376
Dt 21:22 And if a **m** have committed a sin worthy H376
22: 5 pertaineth unto a **m**, neither shall a H1397
5 neither shall a **m** put on a woman's H1397
8 thine house, if any **m** fall from thence. H5307
13 If any **m** take a wife, and go in unto her, H376
16 unto this **m** to wife, and he hateth her; H376
18 city shall take that **m** and chastise him; H376
22 If a **m** be found lying with a woman H376
22 of them die, *both* the **m** that lay with the H376
23 a **m** find her in the city, and lie with her; H376
24 in the city; and the **m**, because he hath H376
25 But if a **m** find a betrothed damsel in the H376
25 in the field, and the **m** force her, and lie H376
25 the **m** only that lay with her shall die: H376
26 death: for as when a **m** riseth against his H376
28 If a **m** find a damsel *that is* a virgin, H376
29 Then the **m** that lay with her shall give H376
30 A **m** shall not take his father's wife, nor H376
23:10 If there be among you any **m**, that is not H376
24: 1 When a **m** hath taken a wife, and H376
5 When a **m** hath taken a new wife, he H376
6 No **m** shall take the nether or the upper
7 If a **m** be found stealing any of his H376
11 Thou shalt stand abroad, and the **m** to H376
12 And if the **m** *be* poor, thou shalt not H376
16 **m** shall be put to death for his own sin. H376
25: 2 And it shall be, if the wicked **m** *be*
7 And if the **m** like not to take his H376
9 it be done unto that **m** that will not build H376
27:15 Cursed *be* the **m** that maketh *any* graven H376
28:26 earth, and no **m** shall fray *them* away.
29 evermore, and no **m** shall save *thee*.
30 a wife, and another **m** shall lie with her: H376
54 *So that* the **m** *that is* tender among you, H376
68 bondwomen, and no **m** shall buy *you*.
29:18 Lest there should be among you **m**, or H376
20 against that **m**, and all the curses that H376
32:25 both the young **m** and the virgin, the H970
25 suckling *also* with the **m** of gray hairs. H376
33: 1 Moses the **m** of God blessed the children H376
34: 6 Beth-peor: but no **m** knoweth of his H376
Jos 1: 5 There shall not any **m** be able to stand H376
2:11 courage in any **m**, because of you: for the H376
3:12 the tribes of Israel, out of every tribe a **m**. H376
4: 2 out of the people, out of every tribe a **m**, H376
4 children of Israel, out of every tribe a **m**: H376
5 take ye up every **m** of you a stone upon H376
5:13 there stood a **m** over against him with H376
6: 5 ascend up every **m** straight before him. H376
20 up into the city, every **m** straight before H376
21 in the city, both **m** and woman, young H376
26 Cursed *be* the **m** before the LORD, that H376
7:14 LORD shall take shall come **m** by man. H1397
14 LORD shall take shall come man by **m**. H1397
17 **m** by man; and Zabdi was taken: H1397
17 man by **m**; and Zabdi was taken: H1397
18 And he brought his household **m** by H1397
18 man by **m**; and Achan, the son H1397
8:17 And there was not a **m** left in Ai or H376
31 over which no **m** hath lift up *any* iron:
10: 8 shall not a **m** of them stand before thee. H376
14 of a **m**: for the LORD fought for Israel. H376
11:14 but every **m** they smote with the H120
14: 6 unto Moses the **m** of God concerning me H376
15 *which Arba was* a great **m** among the H120
17: 1 because he was a **m** of war, therefore he H376
21:44 there stood not a **m** of all their enemies H376
22:20 **m** perished not alone in his iniquity. H376
23: 9 but *as for* you, no **m** hath been able to H376
10 One **m** of you shall chase a thousand: for H376
24:28 So Joshua let the people depart, every **m** H376
Jdg 1:24 And the spies saw a **m** come forth out of H376
25 but they let go the **m** and all his family. H376
26 And the **m** went into the land of the H376
2: 6 Israel went every **m** unto his inheritance H376
3:15 a Benjamite, a **m** lefthanded: and by H376
17 of Moab: and Eglon *was* a very fat **m**. H376
28 and suffered not a **m** to pass over. H376
29 of valour; and there escaped not a **m**. H376
4:16 of the sword; *and* there was not a **m** left. H259
20 it shall be, when any **m** doth come and H376
20 any **m** here? that thou shalt say, No. H376
22 will shew thee the **m** whom thou seekest. H376
5:30 the prey; to every **m** a damsel *or* two; to H1397
6:12 *is* with thee, thou mighty **m** of valour.
16 thou shalt smite the Midianites as one **m**. H376
7: 7 *other* people go every **m** unto his place. H376
8 *rest of* Israel every **m** unto his tent, and H376
13 *there was* a **m** that told a dream unto H376
Jdg 7:14 the son of Joash, a **m** of Israel: *for* into H376
21 And they stood every **m** in his place H376
8:14 And caught a young **m** of the men of H5288
21 fall upon us: for as the **m** *is*, *so is* his H376
24 give me every **m** the earrings of his prey. H376
25 therein every **m** the earrings of his prey. H376
9: 9 **m**, and go to be promoted over the trees? H582
13 **m**, and go to be promoted over the trees? H582
49 cut down every **m** his bough, and H376
54 unto the young **m** his armourbearer, H5288
54 **m** thrust him through, and he died. H5288
55 they departed every **m** unto his place. H376
10: 1 the son of Dodo, a **m** of Issachar; and he H376
18 to another, What **m** *is he* that will begin H376
11: 1 was a mighty **m** of valour, and he *was*
39 no **m**. And it was a custom in Israel, H376
13: 2 And there was a certain **m** of Zorah, of H376
6 saying, A **m** of God came unto me, H376
8 O my Lord, let the **m** of God which thou H376
10 him, Behold, the **m** hath appeared unto H376
11 and came to the **m**, and said unto him, H376
11 him, *Art* thou the **m** that spakest unto H376
16: 7 shall I be weak, and be as another **m**. H120
11 shall I be weak, and be as another **m**. H120
17 become weak, and be like any *other* **m**. H120
19 she called for a **m**, and she caused him H376
17: 1 And there was a **m** of mount Ephraim, H376
5 And the **m** Micah had an house of gods, H376
6 in Israel, *but* every **m** did *that which was* H376
7 And there was a young **m** out of H5288
8 And the **m** departed out of the city from H376
11 to dwell with the **m**; and the young man H376
11 **m** was unto him as one of his sons. H5288
12 and the young **m** became his priest, H5288
18: 3 voice of the young **m** the Levite: and H5288
7 and had no business with *any* **m**. H120
15 of the young **m** the Levite, *even* unto H5288
19 the house of one **m**, or that thou be a H376
28 no business with *any* **m**; and it was in the H120
19: 6 had said unto the **m**, Be content, I pray H376
7 And when the **m** rose up to depart, his H376
9 And when the **m** rose up to depart, he, H376
10 But the **m** would not tarry that night, but H376
15 for *there was* no **m** that took them into H376
16 And, behold, there came an old **m** from H376
17 he saw a wayfaring **m** in the street of the H376
17 city: and the old **m** said, Whither goest H376
18 there *is* no **m** that receiveth me to house. H376
19 and for the young **m** *which is* with thy H5288
20 And the old **m** said, Peace *be* with thee; H376
22 the house, the old **m**, saying, Bring forth H376
22 Bring forth the **m** that came into thine H376
23 And the **m**, the master of the house, went H376
23 seeing that this **m** is come into mine H376
24 but unto this **m** do not so vile a thing. H376
25 to him: so the **m** took his concubine, H376
28 Then the **m** took her *up* upon an H376
28 **m** rose up, and gat him unto his place. H376
20: 1 together as one **m**, from Dan even to H376
8 And all the people arose as one **m**, H376
11 against the city, knit together as one **m**. H376
21:11 and every woman that hath lain by **m**. H2145
12 had known no **m** by lying with any male: H376
21 and catch you every **m** his wife of the H376
22 not to each **m** his wife in the war: H376
24 at that time, every **m** to his tribe and to H376
24 from thence every **m** to his inheritance. H376
25 in Israel: every **m** did *that which was* H376
Ru 1: 1 And a certain **m** of Beth-lehem-judah H376
2 And the name of the **m** *was* Elimelech, H376
2: 1 a mighty **m** of wealth, of the family H376
20 said unto her, The **m** *is* near of kin unto H376
3: 3 known unto the **m**, until he shall have H376
8 at midnight, that the **m** was afraid, and H376
16 told her all that the **m** had done to her. H376
18 will fall: for the **m** will not be in rest, H376
4: 7 all things; a **m** plucked off his shoe, H376
1Sa 1: 1 Now there was a certain **m** of H376
3 And this **m** went up out of his city yearly H376
11 thine handmaid a **m** child, then I will H582
21 And the **m** Elkanah, and all his house, H376
2: 9 for by strength shall no **m** prevail. H376
13 *that*, when any **m** offered sacrifice, the H376
15 and said to the **m** that sacrificed, Give H376
16 And *if* any **m** said unto him, Let them H376
25 If one **m** sin against another, the judge H376
25 judge him: but if a **m** sin against the H376
27 And there came a **m** of God unto Eli, and H376
31 shall not be an old **m** in thine house. H2205

1Sa 2:32 not be an old **m** in thine house for ever. H2205
33 And the **m** of thine, *whom* I shall not cut H376
4:10 they fled every **m** into his tent: and there H376
12 And there ran a **m** of Benjamin out of H376
13 And when the **m** came into the city, and H376
14 And the **m** came in hastily, and told Eli. H376
16 And the **m** said unto Eli, I *am* he that H376
18 for he was an old **m**, and heavy. And he H376
8:22 of Israel, Go ye every **m** unto his city. H376
9: 1 Now there was a **m** of Benjamin, whose H376
1 a Benjamite, a mighty **m** of power. H376
2 a choice young **m**, and a goodly: and H970
6 *is* in this city a **m** of God, and *he is* an H376
6 *he is* an honourable **m**; all that he saith H376
7 shall we bring the **m**? for the bread is H376
7 to bring to the **m** of God: what have we? H376
8 I give to the **m** of God, to tell us our way. H376
9 (Beforetime in Israel, when a **m** went to H376
10 unto the city where the **m** of God *was*. H376
16 I will send thee a **m** out of the land of H376
17 him, Behold the **m** whom I spake to thee H376
10: 6 and shalt be turned into another **m**. H376
22 further, if the **m** should yet come thither. H376
25 the people away, every **m** to his house. H376
27 said, How shall this **m** save us? And they
11: 3 **m** to save us, we will come out to thee.
13 And Saul said, There shall not a **m** be H376
13: 2 of the people he sent every **m** to his tent. H376
14 hath sought him a **m** after his own heart, H376
20 to sharpen every **m** his share, and his H376
14: 1 said unto the young **m** that bare his H5288
6 And Jonathan said to the young **m** that H5288
24 Cursed *be* the **m** that eateth *any* food H376
26 dropped; but no **m** put his hand to his
28 Cursed *be* the **m** that eateth *any* food H376
34 me hither every **m** his ox, and every man H376
34 his ox, and every **m** his sheep, and slay H376
34 brought every **m** his ox with him that H376
36 let us not leave a **m** of them. And they H376
39 *there was* not a **m** among all the people
52 saw any strong **m**, or any valiant man, H376
52 or any valiant **m**, he took him unto him. H1121
15: 3 not; but slay both **m** and woman, infant H376
29 for he *is* not a **m**, that he should repent. H120
16: 7 *the LORD seeth* not as **m** seeth; for man H120
7 not as man seeth; for **m** looketh on the H120
16 thee, to seek out a **m**, *who is* a cunning H376
17 Provide me now a **m** that can play well, H376
18 a mighty valiant **m**, and a man of war,
18 man, and a **m** of war, and prudent H376
17: 8 to Saul? choose you a **m** for you, and let H376
10 give me a **m**, that we may fight together. H376
12 eight sons: and the **m** went among men H376
12 men *for* an old **m** in the days of Saul. H2204
24 **m**, fled from him, and were sore afraid. H376
25 Have ye seen this **m** that is come up? H376
25 it shall be, *that* the **m** who killeth him, H376
26 shall be done to the **m** that killeth this H376
27 shall it be done to the **m** that killeth him. H376
33 youth, and he a **m** of war from his youth. H376
41 **m** that bare the shield *went* before him. H376
58 *art* thou, *thou* young **m**? And David H5288
18:23 that I *am* a poor **m**, and lightly esteemed? H376
20:22 But if I say thus unto the young **m**, H5958
21: 1 Why *art* thou alone, and no **m** with thee? H376
2 unto me, Let no **m** know any thing of the H376
7 Now a certain **m** of the servants of Saul H376
14 Lo, ye see the **m** is mad: wherefore *then* H376
15 to play the mad **m** in my presence? shall
24:19 For if a **m** find his enemy, will he let him H376
25: 2 And *there was* a **m** in Maon, whose H376
2 in Carmel; and the **m** *was* very great, H376
3 Now the name of the **m** *was* Nabal; and H376
3 but the **m** *was* churlish and evil H376
10 break away every **m** from his master. H376
13 Gird ye on every **m** his sword. And they H376
13 girded on every **m** his sword; and David H376
17 of Belial, that *a* **m** cannot speak to him.
25 thee, regard this **m** of Belial, *even* Nabal: H376
29 Yet a **m** is risen to pursue thee, and to H120
26:12 away, and no **m** saw *it*, nor knew *it*,
15 not thou a *valiant* **m**? and who *is* like to H376
23 The LORD render to every **m** his H376
27: 3 his men, every **m** with his household, H376
9 and left neither **m** nor woman alive, and H376
11 And David saved neither **m** nor woman H376
28:14 she said, An old **m** cometh up; and he *is* H376
30: 6 was grieved, every **m** for his sons and for H376
13 I *am* a young **m** of Egypt, servant to H5288

1Sa 30:17 there escaped not a **m** of them, save four H376
22 save to every **m** his wife and his H376
2Sa 1: 2 that, behold, a **m** came out of the camp H376
5 And David said unto the young **m** that H5288
6 And the young **m** that told him said, As H5288
13 And David said unto the young **m** that H5288
2: 3 bring up, every **m** with his household: H376
3:34 put into fetters: as a **m** falleth before H1121
38 and a great **m** fallen this day in Israel? H1419
7:19 *is* this the manner of **m**, O Lord GOD? H120
12: 2 The rich *m* had exceeding many flocks
3 But the poor *m* had nothing, save one
4 unto the rich **m**, and he spared to take H376
4 for the wayfaring **m** that was come unto H732
4 it for the **m** that was come to him. H376
5 against the **m**; and he said to Nathan, H376
5 LORD liveth, the **m** that hath done this H376
7 Thou *art* the **m**. Thus saith the LORD H376
13: 3 and Jonadab *was* a very subtil **m**. H376
9 And they went out every **m** from him. H376
29 **m** gat him up upon his mule, and fled. H376
34 But Absalom fled. And the young **m** H5288
14:16 of the hand of the **m** *that would* destroy H376
21 bring the young **m** Absalom again. H5288
15: 2 was *so*, that when any **m** that had a H376
3 *is* no **m** *deputed* of the king to hear thee.
4 land, that every **m** which hath any suit H376
5 And it was *so*, that when any **m** came H376
30 him covered every **m** his head, and they H376
16: 5 thence came out a **m** of the family of the H376
7 thou bloody **m**, and thou man of Belial: H376
7 thou bloody man, and thou **m** of Belial: H376
8 mischief, because thou *art* a bloody **m**. H376
23 days, *was* as if a **m** had inquired at the H376
17: 3 unto thee: the **m** whom thou seekest H376
8 and thy father *is* a **m** of war, and will not H376
10 father *is* a mighty **m**, and *they* which *be* H1368
18: 5 with the young **m**, *even* with Absalom. H5288
10 And a certain **m** saw *it*, and told Joab, H376
11 And Joab said unto the **m** that told him, H376
12 And the **m** said unto Joab, Though I H376
12 that none *touch* the young **m** Absalom. H5288
24 looked, and behold a **m** running alone. H376
26 And the watchman saw another **m** H376
26 Behold *another* **m** running alone. And H376
27 a good **m**, and cometh with good tidings. H376
29 And the king said, Is the young **m** H5288
32 Is the young **m** Absalom safe? And H5288
32 to do *thee* hurt, be as *that* young **m** *is*. H5288
19: 8 for Israel had fled every **m** to his tent. H376
14 as *the heart of* one **m**; so that they sent H376
22 shall there any **m** be put to death this H376
32 Now Barzillai was a very aged **m**, *even*
32 at Mahanaim; for he *was* a very great **m**. H376
20: 1 And there happened to be there a **m** of H376
1 of Jesse: every **m** to his tents, O Israel. H376
2 So every **m** of Israel went up from after H376
12 And when the **m** saw that all the people H376
21 The matter *is* not so: but a **m** of mount H376
22 the city, every **m** to his tent. And Joab H376
21: 4 us shalt thou kill any **m** in Israel. And he H376
5 And they answered the king, The **m** that H376
20 in Gath, where was a **m** of *great* stature, H376
22:26 **m** thou wilt shew thyself upright.
49 hast delivered me from the violent **m**. H376
23: 1 said, and the **m** *who was* raised up H1397
7 But the **m** *that* shall touch them must be H376
20 son of a valiant **m**, of Kabzeel, who had H376
21 And he slew an Egyptian, a goodly **m**: H376
24:14 and let me not fall into the hand of **m**. H120
1Ki 1: 6 also *was a* very goodly *m;* and *his mother*
42 a valiant **m**, and bringest good tidings. H376
49 and rose up, and went every **m** his way. H376
52 himself a worthy **m**, there shall not an H1121
2: 2 strong therefore, and shew thyself a **m**; H376
4 (said he) a **m** on the throne of Israel. H376
9 for thou *art* a wise **m**, and knowest what H376
4: 7 **m** his month in a year made provision. H259
25 dwelt safely, every **m** under his vine and H376
27 **m** in his month: they lacked nothing. H376
28 were, every **m** according to his charge. H376
7:14 his father *was* a **m** of Tyre, a worker in H376
8:25 not fail thee a **m** in my sight to sit on H376
31 If any **m** trespass against his neighbour, H376
38 be *made* by any **m**, *or* by all thy people H120
38 shall know every **m** the plague of his H376
39 do, and give to every **m** according to his H376
46 (for *there is* no **m** that sinneth not,) and H120
9: 5 fail thee a **m** upon the throne of Israel. H376

1Ki 10:25 And they brought every **m** his present, H376
11:28 And the **m** Jeroboam *was* a mighty man H376
28 And the man Jeroboam *was* a mighty **m**
28 seeing the young **m** that he was H5288
12:22 unto Shemaiah the **m** of God, saying, H376
24 return every **m** to his house; for this H376
13: 1 And, behold, there came a **m** of God out H376
4 the saying of the **m** of God, which had H376
5 to the sign which the **m** of God had given H376
6 and said unto the **m** of God, Entreat now H376
6 me again. And the **m** of God besought H376
7 And the king said unto the **m** of God, H376
8 And the **m** of God said unto the king, If H376
11 all the works that the **m** of God had done H376
12 **m** of God went, which came from Judah. H376
14 And went after the **m** of God, and found H376
14 him, *Art* thou the **m** of God that camest H376
21 And he cried unto the **m** of God that H376
26 he said, It *is* the **m** of God, who was H376
29 the carcase of the **m** of God, and laid it H376
31 wherein the **m** of God *is* buried; lay H376
14:10 a **m** taketh away dung, till it be all gone.
17:18 do with thee, O thou **m** of God? art thou H376
24 that thou *art* a **m** of God, *and* that the H376
20: 7 and see how this *m* seeketh mischief: for
20 And they slew every one his **m**: and the H376
24 the kings away, every **m** out of his place, H376
28 And there came a **m** of God, and spake H376
35 And a certain **m** of the sons of the H376
35 thee. And the **m** refused to smite him. H376
37 Then he found another **m**, and said, H376
37 pray thee. And the **m** smote him, so that H376
39 and, behold, a **m** turned aside, and H376
39 and brought a **m** unto me, and said, H376
39 said, Keep this **m**: if by any means he be H376
42 out of *thy* hand a **m** whom I appointed H376
22: 8 *There is* yet one **m**, Micaiah the son of H376
17 return every **m** to his house in peace. H376
34 And a *certain* **m** drew a bow at a H376
36 the sun, saying, Every **m** to his city, and H376
36 his city, and every **m** to his own country. H376
2Ki 1: 6 And they said unto him, There came a **m** H376
7 What manner of **m** *was he* which came H376
8 *He was* an hairy **m**, and girt with a girdle H376
9 unto him, Thou **m** of God, the king hath H376
10 of fifty, If I *be* a **m** of God, then let fire H376
11 said unto him, O **m** of God, thus hath the H376
12 them, If I *be* a **m** of God, let fire come H376
13 said unto him, O **m** of God, I pray thee, H376
3:25 of land cast every **m** his stone, and filled H376
4: 7 Then she came and told the **m** of God. H376
9 that this *is* an holy **m** of God, which H376
16 Nay, my lord, *thou* **m** of God, do not lie H376
21 on the bed of the **m** of God, and shut *the* H376
22 run to the **m** of God, and come again. H376
25 So she went and came unto the **m** of God H376
25 to pass, when the **m** of God saw her afar H376
27 And when she came to the **m** of God to H376
27 her away. And the **m** of God said, Let her H376
29 if thou meet any **m**, salute him not; and H376
40 out, and said, O *thou* **m** of God, *there is* H376
42 And there came a **m** from Baal-shalisha, H376
42 and brought the **m** of God bread of the H376
5: 1 of Syria, was a great **m** with his master, H376
1 a mighty **m** in valour, *but he was* a leper. H376
7 alive, that this **m** doth send unto me H2088
7 unto me to recover a **m** of his leprosy? H376
8 And it was *so*, when Elisha the **m** of God H376
14 the saying of the **m** of God: and his flesh H376
15 And he returned to the **m** of God, he and H376
20 But Gehazi, the servant of Elisha the **m** H376
26 *thee*, when the **m** turned again from his H376
6: 2 take thence every **m** a beam, and let us H376
6 And the **m** of God said, Where fell it? H376
9 And the **m** of God sent unto the king of H376
10 place which the **m** of God told him and H376
15 And when the servant of the **m** of God H376
17 eyes of the young **m**; and he saw: and, H5288
19 bring you to the **m** whom ye seek. But he H376
32 *the king* sent a **m** from before him: but H376
7: 2 leaned answered the **m** of God, and said, H376
5 of Syria, behold, *there was* no **m** there. H376
10 *there was* no **m** there, neither voice H376
10 neither voice of **m**, but horses tied, and H120
17 and he died, as the **m** of God had said, H376
18 And it came to pass as the **m** of God had H376
19 And that lord answered the **m** of God, H376
8: 2 the saying of the **m** of God: and she went H376
4 the servant of the **m** of God, saying, Tell H376

2Ki 8: 7 saying, The **m** of God is come hither. H376
8 and go, meet the **m** of God, and inquire H376
11 was ashamed: and the **m** of God wept. H376
9: 4 So the young **m**, *even* the young man H5288
4 So the young man, *even* the young **m** H5288
11 Ye know the **m**, and his communication. H376
13 Then they hasted, and took every **m** his H376
10:21 there was not a **m** left that came not. H376
11: 8 about, every **m** with his weapons in H376
9 they took every **m** his men that were to H376
11 And the guard stood, every **m** with his H376
12: 4 money that every **m** is set at, *and* all H5315
5 Let the priests take *it* to them, every **m** of H376
13:19 And the **m** of God was wroth with him, H376
21 they were burying a **m**, that, behold, they H376
21 and they cast the **m** into the sepulchre of H376
21 and when the **m** was let down, and H376
14: 6 **m** shall be put to death for his own sin. H376
12 and they fled every **m** to their tents. H376
15:20 men of wealth, of each **m** fifty shekels of H376
18:21 on which if a **m** lean, it will go into his H376
31 *then* eat ye every **m** of his own vine, and H376
21:13 Jerusalem as *a* **m** wipeth a dish, wiping
22:15 of Israel, Tell the **m** that sent you to me, H376
23:10 Hinnom, that no **m** might make his son H376
16 LORD which the **m** of God proclaimed, H376
17 sepulchre of the **m** of God, which came H376
18 And he said, Let him alone; let no **m** H376
1Ch 11:22 son of a valiant **m** of Kabzeel, who had H376
23 And he slew an Egyptian, a **m** of *great* H376
12: 4 a mighty **m** among the thirty, and H1368
28 And Zadok, a young **m** mighty of H5288
16: 3 one of Israel, both **m** and woman, to H376
21 He suffered no **m** to do them wrong: yea, H376
43 And all the people departed every **m** to H376
17:17 of a **m** of high degree, O LORD God. H120
20: 6 at Gath, where was a **m** of *great* stature, H376
21:13 but let me not fall into the hand of **m**. H120
22: 9 who shall be a **m** of rest; and I will give H376
23: 3 by their polls, **m** by man, was thirty H1397
3 by **m**, was thirty and eight thousand. H1397
14 Now *concerning* Moses the **m** of God, his H376
27:32 a counsellor, a wise **m**, and a scribe: and H376
28: 3 *been* a **m** of war, and hast shed blood. H376
21 every willing skilful **m**, for any manner of
29: 1 *is* not for **m**, but for the LORD God. H120
2Ch 2: 7 Send me now therefore a **m** cunning to H376
13 And now I have sent a cunning **m**, H376
14 and his father *was* a **m** of Tyre, skilful to H376
6: 5 **m** to be a ruler over my people Israel: H376
16 not fail thee a **m** in my sight to sit upon H376
22 If a **m** sin against his neighbour, and an H376
29 be made of any **m**, or of all thy people H120
30 render unto every **m** according unto all H376
36 (for *there is* no **m** which sinneth not,) H120
7:18 not fail thee a **m** *to be* ruler in Israel. H376
8:14 so had David the **m** of God commanded. H376
9:24 And they brought every **m** his present, H376
10:16 the son of Jesse: every **m** to your tents, O H376
11: 2 came to Shemaiah the **m** of God, saying, H376
4 return every **m** to his house: for this H376
14:11 our God; let not **m** prevail against thee. H582
15:13 small or great, whether **m** or woman. H376
17:17 And of Benjamin; Eliada a mighty **m** of H1368
18: 7 *There is* yet one **m**, by whom we may H376
16 *therefore* every **m** to his house in peace. H376
33 And *a certain* **m** drew a bow at a H376
33 said to his chariot **m**, Turn thine hand, H7395
19: 6 for ye judge not for **m**, but for the LORD, H120
20:27 Then they returned, every **m** of Judah H376
23: 7 about, every **m** with his weapons in H376
8 and took every **m** his men that were to H376
10 And he set all the people, every **m** having H376
25: 4 but every **m** shall die for his own sin. H376
7 But there came a **m** of God to him, H376
9 And Amaziah said to the **m** of God, But H376
9 of Israel? And the **m** of God answered, H376
22 Israel, and they fled every **m** to his tent. H376
28: 7 And Zichri, a mighty **m** of Ephraim, H1368
30:16 law of Moses the **m** of God: the priests H376
31: 1 returned, every **m** to his possession, into H376
2 their courses, every **m** according to his H376
32:19 *which were* the work of the hands of **m**. H120
34:23 Israel, Tell ye the **m** that sent you to me, H376
36:17 upon young **m** or maiden, old man, H970
17 or maiden, old **m**, or him that stooped H2205
Ezr 3: 1 together as one **m** to Jerusalem. H376
2 in the law of Moses the **m** of God. H376
8:18 they brought us a **m** of understanding, H376
Neh 1:11 of this **m**. For I was the king's cupbearer. H376
2:10 there was come a **m** to seek the welfare H120
12 neither told I *any* **m** what my God had H120
5:13 shake out every **m** from his house, and H376
6:11 And I said, Should such a **m** as I flee? H376
7: 2 faithful **m**, and feared God above many. H376
8: 1 together as one **m** into the street that H376
9:29 (which if a **m** do, he shall live in them;) H120
12:24 the **m** of God, ward over against ward. H376
36 of David the **m** of God, and Ezra the H376
Est 1:22 that every **m** should bear rule in his H376
4:11 whether **m** or woman, shall come H376
5:12 queen did let no **m** come in with the king
6: 6 shall be done unto the **m** whom the king H376
7 **m** whom the king delighteth to honour, H376
9 may array the **m** *withal* whom the king H376
9 **m** whom the king delighteth to honour. H376
11 **m** whom the king delighteth to honour. H376
8: 8 with the king's ring, may no **m** reverse.
9: 2 their hurt: and no **m** could withstand H376
4 **m** Mordecai waxed greater and greater. H376
Job 1: 1 There was a **m** in the land of Uz, whose H376
1 *was* Job; and that **m** was perfect and H376
3 so that this **m** was the greatest of all H376
8 and an upright **m**, one that feareth God, H376
2: 3 and an upright **m**, one that feareth God, H376
4 all that a **m** hath will he give for his life. H376
3: 3 was said, There is a **m** child conceived. H1397
23 *Why is light given* to a **m** whose way is H1397
4:17 Shall mortal **m** be more just than God? H582
17 a **m** be more pure than his maker? H1397
5: 2 For wrath killeth the foolish **m**, and envy H191
7 Yet **m** is born unto trouble, as the sparks H120
17 Behold, happy *is* the **m** whom God H582
7: 1 *Is there* not an appointed time to **m** H582
17 What *is* **m**, that thou shouldest magnify H582
8:20 **m**, neither will he help the evil doers:
9: 2 but how should **m** be just with God? H582
32 For *he is* not a **m**, as I *am, that* I should H376
10: 4 eyes of flesh? or seest thou as **m** seeth? H582
5 *Are* thy days as the days of **m**? *are* thy H582
11: 2 and should a **m** full of talk be justified? H376
3 shall no **m** make thee ashamed?
12 For vain **m** would be wise, though man H376
12 For vain man would be wise, though **m** H120
12: 4 the just upright *m is* laughed to scorn.
14 up a **m**, and there can be no opening. H376
25 them to stagger like *a* drunken *m*.
13: 9 **m** mocketh another, do ye *so* mock him? H582
14: 1 **M** *that is* born of a woman *is* of few H120
10 But **m** dieth, and wasteth away: yea, H1397
10 **m** giveth up the ghost, and where *is* he? H120
12 So **m** lieth down, and riseth not: till the H376
14 If a **m** die, shall he live *again*? all the H1397
19 earth; and thou destroyest the hope of **m**. H582
15: 2 Should a wise **m** utter vain knowledge, H2450
7 *Art* thou the first **m** *that* was born? or H120
14 What *is* **m**, that he should be clean? and H582
16 *is* **m**, which drinketh iniquity like water? H376
20 The wicked **m** travaileth with pain all
28 in houses which no **m** inhabiteth, which
16:21 O that one might plead for a **m** with H1397
21 God, as a **m** *pleadeth* for his neighbour! H120
17:10 for I cannot find *one* wise *m* among you.
20: 4 Knowest thou *not* this of old, since **m** H120
21 therefore shall no **m** look for his goods.
29 This *is* the portion of a wicked **m** from H120
21: 4 As for me, *is* my complaint to **m**? and if *it* H120
33 him, and every **m** shall draw after him, H120
22: 2 Can a **m** be profitable unto God, as he H1397
8 But *as for* the mighty **m**, he had the H376
8 earth; and the honourable **m** dwelt in it.
24:22 he riseth up, and no *m* is sure of life.
25: 4 How then can **m** be justified with God? H582
6 How much less **m**, *that is* a worm? and H582
6 and the son of **m**, *which is* a worm? H120
27:13 This *is* the portion of a wicked **m** with H120
19 The rich **m** shall lie down, but he shall
28:13 **M** knoweth not the price thereof; neither H582
28 And unto **m** he said, Behold, the fear of H120
32: 8 But *there is* a spirit in **m**: and the H582
13 wisdom: God thrusteth him down, not **m**. H376
21 let me give flattering titles unto **m**. H120
33:12 answer thee, that God is greater than **m**. H582
14 For God speaketh once, yea twice, *yet m*
17 That he may withdraw **m** *from his* H120
17 *his* purpose, and hide pride from **m**. H1397
23 to shew unto **m** his uprightness: H120
26 he will render unto **m** his righteousness. H582
Job 33:29 *things* worketh God oftentimes with **m**, H1397
34: 7 What **m** *is* like Job, *who* drinketh up H1397
9 For he hath said, It profiteth a **m** H1397
11 For the work of a **m** shall he render unto H120
11 every **m** to find according to *his* ways. H376
14 If he set his heart upon **m**, *if* he gather
15 All flesh shall perish together, and **m** H120
21 For his eyes *are* upon the ways of **m**, and H376
23 For he will not lay upon **m** more *than* H376
29 against a nation, or against a **m** only: H120
34 me, and let a wise **m** hearken unto me. H1397
35: 8 Thy wickedness *may hurt* a **m** as thou H376
8 righteousness *may profit* the son of **m**. H120
36:25 Every **m** may see it; man may behold *it* H120
25 Every man may see it; **m** may behold *it* H582
28 do drop *and* distil upon **m** abundantly. H120
37: 7 He sealeth up the hand of every **m**; that H120
20 Shall it be told him that I speak? if a **m** H376
38: 3 Gird up now thy loins like a **m**; for I will H1397
26 earth, *where* no **m** *is; on* the wilderness, H376
26 *on* the wilderness, wherein *there is* no **m**; H120
40: 7 Gird up thy loins now like a **m**: I will H1397
42:11 upon him: every **m** also gave him a piece H376
Ps 1: 1 Blessed *is* the **m** that walketh not in the H376
5: 6 will abhor the bloody and deceitful **m**. H376
8: 4 What is **m**, that thou art mindful of him? H582
4 and the son of **m**, that thou visitest him? H120
9:19 Arise, O LORD; let not **m** prevail: let the H582
10:15 and the evil *m*: seek out his wickedness
18 the **m** of the earth may no more oppress. H582
12: 1 Help, LORD; for the godly **m** ceaseth; H2623
18:25 **m** thou wilt shew thyself upright; H1399
48 hast delivered me from the violent **m**. H376
19: 5 rejoiceth as a strong **m** to run a race. H1368
22: 6 But I *am* a worm, and no **m**; a reproach H376
25:12 What **m** *is* he that feareth the LORD? H376
31:12 I am forgotten as a dead **m** out of H4191
20 from the pride of **m**: thou shalt keep H376
32: 2 Blessed *is* the **m** unto whom the LORD H120
33:16 **m** is not delivered by much strength. H1368
34: 6 This poor **m** cried, and the LORD heard
8 blessed *is* the **m** *that* trusteth in him. H1397
12 What **m** *is he that* desireth life, *and* H376
36: 6 O LORD, thou preservest **m** and beast. H120
37: 7 **m** who bringeth wicked devices to pass. H376
16 A little that a righteous **m** hath *is* better
23 The steps of a *good* **m** are ordered by H1397
37 Mark the perfect *m*, and behold the
37 upright: for the end of *that* **m** *is* peace. H376
38:13 But I, as a deaf *m*, heard not; and *I was*
13 a dumb **m** *that* openeth not his mouth. H483
14 Thus I was as a **m** that heareth not, and H376
39: 5 thee: verily every **m** at his best state *is* H120
6 Surely every **m** walketh in a vain shew: H376
11 When thou with rebukes dost correct **m** H376
11 a moth: surely every **m** *is* vanity. Selah. H120
40: 4 Blessed *is* that **m** that maketh the H1397
43: 1 me from the deceitful and unjust **m**. H376
49:12 Nevertheless **m** *being* in honour abideth H120
20 **M** *that is* in honour, and understandeth H120
52: 1 O mighty **m**? the goodness of God
7 Lo, *this is* the **m** *that* made not God his H1397
55:13 But *it was* thou, a **m** mine equal, my H582
56: 1 Be merciful unto me, O God: for **m** H582
11 not be afraid what **m** can do unto me. H120
58:11 So that a **m** shall say, Verily *there is* a H120
60:11 from trouble: for vain *is* the help of **m**. H120
62: 3 mischief against a **m**? ye shall be slain all H376
12 to every **m** according to his work. H376
65: 4 Blessed *is the* **m** *whom* thou choosest, H376
71: 4 the hand of the unrighteous and cruel **m**.
74: 5 *A* **m** was famous according as he had
22 the foolish **m** reproacheth thee daily. H5036
76:10 Surely the wrath of **m** shall praise thee: H120
78:25 **M** did eat angels' food: he sent them H376
65 **m** that shouteth by reason of wine. H1368
80:17 Let thy hand be upon the **m** of thy right H376
17 **m** *whom* thou madest strong for thyself. H120
84: 5 Blessed *is* the **m** whose strength *is* in H120
12 O LORD of hosts, blessed *is* the **m** that H120
87: 4 with Ethiopia; this *m* was born there.
5 said, This and that **m** was born in her: H376
6 *that* this *m* was born there. Selah.
88: 4 pit: I am as a **m** *that hath* no strength: H1397
89:48 What **m** *is he that* liveth, and shall not H1397
90: 3 Thou turnest **m** to destruction; and H582
ttl A Prayer of Moses the **m** of God. H376
92: 6 A brutish **m** knoweth not; neither doth a H376
94:10 **m** knowledge, *shall not he know*? H120

Ps 94:11 The LORD knoweth the thoughts of **m**, H120
12 Blessed *is* the **m** whom thou H1397
103:15 *As for* **m**, his days *are* as grass: as a H582
104:14 for the service of **m**: that he may bring H120
15 glad the heart of **m**, *and* oil to make *his* H582
23 **M** goeth forth unto his work and to his H120
105:14 He suffered no **m** to do them wrong: yea, H120
17 He sent a **m** before them, *even* Joseph, H376
107:27 a drunken **m**, and are at their wits' end.
108:12 from trouble: for vain *is* the help of **m**. H120
109: 6 Set thou a wicked **m** over him: and let
16 poor and needy **m**, that he might even H376
112: 1 Praise ye the LORD. Blessed *is* the **m** H376
5 A good **m** sheweth favour, and lendeth: H376
118: 6 I will not fear: what can **m** do unto me? H120
8 in the LORD than to put confidence in **m**. H120
119: 9 Wherewithal shall a young **m** cleanse H5288
134 Deliver me from the oppression of **m**: so H120
127: 4 mighty **m**; so *are* children of the youth. H1368
5 Happy *is* the **m** that hath his quiver full H1397
128: 4 Behold, that thus shall the **m** be blessed H1397
135: 8 firstborn of Egypt, both of **m** and beast. H120
140: 1 Deliver me, O LORD, from the evil **m**: H120
1 man: preserve me from the violent **m**; H376
4 from the violent **m**; who have purposed H376
11 hunt the violent **m** to overthrow *him*. H376
142: 4 but *there was* no **m** that would know me:
4 failed me; no **m** cared for my soul.
143: 2 in thy sight shall no **m** living be justified.
144: 3 LORD, what *is* **m**, that thou takest H120
3 of **m**, that thou makest account of him! H582
4 **M** is like to vanity: his days *are* as a H120
146: 3 in the son of **m**, in whom *there is* no help. H120
147:10 he taketh not pleasure in the legs of a **m**. H376
Prv 1: 4 the young **m** knowledge and discretion. H5288
5 A wise *m* will hear, and will increase
5 learning; and a **m** of understanding
24 out my hand, and no **m** regarded;
2:12 the way of the evil *m*, from the man that
12 the **m** that speaketh froward things; H376
3: 4 understanding in the sight of God and **m**. H120
13 Happy *is* the **m** *that* findeth wisdom, H120
13 and the **m** *that* getteth understanding. H120
30 Strive not with a **m** without cause, if he H120
5:21 For the ways of **m** *are* before the eyes of H376
6:11 travelleth, and thy want as an armed **m**. H376
12 A naughty person, a wicked **m**, walketh H376
26 For by means of a whorish woman *a m*
27 Can a **m** take fire in his bosom, and his H376
34 For jealousy *is* the rage of a **m**: H1397
7: 7 a young **m** void of understanding, H5288
8: 4 I call; and my voice *is* to the sons of **m**. H120
34 Blessed *is* the **m** that heareth me, H120
9: 7 a wicked *m getteth* himself a blot.
8 rebuke a wise **m**, and he will love thee. H2450
9 Give *instruction* to a wise *m*, and he will
9 a just *m*, and he will increase in learning.
10:11 The mouth of a righteous *m is* a well of
23 but a **m** of understanding hath wisdom. H376
11: 7 When a wicked **m** dieth, *his* expectation H120
12 a **m** of understanding holdeth his peace. H376
17 The merciful **m** doeth good to his own H376
12: 2 A good *m* obtaineth favour of the LORD:
2 a **m** of wicked devices will he condemn. H376
3 A **m** shall not be established by H120
8 A **m** shall be commended according to H376
10 A righteous *m* regardeth the life of his
14 A **m** shall be satisfied with good by the H376
16 but a prudent *m* covereth shame.
23 A prudent **m** concealeth knowledge: but H120
25 Heaviness in the heart of **m** maketh it H376
27 The slothful *m* roasteth not that which
27 the substance of a diligent **m** *is* precious. H120
13: 2 A **m** shall eat good by the fruit of *his* H376
5 A righteous *m* hateth lying: but a wicked
5 *m* is loathsome, and cometh to shame.
16 Every prudent *m* dealeth with
22 A good *m* leaveth an inheritance to his
14: 7 Go from the presence of a foolish **m**, H376
12 right unto a **m**, but the end thereof H376
14 a good **m** *shall be satisfied* from himself. H376
15 the prudent *m* looketh well to his going.
16 A wise *m* feareth, and departeth from
17 and a **m** of wicked devices is hated. H376
15:18 A wrathful **m** stirreth up strife: but *he* H376
19 The way of the slothful *m is* as an hedge
20 but a foolish **m** despiseth his mother. H120
21 a **m** of understanding walketh uprightly. H376
23 A **m** hath joy by the answer of his H376

Prv 16: 1 The preparations of the heart in **m**, and H120
2 All the ways of a **m** *are* clean in his own H376
14 of death: but a wise **m** will pacify it. H376
25 right unto a **m**, but the end thereof H376
27 An ungodly **m** diggeth up evil: and in his H376
28 A froward **m** soweth strife: and a H376
29 A violent **m** enticeth his neighbour, and H376
17:10 A reproof entereth more into a wise **m** H995
11 An evil *m* seeketh only rebellion:
12 meet a **m**, rather than a fool in his folly. H376
18 A **m** void of understanding striketh H120
23 A wicked *m* taketh a gift out of the
27 his words: *and* a **m** of understanding is H376
28 lips *is esteemed* a **m** of understanding.
18: 1 Through desire a **m**, having separated
12 Before destruction the heart of **m** is H376
14 The spirit of a **m** will sustain his H376
24 A **m** *that hath* friends must shew himself H376
19: 3 The foolishness of **m** perverteth his way: H120
6 **m** *is* a friend to him that giveth gifts.
11 The discretion of a **m** deferreth his H120
19 A **m** of great wrath shall suffer
22 The desire of a **m** *is* his kindness: and a H120
22 and a poor **m** *is* better than a liar.
24 A slothful *m* hideth his hand in *his*
20: 3 *It is* an honour for a **m** to cease from H376
5 Counsel in the heart of **m** *is like* deep H376
5 a **m** of understanding will draw it out. H376
6 goodness: but a faithful **m** who can find? H376
7 The just *m* walketh in his integrity: his
17 Bread of deceit *is* sweet to a **m**; but H376
24 can a **m** then understand his own way? H120
25 *It is* a snare to the **m** *who* devoureth *that* H120
27 The spirit of **m** *is* the candle of the H120
21: 2 Every way of a **m** *is* right in his own H376
8 The way of **m** *is* froward and strange: H376
12 The righteous *m* wisely considereth the
16 The **m** that wandereth out of the way of H120
17 *shall be* a poor **m**: he that loveth wine H376
20 the wise; but a foolish **m** spendeth it up. H120
22 A wise *m* scaleth the city of the mighty,
28 A false witness shall perish: but the **m** H376
29 A wicked **m** hardeneth his face: but *as* H376
22: 3 A prudent *m* foreseeth the evil, and
13 The slothful *m* saith, *There is* a lion
24 Make no friendship with an angry **m**; H1167
24 and with a furious **m** thou shalt not go: H376
29 Seest thou a **m** diligent in his business? H376
23: 2 throat, if thou *be* a **m** given to appetite.
21 drowsiness shall clothe *a m* with rags.
24: 5 A wise **m** *is* strong; yea, a man of H1397
5 A wise man *is* strong; yea, a **m** of H376
12 to *every* **m** according to his works? H120
15 Lay not wait, O wicked *m*, against the
16 For a just *m* falleth seven times, and
20 no reward to the evil *m*; the candle of the
26 *Every m* shall kiss *his* lips that giveth a
29 render to the **m** according to his work. H376
30 of the **m** void of understanding; H120
34 travelleth; and thy want as an armed **m**. H376
25:18 A **m** that beareth false witness against H376
19 Confidence in an unfaithful **m** in time of H898
26 A righteous *m* falling down before the
26:12 Seest thou a **m** wise in his own conceit? H376
13 The slothful *m* saith, *There is* a lion in
18 As a mad *m* who casteth firebrands,
19 So *is* the **m** *that* deceiveth his neighbour, H376
21 so *is* a contentious **m** to kindle strife. H376
27: 2 Let another **m** praise thee, and not H2114
8 so *is* a **m** that wandereth from his place. H376
12 A prudent *m* foreseeth the evil, *and*
17 Iron sharpeneth iron; so a **m** sharpeneth H376
19 to face, so the heart of **m** to man. H120
19 to face, so the heart of man to **m**. H120
20 full; so the eyes of **m** are never satisfied. H120
21 furnace for gold; so *is* a **m** to his praise. H376
28: 1 The wicked flee when no **m** pursueth:
2 thereof: but by a **m** of understanding H120
3 A poor **m** that oppresseth the poor *is* H1397
11 The rich **m** *is* wise in his own conceit; H376
12 but when the wicked rise, a **m** is hidden. H120
14 Happy *is* the **m** that feareth alway: but H120
17 A **m** that doeth violence to the blood of H120
17 shall flee to the pit; let no **m** stay him.
20 A faithful **m** shall abound with H376
21 a piece of bread *that* **m** will transgress. H1397
23 He that rebuketh a **m** afterwards shall H120
29: 5 A **m** that flattereth his neighbour H1397
6 In the transgression of an evil **m** *there is* H376

Prv 29: 9 *If* a wise **m** contendeth with a foolish H376
9 with a foolish **m**, whether he rage or H376
11 A fool uttereth all his mind: but a wise *m*
13 The poor and the deceitful **m** meet H376
20 Seest thou a **m** *that is* hasty in his H376
22 An angry **m** stirreth up strife, and a H376
22 furious **m** aboundeth in transgression. H1167
25 The fear of **m** bringeth a snare: but H120
27 An unjust **m** *is* an abomination to the H376
30: 1 the prophecy: the **m** spake unto Ithiel, H1397
2 Surely I *am* more brutish than *any* **m**, H376
2 and have not the understanding of a **m**. H120
19 sea; and the way of a **m** with a maid. H1397
Ecc 1: 3 What profit hath a **m** of all his labour H120
8 All things *are* full of labour; **m** cannot H376
13 the sons of **m** to be exercised therewith. H120
2:12 for what *can* the **m** *do* that cometh after H120
16 And how dieth the wise *m*? as the fool.
18 it unto the **m** that shall be after me. H120
19 he shall be a wise *m* or a fool? yet shall
21 For there is a **m** whose labour *is* in H120
21 and in equity; yet to a **m** that hath not H120
22 For what hath **m** of all his labour, and of H120
24 *There is* nothing better for a **m**, *than* that H120
26 For *God* giveth to a **m** that *is* good in his H120
3:11 their heart, so that no **m** can find out the H120
12 *a m* to rejoice, and to do good in his life.
13 And also that every **m** should eat and H120
19 breath; so that a **m** hath no preeminence H120
21 Who knoweth the spirit of **m** H1121+H120
22 better, than that a **m** should rejoice in H120
4: 4 work, that for this a **m** is envied of his H376
5:12 The sleep of a labouring **m** *is* sweet, H5647
19 Every **m** also to whom God hath given H120
6: 2 A **m** to whom God hath given riches, H376
3 If a **m** beget an hundred *children*, and H376
7 All the labour of **m** *is* for his mouth, and H120
10 it is known that it *is* **m**: neither may he H120
11 increase vanity, what *is* **m** the better? H120
12 For who knoweth what *is* good for **m** in H120
12 **m** what shall be after him under the sun? H120
7: 5 than for a **m** to hear the song of fools. H376
7 Surely oppression maketh a wise **m** H2450
14 that **m** should find nothing after him. H120
15 there is a just *m* that perisheth in his
15 there is a wicked *m* that prolongeth *his*
20 For *there is* not a just **m** upon earth, that H120
28 but I find not: one **m** among a thousand H120
29 God hath made **m** upright; but they have H120
8: 1 Who *is* as the wise *m*? and who knoweth
6 the misery of **m** *is* great upon him. H120
8 *There is* no **m** that hath power over the H120
9 **m** ruleth over another to his own hurt. H120
15 Then I commended mirth, because a **m** H120
17 of God, that a **m** cannot find out the H120
17 because though a **m** labour to seek *it* H120
17 though a wise *m* think to know *it*, yet
9: 1 hand of God: no **m** knoweth either love H120
12 For **m** also knoweth not his time: as the H120
15 Now there was found in it a poor wise **m**, H376
15 no **m** remembered that same poor man. H120
15 no man remembered that same poor **m**. H376
10:14 A fool also is full of words: a **m** cannot H120
11: 8 But if a **m** live many years, *and* rejoice in H120
9 Rejoice, O young **m**, in thy youth; and let H970
12: 5 shall fail: because **m** goeth to his long H120
13 for this *is* the whole *duty* of **m**. H120
Song 3: 8 in war: every **m** *hath* his sword upon H376
8: 7 floods drown it: if *a* **m** would give all the H376
Isa 2: 9 And the mean **m** boweth down, and the H120
9 and the great **m** humbleth himself: H376
11 The lofty looks of **m** shall be humbled, H120
17 And the loftiness of **m** shall be bowed H120
20 In that day a **m** shall cast his idols of H120
22 Cease ye from **m**, whose breath *is* in his H120
3: 2 The mighty **m**, and the man of war, the H1368
2 The mighty man, and the **m** of war, the H376
3 the honourable **m**, and the counsellor,
6 When a **m** shall take hold of his brother H376
4: 1 take hold of one **m**, saying, We will eat H376
5:15 And the mean **m** shall be brought down, H120
15 and the mighty **m** shall be humbled, and H376
6: 5 because I *am* a **m** of unclean lips, and H376
11 **m**, and the land be utterly desolate, H120
7:21 pass in that day, *that* a **m** shall nourish a H376
9:19 of the fire: no **m** shall spare his brother. H376
20 eat every **m** the flesh of his own arm: H376
10:13 down the inhabitants like a valiant *m*:
13:12 I will make a **m** more precious than fine H582

M

Isa 13:12 a **m** than the golden wedge of Ophir. H120
14 and as a sheep that no **m** taketh up: they
14 up: they shall every **m** turn to his own H376
14:16 *saying, Is* this the **m** that made the earth H376
17: 7 At that day shall a **m** look to his Maker, H120
19:14 as a drunken *m* staggereth in his vomit.
24:10 is shut up, that no **m** may come in.
28:20 For the bed is shorter than that *a m* can
29: 8 It shall even be as when an hungry *m*
8 or as when a thirsty **m** dreameth, and, H6771
21 That make a **m** an offender for a word, H120
31: 7 For in that day every **m** shall cast away H376
8 not of a mighty **m**; and the sword, not of H376
8 not of a mean **m**, shall devour him: but H120
32: 2 And a **m** shall be as an hiding place H376
33: 8 The highways lie waste, the wayfaring **m**
8 despised the cities, he regardeth no **m**. H582
35: 6 Then shall the lame *m* leap as an hart,
36: 6 whereon if a **m** lean, it will go into his H376
38:11 living: I shall behold **m** no more with the H120
41: 2 Who raised up the righteous *m* from the
28 For I beheld, and *there was* no **m**; even H376
42:13 The LORD shall go forth as a mighty **m**, H1368
13 up jealousy like a **m** of war: he shall cry, H376
44:13 the figure of a **m**, according to the beauty H376
13 of a **m**; that it may remain in the house. H120
15 Then shall it be for a **m** to burn: for he H120
45:12 I have made the earth, and created **m** H120
46:11 from the east, the **m** that executeth my H376
47: 3 and I will not meet *thee as* a **m**. H120
49: 7 One, to him whom **m** despiseth, to him H5315
50: 2 *was there* no **m**? when I called, *was there* H376
51:12 be afraid of a **m** *that* shall die, and of H582
12 son of **m** *which* shall be made *as* grass; H120
52:14 more than any **m**, and his form more H376
53: 3 He is despised and rejected of men; a **m** H376
55: 7 the unrighteous **m** his thoughts: and let H376
56: 2 Blessed *is* the **m** *that* doeth this, and the H582
2 and the son of **m** *that* layeth hold on H120
57: 1 The righteous perisheth, and no **m** H376
58: 5 a day for a **m** to afflict his soul? *is* H120
59:16 And he saw that *there was* no **m**, and H376
60:15 hated, so that no **m** went through *thee*, I
62: 5 For *as* a young **m** marrieth a virgin, *so* H970
65:20 days, nor an old **m** that hath not filled H2205
66: 2 LORD: but to this *m* will I look, *even* to
3 He that killeth an ox *is as if* he slew a **m**; H376
7 came, she was delivered of a **m** child.
Jer 2: 6 a land that no **m** passed through, and H376
6 passed through, and where no **m** dwelt? H120
3: 1 They say, If a **m** put away his wife, and H376
4:25 I beheld, and, lo, *there was* no **m**, and all H120
29 *be* forsaken, and not a **m** dwell therein. H376
5: 1 if ye can find a **m**, if there be *any* that H376
7: 5 between a **m** and his neighbour; H376
20 this place, upon **m**, and upon beast, and H120
8: 6 not aright: no **m** repented him of his H376
9:12 Who *is* the wise **m**, that may understand H376
23 Thus saith the LORD, Let not the wise *m*
23 let the mighty *m* glory in his might, let
23 let not the rich *m* glory in his riches:
10:14 Every **m** is brutish in *his* knowledge: H120
23 O LORD, I know that the way of **m** *is* not H120
23 not in **m** that walketh to direct his steps. H376
11: 3 Cursed *be* the **m** that obeyeth not the H376
12:11 desolate, because no **m** layeth *it* to heart. H376
15 them again, every **m** to his heritage, and H376
15 to his heritage, and every **m** to his land. H376
13:11 to the loins of a **m**, so have I caused to H376
14: 8 **m** *that* turneth aside to tarry for a night? H732
9 Why shouldest thou be as a **m** astonied, H376
9 as a mighty **m** *that* cannot save? yet H1368
15:10 hast borne me a **m** of strife and a man H376
10 of strife and a **m** of contention to the H376
16:20 Shall a **m** make gods unto himself, and H120
17: 5 Thus saith the LORD; Cursed *be* the **m** H1397
5 that trusteth in **m**, and maketh flesh his H120
7 Blessed *is* the **m** that trusteth in the H1397
10 even to give every **m** according to his H376
18:14 Will *a m* leave the snow of Lebanon
20:15 Cursed *be* the **m** who brought tidings to H376
15 father, saying, A **m** child is born unto H2145
16 And let that **m** be as the cities which the H376
21: 6 of this city, both **m** and beast: they shall H120
22: 8 they shall say every **m** to his neighbour, H376
28 *Is* this **m** Coniah a despised broken idol? H376
30 Thus saith the LORD, Write ye this **m** H376
30 this man childless, a **m** *that* shall not H1397
30 in his days: for no **m** of his seed shall H376

Jer 23: 9 I am like a drunken **m**, and like a man H376
9 man, and like a **m** whom wine hath H1397
27 they tell every **m** to his neighbour, as H376
34 I will even punish that **m** and his house. H376
26: 3 and turn every **m** from his evil way, that H376
11 saying, This **m** *is* worthy to die; for H376
16 to the prophets; This **m** *is* not worthy to H376
20 And there was also a **m** that prophesied H376
27: 5 I have made the earth, the **m** and the H120
29:26 the LORD, for every **m** *that is* mad, and H376
32 he shall not have a **m** to dwell among H376
30: 6 Ask ye now, and see whether a **m** doth H2145
6 do I see every **m** with his hands on his H1397
17 This *is* Zion, whom no **m** seeketh after.
31:22 the earth, A woman shall compass a **m**. H1397
27 the seed of **m**, and with the seed of beast. H120
30 iniquity: every **m** that eateth the sour H120
34 And they shall teach no more every **m** H376
34 and every **m** his brother, saying, H376
32:43 *is* desolate without **m** or beast; it is given H120
33:10 desolate without **m** and without beast, H120
10 are desolate, without **m**, and without H120
12 is desolate without **m** and without beast, H120
17 shall never want a **m** to sit upon the H376
18 the Levites want a **m** before me to offer H376
34: 9 That every **m** should let his manservant, H376
9 and every **m** his maidservant, *being* H376
14 let ye go every **m** his brother an Hebrew, H376
15 liberty every **m** to his neighbour; and H376
16 and caused every **m** his servant, and H376
16 his servant, and every **m** his handmaid, H376
17 brother, and every **m** to his neighbour: H376
35: 4 son of Igdaliah, a **m** of God, which *was* H376
15 ye now every **m** from his evil way, and H376
19 want a **m** to stand before me for ever. H376
36: 3 may return every **m** from his evil way; H376
19 and let no **m** know where ye be. H376
29 cause to cease from thence **m** and beast? H120
37:10 they rise up every **m** in his tent, and H376
38: 4 thee, let this **m** be put to death: for H376
4 unto them: for this **m** seeketh not the H376
24 Jeremiah, Let no **m** know of these words, H376
40:15 of Nethaniah, and no **m** shall know *it*: H376
41: 4 had slain Gedaliah, and no **m** knew *it*, H376
44: 2 a desolation, and no **m** dwelleth therein,
7 to cut off from you **m** and woman, child H376
26 in the mouth of any **m** of Judah in all the H376
46: 6 nor the mighty **m** escape; they shall H1368
12 land: for the mighty **m** hath stumbled H1368
49: 5 driven out every **m** right forth; and none H376
18 saith the LORD, no **m** shall abide there, H376
18 there, neither shall a son of **m** dwell in it. H120
19 who *is* a chosen *m*, *that* I may appoint
33 there shall no **m** abide there, nor *any* H376
33 abide there, nor *any* son of **m** dwell in it. H120
50: 3 they shall depart, both **m** and beast. H120
9 expert **m**; none shall return in vain.
40 LORD; *so* shall no **m** abide there, neither H376
40 neither shall any son of **m** dwell therein. H120
42 *one* put in array, like a **m** to the battle, H376
44 who *is* a chosen *m*, *that* I may appoint
51: 6 and deliver every **m** his soul: be not cut H376
17 Every **m** is brutish by *his* knowledge; H120
22 With thee also will I break in pieces **m** H376
22 in pieces the young **m** and the maid; H970
43 a land wherein no **m** dwelleth, neither H376
43 neither doth *any* son of **m** pass thereby. H120
45 and deliver ye every **m** his soul from the H376
62 in it, neither **m** nor beast, but that it H120
Lam 3: 1 I *am* the **m** *that* hath seen affliction by H1397
26 *It is* good that *a m* should both hope and
27 *It is* good for a **m** that he bear the yoke H1397
35 To turn aside the right of a **m** before H1397
36 To subvert a **m** in his cause, the Lord H120
39 Wherefore doth a living **m** complain, a H120
39 a **m** for the punishment of his sins? H1397
4: 4 bread, *and* no **m** breaketh *it* unto them.
Ezk 1: 5 appearance; they had the likeness of a **m**. H120
8 And *they had* the hands of a **m** under H120
10 four had the face of a **m**, and the face of a H120
26 as the appearance of a **m** above upon it. H120
2: 1 And he said unto me, Son of **m**, stand H120
3 And he said unto me, Son of **m**, I send H120
6 And thou, son of **m**, be not afraid of H120
8 But thou, son of **m**, hear what I say unto H120
3: 1 Moreover he said unto me, Son of **m**, eat H120
3 And he said unto me, Son of **m**, cause thy H120
4 And he said unto me, Son of **m**, go, get H120
10 Moreover he said unto me, Son of **m**, all H120

Ezk 3:17 Son of **m**, I have made thee a watchman H120
18 life; the same wicked *m* shall die in his
20 Again, When a righteous *m* doth turn
21 warn the righteous *m*, that the righteous
25 But thou, O son of **m**, behold, they shall H120
4: 1 Thou also, son of **m**, take thee a tile, and H120
12 dung that cometh out of **m**, in their sight. H120
16 Moreover he said unto me, Son of **m**, H120
5: 1 And thou, son of **m**, take thee a sharp H120
6: 2 Son of **m**, set thy face toward the H120
7: 2 Also, thou son of **m**, thus saith the Lord H120
8: 5 Then said he unto me, Son of **m**, lift up H120
6 He said furthermore unto me, Son of **m**, H120
8 Then said he unto me, Son of **m**, dig now H120
11 with every **m** his censer in his hand; H376
12 Then said he unto me, Son of **m**, hast H120
12 in the dark, every **m** in the chambers of H376
15 seen *this*, O son of **m**? turn thee yet again, H120
17 seen *this*, O son of **m**? Is it a light thing to H120
9: 1 near, even every **m** *with* his destroying H376
2 north, and every **m** a slaughter weapon H376
2 in his hand; and one **m** among them *was* H376
3 he called to the **m** clothed with linen, H376
6 come not near any **m** upon whom *is* the H376
11 And, behold, the **m** clothed with linen, H376
10: 2 And he spake unto the **m** clothed with H376
3 the house, when the **m** went in; and the H376
6 commanded the **m** clothed with linen, H376
14 *was* the face of a **m**, and the third the H120
21 the hands of a **m** *was* under their wings. H120
11: 2 Then said he unto me, Son of **m**, these H120
4 against them, prophesy, O son of **m**. H120
15 Son of **m**, thy brethren, *even* thy H120
12: 2 Son of **m**, thou dwellest in the midst of a H120
3 Therefore, thou son of **m**, prepare thee H120
9 Son of **m**, hath not the house of Israel, H120
18 Son of **m**, eat thy bread with quaking, H120
22 Son of **m**, what *is* that proverb *that* ye H120
27 Son of **m**, behold, *they of* the house of H120
13: 2 Son of **m**, prophesy against the prophets H120
17 Likewise, thou son of **m**, set thy face H120
14: 3 Son of **m**, these men have set up their H120
4 the Lord GOD; Every **m** of the house of H376
8 And I will set my face against that **m**, H376
13 Son of **m**, when the land sinneth against H120
13 it, and will cut off **m** and beast from it: H120
15 be desolate, that no **m** may pass through
17 so that I cut off **m** and beast from it: H120
19 in blood, to cut off from it **m** and beast: H120
21 to cut off from it **m** and beast? H120
15: 2 Son of **m**, What is the vine tree more H120
16: 2 Son of **m**, cause Jerusalem to know her H120
17: 2 Son of **m**, put forth a riddle, and speak a H120
18: 5 But if a **m** be just, and do that which is H376
8 true judgment between **m** and man, H376
8 true judgment between man and **m**, H376
24 that the wicked *m* doeth, shall he live?
26 When a righteous *m* turneth away from
27 Again, when the wicked *m* turneth away
20: 3 Son of **m**, speak unto the elders of Israel, H120
4 Wilt thou judge them, son of **m**, wilt thou H120
7 ye away every **m** the abominations of H376
8 me: they did not every **m** cast away the H376
11 *if* a **m** do, he shall even live in them. H120
13 which *if* a **m** do, he shall even live H120
21 them, which *if* a **m** do, he shall even live H120
27 Therefore, son of **m**, speak unto the H120
46 Son of **m**, set thy face toward the south, H120
21: 2 Son of **m**, set thy face toward Jerusalem, H120
6 Sigh therefore, thou son of **m**, with the H120
9 Son of **m**, prophesy, and say, Thus saith H120
12 Cry and howl, son of **m**: for it shall be H120
14 Thou therefore, son of **m**, prophesy, and H120
19 Also, thou son of **m**, appoint thee two H120
28 And thou, son of **m**, prophesy and say, H120
22: 2 Now, thou son of **m**, wilt thou judge, wilt H120
18 Son of **m**, the house of Israel is to me H120
24 Son of **m**, say unto her, Thou *art* the land H120
30 And I sought for a **m** among them, that H376
23: 2 Son of **m**, there were two women, the H120
36 unto me; Son of **m**, wilt thou judge H120
24: 2 Son of **m**, write thee the name of the day, H120
16 Son of **m**, behold, I take away from thee H120
25 Also, thou son of **m**, *shall it* not *be* in the H120
25: 2 Son of **m**, set thy face against the H120
13 and will cut off **m** and beast from it; and H120
26: 2 Son of **m**, because that Tyrus hath said H120
27: 2 Now, thou son of **m**, take up a H120
28: 2 Son of **m**, say unto the prince of Tyrus, H120

Ezk 28: 2 the seas; yet thou *art* a **m**, and not God, H120
9 but thou *shalt be* a **m**, and no God, in the H120
12 Son of **m**, take up a lamentation upon H120
21 Son of **m**, set thy face against Zidon, and H120
29: 2 Son of **m**, set thy face against Pharaoh H120
8 thee, and cut off **m** and beast out of thee. H120
11 No foot of **m** shall pass through it, nor H120
18 Son of **m**, Nebuchadrezzar king of H120
30: 2 Son of **m**, prophesy and say, Thus saith H120
21 Son of **m**, I have broken the arm of H120
24 the groanings of a deadly wounded *m*.
31: 2 Son of **m**, speak unto Pharaoh king of H120
32: 2 Son of **m**, take up a lamentation for H120
10 **m** for his own life, in the day of thy fall. H376
13 shall the foot of **m** trouble them any H120
18 Son of **m**, wail for the multitude of Egypt, H120
33: 2 Son of **m**, speak to the children of thy H120
2 of the land take a **m** of their coasts, and H376
7 So thou, O son of **m**, I have set thee a H120
8 When I say unto the wicked, O wicked *m*,
8 his way, that wicked *m* shall die in his
10 Therefore, O thou son of **m**, speak unto H120
12 Therefore, thou son of **m**, say unto the H120
24 Son of **m**, they that inhabit those wastes H120
30 Also, thou son of **m**, the children of thy H120
34: 2 Son of **m**, prophesy against the H120
35: 2 Son of **m**, set thy face against mount Seir, H120
36: 1 Also, thou son of **m**, prophesy unto the H120
11 And I will multiply upon you **m** and H120
17 Son of **m**, when the house of Israel dwelt H120
37: 3 And he said unto me, Son of **m**, can these H120
9 prophesy, son of **m**, and say to the wind, H120
11 Then he said unto me, Son of **m**, these H120
16 Moreover, thou son of **m**, take thee one H120
38: 2 Son of **m**, set thy face against Gog, the H120
14 Therefore, son of **m**, prophesy and say H120
39: 1 Therefore, thou son of **m**, prophesy H120
17 And, thou son of **m**, thus saith the Lord H120
40: 3 *there was* a **m**, whose appearance *was* H376
4 And the **m** said unto me, Son of man, H376
4 And the man said unto me, Son of **m**, H120
41:19 So that the face of a **m** *was* toward the H120
43: 6 out of the house; and the **m** stood by me. H376
7 And he said unto me, Son of **m**, the place H120
10 Thou son of **m**, shew the house to the H120
18 And he said unto me, Son of **m**, thus H120
44: 2 be opened, and no **m** shall enter in by it; H376
5 And the LORD said unto me, Son of **m**, H120
46:18 scattered every **m** from his possession. H376
47: 3 And when the **m** that had the line in his H376
6 And he said unto me, Son of **m**, hast thou H120
20 the border, till a **m** come over against
Dan 2:10 There is not a **m** upon the earth that H606
25 I have found a **m** of the captives of H1400
48 Then the king made Daniel a great **m**, H7236
3:10 a decree, that every **m** that shall hear the H606
5:11 There is a **m** in thy kingdom, in whom H1400
6: 7 of any God or **m** for thirty days, save H606
12 a decree, that every **m** that shall ask *a* H606
12 of any God or **m** within thirty days, save H606
7: 4 as a **m**, and a man's heart was given to it. H606
8 of **m**, and a mouth speaking great things. H606
13 *one* like the Son of **m** came with the H606
8:15 before me as the appearance of a **m**. H1397
16 make this *m* to understand the vision.
17 O son of **m**: for at the time of the H120
9:21 in prayer, even the **m** Gabriel, whom I H376
10: 5 and behold a certain **m** clothed in linen, H376
11 And he said unto me, O Daniel, a **m** H376
18 of a **m**, and he strengthened me, H120
19 And said, O **m** greatly beloved, fear not: H376
12: 6 And *one* said to the **m** clothed in linen, H376
7 And I heard the **m** clothed in linen, H376
Hos 3: 3 for *another* **m**: so *will* I also *be* for thee. H376
4: 4 Yet let no **m** strive, nor reprove another: H376
6: 9 And as troops of robbers wait for a **m**, *so* H376
9: 7 a fool, the spiritual **m** *is* mad, for the H376
12 *shall* not *be* a **m** *left*: yea, woe also to H120
11: 4 I drew them with cords of a **m**, with H120
9 I *am* God, and not **m**; the Holy One in the H376
Am 2: 7 of the meek: and a **m** and his father will H376
4:13 declareth unto **m** what *is* his thought, H120
5:19 As if a **m** did flee from a lion, and a bear H376
Jna 1: 5 and cried every **m** unto his god, and cast H376
3: 7 saying, Let neither **m** nor beast, herd H120
8 But let **m** and beast be covered with H120
Mic 2: 2 so they oppress a **m** and his house, H1397
2 his house, even a **m** and his heritage. H376
11 If a **m** walking in the spirit and H376

Mic 4: 4 But they shall sit every **m** under his vine H376
5: 5 And this *m* shall be the peace, when the
7 for **m**, nor waiteth for the sons of men. H376
6: 8 He hath shewed thee, O **m**, what *is* good; H120
9 the city, and *the* **m** *of* wisdom shall see
7: 2 The good *m* is perished out of the earth:
2 they hunt every **m** his brother with a net. H376
3 reward; and the great *m*, he uttereth his
Nah 3:18 mountains, and no **m** gathereth *them*.
Hab 1:13 *the* **m** *that is* more righteous than he?
2: 5 *he is* a proud **m**, neither keepeth at H1397
Zep 1: 3 I will consume **m** and beast; I will H120
3 off **m** from off the land, saith the LORD. H120
14 the mighty **m** shall cry there bitterly. H1368
3: 6 is no **m**, that there is none inhabitant. H376
Hag 1: 9 and ye run every **m** unto his own house. H376
Zec 1: 8 I saw by night, and behold a **m** riding H376
10 And the **m** that stood among the myrtle H376
21 Judah, so that no **m** did lift up his head: H376
2: 1 a **m** with a measuring line in his hand. H376
4 to this young **m**, saying, Jerusalem shall H5288
3:10 hosts, shall ye call every **m** his neighbour H376
4: 1 as a **m** that is wakened out of his sleep, H376
6:12 saying, Behold the **m** whose name *is* The H376
7: 9 and compassions every **m** to his brother: H376
14 after them, that no **m** passed through
8: 4 **m** with his staff in his hand for very age. H376
10 was no hire for **m**, nor any hire for beast; H120
16 do; Speak ye every **m** the truth to his H376
9: 1 when the eyes of **m**, as of all the tribes of H120
13 made thee as the sword of a mighty **m**. H1368
10: 7 be like a mighty *m*, and their heart shall
12: 1 and formeth the spirit of **m** within him. H120
13: 5 husbandman; for **m** taught me to keep H120
7 and against the **m** *that is* my fellow, H1397
Mal 2:10 every **m** against his brother, H376
12 The LORD will cut off the **m** that doeth H376
3: 8 Will a **m** rob God? Yet ye have robbed H120
17 **m** spareth his own son that serveth him. H376
Mt 1:19 being a just *m*, and not willing to make
4: 4 and said, It is written, M shall not live by G444
5:40 And if any **m** will sue thee at the law,
6:24 No **m** can serve two masters: for either G3762
7: 9 Or what **m** is there of you, whom if his G444
24 **m**, which built his house upon a rock: G435
26 **m**, which built his house upon the sand: G435
8: 4 See thou tell no **m**; but go thy way, shew G3367
9 For I am a **m** under authority, having G444
9 me: and I say to this *m*, Go, and he goeth;
20 Son of **m** hath not where to lay *his* head. G444
27 What manner of **m** is this, that even G4217
28 so that no **m** might pass by that way. G5100
9: 2 And, behold, they brought to him a **m**
3 within themselves, This *m* blasphemeth.
6 But that ye may know that the Son of **m** G444
9 thence, he saw a **m**, named Matthew, G444
16 No **m** putteth a piece of new cloth unto G3762
30 them, saying, See *that* no **m** know *it*. G3367
32 to him a dumb **m** possessed with a devil. G444
10:23 cities of Israel, till the Son of **m** be come. G444
35 For I am come to set a **m** at variance G444
41 a righteous **m** in the name of a G1342
41 name of a righteous **m** shall receive a G1342
11: 8 But what went ye out for to see? A **m** G444
19 The Son of **m** came eating and drinking, G444
19 they say, Behold a **m** gluttonous, and a G444
27 Father: and no **m** knoweth the Son, but G3762
27 knoweth any **m** the Father, save the G5100
12: 8 For the Son of **m** is Lord even of the G444
10 And, behold, there was a **m** which had G444
11 And he said unto them, What **m** shall G444
12 How much then is a **m** better than a G444
13 Then saith he to the **m**, Stretch forth G444
19 any **m** hear his voice in the streets. G5100
29 **m**? and then he will spoil his house. G2478
32 against the Son of **m**, it shall be forgiven G444
35 A good **m** out of the good treasure of the G444
35 good things: and an evil **m** out of the evil G444
40 so shall the Son of **m** be three days and G444
43 is gone out of a **m**, he walketh through G444
45 the last *state* of that **m** is worse than the G444
13:24 a **m** which sowed good seed in his field: G444
31 which a **m** took, and sowed in his field: G444
37 soweth the good seed is the Son of **m**; G444
41 The Son of **m** shall send forth his angels, G444
44 field; the which when a **m** hath found, he G444
45 a merchant **m**, seeking goodly pearls: G444
52 is like unto a **m** *that is* an householder, G444
54 **m** this wisdom, and *these* mighty works?

Mt 13:56 then hath this *m* all these things?
15:11 the mouth defileth a **m**; but that which G444
11 out of the mouth, this defileth a **m**. G444
18 from the heart; and they defile the **m**. G444
20 These are *the things* which defile a **m**: G444
20 with unwashen hands defileth not a **m**. G444
16:13 do men say that I the Son of **m** am? G444
20 tell no **m** that he was Jesus the Christ. G3367
24 disciples, If any *m* will come after me,
26 For what is a **m** profited, if he shall gain G444
26 shall a **m** give in exchange for his soul? G444
27 For the Son of **m** shall come in the glory G444
27 reward every **m** according to his works. G1538
28 see the Son of **m** coming in his kingdom. G444
17: 8 eyes, they saw no **m**, save Jesus only. G3762
9 the vision to no **m**, until the Son of man G3367
9 Son of **m** be risen again from the dead. G444
12 shall also the Son of **m** suffer of them. G444
14 **m**, kneeling down to him, and saying, G444
22 them, The Son of **m** shall be betrayed G444
18: 7 to that **m** by whom the offence cometh! G444
11 For the Son of **m** is come to save that G444
12 How think ye? if a **m** have an hundred G5100
17 thee as an heathen **m** and a publican. G1482
19: 3 a **m** to put away his wife for every cause? G444
5 And said, For this cause shall a **m** leave G444
6 joined together, let not **m** put asunder. G444
10 If the case of the **m** be so with *his* wife, G444
20 The young **m** saith unto him, All these G3495
22 But when the young **m** heard that G3495
23 you, That a rich **m** shall hardly enter G4145
24 **m** to enter into the kingdom of God. G4145
28 when the Son of **m** shall sit in the throne G444
20: 1 is like unto a **m** *that is* an householder, G444
7 They say unto him, Because no **m** hath G3762
9 hour, they received every **m** a penny. G303
10 they likewise received every **m** a penny. G303
18 and the Son of **m** shall be betrayed unto G444
28 Even as the Son of **m** came not to be G444
21: 3 And if any *m* say ought unto you, ye
28 But what think ye? A *certain* **m** had two G444
22:11 **m** which had not on a wedding garment: G444
16 thou for any *m*: for thou regardest not G3762
24 Saying, Master, Moses said, If a **m** die, G5100
46 And no **m** was able to answer him a G3762
46 neither durst any *m* from that day forth
23: 9 And call no *m* your father upon the
24: 4 Take heed that no **m** deceive you. G5100
23 Then if any **m** shall say unto you, Lo, G5100
27 shall also the coming of the Son of **m** be. G444
30 sign of the Son of **m** in heaven: and then G444
30 see the Son of **m** coming in the clouds G444
36 hour knoweth no *m*, no, not the angels G3762
37 shall also the coming of the Son of **m** be. G444
39 shall also the coming of the Son of **m** be. G444
44 as ye think not the Son of **m** cometh. G444
25:13 the hour wherein the Son of **m** cometh. G444
14 For *the kingdom of heaven is* as a **m** G444
15 one; to every **m** according to his several G1538
24 thou art an hard **m**, reaping where thou G444
31 When the Son of **m** shall come in his G444
26: 2 the Son of **m** is betrayed to be crucified. G444
18 the city to such a **m**, and say unto him, G1170
24 The Son of **m** goeth as it is written of G444
24 but woe unto that **m** by whom the Son of G444
24 by whom the Son of **m** is betrayed! it had G444
24 good for that **m** if he had not been born. G846
45 **m** is betrayed into the hands of sinners. G444
64 ye see the Son of **m** sitting on the right G444
72 with an oath, I do not know the **m**. G444
74 the **m**. And immediately the cock crew. G444
27:19 do with that just **m**: for I have suffered G1342
32 And as they came out, they found a **m** of G444
47 heard *that*, said, This *m* calleth for Elias.
57 there came a rich **m** of Arimathaea, G444
Mk 1:23 And there was in their synagogue a **m** G444
44 nothing to any **m**: but go thy way, shew G3367
2: 7 Why doth this *m* thus speak
10 But that ye may know that the Son of **m** G444
21 No **m** also seweth a piece of new cloth G3762
22 And no **m** putteth new wine into old G3762
27 for **m**, and not man for the sabbath: G444
27 for man, and not **m** for the sabbath: G444
28 Therefore the Son of **m** is Lord also of G444
3: 1 a **m** there which had a withered hand. G444
3 And he saith unto the **m** which had the G444
5 he saith unto the **m**, Stretch forth thine G444
27 No **m** can enter into a strong man's G3762
27 **m**; and then he will spoil his house. G2478

Mk 4:23 If any **m** have ears to hear, let him G1536
26 if a **m** should cast seed into the ground; G444
41 What manner of **m** is this, that even G5101
5: 2 of the tombs a **m** with an unclean spirit, G444
3 **m** could bind him, no, not with chains: G3762
4 in pieces: neither could any *m* tame him.
8 For he said unto him, Come out of the **m**, G444
37 And he suffered no **m** to follow him, G3762
43 And he charged them straitly that no **m** G3367
6: 2 whence hath this *m* these things? and
20 that he was a just **m** and an holy, and G435
7:11 But ye say, If a **m** shall say to his father G444
15 There is nothing from without a **m**, that G444
15 of him, those are they that defile the **m**. G444
16 If any **m** have ears to hear, let him G1536
18 entereth into the **m**, *it* cannot defile him; G444
20 out of the **m**, that defileth the man. G444
20 out of the man, that defileth the **m**. G444
23 come from within, and defile the **m**. G444
24 no **m** know *it*: but he could not be hid. G3762
36 they should tell no **m**: but the more he G3367
8: 4 whence can a **m** satisfy these *men* with G5100
22 they bring a blind **m** unto him, and G5185
23 And he took the blind **m** by the hand, G5185
25 was restored, and saw every **m** clearly. G537
30 them that they should tell no **m** of him. G3367
31 that the Son of **m** must suffer many G444
36 For what shall it profit a **m**, if he shall G444
37 Or what shall a **m** give in exchange for G444
38 shall the Son of **m** be ashamed, when he G444
9: 8 they saw no **m** any more, save Jesus G3762
9 should tell no **m** what things they had G3367
9 the Son of **m** were risen from the dead. G444
12 of the Son of **m**, that he must suffer G444
30 would not that any **m** should know *it*. G5100
31 them, The Son of **m** is delivered into the G444
35 unto them, If any **m** desire to be first, G1536
39 not: for there is no **m** which shall do a G3762
10: 2 a **m** to put away *his* wife? tempting him. G435
7 For this cause shall a **m** leave his father G444
9 joined together, let not **m** put asunder. G444
25 **m** to enter into the kingdom of God. G4145
29 you, There is no **m** that hath left house, G3762
33 and the Son of **m** shall be delivered unto G444
45 For even the Son of **m** came not to be G444
49 they call the blind **m**, saying unto him, G5185
51 thee? The blind **m** said unto him, Lord, G5185
11: 2 never **m** sat; loose him, and bring *him*. G444
3 And if any **m** say unto you, Why do ye G5100
14 and said unto it, No **m** eat fruit of thee G3367
16 And would not suffer that any **m** G5100
12: 1 A *certain* **m** planted a vineyard, G444
14 and carest for no **m**: for thou regardest G3762
34 of God. And no **m** after that durst ask G3762
13: 5 say, Take heed lest any **m** deceive you:
21 And then if any **m** shall say to you, Lo, G5100
26 And then shall they see the Son of **m** G444
32 hour knoweth no **m**, no, not the angels G3762
34 *For the Son of m is* as a man taking a far
34 *For the Son of man is* as a **m** taking a far G444
34 servants, and to every **m** his work, and G1538
14:13 shall meet you a **m** bearing a pitcher of G444
21 The Son of **m** indeed goeth, as it is G444
21 but woe to that **m** by whom the Son of G444
21 by whom the Son of **m** is betrayed! good G444
21 it for that **m** if he had never been born. G444
41 **m** is betrayed into the hands of sinners. G444
51 a certain young **m**, having a linen cloth G3495
62 shall see the Son of **m** sitting on the right G444
71 I know not this **m** of whom ye speak. G444
15:24 upon them, what every **m** should take. G5101
39 he said, Truly this **m** was the Son of God. G444
16: 5 they saw a young **m** sitting on the right G3495
8 thing to any *m*; for they were afraid. G3762
Lk 1:18 **m**, and my wife well stricken in years. G4246
27 To a virgin espoused to a **m** whose name G435
34 How shall this be, seeing I know not a **m**? G435
2:25 And, behold, there was a **m** in G444
25 and the same **m** *was* just and devout, G444
52 stature, and in favour with God and **m**. G444
3:14 Do violence to no **m**, neither accuse *any* G3367
4: 4 It is written, That **m** shall not live by G444
33 And in the synagogue there was a **m**, G444
5: 8 from me; for I am a sinful **m**, O Lord. G435
12 city, behold a **m** full of leprosy: who G435
14 And he charged him to tell no **m**: but G3367
18 And, behold, men brought in a bed a **m** G444
20 unto him, **M**, thy sins are forgiven thee. G444
24 But that ye may know that the Son of **m** G444

Lk 5:36 unto them; No **m** putteth a piece of a G3762
37 And no **m** putteth new wine into old G3762
39 No **m** also having drunk old *wine* G3762
6: 5 the Son of **m** is Lord also of the sabbath. G444
6 was a **m** whose right hand was withered. G444
8 and said to the **m** which had the G444
10 all, he said unto the **m**, Stretch forth thy G444
30 Give to every **m** that asketh of thee; G3956
45 A good **m** out of the good treasure of his G444
45 is good; and an evil **m** out of the evil G444
48 He is like a **m** which built an house, and G444
49 and doeth not, is like a **m** that without a G444
7: 8 For I also am a **m** set under authority, G444
12 there was a dead **m** carried out, the G2348
14 said, Young **m**, I say unto thee, Arise. G3495
25 But what went ye out for to see? A **m** G444
34 The Son of **m** is come eating and G444
34 a gluttonous **m**, and a winebibber, a G444
39 saying, This **m**, if he were a prophet, G3778
8:16 No **m**, when he hath lighted a candle, G3762
25 What manner of **m** is this! for he G5101
27 of the city a certain **m**, which had devils G435
29 to come out of the **m**. For oftentimes it G444
33 Then went the devils out of the **m**, and G444
35 and found the **m**, out of whom the devils G444
38 Now the **m** out of whom the devils were G435
41 And, behold, there came a **m** named G435
51 he suffered no **m** to go in, save Peter, G3756
56 they should tell no **m** what was done. G3367
9:21 *them* to tell no **m** that thing; G3367
22 Saying, The Son of **m** must suffer many G444
23 And he said to *them* all, If any *m* will
25 For what is a **m** advantaged, if he gain G444
26 shall the Son of **m** be ashamed, when he G444
36 close, and told no **m** in those days any G3762
38 And, behold, a **m** of the company cried G435
44 ears: for the Son of **m** shall be delivered G444
56 For the Son of **m** is not come to destroy G444
57 in the way, a certain *m* said unto him,
58 Son of **m** hath not where to lay *his* head. G444
62 And Jesus said unto him, No **m**, having G3762
10: 4 nor shoes: and salute no **m** by the way. G3367
22 Father: and no **m** knoweth who the Son G3762
30 And Jesus answering said, A certain *m* G444
11:21 When a strong **m** armed keepeth his G2478
24 is gone out of a **m**, he walketh through G444
26 *state* of that **m** is worse than the first. G444
30 also the Son of **m** be to this generation. G444
33 No **m**, when he hath lighted a candle, G3762
12: 8 **m** also confess before the angels of God: G444
10 against the Son of **m**, it shall be forgiven G444
14 And he said unto him, **M**, who made me G444
16 certain rich **m** brought forth plentifully: G444
40 **m** cometh at an hour when ye think not. G444
13: 6 He spake also this parable; A certain *m*
19 seed, which a **m** took, and cast into his G444
14: 2 And, behold, there was a certain **m** G444
8 When thou art bidden of any *m* to a
8 **m** than thou be bidden of him; G1784
9 say to thee, Give this **m** place; and thou G5129
16 Then said he unto him, A certain **m** G444
26 If any **m** come to me, and hate not his
30 Saying, This **m** began to build, and was G444
15: 2 saying, This **m** receiveth sinners, and G3778
4 What **m** of you, having an hundred G444
11 And he said, A certain **m** had two sons: G444
16 did eat: and no **m** gave unto him. G3762
16: 1 There was a certain rich **m**, which had a G444
16 preached, and every **m** presseth into it. G3956
19 There was a certain rich **m**, which was G444
22 the rich **m** also died, and was buried; G4145
17:22 of the Son of **m**, and ye shall not see *it*. G444
24 so shall also the Son of **m** be in his day. G444
26 it be also in the days of the Son of **m**. G444
30 in the day when the Son of **m** is revealed. G444
18: 2 feared not God, neither regarded **m**: G444
4 Though I fear not God, nor regard **m**; G444
8 when the Son of **m** cometh, shall he find G444
14 I tell you, this **m** went down to his G3778
25 **m** to enter into the kingdom of God. G4145
29 you, There is no **m** that hath left house, G3762
31 the Son of **m** shall be accomplished. G444
35 blind **m** sat by the way side begging: G5185
19: 2 And, behold, *there was* a **m** named G435
7 to be guest with a **m** that is a sinner. G435
8 thing from any **m** by false accusation, G5100
10 For the Son of **m** is come to seek and to G444
14 We will not have this *m* to reign over us.
15 much every **m** had gained by trading. G5101

Lk 19:21 art an austere **m**: thou takest up that G444
22 I was an austere **m**, taking up that I laid G444
30 **m** sat: loose him, and bring *him hither*. G444
31 And if any **m** ask you, Why do ye loose G5100
20: 9 parable; A certain **m** planted a vineyard, G444
21:27 And then shall they see the Son of **m** G444
36 to pass, and to stand before the Son of **m**. G444
22:10 city, there shall a **m** meet you, bearing a G444
22 And truly the Son of **m** goeth, as it was G444
22 unto that **m** by whom he is betrayed! G444
48 betrayest thou the Son of **m** with a kiss? G444
56 and said, This **m** was also with him. G3778
58 of them. And Peter said, **M**, I am not. G444
60 And Peter said, **M**, I know not what thou G444
69 Hereafter shall the Son of **m** sit on the G444
23: 4 *to* the people, I find no fault in this **m**. G444
6 asked whether the **m** were a Galilaean. G444
14 Said unto them, Ye have brought this **m** G444
14 no fault in this **m** touching those things G444
18 this *m*, and release unto us Barabbas:
41 but this **m** hath done nothing amiss. G3778
47 saying, Certainly this was a righteous **m**. G444
50 And, behold, *there was* a **m** named G435
50 *and he was* a good **m**, and a just: G435
52 This *m* went unto Pilate, and begged the
53 wherein never **m** before was laid. G3756
24: 7 Saying, The Son of **m** must be delivered G444
Jn 1: 6 There was a **m** sent from God, whose G444
9 every **m** that cometh into the world. G444
13 the flesh, nor of the will of **m**, but of God. G435
18 No **m** hath seen God at any time; the G3762
30 After me cometh a **m** which is preferred G435
51 and descending upon the Son of **m**. G444
2:10 And saith unto him, Every **m** at the G444
25 of **m**: for he knew what was in man. G444
25 of man: for he knew what was in **m**. G444
3: 1 There was a **m** of the Pharisees, named G444
2 come from God: for no **m** can do these G3762
3 thee, Except a **m** be born again, he G5100
4 him, How can a **m** be born when he is G444
5 thee, Except a **m** be born of water and G5100
13 And no **m** hath ascended up to heaven, G3762
13 *even* the Son of **m** which is in heaven. G444
14 even so must the Son of **m** be lifted up: G444
27 John answered and said, A **m** can G444
32 and no **m** receiveth his testimony. G3762
4:27 woman: yet no **m** said, What seekest G3762
29 Come, see a **m**, which told me all things G444
33 Hath any **m** brought him *ought* to eat?
50 son liveth. And the **m** believed the word G444
5: 5 And a certain **m** was there, which had G444
7 The impotent **m** answered him, Sir, I G770
7 him, Sir, I have no **m**, when the water is G444
9 And immediately the **m** was made G444
12 Then asked they him, What **m** is that G444
15 The **m** departed, and told the Jews that it G444
22 For the Father judgeth no **m**, but hath G3762
27 also, because he is the Son of **m**. G444
34 But I receive not testimony from **m**: but G444
6:27 which the Son of **m** shall give unto you: G444
44 No **m** can come to me, except the G3762
45 of God. Every **m** therefore that hath G3956
46 Not that any **m** hath seen the Father, G5100
50 that a **m** may eat thereof, and not die. G5100
51 heaven: if any **m** eat of this bread, he G5100
52 How can this **m** give us *his* flesh to eat? G3778
53 the flesh of the Son of **m**, and drink his G444
62 *What* and if ye shall see the Son of **m** G444
65 unto you, that no **m** can come unto me, G3762
7: 4 For *there is* no **m** *that* doeth any thing G3762
12 said, He is a good **m**: others said, Nay; G18
13 Howbeit no **m** spake openly of him for G3762
15 this **m** letters, having never learned? G3778
17 If any **m** will do his will, he shall know G5100
22 ye on the sabbath day circumcise a **m**. G444
23 If a **m** on the sabbath day receive G444
23 **m** every whit whole on the sabbath day? G444
27 Howbeit we know this **m** whence he is: G5126
27 cometh, no **m** knoweth whence he is. G3762
30 Then they sought to take him: but no **m** G3762
31 than these which this *m* hath done?
37 saying, If any **m** thirst, let him come G5100
44 him; but no **m** laid hands on him. G3762
46 The officers answered, Never **m** spake G444
46 answered, Never man spake like this **m**. G444
51 Doth our law judge *any* **m**, before it hear G444
53 And every **m** went unto his own house. G1538
8:10 accusers? hath no **m** condemned thee? G3762
11 She said, No **m**, Lord. And Jesus said G3762

Jn 8:15 Ye judge after the flesh; I judge no **m**. G3762
20 temple: and no **m** laid hands on him; G3762
28 lifted up the Son of **m**, then shall ye know G444
33 in bondage to any **m**: how sayest thou, G3762
40 But now ye seek to kill me, a **m** that hath G444
51 Verily, verily, I say unto you, If a **m** G5100
52 thou sayest, If a **m** keep my saying, he G5100
9: 1 And as *Jesus* passed by, he saw a **m** G444
2 who did sin, this **m**, or his parents, that G3778
3 Jesus answered, Neither hath this **m** G3778
4 night cometh, when no **m** can work. G3762
6 the eyes of the blind **m** with the clay, G5185
11 He answered and said, A **m** that is called G444
16 Pharisees, This **m** is not of God, because G444
16 said, How can a **m** that is a sinner do G444
17 They say unto the blind **m** again, What G5185
22 that if any **m** did confess that he G5100
24 Then again called they the **m** that was G444
24 praise: we know that this **m** is a sinner. G444
30 The **m** answered and said unto them, G444
31 sinners: but if any **m** be a worshipper G5100
32 heard that any **m** opened the eyes of G5100
33 If this **m** were not of God, he could do G3778
10: 9 I am the door: by me if any **m** enter in, G5100
18 No **m** taketh it from me, but I lay it G3762
28 shall any ***m*** pluck them out of my hand.
29 than all; and no ***m*** is able to pluck *them*
33 that thou, being a **m**, makest thyself God. G444
41 that John spake of this **m** were true. G5127
11: 1 Now a certain ***m*** was sick, *named*
9 in the day? If any **m** walk in the day, he G5100
10 But if a **m** walk in the night, he G5100
37 Could not this **m**, which opened the G3778
37 that even this **m** should not have died? G3778
47 do we? for this **m** doeth many miracles. G444
50 for us, that one **m** should die for the G444
57 that, if any **m** knew where he were, G5100
12:23 that the Son of **m** should be glorified. G444
26 If any **m** serve me, let him follow me; G5100
26 servant be: if any **m** serve me, him will G5100
34 thou, The Son of **m** must be lifted up? G444
34 must be lifted up? who is this Son of **m**? G444
47 And if any **m** hear my words, and G5100
13:28 Now no **m** at the table knew for what G3762
31 **m** glorified, and God is glorified in him. G444
14: 6 **m** cometh unto the Father, but by me. G3762
23 unto him, If a **m** love me, he will keep G5100
15: 6 If a **m** abide not in me, he is cast forth G5100
13 Greater love hath no **m** than this, that a G3762
13 a **m** lay down his life for his friends. G5100
24 which none other **m** did, they had not G243
16:21 for joy that a **m** is born into the world. G444
22 and your joy no **m** taketh from you. G3762
30 not that any **m** should ask thee: by G5100
32 be scattered, every **m** to his own, and G1538
18:14 that one **m** should die for the people. G444
29 What accusation bring ye against this **m**? G444
31 not lawful for us to put any **m** to death: G3762
40 saying, Not this **m**, but Barabbas. Now G5126
19: 5 *Pilate* saith unto them, Behold the **m**! G444
12 If thou let this **m** go, thou art not G5126
41 wherein was never **m** yet laid. G3762
21:21 Jesus, Lord, and what *shall* this **m** *do*? G3778
Act 1:18 Now this **m** purchased a field with the G3778
20 and let no **m** dwell therein: and his G3588
2: 6 that every **m** heard them speak in G1520
8 And how hear we every **m** in our own G1538
22 Jesus of Nazareth, a **m** approved of God G435
45 them to all *men*, as every **m** had need. G5100
3: 2 And a certain **m** lame from his mother's G435
11 And as the lame **m** which was healed G5560
12 or holiness we had made this **m** to walk? G846
16 hath made this **m** strong, whom ye see G5126
4: 9 **m**, by what means he is made whole; G444
10 this **m** stand here before you whole. G3778
14 And beholding the **m** which was healed G444
17 speak henceforth to no **m** in this name. G444
22 For the **m** was above forty years old, on G444
35 every **m** according as he had need. G1538
5: 1 But a certain **m** named Ananias, with G435
13 And of the rest durst no **m** join himself G3762
23 we had opened, we found no **m** within. G3762
37 After this **m** rose up Judas of Galilee in G5126
6: 5 chose Stephen, a **m** full of faith and of G435
13 which said, This **m** ceaseth not to speak G444
7:56 of **m** standing on the right hand of God. G444
8: 9 But there was a certain **m**, called Simon, G435
10 This **m** is the great power of God. G3778
27 and, behold, a **m** of Ethiopia, an eunuch G435

Act 8:31 And he said, How can I, except some **m** G5100
34 this? of himself, or of some other **m**? G2087
9: 7 hearing a voice, but seeing no **m**. G3367
8 he saw no **m**: but they led him by G3762
12 And hath seen in a vision a **m** named G435
13 by many of this **m**, how much evil he G435
33 And there he found a certain **m** named G444
10: 1 There was a certain **m** in Caesarea G435
2 *A* devout ***m***, and one that feared God
22 centurion, a just **m**, and one that feareth G435
26 saying, Stand up; I myself also am a **m**. G444
28 thing for a **m** that is a Jew to keep G435
28 not call any **m** common or unclean. G444
30 a **m** stood before me in bright clothing, G435
47 Can any **m** forbid water, that these G5100
11:24 For he was a good **m**, and full of the Holy G435
29 Then the disciples, every **m** according G1538
12:22 *It is* the voice of a god, and not of a **m**. G444
13: 7 Paulus, a prudent **m**; who called for G435
21 Saul the son of Cis, a **m** of the tribe of G435
22 the *son* of Jesse, a **m** after mine own G435
38 that through this **m** is preached unto G5127
41 believe, though a **m** declare it unto you. G5100
14: 8 And there sat a certain **m** at Lystra, G435
16: 9 There stood a **m** of Macedonia, and G435
17:31 by *that* **m** whom he hath ordained; G435
18:10 For I am with thee, and no **m** shall set G3762
24 an eloquent **m**, *and* mighty in the G435
25 This **m** was instructed in the way of the G3778
19:16 And the **m** in whom the evil spirit was G444
24 For a certain ***m*** named Demetrius, a
35 men of Ephesus, what **m** is there that G444
38 against any **m**, the law is open, and G5100
20: 9 a certain young **m** named Eutychus, G3494
12 And they brought the young **m** alive, G3816
21: 9 And the same **m** had four daughters, G5129
11 bind the **m** that owneth this girdle, G435
28 help: This is the **m**, that teacheth all *men* G444
39 But Paul said, I am a **m** *which am* a Jew G444
22: 3 I am verily a **m** *which am* a Jew, born in G435
12 And one Ananias, a devout **m** according G435
25 **m** that is a Roman, and uncondemned? G444
26 what thou doest: for this **m** is a Roman. G444
23: 9 find no evil in this **m**: but if a spirit or an G444
17 said, Bring this young **m** unto the chief G3494
18 to bring this young **m** unto thee, who G3494
22 *then* let the young **m** depart, and G3494
22 *him, See thou* tell no **m** that thou hast G3367
27 This **m** was taken of the Jews, and G435
30 laid wait for the **m**, I sent straightway to G435
24: 5 For we have found this **m** *a* pestilent G435
12 with any **m**, neither raising up the G5100
25: 5 this **m**, if there be any wickedness in him. G435
11 accuse me, no **m** may deliver me unto G3762
14 is a certain **m** left in bonds by Felix:' G435
16 to deliver any **m** to die, before that he G444
17 commanded the **m** to be brought forth. G435
22 also hear the **m** myself. To morrow, G444
24 us, ye see this **m**, about whom all the G5126
26:31 saying, This **m** doeth nothing worthy G444
32 Then said Agrippa unto Festus, This **m** G444
28: 4 No doubt this **m** is a murderer, whom, G444
7 of the chief **m** of the island, whose G4413
31 all confidence, no **m** forbidding him.
Ro 1:23 like to corruptible **m**, and to birds, and G444
2: 1 Therefore thou art inexcusable, O **m**, G444
3 And thinkest thou this, O **m**, that judgest G444
6 Who will render to every **m** according G1538
9 upon every soul of **m** that doeth evil, of G444
10 peace, to every **m** that worketh good, G3956
21 a **m** should not steal, dost thou steal?
22 Thou that sayest a **m** should not commit
3: 4 God be true, but every **m** a liar; as it is G444
5 who taketh vengeance? (I speak as a **m**) G444
28 Therefore we conclude that a **m** is G444
4: 6 the blessedness of the **m**, unto whom God G444
8 Blessed *is* the **m** to whom the Lord will G435
5: 7 For scarcely for a righteous **m** will one G1342
7 a good **m** some would even dare to die. G18
12 Wherefore, as by one **m** sin entered into G444
15 *which is* by one **m**, Jesus Christ, hath G444
6: 6 Knowing this, that our old **m** is crucified G444
7: 1 dominion over a **m** as long as he liveth? G444
3 to another **m**, she shall be called an G435
3 though she be married to another **m**. G435
22 in the law of God after the inward **m**: G444
24 O wretched **m** that I am! who shall G444
8: 9 you. Now if any **m** have not the Spirit G1536
24 a **m** seeth, why doth he yet hope for? G5100

Ro 9:20 Nay but, O **m**, who art thou that repliest G444
10: 5 of the law, That the **m** which doeth those G444
10 For with the heart **m** believeth unto
12: 3 unto me, to every **m** that is among you, G3956
3 dealt to every **m** the measure of faith. G1538
17 Recompense to no **m** evil for evil. G3367
13: 8 Owe no **m** any thing, but to love one G3367
14: 5 One **m** esteemeth one day above G3739
5 **m** be fully persuaded in his own mind. G1538
7 to himself, and no **m** dieth to himself. G3762
13 rather, that no **m** put a stumblingblock G3361
20 evil for that **m** who eateth with offence. G444
1Co 2: 9 into the heart of **m**, the things which God G444
11 For what **m** knoweth the things of a G444
11 For what man knoweth the things of a **m**, G444
11 save the spirit of **m** which is in him? G444
11 knoweth no **m**, but the Spirit of God. G3762
14 But the natural **m** receiveth not the G444
15 things, yet he himself is judged of no **m**. G3762
3: 5 even as the Lord gave to every **m**? G1538
8 one: and every **m** shall receive his own G1538
10 But let every **m** take heed how he G1538
11 For other foundation can no **m** lay G3762
12 Now if any **m** build upon this G1536
17 If any **m** defile the temple of God, him G1536
18 Let no **m** deceive himself. If any man G3367
18 Let no man deceive himself. If any **m** G1536
21 Therefore let no **m** glory in men. For all G3367
4: 1 Let a **m** so account of us, as of the G444
2 in stewards, that a **m** be found faithful. G5100
5 then shall every **m** have praise of God. G1538
5:11 keep company, if any **m** that is called a G5100
6: 5 there is not a wise **m** among you? no, G4680
18 Flee fornication. Every sin that a **m** G444
7: 1 *It is* good for a **m** not to touch a woman. G444
2 let every **m** have his own wife, G1538
7 I myself. But every **m** hath his proper G1538
16 O **m**, whether thou shalt save *thy* wife? G435
17 But as God hath distributed to every **m**, G1538
18 Is any **m** called being circumcised? let G5100
20 Let every **m** abide in the same calling G1538
24 Brethren, let every **m**, wherein he is G1538
26 *I say*, that *it is* good for a **m** so to be. G444
36 But if any **m** think that he behaveth G5100
8: 2 And if any **m** think that he knoweth G5100
3 But if any **m** love God, the same is G5100
7 Howbeit *there is* not in every **m** that G3956
10 For if any **m** see thee which hast G5100
9: 8 Say I these things as a **m**? or saith not the G444
15 any **m** should make my glorying void. G5100
25 And every **m** that striveth for the G3956
10:13 as is common to **m**: but God *is* faithful, G442
24 Let no **m** seek his own, but every man G3367
24 Let no man seek his own, but every **m** G1538
28 But if any **m** say unto you, This is G5100
11: 3 the head of every **m** is Christ; and the G435
3 *is* the **m**; and the head of Christ *is* God. G435
4 Every **m** praying or prophesying, having G435
7 For a **m** indeed ought not to cover *his* G435
7 God: but the woman is the glory of the **m**. G435
8 For the **m** is not of the woman; but the G435
8 of the woman; but the woman of the **m**. G435
9 Neither was the **m** created for the G435
9 for the woman; but the woman for the **m**. G435
11 Nevertheless neither is the **m** without G435
11 the woman without the **m**, in the Lord. G435
12 For as the woman *is* of the **m**, even so *is* G435
12 even so *is* the **m** also by the woman; G435
14 you, that, if a **m** have long hair, it is G435
16 But if any **m** seem to be contentious, G5100
28 But let a **m** examine himself, and so let G444
34 And if any **m** hunger, let him eat at G5100
12: 3 that no **m** speaking by the Spirit G3762
3 and *that* no **m** can say that Jesus is G3762
7 is given to every **m** to profit withal. G1538
11 dividing to every **m** severally as he will. G1538
13:11 I became a **m**, I put away childish things. G435
14: 2 but unto God: for no **m** understandeth G3762
27 If any **m** speak in an *unknown* tongue, G5100
37 If any **m** think himself to be a prophet, G1536
38 But if any **m** be ignorant, let him be G5100
15:21 For since by **m** *came* death, by man G444
21 For since by man *came* death, by **m** G444
23 But every **m** in his own order: Christ G1538
35 But some ***m*** will say, How are the dead
45 And so it is written, The first **m** Adam G444
47 The first **m** *is* of the earth, earthy: the G444
47 the second **m** *is* the Lord from heaven. G444
16:11 Let no **m** therefore despise him: but G5100

1Co 16:22 If any **m** love not the Lord Jesus Christ, G1536
2Co 2: 6 Sufficient to such a **m** *is* this G5108
4:16 our outward **m** perish, yet the inward G444
16 yet the inward *m* is renewed day by day.
5:16 Wherefore henceforth know we no **m** G3762
17 Therefore if any **m** *be* in Christ, *he is* a G1536
7: 2 Receive us; we have wronged no **m**, we G3762
2 no **m**, we have defrauded no man. G3762
2 no man, we have defrauded no **m**. G3762
8:12 to that a **m** hath, *and* not according G5100
20 Avoiding this, that no **m** should blame G5100
9: 7 Every **m** according as he purposeth in G1538
10: 7 If any **m** trust to himself that G1536
11: 9 chargeable to no **m**: for that which was G3762
10 As the truth of Christ is in me, no **m** G3756
16 I say again, Let no **m** think me a fool; if G5100
20 For ye suffer, if a **m** bring you into G1536
20 into bondage, if a **m** devour *you*, if a G1536
20 devour *you*, if a **m** take *of you*, if a man G1536
20 take *of you*, if a **m** exalt himself, if a G1536
20 himself, if a **m** smite you on the face. G1536
12: 2 I knew a **m** in Christ above fourteen G444
3 And I knew such a **m**, (whether in the G444
4 which it is not lawful for a **m** to utter. G444
6 I forbear, lest any **m** should think of G5100
Gal 1: 1 of men, neither by **m**, but by Jesus Christ, G444
9 I now again, If any *m* preach any other
11 which was preached of me is not after **m**. G444
12 For I neither received it of **m**, neither was G444
2:16 Knowing that a **m** is not justified by the G444
3:11 But that no **m** is justified by the law in G3762
12 And the law is not of faith: but, The **m** G444
15 no **m** disannulleth, or addeth thereto. G3762
5: 3 For I testify again to every **m** that is G444
6: 1 Brethren, if a **m** be overtaken in a fault, G444
3 For if a **m** think himself to be G5100
4 But let every **m** prove his own work, G1538
5 For every **m** shall bear his own burden. G1538
7 a **m** soweth, that shall he also reap. G444
17 From henceforth let no **m** trouble me: G3367
Eph 2: 9 Not of works, lest any **m** should boast. G5100
15 of twain one new **m**, *so* making peace; G444
3:16 with might by his Spirit in the inner **m**; G444
4:13 unto a perfect **m**, unto the measure of G435
22 the old **m**, which is corrupt according G444
24 And that ye put on the new **m**, which G444
25 lying, speak every **m** truth with his G1538
5: 5 nor covetous **m**, who is an idolater, G4123
6 Let no **m** deceive you with vain words: G3367
29 For no **m** ever yet hated his own flesh; G3762
31 For this cause shall a **m** leave his father G444
6: 8 good thing any **m** doeth, the same shall G1538
Php 2: 4 Look not every **m** on his own things, G1538
4 every **m** also on the things of others. G1538
8 And being found in fashion as a **m**, he G444
20 For I have no **m** likeminded, who will G3762
3: 4 the flesh. If any other **m** thinketh that he G243
Col 1:28 Whom we preach, warning every **m**, and G444
28 teaching every **m** in all wisdom; that we G444
28 present every **m** perfect in Christ Jesus: G444
2: 4 And this I say, lest any **m** should G5100
8 Beware lest any **m** spoil you through G5100
16 Let no **m** therefore judge you in meat, G5100
18 Let no **m** beguile you of your reward in G3367
3: 9 ye have put off the old **m** with his deeds; G444
10 And have put on the new *m*, which is
13 one another, if any **m** have a quarrel G5100
4: 6 know how ye ought to answer every **m**. G1520
1Th 3: 3 That no **m** should be moved by these G3367
4: 6 That no *m* go beyond and defraud his
8 despiseth not **m**, but God, who hath also G444
5:15 for evil unto any *m*; but ever follow that
2Th 2: 3 Let no **m** deceive you by any means: G5100
3 first, and that **m** of sin be revealed, the G444
3:14 And if any **m** obey not our word by this G5100
14 this epistle, note that **m**, and have no G5126
1Ti 1: 8 the law *is* good, if a **m** use it lawfully; G5100
9 for a righteous **m**, but for the lawless G1342
2: 5 God and men, the **m** Christ Jesus; G444
12 authority over the **m**, but to be in silence. G435
3: 1 This *is* a true saying, If a **m** desire the G1536
5 (For if a **m** know not how to rule his G5100
4:12 Let no **m** despise thy youth; but be thou G3367
5: 9 years old, having been the wife of one **m**, G435
16 If any **m** or woman that believeth have G4103
22 Lay hands suddenly on no **m**, neither G3367
6: 3 If any **m** teach otherwise, and consent G1536
11 But thou, O **m** of God, flee these things; G444
16 the light which no **m** can approach unto;
1Ti 6:16 unto; whom no **m** hath seen, nor can G444
2Ti 2: 4 No **m** that warreth entangleth himself G3762
5 And if a **m** also strive for masteries, *yet* G5100
21 If a **m** therefore purge himself from G5100
3:17 That the **m** of God may be perfect, G444
4:16 At my first answer no **m** stood with G3762
Tit 2:15 all authority. Let no **m** despise thee. G3367
3: 2 To speak evil of no **m**, to be no G3367
4 God our Saviour toward **m** appeared, G5363
10 A **m** that is an heretick after the first and G444
Heb 2: 6 saying, What is **m**, that thou art mindful G444
6 or the son of **m**, that thou visitest him? G444
9 of God should taste death for every **m**. G3956
3: 3 For this *m* was counted worthy of more
4 For every house is builded by some *m*;
4:11 that rest, lest any **m** fall after the same G5100
5: 4 And no **m** taketh this honour unto G5100
7: 4 Now consider how great this **m** *was*, G3778
13 no **m** gave attendance at the altar. G3762
24 But this *m*, because he continueth ever,
8: 2 which the Lord pitched, and not **m**. G444
3 this **m** have somewhat also to offer. G5126
11 And they shall not teach every **m** his G1538
11 and every **m** his brother, saying, G1538
10:12 But this **m**, after he had offered one G846
38 live by faith: but if *any m* draw back, my
12:14 without which no **m** shall see the Lord: G3762
15 Looking diligently lest any **m** fail of the G5100
13: 6 I will not fear what **m** shall do unto me. G444
Jas 1: 7 For let not that **m** think that he shall G444
8 A double minded **m** *is* unstable in all his G435
11 shall the rich **m** fade away in his ways. G4145
12 Blessed *is* the **m** that endureth G435
13 Let no **m** say when he is tempted, I am G3367
13 with evil, neither tempteth he any **m**: G3762
14 But every **m** is tempted, when he is G1538
19 brethren, let every **m** be swift to hear, G444
20 For the wrath of **m** worketh not the G435
23 **m** beholding his natural face in a glass: G435
24 forgetteth what manner of **m** he was. G3697
25 this **m** shall be blessed in his deed. G3778
26 If any **m** among you seem to be G1536
2: 2 your assembly a **m** with a gold ring, in G435
2 come in also a poor **m** in vile raiment; G4434
14 though a **m** say he hath faith, and G5100
18 Yea, a **m** may say, Thou hast faith, and G5100
20 But wilt thou know, O vain **m**, that faith G444
24 Ye see then how that by works a **m** is G444
3: 2 offend all. If any **m** offend not in word, G1536
2 the same *is* a perfect **m**, *and* able also to G435
8 But the tongue can no **m** tame; *it is* an G444
13 Who *is* a wise **m** and endued with G4680
5:16 prayer of a righteous **m** availeth much. G1342
17 Elias was a **m** subject to like passions as G444
1Pt 1:24 and all the glory of **m** as the flower of G444
2:13 every ordinance of **m** for the Lord's sake: G442
19 For this *is* thankworthy, if a **m** for G5100
3: 4 But *let it be* the hidden **m** of the heart, in G444
15 an answer to every **m** that asketh you a G3956
4:10 As every **m** hath received the gift, *even* G1538
11 If any **m** speak, *let him speak* as the G1536
11 of God; if any **m** minister, *let him do* G1536
16 Yet if *any m suffer* as a Christian, let
2Pt 1:21 old time by the will of **m**: but holy men of G444
2: 8 (For that righteous **m** dwelling among G1342
19 for of whom a **m** is overcome, of the G5100
1Jn 2: 1 sin not. And if any **m** sin, we have an G5100
15 the world. If any **m** love the world, the G5100
27 need not that any **m** teach you: but as G5100
3: 3 And every **m** that hath this hope in him G3956
7 Little children, let no **m** deceive you: he G3367
4:12 No **m** hath seen God at any time. If we G3762
20 If a **m** say, I love God, and hateth his G5100
5:16 If any **m** see his brother sin a sin *which* G5100
Rev 1:13 like unto the Son of **m**, clothed with a G444
2:17 **m** knoweth saving he that receiveth *it*. G3762
3: 7 that openeth, and no **m** shutteth; and G3762
7 and shutteth, and no **m** openeth; G3762
8 door, and no **m** can shut it: for thou G3762
11 thou hast, that no **m** take thy crown. G3367
20 and knock: if any **m** hear my voice, G5100
4: 7 had a face as a **m**, and the fourth beast G444
5: 3 And no **m** in heaven, nor in earth, G3762
4 And I wept much, because no **m** was G3762
6:15 and every free **m**, hid themselves in the G1658
7: 9 which no **m** could number, of all G3762
9: 5 of a scorpion, when he striketh a **m**. G444
11: 5 And if any **m** will hurt them, fire G1536
5 and if any **m** will hurt them, he must G1536
Rev 12: 5 And she brought forth a **m** child, who G730
13 woman which brought forth the **m** *child*. G730
13: 9 If any **m** have an ear, let him hear. G1536
17 And that no **m** might buy or sell, save G5100
18 is the number of a **m**; and his number *is* G444
14: 3 the elders: and no **m** could learn that G3762
9 loud voice, If any **m** worship the beast G1536
14 unto the Son of **m**, having on his head G444
15: 8 his power; and no **m** was able to enter G3762
16: 3 *m*: and every living soul died in the sea.
18:11 **m** buyeth their merchandise any more: G3762
19:12 that no **m** knew, but he himself. G3762
20:13 every **m** according to their works. G1538
21:17 the measure of a **m**, that is, of the angel. G444
22:12 every **m** according as his work shall be. G1538
18 For I testify unto every **m** that heareth G3956
18 this book, If any **m** shall add unto these G5100
19 And if any **m** shall take away from the G5100

MANAEN
Act 13: 1 of Cyrene, and **M**, which had been G3127

MANAHATH
Gen 36:23 and **M**, and Ebal, Shepho, and Onam. H4506
1Ch 1:40 The sons of Shobal; Alian, and **M**, and H4506
8: 6 of Geba, and they removed them to **M**: H4506

MANAHETHITES
1Ch 2:52 had sons; Haroeh, *and* half of the **M**. H2679
54 of Joab, and half of the **M**, the Zorites. H2680

MANASSEH
Gen 41:51 of the firstborn **M**: For God, *said he*, H4519
46:20 of Egypt were born **M** and Ephraim, H4519
48: 1 him his two sons, **M** and Ephraim. H4519
5 And now thy two sons, Ephraim and **M**, H4519
13 left hand, and **M** in his left hand H4519
14 wittingly; for **M** *was* the firstborn. H4519
20 Ephraim and as **M**: and he set Ephraim H4519
20 and he set Ephraim before **M**. H4519
50:23 Machir the son of **M** were brought up H4519
Nu 1:10 of **M**; Gamaliel the son of Pedahzur. H4519
34 Of the children of **M**, by their H4519
35 of the tribe of **M**, *were* thirty and two H4519
2:20 And by him *shall be* the tribe of **M**: and H4519
20 of the children of **M** *shall be* Gamaliel H4519
7:54 Pedahzur, prince of the children of **M**: H4519
10:23 **M** *was* Gamaliel the son of Pedahzur. H4519
13:11 of the tribe of **M**, Gaddi the son of Susi. H4519
26:28 their families *were* **M** and Ephraim. H4519
29 Of the sons of **M**: of Machir, the family H4519
34 These *are* the families of **M**, and those H4519
27: 1 Machir, the son of **M**, of the families of H4519
1 of the families of **M** the son of Joseph: H4519
32:33 half the tribe of **M** the son of Joseph, H4519
39 of Machir the son of **M** went to Gilead, H4519
40 the son of **M**; and he dwelt therein. H4519
41 And Jair the son of **M** went and took H4519
34:14 of **M** have received their inheritance: H4519
23 of **M**, Hanniel the son of Ephod. H4519
36: 1 the son of **M**, of the families of the H4519
12 of the sons of **M** the son of Joseph, and H4519
Dt 3:13 unto the half tribe of **M**; all the region of H4519
14 Jair the son of **M** took all the country of H4519
29: 8 the Gadites, and to the half tribe of **M**. H4520
33:17 and they *are* the thousands of **M**. H4519
34: 2 of Ephraim, and **M**, and all the land of H4519
Jos 1:12 the tribe of **M**, spake Joshua, saying, H4519
4:12 half the tribe of **M**, passed over armed H4519
12: 6 and the Gadites, and the half tribe of **M**. H4519
13: 7 the nine tribes, and the half tribe of **M**, H4519
29 the half tribe of **M**: and *this* was *the* H4519
29 of the children of **M** by their families. H4519
31 of Machir the son of **M**, *even* to the one H4519
14: 4 were two tribes, **M** and Ephraim: H4519
16: 4 So the children of Joseph, **M** and H4519
9 of **M**, all the cities with their villages. H4519
17: 1 There was also a lot for the tribe of **M**; H4519
1 the firstborn of **M**, the father of Gilead: H4519
2 of the children of **M** by their families; H4519
2 **M** the son of Joseph by their families. H4519
3 Machir, the son of **M**, had no sons, but H4519
5 And there fell ten portions to **M**, beside H4519
6 Because the daughters of **M** had an H4519
7 And the coast of **M** was from Asher to H4519
8 *Now* **M** had the land of Tappuah: but H4519
8 **M** *belonged* to the children of Ephraim; H4519
9 the cities of **M**: the coast of Manasseh H4519
9 the coast of **M** also *was* on the north H4519

Jos 17:11 And M had in Issachar and in Asher H4519
12 Yet the children of M could not drive H4519
17 Ephraim and to M, saying, Thou art a H4519
18: 7 half the tribe of M, have received their H4519
20: 8 Golan in Bashan out of the tribe of M. H4519
21: 5 and out of the half tribe of M, ten cities. H4519
6 tribe of M in Bashan, thirteen cities. H4519
25 And out of the half tribe of M, Tanach H4519
27 other half tribe of M they gave Golan in H4519
22: 1 and the Gadites, and the half tribe of M, H4519
7 Now to the one half of the tribe of M H4519
9 and the half tribe of M returned, and H4519
10 the half tribe of M built there an altar H4519
11 the half tribe of M have built an altar H4519
13 to the half tribe of M, into the land of H4519
15 to the half tribe of M, unto the land of H4519
21 the half tribe of M answered, and said H4519
30 children of M spake, it pleased them. H4519
31 and to the children of M, This day we H4519
Jdg 1:27 Neither did M drive out the inhabitants H4519
6:15 family is poor in M, and I am the least H4519
35 throughout all M; who also was H4519
7:23 all M, and pursued after the Midianites. H4519
11:29 over Gilead, and M, and passed over H4519
18:30 the son of M, he and his sons were H4519
1Ki 4:13 towns of Jair the son of M, which are in H4519
2Ki 20:21 and M his son reigned in his stead. H4519
21: 1 M was twelve years old when he began H4519
9 But they hearkened not: and M H4519
11 Because M king of Judah hath done H4519
16 Moreover M shed innocent blood very H4519
17 Now the rest of the acts of M, and all H4519
18 And M slept with his fathers, and was H4519
20 sight of the LORD, as his father M did. H4519
23:12 the altars which M had made in the H4519
26 that M had provoked him withal. H4519
24: 3 sins of M, according to all that he did; H4519
1Ch 3:13 Ahaz his son, Hezekiah his son, M his H4519
5:18 half the tribe of M, of valiant men, men H4519
23 And the children of the half tribe of M H4519
26 the half tribe of M, and brought them H4519
6:61 of the half tribe of M, by lot, ten cities. H4519
62 tribe of M in Bashan, thirteen cities. H4519
70 And out of the half tribe of M; Aner H4519
71 of the half tribe of M, Golan in Bashan H4519
7:14 The sons of M; Ashriel, whom she bare: H4519
17 Gilead, the son of Machir, the son of M. H4519
29 And by the borders of the children of M, H4519
9: 3 and of the children of Ephraim, and M; H4519
12:19 And there fell some of M to David, H4519
20 fell to him of M, Adnah, and Jozabad, H4519
20 of the thousands that were of M. H4519
31 And of the half tribe of M eighteen H4519
37 of the half tribe of M, with all manner of H4519
26:32 and the half tribe of M, for every matter H4520
27:20 half tribe of M, Joel the son of Pedaiah: H4519
21 Of the half tribe of M in Gilead, Iddo H4519
2Ch 15: 9 of Ephraim and M, and out of Simeon: H4519
30: 1 to Ephraim and M, that they should H4519
10 of Ephraim and M even unto Zebulun: H4519
11 Nevertheless divers of Asher and M H4519
18 of Ephraim, and M, Issachar, and H4519
31: 1 in Ephraim also and M, until they had H4519
32:33 And M his son reigned in his stead. H4519
33: 1 M was twelve years old when he began H4519
9 So M made Judah and the inhabitants H4519
10 And the LORD spake to M, and to his H4519
11 which took M among the thorns, H4519
13 M knew that the LORD he was God. H4519
18 Now the rest of the acts of M, and his H4519
20 So M slept with his fathers, and they H4519
22 of the LORD, as did M his father: for H4519
22 images which M his father had made, H4519
23 before the LORD, as M his father had H4519
34: 6 And so did he in the cities of M, and H4519
9 of the hand of M and Ephraim, and H4519
Ezr 10:30 Bezaleel, and Binnui, and M. H4519
33 Eliphelet, Jeremai, M, and Shimei. H4519
Ps 60: 7 Gilead is mine, and M is mine; H4519
80: 2 Before Ephraim and Benjamin and M H4519
108: 8 Gilead is mine; M is mine; Ephraim H4519
Isa 9:21 M, Ephraim; and Ephraim, Manasseh: H4519
21 Manasseh, Ephraim; and Ephraim, M: H4519
Jer 15: 4 the earth, because of M the son of H4519
Ezk 48: 4 side unto the west side, a portion for M. H4519
5 And by the border of M, from the east H4519

MANASSEH'S
Gen 48:14 his left hand upon M head, guiding his H4519
17 it from Ephraim's head unto M head. H4519
Jos 17: 6 rest of M sons had the land of Gilead. H4519
10 northward it was M, and the sea is his H4519

MANASSES
Mt 1:10 And Ezekias begat M; and Manasses G3128
10 And Ezekias begat Manasses; and M G3128
Rev 7: 6 of M were sealed twelve thousand. G3128

MANASSITES
Dt 4:43 Gadites; and Golan in Bashan, of the M. H4520
Jdg 12: 4 the Ephraimites, and among the M. H4519
2Ki 10:33 and the M, from Aroer, which H4520

MANDRAKES
Gen 30:14 and found m in the field, and brought H1736
14 Give me, I pray thee, of thy son's m. H1736
15 away my son's m also? And Rachel H1736
15 lie with thee to night for thy son's m. H1736
16 son's m. And he lay with her that night. H1736
Song 7:13 The m give a smell, and at our gates H1736

MANEH
Ezk 45:12 shekels, fifteen shekels, shall be your m. H4488

MANGER
Lk 2: 7 and laid him in a m; because there was G5336
12 in swaddling clothes, lying in a m. G5336
16 and Joseph, and the babe lying in a m. G5336

MANIFEST
Ecc 3:18 that God might m them, and that they H1305
Lk 8:17 shall not be made m; neither any thing G5318
Jn 1:31 should be made m to Israel, therefore G5319
3:21 made m, that they are wrought in God. G5319
9: 3 of God should be made m in him. G5319
14:21 will love him, and will m myself to him. G1718
22 is it that thou wilt m thyself unto us, G1718
Act 4:16 done by them is m to all them that G5318
Ro 1:19 be known of God is m in them; for God G5318
10:20 m unto them that asked not after me. G1717
16:26 But now is made m, and by the G5319
1Co 3:13 Every man's work shall be made m: for G5318
4: 5 and will make m the counsels of the G5319
11:19 approved may be made m among you. G5318
14:25 of his heart made m; and so falling G5318
15:27 under him, it is m that he is excepted, G1212
2Co 2:14 Christ, and maketh m the savour of his G5319
4:10 of Jesus might be made m in our body. G5319
11 might be made m in our mortal flesh. G5319
5:11 but we are made m unto God; and I G5319
11 also are made m in your consciences. G5319
11: 6 made m among you in all things. G5319
Gal 5:19 Now the works of the flesh are m, which G5318
Eph 5:13 reproved are made m by the light: for G5319
13 for whatsoever doth make m is light. G5319
Php 1:13 So that my bonds in Christ are m in all G5318
Col 1:26 but now is made m to his saints: G5319
4: 4 That I may make it m, as I ought to G5319
2Th 1: 5 Which is a m token of the righteous
1Ti 3:16 God was m in the flesh, justified G5319
5:25 of some are m beforehand; and they G4271
2Ti 1:10 But is now made m by the appearing of G5319
3: 9 be m unto all men, as theirs also was. G1552
Heb 4:13 that is not m in his sight: but all things G852
9: 8 was not yet made m, while as the first G5319
1Pt 1:20 but was m in these last times for you, G5319
1Jn 2:19 be made m that they were not all of us. G5319
3:10 In this the children of God are m, and G5318
Rev 15: 4 thee; for thy judgments are made m. G5319

MANIFESTATION
Ro 8:19 waiteth for the m of the sons of God. G602
1Co 12: 7 But the m of the Spirit is given to every G5321
2Co 4: 2 God deceitfully; but by m of the truth G5321

MANIFESTED
Mk 4:22 which shall not be m; neither was any G5319
Jn 2:11 of Galilee, and m forth his glory; and G5319
17: 6 I have m thy name unto the men which G5319
Ro 3:21 without the law is m, being witnessed G5319
Tit 1: 3 But hath in due times m his word G5319
1Jn 1: 2 (For the life was m, and we have seen it, G5319
2 with the Father, and was m unto us;) G5319
3: 5 And ye know that he was m to take G5319
8 the Son of God was m, that he might G5319
4: 9 In this was m the love of God toward G5319

MANIFESTLY
2Co 3: 3 Forasmuch as ye are m declared to be G5319

MANIFOLD
Neh 9:19 Yet thou in thy m mercies forsookest H7227
27 according to thy m mercies thou gavest H7227
Ps 104:24 O LORD, how m are thy works! in H7231
Am 5:12 For I know your m transgressions and H7227
Lk 18:30 Who shall not receive m more in this G4179
Eph 3:10 by the church the m wisdom of God, G4182
1Pt 1: 6 in heaviness through m temptations: G4164
4:10 good stewards of the m grace of God. G4164

MANKIND
Lev 18:22 Thou shalt not lie with m, as with H2145
20:13 If a man also lie with m, as he lieth with H2145
Job 12:10 thing, and the breath of all m. H376+H1320
1Co 6: 9 nor abusers of themselves with m, G733
1Ti 1:10 themselves with m, for menstealers, for G733
Jas 3: 7 is tamed, and hath been tamed of m: G5449

MANNA
Ex 16:15 one to another, It is m: for they wist not H4478
31 the name thereof M: and it was like H4478
33 an omer full of m therein, and lay it up H4478
35 And the children of Israel did eat m H4478
35 they did eat m, until they came unto H4478
Nu 11: 6 at all, beside this m, before our eyes. H4478
7 And the m was as coriander seed, and H4478
9 camp in the night, the m fell upon it. H4478
Dt 8: 3 and fed thee with m, which thou H4478
16 Who fed thee in the wilderness with m, H4478
Jos 5:12 And the m ceased on the morrow after H4478
12 children of Israel m any more; but they H4478
Neh 9:20 not thy m from their mouth, and H4478
Ps 78:24 And had rained down m upon them to H4478
Jn 6:31 Our fathers did eat m in the desert; as G3131
49 Your fathers did eat m in the G3131
58 fathers did eat m, and are dead: he that G3131
Heb 9: 4 pot that had m, and Aaron's rod that G3131
Rev 2:17 eat of the hidden m, and will give him a G3131

MANNER
Gen 18:11 to be with Sarah after the m of women. H734
25 That be far from thee to do after this m, H1697
19:31 in unto us after the m of all the earth: H1870
25:23 thy womb, and two m of people shall be
32:19 saying, On this m shall ye speak unto H1697
39:19 saying, After this m did thy servant to H1697
40:13 former m when thou wast his butler. H4941
17 there was of all m of bakemeats for
45:23 And to his father he sent after this m; ten
Ex 1:14 in brick, and in all m of service in the
7:11 did in like m with their enchantments. H3651
12:16 to you; no m of work shall be done
21: 9 deal with her after the m of daughters. H4941
22: 9 For all m of trespass, whether it be for H1697
9 or for any m of lost thing, which
23:11 shall eat. In like m thou shalt deal with H3651
31: 3 and in all m of workmanship,
5 to work in all m of workmanship.
35:29 to bring for all m of work, which the
31 and in all m of workmanship;
33 wood, to make any m of cunning work.
35 of heart, to work all m of work, of the H3605
36: 1 how to work all m of work for the service
Lev 5:10 according to the m: and the priest shall H4941
7:23 no m of fat, of ox, or of sheep, or of goat.
26 Moreover ye shall eat no m of blood,
27 it be that eateth any m of blood, even H3605
9:16 and offered it according to the m. H4941
11:27 paws, among all m of beasts that go on
44 with any m of creeping thing that
14:54 This is the law for all m of plague of
17:10 that eateth any m of blood; I will even
14 eat the blood of no m of flesh: for the life
19:23 have planted all m of trees for food, then
20:25 by fowl, or by any m of living thing that
23:31 Ye shall do no m of work: it shall be a
24:22 Ye shall have one m of law, as well for H4941
Nu 5:13 her, neither she be taken with the m;
9:14 according to the m thereof, so shall he H4941
15:13 these things after this m, in offering an H3541
16 One law and one m shall be for you, H4941
24 according to the m, and one kid of the H4941
28:18 ye shall do no m of servile work therein:
24 After this m ye shall offer daily,
29: 6 unto their m, for a sweet savour, H4941
18 according to their number, after the m: H4941

Nu 29:21 according to their number, after the **m**: H4941
24 according to their number, after the **m**: H4941
27 according to their number, after the **m**: H4941
30 according to their number, after the **m**: H4941
33 according to their number, after the **m**: H4941
37 according to their number, after the **m**: H4941
31:30 of the flocks, of all **m** of beasts, and give
Dt 4:15 for ye saw no **m** of similitude on the
15: 2 And this *is* the **m** of the release: Every H1697
22: 3 In like **m** shalt thou do with his ass; H3651
27:21 Cursed *be* he that lieth with any **m** of
Jos 6:15 after the same **m** seven times: only on H4941
Jdg 8:18 Zalmunna, What **m** of men *were they* H375
11:17 And in like **m** they sent unto the king
18: 7 careless, after the **m** of the Zidonians, H4941
Ru 4: 7 Now this *was the* **m** in former time in
1Sa 8: 9 shew them the **m** of the king that shall H4941
11 And he said, This will be the **m** of the H4941
10:25 Then Samuel told the people the **m** of H4941
17:27 him after this **m**, saying, So shall it be H1697
30 spake after the same **m**: and the people H1697
30 answered him again after the former **m**. H1697
18:24 him, saying, On this **m** spake David. H1697
19:24 Samuel in like **m**, and lay down naked H1571
21: 5 and *the bread is* in a **m** common, yea, H1870
27:11 and so *will be* his **m** all the while he H4941
2Sa 6: 5 the LORD on all **m** of *instruments made*
7:19 And *is* this the **m** of man, O Lord GOD? H8452
14: 3 and speak on this **m** unto him. So Joab H1697
15: 6 And on this **m** did Absalom to all Israel H1697
17: 6 spoken after this **m**: shall we do *after* H1697
1Ki 7:28 And the work of the bases *was* on this *m:*
37 After this *m* he made the ten bases: all of
18:28 after their **m** with knives and lancets, H4941
22:20 **m**, and another said on that manner. H3541
20 manner, and another said on that **m**. H3541
2Ki 1: 7 And he said unto them, What **m** of H4941
11:14 stood by a pillar, as the **m** *was*, and the H4941
17:26 know not the **m** of the God of the land: H4941
26 know not the **m** of the God of the land. H4941
27 them the **m** of the God of the land. H4941
33 gods, after the **m** of the nations whom H4941
40 but they did after their former **m**. H4941
1Ch 6:48 appointed unto all **m** of service of the
12:37 with all **m** of instruments of war
18:10 **m** of vessels of gold and silver and brass.
22:15 timber, and all **m** of cunning men for
15 of cunning men for every **m** of work.
23:29 fried, and for all **m** of measure and size;
24:19 according to their **m**, under Aaron their H4941
28:14 all instruments of all **m** of service; *silver*
21 *be* with thee for all **m** of workmanship
21 man, for any **m** of service: also the
29: 2 colours, and all **m** of precious stones,
5 silver, and for all **m** of work *to be made*
2Ch 2:14 also to grave any **m** of graving, and to
4:20 the **m** before the oracle, of pure gold; H4941
13: 9 you priests after the **m** of the nations of
18:19 saying after this **m**, and another saying H3602
19 and another saying after that **m**. H3602
30:16 place after their **m**, according to the law H4941
32:15 you on this **m**, neither yet believe him:
27 shields, and for all **m** of pleasant jewels;
28 for all **m** of beasts, and cotes for flocks.
34:13 the work in any **m** of service: and of the
Ezr 5: 4 Then said we unto them after this **m**, H3660
Neh 6: 4 and I answered them after the same **m**. H1697
5 unto me in like **m** the fifth time with an H1697
8:18 assembly, according unto the **m**. H4941
10:37 and the fruit of all **m** of trees, of wine
13:15 and figs, and all *m of* burdens, which
16 fish, and all **m** of ware, and sold on
Est 1:13 (for so *was* the king's **m** toward all that H1697
2:12 according to the **m** of the women, (for H1881
Ps 107:18 Their soul abhorreth all **m** of meat; and
144:13 *be* full, affording all **m** of store: *that* our
Song 7:13 at our gates *are* all **m** of pleasant *fruits*,
Isa 5:17 Then shall the lambs feed after their **m**, H1699
10:24 staff against thee, after the **m** of Egypt. H1870
26 shall he lift it up after the **m** of Egypt. H1870
51: 6 shall die in like **m**: but my salvation H3654
Jer 13: 9 Thus saith the LORD, After this **m** will I
22:21 *hath been* thy **m** from thy youth, that H1870
30:18 palace shall remain after the **m** thereof. H4941
Ezk 20:30 ye polluted after the **m** of your fathers? H1870
23:15 look to, after the **m** of the Babylonians H1823
45 them after the **m** of adulteresses, and H4941
45 and after the **m** of women that shed H4941
Dan 6:23 of the den, and no **m** of hurt was found H3606

Am 4:10 after the **m** of Egypt: your young H1870
8:14 liveth; and, The **m** of Beer-sheba liveth; H1870
Mt 4:23 and healing all **m** of sickness and all *G3956*
23 and all **m** of disease among the people. *G3956*
5:11 and shall say all **m** of evil against you *G3956*
6: 9 After this **m** therefore pray ye: Our *G3779*
8:27 But the men marvelled, saying, What **m**
10: 1 and to heal all **m** of sickness and all *G3956*
1 of sickness and all **m** of disease. *G3956*
12:31 Wherefore I say unto you, All **m** of sin
Mk 4:41 to another, What **m** of man is this, that
13: 1 Master, see what **m** of stones and what *G4217*
29 So ye in like **m**, when ye shall see these *G2532*
Lk 1:29 what **m** of salutation this should be. *G4217*
66 saying, What **m** of child shall this be! *G686*
6:23 **m** did their fathers unto the prophets. *G2596*
7:39 who and what **m** of woman *this is* that *G4217*
8:25 to another, What **m** of man is this! for he
9:55 Ye know not what **m** of spirit ye are of. *G3634*
11:42 and rue and all **m** of herbs, and pass *G3956*
20:31 And the third took her; and in like **m** *G5615*
24:17 And he said unto them, What **m** of
Jn 2: 6 of stone, after the **m** of the purifying of
7:36 What *m of* saying is this that he said, Ye
19:40 spices, as the **m** of the Jews is to bury. *G1485*
Act 1:11 **m** as ye have seen him go into heaven. *G5158*
10:12 Wherein were all **m** of fourfooted *G3956*
15: 1 the **m** of Moses, ye cannot be saved. *G1485*
23 by them after this **m**; The apostles and *G3592*
17: 2 And Paul, as his **m** was, went in unto *G1483*
20:18 **m** I have been with you at all seasons, *G4459*
22: 3 to the perfect **m** of the law of the fathers, *G195*
23:25 And he wrote a letter after this **m**: *G5179*
25:16 To whom I answered, It is not the **m** of *G1485*
20 And because I doubted of such **m** of *G4012*
26: 4 My **m** of life from my youth, which was *G981*
Ro 6:19 I speak after the **m** of men because of *G442*
7: 8 wrought in me all **m** of concupiscence.
1Co 7: 7 one after this **m**, and another after that. *G3779*
11:25 After the same **m** also *he took* the cup, *G5615*
15:32 If after the **m** of men I have fought with *G2596*
2Co 7: 9 after a godly **m**, that ye might receive *G2596*
Gal 2:14 livest after the **m** of Gentiles, and not *G1483*
3:15 Brethren, I speak after the **m** of men; *G2596*
1Th 1: 5 as ye know what **m** of men we were *G3034*
9 For they themselves shew of us what **m** *G3697*
1Ti 2: 9 In like **m** also, that women adorn *G5615*
2Ti 3:10 my doctrine, **m** of life, purpose, faith, *G72*
Heb 10:25 together, as the **m** of some *is*; but *G1485*
Jas 1:24 forgetteth what **m** of man he was. *G3697*
1Pt 1:11 Searching what, or what **m** of time the *G4169*
15 so be ye holy in all **m** of conversation; *G3956*
3: 5 For after this **m** in the old time the holy *G3779*
2Pt 3:11 dissolved, what **m** *of persons* ought ye *G4217*
1Jn 3: 1 Behold, what **m** of love the Father hath *G4217*
Jude 7 them in like **m**, giving themselves over *G5158*
Rev 11: 5 hurt them, he must in this **m** be killed. *G3779*
18:12 wood, and all **m** vessels of ivory, and *G3956*
12 of ivory, and all **m** vessels of most *G3956*
21:19 garnished with all **m** of precious stones.
22: 2 life, which bare twelve *m of* fruits, *and*

MANNERS

Lev 20:23 And ye shall not walk in the **m** of the H2708
2Ki 17:34 do after the former **m**: they fear not the H4941
Ezk 11:12 done after the **m** of the heathen that H4941
Act 13:18 suffered he their **m** in the wilderness. *G5159*
1Co 15:33 evil communications corrupt good **m**. *G2239*
Heb 1: 1 and in divers **m** spake in time past *G4187*

MANOAH

Jdg 13: 2 whose name *was* **M**; and his wife *was* H4495
8 Then **M** entreated the LORD, and said, H4495
9 And God hearkened to the voice of **M**; H4495
9 but **M** her husband *was* not with her. H4495
11 And **M** arose, and went after his wife, H4495
12 And **M** said, Now let thy words come to H4495
13 And the angel of the LORD said unto **M**, H4495
15 And **M** said unto the angel of the H4495
16 And the angel of the LORD said unto **M**, H4495
16 the LORD. For **M** knew not that he *was* H4495
17 And **M** said unto the angel of the H4495
19 So **M** took a kid with a meat offering, H4495
19 and **M** and his wife looked on. H4495
20 of the altar. And **M** and his wife looked H4495
21 no more appear to **M** and to his wife. H4495
21 to his wife. Then **M** knew that he *was* H4495
22 And **M** said unto his wife, We shall H4495
16:31 burying-place of **M** his father. And he H4495

MAN'S

Gen 8:21 ground any more for **m** sake; for the H120
21 the imagination of **m** heart *is* evil from H120
9: 5 **m** brother will I require the life of man. H376
6 Whoso sheddeth **m** blood, by man shall H120
16:12 man, and every **m** hand against him;
20: 3 thou hast taken; for she *is* a **m** wife. H1167
42:11 We *are* all one **m** sons; we *are* true *men*, H376
25 to restore every **m** money into his sack, H376
35 that, behold, every **m** bundle of money H376
43:21 and, behold, *every* **m** money *was* in the H376
44: 1 put every **m** money in his sack's mouth. H376
26 we may not see the **m** face, except our H376
Ex 4:11 him, Who hath made **m** mouth? or who H120
12:44 But every **m** servant that is bought for H376
21:35 And if one **m** ox hurt another's, that he H376
22: 5 feed in another **m** field; of the best of his H312
7 stolen out of the **m** house; if the thief be H376
30:32 Upon **m** flesh shall it not be poured, H120
Lev 7: 8 And the priest that offereth any **m** burnt H376
15:16 And if any **m** seed of copulation go out H376
20:10 with *another* **m** wife, *even he* that H376
Nu 5:10 And every **m** hallowed things shall be H376
12 unto them, If any **m** wife go aside, and H376
17: 2 write thou every **m** name upon his rod. H376
5 And it shall come to pass, *that* the **m** H376
33:54 inheritance: every **m** *inheritance* shall be
Dt 20:19 *is* **m** *life*) to employ *them* in the siege: H120
24: 2 she may go and be another **m** *wife*. H376
6 pledge: for he taketh *a* **m** life to pledge.
Jdg 7:16 a trumpet in every **m** hand, with empty
22 the LORD set every **m** sword against his H376
19:26 at the door of the **m** house where her H376
Ru 2:19 and said, The **m** name with whom I H376
1Sa 12: 4 hast thou taken ought of any **m** hand. H376
14:20 and, behold, every **m** sword was against H376
17:32 And David said to Saul, Let no **m** heart H120
2Sa 12: 4 but took the poor **m** lamb, and dressed it H376
17:18 and came to a **m** house in Bahurim, H376
25 Amasa *was* a **m** son, whose name *was* H376
1Ki 18:44 of the sea, like a **m** hand. And he said, H376
2Ki 12: 4 cometh into any **m** heart to bring into H376
23: 8 on a **m** left hand at the gate of the city. H376
25: 9 every great *m* house burnt he with fire.
Est 1: 8 do according to every **m** pleasure. H376
Job 10: 5 days of man? *are* thy years as **m** days, H1397
32:21 Let me not, I pray you, accept any **m** H376
Ps 104:15 and bread *which* strengtheneth **m** heart. H582
Prv 10:15 The rich **m** wealth *is* his strong city: the
12:14 a **m** hands shall be rendered unto him. H120
13: 8 The ransom of a **m** life *are* his riches: H376
16: 7 When a **m** ways please the LORD, he H376
9 A **m** heart deviseth his way: but the H120
18: 4 The words of a **m** mouth *are as* deep H376
11 The rich **m** wealth *is* his strong city, and
16 A **m** gift maketh room for him, and H120
20 A **m** belly shall be satisfied with the fruit H376
19:21 *There are* many devices in a **m** heart; H376
20:24 **M** goings *are* of the LORD; how can a H1397
27: 9 of a **m** friend by hearty counsel.
29:23 A **m** pride shall bring him low: but H120
26 **m** judgment *cometh* from the LORD. H376
Ecc 2:14 The wise **m** eyes *are* in his head; but H2450
8: 1 of a thing? a **m** wisdom maketh his H120
5 thing: and a wise **m** heart discerneth H2450
9:16 the poor **m** wisdom *is* despised, H4542
10: 2 A wise **m** heart *is* at his right hand; but H2450
12 The words of a wise **m** mouth *are* H2450
Isa 8: 1 and write in it with a **m** pen concerning H582
13: 7 be faint, and every **m** heart shall melt: H582
Jer 3: 1 become another **m**, shall he return unto H376
23:36 no more: for every **m** word shall be his H376
Ezk 4:15 cow's dung for **m** dung, and thou shalt H120
10: 8 the form of a **m** hand under their wings. H120
38:21 **m** sword shall be against his brother. H376
39:15 when *any* seeth a **m** bone, then shall he H120
40: 5 about, and in the **m** hand a measuring H376
Dan 4:16 Let his heart be changed from **m**, and let H606
5: 5 forth fingers of a **m** hand, and wrote H606
7: 4 as a man, and a **m** heart was given to it. H606
8:16 And I heard a **m** voice between *the* H120
Am 6:10 And a **m** uncle shall take him up, and he
Jna 1:14 us not perish for this **m** life, and lay not H376
Mic 7: 6 mother in law; a **m** enemies *are* the men H376
Mt 10:36 And a **m** foes *shall be* they of his own *G444*
41 shall receive a righteous **m** reward. *G1342*
12:29 into a strong **m** house, and spoil his *G2478*
Mk 3:27 No man can enter into a strong **m** *G2478*
12:19 Master, Moses wrote unto us, If a **m** *G5100*

Lk 6:22 your name as evil, for the Son of m sake. G444
12:15 for a m life consisteth not in G5100
16:12 which is another m, who shall give you G245
21 fell from the rich m table: moreover the G4145
20:28 unto us, If any m brother die, having G5100
Jn 18:17 of this m disciples? He saith, I am not. G444
Act 5:28 intend to bring this m blood upon us. G444
7:58 a young m feet, whose name was Saul. G3494
11:12 me, and we entered into the m house: G435
13:23 Of this m seed hath God according to G5127
17:29 or stone, graven by art and m device. G444
18: 7 into a certain m house, named Justus,
20:33 I have coveted no m silver, or gold, or G3762
27:22 of any m life among you, but of the ship.
Ro 5:17 For if by one m offence death reigned G1520
19 For as by one m disobedience many G444
14: 4 Who art thou that judgest another m G245
15:20 build upon another m foundation: G245
1Co 2: 4 with enticing words of m wisdom, but in G442
13 in the words which m wisdom teacheth, G442
3:13 Every m work shall be made manifest: G1538
13 try every m work of what sort it is. G1538
14 If any m work abide which he hath G1536
15 If any m work shall be burned, he shall G1536
4: 3 of you, or of m judgment: yea, I judge G442
10:29 liberty judged of another m conscience?
2Co 4: 2 every m conscience in the sight of God. G444
10:16 boast in another m line of things made G245
Gal 2: 6 God accepteth no m person:) for they G444
3:15 Though it be but a m covenant, yet if it G444
2Th 3: 8 Neither did we eat any m bread for G5100
Jas 1:26 his own heart, this m religion is vain. G5127
1Pt 1:17 to every m work, pass the time G1538
2Pt 2:16 ass speaking with m voice forbad the G444

MANSERVANT
Ex 20:10 nor thy daughter, thy m, nor thy H5650
17 wife, nor his m, nor his maidservant, H5650
21:32 If the ox shall push a m or a H5650
Dt 5:14 thy daughter, nor thy m, nor thy H5650
14 within thy gates; that thy m and thy H5650
21 his field, or his m, or his maidservant, H5650
12:18 thy daughter, and thy m, and thy H5650
16:11 thy daughter, and thy m, and thy H5650
14 thy daughter, and thy m, and thy H5650
Job 31:13 If I did despise the cause of my m or of H5650
Jer 34: 9 That every man should let his m, and H5650
10 one should let his m, and every one his H5650

MANSERVANTS
Neh 7:67 Beside their m and their maidservants, H5650

MANSERVANT'S
Ex 21:27 And if he smite out his m tooth, or his H5650

MANSIONS
Jn 14: 2 In my Father's house are many m: if it G3438

MANSLAYER
Nu 35: 6 shall appoint for the m, that he may flee H7523
12 the avenger; that the m die not, until he H7523

MANSLAYERS
1Ti 1: 9 fathers and murderers of mothers, for m, G409

MANTLE
Jdg 4:18 into the tent, she covered him with a m. H8063
1Sa 15:27 hold upon the skirt of his m, and it rent. H4598
28:14 is covered with a m. And Saul perceived H4598
1Ki 19:13 his face in his m, and went out, and H155
19 by him, and cast his m upon him. H155
2Ki 2: 8 And Elijah took his m, and wrapped it H155
13 He took up also the m of Elijah that fell H155
14 And he took the m of Elijah that fell H155
Ezr 9: 3 garment and my m, and plucked off the H4598
5 my garment and my m, I fell upon my H4598
Job 1:20 Then Job arose, and rent his m, and H4598
2:12 rent every one his m, and sprinkled H4598
Ps 109:29 with their own confusion, as with a m. H4598

MANTLES
Isa 3:22 of apparel, and the m, and the wimples, H4595

MANY
Gen 17: 4 thou shalt be a father of m nations. H1995
5 a father of m nations have I made thee. H1995
21:34 in the Philistines' land m days. H7227
37: 3 and he made him a coat of m colours.
23 his coat of m colours that was on him;
37:32 And they sent the coat of m colours, and
34 loins, and mourned for his son m days. H7227
Ex 5: 5 the land now are m, and ye make them H7227
19:21 LORD to gaze, and m of them perish. H7227
23: 2 to decline after m to wrest judgment: H7227
35:22 men and women, as m as were willing
Lev 15:25 an issue of her blood m days out of the H7227
25:51 If there be yet m years behind, H7227
Nu 9:19 upon the tabernacle m days, then the H7227
10:36 LORD, unto the m thousands of Israel. H7233
13:18 they be strong or weak, few or m; H7227
22: 3 because they were m: and Moab was H7227
24: 7 seed shall be in m waters, and his king H7227
26:54 To m thou shalt give the more H7227
56 thereof be divided between m and few. H7227
35: 8 them that have m ye shall give many; H7227
8 ye shall give m; but from them that H7235
Dt 1:11 a thousand times so m more as ye are,
46 So ye abode in Kadesh m days, H7227
2: 1 and we compassed mount Seir m days. H7227
10 great, and m, and tall, as the Anakims; H7227
21 A people great, and m, and tall, as the H7227
3: 5 bars; beside unwalled towns a great m. H7235
7: 1 it, and hath cast out m nations before H7227
15: 6 shalt lend unto m nations, but thou H7227
6 shalt reign over m nations, but they H7227
25: 3 above these with m stripes, then thy H7227
28:12 m nations, and thou shalt not borrow. H7227
31:17 be devoured, and m evils and troubles H7227
21 And it shall come to pass, when m evils H7227
32: 7 the years of m generations: ask thy H1755
Jos 11: 4 with horses and chariots very m. H7227
22: 3 Ye have not left your brethren these m H7227
Jdg 3: 1 by them, even as m of Israel as had not
7: 2 with thee are too m for me to give the H7227
4 people are yet too m; bring them down H7227
8:30 his body begotten: for he had m wives. H7227
9:40 before him, and m were overthrown H7227
16:24 of our country, which slew m of us. H7235
1Sa 2: 5 that hath m children is waxed feeble. H7227
6:19 m of the people with a great slaughter.
14: 6 to the LORD to save by m or by few. H7227
25:10 son of Jesse? there be m servants now a H7231
2Sa 1: 4 the battle, and m of the people also are H7235
2:23 to pass, that as m as came to the place
12: 2 The rich man had exceeding m flocks H7235
22:17 took me; he drew me out of m waters; H7227
23:20 who had done m acts, he slew two H7227
24: 3 the people, how m soever they be, an
1Ki 2:38 And Shimei dwelt in Jerusalem m days. H7227
4:20 Judah and Israel were m, as the sand H7227
7:47 they were exceeding m: neither was the H7230
11: 1 But king Solomon loved m strange H7227
17:15 and he, and her house, did eat m days.
18: 1 And it came to pass after m days, that H7227
25 it first; for ye are m; and call on the H7227
22:16 And the king said unto him, How m
2Ki 9:22 Jezebel and her witchcrafts are so m? H7227
1Ch 4:27 brethren had not m children, neither H7227
5:22 For there fell down m slain, because H7227
7: 4 men: for they had m wives and sons. H7235
22 And Ephraim their father mourned m H7227
8:40 archers, and had m sons, and sons' H7235
11:22 who had done m acts; he slew two H7227
21: 3 an hundred times so m more as they be:
23:11 Beriah had not m sons; therefore they H7235
17 but the sons of Rehabiah were very m. H7235
28: 5 hath given me m sons,) he hath chosen H7227
2Ch 11:23 in abundance. And he desired m wives. H1995
14:11 whether with m, or with them that have H7227
16: 8 huge host, with very m chariots and H7235
18:15 And the king said to him, How m times
26:10 and digged m wells: for he had much H7227
29:31 m as were of a free heart burnt offerings.
30:17 For there were m in the congregation H7227
18 For a multitude of the people, even m H7227
32:23 And m brought gifts unto the LORD to H7227
Ezr 3:12 But m of the priests and Levites and H7227
12 voice; and m shouted aloud for joy: H7227
5:11 was builded these m years ago, which a H7690
10:13 But the people are m, and it is a time of H7227
13 m that have transgressed in this thing. H7235
Neh 5: 2 daughters, are m: therefore we take up H7227
6:17 of Judah sent m letters unto Tobiah, H7235
18 For there were m in Judah sworn unto H7227
7: 2 faithful man, and feared God above m. H7227
9:28 from heaven; and m times didst thou H7227
30 Yet m years didst thou forbear them, H7227
13:26 things? yet among m nations was there H7227
Est 1: 4 his excellent majesty m days, even an H7227
2: 8 was heard, and when m maidens were H7227
4: 3 and m lay in sackcloth and ashes. H7227
8:17 a good day. And m of the people of the H7227
Job 4: 3 Behold, thou hast instructed m, and H7227
11:19 yea, m shall make suit unto thee. H7227
13:23 How m are mine iniquities and sins?
16: 2 I have heard m such things: miserable H7227
23:14 me: and m such things are with him. H7227
41: 3 Will he make m supplications unto H7235
Ps 3: 1 me! m are they that rise up against me. H7227
2 M there be which say of my soul, There H7227
4: 6 There be m that say, Who will shew us H7227
18:16 took me, he drew me out of m waters. H7227
22:12 M bulls have compassed me: strong H7227
25:19 Consider mine enemies; for they are m; H7231
29: 3 the LORD is upon m waters. H7227
31:13 For I have heard the slander of m: fear H7227
32:10 M sorrows shall be to the wicked: but H7227
34:12 loveth m days, that he may see good?
19 M are the afflictions of the righteous: H7227
37:16 is better than the riches of m wicked. H7227
40: 3 unto our God: m shall see it, and fear, H7227
5 M, O LORD my God, are thy wonderful H7227
55:18 against me: for there were m with me. H7227
56: 2 me up: for they be m that fight against H7227
61: 6 life: and his years as m generations. H1755
71: 7 I am as a wonder unto m; but thou art H7227
78:38 them not: yea, m a time turned he his
93: 4 than the noise of m waters, yea, than H7227
106:43 M times did he deliver them; but they H7227
110: 6 wound the heads over m countries. H7227
119:84 How m are the days of thy servant?
157 M are my persecutors and mine H7227
129: 1 M a time have they afflicted me from my
2 M a time have they afflicted me from my
Prv 4:10 and the years of thy life shall be m. H7235
6:35 content, though thou givest m gifts. H7235
7:26 For she hath cast down m wounded: H7227
26 m strong men have been slain by her.
10:21 The lips of the righteous feed m: but H7227
14:20 neighbour: but the rich hath m friends. H7227
19: 4 Wealth maketh m friends; but the poor H7227
6 M will entreat the favour of the prince: H7227
21 There are m devices in a man's heart; H7227
28: 2 For the transgression of a land m are H7227
27 hideth his eyes shall have m a curse. H7227
29:26 M seek the ruler's favour; but every H7227
31:29 M daughters have done virtuously, but H7227
Ecc 5: 7 For in the multitude of dreams and m H7235
6: 3 children, and live m years, so that the H7227
3 of his years be m, and his soul be not H7227
11 Seeing there be m things that increase H7235
7:29 but they have sought out m inventions. H7227
11: 1 for thou shalt find it after m days. H7230
8 But if a man live m years, and rejoice H7235
8 shall be m. All that cometh is vanity. H7235
12: 9 out, and set in order m proverbs. H7235
12 of making m books there is no end; H7235
Song 8: 7 M waters cannot quench love, neither H7227
Isa 1:15 when ye make m prayers, I will not H7235
2: 3 And m people shall go and say, Come H7227
4 and shall rebuke m people: and they H7227
5: 9 of hosts, Of a truth m houses shall be H7227
8: 7 the river, strong and m, even the king of H7227
15 And m among them shall stumble, and H7227
17:12 Woe to the multitude of m people, H7227
13 like the rushing of m waters: but God H7227
22: 9 David, that they are m: and ye gathered H7231
23:16 sweet melody, sing m songs, that thou H7235
24:22 and after m days shall they be visited. H7230
31: 1 because they are m; and in horsemen, H7227
32:10 M days and years shall ye be troubled,
42:20 Seeing m things, but thou observest H7227
52:14 As m were astonied at thee; his visage H7227
15 So shall he sprinkle m nations; the H7227
53:11 m; for he shall bear their iniquities. H7227
12 and he bare the sin of m, and made H7227
58:12 the foundations of m generations; and H1755
60:15 excellency, a joy of m generations. H1755
61: 4 the desolations of m generations. H1755
66:16 and the slain of the LORD shall be m. H7231
Jer 3: 1 the harlot with m lovers; yet return H7227
5: 6 are m, and their backslidings H7231
11:15 lewdness with m, and the holy flesh is H7227
12:10 M pastors have destroyed my H7227
13: 6 And it came to pass after m days, that H7227
14: 7 are m; we have sinned against thee. H7231
16:16 Behold, I will send for m fishers, saith H7227

M

Jer 16:16 will I send for **m** hunters, and they H7227
20:10 For I heard the defaming of **m**, fear on H7227
22: 8 And **m** nations shall pass by this city, H7227
25:14 For **m** nations and great kings shall H7227
27: 7 come: and then **m** nations and great H7227
28: 8 both against **m** countries, and against H7227
32:14 vessel, that they may continue **m** days. H7227
35: 7 that ye may live **m** days in the land H7227
36:32 added besides unto them **m** like words. H7227
37:16 Jeremiah had remained there **m** days; H7227
42: 2 a few of **m**, as thine eyes do behold us:) H7235
46:11 shalt thou use **m** medicines; *for* thou H7235
16 He made **m** to fall, yea, one fell upon H7235
50:41 a great nation, and **m** kings shall be H7227
51:13 O thou that dwellest upon **m** waters, H7227
Lam 1:22 my sighs *are* **m**, and my heart *is* faint. H7227
Ezk 3: 6 Not to **m** people of a strange speech H7227
12:27 He seeth *is* for **m** days *to come*, and H7227
16:41 thee in the sight of **m** women: and I will H7227
17: 7 with great wings and **m** feathers: and, H7227
9 great power or **m** people to pluck it up H7227
17 building forts, to cut off **m** persons: H7227
19:10 full of branches by reason of **m** waters. H7227
22:25 her **m** widows in the midst thereof. H7235
26: 3 and will cause **m** nations to come up H7227
27: 3 of the people for **m** isles, Thus saith the H7227
15 *were* thy merchants; **m** isles *were* the H7227
33 seas, thou filledst **m** people; thou didst H7227
32: 3 a company of **m** people; and they shall H7227
9 I will also vex the hearts of **m** people, H7227
10 Yea, I will make **m** people amazed at H7227
33:24 **m**; the land is given us for inheritance. H7227
37: 2 *there were* very **m** in the open valley; H7227
38: 6 all his bands: *and* **m** people with thee. H7227
8 After **m** days thou shalt be visited: in H7227
8 *is* gathered out of **m** people, against the H7227
9 all thy bands, and **m** people with thee. H7227
15 parts, thou, and **m** people with thee, all H7227
17 in those days *m* years that I would bring
22 and upon the **m** people that *are* with H7227
23 in the eyes of **m** nations, and they shall H7227
39:27 in them in the sight of **m** nations; H7227
43: 2 *was* like a noise of **m** waters: and the H7227
47: 7 river *were* very **m** trees on the one side H7227
10 the fish of the great sea, exceeding **m**. H7227
Dan 2:48 and gave him **m** great gifts, and made H7690
8:25 shall destroy **m**: he shall also stand H7227
26 up the vision; for it *shall be* for **m** days. H7227
9:27 the covenant with **m** for one week: and H7227
10:14 days: for yet the vision *is* for **m** days.
11:12 he shall cast down *m* ten thousands: but
14 And in those times there shall **m** stand H7227
18 and shall take **m**: but a prince for his H7227
26 overflow: and **m** shall fall down slain. H7227
33 shall instruct **m**: yet they shall fall by H7227
33 by captivity, and by spoil, *m* days.
34 **m** shall cleave to them with flatteries. H7227
39 **m**, and shall divide the land for gain. H7227
40 and with **m** ships; and he shall H7227
41 glorious land, and **m** *countries* shall be H7227
44 to destroy, and utterly to make away **m**. H7227
12: 2 And **m** of them that sleep in the dust of H7227
3 they that turn **m** to righteousness as H7227
4 time of the end: **m** shall run to and fro, H7227
10 **M** shall be purified, and made white, H7227
Hos 3: 3 shalt abide for me **m** days; thou shalt H7227
4 For the children of Israel shall abide **m** H7227
8:11 Because Ephraim hath made **m** altars H7235
Joel 2: 2 it, *even* to the years of **m** generations. H1755
Am 8: 3 *there shall be* **m** dead bodies in every H7227
Mic 4: 2 And **m** nations shall come, and say, H7227
3 And he shall judge among **m** people, H7227
11 Now also **m** nations are gathered H7227
13 shalt beat in pieces **m** people: and I will H7227
5: 7 be in the midst of **m** people as a dew H7227
8 in the midst of **m** people as a lion H7227
Nah 1:12 and likewise **m**, yet thus shall they be H7227
3:15 make thyself **m** as the cankerworm, H3513
15 make thyself **m** as the locusts. H3513
Hab 2: 8 Because thou hast spoiled **m** nations, H7227
10 house by cutting off **m** people, and hast H7227
Zec 2:11 And **m** nations shall be joined to the H7227
7: 3 myself, as I have done these so **m** years?
8:20 people, and the inhabitants of **m** cities: H7227
22 Yea, **m** people and strong nations shall H7227
Mal 2: 6 and did turn **m** away from iniquity. H7227
8 ye have caused **m** to stumble at the H7227
Mt 3: 7 But when he saw **m** of the Pharisees *G4183*
7:13 and **m** there be which go in thereat: *G4183*

Mt 7:22 **M** will say to me in that day, Lord, *G4183*
22 in thy name done **m** wonderful works? *G4183*
8:11 And I say unto you, That **m** shall come *G4183*
16 they brought unto him **m** that were *G4183*
30 from them an herd of **m** swine feeding. *G4183*
9:10 the house, behold, **m** publicans and *G4183*
10:31 ye are of more value than **m** sparrows. *G4183*
13: 3 And he spake **m** things unto them in *G4183*
17 For verily I say unto you, That **m** *G4183*
58 And he did not **m** mighty works there *G4183*
14:36 his garment: and as **m** as touched were *G3745*
15:30 maimed, and **m** others, and cast them *G4183*
34 And Jesus saith unto them, How **m** *G4214*
16: 9 and how **m** baskets ye took up? *G4214*
10 and how **m** baskets ye took up? *G4214*
21 and suffer **m** things of the elders *G4183*
19:30 But **m** *that are* first shall be last; and *G4183*
20:16 last: for **m** be called, but few chosen. *G4183*
28 and to give his life a ransom for **m**. *G4183*
22: 9 **m** as ye shall find, bid to the marriage. *G3745*
10 together all as **m** as they found, both *G3745*
14 For **m** are called, but few *are* chosen. *G4183*
24: 5 For **m** shall come in my name, saying, I *G4183*
5 I am Christ; and shall deceive **m**. *G4183*
10 And then shall **m** be offended, and *G4183*
11 And **m** false prophets shall rise, and *G4183*
11 prophets shall rise, and shall deceive **m**. *G4183*
12 abound, the love of **m** shall wax cold. *G4183*
25:21 thee ruler over **m** things: enter thou *G4183*
23 thee ruler over **m** things: enter thou *G4183*
26:28 is shed for **m** for the remission of sins. *G4183*
60 But found none: yea, though **m** false *G4183*
27:13 **m** things they witness against thee? *G4214*
19 I have suffered **m** things this day in a *G4183*
52 And the graves were opened; and **m** *G4183*
53 the holy city, and appeared unto **m**. *G4183*
55 And **m** women were there beholding *G4183*
Mk 1:34 And he healed **m** that were sick of *G4183*
34 and cast out **m** devils; and suffered *G4183*
2: 2 And straightway **m** were gathered *G4183*
15 in his house, **m** publicans and sinners *G4183*
15 there were **m**, and they followed him. *G4183*
3:10 For he had healed **m**; insomuch that *G4183*
10 for to touch him, as **m** as had plagues. *G3745*
4: 2 And he taught them **m** things by *G4183*
33 And with **m** such parables spake he the *G4183*
5: 9 My name *is* Legion: for we are **m**. *G4183*
26 And had suffered **m** things of many *G4183*
26 And had suffered many things of **m** *G4183*
6: 2 synagogue: and **m** hearing *him* were *G4183*
13 And they cast out **m** devils, and *G4183*
13 oil **m** that were sick, and healed *them*. *G4183*
20 he did **m** things, and heard him gladly. *G4183*
31 for there were **m** coming and going, *G4183*
33 departing, and **m** knew him, and ran *G4183*
34 and he began to teach them **m** things. *G4183*
38 He saith unto them, How **m** loaves *G4214*
56 as **m** as touched him were made whole. *G3745*
7: 4 they eat not. And **m** other things there *G4183*
8 and **m** other such like things ye do. *G4183*
13 delivered: and **m** such like things do ye. *G4183*
8: 5 And he asked them, How **m** loaves *G4214*
19 five thousand, how **m** baskets full of *G4214*
20 four thousand, how **m** baskets full of *G4214*
31 of man must suffer **m** things, and be *G4183*
9:12 suffer **m** things, and be set at nought. *G4183*
26 insomuch that **m** said, He is dead. *G4183*
10:31 But **m** *that are* first shall be last; and *G4183*
45 and to give his life a ransom for **m**. *G4183*
48 And **m** charged him that he should *G4183*
11: 8 And **m** spread their garments in the *G4183*
12: 5 him they killed, and **m** others; beating *G4183*
41 and **m** that were rich cast in much. *G4183*
13: 6 For **m** shall come in my name, saying, I *G4183*
6 I am *Christ*; and shall deceive **m**. *G4183*
14:24 the new testament, which is shed for **m**. *G4183*
56 For **m** bare false witness against him, *G4183*
15: 3 And the chief priests accused him of **m** *G4183*
4 **m** things they witness against thee. *G4214*
41 unto him;) and **m** other women which *G4183*
Lk 1: 1 Forasmuch as **m** have taken in hand to *G4183*
14 and **m** shall rejoice at his birth. *G4183*
16 And **m** of the children of Israel shall he *G4183*
2:34 rising again of **m** in Israel; and for a *G4183*
35 thoughts of **m** hearts may be revealed. *G4183*
3:18 And **m** other things in his exhortation *G4183*
4:25 But I tell you of a truth, **m** widows were *G4183*
27 And **m** lepers were in Israel in the time *G4183*
41 And devils also came out of **m**, crying *G4183*

Lk 7:11 city called Nain; and **m** of his disciples *G2425*
21 And in that same hour he cured **m** of *G4183*
21 unto **m** *that were* blind he gave sight. *G4183*
47 sins, which are **m**, are forgiven; for she *G4183*
8: 3 and Susanna, and **m** others, which *G4183*
30 **m** devils were entered into him. *G4183*
32 And there was there an herd of **m** *G2425*
9:22 Saying, The Son of man must suffer **m** *G4183*
10:24 For I tell you, that **m** prophets and *G4183*
41 careful and troubled about **m** things: *G4183*
11: 8 rise and give him as **m** as he needeth. *G3745*
53 to provoke him to speak of **m** things: *G4119*
12: 7 ye are of more value than **m** sparrows. *G4183*
19 goods laid up for **m** years; take thine *G4183*
47 his will, shall be beaten with **m** *stripes*. *G4183*
13:24 at the strait gate: for **m**, I say unto you, *G4183*
14:16 man made a great supper, and bade **m**: *G4183*
15:13 And not **m** days after the younger son *G4183*
17 he said, How **m** hired servants of my *G4214*
29 *his* father, Lo, these **m** years do I serve *G5118*
17:25 But first must he suffer **m** things, and *G4183*
21: 8 not deceived: for **m** shall come in my *G4183*
22:65 And **m** other things blasphemously *G4183*
23: 8 he had heard **m** things of him; and *G4183*
9 Then he questioned with him in **m** *G2425*
Jn 1:12 But as **m** as received him, to them gave *G3745*
2:12 and they continued there not **m** days. *G4183*
23 in the feast *day*, **m** believed in his *G4183*
4:39 And **m** of the Samaritans of that city *G4183*
41 And **m** more believed because of his *G4183*
6: 9 fishes: but what are they among so **m**? *G5118*
60 **M** therefore of his disciples, when they *G4183*
66 From that *time* **m** of his disciples went *G4183*
7:31 And **m** of the people believed on him, *G4183*
40 **M** of the people therefore, when they *G4183*
8:26 I have **m** things to say and to judge of *G4183*
30 As he spake these words, **m** believed on *G4183*
10:20 And **m** of them said, He hath a devil, *G4183*
32 Jesus answered them, **M** good works *G4183*
41 And **m** resorted unto him, and said, *G4183*
42 And **m** believed on him there. *G4183*
11:19 And **m** of the Jews came to Martha and *G4183*
45 Then **m** of the Jews which came to *G4183*
47 do we? for this man doeth **m** miracles. *G4183*
55 nigh at hand: and **m** went out of the *G4183*
12:11 Because that by reason of him **m** of the *G4183*
37 But though he had done so **m** miracles *G5118*
42 chief rulers also **m** believed on him; but *G4183*
14: 2 In my Father's house are **m** mansions: *G4183*
16:12 I have yet **m** things to say unto you, but *G4183*
17: 2 life to as **m** as thou hast given him.
19:20 This title then read **m** of the Jews: for *G4183*
20:30 And **m** other signs truly did Jesus in the *G4183*
21:11 were so **m**, yet was not the net broken. *G5118*
25 And there are also **m** other things *G4183*
Act 1: 3 after his passion by **m** infallible proofs, *G4183*
5 with the Holy Ghost not **m** days hence. *G4183*
2:39 as **m** as the Lord our God shall call. *G3745*
40 And with **m** other words did he testify *G4119*
43 And fear came upon every soul: and **m** *G4183*
3:24 follow after, as **m** as have spoken, have *G3745*
4: 4 Howbeit **m** of them which heard the *G4183*
6 and as **m** as were of the kindred *G3745*
34 them that lacked: for as **m** as were *G3745*
5:11 and upon as **m** as heard these things.
12 the apostles were **m** signs and wonders *G4183*
36 was slain; and all, as **m** as obeyed him, *G3745*
37 as **m** as obeyed him, were dispersed. *G3745*
8: 7 loud voice, came out of **m** that were *G4183*
7 *with them*: and **m** taken with palsies, *G4183*
25 gospel in **m** villages of the Samaritans. *G4183*
9:13 I have heard by **m** of this man, how *G4183*
23 And after that **m** days were fulfilled, *G2425*
42 all Joppa; and **m** believed in the Lord. *G4183*
43 And it came to pass, that he tarried **m** *G2425*
10:27 and found **m** that were come together. *G4183*
45 astonished, as **m** as came with Peter, *G3745*
12:12 **m** were gathered together praying. *G2425*
13:31 And he was seen **m** days of them which *G4119*
43 was broken up, **m** of the Jews and *G4183*
48 the Lord: and as **m** as were ordained to *G3745*
14:21 and had taught **m**, they returned again *G2425*
15:32 with **m** words, and confirmed *them*. *G4183*
35 word of the Lord, with **m** others also. *G4183*
16:18 And this did she **m** days. But Paul, *G1909*
23 And when they had laid **m** stripes upon *G4183*
17:12 Therefore **m** of them believed; also of *G4183*
18: 8 all his house; and **m** of the Corinthians *G4183*
19:18 And **m** that believed came, and *G4183*

Act 19:19 **M** of them also which used curious arts *G2425*
20: 8 And there were **m** lights in the upper *G2425*
19 of mind, and with **m** tears, and *G4183*
21:10 And as we tarried *there* **m** days, there *G4119*
20 brother, how **m** thousands of Jews *G4214*
24:10 thou hast been of **m** years a judge unto *G4183*
17 Now after **m** years I came to bring *G4119*
25: 7 round about, and laid **m** and grievous *G4183*
14 And when they had been there **m** days, *G4119*
26: 9 that I ought to do **m** things contrary to *G4183*
10 in Jerusalem: and **m** of the saints did I *G4183*
27: 7 And when we had sailed slowly **m** *G2425*
20 And when neither sun nor stars in **m** *G4119*
28:10 Who also honoured us with **m** *G4183*
23 a day, there came **m** to him into *his* *G4119*
Ro 2:12 For as **m** as have sinned without law *G3745*
12 law: and as **m** as have sinned in the *G3745*
4:17 thee a father of **m** nations,) before him *G4183*
18 the father of **m** nations, according *G4183*
5:15 the offence of one **m** be dead, much *G4183*
15 Jesus Christ, hath abounded unto **m**. *G4183*
16 gift *is* of **m** offences unto justification. *G4183*
19 For as by one man's disobedience **m** *G4183*
19 of one shall **m** be made righteous. *G4183*
6: 3 Know ye not, that so **m** of us as were *G3745*
8:14 For as **m** as are led by the Spirit of God, *G3745*
29 be the firstborn among **m** brethren. *G4183*
12: 4 For as we have **m** members in one *G4183*
5 So we, *being* **m**, are one body in Christ, *G4183*
15:23 desire these **m** years to come unto you; *G4183*
16: 2 a succourer of **m**, and of myself also. *G4183*
1Co 1:26 how that not **m** wise men after the *G4183*
26 **m** mighty, not many noble, *are called*: *G4183*
26 many mighty, not **m** noble, *are called*: *G4183*
4:15 yet *have ye* not **m** fathers: for in Christ *G4183*
8: 5 (as there be gods **m**, and lords many,) *G4183*
5 (as there be gods many, and lords **m**,) *G4183*
10: 5 But with **m** of them God was not well *G4119*
17 For we *being* **m** are one bread, *and* one *G4183*
33 the *profit* of **m**, that they may be saved. *G4183*
11:30 For this cause **m** *are* weak and sickly *G4183*
30 and sickly among you, and **m** sleep. *G2425*
12:12 For as the body is one, and hath **m** *G4183*
12 being **m**, are one body: so also *is* Christ. *G4183*
14 For the body is not one member, but **m**. *G4183*
20 But now *are they* **m** members, yet but *G4183*
14:10 There are, it may be, so **m** kinds of *G5118*
16: 9 unto me, and *there are* **m** adversaries. *G4183*
2Co 1:11 by the means of **m** persons thanks may *G4183*
11 may be given by **m** on our behalf. *G4183*
2: 4 unto you with **m** tears; not that ye *G4183*
6 punishment, which *was inflicted* of **m**. *G4119*
17 For we are not as **m**, which corrupt the *G4183*
4:15 of **m** redound to the glory of God. *G4119*
6:10 as poor, yet making **m** rich; as having *G4183*
8:22 proved diligent in **m** things, but now *G4183*
9: 2 and your zeal hath provoked very **m**. *G4119*
12 also by **m** thanksgivings unto God; *G4183*
11:18 Seeing that **m** glory after the flesh, I *G4183*
12:21 and *that* I shall bewail **m** which have *G4183*
Gal 1:14 religion above **m** my equals in mine *G4183*
3: 4 Have ye suffered so **m** things in vain? if *G5118*
10 For as **m** as are of the works of the law *G3745*
16 to seeds, as of **m**; but as of one, And *G4183*
27 For as **m** of you as have been baptized *G3745*
4:27 for the desolate hath **m** more children *G4183*
6:12 As **m** as desire to make a fair shew in *G3745*
16 And as **m** as walk according to this *G3745*
Php 1:14 And **m** of the brethren in the Lord, *G4119*
3:15 Let us therefore, as **m** as be perfect, be *G3745*
18 (For **m** walk, of whom I have told you *G4183*
Col 2: 1 **m** as have not seen my face in the flesh; *G3745*
1Ti 6: 1 Let as **m** servants as are under the yoke *G3745*
9 a snare, and *into* **m** foolish and hurtful *G4183*
10 themselves through with **m** sorrows. *G4183*
12 a good profession before **m** witnesses. *G4183*
2Ti 1:18 that day: and in how **m** things he *G3745*
2: 2 of me among **m** witnesses, the same *G4183*
Tit 1:10 For there are **m** unruly and vain talkers *G4183*
Heb 2:10 in bringing **m** sons unto glory, to *G4183*
5:11 Of whom we have **m** things to say, and *G4183*
7:23 And they truly were **m** priests, because *G4119*
9:28 to bear the sins of **m**; and unto them *G4183*
11:12 as good as dead, *so* **m** as the stars of the
12:15 trouble *you*, and thereby **m** be defiled; *G4183*
Jas 3: 1 My brethren, be not **m** masters, *G4183*
2 For in **m** things we offend all. If any *G4183*
2Pt 2: 2 And **m** shall follow their pernicious *G4183*
1Jn 2:18 now are there **m** antichrists; whereby *G4183*
1Jn 4: 1 of God: because **m** false prophets are *G4183*
2Jn 7 For **m** deceivers are entered into the *G4183*
12 Having **m** things to write unto you, I *G4183*
3Jn 13 I had **m** things to write, but I will not *G4183*
Rev 1:15 and his voice as the sound of **m** waters. *G4183*
2:24 rest in Thyatira, as **m** as have not this *G3745*
3:19 As **m** as I love, I rebuke and chasten: *G3745*
5:11 I heard the voice of **m** angels round *G4183*
8:11 wormwood; and **m** men died of the *G4183*
9: 9 chariots of **m** horses running to battle. *G4183*
10:11 again before **m** peoples, and nations, *G4183*
13:15 and cause that as **m** as would not *G3745*
14: 2 as the voice of **m** waters, and as the *G4183*
17: 1 whore that sitteth upon **m** waters: *G4183*
18:17 as **m** as trade by sea, stood afar off, *G3745*
19: 6 as the voice of **m** waters, and as the *G4183*
12 on his head *were* **m** crowns; and he *G4183*

MAOCH
1Sa 27: 2 unto Achish, the son of **M**, king of Gath. H4582

MAON
Jos 15:55 **M**, Carmel, and Ziph, and Juttah, H4584
1Sa 23:24 the wilderness of **M**, in the plain on the H4584
25 in the wilderness of **M**. And when Saul H4584
25 after David in the wilderness of **M**. H4584
25: 2 And *there was* a man in **M**, whose H4584
1Ch 2:45 And the son of Shammai *was* **M**: and H4584
45 and **M** *was* the father of Beth-zur. H4584

MAONITES
Jdg 10:12 and the **M**, did oppress you; and H4584

MAR
Lev 19:27 shalt thou **m** the corners of thy beard. H7843
Ru 4: 6 redeem *it* for myself, lest I **m** mine own H7843
1Sa 6: 5 of your mice that **m** the land; and ye H7843
2Ki 3:19 **m** every good piece of land with stones. H3510
Job 30:13 They **m** my path, they set forward my H5420
Jer 13: 9 After this manner will I **m** the pride of H7843

MARA
Ru 1:20 not Naomi, call me **M**: for the Almighty H4755

MARAH
Ex 15:23 And when they came to **M**, they could H4785
23 of the waters of **M**, for they *were* bitter: H4785
23 therefore the name of it was called **M**. H4785
Nu 33: 8 wilderness of Etham, and pitched in **M**. H4785
9 And they removed from **M**, and came H4785

MARALAH
Jos 19:11 toward the sea, and **M**, and reached to H4831

MARANATHA
1Co 16:22 Jesus Christ, let him be Anathema **M**. *G3134*

MARBLE
1Ch 29: 2 stones, and **m** stones in abundance. H7893
Est 1: 6 and pillars of **m**: the beds *were of* gold H8336
6 red, and blue, and white, and black, **m**. H8336
Song 5:15 His legs *are as* pillars of **m**, set upon H8336
Rev 18:12 wood, and of brass, and iron, and **m**, *G3139*

MARCABOTH See BETH-MARCABOTH.

MARCH
Ps 68: 7 didst **m** through the wilderness; Selah: H6805
Jer 46:22 for they shall **m** with an army, and H3212
Joel 2: 7 war; and they shall **m** every one on his H3212
Hab 1: 6 which shall **m** through the breadth H1980
3:12 Thou didst **m** through the land in H6805

MARCHED
Ex 14:10 the Egyptians **m** after them; and they H5265

MARCHEDST
Jdg 5: 4 of Seir, when thou **m** out of the field of H6805

MARCUS
Col 4:10 saluteth you, and **M**, sister's son to *G3138*
Phlm 24 **M**, Aristarchus, Demas, Lucas, my *G3138*
1Pt 5:13 saluteth you; and *so doth* **M** my son. *G3138*

MARESHAH
Jos 15:44 And Keilah, and Achzib, and **M**; nine H4762
1Ch 2:42 and the sons of **M** the father of Hebron. H4762
4:21 the father of **M**, and the families of H4762
2Ch 11: 8 And Gath, and **M**, and Ziph, H4762
2Ch 14: 9 hundred chariots; and came unto **M**. H4762
10 array in the valley of Zephathah at **M**. H4762
20:37 Then Eliezer the son of Dodavah of **M** H4762
Mic 1:15 O inhabitant of **M**: he shall come unto H4762

MARINERS
Ezk 27: 8 and Arvad were thy **m**: thy wise *men*, O H7751
9 of the sea with their **m** were in thee to H4419
27 merchandise, thy **m**, and thy pilots, thy H4419
29 And all that handle the oar, the **m**, *and* H4419
Jna 1: 5 Then the **m** were afraid, and cried H4419

MARISHES
Ezk 47:11 But the miry places thereof and the **m** H1360

MARK
Gen 4:15 the LORD set a **m** upon Cain, lest any H226
Ru 3: 4 that thou shalt **m** the place where he H3045
1Sa 20:20 the side *thereof*, as though I shot at a **m**. H4307
2Sa 13:28 his servants, saying, **M** ye now when H7200
1Ki 20: 7 land, and said, **M**, I pray you, and see H3045
22 thyself, and **m**, and see what thou H3045
Job 7:20 thou set me as a **m** against thee, so that H4645
16:12 me to pieces, and set me up for his **m**. H4307
18: 2 words? **m**, and afterwards we will speak. H995
21: 5 **M** me, and be astonished, and lay *your* H6437
33:31 **M** well, O Job, hearken unto me: hold H7181
39: 1 canst thou **m** when the hinds do calve? H8104
Ps 37:37 **M** the perfect *man*, and behold the H8104
48:13 **M** ye well her bulwarks, consider her H7896
56: 6 themselves, they **m** my steps, when H8104
130: 3 If thou, LORD, shouldest **m** iniquities, H8104
Lam 3:12 bow, and set me as a **m** for the arrow. H4307
Ezk 9: 4 and set a **m** upon the foreheads H8420
6 upon whom *is* the **m**; and begin at my H8420
44: 5 me, Son of man, **m** well, and behold H7760
5 laws thereof; and **m** well the entering H7760
Act 12:12 surname was **M**; where many were *G3138*
25 with them John, whose surname was **M**. *G3138*
15:37 with them John, whose surname was **M**. *G3138*
39 took **M**, and sailed unto Cyprus; *G3138*
Ro 16:17 Now I beseech you, brethren, **m** them *G4648*
Php 3:14 I press toward the **m** for the prize of the *G4649*
17 of me, and **m** them which walk so *G4648*
2Ti 4:11 Only Luke is with me. Take **M**, and *G3138*
Rev 13:16 and bond, to receive a **m** in their right *G5480*
17 he that had the **m**, or the name of the *G5480*
14: 9 *his* **m** in his forehead, or in his hand, *G5480*
11 whosoever receiveth the **m** of his name. *G5480*
15: 2 and over his **m**, *and* over the number *G5480*
16: 2 men which had the **m** of the beast, and *G5480*
19:20 had received the **m** of the beast, and *G5480*
20: 4 neither had received *his* **m** upon their *G5480*

MARKED
1Sa 1:12 before the LORD, that Eli **m** her mouth. H8104
Job 22:15 Hast thou **m** the old way which wicked H8104
24:16 *which* they had **m** for themselves in the H2856
Jer 2:22 is **m** before me, saith the Lord GOD. H3799
23:18 who hath **m** his word, and heard *it*? H7181
Lk 14: 7 bidden, when he **m** how they chose out *G1907*

MARKEST
Job 10:14 If I sin, then thou **m** me, and thou wilt H8104

MARKET
Ezk 27:13 of men and vessels of brass in thy **m**. H4627
17 they traded in thy **m** wheat of Minnith, H4627
19 cassia, and calamus, were in thy **m**. H4627
25 did sing of thee in thy **m**: and thou wast H4627
Mk 7: 4 And *when they come* from the **m**, except *G58*
Jn 5: 2 by the sheep *m* a pool, which is called
Act 17:17 **m** daily with them that met with him. *G58*

MARKETH
Job 33:11 He putteth my feet in the stocks, he **m** H8104
Isa 44:13 out *his* rule; he **m** it out with a line; he H8388
13 with planes, and he **m** it out with the H8388

MARKETPLACE
Mt 20: 3 and saw others standing idle in the **m**, *G58*
Lk 7:32 sitting in the **m**, and calling one to *G58*
Act 16:19 drew *them* into the **m** unto the rulers, *G58*

MARKETPLACES
Mk 12:38 clothing, and *love* salutations in the **m**, *G58*

MARKETS
Mt 11:16 in the **m**, and calling unto their fellows, *G58*

Mt 23: 7 And greetings in the **m**, and to be called *G58*
Lk 11:43 the synagogues, and greetings in the **m**. *G58*
20:46 greetings in the **m**, and the highest seats *G58*

MARKS
Lev 19:28 print any **m** upon you: I *am* the LORD. H7085
Gal 6:17 in my body the **m** of the Lord Jesus. *G4742*

MAROTH
Mic 1:12 For the inhabitant of **M** waited H4796

MARRED
Isa 52:14 his visage was so **m** more than any H4893
Jer 13: 7 was **m**, it was profitable for nothing. H7843
18: 4 made of clay was **m** in the hand of the H7843
Nah 2: 2 them out, and **m** their vine branches. H7843
Mk 2:22 the bottles will be **m**: but new wine must *G622*

MARRIAGE
Ex 21:10 her duty of **m**, shall he not diminish. H5772
Ps 78:63 and their maidens were not given to **m**. H1984
Mt 22: 2 king, which made a **m** for his son, *G1062*
4 all things *are* ready: come unto the **m**. *G1062*
9 as many as ye shall find, bid to the **m**. *G1062*
30 nor are given in **m**, but are as the angels *G1547*
24:38 and giving in **m**, until the day that Noe *G1547*
25:10 him to the **m**: and the door was shut. *G1062*
Mk 12:25 nor are given in **m**; but are as the angels *G1061*
Lk 17:27 they were given in **m**, until the day that *G1547*
20:34 of this world marry, and are given in **m**: *G1548*
35 neither marry, nor are given in **m**: *G1548*
Jn 2: 1 And the third day there was a **m** in *G1062*
2 was called, and his disciples, to the **m**. *G1062*
1Co 7:38 So then he that giveth *her* in **m** doeth *G1547*
38 that giveth *her* not in **m** doeth better. *G1547*
Heb 13: 4 **M** *is* honourable in all, and the bed *G1062*
Rev 19: 7 to him: for the **m** of the Lamb is come, *G1062*
9 called unto the **m** supper of the Lamb. *G1062*

MARRIAGES
Gen 34: 9 And make ye **m** with us, *and* give your H2859
Dt 7: 3 Neither shalt thou make **m** with them; H2859
Jos 23:12 and shall make **m** with them, and go in H2859

MARRIED
Gen 19:14 in law, which **m** his daughters, and H3947
Ex 21: 3 if he were **m**, then his wife shall H1167+H802
Lev 22:12 If the priest's daughter also be *m* unto a
Nu 12: 1 whom he had **m**: for he had married H3947
1 for he had **m** an Ethiopian woman. H3947
36: 3 And if they be **m** to any of the sons of the H802
11 **m** unto their father's brothers' sons: H802
12 *And* they were **m** into the families of the H802
Dt 22:22 with a woman **m** to an husband, then H1166
24: 1 When a man hath taken a wife, and **m** H1166
1Ch 2:21 of Gilead, whom he **m** when he *was* H3947
2Ch 13:21 But Abijah waxed mighty, and **m** H5375
Neh 13:23 I Jews *that* had **m** wives of Ashdod, of H3427
Prv 30:23 For an odious *woman* when she is **m**; H1166
Isa 54: 1 children of the **m** wife, saith the LORD. H1166
62: 4 in thee, and thy land shall be **m**. H1166
Jer 3:14 LORD; for I am **m** unto you: and I will H1166
Mal 2:11 hath **m** the daughter of a strange god. H1166
Mt 22:25 first, when he had **m** a wife, deceased, *G1060*
Mk 6:17 brother Philip's wife: for he had **m** her. *G1060*
10:12 **m** to another, she committeth adultery. *G1060*
Lk 14:20 And another said, I have **m** a wife, and *G1060*
17:27 They did eat, they drank, they **m** wives, *G1060*
Ro 7: 3 liveth, she be **m** to another man, she *G1096*
3 though she be **m** to another man. *G1096*
4 that ye should be **m** to another, *even* to *G1096*
1Co 7:10 And unto the **m** I command, *yet* not I, *G1060*
33 But he that is **m** careth for the things *G1060*
34 but she that is **m** careth for the things *G1060*
39 **m** to whom she will; only in the Lord. *G1060*

MARRIETH
Isa 62: 5 For *as* a young man **m** a virgin, *so* shall H1166
Mt 19: 9 and whoso **m** her which is put away *G1060*
Lk 16:18 his wife, and **m** another, committeth *G1060*
18 and whosoever **m** her that is put away *G1060*

MARROW
Job 21:24 and his bones are moistened with **m**. H4221
Ps 63: 5 My soul shall be satisfied as *with* **m** H2459
Prv 3: 8 It shall be health to thy navel, and **m** to H8250
Isa 25: 6 of **m**, of wines on the lees well refined. H4229
Heb 4:12 of the joints and **m**, and *is* a discerner *G3452*

MARRY
Gen 38: 8 **m** her, and raise up seed to thy brother. H2992
Nu 36: 6 saying, Let them **m** to whom they think H802
6 of the tribe of their father shall they **m**. H802
Dt 25: 5 dead shall not **m** without unto a H1961+H376
Isa 62: 5 *so* shall thy sons **m** thee: and *as* the H1166
Mt 5:32 whosoever shall **m** her that is divorced *G1060*
19: 9 and shall **m** another, committeth *G1060*
10 be so with *his* wife, it is not good to **m**. *G1060*
22:24 his brother shall **m** his wife, and raise *G1918*
30 For in the resurrection they neither **m**, *G1060*
Mk 10:11 his wife, and **m** another, committeth *G1060*
12:25 dead, they neither **m**, nor are given in *G1060*
Lk 20:34 world **m**, and are given in marriage: *G1060*
35 neither **m**, nor are given in marriage: *G1060*
1Co 7: 9 But if they cannot contain, let them **m**: *G1060*
9 for it is better to **m** than to burn. *G1060*
28 But and if thou **m**, thou hast not sinned; *G1060*
28 and if a virgin **m**, she hath not sinned. *G1060*
36 what he will, he sinneth not: let them **m**. *G1060*
1Ti 4: 3 Forbidding to **m**, *and commanding* to *G1060*
5:11 wax wanton against Christ, they will **m**; *G1060*
14 younger women **m**, bear children, guide *G1060*

MARRYING
Neh 13:27 against our God in **m** strange wives? H3427
Mt 24:38 eating and drinking, **m** and giving in *G1060*

MARS'
Act 17:22 Then Paul stood in the midst of **M** hill, *G697*

MARSENA
Est 1:14 Tarshish, Meres, **M**, *and* Memucan, the H4826

MART
Isa 23: 3 her revenue; and she is a **m** of nations. H5505

MARTHA
Lk 10:38 named **M** received him into her house. *G3136*
40 But **M** was cumbered about much *G3136*
41 and said unto her, **M**, Martha, thou art *G3136*
41 unto her, Martha, **M**, thou art careful *G3136*
Jn 11: 1 the town of Mary and her sister **M**. *G3136*
5 Now Jesus loved **M**, and her sister, and *G3136*
19 And many of the Jews came to **M** and *G3136*
20 Then **M**, as soon as she heard that Jesus *G3136*
21 Then said **M** unto Jesus, Lord, if thou *G3136*
24 **M** saith unto him, I know that he shall *G3136*
30 was in that place where **M** met him. *G3136*
39 Jesus said, Take ye away the stone. **M**, *G3136*
12: 2 There they made him a supper; and **M** *G3136*

MARTYR
Act 22:20 And when the blood of thy **m** Stephen *G3144*
Rev 2:13 *was* my faithful **m**, who was slain *G3144*

MARTYRS
Rev 17: 6 the blood of the **m** of Jesus: and when *G3144*

MARVEL
Ecc 5: 8 in a province, **m** not at the matter: for H8539
Mk 5:20 had done for him: and all *men* did **m**. *G2296*
Jn 3: 7 **M** not that I said unto thee, Ye must be *G2296*
5:20 works than these, that ye may **m**. *G2296*
28 **M** not at this: for the hour is coming, in *G2296*
7:21 I have done one work, and ye all **m**. *G2296*
Act 3:12 of Israel, why **m** ye at this? or why look *G2296*
2Co 11:14 And no **m**; for Satan himself is *G2298*
Gal 1: 6 I **m** that ye are so soon removed from *G2296*
1Jn 3:13 **M** not, my brethren, if the world hate *G2296*
Rev 17: 7 didst thou **m**? I will tell thee the mystery *G2296*

MARVELLED
Gen 43:33 youth: and the men **m** one at another. H8539
Ps 48: 5 They saw *it, and* so they **m**; they were H8539
Mt 8:10 When Jesus heard *it*, he **m**, and said to *G2296*
27 But the men **m**, saying, What manner *G2296*
9: 8 But when the multitudes saw *it*, they **m**, *G2296*
33 the multitudes **m**, saying, It was never *G2296*
21:20 And when the disciples saw *it*, they **m**, *G2296*
22:22 **m**, and left him, and went their way. *G2296*
27:14 insomuch that the governor **m** greatly. *G2296*
Mk 6: 6 And he **m** because of their unbelief. *G2296*
12:17 that are God's. And they **m** at him. *G2296*
15: 5 yet answered nothing; so that Pilate **m**. *G2296*
44 And Pilate **m** if he were already dead: *G2296*
Lk 1:21 **m** that he tarried so long in the temple. *G2296*
63 His name is John. And they **m** all. *G2296*
2:33 And Joseph and his mother **m** at those *G2258*
Lk 7: 9 When Jesus heard these things, he **m** at *G2296*
11:38 And when the Pharisee saw *it*, he **m** *G2296*
20:26 **m** at his answer, and held their peace. *G2296*
Jn 4:27 his disciples, and **m** that he talked with *G2296*
7:15 And the Jews **m**, saying, How knoweth *G2296*
Act 2: 7 And they were all amazed and **m**, *G2296*
4:13 men, they **m**; and they took knowledge *G2296*

MARVELLOUS
1Ch 16:12 Remember his **m** works that he hath H6381
24 his **m** works among all nations. H6381
Job 5: 9 **m** things without number: H6381
10:16 again thou shewest thyself **m** upon me. H6381
Ps 9: 1 heart; I will shew forth all thy **m** works. H6381
17: 7 Shew thy **m** lovingkindness, O thou H6395
31:21 me his **m** kindness in a strong city. H6381
78:12 **M** things did he in the sight of their H6382
98: 1 for he hath done **m** things: his right H6381
105: 5 Remember his **m** works that he hath H6381
118:23 This is the LORD'S doing; it *is* **m** in our H6381
139:14 made: **m** *are* thy works; and H6381
Isa 29:14 proceed to do a **m** work among this H6381
14 people, *even* a **m** work and a wonder: H6381
Dan 11:36 and shall speak **m** things against the H6381
Mic 7:15 of Egypt will I shew unto him **m** *things*. H6381
Zec 8: 6 Thus saith the LORD of hosts; If it be **m** H6381
6 should it also be **m** in mine eyes? saith H6381
Mt 21:42 Lord's doing, and it is **m** in our eyes? *G2298*
Mk 12:11 This was the Lord's doing, and it is **m** *G2298*
Jn 9:30 Why herein is a **m** thing, that ye know *G2298*
1Pt 2: 9 you out of darkness into his **m** light: *G2298*
Rev 15: 1 in heaven, great and **m**, seven angels *G2298*
3 saying, Great and **m** *are* thy works, *G2298*

MARVELLOUSLY
2Ch 26:15 for he was **m** helped, till he was strong. H6381
Job 37: 5 God thundereth **m** with his voice; great H6381
Hab 1: 5 and wonder **m**: for *I* will work a work H8539

MARVELS
Ex 34:10 thy people I will do **m**, such as have not H6381

MARY
Mt 1:16 the husband of **M**, of whom was born *G3137*
18 as his mother **M** was espoused to *G3137*
20 to take unto thee **M** thy wife: for that *G3137*
2:11 young child with **M** his mother, and fell *G3137*
13:55 his mother called **M**? and his brethren, *G3137*
27:56 Among which was **M** Magdalene, and *G3137*
56 Mary Magdalene, and **M** the mother of *G3137*
61 And there was **M** Magdalene, and the *G3137*
61 **M**, sitting over against the sepulchre. *G3137*
28: 1 of the week, came **M** Magdalene and *G3137*
1 and the other **M** to see the sepulchre. *G3137*
Mk 6: 3 Is not this the carpenter, the son of **M**, *G3137*
15:40 whom was **M** Magdalene, and Mary *G3137*
40 Mary Magdalene, and **M** the mother of *G3137*
47 And **M** Magdalene and Mary *the* *G3137*
47 And Mary Magdalene and **M** *the* *G3137*
16: 1 And when the sabbath was past, **M** *G3137*
1 Mary Magdalene, and **M** the *mother* of *G3137*
9 appeared first to **M** Magdalene, out of *G3137*
Lk 1:27 of David; and the virgin's name *was* **M**. *G3137*
30 **M**: for thou hast found favour with God. *G3137*
34 Then said **M** unto the angel, How shall *G3137*
38 And **M** said, Behold the handmaid of *G3137*
39 And **M** arose in those days, and went *G3137*
41 the salutation of **M**, the babe leaped in *G3137*
46 And **M** said, My soul doth magnify the *G3137*
56 And **M** abode with her about three *G3137*
2: 5 To be taxed with **M** his espoused wife, *G3137*
16 haste, and found **M**, and Joseph, and *G3137*
19 But **M** kept all these things, and *G3137*
34 and said unto **M** his mother, Behold, *G3137*
8: 2 and infirmities, **M** called Magdalene, *G3137*
10:39 And she had a sister called **M**, which *G3137*
42 But one thing is needful: and **M** hath *G3137*
24:10 It was **M** Magdalene, and Joanna, and *G3137*
10 and Joanna, and **M** *the mother* of *G3137*
Jn 11: 1 the town of **M** and her sister Martha. *G3137*
2 (It was *that* **M** which anointed the Lord *G3137*
19 to Martha and **M**, to comfort them *G3137*
20 met him: but **M** sat *still* in the house. *G3137*
28 way, and called **M** her sister secretly, *G3137*
31 her, when they saw **M**, that she rose up *G3137*
32 Then when **M** was come where Jesus *G3137*
45 which came to **M**, and had seen the *G3137*
12: 3 Then took **M** a pound of ointment of *G3137*
19:25 mother's sister, **M** the *wife* of Cleophas, *G3137*

Jn 19:25 *wife* of Cleophas, and **M** Magdalene. *G3137*
20: 1 The first *day* of the week cometh **M** *G3137*
11 But **M** stood without at the sepulchre *G3137*
16 Jesus saith unto her, **M**. She turned *G3137*
18 **M** Magdalene came and told the *G3137*
Act 1:14 the women, and **M** the mother of Jesus, *G3137*
12:12 to the house of **M** the mother of John, *G3137*
Ro 16: 6 Greet **M**, who bestowed much labour on *G3137*

MASCHIL
Ps 32:ttl *A Psalm* of David, **M**. H7919
42:ttl To the chief Musician, **M**, for the sons H7919
44:ttl Musician for the sons of Korah, **M**. H7919
45:ttl the sons of Korah, **M**, A Song of loves. H7919
52:ttl To the chief Musician, **M**, *A Psalm* of H7919
53:ttl upon Mahalath, **M**, *A Psalm* of David. H7919
54:ttl To the chief Musician on Neginoth, **M**, H7919
55:ttl To the chief Musician on Neginoth, **M**, H7919
74:ttl **M** of Asaph. H7919
78:ttl **M** of Asaph. H7919
88:ttl Leannoth, **M** of Heman the Ezrahite. H7919
89:ttl **M** of Ethan the Ezrahite. H7919
142:ttl **M** of David; A Prayer when he was in H7919

MASH
Gen 10:23 Aram; Uz, and Hul, and Gether, and **M**. H4851

MASHAL
1Ch 6:74 And out of the tribe of Asher; **M** with H4913

MASONS
2Sa 5:11 **m**: and they built David an house. H2796+H68
2Ki 12:12 And to **m**, and hewers of stone, and to H1443
22: 6 Unto carpenters, and builders, and **m**, H1443
1Ch 14: 1 cedars, with **m** and carpenters, H2796+H7023
22: 2 of Israel; and he set **m** to hew wrought H2672
2Ch 24:12 LORD, and hired **m** and carpenters to H2672
Ezr 3: 7 They gave money also unto the **m**, and H2672

MASREKAH
Gen 36:36 And Hadad died, and Samlah of **M** H4957
1Ch 1:47 Samlah of **M** reigned in his stead. H4957

MASSA
Gen 25:14 And Mishma, and Dumah, and **M**, H4854
1Ch 1:30 Mishma, and Dumah, **M**, Hadad, and H4854

MASSAH
Ex 17: 7 And he called the name of the place **M**, H4532
Dt 6:16 your God, as ye tempted *him* in **M**. H4532
9:22 And at Taberah, and at **M**, and at H4532
33: 8 didst prove at **M**, *and with* whom thou H4532

MAST
Prv 23:34 or as he that lieth upon the top of a **m**. H2260
Isa 33:23 well strengthen their **m**, they could not H8650

MASTER
Gen 24: 9 of Abraham his **m**, and sware to him H113
10 the camels of his **m**, and departed; for all H113
10 all the goods of his **m** *were* in his hand: H113
12 And he said, O LORD God of my **m** H113
12 shew kindness unto my **m** Abraham. H113
14 thou hast shewed kindness unto my **m**. H113
27 LORD God of my **m** Abraham, who hath H113
27 left destitute my **m** of his mercy and his H113
35 And the LORD hath blessed my **m** H113
36 bare a son to my **m** when she was old: H113
37 And my **m** made me swear, saying, H113
39 And I said unto my **m**, Peradventure the H113
42 O LORD God of my **m** Abraham, if now H113
48 the LORD God of my **m** Abraham, which H113
49 and truly with my **m**, tell me: and if not, H113
54 and he said, Send me away unto my **m**. H113
56 send me away that I may go to my **m**. H113
65 *had* said, It *is* my **m**: therefore she took a H113
39: 2 was in the house of his **m** the Egyptian. H113
3 And his **m** saw that the LORD *was* with H113
8 wife, Behold, my **m** wotteth not what *is* H113
19 And it came to pass, when his **m** heard H113
20 And Joseph's **m** took him, and put him H113
Ex 21: 4 If his **m** have given him a wife, and she H113
5 say, I love my **m**, my wife, and my H113
6 Then his **m** shall bring him unto the H113
6 door post; and his **m** shall bore his ear H113
8 If she please not her **m**, who hath H113
32 give unto their **m** thirty shekels of silver, H113
22: 8 If the thief be not found, then the **m** of H1167
Dt 23:15 Thou shalt not deliver unto his **m** the H113
Dt 23:15 which is escaped from his **m** unto thee: H113
Jdg 19:11 said unto his **m**, Come, I pray thee, and H113
12 And his **m** said unto him, We will not H113
22 and spake to the **m** of the house, the H1167
23 And the man, the **m** of the house, went H1167
1Sa 20:38 up the arrows, and came to his **m**. H113
24: 6 do this thing unto my **m**, the LORD'S H113
25:10 that break away every man from his **m**. H113
14 to salute our **m**; and he railed on them. H113
17 against our **m**, and against all his H113
26:16 ye have not kept your **m**, the LORD'S H113
29: 4 himself unto his **m**? *should it* not *be* with H113
30:13 and my **m** left me, because three H113
15 the hands of my **m**, and I will bring thee H113
2Sa 2: 7 ye valiant: for your **m** Saul is dead, and H113
1Ki 22:17 These have no **m**: let them return every H113
2Ki 2: 3 will take away thy **m** from thy head to H113
5 will take away thy **m** from thy head to H113
16 thee, and seek thy **m**: lest peradventure H113
5: 1 a great man with his **m**, and honourable, H113
18 *that* when my **m** goeth into the house H113
20 God, said, Behold, my **m** hath spared H113
22 And he said, All *is* well. My **m** hath sent H113
25 But he went in, and stood before his **m**. H113
6: 5 and said, Alas, **m**! for it was borrowed. H113
15 unto him, Alas, my **m**! how shall we do? H113
22 may eat and drink, and go to their **m**. H113
23 and they went to their **m**. So the bands of H113
8:14 and came to his **m**; who said to him, H113
9: 7 house of Ahab thy **m**, that I may avenge H113
31 said, *Had* Zimri peace, who slew his **m**? H113
10: 9 **m**, and slew him: but who slew all these? H113
18:27 them, Hath my **m** sent me to thy master, H113
27 sent me to thy **m**, and to thee, to speak H113
19: 4 the king of Assyria his **m** hath sent to H113
6 ye say to your **m**, Thus saith the LORD, H113
1Ch 12:19 his **m** Saul to *the jeopardy of* our heads. H113
15:27 Chenaniah the **m** of the song with the H8269
2Ch 18:16 said, These have no **m**; let them return H113
Job 3:19 there; and the servant *is* free from his **m**. H113
Prv 27:18 that waiteth on his **m** shall be honoured. H113
30:10 Accuse not a servant unto his **m**, lest he H113
Isa 24: 2 so with his **m**; as with the maid, so H113
36: 8 I pray thee, to my **m** the king of Assyria, H113
12 But Rabshakeh said, Hath my **m** sent me H113
12 sent me to thy **m** and to thee to speak H113
37: 4 the king of Assyria his **m** hath sent to H113
6 shall ye say unto your **m**, Thus saith the H113
Dan 1: 3 Ashpenaz the **m** of his eunuchs, that H7227
4: 9 O Belteshazzar, **m** of the magicians, H7229
5:11 thy father, made **m** of the magicians, H7229
Mal 1: 6 and a servant his **m**: if then I *be* a father, H113
6 and if I *be* a **m**, where *is* my fear? saith H113
2:12 doeth this, the **m** and the scholar, out H5782
Mt 8:19 and said unto him, **M**, I will follow thee *G1320*
9:11 your **M** with publicans and sinners? *G1320*
10:24 The disciple is not above *his* **m**, nor the *G1320*
25 that he be as his **m**, and the servant as *G1320*
25 they have called the **m** of the house *G1320*
12:38 **M**, we would see a sign from thee. *G1320*
17:24 and said, Doth not your **m** pay tribute? *G1320*
19:16 unto him, Good **M**, what good thing *G1320*
22:16 saying, **M**, we know that thou *G1320*
24 Saying, **M**, Moses said, If a man die, *G1320*
36 **M**, which *is* the great commandment in *G1320*
23: 8 **M**, *even* Christ; and all ye are brethren. *G2519*
10 masters: for one is your **M**, *even* Christ. *G2519*
26:18 say unto him, The **M** saith, My time is *G1320*
25 and said, **M**, is it I? He said unto *G4461*
49 and said, Hail, **m**; and kissed him. *G4461*
Mk 4:38 him, **M**, carest thou not that we perish? *G1320*
5:35 why troublest thou the **M** any further? *G1320*
9: 5 and said to Jesus, **M**, it is good for us to *G4461*
17 and said, **M**, I have brought unto *G1320*
38 And John answered him, saying, **M**, we *G1320*
10:17 asked him, Good **M**, what shall I do that *G1320*
20 and said unto him, **M**, all these have I *G1320*
35 unto him, saying, **M**, we would that *G1320*
11:21 saith unto him, **M**, behold, the fig tree *G4461*
12:14 say unto him, **M**, we know that thou *G1320*
19 **M**, Moses wrote unto us, If a man's *G1320*
32 And the scribe said unto him, Well, **M**, *G1320*
13: 1 saith unto him, **M**, see what manner of *G1320*
35 not when the **m** of the house cometh, *G2962*
14:14 of the house, The **M** saith, Where is the *G1320*
45 and saith, **M**, master; and kissed him. *G4461*
45 and saith, Master, **m**; and kissed him. *G4461*
Lk 3:12 said unto him, **M**, what shall we do? *G1320*
5: 5 said unto him, **M**, we have toiled all the *G1988*
Lk 6:40 The disciple is not above his **m**: but *G1320*
40 one that is perfect shall be as his **m**. *G1320*
7:40 say unto thee. And he saith, **M**, say on. *G1320*
8:24 him, saying, **M**, master, we perish. *G1988*
24 saying, Master, **m**, we perish. Then he *G1988*
45 with him said, **M**, the multitude throng *G1988*
49 daughter is dead; trouble not the **M**. *G1320*
9:33 said unto Jesus, **M**, it is good for us to *G1988*
38 cried out, saying, **M**, I beseech thee, *G1320*
49 And John answered and said, **M**, we *G1988*
10:25 **M**, what shall I do to inherit eternal life? *G1320*
11:45 and said unto him, **M**, thus saying thou *G1320*
12:13 said unto him, **M**, speak to my brother, *G1320*
13:25 When once the **m** of the house is risen *G3617*
14:21 things. Then the **m** of the house being *G3617*
17:13 and said, Jesus, **M**, have mercy on us. *G1988*
18:18 **M**, what shall I do to inherit eternal life? *G1320*
19:39 said unto him, **M**, rebuke thy disciples. *G1320*
20:21 And they asked him, saying, **M**, we *G1320*
28 Saying, **M**, Moses wrote unto us, If any *G1320*
39 answering said, **M**, thou hast well said. *G1320*
21: 7 And they asked him, saying, **M**, but *G1320*
22:11 of the house, The **M** saith unto thee, *G1320*
Jn 1:38 interpreted, **M**,) where dwellest thou? *G1320*
3:10 unto him, Art thou a **m** of Israel, and *G1320*
4:31 his disciples prayed him, saying, **M**, eat. *G4461*
8: 4 They say unto him, **M**, this woman was *G1320*
9: 2 And his disciples asked him, saying, **M**, *G4461*
11: 8 *His* disciples say unto him, **M**, the Jews *G4461*
28 The **M** is come, and calleth for thee. *G1320*
13:13 Ye call me **M** and Lord: and ye say *G1320*
14 If I then, *your* Lord and **M**, have *G1320*
20:16 unto him, Rabboni; which is to say, **M**. *G1320*
Act 27:11 believed the **m** and the owner of the *G2942*
Ro 14: 4 to his own **m** he standeth or falleth. *G2962*
Eph 6: 9 that your **M** also is in heaven; neither *G2962*
Col 4: 1 that ye also have a **M** in heaven. *G2962*

MASTERBUILDER
1Co 3:10 unto me, as a wise **m**, I have laid the *G753*

MASTERIES
2Ti 2: 5 And if a man also strive for **m**, *yet* is he *G118*

MASTERS
Ps 123: 2 the hand of their **m**, *and* as the eyes of a H113
Prv 25:13 him: for he refresheth the soul of his **m**. H113
Ecc 12:11 fastened *by* the **m** of assemblies, *which* H1167
Jer 27: 4 And command them to say unto their **m**, H113
4 of Israel; Thus shall ye say unto your **m**; H113
Am 4: 1 say to their **m**, Bring, and let us drink. H113
Mt 6:24 No man can serve two **m**: for either he *G2962*
23:10 Neither be ye called **m**: for one is your *G2519*
Lk 16:13 No servant can serve two **m**: for either *G2962*
Act 16:16 her **m** much gain by soothsaying: *G2962*
19 And when her **m** saw that the hope of *G2962*
Eph 6: 5 that are *your* **m** according to the flesh, *G2962*
9 And, ye **m**, do the same things unto *G2962*
Col 3:22 Servants, obey in all things *your* **m** *G2962*
4: 1 **M**, give unto *your* servants that which is *G2962*
1Ti 6: 1 yoke count their own **m** worthy of all *G1203*
2 And they that have believing **m**, let *G1203*
Tit 2: 9 unto their own **m**, *and* to please *them* *G1203*
Jas 3: 1 My brethren, be not many **m**, knowing *G1320*
1Pt 2:18 Servants, *be* subject to *your* **m** with all *G1203*

MASTER'S
Gen 24:27 led me to the house of my **m** brethren. H113
36 And Sarah my **m** wife bare a son to my H113
44 LORD hath appointed out for my **m** son. H113
48 my **m** brother's daughter unto his son. H113
51 **m** son's wife, as the LORD hath spoken. H113
39: 7 things, that his **m** wife cast her eyes H113
8 But he refused, and said unto his **m** wife, H113
Ex 21: 4 be her **m**, and he shall go out by himself. H113
1Sa 29:10 morning with thy **m** servants that are H113
2Sa 9: 9 given unto thy **m** son all that pertained H113
10 *the fruits*, that thy **m** son may have food H113
10 Mephibosheth thy **m** son shall eat bread H113
12: 8 And I gave thee thy **m** house, and thy H113
8 house, and thy **m** wives into thy bosom, H113
16: 3 And the king said, And where *is* thy **m** H113
2Ki 6:32 not the sound of his **m** feet behind him? H113
10: 2 to you, seeing your **m** sons *are* with you, H113
3 meetest of your **m** sons, and set *him* on H113
3 throne, and fight for your **m** house. H113
6 of the men your **m** sons, and come to me H113
18:24 of the least of my **m** servants, and put H113
Isa 1: 3 and the ass his **m** crib: *but* Israel doth H1167

Isa 36: 9 of the least of my m servants, and put H113
2Ti 2:21 and meet for the m use, and prepared G1203

MASTERS'
Zep 1: 9 their m houses with violence and deceit. H113
Mt 15:27 crumbs which fall from their m table. G2962

MASTERY
Ex 32:18 that shout for m, neither is it the voice H1369
Dan 6:24 the lions had the m of them, and brake H7981
1Co 9:25 And every man that striveth for the m is G75

MASTS
Ezk 27: 5 from Lebanon to make m for thee. H8650

MATE
Isa 34:15 also be gathered, every one with her m. H7468
16 shall want her m: for my mouth it hath H7468

MATHUSALA
Lk 3:37 Which was the son of M, which was the G3103

MATRED
Gen 36:39 of M, the daughter of Mezahab. H4308
1Ch 1:50 of M, the daughter of Mezahab. H4308

MATRI
1Sa 10:21 the family of M was taken, and Saul H4309

MATRIX
Ex 13:12 that openeth the m, and every firstling H7358
15 that openeth the m, being males; but all H7358
34:19 All that openeth the m is mine; and H7358
Nu 3:12 that openeth the m among the children H7358
18:15 Every thing that openeth the m in all H7358

MATTAN
2Ki 11:18 and slew M the priest of Baal before H4977
2Ch 23:17 M the priest of Baal before the altars. H4977
Jer 38: 1 Then Shephatiah the son of M, and H4977

MATTANAH
Nu 21:18 from the wilderness they went to M: H4980
19 And from M to Nahaliel: and from H4980

MATTANIAH
2Ki 24:17 And the king of Babylon made M his H4983
1Ch 9:15 and Galal, and M the son of Micah, the H4983
25: 4 of Heman; Bukkiah, M, Uzziel, Shebuel, H4983
16 The ninth to M, he, his sons, and his H4983
2Ch 20:14 son of Jeiel, the son of M, a Levite of the H4983
29:13 of the sons of Asaph; Zechariah, and M: H4983
Ezr 10:26 And of the sons of Elam; M, Zechariah, H4983
27 Eliashib, M, and Jeremoth, and H4983
30 Maaseiah, M, Bezaleel, and Binnui, H4983
37 M, Mattenai, and Jaasau, H4983
Neh 11:17 And M the son of Micha, the son of H4983
22 the son of M, the son of Micha. Of H4983
12: 8 Judah, and M, which was over the H4983
25 M, and Bakbukiah, Obadiah, H4983
35 the son of M, the son of Michaiah, H4983
13:13 of Zaccur, the son of M: for they were H4983

MATTATHA
Lk 3:31 was the son of M, which was the son G3160

MATTATHAH
Ezr 10:33 Of the sons of Hashum; Mattenai, M, H4992

MATTATHIAS
Lk 3:25 Which was the son of M, which was the G3161
26 was the son of M, which was the son G3161

MATTENAI
Ezr 10:33 Of the sons of Hashum; M, Mattathah, H4982
37 Mattaniah, M, and Jaasau, H4982
Neh 12:19 And of Joiarib, M; of Jedaiah, Uzzi; H4982

MATTER
Gen 24: 9 and sware to him concerning that m. H1697
30:15 And she said unto her, Is it a small m H4592
Ex 18:16 When they have a m, they come unto H1697
22 be, that every great m they shall bring H1697
22 but every small m they shall judge: so H1697
26 every small m they judged themselves. H1697
23: 7 Keep thee far from a false m; and the H1697
Nu 16:49 them that died about the m of Korah. H1697
25:18 you in the m of Peor, and in the H1697
18 of Peor, and in the m of Cozbi, the H1697
Nu 31:16 the LORD in the m of Peor, and there H1697
Dt 3:26 thee; speak no more unto me of this m. H1697
17: 8 If there arise a m too hard for thee in H1697
19:15 witnesses, shall the m be established. H1697
22:26 and slayeth him, even so is this m: H1697
Ru 3:18 know how the m will fall: for the man H1697
1Sa 10:16 found. But of the m of the kingdom, H1697
20:23 And as touching the m which thou and H1697
39 only Jonathan and David knew the m. H1697
30:24 unto you in this m? but as his part is H1697
2Sa 1: 4 How went the m? I pray thee, tell me. H1697
18:13 life: for there is no m hid from the king, H1697
19:42 ye angry for this m? have we eaten at all H1697
20:18 counsel at Abel: and so they ended the m.
21 The m is not so: but a man of mount H1697
1Ki 8:59 at all times, as the m shall require: H1697
15: 5 save only in the m of Uriah the Hittite. H1697
1Ch 26:32 for every m pertaining to God, H1697
27: 1 the king in any m of the courses, which H1697
2Ch 8:15 any m, or concerning the treasures. H1697
24: 5 m. Howbeit the Levites hastened it not. H1697
Ezr 5: 5 to cease, till the m came to Darius: and H2941
5 answer by letter concerning this m.
17 his pleasure to us concerning this m. H1836
10: 4 Arise; for this m belongeth unto thee: H1697
9 of this m, and for the great rain. H1697
14 our God for this m be turned from us. H1697
15 about this m: and Meshullam and
16 of the tenth month to examine the m. H1697
Neh 6:13 they might have m for an evil report,
Est 2:23 was made of the m, it was found out; H1697
9:26 this m, and which had come unto them, H3602
Job 19:28 seeing the root of the m is found in me? H1697
32:18 For I am full of m, the spirit within me H4405
Ps 45: 1 My heart is inditing a good m: I speak H1697
64: 5 in an evil m: they commune of laying H1697
Prv 11:13 is of a faithful spirit concealeth the m. H1697
16:20 He that handleth a m wisely shall find H1697
17: 9 repeateth a m separateth very friends. H1697
18:13 He that answereth a m before he H1697
25: 2 honour of kings is to search out a m. H1697
Ecc 5: 8 marvel not at the m: for he that is H2656
10:20 that which hath wings shall tell the m. H1697
12:13 of the whole m: Fear God, and keep H1697
Jer 38:27 with him; for the m was not perceived. H1697
Ezk 9:11 his side, reported the m, saying, I have H1697
16:20 Is this of thy whoredoms a small m, H4592
Dan 1:14 So he consented to them in this m, and H1697
2:10 shew the king's m: therefore there is no H4406
23 now made known unto us the king's m. H4406
3:16 are not careful to answer thee in this m. H6600
4:17 This m is by the decree of the watchers, H6600
7:28 Hitherto is the end of the m. As for me H4406
28 in me: but I kept the m in my heart. H4406
9:23 the m, and consider the vision. H1697
Mk 1:45 to blaze abroad the m, insomuch that G3056
10:10 disciples asked him again of the same m.
Act 8:21 Thou hast neither part nor lot in this m: G3056
11: 4 But Peter rehearsed the m from the
15: 6 came together for to consider of this m. G3056
17:32 said, We will hear thee again of this m.
18:14 Jews, If it were a m of wrong or wicked
19:38 with him, have a m against any man, G3056
24:22 I will know the uttermost of your m. G2596
1Co 6: 1 Dare any of you, having a m against G4229
2Co 7:11 yourselves to be clear in this m. G4229
9: 5 m of bounty, and not as of covetousness.
Gal 2: 6 it maketh no m to me: God accepteth G1308
1Th 4: 6 his brother in any m: because that the G4229
Jas 3: 5 how great a m a little fire kindleth! G5208

MATTERS
Ex 24:14 any m to do, let him come unto them. H1697
Dt 17: 8 and stroke, being m of controversy H1697
1Sa 16:18 war, and prudent in m, and a comely H1697
2Sa 11:19 telling the m of the war unto the king, H1697
15: 3 said unto him, See, thy m are good and H1697
19:29 any more of thy m? I have said, Thou H1697
2Ch 19:11 is over you in all m of the LORD; and H1697
11 for all the king's m: also the Levites H1697
Neh 11:24 hand in all m concerning the people. H1697
Est 3: 4 Mordecai's m would stand: for he H1697
9:31 the m of the fastings and their cry. H1697
32 confirmed these m of Purim; and it H1697
Job 33:13 he giveth not account of any of his m. H1697
Ps 35:20 devise deceitful m against them that H1697
131: 1 in great m, or in things too high for me. H1419
Dan 1:20 And in all m of wisdom and H1697
7: 1 the dream, and told the sum of the m. H4406
Mt 23:23 the weightier m of the law, judgment,
Act 18:15 ye to it; for I will be no judge of such m.
19:39 thing concerning other m, it shall be G2087
25:20 and there be judged of these m. G5130
1Co 6: 2 ye unworthy to judge the smallest m? G1646
1Pt 4:15 or as a busybody in other men's m. G244

MATTHAN
Mt 1:15 begat M; and Matthan begat Jacob; G3157
15 begat Matthan; and M begat Jacob; G3157

MATTHAT
Lk 3:24 Which was the son of M, which was the G3158
29 the son of M, which was the son of Levi, G3158

MATTHEW
Mt 9: 9 a man, named M, sitting at the receipt G3156
10: 3 Thomas, and M the publican; James G3156
Mk 3:18 and M, and Thomas, and James G3156
Lk 6:15 M and Thomas, James the son of G3156
Act 1:13 and M, James the son of Alphaeus, G3156

MATTHIAS
Act 1:23 who was surnamed Justus, and M. G3159
26 and the lot fell upon M; and he was G3159

MATTITHIAH
1Ch 9:31 And M, one of the Levites, who was the H4993
15:18 Maaseiah, and M, and Elipheleh, and H4993
21 And M, and Elipheleh, and Mikneiah, H4993
16: 5 and Jehiel, and M, and Eliab, and H4993
25: 3 Hashabiah, and M, six, under the H4993
21 The fourteenth to M, he, his sons, and H4993
Ezr 10:43 Of the sons of Nebo; Jeiel, M, Zabad, H4993
Neh 8: 4 beside him stood M, and Shema, and H4993

MATTOCK
1Sa 13:20 and his coulter, and his axe, and his m. H4281
Isa 7:25 digged with the m, there shall not come H4576

MATTOCKS
1Sa 13:21 Yet they had a file for the m, and for the H4281
2Ch 34: 6 Naphtali, with their m round about. H2719

MAUL
Prv 25:18 is a m, and a sword, and a sharp arrow. H4650

MAW
Dt 18: 3 and the two cheeks, and the m. H6896

MAY See the Appendix.

MAYEST See the Appendix.

MAZZAROTH
Job 38:32 Canst thou bring forth M in his season? H4216

ME See the Appendix.

MEADOW
Gen 41: 2 kine and fatfleshed; and they fed in a m. H260
18 and well favoured; and they fed in a m: H260

MEADOWS
Jdg 20:33 places, even out of the m of Gibeah. H4629

MEAH
Neh 3: 1 unto the tower of M they sanctified it, H3968
12:39 and the tower of M, even unto the sheep H3968

MEAL
Gen 18: 6 measures of fine m, knead it, and make H7058
Nu 5:15 ephah of barley m; he shall pour no oil H7058
1Ki 4:22 flour, and threescore measures of m, H7058
17:12 but an handful of m in a barrel, and a H7058
14 The barrel of m shall not waste, neither H7058
16 And the barrel of m wasted not, neither H7058
2Ki 4:41 But he said, Then bring m. And he cast H7058
1Ch 12:40 oxen, and meat, m, cakes of figs, and H7058
Isa 47: 2 Take the millstones, and grind m: H7058
Hos 8: 7 bud shall yield no m: if so be it yield, H7058
Mt 13:33 of m, till the whole was leavened. G224
Lk 13:21 of m, till the whole was leavened. G224

MEALTIME
Ru 2:14 And Boaz said unto her, At m H6256+H400

MEAN
Gen 21:29 unto Abraham, What m these seven ewe

Ex 12:26 say unto you, What **m** ye by this service?
Dt 6:20 saying, What ***m*** the testimonies, and
Jos 4: 6 saying, What ***m*** ye by these stones?
21 to come, saying, What ***m*** these stones?
1Ki 18:45 And it came to pass in the **m** H5704+H3541
Prv 22:29 kings; he shall not stand before **m** *men.* H2823
Isa 2: 9 And the **m** man boweth down, and the H120
3:15 What **m** ye *that* ye beat my people to
5:15 And the **m** man shall be brought down, H120
31: 8 the sword, not of a **m** man, shall devour H120
Ezk 17:12 what these *things* **m**? tell *them*, Behold,
18: 2 What **m** ye, that ye use this proverb
Mk 9:10 the rising from the dead should **m.** *G2076*
Lk 12: 1 In the **m** time, when there were gathered
Jn 4:31 In the **m** while his disciples prayed *G3342*
Act 10:17 he had seen should **m**, behold, the men *G1498*
17:20 therefore what these things **m.** *G2309+G1511*
21:13 Then Paul answered, What **m** ye to *G4160*
39 a citizen of no **m** city: and, I beseech *G767*
Ro 2:15 *their* thoughts the **m** while accusing or *G3342*
2Co 8:13 For *I* ***m*** not that other men be eased, and

MEANEST
Gen 33: 8 And he said, What ***m*** thou by all this
2Sa 16: 2 And the king said unto Ziba, What **m**
Ezk 37:18 thou not shew us what thou ***m*** by these?
Jna 1: 6 said unto him, What **m** thou, O sleeper?

MEANETH
Dt 29:24 what ***m*** the heat of this great anger?
1Sa 4: 6 they said, What ***m*** the noise of this great
14 crying, he said, What ***m*** the noise of this
15:14 And Samuel said, What ***m*** then this
Isa 10: 7 Howbeit he **m** not so, neither doth his H1819
Mt 9:13 But go ye and learn what *that* **m**, I will *G2076*
12: 7 But if ye had known what *this* **m**, I will *G2076*
Act 2:12 one to another, What **m** this? *G2309+G1511*

MEANING
Dan 8:15 and sought for the **m**, then, behold, there H998
Act 27: 2 we launched, **m** to sail by the coasts *G3195*
1Co 14:11 Therefore if I know not the **m** of the *G1411*

MEANS
Ex 34: 7 and that will by no **m** clear *the guilty;* H5352
Nu 14:18 and by no **m** clearing *the guilty,* H5352
Jdg 5:22 broken by the **m** of the pransings, the
16: 5 *lieth*, and by what ***m*** we may prevail
2Sa 14:14 yet doth he devise **m**, that his banished H4284
1Ki 10:29 did they bring *them* out by their **m.** H3027
20:39 man: if by any **m** he be missing, then H6485
2Ch 1:17 and for the kings of Syria, by their **m.** H3027
Ezr 4:16 set up, by this **m** thou shalt have no H6903
Ps 49: 7 None *of them* can by any **m** redeem his H6299
Prv 6:26 For by **m** of a whorish woman *a man is* H1157
Jer 5:31 bear rule by their **m**; and my people H3027
Mal 1: 9 this hath been by your **m**: will he regard H3027
Mt 5:26 Thou shalt by no **m** come out thence, *G3364*
Lk 5:18 and they sought ***m*** to bring him in, and
8:36 *it* told them by what **m** he that was *G4459*
10:19 and nothing shall by any **m** hurt you. *G3364*
Jn 9:21 But by what **m** he now seeth, we know *G4459*
Act 4: 9 man, by what **m** he is made whole; *G5101*
18:21 I must by all **m** keep this feast that *G3843*
27:12 also, if by any **m** they might attain to *G4458*
Ro 1:10 Making request, if by any **m** now at *G4458*
11:14 If by any **m** I may provoke to *G4458*
1Co 8: 9 But take heed lest by any **m** this liberty *G4458*
9:22 *men*, that I might by all **m** save some. *G3843*
27 lest that by any **m**, when I have *G4458*
2Co 1:11 upon us by the **m** of many persons
11: 3 But I fear, lest by any **m**, as the serpent *G4458*
Gal 2: 2 **m** I should run, or had run, in vain. *G4458*
Php 3:11 If by any **m** I might attain unto the *G4458*
1Th 3: 5 faith, lest by some **m** the tempter have *G4458*
2Th 2: 3 Let no man deceive you by any **m**: for *G5158*
3:16 by all **m.** The Lord *be* with you all. *G5158*
Heb 9:15 that by **m** of death, for the redemption *G1096*
Rev 13:14 on the earth by *the* ***m*** *of* those miracles

MEANT
Gen 50:20 me; *but* God **m** it unto good, to bring H2803
Lk 15:26 and asked what these things **m.** *G1498*
18:36 multitude pass by, he asked what it **m.** *G1498*

MEANWHILE See MEAN and WHILE.

MEARAH
Jos 13: 4 Canaanites, and **M** that *is* beside the H4632

MEASURE
Ex 26: 2 one of the curtains shall have one **m.** H4060
8 the eleven curtains *shall be all* of one **m.** H4060
Lev 19:35 in meteyard, in weight, or in **m.** H4884
Nu 35: 5 And ye shall **m** from without the city H4058
Dt 21: 2 and they shall **m** unto the cities which H4058
25:15 a perfect and just **m** shalt thou have: H374
Jos 3: 4 cubits by **m**: come not near unto H4060
1Ki 6:25 cherubims *were* of one **m** and one size. H4060
7:37 had one casting, one **m**, *and* one size. H4060
2Ki 7: 1 this time *shall* a **m** of fine flour *be sold* H5429
16 of the Syrians. So a **m** of fine flour was H5429
18 for a shekel, and a **m** of fine flour for a H5429
1Ch 23:29 fried, and for all manner of **m** and size; H4884
2Ch 3: 3 after the first **m** *was* threescore cubits, H4060
Job 11: 9 The **m** thereof *is* longer than the earth, H4055
28:25 and he weigheth the waters by **m.** H4060
Ps 39: 4 mine end, and the **m** of my days, what H4060
80: 5 givest them tears to drink in great **m.** H7991
Isa 5:14 mouth without **m**: and their glory, and H2706
27: 8 In **m**, when it shooteth forth, thou wilt H5432
40:12 of the earth in a **m**, and weighed the H7991
65: 7 **m** their former work into their bosom. H4058
Jer 30:11 will correct thee in **m**, and will not leave H4941
46:28 but correct thee in **m**; yet will I not leave H4941
51:13 is come, *and* the **m** of thy covetousness. H520
Ezk 4:11 Thou shalt drink also water by **m**, the H4884
16 water by **m**, and with astonishment: H4884
40:10 three *were* of one **m**: and the posts had H4060
10 one **m** on this side and on that side. H4060
21 were after the **m** of the first gate: the H4060
22 trees, *were* after the **m** of the gate that H4060
41:17 round about within and without, by **m.** H4060
43:10 iniquities: and let them **m** the pattern. H4058
45: 3 And of this **m** shalt thou measure the H4060
3 And of this measure shalt thou **m** the H4058
11 shall be of one **m**, that the bath may H8506
11 the **m** thereof shall be after the homer. H4971
46:22 these four corners *were* of one **m.** H4060
47:18 And the east side ye shall **m** from H4058
Mic 6:10 and the scant **m** *that is* abominable? H374
Zec 2: 2 said unto me, To **m** Jerusalem, to see H4058
Mt 7: 2 and with what **m** ye mete, it shall be *G3358*
23:32 Fill ye up then the **m** of your fathers. *G3358*
Mk 4:24 hear: with what **m** ye mete, it shall be *G3358*
6:51 themselves beyond **m**, and wondered. *G4053*
7:37 And were beyond **m** astonished, *G5249*
10:26 And they were astonished out of **m**, *G4057*
Lk 6:38 unto you; good **m**, pressed down, and *G3358*
38 For with the same **m** that ye mete *G3358*
Jn 3:34 giveth not the Spirit by **m** *unto him.* *G3358*
Ro 12: 3 hath dealt to every man the **m** of faith. *G3358*
2Co 1: 8 were pressed out of **m**, above strength, *G2596*
10:13 of things without *our* **m**, but according to *G280*
13 according to the **m** of the rule which *G3358*
13 to us, a **m** to reach even unto you. *G3358*
14 beyond *our* **m**, as though we reached
15 Not boasting of things without *our* **m**, *G280*
11:23 in stripes above **m**, in prisons more *G5234*
12: 7 And lest I should be exalted above **m** *G5229*
7 me, lest I should be exalted above **m.** *G5229*
Gal 1:13 how that beyond **m** I persecuted the *G5236*
Eph 4: 7 according to the **m** of the gift of Christ. *G3358*
13 **m** of the stature of the fulness of Christ: *G3358*
16 working in the **m** of every part, maketh *G3358*
Rev 6: 6 the four beasts say, A **m** of wheat for a *G5518*
11: 1 saying, Rise, and **m** the temple of God, *G3354*
2 leave out, and **m** it not; for it is given *G3354*
21:15 a golden reed to **m** the city, and the *G3354*
17 *to* the **m** of a man, that is, of the angel. *G3358*

MEASURED
Ru 3:15 when she held it, he **m** six *measures* of H4058
2Sa 8: 2 And he smote Moab, and **m** them with H4058
2 with two lines **m** he to put to death, H4058
Isa 40:12 Who hath **m** the waters in the hollow of H4058
Jer 31:37 above can be **m**, and the foundations H4058
33:22 sand of the sea **m**: so will I multiply the H4058
Ezk 40: 5 breadth: so he **m** the breadth of the H4058
6 thereof, and **m** the threshold of the H4058
8 He **m** also the porch of the gate within, H4058
9 Then **m** he the porch of the gate, eight H4058
11 And he **m** the breadth of the entry of H4058
13 He **m** then the gate from the roof of *one* H4058
19 Then he **m** the breadth from the H4058
20 the north, he **m** the length thereof, H4058
23 **m** from gate to gate an hundred cubits. H4058
24 the south: and he **m** the posts thereof H4058
27 the south: and he **m** from gate to gate H4058
28 south gate: and he **m** the south gate H4058
32 the east: and he **m** the gate according H4058
35 and **m** *it* according to these measures; H4058
47 So he **m** the court, an hundred cubits H4058
48 of the house, and **m** *each* post of the H4058
41: 1 me to the temple, and **m** the posts, six H4058
2 other side: and he **m** the length thereof, H4058
3 Then went he inward, and **m** the post H4058
4 So he **m** the length thereof, twenty H4058
5 After he **m** the wall of the house, six H4058
13 So he **m** the house, an hundred cubits H4058
15 And he **m** the length of the building H4058
42:15 toward the east, and **m** it round about. H4058
16 He **m** the east side with the measuring H4058
17 He **m** the north side, five hundred H4058
18 He **m** the south side, five hundred H4058
19 to the west side, *and* **m** five hundred H4058
20 He **m** it by the four sides: it had a wall H4058
47: 3 eastward, he **m** a thousand cubits, H4058
4 Again he **m** a thousand, and brought H4058
4 the knees. Again he **m** a thousand, and H4058
5 Afterward he **m** a thousand; *and it was* H4058
Hos 1:10 which cannot be **m** nor numbered; and H4058
Hab 3: 6 He stood, and **m** the earth: he beheld, H4128
Mt 7: 2 ye mete, it shall be **m** to you again. *G488*
Mk 4:24 ye mete, it shall be **m** to you: and unto *G3354*
Lk 6:38 ye mete withal it shall be **m** to you again. *G488*
Rev 21:16 the breadth: and he **m** the city with the *G3354*
17 And he **m** the wall thereof, an hundred *G3354*

MEASURES
Gen 18: 6 quickly three **m** of fine meal, knead H5429
Dt 25:14 house divers **m**, a great and a small. H374
Ru 3:15 it, he measured six ***m*** of barley, and laid
17 And she said, These six ***m*** of barley gave
1Sa 25:18 dressed, and five **m** of parched *corn,* H5429
1Ki 4:22 one day was thirty **m** of fine flour, and H3734
22 of fine flour, and threescore **m** of meal, H3734
5:11 twenty thousand **m** of wheat *for* food H3734
11 and twenty **m** of pure oil: thus gave H3734
7: 9 according to the **m** of hewed stones, H4060
11 the **m** of hewed stones, and cedars. H4060
18:32 great as would contain two **m** of seed. H5429
2Ki 7: 1 for a shekel, and two **m** of barley for a H5429
16 for a shekel, and two **m** of barley for a H5429
18 the king, saying, Two **m** of barley for a H5429
2Ch 2:10 twenty thousand **m** of beaten wheat, H3734
10 and twenty thousand **m** of barley, and H3734
27: 5 and ten thousand **m** of wheat, and ten H3734
Ezr 7:22 to an hundred **m** of wheat, and to an H3734
Job 38: 5 Who hath laid the **m** thereof, if thou H4461
Prv 20:10 Divers weights, *and* divers **m**, both of H374
Jer 13:25 This *is* thy lot, the portion of thy **m** H4055
Ezk 40:24 the arches thereof according to these **m.** H4060
28 the south gate according to these **m**; H4060
29 to these **m**: and *there were* windows H4060
32 the gate according to these **m.** H4060
33 to these **m**: and *there were* windows H4060
35 and measured *it* according to these **m**; H4060
43:13 And these *are* the **m** of the altar after H4060
48:16 And these *shall be* the **m** thereof; the H4060
30 four thousand and five hundred **m.** H4060
33 and five hundred **m**: and three gates; H4060
35 *It was* round about eighteen thousand ***m***:
Hag 2:16 an heap of twenty ***m***, there were *but* ten:
Mt 13:33 **m** of meal, till the whole was leavened. *G4568*
Lk 13:21 **m** of meal, till the whole was leavened. *G4568*
16: 6 And he said, An hundred **m** of oil. And *G943*
7 said, An hundred **m** of wheat. And he *G2884*
Rev 6: 6 a penny, and three **m** of barley for a *G5518*

MEASURING
Jer 31:39 And the **m** line shall yet go forth over H4060
Ezk 40: 3 and a **m** reed; and he stood in the gate. H4060
5 the man's hand a **m** reed of six cubits H4060
42:15 Now when he had made an end of **m** H4060
16 He measured the east side with the **m** H4060
16 reeds, with the **m** reed round about. H4060
17 reeds, with the **m** reed round about. H4060
18 five hundred reeds, with the **m** reed. H4060
19 five hundred reeds with the **m** reed. H4060
Zec 2: 1 a man with a **m** line in his hand. H4060
2Co 10:12 but they **m** themselves by themselves, *G3354*

MEAT
Gen 1:29 yielding seed; to you it shall be for **m.** H402
30 every green herb for **m**: and it was so. H402
9: 3 that liveth shall be **m** for you; even as the H402
24:33 And there was set ***m*** before him to eat:

Gen 27: 4 And make me savoury **m**, such as I H4303
7 make me savoury **m**, that I may eat, H4303
9 **m** for thy father, such as he loveth: H4303
14 savoury **m**, such as his father loved. H4303
17 And she gave the savoury **m** and the H4303
31 And he also had made savoury **m**, and H4303
45:23 bread and **m** for his father by the way. H4202
Ex 29:41 according to the **m** offering of the
30: 9 sacrifice, nor **m** offering; neither shall
40:29 offering and the **m** offering; as the LORD
Lev 2: 1 And when any will offer a **m** offering H4503
3 And the remnant of the **m** offering *shall*
4 And if thou bring an oblation of a **m**
5 And if thy oblation *be* a **m** offering
6 and pour oil thereon: it *is* a **m** offering.
7 And if thy oblation *be* a **m** offering
8 And thou shalt bring the **m** offering that
9 And the priest shall take from the **m**
10 And that which is left of the **m** offering
11 No **m** offering, which ye shall bring unto
13 And every oblation of thy **m** offering
13 be lacking from thy **m** offering: with all
14 And if thou offer a **m** offering of thy
14 thou shalt offer for the **m** offering of thy
15 frankincense thereon: it *is* a **m** offering.
5:13 shall be the priest's, as a **m** offering.
6:14 And this *is* the law of the **m** offering: the
15 of the flour of the **m** offering, and of the
15 which *is* upon the **m** offering, and shall
20 of fine flour for a **m** offering perpetual,
21 pieces of the **m** offering shalt thou offer
23 For every **m** offering for the priest shall
7: 9 And all the **m** offering that is baken in
10 And every **m** offering, mingled with oil,
37 offering, of the **m** offering, and of the
9: 4 the LORD; and a **m** offering mingled
17 And he brought the **m** offering, and took
10:12 that were left, Take the **m** offering that
11:34 Of all **m** which may be eaten, *that* on H400
14:10 of fine flour *for* a **m** offering, mingled
20 offering and the **m** offering upon the
21 with oil for a **m** offering, and a log of oil;
31 offering, with the **m** offering: and the
22:11 in his house: they shall eat of his **m**. H3899
13 eat of her father's **m**: but there shall no H3899
23:13 And the **m** offering thereof *shall be* two
16 offer a new **m** offering unto the LORD.
18 LORD, with their **m** offering, and their
37 offering, and a **m** offering, a sacrifice,
25: 6 And the sabbath of the land shall be **m** H402
7 land, shall all the increase thereof be **m**. H398
Nu 4:16 and the daily **m** offering, and the
6:15 **m** offering, and their drink offerings.
17 his **m** offering, and his drink offering.
7:13 flour mingled with oil for a **m** offering:
19 flour mingled with oil for a **m** offering:
25 flour mingled with oil for a **m** offering:
31 flour mingled with oil for a **m** offering:
37 flour mingled with oil for a **m** offering:
43 flour mingled with oil for a **m** offering:
49 flour mingled with oil for a **m** offering:
55 flour mingled with oil for a **m** offering:
61 flour mingled with oil for a **m** offering:
67 flour mingled with oil for a **m** offering:
73 flour mingled with oil for a **m** offering:
79 flour mingled with oil for a **m** offering:
87 twelve, with their **m** offering: and the
8: 8 bullock with his **m** offering, *even* fine
15: 4 the LORD bring a **m** offering of a tenth
6 Or for a ram, thou shalt prepare *for* a **m**
9 Then shall he bring with a bullock a **m**
24 LORD, with his **m** offering, and his drink
18: 9 of theirs, every **m** offering of theirs, and
28: 5 of flour for a **m** offering, mingled with
8 offer at even: as the **m** offering of the
9 deals of flour *for* a **m** offering, mingled
12 And three tenth deals of flour *for* a **m**
12 deals of flour *for* a **m** offering, mingled
13 with oil *for* a **m** offering unto one lamb;
20 And their **m** offering *shall be of* flour
24 seven days, the **m** of the sacrifice made H3899
26 when ye bring a new **m** offering unto the
28 And their **m** offering of flour mingled
31 offering, and his **m** offering, (they shall
29: 3 And their **m** offering *shall be of* flour
6 month, and his **m** offering, and the daily
6 offering, and his **m** offering, and their
9 And their **m** offering *shall be of* flour
11 offering, and the **m** offering of it, and

Nu 29:14 And their **m** offering *shall be of* flour
16 his **m** offering, and his drink offering.
18 And their **m** offering and their drink
19 offering, and the **m** offering thereof, and
21 And their **m** offering and their drink
22 his **m** offering, and his drink offering.
24 Their **m** offering and their drink
25 his **m** offering, and his drink offering.
27 And their **m** offering and their drink
28 his **m** offering, and his drink offering.
30 And their **m** offering and their drink
31 his **m** offering, and his drink offering.
33 And their **m** offering and their drink
34 his **m** offering, and his drink offering.
37 Their **m** offering and their drink
38 his **m** offering, and his drink offering.
39 and for your **m** offerings, and for your
Dt 2: 6 Ye shall buy **m** of them for money, that H400
28 Thou shalt sell me **m** for money, that I H400
20:20 *be* not trees for **m**, thou shalt destroy H3978
28:26 And thy carcase shall be **m** unto all H3978
Jos 22:23 burnt offering or **m** offering, or if to offer
29 burnt offerings, for **m** offerings, or for
Jdg 1: 7 off, gathered *their* **m** under my table: as
13:19 So Manoah took a kid with a **m** offering,
23 offering and a **m** offering at our hands,
14:14 the eater came forth **m**, and out of the H3978
1Sa 20: 5 sit with the king at **m**: but let me go, that H398
24 come, the king sat him down to eat **m**. H3899
27 to **m**, neither yesterday, nor to day? H3899
34 and did eat no **m** the second day of the H3899
2Sa 3:35 David to eat **m** while it was yet day, H3899
11: 8 followed him a mess *of* **m** from the king.
12: 3 it did eat of his own **m**, and drank of his H6595
13: 5 and give me **m**, and dress the meat H3899
5 and dress the **m** in my sight, that I may H1279
7 Amnon's house, and dress him **m**. H1279
10 Tamar, Bring the **m** into the chamber, H1279
1Ki 8:64 offerings, and **m** offerings, and the fat
64 offerings, and **m** offerings, and the fat
10: 5 And the **m** of his table, and the sitting H3978
19: 8 strength of that **m** forty days and forty H396
2Ki 3:20 when the **m** offering was offered,
16:13 offering and his **m** offering, and poured
15 and the evening **m** offering, and the
15 sacrifice, and his **m** offering, with the
15 the land, and their **m** offering, and their
1Ch 12:40 and on oxen, *and* **m**, meal, cakes of figs, H3978
21:23 the wheat for the **m** offering; I give it all.
23:29 the fine flour for **m** offering, and for the
2Ch 7: 7 and the **m** offerings, and the fat.
9: 4 And the **m** of his table, and the sitting H3978
Ezr 3: 7 carpenters; and **m**, and drink, and oil, H3978
7:17 lambs, with their **m** offerings and their
Neh 10:33 for the continual **m** offering, and for the
13: 5 aforetime they laid the **m** offerings, the
9 the **m** offering and the frankincense.
Job 6: 7 refused to touch *are* as my sorrowful **m**. H3899
12:11 try words? and the mouth taste his **m**? H400
20:14 *Yet* his **m** in his bowels is turned, *it is* H3899
21 There shall none of his **m** be left;
30: 4 bushes, and juniper roots *for* their **m**. H3899
33:20 abhorreth bread, and his soul dainty **m**. H3978
34: 3 ear trieth words, as the mouth tasteth **m**. H398
36:31 the people; he giveth **m** in abundance. H400
38:41 cry unto God, they wander for lack of **m**. H400
Ps 42: 3 My tears have been my **m** day and H3899
44:11 *appointed* for **m**; and hast scattered H3978
59:15 Let them wander up and down for **m**, H398
69:21 They gave me also gall for my **m**; and in H1267
74:14 *and* gavest him *to be* **m** to the people H3978
78:18 in their heart by asking **m** for their lust.
25 angels' food: he sent them **m** to the full. H6720
30 while their **m** *was* yet in their mouths, H400
79: 2 they given *to be* **m** unto the fowls of the H3978
104:21 their prey, and seek their **m** from God. H400
27 mayest give *them* their **m** in due season. H400
107:18 Their soul abhorreth all manner of **m**; H400
111: 5 He hath given **m** unto them that fear H2964
145:15 thou givest them their **m** in due season. H400
Prv 6: 8 Provideth her **m** in the summer, *and* H3899
23: 3 of his dainties: for they *are* deceitful **m**. H3899
30:22 and a fool when he is filled with **m**; H3899
25 they prepare their **m** in the summer; H3899
31:15 night, and giveth **m** to her household, H2964
Isa 57: 6 thou hast offered a **m** offering. Should I
62: 8 thy corn *to be* **m** for thine enemies; and H3978
65:25 *be* the serpent's **m**. They shall not hurt H3899
Jer 7:33 people shall be **m** for the fowls of the H3978

Jer 16: 4 carcases shall be **m** for the fowls of H3978
17:26 and sacrifices, and **m** offerings, and
19: 7 will I give to be **m** for the fowls of the H3978
33:18 and to kindle **m** offerings, and to do
34:20 shall be for **m** unto the fowls of the H3978
Lam 1:11 pleasant things for **m** to relieve the soul: H400
19 they sought their **m** to relieve their souls. H400
4:10 they were their **m** in the destruction of H1262
Ezk 4:10 And thy **m** which thou shalt eat *shall* H3978
16:19 My **m** also which I gave thee, fine flour, H3899
29: 5 given thee for **m** to the beasts of the field H402
34: 5 and they became **m** to all the beasts of H402
8 my flock became **m** to every beast of the H402
10 mouth, that they may not be **m** for them. H402
42:13 things, and the **m** offering, and the sin
44:29 They shall eat the **m** offering, and the sin
45:15 of Israel; for a **m** offering, and for a
17 offerings, and **m** offerings, and drink
17 sin offering, and the **m** offering, and the
24 And he shall prepare a **m** offering of an
25 the **m** offering, and according to the oil.
46: 5 And the **m** offering *shall be* an ephah for
5 for a ram, and the **m** offering for the
7 And he shall prepare a **m** offering, an
11 in the solemnities the **m** offering shall be
14 And thou shalt prepare a **m** offering for
14 the fine flour; a **m** offering continually
15 the lamb, and the **m** offering, and the
20 they shall bake the **m** offering; that they
47:12 grow all trees for **m**, whose leaf shall H3978
12 for **m**, and the leaf thereof for medicine. H3978
Dan 1: 5 of the king's **m**, and of the wine which H6598
8 of the king's **m**, nor with the wine which H6598
10 appointed your **m** and your drink: for H3978
13 of the king's **m**: and as thou seest, deal H6598
15 did eat the portion of the king's **m**. H6598
16 portion of their **m**, and the wine that H6598
4:12 and in it *was* **m** for all: the beasts of H4203
21 and in it *was* **m** for all; under which H4203
11:26 the portion of his **m** shall destroy him, H6598
Hos 11: 4 on their jaws, and I laid **m** unto them. H398
Joel 1: 9 The **m** offering and the drink offering is
13 of my God: for the **m** offering and the
16 Is not the **m** cut off before our eyes, *yea*, H400
2:14 him; *even* a **m** offering and a drink
Am 5:22 offerings and your **m** offerings, I will not
Hab 1:16 portion *is* fat, and their **m** plenteous. H3978
3:17 shall yield no **m**; the flock shall be cut H400
Hag 2:12 or oil, or any **m**, shall it be holy? And H3978
Mal 1:12 fruit thereof, *even* his **m**, *is* contemptible. H400
3:10 that there may be **m** in mine house, H2964
Mt 3: 4 and his **m** was locusts and wild honey. *G5160*
6:25 than **m**, and the body than raiment? *G5160*
9:10 And it came to pass, as Jesus sat at **m** in *G345*
10:10 for the workman is worthy of his **m**. *G5160*
14: 9 at **m**, he commanded *it* to be given *her*. *G4873*
15:37 ***m*** that was left seven baskets full.
24:45 to give them **m** in due season? *G5160*
25:35 and ye gave me **m**: I was thirsty, and ye *G5315*
42 ye gave me no **m**: I was thirsty, and ye *G5315*
26: 7 and poured it on his head, as he sat *at* ***m***.
Mk 2:15 as Jesus sat at **m** in his house, many *G2621*
8: 8 broken ***m*** that was left seven baskets.
14: 3 the leper, as he sat at **m**, there came a *G2621*
16:14 as they sat at **m**, and upbraided them *G345*
Lk 3:11 and he that hath **m**, let him do likewise. *G1033*
7:36 the Pharisee's house, and sat down to **m**. *G347*
37 that *Jesus* sat at **m** in the Pharisee's *G345*
49 And they that sat at **m** with him began
8:55 and he commanded to give her **m**. *G5315*
9:13 go and buy **m** for all this people. *G1033*
11:37 him: and he went in, and sat down to **m**. *G377*
12:23 The life is more than **m**, and the body *is* *G5160*
37 **m**, and will come forth and serve them. *G347*
42 *them their* portion of **m** in due season? *G4620*
14:10 presence of them that sit at **m** with thee.
15 And when one of them that sat at **m** with
17: 7 from the field, Go and sit down to **m**? *G377*
22:27 he that sitteth at **m**, or he that serveth? *is* *G345*
27 he that sitteth at **m**? but I am among you *G345*
24:30 And it came to pass, as he sat at **m** *G2625*
41 he said unto them, Have ye here any **m**? *G1034*
Jn 4: 8 were gone away unto the city to buy **m**.) *G5160*
32 But he said unto them, I have **m** to eat *G1035*
34 Jesus saith unto them, My **m** is to do *G1033*
6:27 Labour not for the **m** which perisheth, *G1035*
27 but for that **m** which endureth unto *G1035*
55 For my flesh is **m** indeed, and my *G1035*
21: 5 have ye any **m**? They answered him, No. *G4371*

Act 2:46 did eat their m with gladness and G5160
9:19 And when he had received m, he was G5160
16:34 his house, he set m before them, and
27:33 *them* all to take m, saying, This day is G5160
34 Wherefore I pray you to take *some* m: G5160
36 good cheer, and they also took *some* m. G5160
Ro 14:15 But if thy brother be grieved with *thy* m, G1033
15 him with thy m, for whom Christ died. G1033
17 For the kingdom of God is not m and G1035
20 For m destroy not the work of God. All G1033
1Co 3: 2 and not with m: for hitherto ye were G1033
8: 8 But m commendeth us not to God: for G1033
10 knowledge sit at m in the idol's temple, G2621
13 Wherefore, if m make my brother to G1033
10: 3 And did all eat the same spiritual m; G1033
Col 2:16 Let no man therefore judge you in m, or G1035
Heb 5:12 have need of milk, and not of strong m. G5160
14 But strong m belongeth to them that G5160
12:16 for one morsel of m sold his birthright. G1035

MEAT-OFFERING See MEAT and OFFERING.

MEATS
Prv 23: 6 eye, neither desire thou his dainty m: H4303
Mk 7:19 out into the draught, purging all m? G1033
Act 15:29 That ye abstain from m offered to idols,
1Co 6:13 M for the belly, and the belly for meats: G1033
13 Meats for the belly, and the belly for m: G1033
1Ti 4: 3 to abstain from m, which God hath G1033
Heb 9:10 *Which stood* only in m and drinks, and G1033
13: 9 with grace; not with m, which have not G1033

MEBUNNAI
2Sa 23:27 Abiezer the Anethothite, M the H4012

MECHERATHITE
1Ch 11:36 Hepher the M, Ahijah the Pelonite, H4382

MEDAD
Nu 11:26 the name of the other M: and the spirit H4312
27 Eldad and M do prophesy in the camp. H4312

MEDAN
Gen 25: 2 M, and Midian, and Ishbak, and Shuah. H4091
1Ch 1:32 and Jokshan, and M, and Midian, and H4091

MEDDLE
Dt 2: 5 M not with them; for I will not give you H1624
19 them not, nor m with them: for I will H1624
2Ki 14:10 shouldest thou m to *thy* hurt, that thou H1624
2Ch 25:19 shouldest thou m to *thine* hurt, that H1624
Prv 20:19 secrets: therefore m not with him that H6148
24:21 and the king: *and* m not with them that H6148

MEDDLED
Prv 17:14 off contention, before it be m with. H1566

MEDDLETH
Prv 26:17 He that passeth by, *and* m with strife H5674

MEDDLING
2Ch 35:21 forbear thee from *m with* God, who *is*
Prv 20: 3 from strife: but every fool will be m. H1566

MEDE
Dan 11: 1 Also I in the first year of Darius the M, H4075

MEDEBA
Nu 21:30 unto Nophah, which *reacheth* unto M. H4311
Jos 13: 9 and all the plain of M unto Dibon; H4311
16 of the river, and all the plain by M; H4311
1Ch 19: 7 pitched before M. And the children of H4311
Isa 15: 2 Nebo, and over M: on all their heads H4311

MEDES
2Ki 17: 6 of Gozan, and in the cities of the M. H4074
18:11 of Gozan, and in the cities of the M: H4074
Ezr 6: 2 province of the M, a roll, and therein H4076
Est 1:19 the Persians and the M, that it be not H4074
Isa 13:17 Behold, I will stir up the M against H4074
Jer 25:25 of Elam, and all the kings of the M, H4074
51:11 of the kings of the M: for his device *is* H4074
28 the kings of the M, the captains thereof, H4074
Dan 5:28 and given to the M and Persians. H4076
6: 8 the M and Persians, which altereth not. H4076
12 the M and Persians, which altereth not. H4076
15 that the law of the M and Persians *is*, H4076
9: 1 of the seed of the M, which was made H4074
Act 2: 9 Parthians, and M, and Elamites, and G3370

MEDIA
Est 1: 3 of Persia and M, the nobles and princes H4074
14 of Persia and M, which saw the king's H4074
18 of Persia and M say this day unto all H4074
10: 2 of the kings of M and Persia? H4074
Isa 21: 2 O Elam: besiege, O M; all the sighing H4074
Dan 8:20 horns *are* the kings of M and Persia. H4074

MEDIAN
Dan 5:31 And Darius the M took the kingdom, H4077

MEDIATOR
Gal 3:19 ordained by angels in the hand of a m. G3316
20 Now a m is not *a mediator* of one, but G3316
20 Now a mediator is not *a m* of one, but
1Ti 2: 5 For *there is* one God, and one m G3316
Heb 8: 6 also he is the m of a better covenant, G3316
9:15 And for this cause he is the m of the G3316
12:24 And to Jesus the m of the new G3316

MEDICINE
Prv 17:22 A merry heart doeth good *like* a m: but H1456
Ezk 47:12 be for meat, and the leaf thereof for m. H8644

MEDICINES
Jer 30:13 be bound up: thou hast no healing m. H7499
46:11 many m; *for* thou shalt not be cured. H7499

MEDITATE
Gen 24:63 And Isaac went out to m in the field at H7742
Jos 1: 8 but thou shalt m therein day and night, H1897
Ps 1: 2 in his law doth he m day and night. H1897
63: 6 *and* m on thee in the *night* watches. H1897
77:12 I will m also of all thy work, and talk of H1897
119:15 I will m in thy precepts, and have H7878
23 *but* thy servant did m in thy statutes. H7878
48 have loved; and I will m in thy statutes. H7878
78 a cause: *but* I will m in thy precepts. H7878
148 watches, that I might m in thy word. H7878
143: 5 I remember the days of old; I m on all H1897
Isa 33:18 Thine heart shall m terror. Where *is* H1897
Lk 21:14 not to m before what ye shall answer: G4304
1Ti 4:15 M upon these things; give thyself G3191

MEDITATION
Ps 5: 1 to my words, O LORD, consider my m. H1901
19:14 Let the words of my mouth, and the m H1902
49: 3 of wisdom; and the m of my heart *shall* H1900
104:34 My m of him shall be sweet: I will be H7879
119:97 O how love I thy law! it *is* my m all the H7881
99 teachers: for thy testimonies *are* my m. H7881

MEEK
Nu 12: 3 (Now the man Moses *was* very m, H6035
Ps 22:26 The m shall eat and be satisfied: they H6035
25: 9 The m will he guide in judgment: and H6035
9 and the m will he teach his way. H6035
37:11 But the m shall inherit the earth; and H6035
76: 9 to save all the m of the earth. Selah. H6035
147: 6 The LORD lifteth up the m: he casteth H6035
149: 4 he will beautify the m with salvation. H6035
Isa 11: 4 equity for the m of the earth: and he H6035
29:19 The m also shall increase *their* joy in H6035
61: 1 tidings unto the m; he hath sent me to H6035
Am 2: 7 the way of the m: and a man and his H6035
Zep 2: 3 Seek ye the LORD, all ye m of the earth, H6035
Mt 5: 5 Blessed *are* the m: for they shall inherit G4239
11:29 of me; for I am m and lowly in heart: G4235
21: 5 cometh unto thee, m, and sitting upon G4239
1Pt 3: 4 *the ornament* of a m and quiet spirit, G4239

MEEKNESS
Ps 45: 4 of truth and m *and* righteousness; H6037
Zep 2: 3 seek m: it may be ye shall be H6038
1Co 4:21 a rod, or in love, and *in* the spirit of m? G4236
2Co 10: 1 you by the m and gentleness of Christ, G4236
Gal 5:23 M, temperance: against such there is no G4236
6: 1 in the spirit of m; considering thyself, G4236
Eph 4: 2 With all lowliness and m, with G4236
Col 3:12 humbleness of mind, m, longsuffering; G4236
1Ti 6:11 godliness, faith, love, patience, m. G4236
2Ti 2:25 In m instructing those that oppose G4236
Tit 3: 2 *but* gentle, shewing all m unto all men. G4236
Jas 1:21 and receive with m the engrafted word, G4240
3:13 his works with m of wisdom. G4240
1Pt 3:15 the hope that is in you with m and fear: G4240

MEET
Gen 2:18 I will make him an help m for him. H5828
2:20 there was not found an help m for him. H5828
14:17 And the king of Sodom went out to m H7125
18: 2 *them*, he ran to m them from the tent H7125
19: 1 *them* rose up to m *them*; and he bowed H7125
24:17 And the servant ran to m her, and said, H7125
65 in the field to m us? And the servant H7125
29:13 that he ran to m him, and embraced H7125
30:16 and Leah went out to m him, and said, H7125
32: 6 and also he cometh to m thee, and four H7125
33: 4 And Esau ran to m him, and embraced H7125
46:29 and went up to m Israel his father, to H7125
Ex 4:14 cometh forth to m thee: and when he H7125
27 into the wilderness to m Moses. And he H7125
8:26 And Moses said, It is not m so to do; H3559
18: 7 And Moses went out to m his father in H7125
19:17 of the camp to m with God; and they H7125
23: 4 If thou m thine enemy's ox or his ass H6293
25:22 And there I will m with thee, and I will H3259
29:42 I will m you, to speak there unto thee. H3259
43 And there I will m with the children of H3259
30: 6 the testimony, where I will m with thee. H3259
36 where I will m with thee: it shall be H3259
Nu 17: 4 the testimony, where I will m with you. H3259
22:36 he went out to m him unto a city of H7125
23: 3 will come to m me: and whatsoever H7125
15 offering, while I m *the LORD* yonder. H7136
31:13 forth to m them without the camp. H7125
Dt 3:18 of Israel, all *that are* m for the war. H1121
Jos 2:16 lest the pursuers m you; and hide H6293
9:11 and go to m them, and say unto H7125
Jdg 4:18 And Jael went out to m Sisera, and said H7125
22 Jael came out to m him, and said unto H7125
5:30 on both sides, *m* for the necks of *them*
6:35 Naphtali; and they came up to m them. H7125
11:31 of my house to m me, when I return in H7125
34 came out to m him with timbrels and H7125
19: 3 damsel saw him, he rejoiced to m him. H7125
Ru 2:22 that they m thee not in any other field. H6293
1Sa 10: 3 and there shall m thee three men going H4672
5 city, that thou shalt m a company of H6293
13:10 out to m him, that he might salute him. H7125
15:12 And when Samuel rose early to m Saul H7125
17:48 and drew nigh to m David, that David H7125
48 toward the army to m the Philistine. H7125
18: 6 and dancing, to m king Saul, with H7125
25:32 which sent thee this day to m me: H7125
34 and come to m me, surely there had H7125
30:21 and they went forth to m David, and to H7125
21 David, and to m the people that *were* H7125
2Sa 6:20 of Saul came out to m David, and said, H7125
10: 5 David, he sent to m them, because the H7125
15:32 Archite came to m him with his coat H7125
19:15 came to Gilgal, to go to m the king, to H7125
16 with the men of Judah to m king David. H7125
20 to go down to m my lord the king. H7125
24 came down to m the king, and had H7125
25 to Jerusalem to m the king, that the H7125
1Ki 2: 8 he came down to m me at Jordan, and H7125
19 the king rose up to m her, and bowed H7125
18:16 So Obadiah went to m Ahab, and told H7125
16 told him: and Ahab went to m Elijah. H7125
21:18 Arise, go down to m Ahab king of H7125
2Ki 1: 3 Arise, go up to m the messengers of the H7125
6 came a man up to m us, and said unto H7125
7 up to m you, and told you these words? H7125
2:15 And they came to m him, and bowed H7125
4:26 Run now, I pray thee, to m her, and say H7125
29 thy way: if thou m any man, salute him H4672
31 he went again to m him, and told him, H7125
5:21 chariot to m him, and said, *Is* all well? H7125
26 his chariot to m thee? *Is it* a time to H7125
8: 8 hand, and go, m the man of God, and H7125
9 So Hazael went to m him, and took a H7125
9:17 to m them, and let him say, *Is it* peace? H7125
18 So there went one on horseback to m H7125
10:15 of Rechab *coming* to m him: and he H7125
16:10 And king Ahaz went to Damascus to m H7125
1Ch 12:17 And David went out to m them, and H6440
19: 5 And he sent to m them: for the men H7125
2Ch 15: 2 And he went out to m Asa, and said H6440
19: 2 the seer went out to m him, and said to H6440
Ezr 4:14 and it was not m for us to see the king's H749
Neh 6: 2 Come, let us m together in *some one* H3259
10 he said, Let us m together in the house H3259
Est 2: 9 *which were* m to be given her, out H7200
Job 5:14 They m with darkness in the daytime, H6298
34:31 Surely it is m to be said unto God, I have
39:21 he goeth on to m the armed men. H7125
Prv 7:15 Therefore came I forth to m thee, H7125

M

Prv 11:24 than is **m**, but *it tendeth* to poverty. H3476
17:12 Let a bear robbed of her whelps **m** a H6298
22: 2 The rich and poor **m** together: the H6298
29:13 The poor and the deceitful man **m** H6298
Isa 7: 3 Go forth now to **m** Ahaz, thou, and H7125
14: 9 is moved for thee to **m** *thee* at thy H7125
34:14 desert shall also **m** with the wild beasts H6298
47: 3 and I will not **m** *thee as* a man. H6293
Jer 26:14 me as seemeth good and **m** unto you. H3477
27: 5 it unto whom it seemed **m** unto me. H3474
41: 6 from Mizpah to **m** them, weeping all H7125
51:31 One post shall run to **m** another, and H7125
31 one messenger to **m** another, to shew H7125
Ezk 15: 4 of it is burned. Is it **m** for *any* work? H6743
5 Behold, when it was whole, it was **m** H6213
5 less shall it be **m** yet for *any* work, H6213
Hos 13: 8 I will **m** them as a bear *that is* bereaved H6298
Am 4:12 thee, prepare to **m** thy God, O Israel. H7125
Zec 2: 3 and another angel went out to **m** him, H7125
Mt 3: 8 Bring forth therefore fruits **m** for *G514*
8:34 city came out to **m** Jesus: and when *G4877*
15:26 But he answered and said, It is not **m** *G2570*
25: 1 and went forth to **m** the bridegroom. *G529*
6 bridegroom cometh; go ye out to **m** him. *G529*
Mk 7:27 be filled: for it is not **m** to take the *G2570*
14:13 and there shall **m** you a man bearing a *G528*
Lk 14:31 with ten thousand to **m** him that cometh *G528*
15:32 It was **m** that we should make merry, *G1163*
22:10 there shall a man **m** you, bearing a *G4876*
Jn 12:13 and went forth to **m** him, and cried, *G5222*
Act 26:20 to God, and do works **m** for repentance. *G514*
28:15 of us, they came to **m** us as far as Appii *G529*
Ro 1:27 recompence of their error which was **m**. *G1163*
1Co 15: 9 that am not **m** to be called an apostle, *G2425*
16: 4 And if it be **m** that I go also, they shall go *G514*
Php 1: 7 Even as it is **m** for me to think this of *G1342*
Col 1:12 hath made us **m** to be partakers of the *G2427*
1Th 4:17 in the clouds, to **m** the Lord in the air: *G529*
2Th 1: 3 brethren, as it is **m**, because that your *G514*
2Ti 2:21 sanctified, and **m** for the master's use, *G2173*
Heb 6: 7 forth herbs **m** for them by whom *G2111*
2Pt 1:13 Yea, I think it **m**, as long as I am in this *G1342*

MEETEST
2Ki 10: 3 Look even out the best and **m** of your H3477
Isa 64: 5 Thou **m** him that rejoiceth and H6293

MEETETH
Gen 32:17 Esau my brother **m** thee, and asketh H6298
Nu 35:19 when he **m** him, he shall slay him. H6293
21 slay the murderer, when he **m** him. H6293

MEETING
1Sa 21: 1 was afraid at the **m** of David, and said H7125
Isa 1:13 with; *it is* iniquity, even the solemn **m**. H6116

MEGIDDO
Jos 12:21 of Taanach, one; the king of **M**, one; H4023
17:11 **M** and her towns, *even* three countries. H4023
Jdg 1:27 the inhabitants of **M** and her towns: H4023
5:19 of **M**; they took no gain of money. H4023
1Ki 4:12 Taanach and **M**, and all Beth-shean, H4023
9:15 and Hazor, and **M**, and Gezer. H4023
2Ki 9:27 And he fled to **M**, and died there. H4023
23:29 slew him at **M**, when he had seen him. H4023
30 dead from **M**, and brought him to H4023
1Ch 7:29 and her towns, **M** and her towns, Dor H4023
2Ch 35:22 and came to fight in the valley of **M**. H4023

MEGIDDON
Zec 12:11 of Hadadrimmon in the valley of **M**. H4023

MEHETABEEL
Neh 6:10 Delaiah the son of **M**, who *was* shut up; H4105

MEHETABEL
Gen 36:39 his wife's name *was* **M**, the daughter of H4105
1Ch 1:50 his wife's name *was* **M**, the daughter of H4105

MEHIDA
Ezr 2:52 children of **M**, the children of Harsha, H4240
Neh 7:54 children of **M**, the children of Harsha, H4240

MEHIR
1Ch 4:11 **M**, which *was* the father of Eshton. H4243

MEHOLAH See ABEL-MEHOLAH.

MEHOLATHITE
1Sa 18:19 was given unto Adriel the **M** to wife. H4259
2Sa 21: 8 up for Adriel the son of Barzillai the **M**: H4259

MEHUJAEL
Gen 4:18 and Irad begat **M**: and Mehujael begat H4232
18 Mehujael: and **M** begat Methusael: and H4232

MEHUMAN
Est 1:10 he commanded **M**, Biztha, Harbona, H4104

MEHUNIM
Ezr 2:50 of **M**, the children of Nephusim, H4586

MEHUNIMS
2Ch 26: 7 that dwelt in Gur-baal, and the **M**. H4586

ME-JARKON
Jos 19:46 And **M**, and Rakkon, with the border H4313

MEKONAH
Neh 11:28 And at Ziklag, and at **M**, and in the H4368

MELATIAH
Neh 3: 7 And next unto them repaired **M** the H4424

MELCHI
Lk 3:24 was *the son* of **M**, which was *the son* *G3197*
28 Which was *the son* of **M**, which was *the* *G3197*

MELCHIAH
Jer 21: 1 Pashur the son of **M**, and Zephaniah H4441

MELCHISEDEC
Heb 5: 6 *art* a priest for ever after the order of **M**. *G3198*
10 God an high priest after the order of **M**. *G3198*
6:20 high priest for ever after the order of **M**. *G3198*
7: 1 For this **M**, king of Salem, priest of the *G3198*
10 loins of his father, when **M** met him. *G3198*
11 after the order of **M**, and not be called *G3198*
15 of **M** there ariseth another priest, *G3198*
17 *art* a priest for ever after the order of **M**. *G3198*
21 *art* a priest for ever after the order of **M**:) *G3198*

MELCHISHUA
1Sa 14:49 and Ishui, and **M**: and the names of his H4444

MELCHIZEDEK
Gen 14:18 And **M** king of Salem brought forth H4442
Ps 110: 4 *art* a priest for ever after the order of **M**. H4442

MELEA
Lk 3:31 Which was *the son* of **M**, which was *the* *G3190*

MELECH
1Ch 8:35 Pithon, and **M**, and Tarea, and Ahaz. H4429
9:41 Pithon, and **M**, and Tahrea, *and Ahaz*. H4429

MELICU
Neh 12:14 Of **M**, Jonathan; of Shebaniah, Joseph; H4409

MELITA
Act 28: 1 they knew that the island was called **M**. *G3194*

MELODY
Isa 23:16 make sweet **m**, sing many songs, that H5059
51: 3 thanksgiving, and the voice of **m**. H2172
Am 5:23 for I will not hear the **m** of thy viols. H2172
Eph 5:19 making **m** in your heart to the Lord; *G5567*

MELONS
Nu 11: 5 and the **m**, and the leeks, and the H20

MELT
Ex 15:15 inhabitants of Canaan shall **m** away. H4127
Jos 2:11 our hearts did **m**, neither did there H4549
14: 8 of the people **m**: but I wholly followed H4529
2Sa 17:10 a lion, shall utterly **m**: for all Israel H4549
Ps 58: 7 Let them **m** away as waters *which* run H3988
112:10 his teeth, and **m** away: the desire of H4549
Isa 13: 7 be faint, and every man's heart shall **m**: H4549
19: 1 of Egypt shall **m** in the midst of it. H4549
Jer 9: 7 Behold, I will **m** them, and try them; H6884
Ezk 21: 7 every heart shall **m**, and all hands shall H4549
22:20 the fire upon it, to **m** *it*; so will I gather H5413
20 and I will leave *you there*, and **m** you. H5413
Am 9: 5 land, and it shall **m**, and all that dwell H4127
13 sweet wine, and all the hills shall **m**. H4127
Nah 1: 5 at him, and the hills **m**, and the earth is H4127
2Pt 3:10 the elements shall **m** with fervent heat, *G3089*
12 the elements shall **m** with fervent heat? *G5080*

MELTED
Ex 16:21 and when the sun waxed hot, it **m**. H4549
Jos 5: 1 that their heart **m**, neither was there H4549
7: 5 of the people **m**, and became as water. H4549
Jdg 5: 5 The mountains **m** from before the H5140
1Sa 14:16 the multitude **m** away, and they went H4127
Ps 22:14 wax; it is **m** in the midst of my bowels. H4549
46: 6 he uttered his voice, the earth **m**. H4127
97: 5 The hills **m** like wax at the presence of H4549
107:26 their soul is **m** because of trouble. H4127
Isa 34: 3 mountains shall be **m** with their blood. H4549
Ezk 22:21 and ye shall be **m** in the midst thereof. H5413
22 As silver is **m** in the midst of the H2046
22 so shall ye be **m** in the midst thereof; H5413

MELTETH
Ps 58: 8 As a snail *which* **m**, let *every one of* H8557
68: 2 away: as wax **m** before the fire, *so* let H4549
119:28 My soul **m** for heaviness: strengthen H1811
147:18 He sendeth out his word, and **m** them: H4529
Isa 40:19 The workman **m** a graven image, and H5258
Jer 6:29 the fire; the founder **m** in vain: for the H6884
Nah 2:10 and the heart **m**, and the knees smite H4549

MELTING
Isa 64: 2 As *when* the **m** fire burneth, the fire H2003

MELZAR
Dan 1:11 Then said Daniel to **M**, whom the H4453
16 Thus **M** took away the portion of their H4453

MEMBER
Dt 23: 1 or hath his privy **m** cut off, shall not H8212
1Co 12:14 For the body is not one **m**, but many. *G3196*
19 And if they were all one **m**, where *were* *G3196*
26 And whether one **m** suffer, all the *G3196*
26 with it; or one **m** be honoured, all the *G3196*
Jas 3: 5 Even so the tongue is a little **m**, and *G3196*

MEMBERS
Job 17: 7 sorrow, and all my **m** *are* as a shadow. H3338
Ps 139:16 in thy book all *my* **m** were written, *which*
Mt 5:29 that one of thy **m** should perish, and *G3196*
30 that one of thy **m** should perish, and *G3196*
Ro 6:13 Neither yield ye your **m** *as* instruments *G3196*
13 the dead, and your **m** *as* instruments of *G3196*
19 ye have yielded your **m** servants to *G3196*
19 even so now yield your **m** servants to *G3196*
7: 5 our **m** to bring forth fruit unto death. *G3196*
23 But I see another law in my **m**, warring *G3196*
23 to the law of sin which is in my **m**. *G3196*
12: 4 For as we have many **m** in one body, *G3196*
4 and all **m** have not the same office: *G3196*
5 and every one **m** one of another. *G3196*
1Co 6:15 Know ye not that your bodies are the **m** *G3196*
15 I then take the **m** of Christ, and make *G3196*
15 *them* the **m** of an harlot? God forbid. *G3196*
12:12 and hath many **m**, and all the members *G3196*
12 and all the **m** of that one body, being *G3196*
18 But now hath God set the **m** every one *G3196*
20 But now *are they* many **m**, yet but one *G3196*
22 Nay, much more those **m** of the body, *G3196*
23 And those *m* of the body, which we think
25 body; but *that* the **m** should have the *G3196*
26 suffer, all the **m** suffer with it; or one *G3196*
26 be honoured, all the **m** rejoice with it. *G3196*
27 Now ye are the body of Christ, and **m** *G3196*
Eph 4:25 for we are **m** one of another. *G3196*
5:30 For we are **m** of his body, of his flesh, *G3196*
Col 3: 5 Mortify therefore your **m** which are *G3196*
Jas 3: 6 among our **m**, that it defileth the whole *G3196*
4: 1 *even* of your lusts that war in your **m**? *G3196*

MEMORIAL
Ex 3:15 and this *is* my **m** unto all generations. H2143
12:14 And this day shall be unto you for a **m**; H2146
13: 9 hand, and for a **m** between thine eyes, H2146
17:14 Write this *for* a **m** in a book, and H2146
28:12 *for* stones of **m** unto the children of H2146
12 LORD upon his two shoulders for a **m**. H2146
29 for a **m** before the LORD continually. H2146
30:16 that it may be a **m** unto the children of H2146
39: 7 *be* stones for a **m** to the children of H2146
Lev 2: 2 shall burn the **m** of it upon the altar, H234
9 the meat offering a **m** thereof, and shall H234
16 And the priest shall burn the **m** of it, H234

Lev 5:12 of it, *even* a **m** thereof, and burn *it* H234
6:15 savour, *even* the **m** of it, unto the LORD. H234
23:24 ye have a sabbath, a **m** of blowing of H2146
24: 7 be on the bread for a **m**, *even* an offering H234
Nu 5:15 **m**, bringing iniquity to remembrance. H2146
18 and put the offering of **m** in her hands, H2146
26 offering, *even* the **m** thereof, and burn *it* H234
10:10 be to you for a **m** before your God: I *am* H2146
16:40 *To be* a **m** unto the children of Israel, H2146
31:54 *for* a **m** for the children of Israel H2146
Jos 4: 7 a **m** unto the children of Israel for ever. H2146
Neh 2:20 portion, nor right, nor **m**, in Jerusalem. H2146
Est 9:28 the **m** of them perish from their seed. H2143
Ps 9: 6 cities; their **m** is perished with them. H2143
135:13 **m**, O LORD, throughout all generations. H2143
Hos 12: 5 LORD God of hosts; the LORD *is* his **m**. H2143
Zec 6:14 for a **m** in the temple of the LORD. H2146
Mt 26:13 hath done, be told for a **m** of her. *G3422*
Mk 14: 9 done shall be spoken of for a **m** of her. *G3422*
Act 10: 4 alms are come up for a **m** before God. *G3422*

MEMORY

Ps 109:15 cut off the **m** of them from the earth. H2143
145: 7 They shall abundantly utter the **m** of H2143
Prv 10: 7 The **m** of the just *is* blessed: but the H2143
Ecc 9: 5 reward; for the **m** of them is forgotten. H2143
Isa 26:14 them, and made all their **m** to perish. H2143
1Co 15: 2 if ye keep in **m** what I preached unto *G2722*

MEMPHIS

Hos 9: 6 gather them up, **M** shall bury them: the H4644

MEMUCAN

Est 1:14 Marsena, *and* **M**, the seven princes of H4462
16 And **M** answered before the king and H4462
21 king did according to the word of **M**: H4462

MEN

Gen 4:26 **m** to call upon the name of the LORD. H2490
6: 1 And it came to pass, when **m** began to H120
2 the daughters of **m** that they *were* fair; H120
4 unto the daughters of **m**, and they bare H120
4 **m** which *were* of old, men of renown. H1368
4 men which *were* of old, **m** of renown. H582
11: 5 tower, which the children of **m** builded. H120
12:20 And Pharaoh commanded *his* **m** H582
13:13 But the **m** of Sodom *were* wicked and H582
14:24 Save only that which the young **m** have H5288
24 the portion of the **m** which went with H582
17:23 male among the **m** of Abraham's house; H582
27 And all the **m** of his house, born in the H582
18: 2 and, lo, three **m** stood by him: and when H582
16 And the **m** rose up from thence, and H582
22 And the **m** turned their faces from H582
19: 4 But before they lay down, the **m** of the H582
4 of the city, *even* the **m** of Sodom, H582
5 Where *are* the **m** which came in to thee H582
8 eyes: only unto these **m** do nothing; for H582
10 But the **m** put forth their hand, and H582
11 And they smote the **m** that *were* at the H582
12 And the **m** said unto Lot, Hast thou here H582
16 And while he lingered, the **m** laid hold H582
20: 8 in their ears: and the **m** were sore afraid. H582
22: 3 two of his young **m** with him, and Isaac H5288
5 And Abraham said unto his young **m**, H5288
19 unto his young **m**, and they rose up and H5288
24:13 **m** of the city come out to draw water: H582
54 drink, he and the **m** that *were* with him, H582
59 and Abraham's servant, and his **m**. H582
26: 7 And the **m** of the place asked *him* of his H582
7 lest, *said he*, the **m** of the place should H582
29:22 And Laban gathered together all the **m** H582
32: 6 thee, and four hundred **m** with him. H376
28 God and with **m**, and hast prevailed. H582
33: 1 him four hundred **m**. And he divided the H376
13 *are* with me: and if **m** should overdrive
34: 7 heard *it*: and the **m** were grieved, and H582
20 with the **m** of their city, saying, H582
21 These **m** *are* peaceable with us; therefore H582
22 Only herein will the **m** consent unto us H582
38:21 Then he asked the **m** of that place, H582
22 her; and also the **m** of the place said, H582
39:11 none of the **m** of the house there within. H582
14 That she called unto the **m** of her house, H582
41: 8 Egypt, and all the wise **m** thereof: and H2450
42:11 we *are* true **m**, thy servants are no spies.
19 If ye *be* true **m**, let one of your brethren
31 And we said unto him, We *are* true **m**; we
33 that ye *are* true **m**; leave one of your

Gen 42:34 *that* ye *are* true **m**: *so* will I deliver you
43:15 And the **m** took that present, and they H582
16 his house, Bring *these* **m** home, and slay, H582
16 for *these* **m** shall dine with me at noon. H582
17 man brought the **m** into Joseph's house. H582
18 And the **m** were afraid, because they H582
24 And the man brought the **m** into H582
33 and the **m** marvelled one at another. H582
44: 3 As soon as the morning was light, the **m** H582
4 follow after the **m**; and when thou dost H582
46:32 And the **m** *are* shepherds, for their trade H582
47: 2 **m**, and presented them unto Pharaoh. H582
6 if thou knowest *any* **m** of activity among H582
Ex 1:17 them, but saved the **m** children alive.
18 and have saved the **m** children alive?
2:13 day, behold, two **m** of the Hebrews H582
4:19 all the **m** are dead which sought thy life. H582
5: 9 Let there more work be laid upon the **m**, H582
7:11 Then Pharaoh also called the wise **m** H2450
10: 7 unto us? let the **m** go, that they may H582
11 Not so: go now ye *that are* **m**, and serve H1397
12:33 in haste; for they said, We *be* all dead **m**.
37 on foot *that were* **m**, beside children. H1397
15:15 the mighty **m** of Moab, trembling H352
17: 9 Choose us out **m**, and go out, fight with H582
18:21 of all the people able **m**, such as fear God, H582
21 such as fear God, **m** of truth, hating H582
25 And Moses chose able **m** out of all H582
21:18 And if **m** strive together, and one smite H582
22 If **m** strive, and hurt a woman with H582
22:31 And ye shall be holy **m** unto me: neither H582
24: 5 And he sent young **m** of the children of H5288
32:28 people that day about three thousand **m**. H376
34:23 Thrice in the year shall all your **m**
35:22 And they came, both **m** and women, as H582
36: 4 And all the wise **m**, that wrought all the H2450
38:26 thousand and five hundred and fifty **m**.
Lev 7:25 of the beast, of which **m** offer an offering
18:27 (For all these abominations have the **m** H582
27: 9 And if *it be* a beast, whereof **m** bring H7126
29 shall be devoted of **m**, shall be redeemed; H120
Nu 1: 5 And these *are* the names of the **m** that H582
17 And Moses and Aaron took these **m** H582
44 *being* twelve **m**: each one was for the H376
5: 6 any sin that **m** commit, to do a trespass H120
9: 6 And there were certain **m**, who were H582
7 And those **m** said unto him, We *are* H582
11:16 unto me seventy **m** of the elders of H376
24 the seventy **m** of the elders of the people, H376
26 But there remained two *of the* **m** in the H582
28 *one* of his young **m**, answered and said, H979
12: 3 above all the **m** which *were* upon the H120
13: 2 Send thou **m**, that they may search the H582
3 **m** *were* heads of the children of Israel. H582
16 These *are* the names of the **m** which H582
21 Zin unto Rehob, as **m** come to Hamath.
31 But the **m** that went up with him said, H582
32 that we saw in it *are* **m** of a great stature. H582
14:22 Because all those **m** which have seen my H582
36 And the **m**, which Moses sent to search H582
37 Even those **m** that did bring up the evil H582
38 *which were* of the **m** that went to search H582
16: 1 son of Peleth, sons of Reuben, took **m**:
2 in the congregation, **m** of renown: H582
14 the eyes of these **m**? we will not come up. H582
26 of these wicked **m**, and touch nothing of H582
29 If these **m** die the common death of all
29 death of all **m**, or if they be visited H120
29 all **m**; *then* the LORD hath not sent me. H120
30 that these **m** have provoked the LORD. H582
32 houses, and all the **m** that *appertained* H120
35 and fifty **m** that offered incense. H376
18:15 *whether it be* of **m** or beasts, shall be H120
22: 9 and said, What **m** *are* these with thee? H582
20 unto him, If the **m** come to call thee, rise H582
35 Go with the **m**: but only the word that H582
25: 5 his **m** that were joined unto Baal-peor. H582
26:10 and fifty **m**: and they became a sign. H376
31:11 and all the prey, *both* of **m** and of beasts. H120
21 And Eleazar the priest said unto the **m** H582
28 the LORD of the **m** of war which went H582
32 prey which the **m** of war had caught, H5971
42 Moses divided from the **m** that warred, H582
49 the sum of the **m** of war which *are* under H582
53 (*For* the **m** of war had taken spoil, every H582
32:11 Surely none of the **m** that came up out of H582
14 increase of sinful **m**, to augment yet the H582
34:17 These *are* the names of the **m** which H582
19 And the names of the **m** *are* these: Of the H582

Dt 1:13 Take you wise **m**, and understanding, H582
15 So I took the chief of your tribes, wise **m**, H582
22 said, We will send **m** before us, and they H582
23 I took twelve **m** of you, one of a tribe: H582
35 Surely there shall not one of these **m** of H582
2:14 generation of the **m** of war were wasted H582
16 So it came to pass, when all the **m** of war H582
34 destroyed the **m**, and the women, and H4962
3: 6 **m**, women, and children, of every city. H4962
4: 3 for all the **m** that followed Baal-peor, H376
13:13 *Certain* **m**, the children of Belial, are H582
19:17 Then both the **m**, between whom the H582
21:21 And all the **m** of his city shall stone him H582
22:21 house, and the **m** of her city shall stone H582
25: 1 If there be a controversy between **m**, and H582
11 When **m** strive together one with H582
27:14 unto all the **m** of Israel with a loud voice, H376
29:10 your officers, *with* all the **m** of Israel, H376
25 Then **m** shall say, Because they have
31:12 Gather the people together, **m**, and H582
32:26 of them to cease from among **m**: H582
33: 6 and not die; and let *not* his **m** be few. H4962
Jos 1:14 the mighty **m** of valour, and help them;
2: 1 sent out of Shittim two **m** to spy secretly, H582
2 there came **m** in hither to night of H582
3 Bring forth the **m** that are come to thee, H582
4 And the woman took the two **m**, and hid H582
4 thus, There came **m** unto me, but I wist H582
5 it was dark, that the **m** went out: whither H582
5 went out: whither the **m** went I wot not: H582
7 And the **m** pursued after them the way H582
9 And she said unto the **m**, I know that the H582
14 And the **m** answered her, Our life for H582
17 And the **m** said unto her, We *will be* H582
23 So the two **m** returned, and descended H582
3:12 Now therefore take you twelve **m** out of H376
4: 2 Take you twelve **m** out of the people, out H582
4 Then Joshua called the twelve **m**, whom H376
5: 4 males, *even* all the **m** of war, died in the H582
6 people *that were* **m** of war, which came H582
6: 2 thereof, *and* the mighty **m** of valour. H1368
3 And ye shall compass the city, all *ye* **m** H582
9 And the armed **m** went before the priests
13 and the armed **m** went before them; but
22 But Joshua had said unto the two **m** that H582
23 And the young **m** that were spies went H5288
7: 2 And Joshua sent **m** from Jericho to Ai, H582
2 And the **m** went up and viewed Ai. H582
3 or three thousand **m** go up and smite Ai; H376
4 **m**: and they fled before the men of Ai. H376
4 men: and they fled before the **m** of Ai. H582
5 And the **m** of Ai smote of them about H582
5 thirty and six **m**: for they chased them H376
8: 3 thousand mighty **m** of valour, and sent H376
12 And he took about five thousand **m**, and H376
14 up early, and the **m** of the city went out H582
20 And when the **m** of Ai looked behind H582
21 they turned again, and slew the **m** of Ai. H582
25 that day, both of **m** and women, *were* H376
25 twelve thousand, *even* all the **m** of Ai. H582
9: 6 him, and to the **m** of Israel, We be come H376
7 And the **m** of Israel said unto the H376
14 And the **m** took of their victuals, and H582
10: 2 Ai, and all the **m** thereof *were* mighty. H582
6 And the **m** of Gibeon sent unto Joshua to H582
7 him, and all the mighty **m** of valour.
18 cave, and set **m** by it for to keep them: H582
24 called for all the **m** of Israel, and said H376
24 the captains of the **m** of war which went H582
18: 4 Give out from among you three **m** for H582
8 And the **m** arose, and went away: and H582
9 And the **m** went and passed through the H582
24:11 Jericho: and the **m** of Jericho fought H1167
Jdg 1: 4 slew of them in Bezek ten thousand **m**. H376
3:29 ten thousand **m**, all lusty, and all men H376
29 all lusty, and all **m** of valour; and there H376
31 six hundred **m** with an ox goad: and H376
4: 6 thee ten thousand **m** of the children of H376
10 up with ten thousand **m** at his feet: and H376
14 Tabor, and ten thousand **m** after him. H376
6:27 Then Gideon took ten **m** of his servants, H582
27 and the **m** of the city, that he could H582
28 And when the **m** of the city arose early in H582
30 Then the **m** of the city said unto Joash, H582
7: 6 three hundred **m**: but all the rest of the H376
7 the three hundred **m** that lapped will I H376
8 three hundred **m**: and the host of Midian H376
11 of the armed **m** that *were* in the host. H2571
16 And he divided the three hundred **m** H376

M

Jdg 7:19 So Gideon, and the hundred **m** that *were* H376
23 And the **m** of Israel gathered themselves H376
24 Then all the **m** of Ephraim gathered H376
8: 1 And the **m** of Ephraim said unto him, H376
4 the three hundred **m** that *were* with him, H376
5 And he said unto the **m** of Succoth, Give, H582
8 likewise: and the **m** of Penuel answered H582
8 as the **m** of Succoth had answered *him*. H582
9 And he spake also unto the **m** of Penuel, H582
10 fifteen thousand *m*, all that were left of
10 twenty thousand **m** that drew sword. H376
14 And caught a young man of the **m** of H582
14 *even* threescore and seventeen **m**. H376
15 And he came unto the **m** of Succoth, and H582
15 give bread unto thy **m** *that are* weary? H582
16 with them he taught the **m** of Succoth. H582
17 of Penuel, and slew the **m** of the city. H582
18 What manner of **m** *were they* whom ye H582
22 Then the **m** of Israel said unto Gideon, H376
9: 2 in the ears of all the **m** of Shechem, H1167
3 in the ears of all the **m** of Shechem all H1167
6 And all the **m** of Shechem gathered H1167
7 unto me, ye **m** of Shechem, that God H1167
18 king over the **m** of Shechem, because H1167
20 and devour the **m** of Shechem, and the H1167
20 out from the **m** of Shechem, and from H1167
23 and the **m** of Shechem; and the H1167
23 Shechem; and the **m** of Shechem dealt H1167
24 and upon the **m** of Shechem, which H1167
25 And the **m** of Shechem set liers in wait H1167
26 to Shechem: and the **m** of Shechem put H1167
28 officer? serve the **m** of Hamor the father H582
36 of the mountains as *if they were* **m**. H582
39 And Gaal went out before the **m** of H1167
46 And when all the **m** of the tower of H1167
47 that all the **m** of the tower of Shechem H1167
49 so that all the **m** of the tower of Shechem H582
49 also, about a thousand **m** and women. H376
51 thither fled all the **m** and women, and all H582
54 and slay me, that **m** say not of me, A
55 And when the **m** of Israel saw that H376
57 And all the evil of the **m** of Shechem did H582
11: 3 **m** to Jephthah, and went out with him. H582
12: 1 And the **m** of Ephraim gathered H376
4 together all the **m** of Gilead, and fought H582
4 Ephraim: and the **m** of Gilead smote H582
5 go over; that the **m** of Gilead said unto H582
14:10 a feast; for so used the young **m** to do. H970
18 And the **m** of the city said unto him on H582
19 and slew thirty **m** of them, and took H376
15:10 And the **m** of Judah said, Why are ye H376
11 Then three thousand **m** of Judah went to H376
15 it, and slew a thousand **m** therewith. H376
16 jaw of an ass have I slain a thousand **m**. H376
16: 9 Now *there were* **m** lying in wait, abiding
27 Now the house was full of **m** and H582
27 three thousand **m** and women, that H376
18: 2 family five **m** from their coasts, H582+H1121
2 their coasts, **m** of valour, from H582+H1121
7 Then the five **m** departed, and came to H582
11 **m** appointed with weapons of war. H376
14 Then answered the five **m** that went to H582
16 And the six hundred **m** appointed with H376
17 And the five **m** that went to spy out the H582
17 the six hundred **m** *that were* appointed H376
22 of Micah, the **m** that *were* in the houses H582
19:16 but the **m** of the place *were* Benjamites. H582
22 merry, behold, the **m** of the city, certain H582
25 But the **m** would not hearken to him: so H582
20: 5 And the **m** of Gibeah rose against me, H1167
10 And we will take ten **m** of an hundred H582
11 So all the **m** of Israel were gathered H376
12 And the tribes of Israel sent **m** through H582
13 Now therefore deliver *us* the **m**, the H582
15 and six thousand **m** that drew sword, H376
15 numbered seven hundred chosen **m**. H376
16 hundred chosen **m** lefthanded; every one H376
17 And the **m** of Israel, beside Benjamin, H376
17 hundred thousand **m** that drew sword: H376
17 drew sword: all these *were* **m** of war. H376
20 And the **m** of Israel went out to battle H376
20 Benjamin; and the **m** of Israel put H376
21 that day twenty and two thousand **m**. H376
22 And the people the **m** of Israel H376
25 thousand **m**; all these drew the sword. H376
31 in the field, about thirty **m** of Israel. H376
33 And all the **m** of Israel rose up out of H376
34 thousand chosen **m** out of all Israel, and H376
35 an hundred **m**: all these drew the sword. H376

Jdg 20:36 smitten: for the **m** of Israel gave place H376
38 sign between the **m** of Israel and the H376
39 And when the **m** of Israel retired in the H376
39 *and* kill of the **m** of Israel about thirty H376
41 And when the **m** of Israel turned again, H376
41 turned again, the **m** of Benjamin were H376
42 *backs* before the **m** of Israel unto the H376
44 **m**; all these *were* men of valour. H376
44 men; all these *were* **m** of valour. H582
45 five thousand **m**; and pursued hard after H376
45 and slew two thousand **m** of them. H376
46 and five thousand **m** that drew the H376
46 the sword; all these *were* **m** of valour. H582
47 But six hundred **m** turned and fled to the H376
48 And the **m** of Israel turned again upon H376
48 sword, as well the **m** of *every* city, as H4974
21: 1 Now the **m** of Israel had sworn in H376
10 twelve thousand **m** of the valiantest, and H376
Ru 2: 9 the young **m** that they shall not touch H5288
9 of *that* which the young **m** have drawn. H5288
15 his young **m**, saying, Let her glean H5288
21 **m**, until they have ended all my harvest. H5288
3:10 not young **m**, whether poor or rich. H970
4: 2 And he took ten **m** of the elders of the H582
1Sa 2: 4 The bows of the mighty **m** *are* broken,
17 Wherefore the sin of the young **m** was H5288
17 **m** abhorred the offering of the LORD. H582
26 both with the LORD, and also with **m**. H582
4: 2 army in the field about four thousand **m**. H376
9 Be strong, and quit yourselves like **m**, O H582
9 to you: quit yourselves like **m**, and fight. H582
5: 7 And when the **m** of Ashdod saw that *it* H582
9 and he smote the **m** of the city, both H582
12 And the **m** that died not were smitten H582
6:10 And the **m** did so; and took two milch H582
15 great stone: and the **m** of Beth-shemesh H582
19 And he smote the **m** of Beth-shemesh, H376
19 and threescore and ten **m**: and the people H582
20 And the **m** of Beth-shemesh said, Who is H582
7: 1 And the **m** of Kirjath-jearim came, and H582
11 And the **m** of Israel went out of Mizpeh, H582
8:16 goodliest young **m**, and your asses, and H970
22 said unto the **m** of Israel, Go ye every H582
10: 2 shalt find two **m** by Rachel's sepulchre H582
3 meet thee three **m** going up to God to H582
26 of **m**, whose hearts God had touched. H2428
11: 1 and all the **m** of Jabesh said unto H582
5 told him the tidings of the **m** of Jabesh. H582
8 and the **m** of Judah thirty thousand. H376
9 ye say unto the **m** of Jabesh-gilead, To H376
9 *it* to the **m** of Jabesh; and they were glad. H582
10 Therefore the **m** of Jabesh said, To H582
12 the **m**, that we may put them to death. H582
15 and all the **m** of Israel rejoiced greatly. H582
13: 2 Saul chose him three thousand *m* of
6 When the **m** of Israel saw that they were H376
15 present with him, about six hundred **m**. H376
14: 2 with him *were* about six hundred **m**; H376
8 over unto *these* **m**, and we will discover H582
12 And the **m** of the garrison answered H582
14 was about twenty **m**, within as it were an H376
22 Likewise all the **m** of Israel which had H376
24 And the **m** of Israel were distressed that H376
15: 4 footmen, and ten thousand **m** of Judah. H376
17: 2 And Saul and the **m** of Israel were H376
12 **m** *for* an old man in the days of Saul. H582
19 Now Saul, and they, and all the **m** of H376
24 And all the **m** of Israel, when they saw H376
25 And the **m** of Israel said, Have ye seen H376
26 And David spake to the **m** that stood by H582
28 he spake unto the **m**; and Eliab's anger H582
52 And the **m** of Israel and of Judah arose, H582
18: 5 set him over the **m** of war, and he was H582
27 and went, he and his **m**, and slew of the H582
27 two hundred **m**; and David brought H376
21: 4 if the young **m** have kept themselves H5288
5 of the young **m** are holy, and *the bread* H5288
15 Have I need of mad **m**, that ye have
22: 2 were with him about four hundred **m**. H376
6 and the **m** that *were* with him, H582
19 edge of the sword, both **m** and women, H376
23: 3 And David's **m** said unto him, Behold, H582
5 So David and his **m** went to Keilah, and H582
8 to Keilah, to besiege David and his **m**. H582
11 Will the **m** of Keilah deliver me up into H1167
12 Then said David, Will the **m** of Keilah H1167
12 deliver me and my **m** into the hand of H582
13 Then David and his **m**, *which were* about H582
24 Saul: but David and his **m** *were* in the H582

1Sa 23:25 Saul also and his **m** went to seek *him*. H582
26 and David and his **m** on that side of the H582
26 for Saul and his **m** compassed David H582
26 and his **m** round about to take them. H582
24: 2 thousand chosen **m** out of all Israel, and H376
2 his **m** upon the rocks of the wild goats. H582
3 his **m** remained in the sides of the cave. H582
4 And the **m** of David said unto him, H582
6 And he said unto his **m**, The LORD H582
22 and his **m** gat them up unto the hold. H582
25: 5 And David sent out ten young **m**, and H5288
5 said unto the young **m**, Get you up to H5288
8 Ask thy young **m**, and they will shew H5288
8 let the young **m** find favour in thine H5288
9 And when David's young **m** came, they H5288
11 **m**, whom I know not whence they *be*? H582
12 So David's young **m** turned their way, H5288
13 And David said unto his **m**, Gird ye on H582
13 **m**; and two hundred abode by the stuff. H376
14 But one of the young **m** told Abigail, H5288
15 But the **m** *were* very good unto us, and H582
20 David and his **m** came down against H582
25 **m** of my lord, whom thou didst send. H5288
27 unto the young **m** that follow my lord. H5288
26: 2 thousand chosen **m** of Israel with him, H376
19 *they be* the children of **m**, cursed *be* they H120
22 of the young **m** come over and fetch it. H5288
27: 2 the six hundred **m** that *were* with him H376
3 at Gath, he and his **m**, every man with H582
8 And David and his **m** went up, and H582
28: 1 go out with me to battle, thou and thy **m**. H582
8 he went, and two **m** with him, and they H582
29: 2 but David and his **m** passed on in the H582
4 *it* not *be* with the heads of these **m**? H582
11 So David and his **m** rose up early to H582
30: 1 David and his **m** were come to Ziklag H582
3 So David and his **m** came to the city, H582
9 the six hundred **m** that *were* with him, H376
10 he and four hundred **m**: for two hundred H376
17 **m**, which rode upon camels, and fled. H376
21 And David came to the two hundred **m**, H582
22 Then answered all the wicked **m** and H376
22 the wicked men and *m* of Belial, of those
31 himself and his **m** were wont to haunt. H582
31: 1 Israel: and the **m** of Israel fled from H582
6 and all his **m**, that same day together. H582
7 And when the **m** of Israel that *were* on H582
7 saw that the **m** of Israel fled, and that H582
12 All the valiant **m** arose, and went all H376
2Sa 1:11 likewise all the **m** that *were* with him: H582
15 And David called one of the young **m**, H5288
2: 3 And his **m** that *were* with him did David H582
4 And the **m** of Judah came, and there H582
4 saying, *That* the **m** of Jabesh-gilead *were* H582
5 And David sent messengers unto the **m** H582
14 Let the young **m** now arise, and play H5288
17 **m** of Israel, before the servants of David. H582
21 one of the young **m**, and take thee his H5288
29 And Abner and his **m** walked all that H582
30 David's servants nineteen **m** and Asahel. H376
31 and of Abner's **m**, *so that* three hundred H582
31 three hundred and threescore **m** died. H376
32 And Joab and his **m** went all night, and H582
3:20 and twenty **m** with him. And David H582
20 and the **m** that *were* with him a feast. H582
34 before wicked **m**, *so* fellest thou. And H1121
39 king; and these **m** the sons of Zeruiah H582
4: 2 And Saul's son had two **m** *that were* H582
11 How much more, when wicked **m** have H582
12 And David commanded his young **m**, H5288
5: 6 And the king and his **m** went to H582
21 and David and his **m** burned them. H582
6: 1 *the* chosen *m* of Israel, thirty thousand.
19 to the women as **m**, to every one a cake H376
7: 9 of the great *m* that *are* in the earth.
14 with the rod of **m**, and with the stripes H582
14 and with the stripes of the children of **m**: H120
8: 5 the Syrians two and twenty thousand **m**. H376
13 valley of salt, *being* eighteen thousand *m*.
10: 5 meet them, because the **m** were greatly H582
6 **m**, and of Ish-tob twelve thousand men. H376
6 men, and of Ish-tob twelve thousand **m**. H376
7 Joab, and all the host of the mighty **m**. H1368
9 of all the choice *m* of Israel, and put
12 let us play the **m** for our people, and H2388
18 and David slew *the m of* seven hundred
11:16 where he knew that valiant **m** *were*. H582
17 And the **m** of the city went out, and H582
23 David, Surely the **m** prevailed against H582

2Sa 12: 1 There were two **m** in one city; the one H582
13: 9 said, Have out all **m** from me. And they H376
32 all the young **m** the king's sons; for H5288
15: 1 horses, and fifty **m** to run before him. H376
6 stole the hearts of the **m** of Israel. H582
11 And with Absalom went two hundred **m** H376
13 of the **m** of Israel are after Absalom. H376
18 six hundred **m** which came after him H376
22 over, and all his **m**, and all the little ones H582
16: 2 for the young **m** to eat; and the wine, H5288
6 all the mighty **m** *were* on his right hand H1368
13 And as David and his **m** went by the H582
15 And Absalom, and all the people the **m** H376
18 people, and all the **m** of Israel, choose, H376
17: 1 twelve thousand **m**, and I will arise and H376
8 thy father and his **m**, that they *be* mighty H582
8 they *be* mighty **m**, and they *be* chafed H1368
10 *they* which *be* with him *are* valiant **m**. H1121
12 of him and of all the **m** that *are* with him H582
14 And Absalom and all the **m** of Israel H376
24 he and all the **m** of Israel with him. H376
18: 7 slaughter that day of twenty thousand ***m***.
15 And ten young **m** that bare Joab's H5288
28 delivered up the **m** that lifted up their H582
19:14 And he bowed the heart of all the **m** of H376
16 with the **m** of Judah to meet king David. H376
17 And *there were* a thousand **m** of H376
28 were but dead **m** before my lord the H582
35 voice of singing **m** and singing women? H7891
41 And, behold, all the **m** of Israel came to H376
41 our brethren the **m** of Judah stolen thee H376
41 all David's **m** with him, over Jordan? H582
42 And all the **m** of Judah answered the H376
42 answered the **m** of Israel, Because the H376
43 And the **m** of Israel answered the men of H376
43 And the men of Israel answered the **m** of H376
43 the words of the **m** of Judah were fiercer H376
43 fiercer than the words of the **m** of Israel. H376
20: 2 of Bichri: but the **m** of Judah clave unto H376
4 Assemble me the **m** of Judah within H376
5 So Amasa went to assemble *the* ***m*** *of*
7 And there went out after him Joab's **m**, H582
7 all the mighty **m**: and they went out of H1368
11 And one of Joab's **m** stood by him, and H5288
21: 6 Let seven **m** of his sons be delivered H582
12 his son from the **m** of Jabesh-gilead, H1167
17 him. Then the **m** of David sware unto H582
22: 5 floods of ungodly **m** made me afraid; H1100
23: 3 **m** *must be* just, ruling in the fear of God. H120
8 These *be* the names of the mighty **m** H1368
9 the three mighty **m** with David, when H1368
9 and the **m** of Israel were gone away: H376
16 And the three mighty **m** brake through H1368
17 the blood of the **m** that went in jeopardy H582
17 These things did these three mighty **m**. H1368
20 he slew two lionlike **m** of Moab: he went H739
22 had the name among three mighty **m**. H1368
24: 9 thousand valiant **m** that drew the sword; H376
9 the sword; and the **m** of Judah *were* five H376
9 of Judah *were* five hundred thousand **m**. H376
15 even to Beer-sheba seventy thousand **m**. H376
1Ki 1: 5 and fifty **m** to run before him. H376
8 and the mighty **m** which *belonged* to H1368
9 all the **m** of Judah the king's servants: H582
10 and the mighty **m**, and Solomon his H1368
2:32 who fell upon two **m** more righteous and H582
4:31 For he was wiser than all **m**; than Ethan H120
5:13 and the levy was thirty thousand **m**. H376
8: 2 And all the **m** of Israel assembled H376
39 the hearts of all the children of **m**;) H120
9:22 but they *were* **m** of war, and his H582
10: 8 Happy *are* thy **m**, happy *are* these thy H582
11:18 and they took **m** with them out of Paran, H582
24 And he gathered **m** unto him, and H582
12: 6 with the old **m**, that stood before H2205
8 But he forsook the counsel of the old **m**, H2205
8 with the young **m** that were grown up H3206
10 And the young **m** that were grown up H3206
14 of the young **m**, saying, My father made H3206
21 thousand chosen **m**, which were H977
13:25 And, behold, **m** passed by, and saw the H582
18:13 how I hid an hundred **m** of the LORD'S H376
22 prophets *are* four hundred and fifty **m**. H376
20:14 by the young **m** of the princes of the H5288
15 Then he numbered the young **m** of the H5288
17 And the young **m** of the princes of the H5288
17 There are **m** come out of Samaria. H582
19 So these young **m** of the princes of the H5288
30 thousand of the **m** *that were* left. And H376
1Ki 20:33 Now the **m** did diligently observe H582
21:10 And set two **m**, sons of Belial, before him, H582
11 And the **m** of his city, *even* the elders H582
13 And there came in two **m**, children of H582
13 him: and the **m** of Belial witnessed H582
22: 6 four hundred **m**, and said unto them, H376
2Ki 2: 7 And fifty **m** of the sons of the prophets H376
16 fifty strong **m**; let them go, we H1121+H582
17 sent therefore fifty **m**; and they sought H376
19 And the **m** of the city said unto Elisha, H582
3:26 seven hundred **m** that drew swords, to H376
4:22 thee, one of the young **m**, and one of the H5288
40 So they poured out for the **m** to eat. And H582
43 this before an hundred **m**? He said again, H376
5:22 two young **m** of the sons of the H5288
24 and he let the **m** go, and they departed. H582
6:20 the eyes of these ***m***, that they may see.
7: 3 And there were four leprous **m** at the H582
8:12 and their young **m** wilt thou slay with H970
10: 6 take ye the heads of the **m** your master's H582
6 **m** of the city, which brought them up. H1419
11 and all his great **m**, and his kinsfolks, H1419
14 and forty **m**; neither left he any of them. H376
24 fourscore **m** without, and said, *If* H376
24 and said, *If* any of the **m** whom I have H582
11: 9 every man his **m** that were to come in H582
12:15 Moreover they reckoned not with the **m**, H582
13:21 spied a band *of* ***m***; and they cast the man
15:20 of all the mighty **m** of wealth, of each H1368
25 and with him fifty **m** of the Gileadites: H376
17:24 And the king of Assyria brought ***m*** from
30 And the **m** of Babylon made H582
30 and the **m** of Cuth made Nergal, H582
30 and the **m** of Hamath made Ashima, H582
18:27 *he* not *sent me* to the **m** which sit on the H582
20:14 What said these **m**? and from whence H582
23: 2 LORD, and all the **m** of Judah and all the H376
14 filled their places with the bones of **m**. H120
17 that that I see? And the **m** of the city told H582
24:14 all the mighty **m** of valour, *even* ten H1368
16 And all the **m** of might, *even* seven H582
25: 4 up, and all the **m** of war *fled* by night H582
19 was set over the **m** of war, and five men H582
19 of war, and five **m** of them that were in H582
19 and threescore **m** of the people of the H376
23 they and their **m**, heard that the king H582
23 son of a Maachathite, they and their **m**. H582
24 to them, and to their **m**, and said unto H582
25 came, and ten **m** with him, and smote H582
1Ch 4:12 of Irnahash. These *are* the **m** of Rechah. H582
22 And Jokim, and the **m** of Chozeba, and H582
42 five hundred **m**, went to mount Seir, H582
5:18 of valiant **m**, men able to bear buckler H1121
18 of valiant men, **m** able to bear buckler H582
21 and of **m** an hundred thousand. H120+H5315
24 and Jahdiel, mighty **m** of valour, famous H582
24 of valour, famous **m**, *and* heads of the H582
7: 2 *they were* valiant **m** of might in their H1368
3 and Joel, Ishiah, five: all of them chief **m**.
4 ***m***: for they had many wives and sons.
5 *were* valiant **m** of might, reckoned in
7 fathers, mighty **m** of valour; and were
9 their fathers, mighty **m** of valour, *was* H1368
11 their fathers, mighty **m** of valour, *were*
21 Elead, whom the **m** of Gath *that were* H582
40 *and* mighty **m** of valour, chief of the H1368
40 to battle *was* twenty and six thousand **m**. H582
8:28 chief ***m***. These dwelt in Jerusalem.
40 And the sons of Ulam were mighty **m** of H582
9: 9 and six. All these **m** *were* chief of the H582
13 very able **m** for the work of the H1368
10: 1 Israel; and the **m** of Israel fled from H376
7 And when all the **m** of Israel that *were* in H376
12 They arose, all the valiant **m**, and took H376
11:10 of the mighty **m** whom David had, who H1368
11 And this *is* the number of the mighty **m** H1368
19 the blood of these **m** that have put their H582
22 he slew two lionlike **m** of Moab: also he H739
26 Also the valiant **m** of the armies *were*, H1368
12: 1 the mighty **m**, helpers of the war. H1368
8 to the wilderness **m** of might, *and* men H1368
8 men of might, *and* **m** of war *fit* for the H582
21 *were* all mighty **m** of valour, and were H1368
25 Of the children of Simeon, mighty **m** of H1368
30 hundred, mighty **m** of valour, famous H1368
32 *which were* **m** that had understanding
38 All these **m** of war, that could keep rank, H582
16:31 earth rejoice: and let ***m*** say among the
17: 8 of the great **m** that *are* in the earth. H1419
1Ch 18: 5 the Syrians two and twenty thousand **m**. H376
19: 5 David how the **m** were served. And he H582
5 to meet them: for the **m** were greatly H582
8 Joab, and all the host of the mighty **m**. H1368
18 seven thousand ***m which fought in***
21: 5 hundred thousand **m** that drew sword: H376
5 and ten thousand **m** that drew sword. H376
14 there fell of Israel seventy thousand **m**. H376
22:15 cunning **m** for every manner of work. H2450
24: 4 And there were more chief **m** found of H1397
4 *were* sixteen chief **m** of the house of *their*
26: 6 for they *were* mighty **m** of valour. H1368
7 *were* strong **m**, Elihu, and Semachiah. H1121
8 brethren, able **m** for strength for the H376
9 sons and brethren, strong **m**, eighteen. H1121
12 among the chief **m**, *having* wards one H1397
30 and his brethren, **m** of valour, a H1121
31 mighty **m** of valour at Jazer of Gilead. H1368
32 And his brethren, **m** of valour, *were* H1121
28: 1 and with the mighty **m**, and with all the H1368
1 with all the valiant **m**, unto Jerusalem. H1368
29:24 And all the princes, and the mighty **m**, H1368
2Ch 2: 2 and ten thousand **m** to bear burdens, H376
7 with the cunning **m** that *are* with me in H2450
14 him, with thy cunning **m**, and with the H2450
14 cunning **m** of my lord David thy father. H2450
5: 3 Wherefore all the **m** of Israel assembled H376
6:18 But will God in very deed dwell with **m** H120
30 knowest the hearts of the children of **m**:) H120
8: 9 but they *were* **m** of war, and chief of
9: 7 Happy *are* thy **m**, and happy *are* these
10: 6 with the old **m** that had stood before H2205
8 which the old **m** gave him, and took H2205
8 with the young **m** that were brought up H3206
10 And the young **m** that were brought up H3206
13 forsook the counsel of the old **m**, H2205
14 of the young **m**, saying, My father made H3206
11: 1 thousand chosen ***m***, which were
13: 3 an army of valiant **m** of war, *even* four H1368
3 thousand chosen **m**: Jeroboam also set H376
3 chosen **m**, *being* mighty men of valour. H376
3 chosen men, *being* mighty **m** of valour. H1368
7 And there are gathered unto him vain **m**,
15 Then the **m** of Judah gave a shout: and H376
15 a shout: and as the **m** of Judah shouted, H376
17 Israel five hundred thousand chosen **m**. H376
14: 8 And Asa had an army *of* ***m*** that bare
8 all these *were* mighty **m** of valour. H1368
17:13 of Judah: and the **m** of war, mighty men
13 mighty **m** of valour, *were* in Jerusalem. H1368
14 **m** of valour three hundred thousand. H1368
16 hundred thousand mighty **m** of valour. H1368
17 with him armed **m** with bow and shield
18: 5 four hundred **m**, and said unto them, H376
22: 1 for the band of **m** that came with the H1416
23: 8 every man his **m** that were to come in
24:24 a small company of **m**, and the LORD
25: 5 thousand choice ***m***, *able* to go forth to
6 thousand mighty **m** of valour out of H1368
26:11 host of fighting **m**, that went out to war H6213
12 of the mighty **m** of valour *were* two H1368
15 by cunning **m**, to be on the towers H2803
17 of the LORD, *that were* valiant **m**: H1121
28: 6 *were* all valiant **m**; because they had H1121
14 So the armed **m** left the captives and the
15 And the **m** which were expressed by
31:19 several city, the **m** that were expressed
32: 3 and his mighty **m** to stop the waters of H1368
21 off all the mighty **m** of valour, and the H1368
34:12 And the **m** did the work faithfully: and
30 LORD, and all the **m** of Judah, and the H376
35:25 and all the singing **m** and the singing
36:17 slew their young **m** with the sword in the H970
Ezr 1: 4 he sojourneth, let the **m** of his place help H582
2: 2 number of the **m** of the people of Israel: H582
22 The **m** of Netophah, fifty and six. H582
23 The **m** of Anathoth, an hundred twenty H582
27 The **m** of Michmas, an hundred twenty H582
28 The **m** of Beth-el and Ai, two hundred H582
65 hundred singing **m** and singing women.
3:12 *who were* ancient **m**, that had seen the H2205
4:11 Thy servants the **m** on this side the river, H606
21 to cause these **m** to cease, and that this H1400
5: 4 of the **m** that make this building? H1400
10 of the **m** that *were* the chief of them. H1400
6: 8 unto these **m**, that they be not hindered. H1400
7:28 out of Israel chief **m** to go up with me.
8:16 Meshullam, chief **m**; also for Joiarib, and
16 and for Elnathan, **m** of understanding.

Ezr 10: 1 great congregation of **m** and women and H582
9 Then all the **m** of Judah and Benjamin H582
17 And they made an end with all the **m** H582
Neh 1: 2 he and *certain* **m** of Judah; and I asked H582
2:12 I and some few **m** with me; neither told H582
3: 2 And next unto him builded the **m** of H582
7 the Meronothite, the **m** of Gibeon, and of H582
22 repaired the priests, the **m** of the plain. H582
4:23 servants, nor the **m** of the guard which H582
5: 5 other **m** have our lands and vineyards. H312
7: 7 of the **m** of the people of Israel *was this*; H582
26 The **m** of Beth-lehem and Netophah, an H582
27 The **m** of Anathoth, an hundred twenty H582
28 The **m** of Beth-azmaveth, forty and two. H582
29 The **m** of Kirjath-jearim, Chephirah, and H582
30 The **m** of Ramah and Geba, six hundred H582
31 The **m** of Michmas, an hundred and H582
32 The **m** of Beth-el and Ai, an hundred H582
33 The **m** of the other Nebo, fifty and two. H582
67 and five singing **m** and singing women.
8: 2 both of **m** and women, and all H376
3 before the **m** and the women, and H582
11: 2 And the people blessed all the **m**, that H582
6 hundred threescore and eight valiant **m**. H582
14 And their brethren, mighty **m** of H1368
14 Zabdiel, the son of *one of* the great **m**. H1419
13:16 There dwelt **m** of Tyre also therein,
Est 1:13 Then the king said to the wise **m**, which H2450
6:13 said his wise **m** and Zeresh his wife H2450
9: 6 Jews slew and destroyed five hundred **m**. H376
12 five hundred **m** in Shushan the palace, H376
15 three hundred **m** at Shushan; but on the H376
Job 1: 3 was the greatest of all the **m** of the east. H1121
19 upon the young **m**, and they are dead; H5288
4:13 the night, when deep sleep falleth on **m**, H582
7:20 O thou preserver of **m**? why hast thou set H120
11: 3 Should thy lies make **m** hold their H4962
11 For he knoweth vain **m**: he seeth H4962
15:10 very aged **m**, much elder than thy father.
18 Which wise **m** have told from their
17: 8 Upright *m* shall be astonied at this, and
22:15 old way which wicked **m** have trodden? H4962
29 When *m* are cast down, then thou shalt
24:12 **M** groan from out of the city, and the H4962
27:23 *M* shall clap their hands at him, and
28: 4 are dried up, they are gone away from **m**. H582
29: 8 The young **m** saw me, and hid H5288
21 Unto me *m* gave ear, and waited, and
30: 5 They were driven forth from among *m*,
8 base **m**: they were viler than the earth. H8034
31:31 If the **m** of my tabernacle said not, Oh H4962
32: 1 So these three **m** ceased to answer Job, H582
5 three **m**, then his wrath was kindled. H582
9 Great **m** are not *always* wise: neither do
33:15 upon **m**, in slumberings upon the bed; H582
16 Then he openeth the ears of **m**, and H582
27 He looketh upon **m**, and *if any* say, I H582
34: 2 Hear my words, O ye wise *m*; and give
8 of iniquity, and walketh with wicked **m**. H582
10 Therefore hearken unto me, ye **m** of H582
24 He shall break in pieces mighty **m**
26 He striketh them as wicked **m** in the
34 Let **m** of understanding tell me, and let a H582
36 end because of *his* answers for wicked **m**. H582
35:12 answer, because of the pride of evil **m**.
36:24 thou magnify his work, which **m** behold. H582
37: 7 man; that all **m** may know his work. H582
21 And now *m* see not the bright light
24 **M** do therefore fear him: he respecteth H582
39:21 he goeth on to meet the armed **m**. H5402
Ps 4: 2 O ye sons of **m**, how long *will ye turn* my H376
9:20 may know themselves *to be but* **m**. Selah. H582
11: 4 behold, his eyelids try, the children of **m**. H120
12: 1 fail from among the children of **m**. H120
8 when the vilest **m** are exalted. H1121+H120
14: 2 the children of **m**, to see if there were any H120
17: 4 Concerning the works of **m**, by the word H120
14 From **m** *which are* thy hand, O LORD, H4962
14 O LORD, from **m** of the world, *which* H4962
18: 4 floods of ungodly **m** made me afraid. H1100
21:10 their seed from among the children of **m**. H120
22: 6 of **m**, and despised of the people. H120
26: 9 with sinners, nor my life with bloody **m**: H582
31:19 that trust in thee before the sons of **m**! H120
33:13 heaven; he beholdeth all the sons of **m**. H120
36: 7 the children of **m** put their trust under H120
45: 2 Thou art fairer than the children of **m**: H120
49:10 For he seeth *that* wise **m** die, likewise H2450
18 his soul: and *m* will praise thee, when

Ps 53: 2 the children of **m**, to see if there were *any* H120
55:23 and deceitful **m** shall not live out half H582
57: 4 fire, *even* the sons of **m**, whose teeth *are* H120
58: 1 do ye judge uprightly, O ye sons of **m**? H120
59: 2 of iniquity, and save me from bloody **m**. H582
62: 9 Surely **m** of low degree *are* H1121+H120
9 vanity, *and* **m** of high degree *are* H1121+H120
64: 9 And all **m** shall fear, and shall declare H120
66: 5 *in his* doing toward the children of **m**. H120
12 Thou hast caused **m** to ride over our H582
68:18 hast received gifts for **m**; yea, *for* the H120
72:17 as the sun: and *m* shall be blessed in
73: 5 They *are* not in trouble *as other* **m**; H582
5 neither are they plagued like *other* **m**. H120
76: 5 the **m** of might have found their hands. H582
78:31 and smote down the chosen *m* of Israel.
60 the tent *which* he placed among **m**; H120
63 The fire consumed their young **m**; and H970
82: 7 But ye shall die like **m**, and fall like one H120
83:18 That *m* may know that thou, whose
86:14 of violent *m* have sought after my
89:47 hast thou made all **m** in vain? H1121+H120
90: 3 and sayest, Return, ye children of **m**. H120
105:12 When they were *but* a few **m** in H4962
107: 8 Oh that *m* would praise the LORD *for* his
8 his wonderful works to the children of **m**! H120
15 Oh that *m* would praise the LORD *for* his
15 his wonderful works to the children of **m**! H120
21 Oh that *m* would praise the LORD *for* his
21 his wonderful works to the children of **m**! H120
31 Oh that *m* would praise the LORD *for* his
31 his wonderful works to the children of **m**! H120
115:16 earth hath he given to the children of **m**. H120
116:11 I said in my haste, All **m** *are* liars. H120
124: 2 on our side, when **m** rose up against us: H120
139:19 depart from me therefore, ye bloody **m**. H582
141: 4 wicked works with **m** that work iniquity: H376
145: 6 And *m* shall speak of the might of thy
12 To make known to the sons of **m** his H120
148:12 Both young **m**, and maidens; old men, H970
12 Both young men, and maidens; old **m**, H2205
Prv 2:20 *m*, and keep the paths of the righteous.
4:14 wicked, and go not in the way of evil *m*.
6:30 *M* do not despise a thief, if he steal to
7:26 many strong *m* have been slain by her.
8: 4 Unto you, O **m**, I call; and my voice *is* to H376
31 and my delights *were* with the sons of **m**. H120
10:14 Wise *m* lay up knowledge: but the
11: 7 and the hope of unjust *m* perisheth.
16 honour: and strong *m* retain riches.
12:12 The wicked desireth the net of evil *m*: but
13:20 He that walketh with wise *m* shall be
15:11 then the hearts of the children of **m**? H120
16: 6 the fear of the LORD *m* depart from evil.
17: 6 *are* the crown of old **m**; and the glory of H2205
18:16 him, and bringeth him before great **m**. H1419
20: 6 Most **m** will proclaim every one his own H120
29 The glory of young **m** *is* their strength: H970
29 the beauty of old **m** *is* the gray head. H2205
22:29 kings; he shall not stand before mean *m*.
23:28 increaseth the transgressors among **m**. H120
24: 1 Be not thou envious against evil **m**, H582
9 and the scorner *is* an abomination to **m**. H120
19 Fret not thyself because of evil *m*, neither
25: 1 **m** of Hezekiah king of Judah copied out. H582
6 and stand not in the place of great *m*:
27 *m* to search their own glory *is not* glory.
26:16 than seven **m** that can render a reason.
28: 5 Evil **m** understand not judgment: but H582
7 of riotous *m* shameth his father.
12 When righteous *m* do rejoice, *there is*
28 When the wicked rise, **m** hide H120
29: 8 Scornful **m** bring a city into a snare: but H582
8 a snare: but wise *m* turn away wrath.
30:14 the earth, and the needy from *among* **m**. H120
Ecc 2: 3 for the sons of **m**, which they should do H120
8 I gat me **m** singers and women
8 of the sons of **m**, *as* musical instruments, H120
3:10 to the sons of **m** to be exercised in it. H120
14 doeth *it*, that *m* should fear before him.
18 estate of the sons of **m**, that God might H120
19 For that which befalleth the sons of **m** H120
6: 1 the sun, and it *is* common among **m**: H120
7: 2 **m**; and the living will lay *it* to his heart. H120
19 than ten mighty *m* which are in the city.
8:11 sons of **m** is fully set in them to do evil. H120
14 earth; that there be just *m*, unto whom it
14 there be wicked *m*, to whom it happeneth
9: 3 heart of the sons of **m** is full of evil, and H120

Ecc 9:11 nor yet riches to **m** of understanding,
11 nor yet favour to **m** of skill; but time and
12 so *are* the sons of **m** snared in an evil H120
14 *There was* a little city, and few **m** within H582
17 The words of wise *m* *are* heard in quiet
12: 3 and the strong **m** shall bow themselves, H582
Song 3: 7 **m** *are* about it, of the valiant of Israel. H1368
4: 4 bucklers, all shields of mighty **m**. H1368
Isa 2:11 and the haughtiness of **m** shall be bowed H582
17 the haughtiness of **m** shall be made low: H582
3:25 Thy **m** shall fall by the sword, and thy H4962
5: 3 of Jerusalem, and **m** of Judah, judge, I H376
7 house of Israel, and the **m** of Judah his H376
13 their honourable **m** *are* famished, and H4962
22 **m** of strength to mingle strong drink: H582
6:12 And the LORD have removed **m** far H120
7:13 weary **m**, but will ye weary my God also? H582
24 With arrows and with bows shall *m*
9: 3 as *m* rejoice when they divide the spoil.
17 joy in their young **m**, neither shall have H970
11:15 streams, and make *m* go over dryshod.
13:18 *Their* bows also shall dash the young **m** H5288
19:12 Where *are* they? where *are* thy wise *m*?
21: 9 And, behold, here cometh a chariot of **m**, H376
17 the mighty **m** of the children of Kedar, H1368
22: 2 city: thy slain *m* *are* not slain with the
6 with chariots of **m** *and* horsemen, and H120
23: 4 up young **m**, *nor* bring up virgins. H970
24: 6 of the earth are burned, and few **m** left. H582
26:19 Thy dead **m** shall live, *together with* my
28:14 the LORD, ye scornful **m**, that rule this H582
29:11 is sealed, which *m* deliver to one that is
13 toward me is taught by the precept of **m**: H582
14 of their wise *m* shall perish, and the
14 of their prudent *m* shall be hid.
19 **m** shall rejoice in the Holy One of Israel. H120
31: 3 Now the Egyptians *are* **m**, and not God; H120
8 and his young **m** shall be discomfited. H970
35: 8 **m**, though fools, shall not err *therein*.
36:12 *he* not *sent me* to the **m** that sit upon the H582
38:16 O Lord, by these *things* *m* live, and in all
39: 3 What said these **m**? and from whence H582
40:30 and the young **m** shall utterly fall: H970
41: 9 thee from the chief **m** thereof, and said H678
14 Fear not, thou worm Jacob, *and* ye **m** H4962
43: 4 I give **m** for thee, and people for thy life. H120
44:11 they *are* of **m**: let them all be gathered H120
25 that turneth wise **m** backward, and
45:14 of the Sabeans, **m** of stature, shall come H582
24 *even* to him shall *m* come; and all that
46: 8 Remember this, and shew yourselves **m**: H377
51: 7 **m**, neither be ye afraid of their revilings. H582
52:14 and his form more than the sons of **m**: H120
53: 3 He is despised and rejected of **m**; a man H376
57: 1 and merciful **m** *are* taken away, none H582
59:10 *we are* in desolate places as dead *m*.
60:11 day nor night; that *m* may bring unto
61: 6 Priests of the LORD: *m* shall call you the
64: 4 For since the beginning of the world *m*
66:24 upon the carcases of the **m** that have H582
Jer 4: 3 For thus saith the LORD to the **m** of H376
4 of your heart, ye **m** of Judah and H376
5: 5 I will get me unto the great **m**, and will
16 open sepulchre, they *are* all mighty **m**. H1368
26 are found wicked *m*: they lay wait, as he
26 snares; they set a trap, they catch **m**. H582
6:11 assembly of young **m** together: for even H970
23 set in array as **m** for war against thee, H376
30 Reprobate silver shall *m* call them,
8: 9 The wise *m* are ashamed, they are
9: 2 place of wayfaring **m**; that I might leave H732
2 an assembly of treacherous **m**. H898
10 *them*; neither can *m* hear the voice of
21 *and* the young **m** from the streets. H970
22 the carcases of **m** shall fall as dung upon H120
10: 7 among all the wise *m* of the nations, and
9 they *are* all the work of cunning *m*.
11: 2 speak unto the **m** of Judah, and to the H376
9 is found among the **m** of Judah, and H376
21 Therefore thus saith the LORD of the **m** H582
22 them: the young **m** shall die by the H970
23 bring evil upon the **m** of Anathoth, *even* H582
15: 8 of the young **m** a spoiler at noonday: H970
10 lent on usury, nor **m** have lent to me on
16: 6 neither shall *m* lament for them, nor
7 Neither shall *m* tear *themselves* for them
7 dead; neither shall *m* give them the cup
17:25 their princes, the **m** of Judah, and the H376
18:11 Now therefore go to, speak to the **m** of H376

Jer 18:21 and let their **m** be put to death; *let* their H582
21 young **m** *be* slain by the sword in battle. H970
19:10 in the sight of the **m** that go with thee, H582
26:21 all his mighty **m**, and all the princes, H1368
22 And Jehoiakim the king sent **m** into H582
22 and *certain* **m** with him into Egypt. H582
31:13 dance, both young **m** and old together: H970
32:19 ways of the sons of **m**: to give every one H120
20 and among *other* **m**; and hast made thee H120
32 prophets, and the **m** of Judah, and the H376
44 **M** shall buy fields for money, and
33: 5 the dead bodies of **m**, whom I have slain H120
34:18 And I will give the **m** that have H582
35:13 Go and tell the **m** of Judah and the H376
36:31 and upon the **m** of Judah, all the evil H376
37:10 *but* wounded **m** among them, *yet* should H582
38: 4 the hands of the **m** of war that remain in H582
9 My lord the king, these **m** have done evil H582
10 from hence thirty **m** with thee, and take H582
11 So Ebed-melech took the **m** with him, H582
16 the hand of these **m** that seek thy life. H582
39: 4 them, and all the **m** of war, then they H582
17 hand of the **m** of whom thou *art* afraid. H582
40: 7 they and their **m**, heard that the king H582
7 unto him **m**, and women, and children, H582
8 son of a Maachathite, they and their **m**. H582
9 them and to their **m**, saying, Fear not to H582
41: 1 of the king, even ten **m** with him, came H582
2 and the ten **m** that were with him, H582
3 that were found there, *and* the **m** of war. H582
5 *even* fourscore **m**, having their beards H376
7 pit, he, and the **m** that *were* with him. H582
8 But ten **m** were found among them that H582
9 dead bodies of the **m**, whom he had slain H582
12 Then they took all the **m**, and went to H582
15 eight **m**, and went to the Ammonites. H582
16 *even* mighty **m** of war, and the women, H582
42:17 So shall it be with all the **m** that set their H582
43: 2 Kareah, and all the proud **m**, saying unto H582
6 *Even* **m**, and women, and children, and H1397
9 in the sight of the **m** of Judah; H582
44:15 Then all the **m** which knew that their H582
19 drink offerings unto her, without our **m**? H582
20 the people, to the **m**, and to the women, H1397
27 good: and all the **m** of Judah that *are* in H376
46: 9 and let the mighty **m** come forth; the H1368
15 Why are thy valiant *m* swept away? they
21 Also her hired **m** *are* in the midst of her
47: 2 therein: then the **m** shall cry, and all the H120
48:14 *are* mighty and strong **m** for the war? H582
15 his chosen young **m** are gone down to H970
31 *heart* shall mourn for the **m** of Kir-heres. H582
36 like pipes for the **m** of Kir-heres: because H582
49:15 the heathen, *and* despised among **m**. H120
22 of the mighty **m** of Edom be as the H1368
26 Therefore her young **m** shall fall in her H970
26 streets, and all the **m** of war shall be cut H582
28 to Kedar, and spoil the **m** of the east. H1121
50:30 Therefore shall her young **m** fall in the H970
30 streets, and all her **m** of war shall be cut H582
35 upon her princes, and upon her wise *m*.
36 mighty **m**; and they shall be dismayed. H1368
51: 3 young **m**; destroy ye utterly all her host. H970
14 I will fill thee with **m**, as with caterpillers; H120
30 The mighty **m** of Babylon have forborn H1368
32 fire, and the **m** of war are affrighted. H582
56 and her mighty **m** are taken, every one H1368
57 and her wise *m*, her captains, and her
57 and her mighty **m**: and they shall sleep H1368
52: 7 up, and all the **m** of war fled, and went H582
13 of the great *m*, burned he with fire:
25 the charge of the **m** of war; and seven H582
25 of war; and seven **m** of them that were H582
25 and threescore **m** of the people of the H376
Lam 1:15 foot all my mighty *m* in the midst of me:
15 me to crush my young **m**: the Lord hath H970
18 and my young **m** are gone into captivity. H970
2:15 *Is* this the city that *m* call The perfection
21 and my young **m** are fallen by the sword; H970
3:33 willingly nor grieve the children of **m**. H376
4:14 They have wandered *as* blind *m* in the
14 that **m** could not touch their garments.
5:13 They took the young **m** to grind, and the H970
14 the gate, the young **m** from their musick. H970
Ezk 6: 4 down your slain *m* before your idols.
13 when their slain *m* shall be among their
8:11 And there stood before them seventy **m** H376
16 five and twenty **m**, with their backs H376
9: 2 And, behold, six **m** came from the way H582

Ezk 9: 4 foreheads of the **m** that sigh and that cry H582
6 ancient **m** which *were* before the house. H582
11: 1 five and twenty **m**; among whom I saw H376
2 of man, these *are* the **m** that devise H582
15 thy brethren, the **m** of thy kindred, and H582
12:16 But I will leave a few **m** of them from the H582
14: 3 Son of man, these **m** have set up their H582
14 Though these three **m**, Noah, Daniel, and H582
16 *Though* these three **m** *were* in it, *as* I H582
18 Though these three **m** *were* in it, *as* I H582
15: 3 do any work? or will *m* take a pin of it to
16:17 thyself images of **m**, and didst commit H2145
19: 3 learned to catch the prey; it devoured **m**. H120
6 to catch the prey, *and* devoured **m**. H120
21:14 the sword of the great *m* *that are* slain,
31 hand of brutish **m**, *and* skilful to destroy. H582
22: 9 In thee are **m** that carry tales to shed H582
23: 6 young **m**, horsemen riding upon horses. H970
7 *were* the chosen **m** of Assyria, and with H1121
12 horses, all of them desirable young **m**. H970
14 for when she saw **m** pourtrayed upon H582
23 desirable young **m**, captains and rulers, H970
40 that ye have sent for **m** to come from far, H582
42 her: and with the **m** of the common sort H582
45 And the righteous **m**, they shall judge H582
24:17 not *thy* lips, and eat not the bread of **m**. H582
22 cover *your* lips, nor eat the bread of **m**. H582
25: 4 deliver thee to the **m** of the east for a H1121
10 Unto the **m** of the east with the H1121
26:10 into thy gates, as **m** enter into a city
17 of seafaring **m**, the renowned city, H3220
27: 8 mariners: thy wise *m*, O Tyrus, *that* were
9 The ancients of Gebal and the wise *m*
10 in thine army, thy **m** of war: they hanged H582
11 The **m** of Arvad with thine army *were* H1121
13 of **m** and vessels of brass in thy market. H120
15 The **m** of Dedan *were* thy merchants; H1121
27 and all thy **m** of war, that *are* in thee, H582
30: 5 Chub, and the **m** of the land that is in H1121
17 The young **m** of Aven and of Pi-beseth H970
31:14 of **m**, with them that go down to the pit. H120
34:31 of my pasture, *are* **m**, *and* I *am* your God, H120
35: 8 with his slain *m*: in thy hills, and in thy
36:10 And I will multiply **m** upon you, all the H120
12 Yea, I will cause **m** to walk upon you, H120
12 no more henceforth bereave them *of m*.
13 up **m**, and hast bereaved thy nations; H120
14 Therefore thou shalt devour **m** no more, H120
15 Neither will I cause *m* to hear in thee the
37 I will increase them with **m** like a flock. H120
38 with flocks of **m**: and they shall know H120
38:20 earth, and all the **m** that *are* upon the H120
39:14 And they shall sever out **m** of continual
20 with mighty **m**, and with all men of H1368
20 with all **m** of war, saith the Lord GOD. H376
47:15 the way of Hethlon, as **m** go to Zedad;
Dan 2:12 to destroy all the wise *m* of Babylon.
13 forth that the wise *m* should be slain;
14 gone forth to slay the wise *m* of Babylon:
18 with the rest of the wise *m* of Babylon.
24 to destroy the wise *m* of Babylon: he
24 not the wise *m* of Babylon: bring me
27 cannot the wise *m*, the astrologers, the
38 And wheresoever the children of **m** H606
43 with the seed of **m**: but they shall not H606
48 over all the wise *m* of Babylon.
3:12 Abed-nego; these **m**, O king, have not H1400
13 they brought these **m** before the king. H1400
20 the most mighty **m** that *were* in his H1400
21 Then these **m** were bound in their H1400
22 of the fire slew those **m** that took up H1400
23 And these three **m**, Shadrach, Meshach, H1400
24 Did not we cast three **m** bound into the H1400
25 He answered and said, Lo, I see four **m** H1400
27 saw these **m**, upon whose bodies H1400
4: 6 in all the wise *m* of Babylon before me,
17 in the kingdom of **m**, and giveth it to H606
17 and setteth up over it the basest of **m**. H606
18 as all the wise *m* of my kingdom are
25 That they shall drive thee from **m**, and H606
25 **m**, and giveth it to whomsoever he will. H606
32 And they shall drive thee from **m**, and H606
32 **m**, and giveth it to whomsoever he will. H606
33 was driven from **m**, and did eat grass as H606
5: 7 and said to the wise *m* of Babylon,
8 Then came in all the king's wise *m*: but
15 And now the wise *m*, the astrologers,
21 And he was driven from the sons of **m**; H606
21 ruled in the kingdom of **m**, and *that* he H606

Dan 6: 5 Then said these **m**, We shall not find H1400
11 Then these **m** assembled, and found H1400
15 Then these **m** assembled unto the king, H1400
24 brought those **m** which had accused H1400
26 of my kingdom **m** tremble and fear
9: 7 at this day; to the **m** of Judah, and to the H376
10: 7 the vision: for the **m** that were with me H582
16 of the sons of **m** touched my lips: then H120
Hos 6: 7 But they like **m** have transgressed the H120
10:13 way, in the multitude of thy mighty **m**. H1368
13: 2 Let the **m** that sacrifice kiss the calves. H120
Joel 1: 2 Hear this, ye old **m**, and give ear, all ye H2205
12 joy is withered away from the sons of **m**. H120
2: 7 They shall run like mighty **m**; they shall H1368
7 climb the wall like **m** of war; and they H582
28 your old **m** shall dream dreams, H2205
28 dreams, your young **m** shall see visions: H970
3: 9 up the mighty **m**, let all the men of war H1368
9 **m** of war draw near; let them come up: H582
Am 2:11 and of your young **m** for Nazarites. *Is it* H970
4:10 of Egypt: your young **m** have I slain with H970
6: 9 ten **m** in one house, that they shall die. H582
8:13 fair virgins and young **m** faint for thirst. H970
Oba 7 All the **m** of thy confederacy have H582
7 to the border: the **m** that were at peace H582
8 destroy the wise *m* out of Edom, and
9 And thy mighty *m*, O Teman, shall be
Jna 1:10 Then were the **m** exceedingly afraid, and H582
10 done this? For the **m** knew that he fled H582
13 Nevertheless the **m** rowed hard to bring H582
16 Then the **m** feared the LORD H582
Mic 2: 8 pass by securely as **m** averse from war.
12 noise by reason of *the multitude of* **m**. H120
5: 5 seven shepherds, and eight principal **m**. H120
7 for man, nor waiteth for the sons of **m**. H120
6:12 For the rich **m** thereof are full of
7: 2 upright among **m**: they all lie in wait for H120
6 enemies *are* the **m** of his own house.
Nah 2: 3 The shield of his mighty **m** is made red, H1368
3 red, the valiant **m** *are* in scarlet: the
3:10 for her honourable **m**, and all her great H3513
10 all her great **m** were bound in chains. H1419
Hab 1:14 And makest **m** as the fishes of the sea, as H120
Zep 1:12 and punish the **m** that are settled on H582
17 And I will bring distress upon **m**, that H120
17 walk like blind **m**, because they have
2:11 of the earth; and *m* shall worship him,
Hag 1:11 forth, and upon **m**, and upon cattle, and H120
Zec 2: 4 the multitude of **m** and cattle therein: H120
3: 8 thee: for they *are* **m** wondered at: for, H582
7: 2 and their **m**, to pray before the LORD, H582
7 *m* inhabited the south and the plain?
8: 4 shall yet old **m** and old women dwell H2205
10 all **m** every one against his neighbour. H120
23 *to pass*, that ten **m** shall take hold out of H582
9:17 **m** cheerful, and new wine the maids. H970
10: 5 And they shall be as mighty *m*, which
11: 6 lo, I will deliver the **m** every one into his H120
14:11 And *m* shall dwell in it, and there shall
Mt 2: 1 wise **m** from the east to Jerusalem, *G3097*
7 called the wise **m**, inquired of them *G3097*
16 of the wise **m**, was exceeding wroth, *G3097*
16 had diligently inquired of the wise **m**. *G3097*
4:19 me, and I will make you fishers of **m**. *G444*
5:11 Blessed are ye, when *m* shall revile you,
13 out, and to be trodden under foot of **m**. *G444*
15 Neither do **m** light a candle, and put it
16 Let your light so shine before **m**, that *G444*
19 and shall teach **m** so, he shall be called *G444*
6: 1 your alms before **m**, to be seen of them: *G444*
2 may have glory of **m**. Verily I say unto *G444*
5 may be seen of **m**. Verily I say unto you, *G444*
14 For if ye forgive **m** their trespasses, your *G444*
15 But if ye forgive not **m** their trespasses, *G444*
16 may appear unto **m** to fast. Verily I say *G444*
18 That thou appear not unto **m** to fast, but *G444*
7:12 ye would that **m** should do to you, do *G444*
16 Ye shall know them by their fruits. Do **m**
8:27 But the **m** marvelled, saying, What *G444*
9: 8 which had given such power unto **m**. *G444*
17 Neither do **m** put new wine into old
27 thence, two blind **m** followed him, *G5185*
28 house, the blind **m** came to him: and *G5185*
10:17 But beware of **m**: for they will deliver you *G444*
22 And ye shall be hated of all *m* for my
32 confess me before **m**, him will I confess *G444*
33 But whosoever shall deny me before **m**, *G444*
12:31 be forgiven unto **m**: but the blasphemy *G444*
31 *Holy* Ghost shall not be forgiven unto **m**. *G444*

M

Mt 12:36 idle word that **m** shall speak, they shall G444
41 The **m** of Nineveh shall rise in judgment G435
13:17 and righteous ***m*** have desired to see
25 But while **m** slept, his enemy came and G444
14:21 **m**, beside women and children. G435
35 And when the **m** of that place had G435
15: 9 *for* doctrines the commandments of **m**. G444
38 **m**, beside women and children. G435
16:13 do **m** say that I the Son of man am? G444
23 that be of God, but those that be of **m**. G444
17:22 shall be betrayed into the hands of **m**: G444
19:11 But he said unto them, All ***m*** cannot
12 were made eunuchs of **m**: and there be G444
26 unto them, With **m** this is impossible; G444
20:30 And, behold, two blind **m** sitting by the G5185
21:25 from heaven, or of **m**? And they reasoned G444
26 But if we shall say, Of **m**; we fear the G444
41 those wicked **m**, and will let out *his* G2556
22:16 for thou regardest not the person of **m**. G444
23: 5 do for to be seen of **m**: they make broad G444
7 and to be called of **m**, Rabbi, Rabbi. G444
13 of heaven against **m**: for ye neither go in G444
28 righteous unto **m**, but within ye are full G444
34 and wise **m**, and scribes: and *some* G4680
26:33 him, Though all ***m*** shall be offended
28: 4 did shake, and became as dead ***m***.
Mk 1:17 I will make you to become fishers of **m**. G444
37 they said unto him, All ***m*** seek for thee.
3:28 unto the sons of **m**, and blasphemies G444
5:20 had done for him: and all ***m*** did marvel.
6:12 And they went out, and preached that **m**
44 the loaves were about five thousand **m**. G435
7: 7 *for* doctrines the commandments of **m**. G444
8 the tradition of **m**, *as* the washing of pots G444
21 For from within, out of the heart of **m**, G444
8: 4 ***m*** with bread here in the wilderness?
24 And he looked up, and said, I see **m** as G444
27 unto them, Whom do **m** say that I am? G444
33 be of God, but the things that be of **m**. G444
9:31 into the hands of **m**, and they shall kill G444
10:27 them saith, With **m** *it is* impossible, but G444
11:30 was *it* from heaven, or of **m**? answer me. G444
32 But if we shall say, Of **m**; they feared the G444
32 the people: for all ***m*** counted John, that
12:14 not the person of **m**, but teachest the way G444
13:13 And ye shall be hated of all ***m*** for my
14:51 and the young **m** laid hold on him: G3495
Lk 1:25 *me*, to take away my reproach among **m**. G444
2:14 and on earth peace, good will toward **m**. G444
3:15 and all **m** mused in their hearts G3956
5:10 not; from henceforth thou shalt catch **m**. G444
18 And, behold, **m** brought in a bed a man G435
6:22 Blessed are ye, when **m** shall hate you, G444
26 Woe unto you, when all **m** shall speak G444
31 And as ye would that **m** should do to G444
38 over, shall **m** give into your bosom.
44 fruit. For of thorns **m** do not gather figs,
7:20 When the **m** were come unto him, they G435
31 shall I liken the **m** of this generation? G444
9:14 For they were about five thousand **m**. G435
30 him two **m**, which were Moses and Elias: G435
32 and the two **m** that stood with him. G435
44 shall be delivered into the hands of **m**. G444
11:31 judgment with the **m** of this generation, G435
32 The **m** of Nineve shall rise up in the G435
44 not, and the **m** that walk over *them* G444
46 for ye lade **m** with burdens grievous G444
12: 8 confess me before **m**, him shall the Son of G444
9 But he that denieth me before **m** shall be G444
36 And ye yourselves like unto **m** that wait G444
48 and to whom **m** have committed much,
13: 4 above all **m** that dwelt in Jerusalem? G444
14 six days in which **m** ought to work: in
14:24 For I say unto you, That none of those **m** G435
35 the dunghill; *but* **m** cast it out. He that
16:15 yourselves before **m**; but God knoweth G444
15 **m** is abomination in the sight of God. G444
17:12 **m** that were lepers, which stood afar off: G435
34 there shall be two ***m*** in one bed; the one
36 Two ***m*** shall be in the field; the one shall
18: 1 **m** ought always to pray, and not to faint;
10 Two **m** went up into the temple to pray; G444
11 I am not as other **m** *are*, extortioners, G444
27 with **m** are possible with God. G444
20: 4 of John, was it from heaven, or of **m**? G444
6 But and if we say, Of **m**; all the people G444
20 themselves just **m**, that they might take G1342
21: 1 And he looked up, and saw the rich **m** G4145
17 And ye shall be hated of all ***m*** for my

Lk 22:63 And the **m** that held Jesus mocked him, G435
23:11 And Herod with his **m** of war set him at
24: 4 **m** stood by them in shining garments: G435
7 the hands of sinful **m**, and be crucified, G444
Jn 1: 4 was life; and the life was the light of **m**. G444
7 that all ***m*** through him might believe.
2:10 wine; and when **m** have well drunk, then
24 unto them, because he knew all ***m***,
3:19 the world, and **m** loved darkness rather G444
26 same baptizeth, and all ***m*** come to him.
4:20 is the place where **m** ought to worship.
28 her way into the city, and saith to the **m**, G444
38 no labour: other **m** laboured, and ye are G243
5:23 That all ***m*** should honour the Son, even
41 I receive not honour from **m**. G444
6:10 And Jesus said, Make the **m** sit down. G444
10 grass in the place. So the **m** sat down, in G435
14 Then those **m**, when they had seen the G444
8:17 law, that the testimony of two **m** is true. G444
11:48 If we let him thus alone, all ***m*** will
12:32 from the earth, will draw all ***m*** unto me.
43 For they loved the praise of **m** more than G444
13:35 By this shall all ***m*** know that ye are my
15: 6 and is withered; and **m** gather them, and
17: 6 I have manifested thy name unto the **m** G444
18: 3 Judas then, having received a band *of* ***m***
Act 1:10 two **m** stood by them in white apparel; G435
11 Which also said, Ye **m** of Galilee, why G435
16 **M** *and* brethren, this scripture must G435
21 Wherefore of these **m** which have G435
24 the hearts of all ***m***, shew whether of these
2: 5 **m**, out of every nation under heaven. G435
13 Others mocking said, These **m** are full of
14 said unto them, Ye **m** of Judaea, and all G435
17 and your young **m** shall see visions, G3495
17 and your old **m** shall dream dreams: G4245
22 Ye **m** of Israel, hear these words; Jesus of G435
29 **M** *and* brethren, let me freely speak unto G435
37 **M** *and* brethren, what shall we do? G435
45 them to all ***m***, as every man had need.
3:12 the people, Ye **m** of Israel, why marvel G435
4: 4 of the **m** was about five thousand. G435
12 among **m**, whereby we must be saved. G444
13 and ignorant **m**, they marvelled; and G444
16 Saying, What shall we do to these **m**? for G444
21 ***m*** glorified God for that which was done.
5: 4 thou hast not lied unto **m**, but unto God. G444
6 And the young **m** arose, wound him G3501
10 and the young **m** came in, and found G3495
14 multitudes both of **m** and women.) G435
25 Behold, the **m** whom ye put in prison G435
29 We ought to obey God rather than **m**. G444
35 And said unto them, Ye **m** of Israel, take G435
35 ye intend to do as touching these **m**. G444
36 a number of **m**, about four hundred, G435
38 you, Refrain from these **m**, and let them G444
38 this work be of **m**, it will come to nought: G444
6: 3 among you seven **m** of honest report, G435
11 Then they suborned **m**, which said, We G435
7: 2 And he said, **M**, brethren, and fathers, G435
8: 2 And devout **m** carried Stephen *to his* G435
3 every house, and haling **m** and women G435
12 they were baptized, both **m** and women. G435
9: 2 way, whether they were **m** or women, he G435
7 And the **m** which journeyed with him G435
38 sent unto him two **m**, desiring *him* that G435
10: 5 And now send **m** to Joppa, and call for G435
17 mean, behold, the **m** which were sent G435
19 unto him, Behold, three **m** seek thee. G435
21 Then Peter went down to the **m** which G435
11: 3 Saying, Thou wentest in to **m** G435
11 there were three **m** already come unto G435
13 unto him, Send **m** to Joppa, and call for G435
20 And some of them were **m** of Cyprus and G435
13:15 them, saying, *Ye* **m** *and* brethren, if ye G435
16 *his* hand said, **M** of Israel, and ye that G435
26 **M** *and* brethren, children of the stock of G435
38 Be it known unto you therefore, **m** *and* G435
50 and the chief **m** of the city, and raised G4413
14:11 are come down to us in the likeness of **m**. G444
15 We also are **m** of like passions with G444
15: 1 And certain **m** which came down from G5100
7 and said unto them, **M** *and* brethren, ye G435
13 **M** *and* brethren, hearken unto me: G435
17 That the residue of **m** might seek after G444
22 to send chosen **m** of their own company G435
22 and Silas, chief **m** among the brethren: G435
25 to send chosen **m** unto you with our G435
26 **M** that have hazarded their lives for the G444

Act 16:17 saying, These **m** are the servants of the G444
20 saying, These **m**, being Jews, do G444
35 the serjeants, saying, Let those **m** go. G444
17:12 which were Greeks, and of **m**, not a few. G435
22 hill, and said, *Ye* **m** of Athens, I perceive G435
26 all nations of **m** for to dwell on all the G444
30 all **m** every where to repent: G444
31 assurance unto all ***m***, in that he hath
34 Howbeit certain **m** clave unto him, and G435
18:13 Saying, This *fellow* persuadeth **m** to G444
19: 7 And all the **m** were about twelve. G435
19 them before all ***m***: and they counted the
29 Gaius and Aristarchus, **m** of Macedonia,
35 people, he said, *Ye* **m** of Ephesus, what G435
37 For ye have brought hither these **m**, G435
20:26 that I *am* pure from the blood of all ***m***.
30 Also of your own selves shall **m** arise, G435
21:23 have four **m** which have a vow on them; G435
26 Then Paul took the **m**, and the next day G435
28 Crying out, **M** of Israel, help: This is the G435
28 that teacheth all ***m*** every where against
38 four thousand **m** that were murderers? G435
22: 1 **M**, brethren, and fathers, hear ye my G435
4 into prisons both **m** and women. G435
15 For thou shalt be his witness unto all **m** G444
23: 1 the council, said, **M** *and* brethren, I have G435
6 out in the council, **M** *and* brethren, I am G435
21 more than forty **m**, which have bound G435
24:16 of offence toward God, and *toward* **m**. G444
25:23 and principal **m** of the city, at Festus' G435
24 King Agrippa, and all **m** which are here G435
28:17 he said unto them, **M** *and* brethren, G435
Ro 1:18 of **m**, who hold the truth in G444
27 And likewise also the **m**, leaving the G730
27 toward another; **m** with men working G730
27 another; men with **m** working that G730
2:16 judge the secrets of **m** by Jesus Christ G444
29 whose praise *is* not of **m**, but of God. G444
5:12 upon all **m**, for that all have sinned: G444
18 *came* upon all **m** to condemnation; even G444
18 upon all **m** unto justification of life. G444
6:19 I speak after the manner of **m** because of G442
11: 4 seven thousand **m**, who have not bowed G435
12:16 but condescend to **m** of low estate. Be
17 things honest in the sight of all **m**. G444
18 as lieth in you, live peaceably with all **m**. G444
14:18 *is* acceptable to God, and approved of **m**. G444
16:19 abroad unto all ***m***. I am glad therefore
1Co 1:25 God is wiser than **m**; and the weakness of G444
25 the weakness of God is stronger than **m**. G444
26 not many wise **m** after the flesh, not G4680
2: 5 wisdom of **m**, but in the power of God. G444
3: 3 are ye not carnal, and walk as **m**? G444
21 Therefore let no man glory in **m**. For all G444
4: 6 us not to think *of* ***m*** above that which is
9 unto the world, and to angels, and to **m**. G444
7: 7 For I would that all **m** were even as I G444
23 with a price; be not ye the servants of **m**. G444
9:19 For though I be free from all ***m***, yet have
22 ***m***, that I might by all means save some.
10:15 I speak as to wise **m**; judge ye what I G5429
33 Even as I please all ***m*** in all *things*, not
13: 1 Though I speak with the tongues of **m** G444
14: 2 speaketh not unto **m**, but unto God: for G444
3 speaketh unto **m** *to* edification, and G444
20 ye children, but in understanding be **m**. G5046
21 In the law it is written, With ***m*** *of* other
15:19 Christ, we are of all **m** most miserable. G444
32 If after the manner of **m** I have fought G444
39 one *kind of* flesh of **m**, another flesh of G444
16:13 in the faith, quit you like **m**, be strong. G407
2Co 3: 2 in our hearts, known and read of all **m**: G444
5:11 Lord, we persuade **m**; but we are made G444
8:13 For *I mean* not that other **m** be eased, G243
21 of the Lord, but also in the sight of **m**. G444
9:13 distribution unto them, and unto all ***m***;
Gal 1: 1 Paul, an apostle, (not of **m**, neither by G444
10 For do I now persuade **m**, or God? or do I G444
10 do I seek to please **m**? for if I yet pleased G444
10 **m**, I should not be the servant of Christ. G444
3:15 Brethren, I speak after the manner of **m**; G444
6:10 do good unto all ***m***, especially unto them
Eph 3: 5 unto the sons of **m**, as it is now revealed G444
9 And to make all ***m*** see what *is* the
4: 8 captivity captive, and gave gifts unto **m**. G444
14 by the sleight of **m**, *and* cunning G444
5:28 So ought **m** to love their wives as their G435
6: 7 service, as to the Lord, and not to **m**: G444
Php 2: 7 and was made in the likeness of **m**: G444

Php 4: 5 known unto all **m**. The Lord *is* at hand. G444
Col 2: 8 the tradition of **m**, after the rudiments G444
22 the commandments and doctrines of **m**? G444
3:23 heartily, as to the Lord, and not unto **m**; G444
1Th 1: 5 of **m** we were among you for your sake. G3634
2: 4 **m**, but God, which trieth our hearts. G444
6 Nor of **m** sought we glory, neither of you, G444
13 not *as* the word of **m**, but as it is in truth, G444
15 not God, and are contrary to all **m**: G444
3:12 toward all *m*, even as we *do* toward you:
5:14 the weak, be patient toward all *m*.
15 both among yourselves, and to all *m*.
2Th 3: 2 and wicked **m**: for all *men* have not faith. G444
2 wicked men: for all *m* have not faith.
1Ti 2: 1 *and* giving of thanks, be made for all **m**; G444
4 Who will have all **m** to be saved, and to G444
5 God and **m**, the man Christ Jesus; G444
8 I will therefore that **m** pray every where, G435
4:10 of all **m**, specially of those that believe. G444
5: 1 father; *and* the younger **m** as brethren; G3501
24 judgment; and some *m* they follow after.
6: 5 Perverse disputings of **m** of corrupt G444
9 drown **m** in destruction and perdition. G444
2Ti 2: 2 **m**, who shall be able to teach others also. G444
24 gentle unto all *m*, apt to teach, patient,
3: 2 For **m** shall be lovers of their own selves, G444
8 also resist the truth: **m** of corrupt minds, G444
9 manifest unto all *m*, as theirs also was.
13 But evil **m** and seducers shall wax worse G444
4:16 with me, but all *m* forsook me: *I pray*
Tit 1: 8 of good **m**, sober, just, holy, temperate; G5358
14 of **m**, that turn from the truth. G444
2: 2 That the aged **m** be sober, grave, G4246
6 Young **m** likewise exhort to be sober G3501
11 salvation hath appeared to all **m**, G444
3: 2 gentle, shewing all meekness unto all **m**. G444
8 things are good and profitable unto **m**. G444
Heb 5: 1 taken from among **m** is ordained for G444
1 is ordained for **m** in things *pertaining* G444
6:16 For **m** verily swear by the greater: and G444
7: 8 And here **m** that die receive tithes; but G444
28 For the law maketh **m** high priests which G444
9:17 For a testament *is* of force after **m** are
27 And as it is appointed unto **m** once to G444
12:14 Follow peace with all *m*, and holiness,
23 to the spirits of just **m** made perfect, G1342
Jas 1: 5 God, that giveth to all *m* liberally, and
2: 6 poor. Do not rich **m** oppress you, and G4145
3: 9 therewith curse we **m**, which are made G444
5: 1 Go to now, *ye* rich **m**, weep and howl G4145
1Pt 2: 4 of **m**, but chosen of God, *and* precious, G444
15 put to silence the ignorance of foolish **m**: G444
17 Honour all *m*. Love the brotherhood.
4: 2 to the lusts of **m**, but to the will of God. G444
6 according to **m** in the flesh, but live G444
2Pt 1:21 of man: but holy **m** of God spake *as they* G444
3: 7 of judgment and perdition of ungodly **m**. G444
9 promise, as some **m** count slackness; G5100
1Jn 2:13 unto you, young **m**, because ye have G3495
14 unto you, young **m**, because ye are G3495
5: 9 If we receive the witness of **m**, the G444
3Jn 12 Demetrius hath good report of all *m*, and
Jude 4 For there are certain **m** crept in G444
4 ungodly **m**, turning the grace of G765
Rev 6:15 and the great **m**, and the rich men, and G3175
15 great men, and the rich **m**, and the chief G4145
15 and the mighty **m**, and every bondman, G1415
8:11 and many **m** died of the waters, because G444
9: 4 but only those **m** which have not the G444
6 And in those days shall **m** seek death, G444
7 and their faces *were* as the faces of **m**. G444
10 their power *was* to hurt **m** five months. G444
15 and a year, for to slay the third part of **m**. G444
18 By these three was the third part of **m** G444
20 And the rest of the **m** which were not G444
11:13 were slain of **m** seven thousand: and G444
13:13 heaven on the earth in the sight of **m**, G444
14: 4 from among **m**, *being* the firstfruits G444
16: 2 sore upon the **m** which had the mark G444
8 given unto him to scorch **m** with fire. G444
9 And **m** were scorched with great heat, G444
18 as was not since **m** were upon the earth, G444
21 And there fell upon **m** a great hail out of G444
21 of a talent: and **m** blasphemed God G444
18:13 and chariots, and slaves, and souls of **m**. G444
23 were the great **m** of the earth; for by G3175
19:18 the flesh of mighty **m**, and the flesh of G2478
18 and the flesh of all *m*, *both* free and
21: 3 of God *is* with **m**, and he will dwell with G444

MENAHEM
2Ki 15:14 For **M** the son of Gadi went up from H4505
16 Then **M** smote Tiphsah, and all that H4505
17 of Judah began **M** the son of Gadi to H4505
19 the land: and **M** gave Pul a thousand H4505
20 And **M** exacted the money of Israel, H4505
21 And the rest of the acts of **M**, and all H4505
22 And **M** slept with his fathers; and H4505
23 the son of **M** began to reign over H4505

MENAN
Lk 3:31 was *the son* of **M**, which was *the son* G3104

MEND
2Ch 24:12 and brass to **m** the house of the LORD. H2388

MENDING
Mt 4:21 **m** their nets; and he called them. G2675
Mk 1:19 who also were in the ship **m** their nets. G2675

MENE
Dan 5:25 written, **M**, MENE, TEKEL, UPHARSIN. H4484
25 written, MENE, **M**, TEKEL, UPHARSIN. H4484
26 of the thing: **M**; God hath numbered H4484

MENPLEASERS
Eph 6: 6 Not with eyeservice, as **m**; but as the G441
Col 3:22 with eyeservice, as **m**; but in singleness G441

MEN'S
Gen 24:32 feet, and the **m** feet that *were* with him. H582
44: 1 saying, Fill the **m** sacks *with* food, as H582
Dt 4:28 gods, the work of **m** hands, wood and H120
1Sa 24: 9 hearest thou **m** words, saying, Behold, H120
1Ki 12:13 the old **m** counsel that they gave him; H2205
13: 2 and **m** bones shall be burnt upon thee. H120
2Ki 19:18 but the work of **m** hands, wood and H120
23:20 altars, and burned **m** bones upon them, H120
Ps 115: 4 *are* silver and gold, the work of **m** hands. H120
135:15 *are* silver and gold, the work of **m** hands. H120
Isa 37:19 but the work of **m** hands, wood and H120
Jer 48:41 and the mighty **m** hearts in Moab at H1368
Hab 2: 8 thee; because of **m** blood, and *for* the H120
17 afraid, because of **m** blood, and for the H120
Mt 23: 4 and lay *them* on **m** shoulders; but they G444
27 of dead *m* bones, and of all uncleanness.
Lk 9:56 not come to destroy **m** lives, but to save G444
21:26 **M** hearts failing them for fear, and for G444
Act 17:25 Neither is worshipped with **m** hands, as G444
2Co 10:15 *that is*, of other **m** labours; but having G245
1Ti 5:22 of other **m** sins: keep thyself pure. G245
24 Some **m** sins are open beforehand, going G444
1Pt 4:15 or as a busybody in other **m** matters.
Jude 16 *words*, having **m** persons in admiration

MENSERVANTS
Gen 12:16 oxen, and he asses, and **m**, and H5650
20:14 and oxen, and **m**, and womenservants, H5650
24:35 and gold, and **m**, and maidservants, H5650
30:43 and **m**, and camels, and asses. H5650
32: 5 and asses, flocks, and **m**, and H5650
Ex 21: 7 she shall not go out as the **m** do. H5650
Dt 12:12 and your **m**, and your maidservants, H5650
1Sa 8:16 And he will take your **m**, and your H5650
2Ki 5:26 and oxen, and **m**, and maidservants? H5650
Lk 12:45 begin to beat the **m** and maidens, and G3816

MENSTEALERS
1Ti 1:10 with mankind, for **m**, for liars, for G405

MENSTRUOUS
Isa 30:22 them away as a **m** cloth; thou shalt say H1739
Lam 1:17 is as a **m** woman among them. H5079
Ezk 18: 6 neither hath come near to a **m** woman, H5079

MENTION
Gen 40:14 me, and make **m** of me unto Pharaoh, H2142
Ex 23:13 and make no **m** of the name of other H2142
Jos 23: 7 you; neither make **m** of the name of H2142
1Sa 4:18 And it came to pass, when he made **m** H2142
Job 28:18 No **m** shall be made of coral, or of H2142
Ps 71:16 Lord GOD: I will make **m** of thy H2142
87: 4 I will make **m** of Rahab and Babylon to H2142
Isa 12: 4 make **m** that his name is exalted. H2142
19:17 one that maketh **m** thereof shall be H2142
26:13 thee only will we make **m** of thy name. H2142
48: 1 the LORD, and make **m** of the God of H2142
49: 1 mother hath he made **m** of my name. H2142
62: 6 make **m** of the LORD, keep not silence, H2142
Isa 63: 7 I will **m** the lovingkindnesses of the H2142
Jer 4:16 Make ye **m** to the nations; behold, H2142
20: 9 Then I said, I will not make **m** of him, H2142
23:36 And the burden of the LORD shall ye **m** H2142
Am 6:10 not make **m** of the name of the LORD. H2142
Ro 1: 9 I make **m** of you always in my prayers; G3417
Eph 1:16 you, making **m** of you in my prayers; G3417
1Th 1: 2 all, making **m** of you in our prayers; G3417
Phlm 4 I thank my God, making **m** of thee G3417
Heb 11:22 By faith Joseph, when he died, made **m** G3421

MENTIONED
Jos 21: 9 these cities which are *here* **m** by name, H7121
1Ch 4:38 These **m** by *their* names *were* princes in H935
2Ch 20:34 *is* **m** in the book of the kings of Israel. H5927
Ezk 16:56 For thy sister Sodom was not **m** by thy H8052
18:22 they shall not be **m** unto him: in his H2142
24 done shall not be **m**: in his trespass that H2142
33:16 shall be **m** unto him: he hath done H2142

MEON See BAAL-MEON and BETH-MEON.

MEONENIM
Jdg 9:37 company come along by the plain of **M**. H6049

MEONOTHAI
1Ch 4:14 And **M** begat Ophrah: and Seraiah H4587

MEPHAATH
Jos 13:18 And Jahazah, and Kedemoth, and **M**, H4158
21:37 Kedemoth with her suburbs, and **M** H4158
1Ch 6:79 her suburbs, and **M** with her suburbs: H4158
Jer 48:21 Holon, and upon Jahazah, and upon **M**, H4158

MEPHIBOSHETH
2Sa 4: 4 became lame. And his name *was* **M**. H4648
9: 6 Now when **M**, the son of Jonathan, the H4648
6 And David said, **M**. And he answered, H4648
10 food to eat: but **M** thy master's son H4648
11 servant do. As for **M**, *said the king*, he H4648
12 And **M** had a young son, whose name H4648
12 the house of Ziba *were* servants unto **M**. H4648
13 So **M** dwelt in Jerusalem: for he did eat H4648
16: 1 Ziba the servant of **M** met him, with a H4648
4 that *pertained* unto **M**. And Ziba said, I H4648
19:24 And **M** the son of Saul came down to H4648
25 wentest not thou with me, **M**? H4648
30 And **M** said unto the king, Yea, let him H4648
21: 7 But the king spared **M**, the son of H4648
8 Saul, Armoni and **M**; and the five sons H4648

MERAB
1Sa 14:49 of the firstborn **M**, and the name of the H4764
18:17 elder daughter **M**, her will I give thee H4764
19 But it came to pass at the time when **M** H4764

MERAIAH
Neh 12:12 of Seraiah, **M**; of Jeremiah, Hananiah; H4811

MERAIOTH
1Ch 6: 6 begat Zerahiah, and Zerahiah begat **M**, H4812
7 **M** begat Amariah, and Amariah begat H4812
52 **M** his son, Amariah his son, Ahitub his H4812
9:11 Zadok, the son of **M**, the son of Ahitub, H4812
Ezr 7: 3 the son of Azariah, the son of **M**, H4812
Neh 11:11 Zadok, the son of **M**, the son of Ahitub, H4812
12:15 Of Harim, Adna; of **M**, Helkai; H4812

MERARI
Gen 46:11 sons of Levi; Gershon, Kohath, and **M**. H4847
Ex 6:16 and Kohath, and **M**: and the years of H4847
19 And the sons of **M**; Mahali and Mushi: H4847
Nu 3:17 names; Gershon, and Kohath, and **M**. H4847
20 And the sons of **M** by their families; H4847
33 Of **M** *was* the family of the Mahlites, H4847
33 Mushites: these *are* the families of **M**. H4847
35 of the families of **M** *was* Zuriel the son H4847
36 of the sons of **M** *shall be* the boards H4847
4:29 As for the sons of **M**, thou shalt number H4847
33 of the sons of **M**, according to all their H4847
42 of the sons of **M**, throughout their H4847
45 of the sons of **M**, whom Moses and H4847
7: 8 gave unto the sons of **M**, according unto H4847
10:17 **M** set forward, bearing the tabernacle. H4847
26:57 of **M**, the family of the Merarites. H4847
Jos 21: 7 The children of **M** by their families *had* H4847
34 of the children of **M**, the rest of the H4847
40 So all the cities for the children of **M** by H4847
1Ch 6: 1 sons of Levi; Gershon, Kohath, and **M**. H4847

1Ch 6:16 sons of Levi; Gershom, Kohath, and **M**. H4847
19 The sons of **M**; Mahli, and Mushi. And H4847
29 The sons of **M**; Mahli, Libni his son, H4847
44 And their brethren the sons of **M** *stood* H4847
47 of Mushi, the son of **M**, the son of Levi. H4847
63 Unto the sons of **M** *were given* by lot, H4847
77 Unto the rest of the children of **M** *were* H4847
9:14 the son of Hashabiah, of the sons of **M**; H4847
15: 6 Of the sons of **M**; Asaiah the chief, and H4847
17 and of the sons of **M** their brethren, H4847
23: 6 Levi, *namely*, Gershon, Kohath, and **M**. H4847
21 The sons of **M**; Mahli, and Mushi. The H4847
24:26 The sons of **M** *were* Mahli and Mushi: H4847
27 The sons of **M** by Jaaziah; Beno, and H4847
26:10 Also Hosah, of the children of **M**, had H4847
19 sons of Kore, and among the sons of **M**. H4847
2Ch 29:12 and of the sons of **M**, Kish the son of H4847
34:12 of the sons of **M**; and Zechariah and H4847
Ezr 8:19 **M**, his brethren and their sons, twenty; H4847

MERARITES
Nu 26:57 of Merari, the family of the **M**. H4848

MERATHAIM
Jer 50:21 Go up against the land of **M**, *even* H4850

MERCHANDISE
Dt 21:14 shalt not make **m** of her, because thou H6014
24: 7 and maketh **m** of him, or selleth him; H6014
Prv 3:14 For the **m** of it *is* better than the H5504
14 it *is* better than the **m** of silver, and the H5505
31:18 She perceiveth that her **m** *is* good: her H5504
Isa 23:18 And her **m** and her hire shall be H5504
18 laid up; for her **m** shall be for them that H5504
45:14 of Egypt, and **m** of Ethiopia and of the H5505
Ezk 26:12 a prey of thy **m**: and they shall break H7404
27: 9 mariners were in thee to occupy thy **m**. H4627
15 isles *were* the **m** of thine hand: they H5506
24 and made of cedar, among thy **m**. H4819
27 Thy riches, and thy fairs, thy **m**, thy H4627
27 occupiers of thy **m**, and all thy men of H4627
33 multitude of thy riches and of thy **m**. H4627
34 depths of the waters thy **m** and all thy H4627
28:16 By the multitude of thy **m** they have H7404
Mt 22: 5 ways, one to his farm, another to his **m**: *G1711*
Jn 2:16 not my Father's house an house of **m**. *G1712*
2Pt 2: 3 words make **m** of you: whose judgment *G1710*
Rev 18:11 for no man buyeth their **m** any more: *G1117*
12 The **m** of gold, and silver, and precious *G1117*

MERCHANT
Gen 23:16 of silver, current *money* with the **m**. H5503
Prv 31:24 *it*; and delivereth girdles unto the **m**. H3669
Song 3: 6 with all powders of the **m**? H7402
Isa 23:11 against the **m** *city*, to destroy the H3667
Ezk 27: 3 the sea, *which art* a **m** of the people for H7402
12 Tarshish *was* thy **m** by reason of the H5503
16 Syria *was* thy **m** by reason of the H5503
18 Damascus *was* thy **m** in the multitude H5503
20 Dedan *was* thy **m** in precious clothes H7402
Hos 12: 7 *He is* a **m**, the balances of deceit *are* in H3667
Zep 1:11 for all the **m** people are cut down; H3667
Mt 13:45 unto a **m** man, seeking goodly pearls: *G1713*

MERCHANTMEN
Gen 37:28 Then there passed by Midianites **m**; H5503
1Ki 10:15 Beside *that he had* of the **m**, and H582+H8446

MERCHANTS
1Ki 10:15 of the spice **m**, and of all the kings H7402
28 **m** received the linen yarn at a price. H5503
2Ch 1:16 **m** received the linen yarn at a price. H5503
9:14 Beside *that which* chapmen and **m** H5503
Neh 3:31 and of the **m**, over against the gate H7402
32 gate repaired the goldsmiths and the **m**. H7402
13:20 So the **m** and sellers of all kind of ware H7402
Job 41: 6 him? shall they part him among the **m**? H3669
Isa 23: 2 thou whom the **m** of Zidon, that pass H5503
8 *city*, whose **m** *are* princes, whose H5503
47:15 *even* thy **m**, from thy youth: they H5503
Ezk 17: 4 a land of traffick; he set it in a city of **m**. H7402
27:13 they *were* thy **m**: they traded the H7402
15 The men of Dedan *were* thy **m**; many H7402
17 they *were* thy **m**: they traded in thy H7402
21 and goats: in these *were they* thy **m**. H5503
22 The **m** of Sheba and Raamah, they H7402
22 they *were* thy **m**: they occupied in thy H7402
23 Haran, and Canneh, and Eden, the **m** H7402
23 Asshur, *and* Chilmad, *were* thy **m**. H7402
Ezk 27:24 These *were* thy **m** in all sorts *of things*, H7402
36 The **m** among the people shall hiss at H5503
38:13 Sheba, and Dedan, and the **m** of H5503
Nah 3:16 Thou hast multiplied thy **m** above the H7402
Rev 18: 3 with her, and the **m** of the earth are *G1713*
11 And the **m** of the earth shall weep and *G1713*
15 The **m** of these things, which were *G1713*
23 at all in thee: for thy **m** were the great *G1713*

MERCHANTS'
Prv 31:14 She is like the **m** ships; she bringeth her H5503

MERCIES
Gen 32:10 I am not worthy of the least of all the **m**, H2617
2Sa 24:14 the LORD; for his **m** *are* great: and let H7356
1Ch 21:13 very great *are* his **m**: but let me not fall H7356
2Ch 6:42 remember the **m** of David thy servant. H2617
Neh 9:19 Yet thou in thy manifold **m** forsookest H7356
27 to thy manifold **m** thou gavest them H7356
28 thou deliver them according to thy **m**; H7356
Ps 25: 6 Remember, O LORD, thy tender **m** and H7356
40:11 Withhold not thou thy tender **m** from H7356
51: 1 tender **m** blot out my transgressions. H7356
69:16 to the multitude of thy tender **m**. H7356
77: 9 he in anger shut up his tender **m**? Selah. H7356
79: 8 let thy tender **m** speedily prevent us: H7356
89: 1 I will sing of the **m** of the LORD for H2617
103: 4 thee with lovingkindness and tender **m**; H7356
106: 7 multitude of thy **m**; but provoked *him* H2617
45 according to the multitude of his **m**. H2617
119:41 Let thy **m** come also unto me, O LORD, H2617
77 Let thy tender **m** come unto me, that I H7356
156 Great *are* thy tender **m**, O LORD: H7356
145: 9 and his tender **m** *are* over all his works. H7356
Prv 12:10 the tender **m** of the wicked *are* cruel. H7356
Isa 54: 7 but with great **m** will I gather thee. H7356
55: 3 with you, *even* the sure **m** of David. H2617
63: 7 according to his **m**, and according to H7356
15 thy **m** toward me? are they restrained? H7356
Jer 16: 5 the LORD, *even* lovingkindness and **m**. H7356
42:12 And I will shew **m** unto you, that he H7356
Lam 3:22 *It is of* the LORD'S **m** that we are not H2617
32 according to the multitude of his **m**. H2617
Dan 2:18 That they would desire **m** of the God of H7359
9: 9 To the Lord our God *belong* **m** and H7356
18 righteousnesses, but for thy great **m**. H7356
Hos 2:19 and in lovingkindness, and in **m**. H7356
Zec 1:16 to Jerusalem with **m**: my house shall be H7356
Act 13:34 I will give you the sure **m** of David. *G3741*
Ro 12: 1 brethren, by the **m** of God, that ye *G3628*
2Co 1: 3 Father of **m**, and the God of all comfort; *G3628*
Php 2: 1 of the Spirit, if any bowels and **m**, *G3628*
Col 3:12 bowels of **m**, kindness, humbleness *G3628*

MERCIES'
Neh 9:31 Nevertheless for thy great **m** sake thou H7356
Ps 6: 4 my soul: oh save me for thy **m** sake. H2617
31:16 thy servant: save me for thy **m** sake. H2617
44:26 help, and redeem us for thy **m** sake. H2617

MERCIFUL
Gen 19:16 the LORD being **m** unto him: and they H2551
Ex 34: 6 The LORD God, **m** and gracious, H7349
Dt 4:31 (For the LORD thy God *is* a **m** God;) he H7349
21: 8 Be **m**, O LORD, unto thy people Israel, H3722
32:43 be **m** unto his land, *and* to his people. H3722
2Sa 22:26 With the **m** thou wilt shew thyself H2623
26 thou wilt shew thyself **m**, *and* with the H2616
1Ki 20:31 of Israel *are* **m** kings: let us, I pray H2617
2Ch 30: 9 *is* gracious and **m**, and will not turn H7349
Neh 9:17 gracious and **m**, slow to anger, and H7349
31 for thou *art* a gracious and **m** God. H7349
Ps 18:25 With the **m** thou wilt shew thyself H2623
25 wilt shew thyself **m**; with an upright H2616
26:11 redeem me, and be **m** unto me. H2603
37:26 *He is* ever **m**, and lendeth; and his seed H2603
41: 4 I said, LORD, be **m** unto me: heal my H2603
10 But thou, O LORD, be **m** unto me, and H2603
56: 1 Be **m** unto me, O God: for man would H2603
57: 1 Be **m** unto me, O God, be merciful unto H2603
1 Be merciful unto me, O God, be **m** unto H2603
59: 5 **m** to any wicked transgressors. Selah. H2603
67: 1 God be **m** unto us, and bless us; *and* H2603
86: 3 Be **m** unto me, O Lord: for I cry unto H2603
103: 8 The LORD *is* **m** and gracious, slow to H7349
116: 5 and righteous; yea, our God *is* **m**. H7355
117: 2 For his **m** kindness is great toward us: H2617
119:58 be **m** unto me according to thy word. H2603
76 Let, I pray thee, thy **m** kindness be for H2617
Ps119:132 Look thou upon me, and be **m** unto H2603
Prv 11:17 The **m** man doeth good to his own soul: H2617
Isa 57: 1 *it* to heart: and **m** men *are* taken away, H2617
Jer 3:12 you: for I *am* **m**, saith the LORD, *and* H2623
Joel 2:13 for he *is* gracious and **m**, slow to anger, H7349
Jna 4: 2 God, and **m**, slow to anger, and H7349
Mt 5: 7 Blessed *are* the **m**: for they shall obtain *G1655*
Lk 6:36 Be ye therefore **m**, as your Father also is *G3629*
36 merciful, as your Father also is **m**. *G3629*
18:13 saying, God be **m** to me a sinner. *G2433*
Heb 2:17 that he might be a **m** and faithful high *G1655*
8:12 For I will be **m** to their *G2436*

MERCURIUS
Act 14:12 **M**, because he was the chief speaker. *G2060*

MERCY
Gen 19:19 hast magnified thy **m**, which thou hast H2617
24:27 my master of his **m** and his truth: I H2617
39:21 and shewed him **m**, and gave him H2617
43:14 And God Almighty give you **m** before H7356
Ex 15:13 Thou in thy **m** hast led forth the people H2617
20: 6 And shewing **m** unto thousands of H2617
25:17 And thou shalt make a **m** seat *of* pure H3727
18 them, in the two ends of the **m** seat. H3727
19 end: *even* of the **m** seat shall ye make H3727
20 on high, covering the **m** seat with their H3727
20 toward the **m** seat shall the faces H3727
21 And thou shalt put the **m** seat above H3727
22 from above the **m** seat, from between H3727
26:34 And thou shalt put the **m** seat upon the H3727
30: 6 before the **m** seat that *is* over the H3727
31: 7 and the **m** seat that *is* thereupon, H3727
33:19 shew **m** on whom I will shew mercy. H7355
19 shew mercy on whom I will shew **m**. H7355
34: 7 Keeping **m** for thousands, forgiving H2617
35:12 the **m** seat, and the vail of the covering, H3727
37: 6 And he made the **m** seat *of* pure gold: H3727
7 he them, on the two ends of the **m** seat; H3727
8 that side: out of the **m** seat made he the H3727
9 wings over the **m** seat, with their faces H3727
9 *even* to the **m** seatward were the H3727
39:35 and the staves thereof, and the **m** seat, H3727
40:20 and put the **m** seat above upon the ark: H3727
Lev 16: 2 the vail before the **m** seat, which *is* H3727
2 appear in the cloud upon the **m** seat. H3727
13 may cover the **m** seat that *is* upon the H3727
14 finger upon the **m** seat eastward; and H3727
14 and before the **m** seat shall he sprinkle H3727
15 the **m** seat, and before the mercy seat: H3727
15 the mercy seat, and before the **m** seat: H3727
Nu 7:89 him from off the **m** seat that *was* upon H3727
14:18 and of great **m**, forgiving iniquity and H2617
19 the greatness of thy **m**, and as thou hast H2617
Dt 5:10 And shewing **m** unto thousands of H2617
7: 2 with them, nor shew **m** unto them: H2603
9 covenant and **m** with them that love H2617
12 the **m** which he sware unto thy fathers: H2617
13:17 and shew thee **m**, and have compassion H7356
Jdg 1:24 into the city, and we will shew thee **m**. H2617
2Sa 7:15 But my **m** shall not depart away from H2617
15:20 thy brethren: **m** and truth *be* with thee. H2617
22:51 and sheweth **m** to his anointed, unto H2617
1Ki 3: 6 my father great **m**, according as he H2617
8:23 covenant and **m** with thy servants that H2617
1Ch 16:34 *he is* good; for his **m** *endureth* for ever. H2617
41 because his **m** *endureth* for ever; H2617
17:13 I will not take my **m** away from him, as H2617
28:11 thereof, and of the place of the **m** seat, H3727
2Ch 1: 8 hast shewed great **m** unto David my H2617
5:13 *he is* good; for his **m** *endureth* for ever: H2617
6:14 and *shewest* **m** unto thy servants, that H2617
7: 3 *he is* good; for his **m** *endureth* for ever. H2617
6 because his **m** *endureth* for ever, when H2617
20:21 the LORD; for his **m** *endureth* for ever. H2617
Ezr 3:11 *he is* good, for his **m** *endureth* for ever H2617
7:28 And hath extended **m** unto me before H2617
9: 9 hath extended **m** unto us in the sight H2617
Neh 1: 5 covenant and **m** for them that love him H2617
11 and grant him **m** in the sight of this H7356
9:32 covenant and **m**, let not all the trouble H2617
13:22 me according to the greatness of thy **m**. H2617
Job 37:13 for correction, or for his land, or for **m**. H2617
Ps 4: 1 have **m** upon me, and hear my prayer. H2603
5: 7 multitude of thy **m**: *and* in thy fear will H2617
6: 2 Have **m** upon me, O LORD; for I *am* H2603
9:13 Have **m** upon me, O LORD; consider H2603
13: 5 But I have trusted in thy **m**; my heart H2617
18:50 and sheweth **m** to his anointed, to H2617

Ps 21: 7 and through the **m** of the most High he H2617
23: 6 Surely goodness and **m** shall follow me H2617
25: 7 according to thy **m** remember thou me H2617
10 All the paths of the LORD *are* **m** and H2617
16 Turn thee unto me, and have **m** upon H2603
27: 7 have **m** also upon me, and answer me. H2603
30:10 Hear, O LORD, and have **m** upon me: H2603
31: 7 I will be glad and rejoice in thy **m**: for H2617
9 Have **m** upon me, O LORD, for I am in H2603
32:10 the LORD, **m** shall compass him about. H2617
33:18 fear him, upon them that hope in his **m**; H2617
22 Let thy **m**, O LORD, be upon us, H2617
36: 5 Thy **m**, O LORD, *is* in the heavens; *and* H2617
37:21 the righteous sheweth **m**, and giveth. H2603
51: 1 Have **m** upon me, O God, according to H2603
52: 8 trust in the **m** of God for ever and ever. H2617
57: 3 shall send forth his **m** and his truth. H2617
10 For thy **m** *is* great unto the heavens, H2617
59:10 The God of my **m** shall prevent me: H2617
16 sing aloud of thy **m** in the morning: for H2617
17 *is* my defence, *and* the God of my **m**. H2617
61: 7 **m** and truth, *which* may preserve him. H2617
62:12 Also unto thee, O Lord, *belongeth* **m**: H2617
66:20 away my prayer, nor his **m** from me. H2617
69:13 the multitude of thy **m** hear me, in the H2617
77: 8 Is his **m** clean gone for ever? doth *his* H2617
85: 7 Shew us thy **m**, O LORD, and grant us H2617
10 **M** and truth are met together; H2617
86: 5 in **m** unto all them that call upon thee. H2617
13 For great *is* thy **m** toward me: and thou H2617
15 and plenteous in **m** and truth. H2617
16 O turn unto me, and have **m** upon me; H2603
89: 2 For I have said, **M** shall be built up for H2617
14 **m** and truth shall go before thy face. H2617
24 But my faithfulness and my **m** *shall be* H2617
28 My **m** will I keep for him for evermore, H2617
90:14 O satisfy us early with thy **m**; that we H2617
94:18 When I said, My foot slippeth; thy **m**, O H2617
98: 3 He hath remembered his **m** and his H2617
100: 5 For the LORD *is* good; his **m** *is* H2617
101: 1 I will sing of **m** and judgment: unto H2617
102:13 Thou shalt arise, *and* have **m** upon H7355
103: 8 slow to anger, and plenteous in **m**. H2617
11 is his **m** toward them that fear him. H2617
17 But the **m** of the LORD *is* from H2617
106: 1 *he is* good: for his **m** *endureth* for ever. H2617
107: 1 *he is* good: for his **m** *endureth* for ever. H2617
108: 4 For thy **m** *is* great above the heavens: H2617
109:12 Let there be none to extend **m** unto H2617
16 not to shew **m**, but persecuted the H2617
21 because thy **m** *is* good, deliver thou me. H2617
26 my God: O save me according to thy **m**: H2617
115: 1 for thy **m**, *and* for thy truth's sake. H2617
118: 1 good: because his **m** *endureth* for ever. H2617
2 Let Israel now say, that his **m** *endureth* H2617
3 now say, that his **m** *endureth* for ever. H2617
4 say, that his **m** *endureth* for ever. H2617
29 *he is* good: for his **m** *endureth* for ever. H2617
119:64 The earth, O LORD, is full of thy **m**: H2617
124 unto thy **m**, and teach me thy statutes. H2617
123: 2 our God, until that he have **m** upon us. H2603
3 Have **m** upon us, O LORD, have mercy H2603
3 Have mercy upon us, O LORD, have **m** H2603
130: 7 the LORD *there is* **m**, and with him *is* H2617
136: 1 *he is* good: for his **m** *endureth* for ever. H2617
2 of gods: for his **m** *endureth* for ever. H2617
3 of lords: for his **m** *endureth* for ever. H2617
4 wonders: for his **m** *endureth* for ever. H2617
5 heavens: for his **m** *endureth* for ever. H2617
6 the waters: for his **m** *endureth* for ever. H2617
7 lights: for his **m** *endureth* for ever: H2617
8 The sun to rule by day: for his **m** H2617
9 by night: for his **m** *endureth* for ever. H2617
10 firstborn: for his **m** *endureth* for ever: H2617
11 them: for his **m** *endureth* for ever: H2617
12 out arm: for his **m** *endureth* for ever. H2617
13 into parts: for his **m** *endureth* for ever: H2617
14 midst of it: for his **m** *endureth* for ever: H2617
15 Red sea: for his **m** *endureth* for ever. H2617
16 wilderness: for his **m** *endureth* for ever. H2617
17 kings: for his **m** *endureth* for ever: H2617
18 And slew famous kings: for his **m** H2617
19 Sihon king of the Amorites: for his **m** H2617
20 And Og the king of Bashan: for his **m** H2617
21 heritage: for his **m** *endureth* for ever: H2617
22 servant: for his **m** *endureth* for ever. H2617
23 low estate: for his **m** *endureth* for ever: H2617
24 enemies: for his **m** *endureth* for ever. H2617
25 Who giveth food to all flesh: for his **m** H2617
Ps 136:26 of heaven: for his **m** *endureth* for ever. H2617
138: 8 me: thy **m**, O LORD, *endureth* H2617
143:12 And of thy **m** cut off mine enemies, H2617
145: 8 slow to anger, and of great **m**. H2617
147:11 fear him, in those that hope in his **m**. H2617
Prv 3: 3 Let not **m** and truth forsake thee: bind H2617
14:21 that hath **m** on the poor, happy *is* he. H2603
22 Do they not err that devise evil? but **m** H2617
31 honoureth him hath **m** on the poor. H2603
16: 6 By **m** and truth iniquity is purged: and H2617
20:28 **M** and truth preserve the king: and his H2617
28 king: and his throne is upholden by **m**. H2617
21:21 and **m** findeth life, righteousness, H2617
28:13 and forsaketh *them* shall have **m**. H7355
Isa 9:17 neither shall have **m** on their fatherless H7355
14: 1 For the LORD will have **m** on Jacob, H7355
16: 5 And in **m** shall the throne be H2617
27:11 will not have **m** on them, and he that H7355
30:18 that he may have **m** upon you: for the H7355
47: 6 shew them no **m**; upon the ancient hast H7356
49:10 for he that hath **m** on them shall lead H7355
13 and will have **m** upon his afflicted. H7355
54: 8 will I have **m** on thee, saith the LORD H7355
10 saith the LORD that hath **m** on thee. H7355
55: 7 and he will have **m** upon him; and to H7355
60:10 but in my favour have I had **m** on thee. H7355
Jer 6:23 and have no **m**; their voice roareth H7355
13:14 spare, nor have **m**, but destroy them. H7355
21: 7 them, neither have pity, nor have **m**. H7355
30:18 Jacob's tents, and have **m** on his H7355
31:20 have **m** upon him, saith the LORD. H7355
33:11 *is* good; for his **m** *endureth* for ever: H2617
26 to return, and have **m** on them. H7355
42:12 that he may have **m** upon you, and H7355
50:42 and will not shew **m**: their voice shall H7355
Ezk 39:25 of Jacob, and have **m** upon the whole H7355
Dan 4:27 by shewing **m** to the poor; if it may H2604
9: 4 the covenant and **m** to them that love H2617
Hos 1: 6 will no more have **m** upon the house of H7355
7 But I will have **m** upon the house of H7355
2: 4 And I will not have **m** upon her H7355
23 and I will have **m** upon her that had H7355
23 obtained **m**; and I will H3808+H7355+H3819
4: 1 **m**, nor knowledge of God in the land. H2617
6: 6 For I desired **m**, and not sacrifice; and H2617
10:12 reap in **m**; break up your fallow H2617
12: 6 Therefore turn thou to thy God: keep **m** H2617
14: 3 for in thee the fatherless findeth **m**. H7355
Jna 2: 8 lying vanities forsake their own **m**. H2617
Mic 6: 8 **m**, and to walk humbly with thy God? H2617
7:18 for ever, because he delighteth *in* **m**. H2617
20 to Jacob, *and* the **m** to Abraham, which H2617
Hab 3: 2 make known; in wrath remember **m**. H7355
Zec 1:12 wilt thou not have **m** on Jerusalem and H7355
7: 9 and shew **m** and compassions every H2617
10: 6 them; for I have **m** upon them: and H7355
Mt 5: 7 the merciful: for they shall obtain **m**. G1653
9:13 I will have **m**, and not sacrifice: for G1656
27 *Thou* son of David, have **m** on us. G1653
12: 7 I will have **m**, and not sacrifice, ye G1656
15:22 him, saying, Have **m** on me, O Lord, G1653
17:15 Lord, have **m** on my son: for he is G1653
20:30 **m** on us, O Lord, *thou* son of David. G1653
31 **m** on us, O Lord, *thou* son of David. G1653
23:23 the law, judgment, **m**, and faith: these G1656
Mk 10:47 *thou* son of David, have **m** on me. G1653
48 *Thou* son of David, have **m** on me. G1653
Lk 1:50 And his **m** *is* on them that fear him G1656
54 Israel, in remembrance of *his* **m**; G1656
58 **m** upon her; and they rejoiced with her. G1656
72 To perform the **m** *promised* to our G1656
78 Through the tender **m** of our God; G4698
10:37 And he said, He that shewed **m** on him. G1656
16:24 Abraham, have **m** on me, and send G1653
17:13 and said, Jesus, Master, have **m** on us. G1653
18:38 *thou* son of David, have **m** on me. G1653
39 *Thou* son of David, have **m** on me. G1653
Ro 9:15 For he saith to Moses, I will have **m** on G1653
15 on whom I will have **m**, and I will have G1653
16 runneth, but of God that sheweth **m**. G1653
18 Therefore hath he **m** on whom he will G1653
18 *have* **m**, and whom he will he hardeneth.
23 on the vessels of **m**, which he had afore G1656
11:30 now obtained **m** through their unbelief: G1653
31 your **m** they also may obtain mercy. G1656
31 your mercy they also may obtain **m**. G1653
32 that he might have **m** upon all. G1653
12: 8 he that sheweth **m**, with cheerfulness. G1653
15: 9 glorify God for *his* **m**; as it is written, G1656
1Co 7:25 obtained **m** of the Lord to be faithful. G1653
2Co 4: 1 as we have received **m**, we faint not; G1653
Gal 6:16 and **m**, and upon the Israel of God. G1656
Eph 2: 4 But God, who is rich in **m**, for his great G1656
Php 2:27 but God had **m** on him; and not on G1653
1Ti 1: 2 in the faith: Grace, **m**, *and* peace, from G1656
13 but I obtained **m**, because I did *it* G1653
16 Howbeit for this cause I obtained **m**, G1653
2Ti 1: 2 son: Grace, **m**, *and* peace, from God G1656
16 The Lord give **m** unto the house of G1656
18 that he may find **m** of the Lord in that G1656
Tit 1: 4 faith: Grace, **m**, *and* peace, from God G1656
3: 5 according to his **m** he saved us, by the G1656
Heb 4:16 we may obtain **m**, and find grace to G1656
10:28 **m** under two or three witnesses: G3628
Jas 2:13 For he shall have judgment without **m**, G448
13 hath shewed no **m**; and mercy rejoiceth G1656
13 and **m** rejoiceth against judgment. G1656
3:17 be entreated, full of **m** and good fruits, G1656
5:11 the Lord is very pitiful, and of tender **m**. G3629
1Pt 1: 3 to his abundant **m** hath begotten us G1656
2:10 **m**, but now have obtained mercy. G1653
10 mercy, but now have obtained **m**. G1653
2Jn 3 Grace be with you, **m**, *and* peace, from G1656
Jude 2 **M** unto you, and peace, and love, be G1656
21 looking for the **m** of our Lord Jesus G1656

MERCYSEAT
Heb 9: 5 shadowing the **m**; of which we cannot G2435

MERED
1Ch 4:17 *were*, Jether, and **M**, and Epher, and H4778
18 daughter of Pharaoh, which **M** took. H4778

MEREMOTH
Ezr 8:33 by the hand of **M** the son of Uriah the H4822
10:36 Vaniah, **M**, Eliashib, H4822
Neh 3: 4 And next unto them repaired **M** the H4822
21 After him repaired **M** the son of Urijah H4822
10: 5 Harim, **M**, Obadiah, H4822
12: 3 Shechaniah, Rehum, **M**, H4822

MERES
Est 1:14 Tarshish, **M**, Marsena, *and* Memucan, H4825

MERIBAH
Ex 17: 7 Massah, and **M**, because of the chiding H4809
Nu 20:13 This *is* the water of **M**; because the H4809
24 against my word at the water of **M**. H4809
27:14 **M** in Kadesh in the wilderness of Zin. H4809
Dt 33: 8 thou didst strive at the waters of **M**; H4809
Ps 81: 7 I proved thee at the waters of **M**. Selah. H4809

MERIBAH-KADESH
Dt 32:51 at the waters of **M**, in the H4809+H6946

MERIB-BAAL
1Ch 8:34 And the son of Jonathan *was* **M**; and H4807
34 *was* Merib-baal; and **M** begat Micah. H4807
9:40 And the son of Jonathan *was* **M**: and H4807
40 *was* Merib-baal: and **M** begat Micah. H4810

MERODACH
Jer 50: 2 is confounded, **M** is broken in pieces; H4781

MERODACH-BALADAN
Isa 39: 1 At that time **M**, the son of Baladan, H4757

MEROM
Jos 11: 5 the waters of **M**, to fight against Israel. H4792
7 **M** suddenly; and they fell upon them. H4792

MERON See SHIMRON-MERON and MERONOTHITE.

MERONOTHITE
1Ch 27:30 and over the asses *was* Jehdeiah the **M**: H4824
Neh 3: 7 and Jadon the **M**, the men of Gibeon, H4824

MEROZ
Jdg 5:23 Curse ye **M**, said the angel of the LORD, H4789

MERRILY
Est 5:14 then go thou in **m** with the king unto H8056

MERRY
Gen 43:34 And they drank, and were **m** with him. H7937
Jdg 9:27 *grapes*, and made **m**, and went into the H1974
16:25 their hearts were **m**, that they said, Call H2896
19: 6 tarry all night, and let thine heart be **m**. H3190

Jdg 19: 9 heart may be **m**; and to morrow get H3190
22 their hearts **m**, behold, the men of H3190
Ru 3: 7 and his heart was **m**, he went to lie H3190
1Sa 25:36 Nabal's heart *was* **m** within him, for he H2896
2Sa 13:28 Amnon's heart is **m** with wine, and H2896
1Ki 4:20 eating and drinking, and making **m**. H8056
21: 7 let thine heart be **m**: I will give thee the H3190
2Ch 7:10 their tents, glad and **m** in heart for the H2896
Est 1:10 heart of the king was **m** with wine, he H2896
Prv 15:13 A **m** heart maketh a cheerful H8056
15 is of a **m** heart *hath* a continual feast. H2896
17:22 A **m** heart doeth good *like* a medicine: H8056
Ecc 8:15 drink, and to be **m**: for that shall abide H8055
9: 7 thy wine with a **m** heart; for God now H2896
10:19 **m**: but money answereth all *things*. H8055
Jer 30:19 them that make **m**: and I will multiply H7832
31: 4 in the dances of them that make **m**. H7832
Lk 12:19 take thine ease, eat, drink, *and* be **m**. *G2165*
15:23 calf, and kill *it*; and let us eat, and be **m**: *G2165*
24 and is found. And they began to be **m**. *G2165*
29 that I might make **m** with my friends: *G2165*
32 It was meet that we should make **m**, *G2165*
Jas 5:13 pray. Is any **m**? let him sing psalms. *G2114*
Rev 11:10 them, and make **m**, and shall send gifts *G2165*

MERRYHEARTED
Isa 24: 7 languisheth, all the **m** do sigh. H8056+H3820

MESECH
Ps 120: 5 Woe is me, that I sojourn in **M**, *that* I H4902

MESHA
Gen 10:30 And their dwelling was from **M**, as thou H4852
2Ki 3: 4 And **M** king of Moab was a H4338
1Ch 2:42 Jerahmeel *were*, **M** his firstborn, which H4337
8: 9 and Zibia, and **M**, and Malcham, H4331

MESHACH
Dan 1: 7 of **M**; and to Azariah, of Abed-nego. H4335
2:49 he set Shadrach, **M**, and Abed-nego, H4336
3:12 Shadrach, **M**, and Abed-nego; these H4336
13 to bring Shadrach, **M**, and Abed-nego. H4336
14 *it* true, O Shadrach, **M**, and Abed-nego, H4336
16 Shadrach, **M**, and Abed-nego, H4336
19 against Shadrach, **M**, and Abed-nego: H4336
20 to bind Shadrach, **M**, and Abed-nego, H4336
22 took up Shadrach, **M**, and Abed-nego. H4336
23 And these three men, Shadrach, **M**, and H4336
26 said, Shadrach, **M**, and Abed-nego, ye H4336
26 Then Shadrach, **M**, and Abed-nego, H4336
28 God of Shadrach, **M**, and Abed-nego, H4336
29 God of Shadrach, **M**, and Abed-nego, H4336
30 Then the king promoted Shadrach, **M**, H4336

MESHECH
Gen 10: 2 Javan, and Tubal, and **M**, and Tiras. H4902
1Ch 1: 5 Javan, and Tubal, and **M**, and Tiras. H4902
17 and Uz, and Hul, and Gether, and **M**. H4902
Ezk 27:13 Javan, Tubal, and **M**, they *were* thy H4902
32:26 There *is* **M**, Tubal, and all her H4902
38: 2 the chief prince of **M** and Tubal, and H4902
3 O Gog, the chief prince of **M** and Tubal: H4902
39: 1 O Gog, the chief prince of **M** and Tubal: H4902

MESHELEMIAH
1Ch 9:21 *And* Zechariah the son of **M** *was* porter H4920
26: 1 the Korhites *was* **M** the son of Kore, of H4920
2 And the sons of **M** *were*, Zechariah the H4920
9 And **M** had sons and brethren, strong H4920

MESHEZABEEL
Neh 3: 4 the son of **M**. And next unto them H4898
10:21 **M**, Zadok, Jaddua, H4898
11:24 And Pethahiah the son of **M**, of the H4898

MESHILLEMITH
1Ch 9:12 the son of **M**, the son of Immer; H4921

MESHILLEMOTH
2Ch 28:12 the son of **M**, and Jehizkiah the son H4919
Neh 11:13 Ahasai, the son of **M**, the son of Immer, H4919

MESHOBAB
1Ch 4:34 And **M**, and Jamlech, and Joshah the H4877

MESHULLAM
2Ki 22: 3 the son of **M**, the scribe, to the house H4918
1Ch 3:19 of Zerubbabel; **M**, and Hananiah, and H4918
5:13 Michael, and **M**, and Sheba, and Jorai, H4918
8:17 And Zebadiah, and **M**, and Hezeki, and H4918
9: 7 Sallu the son of **M**, the son of Hodaviah, H4918
8 son of Michri, and **M** the son of H4918
11 the son of **M**, the son of Zadok, the H4918
12 the son of **M**, the son of Meshillemith, H4918
2Ch 34:12 and Zechariah and **M**, of the sons of the H4918
Ezr 8:16 and for **M**, chief men; also for H4918
10:15 this *matter*: and **M** and Shabbethai the H4918
29 And of the sons of Bani; **M**, Malluch, H4918
Neh 3: 4 them repaired **M** the son of Berechiah, H4918
6 of Paseah, and **M** the son of Besodeiah; H4918
30 him repaired **M** the son of Berechiah H4918
6:18 the daughter of **M** the son of Berechiah. H4918
8: 4 and Hashbadana, Zechariah, *and* **M**. H4918
10: 7 **M**, Abijah, Mijamin, H4918
20 Magpiash, **M**, Hezir, H4918
11: 7 Sallu the son of **M**, the son of Joed, the H4918
11 the son of **M**, the son of Zadok, the H4918
12:13 Of Ezra, **M**; of Amariah, Jehohanan; H4918
16 Of Iddo, Zechariah; of Ginnethon, **M**; H4918
25 Obadiah, **M**, Talmon, Akkub, *were* H4918
33 And Azariah, Ezra, and **M**, H4918

MESHULLEMETH
2Ki 21:19 **M**, the daughter of Haruz of Jotbah. H4922

MESOBAITE
1Ch 11:47 Eliel, and Obed, and Jasiel the **M**. H4677

MESOPOTAMIA
Gen 24:10 and went to **M**, unto the city of Nahor. H763
Dt 23: 4 son of Beor of Pethor of **M**, to curse thee. H763
Jdg 3: 8 king of **M**: and the children of H763
10 king of **M** into his hand; and his H758
1Ch 19: 6 and horsemen out of **M**, and out of H763
Act 2: 9 the dwellers in **M**, and in Judaea, and *G3318*
7: 2 was in **M**, before he dwelt in Charran, *G3318*

MESS
Gen 43:34 but Benjamin's **m** was five times so H4864
2Sa 11: 8 him a **m** *of meat* from the king. H4864

MESSAGE
Jdg 3:20 said, I have a **m** from God unto thee. H1697
1Ki 20:12 heard this **m**, as he *was* drinking, H1697
Prv 26: 6 He that sendeth a **m** by the hand of a H1697
Hag 1:13 in the LORD'S **m** unto the people, H4400
Lk 19:14 him, and sent a **m** after him, saying, *G4242*
1Jn 1: 5 This then is the **m** which we have heard *G1860*
3:11 For this is the **m** that ye heard from the *G31*

MESSENGER
Gen 50:16 And they sent a **m** unto Joseph, saying, H6680
1Sa 4:17 And the **m** answered and said, Israel is H1319
23:27 But there came a **m** unto Saul, saying, H4397
2Sa 11:19 And charged the **m**, saying, When thou H4397
22 So the **m** went, and came and shewed H4397
23 And the **m** said unto David, Surely the H4397
25 Then David said unto the **m**, Thus shalt H4397
15:13 And there came a **m** to David, saying, H5046
1Ki 19: 2 Then Jezebel sent a **m** unto Elijah, H4397
22:13 And the **m** that was gone to call H4397
2Ki 5:10 And Elisha sent a **m** unto him, saying, H4397
6:32 him: but ere the **m** came to him, he H4397
32 look, when the **m** cometh, shut the H4397
33 them, behold, the **m** came down unto H4397
9:18 told, saying, The **m** came to them, but H4397
10: 8 And there came a **m**, and told him, H4397
2Ch 18:12 And the **m** that went to call Micaiah H4397
Job 1:14 And there came a **m** unto Job, and H4397
33:23 If there be a **m** with him, an H4397
Prv 13:17 A wicked **m** falleth into mischief: but a H4397
17:11 a cruel **m** shall be sent against him. H4397
25:13 *so is* a faithful **m** to them that send H6735
Isa 42:19 or deaf, as my **m** *that* I sent? who *is* H4397
Jer 51:31 another, and one **m** to meet another, to H5046
Ezk 23:40 far, unto whom a **m** *was* sent; and, lo, H4397
Hag 1:13 Then spake Haggai the LORD'S **m** in H4397
Mal 2: 7 for he *is* the **m** of the LORD of hosts. H4397
3: 1 Behold, I will send my **m**, and he shall H4397
1 his temple, even the **m** of the covenant, H4397
Mt 11:10 Behold, I send my **m** before thy face, *G32*
Mk 1: 2 Behold, I send my **m** before thy face, *G32*
Lk 7:27 Behold, I send my **m** before thy face, *G32*
2Co 12: 7 in the flesh, the **m** of Satan to buffet me, *G32*
Php 2:25 **m**, and he that ministered to my wants. *G652*

MESSENGERS
Gen 32: 3 And Jacob sent **m** before him to Esau H4397
32: 6 And the **m** returned to Jacob, saying, H4397
Nu 20:14 And Moses sent **m** from Kadesh unto H4397
21:21 And Israel sent **m** unto Sihon king of H4397
22: 5 He sent **m** therefore unto Balaam the H4397
24:12 **m** which thou sentest unto me, saying, H4397
Dt 2:26 And I sent **m** out of the wilderness of H4397
Jos 6:17 because she hid the **m** that we sent. H4397
25 **m**, which Joshua sent to spy out Jericho. H4397
7:22 So Joshua sent **m**, and they ran unto the H4397
Jdg 6:35 And he sent **m** throughout all H4397
35 him: and he sent **m** unto Asher, and H4397
7:24 And Gideon sent **m** throughout all H4397
9:31 And he sent **m** unto Abimelech privily, H4397
11:12 And Jephthah sent **m** unto the king of H4397
13 unto the **m** of Jephthah, Because H4397
14 And Jephthah sent **m** again unto the H4397
17 Then Israel sent **m** unto the king of H4397
19 And Israel sent **m** unto Sihon king of H4397
1Sa 6:21 And they sent **m** to the inhabitants of H4397
11: 3 that we may send **m** unto all the coasts H4397
4 Then came the **m** to Gibeah of Saul, H4397
7 by the hands of **m**, saying, Whosoever H4397
9 And they said unto the **m** that came, H4397
9 help. And the **m** came and shewed *it* H4397
16:19 Wherefore Saul sent **m** unto Jesse, and H4397
19:11 Saul also sent **m** unto David's house, to H4397
14 And when Saul sent **m** to take David, H4397
15 And Saul sent the **m** *again* to see H4397
16 And when the **m** were come in, behold, H4397
20 And Saul sent **m** to take David: and H4397
20 **m** of Saul, and they also prophesied. H4397
21 he sent other **m**, and they prophesied H4397
21 And Saul sent **m** again the third time, H4397
25:14 David sent **m** out of the wilderness H4397
42 the **m** of David, and became his wife. H4397
2Sa 2: 5 And David sent **m** unto the men of H4397
3:12 And Abner sent **m** to David on his H4397
14 And David sent **m** to Ish-bosheth H4397
26 David, he sent **m** after Abner, which H4397
5:11 And Hiram king of Tyre sent **m** to H4397
11: 4 And David sent **m**, and took her; and H4397
12:27 And Joab sent **m** to David, and said, I H4397
1Ki 20: 2 And he sent **m** to Ahab king of Israel H4397
5 And the **m** came again, and said, Thus H4397
9 Wherefore he said unto the **m** of H4397
9 may not do. And the **m** departed, and H4397
2Ki 1: 2 was sick: and he sent **m**, and said unto H4397
3 go up to meet the **m** of the king of H4397
5 And when the **m** turned back unto him, H4397
16 as thou hast sent **m** to inquire of H4397
7:15 And the **m** returned, and told the king. H4397
14: 8 Then Amaziah sent **m** to Jehoash, the H4397
16: 7 So Ahaz sent **m** to Tiglath-pileser king H4397
17: 4 for he had sent **m** to So king of Egypt, H4397
19: 9 he sent **m** again unto Hezekiah, saying, H4397
14 of the hand of the **m**, and read it: and H4397
23 By thy **m** thou hast reproached the H4397
1Ch 14: 1 Now Hiram king of Tyre sent **m** to H4397
19: 2 me. And David sent **m** to comfort him H4397
16 Israel, they sent **m**, and drew forth the H4397
2Ch 36:15 to them by his **m**, rising up betimes, H4397
16 But they mocked the **m** of God, and H4397
Neh 6: 3 And I sent **m** unto them, saying, I *am* H4397
Prv 16:14 The wrath of a king *is as* **m** of death: H4397
Isa 14:32 What shall *one* then answer the **m** of H4397
18: 2 Go, ye swift **m**, to a nation scattered H4397
37: 9 heard *it*, he sent **m** to Hezekiah, saying, H4397
14 the hand of the **m**, and read it: and H4397
44:26 the counsel of his **m**; that saith to H4397
57: 9 and didst send thy **m** far off, and didst H6735
Jer 27: 3 by the hand of the **m** which come to H4397
Ezk 23:16 and sent **m** unto them into Chaldea. H4397
30: 9 In that day shall **m** go forth from me in H4397
Nah 2:13 voice of thy **m** shall no more be heard. H4397
Lk 7:24 And when the **m** of John were departed, *G32*
9:52 And sent **m** before his face: and they *G32*
2Co 8:23 of, they are the **m** of the churches, *and* *G652*
Jas 2:25 **m**, and had sent *them* out another way? *G32*

MESSES
Gen 43:34 And he took *and sent* **m** unto them H4864

MESSIAH
Dan 9:25 unto the **M** the Prince *shall be* H4899
26 two weeks shall **M** be cut off, but not H4899

MESSIAS
Jn 1:41 We have found the **M**, which is, being *G3323*
4:25 him, I know that **M** cometh, which is *G3323*

MET
Gen 32: 1 his way, and the angels of God **m** him. H6293
33: 8 all this drove which I **m**? And he said, H6298
Ex 3:18 the Hebrews hath **m** with us: and now H7136
4:24 LORD **m** him, and sought to kill him. H6298
27 And he went, and **m** him in the mount H6298
5: 3 the Hebrews hath **m** with us: let us go, H7122
20 And they **m** Moses and Aaron, who H6293
Nu 23: 4 And God **m** Balaam: and he said unto H7136
16 And the LORD **m** Balaam, and put a H7136
Dt 23: 4 Because they **m** you not with bread and H6923
25:18 How he **m** thee by the way, and smote H7136
Jos 11: 5 And when all these kings were **m** H3259
17:10 border; and they **m** together in Asher H6293
1Sa 10:10 of prophets **m** him; and the spirit H7125
25:20 down against her; and she **m** them. H6298
2Sa 2:13 went out, and **m** together by the pool H6298
16: 1 of Mephibosheth **m** him, with a couple H7125
18: 9 And Absalom **m** the servants of David. H7122
1Ki 13:24 And when he was gone, a lion **m** him H4672
18: 7 behold, Elijah **m** him: and he knew H7125
2Ki 9:21 against Jehu, and **m** him in the portion H4672
10:13 Jehu **m** with the brethren of Ahaziah H4672
Neh 13: 2 Because they **m** not the children of H6923
Ps 85:10 Mercy and truth are **m** together; H6298
Prv 7:10 And, behold, there **m** him a woman H7125
Jer 41: 6 to pass, as he **m** them, he said unto H6298
Am 5:19 a lion, and a bear **m** him; or went into H6293
Mt 8:28 Gergesenes, there **m** him two possessed G5221
28: 9 behold, Jesus **m** them, saying, All hail. G528
Mk 5: 2 immediately there **m** him out of the G528
11: 4 where two ways **m**; and they loose him. G296
Lk 8:27 to land, there **m** him out of the city G5221
9:37 from the hill, much people **m** him. G4876
17:12 village, there **m** him ten men that were G528
Jn 4:51 down, his servants **m** him, and told *him*, G528
11:20 **m** him: but Mary sat *still* in the house. G5221
30 was in that place where Martha **m** him. G5221
12:18 For this cause the people also **m** him, G5221
Act 10:25 in, Cornelius **m** him, and fell down G4876
16:16 spirit of divination **m** us, which brought G528
17:17 daily with them that **m** with him. G3909
20:14 And when he **m** with us at Assos, we G4820
27:41 where two seas **m**, they ran the ship G1337
Heb 7: 1 high God, who **m** Abraham returning G4876
10 of his father, when Melchisedec **m** him. G4876

METE
Ex 16:18 And when they did **m** *it* with an omer, H4058
Ps 60: 6 and **m** out the valley of Succoth. H4058
108: 7 and **m** out the valley of Succoth. H4058
Mt 7: 2 ye **m**, it shall be measured to you again. G3354
Mk 4:24 with what measure ye **m**, it shall be G3354
Lk 6:38 measure that ye **m** withal it shall be G3354

METED
Isa 18: 2 hitherto; a nation **m** out and trodden H6978
7 hitherto; a nation **m** out and trodden H6978
40:12 of his hand, and **m** out heaven with the H8505

METEYARD
Lev 19:35 in **m**, in weight, or in measure. H4060

METHEG-AMMAH
2Sa 8: 1 **M** out of the hand of the Philistines. H4965

METHUSAEL
Gen 4:18 begat **M**: and Methusael begat Lamech. H4967
18 begat Methusael: and **M** begat Lamech. H4967

METHUSELAH
Gen 5:21 lived sixty and five years, and begat **M**: H4968
22 after he begat **M** three hundred years, H4968
25 And **M** lived an hundred eighty and H4968
26 And **M** lived after he begat Lamech H4968
27 And all the days of **M** were nine H4968
1Ch 1: 3 Henoch, **M**, Lamech, H4968

MEUNIM
Neh 7:52 The children of Besai, the children of **M**, H4586

MEZAHAB
Gen 36:39 daughter of Matred, the daughter of **M**. H4314
1Ch 1:50 daughter of Matred, the daughter of **M**. H4314

MIAMIN
Ezr 10:25 and Malchiah, and **M**, and Eleazar, and H4326
Neh 12: 5 **M**, Maadiah, Bilgah, H4326

MIBHAR
1Ch 11:38 Joel the brother of Nathan, **M** the son H4006

MIBSAM
Gen 25:13 and Kedar, and Adbeel, and **M**, H4017
1Ch 1:29 then Kedar, and Adbeel, and **M**, H4017
4:25 Shallum his son, **M** his son, Mishma H4017

MIBZAR
Gen 36:42 Duke Kenaz, duke Teman, duke **M**, H4014
1Ch 1:53 Duke Kenaz, duke Teman, duke **M**, H4014

MICAH
Jdg 17: 1 of mount Ephraim, whose name *was* **M**. H4321
4 image: and they were in the house of **M**. H4321
5 And the man **M** had an house of gods, H4318
8 to the house of **M**, as he journeyed. H4318
9 And **M** said unto him, Whence comest H4318
10 And **M** said unto him, Dwell with me, H4318
12 And **M** consecrated the Levite; and the H4318
12 his priest, and was in the house of **M**. H4318
13 Then said **M**, Now know I that the H4318
18: 2 to the house of **M**, they lodged there. H4318
3 When they *were* by the house of **M**, they H4318
4 and thus dealeth **M** with me, and hath H4318
13 and came unto the house of **M**. H4318
15 unto the house of **M**, and saluted him. H4318
22 from the house of **M**, the men that *were* H4318
23 and said unto **M**, What aileth thee, that H4318
26 way: and when **M** saw that they *were* H4318
27 And they took *the things* which **M** had H4318
1Ch 5: 5 **M** his son, Reaia his son, Baal his son, H4318
8:34 Merib-baal; and Merib-baal begat **M**. H4318
35 And the sons of **M** *were*, Pithon, and H4318
9:15 **M**, the son of Zichri, the son of Asaph; H4316
40 Merib-baal: and Merib-baal begat **M**. H4318
41 And the sons of **M** *were*, Pithon, and H4318
2Ch 34:20 Abdon the son of **M**, and Shaphan the H4318
Jer 26:18 **M** the Morasthite prophesied in the H4320
Mic 1: 1 The word of the LORD that came to **M** H4318

MICAH'S
Jdg 18:18 And these went into **M** house, and H4318
22 houses near to **M** house were gathered H4318
31 And they set them up **M** graven image, H4318

MICAIAH
1Ki 22: 8 *is* yet one man, **M** the son of Imlah, by H4321
9 said, Hasten *hither* **M** the son of Imlah. H4321
13 was gone to call **M** spake unto him, H4321
14 And **M** said, *As* the LORD liveth, what H4321
15 said unto him, **M**, shall we go against H4321
24 near, and smote **M** on the cheek, and H4321
25 And **M** said, Behold, thou shalt see in H4321
26 And the king of Israel said, Take **M**, H4321
28 And **M** said, If thou return at all in H4321
2Ch 18: 7 evil: the same *is* **M** the son of Imla. And H4321
8 said, Fetch quickly **M** the son of Imla. H4319
12 And the messenger that went to call **M** H4321
13 And **M** said, *As* the LORD liveth, even H4321
14 king said unto him, **M**, shall we go to H4318
23 near, and smote **M** upon the cheek, H4321
24 And **M** said, Behold, thou shalt see on H4321
25 Then the king of Israel said, Take ye **M**, H4321
27 And **M** said, If thou certainly return in H4321

MICE
1Sa 6: 4 and five golden **m**, *according to* the H5909
5 images of your **m** that mar the land; H5909
11 the coffer with the **m** of gold and the H5909
18 And the golden **m**, *according to* the H5909

MICHA
2Sa 9:12 whose name *was* **M**. And all that dwelt H4316
Neh 10:11 **M**, Rehob, Hashabiah, H4316
11:17 And Mattaniah the son of **M**, the son of H4316
22 the son of **M**. Of the sons of Asaph, H4316

MICHAEL
Nu 13:13 the tribe of Asher, Sethur the son of **M**. H4317
1Ch 5:13 fathers *were*, **M**, and Meshullam, and H4317
14 of Gilead, the son of **M**, the son of H4317
6:40 The son of **M**, the son of Baaseiah, the H4317
7: 3 sons of Izrahiah; **M**, and Obadiah, and H4317
8:16 And **M**, and Ispah, and Joha, the sons H4317
12:20 and Jediael, and **M**, and Jozabad, and H4317
27:18 David: of Issachar, Omri the son of **M**: H4317
2Ch 21: 2 and Azariah, and **M**, and Shephatiah: H4317
Ezr 8: 8 of **M**, and with him fourscore males. H4317
Dan 10:13 twenty days: but, lo, **M**, one of the chief H4317
21 me in these things, but **M** your prince. H4317
12: 1 And at that time shall **M** stand up, the H4317
Jude 9 Yet **M** the archangel, when contending G3413
Rev 12: 7 And there was war in heaven: **M** and G3413

MICHAH
1Ch 23:20 Of the sons of Uzziel; **M** the first, and H4318
24:24 *Of* the sons of Uzziel; **M**: of the sons of H4318
24 Michah: of the sons of **M**; Shamir. H4318
25 The brother of **M** *was* Isshiah: of the H4318

MICHAIAH
2Ki 22:12 Achbor the son of **M**, and Shaphan the H4320
2Ch 13: 2 name also *was* **M** the daughter of Uriel H4322
17: 7 and to **M**, to teach in the cities of Judah. H4322
Neh 12:35 **M**, the son of Zaccur, the son of Asaph: H4320
41 Miniamin, **M**, Elioenai, Zechariah, H4320
Jer 36:11 When **M** the son of Gemariah, the son H4321
13 Then **M** declared unto them all the H4321

MICHAL
1Sa 14:49 Merab, and the name of the younger **M**: H4324
18:20 And **M** Saul's daughter loved David: H4324
27 Saul gave him **M** his daughter to wife. H4324
28 and *that* **M** Saul's daughter loved him. H4324
19:11 the morning: and **M** David's wife told H4324
12 So **M** let David down through a H4324
13 And **M** took an image, and laid *it* in the H4324
17 And Saul said unto **M**, Why hast thou H4324
17 is escaped? And **M** answered Saul, He H4324
25:44 But Saul had given **M** his daughter, H4324
2Sa 3:13 thou first bring **M** Saul's daughter, H4324
14 *me* my wife **M**, which I espoused to H4324
6:16 the city of David, **M** Saul's daughter H4324
20 household. And **M** the daughter of Saul H4324
21 And David said unto **M**, *It was* before H4324
23 Therefore **M** the daughter of Saul had H4324
21: 8 the five sons of **M** the daughter of Saul, H4324
1Ch 15:29 city of David, that **M** the daughter of H4324

MICHMAS
Ezr 2:27 The men of **M**, an hundred twenty and H4363
Neh 7:31 The men of **M**, an hundred and twenty H4363

MICHMASH
1Sa 13: 2 were with Saul in **M** and in mount H4363
5 pitched in **M**, eastward from Beth-aven. H4363
11 gathered themselves together at **M**; H4363
16 but the Philistines encamped in **M**. H4363
23 went out to the passage of **M**. H4363
14: 5 over against **M**, and the other H4363
31 that day from **M** to Aijalon: and the H4363
Neh 11:31 Geba *dwelt* at **M**, and Aija, and Beth-el, H4363
Isa 10:28 at **M** he hath laid up his carriages: H4363

MICHMETHAH
Jos 16: 6 toward the sea to **M** on the north side; H4366
17: 7 was from Asher to **M**, that *lieth* before H4366

MICHRI
1Ch 9: 8 of Uzzi, the son of **M**, and Meshullam H4381

MICHTAM
Ps 16:ttl **M** of David. H4387
56:ttl **M** of David, when the H4387
57:ttl To the chief Musician, Al-taschith, **M** H4387
58:ttl To the chief Musician, Al-taschith, **M** H4387
59:ttl To the chief Musician, Al-taschith, **M** H4387
60:ttl Shushan-eduth, **M** of David, to teach; H4387

MIDDAY
1Ki 18:29 And it came to pass, when **m** was past, H6672
Neh 8: 3 until **m**, before the men H4276+H3117
Act 26:13 At **m**, O king, I saw in the way a G2250+G3319

MIDDIN
Jos 15:61 In the wilderness, Beth-arabah, **M**, and H4081

MIDDLE
Ex 26:28 And the **m** bar in the midst of the H8484
36:33 And he made the **m** bar to shoot H8484
Jos 12: 2 and from the **m** of the river, and from H8432
Jdg 7:19 the beginning of the **m** watch; and they H8484
9:37 people down by the **m** of the land, and H2872
16:29 And Samson took hold of the two **m** H8432
1Sa 25:29 he sling out, *as out* of the **m** of a sling. H8432
2Sa 10: 4 their garments in the **m**, *even* to their H2677
1Ki 6: 6 broad, and the **m** *was* six cubits broad, H8484

1Ki 6: 8 The door for the **m** chamber *was* in the H8484
8 stairs into the **m** *chamber*, and out of H8484
8 and out of the **m** into the third. H8484
8:64 king hallow the **m** of the court that *was* H8432
2Ki 20: 4 was gone out into the **m** court, that the H8484
2Ch 7: 7 Moreover Solomon hallowed the **m** of H8432
Jer 39: 3 came in, and sat in the **m** gate, *even* H8432
Ezk 1:16 as it were a wheel in the **m** of a wheel. H8432
Eph 2:14 the **m** wall of partition *between us*; *G3320*

MIDDLEMOST
Ezk 42: 5 lower, and than the **m** of the building. H8484
6 the lowest and the **m** from the ground. H8484

MIDIAN
Gen 25: 2 Medan, and **M**, and Ishbak, and Shuah. H4080
4 And the sons of **M**; Ephah, and Epher, H4080
36:35 who smote **M** in the field of Moab, H4080
Ex 2:15 land of **M**: and he sat down by a well. H4080
16 Now the priest of **M** had seven H4080
3: 1 law, the priest of **M**: and he led the flock H4080
4:19 And the LORD said unto Moses in **M**, H4080
18: 1 When Jethro, the priest of **M**, Moses' H4080
Nu 22: 4 And Moab said unto the elders of **M**, H4080
7 and the elders of **M** departed with the H4080
25:15 a people, *and* of a chief house in **M**. H4080
18 of a prince of **M**, their sister, which was H4080
31: 3 Midianites, and avenge the LORD of **M**. H4080
8 And they slew the kings of **M**, beside the H4080
8 five kings of **M**: Balaam also the son H4080
9 *all* the women of **M** captives, and their H4080
Jos 13:21 the princes of **M**, Evi, and Rekem, and H4080
Jdg 6: 1 them into the hand of **M** seven years. H4080
2 And the hand of **M** prevailed against H4080
7: 8 of **M** was beneath him in the valley. H4080
13 into the host of **M**, and came unto a H4080
14 hath God delivered **M**, and all the host. H4080
15 delivered into your hand the host of **M**. H4080
25 and pursued **M**, and brought the heads H4080
8: 3 the princes of **M**, Oreb and Zeeb: and H4080
5 after Zebah and Zalmunna, kings of **M**. H4080
12 took the two kings of **M**, Zebah and H4080
22 hast delivered us from the hand of **M**. H4080
26 *was* on the kings of **M**, and beside the H4080
28 Thus was **M** subdued before the H4080
9:17 and delivered you out of the hand of **M**: H4080
1Ki 11:18 And they arose out of **M**, and came to H4080
1Ch 1:32 and Medan, and **M**, and Ishbak, and H4080
33 And the sons of **M**; Ephah, and Epher, H4080
46 which smote **M** in the field of Moab, H4080
Isa 9: 4 rod of his oppressor, as in the day of **M**. H4080
10:26 to the slaughter of **M** at the rock of H4080
60: 6 dromedaries of **M** and Ephah; all they H4080
Hab 3: 7 curtains of the land of **M** did tremble. H4080

MIDIANITE
Nu 10:29 son of Raguel the **M**, Moses' father in H4084

MIDIANITES
Gen 37:28 Then there passed by **M** merchantmen; H4084
36 And the **M** sold him into Egypt unto H4092
Nu 25:17 Vex the **M**, and smite them: H4084
31: 2 Avenge the children of Israel of the **M**: H4084
3 the **M**, and avenge the LORD of Midian. H4080
7 And they warred against the **M**, as the H4080
Jdg 6: 2 because of the **M** the children of Israel H4080
3 had sown, that the **M** came up, and the H4080
6 because of the **M**; and the children of H4080
7 cried unto the LORD because of the **M**, H4080
11 by the winepress, to hide *it* from the **M**. H4080
13 delivered us into the hands of the **M**. H4080
14 the hand of the **M**: have not I sent thee? H4080
16 thou shalt smite the **M** as one man. H4080
33 Then all the **M** and the Amalekites and H4080
7: 1 the host of the **M** were on the north H4080
2 for me to give the **M** into their hands, H4080
7 and deliver the **M** into thine hand: and H4080
12 And the **M** and the Amalekites and all H4080
23 all Manasseh, and pursued after the **M**. H4080
24 down against the **M**, and take before H4080
25 And they took two princes of the **M**, H4080
8: 1 to fight with the **M**? And they did chide H4080
Ps 83: 9 Do unto them as *unto* the **M**; as *to* H4080

MIDIANITISH
Nu 25: 6 his brethren a **M** woman in the sight H4084
14 that was slain with the **M** woman, *was* H4084
15 And the name of the **M** woman that H4084

MIDNIGHT
Ex 11: 4 LORD, About **m** will I go out H2676+H3915
12:29 And it came to pass, that at **m** H2677+H3915
Jdg 16: 3 And Samson lay till **m**, and H2677+H3915
3 and arose at **m**, and took the H2677+H3915
Ru 3: 8 And it came to pass at **m**, that H2677+H3915
1Ki 3:20 And she arose at **m**, and took H8432+H3915
Job 34:20 be troubled at **m**, and pass H2676+H3915
Ps 119:62 At **m** I will rise to give thanks H2676+H3915
Mt 25: 6 And at **m** there was a cry *G3319+G3571*
Mk 13:35 at even, or at **m**, or at the cockcrowing, *G3317*
Lk 11: 5 go unto him at **m**, and say unto him, *G3317*
Act 16:25 And at **m** Paul and Silas prayed, and *G3317*
20: 7 and continued his speech until **m**. *G3317*
27:27 in Adria, about **m** the shipmen *G3319+G3571*

MIDST
Gen 1: 6 firmament in the **m** of the waters, and H8432
2: 9 of life also in the **m** of the garden, and H8432
3: 3 which *is* in the **m** of the garden, God H8432
15:10 them in the **m**, and laid each piece H8432
19:29 sent Lot out of the **m** of the overthrow, H8432
48:16 into a multitude in the **m** of the earth. H7130
Ex 3: 2 of fire out of the **m** of a bush: and he H8432
4 him out of the **m** of the bush, and said, H8432
20 I will do in the **m** thereof: and after that H7130
8:22 I *am* the LORD in the **m** of the earth. H7130
11: 4 will I go out into the **m** of Egypt: H8432
14:16 dry *ground* through the **m** of the sea. H8432
22 went into the **m** of the sea upon the H8432
23 after them to the **m** of the sea, *even* all H8432
27 the Egyptians in the **m** of the sea. H8432
29 dry *land* in the **m** of the sea; and the H8432
15:19 went on dry *land* in the **m** of the sea. H8432
23:25 take sickness away from the **m** of thee. H7130
24:16 unto Moses out of the **m** of the cloud. H8432
18 And Moses went into the **m** of the H8432
26:28 And the middle bar in the **m** of the H8432
27: 5 net may be even to the **m** of the altar. H2677
28:32 top of it, in the **m** thereof: it shall have H8432
33: 3 not go up in the **m** of thee; for thou *art* H7130
5 will come up into the **m** of thee in a H7130
34:12 lest it be for a snare in the **m** of thee: H7130
38: 4 thereof beneath unto the **m** of it. H2677
39:23 And *there was* an hole in the **m** of the H8432
Lev 16:16 them in the **m** of their uncleanness. H8432
Nu 2:17 of the Levites in the **m** of the camp: as H8432
5: 3 their camps, in the **m** whereof I dwell. H8432
16:47 and ran into the **m** of the congregation; H8432
19: 6 into the **m** of the burning of the heifer. H8432
33: 8 through the **m** of the sea into the H8432
35: 5 the city *shall be* in the **m**: this shall be to H8432
Dt 4:11 with fire unto the **m** of heaven, with H3820
12 you out of the **m** of the fire: ye heard H8432
15 you in Horeb out of the **m** of the fire: H8432
33 out of the **m** of the fire, as thou hast H8432
34 a nation from the **m** of *another* nation, H7130
36 his words out of the **m** of the fire. H8432
5: 4 in the mount out of the **m** of the fire, H8432
22 mount out of the **m** of the fire, of the H8432
23 voice out of the **m** of the darkness, (for H8432
24 voice out of the **m** of the fire: we have H8432
26 the **m** of the fire, as we *have*, and lived? H8432
9:10 **m** of the fire in the day of the assembly. H8432
10: 4 the mount out of the **m** of the fire in the H8432
11: 3 he did in the **m** of Egypt unto Pharaoh H8432
6 their possession, in the **m** of all Israel: H7130
13: 5 put the evil away from the **m** of thee. H7130
16 the spoil of it into the **m** of the street H8432
17:20 he, and his children, in the **m** of Israel. H7130
18:15 a Prophet from the **m** of thee, of thy H7130
19: 2 for thee in the **m** of thy land, which the H8432
23:14 God walketh in the **m** of thy camp, to H7130
32:51 not in the **m** of the children of Israel. H8432
Jos 3:17 dry ground in the **m** of Jordan, and all H8432
4: 3 hence out of the **m** of Jordan, out of the H8432
5 your God into the **m** of Jordan, and H8432
8 stones out of the **m** of Jordan, as the H8432
9 stones in the **m** of Jordan, in the place H8432
10 the ark stood in the **m** of Jordan, until H8432
18 up out of the **m** of Jordan, *and* the soles H8432
7:13 thing in the **m** of thee, O Israel: thou H7130
21 **m** of my tent, and the silver under it. H8432
23 And they took them out of the **m** of the H8432
8:13 went that night into the **m** of the valley. H8432
22 so they were in the **m** of Israel, some on H8432
10:13 sun stood still in the **m** of heaven, and H2677
13: 9 city that *is* in the **m** of the river, and all H8432
16 city that *is* in the **m** of the river, and all H8432

Jdg 15: 4 a firebrand in the **m** between two tails. H8432
18:20 image, and went in the **m** of the people. H7130
20:42 cities they destroyed in the **m** of them. H8432
1Sa 11:11 they came into the **m** of the host in the H8432
16:13 him in the **m** of his brethren: and H7130
18:10 prophesied in the **m** of the house: and H8432
2Sa 1:25 How are the mighty fallen in the **m** of H8432
4: 6 And they came thither into the **m** of the H8432
6:17 in his place, in the **m** of the tabernacle H8432
18:14 he *was* yet alive in the **m** of the oak. H3820
20:12 in blood in the **m** of the highway. And H8432
23:12 But he stood in the **m** of the ground, H8432
20 a lion in the **m** of a pit in time of snow: H8432
24: 5 that *lieth* in the **m** of the river of Gad, H8432
1Ki 3: 8 And thy servant *is* in the **m** of thy H8432
6:27 one another in the **m** of the house. H8432
8:51 from the **m** of the furnace of iron: H8432
20:39 went out into the **m** of the battle; and, H7130
22:35 of the wound into the **m** of the chariot. H2436
2Ki 6:20 behold, *they were* in the **m** of Samaria. H8432
1Ch 11:14 And they set themselves in the **m** of H8432
16: 1 God, and set it in the **m** of the tent that H8432
19: 4 their garments in the **m** hard by their H2677
2Ch 6:13 and had set it in the **m** of the court: and H8432
20:14 the LORD in the **m** of the congregation; H8432
32: 4 ran through the **m** of the land, saying, H8432
Neh 4:11 till we come in the **m** among them, and H8432
9:11 went through the **m** of the sea on the H8432
Est 4: 1 and went out into the **m** of the city, and H8432
Job 21:21 of his months is cut off in the **m**? H2686
Ps 22:14 wax; it is melted in the **m** of my bowels. H8432
22 brethren: in the **m** of the congregation H8432
46: 2 be carried into the **m** of the sea; H3820
5 God *is* in the **m** of her; she shall not be H7130
48: 9 O God, in the **m** of thy temple. H7130
55:10 also and sorrow *are* in the **m** of it. H7130
11 Wickedness *is* in the **m** thereof: deceit H7130
57: 6 me, into the **m** whereof they are fallen H8432
74: 4 Thine enemies roar in the **m** of thy H7130
12 salvation in the **m** of the earth. H7130
78:28 And he let *it* fall in the **m** of their camp, H7130
102:24 me not away in the **m** of my days: thy H2677
110: 2 rule thou in the **m** of thine enemies. H7130
116:19 house, in the **m** of thee, O Jerusalem. H8432
135: 9 wonders into the **m** of thee, O Egypt, H8432
136:14 And made Israel to pass through the **m** H8432
137: 2 upon the willows in the **m** thereof. H8432
138: 7 Though I walk in the **m** of trouble, thou H7130
Prv 4:21 eyes; keep them in the **m** of thine heart. H8432
5:14 I was almost in all evil in the **m** of the H8432
8:20 in the **m** of the paths of judgment: H8432
14:33 *is* in the **m** of fools is made known. H7130
23:34 lieth down in the **m** of the sea, or as he H3820
30:19 of a ship in the **m** of the sea; and the H3820
Song 3:10 of it *of* purple, the **m** thereof being H8432
Isa 4: 4 from the **m** thereof by the spirit H7130
5: 2 a tower in the **m** of it, and also made H8432
8 be placed alone in the **m** of the earth! H7130
25 *were* torn in the **m** of the streets. For all H7130
6: 5 lips, and I dwell in the **m** of a people of H8432
12 a great forsaking in the **m** of the land. H7130
7: 6 in the **m** of it, *even* the son of Tabeal: H8432
10:23 determined, in the **m** of all the land. H7130
12: 6 the Holy One of Israel in the **m** of thee. H7130
16: 3 as the night in the **m** of the noonday; H8432
19: 1 heart of Egypt shall melt in the **m** of it. H7130
3 shall fail in the **m** thereof; and I will H7130
14 spirit in the **m** thereof: and they have H7130
19 the LORD in the **m** of the land of Egypt, H8432
24 *even* a blessing in the **m** of the land: H7130
24:13 When thus it shall be in the **m** of the H7130
18 up out of the **m** of the pit shall be taken H8432
25:11 his hands in the **m** of them, as he that H7130
29:23 mine hands, in the **m** of him, they shall H7130
30:28 shall reach to the **m** of the neck, to sift H2673
41:18 fountains in the **m** of the valleys: I will H8432
52:11 go ye out of the **m** of her; be ye clean, H8432
58: 9 away from the **m** of thee the yoke, the H8432
66:17 one *tree* in the **m**, eating swine's flesh, H8432
Jer 6: 1 to flee out of the **m** of Jerusalem, and H7130
6 *is* wholly oppression in the **m** of her. H7130
9: 6 Thine habitation *is* in the **m** of deceit; H8432
12:16 they be built in the **m** of my people. H8432
14: 9 O LORD, *art* in the **m** of us, and we are H7130
17:11 leave them in the **m** of his days, and at H2677
21: 4 assemble them into the **m** of this city. H8432
29: 8 that *be* in the **m** of you, deceive you, H7130
30:21 proceed from the **m** of them; and I will H7130
37:12 himself thence in the **m** of the people. H8432

Jer 41: 7 they came into the **m** of the city, that H8432
7 *cast them* into the **m** of the pit, he, and H8432
46:21 Also her hired men *are* in the **m** of her H7130
48:45 a flame from the **m** of Sihon, and shall H996
50: 8 Remove out of the **m** of Babylon, and H8432
37 that *are* in the **m** of her; and they shall H8432
51: 1 that dwell in the **m** of them that rise up H3820
6 Flee out of the **m** of Babylon, and H8432
45 My people, go ye out of the **m** of her, H8432
47 all her slain shall fall in the **m** of her. H8432
63 it, and cast it into the **m** of Euphrates: H8432
52:25 that were found in the **m** of the city. H8432
Lam 1:15 *men* in the **m** of me: he hath called H7130
3:45 and refuse in the **m** of the people. H7130
4:13 the blood of the just in the **m** of her, H7130
Ezk 1: 4 it, and out of the **m** thereof as the H8432
4 of amber, out of the **m** of the fire. H8432
5 Also out of the **m** thereof *came* the H8432
5: 2 a third part in the **m** of the city, when H8432
4 cast them into the **m** of the fire, and H8432
5 I have set it in the **m** of the nations and H8432
8 **m** of thee in the sight of the nations. H8432
10 eat the sons in the **m** of thee, and the H8432
12 consumed in the **m** of thee: and a third H8432
6: 7 And the slain shall fall in the **m** of you, H8432
7: 4 shall be in the **m** of thee: and ye shall H8432
9 *that* are in the **m** of thee; and ye shall H8432
8:11 of Israel, and in the **m** of them stood H8432
9: 4 Go through the **m** of the city, through H8432
4 city, through the **m** of Jerusalem, and H8432
4 that be done in the **m** thereof. H8432
10:10 if a wheel had been in the **m** of a wheel. H8432
11: 7 ye have laid in the **m** of it, they *are* the H8432
7 I will bring you forth out of the **m** of it. H8432
9 And I will bring you out of the **m** H8432
11 be the flesh in the **m** thereof; *but* I will H8432
23 went up from the **m** of the city, and H8432
12: 2 Son of man, thou dwellest in the **m** of a H8432
13:14 be consumed in the **m** thereof: and ye H8432
14: 8 him off from the **m** of my people; and H8432
9 him from the **m** of my people Israel. H8432
15: 4 ends of it, and the **m** of it is burned. Is H8432
16:53 of thy captives in the **m** of them: H8432
17:16 him in the **m** of Babylon he shall die. H8432
20: 8 them in the **m** of the land of Egypt. H8432
21:32 shall be in the **m** of the land; thou shalt H8432
22: 3 blood in the **m** of it, that her time may H8432
7 and mother: in the **m** of thee have they H8432
9 in the **m** of thee they commit lewdness. H8432
13 blood which hath been in the **m** of thee. H8432
18 and lead, in the **m** of the furnace; they H8432
19 will gather you into the **m** of Jerusalem. H8432
20 and tin, into the **m** of the furnace, to H8432
21 and ye shall be melted in the **m** thereof. H8432
22 As silver is melted in the **m** of the H8432
22 be melted in the **m** thereof; and ye shall H8432
25 her prophets in the **m** thereof, like a H8432
25 her many widows in the **m** thereof. H8432
27 Her princes in the **m** thereof *are* like H7130
23:39 have they done in the **m** of mine house. H8432
24: 7 For her blood is in the **m** of her; she set H8432
26: 5 of nets in the **m** of the sea: for I have H8432
12 and thy dust in the **m** of the water. H8432
15 the slaughter is made in the **m** of thee? H8432
27: 4 Thy borders *are* in the **m** of the seas, H3820
25 very glorious in the **m** of the seas. H3820
26 hath broken thee in the **m** of the seas. H3820
27 which *is* in the **m** of thee, shall fall into H8432
27 the **m** of the seas in the day of thy ruin. H3820
32 like the destroyed in the **m** of the sea? H8432
34 thy company in the **m** of thee shall fall. H8432
28: 2 the seat of God, in the **m** of the seas; yet H3820
8 *them that are* slain in the **m** of the seas. H3820
14 and down in the **m** of the stones of fire. H8432
16 have filled the **m** of thee with violence, H8432
16 cherub, from the **m** of the stones of fire. H8432
18 forth a fire from the **m** of thee, it shall H8432
22 be glorified in the **m** of thee: and they H8432
23 be judged in the **m** of her by the sword H8432
29: 3 that lieth in the **m** of his rivers, which H8432
4 thee up out of the **m** of thy rivers, and H8432
12 desolate in the **m** of the countries *that* H8432
21 the mouth in the **m** of them; and they H8432
30: 7 And they shall be desolate in the **m** of H8432
7 in the **m** of the cities *that are* wasted. H8432
31:14 of the earth, in the **m** of the children of H8432
17 his shadow in the **m** of the heathen. H8432
18 shalt lie in the **m** of the uncircumcised H8432
32:20 They shall fall in the **m** of *them that are* H8432

Ezk 32:21 to him out of the **m** of hell with them H8432
25 They have set her a bed in the **m** of the H8432
25 he is put in the **m** of *them that be* slain. H8432
28 Yea, thou shalt be broken in the **m** of H8432
32 be laid in the **m** of the uncircumcised H8432
36:23 profaned in the **m** of them; and the H8432
37: 1 **m** of the valley which *was* full of bones, H8432
26 in the **m** of them for evermore. H8432
28 shall be in the **m** of them for evermore. H8432
38:12 goods, that dwell in the **m** of the land. H2872
39: 7 known in the **m** of my people Israel; H8432
41: 7 lowest *chamber* to the highest by the **m**. H8484
43: 7 I will dwell in the **m** of the children of H8432
9 I will dwell in the **m** of them for ever. H8432
46:10 And the prince in the **m** of them, when H8432
48: 8 the sanctuary shall be in the **m** of it. H8432
10 of the LORD shall be in the **m** thereof. H8432
15 and the city shall be in the **m** thereof. H8432
21 of the house *shall be* in the **m** thereof. H8432
22 city, *being* in the **m** *of that* which is the H8432
Dan 3: 6 into the **m** of a burning fiery furnace. H1459
11 into the **m** of a burning fiery furnace. H1459
15 same hour into the **m** of a burning fiery H1459
21 into the **m** of the burning fiery furnace. H1459
23 into the **m** of the burning fiery furnace. H1459
24 men bound into the **m** of the fire? They H1459
25 walking in the **m** of the fire, and they H1459
26 came forth of the **m** of the fire. H1459
4:10 a tree in the **m** of the earth, and the H1459
7:15 in my spirit in the **m** of *my* body, and H1459
9:27 week: and in the **m** of the week he shall H2677
Hos 5: 4 *is* in the **m** of them, and they have H7130
11: 9 Holy One in the **m** of thee: and I will H7130
Joel 2:27 And ye shall know that I *am* in the **m** of H7130
Am 2: 3 And I will cut off the judge from the **m** H7130
3: 9 great tumults in the **m** thereof, and the H7130
9 and the oppressed in the **m** thereof. H8432
6: 4 and the calves out of the **m** of the stall; H8432
7: 8 plumbline in the **m** of my people Israel: H7130
10 thee in the **m** of the house of Israel: H7130
Jna 2: 3 the deep, in the **m** of the seas; and the H3824
Mic 2:12 as the flock in the **m** of their fold: they H8432
5: 7 shall be in the **m** of many people as a H7130
8 the Gentiles in the **m** of many people as H7130
10 horses out of the **m** of thee, and I will H7130
13 images out of the **m** of thee; and thou H7130
14 **m** of thee: so will I destroy thy cities. H7130
6:14 *shall be* in the **m** of thee; and thou shalt H7130
7:14 the wood, in the **m** of Carmel: let them H8432
Nah 3:13 Behold, thy people in the **m** of thee *are* H7130
Hab 2:19 *there is* no breath at all in the **m** of it. H7130
3: 2 thy work in the **m** of the years, in the H7130
2 of the years, in the **m** of the years make H7130
Zep 2:14 And flocks shall lie down in the **m** of H8432
3: 5 The just LORD *is* in the **m** thereof; he H7130
11 away out of the **m** of thee them that H7130
12 I will also leave in the **m** of thee an H7130
15 LORD, *is* in the **m** of thee: thou shalt H7130
17 The LORD thy God in the **m** of thee *is* H7130
Zec 2: 5 and will be the glory in the **m** of her. H8432
10 dwell in the **m** of thee, saith the LORD. H8432
11 I will dwell in the **m** of thee, and thou H8432
5: 4 remain in the **m** of his house, and shall H8432
7 that sitteth in the **m** of the ephah. H8432
8 he cast it into the **m** of the ephah; and H8432
8: 3 will dwell in the **m** of Jerusalem: and H8432
8 shall dwell in the **m** of Jerusalem: and H8432
14: 1 spoil shall be divided in the **m** of thee. H7130
4 shall cleave in the **m** thereof toward the H2677
Mt 10:16 forth as sheep in the **m** of wolves: be ye *G3319*
14:24 But the ship was now in the **m** of the *G3319*
18: 2 him, and set him in the **m** of them, *G3319*
20 my name, there am I in the **m** of them. *G3319*
Mk 6:47 **m** of the sea, and he alone on the land. *G3319*
7:31 the **m** of the coasts of Decapolis. *G3319*
9:36 and set him in the **m** of them: and *G3319*
14:60 And the high priest stood up in the **m**, *G3319*
Lk 2:46 sitting in the **m** of the doctors, both *G3319*
4:30 But he passing through the **m** of them *G3319*
35 thrown him in the **m**, he came out of *G3319*
5:19 with *his* couch into the **m** before Jesus. *G3319*
6: 8 in the **m**. And he arose and stood forth. *G3319*
17:11 through the **m** of Samaria and Galilee. *G3319*
21:21 which are in the **m** of it depart out; and *G3319*
22:55 a fire in the **m** of the hall, and were *G3319*
23:45 the veil of the temple was rent in the **m**. *G3319*
24:36 stood in the **m** of them, and saith *G3319*
Jn 7:14 Now about the **m** of the feast Jesus *G3322*
8: 3 and when they had set her in the **m**, *G3319*

Jn 8: 9 and the woman standing in the **m**. *G3319*
59 the **m** of them, and so passed by. *G3319*
19:18 on either side one, and Jesus in the **m**. *G3319*
20:19 and stood in the **m**, and saith unto *G3319*
26 in the **m**, and said, Peace be unto you. *G3319*
Act 1:15 stood up in the **m** of the disciples, and *G3319*
18 in the **m**, and all his bowels gushed out. *G3319*
2:22 **m** of you, as ye yourselves also know: *G3319*
4: 7 And when they had set them in the **m**, *G3319*
17:22 Then Paul stood in the **m** of Mars' hill, *G3319*
27:21 stood forth in the **m** of them, and said, *G3319*
Php 2:15 rebuke, in the **m** of a crooked and *G3319*
Heb 2:12 brethren, in the **m** of the church will I *G3319*
Rev 1:13 And in the **m** of the seven candlesticks *G3319*
2: 1 the **m** of the seven golden candlesticks; *G3319*
7 is in the **m** of the paradise of God. *G3319*
4: 6 crystal: and in the **m** of the throne, and *G3319*
5: 6 And I beheld, and, lo, in the **m** of the *G3319*
6 four beasts, and in the **m** of the elders, *G3319*
6: 6 And I heard a voice in the **m** of the four *G3319*
7:17 For the Lamb which is in the **m** of the *G3319*
8:13 flying through the **m** of heaven, saying *G3321*
14: 6 And I saw another angel fly in the **m** of *G3321*
19:17 that fly in the **m** of heaven, Come and *G3321*
22: 2 In the **m** of the street of it, and on *G3319*

MIDWIFE
Gen 35:17 labour, that the **m** said unto her, Fear H3205
38:28 *his* hand: and the **m** took and bound H3205
Ex 1:16 ye do the office of a **m** to the Hebrew H3205

MIDWIVES
Ex 1:15 to the Hebrew **m**, of which the name H3205
17 But the **m** feared God, and did not as H3205
18 And the king of Egypt called for the **m**, H3205
19 And the **m** said unto Pharaoh, Because H3205
19 delivered ere the **m** come in unto them. H3205
20 Therefore God dealt well with the **m**: H3205
21 And it came to pass, because the **m** H3205

MIGDAL-EL
Jos 19:38 And Iron, and **M**, Horem, and H4027

MIGDAL-GAD
Jos 15:37 Zenan, and Hadashah, and **M**, H4028

MIGDOL
Ex 14: 2 between **M** and the sea, over against H4024
Nu 33: 7 and they pitched before **M**. H4024
Jer 44: 1 which dwell at **M**, and at Tahpanhes, H4024
46:14 Declare ye in Egypt, and publish in **M**, H4024

MIGHT See the Appendix.

MIGHTEST See the Appendix.

MIGHTIER
Gen 26:16 from us; for thou art much **m** than we. H6105
Ex 1: 9 of Israel *are* more and **m** than we: H6099
Nu 14:12 thee a greater nation and **m** than they. H6099
Dt 4:38 thee greater and **m** than thou *art*, to H6099
7: 1 seven nations greater and **m** than thou; H6099
9: 1 greater and **m** than thyself, cities H6099
14 thee a nation **m** and greater than they. H6099
11:23 greater nations and **m** than yourselves. H6099
Ps 93: 4 The LORD on high *is* **m** than the noise of H117
Ecc 6:10 he contend with him that is **m** than he. H8623
Mt 3:11 after me is **m** than I, whose shoes *G2478*
Mk 1: 7 There cometh one **m** than I after me, *G2478*
Lk 3:16 water; but one **m** than I cometh, the *G2478*

MIGHTIES
1Ch 11:12 Ahohite, who *was one* of the three **m**. H1368
24 and had the name among the three **m**. H1368

MIGHTIEST
1Ch 11:19 drink it. These things did these three **m**. H1368

MIGHTILY
Dt 6: 3 ye may increase **m**, as the LORD God of H3966
Jdg 4: 3 he **m** oppressed the children of Israel. H2393
14: 6 And the spirit of the LORD came **m** H6743
15:14 the LORD came **m** upon him, and the H6743
Jer 25:30 he shall **m** roar upon his habitation; H7580
Jna 3: 8 and cry **m** unto God: yea, let them H2394
Nah 2: 1 *thy* loins strong, fortify *thy* power **m**. H3966
Act 18:28 For he **m** convinced the Jews, *and that* *G2159*
19:20 So **m** grew the word of God and *G2596*
Col 1:29 to his working, which worketh in me **m**. *G1411*

Rev 18: 2 And he cried **m** with a strong voice, *G2479*

MIGHTY

Gen 6: 4 the same *became* **m** men which *were* of H1368
10: 8 he began to be a **m** one in the earth. H1368
9 He was a **m** hunter before the LORD: H1368
9 Nimrod the **m** hunter before the LORD. H1368
18:18 a great and **m** nation, and all the H6099
23: 6 Hear us, my lord: thou *art* a **m** prince H430
49:24 the hands of the **m** *God* of Jacob; (from H46
Ex 1: 7 **m**; and the land was filled with them. H6105
20 people multiplied, and waxed very **m**. H6105
3:19 not let you go, no, not by a **m** hand. H2389
9:28 there be no *more* **m** thunderings and H430
10:19 And the LORD turned a **m** strong west H3966
15:10 them: they sank as lead in the **m** waters. H117
15 shall be amazed; the **m** men of Moab, H352
32:11 with great power, and with a **m** hand? H2389
Lev 19:15 honour the person of the **m**: *but* in H1419
Nu 22: 6 people; for they *are* too **m** for me: H6099
Dt 3:24 and thy **m** hand: for what God H2389
4:34 and by war, and by a **m** hand, and by a H2389
37 sight with his **m** power out of Egypt; H1419
5:15 out thence through a **m** hand and by a H2389
6:21 brought us out of Egypt with a **m** hand: H2389
7: 8 you out with a **m** hand, and redeemed H2389
19 the wonders, and the **m** hand, and the H2389
21 *is* among you, a **m** God and terrible. H1419
23 **m** destruction, until they be destroyed. H1419
9:26 forth out of Egypt with a **m** hand. H2389
29 **m** power and by thy stretched out arm. H1419
10:17 a great God, a **m**, and a terrible, which H1368
11: 2 his **m** hand, and his stretched out arm, H2389
26: 5 there a nation, great, **m**, and populous: H6099
8 of Egypt with a **m** hand, and with an H2389
34:12 And in all that **m** hand, and in all the H2389
Jos 1:14 all the **m** men of valour, and help them; H1368
4:24 LORD, that it *is* **m**: that ye might fear H2389
6: 2 king thereof, *and* the **m** men of valour. H1368
8: 3 thirty thousand **m** men of valour, and H1368
10: 2 Ai, and all the men thereof *were* **m**. H1368
7 with him, and all the **m** men of valour. H1368
Jdg 5:13 made me have dominion over the **m**. H1368
22 the pransings of their **m** ones. H47
23 to the help of the LORD against the **m**. H1368
6:12 *is* with thee, thou **m** man of valour. H1368
11: 1 Now Jephthah the Gileadite was a **m** H1368
Ru 2: 1 her husband's, a **m** man of wealth, of H1368
1Sa 2: 4 The bows of the **m** men *are* broken, H1368
4: 8 the hand of these **m** Gods? these *are* the H117
9: 1 a Benjamite, a **m** man of power. H1368
16:18 in playing, and a **m** valiant man, and a H1368
2Sa 1:19 thy high places: how are the **m** fallen! H1368
21 the shield of the **m** is vilely cast away, H1368
22 slain, from the fat of the **m**, the bow of H1368
25 How are the **m** fallen in the midst of H1368
27 How are the **m** fallen, and the weapons H1368
10: 7 Joab, and all the host of the **m** men. H1368
16: 6 people and all the **m** men *were* on his H1368
17: 8 men, that they *be* **m** men, and they *be* H1368
10 thy father *is* a **m** man, and *they* which H1368
20: 7 and all the **m** men: and they went H1368
23: 8 These *be* the names of the **m** men H1368
9 *one* of the three **m** men with David, H1368
16 And the three **m** men brake through H1368
17 it. These things did these three **m** men. H1368
22 had the name among three **m** men. H1368
1Ki 1: 8 Shimei, and Rei, and the **m** men which H1368
10 Benaiah, and the **m** men, and Solomon H1368
11:28 And the man Jeroboam *was* a **m** man H1368
2Ki 5: 1 a **m** man in valour, *but he was* a leper. H1368
15:20 *even* of all the **m** men of wealth, of each H1368
24:14 and all the **m** men of valour, *even* H1368
15 his officers, and the **m** of the land, *those* H193
1Ch 1:10 he began to be **m** upon the earth. H1368
5:24 and Jahdiel, **m** men of valour, famous H1368
7: 7 of *their* fathers, **m** men of valour; and H1368
9 of their fathers, **m** men of valour, *was* H1368
11 of their fathers, **m** men of valour, *were* H1368
40 house, choice *and* **m** men of valour, H1368
8:40 And the sons of Ulam were **m** men of H1368
11:10 These also *are* the chief of the **m** men H1368
11 And this *is* the number of the **m** men H1368
12: 1 among the **m** men, helpers of the war. H1368
4 And Ismaiah the Gibeonite, a **m** man H1368
21 for they *were* all **m** men of valour, and H1368
25 Of the children of Simeon, **m** men of H1368
28 And Zadok, a young man **m** of valour, H1368
30 and eight hundred, **m** men of valour, H1368
1Ch 19: 8 Joab, and all the host of the **m** men. H1368
26: 6 father: for they *were* **m** men of valour. H1368
31 **m** men of valour at Jazer of Gilead. H1368
27: 6 This *is that* Benaiah, *who was* **m** H1368
28: 1 and with the **m** men, and with all the H1368
29:24 And all the princes, and the **m** men, H1368
2Ch 6:32 name's sake, and thy **m** hand, and thy H2389
13: 3 chosen men, *being* **m** men of valour. H1368
21 But Abijah waxed **m**, and married H2388
14: 8 all these *were* **m** men of valour. H1368
17:13 **m** men of valour, *were* in Jerusalem. H1368
14 and with him **m** men of valour three H1368
16 hundred thousand **m** men of valour. H1368
17 And of Benjamin; Eliada a **m** man of H1368
25: 6 He hired also an hundred thousand **m** H1368
26:12 the fathers of the **m** men of valour *were* H1368
13 made war with **m** power, to help the H2428
27: 6 So Jotham became **m**, because he H2388
28: 7 And Zichri, a **m** man of Ephraim, slew H1368
32: 3 his princes and his **m** men to stop the H1368
21 cut off all the **m** men of valour, and H1368
Ezr 4:20 There have been **m** kings also over H8624
7:28 all the king's **m** princes. And I was H1368
Neh 3:16 was made, and unto the house of the **m**. H1368
9:11 the deeps, as a stone into the **m** waters. H5794
32 the great, the **m**, and the terrible God, H1368
11:14 And their brethren, **m** men of valour, H1368
Job 5:15 mouth, and from the hand of the **m**. H2389
6:23 or, Redeem me from the hand of the **m**? H6184
9: 4 *He is* wise in heart, and **m** in strength: H533
12:19 away spoiled, and overthroweth the **m**. H386
21 and weakeneth the strength of the **m**. H650
21: 7 live, become old, yea, are **m** in power? H1396
22: 8 But *as for* the **m** man, he had the earth; H2220
24:22 He draweth also the **m** with his power: H47
34:20 the **m** shall be taken away without hand. H47
24 He shall break in pieces **m** men H3524
35: 9 cry out by reason of the arm of the **m**. H7227
36: 5 Behold, God *is* **m**, and despiseth not H3524
5 *any: he is* **m** in strength *and* wisdom. H3524
41:25 When he raiseth up himself, the **m** are H410
Ps 24: 8 and **m**, the LORD mighty in battle. H1368
8 and mighty, the LORD **m** in battle. H1368
29: 1 Give unto the LORD, O ye **m**, H1121+H410
33:16 of an host: a **m** man is not delivered H1368
45: 3 *most* **m**, with thy glory and thy majesty. H1368
50: 1 The **m** God, *even* the LORD, hath H410
52: 1 in mischief, O **m** man? the goodness H1368
59: 3 for my soul: the **m** are gathered against H5794
68:33 send out his voice, *and that* a **m** voice. H5797
69: 4 wrongfully, are **m**: then I restored *that* H6105
74:15 and the flood: thou driedst up **m** rivers. H386
78:65 sleep, *and* like a **m** man that shouteth H1368
82: 1 of the **m**; he judgeth among the gods. H410
89: 6 of the **m** can be likened unto the LORD? H410
13 Thou hast a **m** arm: strong is thy hand, H1369
19 upon *one that is* **m**; I have exalted *one* H1368
50 *the reproach of* all the **m** people; H7227
93: 4 waters, *yea, than* the **m** waves of the sea. H117
106: 2 Who can utter the **m** acts of the LORD? H1369
8 might make his **m** power to be known. H1369
112: 2 His seed shall be **m** upon earth: the H1368
120: 4 Sharp arrows of the **m**, with coals of H1368
127: 4 As arrows *are* in the hand of a **m** man; H1368
132: 2 *and* vowed unto the **m** *God* of Jacob; H46
5 an habitation for the **m** *God* of Jacob. H46
135:10 Who smote great nations, and slew **m** H6099
145: 4 another, and shall declare thy **m** acts. H1369
12 the sons of men his **m** acts, and the H1369
150: 2 Praise him for his **m** acts: praise him H1369
Prv 16:32 *is* better than the **m**; and he that ruleth H1368
18:18 to cease, and parteth between the **m**. H6099
21:22 A wise *man* scaleth the city of the **m**, H1368
23:11 For their redeemer *is* **m**; he shall plead H2389
Ecc 7:19 than ten **m** *men* which are in the city. H7989
Song 4: 4 bucklers, all shields of **m** men. H1368
Isa 1:24 LORD of hosts, the **m** One of Israel, Ah, I H46
3: 2 The **m** man, and the man of war, the H1368
25 fall by the sword, and thy **m** in the war. H1369
5:15 down, and the **m** man shall be humbled, H376
22 Woe unto *them that are* **m** to drink H1368
9: 6 Counsellor, The **m** God, The H1368
10:21 the remnant of Jacob, unto the **m** God. H1368
34 iron, and Lebanon shall fall by a **m** one. H117
11:15 sea; and with his **m** wind shall he H5868
13: 3 also called my **m** ones for mine anger, H1368
17:12 a rushing like the rushing of **m** waters! H3524
21:17 of archers, the **m** men of the children H1368
22:17 **m** captivity, and will surely cover thee. H1397
Isa 28: 2 Behold, the Lord hath a **m** and strong H2389
2 as a flood of **m** waters overflowing, H3524
30:29 of the LORD, to the **m** One of Israel. H6697
31: 8 with the sword, not of a **m** man; and the H376
42:13 The LORD shall go forth as a **m** man, H1368
43:16 in the sea, and a path in the **m** waters; H5794
49:24 Shall the prey be taken from the **m**, or H1368
25 the captives of the **m** shall be taken H1368
26 and thy Redeemer, the **m** One of Jacob. H46
60:16 and thy Redeemer, the **m** One of Jacob. H46
63: 1 that speak in righteousness, **m** to save. H7227
Jer 5:15 saith the LORD: it *is* a **m** nation, it *is* an H386
16 an open sepulchre, they *are* all **m** men. H1368
9:23 neither let the **m** *man* glory in his H1368
14: 9 astonied, as a **m** man *that* cannot save? H1368
20:11 But the LORD *is* with me as a **m** H1368
26:21 king, with all his **m** men, and all the H1368
32:18 **M** God, the LORD of hosts, *is* his name, H1368
19 Great in counsel, and **m** in work: for H7227
33: 3 and **m** things, which thou knowest not. H1219
41:16 of Ahikam, *even* **m** men of war, and H1397
46: 5 back? and their **m** ones are beaten H1368
6 Let not the swift flee away, nor the **m** H1368
9 and let the **m** men come forth; the H1368
12 the land: for the **m** man hath stumbled H1368
12 **m**, *and* they are fallen both together. H1368
48:14 How say ye, We *are* **m** and strong men H1368
41 and the **m** men's hearts in Moab H1368
49:22 the heart of the **m** men of Edom be as H1368
50: 9 *shall be* as of a **m** expert man; none H1368
36 **m** men; and they shall be dismayed. H1368
51:30 The **m** men of Babylon have forborn to H1368
56 Babylon, and her **m** men are taken, H1368
57 rulers, and her **m** men: and they shall H1368
Lam 1:15 under foot all my **m** *men* in the midst of H47
Ezk 17:13 he hath also taken the **m** of the land: H352
17 Neither shall Pharaoh with *his* **m** army H1419
20:33 GOD, surely with a **m** hand, and with a H2389
34 scattered, with a **m** hand, and with a H2389
31:11 the hand of the **m** one of the heathen; H410
32:12 By the swords of the **m** will I cause thy H1368
21 The strong among the **m** shall speak to H1368
27 And they shall not lie with the **m** *that* H1368
27 terror of the **m** in the land of the living. H1368
38:15 a great company, and a **m** army: H7227
39:18 Ye shall eat the flesh of the **m**, and H1368
20 chariots, with **m** men, and with all men H1368
Dan 3:20 And he commanded the most **m** men H1401
4: 3 How great *are* his signs! and how **m** H8624
8:24 And his power shall be **m**, but not by H6105
24 destroy the **m** and the holy people. H6099
9:15 land of Egypt with a **m** hand, and hast H2389
11: 3 And a **m** king shall stand up, that shall H1368
25 a very great and **m** army; but he shall H6099
Hos 10:13 way, in the multitude of thy **m** men. H1368
Joel 2: 7 They shall run like **m** men; they shall H1368
3: 9 war, wake up the **m** men, let all the H1368
11 thy **m** ones to come down, O LORD. H1368
Am 2:14 neither shall the **m** deliver himself: H1368
16 among the **m** shall flee away naked H1368
5:12 and your **m** sins: they afflict the H6099
24 and righteousness as a **m** stream. H386
Oba 9 And thy **m** *men*, O Teman, shall be H1368
Jna 1: 4 and there was a **m** tempest in the sea, H1419
Nah 2: 3 The shield of his **m** men is made red, H1368
Hab 1:12 for judgment; and, O **m** God, thou hast H6697
Zep 1:14 the **m** man shall cry there bitterly. H1368
3:17 midst of thee *is* **m**; he will save, he will H1368
Zec 9:13 made thee as the sword of a **m** man. H1368
10: 5 And they shall be as **m** *men*, which H1368
7 And *they of* Ephraim shall be like a **m** H1368
11: 2 fallen; because the **m** are spoiled: howl, H117
Mt 11:20 most of his **m** works were done, *G1411*
21 for if the **m** works, which were *G1411*
23 to hell: for if the **m** works, which have *G1411*
13:54 *man* this wisdom, and *these* **m** works? *G1411*
58 And he did not many **m** works there *G1411*
14: 2 and therefore **m** works do shew forth *G1411*
Mk 6: 2 **m** works are wrought by his hands? *G1411*
5 And he could there do no **m** work, save *G1411*
14 and therefore **m** works do shew forth *G1411*
Lk 1:49 For he that is **m** hath done to me great *G1415*
52 He hath put down the **m** from *their* *G1413*
9:43 And they were all amazed at the **m** *G3168*
10:13 for if the **m** works had been done *G1411*
15:14 all, there arose a **m** famine in that *G2478*
19:37 for all the **m** works that they had seen; *G1411*
24:19 was a prophet **m** in deed and word *G1415*
Act 2: 2 as of a rushing **m** wind, and it filled all *G972*

Act 7:22 and was **m** in words and in deeds. *G1415*
18:24 **m** in the scriptures, came to Ephesus. *G1415*
Ro 15:19 Through **m** signs and wonders, by the *G1411*
1Co 1:26 many **m**, not many noble, *are called*: *G1415*
27 to confound the things which are **m**; *G2478*
2Co 10: 4 not carnal, but **m** through God to the *G1415*
12:12 in signs, and wonders, and **m** deeds. *G1411*
13: 3 you-ward is not weak, but is **m** in you. *G1414*
Gal 2: 8 was **m** in me toward the Gentiles:) *G1754*
Eph 1:19 to the working of his **m** power, *G2904*
2Th 1: 7 from heaven with his **m** angels, *G1411*
1Pt 5: 6 under the **m** hand of God, that he *G2900*
Rev 6:13 figs, when she is shaken of a **m** wind. *G3173*
15 captains, and the **m** men, and every *G1415*
10: 1 And I saw another **m** angel come down *G2478*
16:18 so **m** an earthquake, *and* so great. *G5082*
18:10 city Babylon, that **m** city! for in one *G2478*
21 And a **m** angel took up a stone like a *G2478*
19: 6 as the voice of **m** thunderings, saying, *G2478*
18 and the flesh of **m** men, and the flesh *G2478*

MIGRON
1Sa 14: 2 tree which *is* in **M**: and the people that H4051
Isa 10:28 He is come to Aiath, he is passed to **M**; H4051

MIJAMIN
1Ch 24: 9 The fifth to Malchijah, the sixth to **M**, H4326
Neh 10: 7 Meshullam, Abijah, **M**, H4326

MIKLOTH
1Ch 8:32 And **M** begat Shimeah. And these also H4732
9:37 and Ahio, and Zechariah, and **M**. H4732
38 And **M** begat Shimeam. And they also H4732
27: 4 of his course *was* **M** also the ruler: in H4732

MIKNEIAH
1Ch 15:18 Elipheleh, and **M**, and Obed-edom, and H4737
21 And Mattithiah, and Elipheleh, and **M**, H4737

MILALAI
Neh 12:36 and Azarael, **M**, Gilalai, Maai, H4450

MILCAH
Gen 11:29 of Nahor's wife, **M**, the daughter of H4435
29 the father of **M**, and the father of Iscah. H4435
22:20 saying, Behold, **M**, she hath also born H4435
23 these eight **M** did bear to Nahor, H4435
24:15 to Bethuel, son of **M**, the wife of Nahor, H4435
24 son of **M**, which she bare unto Nahor. H4435
47 son, whom **M** bare unto him: and H4435
Nu 26:33 and Noah, Hoglah, **M**, and Tirzah. H4435
27: 1 Noah, and Hoglah, and **M**, and Tirzah. H4435
36:11 and Hoglah, and **M**, and Noah, the H4435
Jos 17: 3 and Noah, Hoglah, **M**, and Tirzah. H4435

MILCH
Gen 32:15 Thirty **m** camels with their colts, forty H3243
1Sa 6: 7 cart, and take two **m** kine, on which H5763
10 And the men did so; and took two **m** H5763

MILCOM
1Ki 11: 5 **M** the abomination of the Ammonites. H4445
33 of the Moabites, and **M** the god of the H4445
2Ki 23:13 Moabites, and for **M** the abomination H4445

MILDEW
Dt 28:22 blasting, and with **m**; and they shall H3420
1Ki 8:37 blasting, **m**, locust, *or* if there be H3420
2Ch 6:28 there be blasting, or **m**, locusts, or H3420
Am 4: 9 I have smitten you with blasting and **m**: H3420
Hag 2:17 I smote you with blasting and with **m** H3420

MILE
Mt 5:41 thee to go a **m**, go with him twain. *G3400*

MILETUM
2Ti 4:20 but Trophimus have I left at **M** sick. *G3399*

MILETUS
Act 20:15 and the next *day* we came to **M**. *G3399*
17 And from **M** he sent to Ephesus, and *G3399*

MILK
Gen 18: 8 And he took butter, and **m**, and the calf H2461
49:12 with wine, and his teeth white with **m**. H2461
Ex 3: 8 a land flowing with **m** and honey; unto H2461
17 unto a land flowing with **m** and honey. H2461
13: 5 a land flowing with **m** and honey, that H2461
23:19 shalt not seethe a kid in his mother's **m**. H2461
Ex 33: 3 Unto a land flowing with **m** and honey: H2461
34:26 shalt not seethe a kid in his mother's **m**. H2461
Lev 20:24 that floweth with **m** and honey: I *am* H2461
Nu 13:27 **m** and honey; and this *is* the fruit of it. H2461
14: 8 land which floweth with **m** and honey. H2461
16:13 that floweth with **m** and honey, to kill H2461
14 land that floweth with **m** and honey, or H2461
Dt 6: 3 land that floweth with **m** and honey. H2461
11: 9 a land that floweth with **m** and honey. H2461
14:21 shalt not seethe a kid in his mother's **m**. H2461
26: 9 a land that floweth with **m** and honey. H2461
15 a land that floweth with **m** and honey. H2461
27: 3 that floweth with **m** and honey; as the H2461
31:20 that floweth with **m** and honey; and H2461
32:14 Butter of kine, and **m** of sheep, with fat H2461
Jos 5: 6 a land that floweth with **m** and honey. H2461
Jdg 4:19 she opened a bottle of **m**, and gave him H2461
5:25 He asked water, *and* she gave *him* **m**; H2461
Job 10:10 Hast thou not poured me out as **m**, and H2461
21:24 His breasts are full of **m**, and his bones H2461
Prv 27:27 And *thou shalt have* goats' **m** enough H2461
30:33 Surely the churning of **m** bringeth forth H2461
Song 4:11 honey and **m** *are* under thy tongue; H2461
5: 1 my wine with my **m**: eat, O friends; H2461
12 of waters, washed with **m**, *and* fitly set. H2461
Isa 7:22 the abundance of **m** *that* they shall give H2461
28: 9 the **m**, *and* drawn from the breasts. H2461
55: 1 **m** without money and without price. H2461
60:16 Thou shalt also suck the **m** of the H2461
66:11 that ye may **m** out, and be delighted H4711
Jer 11: 5 land flowing with **m** and honey, as *it is* H2461
32:22 a land flowing with **m** and honey; H2461
Lam 4: 7 were whiter than **m**, they were more H2461
Ezk 20: 6 flowing with **m** and honey, which *is* H2461
15 flowing with **m** and honey, which *is* H2461
25: 4 eat thy fruit, and they shall drink thy **m**. H2461
Joel 3:18 shall flow with **m**, and all the rivers of H2461
1Co 3: 2 I have fed you with **m**, and not with *G1051*
9: 7 and eateth not of the **m** of the flock? *G1051*
Heb 5:12 have need of **m**, and not of strong meat. *G1051*
13 For every one that useth **m** *is* unskilful *G1051*
1Pt 2: 2 desire the sincere **m** of the word, that *G1051*

MILL
Ex 11: 5 the **m**; and all the firstborn of beasts. H7347
Mt 24:41 Two *women shall be* grinding at the **m**; *G3459*

MILLET
Ezk 4: 9 and lentiles, and **m**, and fitches, and H1764

MILLIONS
Gen 24:60 of thousands of **m**, and let thy seed H7233

MILLO
Jdg 9: 6 all the house of **M**, and went, and made H4407
20 and the house of **M**; and let fire come H4407
20 the house of **M**, and devour Abimelech. H4407
2Sa 5: 9 built round about from **M** and inward. H4407
1Ki 9:15 his own house, and **M**, and the wall of H4407
24 had built for her: then did he build **M**. H4407
11:27 Solomon built **M**, *and* repaired the H4407
2Ki 12:20 house of **M**, which goeth down to Silla. H4407
1Ch 11: 8 about, even from **M** round about: and H4407
2Ch 32: 5 and repaired **M** *in* the city of David, H4407

MILLS
Nu 11: 8 *it*, and ground *it* in **m**, or beat *it* in a H7347

MILLSTONE
Dt 24: 6 or the upper **m** to pledge: for he taketh H7393
Jdg 9:53 cast a piece of a **m** upon Abimelech's H7393
2Sa 11:21 cast a piece of a **m** upon him from the H7393
Job 41:24 yea, as hard as a piece of the nether **m**.
Mt 18: 6 for him that a **m** were hanged *G3458+G3684*
Mk 9:42 for him that a **m** were hanged *G3037+G3457*
Lk 17: 2 It were better for him that a **m** *G3458+G3684*
Rev 18:21 stone like a great **m**, and cast *it* into the *G3458*
22 **m** shall be heard no more at all in thee; *G3458*

MILLSTONES
Isa 47: 2 Take the **m**, and grind meal: uncover H7347
Jer 25:10 of the **m**, and the light of the candle. H7347

MINCING
Isa 3:16 eyes, walking and **m** *as* they go, and H2952

MIND
Gen 23: 8 If it be your **m** that I should bury my H5315
26:35 Which were a grief of **m** unto Isaac and H7307
Lev 24:12 And they put him in ward, that the **m** H6310
Nu 16:28 *I have* not *done them* of mine own **m**. H3820
24:13 bad of mine own **m**; *but* what the LORD H3820
Dt 18: 6 all the desire of his **m** unto the place H5315
28:65 and failing of eyes, and sorrow of **m**: H5315
30: 1 thou shalt call *them* to **m** among all the H3824
1Sa 2:35 heart and in my **m**: and I will build him H5315
9:20 ago, set not thy **m** on them; for they are H3820
1Ch 22: 7 me, it was in my **m** to build an house H3824
28: 9 and with a willing **m**: for the LORD H5315
Neh 4: 6 for the people had a **m** to work. H3820
Job 23:13 But he *is* in one **m**, and who can turn
34:33 *Should it be* according to thy **m**? he will H5973
Ps 31:12 I am forgotten as a dead man out of **m**: H3820
Prv 21:27 *when* he bringeth it with a wicked **m**? H2154
29:11 A fool uttereth all his **m**: but a wise *man* H7307
Isa 26: 3 peace, *whose* **m** *is* stayed *on thee*: H3336
46: 8 bring *it* again to **m**, O ye transgressors. H3820
65:17 not be remembered, nor come into **m**. H3820
Jer 3:16 shall it come to **m**: neither shall they H3820
15: 1 stood before me, *yet* my **m** *could* not *be* H5315
19: 5 nor spake *it*, neither came *it* into my **m**: H3820
32:35 came it into my **m**, that they should do H3820
44:21 them, and came it *not* into his **m**? H3820
51:50 and let Jerusalem come into your **m**. H3824
Lam 3:21 This I recall to my **m**, therefore have I H3820
Ezk 11: 5 come into your **m**, *every one of* them. H7307
20:32 And that which cometh into your **m** H7307
23:17 and her **m** was alienated from them. H5315
18 then my **m** was alienated from H5315
18 as my **m** was alienated from her sister. H5315
22 from whom thy **m** is alienated, and I H5315
28 *of them* from whom thy **m** is alienated: H5315
38:10 **m**, and thou shalt think an evil thought: H3824
Dan 2:29 came *into thy* **m** upon thy bed, what
5:20 lifted up, and his **m** hardened in pride, H7308
Hab 1:11 Then shall *his* **m** change, and he shall H7307
Mt 22:37 with all thy soul, and with all thy **m**. *G1271*
Mk 5:15 in his right **m**: and they were afraid. *G4993*
12:30 and with all thy **m**, and with all thy *G1271*
14:72 Peter called to **m** the word that Jesus *G363*
Lk 1:29 and cast in her **m** what manner of *G1260*
8:35 in his right **m**: and they were afraid. *G4993*
10:27 all thy **m**; and thy neighbour as thyself. *G1271*
12:29 shall drink, neither be ye of doubtful **m**. *G3349*
Act 17:11 all readiness of **m**, and searched the *G4288*
20:19 Serving the Lord with all humility of **m**, *G5012*
Ro 1:28 to a reprobate **m**, to do those things *G3563*
7:23 the law of my **m**, and bringing me into *G3563*
25 So then with the **m** I myself serve the *G3563*
8: 5 For they that are after the flesh do **m** *G5426*
7 Because the carnal **m** *is* enmity against *G5427*
27 what *is* the **m** of the Spirit, because *G5427*
11:34 For who hath known the **m** of the Lord? *G3563*
12: 2 renewing of your **m**, that ye may prove *G3563*
16 *Be* of the same **m** one toward another. *G5426*
16 toward another. **M** not high things, but *G5426*
14: 5 man be fully persuaded in his own **m**. *G3563*
15: 6 That ye may with one **m** *and* one *G3661*
15 sort, as putting you in **m**, because of the *G1878*
1Co 1:10 the same **m** and in the same judgment. *G3563*
2:16 For who hath known the **m** of the Lord, *G3563*
16 him? But we have the **m** of Christ. *G3563*
2Co 7: 7 your fervent **m** toward me; so that *G2205*
8:12 For if there be first a willing **m**, *it is* *G4288*
19 Lord, and *declaration of* your ready **m**: *G4288*
9: 2 For I know the forwardness of your **m**, *G4288*
13:11 comfort, be of one **m**, live in peace; and *G5426*
Eph 2: 3 flesh and of the **m**; and were by nature *G1271*
4:17 Gentiles walk, in the vanity of their **m**, *G3563*
23 And be renewed in the spirit of your **m**; *G3563*
Php 1:27 spirit, with one **m** striving together for *G5590*
2: 2 love, *being* of one accord, of one **m**. *G5426*
3 in lowliness of **m** let each esteem other *G5012*
5 Let this **m** be in you, which was also in *G5426*
3:16 the same rule, let us **m** the same thing. *G5426*
19 in their shame, who **m** earthly things.) *G5426*
4: 2 that they be of the same **m** in the Lord. *G5426*
Col 1:21 enemies in *your* **m** by wicked works, *G1271*
2:18 seen, vainly puffed up by his fleshly **m**, *G3563*
3:12 of **m**, meekness, longsuffering; *G5012*
2Th 2: 2 That ye be not soon shaken in **m**, or be *G3563*
2Ti 1: 7 power, and of love, and of a sound **m**. *G4995*
Tit 1:15 even their **m** and conscience is defiled. *G3563*
3: 1 Put them in **m** to be subject to *G5279*
Phlm 14 But without thy **m** would I do nothing; *G1106*
Heb 8:10 my laws into their **m**, and write them in *G1271*
1Pt 1:13 Wherefore gird up the loins of your **m**, *G1271*
3: 8 Finally, *be ye* all of one **m**, having *G3675*

1Pt 4: 1 with the same **m**: for he that hath *G1771*
5: 2 not for filthy lucre, but of a ready **m**; *G4290*
Rev 17: 9 And here *is* the **m** which hath wisdom. *G3563*
13 These have one **m**, and shall give their *G1106*

MINDED
Ru 1:18 When she saw that she was stedfastly **m** H553
2Ch 24: 4 was **m** to repair the house of the LORD. H3820
Ezr 7:13 realm, which are **m** of their own freewill
Mt 1:19 was **m** to put her away privily. *G1014*
Act 27:39 which they were **m**, if it were possible, *G1011*
Ro 8: 6 For to be carnally **m** *is* death; but to be *G5427*
6 but to be spiritually **m** *is* life and peace. *G5427*
2Co 1:15 And in this confidence I was **m** to come *G1014*
17 When I therefore was thus **m**, did I use *G1011*
Gal 5:10 will be none otherwise **m**: but he that *G5426*
Php 3:15 perfect, be thus **m**: and if in any thing *G5426*
15 **m**, God shall reveal even this unto you. *G5426*
Tit 2: 6 men likewise exhort to be sober **m**. *G4993*
Jas 1: 8 A double **m** man *is* unstable in all his *G1374*
4: 8 and purify *your* hearts, *ye* double **m**. *G1374*

MINDFUL
1Ch 16:15 Be ye **m** always of his covenant; the H2142
Neh 9:17 And refused to obey, neither were **m** of H2142
Ps 8: 4 What is man, that thou art **m** of him? H2142
111: 5 him: he will ever be **m** of his covenant. H2142
115:12 The LORD hath been **m** of us: he will H2142
Isa 17:10 and hast not been **m** of the rock of thy H2142
2Ti 1: 4 Greatly desiring to see thee, being **m** of *G3415*
Heb 2: 6 that thou art **m** of him? or the son of *G3403*
11:15 And truly, if they had been **m** of that *G3421*
2Pt 3: 2 That ye may be **m** of the words which *G3415*

MINDING
Act 20:13 he appointed, **m** himself to go afoot. *G3195*

MINDS
Jdg 19:30 of it, take advice, and speak *your m*.
2Sa 17: 8 *be* chafed in their **m**, as a bear robbed H5315
2Ki 9:15 said, If it be your **m**, *then* let none go H5315
Ezk 24:25 their **m**, their sons and their daughters, H5315
36: 5 despiteful **m**, to cast it out for a prey. H5315
Act 14: 2 **m** evil affected against the brethren. *G5590*
28: 6 their **m**, and said that he was a god. *G3328*
2Co 3:14 But their **m** were blinded: for until this *G3540*
4: 4 hath blinded the **m** of them which *G3540*
11: 3 subtilty, so your **m** should be corrupted *G3540*
Php 4: 7 hearts and **m** through Christ Jesus. *G3540*
1Ti 6: 5 of men of corrupt **m**, and destitute of *G3563*
2Ti 3: 8 **m**, reprobate concerning the faith. *G3563*
Heb 10:16 hearts, and in their **m** will I write them; *G1271*
12: 3 lest ye be wearied and faint in your **m**. *G5590*
2Pt 3: 1 your pure **m** by way of remembrance: *G1271*

MINE
See the Appendix.

MINGLE
Isa 5:22 and men of strength to **m** strong drink: H4537
Dan 2:43 clay, they shall **m** themselves with the H6151

MINGLED
Ex 9:24 So there was hail, and fire **m** with the H3947
29:40 a tenth deal of flour **m** with the fourth H1101
Lev 2: 4 cakes of fine flour **m** with oil, or H1101
5 be *of* fine flour unleavened, **m** with oil. H1101
7:10 And every meat offering, **m** with oil, H1101
12 unleavened cakes **m** with oil, and H1101
12 cakes **m** with oil, of fine flour, fried. H1101
9: 4 a meat offering **m** with oil: for to day H1101
14:10 offering, **m** with oil, and one log of oil. H1101
21 deal of fine flour **m** with oil for a meat H1101
19:19 sow thy field with **m** seed: neither shall H3610
19 shall a garment **m** of linen and woollen H3610
23:13 tenth deals of fine flour **m** with oil, an H1101
Nu 6:15 cakes of fine flour **m** with oil, and H1101
7:13 flour **m** with oil for a meat offering: H1101
19 flour **m** with oil for a meat offering: H1101
25 flour **m** with oil for a meat offering: H1101
31 flour **m** with oil for a meat offering: H1101
37 flour **m** with oil for a meat offering: H1101
43 flour **m** with oil for a meat offering: H1101
49 flour **m** with oil for a meat offering: H1101
55 flour **m** with oil for a meat offering: H1101
61 flour **m** with oil for a meat offering: H1101
67 flour **m** with oil for a meat offering: H1101
73 flour **m** with oil for a meat offering: H1101
79 flour **m** with oil for a meat offering: H1101
8: 8 *even* fine flour **m** with oil, and another H1101
Nu 15: 4 **m** with the fourth *part* of an hin of oil. H1101
6 **m** with the third *part* of an hin of oil. H1101
9 deals of flour **m** with half an hin of oil. H1101
28: 5 a meat offering, **m** with the fourth *part* H1101
9 *for* a meat offering, **m** with oil, and the H1101
12 *for* a meat offering, **m** with oil, for one H1101
12 meat offering, **m** with oil, for one ram; H1101
13 And a several tenth deal of flour **m** H1101
20 *shall be of* flour **m** with oil: three tenth H1101
28 And their meat offering of flour **m** with H1101
29: 3 *shall be of* flour **m** with oil, three tenth H1101
9 *shall be of* flour **m** with oil, three tenth H1101
14 *shall be of* flour **m** with oil, three tenth H1101
Ezr 9: 2 holy seed have **m** themselves with the H6148
Ps 102: 9 bread, and **m** my drink with weeping, H4537
106:35 But were **m** among the heathen, and H6148
Prv 9: 2 She hath killed her beasts; she hath **m** H4537
5 and drink of the wine *which* I have **m**. H4537
Isa 19:14 The LORD hath **m** a perverse spirit in H4537
Jer 25:20 And all the **m** people, and all the kings H6154
24 of the **m** people that dwell in the desert, H6154
50:37 and upon all the **m** people that *are* in H6154
Ezk 30: 5 Lydia, and all the **m** people, and Chub, H6154
Mt 27:34 They gave him vinegar to drink **m** with *G3396*
Mk 15:23 And they gave him to drink wine **m** *G3396*
Lk 13: 1 Pilate had **m** with their sacrifices. *G3396*
Rev 8: 7 hail and fire **m** with blood, and they *G3396*
15: 2 And I saw as it were a sea of glass **m** *G3396*

MINIAMIN
2Ch 31:15 And next him *were* Eden, and **M**, and H4509
Neh 12:17 Of Abijah, Zichri; of **M**, of Moadiah, H4509
41 And the priests; Eliakim, Maaseiah, **M**, H4509

MINISH
Ex 5:19 said, Ye shall not **m** *ought* from your H1639

MINISHED
Ps 107:39 Again, they are **m** and brought low H4591

MINISTER
Ex 24:13 And Moses rose up, and his **m** Joshua: H8334
28: 1 of Israel, that he may **m** unto me in the
3 he may **m** unto me in the priest's office.
4 he may **m** unto me in the priest's office.
35 And it shall be upon Aaron to **m**: and H8334
41 may **m** unto me in the priest's office.
43 unto the altar to **m** in the holy *place;* H8334
29: 1 to hallow them, to **m** unto me in the
30 congregation to **m** in the holy *place.* H8334
44 his sons, to **m** to me in the priest's office.
30:20 to the altar to **m**, to burn offering made H8334
30 may **m** unto me in the priest's office.
31:10 of his sons, to **m** in the priest's office,
35:19 of his sons, to **m** in the priest's office. H8334
39:26 **m** *in;* as the LORD commanded Moses. H8334
41 garments, to **m** in the priest's office. H8334
40:13 he may **m** unto me in the priest's office.
15 that they may **m** unto me in the priest's
Lev 7:35 to **m** unto the LORD in the priest's office;
16:32 he shall consecrate to **m** in the priest's
Nu 1:50 and they shall **m** unto it, and shall H8334
3: 3 he consecrated to **m** in the priest's office.
6 the priest, that they may **m** unto him. H8334
31 wherewith they **m**, and the hanging, H8334
4: 9 thereof, wherewith they **m** unto it: H8334
12 wherewith they **m** in the sanctuary, H8334
14 wherewith they **m** about it, *even* the H8334
8:26 But shall **m** with their brethren in the H8334
16: 9 the congregation to **m** unto them? H8334
18: 2 unto thee, and **m** unto thee: but thou H8334
2 *shall m* before the tabernacle of witness.
Dt 10: 8 the LORD to **m** unto him, and to bless H8334
17:12 that standeth to **m** there before the H8334
18: 5 tribes, to stand to **m** in the name of the H8334
7 Then he shall **m** in the name of the H8334
21: 5 God hath chosen to **m** unto him, and to H8334
Jos 1: 1 the son of Nun, Moses' **m**, saying, H8334
1Sa 2:11 **m** unto the LORD before Eli the priest. H8334
1Ki 8:11 So that the priests could not stand to **m** H8334
1Ch 15: 2 ark of God, and to **m** unto him for ever. H8334
16: 4 of the Levites to **m** before the ark of the H8334
37 and his brethren, to **m** before the ark H8334
23:13 the LORD, to **m** unto him, and to bless H8334
26:12 to **m** in the house of the LORD. H8334
2Ch 5:14 So that the priests could not stand to **m** H8334
8:14 to praise and **m** before the priests, as H8334
13:10 the priests, which **m** unto the LORD, H8334
23: 6 and they that **m** of the Levites; they H8334
2Ch 24:14 *even* vessels to **m**, and to offer *withal,* H8335
29:11 should **m** unto him, and burn incense. H8334
31: 2 offerings, to **m**, and to give thanks, H8334
Neh 10:36 priests that **m** in the house of our God: H8334
39 the priests that **m**, and the porters, and H8334
Ps 9: 8 he shall **m** judgment to the people H1777
Isa 60: 7 of Nebaioth shall **m** unto thee: they H8334
10 their kings shall **m** unto thee: for in my H8334
Jer 33:22 and the Levites that **m** unto me. H8334
Ezk 40:46 come near to the LORD to **m** unto him. H8334
42:14 wherein they **m**; for they *are* holy; and H8334
43:19 unto me, to **m** unto me, saith the Lord H8334
44:11 stand before them to **m** unto them. H8334
15 near to me to **m** unto me, and they H8334
16 to my table, to **m** unto me, and they H8334
17 them, whiles they **m** in the gates of the H8334
27 the inner court, to **m** in the sanctuary, H8334
45: 4 come near to **m** unto the LORD: and H8334
Mt 20:26 be great among you, let him be your **m**; *G1249*
28 unto, but to **m**, and to give his life a *G1247*
25:44 or in prison, and did not **m** unto thee? *G1247*
Mk 10:43 be great among you, shall be your **m**: *G1249*
45 unto, but to **m**, and to give his life a *G1247*
Lk 4:20 *it* again to the **m**, and sat down. And *G5257*
Act 13: 5 Jews: and they had also John to *their* **m**. *G5257*
24:23 acquaintance to **m** or come unto him. *G5256*
26:16 to make thee a **m** and a witness both *G5257*
Ro 13: 4 For he is the **m** of God to thee for good. *G1249*
4 vain: for he is the **m** of God, a revenger *G1249*
15: 8 Now I say that Jesus Christ was a **m** of *G1249*
16 That I should be the **m** of Jesus Christ *G3011*
25 But now I go unto Jerusalem to **m** unto *G1247*
27 is also to **m** unto them in carnal things. *G3008*
1Co 9:13 Do ye not know that they which **m** *G2038*
2Co 9:10 to the sower both **m** bread for *your* *G5524*
Gal 2:17 Christ the **m** of sin? God forbid. *G1249*
Eph 3: 7 Whereof I was made a **m**, according to *G1249*
4:29 that it may **m** grace unto the hearers. *G1325*
6:21 and faithful **m** in the Lord, shall make *G1249*
Col 1: 7 who is for you a faithful **m** of Christ; *G1249*
23 heaven; whereof I Paul am made a **m**; *G1249*
25 Whereof I am made a **m**, according to *G1249*
4: 7 **m** and fellowservant in the Lord: *G1249*
1Th 3: 2 our brother, and **m** of God, and our *G1249*
1Ti 1: 4 which **m** questions, rather than *G3930*
4: 6 thou shalt be a good **m** of Jesus Christ, *G1249*
Heb 1:14 sent forth to **m** for them who shall *G1248*
6:10 ministered to the saints, and do **m**. *G1247*
8: 2 A **m** of the sanctuary, and of the true *G3011*
1Pt 1:12 unto us they did **m** the things, which *G1247*
4:10 the gift, *even so* **m** the same one to *G1247*
11 of God; if any man **m**, *let him do it* as of *G1247*

MINISTERED
Nu 3: 4 and Ithamar **m** in the priest's office
Dt 10: 6 son **m** in the priest's office in his stead.
1Sa 2:18 But Samuel **m** before the LORD, *being* H8334
3: 1 And the child Samuel **m** unto the H8334
2Sa 13:17 Then he called his servant that **m** unto H8334
1Ki 1: 4 **m** to him: but the king knew her not. H8334
15 the Shunammite **m** unto the king. H8334
19:21 and went after Elijah, and **m** unto him. H8334
2Ki 25:14 wherewith they **m**, took they away. H8334
1Ch 6:32 And they **m** before the dwelling place H8334
28: 1 the companies that **m** to the king by H8334
2Ch 22: 8 that **m** to Ahaziah, he slew them. H8334
Est 2: 2 Then said the king's servants that **m** H8334
6: 3 servants that **m** unto him, There is H8334
Jer 52:18 wherewith they **m**, took they away. H8334
Ezk 44:12 Because they **m** unto them before their H8334
19 wherein they **m**, and lay them in the H8334
Dan 7:10 thousands **m** unto him, and ten H8120
Mt 4:11 behold, angels came and **m** unto him. *G1247*
8:15 her: and she arose, and **m** unto them. *G1247*
20:28 came not to be **m** unto, but to minister, *G1247*
Mk 1:13 beasts; and the angels **m** unto him. *G1247*
31 the fever left her, and she **m** unto them. *G1247*
10:45 came not to be **m** unto, but to minister, *G1247*
15:41 followed him, and **m** unto him;) and *G1247*
Lk 4:39 she arose and **m** unto them. *G1247*
8: 3 which **m** unto him of their substance. *G1247*
Act 13: 2 As they **m** to the Lord, and fasted, the *G3008*
19:22 two of them that **m** unto him, *G1247*
20:34 that these hands have **m** unto my *G5256*
2Co 3: 3 epistle of Christ **m** by us, written not *G1247*
Php 2:25 messenger, and he that **m** to my wants. *G3011*
Col 2:19 nourishment **m**, and knit together, *G2023*
2Ti 1:18 many things he **m** unto me at Ephesus, *G1247*
Phlm 13 **m** unto me in the bonds of the gospel: *G1247*

Heb 6:10 have **m** to the saints, and do minister. *G1247*
2Pt 1:11 For so an entrance shall be **m** unto you *G2023*

MINISTERETH
2Co 9:10 Now he that **m** seed to the sower both *G2023*
Gal 3: 5 He therefore that **m** to you the Spirit, *G2023*

MINISTERING
1Ch 9:28 the charge of the **m** vessels, that they H5656
Ezk 44:11 of the house, and **m** to the house: they H8334
Mt 27:55 Jesus from Galilee, **m** unto him: *G1247*
Ro 12: 7 Or ministry, *let us wait* on *our* **m**: or he *G1248*
15:16 to the Gentiles, **m** the gospel of God, *G2418*
2Co 8: 4 *us* the fellowship of the **m** to the saints. *G1248*
9: 1 For as touching the **m** to the saints, it is *G1248*
Heb 1:14 Are they not all **m** spirits, sent forth to *G3010*
10:11 And every priest standeth daily **m** and *G3008*

MINISTERS
1Ki 10: 5 attendance of his **m**, and their apparel, H8334
2Ch 9: 4 attendance of his **m**, and their apparel; H8334
Ezr 7:24 Nethinims, or **m** of this house of God, H6399
8:17 unto us **m** for the house of our God. H8334
Ps 103:21 hosts; *ye* **m** of his, that do his pleasure. H8334
104: 4 Who maketh his angels spirits; his **m** a H8334
Isa 61: 6 shall call you the **M** of our God: ye shall H8334
Jer 33:21 and with the Levites the priests, my **m**. H8334
Ezk 44:11 Yet they shall be **m** in my sanctuary, H8334
45: 4 for the priests the **m** of the sanctuary, H8334
5 the Levites, the **m** of the house, have H8334
46:24 boil, where the **m** of the house shall H8334
Joel 1: 9 the priests, the LORD'S **m**, mourn. H8334
13 priests: howl, ye **m** of the altar: come, H8334
13 in sackcloth, ye **m** of my God: for the H8334
2:17 Let the priests, the **m** of the LORD, H8334
Lk 1: 2 were eyewitnesses, and **m** of the word; *G5257*
Ro 13: 6 also: for they are God's **m**, attending *G3011*
1Co 3: 5 *is* Apollos, but **m** by whom ye believed, *G1249*
4: 1 Let a man so account of us, as of the **m** *G5257*
2Co 3: 6 Who also hath made us able **m** of the *G1249*
6: 4 ourselves as the **m** of God, in much *G1249*
11:15 Therefore *it is* no great thing if his **m** *G1249*
15 as the **m** of righteousness; whose *G1249*
23 Are they **m** of Christ? (I speak as a fool) *G1249*
Heb 1: 7 angels spirits, and his **m** a flame of fire. *G3011*

MINISTRATION
Lk 1:23 soon as the days of his **m** were *G3009*
Act 6: 1 widows were neglected in the daily **m**. *G1248*
2Co 3: 7 But if the **m** of death, written *and* *G1248*
8 How shall not the **m** of the spirit be *G1248*
9 For if the **m** of condemnation *be* glory, *G1248*
9 the **m** of righteousness exceed in glory. *G1248*
9:13 Whiles by the experiment of this **m** *G1248*

MINISTRY
Nu 4:12 the instruments of **m**, wherewith they H8335
47 the service of the **m**, and the service of H5656
2Ch 7: 6 praised by their **m**; and the priests H3027
Hos 12:10 similitudes, by the **m** of the prophets. H3027
Act 1:17 us, and had obtained part of this **m**. *G1248*
25 That he may take part of this **m** and *G1248*
6: 4 to prayer, and to the **m** of the word. *G1248*
12:25 they had fulfilled *their* **m**, and took with *G1248*
20:24 with joy, and the **m**, which I have *G1248*
21:19 wrought among the Gentiles by his **m**. *G1248*
Ro 12: 7 Or **m**, *let us wait* on *our* ministering: or *G1248*
1Co 16:15 themselves to the **m** of the saints,) *G1248*
2Co 4: 1 Therefore seeing we have this **m**, as we *G1248*
5:18 given to us the **m** of reconciliation; *G1248*
6: 3 in any thing, that the **m** be not blamed: *G1248*
Eph 4:12 **m**, for the edifying of the body of Christ: *G1248*
Col 4:17 Take heed to the **m** which thou hast *G1248*
1Ti 1:12 me faithful, putting me into the **m**; *G1248*
2Ti 4: 5 an evangelist, make full proof of thy **m**. *G1248*
11 for he is profitable to me for the **m**. *G1248*
Heb 8: 6 a more excellent **m**, by how much also *G3009*
9:21 tabernacle, and all the vessels of the **m**. *G3009*

MINNI
Jer 51:27 of Ararat, **M**, and Ashchenaz; appoint H4508

MINNITH
Jdg 11:33 till thou come to **M**, *even* twenty cities, H4511
Ezk 27:17 market wheat of **M**, and Pannag, and H4511

MINSTREL
2Ki 3:15 But now bring me a **m**. And it came to H5059
15 to pass, when the **m** played, that the H5059

MINSTRELS
Mt 9:23 the **m** and the people making a noise, *G834*

MINT
Mt 23:23 for ye pay tithe of **m** and anise and *G2238*
Lk 11:42 for ye tithe **m** and rue and all manner *G2238*

MIPHKAD
Neh 3:31 **M**, and to the going up of the corner. H4663

MIRACLE
Ex 7: 9 saying, Shew a **m** for you: then thou H4159
Mk 6:52 For they considered not *the* **m** of the
9:39 which shall do a **m** in my name, that *G1411*
Lk 23: 8 to have seen some **m** done by him. *G4592*
Jn 4:54 This *is* again the second **m** *that* Jesus *G4592*
6:14 they had seen the **m** that Jesus did, *G4592*
10:41 said, John did no **m**: but all things that *G4592*
12:18 they heard that he had done this **m**. *G4592*
Act 4:16 indeed a notable **m** hath been done by *G4592*
22 whom this **m** of healing was shewed. *G4592*

MIRACLES
Nu 14:22 my glory, and my **m**, which I did in Egypt H226
Dt 11: 3 And his **m**, and his acts, which he did in H226
29: 3 have seen, the signs, and those great **m**: H4159
Jdg 6:13 where *be* all his **m** which our fathers H6381
Jn 2:11 This beginning of **m** did Jesus in Cana *G4592*
23 when they saw the **m** which he did. *G4592*
3: 2 man can do these **m** that thou doest, *G4592*
6: 2 they saw his **m** which he did on them *G4592*
26 ye saw the **m**, but because ye did *G4592*
7:31 will he do more **m** than these which *G4592*
9:16 is a sinner do such **m**? And there was a *G4592*
11:47 do we? for this man doeth many **m**. *G4592*
12:37 But though he had done so many **m** *G4592*
Act 2:22 God among you by **m** and wonders and *G1411*
6: 8 wonders and **m** among the people. *G4592*
8: 6 hearing and seeing the **m** which he did. *G4592*
13 the **m** and signs which were done. *G1411*
15:12 declaring what **m** and wonders God *G4592*
19:11 And God wrought special **m** by the *G1411*
1Co 12:10 To another the working of **m**; to *G1411*
28 after that **m**, then gifts of healings, *G1411*
29 *are* all teachers? *are* all workers of **m**? *G1411*
Gal 3: 5 and worketh **m** among you, *doeth he* *G1411*
Heb 2: 4 and with divers **m**, and gifts of the Holy *G1411*
Rev 13:14 *means of* those **m** which he had power *G4592*
16:14 of devils, working **m**, *which* go forth *G4592*
19:20 that wrought **m** before him, with which *G4592*

MIRE
2Sa 22:43 them as the **m** of the street, *and* did H2916
Job 8:11 Can the rush grow up without **m**? can H1207
30:19 He hath cast me into the **m**, and I am H2563
41:30 sharp pointed things upon the **m**. H2916
Ps 69: 2 I sink in deep **m**, where *there is* no H3121
14 Deliver me out of the **m**, and let me not H2916
Isa 10: 6 them down like the **m** of the streets. H2563
57:20 rest, whose waters cast up **m** and dirt. H7516
Jer 38: 6 but **m**: so Jeremiah sunk in the mire. H2916
6 but mire: so Jeremiah sunk in the **m**. H2916
22 the **m**, *and* they are turned away back. H1206
Mic 7:10 trodden down as the **m** of the streets. H2916
Zec 9: 3 and fine gold as the **m** of the streets. H2916
10: 5 *enemies* in the **m** of the streets in the H2916
2Pt 2:22 was washed to her wallowing in the **m**. *G1004*

MIRIAM
Ex 15:20 And **M** the prophetess, the sister of H4813
21 And **M** answered them, Sing ye to the H4813
Nu 12: 1 And **M** and Aaron spake against Moses H4813
4 Aaron, and unto **M**, Come out ye three H4813
5 and **M**: and they both came forth. H4813
10 and, behold, **M** *became* leprous, *white* H4813
10 upon **M**, and, behold, *she was* leprous. H4813
15 And **M** was shut out from the camp H4813
15 not till **M** was brought in *again*. H4813
20: 1 **M** died there, and was buried there. H4813
26:59 Aaron and Moses, and **M** their sister. H4813
Dt 24: 9 thy God did unto **M** by the way, after H4813
1Ch 4:17 and she bare **M**, and Shammai, and H4813
6: 3 and Moses, and **M**. The sons also of H4813
Mic 6: 4 I sent before thee Moses, Aaron, and **M**. H4813

MIRMA
1Ch 8:10 And Jeuz, and Shachia, and **M**. These H4821

MIRTH
Gen 31:27 thee away with **m**, and with songs, with H8057
Neh 8:12 and to make great **m**, because they had H8057
Ps 137: 3 us *required of us* **m**, *saying*, Sing us *one* H8057
Prv 14:13 and the end of that **m** *is* heaviness. H8057
Ecc 2: 1 I will prove thee with **m**, therefore enjoy H8057
2 I said of laughter, *It is* mad: and of **m**, H8057
7: 4 the heart of fools *is* in the house of **m**. H8057
8:15 Then I commended **m**, because a man H8057
Isa 24: 8 The **m** of tabrets ceaseth, the noise of H4885
11 is darkened, the **m** of the land is gone. H4885
Jer 7:34 the voice of **m**, and the voice of H8342
16: 9 days, the voice of **m**, and the voice of H8342
25:10 them the voice of **m**, and the voice of H8342
Ezk 21:10 we then make **m**? it contemneth the rod H7797
Hos 2:11 I will also cause all her **m** to cease, her H4885

MIRY
Ps 40: 2 pit, out of the **m** clay, and set my feet H3121
Ezk 47:11 But the **m** places thereof and the H1207
Dan 2:41 sawest the iron mixed with **m** clay. H2917
43 iron mixed with **m** clay, they shall H2917

MISCARRYING
Hos 9:14 give them a **m** womb and dry breasts. H7921

MISCHIEF
Gen 42: 4 he said, Lest peradventure **m** befall him. H611
38 he is left alone: if **m** befall him by the H611
44:29 And if ye take this also from me, and **m** H611
Ex 21:22 *her*, and yet no **m** follow: he shall be H611
23 And if *any* **m** follow, then thou shalt give H611
32:12 and say, For **m** did he bring them out, H7451
22 the people, that they *are set* on **m**. H7451
1Sa 23: 9 secretly practised **m** against him; and H7451
2Sa 16: 8 thy **m**, because thou *art* a bloody man. H7451
1Ki 11:25 beside the **m** that Hadad *did:* and H7451
20: 7 this *man* seeketh **m**: for he sent unto me H7451
2Ki 7: 9 light, some **m** will come upon us: H5771
Neh 6: 2 of Ono. But they thought to do me **m**. H7451
Est 8: 3 tears to put away the **m** of Haman the H7451
Job 15:35 They conceive **m**, and bring forth H5999
Ps 7:14 **m**, and brought forth falsehood. H5999
16 His **m** shall return upon his own head, H5999
10: 7 under his tongue *is* **m** and vanity. H5999
14 Thou hast seen *it*; for thou beholdest **m** H5999
26:10 In whose hands *is* **m**, and their right H2154
28: 3 neighbours, but **m** *is* in their hearts. H7451
36: 4 He deviseth **m** upon his bed; he setteth H205
52: 1 Why boastest thou thyself in **m**, O H7451
55:10 **m** also and sorrow *are* in the midst of it. H205
62: 3 How long will ye imagine **m** against a H205
94:20 with thee, which frameth **m** by a law? H5999
119:150 They draw nigh that follow after **m**: H2154
140: 9 let the **m** of their own lips cover them. H5999
Prv 4:16 they have done **m**; and their sleep is H7489
6:14 **m** continually; he soweth discord. H7451
18 feet that be swift in running to **m**, H7451
10:23 *It is* as sport to a fool to do **m**: but a H2154
11:27 that seeketh **m**, it shall come unto him. H7451
12:21 but the wicked shall be filled with **m**. H7451
13:17 A wicked messenger falleth into **m**: but H7451
17:20 hath a perverse tongue falleth into **m**. H7451
24: 2 destruction, and their lips talk of **m**. H5999
16 again: but the wicked shall fall into **m**. H7451
28:14 hardeneth his heart shall fall into **m**. H7451
Isa 47:11 it riseth: and **m** shall fall upon thee; H1943
59: 4 conceive **m**, and bring forth iniquity. H5999
Ezk 7:26 **M** shall come upon mischief, and H1943
26 Mischief shall come upon **m**, and H1943
11: 2 **m**, and give wicked counsel in this city: H205
Dan 11:27 *shall be* to do **m**, and they shall speak H4827
Hos 7:15 yet do they imagine **m** against me. H7451
Act 13:10 And said, O full of all subtilty and all **m**, *G4468*

MISCHIEFS
Dt 32:23 I will heap **m** upon them; I will spend H7451
Ps 52: 2 Thy tongue deviseth **m**; like a sharp H1942
140: 2 Which imagine **m** in *their* heart; H7451

MISCHIEVOUS
Ps 21:11 they imagined a **m** device, *which* they H4209
38:12 my hurt speak **m** things, and imagine H1942
Prv 24: 8 to do evil shall be called a **m** person. H4209
Ecc 10:13 and the end of his talk *is* **m** madness. H7451
Mic 7: 3 his **m** desire: so they wrap it up. H1942

MISERABLE
Job 16: 2 I have heard many such things: **m** H5999

1Co 15:19 in Christ, we are of all men most **m**. *G1652*
Rev 3:17 and **m**, and poor, and blind, and naked: *G1652*

MISERABLY
Mt 21:41 They say unto him, He will **m** destroy *G2560*

MISERIES
Lam 1: 7 and of her **m** all her pleasant things H4788
Jas 5: 1 for your **m** that shall come upon *you*. *G5004*

MISERY
Jdg 10:16 his soul was grieved for the **m** of Israel. H5999
Job 3:20 is in **m**, and life unto the bitter *in* soul; H6001
11:16 Because thou shalt forget *thy* **m**, *and* H5999
Prv 31: 7 poverty, and remember his **m** no more. H5999
Ecc 8: 6 the **m** of man *is* great upon him. H7451
Lam 3:19 and my **m**, the wormwood and the gall. H4788
Ro 3:16 Destruction and **m** *are* in their ways: *G5004*

MISGAB
Jer 48: 1 taken: **M** is confounded and dismayed. H4869

MISHAEL
Ex 6:22 And the sons of Uzziel; **M**, and H4332
Lev 10: 4 And Moses called **M** and Elzaphan, the H4332
Neh 8: 4 Pedaiah, and **M**, and Malchiah, and H4332
Dan 1: 6 Daniel, Hananiah, **M**, and Azariah: H4332
7 of Shadrach; and to **M**, of Meshach; and H4332
11 Daniel, Hananiah, **M**, and Azariah, H4332
19 Hananiah, **M**, and Azariah: therefore H4332
2:17 **M**, and Azariah, his companions: H4333

MISHAL
Jos 21:30 And out of the tribe of Asher, **M** with H4861

MISHAM
1Ch 8:12 The sons of Elpaal; Eber, and **M**, and H4936

MISHEAL
Jos 19:26 And Alammelech, and Amad, and **M**; H4861

MISHMA
Gen 25:14 And **M**, and Dumah, and Massa, H4927
1Ch 1:30 **M**, and Dumah, Massa, Hadad, and H4927
4:25 Shallum his son, Mibsam his son, **M** H4927
26 And the sons of **M**; Hamuel his son, H4927

MISHMANNAH
1Ch 12:10 **M** the fourth, Jeremiah the fifth, H4925

MISHPAT See EN-MISHPAT.

MISHRAITES
1Ch 2:53 and the **M**; of them came the H4954

MISPAR
Ezr 2: 2 Bilshan, **M**, Bigvai, Rehum, Baanah. H4558

MISPERETH
Neh 7: 7 Bilshan, **M**, Bigvai, Nehum, Baanah. H4559

MISREPHOTH-MAIM
Jos 11: 8 Zidon, and unto **M**, and unto the valley H4956
13: 6 Lebanon unto **M**, *and* all the Sidonians, H4956

MISS
Jdg 20:16 stones at an hair *breadth*, and not **m**. H2398
1Sa 20: 6 If thy father at all **m** me, then say, H6485

MISSED
1Sa 20:18 be **m**, because thy seat will be empty. H6485
25:15 not hurt, neither **m** we any thing, as H6485
21 so that nothing was **m** of all that H6485

MISSING
1Sa 25: 7 was there ought **m** unto them, all the H6485
1Ki 20:39 any means he be **m**, then shall thy life H6485

MIST
Gen 2: 6 But there went up a **m** from the earth, H108
Act 13:11 there fell on him a **m** and a darkness; *G887*
2Pt 2:17 the **m** of darkness is reserved for ever. *G2217*

MISTRESS
Gen 16: 4 her **m** was despised in her eyes. H1404
8 said, I flee from the face of my **m** Sarai. H1404
9 **m**, and submit thyself under her hands. H1404
1Ki 17:17 of the woman, the **m** of the house, fell H1172
2Ki 5: 3 And she said unto her **m**, Would God H1404
Ps 123: 2 the hand of her **m**; so our eyes *wait* H1404
Prv 30:23 and an handmaid that is heir to her **m**. H1404
Isa 24: 2 maid, so with her **m**; as with the buyer, H1404
Nah 3: 4 harlot, the **m** of witchcrafts, that H1172

MISUSED
2Ch 36:16 his words, and **m** his prophets, until H8591

MITE
Lk 12:59 till thou hast paid the very last **m**. *G3016*

MITES
Mk 12:42 threw in two **m**, which make a farthing. *G3016*
Lk 21: 2 poor widow casting in thither two **m**. *G3016*

MITHCAH
Nu 33:28 removed from Tarah, and pitched in **M**. H4989
29 And they went from **M**, and pitched in H4989

MITHNITE
1Ch 11:43 son of Maachah, and Joshaphat the **M**, H4981

MITHREDATH
Ezr 1: 8 by the hand of **M** the treasurer, and H4990
4: 7 wrote Bishlam, **M**, Tabeel, and the rest H4990

MITRE
Ex 28: 4 a broidered coat, a **m**, and a girdle: and H4701
37 may be upon the **m**; upon the forefront H4701
37 upon the forefront of the **m** it shall be. H4701
39 shalt make the **m** *of* fine linen, and H4701
29: 6 And thou shalt put the **m** upon his H4701
6 and put the holy crown upon the **m**. H4701
39:28 And a **m** *of* fine linen, and goodly H4701
31 **m**; as the LORD commanded Moses. H4701
Lev 8: 9 And he put the **m** upon his head; also H4701
9 head; also upon the **m**, *even* upon his H4701
16: 4 girdle, and with the linen **m** shall he be H4701
Zec 3: 5 And I said, Let them set a fair **m** upon H6797
5 So they set a fair **m** upon his head, and H6797

MITYLENE
Act 20:14 Assos, we took him in, and came to **M**. *G3412*

MIXED
Ex 12:38 And a **m** multitude went up also with H6154
Neh 13: 3 from Israel all the **m** multitude. H6154
Prv 23:30 the wine; they that go to seek **m** wine. H4469
Isa 1:22 Thy silver is become dross, thy wine **m** H4107
Dan 2:41 thou sawest the iron **m** with miry clay. H6151
43 And whereas thou sawest iron **m** with H6151
43 even as iron is not **m** with clay. H6151
Hos 7: 8 Ephraim, he hath **m** himself among the H1101
Heb 4: 2 **m** with faith in them that heard *it*. *G4786*

MIXT
Nu 11: 4 And the **m** multitude that *was* among

MIXTURE
Ps 75: 8 is red; it is full of **m**; and he poureth out H4538
Jn 19:39 and brought a **m** of myrrh and aloes, *G3395*
Rev 14:10 poured out without **m** into the cup of his *G194*

MIZAR
Ps 42: 6 and of the Hermonites, from the hill **M**. H4706

MIZPAH
Gen 31:49 And **M**; for he said, The LORD watch H4709
1Ki 15:22 with them Geba of Benjamin, and **M**. H4709
2Ki 25:23 to Gedaliah to **M**, even Ishmael the son H4709
25 the Chaldees that were with him at **M**. H4709
2Ch 16: 6 and he built therewith Geba and **M**. H4709
Neh 3: 7 of Gibeon, and of **M**, unto the throne of H4709
15 the ruler of part of **M**; he built it, and H4709
19 the ruler of **M**, another piece over H4709
Jer 40: 6 the son of Ahikam to **M**; and dwelt with H4708
8 Then they came to Gedaliah to **M**, even H4708
10 As for me, behold, I will dwell at **M** to H4709
12 to Gedaliah, unto **M**, and gathered wine H4708
13 in the fields, came to Gedaliah to **M**, H4708
15 to Gedaliah in **M** secretly, saying, Let H4709
41: 1 son of Ahikam to **M**; and there they did H4709
1 there they did eat bread together in **M**. H4708
3 with Gedaliah, at **M**, and the Chaldeans H4709
6 went forth from **M** to meet them, H4709
10 people that *were* in **M**, *even* the king's H4709
10 people that remained in **M**, whom H4709
14 away captive from **M** cast about and H4709
16 of Nethaniah, from **M**, after *that* he had H4709
Hos 5: 1 on **M**, and a net spread upon Tabor. H4709

MIZPEH
Jos 11: 3 Hivite under Hermon in the land of **M**. H4709
8 and unto the valley of **M** eastward; and H4708
15:38 And Dilean, and **M**, and Joktheel, H4708
18:26 And **M**, and Chephirah, and Mozah, H4708
Jdg 10:17 together, and encamped in **M**. H4709
11:11 all his words before the LORD in **M**. H4709
29 and passed over **M** of Gilead, and from H4708
29 of Gilead, and from **M** of Gilead he H4708
34 And Jephthah came to **M** unto his H4709
20: 1 the land of Gilead, unto the LORD in **M**. H4709
3 Israel were gone up to **M**.) Then said the H4709
21: 1 Now the men of Israel had sworn in **M**, H4709
5 up to the LORD to **M**, saying, He shall H4709
8 came not up to **M** to the LORD? And, H4709
1Sa 7: 5 And Samuel said, Gather all Israel to **M**, H4708
6 And they gathered together to **M**, and H4709
6 judged the children of Israel in **M**. H4708
7 gathered together to **M**, the lords of the H4708
11 And the men of Israel went out of **M**, H4709
12 and set *it* between **M** and Shen, and H4709
16 **M**, and judged Israel in all those places. H4709
10:17 people together unto the LORD to **M**; H4709
22: 3 And David went thence to **M** of Moab: H4708

MIZRAIM
Gen 10: 6 And the sons of Ham; Cush, and **M**, and H4714
13 And **M** begat Ludim, and Anamim, H4714
1Ch 1: 8 The sons of Ham; Cush, and **M**, Put, H4714
11 And **M** begat Ludim, and Anamim, H4714

MIZZAH
Gen 36:13 Shammah, and **M**: these were the sons H4199
17 Shammah, duke **M**: these *are* the dukes H4199
1Ch 1:37 Nahath, Zerah, Shammah, and **M**. H4199

MNASON
Act 21:16 with them one **M** of Cyprus, an old *G3416*

MOAB
Gen 19:37 and called his name **M**: the same *is* the H4124
36:35 in the field of **M**, reigned in his stead: H4124
Ex 15:15 mighty men of **M**, trembling shall take H4124
Nu 21:11 *is* before **M**, toward the sunrising. H4124
13 of **M**, between Moab and the Amorites. H4124
13 of Moab, between **M** and the Amorites. H4124
15 of Ar, and lieth upon the border of **M**. H4124
20 *is* in the country of **M**, to the top of H4124
26 the former king of **M**, and taken all his H4124
28 consumed Ar of **M**, *and* the lords of the H4124
29 Woe to thee, **M**! thou art undone, O H4124
22: 1 of **M** on this side Jordan *by* Jericho. H4124
3 And **M** was sore afraid of the people, H4124
3 they *were* many: and **M** was distressed H4124
4 And **M** said unto the elders of Midian, H4124
7 And the elders of **M** and the elders of H4124
8 the princes of **M** abode with Balaam. H4124
10 king of **M**, hath sent unto me, *saying*, H4124
14 And the princes of **M** rose up, and they H4124
21 his ass, and went with the princes of **M**. H4124
36 him unto a city of **M**, which *is* in the H4124
23: 6 sacrifice, he, and all the princes of **M**. H4124
7 Balak the king of **M** hath brought me H4124
17 and the princes of **M** with him. And H4124
24:17 **M**, and destroy all the children of Sheth. H4124
25: 1 whoredom with the daughters of **M**. H4124
26: 3 of **M** by Jordan *near* Jericho, saying, H4124
63 the plains of **M** by Jordan *near* Jericho. H4124
31:12 of **M**, which *are* by Jordan *near* Jericho. H4124
33:44 in Ijeabarim, in the border of **M**. H4124
48 the plains of **M** by Jordan *near* Jericho. H4124
49 unto Abel-shittim in the plains of **M**. H4124
50 of **M** by Jordan *near* Jericho, saying, H4124
35: 1 of **M** by Jordan *near* Jericho, saying, H4124
36:13 the plains of **M** by Jordan *near* Jericho. H4124
Dt 1: 5 On this side Jordan, in the land of **M**, H4124
2: 8 by the way of the wilderness of **M**. H4124
18 through Ar, the coast of **M**, this day: H4124
29: 1 in the land of **M**, beside the covenant H4124
32:49 *is* in the land of **M**, that *is* over against H4124
34: 1 up from the plains of **M** unto the H4124
5 **M**, according to the word of the LORD. H4124
6 valley in the land of **M**, over against H4124
8 in the plains of **M** thirty days: so the H4124
Jos 13:32 in the plains of **M**, on the other side H4124
24: 9 of Zippor, king of **M**, arose and warred H4124
Jdg 3:12 Eglon the king of **M** against Israel, H4124

Jdg 3:14 Eglon the king of **M** eighteen years. H4124
15 sent a present unto Eglon the king of **M**. H4124
17 of **M**: and Eglon *was* a very fat man. H4124
28 **M**, and suffered not a man to pass over. H4124
29 And they slew of **M** at that time about H4124
30 So **M** was subdued that day under the H4124
10: 6 and the gods of **M**, and the gods of the H4124
11:15 away the land of **M**, nor the land of the H4124
17 unto the king of **M**: but he would not H4124
18 and the land of **M**, and came by the east H4124
18 side of the land of **M**, and pitched on H4124
18 **M**: for Arnon *was* the border of Moab. H4124
18 Moab: for Arnon *was* the border of **M**. H4124
25 of Zippor, king of **M**? did he ever strive H4124
Ru 1: 1 of **M**, he, and his wife, and his two sons. H4124
2 the country of **M**, and continued there. H4124
4 of the women of **M**; the name of the one H4125
6 the country of **M**: for she had heard in H4124
6 in the country of **M** how that the LORD H4124
22 of the country of **M**: and they came to H4124
2: 6 with Naomi out of the country of **M**: H4124
4: 3 of the country of **M**, selleth a parcel of H4124
1Sa 12: 9 of **M**, and they fought against them. H4124
14:47 every side, against **M**, and against the H4124
22: 3 And David went thence to Mizpeh of **M**: H4124
3 unto the king of **M**, Let my father and H4124
4 before the king of **M**: and they dwelt H4124
2Sa 8: 2 And he smote **M**, and measured them H4124
12 Of Syria, and of **M**, and of the children H4124
23:20 lionlike men of **M**: he went down also H4124
1Ki 11: 7 the abomination of **M**, in the hill that *is* H4124
2Ki 1: 1 Then **M** rebelled against Israel after the H4124
3: 4 And Mesha king of **M** was a H4124
5 of **M** rebelled against the king of Israel. H4124
7 The king of **M** hath rebelled against H4124
7 go with me against **M** to battle? And he H4124
10 to deliver them into the hand of **M**! H4124
13 to deliver them into the hand of **M**. H4124
23 another: now therefore, **M**, to the spoil. H4124
26 And when the king of **M** saw that the H4124
1Ch 1:46 in the field of **M**, reigned in his stead: H4124
4:22 the dominion in **M**, and Jashubilehem. H4124
8: 8 in the country of **M**, after he had sent H4124
11:22 lionlike men of **M**: also he went down H4124
18: 2 And he smote **M**; and the Moabites H4124
11 from Edom, and from **M**, and from the H4124
2Ch 20: 1 the children of **M**, and the children of H4124
10 of Ammon and **M** and mount Seir, H4124
22 of Ammon, **M**, and mount Seir, which H4124
23 For the children of Ammon and **M** H4124
Neh 13:23 wives of Ashdod, of Ammon, *and* of **M**: H4125
Ps 60: 8 **M** *is* my washpot; over Edom will I cast H4124
83: 6 Ishmaelites; of **M**, and the Hagarenes; H4124
108: 9 **M** *is* my washpot; over Edom will I cast H4124
Isa 11:14 upon Edom and **M**; and the children of H4124
15: 1 The burden of **M**. Because in the night H4124
1 in the night Ar of **M** is laid waste, *and* H4124
1 **M** is laid waste, *and* brought to silence; H4124
2 high places, to weep: **M** shall howl over H4124
4 armed soldiers of **M** shall cry out; his H4124
5 My heart shall cry out for **M**; his H4124
8 the borders of **M**; the howling thereof H4124
9 **M**, and upon the remnant of the land. H4124
16: 2 of **M** shall be at the fords of Arnon. H4124
4 Let mine outcasts dwell with thee, **M**; be H4124
6 We have heard of the pride of **M**; *he is* H4124
7 Therefore shall **M** howl for Moab, H4124
7 Therefore shall Moab howl for **M**, every H4124
11 like an harp for **M**, and mine inward H4124
12 it is seen that **M** is weary on the high H4124
13 spoken concerning **M** since that time. H4124
14 and the glory of **M** shall be contemned, H4124
25:10 the LORD rest, and **M** shall be trodden H4124
Jer 9:26 of Ammon, and **M**, and all *that are* in H4124
25:21 Edom, and **M**, and the children of H4124
27: 3 and to the king of **M**, and to the king of H4124
40:11 the Jews that *were* in **M**, and among the H4124
48: 1 Against **M** thus saith the LORD of H4124
2 *There shall be* no more praise of **M**: in H4124
4 **M** is destroyed; her little ones have H4124
9 Give wings unto **M**, that it may flee and H4124
11 **M** hath been at ease from his youth, H4124
13 And **M** shall be ashamed of Chemosh, H4124
15 **M** is spoiled, and gone up *out of* her H4124
16 The calamity of **M** *is* near to come, and H4124
18 for the spoiler of **M** shall come upon H4124
20 **M** is confounded; for it is broken down: H4124
20 tell ye it in Arnon, that **M** is spoiled, H4124
24 the cities of the land of **M**, far or near. H4124

Jer 48:25 The horn of **M** is cut off, and his arm is H4124
26 the LORD: **M** also shall wallow in H4124
28 O ye that dwell in **M**, leave the cities, H4124
29 We have heard the pride of **M**, (he is H4124
31 Therefore will I howl for **M**, and I will H4124
31 I will cry out for all **M**; *mine heart* shall H4124
33 from the land of **M**; and I have caused H4124
35 Moreover I will cause to cease in **M**, H4124
36 Therefore mine heart shall sound for **M** H4124
38 the housetops of **M**, and in the streets H4124
38 for I have broken **M** like a vessel H4124
39 down! how hath **M** turned the back H4124
39 shame! so shall **M** be a derision and a H4124
40 and shall spread his wings over **M**. H4124
41 men's hearts in **M** at that day shall be H4124
42 And **M** shall be destroyed from *being* a H4124
43 O inhabitant of **M**, saith the LORD. H4124
44 upon it, *even* upon **M**, the year of their H4124
45 the corner of **M**, and the crown of the H4124
46 Woe be unto thee, O **M**! the people of H4124
47 Yet will I bring again the captivity of **M** H4124
47 LORD. Thus far *is* the judgment of **M**. H4124
Ezk 25: 8 GOD; Because that **M** and Seir do say, H4124
9 open the side of **M** from the cities, from H4124
11 And I will execute judgments upon **M**; H4124
Dan 11:41 *even* Edom, and **M**, and the chief of the H4124
Am 2: 1 transgressions of **M**, and for four, I will H4124
2 But I will send a fire upon **M**, and it H4124
2 of Kerioth: and **M** shall die with H4124
Mic 6: 5 Balak king of **M** consulted, and what H4124
Zep 2: 8 I have heard the reproach of **M**, and the H4124
9 of Israel, Surely **M** shall be as Sodom, H4124

MOABITE
Dt 23: 3 An Ammonite or **M** shall not enter into H4125
1Ch 11:46 the sons of Elnaam, and Ithmah the **M**, H4125
Neh 13: 1 and the **M** should not come into H4125

MOABITES
Gen 19:37 *is* the father of the **M** unto this day. H4124
Nu 22: 4 Zippor *was* king of the **M** at that time. H4124
Dt 2: 9 me, Distress not the **M**, neither contend H4124
11 Anakims; but the **M** call them Emims. H4125
29 in Seir, and the **M** which dwell in Ar, H4125
Jdg 3:28 your enemies the **M** into your hand. H4124
2Sa 8: 2 alive. And *so* the **M** became David's H4124
1Ki 11: 1 Pharaoh, women of the **M**, Ammonites, H4125
33 the god of the **M**, and Milcom the god H4124
2Ki 3:18 will deliver the **M** also into your hand. H4124
21 And when all the **M** heard that the H4124
22 the water, and the **M** saw the water on H4124
24 up and smote the **M**, so that they fled H4124
24 smiting the **M**, even in *their* country. H4124
13:20 the bands of the **M** invaded the land at H4124
23:13 of the **M**, and for Milcom the H4124
24: 2 and bands of the **M**, and bands of the H4124
1Ch 18: 2 And he smote Moab; and the **M** H4124
Ezr 9: 1 the **M**, the Egyptians, and the Amorites. H4125

MOABITESS
Ru 1:22 So Naomi returned, and Ruth the **M**, H4125
2: 2 And Ruth the **M** said unto Naomi, Let H4125
21 And Ruth the **M** said, He said unto me H4125
4: 5 buy *it* also of Ruth the **M**, the wife of the H4125
10 Moreover Ruth the **M**, the wife of H4125
2Ch 24:26 and Jehozabad the son of Shimrith a **M**. H4125

MOABITISH
Ru 2: 6 and said, It *is* the **M** damsel that came H4125

MOADIAH
Neh 12:17 Of Abijah, Zichri; of Miniamin, of **M**, H4153

MOAN See BEMOAN.

MOCK
Gen 39:14 unto us to **m** us; he came in unto H6711
17 unto us, came in unto me to **m** me: H6711
Job 13: 9 mocketh another, do ye *so* **m** him? H2048
21: 3 and after that I have spoken, **m** on. H3932
Prv 1:26 I will **m** when your fear cometh; H3932
14: 9 Fools make a **m** at sin: but among the H3887
Jer 38:19 me into their hand, and they **m** me. H5953
Lam 1: 7 saw her, *and* did **m** at her sabbaths. H7832
Ezk 22: 5 far from thee, shall **m** thee, *which art* H7046
Mt 20:19 to the Gentiles to **m**, and to scourge, *G1702*
Mk 10:34 And they shall **m** him, and shall *G1702*
Lk 14:29 *it*, all that behold *it* begin to **m** him, *G1702*

MOCKED
Gen 19:14 as one that **m** unto his sons in law. H6711
Nu 22:29 Because thou hast **m** me: I would there H5953
Jdg 16:10 Behold, thou hast **m** me, and told me H2048
13 thou hast **m** me, and told me lies: H2048
15 me? thou hast **m** me these three times, H2048
1Ki 18:27 at noon, that Elijah **m** them, and said, H2048
2Ki 2:23 of the city, and **m** him, and said unto H7046
2Ch 30:10 laughed them to scorn, and **m** them. H3932
36:16 But they **m** the messengers of God, and H3931
Neh 4: 1 great indignation, and **m** the Jews. H3932
Job 12: 4 I am *as* one **m** of his neighbour, who H7814
Mt 2:16 he saw that he was **m** of the wise men, *G1702*
27:29 **m** him, saying, Hail, King of the Jews! *G1702*
31 And after that they had **m** him, they *G1702*
Mk 15:20 And when they had **m** him, they took *G1702*
Lk 18:32 Gentiles, and shall be **m**, and spitefully *G1702*
22:63 And the men that held Jesus **m** him, *G1702*
23:11 at nought, and **m** *him*, and arrayed *G1702*
36 And the soldiers also **m** him, coming to *G1702*
Act 17:32 of the dead, some **m**: and others said, *G5512*
Gal 6: 7 Be not deceived; God is not **m**: for *G3456*

MOCKER
Prv 20: 1 Wine *is* a **m**, strong drink *is* raging: and H3887

MOCKERS
Job 17: 2 *Are there* not **m** with me? and doth not H2049
Ps 35:16 With hypocritical **m** in feasts, they H3934
Isa 28:22 Now therefore be ye not **m**, lest your H3887
Jer 15:17 I sat not in the assembly of the **m**, nor H7832
Jude 18 there should be **m** in the last time, who *G1703*

MOCKEST
Job 11: 3 **m**, shall no man make thee ashamed? H3932

MOCKETH
Job 13: 9 man **m** another, do ye *so* mock him? H2048
39:22 He **m** at fear, and is not affrighted; H7832
Prv 17: 5 Whoso **m** the poor reproacheth his H3932
30:17 The eye *that* **m** at *his* father, and H3932
Jer 20: 7 I am in derision daily, every one **m** me. H3932

MOCKING
Gen 21: 9 which she had born unto Abraham, **m**. H6711
Ezk 22: 4 the heathen, and a **m** to all countries. H7048
Mt 27:41 Likewise also the chief priests **m** *him*, *G1702*
Mk 15:31 Likewise also the chief priests **m** said *G1702*
Act 2:13 Others **m** said, These men are full of *G5512*

MOCKINGS
Heb 11:36 And others had trial of *cruel* **m** and *G1701*

MODERATELY
Joel 2:23 the former rain **m**, and he will cause to H6666

MODERATION
Php 4: 5 Let your **m** be known unto all men. The *G1933*

MODEST
1Ti 2: 9 adorn themselves in **m** apparel, with *G2887*

MOIST
Nu 6: 3 of grapes, nor eat **m** grapes, or dried. H3892

MOISTENED
Job 21:24 and his bones are **m** with marrow. H8248

MOISTURE
Ps 32: 4 upon me: my **m** is turned into the H3955
Lk 8: 6 it withered away, because it lacked **m**. *G2429*

MOLADAH
Jos 15:26 Amam, and Shema, and **M**, H4137
19: 2 Beer-sheba, or Sheba, and **M**, H4137
1Ch 4:28 And they dwelt at Beer-sheba, and **M**, H4137
Neh 11:26 And at Jeshua, and at **M**, and at H4137

MOLE
Lev 11:30 and the lizard, and the snail, and the **m**. H8580

MOLECH
Lev 18:21 *the fire* to **M**, neither shalt thou profane H4432
20: 2 of his seed unto **M**; he shall surely be H4432
3 given of his seed unto **M**, to defile my H4432
4 of his seed unto **M**, and kill him not: H4432
5 with **M**, from among their people. H4432
1Ki 11: 7 and for **M**, the abomination of H4432
2Ki 23:10 daughter to pass through the fire to **M**. H4432

Jer 32:35 *the fire* unto **M**; which I commanded H4432

MOLES
Isa 2:20 to worship, to the **m** and to the bats; H2661

MOLID
1Ch 2:29 and she bare him Ahban, and **M**. H4140

MOLLIFIED
Isa 1: 6 bound up, neither **m** with ointment. H7401

MOLOCH
Am 5:26 of your **M** and Chiun your images, H4428
Act 7:43 Yea, ye took up the tabernacle of **M**, *G3434*

MOLTEN
Ex 32: 4 he had made it a **m** calf: and they said, H4541
8 have made them a **m** calf, and have H4541
34:17 Thou shalt make thee no **m** gods. H4541
Lev 19: 4 **m** gods: I *am* the LORD your God. H4541
Nu 33:52 destroy all their **m** images, and quite H4541
Dt 9:12 they have made them a **m** image. H4541
16 had made you a **m** calf: ye had turned H4541
27:15 maketh *any* graven or **m** image, an H4541
Jdg 17: 3 image and a **m** image: now therefore H4541
4 image and a **m** image: and they were H4541
18:14 image, and a **m** image? now therefore H4541
17 teraphim, and the **m** image: and the H4541
18 teraphim, and the **m** image. Then said H4541
1Ki 7:16 And he made two chapiters *of* **m** brass, H3332
23 And he made a **m** sea, ten cubits from H3332
30 **m**, at the side of every addition. H3332
33 felloes, and their spokes, *were* all **m**. H3332
14: 9 other gods, and **m** images, to provoke H4551
2Ki 17:16 and made them **m** images, *even* two H4551
2Ch 4: 2 Also he made a **m** sea of ten cubits H3332
28: 2 and made also **m** images for Baalim. H4551
34: 3 the carved images, and the **m** images. H4551
4 images, and the **m** images, he brake in H4551
Neh 9:18 Yea, when they had made them a **m** H4541
Job 28: 2 earth, and brass *is* **m** *out of* the stone. H6694
37:18 *is* strong, *and* as a **m** looking glass? H3332
Ps 106:19 Horeb, and worshipped the **m** image. H4551
Isa 30:22 the ornament of thy **m** images of gold: H4551
41:29 **m** images *are* wind and confusion. H5262
42:17 say to the **m** images, Ye *are* our gods. H4551
44:10 Who hath formed a god, or **m** a graven H5258
48: 5 my **m** image, hath commanded them. H5262
Jer 10:14 image: for his **m** image *is* falsehood, H5262
51:17 image: for his **m** image *is* falsehood, H5262
Ezk 24:11 of it may be **m** in it, *that* the scum H5413
Hos 13: 2 and have made them **m** images of their H4551
Mic 1: 4 And the mountains shall be **m** under H4549
Nah 1:14 image and the **m** image: I will make H4551
Hab 2:18 graven it; the **m** image, and a teacher H4551

MOMENT
Ex 33: 5 midst of thee in a **m**, and consume thee: H7281
Nu 16:21 that I may consume them in a **m**. H7281
45 in a **m**. And they fell upon their faces. H7281
Job 7:18 every morning, *and* try him every **m**? H7281
20: 5 and the joy of the hypocrite *but* for a **m**? H7281
21:13 and in a **m** go down to the grave. H7281
34:20 In a **m** shall they die, and the people H7281
Ps 30: 5 For his anger *endureth but* a **m**; in his H7281
73:19 as in a **m**! they are utterly consumed H7281
Prv 12:19 ever: but a lying tongue *is* but for a **m**. H7280
Isa 26:20 **m**, until the indignation be overpast. H7281
27: 3 I will water it every **m**: lest *any* hurt it, I H7281
47: 9 come to thee in a **m** in one day, the loss H7281
54: 7 For a small **m** have I forsaken thee; but H7281
8 from thee for a **m**; but with everlasting H7281
Jer 4:20 tents spoiled, *and* my curtains in a **m**. H7281
Lam 4: 6 as in a **m**, and no hands stayed on her. H7281
Ezk 26:16 at *every* **m**, and be astonished at thee. H7281
32:10 tremble at *every* **m**, every man for his H7281
Lk 4: 5 kingdoms of the world in a **m** of time. *G4743*
1Co 15:52 In a **m**, in the twinkling of an eye, at the *G823*
2Co 4:17 which is but for a **m**, worketh for us a *G3910*

MONEY
Gen 17:12 or bought with **m** of any stranger, H3701
13 is bought with thy **m**, must needs be H3701
23 bought with his **m**, every male among H3701
27 and bought with **m** of the stranger, H3701
23: 9 field; for as much **m** as it is worth he H3701
13 I will give thee **m** for the field; take *it* H3701
16 of silver, current **m** with the merchant. H3701
31:15 us, and hath quite devoured also our **m**. H3701
Gen 33:19 father, for an hundred pieces of **m**. H7192
42:25 every man's **m** into his sack, and to H3701
27 inn, he espied his **m**; for, behold, it *was* H3701
28 And he said unto his brethren, My **m** is H3701
35 man's bundle of **m** *was* in his sack: and H3701
35 saw the bundles of **m**, they were afraid. H3701
43:12 And take double **m** in your hand; and H3701
12 your hand; and the **m** that was brought H3701
15 they took double **m** in their hand, and H3701
18 Because of the **m** that was returned in H3701
21 *every* man's **m** *was* in the mouth of H3701
21 of his sack, our **m** in full weight: and H3701
22 And other **m** have we brought down in H3701
22 cannot tell who put our **m** in our sacks. H3701
23 sacks: I had your **m**. And he brought H3701
44: 1 put every man's **m** in his sack's mouth. H3701
2 and his corn **m**. And he did according H3701
8 Behold, the **m**, which we found in our H3701
47:14 And Joseph gathered up all the **m** that H3701
14 brought the **m** into Pharaoh's house. H3701
15 And when **m** failed in the land of H3701
15 die in thy presence? for the **m** faileth. H3701
16 I will give you for your cattle, if **m** fail. H3701
18 lord, how that our **m** is spent; my lord H3701
Ex 12:44 that is bought for **m**, when thou hast H3701
21:11 then shall she go out free without **m**. H3701
21 shall not be punished: for he *is* his **m**. H3701
30 If there be laid on him a sum of **m**, then H3724
34 *it* good, *and* give **m** unto the owner of H3701
35 ox, and divide the **m** of it; and the dead H3701
22: 7 his neighbour **m** or stuff to keep, and H3701
17 **m** according to the dowry of virgins. H3701
25 If thou lend **m** to *any of* my people *that* H3701
30:16 And thou shalt take the atonement **m** H3701
Lev 22:11 *any* soul with his **m**, he shall eat of it, H3701
25:37 Thou shalt not give him thy **m** upon H3701
51 out of the **m** that he was bought for. H3701
27:15 the fifth *part* of the **m** of thy estimation H3701
18 unto him the **m** according to the years H3701
19 the fifth *part* of the **m** of thy estimation H3701
Nu 3:48 And thou shalt give the **m**, wherewith H3701
49 And Moses took the redemption **m** of H3701
50 Israel took he the **m**; a thousand three H3701
51 And Moses gave the **m** of them that H3701
18:16 for the **m** of five shekels, after H3701
Dt 2: 6 Ye shall buy meat of them for **m**, that ye H3701
6 water of them for **m**, that ye may drink. H3701
28 Thou shalt sell me meat for **m**, that I H3701
28 give me water for **m**, that I may drink: H3701
14:25 Then shalt thou turn *it* into **m**, and bind H3701
25 and bind up the **m** in thine hand, and H3701
26 And thou shalt bestow that **m** for H3701
21:14 sell her at all for **m**, thou shalt not make H3701
23:19 brother; usury of **m**, usury of victuals, H3701
Jdg 5:19 of Megiddo; they took no gain of **m**. H3701
16:18 unto her, and brought **m** in their hand. H3701
17: 4 Yet he restored the **m** unto his mother; H3701
1Ki 21: 2 thee, I will give thee the worth of it in **m**. H3701
6 thy vineyard for **m**; or else, if it please H3701
15 for **m**: for Naboth is not alive, but dead. H3701
2Ki 5:26 *it* a time to receive **m**, and to receive H3701
12: 4 the priests, All the **m** of the dedicated H3701
4 the LORD, *even* the **m** of every one that H3701
4 *the account,* the **m** that every man is H3701
4 is set at, *and* all the **m** that cometh into H3701
7 therefore receive no *more* **m** of your H3701
8 to receive no *more* **m** of the people, H3701
9 put therein all the **m** *that was* brought H3701
10 *there was* much **m** in the chest, that the H3701
10 bags, and told the **m** that was found in H3701
11 And they gave the **m**, being told, into H3701
13 of silver, of the **m** *that was* brought into H3701
15 they delivered the **m** to be bestowed on H3701
16 The trespass **m** and sin money was not H3701
16 The trespass money and sin **m** was not H3701
15:20 And Menahem exacted the **m** of Israel, H3701
22: 7 with them of the **m** that was delivered H3701
9 have gathered the **m** that was found in H3701
23:35 the land to give the **m** according to the H3701
2Ch 24: 5 of all Israel **m** to repair the house H3701
11 *there was* much **m**, the king's scribe H3701
11 by day, and gathered **m** in abundance. H3701
14 the rest of the **m** before the king and H3701
34: 9 they delivered the **m** that was brought H3701
14 And when they brought out the **m** that H3701
17 And they have gathered together the **m** H3701
Ezr 3: 7 They gave **m** also unto the masons, H3701
7:17 speedily with this **m** bullocks, rams, H3702
Neh 5: 4 have borrowed **m** for the king's tribute, H3701
Neh 5:10 exact of them **m** and corn: I pray you, H3701
11 *part* of the **m**, and of the corn, the H3701
Est 4: 7 of the sum of the **m** that Haman had H3701
Job 31:39 thereof without **m**, or have caused the H3701
42:11 of **m**, and every one an earring of gold. H7192
Ps 15: 5 *He that* putteth not out his **m** to usury, H3701
Prv 7:20 He hath taken a bag of **m** with him, H3701
Ecc 7:12 For wisdom *is* a defence, *and* **m** *is* a H3701
10:19 merry: but **m** answereth all *things*. H3701
Isa 43:24 no sweet cane with **m**, neither hast thou H3701
52: 3 and ye shall be redeemed without **m**. H3701
55: 1 he that hath no **m**; come ye, buy, and H3701
1 and milk without **m** and without price. H3701
2 Wherefore do ye spend **m** for *that* H3701
Jer 32: 9 the **m**, *even* seventeen shekels of silver. H3701
10 weighed *him* the **m** in the balances. H3701
25 thee the field for **m**, and take witnesses; H3701
44 Men shall buy fields for **m**, and H3701
Lam 5: 4 We have drunken our water for **m**; our H3701
Mic 3:11 thereof divine for **m**: yet will they lean H3701
Mt 17:24 received tribute *m* came to Peter, and
27 find a piece of **m**: that take, and give *G4715*
22:19 Shew me the tribute **m**. And they *G3546*
25:18 digged in the earth, and hid his lord's **m**. *G694*
27 to have put my **m** to the exchangers, and *G694*
28:12 they gave large **m** unto the soldiers, *G694*
15 So they took the **m**, and did as they were *G694*
Mk 6: 8 no scrip, no bread, no **m** in *their* purse: *G5475*
12:41 the people cast **m** into the treasury: *G5475*
14:11 to give him **m**. And he sought how *G694*
Lk 9: 3 neither **m**; neither have two coats apiece. *G694*
19:15 he had given the **m**, that he might know *G694*
23 Wherefore then gavest not thou my **m** *G694*
22: 5 glad, and covenanted to give him **m**. *G694*
Jn 2:14 doves, and the changers of **m** sitting: *G2773*
15 changers' **m**, and overthrew the tables; *G2772*
Act 4:37 the **m**, and laid *it* at the apostles' feet. *G5536*
7:16 for a sum of **m** of the sons of Emmor *G694*
8:18 Ghost was given, he offered them **m**, *G5536*
20 But Peter said unto him, Thy **m** perish *G694*
20 gift of God may be purchased with **m**. *G5536*
24:26 He hoped also that **m** should have been *G5536*
1Ti 6:10 For the love of **m** is the root of all evil: *G5365*

MONEYCHANGERS
Mt 21:12 the tables of the **m**, and the seats of *G2855*
Mk 11:15 the tables of the **m**, and the seats of *G2855*

MONSTERS
Lam 4: 3 Even the sea **m** draw out the breast, H8577

MONTH
Gen 7:11 life, in the second **m**, the seventeenth H2320
11 day of the **m**, the same day were H2320
8: 4 And the ark rested in the seventh **m**, on H2320
4 of the **m**, upon the mountains of Ararat. H2320
5 until the tenth **m**: in the tenth *month,* H2320
5 in the tenth *m*, on the first *day* of the H2320
5 **m**, were the tops of the mountains seen. H2320
13 year, in the first *m*, the first *day* of the
13 the first *day* of the **m**, the waters were H2320
14 And in the second **m**, on the seven and H2320
14 day of the **m**, was the earth dried. H2320
29:14 he abode with him the space of a **m**. H2320
Ex 12: 2 This **m** *shall be* unto you the beginning H2320
2 it *shall be* the first **m** of the year to you. H2320
3 tenth *day* of this **m** they shall take to H2320
6 day of the same **m**: and the whole H2320
18 In the first *m*, on the fourteenth day of
18 day of the **m** at even, ye shall eat H2320
18 one and twentieth day of the **m** at even. H2320
13: 4 This day came ye out in the **m** Abib. H2320
5 thou shalt keep this service in this **m**. H2320
16: 1 day of the second **m** after their H2320
19: 1 In the third **m**, when the children of H2320
23:15 appointed of the **m** Abib; for in it thou H2320
34:18 in the time of the **m** Abib: for in the H2320
18 **m** Abib thou camest out from Egypt. H2320
40: 2 On the first day of the first **m** shalt thou H2320
17 And it came to pass in the first **m** in the H2320
17 **m**, *that* the tabernacle was reared up. H2320
Lev 16:29 in the seventh **m**, on the tenth *day* of H2320
29 tenth *day* of the **m**, ye shall afflict your H2320
23: 5 In the fourteenth *day* of the first **m** at H2320
6 And on the fifteenth day of the same **m** H2320
24 In the seventh **m**, in the first *day* of the H2320
24 in the first *day* of the **m**, shall ye have a H2320
27 Also on the tenth *day* of this seventh **m** H2320
32 ninth *day* of the **m** at even, from even H2320

Lev 23:34 of this seventh **m** *shall be* the feast of H2320
39 day of the seventh **m**, when ye have H2320
41 ye shall celebrate it in the seventh **m**. H2320
25: 9 tenth *day* of the seventh **m**, in the day of H2320
27: 6 And if *it be* from a **m** old even unto five H2320
Nu 1: 1 *day* of the second **m**, in the second year H2320
18 *day* of the second **m**, and they declared H2320
3:15 every male from a **m** old and upward H2320
22 the males, from a **m** old and upward, H2320
28 the males, from a **m** old and upward, H2320
34 the males, from a **m** old and upward, H2320
39 the males from a **m** old and upward, H2320
40 of Israel from a **m** old and upward, H2320
43 of names, from a **m** old and upward, of H2320
9: 1 Sinai, in the first **m** of the second year H2320
3 In the fourteenth day of this **m**, at even, H2320
5 day of the first **m** at even in the H2320
11 The fourteenth day of the second **m** at H2320
22 Or *whether it were* two days, or a **m**, or H2320
10:11 *day* of the second **m**, in the second year, H2320
11:20 *But* even a whole **m**, until it come out at H2320
21 flesh, that they may eat a whole **m**. H2320
18:16 be redeemed from a **m** old shalt thou H2320
20: 1 of Zin in the first **m**: and the people H2320
26:62 all males from a **m** old and upward: for H2320
28:14 **m** throughout the months of the year. H2320
16 And in the fourteenth day of the first **m** H2320
17 And in the fifteenth day of this **m** *is* the H2320
29: 1 And in the seventh **m**, on the first *day* of H2320
1 the first *day* of the **m**, ye shall have an H2320
6 Beside the burnt offering of the **m**, and H2320
7 of this seventh **m** an holy convocation; H2320
12 day of the seventh **m** ye shall have an H2320
33: 3 in the first **m**, on the fifteenth day H2320
3 day of the first **m**; on the morrow after H2320
38 of Egypt, in the first *day* of the fifth **m**. H2320
Dt 1: 3 in the eleventh **m**, on the first *day* of the H2320
3 the first *day* of the **m**, *that* Moses spake H2320
16: 1 Observe the **m** of Abib, and keep the H2320
1 thy God: for in the **m** of Abib the LORD H2320
21:13 her mother a full **m**: and after that thou H3991
Jos 4:19 *day* of the first **m**, and encamped in H2320
5:10 the **m** at even in the plains of Jericho. H2320
1Sa 20:27 second *day* of the **m**, that David's place H2320
34 second day of the **m**: for he was grieved H2320
1Ki 4: 7 man his **m** in a year made provision. H2320
27 man in his **m**: they lacked nothing. H2320
5:14 ten thousand a **m** by courses: a month H2320
14 by courses: a **m** they were in Lebanon, H2320
6: 1 over Israel, in the **m** Zif, which *is* the H2320
1 *is* the second **m**, that he began to build H2320
37 house of the LORD laid, in the **m** Zif: H3391
38 And in the eleventh year, in the **m** Bul, H3391
38 *is* the eighth **m**, was the house finished H2320
8: 2 at the feast in the **m** Ethanim, which *is* H3391
2 Ethanim, which *is* the seventh **m**. H2320
12:32 a feast in the eighth **m**, on the fifteenth H2320
32 day of the **m**, like unto the feast that H2320
33 day of the eighth **m**, *even* in the month H2320
33 *even* in the **m** which he had devised H2320
2Ki 15:13 and he reigned a full **m** in Samaria. H3391
25: 1 reign, in the tenth **m**, in the tenth *day* of H2320
1 the tenth *day* of the **m**, *that* H2320
3 And on the ninth *day* of the *fourth* **m** H2320
8 And in the fifth **m**, on the seventh *day* H2320
8 the seventh *day* of the **m**, which *is* the H2320
25 But it came to pass in the seventh **m**, H2320
27 in the twelfth **m**, on the seven and H2320
27 *day* of the **m**, *that* Evil-merodach H2320
1Ch 12:15 over Jordan in the first **m**, when it had H2320
27: 1 came in and went out **m** by month H2320
1 out month by **m** throughout all the H2320
2 Over the first course for the first **m** *was* H2320
3 the captains of the host for the first **m**. H2320
4 And over the course of the second **m** H2320
5 host for the third **m** *was* Benaiah the H2320
7 The fourth *captain* for the fourth **m** H2320
8 The fifth captain for the fifth **m** *was* H2320
9 The sixth *captain* for the sixth **m** *was* H2320
10 The seventh *captain* for the seventh **m** H2320
11 The eighth *captain* for the eighth **m** H2320
12 The ninth *captain* for the ninth **m** *was* H2320
13 The tenth *captain* for the tenth **m** *was* H2320
14 for the eleventh **m** *was* Benaiah the H2320
15 The twelfth *captain* for the twelfth **m** H2320
2Ch 3: 2 **m**, in the fourth year of his reign. H2320
5: 3 in the feast which *was* in the seventh **m**. H2320
7:10 day of the seventh **m** he sent the people H2320
15:10 in the third **m**, in the fifteenth year H2320
29: 3 reign, in the first **m**, opened the doors H2320
17 *day* of the first **m** to sanctify, and on H2320
17 eighth day of the **m** came they to the H2320
17 day of the first **m** they made an end. H2320
30: 2 to keep the passover in the second **m**. H2320
13 second **m**, a very great congregation. H2320
15 *day* of the second **m**: and the priests H2320
31: 7 In the third **m** they began to lay the H2320
7 and finished *them* in the seventh **m**. H2320
35: 1 on the fourteenth *day* of the first **m**. H2320
Ezr 3: 1 And when the seventh **m** was come, H2320
6 From the first day of the seventh **m** H2320
8 in the second **m**, began Zerubbabel the H2320
6:15 third day of the **m** Adar, which was in H3393
19 upon the fourteenth *day* of the first **m**. H2320
7: 8 in the fifth **m**, which *was* in the seventh H2320
9 For upon the first *day* of the first **m** H2320
9 first *day* of the fifth **m** came he to H2320
8:31 *day* of the first **m**, to go unto Jerusalem: H2320
10: 9 It *was* the ninth **m**, on the twentieth *day* H2320
9 *day* of the **m**; and all the people sat H2320
16 of the tenth **m** to examine the matter. H2320
17 wives by the first day of the first **m**. H2320
Neh 1: 1 came to pass in the **m** Chisleu, in the H2320
2: 1 And it came to pass in the **m** Nisan, in H2320
6:15 *day of the* **m** Elul, in fifty and two days.
7:73 when the seventh **m** came, the children H2320
8: 2 upon the first day of the seventh **m**. H2320
14 in booths in the feast of the seventh **m**: H2320
9: 1 and fourth day of this **m** the children of H2320
Est 2:16 royal in the tenth **m**, which *is* the month H2320
16 which *is* the **m** Tebeth, in the seventh H2320
3: 7 In the first **m**, that *is*, the month Nisan, H2320
7 In the first month, that *is*, the **m** Nisan, H2320
7 to day, and from **m** to month, *to* the H2320
7 from month to **m**, *to* the twelfth *month*, H2320
7 *to* the twelfth *m*, that *is*, the month Adar.
7 the twelfth *month*, that *is*, the **m** Adar. H2320
12 day of the first **m**, and there was written H2320
13 *day* of the twelfth **m**, which is the H2320
13 which is the **m** Adar, and *to take* the H2320
8: 9 time in the third **m**, that *is*, the month H2320
9 that *is*, the **m** Sivan, on the three H2320
12 the twelfth **m**, which *is* the month Adar. H2320
12 twelfth month, which *is* the **m** Adar. H2320
9: 1 Now in the twelfth **m**, that *is*, the month H2320
1 that *is*, the **m** Adar, on the thirteenth H2320
15 day also of the **m** Adar, and slew three H2320
17 On the thirteenth day of the **m** Adar; H2320
19 day of the **m** Adar *a day of* gladness H2320
21 day of the **m** Adar, and the fifteenth H2320
22 enemies, and the **m** which was turned H2320
Jer 1: 3 of Jerusalem captive in the fifth **m**. H2320
2:24 in her **m** they shall find her. H2320
28: 1 *and* in the fifth **m**, *that* Hananiah the H2320
17 died the same year in the seventh **m**. H2320
36: 9 in the ninth **m**, *that* they proclaimed H2320
22 in the ninth **m**: and *there was a fire* H2320
39: 1 in the tenth **m**, came Nebuchadrezzar H2320
2 in the fourth **m**, the ninth *day* of the H2320
2 *day* of the **m**, the city was broken up. H2320
41: 1 Now it came to pass in the seventh **m**, H2320
52: 4 reign, in the tenth **m**, in the tenth *day* of H2320
4 the tenth *day* of the **m**, *that* H2320
6 And in the fourth **m**, in the ninth *day* of H2320
6 ninth *day* of the **m**, the famine was sore H2320
12 Now in the fifth **m**, in the tenth *day* of H2320
12 the tenth *day* of the **m**, which *was* the H2320
31 Judah, in the twelfth **m**, in the five and H2320
31 *day* of the **m**, *that* Evil-merodach H2320
Ezk 1: 1 year, in the fourth *m*, in the fifth *day* of
1 fifth *day* of the **m**, as I *was* among the H2320
2 In the fifth *day* of the **m**, which *was* the H2320
8: 1 year, in the sixth *m*, in the fifth *day* of the
1 the fifth *day* of the **m**, *as* I sat in mine H2320
20: 1 year, in the fifth *m*, the tenth *day* of the
1 tenth *day* of the **m**, *that* certain of the H2320
24: 1 Again in the ninth year, in the tenth **m**, H2320
1 the tenth *day* of the **m**, the word of the H2320
26: 1 the first *day* of the **m**, *that* the word of H2320
29: 1 In the tenth year, in the tenth *m*, in the
1 the twelfth *day* of the **m**, the word of the H2320
17 year, in the first *m*, in the first *day* of the
17 in the first *day* of the **m**, the word of the H2320
30:20 year, in the first *m*, in the seventh *day* H2320
20 seventh *day* of the **m**, *that* the word of H2320
31: 1 year, in the third *m*, in the first *day* of the
1 the first *day* of the **m**, *that* the word of H2320
32: 1 in the twelfth **m**, in the first *day* of the H2320
Ezk 32: 1 the first *day* of the **m**, *that* the word of H2320
17 *day* of the **m**, *that* the word of the H2320
33:21 in the tenth *m*, in the fifth *day* of the
21 the fifth *day* of the **m**, *that* one that had H2320
40: 1 the tenth *day* of the **m**, in the fourteenth H2320
45:18 Thus saith the Lord GOD; In the first *m*,
18 the first *day* of the **m**, thou shalt take a H2320
20 seventh *day* of the **m** for every one that H2320
21 In the first *m*, in the fourteenth day of the
21 day of the **m**, ye shall have the H2320
25 In the seventh *m*, in the fifteenth day of
25 day of the **m**, shall he do the like H2320
Dan 10: 4 day of the first **m**, as I was by the side H2320
Hos 5: 7 a **m** devour them with their portions. H2320
Joel 2:23 rain, and the latter rain in the first *m*.
Hag 1: 1 king, in the sixth **m**, in the first day of H2320
1 the first day of the **m**, came the word of H2320
15 day of the sixth **m**, in the second year of H2320
2: 1 In the seventh *m*, in the one and
1 *day* of the **m**, came the word of the H2320
10 *day* of the ninth *m*, in the second year of
18 day of the ninth *m*, *even* from the day
20 four and twentieth *day* of the **m**, saying, H2320
Zec 1: 1 In the eighth **m**, in the second year of H2320
7 of the eleventh **m**, which *is* the month H2320
7 which *is* the **m** Sebat, in the second H2320
7: 1 *day* of the ninth **m**, *even* in Chisleu; H2320
3 I weep in the fifth **m**, separating myself, H2320
5 fifth and seventh *m*, even those seventy
8:19 fast of the fourth *m*, and the fast of the
11: 8 Three shepherds also I cut off in one **m**; H3391
Lk 1:26 And in the sixth **m** the angel Gabriel G3376
36 **m** with her, who was called barren. G3376
Rev 9:15 and a day, and a **m**, and a year, for to G3376
22: 2 her fruit every **m**: and the leaves of the G3376

MONTHLY

Isa 47:13 the stargazers, the **m** prognosticators, H2320

MONTHS

Gen 38:24 And it came to pass about three **m** H2320
Ex 2: 2 *a* goodly *child*, she hid him three **m**. H3391
12: 2 the beginning of **m**: it *shall be* the first H2320
Nu 10:10 of your **m**, ye shall blow with the H2320
28:11 And in the beginnings of your **m** ye H2320
14 month throughout the **m** of the year. H2320
Jdg 11:37 let me alone two **m**, that I may go up H2320
38 her away *for* two **m**: and she went with H2320
39 at the end of two **m**, that she returned H2320
19: 2 and was there four whole **m**. H2320
20:47 and abode in the rock Rimmon four **m**. H2320
1Sa 6: 1 the country of the Philistines seven **m**. H2320
27: 7 Philistines was a full year and four **m**. H2320
2Sa 2:11 of Judah was seven years and six **m**. H2320
5: 5 years and six **m**: and in Jerusalem he H2320
6:11 the Gittite three **m**: and the LORD H2320
24: 8 at the end of nine **m** and twenty days. H2320
13 thou flee three **m** before thine enemies, H2320
1Ki 5:14 in Lebanon, *and* two **m** at home: and H2320
11:16 (For six **m** did Joab remain there with H2320
2Ki 15: 8 reign over Israel in Samaria six **m**. H2320
23:31 he reigned three **m** in Jerusalem. And H2320
24: 8 in Jerusalem three **m**. And his mother's H2320
1Ch 3: 4 years and six **m**: and in Jerusalem he H2320
13:14 in his house three **m**. And the LORD H2320
21:12 Either three years' famine; or three **m** H2320
27: 1 throughout all the **m** of the year, of H2320
2Ch 36: 2 and he reigned three **m** in Jerusalem. H2320
9 and he reigned three **m** and ten days in H2320
Est 2:12 she had been twelve **m**, according to the H2320
12 *to wit*, six **m** with oil of myrrh, and H2320
12 of myrrh, and six **m** with sweet odours, H2320
Job 3: 6 it not come into the number of the **m**. H3391
7: 3 So am I made to possess **m** of vanity, H3391
14: 5 the number of his **m** *are* with thee, H2320
21:21 number of his **m** is cut off in the midst? H2320
29: 2 Oh that I were as *in* **m** past, as *in* the H3391
39: 2 Canst thou number the **m** *that* they H3391
Ezk 39:12 And seven **m** shall the house of Israel H2320
14 the end of seven **m** shall they search. H2320
47:12 fruit according to his **m**, because their H2320
Dan 4:29 At the end of twelve **m** he walked in the H3393
Am 4: 7 *were* yet three **m** to the harvest: and H2320
Lk 1:24 and hid herself five **m**, saying, G3376
56 **m**, and returned to her own house. G3376
4:25 years and six **m**, when great famine G3376
Jn 4:35 Say not ye, There are yet four **m**, and G5072
Act 7:20 up in his father's house three **m**: G3376
18:11 a year and six **m**, teaching the word of G3376

Act 19: 8 for the space of three **m**, disputing and *G3376*
20: 3 And *there* abode three **m**. And when the *G3376*
28:11 And after three **m** we departed in a *G3376*
Gal 4:10 Ye observe days, and **m**, and times, and *G3376*
Heb 11:23 was hid three **m** of his parents, because *G5150*
Jas 5:17 by the space of three years and six **m**. *G3376*
Rev 9: 5 be tormented five **m**: and their torment *G3376*
10 their power *was* to hurt men five **m**. *G3376*
11: 2 they tread under foot forty *and* two **m**. *G3376*
13: 5 unto him to continue forty *and* two **m**. *G3376*

MONUMENTS
Isa 65: 4 and lodge in the **m**, which eat swine's H5341

MOON
Gen 37: 9 the sun and the **m** and the eleven stars H3394
Dt 4:19 the sun, and the **m**, and the stars, *even* H3394
17: 3 either the sun, or **m**, or any of the host H3394
33:14 the precious things put forth by the **m**, H3391
Jos 10:12 and thou, **M**, in the valley of Ajalon. H3394
13 And the sun stood still, and the **m** H3394
1Sa 20: 5 *is* the new **m**, and I should not fail H2320
18 *is* the new **m**: and thou shalt be missed, H2320
24 and when the new **m** was come, the H2320
2Ki 4:23 *it is* neither new **m**, nor sabbath. And H2320
23: 5 sun, and to the **m**, and to the planets, H3394
Job 25: 5 Behold even to the **m**, and it shineth H3394
31:26 shined, or the **m** walking *in* brightness; H3394
Ps 8: 3 of thy fingers, the **m** and the stars, H3394
72: 5 **m** endure, throughout all generations. H3394
7 of peace so long as the **m** endureth. H3394
81: 3 Blow up the trumpet in the new **m**, in H2320
89:37 It shall be established for ever as the **m**, H3394
104:19 He appointed the **m** for seasons: the H3394
121: 6 smite thee by day, nor the **m** by night. H3394
136: 9 The **m** and stars to rule by night: for H3394
148: 3 Praise ye him, sun and **m**: praise him, H3394
Ecc 12: 2 While the sun, or the light, or the **m**, or H3394
Song 6:10 fair as the **m**, clear as the sun, *and* H3842
Isa 3:18 cauls, and *their* round tires like the **m**, H7720
13:10 the **m** shall not cause her light to shine. H3394
24:23 Then the **m** shall be confounded, and H3842
30:26 Moreover the light of the **m** shall be as H3842
60:19 shall the **m** give light unto thee: H3394
20 neither shall thy **m** withdraw itself: for H3391
66:23 from one new **m** to another, and from H2320
Jer 8: 2 the sun, and the **m**, and all the host of H3394
31:35 ordinances of the **m** and of the stars for H3394
Ezk 32: 7 and the **m** shall not give her light. H3394
46: 1 the day of the new **m** it shall be opened. H2320
6 And in the day of the new **m** *it shall be* H2320
Joel 2:10 the sun and the **m** shall be dark, and H3394
31 darkness, and the **m** into blood, before H3394
3:15 The sun and the **m** shall be darkened, H3394
Am 8: 5 Saying, When will the new **m** be gone, H2320
Hab 3:11 The sun *and* **m** stood still in their H3394
Mt 24:29 and the **m** shall not give her light, *G4582*
Mk 13:24 and the **m** shall not give her light, *G4582*
Lk 21:25 sun, and in the **m**, and in the stars; and *G4582*
Act 2:20 darkness, and the **m** into blood, before *G4582*
1Co 15:41 glory of the **m**, and another glory of *G4582*
Col 2:16 or of the new **m**, or of the sabbath *days*: *G3561*
Rev 6:12 of hair, and the **m** became as blood; *G4582*
8:12 third part of the **m**, and the third part of *G4582*
12: 1 the sun, and the **m** under her feet, and *G4582*
21:23 sun, neither of the **m**, to shine in it: for *G4582*

MOONS
1Ch 23:31 in the new **m**, and on the set feasts, H2320
2Ch 2: 4 and on the new **m**, and on the solemn H2320
8:13 and on the new **m**, and on the solemn H2320
31: 3 and for the new **m**, and for the set H2320
Ezr 3: 5 both of the new **m**, and of all the set H2320
Neh 10:33 of the new **m**, for the set feasts, and H2320
Isa 1:13 unto me; the new **m** and sabbaths, the H2320
14 Your new **m** and your appointed feasts H2320
Ezk 45:17 and in the new **m**, and in the sabbaths, H2320
46: 3 in the sabbaths and in the new **m**. H2320
Hos 2:11 days, her new **m**, and her sabbaths, and H2320

MORASTHITE
Jer 26:18 Micah the **M** prophesied in the days of H4183
Mic 1: 1 to Micah the **M** in the days of Jotham, H4183

MORDECAI
Ezr 2: 2 Reelaiah, **M**, Bilshan, Mispar, Bigvai, H4782
Neh 7: 7 Nahamani, **M**, Bilshan, Mispereth, H4782
Est 2: 5 whose name *was* **M**, the son of Jair, the H4782
7 beautiful; whom **M**, when her father H4782
Est 2:10 nor her kindred: for **M** had charged her H4782
11 And **M** walked every day before the H4782
15 the uncle of **M**, who had taken her H4782
19 time, then **M** sat in the king's gate. H4782
20 nor her people; as **M** had charged her: H4782
20 commandment of **M**, like as when she H4782
21 In those days, while **M** sat in the king's H4782
22 And the thing was known to **M**, who H4782
3: 2 **M** bowed not, nor did *him* reverence. H4782
3 gate, said unto **M**, Why transgressest H4782
5 And when Haman saw that **M** bowed H4782
6 to lay hands on **M** alone; for they had H4782
6 him the people of **M**: wherefore Haman H4782
6 of Ahasuerus, *even* the people of **M**. H4782
4: 1 When **M** perceived all that was done, H4782
1 all that was done, **M** rent his clothes, H4782
4 raiment to clothe **M**, and to take away H4782
5 **M**, to know what it *was*, and why it *was*. H4782
6 So Hatach went forth to **M** unto the H4782
7 And **M** told him of all that had H4782
9 came and told Esther the words of **M**. H4782
10 and gave him commandment unto **M**; H4782
12 And they told to **M** Esther's words. H4782
13 Then **M** commanded to answer Esther, H4782
15 Then Esther bade *them* return **M** *this* H4782
17 So **M** went his way, and did according H4782
5: 9 when Haman saw **M** in the king's gate, H4782
9 he was full of indignation against **M**. H4782
13 see **M** the Jew sitting at the king's gate. H4782
14 unto the king that **M** may be hanged H4782
6: 2 And it was found written, that **M** had H4782
3 hath been done to **M** for this? Then H4782
4 the king to hang **M** on the gallows that H4782
10 said, and do even so to **M** the Jew, that H4782
11 and arrayed **M**, and brought him on H4782
12 And **M** came again to the king's gate. H4782
13 his wife unto him, If **M** *be* of the seed of H4782
7: 9 had made for **M**, who had spoken good H4782
10 **M**. Then was the king's wrath pacified. H4782
8: 1 the queen. And **M** came before the H4782
2 and gave it unto **M**. And Esther set H4782
2 Esther set **M** over the house of Haman. H4782
7 the queen and to **M** the Jew, Behold, I H4782
9 to all that **M** commanded unto the H4782
15 And **M** went out from the presence of H4782
9: 3 because the fear of **M** fell upon them. H4782
4 For **M** *was* great in the king's house, H4782
4 this man **M** waxed greater and greater. H4782
20 And **M** wrote these things, and sent H4782
23 and as **M** had written unto them; H4782
29 of Abihail, and **M** the Jew, wrote with H4782
31 according as **M** the Jew and Esther H4782
10: 2 the greatness of **M**, whereunto the king H4782
3 For **M** the Jew *was* next unto king H4782

MORDECAI'S
Est 2:22 certified the king *thereof* in **M** name. H4782
3: 4 to see whether **M** matters would stand: H4782

MORE
Gen 3: 1 Now the serpent was **m** subtil than any
8:12 returned not again unto him any **m**. H5750
21 the ground any **m** for man's sake; for H5750
21 **m** every thing living, as I have done. H5750
9:11 flesh be cut off any **m** by the waters of a H5750
11 any **m** be a flood to destroy the earth. H5750
15 **m** become a flood to destroy all flesh. H5750
17: 5 Neither shall thy name any **m** be called H5750
29:30 he loved also Rachel **m** than Leah, and
32:28 shall be called no **m** Jacob, but Israel: H5750
34:19 and he *was* **m** honourable than all H3513
35:10 not be called any **m** Jacob, but Israel H5750
36: 7 For their riches were **m** than that they H7227
37: 3 Now Israel loved Joseph **m** than all his
4 father loved him **m** than all his brethren,
5 brethren: and they hated him yet the **m**. H3254
8 **m** for his dreams, and for his words. H3254
9 dreamed a dream **m**; and, behold, the H5750
38:26 said, She hath been **m** righteous than I;
26 my son. And he knew her again no **m**. H5750
44:23 with you, ye shall see my face no **m**. H3254
Ex 1: 9 of Israel *are* **m** and mightier than we: H7227
12 But the **m** they afflicted them, the more H3651
12 But the more they afflicted them, the **m** H3651
5: 7 Ye shall no **m** give the people straw to H3254
9 Let there **m** work be laid upon the men,
8:29 deal deceitfully any **m** in not letting the H3254
9:28 that there be no *m* mighty thunderings
29 shall there be any **m** hail; that thou H5750
Ex 9:34 he sinned yet **m**, and hardened his H3254
10:28 see my face no **m**; for in *that* day thou H3254
29 well, I will see thy face again no **m**. H5750
11: 1 I bring one plague *m* upon Pharaoh, and
6 none like it, nor shall be like it any **m**. H3254
14:13 ye shall see them again no **m** for ever. H5750
16:17 so, and gathered, some **m**, some less. H7235
30:15 The rich shall not give **m**, and the poor H7235
36: 5 bring much **m** than enough for the H7235
6 nor woman make any **m** work for the H5750
Lev 6: 5 add the fifth part **m** thereto, *and* give it H3254
11:42 or whatsoever hath **m** feet among all H7235
13: 5 priest shall shut him up seven days **m**: H8145
33 *him that hath* the scall seven days **m**: H8145
54 *is*, and he shall shut it up seven days **m**: H8145
17: 7 And they shall no **m** offer their H5750
26:18 you seven times **m** for your sins. H3254
21 bring seven times **m** plagues upon you H3254
27:20 man, it shall not be redeemed any **m**. H5750
Nu 3:46 of Israel, which are **m** than the Levites; H5736
8:25 service *thereof*, and shall serve no **m**: H5750
18: 5 any **m** upon the children of Israel. H5750
22:15 And Balak sent yet again princes, **m**, H7227
15 more, and **m** honourable than they.
18 of the LORD my God, to do less or **m**. H1419
19 what the LORD will say unto me **m**. H3254
26:54 To many thou shalt give the **m** H7235
33:54 *and* to the **m** ye shall give the more H7227
54 ye shall give the **m** inheritance, and to H7235
Dt 1:11 times so many **m** as ye *are*, and bless H3254
3:26 speak no **m** unto me of this matter. H3254
5:22 and he added no **m**. And he wrote them H3254
25 LORD our God any **m**, then we shall die. H3254
7: 7 because ye were **m** in number than any H7230
17 **m** than I; how can I dispossess them? H7227
10:16 of your heart, and be no **m** stiffnecked. H5750
13:11 and shall do no **m** any such wickedness H3254
17:13 fear, and do no **m** presumptuously. H5750
16 shall henceforth return no **m** that way. H3254
18:16 see this great fire any **m**, that I die not. H5750
19: 9 cities **m** for thee, beside these three: H5750
20 commit no **m** any such evil among you. H3254
20: 1 *and* a people **m** than thou, be not H7227
28:68 shalt see it no **m** again: and there ye H3254
31: 2 this day; I can no **m** go out and come H5750
27 LORD; and how much **m** after my death?
Jos 2:11 did there remain any **m** courage in any H5750
5: 1 any **m**, because of the children of Israel. H5750
12 Israel manna any **m**; but they did eat of H5750
7:12 I be with you any **m**, except ye destroy H3254
10:11 they died: *they were* **m** which died with H7227
23:13 your God will no **m** drive out *any of* H3254
Jdg 2:19 *themselves* **m** than their fathers, in
8:28 up their heads no **m**. And the country H3254
10:13 gods: wherefore I will deliver you no **m**. H3254
13:21 But the angel of the LORD did no **m** H3254
15: 3 Now shall I be **m** blameless than the
16:30 **m** than *they* which he slew in his life. H7227
18:24 and what have I **m**? and what *is* this H5750
Ru 1:11 *are* there yet *any* **m** sons in my womb,
17 do so to me, and **m** also, *if aught* but H3254
3:10 *for* thou hast shewed **m** kindness in the H3190
1Sa 1:18 and her countenance was no **m** *sad*. H5750
2: 3 Talk no **m** so exceeding proudly; let *not* H7235
3:17 do so to thee, and **m** also, if thou hide H3254
7:13 they came no **m** into the coast H3254+H5750
14:30 How much **m**, if haply the people had H637
44 And Saul answered, God do so and **m** H3254
15:35 And Samuel came no **m** to see Saul H3254
18: 2 him go no **m** home to his father's house.
8 *what* can he have **m** but the kingdom? H5750
29 And Saul was yet the **m** afraid of H3254
30 behaved himself **m** wisely than all the
20:13 The LORD do so and much **m** to H3254
22:15 knew nothing of all this, less or **m**. H1490
23: 3 Judah: how much **m** then if we come to
24:17 And he said to David, Thou *art* **m**
25:22 So and **m** also do God unto the enemies H3254
36 less or **m**, until the morning light. H1490
26:21 for I will no **m** do thee harm, because H5750
27: 1 to seek me any **m** in any coast of Israel: H5750
4 and he sought no **m** again for him. H3254
28:15 answereth me no **m**, neither by prophets,
30: 4 until they had no **m** power to weep. H5750
2Sa 2:28 no **m**, neither fought they any more. H5750
28 no more, neither fought they any **m**. H3254
3: 9 So do God to Abner, and **m** also, H3254
35 God to me, and **m** also, if I taste bread, H3254
4:11 How much **m**, when wicked men have

2Sa 5:13 And David took *him* **m** concubines and H5750
6:22 And I will yet be **m** vile than thus, and
7:10 own, and move no **m**; neither shall the H5750
10 afflict them any **m**, as beforetime, H3254
20 And what can David say **m** unto thee? H5750
10:19 to help the children of Ammon any **m**. H5750
11:25 make thy battle **m** strong against the
14:10 he shall not touch thee any **m**. H3254+H5750
11 to destroy any **m**, lest they destroy my H7235
16:11 my life: how much **m** now *may this*
18: 8 wood devoured **m** people that day than H7235
19:13 do so to me, and **m** also, if thou be not H3254
28 have I yet to cry any **m** unto the king? H3254
29 speakest thou any **m** of thy matters? I H5750
35 can I hear any **m** the voice of singing H5750
43 and we have also **m** *right* in David than H5750
20: 6 the son of Bichri do us **m** harm than *did*
21:17 Thou shalt go no **m** out with us to H5750
23:23 He was **m** honourable than the thirty,
1Ki 2:23 do so to me, and **m** also, if Adonijah H3254
32 who fell upon two men **m** righteous and
10: 5 the LORD; there was no **m** spirit in her. H5750
10 there came no **m** such abundance of H5750
16:33 and Ahab did **m** to provoke the LORD H3254
19: 2 do *to me*, and **m** also, if I make not thy H3254
20:10 so unto me, and **m** also, if the dust of H3254
2Ki 2:12 he saw him no **m**: and he took hold of H5750
21 thence any **m** death or barren *land*. H5750
4: 6 *is* not a vessel **m**. And the oil stayed. H5750
6:16 us *are* **m** than they that *be* with them. H7227
23 Syria came no **m** into the land of Israel. H3254
31 Then he said, God do so and **m** also to H3254
9:35 they found no **m** of her than the H3588+H518
12: 7 therefore receive no *m* money of your
8 to receive no *m* money of the people,
21: 8 of Israel move any **m** out of the land H3254
9 them to do **m** evil than did the nations
24: 7 not again any **m** out of his land: for H5750
1Ch 4: 9 And Jabez was **m** honourable than his
11:21 Of the three, he was **m** honourable than
14: 3 And David took **m** wives at Jerusalem: H5750
3 David begat **m** sons and daughters. H5750
17: 9 shall be moved no **m**; neither shall the H5750
9 waste them any **m**, as at the beginning, H3254
18 What can David *speak* **m** to H3254+H5750
19:19 help the children of Ammon any **m**. H5750
21: 3 times so many **m** as they *be*: but, my H3254
23:26 they shall no *m* carry the tabernacle,
24: 4 And there were **m** chief men found of H7227
2Ch 9: 4 the LORD; there was no **m** spirit in her. H5750
10:11 upon you, I will put **m** to your yoke: my H3254
15:19 And there was no *m* war unto the five
20:25 off for themselves, **m** than they could
25: 9 is able to give thee much **m** than this. H7235
28:13 ye intend to add *m* to our sins and to our
22 he trespass yet **m** against the LORD: H3254
29:34 the Levites *were* **m** upright in heart to
32: 7 for *there be* **m** with us than with him: H7227
16 And his servants spake yet *m* against the
33: 8 Neither will I any **m** remove the foot of H3254
23 but Amon trespassed **m** and more.
23 but Amon trespassed more and **m**. H7235
Ezr 7:20 And whatsoever **m** shall be needful for H7606
Neh 2:17 Jerusalem, that we be no **m** a reproach. H5750
13:18 city? yet ye bring **m** wrath upon Israel H3254
21 forth came they no *m* on the sabbath.
Est 1:19 That Vashti come no **m** before king
2:14 in unto the king no **m**, except the king H5750
17 favour in his sight **m** than all the virgins;
4:13 in the king's house, **m** than all the Jews.
6: 6 delight to do honour **m** than to myself? H3148
Job 3:21 and dig for it **m** than for hid treasures;
4:17 Shall mortal man be **m** just than God?
17 shall a man be **m** pure than his maker?
7: 7 *is* wind: mine eye shall no **m** see good. H7725
8 *m*: thine eyes *are* upon me, and I *am* not.
9 down to the grave shall come up no *m*.
10 He shall return no **m** to his house, H5750
10 neither shall his place know him any **m**. H5750
14:12 till the heavens *be* no **m**, they shall not H1115
15:16 How much **m** abominable and filthy *is*
20: 9 shall *see him* no **m**; neither shall his H3254
9 shall his place any **m** behold him. H5750
23:12 of his mouth **m** than my necessary *food*.
24:20 he shall be no **m** remembered; and H5750
32:15 answered no **m**: they left off speaking. H5750
16 not, but stood still, *and* answered no **m**;) H5750
34:19 regardeth the rich **m** than the poor? for H6440
23 For he will not lay upon man **m** *than* H5750
Job 34:31 *chastisement*, I will not offend *any m*:
32 if I have done iniquity, I will do no **m**.
35: 2 My righteousness *is* **m** than God's? H3254
11 Who teacheth us **m** than the beasts of
41: 8 him, remember the battle, do no **m**. H3254
42:12 latter end of Job **m** than his beginning:
Ps 4: 7 Thou hast put gladness in my heart, **m**
10:18 the earth may no **m** oppress. H3254+H5750
19:10 **M** to be desired *are they* than gold, yea,
39:13 strength, before I go hence, and be no **m**. H369
40: 5 they are **m** than can be numbered. H6105
12 to look up; they are **m** than the hairs of H6105
41: 8 *now* that he lieth he shall rise up no **m**. H3254
52: 3 Thou lovest evil **m** than good; *and* lying
69: 4 a cause are **m** than the hairs of mine H7231
71:14 and will yet praise thee **m** and more. H3254
14 and will yet praise thee more and **m**. H3254
73: 7 they have **m** than heart could wish. H5674
74: 9 We see not our signs: *there is* no **m** any H5750
76: 4 Thou *art* **m** glorious *and* excellent than
77: 7 and will he be favourable no **m**? H3254+H5750
78:17 And they sinned yet **m** against him by H5750
83: 4 Israel may be no **m** in remembrance. H5750
87: 2 The LORD loveth the gates of Zion **m**
88: 5 **m**: and they are cut off from thy hand. H5750
103:16 the place thereof shall know it no **m**. H5750
104:35 let the wicked be no **m**. Bless thou the H5750
115:14 The LORD shall increase you **m** and
14 you more and **m**, you and your children.
119:99 I have **m** understanding than all my
100 I understand **m** than the ancients,
130: 6 My soul *waiteth* for the Lord **m** than
6 *m than* they that watch for the morning.
139:18 *If* I should count them, they are **m** in H7235
Prv 3:15 She *is* **m** precious than rubies: and all
4:18 **m** and more unto the perfect day. H1980
18 more and **m** unto the perfect day. H1980
10:25 so *is* the wicked no *m*: but the righteous
11:24 **m** than is meet, but *it tendeth* to poverty.
31 much **m** the wicked and the sinner.
12:26 The righteous *is* **m** excellent than his
15:11 LORD: how much **m** then the hearts of
17:10 A reproof entereth **m** into a wise man
19: 7 him: how much **m** do his friends go far
21: 3 To do justice and judgment *is* **m**
27 how much **m**, *when* he bringeth it
26:12 *there is* **m** hope of a fool than of him.
28:23 shall find **m** favour than he that
29:20 *there is* **m** hope of a fool than of him.
30: 2 Surely I *am* **m** brutish than *any* man,
31: 7 and remember his misery no **m**. H5750
Ecc 1:16 and have gotten **m** wisdom than all H3254
2: 9 So I was great, and increased **m** than all
15 why was I then **m** wise? Then I said in H3148
16 of the wise **m** than of the fool for H5973
25 else can hasten *hereunto*, **m** than I? H2351
4: 2 **m** than the living which are yet alive. H4480
13 king, who will no **m** be admonished. H5750
5: 1 of God, and be **m** ready to hear, than H7138
6: 5 *thing*: this hath **m** rest than the other.
8 For what hath the wise **m** than the fool? H3148
7:19 Wisdom strengtheneth the wise **m** than
26 And I find **m** bitter than death the
9: 5 have they any **m** a reward; for the H5750
6 have they any **m** a portion for ever in H5750
17 *are* heard in quiet **m** than the cry of him
10:10 must he put to **m** strength: but wisdom
Song 1: 4 love **m** than wine: the upright love thee.
5: 9 What *is* thy beloved **m** than *another*
9 *is* thy beloved **m** than *another* beloved,
Isa 1: 5 Why should ye be stricken any **m**? ye H5750
5 ye will revolt **m** and more: the whole
5 revolt more and **m**: the whole head is H3254
13 Bring no **m** vain oblations; incense is H3254
2: 4 neither shall they learn war any **m**. H5750
5: 4 What could have been done **m** to my H5750
9: 1 and afterward did **m** grievously afflict
10:20 of Jacob, shall no **m** again stay upon H3254
13:12 I will make a man **m** precious than fine
15: 9 for I will bring **m** upon Dimon, lions H3254
19: 7 wither, be driven away, and be no *m*.
23:10 of Tarshish: *there is* no **m** strength. H5750
12 And he said, Thou shalt no **m** rejoice, O H3254
26:21 blood, and shall no **m** cover her slain. H5750
30:19 thou shalt weep no **m**: he will be very H1058
20 **m**, but thine eyes shall see thy teachers: H5750
32: 5 The vile person shall be no **m** called H5750
38:11 no **m** with the inhabitants of the world.
47: 1 no **m** be called tender and delicate. H3254
Isa 47: 5 no **m** be called, The lady of kingdoms. H3254
51:22 fury; thou shalt no **m** drink it again: H3254
52: 1 there shall no **m** come into H3254+H5750
14 was so marred **m** than any man, and
14 and his form **m** than the sons of men:
54: 1 with child: for **m** *are* the children of H7227
4 the reproach of thy widowhood any **m**. H5750
9 Noah should no **m** go over the earth; so H5750
56:12 be as this day, *and* much **m** abundant. H3499
60:18 Violence shall no **m** be heard in thy H5750
19 The sun shall be no **m** thy light by day; H5750
20 Thy sun shall no **m** go down; neither H5750
62: 4 Thou shalt no **m** be termed Forsaken; H5750
4 neither shall thy land any **m** be termed H5750
8 Surely I will no **m** give thy corn *to be* H5750
65:19 **m** heard in her, nor the voice of crying. H5750
20 There shall be no **m** thence an infant of H5750
Jer 2:31 are lords; we will come no **m** unto thee? H5750
3:11 herself **m** than treacherous Judah.
16 they shall say no **m**, The ark of the H5750
16 *it*; neither shall *that* be done any **m**. H5750
17 they walk any **m** after the imagination H5750
7:32 that it shall no **m** be called Tophet, nor H5750
10:20 tent any **m**, and to set up my curtains. H5750
11:19 his name may be no **m** remembered. H5750
16:14 that it shall no **m** be said, The LORD H5750
19: 6 this place shall no **m** be called Tophet, H5750
20: 9 nor speak any **m** in his name. But *his* H5750
22:10 return no **m**, nor see his native country. H5750
11 He shall not return thither any **m**: H5750
12 captive, and shall see this land no **m**. H5750
30 of David, and ruling any **m** in Judah. H5750
23: 4 they shall fear no **m**, nor be dismayed, H5750
7 that they shall no **m** say, The LORD H5750
36 ye mention no **m**: for every man's word H5750
25:27 fall, and rise no **m**, because of the sword
30: 8 shall no **m** serve themselves of him: H5750
31:12 and they shall not sorrow any **m** at all. H3254
29 In those days they shall say no **m**, The H5750
34 And they shall teach no **m** every man H5750
34 and I will remember their sin no **m**. H5750
40 up, nor thrown down any **m** for ever. H5750
33:24 should be no **m** a nation before them. H5750
34:10 **m**, then they obeyed, and let *them* go. H5750
38: 9 is: for *there is* no **m** bread in the city. H5750
42:18 and ye shall see this place no **m**. H5750
44:26 my name shall no **m** be named in the H5750
46:23 searched; because they are **m** than the H7231
48: 2 *There shall be* no **m** praise of Moab: in H5750
49: 7 *Is* wisdom no **m** in Teman? is counsel H5750
50:39 and it shall be no **m** inhabited for ever; H5750
51:44 flow together any **m** unto him: yea, the H5750
Lam 2: 9 the law *is* no *m*; her prophets also find
4: 7 milk, they were **m** ruddy in body than
15 They shall no **m** sojourn *there*. H3254
16 them; he will no **m** regard them: they H3254
22 of Zion; he will no **m** carry thee away H3254
Ezk 5: 6 into wickedness **m** than the nations, H4480
6 and my statutes **m** than the countries H4480
7 ye multiplied **m** than the nations that H4480
9 I will not do any **m** the like, because of H5750
6:14 land desolate, yea, **m** desolate than the
12:23 and they shall no **m** use it as a proverb H5750
24 For there shall be no **m** any vain vision H5750
25 it shall be no **m** prolonged: for in your H5750
28 be prolonged any **m**, but the word H5750
13:15 wall *is* no *m*, neither they that daubed it;
21 they shall be no **m** in your hand to be H5750
23 Therefore ye shall see no **m** vanity, nor H5750
14:11 That the house of Israel may go no **m** H5750
11 neither be polluted any **m** with all their H5750
21 GOD; How much **m** when I send my H5750
15: 2 Son of man, What is the vine tree **m**
16:41 and thou also shalt give no hire any **m**. H5750
42 I will be quiet, and will be no **m** angry. H5750
47 corrupted **m** than they in all thy ways.
51 abominations **m** than they, and hast
52 hast committed **m** abominable than
52 than they: they are **m** righteous than
63 open thy mouth any **m** because of thy H5750
18: 3 any **m** to use this proverb in Israel. H5750
19: 9 voice should no **m** be heard upon the H5750
20:39 **m** with your gifts, and with your idols. H5750
21: 5 of his sheath: it shall not return any **m**. H5750
13 rod? it shall be no *m*, saith the Lord GOD.
27 and it shall be no *m*, until he come whose
32 thou shalt be no *m* remembered: for I
23:11 saw *this*, she was **m** corrupt in her
11 **m** than her sister in *her* whoredoms.

M

Ezk 23:27 unto them, nor remember Egypt any **m**. H5750
24:13 thy filthiness any **m**, till I have caused H5750
27 speak, and be no **m** dumb: and thou H5750
26:13 of thy harps shall be no **m** heard. H5750
14 shalt be built no **m**: for I the LORD have H5750
21 and thou *shalt be* no **m**: though thou be
27:36 be a terror, and never *shalt be* any **m**.
28:19 a terror, and never *shalt* thou *be* any **m**.
24 And there shall be no **m** a pricking H5750
29:15 it exalt itself any **m** above the nations: H5750
15 they shall no **m** rule over the nations.
16 And it shall be no **m** the confidence of H5750
30:13 there shall be no **m** a prince of the land H5750
32:13 **m**, nor the hoofs of beasts trouble them. H5750
33:22 was opened, and I was no **m** dumb. H5750
34:10 themselves any **m**; for I will deliver my H5750
22 and they shall no **m** be a prey; and I H5750
28 And they shall no **m** be a prey to the H5750
29 and they shall be no **m** consumed with H5750
29 bear the shame of the heathen any **m**. H5750
36:12 no **m** henceforth bereave them *of men*. H3254
14 Therefore thou shalt devour men no **m**, H5750
14 thy nations any **m**, saith the Lord GOD. H5750
15 of the heathen any **m**, neither shalt thou H5750
15 of the people any **m**, neither shalt thou H5750
15 to fall any **m**, saith the Lord GOD. H5750
30 shall receive no **m** reproach of famine H5750
37:22 they shall be no **m** two nations, neither H5750
22 into two kingdoms any **m** at all: H5750
23 themselves any **m** with their idols, nor H5750
39: 7 holy name any **m**: and the heathen shall H5750
28 have left none of them any **m** there. H5750
29 Neither will I hide my face any **m** from H5750
42: 6 was straitened **m** than the lowest and
43: 7 the house of Israel no **m** defile, *neither* H5750
45: 8 princes shall no **m** oppress my people; H5750
Dan 2:30 that I have **m** than any living, but H4481
3:19 times **m** than it was wont to be heated. H5922
7:20 look *was* **m** stout than his fellows. H5750
11: 8 *m* years than the king of the north.
Hos 1: 6 for I will no **m** have mercy upon the H3254
2:16 me Ishi; and shalt call me no **m** Baali. H5750
17 no **m** be remembered by their name. H5750
6: 6 of God **m** than burnt offerings.
9:15 no **m**: all their princes *are* revolters. H3254
13: 2 And now they sin **m** and more, and have
2 And now they sin more and **m**, and H3254
14: 3 will we say any **m** to the work of our H5750
8 have I to do any **m** with idols? I have H5750
Joel 2: 2 shall be any **m** after it, *even* to the H3254
19 and I will no **m** make you a reproach H5750
3:17 no strangers pass through her any **m**. H5750
Am 5: 2 she shall no **m** rise: she is forsaken H3254
7: 8 I will not again pass by them any **m**: H5750
13 But prophesy not again any **m** at H5750
8: 2 I will not again pass by them any **m**. H5750
9:15 and they shall no **m** be pulled up out of H5750
Jna 4:11 great city, wherein are **m** than sixscore H7235
Mic 4: 3 neither shall they learn war any **m**. H5750
5:12 and thou shalt have no **m** soothsayers:
13 no **m** worship the work of thine hands. H5750
Nah 1:12 afflicted thee, I will afflict thee no **m**. H5750
14 thee, *that* no **m** of thy name be sown: H5750
15 shall no **m** pass through thee; H3254+H5750
2:13 of thy messengers shall no **m** be heard. H5750
Hab 1: 8 the leopards, and are **m** fierce than the
13 *the man that is* **m** righteous than he?
Zep 3:11 thou shalt no **m** be haughty H3254+H5750
15 of thee: thou shalt not see evil any **m**. H5750
Zec 9: 8 **m**: for now have I seen with mine eyes. H5750
11: 6 For I will no **m** pity the inhabitants of H5750
13: 2 and they shall no **m** be remembered: H5750
14:11 there shall be no **m** utter destruction; H5750
21 there shall be no **m** the Canaanite in H5750
Mal 2:13 the offering any **m**, or receiveth *it* with H5750
Mt 5:37 is **m** than these cometh of evil. G4053
47 only, what do ye **m** *than others*? do not G4053
6:25 on. Is not the life **m** than meat, and the G4119
30 much **m** *clothe* you, O ye of little faith? G3123
7:11 how much **m** shall your Father which G3123
10:15 Verily I say unto you, It shall be **m** G414
25 how much **m** *shall they call* them G3123
31 Fear ye not therefore, ye are of **m** value G1308
37 He that loveth father or mother **m** than G5228
37 **m** than me is not worthy of me. G5228
11: 9 I say unto you, and **m** than a prophet. G4055
22 But I say unto you, It shall be **m** G414
24 But I say unto you, That it shall be **m** G414
12:45 seven other spirits **m** wicked than

Mt 13:12 and he shall have **m** abundance: but
18:13 you, he rejoiceth **m** of that *sheep*, than G3123
16 thee one or two **m**, that in the mouth of G2089
19: 6 Wherefore they are no **m** twain, but G3765
20:10 have received **m**; and they likewise G4119
31 but they cried the **m**, saying, Have G3185
21:36 Again, he sent other servants **m** than G4119
22:46 day forth ask him any **m** *questions*. G3765
23:15 **m** the child of hell than yourselves. G1362
25:20 I have gained beside them five talents **m**. G243
26:53 me **m** than twelve legions of angels? G4119
27:23 out the **m**, saying, Let him be crucified. G4057
Mk 1:45 Jesus could no **m** openly enter into the G3371
4:24 unto you that hear shall **m** be given. G4369
6:11 you, It shall be **m** tolerable for Sodom G414
7:12 And ye suffer him no **m** to do ought for G3765
36 no man: but the **m** he charged them, so G3745
36 the **m** a great deal they published *it*; G3123
8:14 in the ship with them **m** than one loaf. G1508
9: 8 any **m**, save Jesus only with themselves. G3765
25 out of him, and enter no **m** into him. G3371
10: 8 they are no **m** twain, but one flesh. G3765
48 but he cried the **m** a great deal, *Thou* G3123
12:33 as himself, is **m** than all whole burnt G4119
43 widow hath cast **m** in, than all they G4119
14: 5 For it might have been sold for **m** than G1833
25 Verily I say unto you, I will drink no **m** G3765
31 But he spake the **m** vehemently, If I G3123
15:14 out the **m** exceedingly, Crucify him. G4056
Lk 3:13 And he said unto them, Exact no **m** G4119
5:15 But so much the **m** went there a fame G3123
7:26 unto you, and much **m** than a prophet. G4055
9:13 said, We have no **m** but five loaves and G4119
10:12 But I say unto you, that it shall be **m** G414
14 But it shall be **m** tolerable for Tyre and G414
35 **m**, when I come again, I will repay thee. G4325
11:13 how much **m** shall *your* heavenly G3123
26 *him* seven other spirits **m** wicked than
12: 4 after that have no **m** that they can do. G4055
7 ye are of **m** value than many sparrows. G1308
23 The life is **m** than meat, and the body G4119
23 meat, and the body *is* **m** than raiment.
24 much **m** are ye better than the fowls? G3123
28 **m** *will he clothe* you, O ye of little faith? G3123
48 much, of him they will ask the **m**. G4055
14: 8 room; lest a **m** honourable man than
15: 7 that repenteth, **m** than over ninety and
19 And am no **m** worthy to be called thy G3765
21 am no **m** worthy to be called thy son. G3765
18:30 Who shall not receive manifold **m** in G4179
39 he cried so much the **m**, *Thou* son of G3123
20:36 Neither can they die any **m**: for they are G2089
21: 3 widow hath cast in **m** than they all: G4119
22:16 For I say unto you, I will not any **m** eat G3765
44 And being in an agony he prayed **m** G1617
23: 5 And they were the **m** fierce, saying, He G2001
Jn 4: 1 and baptized **m** disciples than John, G4119
41 And many **m** believed because of his G4119
5:14 **m**, lest a worse thing come unto thee. G3371
18 Therefore the Jews sought the **m** to kill G3123
6:66 went back, and walked no **m** with him. G3765
7:31 will he do **m** miracles than these G4119
8:11 do I condemn thee: go, and sin no **m**. G3371
10:10 that they might have *it* **m** abundantly.
11:54 Jesus therefore walked no **m** openly G3756
12:43 For they loved the praise of men **m** G3123
14:19 seeth me no **m**; but ye see me: because G2089
15: 2 it, that it may bring forth **m** fruit. G4119
4 no **m** can ye, except ye abide in me. G3779
16:10 I go to my Father, and ye see me no **m**; G3765
21 remembereth no **m** the anguish, for joy G2089
25 when I shall no **m** speak unto you in G3765
17:11 And now I am no **m** in the world, but G3765
19: 8 heard that saying, he was the **m** afraid; G3123
21:15 lovest thou me **m** than these? He saith G4119
Act 4:19 unto you **m** than unto God, judge ye. G3123
5:14 And believers were the **m** added to the G3123
8:39 no **m**: and he went on his way rejoicing. G3765
9:22 But Saul increased the **m** in strength, G3123
13:34 from the dead, *now* no **m** to return to G3371
17:11 These were **m** noble than those in
18:26 unto him the way of God **m** perfectly. G197
19:32 was confused; and the **m** part knew not G4119
20:25 of God, shall see my face no **m**. G3765
35 It is **m** blessed to give than to receive. G3123
38 should see his face no **m**. And they G3765
22: 2 they kept the **m** silence: and he saith,) G3123
23:13 And they were **m** than forty which had G4119
15 would inquire something **m** perfectly G197

Act 23:20 inquire somewhat of him **m** perfectly. G197
21 wait for him of them **m** than forty men, G4119
24:10 do the **m** cheerfully answer for myself: G2115
22 things, having **m** perfect knowledge of G197
25: 6 among them **m** than ten days, he went G4119
27:11 owner of the ship, **m** than those things G3123
12 to winter in, the **m** part advised to G4119
Ro 1:25 the creature **m** than the Creator, who G3844
2:18 the things that are **m** excellent, being
3: 7 For if the truth of God hath **m** abounded
5: 9 Much **m** then, being now justified by G3123
10 of his Son, much **m**, being reconciled, G3123
15 be dead, much **m** the grace of God, and G3123
17 by one; much **m** they which receive G3123
20 abounded, grace did much **m** abound:
6: 9 the dead dieth no **m**; death hath no G3765
9 death hath no **m** dominion over him. G3765
7:17 Now then it is no **m** I that do it, but sin G3765
20 Now if I do that I would not, it is no **m** I G3765
8:37 Nay, in all these things we are **m** than G5245
11: 6 And if by grace, then *is it* no **m** of G3765
6 grace is no **m** grace. But if *it be* of G3765
6 then is it no **m** grace: otherwise work G3765
6 grace: otherwise work is no **m** work. G3765
12 Gentiles; how much **m** their fulness? G3123
24 tree: how much **m** shall these, which be G3123
12: 3 to think *of himself* **m** highly than he G3844
14:13 judge one another any **m**: but judge this G3371
15:15 I have written the **m** boldly unto you in G5112
23 But now having no **m** place in these G3371
1Co 6: 3 much **m** things that pertain to this life? G1065
9:19 unto all, that I might gain the **m**. G4119
12:22 Nay, much **m** those members of the G3123
22 seem to be **m** feeble, are necessary: G3123
23 these we bestow **m** abundant honour; G4055
23 *parts* have **m** abundant comeliness. G4055
24 having given **m** abundant honour to G4055
31 I unto you a **m** excellent way. G2596+G5236
14:18 I speak with tongues **m** than ye all: G3123
15:10 but I laboured **m** abundantly than they G4055
2Co 1:12 world, and **m** abundantly to you-ward. G4056
2: 4 which I have **m** abundantly unto you. G4056
3: 9 *be* glory, much **m** doth the G3123
11 **m** that which remaineth *is* glorious. G3123
4:17 for us a far **m** exceeding *and* G1519+G5236
5:16 yet now henceforth know we *him* no **m**. G3765
7: 7 toward me; so that I rejoiced the **m**. G3123
13 exceedingly the **m** joyed we for the joy G3123
15 And his inward affection is **m** G4056
8:17 but being **m** forward, of his own G4707
22 but now much **m** diligent, upon the G4707
10: 8 For though I should boast somewhat **m** G4055
11:23 as a fool) I *am* **m**; in labours more G5228
23 *am* more; in labours **m** abundant, in G4056
23 in prisons **m** frequent, in deaths oft. G4056
12:15 you; though the **m** abundantly I love G4056
Gal 1:14 mine own nation, being **m** exceedingly G4056
3:18 *be* of the law, *it is* no **m** of promise: but G3765
4: 7 Wherefore thou art no **m** a servant, but G3765
27 hath many **m** children than she which G4183
Eph 2:19 Now therefore ye are no **m** strangers G3765
4:14 That we *henceforth* be no **m** children, G3371
28 Let him that stole steal no **m**: but rather G3371
Php 1: 9 love may abound yet **m** and more in G3123
9 **m** in knowledge and *in* all judgment; G3123
14 **m** bold to speak the word without fear. G4056
24 Nevertheless to abide in the flesh *is* **m** G316
26 That your rejoicing may be **m** abundant
2:12 but now much **m** in my absence, work G3123
28 I sent him therefore the **m** carefully, G3123
3: 4 whereof he might trust in the flesh, I **m**: G3123
1Th 2:17 endeavoured the **m** abundantly to see G4056
4: 1 God, *so* ye would abound **m** and more. G3123
1 God, *so* ye would abound more and **m**. G3123
10 brethren, that ye increase **m** and more; G3123
10 brethren, that ye increase more and **m**; G3123
2Ti 2:16 they will increase unto **m** ungodliness. G4119
3: 4 of pleasures **m** than lovers of God; G3123
Phlm 16 but how much **m** unto thee, both in the G3123
21 that thou wilt also do **m** than I say. G5228
Heb 1: 4 obtained a **m** excellent name than they.
2: 1 Therefore we ought to give the **m** G4056
3: 3 For this *man* was counted worthy of **m** G4119
3 house hath **m** honour than the house. G4119
6:17 Wherein God, willing **m** abundantly to G4054
7:15 And it is yet far **m** evident: for that G4054
8: 6 But now hath he obtained a **m** excellent
12 their iniquities will I remember no **m**. G2089
9:11 by a greater and **m** perfect tabernacle,

Heb 9:14 How much **m** shall the blood of Christ, G3123
10: 2 have had no **m** conscience of sins. G3367
17 and iniquities will I remember no **m**. G2089
18 these *is, there is* no **m** offering for sin. G3765
25 the **m**, as ye see the day approaching. G3123
26 there remaineth no **m** sacrifice for sins, G3765
11: 4 By faith Abel offered unto God a **m**
32 And what shall I **m** say? for the time G2089
12:19 should not be spoken to them any **m**: G4369
25 on earth, much **m** *shall not* we *escape*, G3123
26 saying, Yet once **m** I shake not the earth G530
27 And this *word*, Yet once **m**, signifieth the G530
Jas 4: 6 But he giveth **m** grace. Wherefore he G3187
1Pt 1: 7 faith, being much **m** precious than of
2Pt 1:19 We have also a **m** sure word of
Rev 2:19 and the last *to be* **m** than the first. G4114
3:12 and he shall go no **m** out: and I will G2089
7:16 They shall hunger no **m**, neither thirst G3756
16 neither thirst any **m**; neither shall the G2089
9:12 there come two woes **m** hereafter. G2089
12: 8 was their place found any **m** in heaven. G2089
18:11 man buyeth their merchandise any **m**: G3765
14 and thou shalt find them no **m** at all. G3765
21 down, and shall be found no **m** at all. G2089
22 shall be heard no **m** at all in thee; and G2089
22 be found any **m** in thee; and the sound G2089
22 shall be heard no **m** at all in thee; G2089
23 shall shine no **m** at all in thee; and the G2089
23 shall be heard no **m** at all in thee: for G2089
20: 3 the nations no **m**, till the thousand G3361
21: 1 passed away; and there was no **m** sea. G3756
4 and there shall be no **m** death, neither G3756
4 shall there be any **m** pain: for the G2089
22: 3 And there shall be no **m** curse: but the G3956

MOREH

Gen 12: 6 unto the plain of **M**. And the Canaanite H4176
Dt 11:30 against Gilgal, beside the plains of **M**? H4176
Jdg 7: 1 of them, by the hill of **M**, in the valley. H4176

MOREOVER

Gen 24:25 She said **m** unto him, We have both
32:20 And say ye **m**, Behold, thy servant H1571
45:15 **M** he kissed all his brethren, and wept
47: 4 They said **m** unto Pharaoh, For to
48:22 **M** I have given to thee one portion above
Ex 3: 6 **M** he said, I *am* the God of thy father,
15 And God said **m** unto Moses, Thus H5750
11: 3 of the Egyptians. **M** the man Moses *was*
18:21 **M** thou shalt provide out of all the
26: 1 **M** thou shalt make the tabernacle *with*
30:22 **M** the LORD spake unto Moses, saying,
Lev 7:21 **M** the soul that shall touch any unclean
26 **M** ye shall eat no manner of blood,
14:46 **M** he that goeth into the house all the
18:20 **M** thou shalt not lie carnally with thy
25:45 **M** of the children of the strangers that H1571
Nu 13:28 **m** we saw the children of Anak there. H1571
16:14 **M** thou hast not brought us into a land H637
33:56 **M** it shall come to pass, *that* I shall do
35:31 **M** ye shall take no satisfaction for the
Dt 1:28 up to heaven; and **m** we have seen the H1571
39 **M** your little ones, which ye said should
7:20 **M** the LORD thy God will send the H1571
28:45 **M** all these curses shall come upon thee,
60 **M** he will bring upon thee all the
Jdg 10: 9 **M** the children of Ammon passed over
Ru 4:10 **M** Ruth the Moabitess, the wife of H1571
1Sa 2:19 **M** his mother made him a little coat,
12:23 **M** as for me, God forbid that I should H1571
14:21 **M** the Hebrews *that* were with the
17:37 David said **m**, The LORD that delivered
20: 3 And David sware **m**, and said, Thy H5750
24:11 **M**, my father, see, yea, see the skirt of thy
28:19 **M** the LORD will also deliver Israel H1571
2Sa 7:10 **M** I will appoint a place for my people
12: 8 too little, I would **m** have given unto H3254
15: 4 Absalom said **m**, Oh that I were made
17: 1 **M** Ahithophel said unto Absalom, Let
13 **M**, if he be gotten into a city, then shall H518
21:15 **M** the Philistines had yet war again with
1Ki 1:47 And **m** the king's servants came to bless
2: 5 **M** thou knowest also what Joab the son H1571
14 He said **m**, I have somewhat to say unto
44 The king said **m** to Shimei, Thou
8:41 **M** concerning a stranger, that *is* not of H1571
10:18 **M** the king made a great throne of ivory,
14:14 **M** the LORD shall raise him up a king
2Ki 12:15 **M** they reckoned not with the men, into
2Ki 21:16 **M** Manasseh shed innocent blood very H1571
23:15 **M** the altar that *was* at Beth-el, *and* the H1571
24 **M** the *workers with* familiar spirits, H1571
1Ch 11: 2 And **m** in time past, even when Saul H1571
12:40 **M** they that were nigh them, *even* unto H1571
17:10 my people Israel. **M** I will subdue all
18:12 **M** Abishai the son of Zeruiah slew of the
22:15 **M** *there are* workmen with thee in
23: 5 **M** four thousand *were* porters; and four
25: 1 **M** David and the captains of the host
26: 4 **M** the sons of Obed-edom *were*,
28: 7 **M** I will establish his kingdom for ever,
29: 3 **M**, because I have set my affection to H5750
2Ch 1: 5 **M** the brasen altar, that Bezaleel the son
2:12 Huram said **m**, Blessed *be* the LORD God
4: 1 **M** he made an altar of brass, twenty
20 **M** the candlesticks with their lamps,
6:32 **M** concerning the stranger, which is H1571
7: 7 **M** Solomon hallowed the middle of the
9:17 **M** the king made a great throne of ivory,
17: 6 of the LORD: **m** he took away the high H5750
19: 8 **M** in Jerusalem did Jehoshaphat set of H1571
21:11 **M** he made high places in the mountains
16 **M** the LORD stirred up against Jehoram
23: 9 **M** Jehoiada the priest delivered to the
25: 5 **M** Amaziah gathered Judah together,
26: 9 **M** Uzziah built towers in Jerusalem at
11 **M** Uzziah had an host of fighting men,
27: 4 **M** he built cities in the mountains of
28: 3 **M** he burnt incense in the valley of the
29:19 **M** all the vessels, which king Ahaz in his
30 **M** Hezekiah the king and the princes
31: 4 **M** he commanded the people that dwelt
32:29 **M** he provided him cities, and
35: 1 **M** Josiah kept a passover unto the LORD
36:14 **M** all the chief of the priests, and the H1571
Ezr 6: 8 **M** I make a decree what ye shall do to
10:25 **M** of Israel: of the sons of Parosh;
Neh 2: 7 **M** I said unto the king, If it please the
3: 6 **M** the old gate repaired Jehoiada the son
26 **M** the Nethinims dwelt in Ophel, unto
5:14 **M** from the time that I was appointed H1571
17 **M** *there were* at my table an hundred
6:17 **M** in those days the nobles of Judah H1571
9:12 **M** thou leddest them in the day by a
22 **M** thou gavest them kingdoms and
11:19 **M** the porters, Akkub, Talmon, and their
12: 8 **M** the Levites: Jeshua, Binnui, Kadmiel,
Est 5:12 Haman said **m**, Yea, Esther the queen H637
Job 27: 1 **M** Job continued his parable, and said,
29: 1 **M** Job continued his parable, and said,
35: 1 Elihu spake **m**, and said,
40: 1 **M** the LORD answered Job, and said,
Ps 19:11 **M** by them is thy servant warned: *and* H1571
78:67 **M** he refused the tabernacle of Joseph,
105:16 **M** he called for a famine upon the land:
Ecc 3:16 And **m** I saw under the sun the place of H5750
5: 9 **M** the profit of the earth is for all: the
6: 5 **M** he hath not seen the sun, nor known H1571
12: 9 And **m**, because the preacher was wise, H3148
Isa 3:16 **M** the LORD saith, Because the
7:10 **M** the LORD spake again unto Ahaz,
8: 1 **M** the LORD said unto me, Take thee a
19: 9 **M** they that work in fine flax, and they
29: 5 **M** the multitude of thy strangers shall be
30:26 **M** the light of the moon shall be as the
39: 8 spoken. He said **m**, For there shall be
Jer 1:11 **M** the word of the LORD came unto me,
2: 1 **M** the word of the LORD came to me,
8: 4 **M** thou shalt say unto them, Thus saith
20: 5 **M** I will deliver all the strength of this
25:10 **M** I will take from them the voice of
33: 1 **M** the word of the LORD came unto
23 **M** the word of the LORD came to
37:18 **M** Jeremiah said unto king Zedekiah,
39: 7 **M** he put out Zedekiah's eyes, and
40:13 **M** Johanan the son of Kareah, and all
44:24 **M** Jeremiah said unto all the people, and
48:35 **M** I will cause to cease in Moab, saith
Ezk 3: 1 **M** he said unto me, Son of man, eat that
10 **M** he said unto me, Son of man, all my
4: 3 **M** take thou unto thee an iron pan, and
16 **M** he said unto me, Son of man, behold,
5:14 **M** I will make thee waste, and a
7: 1 **M** the word of the LORD came unto me,
11: 1 **M** the spirit lifted me up, and brought
12:17 **M** the word of the LORD came to me,
16:20 **M** thou hast taken thy sons and thy
29 Thou hast **m** multiplied thy fornication
Ezk 17:11 **M** the word of the LORD came unto me,
19: 1 **M** take thou up a lamentation for the
20:12 **M** also I gave them my sabbaths, to be H1571
45 **M** the word of the LORD came unto me,
22: 1 **M** the word of the LORD came unto me,
23:36 The LORD said **m** unto me; Son of man,
38 **M** this they have done unto me: they H5750
28:11 **M** the word of the LORD came unto me,
35: 1 **M** the word of the LORD came unto me,
36:16 **M** the word of the LORD came unto me,
37:16 **M**, thou son of man, take thee one stick,
26 **M** I will make a covenant of peace with
45: 1 **M**, when ye shall divide by lot the land
46:18 **M** the prince shall not take of the
48:22 **M** from the possession of the Levites,
Zec 4: 8 **M** the word of the LORD came unto me,
5: 6 goeth forth. He said **m**, This *is* their
Mt 6:16 **M** when ye fast, be not, as the G1161
18:15 **M** if thy brother shall trespass against G1161
Lk 16:21 man's table: **m** the dogs came G235+G2532
Act 2:26 glad; **m** also my flesh shall rest in hope: G1161
11:12 nothing doubting. **M** these six brethren G2532
19:26 **M** ye see and hear, that not alone at G2532
Ro 5:20 **M** the law entered, that the offence G1161
8:30 **M** whom he did predestinate, them he G1161
1Co 4: 2 **M** it is required in stewards, G3739+G3063
10: 1 **M**, brethren, I would not that ye should G1161
15: 1 **M**, brethren, I declare unto you the G1161
2Co 1:23 **M** I call God for a record upon my soul, G1161
8: 1 **M**, brethren, we do you to wit of the G1161
1Ti 3: 7 **M** he must have a good report of them G1161
Heb 9:21 **M** he sprinkled with blood both the G3668
11:36 yea, **m** of bonds and imprisonment: G2089
2Pt 1:15 **M** I will endeavour that ye may be able G1161

MORESHETHGATH

Mic 1:14 Therefore shalt thou give presents to **M**: H4182

MORIAH

Gen 22: 2 into the land of **M**; and offer him there H4179
2Ch 3: 1 in mount **M**, where *the LORD* appeared H4179

MORNING

Gen 1: 5 evening and the **m** were the first day. H1242
8 and the **m** were the second day. H1242
13 And the evening and the **m** were the H1242
19 And the evening and the **m** were the H1242
23 And the evening and the **m** were the H1242
31 evening and the **m** were the sixth day. H1242
19:15 And when the **m** arose, then the angels H7837
27 And Abraham gat up early in the **m** to H1242
20: 8 rose early in the **m**, and called all his H1242
21:14 And Abraham rose up early in the **m**, H1242
22: 3 And Abraham rose up early in the **m**, H1242
24:54 rose up in the **m**, and he said, Send me H1242
26:31 And they rose up betimes in the **m**, and H1242
28:18 And Jacob rose up early in the **m**, and H1242
29:25 And it came to pass, that in the **m**, H1242
31:55 And early in the **m** Laban rose up, and H1242
40: 6 in unto them in the **m**, and looked upon H1242
41: 8 And it came to pass in the **m** that his H1242
44: 3 As soon as the **m** was light, the men H1242
49:27 *as* a wolf: in the **m** he shall devour the H1242
Ex 7:15 Get thee unto Pharaoh in the **m**; lo, he H1242
8:20 Rise up early in the **m**, and stand before H1242
9:13 Rise up early in the **m**, and stand before H1242
10:13 **m**, the east wind brought the locusts. H1242
12:10 it remain until the **m**; and that which H1242
10 of it until the **m** ye shall burn with fire. H1242
22 out at the door of his house until the **m**. H1242
14:24 And it came to pass, that in the **m** H1242
27 strength when the **m** appeared; and the H1242
16: 7 And in the **m**, then ye shall see the glory H1242
8 to eat, and in the **m** bread to the full; H1242
12 eat flesh, and in the **m** ye shall be filled H1242
13 **m** the dew lay round about the host. H1242
19 said, Let no man leave of it till the **m**. H1242
20 left of it until the **m**, and it bred worms, H1242
21 And they gathered it every **m**, every H1242
23 lay up for you to be kept until the **m**. H1242
24 And they laid it up till the **m**, as Moses H1242
18:13 by Moses from the **m** unto the evening. H1242
14 stand by thee from **m** unto even? H1242
19:16 the third day in the **m**, that there were H1242
23:18 fat of my sacrifice remain until the **m**. H1242
24: 4 up early in the **m**, and builded an altar H1242
27:21 it from evening to **m** before the LORD: H1242
29:34 remain unto the **m**, then thou shalt H1242
39 The one lamb thou shalt offer in the **m**; H1242

M

Ex 29:41 offering of the **m**, and according to the H1242
30: 7 incense every **m**: when he dresseth the H1242
34: 2 And be ready in the **m**, and come up in H1242
2 come up in the **m** unto mount Sinai, H1242
4 up early in the **m**, and went up unto H1242
25 feast of the passover be left unto the **m**. H1242
36: 3 yet unto him free offerings every **m**. H1242
Lev 6: 9 all night unto the **m**, and the fire of the H1242
12 wood on it every **m**, and lay the burnt H1242
20 of it in the **m**, and half thereof at night. H1242
7:15 he shall not leave any of it until the **m**. H1242
9:17 beside the burnt sacrifice of the **m**. H1242
19:13 abide with thee all night until the **m**. H1242
24: 3 evening unto the **m** before the LORD H1242
Nu 9:12 They shall leave none of it unto the **m**, H1242
15 were the appearance of fire, until the **m**. H1242
21 even unto the **m**, and *that* the cloud H1242
21 taken up in the **m**, then they journeyed: H1242
14:40 And they rose up early in the **m**, and gat H1242
22:13 And Balaam rose up in the **m**, and said H1242
21 And Balaam rose up in the **m**, and H1242
28: 4 The one lamb shalt thou offer in the **m**, H1242
8 meat offering of the **m**, and as the drink H1242
23 burnt offering in the **m**, which *is* for a H1242
Dt 16: 4 at even, remain all night until the **m**. H1242
7 turn in the **m**, and go unto thy tents. H1242
28:67 In the **m** thou shalt say, Would God it H1242
67 God it were **m**! for the fear of thine H1242
Jos 3: 1 And Joshua rose early in the **m**; and H1242
6:12 And Joshua rose early in the **m**, and the H1242
7:14 In the **m** therefore ye shall be brought H1242
16 So Joshua rose up early in the **m**, and H1242
8:10 And Joshua rose up early in the **m**, and H1242
Jdg 6:28 arose early in the **m**, behold, the altar of H1242
31 whilst *it is yet* **m**: if he *be* a god, let him H1242
9:33 And it shall be, *that* in the **m**, as soon as H1242
16: 2 the **m**, when it is day, we shall kill him. H1242
19: 5 arose early in the **m**, that he rose up to H1242
8 And he arose early in the **m** on the fifth H1242
25 the night until the **m**: and when the day H1242
27 And her lord rose up in the **m**, and H1242
20:19 the **m**, and encamped against Gibeah. H1242
Ru 2: 7 even from the **m** until now, that she H1242
3:13 and it shall be in the **m**, *that* if he will H1242
13 the LORD liveth: lie down until the **m**. H1242
14 And she lay at his feet until the **m**: and H1242
1Sa 1:19 And they rose up in the **m** early, and H1242
3:15 And Samuel lay until the **m**, and H1242
5: 4 on the morrow **m**, behold, Dagon *was* H1242
11:11 of the host in the **m** watch, and slew H1242
14:36 them until the **m** light, and let us not H1242
15:12 meet Saul in the **m**, it was told Samuel, H1242
17:16 And the Philistine drew near **m** and H7925
20 And David rose up early in the **m**, and H1242
19: 2 to thyself until the **m**, and abide in a H1242
11 and to slay him in the **m**: and Michal H1242
20:35 And it came to pass in the **m**, that H1242
25:22 to him by the **m** light any that pisseth H1242
34 left unto Nabal by the **m** light any that H1242
36 nothing, less or more, until the **m** light. H1242
37 But it came to pass in the **m**, when the H1242
29:10 Wherefore now rise up early in the **m** H1242
10 early in the **m**, and have light, depart. H1242
11 to depart in the **m**, to return into the H1242
2Sa 2:27 surely then in the **m** the people had H1242
11:14 And it came to pass in the **m**, that H1242
17:22 Jordan: by the **m** light there lacked not H1242
23: 4 And *he shall be* as the light of the **m**, H1242
4 sun riseth, *even* a **m** without clouds; *as* H1242
24:11 For when David was up in the **m**, the H1242
15 Israel from the **m** even to the time H1242
1Ki 3:21 And when I rose in the **m** to give my H1242
21 it in the **m**, behold, it was not my H1242
17: 6 and flesh in the **m**, and bread and flesh H1242
18:26 name of Baal from **m** even until noon, H1242
2Ki 3:20 And it came to pass in the **m**, when the H1242
22 And they rose up early in the **m**, and the H1242
7: 9 peace: if we tarry till the **m** light, some H1242
10: 8 the entering in of the gate until the **m**. H1242
9 And it came to pass in the **m**, that he H1242
16:15 altar burn the **m** burnt offering, and H1242
19:35 **m**, behold, they *were* all dead corpses. H1242
1Ch 9:27 thereof every **m** *pertained* to them. H1242
16:40 continually **m** and evening, and *to* H1242
23:30 And to stand every **m** to thank and H1242
2Ch 2: 4 burnt offerings **m** and evening, on the H1242
13:11 And they burn unto the LORD every **m** H1242
20:20 And they rose early in the **m**, and went H1242
31: 3 *to wit*, for the **m** and evening burnt H1242

Ezr 3: 3 *even* burnt offerings **m** and evening. H1242
Neh 4:21 rising of the **m** till the stars appeared. H7837
8: 3 gate from the **m** until midday, before H216
Job 1: 5 up early in the **m**, and offered burnt H1242
4:20 They are destroyed from **m** to evening: H1242
7:18 every **m**, *and* try him every moment? H1242
21 seek me in the **m**, but I *shall* not *be*. H7836
11:17 shalt shine forth, thou shalt be as the **m**. H1242
24:17 For the **m** *is* to them even as the H1242
38: 7 When the **m** stars sang together, and H1242
12 Hast thou commanded the **m** since thy H1242
41:18 his eyes *are* like the eyelids of the **m**. H7837
Ps 5: 3 My voice shalt thou hear in the **m**, O H1242
3 O LORD; in the **m** will I direct *my* H1242
30: 5 for a night, but joy *cometh* in the **m**. H1242
49:14 over them in the **m**; and their beauty H1242
55:17 Evening, and **m**, and at noon, will I H1242
59:16 thy mercy in the **m**: for thou hast been H1242
65: 8 of the **m** and evening to rejoice. H1242
73:14 I been plagued, and chastened every **m**. H1242
88:13 in the **m** shall my prayer prevent thee. H1242
90: 5 *as* a sleep: in the **m** *they are* like grass H1242
6 In the **m** it flourisheth, and groweth up; H1242
92: 2 the **m**, and thy faithfulness every night, H1242
110: 3 the **m**: thou hast the dew of thy youth. H4891
119:147 I prevented the dawning of the **m**, and H5399
130: 6 that watch for the **m**: *I say, more than* H1242
6 *more than* they that watch for the **m**. H1242
139: 9 *If* I take the wings of the **m**, *and* dwell in H7837
143: 8 in the **m**; for in thee do I trust: H1242
Prv 7:18 the **m**: let us solace ourselves with loves. H1242
27:14 **m**, it shall be counted a curse to him. H1242
Ecc 10:16 *is* a child, and thy princes eat in the **m**! H1242
11: 6 In the **m** sow thy seed, and in the H1242
Song 6:10 Who *is* she *that* looketh forth as the **m**, H7837
Isa 5:11 up early in the **m**, *that* they may follow H1242
14:12 Lucifer, son of the **m**! *how* art thou cut H7837
17:11 grow, and in the **m** shalt thou make thy H1242
14 *and* before the **m** he *is* not. This *is* the H1242
21:12 The watchman said, The **m** cometh, H1242
28:19 shall take you: for by morning shall H1242
19 for morning by **m** shall it pass over, by H1242
33: 2 their arm every **m**, our salvation also in H1242
37:36 **m**, behold, they *were* all dead corpses. H1242
38:13 I reckoned till **m**, *that*, as a lion, so will H1242
50: 4 weary: he wakeneth **m** by morning, he H1242
4 morning by **m**, he wakeneth mine H1242
58: 8 break forth as the **m**, and thine health H7837
Jer 5: 8 They were *as* fed horses in the **m**: every H7904
20:16 in the **m**, and the shouting at noontide; H1242
21:12 judgment in the **m**, and deliver *him that* H1242
Lam 3:23 *They are* new every **m**: great *is* thy H1242
Ezk 7: 7 The **m** is come unto thee, O thou that H6843
10 it is come: the **m** is gone forth; the rod H6843
12: 8 And in the **m** came the word of the H1242
24:18 So I spake unto the people in the **m**: and H1242
18 I did in the **m** as I was commanded. H1242
33:22 he came to me in the **m**; and my mouth H1242
46:13 blemish: thou shalt prepare it every **m**. H1242
14 for it every **m**, the sixth part of an H1242
15 every **m** *for* a continual burnt offering. H1242
Dan 6:19 Then the king arose very early in the **m**, H5053
8:26 evening and the **m** which was told *is* H1242
Hos 6: 3 is prepared as the **m**; and he shall come H7837
4 goodness *is* as a **m** cloud, and as the H1242
7: 6 in the **m** it burneth as a flaming fire. H1242
10:15 wickedness: in a **m** shall the king of H7837
13: 3 Therefore they shall be as the **m** cloud, H1242
Joel 2: 2 darkness, as the **m** spread upon the H7837
Am 4: 4 **m**, *and* your tithes after three years: H1242
13 that maketh the **m** darkness, and H7837
5: 8 of death into the **m**, and maketh the H1242
Jna 4: 7 But God prepared a worm when the **m** H7837
Mic 2: 1 beds! when the **m** is light, they practise H1242
Zep 3: 5 do iniquity: every **m** doth he bring his H1242
Mt 16: 3 And in the **m**, *It will be* foul weather to *G4404*
20: 1 **m** to hire labourers into his vineyard. *G260*
21:18 Now in the **m** as he returned into the *G4405*
27: 1 When the **m** was come, all the chief *G4405*
Mk 1:35 And in the **m**, rising up a great while *G4404*
11:20 And in the **m**, as they passed by, they *G4404*
13:35 or at the cockcrowing, or in the **m**: *G4404*
15: 1 And straightway in the **m** the chief *G4404*
16: 2 And very early in the **m** the first *day* of *G4404*
Lk 21:38 And all the people came early in the **m** *G3719*
24: 1 very early in the **m**, they came unto the *G3722*
Jn 8: 2 And early in the **m** he came again into *G3722*
21: 4 But when the **m** was now come, Jesus *G4405*
Act 5:21 early in the **m**, and taught. But the *G5259*

Act 28:23 *of* the prophets, from **m** till evening. *G4404*
Rev 2:28 And I will give him the **m** star. *G4407*
22:16 of David, *and* the bright and **m** star. *G3720*

MORNING-CLOUD See MORNING and CLOUD.

MORNING-LIGHT See MORNING and LIGHT.

MORNING-STAR See MORNING and STAR.

MORROW

Gen 19:34 And it came to pass on the **m**, that the H4283
Ex 8:10 And he said, To **m**. And he said, *Be it* H4279
23 and thy people: to **m** shall this sign be. H4279
29 his people, to **m**: but let not Pharaoh H4279
9: 5 time, saying, To **m** the LORD shall do H4279
6 And the LORD did that thing on the **m**, H4283
18 Behold, to **m** about this time I will H4279
10: 4 **m** will I bring the locusts into thy coast: H4279
16:23 hath said, To **m** *is* the rest of the holy H4279
17: 9 with Amalek: to **m** I will stand on the H4279
18:13 And it came to pass on the **m**, that H4283
19:10 to **m**, and let them wash their clothes, H4279
32: 5 and said, To **m** *is* a feast to the LORD. H4279
6 And they rose up early on the **m**, and H4283
30 And it came to pass on the **m**, that H4283
Lev 7:16 and on the **m** also the remainder H4283
19: 6 it, and on the **m**: and if ought remain H4283
22:30 none of it until the **m**: I *am* the LORD. H1242
23:11 for you: on the **m** after the sabbath the H4283
15 unto you from the **m** after the sabbath, H4283
16 Even unto the **m** after the seventh H4283
Nu 11:18 against to **m**, and ye shall eat flesh: H4279
14:25 in the valley.) To **m** turn you, and get H4279
16: 5 saying, Even to **m** the LORD will shew H1242
7 the LORD to **m**: and it shall be *that* H4279
16 LORD, thou, and they, and Aaron, to **m**: H4279
41 But on the **m** all the congregation of H4283
17: 8 And it came to pass, that on the **m** H4283
22:41 And it came to pass on the **m**, that H1242
33: 3 month; on the **m** after the passover the H4283
Jos 3: 5 yourselves: for to **m** the LORD will do H4279
5:11 of the land on the **m** after the passover, H4283
12 And the manna ceased on the **m** after H4283
7:13 against to **m**: for thus saith the LORD H4279
11: 6 of them: for to **m** about this time will H4279
22:18 the LORD, that to **m** he will be wroth H4279
Jdg 6:38 up early on the **m**, and thrust the fleece H4283
9:42 And it came to pass on the **m**, that the H4283
19: 9 be merry; and to **m** get you early on H4279
20:28 **m** I will deliver them into thine hand. H4279
21: 4 And it came to pass on the **m**, that the H4283
1Sa 5: 3 arose early on the **m**, behold, Dagon H4283
4 And when they arose early on the **m** H4283
9:16 To **m** about this time I will send thee a H4279
19 me to day, and to **m** I will let thee go, H1242
11: 9 of Jabesh-gilead, To **m**, by *that time* the H4279
10 Therefore the men of Jabesh said, To **m** H4279
11 And it was *so* on the **m**, that Saul put H4283
18:10 And it came to pass on the **m**, that the H4283
19:11 life to night, to **m** thou shalt be slain. H4279
20: 5 Behold, to **m** *is* the new moon, and H4279
12 father about to **m** any time, *or* the third H4279
18 Then Jonathan said to David, To **m** *is* H4279
27 And it came to pass on the **m**, *which* H4283
28:19 Philistines: and to **m** *shalt* thou and thy H4279
31: 8 And it came to pass on the **m**, when the H4283
2Sa 11:12 to day also, and to **m** I will let thee H4279
12 abode in Jerusalem that day, and the **m**. H4283
1Ki 19: 2 of one of them by to **m** about this time. H4279
20: 6 unto thee to **m** about this time, and H4279
2Ki 6:28 to day, and we will eat my son to **m**. H4279
7: 1 the LORD, To **m** about this time *shall* H4279
18 shekel, shall be to **m** about this time in H4279
8:15 And it came to pass on the **m**, that he H4283
10: 6 to Jezreel by to **m** this time. Now the H4279
1Ch 10: 8 And it came to pass on the **m**, when the H4283
29:21 the LORD, on the **m** after that day, H4283
2Ch 20:16 To **m** go ye down against them: behold, H4279
17 be dismayed; to **m** go out against them: H4279
Est 2:14 In the evening she went, and on the **m** H1242
5: 8 I will do to **m** as the king hath said. H4279
12 but myself; and to **m** am I invited unto H4279
14 high, and to **m** speak thou unto the H1242
9:13 in Shushan to do to **m** also according H4279
Prv 3:28 **m** I will give; when thou hast it by thee. H4279
27: 1 Boast not thyself of to **m**; for thou H4279
Isa 22:13 us eat and drink; for to **m** we shall die. H4279
56:12 drink; and to **m** shall be as this day, H4279

Jer 20: 3 And it came to pass on the **m**, that H4283
Zep 3: 3 they gnaw not the bones till the **m**. H1242
Mt 6:30 to day is, and to **m** is cast into the oven, *G839*
34 Take therefore no thought for the **m**: for *G839*
34 morrow: for the **m** shall take thought for *G839*
Mk 11:12 And on the **m**, when they were come *G1887*
Lk 10:35 And on the **m** when he departed, he took *G839*
12:28 day in the field, and to **m** is cast into the *G839*
13:32 **m**, and the third *day* I shall be perfected. *G839*
33 to day, and to **m**, and the *day* following: *G839*
Act 4: 5 And it came to pass on the **m**, that their *G839*
10: 9 On the **m**, as they went on their journey, *G1887*
23 *them*. And on the **m** Peter went away *G1887*
24 And the **m** after they entered into *G1887*
20: 7 to depart on the **m**; and continued his *G1887*
22:30 On the **m**, because he would have *G1887*
23:15 down unto you to **m**, as though ye would *G839*
20 down Paul to **m** into the council, as *G839*
32 On the **m** they left the horsemen to go *G1887*
25:17 without any delay on the **m** I sat on the *G1836*
22 To **m**, said he, thou shalt hear him. *G839*
23 And on the **m**, when Agrippa was come, *G1887*
1Co 15:32 not? let us eat and drink; for to **m** we die. *G839*
Jas 4:13 Go to now, ye that say, To day or to **m** *G839*
14 *shall be* on the **m**. For what *is* your life? *G839*

MORSEL
Gen 18: 5 And I will fetch a **m** of bread, and H6595
Jdg 19: 5 thine heart with a **m** of bread, and H6595
Ru 2:14 and dip thy **m** in the vinegar. And H6595
1Sa 2:36 of silver and a **m** of bread, and shall H3603
28:22 and let me set a **m** of bread before thee; H6595
1Ki 17:11 I pray thee, a **m** of bread in thine hand. H6595
Job 31:17 Or have eaten my **m** myself alone, and H6595
Prv 17: 1 Better *is* a dry **m**, and quietness H6595
23: 8 The **m** *which* thou hast eaten shalt H6595
Heb 12:16 for one **m** of meat sold his birthright. *G1035*

MORSELS
Ps 147:17 He casteth forth his ice like **m**: who can H6595

MORTAL
Job 4:17 Shall **m** man be more just than God? H582
Ro 6:12 Let not sin therefore reign in your **m** *G2349*
8:11 shall also quicken your **m** bodies by his *G2349*
1Co 15:53 and this **m** *must* put on immortality. *G2349*
54 and this **m** shall have put on *G2349*
2Co 4:11 might be made manifest in our **m** flesh. *G2349*

MORTALITY
2Co 5: 4 that **m** might be swallowed up of life. *G2349*

MORTALLY
Dt 19:11 and smite him **m** that he die, and fleeth H5315

MORTAR
Nu 11: 8 or beat *it* in a **m**, and baked *it* in pans, H4085
Prv 27:22 bray a fool in a **m** among wheat with H4388

MORTER
Gen 11: 3 for stone, and slime had they for **m**. H2563
Ex 1:14 hard bondage, in **m**, and in brick, and H2563
Lev 14:42 other **m**, and shall plaister the house. H6083
45 and all the **m** of the house; and he H6083
Isa 41:25 *upon* **m**, and as the potter treadeth clay. H2563
Ezk 13:10 lo, others daubed it with untempered *m*:
11 *it* with untempered *m*, that it shall fall:
14 with untempered *m*, and bring it down to
15 it with untempered *m*, and will say unto
22:28 with untempered *m*, seeing vanity, and
Nah 3:14 tread the **m**, make strong the brickkiln. H2563

MORTGAGED
Neh 5: 3 said, We have **m** our lands, vineyards, H6148

MORTIFY
Ro 8:13 **m** the deeds of the body, ye shall live. *G2289*
Col 3: 5 **M** therefore your members which are *G3499*

MOSERA
Dt 10: 6 of Jaakan to **M**: there Aaron died, and H4149

MOSEROTH
Nu 33:30 from Hashmonah, and encamped at **M**. H4149
31 And they departed from **M**, and pitched H4149

MOSES
Ex 2:10 she called his name **M**: and she said, H4872
11 those days, when **M** was grown, that he H4872
Ex 2:14 the Egyptian? And **M** feared, and said, H4872
15 he sought to slay **M**. But Moses fled H4872
15 to slay Moses. But **M** fled from the face H4872
17 them away: but **M** stood up and helped H4872
21 And **M** was content to dwell with the H4872
21 and he gave **M** Zipporah his daughter. H4872
3: 1 Now **M** kept the flock of Jethro his H4872
3 And **M** said, I will now turn aside, and H4872
4 said, **M**, Moses. And he said, Here *am* I. H4872
4 said, Moses, **M**. And he said, Here *am* I. H4872
6 of Jacob. And **M** hid his face; for he H4872
11 And **M** said unto God, Who *am* I, that I H4872
13 And **M** said unto God, Behold, *when* I H4872
14 And God said unto **M**, I AM THAT I H4872
15 And God said moreover unto **M**, Thus H4872
4: 1 And **M** answered and said, But, H4872
3 a serpent; and **M** fled from before it. H4872
4 And the LORD said unto **M**, Put forth H4872
10 And **M** said unto the LORD, O my H4872
14 kindled against **M**, and he said, *Is* not H4872
18 And **M** went and returned to Jethro his H4872
18 And Jethro said to **M**, Go in peace. H4872
19 And the LORD said unto **M** in Midian, H4872
20 And **M** took his wife and his sons, and H4872
20 and **M** took the rod of God in his hand. H4872
21 And the LORD said unto **M**, When thou H4872
27 to meet **M**. And he went, and met H4872
28 And **M** told Aaron all the words of the H4872
29 And **M** and Aaron went and gathered H4872
30 had spoken unto **M**, and did the signs H4872
5: 1 And afterward **M** and Aaron went in, H4872
4 Wherefore do ye, **M** and Aaron, let the H4872
20 And they met **M** and Aaron, who stood H4872
22 And **M** returned unto the LORD, and H4872
6: 1 Then the LORD said unto **M**, Now shalt H4872
2 And God spake unto **M**, and said unto H4872
9 And **M** spake so unto the children of H4872
9 not unto **M** for anguish of spirit, H4872
10 And the LORD spake unto **M**, saying, H4872
12 And **M** spake before the LORD, saying, H4872
13 And the LORD spake unto **M** and unto H4872
20 him Aaron and **M**: and the years of the H4872
26 These *are* that Aaron and **M**, to whom H4872
27 Egypt: these *are* that **M** and Aaron. H4872
28 spake unto **M** in the land of Egypt, H4872
29 That the LORD spake unto **M**, saying, I H4872
30 And **M** said before the LORD, Behold, I H4872
7: 1 And the LORD said unto **M**, See, I have H4872
6 And **M** and Aaron did as the LORD H4872
7 And **M** *was* fourscore years old, and H4872
8 And the LORD spake unto **M** and unto H4872
10 And **M** and Aaron went in unto H4872
14 And the LORD said unto **M**, Pharaoh's H4872
19 And the LORD spake unto **M**, Say unto H4872
20 And **M** and Aaron did so, as the LORD H4872
8: 1 And the LORD spake unto **M**, Go unto H4872
5 And the LORD spake unto **M**, Say unto H4872
8 Then Pharaoh called for **M** and Aaron, H4872
9 And **M** said unto Pharaoh, Glory over H4872
12 And **M** and Aaron went out from H4872
12 Pharaoh: and **M** cried unto the LORD H4872
13 to the word of **M**; and the frogs died out H4872
16 And the LORD said unto **M**, Say unto H4872
20 And the LORD said unto **M**, Rise up H4872
25 And Pharaoh called for **M** and for H4872
26 And **M** said, It is not meet so to do; for H4872
29 And **M** said, Behold, I go out from thee, H4872
30 And **M** went out from Pharaoh, and H4872
31 to the word of **M**; and he removed the H4872
9: 1 Then the LORD said unto **M**, Go in unto H4872
8 And the LORD said unto **M** and unto H4872
8 furnace, and let **M** sprinkle it toward H4872
10 Pharaoh; and **M** sprinkled it up toward H4872
11 not stand before **M** because of the H4872
12 them; as the LORD had spoken unto **M**. H4872
13 And the LORD said unto **M**, Rise up H4872
22 And the LORD said unto **M**, Stretch H4872
23 And **M** stretched forth his rod toward H4872
27 And Pharaoh sent, and called for **M** H4872
29 And **M** said unto him, As soon as I am H4872
33 And **M** went out of the city from H4872
35 go; as the LORD had spoken by **M**. H4872
10: 1 And the LORD said unto **M**, Go in unto H4872
3 And **M** and Aaron came in unto H4872
8 And **M** and Aaron were brought again H4872
9 And **M** said, We will go with our young H4872
12 And the LORD said unto **M**, Stretch out H4872
13 And **M** stretched forth his rod over the H4872
16 Then Pharaoh called for **M** and Aaron H4872
Ex 10:21 And the LORD said unto **M**, Stretch out H4872
22 And **M** stretched forth his hand toward H4872
24 And Pharaoh called unto **M**, and said, H4872
25 And **M** said, Thou must give us also H4872
29 And **M** said, Thou hast spoken well, I H4872
11: 1 And the LORD said unto **M**, Yet will I H4872
3 the man **M** *was* very great in the H4872
4 And **M** said, Thus saith the LORD, H4872
9 And the LORD said unto **M**, Pharaoh H4872
10 And **M** and Aaron did all these H4872
12: 1 And the LORD spake unto **M** and H4872
21 Then **M** called for all the elders of H4872
28 commanded **M** and Aaron, so did they. H4872
31 And he called for **M** and Aaron by H4872
35 to the word of **M**; and they borrowed H4872
43 And the LORD said unto **M** and Aaron, H4872
50 commanded **M** and Aaron, so did they. H4872
13: 1 And the LORD spake unto **M**, saying, H4872
3 And **M** said unto the people, H4872
19 And **M** took the bones of Joseph with H4872
14: 1 And the LORD spake unto **M**, saying, H4872
11 And they said unto **M**, Because *there* H4872
13 And **M** said unto the people, Fear ye H4872
15 And the LORD said unto **M**, Wherefore H4872
21 And **M** stretched out his hand over the H4872
26 And the LORD said unto **M**, Stretch out H4872
27 And **M** stretched forth his hand over H4872
31 believed the LORD, and his servant **M**. H4872
15: 1 Then sang **M** and the children of Israel H4872
22 So **M** brought Israel from the Red sea, H4872
24 And the people murmured against **M**, H4872
16: 2 against **M** and Aaron in the wilderness: H4872
4 Then said the LORD unto **M**, Behold, I H4872
6 And **M** and Aaron said unto all the H4872
8 And **M** said, *This shall be*, when the H4872
9 And **M** spake unto Aaron, Say unto all H4872
11 And the LORD spake unto **M**, saying, H4872
15 what it *was*. And **M** said unto them, H4872
19 And **M** said, Let no man leave of it till H4872
20 not unto **M**; but some of them left H4872
20 stank: and **M** was wroth with them. H4872
22 of the congregation came and told **M**. H4872
24 the morning, as **M** bade: and it did not H4872
25 And **M** said, Eat that to day; for to day H4872
28 And the LORD said unto **M**, How long H4872
32 And **M** said, This *is* the thing which the H4872
33 And **M** said unto Aaron, Take a pot, H4872
34 As the LORD commanded **M**, so Aaron H4872
17: 2 Wherefore the people did chide with **M**, H4872
2 we may drink. And **M** said unto them, H4872
3 against **M**, and said, Wherefore H4872
4 And **M** cried unto the LORD, saying, H4872
5 And the LORD said unto **M**, Go on H4872
6 may drink. And **M** did so in the sight of H4872
9 And **M** said unto Joshua, Choose us out H4872
10 So Joshua did as **M** had said to him, H4872
10 with Amalek: and **M**, Aaron, and Hur H4872
11 And it came to pass, when **M** held up H4872
14 And the LORD said unto **M**, Write this H4872
15 And **M** built an altar, and called the H4872
18: 1 God had done for **M**, and for Israel his H4872
5 sons and his wife unto **M** into the H4872
6 And he said unto **M**, I thy father in law H4872
7 And **M** went out to meet his father in H4872
8 And **M** told his father in law all that the H4872
13 on the morrow, that **M** sat to judge the H4872
13 **M** from the morning unto the evening. H4872
15 And **M** said unto his father in law, H4872
24 So **M** hearkened to the voice of his H4872
25 And **M** chose able men out of all Israel, H4872
26 they brought unto **M**, but every small H4872
27 And **M** let his father in law depart; and H4872
19: 3 And **M** went up unto God, and the H4872
7 And **M** came and called for the elders H4872
8 we will do. And **M** returned the words H4872
9 And the LORD said unto **M**, Lo, I come H4872
9 thee for ever. And **M** told the words of H4872
10 And the LORD said unto **M**, Go unto the H4872
14 And **M** went down from the mount H4872
17 And **M** brought forth the people out of H4872
19 louder and louder, **M** spake, and God H4872
20 the LORD called **M** *up* to the top of the H4872
20 the top of the mount; and **M** went up. H4872
21 And the LORD said unto **M**, Go down, H4872
23 And **M** said unto the LORD, The people H4872
25 So **M** went down unto the people, and H4872
20:19 And they said unto **M**, Speak thou with H4872
20 And **M** said unto the people, Fear not: H4872
21 And the people stood afar off, and **M** H4872

Ex 20:22 And the LORD said unto **M**, Thus thou H4872
24: 1 And he said unto **M**, Come up unto the H4872
2 And **M** alone shall come near the H4872
3 And **M** came and told the people all the H4872
4 And **M** wrote all the words of the H4872
6 And **M** took half of the blood, and put H4872
8 And **M** took the blood, and sprinkled *it* H4872
9 Then went up **M**, and Aaron, Nadab, H4872
12 And the LORD said unto **M**, Come up to H4872
13 And **M** rose up, and his minister H4872
13 and **M** went up into the mount of God. H4872
15 And **M** went up into the mount, and a H4872
16 unto **M** out of the midst of the cloud. H4872
18 And **M** went into the midst of the H4872
18 the mount: and **M** was in the mount H4872
25: 1 And the LORD spake unto **M**, saying, H4872
30:11 And the LORD spake unto **M**, saying, H4872
17 And the LORD spake unto **M**, saying, H4872
22 Moreover the LORD spake unto **M**, H4872
34 And the LORD said unto **M**, Take unto H4872
31: 1 And the LORD spake unto **M**, saying, H4872
12 And the LORD spake unto **M**, saying, H4872
18 And he gave unto **M**, when he had H4872
32: 1 And when the people saw that **M** H4872
1 us; for *as for* this **M**, the man that H4872
7 And the LORD said unto **M**, Go, get thee H4872
9 And the LORD said unto **M**, I have seen H4872
11 And **M** besought the LORD his God, H4872
15 And **M** turned, and went down from H4872
17 **M**, *There is* a noise of war in the camp. H4872
21 And **M** said unto Aaron, What did this H4872
23 us: for *as for* this **M**, the man that H4872
25 And when **M** saw that the people *were* H4872
26 Then **M** stood in the gate of the camp, H4872
28 to the word of **M**: and there fell of the H4872
29 For **M** had said, Consecrate yourselves H4872
30 on the morrow, that **M** said unto the H4872
31 And **M** returned unto the LORD, and H4872
33 And the LORD said unto **M**, Whosoever H4872
33: 1 And the LORD said unto **M**, Depart, H4872
5 For the LORD had said unto **M**, Say H4872
7 And **M** took the tabernacle, and H4872
8 And it came to pass, when **M** went out H4872
8 and looked after **M**, until he was gone H4872
9 And it came to pass, as **M** entered into H4872
9 and *the LORD* talked with **M**. H4872
11 And the LORD spake unto **M** face to H4872
12 And **M** said unto the LORD, See, thou H4872
17 And the LORD said unto **M**, I will do H4872
34: 1 And the LORD said unto **M**, Hew thee H4872
4 unto the first; and **M** rose up early in H4872
8 And **M** made haste, and bowed his H4872
27 And the LORD said unto **M**, Write thou H4872
29 And it came to pass, when **M** came H4872
29 the mount, that **M** wist not that the H4872
30 of Israel saw **M**, behold, the skin of H4872
31 And **M** called unto them; and Aaron H4872
31 unto him: and **M** talked with them. H4872
33 And *till* **M** had done speaking with H4872
34 But when **M** went in before the LORD H4872
35 Israel saw the face of **M**, that the skin of H4872
35 face shone: and **M** put the vail upon his H4872
35: 1 And **M** gathered all the congregation of H4872
4 And **M** spake unto all the congregation H4872
20 Israel departed from the presence of **M**. H4872
29 to be made by the hand of **M**. H4872
30 And **M** said unto the children of Israel, H4872
36: 2 And **M** called Bezaleel and Aholiab, H4872
3 And they received of **M** all the offering, H4872
5 And they spake unto **M**, saying, The H4872
6 And **M** gave commandment, and they H4872
38:21 commandment of **M**, *for* the service of H4872
22 made all that the LORD commanded **M**. H4872
39: 1 for Aaron; as the LORD commanded **M**. H4872
5 linen; as the LORD commanded **M**. H4872
7 of Israel; as the LORD commanded **M**. H4872
21 ephod; as the LORD commanded **M**. H4872
26 *in;* as the LORD commanded **M**. H4872
29 as the LORD commanded **M**. H4872
31 the mitre; as the LORD commanded **M**. H4872
32 the LORD commanded **M**, so did they. H4872
33 tabernacle unto **M**, the tent, and all his H4872
42 commanded **M**, so the children of Israel H4872
43 And **M** did look upon all the work, and, H4872
43 had they done it: and **M** blessed them. H4872
40: 1 And the LORD spake unto **M**, saying, H4872
16 Thus did **M**: according to all that the H4872
18 And **M** reared up the tabernacle, and H4872
19 upon it; as the LORD commanded **M**. H4872

Ex 40:21 as the LORD commanded **M**. H4872
23 as the LORD had commanded **M**. H4872
25 the LORD; as the LORD commanded **M**. H4872
27 thereon; as the LORD commanded **M**. H4872
29 offering; as the LORD commanded **M**. H4872
31 And **M** and Aaron and his sons washed H4872
32 washed; as the LORD commanded **M**. H4872
33 the court gate. So **M** finished the work. H4872
35 And **M** was not able to enter into the H4872
Lev 1: 1 And the LORD called unto **M**, and H4872
4: 1 And the LORD spake unto **M**, saying, H4872
5:14 And the LORD spake unto **M**, saying, H4872
6: 1 And the LORD spake unto **M**, saying, H4872
8 And the LORD spake unto **M**, saying, H4872
19 And the LORD spake unto **M**, saying, H4872
24 And the LORD spake unto **M**, saying, H4872
7:22 And the LORD spake unto **M**, saying, H4872
28 And the LORD spake unto **M**, saying, H4872
38 Which the LORD commanded **M** in H4872
8: 1 And the LORD spake unto **M**, saying, H4872
4 And **M** did as the LORD commanded H4872
5 And **M** said unto the congregation, H4872
6 And **M** brought Aaron and his sons, H4872
9 crown; as the LORD commanded **M**. H4872
10 And **M** took the anointing oil, and H4872
13 And **M** brought Aaron's sons, and put H4872
13 them; as the LORD commanded **M**. H4872
15 And he slew *it;* and **M** took the blood, H4872
16 fat, and **M** burned *it* upon the altar. H4872
17 the camp; as the LORD commanded **M**. H4872
19 And he killed *it;* and **M** sprinkled the H4872
20 And he cut the ram into pieces; and **M** H4872
21 legs in water; and **M** burnt the whole H4872
21 the LORD; as the LORD commanded **M**. H4872
23 And he slew *it;* and **M** took of the blood H4872
24 And he brought Aaron's sons, and **M** H4872
24 right feet: and **M** sprinkled the blood H4872
28 And **M** took them from off their hands, H4872
29 And **M** took the breast, and waved it H4872
29 part; as the LORD commanded **M**. H4872
30 And **M** took of the anointing oil, and of H4872
31 And **M** said unto Aaron and to his H4872
36 LORD commanded by the hand of **M**. H4872
9: 1 eighth day, *that* **M** called Aaron and H4872
5 And they brought *that* which **M** H4872
6 And **M** said, This *is* the thing which the H4872
7 And **M** said unto Aaron, Go unto the H4872
10 the altar; as the LORD commanded **M**. H4872
21 before the LORD; as **M** commanded. H4872
23 And **M** and Aaron went into the H4872
10: 3 Then **M** said unto Aaron, This *is it* that H4872
4 And **M** called Mishael and Elzaphan, H4872
5 coats out of the camp; as **M** had said. H4872
6 And **M** said unto Aaron, and unto H4872
7 they did according to the word of **M**. H4872
11 spoken unto them by the hand of **M**. H4872
12 And **M** spake unto Aaron, and unto H4872
16 And **M** diligently sought the goat of the H4872
19 And Aaron said unto **M**, Behold, this H4872
20 And when **M** heard *that,* he was H4872
11: 1 And the LORD spake unto **M** and to H4872
12: 1 And the LORD spake unto **M**, saying, H4872
13: 1 And the LORD spake unto **M** and H4872
14: 1 And the LORD spake unto **M**, saying, H4872
33 And the LORD spake unto **M** and unto H4872
15: 1 And the LORD spake unto **M** and to H4872
16: 1 And the LORD spake unto **M** after the H4872
2 And the LORD said unto **M**, Speak unto H4872
34 he did as the LORD commanded **M**. H4872
17: 1 And the LORD spake unto **M**, saying, H4872
18: 1 And the LORD spake unto **M**, saying, H4872
19: 1 And the LORD spake unto **M**, saying, H4872
20: 1 And the LORD spake unto **M**, saying, H4872
21: 1 And the LORD said unto **M**, Speak unto H4872
16 And the LORD spake unto **M**, saying, H4872
24 And **M** told *it* unto Aaron, and to his H4872
22: 1 And the LORD spake unto **M**, saying, H4872
17 And the LORD spake unto **M**, saying, H4872
26 And the LORD spake unto **M**, saying, H4872
23: 1 And the LORD spake unto **M**, saying, H4872
9 And the LORD spake unto **M**, saying, H4872
23 And the LORD spake unto **M**, saying, H4872
26 And the LORD spake unto **M**, saying, H4872
33 And the LORD spake unto **M**, saying, H4872
44 And **M** declared unto the children of H4872
24: 1 And the LORD spake unto **M**, saying, H4872
11 brought him unto **M**: (and his mother's H4872
13 And the LORD spake unto **M**, saying, H4872
23 And **M** spake to the children of Israel, H4872

Lev 24:23 Israel did as the LORD commanded **M**. H4872
25: 1 And the LORD spake unto **M** in mount H4872
26:46 Israel in mount Sinai by the hand of **M**. H4872
27: 1 And the LORD spake unto **M**, saying, H4872
34 commanded **M** for the children of H4872
Nu 1: 1 And the LORD spake unto **M** in the H4872
17 And **M** and Aaron took these men H4872
19 As the LORD commanded **M**, so he H4872
44 were numbered, which **M** and Aaron H4872
48 For the LORD had spoken unto **M**, H4872
54 the LORD commanded **M**, so did they. H4872
2: 1 And the LORD spake unto **M** and unto H4872
33 of Israel; as the LORD commanded **M**. H4872
34 commanded **M**: so they pitched by their H4872
3: 1 of Aaron and **M** in the day *that* the H4872
1 LORD spake with **M** in mount Sinai. H4872
5 And the LORD spake unto **M**, saying, H4872
11 And the LORD spake unto **M**, saying, H4872
14 And the LORD spake unto **M** in the H4872
16 And **M** numbered them according to H4872
38 eastward, *shall be* **M**, and Aaron and H4872
39 of the Levites, which **M** and Aaron H4872
40 And the LORD said unto **M**, Number all H4872
42 And **M** numbered, as the LORD H4872
44 And the LORD spake unto **M**, saying, H4872
49 And **M** took the redemption money of H4872
51 And **M** gave the money of them that H4872
51 the LORD, as the LORD commanded **M**. H4872
4: 1 And the LORD spake unto **M** and unto H4872
17 And the LORD spake unto **M** and unto H4872
21 And the LORD spake unto **M**, saying, H4872
34 And **M** and Aaron and the chief of the H4872
37 which **M** and Aaron did number H4872
37 of the LORD by the hand of **M**. H4872
41 whom **M** and Aaron did number H4872
45 sons of Merari, whom **M** and Aaron H4872
45 the word of the LORD by the hand of **M**. H4872
46 Levites, whom **M** and Aaron and the H4872
49 by the hand of **M**, every one according H4872
49 of him, as the LORD commanded **M**. H4872
5: 1 And the LORD spake unto **M**, saying, H4872
4 unto **M**, so did the children of Israel. H4872
5 And the LORD spake unto **M**, saying, H4872
11 And the LORD spake unto **M**, saying, H4872
6: 1 And the LORD spake unto **M**, saying, H4872
22 And the LORD spake unto **M**, saying, H4872
7: 1 And it came to pass on the day that **M** H4872
4 And the LORD spake unto **M**, saying, H4872
6 And **M** took the wagons and the oxen, H4872
11 And the LORD said unto **M**, They shall H4872
89 And when **M** was gone into the H4872
8: 1 And the LORD spake unto **M**, saying, H4872
3 as the LORD commanded **M**. H4872
4 shewed **M**, so he made the candlestick. H4872
5 And the LORD spake unto **M**, saying, H4872
20 And **M**, and Aaron, and all the H4872
20 commanded **M** concerning the Levites, H4872
22 had commanded **M** concerning the H4872
23 And the LORD spake unto **M**, saying, H4872
9: 1 And the LORD spake unto **M** in the H4872
4 And **M** spake unto the children of H4872
5 **M**, so did the children of Israel. H4872
6 **M** and before Aaron on that day: H4872
8 And **M** said unto them, Stand still, and H4872
9 And the LORD spake unto **M**, saying, H4872
23 of the LORD by the hand of **M**. H4872
10: 1 And the LORD spake unto **M**, saying, H4872
13 of the LORD by the hand of **M**. H4872
29 And **M** said unto Hobab, the son of H4872
35 ark set forward, that **M** said, Rise up, H4872
11: 2 And the people cried unto **M**; and when H4872
2 Moses; and when **M** prayed unto the H4872
10 Then **M** heard the people weep H4872
10 kindled greatly; **M** also was displeased. H4872
11 And **M** said unto the LORD, Wherefore H4872
16 And the LORD said unto **M**, Gather H4872
21 And **M** said, The people, among whom H4872
23 And the LORD said unto **M**, Is the H4872
24 And **M** went out, and told the people H4872
27 man, and told **M**, and said, Eldad and H4872
28 the servant of **M**, *one* of his young men, H4872
28 and said, My lord **M**, forbid them. H4872
29 And **M** said unto him, Enviest thou for H4872
30 And **M** gat him into the camp, he and H4872
12: 1 Aaron spake against **M** because of the H4872
2 spoken only by **M**? hath he not spoken H4872
3 (Now the man **M** *was* very meek, above H4872
4 And the LORD spake suddenly unto **M**, H4872
7 My servant **M** *is* not so, who *is* faithful H4872

Nu 12: 8 afraid to speak against my servant M? H4872
11 And Aaron said unto M, Alas, my lord, H4872
13 And M cried unto the LORD, saying, H4872
14 And the LORD said unto M, If her H4872
13: 1 And the LORD spake unto M, saying, H4872
3 And M by the commandment of the H4872
16 of the men which M sent to spy out the H4872
16 out the land. And M called Oshea the H4872
17 And M sent them to spy out the land of H4872
26 And they went and came to M, and to H4872
30 And Caleb stilled the people before M, H4872
14: 2 against M and against Aaron: H4872
5 Then M and Aaron fell on their faces H4872
11 And the LORD said unto M, How long H4872
13 And M said unto the LORD, Then the H4872
26 And the LORD spake unto M and unto H4872
36 And the men, which M sent to search H4872
39 And M told these sayings unto all the H4872
41 And M said, Wherefore now do ye H4872
44 and M, departed not out of the camp. H4872
15: 1 And the LORD spake unto M, saying, H4872
17 And the LORD spake unto M, saying, H4872
22 which the LORD hath spoken unto M, H4872
23 by the hand of M, from the day that the H4872
23 commanded *M*, and henceforward
33 brought him unto M and Aaron, and H4872
35 And the LORD said unto M, The man H4872
36 he died; as the LORD commanded M. H4872
37 And the LORD spake unto M, saying, H4872
16: 2 And they rose up before M, with certain H4872
3 together against M and against Aaron, H4872
4 And when M heard *it*, he fell upon his H4872
8 And M said unto Korah, Hear, I pray H4872
12 And M sent to call Dathan and H4872
15 And M was very wroth, and said unto H4872
16 And M said unto Korah, Be thou and H4872
18 of the congregation with M and Aaron. H4872
20 And the LORD spake unto M and unto H4872
23 And the LORD spake unto M, saying, H4872
25 And M rose up and went unto Dathan H4872
28 And M said, Hereby ye shall know that H4872
36 And the LORD spake unto M, saying, H4872
40 the LORD said to him by the hand of M. H4872
41 against M and against Aaron, H4872
42 gathered against M and against Aaron, H4872
43 And M and Aaron came before the H4872
44 And the LORD spake unto M, saying, H4872
46 And M said unto Aaron, Take a censer, H4872
47 And Aaron took as M commanded, H4872
50 And Aaron returned unto M unto the H4872
17: 1 And the LORD spake unto M, saying, H4872
6 And M spake unto the children of H4872
7 And M laid up the rods before the H4872
8 that on the morrow M went into the H4872
9 And M brought out all the rods from H4872
10 And the LORD said unto M, Bring H4872
11 And M did *so*: as the LORD H4872
12 Israel spake unto M, saying, Behold, we H4872
18:25 And the LORD spake unto M, saying, H4872
19: 1 And the LORD spake unto M and unto H4872
20: 2 together against M and against Aaron. H4872
3 And the people chode with M, and H4872
6 And M and Aaron went from the H4872
7 And the LORD spake unto M, saying, H4872
9 And M took the rod from before the H4872
10 And M and Aaron gathered the H4872
11 And M lifted up his hand, and with his H4872
12 And the LORD spake unto M and H4872
14 And M sent messengers from Kadesh H4872
23 And the LORD spake unto M and H4872
27 And M did as the LORD commanded: H4872
28 And M stripped Aaron of his garments, H4872
28 of the mount: and M and Eleazar came H4872
21: 5 God, and against M, Wherefore have ye H4872
7 Therefore the people came to M, and H4872
7 from us. And M prayed for the people. H4872
8 And the LORD said unto M, Make thee H4872
9 And M made a serpent of brass, and H4872
16 LORD spake unto M, Gather the people H4872
32 And M sent to spy out Jaazer, and they H4872
34 And the LORD said unto M, Fear him H4872
25: 4 And the LORD said unto M, Take all the H4872
5 And M said unto the judges of Israel, H4872
6 in the sight of M, and in the sight of all H4872
10 And the LORD spake unto M, saying, H4872
16 And the LORD spake unto M, saying, H4872
26: 1 LORD spake unto M and unto Eleazar H4872
3 And M and Eleazar the priest spake H4872
4 commanded M and the children of H4872

Nu 26: 9 strove against M and against Aaron H4872
52 And the LORD spake unto M, saying, H4872
59 Aaron and M, and Miriam their sister. H4872
63 numbered by M and Eleazar the priest, H4872
64 of them whom M and Aaron the priest H4872
27: 2 And they stood before M, and before H4872
5 And M brought their cause before the H4872
6 And the LORD spake unto M, saying, H4872
11 judgment, as the LORD commanded M. H4872
12 And the LORD said unto M, Get thee up H4872
15 And M spake unto the LORD, saying, H4872
18 And the LORD said unto M, Take thee H4872
22 And M did as the LORD commanded H4872
23 LORD commanded by the hand of M. H4872
28: 1 And the LORD spake unto M, saying, H4872
29:40 And M told the children of Israel H4872
40 to all that the LORD commanded M. H4872
30: 1 And M spake unto the heads of the H4872
16 commanded M, between a man and H4872
31: 1 And the LORD spake unto M, saying, H4872
3 And M spake unto the people, saying, H4872
6 And M sent them to the war, a H4872
7 M; and they slew all the males. H4872
12 and the spoil, unto M, and Eleazar the H4872
13 And M, and Eleazar the priest, and all H4872
14 And M was wroth with the officers of H4872
15 And M said unto them, Have ye saved H4872
21 law which the LORD commanded M; H4872
25 And the LORD spake unto M, saying, H4872
31 And M and Eleazar the priest did as H4872
31 priest did as the LORD commanded M. H4872
41 And M gave the tribute, *which was* the H4872
41 the priest, as the LORD commanded M. H4872
42 M divided from the men that warred, H4872
47 Even of the children of Israel's half, M H4872
47 the LORD; as the LORD commanded M. H4872
48 of hundreds, came near unto M: H4872
49 And they said unto M, Thy servants H4872
51 And M and Eleazar the priest took the H4872
54 And M and Eleazar the priest took the H4872
32: 2 and spake unto M, and to Eleazar the H4872
6 And M said unto the children of Gad H4872
20 And M said unto them, If ye will do H4872
25 spake unto M, saying, Thy servants H4872
28 So concerning them M commanded H4872
29 And M said unto them, If the children H4872
33 And M gave unto them, *even* to the H4872
40 And M gave Gilead unto Machir the H4872
33: 1 under the hand of M and Aaron. H4872
2 And M wrote their goings out H4872
50 And the LORD spake unto M in the H4872
34: 1 And the LORD spake unto M, saying, H4872
13 And M commanded the children of H4872
16 And the LORD spake unto M, saying, H4872
35: 1 And the LORD spake unto M in the H4872
9 And the LORD spake unto M, saying, H4872
36: 1 and spake before M, and before the H4872
5 And M commanded the children of H4872
10 Even as the LORD commanded M, so H4872
13 by the hand of M unto the children of H4872
Dt 1: 1 These *be* the words which M spake H4872
3 of the month, *that* M spake unto the H4872
5 began M to declare this law, saying, H4872
4:41 Then M severed three cities on this side H4872
44 And this *is* the law which M set before H4872
45 the judgments, which M spake unto the H4872
46 Heshbon, whom M and the children of H4872
5: 1 And M called all Israel, and said unto H4872
27: 1 And M with the elders of Israel H4872
9 And M and the priests the Levites H4872
11 And M charged the people the same H4872
29: 1 LORD commanded M to make with the H4872
2 And M called unto all Israel, and said H4872
31: 1 And M went and spake these words H4872
7 And M called unto Joshua, and said H4872
9 And M wrote this law, and delivered it H4872
10 And M commanded them, saying, At H4872
14 And the LORD said unto M, Behold, thy H4872
14 a charge. And M and Joshua went, and H4872
16 And the LORD said unto M, Behold, H4872
22 M therefore wrote this song the same H4872
24 And it came to pass, when M had H4872
25 That M commanded the Levites, which H4872
30 And M spake in the ears of all the H4872
32:44 And M came and spake all the words H4872
45 And M made an end of speaking all H4872
48 And the LORD spake unto M that H4872
33: 1 And this *is* the blessing, wherewith M H4872
4 M commanded us a law, *even* the H4872

Dt 34: 1 And M went up from the plains of H4872
5 So M the servant of the LORD died H4872
7 And M *was* an hundred and twenty H4872
8 And the children of Israel wept for M H4872
8 *and* mourning for M were ended. H4872
9 of wisdom; for M had laid his hands H4872
9 and did as the LORD commanded M. H4872
10 M, whom the LORD knew face to face, H4872
12 M shewed in the sight of all Israel. H4872
Jos 1: 1 Now after the death of M the servant of H4872
2 M my servant is dead; now therefore H4872
3 have I given unto you, as I said unto M. H4872
5 life: as I was with M, *so* I will be with H4872
7 to all the law, which M my servant H4872
13 Remember the word which M the H4872
14 in the land which M gave you on this H4872
15 enjoy it, which M the LORD'S servant H4872
17 According as we hearkened unto M in H4872
17 thy God be with thee, as he was with M. H4872
3: 7 as I was with M, *so* I will be with thee. H4872
4:10 to all that M commanded Joshua: H4872
12 of Israel, as M spake unto them: H4872
14 as they feared M, all the days of his life. H4872
8:31 As M the servant of the LORD H4872
31 book of the law of M, an altar of whole H4872
32 copy of the law of M, which he wrote in H4872
33 mount Ebal; as M the servant of the H4872
35 There was not a word of all that M H4872
9:24 his servant M to give you all the land, H4872
11:12 them, as M the servant of the LORD H4872
15 As the LORD commanded M his H4872
15 servant, so did M command Joshua, H4872
15 of all that the LORD commanded M. H4872
20 them, as the LORD commanded M. H4872
23 LORD said unto M; and Joshua gave it H4872
12: 6 Them did M the servant of the LORD H4872
6 Israel smite: and M the servant of the H4872
13: 8 which M gave them, beyond H4872
8 M the servant of the LORD gave them; H4872
12 these did M smite, and cast them out. H4872
15 And M gave unto the tribe of the H4872
21 in Heshbon, whom M smote with the H4872
24 And M gave *inheritance* unto the tribe H4872
29 And M gave *inheritance* unto the half H4872
32 These *are the countries* which M did H4872
33 But unto the tribe of Levi M gave not H4872
14: 2 by the hand of M, for the nine tribes, H4872
3 For M had given the inheritance of two H4872
5 As the LORD commanded M, so the H4872
6 the LORD said unto M the man of God H4872
7 Forty years old *was* I when M the H4872
9 And M sware on that day, saying, H4872
10 this word unto M, while *the children of* H4872
11 *was* in the day that M sent me: as my H4872
17: 4 LORD commanded M to give us an H4872
18: 7 M the servant of the LORD gave them. H4872
20: 2 I spake unto you by the hand of M: H4872
21: 2 by the hand of M to give us cities to H4872
8 LORD commanded by the hand of M. H4872
22: 2 have kept all that M the servant of the H4872
4 possession, which M the servant of the H4872
5 and the law, which M the servant of the H4872
7 the tribe of Manasseh M had given H4872
9 the word of the LORD by the hand of M. H4872
23: 6 book of the law of M, that ye turn not H4872
24: 5 I sent M also and Aaron, and I plagued H4872
Jdg 1:20 unto Caleb, as M said: and he expelled H4872
3: 4 their fathers by the hand of M. H4872
4:11 father in law of M, had severed himself H4872
1Sa 12: 6 that advanced M and Aaron, and that H4872
8 the LORD sent M and Aaron, which H4872
1Ki 2: 3 in the law of M, that thou mayest H4872
8: 9 of stone, which M put there at Horeb, H4872
53 by the hand of M thy servant, when H4872
56 promised by the hand of M his servant. H4872
2Ki 14: 6 book of the law of M, wherein the LORD H4872
18: 4 serpent that M had made: for unto H4872
6 which the LORD commanded M. H4872
12 *and* all that M the servant of the LORD H4872
21: 8 that my servant M commanded them. H4872
23:25 to all the law of M; neither after him H4872
1Ch 6: 3 Aaron, and M, and Miriam. The sons H4872
49 M the servant of God had commanded. H4872
15:15 the staves thereon, as M commanded H4872
21:29 of the LORD, which M made in the H4872
22:13 the LORD charged M with concerning H4872
23:13 The sons of Amram; Aaron and M: and H4872
14 Now *concerning* M the man of God, his H4872
15 The sons of M *were*, Gershom, and H4872

1Ch 26:24 the son of **M**, *was* ruler of the treasures. H4872
2Ch 1: 3 of God, which **M** the servant of the H4872
5:10 the two tables which **M** put *therein* at H4872
8:13 commandment of **M**, on the sabbaths, H4872
23:18 in the law of **M**, with rejoicing and H4872
24: 6 *commandment* of **M** the servant of the H4872
9 the collection *that* **M** the servant of God H4872
25: 4 law in the book of **M**, where the LORD H4872
30:16 to the law of **M** the man of God: the H4872
33: 8 and the ordinances by the hand of **M**. H4872
34:14 of the law of the LORD *given* by **M**. H4872
35: 6 the word of the LORD by the hand of **M**. H4872
12 of **M**. And so *did they* with the oxen. H4872
Ezr 3: 2 written in the law of **M** the man of God. H4872
6:18 as it is written in the book of **M**. H4873
7: 6 in the law of **M**, which the LORD God H4872
Neh 1: 7 thou commandedst thy servant **M**. H4872
8 thy servant **M**, saying, *If* ye transgress, H4872
8: 1 book of the law of **M**, which the LORD H4872
14 commanded by **M**, that the children of H4872
9:14 and laws, by the hand of **M** thy servant: H4872
10:29 was given by **M** the servant of God, H4872
13: 1 On that day they read in the book of **M** H4872
Ps 77:20 a flock by the hand of **M** and Aaron. H4872
90:ttl A Prayer of **M** the man of God. H4872
99: 6 **M** and Aaron among his priests, and H4872
103: 7 He made known his ways unto **M**, his H4872
105:26 He sent **M** his servant; *and* Aaron H4872
106:16 They envied **M** also in the camp, *and* H4872
23 them, had not **M** his chosen stood H4872
32 that it went ill with **M** for their sakes: H4872
Isa 63:11 the days of old, **M**, *and* his people, H4872
12 That led *them* by the right hand of **M** H4872
Jer 15: 1 unto me, Though **M** and Samuel stood H4872
Dan 9:11 in the law of **M** the servant of God, H4872
13 As *it is* written in the law of **M**, all this H4872
Mic 6: 4 sent before thee **M**, Aaron, and Miriam. H4872
Mal 4: 4 Remember ye the law of **M** my servant, H4872
Mt 8: 4 offer the gift that **M** commanded, for a *G3475*
17: 3 them **M** and Elias talking with him. *G3475*
4 thee, and one for **M**, and one for Elias. *G3475*
19: 7 They say unto him, Why did **M** then *G3475*
8 He saith unto them, **M** because of the *G3475*
22:24 Saying, Master, **M** said, If a man die; *G3475*
Mk 1:44 things which **M** commanded, for a *G3475*
7:10 For **M** said, Honour thy father and thy *G3475*
9: 4 **M**: and they were talking with Jesus. *G3475*
5 thee, and one for **M**, and one for Elias. *G3475*
10: 3 them, What did **M** command you? *G3475*
4 And they said, **M** suffered to write a bill *G3475*
12:19 Master, **M** wrote unto us, If a man's *G3475*
26 in the book of **M**, how in the bush God *G3475*
Lk 2:22 to the law of **M** were accomplished, *G3475*
5:14 according as **M** commanded, for a *G3475*
9:30 him two men, which were **M** and Elias: *G3475*
33 thee, and one for **M**, and one for Elias: *G3475*
16:29 Abraham saith unto him, They have **M** *G3475*
31 If they hear not **M** and the prophets, *G3475*
20:28 Saying, Master, **M** wrote unto us, If *G3475*
37 Now that the dead are raised, even **M** *G3475*
24:27 And beginning at **M** and all the *G3475*
44 in the law of **M**, and *in* the prophets, *G3475*
Jn 1:17 For the law was given by **M**, *but* grace *G3475*
45 him, of whom **M** in the law, and the *G3475*
3:14 And as **M** lifted up the serpent in the *G3475*
5:45 you, *even* **M**, in whom ye trust. *G3475*
46 For had ye believed **M**, ye would have *G3475*
6:32 I say unto you, **M** gave you not that *G3475*
7:19 Did not **M** give you the law, and *yet* *G3475*
22 **M** therefore gave unto you *G3475*
22 because it is of **M**, but of the fathers;) *G3475*
23 that the law of **M** should not be broken; *G3475*
8: 5 Now **M** in the law commanded us, that *G3475*
9:29 We know that God spake unto **M**: *as for* *G3475*
Act 3:22 For **M** truly said unto the fathers, A *G3475*
6:11 words against **M**, and *against* God. *G3475*
14 the customs which **M** delivered us. *G3475*
7:20 In which time **M** was born, and was *G3475*
22 And **M** was learned in all the wisdom *G3475*
29 Then fled **M** at this saying, and was a *G3475*
31 When **M** saw *it*, he wondered at the *G3475*
32 **M** trembled, and durst not behold. *G3475*
35 This **M** whom they refused, saying, *G3475*
37 This is that **M**, which said unto the *G3475*
40 us: for *as for* this **M**, which brought us *G3475*
44 speaking unto **M**, that he should make *G3475*
13:39 could not be justified by the law of **M**. *G3475*
15: 1 the manner of **M**, ye cannot be saved. *G3475*
5 to command *them* to keep the law of **M**. *G3475*

Act 15:21 For **M** of old time hath in every city *G3475*
21:21 to forsake **M**, saying that they ought *G3475*
26:22 prophets and **M** did say should come: *G3475*
28:23 both out of the law of **M**, and *out of* the *G3475*
Ro 5:14 from Adam to **M**, even over them that *G3475*
9:15 For he saith to **M**, I will have mercy on *G3475*
10: 5 For **M** describeth the righteousness *G3475*
19 But I say, Did not Israel know? First **M** *G3475*
1Co 9: 9 For it is written in the law of **M**, Thou *G3475*
10: 2 And were all baptized unto **M** in the *G3475*
2Co 3: 7 behold the face of **M** for the glory of his *G3475*
13 And not as **M**, *which* put a veil over his *G3475*
15 But even unto this day, when **M** is *G3475*
2Ti 3: 8 withstood **M**, so do these also resist *G3475*
Heb 3: 2 as also **M** *was faithful* in all his house. *G3475*
3 of more glory than **M**, inasmuch as he *G3475*
5 And **M** verily *was* faithful in all his *G3475*
16 not all that came out of Egypt by **M**. *G3475*
7:14 Juda; of which tribe **M** spake nothing *G3475*
8: 5 things, as **M** was admonished of *G3475*
9:19 For when **M** had spoken every precept *G3475*
11:23 By faith **M**, when he was born, was hid *G3475*
24 By faith **M**, when he was come to years, *G3475*
12:21 And so terrible was the sight, *that* **M** *G3475*
Jude 9 about the body of **M**, durst not bring *G3475*
Rev 15: 3 And they sing the song of **M** the *G3475*

MOSES'

Ex 17:12 But **M** hands *were* heavy; and they H4872
18: 1 When Jethro, the priest of Midian, **M** H4872
2 Then Jethro, **M** father in law, took H4872
2 **M** wife, after he had sent her back, H4872
5 And Jethro, **M** father in law, came with H4872
12 And Jethro, **M** father in law, took a H4872
12 bread with **M** father in law before God. H4872
14 And when **M** father in law saw all that H4872
17 And **M** father in law said unto him, H4872
32:19 the dancing: and **M** anger waxed hot, H4872
34:29 of testimony in **M** hand, when he came H4872
35 that the skin of **M** face shone: and H4872
Lev 8:29 it was **M** part; as the LORD H4872
Nu 10:29 the Midianite, **M** father in law, We are H4872
Jos 1: 1 the son of Nun, **M** minister, saying, H4872
Jdg 1:16 And the children of the Kenite, **M** H4872
Mt 23: 2 scribes and the Pharisees sit in **M** seat: *G3475*
Jn 9:28 art his disciple; but we are **M** disciples. *G3475*
Heb 10:28 He that despised **M** law died without *G3475*

MOST

Gen 14:18 he *was* the priest of the **m** high God. H5945
19 *be* Abram of the **m** high God, possessor H5945
20 And blessed be the **m** high God, which H5945
22 unto the LORD, the **m** high God, the H5945
Ex 26:33 between the holy *place* and the **m** holy. H6944
34 of the testimony in the **m** holy *place*. H6944
29:37 it shall be an altar **m** holy: whatsoever H6944
30:10 it *is* **m** holy unto the LORD. H6944
29 that they may be **m** holy: whatsoever H6944
36 with thee: it shall be unto you **m** holy. H6944
40:10 altar: and it shall be an altar **m** holy. H6944
Lev 2: 3 his sons': *it is* a thing **m** holy of the H6944
10 his sons': *it is* a thing **m** holy of the H6944
6:17 made by fire; it *is* **m** holy, as *is* the sin H6944
25 be killed before the LORD: it *is* **m** holy. H6944
29 priests shall eat thereof: it *is* **m** holy. H6944
7: 1 of the trespass offering: it *is* **m** holy. H6944
6 be eaten in the holy place: it *is* **m** holy. H6944
10:12 leaven beside the altar: for it *is* **m** holy: H6944
17 place, seeing it *is* **m** holy, and *God* hath H6944
14:13 *so is* the trespass offering: it *is* **m** holy: H6944
21:22 *both* of the **m** holy, and of the holy. H6944
24: 9 place: for it *is* **m** holy unto him of the H6944
27:28 thing *is* **m** holy unto the LORD. H6944
Nu 4: 4 congregation, *about* the **m** holy things: H6944
19 unto the **m** holy things: Aaron H6944
18: 9 This shall be thine of the **m** holy things, H6944
9 *be* **m** holy for thee and for thy sons. H6944
10 In the **m** holy *place* shalt thou eat it; H6944
24:16 knowledge of the **m** High, *which* saw H6944
Dt 32: 8 When the **m** High divided to the H6944
2Sa 22:14 and the **m** High uttered his voice. H6944
23:19 Was he not **m** honourable of three?
1Ki 6:16 the oracle, *even* for the **m** holy *place*. H6944
7:50 inner house, the **m** holy *place, and* for H6944
8: 6 of the house, to the **m** holy *place, even* H6944
1Ch 6:49 work of the *place* **m** holy, and to make H6944
23:13 sanctify the **m** holy things, he and H6944
2Ch 3: 8 And he made the **m** holy house, the H6944
10 And in the **m** holy house he made two H6944

2Ch 4:22 thereof for the **m** holy *place*, and the H6944
5: 7 the house, into the **m** holy *place, even* H6944
31:14 of the LORD, and the **m** holy things. H6944
Ezr 2:63 not eat of the **m** holy things, till there H6944
Neh 7:65 not eat of the **m** holy things, till there H6944
Est 6: 9 one of the king's **m** noble princes, that H6579
Job 34:17 wilt thou condemn him that is **m** just? H3524
Ps 7:17 to the name of the LORD **m** high. H5945
9: 2 praise to thy name, O thou **m** High. H5945
21: 6 For thou hast made him **m** blessed for
7 of the **m** High he shall not be moved. H5945
45: 3 Gird thy sword upon *thy* thigh, O **m**
46: 4 *place* of the tabernacles of the **m** High. H5945
47: 2 For the LORD **m** high *is* terrible; *he is* a H5945
50:14 and pay thy vows unto the **m** High: H5945
56: 2 that fight against me, O thou **m** High. H4791
57: 2 I will cry unto God **m** high; unto God H5945
73:11 and is there knowledge in the **m** High? H5945
77:10 years of the right hand of the **m** High. H5945
78:17 the **m** High in the wilderness. H5945
56 Yet they tempted and provoked the **m** H5945
82: 6 all of you *are* children of the **m** High. H5945
83:18 *art* the **m** high over all the earth. H5945
91: 1 secret place of the **m** High shall abide H5945
9 *even* the **m** High, thy habitation; H5945
92: 1 sing praises unto thy name, O **m** High: H5945
8 But thou, LORD, *art* **m** high for
107:11 contemned the counsel of the **m** High: H5945
Prv 20: 6 **M** men will proclaim every one his own H7230
Song 5:11 His head *is as* the **m** fine gold, his locks H3800
16 His mouth *is* **m** sweet: yea, he *is*
8: 6 of fire, *which hath a* **m** vehement flame.
Isa 14:14 of the clouds; I will be like the **m** High. H5945
26: 7 uprightness: thou, **m** upright, dost weigh
Jer 6:26 *as for* an only son, **m** bitter lamentation:
50:31 Behold, I *am* against thee, *O thou* **m**
32 And the **m** proud shall stumble and fall,
Lam 3:35 of a man before the face of the **m** High, H5945
38 Out of the mouth of the **m** High H5945
4: 1 dim! *how* is the **m** fine gold changed! H2896
Ezk 2: 7 will forbear: for they *are* **m** rebellious.
23:12 and rulers clothed **m** gorgeously,
33:28 For I will lay the land **m** desolate, and
29 have laid the land **m** desolate because of
35: 3 thee, and I will make thee **m** desolate.
7 Thus will I make mount Seir **m** H8077
41: 4 said unto me, This *is* the **m** holy *place*. H6944
42:13 shall eat the **m** holy things: there shall H6944
13 shall they lay the **m** holy things, and H6944
43:12 about *shall be* **m** holy. Behold, this *is* H6944
44:13 my holy things, in the **m** holy *place*: but H6944
45: 3 be the sanctuary *and* the **m** holy *place*. H6944
48:12 **m** holy by the border of the Levites. H6944
Dan 3:20 And he commanded the **m** mighty men H2429
26 ye servants of the **m** high God, come H5943
4:17 know that the **m** High ruleth in the H5943
24 *is* the decree of the **m** High, which is H5943
25 know that the **m** High ruleth in the H5943
32 know that the **m** High ruleth in the H5943
34 and I blessed the **m** High, and I praised H5943
5:18 O thou king, the **m** high God gave H5943
21 he knew that the **m** high God ruled in H5943
7:18 But the saints of the **m** High shall take H5946
22 the saints of the **m** High; and the time H5946
25 words against the **m** High, and shall H5943
25 the saints of the **m** High, and think to H5946
27 of the saints of the **m** High, whose H5945
9:24 prophecy, and to anoint the **m** Holy. H6944
11:15 and take the **m** fenced cities: and the
39 Thus shall he do in the **m** strong holds H4581
Hos 7:16 They return, *but* not to the **m** High: H5920
11: 7 **m** High, none at all would exalt *him*. H5920
12:14 Ephraim provoked *him* to anger **m** H8563
Mic 7: 4 The best of them *is* as a brier: the **m**
Mt 11:20 the cities wherein **m** of his mighty *G4118*
Mk 5: 7 *thou* Son of the **m** high God? I adjure *G5310*
Lk 1: 1 which are **m** surely believed among us,
3 thee in order, **m** excellent Theophilus, *G2903*
7:42 which of them will love him **m**? *G4119*
43 whom he forgave **m**. And he said unto *G4119*
8:28 *thou* Son of God **m** high? I beseech *G5310*
Act 7:48 Howbeit the **m** High dwelleth not in *G5310*
16:17 The servants of the **m** high God, which *G5310*
20:38 Sorrowing **m** of all for the words which *G3122*
23:26 Claudius Lysias unto the **m** excellent *G2903*
24: 3 **m** noble Felix, with all thankfulness. *G2903*
26: 5 that after the **m** straitest sect of our
25 But he said, I am not mad, **m** noble *G2903*
1Co 14:27 by two, or at the **m** *by* three, and *that* *G4118*

1Co 15:19 in Christ, we are of all men **m** miserable.
2Co 12: 9 in weakness. **M** gladly therefore will *G2236*
Heb 7: 1 priest of the **m** high God, who met *G5310*
Jude 20 **m** holy faith, praying in the Holy Ghost, *G40*
Rev 18:12 manner vessels of **m** precious wood, and
21:11 like unto a stone **m** precious, even like a

MOST-HIGH See MOST and HIGH.

MOST-HOLY See MOST and HOLY.

MOTE
Mt 7: 3 And why beholdest thou the **m** that is *G2595*
4 me pull out the **m** out of thine eye; and, *G2595*
5 cast out the **m** out of thy brother's eye. *G2595*
Lk 6:41 And why beholdest thou the **m** that is *G2595*
42 let me pull out the **m** that is in thine *G2595*
42 out the **m** that is in thy brother's eye. *G2595*

MOTH
Job 4:19 dust, *which* are crushed before the **m**? H6211
13:28 as a garment that is **m** eaten. H6211
27:18 He buildeth his house as a **m**, and as a H6211
Ps 39:11 a **m**: surely every man *is* vanity. Selah. H6211
Isa 50: 9 as a garment; the **m** shall eat them up. H6211
51: 8 For the **m** shall eat them up like a H6211
Hos 5:12 Ephraim as a **m**, and to the house of H6211
Mt 6:19 earth, where **m** and rust doth corrupt, *G4597*
20 where neither **m** nor rust doth corrupt, *G4597*
Lk 12:33 approacheth, neither **m** corrupteth. *G4597*

MOTHEATEN
Jas 5: 2 corrupted, and your garments are **m**. *G4598*

MOTHER
Gen 2:24 his father and his **m**, and shall cleave H517
3:20 Eve; because she was the **m** of all living. H517
17:16 and she shall be *a m* of nations; kings of
20:12 of my **m**; and she became my wife. H517
21:21 of Paran: and his **m** took him a wife out H517
24:53 brother and to her **m** precious things. H517
55 And her brother and her **m** said, Let the H517
60 our sister, be thou *the m* of thousands of
67 And Isaac brought her into his **m** H517
27:11 And Jacob said to Rebekah his **m**, H517
13 And his **m** said unto him, Upon me *be* H517
14 *them* to his **m**: and his mother made H517
14 mother: and his **m** made savoury meat, H517
28: 5 of Rebekah, Jacob's and Esau's **m**. H517
7 and his **m**, and was gone to Padan-aram; H517
30:14 them unto his **m** Leah. Then Rachel said H517
32:11 smite me, *and* the **m** with the children. H517
37:10 Shall I and thy **m** and thy brethren H517
44:20 is left of his **m**, and his father loveth him. H517
Ex 2: 8 the maid went and called the child's **m**. H517
20:12 Honour thy father and thy **m**: that thy H517
21:15 And he that smiteth his father, or his **m**, H517
17 And he that curseth his father, or his **m**, H517
Lev 18: 7 the nakedness of thy **m**, shalt thou not H517
7 **m**; thou shalt not uncover her nakedness. H517
9 or daughter of thy **m**, *whether she be* H517
19: 3 Ye shall fear every man his **m**, and his H517
20: 9 his father or his **m** shall be surely put to H517
9 or his **m**; his blood *shall be* upon him. H517
14 And if a man take a wife and her **m**, it *is* H517
21: 2 *that is*, for his **m**, and for his father, and H517
11 defile himself for his father, or for his **m**; H517
Nu 6: 7 father, or for his **m**, for his brother, or for H517
26:59 of Levi, whom *her m* bare to Levi in
Dt 5:16 Honour thy father and thy **m**, as the H517
13: 6 If thy brother, the son of thy **m**, or thy H517
21:13 her father and her **m** a full month: and H517
18 or the voice of his **m**, and *that*, when they H517
19 Then shall his father and his **m** lay hold H517
22:15 damsel, and her **m**, take and bring forth H517
27:16 **m**. And all the people shall say, Amen. H517
22 **m**. And all the people shall say, Amen. H517
23 Cursed *be* he that lieth with his **m** in H2859
33: 9 Who said unto his father and to his **m**, I H517
Jos 2:13 my father, and my **m**, and my brethren, H517
18 thy father, and thy **m**, and thy brethren, H517
6:23 her father, and her **m**, and her brethren, H517
Jdg 5: 7 arose, that I arose a **m** in Israel. H517
28 The **m** of Sisera looked out at a window, H517
8:19 the sons of my **m**: *as* the LORD liveth, H517
14: 2 his father and his **m**, and said, I have H517
3 Then his father and his **m** said unto H517
4 But his father and his **m** knew not that it H517
5 his father and his **m**, to Timnath, and H517
Jdg 14: 6 his father or his **m** what he had done. H517
9 to his father and **m**, and he gave them, H517
16 father nor my **m**, and shall I tell *it* thee? H517
17: 2 And he said unto his **m**, The eleven H517
2 I took it. And his **m** said, Blessed *be thou* H517
3 of silver to his **m**, his mother said, I had H517
3 to his mother, his **m** said, I had wholly H517
4 Yet he restored the money unto his **m**; H517
4 his mother; and his **m** took two hundred H517
Ru 1:14 her **m** in law; but Ruth clave unto her. H2545
2:11 done unto thy **m** in law since the death H2545
11 thy father and thy **m**, and the land of thy H517
18 the city: and her **m** in law saw what she H2545
19 And her **m** in law said unto her, Where H2545
19 she shewed her **m** in law with whom H2545
23 harvest; and dwelt with her **m** in law. H2545
3: 1 Then Naomi her **m** in law said unto H2545
6 to all that her **m** in law bade her. H2545
16 And when she came to her **m** in law, H2545
17 to me, Go not empty unto thy **m** in law. H2545
1Sa 2:19 Moreover his **m** made him a little coat, H517
15:33 so shall thy **m** be childless among H517
22: 3 my father and my **m**, I pray thee, come H517
2Sa 17:25 of Nahash, sister to Zeruiah Joab's **m**. H517
19:37 my father and of my **m**. But behold thy H517
20:19 a city and a **m** in Israel: why wilt thou H517
1Ki 1: 6 *man;* and *his m* bare him after Absalom.
11 Bath-sheba the **m** of Solomon, saying, H517
2:13 to Bath-sheba the **m** of Solomon. And H517
19 king's **m**; and she sat on his right hand. H517
20 Ask on, my **m**: for I will not say thee nay. H517
22 and said unto his **m**, And why dost thou H517
3:27 in no wise slay it: she *is* the **m** thereof. H517
15:13 And also Maachah his **m**, even her he H517
17:23 his **m**: and Elijah said, See, thy son liveth. H517
19:20 kiss my father and my **m**, and *then* I will H517
22:52 in the way of his **m**, and in the way of H517
2Ki 3: 2 father, and like his **m**: for he put away H517
13 to the prophets of thy **m**. And the king of H517
4:19 And he said to a lad, Carry him to his **m**. H517
20 brought him to his **m**, he sat on her knees H517
30 And the **m** of the child said, *As* the H517
9:22 the whoredoms of thy **m** Jezebel and her H517
11: 1 And when Athaliah the **m** of Ahaziah H517
24:12 he, and his **m**, and his servants, and H517
15 and the king's **m**, and the king's wives, H517
1Ch 2:26 *was* Atarah; she *was* the **m** of Onam. H517
4: 9 his brethren: and his **m** called his name H517
2Ch 15:16 And also *concerning* Maachah the **m** of H517
22: 3 his **m** was his counsellor to do wickedly. H517
10 But when Athaliah the **m** of Ahaziah H517
Est 2: 7 neither father nor **m**, and the maid *was* H517
7 **m** were dead, took for his own daughter. H517
Job 17:14 the worm, *Thou art* my **m**, and my sister. H517
Ps 27:10 When my father and my **m** forsake me, H517
35:14 heavily, as one that mourneth *for his* **m**. H517
51: 5 and in sin did my **m** conceive me. H517
109:14 let not the sin of his **m** be blotted out. H517
113: 9 joyful **m** of children. Praise ye the LORD. H517
131: 2 his **m**: my soul *is* even as a weaned child. H517
Prv 1: 8 father, and forsake not the law of thy **m**: H517
4: 3 and only *beloved* in the sight of my **m**. H517
6:20 and forsake not the law of thy **m**: H517
10: 1 a foolish son *is* the heaviness of his **m**. H517
15:20 but a foolish man despiseth his **m**. H517
19:26 chaseth away *his m*, *is* a son that causeth H517
20:20 Whoso curseth his father or his **m**, his H517
23:22 and despise not thy **m** when she is old. H517
25 Thy father and thy **m** shall be glad, and H517
28:24 Whoso robbeth his father or his **m**, and H517
29:15 left *to himself* bringeth his **m** to shame. H517
30:11 their father, and doth not bless their **m**. H517
17 to obey *his* **m**, the ravens of the valley H517
31: 1 the prophecy that his **m** taught him. H517
Song 3:11 wherewith his **m** crowned him in the H517
6: 9 *is* the *only* one of her **m**, she *is* the choice H517
8: 1 the breasts of my **m**! *when* I should find H517
5 tree: there thy **m** brought thee forth: H517
Isa 8: 4 cry, My father, and my **m**, the riches of H517
49: 1 **m** hath he made mention of my name. H517
50: 1 your transgressions is your **m** put away. H517
66:13 As one whom his **m** comforteth, so will I H517
Jer 15: 8 them against the **m** of the young men a H517
10 Woe is me, my **m**, that thou hast borne H517
16: 7 to drink for their father or for their **m**. H517
20:14 day wherein my **m** bare me be blessed. H517
17 womb; or that my **m** might have been H517
22:26 And I will cast thee out, and thy **m** that H517
50:12 Your **m** shall be sore confounded; she H517
Ezk 16: 3 *was* an Amorite, and thy **m** an Hittite. H517
44 saying, As *is* the **m**, *so is* her daughter. H517
45 children: your **m** *was* an Hittite, and H517
19: 2 And say, What *is* thy **m**? A lioness: she H517
10 Thy **m** *is* like a vine in thy blood, planted H517
22: 7 light by father and **m**: in the midst of thee H517
23: 2 two women, the daughters of one **m**: H517
44:25 but for father, or for **m**, or for son, or for H517
Hos 2: 2 Plead with your **m**, plead: for she *is* not H517
5 For their **m** hath played the harlot: she H517
4: 5 in the night, and I will destroy thy **m**. H517
10:14 day of battle: the **m** was dashed in pieces H517
Mic 7: 6 up against her **m**, the daughter in law H517
6 in law against her **m** in law; a man's H2545
Zec 13: 3 his father and his **m** that begat him shall H517
3 his father and his **m** that begat him shall H517
Mt 1:18 this wise: When as his **m** Mary was *G3384*
2:11 with Mary his **m**, and fell down, and *G3384*
13 child and his **m**, and flee into Egypt, *G3384*
14 **m** by night, and departed into Egypt: *G3384*
20 child and his **m**, and go into the land *G3384*
21 his **m**, and came into the land of Israel. *G3384*
8:14 his wife's **m** laid, and sick of a fever. *G3994*
10:35 against her **m**, and the daughter in *G3384*
35 daughter in law against her **m** in law. *G3994*
37 He that loveth father or **m** more than *G3384*
12:46 behold, *his* **m** and his brethren stood *G3384*
47 Then one said unto him, Behold, thy **m** *G3384*
48 is my **m**? and who are my brethren? *G3384*
49 said, Behold my **m** and my brethren! *G3384*
50 same is my brother, and sister, and **m**. *G3384*
13:55 son? is not his **m** called Mary? and his *G3384*
14: 8 instructed of her **m**, said, Give me here *G3384*
11 the damsel: and she brought *it* to her **m**. *G3384*
15: 4 thy father and **m**: and, He that curseth *G3384*
4 father or **m**, let him die the death. *G3384*
5 to *his* father or *his* **m**, *It is* a gift, by *G3384*
6 And honour not his father or his **m**, *he* *G3384*
19: 5 leave father and **m**, and shall cleave to *G3384*
19 Honour thy father and *thy* **m**: and, *G3384*
29 or father, or **m**, or wife, or children, *G3384*
20:20 Then came to him the **m** of Zebedee's *G3384*
27:56 and Mary the **m** of James and Joses, *G3384*
56 Joses, and the **m** of Zebedee's children. *G3384*
Mk 1:30 But Simon's wife's **m** lay sick of a fever, *G3994*
3:31 his brethren and his **m**, and, standing *G3384*
32 him, Behold, thy **m** and thy brethren *G3384*
33 saying, Who is my **m**, or my brethren? *G3384*
34 said, Behold my **m** and my brethren! *G3384*
35 is my brother, and my sister, and **m**. *G3384*
5:40 the father and the **m** of the damsel, and *G3384*
6:24 and said unto her **m**, What shall I ask? *G3384*
28 and the damsel gave it to her **m**. *G3384*
7:10 thy father and thy **m**; and, Whoso *G3384*
10 father or **m**, let him die the death: *G3384*
11 to his father or **m**, *It is* Corban, that is *G3384*
12 to do ought for his father or his **m**; *G3384*
10: 7 his father and **m**, and cleave to his wife; *G3384*
19 Defraud not, Honour thy father and **m**. *G3384*
29 or father, or **m**, or wife, or children, *G3384*
15:40 and Mary the **m** of James the less and *G3384*
47 And Mary Magdalene and Mary *the m*
16: 1 and Mary the *m* of James, and Salome,
Lk 1:43 And whence *is* this to me, that the **m** of *G3384*
60 And his **m** answered and said, Not *so;* *G3384*
2:33 And Joseph and his **m** marvelled at *G3384*
34 unto Mary his **m**, Behold, this *child* is *G3384*
43 and Joseph and his **m** knew not *of it*. *G3384*
48 amazed: and his **m** said unto him, Son, *G3384*
51 **m** kept all these sayings in her heart. *G3384*
4:38 And Simon's wife's **m** was taken with a *G3994*
7:12 the only son of his **m**, and she was a *G3384*
15 speak. And he delivered him to his **m**. *G3384*
8:19 Then came to him *his* **m** and his *G3384*
20 which said, Thy **m** and thy brethren *G3384*
21 unto them, My **m** and my brethren are *G3384*
51 the father and the **m** of the maiden. *G3384*
12:53 the father; the **m** against the daughter, *G3384*
53 against the **m**; the mother in law *G3384*
53 the mother; the **m** in law against her *G3994*
53 daughter in law against her **m** in law. *G3994*
14:26 not his father, and **m**, and wife, and *G3384*
18:20 witness, Honour thy father and thy **m**. *G3384*
24:10 and Mary the *m* of James, and other
Jn 2: 1 Galilee; and the **m** of Jesus was there: *G3384*
3 And when they wanted wine, the **m** of *G3384*
5 His **m** saith unto the servants, *G3384*
12 he, and his **m**, and his brethren, and *G3384*
6:42 whose father and **m** we know? how is it *G3384*

Jn 19:25 cross of Jesus his **m**, and his mother's *G3384*
26 When Jesus therefore saw his **m**, and *G3384*
26 unto his **m**, Woman, behold thy son! *G3384*
27 Behold thy **m**! And from that hour *G3384*
Act 1:14 the **m** of Jesus, and with his brethren. *G3384*
12:12 house of Mary the **m** of John, whose *G3384*
Ro 16:13 in the Lord, and his **m** and mine. *G3384*
Gal 4:26 is above is free, which is the **m** of us all. *G3384*
Eph 5:31 his father and **m**, and shall be joined *G3384*
6: 2 Honour thy father and **m**; which is the *G3384*
2Ti 1: 5 Lois, and thy **m** Eunice; and I am *G3384*
Heb 7: 3 Without father, without **m**, without *G282*
Rev 17: 5 GREAT, THE **M** OF HARLOTS AND *G3384*

MOTHER-IN-LAW See MOTHER and LAW.

MOTHERS
Isa 49:23 thy nursing **m**: they shall bow down H3243
Jer 16: 3 concerning their **m** that bare them, and H517
Lam 2:12 They say to their **m**, Where *is* corn and H517
5: 3 We are orphans and fatherless, our **m** H517
Mk 10:30 and sisters, and **m**, and children, and *G3384*
1Ti 1: 9 and murderers of **m**, for manslayers, *G3389*
5: 2 The elder women as **m**; the younger as *G3384*

MOTHER'S
Gen 24:28 told *them of* her **m** house these things. H517
67 Isaac was comforted after his **m** *death.* H517
27:29 and let thy **m** sons bow down to thee: H517
28: 2 of Bethuel thy **m** father; and take thee H517
2 of the daughters of Laban thy **m** brother. H517
29:10 of Laban his **m** brother, and the sheep H517
10 sheep of Laban his **m** brother, that Jacob H517
10 the flock of Laban his **m** brother. H517
43:29 Benjamin, his **m** son, and said, *Is* this H517
Ex 23:19 shalt not seethe a kid in his **m** milk. H517
34:26 shalt not seethe a kid in his **m** milk. H517
Lev 18:13 nakedness of thy **m** sister: for she *is* thy H517
13 sister: for she *is* thy **m** near kinswoman. H517
20:17 daughter, or his **m** daughter, and see her H517
19 the nakedness of thy **m** sister, nor of thy H517
24:11 Moses: (and his **m** name *was* Shelomith, H517
Nu 12:12 when he cometh out of his **m** womb. H517
Dt 14:21 shalt not seethe a kid in his **m** milk. H517
Jdg 9: 1 to Shechem unto his **m** brethren, and H517
1 of the house of his **m** father, saying, H517
3 And his **m** brethren spake of him in the H517
16:17 unto God from my **m** womb: if I be H517
Ru 1: 8 return each to her **m** house: the LORD H517
1Sa 20:30 unto the confusion of thy **m** nakedness? H517
1Ki 11:26 servant, whose **m** name *was* Zeruah, a H517
14:21 **m** name *was* Naamah an Ammonitess. H517
31 of David. And his **m** name *was* Naamah H517
15: 2 And his **m** name *was* Maachah, H517
10 And his **m** name *was* Maachah, H517
22:42 And his **m** name *was* Azubah the H517
2Ki 8:26 And his **m** name *was* Athaliah, H517
12: 1 his **m** name *was* Zibiah of Beer-sheba. H517
14: 2 **m** name *was* Jehoaddan of Jerusalem. H517
15: 2 his **m** name *was* Jecholiah of Jerusalem. H517
33 And his **m** name *was* Jerusha, H517
18: 2 in Jerusalem. His **m** name also *was* Abi, H517
21: 1 And his **m** name *was* Hephzi-bah. H517
19 And his **m** name *was* Meshullemeth, H517
22: 1 And his **m** name *was* Jedidah, H517
23:31 And his **m** name *was* Hamutal, H517
36 And his **m** name *was* Zebudah, H517
24: 8 months. And his **m** name *was* Nehushta, H517
18 And his **m** name *was* Hamutal, H517
2Ch 12:13 **m** name *was* Naamah an Ammonitess. H517
13: 2 in Jerusalem. His **m** name also *was* H517
20:31 And his **m** name *was* Azubah the H517
22: 2 year in Jerusalem. His **m** name also *was* H517
24: 1 **m** name also *was* Zibiah of Beer-sheba. H517
25: 1 **m** name *was* Jehoaddan of Jerusalem. H517
26: 3 **m** name also *was* Jecoliah of Jerusalem. H517
27: 1 in Jerusalem. His **m** name also *was* H517
29: 1 And his **m** name *was* Abijah, the H517
Job 1:21 And said, Naked came I out of my **m** H517
3:10 Because it shut not up the doors of my ***m***
31:18 I have guided her from my **m** womb;) H517
Ps 22: 9 me hope *when I was* upon my **m** breasts. H517
10 thou *art* my God from my **m** belly. H517
50:20 thou slanderest thine own **m** son. H517
69: 8 and an alien unto my **m** children. H517
71: 6 took me out of my **m** bowels: my praise H517
139:13 thou hast covered me in my **m** womb. H517
Ecc 5:15 As he came forth of his **m** womb, naked H517
Song 1: 6 upon me: my **m** children were angry H517
Song 3: 4 him into my **m** house, and into the H517
8: 2 bring thee into my **m** house, *who* would H517
Isa 50: 1 *is* the bill of your **m** divorcement, whom H517
Jer 52: 1 And his **m** name *was* Hamutal H517
Ezk 16:45 Thou *art* thy **m** daughter, that lotheth H517
Mt 19:12 born from *their* **m** womb: and there are *G3384*
Lk 1:15 Holy Ghost, even from his **m** womb. *G3384*
Jn 3: 4 time into his **m** womb, and be born? *G3384*
19:25 mother, and his **m** sister, Mary the *wife* *G3384*
Act 3: 2 And a certain man lame from his **m** *G3384*
14: 8 his **m** womb, who never had walked: *G3384*
Gal 1:15 **m** womb, and called *me* by his grace, *G3384*

MOTHERS'
Lam 2:12 soul was poured out into their **m** bosom. H517

MOTIONS
Ro 7: 5 For when we were in the flesh, the **m** of *G3804*

MOULDY
Jos 9: 5 bread of their provision was dry *and* **m**. H5350
12 but now, behold, it is dry, and it is **m**: H5350

MOUNT
Gen 10:30 thou goest unto Sephar a **m** of the east. H2022
14: 6 And the Horites in their **m** Seir, unto H2042
22:14 In the **m** of the LORD it shall be seen. H2022
31:21 and set his face *toward* the **m** Gilead. H2022
23 and they overtook him in the **m** Gilead. H2022
25 his tent in the **m**: and Laban with his H2022
25 his brethren pitched in the **m** of Gilead. H2022
54 sacrifice upon the **m**, and called his H2022
54 bread, and tarried all night in the **m**. H2022
36: 8 Thus dwelt Esau in **m** Seir: Esau *is* H2022
9 the father of the Edomites in **m** Seir: H2022
Ex 4:27 him in the **m** of God, and kissed him. H2022
18: 5 where he encamped at the **m** of God: H2022
19: 2 and there Israel camped before the **m**. H2022
11 sight of all the people upon **m** Sinai. H2022
12 *ye* go *not* up into the **m**, or touch the H2022
12 the **m** shall be surely put to death: H2022
13 long, they shall come up to the **m**. H2022
14 And Moses went down from the **m** H2022
16 cloud upon the **m**, and the voice of the H2022
17 they stood at the nether part of the **m**. H2022
18 And **m** Sinai was altogether on a H2022
18 and the whole **m** quaked greatly. H2022
20 And the LORD came down upon **m** H2022
20 on the top of the **m**: and the LORD H2022
20 to the top of the **m**; and Moses went up. H2022
23 come up to **m** Sinai: for thou chargedst H2022
23 Set bounds about the **m**, and sanctify it. H2022
24:12 up to me into the **m**, and be there: and I H2022
13 and Moses went up into the **m** of God. H2022
15 And Moses went up into the **m**, and a H2022
15 the mount, and a cloud covered the **m**. H2022
16 abode upon **m** Sinai, and the cloud H2022
17 **m** in the eyes of the children of Israel. H2022
18 him up into the **m**: and Moses was in H2022
18 in the **m** forty days and forty nights. H2022
25:40 which was shewed thee in the **m**. H2022
26:30 which was shewed thee in the **m**. H2022
27: 8 thee in the **m**, so shall they make *it*. H2022
31:18 with him upon **m** Sinai, two tables of H2022
32: 1 down out of the **m**, the people gathered H2022
15 down from the **m**, and the two tables H2022
19 hands, and brake them beneath the **m**. H2022
33: 6 of their ornaments by the **m** Horeb. H2022
34: 2 the morning unto **m** Sinai, and present H2022
2 thyself there to me in the top of the **m**. H2022
3 throughout all the **m**; neither let the H2022
3 the flocks nor herds feed before that **m**. H2022
4 and went up unto **m** Sinai, as the H2022
29 came down from **m** Sinai with the two H2022
29 down from the **m**, that Moses wist not H2022
32 LORD had spoken with him in **m** Sinai. H2022
Lev 7:38 Moses in **m** Sinai, in the day that H2022
25: 1 And the LORD spake unto Moses in **m** H2022
26:46 Israel in **m** Sinai by the hand of Moses. H2022
27:34 for the children of Israel in **m** Sinai. H2022
Nu 3: 1 LORD spake with Moses in **m** Sinai. H2022
10:33 And they departed from the **m** of the H2022
20:22 from Kadesh, and came unto **m** Hor. H2022
23 and Aaron in **m** Hor, by the coast of H2022
25 son, and bring them up unto **m** Hor: H2022
27 they went up into **m** Hor in the sight of H2022
28 in the top of the **m**: and Moses and H2022
28 and Eleazar came down from the **m**. H2022
21: 4 And they journeyed from **m** Hor by the H2022
Nu 27:12 thee up into this **m** Abarim, and see the H2022
28: 6 was ordained in **m** Sinai for a sweet H2022
33:23 Kehelathah, and pitched in **m** Shapher. H2022
24 And they removed from **m** Shapher, H2022
37 **m** Hor, in the edge of the land of Edom. H2022
38 And Aaron the priest went up into **m** H2022
39 three years old when he died in **m** Hor. H2022
41 And they departed from **m** Hor, and H2022
34: 7 sea ye shall point out for you **m** Hor: H2022
8 From **m** Hor ye shall point out *your* H2022
Dt 1: 2 way of **m** Seir unto Kadesh-barnea.) H2022
6 Ye have dwelt long enough in this **m**: H2022
7 and go to the **m** of the Amorites, and H2022
2: 1 and we compassed **m** Seir many days. H2022
5 **m** Seir unto Esau *for* a possession. H2022
3: 8 the river of Arnon unto **m** Hermon; H2022
12 Arnon, and half **m** Gilead, and the H2022
4:48 even unto **m** Sion, which *is* Hermon, H2022
5: 4 in the **m** out of the midst of the fire, H2022
5 fire, and went not up into the **m**;) saying, H2022
22 assembly in the **m** out of the midst of H2022
9: 9 When I was gone up into the **m** to H2022
9 I abode in the **m** forty days and forty H2022
10 with you in the **m** out of the midst of H2022
15 So I turned and came down from the **m**, H2022
15 the mount, and the **m** burned with fire: H2022
21 the brook that descended out of the **m**. H2022
10: 1 the **m**, and make thee an ark of wood. H2022
3 **m**, having the two tables in mine hand. H2022
4 unto you in the **m** out of the midst of H2022
5 down from the **m**, and put the tables in H2022
10 And I stayed in the **m**, according to the H2022
11:29 the blessing upon **m** Gerizim, and the H2022
29 Gerizim, and the curse upon **m** Ebal. H2022
27: 4 you this day, in **m** Ebal, and thou shalt H2022
12 These shall stand upon **m** Gerizim to H2022
13 And these shall stand upon **m** Ebal to H2022
32:49 Abarim, *unto* **m** Nebo, which *is* in the H2022
50 And die in the **m** whither thou goest H2022
50 thy brother died in **m** Hor, and was H2022
33: 2 he shined forth from **m** Paran, and he H2022
Jos 8:30 unto the LORD God of Israel in **m** Ebal, H2022
33 them over against **m** Gerizim, and half H2022
33 of them over against **m** Ebal; as Moses H2022
11:17 *Even* from the **m** Halak, that goeth up H2022
17 of Lebanon under **m** Hermon: and all H2022
12: 1 river Arnon unto **m** Hermon, and all H2022
5 And reigned in **m** Hermon, and in H2022
7 even unto the **m** Halak, that goeth up H2022
13: 5 Baal-gad under **m** Hermon unto the H2022
11 and all **m** Hermon, and all Bashan H2022
19 Zareth-shahar in the **m** of the valley, H2022
15: 9 out to the cities of **m** Ephron; and the H2022
10 westward unto **m** Seir, and passed H2022
10 unto the side of **m** Jearim, which *is* H2022
11 passed along to **m** Baalah, and went H2022
16: 1 up from Jericho throughout **m** Beth-el, H2022
17:15 if **m** Ephraim be too narrow for thee. H2022
19:50 Timnath-serah in **m** Ephraim: and he H2022
20: 7 in Galilee in **m** Naphtali, and Shechem H2022
7 and Shechem in **m** Ephraim, and H2022
21:21 her suburbs in **m** Ephraim, *to be* a city H2022
24: 4 I gave unto Esau **m** Seir, to possess it; H2022
30 which *is* in **m** Ephraim, on the north H2022
33 which was given him in **m** Ephraim. H2022
Jdg 1:35 But the Amorites would dwell in **m** H2022
2: 9 in the **m** of Ephraim, on the H2022
3: 3 that dwelt in **m** Lebanon, from mount H2022
3 Lebanon, from **m** Baal-hermon unto H2022
27 him from the **m**, and he before them. H2022
4: 5 and Beth-el in **m** Ephraim: and the H2022
6 and draw toward **m** Tabor, and take H2022
12 of Abinoam was gone up to **m** Tabor. H2022
14 went down from **m** Tabor, and ten H2022
7: 3 depart early from **m** Gilead. And there H2022
24 throughout all **m** Ephraim, saying, H2022
9: 7 and stood in the top of **m** Gerizim, and H2022
48 And Abimelech gat him up to **m** H2022
10: 1 and he dwelt in Shamir in **m** Ephraim. H2022
12:15 of Ephraim, in the **m** of the Amalekites. H2022
17: 1 And there was a man of **m** Ephraim, H2022
8 and he came to **m** Ephraim to the H2022
18: 2 they came to **m** Ephraim, to the house H2022
13 And they passed thence unto **m** H2022
19: 1 on the side of **m** Ephraim, who took H2022
16 which *was* also of **m** Ephraim; and he H2022
18 toward the side of **m** Ephraim; from H2022
1Sa 1: 1 of **m** Ephraim, and his name H2022
9: 4 And he passed through **m** Ephraim, H2022

1Sa 13: 2 in Michmash and in **m** Beth-el, and a H2022
14:22 hid themselves in **m** Ephraim, *when* H2022
31: 1 and fell down slain in **m** Gilboa. H2022
8 and his three sons fallen in **m** Gilboa. H2022
2Sa 1: 6 by chance upon **m** Gilboa, behold, Saul H2022
15:30 And David went up by the ascent of ***m***
32 to the top *of the m*, where he worshipped
20:21 The matter *is* not so: but a man of **m** H2022
1Ki 4: 8 names: The son of Hur, in **m** Ephraim: H2022
12:25 Then Jeroboam built Shechem in **m** H2022
18:19 to me all Israel unto **m** Carmel, and the H2022
20 the prophets together unto **m** Carmel. H2022
19: 8 forty nights unto Horeb the **m** of God. H2022
11 stand upon the **m** before the LORD. H2022
2Ki 2:25 And he went from thence to **m** Carmel, H2022
4:25 the man of God to **m** Carmel. And it H2022
5:22 be come to me from **m** Ephraim two H2022
19:31 that escape out of **m** Zion: the zeal of H2022
23:13 the right hand of the **m** of corruption, H2022
16 *were* there in the **m**, and sent, and took H2022
1Ch 4:42 men, went to **m** Seir, having for their H2022
5:23 and Senir, and unto **m** Hermon. H2022
6:67 Shechem in **m** Ephraim with her H2022
10: 1 and fell down slain in **m** Gilboa. H2022
8 Saul and his sons fallen in **m** Gilboa. H2022
2Ch 3: 1 at Jerusalem in **m** Moriah, where *the* H2022
13: 4 And Abijah stood up upon **m** H2022
4 which *is* in **m** Ephraim, and said, H2022
15: 8 he had taken from **m** Ephraim, and H2022
19: 4 Beer-sheba to **m** Ephraim, and brought H2022
20:10 and Moab and **m** Seir, whom thou H2022
22 Moab, and **m** Seir, which were come H2022
23 the inhabitants of **m** Seir, utterly to H2022
33:15 had built in the **m** of the house of the H2022
Neh 8:15 Go forth unto the **m**, and fetch olive H2022
9:13 Thou camest down also upon **m** Sinai, H2022
Job 20: 6 Though his excellency **m** up to the H5927
39:27 Doth the eagle **m** up at thy command, H1361
Ps 48: 2 whole earth, *is* **m** Zion, *on* the sides of H2022
11 Let **m** Zion rejoice, let the daughters of H2022
74: 2 this **m** Zion, wherein thou hast dwelt. H2022
78:68 But chose the tribe of Judah, the **m** H2022
107:26 They **m** up to the heaven, they go down H5927
125: 1 the LORD *shall be* as **m** Zion, *which* H2022
Song 4: 1 of goats, that appear from **m** Gilead. H2022
Isa 4: 5 dwelling place of **m** Zion, and upon her H2022
8:18 of hosts, which dwelleth in **m** Zion. H2022
9:18 shall **m** up *like* the lifting up of smoke. H55
10:12 his whole work upon **m** Zion and on H2022
32 hand *against* the **m** of the daughter of H2022
14:13 will sit also upon the **m** of the H2022
16: 1 unto the **m** of the daughter of Zion. H2022
18: 7 of the LORD of hosts, the **m** Zion. H2022
24:23 hosts shall reign in **m** Zion, and in H2022
27:13 the LORD in the holy **m** at Jerusalem. H2022
28:21 For the LORD shall rise up as *in* **m** H2022
29: 3 a **m**, and I will raise forts against thee. H4674
8 nations be, that fight against **m** Zion. H2022
31: 4 for **m** Zion, and for the hill thereof. H2022
37:32 that escape out of **m** Zion: the zeal of H2022
40:31 they shall **m** up with wings as eagles; H5927
Jer 4:15 publisheth affliction from **m** Ephraim. H2022
6: 6 trees, and cast a **m** against Jerusalem: H5550
31: 6 upon the **m** Ephraim shall cry, H2022
50:19 satisfied upon **m** Ephraim and Gilead. H2022
51:53 Though Babylon should **m** up to H5927
Ezk 4: 2 it, and cast a **m** against it; set the camp H5550
10:16 up their wings to **m** up from the earth, H7311
21:22 gates, to cast a **m**, *and* to build a fort. H5550
26: 8 thee, and cast a **m** against thee, and lift H5550
35: 2 Son of man, set thy face against **m** Seir, H2022
3 GOD; Behold, O **m** Seir, I *am* against H2022
7 Thus will I make **m** Seir most desolate, H2022
15 be desolate, O **m** Seir, and all Idumea, H2022
Dan 11:15 and cast up a **m**, and take the most H5550
Joel 2:32 be delivered: for in **m** Zion and in H2022
Oba 8 understanding out of the **m** of Esau? H2022
9 **m** of Esau may be cut off by slaughter. H2022
17 But upon **m** Zion shall be deliverance, H2022
19 shall possess the **m** of Esau; and *they of* H2022
21 And saviours shall come up on **m** Zion H2022
21 Zion to judge the **m** of Esau; and the H2022
Mic 4: 7 **m** Zion from henceforth, even for ever. H2022
Hab 3: 3 the Holy One from **m** Paran. Selah. His H2022
Zec 14: 4 that day upon the **m** of Olives, which *is* H2022
4 on the east, and the **m** of Olives shall H2022
Mt 21: 1 unto the **m** of Olives, then sent *G3735*
24: 3 And as he sat upon the **m** of Olives, the *G3735*
26:30 they went out into the **m** of Olives. *G3735*
Mk 11: 1 Bethany, at the **m** of Olives, he sendeth *G3735*
13: 3 And as he sat upon the **m** of Olives *G3735*
14:26 they went out into the **m** of Olives. *G3735*
Lk 19:29 Bethany, at the **m** called *the mount* of *G3735*
29 ***m*** of Olives, he sent two of his disciples,
37 at the descent of the **m** of Olives, the *G3735*
21:37 **m** that is called *the mount* of Olives. *G3735*
37 the mount that is called *the* **m** of Olives.
22:39 was wont, to the **m** of Olives; and his *G3735*
Jn 8: 1 Jesus went unto the **m** of Olives. *G3735*
Act 1:12 from the **m** called Olivet, which *G3735*
7:30 in the wilderness of **m** Sina an angel of *G3735*
38 to him in the **m** Sina, and *with* our *G3735*
Gal 4:24 the one from the **m** Sinai, which *G3735*
25 For this Agar is **m** Sinai in Arabia, and *G3735*
Heb 8: 5 to the pattern shewed to thee in the **m**. *G3735*
12:18 For ye are not come unto the **m** that *G3735*
22 But ye are come unto **m** Sion, and unto *G3735*
2Pt 1:18 when we were with him in the holy **m**. *G3735*
Rev 14: 1 stood on the **m** Sion, and with him *G3735*

MOUNTAIN

Gen 12: 8 And he removed from thence unto a **m** H2022
14:10 and they that remained fled to the **m**. H2022
19:17 escape to the **m**, lest thou be consumed. H2022
19 the **m**, lest some evil take me, and I die: H2022
30 Zoar, and dwelt in the **m**, and his two H2022
Ex 3: 1 came to the **m** of God, *even* to Horeb. H2022
12 Egypt, ye shall serve God upon this **m**. H2022
15:17 and plant them in the **m** of thine H2022
19: 3 him out of the **m**, saying, Thus shalt H2022
20:18 the trumpet, and the **m** smoking: and H2022
Nu 13:17 *way* southward, and go up into the **m**: H2022
14:40 into the top of the **m**, saying, Lo, we *be* H2022
Dt 1:19 by the way of the **m** of the Amorites, as H2022
20 are come unto the **m** of the Amorites, H2022
24 went up into the **m**, and came unto the H2022
44 dwelt in that **m**, came out against you, H2022
2: 3 Ye have compassed this **m** long H2022
3:25 Jordan, that goodly **m**, and Lebanon. H2022
4:11 stood under the **m**; and the mountain H2022
11 and the **m** burned with fire unto H2022
5:23 the darkness, (for the **m** did burn with H2022
32:49 Get thee up into this **m** Abarim, *unto* H2022
33:19 They shall call the people unto the **m**; H2022
34: 1 of Moab unto the **m** of Nebo, to the top H2022
Jos 2:16 Get you to the **m**, lest the pursuers meet H2022
22 And they went, and came unto the **m**, H2022
23 from the **m**, and passed over, and H2022
11:16 **m** of Israel, and the valley of the same; H2022
14:12 Now therefore give me this **m**, whereof H2022
15: 8 to the top of the **m** that *lieth* before the H2022
17:18 But the **m** shall be thine; for it *is* a H2022
18:16 to the end of the **m** that *lieth* before the H2022
20: 7 which *is* Hebron, in the **m** of Judah. H2022
Jdg 1: 9 **m**, and in the south, and in the valley. H2022
19 *the inhabitants of* the **m**; but could not H2022
34 of Dan into the **m**: for they would not H2022
3:27 a trumpet in the **m** of Ephraim, and the H2022
1Sa 17: 3 And the Philistines stood on a **m** on the H2022
3 Israel stood on a **m** on the other side: H2022
23:14 remained in a **m** in the wilderness of H2022
26 And Saul went on this side of the **m**, H2022
26 on that side of the **m**: and David made H2022
2Ki 2:16 him upon some **m**, or into some valley. H2022
6:17 and, behold, the **m** *was* full of horses H2022
2Ch 2: 2 to hew in the **m**, and three thousand H2022
18 *be* hewers in the **m**, and three thousand H2022
Job 14:18 And surely the **m** falling cometh to H2022
Ps 11: 1 ye to my soul, Flee *as* a bird to your **m**? H2022
30: 7 hast made my **m** to stand strong: thou H2042
48: 1 of our God, *in* the **m** of his holiness. H2022
78:54 **m**, *which* his right hand had purchased. H2022
Song 4: 6 I will get me to the **m** of myrrh, and to H2022
Isa 2: 2 the last days, *that* the **m** of the LORD'S H2022
3 let us go up to the **m** of the LORD, to H2022
11: 9 in all my holy **m**: for the earth shall be H2022
13: 2 Lift ye up a banner upon the high **m**, H2022
25: 6 And in this **m** shall the LORD of hosts H2022
7 And he will destroy in this **m** the face H2022
10 For in this **m** shall the hand of the H2022
30:17 top of a **m**, and as an ensign on an hill. H2022
25 And there shall be upon every high **m**, H2022
29 to come into the **m** of the LORD, to the H2022
40: 4 and every **m** and hill shall be made H2022
9 up into the high **m**; O Jerusalem, that H2022
56: 7 Even them will I bring to my holy **m**, H2022
57: 7 Upon a lofty and high **m** hast thou set H2022
13 the land, and shall inherit my holy **m**; H2022
Isa 65:11 forget my holy **m**, that prepare a table H2022
25 in all my holy **m**, saith the LORD. H2022
66:20 beasts, to my holy **m** Jerusalem, saith H2022
Jer 3: 6 up upon every high **m** and under every H2022
16:16 them from every **m**, and from every hill, H2022
17: 3 O my **m** in the field, I will give thy H2042
26:18 heaps, and the **m** of the house as the H2022
31:23 of justice, *and* **m** of holiness. H2022
50: 6 have gone from **m** to hill, they have H2022
51:25 thee, O destroying **m**, saith the LORD, H2022
25 rocks, and will make thee a burnt **m**. H2022
Lam 5:18 Because of the **m** of Zion, which is H2022
Ezk 11:23 **m** which *is* on the east side of the city. H2022
17:22 plant *it* upon an high **m** and eminent: H2022
23 In the **m** of the height of Israel will I H2022
20:40 For in mine holy **m**, in the mountain of H2022
40 For in mine holy mountain, in the **m** of H2022
28:14 wast upon the holy **m** of God; thou hast H2022
16 profane out of the **m** of God: and I will H2022
40: 2 upon a very high **m**, by which *was* as H2022
43:12 the top of the **m** the whole limit thereof H2022
Dan 2:35 a great **m**, and filled the whole earth. H2906
45 was cut out of the **m** without hands, H2906
9:16 thy holy **m**: because for our sins, H2022
20 my God for the holy **m** of my God; H2022
11:45 the glorious holy **m**; yet he shall come to H2022
Joel 2: 1 an alarm in my holy **m**: let all the H2022
3:17 dwelling in Zion, my holy **m**: then shall H2022
Am 4: 1 that *are* in the **m** of Samaria, which H2022
6: 1 and trust in the **m** of Samaria, *which* H2022
Oba 16 For as ye have drunk upon my holy **m**, H2022
Mic 3:12 heaps, and the **m** of the house as the H2022
4: 1 to pass, *that* the **m** of the house of the H2022
2 let us go up to the **m** of the LORD, and H2022
7:12 sea to sea, and *from* **m** to mountain. H2022
12 sea to sea, and *from* mountain to **m**. H2022
Zep 3:11 more be haughty because of my holy **m**. H2022
Hag 1: 8 Go up to the **m**, and bring wood, and H2022
Zec 4: 7 Who *art* thou, O great **m**? before H2022
8: 3 city of truth; and the **m** of the LORD of H2022
3 of the LORD of hosts the holy **m**. H2022
14: 4 and half of the **m** shall remove toward H2022
Mt 4: 8 an exceeding high **m**, and sheweth him *G3735*
5: 1 he went up into a **m**: and when he was *G3735*
8: 1 When he was come down from the **m**, *G3735*
14:23 he went up into a **m** apart to pray: and *G3735*
15:29 went up into a **m**, and sat down there. *G3735*
17: 1 bringeth them up into an high **m** apart, *G3735*
9 And as they came down from the **m**, *G3735*
20 shall say unto this **m**, Remove hence to *G3735*
21:21 shall say unto this **m**, Be thou removed, *G3735*
28:16 a **m** where Jesus had appointed them. *G3735*
Mk 3:13 And he goeth up into a **m**, and calleth *G3735*
6:46 away, he departed into a **m** to pray. *G3735*
9: 2 up into an high **m** apart by themselves: *G3735*
9 And as they came down from the **m**, he *G3735*
11:23 shall say unto this **m**, Be thou removed, *G3735*
Lk 3: 5 Every valley shall be filled, and every **m** *G3735*
4: 5 up into an high **m**, shewed unto him all *G3735*
6:12 that he went out into a **m** to pray, and *G3735*
8:32 feeding on the **m**: and they besought *G3735*
9:28 James, and went up into a **m** to pray. *G3735*
Jn 4:20 Our fathers worshipped in this **m**; and *G3735*
21 neither in this **m**, nor yet at Jerusalem, *G3735*
6: 3 And Jesus went up into a **m**, and there *G3735*
15 departed again into a **m** himself alone. *G3735*
Heb 12:20 a beast touch the **m**, it shall be stoned, *G3735*
Rev 6:14 and every **m** and island were moved *G3735*
8: 8 as it were a great **m** burning with fire *G3735*
21:10 to a great and high **m**, and shewed me *G3735*

MOUNTAINS

Gen 7:20 prevail; and the **m** were covered. H2022
8: 4 of the month, upon the **m** of Ararat. H2022
5 the month, were the tops of the **m** seen. H2022
22: 2 one of the **m** which I will tell thee of. H2022
Ex 32:12 to slay them in the **m**, and to consume H2022
Nu 13:29 dwell in the **m**: and the Canaanites H2022
23: 7 Aram, out of the **m** of the east, *saying*, H2042
33:47 in the **m** of Abarim, before Nebo. H2022
48 And they departed from the **m** of H2022
Dt 2:37 the cities in the **m**, nor unto whatsoever H2022
12: 2 upon the high **m**, and upon the hills, H2022
32:22 set on fire the foundations of the **m**. H2022
33:15 of the ancient **m**, and for the precious H2042
Jos 10: 6 the **m** are gathered together against us. H2022
11: 2 on the north of the **m**, and of the plains H2022
3 the Jebusite in the **m**, and *to* the Hivite H2022
21 from the **m**, from Hebron, from H2022

Jos 11:21 and from all the **m** of Judah, and from H2022
21 and from all the **m** of Israel: Joshua H2022
12: 8 In the **m**, and in the valleys, and in the H2022
15:48 And in the **m**, Shamir, and Jattir, and H2022
18:12 up through the **m** westward; and the H2022
Jdg 5: 5 The **m** melted from before the LORD, H2022
6: 2 in the **m**, and caves, and strong holds. H2022
9:25 in the top of the **m**, and they robbed all H2022
36 the top of the **m**. And Zebul said unto H2022
36 shadow of the **m** as *if they were* men. H2022
11:37 and down upon the **m**, and bewail my H2022
38 and bewailed her virginity upon the **m**. H2022
1Sa 26:20 one doth hunt a partridge in the **m**. H2022
2Sa 1:21 Ye **m** of Gilboa, *let there be* no dew, H2022
1Ki 5:15 fourscore thousand hewers in the **m**; H2022
19:11 wind rent the **m**, and brake in pieces H2022
2Ki 19:23 to the height of the **m**, to the sides of H2022
1Ch 12: 8 *were* as swift as the roes upon the **m**; H2022
2Ch 18:16 upon the **m**, as sheep that have H2022
21:11 Moreover he made high places in the **m** H2022
26:10 dressers in the **m**, and in Carmel: for H2022
27: 4 Moreover he built cities in the **m** of H2022
Job 9: 5 Which removeth the **m**, and they know H2022
24: 8 They are wet with the showers of the **m**, H2022
28: 9 he overturneth the **m** by the roots. H2022
39: 8 The range of the **m** *is* his pasture, and H2022
40:20 Surely the **m** bring him forth food, H2022
Ps 36: 6 Thy righteousness *is* like the great **m**; H2042
46: 2 **m** be carried into the midst of the sea; H2022
3 *though* the **m** shake with the swelling H2022
50:11 I know all the fowls of the **m**: and the H2022
65: 6 fast the **m**; *being* girded with power: H2022
72: 3 The **m** shall bring peace to the people, H2022
16 the top of the **m**; the fruit thereof shall H2022
76: 4 *and* excellent than the **m** of prey. H2042
83:14 and as the flame setteth the **m** on fire; H2022
87: 1 His foundation *is* in the holy **m**. H2042
90: 2 Before the **m** were brought forth, or H2022
104: 6 garment: the waters stood above the **m**. H2022
8 They go up by the **m**; they go down by H2022
114: 4 The **m** skipped like rams, *and* the little H2022
6 Ye **m**, *that* ye skipped like rams; *and* ye H2022
125: 2 As the **m** *are* round about Jerusalem, H2022
133: 3 upon the **m** of Zion: for there the H2042
144: 5 touch the **m**, and they shall smoke. H2022
147: 8 who maketh grass to grow upon the **m**. H2022
148: 9 **M**, and all hills; fruitful trees, and all H2022
Prv 8:25 Before the **m** were settled, before the H2022
27:25 itself, and herbs of the **m** are gathered. H2022
Song 2: 8 upon the **m**, skipping upon the hills. H2022
17 or a young hart upon the **m** of Bether. H2022
4: 8 lions' dens, from the **m** of the leopards. H2042
8:14 to a young hart upon the **m** of spices. H2022
Isa 2: 2 in the top of the **m**, and shall be exalted H2022
14 And upon all the high **m**, and upon all H2022
13: 4 The noise of a multitude in the **m**, like H2022
14:25 and upon my **m** tread him under foot: H2022
17:13 as the chaff of the **m** before the wind, H2022
18: 3 up an ensign on the **m**; and when he H2022
6 the fowls of the **m**, and to the beasts of H2022
22: 5 down the walls, and of crying to the **m**. H2022
34: 3 the **m** shall be melted with their blood. H2022
37:24 to the height of the **m**, to the sides of H2022
40:12 **m** in scales, and the hills in a balance? H2022
41:15 thou shalt thresh the **m**, and beat *them* H2022
42:11 let them shout from the top of the **m**. H2022
15 I will make waste **m** and hills, and dry H2022
44:23 into singing, ye **m**, O forest, and every H2022
49:11 And I will make all my **m** a way, and H2022
13 into singing, O **m**: for the LORD hath H2022
52: 7 How beautiful upon the **m** are the feet H2022
54:10 For the **m** shall depart, and the hills be H2022
55:12 with peace: the **m** and the hills shall H2022
64: 1 the **m** might flow down at thy presence, H2022
3 the **m** flowed down at thy presence. H2022
65: 7 incense upon the **m**, and blasphemed H2022
9 inheritor of my **m**: and mine elect shall H2022
Jer 3:23 the multitude of **m**: truly in the LORD H2022
4:24 I beheld the **m**, and, lo, they trembled, H2022
9:10 For the **m** will I take up a weeping and H2022
13:16 upon the dark **m**, and, while ye look for H2022
17:26 and from the **m**, and from the south, H2022
31: 5 Thou shalt yet plant vines upon the **m** H2022
32:44 in the cities of the **m**, and in the cities of H2022
33:13 In the cities of the **m**, in the cities of the H2022
46:18 *is* among the **m**, and as Carmel by the H2022
50: 6 them away *on* the **m**: they have gone H2022
Lam 4:19 us upon the **m**, they laid wait for us H2022
Ezk 6: 2 Son of man, set thy face toward the **m** H2022
6: 3 And say, Ye **m** of Israel, hear the word H2022
3 Lord GOD to the **m**, and to the hills, to H2022
13 in all the tops of the **m**, and under every H2022
7: 7 and not the sounding again of the **m**. H2022
16 and shall be on the **m** like doves of the H2022
18: 6 *And* hath not eaten upon the **m**, neither H2022
11 **m**, and defiled his neighbour's wife, H2022
15 *That* hath not eaten upon the **m**, H2022
19: 9 no more be heard upon the **m** of Israel. H2022
22: 9 they eat upon the **m**: in the midst of H2022
31:12 have left him: upon the **m** and in all the H2022
32: 5 And I will lay thy flesh upon the **m**, and H2022
6 **m**; and the rivers shall be full of thee. H2022
33:28 shall cease; and the **m** of Israel shall be H2022
34: 6 My sheep wandered through all the **m**, H2022
13 them upon the **m** of Israel by the rivers, H2022
14 upon the high **m** of Israel shall their H2022
14 shall they feed upon the **m** of Israel. H2022
35: 8 And I will fill his **m** with his slain *men*: H2022
12 against the **m** of Israel, saying, They H2022
36: 1 unto the **m** of Israel, and say, Ye H2022
1 **m** of Israel, hear the word of the LORD: H2022
4 Therefore, ye **m** of Israel, hear the H2022
4 Lord GOD to the **m**, and to the hills, to H2022
6 and say unto the **m**, and to the hills, to H2022
8 But ye, O **m** of Israel, ye shall shoot H2022
37:22 the land upon the **m** of Israel; and one H2022
38: 8 against the **m** of Israel, which have H2022
20 presence, and the **m** shall be thrown H2022
21 throughout all my **m**, saith the Lord H2022
39: 2 will bring thee upon the **m** of Israel: H2022
4 Thou shalt fall upon the **m** of Israel, H2022
17 sacrifice upon the **m** of Israel, that ye H2022
Hos 4:13 They sacrifice upon the tops of the **m**, H2022
10: 8 **m**, Cover us; and to the hills, Fall on us. H2022
Joel 2: 2 spread upon the **m**: a great people and H2022
5 on the tops of **m** shall they leap, like H2022
3:18 in that day, *that* the **m** shall drop down H2022
Am 3: 9 upon the **m** of Samaria, and behold H2022
4:13 For, lo, he that formeth the **m**, and H2022
9:13 seed; and the **m** shall drop sweet wine, H2022
Jna 2: 6 I went down to the bottoms of the **m**; H2022
Mic 1: 4 And the **m** shall be molten under him, H2022
4: 1 in the top of the **m**, and it shall be H2022
6: 1 the **m**, and let the hills hear thy voice. H2022
2 Hear ye, O **m**, the LORD'S controversy, H2022
Nah 1: 5 The **m** quake at him, and the hills melt, H2022
15 Behold upon the **m** the feet of him that H2022
3:18 the **m**, and no man gathereth *them*. H2022
Hab 3: 6 the everlasting **m** were scattered, the H2042
10 The **m** saw thee, *and* they trembled: the H2022
Hag 1:11 and upon the **m**, and upon the corn, H2022
Zec 6: 1 out from between two **m**; and the H2022
1 and the **m** *were* mountains of brass. H2022
1 and the mountains *were* **m** of brass. H2022
14: 5 And ye shall flee *to* the valley of the **m**; H2022
5 for the valley of the **m** shall reach unto H2022
Mal 1: 3 And I hated Esau, and laid his **m** and H2022
Mt 18:12 and goeth into the **m**, and seeketh that *G3735*
24:16 which be in Judaea flee into the **m**: *G3735*
Mk 5: 5 day, he was in the **m**, and in the tombs, *G3735*
11 Now there was there nigh unto the **m** a *G3735*
13:14 let them that be in Judaea flee to the **m**: *G3735*
Lk 21:21 in Judaea flee to the **m**; and let them *G3735*
23:30 Then shall they begin to say to the **m**, *G3735*
1Co 13: 2 **m**, and have not charity, I am nothing. *G3735*
Heb 11:38 **m**, and *in* dens and caves of the earth. *G3735*
Rev 6:15 in the dens and in the rocks of the **m**; *G3735*
16 And said to the **m** and rocks, Fall on *G3735*
16:20 And every island fled away, and the **m** *G3735*
17: 9 seven **m**, on which the woman sitteth. *G3735*

MOUNTED
Ezk 10:19 their wings, and **m** up from the earth in H7426

MOUNTING
Isa 15: 5 old: for by the **m** up of Luhith with H4608

MOUNTS
Jer 32:24 Behold the **m**, they are come unto the H5550
33: 4 down by the **m**, and by the sword; H5550
Ezk 17:17 by casting up **m**, and building forts, H5550

MOURN
Gen 23: 2 to **m** for Sarah, and to weep for her. H5594
1Sa 16: 1 long wilt thou **m** for Saul, seeing I have H56
2Sa 3:31 sackcloth, and **m** before Abner. And H5594
1Ki 13:29 came to the city, to **m** and to bury him. H5594
14:13 And all Israel shall **m** for him, and H5594
Neh 8: 9 LORD your God; **m** not, nor weep. For H56
Job 2:11 to **m** with him and to comfort him. H5110
5:11 which **m** may be exalted to safety. H6937
14:22 pain, and his soul within him shall **m**. H56
Ps 55: 2 Attend unto me, and hear me: I **m** in H7300
Prv 5:11 And thou **m** at the last, when thy flesh H5098
29: 2 the wicked beareth rule, the people **m**. H584
Ecc 3: 4 laugh; a time to **m**, and a time to dance; H5594
Isa 3:26 And her gates shall lament and **m**; and H56
16: 7 shall ye **m**; surely *they are* stricken. H1897
19: 8 The fishers also shall **m**, and all they that H578
38:14 did I chatter: I did **m** as a dove: mine H1897
59:11 We roar all like bears, and **m** sore like H1897
61: 2 of our God; to comfort all that **m**; H57
3 To appoint unto them that **m** in Zion, to H57
66:10 for joy with her, all ye that **m** for her: H56
Jer 4:28 For this shall the earth **m**, and the H56
12: 4 How long shall the land **m**, and the herbs H56
48:31 *heart* shall **m** for the men of Kir-heres. H1897
Lam 1: 4 The ways of Zion do **m**, because none H57
Ezk 7:12 nor the seller **m**: for wrath *is* upon all H56
27 The king shall **m**, and the prince shall be H56
24:16 neither shalt thou **m** nor weep, neither H5594
23 feet: ye shall not **m** nor weep; but ye H5594
23 iniquities, and **m** one toward another. H5098
31:15 Lebanon to **m** for him, and all the H6937
Hos 4: 3 Therefore shall the land **m**, and every H56
10: 5 thereof shall **m** over it, and the priests H56
Joel 1: 9 the priests, the LORD'S ministers, **m**. H56
Am 1: 2 **m**, and the top of Carmel shall wither. H56
8: 8 for this, and every one **m** that dwelleth H56
9: 5 dwell therein shall **m**: and it shall rise up H56
Zec 12:10 and they shall **m** for him, as one H5594
12 And the land shall **m**, every family H5594
Mt 5: 4 Blessed *are* they that **m**: for they shall *G3996*
9:15 of the bridechamber **m**, as long as the *G3996*
24:30 tribes of the earth **m**, and they shall see *G2875*
Lk 6:25 laugh now! for ye shall **m** and weep. *G3996*
Jas 4: 9 Be afflicted, and **m**, and weep: let your *G3996*
Rev 18:11 shall weep and **m** over her; for no man *G3996*

MOURNED
Gen 37:34 his loins, and **m** for his son many days. H56
50: 3 **m** for him threescore and ten days. H1058
10 and there they **m** with a great and very H5594
Ex 33: 4 evil tidings, they **m**: and no man did put H56
Nu 14:39 of Israel: and the people **m** greatly. H56
20:29 was dead, they **m** for Aaron thirty H1058
1Sa 15:35 Samuel **m** for Saul: and the LORD H56
2Sa 1:12 And they **m**, and wept, and fasted until H5594
11:26 was dead, she **m** for her husband. H5594
13:37 And *David* **m** for his son every day. H56
14: 2 that had a long time **m** for the dead: H56
1Ki 13:30 **m** over him, *saying*, Alas, my brother! H5594
14:18 And they buried him; and all Israel **m** H5594
1Ch 7:22 And Ephraim their father **m** many days, H56
2Ch 35:24 all Judah and Jerusalem **m** for Josiah. H56
Ezr 10: 6 nor drink water: for he **m** because of the H56
Neh 1: 4 and wept, and **m** *certain* days, and H56
Zec 7: 5 When ye fasted and **m** in the fifth and H5594
Mt 11:17 **m** unto you, and ye have not lamented. *G2354*
Mk 16:10 been with him, as they **m** and wept. *G3996*
Lk 7:32 have **m** to you, and ye have not wept. *G2354*
1Co 5: 2 have not rather **m**, that he that hath *G3996*

MOURNER
2Sa 14: 2 feign thyself to be a **m**, and put on now H56

MOURNERS
Job 29:25 the army, as one *that* comforteth the **m**. H57
Ecc 12: 5 home, and the **m** go about the streets: H5594
Isa 57:18 restore comforts unto him and to his **m**. H57
Hos 9: 4 as the bread of **m**; all that eat thereof H205

MOURNETH
2Sa 19: 1 the king weepeth and **m** for Absalom. H56
Ps 35:14 heavily, as one that **m** *for his* mother. H57
88: 9 Mine eye **m** by reason of affliction: H1669
Isa 24: 4 The earth **m** *and* fadeth away, the world H56
7 The new wine **m**, the vine languisheth, all H56
33: 9 The earth **m** *and* languisheth: Lebanon H56
Jer 12:11 *being* desolate it **m** unto me; the whole H56
14: 2 Judah **m**, and the gates thereof languish; H56
23:10 swearing the land **m**; the pleasant places H56
Joel 1:10 The field is wasted, the land **m**; for the H56
Zec 12:10 for him, as one **m** for *his* only *son*, and H4553

MOURNFULLY
Mal 3:14 walked **m** before the LORD of hosts? H6941

MOURNING
Gen 27:41 heart, The days of **m** for my father are at H60
37:35 my son **m**. Thus his father wept for him. H57
50: 4 And when the days of his **m** were past, H1068
10 he made a **m** for his father seven days. H60
11 saw the **m** in the floor of Atad, H60
11 This *is* a grievous **m** to the Egyptians: H60
Dt 26:14 I have not eaten thereof in my **m**, neither H205
34: 8 of weeping *and* **m** for Moses were ended. H60
2Sa 11:27 And when the **m** was past, David sent H60
14: 2 and put on now **m** apparel, and anoint H60
19: 2 was *turned* into **m** unto all the people: H60
Est 4: 3 *there was* great **m** among the Jews, and H60
6:12 house **m**, and having his head covered. H57
9:22 to joy, and from **m** into a good day: that H60
Job 3: 8 day, who are ready to raise up their **m**. H3882
30:28 I went **m** without the sun: I stood up, H6937
31 My harp also is *turned* to **m**, and my H60
Ps 30:11 Thou hast turned for me my **m** into H4553
38: 6 down greatly; I go **m** all the day long. H6937
42: 9 me? why go I **m** because of the H6937
43: 2 cast me off? why go I **m** because of the H6937
Ecc 7: 2 *It is* better to go to the house of **m**, than H60
4 The heart of the wise *is* in the house of **m**; H60
Isa 22:12 to weeping, and to **m**, and to baldness, H4553
51:11 joy; *and* sorrow and **m** shall flee away. H585
60:20 and the days of thy **m** shall be ended. H60
61: 3 the oil of joy for **m**, the garment of praise H60
Jer 6:26 ashes: make thee **m**, *as for* an only son, H60
9:17 ye, and call for the **m** women, that they H6969
16: 5 not into the house of **m**, neither go to H4798
7 for them in **m**, to comfort them for H60
31:13 for I will turn their **m** into joy, and will H60
Lam 2: 5 daughter of Judah **m** and lamentation. H8386
5:15 is ceased; our dance is turned into **m**. H60
Ezk 2:10 therein lamentations, and **m**, and woe. H1899
7:16 all of them **m**, every one for his iniquity. H1993
24:17 Forbear to cry, make no **m** for the dead, H60
31:15 grave I caused a **m**: I covered the deep H56
Dan 10: 2 In those days I Daniel was **m** three full H56
Joel 2:12 fasting, and with weeping, and with **m**: H4553
Am 5:16 the husbandman to **m**, and such as are H60
8:10 And I will turn your feasts into **m**, and all H60
10 will make it as the **m** of an only *son*, and H60
Mic 1: 8 like the dragons, and **m** as the owls. H60
11 not forth in the **m** of Beth-ezel; he shall H4553
Zec 12:11 In that day shall there be a great **m** in H4553
11 Jerusalem, as the **m** of Hadadrimmon H4553
Mt 2:18 and great **m**, Rachel weeping *for* *G3602*
2Co 7: 7 desire, your **m**, your fervent mind *G3602*
Jas 4: 9 turned to **m**, and *your* joy to heaviness. *G3997*
Rev 18: 8 day, death, and **m**, and famine; and she *G3997*

MOURNING-WATCH See MORNING and WATCH.

MOUSE
Lev 11:29 the **m**, and the tortoise after his kind, H5909
Isa 66:17 and the **m**, shall be consumed H5909

MOUTH
Gen 4:11 which hath opened her **m** to receive thy H6310
8:11 and, lo, in her **m** *was* an olive leaf H6310
24:57 call the damsel, and inquire at her **m**. H6310
29: 2 a great stone *was* upon the well's **m**. H6310
3 from the well's **m**, and watered the H6310
3 again upon the well's **m** in his place. H6310
8 the well's **m**; then we water the sheep. H6310
10 from the well's **m**, and watered the flock H6310
42:27 for, behold, it *was* in his sack's **m**. H6310
43:12 again in the **m** of your sacks, carry H6310
21 money *was* in the **m** of his sack, our H6310
44: 1 put every man's money in his sack's **m**. H6310
2 cup, in the sack's **m** of the youngest, H6310
45:12 that *it is* my **m** that speaketh unto you. H6310
Ex 4:11 hath made man's **m**? or who maketh the H6310
12 **m**, and teach thee what thou shalt say. H6310
15 put words in his **m**: and I will be with H6310
15 and I will be with thy **m**, and with his H6310
15 **m**, and will teach you what ye shall do. H6310
16 thee instead of a **m**, and thou shalt be to H6310
13: 9 law may be in thy **m**: for with a strong H6310
23:13 neither let it be heard out of thy **m**. H6310
Nu 12: 8 With him will I speak **m** to mouth, H6310
8 With him will I speak mouth to **m**, even H6310
16:30 earth open her **m**, and swallow them H6310
32 And the earth opened her **m**, and H6310
22:28 And the LORD opened the **m** of the ass, H6310
38 God putteth in my **m**, that shall I speak. H6310
23: 5 a word in Balaam's **m**, and said, Return H6310
Nu 23:12 that which the LORD hath put in my **m**? H6310
16 put a word in his **m**, and said, Go again H6310
26:10 And the earth opened her **m**, and H6310
30: 2 to all that proceedeth out of his **m**. H6310
32:24 which hath proceeded out of your **m**. H6310
35:30 to death by the **m** of witnesses: but one H6310
Dt 8: 3 of the **m** of the LORD doth man live. H6310
11: 6 the earth opened her **m**, and swallowed H6310
17: 6 At the **m** of two witnesses, or three H6310
6 to death; *but* at the **m** of one witness he H6310
18:18 my words in his **m**; and he shall speak H6310
19:15 he sinneth: at the **m** of two witnesses, H6310
15 or at the **m** of three witnesses, H6310
23:23 which thou hast promised with thy **m**. H6310
30:14 unto thee, in thy **m**, and in thy heart, H6310
32: 1 and hear, O earth, the words of my **m**. H6310
Jos 1: 8 not depart out of thy **m**; but thou shalt H6310
6:10 out of your **m**, until the day I bid you H6310
9:14 not *counsel* at the **m** of the LORD. H6310
10:18 stones upon the **m** of the cave, and set H6310
22 Then said Joshua, Open the **m** of the H6310
27 **m**, *which remain* until this very day. H6310
Jdg 7: 6 hand to their **m**, were three hundred H6310
9:38 Where *is* now thy **m**, wherewith thou H6310
11:35 I have opened my **m** unto the LORD, H6310
36 hast opened thy **m** unto the LORD, do H6310
36 out of thy **m**; forasmuch as the LORD H6310
18:19 hand upon thy **m**, and go with us, and H6310
1Sa 1:12 the LORD, that Eli marked her **m**. H6310
2: 1 in the LORD: my **m** is enlarged over H6310
3 come out of your **m**: for the LORD *is* a H6310
14:26 to his **m**: for the people feared the oath. H6310
27 to his **m**; and his eyes were enlightened. H6310
17:35 *it* out of his **m**: and when he arose H6310
2Sa 1:16 upon thy head; for thy **m** hath testified H6310
14: 3 him. So Joab put the words in her **m**. H6310
19 words in the **m** of thine handmaid: H6310
17:19 over the well's **m**, and spread ground H6440
18:25 **m**. And he came apace, and drew near. H6310
22: 9 **m** devoured: coals were kindled by it. H6310
1Ki 7:31 And the **m** of it within the chapiter and H6310
31 a cubit: but the **m** thereof *was* round H6310
31 and also upon the **m** of it *were* gravings H6310
8:15 which spake with his **m** unto David my H6310
24 also with thy **m**, and hast fulfilled *it* H6310
13:21 disobeyed the **m** of the LORD, and hast H6310
17:24 the word of the LORD in thy **m** *is* truth. H6310
19:18 every **m** which hath not kissed him. H6310
22:13 the king with one **m**: let thy word, I pray H6310
22 lying spirit in the **m** of all his prophets. H6310
23 a lying spirit in the **m** of all these thy H6310
2Ki 4:34 child, and put his **m** upon his mouth, H6310
34 mouth upon his **m**, and his eyes upon H6310
1Ch 16:12 wonders, and the judgments of his **m**; H6310
2Ch 6: 4 with his **m** to my father David, saying, H6310
15 spakest with thy **m**, and hast fulfilled *it* H6310
18:21 lying spirit in the **m** of all his prophets. H6310
22 a lying spirit in the **m** of these thy H6310
35:22 of Necho from the **m** of God, and came H6310
36:12 *speaking* from the **m** of the LORD. H6310
21 To fulfil the word of the LORD by the **m** H6310
22 *spoken* by the **m** of Jeremiah might be H6310
Ezr 1: 1 the LORD by the **m** of Jeremiah might H6310
Neh 9:20 manna from their **m**, and gavest them H6310
Est 7: 8 king's **m**, they covered Haman's face. H6310
Job 3: 1 After this opened Job his **m**, and cursed H6310
5:15 **m**, and from the hand of the mighty. H6310
16 hath hope, and iniquity stoppeth her **m**. H6310
7:11 Therefore I will not refrain my **m**; I will H6310
8: 2 words of thy **m** *be like* a strong wind? H6310
21 Till he fill thy **m** with laughing, and thy H6310
9:20 If I justify myself, mine own **m** shall H6310
12:11 Doth not the ear try words? and the **m** H2441
15: 5 For thy **m** uttereth thine iniquity, and H6310
6 Thine own **m** condemneth thee, and H6310
13 and lettest *such* words go out of thy **m**? H6310
30 by the breath of his **m** shall he go away. H6310
16: 5 *But* I would strengthen you with my **m**, H6310
10 They have gaped upon me with their **m**; H6310
19:16 no answer; I entreated him with my **m**. H6310
20:12 Though wickedness be sweet in his **m**, H6310
13 it not; but keep it still within his **m**: H2441
21: 5 and lay *your* hand upon *your* **m**. H6310
22:22 Receive, I pray thee, the law from his **m**, H6310
23: 4 him, and fill my **m** with arguments. H6310
12 of his **m** more than my necessary *food*. H6310
29: 9 talking, and laid *their* hand on their **m**. H6310
10 tongue cleaved to the roof of their **m**. H2441
23 their **m** wide *as* for the latter rain. H6310
Job 31:27 enticed, or my **m** hath kissed my hand: H6310
30 Neither have I suffered my **m** to sin by H2441
32: 5 no answer in the **m** of *these* three men, H6310
33: 2 Behold, now I have opened my **m**, my H6310
2 my tongue hath spoken in my **m**. H2441
34: 3 For the ear trieth words, as the **m** H2441
35:16 Therefore doth Job open his **m** in vain; H6310
37: 2 and the sound *that* goeth out of his **m**. H6310
40: 4 thee? I will lay mine hand upon my **m**. H6310
23 that he can draw up Jordan into his **m**. H6310
41:19 Out of his **m** go burning lamps, *and* H6310
21 coals, and a flame goeth out of his **m**. H6310
Ps 5: 9 For *there is* no faithfulness in their **m**; H6310
8: 2 Out of the **m** of babes and sucklings H6310
10: 7 His **m** is full of cursing and deceit and H6310
17: 3 *that* my **m** shall not transgress. H6310
10 fat: with their **m** they speak proudly. H6310
18: 8 **m** devoured: coals were kindled by it. H6310
19:14 Let the words of my **m**, and the H6310
22:21 Save me from the lion's **m**: for thou hast H6310
32: 9 whose **m** must be held in with H5716
33: 6 the host of them by the breath of his **m**. H6310
34: 1 his praise *shall* continually *be* in my **m**. H6310
35:21 Yea, they opened their **m** wide against H6310
36: 3 The words of his **m** *are* iniquity and H6310
37:30 The **m** of the righteous speaketh H6310
38:13 as a dumb man *that* openeth not his **m**. H6310
14 not, and in whose **m** *are* no reproofs. H6310
39: 1 I will keep my **m** with a bridle, while H6310
9 I was dumb, I opened not my **m**; H6310
40: 3 And he hath put a new song in my **m**, H6310
49: 3 My **m** shall speak of wisdom; and the H6310
50:16 shouldest take my covenant in thy **m**? H6310
19 Thou givest thy **m** to evil, and thy H6310
51:15 O Lord, open thou my lips; and my **m** H6310
54: 2 O God; give ear to the words of my **m**. H6310
55:21 *The words* of his **m** were smoother H6310
58: 6 Break their teeth, O God, in their **m**: H6310
59: 7 Behold, they belch out with their **m**: H6310
12 *For* the sin of their **m** *and* the words of H6310
62: 4 their **m**, but they curse inwardly. Selah. H6310
63: 5 my **m** shall praise *thee* with joyful lips: H6310
11 glory: but the **m** of them that speak H6310
66:14 Which my lips have uttered, and my **m** H6310
17 I cried unto him with my **m**, and he was H6310
69:15 and let not the pit shut her **m** upon me. H6310
71: 8 Let my **m** be filled *with* thy praise *and* H6310
15 My **m** shall shew forth thy H6310
73: 9 They set their **m** against the heavens, H6310
78: 1 incline your ears to the words of my **m**. H6310
2 I will open my **m** in a parable: I will H6310
36 him with their **m**, and they lied unto H6310
81:10 open thy **m** wide, and I will fill it. H6310
89: 1 for ever: with my **m** will I make known H6310
103: 5 Who satisfieth thy **m** with good *things;* H5716
105: 5 wonders, and the judgments of his **m**; H6310
107:42 and all iniquity shall stop her **m**. H6310
109: 2 For the **m** of the wicked and the mouth H6310
2 For the mouth of the wicked and the **m** H6310
30 LORD with my **m**; yea, I will praise him H6310
119:13 I declared all the judgments of thy **m**. H6310
43 **m**; for I have hoped in thy judgments. H6310
72 The law of thy **m** *is* better unto me than H6310
88 so shall I keep the testimony of thy **m**. H6310
103 taste! *yea, sweeter* than honey to my **m**! H6310
108 offerings of my **m**, O LORD, and teach H6310
131 I opened my **m**, and panted: for I H6310
126: 2 Then was our **m** filled with laughter, H6310
137: 6 to the roof of my **m**; if I prefer not H2441
138: 4 when they hear the words of thy **m**. H6310
141: 3 Set a watch, O LORD, before my **m**; H6310
7 at the grave's **m**, as when one cutteth H6310
144: 8 Whose **m** speaketh vanity, and their H6310
11 children, whose **m** speaketh vanity, H6310
145:21 My **m** shall speak the praise of the H6310
149: 6 **m**, and a twoedged sword in their hand; H1627
Prv 2: 6 out of his **m** *cometh* knowledge H6310
4: 5 decline from the words of my **m**. H6310
24 Put away from thee a froward **m**, and H6310
5: 3 and her **m** *is* smoother than oil: H2441
7 depart not from the words of my **m**. H6310
6: 2 the words of thy **m**, thou art taken with H6310
2 thou art taken with the words of thy **m**. H6310
12 wicked man, walketh with a froward **m**. H6310
7:24 and attend to the words of my **m**. H6310
8: 7 For my **m** shall speak truth; and H2441
8 All the words of my **m** *are* in H6310
13 evil way, and the froward **m**, do I hate. H6310
10: 6 violence covereth the **m** of the wicked. H6310

M

Prv 10:11 The **m** of a righteous *man is* a well of H6310
11 violence covereth the **m** of the wicked. H6310
14 Wise *men* lay up knowledge: but the **m** H6310
31 The **m** of the just bringeth forth H6310
32 **m** of the wicked *speaketh* frowardness. H6310
11: 9 An hypocrite with *his* **m** destroyeth his H6310
11 it is overthrown by the **m** of the wicked. H6310
12: 6 the **m** of the upright shall deliver them. H6310
14 good by the fruit of *his* **m**: and the H6310
13: 2 by the fruit of *his* **m**: but the soul of the H6310
3 He that keepeth his **m** keepeth his life: H6310
14: 3 In the **m** of the foolish *is* a rod of pride: H6310
15: 2 the **m** of fools poureth out foolishness. H6310
14 but the **m** of fools feedeth H6310+H6440
23 A man hath joy by the answer of his **m**: H6310
28 to answer: but the **m** of the wicked H6310
16:10 his **m** transgresseth not in judgment. H6310
23 The heart of the wise teacheth his **m**, H6310
26 for himself; for his **m** craveth it of him. H6310
18: 4 The words of a man's **m** *are as* deep H6310
6 and his **m** calleth for strokes. H6310
7 A fool's **m** *is* his destruction, and his H6310
20 the fruit of his **m**; *and* with the increase H6310
19:24 not so much as bring it to his **m** again. H6310
28 the **m** of the wicked devoureth iniquity. H6310
20:17 his **m** shall be filled with gravel. H6310
21:23 Whoso keepeth his **m** and his tongue H6310
22:14 The **m** of strange women *is* a deep pit: H6310
24: 7 a fool: he openeth not his **m** in the gate. H6310
26: 7 equal: so *is* a parable in the **m** of fools. H6310
9 so *is* a parable in the **m** of fools. H6310
15 grieveth him to bring it again to his **m**. H6310
28 by it; and a flattering **m** worketh ruin. H6310
27: 2 **m**; a stranger, and not thine own lips. H6310
30:20 and wipeth her **m**, and saith, I have H6310
32 evil, *lay* thine hand upon thy **m**. H6310
31: 8 Open thy **m** for the dumb in the cause H6310
9 Open thy **m**, judge righteously, and H6310
26 She openeth her **m** with wisdom; and H6310
Ecc 5: 2 Be not rash with thy **m**, and let not H6310
6 Suffer not thy **m** to cause thy flesh to H6310
6: 7 All the labour of man *is* for his **m**, and H6310
10:12 The words of a wise man's **m** *are* H6310
13 The beginning of the words of his **m** *is* H6310
Song 1: 2 his **m**: for thy love *is* better than wine. H6310
5:16 His **m** *is* most sweet: yea, he *is* H2441
7: 9 And the roof of thy **m** like the best wine H2441
Isa 1:20 for the **m** of the LORD hath spoken *it*. H6310
5:14 and opened her **m** without measure: H6310
6: 7 And he laid *it* upon my **m**, and said, Lo, H6310
9:12 Israel with open **m**. For all this his H6310
17 and every **m** speaketh folly. For H6310
10:14 the wing, or opened the **m**, or peeped. H6310
11: 4 with the rod of his **m**, and with the H6310
19: 7 the brooks, by the **m** of the brooks, and H6310
29:13 *me* with their **m**, and with their lips H6310
30: 2 have not asked at my **m**; to strengthen H6310
34:16 want her mate: for my **m** it hath H6310
40: 5 for the **m** of the LORD hath spoken *it*. H6310
45:23 is gone out of my **m** *in* righteousness, H6310
48: 3 forth out of my **m**, and I shewed them; H6310
49: 2 And he hath made my **m** like a sharp H6310
51:16 And I have put my words in thy **m**, and H6310
53: 7 he opened not his **m**: he is brought as a H6310
7 is dumb, so he openeth not his **m**. H6310
9 neither *was any* deceit in his **m**. H6310
55:11 forth out of my **m**: it shall not return H6310
57: 4 make ye a wide **m**, *and* draw out the H6310
58:14 for the **m** of the LORD hath spoken *it*. H6310
59:21 I have put in thy **m**, shall not depart out H6310
21 not depart out of thy **m**, nor out of the H6310
21 nor out of the **m** of thy seed, nor out H6310
21 nor out of the **m** of thy seed's seed, H6310
62: 2 which the **m** of the LORD shall name. H6310
Jer 1: 9 and touched my **m**. And the LORD said H6310
9 Behold, I have put my words in thy **m**. H6310
5:14 my words in thy **m** fire, and this people H6310
7:28 is perished, and is cut off from their **m**. H6310
9: 8 his **m**, but in heart he layeth his wait. H6310
12 *is he* to whom the **m** of the LORD hath H6310
20 the word of his **m**, and teach your H6310
12: 2 in their **m**, and far from their reins. H6310
15:19 shalt be as my **m**: let them return unto H6310
23:16 *and* not out of the **m** of the LORD. H6310
32: 4 speak with him **m** to mouth, and his H6310
4 to **m**, and his eyes shall behold his eyes; H6310
34: 3 speak with thee **m** to mouth, and thou H6310
3 to **m**, and thou shalt go to Babylon. H6310
36: 4 wrote from the **m** of Jeremiah all the H6310

Jer 36: 6 written from my **m**, the words of the H6310
17 thou write all these words at his **m**? H6310
18 unto me with his **m**, and I wrote *them* H6310
27 wrote at the **m** of Jeremiah, saying, H6310
32 therein from the **m** of Jeremiah all the H6310
44:17 out of our own **m**, to burn incense unto H6310
26 more be named in the **m** of any man of H6310
45: 1 in a book at the **m** of Jeremiah, in the H6310
48:28 her nest in the sides of the hole's **m**. H6310
51:44 forth out of his **m** that which he hath H6310
Lam 2:16 All thine enemies have opened their **m** H6310
3:29 He putteth his **m** in the dust; if so be H6310
38 Out of the **m** of the most High H6310
4: 4 to the roof of his **m** for thirst: the young H2441
Ezk 2: 8 open thy **m**, and eat that I give thee. H6310
3: 2 So I opened my **m**, and he caused me to H6310
3 it was in my **m** as honey for sweetness. H6310
17 my **m**, and give them warning from me. H6310
26 to the roof of thy **m**, that thou shalt be H2441
27 I will open thy **m**, and thou shalt say H6310
4:14 there abominable flesh into my **m**. H6310
16:56 by thy **m** in the day of thy pride, H6310
63 never open thy **m** any more because of H6310
21:22 to open the **m** in the slaughter, to H6310
24:27 In that day shall thy **m** be opened to H6310
29:21 the opening of the **m** in the midst of H6310
33: 7 at my **m**, and warn them from me. H6310
22 had opened my **m**, until he came to me H6310
22 morning; and my **m** was opened, and I H6310
31 for with their **m** they shew much love, H6310
34:10 **m**, that they may not be meat for them. H6310
35:13 Thus with your **m** ye have boasted H6310
Dan 3:26 came near to the **m** of the burning fiery H8651
4:31 While the word *was* in the king's **m**, H6433
6:17 and laid upon the **m** of the den; and the H6433
7: 5 three ribs in the **m** of it between the H6433
8 of man, and a **m** speaking great things. H6433
20 that had eyes, and a **m** that spake very H6433
10: 3 nor wine in my **m**, neither did I anoint H6310
16 then I opened my **m**, and spake, and H6310
Hos 2:17 Baalim out of her **m**, and they shall no H6310
6: 5 the words of my **m**: and thy judgments H6310
8: 1 *Set* the trumpet to thy **m**. *He shall come* H2441
Joel 1: 5 new wine; for it is cut off from your **m**. H6310
Am 3:12 taketh out of the **m** of the lion two legs, H6310
Mic 4: 4 **m** of the LORD of hosts hath spoken *it*. H6310
6:12 and their tongue *is* deceitful in their **m**. H6310
7: 5 thy **m** from her that lieth in thy bosom. H6310
16 upon *their* **m**, their ears shall be deaf. H6310
Nah 3:12 shall even fall into the **m** of the eater. H6310
Zep 3:13 be found in their **m**: for they shall feed H6310
Zec 5: 8 the weight of lead upon the **m** thereof. H6310
8: 9 words by the **m** of the prophets, which H6310
9: 7 his blood out of his **m**, and his H6310
14:12 tongue shall consume away in their **m**. H6310
Mal 2: 6 The law of truth was in his **m**, and H6310
7 seek the law at his **m**: for he *is* the H6310
Mt 4: 4 that proceedeth out of the **m** of God. *G4750*
5: 2 And he opened his **m**, and taught them, *G4750*
12:34 of the heart the **m** speaketh. *G4750*
13:35 I will open my **m** in parables; I will *G4750*
15: 8 me with their **m**, and honoureth me *G4750*
11 Not that which goeth into the **m** *G4750*
11 out of the **m**, this defileth a man. *G4750*
17 entereth in at the **m** goeth into the *G4750*
18 proceed out of the **m** come forth from *G4750*
17:27 hast opened his **m**, thou shalt find a *G4750*
18:16 two more, that in the **m** of two or three *G4750*
21:16 never read, Out of the **m** of babes and *G4750*
Lk 1:64 And his **m** was opened immediately, *G4750*
70 As he spake by the **m** of his holy *G4750*
4:22 out of his **m**. And they said, Is not *G4750*
6:45 abundance of the heart his **m** speaketh. *G4750*
11:54 of his **m**, that they might accuse him. *G4750*
19:22 Out of thine own **m** will I judge thee, *G4750*
21:15 For I will give you a **m** and wisdom, *G4750*
22:71 we ourselves have heard of his own **m**. *G4750*
Jn 19:29 put *it* upon hyssop, and put *it* to his **m**. *G4750*
Act 1:16 Holy Ghost by the **m** of David spake *G4750*
3:18 shewed by the **m** of all his prophets, *G4750*
21 hath spoken by the **m** of all his holy *G4750*
4:25 Who by the **m** of thy servant David *G4750*
8:32 his shearer, so opened he not his **m**: *G4750*
35 Then Philip opened his **m**, and began at *G4750*
10:34 Then Peter opened *his* **m**, and said, Of a *G4750*
11: 8 hath at any time entered into my **m**. *G4750*
15: 7 Gentiles by my **m** should hear the word *G4750*
27 shall also tell *you* the same things by **m**. *G3056*
18:14 about to open *his* **m**, Gallio said unto *G4750*

Act 22:14 and shouldest hear the voice of his **m**. *G4750*
23: 2 stood by him to smite him on the **m**. *G4750*
Ro 3:14 Whose **m** *is* full of cursing and *G4750*
19 law: that every **m** may be stopped, and *G4750*
10: 8 thee, *even* in thy **m**, and in thy heart: *G4750*
9 That if thou shalt confess with thy **m** *G4750*
10 **m** confession is made unto salvation. *G4750*
15: 6 That ye may with one mind *and* one **m** *G4750*
1Co 9: 9 not muzzle the **m** of the ox that treadeth
2Co 6:11 O *ye* Corinthians, our **m** is open unto *G4750*
13: 1 coming to you. In the **m** of two or three *G4750*
Eph 4:29 out of your **m**, but that which is good *G4750*
6:19 that I may open my **m** boldly, to make *G4750*
Col 3: 8 filthy communication out of your **m**. *G4750*
2Th 2: 8 the spirit of his **m**, and shall destroy *G4750*
2Ti 4:17 I was delivered out of the **m** of the lion. *G4750*
Jas 3:10 Out of the same **m** proceedeth blessing *G4750*
1Pt 2:22 no sin, neither was guile found in his **m**: *G4750*
Jude 16 own lusts; and their **m** speaketh great *G4750*
Rev 1:16 stars: and out of his **m** went a sharp *G4750*
2:16 against them with the sword of my **m**. *G4750*
3:16 nor hot, I will spue thee out of my **m**. *G4750*
9:19 For their power is in their **m**, and in *G4750*
10: 9 but it shall be in thy **m** sweet as honey. *G4750*
10 up; and it was in my **m** sweet as honey: *G4750*
11: 5 out of their **m**, and devoureth their *G4750*
12:15 And the serpent cast out of his **m** water *G4750*
16 earth opened her **m**, and swallowed up *G4750*
16 which the dragon cast out of his **m**. *G4750*
13: 2 of a bear, and his **m** as the mouth of a *G4750*
2 his mouth as the **m** of a lion: and the *G4750*
5 And there was given unto him a **m** *G4750*
6 And he opened his **m** in blasphemy *G4750*
14: 5 And in their **m** was found no guile: for *G4750*
16:13 *come* out of the **m** of the dragon, and *G4750*
13 and out of the **m** of the beast, and out *G4750*
13 and out of the **m** of the false prophet. *G4750*
19:15 And out of his **m** goeth a sharp sword, *G4750*
21 out of his **m**: and all the fowls were *G4750*

MOUTHS

Gen 44: 8 in our sacks' **m**, we brought again unto H6310
Dt 31:19 put it in their **m**, that this song may H6310
21 out of the **m** of their seed: for I know H6310
Ps 22:13 They gaped upon me *with* their **m**, *as* a H6310
78:30 But while their meat *was* yet in their **m**, H6310
115: 5 They have **m**, but they speak not: eyes H6310
135:16 They have **m**, but they speak not; eyes H6310
17 neither is there *any* breath in their **m**. H6310
Isa 52:15 kings shall shut their **m** at him: for *that* H6310
Jer 44:25 spoken with your **m**, and fulfilled with H6310
Lam 3:46 All our enemies have opened their **m** H6310
Dan 6:22 shut the lions' **m**, that they have not H6433
Mic 3: 5 **m**, they even prepare war against him. H6310
Tit 1:11 Whose **m** must be stopped, who *G1993*
Heb 11:33 promises, stopped the **m** of lions, *G4750*
Jas 3: 3 Behold, we put bits in the horses' **m**, *G4750*
Rev 9:17 lions; and out of their **m** issued fire and *G4750*
18 brimstone, which issued out of their **m**. *G4750*

MOVE

Ex 11: 7 shall not a dog **m** his tongue, against H2782
Lev 11:10 rivers, of all that **m** in the waters, and H8318
Dt 23:25 but thou shalt not **m** a sickle unto thy H5130
32:21 vanities: and I will **m** them to jealousy
Jdg 13:25 And the spirit of the LORD began to **m** H6470
2Sa 7:10 of their own, and **m** no more; neither H7264
2Ki 21: 8 Neither will I make the feet of Israel **m** H5110
23:18 alone; let no man **m** his bones. So they H5128
Jer 10: 4 nails and with hammers, that it **m** not. H6328
Mic 7:17 they shall **m** out of their holes like H7264
Mt 23: 4 not **m** them with one of their fingers. *G2795*
Act 17:28 For in him we live, and **m**, and have our *G2795*
20:24 But none of these things **m** me, *G3056+G4160*

MOVEABLE

Prv 5: 6 are **m**, *that* thou canst not know *them*. H5128

MOVED

Gen 1: 2 of God **m** upon the face of the waters. H7363
7:21 And all flesh died that **m** upon the H7430
Dt 32:21 They have **m** me to jealousy with *that*
Jos 10:21 in peace: none **m** his tongue against H2782
15:18 *unto him*, that she **m** him to ask of her H5496
Jdg 1:14 *to him*, that she **m** him to ask of her H5496
Ru 1:19 all the city was **m** about them, and they H1949
1Sa 1:13 only her lips **m**, but her voice was not H5128
2Sa 18:33 And the king was much **m**, and went up H7264
22: 8 **m** and shook, because he was wroth. H7264

2Sa 24: 1 Israel, and he **m** David against them H5496
1Ch 16:30 also shall be stable, that it be not **m**. H4131
17: 9 and shall be **m** no more; neither shall H7264
2Ch 18:31 and God **m** them *to depart* from him. H5496
Ezr 4:15 that they have **m** sedition within the H5648
Est 5: 9 he stood not up, nor **m** for him, he was H2111
Job 37: 1 trembleth, and is **m** out of his place. H5425
41:23 firm in themselves; they cannot be **m**. H4131
Ps 10: 6 be **m**: for *I shall* never *be* in adversity. H4131
13: 4 that trouble me rejoice when I am **m**. H4131
15: 5 doeth these *things* shall never be **m**. H4131
16: 8 *he is* at my right hand, I shall not be **m**. H4131
18: 7 also of the hills **m** and were shaken, H7264
21: 7 of the most High he shall not be **m**. H4131
30: 6 my prosperity I said, I shall never be **m**. H4131
46: 5 she shall not be **m**: God shall help her, H4131
6 kingdoms were **m**: he uttered his voice, H4131
55:22 shall never suffer the righteous to be **m**. H4131
62: 2 *is* my defence; I shall not be greatly **m**. H4131
6 *he is* my defence; I shall not be **m**. H4131
66: 9 life, and suffereth not our feet to be **m**. H4132
68: 8 *even* Sinai itself *was* **m** at the presence of
78:58 high places, and **m** him to jealousy with
93: 1 also is stablished, that it cannot be **m**. H4131
96:10 that it shall not be **m**: he shall judge the H4131
99: 1 the cherubims; let the earth be **m**. H5120
112: 6 Surely he shall not be **m** for ever: the H4131
121: 3 He will not suffer thy foot to be **m**: he H4132
Prv 12: 3 the root of the righteous shall not be **m**. H4131
Song 5: 4 *door*, and my bowels were **m** for him. H1993
Isa 6: 4 And the posts of the door **m** at the H5128
7: 2 And his heart was **m**, and the heart of H5128
2 trees of the wood are **m** with the wind. H5128
10:14 was none that **m** the wing, or opened H5074
14: 9 Hell from beneath is **m** for thee to meet H7264
19: 1 of Egypt shall be **m** at his presence, H5128
24:19 dissolved, the earth is **m** exceedingly. H4131
40:20 a graven image, *that* shall not be **m**. H4131
41: 7 it with nails, *that* it should not be **m**. H4131
Jer 4:24 trembled, and all the hills **m** lightly. H7043
25:16 And they shall drink, and be **m**, and be H1607
46: 7 whose waters are **m** as the rivers? H1607
8 *his* waters are **m** like the rivers; and H1607
49:21 The earth is **m** at the noise of their fall, H7493
50:46 the earth is **m**, and the cry is heard H7493
Dan 8: 7 ram, and he was **m** with choler against
11:11 And the king of the south shall be **m**
Mt 9:36 he was **m** with compassion on *G4697*
14:14 and was **m** with compassion toward *G4697*
18:27 Then the lord of that servant was **m** *G4697*
20:24 And when the ten heard *it*, they were **m** *G23*
21:10 all the city was **m**, saying, Who is this? *G4579*
Mk 1:41 And Jesus, **m** with compassion, put *G4697*
6:34 people, and was **m** with compassion *G4697*
15:11 But the chief priests **m** the people, that *G383*
Act 2:25 my right hand, that I should not be **m**: *G4531*
7: 9 And the patriarchs, **m** with envy, sold *G2206*
17: 5 But the Jews which believed not, **m** *G2206*
21:30 And all the city was **m**, and the people *G2795*
Col 1:23 and *be* not **m** away from the hope *G3334*
1Th 3: 3 That no man should be **m** by these *G4525*
Heb 11: 7 not seen as yet, **m** with fear, prepared *G2125*
12:28 which cannot be **m**, let us have grace, *G761*
2Pt 1:21 *as they were* **m** by the Holy Ghost. *G5342*
Rev 6:14 and island were **m** out of their places. *G2795*

MOVEDST
Job 2: 3 although thou **m** me against him, to H5496

MOVER
Act 24: 5 *fellow*, and a **m** of sedition among all *G2795*

MOVETH
Gen 1:21 living creature that **m**, which the waters H7430
28 living thing that **m** upon the earth. H7430
9: 2 the air, upon all that **m** *upon* the earth, H7430
Lev 11:46 creature that **m** in the waters, and of H7430
Job 40:17 He **m** his tail like a cedar: the sinews of H2654
Ps 69:34 seas, and every thing that **m** therein. H7430
Prv 23:31 in the cup, *when* it **m** itself aright. H1980
Ezk 47: 9 that liveth, which **m**, whithersoever the H8317

MOVING
Gen 1:20 abundantly the **m** creature that hath H8318
9: 3 Every **m** thing that liveth shall be meat H7431
Job 16: 5 my mouth, and the **m** of my lips should H5205
Prv 16:30 **m** his lips he bringeth evil to pass. H7169
Jn 5: 3 waiting for the **m** of the water. *G2796*

MOWER
Ps 129: 7 Wherewith the **m** filleth not his hand; H7114

MOWINGS
Am 7: 1 *was* the latter growth after the king's **m**. H1488

MOWN
Ps 72: 6 like rain upon the **m** grass: as showers H1488

MOZA
1Ch 2:46 **M**, and Gazez: and Haran begat Gazez. H4162
8:36 and Zimri; and Zimri begat **M**, H4162
37 And **M** begat Binea: Rapha *was* his H4162
9:42 and Zimri; and Zimri begat **M**; H4162
43 And **M** begat Binea; and Rephaiah his H4162

MOZAH
Jos 18:26 And Mizpeh, and Chephirah, and **M**, H4681

MUCH
Gen 23: 9 end of his field; for as **m** money as it is H3966
26:16 us; for thou art **m** mightier than we. H3966
30:43 and had **m** cattle, and maidservants, H7227
34:12 Ask me never so **m** dowry and gift, and H3966
41:49 sand of the sea, very **m**, until he left H7235
43:34 was five times so **m** as any of theirs. H7235
44: 1 *with* food, as **m** as they can carry, and H834
50:20 as *it is* this day, to save **m** people alive. H7227
Ex 12:38 flocks, and herds, *even* very **m** cattle. H3515
42 It *is* a night to be **m** observed unto the
14:28 remained not so **m** as one of them. H5704
16: 5 shall be twice as **m** as they gather daily. H834
18 he that gathered **m** had nothing over, H7235
22 gathered twice as **m** bread, two omers H4932
30:23 cinnamon half so **m**, *even* two hundred H4276
36: 5 The people bring **m** more than enough H7235
7 for all the work to make it, and too **m**. H3498
Lev 7:10 of Aaron have, one *as* **m** as another.
13: 7 But if the scab spread **m** abroad in the H6581
22 And if it spread **m** abroad in the skin, H6581
27 *and* if it be spread **m** abroad in the H6581
35 But if the scall spread **m** in the skin H6581
14:21 And if he *be* poor, and cannot get so **m**;
Nu 16: 3 them, *Ye take* too **m** upon you, seeing H7227
7 *take* too **m** upon you, ye sons of Levi. H7227
20:20 with **m** people, and with a strong hand. H3515
21: 4 was **m** discouraged because of the way. H7114
6 the people; and **m** people of Israel died. H7227
Dt 2: 5 land, no, not so **m** as a foot breadth; H5704
3:19 I know that ye have **m** cattle,) shall H7227
28:38 Thou shalt carry **m** seed out into the H7227
31:27 and how **m** more after my death? H7227
Jos 11: 4 hosts with them, **m** people, even as the H7227
13: 1 yet very **m** land to be possessed. H7235
19: 9 of Judah was too **m** for them: therefore H7227
22: 8 Return with **m** riches unto your tents, H7227
8 and with very **m** cattle, with silver, and H7227
8 and with very **m** raiment: divide the H7235
Ru 1:13 for it grieveth me **m** for your sakes that H3966
1Sa 2:16 and *then* take *as* **m** as thy soul desireth;
14:30 How **m** more, if haply the people had H637
30 not been now a **m** greater slaughter
18:30 of Saul; so that his name was **m** set by. H3966
19: 2 But Jonathan Saul's son delighted **m** in H3966
20:13 The LORD do so and **m** more to H3254
23: 3 here in Judah: how **m** more then if we H637
26:24 And, behold, as thy life was **m** set by H1431
24 so let my life be **m** set by in the eyes of H1431
2Sa 4:11 How **m** more, when wicked men have H637
8: 8 king David took exceeding **m** brass. H7235
13:34 there came **m** people by the way of H7227
14:25 there was none to be so **m** praised as H3966
16:11 my life: how **m** more now *may this* H637
17:12 him there shall not be left so **m** as one. H1571
18:33 And the king was **m** moved, and went up
1Ki 4:29 exceeding **m**, and largeness of heart, H7235
8:27 **m** less this house that I have builded? H637
10: 2 spices, and very **m** gold, and precious H7227
12:28 them, It is too **m** for you to go up to H7227
2Ki 5:13 done *it*? how **m** rather then, H637+H3588
10:18 Baal a little; *but* Jehu shall serve him **m**. H7235
12:10 that *there was* **m** money in the chest, H7227
21: 6 he wrought **m** wickedness in the sight H7235
16 innocent blood very **m**, till he had filled H7235
1Ch 18: 8 David very **m** brass, wherewith H7227
20: 2 also exceeding **m** spoil out of the city. H7235
22: 4 Tyre brought **m** cedar wood to David. H7230
8 **m** blood upon the earth in my sight. H7227
2Ch 2:16 of Lebanon, as **m** as thou shalt need: H3605
6:18 how **m** less this house which I have built! H637
14:13 and they carried away very **m** spoil. H7235
14 there was exceeding **m** spoil in them. H7227
17:13 And he had **m** business in the cities of H7227
20:25 in gathering of the spoil, it was so **m**. H7227
24:11 saw that *there was* **m** money, the king's H7227
25: 9 is able to give thee **m** more than this. H7235
13 thousand of them, and took **m** spoil. H7227
26:10 wells: for he had **m** cattle, both in the H7227
27: 3 and on the wall of Ophel he built **m**. H7230
5 of barley. So **m** did the children of H1931
28: 8 took also away **m** spoil from them, and H7227
30:13 And there assembled at Jerusalem **m** H7227
32: 4 So there was gathered **m** people H7227
4 of Assyria come, and find **m** water? H7227
15 fathers: how **m** less shall your H637+H3588
27 And Hezekiah had exceeding **m** riches H7235
29 God had given him substance very **m**. H7227
33: 6 he wrought **m** evil in the sight of the H7235
36:14 transgressed very **m** after all the H7235
Ezr 7:22 oil, and salt without prescribing *how* **m**.
10:13 and *it is* a time of **m** rain, and we are not
Neh 4:10 and *there is* **m** rubbish; so that we H7235
6:16 *things*, they were **m** cast down in their H3966
9:37 And it yieldeth **m** increase unto the H7235
Est 1:18 *there arise* too **m** contempt and wrath. H1767
Job 4:19 How **m** less *in* them that dwell in houses H637
9:14 How **m** less shall I answer him, H637+H3588
15:10 very aged men, **m** elder than thy father. H3524
16 How **m** more abominable and filthy *is*
25: 6 How **m** less man, *that is* a worm? and H637
31:25 and because mine hand had gotten **m**; H3524
34:19 *How* **m** *less to him* that accepteth not the
42:10 gave Job twice as **m** as he had before. H4932
Ps 19:10 gold, yea, than **m** fine gold: sweeter H7227
33:16 man is not delivered by **m** strength. H7230
35:18 I will praise thee among **m** people. H6099
119:14 of thy testimonies, as *m as* in all riches.
107 I am afflicted very **m**: quicken me, O H3966
Prv 7:21 With her **m** fair speech she caused him H7230
11:31 **m** more the wicked and the sinner. H637
13:23 **M** food *is in* the tillage of the poor: but H7230
14: 4 **m** increase *is* by the strength of the ox. H7230
15: 6 In the house of the righteous *is* **m** H7227
11 the LORD: how **m** more then the hearts H637
16:16 How **m** better *is it* to get wisdom than
17: 7 Excellent speech becometh not a fool: **m** H637
19: 7 do hate him: how **m** more do his friends H637
10 Delight is not seemly for a fool; **m** less H637
24 not so **m** as bring it to his mouth again. H1571
21:27 *is* abomination: how **m** more, *when* he H637
25:16 Hast thou found honey? eat so **m** as is H1767
27 *It is* not good to eat **m** honey: so *for* H7235
Ecc 1:18 For in **m** wisdom *is* much grief: and he H7230
18 For in much wisdom *is* **m** grief: and he H7230
5:12 he eat little or **m**: but the abundance H7235
17 **m** sorrow and wrath with his sickness. H7235
20 For he shall not **m** remember the days H7235
7:16 Be not righteous over **m**; neither make H7235
17 Be not over **m** wicked, neither be thou H7235
9:18 war: but one sinner destroyeth **m** good. H7235
10:18 By **m** slothfulness the building decayeth;
12:12 and **m** study *is* a weariness of the flesh. H7235
Song 4:10 *my* spouse! how **m** better is thy love than
Isa 21: 7 he hearkened diligently with **m** heed: H7227
30:33 thereof *is* fire and **m** wood; the breath H7235
56:12 be as this day, *and* **m** more abundant. H3966
Jer 2:22 nitre, and take thee **m** soap, *yet* thine H7235
36 Why gaddest thou about so **m** to H3966
40:12 wine and summer fruits very **m**. H7235
Ezk 14:21 For thus saith the Lord GOD; How **m** H637
15: 5 for no work: how **m** less shall it be meet H7227
17:15 give him horses and **m** people. Shall he H7227
22: 5 thee, *which art* infamous *and* **m** vexed. H7227
23:32 and had in derision; it containeth **m**. H4767
26: 7 and companies, and **m** people. H7227
33:31 mouth they shew **m** love, *but* their heart
Dan 4:12 the fruit thereof **m**, and in it *was* meat H7690
21 the fruit thereof **m**, and in it *was* meat H7690
7: 5 said thus unto it, Arise, devour **m** flesh. H7690
28 my cogitations **m** troubled me, and my H7690
11:13 with a great army and with **m** riches. H7227
Joel 2: 6 Before their face the people shall be **m**
Jna 4:11 and their left hand; and *also* **m** cattle? H7227
Nah 2:10 together, and **m** pain *is* in all loins, H2479
Hag 1: 6 Ye have sown **m**, and bring in little; ye H7235
9 Ye looked for **m**, and, lo, *it came* to H7235
Mal 3:13 What have we spoken *so* **m** against thee?
Mt 6: 7 shall be heard for their **m** speaking. *G4180*

Mt 6:26 them. Are ye not **m** better than they? G3123
30 **m** more *clothe* you, O ye of little faith? G4183
7:11 your children, how **m** more shall your G4214
10:25 Beelzebub, how **m** more *shall they call* G4214
12:12 How **m** then is a man better than a G4214
13: 5 they had not **m** earth: and forthwith G4183
15:33 should we have so **m** bread in the G5118
26: 9 been sold for **m**, and given to the poor. G4183
Mk 1:45 to publish *it* **m**, and to blaze abroad G4183
2: 2 *them*, no, not so **m** as about the door: G3366
3:20 that they could not so **m** as eat bread. G3383
4: 5 ground, where it had not **m** earth; and G4183
5:10 And he besought him **m** that he would G4183
21 the other side, **m** people gathered unto G4183
24 And *Jesus* went with him; and **m** G4183
6:31 and they had no leisure so **m** as to eat.
34 And Jesus, when he came out, saw **m** G4183
7:36 charged them, so **m** the more a great G3123
10:14 But when Jesus saw *it*, he was **m** G23
41 to be **m** displeased with James and John. G23
12:41 and many that were rich cast in **m**. G4183
Lk 5:15 But so **m** the more went there a fame G3123
6: 3 ye not read so **m** as this, what David G3761
34 lend to sinners, to receive as **m** again. G2470
7:11 disciples went with him, and **m** people. G4183
12 and **m** people of the city was with her. G2425
26 unto you, and **m** more than a prophet. G4055
47 for she loved **m**: but to whom little is G4183
8: 4 And when **m** people were gathered G4183
9:37 down from the hill, **m** people met him. G4183
10:40 But Martha was cumbered about **m** G4183
11:13 your children: how **m** more shall *your* G4214
12:19 Soul, thou hast **m** goods laid up for G4183
24 **m** more are ye better than the fowls? G4214
28 the oven; how **m** more *will he clothe* G4214
48 unto whomsoever **m** is given, of him G4183
48 of him shall be **m** required: and to G4183
48 **m**, of him they will ask the more. G4183
16: 5 first, How **m** owest thou unto my lord? G4214
7 Then said he to another, And how **m** G4214
10 least is faithful also in **m**: and he that is G4183
10 is unjust in the least is unjust also in **m**. G4183
18:13 would not lift up so **m** as *his* eyes unto G3761
39 but he cried so **m** the more, *Thou* son G4183
19:15 **m** every man had gained by trading. G5101
24: 4 And it came to pass, as they were **m** G1280
Jn 3:23 because there was **m** water there: and G4183
6:10 Now there was **m** grass in the place. So G4183
11 of the fishes as **m** as they would. G3745
7:12 And there was **m** murmuring among G4183
12: 9 **M** people of the Jews therefore knew G4183
12 On the next day **m** people that were G4183
24 but if it die, it bringeth forth **m** fruit. G4183
14:30 Hereafter I will not talk **m** with you: for G4183
15: 5 bringeth forth **m** fruit: for without me G4183
8 **m** fruit; so shall ye be my disciples. G4183
Act 5: 8 so **m**? And she said, Yea, for so much. G5118
8 so much? And she said, Yea, for so **m**. G5118
37 and drew away **m** people after him: he G2425
7: 5 in it, no, not *so* **m** *as* to set his foot on:
9:13 of this man, how **m** evil he hath done G3745
10: 2 which gave **m** alms to the people, G4183
11:24 **m** people was added unto the Lord. G2425
26 and taught **m** people. And the disciples G2425
14:22 we must through **m** tribulation enter G4183
15: 7 And when there had been **m** disputing, G4183
16:16 her masters **m** gain by soothsaying: G4183
18:10 thee: for I have **m** people in this city. G4183
27 **m** which had believed through grace: G4183
19: 2 We have not so **m** as heard whether G3761
26 and turned away **m** people, saying that G2425
20: 2 **m** exhortation, he came into Greece, G4183
26:24 **m** learning doth make thee mad. G4183
27: 9 Now when **m** time was spent, and G2425
10 be with hurt and **m** damage, not only G4183
16 we had **m** work to come by the boat: G3433
Ro 1:15 So, as **m** as in me is, I am ready to G3588
3: 2 **M** every way: chiefly, because that unto G4183
5: 9 **M** more then, being now justified by G4183
10 the death of his Son, **m** more, being G4183
15 one many be dead, **m** more the grace of G4183
17 reigned by one; **m** more they which G4183
20 abounded, grace did **m** more abound: G5248
9:22 endured with **m** longsuffering the G4183
11:12 the Gentiles; how **m** more their fulness? G4124
24 olive tree: how **m** more shall these, G4214
12:18 If it be possible, as **m** as lieth in you, G3588
15:22 For which cause also I have been **m** G4183
16: 6 Greet Mary, who bestowed **m** labour G4183
Ro 16:12 Persis, which laboured **m** in the Lord. G4183
1Co 2: 3 and in fear, and in **m** trembling. G4183
5: 1 as is not so **m** as named among the G3761
6: 3 **m** more things that pertain to this life? G3386
12:22 Nay, **m** more those members of the G4183
16:19 salute you **m** in the Lord, with the G4183
2Co 2: 4 For out of **m** affliction and anguish of G4183
3: 9 *be* glory, **m** more doth the ministration G4183
11 away *was* glorious, **m** more that which G4183
6: 4 of God, in **m** patience, in afflictions, G4183
8: 4 Praying us with **m** entreaty that we G4183
15 As it is written, He that *had gathered* **m** G4183
22 things, but now **m** more diligent, upon G4183
Php 1:14 by my bonds, are **m** more bold to G4056
2:12 only, but now **m** more in my absence, G4183
1Th 1: 5 Ghost, and in **m** assurance; as ye know G4183
6 **m** affliction, with joy of the Holy Ghost: G4183
2: 2 the gospel of God with **m** contention. G4183
1Ti 3: 8 to **m** wine, not greedy of filthy lucre; G4183
2Ti 4:14 Alexander the coppersmith did me **m** G4183
Tit 2: 3 to **m** wine, teachers of good things; G4183
Phlm 8 Wherefore, though I might be **m** bold G4183
16 to me, but how **m** more unto thee, both G4214
Heb 1: 4 Being made so **m** better than the G5118
7:22 By so **m** was Jesus made a surety of a G5118
8: 6 ministry, by how **m** also he is the G3745
9:14 How **m** more shall the blood of Christ, G4214
10:25 *another*: and so **m** the more, as ye see G5118
29 Of how **m** sorer punishment, suppose G4214
12: 9 shall we not **m** rather be in subjection G4183
20 And if so **m** as a beast touch the G2579
25 spake on earth, **m** more *shall not* we G4183
Jas 5:16 prayer of a righteous man availeth **m**. G4183
1Pt 1: 7 That the trial of your faith, being **m** G4183
2Pt 2:18 the flesh, *through* **m** wantonness, those
Rev 5: 4 And I wept **m**, because no man was G4183
8: 3 was given unto him **m** incense, that he G4183
18: 7 How **m** she hath glorified herself, and G3745
7 deliciously, so **m** torment and sorrow G5118
19: 1 a great voice of **m** people in heaven, G4183

MUFFLERS
Isa 3:19 chains, and the bracelets, and the **m**, H7479

MULBERRY
2Sa 5:23 upon them over against the **m** trees. H1057
24 in the tops of the **m** trees, that then H1057
1Ch 14:14 upon them over against the **m** trees. H1057
15 in the tops of the **m** trees, *that* then H1057

MULBERRY-TREES See MULBERRY and TREES.

MULE
2Sa 13:29 man gat him up upon his **m**, and fled. H6505
18: 9 rode upon a **m**, and the mule went H6505
9 a mule, and the **m** went under the thick H6505
9 the **m** that *was* under him went away. H6505
1Ki 1:33 own **m**, and bring him down to Gihon: H6506
38 David's **m**, and brought him to Gihon. H6506
44 caused him to ride upon the king's **m**: H6506
Ps 32: 9 Be ye not as the horse, *or* as the **m**, H6505
Zec 14:15 the horse, of the **m**, of the camel, and of H6505

MULES
Gen 36:24 that found the **m** in the wilderness, as H3222
1Ki 10:25 horses, and **m**, a rate year by year. H6505
18: 5 **m** alive, that we lose not all the beasts. H6505
1Ch 12:40 on camels, and on **m**, and on oxen, *and* H6505
2Ch 9:24 horses, and **m**, a rate year by year. H6505
Ezr 2:66 six; their **m**, two hundred forty and five; H6505
Neh 7:68 six: their **m**, two hundred forty and five: H6505
Est 8:10 on **m**, camels, *and* young dromedaries: H7409
14 *So* the posts that rode upon **m** *and* H7409
Isa 66:20 in litters, and upon **m**, and upon swift H6505
Ezk 27:14 fairs with horses and horsemen and **m**. H6505

MULES'
2Ki 5:17 to thy servant two **m** burden of earth? H6505

MULTIPLIED
Gen 47:27 therein, and grew, and **m** exceedingly. H7235
Ex 1: 7 abundantly, and **m**, and waxed H7235
12 the more they **m** and grew. And they H7235
20 the people **m**, and waxed very mighty. H7235
11: 9 may be **m** in the land of Egypt. H7235
Dt 1:10 The LORD your God hath **m** you, and, H7235
8:13 **m**, and all that thou hast is multiplied; H7235
13 multiplied, and all that thou hast is **m**; H7235
11:21 That your days may be **m**, and the days H7235
Jos 24: 3 and **m** his seed, and gave him Isaac. H7235
1Ch 5: 9 cattle were **m** in the land of Gilead. H7235
Job 27:14 If his children be **m**, *it is* for the sword: H7235
35: 6 be **m**, what doest thou unto him? H7231
Ps 16: 4 Their sorrows shall be **m** *that* hasten H7235
38:19 they that hate me wrongfully are **m**. H7231
107:38 also, so that they are **m** greatly; and H7235
Prv 9:11 For by me thy days shall be **m**, and the H7235
29:16 When the wicked are **m**, transgression H7235
Isa 9: 3 Thou hast **m** the nation, *and* not H7235
59:12 For our transgressions are **m** before H7231
Jer 3:16 to pass, when ye be **m** and increased in H7235
Ezk 5: 7 GOD; Because ye **m** more than the H1995
11: 6 Ye have **m** your slain in this city, and H7235
16:25 that passed by, and **m** thy whoredoms. H7235
29 Thou hast moreover **m** thy fornication H7235
51 but thou hast **m** thine abominations H7235
21:15 and *their* ruins be **m**: ah! *it is* made H7235
23:19 Yet she **m** her whoredoms, in calling to H7235
31: 5 his boughs were **m**, and his branches H7235
35:13 me, and have **m** your words against H6280
Dan 4: 1 in all the earth; Peace be **m** unto you. H7680
6:25 in all the earth; Peace be **m** unto you. H7680
Hos 2: 8 and wine, and oil, and **m** her silver and H7235
8:14 and Judah hath **m** fenced cities: but I H7235
12:10 and I have **m** visions, and used H7235
Nah 3:16 Thou hast **m** thy merchants above the H7235
Act 6: 1 of the disciples was **m**, there arose a G4129
7 of the disciples **m** in Jerusalem greatly; G4129
7:17 the people grew and **m** in Egypt, G4129
9:31 the comfort of the Holy Ghost, were **m**. G4129
12:24 But the word of God grew and **m**. G4129
1Pt 1: 2 Grace unto you, and peace, be **m**. G4129
2Pt 1: 2 Grace and peace be **m** unto you G4129
Jude 2 unto you, and peace, and love, be **m**. G4129

MULTIPLIEDST
Neh 9:23 Their children also **m** thou as the stars H7235

MULTIPLIETH
Job 9:17 and **m** my wounds without cause. H7235
34:37 us, and **m** his words against God. H7235
35:16 vain; he **m** words without knowledge. H3527

MULTIPLY
Gen 1:22 Be fruitful, and **m**, and fill the waters in H7235
22 in the seas, and let fowl **m** in the earth. H7235
28 Be fruitful, and **m**, and replenish the H7235
3:16 he said, I will greatly **m** thy sorrow and H7235
6: 1 men began to **m** on the face of the H7231
8:17 and be fruitful, and **m** upon the earth. H7235
9: 1 fruitful, and **m**, and replenish the earth. H7235
7 And you, be ye fruitful, and **m**; bring H7235
7 in the earth, and **m** therein. H7235
16:10 unto her, I will **m** thy seed exceedingly, H7235
17: 2 and thee, and will **m** thee exceedingly. H7235
20 fruitful, and will **m** him exceedingly; H7235
22:17 in multiplying I will **m** thy seed as the H7235
26: 4 And I will make thy seed to **m** as the H7235
24 will bless thee, and **m** thy seed for my H7235
28: 3 thee fruitful, and **m** thee, that thou H7235
35:11 be fruitful and **m**; a nation and a H7235
48: 4 thee fruitful, and **m** thee, and I will H7235
Ex 1:10 them; lest they **m**, and it come to pass, H7235
7: 3 heart, and **m** my signs and my H7235
23:29 the beast of the field **m** against thee. H7227
32:13 unto them, I will **m** your seed as the H7235
Lev 26: 9 you fruitful, and **m** you, and establish H7235
Dt 7:13 and bless thee, and **m** thee: he will also H7235
8: 1 that ye may live, and **m**, and go in and H7235
13 And *when* thy herds and thy flocks **m**, H7235
13:17 upon thee, and **m** thee, as he hath H7235
17:16 But he shall not **m** horses to himself, H7235
16 that he should **m** horses: forasmuch H7235
17 Neither shall he **m** wives to himself, H7235
17 he greatly **m** to himself silver and gold. H7235
28:63 you good, and to **m** you; so the LORD H7235
30: 5 good, and **m** thee above thy fathers. H7235
16 mayest live and **m**: and the LORD thy H7235
1Ch 4:27 family **m**, like to the children of Judah. H7235
Job 29:18 and I shall **m** *my* days as the sand. H7235
Jer 30:19 merry: and I will **m** them, and they H7235
33:22 so will I **m** the seed of David my H7235
Ezk 16: 7 I have caused thee to **m** as the bud of H7233
36:10 And I will **m** men upon you, all the H7235
11 And I will **m** upon you man and beast; H7235
30 And I will **m** the fruit of the tree, and H7235
37:26 place them, and **m** them, and will set H7235
Am 4: 4 at Gilgal **m** transgression; and H7235

2Co 9:10 for *your* food, and **m** your seed sown, G4129
Heb 6:14 thee, and multiplying I will **m** thee. G4129

MULTIPLYING

Gen 22:17 bless thee, and in **m** I will multiply thy H7235
Heb 6:14 bless thee, and **m** I will multiply thee. G4129

MULTITUDE

Gen 16:10 that it shall not be numbered for **m**. H7230
28: 3 that thou mayest be a **m** of people; H6951
30:30 increased unto a **m**; and the LORD hath H7230
32:12 sea, which cannot be numbered for **m**. H7230
48: 4 make of thee a **m** of people; and will H6951
16 grow into a **m** in the midst of the earth. H7230
19 his seed shall become a **m** of nations. H4393
Ex 12:38 And a mixed **m** went up also with H7227
23: 2 Thou shalt not follow a **m** to *do* evil; H7227
Lev 25:16 According to the **m** of years thou shalt H7230
Nu 11: 4 And the mixt **m** that *was* among them H628
32: 1 had a very great **m** of cattle: and when H7227
Dt 1:10 this day as the stars of heaven for **m**. H7230
10:22 made thee as the stars of heaven for **m**. H7230
28:62 of heaven for **m**; because thou wouldest H7230
Jos 11: 4 **m**, with horses and chariots very many. H7230
Jdg 4: 7 chariots and his **m**; and I will deliver H1995
6: 5 grasshoppers for **m**; *for* both they and H7230
7:12 grasshoppers for **m**; and their camels H7230
12 as the sand by the sea side for **m**. H7230
1Sa 13: 5 the sea shore in **m**: and they came up, H7230
14:16 and, behold, the **m** melted away, and H1995
2Sa 6:19 among the whole **m** of Israel, as well to H1995
17:11 *is* by the sea for **m**; and that thou go to H7230
1Ki 3: 8 be numbered nor counted for **m**. H7230
4:20 *is* by the sea in **m**, eating and drinking, H7230
8: 5 could not be told nor numbered for **m**. H7230
20:13 thou seen all this great **m**? behold, I will H1995
28 all this great **m** into thine hand, and H1995
2Ki 7:13 they *are* as all the **m** of Israel that are H1995
13 *are* even as all the **m** of the Israelites H1995
19:23 said, With the **m** of my chariots I am H7393
25:11 remnant of the **m**, did Nebuzar-adan H1995
2Ch 1: 9 a people like the dust of the earth in **m**. H7227
5: 6 could not be told nor numbered for **m**. H7230
13: 8 and ye *be* a great **m**, and *there are* with H1995
14:11 we go against this **m**. O LORD, thou *art* H1995
20: 2 cometh a great **m** against thee from H1995
15 **m**; for the battle *is* not yours, but God's. H1995
24 looked unto the **m**, and, behold, they H1995
28: 5 away a great **m** of them captives, and
30:18 For a **m** of the people, *even* many of H4768
32: 7 nor for all the **m** that *is* with him: for H1995
Neh 13: 3 separated from Israel all the mixed **m**. H6154
Est 5:11 riches, and the **m** of his children, and H7230
10: 3 and accepted of the **m** of his brethren, H7230
Job 11: 2 Should not the **m** of words be H7230
31:34 Did I fear a great **m**, or did the H1995
32: 7 I said, Days should speak, and **m** of H7230
33:19 the **m** of his bones with strong *pain*: H7379
35: 9 By reason of the **m** of oppressions they H7230
39: 7 He scorneth the **m** of the city, neither H1995
Ps 5: 7 thy house in the **m** of thy mercy: *and* in H7230
10 cast them out in the **m** of their H7230
33:16 There is no king saved by the **m** of an H7230
42: 4 I had gone with the **m**, I went with them H5519
4 and praise, with a **m** that kept holyday. H1995
49: 6 themselves in the **m** of their riches; H7230
51: 1 unto the **m** of thy tender mercies H7230
68:30 of spearmen, the **m** of the bulls, with H5712
69:13 O God, in the **m** of thy mercy hear me, H7230
16 to the **m** of thy tender mercies. H7230
74:19 unto the **m** *of the wicked*: forget H2416
94:19 In the **m** of my thoughts within me thy H7230
97: 1 let the **m** of isles be glad *thereof*. H7227
106: 7 not the **m** of thy mercies; but H7230
45 according to the **m** of his mercies. H7230
109:30 yea, I will praise him among the **m**. H7227
Prv 10:19 In the **m** of words there wanteth not H7230
11:14 in the **m** of counsellors *there is* safety. H7230
14:28 In the **m** of people *is* the king's honour: H7230
15:22 **m** of counsellors they are established. H7230
20:15 There is gold, and a **m** of rubies: but H7230
24: 6 and in **m** of counsellors *there is* safety. H7230
Ecc 5: 3 For a dream cometh through the **m** of H7230
3 a fool's voice *is known* by **m** of words. H7230
7 For in the **m** of dreams and many H7230
Isa 1:11 To what purpose *is* the **m** of your H7230
5:13 and their **m** dried up with thirst. H1995
14 glory, and their **m**, and their pomp, and H1995
13: 4 The noise of a **m** in the mountains, like H1995
Isa 16:14 with all that great **m**; and the remnant H1995
17:12 Woe to the **m** of many people, *which* H1995
29: 5 Moreover the **m** of thy strangers shall H1995
5 dust, and the **m** of the terrible ones H1995
7 And the **m** of all the nations that fight H1995
8 so shall the **m** of all the nations be, H1995
31: 4 on his prey, when a **m** of shepherds is H4393
32:14 be forsaken; the **m** of the city shall be H1995
37:24 hast said, By the **m** of my chariots am H7230
47: 9 perfection for the **m** of thy sorceries, H7230
12 and with the **m** of thy sorceries, H7230
13 Thou art wearied in the **m** of thy H7230
60: 6 The **m** of camels shall cover thee, the H8229
63: 7 to the **m** of his lovingkindnesses. H7230
Jer 3:23 *and from* the **m** of mountains: truly H1995
10:13 his voice, *there is* a **m** of waters in the H1995
12: 6 they have called a **m** after thee: believe H4392
30:14 a cruel one, for the **m** of thine iniquity; H7230
15 *is* incurable for the **m** of thine iniquity: H7230
44:15 stood by, a great **m**, even all the people H6951
46:25 I will punish the **m** of No, and H527+H528
49:32 be a booty, and the **m** of their cattle a H1995
51:16 *his* voice, *there is* a **m** of waters in the H1995
42 with the **m** of the waves thereof. H1995
52:15 king of Babylon, and the rest of the **m**. H527
Lam 1: 5 her for the **m** of her transgressions: H7230
3:32 according to the **m** of his mercies. H7230
Ezk 7:11 nor of their **m**, nor of any of theirs: H1995
12 for wrath *is* upon all the **m** thereof. H1995
13 the whole **m** thereof, *which* shall H1995
14 for my wrath *is* upon all the **m** thereof. H1995
14: 4 cometh according to the **m** of his idols; H7230
19:11 her height with the **m** of her branches. H7230
23:42 And a voice of a **m** being at ease *was* H1995
27:12 by reason of the **m** of all *kind of* riches; H7230
16 by reason of the **m** of the wares of thy H7230
18 Damascus *was* thy merchant in the **m** H7230
18 making, for the **m** of all riches; in the H7230
33 the earth with the **m** of thy riches and H7230
28:16 By the **m** of thy merchandise they have H7230
18 by the **m** of thine iniquities, H7230
29:19 he shall take her **m**, and take her spoil, H1995
30: 4 take away her **m**, and her foundations H1995
10 I will also make the **m** of Egypt to cease H1995
15 of Egypt; and I will cut off the **m** of No. H1995
31: 2 **m**; Whom art thou like in thy greatness? H1995
5 of the **m** of waters, when he shot forth. H7227
9 I have made him fair by the **m** of his H7230
18 and all his **m**, saith the Lord GOD. H1995
32:12 will I cause thy **m** to fall, the terrible of H1995
12 all the **m** thereof shall be destroyed. H1995
16 and for all her **m**, saith the Lord GOD. H1995
18 Son of man, wail for the **m** of Egypt, H1995
24 There *is* Elam and all her **m** round H1995
25 the slain with all her **m**: her graves *are* H1995
26 There *is* Meshech, Tubal, and all her **m**: H1995
31 over all his **m**, *even* Pharaoh and H1995
32 and all his **m**, saith the Lord GOD. H1995
39:11 Gog and all his **m**: and they shall call *it* H1995
47: 9 be a very great **m** of fish, because these
Dan 10: 6 voice of his words like the voice of a **m**. H1995
11:10 shall assemble a **m** of great forces: and H1995
11 set forth a great **m**; but the multitude H1995
11 but the **m** shall be given into his hand. H1995
12 *And* when he hath taken away the **m**, H1995
13 and shall set forth a **m** greater than the H1995
Hos 9: 7 *is* mad, for the **m** of thine iniquity, and H7230
10: 1 according to the **m** of his fruit he hath H7230
13 in thy way, in the **m** of thy mighty men. H7230
Mic 2:12 great noise by reason of *the* **m** *of* men.
Nah 3: 3 and *there is* a **m** of slain, and a great H7230
4 Because of the **m** of the whoredoms of H7230
Zec 2: 4 for the **m** of men and cattle therein: H7230
Mt 13: 2 and the whole **m** stood on the shore. G3793
34 All these things spake Jesus unto the **m** G3793
36 Then Jesus sent the **m** away, and went G3793
14: 5 he feared the **m**, because they counted G3793
14 and saw a great **m**, and was moved G3793
15 past; send the **m** away, that they may G3793
19 And he commanded the **m** to sit down G3793
19 *his* disciples, and the disciples to the **m**. G3793
15:10 And he called the **m**, and said unto G3793
31 Insomuch that the **m** wondered, when G3793
32 on the **m**, because they continue G3793
33 in the wilderness, as to fill so great a **m**? G3793
35 And he commanded the **m** to sit down G3793
36 his disciples, and the disciples to the **m**. G3793
39 And he sent away the **m**, and took ship, G3793
17:14 And when they were come to the **m**, G3793
Mt 20:29 from Jericho, a great **m** followed him. G3793
31 And the **m** rebuked them, because they G3793
21: 8 And a very great **m** spread their G3793
11 And the **m** said, This is Jesus the G3793
46 **m**, because they took him for a prophet. G3793
22:33 And when the **m** heard *this*, they were G3793
23: 1 Then spake Jesus to the **m**, and to his G3793
26:47 with him a great **m** with swords and G3793
27:20 persuaded the **m** that they should ask G3793
24 *his* hands before the **m**, saying, I am G3793
Mk 2:13 side; and all the **m** resorted unto him, G3793
3: 7 the sea: and a great **m** from Galilee G4128
8 Sidon, a great **m**, when they had heard G4128
9 of the **m**, lest they should throng him. G3793
20 And the **m** cometh together again, so G3793
32 And the **m** sat about him, and they G3793
4: 1 unto him a great **m**, so that he entered G3793
1 whole **m** was by the sea on the land. G3793
36 And when they had sent away the **m**, G3793
5:31 Thou seest the **m** thronging thee, and G3793
7:33 And he took him aside from the **m**, and G3793
8: 1 In those days the **m** being very great, G3793
2 I have compassion on the **m**, because G3793
9:14 he saw a great **m** about them, and the G3793
17 And one of the **m** answered and said, G3793
14:43 with him a great **m** with swords and G3793
15: 8 And the **m** crying aloud began to desire G3793
Lk 1:10 And the whole **m** of the people were G4128
2:13 with the angel a **m** of the heavenly host G4128
3: 7 Then said he to the **m** that came forth G3793
5: 6 a great **m** of fishes: and their net brake. G4128
19 in because of the **m**, they went upon the G3793
6:17 and a great **m** of people out of all G4128
19 And the whole **m** sought to touch him: G3793
8:37 Then the whole **m** of the country of the G4128
45 said, Master, the **m** throng thee and G3793
9:12 him, Send the **m** away, that they may G3793
16 gave to the disciples to set before the **m**. G3793
12: 1 an innumerable **m** of people, insomuch G3461
18:36 And hearing the **m** pass by, he asked G3793
19:37 of Olives, the whole **m** of the disciples G4128
39 from among the **m** said unto him, G3793
22: 6 him unto them in the absence of the **m**. G3793
47 And while he yet spake, behold a **m**, G3793
23: 1 And the whole **m** of them arose, and G4128
Jn 5: 3 In these lay a great **m** of impotent folk, G4128
13 himself away, a **m** being in *that* place. G3793
6: 2 And a great **m** followed him, because G3793
21: 6 not able to draw it for the **m** of fishes. G4128
Act 2: 6 abroad, the **m** came together, and G4128
4:32 And the **m** of them that believed were G4128
5:16 There came also a **m** *out* of the cities G4128
6: 2 Then the twelve called the **m** of the G4128
5 And the saying pleased the whole **m**: G4128
14: 1 that a great **m** both of the Jews and G4128
4 But the **m** of the city was divided: and G4128
15:12 Then all the **m** kept silence, and gave G4128
30 **m** together, they delivered the epistle: G4128
16:22 And the **m** rose up together against G3793
17: 4 **m**, and of the chief women not a few. G4128
19: 9 way before the **m**, he departed from G4128
33 And they drew Alexander out of the **m**, G3793
21:22 What is it therefore? the **m** must needs G4128
34 among the **m**: and when he could G3793
36 For the **m** of the people followed after, G4128
23: 7 the Sadducees: and the **m** was divided. G4128
24:18 neither with **m**, nor with tumult. G3793
25:24 whom all the **m** of the Jews have dealt G4128
Heb 11:12 stars of the sky in **m**, and as the sand G4128
Jas 5:20 from death, and shall hide a **m** of sins. G4128
1Pt 4: 8 for charity shall cover the **m** of sins. G4128
Rev 7: 9 After this I beheld, and, lo, a great **m**, G3793
19: 6 voice of a great **m**, and as the voice of G3793

MULTITUDES

Ezk 32:20 to the sword: draw her and all her **m**. H1995
Joel 3:14 **M**, multitudes in the valley of decision: H1995
14 Multitudes, **m** in the valley of decision: H1995
Mt 4:25 And there followed him great **m** of G3793
5: 1 And seeing the **m**, he went up into a G3793
8: 1 the mountain, great **m** followed him. G3793
18 Now when Jesus saw great **m** about G3793
9: 8 But when the **m** saw *it*, they marvelled, G3793
33 spake: and the **m** marvelled, saying, G3793
36 But when he saw the **m**, he was moved G3793
11: 7 to say unto the **m** concerning John, G3793
12:15 thence: and great **m** followed him, and G3793
13: 2 And great **m** were gathered together G3793
14:22 other side, while he sent the **m** away. G3793

Mt 14:23 And when he had sent the **m** away, he G3793
15:30 And great **m** came unto him, having G3793
19: 2 And great **m** followed him; and he G3793
21: 9 And the **m** that went before, and that G3793
26:55 In that same hour said Jesus to the **m**, G3793
Lk 5:15 of him: and great **m** came together to G3793
14:25 And there went great **m** with him: and G3793
Act 5:14 the Lord, **m** both of men and women.) G4128
13:45 But when the Jews saw the **m**, they were G3793
Rev 17:15 and **m**, and nations, and tongues. G3793

MUNITION
Isa 29: 7 her and her **m**, and that distress her, H4685
Nah 2: 1 thy face: keep the **m**, watch the way, H4694

MUNITIONS
Isa 33:16 *shall be* the **m** of rocks: bread shall H4679

MUPPIM
Gen 46:21 and Rosh, **M**, and Huppim, and Ard. H4649

MURDER
Ps 10: 8 places doth he **m** the innocent: his eyes H2026
94: 6 and the stranger, and **m** the fatherless. H7523
Jer 7: 9 Will ye steal, **m**, and commit adultery, H7523
Hos 6: 9 of priests **m** in the way by consent: H7523
Mt 19:18 Thou shalt do no **m**, Thou shalt not G5407
Mk 15: 7 had committed **m** in the insurrection. G5408
Lk 23:19 city, and for **m**, was cast into prison.) G5408
25 that for sedition and **m** was cast into G5408
Ro 1:29 full of envy, **m**, debate, deceit, G5408

MURDERER
Nu 35:16 so that he die, he *is* a **m**: the murderer H7523
16 the **m** shall surely be put to death. H7523
17 die, and he die, he *is* a **m**: the murderer H7523
17 the **m** shall surely be put to death. H7523
18 die, and he die, he *is* a **m**: the murderer H7523
18 the **m** shall surely be put to death. H7523
19 shall slay the **m**: when he meeteth him, H7523
21 to death; *for* he *is* a **m**: the revenger of H7523
21 shall slay the **m**, when he meeteth him. H7523
30 Whoso killeth any person, the **m** shall H7523
31 for the life of a **m**, which *is* guilty of H7523
2Ki 6:32 ye how this son of a **m** hath sent to take H7523
Job 24:14 The **m** rising with the light killeth the H7523
Hos 9:13 shall bring forth his children to the **m**. H2026
Jn 8:44 will do. He was a **m** from the beginning, G443
Act 3:14 desired a **m** to be granted unto you; G5406
28: 4 this man is a **m**, whom, though he hath G5406
1Pt 4:15 But let none of you suffer as a **m**, or *as* a G5406
1Jn 3:15 Whosoever hateth his brother is a **m**: and G443
15 no **m** hath eternal life abiding in him. G443

MURDERERS
2Ki 14: 6 But the children of the **m** he slew not: H5221
Isa 1:21 righteousness lodged in it; but now **m**. H7523
Jer 4:31 for my soul is wearied because of **m**. H2026
Mt 22: 7 those **m**, and burned up their city. G5406
Act 7:52 ye have been now the betrayers and **m**: G5406
21:38 four thousand men that were **m**? G4607
1Ti 1: 9 and profane, for **m** of fathers and G3964
9 and **m** of mothers, for manslayers, G3389
Rev 21: 8 the abominable, and **m**, and G5406
22:15 and **m**, and idolaters, and G5406

MURDERS
Mt 15:19 proceed evil thoughts, **m**, adulteries, G5408
Mk 7:21 thoughts, adulteries, fornications, **m**, G5408
Gal 5:21 Envyings, **m**, drunkenness, revellings, G5408
Rev 9:21 Neither repented they of their **m**, nor of G5408

MURMUR
Ex 16: 7 and what *are* we, that ye **m** against us? H3885
8 which ye **m** against him: and what H3885
Nu 14:27 which **m** against me? I have H3885
27 of Israel, which they **m** against me. H3885
36 the congregation to **m** against him, by H3885
16:11 what *is* Aaron, that ye **m** against him? H3885
17: 5 of Israel, whereby they **m** against you. H3885
Jn 6:43 unto them, **M** not among yourselves. G1111
1Co 10:10 Neither **m** ye, as some of them also G1111

MURMURED
Ex 15:24 And the people **m** against Moses, H3885
16: 2 children of Israel **m** against Moses and H3885
17: 3 and the people **m** against Moses, and H3885
Nu 14: 2 And all the children of Israel **m** against H3885
29 upward, which have **m** against me, H3885
16:41 children of Israel **m** against Moses and H3885
Dt 1:27 And ye **m** in your tents, and said, H7279
Jos 9:18 congregation **m** against the princes. H3885
Ps 106:25 But **m** in their tents, *and* hearkened not H7279
Isa 29:24 and they that **m** shall learn doctrine. H7279
Mt 20:11 And when they had received *it*, they **m** G1111
Mk 14: 5 to the poor. And they **m** against her. G1690
Lk 5:30 But their scribes and Pharisees **m** G1111
15: 2 And the Pharisees and scribes **m**, G1234
19: 7 And when they saw *it*, they all **m**, G1234
Jn 6:41 The Jews then **m** at him, because he G1111
61 that his disciples **m** at it, he said unto G1111
7:32 The Pharisees heard that the people **m** G1111
1Co 10:10 **m**, and were destroyed of the destroyer. G1111

MURMURERS
Jude 16 These are **m**, complainers, walking G1113

MURMURING
Jn 7:12 And there was much **m** among the G1112
Act 6: 1 there arose a **m** of the Grecians against G1112

MURMURINGS
Ex 16: 7 he heareth your **m** against the LORD: H8519
8 heareth your **m** which ye murmur H8519
8 what *are* we? your **m** *are* not against H8519
9 the LORD: for he hath heard your **m**. H8519
12 I have heard the **m** of the children of H8519
Nu 14:27 I have heard the **m** of the children of H8519
17: 5 from me the **m** of the children of Israel, H8519
10 their **m** from me, that they die not. H8519
Php 2:14 Do all things without **m** and G1112

MURRAIN
Ex 9: 3 sheep: *there shall be* a very grievous **m**. H1698

MUSE
Ps 143: 5 works; I **m** on the work of thy hands. H7878

MUSED
Lk 3:15 and all men **m** in their hearts of John, G1260

MUSHI
Ex 6:19 And the sons of Merari; Mahali and **M**: H4187
Nu 3:20 Mahli, and **M**. These *are* the families H4187
1Ch 6:19 The sons of Merari; Mahli, and **M**. And H4187
47 The son of Mahli, the son of **M**, the son H4187
23:21 The sons of Merari; Mahli, and **M**. The H4187
23 The sons of **M**; Mahli, and Eder, and H4187
24:26 The sons of Merari *were* Mahli and **M**: H4187
30 The sons also of **M**; Mahli, and Eder, H4187

MUSHITES
Nu 3:33 the **M**: these *are* the families of Merari. H4188
26:58 the family of the **M**, the family of the H4188

MUSIC See MUSICK.

MUSICAL
1Ch 16:42 a sound, and with **m** instruments of H7892
Neh 12:36 Hanani, with the **m** instruments of H7892
Ecc 2: 8 *as* **m** instruments, and that of all sorts. H7705

MUSICIAN
Ps 4:ttl To the chief **M** on Neginoth, A Psalm of H5329
5:ttl To the chief **M** upon Nehiloth, A Psalm H5329
6:ttl To the chief **M** on Neginoth upon H5329
8:ttl To the chief **M** upon Gittith, A Psalm of H5329
9:ttl To the chief **M** upon Muth-labben, A H5329
11:ttl To the chief **M**, *A Psalm* of David. H5329
12:ttl To the chief **M** upon Sheminith, A H5329
13:ttl To the chief **M**, A Psalm of David. H5329
14:ttl To the chief **M**, *A Psalm* of David. H5329
18:ttl To the chief **M**, *A Psalm* of David, the H5329
19:ttl To the chief **M**, A Psalm of David. H5329
20:ttl To the chief **M**, A Psalm of David. H5329
21:ttl To the chief **M**, A Psalm of David. H5329
22:ttl To the chief **M** upon Aijeleth Shahar, A H5329
31:ttl To the chief **M**, A Psalm of David. H5329
36:ttl To the chief **M**, *A Psalm* of David the H5329
39:ttl To the chief **M**, *even* to Jeduthun, A H5329
40:ttl To the chief **M**, A Psalm of David. H5329
41:ttl To the chief **M**, A Psalm of David. H5329
42:ttl To the chief **M**, Maschil, for the sons of H5329
44:ttl To the chief **M** for the sons of Korah, H5329
45:ttl To the chief **M** upon Shoshannim, for H5329
46:ttl To the chief **M** for the sons of Korah, A H5329
47:ttl To the chief **M**, A Psalm for the sons of H5329
49:ttl To the chief **M**, A Psalm for the sons of H5329
51:ttl To the chief **M**, A Psalm of David, when H5329
52:ttl To the chief **M**, Maschil, *A Psalm* of H5329
53:ttl To the chief **M** upon Mahalath, H5329
54:ttl To the chief **M** on Neginoth, Maschil, *A* H5329
55:ttl To the chief **M** on Neginoth, Maschil, *A* H5329
56:ttl To the chief **M** upon H5329
57:ttl To the chief **M**, Al-taschith, Michtam of H5329
58:ttl To the chief **M**, Al-taschith, Michtam of H5329
59:ttl To the chief **M**, Al-taschith, Michtam of H5329
60:ttl To the chief **M** upon Shushan-eduth, H5329
61:ttl To the chief **M** upon Neginah, *A Psalm* H5329
62:ttl To the chief **M**, to Jeduthun, A Psalm of H5329
64:ttl To the chief **M**, A Psalm of David. H5329
65:ttl To the chief **M**, A Psalm *and* Song of H5329
66:ttl To the chief **M**, A Song *or* Psalm. H5329
67:ttl To the chief **M** on Neginoth, A Psalm H5329
68:ttl To the chief **M**, A Psalm *or* Song of H5329
69:ttl To the chief **M** upon Shoshannim, *A* H5329
70:ttl To the chief **M**, *A Psalm* of David, to H5329
75:ttl To the chief **M**, Al-taschith, A Psalm *or* H5329
76:ttl To the chief **M** on Neginoth, A Psalm H5329
77:ttl To the chief **M**, to Jeduthun, A Psalm of H5329
80:ttl To the chief **M** upon H5329
81:ttl To the chief **M** upon Gittith, *A Psalm* of H5329
84:ttl To the chief **M** upon Gittith, A Psalm H5329
85:ttl To the chief **M**, A Psalm for the sons of H5329
88:ttl Korah, to the chief **M** upon Mahalath H5329
109:ttl To the chief **M**, A Psalm of David. H5329
139:ttl To the chief **M**, A Psalm of David. H5329
140:ttl To the chief **M**, A Psalm of David. H5329

MUSICIANS
Rev 18:22 And the voice of harpers, and **m**, and of G3451

MUSICK
1Sa 18: 6 with joy, and with instruments of **m**.
1Ch 15:16 instruments of **m**, psalteries and harps H7892
2Ch 5:13 and instruments of **m**, and praised the H7892
7: 6 instruments of **m** of the LORD, which H7892
23:13 instruments of **m**, and such as taught H7892
34:12 all that could skill of instruments of **m**. H7892
Ecc 12: 4 daughters of **m** shall be brought low; H7892
Lam 3:63 down, and their rising up; I *am* their **m**. H4485
5:14 the gate, the young men from their **m**. H5058
Dan 3: 5 and all kinds of **m**, ye fall down and H2170
7 and all kinds of **m**, all the people, the H2170
10 and all kinds of **m**, shall fall down and H2170
15 and all kinds of **m**, ye fall down and H2170
6:18 instruments of **m** brought before him:
Am 6: 5 instruments of **m**, like David; H7892
Lk 15:25 to the house, he heard **m** and dancing. G4858

MUSING
Ps 39: 3 me, while I was **m** the fire burned: *then* H1901

MUST
Gen 17:13 bought with thy money, **m** needs be
24: 5 me unto this land: **m** I needs bring thy
29:26 And Laban said, It **m** not be so done in
30:16 and said, Thou **m** come in unto me; for
43:11 unto them, If *it* **m** *be* so now, do this;
47:29 And the time drew nigh that Israel **m**
Ex 10: 9 go; for we **m** *hold* a feast unto the LORD.
25 And Moses said, Thou **m** give us also
26 behind; for thereof **m** we take to serve
26 not with what we **m** serve the LORD,
12:16 **m** eat, that only may be done of you.
18:20 **m** walk, and the work that they must do.
20 must walk, and the work that they **m** do.
Lev 11:32 work is done, it **m** be put into water, and
23: 6 seven days ye **m** eat unleavened bread.
Nu 6:21 he **m** do after the law of his separation.
18:22 Neither **m** the children of Israel
20:10 **m** we fetch you water out of this rock?
23:12 And he answered and said, **M** I not take
26 All that the LORD speaketh, that I **m** do?
Dt 1:22 by what way we **m** go up, and into what
4:22 But I **m** die in this land, I must not go
22 But I must die in this land, I **m** not go
12:18 But thou **m** eat them before the LORD
31: 7 courage: for thou **m** go with this people
14 that thou **m** die: call Joshua, and
Jos 3: 4 way by which ye **m** go: for ye have not
22:18 But that ye **m** turn away this day from
Jdg 13:16 offering, thou **m** offer it unto the LORD.
21:17 And they said, *There* **m** *be* an
Ru 4: 5 of Naomi, thou **m** buy *it* also of Ruth the
1Sa 14:43 that *was* in mine hand, *and*, lo, I **m** die.
2Sa 14:14 For we **m** needs die, and *are* as water

2Sa 23: 3 men *m be* just, ruling in the fear of God.
7 But the man *that* shall touch them m be
1Ki 18:27 he sleepeth, and m be awaked.
1Ch 17:11 be expired that thou m go *to be* with thy
22: 5 builded for the LORD *m be* exceeding
Ezr 10:12 voice, As thou hast said, so m we do.
Ps 32: 9 whose mouth m be held in with bit and
Prv 18:24 A man *that hath* friends m shew himself
19:19 thou deliver *him*, yet thou m do it again.
Ecc 10:10 whet the edge, then m he put to more
Song 8:12 thou, O Solomon, *m have* a thousand,
Isa 28:10 For precept *m be* upon precept, precept
Jer 10: 5 but speak not: they m needs be borne,
19 said, Truly this *is* a grief, and I m bear it.
Ezk 34:18 pasture, but ye m tread down with your
18 but ye m foul the residue with your feet?
Mt 16:21 how that he m go unto Jerusalem, G1163
17:10 say the scribes that Elias m first come? G1163
18: 7 of offences! for it m needs be that G318
24: 6 m come to pass, but the end is not yet. G1163
26:54 be fulfilled, that thus it m be? G1163
Mk 2:22 but new wine m be put into new bottles.
8:31 the Son of man m suffer many things, G1163
9:11 say the scribes that Elias m first come? G1163
12 of man, that he m suffer many things,
13: 7 for *such things* m needs be; but the end G1163
10 And the gospel m first be published G1163
14:49 not: but the scriptures m be fulfilled. G2443
Lk 2:49 I m be about my Father's business? G1163
4:43 And he said unto them, I m preach the G1163
5:38 But new wine m be put into new bottles;
9:22 Saying, The Son of man m suffer many G1163
13:33 Nevertheless I m walk to day, and to G1163
14:18 of ground, and I m needs go and see it: G2192
17:25 But first m he suffer many things, and G1163
19: 5 for to day I m abide at thy house. G1163
21: 9 for these things m first come to pass; G1163
22: 7 bread, when the passover m be killed. G1163
37 that is written m yet be accomplished G1163
23:17 (For of necessity he m release one unto G2192
24: 7 Saying, The Son of man m be delivered G1163
44 that all things m be fulfilled, which G1163
Jn 3: 7 Marvel not that I said unto thee, Ye m G1163
14 even so m the Son of man be lifted up: G1163
30 He m increase, but I *must* decrease. G1163
30 He must increase, but I *m* decrease.
4: 4 And he m needs go through Samaria.
24 m worship *him* in spirit and in truth. G1163
9: 4 I m work the works of him that sent G1163
10:16 this fold: them also I m bring, and they G1163
12:34 m be lifted up? who is this Son of man? G1163
20: 9 that he m rise again from the dead. G1163
Act 1:16 Men *and* brethren, this scripture m G1163
22 taken up from us, m one be ordained G1163
3:21 Whom the heaven m receive until the G1163
4:12 among men, whereby we m be saved. G1163
9: 6 it shall be told thee what thou m do. G1163
16 things he m suffer for my name's sake. G1163
14:22 the faith, and that we m through much G1163
15:24 souls, saying, *Ye m* be circumcised, and
16:30 and said, Sirs, what m I do to be saved? G1163
17: 3 Opening and alleging, that Christ m G1163
18:21 But bade them farewell, saying, I m by G1163
19:21 I have been there, I m also see Rome. G1163
21:22 What is it therefore? the multitude m G1163
23:11 so m thou bear witness also at Rome. G1163
27:24 Saying, Fear not, Paul; thou m be G1163
26 Howbeit we m be cast upon a certain G1163
Ro 13: 5 Wherefore *ye* m needs be subject, not
1Co 5:10 for then m ye needs go out of the world. G3784
11:19 For there m be also heresies among G1163
15:25 For he m reign, till he hath put all G1163
53 For this corruptible m put on G1163
53 and this mortal *m* put on immortality.
2Co 5:10 For we m all appear before the G1163
11:30 If I m needs glory, I will glory of the G1163
1Ti 3: 2 A bishop then m be blameless, the G1163
7 Moreover he m have a good report of G1163
8 Likewise *m* the deacons *be* grave, not
11 Even so *m their* wives *be* grave, not
2Ti 2: 6 The husbandman that laboureth m be G1163
24 And the servant of the Lord m not G1163
Tit 1: 7 For a bishop m be blameless, as the G1163
11 Whose mouths m be stopped, who G1163
Heb 4: 6 that some m enter therein, and they
9:16 For where a testament *is*, there m also of
26 For then m he often have suffered since G1163
11: 6 cometh to God m believe that he is, G1163
13:17 souls, as they that m give account, that
1Pt 4:17 For the time *is come* that judgment m
2Pt 1:14 Knowing that shortly I m put off *this* G2076
Rev 1: 1 things which m shortly come to pass; G1163
4: 1 shew thee things which m be hereafter. G1163
10:11 And he said unto me, Thou m G1163
11: 5 them, he m in this manner be killed. G1163
13:10 with the sword m be killed with the G1163
17:10 cometh, he m continue a short space. G1163
20: 3 that he m be loosed a little season. G1163
22: 6 the things which m shortly be done. G1163

MUSTARD
Mt 13:31 like to a grain of m seed, which a man G4615
17:20 faith as a grain of m seed, ye shall say G4615
Mk 4:31 *It is* like a grain of m seed, which, when G4615
Lk 13:19 It is like a grain of m seed, which a G4615
17: 6 faith as a grain of m seed, ye might say G4615

MUSTARD-SEED See MUSTARD and SEED.

MUSTERED
2Ki 25:19 of the host, which m the people of the H6633
Jer 52:25 of the host, who m the people of the H6633

MUSTERETH
Isa 13: 4 LORD of hosts m the host of the battle. H6485

MUTABILITY See IMMUTABILITY.

MUTABLE See IMMUTABLE.

MUTH-LABBEN
Ps 9:ttl To the chief Musician upon M, A Psalm H4192

MUTTER
Isa 8:19 peep, and that m: should not a people H1897

MUTTERED
Isa 59: 3 lies, your tongue hath m perverseness. H1897

MUTUAL
Ro 1:12 the m faith both of you and me. G1722+G240

MUZZLE
Dt 25: 4 Thou shalt not m the ox when he H2629
1Co 9: 9 Thou shalt not m the mouth of the ox G5392
1Ti 5:18 Thou shalt not m the ox that treadeth G5392

MY See the Appendix.

MYRA
Act 27: 5 we came to M, *a city* of Lycia. G3460

MYRRH
Gen 37:25 and m, going to carry *it* down to Egypt. H3910
43:11 spices, and m, nuts, and almonds: H3910
Ex 30:23 spices, of pure m five hundred *shekels*, H4753
Est 2:12 with oil of m, and six months with H4753
Ps 45: 8 All thy garments *smell* of m, and aloes, H4753
Prv 7:17 I have perfumed my bed with m, aloes, H4753
Song 1:13 A bundle of m *is* my wellbeloved unto H4753
3: 6 perfumed with m and frankincense, H4753
4: 6 of m, and to the hill of frankincense. H4753
14 m and aloes, with all the chief spices: H4753
5: 1 I have gathered my m with my spice; I H4753
5 dropped *with* m, and my fingers *with* H4753
5 m, upon the handles of the lock. H4753
13 *like* lilies, dropping sweet smelling m. H4753
Mt 2:11 gifts; gold, and frankincense, and m. G4666
Mk 15:23 mingled with m: but he received *it* not. G4669
Jn 19:39 a mixture of m and aloes, about an G4666

MYRTLE
Neh 8:15 branches, and m branches, and palm H1918
Isa 41:19 tree, and the m, and the oil tree; I will H1918
55:13 shall come up the m tree: and it shall H1918
Zec 1: 8 stood among the m trees that *were* in H1918
10 And the man that stood among the m H1918
11 stood among the m trees, and said, We H1918

MYRTLE-TREE See MYRTLE and TREE.

MYSELF See the Appendix.

MYSIA
Act 16: 7 After they were come to M, they G3465
8 And they passing by M came down to G3465

MYSTERIES
Mt 13:11 you to know the m of the kingdom of G3466
Lk 8:10 given to know the m of the kingdom of G3466
1Co 4: 1 Christ, and stewards of the m of God. G3466
13: 2 understand all m, and all knowledge; G3466
14: 2 howbeit in the spirit he speaketh m. G3466

N

MYSTERY
Mk 4:11 given to know the m of the kingdom of G3466
Ro 11:25 be ignorant of this m, lest ye should be G3466
16:25 the revelation of the m, which was kept G3466
1Co 2: 7 But we speak the wisdom of God in a m, G3466
15:51 Behold, I shew you a m; We shall not all G3466
Eph 1: 9 Having made known unto us the m of G3466
3: 3 the m; (as I wrote afore in few words, G3466
4 my knowledge in the m of Christ) G3466
9 the fellowship of the m, which from the G3466
5:32 This is a great m: but I speak G3466
6:19 to make known the m of the gospel, G3466
Col 1:26 *Even* the m which hath been hid from G3466
27 riches of the glory of this m among the G3466
2: 2 of the m of God, and of the Father, G3466
4: 3 to speak the m of Christ, for which G3466
2Th 2: 7 For the m of iniquity doth already G3466
1Ti 3: 9 Holding the m of the faith in a pure G3466
16 And without controversy great is the m G3466
Rev 1:20 The m of the seven stars which thou G3466
10: 7 begin to sound, the m of God should be G3466
17: 5 *was* a name written, M, BABYLON THE G3466
7 I will tell thee the m of the woman, and G3466

N

NAAM
1Ch 4:15 N: and the sons of Elah, even Kenaz. H5277

NAAMAH
Gen 4:22 and the sister of Tubal-cain *was* N. H5279
Jos 15:41 And Gederoth, Beth-dagon, and N, and H5279
1Ki 14:21 mother's name *was* N an Ammonitess. H5279
31 name *was* N an Ammonitess. And H5279
2Ch 12:13 mother's name *was* N an Ammonitess. H5279

NAAMAN
Gen 46:21 Ashbel, Gera, and N, Ehi, and Rosh, H5283
Nu 26:40 And the sons of Bela were Ard and N: *of* H5283
40 *and* of N, the family of the Naamites. H5283
2Ki 5: 1 Now N, captain of the host of the king H5283
6 *therewith* sent N my servant to thee, H5283
9 So N came with his horses and with his H5283
11 But N was wroth, and went away, and H5283
17 And N said, Shall there not then, I pray H5283
20 hath spared N this Syrian, in not H5283
21 So Gehazi followed after N. And when H5283
21 And when N saw *him* running after H5283
23 And N said, Be content, take two H5283
27 The leprosy therefore of N shall cleave H5283
1Ch 8: 4 And Abishua, and N, and Ahoah, H5283
1Ch 8: 7 And N, and Ahiah, and Gera, he H5283
Lk 4:27 was cleansed, saving N the Syrian. G3497

NAAMAN'S
2Ki 5: 2 a little maid; and she waited on N wife. H5283

NAAMATHITE
Job 2:11 and Zophar the N: for they had made H5284
11: 1 Then answered Zophar the N, and said, H5284
20: 1 Then answered Zophar the N, and said, H5284
42: 9 *and* Zophar the N went, and did H5284

NAAMITES
Nu 26:40 *and* of Naaman, the family of the **N**. H5280

NAARAH
1Ch 4: 5 of Tekoa had two wives, Helah and **N**. H5292
6 And **N** bare him Ahuzam, and Hepher, H5292
6 Haahashtari. These *were* the sons of **N**. H5292

NAARAI
1Ch 11:37 Hezro the Carmelite, **N** the son of H5293

NAARAN
1Ch 7:28 and eastward **N**, and westward Gezer, H5295

NAARATH
Jos 16: 7 to Ataroth, and to **N**, and came to H5292

NAASHON
Ex 6:23 sister of **N**, to wife; and she bare H5177

NAASSON
Mt 1: 4 begat **N**; and Naasson begat Salmon; *G3476*
4 begat Naasson; and **N** begat Salmon; *G3476*
Lk 3:32 *son* of Salmon, which was *the son* of **N**, *G3476*

NABAL
1Sa 25: 3 Now the name of the man *was* **N**; and H5037
4 wilderness that **N** did shear his sheep. H5037
5 and go to **N**, and greet him in my name: H5037
9 they spake to **N** according to all those H5037
10 And **N** answered David's servants, and H5037
19 you. But she told not her husband **N**. H5037
25 of Belial, *even* **N**: for as his name *is*, so H5037
25 name *is*, so *is* he; **N** *is* his name, and H5037
26 they that seek evil to my lord, be as **N**. H5037
34 not been left unto **N** by the morning H5037
36 And Abigail came to **N**; and, behold, he H5037
37 was gone out of **N**, and his wife had told H5037
38 that the LORD smote **N**, that he died. H5037
39 And when David heard that **N** was H5037
39 from the hand of **N**, and hath kept his H5037
39 the wickedness of **N** upon his own H5037
30: 5 and Abigail the wife of **N** the Carmelite. H5037
2Sa 3: 3 Abigail the wife of **N** the Carmelite; and H5037

NABAL'S
1Sa 25:14 young men told Abigail, **N** wife, saying, H5037
36 feast of a king; and **N** heart *was* merry H5037
27: 3 and Abigail the Carmelitess, **N** wife. H5037
2Sa 2: 2 and Abigail **N** wife the Carmelite. H5037

NABOTH
1Ki 21: 1 these things, *that* **N** the Jezreelite had a H5022
2 And Ahab spake unto **N**, saying, Give H5022
3 And **N** said to Ahab, The LORD forbid H5022
4 of the word which **N** the Jezreelite had H5022
6 I spake unto **N** the Jezreelite, and said H5022
7 thee the vineyard of **N** the Jezreelite. H5022
8 that *were* in his city, dwelling with **N**. H5022
9 and set **N** on high among the people: H5022
12 They proclaimed a fast, and set **N** on H5022
13 him, *even* against **N**, in the presence of H5022
13 people, saying, **N** did blaspheme God H5022
14 Then they sent to Jezebel, saying, **N** is H5022
15 Jezebel heard that **N** was stoned, and H5022
15 of the vineyard of **N** the Jezreelite, H5022
15 for money: for **N** is not alive, but dead. H5022
16 Ahab heard that **N** was dead, that H5022
16 to the vineyard of **N** the Jezreelite, to H5022
18 in the vineyard of **N**, whither he is gone H5022
19 **N** shall dogs lick thy blood, even thine. H5022
2Ki 9:21 him in the portion of **N** the Jezreelite. H5022
25 of the field of **N** the Jezreelite: for H5022
26 the blood of **N**, and the blood of his H5022

NACHON'S
2Sa 6: 6 And when they came to **N** H5225

NACHOR
Jos 24: 2 father of **N**: and they served other gods. H5152
Lk 3:34 *son* of Thara, which was *the son* of **N**, *G3493*

NADAB
Ex 6:23 **N**, and Abihu, Eleazar, and Ithamar. H5070
24: 1 thou, and Aaron, **N**, and Abihu, and H5070
9 Then went up Moses, and Aaron, **N**, H5070
28: 1 *even* Aaron, **N** and Abihu, Eleazar H5070
Lev 10: 1 And **N** and Abihu, the sons of Aaron, H5070
Nu 3: 2 the sons of Aaron; **N** the firstborn, and H5070
Nu 3: 4 And **N** and Abihu died before the H5070
26:60 And unto Aaron was born **N**, and H5070
61 And **N** and Abihu died, when they H5070
1Ki 14:20 and **N** his son reigned in his stead. H5070
15:25 And **N** the son of Jeroboam began to H5070
27 **N** and all Israel laid siege to Gibbethon. H5070
31 Now the rest of the acts of **N**, and all H5070
1Ch 2:28 the sons of Shammai; **N**, and Abishur. H5070
30 And the sons of **N**; Seled, and Appaim: H5070
6: 3 **N**, and Abihu, Eleazar, and Ithamar. H5070
8:30 and Zur, and Kish, and Baal, and **N**, H5070
9:36 and Kish, and Baal, and Ner, and **N**, H5070
24: 1 **N**, and Abihu, Eleazar, and Ithamar. H5070
2 But **N** and Abihu died before their H5070

NADIB See AMMI-NADIB.

NAGGE
Lk 3:25 *the son* of Esli, which was *the son* of **N**, *G3477*

NAHALAL
Jos 21:35 Dimnah with her suburbs, **N** with her H5096

NAHALIEL
Nu 21:19 And from Mattanah to **N**: and from H5160
19 to Nahaliel: and from **N** to Bamoth: H5160

NAHALLAL
Jos 19:15 And Kattath, and **N**, and Shimron, and H5096

NAHALOL
Jdg 1:30 nor the inhabitants of **N**; but the H5096

NAHAM
1Ch 4:19 the sister of **N**, the father of Keilah H5163

NAHAMANI
Neh 7: 7 Raamiah, **N**, Mordecai, Bilshan, H5167

NAHARAI
2Sa 23:37 Zelek the Ammonite, **N** the Beerothite, H5171
1Ch 11:39 Zelek the Ammonite, **N** the Berothite, H5171

NAHASH
1Sa 11: 1 Then **N** the Ammonite came up, and H5176
1 of Jabesh said unto **N**, Make a covenant H5176
2 And **N** the Ammonite answered them, H5176
12:12 And when ye saw that **N** the king of the H5176
2Sa 10: 2 unto Hanun the son of **N**, as his father H5176
17:25 of **N**, sister to Zeruiah Joab's mother. H5176
27 Shobi the son of **N** of Rabbah of the H5176
1Ch 19: 1 Now it came to pass after this, that **N** H5176
2 Hanun the son of **N**, because his father H5176

NAHATH
Gen 36:13 And these *are* the sons of Reuel; **N**, and H5184
17 Esau's son; duke **N**, duke Zerah, duke H5184
1Ch 1:37 The sons of Reuel; **N**, Zerah, Shammah, H5184
6:26 Zophai his son, and **N** his son, H5184
2Ch 31:13 And Jehiel, and Azaziah, and **N**, and H5184

NAHBI
Nu 13:14 Of the tribe of Naphtali, **N** the son of H5147

NAHOR
Gen 11:22 Serug lived thirty years, and begat **N**: H5152
23 And Serug lived after he begat **N** two H5152
24 And **N** lived nine and twenty years, H5152
25 And **N** lived after he begat Terah an H5152
26 years, and begat Abram, **N**, and Haran. H5152
27 **N**, and Haran; and Haran begat Lot. H5152
29 And Abram and **N** took them wives: H5152
22:20 also born children unto thy brother **N**; H5152
23 did bear to **N**, Abraham's brother. H5152
24:10 to Mesopotamia, unto the city of **N**. H5152
15 the wife of **N**, Abraham's brother, H5152
24 son of Milcah, which she bare unto **N**. H5152
29: 5 son of **N**? And they said, We know *him*. H5152
31:53 The God of Abraham, and the God of **N**, H5152
1Ch 1:26 Serug, **N**, Terah, H5152

NAHOR'S
Gen 11:29 and the name of **N** wife, Milcah, the H5152
24:47 of Bethuel, **N** son, whom Milcah H5152

NAHSHON
Nu 1: 7 Of Judah; **N** the son of Amminadab. H5177
2: 3 their armies: and **N** the son of H5177
7:12 offering the first day was **N** the son of H5177
Nu 7:17 offering of **N** the son of Amminadab. H5177
10:14 his host *was* **N** the son of Amminadab. H5177
Ru 4:20 And Amminadab begat **N**, and H5177
20 begat Nahshon, and **N** begat Salmon, H5177
1Ch 2:10 begat **N**, prince of the children of Judah; H5177
11 And **N** begat Salma, and Salma begat H5177

NAHUM
Nah 1: 1 book of the vision of **N** the Elkoshite. H5151

NAIL
Jdg 4:21 Then Jael Heber's wife took a **n** of the H3489
21 and smote the **n** into his temples, and H3489
22 lay dead, and the **n** *was* in his temples. H3489
5:26 She put her hand to the **n**, and her right H3489
Ezr 9: 8 and to give us a **n** in his holy place, that H3489
Isa 22:23 And I will fasten him *as* a **n** in a sure H3489
25 of hosts, shall the **n** that is fastened in H3489
Zec 10: 4 out of him the **n**, out of him the battle H3489

NAILING
Col 2:14 took it out of the way, **n** it to his cross; *G4338*

NAILS
Dt 21:12 shall shave her head, and pare her **n**; H6856
1Ch 22: 3 in abundance for the **n** for the doors of H4548
2Ch 3: 9 And the weight of the **n** *was* fifty H4548
Ecc 12:11 *are* as goads, and as **n** fastened *by* the H4930
Isa 41: 7 it with **n**, *that* it should not be moved. H4548
Jer 10: 4 **n** and with hammers, that it move not. H4548
Dan 4:33 *feathers*, and his **n** like birds' *claws*. H2953
7:19 *were of* iron, and his **n** *of* brass; *which* H2953
Jn 20:25 the print of the **n**, and put my finger *G2247*
25 the print of the **n**, and thrust my hand *G2247*

NAIN
Lk 7:11 into a city called **N**; and many of his *G3484*

NAIOTH
1Sa 19:18 he and Samuel went and dwelt in **N**. H5121
19 Behold, David *is* at **N** in Ramah. H5121
22 said, Behold, *they be* at **N** in Ramah. H5121
23 And he went thither to **N** in Ramah: H5121
23 until he came to **N** in Ramah. H5121
20: 1 And David fled from **N** in Ramah, and H5121

NAKED
Gen 2:25 And they were both **n**, the man and his H6174
3: 7 that they *were* **n**; and they sewed fig H5903
10 because I *was* **n**; and I hid myself. H5903
11 that thou *wast* **n**? Hast thou eaten of the H5903
Ex 32:25 the people *were* **n**; (for Aaron had made H6544
25 had made them **n** unto *their* shame H6544
1Sa 19:24 and lay down **n** all that day and all H6174
2Ch 28:15 all that were **n** among them, and H4636
19 for he made Judah **n**, and transgressed H6544
Job 1:21 And said, **N** came I out of my mother's H6174
21 womb, and **n** shall I return thither: H6174
22: 6 and stripped the **n** of their clothing. H6174
24: 7 They cause the **n** to lodge without H6174
10 They cause *him* to go **n** without H6174
26: 6 Hell *is* **n** before him, and destruction H6174
Ecc 5:15 mother's womb, **n** shall he return to go H6174
Isa 20: 2 And he did so, walking **n** and barefoot. H6174
3 hath walked **n** and barefoot three H6174
4 young and old, **n** and barefoot, even H6174
58: 7 thou seest the **n**, that thou cover him; H6174
Lam 4:21 be drunken, and shalt make thyself **n**. H6168
Ezk 16: 7 grown, whereas thou *wast* **n** and bare. H5903
22 when thou wast **n** and bare, *and* wast H5903
39 fair jewels, and leave thee **n** and bare. H5903
18: 7 and hath covered the **n** with a garment; H5903
16 and hath covered the **n** with a garment, H5903
23:29 shall leave thee **n** and bare: and the H5903
Hos 2: 3 Lest I strip her **n**, and set her as in the H6174
Am 2:16 away **n** in that day, saith the LORD. H6174
Mic 1: 8 go stripped and **n**: I will make a wailing H6174
11 having thy shame **n**: the inhabitant of H6181
Hab 3: 9 Thy bow was made quite **n**, *according* H5783
Mt 25:36 **N**, and ye clothed me: I was sick, and ye *G1131*
38 took *thee* in? or **n**, and clothed *thee*? *G1131*
43 ye took me not in: **n**, and ye clothed me *G1131*
44 or a stranger, or **n**, or sick, or in prison, *G1131*
Mk 14:51 cast about *his* **n** *body*; and the young *G1131*
52 the linen cloth, and fled from them **n**. *G1131*
Jn 21: 7 was **n**,) and did cast himself into the sea. *G1131*
Act 19:16 fled out of that house **n** and wounded. *G1131*
1Co 4:11 thirst, and are **n**, and are buffeted, and *G1130*
2Co 5: 3 being clothed we shall not be found **n**. *G1131*

Heb 4:13 but all things *are* **n** and opened unto G1131
Jas 2:15 If a brother or sister be **n**, and destitute G1131
Rev 3:17 miserable, and poor, and blind, and **n**: G1131
16:15 lest he walk **n**, and they see his shame. G1131
17:16 her desolate and **n**, and shall eat her G1131

NAKEDNESS

Gen 9:22 of Canaan, saw the **n** of his father, and H6172
23 and covered the **n** of their father; and H6172
23 and they saw not their father's **n**. H6172
42: 9 to see the **n** of the land ye are come. H6172
12 but to see the **n** of the land ye are come. H6172
Ex 20:26 that thy **n** be not discovered thereon. H6172
28:42 to cover their **n**; from the loins even H1320
Lev 18: 6 him, to uncover *their* **n**: I *am* the LORD. H6172
7 The **n** of thy father, or the nakedness of H6172
7 The nakedness of thy father, or the **n** of H6172
7 mother; thou shalt not uncover her **n**. H6172
8 The **n** of thy father's wife shalt thou not H6172
8 thou not uncover: it *is* thy father's **n**. H6172
9 The **n** of thy sister, the daughter of thy H6172
9 *even* their **n** thou shalt not uncover. H6172
10 The **n** of thy son's daughter, or of thy H6172
10 *even* their **n** thou shalt not uncover: H6172
10 not uncover: for theirs *is* thine own **n**. H6172
11 The **n** of thy father's wife's daughter, H6172
11 thy sister, thou shalt not uncover her **n**. H6172
12 Thou shalt not uncover the **n** of thy H6172
13 Thou shalt not uncover the **n** of thy H6172
14 Thou shalt not uncover the **n** of thy H6172
15 Thou shalt not uncover the **n** of thy H6172
15 son's wife; thou shalt not uncover her **n**. H6172
16 Thou shalt not uncover the **n** of thy H6172
16 thy brother's wife: it *is* thy brother's **n**. H6172
17 Thou shalt not uncover the **n** of a H6172
17 to uncover her **n**; *for* they *are* her near H6172
18 her **n**, beside the other in her life *time*. H6172
19 to uncover her **n**, as long as she is put H6172
20:11 his father's **n**: both of them shall surely H6172
17 daughter, and see her **n**, and she see his H6172
17 and she see his **n**; it *is* a wicked thing; H6172
17 his sister's **n**; he shall bear his iniquity. H6172
18 shall uncover her **n**; he hath discovered H6172
19 And thou shalt not uncover the **n** of thy H6172
20 his uncle's **n**: they shall bear their H6172
21 his brother's **n**; they shall be childless. H6172
Dt 28:48 in thirst, and in **n**, and in want of all H5903
1Sa 20:30 unto the confusion of thy mother's **n**? H6172
Isa 47: 3 Thy **n** shall be uncovered, yea, thy H6172
Lam 1: 8 they have seen her **n**: yea, she sigheth, H6172
Ezk 16: 8 and covered thy **n**: yea, I sware unto H6172
36 out, and thy **n** discovered through H6172
37 will discover thy **n** unto them, that they H6172
37 unto them, that they may see all thy **n**. H6172
22:10 their fathers' **n**: in thee have they H6172
23:10 These discovered her **n**: they took her H6172
18 discovered her **n**: then my mind was H6172
29 and bare: and the **n** of thy whoredoms H6172
Hos 2: 9 wool and my flax *given* to cover her **n**. H6172
Nah 3: 5 thy **n**, and the kingdoms thy shame. H4626
Hab 2:15 also, that thou mayest look on their **n**! H4589
Ro 8:35 or famine, or **n**, or peril, or sword? G1132
2Co 11:27 thirst, in fastings often, in cold and **n**. G1132
Rev 3:18 the shame of thy **n** do not appear; and G1132

NAME

Gen 2:11 The **n** of the first *is* Pison: that *is* it H8034
13 And the **n** of the second river *is* Gihon: H8034
14 And the **n** of the third river *is* Hiddekel: H8034
19 living creature, that *was* the **n** thereof. H8034
3:20 And Adam called his wife's **n** Eve; H8034
4:17 and called the **n** of the city, after the H8034
17 of the city, after the **n** of his son, Enoch. H8034
19 two wives: the **n** of the one *was* Adah, H8034
19 Adah, and the **n** of the other Zillah. H8034
21 And his brother's **n** *was* Jubal: he was H8034
25 and called his **n** Seth: For God, *said* H8034
26 and he called his **n** Enos; then began H8034
26 men to call upon the **n** of the LORD. H8034
5: 2 and called their **n** Adam, in the day H8034
3 after his image; and called his **n** Seth: H8034
29 And he called his **n** Noah, saying, This H8034
10:25 born two sons: the **n** of one *was* Peleg; H8034
25 and his brother's **n** *was* Joktan. H8034
11: 4 let us make us a **n**, lest we be scattered H8034
9 Therefore is the **n** of it called Babel; H8034
29 them wives: the **n** of Abram's wife *was* H8034
29 *was* Sarai; and the **n** of Nahor's wife, H8034
12: 2 **n** great; and thou shalt be a blessing: H8034
Gen 12: 8 and called upon the **n** of the LORD. H8034
13: 4 Abram called on the **n** of the LORD. H8034
16: 1 an Egyptian, whose **n** *was* Hagar. H8034
11 and shalt call his **n** Ishmael; because H8034
13 And she called the **n** of the LORD that H8034
15 his son's **n**, which Hagar bare, Ishmael. H8034
17: 5 Neither shall thy **n** any more be called H8034
5 Abram, but thy **n** shall be Abraham; H8034
15 **n** Sarai, but Sarah *shall* her name *be*. H8034
15 name Sarai, but Sarah *shall* her **n** *be*. H8034
19 thou shalt call his **n** Isaac: and I will H8034
19:22 the **n** of the city was called Zoar. H8034
37 and called his **n** Moab: the same *is* the H8034
38 and called his **n** Ben-ammi: the same H8034
21: 3 And Abraham called the **n** of his son H8034
33 the **n** of the LORD, the everlasting God. H8034
22:14 And Abraham called the **n** of that place H8034
24 And his concubine, whose **n** *was* H8034
24:29 And Rebekah had a brother, and his **n** H8034
25: 1 took a wife, and her **n** *was* Keturah. H8034
25 garment; and they called his **n** Esau. H8034
26 heel; and his **n** was called Jacob: and H8034
30 faint: therefore was his **n** called Edom. H8034
26:20 and he called the **n** of the well Esek; H8034
21 also: and he called the **n** of it Sitnah. H8034
22 and he called the **n** of it Rehoboth; and H8034
25 called upon the **n** of the LORD, and H8034
33 And he called it Shebah: therefore the **n** H8034
28:19 And he called the **n** of that place H8034
19 **n** of that city *was called* Luz at the first. H8034
29:16 And Laban had two daughters: the **n** of H8034
16 and the **n** of the younger *was* Rachel. H8034
32 and she called his **n** Reuben: for she H8034
33 *son* also: and she called his **n** Simeon. H8034
34 sons: therefore was his **n** called Levi. H8034
35 she called his **n** Judah; and left bearing. H8034
30: 6 a son: therefore called she his **n** Dan. H8034
8 and she called his **n** Naphtali. H8034
11 cometh: and she called his **n** Gad. H8034
13 me blessed: and she called his **n** Asher. H8034
18 husband: and she called his **n** Issachar. H8034
20 six sons: and she called his **n** Zebulun. H8034
21 a daughter, and called her **n** Dinah. H8034
24 And she called his **n** Joseph; and said, H8034
31:48 Therefore was the **n** of it called Galeed; H8034
32: 2 called the **n** of that place Mahanaim. H8034
27 And he said unto him, What *is* thy **n**? H8034
28 And he said, Thy **n** shall be called no H8034
29 *me*, I pray thee, thy **n**. And he said, H8034
29 after my **n**? And he blessed him there. H8034
30 And Jacob called the **n** of the place H8034
33:17 the **n** of the place is called Succoth. H8034
35: 8 the **n** of it was called Allon-bachuth. H8034
10 And God said unto him, Thy **n** *is* Jacob: H8034
10 name *is* Jacob: thy **n** shall not be called H8034
10 be thy **n**: and he called his name Israel. H8034
10 be thy name: and he called his **n** Israel. H8034
15 And Jacob called the **n** of the place H8034
18 that she called his **n** Ben-oni: but his H8034
36:32 and the **n** of his city *was* Dinhabah. H8034
35 stead: and the **n** of his city *was* Avith. H8034
39 his stead: and the **n** of his city *was* Pau; H8034
39 and his wife's **n** *was* Mehetabel, the H8034
38: 1 Adullamite, whose **n** *was* Hirah. H8034
2 Canaanite, whose **n** *was* Shuah; and he H8034
3 and bare a son; and he called his **n** Er. H8034
4 bare a son; and she called his **n** Onan. H8034
5 and called his **n** Shelah: and he was H8034
6 Er his firstborn, whose **n** *was* Tamar. H8034
29 thee: therefore his **n** was called Pharez. H8034
30 his hand: and his **n** was called Zarah. H8034
41:45 And Pharaoh called Joseph's **n** H8034
51 And Joseph called the **n** of the firstborn H8034
52 And the **n** of the second called he H8034
48: 6 **n** of their brethren in their inheritance. H8034
16 lads; and let my **n** be named on them, H8034
16 on them, and the **n** of my fathers H8034
50:11 wherefore the **n** of it was called H8034
Ex 1:15 of which the **n** of the one *was* Shiphrah, H8034
15 Shiphrah, and the **n** of the other Puah: H8034
2:10 And she called his **n** Moses: and she H8034
22 and he called his **n** Gershom: for he H8034
3:13 *is* his **n**? what shall I say unto them? H8034
15 you: this *is* my **n** for ever, and this *is* H8034
5:23 to speak in thy **n**, he hath done evil to H8034
6: 3 unto Jacob, by *the* **n** *of* God Almighty,
3 **n** JEHOVAH was I not known to them. H8034
9:16 power; and that my **n** may be declared H8034
15: 3 *is* a man of war: the LORD *is* his **n**. H8034
Ex 15:23 therefore the **n** of it was called Marah. H8034
16:31 And the house of Israel called the **n** H8034
17: 7 And he called the **n** of the place H8034
15 and called the **n** of it Jehovah-nissi: H8034
18: 3 And her two sons; of which the **n** of the H8034
4 And the **n** of the other *was* Eliezer; for H8034
20: 7 Thou shalt not take the **n** of the LORD H8034
7 him guiltless that taketh his **n** in vain. H8034
24 where I record my **n** I will come unto H8034
23:13 no mention of the **n** of other gods, H8034
21 your transgressions: for my **n** *is* in him. H8034
28:21 every one with his **n** shall they be H8034
31: 2 See, I have called by **n** Bezaleel the son H8034
33:12 I know thee by **n**, and thou hast also H8034
17 grace in my sight, and I know thee by **n**. H8034
19 and I will proclaim the **n** of the LORD H8034
34: 5 and proclaimed the **n** of the LORD. H8034
14 whose **n** *is* Jealous, *is* a jealous God: H8034
35:30 hath called by **n** Bezaleel the son of Uri, H8034
39:14 his **n**, according to the twelve tribes. H8034
Lev 18:21 the **n** of thy God: I *am* the LORD. H8034
19:12 And ye shall not swear by my **n** falsely, H8034
12 the **n** of thy God: I *am* the LORD. H8034
20: 3 sanctuary, and to profane my holy **n**. H8034
21: 6 not profane the **n** of their God: for the H8034
22: 2 not my holy **n** *in those things* which H8034
32 Neither shall ye profane my holy **n**; but H8034
24:11 blasphemed the **n** *of the LORD*, and H8034
11 (and his mother's **n** *was* Shelomith, the H8034
16 And he that blasphemeth the **n** of the H8034
16 **n** *of the LORD*, shall be put to death. H8034
Nu 4:32 service: and by **n** ye shall reckon the H8034
6:27 And they shall put my **n** upon the H8034
11: 3 And he called the **n** of the place H8034
26 men in the camp, the **n** of the one *was* H8034
26 Eldad, and the **n** of the other Medad: H8034
34 And he called the **n** of that place H8034
17: 2 write thou every man's **n** upon his rod. H8034
3 And thou shalt write Aaron's **n** upon H8034
21: 3 he called the **n** of the place Hormah. H8034
25:14 Now the **n** of the Israelite that was H8034
15 And the **n** of the Midianitish woman H8034
26:46 And the **n** of the daughter of Asher *was* H8034
59 And the **n** of Amram's wife *was* H8034
27: 4 Why should the **n** of our father be done H8034
32:42 and called it Nobah, after his own **n**. H8034
Dt 3:14 **n**, Bashan-havoth-jair, unto this day. H8034
5:11 Thou shalt not take the **n** of the LORD H8034
11 *him* guiltless that taketh his **n** in vain. H8034
6:13 serve him, and shalt swear by his **n**. H8034
7:24 thou shalt destroy their **n** from under H8034
9:14 them, and blot out their **n** from under H8034
10: 8 him, and to bless in his **n**, unto this day. H8034
20 shalt thou cleave, and swear by his **n**. H8034
12: 5 tribes to put his **n** there, *even* unto his H8034
11 to cause his **n** to dwell there; thither H8034
21 chosen to put his **n** there be too far H8034
14:23 to place his **n** there, the tithe of thy H8034
24 shall choose to set his **n** there, when the H8034
16: 2 LORD shall choose to place his **n** there. H8034
6 to place his **n** in, there thou shalt H8034
11 God hath chosen to place his **n** there. H8034
18: 5 to minister in the **n** of the LORD, him H8034
7 Then he shall minister in the **n** of the H8034
19 speak in my **n**, I will require *it* of him. H8034
20 speak a word in my **n**, which I have not H8034
20 shall speak in the **n** of other gods, even H8034
22 When a prophet speaketh in the **n** of H8034
21: 5 and to bless in the **n** of the LORD; and H8034
22:14 bring up an evil **n** upon her, and say, H8034
19 brought up an evil **n** upon a virgin of H8034
25: 6 succeed in the **n** of his brother *which* H8034
6 dead, that his **n** be not put out of Israel. H8034
7 unto his brother a **n** in Israel, he will H8034
10 And his **n** shall be called in Israel, The H8034
26: 2 God shall choose to place his **n** there. H8034
19 in praise, and in **n**, and in honour; and H8034
28:10 art called by the **n** of the LORD; and H8034
58 and fearful **n**, THE LORD THY GOD; H8034
29:20 shall blot out his **n** from under heaven. H8034
32: 3 Because I will publish the **n** of the H8034
Jos 5: 9 Wherefore the **n** of the place is called H8034
7: 9 and cut off our **n** from the earth: and H8034
9 and what wilt thou do unto thy great **n**? H8034
26 Wherefore the **n** of that place was H8034
9: 9 because of the **n** of the LORD thy God: H8034
14:15 And the **n** of Hebron before *was* H8034
15:15 **n** of Debir before *was* Kirjath-sepher. H8034
19:47 Dan, after the **n** of Dan their father. H8034

Jos 21: 9 cities which are *here* mentioned by **n**, H8034
23: 7 mention of the **n** of their gods, nor H8034
Jdg 1:10 Hebron: (now the **n** of Hebron before H8034
11 **n** of Debir before *was* Kirjath-sepher: H8034
17 the **n** of the city was called Hormah. H8034
23 (Now the **n** of the city before *was* Luz.) H8034
26 and called the **n** thereof Luz: which H8034
26 which *is* the **n** thereof unto this day. H8034
2: 5 And they called the **n** of that place H8034
8:31 a son, whose **n** he called Abimelech. H8034
13: 2 Danites, whose **n** *was* Manoah; and his H8034
6 he *was*, neither told he me his **n**: H8034
17 What *is* thy **n**, that when thy sayings H8034
18 thou thus after my **n**, seeing it *is* secret? H8034
24 and called his **n** Samson: and the child H8034
15:19 he called the **n** thereof En-hakkore, H8034
16: 4 valley of Sorek, whose **n** *was* Delilah. H8034
17: 1 mount Ephraim, whose **n** *was* Micah. H8034
18:29 And they called the **n** of the city Dan, H8034
29 the city Dan, after the **n** of Dan their H8034
29 the **n** of the city *was* Laish at the first. H8034
Ru 1: 2 And the **n** of the man *was* Elimelech, H8034
2 and the **n** of his wife Naomi, and H8034
2 wife Naomi, and the **n** of his two sons H8034
4 of Moab; the **n** of the one *was* Orpah, H8034
4 Orpah, and the **n** of the other Ruth: H8034
2: 1 of Elimelech; and his **n** *was* Boaz. H8034
19 **n** with whom I wrought to day *is* Boaz. H8034
4: 5 the **n** of the dead upon his inheritance. H8034
10 to raise up the **n** of the dead upon his H8034
10 that the **n** of the dead be not cut H8034
14 that his **n** may be famous in Israel. H8034
17 gave it a **n**, saying, There is a son H8034
17 they called his **n** Obed: he *is* the father H8034
1Sa 1: 1 Ephraim, and his **n** *was* Elkanah, the H8034
2 And he had two wives; the **n** of the one H8034
2 *was* Hannah, and the **n** of the other H8034
20 son, and called his **n** Samuel, *saying*, H8034
7:12 and called the **n** of it Eben-ezer, saying, H8034
8: 2 Now the **n** of his firstborn was Joel; and H8034
2 was Joel; and the **n** of his second, H8034
9: 1 Benjamin, whose **n** *was* Kish, the son H8034
2 And he had a son, whose **n** *was* Saul, a H8034
14: 4 side: and the **n** of the one *was* Bozez, H8034
4 Bozez, and the **n** of the other Seneh. H8034
49 *were these;* the **n** of the firstborn H8034
49 and the **n** of the younger Michal: H8034
50 And the **n** of Saul's wife *was* Ahinoam, H8034
50 of Ahimaaz: and the **n** of the captain of H8034
16: 3 anoint unto me *him* whom I **n** unto thee. H559
17:12 whose **n** *was* Jesse; and he had H8034
23 Gath, Goliath by **n**, out of the armies of H8034
45 to thee in the **n** of the LORD of hosts, H8034
18:30 of Saul; so that his **n** was much set by. H8034
20:42 both of us in the **n** of the LORD, saying, H8034
21: 7 the LORD; and his **n** *was* Doeg, an H8034
24:21 destroy my **n** out of my father's house. H8034
25: 3 Now the **n** of the man *was* Nabal; and H8034
3 Nabal; and the **n** of his wife Abigail: H8034
5 and go to Nabal, and greet him in my **n**: H8034
9 words in the **n** of David, and ceased. H8034
25 Nabal: for as his **n** *is*, so *is* he; Nabal *is* H8034
25 so *is* he; Nabal *is* his **n**, and folly *is* with H8034
28: 8 me *him* up, whom I shall **n** unto thee. H559
2Sa 3: 7 And Saul had a concubine, whose **n** H8034
4: 2 of bands: the **n** of the one *was* Baanah, H8034
2 Baanah, and the **n** of the other Rechab, H8034
4 lame. And his **n** *was* Mephibosheth. H8034
5:20 called the **n** of that place Baal-perazim. H8034
6: 2 the ark of God, whose **n** is called by the H8034
2 is called by the **n** of the LORD of hosts H8034
8 **n** of the place Perez-uzzah to this day. H8034
18 people in the **n** of the LORD of hosts. H8034
7: 9 made thee a great **n**, like unto the name H8034
9 **n** of the great *men* that *are* in the earth. H8034
13 He shall build an house for my **n**, and I H8034
23 and to make him a **n**, and to do for you H8034
26 And let thy **n** be magnified for ever, H8034
8:13 And David gat *him* a **n** when he H8034
9: 2 a servant whose **n** *was* Ziba. And when H8034
12 young son, whose **n** *was* Micha. And all H8034
12:24 **n** Solomon: and the LORD loved him. H8034
25 his **n** Jedidiah, because of the LORD. H8034
28 take the city, and it be called after my **n**. H8034
13: 1 a fair sister, whose **n** *was* Tamar; and H8034
3 But Amnon had a friend, whose **n** *was* H8034
14: 7 **n** nor remainder upon the earth. H8034
27 daughter, whose **n** *was* Tamar: she was H8034
16: 5 of Saul, whose **n** *was* Shimei, the son H8034

2Sa 17:25 a man's son, whose **n** *was* Ithra an H8034
18:18 no son to keep my **n** in remembrance: H8034
18 after his own **n**: and it is called unto H8034
20: 1 of Belial, whose **n** *was* Sheba, the son H8034
21 the son of Bichri by **n**, hath lifted up his H8034
22:50 and I will sing praises unto thy **n**. H8034
23:18 slew *them*, and had the **n** among three. H8034
22 had the **n** among three mighty men. H8034
1Ki 1:47 God make the **n** of Solomon better than H8034
47 better than thy **n**, and make his throne H8034
3: 2 the **n** of the LORD, until those days. H8034
5: 3 an house unto the **n** of the LORD his H8034
5 an house unto the **n** of the LORD my H8034
5 he shall build an house unto my **n**. H8034
7:21 and called the **n** thereof Jachin: and H8034
21 pillar, and called the **n** thereof Boaz. H8034
8:16 an house, that my **n** might be therein; H8034
17 for the **n** of the LORD God of Israel. H8034
18 an house unto my **n**, thou didst well H8034
19 he shall build the house unto my **n**. H8034
20 for the **n** of the LORD God of Israel. H8034
29 hast said, My **n** shall be there: that H8034
33 and confess thy **n**, and pray, and make H8034
35 and confess thy **n**, and turn from their H8034
42 (For they shall hear of thy great **n**, and H8034
43 may know thy **n**, to fear thee, as *do* thy H8034
43 which I have builded, is called by thy **n**. H8034
44 the house that I have built for thy **n**: H8034
48 the house which I have built for thy **n**: H8034
9: 3 built, to put my **n** there for ever; and H8034
7 hallowed for my **n**, will I cast out of my H8034
10: 1 concerning the **n** of the LORD, she H8034
11:26 whose mother's **n** *was* Zeruah, a widow H8034
36 I have chosen me to put my **n** there. H8034
13: 2 David, Josiah by **n**; and upon thee shall H8034
14:21 of Israel, to put his **n** there. And his H8034
21 **n** *was* Naamah an Ammonitess. H8034
31 And his mother's **n** *was* Naamah an H8034
15: 2 And his mother's **n** *was* Maachah, the H8034
10 And his mother's **n** *was* Maachah, the H8034
16:24 hill, and called the **n** of the city which H8034
24 he built, after the **n** of Shemer, owner H8034
18:24 And call ye on the **n** of your gods, and I H8034
24 I will call on the **n** of the LORD: and the H8034
25 **n** of your gods, but put no fire *under*. H8034
26 *it*, and called on the **n** of Baal from H8034
31 came, saying, Israel shall be thy **n**: H8034
32 an altar in the **n** of the LORD: and he H8034
21: 8 So she wrote letters in Ahab's **n**, and H8034
22:16 *that which is* true in the **n** of the LORD? H8034
42 **n** *was* Azubah the daughter of Shilhi. H8034
2Ki 2:24 them in the **n** of the LORD. And there H8034
5:11 and call on the **n** of the LORD his God, H8034
8:26 And his mother's **n** *was* Athaliah, the H8034
12: 1 mother's **n** *was* Zibiah of Beer-sheba. H8034
14: 2 **n** *was* Jehoaddan of Jerusalem. H8034
7 called the **n** of it Joktheel unto this day. H8034
27 he would blot out the **n** of Israel from H8034
15: 2 mother's **n** *was* Jecholiah of Jerusalem. H8034
33 **n** *was* Jerusha, the daughter of Zadok. H8034
18: 2 His mother's **n** also *was* Abi, the H8034
21: 1 And his mother's **n** *was* Hephzi-bah. H8034
4 said, In Jerusalem will I put my **n**. H8034
7 tribes of Israel, will I put my **n** for ever: H8034
19 And his mother's **n** *was* Meshullemeth, H8034
22: 1 And his mother's **n** *was* Jedidah, the H8034
23:27 of which I said, My **n** shall be there. H8034
31 And his mother's **n** *was* Hamutal, the H8034
34 and turned his **n** to Jehoiakim, and H8034
36 And his mother's **n** *was* Zebudah, the H8034
24: 8 And his mother's **n** *was* Nehushta, the H8034
17 stead, and changed his **n** to Zedekiah. H8034
18 And his mother's **n** *was* Hamutal, the H8034
1Ch 1:19 born two sons: the **n** of the one *was* H8034
19 and his brother's **n** *was* Joktan. H8034
43 and the **n** of his city *was* Dinhabah. H8034
46 stead: and the **n** of his city *was* Avith. H8034
50 his stead: and the **n** of his city *was* Pai; H8034
50 Pai; and his wife's **n** *was* Mehetabel, H8034
2:26 wife, whose **n** *was* Atarah; she *was* H8034
29 And the **n** of the wife of Abishur *was* H8034
34 an Egyptian, whose **n** *was* Jarha. H8034
4: 3 the **n** of their sister *was* Hazelelponi: H8034
9 his mother called his **n** Jabez, saying, H8034
41 And these written by **n** came in the H8034
7:15 whose sister's **n** *was* Maachah;) and H8034
15 Maachah;) and the **n** of the second *was* H8034
16 and she called his **n** Peresh; and the H8034
16 Peresh; and the **n** of his brother *was* H8034

1Ch 7:23 and he called his **n** Beriah, because it H8034
8:29 Gibeon; whose wife's **n** *was* Maachah: H8034
9:35 Jehiel, whose wife's **n** *was* Maachah: H8034
11:20 *them*, and had a **n** among the three. H8034
24 had the **n** among the three mighties. H8034
12:31 by **n**, to come and make David king. H8034
13: 6 the cherubims, whose **n** is called *on it*. H8034
14:11 the **n** of that place Baal-perazim. H8034
16: 2 the people in the **n** of the LORD. H8034
8 call upon his **n**, make known his deeds H8034
10 Glory ye in his holy **n**: let the heart of H8034
29 glory *due* unto his **n**: bring an offering, H8034
35 to thy holy **n**, *and* glory in thy praise. H8034
41 were expressed by **n**, to give thanks to H8034
17: 8 have made thee a **n** like the name of H8034
8 **n** of the great men that *are* in the earth. H8034
21 to make thee a **n** of greatness and H8034
24 Let it even be established, that thy **n** H8034
21:19 which he spake in the **n** of the LORD. H8034
22: 7 house unto the **n** of the LORD my God: H8034
8 an house unto my **n**, because thou hast H8034
9 about: for his **n** shall be Solomon, and H8034
10 He shall build an house for my **n**; and H8034
19 that is to be built to the **n** of the LORD. H8034
23:13 unto him, and to bless in his **n** for ever. H8034
28: 3 an house for my **n**, because thou *hast* H8034
29:13 thank thee, and praise thy glorious **n**. H8034
16 for thine holy **n** *cometh* of thine hand, H8034
2Ch 2: 1 an house for the **n** of the LORD, and an H8034
4 Behold, I build an house to the **n** of the H8034
3:17 the left; and called the **n** of that on the H8034
17 and the **n** of that on the left Boaz. H8034
6: 5 an house, that my **n** might be there; H8034
6 But I have chosen Jerusalem, that my **n** H8034
7 for the **n** of the LORD God of Israel. H8034
8 an house for my **n**, thou didst well in H8034
9 loins, he shall build the house for my **n**. H8034
10 for the **n** of the LORD God of Israel. H8034
20 wouldest put thy **n** there; to hearken H8034
24 and confess thy **n**, and pray and make H8034
26 and confess thy **n**, and turn from their H8034
33 may know thy **n**, and fear thee, as *doth* H8034
33 which I have built is called by thy **n**. H8034
34 the house which I have built for thy **n**; H8034
38 the house which I have built for thy **n**: H8034
7:14 If my people, which are called by my **n**, H8034
16 house, that my **n** may be there for ever: H8034
20 sanctified for my **n**, will I cast out of my H8034
12:13 of Israel, to put his **n** there. And his H8034
13 **n** *was* Naamah an Ammonitess. H8034
13: 2 His mother's **n** also *was* Michaiah H8034
14:11 on thee, and in thy **n** we go against this H8034
18:15 the truth to me in the **n** of the LORD? H8034
20: 8 a sanctuary therein for thy **n**, saying, H8034
9 presence, (for thy **n** *is* in this house,) H8034
26 therefore the **n** of the same place was H8034
31 **n** *was* Azubah the daughter of Shilhi. H8034
22: 2 His mother's **n** also *was* Athaliah the H8034
24: 1 **n** also *was* Zibiah of Beer-sheba. H8034
25: 1 **n** *was* Jehoaddan of Jerusalem. H8034
26: 3 **n** also *was* Jecoliah of Jerusalem. H8034
8 to Uzziah: and his **n** spread abroad H8034
15 withal. And his **n** spread far abroad; H8034
27: 1 His mother's **n** also *was* Jerushah, H8034
28: 9 was there, whose **n** *was* Oded: and he H8034
15 were expressed by **n** rose up, and took H8034
29: 1 And his mother's **n** *was* Abijah, the H8034
31:19 were expressed by **n**, to give portions to H8034
33: 4 In Jerusalem shall my **n** be for ever. H8034
7 tribes of Israel, will I put my **n** for ever: H8034
18 to him in the **n** of the LORD God of H8034
36: 4 and turned his **n** to Jehoiakim. And H8034
Ezr 2:61 Gileadite, and was called after their **n**: H8034
5: 1 **n** of the God of Israel, *even* unto them. H8036
14 unto *one*, whose **n** *was* Sheshbazzar, H8036
6:12 And the God that hath caused his **n** to H8036
8:20 all of them were expressed by **n**. H8034
Neh 1: 9 that I have chosen to set my **n** there. H8034
11 desire to fear thy **n**: and prosper, I pray H8034
7:63 to wife, and was called after their **n**. H8034
9: 5 be thy glorious **n**, which is exalted H8034
7 and gavest him the **n** of Abraham; H8034
10 didst thou get thee a **n**, as *it is* this day. H8034
Est 2: 5 Jew, whose **n** *was* Mordecai, the son H8034
14 in her, and that she were called by **n**. H8034
22 the king *thereof* in Mordecai's **n**. H8034
3:12 language; in the **n** of king Ahasuerus H8034
8: 8 you, in the king's **n**, and seal *it* with the H8034
8 in the king's **n**, and sealed with the H8034

Est 8:10 And he wrote in the king Ahasuerus' **n**, H8034
9:26 Purim after the **n** of Pur. Therefore for H8034
Job 1: 1 land of Uz, whose **n** *was* Job; and that H8034
21 away; blessed be the **n** of the LORD. H8034
18:17 and he shall have no **n** in the street. H8034
42:14 And he called the **n** of the first, H8034
14 first, Jemima; and the **n** of the second, H8034
14 and the **n** of the third, Keren-happuch. H8034
Ps 5:11 also that love thy **n** be joyful in thee. H8034
7:17 praise to the **n** of the LORD most high. H8034
8: 1 excellent *is* thy **n** in all the earth! who H8034
9 how excellent *is* thy **n** in all the earth! H8034
9: 2 sing praise to thy **n**, O thou most High. H8034
5 hast put out their **n** for ever and ever. H8034
10 And they that know thy **n** will put their H8034
18:49 heathen, and sing praises unto thy **n**. H8034
20: 1 the **n** of the God of Jacob defend thee; H8034
5 and in the **n** of our God we will set H8034
7 remember the **n** of the LORD our God. H8034
22:22 I will declare thy **n** unto my brethren: H8034
29: 2 glory due unto his **n**; worship the LORD H8034
33:21 because we have trusted in his holy **n**. H8034
34: 3 with me, and let us exalt his **n** together. H8034
41: 5 When shall he die, and his **n** perish? H8034
44: 5 through thy **n** will we tread them under H8034
8 long, and praise thy **n** for ever. Selah. H8034
20 If we have forgotten the **n** of our God, H8034
45:17 I will make thy **n** to be remembered in H8034
48:10 According to thy **n**, O God, so *is* thy H8034
52: 9 on thy **n**; for *it is* good before thy saints. H8034
54: 1 Save me, O God, by thy **n**, and judge me H8034
6 will praise thy **n**, O LORD; for *it is* good. H8034
61: 5 *me* the heritage of those that fear thy **n**. H8034
8 So will I sing praise unto thy **n** for ever, H8034
63: 4 I live: I will lift up my hands in thy **n**. H8034
66: 2 Sing forth the honour of his **n**: make his H8034
4 thee; they shall sing *to* thy **n**. Selah. H8034
68: 4 Sing unto God, sing praises to his **n**: H8034
4 by his **n** JAH, and rejoice before him. H8034
69:30 I will praise the **n** of God with a song, H8034
36 they that love his **n** shall dwell therein. H8034
72:17 His **n** shall endure for ever: his name H8034
17 His name shall endure for ever: his **n** H8034
19 And blessed *be* his glorious **n** for ever: H8034
74: 7 dwelling place of thy **n** to the ground. H8034
10 the enemy blaspheme thy **n** for ever? H8034
18 foolish people have blasphemed thy **n**. H8034
21 let the poor and needy praise thy **n**. H8034
75: 1 **n** is near thy wondrous works declare. H8034
76: 1 In Judah *is* God known: his **n** *is* great in H8034
79: 6 that have not called upon thy **n**. H8034
9 for the glory of thy **n**: and deliver us, H8034
80:18 quicken us, and we will call upon thy **n**. H8034
83: 4 a nation; that the **n** of Israel may be no H8034
16 that they may seek thy **n**, O LORD. H8034
18 that thou, whose **n** alone *is* JEHOVAH, H8034
86: 9 thee, O Lord; and shall glorify thy **n**. H8034
11 thy truth: unite my heart to fear thy **n**. H8034
12 and I will glorify thy **n** for evermore. H8034
89:12 and Hermon shall rejoice in thy **n**. H8034
16 In thy **n** shall they rejoice all the day: H8034
24 and in my **n** shall his horn be exalted. H8034
91:14 on high, because he hath known my **n**. H8034
92: 1 to sing praises unto thy **n**, O most High: H8034
96: 2 Sing unto the LORD, bless his **n**; shew H8034
8 glory *due unto* his **n**: bring an offering, H8034
99: 3 Let them praise thy great and terrible **n**; H8034
6 that call upon his **n**; they called upon H8034
100: 4 be thankful unto him, *and* bless his **n**. H8034
102:15 So the heathen shall fear the **n** of the H8034
21 To declare the **n** of the LORD in Zion, H8034
103: 1 all that is within me, *bless* his holy **n**. H8034
105: 1 call upon his **n**: make known his deeds H8034
3 Glory ye in his holy **n**: let the heart of H8034
106:47 thy holy **n**, *and* to triumph in thy praise. H8034
109:13 following let their **n** be blotted out. H8034
111: 9 for ever: holy and reverend *is* his **n**. H8034
113: 1 of the LORD, praise the **n** of the LORD. H8034
2 Blessed be the **n** of the LORD from this H8034
3 the same the LORD'S **n** *is* to be praised. H8034
115: 1 us, but unto thy **n** give glory, for thy H8034
116: 4 Then called I upon the **n** of the LORD; H8034
13 and call upon the **n** of the LORD. H8034
17 and will call upon the **n** of the LORD. H8034
118:10 the **n** of the LORD will I destroy them. H8034
11 the **n** of the LORD I will destroy them. H8034
12 the **n** of the LORD I will destroy them. H8034
26 Blessed *be* he that cometh in the **n** of H8034
119:55 I have remembered thy **n**, O LORD, in H8034

Ps119:132 usest to do unto those that love thy **n**. H8034
122: 4 to give thanks unto the **n** of the LORD. H8034
124: 8 Our help *is* in the **n** of the LORD, who H8034
129: 8 you: we bless you in the **n** of the LORD. H8034
135: 1 Praise ye the LORD. Praise ye the **n** of H8034
3 praises unto his **n**; for *it is* pleasant. H8034
13 Thy **n**, O LORD, *endureth* for ever; *and* H8034
138: 2 and praise thy **n** for thy lovingkindness H8034
2 magnified thy word above all thy **n**. H8034
139:20 *and* thine enemies take *thy* **n** in vain.
140:13 give thanks unto thy **n**: the upright shall H8034
142: 7 I may praise thy **n**: the righteous shall H8034
145: 1 and I will bless thy **n** for ever and ever. H8034
2 I will praise thy **n** for ever and ever. H8034
21 flesh bless his holy **n** for ever and ever. H8034
148: 5 Let them praise the **n** of the LORD: for H8034
13 Let them praise the **n** of the LORD: for H8034
13 the LORD: for his **n** alone is excellent; H8034
149: 3 Let them praise his **n** in the dance: let H8034
Prv 10: 7 but the **n** of the wicked shall rot. H8034
18:10 The **n** of the LORD *is* a strong tower: H8034
21:24 Proud *and* haughty scorner *is* his **n**, H8034
22: 1 A *good* **n** *is* rather to be chosen than H8034
30: 4 the earth? what *is* his **n**, and what *is* his H8034
4 what *is* his son's **n**, if thou canst tell? H8034
9 steal, and take the **n** of my God *in vain*. H8034
Ecc 6: 4 his **n** shall be covered with darkness. H8034
7: 1 A good **n** *is* better than precious H8034
Song 1: 3 ointments thy **n** *is as* ointment poured H8034
Isa 4: 1 by thy **n**, to take away our reproach. H8034
7:14 a son, and shall call his **n** Immanuel. H8034
8: 3 me, Call his **n** Maher-shalal-hash-baz. H8034
9: 6 his shoulder: and his **n** shall be called H8034
12: 4 call upon his **n**, declare his doings H8034
4 make mention that his **n** is exalted. H8034
14:22 from Babylon the **n**, and remnant, and H8034
18: 7 to the place of the **n** of the LORD of H8034
24:15 the fires, *even* the **n** of the LORD God of H8034
25: 1 I will praise thy **n**; for thou hast done H8034
26: 8 thy **n**, and to the remembrance of thee. H8034
13 only will we make mention of thy **n**. H8034
29:23 shall sanctify my **n**, and sanctify the H8034
30:27 Behold, the **n** of the LORD cometh H8034
41:25 he call upon my **n**: and he shall come H8034
42: 8 I *am* the LORD: that *is* my **n**: and my H8034
43: 1 have called *thee* by thy **n**; thou *art* mine. H8034
7 *Even* every one that is called by my **n**: H8034
44: 5 shall call *himself* by the **n** of Jacob; and H8034
5 and surname *himself* by the **n** of Israel. H8034
45: 3 call *thee* by thy **n**, *am* the God of Israel. H8034
4 called thee by thy **n**: I have surnamed H8034
47: 4 of hosts *is* his **n**, the Holy One of Israel. H8034
48: 1 are called by the **n** of Israel, and are H8034
1 swear by the **n** of the LORD, and make H8034
2 of Israel; The LORD of hosts *is* his **n**. H8034
11 for how should *my* **n** be polluted? and I
19 gravel thereof; his **n** should not have H8034
49: 1 mother hath he made mention of my **n**. H8034
50:10 **n** of the LORD, and stay upon his God. H8034
51:15 roared: The LORD of hosts *is* his **n**. H8034
52: 5 **n** continually every day *is* blasphemed. H8034
6 Therefore my people shall know my **n**: H8034
54: 5 of hosts *is* his **n**; and thy Redeemer the H8034
55:13 to the LORD for a **n**, for an everlasting H8034
56: 5 a place and a **n** better than of sons H8034
5 everlasting **n**, that shall not be cut off. H8034
6 and to love the **n** of the LORD, to be his H8034
57:15 eternity, whose **n** *is* Holy; I dwell in the H8034
59:19 So shall they fear the **n** of the LORD H8034
60: 9 them, unto the **n** of the LORD thy God, H8034
62: 2 be called by a new **n**, which the mouth H8034
2 which the mouth of the LORD shall **n**. H5344
63:12 them, to make himself an everlasting **n**? H8034
14 thy people, to make thyself a glorious **n**. H8034
16 redeemer; thy **n** *is* from everlasting. H8034
19 them; they were not called by thy **n**. H8034
64: 2 to boil, to make thy **n** known to thine H8034
7 that calleth upon thy **n**, that stirreth up H8034
65: 1 a nation *that* was not called by my **n**. H8034
15 And ye shall leave your **n** for a curse H8034
15 thee, and call his servants by another **n**: H8034
66:22 so shall your seed and your **n** remain. H8034
Jer 3:17 unto it, to the **n** of the LORD, to H8034
7:10 is called by my **n**, and say, We are H8034
11 Is this house, which is called by my **n**, H8034
12 where I set my **n** at the first, and see H8034
14 is called by my **n**, wherein ye trust, and H8034
30 which is called by my **n**, to pollute it. H8034
10: 6 *art* great, and thy **n** *is* great in might. H8034

Jer 10:16 inheritance: The LORD of hosts *is* his **n**. H8034
25 call not on thy **n**: for they have eaten H8034
11:16 The LORD called thy **n**, A green olive H8034
19 his **n** may be no more remembered. H8034
21 not in the **n** of the LORD, that thou H8034
12:16 to swear by my **n**, The LORD liveth; as H8034
13:11 a people, and for a **n**, and for a praise, H8034
14: 9 and we are called by thy **n**; leave us not. H8034
14 lies in my **n**: I sent them not, neither H8034
15 prophesy in my **n**, and I sent them not, H8034
15:16 called by thy **n**, O LORD God of hosts. H8034
16:21 shall know that my **n** *is* The LORD. H8034
20: 3 thy **n** Pashur, but Magor-missabib. H8034
9 any more in his **n**. But *his word* was in H8034
23: 6 and this *is* his **n** whereby he shall be H8034
25 lies in my **n**, saying, I have dreamed, H8034
27 to forget my **n** by their dreams which H8034
27 fathers have forgotten my **n** for Baal. H8034
25:29 is called by my **n**, and should ye be H8034
26: 9 Why hast thou prophesied in the **n** of H8034
16 to us in the **n** of the LORD our God. H8034
20 that prophesied in the **n** of the LORD, H8034
27:15 a lie in my **n**; that I might drive you H8034
29: 9 **n**: I have not sent them, saith the LORD. H8034
21 a lie unto you in my **n**; Behold, I will H8034
23 lying words in my **n**, which I have not H8034
25 sent letters in thy **n** unto all the people H8034
31:35 roar; The LORD of hosts *is* his **n**: H8034
32:18 Mighty God, the LORD of hosts, *is* his **n**, H8034
20 and hast made thee a **n**, as at this day; H8034
34 which is called by my **n**, to defile it. H8034
33: 2 it, to establish it; the LORD *is* his **n**; H8034
9 And it shall be to me a **n** of joy, a praise H8034
16 and this *is the* **n** wherewith she shall
34:15 in the house which is called by my **n**: H8034
16 But ye turned and polluted my **n**, and H8034
37:13 *was* there, whose **n** *was* Irijah, the son H8034
44:16 unto us in the **n** of the LORD, we will H8034
26 by my great **n**, saith the LORD, that H8034
26 the LORD, that my **n** shall no more be H8034
46:18 *As* I live, saith the King, whose **n** *is* the H8034
48:15 the King, whose **n** *is* the LORD of hosts. H8034
17 all ye that know his **n**, say, How is the H8034
50:34 of hosts *is* his **n**: he shall throughly H8034
51:19 inheritance: the LORD of hosts *is* his **n**. H8034
57 the King, whose **n** *is* the LORD of hosts. H8034
52: 1 And his mother's **n** *was* Hamutal the H8034
Lam 3:55 I called upon thy **n**, O LORD, out of the H8034
Ezk 20:29 ye go? And the **n** thereof is called H8034
39 pollute ye my holy **n** no more with your H8034
24: 2 Son of man, write thee the **n** of the day, H8034
36:20 profaned my holy **n**, when they said to H8034
21 But I had pity for mine holy **n**, which H8034
23 And I will sanctify my great **n**, which H8034
39: 7 So will I make my holy **n** known in the H8034
7 pollute my holy **n** any more: and the H8034
16 And also the **n** of the city *shall be* H8034
25 Israel, and will be jealous for my holy **n**; H8034
43: 7 ever, and my holy **n**, shall the house of H8034
8 even defiled my holy **n** by their H8034
48:35 *measures*: and the **n** of the city from H8034
Dan 1: 7 unto Daniel *the* **n** of Belteshazzar; and
2:20 Blessed be the **n** of God for ever and H8036
26 to Daniel, whose **n** *was* Belteshazzar, H8036
4: 8 before me, whose **n** *was* Belteshazzar, H8036
8 according to the **n** of my god, and in H8036
19 Then Daniel, whose **n** *was* H8036
9: 6 which spake in thy **n** to our kings, our H8034
18 is called by thy **n**: for we do not present H8034
19 city and thy people are called by thy **n**. H8034
10: 1 unto Daniel, whose **n** was called H8034
Hos 1: 4 unto him, Call his **n** Jezreel; for yet a H8034
6 unto him, Call her **n** Lo-ruhamah: for I H8034
9 Then said *God*, Call his **n** Lo-ammi: for H8034
2:17 no more be remembered by their **n**. H8034
Joel 2:26 and praise the **n** of the LORD your God, H8034
32 shall call on the **n** of the LORD shall be H8034
Am 2: 7 the *same* maid, to profane my holy **n**: H8034
4:13 The LORD, The God of hosts, *is* his **n**. H8034
5: 8 the face of the earth: The LORD *is* his **n**: H8034
27 the LORD, whose **n** *is* The God of hosts. H8034
6:10 make mention of the **n** of the LORD. H8034
9: 6 the face of the earth: The LORD *is* his **n**. H8034
12 my **n**, saith the LORD that doeth this. H8034
Mic 4: 5 every one in the **n** of his god, and we H8034
5 we will walk in the **n** of the LORD our H8034
5: 4 in the majesty of the **n** of the LORD his H8034
6: 9 shall see thy **n**: hear ye the rod, and H8034
Nah 1:14 no more of thy **n** be sown: out of the H8034

Zep 1: 4 **n** of the Chemarims with the priests; H8034
3: 9 may all call upon the **n** of the LORD, to H8034
12 they shall trust in the **n** of the LORD. H8034
20 I will make you a **n** and a praise among H8034
Zec 5: 4 falsely by my **n**: and it shall remain H8034
6:12 the man whose **n** *is* The BRANCH; and H8034
10:12 up and down in his **n**, saith the LORD. H8034
13: 3 lies in the **n** of the LORD: and his H8034
9 shall call on my **n**, and I will hear them: H8034
14: 9 shall there be one LORD, and his **n** one. H8034
Mal 1: 6 that despise my **n**. And ye say, Wherein H8034
6 ye say, Wherein have we despised thy **n**? H8034
11 of the same my **n** *shall be* great among H8034
11 offered unto my **n**, and a pure offering: H8034
11 offering: for my **n** *shall be* great among H8034
14 my **n** *is* dreadful among the heathen. H8034
2: 2 give glory unto my **n**, saith the LORD of H8034
5 feared me, and was afraid before my **n**. H8034
3:16 the LORD, and that thought upon his **n**. H8034
4: 2 But unto you that fear my **n** shall the H8034
Mt 1:21 thou shalt call his **n** JESUS: for he shall *G3686*
23 they shall call his **n** Emmanuel, which *G3686*
25 son: and he called his **n** JESUS. *G3686*
6: 9 which art in heaven, Hallowed be thy **n**. *G3686*
7:22 prophesied in thy **n**? and in thy name *G3686*
22 thy name? and in thy **n** have cast out *G3686*
22 in thy **n** done many wonderful works? *G3686*
10:41 He that receiveth a prophet in the **n** of *G3686*
41 man in the **n** of a righteous man *G3686*
42 *water* only in the **n** of a disciple, verily *G3686*
12:21 And in his **n** shall the Gentiles trust. *G3686*
18: 5 such little child in my **n** receiveth me. *G3686*
20 my **n**, there am I in the midst of them. *G3686*
21: 9 **n** of the Lord; Hosanna in the highest. *G3686*
23:39 *is* he that cometh in the **n** of the Lord. *G3686*
24: 5 For many shall come in my **n**, saying, I *G3686*
27:32 **n**: him they compelled to bear his cross. *G3686*
28:19 them in the **n** of the Father, and of *G3686*
Mk 5: 9 And he asked him, What *is* thy **n**? And *G3686*
9 My **n** *is* Legion: for we are many. *G3686*
22 Jairus by **n**; and when he saw him, *G3686*
6:14 *of him*; (for his **n** was spread abroad:) *G3686*
9:37 children in my **n**, receiveth me: and *G3686*
38 out devils in thy **n**, and he followeth not *G3686*
39 my **n**, that can lightly speak evil of me. *G3686*
41 to drink in my **n**, because ye belong to *G3686*
11: 9 *is* he that cometh in the **n** of the Lord: *G3686*
10 **n** of the Lord: Hosanna in the highest. *G3686*
13: 6 For many shall come in my **n**, saying, I *G3686*
16:17 that believe; In my **n** shall they cast out *G3686*
Lk 1: 5 of Aaron, and her **n** *was* Elisabeth. *G3686*
13 a son, and thou shalt call his **n** John. *G3686*
27 To a virgin espoused to a man whose **n** *G3686*
27 of David; and the virgin's **n** *was* Mary. *G3686*
31 forth a son, and shalt call his **n** JESUS. *G3686*
49 to me great things; and holy *is* his **n**. *G3686*
59 him Zacharias, after the **n** of his father. *G3686*
61 of thy kindred that is called by this **n**. *G3686*
63 His **n** is John. And they marvelled all. *G3686*
2:21 of the child, his **n** was called JESUS, *G3686*
25 Jerusalem, whose **n** *was* Simeon; and *G3686*
6:22 **n** as evil, for the Son of man's sake. *G3686*
8:30 What is thy **n**? And he said, Legion: *G3686*
9:48 this child in my **n** receiveth me: and *G3686*
49 out devils in thy **n**; and we forbad him, *G3686*
10:17 are subject unto us through thy **n**. *G3686*
11: 2 Hallowed be thy **n**. Thy kingdom come. *G3686*
13:35 *is* he that cometh in the **n** of the Lord. *G3686*
19:38 that cometh in the **n** of the Lord: peace *G3686*
21: 8 shall come in my **n**, saying, I am *Christ*; *G3686*
24:18 And the one of them, whose **n** was *G3686*
47 be preached in his **n** among all nations, *G3686*
Jn 1: 6 man sent from God, whose **n** *was* John. *G3686*
12 God, *even* to them that believe on his **n**: *G3686*
2:23 believed in his **n**, when they saw the *G3686*
3:18 the **n** of the only begotten Son of God. *G3686*
5:43 I am come in my Father's **n**, and ye *G3686*
43 come in his own **n**, him ye will receive. *G3686*
10: 3 own sheep by **n**, and leadeth them out. *G3686*
25 my Father's **n**, they bear witness of me. *G3686*
12:13 Israel that cometh in the **n** of the Lord. *G3686*
28 Father, glorify thy **n**. Then came there a *G3686*
14:13 And whatsoever ye shall ask in my **n**, *G3686*
14 If ye shall ask any thing in my **n**, I will *G3686*
26 will send in my **n**, he shall teach you all *G3686*
15:16 the Father in my **n**, he may give it you. *G3686*
16:23 the Father in my **n**, he will give *it* you. *G3686*
24 Hitherto have ye asked nothing in my **n**: *G3686*
26 At that day ye shall ask in my **n**: and I *G3686*
Jn 17: 6 I have manifested thy **n** unto the men *G3686*
11 thine own **n** those whom thou hast *G3686*
12 I kept them in thy **n**: those that thou *G3686*
26 And I have declared unto them thy **n**, *G3686*
18:10 right ear. The servant's **n** was Malchus. *G3686*
20:31 ye might have life through his **n**. *G3686*
Act 2:21 call on the **n** of the Lord shall be saved. *G3686*
38 one of you in the **n** of Jesus Christ for *G3686*
3: 6 give I thee: In the **n** of Jesus Christ of *G3686*
16 And his **n** through faith in his name *G3686*
16 And his name through faith in his **n** *G3686*
4: 7 power, or by what **n**, have ye done this? *G3686*
10 of Israel, that by the **n** of Jesus Christ of *G3686*
12 is none other **n** under heaven given *G3686*
17 speak henceforth to no man in this **n**. *G3686*
18 speak at all nor teach in the **n** of Jesus. *G3686*
30 be done by the **n** of thy holy child Jesus. *G3686*
5:28 not teach in this **n**? and, behold, ye have *G3686*
40 speak in the **n** of Jesus, and let them go. *G3686*
41 worthy to suffer shame for his **n**. *G3686*
7:58 a young man's feet, whose **n** was Saul. *G2564*
8:12 of God, and the **n** of Jesus Christ, they *G3686*
16 baptized in the **n** of the Lord Jesus.) *G3686*
9:14 priests to bind all that call on thy **n**. *G3686*
15 me, to bear my **n** before the Gentiles, *G3686*
21 called on this **n** in Jerusalem, and came *G3686*
27 boldly at Damascus in the **n** of Jesus. *G3686*
29 And he spake boldly in the **n** of the *G3686*
10:43 that through his **n** whosoever believeth *G3686*
48 be baptized in the **n** of the Lord. Then *G3686*
13: 6 prophet, a Jew, whose **n** *was* Barjesus: *G3686*
8 But Elymas the sorcerer (for so is his **n** *G3686*
15:14 to take out of them a people for his **n**. *G3686*
17 upon whom my **n** is called, saith the *G3686*
26 lives for the **n** of our Lord Jesus Christ. *G3686*
16:18 thee in the **n** of Jesus Christ to come *G3686*
19: 5 baptized in the **n** of the Lord Jesus. *G3686*
13 had evil spirits the **n** of the Lord Jesus, *G3686*
17 the **n** of the Lord Jesus was magnified. *G3686*
21:13 Jerusalem for the **n** of the Lord Jesus. *G3686*
22:16 thy sins, calling on the **n** of the Lord. *G3686*
26: 9 contrary to the **n** of Jesus of Nazareth. *G3686*
28: 7 the island, whose **n** was Publius; who *G3686*
Ro 1: 5 to the faith among all nations, for his **n**: *G3686*
2:24 For the **n** of God is blasphemed among *G3686*
9:17 thee, and that my **n** might be declared *G3686*
10:13 For whosoever shall call upon the **n** of *G3686*
15: 9 the Gentiles, and sing unto thy **n**. *G3686*
1Co 1: 2 call upon the **n** of Jesus Christ our *G3686*
10 Now I beseech you, brethren, by the **n** *G3686*
13 or were ye baptized in the **n** of Paul? *G3686*
15 say that I had baptized in mine own **n**. *G3686*
5: 4 In the **n** of our Lord Jesus Christ, when *G3686*
6:11 are justified in the **n** of the Lord Jesus, *G3686*
Eph 1:21 and every **n** that is named, not only *G3686*
5:20 in the **n** of our Lord Jesus Christ; *G3686*
Php 2: 9 him a **n** which is above every name: *G3686*
9 him a name which is above every **n**: *G3686*
10 That at the **n** of Jesus every knee *G3686*
Col 3:17 deed, *do* all in the **n** of the Lord Jesus, *G3686*
2Th 1:12 That the **n** of our Lord Jesus Christ *G3686*
3: 6 brethren, in the **n** of our Lord Jesus *G3686*
1Ti 6: 1 all honour, that the **n** of God and *his* *G3686*
2Ti 2:19 the **n** of Christ depart from iniquity. *G3686*
Heb 1: 4 obtained a more excellent **n** than they. *G3686*
2:12 Saying, I will declare thy **n** unto my *G3686*
6:10 toward his **n**, in that ye have ministered *G3686*
13:15 fruit of *our* lips giving thanks to his **n**. *G3686*
Jas 2: 7 Do not they blaspheme that worthy **n** *G3686*
5:10 have spoken in the **n** of the Lord, for an *G3686*
14 him with oil in the **n** of the Lord: *G3686*
1Pt 4:14 If ye be reproached for the **n** of Christ, *G3686*
1Jn 3:23 believe on the **n** of his Son Jesus Christ, *G3686*
5:13 that believe on the **n** of the Son of God; *G3686*
13 may believe on the **n** of the Son of God. *G3686*
3Jn 14 salute thee. Greet the friends by **n**. *G3686*
Rev 2:13 holdest fast my **n**, and hast not denied *G3686*
17 in the stone a new **n** written, which no *G3686*
3: 1 hast a **n** that thou livest, and art dead. *G3686*
5 not blot out his **n** out of the book of life, *G3686*
5 I will confess his **n** before my Father, *G3686*
8 my word, and hast not denied my **n**. *G3686*
12 upon him the **n** of my God, and the *G3686*
12 of my God, and the **n** of the city of my *G3686*
12 and *I will write upon him* my new **n**. *G3686*
6: 8 horse: and his **n** that sat on him was *G3686*
8:11 And the **n** of the star is called *G3686*
9:11 pit, whose **n** in the Hebrew tongue *G3686*
11 the Greek tongue hath *his* **n** Apollyon. *G3686*
Rev 11:18 them that fear thy **n**, small and great; *G3686*
13: 1 upon his heads the **n** of blasphemy. *G3686*
6 to blaspheme his **n**, and his tabernacle, *G3686*
17 the mark, or the **n** of the beast, or the *G3686*
17 of the beast, or the number of his **n**. *G3686*
14: 1 Father's **n** written in their foreheads. *G3686*
11 whosoever receiveth the mark of his **n**. *G3686*
15: 2 the number of his **n**, stand on the sea of *G3686*
4 and glorify thy **n**? for *thou* only *art* holy: *G3686*
16: 9 blasphemed the **n** of God, which hath *G3686*
17: 5 And upon her forehead *was* a **n** *G3686*
19:12 and he had a **n** written, that no man *G3686*
13 and his **n** is called The Word of God. *G3686*
16 and on his thigh a **n** written, KING OF *G3686*
22: 4 And they shall see his face; and his **n** *G3686*

NAMED

Gen 23:16 which he had **n** in the audience of the H1696
27:36 And he said, Is not he rightly **n** H7121+H8034
48:16 and let my name be **n** on them, and the H7121
Jos 2: 1 house, **n** Rahab, and lodged there. H8034
1Sa 4:21 And she **n** the child Ichabod, saying, H7121
17: 4 of the Philistines, **n** Goliath, of Gath, H8034
22:20 the son of Ahitub, **n** Abiathar, escaped, H8034
2Ki 17:34 children of Jacob, whom he **n** Israel; H8034
1Ch 23:14 his sons were **n** of the tribe of Levi. H7121
Ecc 6:10 That which hath been is **n** H7121+H8034
Isa 61: 6 But ye shall be **n** the Priests of the H7121
Jer 44:26 shall no more be **n** in the mouth of any H7121
Dan 5:12 whom the king **n** Belteshazzar: now let H8036
Am 6: 1 *which are* **n** chief of the nations, H5344
Mic 2: 7 O *thou that art* **n** the house of Jacob, is H559
Mt 9: 9 he saw a man, **n** Matthew, sitting at *G3004*
27:57 of Arimathaea, **n** Joseph, who also *G5122*
Mk 14:32 And they came to a place which was **n** *G3686*
15: 7 And there was *one* **n** Barabbas, *which* *G3004*
Lk 1: 5 a certain priest **n** Zacharias, of the *G3686*
26 God unto a city of Galilee, **n** Nazareth, *G3739*
2:21 which was so **n** of the angel before he *G2564*
5:27 saw a publican, **n** Levi, sitting at the *G3686*
6:13 chose twelve, whom also he **n** apostles; *G3687*
14 Simon, (whom he also **n** Peter,) and *G3687*
8:41 And, behold, there came a man **n** *G3686*
10:38 **n** Martha received him into her house. *G3686*
16:20 And there was a certain beggar **n** *G3686*
19: 2 And, behold, *there was* a man **n** *G3686*
23:50 And, behold, *there was* a man **n** *G3686*
Jn 3: 1 There was a man of the Pharisees, **n** *G3686*
11: 1 Now a certain *man* was sick, ***n*** Lazarus,
49 And one of them, ***n*** Caiaphas, being the
Act 5: 1 But a certain man **n** Ananias, with *G3686*
34 a Pharisee, **n** Gamaliel, a doctor of *G3686*
9:10 at Damascus, **n** Ananias; and to him *G3686*
12 And hath seen in a vision a man **n** *G3686*
33 And there he found a certain man **n** *G3686*
36 a certain disciple **n** Tabitha, which by *G3686*
11:28 And there stood up one of them **n** *G3686*
12:13 a damsel came to hearken, **n** Rhoda. *G3686*
16: 1 disciple was there, **n** Timotheus, the *G3686*
14 And a certain woman **n** Lydia, a seller *G3686*
17:34 **n** Damaris, and others with them. *G3686*
18: 2 And found a certain Jew **n** Aquila, born *G3686*
7 certain *man's* house, **n** Justus, *one* that *G3686*
24 And a certain Jew **n** Apollos, born at *G3686*
19:24 For a certain *man* **n** Demetrius, a *G3686*
20: 9 young man **n** Eutychus, being fallen *G3686*
21:10 Judaea a certain prophet, **n** Agabus. *G3686*
24: 1 *with* a certain orator ***n*** Tertullus, who
27: 1 unto *one* **n** Julius, a centurion of *G3686*
Ro 15:20 where Christ was **n**, lest I should build *G3687*
1Co 5: 1 as is not so much as **n** among the *G3687*
Eph 1:21 every name that is **n**, not only in this *G3687*
3:15 whole family in heaven and earth is **n**, *G3687*
5: 3 once **n** among you, as becometh saints; *G3687*

NAMELY

Lev 1:10 And if his offering *be* of the flocks, ***n***, of
Nu 1:32 Of the children of Joseph, ***n***, of the
9:15 covered the tabernacle, ***n***, the tent of the
13:11 Of the tribe of Joseph, ***n***, of the tribe of
31: 8 that were slain; ***n***, Evi, and Rekem, and
Dt 4:43 ***N***, Bezer in the wilderness, in the plain
13: 7 ***N***, of the gods of the people which *are*
20:17 But thou shalt utterly destroy them; ***n***,
Jdg 3: 3 ***N***, five lords of the Philistines, and all the
8:35 of Jerubbaal, ***n***, Gideon, according to
1Ch 6:57 the cities of Judah, ***n***, Hebron, *the city* of
61 of the half tribe, ***n***, *out of* the half *tribe* of
9:23 ***n***, the house of the tabernacle, by wards.

1Ch 23: 6 of Levi, *n*, Gershon, Kohath, and Merari.
Ezr 10:18 strange wives: *n*, of the sons of Jeshua
Neh 12:35 with trumpets; *n*, Zechariah the son of
Est 8:12 of king Ahasuerus, *n*, upon the thirteenth
Ecc 5:13 seen under the sun, *n*, riches kept for the
Isa 7:20 razor that is hired, *n*, by them beyond the
Jer 26:22 men into Egypt, *n*, Elnathan the son of
Mk 12:31 And the second *is* like, *n* this, Thou shalt
Act 15:22 Paul and Barnabas; *n*, Judas surnamed
Ro 13: 9 in this saying, **n**, Thou shalt love thy *G1722*

NAMES

Gen 2:20 And Adam gave **n** to all cattle, and to H8034
25:13 And these *are* the **n** of the sons of H8034
13 Ishmael, by their **n**, according to their H8034
16 these *are* their **n**, by their towns, and H8034
26:18 he called their **n** after the names by H8034
18 **n** by which his father had called them. H8034
36:10 These *are* the **n** of Esau's sons; Eliphaz H8034
40 And these *are* the **n** of the dukes *that* H8034
40 places, by their **n**; duke Timnah, duke H8034
46: 8 And these *are* the **n** of the children of H8034
Ex 1: 1 Now these *are* the **n** of the children of H8034
6:16 And these *are* the **n** of the sons of Levi H8034
28: 9 on them the **n** of the children of Israel: H8034
10 Six of their **n** on one stone, and *the* H8034
10 and *the other* six **n** of the rest on the H8034
11 two stones with the **n** of the children of H8034
12 shall bear their **n** before the LORD H8034
21 And the stones shall be with the **n** of H8034
21 according to their **n**, *like* the engravings H8034
29 And Aaron shall bear the **n** of the H8034
39: 6 with the **n** of the children of Israel. H8034
14 And the stones *were* according to the **n** H8034
14 according to their **n**, *like* the engravings H8034
Nu 1: 2 of *their* **n**, every male by their polls; H8034
5 And these *are* the **n** of the men that H8034
17 men which are expressed by *their* **n**: H8034
18 the number of the **n**, from twenty years H8034
20 to the number of the **n**, by their polls, H8034
22 to the number of the **n**, by their polls, H8034
24 the number of the **n**, from twenty years H8034
26 the number of the **n**, from twenty years H8034
28 the number of the **n**, from twenty years H8034
30 the number of the **n**, from twenty years H8034
32 the number of the **n**, from twenty years H8034
34 the number of the **n**, from twenty years H8034
36 the number of the **n**, from twenty years H8034
38 the number of the **n**, from twenty years H8034
40 the number of the **n**, from twenty years H8034
42 the number of the **n**, from twenty years H8034
3: 2 And these *are* the **n** of the sons of H8034
3 These *are* the **n** of the sons of Aaron, H8034
17 **n**; Gershon, and Kohath, and Merari. H8034
18 And these *are* the **n** of the sons of H8034
40 and take the number of their **n**. H8034
43 by the number of **n**, from a month old H8034
13: 4 And these *were* their **n**: of the tribe of H8034
16 These *are* the **n** of the men which H8034
26:33 and the **n** of the daughters of H8034
53 according to the number of **n**. H8034
55 according to the **n** of the tribes of their H8034
27: 1 and these *are* the **n** of his daughters; H8034
32:38 And Nebo, and Baal-meon, (their **n** H8034
38 **n** unto the cities which they builded. H8034
34:17 These *are* the **n** of the men which shall H8034
19 And the **n** of the men *are* these: Of the H8034
Dt 12: 3 destroy the **n** of them out of that place. H8034
Jos 17: 3 and these *are* the **n** of his daughters, H8034
1Sa 14:49 and the **n** of his two daughters H8034
17:13 to the battle: and the **n** of his three sons H8034
2Sa 5:14 And these *be* the **n** of those that were H8034
23: 8 These *be* the **n** of the mighty men H8034
1Ki 4: 8 And these *are* their **n**: The son of Hur, H8034
1Ch 4:38 These mentioned by *their* **n** *were* H8034
6:17 And these *be* the **n** of the sons of H8034
65 these cities, which are called by *their* **n**. H8034
8:38 And Azel had six sons, whose **n** *are* H8034
9:44 And Azel had six sons, whose **n** *are* H8034
14: 4 Now these *are* the **n** of *his* children H8034
23:24 by number of **n** by their polls, that did H8034
Ezr 5: 4 **n** of the men that make this building? H8036
10 We asked their **n** also, to certify thee, H8036
10 might write the **n** of the men that *were* H8036
8:13 of Adonikam, whose **n** *are* these, H8034
10:16 of them by *their* **n**, were separated, and H8034
Ps 16: 4 offer, nor take up their **n** into my lips. H8034
49:11 they call *their* lands after their own **n**. H8034
147: 4 the stars; he calleth them all by *their* **n**. H8034
Isa 40:26 calleth them all by **n** by the greatness of H8034
Ezk 23: 4 And the **n** of them *were* Aholah the H8034
4 Thus *were* their **n**; Samaria *is* Aholah, H8034
48: 1 Now these *are* the **n** of the tribes. From H8034
31 city *shall be* after the **n** of the tribes of H8034
Dan 1: 7 of the eunuchs gave **n**: for he gave unto H8034
Hos 2:17 For I will take away the **n** of Baalim out H8034
Zec 13: 2 I will cut off the **n** of the idols out of the H8034
Mt 10: 2 Now the **n** of the twelve apostles are *G3686*
Lk 10:20 because your **n** are written in heaven. *G3686*
Act 1:15 (the number of **n** together were about *G3686*
18:15 But if it be a question of words and **n**, *G3686*
Php 4: 3 whose **n** *are* in the book of life. *G3686*
Rev 3: 4 Thou hast a few **n** even in Sardis which *G3686*
13: 8 him, whose **n** are not written in the *G3686*
17: 3 beast, full of **n** of blasphemy, having *G3686*
8 wonder, whose **n** were not written in *G3686*
21:12 twelve angels, and **n** written thereon, *G3686*
12 which are *the* **n** of the twelve tribes of
14 **n** of the twelve apostles of the Lamb. *G3686*

NAME'S

1Sa 12:22 for his great **n** sake: because it hath H8034
1Ki 8:41 out of a far country for thy **n** sake; H8034
2Ch 6:32 for thy great **n** sake, and thy mighty H8034
Ps 23: 3 paths of righteousness for his **n** sake. H8034
25:11 For thy **n** sake, O LORD, pardon mine H8034
31: 3 for thy **n** sake lead me, and guide me. H8034
79: 9 purge away our sins, for thy **n** sake. H8034
106: 8 Nevertheless he saved them for his **n** H8034
109:21 the Lord, for thy **n** sake: because thy H8034
143:11 Quicken me, O LORD, for thy **n** sake: H8034
Isa 48: 9 For my **n** sake will I defer mine anger, H8034
66: 5 you out for my **n** sake, said, Let the H8034
Jer 14: 7 us, do thou *it* for thy **n** sake: for our H8034
21 Do not abhor *us*, for thy **n** sake, do not H8034
Ezk 20: 9 But I wrought for my **n** sake, that it H8034
14 But I wrought for my **n** sake, that it H8034
22 wrought for my **n** sake, that it should H8034
44 with you for my **n** sake, not according H8034
36:22 but for mine holy **n** sake, which ye H8034
Mt 10:22 of all *men* for my **n** sake: but he that *G3686*
19:29 or lands, for my **n** sake, shall receive *G3686*
24: 9 be hated of all nations for my **n** sake. *G3686*
Mk 13:13 of all *men* for my **n** sake: but he that *G3686*
Lk 21:12 before kings and rulers for my **n** sake. *G3686*
17 shall be hated of all *men* for my **n** sake. *G3686*
Jn 15:21 unto you for my **n** sake, because they *G3686*
Act 9:16 things he must suffer for my **n** sake. *G3686*
1Jn 2:12 sins are forgiven you for his **n** sake. *G3686*
3Jn 7 Because that for his **n** sake they went *G3686*
Rev 2: 3 and for my **n** sake hast laboured, *G3686*

NAMETH

2Ti 2:19 Let every one that **n** the name of Christ *G3687*

NAOMI

Ru 1: 2 name of his wife **N**, and the name of his H5281
8 And **N** said unto her two daughters in H5281
11 And **N** said, Turn again, my daughters: H5281
19 about them, and they said, *Is* this **N**? H5281
20 And she said unto them, Call me not **N**, H5281
21 why *then* call ye me **N**, seeing the LORD H5281
22 So **N** returned, and Ruth the H5281
2: 1 And **N** had a kinsman of her H5281
2 And Ruth the Moabitess said unto **N**, H5281
6 with **N** out of the country of Moab: H5281
20 And **N** said unto her daughter in law, H5281
20 to the dead. And **N** said unto her, The H5281
22 And **N** said unto Ruth her daughter in H5281
3: 1 Then **N** her mother in law said unto H5281
4: 3 And he said unto the kinsman, **N**, that H5281
5 of the hand of **N**, thou must buy *it* also H5281
9 and Mahlon's, of the hand of **N**. H5281
14 And the women said unto **N**, Blessed *be* H5281
16 And **N** took the child, and laid it in her H5281
17 is a son born to **N**; and they called his H5281

NAOMI'S

Ru 1: 3 And Elimelech **N** husband died; and H5281

NAPHISH

Gen 25:15 Hadar, and Tema, Jetur, **N**, and H5305
1Ch 1:31 Jetur, **N**, and Kedemah. These are the H5305

NAPHTALI

Gen 30: 8 prevailed: and she called his name **N**. H5321
35:25 Rachel's handmaid; Dan, and **N**: H5321
46:24 And the sons of **N**; Jahzeel, and Guni, H5321
49:21 **N** *is* a hind let loose: he giveth goodly H5321
Ex 1: 4 Dan, and **N**, Gad, and Asher. H5321
Nu 1:15 Of **N**; Ahira the son of Enan. H5321
42 Of the children of **N**, throughout their H5321
43 of the tribe of **N**, *were* fifty and three H5321
2:29 Then the tribe of **N**: and the captain of H5321
29 of **N** *shall be* Ahira the son of Enan. H5321
7:78 prince of the children of **N**, *offered*: H5321
10:27 of **N** *was* Ahira the son of Enan. H5321
13:14 Of the tribe of **N**, Nahbi the son of H5321
26:48 *Of* the sons of **N** after their families: of H5321
50 These *are* the families of **N** according H5321
34:28 of **N**, Pedahel the son of Ammihud. H5321
Dt 27:13 and Asher, and Zebulun, Dan, and **N**. H5321
33:23 And of **N** he said, O Naphtali, satisfied H5321
23 And of Naphtali he said, O **N**, satisfied H5321
34: 2 And all **N**, and the land of Ephraim, H5321
Jos 19:32 out to the children of **N**, *even* for the H5321
32 of **N** according to their families. H5321
39 of the children of **N** according to their H5321
20: 7 in Galilee in mount **N**, and Shechem in H5321
21: 6 out of the tribe of **N**, and out of the half H5321
32 And out of the tribe of **N**, Kedesh in H5321
Jdg 1:33 Neither did **N** drive out the inhabitants H5321
4: 6 of **N** and of the children of Zebulun? H5321
10 And Barak called Zebulun and **N** to H5321
5:18 Zebulun and **N** *were* a people *that* H5321
6:35 **N**; and they came up to meet them. H5321
7:23 together out of **N**, and out of Asher, and H5321
1Ki 4:15 Ahimaaz *was* in **N**; he also took H5321
7:14 He *was* a widow's son of the tribe of **N**, H5321
15:20 all Cinneroth, with all the land of **N**. H5321
2Ki 15:29 **N**, and carried them captive to Assyria. H5321
1Ch 2: 2 Dan, Joseph, and Benjamin, **N**, Gad, H5321
6:62 out of the tribe of **N**, and out of the tribe H5321
76 And out of the tribe of **N**; Kedesh in H5321
7:13 The sons of **N**; Jahziel, and Guni, and H5321
12:34 And of **N** a thousand captains, and H5321
40 and Zebulun and **N**, brought bread on H5321
27:19 of **N**, Jerimoth the son of Azriel: H5321
2Ch 16: 4 Abel-maim, and all the store cities of **N**. H5321
34: 6 **N**, with their mattocks round about. H5321
Ps 68:27 of Zebulun, *and* the princes of **N**. H5321
Isa 9: 1 and the land of **N**, and afterward did H5321
Ezk 48: 3 even unto the west side, a *portion for* **N**. H5321
4 And by the border of **N**, from the east H5321
34 of Gad, one gate of Asher, one gate of **N**. H5321

NAPHTUHIM

Gen 10:13 and Anamim, and Lehabim, and **N**, H5320
1Ch 1:11 and Anamim, and Lehabim, and **N**, H5320

NAPKIN

Lk 19:20 pound, which I have kept laid up in a **n**: *G4676*
Jn 11:44 about with a **n**. Jesus saith unto them, *G4676*
20: 7 And the **n**, that was about his head, not *G4676*

NARCISSUS

Ro 16:11 *household* of **N**, which are in the Lord. *G3488*

NARD See SPIKENARD.

NARROW

Nu 22:26 and stood in a **n** place, where *was* no H6862
Jos 17:15 if mount Ephraim be too **n** for thee. H213
1Ki 6: 4 And for the house he made windows of **n** H331
Prv 23:27 ditch; and a strange woman *is* a **n** pit. H6862
Isa 49:19 even now be too **n** by reason of the H3334
Ezk 40:16 And *there were* **n** windows to the little H331
41:16 The door posts, and the **n** windows, and H331
26 And *there were* **n** windows and palm H331
Mt 7:14 Because strait *is* the gate, and **n** *is* the *G2346*

NARROWED

1Ki 6: 6 house he made **n** rests round about, H4052

NARROWER

Isa 28:20 **n** than that he can wrap himself *in it*. H6887

NARROWLY

Job 13:27 and lookest **n** unto all my paths; thou H8104
Isa 14:16 They that see thee shall **n** look upon

NATHAN

2Sa 5:14 and Shobab, and **N**, and Solomon, H5416
7: 2 That the king said unto **N** the prophet, H5416
3 And **N** said to the king, Go, do all that H5416
4 word of the LORD came unto **N**, saying, H5416
17 this vision, so did **N** speak unto David. H5416

N

2Sa 12: 1 And the LORD sent N unto David. And H5416
5 and he said to N, As the LORD liveth, H5416
7 And N said to David, Thou art the H5416
13 And David said unto N, I have sinned H5416
13 the LORD. And N said unto David, The H5416
15 And N departed unto his house. And H5416
25 And he sent by the hand of N the H5416
23:36 Igal the son of N of Zobah, Bani the H5416
1Ki 1: 8 of Jehoiada, and N the prophet, and H5416
10 But N the prophet, and Benaiah, and H5416
11 Wherefore N spake unto Bath-sheba H5416
22 the king, N the prophet also came in. H5416
23 saying, Behold N the prophet. And H5416
24 And N said, My lord, O king, hast thou H5416
32 the priest, and N the prophet, and H5416
34 And let Zadok the priest and N the H5416
38 So Zadok the priest, and N the prophet, H5416
44 the priest, and N the prophet, and H5416
45 And Zadok the priest and N the H5416
4: 5 And Azariah the son of N was over the H5416
5 and Zabud the son of N was principal H5416
1Ch 2:36 And Attai begat N, and Nathan begat H5416
36 And Attai begat Nathan, and N begat H5416
3: 5 and Shobab, and N, and Solomon, four, H5416
11:38 Joel the brother of N, Mibhar the son of H5416
14: 4 and Shobab, N, and Solomon, H5416
17: 1 that David said to N the prophet, Lo, I H5416
2 Then N said unto David, Do all that is H5416
3 that the word of God came to N, saying, H5416
15 this vision, so did N speak unto David. H5416
29:29 and in the book of N the prophet, and H5416
2Ch 9:29 in the book of N the prophet, and in H5416
29:25 king's seer, and N the prophet: for so H5416
Ezr 8:16 Elnathan, and for N, and for Zechariah, H5416
10:39 And Shelemiah, and N, and Adaiah, H5416
Ps 51:ttl of David, when N the prophet came H5416
Zec 12:12 of N apart, and their wives apart; H5416
Lk 3:31 son of N, which was the son of David, G3481

NATHANAEL

Jn 1:45 Philip findeth N, and saith unto him, G3482
46 And N said unto him, Can there any G3482
47 Jesus saw N coming to him, and saith G3482
48 N saith unto him, Whence knowest G3482
49 N answered and saith unto him, Rabbi, G3482
21: 2 Didymus, and N of Cana in Galilee, G3482

NATHAN-MELECH

2Ki 23:11 by the chamber of N the chamberlain, H5419

NATION

Gen 12: 2 And I will make of thee a great n, and I H1471
15:14 And also that n, whom they shall serve, H1471
17:20 he beget, and I will make him a great n. H1471
18:18 great and mighty n, and all the nations H1471
20: 4 Lord, wilt thou slay also a righteous n? H1471
21:13 will I make a n, because he is thy seed. H1471
18 hand; for I will make him a great n. H1471
35:11 and multiply; a n and a company of H1471
46: 3 for I will there make of thee a great n: H1471
Ex 9:24 the land of Egypt since it became a n. H1471
19: 6 and an holy n. These are the words H1471
21: 8 her unto a strange n he shall have no H5971
32:10 them: and I will make of thee a great n. H1471
33:13 and consider that this n is thy people. H1471
34:10 earth, nor in any n: and all the people H1471
Lev 18:26 any of your own n, nor any stranger that H249
20:23 the manners of the n, which I cast out H1471
Nu 14:12 a greater n and mightier than they. H1471
Dt 4: 6 n is a wise and understanding people. H1471
7 For what n is there so great, who hath H1471
8 And what n is there so great, that hath H1471
34 go and take him a n from the midst of H1471
34 midst of another n, by temptations, by H1471
9:14 a n mightier and greater than they. H1471
26: 5 there a n, great, mighty, and populous: H1471
28:33 labours, shall a n which thou knowest H5971
36 over thee, unto a n which neither thou H1471
49 The LORD shall bring a n against thee H1471
49 the eagle flieth; a n whose tongue thou H1471
50 A n of fierce countenance, which shall H1471
32:21 provoke them to anger with a foolish n. H1471
28 For they are a n void of counsel, H1471
2Sa 7:23 And what one n in the earth is like thy H1471
1Ki 18:10 God liveth, there is no n or kingdom, H1471
10 and n, that they found thee not. H1471
2Ki 17:29 Howbeit every n made gods of their H1471
29 n in their cities wherein they dwelt. H1471
1Ch 16:20 And when they went from n to nation, H1471
1Ch 16:20 And when they went from nation to n, H1471
17:21 And what one n in the earth is like thy H1471
2Ch 15: 6 And n was destroyed of nation, and H1471
6 And nation was destroyed of n, and city H1471
32:15 for no god of any n or kingdom was H1471
Job 34:29 against a n, or against a man only: H1471
Ps 33:12 Blessed is the n whose God is the H1471
43: 1 an ungodly n: O deliver me from the H1471
83: 4 off from being a n; that the name of H1471
105:13 When they went from one n to another, H1471
106: 5 gladness of thy n, that I may glory with H1471
147:20 He hath not dealt so with any n: and as H1471
Prv 14:34 Righteousness exalteth a n: but sin is a H1471
Isa 1: 4 Ah sinful n, a people laden with H1471
2: 4 pruninghooks: n shall not lift up sword H1471
4 up sword against n, neither shall they H1471
9: 3 Thou hast multiplied the n, and not H1471
10: 6 an hypocritical n, and against the H1471
14:32 the messengers of the n? That the LORD H1471
18: 2 swift messengers, to a n scattered and H1471
2 hitherto; a n meted out and trodden H1471
7 hitherto; a n meted out and trodden H1471
26: 2 Open ye the gates, that the righteous n H1471
15 Thou hast increased the n, O LORD, H1471
15 hast increased the n: thou art glorified: H1471
49: 7 to him whom the n abhorreth, to a H1471
51: 4 ear unto me, O my n: for a law shall H3816
55: 5 Behold, thou shalt call a n that thou H1471
58: 2 my ways, as a n that did righteousness, H1471
60:12 For the n and kingdom that will not H1471
22 n: I the LORD will hasten it in his time. H1471
65: 1 a n that was not called by my name. H1471
66: 8 one day? or shall a n be born at once? H1471
Jer 2:11 Hath a n changed their gods, which are H1471
5: 9 my soul be avenged on such a n as this? H1471
15 Lo, I will bring a n upon you from far, H1471
15 it is a mighty n, it is an ancient nation, H1471
15 it is an ancient n, a nation whose H1471
15 an ancient nation, a n whose language H1471
29 my soul be avenged on such a n as this? H1471
6:22 and a great n shall be raised from H1471
7:28 them, This is a n that obeyeth not the H1471
9: 9 my soul be avenged on such a n as this? H1471
12:17 up and destroy that n, saith the LORD. H1471
18: 7 speak concerning a n, and concerning a H1471
8 If that n, against whom I have H1471
9 speak concerning a n, and concerning a H1471
25:12 of Babylon, and that n, saith the LORD, H1471
32 go forth from n to nation, and a great H1471
32 from nation to n, and a great whirlwind H1471
27: 8 And it shall come to pass, that the n H1471
8 of Babylon, that n will I punish, saith H1471
13 against the n that will not serve the H1471
31:36 from being a n before me for ever. H1471
33:24 should be no more a n before them. H1471
48: 2 it off from being a n. Also thou shalt be H1471
49:31 Arise, get you up unto the wealthy n, H1471
36 there shall be no n whither the outcasts H1471
50: 3 there cometh up a n against her, which H1471
41 north, and a great n, and many kings H1471
Lam 4:17 watched for a n that could not save us. H1471
Ezk 2: 3 to a rebellious n that hath rebelled H1471
37:22 And I will make them one n in the land H1471
Dan 3:29 That every people, n, and language, H524
8:22 up out of the n, but not in his power. H1471
12: 1 since there was a n even to that same H1471
Joel 1: 6 For a n is come up upon my land, H1471
Am 6:14 up against you a n, O house of Israel, H1471
Mic 4: 3 into pruninghooks: n shall not lift up a H1471
3 up a sword against n, neither shall they H1471
7 far off a strong n: and the LORD shall H1471
Hab 1: 6 bitter and hasty n, which shall march H1471
Zep 2: 1 yea, gather together, O n not desired; H1471
5 the sea coast, the n of the Cherethites! H1471
Hag 2:14 and so is this n before me, saith the H1471
Mal 3: 9 ye have robbed me, even this whole n. H1471
Mt 21:43 to a n bringing forth the fruits thereof. G1484
24: 7 For n shall rise against nation, and G1484
7 For nation shall rise against n, and G1484
Mk 7:26 a Syrophenician by n; and she besought G1085
13: 8 For n shall rise against nation, and G1484
8 For nation shall rise against n, and G1484
Lk 7: 5 For he loveth our n, and he hath built G1484
21:10 Then said he unto them, N shall rise G1484
10 n, and kingdom against kingdom: G1484
23: 2 perverting the n, and forbidding to give G1484
Jn 11:48 and take away both our place and n. G1484
50 and that the whole n perish not. G1484
51 that Jesus should die for that n; G1484
Jn 11:52 And not for that n only, but that also G1484
18:35 I a Jew? Thine own n and the chief G1484
Act 2: 5 men, out of every n under heaven. G1484
7: 7 And the n to whom they shall be in G1484
10:22 report among all the n of the Jews, was G1484
28 one of another n; but God hath shewed G246
35 But in every n he that feareth him, and G1484
24: 2 are done unto this n by thy providence, G1484
10 years a judge unto this n, I do the more G1484
17 to bring alms to my n, and offerings. G1484
26: 4 own n at Jerusalem, know all the Jews; G1484
28:19 not that I had ought to accuse my n of. G1484
Ro 10:19 and by a foolish n I will anger you. G1484
Gal 1:14 in mine own n, being more exceedingly G1085
Php 2:15 and perverse n, among whom ye shine G1074
1Pt 2: 9 an holy n, a peculiar people; that G1484
Rev 5: 9 and tongue, and people, and n; G1484
14: 6 earth, and to every n, and kindred, and G1484

NATIONS

Gen 10: 5 tongue, after their families, in their n. H1471
20 in their countries, and in their n. H1471
31 tongues, in their lands, after their n. H1471
32 in their n: and by these were the H1471
32 n divided in the earth after the flood. H1471
14: 1 king of Elam, and Tidal king of n; H1471
9 and with Tidal king of n, and Amraphel H1471
17: 4 and thou shalt be a father of many n. H1471
5 a father of many n have I made thee. H1471
6 and I will make n of thee, and kings H1471
16 of n; kings of people shall be of her. H1471
18:18 n of the earth shall be blessed in him? H1471
22:18 And in thy seed shall all the n of the H1471
25:16 twelve princes according to their n. H523
23 And the LORD said unto her, Two n H1471
26: 4 shall all the n of the earth be blessed; H1471
27:29 Let people serve thee, and n bow down H3816
35:11 and a company of n shall be of thee, H1471
48:19 his seed shall become a multitude of n. H1471
Ex 34:24 For I will cast out the n before thee, H1471
Lev 18:24 for in all these the n are defiled which I H1471
28 it spued out the n that were before you. H1471
Nu 14:15 one man, then the n which have heard H1471
23: 9 and shall not be reckoned among the n. H1471
24: 8 he shall eat up the n his enemies, and H1471
20 was the first of the n; but his latter end H1471
Dt 2:25 of thee upon the n that are under the H5971
4: 6 in the sight of the n, which shall hear all H5971
19 unto all n under the whole heaven. H5971
27 you among the n, and ye shall be left H5971
38 To drive out n from before thee greater H1471
7: 1 hath cast out many n before thee, the H1471
1 n greater and mightier than thou; H1471
17 If thou shalt say in thine heart, These n H1471
22 will put out those n before thee by little H1471
8:20 As the n which the LORD destroyeth H1471
9: 1 day, to go in to possess n greater and H1471
4 of these n the LORD doth drive H1471
5 of these n the LORD thy God doth H1471
11:23 drive out all these n from before you, H1471
23 n and mightier than yourselves. H1471
12: 2 wherein the n which ye shall possess H1471
29 shall cut off the n from before thee, H1471
30 How did these n serve their gods? even H1471
14: 2 above all the n that are upon the earth. H5971
15: 6 lend unto many n, but thou shalt not H1471
6 n, but they shall not reign over thee. H1471
17:14 me, like as all the n that are about me; H1471
18: 9 to do after the abominations of those n. H1471
14 For these n, which thou shalt possess, H1471
19: 1 hath cut off the n, whose land the LORD H1471
20:15 which are not of the cities of these n. H1471
26:19 And to make thee high above all n H1471
28: 1 thee on high above all n of the earth: H1471
12 many n, and thou shalt not borrow. H1471
37 all n whither the LORD shall lead thee. H5971
65 And among these n shalt thou find no H1471
29:16 through the n which ye passed by; H1471
18 the gods of these n; lest there should be H1471
24 Even all n shall say, Wherefore hath H1471
30: 1 among all the n, whither the LORD thy H1471
3 thee from all the n, whither the LORD H5971
31: 3 will destroy these n from before thee, H1471
32: 8 When the most High divided to the n H1471
43 Rejoice, O ye n, with his people: for he H1471
Jos 12:23 one; the king of the n of Gilgal, one; H1471
23: 3 unto all these n because of you; for H1471
4 you by lot these n that remain, to be an H1471
4 with all the n that I have cut off, even H1471

Jos 23: 7 That ye come not among these **n**, these H1471
9 before you great **n** and strong: but *as* H1471
12 the remnant of these **n**, *even* these that H1471
13 out *any of* these **n** from before you; but H1471
Jdg 2:21 the **n** which Joshua left when he died: H1471
23 Therefore the LORD left those **n**, H1471
3: 1 Now these *are* the **n** which the LORD H1471
1Sa 8: 5 make us a king to judge us like all the **n**. H1471
20 That we also may be like all the **n**; and H1471
27: 8 for those *n were* of old the inhabitants
2Sa 7:23 from Egypt, *from* the **n** and their gods? H1471
8:11 dedicated of all **n** which he subdued; H1471
1Ki 4:31 and his fame was in all **n** round about. H1471
11: 2 Of the **n** *concerning* which the LORD H1471
14:24 of the **n** which the LORD cast H1471
2Ki 17:26 Assyria, saying, The **n** which thou hast H1471
33 the manner of the **n** whom they carried H1471
41 So these **n** feared the LORD, and served H1471
18:33 Hath any of the gods of the **n** delivered H1471
19:12 Have the gods of the **n** delivered them H1471
17 have destroyed the **n** and their lands, H1471
21: 9 evil than did the **n** whom the LORD H1471
1Ch 14:17 brought the fear of him upon all **n**. H1471
16:24 his marvellous works among all **n**. H5971
31 say among the **n**, The LORD reigneth. H1471
17:21 by driving out **n** from before thy H1471
18:11 from all *these* **n**; from Edom, and from H1471
2Ch 7:20 *be* a proverb and a byword among all **n**. H5971
13: 9 the manner of the **n** of *other* lands? so H5971
32:13 the gods of the **n** of those lands any H1471
14 all the gods of those **n** that my fathers H1471
17 As the gods of the **n** of *other* lands have H1471
23 in the sight of all **n** from thenceforth. H1471
Ezr 4:10 And the rest of the **n** whom the great H524
Neh 1: 8 I will scatter you abroad among the **n**: H5971
9:22 kingdoms and **n**, and didst divide them H5971
13:26 yet among many **n** was there no king H1471
Job 12:23 He increaseth the **n**, and destroyeth H1471
23 the **n**, and straiteneth them *again*. H1471
Ps 9:17 into hell, *and* all the **n** that forget God. H1471
20 Put them in fear, O LORD: *that* the **n** H1471
22:27 of the **n** shall worship before thee. H1471
28 and he *is* the governor among the **n**. H1471
47: 3 under us, and the **n** under our feet. H3816
57: 9 I will sing unto thee among the **n**. H3816
66: 7 eyes behold the **n**: let not the rebellious H1471
67: 2 earth, thy saving health among all **n**. H1471
4 O let the **n** be glad and sing for joy: for H3816
4 and govern the **n** upon earth. Selah. H3816
72:11 down before him: all **n** shall serve him. H1471
17 in him: all **n** shall call him blessed. H1471
82: 8 the earth: for thou shalt inherit all **n**. H1471
86: 9 All **n** whom thou hast made shall come H1471
96: 5 For all the gods of the **n** *are* idols: but H5971
106:27 the **n**, and to scatter them in the lands. H1471
34 They did not destroy the **n**, concerning H5971
108: 3 will sing praises unto thee among the **n**. H3816
113: 4 The LORD *is* high above all **n**, *and* his H1471
117: 1 O praise the LORD, all ye **n**: praise him, H1471
118:10 All **n** compassed me about: but in the H1471
135:10 Who smote great **n**, and slew mighty H1471
Prv 24:24 the people curse, **n** shall abhor him: H3816
Isa 2: 2 the hills; and all **n** shall flow unto it. H1471
4 And he shall judge among the **n**, and H1471
5:26 And he will lift up an ensign to the **n** H1471
9: 1 sea, beyond Jordan, in Galilee of the **n**. H1471
10: 7 heart to destroy and cut off **n** not a few. H1471
11:12 And he shall set up an ensign for the **n**, H1471
13: 4 of the kingdoms of **n** gathered together: H1471
14: 6 stroke, he that ruled the **n** in anger, is H1471
9 from their thrones all the kings of the **n**. H1471
12 the ground, which didst weaken the **n**! H1471
18 All the kings of the **n**, *even* all of them, H1471
26 that is stretched out upon all the **n**. H1471
17:12 to the rushing of **n**, *that* make a rushing H3816
13 The **n** shall rush like the rushing of H3816
23: 3 *is* her revenue; and she is a mart of **n**. H1471
25: 3 the city of the terrible **n** shall fear thee. H1471
7 and the vail that is spread over all **n**. H1471
29: 7 And the multitude of all the **n** that fight H1471
8 the **n** be, that fight against mount Zion. H1471
30:28 the neck, to sift the **n** with the sieve of H1471
33: 3 up of thyself the **n** were scattered. H1471
34: 1 Come near, ye **n**, to hear; and hearken, H1471
2 LORD *is* upon all **n**, and *his* fury upon H1471
36:18 of the gods of the **n** delivered his land H1471
37:12 Have the gods of the **n** delivered them H1471
18 laid waste all the **n**, and their countries, H776
40:15 Behold, the **n** *are* as a drop of a bucket, H1471

Isa 40:17 All **n** before him *are* as nothing; and H1471
41: 2 to his foot, gave the **n** before him, and H1471
43: 9 Let all the **n** be gathered together, and H1471
45: 1 holden, to subdue **n** before him; and I H1471
20 *that are* escaped of the **n**: they have no H1471
52:10 the eyes of all the **n**; and all the ends of H1471
15 So shall he sprinkle many **n**; the kings H1471
55: 5 knowest not, and **n** *that* knew not thee H1471
60:12 yea, *those* **n** shall be utterly wasted. H1471
61:11 praise to spring forth before all the **n**. H1471
64: 2 *that* the **n** may tremble at thy presence! H1471
66:18 that I will gather all **n** and tongues; and H1471
19 of them unto the **n**, *to* Tarshish, Pul, H1471
20 LORD out of all **n** upon horses, and in H1471
Jer 1: 5 I ordained thee a prophet unto the **n**. H1471
10 See, I have this day set thee over the **n** H1471
3:17 LORD; and all the **n** shall be gathered H1471
19 of the hosts of **n**? and I said, Thou shalt H1471
4: 2 and the **n** shall bless themselves H1471
16 Make ye mention to the **n**; behold, H1471
6:18 Therefore hear, ye **n**, and know, O H1471
9:26 for all *these* **n** *are* uncircumcised, H1471
10: 7 Who would not fear thee, O King of **n**? H1471
7 the wise *men* of the **n**, and in all their H1471
10 tremble, and the **n** shall not be able to H1471
22: 8 And many **n** shall pass by this city, and H1471
25: 9 against all these **n** round about, and H1471
11 and these **n** shall serve the king H1471
13 hath prophesied against all the **n**. H1471
14 For many **n** and great kings shall serve H1471
15 the **n**, to whom I send thee, to drink it. H1471
17 hand, and made all the **n** to drink, unto H1471
31 with the **n**, he will plead with all H1471
26: 6 this city a curse to all the **n** of the earth. H1471
27: 7 And all **n** shall serve him, and his son, H1471
7 and then many **n** and great kings shall H1471
11 But the **n** that bring their neck under H1471
28:11 the neck of all **n** within the space of H1471
14 neck of all these **n**, that they may serve H1471
29:14 you from all the **n**, and from all the H1471
18 all the **n** whither I have driven them: H1471
30:11 make a full end of all **n** whither I have H1471
31: 7 the chief of the **n**: publish ye, praise ye, H1471
10 Hear the word of the LORD, O ye **n**, and H1471
33: 9 before all the **n** of the earth, which H1471
36: 2 and against all the **n**, from the day I H1471
43: 5 returned from all **n**, whither they had H1471
44: 8 reproach among all the **n** of the earth? H1471
46:12 The **n** have heard of thy shame, and H1471
28 a full end of all the **n** whither I have H1471
50: 2 Declare ye among the **n**, and publish, H1471
9 an assembly of great **n** from the north H1471
12 the hindermost of the **n** *shall be* a H1471
23 become a desolation among the **n**! H1471
46 and the cry is heard among the **n**. H1471
51: 7 drunken: the **n** have drunken of her H1471
7 of her wine; therefore the **n** are mad. H1471
20 in pieces the **n**, and with thee will I H1471
27 among the **n**, prepare the nations H1471
27 prepare the **n** against her, call together H1471
28 Prepare against her the **n** with the H1471
41 become an astonishment among the **n**! H1471
44 up: and the **n** shall not flow together H1471
Lam 1: 1 great among the **n**, *and* princess among H1471
Ezk 5: 5 in the midst of the **n** and countries *that* H1471
6 more than the **n**, and my statutes more H1471
7 more than the **n** that *are* round about H1471
7 of the **n** that *are* round about you; H1471
8 in the midst of thee in the sight of the **n**. H1471
14 among the **n** that *are* round about H1471
15 unto the **n** that *are* round about H1471
6: 8 sword among the **n**, when ye shall be H1471
9 me among the **n** whither they shall be H1471
12:15 **n**, and disperse them in the countries. H1471
19: 4 The **n** also heard of him; he was taken H1471
8 Then the **n** set against him on every H1471
25:10 may not be remembered among the **n**. H1471
26: 3 will cause many **n** to come up against H1471
5 and it shall become a spoil to the **n**. H1471
28: 7 the terrible of the **n**: and they shall draw H1471
29:12 among the **n**, and will disperse them H1471
15 more above the **n**: for I will diminish H1471
15 that they shall no more rule over the **n**. H1471
30:11 the terrible of the **n**, shall be brought to H1471
23 among the **n**, and will disperse them H1471
26 among the **n**, and disperse them among H1471
31: 6 and under his shadow dwelt all great **n**. H1471
12 And strangers, the terrible of the **n**, H1471
16 I made the **n** to shake at the sound of H1471

Ezk 32: 2 a young lion of the **n**, and thou *art* as a H1471
9 among the **n**, into the countries which H1471
12 the terrible of the **n**, all of them: and H1471
16 the daughters of the **n** shall lament her: H1471
18 of the famous **n**, unto the nether parts H1471
35:10 Because thou hast said, These two **n** H1471
36:13 up men, and hast bereaved thy **n**; H1471
14 thy **n** any more, saith the Lord GOD. H1471
15 **n** to fall any more, saith the Lord GOD. H1471
37:22 be no more two **n**, neither shall they be H1471
38: 8 forth out of the **n**, and they shall dwell H5971
12 out of the **n**, which have gotten cattle H1471
23 the eyes of many **n**, and they shall know H1471
39:27 in them in the sight of many **n**; H1471
Dan 3: 4 commanded, O people, **n**, and languages, H524
7 all the people, the **n**, and the languages, H524
4: 1 unto all people, **n**, and languages, that H524
5:19 gave him, all people, **n**, and languages, H524
6:25 unto all people, **n**, and languages, that H524
7:14 that all people, **n**, and languages, should H524
Hos 8:10 hired among the **n**, now will I gather H1471
9:17 they shall be wanderers among the **n**. H1471
Joel 3: 2 I will also gather all **n**, and will bring H1471
2 among the **n**, and parted my land. H1471
Am 6: 1 **n**, to whom the house of Israel came! H1471
9: 9 Israel among all **n**, like as *corn* is sifted H1471
Mic 4: 2 And many **n** shall come, and say, H1471
3 and rebuke strong **n** afar off; and they H1471
11 Now also many **n** are gathered against H1471
7:16 The **n** shall see and be confounded at H1471
Nah 3: 4 that selleth **n** through her whoredoms, H1471
5 I will shew the **n** thy nakedness, and H1471
Hab 1:17 and not spare continually to slay the **n**? H1471
2: 5 all **n**, and heapeth unto him all people: H1471
8 Because thou hast spoiled many **n**, all H1471
3: 6 and drove asunder the **n**; and the H1471
Zep 2:14 the beasts of the **n**: both the cormorant H1471
3: 6 I have cut off the **n**: their towers are H1471
8 *is* to gather the **n**, that I may assemble H1471
Hag 2: 7 And I will shake all **n**, and the desire of H1471
7 the desire of all **n** shall come: and I will H1471
Zec 2: 8 sent me unto the **n** which spoiled you: H1471
11 And many **n** shall be joined to the H1471
7:14 among all the **n** whom they knew not. H1471
8:22 Yea, many people and strong **n** shall H1471
23 languages of the **n**, even shall take hold H1471
12: 9 all the **n** that come against Jerusalem. H1471
14: 2 For I will gather all **n** against Jerusalem H1471
3 fight against those **n**, as when he fought H1471
16 is left of all the **n** which came against H1471
19 punishment of all **n** that come not up H1471
Mal 3:12 And all **n** shall call you blessed: for ye H1471
Mt 24: 9 be hated of all **n** for my name's sake. *G1484*
14 unto all **n**; and then shall the end come. *G1484*
25:32 And before him shall be gathered all **n**: *G1484*
28:19 Go ye therefore, and teach all **n**, *G1484*
Mk 11:17 be called of all **n** the house of prayer? *G1484*
13:10 must first be published among all **n**. *G1484*
Lk 12:30 For all these things do the **n** of the *G1484*
21:24 captive into all **n**: and Jerusalem shall *G1484*
25 earth distress of **n**, with perplexity; the *G1484*
24:47 among all **n**, beginning at Jerusalem. *G1484*
Act 13:19 And when he had destroyed seven **n** in *G1484*
14:16 Who in times past suffered all **n** to *G1484*
17:26 And hath made of one blood all **n** of *G1484*
Ro 1: 5 to the faith among all **n**, for his name: *G1484*
4:17 a father of many **n**,) before him whom *G1484*
18 the father of many **n**, according to that *G1484*
16:26 to all **n** for the obedience of faith: *G1484*
Gal 3: 8 *saying*, In thee shall all **n** be blessed. *G1484*
Rev 2:26 end, to him will I give power over the **n**: *G1484*
7: 9 number, of all **n**, and kindreds, and *G1484*
10:11 peoples, and **n**, and tongues, and kings. *G1484*
11: 9 and tongues and **n** shall see their dead *G1484*
18 And the **n** were angry, and thy wrath is *G1484*
12: 5 was to rule all **n** with a rod of iron: and *G1484*
13: 7 over all kindreds, and tongues, and **n**. *G1484*
14: 8 she made all **n** drink of the wine of *G1484*
15: 4 only *art* holy: for all **n** shall come and *G1484*
16:19 and the cities of the **n** fell: and great *G1484*
17:15 and multitudes, and **n**, and tongues. *G1484*
18: 3 For all **n** have drunk of the wine of the *G1484*
23 for by thy sorceries were all **n** deceived. *G1484*
19:15 he should smite the **n**: and he shall rule *G1484*
20: 3 should deceive the **n** no more, till the *G1484*
8 And shall go out to deceive the **n** which *G1484*
21:24 And the **n** of them which are saved *G1484*
26 the glory and honour of the **n** into it. *G1484*
22: 2 of the tree *were* for the healing of the **n**. *G1484*

NATIVE
Jer 22:10 return no more, nor see his n country. H4138

NATIVITY
Gen 11:28 the land of his n, in Ur of the Chaldees. H4138
Ru 2:11 the land of thy n, and art come unto a H4138
Jer 46:16 of our n, from the oppressing sword. H4138
Ezk 16: 3 Thy birth and thy n *is* of the land of H4138
4 And *as for* thy n, in the day thou wast H4138
21:30 thou wast created, in the land of thy n. H4351
23:15 of Chaldea, the land of their n: H4138

NATURAL
Dt 34: 7 was not dim, nor his n force abated. H3893
Ro 1:26 n use into that which is against nature: G5446
27 men, leaving the n use of the woman, G5446
31 n affection, implacable, unmerciful:
11:21 For if God spared not the n branches, G2596
24 which be the n *branches*, be graffed G2596
1Co 2:14 But the n man receiveth not the things G5591
15:44 It is sown a n body; it is raised a G5591
44 a n body, and there is a spiritual body. G5591
46 n; and afterward that which is spiritual. G5591
2Ti 3: 3 Without n affection, trucebreakers, false
Jas 1:23 a man beholding his n face in a glass: G1078
2Pt 2:12 But these, as n brute beasts, made to G5446

NATURALLY
Php 2:20 who will n care for your state. G1104
Jude 10 what they know n, as brute beasts, in G5447

NATURE
Ro 1:26 natural use into that which is against n: G5449
2:14 have not the law, do by n the things G5449
27 which is by n, if it fulfil the law, judge G5449
11:24 tree which is wild by n, and wert graffed G5449
24 contrary to n into a good olive tree: G5449
1Co 11:14 Doth not even n itself teach you, that, if G5449
Gal 2:15 We *who are* Jews by n, and not sinners G5449
4: 8 unto them which by n are no gods. G5449
Eph 2: 3 n the children of wrath, even as others. G5449
Heb 2:16 For verily he took not on *him the n of*
Jas 3: 6 course of n; and it is set on fire of hell. G1078
2Pt 1: 4 of the divine n, having escaped the G5449

NAUGHT
2Ki 2:19 the water *is* n, and the ground barren. H7451
Prv 20:14 *It is* n, *it is* naught, saith the buyer: but H7451
14 *It is* naught, *it is* n, saith the buyer: but H7451

NAUGHTINESS
1Sa 17:28 thy pride, and the n of thine heart; for H7455
Prv 11: 6 shall be taken in *their own* n. H1942
Jas 1:21 and superfluity of n, and receive with G2549

NAUGHTY
Prv 6:12 A n person, a wicked man, walketh H1100
17: 4 lips; *and* a liar giveth ear to a n tongue. H1942
Jer 24: 2 basket *had* very n figs, which could not H7451

NAUM
Lk 3:25 was *the son* of N, which was *the son* of G3486

NAVEL
Job 40:16 and his force *is* in the n of his belly. H8306
Prv 3: 8 It shall be health to thy n, and marrow H8270
Song 7: 2 Thy n *is like* a round goblet, *which* H8326
Ezk 16: 4 wast born thy n was not cut, neither H8270

NAVES
1Ki 7:33 and their n, and their felloes, and H1354

NAVY
1Ki 9:26 And king Solomon made a n of ships in H590
27 And Hiram sent in the n his servants, H590
10:11 And the n also of Hiram, that brought H590
22 For the king had at sea a n of Tharshish H590
22 Tharshish with the n of Hiram: once in H590
22 years came the n of Tharshish, bringing H590

NAY
Gen 18:15 And he said, N; but thou didst laugh. H3808
19: 2 And they said, N; but we will abide in H3808
23:11 N, my lord, hear me: the field give I H3808
33:10 And Jacob said, N, I pray thee, if now I H408
42:10 And they said unto him, N, my lord, but H3808
12 And he said unto them, N, but to see the H3808
Nu 22:30 to do so unto thee? And he said, N. H3808
Jos 5:14 And he said, N; but *as* captain of the H3808
Jos 24:21 And the people said unto Joshua, N; but H3808
Jdg 12: 5 *Art* thou an Ephraimite? If he said, N; H3808
19:23 said unto them, N, my brethren, *nay*, I H408
23 Nay, my brethren, *n*, I pray you, do not
Ru 1:13 having husbands? n, my daughters; for it H408
1Sa 2:16 answer him, *N;* but thou shalt give *it*
24 N, my sons; for *it is* no good report that I H408
8:19 said, N; but we will have a king over us; H3808
10:19 said unto him, *N*, but set a king over us.
12:12 you, ye said unto me, N; but a king shall H3808
2Sa 13:12 And she answered him, N, my brother, H408
25 And the king said to Absalom, N, my H408
16:18 And Hushai said unto Absalom, N; but H3808
24:24 And the king said unto Araunah, N; but H3808
1Ki 2:17 he will not say thee n,) that he give me H7725
20 *thee*, say me not n. And the king said H7725
20 on, my mother: for I will not say thee n. H7725
30 And he said, N; but I will die here. And H3808
3:22 And the other woman said, N; but the H3808
23 and the other saith, N; but thy son *is* the H3808
2Ki 3:13 said unto him, N: for the LORD hath H408
4:16 son. And she said, N, my lord, *thou* man H408
20:10 down ten degrees: n, but let the shadow H3808
1Ch 21:24 And king David said to Ornan, N; but I H3808
Jer 6:15 abomination? n, they were not at all H1571
8:12 abomination? n, they were not at all H1571
Mt 5:37 be, Yea, yea; N, nay: for whatsoever G3756
37 be, Yea, yea; Nay, n: for whatsoever is G3756
13:29 But he said, N; lest while ye gather up G3756
Lk 12:51 earth? I tell you, N; but rather division: G3780
13: 3 I tell you, N: but, except ye repent, ye G3780
5 I tell you, N: but, except ye repent, ye G3780
16:30 And he said, N, father Abraham: but if G3780
Jn 7:12 said, N; but he deceiveth the people. G3756
Act 16:37 us out privily? n verily; but let them G3756
Ro 3:27 of works? N: but by the law of faith. G3780
7: 7 sin? God forbid. N, I had not known sin, G235
8:37 N, in all these things we are more than G235
9:20 N but, O man, who art thou that G3304
1Co 6: 8 N, ye do wrong, and defraud, and that G235
12:22 N, much more those members of the G235
2Co 1:17 me there should be yea yea, and n nay? G3756
17 me there should be yea yea, and nay n? G3756
18 word toward you was not yea and n. G3756
19 was not yea and n, but in him was yea. G3756
Jas 5:12 n, nay; lest ye fall into condemnation. G3756
12 nay, n; lest ye fall into condemnation. G3756

NAZARENE
Mt 2:23 by the prophets, He shall be called a N. G3480

NAZARENES
Act 24: 5 and a ringleader of the sect of the N: G3480

NAZARETH
Mt 2:23 dwelt in a city called N: that it might be G3478
4:13 And leaving N, he came and dwelt in G3478
21:11 is Jesus the prophet of N of Galilee. G3478
26:71 This *fellow* was also with Jesus of N. G3480
Mk 1: 9 Jesus came from N of Galilee, and was G3478
24 thee, thou Jesus of N? art thou come to G3479
10:47 it was Jesus of N, he began to cry out, G3480
14:67 And thou also wast with Jesus of N. G3479
16: 6 Ye seek Jesus of N, which was crucified: G3479
Lk 1:26 God unto a city of Galilee, named N, G3478
2: 4 out of the city of N, into Judaea, unto G3478
39 into Galilee, to their own city N. G3478
51 and came to N, and was subject unto G3478
4:16 And he came to N, where he had been G3478
34 thee, *thou* Jesus of N? art thou come to G3479
18:37 And they told him, that Jesus of N G3480
24:19 Jesus of N, which was a prophet G3480
Jn 1:45 did write, Jesus of N, the son of Joseph. G3478
46 N? Philip saith unto him, Come and see. G3478
18: 5 They answered him, Jesus of N. Jesus G3480
7 seek ye? And they said, Jesus of N. G3480
19:19 JESUS OF N THE KING OF THE JEWS. G3480
Act 2:22 words; Jesus of N, a man approved of G3480
3: 6 of Jesus Christ of N rise up and walk. G3480
4:10 of Jesus Christ of N, whom ye crucified, G3480
6:14 that this Jesus of N shall destroy this G3480
10:38 How God anointed Jesus of N with the G3478
22: 8 am Jesus of N, whom thou persecutest. G3480
26: 9 contrary to the name of Jesus of N. G3480

NAZARITE
Nu 6: 2 to vow a vow of a N, to separate H5139
13 And this *is* the law of the N, when the H5139
18 And the N shall shave the head of his H5139
Nu 6:19 the hands of the N, after *the hair of* his H5139
20 and after that the N may drink wine. H5139
21 This *is* the law of the N who hath H5139
Jdg 13: 5 child shall be a N unto God from the H5139
7 the child shall be a N to God from the H5139
16:17 for I *have been* a N unto God from my H5139

NAZARITES
Lam 4: 7 Her N were purer than snow, they were H5139
Am 2:11 young men for N. *Is it* not even thus, H5139
12 But ye gave the N wine to drink; and H5139

NEAH
Jos 19:13 goeth out to Remmonmethoar to N; H5269

NEAPOLIS
Act 16:11 to Samothracia, and the next *day* to N; G3496

NEAR
Gen 12:11 he was come n to enter into Egypt, H7126
18:23 And Abraham drew n, and said, Wilt H5066
19: 9 Lot, and came n to break the door. H5066
20 Behold now, this city *is* n to flee unto, H7138
20: 4 But Abimelech had not come n her: H7126
27:21 And Isaac said unto Jacob, Come n, I H5066
22 And Jacob went n unto Isaac his H5066
25 And he said, Bring *it* n to me, and I will H5066
25 And he brought *it* n to him, and he did H5066
26 Come n now, and kiss me, my son. H5066
27 And he came n, and kissed him: and he H5066
29:10 that Jacob went n, and rolled the stone H5066
33: 3 times, until he came n to his brother. H5066
6 Then the handmaidens came n, they H5066
7 with her children came n, and bowed H5066
7 after came Joseph n and Rachel, and H5066
37:18 even before he came n unto them, they H7126
43:19 And they came n to the steward of H5066
44:18 Then Judah came n unto him, and H5066
45: 4 his brethren, Come n to me, I pray you. H5066
4 And they came n. And he said, I *am* H5066
10 and thou shalt be n unto me, thou, and H7138
48:10 he brought them n unto him; and he H5066
13 hand, and brought *them* n unto him. H5066
Ex 12:48 then let him come n and keep it; and he H7126
13:17 although that *was* n; for God said, Lest H7138
14:20 one came not n the other all the night. H7126
16: 9 of Israel, Come n before the LORD: for H7126
19:22 And let the priests also, which come n H5066
20:21 off, and Moses drew n unto the thick H5066
24: 2 And Moses alone shall come n the H5066
28:43 or when they come n unto the altar to H5066
30:20 or when they come n to the altar to H5066
40:32 when they came n unto the altar, they H7126
Lev 9: 5 drew n and stood before the LORD. H7126
10: 4 unto them, Come n, carry your brethren H7126
5 So they went n, and carried them in H7126
18: 6 to any that is n of kin to him, to H7607
12 sister: she *is* thy father's n kinswoman. H7607
13 for she *is* thy mother's n kinswoman. H7607
17 *are* her n kinswomen: it *is* wickedness. H7608
20:19 his n kin: they shall bear their iniquity. H7607
21: 2 But for his kin, that is n unto him, *that* H7138
Nu 3: 6 Bring the tribe of Levi n, and present H7126
5:16 And the priest shall bring her n, and set H7126
16: 5 *him* to come n unto him: even *him* H7126
5 will he cause to come n unto him. H7126
9 to bring you n to himself to do the H7126
10 And he hath brought thee n *to him*, H7126
40 seed of Aaron, come n to offer incense H7126
17:13 Whosoever cometh any thing n unto H7131
26: 3 of Moab by Jordan *n* Jericho, saying,
63 the plains of Moab by Jordan *n* Jericho.
31:12 of Moab, which *are* by Jordan *n* Jericho.
48 of hundreds, came n unto Moses: H7126
32:16 And they came n unto him, and said, H5066
33:48 the plains of Moab by Jordan *n* Jericho.
50 of Moab by Jordan *n* Jericho, saying,
34:15 on this side Jordan *n* Jericho eastward,
35: 1 of Moab by Jordan *n* Jericho, saying,
36: 1 of Joseph, came n, and spake before H7126
13 the plains of Moab by Jordan *n* Jericho.
Dt 1:22 And ye came n unto me every one of H7126
4:11 And ye came n and stood under the H7126
5:23 fire,) that ye came n unto me, *even* all H7126
27 Go thou n, and hear all that the LORD H7126
16:21 grove of any trees n unto the altar of the H681
21: 5 of Levi shall come n; for them the LORD H5066
25:11 of the one draweth n for to deliver her H7126
Jos 3: 4 come not n unto it, that ye may H7126

Jos 10:24 with him, Come n, put your feet upon H7126
24 And they came n, and put their feet H7126
15:46 that lay n Ashdod, with their villages: H3027
17: 4 And they came n before Eleazar the H7126
18:13 to Ataroth-adar, n the hill that lieth on H5921
21: 1 Then came n the heads of the fathers of H5066
Jdg 18:22 were in the houses n to Micah's house H5973
19:13 and let us draw n to one of these places H7126
20:24 And the children of Israel came n H7126
34 but they knew not that evil was n them. H5060
Ru 2:20 her, The man is n of kin unto us, one H7138
3: 9 handmaid; for thou art a n kinsman.
12 And now it is true that I am thy n
1Sa 4:19 was with child, n to be delivered: and
7:10 the Philistines drew n to battle against H5066
9:18 Then Saul drew n to Samuel in the H5066
10:20 n, the tribe of Benjamin was taken. H7126
21 Benjamin to come n by their families, H7126
14:36 priest, Let us draw n hither unto God. H7126
38 And Saul said, Draw ye n hither, all the H5066
17:16 And the Philistine drew n morning and H5066
40 hand: and he drew n to the Philistine. H5066
41 And the Philistine came on and drew n H7131
30:21 came n to the people, he saluted them. H5066
2Sa 1:15 men, and said, Go n, and fall upon him. H5066
14:30 See, Joab's field is n mine, and he hath H413
18:25 And he came apace, and drew n. H7131
19:42 the king is n of kin to us: wherefore H7138
20:16 n hither, that I may speak with thee. H7126
17 And when he was come n unto her, the H7126
1Ki 8:46 unto the land of the enemy, far or n; H7138
18:30 all the people, Come n unto me. And all H5066
30 all the people came n unto him. And he H5066
36 the prophet came n, and said, LORD H5066
21: 2 because it is n unto my house: and H7138
22:24 Chenaanah went n, and smote Micaiah H5066
2Ki 4:27 but Gehazi came n to thrust her away. H5066
5:13 And his servants came n, and spake H5066
2Ch 6:36 away captives unto a land far off or n; H7138
18:23 Chenaanah came n, and smote Micaiah H5066
21:16 Arabians, that were n the Ethiopians: H3027
29:31 the LORD, come n and bring sacrifices H5066
Est 5: 2 n, and touched the top of the sceptre. H7126
9: 1 and his decree drew n to be put in H5060
Job 31:37 as a prince would I go n unto him. H7126
33:22 Yea, his soul draweth n unto the grave, H7126
41:16 One is so n to another, that no air can H5066
Ps 22:11 Be not far from me; for trouble is n; for H7138
32: 9 and bridle, lest they come n unto thee. H7126
73:28 But it is good for me to draw n to God: H7132
75: 1 name is n thy wondrous works declare. H7138
107:18 they draw n unto the gates of death. H5060
119:151 Thou art n, O LORD; and all thy H7138
169 Let my cry come n before thee, O H7126
148:14 people n unto him. Praise ye the LORD. H7138
Prv 7: 8 Passing through the street n her corner; H681
10:14 mouth of the foolish is n destruction. H7138
27:10 that is n than a brother far off. H7138
Isa 13:22 and her time is n to come, and her days H7138
26:17 draweth n the time of her delivery, H7126
29:13 as this people draw n me with their H5066
33:13 ye that are n, acknowledge my might. H7138
34: 1 Come n, ye nations, to hear; and H7126
41: 1 let them come n; then let them speak: H5066
1 let us come n together to judgment. H7126
5 earth were afraid, drew n, and came. H7126
45:20 Assemble yourselves and come; draw n H5066
21 Tell ye, and bring them n; yea, let them H5066
46:13 I bring n my righteousness; it shall not H7126
48:16 Come ye n unto me, hear ye this; I have H7126
50: 8 He is n that justifieth me; who will H7138
8 mine adversary? let him come n to me. H5066
51: 5 My righteousness is n; my salvation is H7138
54:14 terror; for it shall not come n thee. H7126
55: 6 be found, call ye upon him while he is n: H7138
56: 1 for my salvation is n to come, and my H7138
57: 3 But draw n hither, ye sons of the H7126
19 n, saith the LORD; and I will heal him. H7138
65: 5 by thyself, come not n to me; for I am H5066
Jer 12: 2 fruit: thou art n in their mouth, and H7138
25:26 the north, far and n, one with another, H7138
30:21 will cause him to draw n, and he shall H7126
42: 1 the least even unto the greatest, came n, H5066
46: 3 and shield, and draw n to battle. H5066
48:16 The calamity of Moab is n to come, H7138
24 the cities of the land of Moab, far or n. H7138
52:25 of them that were n the king's person, H7200
Lam 3:57 Thou drewest n in the day that I called H7126
4:18 our streets: our end is n, our days are H7126

Ezk 6:12 and he that is n shall fall by the sword; H7138
7: 7 the day of trouble is n, and not the H7138
12 The time is come, the day draweth n: let H5060
9: 1 the city to draw n, even every man with H7126
6 but come not n any man upon whom H5066
11: 3 Which say, It is not n; let us build H7138
18: 6 hath come n to a menstruous woman, H7126
22: 4 thy days to draw n, and art come even H7126
5 Those that be n, and those that be far H7138
30: 3 For the day is n, even the day of the H7138
3 of the LORD is n, a cloudy day; it shall H7138
40:46 n to the LORD to minister unto him. H7131
44:13 And they shall not come n unto me, to H5066
13 me, nor to come n to any of my holy H5066
15 me, they shall come n to me to minister H7126
16 and they shall come n to my table, to H7126
45: 4 which shall come n to minister unto H7131
Dan 3: 8 came n, and accused the Jews. H7127
26 Then Nebuchadnezzar came n to the H7127
6:12 Then they came n, and spake before the H7127
7:13 and they brought him n before him. H7127
16 I came n unto one of them that stood H7127
8:17 So he came n where I stood: and when H681
9: 7 all Israel, that are n, and that are far H7138
Joel 3: 9 men of war draw n; let them come up: H5066
14 the LORD is n in the valley of decision. H7138
Am 6: 3 cause the seat of violence to come n; H5066
Oba 15 For the day of the LORD is n upon all H7138
Zep 1:14 The great day of the LORD is n, it is H7138
14 the LORD is near, it is n, and hasteth H7138
3: 2 the LORD; she drew not n to her God. H7126
Mal 3: 5 And I will come n to you to judgment; H7126
Mt 21:34 And when the time of the fruit drew n, G1448
24:33 know that it is n, even at the doors. G1451
Mk 13:28 forth leaves, ye know that summer is n: G1451
Lk 15: 1 Then drew n unto him all the publicans G2258
18:40 when he was come n, he asked him, G1448
19:41 And when he was come n, he beheld the G1448
21: 8 n: go ye not therefore after them. G1448
22:47 and drew n unto Jesus to kiss him. G1448
24:15 himself drew n, and went with them. G1448
Jn 3:23 in Aenon n to Salim, because there G1451
4: 5 is called Sychar, n to the parcel of G4139
11:54 unto a country n to the wilderness, into G1451
Act 7:31 and as he drew n to behold it, the voice G4334
8:29 Then the Spirit said unto Philip, Go n, G4334
9: 3 And as he journeyed, he came n G1448
10:24 together his kinsmen and n friends. G316
21:33 Then the chief captain came n, and G1448
23:15 or ever he come n, are ready to kill him. G1448
27:27 that they drew n to some country; G4317
Heb 10:22 Let us draw n with a true heart in full G4334

NEARER
Ru 3:12 howbeit there is a kinsman n than I. H7138
Ro 13:11 our salvation n than when we believed. G1452

NEARIAH
1Ch 3:22 and Bariah, and N, and Shaphat, six. H5294
23 And the sons of N; Elioenai, and H5294
4:42 Pelatiah, and N, and Rephaiah, and H5294

NEBAI
Neh 10:19 Hariph, Anathoth, N, H5109

NEBAIOTH
1Ch 1:29 of Ishmael, N; then Kedar, and Adbeel, H5032
Isa 60: 7 thee, the rams of N shall minister unto H5032

NEBAJOTH
Gen 25:13 of Ishmael, N; and Kedar, and Adbeel, H5032
28: 9 son, the sister of N, to be his wife. H5032
36: 3 Ishmael's daughter, sister of N. H5032

NEBALLAT
Neh 11:34 Hadid, Zeboim, N, H5041

NEBAT
1Ki 11:26 And Jeroboam the son of N, an H5028
12: 2 the son of N, who was yet in Egypt, H5028
15 Shilonite unto Jeroboam the son of N. H5028
15: 1 son of N reigned Abijam over Judah. H5028
16: 3 like the house of Jeroboam the son of N. H5028
26 the son of N, and in his sin wherewith H5028
31 the son of N, that he took to wife H5028
21:22 the son of N, and like the house of H5028
22:52 the son of N, who made Israel to sin: H5028
2Ki 3: 3 the son of N, which made Israel H5028
9: 9 the son of N, and like the house of H5028

2Ki 10:29 the son of N, who made Israel to H5028
13: 2 the son of N, which made Israel H5028
11 the son of N, who made Israel sin: H5028
14:24 the son of N, who made Israel to sin. H5028
15: 9 the son of N, who made Israel to sin. H5028
18 the son of N, who made Israel to sin. H5028
24 the son of N, who made Israel to sin. H5028
28 the son of N, who made Israel to sin. H5028
17:21 the son of N king: and Jeroboam H5028
23:15 the son of N, who made Israel to H5028
2Ch 9:29 the seer against Jeroboam the son of N? H5028
10: 2 the son of N, who was in Egypt, whither H5028
15 the Shilonite to Jeroboam the son of N. H5028
13: 6 Yet Jeroboam the son of N, the servant H5028

NEBO
Nu 32: 3 Elealeh, and Shebam, and N, and Beon, H5015
38 And N, and Baal-meon, (their names H5015
33:47 in the mountains of Abarim, before N. H5015
Dt 32:49 unto mount N, which is in the land H5015
34: 1 the mountain of N, to the top of Pisgah, H5015
1Ch 5: 8 in Aroer, even unto N and Baalmeon: H5015
Ezr 2:29 The children of N, fifty and two. H5015
10:43 Of the sons of N; Jeiel, Mattithiah, H5015
Neh 7:33 The men of the other N, fifty and two. H5015
Isa 15: 2 shall howl over N, and over Medeba: on H5015
46: 1 Bel boweth down, N stoopeth, their H5015
Jer 48: 1 of Israel; Woe unto N! for it is spoiled: H5015
22 And upon Dibon, and upon N, and H5015

NEBUCHADNEZZAR
2Ki 24: 1 In his days N king of Babylon came up, H5019
10 At that time the servants of N king of H5019
11 And N king of Babylon came against H5019
25: 1 of the month, that N king of Babylon H5019
8 year of king N king of Babylon, came H5019
22 of Judah, whom N king of Babylon had H5019
1Ch 6:15 Judah and Jerusalem by the hand of N. H5019
2Ch 36: 6 Against him came up N king of H5019
7 N also carried of the vessels of the H5019
10 And when the year was expired, king N H5019
13 And he also rebelled against king N, H5019
Ezr 1: 7 the LORD, which N had brought forth H5019
2: 1 away, whom N the king of Babylon H5019
5:12 into the hand of N the king of Babylon, H5020
14 of God, which N took out of the temple H5020
6: 5 of God, which N took forth out of the H5020
Neh 7: 6 away, whom N the king of Babylon H5019
Est 2: 6 of Judah, whom N the king of Babylon H5019
Jer 27: 6 into the hand of N the king of Babylon, H5019
8 serve the same N the king of Babylon, H5019
20 Which N king of Babylon took not, H5019
28: 3 house, that N king of Babylon took H5019
11 I break the yoke of N king of Babylon H5019
14 they may serve N king of Babylon; and H5019
29: 1 the people whom N had carried away H5019
3 Babylon to N king of Babylon) saying, H5019
34: 1 the LORD, when N king of Babylon, H5019
39: 5 brought him up to N king of Babylon to H5019
Dan 1: 1 of Judah came N king of Babylon unto H5019
18 the eunuchs brought them in before N. H5019
2: 1 year of the reign of N Nebuchadnezzar H5019
1 Nebuchadnezzar N dreamed dreams, H5019
28 known to the king N what shall be in H5020
46 Then the king N fell upon his face, and H5020
3: 1 N the king made an image of gold, H5020
2 Then N the king sent to gather together H5020
2 the image which N the king had set up. H5020
3 of the image that N the king had set up; H5020
3 before the image that N had set up. H5020
5 image that N the king hath set up: H5020
7 image that N the king had set up. H5020
9 They spake and said to the king N, O H5020
13 Then N in his rage and fury H5020
14 N spake and said unto them, Is it true, H5020
16 said to the king, O N, we are not careful H5020
19 Then was N full of fury, and the form H5020
24 Then N the king was astonied, and rose H5020
26 Then N came near to the mouth of the H5020
28 Then N spake, and said, Blessed be the H5020
4: 1 N the king, unto all people, nations, H5020
4 I N was at rest in mine house, and H5020
18 This dream I king N have seen. Now H5020
28 All this came upon the king N. H5020
31 saying, O king N, to thee it is spoken; H5020
33 fulfilled upon N: and he was driven H5020
34 And at the end of the days I N lifted up H5020
37 Now I N praise and extol and honour H5020
5: 2 which his father N had taken out of the H5020

N

Dan 5:11 whom the king N thy father, the king, H5020
18 O thou king, the most high God gave N H5020

NEBUCHADREZZAR
Jer 21: 2 the LORD for us; for N king of Babylon H5019
7 into the hand of N king of Babylon, H5019
22:25 into the hand of N king of Babylon, H5019
24: 1 the LORD, after that N king of Babylon H5019
25: 1 *was* the first year of N king of Babylon; H5019
9 the LORD, and N the king of Babylon, H5019
29:21 into the hand of N king of Babylon; H5019
32: 1 which *was* the eighteenth year of N. H5019
28 N king of Babylon, and he shall take it: H5019
35:11 But it came to pass, when N king of H5019
37: 1 of Jehoiakim, whom N king of Babylon H5019
39: 1 month, came N king of Babylon and H5019
11 Now N king of Babylon gave charge H5019
43:10 I will send and take N the king of H5019
44:30 into the hand of N king of Babylon, his H5019
46: 2 which N king of Babylon smote H5019
13 the prophet, how N king of Babylon H5019
26 into the hand of N king of Babylon, H5019
49:28 of Hazor, which N king of Babylon H5019
30 the LORD; for N king of Babylon hath H5019
50:17 him; and last this N king of Babylon H5019
51:34 N the king of Babylon hath devoured H5019
52: 4 of the month, *that* N king of Babylon H5019
12 nineteenth year of N king of Babylon, H5019
28 This *is* the people whom N carried H5019
29 In the eighteenth year of N he carried H5019
30 In the three and twentieth year of N H5019
Ezk 26: 7 bring upon Tyrus N king of Babylon, a H5019
29:18 Son of man, N king of Babylon caused H5019
19 of Egypt unto N king of Babylon; and H5019
30:10 cease by the hand of N king of Babylon. H5019

NEBUSHASBAN
Jer 39:13 the guard sent, and N, Rab-saris, and H5021

NEBUZAR-ADAN
2Ki 25: 8 king of Babylon, came N, captain of the H5018
11 N the captain of the guard carry away. H5018
20 And N captain of the guard took these, H5018
Jer 39: 9 Then N the captain of the guard H5018
10 But N the captain of the guard left of H5018
11 to N the captain of the guard, saying, H5018
13 So N the captain of the guard sent, and H5018
40: 1 LORD, after that N the captain of the H5018
41:10 in Mizpah, whom N the captain of the H5018
43: 6 every person that N the captain of the H5018
52:12 king of Babylon, came N, captain of the H5018
15 Then N the captain of the guard H5018
16 But N the captain of the guard left H5018
26 So N the captain of the guard took H5018
30 of Nebuchadrezzar N the captain of the H5018

NECESSARY
Job 23:12 of his mouth more than my **n** *food*. H2706
Act 13:46 and said, It was **n** that the word of God *G316*
15:28 no greater burden than these **n** things; *G1876*
28:10 laded *us* with such things as were **n**. *G5532*
1Co 12:22 which seem to be more feeble, are **n**: *G316*
2Co 9: 5 Therefore I thought it **n** to exhort the *G316*
Php 2:25 Yet I supposed it **n** to send to you *G316*
Tit 3:14 for **n** uses, that they be not unfruitful. *G316*
Heb 9:23 *It was* therefore **n** that the patterns of *G318*

NECESSITIES
Act 20:34 my **n**, and to them that were with me. *G5532*
2Co 6: 4 patience, in afflictions, in **n**, in distresses, *G318*
12:10 in reproaches, in **n**, in persecutions, in *G318*

NECESSITY
Lk 23:17 (For of **n** he must release one unto them *G318*
Ro 12:13 Distributing to the **n** of saints; given to *G5532*
1Co 7:37 heart, having no **n**, but hath power over *G318*
9:16 to glory of: for **n** is laid upon me; yea, *G318*
2Co 9: 7 or of **n**: for God loveth a cheerful giver. *G318*
Php 4:16 ye sent once and again unto my **n**. *G5532*
Phlm 14 not be as it were of **n**, but willingly. *G318*
Heb 7:12 is made of **n** a change also of the law. *G318*
8: 3 wherefore *it is* of **n** that this man have *G316*
9:16 also of **n** be the death of the testator. *G318*

NECHO
2Ch 35:20 the temple, N king of Egypt came H5224
22 unto the words of N from the mouth of H5224
36: 4 to Jehoiakim. And N took Jehoahaz his H5224

NECK
Gen 27:16 hands, and upon the smooth of his **n**: H6677
40 thou shalt break his yoke from off thy **n**. H6677
33: 4 his **n**, and kissed him: and they wept. H6677
41:42 linen, and put a gold chain about his **n**; H6677
45:14 Benjamin's **n**, and wept; and Benjamin H6677
14 wept; and Benjamin wept upon his **n**. H6677
46:29 **n**, and wept on his neck a good while. H6677
29 neck, and wept on his **n** a good while. H6677
49: 8 *shall be* in the **n** of thine enemies; thy H6203
Ex 13:13 shalt break his **n**: and all the firstborn H6202
34:20 thou break his **n**. All the firstborn of thy H6202
Lev 5: 8 his **n**, but shall not divide *it* asunder: H6203
Dt 21: 4 off the heifer's **n** there in the valley: H6202
28:48 thy **n**, until he have destroyed thee. H6677
31:27 For I know thy rebellion, and thy stiff **n**: H6203
1Sa 4:18 the gate, and his **n** brake, and he died: H4665
2Ki 17:14 necks, like to the **n** of their fathers, that H6203
2Ch 36:13 but he stiffened his **n**, and hardened his H6203
Neh 9:29 hardened their **n**, and would not hear. H6203
Job 15:26 He runneth upon him, *even* on *his* **n**, H6677
16:12 taken *me* by my **n**, and shaken me to H6203
39:19 hast thou clothed his **n** with thunder? H6677
41:22 In his **n** remaineth strength, and H6677
Ps 75: 5 horn on high: speak *not with* a stiff **n**. H6677
Prv 1: 9 unto thy head, and chains about thy **n**. H1621
3: 3 them about thy **n**; write them upon the H1621
22 be life unto thy soul, and grace to thy **n**. H1621
6:21 thine heart, *and* tie them about thy **n**. H1621
29: 1 hardeneth *his* **n**, shall suddenly be H6203
Song 1:10 *of jewels*, thy **n** with chains *of gold*. H6677
4: 4 Thy **n** *is* like the tower of David builded H6677
9 of thine eyes, with one chain of thy **n**. H6677
7: 4 Thy **n** *is* as a tower of ivory; thine eyes H6677
Isa 8: 8 reach *even* to the **n**; and the stretching H6677
10:27 yoke from off thy **n**, and the yoke shall H6677
30:28 to the midst of the **n**, to sift the nations H6677
48: 4 **n** *is* an iron sinew, and thy brow brass; H6203
52: 2 of thy **n**, O captive daughter of Zion. H6677
66: 3 he cut off a dog's **n**; he that offereth an H6202
Jer 7:26 **n**: they did worse than their fathers. H6203
17:23 but made their **n** stiff, that they might H6203
27: 2 and yokes, and put them upon thy **n**, H6677
8 will not put their **n** under the yoke of H6677
11 But the nations that bring their **n** H6677
28:10 the prophet Jeremiah's **n**, and brake it. H6677
11 of Babylon from the **n** of all nations H6677
12 the **n** of the prophet Jeremiah, saying, H6677
14 of iron upon the **n** of all these nations, H6677
30: 8 yoke from off thy **n**, and will burst thy H6677
Lam 1:14 come up upon my **n**: he hath made my H6677
Ezk 16:11 upon thy hands, and a chain on thy **n**. H1627
Dan 5: 7 of gold about his **n**, and shall be the H6676
16 of gold about thy **n**, and shalt be the H6676
29 chain of gold about his **n**, and made a H6676
Hos 10:11 passed over upon her fair **n**: I will make H6677
Hab 3:13 the foundation unto the **n**. Selah. H6677
Mt 18: 6 hanged about his **n**, and *that* he were *G5137*
Mk 9:42 his **n**, and he were cast into the sea. *G5137*
Lk 15:20 ran, and fell on his **n**, and kissed him. *G5137*
17: 2 hanged about his **n**, and he cast into the *G5137*
Act 15:10 put a yoke upon the **n** of the disciples, *G5137*
20:37 and fell on Paul's **n**, and kissed him, *G5137*

NECKS
Jos 10:24 put your feet upon the **n** of these kings. H6677
24 and put their feet upon the **n** of them. H6677
Jdg 5:30 for the **n** of *them that take* the spoil? H6677
8:21 ornaments that *were* on their camels' **n**. H6677
26 chains that *were* about their camels' **n**. H6677
2Sa 22:41 Thou hast also given me the **n** of mine H6203
2Ki 17:14 but hardened their **n**, like to the neck of H6203
Neh 3: 5 not their **n** to the work of their Lord. H6677
9:16 hardened their **n**, and hearkened not H6203
17 hardened their **n**, and in their rebellion H6203
Ps 18:40 Thou hast also given me the **n** of mine H6203
Isa 3:16 stretched forth **n** and wanton eyes, H1627
Jer 19:15 **n**, that they might not hear my words. H6203
27:12 saying, Bring your **n** under the yoke of H6677
Lam 5: 5 Our **n** *are* under persecution: we H6677
Ezk 21:29 thee upon the **n** of *them that are* slain, H6677
Mic 2: 3 not remove your **n**; neither shall ye go H6677
Ro 16: 4 down their own **n**: unto whom not only *G5137*

NECROMANCER
Dt 18:11 spirits, or a wizard, or a **n**. H1875+H4191

NEDABIAH
1Ch 3:18 Shenazar, Jecamiah, Hoshama, and N. H5072

NEED
Dt 15: 8 for his **n**, *in that* which he wanteth. H4270
1Sa 21:15 Have I **n** of mad men, that ye have H2638
2Ch 2:16 as thou shalt **n**: and we will bring it H6878
20:17 Ye shall not *n* to fight in this *battle:* set
Ezr 6: 9 And that which they have **n** of, both H2818
Prv 31:11 her, so that he shall have no **n** of spoil. H2637
Mt 3:14 But John forbad him, saying, I have **n** *G5532*
6: 8 things ye have **n** of, before ye ask him. *G5532*
32 that ye have **n** of all these things. *G5535*
9:12 that be whole **n** not a physician, but *G2192*
14:16 But Jesus said unto them, They **n** not *G5532*
21: 3 say, The Lord hath **n** of them; and *G5532*
26:65 what further **n** have we of witnesses? *G5532*
Mk 2:17 are whole have no **n** of the physician, *G5532*
25 David did, when he had **n**, and was an *G5532*
11: 3 ye that the Lord hath **n** of him; and *G5532*
14:63 What **n** we any further witnesses? *G5532*
Lk 5:31 that are whole **n** not a physician; but *G5532*
9:11 and healed them that had **n** of healing. *G5532*
12:30 knoweth that ye have **n** of these things. *G5535*
15: 7 just persons, which **n** no repentance. *G2192*
19:31 him, Because the Lord hath **n** of him. *G5532*
34 And they said, The Lord hath **n** of him. *G5532*
22:71 And they said, What **n** we any further *G5532*
Jn 13:29 that we have **n** of against the feast; *G5532*
Act 2:45 them to all *men*, as every man had **n**. *G5532*
4:35 unto every man according as he had **n**. *G5532*
Ro 16: 2 business she hath **n** of you: for she hath *G5535*
1Co 7:36 of *her* age, and **n** so require, let him do *G3784*
12:21 hand, I have no **n** of thee: nor again the *G5532*
21 the head to the feet, I have no **n** of you. *G5532*
24 For our comely *parts* have no **n**: but *G5532*
2Co 3: 1 ourselves? or **n** we, as some *others*, *G5535*
Php 4:12 hungry, both to abound and to suffer **n**. *G5302*
19 But my God shall supply all your **n** *G5532*
1Th 1: 8 so that we **n** not to speak any thing. *G5532*
4: 9 But as touching brotherly love ye **n** not *G2192*
5: 1 ye have no **n** that I write unto you. *G5532*
Heb 4:16 and find grace to help in time of **n**. *G2121*
5:12 teachers, ye have **n** that one teach you *G5532*
12 have **n** of milk, and not of strong meat. *G5532*
7:11 the law,) what further **n** *was there* that *G5532*
10:36 For ye have **n** of patience, that, after ye *G5532*
1Pt 1: 6 for a season, if **n** be, ye are in heaviness *G1163*
1Jn 2:27 in you, and ye **n** not that any man *G5532*
3:17 his brother have **n**, and shutteth up his *G5532*
Rev 3:17 with goods, and have **n** of nothing; and *G5532*
21:23 And the city had no **n** of the sun, *G5532*
22: 5 there; and they **n** no candle, neither *G5532*

NEEDED
Jn 2:25 And **n** not that any should testify of *G5532*
Act 17:25 as though he **n** any thing, seeing he *G4326*

NEEDEST
Jn 16:30 all things, and **n** not that any man *G5532*

NEEDETH
Gen 33:15 And he said, What **n** it? let me find grace
Lk 11: 8 will rise and give him as many as he **n**. *G5535*
Jn 13:10 Jesus saith to him, He that is washed **n** *G5532*
Eph 4:28 that he may have to give to him that **n**. *G5532*
2Ti 2:15 a workman that **n** not to be ashamed, *G422*
Heb 7:27 Who **n** not daily, as those high priests, *G2192*

NEEDFUL
Ezr 7:20 And whatsoever more shall be **n** for the H2819
Lk 10:42 But one thing is **n**: and Mary hath *G5532*
Act 15: 5 That it was **n** to circumcise them, *G1163*
Php 1:24 to abide in the flesh *is* more **n** for you. *G316*
Jas 2:16 are **n** to the body; what *doth it* profit? *G2006*
Jude 3 salvation, it was **n** for me to write unto *G318*

NEEDLE
Mt 19:24 the eye of a **n**, than for a rich man *G4476*
Mk 10:25 the eye of a **n**, than for a rich man *G4476*

NEEDLE'S
Lk 18:25 to go through a **n** eye, than for a rich *G4476*

NEEDLEWORK
Ex 26:36 and fine twined linen, wrought with **n**. H7551
27:16 wrought with **n**: *and* their pillars *shall* H7551
28:39 and thou shalt make the girdle *of* **n**. H7551
36:37 and scarlet, and fine twined linen, of **n**; H7551
38:18 of the court *was* **n**, *of* blue, and purple, H7551
39:29 *of* **n**; as the LORD commanded Moses. H7551
Jdg 5:30 divers colours of **n**, of divers colours of H7553

Jdg 5:30 divers colours of n on both sides, *meet* H7553
Ps 45:14 the king in raiment of n: the virgins her H7553

NEEDS
Gen 17:13 thy money, must n be circumcised: and H4135
19: 9 and he will n be a judge: now will H8199
24: 5 this land: must I n bring thy son again H8199
31:30 And now, *though* thou wouldest n be H1980
2Sa 14:14 For we must n die, and *are* as water H4191
Jer 10: 5 not: they must n be borne, because H5375
Mt 18: 7 for it must n be that offences come; G318
Mk 13: 7 must n be; but the end *shall* not *be* yet. G1163
Lk 14:18 and I must n go and see it: I pray G318
Jn 4: 4 And he must n go through Samaria. G1163
Act 1:16 scripture must n have been fulfilled, G1163
17: 3 that Christ must n have suffered, and G1163
21:22 multitude must n come together: for G3843
Ro 13: 5 Wherefore *ye* must n be subject, not only G318
1Co 5:10 for then must ye n go out of the world. G3784
2Co 11:30 If I must n glory, I will glory of the G1163

NEEDY
Dt 15:11 to thy poor, and to thy n, in thy land. H34
24:14 *that is* poor and n, *whether he be* of thy H34
Job 24: 4 They turn the n out of the way: the poor H34
14 poor and n, and in the night is as a thief. H34
Ps 9:18 For the n shall not alway be forgotten: H34
12: 5 for the sighing of the n, now will I arise, H34
35:10 and the n from him that spoileth him? H34
37:14 down the poor and n, *and* to slay such as H34
40:17 But I *am* poor and n; *yet* the Lord H34
70: 5 But I *am* poor and n: make haste unto H34
72: 4 the children of the n, and shall break in H34
12 For he shall deliver the n when he crieth; H34
13 He shall spare the poor and n, and shall H34
13 needy, and shall save the souls of the n. H34
74:21 let the poor and n praise thy name. H34
82: 3 do justice to the afflicted and n. H7326
4 Deliver the poor and n: rid *them* out of H34
86: 1 O LORD, hear me: for I *am* poor and n. H34
109:16 the poor and n man, that he might H34
22 For I *am* poor and n, and my heart is H34
113: 7 *and* lifteth the n out of the dunghill; H34
Prv 30:14 the earth, and the n from *among* men. H34
31: 9 and plead the cause of the poor and n. H34
20 she reacheth forth her hands to the n. H34
Isa 10: 2 To turn aside the n from judgment, H1800
14:30 shall feed, and the n shall lie down in H34
25: 4 poor, a strength to the n in his distress, a H34
26: 6 feet of the poor, *and* the steps of the n. H1800
32: 7 words, even when the n speaketh right. H34
41:17 *When* the poor and n seek water, and H34
Jer 5:28 and the right of the n do they not judge. H34
22:16 He judged the cause of the poor and n; H34
Ezk 16:49 strengthen the hand of the poor and n. H34
18:12 Hath oppressed the poor and n, hath H34
22:29 vexed the poor and n: yea, they have H34
Am 4: 1 which crush the n, which say to their H34
8: 4 Hear this, O ye that swallow up the n, H34
6 for silver, and the n for a pair of shoes; H34

NEESINGS
Job 41:18 By his n a light doth shine, and his eyes H5846

NEGINAH
Ps 61:ttl To the chief Musician upon N, *A Psalm* H5058

NEGINOTH
Ps 4:ttl To the chief Musician on N, A Psalm of H5058
6:ttl To the chief Musician on N upon H5058
54:ttl To the chief Musician on N, Maschil, *A* H5058
55:ttl To the chief Musician on N, Maschil, *A* H5058
67:ttl To the chief Musician on N, A Psalm *or* H5058
76:ttl To the chief Musician on N, A Psalm *or* H5058

NEGLECT
Mt 18:17 And if he shall n to hear them, tell *it* G3878
17 church: but if he n to hear the church, G3878
1Ti 4:14 N not the gift that is in thee, which was G272
Heb 2: 3 How shall we escape, if we n so great G272

NEGLECTED
Act 6: 1 were n in the daily ministration. G3865

NEGLECTING
Col 2:23 and humility, and n of the body; not in G857

NEGLIGENT
2Ch 29:11 My sons, be not now n: for the LORD H7952
2Pt 1:12 Wherefore I will not be n to put you G272

NEGO See ABED-NEGO.

NEHELAMITE
Jer 29:24 also speak to Shemaiah the N, saying, H5161
31 Shemaiah the N; Because that H5161
32 Shemaiah the N, and his seed: he shall H5161

NEHEMIAH
Ezr 2: 2 Jeshua, N, Seraiah, Reelaiah, Mordecai, H5166
Neh 1: 1 The words of N the son of Hachaliah. H5166
3:16 After him repaired N the son of Azbuk, H5166
7: 7 Who came with Zerubbabel, Jeshua, N, H5166
8: 9 And N, which *is* the Tirshatha, and H5166
10: 1 Now those that sealed *were*, N, the H5166
12:26 and in the days of N the governor, and H5166
47 and in the days of N, gave the portions H5166

NEHILOTH
Ps 5:ttl To the chief Musician upon N, A Psalm H5155

NEHUM
Neh 7: 7 Mispereth, Bigvai, N, Baanah. The H5149

NEHUSHTA
2Ki 24: 8 name *was* N, the daughter of Elnathan H5179

NEHUSHTAN
2Ki 18: 4 burn incense to it: and he called it N. H5180

NEIEL
Jos 19:27 of Beth-emek, and N, and goeth out to H5272

NEIGHBOUR
Ex 3:22 But every woman shall borrow of her n, H7934
11: 2 man borrow of his n, and every woman H7453
2 n, jewels of silver, and jewels of gold. H7468
12: 4 let him and his n next unto his house H7934
20:16 not bear false witness against thy n. H7453
21:14 upon his n, to slay him with guile; H7453
22: 7 If a man shall deliver unto his n money H7453
9 he shall pay double unto his n. H7453
10 If a man deliver unto his n an ass, or H7453
14 And if a man borrow *ought* of his n, H7453
32:27 his companion, and every man his n. H7138
Lev 6: 2 and lie unto his n in that which was H5997
2 by violence, or hath deceived his n; H5997
19:13 Thou shalt not defraud thy n, neither H7453
15 in righteousness shalt thou judge thy n. H5997
16 the blood of thy n: I *am* the LORD. H7453
17 thy n, and not suffer sin upon him. H5997
18 love thy n as thyself: I *am* the LORD. H7453
24:19 And if a man cause a blemish in his n; H5997
25:14 And if thou sell ought unto thy n, or H5997
15 shalt buy of thy n, *and* according unto H5997
Dt 4:42 should kill his n unawares, and hated H7453
5:20 thou bear false witness against thy n. H7453
15: 2 *ought* unto his n shall release *it*; he H7453
2 not exact *it* of his n, or of his brother; H7453
19: 4 Whoso killeth his n ignorantly, whom H7453
5 the wood with his n to hew wood, and H7453
5 lighteth upon his n, that he die; he shall H7453
11 But if any man hate his n, and lie in H7453
22:26 riseth against his n, and slayeth him, H7453
23:25 corn of thy n, then thou mayest pluck H7453
27:24 Cursed *be* he that smiteth his n H7453
Jos 20: 5 he smote his n unwittingly, and hated H7453
Ru 4: 7 n: and this *was* a testimony in Israel. H7453
1Sa 15:28 to a n of thine, *that is* better than thou. H7453
28:17 and given it to thy n, *even* to David: H7453
2Sa 12:11 *them* unto thy n, and he shall lie with H7453
1Ki 8:31 If any man trespass against his n, and H7453
20:35 said unto his n in the word of the H7453
2Ch 6:22 If a man sin against his n, and an oath H7453
Job 12: 4 I am *as* one mocked of his n, who H7453
16:21 with God, as a man *pleadeth* for his n! H7453
Ps 12: 2 They speak vanity every one with his n: H7453
15: 3 nor doeth evil to his n, nor taketh up a H7453
3 nor taketh up a reproach against his n. H7138
101: 5 Whoso privily slandereth his n, him will H7453
Prv 3:28 Say not unto thy n, Go, and come again, H7453
29 Devise not evil against thy n, seeing he H7453
11: 9 mouth destroyeth his n: but through H7453
12 wisdom despiseth his n: but a man of H7453
12:26 excellent than his n: but the way of the H7453
14:20 The poor is hated even of his own n: but H7453
21 He that despiseth his n sinneth: but he H7453
16:29 A violent man enticeth his n, and H7453
Prv 18:17 but his n cometh and searcheth him. H7453
19: 4 but the poor is separated from his n. H7453
21:10 evil: his n findeth no favour in his eyes. H7453
24:28 Be not a witness against thy n without H7453
25: 8 when thy n hath put thee to shame. H7453
9 Debate thy cause with thy n *himself*; H7453
18 against his n *is* a maul, and a sword, H7453
26:19 So *is* the man *that* deceiveth his n, and H7453
27:10 a n *that is* near than a brother far off. H7934
29: 5 A man that flattereth his n spreadeth a H7453
Ecc 4: 4 is envied of his n. This *is* also vanity H7453
Isa 3: 5 and every one by his n: the child shall H7453
19: 2 one against his n; city against city, *and* H7453
41: 6 They helped every one his n; and *every* H7453
Jer 6:21 them; the n and his friend shall perish. H7934
7: 5 judgment between a man and his n; H7453
9: 4 Take ye heed every one of his n, and H7453
4 and every n will walk with slanders. H7453
5 And they will deceive every one his n, H7453
8 peaceably to his n with his mouth, but H7453
20 and every one her n lamentation. H7468
22: 8 every man to his n, Wherefore hath the H7453
23:27 every man to his n, as their fathers have H7453
30 steal my words every one from his n. H7453
35 Thus shall ye say every one to his n, and H7453
31:34 every man his n, and every man his H7453
34:15 every man to his n; and ye had made a H7453
17 every man to his n: behold, I proclaim a H7453
49:18 and the n *cities* thereof, saith H7934
50:40 and the n *cities* thereof, saith H7934
Hab 2:15 Woe unto him that giveth his n drink, H7453
Zec 3:10 n under the vine and under the fig tree. H7453
8:10 for I set all men every one against his n. H7453
16 the truth to his n; execute the judgment H7453
17 hearts against his n; and love no false H7453
14:13 on the hand of his n, and his hand shall H7453
13 shall rise up against the hand of his n. H7453
Mt 5:43 shalt love thy n, and hate thine enemy. G4139
19:19 and, Thou shalt love thy n as thyself. G4139
22:39 unto it, Thou shalt love thy n as thyself. G4139
Mk 12:31 shalt love thy n as thyself. There is G4139
33 and to love *his* n as himself, is more G4139
Lk 10:27 with all thy mind; and thy n as thyself. G4139
29 said unto Jesus, And who is my n? G4139
36 n unto him that fell among the thieves? G4139
Act 7:27 But he that did his n wrong thrust him G4139
Ro 13: 9 Thou shalt love thy n as thyself. G4139
10 Love worketh no ill to his n: therefore G4139
15: 2 Let every one of us please *his* n for *his* G4139
Gal 5:14 in this; Thou shalt love thy n as thyself. G4139
Eph 4:25 n: for we are members one of another. G4139
Heb 8:11 every man his n, and every man his G4139
Jas 2: 8 shalt love thy n as thyself, ye do well: G4139

NEIGHBOURS
Jos 9:16 n, and *that* they dwelt among them. H7138
Ru 4:17 And the women her n gave it a name, H7934
2Ki 4: 3 abroad of all thy n, *even* empty vessels; H7934
Ps 28: 3 their n, but mischief *is* in their hearts. H7453
31:11 among my n, and a fear to mine H7934
44:13 Thou makest us a reproach to our n, a H7934
79: 4 We are become a reproach to our n, a H7934
12 And render unto our n sevenfold into H7934
80: 6 Thou makest us a strife unto our n: and H7934
89:41 way spoil him: he is a reproach to his n. H7934
Jer 12:14 against all mine evil n, that touch the H7934
49:10 his brethren, and his n, and he *is* not. H7934
Ezk 16:26 the Egyptians thy n, great of flesh; and H7934
22:12 gained of thy n by extortion, and hast H7453
23: 5 on her lovers, on the Assyrians *her* n, H7138
12 She doted upon the Assyrians *her* n, H7138
Lk 1:58 And her n and her cousins heard how G4040
14:12 nor *thy* rich n; lest they also bid thee G1069
15: 6 *his* friends and n, saying unto them, G1069
9 *her* friends and *her* n together, saying, G1069
Jn 9: 8 The n therefore, and they which before G1069

NEIGHBOUR'S
Ex 20:17 Thou shalt not covet thy n house, thou H7453
17 thou shalt not covet thy n wife, nor his H7453
17 nor his ass, nor any thing that *is* thy n. H7453
22: 8 he have put his hand unto his n goods. H7453
11 put his hand unto his n goods; and the H7453
26 If thou at all take thy n raiment to H7453
Lev 18:20 thy n wife, to defile thyself with her. H5997
20:10 adultery with his n wife, the adulterer H7453
25:14 buyest *ought* of thy n hand, ye shall not H5997
Dt 5:21 Neither shalt thou desire thy n wife, H7453
21 thou covet thy n house, his field, or his H7453

N

Dt 5:21 ox, or his ass, or any *thing* that *is* thy **n**. H7453
19:14 Thou shalt not remove thy **n** landmark, H7453
22:24 hath humbled his **n** wife: so thou shalt H7453
23:24 When thou comest into thy **n** vineyard, H7453
25 move a sickle unto thy **n** standing corn. H7453
27:17 Cursed *be* he that removeth his **n** H7453
Job 31: 9 or *if* I have laid wait at my **n** door; H7453
Prv 6:29 So he that goeth in to his **n** wife; H7453
25:17 Withdraw thy foot from thy **n** house; H7453
Jer 5: 8 every one neighed after his **n** wife. H7453
22:13 *that* useth his **n** service without wages, H7453
Ezk 18: 6 hath defiled his **n** wife, neither hath H7453
11 the mountains, and defiled his **n** wife, H7453
15 of Israel, hath not defiled his **n** wife, H7453
22:11 with his **n** wife; and another hath H7453
33:26 **n** wife: and shall ye possess the land? H7453
Zec 11: 6 every one into his **n** hand, and into the H7453

NEIGHBOURS'
Jer 29:23 with their **n** wives, and have spoken H7453

NEIGHED
Jer 5: 8 every one **n** after his neighbour's wife. H6670

NEIGHING
Jer 8:16 at the sound of the **n** of his strong ones; H4684

NEIGHINGS
Jer 13:27 I have seen thine adulteries, and thy **n**, H4684

NEITHER
Gen 3: 3 eat of it, **n** shall ye touch it, lest ye die. H3808
8:21 from his youth; **n** will I again smite any H3808
9:11 with you; **n** shall all flesh be cut H3808
11 the waters of a flood; **n** shall there any H3808
17: 5 **N** shall thy name any more be called H3808
19:17 not behind thee, **n** stay thou in all the H408
21:26 done this thing: **n** didst thou tell me, H3808
26 tell me, **n** yet heard I *of it*, but to day. H3808
22:12 hand upon the lad, **n** do thou any thing H408
24:16 upon, a virgin, **n** had any man known H3808
29: 7 And he said, Lo, *it is* yet high day, **n** *is* H3808
39: 9 this house than I; **n** hath he kept back H3808
45: 6 *there shall* **n** *be* earing nor harvest. H369
Ex 4: 8 not believe thee, **n** hearken to the voice H3808
9 these two signs, **n** hearken unto thy H3808
10 I *am* not eloquent, **n** heretofore, nor H1571
5: 2 the LORD, **n** will I let Israel go. H1571+H3808
23 **n** hast thou delivered thy people at all. H3808
7:22 was hardened, **n** did he hearken unto H3808
23 **n** did he set his heart to this also. H3808
8:32 time also, **n** would he let the people go. H3808
9:29 shall cease, **n** shall there be any more H3808
35 was hardened, **n** would he let the H3808
10: 6 Egyptians; which **n** thy fathers, nor thy H3808
14 as they, **n** after them shall be such. H3808
23 They saw not one another, **n** rose any H3808
12:39 not tarry, **n** had they prepared H1571+H3808
46 house; **n** shall ye break a bone thereof. H3808
13: 7 be seen with thee, **n** shall there be H3808
16:24 stink, **n** was there any worm therein. H3808
20:23 **n** shall ye make unto you gods of gold. H3808
26 **N** shalt thou go up by steps unto mine H3808
22:21 Thou shalt **n** vex a stranger, nor H3808
25 **n** shalt thou lay upon him usury. H3808
31 And ye shall be holy men unto me: **n** H3808
23: 2 to *do* evil; **n** shalt thou speak in H3808
3 **N** shalt thou countenance a poor man H3808
13 gods, **n** let it be heard out of thy mouth. H3808
18 leavened bread; **n** shall the fat of my H3808
24: 2 nigh; **n** shall the people go up with him. H3808
30: 9 **n** shall ye pour drink offering thereon. H3808
32 it not be poured, **n** shall ye make *any* H3808
32:18 shout for mastery, **n** *is it* the voice of H369
34: 3 And no man shall come up with thee, **n** H408
3 all the mount; **n** let the flocks nor herds H408
24 thy borders: **n** shall any man desire H3808
25 with leaven; **n** shall the sacrifice of H3808
28 nights; he did **n** eat bread, nor drink H3808
36: 6 the camp, saying, Let **n** man nor woman H408
Lev 2:13 season with salt; **n** shalt thou suffer the H3808
3:17 dwellings, that ye eat **n** fat nor blood. H3808
5:11 put no oil upon it, **n** shall he put *any* H3808
7:18 not be accepted, **n** shall it be imputed H3808
10: 6 not your heads, **n** rend your clothes; H3808
11:43 thing that creepeth, **n** shall ye make H3808
44 holy; for I *am* holy: **n** shall ye defile H3808
17:12 shall eat blood, **n** shall any stranger H3808
18: 3 do: **n** shall ye walk in their ordinances. H3808
Lev 18:17 and her daughter, **n** shalt thou take her H3808
18 **N** shalt thou take a wife to her sister, to H3808
21 *the fire* to Molech, **n** shalt thou profane H3808
23 **N** shalt thou lie with any beast to defile H3808
23 thyself therewith: **n** shall any woman H3808
26 these abominations; *n* any of your own
19: 9 of thy field, **n** shalt thou gather the
10 thy vineyard, **n** shalt thou gather *every* H3808
11 Ye shall not steal, **n** deal falsely, H3808
11 deal falsely, **n** lie one to another. H3808
12 by my name falsely, **n** shalt thou profane
13 thy neighbour, **n** rob *him*: the wages H3808
16 thy people: **n** shalt thou stand against H3808
19 with mingled seed: **n** shall a garment H3808
26 *thing* with the blood: **n** shall ye use H3808
27 of your heads, **n** shalt thou mar the H3808
31 familiar spirits, **n** seek after wizards, to H408
21: 5 upon their head, **n** shall they shave off H3808
7 or profane; **n** shall they take a woman H3808
11 **N** shall he go in to any dead body, nor H3808
12 **N** shall he go out of the sanctuary, nor H3808
15 **N** shall he profane his seed among his H3808
22:24 or broken, or cut; **n** shall ye make *any* H3808
25 **N** from a stranger's hand shall ye offer H3808
32 **N** shall ye profane my holy name; but I H3808
23:14 And ye shall eat **n** bread, nor parched H3808
22 thou reapest, **n** shalt thou gather any H3808
25: 4 **n** sow thy field, nor prune thy vineyard. H3808
5 shalt not reap, **n** gather the grapes of H3808
11 you: ye shall not sow, **n** reap that which H3808
26: 1 idols nor graven image, **n** rear you up a H3808
1 a standing image, **n** shall ye set up *any* H3808
6 **n** shall the sword go through your land. H3808
20 yield her increase, **n** shall the trees of H3808
44 cast them away, **n** will I abhor them, to H3808
27:33 it be good or bad, **n** shall he change it: H3808
Nu 1:49 the tribe of Levi, **n** take the sum of H3808
5:13 her, **n** she be taken *with the manner;* H3808
6: 3 of strong drink, **n** shall he drink any H3808
11:19 five days, **n** ten days, nor twenty days; H3808
14: 9 Only rebel not ye against the LORD, **n** H408
23 unto their fathers, **n** shall any of them H3808
16:15 from them, **n** have I hurt one of them. H3808
18: 3 that **n** they, nor ye also, die. H3808+H1571
20 in their land, **n** shalt thou have any H3808
22 **N** must the children of Israel H3808
32 it the best of it: **n** shall ye pollute the H3808
20: 5 **n** *is* there any water to drink. H369
17 the vineyards, **n** will we drink *of* the H3808
21: 5 *there is* no bread, **n** *is there any* water; H369
23:19 God *is* not a man, that he should lie; **n**
21 He hath not beheld iniquity in Jacob, **n** H3808
23 against Jacob, **n** *is there* any divination H3808
25 And Balak said unto Balaam, **N** curse H3808
35:23 *was* not his enemy, **n** sought his harm: H3808
36: 9 **N** shall the inheritance remove from H3808
Dt 1:21 unto thee; fear not, **n** be discouraged. H408
29 Then I said unto you, Dread not, **n** be H3808
42 them, Go not up, **n** fight; for I *am* not H3808
2: 9 not the Moabites, **n** contend with them H408
27 high way, I will **n** turn unto the right H3808
4: 2 I command you, **n** shall ye diminish H3808
28 **n** see, nor hear, nor eat, nor smell. H3808
31 not forsake thee, **n** destroy thee, nor H3808
5:18 **N** shalt thou commit adultery. H3808
19 **N** shalt thou steal. H3808
20 **N** shalt thou bear false witness against H3808
21 **N** shalt thou desire thy neighbour's H3808
21 neighbour's wife, **n** shalt thou covet thy H3808
7: 3 **N** shalt thou make marriages with H3808
16 no pity upon them: **n** shalt thou serve H3808
26 **N** shalt thou bring an abomination H3808
8: 3 thou knewest not, **n** did thy fathers H3808
4 **n** did thy foot swell, these forty years. H3808
9: 9 I **n** did eat bread nor drink water: H3808
18 and forty nights: I did **n** eat bread, nor H3808
13: 8 unto him; **n** shall thine eye pity H3808
8 thine eye pity him, **n** shalt thou spare, H3808
8 thou spare, **n** shalt thou conceal him: H3808
16: 4 thy coast seven days; **n** shall there *any* H3808
19 respect persons, **n** take a gift: for a gift H3808
22 **N** shalt thou set thee up *any* image; H3808
17:17 **N** shall he multiply wives to himself, H3808
17 heart turn not away: **n** shall he greatly H3808
18:16 LORD my God, **n** let me see this great H3808
20: 3 **n** be ye terrified because of them; H408
21: 4 valley, which is **n** eared nor sown, and H3808
7 shed this blood, **n** have our eyes seen *it*. H3808
22: 5 unto a man, **n** shall a man put on H3808
Dt 24: 5 not go out to war, **n** shall he be charged H3808
15 give *him* his hire, **n** shall the sun go H3808
16 for the children, **n** shall the children be H3808
26:13 **n** have I forgotten *them*: H3808
14 in my mourning, **n** have I taken away H3808
28:36 a nation which **n** thou nor thy fathers H3808
39 *them*, but shalt **n** drink *of* the wine, nor H3808
64 serve other gods, which **n** thou nor thy H3808
65 thou find no ease, **n** shall the sole of thy H3808
29: 6 Ye have not eaten bread, **n** have ye H3808
14 **N** with you only do I make this H3808
30:11 it *is* not hidden from thee, **n** *is* it far off. H3808
13 **N** *is* it beyond the sea, that thou H3808
31: 8 he will not fail thee, **n** forsake thee: fear H3808
8 forsake thee: fear not, **n** be dismayed. H3808
32:28 For they *are* a nation void of counsel, **n** H369
39 I wound, and I heal: **n** *is there any* that H369
33: 9 not seen him; **n** did he acknowledge H3808
Jos 1: 9 be not afraid, **n** be thou dismayed: for H408
2:11 hearts did melt, **n** did there remain any H3808
5: 1 their heart melted, **n** was there spirit in H3808
12 corn of the land; **n** had the children of H3808
6:10 noise with your voice, **n** shall *any* word H3808
7:12 were accursed: **n** will I be with you any H3808
8: 1 Joshua, Fear not, **n** be thou dismayed: H408
11:14 them, **n** left they any to breathe. H3808
23: 7 among you; **n** make mention of the H3808
7 to swear *by them*, **n** serve them, nor H3808
Jdg 1:27 **N** did Manasseh drive out *the* H3808
29 **N** did Ephraim drive out the H3808
30 **N** did Zebulun drive out the H3808
31 **N** did Asher drive out the inhabitants H3808
33 **N** did Naphtali drive out the H3808
2:23 them out hastily; **n** delivered he them H3808
6: 4 for Israel, **n** sheep, nor ox, nor ass.
8:23 not rule over you, **n** shall my son rule H3808
35 **N** shewed they kindness to the house of H3808
11:34 beside her he had **n** son nor daughter. H369
13: 6 whence he *was*, **n** told he me his name: H3808
7 wine nor strong drink, **n** eat any unclean H408
14 cometh of the vine, **n** let her drink wine H408
23 at our hands, **n** would he have shewed H3808
20: 8 **n** will we any *of us* turn into his house. H3808
Ru 2: 8 in another field, **n** go from hence, but H3808
1Sa 1:15 I have drunk **n** wine nor strong drink, H3808
2: 2 thee: **n** *is there* any rock like our God. H369
3: 7 know the LORD, **n** was the word of the H2962
4:20 she answered not, **n** did she regard *it*. H3808
5: 5 Therefore **n** the priests of Dagon, nor H3808
12: 4 us, nor oppressed us, **n** hast thou taken H3808
13:22 that there was **n** sword nor spear found H3808
16: 8 **N** hath the LORD chosen this. H1571+H3808
9 **N** hath the LORD chosen this. H1571+H3808
20:27 Jesse to meat, **n** yesterday, nor to day? H1571
21: 8 for I have **n** brought my sword H1571+H3808
24:11 see that *there is* **n** evil nor transgression H369
25: 7 we hurt them not, **n** was there ought H3808
15 and we were not hurt, **n** missed we any H3808
26:12 saw *it*, nor knew *it*, **n** awaked: for they H369
27: 9 And David smote the land, and left **n** H3608
11 And David saved **n** man nor woman H3608
28: 6 him not, **n** by dreams, nor by Urim, H1571
15 me no more, **n** by prophets, nor by H1571
30:15 God, that thou wilt **n** kill me, nor deliver H518
19 lacking to them, **n** small nor great, H4480
19 small nor great, **n** sons nor daughters, H4480
19 nor daughters, **n** spoil, nor any *thing* H4480
2Sa 1:21 *let there be* no dew, **n** *let there be* rain, H408
2:28 no more, **n** fought they any more. H3808
7:10 move no more; **n** shall the children of H3808
22 *is* none like thee, **n** *is there any* God H369
12:17 not, **n** did he eat bread with them. H3808
13:22 his brother Amnon **n** good nor bad: for H3808
14: 7 *n* name nor remainder upon the earth. H1115
14 up again; **n** doth God respect *any* H3808
18: 3 will not care for us; **n** if half of us die, H518
19: 6 thou regardest **n** princes nor servants: H369
19 iniquity unto me, **n** do thou remember H408
24 the king, and had **n** dressed his feet, H3808
20: 1 have no part in David, **n** have we H3808
21: 4 nor of his house; **n** for us shalt thou kill H369
10 and suffered **n** the birds of the air to H3808
24:24 *it* of thee at a price: **n** will I offer burnt H3808
1Ki 3:11 thyself long life; **n** hast asked riches for H3808
12 thee before thee, **n** after thee shall any H3808
26 Let it be **n** mine nor thine, *but* divide *it*. H3808
5: 4 *there is* **n** adversary nor evil occurrent. H369
6: 7 so that there was **n** hammer nor axe H3808
7:47 exceeding many: **n** was the weight of H3808

1Ki 11: 2 not go in to them, **n** shall they come in H3808
12:16 portion have we in David? **n** *have we* H3808
13: 8 go in with thee, **n** will I eat bread nor H3808
16 go in with thee: **n** will I eat bread nor H3808
16:11 **n** of his kinsfolks, nor of his friends.
17:14 shall not waste, **n** shall the cruse of oil H3808
16 *And* the barrel of meal wasted not, **n** H3808
18:29 that *there was* **n** voice, nor any to H369
22:31 saying, Fight **n** with small nor great, H3808
2Ki 3:17 shall not see wind, **n** shall ye see rain; H3808
4:23 go to him to day? *it is* **n** new moon, nor H3808
31 child; but *there was* **n** voice, nor hearing. H369
5:17 henceforth offer **n** burnt offering nor H3808
6:19 *is* not the way, **n** *is* this the city: follow H3808
7:10 *was* no man there, **n** voice of man, but H369
10:14 and forty men; **n** left he any of them. H3808
12: 8 **n** to repair the breaches of the house. H1115
13: 7 **N** did he leave of the people to H3808
23 not destroy them, **n** cast he them from H3808
17:34 fear not the LORD, **n** do they after their H369
38 not forget; **n** shall ye fear other gods. H3808
18:30 **N** let Hezekiah make you trust in the H408
21: 8 **N** will I make the feet of Israel move H3808
23:25 **n** after him arose there *any* like him. H3808
1Ch 4:27 many children, **n** did all their family H3808
17: 9 moved no more; **n** shall the children of H3808
20 O LORD, *there is* none like thee, **n** *is* H369
19:19 his servants: **n** would the Syrians help H3808
27:24 it against Israel; **n** was the number put H3808
2Ch 1:11 of thine enemies, **n** yet hast asked long H3808
12 *been* before thee, **n** shall there any after H3808
6: 5 might be there; **n** chose I any man to H3808
9: 9 precious stones: **n** was there any such H3808
13:20 **N** did Jeroboam recover strength again H3808
20:12 against us; **n** know we what to do: H3808
25: 4 for the children, **n** shall the children die H3808
26:18 hast trespassed; **n** *shall it be* for thine H3808
30: 3 sufficiently, **n** had the people gathered H3808
32:15 on this manner, **n** yet believe him: for no H408
33: 8 **N** will I any more remove the foot of H3808
34: 2 ***n*** to the right hand, nor to the left. H3808
28 grave in peace, **n** shall thine eyes see H3808
35:18 the prophet; **n** did all the kings of Israel H3808
Ezr 9:12 unto their sons, **n** take their daughters H408
10:13 to stand without, **n** *is this* a work of H3808
Neh 2:12 few men with me; **n** told I *any* man H3808
12 to do at Jerusalem: **n** *was there any* H369
16 or what I did; **n** had I as yet told *it* to H3808
4:11 shall not know, **n** see, till we come in H3808
23 So **n** I, nor my brethren, nor my H369
5: 5 bondage *already*: **n** *is it* in our power *to* H369
16 the work of this wall, **n** bought we any H3808
8:10 unto our Lord: **n** be ye sorry; for the joy H408
11 for the day *is* holy; **n** be ye grieved. H408
9:17 And refused to obey, **n** were mindful of H3808
19 them in the way; **n** the pillar of fire by
34 **N** have our kings, our princes, our H3808
35 **n** turned they from their wicked works. H3808
Est 2: 7 for she had **n** father nor mother, and H369
3: 8 from all people; **n** keep they the king's H369
4:16 fast ye for me, and **n** eat nor drink three H408
Job 3: 4 from above, **n** let the light shine upon it. H408
9 none; **n** let it see the dawning of the day: H408
26 I was not in safety, **n** had I rest, neither H3808
26 I was not in safety, neither had I rest, **n** H3808
5: 4 the gate, **n** *is there* any to deliver *them*. H369
6 forth of the dust, **n** doth trouble spring H3808
21 of the tongue: **n** shalt thou be afraid H3808
22 thou shalt laugh: **n** shalt thou be afraid H408
7:10 He shall return no more to his house, **n** H3808
8:20 *man*, **n** will he help the evil doers: H3808
9:33 **N** is there any daysman betwixt us, H3808
15:29 He shall not be rich, **n** shall his H3808
29 continue, **n** shall he prolong the H3808
18:19 He shall **n** have son nor nephew among H3808
20: 9 **n** shall his place any more behold him. H3808
21: 9 Their houses *are* safe from fear, **n** *is* H3808
23:12 **N** have I gone back from the H3808
17 the darkness, ***n*** hath he covered the
28:13 Man knoweth not the price thereof; **n** is H3808
15 It cannot be gotten for gold, **n** shall H3808
19 it, **n** shall it be valued with pure gold. H3808
31:30 **N** have I suffered my mouth to sin by H3808
32: 9 Great men are not *always* wise: **n** do the
14 **n** will I answer him with your speeches. H3808
21 **n** let me give flattering titles unto man. H3808
33: 7 **n** shall my hand be heavy upon thee. H3808
9 *am* innocent; **n** *is there* iniquity in me. H3808
34:12 Yea, surely God will not do wickedly, **n** H3808

Job 35:13 Surely God will not hear vanity, **n** will H3808
36:26 we know *him* not, **n** can the number of H3808
39: 7 He scorneth the multitude of the city, **n** H3808
17 her of wisdom, **n** hath he imparted to H3808
22 **n** turneth he back from the sword. H3808
24 and rage: **n** believeth he that *it is* H3808
Ps 5: 4 **n** shall evil dwell with thee. H3808
6: 1 **n** chasten me in thy hot displeasure. H3808
16:10 my soul in hell; **n** wilt thou suffer thine H3808
18:37 overtaken them: **n** did I turn again till H3808
22:24 of the afflicted; **n** hath he hid his face H3808
26: 4 I have not sat with vain persons, **n** will H3808
27: 9 **n** forsake me, O God of my salvation. H408
33:17 An horse *is* a vain thing for safety: **n** H3808
35:19 rejoice over me: ***n*** let them wink with the
37: 1 Fret not thyself because of evildoers, **n** H408
38: 1 O LORD, rebuke me not in thy wrath: **n**
3 of thine anger; **n** *is there any* rest in my H369
44: 3 their own sword, **n** did their own arm H3808
6 For I will not trust in my bow, **n** shall H3808
17 **n** have we dealt falsely in thy covenant. H3808
18 Our heart is not turned back, **n** have our
55:12 have borne *it*: **n** *was it* he that hated H3808
69:15 Let not the waterflood overflow me, **n** let H408
73: 5 They *are* not in trouble *as other* men; **n** H3808
74: 9 any prophet: **n** *is there* among us any H3808
75: 6 For promotion *cometh* **n** from the east, H3808
78:37 **n** were they stedfast in his covenant. H3808
81: 9 There shall no strange god be in thee; **n** H3808
82: 5 They know not, **n** will they understand; H3808
86: 8 unto thee, O Lord; **n** *are there any works* H369
91:10 There shall no evil befall thee, **n** shall H3808
92: 6 A brutish man knoweth not; **n** doth a H3808
94: 7 Yet they say, The LORD shall not see, **n** H3808
14 **n** will he forsake his inheritance. H3808
103: 9 He will not always chide: **n** will he keep H3808
109:12 mercy unto him: **n** let there be any to H408
115: 7 not: **n** speak they through their throat. H3808
17 The dead praise not the LORD, **n** any H3808
121: 4 Behold, he that keepeth Israel shall **n** H3804
129: 8 **N** do they which go by say, The H3808
131: 1 mine eyes lofty: **n** do I exercise myself H3808
135:17 They have ears, but they hear not; **n** is H369
Prv 2:19 None that go unto her return again, **n**
3:11 the LORD; **n** be weary of his correction: H408
25 Be not afraid of sudden fear, **n** of the
4: 5 **n** decline from the words of my mouth. H408
6:25 **n** let her take thee with her eyelids. H408
35 He will not regard any ransom; **n** will H3808
15:12 him: **n** will he go unto the wise. H3808
22:22 Rob not the poor, because he *is* poor: **n** H3808
23: 6 evil eye, **n** desire thou his dainty meats: H408
24: 1 Be not thou envious against evil men, **n** H408
19 Fret not thyself because of evil *men*, **n** be H408
27:10 father's friend, forsake not; **n** go into thy H408
30: 3 I **n** learned wisdom, nor have the H3808
8 and lies: give me **n** poverty nor riches; H408
Ecc 1:11 of former *things*; **n** shall there be *any* H3808
4: 8 yea, he hath **n** child nor brother: H1571+H369
8 of all his labour; **n** is his eye satisfied H3808
8 with riches; **n** *saith he*, For whom
5: 6 thy flesh to sin; **n** say thou before the H408
6:10 that it *is* man: **n** may he contend with H3808
7:16 Be not righteous over much; **n** make H408
17 Be not over much wicked, **n** be thou H408
8: 8 to retain the spirit; **n** *hath he* power in H369
8 in *that* war; **n** shall wickedness deliver H3808
13 with the wicked, **n** shall he prolong *his* H3808
16 *there is that* **n** day nor night H1571+H369
9: 5 not any thing, **n** have they any more H369
6 is now perished; **n** have they any more H369
11 to the strong, **n** yet bread to the wise, H3808
Song 8: 7 Many waters cannot quench love, **n** H3808
Isa 1: 6 not been closed, **n** bound up, neither H3808
6 bound up, **n** mollified with ointment. H3808
23 not the fatherless, **n** doth the cause of H3808
2: 4 **n** shall they learn war any more. H3808
7 of silver and gold, **n** *is there any* end of H3808
7 **n** *is there any* end of their chariots: H3808
3: 7 for in my house *is* **n** bread nor clothing: H369
5:12 **n** consider the operation of his hands. H3808
27 slumber nor sleep; **n** shall the girdle of H3808
7: 4 be quiet; fear not, **n** be fainthearted for H408
7 shall not stand, **n** shall it come to pass. H3808
12 But Ahaz said, I will not ask, **n** will I H3808
8:12 **n** fear ye their fear, nor be afraid. H3808
9:13 **n** do they seek the LORD of hosts. H3808
17 their young men, **n** shall have mercy on H3808
10: 7 Howbeit he meaneth not so, **n** doth his H3808

Isa 11: 3 **n** reprove after the hearing of his ears: H3808
13:20 It shall never be inhabited, **n** shall it be H3808
20 to generation: **n** shall the Arabian pitch H3808
20 pitch tent there; **n** shall the shepherds H3808
16:10 shall be no singing, **n** shall there be H3808
17: 8 work of his hands, **n** shall respect *that* H3808
19:15 **N** shall there be *any* work for Egypt, H3808
22:11 the maker thereof, **n** had respect unto H3808
23: 4 forth children, **n** do I nourish up young H3808
26:18 in the earth; **n** have the inhabitants H1077
28:27 instrument, **n** is a cart wheel turned H1077
29:22 **n** shall his face now wax pale. H3808
31: 1 Holy One of Israel, **n** seek the LORD! H3808
33:20 ever be removed, **n** shall any of the H1077
21 oars, **n** shall gallant ship pass thereby. H3808
36:15 **N** let Hezekiah make you trust in the H408
40:28 fainteth not, **n** is weary? *there is* no H3808
42: 8 another, **n** my praise to graven images.
24 **n** were they obedient unto his law. H3808
43: 2 **n** shall the flame kindle upon thee. H3808
10 God formed, **n** shall there be after me. H3808
18 Remember ye not the former things, **n** H408
23 burnt offerings; **n** hast thou honoured H3808
24 cane with money, **n** hast thou filled me H3808
44: 8 Fear ye not, **n** be afraid: have not I told H408
19 And none considereth in his heart, **n** *is* H3808
47: 7 **n** didst remember the latter end of it. H3808
8 **n** shall I know the loss of children: H3808
49:10 They shall not hunger nor thirst; **n** H3808
50: 5 not rebellious, **n** turned away back. H3808
51: 7 of men, **n** be ye afraid of their revilings. H408
18 brought forth; **n** *is there any* that taketh H369
53: 9 **n** *was any* deceit in his mouth. H3808
54: 4 not be ashamed: **n** be thou confounded; H408
10 depart from thee, **n** shall the covenant H3808
55: 8 not your thoughts, **n** *are* your ways my H3808
56: 3 **N** let the son of the stranger, that hath H408
3 me from his people: **n** let the eunuch say, H408
57:16 For I will not contend for ever, **n** will I H3808
59: 1 **n** his ear heavy, that it cannot hear: H3808
6 become garments, **n** shall they cover H3808
9 Therefore is judgment far from us, **n** H3808
60:19 thy light by day; **n** for brightness shall H3808
20 Thy sun shall no more go down; **n** shall H3808
62: 4 termed Forsaken; **n** shall thy land any H3808
64: 4 by the ear, **n** hath the eye seen, O H3808
9 Be not wroth very sore, O LORD, **n** H408
66:19 heard my fame, **n** have seen my glory; H3808
24 worm shall not die, **n** shall their fire be H3808
Jer 2: 6 **N** said they, Where *is* the LORD that H3808
3:16 of the LORD: **n** shall it come to mind: H3808
16 it come to mind: **n** shall they remember H3808
16 they remember it; **n** shall they visit *it*; H3808
16 visit *it*; **n** shall *that* be done any more. H3808
17 to Jerusalem: **n** shall they walk any H3808
4:28 not repent, **n** will I turn back from it. H3808
5:12 and said, *It is* not he; **n** shall evil come H3808
12 us; **n** shall we see sword nor famine: H3808
15 not, **n** understandest what they say. H3808
24 **N** say they in their heart, Let us now H3808
6:15 at all ashamed, **n** could they H1571+H3808
7: 6 **n** walk after other gods to your hurt: H3808
16 for this people, **n** lift up cry nor prayer H408
16 prayer for them, **n** make intercession to H408
31 *them* not, **n** came it into my heart. H3808
8:12 not at all ashamed, **n** could they blush: H3808
9:10 pass through *them*; **n** can *men* hear the H3808
13 not obeyed my voice, **n** walked therein; H3808
16 heathen, whom **n** they nor their fathers H3808
23 in his wisdom, **n** let the mighty *man* H408
10: 5 **n** also *is it* in them to do good. H1571+H369
11:14 for this people, **n** lift up a cry or prayer H408
14:13 shall not see the sword, **n** shall ye have H3808
14 I sent them not, **n** have I commanded H3808
14 them, **n** spake unto them: they H3808
15:10 earth! I have **n** lent on usury, nor men H3808
16: 2 Thou shalt not take thee a wife, **n** shalt H3808
4 shall not be lamented; **n** shall they be H3808
5 house of mourning, **n** go to lament nor H3808
6 not be buried, **n** shall *men* lament for H3808
7 **N** shall *men* tear *themselves* for them H3808
7 them for the dead; **n** shall *men* give H3808
13 that ye know not, ***n*** ye nor your fathers;
17 **n** is their iniquity hid from mine eyes. H3808
17: 8 **n** shall cease from yielding fruit. H3808
16 to follow thee: **n** have I desired the H3808
22 **N** carry forth a burden out of your H3808
22 the sabbath day, **n** do ye any work, but H3808
23 But they obeyed not, **n** inclined their H3808

Jer 18:23 not their iniquity, n blot out their sin H408
19: 4 unto other gods, whom n they nor their H3808
5 nor spake *it*, n came *it* into my mind:
21: 7 them, n have pity, nor have mercy. H3808
22: 3 n shed innocent blood in this place. H408
10 Weep ye not for the dead, n bemoan H408
23: 4 n shall they be lacking, saith the LORD. H3808
25:33 shall not be lamented, n gathered, nor H3808
29: 8 of you, deceive you, n hearken to your H408
32 this people; n shall he behold the H3808
30:10 saith the LORD; n be dismayed, O Israel: H408
32:23 not thy voice, n walked in thy law; they H3808
35 them not, n came it into my mind, H3808
33:18 N shall the priests the Levites want a H3808
22 be numbered, n the sand of the sea H3808
34:14 not unto me, n inclined their ear. H3808
35: 6 no wine, *n ye*, nor your sons for ever:
7 N shall ye build house, nor sow seed, H3808
9 Nor to build houses for us to dwell in: n H3808
36:24 their garments, *n* the king, nor any of
37: 2 But n he, nor his servants, nor the H3808
38:16 put thee to death, n will I give thee into H518
42:13 n obey the voice of the LORD your God, H1115
44: 3 knew not, *n* they, ye, nor your fathers.
10 unto this day, n have they feared, nor H3808
48:11 vessel to vessel, n hath he gone into H3808
49:18 there, n shall a son of man dwell in it. H3808
31 n gates nor bars, *which* dwell alone. H3808
50:39 inhabited for ever; n shall it be dwelt in H3808
40 n shall any son of man dwell therein. H3808
51:43 n doth *any* son of man pass thereby. H3808
62 shall remain in it, n man nor beast, but H1115
Ezk 2: 6 not afraid of them, n be afraid of their H408
3: 9 fear them not, n be dismayed at their H3808
4:14 or is torn in pieces; n came there H3808
5: 7 walked in my statutes, n have kept my H3808
7 my judgments, n have done according H3808
11 diminish *thee*; n shall mine eye spare, H1571
11 mine eye spare, n will I have any pity. H3808
7: 4 And mine eye shall not spare thee, n H3808
9 And mine eye shall not spare, n will I H3808
11 n *shall there be* wailing for them. H3808
13 shall not return; n shall any strengthen H3808
19 satisfy their souls, n fill their bowels: H3808
8:18 shall not spare, n will I have pity: and H3808
9: 5 let not your eye spare, n have ye pity: H408
10 shall not spare, n will I have pity, *but* H3808
11:11 This *city* shall not be your caldron, n
12 walked in my statutes, n executed my H3808
13: 5 Ye have not gone up into the gaps, n
9 of my people, n shall they be written H3808
9 house of Israel, n shall they enter into H3808
15 wall *is no more*, n they that daubed it; H369
14:11 astray from me, n be polluted any H3808
16 they shall deliver n sons nor daughters; H518
18 they shall deliver n sons nor daughters, H3808
20 they shall deliver n son nor daughter; H518
16: 4 navel was not cut, n wast thou washed H3808
16 *things* shall not come, n shall it be *so*. H3808
49 in her daughters, n did she strengthen H3808
51 N hath Samaria committed half of thy H3808
17:17 N shall Pharaoh with *his* mighty army H3808
18: 6 the mountains, n hath lifted up his H3808
6 the house of Israel, n hath defiled his H3808
6 neighbour's wife, n hath come near to H3808
8 forth upon usury, n hath taken any H3808
15 the mountains, n hath lifted up his H3808
16 N hath oppressed any, hath not H3808
16 the pledge, n hath spoiled by violence, H3808
20 of the father, n shall the father bear H3808
20: 8 of their eyes, n did they forsake the H3808
17 destroying them, n did I make an end H3808
18 statutes of your fathers, n observe their H408
21 in my statutes, n kept my judgments H3808
22:26 holy and profane, n have they shewed H3808
23: 8 N left she her whoredoms *brought* H3808
24:14 *it*; I will not go back, n will I spare, H3808
14 will I spare, n will I repent; according H3808
16 with a stroke: yet n shalt thou mourn H3808
16 nor weep, n shall thy tears run down. H3808
29:11 it, n shall it be inhabited forty years. H3808
15 of the kingdoms; n shall it exalt itself H3808
31:14 for their height, n shoot up their top H3808
14 the thick boughs, n their trees stand up H3808
32:13 the great waters; n shall the foot of H3808
33:12 his wickedness; n shall the righteous be H3808
34: 4 not strengthened, n have ye healed that H3808
4 which was sick, n have ye bound up H3808
4 *was* broken, n have ye brought again H3808
Ezk 34: 4 was driven away, n have ye sought that H3808
8 *was* no shepherd, n did my shepherds H3808
10 feeding the flock; n shall the shepherds H3808
28 to the heathen, n shall the beast of the H3808
29 in the land, n bear the shame of the H3808
36:14 men no more, n bereave thy nations H3808
15 N will I cause *men* to hear in thee the H3808
15 any more, n shalt thou bear the H3808
15 people any more, n shalt thou cause H3808
37:22 no more two nations, n shall they be H3808
23 N shall they defile themselves any H3808
38:11 walls, and having n bars nor gates, H369
39:10 out of the field, n cut down *any* out of H3808
29 N will I hide my face any more from H3808
43: 7 no more defile, *n* they, nor their kings,
44:20 N shall they shave their heads, nor H3808
21 N shall any priest drink wine, when H3808
22 N shall they take for their wives a H3808
47:12 leaf shall not fade, n shall the fruit H3808
48:14 And they shall not sell of it, n H3808
Dan 3:27 of their head singed, n were their coats H3809
6: 4 as he *was* faithful, n was there any H3809
18 the night fasting: n were instruments of H3809
8: 4 stand before him, n *was there any* that H369
9: 6 N have we hearkened unto thy servants H3808
10 N have we obeyed the voice of the H3808
10: 3 I ate no pleasant bread, n came flesh H3808
3 in my mouth, n did I anoint myself H3808
17 in me, n is there breath left in me. H3808
11: 6 power of the arm; n shall he stand, nor H3808
15 shall not withstand, n his chosen people, H369
15 his chosen people, n *shall there be any* H369
17 not stand *on his side*, n be for him. H3808
20 be destroyed, n in anger, nor in battle. H3808
37 N shall he regard the God of his H3808
Hos 2: 2 she *is* not my wife, n *am* I her husband: H3808
4:15 come not ye unto Gilgal, n go ye up to H408
9: 4 to the LORD, n shall they be pleasing H3808
14: 3 not ride upon horses: n will we say any H3808
Joel 2: 2 been ever the like, n shall be any more H3808
8 N shall one thrust another; they shall H3808
Am 2:14 n shall the mighty deliver himself: H3808
15 N shall he stand that handleth the bow; H3808
15 deliver *himself*: n shall he that rideth H3808
5:22 will not accept *them*: n will I regard the H3808
7:14 I *was* no prophet, n *was* I a prophet's H3808
Oba 12 he became a stranger; n shouldest thou H408
12 their destruction; n shouldest thou have H408
14 N shouldest thou have stood in the H408
14 that did escape; n shouldest thou have H408
Jna 3: 7 his nobles, saying, Let n man nor beast, H369
4:10 hast not laboured, n madest it grow; H3808
Mic 2: 3 your necks; n shall ye go haughtily: H3808
4: 3 n shall they learn war any more. H3808
12 of the LORD, n understand they his H3808
Hab 2: 5 *he is* a proud man, n keepeth at home, H3808
3:17 shall not blossom, n *shall* fruit *be* in the H369
Zep 1:12 will not do good, n will he do evil. H3808
18 N their silver nor their gold shall be H3808
3:13 nor speak lies; n shall a deceitful H3808
Zec 8:10 any hire for beast; n *was there any* peace H369
11:16 that be cut off, n shall seek the young H3808
13: 4 he hath prophesied; n shall they wear a H3808
Mal 1:10 doors *for nought*? n do ye kindle *fire* on H3808
10 n will I accept an offering at your hand. H3808
3:11 of your ground; n shall your vine cast H3808
4: 1 it shall leave them n root nor branch.
Mt 5:15 N do men light a candle, and put it *G3761*
34 But I say unto you, Swear not at all; n *G3383*
35 it is his footstool: n by Jerusalem; for it *G3383*
36 N shalt thou swear by thy head, *G3383*
6:15 their trespasses, n will your Father *G3761*
20 in heaven, where n moth nor rust doth *G3777*
26 for they sow not, n do they reap, nor *G3761*
28 they grow; they toil not, n do they spin: *G3761*
7: 6 unto the dogs, n cast ye your pearls *G3366*
18 forth evil fruit, n *can* a corrupt tree *G3761*
9:17 N do men put new wine into old *G3761*
10: 9 Provide n gold, nor silver, nor brass in *G3361*
10 Nor scrip for *your* journey, n two coats, *G3366*
10 neither two coats, n shoes, nor yet *G3366*
11:18 For John came n eating nor drinking, *G3383*
27 but the Father; n knoweth any man the *G3761*
12: 4 for him to eat, n for them which were *G3761*
19 He shall not strive, nor cry; n shall any *G3761*
32 not be forgiven him, n in this world, *G3777*
32 in this world, n in the *world* to come. *G3777*
13:13 they hear not, n do they understand. *G3761*
16: 9 Do ye not yet understand, n remember *G3761*
Mt 16:10 N the seven loaves of the four *G3761*
21:27 he said unto them, N tell I you by what *G3761*
22:16 of God in truth, n carest thou for any *G3756*
30 For in the resurrection they n marry, *G3777*
46 him a word, n durst any *man* from *G3761*
23:10 N be ye called masters: for one is your *G3366*
13 men: for ye n go in *yourselves*, neither *G3756*
13 go in *yourselves*, n suffer ye them that *G3761*
24:18 N let him which is in the field return *G3361*
20 not in the winter, n on the sabbath day: *G3366*
25:13 Watch therefore, for ye know n the day *G3756*
Mk 4:22 be manifested; n was any thing kept *G3761*
5: 4 in pieces: n could any *man* tame him. *G2532*
8:14 to take bread, n had they in the ship *G2532*
17 ye not yet, n understand? have ye *G3761*
26 his house, saying, N go into the town, *G3366*
11:26 But if ye do not forgive, n will your *G3761*
33 saith unto them, N do I tell you by *G3761*
12:21 And the second took her, and died, n *G3761*
24 not the scriptures, n the power of God? *G3366*
25 the dead, they n marry, nor are given *G3777*
13:11 ye shall speak, n do ye premeditate: *G3366*
15 into the house, n enter *therein*, to take *G3366*
19 God created unto this time, n shall be. *G3364*
32 in heaven, n the Son, but the Father. *G3761*
14:40 n wist they what to answer him. *G2532*
59 But n so did their witness agree *G3761*
68 But he denied, saying, I know not, n *G3761*
16: 8 and were amazed: n said they any *G2532*
13 unto the residue: n believed they them. *G3761*
Lk 1:15 Lord, and shall drink n wine nor strong *G3364*
3:14 to no man, n accuse *any* falsely; and *G3366*
6:43 corrupt fruit; n doth a corrupt tree *G3761*
7: 7 Wherefore n thought I myself worthy *G3761*
33 For John the Baptist came n eating *G3383*
8:17 made manifest; n *any thing* hid, that *G3761*
27 ware no clothes, n abode in *any* house, *G2532*
43 physicians, n could be healed of any, *G3756*
9: 3 for *your* journey, n staves, nor scrip, *G3383*
3 staves, nor scrip, n bread, neither *G3383*
3 neither bread, n money; neither have *G3383*
3 money; n have two coats apiece. *G3383*
10: 4 Carry n purse, nor scrip, nor shoes: *G3361*
11:33 in a secret place, n under a bushel, but *G3761*
12: 2 n hid, that shall not be known. *G2532*
22 n for the body, what ye shall put on. *G3366*
24 Consider the ravens: for they n sow nor *G3756*
24 nor reap; which n have storehouse nor *G3756*
29 shall drink, n be ye of doubtful mind. *G2532*
33 thief approacheth, n moth corrupteth. *G3761*
47 not *himself*, n did according to his *G3366*
14:12 nor thy brethren, n thy kinsmen, nor *G3366*
35 It is n fit for the land, nor yet for the *G3777*
15:29 do I serve thee, n transgressed I at any *G2532*
16:26 to you cannot; n can they pass to us, *G3366*
31 Moses and the prophets, n will they be *G3761*
17:21 N shall they say, Lo here! or, lo there! *G3761*
18: 2 which feared not God, n regarded man: *G2532*
34 hid from them, n knew they the things *G2532*
20: 8 And Jesus said unto them, N tell I you *G3761*
21 teachest rightly, n acceptest thou the *G2532*
35 n marry, nor are given in marriage: *G3777*
36 N can they die any more: for they are *G3777*
Jn 1:25 that Christ, nor Elias, n that prophet? *G3777*
3:20 hateth the light, n cometh to the light, *G2532*
4:15 that I thirst not, n come hither to draw. *G3366*
21 when ye shall n in this mountain, nor *G3777*
5:37 of me. Ye have n heard his voice at any *G3777*
6:24 was not there, n his disciples, they also *G3761*
7: 5 For n did his brethren believe in him. *G3761*
8:11 said unto her, N do I condemn thee: *G3761*
19 Jesus answered, Ye n know me, nor my *G3777*
42 n came I of myself, but he sent me. *G3761*
9: 3 Jesus answered, N hath this man *G3777*
10:28 shall never perish, n shall any *man* *G2532*
13:16 than his lord; n he that is sent greater *G3761*
14:17 it seeth him not, n knoweth him: but ye *G3761*
27 heart be troubled, n let it be afraid. *G3366*
17:20 N pray I for these alone, but for them *G1161*
Act 2:27 my soul in hell, n wilt thou suffer thine *G3761*
31 in hell, n his flesh did see corruption. *G3761*
4:12 N is there salvation in any other: for *G2532*
32 and of one soul: n said any *of them* *G2532*
34 N was there any among them that *G3761*
8:21 Thou hast n part nor lot in this matter: *G3756*
9: 9 without sight, and n did eat nor drink. *G3756*
15:10 n our fathers nor we were able to bear? *G3777*
16:21 to receive, n to observe, being Romans. *G3761*
17:25 N is worshipped with men's hands, as *G3761*

Act 19:37 men, which are **n** robbers of churches, G3777
20:24 But none of these things move me, **n** G3761
21:21 children, **n** to walk after the customs. G3366
23: 8 is no resurrection, **n** angel, nor spirit: G3366
12 **n** eat nor drink till they had killed Paul. G3383
21 that they will **n** eat nor drink till they G3383
24:12 And they **n** found me in the temple G3777
12 with any man, **n** raising up the people, G2228
12 **n** in the synagogues, nor in the city: G3777
13 **N** can they prove the things whereof G3777
18 **n** with multitude, nor with tumult. G3756
25: 8 While he answered for himself, **N** G3777
8 law of the Jews, **n** against the temple, G3777
27:20 And when **n** sun nor stars in many G3383
28:21 And they said unto him, We **n** received G3777
21 concerning thee, **n** any of the brethren G3777
Ro 1:21 *him* not as God, **n** were thankful; but G2228
2:28 which is one outwardly; **n** *is that* G3761
4:19 old, **n** yet the deadness of Sarah's womb:
6:13 **N** yield ye your members *as* G3366
8: 7 to the law of God, **n** indeed can be. G3761
38 For I am persuaded, that **n** death, nor G3777
9: 7 **N**, because they are the seed of G3761
11 (For *the children* being not yet born, **n** G3366
14:21 *It is* good **n** to eat flesh, nor to drink G3361
1Co 2: 9 nor ear heard, **n** have entered into the G2532
14 unto him: **n** can he know *them*, G2532
3: 2 able *to bear it*, **n** yet now are ye able. G3777
7 So then **n** is he that planteth any thing, G3777
7 any thing, **n** he that watereth; but G3777
5: 8 with old leaven, **n** with the leaven of G3366
6: 9 Be not deceived: **n** fornicators, nor G3777
8: 8 us not to God: for **n**, if we eat, are we the G3777
8 **n**, if we eat not, are we the worse. G3777
9:15 But I have used none of these things: **n** G1161
10: 7 **N** be ye idolaters, as *were* some of G3366
8 **N** let us commit fornication, as some of G3366
9 **N** let us tempt Christ, as some of them G3366
10 **N** murmur ye, as some of them also G3366
32 Give none offence, **n** to the Jews, nor to G2532
11: 9 **N** was the man created for the woman; G2532
11 Nevertheless **n** is the man without the G3777
11 the woman, **n** the woman without G3777
16 no such custom, **n** the churches of God. G3761
15:50 **n** doth corruption inherit incorruption. G3761
Gal 1: 1 Paul, an apostle, (not of men, **n** by G3761
12 For I **n** received it of man, neither was I G3761
12 For I neither received it of man, **n** was I G3777
17 **N** went I up to Jerusalem to them G3761
2: 3 But **n** Titus, who was with me, being a G3761
3:28 There is **n** Jew nor Greek, there is G3756
28 Jew nor Greek, there is **n** bond nor free, G3756
28 nor free, there is **n** male nor female: for G3756
5: 6 For in Jesus Christ **n** circumcision G3777
6:13 For **n** they themselves who are G3761
15 For in Christ Jesus **n** circumcision G3777
Eph 4:27 **N** give place to the devil. G3383
5: 4 **N** filthiness, nor foolish talking, nor G2532
6: 9 **n** is there respect of persons with him. G2532
Php 2:16 not run in vain, **n** laboured in vain. G3761
Col 3:11 Where there is **n** Greek nor Jew, G3756
1Th 2: 5 For **n** at any time used we flattering G3777
6 Nor of men sought we glory, **n** of you, G3777
2Th 2: 2 or be troubled, **n** by spirit, nor by word, G3383
3: 8 **N** did we eat any man's bread for G3761
10 if any would not work, **n** should he eat. G3366
1Ti 1: 4 **N** give heed to fables and endless G3366
7 understanding **n** what they say, nor G3383
5:22 Lay hands suddenly on no man, **n** be G3366
Heb 4:13 **N** is there any creature that is not G2532
7: 3 descent, having **n** beginning of days, G3383
9:12 **N** by the blood of goats and calves, but G3761
18 Whereupon **n** the first *testament* was G3761
10: 8 wouldest not, **n** hadst pleasure *therein*; G3761
Jas 1:13 with evil, **n** tempteth he any man: G1161
17 no variableness, **n** shadow of turning. G2228
5:12 swear not, **n** by heaven, neither by G3383
12 not, neither by heaven, **n** by the earth, G3383
12 by the earth, **n** by any other oath: but G3383
1Pt 2:22 Who did no sin, **n** was guile found in G3761
3:14 not afraid of their terror, **n** be troubled; G3366
5: 3 **N** as being lords over *God's* heritage, G3366
2Pt 1: 8 make *you that ye shall* **n** *be* barren nor G3756
1Jn 2:15 Love not the world, **n** the things *that* G3366
3: 6 hath not seen him, **n** known him. G3761
10 of God, **n** he that loveth not his brother. G2532
18 **n** in tongue; but in deed and in truth. G3366
2Jn 10 into *your* house, **n** bid him God speed: G2532
3Jn 10 content therewith, **n** doth he himself G3777
Rev 3:15 I know thy works, that thou art **n** cold G3777
16 art lukewarm, and **n** cold nor hot, I will G3777
5: 3 And no man in heaven, nor in earth, **n** G3761
3 to open the book, **n** to look thereon. G3761
4 to read the book, **n** to look thereon. G3777
7: 3 Saying, Hurt not the earth, **n** the sea, G3383
16 They shall hunger no more, **n** thirst G3761
16 thirst any more; **n** shall the sun light on G3761
9: 4 grass of the earth, **n** any green thing, G3761
4 any green thing, **n** any tree; but only G3761
20 which **n** can see, nor hear, nor walk: G3777
21 **N** repented they of their murders, nor G2532
12: 8 And prevailed not; **n** was their place G3777
20: 4 the beast, **n** his image, neither had G3777
4 neither his image, **n** had received *his* G3756
21: 4 shall be no more death, **n** sorrow, nor G3777
4 nor crying, **n** shall there be any more G3777
23 And the city had no need of the sun, **n** G3761
27 that defileth, **n** *whatsoever* worketh G2532
22: 5 need no candle, **n** light of the sun; for G2532

NEKEB
Jos 19:33 and Adami, **N**, and Jabneel, unto H5346

NEKODA
Ezr 2:48 The children of Rezin, the children of **N**, H5353
60 children of **N**, six hundred fifty and two. H5353
Neh 7:50 the children of Rezin, the children of **N**, H5353
62 of **N**, six hundred forty and two. H5353

NEMUEL
Nu 26: 9 And the sons of Eliab; **N**, and Dathan, H5241
12 their families: of **N**, the family of the H5241
1Ch 4:24 The sons of Simeon *were*, **N**, and Jamin, H5241

NEMUELITES
Nu 26:12 the family of the **N**: of Jamin, the family H5242

NEPHEG
Ex 6:21 And the sons of Izhar; Korah, and **N**, H5298
2Sa 5:15 Ibhar also, and Elishua, and **N**, and H5298
1Ch 3: 7 And Nogah, and **N**, and Japhia, H5298
14: 6 And Nogah, and **N**, and Japhia, H5298

NEPHEW
Job 18:19 He shall neither have son nor **n** among H5220
Isa 14:22 and son, and **n**, saith the LORD. H5220

NEPHEWS
Jdg 12:14 And he had forty sons and thirty **n**, that H1121
1Ti 5: 4 But if any widow have children or **n**, let G1549

NEPHISH
1Ch 5:19 with Jetur, and **N**, and Nodab. H5305

NEPHISHESIM
Neh 7:52 children of Meunim, the children of **N**, H5300

NEPHTHALIM
Mt 4:13 coast, in the borders of Zabulon and **N**: G3508
15 The land of Zabulon, and the land of **N**, G3508

NEPHTOAH
Jos 15: 9 of the water of **N**, and went out to the H5318
18:15 and went out to the well of waters of **N**: H5318

NEPHUSIM
Ezr 2:50 children of Mehunim, the children of **N**, H5304

NEPTHALIM
Rev 7: 6 Of the tribe of **N** *were* sealed twelve G3508

NER
1Sa 14:50 *was* Abner, the son of **N**, Saul's uncle. H5369
51 And Kish *was* the father of Saul; and **N** H5369
26: 5 Abner the son of **N**, the captain of his H5369
14 Abner the son of **N**, saying, Answerest H5369
2Sa 2: 8 But Abner the son of **N**, captain of H5369
12 And Abner the son of **N**, and the H5369
3:23 Abner the son of **N** came to the king, H5369
25 Thou knowest Abner the son of **N**, that H5369
28 from the blood of Abner the son of **N**: H5369
37 of the king to slay Abner the son of **N**. H5369
1Ki 2: 5 Abner the son of **N**, and unto Amasa H5369
32 Abner the son of **N**, captain of the host H5369
1Ch 8:33 And **N** begat Kish, and Kish begat Saul, H5369
9:36 and Kish, and Baal, and **N**, and Nadab, H5369
39 And **N** begat Kish; and Kish begat Saul; H5369
26:28 Abner the son of **N**, and Joab the son of H5369

NEREUS
Ro 16:15 Salute Philologus, and Julia, **N**, and his G3517

NERGAL
2Ki 17:30 men of Cuth made **N**, and the men of H5370

NERGAL-SHAREZER
Jer 39: 3 the middle gate, *even* **N**, Samgarnebo, H5371
3 Rab-saris, **N**, Rab-mag, with all the H5371
13 Rab-saris, and **N**, Rab-mag, and all the H5371

NERI
Lk 3:27 of Salathiel, which was *the son* of **N**, G3518

NERIAH
Jer 32:12 unto Baruch the son of **N**, the son of H5374
16 of **N**, I prayed unto the LORD, saying, H5374
36: 4 Baruch the son of **N**: and Baruch wrote H5374
8 And Baruch the son of **N** did according H5374
14 Baruch the son of **N** took the roll in his H5374
32 scribe, the son of **N**; who wrote therein H5374
43: 3 But Baruch the son of **N** setteth thee on H5374
6 the prophet, and Baruch the son of **N**. H5374
45: 1 unto Baruch the son of **N**, when he had H5374
51:59 Seraiah the son of **N**, the son of H5374

NEST
Nu 24:21 and thou puttest thy **n** in a rock. H7064
Dt 22: 6 If a bird's **n** chance to be before thee in H7064
32:11 As an eagle stirreth up her **n**, fluttereth H7064
Job 29:18 Then I said, I shall die in my **n**, and I H7064
39:27 command, and make her **n** on high? H7064
Ps 84: 3 and the swallow a **n** for herself, where H7064
Prv 27: 8 As a bird that wandereth from her **n**, so H7064
Isa 10:14 And my hand hath found as a **n** the H7064
16: 2 cast out of the **n**, *so* the daughters of H7064
34:15 There shall the great owl make her **n**, H7077
Jer 22:23 that makest thy **n** in the cedars, how H7077
48:28 her **n** in the sides of the hole's mouth. H7077
49:16 make thy **n** as high as the eagle, H7064
Oba 4 thou set thy **n** among the stars, thence H7064
Hab 2: 9 he may set his **n** on high, that he may H7064

NESTS
Ps 104:17 Where the birds make their **n**: *as for* the H7077
Ezk 31: 6 All the fowls of heaven made their **n** in H7077
Mt 8:20 of the air *have* **n**; but the Son of man G2682
Lk 9:58 of the air *have* **n**; but the Son of man G2682

NET
Ex 27: 4 and upon the **n** shalt thou make four H7568
5 **n** may be even to the midst of the altar. H7568
Job 18: 8 For he is cast into a **n** by his own feet, H7568
19: 6 me, and hath compassed me with his **n**. H4685
Ps 9:15 they made: in the **n** which they hid is H7568
10: 9 poor, when he draweth him into his **n**. H7568
25:15 for he shall pluck my feet out of the **n**. H7568
31: 4 Pull me out of the **n** that they have laid H7568
35: 7 they hid for me their **n** *in* a pit, *which* H7568
8 and let his **n** that he hath hid catch H7568
57: 6 They have prepared a **n** for my steps; H7568
66:11 Thou broughtest us into the **n**; thou H4685
140: 5 have spread a **n** by the wayside; they H7568
Prv 1:17 Surely in vain the **n** is spread in the H7568
12:12 The wicked desireth the **n** of evil *men*: H4685
29: 5 neighbour spreadeth a **n** for his feet. H7568
Ecc 9:12 taken in an evil **n**, and as the birds that H4685
Isa 51:20 as a wild bull in a **n**: they are full of the H4364
Lam 1:13 he hath spread a **n** for my feet, he hath H7568
Ezk 12:13 My **n** also will I spread upon him, and H7568
17:20 And I will spread my **n** upon him, and H7568
19: 8 **n** over him: he was taken in their pit. H7568
32: 3 spread out my **n** over thee with a H7568
3 and they shall bring thee up in my **n**. H2764
Hos 5: 1 Mizpah, and a **n** spread upon Tabor. H7568
7:12 When they shall go, I will spread my **n** H7568
Mic 7: 2 hunt every man his brother with a **n**. H2764
Hab 1:15 them in their **n**, and gather them in H2764
16 Therefore they sacrifice unto their **n**, H2764
17 Shall they therefore empty their **n**, and H2764
Mt 4:18 a **n** into the sea: for they were fishers. G293
13:47 is like unto a **n**, that was cast into the G4522
Mk 1:16 a **n** into the sea: for they were fishers. G293
Lk 5: 5 at thy word I will let down the **n**. G1350
6 multitude of fishes: and their **n** brake. G1350
Jn 21: 6 And he said unto them, Cast the **n** on G1350
8 cubits,) dragging the **n** with fishes. G1350
11 Simon Peter went up, and drew the **n** G1350
11 so many, yet was not the **n** broken. G1350

N

NETHANEEL
Nu 1: 8 Of Issachar; **N** the son of Zuar. H5417
2: 5 of Issachar: and **N** the son of Zuar *shall* H5417
7:18 On the second day **N** the son of Zuar, H5417
23 *was* the offering of **N** the son of Zuar. H5417
10:15 of Issachar *was* **N** the son of Zuar. H5417
1Ch 2:14 **N** the fourth, Raddai the fifth, H5417
15:24 Jehoshaphat, and **N**, and Amasai, and H5417
24: 6 And Shemaiah the son of **N** the scribe, H5417
26: 4 and Sacar the fourth, and **N** the fifth, H5417
2Ch 17: 7 Zechariah, and to **N**, and to Michaiah, H5417
35: 9 Conaniah also, and Shemaiah and **N**, H5417
Ezr 10:22 Ishmael, **N**, Jozabad, and Elasah. H5417
Neh 12:21 Of Hilkiah, Hashabiah; of Jedaiah, **N**. H5417
36 Gilalai, Maai, **N**, and Judah, Hanani, H5417

NETHANIAH
2Ki 25:23 the son of **N**, and Johanan the son H5418
25 the son of **N**, the son of Elishama, H5418
1Ch 25: 2 and Joseph, and **N**, and Asarelah, the H5418
12 The fifth to **N**, *he*, his sons, and his H5418
2Ch 17: 8 Shemaiah, and **N**, and Zebadiah, and H5418
Jer 36:14 sent Jehudi the son of **N**, the son of H5418
40: 8 Ishmael the son of **N**, and Johanan and H5418
14 the son of **N** to slay thee? But Gedaliah H5418
15 the son of **N**, and no man shall know H5418
41: 1 the son of **N** the son of Elishama, H5418
2 Then arose Ishmael the son of **N**, and H5418
6 And Ishmael the son of **N** went forth H5418
7 the son of **N** slew them, *and cast* H5418
9 of **N** filled it with *them that were* slain. H5418
10 the son of **N** carried them away H5418
11 that Ishmael the son of **N** had done, H5418
12 the son of **N**, and found him by the H5418
15 But Ishmael the son of **N** escaped from H5418
16 the son of **N**, from Mizpah, after H5418
18 the son of **N** had slain Gedaliah H5418

NETHER
Ex 19:17 they stood at the **n** part of the mount. H8482
Dt 24: 6 No man shall take the **n** or the upper H7347
Jos 15:19 the upper springs, and the **n** springs. H8482
16: 3 of Beth-horon the **n**, and to Gezer: and H8481
18:13 on the south side of the **n** Beth-horon. H8481
Jdg 1:15 the upper springs and the **n** springs. H8482
1Ki 9:17 built Gezer, and Beth-horon the **n**, H8481
1Ch 7:24 **n**, and the upper, and Uzzen-sherah.) H8481
2Ch 8: 5 Beth-horon the **n**, fenced cities, with H8481
Job 41:24 as hard as a piece of the **n** *millstone*. H8482
Ezk 31:14 unto death, to the **n** parts of the earth, H8482
16 comforted in the **n** parts of the earth. H8482
18 of Eden unto the **n** parts of the earth: H8482
32:18 nations, unto the **n** parts of the earth, H8482
24 into the **n** parts of the earth, which H8482

NETHERMOST
1Ki 6: 6 The **n** chamber *was* five cubits broad, H8481

NETHINIMS
1Ch 9: 2 the priests, Levites, and the **N**. H5411
Ezr 2:43 The **N**: the children of Ziha, the children H5411
58 All the **N**, and the children of Solomon's H5411
70 porters, and the **N**, dwelt in their cities, H5411
7: 7 porters, and the **N**, unto Jerusalem, in H5411
24 singers, porters, **N**, or ministers of this H5412
8:17 to his brethren the **N**, at the place H5411
20 Also of the **N**, whom David and the H5411
20 **N**: all of them were expressed by name. H5411
Neh 3:26 Moreover the **N** dwelt in Ophel, unto H5411
31 unto the place of the **N**, and of the H5411
7:46 The **N**: the children of Ziha, the children H5411
60 All the **N**, and the children of Solomon's H5411
73 people, and the **N**, and all Israel, dwelt H5411
10:28 the singers, the **N**, and all they that had H5411
11: 3 Levites, and the **N**, and the children of H5411
21 But the **N** dwelt in Ophel: and Ziha and H5411
21 and Ziha and Gispa *were* over the **N**. H5411

NETOPHAH
Ezr 2:22 The men of **N**, fifty and six. H5199
Neh 7:26 The men of Beth-lehem and **N**, an H5199

NETOPHATHI
Neh 12:28 Jerusalem, and from the villages of **N**; H5200

NETOPHATHITE
2Sa 23:28 Zalmon the Ahohite, Maharai the **N**, H5200
29 Heleb the son of Baanah, a **N**, Ittai the H5200
2Ki 25:23 of Tanhumeth the **N**, and Jaazaniah the H5200
1Ch 11:30 Maharai the **N**, Heled the son of H5200
30 Heled the son of Baanah the **N**, H5200
27:13 *was* Maharai the **N**, of the Zarhites: and H5200
15 *was* Heldai the **N**, of Othniel: and in his H5200
Jer 40: 8 sons of Ephai the **N**, and Jezaniah the H5200

NETOPHATHITES
1Ch 2:54 and the **N**, Ataroth, the house H5200
9:16 that dwelt in the villages of the **N**. H5200

NETS
1Ki 7:17 *And* **n** of checker work, and wreaths of H7638
Ps 141:10 Let the wicked fall into their own **n**, H4364
Ecc 7:26 heart *is* snares and **n**, *and* her hands *as* H2764
Isa 19: 8 **n** upon the waters shall languish. H4364
Ezk 26: 5 It shall be *a place for* the spreading of **n** H2764
14 *a place* to spread **n** upon; thou shalt be H2764
47:10 to spread forth **n**; their fish shall be H2764
Mt 4:20 And they straightway left *their* **n**, and *G1350*
21 mending their **n**; and he called them. *G1350*
Mk 1:18 And straightway they forsook their **n**, *G1350*
19 also were in the ship mending their **n**. *G1350*
Lk 5: 2 out of them, and were washing *their* **n**. *G1350*
4 and let down your **n** for a draught. *G1350*

NETTLES
Job 30: 7 the **n** they were gathered together. H2738
Prv 24:31 with thorns, *and* **n** had covered the H2738
Isa 34:13 up in her palaces, **n** and brambles in H7057
Hos 9: 6 for their silver, **n** shall possess them: H7057
Zep 2: 9 the breeding of **n**, and saltpits, and a H2738

NETWORK
Ex 27: 4 And thou shalt make for it a grate of **n** H7568
38: 4 a brasen grate of **n** under the compass H7568
1Ki 7:18 upon the one **n**, to cover the chapiters H7639
20 belly which *was* by the **n**: and the H7639
42 for one **n**, to cover the two bowls H7639
Jer 52:22 five cubits, with **n** and pomegranates H7639
23 the **n** *were* an hundred round about. H7639

NETWORKS
1Ki 7:41 and the two **n**, to cover the two bowls H7639
42 for the two **n**, *even* two rows of H7639
Isa 19: 9 they that weave **n**, shall be confounded. H2355

NEVER
Gen 34:12 Ask me **n** so much dowry and gift, and I
41:19 such as I **n** saw in all the land of H3808
Lev 6:13 upon the altar; it shall **n** go out. H3808
Nu 19: 2 blemish, *and* upon which **n** came yoke: H3808
Dt 15:11 For the poor shall **n** cease out of the H3808
Jdg 2: 1 **n** break my covenant with you. H3808+H5769
14: 3 unto him, *Is there* **n** a woman among the H369
16: 7 withs that were **n** dried, then shall I be H3808
11 new ropes that **n** were occupied, then H3808
2Sa 12:10 shall **n** depart from H3808+H5704+H5769
2Ch 18: 7 but I hate him; for he **n** prophesied good H369
21:17 so that there was **n** a son left him, save H369
Job 3:16 not been; as infants *which* **n** saw light. H3808
9:30 water, and make my hands **n** so clean; H1253
21:25 of his soul, and **n** eateth with pleasure. H3808
Ps 10: 6 be moved: for *I shall* **n** *be* in adversity. H1755
11 hideth his face; he will **n** see *it*. H1077+H5331
15: 5 these *things* shall **n** be moved. H3808+H5769
30: 6 I said, I shall **n** be moved. H3808+H5769
31: 1 my trust; let me **n** be ashamed: H408+H5769
49:19 they shall **n** see light. H5704+H5331+H3808
55:22 thee: he shall **n** suffer the H3808+H5769
58: 5 voice of charmers, charming **n** so wisely.
71: 1 let me **n** be put to confusion. H408+H5769
119:93 I will **n** forget thy precepts: for H5769+H3808
Prv 10:30 The righteous shall **n** be H1077+H5769
27:20 Hell and destruction are **n** full; so the H3808
20 full; so the eyes of man are **n** satisfied. H3808
30:15 *things that* are **n** satisfied, *yea*, four H3808
Isa 13:20 It shall **n** be inhabited, neither H3808+H5331
14:20 evildoers shall **n** be renowned. H3808+H5769
25: 2 to be no city; it shall **n** be built. H3808+H5769
56:11 Yea, *they are* greedy dogs *which* can **n** H3808
62: 6 *which* shall **n** hold their peace H3808+H8548
63:19 We are *thine*: thou **n** barest H5769+H3808
Jer 20:11 confusion shall **n** be forgotten. H3808
33:17 For thus saith the LORD; David shall **n** H3808
Ezk 16:63 confounded, and **n** open thy mouth any
26:21 for, yet shalt thou **n** be found H3808+H5769
27:36 and **n** *shalt be* any more. H5704+H5769
28:19 a terror, and **n** *shalt* thou *be* any more. H369
Dan 2:44 which shall **n** be destroyed: H5957+H3809
Dan 12: 1 of trouble, such as **n** was since there H3808
Joel 2:26 my people shall **n** be ashamed. H3808+H5769
27 my people shall **n** be ashamed. H3808+H5769
Am 8: 7 will **n** forget any of their works. H518+H5331
14 they shall fall, and **n** rise up again. H3808
Hab 1: 4 doth **n** go forth: for the H3808+H5331
Mt 7:23 And then will I profess unto them, I **n** *G3763*
9:33 saying, It was **n** so seen in Israel. *G3763*
21:16 Yea; have ye **n** read, Out of the mouth *G3763*
42 Jesus saith unto them, Did ye **n** read in *G3763*
26:33 of thee, *yet* will I **n** be offended. *G3763*
27:14 And he answered him to **n** a word; *G3756*
Mk 2:12 saying, We **n** saw it on this fashion. *G3763*
25 And he said unto them, Have ye **n** read *G3763*
3:29 Holy Ghost hath **n** forgiveness, but is in *G3756*
9:43 into the fire that **n** shall be quenched: *G3756*
45 into the fire that **n** shall be quenched: *G3756*
11: 2 **n** man sat; loose him, and bring *him*. *G3762*
14:21 it for that man if he had **n** been born. *G3756*
Lk 15:29 and yet thou **n** gavest me a kid, that *G3763*
19:30 tied, whereon yet **n** man sat: loose him, *G3762*
23:29 the wombs that **n** bare, and the paps *G3756*
29 bare, and the paps which **n** gave suck. *G3756*
53 stone, wherein **n** man before was laid. *G3764*
Jn 4:14 give him shall **n** thirst; but the water *G3756*
6:35 to me shall **n** hunger; and he that *G3364*
35 he that believeth on me shall **n** thirst. *G4455*
7:15 this man letters, having **n** learned? *G3361*
46 The officers answered, **N** man spake *G3763*
8:33 seed, and were **n** in bondage to any *G4455*
51 keep my saying, he shall **n** see death. *G1519*
52 my saying, he shall **n** taste of death. *G1519*
10:28 life; and they shall **n** perish, neither *G1519*
11:26 in me shall **n** die. Believest thou this? *G1519*
13: 8 Peter saith unto him, Thou shalt **n** *G3756*
19:41 sepulchre, wherein was **n** man yet laid. *G3764*
Act 10:14 Lord; for I have **n** eaten any thing that *G3763*
14: 8 his mother's womb, who **n** had walked: *G3763*
1Co 13: 8 Charity **n** faileth: but whether *there be* *G3763*
2Ti 3: 7 Ever learning, and **n** able to come to *G3368*
Heb 10: 1 image of the things, can **n** with those *G3763*
11 sacrifices, which can **n** take away sins: *G3763*
13: 5 I will **n** leave thee, nor forsake thee. *G3364*
2Pt 1:10 for if ye do these things, ye shall **n** fall: *G4218*

NEVERTHELESS
Ex 32:34 go before thee: **n** in the day when I visit
Lev 11: 4 **N** these shall ye not eat of them that H389
36 **N** a fountain or pit, *wherein there is* H389
Nu 13:28 **N** the people *be* strong that dwell in the H657
14:44 up unto the hill top: **n** the ark of the
18:15 shall be thine: **n** the firstborn of man H389
24:22 **N** the Kenite shall be wasted, until H518
31:23 it shall be clean: **n** it shall be purified H389
Dt 14: 7 **N** these ye shall not eat of them that H389
23: 5 **N** the LORD thy God would not hearken
Jos 13:13 **N** the children of Israel expelled not the
14: 8 **N** my brethren that went up with me
Jdg 1:33 of the land: **n** the inhabitants of
2:16 **N** the LORD raised up judges, which
1Sa 8:19 **N** the people refused to obey the voice of
15:35 day of his death: **n** Samuel mourned H3588
20:26 **N** Saul spake not any thing that day: for
29: 6 this day: **n** the lords favour thee not.
2Sa 5: 7 **N** David took the strong hold of Zion:
17:18 **N** a lad saw them, and told Absalom:
23:16 *it* to David: **n** he would not drink
1Ki 8:19 **N** thou shalt not build the house; but H7535
15: 4 **N** for David's sake did the LORD his H3588
14 not removed: **n** Asa's heart was perfect H7535
23 kings of Judah? **N** in the time of his old H7535
22:43 eyes of the LORD: **n** the high places were H389
2Ki 2:10 a hard thing: *n*, if thou see me *when*
3: 3 **N** he cleaved unto the sins of Jeroboam H7535
13: 6 **N** they departed not from the sins of the H389
23: 9 **N** the priests of the high places came not H389
1Ch 11: 5 not come hither. **N** David took the castle
21: 4 **N** the king's word prevailed against
2Ch 12: 8 **N** they shall be his servants; that they H3588
15:17 away out of Israel: **n** the heart of Asa H7535
19: 3 **N** there are good things found in thee, in H61
30:11 **N** divers of Asher and Manasseh and of H389
33:17 **N** the people did sacrifice still in the high H61
35:22 **N** Josiah would not turn his face from
Neh 4: 9 **N** we made our prayer unto our God,
9:26 **N** they were disobedient, and rebelled
31 **N** for thy great mercies' sake thou didst
13:26 king over all Israel: **n** even him did H1571
Est 5:10 **N** Haman refrained himself: and when

Ps 31:22 before thine eyes: **n** thou heardest the H403
49:12 **N** man *being* in honour abideth not: he
73:23 **N** I *am* continually with thee: thou hast
78:36 **N** they did flatter him with their mouth,
89:33 **N** my lovingkindness will I not utterly
106: 8 **N** he saved them for his name's sake,
44 **N** he regarded their affliction, when he
Prv 19:21 in a man's heart; **n** the counsel of the
Ecc 9:16 than strength: **n** the poor man's wisdom
Isa 9: 1 **N** the dimness *shall* not *be* such as *was* H3588
Jer 5:18 **N** in those days, saith the LORD, I will H1571
26:24 **N** the hand of Ahikam the son of H389
28: 7 **N** hear thou now this word that I speak H389
36:25 **N** Elnathan and Delaiah and Gemariah H1571
Ezk 3:21 **N** if thou warn the righteous *man*, that
16:60 **N** I will remember my covenant with
20:17 **N** mine eye spared them from
22 **N** I withdrew mine hand, and wrought
33: 9 **N**, if thou warn the wicked of his way to
Dan 4:15 **N** leave the stump of his roots in the H1297
Jna 1:13 **N** the men rowed hard to bring *it* to the
Mt 14: 9 And the king was sorry: **n** for the oath's *G1161*
26:39 me: **n** not as I will, but as thou *wilt*. *G4133*
64 Jesus saith unto him, Thou hast said: **n** *G4133*
Mk 14:36 me: **n** not what I will, but what thou wilt. *G235*
Lk 5: 5 **n** at thy word I will let down the net. *G1161*
13:33 **N** I must walk to day, and to morrow, *G4133*
18: 8 them speedily. **N** when the Son of man *G4133*
22:42 me: **n** not my will, but thine, be done. *G4133*
Jn 11:15 ye may believe; **n** let us go unto him. *G235*
12:42 **N** among the chief rulers also many *G3676*
16: 7 **N** I tell you the truth; It is expedient for *G235*
Act 14:17 **N** he left not himself without witness, *G2544*
27:11 **N** the centurion believed the master *G1161*
Ro 5:14 **N** death reigned from Adam to Moses, *G235*
15:15 **N**, brethren, I have written the more *G1161*
1Co 7: 2 **N**, *to avoid* fornication, let every man *G1161*
28 she hath not sinned. **N** such shall have *G1161*
37 **N** he that standeth stedfast in his heart, *G1161*
9:12 *are* not we rather? **N** we have not used *G235*
11:11 **N** neither is the man without the *G4133*
2Co 3:16 **N** when it shall turn to the Lord, the *G1161*
7: 6 **N** God, that comforteth those that are *G235*
12:16 But be it so, I did not burden you: **n**, *G235*
Gal 2:20 I am crucified with Christ: **n** I live; yet *G1161*
4:30 **N** what saith the scripture? Cast out the *G235*
Eph 5:33 **N** let every one of you in particular so *G4133*
Php 1:24 **N** to abide in the flesh *is* more needful *G1161*
3:16 **N**, whereto we have already attained, *G4133*
2Ti 1:12 suffer these things: **n** I am not ashamed: *G235*
2:19 **N** the foundation of God standeth sure, *G3305*
Heb 12:11 but grievous: **n** afterward it yieldeth *G1161*
2Pt 3:13 **N** we, according to his promise, look *G1161*
Rev 2: 4 **N** I have *somewhat* against thee, *G235*

NEW
Ex 1: 8 Now there arose up a **n** king over H2319
Lev 23:16 offer a **n** meat offering unto the LORD. H2319
26:10 and bring forth the old because of the **n**. H2319
Nu 16:30 But if the LORD make a **n** thing, and H1278
28:26 when ye bring a **n** meat offering unto H2319
Dt 20: 5 that hath built a **n** house, and hath not H2319
22: 8 When thou buildest a **n** house, then H2319
24: 5 When a man hath taken a **n** wife, he H2319
32:17 they knew not, to **n** *gods that* came H2319
Jos 9:13 we filled, *were* **n**; and, behold, they be H2319
Jdg 5: 8 They chose **n** gods; then *was* war in the H2319
15:13 him with two **n** cords, and brought H2319
15 And he found a **n** jawbone of an ass, H2961
16:11 bind me fast with **n** ropes that never H2319
12 Delilah therefore took **n** ropes, and H2319
1Sa 6: 7 Now therefore make a **n** cart, and take H2319
20: 5 to morrow *is* the **n** moon, and I should H2320
18 To morrow *is* the **n** moon: and thou H2320
24 and when the **n** moon was come, the H2320
2Sa 6: 3 And they set the ark of God upon a **n** H2319
3 the sons of Abinadab, drave the **n** cart. H2319
21:16 a **n** *sword*, thought to have slain David. H2319
1Ki 11:29 himself with a **n** garment; and they two H2319
30 And Ahijah caught the **n** garment that H2319
2Ki 2:20 And he said, Bring me a **n** cruse, and H2319
4:23 day? *it is* neither **n** moon, nor sabbath. H2320
1Ch 13: 7 And they carried the ark of God in a **n** H2319
23:31 sabbaths, in the **n** moons, and on the H2320
2Ch 2: 4 and on the **n** moons, and on the H2320
8:13 and on the **n** moons, and on the H2320
20: 5 house of the LORD, before the **n** court, H2319
31: 3 and for the **n** moons, and for the H2320
Ezr 3: 5 both of the **n** moons, and of all the H2320
Ezr 6: 4 and a row of **n** timber: and let the H2323
Neh 10:33 sabbaths, of the **n** moons, for the set H2320
39 of the corn, of the **n** wine, and the oil, H8492
13: 5 of the corn, the **n** wine, and the oil, H8492
12 **n** wine and the oil unto the treasuries. H8492
Job 32:19 vent; it is ready to burst like **n** bottles. H2319
Ps 33: 3 Sing unto him a **n** song; play skilfully H2319
40: 3 And he hath put a **n** song in my mouth, H2319
81: 3 Blow up the trumpet in the **n** moon, in H2320
96: 1 O sing unto the LORD a **n** song: sing H2319
98: 1 O sing unto the LORD a **n** song; for he H2319
144: 9 I will sing a **n** song unto thee, O God: H2319
149: 1 unto the LORD a **n** song, *and* his praise H2319
Prv 3:10 thy presses shall burst out with **n** wine. H8492
Ecc 1: 9 and *there is* no **n** *thing* under the sun. H2319
10 said, See, this *is* **n**? it hath been already H2319
Song 7:13 of pleasant *fruits*, **n** and old, *which* I H2319
Isa 1:13 unto me; the **n** moons and sabbaths, H2320
14 Your **n** moons and your appointed H2320
24: 7 The **n** wine mourneth, the vine H8492
41:15 Behold, I will make thee a **n** sharp H2319
42: 9 are come to pass, and **n** things do I H2319
10 Sing unto the LORD a **n** song, *and* his H2319
43:19 Behold, I will do a **n** thing; now it shall H2319
48: 6 I have shewed thee **n** things from this H2319
62: 2 shalt be called by a **n** name, which the H2319
65: 8 Thus saith the LORD, As the **n** wine is H8492
17 For, behold, I create **n** heavens and a H2319
17 heavens and a **n** earth: and the former H2319
66:22 For as the **n** heavens and the new H2319
22 For as the new heavens and the **n** H2319
23 *that* from one **n** moon to another, and H2320
Jer 26:10 of the **n** gate of the LORD'S *house*. H2319
31:22 hath created a **n** thing in the earth, A H2319
31 that I will make a **n** covenant with the H2319
36:10 at the entry of the **n** gate of the LORD'S H2319
Lam 3:23 *They are* **n** every morning: great *is* thy H2319
Ezk 11:19 and I will put a **n** spirit within you; and H2319
18:31 and make you a **n** heart and a new H2319
31 a new heart and a **n** spirit: for why will H2319
36:26 A **n** heart also will I give you, and a H2319
26 will I give you, and a **n** spirit will I put H2319
45:17 feasts, and in the **n** moons, and in the H2320
46: 1 day of the **n** moon it shall be opened. H2320
3 in the sabbaths and in the **n** moons. H2320
6 And in the day of the **n** moon *it shall be* H2320
47:12 it shall bring forth **n** fruit according to H1069
Hos 2:11 her feast days, her **n** moons, and her H2320
4:11 Whoredom and wine and **n** wine take H8492
9: 2 them, and the **n** wine shall fail in her. H8492
Joel 1: 5 **n** wine; for it is cut off from your mouth.
10 **n** wine is dried up, the oil languisheth. H8492
3:18 shall drop down **n** wine, and the hills
Am 8: 5 Saying, When will the **n** moon be gone, H2320
Hag 1:11 and upon the **n** wine, and upon the H8492
Zec 9:17 men cheerful, and **n** wine the maids. H8492
Mt 9:16 No man putteth a piece of **n** cloth unto *G46*
17 Neither do men put **n** wine into old *G3501*
17 but they put **n** wine into new bottles, *G3501*
17 into **n** bottles, and both are preserved. *G2537*
13:52 out of his treasure *things* **n** and old. *G2537*
26:28 For this is my blood of the **n** testament, *G2537*
29 it **n** with you in my Father's kingdom. *G2537*
27:60 And laid it in his own **n** tomb, which he *G2537*
Mk 1:27 thing is this? what **n** doctrine *is* this? *G2537*
2:21 No man also seweth a piece of **n** cloth on *G46*
21 garment: else the **n** piece that filled it *G2537*
22 And no man putteth **n** wine into old *G3501*
22 bottles: else the **n** wine doth burst the *G3501*
22 **n** wine must be put into new bottles. *G3501*
22 new wine must be put into **n** bottles. *G2537*
14:24 **n** testament, which is shed for many. *G2537*
25 that I drink it **n** in the kingdom of God. *G2537*
16:17 devils; they shall speak with **n** tongues; *G2537*
Lk 5:36 a piece of a **n** garment upon an old; *G2537*
36 then both the **n** maketh a rent, and *G2537*
36 out of the **n** agreeth not with the old. *G2537*
37 And no man putteth **n** wine into old *G3501*
37 bottles; else the **n** wine will burst the *G3501*
38 But **n** wine must be put into new *G3501*
38 But new wine must be put into **n** *G2537*
39 **n**: for he saith, The old is better. *G3501*
22:20 This cup *is* the **n** testament in my *G2537*
Jn 13:34 A **n** commandment I give unto you, *G2537*
19:41 in the garden a **n** sepulchre, wherein *G2537*
Act 2:13 said, These men are full of **n** wine. *G1098*
17:19 **n** doctrine, whereof thou speakest, *is*? *G2537*
21 either to tell, or to hear some **n** thing.) *G2537*
1Co 5: 7 that ye may be a **n** lump, as ye are *G3501*
1Co 11:25 This cup is the **n** testament in my *G2537*
2Co 3: 6 ministers of the **n** testament; not of the *G2537*
5:17 in Christ, *he is* a **n** creature: old things *G2537*
17 away; behold, all things are become **n**. *G2537*
Gal 6:15 nor uncircumcision, but a **n** creature. *G2537*
Eph 2:15 of twain one **n** man, *so* making peace; *G2537*
4:24 And that ye put on the **n** man, which *G2537*
Col 2:16 of the **n** moon, or of the sabbath *days*: *G3561*
3:10 And have put on the **n** *man*, which is *G3501*
Heb 8: 8 when I will make a **n** covenant with the *G2537*
13 In that he saith, A **n** *covenant*, he hath *G2537*
9:15 mediator of the **n** testament, that by *G2537*
10:20 By a **n** and living way, which he hath *G4372*
12:24 And to Jesus the mediator of the **n** *G3501*
2Pt 3:13 promise, look for **n** heavens and a new *G2537*
13 new heavens and a **n** earth, wherein *G2537*
1Jn 2: 7 Brethren, I write no **n** commandment *G2537*
8 Again, a **n** commandment I write unto *G2537*
2Jn 5 as though I wrote a **n** commandment *G2537*
Rev 2:17 and in the stone a **n** name written, *G2537*
3:12 of my God, *which is* **n** Jerusalem, which *G2537*
12 and *I will write upon him* my **n** name. *G2537*
5: 9 And they sung a **n** song, saying, Thou *G2537*
14: 3 And they sung as it were a **n** song *G2537*
21: 1 And I saw a **n** heaven and a new earth: *G2537*
1 And I saw a new heaven and a **n** earth: *G2537*
2 And I John saw the holy city, **n** *G2537*
5 I make all things **n**. And he said unto *G2537*

NEWBORN
1Pt 2: 2 As **n** babes, desire the sincere milk of the *G738*

NEWLY
Dt 32:17 **n** up, whom your fathers feared not. H7138
Jdg 7:19 and they had but **n** set the watch: and H6965

NEW-MOON See NEW and MOON.

NEWNESS
Ro 6: 4 even so we also should walk in **n** of life. *G2538*
7: 6 we should serve in **n** of spirit, and not *G2538*

NEWS
Prv 25:25 soul, so *is* good **n** from a far country. H8052

NEXT
Gen 17:21 unto thee at this set time in the **n** year. H312
Ex 12: 4 and his neighbour **n** unto his house H7138
Nu 2: 5 And those that do pitch **n** unto him *shall*
11:32 *that* night, and all the **n** day, and they H4283
27:11 kinsman that is **n** to him of his family, H7138
Dt 21: 3 And it shall be, *that* the city *which is* **n** H7138
6 that city, *that are* **n** unto the slain *man*, H7138
Ru 2:20 of kin unto us, one of our **n** kinsmen.
1Sa 17:13 Eliab the firstborn, and **n** unto him H4932
23:17 and I shall be **n** unto thee; and that H4932
30:17 the evening of the **n** day: and there H4283
2Ki 6:29 unto her on the **n** day, Give thy son, that H312
1Ch 5:12 Joel the chief, and Shapham the **n**, and H4932
16: 5 Asaph the chief, and **n** to him H4932
2Ch 17:15 And **n** to him *was* Jehohanan H5921+H3027
16 And **n** him *was* Amasiah the H5921+H3027
18 And **n** him *was* Jehozabad, H5921+H3027
28: 7 and Elkanah *that was* **n** to the king. H4932
31:12 ruler, and Shimei his brother *was* the **n**. H4932
15 And **n** him *were* Eden, and H5921+H3027
Neh 3: 2 And **n** unto him builded the H5921+H3027
2 Jericho. And **n** to them builded H5921+H3027
4 And **n** unto them repaired H5921+H3027
4 son of Koz. And **n** unto them H5921+H3027
4 And **n** unto them repaired H5921+H3027
5 And **n** unto them the Tekoites H5921+H3027
7 And **n** unto them repaired H5921+H3027
8 **N** unto him repaired Uzziel the H5921+H3027
8 goldsmiths. **N** unto him also H5921+H3027
9 And **n** unto them repaired H5921+H3027
10 And **n** unto them repaired H5921+H3027
10 his house. And **n** unto him H5921+H3027
12 And **n** unto him repaired H5921+H3027
17 the son of Bani. **N** unto him H5921+H3027
19 And **n** to him repaired Ezer the H5921+H3027
13:13 Pedaiah: and **n** to them *was* H5921+H3027
Est 1:14 And the **n** unto him *was* Carshena, H7138
10: 3 For Mordecai the Jew *was* **n** unto king H4932
Jna 4: 7 morning rose the **n** day, and it smote H4283
Mt 27:62 Now the **n** day, that followed the day of *G1887*
Mk 1:38 Let us go into the **n** towns, that I may *G2192*
Lk 9:37 And it came to pass, that on the **n** day, *G1836*
Jn 1:29 The **n** day John seeth Jesus coming *G1887*

Jn 1:35 Again the **n** day after John stood, and G1887
12:12 On the **n** day much people that were G1887
Act 4: 3 unto the **n** day: for it was now eventide. G839
7:26 And the **n** day he shewed himself unto G1966
13:42 be preached to them the **n** sabbath. G3342
44 And the **n** sabbath day came almost G2064
14:20 into the city: and the **n** day he departed G1887
16:11 and the **n** *day* to Neapolis; G1966
20:15 And we sailed thence, and came the **n** G1966
15 Chios; and the **n** *day* we arrived at G2087
15 and the **n** *day* we came to Miletus. G2192
21: 8 And the **n** *day* we that were of Paul's G1887
26 Then Paul took the men, and the **n** day G2192
25: 6 Caesarea; and the **n** day sitting on the G1887
27: 3 And the **n** *day* we touched at Sidon. G2087
18 the **n** *day* they lightened the ship; G1836
28:13 blew, and we came the **n** day to Puteoli: G1206

NEZIAH
Ezr 2:54 The children of **N**, the children of H5335
Neh 7:56 The children of **N**, the children of H5335

NEZIB
Jos 15:43 And Jiphtah, and Ashnah, and **N**, H5334

NIBHAZ
2Ki 17:31 And the Avites made **N** and Tartak, H5026

NIBSHAN
Jos 15:62 And **N**, and the city of Salt, and H5044

NICANOR
Act 6: 5 and Prochorus, and **N**, and Timon, and G3527

NICODEMUS
Jn 3: 1 Pharisees, named **N**, a ruler of the Jews: G3530
4 **N** saith unto him, How can a man be G3530
9 **N** answered and said unto him, How G3530
7:50 **N** saith unto them, (he that came to G3530
19:39 And there came also **N**, which at the G3530

NICOLAITANS
Rev 2: 6 the deeds of the N, which I also hate. G3531
15 doctrine of the N, which thing I hate. G3531

NICOLAS
Act 6: 5 and **N** a proselyte of Antioch: G3532

NICOPOLIS
Tit 3:12 to come unto me to **N**: for I have G3533

NIGER
Act 13: 1 Simeon that was called **N**, and Lucius of G3526

NIGH
Gen 47:29 And the time drew **n** that Israel must H7126
Ex 3: 5 And he said, Draw not **n** hither: put off H7126
14:10 And when Pharaoh drew **n**, the children H7126
24: 2 they shall not come **n**; neither shall the H5066
32:19 soon as he came **n** unto the camp, that H7126
34:30 and they were afraid to come **n** him. H5066
32 of Israel came **n**: and he gave them in H5066
Lev 10: 3 in them that come **n** me, and before all H7138
21: 3 And for his sister a virgin, that is **n** H7138
21 the priest shall come **n** to offer the H5066
21 come **n** to offer the bread of his God. H5066
23 the vail, nor come **n** unto the altar, H5066
25:49 him, or *any* that is **n** of kin unto him of H7607
Nu 1:51 that cometh **n** shall be put to death. H7131
3:10 that cometh **n** shall be put to death. H7131
38 that cometh **n** shall be put to death. H7131
8:19 of Israel come **n** unto the sanctuary. H5066
18: 3 they shall not come **n** the vessels of the H7126
4 a stranger shall not come **n** unto you. H7126
7 that cometh **n** shall be put to death. H7131
22 henceforth come **n** the tabernacle of H7126
24:17 him, but not **n**: there shall come a Star H7138
Dt 1: 7 unto all *the places* **n** thereunto, in the H7934
2:19 And *when* thou comest **n** over against H7126
4: 7 who *hath* God *so* **n** unto them, as the H7138
13: 7 round about you, **n** unto thee, or far off H7138
20: 2 And it shall be, when ye are come **n** H7126
10 When thou comest **n** unto a city to H7126
22: 2 And if thy brother *be* not **n** unto thee, H7138
30:14 But the word *is* very **n** unto thee, in thy H7138
Jos 8:11 up, and drew **n**, and came before the H5066
1Sa 17:48 came and drew **n** to meet David, that H7126
2Sa 10:13 And Joab drew **n**, and the people that H5066
11:20 approached ye so **n** unto the city when H5066
2Sa 11:21 why went ye **n** the wall? then say thou, H5066
15: 5 any man came **n** *to him* to do him H7126
1Ki 2: 1 Now the days of David drew **n** that he H7126
8:59 the LORD, be **n** unto the LORD our H7138
1Ch 12:40 Moreover they that were **n** them, *even* H7138
19:14 with him drew **n** before the Syrians H5066
Est 9:20 of the king Ahasuerus, *both* **n** and far, H7138
Ps 32: 6 waters they shall not come **n** unto him. H5060
34:18 The LORD *is* **n** unto them that are of a H7138
69:18 Draw **n** unto my soul, *and* redeem it: H7126
73: 2 gone; my steps had well **n** slipped. H369
85: 9 Surely his salvation *is* **n** them that fear H7138
88: 3 and my life draweth **n** unto the grave. H5060
91: 7 right hand; *but* it shall not come **n** thee. H5066
10 shall any plague come **n** thy dwelling. H7126
119:150 They draw **n** that follow after mischief: H7126
145:18 The LORD *is* **n** unto all them that call H7138
Prv 5: 8 and come not **n** the door of her house: H7126
Ecc 12: 1 the years draw **n**, when thou shalt say, H5060
Isa 5:19 **n** and come, that we may know *it*! H7126
Joel 2: 1 of the LORD cometh, for *it is* **n** at hand; H7136
Mt 15: 8 This people draweth n unto me with G1448
29 thence, and came **n** unto the sea of G3844
21: 1 And when they drew **n** unto Jerusalem, G1448
24:32 forth leaves, ye know that summer *is* n: G1451
Mk 2: 4 And when they could not come **n** unto G4331
5:11 Now there was there **n** unto the G4314
21 unto him: and he was **n** unto the sea. G3844
11: 1 And when they came **n** to Jerusalem, G1448
13:29 know that it is n, *even* at the doors. G1451
Lk 7:12 Now when he came **n** to the gate of the G1448
10: 9 kingdom of God is come n unto you. G1448
11 kingdom of God is come n unto you. G1448
15:25 as he came and drew n to the house, he G1448
18:35 that as he was come **n** unto Jericho, a G1448
19:11 because he was **n** to Jerusalem, and G1451
29 when he was come **n** to Bethphage and G1448
37 And when he was come **n**, even now at G1448
21:20 know that the desolation thereof is n. G1448
28 heads; for your redemption draweth n. G1448
30 selves that summer is now n at hand. G1451
31 that the kingdom of God is n at hand. G1451
22: 1 drew **n**, which is called the Passover. G1448
24:28 And they drew **n** unto the village, G1448
Jn 6: 4 the passover, a feast of the Jews, was **n**. G1451
19 **n** unto the ship: and they were afraid. G1451
23 from Tiberias **n** unto the place where G1451
11:18 Now Bethany was **n** unto Jerusalem, G1451
55 And the Jews' passover was **n** at hand: G1451
19:20 was crucified was **n** to the city: and it G1451
42 *day*; for the sepulchre was **n** at hand. G1451
Act 7:17 of the promise drew **n**, which God had G1448
9:38 And forasmuch as Lydda was **n** to G1451
10: 9 their journey, and drew **n** unto the city, G1448
22: 6 and was come **n** unto Damascus about G1448
27: 8 **n** whereunto was the city *of* Lasea. G1451
Ro 10: 8 But what saith it? The word is **n** thee, G1451
Eph 2:13 off are made **n** by the blood of Christ. G1451
17 were afar off, and to them that were **n**. G1451
Php 2:27 For indeed he was sick **n** unto death: G1448
30 Because for the work of Christ he was **n** G1448
Heb 6: 8 briers *is* rejected, and *is* **n** unto cursing; G1451
7:19 *did*; by the which we draw **n** unto God. G1448
Jas 4: 8 Draw **n** to God, and he will draw nigh G1448
8 Draw nigh to God, and he will draw **n** G1448
5: 8 for the coming of the Lord draweth **n**. G1448

NIGHT
Gen 1: 5 he called **N**. And the evening and H3915
14 the day from the **n**; and let them be for H3915
16 to rule the **n**: *he made* the stars also. H3915
18 And to rule over the day and over the **n**, H3915
8:22 winter, and day and **n** shall not cease. H3915
14:15 his servants, by **n**, and smote them, and H3915
19: 2 and tarry all **n**, and wash your feet, H3885
2 Nay; but we will abide in the street all **n**.
5 in to thee this **n**? bring them out unto H3915
33 drink wine that **n**: and the firstborn H3915
34 drink wine this **n** also; and go thou in, H3915
35 drink wine that **n** also: and the younger H3915
20: 3 in a dream by **n**, and said to him, H3915
24:54 and tarried all **n**; and they rose up in H3885
26:24 him the same **n**, and said, I *am* the God H3915
28:11 tarried there all **n**, because the sun was H3885
30:15 with thee to **n** for thy son's mandrakes. H3915
16 mandrakes. And he lay with her that **n**. H3915
31:24 in a dream by **n**, and said unto him, H3915
39 it, *whether* stolen by day, or stolen by **n**. H3915
40 me, and the frost by **n**; and my sleep H3915
Gen 31:54 bread, and tarried all **n** in the mount. H3885
32:13 And he lodged there that same **n**; and H3915
21 himself lodged that **n** in the company. H3915
22 And he rose up that **n**, and took his two H3915
40: 5 man his dream in one **n**, each man H3915
41:11 And we dreamed a dream in one **n**, I H3915
46: 2 in the visions of the **n**, and said, Jacob, H3915
49:27 prey, and at **n** he shall divide the spoil. H6153
Ex 10:13 day, and all *that* **n**; *and* when it was H3915
12: 8 And they shall eat the flesh in that **n**, H3915
12 land of Egypt this **n**, and will smite all H3915
30 And Pharaoh rose up in the **n**, he, and H3915
31 and Aaron by **n**, and said, Rise up, *and* H3915
42 It *is* a **n** to be much observed unto the H3915
42 Egypt: this *is* that **n** of the LORD to be H3915
13:21 the way; and by **n** in a pillar of fire, to H3915
21 to give them light; to go by day and **n**: H3915
22 of fire by **n**, *from* before the people. H3915
14:20 but it gave light by **n** *to these:* so that H3915
20 one came not near the other all the **n**. H3915
21 east wind all that **n**, and made the sea H3915
40:38 fire was on it by **n**, in the sight of all the H3915
Lev 6: 9 upon the altar all **n** unto the morning, H3915
20 it in the morning, and half thereof at **n**. H6153
8:35 day and **n** seven days, and keep H3915
11:16 And the owl, and the **n** hawk, and the H8464
19:13 abide with thee all **n** until the morning.
Nu 9:16 *by day*, and the appearance of fire by **n**. H3915
21 *it was* by day or by **n** that the cloud was H3915
11: 9 camp in the **n**, the manna fell upon it. H3915
32 day, and all *that* **n**, and all the next day, H3915
14: 1 and cried; and the people wept that **n**. H3915
14 of a cloud, and in a pillar of fire by **n**. H3915
22: 8 Lodge here this **n**, and I will bring you H3915
19 ye also here this **n**, that I may know H3915
20 And God came unto Balaam at **n**, and H3915
Dt 1:33 tents *in*, in fire by **n**, to shew you by H3915
14:15 And the owl, and the **n** hawk, and the H8464
16: 1 brought thee forth out of Egypt by **n**. H3915
4 at even, remain all **n** until the morning.
21:23 His body shall not remain all **n** upon the
23:10 that chanceth him by **n**, then shall he go H3915
28:66 shalt fear day and **n**, and shalt have H3915
Jos 1: 8 therein day and **n**, that thou mayest H3915
2: 2 men in hither to **n** of the children of H3915
4: 3 place, where ye shall lodge this **n**. H3915
8: 3 of valour, and sent them away by **n**. H3915
9 lodged that **n** among the people. H3915
13 went that **n** into the midst of the valley. H3915
10: 9 *and* went up from Gilgal all **n**. H3915
Jdg 6:25 And it came to pass the same **n**, that the H3915
27 not do *it* by day, that he did *it* by **n**. H3915
40 And God did so that **n**: for it was dry H3915
7: 9 And it came to pass the same **n**, that the H3915
9:32 Now therefore up by **n**, thou and the H3915
34 *were* with him, by **n**, and they laid wait H3915
16: 2 wait for him all **n** in the gate of the city, H3915
2 and were quiet all the **n**, saying, In the H3915
19: 6 tarry all **n**, and let thine heart be merry. H3885
9 I pray you tarry all **n**: behold, the day H3885
10 But the man would not tarry that **n**, but H3885
13 to lodge all **n**, in Gibeah, or in Ramah. H3885
25 abused her all the **n** until the morning: H3915
20: 5 about upon me by **n**, *and* thought to H3915
Ru 1:12 also to **n**, and should also bear sons; H3915
3: 2 barley to **n** in the threshingfloor. H3915
13 Tarry this **n**, and it shall be in the H3915
1Sa 14:34 with him that **n**, and slew *them* there. H3915
36 the Philistines by **n**, and spoil them H3915
15:11 and he cried unto the LORD all **n**. H3915
16 this **n**. And he said unto him, Say on. H3915
19:10 and David fled, and escaped that **n**. H3915
11 life to **n**, to morrow thou shalt be slain. H3915
24 day and all that **n**. Wherefore they say, H3915
25:16 They were a wall unto us both by **n** and H3915
26: 7 to the people by **n**: and, behold, Saul lay H3915
28: 8 to the woman by **n**: and he said, I pray H3915
20 eaten no bread all the day, nor all the **n**. H3915
25 they rose up, and went away that **n**. H3915
31:12 and went all **n**, and took the body of H3915
2Sa 2:29 walked all that **n** through the plain, H3915
32 his men went all **n**, and they came to H3915
4: 7 gat them away through the plain all **n**. H3915
7: 4 And it came to pass that **n**, that the H3915
12:16 went in, and lay all **n** upon the earth.
17: 1 will arise and pursue after David this **n**: H3915
16 Lodge not this **n** in the plains of the H3915
19: 7 one with thee this **n**: and that will be H3915
21:10 by day, nor the beasts of the field by **n**. H3915

1Ki 3: 5 in a dream by **n**: and God said, Ask H3915
19 And this woman's child died in the **n**; H3915
8:29 toward this house **n** and day, *even* H3915
59 our God day and **n**, that he maintain H3915
2Ki 6:14 by **n**, and compassed the city about. H3915
7:12 And the king arose in the **n**, and said H3915
8:21 him: and he rose by **n**, and smote the H3915
19:35 And it came to pass that **n**, that the H3915
25: 4 of war *fled* by **n** by the way of the gate H3915
1Ch 9:33 were employed in *that* work day and **n**. H3915
17: 3 And it came to pass the same **n**, that the H3915
2Ch 1: 7 In that **n** did God appear unto H3915
6:20 this house day and **n**, upon the place H3915
7:12 to Solomon by **n**, and said unto him, H3915
21: 9 him: and he rose up by **n**, and smote the H3915
35:14 and the fat until **n**; therefore the Levites H3915
Neh 1: 6 thee now, day and **n**, for the children of H3915
2:12 And I arose in the **n**, I and some few H3915
13 And I went out by **n** by the gate of the H3915
15 Then went I up in the **n** by the brook, H3915
4: 9 them day and **n**, because of them. H3915
22 that in the **n** they may be a guard H3915
6:10 in the **n** will they come to slay thee. H3915
9:12 pillar; and in the **n** by a pillar of fire, to H3915
19 the pillar of fire by **n**, to shew them H3915
Est 4:16 drink three days, **n** or day: I also and H3915
6: 1 On that **n** could not the king sleep, and H3915
Job 3: 3 I was born, and the **n** *in which* it was H3915
6 As *for* that **n**, let darkness seize upon it; H3915
7 Lo, let that **n** be solitary, let no joyful H3915
4:13 In thoughts from the visions of the **n**, H3915
5:14 and grope in the noonday as in the **n**. H3915
7: 4 I arise, and the **n** be gone? and I am full H6153
17:12 They change the **n** into day: the light *is* H3915
20: 8 be chased away as a vision of the **n**. H3915
24:14 and needy, and in the **n** is as a thief. H3915
26:10 until the day and **n** come to an end. H2822
27:20 a tempest stealeth him away in the **n**. H3915
29:19 and the dew lay all **n** upon my branch. H3885
30:17 My bones are pierced in me in the **n** H3915
33:15 In a dream, in a vision of the **n**, when H3915
34:25 in the **n**, so that they are destroyed. H3915
35:10 my maker, who giveth songs in the **n**; H3915
36:20 Desire not the **n**, when people are cut H3915
Ps 1: 2 in his law doth he meditate day and **n**. H3915
6: 6 I am weary with my groaning; all the **n** H3915
16: 7 reins also instruct me in the **n** seasons. H3915
17: 3 visited *me* in the **n**; thou hast tried me, H3915
19: 2 Day unto day uttereth speech, and **n** H3915
2 and night unto **n** sheweth knowledge. H3915
22: 2 and in the **n** season, and am not silent. H3915
30: 5 for a **n**, but joy *cometh* in the morning. H6153
32: 4 For day and **n** thy hand was heavy H3915
42: 3 My tears have been my meat day and **n**, H3915
8 and in the **n** his song *shall be* with H3915
55:10 Day and **n** they go about it upon the H3915
63: 6 *and* meditate on thee in the *n* watches. H3915
74:16 The day *is* thine, the **n** also *is* thine: H3915
77: 2 my sore ran in the **n**, and ceased not: H3915
6 I call to remembrance my song in the **n**: H3915
78:14 cloud, and all the **n** with a light of fire. H3915
88: 1 I have cried day *and* **n** before thee: H3915
90: 4 when it is past, and *as* a watch in the **n**. H3915
91: 5 **n**; *nor* for the arrow *that* flieth by day; H3915
92: 2 morning, and thy faithfulness every **n**, H3915
104:20 Thou makest darkness, and it is **n**: H3915
105:39 covering; and fire to give light in the **n**. H3915
119:55 LORD, in the **n**, and have kept thy law. H3915
148 Mine eyes prevent the *n* watches, that I
121: 6 smite thee by day, nor the moon by **n**. H3915
134: 1 by **n** stand in the house of the LORD. H3915
136: 9 The moon and stars to rule by **n**: for his H3915
139:11 me; even the **n** shall be light about me. H3915
12 from thee; but the **n** shineth as the day: H3915
Prv 7: 9 in the evening, in the black and dark **n**: H3915
31:15 She riseth also while it is yet **n**, and H3915
18 *is* good: her candle goeth not out by **n**. H3915
Ecc 2:23 not rest in the **n**. This is also vanity. H3915
8:16 day nor **n** seeth sleep with his eyes:) H3915
Song 1:13 he shall lie all **n** betwixt my breasts. H3885
3: 1 By **n** on my bed I sought him whom my H3915
8 upon his thigh because of fear in the **n**. H3915
5: 2 *and* my locks with the drops of the **n**. H3915
Isa 4: 5 of a flaming fire by **n**: for upon all the H3915
5:11 continue until **n**, *till* wine inflame them! H5399
15: 1 The burden of Moab. Because in the **n** H3915
1 because in the **n** Kir of Moab is laid H3915
16: 3 thy shadow as the **n** in the midst of the H3915
21: 4 affrighted me: the **n** of my pleasure H5399
Isa 21:11 of the **n**? Watchman, what of the night? H3915
11 of the night? Watchman, what of the **n**? H3915
12 and also the **n**: if ye will inquire, inquire H3915
26: 9 desired thee in the **n**; yea, with my spirit H3915
27: 3 lest *any* hurt it, I will keep it **n** and day. H3915
28:19 over, by day and by **n**: and it shall be a H3915
29: 7 her, shall be as a dream of a **n** vision. H3915
30:29 Ye shall have a song, as in the **n** *when* a H3915
34:10 It shall not be quenched **n** nor day; the H3915
38:12 *even* to **n** wilt thou make an end of me. H3915
13 *even* to **n** wilt thou make an end of me. H3915
59:10 noonday as in the **n**; *we are* in desolate H5399
60:11 be shut day nor **n**; that *men* may bring H3915
62: 6 peace day nor **n**: ye that make mention H3915
Jer 6: 5 Arise, and let us go by **n**, and let us H3915
9: 1 weep day and **n** for the slain of the H3915
14: 8 man *that* turneth aside to tarry for a **n**? H3885
17 run down with tears **n** and day, and let H3915
16:13 and **n**; where I will not shew you favour. H3915
31:35 stars for a light by **n**, which divideth the H3915
33:20 covenant of the **n**, and that there should H3915
20 not be day and **n** in their season; H3915
25 *be* not with day and **n**, *and if* I have not H3915
36:30 to the heat, and in the **n** to the frost. H3915
39: 4 out of the city by **n**, by the way of the H3915
49: 9 if thieves by **n**, they will destroy till H3915
52: 7 out of the city by **n** by the way of the H3915
Lam 1: 2 She weepeth sore in the **n**, and her tears H3915
2:18 a river day and **n**: give thyself no rest; H3915
19 Arise, cry out in the **n**: in the beginning H3915
Dan 2:19 unto Daniel in a **n** vision. Then Daniel H3916
5:30 In that **n** was Belshazzar the king of the H3916
6:18 and passed the **n** fasting: neither were H956
7: 2 in my vision by **n**, and, behold, the four H3916
7 After this I saw in the **n** visions, and H3916
13 I saw in the **n** visions, and, behold, *one* H3916
Hos 4: 5 in the **n**, and I will destroy thy mother. H3915
7: 6 sleepeth all the **n**; in the morning it H3915
Joel 1:13 the altar: come, lie all **n** in sackcloth, ye H3885
Am 5: 8 the day dark with **n**: that calleth for the H3915
Oba 5 If thieves came to thee, if robbers by **n**, H3915
Jna 4:10 came up in a **n**, and perished in a night: H3915
10 came up in a night, and perished in a **n**: H3915
Mic 3: 6 Therefore **n** *shall be* unto you, that ye H3915
Zec 1: 8 I saw by **n**, and behold a man riding H3915
14: 7 not day, nor **n**: but it shall come to H3915
Mt 2:14 mother by **n**, and departed into Egypt: G3571
14:25 And in the fourth watch of the **n** Jesus G3571
26:31 because of me this **n**: for it is written, I G3571
34 thee, That this **n**, before the cock crow, G3571
27:64 his disciples come by **n**, and steal him G3571
28:13 Saying, Say ye, His disciples came by **n**, G3571
Mk 4:27 And should sleep, and rise **n** and day, G3571
5: 5 And always, **n** and day, he was in the G3571
6:48 watch of the **n** he cometh unto them, G3571
14:27 because of me this **n**: for it is written, I G3571
30 day, *even* in this **n**, before the cock crow G3571
Lk 2: 8 keeping watch over their flock by **n**. G3571
37 with fastings and prayers **n** and day. G3571
5: 5 we have toiled all the **n**, and have taken G3571
6:12 and continued all **n** in prayer to God. G2258
12:20 him, *Thou* fool, this **n** thy soul shall be G3571
17:34 I tell you, in that **n** there shall be two G3571
18: 7 which cry day and **n** unto him, though G3571
21:37 the temple; and at **n** he went out, and G3571
Jn 3: 2 The same came to Jesus by **n**, and said G3571
7:50 came to Jesus by **n**, being one of them,) G3571
9: 4 the **n** cometh, when no man can work. G3571
11:10 But if a man walk in the **n**, he G3571
13:30 sop went immediately out: and it was **n**. G3571
19:39 first came to Jesus by **n**, and brought a G3571
21: 3 and that **n** they caught nothing. G3571
Act 5:19 But the angel of the Lord by **n** opened G3571
9:24 the gates day and **n** to kill him. G3571
25 Then the disciples took him by **n**, and G3571
12: 6 forth, the same **n** Peter was sleeping G3571
16: 9 And a vision appeared to Paul in the **n**; G3571
33 same hour of the **n**, and washed *their* G3571
17:10 Paul and Silas by **n** unto Berea: who G3571
18: 9 Then spake the Lord to Paul in the **n** by G3571
20:31 to warn every one **n** and day with tears. G3571
23:11 And the **n** following the Lord stood by G3571
23 two hundred, at the third hour of the **n**; G3571
31 and brought *him* by **n** to Antipatris. G3571
26: 7 *God* day and **n**, hope to come. For G3571
27:23 For there stood by me this **n** the angel G3571
27 But when the fourteenth **n** was come, G3571
Ro 13:12 The **n** is far spent, the day is at hand: G3571
1Co 11:23 **n** in which he was betrayed took bread: G3571
2Co 11:25 a **n** and a day I have been in the deep; G3574
1Th 2: 9 for labouring **n** and day, because we G3571
3:10 **N** and day praying exceedingly that we G3571
5: 2 of the Lord so cometh as a thief in the **n**. G3571
5 we are not of the **n**, nor of darkness. G3571
7 For they that sleep sleep in the **n**; and G3571
7 that be drunken are drunken in the **n**. G3571
2Th 3: 8 labour and travail **n** and day, that we G3571
1Ti 5: 5 supplications and prayers **n** and day. G3571
2Ti 1: 3 of thee in my prayers **n** and day; G3571
2Pt 3:10 as a thief in the **n**; in the which the G3571
Rev 4: 8 rest not day and **n**, saying, Holy, holy, G3571
7:15 serve him day and **n** in his temple: and G3571
8:12 for a third part of it, and the **n** likewise. G3571
12:10 them before our God day and **n**. G3571
14:11 have no rest day nor **n**, who worship the G3571
20:10 tormented day and **n** for ever and ever. G3571
21:25 all by day: for there shall be no **n** there. G3571
22: 5 And there shall be no **n** there; and they G3571

NIGHT-HAWK See NIGHT and HAWK.

NIGHTS
Gen 7: 4 forty days and forty **n**; and every living H3915
12 upon the earth forty days and forty **n**. H3915
Ex 24:18 in the mount forty days and forty **n**. H3915
34:28 days and forty **n**; he did neither eat H3915
Dt 9: 9 days and forty **n**, I neither did eat bread H3915
11 days and forty **n**, *that* the LORD gave H3915
18 forty days and forty **n**: I did neither eat H3915
25 days and forty **n**, as I fell down *at the* H3915
10:10 forty days and forty **n**; and the LORD H3915
1Sa 30:12 *any* water, three days and three **n**. H3915
1Ki 19: 8 forty **n** unto Horeb the mount of God. H3915
Job 2:13 days and seven **n**, and none spake a H3915
7: 3 wearisome **n** are appointed to me. H3915
Isa 21: 8 and I am set in my ward whole **n**: H3915
Jna 1:17 belly of the fish three days and three **n**. H3915
Mt 4: 2 forty **n**, he was afterward an hungred. G3571
12:40 days and three **n** in the whale's belly; G3571
40 and three **n** in the heart of the earth. G3571

NIGHT-WATCHES See NIGHT and WATCHES.

NIMRAH
Nu 32: 3 Ataroth, and Dibon, and Jazer, and **N**, H5247

NIMRIM
Isa 15: 6 For the waters of **N** shall be desolate: H5249
Jer 48:34 the waters also of **N** shall be desolate. H5249

NIMROD
Gen 10: 8 And Cush begat **N**: he began to be a H5248
9 **N** the mighty hunter before the LORD. H5248
1Ch 1:10 And Cush begat **N**: he began to be H5248
Mic 5: 6 and the land of **N** in the entrances H5248

NIMSHI
1Ki 19:16 And Jehu the son of **N** shalt thou H5250
2Ki 9: 2 the son of **N**, and go in, and make H5250
14 the son of **N** conspired against Joram. H5250
20 the son of **N**; for he driveth furiously. H5250
2Ch 22: 7 Jehu the son of **N**, whom the LORD had H5250

NINE
Gen 5: 5 Adam lived were **n** hundred and thirty H8672
8 And all the days of Seth were **n** H8672
11 And all the days of Enos were **n** H8672
14 And all the days of Cainan were **n** H8672
20 And all the days of Jared were **n** H8672
27 And all the days of Methuselah were **n** H8672
27 sixty and **n** years: and he died. H8672
9:29 And all the days of Noah were **n** H8672
11:19 **n** years, and begat sons and daughters. H8672
24 And Nahor lived **n** and twenty years, H8672
17: 1 years old and **n**, the LORD appeared H8672
24 ninety years old and **n**, when he was H8672
Ex 38:24 was twenty and **n** talents, and seven H8672
Lev 25: 8 shall be unto thee forty and **n** years. H8672
Nu 1:23 and **n** thousand and three hundred. H8672
2:13 and **n** thousand and three hundred. H8672
29:26 And on the fifth day **n** bullocks, two H8672
34:13 unto the **n** tribes, and to the half tribe: H8672
Dt 3:11 of Ammon? **n** cubits *was* the length H8672
Jos 13: 7 unto the **n** tribes, and the half H8672
14: 2 for the **n** tribes, and *for* the half tribe. H8672
15:32 *are* twenty and **n**, with their villages: H8672
44 Mareshah; **n** cities with their villages: H8672
54 and Zior; **n** cities with their villages: H8672

Jos 21:16 n cities out of those two tribes. H8672
Jdg 4: 3 LORD: for he had n hundred chariots H8672
13 his chariots, *even* n hundred chariots H8672
2Sa 24: 8 the end of n months and twenty days. H8672
2Ki 14: 2 twenty and n years in Jerusalem. H8672
15:13 to reign in the n and thirtieth year of H8672
17 In the n and thirtieth year of Azariah H8672
17: 1 to reign in Samaria over Israel n years. H8672
18: 2 twenty and n years in Jerusalem. H8672
1Ch 3: 8 Elishama, and Eliada, and Eliphelet, n. H8672
9: 9 their generations, n hundred and fifty H8672
2Ch 25: 1 twenty and n years in Jerusalem. H8672
29: 1 and he reigned n and twenty years in H8672
Ezr 1: 9 chargers of silver, n and twenty knives, H8672
2: 8 The children of Zattu, n hundred forty H8672
36 Jeshua, n hundred seventy and three. H8672
42 Shobai, *in* all an hundred thirty and n. H8672
Neh 7:38 three thousand n hundred and thirty. H8672
39 Jeshua, n hundred seventy and three. H8672
11: 1 and n parts *to dwell* in *other* cities. H8672
8 And after him Gabbai, Sallai, n H8672
Mt 18:12 the ninety and n, and goeth into the *G1768*
13 ninety and n which went not astray. *G1768*
Lk 15: 4 the ninety and n in the wilderness, and *G1768*
7 over ninety and n just persons, which *G1768*
17:17 not ten cleansed? but where *are* the n? *G1767*

NINE-HUNDRED See NINE and HUNDRED.

NINETEEN
Gen 11:25 an hundred and n years, and H8672+H6240
Jos 19:38 n cities with their villages. H8672+H6240
2Sa 2:30 servants n men and Asahel. H8672+H6240

NINETEENTH
2Ki 25: 8 which *is* the n year of king H8672+H6240
1Ch 24:16 The n to Pethahiah, the H8672+H6240
25:26 The n to Mallothi, *he*, his sons, H8672+H6240
Jer 52:12 which *was* the n year of H8672+H6240

NINETY
Gen 5: 9 And Enos lived n years, and begat H8673
17 hundred n and five years: and he died. H8673
30 five hundred n and five years, and H8673
17: 1 And when Abram was n years old and H8673
17 shall Sarah, that is n years old, bear? H8673
24 And Abraham *was* n years old and H8673
1Sa 4:15 Now Eli was n and eight years old; and H8673
1Ch 9: 6 and their brethren, six hundred and n. H8673
Ezr 2:16 The children of Ater of Hezekiah, n and H8673
20 The children of Gibbar, n and five. H8673
58 *were* three hundred n and two. H8673
8:35 for all Israel, n and six rams, seventy H8673
Neh 7:21 The children of Ater of Hezekiah, n and H8673
25 The children of Gibeon, n and five. H8673
60 *were* three hundred n and two. H8673
Jer 52:23 And there were n and six H8673
Ezk 4: 5 hundred and n days: so shalt thou H8673
9 and n days shalt thou eat thereof. H8673
41:12 about, and the length thereof n cubits. H8673
Dan 12:11 a thousand two hundred and n days. H8673
Mt 18:12 he not leave the n and nine, and goeth *G1768*
13 the n and nine which went not astray. *G1768*
Lk 15: 4 doth not leave the n and nine in the *G1768*
7 more than over n and nine just *G1768*

NINEVE
Lk 11:32 The men of N shall rise up in the *G3535*

NINEVEH
Gen 10:11 N, and the city Rehoboth, and Calah, H5210
12 And Resen between N and Calah: the H5210
2Ki 19:36 and went and returned, and dwelt at N. H5210
Isa 37:37 and went and returned, and dwelt at N. H5210
Jna 1: 2 Arise, go to N, that great city, and cry H5210
3: 2 Arise, go unto N, that great city, and H5210
3 So Jonah arose, and went unto N, H5210
3 of the LORD. Now N was an exceeding H5210
4 forty days, and N shall be overthrown. H5210
5 So the people of N believed God, and H5210
6 For word came unto the king of N, and H5210
7 through N by the decree of the H5210
4:11 And should not I spare N, that great H5210
Nah 1: 1 The burden of N. The book of the vision H5210
2: 8 But N *is* of old like a pool of water: yet H5210
3: 7 thee, and say, N is laid waste: who will H5210
Zep 2:13 and will make N a desolation, *and* dry H5210
Mt 12:41 The men of N shall rise in judgment *G3536*

NINEVITES
Lk 11:30 For as Jonas was a sign unto the N, so *G3536*

NINTH
Lev 23:32 your souls: in the n *day* of the month at H8672
25:22 of old fruit until the n year; until her H8671
Nu 7:60 On the n day Abidan the son of H8671
2Ki 17: 6 In the n year of Hoshea the king of H8671
18:10 that *is* the n year of Hoshea king H8672
25: 1 And it came to pass in the n year of his H8671
3 And on the n *day* of the *fourth* month H8672
1Ch 12:12 Johanan the eighth, Elzabad the n, H8671
24:11 The n to Jeshua, the tenth to H8671
25:16 The n to Mattaniah, *he*, his sons, and H8671
27:12 The n *captain* for the ninth month *was* H8671
12 The ninth *captain* for the n month *was* H8671
2Ch 16:12 And Asa in the thirty and n year of his H8672
Ezr 10: 9 three days. It *was* the n month, on the H8671
Jer 36: 9 king of Judah, in the n month, *that* they H8671
22 in the n month: and *there was* H8671
39: 1 In the n year of Zedekiah king of H8671
2 fourth month, the n *day* of the month, H8672
52: 4 And it came to pass in the n year of his H8671
6 And in the fourth month, in the n *day* H8672
Ezk 24: 1 Again in the n year, in the tenth H8671
Hag 2:10 In the four and twentieth *day* of the n H8671
18 day of the n *month*, *even* from the H8671
Zec 7: 1 *day* of the n month, *even* in Chisleu; H8671
Mt 20: 5 the sixth and n hour, and did likewise. *G1766*
27:45 over all the land unto the n hour. *G1766*
46 And about the n hour Jesus cried with *G1766*
Mk 15:33 over the whole land until the n hour. *G1766*
34 And at the n hour Jesus cried with a *G1766*
Lk 23:44 over all the earth until the n hour. *G1766*
Act 3: 1 at the hour of prayer, *being* the n *hour*. *G1766*
10: 3 about the n hour of the day an angel *G1766*
30 hour; and at the n hour I prayed in my *G1766*
Rev 21:20 eighth, beryl; the n, a topaz; the tenth, a *G1766*

NISAN
Neh 2: 1 And it came to pass in the month N, in H5212
Est 3: 7 In the first month, that *is*, the month N, H5212

NISROCH
2Ki 19:37 in the house of N his god, that H5268
Isa 37:38 in the house of N his god, that H5268

NITRE
Prv 25:20 *as* vinegar upon n, so *is* he that singeth H5427
Jer 2:22 For though thou wash thee with n, and H5427

NO See the Appendix.

NOADIAH
Ezr 8:33 and N the son of Binnui, Levites; H5129
Neh 6:14 on the prophetess N, and the rest of the H5129

NOAH
Gen 5:29 And he called his name N, saying, This H5146
30 And Lamech lived after he begat N five H5146
32 And N was five hundred years old: and H5146
32 and N begat Shem, Ham, and Japheth. H5146
6: 8 But N found grace in the eyes of the H5146
9 These *are* the generations of N: Noah H5146
9 These *are* the generations of Noah: N H5146
9 generations, *and* N walked with God. H5146
10 And N begat three sons, Shem, Ham, H5146
13 And God said unto N, The end of all H5146
22 Thus did N; according to all that God H5146
7: 1 And the LORD said unto N, Come thou H5146
5 And N did according unto all that the H5146
6 And N *was* six hundred years old when H5146
7 And N went in, and his sons, and his H5146
9 There went in two and two unto N into H5146
9 the female, as God had commanded N. H5146
13 In the selfsame day entered N, and H5146
13 the sons of N, and Noah's wife, and H5146
15 And they went in unto N into the ark, H5146
23 the earth: and N only remained *alive*, H5146
8: 1 And God remembered N, and every H5146
6 end of forty days, that N opened the H5146
11 olive leaf pluckt off: so N knew that the H5146
13 from off the earth: and N removed the H5146
15 And God spake unto N, saying, H5146
18 And N went forth, and his sons, and H5146
20 And N builded an altar unto the LORD; H5146
9: 1 And God blessed N and his sons, and H5146
8 And God spake unto N, and to his sons H5146
17 And God said unto N, This *is* the token H5146
Gen 9:18 And the sons of N, that went forth of the H5146
19 These *are* the three sons of N: and of H5146
20 And N began *to be* an husbandman, H5146
24 And N awoke from his wine, and knew H5146
28 And N lived after the flood three H5146
29 And all the days of N were nine H5146
10: 1 of the sons of N, Shem, Ham, and H5146
32 These *are* the families of the sons of N, H5146
Nu 26:33 and N, Hoglah, Milcah, and Tirzah. H5270
27: 1 N, and Hoglah, and Milcah, and Tirzah. H5270
36:11 and Milcah, and N, the daughters of H5270
Jos 17: 3 and N, Hoglah, Milcah, and Tirzah. H5270
1Ch 1: 4 N, Shem, Ham, and Japheth. H5146
Isa 54: 9 For this *is as* the waters of N unto me: H5146
9 that the waters of N should no more go H5146
Ezk 14:14 Though these three men, N, Daniel, and H5146
20 Though N, Daniel, and Job, *were* in it, H5146
Heb 11: 7 By faith N, being warned of God of *G3575*
1Pt 3:20 in the days of N, while the ark was a *G3575*
2Pt 2: 5 world, but saved N the eighth *person*, a *G3575*

NOAH'S
Gen 7:11 In the six hundredth year of N life, in H5146
13 sons of Noah, and N wife, and the three H5146

NOB
1Sa 21: 1 Then came David to N to Ahimelech H5011
22: 9 to N, to Ahimelech the son of Ahitub. H5011
11 that *were* in N: and they came all of H5011
19 And N, the city of the priests, smote he H5011
Neh 11:32 *And* at Anathoth, N, Ananiah, H5011
Isa 10:32 As yet shall he remain at N that day: he H5011

NOBAH
Nu 32:42 And N went and took Kenath, and the H5025
42 and called it N, after his own name. H5025
Jdg 8:11 on the east of N and Jogbehah, and H5025

NOBLE
Ezr 4:10 the great and n Asnappar brought H3358
Est 6: 9 of the king's most n princes, that they H6579
Jer 2:21 Yet I had planted thee a n vine, wholly a
Act 17:11 These were more n than those in *G2104*
24: 3 most n Felix, with all thankfulness. *G2903*
26:25 But he said, I am not mad, most n *G2903*
1Co 1:26 many mighty, not many n, *are called*: *G2104*

NOBLEMAN
Lk 19:12 He said therefore, A certain n went into *G444*
Jn 4:46 n, whose son was sick at Capernaum. *G937*
49 The n saith unto him, Sir, come down *G937*

NOBLES
Ex 24:11 And upon the n of the children of Israel H678
Nu 21:18 The princes digged the well, the n of H5081
Jdg 5:13 dominion over the n among the people: H117
1Ki 21: 8 elders and to the n that *were* in his city, H2715
11 *even* the elders and the n who were the H2715
2Ch 23:20 hundreds, and the n, and the governors H117
Neh 2:16 priests, nor to the n, nor to the rulers, H2715
3: 5 repaired; but their n put not their necks H117
4:14 and said unto the n, and to the rulers, H2715
19 And I said unto the n, and to the rulers, H2715
5: 7 and I rebuked the n, and the rulers, and H2715
6:17 Moreover in those days the n of Judah H2715
7: 5 together the n, and the rulers, and H2715
10:29 They clave to their brethren, their n, and H117
13:17 Then I contended with the n of Judah, H2715
Est 1: 3 and Media, the n and princes of the H6579
Job 29:10 The n held their peace, and their H5057
Ps 83:11 Make their n like Oreb, and like Zeeb: H5081
149: 8 chains, and their n with fetters of iron; H3513
Prv 8:16 By me princes rule, and n, *even* all the H5081
Ecc 10:17 king *is* the son of n, and thy princes eat H2715
Isa 13: 2 that they may go into the gates of the n. H5081
34:12 They shall call the n thereof to the H2715
43:14 down all their n, and the Chaldeans, H1281
Jer 14: 3 And their n have sent their little ones to H117
27:20 and all the n of Judah and Jerusalem; H2715
30:21 And their n shall be of themselves, and H117
39: 6 king of Babylon slew all the n of Judah. H2715
Jna 3: 7 decree of the king and his n, saying, Let H1419
Nah 3:18 of Assyria: thy n shall dwell *in the dust*: H117

NOD
Gen 4:16 in the land of N, on the east of Eden. H5113

NODAB
1Ch 5:19 with Jetur, and Nephish, and N. H5114

NOE
Mt 24:37 But as the days of N *were*, so shall also G3575
38 the day that N entered into the ark, G3575
Lk 3:36 *son* of N, which was *the son* of Lamech, G3575
17:26 And as it was in the days of N, so shall G3575
27 until the day that N entered into the G3575

NOGAH
1Ch 3: 7 And N, and Nepheg, and Japhia, H5052
14: 6 And N, and Nepheg, and Japhia, H5052

NOHAH
1Ch 8: 2 N the fourth, and Rapha the fifth. H5119

NOISE
Ex 20:18 and the **n** of the trumpet, and H6963
32:17 And when Joshua heard the **n** of the H6963
17 Moses, *There is* a **n** of war in the camp. H6963
18 *but* the **n** of *them that* sing do I hear. H6963
Jos 6:10 shout, nor make any **n** with your voice, H8085
Jdg 5:11 *They that are delivered* from the **n** of H6963
1Sa 4: 6 And when the Philistines heard the **n** of H6963
6 *meaneth* the **n** of this great shout in H6963
14 And when Eli heard the **n** of the crying, H6963
14 *meaneth* the **n** of this tumult? And H6963
14:19 the priest, that the **n** that *was* in the H1995
1Ki 1:41 *is this* **n** of the city being in an uproar? H6963
45 again. This *is* the **n** that ye have heard. H6963
2Ki 7: 6 Syrians to hear a **n** of chariots, and a H6963
6 of chariots, and a **n** of horses, *even* the H6963
6 of horses, *even* the **n** of a great host: H6963
11:13 And when Athaliah heard the **n** of the H6963
1Ch 15:28 making a **n** with psalteries and harps. H8085
2Ch 23:12 Now when Athaliah heard the **n** of the H6963
Ezr 3:13 not discern the **n** of the shout of joy H6963
13 of joy from the **n** of the weeping of the H6963
13 shout, and the **n** was heard afar off. H6963
Job 36:29 the clouds, *or* the **n** of his tabernacle? H8663
33 The **n** thereof sheweth concerning it, H7452
37: 2 Hear attentively the **n** of his voice, and H7267
Ps 33: 3 a new song; play skilfully with a loud **n**. H8643
42: 7 Deep calleth unto deep at the **n** of thy H6963
55: 2 mourn in my complaint, and make a **n**; H1949
59: 6 They return at evening: they make a **n** H1993
14 let them make a **n** like a dog, and go H1993
65: 7 Which stilleth the **n** of the seas, the H7588
7 of the seas, the **n** of their waves, and H7588
66: 1 Make a joyful **n** unto God, all ye lands: H7321
81: 1 make a joyful **n** unto the God of Jacob. H7321
93: 4 *is* mightier than the **n** of many waters, H6963
95: 1 a joyful **n** to the rock of our salvation. H7321
2 make a joyful **n** unto him with psalms. H7321
98: 4 Make a joyful **n** unto the LORD, all the H7321
4 a loud **n**, and rejoice, and sing praise. H6476
6 a joyful **n** before the LORD, the King. H7321
100: 1 Make a joyful **n** unto the LORD, all ye H7321
Isa 9: 5 *is* with confused **n**, and garments rolled H7494
13: 4 The **n** of a multitude in the mountains, H6963
4 a tumultuous **n** of the kingdoms of H6963
14:11 to the grave, *and* the **n** of thy viols: the H1998
17:12 *which* make a **n** like the noise of the H1993
12 a noise like the **n** of the seas; and to the H1993
24: 8 The mirth of tabrets ceaseth, the **n** of H7588
18 fleeth from the **n** of the fear shall fall H6963
25: 5 Thou shalt bring down the **n** of H7588
29: 6 and great **n**, with storm and tempest, H6963
31: 4 himself for the **n** of them: so shall the H1995
33: 3 At the **n** of the tumult the people fled; H6963
66: 6 A voice of **n** from the city, a voice from H7588
Jer 4:19 heart maketh a **n** in me; I cannot hold H1993
29 The whole city shall flee for the **n** of the H6963
10:22 Behold, the **n** of the bruit is come, and H6963
11:16 fruit: with the **n** of a great tumult he H6963
25:31 A **n** shall come *even* to the ends of the H7588
46:17 a **n**; he hath passed the time appointed. H7588
47: 3 At the **n** of the stamping of the hoofs of H6963
49:21 The earth is moved at the **n** of their fall, H6963
21 the **n** thereof was heard in the Red sea. H6963
50:46 At the **n** of the taking of Babylon the H6963
51:55 waters, a **n** of their voice is uttered: H7588
Lam 2: 7 they have made a **n** in the house of the H6963
Ezk 1:24 And when they went, I heard the **n** of H6963
24 wings, like the **n** of great waters, as the H6963
24 of speech, as the **n** of an host: when H6963
3:13 *I heard* also the **n** of the wings of the H6963
13 another, and the **n** of the wheels over H6963
13 them, and a **n** of a great rushing. H6963
19: 7 fulness thereof, by the **n** of his roaring. H6963
26:10 shall shake at the **n** of the horsemen, H6963
Ezk 26:13 And I will cause the **n** of thy songs to H1995
37: 7 there was a **n**, and behold a shaking, H6963
43: 2 voice *was* like a **n** of many waters: and H6963
Joel 2: 5 Like the **n** of chariots on the tops of H6963
5 they leap, like the **n** of a flame of fire H6963
Am 5:23 Take thou away from me the **n** of thy H1995
Mic 2:12 **n** by reason of *the multitude of* men. H1949
Nah 3: 2 The **n** of a whip, and the noise of the H6963
2 The noise of a whip, and the **n** of the H6963
Zep 1:10 *there shall be* the **n** of a cry from the H6963
Zec 9:15 drink, *and* make a **n** as through wine; H1993
Mt 9:23 minstrels and the people making a **n**, G2350
2Pt 3:10 away with a great **n**, and the elements G4500
Rev 6: 1 as it were the **n** of thunder, one of the G5456

NOISED
Jos 6:27 fame was *n* throughout all the country.
Mk 2: 1 and it was **n** that he was in the house. G191
Lk 1:65 sayings were **n** abroad throughout G1255
Act 2: 6 Now when this was **n** abroad, G1096+G5408

NOISOME
Ps 91: 3 the fowler, *and* from the **n** pestilence. H1942
Ezk 14:15 If I cause **n** beasts to pass through the H7451
21 the famine, and the **n** beast, and the H7451
Rev 16: 2 and there fell a **n** and grievous sore G2556

NON
1Ch 7:27 N his son, Jehoshua his son. H5126

NONE
Gen 23: 6 bury thy dead; **n** of us shall withhold H3808
28:17 *is* this place! this *is* **n** other but the house H369
39: 9 *There is* **n** greater in this house than I; H369
11 **n** of the men of the house there within. H369
41: 8 but *there was* **n** that could interpret H369
15 and *there is* **n** that can interpret it: H369
24 *there was* **n** that could declare *it* to me. H369
39 *is* **n** so discreet and wise as thou *art*: H369
Ex 8:10 *there is* **n** like unto the LORD our God. H369
9:14 that *there is* **n** like me in all the earth. H369
24 such as there was **n** like it in all the H3808
11: 6 **n** like it, nor shall be like it any more. H3808
12:22 in the bason; and **n** of you shall go out at H376
15:26 statutes, I will put **n** of these diseases H3808
16:26 *is* the sabbath, in it there shall be **n**. H3808
27 day for to gather, and they found **n**. H3808
23:15 and **n** shall appear before me empty:) H3808
34:20 And **n** shall appear before me empty. H3808
Lev 18: 6 N of you shall approach to any H376+H3808
21: 1 them, There shall **n** be defiled for the H3808
22:30 eaten up; ye shall leave **n** of it until the H3808
25:26 And if the man have **n** to redeem it, H3808
26: 6 ye shall lie down, and **n** shall make *you* H369
17 and ye shall flee when **n** pursueth you. H369
36 and they shall fall when **n** pursueth. H369
37 a sword, when **n** pursueth: and ye shall H369
27:29 N devoted, which shall be devoted of H3808
Nu 7: 9 But unto the sons of Kohath he gave **n**: H3808
9:12 They shall leave **n** of it unto the H3808
21:35 until there was **n** left him alive: and H1115
30: 8 she bound her soul, of **n** effect: and the H6565
32:11 Surely **n** of the men that came up out of H518
Dt 2:34 ones, of every city, we left **n** to remain: H3808
3: 3 him until **n** was left to him remaining. H1115
4:35 he *is* God; *there is* **n** else beside him. H369
39 upon the earth beneath: *there is* **n** else. H369
5: 7 Thou shalt have **n** other gods before me.
7:15 and will put **n** of the evil diseases H3808
22:27 cried, and *there was* **n** to save her. H369
28:31 and thou shalt have **n** to rescue *them*. H369
66 and shalt have **n** assurance of thy life: H3808
32:36 is gone, and *there is* **n** shut up, or left. H657
33:26 *There is* **n** like unto the God of Jeshurun, H369
Jos 6: 1 of Israel: **n** went out, and none came in. H369
1 of Israel: none went out, and **n** came in. H369
8:22 they let **n** of them remain or escape. H1115
9:23 and there shall **n** of you be freed from H3808
10:21 in peace: **n** moved his tongue against H3808
28 therein; he let **n** remain: and he did H3808
30 therein; he let **n** remain in it; but did H3808
33 until he had left him **n** remaining. H1115
37 therein; he left **n** remaining, according H3808
39 therein; he left **n** remaining: as he had H3808
40 all their kings: he left **n** remaining, but H3808
11: 8 them, until they left them **n** remaining. H1115
13 Israel burned **n** of them, save Hazor H3808
22 There was **n** of the Anakims left in the H3808
13:14 Only unto the tribe of Levi he gave **n** H3808
Jos 14: 3 he gave **n** inheritance among them. H3808
Jdg 19:28 let us be going. But **n** answered. Then H369
21: 8 behold, there came **n** to the camp from H376
9 behold, *there were* **n** of the inhabitants H376
Ru 4: 4 know: for *there is* **n** to redeem *it* beside H369
1Sa 2: 2 *There is* **n** holy as the LORD: for *there is* H369
2 LORD: for *there is* **n** beside thee: neither H369
3:19 did let **n** of his words fall to the ground. H3808
10:24 that *there is* **n** like him among all the H369
14:24 So **n** of the people tasted *any* food. H3808
21: 9 said, *There is* **n** like that; give it me. H369
22: 8 me, and *there is* **n** that sheweth me that
8 Jesse, and *there is* **n** of you that is sorry H369
2Sa 7:22 God: for *there is* **n** like thee, neither *is* H369
14: 6 and *there was* **n** to part them, but the H369
19 my lord the king, **n** can turn to the right H376
25 But in all Israel there was **n** to be so H376
18:12 that **n** *touch* the young man Absalom.
22:42 They looked, but *there was* **n** to save; H369
1Ki 3:12 so that there was **n** like thee before H3808
8:60 LORD *is* God, *and that there is* **n** else. H369
10:21 *were of* pure gold; **n** *were of* silver: it was H369
12:20 all Israel: there was **n** that followed the H3808
15:22 all Judah; **n** *was* exempted: and H369
21:25 But there was **n** like unto Ahab, which H3808
2Ki 5:16 I will receive **n**. And he urged him to
6:12 And one of his servants said, N, my H3808
9:10 and *there shall be* **n** to bury *her*. And he H369
15 minds, *then* let **n** go forth *nor* escape out H408
10:11 priests, until he left him **n** remaining. H1115
19 and all his priests; let **n** be wanting: for I H376
23 be here with you **n** of the servants of the
25 in, *and* slay them; let **n** come forth. And H376
17:18 was **n** left but the tribe of Judah only. H3808
18: 5 so that after him was **n** like him among H3808
24:14 and smiths: **n** remained, save the H3808
1Ch 15: 2 Then David said, N ought to carry the H3808
17:20 O LORD, *there is* **n** like thee, neither *is* H369
23:17 And Eliezer had **n** other sons; but the H3808
29:15 *are* as a shadow, and *there is* **n** abiding. H369
2Ch 1:12 honour, such as **n** of the kings have H3808
9:11 **n** such seen before in the land of Judah. H3808
20 *were of* pure gold: **n** *were of* silver; it was H369
10:16 and *we have* **n** inheritance in the son H3808
16: 1 that he might let **n** go out or come in to H1115
20: 6 so that **n** is able to withstand thee? H369
24 fallen to the earth, and **n** escaped. H369
23: 6 But let **n** come into the house of the H408
19 of the LORD, that **n** *which was* unclean H3808
Ezr 8:15 and found there **n** of the sons of Levi. H3808
Neh 4:23 followed me, **n** of us put off our clothes, H369
Est 1: 8 to the law; **n** did compel: for so the H369
4: 2 the king's gate: for **n** *might* enter into the H369
Job 1: 8 Job, that *there is* **n** like him in the earth, H369
2: 3 Job, that *there is* **n** like him in the earth, H369
13 seven nights, and **n** spake a word unto H369
3: 9 for light, but *have* **n**; neither let it see the H369
10: 7 *is* **n** that can deliver out of thine hand. H369
11:19 Also thou shalt lie down, and **n** shall H369
18:15 because *it is* **n** of his: brimstone shall H1097
20:21 There shall **n** of his meat be left; H369
29:12 and *him that had* **n** to help him. H3808
32:12 and, behold, *there was* **n** of you that H369
35:10 But **n** saith, Where *is* God my maker, H3808
12 There they cry, but **n** giveth answer, H3808
41:10 N *is so* fierce that dare stir him up: who H3808
Ps 7: 2 *it* in pieces, while *there is* **n** to deliver. H369
10:15 seek out his wickedness *till* thou find **n**. H1077
14: 1 works, *there is* **n** that doeth good. H369
3 *there is* **n** that doeth good, no, not one. H369
18:41 They cried, but *there was* **n** to save H369
22:11 for trouble *is* near; for *there is* **n** to help. H369
29 him: and **n** can keep alive his own soul. H3808
25: 3 Yea, let **n** that wait on thee be H3808
33:10 the devices of the people of **n** effect. H5106
34:22 his servants: and **n** of them that trust H3808
37:31 The law of his God *is* in his heart; **n** of H3808
49: 7 N *of them* can by any means redeem H3808
50:22 *you* in pieces, and *there be* **n** to deliver. H369
53: 1 iniquity: *there is* **n** that doeth good. H369
3 *there is* **n** that doeth good, no, not one. H369
69:20 **n**; and for comforters, but I found none. H369
20 none; and for comforters, but I found **n**. H3808
25 desolate; *and* let **n** dwell in their tents. H408
71:11 take him; for *there is* **n** to deliver *him*. H369
73:25 **n** upon earth *that* I desire beside thee. H3808
76: 5 their sleep: and **n** of the men of might H3808
79: 3 and *there was* **n** to bury *them*. H369
81:11 to my voice; and Israel would **n** of me. H3808

Ps 86: 8 Among the gods *there is* **n** like unto thee, H369
107:12 they fell down, and *there was* **n** to help. H369
109:12 Let there be **n** to extend mercy unto him: H408
139:16 when *as yet there was* **n** of them. H259
Prv 1:25 counsel, and would **n** of my reproof: H3808
30 They would **n** of my counsel: they H3808
2:19 **N** that go unto her return again, H3808
3:31 the oppressor, and choose **n** of his ways. H408
Song 4: 2 bear twins, and **n** *is* barren among them. H369
Isa 1:31 burn together, and **n** shall quench *them*. H369
5:27 **N** shall be weary nor stumble among H369
27 among them; **n** shall slumber nor H3808
29 carry *it* away safe, and **n** shall deliver *it*. H369
10:14 and there was **n** that moved the wing, H3808
14: 6 anger, is persecuted, *and* **n** hindereth. H1097
31 **n** *shall be* alone in his appointed times. H369
17: 2 lie down, and **n** shall make *them* afraid. H369
22:22 he shall open, and **n** shall shut; and he H369
22 and he shall shut, and **n** shall open. H369
34:10 **n** shall pass through it for ever and ever. H369
12 to the kingdom, but **n** *shall be* there, and H369
16 of these shall fail, **n** shall want her mate: H802
41:17 water, and *there is* **n**, *and* their tongue H369
26 yea, *there is* **n** that sheweth, yea, *there* H369
26 yea, *there is* **n** that declareth, yea, *there* H369
26 yea, *there is* **n** that heareth your words. H369
42:22 are for a prey, and **n** delivereth; for a H369
22 for a spoil, and **n** saith, Restore. H369
43:13 I *am* he; and *there is* **n** that can deliver H369
44:19 And **n** considereth in his heart, neither H3808
45: 5 I *am* the LORD, and *there is* **n** else, *there* H369
6 west, that *there is* **n** beside me. I *am* the H657
6 me. I *am* the LORD, and *there is* **n** else. H369
14 thee; and *there is* **n** else, *there is* no God. H369
18 I *am* the LORD; and *there is* **n** else. H369
21 God and a Saviour; *there is* **n** beside me. H369
22 earth: for I *am* God, and *there is* **n** else. H369
46: 9 God, and *there is* **n** else; *I am* God, and H369
9 else; *I am* God, and *there is* **n** like me, H657
47: 8 heart, I *am*, and **n** else beside me; I shall H657
10 thou hast said, **N** seeth me. Thy wisdom H369
10 thine heart, I *am*, and **n** else beside me. H657
15 one to his quarter; **n** shall save thee. H369
50: 2 I called, *was there* **n** to answer? Is my H369
51:18 *There is* **n** to guide her among all the H369
57: 1 *are* taken away, **n** considering that the H369
59: 4 **N** calleth for justice, nor *any* pleadeth H369
11 **n**; for salvation, *but* it is far off from us. H369
63: 3 the people *there was* **n** with me: for I will H376
5 And I looked, and *there was* **n** to help; H369
5 that *there was* **n** to uphold: therefore H369
64: 7 And *there is* **n** that calleth upon thy H369
66: 4 when I called, **n** did answer; when I H369
Jer 4: 4 like fire, and burn that **n** can quench *it*, H369
22 and they have **n** understanding: they H3808
7:33 of the earth; and **n** shall fray *them* away. H369
9:10 burned up, so that **n** can pass through H376
12 a wilderness, that **n** passeth through? H1997
22 harvestman, and **n** shall gather *them*. H369
10: 6 Forasmuch as *there is* **n** like unto thee, O H369
7 their kingdoms, *there is* **n** like unto thee. H369
20 *are* not: *there is* **n** to stretch forth my H369
13:19 shall be shut up, and **n** shall open *them*: H369
14:16 they shall have **n** to bury them, them, H369
21:12 like fire, and burn that **n** can quench *it*, H369
23:14 of evildoers, that **n** doth return from his H376
30: 7 Alas! for that day *is* great, so that **n** *is* H369
10 be quiet, and **n** shall make *him* afraid. H369
13 *There is* **n** to plead thy cause, that thou H369
34: 9 go free; that **n** should serve himself H376
10 go free, that **n** should serve themselves H1115
35:14 day they drink **n**, but obey their father's H3808
36:30 He shall have **n** to sit upon the throne H3808
42:17 pestilence: and **n** of them shall remain H3808
44: 7 out of Judah, to leave you **n** to remain; H1115
14 So that **n** of the remnant of Judah, H3808
14 **n** shall return but such as shall escape. H3808
46:27 at ease, and **n** shall make *him* afraid. H369
48:33 the winepresses: **n** shall tread with H3808
49: 5 **n** shall gather up him that wandereth. H369
50: 3 her land desolate, and **n** shall dwell H3808
9 expert man; **n** shall return in vain. H3808
20 for, and *there shall be* **n**; and the sins of H369
29 it round about; let **n** thereof escape: H408
32 and fall, and **n** shall raise him up: and H369
51:62 to cut it off, that **n** shall remain in it, H1115
Lam 1: 2 her lovers she hath **n** to comfort *her*: all H369
4 The ways of Zion do mourn, because **n** H1997
7 of the enemy, and **n** did help her: the H369
Lam 1:17 hands, *and there is* **n** to comfort her: the H369
21 They have heard that I sigh: *there is* **n** to H369
2:22 of the LORD'S anger **n** escaped nor H3808
5: 8 Servants have ruled over us: *there is* **n** H369
Ezk 7:11 of wickedness: **n** of them *shall remain*, H3808
14 all ready; but **n** goeth to the battle: for H369
25 shall seek peace, and *there shall be* **n**. H369
12:28 GOD; There shall **n** of my words be H3808
16: 5 **N** eye pitied thee, to do any of these H3808
34 whereas **n** followeth thee to commit H3808
18: 7 hath spoiled **n** by violence, hath given H3808
22:30 I should not destroy it: but I found **n**. H3808
31:14 To the end that **n** of all the trees by the H3808
33:16 **N** of his sins that he hath committed H3808
28 be desolate, that **n** shall pass through. H369
34: 6 and **n** did search or seek *after them*. H369
28 safely, and **n** shall make *them* afraid. H369
39:26 in their land, and **n** made *them* afraid. H369
28 and have left **n** of them any more there. H3808
Dan 1:19 all was found **n** like Daniel, Hananiah, H3808
2:11 and there is **n** other that can shew H3809
4:35 of the earth: and **n** can stay his hand, H3809
6: 4 they could find **n** occasion nor fault; H3809
8: 7 and there was **n** that could deliver the H3808
27 at the vision, but **n** understood *it*. H369
10:21 of truth: and *there is* **n** that holdeth with H259
11:16 to his own will, and **n** shall stand before H369
45 come to his end, and **n** shall help him. H369
12:10 do wickedly: and **n** of the wicked shall H3808
Hos 2:10 and **n** shall deliver her out of mine hand. H376
5:14 I will take away, and **n** shall rescue *him*. H369
7: 7 *is* **n** among them that calleth unto me. H369
11: 7 most High, **n** at all would exalt *him*. H3808
12: 8 find **n** iniquity in me that *were* sin. H3808
Joel 2:27 your God, and **n** else: and my people H369
Am 5: 2 upon her land; *there is* **n** to raise her up. H369
6 *it*, and *there be* **n** to quench *it* in Beth-el. H369
Oba 7 thee: *there is* **n** understanding in him. H369
Mic 2: 5 Therefore thou shalt have **n** that shall H3808
3:11 among us? **n** evil can come upon us. H3808
4: 4 his fig tree; and **n** shall make *them* H369
5: 8 and teareth in pieces, and **n** can deliver. H369
7: 2 the earth: and *there is* **n** upright among H369
Nah 2: 8 *shall they cry*; but **n** shall look back. H369
9 of gold: for *there is* **n** end of the store H369
11 lion's whelp, and **n** made *them* afraid? H369
3: 3 and *there is* **n** end of *their* corpses; H369
Zep 2:15 I *am*, and *there is* **n** beside me: how is H657
3: 6 streets waste, that **n** passeth by: their H1097
6 is no man, that there is **n** inhabitant. H369
13 lie down, and **n** shall make *them* afraid. H369
Hag 1: 6 you, but there is **n** warm; and he that H369
Zec 7:10 the poor; and let **n** of you imagine evil H376
8:17 And let **n** of you imagine evil in your H376
Mal 2:15 your spirit, and let **n** deal treacherously H408
Mt 12:43 dry places, seeking rest, and findeth **n**. G3762
15: 6 of God of **n** effect by your tradition. G208
19:17 me good? *there is* **n** good but one, *that* G3762
26:60 But found **n**: yea, though many false G3756
60 **n**. At the last came two false witnesses, G3756
Mk 7:13 Making the word of God of **n** effect G208
10:18 *there is* **n** good but one, *that is*, God. G3762
12:31 as thyself. There is **n** other G3756
32 is one God; and there is **n** other but he: G3756
14:55 Jesus to put him to death; and found **n**. G3756
Lk 1:61 And they said unto her, There is **n** of G3762
3:11 to him that hath **n**; and he that hath G3361
4:26 But unto **n** of them was Elias sent, save G3762
27 Eliseus the prophet; and **n** of them was G3762
11:24 rest; and finding **n**, he saith, I will G3361
13: 6 and sought fruit thereon, and found **n**. G3756
7 fig tree, and find **n**: cut it down; why G3756
14:24 For I say unto you, That **n** of those men G3762
18:19 good? **n** *is* good, save one, *that is*, God. G3762
34 And they understood **n** of these things: G3762
Jn 6:22 that there was **n** other boat there, save G3756
7:19 the law, and *yet* **n** of you keepeth the G3762
8:10 himself, and saw **n** but the woman, he G3367
15:24 the works which **n** other man did, they G3762
16: 5 that sent me; and **n** of you asketh me, G3762
17:12 I have kept, and **n** of them is lost, but G3762
18: 9 which thou gavest me have I lost **n**. G3762
21:12 and dine. And **n** of the disciples durst G3762
Act 3: 6 and gold have I **n**; but such as I have G3756
4:12 other: for there is **n** other name under G3777
7: 5 And he gave him **n** inheritance in it, G3756
8:16 (For as yet he was fallen upon **n** of G3762
24 the Lord for me, that **n** of these things G3357
11:19 the word to **n** but unto the Jews only. G3367
Act 18:17 And Gallio cared for **n** of those things. G3762
20:24 But **n** of these things move me, neither G3762
24:23 he should forbid **n** of his acquaintance G3367
25:11 to die: but if there be **n** of these things G3762
18 up, they brought **n** accusation of such G3762
26:22 and great, saying **n** other things than G3762
26 persuaded that **n** of these things are G3762
Ro 3:10 As it is written, There is **n** righteous, G3756
11 There is **n** that understandeth, there is G3756
11 there is **n** that seeketh after God. G3756
12 there is **n** that doeth good, no, not one. G3756
4:14 void, and the promise made of **n** effect: G2673
8: 9 not the Spirit of Christ, he is **n** of his. G3756
9: 6 of God hath taken **n** effect. For they *are* G1601
14: 7 For **n** of us liveth to himself, and no G3762
1Co 1:14 I thank God that I baptized **n** of you, G3762
17 of Christ should be made of **n** effect. G2758
2: 8 Which **n** of the princes of this world G3762
7:29 have wives be as though they had **n**; G3361
8: 4 and that *there is* **n** other God but one. G3762
9:15 But I have used **n** of these things: G3762
10:32 Give **n** offence, neither to the Jews, nor G677
14:10 and **n** of them *is* without signification. G3762
2Co 1:13 For we write **n** other things unto you, G3756
Gal 1:19 But other of the apostles saw I **n**, save G3756
3:17 it should make the promise of **n** effect. G208
5:10 that ye will be **n** otherwise minded: G3762
1Th 5:15 See that **n** render evil for evil unto any G3361
1Ti 5:14 guide the house, give **n** occasion to the G3367
1Pt 4:15 But let **n** of you suffer as a murderer, or G3361
1Jn 2:10 is **n** occasion of stumbling in him. G3756
Rev 2:10 Fear **n** of those things which thou shalt G3367
24 I will put upon you **n** other burden. G3756

NOON

Gen 43:16 for *these* men shall dine with me at **n**. H6672
25 Joseph came at **n**: for they heard that H6672
2Sa 4: 5 of Ish-bosheth, who lay on a bed at **n**. H6672
1Ki 18:26 even until **n**, saying, O Baal, hear H6672
27 And it came to pass at **n**, that Elijah H6672
20:16 And they went out at **n**. But Ben-hadad H6672
2Ki 4:20 he sat on her knees till **n**, and *then* died. H6672
Ps 55:17 Evening, and morning, and at **n**, will I H6672
Song 1: 7 *thy flock* to rest at **n**: for why should I H6672
Jer 6: 4 and let us go up at **n**. Woe unto us! for H6672
Am 8: 9 sun to go down at **n**, and I will darken H6672
Zep 2: 4 **n** day, and Ekron shall be rooted up. H6672
Act 22: 6 unto Damascus about **n**, suddenly there G3314

NOONDAY

Dt 28:29 And thou shalt grope at **n**, as the blind H6672
Job 5:14 and grope in the **n** as in the night. H6672
11:17 be clearer than the **n**; thou shalt shine H6672
Ps 37: 6 as the light, and thy judgment as the **n**. H6672
91: 6 for the destruction *that* wasteth at **n**. H6672
Isa 16: 3 in the midst of the **n**; hide the outcasts; H6672
58:10 obscurity, and thy darkness *be* as the **n**: H6672
59:10 we stumble at **n** as in the night; *we are* H6672
Jer 15: 8 men a spoiler at **n**: I have caused *him* to H6672

NOONTIDE

Jer 20:16 and the shouting at **n**; H6256+H6672

NOPH

Isa 19:13 the princes of **N** are deceived; they H5297
Jer 2:16 Also the children of **N** and Tahapanes H5297
44: 1 and at **N**, and in the country H5297
46:14 and publish in **N** and in Tahpanhes: H5297
19 into captivity: for **N** shall be waste and H5297
Ezk 30:13 to cease out of **N**; and there shall be no H5297
16 and **N** *shall have* distresses daily. H5297

NOPHAH

Nu 21:30 unto **N**, which *reacheth* unto Medeba. H5302

NOR See the Appendix.

NORTH

Gen 28:14 east, and to the **n**, and to the south: and H6828
Ex 26:20 the **n** side *there shall be* twenty boards: H6828
35 thou shalt put the table on the **n** side. H6828
27:11 And likewise for the **n** side in length H6828
36:25 the **n** corner, he made twenty boards, H6828
38:11 And for the **n** side *the hangings were* H6828
Nu 2:25 *shall be* on the **n** side by their armies: H6828
34: 7 And this shall be your **n** border: from H6828
9 this shall be your **n** border. H6828
35: 5 cubits, and on the **n** side two thousand H6828
Jos 8:11 pitched on the **n** side of Ai: now *there* H6828

Jos 8:13 that *was* on the **n** of the city, and their H6828
11: 2 And to the kings that *were* on the **n** of H6828
15: 5 *their* border in the **n** quarter *was* from H6828
6 along by the **n** of Beth-arabah; and H6828
10 *is* Chesalon, on the **n** side, and went H6828
16: 6 on the **n** side; and the border H6828
17: 9 also *was* on the **n** side of the river, and H6828
10 on the **n**, and in Issachar on the east. H6828
18: 5 shall abide in their coasts on the **n**. H6828
12 And their border on the **n** side was H6828
12 of Jericho on the **n** side, and went up H6828
16 of the giants on the **n**, and descended to H6828
17 And was drawn from the **n**, and went H6828
19 border were at the **n** bay of the salt sea H6828
19:14 And the border compasseth it on the **n** H6828
27 toward the **n** side of Beth-emek, H6828
24:30 on the **n** side of the hill of Gaash. H6828
Jdg 2: 9 on the **n** side of the hill Gaash. H6828
7: 1 were on the **n** side of them, by the H6828
21:19 which *is* on the **n** side of Beth-el, on the H6828
1Ki 7:25 toward the **n**, and three looking toward H6828
2Ki 16:14 and put it on the **n** side of the altar. H6828
1Ch 9:24 toward the east, west, **n**, and south. H6828
2Ch 4: 4 toward the **n**, and three looking toward H6828
Job 26: 7 He stretcheth out the **n** over the empty H6828
37: 9 the whirlwind: and cold out of the **n**. H4215
22 Fair weather cometh out of the **n**: with H6828
Ps 48: 2 sides of the **n**, the city of the great King. H6828
89:12 The **n** and the south thou hast created H6828
107: 3 west, from the **n**, and from the south. H6828
Prv 25:23 The **n** wind driveth away rain: so *doth* H6828
Ecc 1: 6 about unto the **n**; it whirleth about H6828
11: 3 or toward the **n**, in the place where the H6828
Song 4:16 Awake, O **n** wind; and come, thou H6828
Isa 14:13 the congregation, in the sides of the **n**: H6828
31 come from the **n** a smoke, and none H6828
41:25 I have raised up *one* from the **n**, and he H6828
43: 6 I will say to the **n**, Give up; and to the H6828
49:12 lo, these from the **n** and from the west; H6828
Jer 1:13 and the face thereof *is* toward the **n**. H6828
14 me, Out of the **n** an evil shall break H6828
15 kingdoms of the **n**, saith the LORD; and H6828
3:12 words toward the **n**, and say, Return, H6828
18 of the land of the **n** to the land that I H6828
4: 6 evil from the **n**, and a great destruction. H6828
6: 1 out of the **n**, and great destruction. H6828
22 cometh from the **n** country, and a great H6828
10:22 out of the **n** country, to make the H6828
13:20 come from the **n**: where *is* the flock *that* H6828
16:15 the land of the **n**, and from all the lands H6828
23: 8 of Israel out of the **n** country, and from H6828
25: 9 all the families of the **n**, saith the LORD, H6828
26 And all the kings of the **n**, far and near, H6828
31: 8 Behold, I will bring them from the **n** H6828
46: 6 toward the **n** by the river Euphrates. H6828
10 in the **n** country by the river Euphrates. H6828
20 cometh; it cometh out of the **n**. H6828
24 into the hand of the people of the **n**. H6828
47: 2 rise up out of the **n**, and shall be an H6828
50: 3 For out of the **n** there cometh up a H6828
9 nations from the **n** country: and they H6828
41 Behold, a people shall come from the **n**, H6828
51:48 unto her from the **n**, saith the LORD. H6828
Ezk 1: 4 came out of the **n**, a great cloud, and a H6828
8: 3 toward the **n**; where *was* the seat H6828
5 way toward the **n**. So I lifted up mine H6828
5 the way toward the **n**, and behold H6828
14 *was* toward the **n**; and, behold, there sat H6828
9: 2 lieth toward the **n**, and every man a H6828
20:47 south to the **n** shall be burned therein. H6828
21: 4 against all flesh from the south to the **n**: H6828
26: 7 of kings, from the **n**, with horses, and H6828
32:30 There *be* the princes of the **n**, all of H6828
38: 6 Togarmah of the **n** quarters, and all his H6828
15 thy place out of the **n** parts, thou, and H6828
39: 2 to come up from the **n** parts, and will H6828
40:20 looked toward the **n**, he measured the H6828
23 gate toward the **n**, and toward the east; H6828
35 And he brought me to the **n** gate, and H6828
40 up to the entry of the **n** gate, *were* two H6828
44 *was* at the side of the **n** gate; and their H6828
44 gate *having* the prospect toward the **n**. H6828
46 *is* toward the **n** *is* for the priests, the H6828
41:11 door toward the **n**, and another door H6828
42: 1 way toward the **n**: and he brought me H6828
1 *was* before the building toward the **n**. H6828
2 cubits *was* the **n** door, and the breadth H6828
4 one cubit; and their doors toward the **n**. H6828
11 *were* toward the **n**, as long as they, *and* H6828
Ezk 42:13 Then said he unto me, The **n** chambers H6828
17 He measured the **n** side, five hundred H6828
44: 4 Then brought he me the way of the **n** H6828
46: 9 in by the way of the **n** gate to worship H6828
9 by the way of the **n** gate: he shall not H6828
19 looked toward the **n**: and, behold, there H6828
47:15 land toward the **n** side, from the great H6828
17 and the **n** northward, and the H6828
17 of Hamath. And *this is* the **n** side. H6828
48: 1 tribes. From the **n** end to the coast of H6828
10 toward the **n** five and twenty thousand H6828
16 thereof; the **n** side four thousand H6828
17 be toward the **n** two hundred and fifty, H6828
30 of the city on the **n** side, four thousand H6828
Dan 11: 6 come to the king of the **n** to make an H6828
7 of the king of the **n**, and shall deal H6828
8 *more* years than the king of the **n**. H6828
11 the king of the **n**: and he shall set forth H6828
13 For the king of the **n** shall return, and H6828
15 So the king of the **n** shall come, and H6828
40 the king of the **n** shall come against H6828
44 east and out of the **n** shall trouble him: H6828
Am 8:12 to sea, and from the **n** even to the east, H6828
Zep 2:13 his hand against the **n**, and destroy H6828
Zec 2: 6 the land of the **n**, saith the LORD: for H6828
6: 6 go forth into the **n** country; and the H6828
8 that go toward the **n** country have H6828
8 have quieted my spirit in the **n** country. H6828
14: 4 the **n**, and half of it toward the south. H6828
Lk 13:29 and from the **n**, and *from* the south, *G1005*
Act 27:12 lieth toward the south west and **n** west. *G5566*
Rev 21:13 On the east three gates; on the **n** three *G1005*

NORTHERN
Jer 15:12 Shall iron break the **n** iron and the H6828
Joel 2:20 But I will remove far off from you the **n** H6830

NORTHWARD
Gen 13:14 where thou art **n**, and southward, and H6828
Ex 40:22 of the tabernacle **n**, without the vail. H6828
Lev 1:11 the side of the altar **n** before the LORD: H6828
Nu 3:35 pitch on the side of the tabernacle **n**. H6828
Dt 2: 3 this mountain long enough: turn you **n**. H6828
3:27 westward, and **n**, and southward, and H6828
Jos 13: 3 borders of Ekron **n**, *which* is counted to H6828
15: 7 of Achor, and so **n**, looking toward H6828
8 *is* at the end of the valley of the giants **n**: H6828
11 the side of Ekron **n**: and the border was H6828
17:10 Southward *it was* Ephraim's, and **n** *it* H6828
18:18 Arabah **n**, and went down unto Arabah: H6828
19 of Beth-hoglah **n**: and the outgoings of H6828
Jdg 12: 1 and went **n**, and said unto Jephthah, H6828
1Sa 14: 5 The forefront of the one *was* situate **n** H6828
1Ch 26:14 they cast lots; and his lot came out **n**. H6828
17 Eastward *were* six Levites, **n** four a H6828
Ezk 8: 5 north, and behold **n** at the gate of the H6828
40:19 an hundred cubits eastward and **n**. H6828
47: 2 way of the gate **n**, and led me about the H6828
17 and the north **n**, and the border of H6828
48: 1 of Damascus **n**, to the coast of Hamath; H6828
31 of Israel: three gates **n**; one gate of H6828
Dan 8: 4 westward, and **n**, and southward; so H6828

NORTH-WEST See NORTH and WEST.

NOSE
Lev 21:18 hath a flat **n**, or any thing superfluous, H2763
2Ki 19:28 put my hook in thy **n**, and my bridle in H639
Job 40:24 He taketh it with his eyes: *his* **n** pierceth H639
41: 2 Canst thou put an hook into his **n**? or H639
Prv 30:33 and the wringing of the **n** bringeth forth H639
Song 7: 4 of Bath-rabbim: thy **n** *is* as the tower of H639
8 vine, and the smell of thy **n** like apples; H639
Isa 3:21 The rings, and **n** jewels, H639
37:29 I put my hook in thy **n**, and my bridle in H639
65: 5 in my **n**, a fire that burneth all the day. H639
Ezk 8:17 and, lo, they put the branch to their **n**. H639
23:25 shall take away thy **n** and thine ears; H639

NOSE-JEWELS See NOSE and JEWELS.

NOSES
Ps 115: 6 They have ears, but they hear not: **n** H639
Ezk 39:11 it shall stop the *n* of the passengers: and

NOSTRILS
Gen 2: 7 breathed into his **n** the breath of life; H639
7:22 All in whose **n** *was* the breath of life, of H639
Ex 15: 8 And with the blast of thy **n** the waters H639
Nu 11:20 until it come out at your **n**, and it be H639
2Sa 22: 9 There went up a smoke out of his **n**, and H639
16 LORD, at the blast of the breath of his **n**. H639
Job 4: 9 the breath of his **n** are they consumed. H639
27: 3 *is* in me, and the spirit of God *is* in my **n**; H639
39:20 the glory of his **n** *is* terrible. H5170
41:20 Out of his **n** goeth smoke, as *out* of a H5156
Ps 18: 8 There went up a smoke out of his **n**, and H639
15 LORD, at the blast of the breath of thy **n**. H639
Isa 2:22 **n**: for wherein is he to be accounted of? H639
Lam 4:20 The breath of our **n**, the anointed of the H639
Am 4:10 to come up unto your **n**: yet have ye not H639

NOT See the Appendix.

NOTABLE
Dan 8: 5 the goat *had* a **n** horn between his eyes. H2380
8 it came up four **n** ones toward the four H2380
Mt 27:16 And they had then a **n** prisoner, called *G1978*
Act 2:20 that great and **n** day of the Lord come: *G2016*
4:16 for that indeed a **n** miracle hath been *G1110*

NOTE
Isa 30: 8 in a table, and **n** it in a book, that it H2710
Ro 16: 7 who are of **n** among the apostles, *G1978*
2Th 3:14 by this epistle, **n** that man, and have *G4593*

NOTED
Dan 10:21 But I will shew thee that which is **n** in H7559

NOTHING
Gen 11: 6 to do: and now **n** will be H3808+H3605
19: 8 these men do **n**; for therefore H408+H1697
26:29 done unto thee **n** but good, and have H7535
40:15 have I done **n** that they should H3808+H3972
Ex 9: 4 and there shall **n** die of all *that is* the H1697
12:10 And ye shall let **n** of it remain until the H3808
20 Ye shall eat **n** leavened; in all your H3808
16:18 much had **n** over, and he that gathered H3808
21: 2 in the seventh he shall go out free for **n**. H2600
22: 3 have **n**, then he shall be sold for his theft. H369
23:26 There shall **n** cast their young, nor be H3808
Nu 6: 4 shall he eat **n** that is made of the H3808
11: 6 away: *there is* **n** at all, beside H369+H3605
16:26 and touch **n** of theirs, lest ye H408+H3605
22:16 son of Zippor, Let **n**, I pray thee, hinder H408
Dt 2: 7 *hath been* with thee; thou hast lacked **n**. H1697
20:16 save alive **n** that breatheth: H3808+H3605
22:26 But unto the damsel thou shalt do **n**; H1697
28:55 because he hath **n** left him in the siege, H3605
Jos 11:15 did Joshua; he left **n** undone of all that H1697
Jdg 3: 2 the least such as before knew **n** thereof; H3808
7:14 and said, This *is* **n** else save the sword of H369
14: 6 and *he had* **n** in his hand: but H369+H3972
1Sa 3:18 whit, and hid **n** from him. And he said, H3808
20: 2 father will do **n** either great or H3808+1697
22:15 servant knew **n** of all this, less or more. H1697
25:21 so that **n** was missed of all H3808+H3972
36 **n**, less or more, until the morning light. H1697
27: 1 of Saul: *there is* **n** better for me than that H369
30:19 And there was **n** lacking to them, H3808
2Sa 12: 3 But the poor *man* had **n**, save H369+H3605
24:24 doth cost me **n**. So David bought the H2600
1Ki 4:27 every man in his month: they lacked **n**. H1697
8: 9 *There was* **n** in the ark save the two H369
10:21 silver: it was **n** accounted of in H3808+H3972
11:22 **N**: howbeit let me go in any wise. H3808
18:43 said, *There is* **n**. And he said, Go H369+H3972
22:16 that thou tell me **n** but *that which is* H3808
2Ki 10:10 fall unto the earth **n** of the word of the H3808
20:13 there was **n** in his house, nor in H1697
15 have they seen: there is **n** among my H1697
17 **n** shall be left, saith the LORD. H1697
2Ch 5:10 *There was* **n** in the ark save the two H369
9: 2 and there was **n** hid from H3808+H1697
14:11 said, LORD, *it is* **n** with thee to help, H3808
18:15 thee that thou say **n** but the truth to me H3808
Ezr 4: 3 them, Ye have **n** to do with us to build H369
Neh 2: 2 *art* not sick? this *is* **n** *else* but sorrow of H369
5: 8 their peace, and found **n** *to answer.* H1697
12 and will require **n** of them; so will we H3808
8:10 them for whom **n** is prepared: for *this* H3808
9:21 *that* they lacked **n**; their clothes waxed H3808
Est 2:15 king, she required **n** but what Hegai H1697
5:13 Yet all this availeth me **n**, so long as I see H369
6: 3 unto him, There is **n** done for him. H1697
10 let **n** fail of all that thou hast spoken. H1697
Job 6:18 turned aside; they go to **n**, and perish. H8414
21 For now ye are **n**; ye see *my* casting H3808

Job 8: 9 and know **n**, because our days upon H3808
24:25 me a liar, and make my speech **n** worth? H408
26: 7 place, *and* hangeth the earth upon **n**. H1099
34: 9 For he hath said, It profiteth a man **n** H3808
Ps 17: 3 me, *and* shalt find **n**; I am purposed *that* H369
19: 6 and there is **n** hid from the heat thereof. H369
39: 5 and mine age *is* as **n** before thee: verily H369
49:17 he shall carry **n** away: his glory H3808+H3605
119:165 love thy law: and **n** shall offend them. H369
Prv 8: 8 *there is* **n** froward or perverse in them. H369
9:13 *she is* simple, and knoweth **n**. H1077+H4100
10: 2 Treasures of wickedness profit **n**: but H3808
13: 4 desireth, and *hath* **n**: but the soul of the H369
7 rich, yet *hath* **n**: *there is* that maketh H369
20: 4 shall he beg in harvest, and *have* **n**. H369
22:27 If thou hast **n** to pay, why should he take H369
Ecc 2:24 *There is* **n** better for a man, *than* that he H369
3:14 it shall be for ever: **n** can be put to it, nor H369
22 Wherefore I perceive that *there is* **n** H369
5:14 son, and *there is* **n** in his hand. H3808+H3972
15 and shall take **n** of his labour, H3808+H3972
6: 2 so that he wanteth **n** for his soul of all H369
7:14 man should find **n** after him. H3808+H3972
Isa 34:12 *be* there, and all her princes shall be **n**. H657
39: 2 there was **n** in his house, nor in H1697
4 have they seen: there is **n** among my H1697
6 **n** shall be left, saith the LORD. H1697
40:17 All nations before him *are* as **n**; and they H369
17 counted to him less than **n**, and vanity. H657
23 That bringeth the princes to **n**; he H369
41:11 they shall be as **n**; and they that strive H369
12 shall be as **n**, and as a thing of nought. H369
24 Behold, ye *are* of **n**, and your work of H369
29 their works *are* **n**: their molten images H657
44:10 a graven image *that* is profitable for **n**? H1115
Jer 10:24 in thine anger, lest thou bring me to **n**. H4591
13: 7 marred, it was profitable for **n**. H3808+H3605
10 this girdle, which is good for **n**. H3808+H3605
32:17 arm, *and* there is **n** too hard for thee: H1697
23 law; they have done **n** of all that thou H3808
38:14 I will ask thee a thing; hide **n** from me. H1697
39:10 which had **n**, in the land of H369+H3972
42: 4 unto you; I will keep **n** back from you. H1697
50:26 destroy her utterly: let **n** of her be left. H408
Lam 1:12 *Is it* **n** to you, all ye that pass by? H3808
Ezk 13: 3 follow their own spirit, and have seen **n**! H1115
Dan 4:35 earth *are* reputed as **n**: and he doeth H3809
Joel 2: 3 yea, and **n** shall escape them. H3808
Am 3: 4 cry out of his den, if he have taken **n**? H1115
5 from the earth, and have taken **n** at all? H3808
7 Surely the Lord GOD will do **n**, but he H1697
Hag 2: 3 not in your eyes in comparison of it as **n**? H369
Mt 5:13 good for **n**, but to be cast out, and G3762
10:26 Fear them not therefore: for there is **n** G3762
15:32 days, and have **n** to eat: and I will not G3756
17:20 and **n** shall be impossible unto you. G3762
21:19 to it, and found **n** thereon, but leaves G3762
23:16 by the temple, it is **n**; but whosoever G3762
18 by the altar, it is **n**; but whosoever G3762
26:62 him, Answerest thou **n**? what *is it which* G3762
27:12 chief priests and elders, he answered **n**. G3762
19 saying, Have thou **n** to do with that just G3367
24 he could prevail **n**, but *that* rather a G3762
Mk 1:44 And saith unto him, See thou say **n** to G3367
4:22 For there is **n** hid, which shall not be G3756
5:26 was **n** bettered, but rather grew worse, G3367
6: 8 they should take **n** for *their* journey, G3367
36 bread: for they have **n** to eat. G3756
7:15 There is **n** from without a man, that G3762
8: 1 great, and having **n** to eat, Jesus called G3361
2 with me three days, and have **n** to eat: G3756
9:29 forth by **n**, but by prayer and fasting. G3762
11:13 to it, he found **n** but leaves; for the time G3762
14:60 Answerest thou **n**? what *is it which* G3762
61 But he held his peace, and answered **n**. G3762
15: 3 him of many things: but he answered **n**. G3762
4 Answerest thou **n**? behold how many G3762
5 But Jesus yet answered **n**; so that Pilate G3762
Lk 1:37 For with God **n** shall be impossible. G3956
4: 2 days he did eat **n**: and when they were G3762
5: 5 and have taken **n**: nevertheless at thy G3762
6:35 and lend, hoping for **n** again; and your G3367
7:42 And when they had **n** to pay, he frankly G3361
8:17 For **n** is secret, that shall not be made G3756
9: 3 And he said unto them, Take **n** for *your* G3367
10:19 and **n** shall by any means hurt you. G3762
11: 6 to me, and I have **n** to set before him? G3756
12: 2 For there is **n** covered, that shall not be G3762
22:35 lacked ye any thing? And they said, **N**. G3762
Lk 23: 9 in many words; but he answered him **n**. G3762
15 lo, **n** worthy of death is done unto him. G3762
41 deeds: but this man hath done **n** amiss. G3762
Jn 3:27 **n**, except it be given him from heaven. G3762
4:11 Sir, thou hast **n** to draw with, and the G3777
5:19 The Son can do **n** of himself, but what G3762
30 I can of mine own self do **n**: as I hear, I G3762
6:12 fragments that remain, that **n** be lost. G3361
39 me I should lose **n**, but should raise it G3361
63 the flesh profiteth **n**: the words that I G3762
7:26 and they say **n** unto him. Do the rulers G3762
8:28 *he*, and *that* I do **n** of myself; but as my G3762
54 my honour is **n**: it is my Father that G3762
9:33 man were not of God, he could do **n**. G3762
11:49 year, said unto them, Ye know **n** at all, G3756
12:19 **n**? behold, the world is gone after him. G3762
14:30 of this world cometh, and hath **n** in me. G3762
15: 5 much fruit: for without me ye can do **n**. G3762
16:23 And in that day ye shall ask me **n**. G3762
24 Hitherto have ye asked **n** in my name: G3762
18:20 resort; and in secret have I said **n**. G3762
21: 3 and that night they caught **n**. G3762
Act 4:14 with them, they could say **n** against it. G3762
21 let them go, finding **n** how they might G3367
10:20 them, doubting **n**: for I have sent them. G3367
11: 8 But I said, Not so, Lord: for **n** common G3956
12 And the Spirit bade me go with them, **n** G3367
17:21 spent their time in **n** else, but either to G3762
19:36 ought to be quiet, and to do **n** rashly. G3367
20:20 *And* how I kept back **n** that was G3762
21:24 thee, are **n**; but *that* thou thyself G3762
23:14 we will eat **n** until we have slain Paul. G3367
29 law, but to have **n** laid to his charge G3367
25:25 he had committed **n** worthy of death, G3367
26:31 doeth **n** worthy of death or of bonds. G3762
27:33 and continued fasting, having taken **n**. G3367
28:17 I have committed **n** against the people, G3762
Ro 14:14 Jesus, that *there is* **n** unclean of itself: G3762
1Co 1:19 to **n** the understanding of the prudent. G114
4: 4 For I know **n** by myself; yet am I not G3762
5 Therefore judge **n** before the time, until G3361
7:19 Circumcision is **n**, and uncircumcision G3762
19 uncircumcision is **n**, but the keeping of G3762
8: 2 he knoweth **n** yet as he ought to know. G3762
4 that an idol *is* **n** in the world, and that G3762
9:16 the gospel, I have **n** to glory of: for G3756
13: 2 and have not charity, I am **n**. G3762
3 and have not charity, it profiteth me **n**. G3762
2Co 6:10 having **n**, and *yet* possessing all things. G3367
7: 9 ye might receive damage by us in **n**. G3367
8:15 much had **n** over; and he that *had* G3756
12:11 of you: for in **n** am I behind the very G3762
11 the very chiefest apostles, though I be **n**. G3762
13: 8 For we can do **n** against the truth, but G3756
Gal 2: 6 in conference added **n** to me: G3762
4: 1 is a child, differeth **n** from a servant, G3762
5: 2 circumcised, Christ shall profit you **n**. G3762
6: 3 when he is **n**, he deceiveth himself. G3367
Php 1:20 *my* hope, that in **n** I shall be ashamed, G3762
28 And in **n** terrified by your adversaries: G3367
2: 3 *Let* **n** *be done* through strife or G3367
4: 6 Be careful for **n**; but in every thing by G3367
1Th 4:12 without, and *that* ye may have lack of **n**. G3367
1Ti 4: 4 of God *is* good, and **n** to be refused, if it G3762
5:21 before another, doing **n** by partiality. G3367
6: 4 He is proud, knowing **n**, but doting G3367
7 For we brought **n** into *this* world, *and it* G3762
7 *and it is* certain we can carry **n** out. G3761
Tit 1:15 and unbelieving *is* **n** pure; but even G3762
3:13 that **n** be wanting unto them. G3367
Phlm 14 But without thy mind would I do **n**; that G3762
Heb 2: 8 under him, he left **n** *that is* not put G3762
7:14 Moses spake **n** concerning priesthood. G3762
19 For the law made **n** perfect, but the G3762
Jas 1: 4 may be perfect and entire, wanting **n**. G3367
6 But let him ask in faith, **n** wavering. G3367
3Jn 7 went forth, taking **n** of the Gentiles. G3367
Rev 3:17 and have need of **n**; and knowest not G3762

NOTICE
2Sa 3:36 And all the people took **n** *of it*, and it H5234
2Co 9: 5 whereof ye had **n** before, that the same G4293

NOTWITHSTANDING
Ex 16:20 **N** they hearkened not unto Moses; but
21:21 **N**, if he continue a day or two, he shall H389
Lev 25:32 **N** the cities of the Levites, *and* the
27:28 **N** no devoted thing, that a man shall H389
Nu 26:11 **N** the children of Korah died not.
Nu 26:55 **N** the land shall be divided by lot:
Dt 1:26 **N** ye would not go up, but rebelled
12:15 **N** thou mayest kill and eat flesh in all H7535
Jos 22:19 **N**, if the land of your possession *be* H389
Jdg 4: 9 And she said, I will surely go with thee: **n** H657
9: 5 upon one stone: **n** yet Jotham the
1Sa 2:25 entreat for him? **N** they hearkened not
20: 8 the LORD with thee: **n**, if there be in me
29: 9 as an angel of God: **n** the princes of the H389
2Sa 24: 4 **N** the king's word prevailed against
1Ki 11:12 **N** in thy days I will not do it for David H389
2Ki 17:14 **N** they would not hear, but hardened
23:26 **N** the LORD turned not from the H389
2Ch 6: 9 **N** thou shalt not build the house; but H7535
32:26 **N** Hezekiah humbled himself for the
Jer 35:14 commandment: **n** I have spoken unto
Ezk 20:21 **N** the children rebelled against me: they
Mic 7:13 **N** the land shall be desolate because of
Mt 2:22 to go thither: **n**, being warned of God G1161
11:11 John the Baptist: **n** he that is least in G1161
17:27 **N**, lest we should offend them, go thou G1161
Lk 10:11 off against you: **n** be ye sure of this, G4133
20 **N** in this rejoice not, that the spirits are G4133
Act 15:34 **N** it pleased Silas to abide there still. G1161
24: 4 **N**, that I be not further tedious unto G1161
Php 1:18 What then? **n**, every way, whether in G4133
4:14 **N** ye have well done, that ye did G4133
1Ti 2:15 **N** she shall be saved in childbearing, if G1161
2Ti 4:17 **N** the Lord stood with me, and G1161
Jas 2:16 and filled; **n** ye give them not those G1161
Rev 2:20 **N** I have a few things against thee, G235

NOUGHT
Gen 29:15 for **n**? tell me, what *shall* thy wages *be*? H2600
Dt 13:17 And there shall cleave **n** of the cursed H3972
15: 9 thou givest him **n**; and he cry unto the H3808
28:63 and to bring you to **n**; and ye shall be H8045
Neh 4:15 their counsel to **n**, that we returned all H6565
Job 1: 9 and said, Doth Job fear God for **n**? H2600
8:22 place of the wicked shall come to **n**. H369
14:18 falling cometh to **n**, and the rock is H5034
22: 6 from thy brother for **n**, and stripped the H2600
Ps 33:10 of the heathen to **n**: he maketh the H6331
44:12 Thou sellest thy people for **n**, H3808+H1952
Prv 1:25 But ye have set at **n** all my counsel, and H6544
Isa 8:10 it shall come to **n**; speak the word, and H6565
29:20 For the terrible one is brought to **n**, and H656
21 and turn aside the just for a thing of **n**. H8414
41:12 shall be as nothing, and as a thing of **n**. H657
24 and your work of **n**: an abomination *is* H659
49: 4 spent my strength for **n**, and in vain: *yet* H8414
52: 3 sold yourselves for **n**; and ye shall be H2600
5 is taken away for **n**? they that rule over H2600
Jer 14:14 a thing of **n**, and the deceit of their heart. H434
Am 5: 5 captivity, and Beth-el shall come to **n**. H205
6:13 Ye which rejoice in a thing of **n**, which H3808
Mal 1:10 shut the doors *for* **n**? neither do ye kindle
10 on mine altar for **n**. I have no pleasure H2600
Mk 9:12 suffer many things, and be set at **n**. G1847
Lk 23:11 of war set him at **n**, and mocked *him*, G1848
Act 4:11 This is the stone which was set at **n** of G1848
5:36 him, were scattered, and brought to **n**. G3762
38 this work be of men, it will come to **n**: G2647
19:27 in danger to be set at **n**; but also that the G557
Ro 14:10 dost thou set at **n** thy brother? for we G1848
1Co 1:28 are not, to bring to **n** things that are: G2673
2: 6 princes of this world, that come to **n**: G2673
2Th 3: 8 man's bread for **n**; but wrought with G1432
Rev 18:17 great riches is come to **n**. And every G2049

NOURISH
Gen 45:11 And there will I **n** thee; for yet *there are* H3557
50:21 Now therefore fear ye not: I will **n** you, H3557
Isa 7:21 shall **n** a young cow, and two sheep; H2421
23: 4 I **n** up young men, *nor* bring up virgins. H1431
44:14 planteth an ash, and the rain doth **n** *it*. H1431

NOURISHED
Gen 47:12 And Joseph **n** his father, and his H3557
2Sa 12: 3 he had bought and **n** up: and it grew up H2421
Isa 1: 2 hath spoken, I have **n** and brought up H1431
Ezk 19: 2 she **n** her whelps among young lions. H7235
Act 7:20 **n** up in his father's house three months: G396
21 took him up, and **n** him for her own son. G397
12:20 country was **n** by the king's *country*. G5142
1Ti 4: 6 of Jesus Christ, **n** up in the words of G1789
Jas 5: 5 **n** your hearts, as in a day of slaughter. G5142
Rev 12:14 where she is **n** for a time, and times, G5142

NOURISHER
Ru 4:15 of *thy* life, and a **n** of thine old age: for H3557

NOURISHETH
Eph 5:29 his own flesh; but **n** and cherisheth it, *G1625*

NOURISHING
Dan 1: 5 he drank: so **n** them three years, that H1431

NOURISHMENT
Col 2:19 and bands having **n** ministered, and *G2023*

NOVICE
1Ti 3: 6 Not a **n**, lest being lifted up with pride *G3504*

NOW
Gen 2:23 And Adam said, This *is* **n** bone of my H6471
3: 1 **N** the serpent was more subtil than any H6258
22 good and evil: and **n**, lest he put forth H6258
4:11 And **n** *art* thou cursed from the earth,
10: 1 **N** these *are* the generations of the sons
11: 6 they begin to do: and **n** nothing will be H6258
27 **N** these *are* the generations of Terah:
12: 1 **N** the LORD had said unto Abram, Get
11 his wife, Behold **n**, I know that thou *art* H4994
19 her to me to wife: **n** therefore behold H6258
13:14 from him, Lift up **n** thine eyes, and look
15: 5 and said, Look **n** toward heaven, and H4994
16: 1 **N** Sarai Abram's wife bare him no H8297
2 And Sarai said unto Abram, Behold **n**, H4994
18: 3 And said, My Lord, if **n** I have found H4994
11 **N** Abraham and Sarah *were* old *and* well H85
21 I will go down **n**, and see whether they H4994
27 and said, Behold **n**, I have taken upon H4994
31 And he said, Behold **n**, I have taken H4994
19: 2 And he said, Behold **n**, my lords, turn H4994
8 Behold **n**, I have two daughters which H4994
9 needs be a judge: **n** will we deal worse H6288
19 Behold **n**, thy servant hath found grace H4994
20 Behold **n**, this city *is* near to flee unto, H4994
20: 7 **N** therefore restore the man *his* wife; H6258
21:23 **N** therefore swear unto me here by God H6258
22: 2 And he said, Take **n** thy son, thine only H6258
12 thing unto him: for **n** I know that thou H6258
24:42 **n** thou do prosper my way which I go: H6258
49 And **n** if ye will deal kindly and truly H6258
25:12 **N** these *are* the generations of Ishmael,
26:22 and he said, For **n** the LORD hath H6258
28 said, Let there be **n** an oath betwixt us, H4994
29 thou *art* **n** the blessed of the LORD. H6258
27: 2 And he said, Behold **n**, I am old, I know
3 **N** therefore take, I pray thee, thy
8 **N** therefore, my son, obey my voice
9 Go **n** to the flock, and fetch me from
26 him, Come near **n**, and kiss me, my son. H4994
36 and, behold, **n** he hath taken away H6258
37 and what shall I do **n** unto thee, my son? H645
43 **N** therefore, my son, obey my voice; H6258
29:32 **n** therefore my husband will love me. H6258
34 a son; and said, **N** this time will my H6258
35 a son: and she said, **N** will I praise the H6471
30:20 a good dowry; **n** will my husband dwell H6471
30 I *came*, and it is *n* increased unto a
30 my coming: and **n** when shall I provide H6258
31:12 And he said, Lift up **n** thine eyes and H4994
13 a vow unto me: **n** arise, get thee out H6258
16 our children's: **n** then, whatsoever God H6258
25 Then Laban overtook Jacob. **N** Jacob H3290
28 thou hast **n** done foolishly in *so* doing. H6258
30 And **n**, *though* thou wouldest needs be H6258
34 **N** Rachel had taken the images, and H7354
42 sent me away **n** empty. God hath seen H6258
44 **N** therefore come thou, let us make a H6258
32: 4 with Laban, and stayed there until **n**: H6258
10 Jordan; and **n** I am become two bands. H6258
33:10 And Jacob said, Nay, I pray thee, if **n** I H4994
15 And Esau said, Let me **n** leave with H4994
34: 5 his daughter: **n** his sons were with his
35:22 *it.* **N** the sons of Jacob were twelve:
36: 1 **N** these *are* the generations of Esau, who
37: 3 **N** Israel loved Joseph more than all his H3478
20 Come **n** therefore, and let us slay him, H6258
32 **n** whether it *be* thy son's coat or no. H4994
41:33 **N** therefore let Pharaoh look out a man
42: 1 **N** when Jacob saw that there was corn in
43:10 For except we had lingered, surely **n** we H6258
11 If *it must be* so **n**, do this; take of the best H645
44:10 And he said, **N** also *let* it *be* according H6258
30 **N** therefore when I come to thy servant H6258
Gen 44:33 **N** therefore, I pray thee, let thy servant H6258
45: 5 **N** therefore be not grieved, nor angry H6258
8 So **n** *it was* not you *that* sent me hither, H6258
19 **N** thou art commanded, this do ye; take
46:30 And Israel said unto Joseph, **N** let me H6471
34 youth even until **n**, both we, *and* also H6258
47: 4 land of Canaan: **n** therefore, we pray H6258
29 said unto him, If **n** I have found grace in
48: 5 And **n** thy two sons, Ephraim and H6258
10 **N** the eyes of Israel were dim for age, *so*
50: 4 saying, If **n** I have found grace H4994
5 thou bury me. **N** therefore let me go H6258
17 I pray thee **n**, the trespass of thy H4994
17 did unto thee evil: and **n**, we pray thee, H4994
21 **N** therefore fear ye not: I will nourish H6258
Ex 1: 1 **N** these *are* the names of the children of
8 **N** there arose up a new king over Egypt,
2:15 **N** when Pharaoh heard this thing, he
16 **N** the priest of Midian had seven
3: 1 **N** Moses kept the flock of Jethro his
3 And Moses said, I will **n** turn aside, H4994
9 **N** therefore, behold, the cry of the H6258
10 Come **n** therefore, and I will send thee H6258
18 hath met with us: and **n** let us go, we H6258
4: 6 unto him, Put **n** thine hand into thy H4994
12 **N** therefore go, and I will be with thy H6258
5: 5 people of the land **n** *are* many, and ye H6258
18 Go therefore **n**, *and* work; for there shall H6258
6: 1 Then the LORD said unto Moses, **N** H6258
7:11 and the sorcerers: **n** the magicians of
9:15 For **n** I will stretch out my hand, that I H6258
18 the foundation thereof even until **n**. H6258
19 Send therefore **n**, *and* gather thy cattle, H6258
10:11 Not so: go **n** ye *that are* men, and serve
17 **N** therefore forgive, I pray thee, my sin H6258
11: 2 Speak **n** in the ears of the people, and H4994
12:40 **N** the sojourning of the children of
16:36 **N** an omer *is* the tenth *part* of an ephah.
18:11 **N** I know that the LORD *is* greater than H6258
19 Hearken **n** unto my voice, I will give H6258
19: 5 **N** therefore, if ye will obey my voice H6258
21: 1 **N** these *are* the judgments which thou
29:38 **N** this *is that* which thou shalt offer
32:10 **N** therefore let me alone, that my wrath H6258
30 a great sin: and **n** I will go up unto the H6258
32 Yet **n**, if thou wilt forgive their sin—; H6258
34 Therefore **n** go, lead the people unto H6258
33: 5 thee: therefore **n** put off thy ornaments H6258
13 **N** therefore, I pray thee, if I have found H4994
13 in thy sight, shew me **n** thy way, that I H4994
34: 9 And he said, If **n** I have found grace in H4994
Nu 11: 6 But **n** our soul *is* dried away: *there is* H6258
23 thou shalt see **n** whether my word shall H6258
12: 3 (**N** the man Moses *was* very meek, above
6 And he said, Hear **n** my words: If there H4994
13 Heal her **n**, O God, I beseech thee. H4994
13:20 fruit of the land. **N** the time *was* the time
22 of Anak, *were.* (**N** Hebron was built H2275
14:15 **N** *if* thou shalt kill *all* this people as one
17 And **n**, I beseech thee, let the power of H6258
19 this people, from Egypt even until **n**. H2008
22 have tempted me **n** these ten times, H2088
25 (**N** the Amalekites and the Canaanites
41 And Moses said, Wherefore **n** do ye H2088
16: 1 **N** Korah, the son of Izhar, the son of H7141
49 **N** they that died in the plague were
20:10 unto them, Hear **n**, ye rebels; must we H4994
22: 4 elders of Midian, **N** shall this company H6258
6 Come **n** therefore, I pray thee, curse me H6258
11 of the earth: come **n**, curse me them; H6258
19 **N** therefore, I pray you, tarry ye also H6258
22 against him. **N** he was riding upon
29 in mine hand, for **n** would I kill thee. H6258
33 from me, surely **n** also I had slain thee, H6258
34 the way against me: **n** therefore, if it H6258
38 unto thee: have I **n** any power at all to H6258
24:11 Therefore **n** flee thou to thy place: I H6258
14 And **n**, behold, I go unto my people: H6258
17 I shall see him, but not **n**: I shall behold H6258
25:14 **N** the name of the Israelite that was
31:17 **N** therefore kill every male among the H6258
43 (**N** the half *that pertained unto* the
32: 1 **N** the children of Reuben and the
Dt 2:13 **N** rise up, *said I,* and get you over the H6258
4: 1 **N** therefore hearken, O Israel, unto the H6258
32 For ask **n** of the days that are past, H4994
5:25 **N** therefore why should we die? for this H6258
6: 1 **N** these *are* the commandments, the
10:12 And **n**, Israel, what doth the LORD thy H6258
Dt 10:22 ten persons; and **n** the LORD thy God H6258
26:10 And **n**, behold, I have brought the H6258
31:19 **N** therefore write ye this song for you, H6258
21 go about, even **n**, before I have brought H3117
32:39 See **n** that I, *even* I, *am* he, and *there is* H6258
Jos 1: 1 **N** after the death of Moses the servant of
2 Moses my servant is dead; **n** therefore H6258
2:12 **N** therefore, I pray you, swear unto me H6258
3:12 **N** therefore take you twelve men out of H6258
5: 5 **N** all the people that came out were H3588
14 of the LORD am I **n** come. And Joshua H6258
6: 1 **N** Jericho was straitly shut up because H4994
7:19 him; and tell me **n** what thou hast done;
8:11 the north side of Ai: **n** *there was* a valley
9: 6 **n** therefore make ye a league with us. H6258
11 therefore **n** make ye a league with us. H6258
12 but **n**, behold, it is dry, and it is mouldy: H6258
17 on the third day. **N** their cities *were*
19 **n** therefore we may not touch them. H6258
23 **N** therefore ye *are* cursed, and there H6258
25 And **n**, behold, we *are* in thine hand: as H6258
10: 1 **N** it came to pass, when Adoni-zedek
12: 1 **N** these *are* the kings of the land, which
13: 1 **N** Joshua was old *and* stricken in years;
7 **N** therefore divide this land for an H6258
14:10 And **n**, behold, the LORD hath kept me H6258
10 the wilderness: and **n**, lo, I *am* this day H6258
11 so *is* my strength **n**, for war, both to go H6258
12 **N** therefore give me this mountain, H6258
17: 8 *N* Manasseh had the land of Tappuah:
18:21 **N** the cities of the tribe of the children of
22: 4 And **n** the LORD your God hath given H6258
4 them: therefore **n** return ye, and get H6258
7 **N** to the *one* half of the tribe of
26 Therefore we said, Let us **n** prepare to H4994
31 against the LORD: **n** ye have delivered H227
24:14 **N** therefore fear the LORD, and serve H6258
23 **N** therefore put away, *said he,* the H6258
Jdg 1: 1 **N** after the death of Joshua it came to
8 **N** the children of Judah had fought
10 dwelt in Hebron: (**n** the name of Hebron
23 (**N** the name of the city before *was* Luz.)
3: 1 **N** these *are* the nations which the LORD
4:11 **N** Heber the Kenite, *which was* of the
6:13 up from Egypt? but **n** the LORD hath H6258
17 And he said unto him, If **n** I have found H4994
39 the fleece; let it **n** be dry only upon the H4994
7: 3 **N** therefore go to, proclaim in the ears H6288
8: 2 What have I done **n** in comparison of H6288
6 and Zalmunna **n** in thine hand, that H6258
10 **N** Zebah and Zalmunna *were* in Karkor,
15 and Zalmunna **n** in thine hand, that H6258
9:16 **N** therefore, if ye have done truly and H6258
32 **N** therefore up by night, thou and the H6258
38 Then said Zebul unto him, Where *is* **n** H645
38 go out, I pray **n**, and fight with them. H6258
11: 1 **N** Jephthah the Gileadite was a mighty
7 unto me **n** when ye are in distress? H6258
8 turn again to thee **n**, that thou mayest H6258
13 and unto Jordan: **n** therefore restore H6258
23 So **n** the LORD God of Israel hath H6258
25 And **n** *art* thou any thing better than H6258
12: 6 Then said they unto him, Say **n** H4994
13: 3 unto her, Behold **n**, thou *art* barren, H4994
4 **N** therefore beware, I pray thee, and H4994
7 bear a son; and **n** drink no wine nor H6258
12 And Manoah said, **N** let thy words H6258
14: 2 **n** therefore get her for me to wife. H6258
12 And Samson said unto them, I will **n** H4994
15: 3 And Samson said concerning them, **N** H6471
18 thy servant: and **n** shall I die for thirst, H6258
16: 9 **N** *there were* men lying in wait, abiding
10 and told me lies: **n** tell me, I pray thee, H6258
27 **N** the house was full of men and women;
17: 3 **n** therefore I will restore it unto thee. H6258
13 Then said Micah, **N** know I that the H6258
18:14 a molten image? **n** therefore consider H6258
19: 9 unto him, Behold, **n** the day draweth H4994
18 but I *am* *n* going to the house of
22 *N* as they were making their hearts
24 I will bring out **n**, and humble ye them, H4994
20: 3 (**N** the children of Benjamin heard that
9 But **n** this *shall be* the thing which we H6258
13 **N** therefore deliver *us* the men, the H6258
38 **N** there was an appointed sign between
21: 1 **N** the men of Israel had sworn in
Ru 1: 1 **N** it came to pass in the days when the
2: 2 Naomi, Let me **n** go to the field, and H4994
7 **n**, that she tarried a little in the house. H6258

Ru 3: 2 And **n** *is* not Boaz of our kindred, with H6258
11 And **n**, my daughter, fear not; I will do H6258
12 And **n** it is true that I *am thy* near H6258
4: 7 **N** this *was the manner* in former time in
18 **N** these *are* the generations of Pharez:
1Sa 1: 1 **N** there was a certain man of
9 they had drunk. **N** Eli the priest sat upon
13 **N** Hannah, she spake in her heart; only
2:12 **N** the sons of Eli *were* sons of Belial; they
16 give *it me* **n**: and if not, I will H3588+H6258
22 **N** Eli was very old, and heard all that H6258
30 me for ever: but **n** the LORD saith, Be it
3: 7 **N** Samuel did not yet know the LORD,
4: 1 came to all Israel. **N** Israel went out
15 **N** Eli was ninety and eight years old; and
6: 7 **N** therefore make a new cart, and take H6258
8: 2 **N** the name of his firstborn was Joel; and
5 not in thy ways: **n** make us a king to H6258
9 **N** therefore hearken unto their voice: H6258
9: 1 **N** there was a man of Benjamin, whose
3 Saul his son, Take **n** one of the servants H4994
6 And he said unto him, Behold **n**, *there* H4994
6 surely to pass: **n** let us go thither;
9 seer: for *he that is* **n** *called* a Prophet H3117
12 you: make haste **n**, for he came to day H6258
13 that be bidden. **N** therefore get you up; H6258
15 **N** the LORD had told Samuel in his ear a
10:19 set a king over us. **N** therefore present H6258
12: 2 And **n**, behold, the king walketh before H6258
7 **N** therefore stand still, that I may H6258
10 Ashtaroth: but **n** deliver us out of the H6258
13 **N** therefore behold the king whom ye H6258
16 **N** therefore stand and see this great H6258
13:12 will come down **n** upon me to Gilgal, H6258
13 thee: for **n** would the LORD have H6258
14 But **n** thy kingdom shall not continue: H6258
19 **N** there was no smith found throughout
14: 1 **N** it came to pass upon a day, that
17 with him, Number **n**, and see who is H4994
30 had there not been **n** a much greater H6258
49 **N** the sons of Saul were Jonathan, and
15: 1 over Israel: **n** therefore hearken thou H6258
3 **N** go and smite Amalek, and utterly H6258
25 **N** therefore, I pray thee, pardon my H6258
30 *yet* honour me **n**, I pray thee, before the H6258
16:12 And he sent, and brought him in. **N** he
15 unto him, Behold **n**, an evil spirit from H4994
16 Let our lord **n** command thy servants, H4994
17 Provide me **n** a man that can play H4994
17: 1 **N** the Philistines gathered together their
12 **N** David *was* the son of that Ephrathite
17 his son, Take **n** for thy brethren an H4994
19 **N** Saul, and they, and all the men of
29 And David said, What have I **n** done? H6258
18:22 **n** therefore be the king's son in law. H6258
19: 2 to kill thee: **n** therefore, I pray thee, H6258
20:29 me *to be there:* and **n**, if I have found H6258
31 Wherefore **n** send and fetch him H6258
36 lad, Run, find out **n** the arrows which I H6258
21: 3 **N** therefore what is under thine hand? H6258
7 **N** a certain man of the servants of Saul
22: 6 *were* with him, (**n** Saul abode in Gibeah
7 about him, Hear **n**, ye Benjamites; will H4994
12 And Saul said, Hear **n**, thou son of H4994
23:20 **N** therefore, O king, come down H6258
24:20 And **n**, behold, I know well that thou H6258
21 Swear **n** therefore unto me by the H6258
25: 3 **N** the name of the man *was* Nabal; and
7 And **n** I have heard that thou hast H6258
7 that thou hast shearers: **n** thy shepherds
10 be many servants **n** a days that break
17 **N** therefore know and consider what H6258
21 **N** David had said, Surely in vain have I
26 **N** therefore, my lord, *as* the LORD H6258
26 thine own hand, **n** let thine enemies, H6258
27 And **n** this blessing which thine H6258
26: 8 hand this day: **n** therefore let me smite H6258
11 thee, take thou **n** the spear that *is* at his H6258
16 anointed. And **n** see where the king's H6258
19 **N** therefore, I pray thee, let my lord the H6258
20 **N** therefore, let not my blood fall to the H6258
27: 1 And David said in his heart, I shall **n** H6258
5 Achish, If I have **n** found grace in thine H4994
28: 3 **N** Samuel was dead, and all Israel had
22 **N** therefore, I pray thee, hearken thou H6258
29: 1 **N** the Philistines gathered together all
7 Wherefore **n** return, and go in peace, H6258
10 Wherefore **n** rise up early in the H6258
31: 1 **N** the Philistines fought against Israel:

2Sa 1: 1 **N** it came to pass after the death of Saul,
2: 6 And **n** the LORD shew kindness and H6258
7 Therefore **n** let your hands be H6258
14 the young men **n** arise, and play before H4994
3: 1 **N** there was long war between the house
18 **N** then do *it:* for the LORD hath spoken H6258
4:11 I not therefore **n** require his blood of H6258
7: 2 the prophet, See **n**, I dwell in an house H4994
8 **N** therefore so shalt thou say unto my H6258
25 And **n**, O LORD God, the word that thou H6258
28 And **n**, O Lord GOD, thou *art* that God, H6258
29 Therefore **n** let it please thee to bless the
9: 6 **N** when Mephibosheth, the son of
10 alway at my table. **N** Ziba had fifteen
12:10 **N** therefore the sword shall never H6258
23 But **n** he is dead, wherefore should I H6258
28 **N** therefore gather the rest of the H6258
13: 7 to Tamar, saying, Go **n** to thy brother H4994
13 of the fools in Israel. **N** therefore, I pray H6258
17 him, and said, Put **n** this *woman* out H4994
20 thee? but hold **n** thy peace, my sister: H6258
24 and said, Behold **n**, thy servant hath H4994
25 my son, let us not all **n** go, lest we be H4994
28 **N** Absalom had commanded his
28 saying, Mark ye **n** when Amnon's heart H4994
33 **N** therefore let not my lord the king H6258
14: 1 **N** Joab the son of Zeruiah perceived that
2 and put on **n** mourning apparel, H4994
15 **N** therefore that I am come to speak of H6258
15 said, I will **n** speak unto the king; H4994
17 lord the king shall **n** be comfortable: H4994
18 said, Let my lord the king **n** speak. H4994
21 And the king said unto Joab, Behold **n**, I H4994
32 *been* there still: **n** therefore let me see H6258
15:34 hitherto, so *will* I **n** also *be* thy servant: H6258
16:11 how much more **n** *may this* Benjamite H6258
17: 1 Absalom, Let me **n** choose out twelve H4994
5 Then said Absalom, Call **n** Hushai the H4994
9 Behold, he is hid **n** in some pit, or in H6258
16 **N** therefore send quickly, and tell H6258
17 **N** Jonathan and Ahimaaz stayed by
18: 3 care for us: but **n** *thou art* worth ten H6258
3 of us: therefore **n** *it is* better that thou H6258
18 **N** Absalom in his lifetime had taken and
19 of Zadok, Let me **n** run, and bear the H4994
19: 7 **N** therefore arise, go forth, and speak H6258
7 that befell thee from thy youth until **n**. H6258
9 **n** he is fled out of the land for Absalom. H6258
10 us, is dead in battle. **N** therefore why H6258
32 **N** Barzillai was a very aged man, *even*
20: 6 And David said to Abishai, **N** shall H6258
23 **N** Joab *was* over all the host of Israel:
21: 2 said unto them; (**n** the Gibeonites *were*
23: 1 **N** these *be* the last words of David.
24: 2 *was* with him, Go **n** through all the H4994
3 And Joab said unto the king, **N** the
10 I have done: and **n**, I beseech thee, O H6258
13 in thy land? **n** advise, and see what H6258
14 strait: let us fall **n** into the hand of the H4994
16 It is enough: stay **n** thine hand. And the H6258
1Ki 1: 1 **N** king David was old *and* stricken in
12 **N** therefore come, let me, I pray thee, H6258
18 And **n**, behold, Adonijah reigneth; and H6258
18 **n**, my lord the king, thou knowest *it* not:
2: 1 **N** the days of David drew nigh that he
9 **N** therefore hold him not guiltless: for H6258
16 And **n** I ask one petition of thee, deny H6258
24 **N** therefore, *as* the LORD liveth, which H6258
3: 7 And **n**, O LORD my God, thou hast H6258
5: 4 But **n** the LORD my God hath given me H6258
6 **N** therefore command thou that they H6258
8:25 Therefore **n**, LORD God of Israel, keep H6258
26 And **n**, O God of Israel, let thy word, I
9:11 (*N* Hiram the king of Tyre had furnished
10:14 **N** the weight of gold that came to
12: 4 Thy father made our yoke grievous: **n** H6258
11 And **n** whereas my father did lade you H6258
16 your tents, O Israel: **n** see to thine own H6258
26 And Jeroboam said in his heart, **N** shall H6258
13: 6 of God, Entreat **n** the face of the LORD H4994
11 **N** there dwelt an old prophet in Beth-el;
14:14 of Jeroboam that day: but what? even **n**. H6258
29 **N** the rest of the acts of Rehoboam, and
15: 1 **N** in the eighteenth year of king
7 **N** the rest of the acts of Abijam, and all
31 **N** the rest of the acts of Nadab, and all
16: 5 **N** the rest of the acts of Baasha, and
14 **N** the rest of the acts of Elah, and all that
20 **N** the rest of the acts of Zimri, and his

1Ki 16:27 **N** the rest of the acts of Omri which he
17:24 And the woman said to Elijah, **N** by H6258
18: 3 (**N** Obadiah feared the LORD greatly:
11 And **n** thou sayest, Go, tell thy lord, H6258
14 And **n** thou sayest, Go, tell thy lord, H6258
19 **N** therefore send, *and* gather to me all H6258
43 And said to his servant, Go up **n**, look H4994
19: 4 and said, It is enough; **n**, O LORD, take H6258
20:31 unto him, Behold **n**, we have heard that H4994
33 **N** the men did diligently observe
21: 7 him, Dost thou **n** govern the kingdom H6258
22:13 him, saying, Behold **n**, the words of the H4994
23 **N** therefore, behold, the LORD hath put H6258
39 **N** the rest of the acts of Ahab, and all
45 **N** the rest of the acts of Jehoshaphat,
2Ki 1: 4 **N** therefore thus saith the LORD, Thou
5 unto them, Why are ye **n** turned back? H2088
14 let my life **n** be precious in thy sight. H6258
18 **N** the rest of the acts of Ahaziah which
2:16 And they said unto him, Behold **n**, there H4994
3: 1 **N** Jehoram the son of Ahab began to
15 But **n** bring me a minstrel. And it came H6258
23 **n** therefore, Moab, to the spoil. H6258
4: 1 **N** there cried a certain woman of the
9 husband, Behold **n**, I perceive that this H4994
13 And he said unto him, Say **n** unto her, H4994
26 Run **n**, I pray thee, to meet her, and say H6258
5: 1 **N** Naaman, captain of the host of the
6 of Israel, saying, **N** when this letter is H6258
8 let him come **n** to me, and he shall H4994
15 he said, Behold, **n** I know that *there is* H4994
15 but in Israel: **n** therefore, I pray thee, H6258
22 Behold, even **n** there be come to me H6258
6: 1 Elisha, Behold **n**, the place where we H4994
7: 4 here, we die also. **N** therefore come, H6258
9 come upon us: **n** therefore come, that H6258
12 his servants, I will **n** shew you what the H4994
19 of God, and said, **N**, behold, *if* the LORD
8: 6 day that she left the land, even until **n**. H6258
9:12 And they said, *It is* false; tell us **n**. And H4994
14 against Joram. (**N** Joram had kept
26 saith the LORD. **N** therefore take *and* H6258
34 and said, Go, see **n** this cursed *woman*, H4994
10: 2 **N** as soon as this letter cometh to you, H6258
6 to morrow this time. **N** the king's sons,
10 Know **n** that there shall fall unto the H645
19 **N** therefore call unto me all the H6258
34 **N** the rest of the acts of Jehu, and all that
12: 7 of the house? **n** therefore receive no H6258
13: 8 **N** the rest of the acts of Jehoahaz, and all
14 **N** Elisha was fallen sick of his sickness
19 **n** thou shalt smite Syria *but* thrice. H6258
14:15 **N** the rest of the acts of Jehoash which
19 **N** they made a conspiracy against him
28 **N** the rest of the acts of Jeroboam, and
15:36 **N** the rest of the acts of Jotham, and all
16:19 **N** the rest of the acts of Ahaz which he
18: 1 **N** it came to pass in the third year of
13 **N** in the fourteenth year of king
19 them, Speak ye **n** to Hezekiah, Thus H4994
20 for the war. **N** on whom dost thou H6258
21 **N**, behold, thou trustest upon the staff H6258
23 **N** therefore, I pray thee, give pledges to H6258
25 Am I **n** come up without the LORD H6258
19:19 **N** therefore, O LORD our God, I H6258
25 I have formed it? **n** have I brought it to H6258
20: 3 I beseech thee, O LORD, remember **n** H4994
21:17 **N** the rest of the acts of Manasseh, and
25 **N** the rest of the acts of Amon which he
22:14 keeper of the wardrobe; (**n** she dwelt in
23:28 **N** the rest of the acts of Josiah, and all
24: 5 **N** the rest of the acts of Jehoiakim, and
25: 4 the king's garden: (**n** the Chaldees *were*
11 **N** the rest of the people *that were* left in
1Ch 1:32 **N** the sons of Keturah, Abraham's
43 **N** these *are* the kings that reigned in the
2:34 **N** Sheshan had no sons, but daughters.
42 **N** the sons of Caleb the brother of
3: 1 **N** these were the sons of David, which
5: 1 **N** the sons of Reuben the firstborn of
6:54 **N** these *are* their dwelling places
7: 1 **N** the sons of Issachar *were*, Tola, and
8: 1 **N** Benjamin begat Bela his firstborn,
9: 2 **N** the first inhabitants that *dwelt* in their
10: 1 **N** the Philistines fought against Israel;
11:15 **N** three of the thirty captains went down
12: 1 **N** these *are* they that came to David to
14: 1 **N** Hiram king of Tyre sent messengers to
4 **N** these *are* the names of *his* children

1Ch 17: 1 N it came to pass, as David sat in his
7 N therefore thus shalt thou say unto H6258
23 Therefore n, LORD, let the thing that H6258
26 And n, LORD, thou art God, and hast H6258
27 N therefore let it please thee to bless H6258
18: 1 N after this it came to pass, that David
9 N when Tou king of Hamath heard how
19: 1 N it came to pass after this, that Nahash
10 N when Joab saw that the battle was set
21: 8 this thing: but n, I beseech thee, do H6258
12 the coasts of Israel. N therefore advise H6258
13 strait: let me fall n into the hand of the H4994
15 It is enough, stay n thine hand. And the H6258
20 N Ornan was threshing wheat.
22: 5 I will *therefore* n make preparation for H4994
11 N, my son, the LORD be with thee; and H6258
14 N, behold, in my trouble I have prepared
19 N set your heart and your soul to seek H6258
23: 3 N the Levites were numbered from the
14 N *concerning* Moses the man of God, his
24: 1 N *these are* the divisions of the sons of
7 N the first lot came forth to Jehoiarib,
25: 9 N the first lot came forth for Asaph to
27: 1 N the children of Israel after their
28: 8 N therefore in the sight of all Israel the H6258
10 Take heed n; for the LORD hath chosen H6258
29: 2 N I have prepared with all my might for
13 N therefore, our God, we thank thee, H6258
17 these things: and n have I seen with joy H6258
20 all the congregation, N bless the LORD H4994
29 N the acts of David the king, first and
2Ch 1: 9 N, O LORD God, let thy promise unto H6258
10 Give me n wisdom and knowledge, that H6258
2: 7 Send me n therefore a man cunning to H6258
13 And n I have sent a cunning man, H6258
15 N therefore the wheat, and the barley, H6258
3: 3 N these *are the things wherein* Solomon
6: 7 N it was in the heart of David my father
16 N therefore, O LORD God of Israel, H6258
17 N then, O LORD God of Israel, let thy H6258
40 N, my God, let, I beseech thee, thine H6258
41 N therefore arise, O LORD God, into H6258
7: 1 N when Solomon had made an end of
15 N mine eyes shall be open, and mine H6258
16 For n have I chosen and sanctified this H6258
8:16 N all the work of Solomon was prepared
9:13 N the weight of gold that came to
29 N the rest of the acts of Solomon, first
10: 4 Thy father made our yoke grievous: n H6258
16 O Israel: *and* n, David, see to thine H6258
12:15 N the acts of Rehoboam, first and last,
13: 1 N in the eighteenth year of king
8 And n ye think to withstand the
15: 3 N for a long season Israel *hath been*
18: 1 N Jehoshaphat had riches and honour in
22 N therefore, behold, the LORD hath put
30 N the king of Syria had commanded the
19: 7 Wherefore n let the fear of the LORD be
20:10 And n, behold, the children of Ammon
34 N the rest of the acts of Jehoshaphat,
21: 1 N Jehoshaphat slept with his fathers,
4 N when Jehoram was risen up to the
23:12 N when Athaliah heard the noise of the
24:11 N it came to pass, that at what time the
17 N after the death of Jehoiada came the
27 N *concerning* his sons, and the greatness
25: 3 N it came to pass, when the kingdom
14 N it came to pass, after that Amaziah H6258
19 thee up to boast: abide n at home; why
26 N the rest of the acts of Amaziah, first
27 N after the time that Amaziah did turn
26:22 N the rest of the acts of Uzziah, first and
27: 7 N the rest of the acts of Jotham, and all
28:10 And n ye purpose to keep under the H6258
11 N hear me therefore, and deliver the H6258
26 N the rest of his acts and of all his ways,
29: 5 ye Levites, sanctify n yourselves, and H6258
10 N *it is* in mine heart to make a H6258
11 My sons, be not n negligent: for the H6258
17 N they began on the first *day* of the first
31 Then Hezekiah answered and said, N H6258
30: 8 N be ye not stiffnecked, as your fathers H6258
31: 1 N when all this was finished, all Israel
32:15 N therefore let not Hezekiah deceive H6258
32 N the rest of the acts of Hezekiah, and
33:14 N after this he built a wall without the
18 N the rest of the acts of Manasseh, and
34: 8 N in the eighteenth year of his reign,
22 keeper of the wardrobe; (n she dwelt in

2Ch 35: 3 shoulders: serve n the LORD your God, H6258
26 N the rest of the acts of Josiah, and his
36: 8 N the rest of the acts of Jehoiakim, and
22 N in the first year of Cyrus king of
Ezr 1: 1 N in the first year of Cyrus king of
2: 1 N these *are* the children of the province
3: 8 N in the second year of their coming
4: 1 N when the adversaries of Judah and
13 Be it known n unto the king, that, if H3705
14 N because we have maintenance from H3705
21 Give ye n commandment to cause H3705
22 Take heed n that ye fail not to do this:
23 N when the copy of king Artaxerxes' H116
5:16 that time even until n hath it been in H3705
17 N therefore, if *it seem* good to the king, H3705
6: 6 N *therefore*, Tatnai, governor beyond H3705
7: 1 N after these things, in the reign of
11 N this *is* the copy of the letter that the
8: 1 These *are* n the chief of their fathers,
33 N on the fourth day was the silver and
9: 1 N when these things were done, the
8 And n for a little space grace hath been H6258
10 And n, O our God, what shall we say H6258
12 N therefore give not your daughters H6258
10: 1 N when Ezra had prayed, and when he
2 of the land: yet n there is hope in Israel H6258
3 N therefore let us make a covenant H6258
11 N therefore make confession unto the H6258
14 Let n our rulers of all the congregation H4994
Neh 1: 6 Let thine ear n be attentive, and thine H4994
6 I pray before thee n, day and night, for H3117
10 N these *are* thy servants and thy people,
11 O Lord, I beseech thee, let n thine ear H4994
2: 1 gave *it* unto the king. N I had not been
9 the king's letters. N the king had sent
4: 3 N Tobiah the Ammonite *was* by him,
5: 5 Yet n our flesh *is* as the flesh of our H6258
18 N *that* which was prepared *for me* daily
6: 1 N it came to pass, when Sanballat, and
7 in Judah: and n shall it be reported H6258
7 words. Come n therefore, and let us H6258
9 that it be not done. N therefore, *O God*, H6258
7: 1 N it came to pass, when the wall was
4 N the city *was* large and great: but the
9: 1 N in the twenty and fourth day of this
32 N therefore, our God, the great, the H6258
10: 1 N those that sealed *were*, Nehemiah, the
11: 3 N these *are* the chief of the province that
12: 1 N these *are* the priests and the Levites
13: 3 N it came to pass, when they had heard
Est 1: 1 N it came to pass in the days of
2: 5 N in Shushan the palace there was a
12 N when every maid's turn was come to
15 N when the turn of Esther, the daughter
3: 4 N it came to pass, when they spake daily
5: 1 N it came to pass on the third day, that
6: 4 *is* in the court? N Haman was come into
6 to honour? N Haman thought in his
9: 1 N in the twelfth month, that *is*, the
12 king's provinces? n what *is* thy petition?
Job 1: 6 N there was a day when the sons of H4994
11 But put forth thine hand n, and touch H4994
2: 5 But put forth thine hand n, and touch his
11 N when Job's three friends heard of all
3:13 For n should I have lain still and been H6258
4: 5 But n it is come upon thee, and thou H6258
12 N a thing was secretly brought to me,
5: 1 Call n, if there be any that will answer H4994
6: 3 For n it would be heavier than the sand H6258
21 For n ye are nothing; ye see *my* casting H6258
28 N therefore be content, look upon me; H6258
7:21 mine iniquity? for n shall I sleep in the H6258
8: 6 If thou *wert* pure and upright; surely n H6258
9:25 N my days are swifter than a post: they
12: 7 But ask n the beasts, and they shall H4994
13: 6 Hear n my reasoning, and hearken to H4994
18 Behold n, I have ordered *my* cause; I H4994
19 will plead with me? for n, if I hold my H6258
14:16 For n thou numberest my steps: dost H6258
16: 7 But n he hath made me weary: thou H6258
19 Also n, behold, my witness *is* in heaven, H6258
17: 3 Lay down n, put me in a surety with H4994
10 ye return, and come n: for I cannot find H4994
15 And where *is* n my hope? as for my H645
19: 6 Know n that God hath overthrown me, H645
23 Oh that my words were n written! oh H645
22:21 Acquaint n thyself with him, and be at H4994
24:25 And if *it be* not *so* n, who will make me a H645
30: 1 But n *they that are* younger than I have H6258

Job 30: 9 And n am I their song, yea, I am their H6258
16 And n my soul is poured out upon me; H6258
32: 4 N Elihu had waited till Job had spoken,
14 N he hath not directed *his* words against
33: 2 Behold, n I have opened my mouth, my H4994
34:16 If n *thou hast* understanding, hear this:
35:15 But n, because *it is* not *so*, he hath H6258
37:21 And n *men* see not the bright light H6258
38: 3 Gird up n thy loins like a man; for I will H4994
40: 7 Gird up thy loins n like a man: I will H4994
10 Deck thyself n *with* majesty and H4994
15 Behold n behemoth, which I made with H4994
16 Lo n, his strength *is* in his loins, and his H4994
42: 5 of the ear: but n mine eye seeth thee. H6258
8 Therefore take unto you n seven H6258
Ps 2:10 Be wise n therefore, O ye kings: be H6258
12: 5 of the needy, n will I arise, saith the H6258
17:11 They have n compassed us in our H6258
20: 6 N know I that the LORD saveth his H6258
27: 6 And n shall mine head be lifted up H6258
37:25 I have been young, and *n* am old; yet
39: 7 And n, Lord, what wait I for? my hope H6258
41: 8 *n* that he lieth he shall rise up no more.
50:22 N consider this, ye that forget God, lest H4994
71:18 N also when I am old and grayheaded, O
74: 6 But n they break down the carved work H6258
115: 2 the heathen say, Where *is* n their God? H4994
116:14 I will pay my vows unto the LORD n in
18 I will pay my vows unto the LORD n in
118: 2 Let Israel n say, that his mercy H4994
3 Let the house of Aaron n say, that his H4994
4 Let them n that fear the LORD say, that H4994
25 Save n, I beseech thee, O LORD: O H4994
25 I beseech thee, send n prosperity. H4994
119:67 astray: but n have I kept thy word. H6258
122: 8 I will n say, Peace *be* within thee. H4994
124: 1 who was on our side, n may Israel say; H4994
129: 1 me from my youth, may Israel n say: H4994
Prv 5: 7 Hear me n therefore, O ye children, H6258
6: 3 Do this n, my son, and deliver thyself, H645
7:12 N *is she* without, now in the streets, H6471
12 Now *is she* without, n in the streets, H6471
24 Hearken unto me n therefore, O ye H6258
8:32 N therefore hearken unto me, O ye H6258
Ecc 2: 1 I said in mine heart, Go to n, I will H4994
16 seeing that which n *is* in the days to H3528
3:15 That which hath been is n; and that H3528
9: 6 and their envy, is n perished; neither H3528
7 heart; for God n accepteth thy works. H3528
15 N there was found in it a poor wise man,
12: 1 Remember n thy Creator in the days of
Song 3: 2 I will rise n, and go about the city in the H4994
7: 8 boughs thereof: n also thy breasts shall
Isa 1:18 Come n, and let us reason together, H4994
21 lodged in it; but n murderers. H6258
5: 1 N will I sing to my wellbeloved a song H4994
3 And n, O inhabitants of Jerusalem, and H6258
5 And n go to; I will tell you what I will H6258
7: 3 Isaiah, Go forth n to meet Ahaz, thou, H4994
13 And he said, Hear ye n, O house of
8: 7 N therefore, behold, the Lord bringeth
16:14 But n the LORD hath spoken, saying, H6258
19:12 let them tell thee n, and let them know H4994
22: 1 What aileth thee n, that thou art wholly H645
28:22 N therefore be ye not mockers, lest H6258
29:22 Jacob shall not n be ashamed, neither H6258
22 neither shall his face n wax pale. H6258
30: 8 N go, write it before them in a table, H6258
31: 3 N the Egyptians *are* men, and not God;
33:10 N will I rise, saith the LORD; now will I H6258
10 Now will I rise, saith the LORD; n will I H6258
10 will I be exalted; n will I lift up myself. H6258
36: 1 N it came to pass in the fourteenth year
4 unto them, Say ye n to Hezekiah, Thus H4994
5 strength for war: n on whom dost thou H6258
8 N therefore give pledges, I pray thee, to H6258
10 And am I n come up without the LORD H6258
37:20 N therefore, O LORD our God, save us H6258
26 I have formed it? n have I brought it to
38: 3 And said, Remember n, O LORD, I H4994
42:14 *and* refrained myself: *n* will I cry like a
43: 1 But n thus saith the LORD that created H6258
19 Behold, I will do a new thing; n it shall H6258
44: 1 Yet n hear, O Jacob my servant; and H6258
47: 8 Therefore hear n this, *thou that art* H6258
12 Stand n with thine enchantments, and H4994
13 thy counsels. Let n the astrologers, the H4994
48: 7 They are created n, and not from the H6258
16 there *am* I: and n the Lord GOD, and H6258

Isa 49: 5 And n, saith the LORD that formed me H6258
19 shall even n be too narrow by reason H6258
51:21 Therefore hear n this, thou afflicted, H4994
52: 5 N therefore, what have I here, saith the H6258
64: 8 But n, O LORD, thou art our father; we H6258
Jer 2:18 And n what hast thou to do in the way H6258
4:12 shall come unto me: n also will I give H6258
31 saying, Woe is me n! for my soul is H4994
5: 1 and see n, and know, and seek H4994
21 Hear n this, O foolish people, and H4994
24 Neither say they in their heart, Let us n H4994
7:12 But go ye n unto my place which was in H4994
13 And n, because ye have done all these H4994
14:10 accept them; he will n remember their H4994
17:15 is the word of the LORD? let it come n. H4994
18:11 N therefore go to, speak to the men of H6258
11 you: return ye n every one from his H4994
13 saith the LORD; Ask ye n among the H4994
20: 1 N Pashur the son of Immer the priest,
25: 5 They said, Turn ye again n every one H4994
26: 8 N it came to pass, when Jeremiah had
13 Therefore n amend your ways and H6258
27: 6 And n have I given all these lands into H6258
16 house shall n shortly be brought again H6258
18 them, let them n make intercession to H4994
28: 7 Nevertheless hear thou n this word that H4994
15 the prophet, Hear n, Hananiah; The H4994
29: 1 N these are the words of the letter that
27 N therefore why hast thou not reproved
30: 6 Ask ye n, and see whether a man doth H4994
32:16 N when I had delivered the evidence of
36 And n therefore thus saith the LORD, H6258
34:10 N when all the princes, and all the
15 And ye were n turned, and had done H3117
35:15 saying, Return ye n every man from his H4994
36:15 And they said unto him, Sit down n, H4994
16 N it came to pass, when they had heard
17 saying, Tell us n, How didst thou write H4994
22 N the king sat in the winterhouse in the
37: 3 Pray n unto the LORD our God for us. H4994
4 N Jeremiah came in and went out
19 Where are n your prophets which H346
20 Therefore hear n, I pray thee, O my lord
38: 7 N when Ebed-melech the Ethiopian, one
12 Jeremiah, Put n these old cast clouts H4994
25 Declare unto us n what thou hast said H4994
39:11 N Nebuchadrezzar king of Babylon gave
15 N the word of the LORD came unto
40: 3 N the LORD hath brought it, and done
4 And n, behold, I loose thee this day H6258
5 N while he was not yet gone back, he
7 N when all the captains of the forces
41: 1 N it came to pass in the seventh month,
9 N the pit wherein Ishmael had cast all
13 N it came to pass, that when all the H6258
42:15 And n therefore hear the word of the
21 And n I have this day declared it to H6258
22 N therefore know certainly that ye shall H6258
44: 7 Therefore n thus saith the LORD, the
45: 3 Thou didst say, Woe is me n! for the H4994
52: 7 the king's garden; (n the Chaldeans were
12 N in the fifth month, in the tenth day of
Ezk 1: 1 N it came to pass in the thirtieth year, in
15 N as I beheld the living creatures, behold
4:14 youth up even till n have I not eaten of
7: 3 N is the end come upon thee, and I will H6258
8 N will I shortly pour out my fury upon H6258
8: 5 lift up thine eyes n the way toward the H4994
8 me, Son of man, dig n in the wall: and H4994
10: 3 N the cherubims stood on the right side
16: 8 N when I passed by thee, and looked
17:12 Say n to the rebellious house, Know ye H4994
18:14 N, lo, if he beget a son, that seeth all his
25 is not equal. Hear n, O house of Israel; H4994
19: 5 N when she saw that she had waited,
13 And n she is planted in the wilderness, H6258
22: 2 N, thou son of man, wilt thou judge, wilt
23:43 Will they n commit whoredoms H6258
26: 2 shall be replenished, n she is laid waste:
18 N shall the isles tremble in the day of H6258
27: 2 N, thou son of man, take up a
33:22 N the hand of the LORD was upon me in
38:12 places that are n inhabited, and upon
39:25 Therefore thus saith the Lord GOD; N H6258
41:12 N the building that was before the
42: 5 N the upper chambers were shorter: for
15 N when he had made an end of
43: 9 N let them put away their whoredom, H6258
46:12 N when the prince shall prepare a H3588

Ezk 47: 7 N when I had returned, behold, at the
48: 1 N these are the names of the tribes.
Dan 1: 6 N among these were of the children of
9 N God had brought Daniel into favour
18 N at the end of the days that the king
2:23 known unto me n what we desired of H3705
23 thee: for thou hast n made known unto H3705
3:15 N if ye be ready that at what time ye H3705
4:18 have seen. N thou, O Belteshazzar,
37 N I Nebuchadnezzar praise and extol H3705
5:10 N the queen, by reason of the words of
12 Belteshazzar: n let Daniel be called, H3705
15 And n the wise men, the astrologers, H3705
16 dissolve doubts: n if thou canst read H3705
6: 8 N, O king, establish the decree, and sign H3705
10 N when Daniel knew that the writing H1768
16 the den of lions. N the king spake and H116
8:18 N as he was speaking with me, I was in a
22 N that being broken, whereas four stood
9:15 And n, O Lord our God, that hast H6258
17 N therefore, O our God, hear the prayer H6258
22 O Daniel, I am n come forth to give H6258
10:11 for unto thee am I n sent. And when he H6258
14 N I am come to make thee understand
20 unto thee? and n will I return to fight H6258
11: 2 And n will I shew thee the truth. H6258
34 N when they shall fall, they shall be
Hos 1: 8 N when she had weaned Lo-ruhamah,
2: 7 for then was it better with me than n. H6258
10 And n will I discover her lewdness in H6258
4:16 heifer: n the LORD will feed H6258
5: 3 not hid from me: for n, O Ephraim, thou
7 strange children: n shall a month H6258
7: 2 all their wickedness: n their own doings
8: 8 Israel is swallowed up: n shall they be
10 the nations, n will I gather them, and H6258
13 them not; n will he remember their H6258
10: 2 Their heart is divided; n shall they be H6258
3 For n they shall say, We have no king, H6258
13: 2 And n they sin more and more, and H6258
Joel 2:12 Therefore also n, saith the LORD, turn H6258
Am 6: 7 Therefore n shall they go captive with H6258
7:16 N therefore hear thou the word of the H6258
Jna 1: 1 N the word of the LORD came unto
17 N the LORD had prepared a great fish to
3: 3 word of the LORD. N Nineveh was an
4: 3 Therefore n, O LORD, take, I beseech H6258
Mic 4: 9 N why dost thou cry out aloud? is there H6258
10 in travail: for n shalt thou go forth out H6258
11 N also many nations are gathered H6258
5: 1 N gather thyself in troops, O daughter H6258
4 shall abide: for n shall he be great unto H6258
6: 1 Hear ye n what the LORD saith; Arise, H4994
5 O my people, remember n what Balak H4994
7: 4 cometh; n shall be their perplexity. H6258
10 shall behold her: n shall she be trodden H6258
Nah 1:13 For n will I break his yoke from off H6258
Hag 1: 5 N therefore thus saith the LORD of H6258
2: 2 Speak n to Zerubbabel the son of H4994
3 how do ye see it n? is it not in your eyes H6258
4 Yet n be strong, O Zerubbabel, saith H6258
11 Thus saith the LORD of hosts; Ask n H4994
15 And n, I pray you, consider from this H4994
18 Consider n from this day and upward, H4994
Zec 1: 4 of hosts; Turn ye n from your evil H4994
3: 3 N Joshua was clothed with filthy
8 Hear n, O Joshua the high priest, thou, H4994
5: 5 unto me, Lift up n thine eyes, and see H4994
8:11 But n I will not be unto the residue of H6258
9: 8 more: for n have I seen with mine eyes. H6258
Mal 1: 8 it not evil? offer it n unto thy governor; H4994
9 And n, I pray you, beseech God that he H6258
2: 1 And n, O ye priests, this commandment H6258
3:10 and prove me n herewith, saith the H4994
15 And n we call the proud happy; yea, H6258
Mt 1:18 N the birth of Jesus Christ was on this G1161
22 N all this was done, that it might be G1161
2: 1 N when Jesus was born in Bethlehem of G1161
3:10 And n also the axe is laid unto the root G2235
15 Suffer it to be so n: for thus it becometh G737
4:12 N when Jesus had heard that John was G1161
8:18 N when Jesus saw great multitudes G1161
9:18 daughter is even n dead: but come and G737
10: 2 N the names of the twelve apostles are G1161
11: 2 N when John had heard in the prison G1161
12 John the Baptist until n the kingdom of G737
14:15 place, and the time is n past; send the G2235
24 But the ship was n in the midst of the G2235
15:32 continue with me n three days, and G2235

Mt 21:18 N in the morning as he returned into G1161
22:25 N there were with us seven brethren: G1161
24:32 N learn a parable of the fig tree; When G1161
26: 6 N when Jesus was in Bethany, in the G1161
17 N the first day of the feast of G1161
20 N when the even was come, he sat G1161
45 them, Sleep on n, and take your rest: G3063
48 N he that betrayed him gave them a G1161
53 Thinkest thou that I cannot n pray to my G737
59 N the chief priests, and elders, and all G1161
65 behold, n ye have heard his blasphemy. G3568
69 N Peter sat without in the palace: and a G1161
27:15 N at that feast the governor was wont G1161
42 of Israel, let him n come down from the G3568
43 him deliver him n, if he will have him: G3568
45 N from the sixth hour there was G1161
54 N when the centurion, and they that G1161
62 N the next day, that followed the day of G1161
28:11 N when they were going, behold, some G1161
Mk 1:14 N after that John was put in prison, G1161
16 N as he walked by the sea of Galilee, he G1161
4:37 beat into the ship, so that it was n full. G2235
5:11 N there was there nigh unto the G1161
6:35 And when the day was n far spent, his G2235
35 place, and n the time is far passed: G2235
8: 2 because they have n been with me G2235
14 N the disciples had forgotten to take G2532
10:30 But he shall receive an hundredfold n G3568
11:11 upon all things, and n the eventide was G2235
12:20 N there were seven brethren: and the G3767
13:12 N the brother shall betray the brother G1161
28 N learn a parable of the fig tree; When G1161
14:41 them, Sleep on n, and take your rest: G3063
15: 6 N at that feast he released unto them G1161
32 Let Christ the King of Israel descend n G3568
42 And n when the even was come, G2235
16: 9 N when Jesus was risen early the first G1161
Lk 1: 7 they both were n well stricken in years.
57 N Elisabeth's full time came that she G1161
2:15 one to another, Let us n go even unto G1211
29 Lord, n lettest thou thy servant depart G3568
41 N his parents went to Jerusalem every G2532
3: 1 N in the fifteenth year of the reign of G1161
9 And n also the axe is laid unto the root G2235
21 N when all the people were baptized, it G1161
4:40 N when the sun was setting, all they G1161
5: 4 N when he had left speaking, he said G1161
6:21 Blessed are ye that hunger n: for ye G3568
21 are ye that weep n: for ye shall laugh. G3568
25 laugh n! for ye shall mourn and weep. G3568
7: 1 N when he had ended all his sayings in G1161
6 And when he was n not far from the G2235
12 N when he came nigh to the gate of the G1161
39 N when the Pharisee which had bidden G1161
8:11 N the parable is this: The seed is the G1161
22 N it came to pass on a certain day, that G2532
38 N the man out of whom the devils were G1161
9: 7 N Herod the tetrarch heard of all that G1161
10:36 Which n of these three, thinkest thou, G3767
38 N it came to pass, as they went, that he G1161
11: 7 me not: the door is n shut, and my G2235
39 And the Lord said unto him, N do ye G3568
14:17 Come; for all things are n ready. G2235
15:25 N his elder son was in the field: and as G1161
16:25 evil things: but n he is comforted, and G3568
18:22 N when Jesus heard these things, he G1161
19:37 And when he was come nigh, even n at G2235
42 but n they are hid from thine eyes. G3568
20:37 N that the dead are raised, even Moses G1161
21:30 When they n shoot forth, ye see and G2235
30 selves that summer is n nigh at hand. G2235
22: 1 N the feast of unleavened bread drew G1161
36 Then said he unto them, But n, he that G3568
23:47 N when the centurion saw what was G1161
24: 1 N upon the first day of the week, very G1161
Jn 1:44 N Philip was of Bethsaida, the city of G1161
2: 8 And he saith unto them, Draw out n, G3568
10 but thou hast kept the good wine until n. G737
23 N when he was in Jerusalem at the G1161
4: 6 N Jacob's well was there. Jesus G1161
18 and he whom thou n hast is not thy G3568
23 But the hour cometh, and n is, when G3568
42 And said unto the woman, N we G3765
43 N after two days he departed thence, G1161
51 And as he was n going down, his G2235
5: 2 N there is at Jerusalem by the sheep G1161
6 that he had been n a long time in that G2235
25 is coming, and n is, when the dead G3568
6:10 the men sit down. N there was much G1161

Jn 6:16 And when even was n come, his
17 And it was n dark, and Jesus was G2235
7: 2 N the Jews' feast of tabernacles was at G1161
14 N about the midst of the feast Jesus G2235
8: 5 N Moses in the law commanded us, G1161
40 But n ye seek to kill me, a man that G3568
52 Then said the Jews unto him, N we G3568
9:19 was born blind? how then doth he n see? G737
21 But by what means he n seeth, we G3568
25 know, that, whereas I was blind, n I see. G737
31 N we know that God heareth not G1161
41 have no sin: but n ye say, We see; G3568
11: 1 N a certain *man* was sick, *named* G1161
5 N Jesus loved Martha, and her sister, G1161
18 N Bethany was nigh unto Jerusalem, G1161
22 But I know, that even n, whatsoever G3568
30 N Jesus was not yet come into the G1161
57 N both the chief priests and the G1161
12:27 N is my soul troubled; and what shall I G3568
31 N is the judgment of this world: now G3568
31 Now is the judgment of this world: n G3568
13: 1 N before the feast of the passover, G1161
2 the devil having n put into the heart of G2235
7 not n; but thou shalt know hereafter. G737
19 N I tell you before it come, that, when it G575
23 N there was leaning on Jesus' bosom G1161
28 N no man at the table knew for what G1161
31 out, Jesus said, N is the Son of man G3568
33 I go, ye cannot come; so n I say to you. G737
36 n; but thou shalt follow me afterwards. G3568
37 n? I will lay down my life for thy sake. G737
14:29 And n I have told you before it come to G3568
15: 3 N ye are clean through the word which G2235
22 but n they have no cloak for their sin. G3568
24 not had sin: but n have they both seen G3568
16: 5 But n I go my way to him that sent me; G3568
12 say unto you, but ye cannot bear them n. G737
19 N Jesus knew that they were desirous G3767
22 And ye n therefore have sorrow: but I G3568
29 His disciples said unto him, Lo, n G3568
30 N are we sure that thou knowest all G3568
31 Jesus answered them, Do ye n believe? G737
32 Behold, the hour cometh, yea, is n G3568
17: 5 And n, O Father, glorify thou me with G3568
7 N they have known that all things G3568
11 And n I am no more in the world, but G3765
13 And n come I to thee; and these things G3568
18:14 N Caiaphas was he, which gave G1161
24 N Annas had sent him bound unto G3767
36 but n is my kingdom not from hence. G3568
40 Barabbas. N Barabbas was a robber. G1161
19:23 part; and also *his* coat: n the coat was G1161
25 N there stood by the cross of Jesus his G1161
28 all things were n accomplished, that G2235
29 N there was set a vessel full of vinegar: G3767
41 N in the place where he was crucified G1161
21: 4 But when the morning was n come, G2235
6 therefore, and n they were not able to G2089
7 It is the Lord. N when Simon Peter G3767
10 of the fish which ye have n caught. G3568
14 This is n the third time that Jesus G2235
Act 1:18 N this man purchased a field with the G3767
2: 6 N when this was noised abroad, the G1161
33 forth this, which ye n see and hear. G3568
37 N when they heard *this*, they were G1161
3: 1 N Peter and John went up together into G1161
17 And n, brethren, I wot that through G3568
4: 3 unto the next day: for it was n eventide. G2235
13 N when they saw the boldness of Peter G1161
29 And n, Lord, behold their threatenings: G3569
5:24 N when the high priest and the captain G1161
38 And n I say unto you, Refrain from G3569
7: 4 him into this land, wherein ye n dwell. G3568
11 N there came a dearth over all the land G1161
34 n come, I will send thee into Egypt. G3568
52 been n the betrayers and murderers: G3568
8:14 N when the apostles which were at G1161
9:36 N there was at Joppa a certain disciple G1161
10: 5 And n send men to Joppa, and call for G3568
17 N while Peter doubted in himself what G1161
33 thou art come. N therefore are we all G3568
11:19 N they which were scattered abroad G3767
12: 1 N about that time Herod the king G1161
11 himself, he said, N I know of a surety, G3568
18 N as soon as it was day, there was no G1161
13: 1 N there were in the church that was at G1161
11 And n, behold, the hand of the Lord *is* G3568
13 N when Paul and his company loosed G1161
34 up from the dead, n no more to return to

Act 13:43 N when the congregation was broken G1161
15:10 N therefore why tempt ye God, to put a G3568
16: 6 N when they had gone throughout G1161
36 go: n therefore depart, and go in peace. G3568
37 into prison; and n do they thrust us out G3568
17: 1 N when they had passed through G1161
16 N while Paul waited for them at G1161
30 winked at; but n commandeth all men G3569
18:14 And when Paul was n about to open G1161
20:22 And n, behold, I go bound in the spirit G3568
25 And n, behold, I know that ye all, G3568
32 And n, brethren, I commend you to G3569
21: 3 N when we had discovered Cyprus, we G1161
22: 1 my defence *which I make* n unto you. G3568
16 And n why tarriest thou? arise, and be G3568
23:15 N therefore ye with the council signify G3568
21 have killed him: and n are they ready, G3568
24:13 the things whereof they n accuse me. G3568
17 N after many years I came to bring G1161
25: 1 N when Festus was come into the G3767
26: 6 And n I stand and am judged for the G3568
17 the Gentiles, unto whom n I send thee, G3568
27: 9 N when much time was spent, and G1161
9 when sailing was n dangerous, because G2235
9 n already past, Paul admonished *them*, G2235
22 And n I exhort you to be of good cheer: G3569
Ro 1:10 Making request, if by any means n at G2235
13 N I would not have you ignorant, G1161
3:19 N we know that what things soever the G1161
21 But n the righteousness of God without G3570
4: 4 N to him that worketh is the reward G1161
19 not his own body n dead, when he was G2235
23 N it was not written for his sake alone, G1161
5: 9 Much more then, being n justified by G3568
11 we have n received the atonement. G3568
6: 8 N if we be dead with Christ, we believe G1161
19 iniquity; even so n yield your members G3568
21 whereof ye are n ashamed? for the end G3568
22 But n being made free from sin, and G3570
7: 6 But n we are delivered from the law, G3570
17 N then it is no more I that do it, but sin G3570
20 N if I do that I would not, it is no more G1161
8: 1 *There is* therefore n no condemnation G3568
9 of God dwell in you. N if any man have G1161
22 and travaileth in pain together until n. G3568
11:12 N if the fall of them *be* the riches of the G1161
30 God, yet have n obtained mercy G3568
31 Even so have these also n not believed, G3568
13:11 And that, knowing the time, that n *it is* G2235
11 out of sleep: for n *is* our salvation G3568
14:15 with *thy* meat, n walkest thou not G3765
15: 5 N the God of patience and consolation G1161
8 N I say that Jesus Christ was a minister G1161
13 N the God of hope fill you with all joy G1161
23 But n having no more place in these G3570
25 But n I go unto Jerusalem to minister G3570
30 N I beseech you, brethren, for the Lord G1161
33 N the God of peace *be* with you all. G1161
16:17 N I beseech you, brethren, mark them G1161
25 N to him that is of power to stablish G1161
26 But n is made manifest, and by the G3568
1Co 1:10 N I beseech you, brethren, by the name G1161
12 N this I say, that every one of you saith, G1161
2:12 N we have received, not the spirit of the G1161
3: 2 able *to bear it*, neither yet n are ye able. G3568
8 N he that planteth and he that G1161
12 N if any man build upon this G1161
4: 7 thou didst not receive? n if thou didst G1161
8 N ye are full, now ye are rich, ye have G2235
8 Now ye are full, n ye are rich, ye have G2235
18 N some are puffed up, as though I G1161
5:11 But n I have written unto you not to G3570
6: 7 N therefore there is utterly a fault G2235
13 both it and them. N the body *is* not for G1161
7: 1 N concerning the things whereof ye G1161
14 children unclean; but n are they holy. G3568
25 N concerning virgins I have no G1161
8: 1 N as touching things offered unto idols, G1161
9:25 in all things. N they *do it* to obtain G3767
10: 6 N these things were our examples, to G1161
11 N all these things happened unto them G1161
11: 2 N I praise you, brethren, that ye G1161
17 N in this that I declare *unto you* I G1161
12: 1 N concerning spiritual *gifts*, brethren, I G1161
4 N there are diversities of gifts, but the G1161
18 But n hath God set the members every G3570
20 But n *are they* many members, yet but G3568
27 N ye are the body of Christ, and G1161
13:12 For n we see through a glass, darkly; but G737

1Co 13:12 then face to face: n I know in part; but G737
13 And n abideth faith, hope, charity, G3570
14: 6 N, brethren, if I come unto you G3570
15:12 N if Christ be preached that he rose G1161
20 But n is Christ risen from the dead, *and* G3570
50 N this I say, brethren, that flesh and G1161
16: 1 N concerning the collection for the G1161
5 N I will come unto you, when I shall G1161
7 For I will not see you n by the way; but I G737
10 N if Timotheus come, see that he may G1161
2Co 1:21 N he which stablisheth us with you in G1161
2:14 N thanks *be* unto God, which always G1161
3:17 N the Lord is that Spirit: and where the G1161
5: 5 N he that hath wrought us for the G1161
16 n henceforth know we *him* no more. G3568
20 N then we are ambassadors for Christ,
6: 2 thee: behold, n *is* the accepted time; G3568
2 time; behold, n *is* the day of salvation.) G3568
13 N for a recompence in the same, (I G1161
7: 9 N I rejoice, not that ye were made G3568
8:11 N therefore perform the doing *of it*; G3570
14 But by an equality, *that* n at this time G3568
22 in many things, but n much more G3570
9:10 N he that ministereth seed to the sower G1161
10: 1 N I Paul myself beseech you by the G1161
12: 6 say the truth: but n I forbear, lest any
13: 2 and being absent n I write to them G3568
7 N I pray to God that ye do no evil; not G1161
Gal 1: 9 As we said before, so say I n again, If G737
10 For do I n persuade men, or God? or do I G737
20 N the things which I write unto you, G1161
23 us in times past n preacheth the faith G3568
2:20 the life which I n live in the flesh I live G3568
3: 3 are ye n made perfect by the flesh? G3568
16 N to Abraham and his seed were the G1161
20 N a mediator is not *a mediator* of one, G1161
4: 1 N I say, *That* the heir, as long as he is a G1161
9 But n, after that ye have known God, or G3568
20 I desire to be present with you n, and to G737
25 to Jerusalem which n is, and is in G3568
28 N we, brethren, as Isaac was, are the G1161
29 *was born* after the Spirit, even so *it is* n. G3568
5:19 N the works of the flesh are manifest, G1161
Eph 2: 2 the air, the spirit that n worketh in the G3568
13 But n in Christ Jesus ye who sometimes G3570
19 N therefore ye are no more strangers G3767
3: 5 of men, as it is n revealed unto his holy G3568
10 To the intent that n unto the G3568
20 N unto him that is able to do exceeding G1161
4: 9 (N that he ascended, what is it but that G1161
5: 8 For ye were sometimes darkness, but n G3568
Php 1: 5 in the gospel from the first day until n; G3568
20 as always, *so* n also Christ shall be G3568
30 ye saw in me, and n hear *to be* in me. G3568
2:12 presence only, but n much more in my G3568
3:18 you often, and n tell you even weeping, G3568
4:10 the Lord greatly, that n at the last your G2235
15 N ye Philippians know also, that in the G1161
20 N unto God and our Father *be* glory for G1161
Col 1:21 wicked works, yet n hath he reconciled G3570
24 Who n rejoice in my sufferings for you, G3568
26 but n is made manifest to his saints: G3570
3: 8 But n ye also put off all these; anger, G3570
1Th 3: 6 But n when Timotheus came from you G737
8 For n we live, if ye stand fast in the G3568
11 N God himself and our Father, and our G1161
5:14 N we exhort you, brethren, warn them G1161
2Th 2: 1 N we beseech you, brethren, by the G1161
6 And n ye know what withholdeth that G3568
7 work: only he who n letteth *will let*, until G737
16 N our Lord Jesus Christ himself, and G1161
3: 6 N we command you, brethren, in the G1161
12 N them that are such we command G1161
16 N the Lord of peace himself give you G1161
1Ti 1: 5 N the end of the commandment is G1161
17 N unto the King eternal, immortal, G1161
4: 1 N the Spirit speaketh expressly, that in G1161
8 that n is, and of that which is to come. G3568
5: 5 N she that is a widow indeed, and G1161
2Ti 1:10 But is n made manifest by the G3568
3: 8 N as Jannes and Jambres withstood G1161
4: 6 For I am n ready to be offered, and the G2235
Phlm 9 and n also a prisoner of Jesus Christ. G3570
11 but n profitable to thee and to me: G3570
16 Not n as a servant, but above a G3765
Heb 2: 8 put under him. But n we see not yet all G3568
7: 4 N consider how great this man *was*, G1161
8: 1 N of the things which we have spoken G1161
6 But n hath he obtained a more G3570

Heb 8:13 hath made the first old. **N** that which G1161
9: 5 which we cannot **n** speak particularly. G3568
6 **N** when these things were thus G1161
24 into heaven itself, **n** to appear in the G3568
26 of the world: but **n** once in the end of G3568
10:18 **N** where remission of these *is, there is* G1161
38 **N** the just shall live by faith: but if *any* G1161
11: 1 **N** faith is the substance of things hoped G1161
16 But **n** they desire a better *country*, that G3570
12:11 **N** no chastening for the present G1161
26 the earth: but **n** he hath promised, G3568
13:20 **N** the God of peace, that brought again G1161
Jas 2:11 also, Do not kill. **N** if thou commit no G1161
4:13 Go to **n**, ye that say, To day or to G3568
16 But **n** ye rejoice in your boastings: all G3568
5: 1 Go to **n**, *ye* rich men, weep and howl for G3568
1Pt 1: 6 Wherein ye greatly rejoice, though **n** for G737
8 in whom, though **n** ye see *him* not, yet G737
12 things, which are **n** reported unto you G3568
2:10 a people, but *are* **n** the people of God: G3568
10 mercy, but **n** have obtained mercy. G3568
25 astray; but are **n** returned unto the G3568
3:21 baptism doth also **n** save us (not the G3568
2Pt 2: 3 you: whose judgment **n** of a long time
3: 1 This second epistle, beloved, I **n** write G2235
7 earth, which are **n**, by the same word G3568
18 *be* glory both **n** and for ever. Amen. G3568
1Jn 2: 8 is past, and the true light **n** shineth. G2235
9 his brother, is in darkness even until **n**. G737
18 shall come, even **n** are there many G3568
28 And **n**, little children, abide in him; G3568
3: 2 Beloved, **n** are we the sons of God, and G3568
4: 3 and even **n** already is it in the world. G3568
2Jn 5 And **n** I beseech thee, lady, not as G3568
Jude 24 **N** unto him that is able to keep you G1161
25 and power, both **n** and ever. Amen. G3568
Rev 12:10 saying in heaven, **N** is come salvation, G737

NUMBER

Gen 13:16 so that if a man can **n** the dust of the H4487
15: 5 if thou be able to **n** them: and he said H5608
34:30 and I *being* few in **n**, they shall gather H4557
41:49 he left numbering; for *it was* without **n**. H4557
Ex 12: 4 *it* according to the **n** of the souls; every H4373
16:16 *according to* the **n** of your persons; H4557
23:26 thy land: the **n** of thy days I will fulfil. H4557
30:12 Israel after their **n**, then shall they give H6485
Lev 15:13 then he shall **n** to himself seven days H5608
28 then she shall **n** to herself seven days, H5608
23:16 sabbath shall ye **n** fifty days; and ye H5608
25: 8 And thou shalt **n** seven sabbaths of H5608
15 According to the **n** of years after the H4557
15 unto the **n** of years of the fruits H4557
16 *according* to the **n** *of the years* of the H4557
50 unto the **n** of years, according H4557
26:22 **n**; and your *high* ways shall be desolate. H4591
Nu 1: 2 their fathers, with the **n** of *their* names, H4557
3 Aaron shall **n** them by their armies. H6485
18 according to the **n** of the names, from H4557
20 according to the **n** of the names, by H4557
22 according to the **n** of the names, by H4557
24 according to the **n** of the names, from H4557
26 according to the **n** of the names, from H4557
28 according to the **n** of the names, from H4557
30 according to the **n** of the names, from H4557
32 according to the **n** of the names, from H4557
34 according to the **n** of the names, from H4557
36 according to the **n** of the names, from H4557
38 according to the **n** of the names, from H4557
40 according to the **n** of the names, from H4557
42 according to the **n** of the names, from H4557
49 Only thou shalt not **n** the tribe of Levi, H6485
3:15 **N** the children of Levi after the house of H6485
15 old and upward shalt thou **n** them. H6485
22 according to the **n** of all the males, H4557
28 In the **n** of all the males, from a month H4557
34 according to the **n** of all the males, H4557
40 And the LORD said unto Moses, **N** all H6485
40 upward, and take the **n** of their names. H4557
43 And all the firstborn males by the **n** of H4557
48 the odd **n** of them is to be redeemed, H5736
4:23 old shalt thou **n** them; all that enter H6485
29 As for the sons of Merari, thou shalt **n** H6485
30 old shalt thou **n** them, every one that H6485
37 and Aaron did **n** according to the H6485
41 and Aaron did **n** according to the H6485
14:29 to your whole **n**, from twenty years old H4557
34 After the **n** of the days in which ye H4557
15:12 According to the **n** that ye shall H4557
Nu 15:12 ye do to every one according to their **n**. H4557
23:10 of Jacob, and the **n** of the fourth *part* of H4557
26:53 according to the **n** of names. H4557
29:18 according to their **n**, after the manner: H4557
21 according to their **n**, after the manner: H4557
24 according to their **n**, after the manner: H4557
27 according to their **n**, after the manner: H4557
30 according to their **n**, after the manner: H4557
33 according to their **n**, after the manner: H4557
37 according to their **n**, after the manner: H4557
31:36 out to war, was in **n** three hundred H4557
Dt 4:27 ye shall be left few in **n** among the H4557
7: 7 ye were more in **n** than any people; for H7230
16: 9 Seven weeks shalt thou **n** unto thee: H5608
9 thee: begin to **n** the seven weeks from H5608
25: 2 according to his fault, by a certain **n**. H4557
28:62 And ye shall be left few in **n**, whereas ye H4962
32: 8 to the **n** of the children of Israel. H4557
Jos 4: 5 **n** of the tribes of the children of Israel: H4557
8 according to the **n** of the tribes of the H4557
Jdg 6: 5 were without **n**: and they entered into H4557
7: 6 And the **n** of them that lapped, *putting* H4557
12 *were* without **n**, as the sand by the sea H4557
21:23 wives, according to their **n**, of them that H4557
1Sa 6: 4 *according to* the **n** of the lords of the H4557
18 *according to* the **n** of all the cities of the H4557
14:17 *were* with him, **N** now, and see who is H6485
2Sa 2:15 Then there arose and went over by **n** H4557
21:20 in **n**; and he also was born to the giant. H4557
24: 1 them to say, Go, **n** Israel and Judah. H4487
2 Beer-sheba, and **n** ye the people, that I H6485
2 that I may know the **n** of the people. H4557
4 of the king, to **n** the people of Israel. H6485
9 And Joab gave up the sum of the **n** of H4662
1Ki 18:31 according to the **n** of the tribes of the H4557
20:25 And **n** thee an army, like the army that H4487
1Ch 7: 2 whose **n** *was* in the days of David H4557
9 And the **n** of them, after their H3187
40 the princes. And the **n** throughout the H4557
11:11 And this *is* the **n** of the mighty men H4557
21: 1 Israel, and provoked David to **n** Israel. H4487
2 rulers of the people, Go, **n** Israel from H5608
2 **n** of them to me, that I may know *it*. H4557
5 And Joab gave the sum of the **n** of the H4662
22:16 iron, *there is* no **n**. Arise *therefore*, and H4557
23: 3 upward: and their **n** by their polls, man H4557
24 were counted by **n** of names by their H4557
31 on the set feasts, by **n**, according to the H4557
25: 1 cymbals: and the **n** of the workmen H4557
7 So the **n** of them, with their brethren H4557
27: 1 Now the children of Israel after their **n**, H4557
23 But David took not the **n** of them from H4557
24 Joab the son of Zeruiah began to **n**, but H4487
24 neither was the **n** put in the account of H4557
2Ch 12: 3 *were* without **n** that came with him H4557
26:11 according to the **n** of their account by H4557
12 The whole **n** of the chief of the fathers H4557
29:32 And the **n** of the burnt offerings, which H4557
30:24 great **n** of priests sanctified themselves. H7230
35: 7 present, to the **n** of thirty thousand, H4557
Ezr 1: 9 And this *is* the **n** of them: thirty H4557
2: 2 **n** of the men of the people of Israel: H4557
3: 4 burnt offerings by **n**, according to the H4557
6:17 to the **n** of the tribes of Israel. H4510
8:34 By **n** *and* by weight of every one: and H4557
Neh 7: 7 Baanah. The **n**, *I say*, of the men of H4557
Est 9:11 On that day the **n** of those that were H4557
Job 1: 5 *according* to the **n** of them all: for Job H4557
3: 6 let it not come into the **n** of the months. H4557
5: 9 marvellous things without **n**: H4557
9:10 out; yea, and wonders without **n**. H4557
14: 5 Seeing his days *are* determined, the **n** H4557
15:20 **n** of years is hidden to the oppressor. H4557
21:21 **n** of his months is cut off in the midst? H4557
25: 3 Is there any **n** of his armies? and upon H4557
31:37 I would declare unto him the **n** of my H4557
34:24 without **n**, and set others in their stead. H2714
36:26 can the **n** of his years be searched out. H4557
38:21 or *because* the **n** of thy days *is* great? H4557
37 Who can **n** the clouds in wisdom? or H5608
39: 2 Canst thou **n** the months *that* they H5608
Ps 90:12 So teach *us* to **n** our days, that we may H4487
105:12 When they were *but* a few men in **n**; H4557
34 and caterpillers, and that without **n**, H4557
139:18 they are more in **n** than the sand: when
147: 4 He telleth the **n** of the stars; he calleth H4557
Song 6: 8 concubines, and virgins without **n**. H4557
Isa 21:17 And the residue of the **n** of archers, the H4557
40:26 out their host by **n**: he calleth them all H4557
Isa 65:11 furnish the drink offering unto that **n**. H4507
12 Therefore will I **n** you to the sword, and H4487
Jer 2:28 **n** of thy cities are thy gods, O Judah. H4557
32 have forgotten me days without **n**. H4557
11:13 For *according to* the **n** of thy cities were H4557
13 and *according to* the **n** of the streets of H4557
44:28 Yet a small **n** that escape the sword H4557
Ezk 4: 4 *according* to the **n** of the days that thou H4557
5 according to the **n** of the days, three H4557
9 *according* to the **n** of the days that thou H4557
5: 3 Thou shalt also take thereof a few in **n**, H4557
Dan 9: 2 by books the **n** of the years, whereof H4557
Hos 1:10 Yet the **n** of the children of Israel shall H4557
Joel 1: 6 and without **n**, whose teeth *are* the H4557
Nah 3: 3 of slain, and a great **n** of carcases; and
Mk 10:46 disciples and a great **n** of people, blind G2425
Lk 22: 3 Iscariot, being of the **n** of the twelve. G706
Jn 6:10 men sat down, in **n** about five thousand. G706
Act 1:15 and said, (the **n** of names together G3793
4: 4 **n** of the men was about five thousand. G706
5:36 to whom a **n** of men, about four G706
6: 1 And in those days, when the **n** of the G4129
7 God increased; and the **n** of the disciples G706
11:21 **n** believed, and turned unto the Lord. G706
16: 5 in the faith, and increased in **n** daily. G706
Ro 9:27 Israel, Though the **n** of the children of G706
2Co 10:12 make ourselves of the **n**, or compare G1469
1Ti 5: 9 Let not a widow be taken into the **n** G2639
Rev 5:11 the elders: and the **n** of them was ten G706
7: 4 And I heard the **n** of them which were G706
9 no man could **n**, of all nations, and G705
9:16 And the **n** of the army of the horsemen G706
16 thousand: and I heard the **n** of them. G706
13:17 name of the beast, or the **n** of his name. G706
18 count the **n** of the beast: for it is G706
18 the beast: for it is the **n** of a man; and his G706
18 his **n** *is* Six hundred threescore *and* six. G706
15: 2 mark, *and* over the **n** of his name, stand G706
20: 8 the **n** of whom *is* as the sand of the sea. G706

NUMBERED

Gen 13:16 the earth, *then* shall thy seed also be **n**. H4487
16:10 that it shall not be **n** for multitude. H5608
32:12 sea, which cannot be **n** for multitude. H5608
Ex 30:13 them that are **n**, half a shekel after the H6485
14 them that are **n**, from twenty years old H6485
38:25 And the silver of them that were **n** of H6485
26 that went to be **n**, from twenty years old H6485
Nu 1:19 so he **n** them in the wilderness of Sinai. H6485
21 Those that were **n** of them, *even* of the H6485
22 those that were **n** of them, according H6485
23 Those that were **n** of them, *even* of the H6485
25 Those that were **n** of them, *even* of the H6485
27 Those that were **n** of them, *even* of the H6485
29 Those that were **n** of them, *even* of the H6485
31 Those that were **n** of them, *even* of the H6485
33 Those that were **n** of them, *even* of the H6485
35 Those that were **n** of them, *even* of the H6485
37 Those that were **n** of them, *even* of the H6485
39 Those that were **n** of them, *even* of the H6485
41 Those that were **n** of them, *even* of the H6485
43 Those that were **n** of them, *even* of the H6485
44 These *are* those that were **n**, which H6485
44 Moses and Aaron **n**, and the princes of H6485
45 So were all those that were **n** of the H6485
46 Even all they that were **n** were six H6485
47 their fathers were not **n** among them. H6485
2: 4 And his host, and those that were **n** of H6485
6 And his host, and those that were **n** H6485
8 And his host, and those that were **n** H6485
9 All that were **n** in the camp of Judah H6485
11 And his host, and those that were **n** H6485
13 And his host, and those that were **n** of H6485
15 And his host, and those that were **n** of H6485
16 All that were **n** in the camp of Reuben H6485
19 And his host, and those that were **n** of H6485
21 And his host, and those that were **n** of H6485
23 And his host, and those that were **n** of H6485
24 All that were **n** of the camp of Ephraim H6485
26 And his host, and those that were **n** of H6485
28 And his host, and those that were **n** of H6485
30 And his host, and those that were **n** of H6485
31 All they that were **n** in the camp of Dan H6485
32 These *are* those which were **n** of the H6485
32 all those that were **n** of the camps H6485
33 But the Levites were not **n** among the H6485
3:16 And Moses **n** them according to the H6485
22 Those that were **n** of them, according H6485
22 those that were **n** of them *were* seven H6485

Nu 3:34 And those that were **n** of them, H6485
39 All that were **n** of the Levites, which H6485
39 which Moses and Aaron **n** at the H6485
42 And Moses **n**, as the LORD commanded H6485
43 of those that were **n** of them, were H6485
4:34 of the congregation **n** the sons of the H6485
36 And those that were **n** of them by their H6485
37 These *were* they that were **n** of the H6485
38 And those that were **n** of the sons of H6485
40 Even those that were **n** of them, H6485
41 These *are* they that were **n** of the H6485
42 And those that were **n** of the families of H6485
44 Even those that were **n** of them after H6485
45 These *be* those that were **n** of the H6485
45 Moses and Aaron **n** according to the H6485
46 All those that were **n** of the Levites, H6485
46 the chief of Israel **n**, after their families, H6485
48 Even those that were **n** of them, were H6485
49 the LORD they were **n** by the hand of H6485
49 thus were they **n** of him, as the LORD H6485
7: 2 were over them that were **n**, offered: H6485
14:29 and all that were **n** of you, according to H6485
26: 7 they that were **n** of them were forty and H6485
18 to those that were **n** of them, forty H6485
22 according to those that were **n** of them, H6485
25 according to those that were **n** of them, H6485
27 according to those that were **n** of them, H6485
34 those that were **n** of them, fifty and two H6485
37 to those that were **n** of them, thirty and H6485
41 they that were **n** of them *were* forty and H6485
43 to those that were **n** of them, *were* H6485
47 to those that were **n** of them; *who were* H6485
50 they that were **n** of them *were* forty and H6485
51 These *were* the **n** of the children of H6485
54 according to those that were **n** of him. H6485
57 And these *are* they that were **n** of the H6485
62 And those that were **n** of them were H6485
62 for they were not **n** among the children H6485
63 These *are* they that were **n** by Moses H6485
63 the priest, who **n** the children of Israel H6485
64 and Aaron the priest **n**, when they H6485
64 when they **n** the children of Israel H6485
Jos 8:10 in the morning, and **n** the people, and H6485
Jdg 20:15 And the children of Benjamin were **n** at H6485
15 were **n** seven hundred chosen men. H6485
17 beside Benjamin, were **n** four hundred H6485
21: 9 For the people were **n**, and, behold, H6485
1Sa 11: 8 And when he **n** them in Bezek, the H6485
13:15 And Saul **n** the people *that were* H6485
14:17 when they had **n**, behold, Jonathan and H6485
15: 4 together, and **n** them in Telaim, two H6485
2Sa 18: 1 And David **n** the people that *were* with H6485
24:10 him after that he had **n** the people. And H5608
1Ki 3: 8 cannot be **n** nor counted for multitude. H4487
8: 5 could not be told nor **n** for multitude. H4487
20:15 Then he **n** the young men of the princes H6485
15 and after them he **n** all the people, *even* H6485
26 that Ben-hadad **n** the Syrians, and H6485
27 And the children of Israel were **n**, and H6485
2Ki 3: 6 the same time, and **n** all Israel. H6485
1Ch 21:17 the people to be **n**? even I it is that have H4487
23: 3 Now the Levites were **n** from the age of H5608
27 **n** from twenty years old and above: H4557
2Ch 2:17 And Solomon **n** all the strangers that H5608
17 his father had **n** them; and they were H5608
5: 6 could not be told nor **n** for multitude. H4487
25: 5 Benjamin: and he **n** them from twenty H6485
Ezr 1: 8 the treasurer, and **n** them unto H5608
Ps 40: 5 *of them*, they are more than can be **n**. H5608
Ecc 1:15 and that which is wanting cannot be **n**. H4487
Isa 22:10 And ye have **n** the houses of Jerusalem, H5608
53:12 unto death: and he was **n** with the H4487
Jer 33:22 As the host of heaven cannot be **n**, H5608
Dan 5:26 hath **n** thy kingdom, and finished it. H4483
Hos 1:10 be measured nor **n**; and it shall come to H5608
Mt 10:30 But the very hairs of your head are all **n**. *G705*
Mk 15:28 And he was **n** with the transgressors. *G3049*
Lk 12: 7 your head are all **n**. Fear not therefore: ye *G705*
Act 1:17 For he was **n** with us, and had obtained *G2674*
26 and he was **n** with the eleven apostles. *G4785*

NUMBEREST
Ex 30:12 LORD, when thou **n** them; that there be H6485
12 among them, when *thou* **n** them. H6485
Job 14:16 For now thou **n** my steps: dost thou not H5608

NUMBERING
Gen 41:49 he left **n**; for *it was* without number. H5608
2Ch 2:17 of Israel, after the **n** wherewith David H5610

NUMBERS
1Ch 12:23 And these *are* the **n** of the bands *that* H4557
2Ch 17:14 And these *are* the **n** of them according H6486
Ps 71:15 the day; for I know not the **n** *thereof*. H5615

NUN
Ex 33:11 Joshua, the son of **N**, a young man, H5126
Nu 11:28 And Joshua the son of **N**, the servant of H5126
13: 8 tribe of Ephraim, Oshea the son of **N**. H5126
16 called Oshea the son of **N** Jehoshua. H5126
14: 6 And Joshua the son of **N**, and Caleb the H5126
30 of Jephunneh, and Joshua the son of **N**. H5126
38 But Joshua the son of **N**, and Caleb the H5126
26:65 of Jephunneh, and Joshua the son of **N**. H5126
27:18 Joshua the son of **N**, a man in whom *is* H5126
32:12 and Joshua the son of **N**: for they have H5126
28 and Joshua the son of **N**, and the chief H5126
34:17 the priest, and Joshua the son of **N**. H5126
Dt 1:38 *But* Joshua the son of **N**, which standeth H5126
31:23 And he gave Joshua the son of **N** a H5126
32:44 people, he, and Hoshea the son of **N**. H5126
34: 9 And Joshua the son of **N** was full of the H5126
Jos 1: 1 the son of **N**, Moses' minister, saying, H5126
2: 1 And Joshua the son of **N** sent out of H5126
23 to Joshua the son of **N**, and told him all H5126
6: 6 And Joshua the son of **N** called the H5126
14: 1 Joshua the son of **N**, and the heads of H5126
17: 4 Joshua the son of **N**, and before the H5126
19:49 to Joshua the son of **N** among them: H5126
51 Joshua the son of **N**, and the heads of H5126
21: 1 Joshua the son of **N**, and unto the heads H5126
24:29 Joshua the son of **N**, the servant of the H5126
Jdg 2: 8 And Joshua the son of **N**, the servant of H5126
1Ki 16:34 which he spake by Joshua the son of **N**. H5126
Neh 8:17 Jeshua the son of **N** unto that day had H5126

NURSE
Gen 24:59 their sister, and her **n**, and Abraham's H3243
35: 8 But Deborah Rebekah's **n** died, and she H3243
Ex 2: 7 go and call to thee a **n** of the Hebrew H3243
7 that she may **n** the child for thee? H3243
9 child away, and **n** it for me, and I will H3243
Ru 4:16 it in her bosom, and became **n** unto it. H539
2Sa 4: 4 of Jezreel, and his **n** took him up, and H539
2Ki 11: 2 *even* him and his **n**, in the bedchamber H3243
2Ch 22:11 put him and his **n** in a bedchamber. So H3243
1Th 2: 7 even as a **n** cherisheth her children: *G5162*

NURSED
Ex 2: 9 the woman took the child, and **n** it. H5134
Isa 60: 4 and thy daughters shall be **n** at *thy* side. H539

NURSING
Nu 11:12 in thy bosom, as a **n** father beareth the H539
Isa 49:23 And kings shall be thy **n** fathers, and H539
23 their queens thy **n** mothers: they shall H3243

NURTURE
Eph 6: 4 in the **n** and admonition of the Lord. *G3809*

NUTS
Gen 43:11 spices, and myrrh, **n**, and almonds: H992
Song 6:11 I went down into the garden of **n** to see H93

NYMPHAS
Col 4:15 **N**, and the church which is in his house. *G3564*

O

O See the Appendix.

OAK
Gen 35: 4 under the **o** which *was* by Shechem. H424
8 Beth-el under an **o**: and the name of it H437
Jos 24:26 it up there under an **o**, that *was* by the H427
Jdg 6:11 LORD, and sat under an **o** which *was* in H424
19 unto him under the **o**, and presented *it*. H424
2Sa 18: 9 boughs of a great **o**, and his head caught H424
9 caught hold of the **o**, and he was taken H424
10 Behold, I saw Absalom hanged in an **o**. H424
14 he *was* yet alive in the midst of the **o**. H424
1Ki 13:14 sitting under an **o**: and he said unto him, H424
1Ch 10:12 the **o** in Jabesh, and fasted seven days. H424
Isa 1:30 For ye shall be as an **o** whose leaf fadeth, H424
6:13 teil tree, and as an **o**, whose substance *is* H437
44:14 taketh the cypress and the **o**, which he H437
Ezk 6:13 under every thick **o**, the place where they H424

OAKS
Isa 1:29 For they shall be ashamed of the **o** which H352
2:13 lifted up, and upon all the **o** of Bashan, H437
Ezk 27: 6 *Of* the **o** of Bashan have they made thine H437
Hos 4:13 the hills, under **o** and poplars and elms, H437
Am 2: 9 he *was* strong as the **o**; yet I destroyed his H437
Zec 11: 2 spoiled: howl, O ye **o** of Bashan; for the H437

OAR
Ezk 27:29 And all that handle the **o**, the mariners, H4880

OARS
Isa 33:21 go no galley with **o**, neither shall gallant H7885
Ezk 27: 6 they made thine **o**; the company of the H4880

OATH
Gen 24: 8 **o**: only bring not my son thither again. H7621
41 Then shalt thou be clear from *this* my **o**, H423
41 thee *one*, thou shalt be clear from my **o**. H423
26: 3 I will perform the **o** which I sware unto H7621
28 Let there be now an **o** betwixt us, *even* H423
50:25 And Joseph took an **o** of the children of H7650
Ex 22:11 *Then* shall an **o** of the LORD be H7621
Lev 5: 4 with an **o**, and it be hid from him; H7621
Nu 5:19 And the priest shall charge her by an **o**, H7650
21 woman with an **o** of cursing, and the H7621
21 a curse and an **o** among thy people, H7621
30: 2 or swear an **o** to bind his soul with H7621
10 or bound her soul by a bond with an **o**; H7621
13 Every vow, and every binding **o** to H7621
Dt 7: 8 he would keep the **o** which he had H7621
29:12 God, and into his **o**, which the LORD thy H423
14 only do I make this covenant and this **o**; H423
Jos 2:17 **o** which thou hast made us swear. H7621
20 **o** which thou hast made us to swear. H7621
9:20 of the **o** which we sware unto them. H7621
Jdg 21: 5 had made a great **o** concerning him H7621
1Sa 14:26 his mouth: for the people feared the **o**. H7621
27 the people with the **o**: wherefore he put H7650
28 the people with an **o**, saying, Cursed *be* H7650
2Sa 21: 7 of the LORD'S **o** that *was* between H7621
1Ki 2:43 Why then hast thou not kept the **o** of H7621
8:31 neighbour, and an **o** be laid upon him to H423
31 **o** come before thine altar in this house: H423
18:10 *there;* he took an **o** of the kingdom and H7650
2Ki 11: 4 them, and took an **o** of them in the H7650
1Ch 16:16 with Abraham, and of his **o** unto Isaac; H7621
2Ch 6:22 neighbour, and an **o** be laid upon him to H423
22 **o** come before thine altar in this house; H423
15:15 And all Judah rejoiced at the **o**: for they H7621
Neh 5:12 and took an **o** of them, that they should H7650
10:29 a curse, and into an **o**, to walk in God's H7621
Ps 105: 9 with Abraham, and his **o** unto Isaac; H7621
Ecc 8: 2 and *that* in regard of the **o** of God. H7621
9: 2 that sweareth, as *he* that feareth an **o**. H7621
Jer 11: 5 That I may perform the **o** which I have H7621
Ezk 16:59 despised the **o** in breaking the covenant. H423
17:13 and hath taken an **o** of him: he hath also H423
16 him king, whose **o** he despised, and H423
18 Seeing he despised the **o** by breaking the H423
19 *As* I live, surely mine **o** that he hath H423
Dan 9:11 upon us, and the **o** that *is* written in the H7621
Zec 8:17 and love no false **o**: for all these *are* H7621
Mt 14: 7 Whereupon he promised with an **o** to *G3727*
26:72 And again he denied with an **o**, I do not *G3727*
Lk 1:73 The **o** which he sware to our father *G3727*
Act 2:30 had sworn with an **o** to him, that of the *G3727*
23:21 themselves with an **o**, that they will *G332*
Heb 6:16 greater: and an **o** for confirmation *is* *G3727*
17 of his counsel, confirmed *it* by an **o**: *G3727*
7:20 And inasmuch as not without an **o** *he* *G3728*

Heb 7:21 made without an **o**; but this with an *G3728*
21 but this with an **o** by him that said *G3728*
28 the word of the **o**, which was since the *G3728*
Jas 5:12 by any other **o**: but let your yea be yea; *G3727*

OATHS
Ezk 21:23 that have sworn **o**: but he will call to H7621
Hab 3: 9 *according* to the **o** of the tribes, *even* H7621
Mt 5:33 but shalt perform unto the Lord thine **o**: *G3727*

OATH'S
Mt 14: 9 for the **o** sake, and them which *G3727*
Mk 6:26 sorry; *yet* for his **o** sake, and for their *G3727*

OBADIAH
1Ki 18: 3 And Ahab called **O**, which *was* the H5662
3 (Now **O** feared the LORD greatly: H5662
4 of the LORD, that **O** took an hundred H5662
5 And Ahab said unto **O**, Go into the H5662
6 and **O** went another way by himself. H5662
7 And as **O** was in the way, behold, Elijah H5662
16 So **O** went to meet Ahab, and told him: H5662
1Ch 3:21 the sons of **O**, the sons of Shechaniah. H5662
7: 3 Michael, and **O**, and Joel, Ishiah, five: H5662
8:38 Sheariah, and **O**, and Hanan. All these H5662
9:16 And **O** the son of Shemaiah, the son of H5662
44 and Sheariah, and **O**, and Hanan: these H5662
12: 9 Ezer the first, **O** the second, Eliab the H5662
27:19 Of Zebulun, Ishmaiah the son of **O**: of H5662
2Ch 17: 7 to Ben-hail, and to **O**, and to Zechariah, H5662
34:12 *were* Jahath and **O**, the Levites, of the H5662
Ezr 8: 9 Of the sons of Joab; **O** the son of Jehiel, H5662
Neh 10: 5 Harim, Meremoth, **O**, H5662
12:25 Mattaniah, and Bakbukiah, **O**, H5662
Oba 1 The vision of **O**. Thus saith the Lord H5662

OBAL
Gen 10:28 And **O**, and Abimael, and Sheba, H5745

OBED
Ru 4:17 called his name **O**: he *is* the father of H5744
21 Salmon begat Boaz, and Boaz begat **O**, H5744
22 And **O** begat Jesse, and Jesse begat H5744
1Ch 2:12 And Boaz begat **O**, and Obed begat H5744
12 And Boaz begat Obed, and **O** begat H5744
37 begat Ephlal, and Ephlal begat **O**, H5744
38 And **O** begat Jehu, and Jehu begat H5744
11:47 Eliel, and **O**, and Jasiel the Mesobaite. H5744
26: 7 and Rephael, and **O**, Elzabad, whose H5744
2Ch 23: 1 Azariah the son of **O**, and Maaseiah the H5744
Mt 1: 5 begat **O** of Ruth; and Obed begat Jesse; *G5601*
5 begat Obed of Ruth; and **O** begat Jesse; *G5601*
Lk 3:32 was *the son* of **O**, which was *the son* of *G5601*

OBED-EDOM
2Sa 6:10 it aside into the house of **O** the Gittite. H5654
11 in the house of **O** the Gittite three H5654
11 LORD blessed **O**, and all his household. H5654
12 the house of **O**, and all that *pertaineth* H5654
12 **O** into the city of David with gladness. H5654
1Ch 13:13 it aside into the house of **O** the Gittite. H5654
14 with the family of **O** in his house three H5654
14 the house of **O**, and all that he had. H5654
15:18 Mikneiah, and **O**, and Jeiel, the porters. H5654
21 and Mikneiah, and **O**, and Jeiel, and H5654
24 the ark of God: and **O** and Jehiah *were* H5654
25 LORD out of the house of **O** with joy. H5654
16: 5 and Benaiah, and **O**: and Jeiel with H5654
38 And **O** with their brethren, threescore H5654
38 and eight; **O** also the son of Jeduthun H5654
26: 4 Moreover the sons of **O** *were,* H5654
8 All these of the sons of **O**: they and their H5654
8 service, *were* threescore and two of **O**. H5654
15 To **O** southward; and to his sons the H5654
2Ch 25:24 house of God with **O**, and the treasures H5654

OBEDIENCE
Ro 1: 5 apostleship, for **o** to the faith among all *G5218*
5:19 **o** of one shall many be made righteous. *G5218*
6:16 unto death, or of **o** unto righteousness? *G5218*
16:19 For your **o** is come abroad unto all *G5218*
26 known to all nations for the **o** of faith: *G5218*
1Co 14:34 to be under **o**, as also saith the law. *G5293*
2Co 7:15 remembereth the **o** of you all, how with *G5218*
10: 5 every thought to the **o** of Christ; *G5218*
6 disobedience, when your **o** is fulfilled. *G5218*
Phlm 21 Having confidence in thy **o** I wrote *G5218*
Heb 5: 8 Though he were a Son, yet learned he **o** *G5218*
1Pt 1: 2 of the Spirit, unto **o** and sprinkling of *G5218*

OBEDIENT
Ex 24: 7 LORD hath said will we do, and be **o**. H8085
Nu 27:20 of the children of Israel may be **o**. H8085
Dt 4:30 thy God, and shalt be **o** unto his voice; H8085
8:20 **o** unto the voice of the LORD your God. H8085
2Sa 22:45 as they hear, they shall be **o** unto me. H8085
Prv 25:12 *so is* a wise reprover upon an **o** ear. H8085
Isa 1:19 If ye be willing and **o**, ye shall eat the H8085
42:24 ways, neither were they **o** unto his law. H8085
Act 6: 7 of the priests were **o** to the faith. *G5219*
Ro 15:18 make the Gentiles **o**, by word and deed, *G5218*
2Co 2: 9 of you, whether ye be **o** in all things. *G5255*
Eph 6: 5 Servants, be **o** to them that are *your* *G5219*
Php 2: 8 and became **o** unto death, even the *G5255*
Tit 2: 5 keepers at home, good, **o** to their own *G5293*
9 *Exhort* servants to be **o** unto their own *G5293*
1Pt 1:14 As **o** children, not fashioning *G5218*

OBEISANCE
Gen 37: 7 round about, and made **o** to my sheaf. H7812
9 and the eleven stars made **o** to me. H7812
43:28 bowed down their heads, and made **o**. H7812
Ex 18: 7 in law, and did **o**, and kissed him; and H7812
2Sa 1: 2 that he fell to the earth, and did **o**. H7812
14: 4 and did **o**, and said, Help, O king. H7812
15: 5 nigh *to him* to do him **o**, he put forth his H7812
1Ki 1:16 And Bath-sheba bowed, and did **o** unto H7812
2Ch 24:17 of Judah, and made **o** to the king. Then H7812

OBEY
Gen 27: 8 Now therefore, my son, **o** my voice H8085
13 only **o** my voice, and go fetch me *them.* H8085
43 Now therefore, my son, **o** my voice; H8085
Ex 5: 2 that I should **o** his voice to let Israel H8085
19: 5 Now therefore, if ye will **o** my voice H8085
23:21 Beware of him, and **o** his voice, H8085
22 But if thou shalt indeed **o** his voice, and H8085
Dt 11:27 A blessing, if ye **o** the commandments H8085
28 And a curse, if ye will not **o** the H8085
13: 4 and **o** his voice, and ye shall H8085
21:18 which will not **o** the voice of his father, H8085
20 he will not **o** our voice; *he is* a glutton, H8085
27:10 Thou shalt therefore **o** the voice of the H8085
28:62 not **o** the voice of the LORD thy God. H8085
30: 2 LORD thy God, and shalt **o** his voice H8085
8 And thou shalt return and **o** the voice H8085
20 that thou mayest **o** his voice, and that H8085
Jos 24:24 will we serve, and his voice will we **o**. H8085
1Sa 8:19 Nevertheless the people refused to **o** H8085
12:14 and serve him, and **o** his voice, and not H8085
15 But if ye will not **o** the voice of the H8085
15:19 Wherefore then didst thou not **o** the H8085
22 the LORD? Behold, to **o** *is* better than H8085
Neh 9:17 And refused to **o**, neither were mindful H8085
Job 36:11 If they **o** and serve *him*, they shall H8085
12 But if they **o** not, they shall perish by H8085
Ps 18:44 As soon as they hear of me, they shall **o** H8085
Prv 30:17 and despiseth to **o** *his* mother, the H3349
Isa 11:14 the children of Ammon shall **o** them. H4928
Jer 7:23 I them, saying, **O** my voice, and I will H8085
11: 4 furnace, saying, **O** my voice, and do H8085
7 and protesting, saying, **O** my voice. H8085
12:17 But if they will not **o**, I will utterly pluck H8085
18:10 If it do evil in my sight, that it **o** not my H8085
26:13 and your doings, and **o** the voice of the H8085
35:14 they drink none, but **o** their father's H8085
38:20 not deliver *thee*. **O**, I beseech thee, the H8085
42: 6 *it be* evil, we will **o** the voice of the H8085
6 we **o** the voice of the LORD our God. H8085
13 **o** the voice of the LORD your God, H8085
Dan 7:27 all dominions shall serve and **o** him. H8086
9:11 they might not **o** thy voice; therefore H8085
Zec 6:15 **o** the voice of the LORD your God. H8085
Mt 8:27 that even the winds and the sea **o** him! *G5219*
Mk 1:27 the unclean spirits, and they do **o** him. *G5219*
4:41 that even the wind and the sea **o** him? *G5219*
Lk 8:25 the winds and water, and they **o** him. *G5219*
17: 6 planted in the sea; and it should **o** you. *G5219*
Act 5:29 We ought to **o** God rather than men. *G3980*
32 God hath given to them that **o** him. *G3980*
7:39 To whom our fathers would not **o**, but *G1096*
Ro 2: 8 and do not **o** the truth, but obey *G544*
8 obey the truth, but **o** unrighteousness, *G3982*
6:12 that ye should **o** it in the lusts thereof. *G5219*
16 servants to **o**, his servants ye are to *G5218*
16 ye are to whom ye **o**; whether of sin *G5219*
Gal 3: 1 that ye should not **o** the truth, before *G3982*
5: 7 you that ye should not **o** the truth? *G3982*
Eph 6: 1 Children, **o** your parents in the Lord: *G5219*
Col 3:20 Children, **o** *your* parents in all things: *G5219*
22 Servants, **o** in all things *your* masters *G5219*
2Th 1: 8 not God, and that **o** not the gospel of *G5219*
3:14 And if any man **o** not our word by this *G5219*
Tit 3: 1 and powers, to **o** magistrates, to be *G3980*
Heb 5: 9 salvation unto all them that **o** him; *G5219*
13:17 **O** them that have the rule over you, *G3982*
Jas 3: 3 that they may **o** us; and we turn about *G3982*
1Pt 3: 1 that, if any **o** not the word, they also *G544*
4:17 *be* of them that **o** not the gospel of God? *G544*

OBEYED
Gen 22:18 blessed; because thou hast **o** my voice. H8085
26: 5 Because that Abraham **o** my voice, and H8085
28: 7 And that Jacob **o** his father and his H8085
Jos 5: 6 because they **o** not the voice of the H8085
22: 2 you, and have **o** my voice in all that H8085
Jdg 2: 2 not **o** my voice: why have ye done this? H8085
6:10 ye dwell: but ye have not **o** my voice. H8085
1Sa 15:20 Yea, I have **o** the voice of the LORD, H8085
24 I feared the people, and **o** their voice. H8085
28:21 handmaid hath **o** thy voice, and I have H8085
1Ki 20:36 thou hast not **o** the voice of the LORD, H8085
2Ki 18:12 Because they **o** not the voice of the H8085
1Ch 29:23 and prospered; and all Israel **o** him. H8085
2Ch 11: 4 of me. And they **o** the words of the H8085
Prv 5:13 And have not **o** the voice of my H8085
Jer 3:13 have not **o** my voice, saith the LORD. H8085
25 not **o** the voice of the LORD our God. H8085
9:13 not **o** my voice, neither walked therein; H8085
11: 8 Yet they **o** not, nor inclined their ear, H8085
17:23 But they **o** not, neither inclined their H8085
32:23 it; but they **o** not thy voice, neither H8085
34:10 any more, then they **o**, and let *them* go. H8085
35: 8 Thus have we **o** the voice of Jonadab H8085
10 But we have dwelt in tents, and have **o**, H8085
18 Because ye have **o** the commandment H8085
40: 3 and have not **o** his voice, therefore H8085
42:21 but ye have not **o** the voice of the LORD H8085
43: 4 and all the people, **o** not the voice of H8085
7 of Egypt: for they **o** not the voice of the H8085
44:23 and have not **o** the voice of the LORD, H8085
Dan 9:10 Neither have we **o** the voice of the H8085
14 which he doeth: for we **o** not his voice. H8085
Zep 3: 2 She **o** not the voice; she received not H8085
Hag 1:12 of the people, **o** the voice of the LORD H8085
Act 5:36 all, as many as **o** him, were scattered, *G3982*
37 as many as **o** him, were dispersed. *G3982*
Ro 6:17 of sin, but ye have **o** from the heart that *G5219*
10:16 But they have not all **o** the gospel. For *G5219*
Php 2:12 as ye have always **o**, not as in my *G5219*
Heb 11: 8 an inheritance, **o**; and he went out, not *G5219*
1Pt 3: 6 Even as Sara **o** Abraham, calling him *G5219*

OBEYEDST
1Sa 28:18 Because thou **o** not the voice of the H8085
Jer 22:21 thy youth, that thou **o** not my voice. H8085

OBEYETH
Isa 50:10 the LORD, that **o** the voice of his H8085
Jer 7:28 *is* a nation that **o** not the voice of the H8085
11: 3 that **o** not the words of this covenant, H8085

OBEYING
Jdg 2:17 their fathers walked in, **o** the H8085
1Sa 15:22 and sacrifices, as in **o** the voice of the H8085
1Pt 1:22 Seeing ye have purified your souls in **o** *G5218*

OBIL
1Ch 27:30 Over the camels also *was* **O** the H179

OBJECT
Act 24:19 and **o**, if they had ought against me. *G2723*

OBLATION
Lev 2: 4 And if thou bring an **o** of a meat H7133
5 And if thy **o** *be* a meat offering *baken* H7133
7 And if thy **o** *be* a meat offering *baken* H7133
12 As for the **o** of the firstfruits, ye shall H7133
13 And every **o** of thy meat offering shalt H7133
3: 1 And if his **o** *be* a sacrifice of peace H7133
7:14 out of the whole **o** *for* an heave offering H7133
29 shall bring his **o** unto the LORD of the H7133
22:18 that will offer his **o** for all his vows, and H7133
Nu 18: 9 the fire: every **o** of theirs, every meat H7133
31:50 We have therefore brought an **o** for the H7133
Isa 19:21 do sacrifice and **o**; yea, they shall vow H4503
40:20 that he hath no **o** chooseth a tree *that* H8641
66: 3 he that offereth an **o**, *as if he offered* H4503

Jer 14:12 offering and an o, I will not accept H4503
Ezk 44:30 *things*, and every o of all, of every *sort* H8641
45: 1 ye shall offer an o unto the LORD, an H8641
6 over against the o of the holy *portion*: H8641
7 other side of the o of the holy *portion*, H8641
7 of the city, before the o of the holy H8641
13 This *is* the o that ye shall offer; the H8641
16 shall give this o for the prince in Israel. H8641
48: 9 The o that ye shall offer unto the LORD H8641
10 shall be *this* holy o; toward the north H8641
12 And *this* o of the land that is offered H8642
18 over against the o of the holy *portion* H8641
18 over against the o of the holy *portion*; H8641
20 All the o *shall be* five and twenty H8641
20 shall offer the holy o foursquare, with H8641
21 the other of the holy o, and of the H8641
21 thousand of the o toward the east H8641
21 it shall be the holy o; and the sanctuary H8641
Dan 2:46 offer an o and sweet odours unto him. H4504
9:21 me about the time of the evening o. H4503
27 sacrifice and the o to cease, and for the H4503

OBLATIONS
Lev 7:38 to offer their o unto the LORD, in the H7133
2Ch 31:14 to distribute the o of the LORD, and the H8641
Isa 1:13 Bring no more vain o; incense is an H4503
Ezk 20:40 of your o, with all your holy things. H4864
44:30 of every *sort* of your o, shall be the H8641

OBOTH
Nu 21:10 of Israel set forward, and pitched in O. H88
11 And they journeyed from O, and pitched H88
33:43 departed from Punon, and pitched in O. H88
44 And they departed from O, and pitched H88

OBSCURE
Prv 20:20 his lamp shall be put out in o darkness. H380

OBSCURITY
Isa 29:18 shall see out of o, and out of darkness. H652
58:10 o, and thy darkness *be* as the noonday: H2822
59: 9 light, but behold o; for brightness, *but* H2822

OBSERVATION
Lk 17:20 The kingdom of God cometh not with o: G3907

OBSERVE
Ex 12:17 And ye shall o *the feast of* unleavened H8104
17 therefore shall ye o this day in your H8104
24 And ye shall o this thing for an H8104
31:16 keep the sabbath, to o the sabbath H6213
34:11 O thou that which I command thee this H8104
22 And thou shalt o the feast of weeks, of H6213
Lev 19:26 shall ye use enchantment, nor o times. H6049
37 Therefore shall ye o all my statutes, H8104
Nu 28: 2 o to offer unto me in their due season. H8104
Dt 5:32 Ye shall o to do therefore as the LORD H8104
6: 3 Hear therefore, O Israel, and o to do *it*; H8104
25 if we o to do all these commandments H8104
8: 1 this day shall ye o to do, that ye may H8104
11:32 And ye shall o to do all the statutes and H8104
12: 1 which ye shall o to do in the land, H8104
28 O and hear all these words which I H8104
32 What thing soever I command you, o H8104
15: 5 the LORD thy God, to o to do all these H8104
16: 1 O the month of Abib, and keep the H8104
12 and thou shalt o and do these statutes. H8104
13 Thou shalt o the feast of tabernacles H6213
17:10 and thou shalt o to do according to all H8104
24: 8 leprosy, that thou o diligently, and do H8104
8 I commanded them, *so* ye shall o to do. H8104
28: 1 LORD thy God, to o *and* to do all his H8104
13 thee this day, to o and to do *them*: H8104
15 the LORD thy God, to o to do all his H8104
58 If thou wilt not o to do all the words of H8104
31:12 and o to do all the words of this law: H8104
32:46 to o to do, all the words of this law. H8104
Jos 1: 7 that thou mayest o to do according to H8104
8 that thou mayest o to do according to H8104
Jdg 13:14 all that I commanded her let her o. H8104
1Ki 20:33 Now the men did diligently o whether H5172
2Ki 17:37 for you, ye shall o to do for evermore; H8104
21: 8 only if they will o to do according to all H8104
2Ch 7:17 shalt o my statutes and my judgments; H8104
Neh 1: 5 love him and o his commandments: H8104
10:29 servant of God, and to o and do all the H8104
Ps 105:45 That they might o his statutes, and H8104
107:43 Whoso *is* wise, and will o these *things*, H8104
119:34 yea, I shall o it with *my* whole heart. H8104
Prv 23:26 heart, and let thine eyes o my ways. H5341
Jer 8: 7 and the swallow o the time of their H8104
Ezk 20:18 fathers, neither o their judgments, nor H8104
37:24 and o my statutes, and do them. H8104
Hos 13: 7 as a leopard by the way will I o *them*: H7789
Jna 2: 8 They that o lying vanities forsake their H8104
Mt 23: 3 All therefore whatsoever they bid you o, G5083
3 you observe, *that* o and do; but do not G5083
28:20 Teaching them to o all things G5083
Act 16:21 to receive, neither to o, being Romans. G4160
21:25 that they o no such thing, save G5083
Gal 4:10 Ye o days, and months, and times, and G3906
1Ti 5:21 angels, that thou o these things without G5442

OBSERVED
Gen 37:11 envied him; but his father o the saying. H8104
Ex 12:42 It *is* a night to be much o unto the H8107
42 of the LORD to be o of all the children H8107
Nu 15:22 And if ye have erred, and not o all H6213
Dt 33: 9 o thy word, and kept thy covenant. H8104
2Sa 11:16 And it came to pass, when Joab o the H8104
2Ki 21: 6 through the fire, and o times, and used H6049
2Ch 33: 6 of Hinnom: also he o times, and used H6049
Hos 14: 8 have heard *him*, and o him: I *am* like a H7789
Mk 6:20 and an holy, and o him; and when he G4933
10:20 all these have I o from my youth. G5442

OBSERVER
Dt 18:10 o of times, or an enchanter, or a witch, H6049

OBSERVERS
Dt 18:14 hearkened unto o of times, and unto H6049

OBSERVEST
Isa 42:20 Seeing many things, but thou o not; H8104

OBSERVETH
Ecc 11: 4 He that o the wind shall not sow; and H8104

OBSTINATE
Dt 2:30 made his heart o, that he might deliver H553
Isa 48: 4 Because I knew that thou *art* o, and thy H7186

OBTAIN
Gen 16: 2 it may be that I may o children by her. H1129
Prv 8:35 life, and shall o favour of the LORD. H6329
Isa 35:10 heads: they shall o joy and gladness, H5381
51:11 head: they shall o gladness and joy; H5381
Dan 11:21 and o the kingdom by flatteries. H2388
Mt 5: 7 *are* the merciful: for they shall o mercy. G1653
Lk 20:35 worthy to o that world, and the G5177
Ro 11:31 your mercy they also may o mercy. G1653
1Co 9:24 the prize? So run, that ye may o. G2638
25 Now they *do it* to o a corruptible G2983
1Th 5: 9 to o salvation by our Lord Jesus Christ, G4047
2Ti 2:10 that they may also o the salvation G5177
Heb 4:16 that we may o mercy, and find grace G2983
11:35 that they might o a better resurrection: G5177
Jas 4: 2 to have, and cannot o: ye fight and war, G2013

OBTAINED
Neh 13: 6 after certain days o I leave of the king: H7592
Est 2: 9 him, and she o kindness of him; and H5375
15 And Esther o favour in the sight of H5375
17 women, and she o grace and favour in H5375
5: 2 the court, *that* she o favour in his sight: H5375
Hos 2:23 her that had not o mercy; and I will say H5375
Act 1:17 us, and had o part of this ministry. G2975
22:28 With a great sum o I this freedom. And G2932
26:22 Having therefore o help of God, I G5177
27:13 that they had o *their* purpose, loosing G2902
Ro 11: 7 What then? Israel hath not o that G2013
7 hath o it, and the rest were blinded G2018
30 now o mercy through their unbelief: G1653
1Co 7:25 hath o mercy of the Lord to be faithful. G1653
Eph 1:11 In whom also we have o an G2820
1Ti 1:13 injurious: but I o mercy, because I did G1653
16 Howbeit for this cause I o mercy, that G1653
Heb 1: 4 o a more excellent name than they. G2816
6:15 patiently endured, he o the promise. G2013
8: 6 But now hath he o a more excellent G5177
9:12 having o eternal redemption *for us*. G2147
11: 2 For by it the elders o a good report. G3140
4 Cain, by which he o witness that he G3140
33 righteousness, o promises, stopped the G2013
39 And these all, having o a good report G3140
1Pt 2:10 which had not o mercy, but now have G1653
10 mercy, but now have o mercy. G1653
2Pt 1: 1 to them that have o like precious faith G2975

OBTAINETH
Prv 12: 2 A good *man* o favour of the LORD: but H6329
18:22 good *thing*, and o favour of the LORD. H6329

OBTAINING
2Th 2:14 o of the glory of our Lord Jesus Christ. G4047

OCCASION
Gen 43:18 that he may seek o against us, and fall H1556
Jdg 9:33 thou do to them as thou shalt find o. H4672
14: 4 LORD, that he sought an o against the H8385
1Sa 10: 7 do as o serve thee; for God *is* with thee. H4672
2Sa 12:14 hast given great o to the enemies of the
Ezr 7:20 thou shalt have o to bestow, bestow *it* H5308
Jer 2:24 her pleasure; in her o who can turn her H8385
Ezk 18: 3 o any more to use this proverb in Israel.
Dan 6: 4 princes sought to find o against Daniel H5931
4 could find none o nor fault; forasmuch H5931
5 shall not find any o against this Daniel, H5931
Ro 7: 8 But sin, taking o by the commandment, G874
11 For sin, taking o by the commandment, G874
14:13 or an o to fall in *his* brother's way. G4625
2Co 5:12 unto you, but give you o to glory on our G874
8: 8 I speak not by commandment, but by o G1223
11:12 do, that I may cut off o from them which G874
12 them which desire o; that wherein they G874
Gal 5:13 not liberty for an o to the flesh, but by G874
1Ti 5:14 house, give none o to the adversary to G874
1Jn 2:10 there is none o of stumbling in him. G4625

OCCASIONED
1Sa 22:22 tell Saul: I have o *the death* of all the H5437

OCCASIONS
Dt 22:14 And give o of speech against her, and H5949
17 And, lo, he hath given o of speech H5949
Job 33:10 Behold, he findeth o against me, he H8569

OCCUPATION
Gen 46:33 call you, and shall say, What *is* your o? H4639
47: 3 What *is* your o? And they said unto H4639
Jna 1: 8 us; What *is* thine o? and whence comest H4399
Act 18: 3 for by their o they were tentmakers. G5078
19:25 the workmen of like o, and said, Sirs, ye G5108

OCCUPIED
Ex 38:24 All the gold that was o for the work in H6213
Jdg 16:11 never were o, then shall I be H6213+H4399
Ezk 27:16 of thy making: they o in thy fairs with H5414
19 Dan also and Javan going to and fro o H5414
21 of Kedar, they o with thee in lambs, H5503
22 thy merchants: they o in thy fairs with H5414
Heb 13: 9 profited them that have been o therein. G4043

OCCUPIERS
Ezk 27:27 calkers, and the o of thy merchandise, H6148

OCCUPIETH
1Co 14:16 how shall he that o the room of the G378

OCCUPY
Ezk 27: 9 were in thee to o thy merchandise. H6148
Lk 19:13 and said unto them, O till I come. G4231

OCCURRENT
1Ki 5: 4 *there is* neither adversary nor evil o. H6294

OCRAN
Nu 1:13 Of Asher; Pagiel the son of O. H5918
2:27 of Asher *shall be* Pagiel the son of O. H5918
7:72 On the eleventh day Pagiel the son of O, H5918
77 *was* the offering of Pagiel the son of O. H5918
10:26 of Asher *was* Pagiel the son of O. H5918

ODD
Nu 3:48 wherewith the o number of them is to H5736

ODED
2Ch 15: 1 of God came upon Azariah the son of O: H5752
8 the prophecy of O the prophet, he took H5752
28: 9 whose name *was* O: and he went out H5752

ODIOUS
1Ch 19: 6 made themselves o to David, Hanun and H887
Prv 30:23 For an o *woman* when she is married; H8130

ODOUR
Jn 12: 3 was filled with the o of the ointment. G3744
Php 4:18 *sent* from you, an o of a sweet smell, a G3744

ODOURS
Lev 26:31 not smell the savour of your sweet **o**. H5207
2Ch 16:14 filled with sweet **o** and divers kinds *of* H1314
Est 2:12 with sweet **o**, and with *other* things H1314
Jer 34: 5 so shall they burn *o* for thee; and they
Dan 2:46 offer an oblation and sweet **o** unto him. H5208
Rev 5: 8 full of **o**, which are the prayers of saints. *G2368*
18:13 And cinnamon, and **o**, and ointments, *G2368*

OF See the Appendix.

OFF
Gen 7: 4 I destroy from **o** the face of the earth. H5921
8: 3 And the waters returned from **o** the H5921
7 waters were dried up from **o** the earth. H5921
8 abated from **o** the face of the ground; H5921
11 olive leaf pluckt **o**: so Noah knew that H2965
11 waters were abated from **o** the earth. H5921
13 dried up from **o** the earth: and Noah H5921
9:11 shall all flesh be cut **o** any more by the H3772
11: 8 earth: and they left **o** to build the city. H2308
17:14 soul shall be cut **o** from his people; he H3772
22 And he left **o** talking with him, and God H3615
21:16 *him* a good way **o**, as it were a bowshot: H7368
22: 4 up his eyes, and saw the place afar **o**. H7350
24:64 she saw Isaac, she lighted **o** the camel. H5921
27:40 shalt break his yoke from **o** thy neck. H5921
37:18 And when they saw him afar **o**, even H7350
38:14 And she put her widow's garments **o** H5493
40:19 lift up thy head from **o** thee, and shall H5921
19 the birds shall eat thy flesh from **o** thee. H5921
41:42 And Pharaoh took **o** his ring from his H5493
44: 4 *and* not *yet* far **o**, Joseph said unto his H7368
Ex 2: 4 And his sister stood afar **o**, to wit what H7350
3: 5 nigh hither: put **o** thy shoes from off H5394
5 put off thy shoes from **o** thy feet, for the
4:25 stone, and cut **o** the foreskin of her son, H3772
9:15 and thou shalt be cut **o** from the earth. H3582
12:15 that soul shall be cut **o** from Israel. H3772
19 that soul shall be cut **o** from the H3772
14:25 And took **o** their chariot wheels, that H5493
20:18 saw *it*, they removed, and stood afar **o**. H7350
21 And the people stood afar **o**, and Moses H7350
23:23 and the Jebusites: and I will cut them **o**. H3582
24: 1 elders of Israel; and worship ye afar **o**. H7350
30:33 shall even be cut **o** from his people. H3772
38 shall even be cut **o** from his people. H3772
31:14 shall be cut **o** from among his people. H3772
32: 2 And Aaron said unto them, Break **o** the H6561
3 And all the people brake **o** the golden H6561
24 let them break *it* **o**. So they gave *it* me: H6561
33: 5 therefore now put **o** thy ornaments H3381
7 the camp, afar **o** from the camp, and H7368
34:34 he took the vail **o**, until he came out. H5493
Lev 1:15 altar, and wring **o** his head, and burn H4454
3: 9 it shall he take **o** hard by the backbone; H5493
4: 8 And he shall take **o** from it all the fat of H7311
10 As it was taken **o** from the bullock of H7311
31 fat is taken away from **o** the sacrifice of
5: 8 first, and wring **o** his head from his H4454
6:11 And he shall put **o** his garments, and H6584
7:20 that soul shall be cut **o** from his people. H3772
21 that soul shall be cut **o** from his people. H3772
25 eateth *it* shall be cut **o** from his people. H3772
27 that soul shall be cut **o** from his people. H3772
34 of Israel from **o** the sacrifices of their
8:28 And Moses took them from **o** their H5921
13:40 And the man whose hair is fallen **o** his H4803
41 And he that hath his hair fallen **o** from H4803
14: 8 his clothes, and shave **o** all his hair, and
9 shave all his hair **o** his head and his
9 hair he shall shave **o**: and he shall wash
41 **o** without the city into an unclean place:
16:12 coals of fire from **o** the altar before the H5921
23 and shall put **o** the linen garments, H6584
17: 4 shall be cut **o** from among his people: H3772
9 shall be cut **o** from among his people. H3772
10 will cut him **o** from among his people. H3772
14 whosoever eateth it shall be cut **o**. H3772
18:29 shall be cut **o** from among their people. H3772
19: 8 shall be cut **o** from among his people. H3772
20: 3 and will cut him **o** from among his H3772
5 and will cut him **o**, and all that go a H3772
6 will cut him **o** from among his people. H3772
17 they shall be cut **o** in the sight of their H3772
18 shall be cut **o** from among their people. H3772
21: 5 shall they shave **o** the corner of their H1548
22: 3 **o** from my presence: I *am* the LORD. H3772
23:29 shall be cut **o** from among his people. H3772
Nu 2: 2 their father's house: far **o** about the H5048
4:18 Cut ye not **o** the tribe of the families of H3772
7:89 unto him from **o** the mercy seat that H5921
9:10 in a journey afar **o**, yet he shall keep the H7350
13 soul shall be cut **o** from among his H3772
10:11 from **o** the tabernacle of the testimony. H5921
12:10 And the cloud departed from **o** the H5921
15:30 shall be cut **o** from among his people. H5921
31 be cut **o**; his iniquity *shall be* upon him. H3772
16:46 fire therein from **o** the altar, and put on H5921
19:13 soul shall be cut **o** from Israel: because H3772
20 that soul shall be cut **o** from among the H3772
Dt 4:26 perish from **o** the land whereunto H5921
6:15 thee from **o** the face of the earth. H5921
11:17 quickly from **o** the good land which H5921
12:29 When the LORD thy God shall cut **o** the H3772
13: 7 unto thee, or far **o** from thee, from the H7350
19: 1 When the LORD thy God hath cut **o** the H3772
20:15 *which are* very far **o** from thee, which H7350
21: 4 **o** the heifer's neck there in the valley: H6202
13 of her captivity from **o** her, and shall H5921
23: 1 privy member cut **o**, shall not enter into H3772
25: 9 his shoe from **o** his foot, and spit in H5921
12 Then thou shalt cut **o** her hand, thine H7112
28:21 thee from **o** the land, whither thou H5921
63 be plucked from **o** the land whither H5921
30:11 not hidden from thee, neither *is* it far **o**. H7350
Jos 3:13 shall be cut **o** *from* the waters that H3772
16 *and* were cut **o**: and the people passed H3772
4: 7 of Jordan were cut **o** before the ark of H3772
7 of Jordan were cut **o**: and these stones H3772
5: 9 of Egypt from **o** you. Wherefore the H5921
15 thy shoe from **o** thy foot; for the place H5921
7: 9 us round, and cut **o** our name from the H3772
10:27 took them down **o** the trees, and cast H5921
11:21 Joshua, and cut **o** the Anakims from H3772
15:18 and she lighted **o** *her* ass; and Caleb H5921
23: 4 cut **o**, even unto the great sea westward. H3772
13 ye perish from **o** this good land which H5921
15 you from **o** this good land which H5921
16 quickly from **o** the good land which H5921
Jdg 1: 6 cut **o** his thumbs and his great toes. H7112
7 great toes cut **o**, gathered *their meat* H7112
14 she lighted from **o** *her* ass; and Caleb H5921
4:15 **o** *his* chariot, and fled away on his feet. H5921
5:26 Sisera, she smote **o** his head, when she H4277
13:20 heaven from **o** the altar, that the angel H5921
15:14 and his bands loosed from **o** his hands. H5921
16:12 them from **o** his arms like a thread. H5921
19 him to shave **o** the seven locks of his H1548
21: 6 is one tribe cut **o** from Israel this day. H1438
Ru 2:20 who hath not left **o** his kindness to the H5800
4: 7 a man plucked **o** his shoe, and gave *it* H8025
8 Buy *it* for thee. So he drew **o** his shoe. H8025
10 the dead be not cut **o** from among his H3772
1Sa 2:31 Behold, the days come, that I will cut **o** H1438
33 I shall not cut **o** from mine altar, *shall* H3772
4:18 that he fell from **o** the seat backward H5921
5: 4 hands *were* cut **o** upon the threshold; H3772
6: 5 his hand from **o** you, and from off your H5921
5 **o** your gods, and from off your land. H5921
5 off your gods, and from **o** your land. H5921
17:39 *them*. And David put them **o** him. H5921
51 slew him, and cut **o** his head therewith. H3772
19:24 And he stripped **o** his clothes also, and H6584
20:15 But *also* thou shalt not cut **o** thy H3772
15 LORD hath cut **o** the enemies of David H3772
24: 4 cut **o** the skirt of Saul's robe privily. H3772
5 him, because he had cut **o** Saul's skirt. H3772
11 for in that I cut **o** the skirt of thy robe, H3772
21 thou wilt not cut **o** my seed after me, H3772
25:23 and lighted **o** the ass, and fell before H5921
26:13 **o**; a great space *being* between them: H7350
28: 9 how he hath cut **o** those that have H3772
31: 9 And they cut **o** his head, and stripped H3772
9 and stripped **o** his armour, and sent H6584
2Sa 4:12 them, and cut **o** their hands and their H7112
7: 9 and have cut **o** all thine enemies out H3772
10: 4 and shaved **o** the one half of their H1548
4 beards, and cut **o** their garments in the H3772
11: 2 that David arose from **o** his bed, and H5921
24 And the shooters shot from **o** the wall H5921
12:30 And he took their king's crown from **o** H5921
15:17 and tarried in a place that was far **o**.
16: 9 over, I pray thee, and take **o** his head. H5493
20:22 And they cut **o** the head of Sheba the H3772
1Ki 9: 7 Then will I cut **o** Israel out of the land H3772
11:16 until he had cut **o** every male in Edom:) H3772
13:34 even to cut *it* **o**, and to destroy *it* from H3582
1Ki 13:34 to destroy *it* from **o** the face of the earth.
14:10 and will cut **o** from Jeroboam him H3772
14 who shall cut **o** the house of Jeroboam H3772
15:21 that he left **o** building of Ramah, H2308
18: 4 For it was *so*, when Jezebel cut **o** the H3772
20:11 boast himself as he that putteth it **o**. H6605
21:21 and will cut **o** from Ahab him that H3772
2Ki 1:16 not come down **o** that bed on which thou
2: 7 afar **o**: and they two stood by Jordan. H7350
4:25 of God saw her afar **o**, that he said to
9: 8 and I will cut **o** from Ahab him that H3772
16:17 And king Ahaz cut **o** the borders of the H7112
17 the laver from **o** them; and took down
17 down the sea from **o** the brasen oxen H5921
18:16 At that time did Hezekiah cut **o** *the* H7112
23:27 and will cast **o** this city Jerusalem H3988
1Ch 17: 8 and have cut **o** all thine enemies from H3772
19: 4 them, and cut **o** their garments in the H3772
20: 2 of their king from **o** his head, and H5921
28: 9 him, he will cast thee **o** for ever. H2186
2Ch 6:36 captives unto a land far **o** or near; H7350
11:14 had cast them **o** from executing the H2186
16: 5 *it*, that he left **o** building of Ramah, H2308
20:25 they stripped **o** for themselves, more H5337
22: 7 anointed to cut **o** the house of Ahab. H3772
26:21 for he was cut **o** from the house of the H1504
32:21 angel, which cut **o** all the mighty men H3582
Ezr 3:13 shout, and the noise was heard afar **o**. H7350
9: 3 and plucked **o** the hair of my head H4803
Neh 4:23 me, none of us put **o** our clothes, H6584
23 *that* every one put them **o** for washing. H7973
5:10 I pray you, let us leave **o** this usury. H5800
12:43 joy of Jerusalem was heard even afar **o**. H7350
13:25 of them, and plucked **o** their hair, and
Est 8: 2 And the king took **o** his ring, which he H5493
Job 2:12 up their eyes afar **o**, and knew him not, H7350
4: 7 or where were the righteous cut **o**? H3582
6: 9 would let loose his hand, and cut me **o**! H1214
8:14 Whose hope shall be cut **o**, and whose
9:27 **o** my heaviness, and comfort *myself*: H5800
11:10 If he cut **o**, and shut up, or gather H2498
15: 4 Yea, thou castest **o** fear, and H6565
33 He shall shake **o** his unripe grape as H2554
33 and shall cast **o** his flower as the olive. H7993
17:11 **o**, *even* the thoughts of my heart. H5423
18:16 and above shall his branch be cut **o**.
21:21 of his months is cut **o** in the midst?
23:17 Because I was not cut **o** before the H6789
24:24 and cut **o** as the tops of the ears of corn.
32:15 no more: they left **o** speaking. H6275
36:20 when people are cut **o** in their place. H5927
25 may see it; man may behold *it* afar **o**. H7350
39:25 the battle afar **o**, the thunder of the H7350
29 the prey, *and* her eyes behold afar **o**. H7350
Ps 10: 1 Why standest thou afar **o**, O LORD? H7350
12: 3 The LORD shall cut **o** all flattering lips, H3772
30:11 thou hast put **o** my sackcloth, and
31:22 For I said in my haste, I am cut **o** from
34:16 that do evil, to cut **o** the remembrance H3772
36: 3 hath left **o** to be wise, *and* to do good. H2308
37: 9 For evildoers shall be cut **o**: but those H3772
22 *that be* cursed of him shall be cut **o**. H3772
28 but the seed of the wicked shall be cut **o**. H3772
34 the wicked are cut **o**, thou shalt see *it*. H3772
38 the end of the wicked shall be cut **o**. H3772
38:11 my sore; and my kinsmen stand afar **o**. H7350
43: 2 dost thou cast me **o**? why go I mourning
44: 9 But thou hast cast **o**, and put us to
23 O Lord? arise, cast *us* not **o** for ever.
54: 5 mine enemies: cut them **o** in thy truth. H6789
55: 7 Lo, *then* would I wander far **o**, *and* H7368
60: 1 O God, thou hast cast us **o**, thou hast
10 hadst cast us **o**? and *thou*, O God, *which*
65: 5 of them that are afar **o** *upon* the sea: H7350
71: 9 Cast me not **o** in the time of old age; H7993
74: 1 O God, why hast thou cast *us* **o** for ever?
75:10 also will I cut **o**; *but* the horns of the H1438
76:12 He shall cut **o** the spirit of princes: *he is* H1219
77: 7 Will the Lord cast **o** for ever? and will he
83: 4 let us cut them **o** from *being* a nation; H3582
88: 5 and they are cut **o** from thy hand. H1504
14 LORD, why castest thou **o** my soul? *why*
16 over me; thy terrors have cut me **o**. H6789
89:38 But thou hast cast **o** and abhorred, thou
90:10 for it is soon cut **o**, and we fly away. H1468
94:14 For the LORD will not cast **o** his people, H5203
23 and shall cut them **o** in their own H6789
23 the LORD our God shall cut them **o**. H6789
101: 5 him will I cut **o**: him that hath an high H6789

Ps 101: 8 that I may cut **o** all wicked doers from H3772
108:11 *Wilt* not *thou,* O God, *who* hast cast us **o**?
109:13 Let his posterity be cut **o**; *and* in the H3772
15 **o** the memory of them from the earth. H3772
138: 6 lowly: but the proud he knoweth afar **o**. H4801
139: 2 thou understandest my thought afar **o**. H7350
143:12 And of thy mercy cut **o** mine enemies, H6789
Prv 2:22 But the wicked shall be cut **o** from the H3772
17:14 therefore leave **o** contention, before it H5203
23:18 and thine expectation shall not be cut **o**. H3772
24:14 and thy expectation shall not be cut **o**. H3772
26: 6 **o** the feet, *and* drinketh damage. H7096
27:10 *that is* near than a brother far **o**. H7350
30:14 the poor from **o** the earth, and the needy
Ecc 7:24 That which is far **o**, and exceeding H7350
Song 5: 3 I have put **o** my coat; how shall I put it H6584
Isa 6: 6 taken with the tongs from **o** the altar: H5921
9:14 Therefore the LORD will cut **o** from H3772
10: 7 to destroy and cut **o** nations not a few. H3772
27 taken away from **o** thy shoulder, and H5921
27 and his yoke from **o** thy neck, and the H5921
11:13 Judah shall be cut **o**: Ephraim shall not H3772
14:22 of hosts, and cut **o** from Babylon the H3772
25 his yoke depart from **o** them, and his H5921
25 burden depart from **o** their shoulders. H5921
15: 2 *be* baldness, *and* every beard cut **o**. H1438
17:13 they shall flee far **o**, and shall be chased H4801
18: 5 he shall both cut **o** the sprigs with H3772
20: 2 sackcloth from **o** thy loins, and put off H5921
2 thy loins, and put **o** thy shoe from thy H2502
22:25 be cut **o**: for the LORD hath spoken *it*. H3772
23: 7 feet shall carry her afar **o** to sojourn. H7350
25: 8 away tears from **o** all faces; and the H5921
8 he take away from **o** all the earth: for H5921
27:11 shall be broken **o**: the women come, H7665
12 LORD shall beat **o** from the channel of H2251
29:20 and all that watch for iniquity are cut **o**: H3772
33: 9 and Carmel shake **o** *their fruits*. H5287
13 Hear, ye *that are* far **o**, what I have H7350
17 shall behold the land that is very far **o**. H4801
34: 4 as the leaf falleth **o** from the vine, and H5034
38:10 I said in the cutting **o** of my days, I H1824
12 tent: I have cut **o** like a weaver my life: H7088
12 my life: he will cut me **o** with pining H1214
46:13 it shall not be far **o**, and my salvation H7368
47:11 be able to put it **o**: and desolation shall H3722
48: 9 I refrain for thee, that I cut thee not **o**. H3772
19 cut **o** nor destroyed from before me. H3772
50: 6 to them that plucked **o** the hair: I hid not
53: 8 for he was cut **o** out of the land of the H1504
55:13 everlasting sign *that* shall not be cut **o**. H3772
56: 5 name, that shall not be cut **o**. H3772
57: 9 thy messengers far **o**, and didst debase H7350
19 to *him that is* far **o**, and to *him that is* H7350
59:11 for salvation, *but* it is far **o** from us. H7368
14 standeth afar **o**: for truth is fallen in H7350
66: 3 a lamb, *as if* he cut **o** a dog's neck; he H6202
19 *to* the isles afar **o**, that have not heard H7350
Jer 7:28 and is cut **o** from their mouth. H3772
29 Cut **o** thine hair, *O Jerusalem*, and cast H1494
9:21 our palaces, to cut **o** the children from H3772
11:19 and let us cut him **o** from the land of H3772
23:23 saith the LORD, and not a God afar **o**? H7350
24:10 consumed from **o** the land that I gave H5921
28:10 the yoke from **o** the prophet Jeremiah's H5921
12 the yoke from **o** the neck of the prophet H5921
16 I will cast thee from **o** the face of the H5921
30: 8 his yoke from **o** thy neck, and will burst H5921
31:10 *it* in the isles afar **o**, and say, He that H4801
37 I will also cast **o** all the seed of Israel H3988
33:24 hath even cast them **o**? thus they have H3988
38:27 So they left **o** speaking with him; for
44: 7 your souls, to cut **o** from you man and H3772
8 cut yourselves **o**, and that ye might be H3772
11 you for evil, and to cut **o** all Judah. H3772
18 But since we left **o** to burn incense to H2308
46:27 thee from afar **o**, and thy seed from the H7350
47: 4 *and* to cut **o** from Tyrus and Zidon H3772
5 Ashkelon is cut **o** *with* the remnant of H1820
48: 2 and let us cut it **o** from *being* a nation. H3772
25 The horn of Moab is cut **o**, and his arm H1438
49:26 **o** in that day, saith the LORD of hosts. H1826
30 Flee, get you far **o**, dwell deep, O ye
50:16 Cut **o** the sower from Babylon, and him H3772
30 be cut **o** in that day, saith the LORD. H1826
51: 6 his soul: be not cut **o** in her iniquity; for H1826
50 the LORD afar **o**, and let Jerusalem H7350
62 this place, to cut it **o**, that none shall H3772
Lam 2: 3 He hath cut **o** in *his* fierce anger all the H1438
7 The Lord hath cast **o** his altar, he hath H2186
3:17 And thou hast removed my soul far **o** H2186
31 For the Lord will not cast **o** for ever: H2186
53 They have cut **o** my life in the dungeon, H6789
54 over mine head; *then* I said, I am cut **o**. H1504
Ezk 6:12 He that is far **o** shall die of the H7350
8: 6 I should go far **o** from my sanctuary? H7368
10:18 departed from **o** the threshold of the H5921
11:16 I have cast them far **o** among the H7368
12:27 prophesieth of the times *that are* far **o**. H7350
14: 8 and I will cut him **o** from the midst of H3772
13 and will cut **o** man and beast from it: H3772
17 so that I cut **o** man and beast from it: H3772
19 blood, to cut **o** from it man and beast: H3772
21 to cut **o** from it man and beast? H3772
17: 4 He cropped **o** the top of his young H6998
9 thereof, and cut **o** the fruit thereof, that H7082
17 building forts, to cut **o** many persons: H3772
22 set *it*; I will crop **o** from the top of his H6998
18:17 *That* hath taken **o** his hand from the H7725
21: 3 and will cut **o** from thee the righteous H3772
4 Seeing then that I will cut **o** from thee H3772
26 the diadem, and take **o** the crown: this H7311
23:34 thereof, and pluck **o** thine own breasts: H5423
25: 7 and I will cut thee **o** from the people, H3772
13 and will cut **o** man and beast from H3772
16 and I will cut **o** the Cherethims, and H3772
26:16 their robes, and put **o** their broidered H6584
29: 8 and cut **o** man and beast out of thee. H3772
30:15 and I will cut **o** the multitude of No. H3772
31:12 have cut him **o**, and have left him: upon H3772
35: 7 desolate, and cut **o** from it him that H3772
37:11 hope is lost: we are cut **o** for our parts. H1504
44:19 they shall put **o** their garments wherein H6584
Dan 4:14 the tree, and cut **o** his branches, shake H7113
14 his branches, shake **o** his leaves, and H5426
27 unto thee, and break **o** thy sins by H6562
9: 7 near, and *that are* far **o**, through all the H7350
26 Messiah be cut **o**, but not for himself: H3772
Hos 4:10 have left **o** to take heed to the LORD. H5800
8: 3 Israel hath cast **o** *the thing that is* H2186
4 them idols, that they may be cut **o**. H3772
5 Thy calf, O Samaria, hath cast *thee* **o**; H2186
10: 7 *As for* Samaria, her king is cut **o** as the H1820
15 shall the king of Israel utterly be cut **o**. H1820
11: 4 as they that take **o** the yoke on their H7311
Joel 1: 5 wine; for it is cut **o** from your mouth. H3772
9 offering is cut **o** from the house of the H3772
16 Is not the meat cut **o** before our eyes, H3772
2:20 But I will remove far **o** from you the H7368
3: 8 far **o**: for the LORD hath spoken *it*. H7350
Am 1: 5 and cut **o** the inhabitant from H3772
8 And I will cut **o** the inhabitant from H3772
11 and did cast **o** all pity, and his anger H7843
2: 3 And I will cut **o** the judge from the H3772
3:14 shall be cut **o**, and fall to the ground. H1438
5: 7 and leave **o** righteousness in the earth, H3240
9: 8 destroy it from **o** the face of the earth; H5921
Oba 5 (how art thou cut **o**!) would they not H1820
9 of Esau may be cut **o** by slaughter. H3772
10 thee, and thou shalt be cut **o** for ever. H3772
14 crossway, to cut **o** those of his that did H3772
Mic 2: 8 as an enemy: ye pull **o** the robe with the H6584
3: 2 the evil; who pluck **o** their skin from off H1497
2 off their skin from **o** them, and their
2 and their flesh from **o** their bones; H5921
3 their skin from **o** them; and they break H5921
4: 3 nations afar **o**; and they shall beat H7350
7 that was cast far **o** a strong nation: and H1972
5: 9 and all thine enemies shall be cut **o**. H3772
10 that I will cut **o** thy horses out of the H3772
11 And I will cut **o** the cities of thy land, H3772
12 And I will cut **o** witchcrafts out of thine H3772
13 Thy graven images also will I cut **o**, and H3772
Nah 1:13 For now will I break his yoke from **o** H5921
14 thy gods will I cut **o** the graven image H3772
15 pass through thee; he is utterly cut **o**. H3772
2:13 and I will cut **o** thy prey from the earth, H3772
3:15 shall cut thee **o**, it shall eat thee up like H3772
Hab 2:10 house by cutting **o** many people, and H7096
3:17 flock shall be cut **o** from the fold, and H1504
Zep 1: 2 I will utterly consume all *things* from **o** H6440
3 and I will cut **o** man from off the land, H3772
3 man from **o** the land, saith the LORD. H6440
4 and I will cut **o** the remnant of Baal H3772
11 down; all they that bear silver are cut **o**. H3772
3: 6 I have cut **o** the nations: their towers H3772
Zep 3: 7 should not be cut **o**, howsoever I H3772
Zec 5: 3 shall be cut **o** *as* on this side according H5352
3 be cut **o** *as* on that side according to it. H5352
6:15 And they *that are* far **o** shall come and H7350
9: 6 I will cut **o** the pride of the Philistines. H3772
10 And I will cut **o** the chariot from H3772
10 bow shall be cut **o**: and he shall speak H3772
10: 6 had not cast them **o**: for I *am* the LORD H2186
11: 8 Three shepherds also I cut **o** in one H3582
9 that is to be cut **o**, let it be cut off; and H3582
9 cut off, let it be cut **o**; and let the rest eat H3582
16 those that be cut **o**, neither shall seek H3582
13: 2 *that* I will cut **o** the names of the idols H3772
8 shall be cut **o** *and* die; but the third H3772
14: 2 people shall not be cut **o** from the city. H3772
Mal 2:12 The LORD will cut **o** the man that H3772
Mt 5:30 offend thee, cut it **o**, and cast *it* from G1581
8:30 And there was a good way **o** from them G3112
10:14 or city, shake **o** the dust of your feet. G1621
18: 8 thee, cut them **o**, and cast *them* from G1581
26:51 of the high priest's, and smote **o** his ear. G851
58 But Peter followed him afar **o** unto the G575
27:31 they took the robe **o** from him, and put G1562
55 beholding afar **o**, which followed Jesus G575
Mk 5: 6 But when he saw Jesus afar **o**, he ran and G575
6:11 thence, shake **o** the dust under your G1621
9:43 And if thy hand offend thee, cut it **o**: it is G609
45 And if thy foot offend thee, cut it **o**: it is G609
11: 8 cut down branches **o** the trees, and G1537
13 And seeing a fig tree afar **o** having G3113
14:47 of the high priest, and cut **o** his ear. G851
54 And Peter followed him afar **o**, even into G575
15:20 him, they took **o** the purple from him, G1562
40 looking on afar **o**: among whom was G575
Lk 9: 5 of that city, shake **o** the very dust from G660
10:11 on us, we do wipe **o** against you: G631
14:32 other is yet a great way **o**, he sendeth an G4206
15:20 yet a great way **o**, his father saw him, G568
16:23 afar **o**, and Lazarus in his bosom. G575
17:12 that were lepers, which stood afar **o**: G4207
18:13 And the publican, standing afar **o**, G3113
22:50 of the high priest, and cut **o** his right ear. G851
54 house. And Peter followed afar **o**. G3113
23:49 stood afar **o**, beholding these things. G3113
Jn 11:18 unto Jerusalem, about fifteen furlongs **o**: G575
18:10 servant, and cut **o** his right ear. The G609
26 ear Peter cut **o**, saith, Did not I see thee G609
Act 2:39 to all that are afar **o**, *even* as many as G1519
7:33 Then said the Lord to him, Put **o** thy G3089
12: 7 And his chains fell **o** from *his* hands. G1601
13:51 But they shook **o** the dust of their feet G1621
16:22 magistrates rent **o** their clothes, and G4048
22:23 And as they cried out, and cast **o** *their* G4495
27:32 Then the soldiers cut **o** the ropes of the G609
32 the ropes of the boat, and let her fall **o**. G1601
28: 5 And he shook **o** the beast into the fire, G660
Ro 11:17 be broken **o**, and thou, being a wild G1575
19 broken **o**, that I might be graffed in. G1575
20 they were broken **o**, and thou standest G1575
22 otherwise thou also shalt be cut **o**. G1581
13:12 let us therefore cast **o** the works of G659
2Co 11:12 will do, that I may cut **o** occasion from G1581
Gal 5:12 I would they were even cut **o** which G609
Eph 2:13 **o** are made nigh by the blood of Christ. G3112
17 were afar **o**, and to them that were nigh. G3112
4:22 That ye put **o** concerning the former G659
Col 2:11 hands, in putting **o** the body of the sins G555
3: 8 But now ye also put **o** all these; anger, G659
9 have put **o** the old man with his deeds; G554
1Ti 5:12 because they have cast **o** their first faith. G114
Heb 11:13 seen them afar **o**, and were persuaded G4207
2Pt 1: 9 cannot see afar **o**, and hath forgotten G3467
14 Knowing that shortly I must put **o** *this* G595
Rev 18:10 Standing afar **o** for the fear of her G575
15 her, shall stand afar **o** for the fear of her G575
17 as many as trade by sea, stood afar **o**, G575

OFFENCE

1Sa 25:31 unto thee, nor **o** of heart unto my lord, H4383
Isa 8:14 and for a rock of **o** to both the houses H4383
Hos 5:15 acknowledge their **o**, and seek my face: H816
Mt 16:23 Satan: thou art an **o** unto me: for thou G4625
18: 7 to that man by whom the **o** cometh! G4625
Act 24:16 void of **o** toward God, and *toward* men. G677
Ro 5:15 But not as the **o**, so also *is* the free gift. G3900
15 For if through the **o** of one many be G3900
17 For if by one man's **o** death reigned by G3900
18 Therefore as by the **o** of one *judgment* G3900

Ro 5:20 Moreover the law entered, that the **o** G3900
9:33 and rock of **o**: and whosoever believeth G4625
14:20 *it is* evil for that man who eateth with **o**. G4348
1Co 10:32 Give none **o**, neither to the Jews, nor to G677
2Co 6: 3 Giving no **o** in any thing, that the G4349
11: 7 Have I committed an **o** in abasing G266
Gal 5:11 then is the **o** of the cross ceased. G4625
Php 1:10 and without **o** till the day of Christ; G677
1Pt 2: 8 and a rock of **o**, *even to them* which G4625

OFFENCES

Ecc 10: 4 thy place; for yielding pacifieth great **o**. H2399
Mt 18: 7 Woe unto the world because of **o**! for it G4625
7 needs be that **o** come; but woe to that G4625
Lk 17: 1 but that **o** will come: but woe G4625
Ro 4:25 Who was delivered for our **o**, and was G3900
5:16 free gift *is* of many **o** unto justification. G3900
16:17 cause divisions and **o** contrary to the G4625

OFFEND

Job 34:31 *chastisement,* I will not **o** *any more*: H2254
Ps 73:15 **o** *against* the generation of thy children. H898
119:165 love thy law: and nothing shall **o** them. H4383
Jer 2: 3 devour him shall **o**; evil shall come upon H816
50: 7 said, We **o** not, because they have H816
Hos 4:15 *yet* let not Judah **o**; and come not ye unto H816
Hab 1:11 **o**, *imputing* this his power unto his god. H816
Mt 5:29 And if thy right eye **o** thee, pluck it out, G4624
30 And if thy right hand **o** thee, cut it off, G4624
13:41 that **o**, and them which do iniquity; G4625
17:27 Notwithstanding, lest we should **o** G4624
18: 6 But whoso shall **o** one of these little G4624
8 Wherefore if thy hand or thy foot **o** G4624
9 And if thine eye **o** thee, pluck it out, G4624
Mk 9:42 And whosoever shall **o** one of *these* G4624
43 And if thy hand **o** thee, cut it off: it is G4624
45 And if thy foot **o** thee, cut it off: it is G4624
47 And if thine eye **o** thee, pluck it out: it G4624
Lk 17: 2 that he should **o** one of these little ones. G4624
Jn 6:61 it, he said unto them, Doth this **o** you? G4624
1Co 8:13 my brother to **o**, I will eat no flesh while G4624
13 standeth, lest I make my brother to **o**. G4624
Jas 2:10 yet **o** in one *point*, he is guilty of all. G4417
3: 2 For in many things we **o** all. If any man G4417
2 all. If any man **o** not in word, the same G4417

OFFENDED

Gen 20: 9 and what have I **o** thee, that thou hast H2398
40: 1 had **o** their lord the king of Egypt. H2398
2Ki 18:14 saying, I have **o**; return from me: that H2398
2Ch 28:13 for whereas we have **o** against the LORD H819
Prv 18:19 A brother **o** *is harder to be won* than a H6586
Jer 37:18 What have I **o** against thee, or against H2398
Ezk 25:12 **o**, and revenged himself upon them; H816
Hos 13: 1 in Israel; but when he **o** in Baal, he died. H816
Mt 11: 6 *is he*, whosoever shall not be **o** in me. G4624
13:21 because of the word, by and by he is **o**. G4624
57 And they were **o** in him. But Jesus said G4624
15:12 were **o**, after they heard this saying? G4624
24:10 And then shall many be **o**, and shall G4624
26:31 All ye shall be **o** because of me this G4624
33 all *men* shall be **o** because of thee, *yet* G4624
33 because of thee, *yet* will I never be **o**. G4624
Mk 4:17 word's sake, immediately they are **o**. G4624
6: 3 here with us? And they were **o** at him. G4624
14:27 All ye shall be **o** because of me this G4624
29 Although all shall be **o**, yet *will* not I. G4624
Lk 7:23 *is he*, whosoever shall not be **o** in me. G4624
Jn 16: 1 unto you, that ye should not be **o**. G4624
Act 25: 8 against Caesar, have I **o** any thing at all. G264
Ro 14:21 stumbleth, or is **o**, or is made weak. G4624
2Co 11:29 am not weak? who is **o**, and I burn not? G4624

OFFENDER

Isa 29:21 That make a man an **o** for a word, and H2398
Act 25:11 For if I be an **o**, or have committed any G91

OFFENDERS

1Ki 1:21 my son Solomon shall be counted **o**. H2400

OFFER

Gen 22: 2 of Moriah; and **o** him there for a burnt H5927
Ex 22:29 Thou shalt not delay *to* **o** the first of thy
23:18 Thou shalt not **o** the blood of my H2076
29:36 And thou shalt **o** every day a bullock H6213
38 Now this *is that* which thou shalt **o** H6213
39 The one lamb thou shalt **o** in the H6213
39 the other lamb thou shalt **o** at even: H6213
Ex 29:41 And the other lamb thou shalt **o** at H6213
30: 9 Ye shall **o** no strange incense thereon, H5927
34:25 Thou shalt not **o** the blood of my H7819
35:24 Every one that did **o** an offering of H7311
Lev 1: 3 of the herd, let him **o** a male without H7126
3 blemish: he shall **o** it of his own H7126
2: 1 And when any will **o** a meat offering H7126
12 the firstfruits, ye shall **o** them unto the H7126
13 all thine offerings thou shalt **o** salt. H7126
14 And if thou **o** a meat offering of thy H7126
14 the LORD, thou shalt **o** for the meat H7126
3: 1 offering, if he **o** *it* of the herd; whether H7126
1 **o** it without blemish before the LORD. H7126
3 And he shall **o** of the sacrifice of the H7126
6 female, he shall **o** it without blemish. H7126
7 If he **o** a lamb for his offering, then H7126
7 then shall he **o** it before the LORD. H7126
9 And he shall **o** of the sacrifice of the H7126
12 then he shall **o** it before the LORD. H7126
14 And he shall **o** thereof his offering, H7126
4:14 congregation shall **o** a young bullock H7126
5: 8 priest, who shall **o** *that* which *is* for the H7126
10 And he shall **o** the second *for* a burnt H6213
6:14 **o** it before the LORD, before the altar. H7126
20 which they shall **o** unto the LORD in H7126
21 **o** *for* a sweet savour unto the LORD. H7126
22 in his stead shall **o** it: *it is* a statute for H6213
7: 3 And he shall **o** of it all the fat thereof; H7126
11 which he shall **o** unto the LORD. H7126
12 If he **o** it for a thanksgiving, then he H7126
12 then he shall **o** with the sacrifice of H7126
13 Besides the cakes, he shall **o** *for* his H7126
14 And of it he shall **o** one out of the whole H7126
25 of which men **o** an offering made by H7126
38 of Israel to **o** their oblations unto H7126
9: 2 blemish, and **o** *them* before the LORD. H7126
7 the altar, and **o** thy sin offering, and H6213
7 for the people: and **o** the offering of the H6213
12: 7 Who shall **o** it before the LORD, and H7126
14:12 one he lamb, and **o** him for a trespass H7126
19 And the priest shall **o** the sin offering, H6213
20 And the priest shall **o** the burnt H5927
30 And he shall **o** the one of the H6213
15:15 And the priest shall **o** them, the one *for* H6213
30 And the priest shall **o** the one *for* a sin H6213
16: 6 And Aaron shall **o** his bullock of the sin H7126
9 lot fell, and **o** him *for* a sin offering. H6213
24 come forth, and **o** his burnt offering, H6213
17: 4 congregation, to **o** an offering unto the H7126
5 which they **o** in the open field, even H2076
5 unto the priest, and **o** them *for* peace H2076
7 And they shall no more **o** their H2076
9 congregation, to **o** it unto the LORD; H6213
19: 5 And if ye **o** a sacrifice of peace H2076
5 LORD, ye shall **o** it at your own will. H2076
6 It shall be eaten the same day ye **o** it, H2077
21: 6 they do **o**: therefore they shall be holy. H7126
17 not approach to **o** the bread of his God. H7126
21 shall come nigh to **o** the offerings of the H7126
21 come nigh to **o** the bread of his God. H7126
22:15 of Israel, which they **o** unto the LORD; H7311
18 in Israel, that will **o** his oblation for all H7126
18 **o** unto the LORD for a burnt offering; H7126
19 *Ye shall* **o** at your own will a male
20 **o**: for it shall not be acceptable for you. H7126
22 ye shall not **o** these unto the LORD, H7126
23 parts, that mayest thou **o** *for* a freewill H6213
24 Ye shall not **o** unto the LORD that H7126
25 hand shall ye **o** the bread of your God H7126
29 And when ye will **o** a sacrifice of H2076
29 unto the LORD, **o** *it* at your own will. H2076
23: 8 But ye shall **o** an offering made by fire H7126
12 And ye shall **o** that day when ye wave H6213
16 **o** a new meat offering unto the LORD. H7126
18 And ye shall **o** with the bread seven H7126
25 but ye shall **o** an offering made by H7126
27 your souls, and **o** an offering made by H7126
36 Seven days ye shall **o** an offering made H7126
36 you; and ye shall **o** an offering made by H7126
37 convocations, to **o** an offering made by H7126
27:11 which they do not **o** a sacrifice unto the H7126
Nu 5:25 the LORD, and **o** it upon the altar: H7126
6:11 And the priest shall **o** the one for a sin H6213
14 And he shall **o** his offering unto the H7126
16 LORD, and shall **o** his sin offering, and H6213
17 And he shall **o** the ram *for* a sacrifice of H6213
17 the priest shall **o** also his meat offering, H6213
7:11 Moses, They shall **o** their offering, each H7126
Nu 7:18 son of Zuar, prince of Issachar, did **o**: H7126
24 prince of the children of Zebulun, *did* **o**:
30 prince of the children of Reuben, *did* **o**:
36 prince of the children of Simeon, *did* **o**:
8:11 And Aaron shall **o** the Levites before H5130
12 and thou shalt **o** the one *for* a sin H6213
13 **o** them *for* an offering unto the LORD. H5130
15 them, and **o** them *for* an offering. H5130
9: 7 that we may not **o** an offering of the H7126
15: 7 And for a drink offering thou shalt **o** H7126
14 and will **o** an offering made by H6213
19 **o** up an heave offering unto the LORD. H7311
20 Ye shall **o** up a cake of the first of your H7311
24 congregation shall **o** one young bullock H6213
16:40 come near to **o** incense before the H6999
18:12 which they shall **o** unto the LORD, H5414
19 the children of Israel **o** unto the LORD, H7311
24 of Israel, which they **o** *as* an heave H7311
26 then ye shall **o** up an heave offering H7311
28 Thus ye also shall **o** an heave offering H7311
29 Out of all your gifts ye shall **o** every H7311
28: 2 to **o** unto me in their due season. H7126
3 by fire which ye shall **o** unto the LORD; H7126
4 The one lamb shalt thou **o** in the H6213
4 the other lamb shalt thou **o** at even; H6213
8 And the other lamb shalt thou **o** at H6213
8 thereof, thou shalt **o** *it*, a sacrifice H6213
11 months ye shall **o** a burnt offering unto H7126
19 But ye shall **o** a sacrifice made by fire H7126
20 deals shall ye **o** for a bullock, and two H6213
21 A several tenth deal shalt thou **o** for H6213
23 Ye shall **o** these beside the burnt H6213
24 After this manner ye shall **o** daily, H6213
27 But ye shall **o** the burnt offering for a H7126
31 Ye shall **o** *them* beside the continual H6213
29: 2 And ye shall **o** a burnt offering for a H6213
8 But ye shall **o** a burnt offering unto the H7126
13 And ye shall **o** a burnt offering, a H7126
17 And on the second day *ye shall* **o** twelve
36 But ye shall **o** a burnt offering, a H7126
Dt 12:13 Take heed to thyself that thou **o** not thy H5927
14 there thou shalt **o** thy burnt offerings, H5927
27 And thou shalt **o** thy burnt offerings, H6213
18: 3 from them that **o** a sacrifice, whether H2076
27: 6 stones: and thou shalt **o** burnt offerings H5927
7 And thou shalt **o** peace offerings, and H2076
33:19 there they shall **o** sacrifices of H2076
Jos 22:23 the LORD; or if to **o** thereon burnt H5927
23 meat offering, or if to **o** peace offerings H6213
Jdg 3:18 And when he had made an end to **o** the H7126
6:26 bullock, and **o** a burnt sacrifice with H5927
11:31 and I will **o** it up for a burnt offering. H5927
13:16 and if thou wilt **o** a burnt offering, thou H6213
16 thou must **o** it unto the LORD. For H5927
16:23 together for to **o** a great sacrifice unto H2076
1Sa 1:21 house, went up to **o** unto the LORD the H2076
2:19 her husband to **o** the yearly sacrifice. H2076
28 *to be* my priest, to **o** upon mine altar, H5927
10: 8 unto thee, to **o** burnt offerings, *and* H5927
2Sa 24:12 saith the LORD, I **o** thee three *things;* H5190
22 the king take and **o** up what *seemeth* H5927
24 neither will I **o** burnt offerings unto H5927
1Ki 3: 4 did Solomon **o** upon that altar. H5927
9:25 a year did Solomon **o** burnt offerings H5927
13: 2 upon thee shall he **o** the priests of the H2076
2Ki 5:17 will henceforth **o** neither burnt offering H6213
10:24 And when they went in to **o** sacrifices H6213
1Ch 16:40 To **o** burnt offerings unto the LORD H5927
21:10 saith the LORD, I **o** thee three *things:* H5186
24 nor **o** burnt offerings without cost. H5927
23:31 And to **o** all burnt sacrifices unto the H5927
29:14 should be able to **o** so willingly after this
17 are present here, to **o** willingly unto thee.
2Ch 23:18 of the LORD, to **o** the burnt offerings H5927
24:14 minister, and to **o** *withal*, and spoons, H5927
29:21 to **o** *them* on the altar of the LORD. H5927
27 And Hezekiah commanded to **o** the H5927
35:12 of the people, to **o** unto the LORD, as *it* H7126
16 the passover, and to **o** burnt offerings H5927
Ezr 3: 2 the God of Israel, to **o** burnt offerings H5927
6 began they to **o** burnt offerings unto H5927
6:10 That they may **o** sacrifices of sweet H7127
7:17 offerings, and **o** them upon the altar H7127
Job 42: 8 servant Job, and **o** up for yourselves a H5927
Ps 4: 5 **O** the sacrifices of righteousness, and H2076
16: 4 **o**, nor take up their names into my lips. H5258
27: 6 me: therefore will I **o** in his tabernacle H2076
50:14 **O** unto God thanksgiving; and pay thy H2076

Ps 51:19 shall they **o** bullocks upon thine altar. H5927
66:15 I will **o** unto thee burnt sacrifices of H5927
15 I will **o** bullocks with goats. Selah. H6213
72:10 kings of Sheba and Seba shall **o** gifts. H7126
116:17 I will **o** to thee the sacrifice of H2076
Isa 57: 7 thither wentest thou up to **o** sacrifice. H2076
Jer 11:12 unto whom they **o** incense: but they shall
14:12 and when they **o** burnt offering and an H5927
33:18 a man before me to **o** burnt offerings, H5927
Ezk 6:13 did **o** sweet savour to all their idols. H5414
20:31 For when ye **o** your gifts, when ye make H5375
43:18 they shall make it, to **o** burnt offerings H5927
22 And on the second day thou shalt **o** a H7126
23 *it*, thou shalt **o** a young bullock without H7126
24 And thou shalt **o** them before the H7126
24 and they shall **o** them up *for* a burnt H5927
44: 7 house, when ye **o** my bread, the fat and H7126
15 before me to **o** unto me the fat and H7126
27 **o** his sin offering, saith the Lord GOD. H7126
45: 1 ye shall **o** an oblation unto the H7311
13 This *is* the oblation that ye shall **o**; the H7311
14 bath of oil, *ye shall* **o** the tenth part of a
46: 4 the prince shall **o** unto the LORD in the H7126
48: 8 which ye shall **o** of five and twenty H7311
9 The oblation that ye shall **o** unto the H7311
20 thousand: ye shall **o** the holy oblation H7311
Dan 2:46 that they should **o** an oblation and H5260
Hos 9: 4 They shall not **o** wine *offerings* to the H5258
Am 4: 5 And **o** a sacrifice of thanksgiving with H6999
5:22 Though ye **o** me burnt offerings and H5927
Hag 2:14 and that which they **o** there *is* unclean. H7126
Mal 1: 7 Ye **o** polluted bread upon mine altar; H5066
8 And if ye **o** the blind for sacrifice, *is it* H5066
8 not evil? and if ye **o** the lame and sick, H5066
8 and sick, *is it* not evil? **o** it now unto thy H7126
3: 3 that they may **o** unto the LORD an H5066
Mt 5:24 brother, and then come and **o** thy gift. G4374
8: 4 to the priest, and **o** the gift that Moses G4374
Mk 1:44 to the priest, and **o** for thy cleansing G4374
Lk 2:24 And to **o** a sacrifice according to that G1325
5:14 to the priest, and **o** for thy cleansing, G4374
6:29 on the *one* cheek **o** also the other; and G3930
11:12 Or if he shall ask an egg, will he **o** him a G1929
Heb 5: 1 may **o** both gifts and sacrifices for sins: G4374
3 so also for himself, to **o** for sins. G4374
7:27 high priests, to **o** up sacrifice, first for G399
8: 3 For every high priest is ordained to **o** G4374
3 that this man have somewhat also to **o**. G4374
4 priests that **o** gifts according to the law: G4374
9:25 Nor yet that he should **o** himself often, G4374
13:15 By him therefore let us **o** the sacrifice of G399
1Pt 2: 5 an holy priesthood, to **o** up spiritual G399
Rev 8: 3 that he should **o** *it* with the prayers of G1325

OFFERED

Gen 8:20 fowl, and **o** burnt offerings on the altar. H5927
22:13 took the ram, and **o** him up for a burnt H5927
31:54 Then Jacob **o** sacrifice upon the mount, H2076
46: 1 to Beer-sheba, and **o** sacrifices unto the H2076
Ex 24: 5 of Israel, which **o** burnt offerings, and H5927
32: 6 the morrow, and **o** burnt offerings, and H5927
35:22 every man that **o** *offered* an offering H5130
22 *o* an offering of gold unto the LORD. H5130
40:29 congregation, and **o** upon it the burnt H5927
Lev 7: 8 of the burnt offering which he hath **o**. H7126
15 same day that it is **o**; he shall not leave H7133
9:15 and slew it, and **o** it for sin, as the first. H2398
16 and **o** it according to the manner. H6213
10: 1 thereon, and **o** strange fire before the H7126
19 this day have they **o** their sin offering H7126
16: 1 they **o** before the LORD, and died; H7126
Nu 3: 4 LORD, when they **o** strange fire before H7126
7: 2 were over them that were numbered, **o**: H7126
10 And the princes **o** for dedicating of the H7126
10 princes **o** their offering before the altar. H7126
12 And he that **o** his offering the first day H7126
19 He **o** *for* his offering one silver charger, H7126
42 of Deuel, prince of the children of Gad, *o*:
48 prince of the children of Ephraim, *o*:
54 On the eighth day *o* Gamaliel the son of
60 prince of the children of Benjamin, *o*:
66 prince of the children of Dan, *o*:
72 Ocran, prince of the children of Asher, *o*:
78 prince of the children of Naphtali, *o*:
8:21 and Aaron **o** them *as* an offering H5130
16:35 hundred and fifty men that **o** incense. H7126
38 of the altar: for they **o** them before the H7126
39 were burnt had **o**; and they were made H7126
Nu 22:40 And Balak **o** oxen and sheep, and sent H2076
23: 2 **o** on *every* altar a bullock and a ram. H5927
4 **o** upon *every* altar a bullock and a ram. H5927
14 **o** a bullock and a ram on *every* altar. H5927
30 **o** a bullock and a ram on *every* altar. H5927
26:61 they **o** strange fire before the LORD. H7126
28:15 unto the LORD shall be **o**, beside the H6213
24 LORD: it shall be **o** beside the continual H6213
31:52 offering that they **o** up to the LORD, of H7311
Jos 8:31 up *any* iron: and they **o** thereon burnt H5927
Jdg 5: 2 when the people willingly **o** themselves. H5068
9 of Israel, that **o** themselves willingly
6:28 was **o** upon the altar *that was* built. H5927
13:19 a meat offering, and **o** *it* upon a rock H5927
20:26 until even, and **o** burnt offerings and H5927
21: 4 **o** burnt offerings and peace offerings. H5927
1Sa 1: 4 And when the time was that Elkanah **o**, H2076
2:13 when any man **o** sacrifice, the priest's H2076
6:14 wood of the cart, and **o** the kine a burnt H5927
15 of Beth-shemesh **o** burnt offerings and H5927
7: 9 a sucking lamb, and **o** *it for* a burnt H5927
13: 9 offerings. And he **o** the burnt offering. H5927
12 therefore, and **o** a burnt offering. H5927
2Sa 6:17 for it: and David **o** burnt offerings and H5927
15:12 Giloh, while he **o** sacrifices. And the H2076
24:25 the LORD, and **o** burnt offerings and H5927
1Ki 3:15 of the LORD, and **o** up burnt offerings, H5927
15 offerings, and **o** peace offerings, and H6213
8:62 And the king, and all Israel with him, **o** H2076
63 And Solomon **o** a sacrifice of peace H2076
63 which he **o** unto the LORD, two H2076
64 for there he **o** burnt offerings, and H6213
12:32 *is* in Judah, and he **o** upon the altar. So H5927
33 So he **o** upon the altar which he had H5927
33 he **o** upon the altar, and burnt incense. H5927
22:43 *for* the people **o** and burnt incense yet H2076
2Ki 3:20 meat offering was **o**, that, behold, there H5927
27 in his stead, and **o** him *for* a burnt H5927
16:12 approached to the altar, and **o** thereon. H5927
1Ch 6:49 But Aaron and his sons **o** upon the H6999
15:26 they **o** seven bullocks and seven rams. H2076
16: 1 for it: and they **o** burnt sacrifices and H7126
21:26 the LORD, and **o** burnt offerings and H5927
29: 6 the rulers of the king's work, **o** willingly,
9 Then the people rejoiced, for that they **o**
9 with perfect heart they **o** willingly to the
17 I have willingly **o** all these things: and H5068
21 the LORD, and **o** burnt offerings unto H5927
2Ch 1: 6 **o** a thousand burnt offerings upon it. H5927
4: 6 things as they **o** for the burnt offering H4639
7: 4 Then the king and all the people **o** H2076
5 And king Solomon **o** a sacrifice of H2076
7 for there he **o** burnt offerings, and H6213
8:12 Then Solomon **o** burnt offerings unto H5927
15:11 And they **o** unto the LORD the same H2076
17:16 who willingly **o** himself unto the LORD; H5068
24:14 silver. And they **o** burnt offerings in the H5927
29: 7 incense nor **o** burnt offerings in the H5927
Ezr 1: 6 things, beside all *that* was willingly **o**. H5068
2:68 *is* at Jerusalem, **o** freely for the house of
3: 3 and they **o** burnt offerings thereon H5927
4 as *it is* written, and *o* the daily burnt
5 And afterward *o* the continual burnt
5 **o** a freewill offering unto the LORD. H5068
6: 3 place where they **o** sacrifices, and let H1684
17 And **o** at the dedication of this house of H7127
7:15 have freely **o** unto the God of Israel, H5069
8:25 and all Israel *there* present, had **o**: H7311
35 of the captivity, **o** burnt offerings unto H7126
10:19 *o* a ram of the flock for their trespass.
Neh 11: 2 **o** themselves to dwell at Jerusalem. H5068
12:43 Also that day they **o** great sacrifices, H2076
Job 1: 5 in the morning, and **o** burnt offerings H5927
Isa 57: 6 offering, thou hast **o** a meat offering. H5927
66: 3 an oblation, *as if he* **o** swine's blood; he H5927
Jer 32:29 roofs they have **o** incense unto Baal, H6999
Ezk 20:28 trees, and they **o** there their sacrifices, H2076
48:12 And *this* oblation of the land that is **o** H8641
Dan 11:18 cause the reproach **o** by him to cease;
Am 5:25 Have ye **o** unto me sacrifices and H5066
Jna 1:16 exceedingly, and **o** a sacrifice unto the H2076
Mal 1:11 incense *shall be* **o** unto my name, and H5066
Act 7:41 in those days, and **o** sacrifice unto the G321
42 of Israel, have ye **o** to me slain beasts G4374
8:18 Ghost was given, he **o** them money, G4374
15:29 That ye abstain from meats **o** to idols, G1494
21:25 from *things* **o** to idols, and from blood, G1494
26 should be **o** for every one of them. G4374
1Co 8: 1 Now as touching things **o** unto idols, G1494
4 things that are **o** in sacrifice unto idols, G1494
7 eat *it* as a thing **o** unto an idol; and G1494
10 to eat those things which are **o** to idols; G1494
10:19 is **o** in sacrifice to idols is any thing? G1494
28 But if any man say unto you, This is **o** G1494
Php 2:17 Yea, and if I be **o** upon the sacrifice G4689
2Ti 4: 6 For I am now ready to be **o**, and the G4689
Heb 5: 7 flesh, when he had **o** up prayers and G4374
7:27 this he did once, when he *o* up himself.
9: 7 blood, which he **o** for himself, and *for* G4374
9 present, in which were **o** both gifts and G4374
14 the eternal Spirit **o** himself without G4374
28 So Christ was once **o** to bear the sins of G4374
10: 1 which they **o** year by year continually G4374
2 have ceased to be **o**? because that the G4374
8 *therein*; which are **o** by the law; G4374
12 But this man, after he had **o** one G4374
11: 4 By faith Abel **o** unto God a more G4374
17 he was tried, **o** up Isaac: and he that G4374
17 promises **o** up his only begotten *son*, G4374
Jas 2:21 he had **o** Isaac his son upon the altar? G399

OFFERETH

Lev 6:26 The priest that **o** it for sin shall eat it: in H2398
7: 8 And the priest that **o** any man's burnt H7126
9 in the pan, shall be the priest's that **o** it. H7126
16 same day that he **o** his sacrifice: and on H7126
18 unto him that **o** it: it shall be an H7126
29 saying, He that **o** the sacrifice of his H7126
33 He among the sons of Aaron, that **o** the H7126
17: 8 you, that **o** a burnt offering or sacrifice, H5927
21: 8 therefore; for he **o** the bread of thy God: H7126
22:21 And whosoever **o** a sacrifice of peace H7126
Nu 15: 4 Then shall he that **o** his offering unto H7126
Ps 50:23 Whoso **o** praise glorifieth me: and to H2076
Isa 66: 3 a dog's neck; he that **o** an oblation, *as if* H5927
Jer 48:35 LORD, him that **o** in the high places, H5927
Mal 2:12 **o** an offering unto the LORD of hosts. H5066

OFFERING

Gen 4: 3 of the ground an **o** unto the LORD. H4503
4 had respect unto Abel and to his **o**: H4503
5 But unto Cain and to his **o** he had not H4503
22: 2 him there for a burnt **o** upon one of the H5930
3 for the burnt **o**, and rose up, and went H5930
6 wood of the burnt **o**, and laid *it* upon H5930
7 but where *is* the lamb for a burnt **o**? H5930
8 **o**: so they went both of them together. H5930
13 up for a burnt **o** in the stead of his son. H5930
35:14 **o** thereon, and he poured oil thereon. H5262
Ex 18:12 in law, took a burnt **o** and sacrifices for H5930
25: 2 they bring me an **o**: of every man that H8641
2 with his heart ye shall take my **o**. H8641
3 And this *is* the **o** which ye shall take of H8641
29:14 with fire without the camp: it *is* a sin **o**. H2403
18 altar: it *is* a burnt **o** unto the LORD: it H5930
18 an **o** made by fire unto the LORD.
24 them *for* a wave **o** before the LORD. H8573
25 altar for a burnt **o**, for a sweet savour H5930
25 it *is* an **o** made by fire unto the LORD.
26 wave it *for* a wave **o** before the LORD: H8573
27 breast of the wave **o**, and the shoulder H8573
27 of the heave **o**, which is waved, and H8641
28 for it *is* an heave **o**: and it shall be an H8641
28 shall be an heave **o** from the children of H8641
28 *even* their heave **o** unto the LORD. H8641
36 day a bullock *for* a sin **o** for atonement: H2403
40 part of an hin of wine *for* a drink **o**. H5262
41 to the meat **o** of the morning, and H4503
41 to the drink **o** thereof, for a sweet H5262
41 an **o** made by fire unto the LORD. H4503
42 *This shall be* a continual burnt **o** H5930
30: 9 nor meat **o**; neither shall ye pour H4503
9 neither shall ye pour drink **o** thereon. H5262
10 blood of the sin **o** of atonements: once H2403
13 half shekel *shall be* the **o** of the LORD. H8641
14 above, shall give an **o** unto the LORD. H8641
15 when *they* give an **o** unto the LORD, to H8641
20 to burn **o** made by fire unto the LORD:
28 And the altar of burnt **o** with all his H5930
31: 9 And the altar of burnt **o** with all his H5930
35: 5 Take ye from among you an **o** unto the H8641
5 let him bring it, an **o** of the LORD; gold, H8641
16 The altar of burnt **o**, with his brasen H5930
21 the LORD'S **o** to the work of the H8641
22 *offered* an **o** of gold unto the LORD. H8573
24 Every one that did offer an **o** of silver H8641

Ex 35:24 the LORD'S **o**: and every man, with H8641
29 brought a willing **o** unto the LORD, H5071
36: 3 And they received of Moses all the **o**, H8641
6 more work for the **o** of the sanctuary. H8641
38: 1 And he made the altar of burnt **o** *of* H5930
24 the gold of the **o**, was twenty and nine H8573
29 And the brass of the **o** *was* seventy H8573
40: 6 altar of the burnt **o** before the door of H5930
10 altar of the burnt **o**, and all his vessels, H5930
29 And he put the altar of burnt **o** *by* the H5930
29 upon it the burnt **o** and the meat H5930
29 **o**; as the LORD commanded Moses. H4503
Lev 1: 2 of you bring an **o** unto the LORD, ye H7133
2 shall bring your **o** of the cattle, *even* of H7133
3 If his **o** *be* a burnt sacrifice of the herd, H7133
4 the head of the burnt **o**; and it shall be H5930
6 And he shall flay the burnt **o**, and cut it H5930
9 a burnt sacrifice, an **o** made by fire, of a H801
10 And if his **o** *be* of the flocks, *namely*, of H7133
13 a burnt sacrifice, an **o** made by fire, of a H801
14 And if the burnt sacrifice for his **o** to H7133
14 **o** of turtledoves, or of young pigeons. H7133
17 a burnt sacrifice, an **o** made by fire, of a
2: 1 And when any will offer a meat **o** unto H7133
1 the LORD, his **o** shall be *of* fine flour; H7133
2 the altar, *to be* an **o** made by fire, of a
3 And the remnant of the meat **o** *shall be* H4503
4 oblation of a meat **o** baken in the oven, H4503
5 And if thy oblation *be* a meat **o** *baken* H4503
6 and pour oil thereon: it *is* a meat **o**. H4503
7 And if thy oblation *be* a meat **o** *baken* H4503
8 And thou shalt bring the meat **o** that is H4503
9 from the meat **o** a memorial thereof, H4503
9 the altar: *it is* an **o** made by fire, of a H4503
10 And that which is left of the meat **o** H4503
11 No meat **o**, which ye shall bring unto H4503
11 in any **o** of the LORD made by fire. H801
13 And every oblation of thy meat **o** shalt H4503
13 from thy meat **o**: with all thine offerings H4503
14 And if thou offer a meat **o** of thy H4503
14 offer for the meat **o** of thy first-fruits H4503
15 lay frankincense thereon: it *is* a meat **o**. H4503
16 *it is* an **o** made by fire unto the LORD.
3: 1 a sacrifice of peace **o**, if he offer *it* of the H8002
2 the head of his **o**, and kill it *at* the door H7133
3 of the peace **o** an offering made by H8002
3 peace offering an **o** made by fire unto
5 *is* on the fire: *it is* an **o** made by fire, of a
6 And if his **o** for a sacrifice of peace H7133
6 a sacrifice of peace **o** unto the LORD *be* H8002
7 If he offer a lamb for his **o**, then shall he H7133
8 the head of his **o**, and kill it before the H7133
9 of the peace **o** an offering made by H8002
9 peace offering an **o** made by fire unto
11 of the **o** made by fire unto the LORD.
12 And if his **o** *be* a goat, then he shall H7133
14 And he shall offer thereof his **o**, *even* an H7133
14 offering, *even* an **o** made by fire unto the
16 *it is* the food of the **o** made by fire for a
4: 3 blemish unto the LORD for a sin **o**.
7 altar of the burnt **o**, which *is at* the door H5930
8 bullock for the sin **o**; the fat that covereth
10 burn them upon the altar of the burnt **o**. H5930
18 altar of the burnt **o**, which *is at* the door H5930
20 the bullock for a sin **o**, so shall he do with
21 bullock: it *is* a sin **o** for the congregation.
23 he shall bring his **o**, a kid of the goats, a H7133
24 **o** before the LORD: it *is* a sin offering. H5930
24 offering before the LORD: it *is* a sin **o**.
25 the blood of the sin **o** with his finger, and
25 the altar of burnt **o**, and shall pour out H5930
25 at the bottom of the altar of burnt **o**. H5930
28 he shall bring his **o**, a kid of the goats, a H7133
29 the head of the sin **o**, and slay the sin
29 sin **o** in the place of the burnt offering.
29 sin offering in the place of the burnt **o**. H5930
30 the altar of burnt **o**, and shall pour out H5930
32 And if he bring a lamb for a sin **o**, he H7133
33 the head of the sin **o**, and slay it for a sin
33 and slay it for a sin **o** in the place where
33 in the place where they kill the burnt **o**. H5930
34 the blood of the sin **o** with his finger, and
34 the altar of burnt **o**, and shall pour out H5930
5: 6 And he shall bring his trespass **o** unto H817
6 the goats, for a sin **o**; and the priest shall
7 sin **o**, and the other for a burnt offering.
7 sin offering, and the other for a burnt **o**. H5930
8 which *is* for the sin **o** first, and wring off

Lev 5: 9 of the blood of the sin **o** upon the side of
9 out at the bottom of the altar: it *is* a sin **o**.
10 second *for* a burnt **o**, according to the H5930
11 shall bring for his **o** the tenth part of an H7133
11 of fine flour for a sin **o**; he shall put no oil
11 *any* frankincense thereon: for it *is* a sin **o**.
12 made by fire unto the LORD: it *is* a sin **o**.
13 shall be the priest's, as a meat **o**. H4503
15 shekel of the sanctuary, for a trespass **o**: H817
16 trespass **o**, and it shall be forgiven him. H817
18 for a trespass **o**, unto the priest: and H817
19 It *is* a trespass **o**: he hath certainly H817
6: 5 appertaineth, in the day of his trespass **o**. H819
6 And he shall bring his trespass **o** unto H817
6 for a trespass **o**, unto the priest: H817
9 the law of the burnt **o**: It *is* the burnt H5930
9 It *is* the burnt **o**, because of the burning H5930
10 with the burnt **o** on the altar, and he H5930
12 and lay the burnt **o** in order upon it; H5930
14 And this *is* the law of the meat **o**: the H4503
15 the flour of the meat **o**, and of the oil H4503
15 *is* upon the meat **o**, and shall burn *it* H4503
17 *is* the sin **o**, and as the trespass offering.
17 *is* the sin offering, and as the trespass **o**. H817
20 This *is* the **o** of Aaron and of his sons, H7133
20 flour for a meat **o** perpetual, half of it H4503
21 pieces of the meat **o** shalt thou offer *for* H4503
23 For every meat **o** for the priest shall be H4503
25 *is* the law of the sin **o**: In the place where
25 where the burnt **o** is killed shall the sin H5930
25 killed shall the sin **o** be killed before the
30 And no sin **o**, whereof *any* of the blood is
7: 1 Likewise this *is* the law of the trespass **o**: H817
2 In the place where they kill the burnt **o** H5930
2 kill the trespass **o**: and the blood thereof H817
5 the altar *for* an **o** made by fire unto the
5 by fire unto the LORD: it *is* a trespass **o**. H817
7 As the sin **o** *is*, so *is* the trespass offering:
7 As the sin offering *is*, so *is* the trespass **o**: H817
8 any man's burnt **o**, *even* the priest shall H5930
8 of the burnt **o** which he hath offered. H5930
9 And all the meat **o** that is baken in the H4503
10 And every meat **o**, mingled with oil, and H4503
13 he shall offer *for* his **o** leavened bread H7133
14 *for* an heave **o** unto the LORD, *and* H8641
16 But if the sacrifice of his **o** *be* a vow, or H7133
16 or a voluntary **o**, it shall be eaten the H5071
25 men offer an **o** made by fire unto the
30 waved *for* a wave **o** before the LORD. H8573
32 *for* an heave **o** of the sacrifices of your H8641
37 This *is* the law of the burnt **o**, of the H5930
37 of the meat **o**, and of the sin offering, H4503
37 and of the sin **o**, and of the trespass
37 offering, and of the trespass **o**, and of the H817
8: 2 bullock for the sin **o**, and two rams, and
14 And he brought the bullock for the sin **o**:
14 upon the head of the bullock for the sin **o**.
18 And he brought the ram for the burnt **o**: H5930
21 savour, *and* an **o** made by fire unto the
27 them *for* a wave **o** before the LORD. H8573
28 altar upon the burnt **o**: they *were* H5930
28 it *is* an **o** made by fire unto the LORD.
29 it *for* a wave **o** before the LORD: *for* H8573
9: 2 a young calf for a sin **o**, and a ram for a
2 a ram for a burnt **o**, without blemish, H5930
3 of the goats for a sin **o**; and a calf and a
3 year, without blemish, for a burnt **o**; H5930
4 and a meat **o** mingled with oil: for H4503
7 altar, and offer thy sin **o**, and thy burnt
7 offering, and thy burnt **o**, and make an H5930
7 and offer the **o** of the people, and make H7133
8 calf of the sin **o**, which *was* for himself.
10 the liver of the sin **o**, he burnt upon the
12 And he slew the burnt **o**; and Aaron's H5930
13 And they presented the burnt **o** unto H5930
14 *them* upon the burnt **o** on the altar. H5930
15 And he brought the people's **o**, and took H7133
15 which *was* the sin **o** for the people, and
16 And he brought the burnt **o**, and offered H5930
17 And he brought the meat **o**, and took an H4503
21 waved *for* a wave **o** before the LORD; H8573
22 came down from **o** of the sin offering, H6213
22 from offering of the sin **o**, and the burnt
22 and the burnt **o**, and peace offerings. H5930
24 the altar the burnt **o** and the fat: *which* H5930
10:12 Take the meat **o** that remaineth of the H4503
15 wave it *for* a wave **o** before the LORD; H8573
16 the goat of the sin **o**, and, behold, it was

Lev 10:17 Wherefore have ye not eaten the sin **o** in
19 they offered their sin **o** and their burnt
19 and their burnt **o** before the LORD; and H5930
19 *if* I had eaten the sin **o** to day, should it
12: 6 year for a burnt **o**, and a young pigeon, H5930
6 for a sin **o**, unto the door of the
8 one for the burnt **o**, and the other for a H5930
8 the other for a sin **o**: and the priest shall
14:10 **o**, mingled with oil, and one log of oil. H4503
12 him for a trespass **o**, and the log of oil, H817
12 them *for* a wave **o** before the LORD: H8573
13 he shall kill the sin **o** and the burnt
13 and the burnt **o**, in the holy place: for H5930
13 for as the sin **o** *is* the priest's, *so is* the
13 *so is* the trespass **o**: it *is* most holy: H817
14 of the trespass **o**, and the priest shall put H817
17 foot, upon the blood of the trespass **o**: H817
19 And the priest shall offer the sin **o**, and
19 and afterward he shall kill the burnt **o**: H5930
20 And the priest shall offer the burnt **o** H5930
20 and the meat **o** upon the altar: and H4503
21 one lamb *for* a trespass **o** to be waved, to H817
21 with oil for a meat **o**, and a log of oil; H4503
22 be a sin **o**, and the other a burnt offering.
22 a sin offering, and the other a burnt **o**. H5930
24 of the trespass **o**, and the log of oil, and H817
24 them *for* a wave **o** before the LORD: H8573
25 of the trespass **o**, and the priest shall take H817
25 of the trespass **o**, and put *it* upon the tip H817
28 the place of the blood of the trespass **o**: H817
31 the one *for* a sin **o**, and the other *for* a
31 the other *for* a burnt **o**, with the meat H5930
31 with the meat **o**: and the priest shall H4503
15:15 the one *for* a sin **o**, and the other *for* a
15 other *for* a burnt **o**; and the priest shall H5930
30 the one *for* a sin **o**, and the other *for* a
30 other *for* a burnt **o**; and the priest shall H5930
16: 3 a sin **o**, and a ram for a burnt offering.
3 a sin offering, and a ram for a burnt **o**. H5930
5 a sin **o**, and one ram for a burnt offering.
5 sin offering, and one ram for a burnt **o**. H5930
6 bullock of the sin **o**, which *is* for himself,
9 LORD'S lot fell, and offer him *for* a sin **o**.
11 bullock of the sin **o**, which *is* for himself,
11 bullock of the sin **o** which *is* for himself:
15 Then shall he kill the goat of the sin **o**,
24 offer his burnt **o**, and the burnt offering H5930
24 and the burnt **o** of the people, and H5930
25 And the fat of the sin **o** shall he burn
27 And the bullock *for* the sin **o**, and the
27 the goat *for* the sin **o**, whose blood was
17: 4 to offer an **o** unto the LORD before H7133
8 you, that offereth a burnt **o** or sacrifice, H5930
19:21 And he shall bring his trespass **o** unto H817
21 *even* a ram for a trespass **o**. H817
22 ram of the trespass **o** before the LORD H817
22:12 may not eat of an **o** of the holy things. H8641
18 will offer unto the LORD for a burnt **o**; H5930
21 vow, or a freewill **o** in beeves or sheep, H5071
22 nor make an **o** by fire of them upon
23 **o**; but for a vow it shall not be accepted. H5071
24 shall ye make *any* **o** *thereof* in your land.
27 for an **o** made by fire unto the LORD. H7133
23: 8 But ye shall offer an **o** made by fire unto
12 first year for a burnt **o** unto the LORD. H5930
13 And the meat **o** thereof *shall be* two H4503
13 with oil, an **o** made by fire unto the
13 and the drink **o** thereof *shall be* of H5262
14 ye have brought an **o** unto your God: *it* H7133
15 **o**; seven sabbaths shall be complete: H8573
16 offer a new meat **o** unto the LORD. H4503
18 be *for* a burnt **o** unto the LORD, with H5930
18 with their meat **o**, and their drink H4503
18 offerings, *even* an **o** made by fire, of
19 of the goats for a sin **o**, and two lambs of
20 *for* a wave **o** before the LORD, with H8573
25 offer an **o** made by fire unto the LORD.
27 offer an **o** made by fire unto the LORD.
36 Seven days ye shall offer an **o** made by
36 ye shall offer an **o** made by fire unto the
37 to offer an **o** made by fire unto the
37 unto the LORD, a burnt **o**, and a meat H5930
37 and a meat **o**, a sacrifice, and drink H4503
24: 7 *even* an **o** made by fire unto the LORD.
27: 9 men bring an **o** unto the LORD, all H7133
Nu 4:16 the daily meat **o**, and the anointing oil, H4503
5: 9 And every **o** of all the holy things of the H8641
15 he shall bring her **o** for her, the tenth H7133

Nu 5:15 for it *is* an **o** of jealousy, an offering H4503
15 of jealousy, an **o** of memorial, bringing H4503
18 head, and put the **o** of memorial in her H4503
18 *is* the jealousy **o**: and the priest shall H4503
25 take the jealousy **o** out of the woman's H4503
25 and shall wave the **o** before the LORD, H4503
26 an handful of the **o**, *even* the memorial H4503
6:11 the one for a sin **o**, and the other for a H2403
11 the other for a burnt **o**, and make an H5930
12 year for a trespass **o**: but the days that H817
14 And he shall offer his **o** unto the LORD, H7133
14 for a burnt **o**, and one ewe lamb of H5930
14 blemish for a sin **o**, and one ram H2403
15 their meat **o**, and their drink offerings. H4503
16 offer his sin **o**, and his burnt offering: H2403
16 offer his sin offering, and his burnt **o**: H5930
17 also his meat **o**, and his drink offering. H4503
17 also his meat offering, and his drink **o**. H5262
20 them *for* a wave **o** before the LORD: H8573
21 vowed, *and of* his **o** unto the LORD for H7133
7: 3 And they brought their **o** before the H7133
10 princes offered their **o** before the altar. H7133
11 shall offer their **o**, each prince on his H7133
12 And he that offered his **o** the first day H7133
13 And his **o** *was* one silver charger, the H7133
13 fine flour mingled with oil for a meat **o**: H4503
15 one lamb of the first year, for a burnt **o**: H5930
16 One kid of the goats for a sin **o**: H2403
17 **o** of Nahshon the son of Amminadab. H7133
19 He offered *for* his **o** one silver charger, H7133
19 fine flour mingled with oil for a meat **o**: H4503
21 one lamb of the first year, for a burnt **o**: H5930
22 One kid of the goats for a sin **o**: H2403
23 *was* the **o** of Nethaneel the son of Zuar. H7133
25 His **o** *was* one silver charger, the H7133
25 fine flour mingled with oil for a meat **o**: H4503
27 one lamb of the first year, for a burnt **o**: H5930
28 One kid of the goats for a sin **o**: H2403
29 this *was* the **o** of Eliab the son of Helon. H7133
31 His **o** *was* one silver charger of the H7133
31 fine flour mingled with oil for a meat **o**: H4503
33 one lamb of the first year, for a burnt **o**: H5930
34 One kid of the goats for a sin **o**: H2403
35 *was* the **o** of Elizur the son of Shedeur. H7133
37 His **o** *was* one silver charger, the H7133
37 fine flour mingled with oil for a meat **o**: H4503
39 one lamb of the first year, for a burnt **o**: H5930
40 One kid of the goats for a sin **o**: H2403
41 **o** of Shelumiel the son of Zurishaddai. H7133
43 His **o** *was* one silver charger of the H7133
43 fine flour mingled with oil for a meat **o**: H4503
45 one lamb of the first year, for a burnt **o**: H5930
46 One kid of the goats for a sin **o**: H2403
47 *was* the **o** of Eliasaph the son of Deuel. H7133
49 His **o** *was* one silver charger, the H7133
49 fine flour mingled with oil for a meat **o**: H4503
51 one lamb of the first year, for a burnt **o**: H5930
52 One kid of the goats for a sin **o**: H2403
53 the **o** of Elishama the son of Ammihud. H7133
55 His **o** *was* one silver charger of the H7133
55 fine flour mingled with oil for a meat **o**: H4503
57 one lamb of the first year, for a burnt **o**: H5930
58 One kid of the goats for a sin **o**: H2403
59 the **o** of Gamaliel the son of Pedahzur. H7133
61 His **o** *was* one silver charger, the H7133
61 fine flour mingled with oil for a meat **o**: H4503
63 one lamb of the first year, for a burnt **o**: H5930
64 One kid of the goats for a sin **o**: H2403
65 *was* the **o** of Abidan the son of Gideoni. H7133
67 His **o** *was* one silver charger, the H7133
67 fine flour mingled with oil for a meat **o**: H4503
69 one lamb of the first year, for a burnt **o**: H5930
70 One kid of the goats for a sin **o**: H2403
71 **o** of Ahiezer the son of Ammishaddai. H7133
73 His **o** *was* one silver charger, the H7133
73 fine flour mingled with oil for a meat **o**: H4503
75 one lamb of the first year, for a burnt **o**: H5930
76 One kid of the goats for a sin **o**: H2403
77 *was* the **o** of Pagiel the son of Ocran. H7133
79 His **o** *was* one silver charger, the H7133
79 fine flour mingled with oil for a meat **o**: H4503
81 one lamb of the first year, for a burnt **o**: H5930
82 One kid of the goats for a sin **o**: H2403
83 this *was* the **o** of Ahira the son of Enan. H7133
87 All the oxen for the burnt **o** *were* twelve H5930
87 with their meat **o**: and the kids of the H4503
87 the kids of the goats for sin **o** twelve. H2403
8: 8 with his meat **o**, *even* fine flour mingled H4503

Nu 8: 8 bullock shalt thou take for a sin **o**. H2403
11 the LORD *for* an **o** of the children of H8573
12 the one *for* a sin **o**, and the other *for* a H2403
12 other *for* a burnt **o**, unto the LORD, to H5930
13 and offer them *for* an **o** unto the LORD. H8573
15 cleanse them, and offer them *for* an **o**. H8573
21 them *as* an **o** before the LORD; and H8573
9: 7 may not offer an **o** of the LORD in his H7133
13 he brought not the **o** of the LORD in his H7133
15: 3 And will make an **o** by fire unto the
3 the LORD, a burnt **o**, or a sacrifice in H5930
3 or in a freewill **o**, or in your solemn H5071
4 Then shall he that offereth his **o** unto H7133
4 bring a meat **o** of a tenth deal of flour H4503
5 of wine for a drink **o** shalt thou prepare H5262
5 the burnt **o** or sacrifice, for one lamb. H5930
6 *for* a meat **o** two tenth deals of flour H4503
7 And for a drink **o** thou shalt offer the H5262
8 *for* a burnt **o**, or *for* a sacrifice in H5930
9 a bullock a meat **o** of three tenth deals H4503
10 And thou shalt bring for a drink **o** half H5262
10 hin of wine, *for* an **o** made by fire, of a
13 this manner, in **o** an offering made by H7126
13 in offering an **o** made by fire, of a sweet
14 and will offer an **o** made by fire, of a
19 offer up an heave **o** unto the LORD. H8641
20 *for* an heave **o**: as *ye do* the heave H8641
20 offering: as *ye do* the heave **o** of the H8641
21 LORD an heave **o** in your generations. H8641
24 for a burnt **o**, for a sweet savour unto H5930
24 with his meat **o**, and his drink offering, H4503
24 and his drink **o**, according to the H5262
24 and one kid of the goats for a sin **o**. H2403
25 shall bring their **o**, a sacrifice made by H7133
25 **o** before the LORD, for their ignorance: H2403
27 a she goat of the first year for a sin **o**. H2403
16:15 not thou their **o**: I have not taken one H4503
18: 9 theirs, every meat **o** of theirs, and every H4503
9 and every sin **o** of theirs, and every H2403
9 and every trespass **o** of theirs, which H817
11 And this *is* thine; the heave **o** of their H8641
17 burn their fat *for* an **o** made by fire, for a
24 offer *as* an heave **o** unto the LORD, I H8641
26 offer up an heave **o** of it for the LORD, H8641
27 And *this* your heave **o** shall be H8641
28 Thus ye also shall offer an heave **o** unto H8641
28 LORD'S heave **o** to Aaron the priest. H8641
29 offer every heave **o** of the LORD, of all H8641
23: 3 Stand by thy burnt **o**, and I will go: H5930
15 burnt **o**, while I meet *the LORD* yonder. H5930
17 stood by his burnt **o**, and the princes of H5930
28: 2 unto them, My **o**, *and* my bread for my H7133
3 them, This *is* the **o** made by fire which ye
3 day by day, *for* a continual burnt **o**. H5930
5 of flour for a meat **o**, mingled with the H4503
6 *It is* a continual burnt **o**, which was H5930
7 And the drink **o** thereof *shall be* the H5262
7 be poured unto the LORD *for* a drink **o**. H5262
8 at even: as the meat **o** of the morning, H4503
8 and as the drink **o** thereof, thou shalt H5262
9 of flour *for* a meat **o**, mingled with oil, H4503
9 with oil, and the drink **o** thereof: H5262
10 *This is* the burnt **o** of every sabbath, H5930
10 burnt **o**, and his drink offering. H5930
10 burnt offering, and his drink **o**. H5262
11 ye shall offer a burnt **o** unto the LORD; H5930
12 of flour *for* a meat **o**, mingled with oil, H4503
12 a meat **o**, mingled with oil, for one ram; H4503
13 with oil *for* a meat **o** unto one lamb; *for* H4503
13 lamb; *for* a burnt **o** of a sweet savour, a H5930
14 this *is* the burnt **o** of every month H5930
15 And one kid of the goats for a sin **o** H2403
15 burnt **o**, and his drink offering. H5930
15 burnt offering, and his drink **o**. H5262
19 by fire *for* a burnt **o** unto the LORD; H5930
20 And their meat **o** *shall be of* flour H4503
22 And one goat *for* a sin **o**, to make an H2403
23 Ye shall offer these beside the burnt **o** H5930
23 which *is* for a continual burnt **o**. H5930
24 burnt **o**, and his drink offering. H5930
24 burnt offering, and his drink **o**. H5262
26 ye bring a new meat **o** unto the LORD, H4503
27 But ye shall offer the burnt **o** for a H5930
28 And their meat **o** of flour mingled with H4503
31 the continual burnt **o**, and his meat H5930
31 and his meat **o**, (they shall be unto H4503
29: 2 And ye shall offer a burnt **o** for a sweet H5930
3 And their meat **o** *shall be of* flour H4503

Nu 29: 5 And one kid of the goats *for* a sin **o**, to H2403
6 Beside the burnt **o** of the month, and H5930
6 and his meat **o**, and the daily burnt H4503
6 the daily burnt **o**, and his meat offering, H5930
6 and his meat **o**, and their drink H4503
8 But ye shall offer a burnt **o** unto the H5930
9 And their meat **o** *shall be of* flour H4503
11 One kid of the goats *for* a sin **o**; beside H2403
11 beside the sin **o** of atonement, and the H2403
11 the continual burnt **o**, and the meat H5930
11 meat **o** of it, and their drink offerings. H4503
13 And ye shall offer a burnt **o**, a sacrifice H5930
14 And their meat **o** *shall be of* flour H4503
16 And one kid of the goats *for* a sin **o**; H2403
16 the continual burnt **o**, his meat offering, H5930
16 his meat **o**, and his drink offering. H4503
16 his meat offering, and his drink **o**. H5262
18 And their meat **o** and their drink H4503
19 And one kid of the goats *for* a sin **o**; H2403
19 the continual burnt **o**, and the meat H5930
19 **o** thereof, and their drink offerings. H4503
21 And their meat **o** and their drink H4503
22 And one goat *for* a sin **o**; beside the H2403
22 the continual burnt **o**, and his meat H5930
22 and his meat **o**, and his drink offering. H4503
22 and his meat offering, and his drink **o**. H5262
24 Their meat **o** and their drink offerings H4503
25 And one kid of the goats *for* a sin **o**; H2403
25 the continual burnt **o**, his meat offering, H5930
25 his meat **o**, and his drink offering. H4503
25 his meat offering, and his drink **o**. H5262
27 And their meat **o** and their drink H4503
28 And one goat *for* a sin **o**; beside the H2403
28 the continual burnt **o**, and his meat H5930
28 and his meat **o**, and his drink offering. H4503
28 and his meat offering, and his drink **o**. H5262
30 And their meat **o** and their drink H4503
31 And one goat *for* a sin **o**; beside the H2403
31 the continual burnt **o**, his meat offering, H5930
31 his meat **o**, and his drink offering. H4503
31 his meat offering, and his drink **o**. H5262
33 And their meat **o** and their drink H4503
34 And one goat *for* a sin **o**; beside the H2403
34 the continual burnt **o**, his meat offering, H5930
34 his meat **o**, and his drink offering. H4503
34 his meat offering, and his drink **o**. H5262
36 But ye shall offer a burnt **o**, a sacrifice H5930
37 Their meat **o** and their drink offerings H4503
38 And one goat *for* a sin **o**; beside the H2403
38 the continual burnt **o**, and his meat H5930
38 and his meat **o**, and his drink offering. H4503
38 and his meat offering, and his drink **o**. H5262
31:29 the priest, *for* an heave **o** of the LORD. H8641
41 the LORD'S heave **o**, unto Eleazar the H8641
52 And all the gold of the **o** that they H8641
Dt 12:11 and the heave **o** of your hand, and all H8641
17 offerings, or heave **o** of thine hand: H8641
16:10 of a freewill **o** of thine hand, which H5071
23:23 *even* a freewill **o**, according as thou hast H5071
Jos 22:23 thereon burnt **o** or meat offering, or H5930
23 offering or meat **o**, or if to offer peace H4503
26 altar, not for burnt **o**, nor for sacrifice: H5930
Jdg 11:31 and I will offer it up for a burnt **o**. H5930
13:16 wilt offer a burnt **o**, thou must offer it H5930
19 So Manoah took a kid with a meat **o**, H4503
23 received a burnt **o** and a meat offering H5930
23 and a meat **o** at our hands, neither H4503
1Sa 2:17 for men abhorred the **o** of the LORD. H4503
29 sacrifice and at mine **o**, which I have H4503
3:14 be purged with sacrifice nor **o** for ever. H4503
6: 3 him a trespass **o**: then ye shall be healed, H817
4 *be* the trespass **o** which we shall return H817
8 him *for* a trespass **o**, in a coffer by the H817
14 the kine a burnt **o** unto the LORD. H5930
17 *for* a trespass **o** unto the LORD; for H817
7: 9 *it for* a burnt **o** wholly unto the LORD: H5930
10 And as Samuel was **o** up the burnt H5927
10 up the burnt **o**, the Philistines drew H5930
13: 9 And Saul said, Bring hither a burnt **o** to H5930
9 offerings. And he offered the burnt **o**. H5930
10 made an end of **o** the burnt offering, H5927
10 of offering the burnt **o**, behold, Samuel H5930
12 myself therefore, and offered a burnt **o**. H5930
26:19 let him accept an **o**: but if *they be* the H4503
2Sa 6:18 made an end of **o** burnt offerings and H5927
1Ki 18:29 until the *time* of the **o** of the *evening* H5927
36 And it came to pass at *the time of* the **o** H5927
2Ki 3:20 when the meat **o** was offered, that, H4503

O

2Ki 3:27 him *for* a burnt **o** upon the wall. And H5930
5:17 neither burnt **o** nor sacrifice unto other H5930
10:25 made an end of **o** the burnt offering, H6213
25 of offering the burnt **o**, that Jehu said to H5930
16:13 And he burnt his burnt **o** and his meat H5930
13 and his meat **o**, and poured his drink H4503
13 poured his drink **o**, and sprinkled the H5262
15 morning burnt **o**, and the evening meat H5930
15 and the evening meat **o**, and the king's H4503
15 and his meat **o**, with the burnt offering H4503
15 with the burnt **o** of all the people of the H5930
15 land, and their meat **o**, and their drink H4503
15 blood of the burnt **o**, and all the blood H5930
1Ch 6:49 altar of the burnt **o**, and on the altar of H5930
16: 2 And when David had made an end of **o** H5927
29 his name: bring an **o**, and come before H4503
40 the altar of the burnt **o** continually H5930
21:23 the wheat for the meat **o**; I give it all. H4503
26 heaven by fire upon the altar of burnt **o**. H5930
29 altar of the burnt **o**, *were* at that season H5930
22: 1 this *is* the altar of the burnt **o** for Israel. H5930
23:29 the fine flour for meat **o**, and for the H4503
2Ch 4: 6 for the burnt **o** they washed in them; H5930
7: 1 the burnt **o** and the sacrifices; and H5930
8:13 Even after a certain rate every day, **o** H5927
29:18 the altar of burnt **o**, with all the vessels H5930
21 he goats, for a sin **o** for the kingdom,
23 he goats *for* the sin **o** before the king and
24 *that* the burnt **o** and the sin offering H5930
24 the sin **o** *should be made* for all Israel.
27 to offer the burnt **o** upon the altar. And H5930
27 when the burnt **o** began, the song of the H5930
28 until the burnt **o** was finished. H5930
29 And when they had made an end of **o**, H5927
32 these *were* for a burnt **o** to the LORD. H5930
35 for *every* burnt **o**. So the service of the H5930
30:22 feast seven days, **o** peace offerings, and H2076
35:14 *were busied* in **o** of burnt offerings and H5927
Ezr 1: 4 beside the freewill **o** for the house of H5071
3: 5 the continual burnt **o**, both of the new H5930
5 offered a freewill **o** unto the LORD. H5071
6:17 and for a sin **o** for all Israel, twelve
7:16 with the freewill **o** of the people, and of H5069
16 and of the priests, **o** willingly for the
8:25 vessels, *even* the **o** of the house of our H8641
28 **o** unto the LORD God of your fathers. H5071
35 he goats *for* a sin **o**: all *this was* a burnt
35 all *this was* a burnt **o** unto the LORD. H5930
Neh 10:33 continual meat **o**, and for the continual H4503
33 continual burnt **o**, of the sabbaths, of H5930
34 for the wood **o**, to bring *it* into the H7133
39 shall bring the **o** of the corn, of the new H8641
13: 9 with the meat **o** and the frankincense. H4503
31 And for the wood **o**, at times appointed, H7133
Job 42: 8 yourselves a burnt **o**; and my servant H5930
Ps 40: 6 Sacrifice and **o** thou didst not desire; H4503
6 opened: burnt **o** and sin offering hast
6 and sin **o** hast thou not required. H2401
51:16 I give *it*: thou delightest not in burnt **o**.
19 with burnt **o** and whole burnt offering:
19 and whole burnt **o**: then shall they offer
96: 8 bring an **o**, and come into his courts. H4503
Isa 40:16 beasts thereof sufficient for a burnt **o**. H5930
43:23 an **o**, nor wearied thee with incense. H4503
53:10 make his soul an **o** for sin, he shall see
57: 6 poured a drink **o**, thou hast offered a H5262
6 **o**. Should I receive comfort in these? H4503
61: 8 robbery for burnt **o**; and I will direct H5930
65:11 furnish the drink **o** unto that number. H4469
66:20 brethren *for* an **o** unto the LORD out H4503
20 of Israel bring an **o** in a clean vessel H4503
Jer 11:17 me to anger in **o** incense unto Baal.
14:12 they offer burnt **o** and an oblation, I H5930
Ezk 20:28 of their **o**: there also they made H7133
40:38 gates, where they washed the burnt **o**. H5930
39 thereon the burnt **o** and the sin offering H5930
39 and the sin **o** and the trespass offering. H2403
39 and the sin offering and the trespass **o**. H817
42 for the burnt **o**, of a cubit and an half H5930
42 they slew the burnt **o** and the sacrifice. H5930
43 upon the tables *was* the flesh of the **o**. H7133
42:13 and the meat **o**, and the sin offering, H4503
13 and the sin **o**, and the trespass offering; H2403
13 and the trespass **o**; for the place *is* holy. H817
43:19 Lord GOD, a young bullock for a sin **o**. H2403
21 also of the sin **o**, and he shall burn it H2403
22 blemish for a sin **o**; and they shall H2403
24 them up *for* a burnt **o** unto the LORD. H5930
Ezk 43:25 day a goat *for* a sin **o**: they shall also H2403
44:11 slay the burnt **o** and the sacrifice for H5930
27 shall offer his sin **o**, saith the Lord GOD. H2403
29 They shall eat the meat **o**, and the sin H4503
29 and the sin **o**, and the trespass offering; H2403
29 and the trespass **o**; and every dedicated H817
45:15 of Israel; for a meat **o**, and for a burnt H4503
15 and for a burnt **o**, and for peace H5930
17 shall prepare the sin **o**, and the meat H2403
17 and the meat **o**, and the burnt offering, H4503
17 offering, and the burnt **o**, and the peace H5930
19 blood of the sin **o**, and put *it* upon the H2403
22 people of the land a bullock *for* a sin **o**. H2403
23 prepare a burnt **o** to the LORD, seven H5930
23 and a kid of the goats daily *for* a sin **o**. H2403
24 And he shall prepare a meat **o** of an H4503
25 to the sin **o**, according to the burnt H2403
25 to the burnt **o**, and according to the H5930
25 to the meat **o**, and according to the oil. H4503
46: 2 shall prepare his burnt **o** and his peace H5930
4 And the burnt **o** that the prince shall H5930
5 And the meat **o** *shall be* an ephah for a H4503
5 a ram, and the meat **o** for the lambs as H4503
7 And he shall prepare a meat **o**, an H4503
11 the meat **o** shall be an ephah to H4503
12 a voluntary burnt **o** or peace offerings H5930
12 shall prepare his burnt **o** and his peace H5930
13 Thou shalt daily prepare a burnt **o** H5930
14 And thou shalt prepare a meat **o** for it H4503
14 the fine flour; a meat **o** continually by a H4503
15 lamb, and the meat **o**, and the oil, every H4503
15 every morning *for* a continual burnt **o**. H5930
20 boil the trespass **o** and the sin offering, H817
20 and the sin **o**, where they shall bake H2403
20 bake the meat **o**; that they bear *them* H4503
48: 8 side, shall be the **o** which ye shall offer H8641
Joel 1: 9 The meat **o** and the drink offering is H4503
9 The meat offering and the drink **o** is H5262
13 my God: for the meat **o** and the drink H4503
13 and the drink **o** is withholden from H5262
2:14 behind him; *even* a meat **o** and a drink H4503
14 a drink **o** unto the LORD your God? H5262
Zep 3:10 of my dispersed, shall bring mine **o**. H4503
Mal 1:10 neither will I accept an **o** at your hand. H4503
11 name, and a pure **o**: for my name *shall* H4503
13 ye brought an **o**: should I accept this H4503
2:12 offereth an **o** unto the LORD of hosts. H4503
13 he regardeth not the **o** any more, or H4503
3: 3 unto the LORD an **o** in righteousness. H4503
4 Then shall the **o** of Judah and H4503
Lk 23:36 coming to him, and **o** him vinegar, *G4374*
Act 21:26 until that an **o** should be offered for *G4376*
Ro 15:16 of God, that the **o** up of the Gentiles *G4376*
Eph 5: 2 himself for us an **o** and a sacrifice to *G4376*
Heb 10: 5 Sacrifice and **o** thou wouldest not, *G4376*
8 Above when he said, Sacrifice and **o** *G4376*
8 offerings and **o** for sin thou wouldest *G4376*
10 through the **o** of the body of Jesus *G4376*
11 ministering and **o** oftentimes the same *G4374*
14 For by one **o** he hath perfected for ever *G4376*
18 of these *is*, *there is* no more **o** for sin. *G4376*

OFFERINGS

Gen 8:20 fowl, and offered burnt **o** on the altar. H5930
Ex 10:25 and burnt **o**, that we may sacrifice H5930
20:24 thereon thy burnt **o**, and thy peace H5930
24 and thy peace **o**, thy sheep, and thine H8002
24: 5 offered burnt **o**, and sacrificed peace H5930
5 peace **o** of oxen unto the LORD.
29:28 of their peace **o**, *even* their heave H8002
32: 6 and offered burnt **o**, and brought peace H5930
6 and brought peace **o**; and the people sat H8002
36: 3 yet unto him free **o** every morning. H5071
Lev 2: 3 holy of the **o** of the LORD made by fire. H801
10 holy of the **o** of the LORD made by fire. H801
13 with all thine **o** thou shalt offer salt. H7133
4:10 sacrifice of peace **o**: and the priest shall H8002
26 sacrifice of peace **o**: and the priest shall H8002
31 sacrifice of peace **o**; and the priest shall H8002
35 of the peace **o**; and the priest shall H8002
35 according to the **o** made by fire unto the
5:12 according to the **o** made by fire unto the
6:12 burn thereon the fat of the peace **o**. H8002
17 their portion of my **o** made by fire; it *is*
18 concerning the **o** of the LORD made by H801
7:11 **o**, which he shall offer unto the LORD. H8002
13 sacrifice of thanksgiving of his peace **o**. H8002
14 that sprinkleth the blood of the peace **o**. H8002
Lev 7:15 of his peace **o** for thanksgiving shall H8002
18 of his peace **o** be eaten at all on the H8002
20 sacrifice of peace **o**, that *pertain* unto H8002
21 sacrifice of peace **o**, which *pertain* unto H8002
29 of his peace **o** unto the LORD shall H8002
29 the LORD of the sacrifice of his peace **o**. H8002
30 His own hands shall bring the **o** of the H801
32 of the sacrifices of your peace **o**. H8002
33 blood of the peace **o**, and the fat, shall H8002
34 of their peace **o**, and have given them H8002
35 his sons, out of the **o** of the LORD made H801
37 and of the sacrifice of the peace **o**; H8002
9: 4 Also a bullock and a ram for peace **o**, to H8002
18 a sacrifice of peace **o**, which *was* for the H8002
22 and the burnt offering, and peace **o**. H8002
10:12 remaineth of the **o** of the LORD made by H801
14 of peace **o** of the children of Israel. H8002
15 they bring with the **o** made by fire of the
17: 5 offer them *for* peace **o** unto the LORD. H2077
19: 5 And if ye offer a sacrifice of peace **o** H8002
21: 6 of their God: for the **o** of the LORD made H801
21 nigh to offer the **o** of the LORD made by H801
22:18 and for all his freewill **o**, which they will H5071
21 a sacrifice of peace **o** unto the LORD to H8002
23:18 and their drink **o**, *even* an offering H5262
19 the first year for a sacrifice of peace **o**. H8002
37 and drink **o**, every thing upon his day: H5262
38 freewill **o**, which ye give unto the LORD. H5071
24: 9 unto him of the **o** of the LORD made by H801
Nu 6:14 one ram without blemish for peace **o**, H8002
15 their meat offering, and their drink **o**. H5262
17 a sacrifice of peace **o** unto the LORD, H8002
18 *is* under the sacrifice of the peace **o**. H8002
7:17 And for a sacrifice of peace **o**, two oxen, H8002
23 And for a sacrifice of peace **o**, two oxen, H8002
29 And for a sacrifice of peace **o**, two oxen, H8002
35 And for a sacrifice of peace **o**, two oxen, H8002
41 And for a sacrifice of peace **o**, two oxen, H8002
47 And for a sacrifice of peace **o**, two oxen, H8002
53 And for a sacrifice of peace **o**, two oxen, H8002
59 And for a sacrifice of peace **o**, two oxen, H8002
65 And for a sacrifice of peace **o**, two oxen, H8002
71 And for a sacrifice of peace **o**, two oxen, H8002
77 And for a sacrifice of peace **o**, two oxen, H8002
83 And for a sacrifice of peace **o**, two oxen, H8002
88 of the peace **o** *were* twenty and four H8002
10:10 over your burnt **o**, and over the H5930
10 of your peace **o**; that they may be to H8002
15: 8 a vow, or peace **o** unto the LORD: H8002
18: 8 of mine heave **o** of all the hallowed H8641
11 with all the wave **o** of the children of H8573
19 All the heave **o** of the holy things, H8641
28:14 And their drink **o** shall be half an hin of H5262
31 you without blemish) and their drink **o**. H5262
29: 6 and their drink **o**, according unto their H5262
11 meat offering of it, and their drink **o**. H5262
18 and their drink **o** for the bullocks, for H5262
19 meat offering thereof, and their drink **o**. H5262
21 and their drink **o** for the bullocks, for H5262
24 Their meat offering and their drink **o** H5262
27 and their drink **o** for the bullocks, for H5262
30 and their drink **o** for the bullocks, for H5262
33 and their drink **o** for the bullocks, for H5262
37 Their meat offering and their drink **o** H5262
39 and your freewill **o**, for your burnt H5071
39 for your burnt **o**, and for your meat H5930
39 and for your meat **o**, and for your drink H4503
39 drink **o**, and for your peace offerings. H5262
39 drink offerings, and for your peace **o**. H8002
Dt 12: 6 And thither ye shall bring your burnt **o**, H5930
6 tithes, and heave **o** of your hand, and H8641
6 and your freewill **o**, and the firstlings of H5071
11 you; your burnt **o**, and your sacrifices, H5930
13 burnt **o** in every place that thou seest: H5930
14 offer thy burnt **o**, and there thou shalt H5930
17 **o**, or heave offering of thine hand: H5071
27 And thou shalt offer thy burnt **o**, the H5930
18: 1 they shall eat the **o** of the LORD made by H801
27: 6 **o** thereon unto the LORD thy God: H5930
7 And thou shalt offer peace **o**, and shalt H8002
32:38 the wine of their drink **o**? let them rise up
Jos 8:31 thereon burnt **o** unto the LORD, and H5930
31 unto the LORD, and sacrificed peace **o**. H8002
22:23 or if to offer peace **o** thereon, let the H2077
27 him with our burnt **o**, and with our H5930
27 with our peace **o**; that your children H8002
28 not for burnt **o**, nor for sacrifices; but H5930
29 an altar for burnt **o**, for meat offerings, H5930

Jos 22:29 offerings, for meat **o**, or for sacrifices, H4503
Jdg 20:26 **o** and peace offerings before the LORD. H5930
26 offerings and peace **o** before the LORD. H8002
21: 4 offered burnt **o** and peace offerings. H5930
4 offered burnt offerings and peace **o**. H8002
1Sa 2:28 **o** made by fire of the children of Israel?
29 chiefest of all the **o** of Israel my people? H4503
6:15 offered burnt **o** and sacrificed H5930
10: 8 thee, to offer burnt **o**, *and* to sacrifice H5930
8 sacrifices of peace **o**: seven days shalt H8002
11:15 sacrifices of peace **o** before the LORD; H8002
13: 9 **o**. And he offered the burnt offering. H8002
15:22 delight in burnt **o** and sacrifices, as in H5930
2Sa 1:21 you, nor fields of **o**: for there the shield H8641
6:17 **o** and peace offerings before the LORD.
17 offerings and peace **o** before the LORD. H8002
18 of offering burnt **o** and peace offerings,
18 and peace **o**, he blessed the people H8002
24:24 will I offer burnt **o** unto the LORD my
25 and offered burnt **o** and peace offerings.
25 offerings and peace **o**. So the LORD was H8002
1Ki 3: 4 **o** did Solomon offer upon that altar. H5930
15 offered up burnt **o**, and offered peace H5930
15 **o**, and made a feast to all his servants. H8002
8:63 a sacrifice of peace **o**, which he offered H8002
64 he offered burnt **o**, and meat offerings, H5930
64 and meat **o**, and the fat of the peace H4503
64 fat of the peace **o**: because the brasen H8002
64 receive the burnt **o**, and meat offerings, H5930
64 **o**, and the fat of the peace offerings. H4503
64 offerings, and the fat of the peace **o**. H8002
9:25 offer burnt **o** and peace offerings H5930
25 and peace **o** upon the altar which H8002
2Ki 10:24 and burnt **o**, Jehu appointed fourscore H5930
16:13 the blood of his peace **o**, upon the altar. H8002
15 and their drink **o**; and sprinkle upon it H5262
1Ch 16: 1 sacrifices and peace **o** before God. H8002
2 of offering the burnt **o** and the peace H5930
2 and the peace **o**, he blessed the people H8002
40 To offer burnt **o** unto the LORD upon H5930
21:23 oxen *also* for burnt **o**, and the threshing H5930
24 LORD, nor offer burnt **o** without cost. H5930
26 LORD, and offered burnt **o** and peace H5930
26 and peace **o**, and called upon the H8002
29:21 and offered burnt **o** unto the LORD, on H5930
21 with their drink **o**, and sacrifices in H5262
2Ch 1: 6 offered a thousand burnt **o** upon it. H5930
2: 4 and for the burnt **o** morning and H5930
7: 7 he offered burnt **o**, and the fat of the H5930
7 fat of the peace **o**, because the brasen H8002
7 **o**, and the meat offerings, and the fat. H5930
7 offerings, and the meat **o**, and the fat. H4503
8:12 Then Solomon offered burnt **o** unto the H5930
23:18 to offer the burnt **o** of the LORD, as *it is* H5930
24:14 they offered burnt **o** in the house of the H5930
29: 7 nor offered burnt **o** in the holy *place* H5930
31 and thank **o** into the house of the H8426
31 and thank **o**; and as many as were H8426
31 as many as were of a free heart burnt **o**. H5930
32 And the number of the burnt **o**, which H5930
34 not flay all the burnt **o**: wherefore their H5930
35 And also the burnt **o** *were* in H5930
35 the fat of the peace **o**, and the drink H8002
35 and the drink **o** for *every* burnt H5262
30:15 the burnt **o** into the house of the LORD. H5930
22 days, offering peace **o**, and making H2077
31: 2 and Levites for burnt **o** and for peace H5930
2 and for peace **o**, to minister, and to H8002
3 for the burnt **o**, *to wit*, for the morning H5930
3 and evening burnt **o**, and the burnt H5930
3 and the burnt **o** for the sabbaths, and H5930
10 began to bring the **o** into the house of H8641
12 And brought in the **o** and the tithes and H8641
14 over the freewill **o** of God, to distribute H5071
33:16 thereon peace **o** and thank offerings, H2077
16 and thank **o**, and commanded Judah H8426
35: 7 all for the passover **o**, for all that were H6453
8 for the passover **o** two thousand and H6453
9 for passover **o** five thousand *small* H6453
12 And they removed the burnt **o**, that H5930
13 but the *other* holy **o** sod they in pots, and
14 in offering of burnt **o** and the fat until H5930
16 and to offer burnt **o** upon the altar of H5930
Ezr 3: 2 to offer burnt **o** thereon, as *it is* written H5930
3 they offered burnt **o** thereon unto the H5930
3 *even* burnt **o** morning and evening. H5930
4 the daily burnt **o** by number, according H5930
6 they to offer burnt **o** unto the LORD. H5930
Ezr 6: 9 for the burnt **o** of the God of heaven, H5928
7:17 with their meat **o** and their drink H4504
17 and their drink **o**, and offer them upon H5261
8:35 offered burnt **o** unto the God of Israel, H5930
Neh 10:33 *things*, and for the sin **o** to make an H2403
37 dough, and our **o**, and the fruit of all H8641
12:44 treasures, for the **o**, for the first-fruits, H8641
13: 5 they laid the meat **o**, the frankincense, H4503
5 the porters; and the **o** of the priests. H8641
Job 1: 5 and offered burnt **o** *according* to the H5930
Ps 16: 4 *god*: their drink **o** of blood will I not
20: 3 Remember all thy **o**, and accept thy H4503
50: 8 **o**, *to have been* continually before me.
66:13 I will go into thy house with burnt **o**: I
119:108 Accept, I beseech thee, the freewill **o** of H5071
Prv 7:14 *I have* peace **o** with me; this day have I H2077
Isa 1:11 full of the burnt **o** of rams, and the fat H5930
43:23 cattle of thy burnt **o**; neither hast thou H5930
56: 7 their burnt **o** and their sacrifices H5930
Jer 6:20 your burnt **o** *are* not acceptable, H5930
7:18 to pour out drink **o** unto other gods, H5262
21 **o** unto your sacrifices, and eat flesh. H5930
22 Egypt, concerning burnt **o** or sacrifices: H5930
17:26 bringing burnt **o**, and sacrifices, and H5930
26 and meat **o**, and incense, and bringing H4503
19: 5 with fire *for* burnt **o** unto Baal, which I H5930
13 poured out drink **o** unto other gods. H5262
32:29 poured out drink **o** unto other gods, to H5262
33:18 me to offer burnt **o**, and to kindle meat H5930
18 meat **o**, and to do sacrifice continually. H4503
41: 5 themselves, with **o** and incense in their H4503
44:17 and to pour out drink **o** unto her, as we H5262
18 to pour out drink **o** unto her, we have H5262
19 poured out drink **o** unto her, did we H5262
19 out drink **o** unto her, without our men? H5262
25 to pour out drink **o** unto her: ye will H5262
Ezk 20:28 and poured out there their drink **o**. H5262
40 will I require your **o**, and the firstfruits H8641
43:18 it, to offer burnt **o** thereon, and to H5930
27 make your burnt **o** upon the altar, and H5930
27 and your peace **o**; and I will accept you, H8002
45:15 and for peace **o**, to make reconciliation H8002
17 part *to give* burnt **o**, and meat offerings, H5930
17 and meat **o**, and drink offerings, H4503
17 and drink **o**, in the feasts, and in H5262
17 and the peace **o**, to make reconciliation H8002
46: 2 and his peace **o**, and he shall worship H8002
12 offering or peace **o** voluntarily unto the H8002
12 and his peace **o**, as he did on the H8002
Hos 6: 6 knowledge of God more than burnt **o**. H5930
8:13 sacrifices of mine **o**, and eat *it*; *but* the H1890
9: 4 They shall not offer wine *o* to the LORD,
Am 4: 5 publish the free **o**: for this liketh you, O H5071
5:22 Though ye offer me burnt **o** and your H5930
22 and your meat **o**, I will not accept *them*: H4503
22 I regard the peace **o** of your fat beasts. H8002
25 me sacrifices and **o** in the wilderness H4503
Mic 6: 6 with burnt **o**, with calves of a year old? H5930
Mal 3: 8 have we robbed thee? In tithes and **o**. H8641
Mk 12:33 than all whole burnt **o** and sacrifices. *G3646*
Lk 21: 4 cast in unto the **o** of God: but she of her *G1435*
Act 24:17 came to bring alms to my nation, and **o**. *G4376*
Heb 10: 6 In burnt **o** and *sacrifices* for sin thou *G3646*
8 offering and burnt **o** and *offering* for *G3646*

OFFICE

Gen 41:13 unto mine **o**, and him he hanged. H3653
Ex 1:16 And he said, When ye do the **o** of a
28: 1 me in the priest's **o**, *even* Aaron, Nadab H3547
3 may minister unto me in the priest's **o**. H3547
4 may minister unto me in the priest's **o**. H3547
41 may minister unto me in the priest's **o**. H3547
29: 1 me in the priest's **o**: Take one young H3547
9 and the priest's **o** shall be theirs for a H3550
44 sons, to minister to me in the priest's **o**. H3547
30:30 may minister unto me in the priest's **o**. H3547
31:10 of his sons, to minister in the priest's **o**, H3547
35:19 of his sons, to minister in the priest's **o**. H3547
39:41 garments, to minister in the priest's **o**. H3547
40:13 may minister unto me in the priest's **o**. H3547
15 me in the priest's **o**: for their anointing H3547
Lev 7:35 unto the LORD in the priest's **o**; H3547
16:32 in the priest's **o** in his father's stead, H3547
Nu 3: 3 consecrated to minister in the priest's **o**. H3547
4 **o** in the sight of Aaron their father. H3547
10 on their priest's **o**: and the stranger that H3550
4:16 And to the **o** of Eleazar the son of H6486
18: 7 keep your priest's **o** for every thing of H3550
Nu 18: 7 have given your priest's **o** *unto you* as a H3550
Dt 10: 6 ministered in the priest's **o** in his stead. H3547
1Ch 6:10 the priest's **o** in the temple that H3547
32 on their **o** according to their order. H5656
9:22 Samuel the seer did ordain in their set **o**. H530
26 were in *their* set **o**, and were over the H530
31 had the set **o** over the things that H530
23:28 Because their **o** *was* to wait on the sons H4612
24: 2 and Ithamar executed the priest's **o**. H3547
2Ch 11:14 executing the priest's **o** unto the LORD: H3547
24:11 unto the king's **o** by the hand of the H6486
31:15 the priests, in *their* set **o**, to give to their H530
18 **o** they sanctified themselves in holiness: H530
Neh 13:13 **o** *was* to distribute unto their brethren.
Ps 109: 8 days be few; *and* let another take his **o**. H6486
Ezk 44:13 unto me, to do the **o** of a priest unto me,
Lk 1: 8 **o** before God in the order of his course, *G2407*
9 of the priest's **o**, his lot was to burn *G2405*
Ro 11:13 of the Gentiles, I magnify mine **o**: *G1248*
12: 4 and all members have not the same **o**: *G4234*
1Ti 3: 1 **o** of a bishop, he desireth a good work. *G1984*
10 **o** of a deacon, being *found* blameless. *G1247*
13 For they that have used the **o** of a *G1247*
Heb 7: 5 who receive the **o** of the priesthood, *G2405*

OFFICER

Gen 37:36 unto Potiphar, an **o** of Pharaoh's, *and* H5631
39: 1 and Potiphar, an **o** of Pharaoh, captain H5631
Jdg 9:28 and Zebul his **o**? serve the men of H6496
1Ki 4: 5 *was* principal **o**, *and* the king's friend: H3548
19 *was* the only **o** which *was* in the land. H5333
22: 9 Then the king of Israel called an **o**, and H5631
2Ki 8: 6 unto her a certain **o**, saying, Restore all H5631
25:19 And out of the city he took an **o** that H5631
2Ch 24:11 the high priest's **o** came and emptied H6496
Mt 5:25 to the **o**, and thou be cast into prison. *G5257*
Lk 12:58 **o**, and the officer cast thee into prison. *G4233*
58 officer, and the **o** cast thee into prison. *G4233*

OFFICERS

Gen 40: 2 against two *of* his **o**, against the chief of H5631
7 And he asked Pharaoh's **o** that *were* H5631
41:34 let him appoint **o** over the land, and H6496
Ex 5: 6 of the people, and their **o**, saying, H7860
10 out, and their **o**, and they spake to the H7860
14 And the **o** of the children of Israel, H7860
15 Then the **o** of the children of Israel H7860
19 And the **o** of the children of Israel did H7860
Nu 11:16 of the people, and **o** over them; and H7860
31:14 And Moses was wroth with the **o** of the H6485
48 And the **o** which *were* over thousands H6485
Dt 1:15 over tens, and **o** among your tribes. H7860
16:18 Judges and **o** shalt thou make thee in H7860
20: 5 And the **o** shall speak unto the people, H7860
8 And the **o** shall speak further unto the H7860
9 And it shall be, when the **o** have made H7860
29:10 and your **o**, *with* all the men of Israel, H7860
31:28 tribes, and your **o**, that I may speak H7860
Jos 1:10 Then Joshua commanded the **o** of the H7860
3: 2 days, that the **o** went through the host; H7860
8:33 And all Israel, and their elders, and **o**, H7860
23: 2 and for their **o**, and said unto them, H7860
24: 1 and for their **o**; and they presented H7860
1Sa 8:15 and give to his **o**, and to his servants. H5631
1Ki 4: 5 *was* over the **o**: and Zabud the son H5324
7 And Solomon had twelve **o** over all H5324
27 And those **o** provided victual for king H5324
28 the place where *the* **o** were, every man
5:16 Beside the chief of Solomon's **o** which H5324
9:23 These *were* the chief of the **o** that *were* H5324
2Ki 11:15 of the hundreds, the **o** of the host, and H6485
18 **o** over the house of the LORD. H6586
24:12 his princes, and his **o**: and the king of H5631
15 wives, and his **o**, and the mighty of the H5631
1Ch 23: 4 and six thousand *were* **o** and judges: H7860
26:29 business over Israel, for **o** and judges. H7860
30 hundred, *were* **o** among them of Israel H6486
27: 1 and their **o** that served the king H7860
28: 1 of his sons, with the **o**, and with the H5631
2Ch 8:10 of king Solomon's **o**, *even* two hundred H5324
18: 8 for one *of his* **o**, and said, Fetch quickly H5631
19:11 the Levites *shall be* **o** before you. Deal H7860
34:13 *there were* scribes, and **o**, and porters. H7860
Est 1: 8 to all the **o** of his house, that they H7227
2: 3 And let the king appoint **o** in all the H6496
9: 3 the deputies, and **o** of the king, helped H6213
Isa 60:17 I will also make thy **o** peace, and thine H6486
Jer 29:26 that ye should be **o** in the house of the H6496

O

Jn 7:32 and the chief priests sent **o** to take him. *G5257*
45 Then came the **o** to the chief priests *G5257*
46 The **o** answered, Never man spake like *G5257*
18: 3 a band *of men* and **o** from the chief *G5257*
12 Then the band and the captain and **o** *G5257*
18 And the servants and **o** stood there, *G5257*
22 spoken, one of the **o** which stood by *G5257*
19: 6 When the chief priests therefore and **o** *G5257*
Act 5:22 But when the **o** came, and found them *G5257*
26 Then went the captain with the **o**, and *G5257*

OFFICES
1Sa 2:36 **o**, that I may eat a piece of bread. H3550
1Ch 24: 3 according to their **o** in their service. H6486
2Ch 7: 6 And the priests waited on their **o**: the H4931
23:18 Also Jehoiada appointed the **o** of the H6486
Neh 13:14 house of my God, and for the **o** thereof. H4929

OFFSCOURING
Lam 3:45 Thou hast made us *as* the **o** and refuse H5501
1Co 4:13 *are* the **o** of all things unto this day. *G4067*

OFFSPRING
Job 5:25 and thine **o** as the grass of the earth. H6631
21: 8 them, and their **o** before their eyes. H6631
27:14 his **o** shall not be satisfied with bread. H6631
31: 8 eat; yea, let my **o** be rooted out. H6631
Isa 22:24 father's house, the **o** and the issue, all H6631
44: 3 thy seed, and my blessing upon thine **o**: H6631
48:19 the sand, and the **o** of thy bowels like H6631
61: 9 Gentiles, and their **o** among the people: H6631
65:23 of the LORD, and their **o** with them. H6631
Act 17:28 poets have said, For we are also his **o**. *G1085*
29 Forasmuch then as we are the **o** of God, *G1085*
Rev 22:16 am the root and the **o** of David, *and* the *G1085*

OFT
2Ki 4: 8 *so* it was, *that* as **o** as he passed by, he H1767
Job 21:17 How **o** is the candle of the wicked put
17 wicked put out! and *how* **o** cometh their
Ps 78:40 How **o** did they provoke him in the H4100
Mt 9:14 fast **o**, but thy disciples fast not? *G4183*
17:15 into the fire, and **o** into the water. *G4178*
18:21 said, Lord, how **o** shall my brother sin *G4212*
Mk 7: 3 wash *their* hands **o**, eat not, holding the *G4435*
Act 26:11 And I punished them **o** in every *G4178*
1Co 11:25 **o** as ye drink *it*, in remembrance of me. *G3740*
2Co 11:23 in prisons more frequent, in deaths **o**. *G4178*
2Ti 1:16 for he **o** refreshed me, and was *G4178*
Heb 6: 7 the rain that cometh **o** upon it, and *G4178*

OFTEN
Prv 29: 1 He, that being **o** reproved hardeneth *his*
Mal 3:16 Then they that feared the LORD spake **o**
Mt 23:37 unto thee, how **o** would I have gathered *G4212*
Mk 5: 4 Because that he had been **o** bound with *G4178*
Lk 5:33 of John fast **o**, and make prayers, *G4437*
13:34 unto thee; how **o** would I have gathered *G4212*
1Co 11:26 For as **o** as ye eat this bread, and drink *G4178*
2Co 11:26 *In* journeyings **o**, *in* perils of waters, *in* *G4178*
27 in watchings **o**, in hunger and thirst, *G4178*
27 in fastings **o**, in cold and nakedness. *G4178*
Php 3:18 I have told you **o**, and now tell you even *G4178*
1Ti 5:23 stomach's sake and thine **o** infirmities. *G4437*
Heb 9:25 Nor yet that he should offer himself **o**, *G4178*
26 For then must he **o** have suffered since *G4178*
Rev 11: 6 earth with all plagues, as **o** as they will. *G3740*

OFTENER
Act 24:26 for him the **o**, and communed with him. *G4437*

OFTENTIMES
Job 33:29 worketh God **o** with man, H6471+H7969
Ecc 7:22 For **o** also thine own heart H6471+H7227
Lk 8:29 of the man. For **o** it had caught him: *G4183*
Ro 1:13 brethren, that **o** I purposed to come *G4178*
2Co 8:22 whom we have **o** proved diligent in *G4178*
Heb 10:11 and offering **o** the same sacrifices, *G4178*

OFTTIMES
Mt 17:15 sore vexed: for **o** he falleth into the fire, *G4178*
Mk 9:22 And **o** it hath cast him into the fire, *G4178*
Jn 18: 2 **o** resorted thither with his disciples. *G4178*

OG
Nu 21:33 of Bashan: and **O** the king of Bashan H5747
32:33 the kingdom of **O** king of Bashan, the H5747
Dt 1: 4 in Heshbon, and **O** the king of Bashan, H5747
Dt 3: 1 to Bashan: and **O** the king of Bashan H5747
3 into our hands **O** also, the king of H5747
4 of Argob, the kingdom of **O** in Bashan. H5747
10 cities of the kingdom of **O** in Bashan. H5747
11 For only **O** king of Bashan remained of H5747
13 the kingdom of **O**, gave I unto the half H5747
4:47 and the land of **O** king of Bashan, two H5747
29: 7 of Heshbon, and **O** the king of Bashan, H5747
31: 4 did to Sihon and to **O**, kings of the H5747
Jos 2:10 and **O**, whom ye utterly destroyed. H5747
9:10 of Heshbon, and to **O** king of Bashan, H5747
12: 4 And the coast of **O** king of Bashan, H5747
13:12 All the kingdom of **O** in Bashan, which H5747
30 all the kingdom of **O** king of Bashan, H5747
31 of the kingdom of **O** in Bashan, *were* H5747
1Ki 4:19 the Amorites, and of **O** king of Bashan; H5747
Neh 9:22 and the land of **O** king of Bashan. H5747
Ps 135:11 Sihon king of the Amorites, and **O** king H5747
136:20 And **O** the king of Bashan: for his H5747

OH
Gen 18:30 And he said *unto him*, **O** let not the H4994
32 And he said, **O** let not the Lord be H4994
19:18 And Lot said unto them, **O**, not so, my H4994
20 it *is* a little one: **O**, let me escape thither, H4994
44:18 unto him, and said, **O** my lord, let thy H994
Ex 32:31 the LORD, and said, **O**, this people have H577
Jdg 6:13 And Gideon said unto him, **O** my Lord, if H994
15 And he said unto him, **O** my Lord, H994
1Sa 1:26 And she said, **O** my lord, *as* thy soul H994
2Sa 15: 4 Absalom said moreover, **O** that I were
23:15 And David longed, and said, **O** that one
1Ch 4:10 of Israel, saying, **O** that thou wouldest H518
11:17 And David longed, and said, **O** that one
Job 6: 2 **O** that my grief were throughly H3863
8 **O** that I might have my request; and that
10:18 out of the womb? **O** that I had given up
11: 5 But **o** that God would speak, and open
19:23 **O** that my words were now written! oh
23 Oh that my words were now written! **o**
23: 3 **O** that I knew where I might find him!
29: 2 **O** that I were as *in* months past, as *in* the
31:31 If the men of my tabernacle said not, **O**
35 **O** that one would hear me! behold, my
Ps 6: 4 Return, O LORD, deliver my soul: **o** save
7: 9 **O** let the wickedness of the wicked H4994
14: 7 **O** that the salvation of Israel *were come*
31:19 **O** how great *is* thy goodness, which thou
53: 6 **O** that the salvation of Israel *were come*
55: 6 And I said, **O** that I had wings like a
81:13 **O** that my people had hearkened unto H3863
107: 8 **O** that *men* would praise the LORD *for*
15 **O** that *men* would praise the LORD *for*
21 **O** that *men* would praise the LORD *for*
31 **O** that *men* would praise the LORD *for*
Isa 64: 1 **O** that thou wouldest rend the heavens, H3863
Jer 9: 1 **O** that my head were waters, and mine
2 **O** that I had in the wilderness a lodging
44: 4 *them*, saying, **O**, do not this abominable H4994

OHAD
Gen 46:10 and Jamin, and **O**, and Jachin, and H161
Ex 6:15 and Jamin, and **O**, and Jachin, and H161

OHEL
1Ch 3:20 And Hashubah, and **O**, and Berechiah, H169

OIL
Gen 28:18 pillar, and poured **o** upon the top of it. H8081
35:14 thereon, and he poured **o** thereon. H8081
Ex 25: 6 **O** for the light, spices for anointing oil, H8081
6 Oil for the light, spices for anointing **o**, H8081
27:20 bring thee pure **o** olive beaten for the H8081
29: 2 tempered with **o**, and wafers H8081
2 anointed with **o**: *of* wheaten flour shalt H8081
7 Then shalt thou take the anointing **o**, H8081
21 of the anointing **o**, and sprinkle *it* upon H8081
40 an hin of beaten **o**; and the fourth part H8081
30:24 of the sanctuary, and of **o** olive an hin: H8081
25 And thou shalt make it an **o** of holy H8081
25 it shall be an holy anointing **o**. H8081
31 be an holy anointing **o** unto me H8081
31:11 And the anointing **o**, and sweet incense H8081
35: 8 And **o** for the light, and spices for H8081
8 anointing **o**, and for the sweet incense, H8081
14 and his lamps, with the **o** for the light, H8081
15 and the anointing **o**, and the sweet H8081
28 And spice, and **o** for the light, and for H8081
Ex 35:28 anointing **o**, and for the sweet incense. H8081
37:29 And he made the holy anointing **o**, and H8081
39:37 the vessels thereof, and the **o** for light, H8081
38 and the anointing **o**, and the sweet H8081
40: 9 And thou shalt take the anointing **o**, H8081
Lev 2: 1 and he shall pour **o** upon it, and put H8081
2 thereof, and of the **o** thereof, with all H8081
4 mingled with **o**, or unleavened wafers H8081
4 or unleavened wafers anointed with **o**. H8081
5 fine flour unleavened, mingled with **o**. H8081
6 Thou shalt part it in pieces, and pour **o** H8081
7 it shall be made *of* fine flour with **o**. H8081
15 And thou shalt put **o** upon it, and lay H8081
16 and *part* of the **o** thereof, with all the H8081
5:11 he shall put no **o** upon it, neither shall H8081
6:15 and of the **o** thereof, and all the H8081
21 In a pan it shall be made with **o**; *and* H8081
7:10 mingled with **o**, and dry, shall all the H8081
12 mingled with **o**, and unleavened wafers H8081
12 anointed with **o**, and cakes mingled H8081
12 mingled with **o**, of fine flour, fried. H8081
8: 2 and the anointing **o**, and a bullock for H8081
10 And Moses took the anointing **o**, and H8081
12 And he poured of the anointing **o** upon H8081
30 And Moses took of the anointing **o**, and H8081
9: 4 mingled with **o**: for to day the LORD H8081
10: 7 for the anointing **o** of the LORD *is* upon H8081
14:10 mingled with **o**, and one log of oil. H8081
10 mingled with oil, and one log of **o**. H8081
12 and the log of **o**, and wave them *for* H8081
15 *some* of the log of **o**, and pour *it* into the H8081
16 his right finger in the **o** that *is* in his left H8081
16 sprinkle of the **o** with his finger seven H8081
17 And of the rest of the **o** that *is* in his H8081
18 And the remnant of the **o** that *is* in the H8081
21 **o** for a meat offering, and a log of oil; H8081
21 oil for a meat offering, and a log of **o**; H8081
24 and the log of **o**, and the priest shall H8081
26 And the priest shall pour of the **o** into H8081
27 finger *some* of the **o** that *is* in his left H8081
28 And the priest shall put of the **o** that *is* H8081
29 And the rest of the **o** that *is* in the H8081
21:10 the anointing **o** was poured, and that H8081
12 of the anointing **o** of his God *is* upon H8081
23:13 mingled with **o**, an offering made by H8081
24: 2 unto thee pure **o** olive beaten for the H8081
Nu 4: 9 and all the **o** vessels thereof, wherewith H8081
16 *pertaineth* the **o** for the light, and the H8081
16 and the anointing **o**, *and* the oversight H8081
5:15 he shall pour no **o** upon it, nor put H8081
6:15 flour mingled with **o**, and wafers of H8081
15 bread anointed with **o**, and their meat H8081
7:13 mingled with **o** for a meat offering: H8081
19 mingled with **o** for a meat offering: H8081
25 mingled with **o** for a meat offering: H8081
31 mingled with **o** for a meat offering: H8081
37 mingled with **o** for a meat offering: H8081
43 mingled with **o** for a meat offering: H8081
49 mingled with **o** for a meat offering: H8081
55 mingled with **o** for a meat offering: H8081
61 mingled with **o** for a meat offering: H8081
67 mingled with **o** for a meat offering: H8081
73 mingled with **o** for a meat offering: H8081
79 mingled with **o** for a meat offering: H8081
8: 8 mingled with **o**, and another young H8081
11: 8 the taste of it was as the taste of fresh **o**. H8081
15: 4 with the fourth *part* of an hin of **o**. H8081
6 with the third *part* of an hin of **o**. H8081
9 of flour mingled with half an hin of **o**. H8081
18:12 All the best of the **o**, and all the best of H3323
28: 5 the fourth *part* of an hin of beaten **o**. H8081
9 with **o**, and the drink offering thereof: H8081
12 mingled with **o**, for one bullock; and H8081
12 offering, mingled with **o**, for one ram; H8081
13 mingled with **o** *for* a meat offering H8081
20 mingled with **o**: three tenth deals shall H8081
28 mingled with **o**, three tenth deals unto H8081
29: 3 mingled with **o**, three tenth deals for H8081
9 mingled with **o**, three tenth deals to H8081
14 mingled with **o**, three tenth deals unto H8081
35:25 which was anointed with the holy **o**. H8081
Dt 7:13 wine, and thine **o**, the increase of thy H3323
8: 8 a land of **o** olive, and honey; H8081
11:14 in thy corn, and thy wine, and thine **o**. H3323
12:17 thy wine, or of thy **o**, or the firstlings of H3323
14:23 wine, and of thine **o**, and the firstlings H3323
18: 4 wine, and of thine **o**, and the first of the H3323
28:40 the **o**; for thine olive shall cast *his fruit*. H8081

Dt 28:51 corn, wine, or **o**, *or* the increase of thy H3323
32:13 of the rock, and **o** out of the flinty rock; H8081
33:24 brethren, and let him dip his foot in **o**. H8081
1Sa 10: 1 Then Samuel took a vial of **o**, and H8081
16: 1 fill thine horn with **o**, and go, I will send H8081
13 Then Samuel took the horn of **o**, and H8081
2Sa 1:21 *he had* not *been* anointed with **o**. H8081
14: 2 not thyself with **o**, but be as a woman H8081
1Ki 1:39 And Zadok the priest took an horn of **o** H8081
5:11 measures of pure **o**: thus gave Solomon H8081
17:12 a barrel, and a little **o** in a cruse: and, H8081
14 shall the cruse of **o** fail, until the day H8081
16 did the cruse of **o** fail, according to the H8081
2Ki 4: 2 any thing in the house, save a pot of **o**. H8081
6 *is* not a vessel more. And the **o** stayed. H8081
7 he said, Go, sell the **o**, and pay thy debt, H8081
9: 1 take this box of **o** in thine hand, and go H8081
3 Then take the box of **o**, and pour *it* on H8081
6 and he poured the **o** on his head, and H8081
18:32 a land of **o** olive and of honey, H3323
1Ch 9:29 **o**, and the frankincense, and the spices. H8081
12:40 and wine, and **o**, and oxen, and sheep H8081
27:28 and over the cellars of **o** *was* Joash: H8081
2Ch 2:10 wine, and twenty thousand baths of **o**. H8081
15 the barley, the **o**, and the wine, which H8081
11:11 and store of victual, and of **o** and wine. H8081
31: 5 of corn, wine, and **o**, and honey, and of H3323
32:28 corn, and wine, and **o**; and stalls for all H3323
Ezr 3: 7 and drink, and **o**, unto them of Zidon, H8081
6: 9 salt, wine, and **o**, according to the H4887
7:22 an hundred baths of **o**, and salt without H4887
Neh 5:11 wine, and the **o**, that ye exact of them. H3323
10:37 of wine and of **o**, unto the priests, to H3323
39 the new wine, and the **o**, unto the H3323
13: 5 the new wine, and the **o**, which was H3323
12 new wine and the **o** unto the treasuries. H3323
Est 2:12 six months with **o** of myrrh, and six H8081
Job 24:11 *Which* make **o** within their walls, *and* H6671
29: 6 and the rock poured me out rivers of **o**; H8081
Ps 23: 5 my head with **o**; my cup runneth over. H8081
45: 7 the **o** of gladness above thy fellows. H8081
55:21 than **o**, yet *were* they drawn swords. H8081
89:20 with my holy **o** have I anointed him: H8081
92:10 I shall be anointed with fresh **o**. H8081
104:15 heart of man, *and* **o** to make *his* face to H8081
109:18 like water, and like **o** into his bones. H8081
141: 5 *be* an excellent **o**, *which* shall not break H8081
Prv 5: 3 and her mouth *is* smoother than **o**: H8081
21:17 loveth wine and **o** shall not be rich. H8081
20 *There is* treasure to be desired and **o** in H8081
Isa 41:19 myrtle, and the **o** tree; I will set in the H8081
61: 3 for ashes, the **o** of joy for mourning, H8081
Jer 31:12 for wine, and for **o**, and for the young of H3323
40:10 fruits, and **o**, and put *them* in your H8081
41: 8 of barley, and of **o**, and of honey. So he H8081
Ezk 16: 9 from thee, and I anointed thee with **o**. H8081
13 flour, and honey, and **o**: and thou wast H8081
18 mine **o** and mine incense before them. H8081
19 fine flour, and **o**, and honey, *wherewith* H8081
23:41 thou hast set mine incense and mine **o**. H8081
27:17 Pannag, and honey, and **o**, and balm. H8081
32:14 rivers to run like **o**, saith the Lord GOD. H8081
45:14 Concerning the ordinance of **o**, the bath H8081
14 of oil, the bath of **o**, *ye shall offer* the H8081
24 a ram, and an hin of **o** for an ephah. H8081
25 meat offering, and according to the **o**. H8081
46: 5 to give, and an hin of **o** to an ephah. H8081
7 unto, and an hin of **o** to an ephah. H8081
11 to give, and an hin of **o** to an ephah. H8081
14 part of an hin of **o**, to temper with the H8081
15 offering, and the **o**, every morning *for* a H8081
Hos 2: 5 and my flax, mine **o** and my drink. H8081
8 and wine, and **o**, and multiplied her H3323
22 and the **o**; and they shall hear Jezreel. H3323
12: 1 Assyrians, and **o** is carried into Egypt. H8081
Joel 1:10 wine is dried up, the **o** languisheth. H3323
2:19 corn, and wine, and **o**, and ye shall be H3323
24 the fats shall overflow with wine and **o**. H3323
Mic 6: 7 of rivers of **o**? shall I give my firstborn H8081
15 anoint thee with **o**; and sweet wine, but H8081
Hag 1:11 and upon the **o**, and upon *that* which H3323
2:12 or wine, or **o**, or any meat, shall it H8081
Zec 4:12 empty the golden *o* out of themselves?
Mt 25: 3 their lamps, and took no **o** with them: *G1637*
4 But the wise took **o** in their vessels with *G1637*
8 of your **o**; for our lamps are gone out. *G1637*
Mk 6:13 and anointed with **o** many that were *G1637*
Lk 7:46 My head with **o** thou didst not anoint: *G1637*
Lk 10:34 pouring in **o** and wine, and set him *G1637*
16: 6 measures of **o**. And he said unto him, *G1637*
Heb 1: 9 the **o** of gladness above thy fellows. *G1637*
Jas 5:14 him with **o** in the name of the Lord: *G1637*
Rev 6: 6 *see* thou hurt not the **o** and the wine. *G1637*
18:13 and wine, and **o**, and fine flour, and *G1637*

OILED

Ex 29:23 and one cake of **o** bread, and one wafer H8081
Lev 8:26 and a cake of **o** bread, and one wafer, H8081

OINTMENT

Ex 30:25 And thou shalt make it an oil of holy **o**, H4888
25 of holy ointment, an **o** compound after H7545
2Ki 20:13 and the precious **o**, and *all* the house of H8081
1Ch 9:30 of the priests made the **o** of the spices. H4842
Job 41:31 a pot: he maketh the sea like a pot of **o**. H4841
Ps 133: 2 *It is* like the precious **o** upon the head, H8081
Prv 27: 9 **O** and perfume rejoice the heart: so H8081
16 the wind, and the **o** of his right hand, H8081
Ecc 7: 1 A good name *is* better than precious **o**; H8081
9: 8 white; and let thy head lack no **o**. H8081
10: 1 Dead flies cause the **o** of the H8081
Song 1: 3 thy name *is as* **o** poured forth, H8081
Isa 1: 6 bound up, neither mollified with **o**. H8081
39: 2 and the precious **o**, and all the house of H8081
57: 9 And thou wentest to the king with **o**, H8081
Mt 26: 7 of very precious **o**, and poured it on his *G3464*
9 For this **o** might have been sold for *G3464*
12 For in that she hath poured this **o** on *G3464*
Mk 14: 3 an alabaster box of **o** of spikenard very *G3464*
4 Why was this waste of the **o** made? *G3464*
Lk 7:37 house, brought an alabaster box of **o**, *G3464*
38 his feet, and anointed *them* with the **o**. *G3464*
46 woman hath anointed my feet with **o**. *G3464*
Jn 11: 2 the Lord with **o**, and wiped his feet with *G3464*
12: 3 Then took Mary a pound of **o** of *G3464*
3 house was filled with the odour of the **o**. *G3464*
5 Why was not this **o** sold for three *G3464*

OINTMENTS

Song 1: 3 Because of the savour of thy good **o** thy H8081
4:10 and the smell of thine **o** than all spices! H8081
Am 6: 6 with the chief **o**: but they are not H8081
Lk 23:56 spices and **o**; and rested the sabbath *G3464*
Rev 18:13 And cinnamon, and odours, and **o**, and *G3464*

OLD

Gen 5:32 And Noah was five hundred years **o**: H1121
6: 4 men which *were* of **o**, men of renown. H5769
7: 6 And Noah *was* six hundred years **o** H1121
11:10 *was* an hundred years **o**, and begat H1121
12: 4 **o** when he departed out of Haran. H1121
15: 9 of three years **o**, and a she goat of three H8027
9 goat of three years **o**, and a ram of three H8027
9 ram of three years **o**, and a turtledove, H8027
15 thou shalt be buried in a good **o** age. H7872
16:16 **o**, when Hagar bare Ishmael to Abram. H1121
17: 1 And when Abram was ninety years **o** H1121
12 And he that is eight days **o** shall be H1121
17 is an hundred years **o**? and shall Sarah, H1121
17 shall Sarah, that is ninety years **o**, bear? H1323
24 And Abraham *was* ninety years **o** and H1121
25 son *was* thirteen years **o**, when he was H1121
18:11 Now Abraham and Sarah *were* **o** *and* H2205
12 saying, After I am waxed **o** shall I have H1086
12 I have pleasure, my lord being **o** also? H2204
13 I of a surety bear a child, which am **o**? H2204
19: 4 house round, both **o** and young, all the H2205
31 Our father *is* **o**, and *there is* not a man H2204
21: 2 a son in his **o** age, at the set time H2208
4 days **o**, as God had commanded him. H1121
5 And Abraham was an hundred years **o**, H1121
7 for I have born *him* a son in his **o** age. H2208
23: 1 and twenty years **o**: *these were* the H2416
24: 1 And Abraham was **o**, *and* well stricken H2204
36 when she was **o**: and unto him hath H2209
25: 8 died in a good **o** age, an old man, and H7872
8 in a good old age, an **o** man, and full *of* H2205
20 And Isaac was forty years **o** when he H1121
26 threescore years **o** when she bare them. H1121
26:34 And Esau was forty years **o** when he H1121
27: 1 when Isaac was **o**, and his eyes were H2204
2 And he said, Behold now, I am **o**, I H2204
35:29 his people, *being* **o** and full of days: H2205
37: 2 seventeen years **o**, was feeding the flock H1121
3 *was* the son of his **o** age: and he made H2208
41:46 And Joseph *was* thirty years **o** when he H1121
Gen 43:27 your father well, the **o** man of whom ye H2205
44:20 have a father, an **o** man, and a child of H2205
20 and a child of his **o** age, a little one; H2208
47: 8 How **o** *art* thou? H3117+H8140+H3117
49: 9 as an **o** lion; who shall rouse him up? H3833
50:26 and ten years **o**: and they embalmed H1121
Ex 7: 7 And Moses *was* fourscore years **o**, and H1121
7 years **o**, when they spake unto Pharaoh. H1121
10: 9 and with our **o**, with our sons and with H2205
30:14 from twenty years **o** and above, shall H1121
38:26 from twenty years **o** and upward, for H1121
Lev 13:11 It *is* an **o** leprosy in the skin of his flesh, H3462
19:32 the face of the **o** man, and fear thy God: H2205
25:22 and eat *yet* of **o** fruit until the ninth H3465
22 come in ye shall eat *of* the **o** *store*. H3465
26:10 And ye shall eat **o** store, and bring H3465
10 bring forth the **o** because of the new. H3465
27: 3 from twenty years **o** even unto sixty H1121
3 unto sixty years **o**, even thy estimation H1121
5 And if *it be* from five years **o** even unto H1121
5 even unto twenty years **o**, then thy H1121
6 And if *it be* from a month **o** even unto H1121
6 unto five years **o**, then thy estimation H1121
7 And if *it be* from sixty years **o** and H1121
Nu 1: 3 From twenty years **o** and upward, all H1121
18 years **o** and upward, by their polls. H1121
20 from twenty years **o** and upward, all H1121
22 from twenty years **o** and upward, all H1121
24 from twenty years **o** and upward, all H1121
26 from twenty years **o** and upward, all H1121
28 from twenty years **o** and upward, all H1121
30 from twenty years **o** and upward, all H1121
32 from twenty years **o** and upward, all H1121
34 from twenty years **o** and upward, all H1121
36 from twenty years **o** and upward, all H1121
38 from twenty years **o** and upward, all H1121
40 from twenty years **o** and upward, all H1121
42 from twenty years **o** and upward, all H1121
45 from twenty years **o** and upward, all H1121
3:15 from a month **o** and upward shalt thou H1121
22 from a month **o** and upward, *even* H1121
28 from a month **o** and upward, *were* H1121
34 from a month **o** and upward, *were* six H1121
39 from a month **o** and upward, *were* H1121
40 from a month **o** and upward, and take H1121
43 from a month **o** and upward, of those H1121
4: 3 From thirty years **o** and upward even H1121
3 until fifty years **o**, all that enter into the H1121
23 From thirty years **o** and upward until H1121
23 until fifty years **o** shalt thou number H1121
30 From thirty years **o** and upward even H1121
30 unto fifty years **o** shalt thou number H1121
35 From thirty years **o** and upward even H1121
35 even unto fifty years **o**, every one that H1121
39 From thirty years **o** and upward even H1121
39 even unto fifty years **o**, every one that H1121
43 From thirty years **o** and upward even H1121
43 even unto fifty years **o**, every one that H1121
47 From thirty years **o** and upward even H1121
47 unto fifty years **o**, every one that came H1121
8:24 and five years **o** and upward they shall H1121
14:29 from twenty years **o** and upward, H1121
18:16 from a month **o** shalt thou redeem, H1121
26: 2 from twenty years **o** and upward, H1121
4 from twenty years **o** and upward; as H1121
62 from a month **o** and upward: for they H1121
32:11 from twenty years **o** and upward, shall H1121
33:39 years **o** when he died in mount Hor. H1121
Dt 2:20 giants dwelt therein in **o** time; and the H6440
8: 4 Thy raiment waxed not **o** upon thee, H1086
19:14 which they of **o** time have set in thine H7223
28:50 of the **o**, nor shew favour to the young: H2205
29: 5 are not waxen **o** upon you, and thy H1086
5 thy shoe is not waxen **o** upon thy foot. H1086
31: 2 and twenty years **o** this day; I can no H1121
32: 7 Remember the days of **o**, consider the H5769
34: 7 and twenty years **o** when he died: his H1121
Jos 5:11 And they did eat of the **o** corn of the H15669
12 had eaten of the **o** corn of the land; H15669
6:21 young and **o**, and ox, and sheep, H2205
9: 4 and took **o** sacks upon their asses, H1087
4 wine bottles, **o**, and rent, and bound up; H1087
5 And **o** shoes and clouted upon their H1087
5 their feet, and **o** garments upon them; H1087
13 **o** by reason of the very long journey. H1086
13: 1 Now Joshua was **o** *and* stricken in H2204
1 him, Thou art **o** *and* stricken in years, H2204
14: 7 Forty years **o** *was* I when Moses the H1121

O

Jos 14:10 I *am* this day fourscore and five years **o**. H1121
23: 1 Joshua waxed **o** *and* stricken in age. H2204
2 unto them, I am **o** *and* stricken in age: H2204
24: 2 side of the flood in **o** time, *even* Terah, H5769
29 died, *being* an hundred and ten years **o**. H1121
Jdg 2: 8 died, *being* an hundred and ten years **o**. H1121
6:25 of seven years **o**, and throw down the
8:32 died in a good **o** age, and was buried H7872
19:16 And, behold, there came an **o** man H2205
17 street of the city: and the **o** man said, H2205
20 And the **o** man said, Peace *be* with H2205
22 of the house, the **o** man, saying, Bring H2205
Ru 1:12 *your way;* for I am too **o** to have an H2204
4:15 a nourisher of thine **o** age: for thy H7872
1Sa 2:22 Now Eli was very **o**, and heard all that H2204
31 shall not be an **o** man in thine house. H2205
32 be an **o** man in thine house for ever. H2205
4:15 Now Eli was ninety and eight years **o**; H1121
18 for he was an **o** man, and heavy. And H2204
8: 1 when Samuel was **o**, that he made his H2204
5 And said unto him, Behold, thou art **o**, H2204
12: 2 you: and I am **o** and grayheaded; and, H2204
17:12 men *for* an **o** man in the days of Saul. H2204
27: 8 *nations were* of **o** the inhabitants of the H5769
28:14 of? And she said, An **o** man cometh up; H2205
2Sa 2:10 son *was* forty years **o** when he began to H1121
4: 4 He was five years **o** when the tidings H1121
5: 4 David *was* thirty years **o** when he H1121
19:32 fourscore years **o**: and he had provided H1121
35 I *am* this day fourscore years **o**: *and* can H1121
20:18 wont to speak in **o** time, saying, They H7223
1Ki 1: 1 Now king David was **o** *and* stricken in H2204
15 the king was very **o**; and Abishag the H2204
11: 4 Solomon was **o**, *that* his wives turned H2209
12: 6 consulted with the **o** men, that stood H2205
8 But he forsook the counsel of the **o** H2205
13 the **o** men's counsel that they gave him; H2205
13:11 Now there dwelt an **o** prophet in H2205
25 *it* in the city where the **o** prophet dwelt. H2205
29 it back: and the **o** prophet came to the H2205
14:21 forty and one years **o** when he began to H1121
15:23 of his **o** age he was diseased in his feet. H2209
22:42 Jehoshaphat *was* thirty and five years **o** H1121
2Ki 4:14 she hath no child, and her husband is **o**. H2204
8:17 Thirty and two years **o** was he when he H1121
26 Two and twenty years **o** *was* Ahaziah H1121
11:21 Seven years **o** *was* Jehoash when he H1121
14: 2 He was twenty and five years **o** when H1121
21 *was* sixteen years **o**, and made him king H1121
15: 2 Sixteen years **o** was he when he began H1121
33 Five and twenty years **o** was he when H1121
16: 2 Twenty years **o** *was* Ahaz when he H1121
18: 2 Twenty and five years **o** was he when H1121
21: 1 Manasseh *was* twelve years **o** when he H1121
19 Amon *was* twenty and two years **o** H1121
22: 1 Josiah *was* eight years **o** when he began H1121
23:31 Jehoahaz *was* twenty and three years **o** H1121
36 Jehoiakim *was* twenty and five years **o** H1121
24: 8 Jehoiachin *was* eighteen years **o** when H1121
18 Zedekiah *was* twenty and one years **o** H1121
1Ch 2:21 years **o**; and she bare him Segub. H1121
4:40 for *they* of Ham had dwelt there of **o**. H6440
23: 1 So when David was **o** and full of days, H2204
27 from twenty years **o** and above: H1121
27:23 them from twenty years **o** and under: H1121
29:28 And he died in a good **o** age, full of H7872
2Ch 10: 6 counsel with the **o** men that had stood H2205
8 But he forsook the counsel which the **o** H2205
13 forsook the counsel of the **o** men, H2205
12:13 one and forty years **o** when he began to H1121
20:31 and five years **o** when he began to H1121
21: 5 Jehoram *was* thirty and two years **o** H1121
20 Thirty and two years **o** was he when he H1121
22: 2 Forty and two years **o** *was* Ahaziah H1121
24: 1 Joash *was* seven years **o** when he began H1121
15 But Jehoiada waxed **o**, and was full of H2204
15 and thirty years **o** *was he* when he died. H1121
25: 1 Amaziah *was* twenty and five years **o** H1121
5 from twenty years **o** and above, and H1121
26: 1 *was* sixteen years **o**, and made him king H1121
3 Sixteen years **o** *was* Uzziah when he H1121
27: 1 Jotham *was* twenty and five years **o** H1121
8 He was five and twenty years **o** when H1121
28: 1 Ahaz *was* twenty years **o** when he H1121
29: 1 and twenty years **o**, and he reigned nine H1121
31:16 from three years **o** and upward, *even* H1121
17 from twenty years **o** and upward, in H1121
33: 1 Manasseh *was* twelve years **o** when he H1121
2Ch 33:21 Amon *was* two and twenty years **o** H1121
34: 1 Josiah *was* eight years **o** when he began H1121
36: 2 Jehoahaz *was* twenty and three years **o** H1121
5 Jehoiakim *was* twenty and five years **o** H1121
9 Jehoiachin *was* eight years **o** when he H1121
11 Zedekiah *was* one and twenty years **o** H1121
17 man or maiden, **o** man, or him that H2205
Ezr 3: 8 from twenty years **o** and upward, to set H1121
4:15 within the same of **o** time: for which H5957
19 that this city of **o** time hath made H5957
Neh 3: 6 Moreover the **o** gate repaired Jehoiada H3465
9:21 waxed not **o**, and their feet swelled not. H1086
12:39 and above the **o** gate, and above the H3465
46 and Asaph of **o** *there were* chief of the H6924
Est 3:13 both young and **o**, little children and H2205
Job 4:11 The **o** lion perisheth for lack of prey, and
14: 8 Though the root thereof wax **o** in the H2204
20: 4 Knowest thou *not* this of **o**, since man H5703
21: 7 become **o**, yea, are mighty in power? H6275
22:15 Hast thou marked the **o** way which H5769
30: 2 *profit* me, in whom **o** age was perished?
32: 6 and ye *are* very **o**; wherefore I was H3453
42:17 So Job died, *being* **o** and full of days. H2205
Ps 6: 7 waxeth **o** because of all mine enemies. H6275
25: 6 for they *have been* ever of **o**. H5769
32: 3 When I kept silence, my bones waxed **o** H1086
37:25 I have been young, and *now* am **o**; yet H2204
44: 1 didst in their days, in the times of **o**. H6924
55:19 he that abideth of **o**. Selah. Because H6924
68:33 *which were* of **o**; lo, he doth send out H6924
71: 9 Cast me not off in the time of **o** age; H2209
18 Now also when I am **o** and H2209
74: 2 hast purchased of **o**; the rod of thine H6924
12 For God *is* my King of **o**, working H6924
77: 5 I have considered the days of **o**, the H6924
11 I will remember thy wonders of **o**. H6924
78: 2 a parable: I will utter dark sayings of **o**: H6924
92:14 They shall still bring forth fruit in **o** H7872
93: 2 Thy throne *is* established of **o**: thou *art* H227
102:25 Of **o** hast thou laid the foundation of H6440
26 of them shall wax **o** like a garment; as H1086
119:52 I remembered thy judgments of **o**, O H5769
152 **o** that thou hast founded them for ever. H6924
143: 5 I remember the days of **o**; I meditate on H6924
148:12 Both young men, and maidens; **o** men, H2205
Prv 8:22 of his way, before his works of **o**. H227
17: 6 Children's children *are* the crown of **o** H2205
20:29 the beauty of **o** men *is* the gray head. H2205
22: 6 when he is **o**, he will not depart from it. H2204
23:10 Remove not the **o** landmark; and enter H5769
22 despise not thy mother when she is **o**. H2204
Ecc 1:10 already of **o** time, which was before us. H5769
4:13 a wise child than an **o** and foolish king, H2205
Song 7:13 *fruits*, new and **o**, *which* I have laid up H3465
Isa 15: 5 of three years **o**: for by the mounting H7992
20: 4 young and **o**, naked and barefoot, H2205
22:11 the water of the **o** pool: but ye have not H3465
25: 1 of **o** *are* faithfulness *and* truth. H7350
30: 6 the young and **o** lion, the viper and H3918
33 For Tophet *is* ordained of **o**; yea, for the H865
43:18 things, neither consider the things of **o**. H6931
46: 4 And *even* to *your* **o** age I *am* he; and H2209
9 Remember the former things of **o**: for I H5769
50: 9 they all shall wax **o** as a garment; the H1086
51: 6 earth shall wax **o** like a garment, and H1086
9 the generations of **o**. *Art* thou not it that H5769
57:11 even of **o**, and thou fearest me not? H5769
58:12 shall build the **o** waste places: thou H5769
61: 4 And they shall build the **o** wastes, they H5769
63: 9 and carried them all the days of **o**. H5769
11 Then he remembered the days of **o**, H5769
65:20 of days, nor an **o** man that hath not H2205
20 die an hundred years **o**; but the sinner H1121
20 an hundred years **o** shall be accursed. H1121
Jer 2:20 For of **o** time I have broken thy yoke, H5769
6:16 and ask for the **o** paths, where *is* the H5769
28: 8 and before thee of **o** prophesied both H5769
31: 3 The LORD hath appeared of **o** unto me, H7350
13 young men and **o** together: for I will H2205
38:11 and took thence **o** cast clouts and old H1094
11 cast clouts and **o** rotten rags, and let H1094
12 Put now *these* **o** cast clouts and rotten H1094
46:26 as in the days of **o**, saith the LORD. H6924
48:34 of three years **o**: for the waters also of H7992
51:22 I break in pieces **o** and young; and with H2205
52: 1 Zedekiah *was* one and twenty years **o** H1121
Lam 1: 7 had in the days of **o**, when her people H6924
2:17 in the days of **o**: he hath thrown down, H6924
Lam 2:21 The young and the **o** lie on the ground H2205
3: 4 My flesh and my skin hath he made **o**; H1086
6 dark places, as *they that be* dead of **o**. H5769
5:21 shall be turned; renew our days as of **o**. H6924
Ezk 9: 6 Slay utterly **o** *and* young, both maids, H2205
23:43 Then said I unto *her that was* **o** in H1087
25:15 heart, to destroy *it* for the **o** hatred; H5769
26:20 with the people of **o** time, and shall set H5769
20 places desolate of **o**, with them that go H5769
36:11 you after your **o** estates, and will do H6927
38:17 I have spoken in **o** time by my servants H6931
Dan 5:31 *being* about threescore and two years **o**. H1247
Joel 1: 2 Hear this, ye **o** men, and give ear, all ye H2205
2:28 prophesy, your **o** men shall dream H2205
Am 9:11 and I will build it as in the days of **o**: H5769
Mic 5: 2 *have been* from of **o**, from everlasting. H6924
6: 6 burnt offerings, with calves of a year **o**? H1121
7:14 Bashan and Gilead, as in the days of **o**. H5769
20 unto our fathers from the days of **o**. H6924
Nah 2: 8 But Nineveh *is* of **o** like a pool of water: H3117
11 the lion, *even* the **o** lion, walked, *and* the
Zec 8: 4 There shall yet **o** men and old women H2205
4 yet old men and **o** women dwell in the H2205
Mal 3: 4 in the days of **o**, and as in former years. H5769
Mt 2:16 from two years **o** and under, according *G1332*
5:21 said by them of **o** time, Thou shalt not *G744*
27 **o** time, Thou shalt not commit adultery: *G744*
33 said by them of **o** time, Thou shalt not *G744*
9:16 new cloth unto an **o** garment, for that *G3820*
17 Neither do men put new wine into **o** *G3820*
13:52 out of his treasure *things* new and **o**. *G3820*
Mk 2:21 of new cloth on an **o** garment: else the *G3820*
21 from the **o**, and the rent is made worse. *G3820*
22 And no man putteth new wine into **o** *G3820*
Lk 1:18 this? for I am an **o** man, and my wife *G4246*
36 a son in her **o** age: and this is the *G1094*
2:42 And when he was twelve years **o**, they
5:36 garment upon an **o**; if otherwise, then *G3820*
36 out of the new agreeth not with the **o**. *G3820*
37 And no man putteth new wine into **o** *G3820*
39 No man also having drunk **o** *wine* *G3820*
39 new: for he saith, The **o** is better. *G3820*
9: 8 one of the **o** prophets was risen again. *G744*
19 that one of the **o** prophets is risen again. *G744*
12:33 bags which wax not **o**, a treasure in the *G3822*
Jn 3: 4 be born when he is **o**? can he enter the *G1088*
8:57 years **o**, and hast thou seen Abraham? *G2094*
21:18 thou shalt be **o**, thou shalt stretch forth *G1095*
Act 2:17 and your **o** men shall dream dreams: *G4245*
4:22 For the man was above forty years **o**, on
7:23 And when he was full forty years **o**, it *G5550*
15:21 For Moses of **o** time hath in every city *G744*
21:16 **o** disciple, with whom we should lodge. *G744*
Ro 4:19 an hundred years **o**, neither yet the *G1541*
6: 6 Knowing this, that our **o** man is *G3820*
1Co 5: 7 Purge out therefore the **o** leaven, that *G3820*
8 the feast, not with **o** leaven, neither *G3820*
2Co 3:14 the reading of the **o** testament; which *G3820*
5:17 *he is* a new creature: **o** things are passed *G744*
Eph 4:22 conversation the **o** man, which is *G3820*
Col 3: 9 have put off the **o** man with his deeds; *G3820*
1Ti 4: 7 But refuse profane and **o** wives' fables, *G1126*
5: 9 years **o**, having been the wife of one man,
Heb 1:11 they all shall wax **o** as doth a garment; *G3822*
8:13 hath made the first **o**. Now that which *G3822*
13 and waxeth **o** *is* ready to vanish away. *G1095*
1Pt 3: 5 For after this manner in the **o** time the *G4218*
2Pt 1: 9 that he was purged from his **o** sins. *G3819*
21 For the prophecy came not in **o** time by *G4218*
2: 5 And spared not the **o** world, but saved *G744*
3: 5 the heavens were of **o**, and the earth *G1597*
1Jn 2: 7 unto you, but an **o** commandment *G3820*
7 beginning. The **o** commandment is the *G3820*
Jude 4 who were before of **o** ordained to this *G3819*
Rev 12: 9 was cast out, that **o** serpent, called the *G744*
20: 2 And he laid hold on the dragon, that **o** *G744*

OLD AGE See OLD and AGE.

OLDNESS
Ro 7: 6 of spirit, and not *in* the **o** of the letter. *G3821*

OLIVE
Gen 8:11 her mouth *was* an **o** leaf pluckt off: so H2132
Ex 27:20 they bring thee pure oil **o** beaten for the H2132
30:24 of the sanctuary, and of oil **o** an hin: H2132
Lev 24: 2 unto thee pure oil **o** beaten for the H2132
Dt 6:11 not, vineyards and **o** trees, which thou H2132

Dt 8: 8 a land of oil **o**, and honey; H2132
24:20 When thou beatest thine **o** tree, thou H2132
28:40 Thou shalt have **o** trees throughout all H2132
40 the oil; for thine **o** shall cast *his fruit.* H2132
Jdg 9: 8 unto the **o** tree, Reign thou over us. H2132
9 But the **o** tree said unto them, Should I H2132
1Ki 6:23 *of* **o** tree, *each* ten cubits high. H8081
31 he made doors *of* **o** tree: the lintel *and* H8081
32 The two doors also *were of* **o** tree; and H8081
33 posts *of* **o** tree, a fourth part *of the wall.* H8081
2Ki 18:32 a land of oil **o** and of honey, that ye H2132
1Ch 27:28 And over the **o** trees and the sycomore H3121
Neh 8:15 mount, and fetch **o** branches, and pine H2132
Job 15:33 and shall cast off his flower as the **o**. H2132
Ps 52: 8 But I *am* like a green **o** tree in the H2132
128: 3 like **o** plants round about thy table. H2132
Isa 17: 6 as the shaking of an **o** tree, two *or* three H2132
24:13 as the shaking of an **o** tree, *and* as the H2132
Jer 11:16 The LORD called thy name, A green **o** H2132
Hos 14: 6 as the **o** tree, and his smell as Lebanon. H2132
Am 4: 9 fig trees and your **o** trees increased, the H2132
Hab 3:17 the labour of the **o** shall fail, and the H2132
Hag 2:19 and the **o** tree, hath not brought H2132
Zec 4: 3 And two **o** trees by it, one upon the H2132
11 *are* these two **o** trees upon the right H2132
12 What *be these* two **o** branches which H2132
Ro 11:17 thou, being a wild **o** tree, wert graffed in *G65*
17 of the root and fatness of the **o** tree; *G1636*
24 For if thou wert cut out of the **o** tree *G65*
24 to nature into a good **o** tree: how much *G2565*
24 be graffed into their own **o** tree? *G1636*
Jas 3:12 Can the fig tree, my brethren, bear **o** *G1636*
Rev 11: 4 These are the two **o** trees, and the two *G1636*

OLIVE-BERRIES See OLIVE and BERRIES.

OLIVE-BRANCHES See OLIVE and BRANCHES.

OLIVE-LEAF See OLIVE and LEAF.

OLIVES
Jdg 15: 5 corn, with the vineyards *and* **o**. H2132
Mic 6:15 shalt tread the **o**, but thou shalt not H2132
Zec 14: 4 upon the mount of **O**, which *is* before H2132
4 and the mount of **O** shall cleave in the H2132
Mt 21: 1 of **O**, then sent Jesus two disciples, *G1636*
24: 3 And as he sat upon the mount of **O**, the *G1636*
26:30 they went out into the mount of **O**. *G1636*
Mk 11: 1 **O**, he sendeth forth two of his disciples, *G1636*
13: 3 And as he sat upon the mount of **O** *G1636*
14:26 they went out into the mount of **O**. *G1636*
Lk 19:29 *mount* of **O**, he sent two of his disciples, *G1636*
37 of the mount of **O**, the whole multitude *G1636*
21:37 the mount that is called *the mount* of **O**. *G1636*
22:39 **O**; and his disciples also followed him. *G1636*
Jn 8: 1 Jesus went unto the mount of **O**. *G1636*

OLIVET
2Sa 15:30 ascent of *mount* **O**, and wept as he went H2132
Act 1:12 from the mount called **O**, which is from *G1638*

OLIVEYARD
Ex 23:11 deal with thy vineyard, *and* with thy **o**. H2132

OLIVEYARDS
Jos 24:13 and **o** which ye planted not do ye eat. H2132
1Sa 8:14 and your **o**, *even* the best *of them,* H2132
2Ki 5:26 garments, and **o**, and vineyards, and H2132
Neh 5:11 vineyards, their **o**, and their houses, H2132
9:25 vineyards, and **o**, and fruit trees in H2132

OLYMPAS
Ro 16:15 and his sister, and **O**, and all the saints *G3652*

OMAR
Gen 36:11 And the sons of Eliphaz were Teman, **O**, H201
15 duke **O**, duke Zepho, duke Kenaz, H201
1Ch 1:36 The sons of Eliphaz; Teman, and **O**, H201

OMEGA
Rev 1: 8 I am Alpha and **O**, the beginning and *G5598*
11 Saying, I am Alpha and **O**, the first and *G5598*
21: 6 I am Alpha and **O**, the beginning and *G5598*
22:13 I am Alpha and **O**, the beginning and *G5598*

OMER
Ex 16:16 to his eating, an **o** for every man, H6016
18 And when they did mete *it* with an **o**, he H6016
16:32 Fill an **o** of it to be kept for your H6016
33 Take a pot, and put an **o** full of manna H6016
36 Now an **o** *is* the tenth *part* of an ephah. H6016

OMERS
Ex 16:22 as much bread, two **o** for one *man:* and H6016

OMITTED
Mt 23:23 and cummin, and have **o** the weightier *G863*

OMNIPOTENT
Rev 19: 6 Alleluia: for the Lord God **o** reigneth. *G3841*

OMRI
1Ki 16:16 all Israel made **O**, the captain of the H6018
17 And **O** went up from Gibbethon, and H6018
21 to make him king; and half followed **O**. H6018
22 But the people that followed **O** H6018
22 Ginath: so Tibni died, and **O** reigned. H6018
23 of Judah began **O** to reign over Israel, H6018
25 But **O** wrought evil in the eyes of the H6018
27 Now the rest of the acts of **O** which he H6018
28 So **O** slept with his fathers, and was H6018
29 Ahab the son of **O** to reign over Israel: H6018
29 Ahab the son of **O** reigned over Israel H6018
30 And Ahab the son of **O** did evil in the H6018
2Ki 8:26 the daughter of **O** king of Israel. H6018
1Ch 7: 8 and Elioenai, and **O**, and Jerimoth, and H6018
9: 4 the son of **O**, the son of Imri, the H6018
27:18 of Issachar, **O** the son of Michael: H6018
2Ch 22: 2 also *was* Athaliah the daughter of **O**. H6018
Mic 6:16 For the statutes of **O** are kept, and all H6018

ON See the Appendix.

ONAM
Gen 36:23 and Manahath, and Ebal, Shepho, and **O**. H208
1Ch 1:40 and Ebal, Shephi, and **O**. And the sons of H208
2:26 *was* Atarah; she *was* the mother of **O**. H208
28 And the sons of **O** were, Shammai, and H208

ONAN
Gen 38: 4 bare a son; and she called his name **O**. H209
8 And Judah said unto **O**, Go in unto thy H209
9 And **O** knew that the seed should not be H209
46:12 And the sons of Judah; Er, and **O**, and H209
12 Zerah: but Er and **O** died in the land of H209
Nu 26:19 The sons of Judah *were* Er and **O**: and Er H209
19 Er and **O** died in the land of Canaan. H209
1Ch 2: 3 The sons of Judah; Er, and **O**, and H209

ONCE
Gen 18:32 speak yet but this **o**: Peradventure ten H6471
Ex 10:17 thee, my sin only this **o**, and entreat the H6471
30:10 the horns of it **o** in a year with the blood H259
10 of atonements: **o** in the year shall he H259
Lev 16:34 for all their sins **o** a year. And he did as H259
Nu 13:30 Let us go up at **o**, and possess it; for we H5927
Dt 7:22 consume them at **o**, lest the beasts of H4118
Jos 6: 3 the city **o**. Thus shalt thou do six days. H259
11 city, going about *it* **o**: and they came into H259
14 compassed the city **o**, and returned into H259
Jdg 6:39 I will speak but this **o**: let me prove, I H6471
39 pray thee, but this **o** with the fleece; let H6471
16:18 Come up this **o**, for he hath shewed H6471
28 thee, only this **o**, O God, that I may be H6471
28 God, that I may be at **o** avenged of the H259
1Sa 26: 8 to the earth at **o**, and I will not H6471+H259
1Ki 10:22 the navy of Hiram: **o** in three years came H259
2Ki 6:10 and saved himself there, not **o** nor twice. H259
2Ch 9:21 every three years **o** came the ships of H259
Neh 5:18 for me, and **o** in ten days store of all H996
13:20 lodged without Jerusalem **o** or twice. H6471
Job 33:14 For God speaketh **o**, yea twice, *yet man* H259
40: 5 **O** have I spoken; but I will not answer: H259
Ps 62:11 God hath spoken **o**; twice have I heard H259
74: 6 thereof at **o** with axes and hammers. H3162
76: 7 in thy sight when **o** thou art angry? H227
89:35 **O** have I sworn by my holiness that I will H259
Prv 28:18 *that is* perverse *in his* ways shall fall at **o**. H259
Isa 42:14 woman; I will destroy and devour at **o**. H3162
66: 8 nation be born at **o**? for as soon as Zion H6471
Jer 10:18 of the land at this **o**, and will distress H6471
13:27 not be made clean? when *shall it* **o** *be*? H5750
16:21 Therefore, behold, I will this **o** cause H6471
Hag 2: 6 For thus saith the LORD of hosts; Yet **o**, it H259
Lk 13:25 When **o** the master of the house is risen *G575*
23:18 And they cried out all at **o**, saying, *G3826*
Ro 6:10 For in that he died, he died unto sin **o**: *G2178*
7: 9 For I was alive without the law **o**: but *G4218*
1Co 15: 6 brethren at **o**; of whom the greater *G2178*
2Co 11:25 Thrice was I beaten with rods, **o** was I *G530*
Gal 1:23 the faith which **o** he destroyed. *G4218*
Eph 5: 3 let it not be **o** named among you, *G3366*
Php 4:16 For even in Thessalonica ye sent **o** and *G530*
1Th 2:18 **o** and again; but Satan hindered us. *G530*
Heb 6: 4 For *it is* impossible for those who were **o** *G530*
7:27 he did **o**, when he offered up himself. *G2178*
9: 7 the high priest alone **o** every year, not *G530*
12 he entered in **o** into the holy place, *G2178*
26 of the world: but now **o** in the end of the *G530*
27 And as it is appointed unto men **o** to die, *G530*
28 So Christ was **o** offered to bear the sins *G530*
10: 2 the worshippers **o** purged should have *G530*
10 of the body of Jesus Christ **o** *for all.* *G2178*
12:26 saying, Yet **o** more I shake not the *G530*
27 And this *word,* Yet **o** more, signifieth the *G530*
1Pt 3:18 For Christ also hath **o** suffered for sins, *G530*
20 disobedient, when **o** the longsuffering of *G530*
Jude 3 which was **o** delivered unto the saints. *G530*
5 though ye **o** knew this, how that *G530*

ONE
Gen 1: 9 together unto **o** place, and let the dry H259
2:21 he slept: and he took **o** of his ribs, and H259
24 unto his wife: and they shall be **o** flesh. H259
3: 6 desired to make *o* wise, she took of the H7919
22 man is become as **o** of us, to know good H259
4:14 every **o** that findeth me shall slay me.
19 the name of the **o** *was* Adah, and the H259
10: 5 in their lands; every **o** after his tongue, H376
8 he began to be a mighty **o** in the earth. H1368
25 sons: the name of **o** *was* Peleg; for in his H259
11: 1 And the whole earth was of **o** language, H259
1 was of one language, and of **o** speech. H259
3 And they said **o** to another, Go to, let us H376
6 the people *is* **o**, and they have all one H259
6 and they have all **o** language; and this H259
7 may not understand **o** another's speech. H376
13:11 themselves the **o** from the other. H376
14:13 And there came **o** that had escaped, and
15: 3 lo, **o** born in my house is mine heir. H1121
10 and laid each piece **o** against another:
19: 9 they said *again,* This **o** *fellow* came in to H259
14 as **o** that mocked unto his sons in law.
20 and it *is* a little **o**: Oh, let me escape H4705
20 it not a little **o**?) and my soul shall live. H4705
21:15 she cast the child under **o** of the shrubs. H259
22: 2 offering upon **o** of the mountains which H259
24:41 thee *o*, thou shalt be clear from my oath.
25:23 thy bowels; and *the* **o** people shall be H3816
26:10 hast done unto us? **o** of the people might H259
26 and Ahuzzath **o** of his friends, and H259
31 and sware **o** to another: and Isaac H376
27:29 cursed *be* every **o** that curseth thee, and
38 Hast thou but **o** blessing, my father? H259
45 I be deprived also of you both in **o** day? H259
30:33 thy face: every **o** that *is* not speckled H3605
35 and spotted, *and* every **o** that had *some*
31:49 when we are absent **o** from another. H376
32: 8 And said, If Esau come to the **o** H259
33:13 them **o** day, all the flock will die. H259
34:14 thing, to give our sister to **o** that is H376
16 with you, and we will become **o** people. H259
22 to dwell with us, to be **o** people, if every H259
37:19 And they said **o** to another, Behold, this H376
38:28 travailed, that *the* **o** put out *his* hand: H5414
40: 5 man his dream in **o** night, each man H259
41: 5 came up upon **o** stalk, rank and good. H259
11 And we dreamed a dream in **o** night, I H259
22 ears came up in **o** stalk, full and good: H259
25 dream of Pharaoh *is* **o**: God hath shewed H259
26 ears *are* seven years: the dream *is* **o**. H259
38 Can we find *such a* **o** as this *is,* a man in H259
42: 1 sons, Why do ye look **o** upon another? H7200
11 We *are* all **o** man's sons; we *are* true H259
13 the sons of **o** man in the land of Canaan; H259
13 *is* this day with our father, and **o** *is* not. H259
16 Send **o** of you, and let him fetch your H259
19 If ye *be* true *men,* let **o** of your brethren H259
21 And they said **o** to another, We *are* H376
27 And as **o** of them opened his sack to give H259
28 were afraid, saying **o** to another, What *is* H376
32 sons of our father; **o** *is* not, and the H259
33 ye *are* true *men;* leave **o** of your brethren H259
43:33 and the men marvelled **o** at another. H376

Gen 44:20 his old age, a little **o**; and his brother is H6996
28 And the **o** went out from me, and I said, H259
47:21 to cities from *o* end of the borders of H7097
48: 1 these things, that *o* told Joseph, Behold,
2 And *o* told Jacob, and said, Behold, thy
22 Moreover I have given to thee **o** portion H259
49:16 Dan shall judge his people, as **o** of the H259
28 them; every **o** according to his blessing H376
Ex 1:15 the name of the **o** *was* Shiphrah, and the H259
2: 6 said, This *is o* of the Hebrews' children.
11 smiting an Hebrew, **o** of his brethren.
6:25 And Eleazar Aaron's son took him *o* of
8:31 from his people; there remained not **o**. H259
9: 6 cattle of the children of Israel died not **o**. H259
7 there was not **o** of the cattle of the H259
10: 5 of the earth, that **o** cannot be able to see
19 not **o** locust in all the coasts of Egypt. H259
23 They saw not **o** another, neither rose any H376
11: 1 Yet will I bring **o** plague *more* upon H259
12:18 bread, until the **o** and twentieth day of H259
30 not a house where *there was* not **o** dead.
46 In **o** house shall it be eaten; thou shalt H259
48 it; and he shall be as **o** that is born in the
49 **O** law shall be to him that is homeborn, H259
14: 7 and captains over every **o** of them.
20 **o** came not near the other all the night. H2088
28 remained not so much as **o** of them. H259
16:15 Israel saw *it*, they said **o** to another, It *is* H376
22 two omers for **o** *man*: and all the rulers H259
17:12 up his hands, the **o** on the one side, and H259
12 the one on the **o** side, and the other H2088
18: 3 the name of the **o** *was* Gershom; for he H259
16 I judge between **o** and another, and I do H376
21:18 And if men strive together, and **o** smite H376
35 And if **o** man's ox hurt another's, that he
23:29 from before thee in **o** year; lest the land H259
24: 3 answered with **o** voice, and said, All the H259
25:12 *shall be* in the **o** side of it, and two rings H259
19 And make **o** cherub on the one end, and H259
19 And make one cherub on the **o** end, H2088
20 faces *shall look* **o** to another; toward the H376
32 out of the **o** side, and three branches H259
33 and a flower in **o** branch; and three H259
36 all it *shall be* **o** beaten work *of* pure gold. H259
26: 2 The length of **o** curtain *shall be* eight H259
2 and the breadth of **o** curtain four cubits: H259
2 **o** of the curtains shall have one measure. H259
2 one of the curtains shall have **o** measure. H259
3 coupled together **o** to another; and *other* H802
3 curtains *shall be* coupled **o** to another. H802
4 upon the edge of the **o** curtain from the H259
5 Fifty loops shalt thou make in the **o** H259
5 the loops may take hold **o** of another. H802
6 the taches: and it shall be **o** tabernacle. H259
8 The length of **o** curtain *shall be* thirty H259
8 and the breadth of **o** curtain four cubits: H259
8 eleven curtains *shall be all* of **o** measure. H259
10 loops on the edge of the **o** curtain *that is* H259
11 couple the tent together, that it may be **o**. H259
13 And a cubit on the **o** side, and a cubit on
16 a half *shall be* the breadth of **o** board. H259
17 Two tenons *shall there be* in **o** board, set H259
17 board, set in order **o** against another: H802
19 two sockets under **o** board for his two H259
21 two sockets under **o** board, and two H259
24 the head of it unto **o** ring: thus shall it be H259
25 two sockets under **o** board, and two H259
26 boards of the **o** side of the tabernacle, H259
27: 9 of an hundred cubits long for **o** side: H259
14 The hangings of **o** side *of the gate shall*
28:10 Six of their names on **o** stone, and *the* H259
21 of a signet; every **o** with his name shall H376
29: 1 office: Take **o** young bullock, and two H259
3 And thou shalt put them into **o** basket, H259
15 Thou shalt also take **o** ram; and Aaron H259
23 And **o** loaf of bread, and one cake of H259
23 And one loaf of bread, and **o** cake of H259
23 of oiled bread, and **o** wafer out of the H259
39 The **o** lamb thou shalt offer in the H259
40 And with the **o** lamb a tenth deal of flour H259
30:13 This they shall give, every **o** that passeth
14 Every **o** that passeth among them that
31:14 unto you: every **o** that defileth it shall
32:15 both their sides; on the **o** side and on the
33: 7 to pass, *that* every **o** which sought the
34:15 *o* call thee, and thou eat of his sacrifice;
35:21 And they came, every **o** whose heart H376
21 him up, and every **o** whom his spirit

Ex 35:24 Every **o** that did offer an offering of
36: 2 *even* every **o** whose heart stirred
9 The length of **o** curtain *was* twenty and H259
9 and the breadth of **o** curtain four cubits: H259
9 cubits: the curtains *were* all of **o** size. H259
10 And he coupled the five curtains **o** unto H259
10 five curtains he coupled **o** unto another. H259
11 of blue on the edge of **o** curtain from the H259
12 Fifty loops made he in **o** curtain, and H259
12 the loops held **o** *curtain* to another. H259
13 the curtains **o** unto another with the H259
13 the taches: so it became **o** tabernacle. H259
15 The length of **o** curtain *was* thirty cubits, H259
15 *was* the breadth of **o** curtain: the eleven H259
15 the eleven curtains *were* of **o** size. H259
18 the tent together, that it might be **o**. H259
21 breadth of a board **o** cubit and a half.
22 **O** board had two tenons, equally distant H259
22 equally distant **o** from another: thus did H259
24 two sockets under **o** board for his two H259
26 two sockets under **o** board, and two H259
29 the head thereof, to **o** ring: thus he did to H259
31 boards of the **o** side of the tabernacle, H259
33 the boards from the **o** end to the other. H259
37: 3 two rings upon the **o** side of it, and two H259
6 **o** cubit and a half the breadth thereof.
7 *of* gold, beaten out of **o** piece made he
8 **O** cherub on the end on this side, and H259
9 with their faces **o** to another; *even* to the H376
18 out of the **o** side thereof, and three H259
19 of almonds in **o** branch, a knop and H259
22 all of it *was* **o** beaten work *of* pure gold. H259
38:14 The hangings of the **o** side *of the gate*
26 for every **o** that went to be numbered,
39:14 of a signet, every **o** with his name, H376
Lev 4:27 And if any **o** of the common people sin H5315
5: 4 *of it*, then he shall be guilty in **o** of these. H259
5 shall be guilty in **o** of these *things*, that H259
7 unto the LORD; **o** for a sin offering, and H259
13 he hath sinned in **o** of these, and it shall H259
6:18 every **o** that toucheth them shall be holy.
7: 7 offering: *there is* **o** law for them: the H259
10 of Aaron have, **o** *as much* as another. H376
14 And of it he shall offer **o** out of the whole H259
8:26 the LORD, he took **o** unleavened cake, H259
26 of oiled bread, and **o** wafer, and put H259
11:26 **o** that toucheth them shall be unclean.
12: 8 two young pigeons; the **o** for the burnt H259
13: 2 priest, or unto **o** of his sons the priests: H259
14: 5 And the priest shall command that **o** of H259
10 blemish, and **o** ewe lamb of the first H259
10 mingled with oil, and **o** log of oil. H259
12 And the priest shall take **o** he lamb, and H259
21 then he shall take **o** lamb *for* a trespass H259
21 for him, and **o** tenth deal of fine flour H259
22 is able to get; and the **o** shall be a sin H259
30 And he shall offer the **o** of the H259
31 *Even* such as he is able to get, the **o** *for* a H259
50 And he shall kill the **o** of the birds in an H259
15:15 And the priest shall offer them, the **o** *for* H259
30 And the priest shall offer the **o** *for* a sin H259
16: 5 offering, and **o** ram for a burnt offering. H259
8 the two goats; **o** lot for the LORD, and H259
27 holy *place*, shall **o** carry forth without
29 work at all, *whether it be* **o** of your own
17:15 *whether it be* **o** of your own country,
18:30 that *ye* commit not *any* **o** of these
19: 8 Therefore *every* **o** that eateth it shall
11 deal falsely, neither lie **o** to another. H376
34 be unto you as **o** born among you, and
20: 9 For every **o** that curseth his father or his H376
22:28 not kill it and her young both in **o** day. H259
23:18 the first year, and **o** young bullock, and H259
19 Then ye shall sacrifice **o** kid of the goats H259
24: 5 two tenth deals shall be in **o** cake. H259
22 Ye shall have **o** manner of law, as well H259
22 for the stranger, as for **o** of your own H259
25:14 hand, ye shall not oppress **o** another: H376
17 Ye shall not therefore oppress **o** another; H376
46 shall not rule **o** over another with rigour. H376
48 **o** of his brethren may redeem him: H259
26:26 bake your bread in **o** oven, and they H259
37 And they shall fall **o** upon another, as it H376
Nu 1: 4 every **o** head of the house of his fathers. H376
41 forty and **o** thousand and five hundred. H259
44 each **o** was for the house of his fathers. H259
2:16 and fifty and **o** thousand and four H259
28 forty and **o** thousand and five hundred. H259

Nu 2:34 set forward, every **o** after their families, H376
4:19 every **o** to his service and to his burden: H376
30 them, every **o** that entereth into the
35 years old, every **o** that entereth into the
39 years old, every **o** that entereth into the
43 years old, every **o** that entereth into the
47 years old, every **o** that came to do the
49 hand of Moses, every **o** according to his H376
5: 2 leper, and every **o** that hath an issue,
6:11 And the priest shall offer the **o** for a sin H259
14 unto the LORD, **o** he lamb of the first H259
14 a burnt offering, and **o** ewe lamb of the H259
14 for a sin offering, and **o** ram without H259
19 of the ram, and **o** unleavened cake out H259
19 of the basket, and **o** unleavened wafer, H259
7: 3 and for each **o** an ox: and they brought H259
13 And his offering *was* **o** silver charger, H259
13 and thirty *shekels*, **o** silver bowl of H259
14 **O** spoon of ten *shekels* of gold, full of H259
15 **O** young bullock, one ram, one lamb of H259
15 One young bullock, **o** ram, one lamb of H259
15 One young bullock, one ram, **o** lamb of H259
16 **O** kid of the goats for a sin offering: H259
19 He offered *for* his offering **o** silver H259
19 and thirty *shekels*, **o** silver bowl of H3701
20 **O** spoon of gold of ten *shekels*, full of H259
21 **O** young bullock, one ram, one lamb of H259
21 One young bullock, **o** ram, one lamb of H259
21 One young bullock, one ram, **o** lamb of H259
22 **O** kid of the goats for a sin offering: H259
25 His offering *was* **o** silver charger, the H259
25 and thirty *shekels*, **o** silver bowl of H259
26 **O** golden spoon of ten *shekels*, full of H259
27 **O** young bullock, one ram, one lamb of H259
27 One young bullock, **o** ram, one lamb of H259
27 One young bullock, one ram, **o** lamb of H259
28 **O** kid of the goats for a sin offering: H259
31 His offering *was* **o** silver charger of the H259
31 and thirty *shekels*, **o** silver bowl of H259
32 **O** golden spoon of ten *shekels*, full of H259
33 **O** young bullock, one ram, one lamb of H259
33 One young bullock, **o** ram, one lamb of H259
33 One young bullock, one ram, **o** lamb of H259
34 **O** kid of the goats for a sin offering: H259
37 His offering *was* **o** silver charger, the H259
37 and thirty *shekels*, **o** silver bowl of H259
38 **O** golden spoon of ten *shekels*, full of H259
39 **O** young bullock, one ram, one lamb of H259
39 One young bullock, **o** ram, one lamb of H259
39 One young bullock, one ram, **o** lamb of H259
40 **O** kid of the goats for a sin offering: H259
43 His offering *was* **o** silver charger of the H259
44 **O** golden spoon of ten *shekels*, full of H259
45 **O** young bullock, one ram, one lamb of H259
45 One young bullock, **o** ram, one lamb of H259
45 One young bullock, one ram, **o** lamb of H259
46 **O** kid of the goats for a sin offering: H259
49 His offering *was* **o** silver charger, the H259
49 and thirty *shekels*, **o** silver bowl of H259
50 **O** golden spoon of ten *shekels*, full of H259
51 **O** young bullock, one ram, one lamb of H259
51 One young bullock, **o** ram, one lamb of H259
51 One young bullock, one ram, **o** lamb of H259
52 **O** kid of the goats for a sin offering: H259
55 His offering *was* **o** silver charger of the H259
55 and thirty *shekels*, **o** silver bowl of H259
56 **O** golden spoon of ten *shekels*, full of H259
57 **O** young bullock, one ram, one lamb of H259
57 One young bullock, **o** ram, one lamb of H259
57 One young bullock, one ram, **o** lamb of H259
58 **O** kid of the goats for a sin offering: H259
61 His offering *was* **o** silver charger, the H259
61 and thirty *shekels*, **o** silver bowl of H259
62 **O** golden spoon of ten *shekels*, full of H259
63 **O** young bullock, one ram, one lamb of H259
63 One young bullock, **o** ram, one lamb of H259
63 One young bullock, one ram, **o** lamb of H259
64 **O** kid of the goats for a sin offering: H259
67 His offering *was* **o** silver charger, the H259
67 and thirty *shekels*, **o** silver bowl of H259
68 **O** golden spoon of ten *shekels*, full of H259
69 **O** young bullock, one ram, one lamb of H259
69 One young bullock, **o** ram, one lamb of H259
69 One young bullock, one ram, **o** lamb of H259
70 **O** kid of the goats for a sin offering: H259
73 His offering *was* **o** silver charger, the H259
73 and thirty *shekels*, **o** silver bowl of H259
74 **O** golden spoon of ten *shekels*, full of H259

Nu 7:75 **O** young bullock, one ram, one lamb of H259
75 One young bullock, **o** ram, one lamb of H259
75 One young bullock, one ram, **o** lamb of H259
76 **O** kid of the goats for a sin offering: H259
79 His offering *was* **o** silver charger, the H259
79 and thirty *shekels,* **o** silver bowl of H259
80 **O** golden spoon of ten *shekels,* full of H259
81 **O** young bullock, one ram, one lamb of H259
81 One young bullock, **o** ram, one lamb of H259
81 One young bullock, one ram, **o** lamb of H259
82 **O** kid of the goats for a sin offering: H259
89 heard the voice of **o** speaking unto him
8:12 thou shalt offer the **o** *for* a sin offering, H259
9:14 do: ye shall have **o** ordinance, both for H259
10: 4 And if they blow *but* with **o** *trumpet,* H259
11:19 Ye shall not eat **o** day, nor two days, nor H259
26 the name of the **o** *was* Eldad, and the H259
28 servant of Moses, ***o*** of his young men,
12:12 Let her not be as **o** dead, of whom the H4191
13: 2 a man, every **o** a ruler among them.
23 a branch with **o** cluster of grapes, and H259
14: 4 And they said **o** to another, Let us make H376
15 Now *if* thou shalt kill *all* this people as **o** H259
15: 5 burnt offering or sacrifice, for **o** lamb. H259
11 Thus shall it be done for **o** bullock, or for H259
11 or for **o** ram, or for a lamb, or a kid. H259
12 do to every **o** according to their number. H259
15 **O** ordinance *shall be both* for you of the H259
16 **O** law and one manner shall be for you, H259
16 One law and **o** manner shall be for you, H259
24 shall offer **o** young bullock for a H259
24 and **o** kid of the goats for a sin offering. H259
29 Ye shall have **o** law for him that sinneth H259
16: 3 *are* holy, every **o** of them, and the LORD
15 I have not taken **o** ass from them, H259
15 them, neither have I hurt **o** of them. H259
22 of all flesh, shall **o** man sin, and wilt H259
17: 2 Israel, and take of every **o** of them a rod
3 the rod of Levi: for **o** rod *shall be* for the H259
6 of Israel, and every **o** of their princes
6 for each prince **o**, according to their H259
18:11 **o** that is clean in thy house shall eat of it.
13 be thine; every **o** that is clean in thine
19: 3 and ***o*** shall slay her before his face:
5 And ***o*** shall burn the heifer in his sight;
16 And whosoever toucheth **o** that is slain
18 or **o** slain, or one dead, or a grave: H2491
18 or one slain, or **o** dead, or a grave: H4191
21: 8 to pass, that every **o** that is bitten, when
25: 5 Slay ye every **o** his men that were joined H376
6 And, behold, **o** of the children of Israel H376
26:54 to every **o** shall his inheritance H376
28: 4 The **o** lamb shalt thou offer in the H259
7 *part* of an hin for the **o** lamb: in the holy H259
11 bullocks, and **o** ram, seven lambs of H259
12 with oil, for **o** bullock; and two tenth H259
12 offering, mingled with oil, for **o** ram; H259
13 a meat offering unto **o** lamb; *for* a burnt H259
15 And **o** kid of the goats for a sin offering H259
19 bullocks, and **o** ram, and seven lambs H259
22 And **o** goat *for* a sin offering, to make an H259
27 **o** ram, seven lambs of the first year; H259
28 **o** bullock, two tenth deals unto one ram, H259
28 one bullock, two tenth deals unto **o** ram, H259
29 A several tenth deal unto **o** lamb, H259
30 *And* **o** kid of the goats, to make an H259
29: 2 unto the LORD; **o** young bullock, one H259
2 one young bullock, **o** ram, *and* seven H259
4 And **o** tenth deal for one lamb, H259
4 And one tenth deal for **o** lamb, H259
5 And **o** kid of the goats *for* a sin offering, H259
8 *for* a sweet savour; **o** young bullock, one H259
8 one young bullock, **o** ram, *and* seven H259
9 a bullock, *and* two tenth deals to **o** ram, H259
10 A several tenth deal for **o** lamb, H259
11 **O** kid of the goats *for* a sin offering; H259
16 And **o** kid of the goats *for* a sin offering; H259
19 And **o** kid of the goats *for* a sin offering; H259
22 And **o** goat *for* a sin offering; beside the H259
25 And **o** kid of the goats *for* a sin offering; H259
28 And **o** goat *for* a sin offering; beside the H259
31 And **o** goat *for* a sin offering; beside the H259
34 And **o** goat *for* a sin offering; beside the H259
36 unto the LORD: **o** bullock, one ram, H259
36 one bullock, **o** ram, seven lambs of H259
38 And **o** goat *for* a sin offering; beside the H259
31:28 which went out to battle: **o** soul of five H259
30 thou shalt take **o** portion of fifty, of the H259

Nu 31:34 And threescore and **o** thousand asses, H259
39 the LORD'S tribute *was* threescore and **o**. H259
47 half, Moses took **o** portion of fifty, *both* H259
49 and there lacketh not **o** man of us. H259
34:18 And ye shall take **o** prince of every tribe, H259
35: 8 give few: every **o** shall give of his cities H376
15 them: that every **o** that killeth any
30 of witnesses: but **o** witness shall not H259
36: 7 to tribe: for every **o** of the children of H376
8 shall be wife unto **o** of the family of the H259
9 remove from ***o*** tribe to another tribe; H4294
9 tribe; but every **o** of the tribes of the H376
Dt 1:22 And ye came near unto me every **o** of
23 I took twelve men of you, **o** of a tribe: H259
35 Surely there shall not **o** of these men of H376
2:36 there was not **o** city too strong for us:
4: 4 God *are* alive every **o** of you this day.
32 and *ask* from the **o** side of heaven unto H7097
42 unto **o** of these cities he might live: H259
6: 4 Hear, O Israel: The LORD our God *is* **o** H259
12:14 shall choose in **o** of thy tribes, there thou H259
13: 7 thee, from the ***o*** end of the earth even H7097
12 If thou shalt hear *say* in **o** of thy cities, H259
15: 7 If there be among you a poor man of **o** of H259
17: 6 of **o** witness he shall not be put to death. H259
15 thy God shall choose: ***o*** from among thy
18:10 among you *any* ***o*** that maketh his son
19: 5 shall flee unto **o** of those cities, and live: H259
11 he die, and fleeth into **o** of these cities: H259
15 **O** witness shall not rise up against a H259
21: 1 If ***o*** be found slain in the land which the
15 If a man have two wives, **o** beloved, and H259
23:16 he shall choose in **o** of thy gates, where it H259
24: 5 be free at home **o** year, and shall cheer H259
25: 5 If brethren dwell together, and **o** of them H259
11 When men strive together **o** with H376
11 and the wife of the **o** draweth near for to H259
28: 7 **o** way, and flee before thee seven ways. H259
25 thou shalt go out **o** way against them, H259
57 And toward her young **o** that cometh H7988
64 all people, from the **o** end of the earth H7097
32:30 How should **o** chase a thousand, and H259
33: 3 feet; *every* ***o*** shall receive of thy words.
8 *be* with thy holy **o**, whom thou didst H376
Jos 9: 2 Joshua and with Israel, with **o** accord. H259
10: 2 *was* a great city, as **o** of the royal cities, H259
42 did Joshua take at **o** time, because the H259
12: 9 The king of Jericho, **o**; the king of Ai, H259
9 the king of Ai, which *is* beside Beth-el, **o**; H259
10 The king of Jerusalem, **o**; the king of H259
10 of Jerusalem, one; the king of Hebron, **o**; H259
11 The king of Jarmuth, **o**; the king of H259
11 of Jarmuth, one; the king of Lachish, **o**; H259
12 The king of Eglon, **o**; the king of Gezer, H259
12 king of Eglon, one; the king of Gezer, **o**; H259
13 The king of Debir, **o**; the king of Geder, H259
13 king of Debir, one; the king of Geder, **o**; H259
14 The king of Hormah, **o**; the king of Arad, H259
14 king of Hormah, one; the king of Arad, **o**; H259
15 The king of Libnah, **o**; the king of H259
15 of Libnah, one; the king of Adullam, **o**; H259
16 The king of Makkedah, **o**; the king of H259
16 of Makkedah, one; the king of Beth-el, **o**; H259
17 The king of Tappuah, **o**; the king of H259
17 of Tappuah, one; the king of Hepher, **o**; H259
18 The king of Aphek, **o**; the king of H259
18 of Aphek, one; the king of Lasharon, **o**; H259
19 The king of Madon, **o**; the king of Hazor, H259
19 king of Madon, one; the king of Hazor, **o**; H259
20 The king of Shimron-meron, **o**; the king H259
20 one; the king of Achshaph, **o**; H259
21 The king of Taanach, **o**; the king of H259
21 of Taanach, one; the king of Megiddo, **o**; H259
22 The king of Kedesh, **o**; the king of H259
22 one; the king of Jokneam of Carmel, **o**; H259
23 The king of Dor in the coast of Dor, **o**; the H259
23 one; the king of the nations of Gilgal, **o**; H259
24 The king of Tirzah, **o**: all the kings thirty H259
24 of Tirzah, one: all the kings thirty and **o**. H259
13:31 *even* to the ***o*** half of the children of
17:14 thou given me *but* **o** lot and one portion H259
14 me *but* one lot and **o** portion to inherit, H259
17 power: thou shalt not have **o** lot *only*: H259
20: 4 And when he that doth flee unto **o** of H259
21:42 These cities were every **o** with their
22: 7 Now to the ***o*** half of the tribe of H2677
14 of Israel; and each **o** *was* an head of the H376
23:10 **O** man of you shall chase a thousand: for H259

Jos 23:14 souls, that not **o** thing hath failed of all H259
14 you, *and* not **o** thing hath failed thereof. H259
Jdg 6:16 shalt smite the Midianites as **o** man. H259
29 And they said **o** to another, Who hath H376
31 because ***o*** hath cast down his altar.
7: 5 unto Gideon, Every **o** that lappeth of the
5 likewise every **o** that boweth down upon
8:18 each **o** resembled the children of a king. H259
9: 2 reign over you, or that **o** reign over you? H259
5 and ten persons, upon **o** stone: H259
18 and ten persons, upon **o** stone, and have H259
10:18 of Gilead said **o** to another, What man H376
11:35 low, and thou art **o** of them that trouble
12: 7 was buried in **o** *of* the cities of Gilead.
16: 5 **o** of us eleven hundred *pieces* of silver. H376
29 borne up, of the **o** with his right hand, H259
17: 5 **o** of his sons, who became his priest. H259
11 man was unto him as **o** of his sons. H259
18:19 unto the house of **o** man, or that thou be H259
19:13 let us draw near to **o** of these places to H259
20: 1 together as **o** man, from Dan even H259
8 And all the people arose as **o** man, H259
11 against the city, knit together as **o** man. H259
16 lefthanded; every **o** could sling stones at
31 the highways, of which **o** goeth up to the H259
21: 3 be to day **o** tribe lacking in Israel? H259
6 is **o** tribe cut off from Israel this day. H259
8 And they said, What **o** *is there* of the H259
Ru 1: 4 the name of the **o** *was* Orpah, and the H259
2:13 be not like unto **o** of thine handmaidens. H259
20 of kin unto us, **o** of our next kinsmen.
3:14 and she rose up before **o** could know H376
4: 1 he said, Ho, such a **o**! turn aside, sit H492
1Sa 1: 2 And he had two wives; the name of the **o** H259
24 three bullocks, and **o** ephah of flour, and H259
2:25 If **o** man sin against another, the judge
34 in **o** day they shall die both of them. H259
36 And it shall come to pass, *that* every **o**
36 I pray thee, into **o** of the priests' offices, H259
3:11 of every **o** that heareth it shall tingle.
6: 4 the Philistines: for **o** plague *was* on you H259
17 LORD; for Ashdod **o**, for Gaza one, for H259
17 one, for Gaza **o**, for Askelon one, for H259
17 Askelon **o**, for Gath one, for Ekron one; H259
17 Askelon one, for Gath **o**, for Ekron one; H259
17 Askelon one, for Gath one, for Ekron **o**; H259
9: 3 his son, Take now **o** of the servants with H259
10: 3 to God to Beth-el, **o** carrying three kids, H259
11 the people said **o** to another, What *is* H376
12 And **o** of the same place answered and H376
11: 7 and they came out with **o** consent. H259
13: 1 Saul reigned **o** year; and when he had
17 in three companies: **o** company turned H259
14: 4 a sharp rock on the **o** side, and a sharp H2088
4 the name of the **o** *was* Bozez, and the H259
5 The forefront of the **o** *was* situate H259
16 they went on beating down ***o another.***
28 Then answered **o** of the people, and H376
40 Then said he unto all Israel, Be ye on **o** H259
45 there shall not **o** hair of his head fall
16:18 Then answered **o** of the servants, and H259
17: 3 on a mountain on the **o** side, and Israel H2088
7 and **o** bearing a shield went before him.
36 shall be as **o** of them, seeing he hath H259
18: 7 And the women answered ***o another*** as
21 be my son in law in *the **o** of* the twain.
19:22 and David? And ***o*** said, Behold, *they be*
20:15 David every **o** from the face of the earth. H376
41 and they kissed **o** another, and wept one H376
41 **o** with another, until David exceeded. H376
21:11 did they not sing **o** to another of him in
22: 2 And every **o** *that was* in distress, and H376
2 in distress, and every **o** that *was* in debt, H376
2 *was* in debt, and every **o** *that was* H376
7 of Jesse give every **o** of you fields and
20 And **o** of the sons of Ahimelech the son H259
25:14 But **o** of the young men told Abigail, H259
26:15 king? for there came **o** of the people in to H259
20 a flea, as when **o** doth hunt a partridge
22 spear! and let **o** of the young men come H259
27: 1 I shall now perish **o** day by the hand of H259
29: 5 *Is* not this David, of whom they sang **o** to
2Sa 1:15 And David called **o** of the young men, H259
2:13 they sat down, the **o** on the one side of H428
13 the one on the **o** side of the pool, and H2088
16 And they caught every **o** his fellow by the H376
21 lay thee hold on **o** of the young men, and H259
25 **o** troop, and stood on the top of an hill. H259

O

2Sa 2:27 up every **o** from following his brother. H376
3:13 with thee: but **o** thing I require of thee, H259
29 the house of Joab **o** that hath an issue, or
4: 2 the name of the **o** *was* Baanah, and the H259
10 When **o** told me, saying, Behold, Saul is
6:19 as men, to every **o** a cake of bread, and H376
19 the people departed every **o** to his house. H376
20 of his servants, as **o** of the vain fellows H259
7:23 And what **o** nation in the earth *is* like thy H259
8: 2 put to death, and with **o** full line to keep
9:11 eat at my table, as **o** of the king's sons. H259
10: 4 and shaved off the **o** half of their beards,
11: 3 after the woman. And **o** said, *Is* not this
25 sword devoureth **o** as well as another: H2088
12: 1 **o** city; the one rich, and the other poor. H259
1 one city; the **o** rich, and the other poor. H259
3 But the poor *man* had nothing, save **o** H259
13:13 thou shalt be as **o** of the fools in Israel. H259
30 sons, and there is not **o** of them left. H259
14: 6 but the **o** smote the other, and slew him. H259
11 not **o** hair of thy son fall to the earth.
12 I pray thee, speak *o* word unto my lord
13 speak this thing as **o** which is faulty, in
27 three sons, and **o** daughter, whose name H259
15: 2 Thy servant *is* of **o** of the tribes of Israel. H259
31 And **o** told David, saying, Ahithophel *is*
17:12 him there shall not be left so much as **o**. H259
13 there be not **o** small stone found there. H1571
22 **o** of them that was not gone over Jordan. H259
18:17 and all Israel fled every **o** to his tent. H376
19: 7 forth, there will not tarry **o** with thee this H376
14 as *the heart of* **o** man; so that they sent H259
20:11 And **o** of Joab's men stood by him, and H376
12 that every **o** that came by him stood still.
19 I *am o of them that are* peaceable *and*
23: 8 eight hundred, whom he slew at **o** time. H259
9 Dodo the Ahohite, *o* of the three mighty
15 And David longed, and said, Oh that **o**
24 Asahel the brother of Joab *was* **o** of the
24:12 **o** of them, that I may *do it* unto thee. H259
1Ki 1:48 which hath given *o* to sit on my throne
2:16 And now I ask **o** petition of thee, deny H259
20 Then she said, I desire **o** small petition H259
3:17 And the **o** woman said, O my lord, I and H259
17 this woman dwell in **o** house; and I was H259
23 Then said the king, The **o** saith, This *is* H2063
25 give half to the **o**, and half to the other. H259
4:22 And Solomon's provision for **o** day was H259
6:24 And five cubits *was* the **o** wing of the H259
24 part of the **o** wing unto the uttermost
25 *were* of **o** measure and one size. H259
25 *were* of one measure and **o** size. H259
26 The height of the **o** cherub *was* ten H259
27 the wing of the **o** touched the *one* wall, H259
27 one touched the *o* wall, and the wing of
27 **o** another in the midst of the house. H3671
34 the two leaves of the **o** door *were* folding, H259
7: 7 from **o** side of the floor to the other.
16 the height of the **o** chapiter *was* five H259
17 seven for the **o** chapiter, and seven H259
18 about upon the **o** network, to cover the H259
23 ten cubits from the **o** brim to the other: *it*
27 *was* the length of **o** base, and four cubits H259
34 to the four corners of **o** base: *and* the H259
36 of every **o**, and additions round about. H376
37 **o** casting, one measure, *and* one size. H259
37 one casting, **o** measure, *and* one size. H259
37 one casting, one measure, *and* **o** size. H259
38 Then made he ten lavers of brass: **o** H259
38 upon every **o** of the ten bases one laver. H259
38 upon every one of the ten bases **o** laver. H259
42 of pomegranates for **o** network, to cover H259
44 And **o** sea, and twelve oxen under the H259
8:56 hath not failed **o** word of all his good H259
9: 8 And at this house, *which* is high, every **o**
10:14 to Solomon in **o** year was six hundred H259
16 hundred *shekels* of gold went to **o** target. H259
17 of gold went to **o** shield: and the king H259
20 And twelve lions stood there on the **o** H2088
11:13 *but* will give **o** tribe to thy son for David H259
32 (But he shall have **o** tribe for my servant H259
36 And unto his son will I give **o** tribe, that H259
12:29 And he set the **o** in Beth-el, and the other H259
30 *to worship* before the **o**, *even* unto Dan. H259
13:33 **o** of the priests of the high places.
14:21 *was* forty and **o** years old when he began H259
15:10 And forty and **o** years reigned he in H259
16:11 he left him not **o** that pisseth against

1Ki 18: 6 it: Ahab went **o** way by himself, and H259
23 and let them choose **o** bullock for H259
25 of Baal, Choose you **o** bullock for H259
40 of Baal; let not **o** of them escape. And H376
19: 2 **o** of them by to morrow about this time. H259
20:20 And they slew every **o** his man: and the H376
29 And they pitched **o** over against the H428
29 an hundred thousand footmen in **o** day. H259
22: 8 *There is* yet **o** man, Micaiah the son H259
13 good unto the king with **o** mouth: let thy H259
13 **o** of them, and speak *that which is* good. H259
20 And **o** said on this manner,
28 said, Hearken, O people, every **o** of you.
38 And *o* washed the chariot in the pool of
2Ki 3:11 by him? And **o** of the king of Israel's H259
23 and they have smitten **o** another: now H376
4:22 me, I pray thee, **o** of the young men, and H259
22 the young men, and **o** of the asses, that I H259
39 And **o** went out into the field to gather H259
5: 4 And *o* went in, and told his lord, saying,
6: 3 And **o** said, Be content, I pray thee, and H259
5 But as **o** was felling a beam, the axe H259
12 And **o** of his servants said, None, my H259
7: 3 gate: and they said **o** to another, Why sit H376
6 host: and they said **o** to another, Lo, the H376
8 they went into **o** tent, and did eat and H259
9 Then they said **o** to another, We do not H376
13 And **o** of his servants answered and H259
8:26 and he reigned **o** year in Jerusalem. And H259
9: 1 And Elisha the prophet called **o** of the H259
11 of his lord: and *o* said unto him, *Is* all
18 So there went **o** on horseback to meet
10:21 of Baal was full from **o** end to another.
12: 4 the money of every **o** that passeth *the* H376
9 on the right side as **o** cometh into the H376
14: 8 Come, let us look **o** another in the face.
11 of Judah looked **o** another in the face at
23 Samaria, *and reigned* forty and **o** years. H259
17:27 Carry thither **o** of the priests whom H259
28 Then **o** of the priests whom they had H259
18:24 away the face of **o** captain of the least of H259
31 own vine, and every **o** of his fig tree, and H376
31 drink ye every **o** the waters of his cistern: H376
19:22 high? *even* against the Holy *O* of Israel.
21:16 Jerusalem from **o** end to another; beside
22: 1 reigned thirty and **o** years in Jerusalem. H259
23:35 of the land, of every **o** according to his H376
24:18 Zedekiah *was* twenty and **o** years old H259
25:16 The two pillars, **o** sea, and the bases H259
17 The height of the **o** pillar *was* eighteen H259
1Ch 1:19 the name of the **o** *was* Peleg; because in H259
9:31 And Mattithiah, *o* of the Levites, who
10:13 asking *counsel* of *o that had* a familiar
11:11 three hundred slain *by him* at **o** time. H259
12 who *was o* of the three mighties.
17 And David longed, and said, Oh that **o**
12:14 of the host: **o** of the least *was* over H259
25 the war, seven thousand and **o** hundred.
38 *were* of **o** heart to make David king. H259
16: 3 And he dealt to every **o** of Israel, both H376
3 woman, to every **o** a loaf of bread, and H376
20 and from *o* kingdom to another people;
17: 5 tent, and from **o** tabernacle *to another.*
21 And what **o** nation in the earth *is* like thy H259
21:10 **o** of them, that I may do *it* unto thee. H259
23:11 they were in **o** reckoning, according H259
24: 5 Thus were they divided by lot, **o** sort H428
6 the scribe, *o* of the Levites, wrote
6 and Levites: **o** principal household H259
6 for Eleazar, and *o* taken for Ithamar.
17 The **o** and twentieth to Jachin, the two H259
25:28 The **o** and twentieth to Hothir, *he*, his H259
26:12 men, *having* wards **o** against another, to
27:18 Of Judah, Elihu, *o* of the brethren of
29: 7 and **o** hundred thousand talents of iron.
2Ch 3:11 twenty cubits long: **o** wing *of the one* H259
11 one wing *of the o* cherub was five cubits,
12 And *o* wing of the other cherub *was* five
17 before the temple, **o** on the right hand, H259
4:15 **O** sea, and twelve oxen under it. H259
5:13 singers *were* as **o**, to make one sound to H259
13 as one, to make **o** sound to be heard in H259
6:29 Israel, when every **o** shall know his own H376
7:21 to every **o** that passeth by it; so
9: 6 seen *it:* and, behold, the **o** half of the
13 to Solomon in **o** year was six hundred H259
15 *shekels* of beaten gold went to **o** target. H259
16 of gold went to **o** shield. And the king H259

2Ch 9:19 And twelve lions stood there on the **o**
12:13 for Rehoboam *was* **o** and forty years old H259
16:13 in the **o** and fortieth year of his reign. H259
18: 7 *There is* yet **o** man, by whom we may H259
8 And the king of Israel called for **o** *of his* H259
12 to the king with **o** assent; let thy word H259
12 be like **o** of theirs, and speak thou good. H259
19 And **o** spake saying after this
20:23 Seir, every **o** helped to destroy another. H376
22: 2 and he reigned **o** year in Jerusalem. His H259
25:17 Come, let us see **o** another in the face.
21 up; and they saw **o** another in the face,
26:11 of Hananiah, *o* of the king's captains.
28: 6 thousand in **o** day, *which were* all H259
30:12 God was to give them **o** heart to do the H259
17 passovers for every **o** *that was* not clean,
18 saying, The good LORD pardon every **o**
31:16 *even* unto every **o** that entereth into the
32:12 before **o** altar, and burn incense upon it? H259
34: 1 reigned in Jerusalem **o** and thirty years. H259
35:24 and was buried in *o of* the sepulchres of
36:11 Zedekiah *was* **o** and twenty years old H259
Ezr 2: 1 and Judah, every **o** unto his city; H376
26 and Gaba, six hundred twenty and **o**. H259
69 threescore and **o** thousand drams of
69 silver, and **o** hundred priests' garments.
3: 1 together as **o** man to Jerusalem. H259
5 and of every **o** that willingly offered
5:14 were delivered unto *o*, whose name *was*
6: 5 *is* at Jerusalem, *every o* to his place, and
8:34 By number *and* by weight of every **o**: and
9: 4 Then were assembled unto me every **o**
11 **o** end to another with their uncleanness.
10: 2 And Shechaniah the son of Jehiel, *o* of
13 *is this* a work of **o** day or two: for we are H259
Neh 1: 2 That Hanani, **o** of my brethren, came, he H259
3: 8 the son of *o of* the apothecaries,
28 priests, every **o** over against his house. H376
4:15 of us to the wall, every **o** unto his work. H376
17 that laded, *every o* with one of his hands
17 *every one* with **o** of his hands wrought H259
18 For the builders, every **o** had his sword H376
19 upon the wall, **o** far from another. H376
22 the people, Let every **o** with his servant H376
23 *that* every **o** put them off for washing. H376
5: 7 exact usury, every **o** of his brother. And I H376
18 *for me* daily *was* **o** ox *and* six choice H259
6: 2 together in *some o of* the villages in the
7: 3 of Jerusalem, every **o** in his watch, and H376
3 and every **o** *to be* over against his house. H376
6 and to Judah, every **o** unto his city; H376
30 and Geba, six hundred twenty and **o**. H259
37 and Ono, seven hundred twenty and **o**. H259
63 which took *o* of the daughters of
8: 1 together as **o** man into the street that H259
16 booths, every **o** upon the roof of his H376
9: 3 LORD their God *o* fourth part of the day;
10:28 daughters, every **o** having knowledge,
11: 1 also cast lots, to bring **o** of ten to dwell in H259
3 Judah dwelt every **o** in his possession in H376
14 Zabdiel, the son of *o of* the great men.
20 of Judah, every **o** in his inheritance. H376
12:31 *gave* thanks, *whereof o* went on the right
13:10 the work, were fled every **o** to his field. H376
28 And *o* of the sons of Joiada, the son of
30 and the Levites, every **o** in his business; H376
Est 1: 7 being diverse **o** from another,) and H3627
3:13 and women, in **o** day, *even* upon the H259
4: 5 Then called Esther for Hatach, *o* of the
11 is not called, *there is* **o** law of his to put H259
6: 9 to the hand of **o** of the king's most noble H376
7: 9 And Harbonah, **o** of the chamberlains, H259
8:12 Upon **o** day in all the provinces of king H259
9:19 and of sending portions **o** to another. H376
22 **o** to another, and gifts to the poor. H376
Job 1: 1 **o** that feared God, and eschewed evil.
4 *in their* houses, every **o** his day; and sent H376
8 **o** that feareth God, and escheweth evil?
2: 3 an upright man, **o** that feareth God, and
10 But he said unto her, Thou speakest as **o** H259
11 they came every **o** from his own place; H376
12 and they rent every **o** his mantle, and H376
5: 2 man, and envy slayeth the silly **o**. H6601
6:10 not concealed the words of the Holy **O**. H6918
26 **o** that is desperate, *which are* as wind?
9: 3 he cannot answer him **o** of a thousand. H259
22 This *is* **o** *thing*, therefore I said *it*, He H259
12: 4 I am *as* **o** mocked of his neighbour, who

Job 13: 9 you out? or as **o** man mocketh another,
14: 3 eyes upon such an **o**, and bringest me
4 a clean *thing* out of an unclean? not **o**. H259
16:21 O that **o** might plead for a man with
17:10 for I cannot find *o* wise *man* among you.
19:11 me unto him as **o** *of* his enemies.
21:23 **O** dieth in his full strength, being wholly
23:13 But he *is* in **o** *mind*, and who can turn H259
24: 6 They reap *every* **o** his corn in the field:
17 shadow of death: if *o* know *them, they*
29:25 as **o** *that* comforteth the mourners.
31:15 and did not **o** fashion us in the womb? H259
35 Oh that **o** would hear me! behold, my
33:23 an interpreter, **o** among a thousand, H259
40:11 every **o** *that is* proud, and abase him.
12 Look on every **o** *that is* proud, *and* bring
41: 9 *o* be cast down even at the sight of him?
16 **O** is so near to another, that no air can H259
17 They are joined **o** to another, they stick H376
32 He maketh a path to shine after him; *o*
42:11 money, and every **o** an earring of gold. H376
Ps 12: 2 They speak vanity every **o** with his H376
14: 3 *there is* none that doeth good, no, not **o**. H259
16:10 suffer thine Holy **O** to see corruption. H2623
27: 4 **O** *thing* have I desired of the LORD, that H259
29: 9 temple doth every **o** speak of *his* glory.
32: 6 For this shall every **o** that is godly pray
34:20 He keepeth all his bones: not **o** of them is H259
35:14 as **o** that mourneth *for his* mother.
49:16 Be not thou afraid when **o** is made rich, H376
50:21 altogether *such an o* as thyself: *but* I will
53: 3 Every **o** of them is gone back: they are
3 *there is* none that doeth good, no, not **o**. H259
58: 8 As a snail *which* melteth, let *every o of*
63:11 But the king shall rejoice in God; every **o**
64: 6 every **o** *of them*, and the heart, *is* deep. H376
68:21 an **o** as goeth on still in his trespasses.
30 people, *till every o* submit himself with
71:18 *and* thy power to every **o** *that* is to come.
22 with the harp, O thou Holy **O** of Israel. H6918
73:20 As a dream when **o** awaketh; *so*, O Lord,
75: 7 But God *is* the judge: he putteth down **o**,
78:41 God, and limited the Holy **O** of Israel. H6918
65 Then the Lord awaked as **o** out of sleep,
82: 7 But ye shall die like men, and fall like **o** H259
83: 5 For they have consulted together with **o**
84: 7 *o of them* in Zion appeareth before God.
89:10 Thou hast broken Rahab in pieces, as **o**
18 and the Holy **O** of Israel *is* our king. H6918
19 vision to thy holy **o**, and saidst, I have H2623
19 laid help upon *o that is* mighty; I have
19 have exalted *o* chosen out of the people.
105:13 When they went from **o** nation to
13 from *o* kingdom to another people;
37 not **o** feeble *person* among their tribes.
106:11 enemies: there was not **o** of them left. H259
115: 8 them; *so is* every **o** that trusteth in them.
119:160 and every **o** of thy righteous judgments
162 I rejoice at thy word, as **o** that findeth
128: 1 Blessed *is* every **o** that feareth the LORD;
135:18 them: *so is* every **o** that trusteth in them.
137: 3 *saying*, Sing us *o* of the songs of Zion.
141: 7 mouth, as when **o** cutteth and cleaveth
145: 4 **O** generation shall praise thy works to
Prv 1:14 Cast in thy lot among us; let us all have **o** H259
19 So *are* the ways of every **o** that is greedy
3:18 and happy *is every o* that retaineth her.
6:11 So shall thy poverty come as **o** that
28 Can **o** go upon hot coals, and his feet not H376
8:30 Then I was by him, *as* **o** brought up *with*
15:12 A scorner loveth not **o** that reproveth
16: 5 Every **o** *that is* proud in heart *is* an
17:14 The beginning of strife *is as* when **o**
19:25 and reprove **o** that hath understanding,
20: 6 Most men will proclaim every **o** his own H376
21: 5 but of every **o** *that is* hasty only to want.
22:26 Be not thou *o* of them that strike hands,
24:34 So shall thy poverty come *as* **o** that
26:17 *is like* **o** that taketh a dog by the ears.
Ecc 1: 4 *O* generation passeth away, and *another*
2:14 also that **o** event happeneth to them all. H259
3:19 beasts; even **o** thing befalleth them: H259
19 them: as the **o** dieth, so dieth the other; H2088
19 yea, they have all **o** breath; so that a H259
20 All go unto **o** place; all are of the dust, H259
4: 8 There is **o** *alone*, and *there is* not a H259
9 Two *are* better than **o**; because they have H259
10 For if they fall, the **o** will lift up his H259
Ecc 4:11 heat: but how can **o** be warm *alone*? H259
12 And if **o** prevail against him, two shall H259
5:18 and comely *for o* to eat and to drink,
6: 6 he seen no good: do not all go to **o** place? H259
7:14 God also hath set the **o** over against the H2088
27 **o** by one, to find out the account: H259
27 one by **o**, to find out the account: H259
28 but I find not: **o** man among a thousand H259
8: 9 *is* a time wherein **o** man ruleth over
9: 2 All *things come* alike to all: *there is* **o** H259
3 sun, that *there is* **o** event unto all: yea, H259
18 war: but **o** sinner destroyeth much good. H259
10: 3 and he saith to every **o** *that* he *is* a fool.
15 wearieth every **o** of them, because he
12:11 *which* are given from **o** shepherd. H259
Song 1: 7 why should I be as **o** that turneth aside
2:10 up, my love, my fair **o**, and come away. H3303
13 my love, my fair **o**, and come away. H3303
4: 2 whereof every **o** bear twins, and none
9 my heart with **o** of thine eyes, with one H259
9 of thine eyes, with **o** chain of thy neck. H259
6: 6 whereof every **o** beareth twins, and *there* H259
6 and *there is* not **o** barren among them. H259
9 My dove, my undefiled is *but* **o**; she *is* the H259
9 one; she *is* the *only* **o** of her mother, she H259
9 she *is* the choice *o* of her that bare her. H259
8:10 was I in his eyes as **o** that found favour. H259
11 keepers; every **o** for the fruit thereof was H376
Isa 1: 4 the Holy **O** of Israel unto anger, H6918
23 of thieves: every **o** loveth gifts, and
24 of hosts, the mighty **O** of Israel, Ah, I will
2:12 *be* upon every *o that is* proud and lofty,
12 and upon every **o** *that is* lifted up; and
20 they made *each o* for himself to worship,
3: 5 oppressed, every **o** by another, and every H376
5 another, and every **o** by his neighbour: H376
4: 1 shall take hold of **o** man, saying, We will H259
3 holy, *even* every **o** that is written among
5:10 Yea, ten acres of vineyard shall yield **o** H259
19 of the Holy **O** of Israel draw nigh H6918
24 the word of the Holy **O** of Israel. H6918
30 of the sea: and if *o* look unto the land,
6: 2 Above it stood the seraphims: each **o** H259
3 And **o** cried unto another, and said,
6 Then flew **o** of the seraphims unto me, H259
7:22 shall every **o** eat that is left in the land.
9:14 head and tail, branch and rush, in **o** day. H259
17 widows: for every **o** *is* an hypocrite and
10:14 the people: and as **o** gathereth eggs *that*
17 fire, and his Holy **O** for a flame: and it H6918
17 his thorns and his briers in **o** day; H259
20 LORD, the Holy **O** of Israel, in truth. H6918
34 and Lebanon shall fall by a mighty **o**. H117
12: 6 Holy **O** of Israel in the midst of thee. H6918
13: 8 shall be amazed **o** at another; their faces H376
14 and flee every **o** into his own land. H376
15 Every **o** that is found shall be thrust
15 through; and every **o** that is joined *unto*
14:18 lie in glory, every **o** in his own house. H376
32 What shall *o* then answer the
15: 3 every **o** shall howl, weeping abundantly.
16: 7 for Moab, every **o** shall howl: for the
17: 7 have respect to the Holy **O** of Israel. H6918
19: 2 shall fight every **o** against his brother, H376
2 his brother, and every **o** against his H376
17 terror unto Egypt, every **o** that maketh
18 **o** shall be called, The city of destruction. H259
20 a great **o**, and he shall deliver them. H7227
23:15 to the days of **o** king: after the end of H259
27:12 **o** by one, O ye children of Israel. H259
12 gathered one by **o**, O ye children of Israel. H259
28: 2 mighty and strong **o**, *which* as a tempest
29: 4 thy voice shall be, as of **o** that hath a
11 *men* deliver to **o** that is learned, saying,
19 shall rejoice in the Holy **O** of Israel. H6918
20 For the terrible **o** is brought to nought, H6184
23 sanctify the Holy **O** of Jacob, and shall H6918
30:11 **O** of Israel to cease from before us. H6918
12 Wherefore thus saith the Holy **O** of H6918
15 GOD, the Holy **O** of Israel; In returning H6918
17 **O** thousand *shall flee* at the rebuke of H259
17 at the rebuke of **o**; at the rebuke of five H259
29 of heart, as when **o** goeth with a pipe to
29 of the LORD, to the mighty **O** of Israel. H6697
31: 1 **O** of Israel, neither seek the LORD! H6918
33:20 not be taken down; not **o** of the stakes
34:15 also be gathered, every **o** with her mate. H802
16 and read: no **o** of these shall fail, none H259
Isa 36: 9 away the face of **o** captain of the least of H259
16 and eat ye every **o** of his vine, and every H376
16 his vine, and every **o** of his fig tree, and H376
16 ye every **o** the waters of his own cistern; H376
37:23 high? *even* against the Holy **O** of Israel. H6918
40:25 me, or shall I be equal? saith the Holy **O**. H6918
26 that *he is* strong in power; not **o** faileth. H376
41: 6 They helped every **o** his neighbour; and H376
6 and *every o* said to his brother, Be H376
14 and thy redeemer, the Holy **O** of Israel. H6918
16 *and* shalt glory in the Holy **O** of Israel. H6918
20 and the Holy **O** of Israel hath created it. H6918
25 I have raised up **o** from the north, and
27 Jerusalem **o** that bringeth good tidings.
43: 3 For I *am* the LORD thy God, the Holy **O** H6918
7 *Even* every **o** that is called by my name: H3605
14 the Holy **O** of Israel; For your sake H6918
15 I *am* the LORD, your Holy **O**, the H6918
44: 5 **O** shall say, I *am* the LORD'S; and
45:11 Thus saith the LORD, the Holy **O** of H6918
24 Surely, shall *o* say, in the LORD have I
46: 7 he not remove: yea, *o* shall cry unto him,
47: 4 hosts *is* his name, the Holy **O** of Israel. H6918
9 thee in a moment in **o** day, the loss of H259
15 **o** to his quarter; none shall save thee. H376
48:17 the Holy **O** of Israel; I *am* the LORD H6918
49: 7 *and* his Holy **O**, to him whom man H6918
7 **O** of Israel, and he shall choose thee. H6918
26 thy Redeemer, the mighty **O** of Jacob.
53: 6 have turned every **o** to his own way; and H376
54: 5 the Holy **O** of Israel; The God of H6918
55: 1 Ho, every **o** that thirsteth, come ye to the
5 **O** of Israel; for he hath glorified thee. H6918
56: 6 be his servants, every **o** that keepeth the
11 every **o** for his gain, from his quarter. H376
57: 2 beds, *each o* walking *in* his uprightness.
15 For thus saith the high and lofty **O** that
60: 9 and to the Holy **O** of Israel, because he H6918
14 LORD, The Zion of the Holy **O** of Israel. H6918
16 thy Redeemer, the mighty **O** of Jacob.
22 A little **o** shall become a thousand, and H6996
22 and a small **o** a strong nation: I the H6810
65: 8 in the cluster, and *o* saith, Destroy it not;
66: 8 to bring forth in **o** day? *or* shall a nation H259
13 As **o** whom his mother comforteth, so H376
17 the gardens behind *o tree* in the midst, H259
23 And it shall come to pass, *that* from **o**
23 another, and from **o** sabbath to another,
Jer 1:15 they shall set every **o** his throne at the H376
3:14 and I will take you **o** of a city, and two of H259
5: 6 their cities: every **o** that goeth out thence
8 **o** neighed after his neighbour's wife. H376
6: 3 they shall feed every **o** in his place. H376
13 of them every **o** *is* given to covetousness;
13 unto the priest every **o** dealeth falsely.
8: 6 What have I done? every **o** turned to his
10 *them*: for every **o** from the least even
10 unto the priest every **o** dealeth falsely.
9: 4 Take ye heed every **o** of his neighbour, H376
5 And they will deceive every **o** his H376
8 it speaketh deceit: *o* speaketh peaceably
20 and every **o** her neighbour lamentation. H802
10: 3 *are* vain: for *o* cutteth a tree out of
11: 8 but walked every **o** in the imagination of H376
12:12 devour from the *o* end of the land even
13:14 And I will dash them **o** against another, H376
15:10 *yet* every **o** of them doth curse me.
16:12 ye walk every **o** after the imagination H376
18:11 ye now every **o** from his evil way, and H376
12 **o** do the imagination of his evil heart. H376
16 hissing; every **o** that passeth thereby
19: 8 an hissing; every **o** that passeth thereby
9 and they shall eat every **o** the flesh of his H376
11 and this city, as *o* breaketh a potter's
20: 7 in derision daily, every **o** mocketh me.
11 as a mighty terrible **o**: therefore my H6184
22: 7 against thee, every **o** with his weapons: H376
23:17 say unto every **o** that walketh after the
30 my words every **o** from his neighbour. H376
35 Thus shall ye say every **o** to his H376
35 and every **o** to his brother, What H376
24: 2 **O** basket *had* very good figs, *even* like H259
25: 5 They said, Turn ye again now every **o** H376
26 far and near, **o** with another, and all H376
33 be at that day from *o* end of the earth
30:14 of a cruel **o**, for the multitude of H394
16 adversaries, every **o** of them, shall go
31:30 But every **o** shall die for his own H376

Jer 32:19 of men: to give every **o** according to his H376
39 And I will give them **o** heart, and one H259
39 And I will give them one heart, and **o** H259
34:10 heard that every **o** should let his H376
10 and every **o** his maidservant, go H376
17 liberty, every **o** to his brother, and every H376
35: 2 of the LORD, into **o** of the chambers, H259
36: 7 will return every **o** from his evil way: for H376
16 were afraid both **o** and other, and said H376
38: 7 Now when Ebed-melech the Ethiopian, **o** H376
46:16 He made many to fall, yea, **o** fell upon H376
49:17 Also Edom shall be a desolation: every **o**
50:13 desolate: every **o** that goeth by Babylon
16 shall turn every **o** to his people, and they H376
16 they shall flee every **o** to his own land. H376
29 the LORD, against the Holy **O** of Israel. H6918
42 upon horses, *every o* put in array, like a
51: 5 with sin against the Holy **O** of Israel. H6918
9 her, and let us go every **o** into his own H376
31 **O** post shall run to meet another, and
31 meet another, and **o** messenger to meet
31 of Babylon that his city is taken at *o* end,
46 shall both come *o* year, and after that
56 men are taken, every **o** of their bows is
52: 1 Zedekiah *was* **o** and twenty years old H259
20 The two pillars, **o** sea, and twelve brasen H259
21 the height of **o** pillar *was* eighteen cubits; H259
22 it; and the height of **o** chapiter *was* five H259
Ezk 1: 6 And every **o** had four faces, and every H259
6 four faces, and every **o** had four wings. H259
9 Their wings *were* joined **o** to another; H802
9 they went every **o** straight forward. H376
11 two *wings* of every **o** *were* joined one to H376
11 one *were* joined **o** to another, and two H376
12 And they went every **o** straight forward: H376
15 creatures, behold **o** wheel upon the earth H259
16 and they four had **o** likeness: and their H259
23 wings straight, the **o** toward the other: H802
23 toward the other: every **o** had two, which H376
23 on this side, and every **o** had two, which H376
28 face, and I heard a voice of **o** that spake.
3:13 that touched **o** another, and the noise H802
4: 8 not turn thee from **o** side to another, till
9 and put them in **o** vessel, and make thee H259
17 and be astonied **o** with another, and H376
7:16 them mourning, every **o** for his iniquity. H376
9: 2 in his hand; and **o** man among them H259
10: 7 And *o* cherub stretched forth his hand
9 wheels by the cherubims, **o** wheel by one H259
9 one wheel by **o** cherub, and another H259
10 they four had **o** likeness, as if a wheel H259
14 And every **o** had four faces: the first face H259
19 them, and *every o* stood at the door of
21 Every **o** had four faces apiece, and every H259
21 apiece, and every **o** four wings; and the H259
22 they went every **o** straight forward. H376
11: 5 come into your mind, *every o of* them.
19 And I will give them **o** heart, and I will H259
13:10 *was* no peace; and **o** built up a wall, and,
14: 7 For every **o** of the house of Israel, or of H376
15: 7 shall go out from *o* fire, and *another* fire
16:15 on every **o** that passed by; his it was.
25 thy feet to every **o** that passed by, and
44 Behold, every **o** that useth proverbs shall
17:22 twigs a tender **o**, and will plant *it* upon H7390
18:10 doeth the like to *any* **o** of these *things*, H259
30 of Israel, every **o** according to his ways, H376
19: 3 And she brought up **o** of her whelps: it H259
20:39 Go ye, serve ye every **o** his idols, and H376
21:16 Go thee **o** way or other, *either* on the
19 come forth out of **o** land: and choose H259
22: 6 Behold, the princes of Israel, every **o** H376
11 And **o** hath committed abomination H376
23: 2 two women, the daughters of **o** mother: H259
13 was defiled, *that* they *took* both **o** way, H259
24:23 iniquities, and mourn **o** toward another. H376
31:11 hand of the mighty **o** of the heathen; he
33:20 I will judge you every **o** after his ways. H376
21 of the month, *that* **o** that had escaped
24 Abraham was **o**, and he inherited the H259
26 and ye defile every **o** his neighbour's H376
30 houses, and speak **o** to another, every H2297
30 one to another, every **o** to his brother, H376
32 very lovely song of **o** that hath a pleasant
34:23 And I will set up **o** shepherd over them, H259
37:16 Moreover, thou son of man, take thee **o** H259
17 And join them **o** to another into one H259
17 And join them one to another into **o** H259

Ezk 37:17 and they shall become **o** in thine hand. H259
19 and make them **o** stick, and they shall H259
19 stick, and they shall be **o** in mine hand. H259
22 And I will make them **o** nation in the H259
22 of Israel; and **o** king shall be king to H259
24 they all shall have **o** shepherd: they shall H259
39: 7 I *am* the LORD, the Holy **O** in Israel. H6918
40: 5 **o** reed; and the height, one reed. H259
5 one reed; and the height, **o** reed. H259
6 gate, *which was* **o** reed broad; and the H259
6 *of the gate, which was* **o** reed broad. H259
7 And *every* little chamber *was* **o** reed H259
7 one reed long, and **o** reed broad; and H259
7 the porch of the gate within *was* **o** reed. H259
8 also the porch of the gate within, **o** reed. H259
10 they three *were* of **o** measure: and the H259
10 **o** measure on this side and on that side. H259
12 chambers *was* **o** cubit *on this side*, and H259
12 and the space *was* **o** cubit on that side: H259
13 from the roof of *o* little chamber to the
26 and it had palm trees, **o** on this side, and H259
40 And at the side without, as **o** goeth up to
42 and an half broad, and **o** cubit high: H259
44 *was* toward the south: **o** at the side of the H259
49 **o** on this side, and another on that side. H259
41: 1 broad on the **o** side, and six cubits broad
2 five cubits on the **o** side, and five cubits
6 And the side chambers *were* three, **o**
11 *the place that was* left, **o** door toward the H259
15 thereof on the **o** side and on the other
19 palm tree on the **o** side, and the face of
21 *of the* **o** as the appearance *of the other.*
24 two *leaves* for the **o** door, and two leaves H259
26 palm trees on the **o** side and on the other
42: 4 inward, a way of **o** cubit; and their doors H259
9 **o** goeth into them from the utter court.
12 toward the east, as **o** entereth into them.
43:14 and the breadth **o** cubit; and from the H259
14 *be* four cubits, and the breadth *o* cubit.
45: 7 the prince on the **o** side and on the other
7 *be* over against **o** of the portions, from H259
11 The ephah and the bath shall be of **o** H259
15 And **o** lamb out of the flock, out of two H259
20 month for every **o** that erreth, and for H376
46:12 unto the LORD, *o* shall then open him
12 his going forth *o* shall shut the gate.
17 his inheritance to **o** of his servants, then H259
22 these four corners *were* of **o** measure. H259
47: 7 trees on the **o** side and on the other.
14 And ye shall inherit it, **o** as well as H376
48: 1 way of Hethlon, as **o** goeth to Hamath,
8 and *in* length as **o** of the *other* parts, H259
21 for the prince, on the **o** side and on the
31 gates northward; **o** gate of Reuben, one H259
31 **o** gate of Judah, one gate of Levi. H259
31 one gate of Judah, **o** gate of Levi. H259
32 three gates; and **o** gate of Joseph, one H259
32 **o** gate of Benjamin, one gate of Dan. H259
32 one gate of Benjamin, **o** gate of Dan. H259
33 and three gates; **o** gate of Simeon, one H259
33 **o** gate of Issachar, one gate of Zebulun. H259
33 one gate of Issachar, **o** gate of Zebulun. H259
34 their three gates; **o** gate of Gad, one gate H259
34 **o** gate of Asher, one gate of Naphtali. H259
34 one gate of Asher, **o** gate of Naphtali. H259
Dan 2: 9 *there is but* **o** decree for you: for ye H2298
43 shall not cleave **o** to another, even as H1836
3:19 heat the furnace **o** seven times more H2298
4:13 an holy **o** came down from heaven; H6922
19 was astonied for **o** hour, and his H2298
23 and an holy **o** coming down from H6922
5: 6 and his knees smote **o** against another. H1668
7: 3 from the sea, diverse **o** from another. H1668
5 it raised up itself on **o** side, and *it had* H2298
13 I saw in the night visions, and, behold, *o*
16 I came near unto **o** of them that stood H2298
8: 3 *were* high; but **o** *was* higher than the H259
9 And out of **o** of them came forth a little H259
13 Then I heard **o** saint speaking, and H259
9:27 with many for **o** week: and in the midst H259
10:13 withstood me **o** and twenty days: but, H259
13 but, lo, Michael, **o** of the chief princes, H259
16 And, behold, *o* like the similitude of the
18 and touched me *o* like the appearance
11: 5 be strong, and *o* of his princes; and he
7 But out of a branch of her roots shall *o*
10 of great forces: and *o* shall certainly
27 shall speak lies at **o** table; but it shall not H259

Dan 12: 1 **o** that shall be found written in the book.
5 other two, the **o** on this side of the bank H259
6 And *o* said to the man clothed in linen,
Hos 1:11 themselves **o** head, and they shall H259
4: 3 land mourn, and every **o** that dwelleth
11: 9 not man; the Holy **O** in the midst of H6918
Joel 2: 7 shall march every **o** on his ways, and H376
8 Neither shall **o** thrust another; they shall H376
8 they shall walk every **o** in his path: and H1397
Am 3: 5 *is* for him? shall *o* take up a snare from
4: 7 it to rain upon **o** city, and caused it not H259
7 upon another city: **o** piece was rained H259
8 So two *or* three cities wandered unto **o** H259
6: 9 ten men in **o** house, that they shall die. H259
12 Shall horses run upon the rock? will *o*
8: 8 tremble for this, and every **o** mourn that
Oba 9 to the end that every **o** of the mount of H376
11 Jerusalem, even thou *wast* as **o** of them. H259
Jna 1: 7 And they said every **o** to his fellow, H376
3: 8 let them turn every **o** from his evil way, H376
Mic 2: 4 In that day shall *o* take up a parable
4: 5 For all people will walk every **o** in the H376
Nah 1:11 There is *o* come out of thee, that
2: 4 they shall justle **o** against another in the
Hab 1:12 God, mine Holy **O**? we shall not die. O H6918
3: 3 God came from Teman, and the Holy **O** H6918
Zep 2:11 worship him, every **o** from his place, H376
15 lie down in! every **o** that passeth by her
3: 9 the LORD, to serve him with **o** consent. H259
Hag 2: 1 In the seventh *month*, in the **o** and H259
12 If **o** bear holy flesh in the skirt of his H376
13 Then said Haggai, If *o that is* unclean by
16 Since those *days* were, when *o* came to
16 there were *but* ten: when *o* came to the
22 every **o** by the sword of his brother. H376
Zec 3: 9 Joshua; upon **o** stone *shall be* seven H259
9 the iniquity of that land in **o** day. H259
4: 3 And two olive trees by it, **o** upon the H259
5: 3 earth: for every **o** that stealeth shall be
3 to it; and every **o** that sweareth shall be
8:10 all men every **o** against his neighbour. H376
21 And the inhabitants of **o** *city* shall go to H259
10: 1 of rain, to every **o** grass in the field. H376
11: 6 the men every **o** into his neighbour's H376
7 me two staves; the **o** I called Beauty, and H259
8 Three shepherds also I cut off in **o** H259
9 the rest eat every **o** the flesh of another. H802
16 seek the young **o**, nor heal that that is H5289
12:10 mourn for him, as **o** mourneth for *his*
10 as **o** that is in bitterness for *his* firstborn.
13: 4 be ashamed every **o** of his vision, when H376
6 And *o* shall say unto him, What *are*
14: 7 But it shall be **o** day which shall be H259
9 there be **o** LORD, and his name one. H259
9 shall there be one LORD, and his name **o**. H259
13 shall lay hold every **o** on the hand of his H376
16 And it shall come to pass, *that* every **o**
Mal 2: 3 feasts; and **o** shall take you away with it.
10 Have we not all **o** father? hath not one H259
10 Have we not all one father? hath not **o** H259
15 And did not he make **o**? Yet had he the H259
15 And wherefore **o**? That he might seek a H259
16 putting away: for *o* covereth violence
17 ye say, Every **o** that doeth evil *is* good
3:16 LORD spake often **o** to another: and the H376
Mt 3: 3 The voice of **o** crying in the wilderness,
5:18 and earth pass, **o** jot or one tittle shall *G1520*
18 pass, one jot or **o** tittle shall in no wise *G3391*
19 Whosoever therefore shall break **o** of *G3391*
29 for thee that **o** of thy members should *G1520*
30 for thee that **o** of thy members should *G1520*
36 canst not make **o** hair white or black. *G3391*
6:24 he will hate the **o**, and love the other; *G1520*
24 he will hold to the **o**, and despise the *G1520*
27 can add **o** cubit unto his stature? *G1520*
29 glory was not arrayed like **o** of these. *G1520*
7: 8 For every **o** that asketh receiveth; and *G3956*
21 Not every **o** that saith unto me, Lord, *G3956*
26 And every **o** that heareth these sayings *G3956*
29 For he taught them as *o* having
10:29 a farthing? and **o** of them shall not fall *G1520*
42 give to drink unto **o** of these little ones *G1520*
12: 6 But I say unto you, That in this place is *o*
11 that shall have **o** sheep, and if it fall *G1520*
22 Then was brought unto him **o** possessed
29 Or else how can **o** enter into a strong *G5100*
47 Then **o** said unto him, Behold, thy *G5100*
13:19 When any **o** heareth the word of the *G3956*

Mt 13:19 cometh the wicked *o*, and catcheth away
38 the tares are the children of the wicked *o*;
46 Who, when he had found **o** pearl of G1520
16:14 others, Jeremias, or **o** of the prophets. G1520
17: 4 three tabernacles; **o** for thee, and one G3391
4 and **o** for Moses, and one for Elias. G3391
4 and one for Moses, and **o** for Elias. G3391
18: 5 And whoso shall receive **o** such little G1520
6 But whoso shall offend **o** of these little G1520
9 to enter into life with **o** eye, rather than G3442
10 Take heed that ye despise not **o** of G1520
12 sheep, and **o** of them be gone astray, G1520
14 that **o** of these little ones should perish. G1520
16 take with thee **o** or two more, that in G1520
24 And when he had begun to reckon, **o** G1520
28 out, and found **o** of his fellowservants, G1520
35 not every **o** his brother their trespasses. G1538
19: 5 wife: and they twain shall be **o** flesh? G1519
6 more twain, but **o** flesh. What therefore G3391
16 And, behold, **o** came and said unto G1520
17 *is* none good but **o**, *that is*, God: but if G1520
29 And every **o** that hath forsaken houses, G3956
20:12 Saying, These last have wrought *but* **o** G3391
13 But he answered **o** of them, and said, G1520
21 sons may sit, the **o** on thy right hand, G1520
21:24 I also will ask you **o** thing, which if ye G1520
35 his servants, and beat **o**, and killed G3739
22: 5 went their ways, **o** to his farm, another G3588
35 Then **o** of them, *which was* a lawyer, G1520
23: 4 not move them with **o** of their fingers.
8 But be not ye called Rabbi: for **o** is your G1520
9 for **o** is your Father, which is in heaven. G1520
10 Neither be ye called masters: for **o** is G1520
15 sea and land to make **o** proselyte, and G1520
24: 2 not be left here **o** stone upon another,
10 **o** another, and shall hate one another. G240
10 one another, and shall hate **o** another. G240
31 from **o** end of heaven to the other.
40 Then shall two be in the field; the **o** G1520
41 the **o** shall be taken, and the other left. G3391
25:15 And unto **o** he gave five talents, to G3739
15 two, and to another *o*; to every man G1520
18 But he that had received **o** went and G1520
24 Then he which had received the **o** G1520
29 For unto every **o** that hath shall be G3956
32 shall separate them **o** from another, as a G240
40 have done *it* unto **o** of the least of these G1520
45 as ye did *it* not to **o** of the least of these, G1520
26:14 Then **o** of the twelve, called Judas G1520
21 unto you, that **o** of you shall betray me. G1520
22 **o** of them to say unto him, Lord, is it I? G1538
40 could ye not watch with me **o** hour? G3391
47 And while he yet spake, lo, Judas, **o** of G1520
51 And, behold, **o** of them which were G1520
73 thou also art *o* of them; for thy speech
27:38 with him, **o** on the right hand, and G1520
48 And straightway **o** of them ran, and G1520
Mk 1: 3 The voice of **o** crying in the wilderness,
7 And preached, saying, There cometh **o**
22 he taught them as **o** that had authority,
24 thee who thou art, the Holy **O** of God. G40
2: 3 And they come unto him, bringing **o** sick
4:41 And they feared exceedingly, and said **o** G240
5:22 And, behold, there cometh **o** of the G1520
6:15 it is a prophet, or as **o** of the prophets. G1520
7:14 me every **o** *of you*, and understand: G3956
32 And they bring unto him **o** that was
8:14 in the ship with them more than **o** loaf. G1520
28 Elias; and others, **O** of the prophets. G1520
9: 5 three tabernacles; **o** for thee, and one G3391
5 and **o** for Moses, and one for Elias. G3391
5 and one for Moses, and **o** for Elias. G3391
10 questioning **o** with another what the
17 And **o** of the multitude answered and G1520
26 of him: and he was as **o** dead; insomuch
37 Whosoever shall receive **o** of such G1520
38 Master, we saw **o** casting out devils in G5100
42 And whosoever shall offend **o** of *these* G1520
47 of God with **o** eye, than having two G3442
49 For every **o** shall be salted with fire, G3956
50 and have peace **o** with another. G240
10: 8 And they twain shall be **o** flesh: so then G3391
8 they are no more twain, but **o** flesh. G3391
17 the way, there came **o** running, and G1520
18 *there is* none good but **o**, *that is*, God. G1520
21 said unto him, **O** thing thou lackest: G1520
37 us that we may sit, **o** on thy right hand, G1520
11:29 also ask of you **o** question, and answer G1520

Mk 12: 6 Having yet therefore **o** son, his G1520
28 And **o** of the scribes came, and having G1520
29 O Israel; The Lord our God is **o** Lord: G1520
32 **o** God; and there is none other but he: G1520
13: 1 And as he went out of the temple, **o** of G1520
2 shall not be left **o** stone upon another,
14:10 And Judas Iscariot, **o** of the twelve, G1520
18 I say unto you, **O** of you which eateth G1520
19 to say unto him **o** by one, *Is* it I? and G1520
19 by **o**, *Is* it I? and another *said*, *Is* it I? G1527
20 unto them, *It is* **o** of the twelve, that G1520
37 thou? couldest not thou watch **o** hour? G3391
43 cometh Judas, **o** of the twelve, and with G1520
47 And **o** of them that stood by drew a G1520
66 **o** of the maids of the high priest: G3391
69 to them that stood by, This is *o* of them.
70 Surely thou art *o* of them: for thou art
15: 6 **o** prisoner, whomsoever they desired. G1520
7 And there was *o* named Barabbas,
21 And they compel **o** Simon a Cyrenian, G5100
27 two thieves; the **o** on his right hand, G1520
36 And **o** ran and filled a spunge full of G1520
Lk 2: 3 And all went to be taxed, every **o** into G1538
15 the shepherds said **o** to another, Let us G240
36 And there was **o** Anna, a prophetess, the
3: 4 The voice of **o** crying in the wilderness,
16 you with water; but **o** mightier than I
4:34 thee who thou art; the Holy **O** of God. G40
40 on every **o** of them, and healed them. G1520
5: 3 And he entered into **o** of the ships, G1520
6: 9 I will ask you **o** thing; Is it lawful on G5100
11 and communed **o** with another what G240
29 And unto him that smiteth thee on the *o*
40 **o** that is perfect shall be as his master. G3956
7: 8 and I say unto **o**, Go, and he goeth; and G5129
32 and calling **o** to another, and saying, G240
36 And **o** of the Pharisees desired him that G5100
41 two debtors: the **o** owed five hundred G1520
8:25 wondered, saying **o** to another, What G240
42 For he had **o** only daughter, about
49 While he yet spake, there cometh **o** G5100
9: 8 **o** of the old prophets was risen again. G1520
19 **o** of the old prophets is risen again. G5100
33 three tabernacles; **o** for thee, and one G3391
33 one for thee, and **o** for Moses, and one G3391
33 **o** for Elias: not knowing what he said. G3391
43 wondered every **o** at all things which G3956
49 Master, we saw **o** casting out devils in G5100
10:42 But **o** thing is needful: and Mary hath G1520
11: 1 when he ceased, **o** of his disciples said G5100
4 also forgive every **o** that is indebted to G3956
10 For every **o** that asketh receiveth; and G3956
45 Then answered **o** of the lawyers, and G5100
46 not the burdens with **o** of your fingers. G1520
12: 1 that they trode **o** upon another, he began G240
6 not **o** of them is forgotten before God? G1520
13 And **o** of the company said unto him, G5100
25 thought can add to his stature **o** cubit? G1520
27 glory was not arrayed like **o** of these. G1520
52 shall be five in **o** house divided, three G1520
13:10 And he was teaching in **o** of the G3391
15 doth not each **o** of you on the sabbath G1538
23 Then said **o** unto him, Lord, are there G5100
14: 1 went into the house of **o** of the chief G5100
15 And when **o** of them that sat at meat G5100
18 And they all with **o** *consent* began to G3391
15: 4 sheep, if he lose **o** of them, doth not G1520
7 shall be in heaven over **o** sinner that G1520
8 silver, if she lose **o** piece, doth not light G3391
10 of God over **o** sinner that repenteth. G1520
19 make me as **o** of thy hired servants. G1520
26 And he called **o** of the servants, and G1520
16: 5 So he called every **o** of his lord's G1520
13 he will hate the **o**, and love the other; G1520
13 he will hold to the **o**, and despise the G1520
17 to pass, than **o** tittle of the law to fail. G3391
30 Abraham: but if **o** went unto them G5100
31 though **o** rose from the dead. G5100
17: 2 he should offend **o** of these little ones. G1520
15 And **o** of them, when he saw that he G1520
22 shall desire to see **o** of the days of the G3391
24 out of the **o** *part* under heaven, G3588
34 be two *men* in **o** bed; the one shall be G3391
34 in one bed; the **o** shall be taken, and G1520
35 the **o** shall be taken, and the other left. G3391
36 Two *men* shall be in the field; the **o** G1520
18:10 **o** a Pharisee, and the other a publican. G1520
14 other: for every **o** that exalteth himself G3956

Lk 18:19 good? none *is* good, save **o**, *that is*, God. G1520
22 Yet lackest thou **o** thing: sell all that thou
19:26 For I say unto you, That unto every **o** G3956
44 not leave in thee **o** stone upon another;
20: 1 And it came to pass, *that* on **o** of those G3391
3 also ask you **o** thing; and answer me: G1520
21: 6 shall not be left **o** stone upon another,
22:36 let him sell his garment, and buy **o**.
47 was called Judas, **o** of the twelve, went G1520
50 And **o** of them smote the servant of the G1520
59 And about the space of **o** hour after G3391
23:14 man unto me, as **o** that perverteth the
17 (For of necessity he must release **o** G1520
26 laid hold upon **o** Simon, a Cyrenian, G5100
33 the malefactors, **o** on the right hand, G3303
39 And **o** of the malefactors which were G1520
24:17 **o** to another, as ye walk, and are sad? G240
18 And the **o** of them, whose name was G1520
32 And they said **o** to another, Did not our G240
Jn 1:23 He said, I *am* the voice of **o** crying in the
26 **o** among you, whom ye know not; G2476
40 **O** of the two which heard John *speak*, G1520
3: 8 so is every **o** that is born of the Spirit. G3956
20 For every **o** that doeth evil hateth the G3956
4:33 Therefore said the disciples **o** to another, G240
37 And herein is that saying true, **O** soweth, G243
5:44 receive honour **o** of another, and seek G240
45 the Father: there is *o* that accuseth you,
6: 7 that every **o** of them may take a little. G1538
8 **O** of his disciples, Andrew, Simon G1520
22 boat there, save that **o** whereinto his G1520
40 me, that every **o** which seeth the Son, G3956
70 you twelve, and **o** of you is a devil? G1520
71 betray him, being **o** of the twelve. G1520
7:21 I have done **o** work, and ye all marvel. G1520
50 to Jesus by night, being **o** of them,) G1520
8: 9 went out **o** by one, beginning at G1520
9 went out one by **o**, beginning at the G1527
18 I am **o** that bear witness of myself, and
41 we have **o** Father, *even* God. G1520
50 And I seek not mine own glory: there is **o**
9:25 *or no*, I know not: **o** thing I know, that, G1520
32 the eyes of **o** that was born blind.
10:16 there shall be **o** fold, *and* one shepherd. G3391
16 there shall be one fold, *and* **o** shepherd. G1520
30 I and *my* Father are **o**. G1520
11:49 And **o** of them, *named* Caiaphas, being G1520
50 for us, that **o** man should die for G1520
52 gather together in **o** the children of God G1520
12: 2 **o** of them that sat at the table with him. G1520
4 Then saith **o** of his disciples, Judas G1520
48 my words, hath **o** that judgeth him: the
13:14 ye also ought to wash **o** another's feet. G240
21 unto you, that **o** of you shall betray me. G1520
22 Then the disciples looked **o** on another, G240
23 **o** of his disciples, whom Jesus loved. G1520
34 you, That ye love **o** another; as I have G240
34 loved you, that ye also love **o** another. G240
35 disciples, if ye have love **o** to another. G240
15:12 ye love **o** another, as I have loved you. G240
17 I command you, that ye love **o** another. G240
17:11 given me, that they may be **o**, as we *are*. G1520
21 That they all may be **o**; as thou, Father, G1520
21 they also may be **o** in us: that the world G1520
22 that they may be **o**, even as we are one: G1520
22 that they may be one, even as we are **o**: G1520
23 be made perfect in **o**; and that the world G1520
18:14 that **o** man should die for the people. G1520
17 Peter, Art not thou also *o* of this man's
22 And when he had thus spoken, **o** of the G1520
25 Art not thou also *o* of his disciples? He
26 **O** of the servants of the high priest, G1520
37 **o** that is of the truth heareth my voice. G3956
39 release unto you **o** at the passover: will G1520
19:18 on either side **o**, and Jesus in the midst. G1782
34 But **o** of the soldiers with a spear G1520
20:12 white sitting, the **o** at the head, and the G1520
24 But Thomas, **o** of the twelve, called G1520
21:25 be written every **o**, I suppose that even G2596
Act 1:14 These all continued with **o** accord in G3661
22 up from us, must **o** be ordained to be a G1520
2: 1 were all with **o** accord in one place. G3661
1 all with one accord in **o** place. G3858+G848
7 marvelled, saying **o** to another, Behold, G240
12 saying **o** to another, What meaneth this? G243
27 suffer thine Holy **O** to see corruption. G3741
38 be baptized every **o** of you in the name G1538
46 And they, continuing daily with **o** G3661

O

Act 3:14 But ye denied the Holy **O** and the Just, G40
26 away every **o** of you from his iniquities. G1538
4:24 voice to God with **o** accord, and said, G3661
32 that believed were of **o** heart and of one G3391
32 of one heart and of **o** soul: neither said G3391
5:12 all with **o** accord in Solomon's porch. G3661
16 spirits: and they were healed every **o**. G537
25 Then came **o** and told them, saying, G5100
34 Then stood there up **o** in the council, a G5100
7:24 And seeing **o** *of them* suffer wrong, he G5100
26 have set them at **o** again, saying, Sirs, G5151
26 brethren; why do ye wrong **o** to another? G240
52 coming of the Just **O**; of whom ye have G1342
57 ears, and ran upon him with **o** accord, G3661
8: 6 And the people with **o** accord gave G3661
9 out that himself was some great **o**: G3173
9:11 the house of Judas for *o* called Saul, of
43 days in Joppa with **o** Simon a tanner. G5100
10: 2 *A* devout *man*, and **o** that feared God
5 for *o* Simon, whose surname is Peter:
6 He lodgeth with **o** Simon a tanner, G5100
22 a just man, and **o** that feareth God, and
28 or come unto **o** of another nation; but
32 in the house of *o* Simon a tanner by the
11:28 And there stood up **o** of them named G1520
12:10 on through **o** street; and forthwith G3391
20 they came with **o** accord to him, and, G3661
13:25 there cometh **o** after me, whose shoes G2064
35 suffer thine Holy **O** to see corruption. G3741
15:25 being assembled with **o** accord, to send G3661
39 departed asunder **o** from the other: and G240
17: 7 that there is another king, *o* Jesus.
26 And hath made of **o** blood all nations G1520
27 though he be not far from every **o** of us: G1520
18: 7 named Justus, *o* that worshipped God,
12 insurrection with **o** accord against G3361
19: 9 daily in the school of **o** Tyrannus. G5100
14 And there were seven sons of *o* Sceva, a
29 rushed with **o** accord into the theatre. G3661
32 Some therefore cried **o** thing, and some G3303
34 he was a Jew, all with **o** voice about the G3391
38 deputies: let them implead **o** another. G240
20:31 warn every **o** night and day with tears. G1520
21: 6 And when we had taken our leave **o** of G240
7 brethren, and abode with them **o** day. G3391
8 was *o* of the seven; and abode with him.
16 with them **o** Mnason of Cyprus, G5100
26 should be offered for every **o** of them. G1520
34 And some cried **o** thing, some another,
22:12 And **o** Ananias, a devout man G5100
14 and see that Just **O**, and shouldest hear G1342
23: 6 But when Paul perceived that the **o** G1520
17 Then Paul called **o** of the centurions G1520
24:21 Except it be for this **o** voice, that I cried G3391
25:19 and of **o** Jesus, which was dead, G5100
27: 1 other prisoners unto *o* named Julius, a
2 by the coasts of Asia; *o* Aristarchus, a
28: 2 and received us every **o**, because of the G3956
13 and after **o** day the south wind G3391
25 Paul had spoken **o** word, Well spake G1520
Ro 1:16 salvation to every **o** that believeth; to G3956
27 in their lust **o** toward another; men G240
2:15 accusing or else excusing **o** another;) G240
28 For he is not a Jew, which is **o**
29 But he *is* a Jew, which is **o** inwardly; and
3:10 There is none righteous, no, not **o**: G1520
12 there is none that doeth good, no, not **o**. G2076
30 Seeing *it is* **o** God, which shall justify G1520
5: 7 For scarcely for a righteous man will **o** G5100
12 Wherefore, as by **o** man sin entered G1520
15 the offence of **o** many be dead, much G1520
15 grace, *which is* by **o** man, Jesus Christ, G1520
16 And not as *it was* by **o** that sinned, *so is* G1520
16 judgment *was* by **o** to condemnation, G1520
17 For if by **o** man's offence death reigned G1520
17 death reigned by **o**; much more they G1520
17 shall reign in life by **o**, Jesus Christ.) G1520
18 Therefore as by the offence of **o** G1520
18 righteousness of **o** *the free gift came* G1520
19 For as by **o** man's disobedience many G1520
19 of **o** shall many be made righteous. G1520
9:10 by **o**, *even* by our father Isaac; G1520
21 lump to make **o** vessel unto honour, G3739
10: 4 righteousness to every **o** that believeth. G3956
12: 4 For as we have many members in **o** G1520
5 So we, *being* many, are **o** body in G1520
5 and every **o** members one of another. G1520
5 and every one members **o** of another. G240
Ro 12:10 *Be* kindly affectioned **o** to another with G240
10 love; in honour preferring **o** another; G240
16 *Be* of the same mind **o** toward another. G240
13: 8 Owe no man any thing, but to love **o** G240
14: 2 For **o** believeth that he may eat all G3739
5 **O** man esteemeth one day G3739+G3303
5 One man esteemeth **o** day above
12 So then every **o** of us shall give account G1538
13 Let us not therefore judge **o** another any G240
19 things wherewith **o** may edify another. G240
15: 2 Let every **o** of us please *his* neighbour G1538
5 you to be likeminded **o** toward another G240
6 That ye may with **o** mind *and* one G3661
6 That ye may with one mind *and* **o** G1520
7 Wherefore receive ye **o** another, as G240
14 able also to admonish **o** another. G240
16:16 Salute **o** another with an holy kiss. The G240
1Co 1:12 Now this I say, that every **o** of you G1538
3: 4 For while **o** saith, I am of Paul; and G5100
8 he that watereth are **o**: and every man G1520
4: 6 is written, that no **o** of you be puffed up G1520
6 you be puffed up for **o** against another. G1520
5: 1 that **o** should have his father's wife. G5100
5 To deliver such an **o** unto Satan for the G5108
11 with such an **o** no not to eat. G5108
6: 5 you? no, not **o** that shall be able to G1520
7 ye go to law **o** with another. Why G1438
16 to an harlot is **o** body? for two, saith G1520
16 body? for two, saith he, shall be **o** flesh. G3391
17 But he that is joined unto the Lord is **o** G1520
7: 5 Defraud ye not **o** the other, except *it be* G240
7 proper gift of God, **o** after this manner, G3739
17 hath called every **o**, so let him walk. G1538
25 my judgment, as **o** that hath obtained
8: 4 and that *there is* none other God but **o**. G1520
6 But to us *there is but* **o** God, the Father, G1520
6 we in him; and **o** Lord Jesus Christ, by G1520
9:24 a race run all, but **o** receiveth the prize? G1520
26 so fight I, not as **o** that beateth the air:
10: 8 in **o** day three and twenty thousand. G3391
17 For we *being* many are **o** bread, *and* G1520
17 one bread, *and* **o** body: for we are all G1520
17 for we are all partakers of that **o** bread. G1520
11: 5 that is even all **o** as if she were shaven. G1520
20 When ye come together therefore into **o**
21 For in eating every **o** taketh G3588+G846
21 supper: and **o** is hungry, and G3739+G3303
33 come together to eat, tarry **o** for another. G240
12: 8 For to **o** is given by the Spirit G3739+G3303
11 But all these worketh that **o** and the G1520
12 For as the body is **o**, and hath many G1520
12 members of that **o** body, being many, G1520
12 many, are **o** body: so also *is* Christ. G1520
13 For by **o** Spirit are we all baptized into G1520
13 all baptized into **o** body, whether *we be* G1520
13 been all made to drink into **o** Spirit. G1520
14 For the body is not **o** member, but G1520
18 members every **o** of them in the body, G1520
19 And if they were all **o** member, where G1520
20 *they* many members, yet but **o** body. G1520
25 should have the same care **o** for another. G240
26 And whether **o** member suffer, all the G1520
26 suffer with it; or **o** member be G1520
14:23 together into **o** place, and all G3588+846
24 But if all prophesy, and there come in **o** G5100
24 that believeth not, or *o* unlearned, he is
26 together, every **o** of you hath a psalm, G1538
27 and *that* by course; and let **o** interpret. G1520
31 For ye may all prophesy **o** by one, that
31 For ye may all prophesy one by **o**, that G2596
15: 8 of me also, as of **o** born out of due time.
39 flesh: but *there is* **o** *kind of* flesh of men, G243
40 of the celestial *is* **o**, and the *glory* of the G2087
41 *There is* **o** glory of the sun, and another G243
41 of the stars: for *o* star differeth from
16: 2 the week let every **o** of you lay by him G1538
16 **o** that helpeth with *us*, and laboureth. G3956
20 All the brethren greet you. Greet ye **o** G240
2Co 2: 7 perhaps such a **o** should be swallowed G5108
16 To the **o** *we are* the savour of death G3739
5:10 of Christ; that every **o** may receive the G1538
14 that if **o** died for all, then were all dead: G1520
10:11 Let such an **o** think this, that, such as G5108
11: 2 espoused you to **o** husband, that I may G1520
24 five times received I forty *stripes* save **o**. G3391
12: 2 an **o** caught up to the third heaven. G5108
5 Of such an **o** will I glory: yet of myself I G5108
13:11 comfort, be of **o** mind, live in peace; G846
2Co 13:12 Greet **o** another with an holy kiss. G240
Gal 3:10 Cursed *is* every **o** that continueth not G3956
13 *is* every **o** that hangeth on a tree: G3956
16 as of **o**, And to thy seed, which is Christ. G1520
20 Now a mediator is not *a mediator* of **o**, G1520
20 is not *a mediator* of one, but God is **o**. G1520
28 female: for ye are all **o** in Christ Jesus. G1520
4:22 had two sons, the **o** by a bondmaid, the G1520
24 covenants; the **o** from the mount Sinai, G3391
5:13 to the flesh, but by love serve **o** another. G240
14 For all the law is fulfilled in **o** word, G1520
15 But if ye bite and devour **o** another, take G240
15 that ye be not consumed **o** of another. G240
17 are contrary the **o** to the other: so that G240
26 **o** another, envying one another. G240
26 one another, envying **o** another.
6: 1 restore such an **o** in the spirit of G5108
2 Bear ye **o** another's burdens, and so G240
Eph 1:10 gather together in **o** all things in Christ, G346
2:14 hath made both **o**, and hath broken G1520
15 of twain **o** new man, *so* making peace; G1520
16 both unto God in **o** body by the cross, G1520
18 have access by **o** Spirit unto the Father. G1520
4: 2 forbearing **o** another in love; G240
4 *There is* **o** body, and one Spirit, even as G1520
4 *There is* one body, and **o** Spirit, even as G1520
4 ye are called in **o** hope of your calling; G3391
5 **O** Lord, one faith, one baptism, G1520
5 One Lord, **o** faith, one baptism, G3391
5 One Lord, one faith, **o** baptism, G1520
6 **O** God and Father of all, who *is* above G1520
7 But unto every **o** of us is given grace G1520
25 for we are members **o** of another. G240
32 And be ye kind **o** to another, G240
32 forgiving **o** another, even as God G1438
5:21 Submitting yourselves **o** to another in G240
31 his wife, and they two shall be **o** flesh. G3391
33 Nevertheless let every **o** of you in G1538
Php 1:16 The **o** preach Christ of contention, not G3588
27 ye stand fast in **o** spirit, with one mind G1520
27 fast in one spirit, with **o** mind striving G3391
2: 2 love, *being* of **o** accord, of one mind. G4861
2 *being* of one accord, of **o** mind. G3888+G1520
3:13 but *this* **o** thing *I do*, forgetting G1520
Col 3: 9 Lie not **o** to another, seeing that ye have G240
13 Forbearing **o** another, and forgiving one G240
13 and forgiving **o** another, if any man G1438
15 called in **o** body; and be ye thankful. G1520
16 and admonishing **o** another in psalms G1438
4: 9 brother, who is *o* of you. They shall
12 Epaphras, who is *o* of you, a servant of
1Th 2:11 **o** of you, as a father *doth* his children, G1520
3:12 abound in love **o** toward another, and G240
4: 4 That every **o** of you should know how G1538
9 are taught of God to love **o** another. G240
18 Wherefore comfort **o** another with these G240
5:11 and edify **o** another, even as also ye do. G1520
2Th 1: 3 the charity of every **o** of you all toward G1520
1Ti 2: 5 For *there is* **o** God, and one mediator G1520
5 For *there is* one God, and **o** mediator G1520
3: 2 the husband of **o** wife, vigilant, sober, G3391
4 **O** that ruleth well his own house, having
12 Let the deacons be the husbands of **o** G3391
5: 9 old, having been the wife of **o** man, G1520
21 without preferring **o** before another,
2Ti 2:19 And, Let every **o** that nameth the name G3956
Tit 1: 6 If any be blameless, the husband of **o** G3391
12 **O** of themselves, *even* a prophet of G5100
3: 3 and envy, hateful, *and* hating **o** another. G240
Phlm 9 being such an **o** as Paul the aged, and G5108
Heb 2: 6 But **o** in a certain place testified, G5100
11 *are* all of **o**: for which cause he is G1520
3:13 But exhort **o** another daily, while it is G1438
5:12 ye have need that **o** teach you again
13 For every **o** that useth milk *is* unskilful G3956
6:11 And we desire that every **o** of you do G1538
10:12 But this man, after he had offered **o** G3391
14 For by **o** offering he hath perfected for G3391
24 And let us consider **o** another to provoke G240
25 *is*; but exhorting *o another*: and so much
11:12 Therefore sprang there even of **o**, and G1520
12:16 for **o** morsel of meat sold his birthright. G3391
13:14 continuing city, but we seek **o** to come. G3588
Jas 2:10 yet offend in **o** *point*, he is guilty of all. G1520
16 And **o** of you say unto them, Depart in G5100
19 Thou believest that there is **o** God; thou G1520
4:11 Speak not evil **o** of another, brethren. He G240
12 There is **o** lawgiver, who is able to save G1520

Jas 5: 9 Grudge not o against another, brethren, G240
16 Confess your faults o to another, and G240
16 another, and pray o for another, that ye G240
19 err from the truth, and o convert him; G5100
1Pt 1:22 o another with a pure heart fervently: G240
3: 8 Finally, be ye all of o mind, having G3675
8 having compassion o of another, love as
4: 9 Use hospitality o to another without G240
10 so minister the same o to another, as G1438
5: 5 all of you be subject o to another, and be G240
14 Greet ye o another with a kiss of charity. G240
2Pt 3: 8 But, beloved, be not ignorant of this o G3675
8 one thing, that o day is with the Lord G3391
8 years, and a thousand years as o day. G3391
1Jn 1: 7 we have fellowship o with another, and G3391
2:13 the wicked o. I write unto you, little G4190
14 and ye have overcome the wicked o. G4190
20 But ye have an unction from the Holy O, G40
29 ye know that every o that doeth G3956
3:11 that we should love o another. G240
12 Not as Cain, who was of that wicked o, G4190
23 o another, as he gave us commandment. G240
4: 7 Beloved, let us love o another: for love is G240
7 of God; and every o that loveth is born G3956
11 us, we ought also to love o another. G240
12 time. If we love o another, God dwelleth G240
5: 1 of God: and every o that loveth him G3956
7 the Holy Ghost: and these three are o. G1520
8 the blood: and these three agree in o. G1520
18 and that wicked o toucheth him not. G4190
2Jn 5 the beginning, that we love o another. G240
Rev 1:13 seven candlesticks o like unto the Son of
2:23 every o of you according to your works. G1538
4: 2 set in heaven, and o sat on the throne.
5: 5 And o of the elders saith unto me, G1520
8 having every o of them harps, and
6: 1 And I saw when the Lamb opened o of G3391
1 noise of thunder, o of the four beasts G1520
4 they should kill o another: and there was G240
11 And white robes were given unto every o
7:13 And o of the elders answered, saying G1520
9:12 O woe is past; and, behold, there come G3391
11:10 shall send gifts o to another; because G240
13: 3 And I saw o of his heads as it were G3391
14:14 upon the cloud o sat like unto the Son
15: 7 And o of the four beasts gave unto the G1520
17: 1 And there came o of the seven angels G1520
10 are fallen, and o is, and the other is not G1520
12 power as kings o hour with the beast. G3391
13 These have o mind, and shall give their G3391
18: 8 Therefore shall her plagues come in o G3391
10 for in o hour is thy judgment come. G3391
17 For in o hour so great riches is come to G3391
19 for in o hour is she made desolate. G3391
21: 9 And there came unto me o of the seven G1520
21 gate was of o pearl: and the street G1520

ONES

Gen 34:29 and all their little o, and their wives H2945
43: 8 both we, and thou, and also our little o. H2945
45:19 for your little o, and for your wives, H2945
46: 5 and their little o, and their wives, in the H2945
47:24 and for food for your little o. H2945
50: 8 only their little o, and their flocks, and H2945
21 you, and your little o. And he comforted H2945
Ex 10:10 little o: look to it; for evil is before you. H2945
24 let your little o also go with you. H2945
Nu 14:31 But your little o, which ye said should H2945
31: 9 and their little o, and took the spoil of H2945
17 male among the little o, and kill every H2945
32:16 for our cattle, and cities for our little o: H2945
17 and our little o shall dwell in the fenced H2945
24 Build you cities for your little o, and H2945
26 Our little o, our wives, our flocks, and H2945
Dt 1:39 Moreover your little o, which ye said H2945
2:34 o, of every city, we left none to remain: H2945
3:19 But your wives, and your little o, and H2945
20:14 But the women, and the little o, and the H2945
22: 6 they be young o, or eggs, and the dam
29:11 Your little o, your wives, and thy H2945
Jos 1:14 Your wives, your little o, and your H2945
8:35 and the little o, and the strangers that H2945
Jdg 5:22 the pransings of their mighty o. H47
18:21 and put the little o and the cattle and H2945
2Sa 15:22 and all the little o that were with him. H2945
1Ch 16:13 ye children of Jacob, his chosen o. H972
2Ch 20:13 little o, their wives, and their children. H2945
31:18 And to the genealogy of all their little o, H2945

Ezr 8:21 our little o, and for all our substance. H2945
Est 8:11 them, both little o and women, and to H2945
Job 21:11 They send forth their little o like a H5759
38:41 when his young o cry unto God, they H3206
39: 3 young o, they cast out their sorrows. H3206
4 Their young o are in good liking, they H1121
16 She is hardened against her young o, as H1121
30 Her young o also suck up blood: and
Ps 10:10 that the poor may fall by his strong o. H6099
83: 3 and consulted against thy hidden o. H6845
137: 9 dasheth thy little o against the stones. H5768
Prv 1:22 How long, ye simple o, will ye love H6612
7: 7 And beheld among the simple o, I H6612
Isa 5:17 places of the fat o shall strangers eat. H4220
10:16 send among his fat o leanness; and
33 and the high o of stature shall be hewn H7311
11: 7 shall feed; their young o shall lie down H3206
13: 3 I have commanded my sanctified o, I H6942
3 called my mighty o for mine anger, H1368
14: 9 even all the chief o of the earth; it hath H6260
24:21 host of the high o that are on high, and H4791
25: 4 terrible o is as a storm against the wall. H6184
5 of the terrible o shall be brought low. H6184
29: 5 of the terrible o shall be as chaff that H6184
32:11 ye careless o: strip you, and make H982
33: 7 Behold, their valiant o shall cry without: H691
57:15 and to revive the heart of the contrite o. H1792
Jer 2:33 thou also taught the wicked o thy ways. H7451
8:16 of his strong o; for they are come, and H47
14: 3 And their nobles have sent their little o H6810
46: 5 and their mighty o are beaten down, H1368
48: 4 Moab is destroyed; her little o have H6810
45 crown of the head of the tumultuous o. H1121
Lam 4: 3 to their young o: the daughter of my H1482
Dan 4:17 word of the holy o: to the intent that the H6922
8: 8 o toward the four winds of heaven. H2380
11:17 and upright o with him; thus shall H3477
Joel 3:11 thy mighty o to come down, O LORD. H1368
Zec 4:14 the two anointed o, that stand by the H1121
13: 7 I will turn mine hand upon the little o. H6819
Mt 10:42 one of these little o a cup of cold water G3398
18: 6 one of these little o which believe in G3398
10 one of these little o; for I say unto you, G3398
14 that one of these little o should perish. G3398
Mk 9:42 one of these little o that believe in me, G3398
10:42 great o exercise authority upon them. G3173
Lk 17: 2 he should offend one of these little o. G3398

ONE'S

Ecc 7: 1 the day of death than the day of o birth.
Act 16:26 and every o bands were loosed. G3956

ONESIMUS

Col 4: 9 With O, a faithful and beloved brother, G3682
Phlm 10 I beseech thee for my son O, whom I G3682

ONESIPHORUS

2Ti 1:16 unto the house of O; for he oft refreshed G3683
4:19 and Aquila, and the household of O. G3683

ONI See BEN-ONI.

ONIONS

Nu 11: 5 the leeks, and the o, and the garlick: H1211

ONLY

Gen 6: 5 of his heart was o evil continually. H7535
7:23 earth: and Noah o remained alive, and H389
14:24 Save o that which the young men have
19: 8 good in your eyes: o unto these men do
22: 2 And he said, Take now thy son, thine o H3173
12 withheld thy son, thine o son from me. H3173
16 hast not withheld thy son, thine o son: H3173
24: 8 oath: o bring not my son thither again.
27:13 o obey my voice, and go fetch me them.
34:22 O herein will the men consent unto us H389
23 of theirs be ours? o let us consent unto H389
41:40 people be ruled: o in the throne will I H7535
47:22 O the land of the priests bought he not; H7535
26 priests o, which became not Pharaoh's. H905
50: 8 his father's house: o their little ones, H7535
Ex 8: 9 that they may remain in the river o?
11 people; they shall remain in the river o. H7535
28 in the wilderness; o ye shall not go very
9:26 O in the land of Goshen, where the H7535
10:17 I pray thee, my sin o this once, and
17 he may take away from me this death o.
24 ye, serve the LORD; o let your flocks and

Ex 12:16 must eat, that o may be done of you.
21:19 him be quit: o he shall pay for the H7535
22:20 the LORD o, he shall be utterly destroyed. H905
27 For that is his covering o, it is his H905
Lev 21:23 O he shall not go in unto the vail, nor H389
27:26 O the firstling of the beasts, which H389
Nu 1:49 O thou shalt not number the tribe of H389
12: 2 indeed spoken o by Moses? hath he not H7535
14: 9 O rebel not ye against the LORD, neither H389
18: 3 all the tabernacle: o they shall not come H389
20:19 pay for it: I will o, without doing any H7535
22:35 with the men: but o the word that I shall H657
31:22 O the gold, and the silver, the brass, the H389
36: 6 they think best; o to the family of the H389
Dt 2:28 drink: o I will pass through on my feet; H7535
35 O the cattle we took for a prey unto H7535
37 O unto the land of the children of H7535
3:11 For o Og king of Bashan remained of H7535
4: 9 O take heed to thyself, and keep thy H7535
12 saw no similitude; o ye heard a voice. H2108
8: 3 not live by bread o, but by every word H905
10:15 O the LORD had a delight in thy fathers H7535
12:16 O ye shall not eat the blood; ye shall H7535
23 O be sure that thou eat not the blood: H7535
26 O thy holy things which thou hast, and H7535
15: 5 O if thou carefully hearken unto the H7535
23 O thou shalt not eat the blood thereof; H7535
20:20 O the trees which thou knowest that H7535
22:25 the man o that lay with her shall die: H905
28:13 shalt be above o, and thou shalt not be H7535
29 ways: and thou shalt be o oppressed and H389
33 shalt be o oppressed and crushed alway:
29:14 Neither with you o do I make this H905
Jos 1: 7 O be thou strong and very courageous, H7535
17 unto thee: o the LORD thy God be H7535
18 o be strong and of a good courage. H7535
6:15 manner seven times: o on that day they H7535
17 to the LORD: o Rahab the harlot shall H7535
24 that was therein: o the silver, and the H7535
8: 2 and her king: o the spoil thereof, and H7535
27 O the cattle and the spoil of that city H7535
11:13 save Hazor o; that did Joshua burn. H905
22 children of Israel: o in Gaza, in Gath, H7535
13: 6 children of Israel: o divide thou it by lot H7535
14 O unto the tribe of Levi he gave none H7535
17:17 power: thou shalt not have one lot o:
Jdg 3: 2 O that the generations of the children H7535
6:37 be on the fleece o, and it be dry upon all H905
39 let it now be dry o upon the fleece, and H905
40 o, and there was dew on all the ground. H905
10:15 thee; deliver us o, we pray thee, this day. H389
11:34 and she was his o child; beside her he H3173
16:28 me, I pray thee, o this once, O God, that H389
19:20 lie upon me; o lodge not in the street. H7535
1Sa 1:13 Now Hannah, she spake in her heart; o H7535
23 have weaned him; o the LORD establish H389
5: 4 o the stump of Dagon was left to him. H7535
7: 3 and serve him o: and he will deliver you H905
4 and Ashtaroth, and served the LORD o. H905
12:24 O fear the LORD, and serve him in truth H389
18:17 I give thee to wife: o be thou valiant for H389
20:14 And thou shalt not o while yet I live
39 But the lad knew not any thing: o H389
2Sa 13:32 sons; for Amnon o is dead: for by the H905
33 sons are dead: for Amnon o is dead. H905
17: 2 him shall flee; and I will smite the king o: H905
20:21 David: deliver him o, and I will depart
23:10 the people returned after him o to spoil. H389
1Ki 3: 2 O the people sacrificed in high places, H7535
3 of David his father: o he sacrificed and H7535
4:19 was the o officer which was in the land. H259
8:39 thou, even thou o, knowest the hearts of H905
12:20 house of David, but the tribe of Judah o. H905
14: 8 do that o which was right in mine eyes; H7535
13 and bury him: for he o of Jeroboam shall H905
15: 5 o in the matter of Uriah the Hittite. H7535
18:22 people, I, even I o, remain a prophet of H905
19:10 and I, even I o, am left; and they seek H905
14 and I, even I o, am left; and they seek H905
22:31 nor great, save o with the king of Israel. H905
2Ki 3:25 all the good trees: o in Kir-haraseth left
10:23 the LORD, but the worshippers of Baal o. H905
17:18 was none left but the tribe of Judah o. H905
19:19 that thou art the LORD God, even thou o. H905
21: 8 gave their fathers; o if they will observe H7535
1Ch 22:12 O the LORD give thee wisdom and
2Ch 2: 6 save o to burn sacrifice before him? H518
6:30 knowest; (for thou o knowest the hearts

O

2Ch 18:30 or great, save o with the king of Israel. H905
33:17 places, *yet* unto the LORD their God o. H7535
Ezr 10:15 O Jonathan the son of Asahel and H389
Est 1:16 wrong to the king o, but also to all the H905
Job 1:12 *is* in thy power; o upon himself put not H3535
15 and I o am escaped alone to tell thee. H7535
16 and I o am escaped alone to tell thee. H7535
17 and I o am escaped alone to tell thee. H7535
19 and I o am escaped alone to tell thee. H7535
13:20 O do not two *things* unto me: then will I H389
34:29 against a nation, or against a man o: H3162
Ps 4: 8 LORD, o makest me dwell in safety. H910
51: 4 Against thee, thee o, have I sinned, and H905
62: 2 He o *is* my rock and my salvation; *he is* H389
4 They o consult to cast *him* down from H389
5 My soul, wait thou o upon God; for my H389
6 He o *is* my rock and my salvation: *he is* H389
71:16 of thy righteousness, *even* of thine o. H905
72:18 of Israel, who o doeth wondrous things. H905
91: 8 O with thine eyes shalt thou behold H7535
Prv 4: 3 For I was my father's son, tender and o H3173
5:17 Let them be o thine own, and not
11:23 The desire of the righteous *is* o good: *but* H389
13:10 O by pride cometh contention: but with H7535
14:23 the talk of the lips *tendeth* o to penury. H389
17:11 An evil *man* seeketh o rebellion: H389
21: 5 The thoughts of the diligent *tend* o to H389
5 but of every one *that is* hasty o to want. H389
Ecc 7:29 Lo, this o have I found, that God hath H905
Song 6: 9 *but* one; she *is* the o one of her mother,
Isa 4: 1 our own apparel: o let us be called by H7535
26:13 o will we make mention of thy name. H905
28:19 a vexation o *to* understand the report. H7535
37:20 that thou *art* the LORD, *even* thou o. H905
Jer 3:13 O acknowledge thine iniquity, that thou H389
6:26 mourning, *as for* an o son, most bitter H3173
32:30 of Judah have o done evil before me H389
30 of Israel have o provoked me to anger H389
Ezk 7: 5 Thus saith the Lord GOD; An evil, an o H259
14:16 daughters; they o shall be delivered, but H905
18 but they o shall be delivered themselves. H905
44:20 grow long; they shall o poll their heads. H3697
Am 3: 2 You o have I known of all the families H7535
8:10 the mourning of an o *son*, and the end H3173
Zec 12:10 mourneth for *his* o *son*, and shall be in H3173
Mt 4:10 thy God, and him o shalt thou serve. G3441
5:47 And if ye salute your brethren o, what G3440
8: 8 word o, and my servant shall be healed. G3440
10:42 a cup of cold *water* o in the name of a G3440
12: 4 were with him, but o for the priests? G3441
14:36 And besought him that they might o G3440
17: 8 eyes, they saw no man, save Jesus o. G3441
21:19 but leaves o, and said unto it, Let G3440
21 not, ye shall not o do this *which is done* G3440
24:36 the angels of heaven, but my Father o. G3441
Mk 2: 7 who can forgive sins but God o? G1520
5:36 the synagogue, Be not afraid, o believe. G3440
6: 8 save a staff o; no scrip, no bread, G3440
9: 8 more, save Jesus o with themselves. G3441
Lk 4: 8 thy God, and him o shalt thou serve. G3441
7:12 carried out, the o son of his mother, G3439
8:42 For he had one o daughter, about G3439
50 believe o, and she shall be made whole. G3440
9:38 upon my son: for he is mine o child. G3439
24:18 unto him, Art thou o a stranger in G3441
Jn 1:14 the glory as of the o begotten of the G3439
18 at any time; the o begotten Son, which G3439
3:16 that he gave his o begotten Son, that G3439
18 the name of the o begotten Son of God. G3439
5:18 him, because he not o had broken the G3440
44 not the honour that *cometh* from God o? G3441
11:52 And not for that nation o, but that also G3440
12: 9 came not for Jesus' sake o, but that they G3440
13: 9 feet o, but also *my* hands and *my* head. G3440
17: 3 know thee the o true God, and Jesus G3441
Act 8:16 none of them: o they were baptized G3440
11:19 the word to none but unto the Jews o. G3440
18:25 Lord, knowing o the baptism of John. G3440
19:27 So that not o this our craft is in danger G3440
21:13 not to be bound o, but also to die at G3440
25 no such thing, save o that they keep G1508
26:29 to God, that not o thou, but also all that G3440
27:10 damage, not o of the lading and ship, G3440
Ro 1:32 of death, not o do the same, but have G3440
3:29 *Is he* the God of the Jews o? *is he* not G3440
4: 9 upon the circumcision *o*, or upon the
12 the circumcision o, but who also walk G3440
16 seed; not to that o which is of the law, G3440
Ro 5: 3 And not o *so*, but we glory in G3440
11 And not o *so*, but we also joy in God G3440
8:23 And not o *they*, but ourselves also, G3440
9:10 And not o *this*; but when Rebecca also G3440
24 of the Jews o, but also of the Gentiles? G3440
13: 5 be subject, not o for wrath, but also for G3440
16: 4 unto whom not o I give thanks, but G3441
27 To God o wise, *be* glory through Jesus G3441
1Co 7:39 to whom she will; o in the Lord. G3440
9: 6 Or I o and Barnabas, have not we G3441
14:36 out from you? or came it unto you o? G3441
15:19 If in this life o we have hope in Christ, G3440
2Co 7: 7 And not by his coming o, but by the G3440
8:10 begun before, not o to do, but also to G3440
19 And not *that* o, but who was also G3440
21 Providing for honest things, not o in G3440
9:12 of this service not o supplieth the want G3440
Gal 1:23 But they had heard o, That he which G3440
2:10 O *they would* that we should remember G3440
3: 2 This o would I learn of you, Received G3440
4:18 and not o when I am present with you. G3440
5:13 unto liberty; o *use* not liberty for an G3440
6:12 to be circumcised; o lest they should G3440
Eph 1:21 that is named, not o in this world, but G3440
Php 1:27 O let your conversation be as it G3440
29 of Christ, not o to believe on him, but G3440
2:12 not as in my presence o, but now much G3440
27 and not on him o, but on me also, lest G3440
4:15 giving and receiving, but ye o. G3441
Col 4:11 These o *are my* fellowworkers G3441
1Th 1: 5 unto you in word o, but also in power, G3440
8 of the Lord not o in Macedonia and G3440
2: 8 the gospel of God o, but also our own G3440
2Th 2: 7 already work: o he who now letteth G3440
1Ti 1:17 invisible, the o wise God, *be* honour G3441
5:13 to house; and not o idle, but tattlers G3440
6:15 *is* the blessed and o Potentate, the King G3441
16 Who o hath immortality, dwelling in G3441
2Ti 2:20 But in a great house there are not o G3440
4: 8 and not to me o, but unto all them also G3440
11 O Luke is with me. Take Mark, and G3441
Heb 9:10 *Which stood* o in meats and drinks, G3440
11:17 promises offered up his o begotten *son*, G3439
12:26 I shake not the earth o, but also heaven. G3440
Jas 1:22 hearers o, deceiving your own selves. G3440
2:24 a man is justified, and not by faith o. G3440
1Pt 2:18 with all fear; not o to the good and G3440
1Jn 2: 2 and not for ours o, but also for *the sins* G3440
4: 9 that God sent his o begotten Son into G3439
5: 6 not by water o, but by water and blood. G3440
2Jn 1 truth; and not I o, but also all they that G3441
Jude 4 o Lord God, and our Lord Jesus Christ. G3441
25 To the o wise God our Saviour, *be* glory G3441
Rev 9: 4 any tree; but o those men which have G3441
15: 4 thy name? for *thou* o *art* holy: for all G3441

ONLY-BEGOTTEN See ONLY and BEGOTTEN.

ONO
1Ch 8:12 built O, and Lod, with the towns thereof: H207
Ezr 2:33 The children of Lod, Hadid, and O, seven H207
Neh 6: 2 of O. But they thought to do me mischief. H207
7:37 The children of Lod, Hadid, and O, seven H207
11:35 Lod, and O, the valley of craftsmen. H207

ONWARD
Ex 40:36 of Israel went o in all their journeys: H5265

ONYCHA
Ex 30:34 spices, stacte, and o, and galbanum; H7827

ONYX
Gen 2:12 good: there *is* bdellium and the o stone. H7718
Ex 25: 7 O stones, and stones to be set in the H7718
28: 9 And thou shalt take two o stones, and H7718
20 And the fourth row a beryl, and an o, H7718
35: 9 And o stones, and stones to be set for H7718
27 And the rulers brought o stones, and H7718
39: 6 And they wrought o stones inclosed in H7718
13 And the fourth row, a beryl, an o, and a H7718
1Ch 29: 2 *things* of wood; o stones, and *stones* to H7718
Job 28:16 with the precious o, or the sapphire. H7718
Ezk 28:13 the beryl, the o, and the jasper, the H7718

OPEN
Gen 1:20 the earth in the o firmament of heaven. H6440
38:14 and sat in an o place, which *is* by the H5869
Ex 21:33 And if a man shall o a pit, or if a man H6605
Lev 14: 7 let the living bird loose into the o field. H6440
53 of the city into the o fields, and make H6440
17: 5 they offer in the o field, even that they H6440
Nu 8:16 instead of such as o every womb, *even* H6363
16:30 thing, and the earth o her mouth, and H6475
19:15 And every o vessel, which hath no H6605
16 a sword in the o fields, or a dead body, H6440
24: 3 the man whose eyes are o hath said: H8365
4 *into a trance,* but having his eyes o: H1540
15 the man whose eyes are o hath said: H8365
16 *into a trance,* but having his eyes o: H1540
Dt 15: 8 But thou shalt o thine hand wide unto H6605
11 saying, Thou shalt o thine hand wide H6605
20:11 of peace, and o unto thee, then it shall H6605
28:12 The LORD shall o unto thee his good H6605
Jos 8:17 left the city o, and pursued after Israel. H6605
10:22 Then said Joshua, O the mouth of the H6605
1Sa 3: 1 in those days; *there was* no o vision. H6555
2Sa 11:11 encamped in the o fields; shall I then H6440
1Ki 6:18 with knops and o flowers: all *was* H6358
29 and o flowers, within and without. H6358
32 palm trees and o flowers, and overlaid H6358
35 palm trees and o flowers: and covered H6358
8:29 That thine eyes may be o toward this H6605
52 That thine eyes may be o unto the H6605
2Ki 6:17 I pray thee, o his eyes, that he may H6491
20 said, LORD, o the eyes of these *men*, H6491
9: 3 o the door, and flee, and tarry not. H6605
13:17 And he said, O the window eastward. H6605
19:16 ear, and hear: o, LORD, thine eyes, and H6491
2Ch 6:20 That thine eyes may be o upon this H6605
40 thee, thine eyes be o, and *let* thine ears H6605
7:15 Now mine eyes shall be o, and mine H6605
Neh 1: 6 and thine eyes o, that thou mayest hear H6605
6: 5 fifth time with an o letter in his hand; H6605
Job 11: 5 But oh that God would speak, and o his H6605
14: 3 And dost thou o thine eyes upon such H6491
32:20 refreshed: I will o my lips and answer. H6605
34:26 as wicked men in the o sight of others; H4725
35:16 Therefore doth Job o his mouth in vain; H6475
41:14 Who can o the doors of his face? his H6605
Ps 5: 9 their throat *is* an o sepulchre; they H6605
34:15 and his ears *are* o unto their cry.
49: 4 I will o my dark saying upon the harp. H6605
51:15 O Lord, o thou my lips; and my mouth H6605
78: 2 I will o my mouth in a parable: I will H6605
81:10 Egypt: o thy mouth wide, and I will fill it.
118:19 O to me the gates of righteousness: I H6605
119:18 O thou mine eyes, that I may behold H1540
Prv 13:16 knowledge: but a fool layeth o *his* folly. H6566
20:13 come to poverty; o thine eyes, *and* thou H6491
27: 5 O rebuke *is* better than secret love. H1540
31: 8 O thy mouth for the dumb in the cause H6605
9 O thy mouth, judge righteously, and H6605
Song 5: 2 knocketh, *saying*, O to me, my sister, H6605
5 I rose up to o to my beloved; and my H6605
Isa 9:12 devour Israel with o mouth. For all this H3605
22:22 so he shall o, and none shall shut; H6605
22 and he shall shut, and none shall o. H6605
24:18 from on high are o, and the foundations H6605
26: 2 O ye the gates, that the righteous H6605
28:24 he o and break the clods of his ground? H6605
37:17 Incline thine ear, O LORD, and hear; o H6491
41:18 I will o rivers in high places, and H6605
42: 7 To o the blind eyes, to bring out the H6491
45: 1 loins of kings, to o before him the two H6605
8 let the earth o, and let them bring forth H6605
60:11 Therefore thy gates shall be o H6605
Jer 5:16 Their quiver *is* as an o sepulchre, they H6605
9:22 fall as dung upon the o field, and as the H6440
13:19 up, and none shall o *them*: Judah shall H6605
32:11 law and custom, and that which was o: H1540
14 evidence which is o; and put them in an H1540
19 for thine eyes *are* o upon all the ways of H6491
50:26 utmost border, o her storehouses: cast H6605
Ezk 2: 8 o thy mouth, and eat that I give thee. H6475
3:27 But when I speak with thee, I will o thy H6605
16: 5 cast out in the o field, to the lothing H6440
63 and never o thy mouth any more H6610
21:22 appoint captains, to o the mouth in the H6605
25: 9 Therefore, behold, I will o the side of H6605
29: 5 shalt fall upon the o fields; thou shalt H6440
32: 4 forth upon the o field, and will cause H6440
33:27 him that *is* in the o field will I give to H6440
37: 2 the o valley; and, lo, *they were* very dry. H6440
12 O my people, I will o your graves, and H6605
39: 5 Thou shalt fall upon the o field: for I H6440
46:12 *one* shall then o him the gate that H6605

Dan 6:10 his windows being **o** in his chamber H6606
9:18 ear, and hear; **o** thine eyes, and behold H6491
Nah 3:13 shall be set wide **o** unto thine enemies: H6605
Zec 11: 1 **O** thy doors, O Lebanon, that the fire H6605
12: 4 and I will **o** mine eyes upon the H6491
Mal 3:10 hosts, if I will not **o** you the windows of H6605
Mt 13:35 saying, I will **o** my mouth in parables; *G455*
25:11 other virgins, saying, Lord, Lord, **o** to us. *G455*
Lk 12:36 they may **o** unto him immediately. *G455*
13:25 saying, Lord, Lord, **o** unto us; and he *G455*
Jn 1:51 ye shall see heaven **o**, and the angels of *G455*
10:21 devil. Can a devil **o** the eyes of the blind? *G455*
Act 16:27 seeing the prison doors **o**, he drew out his *G455*
18:14 And when Paul was now about to **o** *his* *G455*
19:38 man, the law is **o**, and there are deputies: *G71*
26:18 To **o** their eyes, *and* to turn *them* from *G455*
Ro 3:13 Their throat *is* an **o** sepulchre; with their *G455*
2Co 3:18 But we all, with **o** face beholding as in a *G343*
6:11 O *ye* Corinthians, our mouth is **o** unto *G455*
Eph 6:19 me, that I may **o** my mouth boldly, to *G457*
Col 4: 3 us, that God would **o** unto us a door of *G455*
1Ti 5:24 Some men's sins are **o** beforehand, *G4271*
Heb 6: 6 afresh, and put *him* to an **o** shame. *G3856*
1Pt 3:12 and his ears *are* **o** unto their prayers: but
Rev 3: 8 set before thee an **o** door, and no man *G455*
20 hear my voice, and **o** the door, I will *G455*
5: 2 Who is worthy to **o** the book, and to *G455*
3 to **o** the book, neither to look thereon. *G455*
4 found worthy to **o** and to read the book, *G455*
5 hath prevailed to **o** the book, and to *G455*
9 the book, and to **o** the seals thereof: for *G455*
10: 2 And he had in his hand a little book **o**: *G455*
8 little book which is **o** in the hand of the *G455*

OPENED

Gen 3: 5 your eyes shall be **o**, and ye shall be as H6491
7 And the eyes of them both were **o**, and H6491
4:11 the earth, which hath **o** her mouth to H6475
7:11 up, and the windows of heaven were **o**. H6605
8: 6 days, that Noah **o** the window of the H6605
21:19 And God **o** her eyes, and she saw a well H6491
29:31 he **o** her womb: but Rachel *was* barren. H6605
30:22 hearkened to her, and **o** her womb. H6605
41:56 the earth: And Joseph **o** all the H6605
42:27 And as one of them **o** his sack to give H6605
43:21 to the inn, that we **o** our sacks, and, H6605
44:11 the ground, and **o** every man his sack. H6605
Ex 2: 6 And when she had **o** *it*, she saw the H6605
Nu 16:32 And the earth **o** her mouth, and H6605
22:28 And the LORD **o** the mouth of the ass, H6605
31 Then the LORD **o** the eyes of Balaam, H1540
26:10 And the earth **o** her mouth, and H6605
Dt 11: 6 how the earth **o** her mouth, and H6475
Jdg 3:25 and, behold, he **o** not the doors of the H6605
25 took a key, and **o** *them*: and, behold, H6605
4:19 thirsty. And she **o** a bottle of milk, and H6605
11:35 me: for I have **o** my mouth unto the H6475
36 *if* thou hast **o** thy mouth unto the H6475
19:27 in the morning, and **o** the doors of the H6605
1Sa 3:15 the morning, and **o** the doors of the H6605
2Ki 4:35 seven times, and the child **o** his eyes. H6491
6:17 And the LORD **o** the eyes of the young H6491
20 And the LORD **o** their eyes, and they H6491
9:10 bury *her*. And he **o** the door, and fled. H6605
13:17 eastward. And he **o** *it*. Then Elisha H6605
15:16 because they **o** not *to him*, therefore H6605
2Ch 29: 3 in the first month, **o** the doors of the H6605
Neh 7: 3 of Jerusalem be **o** until the sun be hot; H6605
8: 5 And Ezra **o** the book in the sight of all H6605
5 when he **o** it, all the people stood up: H6605
13:19 that they should not be **o** till after the H6605
Job 3: 1 After this **o** Job his mouth, and cursed H6605
29:23 the rain; and they **o** their mouth wide H6473
31:32 street: *but* I **o** my doors to the traveller. H6605
33: 2 Behold, now I have **o** my mouth, my H6605
38:17 Have the gates of death been **o** unto H1540
Ps 35:21 Yea, they **o** their mouth wide against
39: 9 I was dumb, I **o** not my mouth; H6605
40: 6 ears hast thou **o**: burnt offering and sin H3738
78:23 from above, and **o** the doors of heaven, H6605
105:41 He **o** the rock, and the waters gushed H6605
106:17 The earth **o** and swallowed up Dathan, H6605
109: 2 of the deceitful are **o** against me: they H6605
119:131 I **o** my mouth, and panted: for I longed H6473
Song 5: 6 I **o** to my beloved; but my beloved had H6605
Isa 5:14 herself, and **o** her mouth without H6473
10:14 the wing, or **o** the mouth, or peeped. H6475
14:17 *that* **o** not the house of his prisoners? H6605
Isa 35: 5 Then the eyes of the blind shall be **o**, H6491
48: 8 *that* thine ear was not **o**: for I knew that H6605
50: 5 The Lord GOD hath **o** mine ear, and I H6605
53: 7 afflicted, yet he **o** not his mouth: he is H6605
Jer 20:12 them: for unto thee have I **o** my cause. H1540
50:25 The LORD hath **o** his armoury, and H6605
Lam 2:16 All thine enemies have **o** their mouth H6475
3:46 All our enemies have **o** their mouths H6475
Ezk 1: 1 were **o**, and I saw visions of God. H6605
3: 2 So I **o** my mouth, and he caused me to H6605
16:25 and hast **o** thy feet to every one H6589
24:27 In that day shall thy mouth be **o** to him H6605
33:22 came; and had **o** my mouth, until he H6605
22 mouth was **o**, and I was no more dumb. H6605
37:13 when I have **o** your graves, O my H6605
44: 2 it shall not be **o**, and no man shall enter H6605
46: 1 sabbath it shall be **o**, and in the day of H6605
1 in the day of the new moon it shall be **o**. H6605
Dan 7:10 was set, and the books were **o**. H6606
10:16 my lips: then I **o** my mouth, and spake, H6605
Nah 2: 6 The gates of the rivers shall be **o**, and H6605
Zec 13: 1 In that day there shall be a fountain **o** H6605
Mt 2:11 and when they had **o** their treasures, *G455*
3:16 lo, the heavens were **o** unto him, and he *G455*
5: 2 And he **o** his mouth, and taught them, *G455*
7: 7 find; knock, and it shall be **o** unto you: *G455*
8 and to him that knocketh it shall be **o**. *G455*
9:30 And their eyes were **o**; and Jesus straitly *G455*
17:27 when thou hast **o** his mouth, thou shalt *G455*
20:33 unto him, Lord, that our eyes may be **o**. *G455*
27:52 And the graves were **o**; and many bodies *G455*
Mk 1:10 saw the heavens **o**, and the Spirit like a *G4977*
7:34 unto him, Ephphatha, that is, Be **o**. *G1272*
35 And straightway his ears were **o**, and *G1272*
Lk 1:64 And his mouth was **o** immediately, and *G455*
3:21 baptized, and praying, the heaven was **o**, *G455*
4:17 And when he had **o** the book, he found *G380*
11: 9 find; knock, and it shall be **o** unto you. *G455*
10 and to him that knocketh it shall be **o**. *G455*
24:31 And their eyes were **o**, and they knew *G1272*
32 and while he **o** to us the scriptures? *G1272*
45 Then **o** he their understanding, that *G1272*
Jn 9:10 they unto him, How were thine eyes **o**? *G455*
14 Jesus made the clay, and **o** his eyes. *G455*
17 **o** thine eyes? He said, He is a prophet. *G455*
21 not; or who hath **o** his eyes, we know *G455*
26 did he to thee? how **o** he thine eyes? *G455*
30 he is, and *yet* he hath **o** mine eyes. *G455*
32 **o** the eyes of one that was born blind. *G455*
11:37 this man, which **o** the eyes of the blind, *G455*
Act 5:19 But the angel of the Lord by night **o** the *G455*
23 when we had **o**, we found no man within. *G455*
7:56 And said, Behold, I see the heavens **o**, *G455*
8:32 his shearer, so **o** he not his mouth: *G455*
35 Then Philip **o** his mouth, and began at *G455*
9: 8 when his eyes were **o**, he saw no man: *G455*
40 arise. And she **o** her eyes: and when she *G455*
10:11 And saw heaven **o**, and a certain vessel *G455*
34 Then Peter **o** *his* mouth, and said, Of a *G455*
12:10 unto the city; which **o** to them of his own *G455*
14 And when she knew Peter's voice, she **o** *G455*
16 and when they had **o** *the door*, and saw *G455*
14:27 had **o** the door of faith unto the Gentiles. *G455*
16:14 heart the Lord **o**, that she attended unto *G1272*
26 **o**, and every one's bands were loosed. *G455*
1Co 16: 9 For a great door and effectual is **o** unto *G455*
2Co 2:12 and a door was **o** unto me of the Lord, *G455*
Heb 4:13 *are* naked and **o** unto the eyes of him *G5136*
Rev 4: 1 behold, a door *was* **o** in heaven: and the *G455*
6: 1 And I saw when the Lamb **o** one of the *G455*
3 And when he had **o** the second seal, I *G455*
5 And when he had **o** the third seal, I *G455*
7 And when he had **o** the fourth seal, I *G455*
9 And when he had **o** the fifth seal, I saw *G455*
12 And I beheld when he had **o** the sixth *G455*
8: 1 And when he had **o** the seventh seal, *G455*
9: 2 And he **o** the bottomless pit; and there *G455*
11:19 And the temple of God was **o** in heaven, *G455*
12:16 woman, and the earth **o** her mouth, and *G455*
13: 6 And he **o** his mouth in blasphemy *G455*
15: 5 of the testimony in heaven was **o**: *G455*
19:11 And I saw heaven **o**, and behold a white *G455*
20:12 the books were **o**: and another book was *G455*
12 another book was **o**, which is *the book* of *G455*

OPENEST

Ps 104:28 **o** thine hand, they are filled with good. H6605
145:16 Thou **o** thine hand, and satisfiest the H6605

OPENETH

Ex 13: 2 whatsoever **o** the womb among the H6363
12 the LORD all that **o** the matrix, and H6363
15 the LORD all that **o** the matrix, being H6363
34:19 All that **o** the matrix *is* mine; and every H6363
Nu 3:12 the firstborn that **o** the matrix among H6363
18:15 Every thing that **o** the matrix in all H6363
Job 27:19 gathered: he **o** his eyes, and he *is* not. H6491
33:16 Then he **o** the ears of men, and sealeth H1540
36:10 He **o** also their ear to discipline, and H1540
15 and **o** their ears in oppression. H1540
Ps 38:13 as a dumb man *that* **o** not his mouth. H6605
146: 8 The LORD **o** *the eyes of* the blind: the H6491
Prv 13: 3 **o** wide his lips shall have destruction. H6589
24: 7 Wisdom *is* too high for a fool: he **o** not H6605
31:26 She **o** her mouth with wisdom; and in H6605
Isa 53: 7 is dumb, so he **o** not his mouth. H6605
Ezk 20:26 *the fire* all that **o** the womb, that I H6363
Lk 2:23 Every male that **o** the womb shall be *G1272*
Jn 10: 3 To him the porter **o**; and the sheep hear *G455*
Rev 3: 7 of David, he that **o**, and no man shutteth; *G455*
7 shutteth; and shutteth, and no man **o**; *G455*

OPENING

1Ch 9:27 them, and the **o** thereof every morning H4668
Job 12:14 up a man, and there can be no **o**. H6605
Prv 8: 6 the **o** of my lips *shall be* right things. H4669
Isa 42:20 not; **o** the ears, but he heareth not. H6491
61: 1 **o** of the prison to *them that are* bound; H6495
Ezk 29:21 I will give thee the **o** of the mouth in the H6610
Act 17: 3 **O** and alleging, that Christ must needs *G1272*

OPENINGS

Prv 1:21 concourse, in the **o** of the gates: in the H6607

OPENLY

Gen 38:21 harlot, that *was* **o** by the way side? And H5869
Ps 98: 2 he **o** shewed in the sight of the heathen.
Mt 6: 4 in secret himself shall reward thee **o**. *G1722*
6 seeth in secret shall reward thee **o**. *G1722*
18 seeth in secret, shall reward thee **o**. *G1722*
Mk 1:45 could no more **o** enter into the city, but *G5320*
8:32 And he spake that saying **o**. And Peter *G3954*
Jn 7: 4 to be known **o**. If thou do these things, *G1722*
10 the feast, not **o**, but as it were in secret. *G5320*
13 Howbeit no man spake **o** of him for *G3954*
11:54 Jesus therefore walked no more **o** *G3954*
18:20 Jesus answered him, I spake **o** to the *G3954*
Act 10:40 up the third day, and shewed him **o**; *G1325*
16:37 have beaten us **o** uncondemned, being *G1219*
Col 2:15 of them **o**, triumphing over them in it. *G1722*

OPERATION

Ps 28: 5 of the LORD, nor the **o** of his hands, he H4639
Isa 5:12 neither consider the **o** of his hands. H4639
Col 2:12 the faith of the **o** of God, who hath *G1753*

OPERATIONS

1Co 12: 6 And there are diversities of **o**, but it is *G1755*

OPHEL

2Ch 27: 3 and on the wall of **O** he built much. H6077
33:14 compassed about **O**, and raised it up a H6077
Neh 3:26 Moreover the Nethinims dwelt in **O**, H6077
27 that lieth out, even unto the wall of **O**. H6077
11:21 But the Nethinims dwelt in **O**: and Ziha H6077

OPHIR

Gen 10:29 And **O**, and Havilah, and Jobab: all these H211
1Ki 9:28 And they came to **O**, and fetched from H211
10:11 brought gold from **O**, brought in from H211
11 brought in from **O** great plenty of almug H211
22:48 of Tharshish to go to **O** for gold: but they H211
1Ch 1:23 And **O**, and Havilah, and Jobab. All these H211
29: 4 of gold, of the gold of **O**, and seven H211
2Ch 8:18 of Solomon to **O**, and took thence four H211
9:10 brought gold from **O**, brought algum H211
Job 22:24 the *gold* of **O** as the stones of the brooks. H211
28:16 It cannot be valued with the gold of **O**, H211
Ps 45: 9 hand did stand the queen in gold of **O**. H211
Isa 13:12 even a man than the golden wedge of **O**. H211

OPHNI

Jos 18:24 And Chephar-haammonai, and **O**, and H6078

OPHRAH

Jos 18:23 And Avim, and Parah, and **O**, H6084
Jdg 6:11 an oak which *was* in **O**, that *pertained* H6084

Jdg 6:24 this day it *is* yet in **O** of the Abi-ezrites. H6084
8:27 in his city, *even* in **O**: and all Israel went H6084
32 Joash his father, in **O** of the Abi-ezrites. H6084
9: 5 his father's house at **O**, and slew his H6084
1Sa 13:17 *leadeth to* **O**, unto the land of Shual: H6084
1Ch 4:14 And Meonothai begat **O**: and Seraiah H6084

OPINION
Job 32: 6 afraid, and durst not shew you mine **o**. H1843
10 Hearken to me; I also will shew mine **o**. H1843
17 also my part, I also will shew mine **o**. H1843

OPINIONS
1Ki 18:21 ye between two **o**? if the LORD *be* God, H5587

OPPORTUNITY
Mt 26:16 And from that time he sought **o** to *G2120*
Lk 22: 6 And he promised, and sought **o** to *G2120*
Gal 6:10 As we have therefore **o**, let us do good *G2540*
Php 4:10 ye were also careful, but ye lacked **o**. *G170*
Heb 11:15 might have had **o** to have returned. *G2540*

OPPOSE
2Ti 2:25 In meekness instructing those that **o** *G475*

OPPOSED
Act 18: 6 And when they **o** themselves, and *G498*

OPPOSEST
Job 30:21 strong hand thou **o** thyself against me. H7852

OPPOSETH
2Th 2: 4 Who **o** and exalteth himself above all *G480*

OPPOSITIONS
1Ti 6:20 and **o** of science falsely so called: *G477*

OPPRESS
Ex 3: 9 wherewith the Egyptians **o** them. H3905
22:21 vex a stranger, nor **o** him: for ye were H3905
23: 9 Also thou shalt not **o** a stranger: for ye H3905
Lev 25:14 hand, ye shall not **o** one another: H3238
17 Ye shall not therefore **o** one another; H3238
Dt 23:16 it liketh him best: thou shalt not **o** him. H3238
24:14 Thou shalt not **o** an hired servant *that* H6231
Jdg 10:12 the Maonites, did **o** you; and ye cried to H3905
Job 10: 3 thou shouldest **o**, that thou shouldest H6231
Ps 10:18 the man of the earth may no more **o**. H6206
17: 9 From the wicked that **o** me, *from* my H7703
119:122 for good: let not the proud **o** me. H6231
Prv 22:22 poor: neither **o** the afflicted in the gate: H1792
Isa 49:26 And I will feed them that **o** thee with H3238
Jer 7: 6 *If* ye **o** not the stranger, the fatherless, H6231
30:20 me, and I will punish all that **o** them. H3905
Ezk 45: 8 shall no more **o** my people; and *the* H3238
Hos 12: 7 of deceit *are* in his hand: he loveth to **o**. H6231
Am 4: 1 of Samaria, which **o** the poor, which H6231
Mic 2: 2 away: so they **o** a man and his house, H6231
Zec 7:10 And **o** not the widow, nor the H6231
Mal 3: 5 against those that **o** the hireling in *his* H6231
Jas 2: 6 Do not rich men **o** you, and draw you *G2616*

OPPRESSED
Dt 28:29 and thou shalt be only **o** and spoiled H6231
33 shalt be only **o** and crushed alway: H6231
Jdg 2:18 of them that **o** them and vexed them. H3905
4: 3 he mightily **o** the children of Israel. H3905
6: 9 hand of all that **o** you, and drave them H3905
10: 8 And that year they vexed and **o** the H7533
1Sa 10:18 all kingdoms, *and* of them that **o** you: H3905
12: 3 whom have I **o**? or of whose hand have H7533
4 not defrauded us, nor **o** us, neither hast H7533
2Ki 13: 4 because the king of Syria **o** them. H3905
22 But Hazael king of Syria **o** Israel all the H3905
2Ch 16:10 **o** *some* of the people the same time. H7533
Job 20:19 Because he hath **o** *and* hath forsaken H7533
35: 9 they make *the* **o** to cry: they cry out by
Ps 9: 9 for the **o**, a refuge in times of trouble. H1790
10:18 To judge the fatherless and the **o**, that H1790
74:21 O let not the **o** return ashamed: let the H1790
103: 6 and judgment for all that are **o**. H6231
106:42 Their enemies also **o** them, and they H3905
146: 7 Which executeth judgment for the **o**: H6231
Ecc 4: 1 tears of *such as were* **o**, and they had no H6231
Isa 1:17 relieve the **o**, judge the fatherless, H2541
3: 5 And the people shall be **o**, every one by H5065
23:12 rejoice, O thou **o** virgin, daughter of H6231
38:14 O LORD, I am **o**; undertake for me. H6234

Isa 52: 4 the Assyrian **o** them without cause. H6231
53: 7 He was **o**, and he was afflicted, yet he H5065
58: 6 **o** go free, and that ye break every yoke? H7533
Jer 50:33 of Judah *were* **o** together: and all that H6231
Ezk 18: 7 And hath not **o** any, *but* hath restored H3238
12 Hath **o** the poor and needy, hath H3238
16 Neither hath **o** any, hath not H3238
18 *As for* his father, because he cruelly **o**, H6231
22:29 they have **o** the stranger wrongfully. H6231
Hos 5:11 Ephraim *is* **o** *and* broken in judgment, H6231
Am 3: 9 thereof, and the **o** in the midst thereof. H6217
Act 7:24 that was **o**, and smote the Egyptian: *G2669*
10:38 **o** of the devil; for God was with him. *G2616*

OPPRESSETH
Nu 10: 9 the enemy that **o** you, then ye shall H6887
Ps 56: 1 swallow me up; he fighting daily **o** me. H3905
Prv 14:31 He that **o** the poor reproacheth his H6231
22:16 He that **o** the poor to increase his H6231
28: 3 A poor man that **o** the poor *is like* a H6231

OPPRESSING
Jer 46:16 land of our nativity, from the **o** sword. H3238
50:16 for fear of the **o** sword they shall turn H3238
Zep 3: 1 that is filthy and polluted, to the **o** city! H3238

OPPRESSION
Ex 3: 9 I have also seen the **o** wherewith the H3906
Dt 26: 7 affliction, and our labour, and our **o**: H3906
2Ki 13: 4 for he saw the **o** of Israel, because the H3906
Job 36:15 affliction, and openeth their ears in **o**. H3906
Ps 12: 5 For the **o** of the poor, for the sighing of H7701
42: 9 because of the **o** of the enemy? H3906
43: 2 because of the **o** of the enemy? H3906
44:24 *and* forgettest our affliction and our **o**? H3906
55: 3 because of the **o** of the wicked: for they H6125
62:10 Trust not in **o**, and become not vain in H6233
73: 8 *concerning* **o**: they speak loftily. H6233
107:39 low through **o**, affliction, and sorrow. H6115
119:134 Deliver me from the **o** of man: so will I H6233
Ecc 5: 8 If thou seest the **o** of the poor, and H6233
7: 7 Surely **o** maketh a wise man mad; and H6233
Isa 5: 7 **o**; for righteousness, but behold a cry. H4939
30:12 **o** and perverseness, and stay thereon: H6233
54:14 shalt be far from **o**; for thou shalt not H6233
59:13 from our God, speaking **o** and revolt, H6233
Jer 6: 6 she *is* wholly **o** in the midst of her. H6233
22:17 and for **o**, and for violence, to do *it*. H6233
Ezk 22: 7 have they dealt by **o** with the stranger: H6233
29 The people of the land have used **o**, and H6233
46:18 inheritance by **o**, to thrust them out of H3238

OPPRESSIONS
Job 35: 9 By reason of the multitude of **o** they H6217
Ecc 4: 1 So I returned, and considered all the **o** H6217
Isa 33:15 the gain of **o**, that shaketh his hands

OPPRESSOR
Job 3:18 they hear not the voice of the **o**. H5065
15:20 the number of years is hidden to the **o**. H6184
Ps 72: 4 needy, and shall break in pieces the **o**. H6231
Prv 3:31 Envy thou not the **o**, and choose H376+H2555
28:16 *is* also a great **o**: *but* he that hateth H4642
Isa 9: 4 the rod of his **o**, as in the day of Midian. H5065
14: 4 the **o** ceased! the golden city ceased! H5065
51:13 of the fury of the **o**, as if he were ready H6693
13 destroy? and where *is* the fury of the **o**? H6693
Jer 21:12 of the hand of the **o**, lest my fury go out H6231
22: 3 of the hand of the **o**: and do no wrong, H6216
25:38 of the **o**, and because of his fierce anger. H3238
Zec 9: 8 returneth: and no **o** shall pass through H5065
10: 4 battle bow, out of him every **o** together. H5065

OPPRESSORS
Job 27:13 and the heritage of **o**, *which* they shall H6184
Ps 54: 3 against me, and **o** seek after my soul: H6184
119:121 and justice: leave me not to mine **o**. H6231
Ecc 4: 1 the side of their **o** *there was* power; but H6231
Isa 3:12 *As for* my people, children *are* their **o**, H5065
14: 2 were; and they shall rule over their **o**. H5065
16: 4 the **o** are consumed out of the land. H7429
19:20 because of the **o**, and he shall send H3905

OR See the Appendix.

ORACLE
2Sa 16:23 inquired at the **o** of God: so *was* all the H1697
1Ki 6: 5 **o**: and he made chambers round about: H1687
6:16 for the **o**, *even* for the most holy *place*. H1687
19 And the **o** he prepared in the house H1687
20 And the **o** in the forepart *was* twenty H1687
21 the **o**; and he overlaid it with gold. H1687
22 that *was* by the **o** he overlaid with gold. H1687
23 And within the **o** he made two H1687
31 And for the entering of the **o** he made H1687
7:49 the left, before the **o**, with the flowers, H1687
8: 6 his place, into the **o** of the house, to the H1687
8 *place* before the **o**, and they were not H1687
2Ch 3:16 And he made chains, *as* in the **o**, and H1687
4:20 the manner before the **o**, of pure gold; H1687
5: 7 his place, to the **o** of the house, into the H1687
9 the ark before the **o**; but they were not H1687
Ps 28: 2 I lift up my hands toward thy holy **o**. H1687

ORACLES
Act 7:38 received the lively **o** to give unto us: *G3051*
Ro 3: 2 them were committed the **o** of God. *G3051*
Heb 5:12 first principles of the **o** of God; and are *G3051*
1Pt 4:11 *him speak* as the **o** of God; if any man *G3051*

ORATION
Act 12:21 his throne, and made an **o** unto them. *G1215*

ORATOR
Isa 3: 3 cunning artificer, and the eloquent **o**. H3908
Act 24: 1 and *with* a certain **o** *named* Tertullus, *G4489*

ORCHARD
Song 4:13 Thy plants *are* an **o** of pomegranates, H6508

ORCHARDS
Ecc 2: 5 I made me gardens and **o**, and I planted H6508

ORDAIN
1Ch 9:22 Samuel the seer did **o** in their set office. H3245
17: 9 Also I will **o** a place for my people H7760
Isa 26:12 LORD, thou wilt **o** peace for us: for H8239
1Co 7:17 let him walk. And so **o** I in all churches. *G1299*
Tit 1: 5 are wanting, and **o** elders in every city, *G2525*

ORDAINED
Nu 28: 6 which was **o** in mount Sinai for a H6213
1Ki 12:32 And Jeroboam **o** a feast in the eighth H6213
33 his own heart; and **o** a feast unto the H6213
2Ki 23: 5 of Judah had **o** to burn incense in the H5414
2Ch 11:15 And he **o** him priests for the high H5975
23:18 and with singing, *as it was* **o** by David.
29:27 instruments ***o*** by David king of Israel.
Est 9:27 The Jews **o**, and took upon them, and H6965
Ps 8: 2 hast thou **o** strength because of H3245
3 moon and the stars, which thou hast **o**; H3559
81: 5 This he **o** in Joseph *for* a testimony, H7760
132:17 I have **o** a lamp for mine anointed. H6186
Isa 30:33 For Tophet *is* **o** of old; yea, for the king H6186
Jer 1: 5 I **o** thee a prophet unto the nations. H5414
Dan 2:24 the king had **o** to destroy the wise H4483
Hab 1:12 LORD, thou hast **o** them for judgment; H7760
Mk 3:14 And he **o** twelve, that they should be *G4160*
Jn 15:16 chosen you, and **o** you, that ye should *G5087*
Act 1:22 us, must one be **o** to be a witness with *G1096*
10:42 it is he which was **o** of God *to be* the *G3724*
13:48 many as were **o** to eternal life believed. *G5021*
14:23 And when they had **o** them elders in *G5500*
16: 4 to keep, that were **o** of the apostles and *G2919*
17:31 whom he hath **o**; *whereof* he hath given *G3724*
Ro 7:10 And the commandment, which *was* **o** to
13: 1 of God: the powers that be are **o** of God. *G5021*
1Co 2: 7 God **o** before the world unto our glory: *G4309*
9:14 Even so hath the Lord **o** that they *G1299*
Gal 3:19 **o** by angels in the hand of a mediator. *G1299*
Eph 2:10 before **o** that we should walk in them. *G4282*
1Ti 2: 7 Whereunto I am **o** a preacher, and an *G5087*
Heb 5: 1 from among men is **o** for men in things *G2525*
8: 3 For every high priest is **o** to offer gifts *G2525*
9: 6 Now when these things were thus **o**, the *G2680*
Jude 4 who were before of old **o** to this *G4270*

ORDAINETH
Ps 7:13 **o** his arrows against the persecutors. H6466

ORDER
Gen 22: 9 laid the wood in **o**, and bound Isaac his H6186
Ex 26:17 in one board, set in **o** one against H7947
27:21 and his sons shall **o** it from evening to H6186
39:37 lamps to be set in **o**, and all the vessels H4634
40: 4 table, and set in **o** the things that are to H6186

Ex 40: 4 that are to be set in **o** upon it; and thou H6187
23 And he set the bread in **o** upon it before H6186
Lev 1: 7 and lay the wood in **o** upon the fire: H6186
8 and the fat, in **o** upon the wood that H6186
12 shall lay them in **o** on the wood that *is* H6186
6:12 burnt offering in **o** upon it; and he shall H6186
24: 3 shall Aaron **o** it from the evening H6186
4 He shall **o** the lamps upon the pure H6186
8 Every sabbath he shall set it in **o** before H6186
Jos 2: 6 which she had laid in **o** upon the roof. H6186
Jdg 13:12 How shall we **o** the child, and *how* shall H4941
2Sa 17:23 his household in **o**, and hanged himself, H6680
1Ki 18:33 And he put the wood in **o**, and cut the H6186
20:14 **o** the battle? And he answered, Thou. H631
2Ki 20: 1 in **o**; for thou shalt die, and not live. H6680
23: 4 of the second **o**, and the keepers of the H4932
1Ch 6:32 on their office according to their **o**. H4941
15:13 that we sought him not after the due **o**. H4941
23:31 according to the **o** commanded unto H4941
25: 2 according to the **o** of the king. H3027
6 **o** to Asaph, Jeduthun, and Heman. H3027
2Ch 8:14 And he appointed, according to the **o** H4941
13:11 also *set they in o* upon the pure table;
29:35 of the house of the LORD was set in **o**. H3559
Job 10:22 **o**, and *where* the light *is* as darkness. H5468
23: 4 I would **o** *my* cause before him, and fill H6186
33: 5 set *thy words* in **o** before me, stand up. H6186
37:19 **o** *our speech* by reason of darkness. H6186
Ps 40: 5 be reckoned up in **o** unto thee: *if* I H6186
50:21 and set *them* in **o** before thine eyes. H6186
110: 4 for ever after the **o** of Melchizedek. H1700
119:133 **O** my steps in thy word: and let not any H3559
Ecc 12: 9 out, *and* set in **o** many proverbs. H8626
Isa 9: 7 his kingdom, to **o** it, and to establish it H3559
38: 1 in **o**: for thou shalt die, and not live. H6680
44: 7 declare it, and set it in **o** for me, since I H6186
Jer 46: 3 **O** ye the buckler and shield, and draw H6186
Ezk 41: 6 and thirty in **o**; and they entered into H6471
Lk 1: 1 in hand to set forth in **o** a declaration of *G392*
3 thee in **o**, most excellent Theophilus, *G2517*
8 office before God in the **o** of his course, *G5010*
Act 11: 4 expounded *it* by **o** unto them, saying, *G2517*
18:23 in **o**, strengthening all the disciples. *G2517*
1Co 11:34 And the rest will I set in **o** when I come. *G1299*
14:40 Let all things be done decently and in **o**. *G5010*
15:23 But every man in his own **o**: Christ the *G5001*
16: 1 as I have given **o** to the churches of *G1299*
Col 2: 5 beholding your **o**, and the stedfastness *G5010*
Tit 1: 5 shouldest set in **o** the things that are *G1930*
Heb 5: 6 for ever after the **o** of Melchisedec. *G5010*
10 Called of God an high priest after the **o** *G5010*
6:20 for ever after the **o** of Melchisedec. *G5010*
7:11 rise after the **o** of Melchisedec, and *G5010*
11 and not be called after the **o** of Aaron? *G5010*
17 for ever after the **o** of Melchisedec. *G5010*
21 for ever after the **o** of Melchisedec:) *G5010*

ORDERED
Jdg 6:26 of this rock, in the **o** place, and take the H4634
2Sa 23: 5 covenant, **o** in all *things*, and sure: H6186
Job 13:18 Behold now, I have **o** *my* cause; I know H6186
Ps 37:23 The steps of a *good* man are **o** by the H3559

ORDERETH
Ps 50:23 me: and to him that **o** *his* conversation H7760

ORDERINGS
1Ch 24:19 These *were* the **o** of them in their H6486

ORDERLY
Act 21:24 also walkest **o**, and keepest the law. *G4748*

ORDINANCE
Ex 12:14 ye shall keep it a feast by an **o** for ever. H2708
17 in your generations by an **o** for ever. H2708
24 And ye shall observe this thing for an **o** H2706
43 Aaron, This *is* the **o** of the passover: H2708
13:10 Thou shalt therefore keep this **o** in his H2708
15:25 and an **o**, and there he proved them, H4941
Lev 18:30 Therefore shall ye keep mine **o**, that *ye* H4931
22: 9 They shall therefore keep mine **o**, lest H4931
Nu 9:14 according to the **o** of the passover, and H2708
14 do: ye shall have one **o**, both for the H2708
10: 8 be to you for an **o** for ever throughout H2708
15:15 One **o** *shall be both* for you of the H2708
15 *with you*, an **o** for ever in your H2708
18: 8 and to thy sons, by an **o** for ever. H2706
19: 2 This *is* the **o** of the law which the LORD H2708
Nu 31:21 battle, This *is* the **o** of the law which the H2708
Jos 24:25 them a statute and an **o** in Shechem. H4941
1Sa 30:25 and an **o** for Israel unto this day. H4941
2Ch 2: 4 our God. This *is an* **o** for ever to Israel.
35:13 according to the **o**: but the *other* holy H4941
25 made them an **o** in Israel: and, behold, H2706
Ezr 3:10 after the **o** of David king of Israel. H3027
Ps 99: 7 and the **o** *that* he gave them. H2706
Isa 24: 5 the **o**, broken the everlasting covenant. H2706
58: 2 forsook not the **o** of their God: they ask H4941
Ezk 45:14 Concerning the **o** of oil, the bath of oil, H2706
46:14 by a perpetual **o** unto the LORD. H2708
Mal 3:14 we have kept his **o**, and that we have H4931
Ro 13: 2 resisteth the **o** of God: and they that *G1296*
1Pt 2:13 Submit yourselves to every **o** of man *G2937*

ORDINANCES
Ex 18:20 And thou shalt teach them **o** and laws, H2706
Lev 18: 3 not do: neither shall ye walk in their **o**. H2708
4 and keep mine **o**, to walk therein: I *am* H2708
Nu 9:12 the **o** of the passover they shall keep it. H2708
2Ki 17:34 or after their **o**, or after the law and H4941
37 And the statutes, and the **o**, and the H4941
2Ch 33: 8 and the **o** by the hand of Moses. H4941
Neh 10:32 Also we made **o** for us, to charge H4687
Job 38:33 Knowest thou the **o** of heaven? canst H2708
Ps 119:91 to thine **o**: for all *are* thy servants. H4941
Isa 58: 2 they ask of me the **o** of justice; they H4941
Jer 31:35 by day, *and* the **o** of the moon and of H2708
36 If those **o** depart from before me, saith H2706
33:25 appointed the **o** of heaven and earth; H2708
Ezk 11:20 and keep mine **o**, and do them: and H4941
43:11 and all the **o** thereof, and all the H2708
11 and all the **o** thereof, and do them. H2708
18 These *are* the **o** of the altar in the day H2708
44: 5 concerning all the **o** of the house of the H2708
Mal 3: 7 away from mine **o**, and have not kept H2706
Lk 1: 6 and **o** of the Lord blameless. *G1345*
1Co 11: 2 keep the **o**, as I delivered *them* to you. *G3862*
Eph 2:15 *contained* in **o**; for to make in himself *G1378*
Col 2:14 Blotting out the handwriting of **o** that *G1378*
20 living in the world, are ye subject to **o**, *G1379*
Heb 9: 1 *covenant* had also **o** of divine service, *G1345*
10 and carnal **o**, imposed *on them* until *G1345*

ORDINARY
Ezk 16:27 diminished thine **o** *food*, and delivered H2706

OREB
Jdg 7:25 of the Midianites, **O** and Zeeb; and they H6159
25 and they slew **O** upon the rock Oreb, H6159
25 upon the rock **O**, and Zeeb they slew H6159
25 the heads of **O** and Zeeb to Gideon H6159
8: 3 the princes of Midian, **O** and Zeeb: and H6159
Ps 83:11 Make their nobles like **O**, and like Zeeb: H6159
Isa 10:26 at the rock of **O**: and *as* his rod *was* H6159

OREGIM See JAARE-OREGIM.

OREN
1Ch 2:25 Bunah, and **O**, and Ozem, *and* Ahijah. H767

ORGAN
Gen 4:21 of all such as handle the harp and **o**. H5748
Job 21:12 harp, and rejoice at the sound of the **o**. H5748
30:31 my **o** into the voice of them that weep. H5748

ORGANS
Ps 150: 4 him with stringed instruments and **o**. H5748

ORION
Job 9: 9 Which maketh Arcturus, **O**, and H3685
38:31 of Pleiades, or loose the bands of **O**? H3685
Am 5: 8 the seven stars and **O**, and turneth the H3685

ORNAMENT
Prv 1: 9 For they *shall be* an **o** of grace unto thy H3880
4: 9 She shall give to thine head an **o** of H3880
25:12 *As* an earring of gold, and an **o** of fine H2481
Isa 30:22 of silver, and the **o** of thy molten images H642
49:18 all, as with an **o**, and bind them *on* H5716
Ezk 7:20 As for the beauty of his **o**, he set it in H5716
1Pt 3: 4 *even the* **o** of a meek and quiet

ORNAMENTS
Ex 33: 4 and no man did put on him his **o**. H5716
5 now put off thy **o** from thee, that I may H5716
6 of their **o** by the mount Horeb. H5716
Jdg 8:21 the **o** that *were* on their camels' necks. H7720
26 of gold; beside **o**, and collars, and H7720
2Sa 1:24 put on **o** of gold upon your apparel. H5716
Isa 3:18 of *their* tinkling **o** *about their feet*, and H5914
20 The bonnets, and the **o** of the legs, and H6807
61:10 *himself* with **o**, and as a bride adorneth H6287
Jer 2:32 Can a maid forget her **o**, *or* a bride her H5716
4:30 deckest thee with **o** of gold, though H5716
Ezk 16: 7 art come to excellent **o**: *thy* breasts are H5716
11 I decked thee also with **o**, and I put H5716
23:40 thy eyes, and deckedst thyself with **o**, H5716

ORNAN
1Ch 21:15 by the threshingfloor of **O** the Jebusite. H771
18 in the threshingfloor of **O** the Jebusite. H771
20 And **O** turned back, and saw the angel; H771
20 themselves. Now **O** was threshing wheat. H771
21 And as David came to **O**, Ornan looked H771
21 And as David came to Ornan, **O** looked H771
22 Then David said to **O**, Grant me the place H771
23 And **O** said unto David, Take *it* to thee, H771
24 And king David said to **O**, Nay; but I will H771
25 So David gave to **O** for the place six H771
28 **O** the Jebusite, then he sacrificed there. H771
2Ch 3: 1 in the threshingfloor of **O** the Jebusite. H771

ORPAH
Ru 1: 4 of the one *was* **O**, and the name of the H6204
14 wept again: and **O** kissed her mother in H6204

ORPHANS
Lam 5: 3 We are **o** and fatherless, our mothers H3490

OSEE
Ro 9:25 As he saith also in **O**, I will call them my *G5617*

OSHEA
Nu 13: 8 Of the tribe of Ephraim, **O** the son of H1954
16 called **O** the son of Nun Jehoshua. H1954

OSPRAY
Lev 11:13 the eagle, and the ossifrage, and the **o**, H5822
Dt 14:12 the eagle, and the ossifrage, and the **o**, H5822

OSSIFRAGE
Lev 11:13 the eagle, and the **o**, and the ospray, H6538
Dt 14:12 the eagle, and the **o**, and the ospray, H6538

OSTRICH
Job 39:13 or wings and feathers unto the **o**? H5133

OSTRICHES
Lam 4: 3 cruel, like the **o** in the wilderness. H3283

OTHER
Gen 4:19 Adah, and the name of the **o** Zillah. H8145
8:10 And he stayed yet **o** seven days; and H312
12 And he stayed yet **o** seven days; and sent H312
13:11 separated themselves the one from the **o**. H251
20:16 and with all **o**: thus she was reproved.
25:23 be stronger than *the* **o** people; and the H3816
28:17 this place! this *is* none **o** but the house of
29:27 shalt serve with me yet seven **o** years. H312
30 and served with him yet seven **o** years. H312
31:50 or if thou shalt take **o** wives beside my
32: 8 the **o** company which is left shall escape.
41: 3 And, behold, seven **o** kine came up after H312
3 the **o** kine upon the brink of the river. H6510
19 And, behold, seven **o** kine came up after H312
43:14 may send away your **o** brother, and H312
22 And **o** money have we brought down in H312
47:21 of Egypt even to the **o** end thereof. H7097
Ex 1:15 Shiphrah, and the name of the **o** Puah: H8145
4: 7 it was turned again as his **o** flesh.
14:20 one came not near the **o** all the night. H2088
17:12 the one side, and the **o** on the other side; H259
12 the other on the **o** side; and his hands H2088
18: 4 And the name of the **o** *was* Eliezer; for H259
7 they asked each **o** of *their* welfare; and H7453
20: 3 Thou shalt have no **o** gods before me. H312
23:13 of the name of **o** gods, neither let it be H312
25:12 of it, and two rings in the **o** side of it. H8145
19 one end, and the **o** cherub on the other H259
19 cherub on the **o** end: *even* of the mercy H2088
32 of the candlestick out of the **o** side: H8145
33 like almonds in the **o** branch, *with* a H259
26: 3 to another; and **o** five curtains *shall be*
13 and a cubit on the **o** side of that which H2088

Ex 26:27 And five bars for the boards of the **o** H8145
27:15 And on the **o** side *shall be* hangings H8145
28:10 on one stone, and *the o* six names of the
10 on the **o** stone, according to their birth. H8145
25 And *the o* two ends of the two wreathen
27 And two *o* rings of gold thou shalt make,
27 over against the *o* coupling thereof,
29:19 And thou shalt take the **o** ram; and H8145
39 and the **o** lamb thou shalt offer at even: H8145
41 And the **o** lamb thou shalt offer at H8145
30:32 shall ye make *any o* like it, after the
32:15 side and on the **o** *were* they written. H2088
34:14 For thou shalt worship no **o** god: for the H312
36:10 unto another: and *the o* five curtains he
25 And for the **o** side of the tabernacle, H8145
32 And five bars for the boards of the **o** H8145
33 the boards from the one end to the **o**. H7097
37: 3 it, and two rings upon the **o** side of it. H8145
8 cherub on the *o* end on that side: out
18 candlestick out of the **o** side thereof: H8145
38:15 And for the **o** side of the court gate, on H8145
39:20 And they made two *o* golden rings, and
20 of it, over against the *o* coupling thereof,
Lev 5: 7 offering, and the **o** for a burnt offering. H259
6:11 and put on **o** garments, and carry H312
7:24 **o** use: but ye shall in no wise eat of it. H4399
8:22 And he brought the **o** ram, the ram of H8145
11:23 But all *o* flying creeping things, which H5775
12: 8 offering, and the **o** for a sin offering: and H259
13:26 *be* no lower than the *o* skin, but *be*
14:22 a sin offering, and the **o** a burnt offering. H259
31 offering, and the **o** *for* a burnt offering, H259
42 And they shall take **o** stones, and put H312
42 **o** morter, and shall plaister the house. H312
15:15 offering, and the *o for* a burnt offering; H259
30 offering, and the **o** *for* a burnt offering; H259
16: 8 LORD, and the **o** lot for the scapegoat. H259
18:18 nakedness, beside the **o** in her life *time*.
20:24 have separated you from *o* people.
26 from *o* people, that ye should be mine.
25:53 with him: *and the o* shall not rule with
Nu 6:11 offering, and the **o** for a burnt offering, H259
8:12 offering, and the *o for* a burnt offering, H259
10:21 the sanctuary: and *the o* did set up the
11:26 and the name of the **o** Medad: and the H8145
31 journey on the **o** side, round about the H3541
21:13 pitched on the **o** side of Arnon, which H5676
24: 1 he went not, as at **o** times, to seek for
28: 4 and the **o** lamb shalt thou offer at even; H8145
8 And the **o** lamb shalt thou offer at H8145
32:38 Shibmah: and gave **o** names unto the
36: 3 any of the sons of the *o* tribes of the H7626
Dt 4:32 and *of* heaven unto the **o**, whether there hath
5: 7 Thou shalt have none **o** gods before me. H312
6:14 Ye shall not go after **o** gods, of the gods H312
7: 4 they may serve **o** gods: so will the anger H312
8:19 and walk after **o** gods, and serve them, H312
11:16 and serve **o** gods, and worship them; H312
28 after **o** gods, which ye have not known. H312
30 *Are* they not on the **o** side Jordan, by H5676
13: 2 Let us go after **o** gods, which thou hast H312
6 Let us go and serve **o** gods, which thou H312
7 earth even unto the *o* end of the earth; H7097
13 serve **o** gods, which ye have not known; H312
17: 3 And hath gone and served **o** gods, and H312
18:20 of **o** gods, even that prophet shall die. H312
28:14 the left, to go after **o** gods to serve them. H312
36 shalt thou serve **o** gods, wood and stone. H312
64 even unto the **o**; and there thou shalt
64 thou shalt serve **o** gods, which neither H312
29:26 For they went and served **o** gods, and H312
30:17 and worship **o** gods, and serve them; H312
31:18 in that they are turned unto **o** gods. H312
20 will they turn unto **o** gods, and serve H312
Jos 2:10 that *were* on the **o** side Jordan, Sihon H5676
7: 7 and dwelt on the **o** side Jordan! H5676
8:22 And the **o** issued out of the city against H428
11:19 of Gibeon: all **o** they took in battle.
12: 1 their land on the **o** side Jordan toward H5676
13:27 on the **o** side Jordan eastward. H5676
32 the **o** side Jordan, by Jericho, eastward. H5676
14: 3 half tribe on the **o** side Jordan: but unto H5676
17: 5 which *were* on the **o** side Jordan; H5676
20: 8 And on the **o** side Jordan by Jericho H5676
21:27 the Levites, out of the *o* half tribe of
22: 4 LORD gave you on the **o** side Jordan. H5676
7 but unto the *o* half thereof gave Joshua
23:16 have gone and served **o** gods, and bowed H312

Jos 24: 2 dwelt on the **o** side of the flood in old H5676
2 of Nachor: and they served **o** gods. H312
3 from the **o** side of the flood, and H5676
8 dwelt on the **o** side Jordan; and they H5676
14 served on the **o** side of the flood, and H5676
15 that *were* on the **o** side of the flood, or H5676
16 forsake the LORD, to serve **o** gods; H312
Jdg 2:12 and followed **o** gods, of the gods of the H312
17 went a whoring after **o** gods, and bowed H312
19 in following **o** gods to serve them, H312
7: 7 *o* people go every man unto his place.
25 Zeeb to Gideon on the **o** side Jordan. H5676
9:44 city: and the two *o* companies ran upon
10: 8 that *were* on the **o** side Jordan in the H5676
13 Yet ye have forsaken me, and served **o** H312
11:18 and pitched on the **o** side of Arnon, but H5676
13:10 unto me, that came unto me the *o* day. H3117
16:17 become weak, and be like any *o* man. H120
20 I will go out as at **o** times before, and
29 his right hand, and of the **o** with his left. H259
20:30 in array against Gibeah, as at **o** times.
31 *and* kill, as at **o** times, in the highways,
31 of God, and the **o** to Gibeah in the field, H259
Ru 1: 4 and the name of the **o** Ruth: and they H8145
2:22 that they meet thee not in any **o** field. H312
1Sa 1: 2 and the name of the **o** Peninnah: and H8145
3:10 stood, and called as at **o** times, Samuel,
8: 8 served **o** gods, so do they also unto thee. H312
14: 1 on the **o** side. But he told not his father. H5676
4 sharp rock on the **o** side: and the name H2088
4 *was* Bozez, and the name of the **o** Seneh. H259
5 the **o** southward over against Gibeah. H259
40 son will be on the **o** side. And the people H259
17: 3 on a mountain on the **o** side: and *there* H2088
18:10 his hand, as at **o** times: and *there was*
19:21 And when it was told Saul, he sent **o** H312
20:25 And the king sat upon his seat, as at **o**
21: 9 *it*: for *there is* no **o** save that here. And H312
26:13 Then David went over to the **o** side, H5676
19 of the LORD, saying, Go, serve **o** gods. H312
28: 8 and put on **o** raiment, and he went, H312
30:20 **o** cattle, and said, This *is* David's spoil.
31: 7 that *were* on the **o** side of the valley, H5676
7 that *were* on the **o** side Jordan, saw H5676
2Sa 1:24 you in scarlet, with *o* delights, who put
2:13 and the **o** on the other side of the pool. H428
13 and the other on the **o** side of the pool. H2088
4: 2 the name of the **o** Rechab, the sons of H8145
12: 1 in one city; the one rich, and the **o** poor. H259
13:16 *is* greater than the **o** that thou didst unto H312
14: 6 but the one smote the **o**, and slew him. H259
17: 9 pit, or in some **o** place: and it will come
24:22 and *o* instruments of the oxen for wood.
1Ki 3:22 And the **o** woman said, Nay; but the H312
23 the dead: and the **o** saith, Nay; but thy H2063
25 and give half to the one, and half to the **o**. H259
26 slay it. But the **o** said, Let it be neither H2063
6:24 and five cubits the **o** wing of the H8145
24 uttermost part of the **o** *were* ten cubits. H3671
25 And the **o** cherub *was* ten cubits: both H8145
26 cubits, and so *was it* of the **o** cherub. H8145
27 the wing of the **o** cherub touched the H8145
27 touched the **o** wall; and their wings H8145
34 two leaves of the **o** door *were* folding. H8145
7: 6 them: and the *o* pillars and the thick
7 cedar from one side of the floor to the **o**. H7172
16 height of the **o** chapiter *was* five cubits: H8145
17 chapiter, and seven for the **o** chapiter. H8145
18 and so did he for the **o** chapiter. H8145
20 rows round about upon the **o** chapiter. H8145
23 the one brim to the **o**: *it was* round all H8193
9: 6 go and serve **o** gods, and worship them: H312
9 have taken hold upon **o** gods, and have H312
10:20 side and on the **o** upon the six steps: H2088
11: 4 his heart after **o** gods: and his heart was H312
10 should not go after **o** gods: but he kept H312
12:29 And he set the one in Beth-el, and the **o** H259
14: 9 gone and made thee **o** gods, and molten H312
18:23 and I will dress the **o** bullock, and lay *it* H259
20:29 And they pitched one over against the **o** H428
2Ki 3:22 the water on the **o** side *as* red as blood: H5048
5:17 unto **o** gods, but unto the LORD. H312
12: 7 the priest, and the *o* priests, and said
17: 7 king of Egypt, and had feared **o** gods, H312
35 saying, Ye shall not fear **o** gods, nor bow H312
37 evermore; and ye shall not fear **o** gods. H312
38 not forget; neither shall ye fear **o** gods. H312
22:17 incense unto **o** gods, that they might H312

1Ch 6:78 And on the **o** side Jordan by Jericho, on H5676
9:32 And *o* of their brethren, of the sons of
12:37 And on the **o** side of Jordan, of the H5676
23:17 Eliezer had none **o** sons; but the sons of H312
2Ch 3:11 the house: and the **o** wing *was likewise* H312
11 reaching to the wing of the **o** cherub. H312
12 And *one* wing of the **o** cherub *was* five H259
12 the house: and the **o** wing *was* five cubits H312
12 *also*, joining to the wing of the **o** cherub. H312
17 hand, and the **o** on the left; and called H259
7:19 go and serve **o** gods, and worship them; H312
22 and laid hold on **o** gods, and worshipped H312
9:19 side and on the **o** upon the six steps. H2088
13: 9 manner of the nations of *o* lands? so that
20: 1 and with them *o* beside the Ammonites,
25:12 And *o* ten thousand *left* alive did the
28:25 burn incense unto **o** gods, and provoked H312
29:34 and until the *o* priests had sanctified
30:23 counsel to keep **o** seven days: and they H312
23 they kept *o* seven days with gladness.
32:13 all the people of *o* lands? were the gods
17 gods of the nations of *o* lands have not
22 of all *o*, and guided them on every side.
34:12 to set *it* forward; and *o of* the Levites, all
25 incense unto **o** gods, that they might H312
35:13 ordinance: but the *o* holy *offerings* sod
Ezr 1:10 and ten, *and* **o** vessels a thousand. H312
2:31 The children of the **o** Elam, a thousand H312
Neh 3:11 **o** piece, and the tower of the furnaces. H8145
20 repaired the **o** piece, from the turning H8145
4:16 in the work, and the **o** half of them held
17 and with the **o** *hand* held a weapon. H259
5: 5 for **o** men have our lands and vineyards. H312
7:33 The men of the **o** Nebo, fifty and two. H312
34 The children of the **o** Elam, a thousand H312
11: 1 city, and nine parts *to dwell* in *o* cities.
12:38 And the **o** *company of them that gave* H8145
Est 2:12 *o* things for the purifying of the women;)
9:16 But the **o** Jews that *were* in the king's H7605
Job 8:12 cut down, it withereth before any *o* herb.
24:24 of the way as all *o*, and cut off as the tops
Ps 73: 5 They *are* not in trouble *as o* men; neither
5 neither are they plagued like *o* men.
85:10 and peace have kissed *each o*.
Ecc 3:19 dieth, so dieth the **o**; yea, they have all H2088
6: 5 *thing*: this hath more rest than the **o**. H2088
7:14 over against the **o**, to the end that man H2088
Isa 26:13 O LORD our God, *o* lords beside thee
49:20 thou hast lost the **o**, shall say again in
Jer 1:16 incense unto **o** gods, and worshipped H312
7: 6 neither walk after **o** gods to your hurt: H312
9 walk after **o** gods whom ye know not; H312
18 offerings unto **o** gods, that they may H312
11:10 they went after **o** gods to serve them: H312
12:12 the land even to the *o* end of the land: no
13:10 and walk after **o** gods, to serve them, H312
16:11 and have walked after **o** gods, and have H312
13 and there shall ye serve **o** gods day and H312
19: 4 incense in it unto **o** gods, whom neither H312
13 poured out drink offerings unto **o** gods. H312
22: 9 worshipped **o** gods, and served them. H312
24: 2 *are* first ripe: and the **o** basket *had* very H259
25: 6 And go not after **o** gods to serve them, H312
33 even unto the **o** end of the earth: they
32:20 in Israel, and among *o* men; and hast
29 unto **o** gods, to provoke me to anger. H312
35:15 and go not after **o** gods to serve them, H312
36:16 both one and **o**, and said unto Baruch, H7453
44: 3 *and* to serve **o** gods, whom they knew H312
5 to burn no incense unto **o** gods. H312
8 incense unto **o** gods in the land of Egypt, H312
15 incense unto **o** gods, and all the women H312
Ezk 1:23 the one toward the **o**: every one had two, H269
16:34 And the contrary is in thee from *o*
21:16 Go thee one way or **o**, *either* on the right H258
40: 6 broad; and the **o** threshold *of the gate*, H259
40 tables; and on the **o** side, which *was* at H312
41: 1 broad on the **o** side, *which was* the H6311
2 and five cubits on the **o** side: and he H6311
15 one side and on the **o** side, an hundred H6311
19 palm tree on the **o** side: *it was* made H6311
21 *of the one* as the appearance *of the o*.
24 one door, and two leaves for the **o** *door*. H312
26 side and on the **o** side, on the sides of H6311
42:14 and shall put on **o** garments, and shall H312
44:19 they shall put on **o** garments; and they H312
45: 7 side and on the **o** side of the oblation H2088
47: 7 trees on the one side and on the **o**. H2088

Ezk 48: 8 as one of the *o* parts, from the east
21 side and on the **o** of the holy oblation, H2088
Dan 2:11 and there is none **o** that can shew it H321
44 shall not be left to **o** people, *but* it shall H321
3:21 hats, and their *o* garments, and were
29 no **o** God that can deliver after this sort. H321
7:20 head, and *of* the **o** which came up, and H317
8: 3 than the **o**, and the higher came up last. H8145
12: 5 behold, there stood **o** two, the one on H312
5 **o** on that side of the bank of the river. H259
Hos 3: 1 look to **o** gods, and love flagons of wine. H312
9: 1 Rejoice not, O Israel, for joy, as *o* people:
13:10 I will be thy king: where *is any o* that
Oba 11 In the day that thou stoodest on the **o** H5048
Zec 4: 3 and the **o** upon the left *side* thereof. H259
11: 7 the **o** I called Bands; and I fed the flock. H259
14 Then I cut asunder mine **o** staff, *even* H8145
Mt 4:21 And going on from thence, he saw **o** two G243
5:39 thy right cheek, turn to him the **o** also. G243
6:24 one, and love the **o**; or else he will hold G2087
24 **o**. Ye cannot serve God and mammon. G2087
8:18 to depart unto the **o** side. G4008
28 And when he was come to the **o** side G4008
12:13 and it was restored whole, like as the **o**. G243
45 himself seven **o** spirits more wicked G2087
13: 8 But **o** fell into good ground, and brought G243
14:22 him unto the **o** side, while he sent the G4008
16: 5 were come to the **o** side, they had G4008
20:21 and the **o** on the left, in thy kingdom. G1520
21:36 Again, he sent **o** servants more than the G243
41 *his* vineyard unto **o** husbandmen, which G243
22: 4 Again, he sent forth **o** servants, saying, G243
23:23 done, and not to leave the **o** undone. G2548
24:31 winds, from one end of heaven to the **o**. G206
40 the one shall be taken, and the **o** left. G1520
41 the one shall be taken, and the **o** left. G3391
25:11 Afterward came also the **o** virgins, G3062
16 the same, and made *them* **o** five talents. G243
17 *had received* two, he also gained **o** two. G243
20 came and brought **o** five talents, saying, G243
22 I have gained two **o** talents beside them. G243
27:61 and the **o** Mary, sitting over against G243
28: 1 and the **o** Mary to see the sepulchre. G243
Mk 3: 5 his hand was restored whole as the **o**. G243
4: 8 And **o** fell on good ground, and did yield G243
19 and the lusts of **o** things entering in, G3062
35 them, Let us pass over unto the **o** side. G4008
36 there were also with him **o** little ships. G243
5: 1 And they came over unto the **o** side of G4008
21 by ship unto the **o** side, much people G4008
6:45 ship, and to go to the **o** side before unto G4008
7: 4 eat not. And many **o** things there be, G243
8 cups: and many **o** such like things ye do. G243
8:13 the ship again departed to the **o** side. G4008
10:37 and the **o** on thy left hand, in thy glory. G1520
12:31 **o** commandment greater than these. G243
32 is one God; and there is none **o** but he: G243
15:27 on his right hand, and the **o** on his left. G1520
41 him;) and many **o** women which came G243
Lk 3:18 And many **o** things in his exhortation G2087
4:43 to **o** cities also: for therefore am I sent. G2087
5: 7 which were in the **o** ship, that they G2087
6:10 his hand was restored whole as the **o**. G243
29 *one* cheek offer also the **o**; and him that G243
7:41 five hundred pence, and the **o** fifty. G2087
8: 8 And **o** fell on good ground, and sprang G2087
22 go over unto the **o** side of the lake. And G4008
10: 1 After these things the Lord appointed **o** G2087
31 he saw him, he passed by on the **o** side. G492
32 *on him*, and passed by on the **o** side. G492
11:26 *to him* seven **o** spirits more wicked G2087
42 done, and not to leave the **o** undone. G2548
14:32 Or else, while the **o** is yet a great way off, G846
16:13 one, and love the **o**; or else he will hold G2087
13 **o**. Ye cannot serve God and mammon. G2087
17:24 shineth unto the **o** *part* under heaven; G3588
34 shall be taken, and the **o** shall be left. G2087
35 the one shall be taken, and the **o** left. G2087
36 the one shall be taken, and the **o** left. G2087
18:10 one a Pharisee, and the **o** a publican. G2087
11 thee, that I am not as **o** men *are*, G3062
14 *rather* than the **o**: for every one that G1565
22:65 And many **o** things blasphemously G2087
23:32 And there were also two **o**, malefactors, G2087
33 on the right hand, and the **o** on the left. G3739
40 But the **o** answering rebuked him, G2087
24:10 of James, and **o** *women that were* with G3062
Jn 4:38 no labour: **o** men laboured, and ye G243
6:22 stood on the **o** side of the sea saw that G4008
22 there was none **o** boat there, save that G243
23 (Howbeit there came **o** boats from G243
25 And when they had found him on the **o** G4008
10: 1 **o** way, the same is a thief and a robber. G237
16 And **o** sheep I have, which are not of this G243
15:24 works which none **o** man did, they had G243
18:16 Then went out that **o** disciple, which was G243
19:18 Where they crucified him, and two **o** G243
32 of the **o** which was crucified with him. G243
20: 2 Peter, and to the **o** disciple, whom Jesus G243
3 Peter therefore went forth, and that **o** G243
4 So they ran both together: and the **o** G243
8 Then went in also that **o** disciple, which G243
12 at the head, and the **o** at the feet, where G1520
25 The **o** disciples therefore said unto him, G243
30 And many **o** signs truly did Jesus in the G243
21: 2 of Zebedee, and two **o** of his disciples. G243
8 And the **o** disciples came in a little ship; G243
25 And there are also many **o** things which G243
Act 2: 4 to speak with **o** tongues, as the Spirit G2087
40 And with many **o** words did he testify G2087
4:12 Neither is there salvation in any **o**: for G243
12 for there is none **o** name under heaven G2087
5:29 Then Peter and the **o** apostles answered
8:34 this? of himself, or of some **o** man? G2087
15: 2 and certain **o** of them, should go up G243
39 one from the **o**: and so Barnabas took G575
17: 9 of Jason, and of the **o**, they let them go. G3062
18 this babbler say? **o** some, He seemeth G1161
19:39 thing concerning **o** matters, it shall be G2087
23: 6 and the **o** Pharisees, he cried G2087
26:22 great, saying none **o** things than those G1622
27: 1 Paul and certain **o** prisoners unto *one* G2087
Ro 1:13 you also, even as among **o** Gentiles. G3062
8:39 Nor height, nor depth, nor any **o** G2087
13: 9 if *there be* any **o** commandment, it is G2087
1Co 1:16 I know not whether I baptized any **o**. G243
3:11 For **o** foundation can no man lay than G243
7: 5 Defraud ye not one the **o**, except *it be* G240
8: 4 and that *there is* none **o** God but one. G2087
9: 5 a wife, as well as **o** apostles, and *as* the G3062
10:29 own, but of the **o**: for why is my liberty G2087
11:21 For in eating every one taketh before **o**
14:17 thanks well, but the **o** is not edified. G2087
21 In the law it is written, With *men of* **o** G2084
21 *of* other tongues and **o** lips will I speak G1722
29 speak two or three, and let the **o** judge. G243
15:37 chance of wheat, or of some **o** *grain*: G3062
2Co 1:13 For we write none **o** things unto you, G243
2:16 death; and to the **o** the savour of life G3739
8:13 For *I mean* not that **o** men be eased, and G243
10:15 measure, *that is*, of **o** men's labours; but G245
11: 8 I robbed **o** churches, taking wages *of* G243
12:13 ye were inferior to **o** churches, except *it* G3062
13: 2 **o**, that, if I come again, I will not spare: G3062
Gal 1: 8 preach any **o** gospel unto you than
9 any *man* preach any **o** gospel unto you G3844
19 But **o** of the apostles saw I none, save G2087
2:13 And the **o** Jews dissembled likewise G3062
4:22 by a bondmaid, the **o** by a freewoman. G1520
5:17 the one to the **o**: so that ye cannot do G240
Eph 3: 5 Which in **o** ages was not made known G2087
4:17 walk not as **o** Gentiles walk, in the G3062
Php 1:13 in all the palace, and in all **o** *places*; G3062
17 But the **o** of love, knowing that I am set G3588
2: 3 let each esteem **o** better than themselves. G240
3: 4 in the flesh. If any **o** man thinketh that G243
4: 3 also, and *with* **o** my fellowlabourers, G3062
2Th 1: 3 one of you all toward each **o** aboundeth; G240
1Ti 1: 3 some that they teach no **o** doctrine, G2085
10 if there be any **o** thing that is contrary G2087
5:22 of **o** men's sins: keep thyself pure. G245
Jas 5:12 neither by any **o** oath: but let your yea G243
1Pt 4:15 or as a busybody in **o** men's matters. G244
2Pt 3:16 as *they do* also the **o** scriptures, unto G3062
Rev 2:24 I will put upon you none **o** burden. G243
8:13 by reason of the **o** voices of the trumpet G3062
17:10 and one is, *and* the **o** is not yet come; G243

OTHERS

Job 8:19 way, and out of the earth shall **o** grow. H312
31:10 another, and let **o** bow down upon her. H312
34:24 without number, and set **o** in their stead. H312
26 as wicked men in the open sight of **o**;
Ps 49:10 perish, and leave their wealth to **o**. H312
Prv 5: 9 Lest thou give thine honour unto **o**, and H312
Ecc 7:22 that thou thyself likewise hast cursed **o**. H312
Isa 56: 8 Yet will I gather *o* to him, beside those
Jer 6:12 And their houses shall be turned unto **o**, H312
8:10 Therefore will I give their wives unto **o**, H312
Ezk 9: 5 And to the **o** he said in mine hearing, Go H428
13: 6 and they have made *o* to hope that they
10 lo, **o** daubed it with untempered *morter*:
Dan 7:19 from all the **o**, exceeding dreadful,
11: 4 be plucked up, even for **o** beside those. H312
Mt 5:47 *than o*? do not even the publicans so?
15:30 and many **o**, and cast them down G2087
16:14 and **o**, Jeremias, or one of the prophets. G2087
20: 3 saw **o** standing idle in the marketplace, G243
6 out, and found **o** standing idle, and saith G243
21: 8 in the way; **o** cut down branches from G243
26:67 buffeted him; and **o** smote *him* with G3588
27:42 He saved **o**; himself he cannot save. If he G243
Mk 6:15 **O** said, That it is Elias. And others said, G243
15 Others said, That it is Elias. And **o** said, G243
8:28 *say*, Elias; and **o**, One of the prophets. G243
11: 8 in the way: and **o** cut down branches off G243
12: 5 many **o**; beating some, and killing some. G243
9 and will give the vineyard unto **o**. G243
15:31 He saved **o**; himself he cannot save. G243
Lk 5:29 and of **o** that sat down with them. G243
8: 3 and many **o**, which ministered unto G2087
10 of God: but to **o** in parables; that seeing G3062
9: 8 appeared; and of **o**, that one of the old G243
19 *say*, Elias; and **o** *say*, that one of the old G243
11:16 And **o**, tempting *him*, sought of him a G2087
18: 9 they were righteous, and despised **o**: G3062
20:16 the vineyard to **o**. And when they heard G243
23:35 saying, He saved **o**; let him save himself, G243
24: 1 had prepared, and certain *o* with them.
Jn 7:12 **o** said, Nay; but he deceiveth the people. G243
41 **O** said, This is the Christ. But some said, G243
9: 9 Some said, This is he: **o** *said*, He is like G243
16 the sabbath day. **O** said, How can a man G243
10:21 **O** said, These are not the words of him G243
12:29 **o** said, An angel spake to him. G243
18:34 of thyself, or did **o** tell it thee of me? G243
Act 2:13 **O** mocking said, These men are full of G2087
15:35 the word of the Lord, with many **o** also. G2087
17:32 mocked: and **o** said, We will hear thee G3588
34 named Damaris, and **o** with them. G2087
28: 9 So when this was done, **o** also, which G3062
1Co 9: 2 If I be not an apostle unto **o**, yet G243
12 If **o** be partakers of *this* power over you, G243
27 to **o**, I myself should be a castaway. G243
14:19 *my voice* I might teach **o** also, than ten G243
2Co 3: 1 or need we, as some *o*, epistles of
8: 8 the forwardness of **o**, and to prove the G2087
Eph 2: 3 nature the children of wrath, even as **o**. G3062
Php 2: 4 but every man also on the things of **o**. G2087
1Th 2: 6 of you, nor *yet* of **o**, when we might have G243
4:13 not, even as **o** which have no hope. G3062
5: 6 Therefore let us not sleep, as *do* **o**; but G3062
1Ti 5:20 Them that sin rebuke before all, that **o** G3062
2Ti 2: 2 men, who shall be able to teach **o** also. G2087
Heb 9:25 the holy place every year with blood of **o**; G245
11:35 to life again: and **o** were tortured, not G243
36 And **o** had trial of *cruel* mockings and G2087
Jude 23 And **o** save with fear, pulling *them* out G3739

OTHERWISE

2Sa 18:13 **O** I should have wrought falsehood H176
1Ki 1:21 **O** it shall come to pass, when my lord
2Ch 30:18 eat the passover **o** than it was written. H3808
Ps 38:16 For I said, *Hear me*, lest *o* they should
Mt 6: 1 be seen of them: **o** ye have no reward of G1490
Lk 5:36 upon an old; if **o**, then both the new G1490
Ro 11: 6 *it* no more of works: **o** grace is no more G1893
6 more grace: **o** work is no more work. G1893
22 goodness: **o** thou also shalt be cut off. G1893
2Co 11:16 think me a fool; if **o**, yet as a fool receive G1490
Gal 5:10 ye will be none **o** minded: but he that G243
Php 3:15 in any thing ye be **o** minded, God shall G2088
1Ti 5:25 and they that are **o** cannot be hid. G247
6: 3 If any man teach **o**, and consent not to G2085
Heb 9:17 men are dead: **o** it is of no strength at G1893

OTHNI

1Ch 26: 7 The sons of Shemaiah; **O**, and Rephael, H6273

OTHNIEL

Jos 15:17 And **O** the son of Kenaz, the brother of H6274
Jdg 1:13 And **O** the son of Kenaz, Caleb's H6274
3: 9 them, *even* **O** the son of Kenaz, Caleb's H6274
11 years. And **O** the son of Kenaz died. H6274

1Ch 4:13 And the sons of Kenaz; O, and Seraiah: H6274
13 Seraiah: and the sons of O; Hathath. H6274
27:15 Netophathite, of O: and in his course H6274

OUCHES
Ex 28:11 shalt make them to be set in o of gold. H4865
13 And thou shalt make o of gold; H4865
14 and fasten the wreathen chains to the o. H4865
25 fasten in the two o, and put them on the H4865
39: 6 stones inclosed in o of gold, graven, as H4865
13 inclosed in o of gold in their inclosings. H4865
16 And they made two o of gold, and two H4865
18 in the two o, and put them on the H4865

OUGHT
Gen 20: 9 deeds unto me that o not to be done.
34: 7 daughter; which thing o not to be done.
39: 6 and he knew not o he had, save the H3972
47:18 of cattle; there is not o left in the sight of
Ex 5: 8 shall not diminish o thereof: for they be
11 not o of your work shall be diminished. H1697
19 o from your bricks of your daily task.
12:46 not carry forth o of the flesh abroad out
22:14 And if a man borrow o of his neighbour,
29:34 And if o of the flesh of the consecrations,
Lev 4: 2 things which o not to be done, and
27 which o not to be done, and be guilty;
11:25 And whosoever beareth o of the carcase
19: 6 on the morrow: and if o remain until the
25:14 And if thou sell o unto thy neighbour, H4465
14 or buyest o of thy neighbour's hand,
27:31 And if a man will at all redeem o of his
Nu 15:24 Then it shall be, if o be committed by
30 But the soul that doeth o
30: 6 she vowed, or uttered o out of her lips,
Dt 4: 2 shall ye diminish o from it, that ye may
15: 2 that lendeth o unto his neighbour shall
26:14 have I taken away o thereof for any
14 use, nor given o thereof for the dead:
Jos 21:45 There failed not o of any good thing H1697
1Sa 12: 4 hast thou taken o of any man's hand. H3972
5 ye have not found o in my hand. And H3972
25: 7 neither was there o missing unto them, H3972
30:22 will not give them o of the spoil that we
2Sa 3:35 bread, or o else, till the sun be down. H3972
13:12 for no such thing o to be done in Israel:
14:10 And the king said, Whosoever saith o
19 or to the left from o that my lord the
1Ch 12:32 to know what Israel o to do; the heads of
15: 2 Then David said, None o to carry the ark
2Ch 13: 5 O ye not to know that the LORD God of
Neh 5: 9 Also I said, It is not good that ye do: o ye
Ps 76:11 presents unto him that o to be feared.
Mt 5:23 that thy brother hath o against thee; G5100
21: 3 And if any man say o unto you, ye shall G5100
23:23 and faith: these o ye to have done, and G1163
Mk 7:12 And ye suffer him no more to do o for G3762
8:23 upon him, he asked him if he saw o. G5100
11:25 forgive, if ye have o against any: that G5100
13:14 standing where it o not, (let him that G1163
Lk 11:42 love of God: these o ye to have done, G1163
12:12 you in the same hour what ye o to say. G1163
13:14 days in which men o to work: in them G1163
16 And o not this woman, being a G1163
18: 1 men o always to pray, and not to faint; G1163
24:26 O not Christ to have suffered these G1163
Jn 4:20 is the place where men o to worship. G1163
33 Hath any man brought him o to eat?
13:14 ye also o to wash one another's feet. G3784
19: 7 and by our law he o to die, because he G3784
Act 4:32 any of them that o of the things which G5100
5:29 We o to obey God rather than men. G1163
17:29 of God, we o not to think that the G3784
19:36 o to be quiet, and to do nothing rashly. G1163
20:35 so labouring ye o to support the weak, G1163
21:21 saying that they o not to circumcise their
24:19 Who o to have been here before thee, G1163
19 and object, if they had o against me. G1536
25:10 seat, where I o to be judged: to the G1163
24 crying that he o not to live any longer. G1163
26: 9 I verily thought with myself, that I o to G1163
28:19 not that I had o to accuse my nation of. G5100
Ro 8:26 pray for as we o: but the Spirit itself G1163
12: 3 highly than he o to think; but to think G1163
15: 1 We then that are strong o to bear the G3784
1Co 8: 2 knoweth nothing yet as he o to know. G1163
11: 7 For a man indeed o not to cover his G3784
10 For this cause o the woman to have G3784
2Co 2: 3 them of whom I o to rejoice; having G1163
7 So that contrariwise ye o rather to
12:11 me: for I o to have been commended G3784
14 for the children o not to lay up for the G3784
Eph 5:28 So o men to love their wives as their G3784
6:20 I may speak boldly, as I o to speak. G1163
Col 4: 4 That I may make it manifest, as I o to G1163
6 know how ye o to answer every man. G1163
1Th 4: 1 of us how ye o to walk and to please G1163
2Th 3: 7 For yourselves know how ye o to follow G1163
1Ti 5:13 speaking things which they o not. G1163
Tit 1:11 which they o not, for filthy lucre's sake. G1163
Phlm 18 oweth thee o, put that on mine account; G5100
Heb 2: 1 Therefore we o to give the more earnest G1163
5: 3 And by reason hereof he o, as for the G3784
12 For when for the time ye o to be G3784
Jas 3:10 brethren, these things o not so to be. G5534
4:15 For that ye o to say, If the Lord will, we
2Pt 3:11 manner of persons o ye to be in all holy G1163
1Jn 2: 6 He that saith he abideth in him o G3784
3:16 o to lay down our lives for the brethren. G3784
4:11 Beloved, if God so loved us, we o also G3784
3Jn 8 We therefore o to receive such, that we G3784

OUGHTEST
1Ki 2: 9 knowest what thou o to do unto him; but
Mt 25:27 Thou o therefore to have put my G1163
Act 10: 6 he shall tell thee what thou o to do. G1163
1Ti 3:15 know how thou o to behave thyself in G1163

OUR See the Appendix.

OURS See the Appendix.

OURSELVES See the Appendix.

OUT See the Appendix.

OUTCAST
Jer 30:17 called thee an O, saying, This is Zion, H5080

OUTCASTS
Ps 147: 2 he gathereth together the o of Israel. H1760
Isa 11:12 and shall assemble the o of Israel, and H1760
16: 3 the o; bewray not him that wandereth. H5080
4 Let mine o dwell with thee, Moab; be H5080
27:13 Assyria, and the o in the land of Egypt, H5080
56: 8 The Lord GOD which gathereth the o of H1760
Jer 49:36 whither the o of Elam shall not come. H5080

OUTER
Ezk 10: 5 heard even to the o court, as the voice H2435
Mt 8:12 be cast out into o darkness: there shall G1857
22:13 and cast him into o darkness; there G1857
25:30 servant into o darkness: there shall G1857

OUTGOINGS
Jos 17: 9 the river, and the o of it were at the sea: H8444
18 it down: and the o of it shall be thine: H8444
18:19 and the o of the border were at H8444
19:14 and the o thereof are in the valley H8444
22 and the o of their border were H8444
29 to Hosah; and the o thereof are at the H8444
33 and the o thereof were at Jordan: H8444
Ps 65: 8 thou makest the o of the morning and H4161

OUTLANDISH
Neh 13:26 even him did o women cause to sin. H5237

OUTLIVED
Jdg 2: 7 elders that o Joshua, who H748+H3117+H310

OUTMOST
Ex 26:10 one curtain that is o in the coupling, H7020
Nu 34: 3 be the o coast of the salt sea eastward: H7097
Dt 30: 4 If any of thine be driven out unto the o H7097
Isa 17: 6 four or five in the o fruitful branches

OUTRAGEOUS
Prv 27: 4 Wrath is cruel, and anger is o; but who H7858

OUTRUN
Jn 20: 4 other disciple did o Peter, and came G4390

OUTSIDE
Jdg 7:11 servant unto the o of the armed men H7097
17 I come to the o of the camp, it shall H7097
19 came unto the o of the camp in the H7097
1Ki 7: 9 and so on the o toward the great court. H2351
Ezk 40: 5 And behold a wall on the o of the house H2351
Mt 23:25 ye make clean the o of the cup and of G1855
26 that the o of them may be clean also. G1622
Lk 11:39 make clean the o of the cup and the G1855

OUTSTRETCHED
Dt 26: 8 hand, and with an o arm, and with H5186
Jer 21: 5 you with an o hand and with a strong H5186
27: 5 power and by my o arm, and have H5186

OUTWARD
Nu 35: 4 and o a thousand cubits round about. H2351
1Sa 16: 7 looketh on the o appearance, but the H5869
1Ch 26:29 his sons were for the o business over H2435
Neh 11:16 of the o business of the house of God. H2435
Est 6: 4 was come into the o court of the king's H2435
Ezk 40:17 Then brought he me into the o court, H2435
20 And the gate of the o court that looked H2435
34 were toward the o court; and palm H2435
44: 1 of the gate of the o sanctuary which H2435
Mt 23:27 appear beautiful o, but are within full of G1855
Ro 2:28 circumcision, which is o in the flesh: G1722
2Co 4:16 but though our o man perish, yet the G1854
10: 7 Do ye look on things after the o G4383
1Pt 3: 3 Whose adorning let it not be that o G1855

OUTWARDLY
Mt 23:28 Even so ye also o appear righteous G1855
Ro 2:28 For he is not a Jew, which is one o; G1722

OUTWENT
Mk 6:33 o them, and came together unto him. G4281

OVEN
Lev 2: 4 baken in the o, it shall be unleavened H8574
7: 9 is baken in the o, and all that is dressed H8574
11:35 whether it be o, or ranges for pots, they H8574
26:26 bake your bread in one o, and they shall H8574
Ps 21: 9 Thou shalt make them as a fiery o in H8574
Lam 5:10 Our skin was black like an o because of H8574
Hos 7: 4 They are all adulterers, as an o heated H8574
6 their heart like an o, whiles they lie in H8574
7 They are all hot as an o, and have H8574
Mal 4: 1 shall burn as an o; and all the proud, H8574
Mt 6:30 is cast into the o, shall he not much G2823
Lk 12:28 is cast into the o; how much more will G2823

OVENS
Ex 8: 3 thine o, and into thy kneadingtroughs: H8574

OVER See the Appendix.

OVERCAME
Act 19:16 on them, and o them, and prevailed G2634
Rev 3:21 even as I also o, and am set down with G3528
12:11 And they o him by the blood of the G3528

OVERCHARGE
2Co 2: 5 but in part: that I may not o you all. G1912

OVERCHARGED
Lk 21:34 your hearts be o with surfeiting, and G925

OVERCOME
Gen 49:19 Gad, a troop shall o him: but he shall H1464
19 him: but he shall o at the last. H1464
Ex 32:18 that cry for being o: but the noise of H2476
Nu 13:30 possess it; for we are well able to o it. H3201
22:11 be able to o them, and drive them out. H3898
2Ki 16: 5 besieged Ahaz, but could not o him. H3898
Song 6: 5 me, for they have o me: thy hair is as a H7292
Isa 28: 1 fat valleys of them that are o with wine! H1986
Jer 23: 9 man whom wine hath o, because of the H5674
Lk 11:22 upon him, and o him, he taketh from G3528
Jn 16:33 be of good cheer; I have o the world. G3528
Ro 3: 4 and mightest o when thou art judged. G3528
12:21 Be not o of evil, but overcome evil with G3528
21 Be not overcome of evil, but o evil with G3528
2Pt 2:19 o, of the same is he brought in bondage. G2274
20 therein, and o, the latter end is worse G2274
1Jn 2:13 because ye have o the wicked one. I G3528
14 in you, and ye have o the wicked one. G3528
4: 4 and have o them: because greater G3528
Rev 11: 7 them, and shall o them, and kill them. G3528
13: 7 the saints, and to o them: and power G3528
17:14 the Lamb shall o them: for he is Lord G3528

OVERCOMETH
1Jn 5: 4 For whatsoever is born of God **o** the *G3528*
4 victory that **o** the world, *even* our faith. *G3528*
5 Who is he that **o** the world, but he that *G3528*
Rev 2: 7 To him that **o** will I give to eat of the *G3528*
11 **o** shall not be hurt of the second death. *G3528*
17 To him that **o** will I give to eat of the *G3528*
26 And he that **o**, and keepeth my works *G3528*
3: 5 He that **o**, the same shall be clothed in *G3528*
12 Him that **o** will I make a pillar in the *G3528*
21 To him that **o** will I grant to sit with me *G3528*
21: 7 He that **o** shall inherit all things; and I *G3528*

OVERDRIVE
Gen 33:13 **o** them one day, all the flock will die. H1849

OVERFLOW
Dt 11: 4 water of the Red sea to **o** them as they H6687
Ps 69: 2 deep waters, where the floods **o** me. H7857
15 Let not the waterflood **o** me, neither let H7857
Isa 8: 8 Judah; he shall **o** and go over, he shall H7857
10:22 decreed shall **o** with righteousness. H7857
28:17 and the waters shall **o** the hiding place. H7857
43: 2 rivers, they shall not **o** thee: when thou H7857
Jer 47: 2 flood, and shall **o** the land, and all that H7857
Dan 11:10 come, and **o**, and pass through: then H7857
26 shall **o**: and many shall fall down slain. H7857
40 countries, and shall **o** and pass over. H7857
Joel 2:24 and the fats shall **o** with wine and oil. H7783
3:13 the fats **o**; for their wickedness *is* great. H7783

OVERFLOWED
Ps 78:20 and the streams **o**; can he give bread H7857
2Pt 3: 6 then was, being **o** with water, perished: *G2626*

OVERFLOWETH
Jos 3:15 **o** all his banks all the time of harvest,) H4390

OVERFLOWING
Job 28:11 He bindeth the floods from **o**; and *the* H1065
38:25 for the **o** of waters, or a way H7858
Isa 28: 2 of mighty waters **o**, shall cast down to H7857
15 when the **o** scourge shall pass through, H7857
18 stand; when the **o** scourge shall pass H7857
30:28 And his breath, as an **o** stream, shall H7857
Jer 47: 2 and shall be an **o** flood, and shall H7857
Ezk 13:11 there shall be an **o** shower; and ye, O H7857
13 and there shall be an **o** shower in mine H7857
38:22 that *are* with him, an **o** rain, and great H7857
Hab 3:10 *and* they trembled: the **o** of the water H2230

OVERFLOWN
1Ch 12:15 when it had **o** all his banks; and they H4390
Job 22:16 whose foundation was **o** with a flood: H3332
Dan 11:22 a flood shall they be **o** from before him, H7857

OVERLAID
Ex 26:32 of shittim *wood* **o** with gold: their H6823
36:34 And he **o** the boards with gold, and H6823
34 for the bars, and **o** the bars with gold. H6823
36 *of* shittim *wood,* and **o** them with gold: H6823
38 hooks: and he **o** their chapiters and H6823
37: 2 And he **o** it with pure gold within and H6823
4 *of* shittim wood, and **o** them with gold. H6823
11 And he **o** it with pure gold, and made H6823
15 and **o** them with gold, to bear the table. H6823
26 And he **o** it with pure gold, *both* the top H6823
28 *of* shittim wood, and **o** them with gold. H6823
38: 2 of the same: and he **o** it with brass. H6823
6 shittim wood, and **o** them with brass. H6823
28 **o** their chapiters, and filleted them. H6823
1Ki 3:19 child died in the night; because she **o** it. H7901
6:20 thereof: and he **o** it with pure gold; and H6823
21 So Solomon **o** the house within with H6823
21 before the oracle; and he **o** it with gold. H6823
22 And the whole house he **o** with gold, H6823
22 that *was* by the oracle he **o** with gold. H6823
28 And he **o** the cherubims with gold. H6823
30 And the floor of the house he **o** with H6823
32 open flowers, and **o** *them* with gold, H6823
10:18 of ivory, and **o** it with the best gold. H6823
2Ki 18:16 **o**, and gave it to the king of Assyria. H6823
2Ch 3: 4 and he **o** it within with pure gold. H6823
5 fir tree, which he **o** with fine gold, and H2645
7 He **o** also the house, the beams, the H2645
8 cubits: and he **o** it with fine gold, H2645
9 he **o** the upper chambers with gold. H2645
10 of image work, and **o** them with gold. H6823
2Ch 4: 9 and **o** the doors of them with brass. H6823
9:17 throne of ivory, and **o** it with pure gold. H6823
Song 5:14 *is as* bright ivory **o** *with* sapphires. H5968
Heb 9: 4 ark of the covenant **o** round about with *G4028*

OVERLAY
Ex 25:11 And thou shalt **o** it with pure gold, H6823
11 without shalt thou **o** it, and shalt make H6823
13 *of* shittim wood, and **o** them with gold. H6823
24 And thou shalt **o** it with pure gold, and H6823
28 *of* shittim wood, and **o** them with gold, H6823
26:29 And thou shalt **o** the boards with gold, H6823
29 and thou shalt **o** the bars with gold. H6823
37 *of* shittim *wood,* and **o** them with gold, H6823
27: 2 same: and thou shalt **o** it with brass. H6823
6 shittim wood, and **o** them with brass. H6823
30: 3 And thou shalt **o** it with pure gold, the H6823
5 *of* shittim wood, and **o** them with gold. H6823
1Ch 29: 4 to **o** the walls of the houses *withal:* H2902

OVERLAYING
Ex 38:17 *of* silver; and the **o** of their chapiters *of* H6826
19 *of* silver, and the **o** of their chapiters H6826

OVERLIVED
Jos 24:31 elders that **o** Joshua, and H748+H3117+H310

OVERMUCH
2Co 2: 7 should be swallowed up with **o** sorrow. *G4055*

OVERPASS
Jer 5:28 they shine: yea, they **o** the deeds of the H5674

OVERPAST
Ps 57: 1 my refuge, until *these* calamities be **o**. H5674
Isa 26:20 moment, until the indignation be **o**. H5674

OVERPLUS
Lev 25:27 and restore the **o** unto the man to H5736

OVERRAN
2Sa 18:23 by the way of the plain, and **o** Cushi. H5674

OVERRUNNING
Nah 1: 8 But with an **o** flood he will make an H5674

OVERSEE
1Ch 9:29 *Some* of them also *were* appointed to **o**
2Ch 2: 2 thousand and six hundred to **o** them. H5329

OVERSEER
Gen 39: 4 and he made him **o** over his house, and H6485
5 he had made him **o** in his house, and H6485
Neh 11: 9 And Joel the son of Zichri *was* their **o**: H6496
14 eight: and their **o** *was* Zabdiel, the son H6496
22 The **o** also of the Levites at Jerusalem H6496
12:42 sang loud, with Jezrahiah *their* **o**. H6496
Prv 6: 7 Which having no guide, **o**, or ruler, H7860

OVERSEERS
2Ch 2:18 six hundred **o** to set the people a work. H5329
31:13 and Benaiah, *were* **o** under the hand of H6496
34:12 work faithfully: and the **o** of them *were* H6485
13 and *were* **o** of all that wrought the H5329
17 the **o**, and to the hand of the workmen. H6485
Act 20:28 hath made you **o**, to feed the church of *G1985*

OVERSHADOW
Lk 1:35 the Highest shall **o** thee: therefore also *G1982*
Act 5:15 Peter passing by might **o** some of them. *G1982*

OVERSHADOWED
Mt 17: 5 a bright cloud **o** them: and behold a *G1982*
Mk 9: 7 And there was a cloud that **o** them: and *G1982*
Lk 9:34 came a cloud, and **o** them: and they *G1982*

OVERSIGHT
Gen 43:12 in your hand; peradventure it *was* an **o**: H4870
Nu 3:32 *and have* the **o** of them that keep the H6486
4:16 oil, *and* the **o** of all the tabernacle, H6486
2Ki 12:11 work, that had the **o** of the house of the H6485
22: 5 that have the **o** of the house of the H6485
9 have the **o** of the house of the LORD. H6485
1Ch 9:23 So they and their children *had* the **o** of H5921
2Ch 34:10 that had the **o** of the house of the H6485
Neh 11:16 the Levites, *had* the **o** of the outward H5921
13: 4 priest, having the **o** of the chamber of H5414
1Pt 5: 2 among you, taking the **o** *thereof,* not by *G1983*

OVERSPREAD
Gen 9:19 and of them was the whole earth **o**. H5310

OVERSPREADING
Dan 9:27 cease, and for the **o** of abominations he H3671

OVERTAKE
Gen 44: 4 when thou dost **o** them, say unto them, H5381
Ex 15: 9 The enemy said, I will pursue, I will **o**, I H5381
Dt 19: 6 his heart is hot, and **o** him, because the H5381
28: 2 come on thee, and **o** thee, if thou shalt H5381
15 shall come upon thee, and **o** thee: H5381
45 pursue thee, and **o** thee, till thou be H5381
Jos 2: 5 after them quickly; for ye shall **o** them. H5381
1Sa 30: 8 after this troop? shall I **o** them? And he H5381
8 **o** *them,* and without fail recover *all.* H5381
2Sa 15:14 to depart, lest he **o** us suddenly, and H5381
Isa 59: 9 doth justice **o** us: we wait for light, H5381
Jer 42:16 ye feared, shall **o** you there in the land H5381
Hos 2: 7 but she shall not **o** them; and she shall H5381
10: 9 the children of iniquity did not **o** them. H5381
Am 9:10 say, The evil shall not **o** nor prevent us. H5066
13 the plowman shall **o** the reaper, and H5066
1Th 5: 4 that that day should **o** you as a thief. *G2638*

OVERTAKEN
Ps 18:37 I have pursued mine enemies, and **o** H5381
Gal 6: 1 Brethren, if a man be **o** in a fault, ye *G4301*

OVERTAKETH
1Ch 21:12 of thine enemies **o** *thee;* or else three H5381

OVERTHREW
Gen 19:25 And he **o** those cities, and all the plain, H2015
29 he **o** the cities in the which Lot dwelt. H2015
Ex 14:27 **o** the Egyptians in the midst of the sea. H5287
Dt 29:23 LORD **o** in his anger, and in his wrath: H2015
Ps 136:15 But **o** Pharaoh and his host in the Red H5287
Isa 13:19 as when God **o** Sodom and Gomorrah. H4114
Jer 20:16 which the LORD **o**, and repented not: H2015
50:40 As God **o** Sodom and Gomorrah and H4114
Am 4:11 *some* of you, as God **o** Sodom and H4114
Mt 21:12 in the temple, and **o** the tables of the *G2690*
Mk 11:15 in the temple, and **o** the tables of the *G2690*
Jn 2:15 the changers' money, and **o** the tables; *G390*

OVERTHROW
Gen 19:21 that I will not **o** this city, for the which H2015
29 out of the midst of the **o**, when he H2018
Ex 23:24 but thou shalt utterly **o** them, and quite H2040
Dt 12: 3 And ye shall **o** their altars, and break H5422
29:23 therein, like the **o** of Sodom, and H4114
2Sa 10: 3 the city, and to spy it out, and to **o** it? H2015
11:25 city, and **o** it: and encourage thou him. H2040
1Ch 19: 3 and to **o**, and to spy out the land? H2015
Ps 106:26 them, to **o** them in the wilderness: H5307
27 To **o** their seed also among the nations, H5307
140: 4 who have purposed to **o** my goings. H1760
11 shall hunt the violent man to **o** *him.* H4073
Prv 18: 5 wicked, to **o** the righteous in judgment. H5186
Jer 49:18 As in the **o** of Sodom and Gomorrah H4114
Hag 2:22 And I will **o** the throne of kingdoms, H2015
22 and I will **o** the chariots, and those H2015
Act 5:39 But if it be of God, ye cannot **o** it; lest *G2647*
2Ti 2:18 is past already; and **o** the faith of some. *G396*
2Pt 2: 6 *them* with an **o**, making *them* an *G2692*

OVERTHROWETH
Job 12:19 He leadeth princes away spoiled, and **o** H5557
Prv 13: 6 the way: but wickedness **o** the sinner. H5557
21:12 *God* **o** the wicked for *their* wickedness. H5557
22:12 and he **o** the words of the transgressor. H5557
29: 4 the land: but he that receiveth gifts **o** it. H2040

OVERTHROWN
Ex 15: 7 thou hast **o** them that rose up against H2040
Jdg 9:40 and many were **o** *and* wounded, *even* H5307
2Sa 17: 9 some of them be **o** at the first, that H5307
2Ch 14:13 Ethiopians were **o**, that they could not H5307
Job 19: 6 Know now that God hath **o** me, and H5791
Ps 141: 6 When their judges are **o** in stony H8058
Prv 11:11 but it is **o** by the mouth of the wicked. H2040
12: 7 The wicked are **o**, and *are* not: but the H2015
14:11 The house of the wicked shall be **o**: but H8045
Isa 1: 7 and *it is* desolate, as **o** by strangers. H4114
Jer 18:23 but let them be **o** before thee; deal *thus* H3782
Lam 4: 6 of Sodom, that was **o** as in a moment, H2015
Dan 11:41 *countries* shall be **o**: but these shall H3782

Am 4:11 I have **o** *some* of you, as God overthrew H2015
Jna 3: 4 Yet forty days, and Nineveh shall be **o**. H2015
1Co 10: 5 for they were **o** in the wilderness. *G2693*

OVERTOOK
Gen 31:23 and they **o** him in the mount Gilead. H1692
25 Then Laban **o** Jacob. Now Jacob had H5381
44: 6 And he **o** them, and he spake unto H5381
Ex 14: 9 And his army, and **o** them encamping H5381
Jdg 18:22 together, and **o** the children of Dan. H1692
20:42 but the battle **o** them; and them which H1692
2Ki 25: 5 after the king, and **o** him in the plains H5381
Jer 39: 5 after them, and **o** Zedekiah in the H5381
52: 8 after the king, and **o** Zedekiah in the H5381
Lam 1: 3 persecutors **o** her between the straits. H5381

OVERTURN
Job 12:15 sendeth them out, and they **o** the earth. H2015
Ezk 21:27 I will **o**, overturn, overturn, it: and it H5754
27 I will overturn, **o**, overturn, it: and it H5754
27 I will overturn, overturn, **o**, it: and it H5754

OVERTURNED
Jdg 7:13 it fell, and **o** it, that the tent lay along. H2015

OVERTURNETH
Job 9: 5 know not: which **o** them in his anger. H2015
28: 9 rock; he **o** the mountains by the roots. H2015
34:25 works, and he **o** *them* in the night, so H2015

OVERWHELM
Job 6:27 Yea, ye **o** the fatherless, and ye dig *a pit* H5307

OVERWHELMED
Ps 55: 5 come upon me, and horror hath **o** me. H3680
61: 2 when my heart is **o**: lead me to the rock H5848
77: 3 complained, and my spirit was **o**. Selah. H5848
78:53 feared not: but the sea **o** their enemies. H3680
102:ttl A Prayer of the afflicted, when he is **o**, H5848
124: 4 Then the waters had **o** us, the stream H7857
142: 3 When my spirit was **o** within me, then H5848
143: 4 Therefore is my spirit **o** within me; my H5848

OWE
Ro 13: 8 **O** no man any thing, but to love one *G3784*

OWED
Mt 18:24 him, which **o** him ten thousand talents. *G3781*
28 which **o** him an hundred pence: *G3784*
Lk 7:41 debtors: the one **o** five hundred pence, *G3784*

OWEST
Mt 18:28 the throat, saying, Pay me that thou **o**. *G3784*
Lk 16: 5 first, How much **o** thou unto my lord? *G3784*
7 And how much **o** thou? And he said, *G3784*
Phlm 19 **o** unto me even thine own self besides. *G4359*

OWETH
Phlm 18 If he hath wronged thee, or **o** *thee* *G3784*

OWL
Lev 11:16 And the **o**, and the night hawk, and the H3284
17 And the little **o**, and the cormorant, and H3563
17 and the cormorant, and the great **o**, H3244
Dt 14:15 And the **o**, and the night hawk, H1323+H3284
16 The little **o**, and the great owl, and the H3563
16 The little owl, and the great **o**, and the H3244
Ps 102: 6 wilderness: I am like an **o** of the desert. H3563
Isa 34:11 possess it; the **o** also and the raven H3244
14 his fellow; the screech **o** also shall rest H3917
15 There shall the great **o** make her nest, H7091

OWLS
Job 30:29 and a companion to **o**. H1323+H3284
Isa 13:21 and **o** shall dwell there, H1323+H3284
34:13 of dragons, *and* a court for **o**. H1323+H3284
43:20 and the **o**: because I give H1323+H3284
Jer 50:39 *there*, and the **o** shall dwell H1323+H3284
Mic 1: 8 and mourning as the **o**. H1323+H3284

OWN
Gen 1:27 So God created man in his *o* image, in H6754
5: 3 begat *a son* in his **o** likeness, after his H1823
14:14 born in his **o** house, three hundred
15: 4 of thine **o** bowels shall be thine heir. H4578
30:25 unto mine **o** place, and to my country. H4725
30 shall I provide for mine **o** house also? H1004
40 and he put his **o** flocks by themselves, H5739
Gen 47:24 parts shall be your **o**, for seed of the field,
Ex 5:16 beaten; but the fault *is* in thine **o** people.
18:27 and he went his way into his **o** land.
21:36 pay ox for ox; and the dead shall be his **o**.
22: 5 of the best of his **o** field, and of the best
5 his **o** vineyard, shall he make restitution.
32:13 swarest by thine **o** self, and saidst unto
Lev 1: 3 shall offer it of his **o** voluntary will at the
7:30 His **o** hands shall bring the offerings of H3027
14:15 pour *it* into the palm of his **o** left hand: H3548
26 the oil into the palm of his **o** left hand: H3548
16:29 *it be* one of your **o** country, or a stranger H249
17:15 *whether it be* one of your **o** country, or a H249
18:10 uncover: for theirs *is* thine **o** nakedness.
26 *neither* any of your **o** nation, nor any H249
19: 5 the LORD, ye shall offer it at your **o** will.
21:14 shall take a virgin of his **o** people to wife.
22:19 *Ye shall offer* at your **o** will a male
29 unto the LORD, offer *it* at your **o** will.
24:22 **o** country: for I *am* the LORD your God. H249
25: 5 That which groweth of its **o** accord of thy
41 return unto his **o** family, and unto the
Nu 1:52 every man by his **o** camp, and every H4264
52 his **o** standard, throughout their hosts. H1714
2: 2 shall pitch by his **o** standard, with the H1714
10:30 to mine **o** land, and to my kindred. H776
13:33 we were in our **o** sight as grasshoppers, H5869
15:39 not after your **o** heart and your own H3824
39 heart and your **o** eyes, after which ye H5869
16:28 *I have* not *done them* of mine **o** mind.
38 against their **o** souls, let them make
24:13 or bad of mine **o** mind; *but* what the H3820
27: 3 but died in his **o** sin, and had no sons. H2399
32:42 and called it Nobah, after his **o** name. H8034
36: 9 shall keep himself to his **o** inheritance. H5159
Dt 3:14 called them after his **o** name, H8034
12: 8 man whatsoever *is* right in his **o** eyes. H5869
13: 6 which *is* as thine **o** soul, entice thee H5315
22: 2 bring it unto thine **o** house, and it shall
23:24 thy fill at thine **o** pleasure; but thou shalt
24:13 he may sleep in his **o** raiment, and bless
16 man shall be put to death for his **o** sin. H2399
28:53 And thou shalt eat the fruit of thine **o** H990
33: 9 nor knew his **o** children: for they have H1121
Jos 7:11 have put *it* even among their **o** stuff. H3627
20: 6 and come unto his **o** city, and unto his H5892
6 city, and unto his **o** house, unto the city H1004
Jdg 2:19 **o** doings, nor from their stubborn way.
7: 2 saying, Mine **o** hand hath saved me. H3027
8:29 of Joash went and dwelt in his **o** house. H1004
17: 6 did *that which was* right in his **o** eyes. H5869
21:25 did *that which was* right in his **o** eyes. H5869
Ru 4: 6 lest I mar mine **o** inheritance: redeem H5159
1Sa 2:20 LORD. And they went unto their **o** home.
5:11 it go again to his **o** place, that it slay us
6: 9 And see, if it goeth up by the way of his **o**
13:14 a man after his **o** heart, and the LORD
14:46 and the Philistines went to their **o** place.
15:17 *wast* little in thine **o** sight, *wast* thou not
18: 1 and Jonathan loved him as his **o** soul.
3 because he loved him as his **o** soul.
20:17 for he loved him as he loved his **o** soul.
30 of Jesse to thine **o** confusion, and unto
25:26 thyself with thine **o** hand, now let thine
33 from avenging myself with mine **o** hand.
39 of Nabal upon his **o** head. And David
28: 3 Ramah, even in his **o** city. And Saul had
2Sa 4:11 person in his **o** house upon his bed?
6:22 will be base in mine **o** sight: and of the
7:10 in a place of their **o**, and move no more;
21 according to thine **o** heart, hast thou
12: 3 it did eat of his **o** meat, and drank of his
3 and drank of his **o** cup, and lay in his
4 to take of his **o** flock and of his own
4 flock and of his **o** herd, to dress for the
11 thee out of thine **o** house, and I will take
20 he came to his **o** house; and when he
14:24 And the king said, Let him turn to his **o**
24 his **o** house, and saw not the king's face.
17:11 that thou go to battle in thine **o** person.
18:13 against mine **o** life: for there is no matter
18 the pillar after his **o** name: and it is
19:28 that did eat at thine **o** table. What right
30 is come again in peace unto his **o** house.
37 I may die in mine **o** city, *and be buried*
39 him; and he returned unto his **o** place.
23:21 hand, and slew him with his **o** spear.
1Ki 1:12 **o** life, and the life of thy son Solomon.
1Ki 1:33 **o** mule, and bring him down to Gihon:
2:23 not spoken this word against his **o** life.
26 unto thine **o** fields; for thou *art* worthy
32 his blood upon his **o** head, who fell upon
34 buried in his **o** house in the wilderness.
37 thy blood shall be upon thine **o** head.
44 thy wickedness upon thine **o** head;
3: 1 an end of building his **o** house, and the
7: 1 But Solomon was building his **o** house
8:38 the plague of his **o** heart, and spread
9:15 of the LORD, and his **o** house, and Millo,
10: 6 **o** land of thy acts and of thy wisdom.
13 to her **o** country, she and her servants.
11:19 **o** wife, the sister of Tahpenes the queen.
21 depart, that I may go to mine **o** country.
22 seekest to go to thine **o** country? And he
12:16 now see to thine **o** house, David. So
33 had devised of his **o** heart; and ordained
13:30 And he laid his carcase in his **o** grave;
14:12 Arise thou therefore, get thee to thine **o**
17:19 he abode, and laid him upon his **o** bed.
22:36 his city, and every man to his **o** country.
2Ki 2:12 **o** clothes, and rent them in two pieces.
3:27 from him, and returned to *their* **o** land.
4:13 answered, I dwell among mine **o** people.
12:18 dedicated, and his **o** hallowed things,
14: 6 man shall be put to death for his **o** sin.
17:23 of their **o** land to Assyria unto this day.
29 made gods of their **o**, and put *them* in the
33 LORD, and served their **o** gods, after the
18:27 they may eat their **o** dung, and drink
27 dung, and drink their **o** piss with you?
31 eat ye every man of his **o** vine, and every
32 to a land like your **o** land, a land of corn
19: 7 and shall return to his **o** land; and I will
7 him to fall by the sword in his **o** land.
34 **o** sake, and for my servant David's sake.
20: 6 **o** sake, and for my servant David's sake.
21:18 the garden of his **o** house, in the garden
23 him, and slew the king in his **o** house.
23:30 buried him in his **o** sepulchre. And the
1Ch 11:23 hand, and slew him with his **o** spear.
17:19 according to thine **o** heart, hast thou
21 to redeem *to be* his **o** people, to make
22 thou make thine **o** people for ever; and
29: 3 I have of mine **o** proper good, of gold
14 thee, and of thine **o** have we given thee. H3027
16 *cometh* of thine hand, and *is* all thine **o**.
2Ch 6:23 his way upon his **o** head; and by
29 one shall know his **o** sore and his own
29 his own sore and his **o** grief, and shall
7:11 in his **o** house, he prosperously effected.
8: 1 the house of the LORD, and his **o** house,
9: 5 **o** land of thine acts, and of thy wisdom:
12 to her **o** land, she and her servants.
10:16 **o** house. So all Israel went to their tents.
16:14 And they buried him in his **o** sepulchres,
24:25 great diseases,) his **o** servants conspired
25: 4 but every man shall die for his **o** sin.
15 deliver their **o** people out of thine hand?
31: 1 man to his possession, into their **o** cities.
32:21 of face to his **o** land. And when he was
21 **o** bowels slew him there with the sword.
33:20 buried him in his **o** house: and Amon his
24 him, and slew him in his **o** house.
Ezr 7:13 are minded of their **o** freewill to go up to
Neh 4: 4 upon their **o** head, and give them
6: 8 thou feignest them out of thine **o** heart.
16 much cast down in their **o** eyes: for they
Est 1:22 bear rule in his **o** house, and that *it*
2: 7 were dead, took for his **o** daughter.
9:25 return upon his **o** head, and that he and
Job 2:11 every one from his **o** place; Eliphaz the
5:13 He taketh the wise in their **o** craftiness:
9:20 If I justify myself, mine **o** mouth shall
31 and mine **o** clothes shall abhor me.
13:15 I will maintain mine **o** ways before him.
15: 6 Thine **o** mouth condemneth thee, and
6 I: yea, thine **o** lips testify against thee.
18: 7 and his **o** counsel shall cast him down.
8 For he is cast into a net by his **o** feet, and
19:17 for the children's *sake* of mine **o** body.
20: 7 *Yet* he shall perish for ever like his **o**
32: 1 because he *was* righteous in his **o** eyes.
40:14 that thine **o** right hand can save thee.
Ps 4: 4 with your **o** heart upon your bed,
5:10 them fall by their **o** counsels; cast them
7:16 His mischief shall return upon his **o**

Ps 7:16 shall come down upon his **o** pate.
9:15 net which they hid is their **o** foot taken.
16 the work of his **o** hands. Higgaion. Selah.
12: 4 our lips *are* our **o**: who *is* lord over us?
15: 4 to *his* **o** hurt, and changeth not.
17:10 They are inclosed in their **o** fat: with
20: 4 Grant thee according to thine **o** heart,
21:13 Be thou exalted, LORD, in thine **o**
22:29 him: and none can keep alive his **o** soul.
33:12 he hath chosen for his **o** inheritance.
35:13 my prayer returned into mine **o** bosom.
36: 2 For he flattereth himself in his **o** eyes,
37:15 Their sword shall enter into their **o**
41: 9 Yea, mine **o** familiar friend, in whom I
44: 3 possession by their **o** sword, neither did
3 neither did their **o** arm save them: but
45:10 thine **o** people, and thy father's house;
49:11 they call *their* lands after their **o** names.
50:20 thou slanderest thine **o** mother's son.
64: 8 So they shall make their **o** tongue to fall
67: 6 *and* God, *even* our **o** God, shall bless us.
74:22 Arise, O God, plead thine **o** cause:
77: 6 with mine **o** heart: and my spirit
78:29 filled: for he gave them their **o** desire;
52 But made his **o** people to go forth like
81:12 So I gave them up unto their **o** hearts'
12 lust: *and* they walked in their **o** counsels.
94:23 And he shall bring upon them their **o**
23 them off in their **o** wickedness; *yea*, the
106:39 Thus were they defiled with their **o**
39 went a whoring with their **o** inventions.
40 that he abhorred his **o** inheritance.
109:29 with their **o** confusion, as with a mantle.
138: 8 forsake not the works of thine **o** hands.
140: 9 the mischief of their **o** lips cover them.
141:10 Let the wicked fall into their **o** nets,
Prv 1:18 And they lay wait for their **o** blood; they
18 blood; they lurk privily for their **o** lives.
31 of the fruit of their **o** way, and be filled
31 way, and be filled with their **o** devices.
3: 5 lean not unto thine **o** understanding.
7 Be not wise in thine **o** eyes: fear the
5:15 Drink waters out of thine **o** cistern, and
15 and running waters out of thine **o** well.
17 Let them be only thine **o**, and not
22 His **o** iniquities shall take the wicked
6:32 he *that* doeth it destroyeth his **o** soul.
8:36 **o** soul: all they that hate me love death.
11: 5 the wicked shall fall by his **o** wickedness.
6 shall be taken in *their* **o** naughtiness.
17 The merciful man doeth good to his **o**
17 but *he that is* cruel troubleth his **o** flesh.
19 pursueth evil *pursueth it* to his **o** death.
29 He that troubleth his **o** house shall
12:15 The way of a fool *is* right in his **o** eyes:
14:10 The heart knoweth his **o** bitterness; H5315
14 be filled with his **o** ways: and a good
20 The poor is hated even of his **o**
15:27 He that is greedy of gain troubleth his **o**
32 despiseth his **o** soul: but he that heareth
16: 2 All the ways of a man *are* clean in his **o**
18:11 city, and as an high wall in his **o** conceit.
17 *He that is* first in his **o** cause *seemeth*
19: 8 He that getteth wisdom loveth his **o** soul:
16 keepeth his **o** soul; *but* he that despiseth
20: 2 him to anger sinneth *against* his **o** soul.
6 Most men will proclaim every one his **o**
24 can a man then understand his **o** way?
21: 2 Every way of a man *is* right in his **o** eyes:
23: 4 Labour not to be rich: cease from thine **o**
25:27 *men* to search their **o** glory *is not* glory.
28 He that *hath* no rule over his **o** spirit *is*
26: 5 his folly, lest he be wise in his **o** conceit.
12 Seest thou a man wise in his **o** conceit?
16 The sluggard *is* wiser in his **o** conceit
27: 2 thee, and not thine **o** mouth; a stranger,
2 mouth; a stranger, and not thine **o** lips.
10 Thine **o** friend, and thy father's friend,
28:10 fall himself into his **o** pit: but the upright
11 The rich man *is* wise in his **o** conceit; but
26 He that trusteth in his **o** heart is a fool:
29:24 with a thief hateth his **o** soul: he heareth
30:12 *are* pure in their **o** eyes, and *yet* is not
31:31 let her **o** works praise her in the gates.
Ecc 1:16 I communed with mine **o** heart, saying,
3:22 rejoice in his **o** works; for that *is* his
4: 5 hands together, and eateth his **o** flesh.
7:22 For oftentimes also thine **o** heart

Ecc 8: 9 man ruleth over another to his **o** hurt.
Song 1: 6 *but* mine **o** vineyard have I not kept.
Isa 2: 8 the work of their **o** hands, that which
8 that which their **o** fingers have made:
4: 1 We will eat our **o** bread, and wear our
1 and wear our **o** apparel: only let us be
5:21 Woe unto *them that are* wise in their **o**
21 own eyes, and prudent in their **o** sight!
9:20 eat every man the flesh of his **o** arm:
13:14 man turn to his **o** people, and flee every
14 and flee every one into his **o** land.
14: 1 and set them in their **o** land: and the
18 lie in glory, every one in his **o** house.
23: 7 **o** feet shall carry her afar off to sojourn.
31: 7 **o** hands have made unto you *for* a sin.
36:12 they may eat their **o** dung, and drink
12 dung, and drink their **o** piss with you?
16 ye every one the waters of his **o** cistern;
17 to a land like your **o** land, a land of corn
37: 7 and return to his **o** land; and I will cause
7 him to fall by the sword in his **o** land.
35 **o** sake, and for my servant David's sake.
43:25 **o** sake, and will not remember thy sins.
44: 9 and they *are* their **o** witnesses; they see
48:11 For mine **o** sake, *even* for mine own
11 For mine own sake, *even* for mine **o**
49:26 thee with their **o** flesh; and they shall
26 be drunken with their **o** blood, as with
53: 6 every one to his **o** way; and the LORD
56:11 all look to their **o** way, every one for his
58: 7 thou hide not thyself from thine **o** flesh?
13 not doing thine **o** ways, nor finding thine
13 ways, nor finding thine **o** pleasure, nor
13 pleasure, nor speaking *thine* **o** words:
63: 5 therefore mine **o** arm brought salvation
65: 2 *that was* not good, after their **o** thoughts;
66: 3 have chosen their **o** ways, and their soul
Jer 1:16 worshipped the works of their **o** hands.
2:19 Thine **o** wickedness shall correct thee,
30 no correction: your **o** sword hath
7:19 to the confusion of their **o** faces?
9:14 of their **o** heart, and after Baalim,
18:12 will walk after our **o** devices, and we will
23: 8 and they shall dwell in their **o** land.
16 a vision of their **o** heart, *and* not out of
17 his **o** heart, No evil shall come upon you.
26 prophets of the deceit of their **o** heart;
25: 7 the works of your hands to your **o** hurt.
14 according to the works of their **o** hands.
27:11 still in their **o** land, saith the LORD;
30:18 builded upon her **o** heap, and the palace
31:17 shall come again to their **o** border.
30 But every one shall die for his **o** iniquity:
37: 7 shall return to Egypt into their **o** land.
42:12 and cause you to return to your **o** land.
44: 9 wives, and your **o** wickedness, and the
17 goeth forth out of our **o** mouth, to burn
46:16 us go again to our **o** people, and to the
50:16 they shall flee every one to his **o** land.
51: 9 go every one into his **o** country: for her
52:27 carried away captive out of his **o** land.
Lam 4:10 have sodden their **o** children: they were
Ezk 11:21 upon their **o** heads, saith the Lord GOD.
13: 2 **o** hearts, Hear ye the word of the LORD;
3 their **o** spirit, and have seen nothing!
17 out of their **o** heart; and prophesy
14: 5 of Israel in their **o** heart, because they
14 should deliver *but* their **o** souls by their
20 their **o** souls by their righteousness.
16: 6 polluted in thine **o** blood, I said unto
15 But thou didst trust in thine **o** beauty,
52 sisters, bear thine **o** shame for thy sins
54 That thou mayest bear thine **o** shame,
17:19 it will I recompense upon his **o** head.
20:26 And I polluted them in their **o** gifts, in
43 yourselves in your **o** sight for all your
22:31 fire of my wrath: their **o** way have I
23:34 and pluck off thine **o** breasts: for I have
29: 3 *is* mine **o**, and I have made *it* for myself.
32:10 man for his **o** life, in the day of thy fall.
33: 4 his blood shall be upon his **o** head.
13 if he trust to his **o** righteousness, and
34:13 will bring them to their **o** land, and feed
36:17 dwelt in their **o** land, they defiled it by
17 defiled it by their **o** way and by their
24 and will bring you into your **o** land.
31 Then shall ye remember your **o** evil
31 lothe yourselves in your **o** sight for your

Ezk 36:32 for your **o** ways, O house of Israel.
37:14 place you in your **o** land: then shall ye
21 side, and bring them into their **o** land:
39:28 them unto their **o** land, and have left
46:18 out of his **o** possession: that my
Dan 3:28 nor worship any god, except their **o** God.
6:17 sealed it with his **o** signet, and with the
8:24 but not by his **o** power: and he shall
9:19 defer not, for thine **o** sake, O my God: for
11: 9 and shall return into his **o** land.
16 according to his **o** will, and none shall H7522
18 but a prince for his **o** behalf shall cause
18 to cease; without his **o** reproach he shall
19 toward the fort of his **o** land: but he shall
28 do *exploits*, and return to his **o** land.
Hos 7: 2 now their **o** doings have beset them
10: 6 Israel shall be ashamed of his **o** counsel.
11: 6 *them*, because of their **o** counsels.
13: 2 according to their **o** understanding, all
Joel 3: 4 your recompence upon your **o** head;
7 your recompence upon your **o** head:
Am 6:13 not taken to us horns by our **o** strength?
7:11 be led away captive out of their **o** land.
Oba 15 reward shall return upon thine **o** head.
Jna 2: 8 lying vanities forsake their **o** mercy.
Mic 7: 6 enemies *are* the men of his **o** house.
Hag 1: 9 and ye run every man unto his **o** house.
Zec 5:11 and set there upon her **o** base.
11: 5 and their **o** shepherds pity them not.
12: 6 again in her **o** place, *even* in Jerusalem.
Mal 3:17 man spareth his **o** son that serveth him.
Mt 2:12 into their **o** country another way. *G846*
7: 3 not the beam that is in thine **o** eye? *G4674*
4 and, behold, a beam *is* in thine **o** eye? *G4675*
5 beam out of thine **o** eye; and then shalt *G4675*
9: 1 passed over, and came into his **o** city. *G2398*
10:36 And a man's foes *shall be* they of his **o** *G846*
13:54 And when he was come into his **o** *G846*
57 in his **o** country, and in his own house. *G846*
57 in his own country, and in his **o** house. *G846*
16:26 world, and lose his **o** soul? or what shall *G846*
17:25 of their **o** children, or of strangers? *G846*
20:15 **o**? Is thine eye evil, because I am good? *G1699*
25:14 country, *who* called his **o** servants, and *G2398*
27 have received mine **o** with usury. *G1699*
27:31 him, and put his **o** raiment on him, and *G846*
60 And laid it in his **o** new tomb, which he *G846*
Mk 6: 1 **o** country; and his disciples follow him. *G846*
4 honour, but in his **o** country, and among *G846*
4 among his **o** kin, and in his own house.
4 among his own kin, and in his **o** house. *G846*
7: 9 God, that ye may keep your **o** tradition. *G5216*
8: 3 fasting to their **o** houses, they will faint *G846*
36 the whole world, and lose his **o** soul? *G846*
15:20 him, and put his **o** clothes on him, and *G2398*
Lk 1:23 he departed to his **o** house. *G846*
56 months, and returned to her **o** house. *G846*
2: 3 to be taxed, every one into his **o** city. *G2398*
35 pierce through thy **o** soul also,) that the *G4675*
39 into Galilee, to their **o** city Nazareth. *G846*
4:24 No prophet is accepted in his **o** country. *G846*
5:25 departed to his **o** house, glorifying God. *G846*
29 And Levi made him a great feast in his **o** *G846*
6:41 not the beam that is in thine **o** eye? *G2398*
42 that is in thine **o** eye? Thou hypocrite, *G4675*
42 beam out of thine **o** eye, and then shalt *G4675*
44 For every tree is known by his **o** fruit. *G2398*
8:39 Return to thine **o** house, and shew how *G4675*
9:26 he shall come in his **o** glory, and *in his* *G846*
10:34 wine, and set him on his **o** beast, and *G2398*
14:26 **o** life also, he cannot be my disciple. *G1438*
16:12 who shall give you that which is your **o**? *G5212*
18: 7 And shall not God avenge his **o** elect, *G846*
19:22 And he saith unto him, Out of thine **o** *G4675*
23 might have required mine **o** with usury? *G846*
21:30 and know of your **o** selves that summer
22:71 we ourselves have heard of his **o** mouth. *G846*
Jn 1:11 He came unto his **o**, and his own *G2398*
11 He came unto his own, and his **o** *G2398*
41 He first findeth his **o** brother Simon, *G2398*
4:41 more believed because of his **o** word; *G846*
44 hath no honour in his **o** country. *G2398*
5:30 I can of mine **o** self do nothing: as I hear,
30 I seek not mine **o** will, but the will of *G1699*
43 in his **o** name, him ye will receive. *G2398*
6:38 **o** will, but the will of him that sent me. *G1699*
7:18 seeketh his **o** glory: but he that seeketh *G2398*
53 And every man went unto his **o** house. *G846*

Jn 8: 9 convicted by *their* **o** conscience, went
44 his **o**: for he is a liar, and the father of it. G2398
50 And I seek not mine **o** glory: there is G3450
10: 3 and he calleth his **o** sheep by name, G2398
4 And when he putteth forth his **o** sheep, G2398
12 shepherd, whose **o** the sheep are not, G2398
13: 1 having loved his **o** which were in the G2398
15:19 would love his **o**: but because ye are not G2398
16:32 every man to his **o**, and shall leave me G2398
17: 5 thou me with thine **o** self with the glory G4572
11 through thine **o** name those whom G4675
18:35 Pilate answered, Am I a Jew? Thine **o** G4674
20:27 that disciple took her unto his **o** *home*. G2398
20:10 went away again unto their **o** home. G1438
Act 1: 7 the Father hath put in his **o** power. G2398
25 fell, that he might go to his **o** place. G2398
2: 6 heard them speak in his **o** language. G2398
8 And how hear we every man in our **o** G2398
3:12 as though by our **o** power or holiness G2398
4:23 And being let go, they went to their **o** G2398
32 his **o**; but they had all things common. G2398
5: 4 Whiles it remained, was it not thine **o**? G4671
4 was it not in thine **o** power? why hast G4674
7:21 up, and nourished him for her **o** son. G1438
41 rejoiced in the works of their **o** hands. G846
12:10 to them of his **o** accord: and they went G848
13:22 **o** heart, which shall fulfil all my will. G3450
36 For David, after he had served his **o** G2398
14:16 all nations to walk in their **o** ways. G846
15:22 men of their **o** company to Antioch
17:28 also of your **o** poets have said, For G2596
18: 6 *be* upon your **o** heads; I *am* clean: from G5216
20:28 he hath purchased with his **o** blood. G2398
30 Also of your **o** selves shall men arise,
21:11 and bound his **o** hands and feet, and G846
25:19 him of their **o** superstition, and of G2398
26: 4 the first among mine **o** nation at G3450
27:19 And the third *day* we cast out with our **o** G849
28:30 whole years in his **o** hired house, and G2398
Ro 1:24 the lusts of their **o** hearts, to dishonour G846
24 their **o** bodies between themselves: G846
4:19 considered not his **o** body now dead, G1438
8: 3 God sending his **o** Son in the likeness of G1438
32 He that spared not his **o** Son, but G2398
10: 3 to establish their **o** righteousness, have G2398
11:24 be graffed into their **o** olive tree? G2398
25 should be wise in your **o** conceits; that G1438
12:16 estate. Be not wise in your **o** conceits. G1438
14: 4 servant? to his **o** master he standeth G2398
5 man be fully persuaded in his **o** mind. G2398
16: 4 Who have for my life laid down their **o** G1438
18 Christ, but their **o** belly; and by good G1438
1Co 1:15 that I had baptized in mine **o** name. G1699
3: 8 **o** reward according to his own labour. G2398
8 own reward according to his **o** labour. G2398
19 He taketh the wise in their **o** craftiness. G846
4: 3 judgment: yea, I judge not mine **o** self. G1683
12 And labour, working with our **o** hands: G2398
6:14 and will also raise up us by his **o** power. G846
18 fornication sinneth against his **o** body. G2398
19 ye have of God, and ye are not your **o**? G1438
7: 2 man have his **o** wife, and let every G1438
2 let every woman have her **o** husband. G2398
4 The wife hath not power of her **o** body, G2398
4 not power of his **o** body, but the wife. G2398
35 And this I speak for your **o** profit; not G5216
37 hath power over his **o** will, and hath so G2398
9: 7 Who goeth a warfare any time at his **o** G2398
10:24 Let no man seek his **o**, but every man G1438
29 Conscience, I say, not thine **o**, but of the G1438
33 not seeking mine **o** profit, but the *profit* G1683
11:21 before *other* his **o** supper: and one is G2398
13: 5 seeketh not her **o**, is not easily G1438
15:23 But every man in his **o** order: Christ the G2398
38 him, and to every seed his **o** body. G2398
16:21 The salutation of *me* Paul with mine **o** G1699
2Co 6:12 but ye are straitened in your **o** bowels. G5216
8: 5 but first gave their **o** selves to the Lord,
17 of his **o** accord he went unto you. G830
11:26 *in* perils by *mine* **o** countrymen, *in* perils
13: 5 faith; prove your **o** selves. Know ye not
5 Know ye not your **o** selves, how that
Gal 1:14 my equals in mine **o** nation, being G3450
4:15 **o** eyes, and have given them to me. G5216
6: 4 But let every man prove his **o** work, G1438
5 For every man shall bear his **o** burden. G2398
11 written unto you with mine **o** hand. G1699
Eph 1:11 all things after the counsel of his **o** will: G846
Eph 1:20 his **o** right hand in the heavenly *places*, G846
5:22 Wives, submit yourselves unto your **o** G2398
24 *be* to their **o** husbands in every thing. G2398
28 wives as their **o** bodies. He that loveth G1438
29 For no man ever yet hated his **o** flesh; G1438
Php 2: 4 Look not every man on his **o** things, G1438
12 **o** salvation with fear and trembling. G1438
21 For all seek their **o**, not the things which G1438
3: 9 him, not having mine **o** righteousness, G1699
Col 3:18 Wives, submit yourselves unto your **o** G2398
1Th 2: 8 **o** souls, because ye were dear unto us. G1438
14 like things of your **o** countrymen, even G2398
15 Jesus, and their **o** prophets, and have G2398
4:11 and to do your **o** business, and to work G2398
11 your **o** hands, as we commanded you; G2398
2Th 3:12 they work, and eat their **o** bread. G1438
17 The salutation of Paul with mine **o** G1699
1Ti 1: 2 Unto Timothy, *my* **o** son in the faith: G1103
3: 4 One that ruleth well his **o** house, G2398
5 how to rule his **o** house, how shall he G2398
12 their children and their **o** houses well. G2398
5: 8 But if any provide not for his **o**, and G2398
8 for those of his **o** house, he hath denied G2398
6: 1 yoke count their **o** masters worthy of G2398
2Ti 1: 9 according to his **o** purpose and grace, G2398
3: 2 For men shall be lovers of their **o** selves,
4: 3 but after their **o** lusts shall they heap G2398
Tit 1: 4 To Titus, *mine* **o** son after the common G1103
12 a prophet of their **o**, said, The Cretians G2398
2: 5 obedient to their **o** husbands, that the G2398
9 unto their **o** masters, *and* to please G2398
Phlm 12 receive him, that is, mine **o** bowels: G1699
19 I Paul have written *it* with mine **o** G1699
19 owest unto me even thine **o** self besides.
Heb 2: 4 the Holy Ghost, according to his **o** will? G846
3: 6 But Christ as a son over his **o** house; G846
4:10 from his **o** works, as God *did* from his. G846
7:27 first for his **o** sins, and then for the G2398
9:12 calves, but by his **o** blood he entered in G2398
12:10 *us* after their **o** pleasure; but he for G846
13:12 his **o** blood, suffered without the gate. G2398
Jas 1:14 drawn away of his **o** lust, and enticed. G2398
18 Of his **o** will begat he us with the word of
22 hearers only, deceiving your **o** selves.
26 his **o** heart, this man's religion *is* vain. G846
1Pt 2:24 Who his **o** self bare our sins in his own G848
24 Who his own self bare our sins in his **o**
3: 1 subjection to your **o** husbands; that, if G2398
5 in subjection unto their **o** husbands: G2398
2Pt 2:12 shall utterly perish in their **o** corruption; G846
13 **o** deceivings while they feast with you; G846
22 *is* turned to his **o** vomit again; and the G2398
3: 3 scoffers, walking after their **o** lusts, G2398
16 scriptures, unto their **o** destruction. G2398
17 wicked, fall from your **o** stedfastness. G2398
1Jn 3:12 him? Because his **o** works were evil, and G846
Jude 6 but left their **o** habitation, he hath G2398
13 foaming out their **o** shame; wandering G1438
16 walking after their **o** lusts; and their G846
18 should walk after their **o** ungodly lusts. G1438
Rev 1: 5 washed us from our sins in his **o** blood, G846

OWNER

Ex 21:28 eaten; but the **o** of the ox *shall be* quit. H1167
29 testified to his **o**, and he hath not kept H1167
29 and his **o** also shall be put to death. H1167
34 The **o** of the pit shall make *it* good, *and* H1167
34 give money unto the **o** of them; and the H1167
36 time past, and his **o** hath not kept him H1167
22:11 goods; and the **o** of it shall accept H1167
12 make restitution unto the **o** thereof. H1167
14 be hurt, or die, the **o** thereof *being* not H1167
15 *But* if the **o** thereof *be* with it, he shall H1167
1Ki 16:24 name of Shemer, **o** of the hill, Samaria. H113
Isa 1: 3 The ox knoweth his **o**, and the ass his H7069
Act 27:11 the master and the **o** of the ship, more G3490

OWNERS

Job 31:39 caused the **o** thereof to lose their life: H1167
Prv 1:19 taketh away the life of the **o** thereof. H1167
Ecc 5:11 *is there* to the **o** thereof, saving the H1167
13 kept for the **o** thereof to their hurt. H1167
Lk 19:33 And as they were loosing the colt, the **o** G2962

OWNETH

Lev 14:35 And he that **o** the house shall come and
Act 21:11 bind the man that **o** this girdle, and G2076

OX

Ex 20:17 nor his **o**, nor his ass, nor any H7794
21:28 If an **o** gore a man or a woman, that H7794
28 that they die: then the **o** shall be surely H7794
28 but the owner of the **o** *shall be* quit. H7794
29 But if the **o** were wont to push with his H7794
29 or a woman; the **o** shall be stoned, and H7794
32 If the **o** shall push a manservant or a H7794
32 of silver, and the **o** shall be stoned. H7794
33 cover it, and an **o** or an ass fall therein; H7794
35 And if one man's **o** hurt another's, that H7794
35 they shall sell the live **o**, and divide the H7794
35 and the dead *o* also they shall divide. H7794
36 Or if it be known that the **o** hath used H7794
36 **o** for ox; and the dead shall be his own. H7794
36 ox for **o**; and the dead shall be his own. H7794
22: 1 If a man shall steal an **o**, or a sheep, H7794
1 for an **o**, and four sheep for a sheep. H7794
4 whether it be **o**, or ass, or sheep; he H7794
9 *whether it be* for **o**, for ass, for sheep, H7794
10 an ass, or an **o**, or a sheep, or any beast, H7794
23: 4 If thou meet thine enemy's **o** or his ass H7794
12 rest: that thine **o** and thine ass may H7794
34:19 cattle, *whether* **o** or sheep, *that is male*. H7794
Lev 7:23 of fat, of **o**, or of sheep, or of goat. H7794
17: 3 that killeth an **o**, or lamb, or goat, in H7794
27:26 *it be* **o**, or sheep: it *is* the LORD'S. H7794
Nu 7: 3 and for each one an **o**: and they brought H7794
22: 4 about us, as the **o** licketh up the grass H7794
Dt 5:14 nor thine **o**, nor thine ass, nor any H7794
21 maidservant, his **o**, or his ass, or any H7794
14: 4 shall eat: the **o**, the sheep, and the goat, H7794
5 and the wild **o**, and the chamois. H8377
18: 3 whether *it be* **o** or sheep; and they shall H7794
22: 1 Thou shalt not see thy brother's **o** or H7794
4 ass or his **o** fall down by the way, H7794
10 Thou shalt not plow with an **o** and an H7794
25: 4 Thou shalt not muzzle the **o** when he H7794
28:31 Thine **o** *shall be* slain before thine eyes, H7794
Jos 6:21 and old, and **o**, and sheep, and ass, H7794
Jdg 3:31 an **o** goad: and he also delivered Israel. H1241
6: 4 for Israel, neither sheep, nor **o**, nor ass. H7794
1Sa 12: 3 his anointed: whose **o** have I taken? or H7794
14:34 every man his **o**, and every man his H7794
34 every man his **o** with him that night, H7794
15: 3 suckling, **o** and sheep, camel and ass. H7794
Neh 5:18 *for me* daily *was* one **o** *and* six choice H7794
Job 6: 5 grass? or loweth the **o** over his fodder? H7794
24: 3 they take the widow's **o** for a pledge. H7794
40:15 made with thee; he eateth grass as an **o**. H1241
Ps 69:31 **o** *or* bullock that hath horns and hoofs. H7794
106:20 the similitude of an **o** that eateth grass. H7794
Prv 7:22 He goeth after her straightway, as an **o** H7794
14: 4 increase *is* by the strength of the **o**. H7794
15:17 than a stalled **o** and hatred therewith. H7794
Isa 1: 3 The **o** knoweth his owner, and the ass H7794
11: 7 and the lion shall eat straw like the **o**. H1241
32:20 *thither* the feet of the **o** and the ass. H7794
66: 3 He that killeth an **o** *is as if* he slew a H7794
Jer 11:19 But I *was* like a lamb *or* an **o** *that* is H441
Ezk 1:10 had the face of an **o** on the left side; H7794
Lk 13:15 sabbath loose his **o** or *his* ass from the G1016
14: 5 have an ass or an **o** fallen into a pit, G1016
1Co 9: 9 the mouth of the **o** that treadeth out the G1016
1Ti 5:18 not muzzle the **o** that treadeth out the G1016

OXEN

Gen 12:16 he had sheep, and **o**, and he asses, and H1241
20:14 And Abimelech took sheep, and **o**, and H1241
21:27 And Abraham took sheep and **o**, and H1241
32: 5 And I have **o**, and asses, flocks, and H7794
34:28 They took their sheep, and their **o**, and H1241
Ex 9: 3 the camels, upon the **o**, and upon the H1241
20:24 sheep, and thine **o**: in all places where I H1241
22: 1 **o** for an ox, and four sheep for a sheep. H1241
30 Likewise shalt thou do with thine **o**, *and* H7794
24: 5 peace offerings of **o** unto the LORD. H6499
Nu 7: 3 and twelve **o**; a wagon for two of H1241
6 And Moses took the wagons and the **o**, H1241
7 Two wagons and four **o** he gave unto H1241
8 And four wagons and eight **o** he gave H1241
17 peace offerings, two **o**, five rams, five he H1241
23 peace offerings, two **o**, five rams, five he H1241
29 peace offerings, two **o**, five rams, five he H1241
35 peace offerings, two **o**, five rams, five he H1241
41 peace offerings, two **o**, five rams, five he H1241
47 peace offerings, two **o**, five rams, five he H1241
53 peace offerings, two **o**, five rams, five he H1241

Nu 7:59 peace offerings, two **o**, five rams, five he H1241
65 peace offerings, two **o**, five rams, five he H1241
71 peace offerings, two **o**, five rams, five he H1241
77 peace offerings, two **o**, five rams, five he H1241
83 peace offerings, two **o**, five rams, five he H1241
87 All the **o** for the burnt offering *were* H1241
88 And all the **o** for the sacrifice of the H1241
22:40 And Balak offered **o** and sheep, and H1241
23: 1 me here seven **o** and seven rams. H6499
Dt 14:26 lusteth after, for **o**, or for sheep, or for H1241
Jos 7:24 and his **o**, and his asses, and his H7794
1Sa 11: 7 And he took a yoke of **o**, and hewed H1241
7 it be done unto his **o**. And the fear of the H1241
14:14 of land, *which* a yoke *of* **o** *might plow.*
32 took sheep, and **o**, and calves, and slew H1241
15: 9 sheep, and of the **o**, and of the fatlings, H1241
14 and the lowing of the **o** which I hear? H1241
15 sheep and of the **o**, to sacrifice unto the H1241
21 the spoil, sheep and **o**, the chief of the H1241
22:19 sucklings, and **o**, and asses, and sheep, H7794
27: 9 the sheep, and the **o**, and the asses, and H1241
2Sa 6: 6 and took hold of it; for the **o** shook *it.* H1241
13 six paces, he sacrificed **o** and fatlings. H7794
24:22 behold, *here be* **o** for burnt sacrifice, H1241
22 *other* instruments of the **o** for wood. H1241
24 and the **o** for fifty shekels of silver. H1241
1Ki 1: 9 And Adonijah slew sheep and **o** and fat H1241
19 And he hath slain **o** and fat cattle and H7794
25 day, and hath slain **o** and fat cattle and H7794
4:23 Ten fat **o**, and twenty oxen out of the H1241
23 Ten fat oxen, and twenty **o** out of the H1241
7:25 It stood upon twelve **o**, three looking H1241
29 the ledges *were* lions, **o**, and cherubims: H1241

1Ki 7:29 the lions and **o** *were* certain additions H1241
44 And one sea, and twelve **o** under the H1241
8: 5 sheep and **o**, that could not be told H1241
63 twenty thousand **o**, and an hundred H1241
19:19 *with* twelve yoke *of* **o** before him, and he
20 And he left the **o**, and ran after Elijah, H1241
21 and took a yoke of **o**, and slew them, H1241
21 instruments of the **o**, and gave unto the H1241
2Ki 5:26 **o**, and menservants, and maidservants? H1241
16:17 off the brasen **o** that *were* under it, and H1241
1Ch 12:40 on mules, and on **o**, *and* meat, meal, H1241
40 and wine, and oil, and **o**, and sheep H1241
13: 9 to hold the ark; for the **o** stumbled. H1241
21:23 eyes: lo, I give *thee* the **o** *also* for burnt H1241
2Ch 4: 3 And under it *was* the similitude of **o**, H1241
3 rows of **o** *were* cast, when it was cast. H1241
4 It stood upon twelve **o**, three looking H1241
15 One sea, and twelve **o** under it. H1241
5: 6 sheep and **o**, which could not be H1241
7: 5 and two thousand **o**, and an hundred H1241
15:11 hundred **o** and seven thousand sheep. H1241
18: 2 Ahab killed sheep and **o** for him in H1241
29:33 hundred **o** and three thousand sheep. H1241
31: 6 in the tithe of **o** and sheep, and the H1241
35: 8 *small cattle,* and three hundred **o**. H1241
9 *small cattle,* and five hundred **o**. H1241
12 of Moses. And so *did they* with the **o**. H1241
Job 1: 3 hundred yoke of **o**, and five hundred H1241
14 Job, and said, The **o** were plowing, and H1241
42:12 yoke of **o**, and a thousand she asses. H1241
Ps 8: 7 All sheep and **o**, yea, and the beasts of H504
144:14 *That* our **o** *may be* strong to labour; *that* H441
Prv 14: 4 Where no **o** *are,* the crib *is* clean: but H504

Isa 7:25 **o**, and for the treading of lesser cattle. H7794
22:13 And behold joy and gladness, slaying **o**, H1241
30:24 The **o** likewise and the young asses that H504
Jer 51:23 and his yoke of **o**; and with thee will I
Dan 4:25 to eat grass as **o**, and they shall wet thee H8450
32 to eat grass as **o**, and seven times shall H8450
33 did eat grass as **o**, and his body was wet H8450
5:21 with grass like **o**, and his body was wet H8450
Am 6:12 plow *there* with **o**? for ye have turned H1241
Mt 22: 4 my dinner: my **o** and *my* fatlings *are* *G5022*
Lk 14:19 five yoke of **o**, and I go to prove them: *G1016*
Jn 2:14 those that sold **o** and sheep and doves, *G1016*
15 the sheep, and the **o**; and poured out *G1016*
Act 14:13 their city, brought **o** and garlands unto *G5022*
1Co 9: 9 out the corn. Doth God take care for **o**? *G1016*

OX-GOAD See OX and GOAD.

OZEM
1Ch 2:15 **O** the sixth, David the seventh: H684
25 Bunah, and Oren, and **O**, *and* Ahijah. H684

OZIAS
Mt 1: 8 begat Joram; and Joram begat **O**; *G3604*
9 And **O** begat Joatham; and Joatham *G3604*

OZNI
Nu 26:16 Of **O**, the family of the Oznites: of Eri, the H244

OZNITES
Nu 26:16 Of Ozni, the family of the **O**: of Eri, the H244

P

PAANEAH See ZAPHNATH-PAANEAH.

PAARAI
2Sa 23:35 Hezrai the Carmelite, **P** the Arbite, H6474

PACES
2Sa 6:13 six **p**, he sacrificed oxen and fatlings. H6806

PACIFIED
Est 7:10 Mordecai. Then was the king's wrath **p**. H7918
Ezk 16:63 shame, when I am **p** toward thee for all H3722

PACIFIETH
Prv 21:14 A gift in secret **p** anger: and a reward H3711
Ecc 10: 4 thy place; for yielding **p** great offences. H3240

PACIFY
Prv 16:14 of death: but a wise man will **p** it. H3722

PADAN
Gen 48: 7 And as for me, when I came from **P**, H6307

PADAN-ARAM
Gen 25:20 of **P**, the sister to Laban the Syrian. H6307
28: 2 Arise, go to **P**, to the house of Bethuel H6307
5 and he went to **P** unto Laban, son of H6307
6 sent him away to **P**, to take him a wife H6307
7 and his mother, and was gone to **P**; H6307
31:18 he had gotten in **P**, for to go to Isaac his H6307
33:18 **P**; and pitched his tent before the city. H6307
35: 9 he came out of **P**, and blessed him. H6307
26 of Jacob, which were born to him in **P**. H6307
46:15 bare unto Jacob in **P**, with his daughter H6307

PADDLE
Dt 23:13 And thou shalt have a **p** upon thy H3489

PADON
Ezr 2:44 the children of Siaha, the children of **P**, H6303
Neh 7:47 the children of Sia, the children of **P**, H6303

PAGIEL
Nu 1:13 Of Asher; **P** the son of Ocran. H6295
2:27 of Asher *shall be* **P** the son of Ocran. H6295
7:72 On the eleventh day **P** the son of Ocran, H6295
77 *was* the offering of **P** the son of Ocran. H6295
10:26 of Asher *was* **P** the son of Ocran. H6295

PAHATH-MOAB
Ezr 2: 6 The children of **P**, of the children of H6355
8: 4 Of the sons of **P**; Elihoenai the son of H6355
10:30 And of the sons of **P**; Adna, and Chelal, H6355
Neh 3:11 Hashub the son of **P**, repaired the other H6355
7:11 The children of **P**, of the children of H6355
10:14 The chief of the people; Parosh, **P**, H6355

PAI
1Ch 1:50 of his city *was* **P**; and his wife's name H6464

PAID
Ezr 4:20 tribute, and custom, was **p** unto them. H3052
Jna 1: 3 to Tarshish: so he **p** the fare thereof, H5414
Mt 5:26 till thou hast **p** the uttermost farthing. *G591*
Lk 12:59 thence, till thou hast **p** the very last mite. *G591*

PAIN
Job 14:22 But his flesh upon him shall have **p**, H3510
15:20 The wicked man travaileth with **p** all *his*
33:19 He is chastened also with **p** upon his H4341
19 the multitude of his bones with strong *p*:
Ps 25:18 Look upon mine affliction and my **p**; H5999
48: 6 Fear took hold upon them there, *and* **p**, H2427
Isa 13: 8 they shall be in **p** as a woman that H2342
21: 3 Therefore are my loins filled with **p**: H2479
26:17 of her delivery, is in **p**, *and* crieth out in H2342
18 we have been in **p**, we have as it were H2342
66: 7 forth; before her **p** came, she was H2256
Jer 6:24 of us, *and* **p**, as of a woman in travail. H2427
12:13 put themselves to **p**, *but* shall not profit: H2470
15:18 Why is my **p** perpetual, and my wound H3511
22:23 thee, the **p** as of a woman in travail! H2427
30:23 fall with **p** upon the head of the wicked. H2342
51: 8 for her **p**, if so be she may be healed. H4341
Ezk 30: 4 Egypt, and great **p** shall be in Ethiopia, H2479
9 afraid, and great **p** shall come upon H2479
16 shall have great **p**, and No shall be rent H2342
Mic 4:10 Be in **p**, and labour to bring forth, O H2342
Nah 2:10 and much **p** *is* in all loins, and the H2479
Ro 8:22 and travaileth in **p** together until now.
Rev 16:10 and they gnawed their tongues for **p**, *G4192*
21: 4 there be any more **p**: for the former *G4192*

PAINED
Ps 55: 4 My heart is sore **p** within me: and the H2342
Isa 23: 5 they be sorely **p** at the report of Tyre. H2342
Jer 4:19 My bowels, my bowels! I am **p** at my H3176
Joel 2: 6 much **p**: all faces shall gather blackness. H2342

Rev 12: 2 travailing in birth, and **p** to be delivered. *G928*

PAINFUL
Ps 73:16 to know this, it *was* too **p** for me; H5999

PAINFULNESS
2Co 11:27 In weariness and **p**, in watchings often, *G3449*

PAINS
1Sa 4:19 and travailed; for her **p** came upon her. H6735
Ps 116: 3 me, and the **p** of hell gat hold upon H4712
Act 2:24 having loosed the **p** of death: because it *G5604*
Rev 16:11 because of their **p** and their sores, and *G4192*

PAINTED
2Ki 9:30 *of it;* and she **p** her face, and H7760+H6320
Jer 22:14 with cedar, and **p** with vermilion. H4886

PAINTEDST
Ezk 23:40 wash thyself, **p** thy eyes, and deckedst H3583

PAINTING
Jer 4:30 thy face with **p**, in vain shalt thou make H6320

PAIR
Am 2: 6 for silver, and the poor for a **p** of shoes;
8: 6 and the needy for a **p** of shoes; *yea,* and
Lk 2:24 **p** of turtledoves, or two young pigeons. *G2201*
Rev 6: 5 on him had a **p** of balances in his hand. *G2218*

PALACE
1Ki 16:18 he went into the **p** of the king's house, H759
21: 1 hard by the **p** of Ahab king of Samaria. H1964
2Ki 15:25 in Samaria, in the **p** of the king's house, H759
20:18 in the **p** of the king of Babylon. H1964
1Ch 29: 1 *is* great: for the **p** *is* not for man, but H1002
19 **p**, *for* the which I have made provision. H1002
2Ch 9:11 and to the king's **p**, and harps and H1004
Ezr 4:14 from *the king's* **p**, and it was not meet H1965
6: 2 at Achmetha, in the **p** that *is* in the H1002
Neh 1: 1 year, as I was in Shushan the **p**, H1002
2: 8 beams for the gates of the **p** which H1002
7: 2 Hananiah the ruler of the **p**, charge over H1002
Est 1: 2 kingdom, which *was* in Shushan the **p**, H1002
5 in Shushan the **p**, both unto great and H1002
5 the court of the garden of the king's **p**; H1055
2: 3 unto Shushan the **p**, to the house of the H1002
5 *Now* in Shushan the **p** there was a H1002
8 unto Shushan the **p**, to the custody of H1002

Est 3:15 in Shushan the **p**. And the king and H1002
7: 7 *went* into the **p** garden: and Haman H1055
8 Then the king returned out of the **p** H1055
8:14 the decree was given at Shushan the **p**. H1002
9: 6 And in Shushan the **p** the Jews slew H1002
11 the **p** was brought before the king. H1002
12 in Shushan the **p**, and the ten sons of H1002
Ps 45:15 they shall enter into the king's **p**. H1964
144:12 polished *after* the similitude of a **p**: H1964
Song 8: 9 build upon her a **p** of silver: and if she H2918
Isa 25: 2 city a ruin: a **p** of strangers to be no H759
39: 7 in the **p** of the king of Babylon. H1964
Jer 30:18 **p** shall remain after the manner thereof. H759
Dan 1: 4 to stand in the king's **p**, and whom they H1964
4: 4 in mine house, and flourishing in my **p**: H1965
29 in the **p** of the kingdom of Babylon. H1965
5: 5 wall of the king's **p**: and the king saw H1965
6:18 Then the king went to his **p**, and passed H1965
8: 2 *was* at Shushan *in* the **p**, which *is* in the H1002
11:45 tabernacles of his **p** between the seas in H643
Am 4: 3 cast *them* into the **p**, saith the LORD. H2038
Nah 2: 6 opened, and the **p** shall be dissolved. H1964
Mt 26: 3 people, unto the **p** of the high priest, who *G833*
58 the high priest's **p**, and went in, and sat *G833*
69 Now Peter sat without in the **p**: and a *G833*
Mk 14:54 off, even into the **p** of the high priest: *G833*
66 And as Peter was beneath in the **p**, there *G833*
Lk 11:21 When a strong man armed keepeth his **p**, *G833*
Jn 18:15 in with Jesus into the **p** of the high priest. *G833*
Php 1:13 in all the **p**, and in all other *places*; *G4232*

PALACES
2Ch 36:19 and burnt all the **p** thereof with fire, and H759
Ps 45: 8 **p**, whereby they have made thee glad. H1964
48: 3 God is known in her **p** for a refuge. H759
13 consider her **p**; that ye may tell *it* to H759
78:69 And he built his sanctuary like high **p**,
122: 7 thy walls, *and* prosperity within thy **p**. H759
Prv 30:28 hold with her hands, and is in kings' **p**. H1964
Isa 13:22 in *their* pleasant **p**: and her time *is* near H1964
23:13 the **p** thereof; *and* he brought it to ruin. H759
32:14 Because the **p** shall be forsaken; the H759
34:13 And thorns shall come up in her **p**, H759
Jer 6: 5 us go by night, and let us destroy her **p**. H759
9:21 *and* is entered into our **p**, to cut off the H759
17:27 it shall devour the **p** of Jerusalem, and it H759
49:27 it shall consume the **p** of Ben-hadad. H759
Lam 2: 5 up all her **p**: he hath destroyed his H759
7 the walls of her **p**; they have made a H759
Ezk 19: 7 And he knew their desolate **p**, and he laid H490
25: 4 they shall set their **p** in thee, and make H2918
Hos 8:14 cities, and it shall devour the **p** thereof. H759
Am 1: 4 which shall devour the **p** of Ben-hadad. H759
7 Gaza, which shall devour the **p** thereof: H759
10 Tyrus, which shall devour the **p** thereof. H759
12 which shall devour the **p** of Bozrah. H759
14 and it shall devour the **p** thereof, with H759
2: 2 and it shall devour the **p** of Kerioth: and H759
5 and it shall devour the **p** of Jerusalem. H759
3: 9 Publish in the **p** at Ashdod, and in the H759
9 at Ashdod, and in the **p** in the land of H759
10 store up violence and robbery in their **p**. H759
11 from thee, and thy **p** shall be spoiled. H759
6: 8 of Jacob, and hate his **p**: therefore will I H759
Mic 5: 5 shall tread in our **p**, then shall we raise H759

PALAL
Neh 3:25 **P** the son of Uzai, over against the H6420

PALE
Isa 29:22 neither shall his face now wax **p**. H2357
Rev 6: 8 And I looked, and behold a **p** horse: *G5515*

PALENESS
Jer 30: 6 travail, and all faces are turned into **p**? H3420

PALESTINA
Ex 15:14 shall take hold on the inhabitants of **P**. H6429
Isa 14:29 Rejoice not thou, whole **P**, because the H6429
31 Howl, O gate; cry, O city; thou, whole **P**, H6429

PALESTINE
Joel 3: 4 all the coasts of **P**? will ye render me a H6429

PALLU
Ex 6:14 Hanoch, and **P**, Hezron, and Carmi: H6396
Nu 26: 5 of **P**, the family of the Palluites: H6396
8 And the sons of **P**; Eliab. H6396
1Ch 5: 3 Hanoch, and **P**, Hezron, and Carmi. H6396

PALLUITES
Nu 26: 5 of Pallu, the family of the **P**: H6384

PALM
Ex 15:27 and ten **p** trees: and they encamped H8558
Lev 14:15 pour *it* into the **p** of his own left hand: H3709
26 the oil into the **p** of his own left hand: H3709
23:40 trees, branches of **p** trees, and the H8558
Nu 33: 9 and ten **p** trees; and they pitched there. H8558
Dt 34: 3 Jericho, the city of **p** trees, unto Zoar. H8558
Jdg 1:16 up out of the city of **p** trees with the H8558
3:13 Israel, and possessed the city of **p** trees. H8558
4: 5 And she dwelt under the **p** tree of H8560
1Ki 6:29 of cherubims and **p** trees and open H8561
32 of cherubims and **p** trees and open H8561
32 the cherubims, and upon the **p** trees. H8561
35 cherubims and **p** trees and open H8561
7:36 lions, and **p** trees, according to the H8561
2Ch 3: 5 and set thereon **p** trees and chains. H8561
28:15 to Jericho, the city of **p** trees, to their H8558
Neh 8:15 myrtle branches, and **p** branches, and H8558
Ps 92:12 The righteous shall flourish like the **p** H8558
Song 7: 7 This thy stature is like to a **p** tree, and H8558
8 I said, I will go up to the **p** tree, I will H8558
Jer 10: 5 They *are* upright as the **p** tree, but H8560
Ezk 40:16 and upon *each* post *were* **p** trees. H8561
22 arches, and their **p** trees, *were* after the H8561
26 them: and it had **p** trees, one on this H8561
31 utter court; and **p** trees *were* upon the H8561
34 court; and **p** trees *were* upon the H8561
37 utter court; and **p** trees *were* upon the H8561
41:18 And *it was* made with cherubims and **p** H8561
18 trees, so that a **p** tree *was* between a H8561
19 *was* toward the **p** tree on the one side, H8561
19 lion toward the **p** tree on the other side: H8561
20 cherubims and **p** trees made, and *on* H8561
25 cherubims and **p** trees, like as *were* H8561
26 And *there were* narrow windows and **p** H8561
Joel 1:12 tree, the **p** tree also, and the apple H8558
Jn 12:13 Took branches of **p** trees, and went *G5404*
18:22 Jesus with the **p** of his hand, saying, *G4475*

PALM-BRANCHES See PALM and BRANCHES.

PALMERWORM
Joel 1: 4 That which the **p** hath left hath the H1501
2:25 and the **p**, my great army which H1501
Am 4: 9 increased, the **p** devoured *them*: yet H1501

PALMS
1Sa 5: 4 and both the **p** of his hands *were* cut H3709
2Ki 9:35 and the feet, and the **p** of *her* hands. H3709
Isa 49:16 Behold, I have graven thee upon the **p** H3709
Dan 10:10 my knees and *upon* the **p** of my hands. H3709
Mt 26:67 smote *him* with the **p** of their hands, *G4474*
Mk 14:65 strike him with the **p** of their hands. *G4475*
Rev 7: 9 with white robes, and **p** in their hands; *G5404*

PALM-TREE See PALM and TREE.

PALSIES
Act 8: 7 **p**, and that were lame, were healed. *G3886*

PALSY
Mt 4:24 that had the **p**; and he healed them. *G3885*
8: 6 sick of the **p**, grievously tormented. *G3885*
9: 2 a man sick of the **p**, lying on a bed: and *G3885*
2 the sick of the **p**; Son, be of good cheer; *G3885*
6 he to the sick of the **p**,) Arise, take up thy *G3885*
Mk 2: 3 sick of the **p**, which was borne of four. *G3885*
4 the bed wherein the sick of the **p** lay. *G3885*
5 of the **p**, Son, thy sins be forgiven thee. *G3885*
9 to the sick of the **p**, *Thy* sins be forgiven *G3885*
10 sins, (he saith to the sick of the **p**,) *G3885*
Lk 5:18 was taken with a **p**: and they sought *G3886*
24 the sick of the **p**,) I say unto thee, Arise, *G3886*
Act 9:33 bed eight years, and was sick of the **p**. *G3886*

PALTI
Nu 13: 9 Of the tribe of Benjamin, **P** the son of H6406

PALTIEL
Nu 34:26 of Issachar, **P** the son of Azzan. H6409

PALTITE
2Sa 23:26 Helez the **P**, Ira the son of Ikkesh the H6407

PAMPHYLIA
Act 2:10 Phrygia, and **P**, in Egypt, and in the *G3828*
13:13 came to Perga in **P**: and John departing *G3828*
14:24 throughout Pisidia, they came to **P**. *G3828*
15:38 **P**, and went not with them to the work. *G3828*
27: 5 and **P**, we came to Myra, *a city* of Lycia. *G3828*

PAN
Lev 2: 5 *baken* in a **p**, it shall be *of* fine flour H4227
6:21 In a **p** it shall be made with oil; *and* H4227
7: 9 **p**, shall be the priest's that offereth it. H4227
1Sa 2:14 And he struck *it* into the **p**, or kettle, or H3595
2Sa 13: 9 And she took a **p**, and poured *them* out H4958
1Ch 23:29 *is baked in* the **p**, and for that which is H4227
Ezk 4: 3 Moreover take thou unto thee an iron **p**, H4227

PANGS
Isa 13: 8 And they shall be afraid: **p** and sorrows H6735
21: 3 filled with pain: **p** have taken hold H6735
3 upon me, as the **p** of a woman that H6735
26:17 crieth out in her **p**; so have we been in H2256
Jer 22:23 thou be when **p** come upon thee, the H2256
48:41 be as the heart of a woman in her **p**. H6887
49:22 be as the heart of a woman in her **p**. H6887
50:43 of him, *and* **p** as of a woman in travail. H2427
Mic 4: 9 perished? for **p** have taken thee as a H2427

PANNAG
Ezk 27:17 and **P**, and honey, and oil, and balm. H6436

PANS
Ex 27: 3 And thou shalt make his **p** to receive H5518
Nu 11: 8 and baked *it* in **p**, and made cakes of H6517
1Ch 9:31 over the things that were made in the **p**. H2281
2Ch 35:13 in caldrons, and in **p**, and divided *them* H6745

PANT
Am 2: 7 That **p** after the dust of the earth on the H7602

PANTED
Ps119:131 I opened my mouth, and **p**: for I longed H7602
Isa 21: 4 My heart **p**, fearfulness affrighted me: H8582

PANTETH
Ps 38:10 My heart **p**, my strength faileth me: as H5503
42: 1 As the hart **p** after the water brooks, so H6165
1 brooks, so **p** my soul after thee, O God. H6165

PAPER
Isa 19: 7 The **p** reeds by the brooks, by the H6169
2Jn 12 not *write* with **p** and ink: but I trust *G5489*

PAPER-REEDS See PAPER and REEDS.

PAPHOS
Act 13: 6 the isle unto **P**, they found a certain *G3974*
13 loosed from **P**, they came to Perga *G3974*

PAPS
Ezk 23:21 by the Egyptians for the **p** of thy youth. H7699
Lk 11:27 and the **p** which thou hast sucked. *G3149*
23:29 bare, and the **p** which never gave suck. *G3149*
Rev 1:13 girt about the **p** with a golden girdle. *G3149*

PARABLE
Nu 23: 7 And he took up his **p**, and said, Balak H4912
18 And he took up his **p**, and said, Rise up, H4912
24: 3 And he took up his **p**, and said, Balaam H4912
15 And he took up his **p**, and said, Balaam H4912
20 he took up his **p**, and said, Amalek *was* H4912
21 and took up his **p**, and said, Strong is H4912
23 And he took up his **p**, and said, Alas, H4912
Job 27: 1 Moreover Job continued his **p**, and said, H4912
29: 1 Moreover Job continued his **p**, and said, H4912
Ps 49: 4 I will incline mine ear to a **p**: I will open H4912
78: 2 I will open my mouth in a **p**: I will utter H4912
Prv 26: 7 equal: so *is* a **p** in the mouth of fools. H4912
9 so *is* a **p** in the mouth of fools. H4912
Ezk 17: 2 and speak a **p** unto the house of Israel; H4912
24: 3 And utter a **p** unto the rebellious H4912
Mic 2: 4 In that day shall *one* take up a **p** H4912
Hab 2: 6 Shall not all these take up a **p** against H4912
Mt 13:18 Hear ye therefore the **p** of the sower. *G3850*
24 Another **p** put he forth unto them, *G3850*
31 Another **p** put he forth unto them, *G3850*
33 Another **p** spake he unto them; The *G3850*
34 without a **p** spake he not unto them: *G3850*
36 unto us the **p** of the tares of the field. *G3850*
15:15 said unto him, Declare unto us this **p**. *G3850*
21:33 Hear another **p**: There was a certain *G3850*
24:32 Now learn a **p** of the fig tree; When his *G3850*

Mk 4:10 him with the twelve asked of him the **p**. G3850
13 Know ye not this **p**? and how then will G3850
34 But without a **p** spake he not unto G3850
7:17 disciples asked him concerning the **p**. G3850
12:12 he had spoken the **p** against them: and G3850
13:28 Now learn a **p** of the fig tree; When her G3850
Lk 5:36 And he spake also a **p** unto them; No G3850
6:39 And he spake a **p** unto them, Can the G3850
8: 4 to him out of every city, he spake by a **p**: G3850
9 him, saying, What might this **p** be? G3850
11 Now the **p** is this: The seed is the word G3850
12:16 And he spake a **p** unto them, saying, G3850
41 thou this **p** unto us, or even to all? G3850
13: 6 He spake also this **p**; A certain *man* had G3850
14: 7 And he put forth a **p** to those which G3850
15: 3 And he spake this **p** unto them, saying, G3850
18: 1 And he spake a **p** unto them *to this* G3850
9 And he spake this **p** unto certain which G3850
19:11 and spake a **p**, because he was nigh G3850
20: 9 to the people this **p**; A certain man G3850
19 he had spoken this **p** against them. G3850
21:29 And he spake to them a **p**; Behold the G3850
Jn 10: 6 This **p** spake Jesus unto them: but they G3942

PARABLES
Ezk 20:49 they say of me, Doth he not speak **p**? H4912
Mt 13: 3 unto them in **p**, saying, Behold, a sower G3850
10 Why speakest thou unto them in **p**? G3850
13 Therefore speak I to them in **p**: because G3850
34 unto the multitude in **p**; and without a G3850
35 open my mouth in **p**; I will utter things G3850
53 finished these **p**, he departed thence. G3850
21:45 **p**, they perceived that he spake of them. G3850
22: 1 spake unto them again by **p**, and said, G3850
Mk 3:23 in **p**, How can Satan cast out Satan? G3850
4: 2 And he taught them many things by **p**, G3850
11 without, all *these* things are done in **p**: G3850
13 and how then will ye know all **p**? G3850
33 And with many such **p** spake he the G3850
12: 1 And he began to speak unto them by **p**. G3850
Lk 8:10 God: but to others in **p**; that seeing they G3850

PARADISE
Lk 23:43 thee, To day shalt thou be with me in **p**. G3857
2Co 12: 4 How that he was caught up into **p**, and G3857
Rev 2: 7 which is in the midst of the **p** of God. G3857

PARAH
Jos 18:23 And Avim, and **P**, and Ophrah, H6511

PARAMOURS
Ezk 23:20 For she doted upon their **p**, whose flesh H6370

PARAN
Gen 21:21 And he dwelt in the wilderness of **P**: and H6290
Nu 10:12 the cloud rested in the wilderness of **P**. H6290
12:16 and pitched in the wilderness of **P**. H6290
13: 3 the wilderness of **P**: all those men *were* H6290
26 the wilderness of **P**, to Kadesh; and H6290
Dt 1: 1 Red *sea*, between **P**, and Tophel, and H6290
33: 2 forth from mount **P**, and he came with H6290
1Sa 25: 1 and went down to the wilderness of **P**. H6290
1Ki 11:18 and came to **P**: and they took men H6290
18 with them out of **P**, and they came to H6290
Hab 3: 3 One from mount **P**. Selah. His glory H6290

PARBAR
1Ch 26:18 At **P** westward, four at the causeway, H6503
18 four at the causeway, *and* two at **P**. H6503

PARCEL
Gen 33:19 And he bought a **p** of a field, where he H2513
Jos 24:32 in Shechem, in a **p** of ground which H2513
Ru 4: 3 of Moab, selleth a **p** of land, which *was* H2513
1Ch 11:13 where was a **p** of ground full of barley; H2513
14 in the midst of *that* **p**, and delivered it, H2513
Jn 4: 5 near to the **p** of ground that Jacob G5564

PARCHED
Lev 23:14 And ye shall eat neither bread, nor **p** H7039
Jos 5:11 cakes, and **p** *corn* in the selfsame day. H7033
Ru 2:14 he reached her **p** *corn*, and she did eat, H7039
1Sa 17:17 an ephah of this **p** *corn*, and these ten H7039
25:18 and five measures of **p** *corn*, and an H7039
2Sa 17:28 and flour, and **p** *corn*, and beans, and H7039
28 and beans, and lentiles, and **p** *pulse*, H7039
Isa 35: 7 And the **p** ground shall become a pool, H8273
Jer 17: 6 but shall inhabit the **p** places in the H2788

PARCHMENTS
2Ti 4:13 and the books, *but* especially the **p**. G3200

PARDON
Ex 23:21 him not; for he will not **p** your H5375
34: 9 people; and **p** our iniquity and our H5545
Nu 14:19 **P**, I beseech thee, the iniquity of this H5545
1Sa 15:25 Now therefore, I pray thee, **p** my sin, H5375
2Ki 5:18 In this thing the LORD **p** thy servant, H5545
18 the LORD **p** thy servant in this thing. H5545
24: 4 blood; which the LORD would not **p**. H5545
2Ch 30:18 saying, The good LORD **p** every one H3722
Neh 9:17 thou *art* a God ready to **p**, gracious and H5547
Job 7:21 And why dost thou not **p** my H5375
Ps 25:11 For thy name's sake, O LORD, **p** mine H5545
Isa 55: 7 to our God, for he will abundantly **p**. H5545
Jer 5: 1 that seeketh the truth; and I will **p** it. H5545
7 How shall I **p** thee for this? thy children H5545
33: 8 me; and I will **p** all their iniquities, H5545
50:20 for I will **p** them whom I reserve. H5545

PARDONED
Nu 14:20 And the LORD said, I have **p** according H5545
Isa 40: 2 that her iniquity is **p**: for she hath H7521
Lam 3:42 and have rebelled: thou hast not **p**. H5545

PARDONETH
Mic 7:18 Who *is* a God like unto thee, that **p** H5375

PARE
Dt 21:12 shall shave her head, and **p** her nails; H6213

PARENTS
Mt 10:21 **p**, and cause them to be put to death. G1118
Mk 13:12 up against *their* **p**, and shall cause them G1118
Lk 2:27 and when the **p** brought in the child G1118
41 Now his **p** went to Jerusalem every year G1118
8:56 And her **p** were astonished: but he G1118
18:29 hath left house, or **p**, or brethren, or G1118
21:16 And ye shall be betrayed both by **p**, and G1118
Jn 9: 2 man, or his **p**, that he was born blind? G1118
3 sinned, nor his **p**: but that the works of G1118
18 the **p** of him that had received his sight. G1118
20 His **p** answered them and said, We G1118
22 These *words* spake his **p**, because they G1118
23 Therefore said his **p**, He is of age; ask G1118
Ro 1:30 of evil things, disobedient to **p**, G1118
2Co 12:14 the **p**, but the parents for the children. G1118
14 the parents, but the **p** for the children. G1118
Eph 6: 1 Children, obey your **p** in the Lord: for G1118
Col 3:20 Children, obey *your* **p** in all things: for G1118
1Ti 5: 4 to requite their **p**: for that is good and G4269
2Ti 3: 2 disobedient to **p**, unthankful, unholy, G1118
Heb 11:23 months of his **p**, because they saw *he* G3962

PAREZ See RIMMON-PAREZ.

PARLOUR
Jdg 3:20 sitting in a summer **p**, which he had for H5944
23 of the **p** upon him, and locked them. H5944
24 the doors of the **p** *were* locked, they H5944
25 the doors of the **p**; therefore they took H5944
1Sa 9:22 them into the **p**, and made them sit H3957

PARLOURS
1Ch 28:11 and of the inner **p** thereof, and of the H2315

PARMASHTA
Est 9: 9 And **P**, and Arisai, and Aridai, and H6534

PARMENAS
Act 6: 5 **P**, and Nicolas a proselyte of Antioch: G3937

PARNACH
Nu 34:25 of Zebulun, Elizaphan the son of **P**. H6535

PAROSH
Ezr 2: 3 The children of **P**, two thousand an H6551
10:25 Moreover of Israel: of the sons of **P**; H6551
Neh 3:25 prison. After him Pedaiah the son of **P**. H6551
7: 8 The children of **P**, two thousand an H6551
10:14 The chief of the people; **P**, H6551

PARSHANDATHA
Est 9: 7 And **P**, and Dalphon, and Aspatha, H6577

PART
Gen 41:34 take up the fifth **p** of the land of Egypt H2567
47:24 shall give the fifth *p* unto Pharaoh, and H2549
Gen 47:26 have the fifth *p*; except the land of the H2569
Ex 16:36 Now an omer *is* the tenth *p* of an ephah.
19:17 stood at the nether **p** of the mount. H8482
29:26 before the LORD: and it shall be thy **p**. H4490
40 with the fourth **p** of an hin of beaten oil;
40 **p** of an hin of wine *for* a drink offering.
Lev 1:16 on the east **p**, by the place of the ashes:
2: 6 Thou shalt **p** it in pieces, and pour oil H6626
16 the memorial of it, *p* of the beaten corn
16 corn thereof, and *p* of the oil thereof,
5:11 offering the tenth **p** of an ephah of fine
16 shall add the fifth **p** thereto, and give it H2549
6: 5 shall add the fifth **p** more thereto, *and* H2549
20 anointed; the tenth **p** of an ephah of fine
7:33 shall have the right shoulder for *his* **p**. H4490
8:29 **p**; as the LORD commanded Moses. H4490
11:35 And every *thing* whereupon *any* **p** of
37 And if *any* **p** of their carcase fall upon
38 the seed, and *any* **p** of their carcase fall
13:41 fallen off from the **p** of his head toward H6285
22:14 shall put the fifth *p* thereof unto it, and
23:13 *shall be* of wine, the fourth **p** of an hin.
27:13 add a fifth *p* thereof unto thy estimation.
15 shall add the fifth *p* of the money of thy
16 unto the LORD *some* **p** of a field of his
19 shall add the fifth *p* of the money of thy
27 shall add a fifth *p* of it thereto: or if it be
31 he shall add thereto the fifth *p* thereof.
Nu 5: 7 add unto it the fifth *p* thereof, and give *it*
15 for her, the tenth *p* of an ephah of barley
15: 4 with the fourth *p* of an hin of oil.
5 And the fourth *p* of an hin of wine for a
6 mingled with the third *p* of an hin of oil.
7 offer the third *p* of an hin of wine, *for*
18:20 thou have any **p** among them: I *am* thy H2506
20 them: I *am* thy **p** and thine inheritance H2506
26 the LORD, *even* a tenth **p** of the tithe. H2506
29 *even* the hallowed **p** thereof out of it. H4720
22:41 he might see the utmost *p* of the people.
23:10 of the fourth *p* of Israel? Let me die
13 see but the utmost **p** of them, and shalt H7097
28: 5 And a tenth **p** of an ephah of flour for a
5 with the fourth *p* of an hin of beaten oil.
7 *shall be* the fourth **p** of an hin for the one
14 and the third *p* of an hin unto a ram,
14 a ram, and a fourth *p* of an hin unto a
Dt 10: 9 Wherefore Levi hath no **p** nor H2506
12:12 he hath no **p** nor inheritance with you. H2506
14:27 he hath no **p** nor inheritance with thee. H2506
29 And the Levite, (because he hath no **p** H2506
18: 1 shall have no **p** nor inheritance with H2506
33:21 And he provided the first **p** for himself, H7225
Jos 14: 4 they gave no **p** unto the Levites in the H2506
15: 1 *was* the uttermost **p** of the south coast. H7097
5 of the sea at the uttermost *p* of Jordan: H7097
13 he gave a **p** among the children H2506
18: 7 But the Levites have no **p** among you; H2506
19: 9 of Simeon: for the **p** of the children of H2506
22:25 of Gad; ye have no **p** in the LORD: so H2506
27 to come, Ye have no **p** in the LORD. H2506
Ru 1:17 also, *if aught* but death **p** thee and me. H6504
2: 3 hap was to light on a **p** of the field H2513
3:13 unto thee the **p** of a kinsman, well; let
13 do the kinsman's **p**: but if he will not do H1350
13 if he will not do the **p** of a kinsman to
13 then will I do the **p** of a kinsman to thee,
1Sa 9: 8 at hand the fourth *p* of a shekel of silver:
14: 2 And Saul tarried in the uttermost **p** of H7097
23:20 down; and our **p** *shall be* to deliver him
30:24 matter? but as his **p** *is* that goeth down H2506
24 battle, so *shall* his **p** *be* that tarrieth by H2506
24 tarrieth by the stuff: they shall **p** alike. H2505
2Sa 14: 6 *there was* none to **p** them, but the one H5337
18: 2 And David sent forth a third **p** of the H7992
2 Joab, and a third **p** under the hand of H7992
2 and a third **p** under the hand of Ittai H7992
20: 1 said, We have no **p** in David, neither H2506
1Ki 6:24 the uttermost **p** of the one wing unto H7098
24 **p** of the other *were* ten cubits. H7098
31 *and* side posts *were* a fifth **p** *of the wall*. H2549
33 posts *of* olive tree, a fourth **p** *of the wall*.
2Ki 6:25 and the fourth **p** of a cab of dove's dung
7: 5 to the uttermost **p** of the camp of Syria, H7097
8 to the uttermost **p** of the camp, they H7097
11: 5 shall do; A third **p** of you that enter in H7992
6 And a third **p** *shall be* at the gate of H7992
6 of Sur; and a third **p** at the gate behind H7992
18:23 be able on thy **p** to set riders upon them.
1Ch 12:29 the greatest **p** of them had kept the H4768

2Ch 23: 4 ye shall do; A third **p** of you entering on H7992
5 And a third **p** *shall be* at the king's H7992
5 house; and a third **p** at the gate of the H7992
29:16 And the priests went into the inner **p** of H6441
Neh 1: 9 the uttermost **p** of the heaven, *yet* will H7097
3: 9 the ruler of the half **p** of Jerusalem. H6418
12 **p** of Jerusalem, he and his daughters. H6418
14 the ruler of **p** of Beth-haccerem; he H6418
15 the ruler of **p** of Mizpah; he built H6418
16 ruler of the half **p** of Beth-zur, unto *the* H6418
17 ruler of the half **p** of Keilah, in his part. H6418
17 ruler of the half part of Keilah, in his **p**. H6418
18 the ruler of the half **p** of Keilah. H6418
5:11 also the hundredth *p* of the money, and
9: 3 God *one* fourth **p** of the day; and *another*
3 and *another* fourth **p** they confessed,
10:32 with the third **p** of a shekel for the H7992
Job 32:17 *I said*, I will answer also my **p**, I also H2506
41: 6 shall they **p** him among the merchants? H2673
Ps 5: 9 their inward **p** *is* very wickedness; their
22:18 They **p** my garments among them, and H2505
51: 6 *p* thou shalt make me to know wisdom.
118: 7 The LORD taketh my **p** with them that
Prv 8:26 the highest **p** of the dust of the world. H7218
31 Rejoicing in the habitable **p** of his H8398
17: 2 and shall have **p** of the inheritance H2505
Isa 7:18 *is* in the uttermost **p** of the rivers of H7097
24:16 From the uttermost **p** of the earth have H3671
36: 8 be able on thy **p** to set riders upon them.
44:16 He burneth **p** thereof in the fire; with H2677
16 in the fire; with **p** thereof he eateth H2677
19 to say, I have burned **p** of it in the fire; H2677
Ezk 4:11 by measure, the sixth **p** of an hin: from H8345
5: 2 Thou shalt burn with fire a third **p** in H7992
2 shalt take a third **p**, *and* smite about it H7992
2 a knife: and a third **p** thou shalt scatter H7992
12 A third **p** of thee shall die with the H7992
12 of thee: and a third **p** shall fall by the H7992
12 will scatter a third **p** into all the winds, H7992
39: 2 leave but the sixth **p** of thee, and will H8338
45:11 contain the tenth **p** of an homer, and H4643
11 the ephah the tenth **p** of an homer: the
13 offer; the sixth **p** of an ephah of an H8345
13 **p** of an ephah of an homer of barley: H8341
14 *offer* the tenth **p** of a bath out of the H4643
17 And it shall be the prince's **p** *to give*
46:14 morning, the sixth **p** of an ephah, and H8345
14 and the third **p** of an hin of oil, to H7992
Dan 1: 2 his hand, with **p** of the vessels of the H7117
2:33 His legs of iron, his feet **p** of iron and H4481
33 iron, his feet part of iron and **p** of clay. H4481
41 the feet and toes, **p** of potters' clay, and H4481
41 of potters' clay, and **p** of iron, the H4481
42 And *as* the toes of the feet *were* **p** of H4481
42 *were* part of iron, and **p** of clay, *so* the H4481
5: 5 king saw the **p** of the hand that wrote. H6447
24 Then was the **p** of the hand sent from H6447
11:31 And arms shall stand on his **p**, and they
Joel 2:20 and his hinder **p** toward the utmost H5490
Am 7: 4 the great deep, and did eat up a **p**. H2506
Zec 13: 9 And I will bring the third **p** through the H7992
Mk 4:38 And he was in the hinder **p** of the ship,
9:40 For he that is not against us is on our **p**. G5228
13:27 from the uttermost **p** of the earth to the G206
27 of the earth to the uttermost **p** of heaven. G206
Lk 10:42 chosen that good **p**, which shall not be G3310
11:36 of light, having no **p** dark, the whole G3313
39 **p** is full of ravening and wickedness. G2081
17:24 out of the one *p* under heaven, shineth
24 unto the other *p* under heaven; so shall
Jn 13: 8 wash thee not, thou hast no **p** with me. G3313
19:23 to every soldier a **p**; and also *his* coat: G3313
Act 1: 8 and unto the uttermost **p** of the earth. G2078
17 and had obtained **p** of this ministry. G2819
25 That he may take **p** of this ministry G2819
5: 2 And kept back *p* of the price, his wife
2 **p**, and laid *it* at the apostles' feet. G3313
3 to keep back *p* of the price of the land?
8:21 Thou hast neither **p** nor lot in this G3310
14: 4 was divided: and **p** held with the Jews, G3588
4 with the Jews, and **p** with the apostles. G3588
16:12 chief city of that **p** of Macedonia, *and* G3310
19:32 and the more **p** knew not wherefore G4119
23: 6 But when Paul perceived that the one **p** G3313
9 of the Pharisees' **p** arose, and strove, G3313
27:12 in, the more **p** advised to depart thence G4119
41 but the hinder **p** was broken with the G4403
Ro 11:25 that blindness in **p** is happened to G3313
1Co 12:24 honour to that *p* which lacked:
1Co 13: 9 For we know in **p**, and we prophesy in G3313
9 we know in part, and we prophesy in **p**. G3313
10 that which is in **p** shall be done away. G3313
12 now I know in **p**; but then shall I know G3313
15: 6 of whom the greater **p** remain unto this G4119
16:17 lacking on your **p** they have supplied. G5216
2Co 1:14 As also ye have acknowledged us in **p**, G3313
2: 5 in **p**: that I may not overcharge you all. G575
6:15 **p** hath he that believeth with an infidel? G3310
Eph 4:16 measure of every **p**, maketh increase of G3313
Tit 2: 8 is of the contrary **p** may be ashamed, G1727
Heb 2:14 likewise took **p** of the same; that G3348
7: 2 To whom also Abraham gave a tenth **p** G1181
1Pt 4:14 upon you: on their **p** he is evil spoken G2596
14 spoken of, but on your **p** he is glorified. G2596
Rev 6: 8 over the fourth **p** of the earth, to kill G5067
8: 7 and the third **p** of trees was burnt up, G5154
8 the third **p** of the sea became blood; G5154
9 And the third **p** of the creatures which G5154
9 the third **p** of the ships were destroyed. G5154
10 it fell upon the third **p** of the rivers, and G5154
11 and the third **p** of the waters became G5154
12 and the third **p** of the sun was smitten, G5154
12 and the third **p** of the moon, and the G5154
12 and the third **p** of the stars; so as the G5154
12 so as the third **p** of them was darkened, G5154
12 a third **p** of it, and the night likewise. G5154
9:15 a year, for to slay the third **p** of men. G5154
18 By these three was the third **p** of men G5154
11:13 and the tenth **p** of the city fell, and in G1182
12: 4 And his tail drew the third **p** of the G5154
20: 6 Blessed and holy *is* he that hath **p** in G3313
21: 8 shall have their **p** in the lake which G3313
22:19 take away his **p** out of the book of life, G3313

PARTAKER
Ps 50:18 him, and hast been **p** with adulterers. H2506
1Co 9:10 in hope should be **p** of his hope. G3348
23 that I might be **p** thereof with *you*. G4791
10:30 For if I by grace be a **p**, why am I evil G3348
1Ti 5:22 **p** of other men's sins: keep thyself pure. G2841
2Ti 1: 8 but be thou **p** of the afflictions of G4777
2: 6 laboureth must be first **p** of the fruits. G3335
1Pt 5: 1 a **p** of the glory that shall be revealed: G2844
2Jn 11 For he that biddeth him God speed is **p** G2841

PARTAKERS
Mt 23:30 not have been **p** with them in the blood G2844
Ro 15:27 have been made **p** of their spiritual G2841
1Co 9:12 If others be **p** of *this* power over you, G3348
13 wait at the altar are **p** with the altar? G4829
10:17 body: for we are all **p** of that one bread. G3348
18 eat of the sacrifices **p** of the altar? G2844
21 ye cannot be **p** of the Lord's table, G3348
2Co 1: 7 that as ye are **p** of the sufferings, so G2844
Eph 3: 6 **p** of his promise in Christ by the gospel: G4830
5: 7 Be not ye therefore **p** with them. G4830
Php 1: 7 of the gospel, ye all are **p** of my grace. G4791
Col 1:12 us meet to be **p** of the inheritance of G3310
1Ti 6: 2 and beloved, **p** of the benefit. These G482
Heb 2:14 Forasmuch then as the children are **p** G2841
3: 1 Wherefore, holy brethren, **p** of the G3353
14 For we are made **p** of Christ, if we hold G3353
6: 4 and were made **p** of the Holy Ghost, G3353
12: 8 **p**, then are ye bastards, and not sons. G3353
10 that *we* might be **p** of his holiness. G3335
1Pt 4:13 But rejoice, inasmuch as ye are **p** of G2841
2Pt 1: 4 by these ye might be **p** of the divine G2844
Rev 18: 4 that ye be not **p** of her sins, and that G4790

PARTAKEST
Ro 11:17 and with them **p** of the root and fatness G4791

PARTED
Gen 2:10 it was **p**, and became into four heads. H6504
2Ki 2:11 and horses of fire, and **p** them both H6504
14 the waters, they **p** hither and thither: H2673
Job 38:24 By what way is the light **p**, *which* H2505
Joel 3: 2 among the nations, and **p** my land. H2505
Mt 27:35 And they crucified him, and **p** his G1266
35 by the prophet, They **p** my garments G1266
Mk 15:24 him, they **p** his garments, casting G1266
Lk 23:34 And they **p** his raiment, and cast lots. G1266
24:51 them, he was **p** from them, and carried G1339
Jn 19:24 which saith, They **p** my raiment among G1266
Act 2:45 and goods, and **p** them to all *men*, as G1266

PARTETH
Lev 11: 3 Whatsoever **p** the hoof, and is H6536
Dt 14: 6 And every beast that **p** the hoof, and H6536
Prv 18:18 to cease, and **p** between the mighty. H6504

PARTHIANS
Act 2: 9 **P**, and Medes, and Elamites, and the G3934

PARTIAL
Mal 2: 9 my ways, but have been **p** in the law. H6440
Jas 2: 4 Are ye not then **p** in yourselves, and G2532

PARTIALITY
1Ti 5:21 one before another, doing nothing by **p**. G4346
Jas 3:17 fruits, without **p**, and without hypocrisy. G87

PARTICULAR
1Co 12:27 the body of Christ, and members in **p**. G3313
Eph 5:33 Nevertheless let every one of you in **p** G2596

PARTICULARLY
Act 21:19 them, he declared **p** what things God G2596
Heb 9: 5 of which we cannot now speak **p**. G2596

PARTIES
Ex 22: 9 the cause of both **p** shall come before H8147

PARTING
Ezk 21:21 For the king of Babylon stood at the **p** of H517

PARTITION
1Ki 6:21 and he made a **p** by the chains of gold H5674
Eph 2:14 down the middle wall of **p** *between us*; G5418

PARTLY
Dan 2:42 shall be **p** strong, and partly broken. H7118
42 shall be partly strong, and **p** broken. H7118
1Co 11:18 among you; and I **p** believe it. G3313+G5100
Heb 10:33 **P**, whilst ye were made a G5124+G3303
33 and afflictions; and **p**, whilst ye became G5124

PARTNER
Prv 29:24 Whoso is **p** with a thief hateth his own H2505
2Co 8:23 of Titus, *he is* my **p** and fellowhelper G2844
Phlm 17 If thou count me therefore a **p**, receive G2844

PARTNERS
Lk 5: 7 And they beckoned unto *their* **p**, which G3353
10 which were **p** with Simon. And Jesus G2844

PARTRIDGE
1Sa 26:20 one doth hunt a **p** in the mountains. H7124
Jer 17:11 *As* the **p** sitteth *on eggs*, and hatcheth H7124

PARTS
Gen 47:24 Pharaoh, and four **p** shall be your own, H3027
Ex 33:23 my back **p**: but my face shall not be seen. H268
Lev 1: 8 sons, shall lay the **p**, the head, and the H5409
22:23 or lacking in his **p**, that mayest thou H7038
Nu 10: 5 that lie on the east **p** shall go forward. H6924
11: 1 *were* in the uttermost **p** of the camp. H7097
31:27 And divide the prey into two **p**; between
Dt 19: 3 **p**, that every slayer may flee thither. H8027
30: 4 out unto the outmost *p* of heaven, from
Jos 18: 5 And they shall divide it into seven **p**: H2506
6 the land *into* seven **p**, and bring *the* H2506
9 cities into seven **p** in a book, and came H2506
1Sa 5: 9 and they had emerods in their secret **p**. H8368
2Sa 19:43 said, We have ten **p** in the king, and we H3027
1Ki 6:38 throughout all the **p** thereof, and H1697
7:25 and all their hinder **p** *were* inward. H268
16:21 divided into two **p**: half of the people H2677
2Ki 11: 7 And two **p** of all you that go forth on H3027
2Ch 4: 4 and all their hinder **p** *were* inward. H268
Neh 11: 1 city, and nine **p** *to dwell* in *other* cities. H3027
Job 26:14 Lo, these *are* **p** of his ways: but how H7098
38:36 Who hath put wisdom in the inward **p**? H2910
41:12 I will not conceal his **p**, nor his power, H907
Ps 2: 8 **p** of the earth *for* thy possession. H657
51: 6 in the inward **p**: and in the hidden *part* H2910
63: 9 *it*, shall go into the lower **p** of the earth. H8482
65: 8 They also that dwell in the uttermost **p**
78:66 **p**: he put them to a perpetual reproach. H268
136:13 into **p**: for his mercy *endureth* for ever: H1506
139: 9 *and* dwell in the uttermost **p** of the sea; H319
15 wrought in the lowest **p** of the earth. H8482
Prv 18: 8 down into the innermost **p** of the belly. H2315
20:27 searching all the inward **p** of the belly. H2315
30 so *do* stripes the inward **p** of the belly. H2315
26:22 down into the innermost **p** of the belly. H2315
Isa 3:17 the LORD will discover their secret **p**. H6596

Isa 16:11 and mine inward **p** for Kir-haresh. H7130
44:23 *it*: shout, ye lower **p** of the earth: break H8482
Jer 31:33 in their inward **p**, and write it in their H7130
34:18 and passed between the **p** thereof, H1335
19 which passed between the **p** of the calf; H1335
Ezk 26:20 set thee in the low **p** of the earth, in H8482
31:14 to the nether **p** of the earth, in the H8482
16 comforted in the nether **p** of the earth. H8482
18 unto the nether **p** of the earth: thou H8482
32:18 unto the nether **p** of the earth, with H8482
24 into the nether **p** of the earth, which H8482
37:11 our hope is lost: we are cut off for our **p**.
38:15 out of the north **p**, thou, and many H3411
39: 2 up from the north **p**, and will bring thee H3411
48: 8 as one of the *other* **p**, from the east side H2506
Zec 13: 8 the LORD, two **p** therein shall be cut H6310
Mt 2:22 he turned aside into the **p** of Galilee: *G3313*
12:42 the uttermost **p** of the earth to hear *G4009*
Mk 8:10 and came into the **p** of Dalmanutha. *G3313*
Lk 11:31 from the utmost **p** of the earth to hear *G4009*
Jn 19:23 and made four **p**, to every soldier a *G3313*
Act 2:10 in Egypt, and in the **p** of Libya about *G3313*
20: 2 And when he had gone over those **p**, *G3313*
Ro 15:23 place in these **p**, and having a great *G2824*
1Co 12:23 ***p*** have more abundant comeliness.
24 For our comely ***p*** have no need: but God
Eph 4: 9 first into the lower **p** of the earth? *G3313*
Rev 16:19 divided into three **p**, and the cities of *G3313*

PARUAH
1Ki 4:17 Jehoshaphat the son of **P**, in Issachar: H6515

PARVAIM
2Ch 3: 6 for beauty: and the gold *was* gold of **P**. H6516

PASACH
1Ch 7:33 And the sons of Japhlet; **P**, and Bimhal, H6457

PAS-DAMMIM
1Ch 11:13 He was with David at **P**, and there the H6450

PASEAH
1Ch 4:12 And Eshton begat Beth-rapha, and **P**, H6454
Ezr 2:49 The children of Uzza, the children of **P**, H6454
Neh 3: 6 the son of **P**, and Meshullam the H6454

PASHUR
1Ch 9:12 the son of **P**, the son of Malchijah, H6583
Ezr 2:38 The children of **P**, a thousand two H6583
10:22 And of the sons of **P**; Elioenai, H6583
Neh 7:41 The children of **P**, a thousand two H6583
10: 3 **P**, Amariah, Malchijah, H6583
11:12 the son of **P**, the son of Malchiah, H6583
Jer 20: 1 Now **P** the son of Immer the priest, H6583
2 Then **P** smote Jeremiah the prophet, H6583
3 on the morrow, that **P** brought forth H6583
3 thy name **P**, but Magor-missabib. H6583
6 And thou, **P**, and all that dwell in thine H6583
21: 1 sent unto him **P** the son of Melchiah, H6583
38: 1 the son of **P**, and Jucal the son of H6583
1 son of Shelemiah, and **P** the son of H6583

PASS
Gen 4: 3 And in process of time it came to **p**, that
8 and it came to **p**, when they were in the
14 it shall come to **p**, *that* every one that H1961
6: 1 And it came to **p**, when men began to
7:10 And it came to **p** after seven days, that
8: 1 made a wind to **p** over the earth, and H5674
6 And it came to **p** at the end of forty days,
13 And it came to **p** in the six hundredth
9:14 And it shall come to **p**, when I bring a H5674
11: 2 And it came to **p**, as they journeyed from
12:11 And it came to **p**, when he was come
12 Therefore it shall come to **p**, when the
14 And it came to **p**, that, when Abram was
14: 1 And it came to **p** in the days of
15:17 And it came to **p**, that, when the sun
18: 3 in thy sight, **p** not away, I pray thee, H5674
5 after that ye shall **p** on: for therefore H5674
19:17 And it came to **p**, when they had brought
29 And it came to **p**, when God destroyed
34 And it came to **p** on the morrow, that the
20:13 And it came to **p**, when God caused me to
21:22 And it came to **p** at that time, that
22: 1 And it came to **p** after these things, that
20 And it came to **p** after these things, that
24:14 And let it come to **p**, that the damsel to
15 And it came to **p**, before he had done
Gen 24:22 And it came to **p**, as the camels had done
30 And it came to **p**, when he saw the
43 it shall come to **p**, that when the virgin
52 And it came to **p**, that, when Abraham's
25:11 And it came to **p** after the death of
26: 8 And it came to **p**, when he had been there
32 And it came to **p** the same day, that
27: 1 And it came to **p**, that when Isaac was H1961
30 And it came to **p**, as soon as Isaac had
40 it shall come to **p** when thou shalt have
29:10 And it came to **p**, when Jacob saw Rachel
13 And it came to **p**, when Laban heard the
23 And it came to **p** in the evening, that he
25 And it came to **p**, that in the morning,
30:25 And it came to **p**, when Rachel had born
32 I will **p** through all thy flock to day, H5674
41 And it came to **p**, whensoever the
31:10 And it came to **p** at the time that the
52 that I will not **p** over this heap to thee, H5674
52 thou shalt not **p** over this heap and H5674
32:16 unto his servants, **P** over before me, H5674
33:14 Let my lord, I pray thee, **p** over before H5674
34:25 And it came to **p** on the third day, when
35:17 And it came to **p**, when she was in hard
18 And it came to **p**, as her soul was in
22 And it came to **p**, when Israel dwelt in
37:23 And it came to **p**, when Joseph was come
38: 1 And it came to **p** at that time, that Judah
9 be his; and it came to **p**, when he went in
24 And it came to **p** about three months
27 And it came to **p** in the time of her
28 And it came to **p**, when she travailed,
29 And it came to **p**, as he drew back his
39: 5 And it came to **p** from the time *that* he
7 And it came to **p** after these things, that
10 And it came to **p**, as she spake to Joseph
11 And it came to **p** about this time, that
13 And it came to **p**, when she saw that he
15 And it came to **p**, when he heard that I
18 And it came to **p**, as I lifted up my voice
19 And it came to **p**, when his master heard
40: 1 And it came to **p** after these things, *that*
20 And it came to **p** the third day, *which*
41: 1 And it came to **p** at the end of two full
8 And it came to **p** in the morning that his
13 And it came to **p**, as he interpreted to us,
32 God, and God will shortly bring it to **p**. H6213
42:35 And it came to **p** as they emptied their
43: 2 And it came to **p**, when they had eaten
21 And it came to **p**, when we came to the
44:24 And it came to **p** when we came up unto
31 It shall come to **p**, when he seeth that the
46:33 And it shall come to **p**, when Pharaoh
47:24 And it shall come to **p** in the increase,
48: 1 And it came to **p** after these things, that
50:20 good, to bring to **p**, as *it is* this day, to H6213
Ex 1:10 and it come to **p**, that, when there falleth
21 And it came to **p**, because the midwives
2:11 And it came to **p** in those days, when
23 And it came to **p** in process of time, that
3:21 it shall come to **p**, that, when ye go, ye
4: 8 And it shall come to **p**, if they will not
9 And it shall come to **p**, if they will not
24 And it came to **p** by the way in the inn,
6:28 And it came to **p** on the day *when* the
12:12 For I will **p** through the land of Egypt H5674
13 see the blood, I will **p** over you, and the H6452
23 For the LORD will **p** through to smite H5674
23 the LORD will **p** over the door, and will H6452
25 And it shall come to **p**, when ye be come
26 And it shall come to **p**, when your
29 And it came to **p**, that at midnight the
41 And it came to **p** at the end of the four
41 day it came to **p**, that all the hosts of the
51 And it came to **p** the selfsame day, *that*
13:15 And it came to **p**, when Pharaoh would
17 And it came to **p**, when Pharaoh had let
14:24 And it came to **p**, that in the morning
15:16 till thy people **p** over, O LORD, till the H5674
16 **p** over, *which* thou hast purchased. H5674
16: 5 And it shall come to **p**, that on the sixth
10 And it came to **p**, as Aaron spake unto
13 And it came to **p**, that at even the quails
22 And it came to **p**, *that* on the sixth day
27 And it came to **p**, *that* there went out
17:11 And it came to **p**, when Moses held up
18:13 And it came to **p** on the morrow, that
19:16 And it came to **p** on the third day in the
22:27 it shall come to **p**, when he crieth unto
Ex 32:19 And it came to **p**, as soon as he came
30 And it came to **p** on the morrow, that
33: 7 And it came to **p**, *that* every one which
8 And it came to **p**, when Moses went out
9 And it came to **p**, as Moses entered into
19 all my goodness **p** before thee, and I H5674
22 And it shall come to **p**, while my glory
22 cover thee with my hand while I **p** by: H5674
34:29 And it came to **p**, when Moses came
40:17 And it came to **p** in the first month in the
Lev 9: 1 And it came to **p** on the eighth day, *that*
18:21 And thou shalt not let any of thy seed **p** H5674
Nu 5:27 it shall come to **p**, *that*, if she be defiled,
7: 1 And it came to **p** on the day that Moses
10:11 And it came to **p** on the twentieth *day* of
35 And it came to **p**, when the ark set
11:23 word shall come to **p** unto thee or not. H7136
25 and it came to **p**, *that*, when the spirit
16:31 And it came to **p**, as he had made an end
42 And it came to **p**, when the congregation
17: 5 And it shall come to **p**, *that* the man's
8 And it came to **p**, that on the morrow
20:17 Let us **p**, I pray thee, through thy H5674
17 we will not **p** through the fields, or H5674
18 Thou shalt not **p** by me, lest I come out H5674
21: 8 it shall come to **p**, that every one that is
9 and it came to **p**, that if a serpent had
22 Let me **p** through thy land: we will not H5674
23 And Sihon would not suffer Israel to **p** H5674
22:41 And it came to **p** on the morrow, that
26: 1 And it came to **p** after the plague, that
27: 7 of their father to **p** unto them. H5674
8 his inheritance to **p** unto his daughter. H5674
32:27 But thy servants will **p** over, every man H5674
29 of Reuben will **p** with you over Jordan, H5674
30 But if they will not **p** over with you H5674
32 We will **p** over armed before the LORD H5674
33:55 it shall come to **p**, that those which ye
56 Moreover it shall come to **p**, *that* I shall
34: 4 of Akrabbim, and **p** on to Zin: and the H5674
4 to Hazar-addar, and **p** on to Azmon: H5674
Dt 1: 3 And it came to **p** in the fortieth year, in
2: 4 saying, Ye *are* to **p** through the coast of H5674
16 So it came to **p**, when all the men of war H5674
18 Thou art to **p** over through Ar, the H5674
24 Rise ye up, take your journey, and **p** H5674
27 Let me **p** through thy land: I will go H5674
28 drink: only I will **p** through on my feet; H5674
29 me;) until I shall **p** over Jordan into the H5674
30 would not let us **p** by him: for the H5674
3:18 possess it: ye shall **p** over armed before H5674
5:23 And it came to **p**, when ye heard the
7:12 Wherefore it shall come to **p**, if ye
9: 1 Hear, O Israel: Thou *art* to **p** over H5674
11 And it came to **p** at the end of forty days
11:13 And it shall come to **p**, if ye shall hearken
29 And it shall come to **p**, when the LORD
31 For ye shall **p** over Jordan to go in to H5674
13: 2 And the sign or the wonder come to **p**, H935
18:10 or his daughter to **p** through the fire, *or* H5674
19 And it shall come to **p**, *that* whosoever
22 not, nor come to **p**, that *is* the thing H935
24: 1 her, and it come to **p** that she find no
27: 2 day when ye shall **p** over Jordan unto H5674
28: 1 And it shall come to **p**, if thou shalt
15 But it shall come to **p**, if thou wilt not
63 And it shall come to **p**, *that* as the LORD
29:19 And it come to **p**, when he heareth the
30: 1 And it shall come to **p**, when all these
31:21 And it shall come to **p**, when many evils
24 And it came to **p**, when Moses had made
Jos 1: 1 LORD it came to **p**, that the LORD spake
11 **P** through the host, and command the H5674
11 three days ye shall **p** over this Jordan, H5674
14 but ye shall **p** before your brethren H5674
2: 5 And it came to **p** *about the time* of
3: 2 And it came to **p** after three days, that
6 of the covenant, and **p** over before the H5674
13 And it shall come to **p**, as soon as the
14 And it came to **p**, when the people H5674
14 their tents, to **p** over Jordan, and the H5674
4: 1 And it came to **p**, when all the people
5 And Joshua said unto them, **P** over H5674
11 And it came to **p**, when all the people
18 And it came to **p**, when the priests that
5: 1 And it came to **p**, when all the kings of
8 And it came to **p**, when they had done
13 And it came to **p**, when Joshua was by
6: 5 And it shall come to **p**, that when they

Jos 6: 7 And he said unto the people, **P** on, and H5674
7 **p** on before the ark of the LORD. H5674
8 And it came to **p**, when Joshua had
15 And it came to **p** on the seventh day,
16 And it came to **p** at the seventh time,
20 and it came to **p**, when the people heard
8: 5 it shall come to **p**, when they come out
14 And it came to **p**, when the king of Ai saw
24 And it came to **p**, when Israel had made
9: 1 And it came to **p**, when all the kings
16 And it came to **p** at the end of three days
10: 1 Now it came to **p**, when Adoni-zedek
11 And it came to **p**, as they fled from before
20 And it came to **p**, when Joshua and the
24 And it came to **p**, when they brought out
27 And it came to **p** at the time of the going
11: 1 And it came to **p**, when Jabin king of
15:18 And it came to **p**, as she came *unto him,*
17:13 Yet it came to **p**, when the children of
21:45 unto the house of Israel; all came to **p**. H935
22:19 *be* unclean, *then* **p** ye over unto the H5674
23: 1 And it came to **p** a long time after that
14 all are come to **p** unto you, *and* not one H935
15 Therefore it shall come to **p**, *that* as all
24:29 And it came to **p** after these things, that
Jdg 1: 1 Joshua it came to **p**, that the children of
14 And it came to **p**, when she came *to him,*
28 And it came to **p**, when Israel was H5674
2: 4 And it came to **p**, when the angel of the
19 And it came to **p**, when the judge was
3:27 And it came to **p**, when he was come,
28 Moab, and suffered not a man to **p** over.
6: 7 And it came to **p**, when the children of
25 And it came to **p** the same night, that the
7: 9 And it came to **p** the same night, that the
8:33 And it came to **p**, as soon as Gideon was
9:42 And it came to **p** on the morrow, that the
11: 4 And it came to **p** in process of time, that
17 me, I pray thee, **p** through thy land: but H5674
19 said unto him, Let us **p**, we pray thee, H5674
20 But Sihon trusted not Israel to **p** H5674
35 And it came to **p**, when he saw her, that
39 And it came to **p** at the end of two
13:12 thy words come to **p**. How shall we order H935
17 come to **p** we may do thee honour? H935
20 For it came to **p**, when the flame went up
14:11 And it came to **p**, when they saw him,
15 And it came to **p** on the seventh day,
17 and it came to **p** on the seventh day,
15: 1 But it came to **p** within a while after, in
17 And it came to **p**, when he had made an
16: 4 And it came to **p** afterward, that he
16 And it came to **p**, when she pressed him
25 And it came to **p**, when their hearts were
19: 1 And it came to **p** in those days, when
5 And it came to **p** on the fourth day,
12 of Israel; we will **p** over to Gibeah. H5674
21: 3 why is this come to **p** in Israel, that there
4 And it came to **p** on the morrow, that the
Ru 1: 1 Now it came to **p** in the days when the
19 And it came to **p**, when they were come
3: 8 And it came to **p** at midnight, that the
1Sa 1:12 And it came to **p**, as she continued
20 Wherefore it came to **p**, when the time
2:36 And it shall come to **p**, *that* every one
3: 2 And it came to **p** at that time, when Eli
4:18 And it came to **p**, when he made mention
5:10 And it came to **p**, as the ark of God came
7: 2 And it came to **p**, while the ark abode in
8: 1 And it came to **p**, when Samuel was old,
9: 6 cometh surely to **p**: now let us go thither; H935
26 And they arose early: and it came to **p**
27 Bid the servant **p** on before us, (and he H5674
10: 5 it shall come to **p**, when thou art come
9 and all those signs came to **p** that day. H935
11 And it came to **p**, when all that knew him
11:11 the day: and it came to **p**, that they which
13:10 And it came to **p**, that as soon as he had
22 So it came to **p** in the day of battle, that
14: 1 Now it came to **p** upon a day, that
8 Then said Jonathan, Behold, we will **p** H5674
19 And it came to **p**, while Saul talked unto
16: 6 And it came to **p**, when they were come,
8 and made him **p** before Samuel. And H5674
9 Then Jesse made Shammah to **p** by. H5674
10 of his sons to **p** before Samuel. And H5674
16 it shall come to **p**, when the evil spirit
23 And it came to **p**, when the *evil* spirit
17:48 And it came to **p**, when the Philistine

1Sa 18: 1 And it came to **p**, when he had made an
6 And it came to **p** as they came, when
10 And it came to **p** on the morrow, that the
19 But it came to **p** at the time when Merab
30 and it came to **p**, after they went forth,
20:27 And it came to **p** on the morrow, *which*
35 And it came to **p** in the morning, that
23: 6 And it came to **p**, when Abiathar the son
23 it shall come to **p**, if he be in the land,
24: 1 And it came to **p**, when Saul was
5 And it came to **p** afterward, that David's
16 And it came to **p**, when David had made
25:30 And it shall come to **p**, when the LORD
37 But it came to **p** in the morning, when
38 And it came to **p** about ten days *after,*
28: 1 And it came to **p** in those days, that the
30: 1 And it came to **p**, when David and his
31: 8 And it came to **p** on the morrow, when
2Sa 1: 1 Now it came to **p** after the death of Saul,
2 It came even to **p** on the third day, that,
2: 1 And it came to **p** after this, that David
23 and it came to **p**, *that* as many as came
3: 6 And it came to **p**, while there was war
4: 4 fled: and it came to **p**, as she made haste
7: 1 And it came to **p**, when the king sat in his
4 And it came to **p** that night, that the
8: 1 And after this it came to **p**, that David
10: 1 And it came to **p** after this, that the king
11: 1 And it came to **p**, after the year was
2 And it came to **p** in an eveningtide, that
14 And it came to **p** in the morning, that
16 And it came to **p**, when Joab observed the
12:18 And it came to **p** on the seventh day,
31 iron, and made them **p** through the H5674
13: 1 And it came to **p** after this, that Absalom
23 And it came to **p** after two full years,
30 And it came to **p**, while they were in the
36 And it came to **p**, as soon as he had made
15: 1 And it came to **p** after this, that Absalom
7 And it came to **p** after forty years, that
22 And David said to Ittai, Go and **p** over. H5674
32 And it came to **p**, that *when* David was
16:16 And it came to **p**, when Hushai the
17: 9 and it will come to **p**, when some of them
16 but speedily **p** over; lest the king be H5674
21 And it came to **p**, after they were
21 David, Arise, and **p** quickly over the H5674
27 And it came to **p**, when David was come
19:25 And it came to **p**, when he was come to
21:18 And it came to **p** after this, that there
1Ki 1:21 Otherwise it shall come to **p**, when my
2:39 And it came to **p** at the end of three
3:18 And it came to **p** the third day after that
5: 7 And it came to **p**, when Hiram heard the
6: 1 And it came to **p** in the four hundred
8:10 And it came to **p**, when the priests were
9: 1 And it came to **p**, when Solomon had
10 And it came to **p** at the end of twenty
11: 4 For it came to **p**, when Solomon was old,
15 For it came to **p**, when David was in
29 And it came to **p** at that time when
12: 2 And it came to **p**, when Jeroboam the son
20 And it came to **p**, when all Israel heard
13: 4 And it came to **p**, when king Jeroboam
20 And it came to **p**, as they sat at the table,
23 And it came to **p**, after he had eaten
31 And it came to **p**, after he had buried
32 cities of Samaria, shall surely come to **p**.
14:25 And it came to **p** in the fifth year of king
15:21 And it came to **p**, when Baasha heard
29 And it came to **p**, when he reigned, *that*
16:11 And it came to **p**, when he began to
18 And it came to **p**, when Zimri saw that
31 And it came to **p**, as if it had been a light
17: 7 And it came to **p** after a while, that the
17 And it came to **p** after these things, *that*
18: 1 And it came to **p** *after* many days, that
6 between them to **p** throughout it: Ahab H5674
12 And it shall come to **p**, *as soon as* I am
17 And it came to **p**, when Ahab saw Elijah,
27 And it came to **p** at noon, that Elijah
29 And it came to **p**, when midday was past,
36 And it came to **p** at *the time of* the
44 And it came to **p** at the seventh time,
45 And it came to **p** in the mean while, that
19:17 And it shall come to **p**, *that* him that
20:12 And it came to **p**, when *Ben-hadad* heard
26 And it came to **p** at the return of the
21: 1 And it came to **p** after these things, *that*

1Ki 21:15 And it came to **p**, when Jezebel heard
16 And it came to **p**, when Ahab heard that
27 And it came to **p**, when Ahab heard those
22: 2 And it came to **p** in the third year, that
32 And it came to **p**, when the captains of
33 And it came to **p**, when the captains of
2Ki 2: 1 And it came to **p**, when the LORD would
9 And it came to **p**, when they were gone
11 And it came to **p**, as they still went on,
3: 5 But it came to **p**, when Ahab was dead,
15 And it came to **p**, when the minstrel
20 And it came to **p** in the morning, when
4: 6 And it came to **p**, when the vessels were
25 And it came to **p**, when the man of God
40 eat. And it came to **p**, as they were eating
5: 7 And it came to **p**, when the king of Israel
6: 9 Beware that thou **p** not such a place; H5674
20 And it came to **p**, when they were come
24 And it came to **p** after this, that
30 And it came to **p**, when the king heard
7:18 And it came to **p** as the man of God had
8: 3 And it came to **p** at the seven years' end,
5 And it came to **p**, as he was telling the
15 And it came to **p** on the morrow, that he
9:22 And it came to **p**, when Joram saw Jehu,
10: 7 And it came to **p**, when the letter came to
9 And it came to **p** in the morning, that he
25 And it came to **p**, as soon as he had made
13:21 And it came to **p**, as they were burying a
14: 5 And it came to **p**, as soon as the kingdom
15:12 fourth *generation.* And so it came to **p**.
16: 3 and made his son to **p** through the fire, H5674
17:17 their daughters to **p** through the fire, H5674
18: 1 Now it came to **p** in the third year of
9 And it came to **p** in the fourth year of
19: 1 And it came to **p**, when king Hezekiah
25 now have I brought it to **p**, that thou H935
35 And it came to **p** that night, that the
37 And it came to **p**, as he was worshipping
20: 4 And it came to **p**, afore Isaiah was gone
21: 6 And he made his son **p** through the H5674
22: 3 And it came to **p** in the eighteenth year
11 And it came to **p**, when the king had
23:10 to **p** through the fire to Molech. H5674
24:20 the LORD it came to **p** in Jerusalem and
25: 1 And it came to **p** in the ninth year of his
25 But it came to **p** in the seventh month,
27 And it came to **p** in the seven and
1Ch 10: 8 And it came to **p** on the morrow, when
15:26 And it came to **p**, when God helped the
29 And it came to **p**, *as* the ark of the
17: 1 Now it came to **p**, as David sat in his
3 And it came to **p** the same night, that the
11 And it shall come to **p**, when thy days be
18: 1 Now after this it came to **p**, that David
19: 1 Now it came to **p** after this, that Nahash
20: 1 And it came to **p**, that after the year was
4 And it came to **p** after this, that there
2Ch 5:11 And it came to **p**, when the priests were
13 It came even to **p**, as the trumpeters and
8: 1 And it came to **p** at the end of twenty
10: 2 And it came to **p**, when Jeroboam the son
12: 1 And it came to **p**, when Rehoboam had
2 And it came to **p**, *that* in the fifth year of
13:15 shouted, it came to **p**, that God smote
16: 5 And it came to **p**, when Baasha heard *it,*
18:31 And it came to **p**, when the captains of
32 For it came to **p**, that, when the captains
20: 1 It came to **p** after this also, *that* the
21:19 And it came to **p**, that in process of time,
22: 8 And it came to **p**, that, when Jehu was
24: 4 And it came to **p** after this, *that* Joash
11 Now it came to **p**, that at what time the
23 And it came to **p** at the end of the year,
25: 3 Now it came to **p**, when the kingdom was
14 Now it came to **p**, after that Amaziah
16 And it came to **p**, as he talked with him,
33: 6 And he caused his children to **p** H5674
34:19 And it came to **p**, when the king had
Neh 1: 1 And it came to **p** in the month Chisleu,
4 And it came to **p**, when I heard these
2: 1 And it came to **p** in the month Nisan, in
14 for the beast *that was* under me to **p**. H5674
4: 1 But it came to **p**, that when Sanballat
7 But it came to **p**, *that* when Sanballat,
12 And it came to **p**, that when the Jews
15 And it came to **p**, when our enemies
16 And it came to **p** from that time forth,
6: 1 Now it came to **p**, when Sanballat, and

Neh 6:16 And it came to **p**, that when all our
7: 1 Now it came to **p**, when the wall was
13: 3 Now it came to **p**, when they had heard
19 And it came to **p**, that when the gates of
Est 1: 1 Now it came to **p** in the days of
2: 8 So it came to **p**, when the king's
3: 4 Now it came to **p**, when they spake daily
5: 1 Now it came to **p** on the third day, that
Job 6:15 as the stream of brooks they **p** away; H5674
11:16 remember *it* as waters *that* **p** away: H5674
14: 5 appointed his bounds that he cannot **p**; H5674
19: 8 my way that I cannot **p**, and he hath set H5674
34:20 at midnight, and **p** away: and the H5674
Ps 37: 5 also in him; and he shall bring *it* to **p**. H6213
7 man who bringeth wicked devices to **p**. H6213
58: 8 let *every one of them* **p** away: *like* the H1980
78:13 and caused them to **p** through; and he H5674
80:12 they which **p** by the way do pluck her? H5674
89:41 All that **p** by the way spoil him: he is a H5674
104: 9 that they may not **p** over; that they turn H5674
136:14 And made Israel to **p** through the H5674
148: 6 hath made a decree which shall not **p**. H5674
Prv 4:15 Avoid it, **p** not by it, turn from it, and H5674
15 not by it, turn from it, and **p** away. H5674
8:29 the waters should not **p** his H5674
16:30 moving his lips he bringeth evil to **p**. H3615
19:11 *it is* his glory to **p** over a transgression. H5674
22: 3 but the simple **p** on, and are punished. H5674
27:12 *but* the simple **p** on, *and* are punished. H5674
Isa 2: 2 And it shall come to **p** in the last days,
3:24 And it shall come to **p**, *that* instead of
4: 3 And it shall come to **p**, *that he that is* left
7: 1 And it came to **p** in the days of Ahaz the
7 shall not stand, neither shall it come to **p**.
18 And it shall come to **p** in that day, *that*
21 And it shall come to **p** in that day, *that* a
22 And it shall come to **p**, for the abundance
23 And it shall come to **p** in that day, *that*
8: 8 And he shall **p** through Judah; he shall H2498
21 And they shall **p** through it, hardly H5674
21 it shall come to **p**, that when they shall
10:12 Wherefore it shall come to **p**, *that* when
20 And it shall come to **p** in that day, *that*
27 And it shall come to **p** in that day, *that*
11:11 And it shall come to **p** in that day, *that*
14: 3 And it shall come to **p** in the day that the
24 so shall it come to **p**; and as I have
16:12 And it shall come to **p**, when it is seen
17: 4 And in that day it shall come to **p**, *that*
21: 1 in the south **p** through; *so* it cometh H2498
22: 7 And it shall come to **p**, *that* thy choicest
20 And it shall come to **p** in that day, that I
23: 2 that **p** over the sea, have replenished. H5674
6 **P** ye over to Tarshish; howl, ye H5674
10 **P** through thy land as a river, O H5674
12 of Zidon: arise, **p** over to Chittim; there H5674
15 And it shall come to **p** in that day, that
17 And it shall come to **p** after the end of
24:18 And it shall come to **p**, *that* he who fleeth
21 And it shall come to **p** in that day, *that*
27:12 And it shall come to **p** in that day, *that*
13 And it shall come to **p** in that day, *that*
28:15 scourge shall **p** through, it shall not H5674
18 scourge shall **p** through, then ye shall H5674
19 morning shall it **p** over, by day and by H5674
21 and bring to **p** his act, his strange act. H5647
30:32 staff shall **p**, which the LORD shall H4569
31: 9 And he shall **p** over to his strong hold H5674
33:21 neither shall gallant ship **p** thereby. H5674
34:10 shall **p** through it for ever and ever. H5674
35: 8 unclean shall not **p** over it; but it *shall* H5674
36: 1 Now it came to **p** in the fourteenth year
37: 1 And it came to **p**, when king Hezekiah
26 now have I brought it to **p**, that thou H935
38 And it came to **p**, as he was worshipping
42: 9 Behold, the former things are come to **p**, H935
46:11 to **p**; I have purposed *it*, I will also do it. H935
47: 2 uncover the thigh, **p** over the rivers. H5674
48: 3 I did *them* suddenly, and they came to **p**. H935
5 before it came to **p** I shewed *it* thee: lest H935
51:10 sea a way for the ransomed to **p** over? H5674
65:24 And it shall come to **p**, that before they
66:23 And it shall come to **p**, *that* from one new
Jer 2:10 For **p** over the isles of Chittim, and see; H5674
3: 9 And it came to **p** through the lightness of
16 And it shall come to **p**, when ye be
4: 9 And it shall come to **p** at that day, saith
5:19 And it shall come to **p**, when ye shall say,
22 that it cannot **p** it: and though the H5674

Jer 5:22 they roar, yet can they not **p** over it? H5674
8:13 given them shall **p** away from them. H5674
9:10 up, so that none can **p** through *them*; H5674
12:15 And it shall come to **p**, after that I have
16 And it shall come to **p**, if they will
13: 6 And it came to **p** after many days, that
15: 2 And it shall come to **p**, if they say unto
14 And I will make *thee* to **p** with thine H5674
16:10 And it shall come to **p**, when thou shalt
17:24 And it shall come to **p**, if ye diligently
20: 3 And it came to **p** on the morrow, that
22: 8 And many nations shall **p** by this city, H5674
25:12 And it shall come to **p**, when seventy
26: 8 Now it came to **p**, when Jeremiah had
27: 8 And it shall come to **p**, *that* the nation
28: 1 And it came to **p** the same year, in the
9 shall come to **p**, *then* shall the prophet H935
30: 8 For it shall come to **p** in that day, saith
31:28 And it shall come to **p**, *that* like as I have
32:24 is come to **p**; and, behold, thou seest *it*.
35 their daughters to **p** through *the fire* H5674
33:13 shall the flocks **p** again under the H5674
35:11 But it came to **p**, when Nebuchadrezzar
36: 1 And it came to **p** in the fourth year of
9 And it came to **p** in the fifth year of
16 Now it came to **p**, when they had heard
23 And it came to **p**, *that* when Jehudi had
37:11 And it came to **p**, that when the army of
39: 4 And it came to **p**, *that* when Zedekiah the
41: 1 Now it came to **p** in the seventh month,
4 And it came to **p** the second day after he
6 and it came to **p**, as he met them, he said
13 Now it came to **p**, *that* when all the
42: 4 it shall come to **p**, *that* whatsoever thing
7 And it came to **p** after ten days, that the
16 Then it shall come to **p**, *that* the sword,
43: 1 And it came to **p**, *that* when Jeremiah
49:39 But it shall come to **p** in the latter days,
51:43 neither doth *any* son of man **p** thereby. H5674
52: 3 the LORD it came to **p** in Jerusalem and
4 And it came to **p** in the ninth year of his
31 And it came to **p** in the seven and
Lam 1:12 *Is it* nothing to you, all ye that **p** by? H5674
2:15 All that **p** by clap *their* hands at thee; H5674
3:37 Who *is* he *that* saith, and it cometh to **p**,
44 that *our* prayer should not **p** through. H5674
4:21 the cup also shall **p** through unto thee: H5674
Ezk 1: 1 Now it came to **p** in the thirtieth year, in
3:16 And it came to **p** at the end of seven
5: 1 and cause *it* to **p** upon thine head and H5674
14 about thee, in the sight of all that **p** by. H5674
17 and blood shall **p** through thee; and I H5674
8: 1 And it came to **p** in the sixth year, in the
9: 8 And it came to **p**, while they were slaying
10: 6 And it came to **p**, *that* when he had
11:13 And it came to **p**, when I prophesied, that
12:25 shall come to **p**; it shall be no more H6213
14:15 If I cause noisome beasts to **p** through H5674
15 may **p** through because of the beasts: H5674
16:21 them to **p** through *the fire* for them? H5674
23 And it came to **p** after all thy
20: 1 And it came to **p** in the seventh year, in
26 they caused to **p** through *the fire* all H5674
31 make your sons to **p** through the fire, H5674
37 And I will cause you to **p** under the rod, H5674
21: 7 be brought to **p**, saith the Lord GOD. H1961
23:37 bare unto me, to **p** for them through H5674
24:14 *it*: it shall come to **p**, and I will do *it*; I will H935
26: 1 And it came to **p** in the eleventh year, in
29:11 No foot of man shall **p** through it, nor H5674
11 foot of beast shall **p** through it, neither H5674
17 And it came to **p** in the seven and
30:20 And it came to **p** in the eleventh year, in
31: 1 And it came to **p** in the eleventh year, in
32: 1 And it came to **p** in the twelfth year, in
17 It came to **p** also in the twelfth year, in
19 Whom dost thou **p** in beauty? go down,
33:21 And it came to **p** in the twelfth year of
28 be desolate, that none shall **p** through. H5674
33 And when this cometh to **p**, (lo, it will H935
37: 2 And caused me to **p** by them round H5674
38:10 It shall also come to **p**, *that* at the same
18 And it shall come to **p** at the same time
39:11 And it shall come to **p** in that day, *that* I
15 And the passengers *that* **p** through the H5674
44:17 And it shall come to **p**, *that* when they
46:21 and caused me to **p** by the four corners H5674
47: 5 that I could not **p** over: for the waters H5674
9 And it shall come to **p**, *that* every thing

Ezk 47:10 And it shall come to **p**, *that* the fishers
22 And it shall come to **p**, *that* ye shall
23 And it shall come to **p**, *that* in what tribe
Dan 2:29 should come to **p** hereafter: and he that H1934
29 known to thee what shall come to **p**. H1934
45 what shall come to **p** hereafter: and the H1934
4:16 him; and let seven times **p** over him. H2499
23 of the field, till seven times **p** over him; H2499
25 seven times shall **p** over thee, till thou H2499
32 and seven times shall **p** over thee, until H2499
7:14 which shall not **p** away, and his H5709
8: 2 And I saw in a vision; and it came to **p**,
15 And it came to **p**, when I, *even* I Daniel,
11:10 and overflow, and **p** through: then H5674
40 and shall overflow and **p** over. H5674
Hos 1: 5 And it shall come to **p** at that day, that I
10 it shall come to **p**, *that* in the place where
2:21 And it shall come to **p** in that day, I will
Joel 2:28 And it shall come to **p** afterward, *that* I
32 And it shall come to **p**, *that* whosoever
3:17 no strangers **p** through her any more. H5674
18 And it shall come to **p** in that day, *that*
Am 5: 5 into Gilgal, and **p** not to Beer-sheba: H5674
17 I will **p** through thee, saith the LORD. H5674
6: 2 **P** ye unto Calneh, and see; and from H5674
9 And it shall come to **p**, if there remain
7: 2 And it came to **p**, *that* when they had
8 I will not again **p** by them any more: H5674
8: 2 I will not again **p** by them any more. H5674
9 And it shall come to **p** in that day, saith
Jna 4: 8 And it came to **p**, when the sun did arise,
Mic 1:11 **P** ye away, thou inhabitant of Saphir, H5674
2: 8 **p** by securely as men averse from war. H5674
13 their king shall **p** before them, and the H5674
4: 1 But in the last days it shall come to **p**,
5:10 And it shall come to **p** in that day, saith
Nah 1:12 when he shall **p** through. Though I H5674
15 **p** through thee; he is utterly cut off. H5674
3: 7 And it shall come to **p**, *that* all they that
Hab 1:11 change, and he shall **p** over, and offend,
Zep 1: 8 And it shall come to **p** in the day of the H5674
10 And it shall come to **p** in that day, saith
12 And it shall come to **p** at that time, *that* I
2: 2 *before* the day **p** as the chaff, before H5674
Zec 3: 4 thine iniquity to **p** from thee, and I will H5674
6:15 *this* shall come to **p**, if ye will diligently
7: 1 And it came to **p** in the fourth year of
13 Therefore it is come to **p**, *that* as he cried,
8:13 And it shall come to **p**, *that* as ye were a
20 *It shall* yet *come to* **p**, that there shall
23 *it shall come to* **p**, that ten men shall take
9: 8 no oppressor shall **p** through them any H5674
10:11 And he shall **p** through the sea with H5674
12: 9 And it shall come to **p** in that day, *that* I
13: 2 And it shall come to **p** in that day, saith
2 the unclean spirit to **p** out of the land. H5674
3 And it shall come to **p**, *that* when any
4 And it shall come to **p** in that day, *that*
8 And it shall come to **p**, *that* in all the
14: 6 And it shall come to **p** in that day, *that*
7 to **p**, *that* at evening time it shall be light.
13 And it shall come to **p** in that day, *that* a
16 And it shall come to **p**, *that* every one
Mt 5:18 heaven and earth **p**, one jot or one tittle *G3928*
18 wise **p** from the law, till all be fulfilled. *G3928*
7:28 And it came to **p**, when Jesus had ended *G1096*
8:28 so that no man might **p** by that way. *G3928*
9:10 And it came to **p**, as Jesus sat at meat in *G1096*
11: 1 And it came to **p**, when Jesus had made *G1096*
13:53 And it came to **p**, *that* when Jesus had *G1096*
19: 1 And it came to **p**, *that* when Jesus had *G1096*
24: 6 must come to **p**, but the end is not yet. *G1096*
34 not **p**, till all these things be fulfilled. *G3928*
35 Heaven and earth shall **p** away, but my *G3928*
35 away, but my words shall not **p** away. *G3928*
26: 1 And it came to **p**, when Jesus had *G1096*
39 let this cup **p** from me: nevertheless *G3928*
42 if this cup may not **p** away from me, *G3928*
Mk 1: 9 And it came to **p** in those days, that *G1096*
2:15 And it came to **p**, that, as Jesus sat at *G1096*
23 And it came to **p**, that he went through *G1096*
4: 4 And it came to **p**, as he sowed, some fell *G1096*
35 them, Let us **p** over unto the other side. *G1330*
11:23 to **p**; he shall have whatsoever he saith. *G1096*
13:29 things come to **p**, know that it is nigh, *G1096*
30 shall not **p**, till all these things be done. *G3928*
31 Heaven and earth shall **p** away: but my *G3928*
31 away: but my words shall not **p** away. *G3928*
14:35 possible, the hour might **p** from him. *G3928*

Lk 1: 8 And it came to **p**, that while he executed *G1096*
23 And it came to **p**, that, as soon as the *G1096*
41 And it came to **p**, that, when Elisabeth *G1096*
59 And it came to **p**, that on the eighth day *G1096*
2: 1 And it came to **p** in those days, that *G1096*
15 And it came to **p**, as the angels were *G1096*
15 which is come to **p**, which the Lord hath *G1096*
46 And it came to **p**, that after three days *G1096*
3:21 it came to **p**, that Jesus also being *G1096*
5: 1 And it came to **p**, that, as the people *G1096*
12 And it came to **p**, when he was in a *G1096*
17 And it came to **p** on a certain day, as *G1096*
6: 1 And it came to **p** on the second *G1096*
6 And it came to **p** also on another *G1096*
12 And it came to **p** in those days, that he *G1096*
7:11 And it came to **p** the day after, that he *G1096*
8: 1 And it came to **p** afterward, that he *G1096*
22 Now it came to **p** on a certain day, that *G1096*
40 And it came to **p**, that, when Jesus was *G1096*
9:18 And it came to **p**, as he was alone *G1096*
28 And it came to **p** about an eight days *G1096*
33 And it came to **p**, as they departed from *G1096*
37 And it came to **p**, that on the next day, *G1096*
51 And it came to **p**, when the time was *G1096*
57 And it came to **p**, that, as they went in *G1096*
10:38 Now it came to **p**, as they went, that he *G1096*
11: 1 And it came to **p**, that, as he was *G1096*
14 And it came to **p**, when the devil was *G1096*
27 And it came to **p**, as he spake these *G1096*
42 of herbs, and **p** over judgment and *G3928*
12:55 There will be heat; and it cometh to **p**. *G1096*
14: 1 And it came to **p**, as he went into the *G1096*
16:17 to **p**, than one tittle of the law to fail. *G3928*
22 And it came to **p**, that the beggar died, *G1096*
26 they which would **p** from hence to you *G1224*
26 **p** to us, that *would come* from thence. *G1276*
17:11 And it came to **p**, as he went to *G1096*
14 And it came to **p**, that, as they went, *G1096*
18:35 And it came to **p**, that as he was come *G1096*
36 And hearing the multitude **p** by, he *G1279*
19: 4 to see him: for he was to **p** that *way*. *G1330*
15 And it came to **p**, that when he was *G1096*
29 And it came to **p**, when he was come *G1096*
20: 1 And it came to **p**, *that* on one of those *G1096*
21: 7 *be* when these things shall come to **p**? *G1096*
9 come to **p**; but the end *is* not by and by. *G1096*
28 begin to come to **p**, then look up, and *G1096*
31 these things come to **p**, know ye that the *G1096*
32 shall not **p** away, till all be fulfilled. *G3928*
33 Heaven and earth shall **p** away: but my *G3928*
33 away: but my words shall not **p** away. *G3928*
36 **p**, and to stand before the Son of man. *G1096*
24: 4 And it came to **p**, as they were much *G1096*
12 in himself at that which was come to **p**. *G1096*
15 And it came to **p**, that, while they *G1096*
18 are come to **p** there in these days? *G1096*
30 And it came to **p**, as he sat at meat with *G1096*
51 And it came to **p**, while he blessed *G1096*
Jn 13:19 come to **p**, ye may believe that I am *he*. *G1096*
14:29 you before it come to **p**, that, when it is *G1096*
29 when it is come to **p**, ye might believe. *G1096*
15:25 But *this cometh to* **p**, that the word might
Act 2:17 And it shall come to **p** in the last days, *G2071*
21 And it shall come to **p**, *that* whosoever *G2071*
3:23 And it shall come to **p**, *that* every soul, *G2071*
4: 5 And it came to **p** on the morrow, that *G1096*
9:32 And it came to **p**, as Peter passed *G1096*
37 And it came to **p** in those days, that she *G1096*
43 And it came to **p**, that he tarried many *G1096*
11:26 And it came to **p**, that a whole year they *G1096*
28 to **p** in the days of Claudius Caesar. *G1096*
14: 1 And it came to **p** in Iconium, that they *G1096*
16:16 And it came to **p**, as we went to prayer, *G1096*
18:27 And when he was disposed to **p** into *G1330*
19: 1 And it came to **p**, that, while Apollos *G1096*
21: 1 And it came to **p**, that after we were *G1096*
22: 6 And it came to **p**, that, as I made my *G1096*
17 And it came to **p**, that, when I was come *G1096*
27:44 to **p**, that they escaped all safe to land. *G1096*
28: 8 And it came to **p**, that the father of *G1096*
17 And it came to **p**, that after three days *G1096*
Ro 9:26 And it shall come to **p**, *that* in the place *G2071*
1Co 7:36 his virgin, if she **p** the flower of *her* age, *G5230*
15:54 shall be brought to **p** the saying that is *G1096*
16: 5 unto you, when I shall **p** through *G1330*
5 for I do **p** through Macedonia. *G1330*
2Co 1:16 And to **p** by you into Macedonia, and *G1330*
1Th 3: 4 even as it came to **p**, and ye know. *G1096*
Jas 1:10 the flower of the grass he shall **p** away. *G3928*
1Pt 1:17 to every man's work, **p** the time of your *G390*
2Pt 3:10 the heavens shall **p** away with a great *G3928*
Rev 1: 1 must shortly come to **p**; and he sent and *G1096*

PASSAGE

Nu 20:21 Thus Edom refused to give Israel **p** H5674
Jos 22:11 at the **p** of the children of Israel. H5676
1Sa 13:23 went out to the **p** of Michmash. H4569
Isa 10:29 They are gone over the **p**: they have H4569

PASSAGES

Jdg 12: 5 And the Gileadites took the **p** of Jordan H4569
6 slew him at the **p** of Jordan: and there H4569
1Sa 14: 4 And between the **p**, by which Jonathan H4569
Jer 22:20 the **p**: for all thy lovers are destroyed. H5676
51:32 And that the **p** are stopped, and the H4569

PASSED

Gen 12: 6 And Abram **p** through the land unto H5674
15:17 lamp that **p** between those pieces. H5674
31:21 he rose up, and **p** over the river, and set H5674
32:10 for with my staff I **p** over this Jordan; H5674
22 sons, and **p** over the ford Jabbok. H5674
31 And as he **p** over Penuel the sun rose H5674
33: 3 And he **p** over before them, and bowed H5674
37:28 Then there **p** by Midianites H5674
Ex 12:27 passover, who **p** over the houses of the H6452
34: 6 And the LORD **p** by before him, and H5674
Nu 14: 7 land, which we **p** through to search it, H5674
20:17 to the left, until we have **p** thy borders. H5674
33: 8 Pi-hahiroth, and **p** through the midst H5674
51 **p** over Jordan into the land of Canaan; H5674
Dt 2: 8 And when we **p** by from our brethren H5674
8 **p** by the way of the wilderness of Moab. H5674
27: 3 when thou art **p** over, that thou mayest H5674
29:16 through the nations which ye **p** by; H5674
Jos 2:23 the mountain, and **p** over, and came to H5674
3: 1 and lodged there before they **p** over. H5674
4 for ye have not **p** *this* way heretofore. H5674
16 the people **p** over right against Jericho. H5674
17 all the Israelites **p** over on dry ground, H5674
17 all the people were **p** clean over Jordan. H5674
4: 1 people were clean **p** over Jordan, that H5674
7 of the LORD; when it **p** over Jordan, the H5674
10 and the people hasted and **p** over. H5674
11 people were clean **p** over, that the ark H5674
11 the ark of the LORD **p** over, and the H5674
12 of Manasseh, **p** over armed before the H5674
13 prepared for war **p** over before the H5674
23 you, until ye were **p** over, as the LORD H5674
5: 1 until we were **p** over, that their heart H5674
6: 8 of rams' horns **p** on before the LORD, H5674
10:29 Then Joshua **p** from Makkedah, and all H5674
31 And Joshua **p** from Libnah, and all H5674
34 And from Lachish Joshua **p** unto H5674
15: 3 and **p** along to Zin, and ascended H5674
3 and **p** along to Hezron, and H5674
4 *From thence* it **p** toward Azmon, and H5674
6 Beth-hogla, and **p** along by the north of H5674
7 and the border **p** toward the waters of H5674
10 mount Seir, and **p** along unto the side H5674
10 to Beth-shemesh, and **p** on to Timnah: H5674
11 to Shicron, and **p** along to mount H5674
16: 6 and **p** by it on the east to Janohah; H5674
18: 9 And the men went and **p** through the H5674
18 And **p** along toward the side over H5674
19 And the border **p** along to the side of H5674
24:17 all the people through whom we **p**: H5674
Jdg 3:26 while they tarried, and **p** beyond the H5674
8: 4 And Gideon came to Jordan, *and* **p** H5674
10: 9 Moreover the children of Ammon **p** H5674
11:29 Jephthah, and he **p** over Gilead, and H5674
29 and Manasseh, and **p** over Mizpeh of H5674
29 he **p** over *unto* the children of Ammon. H5674
32 So Jephthah **p** over unto the children of H5674
12: 3 in my hands, and **p** over against the H5674
18:13 And they **p** thence unto mount H5674
19:14 And they **p** on and went their way; and H5674
1Sa 9: 4 And he **p** through mount Ephraim, and H5674
4 Ephraim, and **p** through the land of H5674
4 not: then they **p** through the land of H5674
4 *were* not: and he **p** through the land of H5674
27 on before us, (and he **p** on,) but stand H5674
14:23 and the battle **p** over unto Beth-aven. H5674
15:12 and **p** on, and gone down to Gilgal. H5674
27: 2 And David arose, and he **p** over with H5674
29: 2 And the lords of the Philistines **p** on by H5674
2 men **p** on in the rearward with Achish. H5674
2Sa 2:29 the plain, and **p** over Jordan, and went H5674
10:17 together, and **p** over Jordan, and came H5674
15:18 And all his servants **p** on beside him; H5674
18 him from Gath, **p** on before the king. H5674
22 Ittai the Gittite **p** over, and all his men, H5674
23 and all the people **p** over: the king also H5674
23 the king also himself **p** over the brook H5674
23 and all the people **p** over, toward the H5674
17:22 him, and they **p** over Jordan: by the H5674
24 And Absalom **p** over Jordan, he and H5674
24: 5 And they **p** over Jordan, and pitched in H5674
1Ki 13:25 And, behold, men **p** by, and saw the H5674
19:11 behold, the LORD **p** by, and a great H5674
19 twelfth: and Elijah **p** by him, and cast H5674
20:39 And as the king **p** by, he cried unto the H5674
2Ki 4: 8 And it fell on a day, that Elisha **p** to H5674
8 **p** by, he turned in thither to eat bread. H5674
31 And Gehazi **p** on before them, and laid H5674
6:30 his clothes; and he **p** by upon the wall, H5674
14: 9 to wife: and there **p** by a wild beast that H5674
1Ch 19:17 all Israel, and **p** over Jordan, and came H5674
2Ch 9:22 And king Solomon **p** all the kings of the H1431
25:18 to wife: and there **p** by a wild beast that H5674
30:10 So the posts **p** from city to city through H5674
Job 4:15 Then a spirit **p** before my face; the hair H2498
9:26 They are **p** away as the swift ships: as H2498
15:19 given, and no stranger **p** among them. H5674
28: 8 trodden it, nor the fierce lion **p** by it. H5710
Ps 18:12 clouds **p**, hail *stones* and coals of fire. H5674
37:36 Yet he **p** away, and, lo, he *was* not: yea, H5674
48: 4 were assembled, they **p** by together. H5674
90: 9 For all our days are **p** away in thy H6437
Song 3: 4 *It was* but a little that I **p** from them, H5674
Isa 10:28 He is come to Aiath, he is **p** to Migron; H5674
40:27 my judgment is **p** over from my God? H5674
41: 3 He pursued them, *and* **p** safely; *even* by H5674
Jer 2: 6 **p** through, and where no man dwelt? H5674
11:15 the holy flesh is **p** from thee? when thou H5674
34:18 twain, and **p** between the parts thereof, H5674
19 which **p** between the parts of the calf; H5674
46:17 a noise; he hath **p** the time appointed. H5674
Ezk 16: 6 And when I **p** by thee, and saw thee H5674
8 Now when I **p** by thee, and looked H5674
15 on every one that **p** by; his it was. H5674
25 **p** by, and multiplied thy whoredoms. H5674
36:34 lay desolate in the sight of all that **p** by. H5674
47: 5 in, a river that could not be **p** over. H5674
Dan 3:27 nor the smell of fire had **p** on them. H5709
6:18 Then the king went to his palace, and **p**
Hos 10:11 out *the corn*; but I **p** over upon her fair H5674
Jna 2: 3 thy billows and thy waves **p** over me. H5674
Mic 2:13 up, and have **p** through the gate, and H5674
Nah 3:19 hath not thy wickedness **p** continually? H5674
Hab 3:10 of the water **p** by: the deep uttered H5674
Zec 7:14 that no man **p** through nor returned: H5674
Mt 9: 1 And he entered into a ship, and **p** over, *G1276*
9 And as Jesus **p** forth from thence, he *G3855*
20:30 heard that Jesus **p** by, cried out, saying, *G3855*
27:39 And they that **p** by reviled him, *G3899*
Mk 2:14 And as he **p** by, he saw Levi the *son* of *G3855*
5:21 And when Jesus was **p** over again by *G1276*
6:35 desert place, and now the time *is* far **p**: *G4183*
48 the sea, and would have **p** by them. *G3928*
53 And when they had **p** over, they came *G1276*
9:30 And they departed thence, and **p** *G3899*
11:20 And in the morning, as they **p** by, they *G3899*
15:21 a Cyrenian, who **p** by, coming out of *G3855*
29 And they that **p** by railed on him, *G3899*
Lk 10:31 he saw him, he **p** by on the other side. *G492*
32 *on him*, and **p** by on the other side. *G492*
17:11 Jerusalem, that he **p** through the midst *G1330*
19: 1 And *Jesus* entered and **p** through *G1330*
Jn 5:24 but is **p** from death unto life. *G3327*
8:59 through the midst of them, and so **p** by. *G3855*
9: 1 And as *Jesus* **p** by, he saw a man which *G3855*
Act 9:32 And it came to pass, as Peter **p** *G1330*
12:10 went out, and **p** on through one street; *G4281*
14:24 And after they had **p** throughout *G1330*
15: 3 the church, they **p** through Phenice and *G1330*
17: 1 Now when they had **p** through *G1353*
23 For as I **p** by, and beheld your *G1330*
19: 1 Paul having **p** through the upper coasts *G1330*
21 when he had **p** through Macedonia *G1330*
Ro 5:12 sin; and so death **p** upon all men, for *G1330*
1Co 10: 1 the cloud, and all **p** through the sea; *G1330*
2Co 5:17 old things are **p** away; behold, all *G3928*
Heb 4:14 high priest, that is **p** into the heavens, *G1330*
11:29 By faith they **p** through the Red sea as *G1224*
1Jn 3:14 We know that we have **p** from death *G3327*
Rev 21: 1 **p** away; and there was no more sea. *G3928*

Rev 21: 4 pain: for the former things are **p** away. G565

PASSEDST

Jdg 12: 1 Wherefore **p** thou over to fight against H5674

PASSENGERS

Prv 9:15 To call **p** who go right on their H5674+H1870
Ezk 39:11 the valley of the **p** on the east of the H5674
11 the *noses* of the **p**: and there shall they H5674
14 to bury with the **p** those that remain H5674
15 And the **p** *that* pass through the land, H5674

PASSEST

Dt 3:21 unto all the kingdoms whither thou **p**. H5674
30:18 thou **p** over Jordan to go to possess it. H5674
2Sa 15:33 Unto whom David said, If thou **p** on H5674
1Ki 2:37 goest out, and **p** over the brook Kidron, H5674
Isa 43: 2 When thou **p** through the waters, I *will* H5674

PASSETH

Ex 30:13 This they shall give, every one that **p** H5674
14 Every one that **p** among them that are H5674
33:22 while my glory **p** by, that I will put thee H5674
Lev 27:32 of whatsoever **p** under the rod, the H5674
Jos 3:11 the earth **p** over before you into Jordan. H5674
16: 2 to Luz, and **p** along unto the borders H5674
19:13 And from thence **p** on along on the east H5674
1Ki 9: 8 high, every one that **p** by it shall be H5674
2Ki 4: 9 man of God, which **p** by us continually. H5674
12: 4 of every one that **p** *the account,* the H5674
2Ch 7:21 to every one that **p** by it; so that he H5674
Job 9:11 he **p** on also, but I perceive him not. H2498
14:20 him, and he **p**: thou changest his H1980
30:15 and my welfare **p** away as a cloud. H5674
37:21 but the wind **p**, and cleanseth them. H5674
Ps 8: 8 **p** through the paths of the seas. H5674
78:39 that **p** away, and cometh not again. H1980
103:16 For the wind **p** over it, and it is gone; H5674
144: 4 his days *are* as a shadow that **p** away. H5674
Prv 10:25 As the whirlwind **p**, so *is* the wicked no H5674
26:17 He that **p** by, *and* meddleth with strife H5674
Ecc 1: 4 *One* generation **p** away, and *another* H1980
Isa 29: 5 *be* as chaff that **p** away: yea, it shall be H5674
Jer 9:12 like a wilderness, that none **p** through? H5674
13:24 **p** away by the wind of the wilderness. H5674
18:16 every one that **p** thereby shall be H5674
19: 8 every one that **p** thereby shall be H5674
Ezk 35: 7 him that **p** out and him that returneth. H5674
Hos 13: 3 the early dew that **p** away, as the chaff H1980
Mic 7:18 iniquity, and **p** by the transgression H5674
Zep 2:15 **p** by her shall hiss, *and* wag his hand. H5674
3: 6 waste, that none **p** by: their cities are H5674
Zec 9: 8 of him that **p** by, and because of him H5674
Lk 18:37 told him, that Jesus of Nazareth **p** by. G3928
1Co 7:31 *it*: for the fashion of this world **p** away. G3855
Eph 3:19 And to know the love of Christ, which **p** G5235
Php 4: 7 And the peace of God, which **p** all G5242
1Jn 2:17 And the world **p** away, and the lust G3855

PASSING

Jdg 19:18 And he said unto him, We *are* **p** from H5674
2Sa 1:26 me was wonderful, **p** the love of women.
15:24 the people had done **p** out of the city. H5674
2Ki 6:26 And as the king of Israel was **p** by upon H5674
Ps 84: 6 *Who* **p** through the valley of Baca make H5674
Prv 7: 8 **P** through the street near her corner; H5674
Isa 31: 5 deliver *it; and* **p** over he will preserve it. H5674
Ezk 39:14 employment, **p** through the land to H5674
Lk 4:30 But he **p** through the midst of them G1330
Act 5:15 **p** by might overshadow some of them. G2064
8:40 But Philip was found at Azotus: and **p** G1330
16: 8 And they **p** by Mysia came down to G3928
27: 8 And, hardly **p** it, came unto a place G3881

PASSION

Act 1: 3 alive after his **p** by many infallible G3958

PASSIONS

Act 14:15 are men of like **p** with you, and preach G3663
Jas 5:17 Elias was a man subject to like **p** as we G3663

PASSOVER

Ex 12:11 shall eat it in haste: it *is* the LORD'S **p**. H6453
21 to your families, and kill the **p**. H6453
27 of the LORD'S **p**, who passed over the H6453
43 **p**: There shall no stranger eat thereof: H6453
48 and will keep the **p** to the LORD, let all H6453
34:25 feast of the **p** be left unto the morning. H6453
Lev 23: 5 the first month at even *is* the LORD'S **p**. H6453
Nu 9: 2 keep the **p** at his appointed season. H6453
4 of Israel, that they should keep the **p**. H6453
5 And they kept the **p** on the fourteenth H6453
6 could not keep the **p** on that day: and H6453
10 yet he shall keep the **p** unto the LORD. H6453
12 ordinances of the **p** they shall keep it. H6453
13 to keep the **p**, even the same soul H6453
14 and will keep the **p** unto the LORD; H6453
14 ordinance of the **p**, and according to the H6453
28:16 of the first month *is* the **p** of the LORD. H6453
33: 3 the morrow after the **p** the children of H6453
Dt 16: 1 and keep the **p** unto the LORD thy H6453
2 Thou shalt therefore sacrifice the **p** H6453
5 Thou mayest not sacrifice the **p** within H6453
6 thou shalt sacrifice the **p** at even, at the H6453
Jos 5:10 and kept the **p** on the fourteenth day H6453
11 morrow after the **p**, unleavened cakes, H6453
2Ki 23:21 saying, Keep the **p** unto the LORD your H6453
22 Surely there was not holden such a **p** H6453
23 *wherein* this **p** was holden to the LORD H6453
2Ch 30: 1 the **p** unto the LORD God of Israel. H6453
2 to keep the **p** in the second month. H6453
5 come to keep the **p** unto the LORD God H6453
15 Then they killed the **p** on the H6453
18 did they eat the **p** otherwise than it was H6453
35: 1 Moreover Josiah kept a **p** unto the H6453
1 and they killed the **p** on the fourteenth H6453
6 So kill the **p**, and sanctify yourselves, H6453
7 kids, all for the **p** offerings, for all that H6453
8 unto the priests for the **p** offerings two H6453
9 unto the Levites for **p** offerings five H6453
11 And they killed the **p**, and the priests H6453
13 And they roasted the **p** with fire H6453
16 day, to keep the **p**, and to offer burnt H6453
17 present kept the **p** at that time, and the H6453
18 And there was no **p** like to that kept in H6453
18 Israel keep such a **p** as Josiah kept, and H6453
19 of the reign of Josiah was this **p** kept. H6453
Ezr 6:19 the captivity kept the **p** upon the H6453
20 and killed the **p** for all the children of H6453
Ezk 45:21 ye shall have the **p**, a feast of seven H6453
Mt 26: 2 is *the feast of* the **p**, and the Son of man G3957
17 that we prepare for thee to eat the **p**? G3957
18 the **p** at thy house with my disciples. G3957
19 them; and they made ready the **p**. G3957
Mk 14: 1 After two days was *the feast of* the **p**, G3957
12 they killed the **p**, his disciples said unto G3957
12 and prepare that thou mayest eat the **p**? G3957
14 I shall eat the **p** with my disciples? G3957
16 unto them: and they made ready the **p**. G3957
Lk 2:41 every year at the feast of the **p**. G3957
22: 1 bread drew nigh, which is called the **P**. G3957
7 bread, when the **p** must be killed. G3957
8 and prepare us the **p**, that we may eat. G3957
11 I shall eat the **p** with my disciples? G3957
13 unto them: and they made ready the **p**. G3957
15 to eat this **p** with you before I suffer: G3957
Jn 2:13 And the Jews' **p** was at hand, and Jesus G3957
23 Now when he was in Jerusalem at the **p**, G3957
6: 4 And the **p**, a feast of the Jews, was nigh. G3957
11:55 And the Jews' **p** was nigh at hand: and G3957
55 before the **p**, to purify themselves. G3957
12: 1 Then Jesus six days before the **p** came G3957
13: 1 Now before the feast of the **p**, when G3957
18:28 be defiled; but that they might eat the **p**. G3957
39 you one at the **p**: will ye therefore that G3957
19:14 And it was the preparation of the **p**, and G3957
1Co 5: 7 even Christ our **p** is sacrificed for us: G3957
Heb 11:28 Through faith he kept the **p**, and the G3957

PASSOVERS

2Ch 30:17 of the killing of the **p** for every one *that* H6453

PAST

Gen 50: 4 mourning were **p**, Joseph spake unto H5674
Ex 21:29 his horn in time **p**, and it hath been H8032
36 to push in time **p**, and his owner hath H8032
Nu 21:22 *high* way, until we be **p** thy borders. H5674
Dt 2:10 The Emims dwelt therein in times **p**, a H6440
4:32 For ask now of the days that are **p**, H7223
42 him not in times **p**; and that fleeing H8032
19: 4 whom he hated not in time **p**; H8032
6 as he hated him not in time **p**. H8032
1Sa 15:32 said, Surely the bitterness of death is **p**. H5493
19: 7 he was in his presence, as in times **p**. H8032
2Sa 3:17 David in times **p** *to be* king over you: H8032
5: 2 Also in time **p**, when Saul was king over H8032
11:27 And when the mourning was **p**, David H5493
16: 1 And when David was a little **p** the top H5674
1Ki 18:29 pass, when midday was **p**, and they H5674
1Ch 9:20 in time **p**, *and* the LORD *was* with him. H6440
11: 2 And moreover in time **p**, even when H8032
Job 9:10 Which doeth great things **p** finding out; H369
14:13 until thy wrath be **p**, that thou wouldest H7725
17:11 My days are **p**, my purposes are broken H5674
29: 2 Oh that I were as *in* months **p**, as *in* the H6924
Ps 90: 4 it is **p**, and *as* a watch in the night. H5674
Ecc 3:15 and God requireth that which is **p**. H7291
Song 2:11 For, lo, the winter is **p**, the rain is over H5674
Jer 8:20 The harvest is **p**, the summer is ended, H5674
Mt 14:15 the time is now **p**; send the multitude G3928
Mk 16: 1 And when the sabbath was **p**, Mary G1230
Lk 9:36 And when the voice was **p**, Jesus was G1096
Act 12:10 When they were **p** the first and the G1330
14:16 Who in times **p** suffered all nations to G3944
27: 9 now already **p**, Paul admonished *them*, G3928
Ro 3:25 are **p**, through the forbearance of God; G4266
11:30 For as ye in times **p** have not believed G4218
33 judgments, and his ways **p** finding out! G421
Gal 1:13 in time **p** in the Jews' religion, G4218
23 us in times **p** now preacheth the faith G4218
5:21 told *you* in time **p**, that they which do G4277
Eph 2: 2 Wherein in time **p** ye walked according G4218
3 in times **p** in the lusts of our flesh, G4218
11 ye *being* in time **p** Gentiles in the flesh, G4218
4:19 Who being **p** feeling have given G524
2Ti 2:18 that the resurrection is **p** already; and G1096
Phlm 11 Which in time **p** was to thee G4218
Heb 1: 1 **p** unto the fathers by the prophets, G3819
11:11 child when she was **p** age, because she G3844
1Pt 2:10 Which in time **p** *were* not a people, but G4218
4: 3 For the time **p** of *our* life may suffice us G3928
1Jn 2: 8 is **p**, and the true light now shineth. G3855
Rev 9:12 One woe is **p**; *and*, behold, there come G565
11:14 The second woe is **p**; *and*, behold, the G565

PASTOR

Jer 17:16 from *being* a **p** to follow thee: neither H7462

PASTORS

Jer 2: 8 knew me not: the **p** also transgressed H7462
3:15 And I will give you **p** according to mine H7462
10:21 For the **p** are become brutish, and have H7462
12:10 Many **p** have destroyed my vineyard, H7462
22:22 The wind shall eat up all thy **p**, and thy H7462
23: 1 Woe be unto the **p** that destroy and H7462
2 of Israel against the **p** that feed my H7462
Eph 4:11 evangelists; and some, **p** and teachers; G4166

PASTURE

Gen 47: 4 servants have no **p** for their flocks; for H4829
1Ch 4:39 of the valley, to seek **p** for their flocks. H4829
40 And they found fat **p** and good, and the H4829
41 *there was* **p** there for their flocks. H4829
Job 39: 8 The range of the mountains *is* his **p**, H4829
Ps 74: 1 anger smoke against the sheep of thy **p**? H4830
79:13 So we thy people and sheep of thy **p** H4830
95: 7 the people of his **p**, and the sheep of his H4830
100: 3 *are* his people, and the sheep of his **p**. H4830
Isa 32:14 ever, a joy of wild asses, a **p** of flocks; H4829
Jer 23: 1 the sheep of my **p**! saith the LORD. H4830
25:36 for the LORD hath spoiled their **p**. H4830
Lam 1: 6 harts *that* find no **p**, and they are gone H4829
Ezk 34:14 I will feed them in a good **p**, and upon H4829
14 fold, and *in* a fat **p** shall they feed upon H4829
18 eaten up the good **p**, but ye must tread H4829
31 And ye my flock, the flock of my **p**, *are* H4830
Hos 13: 6 According to their **p**, so were they filled; H4830
Joel 1:18 they have no **p**; yea, the flocks of sheep H4829
Jn 10: 9 and shall go in and out, and find **p**. G3542

PASTURES

1Ki 4:23 oxen out of the **p**, and an hundred H7471
Ps 23: 2 He maketh me to lie down in green **p**: H4999
65:12 They drop *upon* the **p** of the H4999
13 The **p** are clothed with flocks; the H3733
Isa 30:23 that day shall thy cattle feed in large **p**. H3733
49: 9 and their **p** *shall be* in all high places. H4830
Ezk 34:18 residue of your **p**? and to have drunk of H4829
45:15 out of the fat **p** of Israel; for a meat H4945
Joel 1:19 hath devoured the **p** of the wilderness, H4999
20 hath devoured the **p** of the wilderness. H4999
2:22 of the field: for the **p** of the wilderness H4999

PATARA

Act 21: 1 unto Rhodes, and from thence unto **P**: G3959

PATE
Ps 7:16 shall come down upon his own **p**. H6936

PATH
Gen 49:17 an adder in the **p**, that biteth the horse H734
Nu 22:24 But the angel of the LORD stood in a **p** H4934
Job 28: 7 *There is* a **p** which no fowl knoweth, H5410
30:13 They mar my **p**, they set forward my H5410
41:32 He maketh a **p** to shine after him; *one* H5410
Ps 16:11 Thou wilt shew me the **p** of life: in thy H734
27:11 in a plain **p**, because of mine enemies. H734
77:19 Thy way *is* in the sea, and thy **p** in the H7635
119:35 Make me to go in the **p** of thy H5410
105 unto my feet, and a light unto my **p**. H5410
139: 3 Thou compassest my **p** and my lying H734
142: 3 thou knewest my **p**. In the way wherein H5410
Prv 1:15 with them; refrain thy foot from their **p**: H5410
2: 9 and equity; *yea*, every good **p**. H4570
4:14 Enter not into the **p** of the wicked, and H734
18 But the **p** of the just *is* as the shining H734
26 Ponder the **p** of thy feet, and let all thy H4570
5: 6 Lest thou shouldest ponder the **p** of life, H734
Isa 26: 7 upright, dost weigh the **p** of the just. H4570
30:11 aside out of the **p**, cause the Holy One of H734
40:14 taught him in the **p** of judgment, and H734
43:16 the sea, and a **p** in the mighty waters; H5410
Joel 2: 8 every one in his **p**: and *when* they fall H4546

PATHROS
Isa 11:11 Egypt, and from **P**, and from Cush, and H6624
Jer 44: 1 Noph, and in the country of **P**, saying, H6624
15 Egypt, in **P**, answered Jeremiah, saying, H6624
Ezk 29:14 *into* the land of **P**, into the land of their H6624
30:14 And I will make **P** desolate, and will set H6624

PATHRUSIM
Gen 10:14 And **P**, and Casluhim, (out of whom H6625
1Ch 1:12 And **P**, and Casluhim, (of whom came H6625

PATHS
Job 6:18 The **p** of their way are turned aside; they H734
8:13 So *are* the **p** of all that forget God; and H734
13:27 unto all my **p**; thou settest a print upon H734
19: 8 pass, and he hath set darkness in my **p**. H5410
24:13 thereof, nor abide in the **p** thereof. H5410
33:11 feet in the stocks, he marketh all my **p**. H734
38:20 know the **p** *to* the house thereof? H5410
Ps 8: 8 passeth through the **p** of the seas. H734
17: 4 kept *me from* the **p** of the destroyer. H734
5 Hold up my goings in thy **p**, *that* my H4570
23: 3 **p** of righteousness for his name's sake. H4570
25: 4 me thy ways, O LORD; teach me thy **p**. H734
10 All the **p** of the LORD *are* mercy and H734
65:11 thy goodness; and thy **p** drop fatness. H4570
Prv 2: 8 He keepeth the **p** of judgment, and H734
13 Who leave the **p** of uprightness, to walk H734
15 crooked, and *they* froward in their **p**: H4570
18 unto death, and her **p** unto the dead. H4570
19 neither take they hold of the **p** of life. H734
20 *men*, and keep the **p** of the righteous. H734
3: 6 him, and he shall direct thy **p**. H734
17 pleasantness, and all her **p** *are* peace. H5410
4:11 of wisdom; I have led thee in right **p**. H4570
7:25 to her ways, go not astray in her **p**. H5410
8: 2 places, by the way in the places of the **p**. H5410
20 in the midst of the **p** of judgment: H5410
Isa 2: 3 we will walk in his **p**: for out of Zion shall H734
3:12 *thee* to err, and destroy the way of thy **p**. H734
42:16 I will lead them in **p** *that* they have not H5410
58:12 breach, The restorer of **p** to dwell in. H5410
59: 7 wasting and destruction *are* in their **p**. H4546
8 made them crooked **p**: whosoever goeth H5410
Jer 6:16 ask for the old **p**, where *is* the good way, H5410
18:15 *from* the ancient **p**, to walk in paths, *in* H7635
15 to walk in **p**, *in* a way not cast up; H5410
Lam 3: 9 stone, he hath made my **p** crooked. H5410
Hos 2: 6 a wall, that she shall not find her **p**. H5410
Mic 4: 2 we will walk in his **p**: for the law shall go H734
Mt 3: 3 way of the Lord, make his **p** straight. G5147
Mk 1: 3 way of the Lord, make his **p** straight. G5147
Lk 3: 4 way of the Lord, make his **p** straight. G5147
Heb 12:13 And make straight **p** for your feet, lest G5163

PATHWAY
Prv 12:28 **p** *thereof there is* no death. H1870+H5410a

PATIENCE
Mt 18:26 have **p** with me, and I will pay thee all. G3114
29 Have **p** with me, and I will pay thee all. G3114
Lk 8:15 keep *it*, and bring forth fruit with **p**. G5281
21:19 In your **p** possess ye your souls. G5281
Ro 5: 3 knowing that tribulation worketh **p**; G5281
4 And **p**, experience; and experience, G5281
8:25 see not, *then* do we with **p** wait for *it*. G5281
15: 4 that we through **p** and comfort of the G5281
5 Now the God of **p** and consolation G5281
2Co 6: 4 of God, in much **p**, in afflictions, in G5281
12:12 among you in all **p**, in signs, and G5281
Col 1:11 all **p** and longsuffering with joyfulness; G5281
1Th 1: 3 of love, and **p** of hope in our Lord G5281
2Th 1: 4 of God for your **p** and faith in all your G5281
1Ti 6:11 godliness, faith, love, **p**, meekness. G5281
2Ti 3:10 purpose, faith, longsuffering, charity, **p**, G5281
Tit 2: 2 sound in faith, in charity, in **p**. G5281
Heb 6:12 faith and **p** inherit the promises. G3115
10:36 For ye have need of **p**, that, after ye G5281
12: 1 run with **p** the race that is set before us, G5281
Jas 1: 3 that the trying of your faith worketh **p**. G5281
4 But let **p** have *her* perfect work, that ye G5281
5: 7 and hath long **p** for it, until he receive G3114
10 of suffering affliction, and of **p**. G3115
11 Ye have heard of the **p** of Job, and have G5281
2Pt 1: 6 **p**; and to patience godliness; G5281
6 patience; and to **p** godliness; G5281
Rev 1: 9 the kingdom and **p** of Jesus Christ, was G5281
2: 2 labour, and thy **p**, and how thou canst G5281
3 And hast borne, and hast **p**, and for my G5281
19 and faith, and thy **p**, and thy works; G5281
3:10 the word of my **p**, I also will keep thee G5281
13:10 Here is the **p** and the faith of the saints. G5281
14:12 Here is the **p** of the saints: here *are* they G5281

PATIENT
Ecc 7: 8 thereof: *and* the **p** in spirit *is* better than H750
Ro 2: 7 To them who by **p** continuance in well G5281
12:12 Rejoicing in hope; **p** in tribulation; G5278
1Th 5:14 support the weak, be **p** toward all *men*. G3114
2Th 3: 5 God, and into the **p** waiting for Christ. G5281
1Ti 3: 3 but **p**, not a brawler, not covetous; G1933
2Ti 2:24 be gentle unto all *men*, apt to teach, **p**, G420
Jas 5: 7 Be **p** therefore, brethren, unto the G3114
8 Be ye also **p**; stablish your hearts: for G3114

PATIENTLY
Ps 37: 7 Rest in the LORD, and wait **p** for him: H2342
40: 1 I waited **p** for the LORD; and he H6960
Act 26: 3 wherefore I beseech thee to hear me **p**. G3116
Heb 6:15 And so, after he had **p** endured, he G3114
1Pt 2:20 ye shall take it **p**? but if, when ye do G5278
20 ye take it **p**, this *is* acceptable with God. G5278

PATMOS
Rev 1: 9 isle that is called **P**, for the word of God, G3963

PATRIARCH
Act 2:29 unto you of the **p** David, that he is both G3966
Heb 7: 4 **p** Abraham gave the tenth of the spoils. G3966

PATRIARCHS
Act 7: 8 Jacob; and Jacob *begat* the twelve **p**. G3966
9 And the **p**, moved with envy, sold G3966

PATRIMONY
Dt 18: 8 that which cometh of the sale of his **p**. H1

PATROBAS
Ro 16:14 Salute Asyncritus, Phlegon, Hermas, **P**, G3969

PATTERN
Ex 25: 9 thee, *after* the **p** of the tabernacle, and H8403
9 and the **p** of all the instruments H8403
40 **p**, which was shewed thee in the mount. H8403
Nu 8: 4 unto the **p** which the LORD had H4758
Jos 22:28 *again*, Behold the **p** of the altar of the H8403
2Ki 16:10 the altar, and the **p** of it; according to H8403
1Ch 28:11 his son the **p** of the porch, and of H8403
12 And the **p** of all that he had by the H8403
18 and gold for the **p** of the chariot of the H8403
19 upon me, *even* all the works of this **p**. H8403
Ezk 43:10 iniquities: and let them measure the **p**. H8508
1Ti 1:16 for a **p** to them which should G5296
Tit 2: 7 In all things shewing thyself a **p** of G5179
Heb 8: 5 to the **p** shewed to thee in the mount. G5179

PATTERNS
Heb 9:23 *It was* therefore necessary that the **p** of G5262

PAU
Gen 36:39 of his city *was* **P**; and his wife's name H6464

PAUL
Act 13: 9 Then Saul, (who also *is called* **P**,) filled G3972
13 Now when **P** and his company loosed G3972
16 Then **P** stood up, and beckoning with G3972
43 followed **P** and Barnabas: who, G3972
45 by **P**, contradicting and blaspheming. G3972
46 Then **P** and Barnabas waxed bold, and G3972
50 against **P** and Barnabas, and G3972
14: 9 The same heard **P** speak: who G3972
11 And when the people saw what **P** had G3972
12 Jupiter; and **P**, Mercurius, because G3972
14 Barnabas and **P**, heard *of*, they rent G3972
19 having stoned **P**, drew *him* out of the G3972
15: 2 When therefore **P** and Barnabas had G3972
2 determined that **P** and Barnabas, and G3972
12 to Barnabas and **P**, declaring what G3972
22 to Antioch with **P** and Barnabas; G3972
25 you with our beloved Barnabas and **P**, G3972
35 **P** also and Barnabas continued in G3972
36 And some days after **P** said unto G3972
38 But **P** thought not good to take him G3972
40 And **P** chose Silas, and departed, being G3972
16: 3 Him would **P** have to go forth with G3972
9 And a vision appeared to **P** in the G3972
14 unto the things which were spoken of **P**. G3972
17 The same followed **P** and us, and cried, G3972
18 And this did she many days. But **P**, G3972
19 was gone, they caught **P** and Silas, and G3972
25 And at midnight **P** and Silas prayed, G3972
28 But **P** cried with a loud voice, saying, G3972
29 and fell down before **P** and Silas, G3972
36 told this saying to **P**, The magistrates G3972
37 But **P** said unto them, They have G3972
17: 2 And **P**, as his manner was, went in unto G3972
4 consorted with **P** and Silas; and of the G3972
10 sent away **P** and Silas by night unto G3972
13 was preached of **P** at Berea, they came G3972
14 sent away **P** to go as it were to the G3972
15 And they that conducted **P** brought G3972
16 Now while **P** waited for them at G3972
22 Then **P** stood in the midst of Mars' hill, G3972
33 So **P** departed from among them. G3972
18: 1 After these things **P** departed from G3972
5 from Macedonia, **P** was pressed in the G3972
9 Then spake the Lord to **P** in the night G3972
12 accord against **P**, and brought him to G3972
14 And when **P** was now about to open *his* G3972
18 And **P** *after this* tarried *there* yet a G3972
19: 1 was at Corinth, **P** having passed G3972
4 Then said **P**, John verily baptized with G3972
6 And when **P** had laid *his* hands upon G3972
11 special miracles by the hands of **P**: G3972
13 adjure you by Jesus whom **P** preacheth. G3972
15 I know, and **P** I know; but who are ye? G3972
21 After these things were ended, **P** G3972
26 all Asia, this **P** hath persuaded and G3972
30 And when **P** would have entered in G3972
20: 1 And after the uproar was ceased, **P** G3972
7 to break bread, **P** preached unto them, G3972
9 a deep sleep: and as **P** was long G3972
10 And **P** went down, and fell on him, and G3972
13 to take in **P**: for so had he appointed, G3972
16 For **P** had determined to sail by G3972
21: 4 days: who said to **P** through the Spirit, G3972
13 Then **P** answered, What mean ye to G3972
18 And the *day* following **P** went in with G3972
26 Then **P** took the men, and the next day G3972
29 that **P** had brought into the temple.) G3972
30 and they took **P**, and drew him out of G3972
32 and the soldiers, they left beating of **P**. G3972
37 And as **P** was to be led into the castle, G3972
39 But **P** said, I am a man *which am* a Jew G3972
40 And when he had given him licence, **P** G3972
22:25 And as they bound him with thongs, **P** G3972
28 And **P** said, But I was *free* born. G3972
30 **P** down, and set him before them. G3972
23: 1 And **P**, earnestly beholding the council, G3972
3 Then said **P** unto him, God shall smite G3972
5 Then said **P**, I wist not, brethren, that G3972
6 But when **P** perceived that the one part G3972
10 fearing lest **P** should have been pulled G3972
11 Be of good cheer, **P**: for as thou hast G3972
12 eat nor drink till they had killed **P**. G3972
14 will eat nothing until we have slain **P**. G3972
16 and entered into the castle, and told **P**. G3972
17 Then **P** called one of the centurions G3972

Act 23:18 captain, and said, P the prisoner called G3972
20 bring down P to morrow into the G3972
24 that they may set P on, and bring *him* G3972
31 them, took P, and brought *him* by G3972
33 governor, presented P also before him. G3972
24: 1 who informed the governor against P. G3972
10 Then P, after that the governor had G3972
23 centurion to keep P, and to let *him* have G3972
24 a Jewess, he sent for P, and heard him G3972
26 been given him of P, that he might loose G3972
27 shew the Jews a pleasure, left P bound. G3972
25: 2 him against P, and besought him, G3972
4 But Festus answered, that P should be G3972
6 seat commanded P to be brought. G3972
7 against P, which they could not prove. G3972
9 answered P, and said, Wilt thou G3972
10 Then said P, I stand at Caesar's G3972
19 was dead, whom P affirmed to be alive. G3972
21 But when P had appealed to be G3972
23 commandment P was brought forth. G3972
26: 1 Then Agrippa said unto P, Thou art G3972
1 for thyself. Then P stretched forth the G3972
24 with a loud voice, P, thou art beside G3972
28 Then Agrippa said unto P, Almost thou G3972
29 And P said, I would to God, that not G3972
27: 1 they delivered P and certain other G3972
3 entreated P, and gave *him* liberty G3972
9 now already past, P admonished *them*, G3972
11 those things which were spoken by P. G3972
21 But after long abstinence P stood forth G3972
24 Saying, Fear not, P; thou must be G3972
31 P said to the centurion and to the G3972
33 And while the day was coming on, P G3972
43 But the centurion, willing to save P, G3972
28: 3 And when P had gathered a bundle of G3972
8 bloody flux: to whom P entered in, and G3972
15 whom when P saw, he thanked God, G3972
16 of the guard: but P was suffered to G3972
17 after three days P called the chief of the G3972
25 after that P had spoken one word, G3972
30 And P dwelt two whole years in his G3972
Ro 1: 1 P, a servant of Jesus Christ, called *to be* G3972
1Co 1: 1 P, called *to be* an apostle of Jesus Christ G3972
12 of you saith, I am of P; and I of Apollos; G3972
13 Is Christ divided? was P crucified for G3972
13 or were ye baptized in the name of P? G3972
3: 4 For while one saith, I am of P; and G3972
5 Who then is P, and who *is* Apollos, but G3972
22 Whether P, or Apollos, or Cephas, or G3972
16:21 The salutation of *me* P with mine own G3972
2Co 1: 1 P, an apostle of Jesus Christ by the will G3972
10: 1 Now I P myself beseech you by the G3972
Gal 1: 1 P, an apostle, (not of men, neither by G3972
5: 2 Behold, I P say unto you, that if ye be G3972
Eph 1: 1 P, an apostle of Jesus Christ by the will G3972
3: 1 For this cause I P, the prisoner of Jesus G3972
Php 1: 1 P and Timotheus, the servants of Jesus G3972
Col 1: 1 P, an apostle of Jesus Christ by the will G3972
23 whereof I P am made a minister; G3972
4:18 The salutation by the hand of me P. G3972
1Th 1: 1 P, and Silvanus, and Timotheus, unto G3972
2:18 unto you, even I P, once and again; but G3972
2Th 1: 1 P, and Silvanus, and Timotheus, unto G3972
3:17 The salutation of P with mine own G3972
1Ti 1: 1 P, an apostle of Jesus Christ by the G3972
2Ti 1: 1 P, an apostle of Jesus Christ by the will G3972
Tit 1: 1 P, a servant of God, and an apostle of G3972
Phlm 1 P, a prisoner of Jesus Christ, and G3972
9 such an one as P the aged, and now G3972
19 I P have written *it* with mine own G3972
2Pt 3:15 beloved brother P also according to the G3972

PAUL'S

Act 19:29 of Macedonia, P companions in travel, G3972
20:37 And they all wept sore, and fell on P G3972
21: 8 And the next *day* we that were of P G3972
11 unto us, he took P girdle, and bound G3972
23:16 And when P sister's son heard of their G3972
25:14 Festus declared P cause unto the king, G3972

PAULUS

Act 13: 7 country, Sergius P, a prudent man; who G3972

PAVED

Ex 24:10 feet as it were a p work of a sapphire H3840
Song 3:10 midst thereof being p *with* love, for the H7528

PAVEMENT

2Ki 16:17 under it, and put it upon a p of stones. H4837
2Ch 7: 3 ground upon the p, and worshipped, H7531
Est 1: 6 and silver, upon a p of red, and blue, H7531
Ezk 40:17 chambers, and a p made for the court H7531
17 thirty chambers *were* upon the p. H7531
18 And the p by the side of the gates over H7531
18 the length of the gates *was* the lower p. H7531
42: 3 over against the p which *was* for the H7531
Jn 19:13 the P, but in the Hebrew, Gabbatha. G3038

PAVILION

Ps 18:11 his secret place; his p round about him H5521
27: 5 hide me in his p: in the secret of his H5520
31:20 in a p from the strife of tongues. H5521
Jer 43:10 he shall spread his royal p over them. H8237

PAVILIONS

2Sa 22:12 And he made darkness p round about H5521
1Ki 20:12 the kings in the p, that he said unto his H5521
16 drunk in the p, he and the kings, the H5521

PAW

1Sa 17:37 me out of the p of the lion, and out H3027
37 and out of the p of the bear, he will H3027

PAWETH

Job 39:21 He p in the valley, and rejoiceth in *his* H2658

PAWS

Lev 11:27 And whatsoever goeth upon his p, H3709

PAY

Ex 21:19 quit: only he shall p *for* the loss of his H5414
22 and he shall p as the judges *determine*. H5414
36 in; he shall surely p ox for ox; and the H7999
22: 7 if the thief be found, let him p double. H7999
9 he shall p double unto his neighbour. H7999
17 unto him, he shall p money according H8254
Nu 20:19 then I will p for it: I will only, H5414+H4377
Dt 23:21 shalt not slack to p it: for the LORD thy H7999
2Sa 15: 7 let me go and p my vow, which I have H7999
1Ki 20:39 or else thou shalt p a talent of silver. H8254
2Ki 4: 7 Go, sell the oil, and p thy debt, and live H7999
2Ch 8: 8 make to p tribute until this day. H5927
27: 5 of Ammon p unto him, both the H7725
Ezr 4:13 *then* will they not p toll, tribute, and H5415
Est 3: 9 and I will p ten thousand talents H8254
4: 7 Haman had promised to p to the king's H8254
Job 22:27 hear thee, and thou shalt p thy vows. H7999
Ps 22:25 p my vows before them that fear him. H7999
50:14 Offer unto God thanksgiving; and p thy H7999
66:13 burnt offerings: I will p thee my vows, H7999
76:11 Vow, and p unto the LORD your God: H7999
116:14 I will p my vows unto the LORD now in H7999
18 I will p my vows unto the LORD now in H7999
Prv 19:17 he hath given will he p him again. H7999
22:27 If thou hast nothing to p, why should he H7999
Ecc 5: 4 God, defer not to p it; for *he hath* no H7999
4 in fools: p that which thou hast vowed. H7999
5 than that thou shouldest vow and not p. H7999
Jna 2: 9 I will p *that* that I have vowed. H7999
Mt 17:24 said, Doth not your master p tribute? G5055
18:25 But forasmuch as he had not to p, his G591
26 patience with me, and I will p thee all. G591
28 the throat, saying, P me that thou owest. G591
29 patience with me, and I will p thee all. G591
30 him into prison, till he should p the debt. G591
34 he should p all that was due unto him. G591
23:23 hypocrites! for ye p tithe of mint and G586
Lk 7:42 And when they had nothing to p, he G591
Ro 13: 6 For for this cause p ye tribute also: for G5055

PAYED

Prv 7:14 with me; this day have I p my vows. H7999
Heb 7: 9 receiveth tithes, p tithes in Abraham. G1183

PAYETH

Ps 37:21 The wicked borroweth, and p not H7999

PAYMENT

Mt 18:25 and all that he had, and p to be made. G591

PAZZAZ See BETH-PAZZEZ.

PEACE

Gen 15:15 And thou shalt go to thy fathers in p; H7965
24:21 at her held his p, to wit whether the H2790
26:29 sent thee away in p: thou *art* now the H7965
31 away, and they departed from him in p. H7965
28:21 in p; then shall the LORD be my God: H7965
Gen 34: 5 Jacob held his p until they were come. H2790
41:16 God shall give Pharaoh an answer of p. H7965
43:23 And he said, P *be* to you, fear not: your H7965
44:17 you, get you up in p unto your father. H7965
Ex 4:18 alive. And Jethro said to Moses, Go in p. H7965
14:14 fight for you, and ye shall hold your p. H2790
18:23 people shall also go to their place in p. H7965
20:24 burnt offerings, and thy p offerings, thy H8002
24: 5 p offerings of oxen unto the LORD. H8002
29:28 sacrifice of their p offerings, *even* their H8002
32: 6 and brought p offerings; and the H8002
Lev 3: 1 And if his oblation *be* a sacrifice of p H8002
3 of the sacrifice of the p offering an H8002
6 And if his offering for a sacrifice of p H8002
9 of the sacrifice of the p offering an H8002
4:10 of the sacrifice of p offerings: and the H8002
26 of the sacrifice of p offerings: and the H8002
31 off the sacrifice of p offerings; and the H8002
35 the sacrifice of the p offerings; and the H8002
6:12 burn thereon the fat of the p offerings. H8002
7:11 And this *is* the law of the sacrifice of p H8002
13 of thanksgiving of his p offerings. H8002
14 sprinkleth the blood of the p offerings. H8002
15 And the flesh of the sacrifice of his p H8002
18 the sacrifice of his p offerings be eaten H8002
20 flesh of the sacrifice of p offerings, that H8002
21 of the sacrifice of p offerings, which H8002
29 the sacrifice of his p offerings unto the H8002
29 LORD of the sacrifice of his p offerings. H8002
32 of the sacrifices of your p offerings. H8002
33 the blood of the p offerings, and the fat, H8002
34 sacrifices of their p offerings, and have H8002
37 and of the sacrifice of the p offerings; H8002
9: 4 Also a bullock and a ram for p H8002
18 *for* a sacrifice of p offerings, which *was* H8002
22 and the burnt offering, and p offerings. H8002
10: 3 I will be glorified. And Aaron held his p. H1826
14 of p offerings of the children of Israel. H8002
17: 5 them *for* p offerings unto the LORD. H8002
19: 5 And if ye offer a sacrifice of p offerings H8002
22:21 And whosoever offereth a sacrifice of p H8002
23:19 first year for a sacrifice of p offerings. H8002
26: 6 And I will give p in the land, and ye H7965
Nu 6:14 ram without blemish for p offerings, H8002
17 *for* a sacrifice of p offerings unto the H8002
18 *is* under the sacrifice of the p offerings. H8002
26 upon thee, and give thee p. H7965
7:17 And for a sacrifice of p offerings, two H8002
23 And for a sacrifice of p offerings, two H8002
29 And for a sacrifice of p offerings, two H8002
35 And for a sacrifice of p offerings, two H8002
41 And for a sacrifice of p offerings, two H8002
47 And for a sacrifice of p offerings, two H8002
53 And for a sacrifice of p offerings, two H8002
59 And for a sacrifice of p offerings, two H8002
65 And for a sacrifice of p offerings, two H8002
71 And for a sacrifice of p offerings, two H8002
77 And for a sacrifice of p offerings, two H8002
83 And for a sacrifice of p offerings, two H8002
88 for the sacrifice of the p offerings *were* H8002
10:10 sacrifices of your p offerings; that they H8002
15: 8 a vow, or p offerings unto the LORD: H8002
25:12 I give unto him my covenant of p: H7965
29:39 offerings, and for your p offerings. H8002
30: 4 shall hold his p at her: then all her H2790
7 *it*, and held his p at her in the day that H2790
11 *it*, and held his p at her, *and* disallowed H2790
14 hold his p at her from day to day; H2790
14 p at her in the day that he heard *them*. H2790
Dt 2:26 of Heshbon with words of p, saying, H7965
20:10 fight against it, then proclaim p unto it. H7965
11 thee answer of p, and open unto thee, H7965
12 And if it will make no p with thee, but H7999
23: 6 Thou shalt not seek their p nor their H7965
27: 7 And thou shalt offer p offerings, and H8002
29:19 I shall have p, though I walk in the H7965
Jos 8:31 the LORD, and sacrificed p offerings. H8002
9:15 And Joshua made p with them, and H7965
10: 1 p with Israel, and were among them; H7999
4 for it hath made p with Joshua and H7999
21 at Makkedah in p: none moved his H7965
11:19 There was not a city that made p with H7999
22:23 or if to offer p offerings thereon, let H8002
27 and with our p offerings; that your H8002
Jdg 4:17 for *there was* p between Jabin the king H7965
6:23 And the LORD said unto him, P *be* H7965
8: 9 again in p, I will break down this tower. H7965
11:31 when I return in p from the children of H7965
18: 6 And the priest said unto them, Go in p: H7965

P

Jdg 18:19 And they said unto him, Hold thy **p**, lay H2790
19:20 And the old man said, **P** *be* with thee; H7965
20:26 and **p** offerings before the LORD. H8002
21: 4 offered burnt offerings and **p** offerings. H8002
1Sa 1:17 Then Eli answered and said, Go in **p**: H7965
7:14 was **p** between Israel and the Amorites. H7965
10: 8 sacrifices of **p** offerings: seven days H8002
27 him no presents. But he held his **p**. H2790
11:15 sacrifices of **p** offerings before the H8002
13: 9 to me, and **p** offerings. And he offered H8002
20: 7 servant shall have **p**: but if he be very H7965
13 thou mayest go in **p**: and the LORD be H7965
21 thou: for *there is* **p** to thee, and no hurt; H7965
42 And Jonathan said to David, Go in **p**, H7965
25: 6 *in prosperity*, **P** *be* both to thee, and H7965
6 both to thee, and **p** *be* to thine house, H7965
6 house, and **p** *be* unto all that thou hast. H7965
35 unto her, Go up in **p** to thine house; H7965
29: 7 Wherefore now return, and go in **p**, that H7965
2Sa 3:21 sent Abner away; and he went in **p**. H7965
22 sent him away, and he was gone in **p**. H7965
23 sent him away, and he is gone in **p**. H7965
6:17 and **p** offerings before the LORD. H8002
18 offerings and **p** offerings, he blessed H8002
10:19 Israel, they made **p** with Israel, and H7999
13:20 but hold now thy **p**, my sister: he *is* thy H2790
15: 9 And the king said unto him, Go in **p**. So H7965
27 into the city in **p**, and your two sons H7965
17: 3 returned: *so* all the people shall be in **p**. H7965
19:24 until the day he came *again* in **p**. H7965
30 is come again in **p** unto his own house. H7965
24:25 offerings and **p** offerings. So the LORD H8002
1Ki 2: 5 blood of war in **p**, and put the blood of H7965
6 his hoar head go down to the grave in **p**. H7965
33 there be **p** for ever from the LORD. H7965
3:15 and offered **p** offerings, and made H8002
4:24 he had **p** on all sides round about him. H7965
5:12 and there was **p** between Hiram and H7965
8:63 And Solomon offered a sacrifice of **p** H8002
64 and the fat of the **p** offerings: because H8002
64 offerings, and the fat of the **p** offerings. H8002
9:25 offerings and **p** offerings upon the altar H8002
20:18 be come out for **p**, take them alive; or H7965
22:17 return every man to his house in **p**. H7965
27 water of affliction, until I come in **p**. H7965
28 return at all in **p**, the LORD hath not H7965
44 And Jehoshaphat made **p** with the king H7999
2Ki 2: 3 he said, Yea, I know *it;* hold ye your **p**. H2814
5 Yea, I know *it;* hold ye your **p**. H2814
5:19 And he said unto him, Go in **p**. So he H7965
7: 9 and we hold our **p**: if we tarry till the H2814
9:17 to meet them, and let him say, *Is it* **p**? H7965
18 saith the king, *Is it* **p**? And Jehu said, H7965
18 thou to do with **p**? turn thee behind me. H7965
19 Thus saith the king, *Is it* **p**? And Jehu H7965
19 thou to do with **p**? turn thee behind me. H7965
22 Jehu, that he said, *Is it* **p**, Jehu? And he H7965
22 he answered, What **p**, so long as the H7965
31 said, *Had* Zimri **p**, who slew his master? H7965
16:13 blood of his **p** offerings, upon the altar. H8002
18:36 But the people held their **p**, and H2790
20:19 not *good*, if **p** and truth be in my days? H7965
22:20 into thy grave in **p**; and thine eyes shall H7965
1Ch 12:18 thou son of Jesse: **p**, peace *be* unto thee, H7965
18 son of Jesse: peace, **p** *be* unto thee, and H7965
18 *be* unto thee, and **p** *be* to thine helpers; H7965
16: 1 sacrifices and **p** offerings before God. H8002
2 burnt offerings and the **p** offerings, he H8002
19:19 Israel, they made **p** with David, and H7999
21:26 offerings and **p** offerings, and called H8002
22: 9 **p** and quietness unto Israel in his days. H7965
2Ch 7: 7 and the fat of the **p** offerings, because H8002
15: 5 And in those times *there was* no **p** to H7965
18:16 *therefore* every man to his house in **p**. H7965
26 water of affliction, until I return in **p**. H7965
27 certainly return in **p**, *then* hath not the H7965
19: 1 returned to his house in **p** to Jerusalem. H7965
29:35 with the fat of the **p** offerings, and the H8002
30:22 days, offering **p** offerings, and making H8002
31: 2 burnt offerings and for **p** offerings, to H8002
33:16 and sacrificed thereon **p** offerings and H8002
34:28 to thy grave in **p**, neither shall thine H7965
Ezr 4:17 beyond the river, **P**, and at such a time. H8001
5: 7 thus; Unto Darius the king, all **p**. H8001
7:12 of heaven, perfect *p*, and at such a time.
9:12 nor seek their **p** or their wealth for H7965
Neh 5: 8 their **p**, and found nothing *to answer.* H2790
8:11 saying, Hold your **p**, for the day *is* holy; H2013
Est 4:14 For if thou altogether holdest thy **p** at H2790
Est 9:30 Ahasuerus, *with* words of **p** and truth, H7965
10: 3 people, and speaking **p** to all his seed. H7965
Job 5:23 of the field shall be at **p** with thee. H7999
24 *shall be* in **p**; and thou shalt visit H7965
11: 3 Should thy lies make men hold their **p**? H2790
13: 5 O that ye would altogether hold your **p**! H2790
13 Hold your **p**, let me alone, that I may H2790
22:21 at **p**: thereby good shall come unto thee. H7999
25: 2 him, he maketh **p** in his high places. H7965
29:10 The nobles held their **p**, and their H6963
33:31 unto me: hold thy **p**, and I will speak. H2790
33 If not, hearken unto me: hold thy **p**, and H2790
Ps 4: 8 I will both lay me down in **p**, and sleep: H7965
7: 4 him that was at **p** with me; (yea, I have H7999
28: 3 which speak **p** to their neighbours, H7965
29:11 the LORD will bless his people with **p**. H7965
34:14 Depart from evil, and do good; seek **p**, H7965
35:20 For they speak not **p**: but they devise H7965
37:11 themselves in the abundance of **p**. H7965
37 the upright: for the end of *that* man *is* **p**. H7965
39: 2 I was dumb with silence, I held my **p**, H2814
12 cry; hold not thy **p** at my tears: for I *am* H2790
55:18 He hath delivered my soul in **p** from H7965
20 such as be at **p** with him: he hath H7965
72: 3 The mountains shall bring **p** to the H7965
7 of **p** so long as the moon endureth. H7965
83: 1 hold not thy **p**, and be not still, O God. H2790
85: 8 for he will speak **p** unto his people, and H7965
10 and **p** have kissed *each other.* H7965
109: 1 Hold not thy **p**, O God of my praise; H2790
119:165 Great **p** have they which love thy law: H7965
120: 6 hath long dwelt with him that hateth **p**. H7965
7 I *am for* **p**: but when I speak, they *are* H7965
122: 6 Pray for the **p** of Jerusalem: they shall H7965
7 **P** be within thy walls, *and* prosperity H7965
8 sakes, I will now say, **P** *be* within thee. H7965
125: 5 of iniquity: *but* **p** *shall be* upon Israel. H7965
128: 6 children's children, *and* **p** upon Israel. H7965
147:14 He maketh **p** *in* thy borders, *and* filleth H7965
Prv 3: 2 For length of days, and long life, and **p**, H7965
17 of pleasantness, and all her paths *are* **p**. H7965
7:14 *I have* **p** offerings with me; this day H8002
11:12 a man of understanding holdeth his **p**. H2790
12:20 evil: but to the counsellors of **p** *is* joy. H7965
16: 7 even his enemies to be at **p** with him. H7999
17:28 Even a fool, when he holdeth his **p**, is H2790
Ecc 3: 8 to hate; a time of war, and a time of **p**. H7965
Isa 9: 6 The everlasting Father, The Prince of **P**. H7965
7 *his* government and **p** *there shall be* no H7965
26: 3 Thou wilt keep *him* in perfect **p**, *whose* H7965
12 LORD, thou wilt ordain **p** for us: for H7965
27: 5 *that* he may make **p** with me; *and* he H7965
5 with me; *and* he shall make **p** with me. H7965
32:17 shall be **p**; and the effect of H7965
33: 7 ambassadors of **p** shall weep bitterly. H7965
36:21 But they held their **p**, and answered H2790
38:17 Behold, for **p** I had great bitterness: but H7965
39: 8 there shall be **p** and truth in my days. H7965
42:14 I have long time holden my **p**; I have H2814
45: 7 darkness: I make **p**, and create evil: I H7965
48:18 then had thy **p** been as a river, and H7965
22 *There is* no **p**, saith the LORD, unto the H7965
52: 7 that publisheth **p**; that bringeth good H7965
53: 5 of our **p** *was* upon him; and H7965
54:10 covenant of my **p** be removed, saith the H7965
13 and great *shall be* the **p** of thy children. H7965
55:12 be led forth with **p**: the mountains and H7965
57: 2 He shall enter into **p**: they shall rest in H7965
11 **p** even of old, and thou fearest me not? H2814
19 I create the fruit of the lips; **P**, peace to H7965
19 I create the fruit of the lips; Peace, **p** to H7965
21 *There is* no **p**, saith my God, to the H7965
59: 8 The way of **p** they know not; and *there* H7965
8 goeth therein shall not know **p**. H7965
60:17 **p**, and thine exactors righteousness. H7965
62: 1 For Zion's sake will I not hold my **p**, H2814
6 never hold their **p** day nor night: ye H2814
64:12 thou hold thy **p**, and afflict us very sore? H2814
66:12 I will extend **p** to her like a river, and H7965
Jer 4:10 Ye shall have **p**; whereas the sword H7965
19 I cannot hold my **p**, because thou hast H2790
6:14 **P**, peace; when *there is* no peace. H7965
14 Peace, **p**; when *there is* no peace. H7965
14 Peace, peace; when *there is* no **p**. H7965
8:11 **P**, peace; when *there is* no peace. H7965
11 Peace, **p**; when *there is* no peace. H7965
11 Peace, peace; when *there is* no **p**. H7965
15 We looked for **p**, but no good *came; and* H7965
12: 5 and *if* in the land of **p**, *wherein* thou H7965
Jer 12:12 end of the land: no flesh shall have **p**. H7965
14:13 I will give you assured **p** in this place. H7965
19 for us? we looked for **p**, and *there is* no H7965
16: 5 taken away my **p** from this people, H7965
23:17 said, Ye shall have **p**; and they say unto H7965
28: 9 The prophet which prophesieth of **p**, H7965
29: 7 And seek the **p** of the city whither I H7965
7 for in the **p** thereof shall ye have peace. H7965
7 for in the peace thereof shall ye have **p**. H7965
11 thoughts of **p**, and not of evil, to give H7965
30: 5 voice of trembling, of fear, and not of **p**. H7965
33: 6 them the abundance of **p** and truth. H7965
34: 5 *But* thou shalt die in **p**: and with the H7965
43:12 and he shall go forth from thence in **p**. H7965
Lam 3:17 soul far off from **p**: I forgat prosperity. H7965
Ezk 7:25 shall seek **p**, and *there shall be* none. H7965
13:10 my people, saying, **P**; and *there was* no H7965
10 and *there was* no **p**; and one built up a H7965
16 see visions of **p** for her, and *there is* H7965
16 and *there is* no **p**, saith the Lord GOD. H7965
34:25 a covenant of **p**, and will cause the evil H7965
37:26 Moreover I will make a covenant of **p** H7965
43:27 altar, and your **p** offerings; and I will H8002
45:15 offering, and for **p** offerings, to make H8002
17 offering, and the **p** offerings, to make H8002
46: 2 offering and his **p** offerings, and he H8002
12 voluntary burnt offering or **p** offerings H8002
12 offering and his **p** offerings, as he did H8002
Dan 4: 1 all the earth; **P** be multiplied unto you. H8001
6:25 all the earth; **P** be multiplied unto you. H8001
8:25 his heart, and by **p** shall destroy many: H7962
10:19 beloved, fear not: **p** *be* unto thee, be H7965
Am 5:22 the **p** offerings of your fat beasts. H8002
Oba 7 the men that were at **p** with thee have H7965
Mic 3: 5 teeth, and cry, **P**; and he that putteth H7965
5: 5 And this *man* shall be the **p**, when the H7965
Nah 1:15 that publisheth **p**! O Judah, keep thy H7965
Zep 1: 7 Hold thy **p** at the presence of the Lord H2013
Hag 2: 9 will I give **p**, saith the LORD of hosts. H7965
Zec 6:13 of **p** shall be between them both. H7965
8:10 *was there any* **p** to him that went out H7965
16 judgment of truth and **p** in your gates: H7965
19 feasts; therefore love the truth and **p**. H7965
9:10 and he shall speak **p** unto the heathen: H7965
Mal 2: 5 My covenant was with him of life and **p**; H7965
6 he walked with me in **p** and equity, and H7965
Mt 10:13 And if the house be worthy, let your **p** *G1515*
13 be not worthy, let your **p** return to you. *G1515*
34 Think not that I am come to send **p** on *G1515*
34 I came not to send **p**, but a sword. *G1515*
20:31 should hold their **p**: but they cried the *G4623*
26:63 But Jesus held his **p**. And the high priest *G4623*
Mk 1:25 Hold thy **p**, and come out of him. *G5392*
3: 4 save life, or to kill? But they held their **p**. *G4623*
4:39 said unto the sea, **P**, be still. And the *G4623*
5:34 go in **p**, and be whole of thy plague. *G1515*
9:34 But they held their **p**: for by the way *G4623*
50 and have **p** one with another. *G1514*
10:48 he should hold his **p**: but he cried the *G4623*
14:61 But he held his **p**, and answered *G4623*
Lk 1:79 to guide our feet into the way of **p**. *G1515*
2:14 and on earth **p**, good will toward men. *G1515*
29 depart in **p**, according to thy word: *G1515*
4:35 saying, Hold thy **p**, and come out of *G5392*
7:50 Thy faith hath saved thee; go in **p**. *G1515*
8:48 thy faith hath made thee whole; go in **p**. *G1515*
10: 5 ye enter, first say, **P** *be* to this house. *G1515*
6 And if the son of **p** be there, your peace *G1515*
6 And if the son of peace be there, your **p** *G1515*
11:21 keepeth his palace, his goods are in **p**: *G1515*
12:51 Suppose ye that I am come to give **p** on *G1515*
14: 4 And they held their **p**. And he took *him*, *G2270*
32 and desireth conditions of **p**. *G1515*
18:39 he should hold his **p**: but he cried so *G4623*
19:38 **p** in heaven, and glory in the highest. *G1515*
40 should hold their **p**, the stones would *G4623*
42 **p**! but now they are hid from thine eyes. *G1515*
20:26 at his answer, and held their **p**. *G4601*
24:36 and saith unto them, **P** *be* unto you. *G1515*
Jn 14:27 **P** I leave with you, my peace I give unto *G1515*
27 Peace I leave with you, my **p** I give unto *G1515*
16:33 in me ye might have **p**. In the world ye *G1515*
20:19 and saith unto them, **P** *be* unto you. *G1515*
21 Then said Jesus to them again, **P** *be* *G1515*
26 in the midst, and said, **P** *be* unto you. *G1515*
Act 10:36 **p** by Jesus Christ: (he is Lord of all:) *G1515*
11:18 they held their **p**, and glorified God, *G2270*
12:17 the hand to hold their **p**, declared unto *G4601*
20 friend, desired **p**; because their country *G1515*

Act 15:13 And after they had held their **p**, James G4601
33 **p** from the brethren unto the apostles. G1515
16:36 go: now therefore depart, and go in **p**. G1515
18: 9 afraid, but speak, and hold not thy **p**: G4623
Ro 1: 7 Grace to you and **p** from God our G1515
2:10 But glory, honour, and **p**, to every man G1515
3:17 And the way of **p** have they not known: G1515
5: 1 by faith, we have **p** with God through G1515
8: 6 to be spiritually minded *is* life and **p**. G1515
10:15 **p**, and bring glad tidings of good things! G1515
14:17 and **p**, and joy in the Holy Ghost. G1515
19 things which make for **p**, and things G1515
15:13 with all joy and **p** in believing, that ye G1515
33 Now the God of **p** *be* with you all. G1515
16:20 And the God of **p** shall bruise Satan G1515
1Co 1: 3 Grace *be* unto you, and **p**, from God our G1515
7:15 such *cases*: but God hath called us to **p**. G1515
14:30 that sitteth by, let the first hold his **p**. G4601
33 but of **p**, as in all churches of the saints. G1515
16:11 him forth in **p**, that he may come unto G1515
2Co 1: 2 Grace *be* to you and **p** from God our G1515
13:11 one mind, live in **p**; and the God of love G1514
11 the God of love and **p** shall be with you. G1515
Gal 1: 3 Grace *be* to you and **p** from God the G1515
5:22 But the fruit of the Spirit is love, joy, **p**, G1515
6:16 to this rule, **p** *be* on them, and mercy, G1515
Eph 1: 2 Grace *be* to you, and **p**, from God our G1515
2:14 For he is our **p**, who hath made both G1515
15 of twain one new man, *so* making **p**; G1515
17 And came and preached **p** to you G1515
4: 3 the unity of the Spirit in the bond of **p**. G1515
6:15 with the preparation of the gospel of **p**; G1515
23 **P** *be* to the brethren, and love with G1515
Php 1: 2 Grace *be* unto you, and **p**, from God our G1515
4: 7 And the **p** of God, which passeth all G1515
9 do: and the God of **p** shall be with you. G1515
Col 1: 2 Grace *be* unto you, and **p**, from God our G1515
20 And, having made **p** through the blood G1517
3:15 And let the **p** of God rule in your G1515
1Th 1: 1 Grace *be* unto you, and **p**, from God our G1515
5: 3 For when they shall say, **P** and safety; G1515
13 sake. *And* be at **p** among yourselves. G1514
23 And the very God of **p** sanctify you G1515
2Th 1: 2 Grace unto you, and **p**, from God our G1515
3:16 Now the Lord of **p** himself give you G1515
16 himself give you **p** always by all means. G1515
1Ti 1: 2 Grace, mercy, *and* **p**, from God our G1515
2Ti 1: 2 son: Grace, mercy, *and* **p**, from God the G1515
2:22 faith, charity, **p**, with them that call G1515
Tit 1: 4 Grace, mercy, *and* **p**, from God the G1515
Phlm 3 Grace to you, and **p**, from God our G1515
Heb 7: 2 also King of Salem, which is, King of **p**; G1515
11:31 when she had received the spies with **p**. G1515
12:14 Follow **p** with all *men*, and holiness, G1515
13:20 Now the God of **p**, that brought again G1515
Jas 2:16 them, Depart in **p**, be *ye* warmed and G1515
3:18 is sown in **p** of them that make peace. G1515
18 is sown in peace of them that make **p**. G1515
1Pt 1: 2 Grace unto you, and **p**, be multiplied. G1515
3:11 do good; let him seek **p**, and ensue it. G1515
5:14 a kiss of charity. **P** *be* with you all that G1515
2Pt 1: 2 Grace and **p** be multiplied unto you G1515
3:14 him in **p**, without spot, and blameless. G1515
2Jn 3 Grace be with you, mercy, *and* **p**, from G1515
3Jn 14 speak face to face. **P** *be* to thee. *Our* G1515
Jude 2 Mercy unto you, and **p**, and love, be G1515
Rev 1: 4 *be* unto you, and **p**, from him which is, G1515
6: 4 thereon to take **p** from the earth, and G1515

PEACEABLE
Gen 34:21 These men *are* **p** with us; therefore let H8003
2Sa 20:19 I *am one of them that are* **p** *and* H7999
1Ch 4:40 and quiet, and **p**; for *they* of Ham had H7961
Isa 32:18 And my people shall dwell in a **p** H7965
Jer 25:37 And the **p** habitations are cut down H7965
1Ti 2: 2 and **p** life in all godliness and honesty. G2272
Heb 12:11 it yieldeth the **p** fruit of righteousness G1516
Jas 3:17 is first pure, then **p**, gentle, *and* easy to G1516

PEACEABLY
Gen 37: 4 him, and could not speak **p** unto him. H7965
Jdg 11:13 therefore restore those *lands* again **p**. H7965
21:13 rock Rimmon, and to call **p** unto them. H7965
1Sa 16: 4 at his coming, and said, Comest thou **p**? H7965
5 And he said, **P**: I am come to sacrifice H7965
1Ki 2:13 Comest thou **p**? And he said, Peaceably. H7965
13 Comest thou peaceably? And he said, **P**. H7965
1Ch 12:17 If ye be come **p** unto me to help me, H7965
Jer 9: 8 *one* speaketh **p** to his neighbour with H7965

Dan 11:21 **p**, and obtain the kingdom by flatteries. H7962
24 He shall enter **p** even upon the fattest H7962
Ro 12:18 as lieth in you, live **p** with all men. G1514

PEACEMAKERS
Mt 5: 9 Blessed *are* the **p**: for they shall be G1518

PEACE-OFFERING See PEACE and OFFERING.

PEACOCKS
1Ki 10:22 gold, and silver, ivory, and apes, and **p**. H8500
2Ch 9:21 gold, and silver, ivory, and apes, and **p**. H8500
Job 39:13 wings unto the **p**? or wings and feathers H5965

PEARL
Mt 13:46 Who, when he had found one **p** of great G3135
Rev 21:21 gate was of one **p**: and the street of the G3135

PEARLS
Job 28:18 of coral, or of **p**: for the price of wisdom H1378
Mt 7: 6 cast ye your **p** before swine, lest they G3135
13:45 a merchant man, seeking goodly **p**: G3135
1Ti 2: 9 hair, or gold, or **p**, or costly array; G3135
Rev 17: 4 stones and **p**, having a golden cup G3135
18:12 stones, and of **p**, and fine linen, and G3135
16 with gold, and precious stones, and **p**! G3135
21:21 And the twelve gates *were* twelve **p**; G3135

PECULIAR
Ex 19: 5 then ye shall be a **p** treasure unto me H5459
Dt 14: 2 thee to be a **p** people unto himself, H5459
26:18 this day to be his **p** people, as he hath H5459
Ps 135: 4 himself, *and* Israel for his **p** treasure. H5459
Ecc 2: 8 and gold, and the **p** treasure of kings H5459
Tit 2:14 a **p** people, zealous of good works. G4041
1Pt 2: 9 an holy nation, a **p** people; that ye G1519

PEDAHEL
Nu 34:28 of Naphtali, **P** the son of Ammihud. H6300

PEDAHZUR
Nu 1:10 of Manasseh; Gamaliel the son of **P**. H6301
2:20 *shall be* Gamaliel the son of **P**. H6301
7:54 **P**, prince of the children of Manasseh: H6301
59 the offering of Gamaliel the son of **P**. H6301
10:23 of Manasseh *was* Gamaliel the son of **P**. H6301

PEDAIAH
2Ki 23:36 Zebudah, the daughter of **P** of Rumah. H6305
1Ch 3:18 Malchiram also, and **P**, and Shenazar, H6305
19 And the sons of **P** *were*, Zerubbabel, H6305
27:20 tribe of Manasseh, Joel the son of **P**: H6305
Neh 3:25 prison. After him **P** the son of Parosh. H6305
8: 4 on his left hand, **P**, and Mishael, and H6305
11: 7 of Joed, the son of **P**, the son of Kolaiah, H6305
13:13 and of the Levites, **P**: and next to them H6305

PEDIGREES
Nu 1:18 declared their **p** after their families, H3205

PEELED
Isa 18: 2 scattered and **p**, to a people terrible H4178
7 scattered and **p**, and from a people H4178
Ezk 29:18 shoulder *was* **p**: yet had he no wages, H4803

PEEP
Isa 8:19 unto wizards that **p**, and that mutter: H6850

PEEPED
Isa 10:14 the wing, or opened the mouth, or **p**. H6850

PEKAH
2Ki 15:25 But **P** the son of Remaliah, a captain of H6492
27 king of Judah **P** the son of Remaliah H6492
29 In the days of **P** king of Israel came H6492
30 against **P** the son of Remaliah, H6492
31 And the rest of the acts of **P**, and all that H6492
32 In the second year of **P** the son of H6492
37 of Syria, and **P** the son of Remaliah. H6492
16: 1 In the seventeenth year of **P** the son of H6492
5 Then Rezin king of Syria and **P** son of H6492
2Ch 28: 6 For **P** the son of Remaliah slew in H6492
Isa 7: 1 the king of Syria, and **P** the son of H6492

PEKAHIAH
2Ki 15:22 and **P** his son reigned in his stead. H6494
23 king of Judah **P** the son of Menahem H6494
26 And the rest of the acts of **P**, and all that H6494

PEKOD
Jer 50:21 the inhabitants of **P**: waste and utterly H6489
Ezk 23:23 and all the Chaldeans, **P**, and Shoa, and H6489

PELAIAH
1Ch 3:24 and Eliashib, and **P**, and Akkub, and H6411
Neh 8: 7 Jozabad, Hanan, **P**, and the Levites, H6411
10:10 Shebaniah, Hodijah, Kelita, **P**, Hanan, H6411

PELALIAH
Neh 11:12 the son of **P**, the son of Amzi, the H6421

PELATIAH
1Ch 3:21 And the sons of Hananiah; **P**, and H6410
4:42 for their captains **P**, and Neariah, and H6410
Neh 10:22 **P**, Hanan, Anaiah, H6410
Ezk 11: 1 son of Azur, and **P** the son of Benaiah, H6410
13 I prophesied, that **P** the son of Benaiah H6410

PELEG
Gen 10:25 name of one *was* **P**; for in his days was H6389
11:16 lived four and thirty years, and begat **P**: H6389
17 And Eber lived after he begat **P** four H6389
18 And **P** lived thirty years, and begat H6389
19 And **P** lived after he begat Reu two H6389
1Ch 1:19 of the one *was* **P**; because in his days H6389
25 Eber, **P**, Reu, H6389

PELET
1Ch 2:47 and **P**, and Ephah, and Shaaph. H6404
12: 3 and Jeziel, and **P**, the sons of Azmaveth; H6404

PELETH
Nu 16: 1 the son of **P**, sons of Reuben, took *men*: H6431
1Ch 2:33 And the sons of Jonathan; **P**, and Zaza. H6431

PELETHITES
2Sa 8:18 **P**; and David's sons were chief rulers. H6432
15:18 and all the **P**, and all the Gittites, H6432
20: 7 and the **P**, and all the mighty men: H6432
23 *was* over the Cherethites and over the **P**: H6432
1Ki 1:38 and the **P**, went down, and caused H6432
44 and the **P**, and they have caused H6432
1Ch 18:17 and the **P**; and the sons of David H6432

PELICAN
Lev 11:18 And the swan, and the **p**, and the gier H6893
Dt 14:17 And the **p**, and the gier eagle, and the H6893
Ps 102: 6 I am like a **p** of the wilderness: I am H6893

P

PELONITE
1Ch 11:27 Shammoth the Harorite, Helez the **P**, H6397
36 Hepher the Mecherathite, Ahijah the **P**, H6397
27:10 *was* Helez the **P**, of the children of H6397

PEN
Jdg 5:14 they that handle the **p** of the writer. H7626
Job 19:24 That they were graven with an iron **p** H5842
Ps 45: 1 my tongue *is* the **p** of a ready writer. H5842
Isa 8: 1 **p** concerning Maher-shalal-hash-baz. H2747
Jer 8: 8 he *it*; the **p** of the scribes *is* in vain. H5842
17: 1 The sin of Judah *is* written with a **p** of H5842
3Jn 13 will not with ink and **p** write unto thee: G2563

PENCE
Mt 18:28 him an hundred **p**: and he laid hands G1220
Mk 14: 5 three hundred **p**, and have been given G1220
Lk 7:41 five hundred **p**, and the other fifty. G1220
10:35 he took out two **p**, and gave *them* to the G1220
Jn 12: 5 three hundred **p**, and given to the poor? G1220

PENIEL
Gen 32:30 name of the place **P**: for I have seen God H6439

PENINNAH
1Sa 1: 2 name of the other **P**: and Peninnah had H6444
2 Peninnah: and **P** had children, but H6444
4 offered, he gave to **P** his wife, and to all H6444

PENKNIFE
Jer 36:23 he cut it with the **p**, and cast *it* into the H8593

PENNY
Mt 20: 2 **p** a day, he sent them into his vineyard. G1220
9 hour, they received every man a **p**. G1220
10 they likewise received every man a **p**. G1220
13 didst not thou agree with me for a **p**? G1220
22:19 money. And they brought unto him a **p**. G1220
Mk 12:15 ye me? bring me a **p**, that I may see *it*. G1220

Lk 20:24 Shew me a **p**. Whose image and G1220
Rev 6: 6 of wheat for a **p**, and three measures G1220
6 of barley for a **p**; and *see* thou hurt not G1220

PENNYWORTH
Mk 6:37 **p** of bread, and give them to eat? G1220
Jn 6: 7 Philip answered him, Two hundred **p** G1220

PENTECOST
Act 2: 1 And when the day of **P** was fully come, G4005
20:16 for him, to be at Jerusalem the day of **P**. G4005
1Co 16: 8 But I will tarry at Ephesus until **P**. G4005

PENUEL
Gen 32:31 And as he passed over **P** the sun rose H6439
Jdg 8: 8 And he went up thence to **P**, and spake H6439
8 and the men of **P** answered him as the H6439
9 And he spake also unto the men of **P**, H6439
17 And he beat down the tower of **P**, and H6439
1Ki 12:25 and went out from thence, and built **P**. H6439
1Ch 4: 4 And **P** the father of Gedor, and Ezer the H6439
8:25 And Iphedeiah, and **P**, the sons of H6439

PENURY
Prv 14:23 but the talk of the lips *tendeth* only to **p**. H4270
Lk 21: 4 but she of her **p** hath cast in all the G5303

PEOPLE
Gen 11: 6 And the LORD said, Behold, the **p** *is* H5971
14:16 goods, and the women also, and the **p**. H5971
17:14 his **p**; he hath broken my covenant. H5971
16 of nations; kings of **p** shall be of her. H5971
19: 4 young, all the **p** from every quarter: H5971
23: 7 himself to the **p** of the land, *even* to H5971
11 of my **p** give I it thee: bury thy dead. H5971
12 down himself before the **p** of the land. H5971
13 audience of the **p** of the land, saying, H5971
25: 8 full *of years;* and was gathered to his **p**. H5971
17 and died; and was gathered unto his **p**. H5971
23 two manner of **p** shall be separated H3816
23 and *the one* **p** shall be stronger than H3816
23 **p**; and the elder shall serve the younger. H3816
26:10 us? one of the **p** might lightly have lien H5971
11 And Abimelech charged all *his* **p**, H5971
27:29 Let **p** serve thee, and nations bow H5971
28: 3 that thou mayest be a multitude of **p**; H5971
29: 1 came into the land of the **p** of the east. H1121
32: 7 he divided the **p** that *was* with him, H5971
34:16 with you, and we will become one **p**. H5971
22 dwell with us, to be one **p**, if every male H5971
35: 6 he and all the **p** that *were* with him. H5971
29 gathered unto his **p**, *being* old and full H5971
41:40 word shall all my **p** be ruled: only in the H5971
55 was famished, the **p** cried to Pharaoh H5971
42: 6 that sold to all the **p** of the land: and H5971
47:21 And as for the **p**, he removed them to H5971
23 Then Joseph said unto the **p**, Behold, I H5971
48: 4 a multitude of **p**; and will give this land H5971
19 shall become a **p**, and he also shall be H5971
49:10 him *shall* the gathering of the **p** *be*. H5971
16 Dan shall judge his **p**, as one of the H5971
29 gathered unto my **p**: bury me with my H5971
33 the ghost, and was gathered unto his **p**. H5971
50:20 as *it is* this day, to save much **p** alive. H5971
Ex 1: 9 And he said unto his **p**, Behold, the H5971
9 Behold, the **p** of the children of Israel H5971
20 **p** multiplied, and waxed very mighty. H5971
22 And Pharaoh charged all his **p**, saying, H5971
3: 7 affliction of my **p** which *are* in Egypt, H5971
10 **p** the children of Israel out of Egypt. H5971
12 brought forth the **p** out of Egypt, ye H5971
21 And I will give this **p** favour in the sight H5971
4:16 unto the **p**: and he shall be, *even* H5971
21 his heart, that he shall not let the **p** go. H5971
30 and did the signs in the sight of the **p**. H5971
31 And the **p** believed: and when they H5971
5: 1 of Israel, Let my **p** go, that they may H5971
4 and Aaron, let the **p** from their works? H5971
5 And Pharaoh said, Behold, the **p** of the H5971
6 of the **p**, and their officers, saying, H5971
7 Ye shall no more give the **p** straw to H5971
10 And the taskmasters of the **p** went out, H5971
10 they spake to the **p**, saying, Thus saith H5971
12 So the **p** were scattered abroad H5971
16 beaten; but the fault *is* in thine own **p**. H5971
22 this **p**? why *is* it *that* thou hast sent me? H5971
23 done evil to this **p**; neither hast thou H5971
23 neither hast thou delivered thy **p** at all. H5971
6: 7 And I will take you to me for a **p**, and I H5971

Ex 7: 4 armies, *and* my **p** the children of Israel, H5971
14 *is* hardened, he refuseth to let the **p** go. H5971
16 saying, Let my **p** go, that they may H5971
8: 1 Let my **p** go, that they may serve me. H5971
3 and upon thy **p**, and into thine ovens, H5971
4 upon thy **p**, and upon all thy servants. H5971
8 me, and from my **p**; and I will let the H5971
8 and I will let the **p** go, that they may do H5971
9 and for thy **p**, to destroy the frogs H5971
11 **p**; they shall remain in the river only. H5971
20 Let my **p** go, that they may serve me. H5971
21 Else, if thou wilt not let my **p** go, H5971
21 and upon thy **p**, and into thy houses: H5971
22 in which my **p** dwell, that no swarms H5971
23 And I will put a division between my **p** H5971
23 and thy **p**: to morrow shall this sign be. H5971
29 and from his **p**, to morrow: but let not H5971
29 the **p** go to sacrifice to the LORD. H5971
31 and from his **p**; there remained not one. H5971
32 time also, neither would he let the **p** go. H5971
9: 1 Let my **p** go, that they may serve me. H5971
7 hardened, and he did not let the **p** go. H5971
13 Let my **p** go, that they may serve me. H5971
14 and upon thy **p**; that thou mayest know H5971
15 smite thee and thy **p** with pestilence; H5971
17 my **p**, that thou wilt not let them go? H5971
27 righteous, and I and my **p** *are* wicked. H5971
10: 3 let my **p** go, that they may serve me. H5971
4 Else, if thou refuse to let my **p** go, H5971
11: 2 Speak now in the ears of the **p**, and let H5971
3 And the LORD gave the **p** favour in the H5971
3 servants, and in the sight of the **p**. H5971
8 out, and all the **p** that follow thee: and H5971
12:27 the **p** bowed the head and worshipped. H5971
31 from among my **p**, both ye and the H5971
33 urgent upon the **p**, that they might send H5971
34 And the **p** took their dough before it H5971
36 And the LORD gave the **p** favour in the H5971
13: 3 And Moses said unto the **p**, Remember H5971
17 had let the **p** go, that God led them H5971
17 peradventure the **p** repent when they H5971
18 But God led the **p** about, *through* the H5971
22 pillar of fire by night, *from* before the **p**. H5971
14: 5 of Egypt that the **p** fled: and the heart H5971
5 was turned against the **p**, and they said, H5971
6 his chariot, and took his **p** with him: H5971
13 And Moses said unto the **p**, Fear ye not, H5971
31 and the **p** feared the LORD, and H5971
15:13 Thou in thy mercy hast led forth the **p** H5971
14 The **p** shall hear, *and* be afraid: sorrow H5971
16 as a stone; till thy **p** pass over, O LORD, H5971
16 O LORD, till the **p** pass over, *which* H5971
24 And the **p** murmured against Moses, H5971
16: 4 for you; and the **p** shall go out and H5971
27 out *some* of the **p** on the seventh day H5971
30 So the **p** rested on the seventh day. H5971
17: 1 *there was* no water for the **p** to drink. H5971
2 Wherefore the **p** did chide with Moses, H5971
3 And the **p** thirsted there for water; and H5971
3 for water; and the **p** murmured against H5971
4 **p**? they be almost ready to stone me. H5971
5 Go on before the **p**, and take with thee H5971
6 out of it, that the **p** may drink. And H5971
13 and his **p** with the edge of the sword. H5971
18: 1 and for Israel his **p**, *and* that the LORD H5971
10 hath delivered the **p** from under the H5971
13 sat to judge the **p**: and the people stood H5971
13 people: and the **p** stood by Moses from H5971
14 all that he did to the **p**, he said, What *is* H5971
14 thou doest to the **p**? why sittest thou H5971
14 alone, and all the **p** stand by thee from H5971
15 the **p** come unto me to inquire of God: H5971
18 thou, and this **p** that *is* with thee: for H5971
19 Be thou for the **p** to God-ward, that H5971
21 out of all the **p** able men, such as fear H5971
22 And let them judge the **p** at all seasons: H5971
23 **p** shall also go to their place in peace. H5971
25 heads over the **p**, rulers of thousands, H5971
26 And they judged the **p** at all seasons: H5971
19: 5 me above all **p**: for all the earth *is* mine: H5971
7 the elders of the **p**, and laid before their H5971
8 And all the **p** answered together, and H5971
8 the words of the **p** unto the LORD. H5971
9 thick cloud, that the **p** may hear when I H5971
9 told the words of the **p** unto the LORD. H5971
10 Go unto the **p**, and sanctify them to H5971
11 the sight of all the **p** upon mount Sinai. H5971
12 And thou shalt set bounds unto the **p** H5971
14 mount unto the **p**, and sanctified the H5971

Ex 19:14 the **p**; and they washed their clothes. H5971
15 And he said unto the **p**, Be ready H5971
16 the **p** that *was* in the camp trembled. H5971
17 And Moses brought forth the **p** out of H5971
21 Go down, charge the **p**, lest they break H5971
23 And Moses said unto the LORD, The **p** H5971
24 the priests and the **p** break through to H5971
25 So Moses went down unto the **p**, and H5971
20:18 And all the **p** saw the thunderings, and H5971
18 and when the **p** saw *it*, they removed, H5971
20 And Moses said unto the **p**, Fear not: H5971
21 And the **p** stood afar off, and Moses H5971
22:25 If thou lend money to *any of* my **p** *that* H5971
28 the gods, nor curse the ruler of thy **p**. H5971
23:11 the poor of thy **p** may eat: and what H5971
27 and will destroy all the **p** to whom thou H5971
24: 2 neither shall the **p** go up with him. H5971
3 And Moses came and told the **p** all the H5971
3 and all the **p** answered with one H5971
7 the audience of the **p**: and they said, All H5971
8 sprinkled *it* on the **p**, and said, Behold H5971
30:33 shall even be cut off from his **p**. H5971
38 thereto, shall even be cut off from his **p**. H5971
31:14 soul shall be cut off from among his **p**. H5971
32: 1 And when the **p** saw that Moses H5971
1 out of the mount, the **p** gathered H5971
3 And all the **p** brake off the golden H5971
6 offerings; and the **p** sat down to eat H5971
7 get thee down; for thy **p**, which thou H5971
9 I have seen this **p**, and, behold, it *is* a H5971
9 and, behold, it *is* a stiffnecked **p**: H5971
11 wax hot against thy **p**, which thou hast H5971
12 and repent of this evil against thy **p**. H5971
14 evil which he thought to do unto his **p**. H5971
17 the noise of the **p** as they shouted, he H5971
21 What did this **p** unto thee, that thou H5971
22 the **p**, that they *are set* on mischief. H5971
25 And when Moses saw that the **p** *were* H5971
28 **p** that day about three thousand men. H5971
30 said unto the **p**, Ye have sinned a great H5971
31 and said, Oh, this **p** have sinned a great H5971
34 Therefore now go, lead the **p** unto *the* H5971
35 And the LORD plagued the **p**, because H5971
33: 1 hence, thou and the **p** which thou hast H5971
3 **p**: lest I consume thee in the way. H5971
4 And when the **p** heard these evil H5971
5 *are* a stiffnecked **p**: I will come up into H5971
8 *that* all the **p** rose up, and stood every H5971
10 And all the **p** saw the cloudy pillar H5971
10 door: and all the **p** rose up and H5971
12 me, Bring up this **p**: and thou hast not H5971
13 and consider that this nation *is* thy **p**. H5971
16 here that I and thy **p** have found grace H5971
16 I and thy **p**, from all the people H5971
16 **p** that *are* upon the face of the earth. H5971
34: 9 for it *is* a stiffnecked **p**; and pardon our H5971
10 before all thy **p** I will do marvels, such H5971
10 any nation: and all the **p** among which H5971
36: 5 saying, The **p** bring much more than H5971
6 So the **p** were restrained from bringing. H5971
Lev 4: 3 to the sin of the **p**; then let him bring for H5971
27 And if any one of the common **p** sin H5971
7:20 that soul shall be cut off from his **p**. H5971
21 even that soul shall be cut off from his **p**.
25 that eateth *it* shall be cut off from his **p**. H5971
27 that soul shall be cut off from his **p**. H5971
9: 7 and for the **p**: and offer the offering H5971
7 offer the offering of the **p**, and make an H5971
15 sin offering for the **p**, and slew it, and H5971
18 which *was* for the **p**: and Aaron's sons H5971
22 hand toward the **p**, and blessed them, H5971
23 and blessed the **p**: and the glory of the H5971
23 of the LORD appeared unto all the **p**. H5971
24 when all the **p** saw, they shouted, and H5971
10: 3 and before all the **p** I will be glorified. H5971
6 wrath come upon all the **p**: but let your H5712
16:15 that *is* for the **p**, and bring his blood H5971
24 burnt offering of the **p**, and make an H5971
24 an atonement for himself, and for the **p**. H5971
33 and for all the **p** of the congregation. H5971
17: 4 man shall be cut off from among his **p**: H5971
9 man shall be cut off from among his **p**. H5971
10 and will cut him off from among his **p**. H5971
18:29 shall be cut off from among their **p**. H5971
19: 8 soul shall be cut off from among his **p**. H5971
16 among thy **p**: neither shalt thou stand H5971
18 the children of thy **p**, but thou shalt love H5971
20: 2 be put to death: the **p** of the land shall H5971
3 off from among his **p**; because he hath H5971

Lev 20: 4 And if the **p** of the land do any ways H5971
5 with Molech, from among their **p**. H5971
6 and will cut him off from among his **p**. H5971
17 the sight of their **p**: he hath uncovered H5971
18 shall be cut off from among their **p**. H5971
24 which have separated you from *other* **p**. H5971
26 from *other* **p**, that ye should be mine. H5971
21: 1 be defiled for the dead among his **p**: H5971
4 man among his **p**, to profane himself. H5971
14 shall take a virgin of his own **p** to wife. H5971
15 his **p**: for I the LORD do sanctify him. H5971
23:29 he shall be cut off from among his **p**. H5971
30 soul will I destroy from among his **p**. H5971
26:12 will be your God, and ye shall be my **p**. H5971
Nu 5:21 oath among thy **p**, when the LORD doth H5971
27 woman shall be a curse among her **p**. H5971
9:13 from among his **p**: because he brought H5971
11: 1 And *when* the **p** complained, it H5971
2 And the **p** cried unto Moses; and when H5971
8 *And* the **p** went about, and gathered *it*, H5971
10 Then Moses heard the **p** weep H5971
11 layest the burden of all this **p** upon me? H5971
12 Have I conceived all this **p**? have I H5971
13 give unto all this **p**? for they weep unto H5971
14 I am not able to bear all this **p** alone, H5971
16 be the elders of the **p**, and officers over H5971
17 the burden of the **p** with thee, that thou H5971
18 And say thou unto the **p**, Sanctify H5971
21 And Moses said, The **p**, among whom I H5971
24 And Moses went out, and told the **p** the H5971
24 men of the elders of the **p**, and set them H5971
29 all the LORD'S **p** were prophets, *and* H5971
32 And the **p** stood up all that day, and all H5971
33 against the **p**, and the LORD smote H5971
33 smote the **p** with a very great plague. H5971
34 there they buried the **p** that lusted. H5971
35 *And* the **p** journeyed from H5971
12:15 seven days: and the **p** journeyed not till H5971
16 And afterward the **p** removed from H5971
13:18 And see the land, what it *is*; and the **p** H5971
28 Nevertheless the **p** *be* strong that dwell H5971
30 And Caleb stilled the **p** before Moses, H5971
31 the **p**; for they *are* stronger than we. H5971
32 and all the **p** that we saw in it *are* H5971
14: 1 and cried; and the **p** wept that night. H5971
9 neither fear ye the **p** of the land; for H5971
11 How long will this **p** provoke me? and H5971
13 this **p** in thy might from among them;) H5971
14 *art* among this **p**, that thou LORD art H5971
15 Now *if* thou shalt kill *all* this **p** as one H5971
16 able to bring this **p** into the land which H5971
19 the iniquity of this **p** according unto H5971
19 this **p**, from Egypt even until now. H5971
39 of Israel: and the **p** mourned greatly. H5971
15:26 seeing all the **p** *were* in ignorance. H5971
30 soul shall be cut off from among his **p**. H5971
16:41 Ye have killed the **p** of the LORD. H5971
47 was begun among the **p**: and he put on H5971
47 and made an atonement for the **p**. H5971
20: 1 month: and the **p** abode in Kadesh; H5971
3 And the **p** chode with Moses, and H5971
20 with much **p**, and with a strong hand. H5971
24 Aaron shall be gathered unto his **p**: for H5971
26 gathered *unto his* **p**, and shall die there.
21: 2 wilt indeed deliver this **p** into my hand, H5971
4 Edom: and the soul of the **p** was much H5971
5 And the **p** spake against God, and H5971
6 among the **p**, and they bit the people; H5971
6 the **p**; and much people of Israel died. H5971
6 the people; and much **p** of Israel died. H5971
7 Therefore the **p** came to Moses, and H5971
7 from us. And Moses prayed for the **p**. H5971
16 **p** together, and I will give them water. H5971
18 the nobles of the **p** digged it, by *the* H5971
23 gathered all his **p** together, and went H5971
29 art undone, O **p** of Chemosh: he hath H5971
33 he, and all his **p**, to the battle at Edrei. H5971
34 hand, and all his **p**, and his land; and H5971
35 sons, and all his **p**, until there was none H5971
22: 3 And Moab was sore afraid of the **p**, H5971
5 the children of his **p**, to call him, saying, H5971
5 Behold, there is a **p** come out from H5971
6 curse me this **p**; for they *are* too mighty H5971
11 Behold, *there is* a **p** come out of Egypt, H5971
12 not curse the **p**: for they *are* blessed. H5971
17 therefore, I pray thee, curse me this **p**. H5971
41 he might see the utmost *part* of the **p**. H5971
23: 9 him: lo, the **p** shall dwell alone, and H5971
24 Behold, the **p** shall rise up as a great H5971

Nu 24:14 And now, behold, I go unto my **p**: come H5971
14 thee what this **p** shall do to thy people H5971
14 shall do to thy **p** in the latter days. H5971
25: 1 And Israel abode in Shittim, and the **p** H5971
2 And they called the **p** unto the H5971
2 gods: and the **p** did eat, and bowed H5971
4 the heads of the **p**, and hang them up H5971
15 over a **p**, *and* of a chief house in Midian. H523
26: 4 *Take the sum of the* **p**, from twenty years
27:13 **p**, as Aaron thy brother was gathered. H5971
31: 2 shalt thou be gathered unto thy **p**. H5971
3 And Moses spake unto the **p**, saying, H5971
32:15 and ye shall destroy all this **p**. H5971
33:14 where was no water for the **p** to drink. H5971
Dt 1:28 our heart, saying, The **p** *is* greater and H5971
2: 4 And command thou the **p**, saying, Ye H5971
10 in times past, a **p** great, and many, and H5971
16 consumed and dead from among the **p**, H5971
21 A **p** great, and many, and tall, as the H5971
32 us, he and all his **p**, to fight at Jahaz. H5971
33 smote him, and his sons, and all his **p**. H5971
3: 1 us, he and all his **p**, to battle at Edrei. H5971
2 him, and all his **p**, and his land, into thy H5971
3 and all his **p**: and we smote him until H5971
28 go over before this **p**, and he shall cause H5971
4: 6 nation *is* a wise and understanding **p**. H5971
10 me, Gather me the **p** together, and I H5971
20 a **p** of inheritance, as *ye are* this day. H5971
33 Did *ever* **p** hear the voice of God H5971
5:28 of the words of this **p**, which they have H5971
6:14 of the **p** which *are* round about you; H5971
7: 6 For thou *art* an holy **p** unto the LORD H5971
6 to be a special **p** unto himself, above H5971
6 all **p** that *are* upon the face of the earth. H5971
7 **p**; for ye *were* the fewest of all people: H5971
7 people; for ye *were* the fewest of all **p**: H5971
14 Thou shalt be blessed above all **p**: there H5971
16 And thou shalt consume all the **p** H5971
19 unto all the **p** of whom thou art afraid. H5971
9: 2 A **p** great and tall, the children of the H5971
6 for thou *art* a stiffnecked **p**. H5971
12 from hence; for thy **p** which thou hast H5971
13 I have seen this **p**, and, behold, it *is* a H5971
13 and, behold, it *is* a stiffnecked **p**: H5971
26 GOD, destroy not thy **p** and thine H5971
27 of this **p**, nor to their wickedness, H5971
29 Yet they *are* thy **p** and thine H5971
10:11 journey before the **p**, that they may go H5971
15 *even* you above all **p**, as *it is* this day. H5971
13: 7 *Namely*, of the gods of the **p** which *are* H5971
9 and afterwards the hand of all the **p**. H5971
14: 2 For thou *art* an holy **p** unto the LORD H5971
2 to be a peculiar **p** unto himself, above H5971
21 thou *art* an holy **p** unto the LORD thy H5971
16:18 shall judge the **p** with just judgment. H5971
17: 7 hands of all the **p**. So thou shalt put the H5971
13 And all the **p** shall hear, and fear, and H5971
16 nor cause the **p** to return to Egypt, to H5971
18: 3 due from the **p**, from them that offer H5971
20: 1 chariots, *and* a **p** more than thou, be H5971
2 shall approach and speak unto the **p**, H5971
5 And the officers shall speak unto the **p**, H5971
8 further unto the **p**, and they shall say, H5971
9 of speaking unto the **p**, that they shall H5971
9 captains of the armies to lead the **p**. H5971
11 be, *that* all the **p** *that is* found therein H5971
16 But of the cities of these **p**, which the H5971
21: 8 Be merciful, O LORD, unto thy **p** Israel, H5971
8 blood unto thy **p** of Israel's charge. And H5971
26:15 and bless thy **p** Israel, and the land H5971
18 day to be his peculiar **p**, as he hath H5971
19 mayest be an holy **p** unto the LORD thy H5971
27: 1 commanded the **p**, saying, Keep all the H5971
9 art become the **p** of the LORD thy God. H5971
11 And Moses charged the **p** the same H5971
12 to bless the **p**, when ye are come over H5971
15 all the **p** shall answer and say, Amen. H5971
16 mother. And all the **p** shall say, Amen. H5971
17 And all the **p** shall say, Amen. H5971
18 the way. And all the **p** shall say, Amen. H5971
19 widow. And all the **p** shall say, Amen. H5971
20 skirt. And all the **p** shall say, Amen. H5971
21 of beast. And all the **p** shall say, Amen. H5971
22 mother. And all the **p** shall say, Amen. H5971
23 in law. And all the **p** shall say, Amen. H5971
24 secretly. And all the **p** shall say, Amen. H5971
25 person. And all the **p** shall say, Amen. H5971
26 do them. And all the **p** shall say, Amen. H5971
28: 9 thee an holy **p** unto himself, as he H5971

Dt 28:10 And all **p** of the earth shall see that H5971
32 unto another **p**, and thine eyes shall H5971
64 thee among all **p**, from the one end of H5971
29:13 thee to day for a **p** unto himself, and H5971
31: 7 thou must go with this **p** unto the land H5971
12 Gather the **p** together, men, and H5971
16 fathers; and this **p** will rise up, and go H5971
32: 6 LORD, O foolish **p** and unwise? *is* not H5971
8 set the bounds of the **p** according to the H5971
9 For the LORD'S portion *is* his **p**; Jacob *is* H5971
21 *which are* not a **p**; I will provoke them H5971
36 For the LORD shall judge his **p**, and H5971
43 Rejoice, O ye nations, *with* his **p**: for he H5971
43 be merciful unto his land, *and* to his **p**. H5971
44 of the **p**, he, and Hoshea the son of Nun. H5971
50 be gathered unto thy **p**; as Aaron thy H5971
50 Hor, and was gathered unto his **p**: H5971
33: 3 Yea, he loved the **p**; all his saints *are* in H5971
5 the heads of the **p** *and* the tribes of H5971
7 bring him unto his **p**: let his hands be H5971
17 he shall push the **p** together to the ends H5971
19 They shall call the **p** unto the H5971
21 with the heads of the **p**, he executed the H5971
29 who *is* like unto thee, O **p** saved by the H5971
Jos 1: 2 thou, and all this **p**, unto the land which H5971
6 for unto this **p** shalt thou divide for H5971
10 the officers of the **p**, saying, H5971
11 and command the **p**, saying, Prepare H5971
3: 3 And they commanded the **p**, saying, H5971
5 And Joshua said unto the **p**, Sanctify H5971
6 over before the **p**. And they took up the H5971
6 of the covenant, and went before the **p**. H5971
14 And it came to pass, when the **p** H5971
14 the ark of the covenant before the **p**; H5971
16 the **p** passed over right against Jericho. H5971
17 the **p** were passed clean over Jordan. H1471
4: 1 And it came to pass, when all the **p** H1471
2 Take you twelve men out of the **p**, out of H5971
10 to speak unto the **p**, according to all H5971
10 and the **p** hasted and passed over. H5971
11 And it came to pass, when all the **p** H5971
11 and the priests, in the presence of the **p**. H5971
19 And the **p** came up out of Jordan on the H5971
24 That all the **p** of the earth might know H5971
5: 4 circumcise: All the **p** that came out of H5971
5 Now all the **p** that came out were H5971
5 but all the **p** *that were* born in the H5971
6 till all the **p** *that were* men of war, H1471
8 all the **p**, that they abode in their H1471
6: 5 the trumpet, all the **p** shall shout with a H5971
5 down flat, and the **p** shall ascend up H5971
7 And he said unto the **p**, Pass on, and H5971
8 had spoken unto the **p**, that the seven H5971
10 And Joshua had commanded the **p**, H5971
16 said unto the **p**, Shout; for the LORD H5971
20 So the **p** shouted when *the priests* blew H5971
20 to pass, when the **p** heard the sound of H5971
20 the trumpet, and the **p** shouted with a H5971
20 flat, so that the **p** went up into the city, H5971
7: 3 Let not all the **p** go up; but let about H5971
3 make not all the **p** to labour thither; for H5971
4 So there went up thither of the **p** about H5971
5 of the **p** melted, and became as water. H5971
7 at all brought this **p** over Jordan, to H5971
13 Up, sanctify the **p**, and say, Sanctify H5971
8: 1 take all the **p** of war with thee, and H5971
1 Ai, and his **p**, and his city, and his land: H5971
3 So Joshua arose, and all the **p** of war, to H5971
5 And I, and all the **p** that *are* with me, H5971
9 Joshua lodged that night among the **p**. H5971
10 and numbered the **p**, and went up, he H5971
10 the elders of Israel, before the **p** to Ai. H5971
11 And all the **p**, *even the people* of war H5971
11 And all the people, *even the* **p** of war
13 And when they had set the **p**, *even* all H5971
14 he and all his **p**, at a time appointed, H5971
16 And all the **p** that *were* in Ai were H5971
20 or that way: and the **p** that fled to the H5971
33 that they should bless the **p** of Israel. H5971
10: 7 he, and all the **p** of war with him, and H5971
13 moon stayed, until the **p** had avenged H1471
21 And all the **p** returned to the camp to H5971
33 **p**, until he had left him none remaining. H5971
11: 4 with them, much **p**, even as the sand H5971
7 So Joshua came, and all the **p** of war H5971
14: 8 the heart of the **p** melt: but I wholly H5971
17:14 I *am* a great **p**, forasmuch as the LORD H5971
15 If thou *be* a great **p**, *then* get thee up to H5971
17 Thou *art* a great **p**, and hast great H5971

Jos 24: 2 And Joshua said unto all the **p**, Thus H5971
16 And the **p** answered and said, God H5971
17 all the **p** through whom we passed: H5971
18 before us all the **p**, even the Amorites H5971
19 And Joshua said unto the **p**, Ye cannot H5971
21 And the **p** said unto Joshua, Nay; but H5971
22 And Joshua said unto the **p**, Ye *are* H5971
24 And the **p** said unto Joshua, The LORD H5971
25 So Joshua made a covenant with the **p** H5971
27 And Joshua said unto all the **p**, Behold, H5971
28 So Joshua let the **p** depart, every man H5971
Jdg 1:16 and they went and dwelt among the **p**. H5971
2: 4 the **p** lifted up their voice, and wept. H5971
6 And when Joshua had let the **p** go, the H5971
7 And the **p** served the LORD all the days H5971
12 of the gods of the **p** that *were* round H5971
20 Because that this **p** hath transgressed H1471
3:18 sent away the **p** that bare the present. H5971
4:13 of iron, and all the **p** that *were* with H5971
5: 2 the **p** willingly offered themselves. H5971
9 among the **p**. Bless ye the LORD. H5971
11 the **p** of the LORD go down to the gates. H5971
13 nobles among the **p**: the LORD made H5971
14 among thy **p**; out of Machir came H5971
18 Zebulun and Naphtali *were* a **p** *that* H5971
7: 1 and all the **p** that *were* with him, H5971
2 And the LORD said unto Gideon, The **p** H5971
3 in the ears of the **p**, saying, Whosoever H5971
3 there returned of the **p** twenty and two H5971
4 And the LORD said unto Gideon, The **p** H5971
5 So he brought down the **p** unto the H5971
6 all the rest of the **p** bowed down upon H5971
7 *other* **p** go every man unto his place. H5971
8 So the **p** took victuals in their hand, H5971
8: 5 of bread unto the **p** that follow me; for H5971
9:29 And would to God this **p** were under H5971
32 thou and the **p** that *is* with thee, and H5971
33 *when* he and the **p** that *is* with him H5971
34 And Abimelech rose up, and all the **p** H5971
35 rose up, and the **p** that *were* with him, H5971
36 And when Gaal saw the **p**, he said to H5971
36 there come **p** down from the top H5971
37 See there come **p** down by the middle H5971
38 him? *is* not this the **p** that thou hast H5971
42 morrow, that the **p** went out into the H5971
43 And he took the **p**, and divided them H5971
43 and, behold, the **p** *were* come forth out H5971
44 **p** that *were* in the fields, and slew them.
45 city, and slew the **p** that *was* therein, H5971
48 he and all the **p** that *were* with him; H5971
48 and said unto the **p** that *were* with him, H5971
49 And all the **p** likewise cut down every H5971
10:18 And the **p** *and* princes of Gilead said H5971
11:11 of Gilead, and the **p** made him head H5971
20 gathered all his **p** together, and pitched H5971
21 Sihon and all his **p** into the hand of H5971
23 **p** Israel, and shouldest thou possess it? H5971
12: 2 them, I and my **p** were at great strife H5971
14: 3 or among all my **p**, that thou goest to H5971
16 the children of my **p**, and hast not told H5971
17 told the riddle to the children of her **p**. H5971
16:24 And when the **p** saw him, they praised H5971
30 and upon all the **p** that *were* therein. So H5971
18: 7 and saw the **p** that *were* therein, how H5971
10 When ye go, ye shall come unto a **p** H5971
20 image, and went in the midst of the **p**. H5971
27 unto Laish, unto a **p** *that were* at quiet H5971
20: 2 And the chief of all the **p**, *even* of all the H5971
2 assembly of the **p** of God, four hundred H5971
8 And all the **p** arose as one man, saying, H5971
10 fetch victual for the **p**, that they may do, H5971
16 Among all this **p** *there were* seven H5971
22 And the **p** the men of Israel encouraged H5971
26 Israel, and all the **p**, went up, and came H5971
31 out against the **p**, *and* were drawn away H5971
31 to smite of the **p**, *and* kill, as at other H5971
21: 2 And the **p** came to the house of God, H5971
4 morrow, that the **p** rose early, and built H5971
9 For the **p** were numbered, and, behold, H5971
15 And the **p** repented them for Benjamin, H5971
Ru 1: 6 had visited his **p** in giving them bread. H5971
10 we will return with thee unto thy **p**. H5971
15 back unto her **p**, and unto her gods: H5971
16 I will lodge: thy **p** *shall be* my people, H5971
16 *shall be* my **p**, and thy God my God: H5971
2:11 a **p** which thou knewest not heretofore. H5971
3:11 all the city of my **p** doth know that thou H5971
4: 4 the elders of my **p**. If thou wilt redeem H5971
9 and *unto* all the **p**, Ye *are* witnesses this H5971

Ru 4:11 And all the **p** that *were* in the gate, and H5971
1Sa 2:13 And the priests' custom with the **p** *was*, H5971
23 I hear of your evil dealings by all this **p**. H5971
24 ye make the LORD'S **p** to transgress. H5971
29 of all the offerings of Israel my **p**? H5971
4: 3 And when the **p** were come into the H5971
4 So the **p** sent to Shiloh, that they might H5971
17 among the **p**, and thy two sons also, H5971
5:10 God of Israel to us, to slay us and our **p**. H5971
11 slay us not, and our **p**: for there was a H5971
6: 6 they not let the **p** go, and they departed?
19 he smote of the **p** fifty thousand and H5971
19 ten men: and the **p** lamented, because H5971
19 *many* of the **p** with a great slaughter. H5971
8: 7 the voice of the **p** in all that they say H5971
10 unto the **p** that asked of him a king. H5971
19 Nevertheless the **p** refused to obey the H5971
21 all the words of the **p**, and he rehearsed H5971
9: 2 *he was* higher than any of the **p**. H5971
12 of the **p** to day in the high place: H5971
13 to eat: for the **p** will not eat until he H5971
16 captain over my **p** Israel, that he may H5971
16 he may save my **p** out of the hand of H5971
16 **p**, because their cry is come unto me. H5971
17 thee of! this same shall reign over my **p**. H5971
24 **p**. So Saul did eat with Samuel that day. H5971
10:11 the prophets, then the **p** said one to H5971
17 And Samuel called the **p** together unto H5971
23 stood among the **p**, he was higher than H5971
23 the **p** from his shoulders and upward. H5971
24 And Samuel said to all the **p**, See ye him H5971
24 him among all the **p**? And all the people H5971
24 **p** shouted, and said, God save the king. H5971
25 Then Samuel told the **p** the manner of H5971
25 all the **p** away, every man to his house. H5971
11: 4 in the ears of the **p**: and all the people H5971
4 the **p** lifted up their voices, and wept. H5971
5 What *aileth* the **p** that they weep? And H5971
7 **p**, and they came out with one consent. H5971
11 that Saul put the **p** in three companies; H5971
12 And the **p** said unto Samuel, Who *is* he H5971
14 Then said Samuel to the **p**, Come, and H5971
15 And all the **p** went to Gilgal; and there H5971
12: 6 And Samuel said unto the **p**, *It is* the H5971
18 **p** greatly feared the LORD and Samuel. H5971
19 And all the **p** said unto Samuel, Pray H5971
20 And Samuel said unto the **p**, Fear not: H5971
22 For the LORD will not forsake his **p** for H5971
22 pleased the LORD to make you his **p**. H5971
13: 2 of the **p** he sent every man to his tent. H5971
4 And the **p** were called together H5971
5 horsemen, and **p** as the sand which *is* H5971
6 in a strait, (for the **p** were distressed,) H5971
6 then the **p** did hide themselves H5971
7 and all the **p** followed him trembling. H5971
8 and the **p** were scattered from him. H5971
11 I saw that the **p** were scattered from H5971
14 *be* captain over his **p**, because thou hast H5971
15 numbered the **p** *that were* present with H5971
16 his son, and the **p** *that were* present H5971
22 the hand of any of the **p** that *were* with H5971
14: 2 Migron: and the **p** that *were* with him H5971
3 **p** knew not that Jonathan was gone. H5971
15 and among all the **p**: the garrison, and H5971
17 Then said Saul unto the **p** that *were* H5971
20 And Saul and all the **p** that *were* with H5971
24 had adjured the **p**, saying, Cursed *be* H5971
24 So none of the **p** tasted *any* food. H5971
26 And when the **p** were come into the H5971
26 to his mouth: for the **p** feared the oath. H5971
27 his father charged the **p** with the oath: H5971
28 Then answered one of the **p**, and said, H5971
28 charged the **p** with an oath, saying, H5971
28 *any* food this day. And the **p** were faint. H5971
30 How much more, if haply the **p** had H5971
31 to Aijalon: and the **p** were very faint. H5971
32 And the **p** flew upon the spoil, and took H5971
32 and the **p** did eat *them* with the blood. H5971
33 Behold, the **p** sin against the LORD, H5971
34 among the **p**, and say unto them, H5971
34 blood. And all the **p** brought every man H5971
38 all the chief of the **p**: and know and see H5971
39 among all the **p** *that* answered him. H5971
40 side. And the **p** said unto Saul, Do what H5971
41 were taken: but the **p** escaped. H5971
45 And the **p** said unto Saul, Shall H5971
45 **p** rescued Jonathan, that he died not. H5971
15: 1 *to be* king over his **p**, over Israel: now H5971
4 And Saul gathered the **p** together, and H5971

1Sa 15: 8 all the **p** with the edge of the sword. H5971
9 But Saul and the **p** spared Agag, and H5971
15 for the **p** spared the best of the H5971
21 But the **p** took of the spoil, sheep and H5971
24 I feared the **p**, and obeyed their voice. H5971
30 the elders of my **p**, and before Israel, H5971
17:27 And the **p** answered him after this H5971
30 manner: and the **p** answered him again H5971
18: 5 in the sight of all the **p**, and also in the H5971
13 he went out and came in before the **p**. H5971
23: 8 And Saul called all the **p** together to H5971
26: 5 and the **p** pitched round about him. H5971
7 So David and Abishai came to the **p** by H5971
7 Abner and the **p** lay round about him. H5971
14 And David cried to the **p**, and to Abner H5971
15 of the **p** in to destroy the king thy lord. H5971
27:12 He hath made his **p** Israel utterly to H5971
30: 4 Then David and the **p** that *were* with H5971
6 distressed; for the **p** spake of stoning H5971
6 the soul of all the **p** was grieved, every H5971
21 and to meet the **p** that *were* with him: H5971
21 came near to the **p**, he saluted them. H5971
31: 9 house of their idols, and among the **p**. H5971
2Sa 1: 4 That the **p** are fled from the battle, H5971
4 and many of the **p** also are fallen and H5971
12 son, and for the **p** of the LORD, and for H5971
2:26 **p** return from following their brethren? H5971
27 in the morning the **p** had gone up every H5971
28 So Joab blew a trumpet, and all the **p** H5971
30 had gathered all the **p** together, there H5971
3:18 I will save my **p** Israel out of the hand H5971
31 And David said to Joab, and to all the **p** H5971
32 the grave of Abner; and all the **p** wept. H5971
34 And all the **p** wept again over him. H5971
35 And when all the **p** came to cause H5971
36 And all the **p** took notice *of it*, and it H5971
36 the king did pleased all the **p**. H5971
37 For all the **p** and all Israel understood H5971
5: 2 shalt feed my **p** Israel, and thou shalt H5971
12 his kingdom for his **p** Israel's sake. H5971
6: 2 went with all the **p** that *were* with him H5971
18 the **p** in the name of the LORD of hosts. H5971
19 And he dealt among all the **p**, *even* H5971
19 the **p** departed every one to his house. H5971
21 me ruler over the **p** of the LORD, over H5971
7: 7 to feed my **p** Israel, saying, Why H5971
8 sheep, to be ruler over my **p**, over Israel: H5971
10 a place for my **p** Israel, and will plant H5971
11 *to be* over my **p** Israel, and have caused H5971
23 the earth *is* like thy **p**, *even* like Israel, H5971
23 to redeem for a **p** to himself, and to H5971
23 thy land, before thy **p**, which thou H5971
24 to thyself thy **p** Israel *to be* a people H5971
24 Israel *to be* a **p** unto thee for ever: and H5971
8:15 judgment and justice unto all his **p**. H5971
10:10 And the rest of the **p** he delivered into H5971
12 the men for our **p**, and for the cities of H5971
13 And Joab drew nigh, and the **p** that H5971
11: 7 the **p** did, and how the war prospered. H5971
17 fell *some* of the **p** of the servants of H5971
12:28 Now therefore gather the rest of the **p** H5971
29 And David gathered all the **p** together, H5971
31 And he brought forth the **p** that *were* H5971
31 and all the **p** returned unto Jerusalem. H5971
13:34 there came much **p** by the way of the H5971
14:13 thing against the **p** of God? for the king H5971
15 king, *it is* because the **p** have made me H5971
15:12 **p** increased continually with Absalom. H5971
17 And the king went forth, and all the **p** H5971
23 voice, and all the **p** passed over: the H5971
23 and all the **p** passed over, toward H5971
24 the **p** had done passing out of the city. H5971
30 and all the **p** that *was* with him covered H5971
16: 6 David: and all the **p** and all the mighty H5971
14 And the king, and all the **p** that *were* H5971
15 And Absalom, and all the **p** the men of H5971
18 LORD, and this **p**, and all the men of H5971
17: 2 afraid: and all the **p** that *are* with him H5971
3 And I will bring back all the **p** unto H5971
3 returned: *so* all the **p** shall be in peace. H5971
8 of war, and will not lodge with the **p**. H5971
9 among the **p** that follow Absalom. H5971
16 up, and all the **p** that *are* with him. H5971
22 Then David arose, and all the **p** that H5971
29 for David, and for the **p** that *were* with H5971
29 eat: for they said, The **p** *is* hungry, and H5971
18: 1 And David numbered the **p** that *were* H5971
2 a third part of the **p** under the hand of H5971
2 the king said unto the **p**, I will surely go H5971

2Sa 18: 3 But the **p** answered, Thou shalt not go H5971
4 gate side, and all the **p** came out by H5971
5 And all the **p** heard when the king H5971
6 So the **p** went out into the field against H5971
7 Where the **p** of Israel were slain before H5971
8 **p** that day than the sword devoured. H5971
16 And Joab blew the trumpet, and the **p** H5971
16 after Israel: for Joab held back the **p**. H5971
19: 2 unto all the **p**: for the people heard H5971
2 the people: for the **p** heard say that day H5971
3 And the **p** gat them by stealth that day H5971
3 into the city, as **p** being ashamed steal H5971
8 told unto all the **p**, saying, Behold, the H5971
8 the gate. And all the **p** came before the H5971
9 And all the **p** were at strife throughout H5971
39 And all the **p** went over Jordan. And H5971
40 him: and all the **p** of Judah conducted H5971
40 the king, and also half the **p** of Israel. H5971
20:12 man saw that all the **p** stood still, he H5971
13 highway, all the **p** went on after Joab, to H376
15 the trench: and all the **p** that *were* with H5971
22 Then the woman went unto all the **p** in H5971
22:28 And the afflicted **p** thou wilt save: but H5971
44 strivings of my **p**, thou hast kept me *to* H5971
44 a **p** *which* I knew not shall serve me. H5971
48 that bringeth down the **p** under me, H5971
23:10 the **p** returned after him only to spoil. H5971
11 and the **p** fled from the Philistines. H5971
24: 2 number ye the **p**, that I may know the H5971
2 that I may know the number of the **p**. H5971
3 God add unto the **p**, how many soever H5971
4 of the king, to number the **p** of Israel. H5971
9 the number of the **p** unto the king: and H5971
10 he had numbered the **p**. And David said H5971
15 there died of the **p** from Dan even to H5971
16 that destroyed the **p**, It is enough: stay H5971
17 that smote the **p**, and said, Lo, I have H5971
21 the plague may be stayed from the **p**. H5971
1Ki 1:39 all the **p** said, God save king Solomon. H5971
40 And all the **p** came up after him, and H5971
40 after him, and the **p** piped with pipes, H5971
3: 2 Only the **p** sacrificed in high places, H5971
8 And thy servant *is* in the midst of thy **p** H5971
8 hast chosen, a great **p**, that cannot be H5971
9 heart to judge thy **p**, that I may H5971
9 is able to judge this thy so great a **p**? H5971
4:34 And there came of all **p** to hear the H5971
5: 7 unto David a wise son over this great **p**. H5971
16 over the **p** that wrought in the work. H5971
6:13 Israel, and will not forsake my **p** Israel. H5971
8:16 Since the day that I brought forth my **p** H5971
16 I chose David to be over my **p** Israel. H5971
30 and of thy **p** Israel, when they shall H5971
33 When thy **p** Israel be smitten down H5971
34 the sin of thy **p** Israel, and bring them H5971
36 and of thy **p** Israel, that thou teach H5971
36 hast given to thy **p** for an inheritance. H5971
38 man, *or* by all thy **p** Israel, which shall H5971
41 that *is* not of thy **p** Israel, but cometh H5971
43 to thee for: that all **p** of the earth may H5971
43 thee, as *do* thy **p** Israel; and that they H5971
44 If thy **p** go out to battle against their H5971
50 And forgive thy **p** that have sinned H5971
51 For they *be* thy **p**, and thine H5971
52 of thy **p** Israel, to hearken unto H5971
53 among all the **p** of the earth, *to be* thine H5971
56 given rest unto his **p** Israel, according H5971
59 the cause of his **p** Israel at all times, as H5971
60 That all the **p** of the earth may know H5971
66 On the eighth day he sent the **p** away: H5971
66 David his servant, and for Israel his **p**. H5971
9: 7 be a proverb and a byword among all **p**: H5971
20 *And* all the **p** *that were* left of the H5971
23 over the **p** that wrought in the work. H5971
12: 5 come again to me. And the **p** departed. H5971
6 do ye advise that I may answer this **p**? H5971
7 a servant unto this **p** this day, and wilt H5971
9 may answer this **p**, who have spoken to H5971
10 speak unto this **p** that spake unto thee, H5971
12 So Jeroboam and all the **p** came to H5971
13 And the king answered the **p** roughly, H5971
15 not unto the **p**; for the cause was from H5971
16 unto them, the **p** answered the king, H5971
23 and to the remnant of the **p**, saying, H5971
27 If this **p** go up to do sacrifice in the H5971
27 the heart of this **p** turn again unto their H5971
30 And this thing became a sin: for the **p** H5971
31 **p**, which were not of the sons of Levi. H5971
13:33 of the lowest of the **p** priests of the high H5971

1Ki 14: 2 me that *I should be* king over this **p**. H5971
7 thee from among the **p**, and made thee H5971
7 and made thee prince over my **p** Israel, H5971
16: 2 prince over my **p** Israel; and thou hast H5971
2 and hast made my **p** Israel to sin, to H5971
15 in Tirzah. And the **p** *were* encamped H5971
16 And the **p** *that were* encamped heard H5971
21 Then were the **p** of Israel divided into H5971
21 parts: half of the **p** followed Tibni the H5971
22 But the **p** that followed Omri prevailed H5971
22 against the **p** that followed Tibni H5971
18:21 And Elijah came unto all the **p**, and H5971
21 And the **p** answered him not a word. H5971
22 Then said Elijah unto the **p**, I, *even* I H5971
24 **p** answered and said, It is well spoken. H5971
30 And Elijah said unto all the **p**, Come H5971
30 me. And all the **p** came near unto him. H5971
37 Hear me, O LORD, hear me, that this **p** H5971
39 And when all the **p** saw *it*, they fell on H5971
19:21 and gave unto the **p**, and they did eat. H5971
20: 8 And all the elders and all the **p** said H5971
10 handfuls for all the **p** that follow me. H5971
15 he numbered all the **p**, *even* all the H5971
42 go for his life, and thy **p** for his people. H5971
42 go for his life, and thy people for his **p**. H5971
21: 9 and set Naboth on high among the **p**: H5971
12 and set Naboth on high among the **p**. H5971
13 presence of the **p**, saying, Naboth did H5971
22: 4 *am* as thou *art*, my **p** as thy people, my H5971
4 as thy **p**, my horses as thy horses. H5971
28 he said, Hearken, O **p**, every one of you. H5971
43 taken away; *for* the **p** offered and burnt H5971
2Ki 3: 7 as thou *art*, my **p** as thy people, *and* my H5971
7 as thy **p**, *and* my horses as thy horses. H5971
4:13 answered, I dwell among mine own **p**. H5971
41 Pour out for the **p**, that they may eat. H5971
42 said, Give unto the **p**, that they may eat. H5971
43 again, Give the **p**, that they may eat: for H5971
6:18 and said, Smite this **p**, I pray thee, with H1471
30 the wall, and the **p** looked, and, behold, H5971
7:16 And the **p** went out, and spoiled the H5971
17 the gate: and the **p** trode upon him in H5971
20 And so it fell out unto him: for the **p** H5971
8:21 chariots: and the **p** fled into their tents. H5971
9: 6 the **p** of the LORD, *even* over Israel. H5971
10: 9 and said to all the **p**, Ye *be* righteous: H5971
18 And Jehu gathered all the **p** together, H5971
11:13 the guard *and* of the **p**, she came to the H5971
13 to the **p** into the temple of the LORD. H5971
14 king, and all the **p** of the land rejoiced, H5971
17 the king and the **p**, that they should be H5971
17 **p**; between the king also and the people. H5971
17 people; between the king also and the **p**. H5971
18 And all the **p** of the land went into the H5971
19 guard, and all the **p** of the land; and H5971
20 And all the **p** of the land rejoiced, and H5971
12: 3 taken away: the **p** still sacrificed and H5971
8 money of the **p**, neither to repair the H5971
13: 7 Neither did he leave of the **p** to H5971
14: 4 away: as yet the **p** did sacrifice and H5971
21 And all the **p** of Judah took Azariah, H5971
15: 4 were not removed: the **p** sacrificed and H5971
5 the house, judging the **p** of the land. H5971
10 him before the **p**, and slew him, and H5971
35 were not removed: the **p** sacrificed and H5971
16: 9 *the p of* it captive to Kir, and slew Rezin.
15 offering of all the **p** of the land, and H5971
18:26 in the ears of the **p** that *are* on the wall. H5971
36 But the **p** held their peace, and H5971
20: 5 the captain of my **p**, Thus saith the H5971
21:24 And the **p** of the land slew all them that H5971
24 king Amon; and the **p** of the land made H5971
22: 4 of the door have gathered of the **p**: H5971
13 for me, and for the **p**, and for all Judah, H5971
23: 2 and all the **p**, both small and great: H5971
3 And all the **p** stood to the covenant. H5971
6 upon the graves of the children of the **p**. H5971
21 And the king commanded all the **p**, H5971
30 And the **p** of the land took Jehoahaz H5971
35 the gold of the **p** of the land, of every H5971
24:14 the poorest sort of the **p** of the land. H5971
25: 3 was no bread for the **p** of the land. H5971
11 Now the rest of the **p** *that were* left in H5971
19 which mustered the **p** of the land, and H5971
19 men of the **p** of the land *that were* H5971
22 And *as for* the **p** that remained in the H5971
26 And all the **p**, both small and great, and H5971
1Ch 5:25 the gods of the **p** of the land, whom H5971
10: 9 tidings unto their idols, and to the **p**. H5971

1Ch 11: 2 shalt feed my **p** Israel, and thou shalt H5971
2 thou shalt be ruler over my **p** Israel. H5971
13 the **p** fled from before the Philistines. H5971
13: 4 thing was right in the eyes of all the **p**. H5971
14: 2 up on high, because of his **p** Israel. H5971
16: 2 blessed the **p** in the name of the LORD. H5971
8 make known his deeds among the **p**. H5971
20 and from *one* kingdom to another **p**; H5971
26 For all the gods of the **p** *are* idols: but H5971
28 ye kindreds of the **p**, give unto the H5971
36 **p** said, Amen, and praised the LORD. H5971
43 And all the **p** departed every man to his H5971
17: 6 to feed my **p**, saying, Why have ye H5971
7 shouldest be ruler over my **p** Israel: H5971
9 Also I will ordain a place for my **p** H5971
10 *to be* over my **p** Israel. Moreover I will H5971
21 the earth *is* like thy **p** Israel, whom God H5971
21 *to be* his own **p**, to make thee a name H5971
21 from before thy **p**, whom thou hast H5971
22 For thy **p** Israel didst thou make thine H5971
22 make thine own **p** for ever; and thou, H5971
18:14 judgment and justice among all his **p**. H5971
19: 7 of Maachah and his **p**; who came and H5971
11 And the rest of the **p** he delivered unto H5971
13 valiantly for our **p**, and for the cities of H5971
14 So Joab and the **p** that *were* with him H5971
20: 3 And he brought out the **p** that *were* in H5971
3 and all the **p** returned to Jerusalem. H5971
21: 2 to the rulers of the **p**, Go, number Israel H5971
3 LORD make his **p** an hundred times so H5971
5 of the number of the **p** unto David. And H5971
17 commanded the **p** to be numbered? H5971
17 on thy **p**, that they should be plagued. H5971
22 the plague may be stayed from the **p**. H5971
22:18 before the LORD, and before his **p**. H5971
23:25 given rest unto his **p**, that they may H5971
28: 2 brethren, and my **p**: *As for me*, I *had* in H5971
21 **p** *will be* wholly at thy commandment. H5971
29: 9 Then the **p** rejoiced, for that they H5971
14 But who *am* I, and what *is* my **p**, that H5971
17 I seen with joy thy **p**, which are present H5971
18 **p**, and prepare their heart unto thee: H5971
2Ch 1: 9 me king over a **p** like the dust of the H5971
10 in before this **p**: for who can judge this H5971
10 can judge this thy **p**, *that is so* great? H5971
11 **p**, over whom I have made thee king: H5971
2:11 **p**, he hath made thee king over them. H5971
18 hundred overseers to set the **p** a work. H5971
6: 5 Since the day that I brought forth my **p** H5971
5 any man to be a ruler over my **p** Israel: H5971
6 chosen David to be over my **p** Israel. H5971
21 and of thy **p** Israel, which they shall H5971
24 And if thy **p** Israel be put to the worse H5971
25 the sin of thy **p** Israel, and bring them H5971
27 and of thy **p** Israel, when thou hast H5971
27 given unto thy **p** for an inheritance. H5971
29 man, or of all thy **p** Israel, when every H5971
32 which is not of thy **p** Israel, but is come H5971
33 to thee for; that all **p** of the earth may H5971
33 fear thee, as *doth* thy **p** Israel, and may H5971
34 If thy **p** go out to war against their H5971
39 thy **p** which have sinned against thee. H5971
7: 4 Then the king and all the **p** offered H5971
5 all the **p** dedicated the house of God. H5971
10 month he sent the **p** away into their H5971
10 and to Solomon, and to Israel his **p**. H5971
13 or if I send pestilence among my **p**; H5971
14 If my **p**, which are called by my name, H5971
8: 7 *As for* all the **p** *that were* left of the H5971
10 and fifty, that bare rule over the **p**. H5971
10: 5 after three days. And the **p** departed. H5971
6 give ye *me* to return answer to this **p**? H5971
7 be kind to this **p**, and please them, and H5971
9 answer to this **p**, which have spoken H5971
10 thou answer the **p** that spake unto H5971
12 So Jeroboam and all the **p** came to H5971
15 So the king hearkened not unto the **p**: H5971
16 unto them, the **p** answered the king, H5971
12: 3 and the **p** *were* without number H5971
13:17 And Abijah and his **p** slew them with a H5971
14:13 And Asa and the **p** that *were* with him H5971
16:10 oppressed *some* of the **p** the same time. H5971
17: 9 all the cities of Judah, and taught the **p**. H5971
18: 2 and for the **p** that *he had* with him, H5971
3 thou *art*, and my **p** as thy people; and H5971
3 **p**; and *we will be* with thee in the war. H5971
27 by me. And he said, Hearken, all ye **p**. H5971
19: 4 again through the **p** from Beer-sheba H5971
20: 7 land before thy **p** Israel, and gavest it H5971

P

2Ch 20:21 And when he had consulted with the **p**, H5971
25 And when Jehoshaphat and his **p** came H5971
33 for as yet the **p** had not prepared their H5971
21:14 the LORD smite thy **p**, and thy children, H5971
19 diseases. And his **p** made no burning H5971
23: 5 and all the **p** *shall be* in the courts H5971
6 the **p** shall keep the watch of the LORD. H5971
10 And he set all the **p**, every man having H5971
12 the noise of the **p** running and praising H5971
12 to the **p** into the house of the LORD: H5971
13 king: and all the **p** of the land rejoiced, H5971
16 between all the **p**, and between the king, H5971
16 king, that they should be the LORD'S **p**. H5971
17 Then all the **p** went to the house of H5971
20 governors of the **p**, and all the people of H5971
20 people, and all the **p** of the land, and H5971
21 And all the **p** of the land rejoiced: and H5971
24:10 And all the princes and all the **p** H5971
20 stood above the **p**, and said unto them, H5971
23 all the princes of the **p** from among the H5971
23 from among the **p**, and sent all the spoil H5971
25:11 and led forth his **p**, and went to the H5971
15 after the gods of the **p**, which could not H5971
15 deliver their own **p** out of thine hand? H5971
26: 1 Then all the **p** of Judah took Uzziah, H5971
21 king's house, judging the **p** of the land. H5971
27: 2 the LORD. And the **p** did yet corruptly. H5971
29:36 And Hezekiah rejoiced, and all the **p**, H5971
36 the **p**: for the thing was *done* suddenly. H5971
30: 3 neither had the **p** gathered themselves H5971
13 Jerusalem much **p** to keep the feast of H5971
18 For a multitude of the **p**, *even* many of H5971
20 to Hezekiah, and healed the **p**. H5971
27 and blessed the **p**: and their voice was H5971
31: 4 Moreover he commanded the **p** that H5971
8 blessed the LORD, and his **p** Israel. H5971
10 and said, Since *the* **p** began to bring the
10 hath blessed his **p**; and that which is left H5971
32: 4 So there was gathered much **p** H5971
6 And he set captains of war over the **p**, H5971
8 battles. And the **p** rested themselves H5971
13 done unto all the **p** of *other* lands? were H5971
14 could deliver his **p** out of mine hand, H5971
15 able to deliver his **p** out of mine hand, H5971
17 not delivered their **p** out of mine hand, H5971
17 deliver his **p** out of mine hand. H5971
18 speech unto the **p** of Jerusalem that H5971
19 the gods of the **p** of the earth, *which* H5971
33:10 to his **p**: but they would not hearken. H5971
17 Nevertheless the **p** did sacrifice still in H5971
25 But the **p** of the land slew all them that H5971
25 king Amon; and the **p** of the land made H5971
34:30 and all the **p**, great and small: and H5971
35: 3 the LORD your God, and his **p** Israel, H5971
5 brethren the **p**, and *after* the H1121+5971
7 And Josiah gave to the **p**, of the flock, H5971
8 willingly unto the **p**, to the priests, and H5971
12 families of the **p**, to offer unto H1121+H5971
13 *them* speedily among all the **p**. H1121+H5971
36: 1 Then the **p** of the land took Jehoahaz H5971
14 the priests, and the **p**, transgressed very H5971
15 on his **p**, and on his dwelling place: H5971
16 against his **p**, till *there was* no remedy. H5971
23 you of all his **p**? The LORD his God H5971
Ezr 1: 3 Who *is there* among you of all his **p**? his H5971
2: 2 number of the men of the **p** of Israel: H5971
70 and *some* of the **p**, and the singers, and H5971
3: 1 in the cities, the **p** gathered themselves H5971
3 because of the **p** of those countries: and H5971
11 Israel. And all the **p** shouted with a H5971
13 So that the **p** could not discern the H5971
13 of the weeping of the **p**: for the people H5971
13 of the people: for the **p** shouted with a H5971
4: 4 Then the **p** of the land weakened the H5971
4 the hands of the **p** of Judah, and H5971
5:12 and carried the **p** away into Babylon. H5972
6:12 all kings and **p**, that shall put to their H5972
7:13 I make a decree, that all they of the **p** of H5972
16 offering of the **p**, and of the priests, H5972
25 may judge all the **p** that *are* beyond the H5972
8:15 and I viewed the **p**, and the priests, and H5971
36 furthered the **p**, and the house of God. H5971
9: 1 to me, saying, The **p** of Israel, and the H5971
1 from the **p** of the lands, *doing* H5971
2 with the **p** of *those* lands: yea, H5971
11 the filthiness of the **p** of the lands, with H5971
14 join in affinity with the **p** of these H5971
10: 1 and children: for the **p** wept very sore. H5971
2 wives of the **p** of the land: yet now H5971
Ezr 10: 9 month; and all the **p** sat in the street of H5971
11 from the **p** of the land, and from H5971
13 But the **p** *are* many, and *it is* a time of H5971
Neh 1:10 Now these *are* thy servants and thy **p**, H5971
4: 6 thereof: for the **p** had a mind to work. H5971
13 I even set the **p** after their families H5971
14 to the rest of the **p**, Be not ye afraid of H5971
19 to the rest of the **p**, The work *is* great H5971
22 said I unto the **p**, Let every one with his H5971
5: 1 And there was a great cry of the **p** and H5971
13 the **p** did according to this promise. H5971
15 unto the **p**, and had taken of them H5971
15 bare rule over the **p**: but so did not I, H5971
18 the bondage was heavy upon this **p**. H5971
19 to all that I have done for this **p**. H5971
7: 4 and great: but the **p** *were* few therein, H5971
5 the rulers, and the **p**, that they might be H5971
7 of the men of the **p** of Israel *was this*; H5971
72 And *that* which the rest of the **p** gave H5971
73 and *some* of the **p**, and the Nethinims, H5971
8: 1 And all the **p** gathered themselves H5971
3 the ears of all the **p** *were attentive* unto H5971
5 the sight of all the **p**; (for he was above H5971
5 he was above all the **p**;) and when he H5971
5 when he opened it, all the **p** stood up: H5971
6 God. And all the **p** answered, Amen, H5971
7 caused the **p** to understand the law: H5971
7 the law: and the **p** *stood* in their place. H5971
9 that taught the **p**, said unto all the H5971
9 said unto all the **p**, This day *is* holy unto H5971
9 nor weep. For all the **p** wept, when they H5971
11 So the Levites stilled all the **p**, saying, H5971
12 And all the **p** went their way to eat, and H5971
13 fathers of all the **p**, the priests, and the H5971
16 So the **p** went forth, and brought *them*, H5971
9:10 and on all the **p** of his land: for thou H5971
24 kings, and the **p** of the land, that they H5971
30 into the hand of the **p** of the lands. H5971
32 and on all thy **p**, since the time of the H5971
10:14 The chief of the **p**; Parosh, H5971
28 And the rest of the **p**, the priests, the H5971
28 from the **p** of the lands unto the H5971
30 unto the **p** of the land, nor take H5971
31 And *if* the **p** of the land bring ware or H5971
34 the Levites, and the **p**, for the wood H5971
11: 1 And the rulers of the **p** dwelt at H5971
1 the rest of the **p** also cast lots, to bring H5971
2 And the **p** blessed all the men, that H5971
24 hand in all matters concerning the **p**. H5971
12:30 the **p**, and the gates, and the wall. H5971
38 and the half of the **p** upon the wall, H5971
13: 1 the audience of the **p**; and therein was H5971
24 but according to the language of each **p**. H5971
Est 1: 5 a feast unto all the **p** that were present H5971
11 royal, to shew the **p** and the princes her H5971
16 and to all the **p** that *are* in all the H5971
22 and to every **p** after their language, H5971
22 according to the language of every **p**. H5971
2:10 Esther had not shewed her **p** nor her H5971
20 her kindred nor her **p**; as Mordecai had H5971
3: 6 had shewed him the **p** of Mordecai: H5971
6 of Ahasuerus, *even* the **p** of Mordecai. H5971
8 There is a certain **p** scattered abroad H5971
8 among the **p** in all the provinces H5971
8 diverse from all **p**; neither keep they the H5971
11 *is* given to thee, the **p** also, to do with H5971
12 the rulers of every **p** of every province H5971
12 and *to* every **p** after their language; H5971
14 published unto all **p**, that they should H5971
4: 8 to make request before him for her **p**. H5971
11 All the king's servants, and the **p** of the H5971
7: 3 my petition, and my **p** at my request: H5971
4 For we are sold, I and my **p**, to be H5971
8: 6 come unto my **p**? or how can I endure H5971
9 and unto every **p** after their language, H5971
11 all the power of the **p** and province that H5971
13 published unto all **p**, and that the Jews H5971
17 And many of the **p** of the land became H5971
9: 2 for the fear of them fell upon all **p**. H5971
10: 3 **p**, and speaking peace to all his seed. H5971
Job 12: 2 No doubt but ye *are* the **p**, and wisdom H5971
24 of the chief of the **p** of the earth, and H5971
17: 6 the **p**; and aforetime I was as a tabret. H5971
18:19 **p**, nor any remaining in his dwellings. H5971
34:20 In a moment shall they die, and the **p** H5971
30 That the hypocrite reign not, lest the **p** H5971
36:20 Desire not the night, when **p** are cut off H5971
31 For by them judgeth he the **p**; he giveth H5971
Ps 2: 1 Why do the heathen rage, and the **p** H3816
Ps 3: 6 of ten thousands of **p**, that have set H5971
8 LORD: thy blessing *is* upon thy **p**. Selah. H5971
7: 7 So shall the congregation of the **p** H3816
8 The LORD shall judge the **p**: judge me, H5971
9: 8 judgment to the **p** in uprightness. H3816
11 Zion: declare among the **p** his doings. H5971
14: 4 who eat up my **p** *as* they eat bread, and H5971
7 back the captivity of his **p**, Jacob shall H5971
18:27 For thou wilt save the afflicted **p**; but H5971
43 the strivings of the **p**; *and* thou hast H5971
43 of the heathen: a **p** *whom* I have not H5971
47 me, and subdueth the **p** under me. H5971
22: 6 reproach of men, and despised of the **p**. H5971
31 unto a **p** that shall be born, that H5971
28: 9 Save thy **p**, and bless thine inheritance: H5971
29:11 The LORD will give strength unto his **p**; H5971
11 the LORD will bless his **p** with peace. H5971
33:10 the devices of the **p** of none effect. H5971
12 *is* the LORD; *and* the **p** *whom* he hath H5971
35:18 I will praise thee among much **p**. H5971
44: 2 didst afflict the **p**, and cast them out. H3816
12 Thou sellest thy **p** for nought, and dost H5971
14 a shaking of the head among the **p**. H3816
45: 5 enemies; *whereby* the **p** fall under thee. H5971
10 thine own **p**, and thy father's house; H5971
12 among the **p** shall entreat thy favour. H5971
17 the **p** praise thee for ever and ever. H5971
47: 1 O clap your hands, all ye **p**; shout unto H5971
3 He shall subdue the **p** under us, and H5971
9 The princes of the **p** are gathered H5971
9 together, *even* the **p** of the God of H5971
49: 1 Hear this, all *ye* **p**; give ear, all *ye* H5971
50: 4 to the earth, that he may judge his **p**. H5971
7 Hear, O my **p**, and I will speak; O Israel, H5971
53: 4 who eat up my **p** *as* they eat bread: H5971
6 back the captivity of his **p**, Jacob shall H5971
56: 7 in *thine* anger cast down the **p**, O God. H5971
57: 9 I will praise thee, O Lord, among the **p**: H5971
59:11 Slay them not, lest my **p** forget: scatter H5971
60: 3 Thou hast shewed thy **p** hard things: H5971
62: 8 Trust in him at all times; *ye* **p**, pour out H5971
65: 7 of their waves, and the tumult of the **p**. H3816
66: 8 O bless our God, ye **p**, and make the H5971
67: 3 Let the **p** praise thee, O God; let all the H5971
3 thee, O God; let all the **p** praise thee. H5971
4 thou shalt judge the **p** righteously, and H5971
5 Let the **p** praise thee, O God; let all the H5971
5 thee, O God; let all the **p** praise thee. H5971
68: 7 forth before thy **p**, when thou didst H5971
22 *my* **p** again from the depths of the sea:
30 the calves of the **p**, *till every one* submit H5971
30 scatter thou the **p** *that* delight in war. H5971
35 and power unto *his* **p**. Blessed *be* God. H5971
72: 2 He shall judge thy **p** with H5971
3 **p**, and the little hills, by righteousness. H5971
4 He shall judge the poor of the **p**, he shall H5971
73:10 Therefore his **p** return hither: and H5971
74:14 to the **p** inhabiting the wilderness. H5971
18 foolish **p** have blasphemed thy name. H5971
77:14 hast declared thy strength among the **p**. H5971
15 **p**, the sons of Jacob and Joseph. Selah. H5971
20 Thou leddest thy **p** like a flock by the H5971
78: 1 Give ear, O my **p**, *to* my law: incline H5971
20 also? can he provide flesh for his **p**? H5971
52 But made his own **p** to go forth like H5971
62 He gave his **p** over also unto the sword; H5971
71 Jacob his **p**, and Israel his inheritance. H5971
79:13 So we thy **p** and sheep of thy pasture H5971
80: 4 be angry against the prayer of thy **p**? H5971
81: 8 Hear, O my **p**, and I will testify unto H5971
11 But my **p** would not hearken to my H5971
13 Oh that my **p** had hearkened unto me, H5971
83: 3 against thy **p**, and consulted against H5971
85: 2 Thou hast forgiven the iniquity of thy **p**, H5971
6 again: that thy **p** may rejoice in thee? H5971
8 peace unto his **p**, and to his saints: but H5971
87: 6 **p**, *that* this *man* was born there. Selah. H5971
89:15 Blessed *is* the **p** that know the joyful H5971
19 I have exalted *one* chosen out of the **p**. H5971
50 bosom *the reproach of* all the mighty **p**; H5971
94: 5 They break in pieces thy **p**, O LORD, H5971
8 Understand, ye brutish among the **p**: H5971
14 For the LORD will not cast off his **p**, H5971
95: 7 For he *is* our God; and we *are* the **p** of H5971
10 and said, It *is* a **p** that do err in their H5971
96: 3 the heathen, his wonders among all **p**. H5971
7 O ye kindreds of the **p**, give unto the H5971
10 he shall judge the **p** righteously. H5971
13 righteousness, and the **p** with his truth. H5971

Ps 97: 6 and all the **p** see his glory. H5971
98: 9 judge the world, and the **p** with equity. H5971
99: 1 The LORD reigneth; let the **p** tremble: H5971
2 in Zion; and he *is* high above all the **p**. H5971
100: 3 *are* his **p**, and the sheep of his pasture. H5971
102:18 to come: and the **p** which shall be H5971
22 When the **p** are gathered together, and H5971
105: 1 make known his deeds among the **p**. H5971
13 from *one* kingdom to another **p**; H5971
20 the ruler of the **p**, and let him go free. H5971
24 And he increased his **p** greatly; and H5971
25 He turned their heart to hate his **p**, to H5971
40 *The* **p** asked, and he brought quails, and
43 And he brought forth his **p** with joy, H5971
44 and they inherited the labour of the **p**; H3816
106: 4 thy **p**: O visit me with thy salvation; H5971
40 kindled against his **p**, insomuch that he H5971
48 the **p** say, Amen. Praise ye the LORD. H5971
107:32 of the **p**, and praise him in the H5971
108: 3 O LORD, among the **p**: and I will sing H5971
110: 3 Thy **p** *shall be* willing in the day of thy H5971
111: 6 He hath shewed his **p** the power of his H5971
9 He sent redemption unto his **p**: he hath H5971
113: 8 princes, *even* with the princes of his **p**. H5971
114: 1 of Jacob from a **p** of strange language; H5971
116:14 LORD now in the presence of all his **p**. H5971
18 LORD now in the presence of all his **p**, H5971
117: 1 LORD, all ye nations: praise him, all ye **p**. H523
125: 2 his **p** from henceforth even for ever. H5971
135:12 heritage, an heritage unto Israel his **p**. H5971
14 For the LORD will judge his **p**, and he H5971
136:16 To him which led his **p** through the H5971
144: 2 I trust; who subdueth my **p** under me. H5971
15 Happy *is that* **p**, that is in such a case: H5971
15 *is that* **p**, whose God *is* the LORD. H5971
148:11 Kings of the earth, and all **p**; princes, H3816
14 He also exalteth the horn of his **p**, the H5971
14 a **p** near unto him. Praise ye the LORD. H5971
149: 4 For the LORD taketh pleasure in his **p**: H5971
7 heathen, *and* punishments upon the **p**; H3816
Prv 11:14 Where no counsel *is*, the **p** fall: but in H5971
26 He that withholdeth corn, the **p** shall H3816
14:28 In the multitude of **p** *is* the king's H5971
28 of **p** *is* the destruction of the prince. H3816
34 a nation: but sin *is* a reproach to any **p**. H3816
24:24 the **p** curse, nations shall abhor him: H5971
28:15 *so is* a wicked ruler over the poor **p**. H5971
29: 2 in authority, the **p** rejoice: but when the H5971
2 the wicked beareth rule, the **p** mourn. H5971
18 Where *there is* no vision, the **p** perish: H5971
30:25 The ants *are* a **p** not strong, yet they H5971
Ecc 4:16 *There is* no end of all the **p**, *even* of all H5971
12: 9 he still taught the **p** knowledge; yea, he H5971
Isa 1: 3 not know, my **p** doth not consider. H5971
4 Ah sinful nation, a **p** laden with H5971
10 the law of our God, ye **p** of Gomorrah. H5971
2: 3 And many **p** shall go and say, Come ye, H5971
4 and shall rebuke many **p**: and they shall H5971
6 Therefore thou hast forsaken thy **p** the H5971
3: 5 And the **p** shall be oppressed, every one H5971
7 clothing: make me not a ruler of the **p**. H5971
12 *As for* my **p**, children *are* their H5971
12 over them. O my **p**, they which lead thee H5971
13 to plead, and standeth to judge the **p**. H5971
14 the ancients of his **p**, and the princes H5971
15 What mean ye *that* ye beat my **p** to H5971
5:13 Therefore my **p** are gone into captivity, H5971
25 against his **p**, and he hath stretched H5971
6: 5 in the midst of a **p** of unclean lips: for H5971
9 And he said, Go, and tell this **p**, Hear ye H5971
10 Make the heart of this **p** fat, and make H5971
7: 2 and the heart of his **p**, as the trees of the H5971
8 Ephraim be broken, that it be not a **p**. H5971
17 and upon thy **p**, and upon thy father's H5971
8: 6 Forasmuch as this **p** refuseth the H5971
9 Associate yourselves, O ye **p**, and ye H5971
11 not walk in the way of this **p**, saying, H5971
12 *them to* whom this **p** shall say, A H5971
19 should not a **p** seek unto their God? H5971
9: 2 The **p** that walked in darkness have H5971
9 And all the **p** shall know, *even* Ephraim H5971
13 For the **p** turneth not unto him that H5971
16 For the leaders of this **p** cause *them* to H5971
19 darkened, and the **p** shall be as the fuel H5971
10: 2 the poor of my **p**, that widows may be H5971
6 and against the **p** of my wrath will I H5971
13 the bounds of the **p**, and have robbed H5971
14 the riches of the **p**: and as one gathereth H5971
22 For though thy **p** Israel be as the sand H5971

Isa 10:24 of hosts, O my **p** that dwellest in Zion, H5971
11:10 for an ensign of the **p**; to it shall the H5971
11 the remnant of his **p**, which shall be left, H5971
16 the remnant of his **p**, which shall be left, H5971
12: 4 his doings among the **p**, make mention H5971
13: 4 like as of a great **p**; a tumultuous noise H5971
14 **p**, and flee every one into his own land. H5971
14: 2 And the **p** shall take them, and bring H5971
6 He who smote the **p** in wrath with a H5971
20 *and* slain thy **p**: the seed of evildoers H5971
32 and the poor of his **p** shall trust in it. H5971
17:12 Woe to the multitude of many **p**, *which* H5971
18: 2 and peeled, to a **p** terrible from their H5971
7 of hosts of a **p** scattered and peeled, H5971
7 peeled, and from a **p** terrible from their H5971
19:25 *be* Egypt my **p**, and Assyria the work H5971
22: 4 of the spoiling of the daughter of my **p**. H5971
23:13 the Chaldeans; this **p** was not, *till* the H5971
24: 2 And it shall be, as with the **p**, so with H5971
4 the haughty **p** of the earth do languish. H5971
13 land among the **p**, *there shall be* as the H5971
25: 3 Therefore shall the strong **p** glorify H5971
6 make unto all **p** a feast of fat things, H5971
7 cast over all **p**, and the vail that is H5971
8 the rebuke of his **p** shall he take away H5971
26:11 *their* envy at the **p**; yea, the fire of thine H5971
20 Come, my **p**, enter thou into thy H5971
27:11 them on fire: for it *is* a **p** of no H5971
28: 5 of beauty, unto the residue of his **p**, H5971
11 another tongue will he speak to this **p**. H5971
14 that rule this **p** which *is* in Jerusalem. H5971
29:13 Forasmuch as this **p** draw near *me* H5971
14 work among this **p**, *even* a marvellous H5971
30: 5 They were all ashamed of a **p** *that* H5971
6 to a **p** *that* shall not profit *them*. H5971
9 That this *is* a rebellious **p**, lying H5971
19 For the **p** shall dwell in Zion at H5971
26 up the breach of his **p**, and healeth the H5971
28 in the jaws of the **p**, causing *them* to err. H5971
32:13 Upon the land of my **p** shall come up H5971
18 And my **p** shall dwell in a peaceable H5971
33: 3 At the noise of the tumult the **p** fled; at H5971
12 And the **p** shall be *as* the burnings of H5971
19 Thou shalt not see a fierce **p**, a people of H5971
19 Thou shalt not see a fierce people, a **p** H5971
24 say, I am sick: the **p** that dwell therein H5971
34: 1 and hearken, ye **p**: let the earth hear, H3816
5 upon the **p** of my curse, to judgment. H5971
36:11 in the ears of the **p** that *are* on the wall. H5971
40: 1 Comfort ye, comfort ye my **p**, saith your H5971
7 bloweth upon it: surely the **p** *is* grass. H5971
41: 1 and let the **p** renew *their* strength: H3816
42: 5 breath unto the **p** upon it, and spirit to H5971
6 of the **p**, for a light of the Gentiles; H5971
22 But this *is* a **p** robbed and spoiled; *they* H5971
43: 4 I give men for thee, and **p** for thy life. H3816
8 Bring forth the blind **p** that have eyes, H5971
9 and let the **p** be assembled: who H3816
20 to give drink to my **p**, my chosen. H5971
21 This **p** have I formed for myself; they H5971
44: 7 the ancient **p**? and the things that H5971
47: 6 I was wroth with my **p**, I have polluted H5971
49: 1 and hearken, ye **p**, from far; The LORD H3816
8 for a covenant of the **p**, to establish the H5971
13 comforted his **p**, and will have mercy H5971
22 standard to the **p**: and they shall bring H5971
51: 4 Hearken unto me, my **p**; and give ear H5971
4 my judgment to rest for a light of the **p**. H5971
5 shall judge the **p**; the isles shall wait H5971
7 righteousness, the **p** in whose heart *is* H5971
16 and say unto Zion, Thou *art* my **p**. H5971
22 the cause of his **p**, Behold, I have taken H5971
52: 4 For thus saith the Lord GOD, My **p** H5971
5 the LORD, that my **p** is taken away for H5971
6 Therefore my **p** shall know my name: H5971
9 his **p**, he hath redeemed Jerusalem. H5971
53: 8 transgression of my **p** was he stricken. H5971
55: 4 *for* a witness to the **p**, a leader and H3816
4 a leader and commander to the **p**. H3816
56: 3 me from his **p**: neither let the eunuch H5971
7 be called an house of prayer for all **p**. H5971
57:14 stumblingblock out of the way of my **p**. H5971
58: 1 and shew my **p** their transgression, H5971
60: 2 darkness the **p**: but the LORD shall H3816
21 Thy **p** also *shall be* all righteous: they H5971
61: 9 among the **p**: all that see them shall H5971
62:10 ye the way of the **p**; cast up, cast up the H5971
10 the stones; lift up a standard for the **p**. H5971
12 And they shall call them, The holy **p**, H5971

Isa 63: 3 alone; and of the **p** *there was* none with H5971
6 And I will tread down the **p** in mine H5971
8 For he said, Surely they *are* my **p**, H5971
11 Moses, *and* his **p**, *saying*, Where *is* he H5971
14 thy **p**, to make thyself a glorious name. H5971
18 The **p** of thy holiness have possessed *it* H5971
64: 9 see, we beseech thee, we *are* all thy **p**. H5971
65: 2 unto a rebellious **p**, which walketh in a H5971
3 A **p** that provoketh me to anger H5971
10 down in, for my **p** that have sought me. H5971
18 Jerusalem a rejoicing, and her **p** a joy. H5971
19 and joy in my **p**: and the voice of H5971
22 *are* the days of my **p**, and mine elect H5971
Jer 1:18 thereof, and against the **p** of the land. H5971
2:11 no gods? but my **p** have changed their H5971
13 For my **p** have committed two evils; H5971
31 wherefore say my **p**, We are lords; we H5971
32 her attire? yet my **p** have forgotten me H5971
4:10 deceived this **p** and Jerusalem, saying, H5971
11 At that time shall it be said to this **p** H5971
11 of my **p**, not to fan, nor to cleanse, H5971
22 For my **p** *is* foolish, they have not H5971
5:14 this **p** wood, and it shall devour them. H5971
21 Hear now this, O foolish **p**, and without H5971
23 But this **p** hath a revolting and a H5971
26 For among my **p** are found wicked H5971
31 means; and my **p** love *to have it* so: H5971
6:14 *the daughter* of my **p** slightly, saying, H5971
19 evil upon this **p**, *even* the fruit of their H5971
21 before this **p**, and the fathers and H5971
22 Thus saith the LORD, Behold, a **p** H5971
26 O daughter of my **p**, gird *thee* with H5971
27 among my **p**, that thou mayest know H5971
7:12 to it for the wickedness of my **p** Israel. H5971
16 Therefore pray not thou for this **p**, H5971
23 and ye shall be my **p**: and walk ye in all H5971
33 And the carcases of this **p** shall be meat H5971
8: 5 Why *then* is this **p** of Jerusalem slidden H5971
7 **p** know not the judgment of the LORD. H5971
11 the daughter of my **p** slightly, saying, H5971
19 daughter of my **p** because of them that H5971
21 For the hurt of the daughter of my **p** H5971
22 of the daughter of my **p** recovered? H5971
9: 1 for the slain of the daughter of my **p**! H5971
2 I might leave my **p**, and go from them! H5971
7 how shall I do for the daughter of my **p**? H5971
15 them, *even* this **p**, with wormwood, and H5971
10: 3 For the customs of the **p** *are* vain: for H5971
11: 4 shall ye be my **p**, and I will be your God: H5971
14 Therefore pray not thou for this **p**, H5971
12:14 I have caused my **p** Israel to inherit; H5971
16 the ways of my **p**, to swear by my name, H5971
16 as they taught my **p** to swear by Baal; H5971
16 shall they be built in the midst of my **p**. H5971
13:10 This evil **p**, which refuse to hear my H5971
11 be unto me for a **p**, and for a name, and H5971
14:10 Thus saith the LORD unto this **p**, Thus H5971
11 me, Pray not for this **p** for *their* good. H5971
16 And the **p** to whom they prophesy shall H5971
17 daughter of my **p** is broken with a great H5971
15: 1 not *be* toward this **p**: cast *them* out of H5971
7 I will destroy my **p**, *since* they return H5971
20 And I will make thee unto this **p** a H5971
16: 5 peace from this **p**, saith the LORD, *even* H5971
10 shalt shew this **p** all these words, and H5971
17:19 the children of the **p**, whereby the kings H5971
18:15 Because my **p** hath forgotten me, they H5971
19: 1 the **p**, and of the ancients of the priests; H5971
11 so will I break this **p** and this city, as H5971
14 the LORD'S house; and said to all the **p**, H5971
21: 7 servants, and the **p**, and such as are left H5971
8 And unto this **p** thou shalt say, Thus H5971
22: 2 and thy **p** that enter in by these gates: H5971
4 horses, he, and his servants, and his **p**. H5971
23: 2 that feed my **p**; Ye have scattered my H5971
13 in Baal, and caused my **p** Israel to err. H5971
22 had caused my **p** to hear my words, H5971
27 Which think to cause my **p** to forget my H5971
32 and cause my **p** to err by their lies, and H5971
32 not profit this **p** at all, saith the LORD. H5971
33 And when this **p**, or the prophet, or a H5971
34 the priest, and the **p**, that shall say, The H5971
24: 7 they shall be my **p**, and I will be their H5971
25: 1 concerning all the **p** of Judah in the H5971
2 spake unto all the **p** of Judah, and to all H5971
19 servants, and his princes, and all his **p**; H5971
20 And all the mingled **p**, and all the kings
24 of the mingled **p** that dwell in the desert,
26: 7 and all the **p** heard Jeremiah speaking H5971

Jer 26: 8 to speak unto all the **p**, that the priests H5971
8 and all the **p** took him, saying, Thou H5971
9 And all the **p** were gathered against H5971
11 and to all the **p**, saying, This man *is* H5971
12 and to all the **p**, saying, The LORD sent H5971
16 Then said the princes and all the **p** H5971
17 to all the assembly of the **p**, saying, H5971
18 and spake to all the **p** of Judah, saying, H5971
23 body into the graves of the common **p**. H5971
24 the hand of the **p** to put him to death. H5971
27:12 and serve him and his **p**, and live. H5971
13 Why will ye die, thou and thy **p**, by the H5971
16 and to all this **p**, saying, Thus saith the H5971
28: 1 of the priests and of all the **p**, saying, H5971
5 **p** that stood in the house of the LORD, H5971
7 thine ears, and in the ears of all the **p**; H5971
11 presence of all the **p**, saying, Thus saith H5971
15 but thou makest this **p** to trust in a lie. H5971
29: 1 and to all the **p** whom Nebuchadnezzar H5971
16 and of all the **p** that dwelleth in this H5971
25 thy name unto all the **p** that *are* at H5971
32 to dwell among this **p**; neither shall he H5971
32 that I will do for my **p**, saith the LORD; H5971
30: 3 the captivity of my **p** Israel and Judah, H5971
22 And ye shall be my **p**, and I will be your H5971
31: 1 of Israel, and they shall be my **p**. H5971
2 Thus saith the LORD, The **p** *which* H5971
7 save thy **p**, the remnant of Israel. H5971
14 fatness, and my **p** shall be satisfied H5971
33 be their God, and they shall be my **p**. H5971
32:21 And hast brought forth thy **p** Israel out H5971
38 And they shall be my **p**, and I will be H5971
42 evil upon this **p**, so will I bring upon H5971
33:24 Considerest thou not what this **p** have H5971
24 have despised my **p**, that they should be H5971
34: 1 and all the **p**, fought against Jerusalem, H5971
8 with all the **p** which *were* at Jerusalem, H5971
10 Now when all the princes, and all the **p**, H5971
19 priests, and all the **p** of the land, which H5971
35:16 but this **p** hath not hearkened unto me: H5971
36: 6 in the ears of the **p** in the LORD'S H5971
7 LORD hath pronounced against this **p**. H5971
9 LORD to all the **p** in Jerusalem, and to H5971
9 and to all the **p** that came from the H5971
10 LORD'S house, in the ears of all the **p**. H5971
13 read the book in the ears of the **p**. H5971
14 read in the ears of the **p**, and come. So H5971
37: 2 his servants, nor the **p** of the land, did H5971
4 **p**: for they had not put him into prison. H5971
12 himself thence in the midst of the **p**. H5971
18 this **p**, that ye have put me in prison? H5971
38: 1 had spoken unto all the **p**, saying, H5971
4 the hands of all the **p**, in speaking such H5971
4 not the welfare of this **p**, but the hurt. H5971
39: 8 the houses of the **p**, with fire, and brake H5971
9 remnant of the **p** that remained in the H5971
9 with the rest of the **p** that remained. H5971
10 of the poor of the **p**, which had nothing, H5971
14 him home: so he dwelt among the **p**. H5971
40: 5 him among the **p**: or go wheresoever it H5971
6 among the **p** that were left in the land. H5971
41:10 all the residue of the **p** that *were* in H5971
10 and all the **p** that remained in Mizpah, H5971
13 *that* when all the **p** which *were* with H5971
14 So all the **p** that Ishmael had carried H5971
16 the remnant of the **p** whom he had H5971
42: 1 and all the **p** from the least even H5971
8 **p** from the least even to the greatest, H5971
43: 1 unto all the **p** all the words of the H5971
4 the forces, and all the **p**, obeyed not the H5971
44:15 even all the **p** that dwelt in the land H5971
20 Then Jeremiah said unto all the **p**, to H5971
20 and to all the **p** which had given him H5971
21 princes, and the **p** of the land, did not H5971
24 Moreover Jeremiah said unto all the **p**, H5971
46:16 again to our own **p**, and to the land of H5971
24 into the hand of the **p** of the north. H5971
48:42 from *being* a **p**, because he hath H5971
46 Woe be unto thee, O Moab! the **p** of H5971
49: 1 Gad, and his **p** dwell in his cities? H5971
50: 6 My **p** hath been lost sheep: their H5971
16 every one to his **p**, and they shall flee H5971
37 all the mingled **p** that *are* in the midst
41 Behold, a **p** shall come from the north, H5971
51:45 My **p**, go ye out of the midst of her, and H5971
58 with fire; and the **p** shall labour in H5971
52: 6 was no bread for the **p** of the land. H5971
15 of the poor of the **p**, and the residue of H5971
15 the residue of the **p** that remained in H5971
Jer 52:25 who mustered the **p** of the land; and H5971
25 men of the **p** of the land, that were H5971
28 This *is* the **p** whom Nebuchadrezzar H5971
Lam 1: 1 *that was* full of **p**! *how* is she become H5971
7 of old, when her **p** fell into the hand of H5971
11 All her **p** sigh, they seek bread; they H5971
18 I pray you, all **p**, and behold my sorrow: H5971
2:11 daughter of my **p**; because the children H5971
3:14 I was a derision to all my **p**; *and* their H5971
45 and refuse in the midst of the **p**. H5971
48 the destruction of the daughter of my **p**. H5971
4: 3 daughter of my **p** *is become* cruel, like H5971
6 daughter of my **p** is greater than the H5971
10 the destruction of the daughter of my **p**. H5971
Ezk 3: 5 For thou *art* not sent to a **p** of a strange H5971
6 Not to many **p** of a strange speech and H5971
11 the children of thy **p**, and speak unto H5971
7:27 the hands of the **p** of the land shall be H5971
11: 1 the son of Benaiah, princes of the **p**. H5971
17 you from the **p**, and assemble you out H5971
20 shall be my **p**, and I will be their God. H5971
12:19 And say unto the **p** of the land, Thus H5971
13: 9 assembly of my **p**, neither shall they be H5971
10 have seduced my **p**, saying, Peace; and H5971
17 daughters of thy **p**, which prophesy out H5971
18 the souls of my **p**, and will ye save the H5971
19 And will ye pollute me among my **p** for H5971
19 your lying to my **p** that hear *your* lies? H5971
21 and deliver my **p** out of your hand, and H5971
23 for I will deliver my **p** out of your hand: H5971
14: 8 the midst of my **p**; and ye shall know H5971
9 him from the midst of my **p** Israel. H5971
11 they may be my **p**, and I may be their H5971
17: 9 **p** to pluck it up by the roots thereof. H5971
15 horses and much **p**. Shall he prosper? H5971
18:18 **p**, lo, even he shall die in his iniquity. H5971
20:34 And I will bring you out from the **p**, and H5971
35 the wilderness of the **p**, and there will I H5971
41 you out from the **p**, and gather you out H5971
21:12 shall be upon my **p**, it *shall be* upon all H5971
12 my **p**: smite therefore upon *thy* thigh. H5971
22:29 The **p** of the land have used H5971
23:24 with an assembly of **p**, *which* shall set H5971
24:18 So I spake unto the **p** in the morning: H5971
19 And the **p** said unto me, Wilt thou not H5971
25: 7 thee off from the **p**, and I will cause thee H5971
14 by the hand of my **p** Israel: and they H5971
26: 2 the gates of the **p**: she is turned unto H5971
7 and companies, and much **p**. H5971
11 he shall slay thy **p** by the sword, and H5971
20 the pit, with the **p** of old time, and shall H5971
27: 3 *art* a merchant of the **p** for many isles, H5971
33 thou filledst many **p**; thou didst enrich H5971
36 The merchants among the **p** shall hiss H5971
28:19 All they that know thee among the **p** H5971
25 of Israel from the **p** among whom they H5971
29:13 from the **p** whither they were scattered: H5971
30: 5 all the mingled **p**, and Chub, and the men
11 He and his **p** with him, the terrible of H5971
31:12 land; and all the **p** of the earth are gone H5971
32: 3 a company of many **p**; and they shall H5971
9 I will also vex the hearts of many **p**, H5971
10 Yea, I will make many **p** amazed at H5971
33: 2 to the children of thy **p**, and say unto H5971
2 upon a land, if the **p** of the land take a H5971
3 he blow the trumpet, and warn the **p**; H5971
6 trumpet, and the **p** be not warned; if H5971
12 the children of thy **p**, The righteousness H5971
17 Yet the children of thy **p** say, The way H5971
30 the children of thy **p** still are talking H5971
31 And they come unto thee as the **p** H5971
31 before thee *as* my **p**, and they hear thy H5971
34:13 And I will bring them out from the **p**, H5971
30 of Israel, *are* my **p**, saith the Lord GOD. H5971
36: 3 of talkers, and *are* an infamy of the **p**: H5971
8 your fruit to my **p** of Israel; for they are H5971
12 you, *even* my **p** Israel; and they shall H5971
15 the reproach of the **p** any more, neither H5971
20 These *are* the **p** of the LORD, and are H5971
28 ye shall be my **p**, and I will be your God. H5971
37:12 Behold, O my **p**, I will open your graves, H5971
13 your graves, O my **p**, and brought you H5971
18 And when the children of thy **p** shall H5971
23 they be my **p**, and I will be their God. H5971
27 be their God, and they shall be my **p**. H5971
38: 6 all his bands: *and* many **p** with thee. H5971
8 out of many **p**, against the mountains H5971
9 all thy bands, and many **p** with thee. H5971
12 and upon the **p** *that are* gathered out H5971
Ezk 38:14 that day when my **p** of Israel dwelleth H5971
15 thou, and many **p** with thee, all of them H5971
16 And thou shalt come up against my **p** H5971
22 upon the many **p** that *are* with him, an H5971
39: 4 bands, and the **p** that *is* with thee: I will H5971
7 in the midst of my **p** Israel; and I will H5971
13 Yea, all the **p** of the land shall bury H5971
27 again from the **p**, and gathered them H5971
42:14 to *those things* which *are* for the **p**. H5971
44:11 sacrifice for the **p**, and they shall stand H5971
19 utter court to the **p**, they shall put off H5971
19 not sanctify the **p** with their garments. H5971
23 And they shall teach my **p** *the* H5971
45: 8 more oppress my **p**; and *the rest of* the H5971
9 from my **p**, saith the Lord GOD. H5971
16 All the **p** of the land shall give this H5971
22 and for all the **p** of the land a bullock H5971
46: 3 Likewise the **p** of the land shall H5971
9 But when the **p** of the land shall come H5971
18 that my **p** be not scattered every H5971
20 into the utter court, to sanctify the **p**. H5971
24 house shall boil the sacrifice of the **p**. H5971
Dan 2:44 not be left to other **p**, *but* it shall break H5972
3: 4 O **p**, nations, and languages, H5972
7 Therefore at that time, when all the **p** H5972
7 of musick, all the **p**, the nations, and H5972
29 a decree, That every **p**, nation, and H5972
4: 1 Nebuchadnezzar the king, unto all **p**, H5972
5:19 that he gave him, all **p**, nations, and H5972
6:25 Then king Darius wrote unto all **p**, H5972
7:14 a kingdom, that all **p**, nations, and H5972
27 be given to the **p** of the saints of the H5972
8:24 shall destroy the mighty and the holy **p**. H5971
9: 6 our fathers, and to all the **p** of the land. H5971
15 hast brought thy **p** forth out of the land H5971
16 Jerusalem and thy **p** *are become* a H5971
19 city and thy **p** are called by thy name. H5971
20 sin and the sin of my **p** Israel, and H5971
24 upon thy **p** and upon thy holy city, H5971
26 for himself: and the **p** of the prince that H5971
10:14 shall befall thy **p** in the latter days: for H5971
11:14 also the robbers of thy **p** shall exalt H5971
15 neither his chosen **p**, neither *shall there* H5971
23 and shall become strong with a small **p**. H1471
32 flatteries: but the **p** that do know their H5971
33 And they that understand among the **p** H5971
12: 1 the children of thy **p**: and there shall be H5971
1 at that time thy **p** shall be delivered, H5971
7 holy **p**, all these *things* shall be finished. H5971
Hos 1: 9 not my **p**, and I will not be your *God*. H5971
10 Ye *are* not my **p**, *there* it shall be said H5971
2:23 *were* not my **p**, Thou *art* my people; H5971
23 **p**; and they shall say, *Thou art* my God. H5971
4: 4 **p** *are* as they that strive with the priest. H5971
6 My **p** are destroyed for lack of H5971
8 They eat up the sin of my **p**, and they H5971
9 And there shall be, like **p**, like priest: H5971
12 My **p** ask counsel at their stocks, and H5971
14 **p** *that* doth not understand shall fall. H5971
6:11 when I returned the captivity of my **p**. H5971
7: 8 the **p**; Ephraim is a cake not turned. H5971
9: 1 Rejoice not, O Israel, for joy, as *other* **p**: H5971
10: 5 of Beth-aven: for the **p** thereof shall H5971
10 them; and the **p** shall be gathered H5971
14 arise among thy **p**, and all thy fortresses H5971
11: 7 And my **p** are bent to backsliding from H5971
Joel 2: 2 a great **p** and a strong; there H5971
5 as a strong **p** set in battle array. H5971
6 Before their face the **p** shall be much H5971
16 Gather the **p**, sanctify the congregation, H5971
17 say, Spare thy **p**, O LORD, and give not H5971
17 say among the **p**, Where *is* their God? H5971
18 be jealous for his land, and pity his **p**. H5971
19 and say unto his **p**, Behold, I will send H5971
26 you: and my **p** shall never be ashamed. H5971
27 else: and my **p** shall never be ashamed. H5971
3: 2 with them there for my **p** and *for* my H5971
3 And they have cast lots for my **p**; and H5971
8 **p** far off: for the LORD hath spoken *it*. H1471
16 *be* the hope of his **p**, and the strength of H5971
Am 1: 5 of Eden: and the **p** of Syria shall go into H5971
3: 6 the city, and the **p** not be afraid? shall H5971
7: 8 in the midst of my **p** Israel: I will not H5971
15 me, Go, prophesy unto my **p** Israel. H5971
8: 2 is come upon my **p** of Israel; I will not H5971
9:10 All the sinners of my **p** shall die by the H5971
14 the captivity of my **p** of Israel, and they H5971
Oba 13 into the gate of my **p** in the day of their H5971
Jna 1: 8 *is* thy country? and of what **p** *art* thou? H5971

Jna 3: 5 So the **p** of Nineveh believed God, and H582
Mic 1: 2 Hear, all ye **p**; hearken, O earth, and all H5971
9 the gate of my **p**, *even* to Jerusalem. H5971
2: 4 the portion of my **p**: how hath he H5971
8 Even of late my **p** is risen up as an H5971
9 The women of my **p** have ye cast out H5971
11 he shall even be the prophet of this **p**. H5971
3: 3 Who also eat the flesh of my **p**, and flay H5971
5 that make my **p** err, that bite with their H5971
4: 1 above the hills; and **p** shall flow unto it. H5971
3 And he shall judge among many **p**, and H5971
5 For all **p** will walk every one in the H5971
13 in pieces many **p**: and I will consecrate H5971
5: 7 the midst of many **p** as a dew from the H5971
8 in the midst of many **p** as a lion among H5971
6: 2 with his **p**, and he will plead with Israel. H5971
3 O my **p**, what have I done unto thee? H5971
5 O my **p**, remember now what Balak H5971
16 ye shall bear the reproach of my **p**. H5971
7:14 Feed thy **p** with thy rod, the flock of H5971
Nah 3:13 Behold, thy **p** in the midst of thee *are* H5971
18 *in the dust*: thy **p** is scattered upon the H5971
Hab 2: 5 all nations, and heapeth unto him all **p**: H5971
8 the remnant of the **p** shall spoil thee; H5971
10 **p**, and hast sinned *against* thy soul. H5971
13 of hosts that the **p** shall labour in the H5971
13 the very fire, and the **p** shall weary H3816
3:13 the salvation of thy **p**, *even* for salvation H5971
16 **p**, he will invade them with his troops. H5971
Zep 1:11 for all the merchant **p** are cut down; all H5971
2: 8 have reproached my **p**, and magnified H5971
9 the residue of my **p** shall spoil them, H5971
9 remnant of my **p** shall possess them. H1471
10 against the **p** of the LORD of hosts. H5971
3: 9 For then will I turn to the **p** a pure H5971
12 an afflicted and poor **p**, and they shall H5971
20 a praise among all **p** of the earth, when H5971
Hag 1: 2 of hosts, saying, This **p** say, The time is H5971
12 remnant of the **p**, obeyed the voice of H5971
12 and the **p** did fear before the LORD. H5971
13 message unto the **p**, saying, I *am* with H5971
14 remnant of the **p**; and they came and H5971
2: 2 and to the residue of the **p**, saying, H5971
4 be strong, all ye **p** of the land, saith the H5971
14 said, So *is* this **p**, and so *is* this nation H5971
Zec 2:11 and shall be my **p**: and I will dwell in H5971
7: 5 Speak unto all the **p** of the land, and to H5971
8: 6 remnant of this **p** in these days, should H5971
7 I will save my **p** from the east country, H5971
8 they shall be my **p**, and I will be their H5971
11 the residue of this **p** as in the former H5971
12 of this **p** to possess all these *things*. H5971
20 **p**, and the inhabitants of many cities: H5971
22 Yea, many **p** and strong nations shall H5971
9:16 as the flock of his **p**: for they *shall be as* H5971
10: 9 And I will sow them among the **p**: and H5971
11:10 which I had made with all the **p**. H5971
12: 2 unto all the **p** round about, when H5971
3 stone for all **p**: all that burden H5971
3 pieces, though all the **p** of the earth be H1471
4 every horse of the **p** with blindness. H5971
6 devour all the **p** round about, on the H5971
13: 9 I will say, It *is* my **p**: and they shall say, H5971
14: 2 the **p** shall not be cut off from the city. H5971
12 will smite all the **p** that have fought H5971
Mal 1: 4 and, The **p** against whom the LORD H5971
2: 9 base before all the **p**, according as ye H5971
Mt 1:21 for he shall save his **p** from their sins. *G2992*
2: 4 priests and scribes of the **p** together, he *G2992*
6 a Governor, that shall rule my **p** Israel. *G2992*
4:16 The **p** which sat in darkness saw great *G2992*
23 and all manner of disease among the **p**. *G2992*
24 unto him all sick **p** that were taken *G3588*
25 multitudes of **p** from Galilee, and *from* *G3793*
7:28 the **p** were astonished at his doctrine: *G3793*
9:23 minstrels and the **p** making a noise, *G3793*
25 But when the **p** were put forth, he went *G3793*
35 and every disease among the **p**. *G2992*
12:23 And all the **p** were amazed, and said, Is *G3793*
46 While he yet talked to the **p**, behold, *his* *G3793*
14:13 and when the **p** had heard *thereof*, they *G3793*
15: 8 This **p** draweth nigh unto me with their *G2992*
21:23 the elders of the **p** came unto him as he *G2992*
26 the **p**; for all hold John as a prophet. *G3793*
26: 3 the elders of the **p**, unto the palace of *G2992*
5 lest there be an uproar among the **p**. *G2992*
47 the chief priests and elders of the **p**. *G2992*
27: 1 priests and elders of the **p** took counsel *G2992*
15 the **p** a prisoner, whom they would. *G3793*

Mt 27:25 Then answered all the **p**, and said, His *G2992*
64 and say unto the **p**, He is risen from the *G2992*
Mk 5:21 other side, much **p** gathered unto him: *G3793*
24 And *Jesus* went with him; and much **p** *G3793*
6:33 And the **p** saw them departing, and *G3793*
34 out, saw much **p**, and was moved with *G3793*
45 Bethsaida, while he sent away the **p**. *G3793*
7: 6 it is written, This **p** honoureth me with *G2992*
14 And when he had called all the **p** *unto* *G3793*
17 house from the **p**, his disciples asked *G3793*
8: 6 And he commanded the **p** to sit down *G3793*
6 and they did set *them* before the **p**. *G3793*
34 And when he had called the **p** *unto him* *G3793*
9:15 And straightway all the **p**, when they *G3793*
25 When Jesus saw that the **p** came *G3793*
10: 1 of Jordan: and the **p** resort unto him *G3793*
46 a great number of **p**, blind Bartimaeus, *G3793*
11:18 the **p** was astonished at his doctrine. *G3793*
32 they feared the **p**: for all *men* counted *G2992*
12:12 but feared the **p**: for they knew that he *G3793*
37 And the common **p** heard him gladly. *G3793*
41 beheld how the **p** cast money into the *G3793*
14: 2 *day*, lest there be an uproar of the **p**. *G2992*
15:11 But the chief priests moved the **p**, that *G3793*
15 And *so* Pilate, willing to content the **p**, *G3793*
Lk 1:10 And the whole multitude of the **p** were *G2992*
17 make ready a **p** prepared for the Lord. *G2992*
21 And the **p** waited for Zacharias, and *G2992*
68 for he hath visited and redeemed his **p**, *G2992*
77 his **p** by the remission of their sins, *G2992*
2:10 of great joy, which shall be to all **p**. *G2992*
31 hast prepared before the face of all **p**; *G2992*
32 Gentiles, and the glory of thy **p** Israel. *G2992*
3:10 And the **p** asked him, saying, What *G3793*
15 And as the **p** were in expectation, and *G2992*
18 his exhortation preached he unto the **p**. *G2992*
21 Now when all the **p** were baptized, it *G2992*
4:42 place: and the **p** sought him, and came *G3793*
5: 1 And it came to pass, that, as the **p** *G3793*
3 down, and taught the **p** out of the ship. *G3793*
6:17 a great multitude of **p** out of all Judaea *G2992*
7: 1 of the **p**, he entered into Capernaum. *G2992*
9 and said unto the **p** that followed him, *G3793*
11 disciples went with him, and much **p**. *G3793*
12 and much **p** of the city was with her. *G3793*
16 us; and, That God hath visited his **p**. *G2992*
24 to speak unto the **p** concerning John, *G3793*
29 And all the **p** that heard *him*, and the *G2992*
8: 4 And when much **p** were gathered *G3793*
40 was returned, the **p** *gladly* received *G3793*
42 But as he went the **p** thronged him. *G3793*
47 him before all the **p** for what cause she *G2992*
9:11 And the **p**, when they knew *it*, followed *G3793*
13 should go and buy meat for all this **p**. *G2992*
18 saying, Whom say the **p** that I am? *G3793*
37 down from the hill, much **p** met him. *G3793*
11:14 the dumb spake; and the **p** wondered. *G3793*
29 And when the **p** were gathered thick *G3793*
12: 1 multitude of **p**, insomuch that they *G3793*
54 And he said also to the **p**, When ye see a *G3793*
13:14 and said unto the **p**, There are six days *G3793*
17 and all the **p** rejoiced for all the *G3793*
18:43 God: and all the **p**, when they saw *it*, *G2992*
19:47 chief of the **p** sought to destroy him, *G2992*
48 the **p** were very attentive to hear him. *G2992*
20: 1 as he taught the **p** in the temple, and *G2992*
6 But and if we say, Of men; all the **p** will *G2992*
9 Then began he to speak to the **p** this *G2992*
19 they feared the **p**: for they perceived *G2992*
26 words before the **p**: and they marvelled *G2992*
45 Then in the audience of all the **p** he *G2992*
21:23 in the land, and wrath upon this **p**. *G2992*
38 And all the **p** came early in the *G2992*
22: 2 might kill him; for they feared the **p**. *G2992*
66 the elders of the **p** and the chief priests *G2992*
23: 4 and *to* the **p**, I find no fault in this man. *G3793*
5 saying, He stirreth up the **p**, teaching *G2992*
13 chief priests and the rulers and the **p**, *G2992*
14 perverteth the **p**: and, behold, I, having *G2992*
27 a great company of **p**, and of women, *G2992*
35 And the **p** stood beholding. And the *G2992*
48 And all the **p** that came together to that *G3793*
24:19 deed and word before God and all the **p**: *G2992*
Jn 6:22 The day following, when the **p** which *G3793*
24 When the **p** therefore saw that Jesus *G3793*
7:12 among the **p** concerning him: for *G3793*
12 others said, Nay; but he deceiveth the **p**. *G3793*
20 The **p** answered and said, Thou hast a *G3793*
31 And many of the **p** believed on him, *G3793*

Jn 7:32 The Pharisees heard that the **p** *G3793*
40 Many of the **p** therefore, when they *G3793*
43 So there was a division among the **p** *G3793*
49 But this **p** who knoweth not the law are *G3793*
8: 2 and all the **p** came unto him; and *G2992*
11:42 but because of the **p** which stand by I *G3793*
50 **p**, and that the whole nation perish not. *G2992*
12: 9 Much **p** of the Jews therefore knew that *G3793*
12 On the next day much **p** that were *G3793*
17 The **p** therefore that was with him *G3793*
18 For this cause the **p** also met him, for *G3793*
29 The **p** therefore, that stood by, and *G3793*
34 The **p** answered him, We have heard *G3793*
18:14 that one man should die for the **p**. *G2992*
Act 2:47 favour with all the **p**. And the Lord *G2992*
3: 9 And all the **p** saw him walking and *G2992*
11 and John, all the **p** ran together unto *G2992*
12 answered unto the **p**, Ye men of Israel, *G2992*
23 shall be destroyed from among the **p**. *G2992*
4: 1 And as they spake unto the **p**, the *G2992*
2 Being grieved that they taught the **p**, *G2992*
8 Ye rulers of the **p**, and elders of Israel, *G2992*
10 all, and to all the **p** of Israel, that by the *G2992*
17 no further among the **p**, let us straitly *G2992*
21 because of the **p**: for all *men* glorified *G2992*
25 rage, and the **p** imagine vain things? *G2992*
27 the **p** of Israel, were gathered together, *G2992*
5:12 among the **p**; (and they were all with *G2992*
13 to them: but the **p** magnified them. *G2992*
20 temple to the **p** all the words of this life. *G2992*
25 in the temple, and teaching the **p**. *G2992*
26 **p**, lest they should have been stoned. *G2992*
34 among all the **p**, and commanded to *G2992*
37 drew away much **p** after him: he also *G2992*
6: 8 wonders and miracles among the **p**. *G2992*
12 And they stirred up the **p**, and the *G2992*
7:17 the **p** grew and multiplied in Egypt, *G2992*
34 the affliction of my **p** which is in Egypt, *G2992*
8: 6 And the **p** with one accord gave heed *G3793*
9 and bewitched the **p** of Samaria, giving *G1484*
10: 2 alms to the **p**, and prayed to God alway. *G2992*
41 Not to all the **p**, but unto witnesses *G2992*
42 to preach unto the **p**, and to testify that *G2992*
11:24 and much **p** was added unto the Lord. *G3793*
26 and taught much **p**. And the disciples *G3793*
12: 4 after Easter to bring him forth to the **p**. *G2992*
11 all the expectation of the **p** of the Jews. *G2992*
22 And the **p** gave a shout, *saying, It is* the *G1218*
13:15 word of exhortation for the **p**, say on. *G2992*
17 The God of this **p** of Israel chose our *G2992*
17 and exalted the **p** when they dwelt as *G2992*
24 of repentance to all the **p** of Israel. *G2992*
31 who are his witnesses unto the **p**. *G2992*
14:11 And when the **p** saw what Paul had *G3793*
13 would have done sacrifice with the **p**. *G3793*
14 and ran in among the **p**, crying out, *G3793*
18 they the **p**, that they had not done *G3793*
19 persuaded the **p**, and, having stoned *G3793*
15:14 to take out of them a **p** for his name. *G2992*
17: 5 and sought to bring them out to the **p**. *G1218*
8 And they troubled the **p** and the rulers *G3793*
13 came thither also, and stirred up the **p**. *G3793*
18:10 hurt thee: for I have much **p** in this city. *G2992*
19: 4 saying unto the **p**, that they should *G2992*
26 away much **p**, saying that they be *G3793*
30 the **p**, the disciples suffered him not. *G1218*
33 have made his defence unto the **p**. *G1218*
35 had appeased the **p**, he said, *Ye* men of *G3793*
21:27 up all the **p**, and laid hands on him, *G3793*
28 where against the **p**, and the law, and *G2992*
30 And all the city was moved, and the **p** *G2992*
35 of the soldiers for the violence of the **p**. *G3793*
36 For the multitude of the **p** followed *G2992*
39 thee, suffer me to speak unto the **p**. *G2992*
40 the hand unto the **p**. And when there *G2992*
23: 5 shalt not speak evil of the ruler of thy **p**. *G2992*
24:12 neither raising up the **p**, neither in the *G3793*
26:17 Delivering thee from the **p**, and *from* *G2992*
23 light unto the **p**, and to the Gentiles. *G2992*
28: 2 And the barbarous **p** shewed us no little *G915*
17 against the **p**, or customs of our fathers, *G2992*
26 Saying, Go unto this **p**, and say, *G2992*
27 For the heart of this **p** is waxed gross, *G2992*
Ro 9:25 I will call them my **p**, which were not *G2992*
25 were not my **p**; and her beloved, which *G2992*
26 Ye *are* not my **p**; there shall they be *G2992*
10:19 by *them that are* no **p**, *and* by a foolish *G1484*
21 unto a disobedient and gainsaying **p**. *G2992*
11: 1 I say then, Hath God cast away his **p**? *G2992*

Ro 11: 2 God hath not cast away his **p** which he G2992
15:10 he saith, Rejoice, ye Gentiles, with his **p**. G2992
11 all ye Gentiles; and laud him, all ye **p**. G2992
1Co 10: 7 it is written, The **p** sat down to eat and G2992
14:21 I speak unto this **p**; and yet for all that G2992
2Co 6:16 be their God, and they shall be my **p**. G2992
Tit 2:14 a peculiar **p**, zealous of good works. G2992
Heb 2:17 reconciliation for the sins of the **p**. G2992
4: 9 therefore a rest to the **p** of God. G2992
5: 3 **p**, so also for himself, to offer for sins. G2992
7: 5 to take tithes of the **p** according to the G2992
11 (for under it the **p** received the law,) G2992
8:10 them a God, and they shall be to me a **p**: G2992
9: 7 for himself, and *for* the errors of the **p**: G2992
19 precept to all the **p** according to the G2992
19 sprinkled both the book, and all the **p**, G2992
10:30 And again, The Lord shall judge his **p**. G2992
11:25 affliction with the **p** of God, than to G2992
13:12 he might sanctify the **p** with his own G2992
1Pt 2: 9 holy nation, a peculiar **p**; that ye should G2992
10 Which in time past *were* not a **p**, but G2992
10 but *are* now the **p** of God: which had G2992
2Pt 2: 1 also among the **p**, even as there shall be G2992
Jude 5 having saved the **p** out of the land of G2992
Rev 5: 9 kindred, and tongue, and **p**, and nation; G2992
7: 9 kindreds, and **p**, and tongues, G2992
11: 9 And they of the **p** and kindreds and G2992
14: 6 nation, and kindred, and tongue, and **p**, G2992
18: 4 Come out of her, my **p**, that ye be not G2992
19: 1 voice of much **p** in heaven, saying, G3793
21: 3 and they shall be his **p**, and God himself G2992

PEOPLES
Rev 10:11 **p**, and nations, and tongues, and kings. G2992
17:15 whore sitteth, are **p**, and multitudes, G2992

PEOPLE'S
Lev 9:15 And he brought the **p** offering, and H5971
Ezk 46:18 shall not take of the **p** inheritance by H5971
Mt 13:15 For this **p** heart is waxed gross, and G2992
Heb 7:27 and then for the **p**: for this he did once, G2992

PEOR
Nu 23:28 top of **P**, that looketh toward Jeshimon. H6465
25:18 in the matter of **P**, and in the matter of H6465
31:16 in the matter of **P**, and there was a H6465
Jos 22:17 *Is* the iniquity of **P** too little for us, H6465

PEOR'S
Nu 25:18 in the day of the plague for **P** sake. H6465

PERADVENTURE
Gen 18:24 **P** there be fifty righteous within the city: H194
28 **P** there shall lack five of the fifty H194
29 yet again, and said, **P** there be forty H194
30 and I will speak: **P** there shall thirty be H194
31 unto the Lord: **P** there shall be twenty H194
32 yet but this once: **P** ten shall be found H194
24: 5 And the servant said unto him, **P** the
39 And I said unto my master, **P** the
27:12 My father **p** will feel me, and I shall
31:31 afraid: for I said, **P** thou wouldest take H6435
32:20 I will see his face; **p** he will accept of me. H194
38:11 for he said, Lest **p** he die also, as his
42: 4 for he said, Lest **p** mischief befall him. H6435
43:12 in your hand; **p** it *was* an oversight: H194
44:34 *be* not with me? lest **p** I see the evil that
50:15 said, Joseph will **p** hate us, and will H3863
Ex 13:17 for God said, Lest **p** the people repent
32:30 go up unto the LORD; **p** I shall make an H194
Nu 22: 6 too mighty for me: **p** I shall prevail, *that* H194
11 now, curse me them; **p** I shall be able to H194
23: 3 and I will go: **p** the LORD will come H194
27 another place; **p** it will please God that H194
Jos 9: 7 unto the Hivites, **P** ye dwell among us; H194
1Sa 6: 5 the God of Israel: **p** he will lighten his H194
9: 6 let us go thither; **p** he can shew us our H194
1Ki 18: 5 unto all brooks: **p** we may find grass to H194
27 *or* **p** he sleepeth, and must be awaked. H194
20:31 the king of Israel: **p** he will save thy life. H194
2Ki 2:16 thy master: lest **p** the spirit of the LORD
Jer 20:10 my halting, *saying*, **P** he will be enticed, H194
Ro 5: 7 will one die: yet **p** for a good man some G5029
2Ti 2:25 themselves; if God **p** will give them G3379

PERAZIM
Isa 28:21 up as *in* mount **P**, he shall be wroth as

PERCEIVE
Dt 29: 4 you an heart to **p**, and eyes to see, and H3045
Jos 22:31 This day we **p** that the LORD *is* among H3045
1Sa 12:17 rain; that ye may **p** and see that your H3045
2Sa 19: 6 for this day I **p**, that if Absalom had H3045
2Ki 4: 9 Behold now, I **p** that this *is* an holy H3045
Job 9:11 not: he passeth on also, but I **p** him not. H995
23: 8 and backward, but I cannot **p** him: H995
Prv 1: 2 To know wisdom and instruction; to **p** H995
Ecc 3:22 Wherefore I **p** that *there is* nothing H7200
Isa 6: 9 not; and see ye indeed, but **p** not. H3045
33:19 than thou canst **p**; of a stammering H8085
Mt 13:14 and seeing ye shall see, and shall not **p**: G1492
Mk 4:12 That seeing they may see, and not **p**; G1492
7:18 also? Do ye not **p**, that whatsoever thing G3539
8:17 ye have no bread? **p** ye not yet, neither G3539
Lk 8:46 for I **p** that virtue is gone out of me. G1097
Jn 4:19 The woman saith unto him, Sir, I **p** G2334
12:19 among themselves, **P** ye how ye prevail G2334
Act 8:23 For I **p** that thou art in the gall of G3708
10:34 I **p** that God is no respecter of persons: G2638
17:22 men of Athens, I **p** that in all things ye G2334
27:10 And said unto them, Sirs, I **p** that this G2334
28:26 and seeing ye shall see, and not **p**: G1492
2Co 7: 8 I did repent: for I **p** that the same epistle G991
1Jn 3:16 Hereby **p** we the love *of God*, because G1097

PERCEIVED
Gen 19:33 her father; and he **p** not when she lay H3045
35 with him; and he **p** not when she lay H3045
Jdg 6:22 And when Gideon **p** that he *was* an H7200
1Sa 3: 8 Eli **p** that the LORD had called the child. H995
28:14 mantle. And Saul **p** that it *was* Samuel, H3045
2Sa 5:12 And David **p** that the LORD had H3045
12:19 whispered, David **p** that the child was H995
14: 1 Now Joab the son of Zeruiah **p** that the H3045
1Ki 22:33 of the chariots **p** that it *was* not the H7200
1Ch 14: 2 And David **p** that the LORD had H3045
2Ch 18:32 of the chariots **p** that it was not the H7200
Neh 6:12 And, lo, I **p** that God had not sent him; H5234
16 own eyes: for they **p** that this work was H3045
13:10 And I **p** that the portions of the Levites H3045
Est 4: 1 When Mordecai **p** all that was done, H3045
Job 38:18 Hast thou **p** the breadth of the earth? H995
Ecc 1:17 I **p** that this also is vexation of spirit. H3045
2:14 and I myself **p** also that one event H3045
Isa 64: 4 not heard, nor **p** by the ear, neither hath H238
Jer 23:18 LORD, and hath **p** and heard his word? H7200
38:27 with him; for the matter was not **p**. H8085
Mt 16: 8 *Which* when Jesus **p**, he said unto them, G1097
21:45 parables, they **p** that he spake of them. G1097
22:18 But Jesus **p** their wickedness, and said, G1097
Mk 2: 8 And immediately when Jesus **p** in his G1921
Lk 1:22 them: and they **p** that he had seen a G1921
5:22 But when Jesus **p** their thoughts, he G1921
9:45 them, that they **p** it not: and they feared G143
20:19 people: for they **p** that he had spoken G1097
23 But he **p** their craftiness, and said unto G2657
Jn 6:15 When Jesus therefore **p** that they would G1097
Act 4:13 Peter and John, and **p** that they were G2638
23: 6 But when Paul **p** that the one part were G1097
29 Whom I **p** to be accused of questions of G2147
Gal 2: 9 to be pillars, **p** the grace that was given G1097

PERCEIVEST
Prv 14: 7 **p** not *in him* the lips of knowledge. H3045
Lk 6:41 brother's eye, but **p** not the beam that G2657

PERCEIVETH
Job 14:21 are brought low, but he **p** *it* not of them. H995
33:14 once, yea twice, *yet man* **p** it not. H7789
Prv 31:18 She **p** that her merchandise *is* good: H2938

PERCEIVING
Mk 12:28 together, and **p** that he had answered G1492
Lk 9:47 And Jesus, **p** the thought of their heart, G1492
Act 14: 9 and **p** that he had faith to be healed, G1492

PERDITION
Jn 17:12 of **p**; that the scripture might be fulfilled. G684
Php 1:28 them an evident token of **p**, but to you of G684
2Th 2: 3 that man of sin be revealed, the son of **p**; G684
1Ti 6: 9 which drown men in destruction and **p**. G684
Heb 10:39 who draw back unto **p**; but of them that G684
2Pt 3: 7 day of judgment and **p** of ungodly men. G684
Rev 17: 8 pit, and go into **p**: and they that dwell on G684
11 and is of the seven, and goeth into **p**. G684

PERES
Dan 5:28 **P**; Thy kingdom is divided, and given to H6537

PERESH
1Ch 7:16 called his name **P**; and the name of his H6570

PEREZ
1Ch 27: 3 Of the children of **P** *was* the chief of all H6557
Neh 11: 4 son of Mahalaleel, of the children of **P**; H6557
6 All the sons of **P** that dwelt at H6557

PEREZ-UZZA
1Ch 13:11 that place is called **P** to this day. H6560

PEREZ-UZZAH
2Sa 6: 8 the name of the place **P** to this day. H6560

PERFECT
Gen 6: 9 a just man *and* **p** in his generations, H8549
17: 1 God; walk before me, and be thou **p**. H8549
Lev 22:21 or sheep, it shall be **p** to be accepted; H8549
Dt 18:13 Thou shalt be **p** with the LORD thy H8549
25:15 *But* thou shalt have a **p** and just H8003
15 and just weight, a **p** and just measure H8003
32: 4 *He is* the Rock, his work *is* **p**: for all his H8549
1Sa 14:41 of Israel, Give a **p** *lot*. And Saul and H8549
2Sa 22:31 *As for* God, his way *is* **p**; the word of the H8549
33 *and* power: and he maketh my way **p**. H8549
1Ki 8:61 Let your heart therefore be **p** with the H8003
11: 4 his heart was not **p** with the LORD his H8003
15: 3 his heart was not **p** with the LORD his H8003
14 heart was **p** with the LORD all his days. H8003
2Ki 20: 3 in truth and with a **p** heart, and have H8003
1Ch 12:38 rank, came with a **p** heart to Hebron, H8003
28: 9 serve him with a **p** heart and with a H8003
29: 9 because with **p** heart they offered H8003
19 And give unto Solomon my son a **p** H8003
2Ch 4:21 *made he of* gold, *and* that **p** gold; H4357
15:17 the heart of Asa was **p** all his days. H8003
16: 9 whose heart *is* **p** toward him. Herein H8003
19: 9 LORD, faithfully, and with a **p** heart. H8003
25: 2 of the LORD, but not with a **p** heart. H8003
Ezr 7:12 of heaven, **p** *peace*, and at such a time. H1585
Job 1: 1 and that man was **p** and upright, and H8535
8 him in the earth, a **p** and an upright H8535
2: 3 him in the earth, a **p** and an upright H8535
8:20 Behold, God will not cast away a **p** H8535
9:20 I *am* **p**, it shall also prove me perverse. H8535
21 *Though* I *were* **p**, *yet* would I not know H8535
22 *it*, He destroyeth the **p** and the wicked. H8535
22: 3 *to him*, that thou makest thy ways **p**? H8552
36: 4 he that is **p** in knowledge *is* with thee. H8549
37:16 works of him which is **p** in knowledge? H8549
Ps 18:30 *As for* God, his way *is* **p**: the word of the H8549
32 with strength, and maketh my way **p**. H8549
19: 7 The law of the LORD *is* **p**, converting H8549
37:37 Mark the **p** *man*, and behold the H8535
64: 4 That they may shoot in secret at the **p**: H8535
101: 2 I will behave myself wisely in a **p** way. H8549
2 walk within my house with a **p** heart. H8537
6 walketh in a **p** way, he shall serve me. H8549
138: 8 The LORD will **p** *that which* concerneth H1584
139:22 I hate them with **p** hatred: I count them H8503
Prv 2:21 the land, and the **p** shall remain in it. H8549
4:18 shineth more and more unto the **p** day. H3559
11: 5 The righteousness of the **p** shall direct H8549
Isa 18: 5 when the bud is **p**, and the sour grape H8552
26: 3 Thou wilt keep *him* in **p** peace, *whose* H7965
38: 3 in truth and with a **p** heart, and have H8003
42:19 *is* **p**, and blind as the LORD'S servant? H7999
Ezk 16:14 thy beauty: for it *was* **p** through my H3632
27: 3 Tyrus, thou hast said, I *am* of **p** beauty. H3632
11 about; they have made thy beauty **p**. H3634
28:12 sum, full of wisdom, and **p** in beauty. H3632
15 Thou *wast* **p** in thy ways from the day H8549
Mt 5:48 Be ye therefore **p**, even as your Father G5046
48 as your Father which is in heaven is **p**. G5046
19:21 Jesus said unto him, If thou wilt be **p**, G5046
Lk 1: 3 It seemed good to me also, having had **p** G199
6:40 one that is **p** shall be as his master. G2675
Jn 17:23 they may be made **p** in one; and that G5048
Act 3:16 **p** soundness in the presence of you all. G3647
22: 3 according to the **p** manner of the law of G195
24:22 having more **p** knowledge of *that* way, G197
Ro 12: 2 and acceptable, and **p**, will of God. G5046
1Co 2: 6 them that are **p**: yet not the wisdom G5046
13:10 But when that which is **p** is come, then G5046
2Co 12: 9 strength is made **p** in weakness. Most G5048
13:11 Finally, brethren, farewell. Be **p**, be of G2675

Gal 3: 3 Spirit, are ye now made **p** by the flesh? G2005
Eph 4:13 the Son of God, unto a **p** man, unto the G5046
Php 3:12 were already **p**: but I follow after, if G5048
15 Let us therefore, as many as be **p**, be G5046
Col 1:28 present every man **p** in Christ Jesus: G5046
4:12 **p** and complete in all the will of God. G5046
1Th 3:10 **p** that which is lacking in your faith? G2675
2Ti 3:17 That the man of God may be **p**, throughly G739
Heb 2:10 of their salvation **p** through sufferings. G5048
5: 9 And being made **p**, he became the G5048
7:19 For the law made nothing **p**, but the G5048
9: 9 **p**, as pertaining to the conscience; G5048
11 a greater and more **p** tabernacle, not G5046
10: 1 make the comers thereunto **p**. G5048
11:40 they without us should not be made **p**. G5048
12:23 and to the spirits of just men made **p**, G5048
13:21 Make you **p** in every good work to do G2675
Jas 1: 4 But let patience have *her* **p** work, that G5046
4 may be **p** and entire, wanting nothing. G5046
17 Every good gift and every **p** gift is from G5046
25 But whoso looketh into the **p** law of G5046
2:22 works, and by works was faith made **p**? G5048
3: 2 the same *is* a **p** man, *and* able also G5046
1Pt 5:10 you **p**, stablish, strengthen, settle *you*. G2675
1Jn 4:17 Herein is our love made **p**, that we may G5048
18 There is no fear in love; but **p** love G5046
18 He that feareth is not made **p** in love. G5048
Rev 3: 2 not found thy works **p** before God. G4137

PERFECTED
2Ch 8:16 *So* the house of the LORD was **p**. H8003
24:13 and the work was **p** by them, and they H724
Ezk 27: 4 seas, thy builders have **p** thy beauty. H3634
Mt 21:16 and sucklings thou hast **p** praise? G2675
Lk 13:32 morrow, and the third *day* I shall be **p**. G5048
Heb 10:14 For by one offering he hath **p** for ever G5048
1Jn 2: 5 **p**: hereby know we that we are in him. G5048
4:12 dwelleth in us, and his love is **p** in us. G5048

PERFECTING
2Co 7: 1 spirit, **p** holiness in the fear of God. G2005
Eph 4:12 For the **p** of the saints, for the work of G2677

PERFECTION
Job 11: 7 thou find out the Almighty unto **p**? H8503
15:29 prolong the **p** thereof upon the earth. H4512
28: 3 and searcheth out all **p**: the stones of H8503
Ps 50: 2 Out of Zion, the **p** of beauty, God hath H4359
119:96 I have seen an end of all **p**: *but* thy H8502
Isa 47: 9 upon thee in their **p** for the multitude H8537
Lam 2:15 **p** of beauty, The joy of the whole earth? H3632
Lk 8:14 of *this* life, and bring no fruit to **p**. G5052
2Co 13: 9 and this also we wish, *even* your **p**. G2676
Heb 6: 1 let us go on unto **p**; not laying again the G5047
7:11 If therefore **p** were by the Levitical G5050

PERFECTLY
Jer 23:20 in the latter days ye shall consider it **p**. H998
Mt 14:36 many as touched were made **p** whole. G1295
Act 18:26 unto him the way of God more **p**. G197
23:15 something more **p** concerning him: and G197
20 would inquire somewhat of him more **p**. G197
1Co 1:10 you; but *that* ye be **p** joined together in G2675
1Th 5: 2 For yourselves know **p** that the day of G199

PERFECTNESS
Col 3:14 *put on* charity, which is the bond of **p**. G5047

PERFORM
Gen 26: 3 and I will **p** the oath which I sware H6965
Ex 18:18 thou art not able to **p** it thyself alone. H6213
Nu 4:23 all that enter in to **p** the service, to do H6633
Dt 4:13 you to **p**, *even* ten commandments; H6213
9: 5 and that he may **p** the word which the H6965
23:23 thou shalt keep and **p**; *even* a freewill H6213
25: 5 her to him to wife, and **p** the duty of an
7 not **p** the duty of my husband's brother.
Ru 3:13 *that* if he will **p** unto thee the part of
1Sa 3:12 In that day I will **p** against Eli all *things* H6965
2Sa 14:15 will **p** the request of his handmaid. H6213
1Ki 6:12 them; then will I **p** my word with thee, H6965
12:15 that he might **p** his saying, which the H6965
2Ki 23: 3 and all *their* soul, to **p** the words of this H6965
24 that he might **p** the words of the law H6965
2Ch 10:15 the LORD might **p** his word, which he H6965
34:31 with all his soul, to **p** the words of the H6213
Est 5: 8 petition, and to **p** my request, let the H6213
Job 5:12 their hands cannot **p** *their* enterprise. H6213
Ps 21:11 device, *which* they are not able *to* **p**.
Ps 61: 8 for ever, that I may daily **p** my vows. H7999
119:106 I have sworn, and I will **p** *it*, that I will H6965
112 I have inclined mine heart to **p** thy H6213
Isa 9: 7 zeal of the LORD of hosts will **p** this. H6213
19:21 vow a vow unto the LORD, and **p** *it*. H7999
44:28 and shall **p** all my pleasure: even H7999
Jer 1:12 seen: for I will hasten my word to **p** it. H6213
11: 5 That I may **p** the oath which I have H6965
28: 6 do so: the LORD **p** thy words which H6965
29:10 I will visit you, and **p** my good word H6965
33:14 the LORD, that I will **p** that good thing H6965
44:25 We will surely **p** our vows that we have H6213
25 your vows, and surely **p** your vows. H6213
Ezk 12:25 word, and will **p** it, saith the Lord GOD. H6213
Mic 7:20 Thou wilt **p** the truth to Jacob, *and* the H5414
Nah 1:15 thy solemn feasts, **p** thy vows: for the H7999
Mt 5:33 but shalt **p** unto the Lord thine oaths: G591
Lk 1:72 To **p** the mercy *promised* to our G4160
Ro 4:21 he had promised, he was able also to **p**. G4160
7:18 *how* to **p** that which is good I find not. G2716
2Co 8:11 Now therefore **p** the doing *of it*; that as G2005
Php 1: 6 will **p** *it* until the day of Jesus Christ: G2005

PERFORMANCE
Lk 1:45 for there shall be a **p** of those things G5050
2Co 8:11 *be* a **p** also out of that which ye have. G2005

PERFORMED
1Sa 15:11 following me, and hath not **p** my H6965
13 **p** the commandment of the LORD. H6965
2Sa 21:14 his father: and they **p** all that the king H6213
1Ki 8:20 And the LORD hath **p** his word that he H6965
2Ch 6:10 The LORD therefore hath **p** his word H6965
Neh 9: 8 **p** thy words; for thou *art* righteous: H6965
Est 1:15 she hath not **p** the commandment H6213
5: 6 to the half of the kingdom it shall be **p**. H6213
7: 2 be **p**, *even* to the half of the kingdom. H6213
Ps 65: 1 Sion: and unto thee shall the vow be **p**. H7999
Isa 10:12 the Lord hath **p** his whole work upon H1214
Jer 23:20 and till he have **p** the thoughts of his H6965
30:24 *it*, and until he have **p** the intents of his H6965
34:18 which have not **p** the words of the H6965
35:14 to drink wine, are **p**; for unto this day H6965
16 of Rechab have **p** the commandment H6965
51:29 the LORD shall be **p** against Babylon, H6965
Ezk 37:14 spoken *it*, and **p** *it*, saith the LORD. H6213
Lk 1:20 things shall be **p**, because thou believest G1096
2:39 And when they had **p** all things G5055
Ro 15:28 When therefore I have **p** this, and have G2005

PERFORMETH
Neh 5:13 his labour, that **p** not this promise, H6965
Job 23:14 For he **p** *the thing that is* appointed for H7999
Ps 57: 2 high; unto God that **p** *all things* for me. H1584
Isa 44:26 of his servant, and **p** the counsel of his H7999

PERFORMING
Nu 15: 3 or a sacrifice in **p** a vow, or in a freewill H6381
8 or *for* a sacrifice in **p** a vow, or peace H6381

PERFUME
Ex 30:35 And thou shalt make it a **p**, a confection H7004
37 And *as for* the **p** which thou shalt H7004
Prv 27: 9 Ointment and **p** rejoice the heart: so H7004

PERFUMED
Prv 7:17 I have **p** my bed with myrrh, aloes, and H5130
Song 3: 6 like pillars of smoke, **p** with myrrh and H6999

PERFUMES
Isa 57: 9 didst increase thy **p**, and didst send thy H7547

PERGA
Act 13:13 they came to **P** in Pamphylia: and G4011
14 But when they departed from **P**, they G4011
14:25 word in **P**, they went down into Attalia: G4011

PERGAMOS
Rev 1:11 unto Smyrna, and unto **P**, and unto G4010
2:12 And to the angel of the church in **P** G4010

PERHAPS
Act 8:22 and pray God, if **p** the thought of thine G686
2Co 2: 7 comfort *him*, lest **p** such a one should G3381
Phlm 15 For **p** he therefore departed for a G5029

PERIDA
Neh 7:57 children of Sophereth, the children of **P**, H6514

PERIL
Lam 5: 9 We gat our bread with *the* **p** *of* our lives
Ro 8:35 famine, or nakedness, or **p**, or sword? G2794

PERILOUS
2Ti 3: 1 This know also, that in the last days **p** G5467

PERILS
2Co 11:26 *In* journeyings often, *in* **p** of waters, *in* G2794
26 *in* perils of waters, *in* **p** of robbers, *in* G2794
26 perils of robbers, *in* **p** by *mine own* G2794
26 countrymen, *in* **p** by the heathen, *in* G2794
26 by the heathen, *in* **p** in the city, *in* perils G2794
26 in the city, *in* **p** in the wilderness, *in* G2794
26 the wilderness, *in* **p** in the sea, *in* perils G2794
26 in the sea, *in* **p** among false brethren; G2794

PERISH
Gen 41:36 that the land **p** not through the famine. H3772
Ex 19:21 the LORD to gaze, and many of them **p**. H5307
21:26 of his maid, that it **p**; he shall let him go H7843
Lev 26:38 And ye shall **p** among the heathen, and H6
Nu 17:12 Behold, we die, we **p**, we all perish. H6
12 Behold, we die, we perish, we all **p**. H6
24:20 his latter end *shall be* that he **p** for ever. H8
24 afflict Eber, and he also shall **p** for ever. H8
Dt 4:26 ye shall soon utterly **p** from off the land H6
8:19 you this day that ye shall surely **p**. H6
20 face, so shall ye **p**; because ye would not H6
11:17 fruit; and *lest* ye **p** quickly from off the H6
26: 5 A Syrian ready to **p** *was* my father, and H6
28:20 and until thou **p** quickly; because of the H6
22 and they shall pursue thee until thou **p**. H6
30:18 that ye shall surely **p**, *and that* ye shall H6
Jos 23:13 your eyes, until ye **p** from off this good H6
16 you, and ye shall **p** quickly from off the H6
Jdg 5:31 So let all thine enemies **p**, O LORD: but H6
1Sa 26:10 or he shall descend into battle, and **p**. H5595
27: 1 his heart, I shall now **p** one day by the H5595
2Ki 9: 8 For the whole house of Ahab shall **p**: and H6
Est 3:13 and to cause to **p**, all Jews, both young H6
4:16 according to the law: and if I **p**, I perish. H6
16 according to the law: and if I perish, I **p**. H6
7: 4 to be slain, and to **p**. But if we had been H6
8:11 and to cause to **p**, all the power of the H6
9:28 memorial of them **p** from their seed. H5486
Job 3: 3 Let the day **p** wherein I was born, and H6
4: 9 By the blast of God they **p**, and by the H6
20 they **p** for ever without any regarding *it*. H6
6:18 turned aside; they go to nothing, and **p**. H6
8:13 God; and the hypocrite's hope shall **p**: H6
18:17 His remembrance shall **p** from the earth, H6
20: 7 *Yet* he shall **p** for ever like his own dung: H6
29:13 The blessing of him that was ready to **p** H6
31:19 If I have seen any **p** for want of clothing, H6
34:15 All flesh shall **p** together, and man H1478
36:12 But if they obey not, they shall **p** by the H5674
Ps 1: 6 but the way of the ungodly shall **p**. H6
2:12 Kiss the Son, lest he be angry, and ye **p** H6
9: 3 they shall fall and **p** at thy presence. H6
18 of the poor shall *not* **p** for ever. H6
37:20 But the wicked shall **p**, and the enemies H6
41: 5 me, When shall he die, and his name **p**? H6
49:10 **p**, and leave their wealth to others. H6
12 abideth not: he is like the beasts *that* **p**. H1820
20 not, is like the beasts *that* **p**. H1820
68: 2 let the wicked **p** at the presence of God. H6
73:27 far from thee shall **p**: thou hast destroyed H6
80:16 they **p** at the rebuke of thy countenance. H6
83:17 yea, let them be put to shame, and **p**: H6
92: 9 thine enemies shall **p**; all the workers of H6
102:26 They shall **p**, but thou shalt endure: yea, H6
112:10 away: the desire of the wicked shall **p**. H6
146: 4 his earth; in that very day his thoughts **p**. H6
Prv 10:28 but the expectation of the wicked shall **p**. H6
11: 7 **p**: and the hope of unjust *men* perisheth. H6
10 and when the wicked **p**, *there is* shouting. H6
19: 9 and *he that* speaketh lies shall **p**. H6
21:28 A false witness shall **p**: but the man that H6
28:28 but when they **p**, the righteous increase. H6
29:18 Where *there is* no vision, the people **p**: H6544
31: 6 that is ready to **p**, and wine unto those H6
Ecc 5:14 But those riches **p** by evil travail: and he H6
Isa 26:14 them, and made all their memory to **p**. H6
27:13 were ready to **p** in the land of Assyria, H6
29:14 wise *men* shall **p**, and the understanding H6
41:11 and they that strive with thee shall **p**. H6
60:12 not serve thee shall **p**; yea, *those* nations H6
Jer 4: 9 of the king shall **p**, and the heart of the H6

P

Jer 6:21 the neighbour and his friend shall p. H6
10:11 *even* they shall p from the earth, and H7
15 in the time of their visitation they shall p. H6
18:18 the law shall not p from the priest, nor H6
27:10 I should drive you out, and ye should p. H6
15 and that ye might p, ye, and the prophets H6
40:15 scattered, and the remnant in Judah p? H6
48: 8 valley also shall p, and the plain shall be H6
51:18 in the time of their visitation they shall p. H6
Ezk 7:26 but the law shall p from the priest, and H6
25: 7 I will cause thee to p out of the countries: H6
Dan 2:18 fellows should not p with the rest of the H7
Am 1: 8 Philistines shall p, saith the Lord GOD. H6
2:14 Therefore the flight shall p from the H6
3:15 of ivory shall p, and the great houses H6
Jna 1: 6 God will think upon us, that we p not. H6
14 thee, let us not p for this man's life, and H6
3: 9 from his fierce anger, that we p not? H6
Zec 9: 5 and the king shall p from Gaza, and H6
Mt 5:29 thy members should p, and not *that* thy G622
30 thy members should p, and not *that* thy G622
8:25 awoke him, saying, Lord, save us: we p. G622
9:17 and the bottles p: but they put new wine G622
18:14 that one of these little ones should p. G622
26:52 take the sword shall p with the sword. G622
Mk 4:38 him, Master, carest thou not that we p? G622
Lk 5:37 and be spilled, and the bottles shall p. G622
8:24 Master, master, we p. Then he arose, and G622
13: 3 except ye repent, ye shall all likewise p. G622
5 except ye repent, ye shall all likewise p. G622
33 be that a prophet p out of Jerusalem. G622
15:17 and to spare, and I p with hunger! G622
21:18 there shall not an hair of your head p. G622
Jn 3:15 in him should not p, but have eternal life. G622
16 should not p, but have everlasting life. G622
10:28 they shall never p, neither shall any *man* G622
11:50 people, and that the whole nation p not. G622
Act 8:20 But Peter said unto him, Thy money p G1498
13:41 Behold, ye despisers, and wonder, and p: G853
Ro 2:12 law shall also p without law: and as G622
1Co 1:18 is to them that p foolishness; but unto G622
8:11 weak brother p, for whom Christ died? G622
2Co 2:15 them that are saved, and in them that p: G622
4:16 our outward man p, yet the inward G1311
Col 2:22 Which all are to p with the using;) after G1519
2Th 2:10 in them that p; because they received G622
Heb 1:11 They shall p; but thou remainest; and G622
2Pt 2:12 shall utterly p in their own corruption; G2704
3: 9 that any should p, but that all should G622

PERISHED
Nu 16:33 they p from among the congregation. H6
21:30 We have shot at them; Heshbon is p H6
Jos 22:20 that man p not alone in his iniquity. H1478
2Sa 1:27 mighty fallen, and the weapons of war p! H6
Job 4: 7 Remember, I pray thee, who *ever* p, H6
30: 2 hands *profit* me, in whom old age was p? H6
Ps 9: 6 cities; their memorial is p with them. H6
10:16 ever: the heathen are p out of his land. H6
83:10 *Which* p at En-dor: they became *as* H8045
119:92 I should then have p in mine affliction. H6
Ecc 9: 6 their envy, is now p; neither have they H6
Jer 7:28 is p, and is cut off from their mouth. H6
48:36 the riches *that* he hath gotten are p. H6
49: 7 Teman? is counsel p from the prudent? H6
Lam 3:18 and my hope is p from the LORD: H6
Joel 1:11 because the harvest of the field is p. H6
Jna 4:10 came up in a night, and p in a night: H6
Mic 4: 9 is thy counsellor p? for pangs have taken H6
7: 2 The good *man* is p out of the earth: and H6
Mt 8:32 place into the sea, and p in the waters. G599
Lk 11:51 of Zacharias, which p between the altar G622
Act 5:37 after him: he also p; and all, *even* as G622
1Co 15:18 which are fallen asleep in Christ are p. G622
Heb 11:31 By faith the harlot Rahab p not with G4881
2Pt 3: 6 was, being overflowed with water, p: G622
Jude 11 reward, and p in the gainsaying of Core. G622

PERISHETH
Job 4:11 The old lion p for lack of prey, and the H6
Prv 11: 7 perish: and the hope of unjust *men* p. H6
Ecc 7:15 is a just *man* that p in his righteousness, H6
Isa 57: 1 The righteous p, and no man layeth *it* to H6
Jer 9:12 for what the land p *and* is burned up like H6
48:46 the people of Chemosh p: for thy sons are H6
Jn 6:27 Labour not for the meat which p, but for G622
Jas 1:11 of the fashion of it p: so also shall the rich G622
1Pt 1: 7 than of gold that p, though it be tried G622

PERISHING
Job 33:18 pit, and his life from p by the sword. H5674

PERIZZITE
Gen 13: 7 and the P dwelled then in the land. H6522
Ex 33: 2 and the P, the Hivite, and the Jebusite: H6522
34:11 the P, and the Hivite, and the Jebusite. H6522
Jos 9: 1 the Canaanite, the P, the Hivite, and the H6522
11: 3 Hittite, and the P, and the Jebusite in H6522

PERIZZITES
Gen 15:20 And the Hittites, and the P, and the H6522
34:30 and the P: and I *being* few in number, H6522
Ex 3: 8 P, and the Hivites, and the Jebusites. H6522
17 Amorites, and the P, and the Hivites, H6522
23:23 Hittites, and the P, and the Canaanites, H6522
Dt 7: 1 and the P, and the Hivites, and H6522
20:17 and the P, the Hivites, and the H6522
Jos 3:10 Hivites, and the P, and the Girgashites, H6522
12: 8 the P, the Hivites, and the Jebusites: H6522
17:15 in the land of the P and of the giants, if H6522
24:11 the Amorites, and the P, and the H6522
Jdg 1: 4 and the P into their hand: and H6522
5 and they slew the Canaanites and the P. H6522
3: 5 and P, and Hivites, and Jebusites: H6522
1Ki 9:20 Hittites, P, Hivites, and Jebusites, H6522
2Ch 8: 7 Amorites, and the P, and the Hivites, H6522
Ezr 9: 1 the Hittites, the P, the Jebusites, the H6522
Neh 9: 8 Amorites, and the P, and the Jebusites, H6522

PERJURED
1Ti 1:10 for liars, for p persons, and if there G1965

PERMISSION
1Co 7: 6 But I speak this by p, *and* not of G4774

PERMIT
1Co 16: 7 to tarry a while with you, if the Lord p. G2010
Heb 6: 3 And this will we do, if God p. G2010

PERMITTED
Act 26: 1 Paul, Thou art p to speak for thyself. G2010
1Co 14:34 for it is not p unto them to speak; G2010

PERNICIOUS
2Pt 2: 2 And many shall follow their p ways; by G684

PERPETUAL
Gen 9:12 that *is* with you, for p generations: H5769
Ex 29: 9 be theirs for a p statute: and thou shalt H5769
30: 8 incense upon it, a p incense before the H8548
31:16 their generations, *for* a p covenant. H5769
Lev 3:17 *It shall be* a p statute for your H5769
6:20 for a meat offering p, half of it in the H8548
24: 9 the LORD made by fire by a p statute. H5769
25:34 not be sold; for it *is* their p possession. H5769
Nu 19:21 And it shall be a p statute unto them, H5769
Ps 9: 6 are come to a p end: and thou hast H5331
74: 3 Lift up thy feet unto the p desolations; H5331
78:66 parts: he put them to a p reproach. H5769
Jer 5:22 of the sea by a p decree, that it cannot H5769
8: 5 slidden back by a p backsliding? they H5329
15:18 Why is my pain p, and my wound H5331
18:16 To make their land desolate, *and* a p H5769
23:40 p shame, which shall not be forgotten. H5769
25: 9 and an hissing, and p desolations. H5769
12 and will make it p desolations. H5769
49:13 all the cities thereof shall be p wastes. H5769
50: 5 p covenant *that* shall not be forgotten. H5769
51:39 p sleep, and not wake, saith the LORD. H5769
57 and they shall sleep a p sleep, and not H5769
Ezk 35: 5 Because thou hast had a p hatred, and H5769
9 I will make thee p desolations, and thy H5769
46:14 by a p ordinance unto the LORD. H5769
Hab 3: 6 scattered, the p hills did bow: his ways H5769
Zep 2: 9 saltpits, and a p desolation: the residue H5769

PERPETUALLY
1Ki 9: 3 mine heart shall be there p. H3605+H3117
2Ch 7:16 mine heart shall be there p. H3605+H3117
Am 1:11 tear p, and he kept his wrath for ever: H5703

PERPLEXED
Est 3:15 to drink; but the city Shushan was p. H943
Joel 1:18 herds of cattle are p, because they have H943
Lk 9: 7 him: and he was p, because that it was G1280
24: 4 they were much p thereabout, behold, G1280
2Co 4: 8 distressed; *we are* p, but not in despair; G639

PERPLEXITY
Isa 22: 5 down, and of p by the Lord GOD of H3998
Mic 7: 4 visitation cometh; now shall be their p. H3998
Lk 21:25 with p; the sea and the waves roaring; G640

PERSECUTE
Job 19:22 Why do ye p me as God, and are not H7291
28 But ye should say, Why p we him, H7291
Ps 7: 1 all them that p me, and deliver me: H7291
5 Let the enemy p my soul, and take *it*; H7291
10: 2 The wicked in *his* pride doth p the H1814
31:15 enemies, and from them that p me. H7291
35: 3 against them that p me: say unto my H7291
6 and let the angel of the LORD p them. H7291
69:26 For they p *him* whom thou hast H7291
71:11 Saying, God hath forsaken him: p and H7291
83:15 So p them with thy tempest, and make H7291
119:84 execute judgment on them that p me? H7291
86 they p me wrongfully; help thou me. H7291
Jer 17:18 Let them be confounded that p me, but H7291
29:18 And I will p them with the H7291+H310
Lam 3:66 P and destroy them in anger from H7291
Mt 5:11 revile you, and p *you*, and shall say all G1377
44 which despitefully use you, and p you; G1377
10:23 But when they p you in this city, flee ye G1377
23:34 and p *them* from city to city: G1377
Lk 11:49 and *some* of them they shall slay and p: G1559
21:12 on you, and p *you*, delivering *you* G1377
Jn 5:16 And therefore did the Jews p Jesus, and G1377
15:20 me, they will also p you; if they have G1377
Ro 12:14 Bless them which p you: bless, and G1377

PERSECUTED
Dt 30: 7 on them that hate thee, which p thee. H7291
Ps 109:16 shew mercy, but p the poor and needy H7291
119:161 Princes have p me without a cause: but H7291
143: 3 For the enemy hath p my soul; he hath H7291
Isa 14: 6 in anger, is p, *and* none hindereth. H4783
Lam 3:43 Thou hast covered with anger, and p H7291
Mt 5:10 Blessed *are* they which are p for G1377
12 in heaven: for so p they the prophets G1377
Jn 15:20 lord. If they have p me, they will also G1377
Act 7:52 not your fathers p? and they have slain G1377
22: 4 And I p this way unto the death, G1377
26:11 I p *them* even unto strange cities. G1377
1Co 4:12 reviled, we bless; being p, we suffer it: G1377
15: 9 apostle, because I p the church of God. G1377
2Co 4: 9 P, but not forsaken; cast down, but not G1377
Gal 1:13 I p the church of God, and wasted it: G1377
23 That he which p us in times past now G1377
4:29 after the flesh p him *that was born* G1377
1Th 2:15 and have p us; and they please G1559
Rev 12:13 unto the earth, he p the woman which G1377

PERSECUTEST
Act 9: 4 unto him, Saul, Saul, why p thou me? G1377
5 Jesus whom thou p: *it is* hard for thee to G1377
22: 7 unto me, Saul, Saul, why p thou me? G1377
8 I am Jesus of Nazareth, whom thou p. G1377
26:14 Saul, Saul, why p thou me? *it is* hard G1377
15 And he said, I am Jesus whom thou p. G1377

PERSECUTING
Php 3: 6 Concerning zeal, p the church; G1377

PERSECUTION
Lam 5: 5 Our necks *are* under p: we labour, *and* H7291
Mt 13:21 tribulation or p ariseth because of the G1375
Mk 4:17 when affliction or p ariseth for the G1375
Act 8: 1 there was a great p against the church G1375
11:19 abroad upon the p that arose about G2347
13:50 the city, and raised p against Paul and G1375
Ro 8:35 or distress, or p, or famine, or G1375
Gal 5:11 why do I yet suffer p? then is the offence G1377
6:12 should suffer p for the cross of Christ. G1377
2Ti 3:12 live godly in Christ Jesus shall suffer p. G1377

PERSECUTIONS
Mk 10:30 p; and in the world to come eternal life. G1375
2Co 12:10 in necessities, in p, in distresses for G1375
2Th 1: 4 your p and tribulations that ye endure: G1375
2Ti 3:11 P, afflictions, which came unto me at G1375
11 at Lystra; what p I endured: but out of G1375

PERSECUTOR
1Ti 1:13 Who was before a blasphemer, and a p, G1376

PERSECUTORS
Neh 9:11 land; and their p thou threwest into the H7291

Ps 7:13 he ordaineth his arrows against the p. H1814
119:157 Many *are* my p and mine enemies; *yet* H7291
142: 6 from my p; for they are stronger than I. H7291
Jer 15:15 revenge me of my p; take me not away H7291
20:11 one: therefore my p shall stumble, and H7291
Lam 1: 3 her p overtook her between the straits. H7291
4:19 Our p are swifter than the eagles of the H7291

PERSEVERANCE
Eph 6:18 all p and supplication for all saints; *G4343*

PERSIA
2Ch 36:20 sons until the reign of the kingdom of P: H6539
22 Now in the first year of Cyrus king of P, H6539
22 spirit of Cyrus king of P, that he made a H6539
23 Thus saith Cyrus king of P, All the H6539
Ezr 1: 1 Now in the first year of Cyrus king of P, H6539
1 spirit of Cyrus king of P, that he made a H6539
2 Thus saith Cyrus king of P, The LORD H6539
8 Even those did Cyrus king of P bring H6539
3: 7 grant that they had of Cyrus king of P. H6539
4: 3 the king of P hath commanded us. H6539
5 of Cyrus king of P, even until the reign H6539
5 even until the reign of Darius king of P. H6539
7 Artaxerxes king of P; and the writing of H6539
24 year of the reign of Darius king of P. H6540
6:14 and Darius, and Artaxerxes king of P. H6540
7: 1 of Artaxerxes king of P, Ezra the son of H6539
9: 9 of the kings of P, to give us a reviving, H6539
Est 1: 3 the power of P and Media, the nobles H6539
14 seven princes of P and Media, which H6539
18 *Likewise* shall the ladies of P and H6539
10: 2 chronicles of the kings of Media and P? H6539
Ezk 27:10 They of P and of Lud and of Phut were H6539
38: 5 P, Ethiopia, and Libya with them; all of H6539
Dan 8:20 *two* horns *are* the kings of Media and P. H6539
10: 1 In the third year of Cyrus king of P a H6539
13 But the prince of the kingdom of P H6539
13 I remained there with the kings of P. H6539
20 with the prince of P: and when I am H6539
11: 2 yet three kings in P; and the fourth shall H6539

PERSIAN
Neh 12:22 the priests, to the reign of Darius the P. H6542
Dan 6:28 Darius, and in the reign of Cyrus the P. H6543

PERSIANS
Est 1:19 the laws of the P and the Medes, that H6539
Dan 5:28 divided, and given to the Medes and P. H6540
6: 8 of the Medes and P, which altereth not. H6540
12 of the Medes and P, which altereth not. H6540
15 of the Medes and P *is*, That no decree H6540

PERSIS
Ro 16:12 P, which laboured much in the Lord. *G4069*

PERSON
Gen 39: 6 was *a* goodly *p*, and well favoured.
Ex 12:48 for no uncircumcised p shall eat thereof.
Lev 19:15 shalt not respect the p of the poor, nor H6440
15 nor honour the p of the mighty: *but* in H6440
Nu 5: 6 against the LORD, and that p be guilty; H5315
19:17 And for an unclean *p* they shall take of
18 And a clean p shall take hyssop, H376+H120
19 And the clean *p* shall sprinkle upon the
22 And whatsoever the unclean *p* H5060
31:19 hath killed any p, and whosoever hath H5315
35:11 which killeth any p at unawares. H5315
15 any p unawares may flee thither. H5315
30 Whoso killeth any p, the murderer shall H5315
30 against any p *to cause him* to die. H5315
Dt 15:22 and the clean p *shall eat it* alike, as the
27:25 p. And all the people shall say, Amen. H5315
28:50 not regard the p of the old, nor shew H6440
Jos 20: 3 That the slayer that killeth *any* p H5315
9 killeth *any* p at unawares might H5315
1Sa 9: 2 of Israel a goodlier p than he: from his H376
16:18 a comely p, and the LORD *is* with him. H376
25:35 to thy voice, and have accepted thy p. H6440
2Sa 4:11 slain a righteous p in his own house H376
14:14 God respect *any* p: yet doth he devise H5315
17:11 that thou go to battle in thine own p. H6440
Job 13: 8 Will ye accept his p? will ye contend for H6440
22:29 up; and he shall save the humble p.
32:21 accept any man's p, neither let me give H6440
Ps 15: 4 In whose eyes a vile p is contemned; but
49:10 fool and the brutish p perish, and leave H1198
101: 4 from me: I will not know a wicked *p*.
105:37 *was* not one feeble *p* among their tribes.

Prv 6:12 A naughty p, a wicked man, walketh with H120
18: 5 *It is* not good to accept the p of the H6440
24: 8 do evil shall be called a mischievous p. H1167
28:17 the blood of *any* p shall flee to the pit; H5315
Isa 32: 5 The vile p shall be no more called H5036
6 For the vile p will speak villany, and his H5036
Jer 43: 6 and every p that Nebuzar-adan H5315
52:25 near the king's p, which were found in H6440
Ezk 16: 5 of thy p, in the day that thou wast born. H5315
33: 6 and take *any* p from among them, H5315
44:25 And they shall come at no dead p to H120
Dan 11:21 And in his estate shall stand up a vile p, H959
Mal 1: 8 accept thy p? saith the LORD of hosts. H6440
Mt 22:16 for thou regardest not the p of men. *G4383*
27:24 of the blood of this just p: see ye *to it*. *G1342*
Mk 12:14 thou regardest not the p of men, but *G4383*
Lk 20:21 neither acceptest thou the p *of any*, but *G4383*
1Co 5:13 from among yourselves that wicked p. *G4190*
2Co 2:10 sakes *forgave I it* in the p of Christ; *G4383*
Gal 2: 6 no man's p:) for they who seemed *G4383*
Eph 5: 5 nor unclean p, nor covetous man, who *G169*
Heb 1: 3 image of his p, and upholding all things *G5287*
12:16 or profane p, as Esau, who for one *G952*
2Pt 2: 5 saved Noah the eighth *p*, a preacher of

PERSONS
Gen 14:21 me the p, and take the goods to thyself. H5315
36: 6 and all the p of his house, and his H5315
Ex 16:16 number of your p; take ye every man H5315
Lev 27: 2 a singular vow, the p *shall be* for the H5315
Nu 19:18 and upon the p that were there, and H5315
31:28 *both* of the p, and of the beeves, and H120
30 of fifty, of the p, of the beeves, of the H120
35 And thirty and two thousand p H5315+H120
40 And the p *were* sixteen H5315+H120
40 tribute *was* thirty and two p. H5315+H120
46 And sixteen thousand p;) H5315+H120
Dt 1:17 Ye shall not respect p in judgment; *but* H6440
10:17 regardeth not p, nor taketh reward: H6440
22 and ten p; and now the LORD H5315
16:19 shalt not respect p, neither take a gift: H6440
Jdg 9: 2 threescore and ten p, reign over you, or H376
4 vain and light p, which followed him. H582
5 threescore and ten p, upon one stone: H376
18 threescore and ten p, upon one stone, H376
20:39 Israel about thirty p: for they said, Surely H376
1Sa 9:22 were bidden, which *were* about thirty p. H376
22:18 and five p that did wear a linen ephod. H376
22 *death* of all the p of thy father's house. H5315
2Ki 10: 6 *being* seventy p, *were* with the great men H376
7 and slew seventy p, and put their heads H376
2Ch 19: 7 nor respect of p, nor taking of gifts. H6440
Job 13:10 reprove you, if ye do secretly accept p. H6440
34:19 that accepteth not the p of princes, nor H6440
Ps 26: 4 I have not sat with vain p, neither will I H4962
82: 2 and accept the p of the wicked? Selah. H6440
Prv 12:11 vain *p is* void of understanding.
24:23 good to have respect of p in judgment. H6440
28:19 after vain *p* shall have poverty enough.
21 To have respect of p *is* not good: for for H6440
Jer 52:29 eight hundred thirty and two p: H5315
30 forty and five p: all the persons *were* H5315
30 p *were* four thousand and six hundred. H5315
Lam 4:16 respected not the p of the priests, they H6440
Ezk 17:17 and building forts, to cut off many p: H5315
27:13 they traded the p of men and vessels H5315
Jna 4:11 sixscore thousand p that cannot discern H120
Zep 3: 4 Her prophets *are* light *and* treacherous p: H582
Mal 1: 9 regard your p? saith the LORD of hosts. H6440
Lk 15: 7 nine just p, which need no repentance. *G1342*
Act 10:34 I perceive that God is no respecter of p: *G4381*
17:17 with the devout p, and in the market *G4576*
Ro 2:11 For there is no respect of p with God. *G4382*
2Co 1:11 means of many p thanks may be given *G4383*
Eph 6: 9 neither is there respect of p with him. *G4382*
Col 3:25 hath done: and there is no respect of p. *G4382*
1Ti 1:10 liars, for perjured p, and if there be any *G1965*
Jas 2: 1 *the Lord* of glory, with respect of p. *G4382*
9 But if ye have respect to p, ye commit *G4380*
1Pt 1:17 without respect of p judgeth according *G678*
2Pt 3:11 what manner *of* p ought ye to be in *all*
Jude 16 p in admiration because of advantage. *G4383*

PERSUADE
1Ki 22:20 And the LORD said, Who shall p Ahab, H6601
21 the LORD, and said, I will p him. H6601
22 he said, Thou shalt p *him*, and prevail H6601
2Ch 32:11 Doth not Hezekiah p you to give over H5496
15 deceive you, nor p you on this manner, H5496

Isa 36:18 *Beware* lest Hezekiah p you, saying, H5496
Mt 28:14 ears, we will p him, and secure you. *G3982*
2Co 5:11 of the Lord, we p men; but we are *G3982*
Gal 1:10 For do I now p men, or God? or do I *G3982*

PERSUADED
2Ch 18: 2 *had* with him, and p him to go up *with* H5496
Prv 25:15 By long forbearing is a prince p, and a H6601
Mt 27:20 But the chief priests and elders p the *G3982*
Lk 16:31 be p, though one rose from the dead. *G3982*
20: 6 for they be p that John was a prophet. *G3982*
Act 13:43 p them to continue in the grace of God. *G3982*
14:19 and Iconium, who p the people, and, *G3982*
18: 4 and p the Jews and the Greeks. *G3982*
19:26 Asia, this Paul hath p and turned away *G3982*
21:14 And when he would not be p, we *G3982*
26:26 freely: for I am p that none of these *G3982*
Ro 4:21 And being fully p that, what he had *G4135*
8:38 For I am p, that neither death, nor life, *G3982*
14: 5 every man be fully p in his own mind. *G4135*
14 I know, and am p by the Lord Jesus, *G3982*
15:14 And I myself also am p of you, my *G3982*
2Ti 1: 5 Eunice; and I am p that in thee also. *G3982*
12 believed, and am p that he is able to *G3982*
Heb 6: 9 But, beloved, we are p better things of *G3982*
11:13 them afar off, and were p of *them*, and *G3982*

PERSUADEST
Act 26:28 Almost thou p me to be a Christian. *G3982*

PERSUADETH
2Ki 18:32 when he p you, saying, The LORD H5496
Act 18:13 Saying, This *fellow* p men to worship *G374*

PERSUADING
Act 19: 8 disputing and p the things concerning *G3982*
28:23 kingdom of God, p them concerning *G3982*

PERSUASION
Gal 5: 8 This p *cometh* not of him that calleth *G3988*

PERTAIN
Lev 7:20 offerings, that *p* unto the LORD, having
21 offerings, which *p* unto the LORD, even
1Sa 25:22 if I leave of all that *p* to him by the
Ro 15:17 Christ in those things which p to God.
1Co 6: 3 how much more things that p to this life?
2Pt 1: 3 unto us all things that *p* unto life and

PERTAINED
Nu 31:43 (Now the half *that p unto* the
Jos 24:33 him in a hill *that p to* Phinehas his son,
Jdg 6:11 *was* in Ophrah, that *p* unto Joash the
1Sa 25:21 missed of all that *p* unto him: and he
2Sa 2:15 of Benjamin, which *p* to Ish-bosheth the
9: 9 all that p to Saul and to all his house. H1961
16: 4 thine *are* all that *p* unto Mephibosheth.
1Ki 4:10 The son of Hesed, in Aruboth; to him *p*
12 Baana the son of Ahilud; *to him p*
13 to him *p* the towns of Jair the
13 in Gilead; to him *also p* the region of
7:48 And Solomon made all the vessels that *p*
2Ki 24: 7 Euphrates all that p to the king of Egypt.
1Ch 9:27 thereof every morning *p* to them.
11:31 Ithai the son of Ribai of Gibeah, *that p* to
2Ch 12: 4 And he took the fenced cities which *p* to
34:33 all the countries that *p* to the children of

PERTAINETH
Lev 14:32 able to get *that which* p to his cleansing.
Nu 4:16 of Aaron the priest *p* the oil for the light,
Dt 22: 5 wear that which p unto a man, neither H3627
1Sa 27: 6 wherefore Ziklag p unto the kings of H1961
2Sa 6:12 and all that *p* unto him, because of
Ro 9: 4 Who are Israelites; to whom *p* the
Heb 7:13 things are spoken p to another tribe, of *G3348*

PERTAINING
Jos 13:31 in Bashan, *were* p unto the children of
1Ch 26:32 matter p to God, and affairs of the king.
Act 1: 3 of the things p to the kingdom of God: *G4012*
Ro 4: 1 father, as p to the flesh, hath found? *G2596*
1Co 6: 4 If then ye have judgments of things p to
Heb 2:17 high priest in things *p* to God, to make
5: 1 for men in things *p* to God, that he may
9: 9 service perfect, as p to the conscience;

PERUDA
Ezr 2:55 children of Sophereth, the children of P, H6514

PERVERSE
Nu 22:32 thee, because *thy* way is **p** before me: H3399
Dt 32: 5 *they are* a **p** and crooked generation. H6141
1Sa 20:30 Thou son of the **p** rebellious *woman,* H5753
Job 6:30 cannot my taste discern **p** things? H1942
9:20 I *am* perfect, it shall also prove me **p**. H6140
Prv 4:24 mouth, and **p** lips put far from thee. H3891
8: 8 *there is* nothing froward or **p** in them. H6141
12: 8 he that is of a **p** heart shall be despised. H5753
14: 2 *he that is* **p** in his ways despiseth him. H3868
17:20 hath a **p** tongue falleth into mischief. H2015
19: 1 *he that is* **p** in his lips, and is a fool. H6141
23:33 and thine heart shall utter **p** things. H8319
28: 6 *that is* **p** *in his* ways, though he *be* rich. H6141
18 *that is* **p** *in his* ways shall fall at once. H6140
Isa 19:14 The LORD hath mingled a **p** spirit in H5773
Mt 17:17 O faithless and **p** generation, how long G1294
Lk 9:41 O faithless and **p** generation, how long G1294
Act 20:30 arise, speaking **p** things, to draw away G1294
Php 2:15 of a crooked and **p** nation, among G1294
1Ti 6: 5 **P** disputings of men of corrupt minds, G3859

PERVERSELY
2Sa 19:19 thy servant did **p** the day that my lord H5753
1Ki 8:47 **p**, we have committed wickedness; H5753
Ps 119:78 for they dealt **p** with me without a H5791

PERVERSENESS
Nu 23:21 hath he seen **p** in Israel: the LORD H5999
Prv 11: 3 **p** of transgressors shall destroy them. H5558
15: 4 but **p** therein *is* a breach in the spirit. H5558
Isa 30:12 in oppression and **p**, and stay thereon: H3868
59: 3 lies, your tongue hath muttered **p**. H5766
Ezk 9: 9 and the city full of **p**: for they say, The H4297

PERVERT
Dt 16:19 wise, and **p** the words of the righteous. H5557
24:17 Thou shalt not **p** the judgment of the H5186
Job 8: 3 Doth God **p** judgment? or doth the H5791
3 or doth the Almighty **p** justice? H5791
34:12 neither will the Almighty **p** judgment. H5791
Prv 17:23 the bosom to **p** the ways of judgment. H5186
31: 5 **p** the judgment of any of the afflicted. H8138
Mic 3: 9 that abhor judgment, and **p** all equity. H6140
Act 13:10 cease to **p** the right ways of the Lord? G1294
Gal 1: 7 you, and would **p** the gospel of Christ. G3344

PERVERTED
1Sa 8: 3 and took bribes, and **p** judgment. H5186
Job 33:27 I have sinned, and **p** *that which was* H5753
Isa 47:10 thy knowledge, it hath **p** thee; and thou H7725
Jer 3:21 for they have **p** their way, *and* they H5753
23:36 for ye have **p** the words of the living H2015

PERVERTETH
Ex 23: 8 wise, and **p** the words of the righteous. H5557
Dt 27:19 Cursed *be* he that **p** the judgment of the H5186
Prv 10: 9 but he that **p** his ways shall be known. H6140
19: 3 The foolishness of man **p** his way: and H5557
Lk 23:14 unto me, as one that **p** the people: and, G654

PERVERTING
Ecc 5: 8 the poor, and violent **p** of judgment and
Lk 23: 2 We found this *fellow* **p** the nation, and G1294

PESTILENCE
Ex 5: 3 fall upon us with **p**, or with the sword. H1698
9:15 thy people with **p**; and thou shalt be cut H1698
Lev 26:25 I will send the **p** among you; and ye H1698
Nu 14:12 I will smite them with the **p**, and H1698
Dt 28:21 The LORD shall make the **p** cleave unto H1698
2Sa 24:13 there be three days' **p** in thy land? now H1698
15 So the LORD sent a **p** upon Israel from H1698
1Ki 8:37 famine, if there be **p**, blasting, mildew, H1698
1Ch 21:12 LORD, even the **p**, in the land, and the H1698
14 So the LORD sent **p** upon Israel: and H1698
2Ch 6:28 land, if there be **p**, if there be blasting, H1698
7:13 land, or if I send **p** among my people; H1698
20: 9 judgment, or **p**, or famine, we stand H1698
Ps 78:50 death, but gave their life over to the **p**; H1698
91: 3 of the fowler, *and* from the noisome **p**. H1698
6 *Nor* for the **p** *that* walketh in darkness; H1698
Jer 14:12 sword, and by the famine, and by the **p**. H1698
21: 6 and beast: they shall die of a great **p**. H1698
7 in this city from the **p**, from the sword, H1698
9 and by the **p**: but he that goeth out, H1698
24:10 the famine, and the **p**, among them, till H1698
27: 8 and with the **p**, until I have consumed H1698
13 and by the **p**, as the LORD hath spoken H1698
Jer 28: 8 kingdoms, of war, and of evil, and of **p**. H1698
29:17 famine, and the **p**, and will make them H1698
18 and with the **p**, and will deliver them H1698
32:24 the famine, and of the **p**: and what thou H1698
36 sword, and by the famine, and by the **p**; H1698
34:17 the sword, to the **p**, and to the famine; H1698
38: 2 and by the **p**: but he that goeth forth H1698
42:17 and by the **p**: and none of them shall H1698
22 and by the **p**, in the place whither H1698
44:13 the sword, by the famine, and by the **p**: H1698
Ezk 5:12 A third part of thee shall die with the **p**, H1698
17 bereave thee; and **p** and blood shall H1698
6:11 the sword, by the famine, and by the **p**. H1698
12 He that is far off shall die of the **p**; and H1698
7:15 The sword *is* without, and the **p** and H1698
15 city, famine and **p** shall devour him. H1698
12:16 and from the **p**; that they may declare H1698
14:19 Or *if* I send a **p** into that land, and pour H1698
21 the **p**, to cut off from it man and beast? H1698
28:23 For I will send into her **p**, and blood H1698
33:27 forts and in the caves shall die of the **p**. H1698
38:22 And I will plead against him with **p** H1698
Am 4:10 I have sent among you the **p** after the H1698
Hab 3: 5 Before him went the **p**, and burning H1698

PESTILENCES
Mt 24: 7 **p**, and earthquakes, in divers places. G3061
Lk 21:11 and famines, and **p**; and fearful sights G3061

PESTILENT
Act 24: 5 For we have found this man *a* **p** *fellow,* G3061

PESTLE
Prv 27:22 among wheat with a **p**, *yet* will not his H5940

PETER
Mt 4:18 Simon called **P**, and Andrew his G4074
10: 2 Simon, who is called **P**, and Andrew his G4074
14:28 And **P** answered him and said, Lord, if G4074
29 And he said, Come. And when **P** was G4074
15:15 Then answered **P** and said unto him, G4074
16:16 And Simon **P** answered and said, Thou G4074
18 That thou art **P**, and upon this rock G4074
22 Then **P** took him, and began to rebuke G4074
23 But he turned, and said unto **P**, Get thee G4074
17: 1 And after six days Jesus taketh **P**, G4074
4 Then answered **P**, and said unto Jesus, G4074
24 *money* came to **P**, and said, Doth not G4074
26 **P** saith unto him, Of strangers. Jesus G4074
18:21 Then came **P** to him, and said, Lord, G4074
19:27 Then answered **P** and said unto him, G4074
26:33 **P** answered and said unto him, Though G4074
35 **P** said unto him, Though I should die G4074
37 And he took with him **P** and the two G4074
40 and saith unto **P**, What, could ye not G4074
58 But **P** followed him afar off unto the G4074
69 Now **P** sat without in the palace: and a G4074
73 by, and said to **P**, Surely thou also art G4074
75 And **P** remembered the word of Jesus, G4074
Mk 3:16 And Simon he surnamed **P**; G4074
5:37 to follow him, save **P**, and James, and G4074
8:29 say ye that I am? And **P** answereth and G4074
32 **P** took him, and began to rebuke him. G4074
33 he rebuked **P**, saying, Get thee behind G4074
9: 2 taketh *with him* **P**, and James, and G4074
5 And **P** answered and said to Jesus, G4074
10:28 Then **P** began to say unto him, Lo, we G4074
11:21 And **P** calling to remembrance saith G4074
13: 3 the temple, **P** and James and John G4074
14:29 But **P** said unto him, Although all shall G4074
33 And he taketh with him **P** and James G4074
37 and saith unto **P**, Simon, sleepest thou? G4074
54 And **P** followed him afar off, even into G4074
66 And as **P** was beneath in the palace, G4074
67 And when she saw **P** warming himself, G4074
70 by said again to **P**, Surely thou art *one* G4074
72 the cock crew. And **P** called to mind the G4074
16: 7 his disciples and **P** that he goeth before G4074
Lk 5: 8 When Simon **P** saw *it*, he fell down at G4074
6:14 Simon, (whom he also named **P**,) and G4074
8:45 When all denied, **P** and they that were G4074
51 no man to go in, save **P**, and James, and G4074
9:20 **P** answering said, The Christ of God. G4074
28 sayings, he took **P** and John and James, G4074
32 But **P** and they that were with him were G4074
33 from him, **P** said unto Jesus, Master, G4074
12:41 Then **P** said unto him, Lord, speakest G4074
18:28 Then **P** said, Lo, we have left all, and G4074
22: 8 And he sent **P** and John, saying, Go G4074
Lk 22:34 And he said, I tell thee, **P**, the cock shall G4074
54 priest's house. And **P** followed afar off. G4074
55 together, **P** sat down among them. G4074
58 of them. And **P** said, Man, I am not. G4074
60 And **P** said, Man, I know not what thou G4074
61 turned, and looked upon **P**. And Peter G4074
61 upon Peter. And **P** remembered the G4074
62 And **P** went out, and wept bitterly. G4074
24:12 Then arose **P**, and ran unto the G4074
Jn 1:44 of Bethsaida, the city of Andrew and **P**. G4074
6:68 Then Simon **P** answered him, Lord, to G4074
13: 6 Then cometh he to Simon **P**: and Peter G4074
6 Then cometh he to Simon Peter: and **P** G1565
8 **P** saith unto him, Thou shalt never G4074
9 Simon **P** saith unto him, Lord, not my G4074
24 Simon **P** therefore beckoned to him, G4074
36 Simon **P** said unto him, Lord, whither G4074
37 **P** said unto him, Lord, why cannot I G4074
18:10 Then Simon **P** having a sword drew it, G4074
11 Then said Jesus unto **P**, Put up thy G4074
15 And Simon **P** followed Jesus, and *so* G4074
16 But **P** stood at the door without. Then G4074
16 that kept the door, and brought in **P**. G4074
17 the door unto **P**, Art not thou also *one* G4074
18 themselves: and **P** stood with them, G4074
25 And Simon **P** stood and warmed G4074
26 whose ear **P** cut off, saith, Did not G4074
27 **P** then denied again: and immediately G4074
20: 2 cometh to Simon **P**, and to the other G4074
3 **P** therefore went forth, and that other G4074
4 **P**, and came first to the sepulchre. G4074
6 Then cometh Simon **P** following him, G4074
21: 2 There were together Simon **P**, and G4074
3 Simon **P** saith unto them, I go a G4074
7 loved saith unto **P**, It is the Lord. Now G4074
7 Now when Simon **P** heard that it was G4074
11 Simon **P** went up, and drew the net to G4074
15 saith to Simon **P**, Simon, *son* of Jonas, G4074
17 lovest thou me? **P** was grieved because G4074
20 Then **P**, turning about, seeth the G4074
21 **P** seeing him saith to Jesus, Lord, and G4074
Act 1:13 where abode both **P**, and James, and G4074
15 And in those days **P** stood up in the G4074
2:14 But **P**, standing up with the eleven, G4074
37 and said unto **P** and to the rest of the G4074
38 Then **P** said unto them, Repent, and be G4074
3: 1 Now **P** and John went up together into G4074
3 Who seeing **P** and John about to go G4074
4 And **P**, fastening his eyes upon him G4074
6 Then **P** said, Silver and gold have I G4074
11 was healed held **P** and John, all the G4074
12 And when **P** saw *it*, he answered unto G4074
4: 8 Then **P**, filled with the Holy Ghost, said G4074
13 Now when they saw the boldness of **P** G4074
19 But **P** and John answered and said G4074
5: 3 But **P** said, Ananias, why hath Satan G4074
8 And **P** answered unto her, Tell me G4074
9 Then **P** said unto her, How is it that ye G4074
15 least the shadow of **P** passing by might G4074
29 Then **P** and the *other* apostles G4074
8:14 God, they sent unto them **P** and John: G4074
20 But **P** said unto him, Thy money perish G4074
9:32 And it came to pass, as **P** passed G4074
34 And **P** said unto him, Aeneas, Jesus G4074
38 had heard that **P** was there, they sent G4074
39 Then **P** arose and went with them. G4074
40 But **P** put them all forth, and kneeled G4074
40 eyes: and when she saw **P**, she sat up. G4074
10: 5 call for *one* Simon, whose surname is **P**: G4074
9 nigh unto the city, **P** went up upon the G4074
13 And there came a voice to him, Rise, **P**; G4074
14 But **P** said, Not so, Lord; for I have G4074
17 Now while **P** doubted in himself what G4074
18 was surnamed **P**, were lodged there. G4074
19 While **P** thought on the vision, the G4074
21 Then **P** went down to the men which G4074
23 on the morrow **P** went away with them, G4074
25 And as **P** was coming in, Cornelius met G4074
26 But **P** took him up, saying, Stand up; I G4074
32 whose surname is **P**; he is lodged in the G4074
34 Then **P** opened *his* mouth, and said, Of G4074
44 While **P** yet spake these words, the G4074
45 as came with **P**, because that on the G4074
46 and magnify God. Then answered **P**, G4074
11: 2 And when **P** was come up to Jerusalem, G4074
4 But **P** rehearsed *the matter* from the G4074
7 saying unto me, Arise, **P**; slay and eat. G4074
13 and call for Simon, whose surname is **P**; G4074
12: 3 further to take **P** also. (Then were the G4074

Act 12: 5 **P** therefore was kept in prison: but *G4074*
6 the same night **P** was sleeping between *G4074*
7 and he smote **P** on the side, and raised *G4074*
11 And when **P** was come to himself, he *G4074*
13 And as **P** knocked at the door of the *G4074*
14 and told how **P** stood before the gate. *G4074*
16 But **P** continued knocking: and when *G4074*
18 the soldiers, what was become of **P**. *G4074*
15: 7 much disputing, **P** rose up, and said *G4074*
Gal 1:18 see **P**, and abode with him fifteen days. *G4074*
2: 7 *gospel* of the circumcision *was* unto **P**; *G4074*
8 (For he that wrought effectually in **P** to *G4074*
11 But when **P** was come to Antioch, I *G4074*
14 gospel, I said unto **P** before *them* all, If *G4074*
1Pt 1: 1 **P**, an apostle of Jesus Christ, to the *G4074*
2Pt 1: 1 Simon **P**, a servant and an apostle of *G4074*

PETER'S
Mt 8:14 And when Jesus was come into **P** *G4074*
Jn 1:40 him, was Andrew, Simon **P** brother. *G4074*
6: 8 One of his disciples, Andrew, Simon **P** *G4074*
Act 12:14 And when she knew **P** voice, she *G4074*

PETHAHIAH
1Ch 24:16 The nineteenth to **P**, the twentieth to H6611
Ezr 10:23 same *is* Kelita,) **P**, Judah, and Eliezer. H6611
Neh 9: 5 Shebaniah, *and* **P**, said, Stand up *and* H6611
11:24 And **P** the son of Meshezabeel, of the H6611

PETHOR
Nu 22: 5 the son of Beor to **P**, which *is* by the H6604
Dt 23: 4 of **P** of Mesopotamia, to curse thee. H6604

PETHUEL
Joel 1: 1 the LORD that came to Joel the son of **P**. H6602

PETITION
1Sa 1:17 *thee* thy **p** that thou hast asked of him. H7596
27 given me my **p** which I asked of him: H7596
1Ki 2:16 And now I ask one **p** of thee, deny me H7596
20 Then she said, I desire one small **p** of H7596
Est 5: 6 of wine, What *is* thy **p**? and it shall be H7596
7 Then answered Esther, and said, My **p** H7596
8 king to grant my **p**, and to perform my H7596
7: 2 wine, What *is* thy **p**, queen Esther? and H7596
3 at my **p**, and my people at my request: H7596
9:12 now what *is* thy **p**? and it shall be H7596
Dan 6: 7 shall ask a **p** of any God or man H1159
12 that shall ask *a* **p** of any God or man
13 but maketh his **p** three times a day. H1159

PETITIONS
Ps 20: 5 *our* banners: the LORD fulfil all thy **p**. H4862
1Jn 5:15 we have the **p** that we desired of him. *G155*

PEULTHAI
1Ch 26: 5 **P** the eighth: for God blessed him. H6469

PHALEC
Lk 3:35 was *the son* of **P**, which was *the son* of *G5317*

PHALLU
Gen 46: 9 and **P**, and Hezron, and Carmi. H6396

PHALTI
1Sa 25:44 David's wife, to **P** the son of Laish, H6406

PHALTIEL
2Sa 3:15 husband, *even* from **P** the son of Laish. H6409

PHANUEL
Lk 2:36 the daughter of **P**, of the tribe of Aser: *G5323*

PHARAOH
Gen 12:15 The princes also of **P** saw her, and H6547
15 her before **P**: and the woman was H6547
17 And the LORD plagued **P** and his H6547
18 And **P** called Abram, and said, What *is* H6547
20 And **P** commanded *his* men H6547
39: 1 an officer of **P**, captain of the guard, H6547
40: 2 And **P** was wroth against two *of* his H6547
13 Yet within three days shall **P** lift up H6547
14 unto **P**, and bring me out of this house: H6547
17 of bakemeats for **P**; and the birds did H6547
19 Yet within three days shall **P** lift up thy H6547
41: 1 two full years, that **P** dreamed: and, H6547
4 well favoured and fat kine. So **P** awoke. H6547
7 **P** awoke, and, behold, *it was* a dream. H6547
8 wise men thereof: and **P** told them his H6547
Gen 41: 8 none that could interpret them unto **P**. H6547
9 Then spake the chief butler unto **P**, H6547
10 **P** was wroth with his servants, and put H6547
14 Then **P** sent and called Joseph, and H6547
14 his raiment, and came in unto **P**. H6547
15 And **P** said unto Joseph, I have H6547
16 And Joseph answered **P**, saying, *It is* H6547
16 God shall give **P** an answer of peace. H6547
17 And **P** said unto Joseph, In my dream, H6547
25 And Joseph said unto **P**, The dream of H6547
25 The dream of **P** *is* one: God hath H6547
25 hath shewed **P** what he *is* about to do. H6547
28 have spoken unto **P**: What God *is* about H6547
28 God *is* about to do he sheweth unto **P**. H6547
32 was doubled unto **P** twice; *it is* because H6547
33 Now therefore let **P** look out a man H6547
34 Let **P** do *this*, and let him appoint H6547
35 **P**, and let them keep food in the cities. H6547
37 And the thing was good in the eyes of **P**, H6547
38 And **P** said unto his servants, Can we H6547
39 And **P** said unto Joseph, Forasmuch as H6547
41 And **P** said unto Joseph, See, I have set H6547
42 And **P** took off his ring from his hand, H6547
44 And **P** said unto Joseph, I *am* Pharaoh, H6547
44 And Pharaoh said unto Joseph, I *am* **P**, H6547
45 And **P** called Joseph's name H6547
46 he stood before **P** king of Egypt. And H6547
46 the presence of **P**, and went throughout H6547
55 the people cried to **P** for bread: and H6547
55 for bread: and **P** said unto all the H6547
42:15 By the life of **P** ye shall not go forth H6547
16 else by the life of **P** surely ye *are* spies. H6547
44:18 thy servant: for thou *art* even as **P**. H6547
45: 2 Egyptians and the house of **P** heard. H6547
8 me a father to **P**, and lord of all his H6547
16 and it pleased **P** well, and his servants. H6547
17 And **P** said unto Joseph, Say unto thy H6547
21 **P**, and gave them provision for the way. H6547
46: 5 wagons which **P** had sent to carry him. H6547
31 go up, and shew **P**, and say unto him, H6547
33 And it shall come to pass, when **P** shall H6547
47: 1 Then Joseph came and told **P**, and said, H6547
2 five men, and presented them unto **P**. H6547
3 And **P** said unto his brethren, What is H6547
3 And they said unto **P**, Thy servants *are* H6547
4 They said moreover unto **P**, For to H6547
5 And **P** spake unto Joseph, saying, Thy H6547
7 before **P**: and Jacob blessed Pharaoh. H6547
7 before Pharaoh: and Jacob blessed **P**. H6547
8 And **P** said unto Jacob, How old *art* H6547
9 And Jacob said unto **P**, The days of the H6547
10 And Jacob blessed **P**, and went out from H6547
10 Pharaoh, and went out from before **P**. H6547
11 of Rameses, as **P** had commanded. H6547
19 be servants unto **P**: and give *us* seed, H6547
20 land of Egypt for **P**; for the Egyptians H6547
22 *assigned them* of **P**, and did eat their H6547
22 portion which **P** gave them: wherefore H6547
23 and your land for **P**: lo, *here is* seed for H6547
24 give the fifth *part* unto **P**, and four parts H6547
26 unto this day, *that* **P** should have the H6547
50: 4 unto the house of **P**, saying, If now I H6547
4 I pray you, in the ears of **P**, saying, H6547
6 And **P** said, Go up, and bury thy father, H6547
7 up all the servants of **P**, the elders of his H6547
Ex 1:11 **P** treasure cities, Pithom and Raamses. H6547
19 And the midwives said unto **P**, Because H6547
22 And **P** charged all his people, saying, H6547
2: 5 And the daughter of **P** came down to H6547
15 Now when **P** heard this thing, he H6547
15 from the face of **P**, and dwelt in the land H6547
3:10 will send thee unto **P**, that thou mayest H6547
11 I should go unto **P**, and that I should H6547
4:21 wonders before **P**, which I have put in H6547
22 And thou shalt say unto **P**, Thus saith H6547
5: 1 went in, and told **P**, Thus saith the H6547
2 And **P** said, Who *is* the LORD, that I H6547
5 And **P** said, Behold, the people of the H6547
6 And **P** commanded the same day the H6547
10 Thus saith **P**, I will not give you straw. H6547
15 and cried unto **P**, saying, Wherefore H6547
20 in the way, as they came forth from **P**: H6547
21 in the eyes of **P**, and in the eyes of his H6547
23 For since I came to **P** to speak in thy H6547
6: 1 see what I will do to **P**: for with a strong H6547
11 Go in, speak unto **P** king of Egypt, that H6547
12 how then shall **P** hear me, who *am* of H6547
13 of Israel, and unto **P** king of Egypt, to H6547
27 These *are* they which spake to **P** king of H6547
Ex 6:29 **P** king of Egypt all that I say unto thee. H6547
30 lips, and how shall **P** hearken unto me? H6547
7: 1 thee a god to **P**: and Aaron thy brother H6547
2 shall speak unto **P**, that he send the H6547
4 But **P** shall not hearken unto you, that I H6547
7 years old, when they spake unto **P**. H6547
9 When **P** shall speak unto you, saying, H6547
9 before **P**, *and* it shall become a serpent. H6547
10 And Moses and Aaron went in unto **P**, H6547
10 down his rod before **P**, and before his H6547
11 Then **P** also called the wise men and H6547
15 Get thee unto **P** in the morning; lo, he H6547
20 in the sight of **P**, and in the sight of his H6547
23 And **P** turned and went into his house, H6547
8: 1 Moses, Go unto **P**, and say unto him, H6547
8 Then **P** called for Moses and Aaron, H6547
9 And Moses said unto **P**, Glory over me: H6547
12 And Moses and Aaron went out from **P**: H6547
12 frogs which he had brought against **P**. H6547
15 But when **P** saw that there was respite, H6547
19 Then the magicians said unto **P**, This *is* H6547
20 and stand before **P**; lo, he cometh forth H6547
24 *flies* into the house of **P**, and *into* his H6547
25 And **P** called for Moses and for Aaron, H6547
28 And **P** said, I will let you go, that ye H6547
29 may depart from **P**, from his servants, H6547
29 but let not **P** deal deceitfully any H6547
30 And Moses went out from **P**, and H6547
31 *of flies* from **P**, from his servants, and H6547
32 And **P** hardened his heart at this time H6547
9: 1 Moses, Go in unto **P**, and tell him, Thus H6547
7 And **P** sent, and, behold, there was not H6547
7 And the heart of **P** was hardened, and H6547
8 it toward the heaven in the sight of **P**. H6547
10 furnace, and stood before **P**; and Moses H6547
12 And the LORD hardened the heart of **P**, H6547
13 and stand before **P**, and say unto him, H6547
20 the servants of **P** made his servants H6547
27 And **P** sent, and called for Moses and H6547
33 And Moses went out of the city from **P**, H6547
34 And when **P** saw that the rain and the H6547
35 And the heart of **P** was hardened, H6547
10: 1 unto Moses, Go in unto **P**: for I have H6547
3 And Moses and Aaron came in unto **P**, H6547
6 he turned himself, and went out from **P**. H6547
8 again unto **P**: and he said unto them, H6547
16 Then **P** called for Moses and Aaron in H6547
18 And he went out from **P**, and entreated H6547
24 And **P** called unto Moses, and said, Go H6547
28 And **P** said unto him, Get thee from H6547
11: 1 plague *more* upon **P**, and upon Egypt; H6547
5 the firstborn of **P** that sitteth upon his H6547
8 he went out from **P** in a great anger. H6547
9 And the LORD said unto Moses, **P** shall H6547
10 these wonders before **P**: and the LORD H6547
12:29 the firstborn of **P** that sat on his throne H6547
30 And **P** rose up in the night, he, and all H6547
13:15 And it came to pass, when **P** would H6547
17 And it came to pass, when **P** had let the H6547
14: 3 For **P** will say of the children of Israel, H6547
4 be honoured upon **P**, and upon all his H6547
5 and the heart of **P** and of his servants H6547
8 And the LORD hardened the heart of **P** H6547
9 *and* chariots of **P**, and his horsemen, H6547
10 And when **P** drew nigh, the children of H6547
17 get me honour upon **P**, and upon all his H6547
18 me honour upon **P**, upon his chariots, H6547
28 *and* all the host of **P** that came into the H6547
15:19 For the horse of **P** went in with his H6547
18: 4 and delivered me from the sword of **P**: H6547
8 had done unto **P** and to the Egyptians H6547
10 out of the hand of **P**, who hath delivered H6547
Dt 6:22 upon Egypt, upon **P**, and upon all his H6547
7: 8 from the hand of **P** king of Egypt. H6547
18 thy God did unto **P**, and unto all Egypt; H6547
11: 3 of Egypt unto **P** the king of Egypt, and H6547
29: 2 land of Egypt unto **P**, and unto all his H6547
34:11 the land of Egypt to **P**, and to all his H6547
1Sa 6: 6 as the Egyptians and **P** hardened their H6547
1Ki 3: 1 And Solomon made affinity with **P** H6547
9:16 *For* **P** king of Egypt had gone up, and H6547
11: 1 with the daughter of **P**, women of the H6547
18 to Egypt, unto **P** king of Egypt; which H6547
19 in the sight of **P**, so that he gave him H6547
20 household among the sons of **P**. H6547
21 Hadad said to **P**, Let me depart, that H6547
22 Then **P** said unto him, But what hast H6547
2Ki 17: 7 under the hand of **P** king of Egypt, and H6547
18:21 and pierce it: so *is* **P** king of Egypt unto H6547

2Ki 23:35 and the gold to P; but he taxed the land H6547
35 the commandment of P: he exacted the H6547
1Ch 4:18 the daughter of P, which Mered took. H6547
2Ch 8:11 up the daughter of P out of the city of H6547
Neh 9:10 and wonders upon P, and on all his H6547
Ps 135: 9 upon P, and upon all his servants. H6547
136:15 But overthrew P and his host in the H6547
Isa 19:11 counsellors of P is become brutish: H6547
11 how say ye unto P, I *am* the son of the H6547
30: 2 P, and to trust in the shadow of Egypt! H6547
3 Therefore shall the strength of P be H6547
36: 6 P king of Egypt to all that trust in him. H6547
Jer 25:19 P king of Egypt, and his servants, and H6547
46:17 They did cry there, P king of Egypt *is* H6547
25 of No, and P, and Egypt, with their H6547
25 even P, and *all* them that trust in him: H6547
47: 1 Philistines, before that P smote Gaza. H6547
Ezk 17:17 Neither shall P with *his* mighty army H6547
29: 2 Son of man, set thy face against P king H6547
3 I *am* against thee, P king of Egypt, the H6547
30:21 Son of man, I have broken the arm of P H6547
22 I *am* against P king of Egypt, and will H6547
25 and the arms of P shall fall down; and H6547
31: 2 Son of man, speak unto P king of H6547
18 by the sword. This *is* P and all his H6547
32: 2 a lamentation for P king of Egypt, and H6547
31 P shall see them, and shall be H6547
31 his multitude, *even* P and all his army H6547
32 with the sword, *even* P and all his H6547
Act 7:10 in the sight of P king of Egypt; and he *G5328*
13 kindred was made known unto P. *G5328*
Ro 9:17 For the scripture saith unto P, Even for *G5328*

PHARAOH-HOPHRA
Jer 44:30 Behold, I will give P king of Egypt into H6548

PHARAOH-NECHO
Jer 46: 2 Against Egypt, against the army of P H6549

PHARAOH-NECHOH
2Ki 23:29 In his days P king of Egypt went up H6549
33 And P put him in bands at Riblah in H6549
34 And P made Eliakim the son of Josiah H6549
35 to his taxation, to give *it* unto P. H6549

PHARAOH'S
Gen 12:15 the woman was taken into P house. H6547
37:36 officer of P, *and* captain of the guard. H6547
40: 7 And he asked P officers that *were* with H6547
11 And P cup *was* in my hand: and I took H6547
11 pressed them into P cup, and I gave the H6547
11 cup, and I gave the cup into P hand. H6547
13 thou shalt deliver P cup into his hand, H6547
20 day, *which was* P birthday, that he H6547
21 again; and he gave the cup into P hand: H6547
45:16 And the fame thereof was heard in P H6547
47:14 brought the money into P house. H6547
20 over them: so the land became P. H6547
25 of my lord, and we will be P servants. H6547
26 of the priests only, *which* became not P. H6547
Ex 2: 7 Then said his sister to P daughter, H6547
8 And P daughter said to her, Go. And H6547
9 And P daughter said unto her, Take H6547
10 brought him unto P daughter, and he H6547
5:14 of Israel, which P taskmasters had set H6547
7: 3 And I will harden P heart, and multiply H6547
13 And he hardened P heart, that he H6547
14 And the LORD said unto Moses, P H6547
22 and P heart was hardened, H6547
8:19 the finger of God: and P heart was H6547
10: 7 And P servants said unto him, How H6547
11 they were driven out from P presence. H6547
20 But the LORD hardened P heart, so H6547
27 But the LORD hardened P heart, and H6547
11: 3 in the sight of P servants, and in the H6547
10 the LORD hardened P heart, so that he H6547
14: 4 And I will harden P heart, that he shall H6547
23 midst of the sea, *even* all P horses, his H6547
15: 4 P chariots and his host hath he cast H6547
Dt 6:21 thy son, We were P bondmen in Egypt; H6547
1Sa 2:27 when they were in Egypt in P house? H6547
1Ki 3: 1 of Egypt, and took P daughter, and H6547
7: 8 also an house for P daughter, whom he H6547
9:24 But P daughter came up out of the city H6547
11:20 weaned in P house: and Genubath H6547
20 Genubath was in P household among H6547
Song 1: 9 to a company of horses in P chariots. H6547
Jer 37: 5 Then P army was come forth out of H6547
7 of me; Behold, P army, which is come H6547
37:11 up from Jerusalem for fear of P army, H6547
43: 9 *is* at the entry of P house in Tahpanhes, H6547
Ezk 30:24 but I will break P arms, and he shall H6547
Act 7:21 And when he was cast out, P daughter *G5328*
Heb 11:24 to be called the son of P daughter; *G5328*

PHARES
Mt 1: 3 And Judas begat P and Zara of *G5329*
3 of Thamar; and P begat Esrom; and *G5329*
Lk 3:33 *the son* of P, which was *the son* of Juda, *G5329*

PHAREZ
Gen 38:29 thee: therefore his name was called P. H6557
46:12 and Shelah, and P, and Zerah: but Er H6557
12 the sons of P were Hezron and Hamul. H6557
Nu 26:20 of the Shelanites: of P, the family of the H6557
21 And the sons of P were; of Hezron, the H6557
Ru 4:12 And let thy house be like the house of P, H6557
18 Now these *are* the generations of P: H6557
18 generations of Pharez: P begat Hezron, H6557
1Ch 2: 4 in law bare him P and Zerah. All the H6557
5 The sons of P; Hezron, and Hamul. H6557
4: 1 The sons of Judah; P, Hezron, and H6557
9: 4 of the children of P the son of Judah. H6557

PHARISEE
Mt 23:26 *Thou* blind P, cleanse first that *which is* *G5330*
Lk 7:39 Now when the P which had bidden him *G5330*
11:37 And as he spake, a certain P besought *G5330*
38 And when the P saw *it*, he marvelled *G5330*
18:10 the one a P, and the other a publican. *G5330*
11 The P stood and prayed thus with *G5330*
Act 5:34 in the council, a P, named Gamaliel, a *G5330*
23: 6 *and* brethren, I am a P, the son of a *G5330*
6 Pharisee, the son of a P: of the hope and *G5330*
26: 5 straitest sect of our religion I lived a P. *G5330*
Php 3: 5 the Hebrews; as touching the law, a P; *G5330*

PHARISEES
Mt 3: 7 But when he saw many of the P and *G5330*
5:20 of the scribes and P, ye shall in no case *G5330*
9:11 And when the P saw *it*, they said unto *G5330*
14 the P fast oft, but thy disciples fast not? *G5330*
34 But the P said, He casteth out devils *G5330*
12: 2 But when the P saw *it*, they said unto *G5330*
14 Then the P went out, and held a *G5330*
24 But when the P heard *it*, they said, This *G5330*
38 Then certain of the scribes and of the P *G5330*
15: 1 Then came to Jesus scribes and P, *G5330*
12 thou that the P were offended, after *G5330*
16: 1 The P also with the Sadducees came, *G5330*
6 leaven of the P and of the Sadducees. *G5330*
11 leaven of the P and of the Sadducees? *G5330*
12 doctrine of the P and of the Sadducees. *G5330*
19: 3 The P also came unto him, tempting *G5330*
21:45 And when the chief priests and P had *G5330*
22:15 Then went the P, and took counsel how *G5330*
34 But when the P had heard that he had *G5330*
41 While the P were gathered together, *G5330*
23: 2 Saying, The scribes and the P sit in *G5330*
13 But woe unto you, scribes and P, *G5330*
14 Woe unto you, scribes and P, *G5330*
15 Woe unto you, scribes and P, *G5330*
23 Woe unto you, scribes and P, *G5330*
25 Woe unto you, scribes and P, *G5330*
27 Woe unto you, scribes and P, *G5330*
29 Woe unto you, scribes and P, *G5330*
27:62 and P came together unto Pilate, *G5330*
Mk 2:16 And when the scribes and P saw him *G5330*
18 And the disciples of John and of the P *G5330*
18 of the P fast, but thy disciples fast not? *G5330*
24 And the P said unto him, Behold, why *G5330*
3: 6 And the P went forth, and straightway *G5330*
7: 1 Then came together unto him the P, *G5330*
3 For the P, and all the Jews, except they *G5330*
5 Then the P and scribes asked him, *G5330*
8:11 And the P came forth, and began to *G5330*
15 of the P, and *of* the leaven of Herod. *G5330*
10: 2 And the P came to him, and asked him, *G5330*
12:13 unto him certain of the P and of the *G5330*
Lk 5:17 that there were P and doctors of the *G5330*
21 And the scribes and the P began to *G5330*
30 But their scribes and P murmured *G5330*
33 of the P; but thine eat and drink? *G5330*
6: 2 And certain of the P said unto them, *G5330*
7 And the scribes and P watched him, *G5330*
7:30 But the P and lawyers rejected the *G5330*
36 And one of the P desired him that he *G5330*
11:39 unto him, Now do ye P make clean the *G5330*
Lk 11:42 But woe unto you, P! for ye tithe mint *G5330*
43 Woe unto you, P! for ye love the *G5330*
44 Woe unto you, scribes and P, *G5330*
53 the scribes and the P began to urge *him* *G5330*
12: 1 the leaven of the P, which is hypocrisy. *G5330*
13:31 certain of the P, saying unto him, Get *G5330*
14: 1 of one of the chief P to eat bread on the *G5330*
3 the lawyers and P, saying, Is it lawful to *G5330*
15: 2 And the P and scribes murmured, *G5330*
16:14 And the P also, who were covetous, *G5330*
17:20 And when he was demanded of the P, *G5330*
19:39 And some of the P from among the *G5330*
Jn 1:24 And they which were sent were of the P. *G5330*
3: 1 There was a man of the P, named *G5330*
4: 1 knew how the P had heard that Jesus *G5330*
7:32 The P heard that the people murmured *G5330*
32 him; and the P and the chief priests *G5330*
45 chief priests and P; and they said unto *G5330*
47 Then answered them the P, Are ye also *G5330*
48 Have any of the rulers or of the P *G5330*
8: 3 And the scribes and P brought unto *G5330*
13 The P therefore said unto him, Thou *G5330*
9:13 They brought to the P him that *G5330*
15 Then again the P also asked him how *G5330*
16 Therefore said some of the P, This man *G5330*
40 And *some* of the P which were with *G5330*
11:46 their ways to the P, and told them what *G5330*
47 priests and the P a council, and said, *G5330*
57 Now both the chief priests and the P *G5330*
12:19 The P therefore said among *G5330*
42 him; but because of the P they did not *G5330*
18: 3 chief priests and P, cometh thither with *G5330*
Act 15: 5 of the sect of the P which believed, *G5330*
23: 6 and the other P, he cried out in the *G5330*
7 between the P and the Sadducees: *G5330*
8 nor spirit: but the P confess both. *G5330*

PHARISEE'S
Lk 7:36 the P house, and sat down to meat. *G5330*
37 sat at meat in the P house, brought an *G5330*

PHARISEES'
Act 23: 9 *that were* of the P part arose, and *G5330*

PHAROSH
Ezr 8: 3 of the sons of P; Zechariah: and with H6551

PHARPAR
2Ki 5:12 *Are* not Abana and P, rivers of H6554

PHARZITES
Nu 26:20 P: of Zerah, the family of the Zarhites. H6558

PHASEAH
Neh 7:51 the children of Uzza, the children of P, H6454

PHEBE
Ro 16: 1 I commend unto you P our sister, *G5402*

PHELET See BETH-PHELET.

PHENICE
Act 11:19 travelled as far as P, and Cyprus, and *G5403*
15: 3 they passed through P and Samaria, *G5403*
27:12 might attain to P, *and there* to winter; *G5405*

PHENICIA
Act 21: 2 And finding a ship sailing over unto P, *G5403*

PHICHOL
Gen 21:22 Abimelech and P the chief captain of H6369
32 rose up, and P the chief captain of H6369
26:26 and P the chief captain of his army. H6369

PHILADELPHIA
Rev 1:11 Sardis, and unto P, and unto Laodicea. *G5359*
3: 7 And to the angel of the church in P *G5359*

PHILEMON
Phlm 1 *our* brother, unto P our dearly beloved, *G5371*

PHILETUS
2Ti 2:17 canker: of whom is Hymenaeus and P; *G5372*

PHILIP
Mt 10: 3 P, and Bartholomew; Thomas, and *G5376*
Mk 3:18 And Andrew, and P, and Bartholomew, *G5376*
Lk 3: 1 and his brother P tetrarch of Ituraea *G5376*
6:14 James and John, P and Bartholomew, *G5376*

Jn 1:43 P, and saith unto him, Follow me. G5376
44 Now P was of Bethsaida, the city of G5376
45 P findeth Nathanael, and saith unto G5376
46 P saith unto him, Come and see. G5376
48 him, Before that P called thee, when G5376
6: 5 him, he saith unto P, Whence shall we G5376
7 P answered him, Two hundred G5376
12:21 The same came therefore to P, which G5376
22 P cometh and telleth Andrew: and G5376
22 and again Andrew and P tell Jesus. G5376
14: 8 P saith unto him, Lord, shew us the G5376
9 not known me, P? he that hath seen me G5376
Act 1:13 John, and Andrew, P, and Thomas, G5376
6: 5 Holy Ghost, and P, and Prochorus, and G5376
8: 5 Then P went down to the city of G5376
6 things which P spake, hearing and G5376
12 But when they believed P preaching the G5376
13 he continued with P, and wondered, G5376
26 And the angel of the Lord spake unto P, G5376
29 Then the Spirit said unto P, Go near, G5376
30 And P ran thither to *him*, and heard G5376
31 And he desired P that he would come G5376
34 And the eunuch answered P, and said, I G5376
35 Then P opened his mouth, and began G5376
37 And P said, If thou believest with all G5376
38 the water, both P and the eunuch; and G5376
39 Lord caught away P, that the eunuch G5376
40 But P was found at Azotus: and G5376
21: 8 into the house of P the evangelist, G5376

PHILIPPI
Mt 16:13 the coasts of Caesarea P, he asked his G5376
Mk 8:27 towns of Caesarea P: and by the way he G5376
Act 16:12 And from thence to P, which is the chief G5375
20: 6 And we sailed away from P after the G5375
Php 1: 1 are at P, with the bishops and deacons: G5375
1Th 2: 2 as ye know, at P, we were bold in our G5375

PHILIPPIANS
Php 4:15 Now ye P know also, that in the G5374

PHILIP'S
Mt 14: 3 for Herodias' sake, his brother P wife. G5376
Mk 6:17 brother P wife: for he had married her. G5376
Lk 3:19 his brother P wife, and for all the G5376

PHILISTIA
Ps 60: 8 shoe: P, triumph thou because of me. H6429
87: 4 that know me: behold P, and Tyre, with H6429
108: 9 cast out my shoe; over P will I triumph. H6429

PHILISTIM
Gen 10:14 (out of whom came P,) and Caphtorim. H6430

PHILISTINE
1Sa 17: 8 array? *am* not I a P, and ye servants to H6430
10 And the P said, I defy the armies of H6430
11 heard those words of the P, they were H6430
16 And the P drew near morning and H6430
23 the champion, the P of Gath, Goliath H6430
26 that killeth this P, and taketh away the H6430
26 uncircumcised P, that he should defy H6430
32 thy servant will go and fight with this P. H6430
33 to go against this P to fight with him: H6430
36 this uncircumcised P shall be as one of H6430
37 out of the hand of this P. And Saul said H6430
40 in his hand: and he drew near to the P. H6430
41 And the P came on and drew near unto H6430
42 And when the P looked about, and saw H6430
43 And the P said unto David, *Am* I a dog, H6430
43 And the P cursed David by his gods. H6430
44 And the P said to David, Come to me, H6430
45 Then said David to the P, Thou comest H6430
48 And it came to pass, when the P arose, H6430
48 and ran toward the army to meet the P. H6430
49 *it*, and smote the P in his forehead, that H6430
50 So David prevailed over the P with a H6430
50 and smote the P, and slew him; but H6430
51 stood upon the P, and took his sword, H6430
54 And David took the head of the P, and H6430
55 forth against the P, he said unto Abner, H6430
57 slaughter of the P, Abner took him, and H6430
57 Saul with the head of the P in his hand. H6430
18: 6 the slaughter of the P, that the women H6430
19: 5 and slew the P, and the LORD wrought H6430
21: 9 of Goliath the P, whom thou slewest H6430
22:10 gave him the sword of Goliath the P. H6430
2Sa 21:17 and smote the P, and killed him. Then H6430

PHILISTINES
Gen 21:32 and they returned into the land of the P. H6430
26: 1 Abimelech king of the P unto Gerar. H6430
8 king of the P looked out at a window, H6430
14 store of servants: and the P envied him. H6430
15 his father, the P had stopped them, H6430
18 his father; for the P had stopped them H6430
Ex 13:17 of the land of the P, although that *was* H6430
23:31 even unto the sea of the P, and from the H6430
Jos 13: 2 all the borders of the P, and all Geshuri, H6430
3 five lords of the P; the Gazathites, and H6430
Jdg 3: 3 *Namely*, five lords of the P, and all the H6430
31 which slew of the P six hundred men H6430
10: 6 and the gods of the P, and forsook the H6430
7 the hands of the P, and into the hands H6430
11 the children of Ammon, and from the P? H6430
13: 1 them into the hand of the P forty years. H6430
5 to deliver Israel out of the hand of the P. H6430
14: 1 in Timnath of the daughters of the P. H6430
2 P: now therefore get her for me to wife. H6430
3 the uncircumcised P? And Samson said H6430
4 against the P: for at that time the H6430
4 time the P had dominion over Israel. H6430
15: 3 the P, though I do them a displeasure. H6430
5 corn of the P, and burnt up both the H6430
6 Then the P said, Who hath done this? H6430
6 And the P came up, and burnt H6430
9 Then the P went up, and pitched in H6430
11 thou not that the P *are* rulers over us? H6430
12 the hand of the P. And Samson said H6430
14 *And* when he came unto Lehi, the P H6430
20 Israel in the days of the P twenty years. H6430
16: 5 And the lords of the P came up unto H6430
8 Then the lords of the P brought up to H6430
9 unto him, The P *be* upon thee, Samson. H6430
12 unto him, The P *be* upon thee, Samson. H6430
14 unto him, The P *be* upon thee, Samson. H6430
18 for the lords of the P, saying, Come up H6430
18 the lords of the P came up unto her, H6430
20 And she said, The P *be* upon thee, H6430
21 But the P took him, and put out his H6430
23 Then the lords of the P gathered them H6430
27 all the lords of the P *were* there; and H6430
28 once avenged of the P for my two eyes. H6430
30 Let me die with the P. And he bowed H6430
1Sa 4: 1 out against the P to battle, and pitched H6430
1 Eben-ezer: and the P pitched in Aphek. H6430
2 And the P put themselves in array H6430
2 smitten before the P: and they slew of H6430
3 to day before the P? Let us fetch the ark H6430
6 And when the P heard the noise of the H6430
7 And the P were afraid, for they said, H6430
9 like men, O ye P, that ye be not servants H6430
10 And the P fought, and Israel was H6430
17 is fled before the P, and there hath been H6430
5: 1 And the P took the ark of God, and H6430
2 When the P took the ark of God, they H6430
8 all the lords of the P unto them, and H6430
11 all the lords of the P, and said, Send H6430
6: 1 in the country of the P seven months. H6430
2 And the P called for the priests and the H6430
4 of the lords of the P: for one plague *was* H6430
12 the lords of the P went after them unto H6430
16 And when the five lords of the P had H6430
17 which the P returned *for* a trespass H6430
18 of all the cities of the P *belonging* to the H6430
21 saying, The P have brought again H6430
7: 3 will deliver you out of the hand of the P. H6430
7 And when the P heard that the children H6430
7 the lords of the P went up against H6430
7 heard *it*, they were afraid of the P. H6430
8 he will save us out of the hand of the P. H6430
10 the burnt offering, the P drew near to H6430
10 that day upon the P, and discomfited H6430
11 and pursued the P, and smote them, H6430
13 So the P were subdued, and they came H6430
13 against the P all the days of Samuel. H6430
14 And the cities which the P had taken H6430
14 the hands of the P. And there was peace H6430
9:16 of the hand of the P: for I have looked H6430
10: 5 the garrison of the P: and it shall come H6430
12: 9 the hand of the P, and into the hand of H6430
13: 3 the garrison of the P that *was* in Geba, H6430
3 *was* in Geba, and the P heard *of it*. And H6430
4 a garrison of the P, and *that* Israel also H6430
4 with the P. And the people were H6430
5 And the P gathered themselves H6430
11 and *that* the P gathered themselves H6430
12 Therefore said I, The P will come down H6430
1Sa 13:16 but the P encamped in Michmash. H6430
17 out of the camp of the P in three H6430
19 land of Israel: for the P said, Lest the H6430
20 went down to the P, to sharpen every H6430
23 And the garrison of the P went out to H6430
14:11 the garrison of the P: and the Philistines H6430
11 and the P said, Behold, the Hebrews H6430
19 *was* in the host of the P went on and H6430
21 *that* were with the P before that time, H6430
22 heard that the P fled, even they also H6430
30 a much greater slaughter among the P? H6430
31 And they smote the P that day from H6430
36 go down after the P by night, and spoil H6430
37 I go down after the P? wilt thou deliver H6430
46 up from following the P: and the H6430
46 and the P went to their own place. H6430
47 and against the P: and whithersoever H6430
52 And there was sore war against the P H6430
17: 1 Now the P gathered together their H6430
2 and set the battle in array against the P. H6430
3 And the P stood on a mountain on the H6430
4 of the camp of the P, named Goliath, of H6430
19 in the valley of Elah, fighting with the P. H6430
21 For Israel and the P had put the battle H6430
23 of the armies of the P, and spake H6430
46 of the host of the P this day unto the H6430
51 And when the P saw their champion H6430
52 and pursued the P, until thou come to H6430
52 wounded of the P fell down by the way H6430
53 after the P, and they spoiled their tents. H6430
18:17 but let the hand of the P be upon him. H6430
21 the hand of the P may be against him. H6430
25 foreskins of the P, to be avenged of the H6430
25 to make David fall by the hand of the P. H6430
27 and slew of the P two hundred men; H6430
30 Then the princes of the P went forth: H6430
19: 8 fought with the P, and slew them with H6430
23: 1 Behold, the P fight against Keilah, H6430
2 and smite these P? And the LORD said H6430
2 Go, and smite the P, and save Keilah. H6430
3 to Keilah against the armies of the P? H6430
4 for I will deliver the P into thine hand. H6430
5 fought with the P, and brought away H6430
27 come; for the P have invaded the land. H6430
28 went against the P: therefore they called H6430
24: 1 from following the P, that it was told H6430
27: 1 the land of the P; and Saul shall despair H6430
7 the P was a full year and four months. H6430
11 he dwelleth in the country of the P. H6430
28: 1 days, that the P gathered their armies H6430
4 And the P gathered themselves H6430
5 And when Saul saw the host of the P, he H6430
15 distressed; for the P make war against H6430
19 the hand of the P: and to morrow *shalt* H6430
19 the host of Israel into the hand of the P. H6430
29: 1 Now the P gathered together all their H6430
2 And the lords of the P passed on by H6430
3 Then said the princes of the P, What *do* H6430
3 the princes of the P, *Is* not this David, H6430
4 And the princes of the P were wroth H6430
4 and the princes of the P said unto him, H6430
7 thou displease not the lords of the P. H6430
9 the princes of the P have said, He shall H6430
11 the land of the P. And the Philistines H6430
11 And the P went up to Jezreel. H6430
30:16 of the P, and out of the land of Judah. H6430
31: 1 Now the P fought against Israel: and H6430
1 P, and fell down slain in mount Gilboa. H6430
2 And the P followed hard upon Saul and H6430
2 his sons; and the P slew Jonathan, and H6430
7 and the P came and dwelt in them. H6430
8 morrow, when the P came to strip the H6430
9 into the land of the P round about, to H6430
11 of that which the P had done to Saul; H6430
2Sa 1:20 the daughters of the P rejoice, lest the H6430
3:14 to me for an hundred foreskins of the P. H6430
18 out of the hand of the P, and out of the H6430
5:17 But when the P heard that they had H6430
17 over Israel, all the P came up to seek H6430
18 The P also came and spread H6430
19 I go up to the P? wilt thou deliver them H6430
19 doubtless deliver the P into thine hand. H6430
22 And the P came up yet again, and H6430
24 before thee, to smite the host of the P. H6430
25 P from Geba until thou come to Gazer. H6430
8: 1 David smote the P, and subdued them: H6430
1 out of the hand of the P. H6430
12 and of the P, and of Amalek, and H6430
19: 9 of the hand of the P; and now he is fled H6430

2Sa 21:12 where the **P** had hanged them, when H6430
12 when the **P** had slain Saul in Gilboa: H6430
15 Moreover the **P** had yet war again with H6430
15 against the **P**: and David waxed faint. H6430
18 again a battle with the **P** at Gob: then H6430
19 in Gob with the **P**, where Elhanan the H6430
23: 9 when they defied the **P** *that* were there H6430
10 He arose, and smote the **P** until his H6430
11 the Hararite. And the **P** were gathered H6430
11 lentiles: and the people fled from the **P**. H6430
12 it, and slew the **P**: and the LORD H6430
13 the **P** pitched in the valley of Rephaim. H6430
14 of the **P** *was* then *in* Beth-lehem. H6430
16 the host of the **P**, and drew water out H6430
1Ki 4:21 the land of the **P**, and unto the border H6430
15:27 *belonged* to the **P**; for Nadab and all H6430
16:15 Gibbethon, which *belonged* to the **P**. H6430
2Ki 8: 2 in the land of the **P** seven years. H6430
3 of the land of the **P**: and she went forth H6430
18: 8 He smote the **P**, *even* unto Gaza, and H6430
1Ch 1:12 (of whom came the **P**,) and Caphthorim. H6430
10: 1 Now the **P** fought against Israel; and H6430
1 **P**, and fell down slain in mount Gilboa. H6430
2 And the **P** followed hard after Saul, and H6430
2 his sons; and the **P** slew Jonathan, and H6430
7 and the **P** came and dwelt in them. H6430
8 morrow, when the **P** came to strip the H6430
9 the land of the **P** round about, to carry H6430
11 heard all that the **P** had done to Saul, H6430
11:13 and there the **P** were gathered together H6430
13 and the people fled from before the **P**. H6430
14 it, and slew the **P**; and the LORD saved H6430
15 **P** encamped in the valley of Rephaim. H6430
18 the host of the **P**, and drew water out H6430
12:19 he came with the **P** against Saul to H6430
19 for the lords of the **P** upon advisement H6430
14: 8 And when the **P** heard that David was H6430
8 over all Israel, all the **P** went up to seek H6430
9 And the **P** came and spread themselves H6430
10 I go up against the **P**? and wilt thou H6430
13 And the **P** yet again spread themselves H6430
15 before thee to smite the host of the **P**. H6430
16 of the **P** from Gibeon even to Gazer. H6430
18: 1 David smote the **P**, and subdued them, H6430
1 and her towns out of the hand of the **P**. H6430
11 and from the **P**, and from Amalek. H6430
20: 4 war at Gezer with the **P**; at which time H6430
5 And there was war again with the **P**; H6430
2Ch 9:26 of the **P**, and to the border of Egypt. H6430
17:11 Also *some* of the **P** brought H6430
21:16 the spirit of the **P**, and of the Arabians, H6430
26: 6 against the **P**, and brake down the H6430
6 cities about Ashdod, and among the **P**. H6430
7 And God helped him against the **P**, and H6430
28:18 The **P** also had invaded the cities of the H6430
Ps 56:ttl of David, when the **P** took him in Gath. H6430
83: 7 Gebal, and Ammon, and Amalek; the **P** H6429
Isa 2: 6 like the **P**, and they please themselves H6430
9:12 The Syrians before, and the **P** behind; H6430
11:14 the shoulders of the **P** toward the west; H6430
Jer 25:20 of the land of the **P**, and Ashkelon, and H6430
47: 1 the **P**, before that Pharaoh smote Gaza. H6430
4 to spoil all the **P**, *and* to cut off from H6430
4 will spoil the **P**, the remnant of the H6430
Ezk 16:27 **P**, which are ashamed of thy lewd way. H6430
57 the **P**, which despise thee round about. H6430
25:15 Lord GOD; Because the **P** have dealt by H6430
16 hand upon the **P**, and I will cut off the H6430
Am 1: 8 the **P** shall perish, saith the Lord GOD. H6430
6: 2 to Gath of the **P**: *be they* better than H6430
9: 7 of Egypt? and the **P** from Caphtor, and H6430
Oba 19 *they of* the plain the **P**: and they shall H6430
Zep 2: 5 the land of the **P**, I will even destroy H6430
Zec 9: 6 and I will cut off the pride of the **P**. H6430

PHILISTINES'
Gen 21:34 And Abraham sojourned in the **P** land H6430
1Sa 14: 1 us go over to the **P** garrison, that *is* on H6430
4 go over unto the **P** garrison, *there was* H6430
1Ch 11:16 the **P** garrison *was* then at Beth-lehem. H6430

PHILOLOGUS
Ro 16:15 Salute **P**, and Julia, Nereus, and his *G5378*

PHILOSOPHERS
Act 17:18 Then certain **p** of the Epicureans, and *G5386*

PHILOSOPHY
Col 2: 8 spoil you through **p** and vain deceit, *G5385*

PHINEHAS
Ex 6:25 and she bare him **P**: these *are* the heads H6372
Nu 25: 7 And when **P**, the son of Eleazar, the son H6372
11 **P**, the son of Eleazar, the son of Aaron H6372
31: 6 tribe, them and **P** the son of Eleazar the H6372
Jos 22:13 Gilead, **P** the son of Eleazar the priest, H6372
30 And when **P** the priest, and the princes H6372
31 And **P** the son of Eleazar the priest said H6372
32 And **P** the son of Eleazar the priest, H6372
24:33 *that pertained to* **P** his son, which was H6372
Jdg 20:28 And **P**, the son of Eleazar, the son of H6372
1Sa 1: 3 **P**, the priests of the LORD, *were* there. H6372
2:34 on Hophni and **P**; in one day they shall H6372
4: 4 of Eli, Hophni and **P**, *were* there with H6372
11 sons of Eli, Hophni and **P**, were slain. H6372
17 **P**, are dead, and the ark of God is taken. H6372
14: 3 brother, the son of **P**, the son of Eli, the H6372
1Ch 6: 4 Eleazar begat **P**, Phinehas begat H6372
4 Eleazar begat Phinehas, **P** begat H6372
50 his son, **P** his son, Abishua his son, H6372
9:20 And **P** the son of Eleazar was the ruler H6372
Ezr 7: 5 The son of Abishua, the son of **P**, the H6372
8: 2 Of the sons of **P**; Gershom: of the sons H6372
33 Eleazar the son of **P**; and with them *was* H6372
Ps 106:30 Then stood up **P**, and executed H6372

PHINEHAS'
1Sa 4:19 And his daughter in law, **P** wife, was H6372

PHLEGON
Ro 16:14 Salute Asyncritus, **P**, Hermas, Patrobas, *G5393*

PHOEBE See PHEBE.

PHOENICE See PHENICE.

PHOENICIA See PHENICIA.

PHRYGIA
Act 2:10 **P**, and Pamphylia, in Egypt, and in the *G5435*
16: 6 Now when they had gone throughout **P** *G5435*
18:23 country of Galatia and **P** in order, *G5435*

PHURAH
Jdg 7:10 with **P** thy servant down to the host: H6513
11 he down with **P** his servant unto the H6513

PHUT
Gen 10: 6 and Mizraim, and **P**, and Canaan. H6316
Ezk 27:10 They of Persia and of Lud and of **P** H6316

PHUVAH
Gen 46:13 And the sons of Issachar; Tola, and **P**, H6312

PHYGELLUS
2Ti 1:15 me; of whom are **P** and Hermogenes. *G5436*

PHYLACTERIES
Mt 23: 5 make broad their **p**, and enlarge the *G5440*

PHYSICIAN
Jer 8:22 *Is there* no balm in Gilead; *is there* no **p** H7495
Mt 9:12 need not a **p**, but they that are sick. *G2395*
Mk 2:17 no need of the **p**, but they that are sick: *G2395*
Lk 4:23 unto me this proverb, **P**, heal thyself: *G2395*
5:31 need not a **p**; but they that are sick. *G2395*
Col 4:14 Luke, the beloved **p**, and Demas, greet *G2395*

PHYSICIANS
Gen 50: 2 his servants the **p** to embalm his H7495
2 his father: and the **p** embalmed Israel. H7495
2Ch 16:12 he sought not to the LORD, but to the **p**. H7495
Job 13: 4 But ye *are* forgers of lies, ye *are* all **p** of H7495
Mk 5:26 things of many **p**, and had spent all that *G2395*
Lk 8:43 upon **p**, neither could be healed of any, *G2395*

PI-BESETH
Ezk 30:17 The young men of Aven and of **P** shall H6364

PICK
Prv 30:17 of the valley shall **p** it out, and the H5365

PICTURES
Nu 33:52 destroy all their **p**, and destroy all their H4906
Prv 25:11 *is like* apples of gold in **p** of silver. H4906
Isa 2:16 of Tarshish, and upon all pleasant **p**. H7914

PIECE
Gen 15:10 and laid each **p** one against another: H1335
Ex 37: 7 beaten out of one **p** made he them, on H4749
Nu 10: 2 of silver; of a whole **p** shalt thou make H4749
Jdg 9:53 And a certain woman cast a **p** of a H6400
1Sa 2:36 *and* crouch to him for a **p** of silver and a H95
36 offices, that I may eat a **p** of bread. H6595
30:12 And they gave him a **p** of a cake of figs, H6400
2Sa 6:19 of bread, and a good **p** *of flesh*, and a H829
11:21 a woman cast a **p** of a millstone upon H6400
23:11 where was a **p** of ground full of lentiles: H2513
2Ki 3:19 mar every good **p** of land with stones. H2513
25 and on every good **p** of land cast every H2513
1Ch 16: 3 a good **p** of flesh, and a flagon *of wine*. H829
Neh 3:11 other **p**, and the tower of the furnaces. H4060
19 of Mizpah, another **p** over against the H4060
20 repaired the other **p**, from the turning H4060
21 of Koz another **p**, from the door of the H4060
24 Henadad another **p**, from the house of H4060
27 repaired another **p**, over against the H4060
30 Zalaph, another **p**. After him repaired H4060
Job 41:24 as hard as a **p** of the nether *millstone*. H6400
42:11 also gave him a **p** of money, and every
Prv 6:26 *man is brought* to a **p** of bread: and the H3603
28:21 a **p** of bread *that* man will transgress. H6595
Song 4: 3 a **p** of a pomegranate within thy locks. H6400
6: 7 As a **p** of a pomegranate *are* thy H6400
Jer 37:21 give him daily a **p** of bread out of the H3603
Ezk 24: 4 it, *even* every good **p**, the thigh, and the H5409
6 it out **p** by piece; let no lot fall upon it. H5409
6 it out piece by **p**; let no lot fall upon it. H5409
Am 3:12 lion two legs, or a **p** of an ear; so shall H915
4: 7 another city: one **p** was rained upon, H2513
7 **p** whereupon it rained not withered. H2513
Mt 9:16 No man putteth a **p** of new cloth unto *G1915*
17:27 thou shalt find a **p** of money: that take,
Mk 2:21 No man also seweth a **p** of new cloth *G1915*
21 else the new **p** that filled it up taketh *G2537*
Lk 5:36 No man putteth a **p** of a new garment *G1915*
36 a rent, and the **p** that was *taken* out *G1915*
14:18 I have bought a **p** of ground, and I must
15: 8 if she lose one **p**, doth not light a candle, *G1406*
9 for I have found the **p** which I had lost. *G1406*
24:42 And they gave him a **p** of a broiled fish, *G3313*

PIECES
Gen 15:17 lamp that passed between those **p**. H1506
20:16 a thousand **p** of silver: behold, he
33:19 father, for an hundred **p** of money.
37:28 for twenty *p* of silver: and they brought
33 him; Joseph is without doubt rent in **p**. H2963
44:28 he is torn in **p**; and I saw him not since: H2963
45:22 **p** of silver, and five changes of raiment.
Ex 15: 6 O LORD, hath dashed in **p** the enemy. H7492
22:13 If it be torn in **p**, *then* let him bring it H2963
29:17 And thou shalt cut the ram in **p**, and H5409
17 put *them* unto his **p**, and unto his head. H5409
Lev 1: 6 the burnt offering, and cut it into his **p**. H5409
12 And he shall cut it into his **p**, with his H5409
2: 6 Thou shalt part it in **p**, and pour oil H6595
6:21 it in: *and* the baken **p** of the meat H6595
8:20 And he cut the ram into **p**; and Moses H5409
20 burnt the head, and the **p**, and the fat. H5409
9:13 unto him, with the **p** thereof, and the H5409
Jos 24:32 for an hundred **p** of silver: and it became
Jdg 9: 4 And they gave him threescore and ten *p*
16: 5 one of us eleven hundred *p* of silver.
19:29 bones, into twelve **p**, and sent her into H5409
20: 6 and cut her in **p**, and sent her H5408
1Sa 2:10 shall be broken to **p**; out of heaven shall H2865
11: 7 and hewed them in **p**, and sent *them* H5408
15:33 Agag in **p** before the LORD in Gilgal. H8158
1Ki 11:30 that *was* on him, and rent it *in* twelve **p**: H7168
31 Take thee ten **p**: for thus saith the H7168
18:23 and cut it in **p**, and lay *it* on wood, H5408
33 cut the bullock in **p**, and laid *him* on the H5408
19:11 and brake in **p** the rocks before the H7665
2Ki 2:12 his own clothes, and rent them in two **p**. H7168
5: 5 *p* of gold, and ten changes of raiment.
6:25 *sold* for fourscore *p* of silver, and the
25 a cab of dove's dung for five *p* of silver.
11:18 brake they in **p** thoroughly, and slew H7665
18: 4 and brake in **p** the brasen serpent H3807
23:14 And he brake in **p** the images, and cut
24:13 house, and cut in **p** all the vessels of H7112
25:13 the Chaldees break in **p**, and carried the H7665
2Ch 23:17 and his images in **p**, and slew Mattan H7665
25:12 the rock, that they all were broken in **p**. H1234
28:24 of God, and cut in **p** the vessels of the H7112
31: 1 the images in **p**, and cut down the groves,
34: 4 he brake in **p**, and made dust *of them*, H7665

Job 16:12 me to **p**, and set me up for his mark.
19: 2 my soul, and break me in **p** with words?
34:24 He shall break in **p** mighty men without
40:18 His bones *are as* strong **p** of brass; his
Ps 2: 9 dash them in **p** like a potter's vessel.
7: 2 *it* in **p**, while *there is* none to deliver. H6561
50:22 *you* in **p**, and *there be* none to deliver. H2963
58: 7 his arrows, let them be as cut in **p**. H4135
68:30 himself with **p** of silver: scatter thou H7518
72: 4 and shall break in **p** the oppressor. H1792
74:14 Thou brakest the heads of leviathan in **p**,
89:10 Thou hast broken Rahab in **p**, as one
94: 5 They break in **p** thy people, O LORD, H1792
Song 8:11 was to bring a thousand ***p*** of silver.
Isa 3:15 beat my people to **p**, and grind the faces
8: 9 shall be broken in **p**; and give ear, all ye H2865
9 ye shall be broken in **p**; gird yourselves, H2865
9 yourselves, and ye shall be broken in **p**. H2865
13:16 Their children also shall be dashed to **p** H7376
18 the young men to **p**; and they shall have H7376
30:14 that is broken in **p**; he shall not spare: H3807
45: 2 I will break in **p** the gates of brass, and H7665
Jer 5: 6 thence shall be torn in **p**: because their H2963
23:29 a hammer *that* breaketh the rock in **p**? H6327
50: 2 Merodach is broken in **p**; her idols are H2865
2 her images are broken in **p**. H2865
51:20 will I break in **p** the nations, and with H5310
21 And with thee will I break in **p** the H5310
21 I break in **p** the chariot and his rider; H5310
22 With thee also will I break in **p** man H5310
22 will I break in **p** old and young; and H5310
22 in **p** the young man and the maid; H5310
23 I will also break in **p** with thee the H5310
23 will I break in **p** the husbandman and H5310
23 will I break in **p** captains and rulers. H5310
Lam 3:11 me in **p**: he hath made me desolate. H6582
Ezk 4:14 itself, or is torn in **p**; neither came there H2966
13:19 of barley and for **p** of bread, to slay the H6595
24: 4 Gather the **p** thereof into it, *even* every H5409
Dan 2: 5 ye shall be cut in **p**, and your houses H1917
34 of iron and clay, and brake them to **p**. H1855
35 and the gold, broken to **p** together, and
40 as iron breaketh in **p** and subdueth all H1855
40 all these, shall it break in **p** and bruise. H1855
44 *but* it shall break in **p** and consume all H1855
45 that it brake in **p** the iron, the brass, H1855
3:29 shall be cut in **p**, and their houses shall H1917
6:24 all their bones in **p** or ever they came at H1855
7: 7 and brake in **p**, and stamped the H1855
19 brake in **p**, and stamped the residue H1855
23 shall tread it down, and break it in **p**. H1855
Hos 3: 2 So I bought her to me for fifteen ***p*** of
8: 6 the calf of Samaria shall be broken in **p**. H7616
10:14 was dashed in **p** upon *her* children. H7376
13:16 shall be dashed in **p**, and their women H7376
Mic 1: 7 shall be beaten to **p**, and all the hires H3807
3: 3 and chop them in **p**, as for the pot, and H6566
4:13 thou shalt beat in **p** many people: and I H1854
5: 8 and teareth in **p**, and none can deliver. H2963
Nah 2: 1 He that dasheth in **p** is come up before H6327
12 The lion did tear in **p** enough for his H2963
3:10 were dashed in **p** at the top of all the H7376
Zec 11:12 weighed for my price thirty ***p*** of silver.
13 And I took the thirty ***p*** of silver, and cast
16 of the fat, and tear their claws in **p**. H6561
12: 3 it shall be cut in **p**, though all the people H8295
Mt 26:15 with him for thirty **p** of silver.
27: 3 **p** of silver to the chief priests and elders,
5 And he cast down the **p** of silver in the
6 And the chief priests took the silver **p**, *G694*
9 they took the thirty **p** of silver, the price
Mk 5: 4 in **p**: neither could any *man* tame him. *G4937*
Lk 15: 8 Either what woman having ten **p** of *G1406*
Act 19:19 and found *it* fifty thousand ***p*** of silver.
23:10 been pulled in **p** of them, commanded *G1288*
27:44 some on *broken* **p** of the ship. And so it

PIERCE
Nu 24: 8 and **p** *them* through with his arrows. H4272
2Ki 18:21 into his hand, and **p** it: so *is* Pharaoh H5344
Isa 36: 6 into his hand, and **p** it: so *is* Pharaoh H5344
Lk 2:35 (Yea, a sword shall **p** through thy own *G1330*

PIERCED
Jdg 5:26 **p** and stricken through his temples. H4272
Job 30:17 My bones are **p** in me in the night H5365
Ps 22:16 me: they **p** my hands and my feet. H738
Zec 12:10 me whom they have **p**, and they shall H1856
Jn 19:34 But one of the soldiers with a spear **p** *G3572*
Jn 19:37 They shall look on him whom they **p**. *G1574*
1Ti 6:10 the faith, and **p** themselves through *G4044*
Rev 1: 7 they *also* which **p** him: and all kindreds *G1574*

PIERCETH
Job 40:24 He taketh it with his eyes: *his* nose **p** H5344

PIERCING
Isa 27: 1 leviathan the **p** serpent, even leviathan H1281
Heb 4:12 twoedged sword, **p** even to the dividing *G1338*

PIERCINGS
Prv 12:18 There is that speaketh like the **p** of a H4094

PIETY
1Ti 5: 4 learn first to shew **p** at home, and to *G2151*

PIGEON
Gen 15: 9 old, and a turtledove, and a young **p**. H1469
Lev 12: 6 and a young **p**, or a turtledove, for H3123

PIGEONS
Lev 1:14 offering of turtledoves, or of young **p**. H3123
5: 7 or two young **p**, unto the LORD; one H3123
11 or two young **p**, then he that sinned H3123
12: 8 or two young **p**; the one for the burnt H3123
14:22 And two turtledoves, or two young **p**, H3123
30 or of the young **p**, such as he can get; H3123
15:14 or two young **p**, and come before the H3123
29 or two young **p**, and bring them unto H3123
Nu 6:10 or two young **p**, to the priest, to the H3123
Lk 2:24 A pair of turtledoves, or two young **p**. *G4058*

PI-HAHIROTH
Ex 14: 2 encamp before **P**, between Migdol and H6367
9 the sea, beside **P**, before Baal-zephon. H6367
Nu 33: 7 turned again unto **P**, which *is* before H6367
8 And they departed from before **P**, and H6367

PILATE
Mt 27: 2 him to Pontius **P** the governor. *G4091*
13 Then said **P** unto him, Hearest thou *G4091*
17 gathered together, **P** said unto them, *G4091*
22 **P** saith unto them, What shall I do then *G4091*
24 When **P** saw that he could prevail *G4091*
58 He went to **P**, and begged the body of *G4091*
58 of Jesus. Then **P** commanded the body *G4091*
62 and Pharisees came together unto **P**, *G4091*
65 **P** said unto them, Ye have a watch: go *G4091*
Mk 15: 1 *him* away, and delivered *him* to **P**. *G4091*
2 And **P** asked him, Art thou the King of *G4091*
4 And **P** asked him again, saying, *G4091*
5 answered nothing; so that **P** marvelled. *G4091*
9 But **P** answered them, saying, Will ye *G4091*
12 And **P** answered and said again unto *G4091*
14 Then **P** said unto them, Why, what evil *G4091*
15 And *so* **P**, willing to content the people, *G4091*
43 unto **P**, and craved the body of Jesus. *G4091*
44 And **P** marvelled if he were already *G4091*
Lk 3: 1 Caesar, Pontius **P** being governor of *G4091*
13: 1 **P** had mingled with their sacrifices. *G4091*
23: 1 of them arose, and led him unto **P**. *G4091*
3 And **P** asked him, saying, Art thou the *G4091*
4 Then said **P** to the chief priests and *to* *G4091*
6 When **P** heard of Galilee, he asked *G4091*
11 gorgeous robe, and sent him again to **P**. *G4091*
12 And the same day **P** and Herod were *G4091*
13 And **P**, when he had called together the *G4091*
20 **P** therefore, willing to release Jesus, *G4091*
24 And **P** gave sentence that it should be *G4091*
52 This *man* went unto **P**, and begged the *G4091*
Jn 18:29 **P** then went out unto them, and said, *G4091*
31 Then said **P** unto them, Take ye him, *G4091*
33 Then **P** entered into the judgment hall *G4091*
35 **P** answered, Am I a Jew? Thine own *G4091*
37 **P** therefore said unto him, Art thou a *G4091*
38 **P** saith unto him, What is truth? And *G4091*
19: 1 Then **P** therefore took Jesus, and *G4091*
4 **P** therefore went forth again, and saith *G4091*
5 And ***P*** saith unto them, Behold the man!
6 *him*, crucify *him*. **P** saith unto them, *G4091*
8 When **P** therefore heard that saying, he *G4091*
10 Then saith **P** unto him, Speakest thou *G4091*
12 And from thenceforth **P** sought to *G4091*
13 When **P** therefore heard that saying, he *G4091*
15 *him*, crucify him. **P** saith unto them, *G4091*
19 And **P** wrote a title, and put *it* on the *G4091*
21 of the Jews to **P**, Write not, The King *G4091*
22 **P** answered, What I have written I have *G4091*
Jn 19:31 day,) besought **P** that their legs might *G4091*
38 the Jews, besought **P** that he might take *G4091*
38 body of Jesus: and **P** gave *him* leave. *G4091*
Act 3:13 him in the presence of **P**, when he was *G4091*
4:27 and Pontius **P**, with the Gentiles, and *G4091*
13:28 desired they **P** that he should be slain. *G4091*
1Ti 6:13 Pontius **P** witnessed a good confession; *G4091*

PILDASH
Gen 22:22 And Chesed, and Hazo, and **P**, and H6394

PILE
Isa 30:33 deep *and* large: the **p** thereof *is* fire and H4071
Ezk 24: 9 I will even make the **p** for fire great. H4071

PILEHA
Neh 10:24 Hallohesh, **P**, Shobek, H6401

PILESER See TIGLATH-PILESER.

PILGRIMAGE
Gen 47: 9 of the years of my **p** *are* an hundred H4033
9 life of my fathers in the days of their **p**. H4033
Ex 6: 4 of their **p**, wherein they were strangers. H4033
Ps 119:54 been my songs in the house of my **p**. H4033

PILGRIMS
Heb 11:13 they were strangers and **p** on the earth. *G3927*
1Pt 2:11 as strangers and **p**, abstain from fleshly *G3927*

PILLAR
Gen 19:26 him, and she became a **p** of salt. H5333
28:18 a **p**, and poured oil upon the top of it. H4676
22 And this stone, which I have set *for* a **p**, H4676
31:13 thou anointedst the **p**, *and* where thou H4676
45 Jacob took a stone, and set it up *for* a **p**. H4676
51 and behold *this* **p**, which I have cast H4676
52 This heap *be* witness, and *this* **p** *be* H4676
52 this heap and this **p** unto me, for harm. H4676
35:14 And Jacob set up a **p** in the place where H4676
14 with him, *even* a **p** of stone: and he H4678
20 And Jacob set a **p** upon her grave: that H4676
20 *is* the **p** of Rachel's grave unto this day. H4678
Ex 13:21 them by day in a **p** of a cloud, to lead H5982
21 and by night in a **p** of fire, to give them H5982
22 He took not away the **p** of the cloud by H5982
22 by day, nor the **p** of fire by night, *from* H5982
14:19 them; and the **p** of the cloud went from H5982
24 through the **p** of fire and of the cloud, H5982
33: 9 the cloudy **p** descended, and stood H5982
10 And all the people saw the cloudy **p** H5982
Nu 12: 5 And the LORD came down in the **p** of H5982
14:14 by day time in a **p** of a cloud, and in a H5982
14 of a cloud, and in a **p** of fire by night. H5982
Dt 31:15 tabernacle in a **p** of a cloud: and the H5982
15 of a cloud: and the **p** of the cloud stood H5982
Jdg 9: 6 the plain of the **p** that *was* in Shechem. H5324
20:40 out of the city with a **p** of smoke, the H5982
2Sa 18:18 up for himself a **p**, which *is* in the king's H4678
18 and he called the **p** after his own name: H4678
1Ki 7:21 and he set up the right **p**, and called the H5982
21 **p**, and called the name thereof Boaz. H5982
2Ki 11:14 king stood by a **p**, as the manner *was*, H5982
23: 3 And the king stood by a **p**, and made a H5982
25:17 The height of the one **p** *was* eighteen H5982
17 had the second **p** with wreathen work. H5982
2Ch 23:13 king stood at his **p** at the entering in, H5982
Neh 9:12 day by a cloudy **p**; and in the night by H5982
12 in the night by a **p** of fire, to give them H5982
19 wilderness: the **p** of the cloud departed H5982
19 way; neither the **p** of fire by night, to H5982
Ps 99: 7 He spake unto them in the cloudy **p**: H5982
Isa 19:19 a **p** at the border thereof to the LORD. H4676
Jer 1:18 city, and an iron **p**, and brasen walls H5982
52:21 the height of one **p** *was* eighteen cubits; H5982
22 *of* brass. The second **p** also and the H5982
1Ti 3:15 God, the **p** and ground of the truth. *G4769*
Rev 3:12 Him that overcometh will I make a **p** in *G4769*

PILLARS
Ex 24: 4 the hill, and twelve **p**, according to the H4676
26:32 And thou shalt hang it upon four **p** of H5982
37 the hanging five **p** of shittim *wood*, and H5982
27:10 And the twenty **p** thereof and their H5982
10 the **p** and their fillets *shall be of* silver. H5982
11 long, and his twenty **p** and their twenty H5982
11 hooks of the **p** and their fillets *of* silver. H5982
12 their **p** ten, and their sockets ten. H5982
14 their **p** three, and their sockets three. H5982

Ex 27:15 their **p** three, and their sockets three. H5982
16 **p** *shall be* four, and their sockets four. H5982
17 All the **p** round about the court *shall be* H5982
35:11 boards, his bars, his **p**, and his sockets, H5982
17 The hangings of the court, his **p**, and H5982
36:36 And he made thereunto four **p** *of* H5982
38 And the five **p** of it with their hooks: H5982
38:10 Their **p** *were* twenty, and their brasen H5982
10 of the **p** and their fillets *were of* silver. H5982
11 cubits, their **p** *were* twenty, and their H5982
11 hooks of the **p** and their fillets *of* silver. H5982
12 of fifty cubits, their **p** ten, and their H5982
12 hooks of the **p** and their fillets *of* silver. H5982
14 their **p** three, and their sockets three. H5982
15 their **p** three, and their sockets three. H5982
17 And the sockets for the **p** *were of* brass; H5982
17 the hooks of the **p** and their fillets *of* H5982
17 **p** of the court *were* filleted with silver. H5982
19 And their **p** *were* four, and their H5982
28 hooks for the **p**, and overlaid their H5982
39:33 his bars, and his **p**, and his sockets, H5982
40 The hangings of the court, his **p**, and H5982
40:18 in the bars thereof, and reared up his **p**. H5982
Nu 3:36 bars thereof, and the **p** thereof, and the H5982
37 And the **p** of the court round about, H5982
4:31 and the **p** thereof, and sockets thereof, H5982
32 And the **p** of the court round about, H5982
Dt 12: 3 altars, and break their **p**, and burn their H4676
Jdg 16:25 sport: and they set him between the **p**. H5982
26 me that I may feel the **p** whereupon the H5982
29 of the two middle **p** upon which the H5982
1Sa 2: 8 of glory: for the **p** of the earth *are* the H4690
1Ki 7: 2 **p**, with cedar beams upon the pillars. H5982
2 pillars, with cedar beams upon the **p**. H5982
3 that *lay* on forty five **p**, fifteen *in* a row. H5982
6 And he made a porch of **p**; the length H5982
6 and the *other* **p** and the thick beam H5982
15 For he cast two **p** of brass, of eighteen H5982
16 the tops of the **p**: the height of the one H5982
17 upon the top of the **p**; seven for the one H5982
18 And he made the **p**, and two rows H5982
19 the top of the **p** *were* of lily work in H5982
20 And the chapiters upon the two **p** *had* H5982
21 And he set up the **p** in the porch of the H5982
22 And upon the top of the **p** *was* lily H5982
22 so was the work of the **p** finished. H5982
41 The two **p**, and the *two* bowls of the H5982
41 on the top of the two **p**; and the two H5982
41 which *were* upon the top of the **p**; H5982
42 of the chapiters that *were* upon the **p**; H5982
10:12 And the king made of the almug trees **p** H4552
2Ki 18:16 and *from* the **p** which Hezekiah king H547
25:13 And the **p** of brass that *were* in the H5982
16 The two **p**, one sea, and the bases which H5982
1Ch 18: 8 sea, and the **p**, and the vessels of brass. H5982
2Ch 3:15 Also he made before the house two **p** of H5982
16 on the heads of the **p**; and made an H5982
17 And he reared up the **p** before the H5982
4:12 *To wit*, the two **p**, and the pommels, H5982
12 on the top of the two **p**, and the two H5982
12 which *were* on the top of the **p**; H5982
13 of the chapiters which *were* upon the **p**. H5982
Est 1: 6 to silver rings and **p** of marble: the H5982
Job 9: 6 of her place, and the **p** thereof tremble. H5982
26:11 The **p** of heaven tremble and are H5982
Ps 75: 3 dissolved: I bear up the **p** of it. Selah. H5982
Prv 9: 1 house, she hath hewn out her seven **p**: H5982
Song 3: 6 of the wilderness like **p** of smoke, H8490
10 He made the **p** thereof *of* silver, the H5982
5:15 His legs *are as* **p** of marble, set upon H5982
Jer 27:19 concerning the **p**, and concerning the H5982
52:17 Also the **p** of brass that *were* in the H5982
20 The two **p**, one sea, and twelve brasen H5982
21 And *concerning* the **p**, the height of one H5982
Ezk 40:49 to it: and *there were* **p** by the posts, one H5982
42: 6 but had not **p** as the pillars of the H5982
6 had not pillars as the **p** of the courts: H5982
Joel 2:30 earth, blood, and fire, and **p** of smoke. H8490
Gal 2: 9 who seemed to be **p**, perceived the grace *G4769*
Rev 10: 1 it were the sun, and his feet as **p** of fire: *G4769*

PILLED
Gen 30:37 chesnut tree; and **p** white strakes in H6478
38 And he set the rods which he had **p** H6478

PILLOW
1Sa 19:13 the bed, and put a **p** of goats' *hair* for H3523
16 with a **p** of goats' *hair* for his bolster. H3523
Mk 4:38 the ship, asleep on a **p**: and they awake *G4344*

PILLOWS
Gen 28:11 **p**, and lay down in that place to sleep. H4763
18 he had put *for* his **p**, and set it up *for* a H4763
Ezk 13:18 *women* that sew **p** to all armholes, and H3704
20 I *am* against your **p**, wherewith ye there H3704

PILNESER See TILGATH-PILNESER.

PILOTS
Ezk 27: 8 O Tyrus, *that* were in thee, were thy **p**. H2259
27 mariners, and thy **p**, thy calkers, and H2259
28 shake at the sound of the cry of thy **p**. H2259
29 *and* all the **p** of the sea, shall come H2259

PILTAI
Neh 12:17 Zichri; of Miniamin, of Moadiah, **P**; H6408

PIN
Jdg 16:14 And she fastened *it* with the **p**, and said H3489
14 the **p** of the beam, and with the web. H3489
Ezk 15: 3 a **p** of it to hang any vessel thereon? H3489

PINE
Lev 26:39 And they that are left of you shall **p** H4743
39 fathers shall they **p** away with them. H4743
Neh 8:15 branches, and **p** branches, and myrtle H8081
Isa 41:19 *and* the **p**, and the box tree together: H8410
60:13 thee, the fir tree, the **p** tree, and the box H8410
Lam 4: 9 with hunger: for these **p** away, stricken H2100
Ezk 24:23 nor weep; but ye shall **p** away for your H4743
33:10 upon us, and we **p** away in them, how H4743

PINETH
Mk 9:18 with his teeth, and **p** away: and I spake *G3583*

PINING
Isa 38:12 cut me off with **p** sickness: from day H1803

PINNACLE
Mt 4: 5 and setteth him on a **p** of the temple, *G4419*
Lk 4: 9 and set him on a **p** of the temple, and *G4419*

PINON
Gen 36:41 Duke Aholibamah, duke Elah, duke **P**, H6373
1Ch 1:52 Duke Aholibamah, duke Elah, duke **P**, H6373

PINS
Ex 27:19 and all the **p** thereof, and all the H3489
19 all the **p** of the court, *shall be of* brass. H3489
35:18 The **p** of the tabernacle, and the pins of H3489
18 The pins of the tabernacle, and the **p** of H3489
38:20 And all the **p** of the tabernacle, and of H3489
31 gate, and all the **p** of the tabernacle, H3489
31 and all the **p** of the court round about. H3489
39:40 his cords, and his **p**, and all the vessels H3489
Nu 3:37 sockets, and their **p**, and their cords. H3489
4:32 sockets, and their **p**, and their cords, H3489
Isa 3:22 and the wimples, and the crisping **p**, H2754

PIPE
1Sa 10: 5 a tabret, and a **p**, and a harp, before H2485
Isa 5:12 the tabret, and **p**, and wine, are in their H2485
30:29 one goeth with a **p** to come into the H2485
1Co 14: 7 sound, whether **p** or harp, except they *G836*

PIPED
1Ki 1:40 him, and the people **p** with pipes, and H2490
Mt 11:17 And saying, We have **p** unto you, and ye *G832*
Lk 7:32 saying, We have **p** unto you, and ye have *G832*
1Co 14: 7 shall it be known what is **p** or harped? *G832*

PIPERS
Rev 18:22 musicians, and of **p**, and trumpeters, *G834*

PIPES
1Ki 1:40 people piped with **p**, and rejoiced with H2485
Jer 48:36 for Moab like **p**, and mine heart shall H2485
36 heart shall sound like **p** for the men of H2485
Ezk 28:13 tabrets and of thy **p** was prepared in H5345
Zec 4: 2 and seven **p** to the seven lamps, H4166
12 the two golden **p** empty the golden *oil* H6804

PIRAM
Jos 10: 3 of Hebron, and unto **P** king of Jarmuth, H6502

PIRATHON
Jdg 12:15 died, and was buried in **P** in the land of H6552

PIRATHONITE
Jdg 12:13 the son of Hillel, a **P**, judged Israel. H6553
15 And Abdon the son of Hillel the **P** died, H6553
2Sa 23:30 Benaiah the **P**, Hiddai of the brooks of H6553
1Ch 11:31 children of Benjamin, Benaiah the **P**, H6553
27:14 *was* Benaiah the **P**, of the children of H6553

PISGAH
Nu 21:20 of **P**, which looketh toward Jeshimon. H6449
23:14 to the top of **P**, and built seven altars, H6449
Dt 3:27 Get thee up into the top of **P**, and lift up H6449
4:49 sea of the plain, under the springs of **P**. H6449
34: 1 of Nebo, to the top of **P**, that *is* over H6449

PISIDIA
Act 13:14 came to Antioch in **P**, and went into the *G4099*
14:24 throughout **P**, they came to Pamphylia. *G4099*

PISON
Gen 2:11 The name of the first *is* **P**: that *is* it H6376

PISPAH
1Ch 7:38 of Jether; Jephunneh, and **P**, and Ara. H6462

PISS
2Ki 18:27 dung, and drink their own **p** with you? H7890
Isa 36:12 dung, and drink their own **p** with you? H7890

PISSETH
1Sa 25:22 light any that **p** against the wall. H8366
34 light any that **p** against the wall. H8366
1Ki 14:10 him that **p** against the wall, *and* H8366
16:11 left him not one that **p** against a wall, H8366
21:21 Ahab him that **p** against the wall, and H8366
2Ki 9: 8 Ahab him that **p** against the wall, and H8366

PIT
Gen 37:20 cast him into some **p**, and we will say, H953
22 *but* cast him into this **p** that *is* in the H953
24 cast him into a **p**: and the pit *was* empty, H953
24 **p** *was* empty, *there was* no water in it. H953
28 up Joseph out of the **p**, and sold Joseph to H953
29 And Reuben returned unto the **p**; and, H953
29 *was* not in the **p**; and he rent his clothes. H953
Ex 21:33 And if a man shall open a **p**, or if a man H953
33 or if a man shall dig a **p**, and not cover it, H953
34 The owner of the **p** shall make *it* good, H953
Lev 11:36 Nevertheless a fountain or **p**, *wherein* H953
Nu 16:30 down quick into the **p**; then ye shall H7585
33 alive into the **p**, and the earth closed H7585
2Sa 17: 9 Behold, he is hid now in some **p**, or in H6354
18:17 him into a great **p** in the wood, and H6354
23:20 a lion in the midst of a **p** in time of snow: H953
2Ki 10:14 slew them at the **p** of the shearing house, H953
1Ch 11:22 and slew a lion in a **p** in a snowy day. H953
Job 6:27 fatherless, and ye dig *a* **p** for your friend.
17:16 They shall go down to the bars of the **p**, H7585
33:18 He keepeth back his soul from the **p**, H7845
24 down to the **p**: I have found a ransom. H7845
28 into the **p**, and his life shall see the light. H7845
30 To bring back his soul from the **p**, to be H7845
Ps 7:15 He made a **p**, and digged it, and is fallen H953
9:15 The heathen are sunk down in the **p** H7845
28: 1 like them that go down into the **p**. H953
30: 3 alive, that I should not go down to the **p**. H953
9 I go down to the **p**? Shall the dust praise H7845
35: 7 me their net *in* a **p**, *which* without cause H7845
40: 2 out of an horrible **p**, out of the miry clay, H953
55:23 down into the **p** of destruction: bloody H875
57: 6 have digged a **p** before me, into the H7882
69:15 let not the **p** shut her mouth upon me. H875
88: 4 **p**: I am as a man *that hath* no strength: H953
6 Thou hast laid me in the lowest **p**, in H953
94:13 until the **p** be digged for the wicked. H7845
143: 7 like unto them that go down into the **p**. H953
Prv 1:12 whole, as those that go down into the **p**: H953
22:14 women *is* a deep **p**: he that is abhorred H7745
23:27 and a strange woman *is* a narrow **p**. H875
26:27 Whoso diggeth a **p** shall fall therein: H7845
28:10 into his own **p**: but the upright shall H7816
17 shall flee to the **p**; let no man stay him. H953
Ecc 10: 8 He that diggeth a **p** shall fall into it; H1475
Isa 14:15 down to hell, to the sides of the **p**. H953
19 of the **p**; as a carcase trodden under feet. H953
24:17 Fear, and the **p**, and the snare, *are* upon H6354
18 shall fall into the **p**; and he that cometh H6354
18 of the midst of the **p** shall be taken in H6354
22 are gathered in the **p**, and shall be shut H953
30:14 or to take water *withal* out of the **p**. H1360

Isa 38:17 *it* from the **p** of corruption: for thou H7845
18 into the **p** cannot hope for thy truth. H953
51: 1 the hole of the **p** *whence* ye are digged. H953
14 in the **p**, nor that his bread should fail. H7845
Jer 18:20 they have digged a **p** for my soul. H7745
22 have digged a **p** to take me, H7745+H7882
41: 7 **p**, he, and the men that *were* with him. H953
9 Now the **p** wherein Ishmael had cast all H953
48:43 Fear, and the **p**, and the snare, *shall be* H6354
44 shall fall into the **p**; and he that getteth H6354
44 up out of the **p** shall be taken in the H6354
Ezk 19: 4 was taken in their **p**, and they brought H7845
8 net over him: he was taken in their **p**. H7845
26:20 descend into the **p**, with the people of old H953
20 that go down to the **p**, that thou be not H953
28: 8 They shall bring thee down to the **p**, H7845
31:14 of men, with them that go down to the **p**. H953
16 descend into the **p**: and all the trees of H953
32:18 earth, with them that go down into the **p**. H953
23 in the sides of the **p**, and her company is H953
24 shame with them that go down to the **p**. H953
25 go down to the **p**: he is put in the midst H953
29 and with them that go down to the **p**. H953
30 shame with them that go down to the **p**. H953
Zec 9:11 out of the **p** wherein *is* no water. H953
Mt 12:11 and if it fall into a **p** on the sabbath day, G999
Lk 14: 5 or an ox fallen into a **p**, and will not G5421
Rev 9: 1 was given the key of the bottomless **p**. G5421
2 And he opened the bottomless **p**; and G5421
2 a smoke out of the **p**, as the smoke of a G5421
2 by reason of the smoke of the **p**. G5421
11 of the bottomless **p**, whose name in the G12
11: 7 out of the bottomless **p** shall make war G12
17: 8 out of the bottomless **p**, and go into G12
20: 1 **p** and a great chain in his hand. G12
3 And cast him into the bottomless **p**, and G12

PITCH
Gen 6:14 **p** it within and without with pitch. H3722
14 shalt pitch it within and without with **p**. H3724
Ex 2: 3 with slime and with **p**, and put the child H2203
Nu 1:52 And the children of Israel shall **p** their H2583
53 But the Levites shall **p** round about the H2583
2: 2 of Israel shall **p** by his own standard, H2583
2 of the congregation shall they **p**. H2583
3 the camp of Judah **p** throughout their H2583
5 And those that do **p** next unto him H2583
12 And those which **p** by him *shall be* the H2583
3:23 The families of the Gershonites shall **p** H2583
29 of Kohath shall **p** on the side of the H2583
35 Abihail: *these* shall **p** on the side of the H2583
Dt 1:33 you out a place to **p** your tents *in*, in H2583
Jos 4:20 out of Jordan, did Joshua **p** in Gilgal. H6965
Isa 13:20 shall the Arabian **p** tent there; neither
34: 9 be turned into **p**, and the dust thereof H2203
9 land thereof shall become burning **p**. H2203
Jer 6: 3 her; they shall **p** *their* tents against her H8628

PITCHED
Gen 12: 8 east of Beth-el, and **p** his tent, *having* H5186
13:12 the plain, and **p** *his* tent toward Sodom.
26:17 And Isaac departed thence, and **p** his H2583
25 of the LORD, and **p** his tent there: and H5186
31:25 Now Jacob had **p** his tent in the mount: H8628
25 his brethren **p** in the mount of Gilead. H8628
33:18 and **p** his tent before the city. H2583
Ex 17: 1 of the LORD, and **p** in Rephidim: and H2583
19: 2 of Sinai, and had **p** in the wilderness; H2583
33: 7 And Moses took the tabernacle, and **p** H5186
Nu 1:51 tabernacle is to be **p**, the Levites shall H2583
2:34 Moses: so they **p** by their standards, H2583
9:17 the children of Israel **p** their tents. H2583
18 of the LORD they **p**: as long as the cloud H2583
12:16 and **p** in the wilderness of Paran. H2583
21:10 of Israel set forward, and **p** in Oboth. H2583
11 And they journeyed from Oboth, and **p** H2583
12 From thence they removed, and **p** in H2583
13 From thence they removed, and **p** on H2583
22: 1 set forward, and **p** in the plains of H2583
33: 5 from Rameses, and **p** in Succoth. H2583
6 And they departed from Succoth, and **p** H2583
7 and they **p** before Migdol. H2583
8 wilderness of Etham, and **p** in Marah. H2583
9 and ten palm trees; and they **p** there. H2583
15 and **p** in the wilderness of Sinai. H2583
16 of Sinai, and **p** at Kibroth-hattaavah. H2583
18 from Hazeroth, and **p** in Rithmah. H2583
19 Rithmah, and **p** at Rimmon-parez. H2583
20 from Rimmon-parez, and **p** in Libnah. H2583
Nu 33:21 And they removed from Libnah, and **p** H2583
22 And they journeyed from Rissah, and **p** H2583
23 And they went from Kehelathah, and **p** H2583
25 from Haradah, and **p** in Makheloth. H2583
27 And they departed from Tahath, and **p** H2583
28 And they removed from Tarah, and **p** H2583
29 And they went from Mithcah, and **p** in H2583
31 from Moseroth, and **p** in Bene-jaakan. H2583
33 Hor-hagidgad, and **p** in Jotbathah. H2583
36 Ezion-gaber, and **p** in the wilderness of H2583
37 And they removed from Kadesh, and **p** H2583
41 from mount Hor, and **p** in Zalmonah. H2583
42 from Zalmonah, and **p** in Punon. H2583
43 And they departed from Punon, and **p** H2583
44 And they departed from Oboth, and **p** H2583
45 And they departed from Iim, and **p** in H2583
47 and **p** in the mountains of H2583
48 of Abarim, and **p** in the plains of Moab H2583
49 And they **p** by Jordan, from H2583
Jos 8:11 the city, and **p** on the north side of H2583
11: 5 they came and **p** together at the waters H2583
Jdg 4:11 the Kenites, and **p** his tent unto the H5186
6:33 over, and **p** in the valley of Jezreel. H2583
7: 1 rose up early, and **p** beside the well of H2583
11:18 land of Moab, and **p** on the other side H2583
20 **p** in Jahaz, and fought against Israel. H2583
15: 9 Then the Philistines went up, and **p** in H2583
18:12 And they went up, and **p** in H2583
1Sa 4: 1 to battle, and **p** beside Eben-ezer: and H2583
1 and the Philistines **p** in Aphek. H2583
13: 5 and they came up, and **p** in Michmash, H2583
17: 1 to Judah, and **p** between Shochoh and H2583
2 together, and **p** by the valley of Elah, H2583
26: 3 And Saul **p** in the hill of Hachilah, H2583
5 where Saul had **p**: and David beheld the H2583
5 and the people **p** round about him. H2583
28: 4 and came and **p** in Shunem: and Saul H2583
4 Israel together, and they **p** in Gilboa. H2583
29: 1 **p** by a fountain which *is* in Jezreel. H2583
2Sa 6:17 that David had **p** for it: and David H5186
17:26 So Israel and Absalom **p** in the land of H2583
23:13 Philistines **p** in the valley of Rephaim. H2583
24: 5 And they passed over Jordan, and **p** in H2583
1Ki 20:27 the children of Israel **p** before them like H2583
29 And they **p** one over against the other H2583
2Ki 25: 1 Jerusalem, and **p** against it; and they H2583
1Ch 15: 1 for the ark of God, and **p** for it a tent. H5186
16: 1 tent that David had **p** for it: and they H5186
19: 7 who came and **p** before Medeba. And H2583
2Ch 1: 4 for he had **p** a tent for it at Jerusalem. H5186
Jer 52: 4 Jerusalem, and **p** against it, and built H2583
Heb 8: 2 which the Lord **p**, and not man. G4078

PITCHER
Gen 24:14 say, Let down thy **p**, I pray thee, that I H3537
15 brother, with her **p** upon her shoulder. H3537
16 the well, and filled her **p**, and came up. H3537
17 I pray thee, drink a little water of thy **p**. H3537
18 **p** upon her hand, and gave him drink. H3537
20 And she hasted, and emptied her **p** into H3537
43 thee, a little water of thy **p** to drink; H3537
45 forth with her **p** on her shoulder; and H3537
46 and let down her **p** from her *shoulder,* H3537
Ecc 12: 6 be broken, or the **p** be broken at the H3537
Mk 14:13 a man bearing a **p** of water: follow him. G2765
Lk 22:10 you, bearing a **p** of water; follow him G2765

PITCHERS
Jdg 7:16 empty **p**, and lamps within the pitchers. H3537
16 empty pitchers, and lamps within the **p**. H3537
19 brake the **p** that *were* in their hands. H3537
20 and brake the **p**, and held the lamps H3537
Lam 4: 2 **p**, the work of the hands of the potter! H5035

PITHOM
Ex 1:11 treasure cities, **P** and Raamses. H6619

PITHON
1Ch 8:35 And the sons of Micah *were*, **P**, and H6377
9:41 And the sons of Micah *were*, **P**, and H6377

PITIED
Ps 106:46 He made them also to be **p** of all those H7356
Lam 2: 2 and hath not **p**: he hath thrown down H2550
17 and hath not **p**: and he hath caused H2550
21 thine anger; thou hast killed, *and* not **p**. H2550
3:43 us: thou hast slain, thou hast not **p**. H2550
Ezk 16: 5 None eye **p** thee, to do any of these H2347

PITIETH
Ps 103:13 Like as a father **p** *his* children, *so* the H7355
13 *so* the LORD **p** them that fear him. H7355
Ezk 24:21 which your soul **p**; and your sons and H4263

PITIFUL
Lam 4:10 The hands of the **p** women have H7362
Jas 5:11 the Lord is very **p**, and of tender mercy. G4184
1Pt 3: 8 love as brethren, *be* **p**, *be* courteous: G2155

PITS
1Sa 13: 6 in rocks, and in high places, and in **p**. H953
Ps 119:85 The proud have digged **p** for me, which H7882
140:10 into deep **p**, that they rise not up again. H4113
Jer 2: 6 of deserts and of **p**, through a land of H7745
14: 3 they came to the **p**, *and* found no water; H1356
Lam 4:20 was taken in their **p**, of whom we said, H7825

PITY
Dt 7:16 eye shall have no **p** upon them: neither H2347
13: 8 shall thine eye **p** him, neither shalt H2347
19:13 Thine eye shall not **p** him, but thou H2347
21 And thine eye shall not **p**; *but* life *shall* H2347
25:12 off her hand, thine eye shall not **p** *her.* H2347
2Sa 12: 6 did this thing, and because he had no **p**. H2550
Job 6:14 To him that is afflicted **p** *should be* H2617
19:21 Have **p** upon me, have pity upon me, O H2603
21 Have pity upon me, have **p** upon me, O H2603
Ps 69:20 *for some* to take **p**, but *there was* none; H5110
Prv 19:17 He that hath **p** upon the poor lendeth H2603
28: 8 gather it for him that will **p** the poor. H2603
Isa 13:18 they shall have no **p** on the fruit of the H7355
63: 9 in his love and in his **p** he redeemed H2551
Jer 13:14 LORD: I will not **p**, nor spare, nor have H2550
15: 5 For who shall have **p** upon thee, O H2550
21: 7 them, neither have **p**, nor have mercy. H2550
Ezk 5:11 eye spare, neither will I have any **p**. H2550
7: 4 thee, neither will I have **p**: but I will H2550
9 neither will I have **p**: I will recompense H2550
8:18 neither will I have **p**: and though they H2550
9: 5 not your eye spare, neither have ye **p**: H2550
10 spare, neither will I have **p**, *but* I will H2550
36:21 But I had **p** for mine holy name, which H2550
Joel 2:18 jealous for his land, and **p** his people. H2550
Am 1:11 and did cast off all **p**, and his anger did H7356
Jna 4:10 Then said the LORD, Thou hast had **p** H2347
Zec 11: 5 and their own shepherds **p** them not. H2550
6 For I will no more **p** the inhabitants of H2550
Mt 18:33 fellowservant, even as I had **p** on thee? G1653

PLACE
Gen 1: 9 together unto one **p**, and let the dry H4725
12: 6 the land unto the **p** of Sichem, unto the H4725
13: 3 Beth-el, unto the **p** where his tent had H4725
4 Unto the **p** of the altar, which he had H4725
14 and look from the **p** where thou art H4725
18:24 destroy and not spare the **p** for the fifty H4725
26 I will spare all the **p** for their sakes. H4725
33 and Abraham returned unto his **p**. H4725
19:12 hast in the city, bring *them* out of this **p**: H4725
13 For we will destroy this **p**, because the H4725
14 get you out of this **p**; for the LORD will H4725
27 the **p** where he stood before the LORD: H4725
20:11 of God *is* not in this **p**; and they will slay H4725
13 unto me; at every **p** whither we shall H4725
21:31 Wherefore he called that **p** Beer-sheba; H4725
22: 3 unto the **p** of which God had told him. H4725
4 up his eyes, and saw the **p** afar off. H4725
9 And they came to the **p** which God had H4725
14 the name of that **p** Jehovah-jireh: as it is H4725
26: 7 And the men of the **p** asked *him* of his H4725
7 *he*, the men of the **p** should kill me for H4725
28:11 And he lighted upon a certain **p**, and H4725
11 of the stones of that **p**, and put *them for* H4725
11 and lay down in that **p** to sleep. H4725
16 the LORD is in this **p**; and I knew *it* not. H4725
17 dreadful *is* this **p**! this *is* none other but H4725
19 And he called the name of that **p** H4725
29: 3 again upon the well's mouth in his **p**. H4725
22 all the men of the **p**, and made a feast. H4725
30:25 unto mine own **p**, and to my country. H4725
31:55 departed, and returned unto his **p**. H4725
32: 2 called the name of that **p** Mahanaim. H4725
30 And Jacob called the name of the **p** H4725
33:17 the name of the **p** is called Succoth. H4725
35: 7 and called the **p** El-beth-el: because H4725
13 And God went up from him in the **p** H4725
14 And Jacob set up a pillar in the **p** where H4725
15 And Jacob called the name of the **p** H4725

P

Gen 38:14 sat in an open **p**, which *is* by the way H6607
21 Then he asked the men of that **p**, H4725
21 they said, There was no harlot in this ***p***. H4725
22 the men of the **p** said, *that* there was H4725
22 said, *that* there was no harlot in this ***p***. H4725
39:20 into the prison, a **p** where the king's H4725
40: 3 prison, the **p** where Joseph *was* bound. H4725
13 thee unto thy **p**: and thou shalt deliver H3653
48: 9 given me in this ***p***. And he said, Bring
50:19 them, Fear not: for *am* I in the **p** of God?
Ex 3: 5 off thy feet, for the **p** whereon thou H4725
8 honey; unto the **p** of the Canaanites, H4725
10:23 rose any from his **p** for three days: but H8478
13: 3 ***p***: there shall no leavened bread be eaten.
15:17 inheritance, *in* the **p**, O LORD, *which* H4349
16:29 every man in his **p**, let no man go out of H8478
29 man go out of his **p** on the seventh day. H4725
17: 7 And he called the name of the **p** H4725
18:21 covetousness; and **p** *such* over them, *to* H7760
23 people shall also go to their **p** in peace. H4725
21:13 appoint thee a **p** whither he shall flee. H4725
23:20 thee into the **p** which I have prepared. H4725
26:33 between the holy ***p*** and the most holy.
34 ark of the testimony in the most holy ***p***.
28:29 in unto the holy ***p***, for a memorial before
35 in unto the holy ***p*** before the LORD, and
43 in the holy ***p***; that they bear not iniquity,
29:30 congregation to minister in the holy ***p***.
31 and seethe his flesh in the holy **p**. H4725
31:11 for the holy ***p***: according to all that
32:34 the people unto *the* **p** of which I have
33:21 Behold, *there is* a **p** by me, and thou H4725
35:19 service in the holy ***p***, the holy garments
38:24 work of the holy ***p***, even the gold of the
39: 1 service in the holy ***p***, and made the holy
41 do service in the holy ***p***, and the holy
Lev 1:16 on the east part, by the **p** of the ashes: H4725
4:12 camp unto a clean **p**, where the ashes H4725
24 and kill it in the **p** where they kill the H4725
29 offering in the **p** of the burnt offering. H4725
33 the **p** where they kill the burnt offering. H4725
6:11 ashes without the camp unto a clean **p**. H4725
16 eaten in the holy **p**; in the court of the H4725
25 sin offering: In the **p** where the burnt H4725
26 eat it: in the holy **p** shall it be eaten, in H4725
27 whereon it was sprinkled in the holy **p**. H4725
30 *withal* in the holy ***p***, shall be eaten: it
7: 2 In the **p** where they kill the burnt H4725
6 be eaten in the holy **p**: it *is* most holy. H4725
10:13 And ye shall eat it in the holy **p**, because H4725
14 ye eat in a clean **p**; thou, and thy sons, H4725
17 in the holy **p**, seeing it *is* most holy, H4725
18 in within the holy ***p***: ye should indeed
18 eaten it in the holy ***p***, as I commanded.
13:19 And in the **p** of the boil there be a white H4725
23 But if the bright spot stay in his **p**, *and* H8478
28 And if the bright spot stay in his **p**, *and* H8478
14:13 And he shall slay the lamb in the **p** H4725
13 in the holy **p**: for as the sin offering H4725
28 **p** of the blood of the trespass offering: H4725
40 into an unclean **p** without the city: H4725
41 off without the city into an unclean **p**: H4725
42 put *them* in the **p** of those stones; and H8478
45 forth out of the city into an unclean **p**. H4725
16: 2 into the holy ***p*** within the vail before H1004
3 Thus shall Aaron come into the holy ***p***:
16 atonement for the holy ***p***, because of the
17 in the holy ***p***, until he come out, and
20 the holy ***p***, and the tabernacle of
23 the holy ***p***, and shall leave them there:
24 with water in the holy **p**, and put on his H4725
27 in the holy ***p***, shall *one* carry forth
24: 9 eat it in the holy **p**: for it *is* most holy H4725
Nu 2:17 every man in his **p** by their standards. H3027
9:17 and in the **p** where the cloud abode, H4725
10:14 In the first ***p*** went the standard of the
29 unto the **p** of which the LORD H4725
33 to search out a resting **p** for them. H4496
11: 3 And he called the name of the **p** H4725
34 And he called the name of that **p** H4725
13:24 The **p** was called the brook Eshcol, H4725
14:40 go up unto the **p** which the LORD hath H4725
18:10 In the most holy ***p*** shalt thou eat it; every
31 And ye shall eat it in every **p**, ye and H4725
19: 9 camp in a clean **p**, and it shall be kept H4725
20: 5 us in unto this evil **p**? it *is* no place of H4725
5 evil place? it *is* no **p** of seed, or of figs, H4725
21: 3 he called the name of the **p** Hormah. H4725
22:26 stood in a narrow **p**, where *was* no way H4725

Nu 23: 3 will tell thee. And he went to an high **p**. H8205
13 me unto another **p**, from whence thou H4725
27 thee unto another **p**; peradventure it H4725
24:11 Therefore now flee thou to thy **p**: I H4725
25 to his **p**: and Balak also went his way. H4725
28: 7 lamb: in the holy ***p*** shalt thou cause the
32: 1 behold, the **p** *was* a place for cattle; H4725
1 behold, the place *was* a **p** for cattle; H4725
17 them unto their **p**: and our little ones H4725
33:54 shall be in the **p** where his lot falleth;
Dt 1:31 that ye went, until ye came into this **p**. H4725
33 search you out a **p** to pitch your tents H4725
2:37 not, *nor* unto any **p** of the river Jabbok, H3027
9: 7 until ye came unto this **p**, ye have been H4725
11: 5 wilderness, until ye came into this **p**; H4725
24 Every **p** whereon the soles of your feet H4725
12: 3 destroy the names of them out of that **p**. H4725
5 But unto the **p** which the LORD your H4725
11 Then there shall be a **p** which the H4725
13 offerings in every **p** that thou seest: H4725
14 But in the **p** which the LORD shall H4725
18 thy God in the **p** which the LORD thy H4725
21 If the **p** which the LORD thy God hath H4725
26 the **p** which the LORD shall choose: H4725
14:23 thy God, in the **p** which he shall choose H4725
23 he shall choose to **p** his name there, the H7931
24 carry it; *or* if the **p** be too far from thee, H4725
25 shalt go unto the **p** which the LORD thy H4725
15:20 year by year in the **p** which the LORD H4725
16: 2 the herd, in the **p** which the LORD shall H4725
2 LORD shall choose to **p** his name there. H7931
6 But at the **p** which the LORD thy God H4725
6 shall choose to **p** his name in, there H7931
7 And thou shalt roast and eat *it* in the **p** H4725
11 among you, in the **p** which the LORD H4725
11 God hath chosen to **p** his name there. H7931
15 thy God in the **p** which the LORD shall H4725
16 thy God in the **p** which he shall choose; H4725
17: 8 thee up into the **p** which the LORD thy H4725
10 which they of that **p** which the LORD H4725
18: 6 the **p** which the LORD shall choose; H4725
21:19 of his city, and unto the gate of his **p**; H4725
23:12 Thou shalt have a **p** also without the H3027
16 you, in that **p** which he shall choose H4725
26: 2 shalt go unto the **p** which the LORD thy H4725
2 God shall choose to **p** his name there. H7931
9 And he hath brought us into this **p**, and H4725
27:15 *it* in *a* secret ***p***. And all the people shall
29: 7 And when ye came unto this **p**, Sihon H4725
31:11 thy God in the **p** which he shall choose, H4725
Jos 1: 3 Every **p** that the sole of your foot shall H4725
3: 3 remove from your **p**, and go after it. H4725
4: 3 of Jordan, out of the **p** where the priests'
3 **p**, where ye shall lodge this night. H4411
8 with them unto the **p** where they lodged,
9 of Jordan, in the **p** where the feet of the
18 unto their **p**, and flowed over all H4725
5: 9 of the **p** is called Gilgal unto this day. H4725
15 off thy foot; for the **p** whereon thou H4725
7:26 the name of that **p** was called, The H4725
8:19 out of their **p**, and they ran as soon H4725
9:27 day, in the **p** which he should choose. H4725
20: 4 a **p**, that he may dwell among them. H4725
Jdg 2: 5 And they called the name of that **p** H4725
6:26 in the ordered **p**, and take the second H4634
7: 7 *other* people go every man unto his **p**. H4725
21 And they stood every man in his **p** H8478
9:55 they departed every man unto his **p**. H4725
11:19 pray thee, through thy land into my **p**. H4725
15:17 hand, and called that **p** Ramath-lehi. H4725
19 But God clave an hollow **p** that *was* in H4388
17: 8 he could find *a* ***p***: and he came to mount
9 and I go to sojourn where I may find *a* ***p***.
18: 3 thou in this ***p***? and what hast thou here?
10 into your hands; a **p** where *there is* no H4725
12 they called that **p** Mahaneh-dan unto H4725
19:16 but the men of the **p** *were* Benjamites. H4725
28 man rose up, and gat him unto his **p**. H4725
20:22 again in array in the **p** where they put H4725
33 up out of their **p**, and put themselves H4725
36 men of Israel gave **p** to the Benjamites, H4725
21:19 Shiloh yearly *in a* **p** which *is* on the north
Ru 1: 7 Wherefore she went forth out of the **p** H4725
3: 4 shalt mark the **p** where he shall lie, and H4725
4:10 gate of his **p**: ye *are* witnesses this day. H4725
1Sa 3: 2 laid down in his **p**, and his eyes began H4725
9 So Samuel went and lay down in his **p**. H4725
5: 3 took Dagon, and set him in his **p** again. H4725
11 again to his own **p**, that it slay us not, H4725

1Sa 6: 2 us wherewith we shall send it to his **p**. H4725
9:12 of the people to day in the high **p**: H1116
13 he go up to the high **p** to eat: for the H1116
14 against them, for to go up to the high **p**. H1116
19 me unto the high **p**; for ye shall eat with H1116
22 sit in the chiefest **p** among them that H4725
25 from the high **p** into the city, *Samuel* H1116
10: 5 from the high **p** with a psaltery, and H1116
12 And one of the same **p** answered and
13 of prophesying, he came to the high **p**. H1116
12: 8 Egypt, and made them dwell in this **p**. H4725
14: 9 in our **p**, and will not go up unto them. H8478
46 and the Philistines went to their own **p**. H4725
15:12 he set him up a **p**, and is gone about, H3027
19: 2 and abide in a secret ***p***, and hide thyself:
20:19 and come to the **p** where thou didst H4725
25 Saul's side, and David's **p** was empty. H4725
27 that David's **p** was empty: and Saul H4725
37 And when the lad was come to the **p** of H4725
41 arose out of *a* **p** toward the south, and
21: 2 *my* servants to such and such a **p**. H4725
23:22 know and see his **p** where his haunt is, H4725
28 they called that **p** Sela-hammahlekoth. H4725
26: 5 And David arose, and came to the **p** H4725
5 David beheld the **p** where Saul lay, and H4725
25 on his way, and Saul returned to his **p**. H4725
27: 5 let them give me a **p** in some town in H4725
29: 4 may go again to his **p** which thou hast H4725
2Sa 2:16 together: wherefore that **p** was called H4725
23 died in the same **p**: and it came to pass, H8478
23 as came to the **p** where Asahel fell H4725
5:20 the name of that **p** Baal-perazim. H4725
6: 8 name of the **p** Perez-uzzah to this day. H4725
17 and set it in his **p**, in the midst of the H4725
7:10 Moreover I will appoint a **p** for my H4725
10 they may dwell in a **p** of their own, and H4725
11:16 Uriah unto a **p** where he knew that H4725
15:17 him, and tarried in a **p** that was far off. H1004
19 us? return to thy **p**, and abide with the H4725
21 surely in what **p** my lord the king shall H4725
17: 9 or in some *other* **p**: and it will come to H4725
12 So shall we come upon him in some **p** H4725
18:18 it is called unto this day, Absalom's **p**. H3027
19:39 him; and he returned unto his own **p**. H4725
22:20 He brought me forth also into a large **p**: H4800
23: 7 utterly burned with fire in the *same* **p**. H7675
1Ki 3: 4 *was* the great high **p**: a thousand burnt H1116
4:12 *even* unto *the* **p** *that is* beyond Jokneam:
28 they unto the **p** where *the officers* were, H4725
5: 9 sea in floats unto the **p** that thou shalt H4725
6:16 for the oracle, *even* for the most holy ***p***.
7:50 the most holy ***p***, *and* for the doors of
8: 6 the LORD unto his **p**, into the oracle of H4725
6 to the most holy ***p***, *even* under the H4725
7 two wings over the **p** of the ark, and the H4725
8 out in the holy ***p*** before the oracle, and
10 out of the holy ***p***, that the cloud filled
13 a settled **p** for thee to abide in for ever. H4349
21 And I have set there a **p** for the ark, H4725
29 *even* toward the **p** of which thou hast H4725
29 thy servant shall make toward this **p**. H4725
30 pray toward this **p**: and hear thou in H4725
30 **p**: and when thou hearest, forgive. H4725
35 they pray toward this **p**, and confess thy H4725
39 thy dwelling **p**, and forgive, and do, H4349
43 Hear thou in heaven thy dwelling **p**, H4349
49 dwelling **p**, and maintain their cause, H4349
10:19 either side on the **p** of the seat, and two H4725
11: 7 Then did Solomon build an high **p** for H1116
13: 8 I eat bread nor drink water in this **p**: H4725
16 nor drink water with thee in this **p**: H4725
22 water in the **p**, of the which *the LORD* H4725
20:24 his **p**, and put captains in their rooms: H4725
21:19 the LORD, In the **p** where dogs licked H4725
22:10 robes, in a void **p** in the entrance of the H1637
2Ki 5:11 hand over the **p**, and recover the leper. H4725
6: 1 Behold now, the **p** where we dwell with H4725
2 let us make us a **p** there, where we may H4725
6 shewed him the **p**. And he cut down a H4725
8 In such and such a **p** *shall be* my camp. H4725
9 thou pass not such a **p**; for thither the H4725
10 And the king of Israel sent to the **p** H4725
18:25 LORD against this **p** to destroy it? The H4725
22:16 bring evil upon this **p**, and upon the H4725
17 this **p**, and shall not be quenched. H4725
19 I spake against this **p**, and against the H4725
20 bring upon this **p**. And they brought the H4725
23:15 *and* the high **p** which Jeroboam the H1116
15 altar and the high **p** he brake down, H1116

2Ki 23:15 and burned the high **p**, *and* stamped *it* H1116
1Ch 6:32 the dwelling **p** of the tabernacle of H4908
49 all the work of the **p** most holy, and to
13:11 that **p** is called Perez-uzza to this day. H4725
14:11 the name of that **p** Baal-perazim. H4725
15: 1 and prepared a **p** for the ark of God, H4725
3 his **p**, which he had prepared for it. H4725
12 unto *the* **p** *that* I have prepared for it.
16:27 strength and gladness *are* in his **p**. H4725
39 LORD in the high **p** that *was* at Gibeon, H1116
17: 9 Also I will ordain a **p** for my people H4725
9 they shall dwell in their **p**, and shall be H4725
21:22 Grant me the **p** of *this* threshingfloor, H4725
25 So David gave to Ornan for the **p** six H4725
29 at that season in the high **p** at Gibeon. H1116
23:32 charge of the holy *p*, and the charge of
28:11 thereof, and of the **p** of the mercy seat, H1004
2Ch 1: 3 went to the high **p** that *was* at Gibeon; H1116
4 to *the* **p** *which* David had prepared
13 to the high **p** that *was* at Gibeon H1116
3: 1 his father, in the **p** that David had H4725
4:22 for the most holy *p*, and the doors of the
5: 7 the LORD unto his **p**, to the oracle of the H4725
7 into the most holy *p*, *even* under the H4725
8 wings over the **p** of the ark, and the H4725
11 out of the holy *p*: (for all the priests *that*
6: 2 thee, and a **p** for thy dwelling for ever. H4349
20 night, upon the **p** whereof thou hast H4725
20 thy servant prayeth toward this **p**. H4725
21 make toward this **p**: hear thou from thy H4725
21 from thy dwelling **p**, *even* from heaven; H4725
26 they pray toward this **p**, and confess thy H4725
30 thy dwelling **p**, and forgive, and render H4349
33 from thy dwelling **p**, and do according H4349
39 from thy dwelling **p**, their prayer and H4349
40 unto the prayer *that is made* in this **p**. H4725
41 into thy resting **p**, thou, and the ark of
7:12 **p** to myself for an house of sacrifice. H4725
15 unto the prayer *that is made* in this **p**. H4725
9:18 **p**, and two lions standing by the stays: H4725
18: 9 they sat in a void **p** at the entering in of H1637
20:26 the name of the same **p** was called, The H4725
24:11 carried it to his **p** again. Thus they did H4725
29: 5 forth the filthiness out of the holy *p*.
7 in the holy *p* unto the God of Israel.
30:16 And they stood in their **p** after their H5977
27 his holy dwelling **p**, *even* unto heaven. H4583
34:24 bring evil upon this **p**, and upon the H4725
25 upon this **p**, and shall not be quenched. H4725
27 words against this **p**, and against the H4725
28 will bring upon this **p**, and upon the H4725
31 And the king stood in his **p**, and made a H5977
35: 5 And stand in the holy *p* according to the
10 stood in their **p**, and the Levites in their H5977
15 Asaph *were* in their **p**, according to the H4612
36:15 on his people, and on his dwelling **p**: H4583
Ezr 1: 4 And whosoever remaineth in any **p** H4725
4 let the men of his **p** help him with H4725
2:68 for the house of God to set it up in his **p**: H4349
5:15 let the house of God be builded in his **p**. H870
6: 3 be builded, the **p** where they offered H870
5 **p**, and place *them* in the house of God. H870
5 place, and **p** *them* in the house of God. H5182
7 the Jews build this house of God in his **p**. H870
8:17 the chief at the **p** Casiphia, and I told H4725
17 Nethinims, at the **p** Casiphia, that they H4725
9: 8 us a nail in his holy **p**, that our God may H4725
Neh 1: 9 them unto the **p** that I have chosen to H4725
2: 3 sad, when the city, the **p** of my fathers' H1004
14 but *there was* no **p** for the beast *that* H4725
3:16 of Beth-zur, unto *the* **p** over against the
26 in Ophel, unto *the* **p** over against the
31 son unto the **p** of the Nethinims, and H1004
4:20 In what **p** *therefore* ye hear the sound H4725
8: 7 the law: and the people *stood* in their **p**. H5977
9: 3 And they stood up in their **p**, and read H5977
13:11 them together, and set them in their **p**. H5977
Est 2: 9 the best *p* of the house of the women.
4:14 Jews from another **p**; but thou and thy H4725
7: 8 garden into the **p** of the banquet of H1004
Job 2:11 every one from his own **p**; Eliphaz the H4725
6:17 is hot, they are consumed out of their **p**. H4725
7:10 neither shall his **p** know him any more. H4725
8:17 the heap, *and* seeth the **p** of stones. H1004
18 If he destroy him from his **p**, then *it* H4725
22 **p** of the wicked shall come to nought. H168
9: 6 Which shaketh the earth out of her **p**, H4725
14:18 and the rock is removed out of his **p**. H4725
16:18 my blood, and let my cry have no **p**. H4725

Job 18: 4 shall the rock be removed out of his **p**? H4725
21 *is* the **p** *of him that* knoweth not God. H4725
20: 9 shall his **p** any more behold him. H4725
26: 7 **p**, *and* hangeth the earth upon nothing. H8414
27:21 and as a storm hurleth him out of his **p**. H4725
23 at him, and shall hiss him out of his **p**. H4725
28: 1 and a **p** for gold *where* they fine *it*. H4725
6 The stones of it *are* the **p** of sapphires: H4725
12 and where *is* the **p** of understanding? H4725
20 and where *is* the **p** of understanding? H4725
23 thereof, and he knoweth the **p** thereof. H4725
36:16 strait *into* a broad **p**, where *there is* no H7338
20 night, when people are cut off in their **p**. H8478
37: 1 trembleth, and is moved out of his **p**. H4725
38:10 And brake up for it my decreed *p*, and set
12 caused the dayspring to know his **p**; H4725
19 *as for* darkness, where *is* the **p** thereof, H4725
39:28 the crag of the rock, and the strong **p**. H4686
40:12 and tread down the wicked in their **p**. H8478
Ps 18:11 He made darkness his secret **p**; his
19 He brought me forth also into a large **p**; H4800
24: 3 LORD? or who shall stand in his holy **p**? H4725
26: 8 and the **p** where thine honour dwelleth. H4725
12 My foot standeth in an even **p**: in the H4334
32: 7 Thou *art* my hiding **p**; thou shalt
33:14 From the **p** of his habitation he looketh H4349
37:10 consider his **p**, and it *shall* not *be*. H4725
44:19 sore broken us in the **p** of dragons, and H4725
46: 4 *p* of the tabernacles of the most High.
52: 5 out of *thy* dwelling **p**, and root thee out of H168
66:12 thou broughtest us out into a wealthy *p*.
68:17 *is* among them, *as in* Sinai, in the holy *p*.
74: 7 dwelling **p** of thy name to the ground. H4908
76: 2 tabernacle, and his dwelling **p** in Zion. H4585
79: 7 Jacob, and laid waste his dwelling **p**.
81: 7 thee in the secret **p** of thunder: I proved
90: 1 Lord, thou hast been our dwelling **p** in H4583
91: 1 He that dwelleth in the secret **p** of the
103:16 the **p** thereof shall know it no more. H4725
104: 8 **p** which thou hast founded for them. H4725
118: 5 answered me, *and set me* in a large **p**. H4800
119:114 Thou *art* my hiding **p** and my shield: I
132: 5 Until I find out a **p** for the LORD, an H4725
Prv 1:21 She crieth in the chief **p** of concourse, H7218
14:26 and his children shall have a **p** of refuge.
15: 3 The eyes of the LORD *are* in every **p**, H4725
24:15 of the righteous; spoil not his resting **p**: H7258
25: 6 and stand not in the **p** of great *men*: H4725
27: 8 so *is* a man that wandereth from his **p**. H4725
Ecc 1: 5 and hasteth to his **p** where he arose. H4725
7 *is* not full; unto the **p** from whence the H4725
3:16 under the sun the **p** of judgment, *that* H4725
16 *was* there; and the **p** of righteousness, H4725
20 All go unto one **p**; all are of the dust, H4725
6: 6 he seen no good: do not all go to one **p**? H4725
8:10 and gone from the **p** of the holy, and H4725
10: 4 **p**; for yielding pacifieth great offences. H4725
6 great dignity, and the rich sit in low **p**. H8216
11: 3 the north, in the **p** where the tree H4725
Isa 4: 5 every dwelling **p** of mount Zion, and H4349
6 the heat, and for a **p** of refuge, and for a
5: 8 field, till *there be* no **p**, that they may be H4725
7:23 day, *that* every **p** shall be, where there H4725
13:13 remove out of her **p**, in the wrath of the H4725
14: 2 them to their **p**: and the house of Israel H4725
16:12 weary on the high **p**, that he shall come H1116
18: 4 in my dwelling **p** like a clear heat upon H4349
7 spoiled, to the **p** of the name of the H4725
22:23 *as* a nail in a sure **p**; and he shall be for H4725
25 in the sure **p** be removed, and be H4725
25: 5 the heat in a dry **p**; *even* the heat with H6724
26:21 cometh out of his **p** to punish the H4725
28: 8 filthiness, *so that there is* no **p** *clean*. H4725
17 the waters shall overflow the hiding **p**. H5643
25 appointed barley and the rie in their **p**? H1367
30:32 And *in* every **p** where the grounded H3605
32: 2 And a man shall be as an hiding **p** H4224
2 of water in a dry **p**, as the shadow of a H6724
19 and the city shall be low in a low **p**. H8218
33:16 He shall dwell on high: his **p** of defence
21 *will be* unto us a **p** of broad rivers *and* H4725
34:14 rest there, and find for herself a **p** of rest.
35: 1 The wilderness and the solitary **p** shall H6723
45:19 I have not spoken in secret, in a dark **p** H4725
46: 7 and set him in his **p**, and he standeth; H8478
7 he standeth; from his **p** shall he not H4725
13 **p** salvation in Zion for Israel my glory. H5414
49:20 in thine ears, The **p** *is* too strait for me: H4725
20 for me: give **p** to me that I may dwell. H5066

Isa 54: 2 Enlarge the **p** of thy tent, and let them H4725
56: 5 within my walls a **p** and a name better H3027
57:15 the high and holy *p*, with him also *that is*
60:13 to beautify the **p** of my sanctuary; and H4725
13 I will make the **p** of my feet glorious. H4725
65:10 valley of Achor a **p** for the herds to lie
66: 1 unto me? and where *is* the **p** of my rest? H4725
Jer 4: 7 gone forth from his **p** to make thy land H4725
26 I beheld, and, lo, the fruitful **p** *was* a
6: 3 about; they shall feed every one in his **p**. H3027
7: 3 and I will cause you to dwell in this **p**. H4725
6 blood in this **p**, neither walk after other H4725
7 Then will I cause you to dwell in this **p**, H4725
12 But go ye now unto my **p** which *was* in H4725
14 and unto the **p** which I gave to you H4725
20 out upon this **p**, upon man, and upon H4725
32 shall bury in Tophet, till there be no **p**. H4725
9: 2 a lodging **p** of wayfaring men; that H4411
13: 7 the girdle from the **p** where I had hid it: H4725
14:13 I will give you assured peace in this **p**. H4725
16: 2 thou have sons or daughters in this **p**. H4725
3 are born in this **p**, and concerning their H4725
9 cease out of this **p** in your eyes, and in H4725
17:12 the beginning *is* the **p** of our sanctuary. H4725
18:14 that come from another **p** be forsaken? H2114
19: 3 evil upon this **p**, the which whosoever H4725
4 have estranged this **p**, and have burned H4725
4 this **p** with the blood of innocents; H4725
6 the LORD, that this **p** shall no more be H4725
7 and Jerusalem in this **p**; and I will cause H4725
11 in Tophet, till *there be* no **p** to bury. H4725
12 Thus will I do unto this **p**, saith the H4725
13 be defiled as the **p** of Tophet, because H4725
22: 3 neither shed innocent blood in this **p**. H4725
11 **p**; He shall not return thither any more: H4725
12 But he shall die in the **p** whither they H4725
24: 5 sent out of this **p** into the land of the H4725
27:22 them up, and restore them to this **p**. H4725
28: 3 again into this **p** all the vessels of the H4725
3 this **p**, and carried them to Babylon: H4725
4 And I will bring again to this **p** H4725
6 away captive, from Babylon into this **p**. H4725
29:10 you, in causing you to return to this **p**. H4725
14 you again into the **p** whence I caused H4725
32:37 **p**, and I will cause them to dwell safely: H4725
33:10 be heard in this **p**, which ye say *shall be* H4725
12 hosts; Again in this **p**, which is desolate H4725
38: 9 die for hunger in the **p** where he is: for H8478
40: 2 hath pronounced this evil upon this **p**. H4725
42:18 and ye shall see this **p** no more. H4725
22 pestilence, in the **p** whither ye desire to H4725
44:29 punish you in this **p**, that ye may know H4725
51:62 against this **p**, to cut it off, that none H4725
Ezk 3:12 *be* the glory of the LORD from his **p**. H4725
6:13 thick oak, the **p** where they did offer H4725
7:22 pollute my secret *p*: for the robbers shall
10:11 went, but to the **p** whither the head H4725
12: 3 remove from thy **p** to another place in H4725
3 place to another **p** in their sight: it may H4725
16:24 thee an eminent **p**, and hast made thee H1354
24 made thee an high **p** in every street. H7413
25 Thou hast built thy high **p** at every H7413
31 In that thou buildest thine eminent **p** H1354
31 makest thine high **p** in every street; H7413
39 thine eminent **p**, and shall break down H1354
17:16 GOD, surely in the **p** *where* the king H4725
20:29 What *is* the high **p** whereunto ye go? H1116
21:19 and choose thou a **p**, choose *it* at the H3027
30 will judge thee in the **p** where thou wast H4725
26: 5 It shall be *a* **p** *for* the spreading of nets in
14 thou shalt be *a* **p** to spread nets upon;
37:14 shall live, and I shall **p** you in your own H3240
26 them: and I will **p** them, and multiply H5414
38:15 And thou shalt come from thy **p** out of H4725
39:11 will give unto Gog a **p** there of graves in H4725
41: 4 he said unto me, This *is* the most holy *p*.
9 *was* left *was* the **p** of the side chambers H1004
11 *were* toward *the* **p** *that was* left, one door
11 the breadth of the **p** that was left *was* H4725
12 the separate **p** at the end toward the H1508
13 and the separate **p**, and the building, H1508
14 **p** toward the east, an hundred cubits. H1508
15 the separate **p** which *was* behind it, H1508
42: 1 the separate **p**, and which *was* before H1508
10 **p**, and over against the building. H1508
13 the separate **p**, they *be* holy chambers, H1508
13 the trespass offering; for the **p** *is* holy. H4725
14 go out of the holy *p* into the utter court,
20 the sanctuary and the profane **p**.

Ezk 43: 7 And he said unto me, Son of man, the **p** H4725
7 my throne, and the **p** of the soles of my H4725
13 this *shall be* the higher **p** of the altar. H1354
21 **p** of the house, without the sanctuary. H4662
44:13 in the most holy *p*: but they shall bear
45: 3 be the sanctuary *and* the most holy *p*.
4 and it shall be a **p** for their houses, and H4725
4 and an holy **p** for the sanctuary. H4720
46:19 *was* a **p** on the two sides westward. H4725
20 Then said he unto me, This *is* the **p** H4725
47:10 they shall be a *p* to spread forth nets;
48:15 shall be a profane *p* for the city, for
Dan 2:35 away, that no **p** was found for them: H870
8:11 the **p** of his sanctuary was cast down. H4349
11:31 and they shall **p** the abomination that H5414
Hos 1:10 to pass, *that* in the **p** where it was said H4725
4:16 will feed them as a lamb in a large **p**. H4800
5:15 I will go *and* return to my **p**, till they H4725
9:13 in a pleasant **p**: but Ephraim shall bring H5116
11:11 **p** them in their houses, saith the LORD. H3427
13:13 in *the p of* the breaking forth of children.
Joel 3: 7 Behold, I will raise them out of the **p** H4725
Am 8: 3 bodies in every **p**; they shall cast *them* H4725
Mic 1: 3 forth out of his **p**, and will come down, H4725
4 waters *that are* poured down a steep **p**. H4174
Nah 1: 8 make an utter end of the **p** thereof, and H4725
3:17 their **p** is not known where they *are*. H4725
Zep 1: 4 of Baal from this **p**, *and* the name of the H4725
2:11 his **p**, *even* all the isles of the heathen. H4725
15 a desolation, a **p** for beasts to lie down
Hag 2: 9 of hosts: and in this **p** will I give peace, H4725
Zec 6:12 grow up out of his **p**, and he shall build H8478
10: 6 them again to **p** them; for I have mercy H3427
10 and *p* shall not be found for them.
12: 6 again in her own **p**, *even* in Jerusalem. H8478
14:10 inhabited in her **p**, from Benjamin's H8478
10 gate unto the **p** of the first gate, unto H4725
Mal 1:11 and in every **p** incense *shall be* offered H4725
Mt 8:32 down a steep **p** into the sea, and *G2911*
9:24 He said unto them, Give **p**: for the maid *G402*
12: 6 But I say unto you, That in this **p** is *one* *G5602*
14:13 by ship into a desert **p** apart: and when *G5117*
15 This is a desert **p**, and the time is now *G5117*
35 And when the men of that **p** had *G5117*
17:20 hence to yonder **p**; and it shall remove; *G1563*
24:15 **p**, (whoso readeth, let him understand:) *G5117*
26:36 Then cometh Jesus with them unto a **p** *G5564*
52 thy sword into his **p**: for all they that *G5117*
27:33 And when they were come unto a **p** *G5117*
33 Golgotha, that is to say, a **p** of a skull, *G5117*
28: 6 Come, see the **p** where the Lord lay. *G5117*
Mk 1:35 into a solitary **p**, and there prayed. *G5117*
5:13 down a steep **p** into the sea, (they were *G2911*
6:10 And he said unto them, In what **p** *G3699*
10 there abide till ye depart from that **p**. *G1564*
31 apart into a desert **p**, and rest a while: *G5117*
32 And they departed into a desert **p** by *G5117*
35 **p**, and now the time *is* far passed: *G5117*
11: 4 door without in a **p** where two ways met;
12: 1 *it*, and digged *a p for* the winefat, and
14:32 And they came to a **p** which was *G5564*
15:22 And they bring him unto the **p** *G5117*
22 is, being interpreted, The **p** of a skull. *G5117*
16: 6 here: behold the **p** where they laid him. *G5117*
Lk 4:17 he found the **p** where it was written, *G5117*
37 every **p** of the country round about. *G5117*
42 and went into a desert **p**: and the people *G5117*
8:33 steep **p** into the lake, and were choked. *G2911*
9:10 into a desert **p** belonging to the city *G5117*
12 victuals: for we are here in a desert **p**. *G5117*
10: 1 and **p**, whither he himself would come. *G5117*
32 he was at the **p**, came and looked *on* *G5117*
11: 1 in a certain **p**, when he ceased, one *G5117*
33 *it* in a secret **p**, neither under a bushel, *G2927*
14: 9 Give this man **p**; and thou begin with *G5117*
16:28 they also come into this **p** of torment. *G5117*
19: 5 And when Jesus came to the **p**, he *G5117*
22:40 And when he was at the **p**, he said unto *G5117*
23: 5 Jewry, beginning from Galilee to this **p**. *G5602*
33 And when they were come to the **p**, *G5117*
Jn 4:20 is the **p** where men ought to worship. *G5117*
5:13 away, a multitude being in *that* **p**. *G5117*
6:10 was much grass in the **p**. So the men sat *G5117*
23 nigh unto the **p** where they did eat *G5117*
8:37 me, because my word hath no **p** in you. *G5562*
10:40 Jordan into the **p** where John at first *G5117*
11: 6 days still in the same **p** where he was. *G5117*
30 was in that **p** where Martha met him. *G5117*
41 the stone *from the p* where the dead was

Jn 11:48 and take away both our **p** and nation. *G5117*
14: 2 told you. I go to prepare a **p** for you. *G5117*
3 And if I go and prepare a **p** for you, I *G5117*
18: 2 him, knew the **p**: for Jesus ofttimes *G5117*
19:13 seat in a **p** that is called the Pavement, *G5117*
17 went forth into a **p** called *the place* of a *G5117*
17 a place called *the* **p** of a skull, which is
20 of the Jews: for the **p** where Jesus was *G5117*
41 Now in the **p** where he was crucified *G5117*
20: 7 but wrapped together in a **p** by itself. *G5117*
Act 1:25 fell, that he might go to his own **p**. *G5117*
2: 1 they were all with one accord in one **p**. *G846*
4:31 And when they had prayed, the **p** was *G5117*
6:13 words against this holy **p**, and the law: *G5117*
14 shall destroy this **p**, and shall change *G5117*
7: 7 they come forth, and serve me in this **p**. *G5117*
33 **p** where thou standest is holy ground. *G5117*
49 the Lord: or what *is* the **p** of my rest? *G5117*
8:32 The **p** of the scripture which he read *G4042*
12:17 he departed, and went into another **p**. *G5117*
21:12 and they of that **p**, besought him not to *G1786*
28 the law, and this **p**: and further brought *G5117*
28 temple, and hath polluted this holy **p**. *G5117*
25:23 entered into the **p** of hearing, with the *G201*
27: 8 And, hardly passing it, came unto a **p** *G5117*
41 And falling into a **p** where two seas *G5117*
Ro 9:26 And it shall come to pass, *that* in the **p** *G5117*
12:19 but *rather* give **p** unto wrath: for it is *G5117*
15:23 But now having no more **p** in these *G5117*
1Co 1: 2 all that in every **p** call upon the name *G5117*
11:20 one **p**, *this* is not to eat the Lord's supper. *G846*
14:23 together into one **p**, and all speak with *G846*
2Co 2:14 of his knowledge by us in every **p**. *G5117*
Gal 2: 5 To whom we gave **p** by subjection, no, *G1502*
Eph 4:27 Neither give **p** to the devil. *G5117*
1Th 1: 8 but also in every **p** your faith to *G5117*
Heb 2: 6 But one in a certain **p** testified, saying, *G4225*
4: 4 For he spake in a certain **p** of the *G4225*
5 And in this *p* again, If they shall enter
5: 6 As he saith also in another *p*, Thou *art* a
8: 7 no **p** have been sought for the second. *G5117*
9:12 in once into the holy **p**, having obtained *G39*
25 holy **p** every year with blood of others; *G39*
11: 8 to go out into a **p** which he should after *G5117*
12:17 for he found no **p** of repentance, *G5117*
Jas 2: 3 here in a good **p**; and say to the poor, *G2573*
3:11 at the same **p** sweet *water* and bitter? *G3692*
2Pt 1:19 shineth in a dark **p**, until the day dawn, *G5117*
Rev 2: 5 out of his **p**, except thou repent. *G5117*
12: 6 where she hath a **p** prepared of God, *G5117*
8 And prevailed not; neither was their **p** *G5117*
14 into her **p**, where she is nourished *G5117*
16:16 And he gathered them together into a **p** *G5117*
20:11 and there was found no **p** for them. *G5117*

PLACED

Gen 3:24 So he drove out the man; and he **p** at H7931
47:11 And Joseph **p** his father and his H3427
1Ki 12:32 he had made: and he **p** in Beth-el the H5975
2Ki 17: 6 into Assyria, and **p** them in Halah and H3427
24 Sepharvaim, and **p** *them* in the cities of H3427
26 hast removed, and **p** in the cities of H3427
2Ch 1:14 which he **p** in the chariot cities, H3240
4: 8 He made also ten tables, and **p** *them* in H3240
17: 2 And he **p** forces in all the fenced cities H5414
Job 20: 4 of old, since man was **p** upon earth, H7760
Ps 78:60 the tent *which* he **p** among men; H7931
Isa 5: 8 be **p** alone in the midst of the earth! H3427
Jer 5:22 which have **p** the sand *for* the bound H7760
Ezk 17: 5 a fruitful field; he **p** *it* by great waters, H3947

PLACES

Gen 28:15 will keep thee in all *p* whither thou goest,
36:40 after their **p**, by their names; duke H4725
Ex 20:24 thine oxen: in all **p** where I record my H4725
25:27 be for **p** of the staves to bear the table. H1004
26:29 rings *of* gold *for* **p** for the bars: and H1004
30: 4 be for **p** for the staves to bear it withal. H1004
36:34 rings *of* gold *to be* **p** for the bars, and H1004
37:14 the **p** for the staves to bear the table. H1004
27 to be **p** for the staves to bear it withal. H1004
38: 5 grate of brass, *to be* **p** for the staves. H1004
Lev 26:30 And I will destroy your high **p**, and cut H1116
Nu 21:28 *and* the lords of the high **p** of Arnon. H1116
22:41 up into the high **p** of Baal, that thence H1116
33:52 and quite pluck down all their high **p**: H1116
Dt 1: 7 and unto all *the p* nigh thereunto, in the
12: 2 Ye shall utterly destroy all the **p**, H4725
32:13 He made him ride on the high **p** of the H1116

Dt 33:29 and thou shalt tread upon their high **p**. H1116
Jos 5: 8 **p** in the camp, till they were whole. H8478
Jdg 5:11 of archers in the **p** of drawing water,
18 unto the death in the high **p** of the field. H4791
19:13 to one of these **p** to lodge all night, in H4725
20:33 **p**, *even* out of the meadows of Gibeah. H4725
1Sa 7:16 Mizpeh, and judged Israel in all those **p**. H4725
13: 6 and in rocks, and in high **p**, and in pits. H6877
23:23 of all the lurking **p** where he hideth
30:31 and to all the **p** where David himself H4725
2Sa 1:19 thy high **p**: how are the mighty fallen! H1116
25 *thou wast* slain in thine high **p**. H1116
7: 7 In all *the p* wherein I have walked with
22:34 *feet:* and setteth me upon my high **p**. H1116
46 they shall be afraid out of their close **p**. H4526
1Ki 3: 2 Only the people sacrificed in high **p**, H1116
3 sacrificed and burnt incense in high **p**. H1116
12:31 And he made an house of high **p**, and H1116
32 of the high **p** which he had made. H1116
13: 2 priests of the high **p** that burn incense H1116
32 houses of the high **p** which *are* in the H1116
33 priests of the high **p**: whosoever would, H1116
33 became *one* of the priests of the high **p**. H1116
14:23 For they also built them high **p**, and H1116
15:14 But the high **p** were not removed: H1116
22:43 the high **p** were not taken away; H1116
43 and burnt incense yet in the high **p**. H1116
2Ki 12: 3 But the high **p** were not taken away: H1116
3 and burnt incense in the high **p**. H1116
14: 4 Howbeit the high **p** were not taken H1116
4 and burnt incense on the high **p**. H1116
15: 4 Save that the high **p** were not removed: H1116
4 and burnt incense still on the high **p**. H1116
35 Howbeit the high **p** were not removed: H1116
35 still in the high **p**. He built the higher H1116
16: 4 in the high **p**, and on the hills, and H1116
17: 9 they built them high **p** in all their cities, H1116
11 in all the high **p**, as *did* the heathen H1116
29 the houses of the high **p** which the H1116
32 priests of the high **p**, which sacrificed H1116
32 for them in the houses of the high **p**. H1116
18: 4 He removed the high **p**, and brake the H1116
22 that he, whose high **p** and whose altars H1116
19:24 I dried up all the rivers of besieged **p**.
21: 3 For he built up again the high **p** which H1116
23: 5 in the high **p** in the cities of Judah, H1116
5 of Judah, and in the **p** round about
8 defiled the high **p** where the priests had H1116
8 down the high **p** of the gates that *were* H1116
9 Nevertheless the priests of the high **p** H1116
13 And the high **p** that *were* before H1116
14 filled their **p** with the bones of men. H4725
19 And all the houses also of the high **p** H1116
20 And he slew all the priests of the high **p** H1116
1Ch 6:54 Now these *are* their dwelling **p** H4186
2Ch 8:11 of Israel, because *the p are* holy,
11:15 for the high **p**, and for the devils, and H1116
14: 3 *gods*, and the high **p**, and brake down H1116
5 of Judah the high **p** and the images: H1116
15:17 But the high **p** were not taken away out H1116
17: 6 the high **p** and groves out of Judah. H1116
20:33 Howbeit the high **p** were not taken H1116
21:11 Moreover he made high **p** in the H1116
28: 4 in the high **p**, and on the hills, and H1116
25 he made high **p** to burn incense unto H1116
31: 1 down the high **p** and the altars out of H1116
32:12 away his high **p** and his altars, and H1116
33: 3 For he built again the high **p** which H1116
17 **p**, *yet* unto the LORD their God only. H1116
19 his trespass, and the **p** wherein he built H4725
19 he built high **p**, and set up groves and H1116
34: 3 from the high **p**, and the groves, and H1116
Neh 4:12 ten times, From all **p** whence ye shall H4725
13 Therefore set I in the lower **p** behind H4725
13 wall, *and* on the higher **p**, I even set the H4725
12:27 out of all their **p**, to bring them to H4725
Job 3:14 which built desolate **p** for themselves; H2723
20:26 All darkness *shall be* hid in his secret **p**: H6845
21:28 where *are* the dwelling **p** of the wicked? H168
25: 2 him, he maketh peace in his high **p**. H4791
37: 8 go into dens, and remain in their **p**. H4585
Ps 10: 8 He sitteth in the lurking **p** of the H3993
8 in the secret **p** doth he murder the H4565
16: 6 pleasant *p*; yea, I have a goodly heritage.
17:12 it were a young lion lurking in secret **p**. H4565
18:33 *feet*, and setteth me upon my high **p**. H1116
45 away, and be afraid out of their close **p**. H4526
49:11 *and* their dwelling **p** to all generations; H4908
68:35 out of thy holy **p**: the God of Israel *is* H4720

Ps 73:18 Surely thou didst set them in slippery **p**:
74:20 for the dark **p** of the earth are full H4285
78:58 with their high **p**, and moved him to H1116
95: 4 In his hand *are* the deep **p** of the earth: H4278
103:22 Bless the LORD, all his works in all **p** of H4725
105:41 out; they ran in the dry **p** *like* a river. H6723
109:10 *their bread* also out of their desolate **p**. H2723
110: 6 he shall fill *the* **p** with the dead bodies;
135: 6 and in earth, in the seas, and all deep **p**. H8415
141: 6 in stony **p**, they shall hear my words; H3027
Prv 8: 2 She standeth in the top of high **p**, by the H4791
2 places, by the way in the **p** of the paths. H1004
9: 3 she crieth upon the highest **p** of the city,
14 on a seat in the high **p** of the city, H4791
Song 2:14 rock, in the secret *p* of the stairs, let me
Isa 5:17 **p** of the fat ones shall strangers eat. H2723
15: 2 to Dibon, the high **p**, to weep: Moab H1116
32:18 in sure dwellings, and in quiet resting **p**; H4496
36: 7 not he, whose high **p** and whose altars H1116
37:25 I dried up all the rivers of the besieged **p**.
40: 4 made straight, and the rough **p** plain: H7406
41:18 I will open rivers in high **p**, and H8205
44:26 I will raise up the decayed **p** thereof: H2723
45: 2 and make the crooked **p** straight: I will H1921
3 riches of secret **p**, that thou mayest H4565
49: 9 and their pastures *shall be* in all high **p**. H8205
19 For thy waste and thy desolate **p**, and H8074
51: 3 all her waste **p**; and he will make her H2723
52: 9 together, ye waste **p** of Jerusalem: for H2723
58:12 the old waste **p**: thou shalt raise up H2723
14 ride upon the high **p** of the earth, and H1116
59:10 night; *we are* in desolate **p** as dead *men*.
Jer 3: 2 Lift up thine eyes unto the high **p**, and H8205
21 A voice was heard upon the high **p**, H8205
4:11 dry wind of the high **p** in the wilderness H8205
12 *Even* a full wind from those *p* shall come
5: 1 seek in the broad **p** thereof, if ye can H7339
7:29 on high **p**; for the LORD hath rejected H8205
31 And they have built the high **p** of H1116
8: 3 remain in all the **p** whither I have H4725
12:12 The spoilers are come upon all high **p** H8205
13:17 weep in secret **p** for *your* pride; and H4565
14: 6 stand in the high **p**, they snuffed up the H8205
17: 3 **p** for sin, throughout all thy borders. H1116
6 the parched **p** in the wilderness, *in* H2788
26 and from the **p** about Jerusalem, and H5639
19: 5 They have built also the high **p** of Baal, H1116
23:10 the pleasant **p** of the wilderness are H4999
24 Can any hide himself in secret **p** that I H4565
24: 9 in all **p** whither I shall drive them. H4725
26:18 of the house as the high **p** of a forest. H1116
29:14 and from all the **p** whither I have H4725
32:35 And they built the high **p** of Baal, H1116
44 and in the **p** about Jerusalem, and
33:13 and in the **p** about Jerusalem, and
40:12 Even all the Jews returned out of all **p** H4725
45: 5 for a prey in all **p** whither thou goest. H4725
48:35 in the high **p**, and him that burneth H1116
49:10 his secret **p**, and he shall not be H4565
Lam 2: 6 hath destroyed his **p** of the assembly: the
3: 6 He hath set me in dark **p**, as *they that* H4285
10 lying in wait, *and as* a lion in secret **p**. H4565
Ezk 6: 3 you, and I will destroy your high **p**. H1116
6 and the high **p** shall be desolate; that H1116
7:24 cease; and their holy **p** shall be defiled. H6942
16:16 and deckedst thy high **p** with divers H1116
39 down thy high **p**: they shall strip thee H7413
21: 2 *word* toward the holy **p**, and prophesy H4720
26:20 of the earth, in **p** desolate of old, with
34:12 them out of all **p** where they have been H4725
13 in all the inhabited **p** of the country. H4186
26 And I will make them and the **p** round
36: 2 ancient high **p** are ours in possession: H1116
36 build the ruined *p*, *and* plant that that
38:12 hand upon the desolate **p** *that are now* H2723
20 and the steep **p** shall fall, and every H4095
43: 7 the carcases of their kings in their high **p**.
46:23 boiling **p** under the rows round about. H4018
24 Then said he unto me, These *are* the **p** H1004
47:11 But the miry **p** thereof and the H1207
Dan 11:24 upon the fattest **p** of the province; and
Hos 9: 6 them: the pleasant *p* for their silver,
10: 8 The high **p** also of Aven, the sin of H1116
Am 4: 6 of bread in all your **p**: yet have ye not H4725
13 upon the high **p** of the earth, The H1116
7: 9 And the high **p** of Isaac shall be H1116
Mic 1: 3 and tread upon the high **p** of the earth. H1116
5 **p** of Judah? *are they* not Jerusalem? H1116
3:12 of the house as the high **p** of the forest. H1116
Hab 3:19 upon mine high **p**. To the chief singer H1116
Zec 3: 7 **p** to walk among these that stand by.
Mal 1: 4 and build the desolate **p**; thus saith the H2723
Mt 12:43 dry **p**, seeking rest, and findeth none. *G5117*
13: 5 Some fell upon stony **p**, where they had *G4075*
20 seed into stony **p**, the same is he that *G4075*
24: 7 and earthquakes, in divers **p**. *G2596*
Mk 1:45 without in desert **p**: and they came to *G5117*
13: 8 in divers **p**, and there shall be famines *G2596*
Lk 11:24 through dry **p**, seeking rest; and finding *G5117*
21:11 shall be in divers **p**, and famines, and *G2596*
Act 24: 3 We accept *it* always, and in all **p**, most *G3837*
Eph 1: 3 blessings in heavenly *p* in Christ:
20 at his own right hand in the heavenly *p*,
2: 6 sit together in heavenly *p* in Christ Jesus:
3:10 in heavenly *p* might be known by the
6:12 against spiritual wickedness in high *p*.
Php 1:13 in all the palace, and in all other *p*;
Heb 9:24 For Christ is not entered into the holy **p** *G39*
Rev 6:14 and island were moved out of their **p**. *G5117*

PLAGUE

Ex 11: 1 will I bring one **p** *more* upon Pharaoh, H5061
12:13 over you, and the **p** shall not be upon H5063
30:12 that there be no **p** among them, when H5063
Lev 13: 2 of his flesh *like* the **p** of leprosy; then he H5061
3 And the priest shall look on the **p** in the H5061
3 the hair in the **p** is turned white, and H5061
3 white, and the **p** in sight *be* deeper than H5061
3 of his flesh, it *is* a **p** of leprosy: and the H5061
4 shut up *him that hath* the **p** seven days: H5061
5 and, behold, *if* the **p** in his sight be at a H5061
5 be at a stay, *and* the **p** spread not in the H5061
6 day: and, behold, *if* the **p** *be* somewhat H5061
6 dark, *and* the **p** spread not in the skin, H5061
9 When the **p** of leprosy is in a man, then H5061
12 *him that hath* the **p** from his head even H5061
13 the **p**: it is all turned white: he *is* clean. H5061
17 and, behold, *if* the **p** be turned into H5061
17 *him* clean *that hath* the **p**: he *is* clean. H5061
20 *is* a **p** of leprosy broken out of the boil. H5061
22 shall pronounce him unclean: it *is* a **p**. H5061
25 him unclean: it *is* the **p** of leprosy. H5061
27 him unclean: it *is* the **p** of leprosy. H5061
29 If a man or woman have a **p** upon the H5061
30 Then the priest shall see the **p**: and, H5061
31 And if the priest look on the **p** of the H5061
31 *that hath* the **p** of the scall seven days: H5061
32 shall look on the **p**: and, behold, *if* the H5061
44 utterly unclean; his **p** *is* in his head. H5061
45 And the leper in whom the **p** *is*, his H5061
46 All the days wherein the **p** *shall be* in H5061
47 The garment also that the **p** of leprosy H5061
49 And if the **p** be greenish or reddish in H5061
49 of skin; it *is* a **p** of leprosy, and shall H5061
50 And the priest shall look upon the **p**, H5061
50 shut up *it that hath* the **p** seven days: H5061
51 And he shall look on the **p** on the H5061
51 seventh day: if the **p** be spread in the H5061
51 the **p** *is* a fretting leprosy; it *is* unclean. H5061
52 skin, wherein the **p** is: for it *is* a fretting H5061
53 and, behold, the **p** be not spread in the H5061
54 *the thing* wherein the **p** *is*, and he shall H5061
55 And the priest shall look on the **p**, after H5061
55 and, behold, *if* the **p** have not changed H5061
55 his colour, and the **p** be not spread; it *is* H5061
56 and, behold, the **p** *be* somewhat dark H5061
57 it *is* a spreading *p*: thou shalt burn that
57 burn that wherein the **p** *is* with fire. H5061
58 shalt wash, if the **p** be departed from H5061
59 This *is* the law of the **p** of leprosy in a H5061
14: 3 the **p** of leprosy be healed in the leper; H5061
32 This *is* the law *of him* in whom *is* the **p** H5061
34 and I put the **p** of leprosy in a house H5061
35 me *there is* as it were a **p** in the house: H5061
36 *into it* to see the **p**, that all that *is* in the H5061
37 And he shall look on the **p**, and, behold, H5061
37 and, behold, *if* the **p** *be* in the walls of H5061
39 **p** be spread in the walls of the house; H5061
40 in which the **p** *is*, and they shall cast H5061
43 And if the **p** come again, and break out H5061
44 and, behold, *if* the **p** be spread in the H5061
48 and, behold, the **p** hath not spread in H5061
48 house clean, because the **p** is healed. H5061
54 This *is* the law for all manner of **p** of H5061
Nu 8:19 that there be no **p** among the children H5063
11:33 smote the people with a very great **p**. H4347
14:37 land, died by the **p** before the LORD. H4046
16:46 out from the LORD; the **p** is begun. H5063
Nu 16:47 and, behold, the **p** was begun among H5063
48 and the living; and the **p** was stayed. H4046
49 Now they that died in the **p** were H4046
50 congregation: and the **p** was stayed. H4046
25: 8 her belly. So the **p** was stayed from the H4046
9 And those that died in the **p** were H4046
18 slain in the day of the **p** for Peor's sake. H4046
26: 1 And it came to pass after the **p**, that the H4046
31:16 Peor, and there was a **p** among the H4046
Dt 24: 8 Take heed in the **p** of leprosy, that thou H5061
28:61 Also every sickness, and every **p**, which H4347
Jos 22:17 a **p** in the congregation of the LORD, H5063
1Sa 6: 4 **p** *was* on you all, and on your lords. H4046
2Sa 24:21 the **p** may be stayed from the people. H4046
25 land, and the **p** was stayed from Israel. H4046
1Ki 8:37 **p**, whatsoever sickness *there be;* H5061
38 every man the **p** of his own heart, and H5061
1Ch 21:22 the **p** may be stayed from the people. H4046
2Ch 21:14 Behold, with a great **p** will the LORD H4046
Ps 89:23 his face, and **p** them that hate him. H5062
91:10 shall any **p** come nigh thy dwelling. H5061
106:29 and the **p** brake in upon them. H4046
30 judgment: and *so* the **p** was stayed. H4046
Zec 14:12 And this shall be the **p** wherewith the H4046
15 And so shall be the **p** of the horse, of H4046
15 that shall be in these tents, as this **p**. H4046
18 *rain*; there shall be the **p**, wherewith the H4046
Mk 5:29 *her* body that she was healed of that **p**. *G3148*
34 go in peace, and be whole of thy **p**. *G3148*
Rev 16:21 God because of the **p** of the hail; for the *G4127*
21 for the **p** thereof was exceeding great. *G4127*

PLAGUED

Gen 12:17 And the LORD **p** Pharaoh and his H5060
Ex 32:35 And the LORD **p** the people, because H5062
Jos 24: 5 I sent Moses also and Aaron, and I **p** H5062
1Ch 21:17 not on thy people, that they should be **p**. H4046
Ps 73: 5 men; neither are they **p** like *other* men. H5060
14 For all the day long have I been **p**, and H5060

PLAGUES

Gen 12:17 great **p** because of Sarai Abram's wife. H5061
Ex 9:14 For I will at this time send all my **p** H4046
Lev 26:21 **p** upon you according to your sins. H4347
Dt 28:59 Then the LORD will make thy **p** H4347
59 and the **p** of thy seed, *even* great H4347
59 thy seed, *even* great **p**, and of long
29:22 when they see the **p** of that land, and H4347
1Sa 4: 8 with all the **p** in the wilderness. H4347
Jer 19: 8 and hiss because of all the **p** thereof. H4347
49:17 and shall hiss at all the **p** thereof. H4347
50:13 be astonished, and hiss at all her **p**. H4347
Hos 13:14 death, I will be thy **p**; O grave, I will be H1698
Mk 3:10 him for to touch him, as many as had **p**. *G3148*
Lk 7:21 infirmities and **p**, and of evil spirits; *G3148*
Rev 9:20 not killed by these **p** yet repented not of *G4127*
11: 6 earth with all **p**, as often as they will. *G4127*
15: 1 the seven last **p**; for in them is filled *G4127*
6 having the seven **p**, clothed in pure and *G4127*
8 **p** of the seven angels were fulfilled. *G4127*
16: 9 power over these **p**: and they repented *G4127*
18: 4 sins, and that ye receive not of her **p**. *G4127*
8 Therefore shall her **p** come in one day, *G4127*
21: 9 of the seven last **p**, and talked with me, *G4127*
22:18 him the **p** that are written in this book: *G4127*

PLAIN

Gen 11: 2 east, that they found a **p** in the land of H1237
12: 6 of Sichem, unto the **p** of Moreh. And the H436
13:10 and beheld all the **p** of Jordan, that it H3603
11 Then Lot chose him all the **p** of Jordan; H3603
12 **p**, and pitched *his* tent toward Sodom. H3603
18 and dwelt in the **p** of Mamre, which *is* H436
14:13 for he dwelt in the **p** of Mamre the H436
19:17 stay thou in all the **p**; escape to the H3603
25 those cities, and all the **p**, and all the H3603
28 all the land of the **p**, and beheld, and, H3603
29 destroyed the cities of the **p**, that God H3603
25:27 Jacob *was* a **p** man, dwelling in tents. H8535
Dt 1: 1 wilderness, in the **p** over against the H6160
7 thereunto, in the **p**, in the hills, and in H6160
2: 8 the way of the **p** from Elath, and from H6160
3:10 All the cities of the **p**, and all Gilead, H4334
17 The **p** also, and Jordan, and the coast H6160
17 unto the sea of the **p**, *even* the salt sea, H6160
4:43 the wilderness, in the **p** country, of the H4334
49 And all the **p** on this side Jordan H6160
49 of the **p**, under the springs of Pisgah. H6160
34: 3 And the south, and the **p** of the valley H3603

Jos 3:16 the sea of the **p**, *even* the salt sea, failed, H6160
8:14 before the **p**; but he wist not that H6160
11:16 the valley, and the **p**, and the mountain H6160
12: 1 Hermon, and all the **p** on the east: H6160
3 And from the **p** to the sea of H6160
3 unto the sea of the **p**, *even* the salt sea H6160
13: 9 and all the **p** of Medeba unto Dibon; H4334
16 of the river, and all the **p** by Medeba; H4334
17 cities that *are* in the **p**; Dibon, and H4334
21 And all the cities of the **p**, and all the H4334
20: 8 upon the **p** out of the tribe of Reuben, H4334
Jdg 4:11 the **p** of Zaanaim, which *is* by Kedesh. H436
9: 6 the **p** of the pillar that *was* in Shechem. H436
37 come along by the **p** of Meonenim. H436
11:33 cities, and unto the **p** of the vineyards, H58
1Sa 10: 3 shalt come to the **p** of Tabor, and there H436
23:24 in the **p** on the south of Jeshimon. H6160
2Sa 2:29 night through the **p**, and passed over H6160
4: 7 gat them away through the **p** all night. H6160
15:28 See, I will tarry in the **p** of the H6160
18:23 by the way of the **p**, and overran Cushi. H3603
1Ki 7:46 In the **p** of Jordan did the king cast H3603
20:23 them in the **p**, and surely we shall H4334
25 them in the **p**, *and* surely we shall H4334
2Ki 14:25 unto the sea of the **p**, according to the H6160
25: 4 and *the king* went the way toward the **p**. H6160
2Ch 4:17 In the **p** of Jordan did the king cast H3603
Neh 3:22 repaired the priests, the men of the **p**. H3603
6: 2 *of* the villages in the **p** of Ono. But they H1237
12:28 both out of the **p** country round about H3603
Ps 27:11 in a **p** path, because of mine enemies. H4334
Prv 8: 9 They *are* all **p** to him that H5228
15:19 but the way of the righteous *is* made **p**. H5549
Isa 28:25 When he hath made **p** the face thereof, H7737
40: 4 made straight, and the rough places **p**: H1237
Jer 17:26 Benjamin, and from the **p**, and from the H8219
21:13 *and* rock of the **p**, saith the LORD; H4334
39: 4 walls: and he went out the way of the **p**. H6160
48: 8 perish, and the **p** shall be destroyed, H4334
21 And judgment is come upon the **p** H4334
52: 7 and they went by the way of the **p**. H6160
Ezk 3:22 the **p**, and I will there talk with thee. H1237
23 Then I arose, and went forth into the **p**: H1237
8: 4 to the vision that I saw in the **p**. H1237
Dan 3: 1 **p** of Dura, in the province of Babylon. H1236
Am 1: 5 from the **p** of Aven, and him that H1237
Oba 19 and *they of* the **p** the Philistines: and H8219
Hab 2: 2 vision, and make *it* **p** upon tables, that H874
Zec 4: 7 *shalt become* a **p**: and he shall bring H4334
7: 7 *men* inhabited the south and the **p**? H8219
14:10 All the land shall be turned as a **p** from H6160
Mk 7:35 his tongue was loosed, and he spake **p**. *G3723*
Lk 6:17 and stood in the **p**, and the company of *G3977*

PLAINLY
Ex 21: 5 And if the servant shall **p** say, I love my H559
Dt 27: 8 stones all the words of this law very **p**. H874
1Sa 2:27 the LORD, Did I **p** appear unto the H1540
10:16 uncle, He told us **p** that the asses were H5046
Ezr 4:18 unto us hath been **p** read before me. H6568
Isa 32: 4 stammerers shall be ready to speak **p**. H6703
Jn 10:24 to doubt? If thou be the Christ, tell us **p**. *G3954*
11:14 Then said Jesus unto them **p**, Lazarus is *G3954*
16:25 but I shall shew you **p** of the Father. *G3954*
29 thou **p**, and speakest no proverb. *G3954*
Heb 11:14 For they that say such things declare **p** *G1718*

PLAINNESS
2Co 3:12 such hope, we use great **p** of speech: *G3954*

PLAINS
Gen 18: 1 unto him in the **p** of Mamre: and he sat H436
Nu 22: 1 and pitched in the **p** of Moab on this H6160
26: 3 with them in the **p** of Moab by Jordan H6160
63 the **p** of Moab by Jordan *near* Jericho. H6160
31:12 the camp at the **p** of Moab, which *are* H6160
33:48 the **p** of Moab by Jordan *near* Jericho. H6160
49 unto Abel-shittim in the **p** of Moab. H6160
50 unto Moses in the **p** of Moab by Jordan H6160
35: 1 unto Moses in the **p** of Moab by Jordan H6160
36:13 the **p** of Moab by Jordan *near* Jericho. H6160
Dt 11:30 against Gilgal, beside the **p** of Moreh? H436
34: 1 And Moses went up from the **p** of H6160
8 for Moses in the **p** of Moab thirty days: H6160
Jos 4:13 LORD unto battle, to the **p** of Jericho. H6160
5:10 of the month at even in the **p** of Jericho. H6160
11: 2 and of the **p** south of Chinneroth, H6160
12: 8 valleys, and in the **p**, and in the springs, H6160
13:32 for inheritance in the **p** of Moab, on the H6160
2Sa 17:16 this night in the **p** of the wilderness, H6160
2Ki 25: 5 him in the **p** of Jericho: and all his H6160
1Ch 27:28 *were* in the low **p** *was* Baal-hanan the H8219
2Ch 9:27 that *are* in the low **p** in abundance. H8219
26:10 and in the **p**: husbandmen *also*, and H4334
Jer 39: 5 Zedekiah in the **p** of Jericho: and when H6160
52: 8 Zedekiah in the **p** of Jericho; and all his H6160

PLAISTER
Lev 14:42 other morter, and shall **p** the house. H2902
Dt 27: 2 great stones, and **p** them with plaister: H7874
2 great stones, and plaister them with **p**: H7875
4 and thou shalt **p** them with plaister. H7874
4 and thou shalt plaister them with **p**. H7875
Isa 38:21 a **p** upon the boil, and he shall recover. H4799
Dan 5: 5 upon the **p** of the wall of the king's H1528

PLAISTERED
Lev 14:43 scraped the house, and after it is **p**; H2902
48 the house was **p**: then the priest shall H2902

PLAITING
1Pt 3: 3 *adorning* of **p** the hair, and of wearing *G1708*

PLANES
Isa 44:13 he fitteth it with **p**, and he marketh it H4741

PLANETS
2Ki 23: 5 to the **p**, and to all the host of heaven. H4208

PLANKS
1Ki 6:15 the floor of the house with **p** of fir. H6763
Ezk 41:25 **p** upon the face of the porch without. H6086
26 chambers of the house, and thick **p**. H5646

PLANT
Gen 2: 5 And every **p** of the field before it was in H7880
Ex 15:17 Thou shalt bring them in, and **p** them H5193
Dt 16:21 Thou shalt not **p** thee a grove of any H5193
28:30 therein: thou shalt **p** a vineyard, and H5193
39 Thou shalt **p** vineyards, and dress H5193
2Sa 7:10 Israel, and will **p** them, that they may H5193
2Ki 19:29 **p** vineyards, and eat the fruits thereof. H5193
1Ch 17: 9 Israel, and will **p** them, and they shall H5193
Job 14: 9 bud, and bring forth boughs like a **p**. H5194
Ps 107:37 And sow the fields, and **p** vineyards, H5193
Ecc 3: 2 to die; a time to **p**, and a time to pluck H5193
Isa 5: 7 Judah his pleasant **p**: and he looked for H5194
17:10 shalt thou **p** pleasant plants, and H5193
11 In the day shalt thou make thy **p** to H5194
37:30 **p** vineyards, and eat the fruit thereof. H5193
41:19 I will **p** in the wilderness the cedar, the H5414
51:16 hand, that I may **p** the heavens, and H5193
53: 2 him as a tender **p**, and as a root out of H3126
65:21 **p** vineyards, and eat the fruit of them. H5193
22 they shall not **p**, and another eat: for H5193
Jer 1:10 and to throw down, to build, and to **p**. H5193
2:21 degenerate **p** of a strange vine unto me?
18: 9 a kingdom, to build and to **p** *it*; H5193
24: 6 I will **p** them, and not pluck *them* up. H5193
29: 5 **p** gardens, and eat the fruit of them; H5193
28 **p** gardens, and eat the fruit of them. H5193
31: 5 Thou shalt yet **p** vines upon the H5193
5 the planters shall **p**, and shall eat *them* H5193
28 to build, and to **p**, saith the LORD. H5193
32:41 good, and I will **p** them in this land H5193
35: 7 nor sow seed, nor **p** vineyard, nor have H5193
42:10 down, and I will **p** you, and not pluck H5193
Ezk 17:22 tender one, and will **p** *it* upon an high H8362
23 of Israel will I **p** it: and it shall bring H8362
28:26 build houses, and **p** vineyards; yea, H5193
34:29 And I will raise up for them a **p** of H4302
36:36 the ruined *places, and* **p** that that was H5193
Dan 11:45 And he shall **p** the tabernacles of his H5193
Am 9:14 and they shall **p** vineyards, and drink H5193
15 And I will **p** them upon their land, and H5193
Zep 1:13 and they shall **p** vineyards, but not H5193
Mt 15:13 But he answered and said, Every **p**, *G5451*

PLANTATION
Ezk 17: 7 might water it by the furrows of her **p**. H4302

PLANTED
Gen 2: 8 And the LORD God **p** a garden H5193
9:20 an husbandman, and he **p** a vineyard: H5193
21:33 And *Abraham* **p** a grove in Beer-sheba, H5193
Lev 19:23 and shall have **p** all manner of trees H5193
Nu 24: 6 **p**, *and* as cedar trees beside the waters. H5193
Dt 20: 6 And what man *is he* that hath **p** a H5193
Jos 24:13 oliveyards which ye **p** not do ye eat. H5193
Ps 1: 3 And he shall be like a tree **p** by the H8362
80: 8 hast cast out the heathen, and **p** it. H5193
15 right hand hath **p**, and the branch *that* H5193
92:13 Those that be **p** in the house of the H8362
94: 9 He that **p** the ear, shall he not hear? he H5193
104:16 the cedars of Lebanon, which he hath **p**; H5193
Ecc 2: 4 I builded me houses; I **p** me vineyards: H5193
5 I **p** trees in them of all *kind of* fruits: H5193
3: 2 and a time to pluck up *that which is* **p**; H5193
Isa 5: 2 thereof, and **p** it with the choicest H5193
40:24 Yea, they shall not be **p**; yea, they shall H5193
Jer 2:21 Yet I had **p** thee a noble vine, wholly a H5193
11:17 For the LORD of hosts, that **p** thee, H5193
12: 2 Thou hast **p** them, yea, they have taken H5193
17: 8 For he shall be as a tree **p** by the H8362
45: 4 **p** I will pluck up, even this whole land. H5193
Ezk 17: 5 of the land, and **p** it in a fruitful field; H5414
8 It was **p** in a good soil by great waters, H8362
10 Yea, behold, *being* **p**, shall it prosper? H8362
19:10 a vine in thy blood, **p** by the waters: she H8362
13 And now she *is* **p** in the wilderness, in a H8362
Hos 9:13 Ephraim, as I saw Tyrus, *is* **p** in a H8362
Am 5:11 in them; ye have **p** pleasant vineyards, H5193
Mt 15:13 Father hath not **p**, shall be rooted up. *G5452*
21:33 which **p** a vineyard, and hedged *G5452*
Mk 12: 1 A *certain* man **p** a vineyard, and set *G5452*
Lk 13: 6 *man* had a fig tree **p** in his vineyard; *G5452*
17: 6 **p** in the sea; and it should obey you. *G5452*
28 bought, they sold, they **p**, they builded; *G5452*
20: 9 A certain man **p** a vineyard, and let *G5452*
Ro 6: 5 For if we have been **p** together in the *G4854*
1Co 3: 6 I have **p**, Apollos watered; but God gave *G5452*

PLANTEDST
Dt 6:11 trees, which thou **p** not; when thou H5193
Ps 44: 2 thy hand, and **p** them; *how* thou didst H5193

PLANTERS
Jer 31: 5 of Samaria: the **p** shall plant, and shall H5193

PLANTETH
Prv 31:16 the fruit of her hands she **p** a vineyard. H5193
Isa 44:14 **p** an ash, and the rain doth nourish *it*. H5193
1Co 3: 7 So then neither is he that **p** any thing, *G5452*
8 Now he that **p** and he that watereth are *G5452*
9: 7 own charges? who **p** a vineyard, and *G5452*

PLANTING
Isa 60:21 the branch of my **p**, the work of my H4302
61: 3 righteousness, the **p** of the LORD, that H4302

PLANTINGS
Mic 1: 6 of the field, *and* as **p** of a vineyard: and H4302

PLANTS
1Ch 4:23 that dwelt among **p** and hedges: there H5196
Ps 128: 3 like olive **p** round about thy table. H8363
144:12 That our sons *may be* as **p** grown up in H5195
Song 4:13 Thy **p** *are* an orchard of pomegranates, H7973
Isa 16: 8 the principal **p** thereof, they are come H8291
17:10 **p**, and shalt set it with strange slips: H5194
Jer 48:32 of Jazer: thy **p** are gone over the sea, H5189
Ezk 31: 4 round about his **p**, and sent out her H4302

PLASTER See PLAISTER.

PLAT
2Ki 9:26 thee in this **p**, saith the LORD. Now H2513
26 *and* cast him into the **p** *of ground*, H2513

PLATE
Ex 28:36 And thou shalt make a **p** *of* pure gold, H6731
39:30 And they made the **p** of the holy crown H6731
Lev 8: 9 he put the golden **p**, the holy crown; as H6731

PLATES
Ex 39: 3 And they did beat the gold into thin **p**, H6341
Nu 16:38 make them broad **p** *for* a covering of H6341
39 made broad **p** *for* a covering of the altar:
1Ki 7:30 wheels, and **p** of brass: and the four H5633
36 For on the **p** of the ledges thereof, and H3871
Jer 10: 9 Silver spread into **p** is brought from H7554

PLATTED
Mt 27:29 And when they had **p** a crown of *G4120*
Mk 15:17 with purple, and **p** a crown of thorns, *G4120*
Jn 19: 2 And the soldiers **p** a crown of thorns, *G4120*

PLATTER
Mt 23:25 the cup and of the **p**, but within they are *G3953*
26 the cup and **p**, that the outside of them *G3953*
Lk 11:39 of the cup and the **p**; but your inward *G4094*

PLAY
Ex 32: 6 to eat and to drink, and rose up to **p**. H6711
Dt 22:21 folly in Israel, to **p** the whore in her
1Sa 16:16 **p** with his hand, and thou shalt be well. H5059
17 that can **p** well, and bring *him* to me. H5059
21:15 this *fellow* to **p** the mad man in my
2Sa 2:14 now arise, and **p** before us. And Joab H7832
6:21 therefore will I **p** before the LORD. H7832
10:12 Be of good courage, and let us **p** the men
Job 40:20 food, where all the beasts of the field **p**. H7832
41: 5 Wilt thou **p** with him as *with* a bird? or H7832
Ps 33: 3 Sing unto him a new song; **p** skilfully H5059
104:26 *whom* thou hast made to **p** therein. H7832
Isa 11: 8 And the sucking child shall **p** on the H8173
Ezk 33:32 voice, and can **p** well on an instrument: H5059
Hos 3: 3 thou shalt not **p** the harlot, and thou
4:15 Though thou, Israel, **p** the harlot, *yet* let
1Co 10: 7 to eat and drink, and rose up to **p**. *G3815*

PLAYED
Gen 38:24 in law hath **p** the harlot; and also,
Jdg 19: 2 And his concubine **p** the whore against
1Sa 16:23 took an harp, and **p** with his hand: so H5059
18: 7 *another* as they **p**, and said, Saul hath H7832
10 house: and David **p** with his hand, as H5059
19: 9 his hand: and David **p** with *his* hand. H5059
26:21 **p** the fool, and have erred exceedingly.
2Sa 6: 5 And David and all the house of Israel **p** H7832
2Ki 3:15 when the minstrel **p**, that the hand of H5059
1Ch 13: 8 And David and all Israel **p** before God H7832
Jer 3: 1 but thou hast **p** the harlot with many
6 green tree, and there hath **p** the harlot.
8 not, but went and **p** the harlot also.
Ezk 16:28 Thou hast **p** the whore also with the
28 yea, thou hast **p** the harlot with them,
23: 5 And Aholah **p** the harlot when she was
19 she had **p** the harlot in the land of Egypt.
Hos 2: 5 For their mother hath **p** the harlot: she

PLAYEDST
Ezk 16:15 own beauty, and **p** the harlot because of
16 with divers colours, and **p** the harlot

PLAYER
1Sa 16:16 *who is* a cunning **p** on an harp: and it H5059

PLAYERS
Ps 68:25 The singers went before, the **p** on H5059
87: 7 As well the singers as the **p** on H2490

PLAYETH
Ezk 23:44 unto a woman that **p** the harlot: so went

PLAYING
Lev 21: 9 she profane herself by **p** the whore, she
1Sa 16:18 *that is* cunning in **p**, and a mighty H5059
1Ch 15:29 **p**: and she despised him in her heart. H7832
Ps 68:25 *them were* the damsels **p** with timbrels.
Jer 2:20 green tree thou wanderest, **p** the harlot.
Ezk 16:41 thee to cease from **p** the harlot, and thou
Zec 8: 5 boys and girls **p** in the streets thereof. H7832

PLEA
Dt 17: 8 and blood, between **p** and plea, and H1779
8 between plea and **p**, and between stroke H1779

PLEAD
Jdg 6:31 him, Will ye **p** for Baal? will ye save H7378
31 him? he that will **p** for him, let him be H7378
31 *be* a god, let him **p** for himself, because H7378
32 saying, Let Baal **p** against him, because H7378
1Sa 24:15 and thee, and see, and **p** my cause, and H7378
Job 9:19 judgment, who shall set me a time *to p*?
13:19 Who *is* he *that* will **p** with me? for now, H7378
16:21 O that one might **p** for a man with God, H3198
19: 5 me, and **p** against me my reproach: H3198
23: 6 Will he **p** against me with *his* great H7378
Ps 35: 1 **P** *my cause*, O LORD, with them that H7378
43: 1 Judge me, O God, and **p** my cause H7378
74:22 Arise, O God, **p** thine own cause: H7378
119:154 **P** my cause, and deliver me: quicken H7378
Prv 22:23 For the LORD will **p** their cause, and H7378
23:11 For their redeemer *is* mighty; he shall **p** H7378
31: 9 and **p** the cause of the poor and needy. H1777
Isa 1:17 judge the fatherless, **p** for the widow. H7378
3:13 The LORD standeth up to **p**, and H7378
43:26 Put me in remembrance: let us **p** H8199
66:16 will the LORD **p** with all flesh: and the H8199
Jer 2: 9 Wherefore I will yet **p** with you, saith H7378
9 with your children's children will I **p**. H7378
29 Wherefore will ye **p** with me? ye all H7378
35 me. Behold, I will **p** with thee, because H8199
12: 1 Righteous *art* thou, O LORD, when I **p** H7378
25:31 nations, he will **p** with all flesh; he will H8199
30:13 *There is* none to **p** thy cause, that thou H1777
50:34 he shall throughly **p** their cause, that H7378
51:36 Behold, I will **p** thy cause, and take H7378
Ezk 17:20 Babylon, and will **p** with him there for H8199
20:35 and there will I **p** with you face to face. H8199
36 will I **p** with you, saith the Lord GOD. H8199
38:22 And I will **p** against him with H8199
Hos 2: 2 **P** with your mother, plead: for she *is* H7378
2 Plead with your mother, **p**: for she *is* H7378
Joel 3: 2 and will **p** with them there for H8199
Mic 6: 2 his people, and he will **p** with Israel. H3198
7: 9 him, until he **p** my cause, and execute H7378

PLEADED
1Sa 25:39 the LORD, that hath **p** the cause of my H7378
Lam 3:58 O Lord, thou hast **p** the causes of my H7378
Ezk 20:36 Like as I **p** with your fathers in the H8199

PLEADETH
Job 16:21 with God, as a man *p* for his neighbour!
Isa 51:22 and thy God *that* **p** the cause of his H7378
59: 4 None calleth for justice, nor *any* **p** for H8199

PLEADINGS
Job 13: 6 and hearken to the **p** of my lips. H7379

PLEASANT
Gen 2: 9 every tree that is **p** to the sight, and H2530
3: 6 and that it *was* **p** to the eyes, and a tree H8378
49:15 the land that *it was* **p**; and bowed his H5276
2Sa 1:23 Saul and Jonathan *were* lovely and **p** in H5273
26 Jonathan: very **p** hast thou been unto H5276
1Ki 20: 6 *that* whatsoever is **p** in thine eyes, they H4261
2Ki 2:19 of this city *is* **p**, as my lord seeth: but H2896
2Ch 32:27 shields, and for all manner of **p** jewels; H2532
Ps 16: 6 The lines are fallen unto me in **p** H5273
81: 2 timbrel, the **p** harp with the psaltery. H5273
106:24 Yea, they despised the **p** land, they H2532
133: 1 Behold, how good and how **p** *it is* for H5273
135: 3 sing praises unto his name; for *it is* **p**. H5273
147: 1 God; for *it is* **p**; *and* praise is comely. H5273
Prv 2:10 and knowledge is **p** unto thy soul; H5276
5:19 *Let her be as* the loving hind and **p** roe; H2580
9:17 sweet, and bread *eaten* in secret is **p**. H5276
15:26 but *the words* of the pure *are* **p** words. H5278
16:24 **P** words *are as* an honeycomb, sweet to H5278
22:18 For *it is* a **p** thing if thou keep them H5273
24: 4 be filled with all precious and **p** riches. H5273
Ecc 11: 7 Truly the light *is* sweet, and a **p** *thing it* H2896
Song 1:16 beloved, yea, **p**: also our bed *is* green. H5273
4:13 **p** fruits; camphire, with spikenard, H4022
16 into his garden, and eat his **p** fruits. H4022
7: 6 How fair and how **p** art thou, O love, H5276
13 *are* all manner of **p** *fruits*, new and old, H4022
Isa 2:16 of Tarshish, and upon all **p** pictures. H2532
5: 7 the men of Judah his **p** plant: and he H8191
13:22 and dragons in *their* **p** palaces: and her H6027
17:10 shalt thou plant **p** plants, and shalt set H5282
32:12 for the **p** fields, for the fruitful vine. H2531
54:12 and all thy borders of **p** stones. H2656
64:11 fire: and all our **p** things are laid waste. H4261
Jer 3:19 and give thee a **p** land, a goodly H2532
12:10 my **p** portion a desolate wilderness. H2532
23:10 land mourneth; the **p** places of the H4999
25:34 and ye shall fall like a **p** vessel. H2532
31:20 *Is* Ephraim my dear son? *is he* a **p** H8191
Lam 1: 7 miseries all her **p** things that she had H4262
10 his hand upon all her **p** things: for she H4621
11 have given their **p** things for meat to H4622
2: 4 slew all *that were* **p** to the eye in the H4261
Ezk 26:12 and destroy thy **p** houses: and they H2532
33:32 of one that hath a **p** voice, and can play H3303
Dan 8: 9 toward the east, and toward the **p** *land*. H6643
10: 3 I ate no **p** bread, neither came flesh nor H2532
11:38 and with precious stones, and **p** things. H2530
Hos 9: 6 bury them: the **p** *places* for their silver, H4261
13 *is* planted in a **p** place: but Ephraim H5116
13:15 shall spoil the treasure of all **p** vessels. H2532
Joel 3: 5 into your temples my goodly **p** things: H4261
Am 5:11 ye have planted **p** vineyards, but ye H2531
Mic 2: 9 cast out from their **p** houses; from their H8588
Nah 2: 9 *and* glory out of all the **p** furniture. H2532
Zec 7:14 for they laid the **p** land desolate. H2532
Mal 3: 4 and Jerusalem be **p** unto the LORD, as H6149

PLEASANTNESS
Prv 3:17 Her ways *are* ways of **p**, and all her H5278

PLEASE
Ex 21: 8 If she **p** not her master, who H7451+H5869
Nu 23:27 it will **p** God that thou mayest H3477+H5869
1Sa 20:13 to Jonathan: but if it **p** my father *to do* H3190
2Sa 7:29 Therefore now let it **p** thee to bless the H2974
1Ki 21: 6 or else, if it **p** thee, I will give thee H2655
1Ch 17:27 Now therefore let it **p** thee to bless the H2974
2Ch 10: 7 to this people, and **p** them, and speak H7521
Neh 2: 5 And I said unto the king, If it **p** the H2895
7 Moreover I said unto the king, If it **p** H2895
Est 1:19 If it **p** the king, let there go a royal H2895
3: 9 If it **p** the king, let it be written that H2895
5: 8 of the king, and if it **p** the king to grant H2895
7: 3 O king, and if it **p** the king, let my life H2895
8: 5 And said, If it **p** the king, and if I have H2896
9:13 Then said Esther, If it **p** the king, let it H2896
Job 6: 9 Even that it would **p** God to destroy H2974
20:10 His children shall seek to **p** the poor, H7521
Ps 69:31 *This* also shall **p** the LORD better than H3190
Prv 16: 7 When a man's ways **p** the LORD, he H7521
Song 2: 7 stir not up, nor awake *my* love, till he **p**. H2654
3: 5 stir not up, nor awake *my* love, till he **p**. H2654
8: 4 not up, nor awake *my* love, until he **p**. H2654
Isa 2: 6 and they **p** themselves in the children H5606
55:11 that which I **p**, and it shall prosper H2654
56: 4 **p** me, and take hold of my covenant; H2654
Jn 8:29 for I do always those things that **p** him. *G701*
Ro 8: 8 they that are in the flesh cannot **p** God. *G700*
15: 1 of the weak, and not to **p** ourselves. *G700*
2 Let every one of us **p** *his* neighbour for *G700*
1Co 7:32 to the Lord, how he may **p** the Lord: *G700*
33 are of the world, how he may **p** *his* wife. *G700*
34 the world, how she may **p** *her* husband. *G700*
10:33 Even as I **p** all *men* in all *things*, not *G700*
Gal 1:10 or do I seek to **p** men? for if I yet pleased *G700*
1Th 2:15 **p** not God, and are contrary to all men: *G700*
4: 1 ought to walk and to **p** God, *so* ye would *G700*
2Ti 2: 4 life; that he may **p** him who hath chosen *G700*
Tit 2: 9 *and* to **p** *them* well in all *G2001+G1511*
Heb 11: 6 But without faith *it is* impossible to **p** *G2100*

PLEASED
Gen 28: 8 of Canaan **p** not Isaac his father; H5869
33:10 face of God, and thou wast **p** with me. H7521
34:18 And their words **p** Hamor, and H3190+H5869
45:16 come: and it **p** Pharaoh well, H3190+H5869
Nu 24: 1 And when Balaam saw that it **p** the H2895
Dt 1:23 And the saying **p** me well: and I took H3190
Jos 22:30 of Manasseh spake, it **p** them. H3190+H5869
33 And the thing **p** the children of H3190+H5869
Jdg 13:23 If the LORD were **p** to kill us, he would H2654
14: 7 and she **p** Samson well. H3477+H5869
1Sa 12:22 **p** the LORD to make you his people. H2974
18:20 told Saul, and the thing **p** him. H3477+H5869
26 words, it **p** David well to be H3477+H5869
2Sa 3:36 notice *of it*, and it **p** them: as H3190+H5869
36 the king did **p** all the people. H2896+H5869
17: 4 And the saying **p** Absalom H3477+H5869
19: 6 day, then it had **p** thee well. H3477+H5869
1Ki 3:10 And the speech **p** the Lord, H3190+H5869
9: 1 Solomon's desire which he was **p** to do, H2654
12 given him; and they **p** him not. H3474+H5869
2Ch 30: 4 And the thing **p** the king and H3477+H5869
Neh 2: 6 thou return? So it **p** the king to send H3190
Est 1:21 And the saying **p** the king and H3190+H5869
2: 4 thing **p** the king; and he did so. H3190+H5869
9 And the maiden **p** him, and H3190+H5869
5:14 And the thing **p** Haman; and he caused H3190
Ps 40:13 Be **p**, O LORD, to deliver me: O LORD, H7521
51:19 Then shalt thou be **p** with the sacrifices H2654
115: 3 he hath done whatsoever he hath **p**. H2654
135: 6 Whatsoever the LORD **p**, *that* did he in H2654
Isa 42:21 The LORD is well **p** for his H2654
53:10 Yet it **p** the LORD to bruise him; he H2654
Dan 6: 1 It **p** Darius to set over the kingdom an H8232
Jna 1:14 thou, O LORD, hast done as it **p** thee. H2654
Mic 6: 7 Will the LORD be **p** with thousands of H7521
Mal 1: 8 will he be **p** with thee, or accept H7521
Mt 3:17 my beloved Son, in whom I am well **p**. *G2106*
12:18 my soul is well **p**: I will put my spirit *G2106*

Mt 14: 6 danced before them, and **p** Herod. G700
17: 5 Son, in whom I am well **p**; hear ye him. G2106
Mk 1:11 my beloved Son, in whom I am well **p**. G2106
6:22 and danced, and **p** Herod and them that G700
Lk 3:22 art my beloved Son; in thee I am well **p**. G2106
Act 6: 5 And the saying **p** the whole multitude: G700
12: 3 And because he saw it **p** the Jews, he G2076
15:22 Then **p** it the apostles and elders, with G1380
34 Notwithstanding it **p** Silas to abide G1380
Ro 15: 3 For even Christ **p** not himself; but, as it G700
26 For it hath **p** them of Macedonia and G2106
27 It hath **p** them verily; and their debtors G2106
1Co 1:21 wisdom knew not God, it **p** God by the G2106
7:12 not, and she be **p** to dwell with him, let G4909
13 not, and if he be **p** to dwell with her, let G4909
10: 5 them God was not well **p**: for they were G2106
12:18 of them in the body, as it hath **p** him. G2309
15:38 But God giveth it a body as it hath **p** G2309
Gal 1:10 men? for if I yet **p** men, I should not be G700
15 But when it **p** God, who separated me G2106
Col 1:19 For it **p** *the Father* that in him should G2106
Heb 11: 5 he had this testimony, that he **p** God. G2100
13:16 for with such sacrifices God is well **p**. G2100
2Pt 1:17 my beloved Son, in whom I am well **p**. G2106

PLEASETH
Gen 16: 6 do to her as it **p** thee. And H2896+H5869
20:15 thee: dwell where it **p** thee. H2896+H5869
Jdg 14: 3 her for me; for she **p** me well. H3477+H5869
Est 2: 4 And let the maiden which **p** H3190+H5869
Ecc 7:26 *as* bands: whoso **p** God shall H2896+H6440
8: 3 thing; for he doeth whatsoever **p** him. H2654

PLEASING
Est 8: 5 the king, and I *be* **p** in his eyes, let it be H2896
Hos 9: 4 neither shall they be **p** unto him: their H6149
Col 1:10 of the Lord unto all **p**, being fruitful in G699
3:20 things: for this is well **p** unto the Lord. G2101
1Th 2: 4 **p** men, but God, which trieth our hearts. G700
1Jn 3:22 do those things that are **p** in his sight. G701

PLEASURE
Gen 18:12 shall I have **p**, my lord being old also? H5730
Dt 23:24 fill at thine own **p**; but thou shalt not H5315
1Ch 29:17 heart, and hast **p** in uprightness. As for H7521
Ezr 5:17 send his **p** to us concerning this matter. H7470
10:11 and do his **p**: and separate yourselves H7522
Neh 9:37 at their **p**, and we *are* in great distress. H7522
Est 1: 8 should do according to every man's **p**. H7522
Job 21:21 For what **p** *hath* he in his house after H2656
25 of his soul, and never eateth with **p**. H2896
22: 3 *Is it* any **p** to the Almighty, that thou H2656
Ps 5: 4 For thou *art* not a God that hath **p** in H2655
35:27 hath **p** in the prosperity of his servant. H2655
51:18 Do good in thy good **p** unto Zion: build H7522
102:14 For thy servants take **p** in her stones, H7521
103:21 hosts; *ye* ministers of his, that do his **p**. H7522
105:22 To bind his princes at his **p**; and teach H5315
111: 2 out of all them that have **p** therein. H2656
147:10 he taketh not **p** in the legs of a man. H7521
11 The LORD taketh **p** in them that fear H7521
149: 4 For the LORD taketh **p** in his people: he H7521
Prv 21:17 He that loveth **p** *shall be* a poor man: H8057
Ecc 2: 1 enjoy **p**: and, behold, this also *is* vanity. H2896
5: 4 it; for *he hath* no **p** in fools: pay that H2656
12: 1 thou shalt say, I have no **p** in them; H2656
Isa 21: 4 my **p** hath he turned into fear unto me. H2837
44:28 shall perform all my **p**: even saying to H2656
46:10 shall stand, and I will do all my **p**: H2656
48:14 him: he will do his **p** on Babylon, and H2656
53:10 *his* days, and the **p** of the LORD shall H2656
58: 3 ye find **p**, and exact all your labours. H2656
13 *from* doing thy **p** on my holy day; and H2656
13 own **p**, nor speaking *thine own* words: H2656
Jer 2:24 up the wind at her **p**; in her occasion who H185
22:28 wherein *is* no **p**? wherefore are they H2656
34:16 set at liberty at their **p**, to return, and H5315
48:38 vessel wherein *is* no **p**, saith the LORD. H2656
Ezk 16:37 thou hast taken **p**, and all *them* that H6149
18:23 Have I any **p** at all that the wicked H2654
32 For I have no **p** in the death of him that H2654
33:11 GOD, I have no **p** in the death of the H2654
Hos 8: 8 the Gentiles as a vessel wherein *is* no **p**. H2656
Hag 1: 8 and I will take **p** in it, and I will be H7521
Mal 1:10 for nought. I have no **p** in you, saith the H2656
Lk 12:32 good **p** to give you the kingdom. G2106
Act 24:27 to shew the Jews a **p**, left Paul bound. G5485
25: 9 But Festus, willing to do the Jews a **p**, G5485
Ro 1:32 same, but have **p** in them that do them. G4909
2Co 12:10 Therefore I take **p** in infirmities, in G2106
Eph 1: 5 according to the good **p** of his will, G2107
9 **p** which he hath purposed in himself: G2107
Php 2:13 you both to will and to do of *his* good **p**. G2107
2Th 1:11 fulfil all the good **p** of *his* goodness, G2107
2:12 truth, but had **p** in unrighteousness. G2106
1Ti 5: 6 But she that liveth in **p** is dead while G4684
Heb 10: 6 *sacrifices* for sin thou hast had no **p**. G2106
8 **p** *therein*; which are offered by the law; G2106
38 back, my soul shall have no **p** in him. G2106
12:10 *us* after their own **p**; but he for *our* G1380
Jas 5: 5 Ye have lived in **p** on the earth, and G5171
2Pt 2:13 *as* they that count it **p** to riot in the day G2237
Rev 4:11 for thy **p** they are and were created. G2307

PLEASURES
Job 36:11 days in prosperity, and their years in **p**. H5273
Ps 16:11 right hand *there are* **p** for evermore. H5273
36: 8 make them drink of the river of thy **p**. H5730
Isa 47: 8 *thou that art* given to **p**, that dwellest H5719
Lk 8:14 and riches and **p** of *this* life, and bring G2237
2Ti 3: 4 lovers of **p** more than lovers of God; G5369
Tit 3: 3 divers lusts and **p**, living in malice and G2237
Heb 11:25 than to enjoy the **p** of sin for a season; G2192

PLEDGE
Gen 38:17 Wilt thou give *me* a **p**, till thou send *it*? H6162
18 And he said, What **p** shall I give thee? H6162
20 to receive *his* **p** from the woman's H6162
Ex 22:26 raiment to **p**, thou shalt deliver it H2254
Dt 24: 6 to **p**: for he taketh *a man's* life to pledge. H2254
6 to pledge: for he taketh *a man's* life to **p**. H2254
10 not go into his house to fetch his **p**. H5667
11 shall bring out the **p** abroad unto thee. H5667
12 *be* poor, thou shalt not sleep with his **p**: H5667
13 In any case thou shalt deliver him the **p** H5667
17 nor take a widow's raiment to **p**: H2254
1Sa 17:18 how thy brethren fare, and take their **p**. H6161
Job 22: 6 For thou hast taken a **p** from thy H2254
24: 3 they take the widow's ox for a **p**. H2254
9 the breast, and take a **p** of the poor. H2254
Prv 20:16 take a **p** of him for a strange woman. H2254
27:13 take a **p** of him for a strange woman. H2254
Ezk 18: 7 to the debtor his **p**, hath spoiled none H2258
12 not restored the **p**, and hath lifted up H2258
16 withholden the **p**, neither hath spoiled H2258
33:15 *If* the wicked restore the **p**, give again H2258
Am 2: 8 clothes laid to **p** by every altar, and H2254

PLEDGES
2Ki 18:23 Now therefore, I pray thee, give **p** to my H6148
Isa 36: 8 Now therefore give **p**, I pray thee, to my H6148

PLEIADES
Job 9: 9 Which maketh Arcturus, Orion, and **P**, H3598
38:31 of **P**, or loose the bands of Orion? H3598

PLENISH
See REPLENISH.

PLENTEOUS
Gen 41:34 the land of Egypt in the seven **p** years. H7647
47 And in the seven **p** years the earth H7647
Dt 28:11 And the LORD shall make thee **p** in H3498
30: 9 will make thee **p** in every work of thine H3498
2Ch 1:15 at Jerusalem *as* **p** as stones, and cedar
Ps 86: 5 to forgive; and **p** in mercy unto all H7227
15 and **p** in mercy and truth. H7227
103: 8 slow to anger, and **p** in mercy. H7227
130: 7 mercy, and with him *is* **p** redemption. H7235
Isa 30:23 it shall be fat and **p**: in that day shall H8082
Hab 1:16 their portion *is* fat, and their meat **p**. H1277
Mt 9:37 truly *is* **p**, but the labourers *are* few; G4183

PLENTEOUSNESS
Gen 41:53 And the seven years of **p**, that was in H7647
Prv 21: 5 *tend* only to **p**; but of every one *that* H4195

PLENTIFUL
Ps 68: 9 Thou, O God, didst send a **p** rain, H5071
Isa 16:10 and joy out of the **p** field; and in the H3759
Jer 2: 7 And I brought you into a **p** country, to H3759
48:33 is taken from the **p** field, and from the H3759

PLENTIFULLY
Job 26: 3 hast thou **p** declared the thing as it is? H7230
Ps 31:23 and **p** rewardeth the proud doer. H3499
Lk 12:16 of a certain rich man brought forth **p**: G2164

PLENTY
Gen 27:28 of the earth, and **p** of corn and wine: H7230
41:29 **p** throughout all the land of Egypt: H7647
30 and all the **p** shall be forgotten in H7647
31 And the **p** shall not be known in the H7647
Lev 11:36 pit, *wherein there is* **p** of water, shall be H4723
1Ki 10:11 **p** of almug trees, and precious stones. H7235
2Ch 31:10 eat, and have left **p**: for the LORD hath H7230
Job 22:25 and thou shalt have **p** of silver. H8443
37:23 and in **p** of justice: he will not afflict. H7230
Prv 3:10 So shall thy barns be filled with **p**, and H7647
28:19 He that tilleth his land shall have **p** of H7646
Jer 44:17 for *then* had we **p** of victuals, and were H7646
Joel 2:26 And ye shall eat in **p**, and be satisfied, H398

PLOT
See PLAT.

PLOTTETH
Ps 37:12 The wicked **p** against the just, and H2161

PLOUGH
Lk 9:62 put his hand to the **p**, and looking back, G723

PLOW
Dt 22:10 Thou shalt not **p** with an ox and an ass H2790
1Sa 14:14 of land, *which* a yoke *of oxen might* **p**. H2790
Job 4: 8 Even as I have seen, they that **p** H2790
Prv 20: 4 The sluggard will not **p** by reason of the H2790
Isa 28:24 Doth the plowman **p** all day to sow? H2790
Hos 10:11 shall **p**, *and* Jacob shall break his clods. H2790
Am 6:12 the rock? will *one* **p** *there* with oxen? for H2790
1Co 9:10 ploweth should **p** in hope; and that he G722

PLOWED
Jdg 14:18 If ye had not **p** with my heifer, ye had H2790
Ps 129: 3 The plowers **p** upon my back: they H2790
Jer 26:18 hosts; Zion shall be **p** *like* a field, and H2790
Hos 10:13 Ye have **p** wickedness, ye have reaped H2790
Mic 3:12 Therefore shall Zion for your sake be **p** H2790

PLOWERS
Ps 129: 3 The **p** plowed upon my back: they H2790

PLOWETH
1Co 9:10 that he that **p** should plow in hope; G722

PLOWING
1Ki 19:19 Shaphat, who *was* **p** *with* twelve yoke H2790
Job 1:14 **p**, and the asses feeding beside them: H2790
Prv 21: 4 heart, *and* the **p** of the wicked, *is* sin. H5215
Lk 17: 7 But which of you, having a servant **p** or G722

PLOWMAN
Isa 28:24 Doth the **p** plow all day to sow? doth he H2790
Am 9:13 the LORD, that the **p** shall overtake the H2790

PLOWMEN
Isa 61: 5 *shall be* your **p** and your vinedressers. H406
Jer 14: 4 in the earth, the **p** were ashamed, they H406

PLOWSHARES
Isa 2: 4 their swords into **p**, and their spears into H855
Joel 3:10 Beat your **p** into swords, and your H855
Mic 4: 3 their swords into **p**, and their spears into H855

PLUCK
Lev 1:16 And he shall **p** away his crop with his H5493
Nu 33:52 and quite **p** down all their high places: H8045
Dt 23:25 then thou mayest **p** the ears with thine H6998
2Ch 7:20 Then will I **p** them up by the roots out H5428
Job 24: 9 They **p** the fatherless from the breast, H1497
Ps 25:15 for he shall **p** my feet out of the net. H3318
52: 5 take thee away, and **p** thee out of *thy* H5255
74:11 thy right hand? **p** *it* out of thy bosom. H3615
80:12 all they which pass by the way do **p** her? H717
Ecc 3: 2 a time to **p** up *that which is* planted; H6131
Jer 12:14 Behold, I will **p** them out of their land, H5428
14 of their land, and **p** out the house of H5428
17 But if they will not obey, I will utterly **p** H5428
18: 7 a kingdom, to **p** up, and to pull down, H5428
22:24 right hand, yet would I **p** thee thence; H5423
24: 6 I will plant them, and not **p** *them* up. H5428
31:28 over them, to **p** up, and to break down, H5428
42:10 will plant you, and not **p** *you* up: for I H5428
45: 4 I will **p** up, even this whole land. H5428
Ezk 17: 9 people to **p** it up by the roots thereof. H5375
23:34 thereof, and **p** off thine own breasts: H5423
Mic 3: 2 love the evil; who **p** off their skin from H1497
5:14 And I will **p** up thy groves out of the H5428

Mt 5:29 And if thy right eye offend thee, p it G1807
12: 1 began to p the ears of corn, and to eat. G5089
18: 9 And if thine eye offend thee, p it out, G1807
Mk 2:23 as they went, to p the ears of corn. G5089
9:47 And if thine eye offend thee, p it out: it G1544
Jn 10:28 shall any man p them out of my hand. G726
29 able to p them out of my Father's hand. G726

PLUCKED
Ex 4: 7 his bosom again; and p it out of his H3318
Dt 28:63 and ye shall be p from off the land H5255
Ru 4: 7 all things; a man p off his shoe, and H8025
2Sa 23:21 with a staff, and p the spear out of the H1497
1Ch 11:23 with a staff, and p the spear out of the H1497
Ezr 9: 3 my mantle, and p off the hair of my H4803
Neh 13:25 of them, and p off their hair, and made H4803
Job 29:17 wicked, and p the spoil out of his teeth. H7993
Isa 50: 6 to them that p off the hair: I hid not H4803
Jer 6:29 in vain: for the wicked are not p away. H5423
12:15 pass, after that I have p them out I will H5428
31:40 it shall not be p up, nor thrown down H5428
Ezk 19:12 But she was p up in fury, she was cast H5428
Dan 7: 4 thereof were p, and it was lifted up H4804
8 of the first horns p up by the roots: H6132
11: 4 be p up, even for others beside those. H5428
Am 4:11 as a firebrand p out of the burning: H5337
Zec 3: 2 is not this a brand p out of the fire? H5337
Mk 5: 4 chains had been p asunder by him, and G1288
Lk 6: 1 and his disciples p the ears of corn, G5089
17: 6 tree, Be thou p up by the root, and G1610
Gal 4:15 ye would have p out your own eyes, G1846
Jude 12 fruit, twice dead, p up by the roots; G1610

PLUCKETH
Prv 14: 1 the foolish p it down with her hands. H2040

PLUCKT
Gen 8:11 was an olive leaf p off: so Noah knew H2965

PLUMBLINE
Am 7: 7 by a p, with a plumbline in his hand. H594
7 by a plumbline, with a p in his hand. H594
8 seest thou? And I said, A p. Then said the H594
8 Behold, I will set a p in the midst of my H594

PLUMMET
2Ki 21:13 of Samaria, and the p of the house of H4949
Isa 28:17 to the p: and the hail shall sweep H4949
Zec 4:10 and shall see the p in the hand of H68+H913

PLUNGE
Job 9:31 Yet shalt thou p me in the ditch, and H2881

POCHERETH
Ezr 2:57 of P of Zebaim, the children of Ami. H6380
Neh 7:59 of P of Zebaim, the children of Amon. H6380

POETS
Act 17:28 also of your own p have said, For we G4163

POINT
Gen 25:32 And Esau said, Behold, I am at the p to H1980
Nu 34: 7 sea ye shall p out for you mount Hor: H8376
8 From mount Hor ye shall p out your H8376
10 And ye shall p out your east border from H184
Jer 17: 1 iron, and with the p of a diamond: it is H6856
Ezk 21:15 I have set the p of the sword against all H19
Mk 5:23 lieth at the p of death: I pray thee, G2079
Jn 4:47 his son: for he was at the p of death. G3195
Jas 2:10 and yet offend in one p, he is guilty of all.

POINTED
Job 41:30 sharp p things upon the mire. H2742

POINTS
Ecc 5:16 And this also is a sore evil, that in all p H5980
Heb 4:15 but was in all p tempted like as we are, G3956

POISON
Dt 32:24 with the p of serpents of the dust. H2534
33 Their wine is the p of dragons, and the H2534
Job 6: 4 are within me, the p whereof drinketh H2534
20:16 He shall suck the p of asps: the viper's H7219
Ps 58: 4 Their p is like the poison of a serpent: H2534
4 Their poison is like the p of a serpent: H2534
140: 3 adders' p is under their lips. Selah. H2534
Ro 3:13 deceit; the p of asps is under their lips: G2447
Jas 3: 8 it is an unruly evil, full of deadly p. G2447

POLE
Nu 21: 8 and set it upon a p: and it shall come to H5251
9 and put it upon a p, and it came to H5251

POLICY
Dan 8:25 And through his p also he shall cause H7922

POLISHED
Ps 144:12 p after the similitude of a palace: H2404
Isa 49: 2 a p shaft; in his quiver hath he hid me; H1305
Dan 10: 6 like in colour to p brass, and the voice H7044

POLISHING
Lam 4: 7 than rubies, their p was of sapphire: H1508

POLL
Nu 3:47 apiece by the p, after the shekel of the H1538
Ezk 44:20 long; they shall only p their heads. H3697
Mic 1:16 Make thee bald, and p thee for thy H1494

POLLED
2Sa 14:26 And when he p his head, (for it was at H1548
26 year's end that he p it: because the hair H1548
26 him, therefore he p it:) he weighed the H1548

POLLS
Nu 1: 2 of their names, every male by their p; H1538
18 years old and upward, by their p. H1538
20 the names, by their p, every male from H1538
22 the names, by their p, every male from H1538
1Ch 23: 3 number by their p, man by man, was H1538
24 of names by their p, that did the work H1538

POLLUTE
Nu 18:32 it: neither shall ye p the holy things of H2490
35:33 So ye shall not p the land wherein ye H2610
Jer 7:30 which is called by my name, to p it. H2930
Ezk 7:21 the earth for a spoil; and they shall p it. H2490
22 and they shall p my secret place: for H2490
13:19 And will ye p me among my people for H2490
20:31 the fire, ye p yourselves with all your H2930
39 unto me: but p ye my holy name no H2490
39: 7 I will not let them p my holy name any H2490
44: 7 my sanctuary, to p it, even my house, H2490
Dan 11:31 part, and they shall p the sanctuary of H2490

POLLUTED
Ex 20:25 lift up thy tool upon it, thou hast p it. H2490
2Ki 23:16 the altar, and p it, according to the H2930
2Ch 36:14 of the heathen; and p the house of the H2930
Ezr 2:62 they, as p, put from the priesthood. H1351
Neh 7:64 they, as p, put from the priesthood. H1351
Ps 106:38 and the land was p with blood. H2610
Isa 47: 6 I was wroth with my people, I have p H2490
48:11 my name be p? and I will not give my H2490
Jer 2:23 How canst thou say, I am not p, I have H2930
3: 1 land be greatly p? but thou hast played H2610
2 and thou hast p the land with thy H2610
34:16 But ye turned and p my name, and H2490
Lam 2: 2 p the kingdom and the princes thereof. H2490
4:14 the streets, they have p themselves with H1351
Ezk 4:14 soul hath not been p: for from my youth H2930
14:11 me, neither be p any more with all H2930
16: 6 thee, and saw thee p in thine own blood, H947
22 and bare, and wast p in thy blood. H947
20: 9 it should not be p before the heathen, H2490
13 they greatly p: then I said, I would H2490
14 it should not be p before the heathen, H2490
16 in my statutes, but p my sabbaths: for H2490
21 live in them; they p my sabbaths: then I H2490
22 it should not be p in the sight of the H2490
24 statutes, and had p my sabbaths, and H2490
26 And I p them in their own gifts, in that H2930
30 Lord GOD; Are ye p after the manner of H2930
23:17 and she was p with them, and her H2930
30 and because thou art p with their idols. H2930
36:18 for their idols wherewith they had p it: H2930
Hos 6: 8 that work iniquity, and is p with blood. H6121
9: 4 eat thereof shall be p: for their bread for H2930
Am 7:17 thou shalt die in a p land: and Israel H2931
Mic 2:10 rest: because it is p, it shall destroy you, H2930
Zep 3: 1 Woe to her that is filthy and p, to the H1351
4 her priests have p the sanctuary, they H2490
Mal 1: 7 Ye offer p bread upon mine altar; and H1351
7 Wherein have we p thee? In that ye say, H1351
12 of the LORD is p; and the fruit thereof, H1351
Act 21:28 the temple, and hath p this holy place. G2840

POLLUTING
Isa 56: 2 the sabbath from p it, and keepeth his H2490
6 p it, and taketh hold of my covenant; H2490

POLLUTION
Ezk 22:10 humbled her that was set apart for p. H2931

POLLUTIONS
Act 15:20 they abstain from p of idols, and from G234
2Pt 2:20 For if after they have escaped the p of G3393

POLLUX
Act 28:11 the isle, whose sign was Castor and P. G1359

POMEGRANATE
Ex 28:34 A golden bell and a p, a golden bell and H7416
34 a golden bell and a p, upon the hem of H7416
39:26 A bell and a p, a bell and a H7416
26 a bell and a p, round about the hem H7416
1Sa 14: 2 of Gibeah under a p tree which is in H7416
Song 4: 3 are like a piece of a p within thy locks. H7416
6: 7 As a piece of a p are thy temples within H7416
8: 2 of spiced wine of the juice of my p. H7416
Joel 1:12 languisheth; the p tree, the palm tree H7416
Hag 2:19 fig tree, and the p, and the olive tree, H7416

POMEGRANATES
Ex 28:33 of it thou shalt make p of blue, and of H7416
39:24 hems of the robe p of blue, and purple, H7416
25 bells between the p upon the hem of H7416
25 of the robe, round about between the p; H7416
Nu 13:23 they brought of the p, and of the figs. H7416
20: 5 of p; neither is there any water to drink. H7416
Dt 8: 8 and p; a land of oil olive, and honey; H7416
1Ki 7:18 p: and so did he for the other chapiter. H7416
20 the two pillars had p also above, over
20 network: and the p were two hundred H7416
42 And four hundred p for the two H7416
42 even two rows of p for one network, to H7416
2Ki 25:17 work, and p upon the chapiter round H7416
2Ch 3:16 hundred p, and put them on the chains. H7416
4:13 And four hundred p on the two H7416
13 two rows of p on each wreath, to cover H7416
Song 4:13 Thy plants are an orchard of p, with H7416
6:11 the vine flourished, and the p budded. H7416
7:12 appear, and the p bud forth: there will H7416
Jer 52:22 with network and p upon the chapiters H7416
22 also and the p were like unto these. H7416
23 And there were ninety and six p on a H7416
23 a side; and all the p upon the network H7416

POMEGRANATE-TREE See POMEGRANATE and TREE.

POMMELS
2Ch 4:12 To wit, the two pillars, and the p, and H1543
12 to cover the two p of the chapiters H1543
13 to cover the two p of the chapiters H1543

POMP
Isa 5:14 and their p, and he that rejoiceth, H7588
14:11 Thy p is brought down to the grave, H1347
Ezk 7:24 I will also make the p of the strong to H1347
30:18 of Egypt: and the p of her strength shall H1347
32:12 shall spoil the p of Egypt, and all the H1347
33:28 desolate, and the p of her strength shall H1347
Act 25:23 with great p, and was entered into G5325

PONDER
Prv 4:26 P the path of thy feet, and let all thy H6424
5: 6 Lest thou shouldest p the path of life, H6424

PONDERED
Lk 2:19 But Mary kept all these things, and p G4820

PONDERETH
Prv 5:21 of the LORD, and he p all his goings. H6424
21: 2 own eyes: but the LORD p the hearts. H8505
24:12 doth not he that p the heart consider it? H8505

PONDS
Ex 7:19 and upon their p, and upon all their H98
8: 5 and over the p, and cause frogs to come H98
Isa 19:10 all that make sluices and p for fish. H99

PONTIUS
Mt 27: 2 delivered him to P Pilate the governor. G4194
Lk 3: 1 of Tiberius Caesar, P Pilate being G4194
Act 4:27 both Herod, and P Pilate, with the G4194
1Ti 6:13 P Pilate witnessed a good confession; G4194

PONTUS
Act 2: 9 and Cappadocia, in **P**, and Asia, *G4195*
18: 2 Aquila, born in **P**, lately come from *G4193*
1Pt 1: 1 throughout **P**, Galatia, Cappadocia, *G4195*

POOL
2Sa 2:13 together by the **p** of Gibeon: and they H1295
13 the one side of the **p**, and the other on H1295
13 and the other on the other side of the **p**. H1295
4:12 *them* up over the **p** in Hebron. But they H1295
1Ki 22:38 And *one* washed the chariot in the **p** of H1295
2Ki 18:17 of the upper **p**, which *is* in the highway H1295
20:20 how he made a **p**, and a conduit, and H1295
Neh 2:14 and to the king's **p**: but *there was* no H1295
3:15 and the wall of the **p** of Siloah by the H1295
16 David, and to the **p** that was made, and H1295
Isa 7: 3 **p** in the highway of the fuller's field; H1295
22: 9 together the waters of the lower **p**. H1295
11 the water of the old **p**: but ye have not H1295
35: 7 shall become a **p**, and the thirsty land H98
36: 2 **p** in the highway of the fuller's field. H1295
41:18 the wilderness a **p** of water, and the dry H98
Nah 2: 8 But Nineveh *is* of old like a **p** of water: H1295
Jn 5: 2 sheep *market* a **p**, which is called in the *G2861*
4 season into the **p**, and troubled the *G2861*
7 to put me into the **p**: but while I am *G2861*
9: 7 And said unto him, Go, wash in the **p** *G2861*
11 unto me, Go to the **p** of Siloam, and *G2861*

POOLS
Ex 7:19 and upon all their **p** of water, that they H4723
Ps 84: 6 make it a well; the rain also filleth the **p**. H1293
Ecc 2: 6 I made me **p** of water, to water H1295
Isa 14:23 for the bittern, and **p** of water: and I will H98
42:15 the rivers islands, and I will dry up the **p**. H98

POOR
Gen 41:19 up after them, **p** and very ill favoured H1803
Ex 22:25 my people *that is* **p** by thee, thou shalt H6041
23: 3 Neither shalt thou countenance a **p** H1800
6 wrest the judgment of thy **p** in his cause. H34
11 lie still; that the **p** of thy people may eat: H34
30:15 The rich shall not give more, and the **p** H1800
Lev 14:21 And if he *be* **p**, and cannot get so much; H1800
19:10 leave them for the **p** and stranger: I *am* H6041
15 the person of the **p**, nor honour the H1800
23:22 them unto the **p**, and to the stranger: H6041
25:25 If thy brother be waxen **p**, and hath sold H4134
35 And if thy brother be waxen **p**, and H4134
39 by thee be waxen **p**, and be sold unto H4134
47 by him wax **p**, and sell himself unto H4134
Dt 15: 4 Save when there shall be no **p** among H34
7 If there be among you a **p** man of one of H34
7 nor shut thine hand from thy **p** brother: H34
9 be evil against thy **p** brother, and thou H34
11 For the **p** shall never cease out of the H34
11 to thy **p**, and to thy needy, in thy land. H6041
24:12 And if the man *be* **p**, thou shalt not H6041
14 servant *that is* **p** and needy, *whether* H6041
15 upon it; for he *is* **p**, and setteth his heart H6041
Jdg 6:15 my family *is* **p** in Manasseh, and I H1800
Ru 3:10 not young men, whether **p** or rich. H1800
1Sa 2: 7 The LORD maketh **p**, and maketh rich: H3423
8 He raiseth up the **p** out of the dust, *and* H1800
18:23 I *am* a **p** man, and lightly esteemed? H7326
2Sa 12: 1 one city; the one rich, and the other **p**. H7326
3 But the **p** *man* had nothing, save one H7326
4 him; but took the **p** man's lamb, and H7326
2Ki 25:12 the guard left of the **p** of the land *to be* H1803
Est 9:22 one to another, and gifts to the **p**. H34
Job 5:15 But he saveth the **p** from the sword, H34
16 So the **p** hath hope, and iniquity H1800
20:10 His children shall seek to please the **p**, H1800
19 hath forsaken the **p**; *because* he hath H1800
24: 4 **p** of the earth hide themselves together. H6035
9 the breast, and take a pledge of the **p**. H6041
14 light killeth the **p** and needy, and in the H6041
29:12 Because I delivered the **p** that cried, H6041
16 I *was* a father to the **p**: and the cause H34
30:25 was *not* my soul grieved for the **p**? H34
31:16 If I have withheld the **p** from *their* H1800
19 of clothing, or any **p** without covering; H34
34:19 **p**? for they all *are* the work of his hands. H1800
28 So that they cause the cry of the **p** to H1800
36: 6 of the wicked: but giveth right to the **p**. H6041
15 He delivereth the **p** in his affliction, H6041
Ps 9:18 of the **p** shall *not* perish for ever. H6041
10: 2 doth persecute the **p**: let them be taken H6041
8 his eyes are privily set against the **p**. H2489
Ps 10: 9 in wait to catch the **p**: he doth catch the H6041
9 **p**, when he draweth him into his net. H6041
10 that the **p** may fall by his strong ones. H2489
14 *it* with thy hand: the **p** committeth H2489
12: 5 For the oppression of the **p**, for the H6041
14: 6 Ye have shamed the counsel of the **p**, H6041
34: 6 This **p** man cried, and the LORD heard H6041
35:10 deliverest the **p** from him that is too H6041
10 for him, yea, the **p** and the needy from H6041
37:14 to cast down the **p** and needy, *and* to H6041
40:17 But I *am* **p** and needy; *yet* the Lord H6041
41: 1 Blessed *is* he that considereth the **p**: the H1800
49: 2 Both low and high, rich and **p**, together. H34
68:10 hast prepared of thy goodness for the **p**. H6041
69:29 But I *am* **p** and sorrowful: let thy H6041
33 For the LORD heareth the **p**, and H34
70: 5 But I *am* **p** and needy: make haste unto H6041
72: 2 and thy **p** with judgment. H6041
4 He shall judge the **p** of the people, he H6041
12 **p** also, and *him* that hath no helper. H6041
13 He shall spare the **p** and needy, and H1800
74:19 not the congregation of thy **p** for ever. H6041
21 let the **p** and needy praise thy name. H6041
82: 3 Defend the **p** and fatherless: do justice H1800
4 Deliver the **p** and needy: rid *them* out H1800
86: 1 LORD, hear me: for I *am* **p** and needy. H6041
107:41 Yet setteth he the **p** on high from H34
109:16 but persecuted the **p** and needy man, H6041
22 For I *am* **p** and needy, and my heart is H6041
31 the right hand of the **p**, to save *him* from H34
112: 9 He hath dispersed, he hath given to the **p**; H34
113: 7 He raiseth up the **p** out of the dust, *and* H1800
132:15 provision: I will satisfy her **p** with bread. H34
140:12 of the afflicted, *and* the right of the **p**. H34
Prv 10: 4 He becometh **p** that dealeth *with* a H7326
15 the destruction of the **p** *is* their poverty. H1800
13: 7 maketh himself **p**, yet *hath* great riches. H7326
8 riches: but the **p** heareth not rebuke. H7326
23 Much food *is in* the tillage of the **p**: but H7326
14:20 The **p** is hated even of his own H7326
21 mercy on the **p**, happy *is* he. H6035+H6041
31 He that oppresseth the **p** reproacheth H1800
31 that honoureth him hath mercy on the **p**. H34
17: 5 Whoso mocketh the **p** reproacheth his H7326
18:23 The **p** useth entreaties; but the rich H7326
19: 1 Better *is* the **p** that walketh in his H7326
4 Wealth maketh many friends; but the **p** H1800
7 All the brethren of the **p** do hate him: H7326
17 He that hath pity upon the **p** lendeth H1800
22 and a **p** man *is* better than a liar. H7326
21:13 ears at the cry of the **p**, he also shall cry H1800
17 He that loveth pleasure *shall be* a **p** H4270
22: 2 The rich and **p** meet together: the H7326
7 The rich ruleth over the **p**, and the H7326
9 for he giveth of his bread to the **p**. H1800
16 He that oppresseth the **p** to increase his H1800
22 Rob not the **p**, because he *is* poor: H1800
22 Rob not the poor, because he *is* **p**: H1800
28: 3 A **p** man that oppresseth the poor *is* H7326
3 A poor man that oppresseth the **p** *is* H1800
6 Better *is* the **p** that walketh in his H7326
8 gather it for him that will pity the **p**. H1800
11 own conceit; but the **p** that hath H1800
15 *so is* a wicked ruler over the **p** people. H1800
27 He that giveth unto the **p** shall not lack: H7326
29: 7 the cause of the **p**: *but* the wicked H1800
13 The **p** and the deceitful man meet H7326
14 The king that faithfully judgeth the **p**, H1800
30: 9 LORD? or lest I be **p**, and steal, and take H3423
14 to devour the **p** from off the earth, and H6041
31: 9 and plead the cause of the **p** and needy. H6041
20 She stretcheth out her hand to the **p**; H6041
Ecc 4:13 Better *is* a **p** and a wise child than an H4542
14 *that is* born in his kingdom becometh **p**. H7326
5: 8 If thou seest the oppression of the **p**, H7326
6: 8 what hath the **p**, that knoweth to walk H6041
9:15 Now there was found in it a **p** wise H4542
15 no man remembered that same **p** man. H4542
16 nevertheless the **p** man's wisdom *is* H4542
Isa 3:14 the spoil of the **p** *is* in your houses. H6041
15 of the **p**? saith the Lord GOD of hosts. H6041
10: 2 the right from the **p** of my people, that H6041
30 to be heard unto Laish, O **p** Anathoth. H6041
11: 4 shall he judge the **p**, and reprove with H1800
14:30 And the firstborn of the **p** shall feed, H1800
32 and the **p** of his people shall trust in it. H6041
25: 4 For thou hast been a strength to the **p**, a H1800
26: 6 feet of the **p**, *and* the steps of the needy. H6041
29:19 in the LORD, and the **p** among men shall H34
Isa 32: 7 to destroy the **p** with lying H6041+H6035
41:17 *When* the **p** and needy seek water, and H6041
58: 7 thou bring the **p** that are cast out to H6041
66: 2 *even* to *him that is* **p** and of a contrite H6041
Jer 2:34 of the souls of the **p** innocents: I have H34
5: 4 Therefore I said, Surely these *are* **p**; H1800
20:13 soul of the **p** from the hand of evildoers. H34
22:16 He judged the cause of the **p** and H6041
39:10 guard left of the **p** of the people, which H1800
40: 7 and of the **p** of the land, of them H1803
52:15 *certain* of the **p** of the people, and the H1803
16 left *certain* of the **p** of the land for H1803
Ezk 16:49 the hand of the **p** and needy. H6041
18:12 Hath oppressed the **p** and needy, hath H6041
17 off his hand from the **p**, *that* hath not H6041
22:29 have vexed the **p** and needy: yea, they H6041
Dan 4:27 shewing mercy to the **p**; if it may be a H6033
Am 2: 6 for silver, and the **p** for a pair of shoes; H34
7 on the head of the **p**, and turn aside the H1800
4: 1 which oppress the **p**, which crush the H1800
5:11 *is* upon the **p**, and ye take from him H1800
12 aside the **p** in the gate *from their right*. H34
8: 4 make the **p** of the land to fail, H6041+H6035
6 That we may buy the **p** for silver, and H1800
Hab 3:14 *was* as to devour the **p** secretly. H6041
Zep 3:12 thee an afflicted and **p** people, and they H1800
Zec 7:10 stranger, nor the **p**; and let none of you H6041
11: 7 *even* you, O **p** of the flock. And I took H6041
11 that day: and so the **p** of the flock that H6041
Mt 5: 3 Blessed *are* the **p** in spirit: for theirs is *G4434*
11: 5 **p** have the gospel preached to them. *G4434*
19:21 and give to the **p**, and thou shalt have *G4434*
26: 9 been sold for much, and given to the **p**. *G4434*
11 For ye have the **p** always with you; but *G4434*
Mk 10:21 and give to the **p**, and thou shalt have *G4434*
12:42 And there came a certain **p** widow, and *G4434*
43 you, That this **p** widow hath cast more *G4434*
14: 5 the **p**. And they murmured against her. *G4434*
7 For ye have the **p** with you always, and *G4434*
Lk 4:18 the gospel to the **p**; he hath sent me to *G4434*
6:20 *ye* **p**: for yours is the kingdom of God. *G4434*
7:22 raised, to the **p** the gospel is preached. *G4434*
14:13 the **p**, the maimed, the lame, the blind: *G4434*
21 bring in hither the **p**, and the maimed, *G4434*
18:22 unto the **p**, and thou shalt have *G4434*
19: 8 goods I give to the **p**; and if I have taken *G4434*
21: 2 And he saw also a certain **p** widow *G3998*
3 unto you, that this **p** widow hath cast *G4434*
Jn 12: 5 hundred pence, and given to the **p**? *G4434*
6 This he said, not that he cared for the **p**; *G4434*
8 For the **p** always ye have with you; but *G4434*
13:29 that he should give something to the **p**. *G4434*
Ro 15:26 for the **p** saints which are at Jerusalem. *G4434*
1Co 13: 3 goods to feed *the* **p**, and though I give my
2Co 6:10 As sorrowful, yet alway rejoicing; as **p**, *G4434*
8: 9 sakes he became **p**, that ye through his *G4433*
9: 9 **p**: his righteousness remaineth for ever. *G3993*
Gal 2:10 remember the **p**; the same which I also *G4434*
Jas 2: 2 come in also a **p** man in vile raiment; *G4434*
3 and say to the **p**, Stand thou there, or *G4434*
5 God chosen the **p** of this world rich in *G4434*
6 But ye have despised the **p**. Do not rich *G4434*
Rev 3:17 miserable, and **p**, and blind, and naked: *G4434*
13:16 and great, rich and **p**, free and bond, to *G4434*

POORER
Lev 27: 8 But if he be **p** than thy estimation, then H4134

POOREST
2Ki 24:14 the **p** sort of the people of the land. H1803

POPLAR
Gen 30:37 And Jacob took him rods of green **p**, H3839

POPLARS
Hos 4:13 under oaks and **p** and elms, because H3839

POPULOUS
Dt 26: 5 there a nation, great, mighty, and **p**: H7227
Nah 3: 8 Art thou better than **p** No, that was H527

PORATHA
Est 9: 8 And **P**, and Adalia, and Aridatha, H6334

PORCH
Jdg 3:23 Then Ehud went forth through the **p**, H4528
1Ki 6: 3 And the **p** before the temple of the H197
7: 6 And he made a **p** of pillars; the length H197
6 cubits: and the **p** *was* before them: and H197

1Ki 7: 7 Then he made a **p** for the throne where H197
7 judge, *even* the **p** of judgment: and *it* H197
8 court within the **p**, *which* was of the like H197
8 he had taken *to wife*, like unto this **p**. H197
12 of the LORD, and for the **p** of the house. H197
19 *were* of lily work in the **p**, four cubits. H197
21 And he set up the pillars in the **p** of the H197
1Ch 28:11 the pattern of the **p**, and of the houses H197
2Ch 3: 4 And the **p** that *was* in the front *of the* H197
8:12 LORD, which he had built before the **p**, H197
15: 8 that *was* before the **p** of the LORD. H197
29: 7 Also they have shut up the doors of the **p**, H197
17 came they to the **p** of the LORD: so they H197
Ezk 8:16 between the **p** and the altar, *were* about H197
40: 7 by the **p** of the gate within *was* one reed. H197
8 He measured also the **p** of the gate H197
9 Then measured he the **p** of the gate, H197
9 cubits; and the **p** of the gate *was* inward. H197
15 the **p** of the inner gate *were* fifty cubits. H197
39 And in the **p** of the gate *were* two tables H197
40 *was* at the **p** of the gate, *were* two tables. H197
48 And he brought me to the **p** of the house, H197
48 *each* post of the **p**, five cubits on this H197
49 The length of the **p** *was* twenty cubits, H197
41:25 planks upon the face of the **p** without. H197
26 on the sides of the **p**, and *upon* the side H197
44: 3 by the way of the **p** of *that* gate, and H197
46: 2 by the way of the **p** of *that* gate without, H197
8 by the way of the **p** of *that* gate, and he H197
Joel 2:17 weep between the **p** and the altar, and H197
Mt 26:71 And when he was gone out into the **p**, *G4440*
Mk 14:68 went out into the **p**; and the cock crew. *G4259*
Jn 10:23 walked in the temple in Solomon's **p**. *G4745*
Act 3:11 unto them in the **p** that is called *G4745*
5:12 all with one accord in Solomon's **p**. *G4745*

PORCHES
Ezk 41:15 the inner temple, and the **p** of the court; H197
Jn 5: 2 Hebrew tongue Bethesda, having five **p**. *G4745*

PORCIUS
Act 24:27 But after two years **P** Festus came into *G4201*

PORT
Neh 2:13 and to the dung **p**, and viewed the walls H8179

PORTER
2Sa 18:26 called unto the **p**, and said, Behold H7778
2Ki 7:10 So they came and called unto the **p** of H7778
1Ch 9:21 Meshelemiah *was* **p** of the door of the H7778
2Ch 31:14 the Levite, the **p** toward the east, *was* H7778
Mk 13:34 work, and commanded the **p** to watch. *G2377*
Jn 10: 3 To him the **p** openeth; and the sheep *G2377*

PORTERS
2Ki 7:11 And he called the **p**; and they told *it* to H7778
1Ch 9:17 And the **p** *were*, Shallum, and Akkub, H7778
18 they *were* **p** in the companies of H7778
22 All these *which were* chosen to be **p** in H7778
24 In four quarters were the **p**, toward the H7778
26 For these Levites, the four chief **p**, were H7778
15:18 and Obed-edom, and Jeiel, the **p**. H7778
16:38 the son of Jeduthun and Hosah *to be* **p**: H7778
42 God. And the sons of Jeduthun *were* **p**. H8179
23: 5 Moreover four thousand *were* **p**; and H7778
26: 1 Concerning the divisions of the **p**: Of the H7778
12 divisions of the **p**, *even* among the chief H7778
19 These *are* the divisions of the **p** among H7778
2Ch 8:14 every day required: the **p** also by their H7778
23: 4 of the Levites, *shall be* **p** of the doors; H7778
19 And he set the **p** at the gates of the H7778
34:13 *there were* scribes, and officers, and **p**. H7778
35:15 seer; and the **p** *waited* at every gate; H7778
Ezr 2:42 The children of the **p**: the children of H7778
70 singers, and the **p**, and the Nethinims, H7778
7: 7 singers, and the **p**, and the Nethinims, H7778
24 and Levites, singers, **p**, Nethinims, or H8652
10:24 of the **p**; Shallum, and Telem, and Uri. H7778
Neh 7: 1 up the doors, and the **p** and the singers H7778
45 The **p**: the children of Shallum, the H7778
73 Levites, and the **p**, and the singers, and H7778
10:28 the Levites, the **p**, the singers, the H7778
39 minister, and the **p**, and the singers: H7778
11:19 Moreover the **p**, Akkub, Talmon, and H7778
12:25 Akkub, *were* **p** keeping the ward at H7778
45 And both the singers and the **p** kept the H7778
47 singers and the **p**, every day his portion: H7778
13: 5 the **p**; and the offerings of the priests. H7778

PORTION
Gen 14:24 eaten, and the **p** of the men which went H2506
24 and Mamre; let them take their **p**. H2506
31:14 *Is there* yet any **p** or inheritance for us H2506
47:22 for the priests had a **p** *assigned them* of H2706
22 and did eat their **p** which Pharaoh gave H2706
48:22 Moreover I have given to thee one **p** H7926
Lev 6:17 *them for* their **p** of my offerings made H2506
7:35 This *is the* **p** of the anointing of Aaron,
Nu 31:30 half, thou shalt take one **p** of fifty, of the H270
36 And the half, *which was* the **p** of them H2506
47 Moses took one **p** of fifty, *both* of man H270
Dt 21:17 him a double **p** of all that he hath: for H6310
32: 9 For the LORD'S **p** *is* his people; Jacob *is* H2506
33:21 there, *in* a **p** of the lawgiver, *was* H2513
Jos 17:14 one lot and one **p** to inherit, seeing I H2256
19: 9 Out of the **p** of the children of Judah H2256
1Sa 1: 5 But unto Hannah he gave a worthy **p**; H4490
9:23 cook, Bring the **p** which I gave thee, of H4490
1Ki 12:16 king, saying, What **p** have we in David? H2506
2Ki 2: 9 let a double **p** of thy spirit be upon me. H6310
9:10 And the dogs shall eat Jezebel in the **p** H2506
21 him in the **p** of Naboth the Jezreelite. H2513
25 cast him in the **p** of the field of Naboth H2513
36 saying, In the **p** of Jezreel shall dogs H2506
37 of the field in the **p** of Jezreel; *so* that H2506
2Ch 10:16 saying, What **p** have we in David? and H2506
28:21 For Ahaz took away a **p** *out* of the H2505
31: 3 *He appointed* also the king's **p** of his H4521
4 to give the **p** of the priests and the H4521
16 LORD, his daily **p** for their service in H1697
Ezr 4:16 shalt have no **p** on this side the river. H2508
Neh 2:20 build: but ye have no **p**, nor right, nor H2506
11:23 them, that a certain **p** should be for the H548
12:47 every day his **p**: and they sanctified H1697
Job 20:29 This *is* the **p** of a wicked man from H2506
24:18 He *is* swift as the waters; their **p** is H2513
26:14 but how little a **p** is heard of him? but H1697
27:13 This *is* the **p** of a wicked man with God, H2506
31: 2 For what **p** of God *is there* from above? H2506
Ps 11: 6 tempest: *this shall be* the **p** of their cup. H4521
16: 5 The LORD *is* the **p** of mine inheritance H4490
17:14 *which have* their **p** in *this* life, and H2506
63:10 the sword: they shall be a **p** for foxes. H4521
73:26 of my heart, and my **p** for ever. H2506
119:57 *Thou art* my **p**, O LORD: I have said H2506
142: 5 *and* my **p** in the land of the living. H2506
Prv 31:15 her household, and a **p** to her maidens. H2706
Ecc 2:10 and this was my **p** of all my labour. H2506
21 **p**. This also *is* vanity and a great evil. H2506
3:22 for that *is* his **p**: for who shall bring H2506
5:18 which God giveth him: for it *is* his **p**. H2506
19 and to take his **p**, and to rejoice in his H2506
9: 6 they any more a **p** for ever in any *thing* H2506
9 for that *is* thy **p** in *this* life, and in thy H2506
11: 2 Give a **p** to seven, and also to eight; for H2506
Isa 17:14 *is* not. This *is* the **p** of them that spoil H2506
53:12 Therefore will I divide him *a* **p** with the
57: 6 of the stream *is* thy **p**; they, they *are* thy H2506
61: 7 rejoice in their **p**: therefore in their land H2506
Jer 10:16 The **p** of Jacob *is* not like them: for he *is* H2506
12:10 have trodden my **p** under foot, they H2513
10 my pleasant **p** a desolate wilderness. H2513
13:25 This *is* thy lot, the **p** of thy measures H4490
51:19 The **p** of Jacob *is* not like them; for he *is* H2506
52:34 every day a **p** until the day of his H1697
Lam 3:24 The LORD *is* my **p**, saith my soul; H2506
Ezk 45: 1 the LORD, an holy **p** of the land: the H6944
4 The holy *p* of the land shall be for the
6 **p**: it shall be for the whole house of Israel.
7 And a *p shall be* for the prince on the
7 of the holy *p*, and of the possession
7 of the holy *p*, and before the possession
48: 1 are his sides east *and* west; a *p for* Dan.
2 side unto the west side, a *p for* Asher.
3 even unto the west side, a *p for* Naphtali.
4 unto the west side, a *p for* Manasseh.
5 side unto the west side, a *p for* Ephraim.
6 even unto the west side, a *p for* Reuben.
7 side unto the west side, a *p for* Judah.
18 of the holy *p shall be* ten thousand
18 of the holy *p*; and the increase thereof
23 the west side, Benjamin *shall have* a *p*.
24 the west side, Simeon *shall have* a *p*.
25 east side unto the west side, Issachar a *p*.
26 east side unto the west side, Zebulun a *p*.
27 the east side unto the west side, Gad a *p*.
Dan 1: 8 himself with the **p** of the king's meat, H6598
13 that eat of the **p** of the king's meat: and H6598
Dan 1:15 which did eat the **p** of the king's meat. H6598
16 Thus Melzar took away the **p** of their H6598
4:15 and *let* his **p** *be* with the beasts in H2508
23 and *let* his **p** *be* with the beasts of H2508
11:26 Yea, they that feed of the **p** of his meat H6598
Mic 2: 4 hath changed the **p** of my people: how H2506
Hab 1:16 their **p** *is* fat, and their meat plenteous. H2506
Zec 2:12 And the LORD shall inherit Judah his **p** H2506
Mt 24:51 appoint *him* his **p** with the hypocrites: *G3313*
Lk 12:42 *them their* **p** of meat in due season? *G4620*
46 appoint him his **p** with the unbelievers. *G3313*
15:12 give me the **p** of goods that falleth *G3313*

PORTIONS
Dt 18: 8 They shall have like **p** to eat, beside H2506
Jos 17: 5 And there fell ten **p** to Manasseh, H2256
1Sa 1: 4 to all her sons and her daughters, **p**: H4490
2Ch 31:19 by name, to give **p** to all the males H4490
Neh 8:10 sweet, and send **p** unto them for whom H4490
12 drink, and to send **p**, and to make great H4490
12:44 of the cities the **p** of the law for the H4521
47 gave the **p** of the singers and the H4521
13:10 And I perceived that the **p** of the H4521
Est 9:19 day, and of sending **p** one to another. H4490
22 **p** one to another, and gifts to the poor. H4490
Ezk 45: 7 over against one of the **p**, from the west H2506
47:13 tribes of Israel: Joseph *shall have two* **p**. H2256
48:21 over against the **p** for the prince: and it H2506
29 these *are* their **p**, saith the Lord GOD. H4256
Hos 5: 7 shall a month devour them with their **p**. H2506

PORTRAY See POURTRAY.

POSSESS
Gen 22:17 thy seed shall **p** the gate of his enemies; H3423
24:60 **p** the gate of those which hate them. H3423
Lev 20:24 will give it unto you to **p** it, a land that H3423
Nu 13:30 **p** it; for we are well able to overcome it. H3423
14:24 he went; and his seed shall **p** it. H3423
27:11 and he shall **p** it: and it shall be unto H3423
33:53 for I have given you the land to **p** it. H3423
Dt 1: 8 you: go in and **p** the land which the H3423
21 thee: go up *and* **p** *it*, as the LORD God H3423
39 them will I give it, and they shall **p** it. H3423
2:24 to **p** *it*, and contend with him in battle. H3423
31 to **p**, that thou mayest inherit his land. H3423
3:18 you this land to **p** it: ye shall pass over H3423
20 and *until* they also **p** the land which the H3423
4: 1 live, and go in and **p** the land which the H3423
5 do so in the land whither ye go to **p** it. H3423
14 in the land whither ye go over to **p** it. H3423
22 ye shall go over, and **p** that good land. H3423
26 ye go over Jordan to **p** it; ye shall not H3423
5:31 in the land which I give them to **p** it. H3423
33 *your* days in the land which ye shall **p**. H3423
6: 1 *them* in the land whither ye go to **p** it: H3423
18 thou mayest go in and **p** the good land H3423
7: 1 thou goest to **p** it, and hath cast out H3423
8: 1 and go in and **p** the land which the H3423
9: 1 day, to go in to **p** nations greater and H3423
4 brought me in to **p** this land: but for H3423
5 dost thou go to **p** their land: but for the H3423
6 not this good land to **p** it for thy H3423
23 saying, Go up and **p** the land which I H3423
10:11 they may go in and **p** the land, which I H3423
11: 8 **p** the land, whither ye go to possess it; H3423
8 possess the land, whither ye go to **p** it; H3423
10 For the land, whither thou goest in to **p** H3423
11 But the land, whither ye go to **p** it, *is* a H3423
23 you, and ye shall **p** greater nations and H3423
29 thou goest to **p** it, that thou shalt put H3423
31 Jordan to go in to **p** the land which the H3423
31 and ye shall **p** it, and dwell therein. H3423
12: 1 giveth thee to **p** it, all the days that H3423
2 which ye shall **p** served their gods, H3423
29 whither thou goest to **p** them, and thou H3423
15: 4 giveth thee *for* an inheritance to **p** it: H3423
17:14 thee, and shalt **p** it, and shalt dwell H3423
18:14 For these nations, which thou shalt **p**, H3423
19: 2 the LORD thy God giveth thee to **p** it. H3423
14 the LORD thy God giveth thee to **p** it. H3423
21: 1 thy God giveth thee to **p** it, lying in the H3423
23:20 to in the land whither thou goest to **p** it. H3423
25:19 an inheritance to **p** it, *that* thou shalt H3423
28:21 off the land, whither thou goest to **p** it. H3423
63 off the land whither thou goest to **p** it. H3423
30: 5 and thou shalt **p** it; and he will do thee H3423
16 in the land whither thou goest to **p** it. H3423
18 thou passest over Jordan to go to **p** it. H3423

Dt 31: 3 and thou shalt **p** them: *and* Joshua, he H3423
13 land whither ye go over Jordan to **p** it. H3423
32:47 land, whither ye go over Jordan to **p** it. H3423
33:23 LORD: **p** thou the west and the south. H3423
Jos 1:11 Jordan, to go in to **p** the land, which H3423
11 the LORD your God giveth you to **p** it. H3423
18: 3 ye slack to go to **p** the land, which the H3423
23: 5 sight; and ye shall **p** their land, as the H3423
24: 4 mount Seir, to **p** it; but Jacob and his H3423
8 hand, that ye might **p** their land; and I H3423
Jdg 2: 6 man unto his inheritance to **p** the land. H3423
11:23 people Israel, and shouldest thou **p** it? H3423
24 Wilt not thou **p** that which Chemosh H3423
24 god giveth thee to **p**? So whomsoever the H3423
24 out from before us, them will we **p**. H3423
18: 9 to go, *and* to enter to **p** the land. H3423
1Ki 21:18 whither he is gone down to **p** it. H3423
1Ch 28: 8 God: that ye may **p** this good land, and H3423
Ezr 9:11 which ye go to **p** it, is an unclean land H3423
Neh 9:15 should go in to **p** the land which thou H3423
23 fathers, that they should go in to **p** *it*. H3423
Job 7: 3 So am I made to **p** months of vanity, H5157
13:26 me to **p** the iniquities of my youth. H3423
Isa 14: 2 of Israel shall **p** them in the land of H5157
21 do not rise, nor **p** the land, nor fill the H3423
34:11 the bittern shall **p** it; the owl also and H3423
17 by line: they shall **p** it for ever, from H3423
57:13 trust in me shall **p** the land, and shall H5157
61: 7 their land they shall **p** the double: H3423
Jer 30: 3 to their fathers, and they shall **p** it. H3423
Ezk 7:24 and they shall **p** their houses: I will also H3423
33:25 shed blood: and shall ye **p** the land? H3423
26 wife: and shall ye **p** the land? H3423
35:10 will **p** it; whereas the LORD was there: H3423
36:12 and they shall **p** thee, and thou shalt H3423
Dan 7:18 the kingdom, and **p** the kingdom for H2631
Hos 9: 6 silver, nettles shall **p** them: thorns *shall* H3423
Am 2:10 to **p** the land of the Amorite. H3423
9:12 That they may **p** the remnant of Edom, H3423
Oba 17 of Jacob shall **p** their possessions. H3423
19 And *they of* the south shall **p** the H3423
19 and they shall **p** the fields of Ephraim, H3423
19 Samaria: and Benjamin *shall* **p** Gilead. H3423
20 of Israel *shall* **p** that of the Canaanites,
20 shall **p** the cities of the south. H3423
Hab 1: 6 **p** the dwellingplaces *that are* not theirs. H3423
Zep 2: 9 the remnant of my people shall **p** them. H5157
Zec 8:12 of this people to **p** all these *things*. H5157
Lk 18:12 in the week, I give tithes of all that I **p**. *G2932*
21:19 In your patience **p** ye your souls. *G2932*
1Th 4: 4 should know how to **p** his vessel in *G2932*

POSSESSED
Nu 21:24 edge of the sword, and **p** his land from H3423
35 none left him alive: and they **p** his land. H3423
Dt 3:12 And this land, *which* we **p** at that time, H3423
4:47 And they **p** his land, and the land of Og H3423
30: 5 land which thy fathers **p**, and thou shalt H3423
Jos 1:15 and they also have **p** the land which the H3423
12: 1 of Israel smote, and **p** their land on the H3423
13: 1 remaineth yet very much land to be **p**. H3423
19:47 edge of the sword, and **p** it, and dwelt H3423
21:43 and they **p** it, and dwelt therein. H3423
22: 9 whereof they were **p**, according to the H270
Jdg 3:13 Israel, and **p** the city of palm trees. H3423
11:21 them: so Israel **p** all the land of the H3423
22 And they **p** all the coasts of the H3423
2Ki 17:24 of Israel: and they **p** Samaria, and H3423
Neh 9:22 corners: so they **p** the land of Sihon, H3423
24 So the children went in and **p** the land, H3423
25 and a fat land, and **p** houses full of all H3423
Ps 139:13 For thou hast **p** my reins: thou hast H7069
Prv 8:22 The LORD **p** me in the beginning of his H7069
Isa 63:18 The people of thy holiness have **p** *it* but H3423
Jer 32:15 vineyards shall be **p** again in this land. H7069
23 And they came in, and **p** it; but they H3423
Dan 7:22 came that the saints **p** the kingdom. H2631
Mt 4:24 those which were **p** with devils, and *G1139*
8:16 many that were **p** with devils: and he *G1139*
28 there met him two **p** with devils, *G1139*
33 what was befallen to the **p** of the devils. *G1139*
9:32 to him a dumb man **p** with a devil. *G1139*
12:22 Then was brought unto him one **p** with *G1139*
Mk 1:32 and them that were **p** with devils. *G1139*
5:15 see him that was **p** with the devil, and *G1139*
16 to him that was **p** with the devil, and *G1139*
18 ship, he that had been **p** with the devil *G1139*
Lk 8:36 he that was **p** of the devils was healed. *G1139*
Act 4:32 the things which he **p** was his own; but *G5224*
Act 8: 7 of many that were **p** *with them*: and *G2192*
16:16 a certain damsel **p** with a spirit of *G2192*
1Co 7:30 they that buy, as though they **p** not; *G2722*

POSSESSEST
Dt 26: 1 and **p** it, and dwellest therein; H3423

POSSESSETH
Nu 36: 8 And every daughter, that **p** an H3423
Lk 12:15 the abundance of the things which he **p**. *G5224*

POSSESSING
2Co 6:10 as having nothing, and *yet* **p** all things. *G2722*

POSSESSION
Gen 17: 8 an everlasting **p**; and I will be their God. H272
23: 4 you: give me a **p** of a buryingplace with H272
9 for a **p** of a buryingplace amongst you. H272
18 Unto Abraham for a **p** in the presence H4736
20 **p** of a burying-place by the sons of Heth. H272
26:14 For he had **p** of flocks, and possession H4735
14 For he had possession of flocks, and **p** H4735
36:43 **p**: he *is* Esau the father of the Edomites. H272
47:11 and gave them a **p** in the land of Egypt, H272
48: 4 to thy seed after thee *for* an everlasting **p**. H272
49:30 the Hittite for a **p** of a buryingplace. H272
50:13 with the field for a **p** of a buryingplace of H272
Lev 14:34 I give to you for a **p**, and I put the plague H272
34 leprosy in a house of the land of your **p**; H272
25:10 every man unto his **p**, and ye shall return H272
13 ye shall return every man unto his **p**. H272
24 And in all the land of your **p** ye shall H272
25 away *some* of his **p**, and if any of his kin H272
27 he sold it; that he may return unto his **p**. H272
28 go out, and he shall return unto his **p**. H272
32 **p**, may the Levites redeem at any time. H272
33 and the city of his **p**, shall go out in *the* H272
33 *are* their **p** among the children of Israel. H272
34 not be sold; for it *is* their perpetual **p**. H272
41 unto the **p** of his fathers shall he return. H272
45 in your land: and they shall be your **p**. H272
46 to inherit *them for* a **p**; they shall be your H272
27:16 of a field of his **p**, then thy estimation H272
21 the **p** thereof shall be the priest's. H272
22 bought, which *is* not of the fields of his **p**; H272
24 to whom the **p** of the land *did belong*. H272
28 and of the field of his **p**, shall be sold or H272
Nu 24:18 And Edom shall be a **p**, Seir also shall H3424
18 Seir also shall be a **p** for his enemies; H3424
26:56 According to the lot shall the **p** thereof H5159
27: 4 a **p** among the brethren of our father. H272
7 surely give them a **p** of an inheritance H272
32: 5 for a **p**, *and* bring us not over Jordan. H272
22 land shall be your **p** before the LORD. H272
29 shall give them the land of Gilead for a **p**: H272
32 of Canaan, that the **p** of our inheritance H272
35: 2 of their **p** cities to dwell in; and H272
8 give *shall be* of the **p** of the children of H272
28 slayer shall return into the land of his **p**. H272
Dt 2: 5 given mount Seir unto Esau *for* a **p**. H3425
9 thee of their land *for* a **p**; because I have H3425
9 Ar unto the children of Lot *for* a **p**. H3425
12 his **p**, which the LORD gave unto them. H3425
19 of Ammon *any* **p**; because I have given H3425
19 given it unto the children of Lot *for* a **p**. H3425
3:20 man unto his **p**, which I have given you. H3425
11: 6 *was* in their **p**, in the midst of all Israel: H7272
32:49 I give unto the children of Israel for a **p**: H272
Jos 1:15 the land of your **p**, and enjoy it, which H3425
12: 6 the LORD gave it *for* a **p** unto the H3425
7 *for* a **p** according to their divisions; H3425
13:29 and *this* was *the* **p** of the half tribe of the
21:12 to Caleb the son of Jephunneh for his **p**. H272
41 All the cities of the Levites within the **p** H272
22: 4 unto the land of your **p**, which Moses the H272
7 Moses had given **p** in Bashan: but unto
9 to the land of their **p**, whereof they were H272
19 Notwithstanding, if the land of your **p** *be* H272
19 the land of the **p** of the LORD, wherein H272
19 dwelleth, and take **p** among us: but rebel H270
1Ki 21:15 Ahab, Arise, take **p** of the vineyard of H3423
16 of Naboth the Jezreelite, to take **p** of it. H3423
19 and also taken **p**? And thou shalt speak H3423
1Ch 28: 1 the substance and **p** of the king, and of H4735
2Ch 11:14 suburbs and their **p**, and came to Judah H272
20:11 **p**, which thou hast given us to inherit. H3425
31: 1 every man to his **p**, into their own cities. H272
Neh 11: 3 every one in his **p** in their cities, *to wit*, H272
Ps 2: 8 the uttermost parts of the earth *for* thy **p**. H272
Ps 44: 3 For they got not the land in **p** by their H3423
69:35 they may dwell there, and have it in **p**. H3423
83:12 take to ourselves the houses of God in **p**. H3423
Prv 28:10 the upright shall have good *things* in **p**. H5157
Isa 14:23 I will also make it a **p** for the bittern, H4180
Ezk 11:15 LORD: unto us is this land given in **p**. H4181
25: 4 of the east for a **p**, and they shall set H4181
10 will give them in **p**, that the Ammonites H4181
36: 2 the ancient high places are ours in **p**: H4181
3 that ye might be a **p** unto the residue of H4181
5 my land into their **p** with the joy of all H4181
44:28 no **p** in Israel: I *am* their possession. H272
28 no possession in Israel: I *am* their **p**. H272
45: 5 themselves, for a **p** for twenty chambers. H272
6 And ye shall appoint the **p** of the city five H272
7 *portion*, and of the **p** of the city, before H272
7 and before the **p** of the city, from the H272
8 In the land shall be his **p** in Israel: and H272
46:16 sons'; it *shall be* their **p** by inheritance. H272
18 them out of their **p**; *but* he shall give his H272
18 out of his own **p**: that my people be not H272
18 be not scattered every man from his **p**. H272
48:20 foursquare, with the **p** of the city. H272
21 and of the **p** of the city, over against H272
22 Moreover from the **p** of the Levites, and H272
22 and from the **p** of the city, *being* in the H272
Act 5: 1 with Sapphira his wife, sold a **p**, *G2933*
7: 5 give it to him for a **p**, and to his seed *G2697*
45 in with Jesus into the **p** of the Gentiles, *G2697*
Eph 1:14 **p**, unto the praise of his glory. *G4047*

POSSESSIONS
Gen 34:10 trade ye therein, and get you **p** therein. H270
47:27 and they had **p** therein, and grew, and H270
Nu 32:30 **p** among you in the land of Canaan. H270
1Sa 25: 2 in Maon, whose **p** *were* in Carmel; and H4639
1Ch 7:28 And their **p** and habitations *were*, Beth-el H272
9: 2 that *dwelt* in their **p** in their cities *were*, H272
2Ch 32:29 Moreover he provided him cities, and **p** H4735
Ecc 2: 7 also I had great **p** of great and small H4735
Oba 17 the house of Jacob shall possess their **p**. H4180
Mt 19:22 away sorrowful: for he had great **p**. *G2933*
Mk 10:22 went away grieved: for he had great **p**. *G2933*
Act 2:45 And sold their **p** and goods, and parted *G2933*
28: 7 In the same quarters were **p** of the chief *G5564*

POSSESSOR
Gen 14:19 most high God, **p** of heaven and earth: H7069
22 high God, the **p** of heaven and earth, H7069

POSSESSORS
Zec 11: 5 Whose **p** slay them, and hold H7069
Act 4:34 as many as were **p** of lands or houses *G2935*

POSSIBLE
Mt 19:26 but with God all things are **p**. *G1415*
24:24 *were* **p**, they shall deceive the very elect. *G1415*
26:39 O my Father, if it be **p**, let this cup pass *G1415*
Mk 9:23 all things *are* **p** to him that believeth. *G1415*
10:27 with God: for with God all things are **p**. *G1415*
13:22 to seduce, if *it were* **p**, even the elect. *G1415*
14:35 were **p**, the hour might pass from him. *G1415*
36 all things *are* **p** unto thee; take away *G1415*
Lk 18:27 impossible with men are **p** with God. *G1415*
Act 2:24 not **p** that he should be holden of it. *G1415*
20:16 he hasted, if it were **p** for him, to be at *G1415*
27:39 if it were **p**, to thrust in the ship. *G1410*
Ro 12:18 If it be **p**, as much as lieth in you, live *G1415*
Gal 4:15 that, if *it had been* **p**, ye would have *G1415*
Heb 10: 4 For *it is* not **p** that the blood of bulls and *G102*

POST
Ex 12: 7 and on the upper door **p** of the houses, H4947
21: 6 or unto the door **p**; and his master shall H4201
1Sa 1: 9 a seat by a **p** of the temple of the LORD. H4201
Job 9:25 Now my days are swifter than a **p**: they H7323
Jer 51:31 One **p** shall run to meet another, and H7323
Ezk 40:14 the **p** of the court round about the gate. H352
16 and upon *each* **p** *were* palm trees. H352
48 and measured *each* **p** of the porch, five H352
41: 3 and measured the **p** of the door, two H352
43: 8 and their **p** by my posts, and the H4201
46: 2 shall stand by the **p** of the gate, and the H4201

POSTERITY
Gen 45: 7 to preserve you a **p** in the earth, and to H7611
Nu 9:10 of you or of your **p** shall be unclean by H1755
1Ki 16: 3 Behold, I will take away the **p** of Baasha, H310
3 of Baasha, and the **p** of his house; and H310

1Ki 21:21 will take away thy **p**, and will cut off from H310
Ps 49:13 This their way *is* their folly: yet their **p** H310
109:13 Let his **p** be cut off; *and* in the H319
Dan 11: 4 and not to his **p**, nor according to his H319
Am 4: 2 with hooks, and your **p** with fishhooks. H319

POSTS
Ex 12: 7 *it* on the two side **p** and on the upper H4201
22 and the two side **p** with the blood that H4201
23 on the two side **p**, the LORD will pass H4201
Dt 6: 9 And thou shalt write them upon the **p** H4201
11:20 **p** of thine house, and upon thy gates: H4201
Jdg 16: 3 city, and the two **p**, and went away with H4201
1Ki 6:31 *and* side **p** *were* a fifth part *of the wall.* H4201
33 **p** *of* olive tree, a fourth part *of the wall.* H4201
7: 5 And all the doors and **p** *were* square, H4201
2Ch 3: 7 the beams, the **p**, and the walls thereof, H5592
30: 6 So the **p** went with the letters from the H7323
10 So the **p** passed from city to city H7323
Est 3:13 And the letters were sent by **p** into all H7323
15 The **p** went out, being hastened by the H7323
8:10 and sent letters by **p** on horseback, *and* H7323
14 *So* the **p** that rode upon mules *and* H7323
Prv 8:34 my gates, waiting at the **p** of my doors. H4201
Isa 6: 4 And the **p** of the door moved at the voice H520
57: 8 Behind the doors also and the **p** hast H4201
Ezk 40: 9 cubits; and the **p** thereof, two cubits; and H352
10 measure: and the **p** had one measure on H352
14 He made also **p** of threescore cubits, H352
16 and to their **p** within the gate round H352
21 on that side; and the **p** thereof and the H352
24 and he measured the **p** thereof and the H352
26 another on that side, upon the **p** thereof. H352
29 thereof, and the **p** thereof, and the H352
31 *were* upon the **p** thereof: and the going H352
33 thereof, and the **p** thereof, and the H352
34 *were* upon the **p** thereof, on this side, H352
36 The little chambers thereof, the **p** H352
37 And the **p** thereof *were* toward the utter H352
37 *were* upon the **p** thereof, on this side, H352
38 thereof *were* by the **p** of the gates, where H352
49 *were* pillars by the **p**, one on this side, H352
41: 1 and measured the **p**, six cubits broad on H352
16 The door **p**, and the narrow windows, H5592
21 The **p** of the temple *were* squared, *and* H4201
43: 8 and their post by my **p**, and the wall H4201
45:19 and put *it* upon the **p** of the house, and H4201
19 the **p** of the gate of the inner court. H4201
Am 9: 1 the door, that the **p** may shake: and cut H5592

POT
Ex 16:33 And Moses said unto Aaron, Take a **p**, H6803
Lev 6:28 in a brasen **p**, it shall be both scoured, H3627
Jdg 6:19 put the broth in a **p**, and brought *it* out H6517
1Sa 2:14 or caldron, or **p**; all that the fleshhook H6517
2Ki 4: 2 any thing in the house, save a **p** of oil. H610
38 Set on the great **p**, and seethe pottage H5518
39 **p** of pottage: for they knew *them* not. H5518
40 in the **p**. And they could not eat *thereof.* H5518
41 he cast *it* into the **p**; and he said, Pour H5518
41 eat. And there was no harm in the **p**. H5518
Job 41:20 as *out* of a seething **p** or caldron. H1731
31 He maketh the deep to boil like a **p**: he H5518
31 he maketh the sea like a **p** of ointment. H5518
Prv 17: 3 The fining **p** *is* for silver, and the H4715
27:21 *As* the fining **p** for silver, and the H4715
Ecc 7: 6 For as the crackling of thorns under a **p**, H5518
Jer 1:13 I see a seething **p**; and the face thereof H5518
Ezk 24: 3 **p**, set *it* on, and also pour water into it: H5518
6 the bloody city, to the **p** whose scum *is* H5518
Mic 3: 3 the **p**, and as flesh within the caldron. H5518
Zec 14:21 Yea, every **p** in Jerusalem and in Judah H5518
Heb 9: 4 *was* the golden **p** that had manna, and *G4713*

POTENT See IMPOTENT.

POTENTATE
1Ti 6:15 **P**, the King of kings, and Lord of lords; *G1413*

POTI See POTI-PHERAH.

POTIPHAR
Gen 37:36 him into Egypt unto **P**, an officer of H6318
39: 1 to Egypt; and **P**, an officer of Pharaoh, H6318

POTI-PHERAH
Gen 41:45 the daughter of **P** priest of On. And H6319
50 of **P** priest of On bare unto him. H6319
46:20 of **P** priest of On bare unto him. H6319

POTS
Ex 16: 3 we sat by the flesh **p**, *and* when we did H5518
38: 3 of the altar, the **p**, and the shovels, and H5518
Lev 11:35 *be* oven, or ranges for **p**, they shall be
1Ki 7:45 And the **p**, and the shovels, and the H5518
2Ki 25:14 And the **p**, and the shovels, and the H5518
2Ch 4:11 And Huram made the **p**, and the H5518
16 The **p** also, and the shovels, and the H5518
35:13 sod they in **p**, and in caldrons, and H5518
Ps 58: 9 Before your **p** can feel the thorns, he H5518
68:13 Though ye have lien among the **p**, *yet* H8240
81: 6 his hands were delivered from the **p**. H1731
Jer 35: 5 of the Rechabites **p** full of wine, and H1375
Zec 14:20 LORD; and the **p** in the LORD'S house H5518
Mk 7: 4 and **p**, brasen vessels, and of tables. *G3582*
8 men, *as* the washing of **p** and cups: and *G3582*

POTSHERD
Job 2: 8 And he took him a **p** to scrape himself H2789
Ps 22:15 My strength is dried up like a **p**; and my H2789
Prv 26:23 *are like* a **p** covered with silver dross. H2789
Isa 45: 9 his Maker! *Let* the **p** *strive* with the H2789

POTSHERDS
Isa 45: 9 *strive* with the **p** of the earth. Shall the H2789

POTTAGE
Gen 25:29 And Jacob sod **p**: and Esau came from H5138
30 thee, with that same red **p**; for I *am* faint:
34 Then Jacob gave Esau bread and **p** of H5138
2Ki 4:38 seethe **p** for the sons of the prophets. H5138
39 the pot of **p**: for they knew *them* not. H5138
40 were eating of the **p**, that they cried out, H5138
Hag 2:12 do touch bread, or **p**, or wine, or oil, or H5138

POTTER
Isa 41:25 morter, and as the **p** treadeth clay. H3335
64: 8 **p**; and we all *are* the work of thy hand. H3335
Jer 18: 4 in the hand of the **p**: so he made it again H3335
4 as seemed good to the **p** to make *it.* H3335
6 do with you as this **p**? saith the LORD. H3335
Lam 4: 2 pitchers, the work of the hands of the **p**! H3335
Zec 11:13 Cast it unto the **p**: a goodly price that H3335
13 them to the **p** in the house of the LORD. H3335
Ro 9:21 Hath not the **p** power over the clay, of *G2763*
Rev 2:27 iron; as the vessels of a **p** shall they be *G2764*

POTTERS
1Ch 4:23 These *were* the **p**, and those that dwelt H3335

POTTER'S
Ps 2: 9 dash them in pieces like a **p** vessel. H3335
Isa 29:16 be esteemed as the **p** clay: for shall the H3335
Jer 18: 2 Arise, and go down to the **p** house, and H3335
3 Then I went down to the **p** house, and, H3335
6 as the clay *is* in the **p** hand, so *are* ye in H3335
19: 1 Thus saith the LORD, Go and get a **p** H3335
11 as *one* breaketh a **p** vessel, that cannot H3335
Mt 27: 7 them the **p** field, to bury strangers in. *G2763*
10 And gave them for the **p** field, as the *G2763*

POTTERS'
Isa 30:14 breaking of the **p** vessel that is broken H3335
Dan 2:41 feet and toes, part of **p** clay, and part of H6353

POUND
1Ki 10:17 beaten gold; three **p** of gold went to one H4488
Ezr 2:69 and five thousand **p** of silver, and one H4488
Neh 7:71 thousand and two hundred **p** of silver. H4488
72 gold, and two thousand **p** of silver, and H4488
Lk 19:16 Then came the first, saying, Lord, thy **p** *G3414*
18 Lord, thy **p** hath gained five pounds. *G3414*
20 behold, *here is* thy **p**, which I have kept *G3414*
24 from him the **p**, and give *it* to him that *G3414*
Jn 12: 3 Then took Mary a **p** of ointment of *G3046*
19:39 and aloes, about an hundred **p** *weight.* *G3046*

POUNDS
Lk 19:13 them ten **p**, and said unto them, *G3414*
16 Lord, thy pound hath gained ten **p**. *G3414*
18 Lord, thy pound hath gained five **p**. *G3414*
24 and give *it* to him that hath ten **p**. *G3414*
25 they said unto him, Lord, he hath ten **p**.) *G3414*

POUR
Ex 4: 9 of the river, and **p** *it* upon the dry *land:* H8210
29: 7 **p** *it* upon his head, and anoint him. H3332
12 thy finger, and **p** all the blood beside H8210
30: 9 shall ye **p** drink offering thereon. H5258
Lev 2: 1 flour; and he shall **p** oil upon it, and H3332
6 Thou shalt part it in pieces, and **p** oil H3332
4: 7 and shall **p** all the blood of the H8210
18 and shall **p** out all the blood at H8210
25 offering, and shall **p** out his blood at H8210
30 offering, and shall **p** out all the blood H8210
34 offering, and shall **p** out all the blood H8210
14:15 **p** *it* into the palm of his own left hand: H3332
18 hand he shall **p** upon the head of him H5414
26 And the priest shall **p** of the oil into the H3332
41 and they shall **p** out the dust that they H8210
17:13 he shall even **p** out the blood thereof, H8210
Nu 5:15 meal; he shall **p** no oil upon it, nor put H3332
24: 7 He shall **p** the water out of his buckets, H5140
Dt 12:16 ye shall **p** it upon the earth as water. H8210
24 Thou shalt not eat it; thou shalt **p** it H8210
15:23 shalt **p** it upon the ground as water. H8210
Jdg 6:20 and **p** out the broth. And he did so. H8210
1Ki 18:33 with water, and **p** *it* on the burnt H3332
2Ki 4: 4 thy sons, and shalt **p** out into all those H3332
41 pot; and he said, **P** out for the people, H3332
9: 3 Then take the box of oil, and **p** *it* on his H3332
Job 36:27 of water: they **p** down rain according H2212
Ps 42: 4 When I remember these *things*, I **p** out H8210
62: 8 Trust in him at all times; *ye* people, **p** H8210
69:24 **P** out thine indignation upon them, H8210
79: 6 **P** out thy wrath upon the heathen that H8210
Prv 1:23 Turn you at my reproof: behold, I will **p** H5042
Isa 44: 3 For I will **p** water upon him that is H3332
3 dry ground: I will **p** my spirit upon thy H3332
45: 8 and let the skies **p** down righteousness: H5140
Jer 6:11 with holding in: I will **p** it out upon the H8210
7:18 of heaven, and to **p** out drink offerings H5258
10:25 **P** out thy fury upon the heathen that H8210
14:16 I will **p** their wickedness upon them. H8210
18:21 to the famine, and **p** out their *blood* by H5064
44:17 of heaven, and to **p** out drink offerings H5258
18 of heaven, and to **p** out drink offerings H5258
19 worship her, and **p** out drink offerings H5258
25 of heaven, and to **p** out drink offerings H5258
Lam 2:19 of the watches **p** out thine heart like H8210
Ezk 7: 8 Now will I shortly **p** out my fury upon H8210
14:19 that land, and **p** out my fury upon it H8210
20: 8 then I said, I will **p** out my fury upon H8210
13 then I said, I would **p** out my fury upon H8210
21 then I said, I would **p** out my fury upon H8210
21:31 And I will **p** out mine indignation upon H8210
24: 3 a pot, set *it* on, and also **p** water into it: H3332
30:15 And I will **p** my fury upon Sin, the H8210
Hos 5:10 **p** out my wrath upon them like water. H8210
Joel 2:28 *that* I will **p** out my spirit upon H8210
29 in those days will I **p** out my spirit. H8210
Mic 1: 6 and I will **p** down the stones thereof H5064
Zep 3: 8 the kingdoms, to **p** upon them mine H8210
Zec 12:10 And I will **p** upon the house of David, H8210
Mal 3:10 of heaven, and **p** you out a blessing, H7324
Act 2:17 saith God, I will **p** out of my Spirit *G1632*
18 I will **p** out in those days of *G1632*
Rev 16: 1 Go your ways, and **p** out the vials of the *G1632*

POURED
Gen 28:18 *for* a pillar, and **p** oil upon the top of it. H3332
35:14 of stone: and he **p** a drink offering H5258
14 offering thereon, and he **p** oil thereon. H3332
Ex 9:33 and the rain was not **p** upon the earth. H5413
30:32 Upon man's flesh shall it not be **p**, H3251
Lev 4:12 the ashes are **p** out, and burn him on H8211
12 the ashes are **p** out shall he be burnt. H8211
8:12 And he **p** of the anointing oil upon H3332
15 the altar, and **p** the blood at the bottom H3332
9: 9 of the altar, and **p** out the blood at the H3332
21:10 the anointing oil was **p**, and that is H3332
Nu 28: 7 **p** unto the LORD *for* a drink offering. H5258
Dt 12:27 sacrifices shall be **p** out upon the altar H8210
1Sa 1:15 have **p** out my soul before the LORD. H8210
7: 6 and drew water, and **p** *it* out before the H8210
10: 1 Then Samuel took a vial of oil, and **p** *it* H3332
2Sa 13: 9 And she took a pan, and **p** *them* out H3332
23:16 thereof, but **p** it out unto the LORD. H5258
1Ki 13: 3 ashes that *are* upon it shall be **p** out. H8210
5 and the ashes **p** out from the altar, H8210
2Ki 3:11 which **p** water on the hands of Elijah. H3332
4: 5 *the vessels* to her; and she **p** out. H3332
40 So they **p** out for the men to eat. And it H3332
9: 6 the house; and he **p** the oil on his head, H3332
16:13 offering, and **p** his drink offering, and H5258
1Ch 11:18 drink *of* it, but **p** it out to the LORD, H5258
2Ch 12: 7 my wrath shall not be **p** out upon H5413
34:21 of the LORD that is **p** out upon us, H5413

P

2Ch 34:25 my wrath shall be **p** out upon this H5413
Job 3:24 my roarings are **p** out like the waters. H5413
10:10 Hast thou not **p** me out as milk, and H5413
29: 6 and the rock **p** me out rivers of oil; H6694
30:16 And now my soul is **p** out upon me; the H8210
Ps 22:14 I am **p** out like water, and all my bones H8210
45: 2 of men: grace is **p** into thy lips: H3332
77:17 The clouds **p** out water: the skies sent H2229
142: 2 I **p** out my complaint before him; I H8210
Song 1: 3 *is as* ointment **p** forth, therefore do the H7324
Isa 26:16 visited thee, they **p** out a prayer *when* H6694
29:10 For the LORD hath **p** out upon you the H5258
32:15 Until the spirit be **p** upon us from on H6168
42:25 Therefore he hath **p** upon him the fury H8210
53:12 because he hath **p** out his soul unto H6168
57: 6 to them hast thou **p** a drink offering, H8210
Jer 7:20 my fury shall be **p** out upon this place, H5413
19:13 **p** out drink offerings unto other gods. H5258
32:29 unto Baal, and **p** out drink offerings H5258
42:18 my fury hath been **p** forth upon the H5413
18 so shall my fury be **p** forth upon you, H5413
44: 6 and mine anger was **p** forth, and was H5413
19 of heaven, and **p** out drink offerings H5258
Lam 2: 4 of Zion: he **p** out his fury like fire. H8210
11 my liver is **p** upon the earth, for H8210
12 was **p** out into their mothers' bosom. H8210
4: 1 are **p** out in the top of every street. H8210
11 his fury; he hath **p** out his fierce anger, H8210
Ezk 16:36 thy filthiness was **p** out, and thy H8210
20:28 and **p** out there their drink offerings. H5258
33 with fury **p** out, will I rule over you: H8210
34 stretched out arm, and with fury **p** out. H8210
22:22 LORD have **p** out my fury upon you. H8210
31 Therefore have I **p** out mine H8210
23: 8 and **p** their whoredom upon her. H8210
24: 7 the top of a rock; she **p** it not upon the H8210
36:18 Wherefore I **p** my fury upon them for H8210
39:29 them: for I have **p** out my spirit upon H8210
Dan 9:11 the curse is **p** upon us, and the oath H5413
27 shall be **p** upon the desolate. H5413
Mic 1: 4 waters *that are* **p** down a steep place. H5064
Nah 1: 6 anger? his fury is **p** out like fire, and the H5413
Zep 1:17 blood shall be **p** out as dust, and their H8210
Mt 26: 7 and **p** it on his head, as he sat *at meat*. *G2708*
12 For in that she hath **p** this ointment on *G906*
Mk 14: 3 she brake the box, and **p** *it* on his head. *G2708*
Jn 2:15 and the oxen; and **p** out the changers' *G1632*
Act 10:45 was **p** out the gift of the Holy Ghost. *G1632*
Rev 14:10 of God, which is **p** out without mixture *G2767*
16: 2 And the first went, and **p** out his vial *G1632*
3 And the second angel **p** out his vial *G1632*
4 And the third angel **p** out his vial upon *G1632*
8 And the fourth angel **p** out his vial *G1632*
10 And the fifth angel **p** out his vial upon *G1632*
12 And the sixth angel **p** out his vial upon *G1632*
17 And the seventh angel **p** out his vial *G1632*

POUREDST
Ezk 16:15 thy renown, and **p** out thy fornications H8210

POURETH
Job 12:21 He **p** contempt upon princes, and H8210
16:13 he **p** out my gall upon the ground. H8210
20 My friends scorn me: *but* mine eye **p** H1811
Ps 75: 8 of mixture; and he **p** out of the same: H5064
102:ttl **p** out his complaint before the LORD. H8210
107:40 He **p** contempt upon princes, and H8210
Prv 15: 2 the mouth of fools **p** out foolishness. H5042
28 mouth of the wicked **p** out evil things. H5042
Am 5: 8 of the sea, and **p** them out upon the H8210
9: 6 of the sea, and **p** them out upon the H8210
Jn 13: 5 After that he **p** water into a bason, and *G906*

POURING
Ezk 9: 8 thy **p** out of thy fury upon Jerusalem? H8210
Lk 10:34 up his wounds, **p** in oil and wine, and

POURTRAY
Ezk 4: 1 and **p** upon it the city, *even* Jerusalem: H2710

POURTRAYED
Ezk 8:10 of Israel, **p** upon the wall round about. H2707
23:14 when she saw men **p** upon the wall, the H2707
14 of the Chaldeans **p** with vermilion, H2710

POVERTY
Gen 45:11 and all that thou hast, come to **p**. H3423
Prv 6:11 So shall thy **p** come as one that H7389
10:15 the destruction of the poor *is* their **p**. H7389
11:24 more than is meet, but *it tendeth* to **p**. H4270
13:18 **P** and shame *shall be to* him that H7389
20:13 Love not sleep, lest thou come to **p**; H3423
23:21 shall come to **p**: and drowsiness shall H3423
24:34 So shall thy **p** come *as* one that H7389
28:19 after vain *persons* shall have **p** enough. H7389
22 not that **p** shall come upon him. H2639
30: 8 give me neither **p** nor riches; feed me H7389
31: 7 Let him drink, and forget his **p**, and H7389
2Co 8: 2 joy and their deep **p** abounded unto the *G4432*
9 that ye through his **p** might be rich. *G4432*
Rev 2: 9 tribulation, and **p**, (but thou art rich) *G4432*

POWDER
Ex 32:20 and ground *it* to **p**, and strawed *it* upon H1854
Dt 28:24 the rain of thy land **p** and dust: from H80
2Ki 23: 6 *it* small to **p**, and cast the powder H6083
6 and cast the **p** thereof upon the graves H6083
15 *it* small to **p**, and burned the grove. H6083
2Ch 34: 7 images into **p**, and cut down all the H1854
Mt 21:44 it shall fall, it will grind him to **p**. *G3039*
Lk 20:18 it shall fall, it will grind him to **p**. *G3039*

POWDERS
Song 3: 6 frankincense, with all **p** of the merchant? H81

POWER
Gen 31: 6 And ye know that with all my **p** I have H3581
29 It is in the **p** of my hand to do you hurt: H410
32:28 a prince hast thou **p** with God and with H8280
49: 3 of dignity, and the excellency of **p**: H5794
Ex 9:16 to shew *in* thee my **p**; and that my name H3581
15: 6 glorious in **p**: thy right hand, O LORD, H3581
21: 8 he shall have no **p**, seeing he hath dealt H4910
32:11 with great **p**, and with a mighty hand? H3581
Lev 26:19 And I will break the pride of your **p**; H5797
37 have no **p** to stand before your enemies.
Nu 14:17 And now, I beseech thee, let the **p** of H3581
22:38 thee: have I now any **p** at all to say any H3201
Dt 4:37 sight with his mighty **p** out of Egypt; H3581
8:17 And thou say in thine heart, My **p** and H3581
18 he that giveth thee **p** to get wealth, that H3581
9:29 mighty **p** and by thy stretched out arm. H3581
32:36 he seeth that *their* **p** is gone, and *there* H3027
Jos 8:20 and they had no **p** to flee this way or H3027
17:17 **p**: thou shalt not have one lot *only*: H3581
1Sa 9: 1 a Benjamite, a mighty man of **p**. H2428
30: 4 until they had no more **p** to weep. H3581
2Sa 22:33 God *is* my strength *and* **p**: and he H2428
2Ki 17:36 Egypt with great **p** and a stretched out H3581
19:26 were of small **p**, they were dismayed H3027
1Ch 20: 1 Joab led forth the **p** of the army, and H2428
29:11 greatness, and the **p**, and the glory, and H1369
12 in thine hand *is* **p** and might; and in H3581
2Ch 14:11 them that have no **p**: help us, O LORD H3581
20: 6 hand *is there not* **p** and might, so that H3581
22: 9 had no **p** to keep still the kingdom. H3581
25: 8 God hath **p** to help, and to cast down. H3581
26:13 **p**, to help the king against the enemy. H3581
32: 9 and all his **p** with him,) unto Hezekiah H4475
Ezr 4:23 and made them to cease by force and **p**. H2429
8:22 seek him; but his **p** and his wrath *is* H5797
Neh 1:10 by thy great **p**, and by thy strong hand. H3581
5: 5 neither *is it* in our **p** *to redeem them*; H3027
Est 1: 3 his servants; the **p** of Persia and Media, H2428
8:11 to perish, all the **p** of the people and H2428
9: 1 hoped to have **p** over them, (though H7980
10: 2 And all the acts of his **p** and of his H8633
Job 1:12 he hath *is* in thy **p**; only upon himself H3027
5:20 and in war from the **p** of the sword. H3027
21: 7 live, become old, yea, are mighty in **p**? H2428
23: 6 **p**? No; but he would put *strength* in me. H3581
24:22 He draweth also the mighty with his **p**: H3581
26: 2 *that is* without **p**? *how* savest thou the H3581
12 He divideth the sea with his **p**, and by H3581
14 thunder of his **p** who can understand? H1369
36:22 Behold, God exalteth by his **p**: who H3581
37:23 *he is* excellent in **p**, and in judgment, H3581
41:12 I will not conceal his parts, nor his **p**, H1369
Ps 21:13 *so* will we sing and praise thy **p**. H1369
22:20 my darling from the **p** of the dog. H3027
37:35 I have seen the wicked in great **p**, and H6184
49:15 my soul from the **p** of the grave: for he H3027
59:11 them by thy **p**; and bring them down, H2428
16 But I will sing of thy **p**; yea, I will sing H5797
62:11 I heard this; that **p** *belongeth* unto God. H5797
63: 2 To see thy **p** and thy glory, so *as* I have H5797
65: 6 fast the mountains; *being* girded with **p**: H1369
66: 3 greatness of thy **p** shall thine enemies H5797
66: 7 He ruleth by his **p** for ever; his eyes H1369
68:35 and **p** unto *his* people. Blessed *be* God. H8592
71:18 *and* thy **p** to every one *that* is to come. H1369
78:26 by his **p** he brought in the south wind. H5797
79:11 greatness of thy **p** preserve thou those H2220
90:11 Who knoweth the **p** of thine anger? H5797
106: 8 might make his mighty **p** to be known. H1369
110: 3 in the day of thy **p**, in the beauties of H2428
111: 6 He hath shewed his people the **p** of his H3581
145:11 glory of thy kingdom, and talk of thy **p**; H1369
147: 5 Great *is* our Lord, and of great **p**: his H3581
150: 1 praise him in the firmament of his **p**. H5797
Prv 3:27 when it is in the **p** of thine hand to do *it*. H410
18:21 Death and life *are* in the **p** of the H3027
Ecc 4: 1 *there was* **p**; but they had no comforter. H3581
5:19 hath given him **p** to eat thereof, and to H7980
6: 2 giveth him not **p** to eat thereof, but a H7980
8: 4 Where the word of a king *is, there is* **p**: H7983
8 *There is* no man that hath **p** over the H7989
8 neither *hath he* **p** in the day of death: H7983
Isa 37:27 *were* of small **p**, they were dismayed H3027
40:26 that *he is* strong in **p**; not one faileth. H3581
29 He giveth **p** to the faint; and to *them* H3581
43:17 the army and the **p**; they shall lie down H5808
47:14 from the **p** of the flame: *there shall* H3027
50: 2 or have I no **p** to deliver? behold, at H3581
Jer 10:12 He hath made the earth by his **p**, he H3581
27: 5 by my great **p** and by my outstretched H3581
32:17 earth by thy great **p** and stretched out H3581
51:15 He hath made the earth by his **p**, he H3581
Ezk 17: 9 even without great **p** or many people to H2220
22: 6 were in thee to their **p** to shed blood. H2220
30: 6 the pride of her **p** shall come down: H5797
Dan 2:37 a kingdom, **p**, and strength, and glory. H2632
3:27 the fire had no **p**, nor was an hair of H7981
4:30 **p**, and for the honour of my majesty? H2632
6:27 Daniel from the **p** of the lions. H3028
8: 6 and ran unto him in the fury of his **p**. H3581
7 and there was no **p** in the ram to stand H3581
22 up out of the nation, but not in his **p**. H3581
24 And his **p** shall be mighty, but not by H3581
24 but not by his own **p**: and he shall H3581
11: 6 not retain the **p** of the arm; neither H3581
25 And he shall stir up his **p** and his H3581
43 But he shall have **p** over the treasures H4910
12: 7 to scatter the **p** of the holy people, all H3027
Hos 12: 3 and by his strength he had **p** with God: H8280
4 Yea, he had **p** over the angel, and H7786
13:14 I will ransom them from the **p** of the H3027
Mic 2: 1 it, because it is in the **p** of their hand. H410
3: 8 But truly I am full of **p** by the spirit of H3581
Nah 1: 3 and great in **p**, and will not at all acquit H3581
2: 1 *thy* loins strong, fortify *thy* **p** mightily. H3581
Hab 1:11 *imputing* this his **p** unto his god. H3581
2: 9 he may be delivered from the **p** of evil! H3709
3: 4 hand: and there *was* the hiding of his **p**. H5797
Zec 4: 6 by might, nor by **p**, but by my spirit, H3581
9: 4 he will smite her **p** in the sea; and she H2428
Mt 6:13 the **p**, and the glory, for ever. Amen. *G1411*
9: 6 Son of man hath **p** on earth to forgive *G1849*
8 which had given such **p** unto men. *G1849*
10: 1 he gave them **p** *against* unclean spirits, *G1849*
22:29 the scriptures, nor the **p** of God. *G1411*
24:30 of heaven with **p** and great glory. *G1411*
26:64 **p**, and coming in the clouds of heaven. *G1411*
28:18 them, saying, All **p** is given unto me in *G1849*
Mk 2:10 Son of man hath **p** on earth to forgive *G1849*
3:15 And to have **p** to heal sicknesses, and *G1849*
6: 7 and gave them **p** over unclean spirits; *G1849*
9: 1 seen the kingdom of God come with **p**. *G1411*
12:24 not the scriptures, neither the **p** of God? *G1411*
13:26 in the clouds with great **p** and glory. *G1411*
14:62 **p**, and coming in the clouds of heaven. *G1411*
Lk 1:17 in the spirit and **p** of Elias, to turn the *G1411*
35 thee, and the **p** of the Highest shall *G1411*
4: 6 And the devil said unto him, All this **p** *G1849*
14 And Jesus returned in the **p** of the *G1411*
32 at his doctrine: for his word was with **p**. *G1849*
36 authority and **p** he commandeth the *G1411*
5:17 **p** of the Lord was *present* to heal them. *G1411*
24 the Son of man hath **p** upon earth to *G1849*
9: 1 and gave them **p** and authority over *G1411*
43 at the mighty **p** of God. But while they *G3168*
10:19 Behold, I give unto you **p** to tread on *G1849*
19 and over all the **p** of the enemy: and *G1411*
12: 5 hath killed hath **p** to cast into hell; yea, *G1849*
20:20 the **p** and authority of the governor. *G746*
21:27 in a cloud with **p** and great glory. *G1411*
22:53 is your hour, and the **p** of darkness. *G1849*

Lk 22:69 sit on the right hand of the p of God. G1411
24:49 until ye be endued with p from on high. G1411
Jn 1:12 to them gave he p to become the sons G1849
10:18 of myself. I have p to lay it down, and G1849
18 it down, and I have p to take it again. G1849
17: 2 As thou hast given him p over all flesh, G1849
19:10 not that I have p to crucify thee, and G1849
10 thee, and have p to release thee? G1849
11 couldest have no p at all against me, G1849
Act 1: 7 which the Father hath put in his own p. G1849
8 But ye shall receive p, after that the G1411
3:12 by our own p or holiness we had G1411
4: 7 p, or by what name, have ye done this? G1411
33 And with great p gave the apostles G1411
5: 4 was it not in thine own p? why hast thou G1849
6: 8 And Stephen, full of faith and p, did G1411
8:10 saying, This man is the great p of God. G1411
19 Saying, Give me also this p, that on G1849
10:38 Holy Ghost and with p: who went about G1411
26:18 and from the p of Satan unto God, G1849
Ro 1: 4 the Son of God with p, according to the G1411
16 of Christ: for it is the p of God unto G1411
20 even his eternal p and Godhead; so G1411
9:17 I might shew my p in thee, and that my G1411
21 Hath not the potter p over the clay, of G1849
22 and to make his p known, endured G1415
13: 1 For there is no p but of God: the powers G1849
2 Whosoever therefore resisteth the p, G1849
3 not be afraid of the p? do that which is G1849
15:13 hope, through the p of the Holy Ghost. G1411
19 wonders, by the p of the Spirit of God; G1411
16:25 Now to him that is of p to stablish you G1410
1Co 1:18 us which are saved it is the p of God. G1411
24 the p of God, and the wisdom of God. G1411
2: 4 in demonstration of the Spirit and of p: G1411
5 the wisdom of men, but in the p of God. G1411
4:19 of them which are puffed up, but the p. G1411
20 kingdom of God is not in word, but in p. G1411
5: 4 with the p of our Lord Jesus Christ, G1411
6:12 will not be brought under the p of any. G1850
14 and will also raise up us by his own p. G1411
7: 4 The wife hath not p of her own body, G1850
4 not p of his own body, but the wife. G1850
37 but hath p over his own will, and G1849
9: 4 Have we not p to eat and to drink? G1849
5 Have we not p to lead about a sister, a G1849
6 Or I only and Barnabas, have not we p G1849
12 If others be partakers of this p over G1849
12 we have not used this p; but suffer all G1849
18 that I abuse not my p in the gospel. G1849
11:10 p on her head because of the angels. G1849
15:24 down all rule and all authority and p. G1411
43 it is sown in weakness; it is raised in p: G1411
2Co 4: 7 of the p may be of God, and not of us. G1411
6: 7 By the word of truth, by the p of God, G1411
8: 3 For to their p, I bear record, yea, and G1411
3 their p they were willing of themselves; G1411
12: 9 that the p of Christ may rest upon me. G1411
13: 4 he liveth by the p of God. For we also G1411
4 with him by the p of God toward you. G1411
10 according to the p which the Lord hath G1849
Eph 1:19 greatness of his p to us-ward who G1411
19 to the working of his mighty p, G2479
21 Far above all principality, and p, and G1849
2: 2 the prince of the p of the air, the spirit G1849
3: 7 me by the effectual working of his p. G1411
20 according to the p that worketh in us, G1411
6:10 in the Lord, and in the p of his might. G2904
Php 3:10 That I may know him, and the p of his G1411
Col 1:11 to his glorious p, unto all patience and G2904
13 Who hath delivered us from the p of G1849
2:10 is the head of all principality and p: G1849
1Th 1: 5 only, but also in p, and in the Holy G1411
2Th 1: 9 of the Lord, and from the glory of his p; G2479
11 goodness, and the work of faith with p: G1411
2: 9 with all p and signs and lying wonders, G1411
3: 9 Not because we have not p, but to make G1849
1Ti 6:16 be honour and p everlasting. Amen. G2904
2Ti 1: 7 of p, and of love, and of a sound mind. G1411
8 of the gospel according to the p of God; G1411
3: 5 the p thereof: from such turn away. G1411
Heb 1: 3 by the word of his p, when he had by G1411
2:14 had the p of death, that is, the devil; G2904
7:16 but after the p of an endless life. G1411
1Pt 1: 5 Who are kept by the p of God through G1411
2Pt 1: 3 According as his divine p hath given G1411
16 unto you the p and coming of our Lord G1411
2:11 Whereas angels, which are greater in p G2479
Jude 25 and p, both now and ever. Amen. G1849

Rev 2:26 to him will I give p over the nations: G1849
4:11 glory and honour and p: for thou hast G1411
5:12 was slain to receive p, and riches, and G1411
13 and glory, and p, be unto him that G2904
6: 4 that was red: and p was given to him
8 with him. And p was given unto them G1849
7:12 and honour, and p, and might, be unto G1411
9: 3 them was given p, as the scorpions of G1849
3 as the scorpions of the earth have p. G1849
10 their p was to hurt men five months. G1849
19 For their p is in their mouth, and in G1849
11: 3 And I will give p unto my two witnesses,
6 These have p to shut heaven, that it G1849
6 and have p over waters to turn G1849
17 to thee thy great p, and hast reigned. G1411
12:10 our God, and the p of his Christ: for the G1849
13: 2 his p, and his seat, and great authority. G1411
4 which gave p unto the beast: and G1849
5 blasphemies; and p was given unto G1849
7 them: and p was given him over G1849
12 And he exerciseth all the p of the first G1849
14 which he had p to do in the sight of G1325
15 And he had p to give life unto the G1325
14:18 altar, which had p over fire; and cried G1849
15: 8 God, and from his p; and no man was G1411
16: 8 upon the sun; and p was given unto him
9 God, which hath p over these plagues: G1849
17:12 p as kings one hour with the beast. G1849
13 their p and strength unto the beast. G1411
18: 1 having great p; and the earth was G1849
19: 1 honour, and p, unto the Lord our God: G1411
20: 6 death hath no p, but they shall be G1849

POWERFUL
Ps 29: 4 The voice of the LORD is p; the voice of H3581
2Co 10:10 they, are weighty and p; but his bodily G2478
Heb 4:12 For the word of God is quick, and p, G1756

POWERS
Mt 24:29 the p of the heavens shall be shaken: G1411
Mk 13:25 p that are in heaven shall be shaken. G1411
Lk 12:11 magistrates, and p, take ye no thought G1849
21:26 for the p of heaven shall be shaken. G1411
Ro 8:38 principalities, nor p, nor things present, G1411
13: 1 unto the higher p. For there is no power G1849
1 God: the p that be are ordained of God. G1849
Eph 3:10 principalities and p in heavenly places G1849
6:12 against p, against the rulers of G1849
Col 1:16 or principalities, or p: all things were G1849
2:15 principalities and p, he made a shew of G1849
Tit 3: 1 to principalities and p, to obey G1849
Heb 6: 5 of God, and the p of the world to come, G1411
1Pt 3:22 and p being made subject unto him. G1411

PRACTICES
2Pt 2:14 with covetous p; cursed children: G4124

PRACTISE
Ps 141: 4 any evil thing, to p wicked works with H5953
Isa 32: 6 work iniquity, to p hypocrisy, and to H6213
Dan 8:24 shall prosper, and p, and shall destroy H6213
Mic 2: 1 is light, they p it, because it is in the H6213

PRACTISED
1Sa 23: 9 And David knew that Saul secretly p H2790
Dan 8:12 to the ground; and it p, and prospered. H6213

PRAETORIUM
Mk 15:16 the hall, called P; and they call together G4232

PRAISE
Gen 29:35 said, Now will I p the LORD: therefore H3034
49: 8 thy brethren shall p: thy hand shall be H3034
Lev 19:24 shall be holy to p the LORD withal. H1974
Dt 10:21 He is thy p, and he is thy God, that hath H8416
26:19 he hath made, in p, and in name, and H8416
Jdg 5: 2 P ye the LORD for the avenging of H1288
3 I will sing p to the LORD God of Israel.
1Ch 16: 4 to thank and p the LORD God of Israel: H1984
35 to thy holy name, and glory in thy p. H8416
23: 5 I made, said David, to p therewith. H1984
30 and p the LORD, and likewise at even; H1984
25: 3 to give thanks and to p the LORD. H1984
29:13 thank thee, and p thy glorious name. H1984
2Ch 7: 6 king had made to p the LORD, because H3034
8:14 their charges, to p and minister before H1984
20:19 stood up to p the LORD God of Israel H1984
21 LORD, and that should p the beauty of H1984
21 army, and to say, P the LORD; for his H3034

2Ch 20:22 And when they began to sing and to p, H8416
23:13 as taught to sing p. Then Athaliah rent H1984
29:30 the Levites to sing p unto the LORD H1984
31: 2 p in the gates of the tents of the LORD. H1984
Ezr 3:10 with cymbals, to p the LORD, after the H1984
Neh 9: 5 is exalted above all blessing and p. H8416
12:24 against them, to p and to give thanks, H1984
46 songs of p and thanksgiving unto God. H8416
Ps 7:17 I will p the LORD according to his H3034
17 p to the name of the LORD most high. H2167
9: 1 I will p thee, O LORD, with my whole H3034
2 sing p to thy name, O thou most High. H2167
14 That I may shew forth all thy p in the H8416
21:13 so will we sing and p thy power. H2167
22:22 midst of the congregation will I p thee. H1984
23 Ye that fear the LORD, p him; all ye the H1984
25 My p shall be of thee in the great H8416
26 they shall p the LORD that seek H1984
28: 7 and with my song will I p him. H3034
30: 9 dust p thee? shall it declare thy truth? H3034
12 To the end that my glory may sing p to H2167
33: 1 for p is comely for the upright. H8416
2 P the LORD with harp: sing unto him H3034
34: 1 I will bless the LORD at all times: his p H8416
35:18 I will p thee among much people. H1984
28 and of thy p all the day long. H8416
40: 3 my mouth, even p unto our God: many H8416
42: 4 p, with a multitude that kept holyday. H8426
5 p him for the help of his countenance. H3034
11 in God: for I shall yet p him, who is the H3034
43: 4 the harp will I p thee, O God my God. H3034
5 in God: for I shall yet p him, who is the H3034
44: 8 In God we boast all the day long, and p H3034
45:17 the people p thee for ever and ever. H3034
48:10 O God, so is thy p unto the ends of the H8416
49:18 p thee, when thou doest well to thyself. H3034
50:23 Whoso offereth p glorifieth me: and to H8426
51:15 and my mouth shall shew forth thy p. H8416
52: 9 I will p thee for ever, because thou hast H3034
54: 6 I will freely sacrifice unto thee: I will p H3034
56: 4 In God I will p his word, in God I have H1984
10 In God will I p his word: in the LORD H1984
10 his word: in the LORD will I p his word. H1984
57: 7 my heart is fixed: I will sing and give p. H2167
9 I will p thee, O Lord, among the people: H3034
61: 8 So will I sing p unto thy name for ever, H2167
63: 3 is better than life, my lips shall p thee. H7623
5 my mouth shall p thee with joyful lips: H1984
65: 1 P waiteth for thee, O God, in Sion: and H8416
66: 2 of his name: make his p glorious. H8416
8 make the voice of his p to be heard: H8416
67: 3 Let the people p thee, O God; let all the H3034
3 thee, O God; let all the people p thee. H3034
5 Let the people p thee, O God; let all the H3034
5 thee, O God; let all the people p thee. H3034
69:30 I will p the name of God with a song, H1984
34 Let the heaven and earth p him, the H1984
71: 6 my p shall be continually of thee. H8416
8 Let my mouth be filled with thy p and H8416
14 and will yet p thee more and more. H8416
22 I will also p thee with the psaltery, even H3034
74:21 let the poor and needy p thy name. H1984
76:10 Surely the wrath of man shall p thee: H3034
79:13 will shew forth thy p to all generations. H8416
86:12 I will p thee, O Lord my God, with all H3034
88:10 shall the dead arise and p thee? Selah. H3034
89: 5 And the heavens shall p thy wonders, O H3034
98: 4 a loud noise, and rejoice, and sing p. H2167
99: 3 Let them p thy great and terrible name; H3034
100: 4 his courts with p: be thankful unto him, H8416
ttl A Psalm of p. H8426
102:18 shall be created shall p the LORD. H1984
21 LORD in Zion, and his p in Jerusalem; H8416
104:33 p to my God while I have my being. H2167
35 the LORD, O my soul. P ye the LORD. H1984
105:45 and keep his laws. P ye the LORD. H1984
106: 1 P ye the LORD. O give thanks unto the H1984
2 the LORD? who can shew forth all his p? H8416
12 believed they his words; they sang his p. H8416
47 thy holy name, and to triumph in thy p. H8416
48 the people say, Amen. P ye the LORD. H1984
107: 8 Oh that men would p the LORD for his H3034
15 Oh that men would p the LORD for his H3034
21 Oh that men would p the LORD for his H3034
31 Oh that men would p the LORD for his H3034
32 p him in the assembly of the elders. H1984
108: 1 will sing and give p, even with my glory. H2167
3 I will p thee, O LORD, among the H3034
109: 1 Hold not thy peace, O God of my p; H8416

P

Ps 109:30 I will greatly **p** the LORD with my H3034
30 yea, I will **p** him among the multitude. H1984
111: 1 **P** ye the LORD. I will praise the LORD H1984
1 Praise ye the LORD. I will **p** the LORD H3034
10 his **p** endureth for ever. H8416
112: 1 **P** ye the LORD. Blessed *is* the man *that* H1984
113: 1 **P** ye the LORD. Praise, O ye servants of H1984
1 Praise ye the LORD. **P**, O ye servants of H1984
1 of the LORD, **p** the name of the LORD. H1984
9 mother of children. **P** ye the LORD. H1984
115:17 The dead **p** not the LORD, neither any H1984
18 forth and for evermore. **P** the LORD. H1984
116:19 of thee, O Jerusalem. **P** ye the LORD. H1984
117: 1 O **p** the LORD, all ye nations: praise H1984
1 O praise the LORD, all ye nations: **p** H7623
2 *endureth* for ever. **P** ye the LORD. H1984
118:19 go into them, *and* I will **p** the LORD: H3034
21 I will **p** thee: for thou hast heard me, H3034
28 Thou *art* my God, and I will **p** thee: H3034
119: 7 I will **p** thee with uprightness of heart, H3034
164 Seven times a day do I **p** thee because H1984
171 My lips shall utter **p**, when thou hast H8416
175 Let my soul live, and it shall **p** thee; H1984
135: 1 **P** ye the LORD. Praise ye the name of H1984
1 Praise ye the LORD. **P** ye the name of H1984
1 **p** *him*, O ye servants of the LORD. H1984
3 **P** the LORD; for the LORD *is* good: sing H1984
21 dwelleth at Jerusalem. **P** ye the LORD. H1984
138: 1 I will **p** thee with my whole heart: H3034
1 before the gods will I sing **p** unto thee. H2167
2 holy temple, and **p** thy name for thy H3034
4 All the kings of the earth shall **p** thee, O H3034
139:14 I will **p** thee; for I am fearfully *and* H3034
142: 7 of prison, that I may **p** thy name: the H3034
145: 2 Every day will I bless thee; and I will **p** H1984
4 One generation shall **p** thy works to H7623
10 All thy works shall **p** thee, O LORD; H3034
21 My mouth shall speak the **p** of the H8416
ttl David's *Psalm* of **p**. H8416
146: 1 **P** ye the LORD. Praise the LORD, O my H1984
1 Praise ye the LORD. **P** the LORD, O my H1984
2 While I live will I **p** the LORD: I will H1984
10 unto all generations. **P** ye the LORD. H1984
147: 1 **P** ye the LORD: for *it is* good to sing H1984
1 God; for *it is* pleasant; *and* **p** is comely. H8416
7 sing **p** upon the harp unto our God: H2167
12 **P** the LORD, O Jerusalem; praise thy H7623
12 Praise the LORD, O Jerusalem; **p** thy H1984
20 have not known them. **P** ye the LORD. H1984
148: 1 **P** ye the LORD. Praise ye the LORD H1984
1 Praise ye the LORD. **P** ye the LORD H1984
1 from the heavens: **p** him in the heights. H1984
2 **P** ye him, all his angels: praise ye him, H1984
2 Praise ye him, all his angels: **p** ye him, H1984
3 **P** ye him, sun and moon: praise him, H1984
3 Praise ye him, sun and moon: **p** him, H1984
4 **P** him, ye heavens of heavens, and ye H1984
5 Let them **p** the name of the LORD: for H1984
7 **P** the LORD from the earth, ye dragons, H1984
13 Let them **p** the name of the LORD: for H1984
14 of his people, the **p** of all his saints; H8416
14 people near unto him. **P** ye the LORD. H1984
149: 1 **P** ye the LORD. Sing unto the LORD a H1984
1 *and* his **p** in the congregation of saints. H8416
3 Let them **p** his name in the dance: let H1984
9 have all his saints. **P** ye the LORD. H1984
150: 1 **P** ye the LORD. Praise God in his H1984
1 Praise ye the LORD. **P** God in his H1984
1 **p** him in the firmament of his power. H1984
2 **P** him for his mighty acts: praise him H1984
2 Praise him for his mighty acts: **p** him H1984
3 **P** him with the sound of the trumpet: H1984
3 **p** him with the psaltery and harp. H1984
4 **P** him with the timbrel and dance: H1984
4 timbrel and dance: **p** him with stringed H1984
5 **P** him upon the loud cymbals: praise H1984
5 Praise him upon the loud cymbals: **p** H1984
6 Let every thing that hath breath **p** the H1984
6 praise the LORD. **P** ye the LORD. H1984
Prv 27: 2 Let another man **p** thee, and not thine H1984
21 furnace for gold; so *is* a man to his **p**. H4110
28: 4 They that forsake the law **p** the wicked: H1984
31:31 let her own works **p** her in the gates. H1984
Isa 12: 1 say, O LORD, I will **p** thee: though thou H3034
4 And in that day shall ye say, **P** the H3034
25: 1 exalt thee, I will **p** thy name; for thou H3034
38:18 For the grave cannot **p** thee, death can H3034
19 The living, the living, he shall **p** thee, as H3034
42: 8 neither my **p** to graven images. H8416
Isa 42:10 new song, *and* his **p** from the end of the H8416
12 LORD, and declare his **p** in the islands. H8416
43:21 for myself; they shall shew forth my **p**. H8416
48: 9 anger, and for my **p** will I refrain for H8416
60:18 call thy walls Salvation, and thy gates **P**. H8416
61: 3 the garment of **p** for the spirit of H8416
11 **p** to spring forth before all the nations. H8416
62: 7 till he make Jerusalem a **p** in the earth. H8416
9 it shall eat it, and **p** the LORD; and they H1984
Jer 13:11 a name, and for a **p**, and for a glory: but H8416
17:14 and I shall be saved: for thou *art* my **p**. H8416
26 of **p**, unto the house of the LORD. H8426
20:13 Sing unto the LORD, **p** ye the LORD: H1984
31: 7 publish ye, **p** ye, and say, O LORD, H1984
33: 9 And it shall be to me a name of joy, a **p** H8416
11 that shall say, **P** the LORD of hosts: H3034
11 the sacrifice of **p** into the house of the H8426
48: 2 *There shall be* no more **p** of Moab: in H8416
49:25 How is the city of **p** not left, the city of H8416
51:41 and how is the **p** of the whole earth H8416
Dan 2:23 I thank thee, and **p** thee, O thou God of H7624
4:37 Now I Nebuchadnezzar **p** and extol H7624
Joel 2:26 and be satisfied, and **p** the name of the H1984
Hab 3: 3 heavens, and the earth was full of his **p**. H8416
Zep 3:19 and I will get them **p** and fame in every H8416
20 you a name and a **p** among all people H8416
Mt 21:16 and sucklings thou hast perfected **p**? *G136*
Lk 18:43 when they saw *it*, gave **p** unto God. *G136*
19:37 to rejoice and **p** God with a loud voice *G134*
Jn 9:24 **p**: we know that this man is a sinner. *G1391*
12:43 For they loved the **p** of men more than *G1391*
43 praise of men more than the **p** of God. *G1391*
Ro 2:29 whose **p** *is* not of men, but of God. *G1868*
13: 3 and thou shalt have **p** of the same: *G1868*
15:11 And again, **P** the Lord, all ye Gentiles; *G134*
1Co 4: 5 then shall every man have **p** of God. *G1868*
11: 2 Now I **p** you, brethren, that ye *G1867*
17 Now in this that I declare *unto you* I **p** *G1867*
22 shall I **p** you in this? I praise *you* not. *G1867*
22 shall I praise you in this? I **p** *you* not. *G1867*
2Co 8:18 the brother, whose **p** *is* in the gospel *G1868*
Eph 1: 6 To the **p** of the glory of his grace, *G1868*
12 That we should be to the **p** of his glory, *G1868*
14 possession, unto the **p** of his glory. *G1868*
Php 1:11 Christ, unto the glory and **p** of God. *G1868*
4: 8 if *there be* any **p**, think on these things. *G1868*
Heb 2:12 of the church will I sing **p** unto thee. *G5214*
13:15 the sacrifice of **p** to God continually, that *G133*
1Pt 1: 7 be found unto **p** and honour and glory *G1868*
2:14 and for the **p** of them that do well. *G1868*
4:11 to whom be **p** and dominion for ever *G1391*
Rev 19: 5 the throne, saying, **P** our God, all ye his *G134*

PRAISED

Jdg 16:24 And when the people saw him, they **p** H1984
2Sa 14:25 to be so much **p** as Absalom for his H1984
22: 4 *is* worthy to be **p**: so shall I be saved H1984
1Ch 16:25 **p**: he also *is* to be feared above all gods. H1984
36 people said, Amen, and **p** the LORD. H1984
23: 5 four thousand **p** the LORD with the H1984
2Ch 5:13 of musick, and **p** the LORD, *saying*, For H1984
7: 3 worshipped, and **p** the LORD, *saying*, H3034
6 ever, when David **p** by their ministry; H1984
30:21 and the priests **p** the LORD day by day, H1984
Ezr 3:11 shout, when they **p** the LORD, because H1984
Neh 5:13 said, Amen, and **p** the LORD. And the H1984
Ps 18: 3 *is worthy* to be **p**: so shall I be saved H1984
48: 1 Great *is* the LORD, and greatly to be **p** H1984
72:15 him continually; *and* daily shall he be **p**. H1288
96: 4 be **p**: he *is* to be feared above all gods. H1984
113: 3 of the same the LORD'S name *is* to be **p**. H1984
145: 3 Great *is* the LORD, and greatly to be **p**; H1984
Prv 31:30 *that* feareth the LORD, she shall be **p**. H1984
Ecc 4: 2 Wherefore I **p** the dead which are H7623
Song 6: 9 and the concubines, and they **p** her. H1984
Isa 64:11 where our fathers **p** thee, is burned up H1984
Dan 4:34 most High, and I **p** and honoured him H7624
5: 4 They drank wine, and **p** the gods of H7624
23 and thou hast **p** the gods of silver, and H7624
Lk 1:64 *loosed*, and he spake, and **p** God. *G2127*

PRAISES

Ex 15:11 in holiness, fearful *in* **p**, doing wonders? H8416
2Sa 22:50 and I will sing **p** unto thy name. H2167
2Ch 29:30 And they sang **p** with gladness, and H1984
Ps 9:11 Sing **p** to the LORD, which dwelleth in H2167
18:49 the heathen, and sing **p** unto thy name. H2167
22: 3 *O thou* that inhabitest the **p** of Israel. H8416
27: 6 sing, yea, I will sing **p** unto the LORD. H2167
Ps 47: 6 Sing **p** to God, sing praises: sing H2167
6 Sing praises to God, sing **p**: sing praises H2167
6 sing **p** unto our King, sing praises. H2167
6 sing praises unto our King, sing **p**. H2167
7 earth: sing ye **p** with understanding. H2167
56:12 me, O God: I will render **p** unto thee. H8426
68: 4 Sing unto God, sing **p** to his name: H2167
32 earth; O sing **p** unto the Lord; Selah: H2167
75: 9 But I will declare for ever; I will sing **p** H2167
78: 4 to come the **p** of the LORD, and his H8416
92: 1 to sing **p** unto thy name, O most High: H2167
108: 3 sing **p** unto thee among the nations. H2167
135: 3 sing **p** unto his name; for *it is* pleasant. H2167
144: 9 of ten strings will I sing **p** unto thee. H2167
146: 2 **p** unto my God while I have any being. H2167
147: 1 *it is* good to sing **p** unto our God; for *it* H2167
149: 3 **p** unto him with the timbrel and harp. H2167
6 *Let* the high **p** of God *be* in their mouth,
Isa 60: 6 shall shew forth the **p** of the LORD. H8416
63: 7 of the LORD, *and* the **p** of the LORD, H8416
Act 16:25 prayed, and sang **p** unto God: and the *G5214*
1Pt 2: 9 shew forth the **p** of him who hath called *G703*

PRAISETH

Prv 31:28 her husband *also*, and he **p** her. H1984

PRAISING

2Ch 5:13 to be heard in **p** and thanking the H1984
23:12 running and **p** the king, she came to H1984
Ezr 3:11 And they sang together by course in **p** H1984
Ps 84: 4 house: they will be still **p** thee. Selah. H1984
Lk 2:13 of the heavenly host **p** God, and saying, *G134*
20 glorifying and **p** God for all the things *G134*
24:53 And were continually in the temple, **p** *G134*
Act 2:47 **P** God, and having favour with all the *G134*
3: 8 walking, and leaping, and **p** God. *G134*
9 the people saw him walking and **p** God: *G134*

PRANSING

Nah 3: 2 **p** horses, and of the jumping chariots. H1725

PRANSINGS

Jdg 5:22 **p**, the pransings of their mighty ones. H1726
22 pransings, the **p** of their mighty ones. H1726

PRATING

Prv 10: 8 commandments: but a **p** fool shall fall. H8193
10 causeth sorrow: but a **p** fool shall fall. H8193
3Jn 10 which he doeth, **p** against us with *G5396*

PRAY

Gen 12:13 Say, I **p** thee, thou *art* my sister: that it H4994
13: 8 be no strife, I **p** thee, between me and H4994
9 separate thyself, I **p** thee, from me: if H4994
16: 2 from bearing: I **p** thee, go in unto my H4994
18: 3 not away, I **p** thee, from thy servant: H4994
4 Let a little water, I **p** you, be fetched, H4994
19: 2 my lords, turn in, I **p** you, into your H4994
7 And said, I **p** you, brethren, do not so H4994
8 man; let me, I **p** you, bring them out H4994
20: 7 and he shall **p** for thee, and thou shalt H6419
23:13 if thou *wilt give it*, I **p** thee, hear me: I H3863
24: 2 Put, I **p** thee, thy hand under my thigh:
12 master Abraham, I **p** thee, send me good
14 Let down thy pitcher, I **p** thee, that I may
17 **p** thee, drink a little water of thy pitcher.
23 *art* thou? tell me, I **p** thee: is there room
43 to her, Give me, I **p** thee, a little water H4994
45 I said unto her, Let me drink, I **p** thee.
25:30 And Esau said to Jacob, Feed me, I **p** H4994
27: 3 Now therefore take, I **p** thee, thy H4994
19 badest me: arise, I **p** thee, sit and eat of H4994
21 Come near, I **p** thee, that I may feel H4994
30:14 me, I **p** thee, of thy son's mandrakes. H4994
27 And Laban said unto him, I **p** thee, if I H4994
32:11 Deliver me, I **p** thee, from the hand of H4994
29 said, Tell *me*, I **p** thee, thy name. And H4994
33:10 And Jacob said, Nay, I **p** thee, if now I H4994
11 Take, I **p** thee, my blessing that is H4994
14 Let my lord, I **p** thee, pass over before H4994
34: 8 daughter: I **p** you give her him to wife. H4994
37: 6 And he said unto them, Hear, I **p** you, H4994
14 And he said to him, Go, I **p** thee, see H4994
16 I **p** thee, where they feed *their flocks*. H4994
38:16 and said, Go to, I **p** thee, let me come in H4994
25 she said, Discern, I **p** thee, whose *are*
40: 8 *belong* to God? tell me *them*, I **p** you. H4994
14 shew kindness, I **p** thee, unto me, and H4994
44:18 let thy servant, I **p** thee, speak a word in

Gen 44:33 Now therefore, I **p** thee, let thy servant H4994
45: 4 near to me, I **p** you. And they came H4994
47: 4 now therefore, we **p** thee, let thy H4994
29 in thy sight, put, I **p** thee, thy hand H4994
29 me; bury me not, I **p** thee, in Egypt: H4994
48: 9 I **p** thee, unto me, and I will bless them.
50: 4 I **p** you, in the ears of Pharaoh, saying, H4994
5 let me go up, I **p** thee, and bury my H4994
17 So shall ye say unto Joseph, Forgive, I **p** H577
17 evil: and now, we **p** thee, forgive the H4994
Ex 4:13 And he said, O my Lord, send, I **p** thee, H4994
18 him, Let me go, I **p** thee, and return H4994
5: 3 with us: let us go, we **p** thee, three days' H4994
10:17 Now therefore forgive, I **p** thee, my sin H4994
32:32 if not, blot me, I **p** thee, out of thy book H4994
33:13 Now therefore, I **p** thee, if I have found H4994
34: 9 let my Lord, I **p** thee, go among us; H4994
Nu 10:31 And he said, Leave us not, I **p** thee; H4994
11:15 with me, kill me, I **p** thee, out of hand, H4994
16: 8 And Moses said unto Korah, Hear, I **p** H4994
26 saying, Depart, I **p** you, from the tents H4994
20:17 Let us pass, I **p** thee, through thy H4994
21: 7 and against thee; **p** unto the LORD, H6419
22: 6 Come now therefore, I **p** thee, curse me H4994
16 Let nothing, I **p** thee, hinder thee from H4994
17 I **p** thee, curse me this people. H4994
19 Now therefore, I **p** you, tarry ye also H4994
23:13 And Balak said unto him, Come, I **p** H4994
27 Balaam, Come, I **p** thee, I will bring H4994
Dt 3:25 I **p** thee, let me go over, and see the H4994
Jos 2:12 Now therefore, I **p** you, swear unto me H4994
7:19 My son, give, I **p** thee, glory to the H4994
Jdg 1:24 him, Shew us, we **p** thee, the entrance H4994
4:19 And he said unto her, Give me, I **p** thee, H4994
6:18 Depart not hence, I **p** thee, until I come H4994
39 let me prove, I **p** thee, but this once H4994
8: 5 men of Succoth, Give, I **p** you, loaves of H4994
9: 2 Speak, I **p** you, in the ears of all the H4994
38 go out, I **p** now, and fight with them. H4994
10:15 deliver us only, we **p** thee, this day. H4994
11:17 saying, Let me, I **p** thee, pass through H4994
19 **p** thee, through thy land into my place. H4994
13: 4 Now therefore beware, I **p** thee, and H4994
15 of the LORD, I **p** thee, let us detain H4994
15: 2 she? take her, I **p** thee, instead of her. H4994
16: 6 Tell me, I **p** thee, wherein thy great H4994
10 lies: now tell me, I **p** thee, wherewith H4994
28 remember me, I **p** thee, and strengthen H4994
28 strengthen me, I **p** thee, only this once, H4994
18: 5 Ask counsel, we **p** thee, of God, that we H4994
19: 6 man, Be content, I **p** thee, and tarry all H4994
8 thine heart, I **p** thee. And they tarried H4994
9 toward evening, I **p** you tarry all night: H4994
11 master, Come, I **p** thee, and let us turn H4994
23 my brethren, *nay*, I **p** you, do not *so* H4994
Ru 2: 7 And she said, I **p** you, let me glean and H4994
1Sa 2:36 say, Put me, I **p** thee, into one of the H4994
3:17 said unto thee? I **p** thee hide *it* not from H4994
7: 5 and I will **p** for you unto the LORD. H6419
9:18 me, I **p** thee, where the seer's house *is*. H4994
10:15 And Saul's uncle said, Tell me, I **p** thee, H4994
12:19 And all the people said unto Samuel, **P** H6419
23 in ceasing to **p** for you: but I will teach H6419
14:29 the land: see, I **p** you, how mine eyes H4994
15:25 Now therefore, I **p** thee, pardon my sin, H4994
30 *yet* honour me now, I **p** thee, before the H4994
16:22 Let David, I **p** thee, stand before me; H4994
19: 2 now therefore, I **p** thee, take heed to H4994
20:29 And he said, Let me go, I **p** thee; for our H4994
29 let me get away, I **p** thee, and see my H4994
22: 3 and my mother, I **p** thee, come forth, H4994
23:22 Go, I **p** you, prepare yet, and know and H4994
25: 8 a good day: give, I **p** thee, whatsoever H4994
24 let thine handmaid, I **p** thee, speak in H4994
25 Let not my lord, I **p** thee, regard this H4994
28 I **p** thee, forgive the trespass of thine
26: 8 me smite him, I **p** thee, with the spear H4994
11 anointed: but, I **p** thee, take thou now H4994
19 Now therefore, I **p** thee, let my lord the H4994
28: 8 and he said, I **p** thee, divine unto me H4994
22 Now therefore, I **p** thee, hearken thou H4994
30: 7 Ahimelech's son, I **p** thee, bring me H4994
2Sa 1: 4 went the matter? I **p** thee, tell me. And H4994
9 He said unto me again, Stand, I **p** thee, H4994
7:27 in his heart to **p** this prayer unto thee. H6419
13: 5 say unto him, I **p** thee, let my sister H4994
6 unto the king, I **p** thee, let Tamar my H4994
13 Now therefore, I **p** thee, speak unto the H4994
26 Then said Absalom, If not, I **p** thee, let H4994

2Sa 14: 2 said unto her, I **p** thee, feign thyself to H4994
11 Then said she, I **p** thee, let the king H4994
12 thine handmaid, I **p** thee, speak *one* H4994
18 not from me, I **p** thee, the thing that H4994
15: 7 unto the king, I **p** thee, let me go and H4994
31 said, O LORD, I **p** thee, turn the counsel
16: 9 go over, I **p** thee, and take off his head. H4994
18:22 let me, I **p** thee, also run after H4994
19:37 Let thy servant, I **p** thee, turn back H4994
20:16 Hear, hear; say, I **p** you, unto Joab, H4994
24:17 let thine hand, I **p** thee, be against me, H4994
1Ki 1:12 Now therefore come, let me, I **p** thee, H4994
2:17 And he said, Speak, I **p** thee, unto H4994
20 petition of thee; *I p thee*, say me not nay.
8:26 let thy word, I **p** thee, be verified, which H4994
30 when they shall **p** toward this place: H6419
33 confess thy name, and **p**, and make H6419
35 thee; if they **p** toward this place, and H6419
42 he shall come and **p** toward this house; H6419
44 send them, and shall **p** unto the LORD H6419
48 away captive, and **p** unto thee toward H6419
13: 6 thy God, and **p** for me, that my hand H6419
14: 2 to his wife, Arise, I **p** thee, and disguise H4994
17:10 said, Fetch me, I **p** thee, a little water in H4994
11 **p** thee, a morsel of bread in thine hand. H4994
21 LORD my God, I **p** thee, let this child's H4994
19:20 said, Let me, I **p** thee, kiss my father H4994
20: 7 and said, Mark, I **p** you, and see how H4994
31 kings: let us, I **p** thee, put sackcloth H4994
32 saith, I **p** thee, let me live. And H4994
35 LORD, Smite me, I **p** thee. And the man
37 said, Smite me, I **p** thee. And the man H4994
22: 5 **p** thee, at the word of the LORD to day. H4994
13 let thy word, I **p** thee, be like the word H4994
2Ki 1:13 O man of God, I **p** thee, let my life, and H4994
2: 2 Tarry here, I **p** thee; for the LORD H4994
4 tarry here, I **p** thee; for the LORD H4994
6 And Elijah said unto him, Tarry, I **p** H4994
9 And Elisha said, I **p** thee, let a double H4994
16 let them go, we **p** thee, and seek thy
19 Elisha, Behold, I **p** thee, the situation of H4994
4:10 Let us make a little chamber, I **p** thee, H4994
22 and said, Send me, I **p** thee, one of the H4994
26 Run now, I **p** thee, to meet her, and say H4994
5: 7 consider, I **p** you, and see how he H4994
15 I **p** thee, take a blessing of thy servant. H4994
17 there not then, I **p** thee, be given to thy H4994
22 give them, I **p** thee, a talent of silver, H4994
6: 2 Let us go, we **p** thee, unto Jordan, and H4994
3 And one said, Be content, I **p** thee, and
17 And Elisha prayed, and said, LORD, I **p** H4994
18 this people, I **p** thee, with blindness. H4994
7:13 said, Let *some* take, I **p** thee, five of the H4994
8: 4 saying, Tell me, I **p** thee, all the great H4994
18:23 Now therefore, I **p** thee, give pledges to H4994
26 Speak, I **p** thee, to thy servants H6419
1Ch 17:25 found *in his heart* to **p** before thee. H6419
21:17 let thine hand, I **p** thee, O LORD my H4994
2Ch 6:24 confess thy name, and **p** and make H6419
26 thee; *yet* if they **p** toward this place, H6419
32 arm; if they come and **p** in this house; H6419
34 them, and they **p** unto thee toward this H6419
37 and turn and **p** unto thee in the land H2603
38 captives, and **p** toward their land, H6419
7:14 themselves, and **p**, and seek my face, H6419
18: 4 **p** thee, at the word of the LORD to day. H4994
12 word therefore, I **p** thee, be like one of H4994
Ezr 6:10 of heaven, and **p** for the life of the king, H6739
Neh 1: 6 servant, which I **p** before thee now, day H6419
11 and prosper, I **p** thee, thy servant this H4994
5:10 corn: I **p** you, let us leave off this usury. H4994
11 Restore, I **p** you, to them, even this day, H4994
Job 4: 7 Remember, I **p** thee, who *ever* perished,
6:29 Return, I **p** you, let it not be iniquity; H4994
8: 8 For inquire, I **p** thee, of the former age, H4994
21:15 should we have, if we **p** unto him? H6293
22:22 Receive, I **p** thee, the law from his H4994
32:21 Let me not, I **p** you, accept any man's H4994
33: 1 Wherefore, Job, I **p** thee, hear my H4994
26 He shall **p** unto God, and he will be H6279
42: 8 servant Job shall **p** for you: for him will H6419
Ps 5: 2 and my God: for unto thee will I **p**. H6419
32: 6 For this shall every one that is godly **p** H6419
55:17 and at noon, will I **p**, and cry aloud: H7878
119:76 Let, I **p** thee, thy merciful kindness be
122: 6 **P** for the peace of Jerusalem: they shall H7592
Isa 5: 3 I **p** you, betwixt me and my vineyard. H4994
16:12 sanctuary to **p**; but he shall not prevail. H6419
29:11 Read this, I **p** thee: and he saith, I H4994

Isa 29:12 I **p** thee: and he saith, I am not learned.
36: 8 Now therefore give pledges, I **p** thee, to H4994
11 Speak, I **p** thee, unto thy servants H4994
45:20 and **p** unto a god *that* cannot save. H6419
Jer 7:16 Therefore **p** not thou for this people, H6419
11:14 Therefore **p** not thou for this people, H6419
14:11 Then said the LORD unto me, **P** not for H6419
21: 2 Inquire, I **p** thee, of the LORD for us; H4994
29: 7 captives, and **p** unto the LORD for it: H6419
12 ye shall go and **p** unto me, and I will H6419
32: 8 me, Buy my field, I **p** thee, that *is* in H4994
37: 3 **P** now unto the LORD our God for us. H6419
20 Therefore hear now, I **p** thee, O my lord H4994
20 my supplication, I **p** thee, be accepted H4994
40:15 Let me go, I **p** thee, and I will slay
42: 2 before thee, and **p** for us unto the H6419
4 *you*; behold, I will **p** unto the LORD H6419
20 your God, saying, **P** for us unto the H6419
Lam 1:18 hear, I **p** you, all people, and H4994
Ezk 33:30 saying, Come, I **p** you, and hear what H4994
Jna 1: 8 Then said they unto him, Tell us, we **p** H4994
4: 2 LORD, and said, I **p** thee, O LORD, *was* H577
Mic 3: 1 And I said, Hear, I **p** you, O heads of H4994
9 Hear this, I **p** you, ye heads of the H4994
Hag 2:15 And now, I **p** you, consider from this H4994
Zec 7: 2 and their men, to **p** before the LORD, H2470
8:21 us go speedily to **p** before the LORD, H2470
22 Jerusalem, and to **p** before the LORD. H2470
Mal 1: 9 And now, I **p** you, beseech God that he H4994
Mt 5:44 that hate you, and **p** for them which G4336
6: 5 *are*: for they love to **p** standing in the G4336
6 shut thy door, **p** to thy Father which G4336
7 But when ye **p**, use not vain repetitions, G4336
9 After this manner therefore **p** ye: Our G4336
9:38 **P** ye therefore the Lord of the harvest, G1189
14:23 a mountain apart to **p**: and when the G4336
19:13 and **p**: and the disciples rebuked them. G4336
24:20 But **p** ye that your flight be not in the G4336
26:36 Sit ye here, while I go and **p** yonder. G4336
41 Watch and **p**, that ye enter not into G4336
53 Thinkest thou that I cannot now **p** to G3870
Mk 5:17 And they began to **p** him to depart out G3870
23 the point of death: *I p thee*, come and lay
6:46 he departed into a mountain to **p**. G4336
11:24 ye desire, when ye **p**, believe that ye G4336
13:18 And **p** ye that your flight be not in the G4336
33 Take ye heed, watch and **p**: for ye know G4336
14:32 his disciples, Sit ye here, while I shall **p**. G4336
38 Watch ye and **p**, lest ye enter into G4336
Lk 6:12 into a mountain to **p**, and continued all G4336
28 Bless them that curse you, and **p** for G4336
9:28 and went up into a mountain to **p**. G4336
10: 2 labourers *are* few: **p** ye therefore the G1189
11: 1 to **p**, as John also taught his disciples. G4336
2 And he said unto them, When ye **p**, say, G4336
14:18 go and see it: I **p** thee have me excused. G2065
19 prove them: I **p** thee have me excused. G2065
16:27 Then he said, I **p** thee therefore, father, G2065
18: 1 men ought always to **p**, and not to faint; G4336
10 Two men went up into the temple to **p**; G4336
21:36 Watch ye therefore, and **p** always, that G1189
22:40 **P** that ye enter not into temptation. G4336
46 rise and **p**, lest ye enter into temptation. G4336
Jn 14:16 And I will **p** the Father, and he shall G2065
16:26 you, that I will **p** the Father for you: G2065
17: 9 I **p** for them: I pray not for the world, G2065
9 I pray for them: I **p** not for the world, G2065
15 I **p** not that thou shouldest take them G2065
20 Neither **p** I for these alone, but for G2065
Act 8:22 wickedness, and **p** God, if perhaps the G1189
24 Then answered Simon, and said, **P** ye G1189
34 Philip, and said, I **p** thee, of whom G1189
10: 9 the housetop to **p** about the sixth hour: G4336
24: 4 unto thee, I **p** thee that thou wouldest G3870
27:34 Wherefore I **p** you to take *some* meat: G3870
Ro 8:26 what we should **p** for as we ought: but G4336
1Co 11:13 that a woman **p** unto God uncovered? G4336
14:13 tongue **p** that he may interpret. G4336
14 For if I **p** in an *unknown* tongue, my G4336
15 What is it then? I will **p** with the spirit, G4336
15 the spirit, and I will **p** with the G4336
2Co 5:20 *you* by us: we **p** *you* in Christ's stead, G1189
13: 7 Now I **p** to God that ye do no evil; not G2172
Php 1: 9 And this I **p**, that your love may abound G4336
Col 1: 9 *it*, do not cease to **p** for you, and to G4336
1Th 5:17 **P** without ceasing. G4336
23 you wholly; and *I p God* your whole
25 Brethren, **p** for us. G4336
2Th 1:11 Wherefore also we **p** always for you, G4336

2Th 3: 1 Finally, brethren, p for us, that the G4336
1Ti 2: 8 I will therefore that men p every where, G4336
2Ti 4:16 *men* forsook me: *I p God* that it may not
Heb 13:18 P for us: for we trust we have a good G4336
Jas 5:13 Is any among you afflicted? let him p. Is G4336
14 and let them p over him, anointing G4336
16 to another, and p one for another, that G2172
1Jn 5:16 death: I do not say that he shall p for it. G2065

PRAYED

Gen 20:17 So Abraham p unto God: and God H6419
Nu 11: 2 and when Moses p unto the LORD, the H6419
21: 7 from us. And Moses p for the people. H6419
Dt 9:20 and I p for Aaron also the same time. H6419
26 I p therefore unto the LORD, and said, H6419
1Sa 1:10 and p unto the LORD, and wept sore. H6419
27 For this child I p; and the LORD hath H6419
2: 1 And Hannah p, and said, My heart H6419
8: 6 us. And Samuel p unto the LORD. H6419
2Ki 4:33 them twain, and p unto the LORD. H6419
6:17 And Elisha p, and said, LORD, I pray H6419
18 to him, Elisha p unto the LORD, and H6419
19:15 And Hezekiah p before the LORD, and H6419
20 *That* which thou hast p to me against H6419
20: 2 the wall, and p unto the LORD, saying, H6419
2Ch 30:18 But Hezekiah p for them, saying, The H6419
32:20 son of Amoz, p and cried to heaven. H6419
24 to the death, and p unto the LORD: and H6419
33:13 And p unto him: and he was entreated H6419
Ezr 10: 1 Now when Ezra had p, and when he H6419
Neh 1: 4 fasted, and p before the God of heaven, H6419
2: 4 request? So I p to the God of heaven. H6419
Job 42:10 of Job, when he p for his friends: also H6419
Isa 37:15 And Hezekiah p unto the LORD, H6419
21 thou hast p to me against Sennacherib H6419
38: 2 toward the wall, and p unto the LORD, H6419
Jer 32:16 of Neriah, I p unto the LORD, saying, H6419
Dan 6:10 times a day, and p, and gave thanks H6739
9: 4 And I p unto the LORD my God, and H6419
Jna 2: 1 Then Jonah p unto the LORD his God H6419
4: 2 And he p unto the LORD, and said, I H6419
Mt 26:39 on his face, and p, saying, O my Father, G4336
42 the second time, and p, saying, O my G4336
44 went away again, and p the third time, G4336
Mk 1:35 into a solitary place, and there p. G4336
5:18 devil p him that he might be with him. G3870
14:35 on the ground, and p that, if it were G4336
39 And again he went away, and p, and G4336
Lk 5: 3 was Simon's, and p him that he would G2065
16 himself into the wilderness, and p. G4336
9:29 And as he p, the fashion of his G4336
18:11 The Pharisee stood and p thus with G4336
22:32 But I have p for thee, that thy faith fail G1189
41 stone's cast, and kneeled down, and p, G4336
44 And being in an agony he p more G4336
Jn 4:31 In the mean while his disciples p him, G2065
Act 1:24 And they p, and said, Thou, Lord, G4336
4:31 And when they had p, the place was G1189
6: 6 had p, they laid *their* hands on them. G4336
8:15 Who, when they were come down, p for G4336
9:40 down, and p; and turning *him* to G4336
10: 2 alms to the people, and p to God alway. G1189
30 at the ninth hour I p in my house, and, G4336
48 Then p they him to tarry certain days. G2065
13: 3 And when they had fasted and p, and G4336
14:23 church, and had p with fasting, they G4336
16: 9 Macedonia, and p him, saying, Come G3870
25 And at midnight Paul and Silas p, and G4336
20:36 he kneeled down, and p with them all. G4336
21: 5 we kneeled down on the shore, and p. G4336
22:17 I p in the temple, I was in a trance; G4336
23:18 me unto *him*, and p me to bring this G2065
28: 8 entered in, and p, and laid his hands on G4336
Jas 5:17 as we are, and he p earnestly that it G4336
18 And he p again, and the heaven gave G4336

PRAYER

2Sa 7:27 in his heart to pray this p unto thee. H8605
1Ki 8:28 Yet have thou respect unto the p of thy H8605
28 the cry and to the p, which thy servant H8605
29 hearken unto the p which thy servant H8605
38 What p and supplication soever be H8605
45 Then hear thou in heaven their p and H8605
49 Then hear thou their p and their H8605
54 of praying all this p and supplication H8605
9: 3 him, I have heard thy p and thy H8605
2Ki 19: 4 up *thy* p for the remnant that are left. H8605
20: 5 I have heard thy p, I have seen thy H8605
2Ch 6:19 Have respect therefore to the p of thy H8605
2Ch 6:19 the cry and the p which thy servant H8605
20 hearken unto the p which thy servant H8605
29 *Then* what p *or* what supplication H8605
35 from the heavens their p and their H8605
39 place, their p and their supplications, H8605
40 unto the p *that is made* in this place. H8605
7:12 I have heard thy p, and have chosen H8605
15 unto the p *that is made* in this place. H8605
30:27 heard, and their p came *up* to his holy H8605
33:18 and his p unto his God, and the H8605
19 His p also, and *how God* was entreated H8605
Neh 1: 6 mayest hear the p of thy servant, which H8605
11 be attentive to the p of thy servant, and H8605
11 and to the p of thy servants, who H8605
4: 9 Nevertheless we made our p unto our H6419
11:17 thanksgiving in p: and Bakbukiah the H8605
Job 15: 4 off fear, and restrainest p before God. H7881
16:17 in mine hands: also my p *is* pure. H8605
22:27 Thou shalt make thy p unto him, and H6279
Ps 4: 1 have mercy upon me, and hear my p. H8605
5: 3 I direct *my* p unto thee, and will look up.
6: 9 the LORD will receive my p. H8605
17: 1 my p, *that goeth* not out of feigned lips. H8605
ttl A P of David. H8605
35:13 my p returned into mine own bosom. H8605
39:12 Hear my p, O LORD, and give ear unto H8605
42: 8 me, *and* my p unto the God of my life. H8605
54: 2 Hear my p, O God; give ear to the words H8605
55: 1 Give ear to my p, O God; and hide not H8605
61: 1 Hear my cry, O God; attend unto my p. H8605
64: 1 Hear my voice, O God, in my p: H7879
65: 2 O thou that hearest p, unto thee shall all H8605
66:19 he hath attended to the voice of my p. H8605
20 away my p, nor his mercy from me. H8605
69:13 But as for me, my p *is* unto thee, O H8605
72:15 the gold of Sheba: p also shall be made H6419
80: 4 be angry against the p of thy people? H8605
84: 8 O LORD God of hosts, hear my p: give H8605
86: 6 Give ear, O LORD, unto my p; and H8605
ttl A P of David. H8605
88: 2 Let my p come before thee: incline H8605
13 in the morning shall my p prevent thee. H8605
90: ttl A P of Moses the man of God. H8605
102: 1 Hear my p, O LORD, and let my cry H8605
17 He will regard the p of the destitute, H8605
17 of the destitute, and not despise their p. H8605
ttl A P of the afflicted, when he is H8605
109: 4 adversaries: but I *give myself unto* p. H8605
7 condemned: and let his p become sin. H8605
141: 2 Let my p be set forth before thee *as* H8605
5 my p also *shall be* in their calamities. H8605
142: ttl Maschil of David; A P when he was in H8605
143: 1 Hear my p, O LORD, give ear to my H8605
Prv 15: 8 but the p of the upright *is* his delight. H8605
29 but he heareth the p of the righteous. H8605
28: 9 law, even his p *shall be* abomination. H8605
Isa 26:16 p *when* thy chastening *was* upon them. H3908
37: 4 lift up *thy* p for the remnant that is left. H8605
38: 5 I have heard thy p, I have seen thy H8605
56: 7 in my house of p: their burnt offerings H8605
7 be called an house of p for all people. H8605
Jer 7:16 lift up cry nor p for them, neither make H8605
11:14 lift up a cry or p for them: for I will not H8605
Lam 3: 8 I cry and shout, he shutteth out my p. H8605
44 that *our* p should not pass through. H8605
Dan 9: 3 God, to seek by p and supplications, H8605
13 yet made we not our p before the LORD H2470
17 Now therefore, O our God, hear the p of H8605
21 Yea, whiles I *was* speaking in p, even H8605
Jna 2: 7 the LORD: and my p came in unto thee, H8605
Hab 3: 1 A p of Habakkuk the prophet upon H8605
Mt 17:21 goeth not out but by p and fasting. G4335
21:13 p; but ye have made it a den of thieves. G4335
22 ask in p, believing, ye shall receive. G4335
23:14 make long p: therefore ye shall receive G4336
Mk 9:29 forth by nothing, but by p and fasting. G4335
11:17 p? but ye have made it a den of thieves. G4335
Lk 1:13 Zacharias: for thy p is heard; and thy G1162
6:12 and continued all night in p to God. G4335
19:46 p: but ye have made it a den of thieves. G4335
22:45 And when he rose up from p, and was G4335
Act 1:14 with one accord in p and supplication, G4335
3: 1 at the hour of p, *being* the ninth *hour*. G4335
6: 4 to p, and to the ministry of the word. G4335
10:31 And said, Cornelius, thy p is heard, G4335
12: 5 kept in prison: but p was made without G4335
16:13 by a river side, where p was wont to be G4335
16 And it came to pass, as we went to p, a G4335
Ro 10: 1 Brethren, my heart's desire and p to G1162
Ro 12:12 in tribulation; continuing instant in p; G4335
1Co 7: 5 to fasting and p; and come together G4335
2Co 1:11 Ye also helping together by p for us, G1162
9:14 And by their p for you, which long after G1162
Eph 6:18 Praying always with all p and G4335
Php 1: 4 Always in every p of mine for you all G1162
19 through your p, and the supply of the G1162
4: 6 in every thing by p and supplication G4335
Col 4: 2 Continue in p, and watch in the same G4335
1Ti 4: 5 is sanctified by the word of God and p. G1783
Jas 5:15 And the p of faith shall save the sick, G2171
16 p of a righteous man availeth much. G1162
1Pt 4: 7 be ye therefore sober, and watch unto p. G4335

PRAYERS

Ps 72:20 The p of David the son of Jesse are H8605
Isa 1:15 ye make many p, I will not hear: your H8605
Mk 12:40 make long p: these shall receive greater G4336
Lk 2:37 *God* with fastings and p night and day. G1162
5:33 fast often, and make p, and likewise *the* G1162
20:47 for a shew make long p: the same shall G4336
Act 2:42 and in breaking of bread, and in p. G4335
10: 4 unto him, Thy p and thine alms are G4335
Ro 1: 9 I make mention of you always in my p; G4335
15:30 with me in *your* p to God for me; G4335
Eph 1:16 you, making mention of you in my p; G4335
Col 4:12 for you in p, that ye may stand perfect G4335
1Th 1: 2 all, making mention of you in our p; G4335
1Ti 2: 1 all, supplications, p, intercessions, *and* G4335
5: 5 in supplications and p night and day. G4335
2Ti 1: 3 of thee in my p night and day; G1162
Phlm 4 mention of thee always in my p, G4335
22 your p I shall be given unto you. G4335
Heb 5: 7 he had offered up p and supplications G1162
1Pt 3: 7 of life; that your p be not hindered. G4335
12 *are open* unto their p: but the face of the G1162
Rev 5: 8 full of odours, which are the p of saints. G4335
8: 3 offer *it* with the p of all saints upon the G4335
4 *came* with the p of the saints, ascended G4335

PRAYEST

Mt 6: 5 And when thou p, thou shalt not be as G4336
6 But thou, when thou p, enter into thy G4336

PRAYETH

1Ki 8:28 which thy servant p before thee to day: H6419
2Ch 6:19 prayer which thy servant p before thee: H6419
20 which thy servant p toward this place. H6419
Isa 44:17 *it*, and p unto it, and saith, Deliver H6419
Act 9:11 called Saul, of Tarsus: for, behold, he p, G4336
1Co 11: 5 But every woman that p or prophesieth G4336
14:14 p, but my understanding is unfruitful. G4336

PRAYING

1Sa 1:12 as she continued p before the LORD, H6419
26 stood by thee here, p unto the LORD. H6419
1Ki 8:54 made an end of p all this prayer and H6419
2Ch 7: 1 made an end of p, the fire came down H6419
Dan 6:11 and found Daniel p and making H1156
9:20 And whiles I *was* speaking, and p, and H6419
Mk 11:25 And when ye stand p, forgive, if ye have G4336
Lk 1:10 were p without at the time of incense. G4336
3:21 and p, the heaven was opened, G4336
9:18 And it came to pass, as he was alone p, G4336
11: 1 And it came to pass, that, as he was p G4336
Act 11: 5 I was in the city of Joppa p: and in a G4336
12:12 where many were gathered together p. G4336
1Co 11: 4 Every man p or prophesying, having G4336
2Co 8: 4 P us with much entreaty that we would G1189
Eph 6:18 P always with all prayer and G4336
Col 1: 3 our Lord Jesus Christ, p always for you, G4336
4: 3 Withal p also for us, that God would G4336
1Th 3:10 Night and day p exceedingly that we G1189
Jude 20 most holy faith, p in the Holy Ghost, G4336

PREACH

Neh 6: 7 prophets to p of thee at Jerusalem, H7121
Isa 61: 1 anointed me to p good tidings unto the H1319
Jna 3: 2 p unto it the preaching that I bid thee. H7121
Mt 4:17 From that time Jesus began to p, and to G2784
10: 7 And as ye go, p, saying, The kingdom of G2784
27 the ear, *that* p ye upon the housetops. G2784
11: 1 thence to teach and to p in their cities. G2784
Mk 1: 4 the wilderness, and p the baptism of G2784
38 p there also: for therefore came I forth. G2784
3:14 and that he might send them forth to p, G2784
16:15 and p the gospel to every creature. G2784
Lk 4:18 hath anointed me to p the gospel to the G2097
18 brokenhearted, to p deliverance to the G2784

Lk 4:19 To p the acceptable year of the Lord. G2784
43 And he said unto them, I must p the G2097
9: 2 And he sent them to p the kingdom of G2784
60 but go thou and p the kingdom of God. G1229
Act 5:42 ceased not to teach and p Jesus Christ. G2097
10:42 And he commanded us to p unto the G2784
14:15 with you, and p unto you that ye G2097
15:21 city them that p him, being read in the G2784
16: 6 of the Holy Ghost to p the word in Asia, G2980
10 called us for to p the gospel unto them. G2097
17: 3 Jesus, whom I p unto you, is Christ. G2605
Ro 1:15 me is, I am ready to p the gospel to you G2097
10: 8 that is, the word of faith, which we p; G2784
15 And how shall they p, except they be G2784
15 feet of them that p the gospel of peace, G2097
15:20 Yea, so have I strived to p the gospel, G2097
1Co 1:17 to baptize, but to p the gospel: not with G2097
23 But we p Christ crucified, unto the Jews G2784
9:14 p the gospel should live of the gospel. G2605
16 For though I p the gospel, I have G2097
16 woe is unto me, if I p not the gospel! G2097
18 that, when I p the gospel, I may make G2097
15:11 I or they, so we p, and so ye believed. G2784
2Co 2:12 I came to Troas to *p* Christ's gospel, G2784
4: 5 For we p not ourselves, but Christ Jesus G2784
10:16 To p the gospel in the *regions* beyond G2097
Gal 1: 8 from heaven, p any other gospel unto G2097
9 again, If any *man* p any other gospel G2097
16 To reveal his Son in me, that I might p G2097
2: 2 gospel which I p among the Gentiles, G2784
5:11 And I, brethren, if I yet p circumcision, G2784
Eph 3: 8 that I should p among the Gentiles G2097
Php 1:15 Some indeed p Christ even of envy and G2784
16 The one p Christ of contention, not G2605
Col 1:28 Whom we p, warning every man, and G2605
2Ti 4: 2 P the word; be instant in season, out of G2784
Rev 14: 6 gospel to p unto them that dwell G2097

PREACHED

Ps 40: 9 I have p righteousness in the great H1319
Mt 11: 5 and the poor have the gospel p to them. G2097
24:14 kingdom shall be p in all the world for G2784
26:13 gospel shall be p in the whole world, G2784
Mk 1: 7 And p, saying, There cometh one G2784
39 And he p in their synagogues G2258
2: 2 the door: and he p the word unto them. G2980
6:12 And they went out, and p that men G2784
14: 9 gospel shall be p throughout the whole G2784
16:20 And they went forth, and p every G2784
Lk 3:18 in his exhortation p he unto the people. G2097
4:44 And he p in the synagogues of Galilee. G2258
7:22 are raised, to the poor the gospel is p. G2097
16:16 is p, and every man presseth into it. G2097
20: 1 in the temple, and p the gospel, the G2097
24:47 of sins should be p in his name among G2784
Act 3:20 Christ, which before was p unto you: G4296
4: 2 the people, and p through Jesus the G2605
8: 5 of Samaria, and p Christ unto them. G2784
25 they had testified and p the word of the G2980
25 to Jerusalem, and p the gospel in many G2097
35 same scripture, and p unto him Jesus. G2097
40 through he p in all the cities, till he G2097
9:20 And straightway he p Christ in the G2784
27 and how he had p boldly at Damascus G3954
10:37 Galilee, after the baptism which John p; G2784
13: 5 And when they were at Salamis, they p G2605
24 When John had first p before his G4296
38 is p unto you the forgiveness of sins: G2605
42 might be p to them the next sabbath. G2980
14: 7 And there they p the gospel. G2097
21 And when they had p the gospel to that G2097
25 And when they had p the word in G2980
15:36 where we have p the word of the Lord, G2605
17:13 the word of God was p of Paul at Berea, G2605
18 gods: because he p unto them Jesus, G2097
20: 7 break bread, Paul p unto them, ready G1256
Ro 15:19 I have fully p the gospel of Christ. G4137
1Co 9:27 when I have p to others, I myself G2784
15: 1 the gospel which I p unto you, which G2097
2 in memory what I p unto you, unless ye G2097
12 Now if Christ be p that he rose from the G2784
2Co 1:19 Christ, who was p among you by us, G2784
11: 4 we have not p, or *if* ye receive another G2784
7 I have p to you the gospel of God freely? G2097
Gal 1: 8 have p unto you, let him be accursed. G2097
11 which was p of me is not after man. G2097
3: 8 through faith, p before the gospel unto G4283
4:13 flesh I p the gospel unto you at the first. G2097
Eph 2:17 And came and p peace to you which G2097
Php 1:18 or in truth, Christ is p; and I therein do G2605
Col 1:23 *and* which was p to every creature G2784
1Th 2: 9 you, we p unto you the gospel of God. G2784
1Ti 3:16 seen of angels, p unto the Gentiles, G2784
Heb 4: 2 For unto us was the gospel p, as well as G2097
2 unto them: but the word p did not profit G189
6 p entered not in because of unbelief: G2097
1Pt 1:12 by them that have p the gospel unto G2097
25 word which by the gospel is p unto you. G2097
3:19 By which also he went and p unto the G2784
4: 6 For for this cause was the gospel p also G2097

PREACHER

Ecc 1: 1 The words of the P, the son of David, H6953
2 Vanity of vanities, saith the P, vanity of H6953
12 I the P was king over Israel in H6953
7:27 Behold, this have I found, saith the p, H6953
12: 8 Vanity of vanities, saith the p; all *is* H6953
9 And moreover, because the p was wise, H6953
10 The p sought to find out acceptable H6953
Ro 10:14 and how shall they hear without a p? G2784
1Ti 2: 7 Whereunto I am ordained a p, and an G2783
2Ti 1:11 Whereunto I am appointed a p, and an G2783
2Pt 2: 5 the eighth *person*, a p of righteousness, G2783

PREACHEST

Ro 2:21 thyself? thou that p a man should not G2784

PREACHETH

Act 19:13 We adjure you by Jesus whom Paul p. G2784
2Co 11: 4 For if he that cometh p another Jesus, G2784
Gal 1:23 p the faith which once he destroyed. G2097

PREACHING

Jna 3: 2 and preach unto it the p that I bid thee. H7150
Mt 3: 1 In those days came John the Baptist, p G2784
4:23 synagogues, and p the gospel of the G2784
9:35 synagogues, and p the gospel of the G2784
12:41 repented at the p of Jonas; and, behold, G2782
Mk 1:14 p the gospel of the kingdom of God, G2784
Lk 3: 3 country about Jordan, p the baptism of G2784
8: 1 city and village, p and shewing the glad G2784
9: 6 p the gospel, and healing every where. G2097
11:32 repented at the p of Jonas; and, behold, G2782
Act 8: 4 abroad went every where p the word. G2097
12 But when they believed Philip p the G2097
10:36 the children of Israel, p peace by Jesus G2097
11:19 and Antioch, p the word to none but G2980
20 unto the Grecians, p the Lord Jesus. G2097
15:35 teaching and p the word of the Lord, G2097
20: 9 as Paul was long p, he sunk down with G1256
25 whom I have gone p the kingdom of G2784
28:31 P the kingdom of God, and teaching G2784
Ro 16:25 my gospel, and the p of Jesus Christ, G2782
1Co 1:18 For the p of the cross is to them that G3056
21 of p to save them that believe. G2782
2: 4 And my speech and my p *was* not with G2782
15:14 And if Christ be not risen, then *is* our p G2782
2Co 10:14 as to you also in *p* the gospel of Christ:
2Ti 4:17 that by me the p might be fully known, G2782
Tit 1: 3 his word through p, which is committed G2782

PRECEPT

Isa 28:10 For p *must be* upon precept, precept H6673
10 For precept *must be* upon p, precept H6673
10 For precept *must be* upon precept, p H6673
10 precept upon p; line upon line, line H6673
13 was unto them p upon precept, precept H6673
13 precept upon p, precept upon precept; H6673
13 upon precept, p upon precept; line H6673
13 precept upon p; line upon line, line H6673
29:13 toward me is taught by the p of men: H4687
Mk 10: 5 of your heart he wrote you this p. G1785
Heb 9:19 For when Moses had spoken every p to G1785

PRECEPTS

Neh 9:14 them p, statutes, and laws, H4687
Ps 119: 4 commanded *us* to keep thy p diligently. H6490
15 I will meditate in thy p, and have H6490
27 p: so shall I talk of thy wondrous works. H6490
40 Behold, I have longed after thy p: H6490
45 I will walk at liberty: for I seek thy p. H6490
56 This I had, because I kept thy p. H6490
63 fear thee, and of them that keep thy p. H6490
69 I will keep thy p with *my* whole heart. H6490
78 a cause: *but* I will meditate in thy p. H6490
87 me upon earth; but I forsook not thy p. H6490
93 I will never forget thy p: for with them H6490
94 thine, save me; for I have sought thy p. H6490
Ps119:100 than the ancients, because I keep thy p. H6490
104 Through thy p I get understanding: H6490
110 snare for me: yet I erred not from thy p. H6490
128 Therefore I esteem all *thy* p *concerning* H6490
134 oppression of man: so will I keep thy p. H6490
141 and despised: *yet* do not I forget thy p. H6490
159 Consider how I love thy p: quicken me, H6490
168 I have kept thy p and thy testimonies: H6490
173 hand help me; for I have chosen thy p. H6490
Jer 35:18 and kept all his p, and done according H4687
Dan 9: 5 from thy p and from thy judgments: H4687

PRECIOUS

Gen 24:53 her brother and to her mother p things. H4030
Dt 33:13 his land, for the p things of heaven, for H4022
14 And for the p fruits *brought forth* by H4022
14 for the p things put forth by the moon, H4022
15 and for the p things of the lasting hills, H4022
16 And for the p things of the earth and H4022
1Sa 3: 1 of the LORD was p in those days; *there* H3368
26:21 my soul was p in thine eyes this day: H3365
2Sa 12:30 of gold with the p stones: and it was *set* H3368
1Ki 10: 2 much gold, and p stones: and when she H3368
10 great store, and p stones: there came H3368
11 plenty of almug trees, and p stones. H3368
2Ki 1:13 fifty thy servants, be p in thy sight. H3365
14 let my life now be p in thy sight. H3365
20:13 all the house of his p things, the silver, H5238
13 the spices, and the p ointment, and *all* H2896
1Ch 20: 2 and *there were* p stones in it; and it H3368
29: 2 and all manner of p stones, and marble H3368
8 And they with whom *p* stones were
2Ch 3: 6 And he garnished the house with p H3368
9: 1 in abundance, and p stones: and when H3368
9 abundance, and p stones: neither was H3368
10 brought algum trees and p stones. H3368
20:25 dead bodies, and p jewels, which they H2530
21: 3 of gold, and of p things, with fenced H4030
32:27 and for gold, and for p stones, and for H3368
Ezr 1: 6 beasts, and with p things, beside all H4030
8:27 two vessels of fine copper, p as gold. H2530
Job 28:10 rocks; and his eye seeth every p thing. H3366
16 Ophir, with the p onyx, or the sapphire. H3368
Ps 49: 8 (For the redemption of their soul *is* p, H3365
72:14 and p shall their blood be in his sight. H3365
116:15 P in the sight of the LORD *is* the death H3368
126: 6 and weepeth, bearing p seed, shall H4901
133: 2 *It is* like the p ointment upon the head, H2896
139:17 How p also are thy thoughts unto me, H3365
Prv 1:13 We shall find all p substance, we shall H3368
3:15 She *is* more p than rubies: and all the H3368
6:26 the adulteress will hunt for the p life. H3368
12:27 but the substance of a diligent man *is* p. H3368
17: 8 A gift *is as* a p stone in the eyes of him H2580
20:15 but the lips of knowledge *are* a p jewel. H3366
24: 4 be filled with all p and pleasant riches. H3368
Ecc 7: 1 A good name *is* better than p ointment; H2896
Isa 13:12 I will make a man more p than fine H3365
28:16 a tried stone, a p corner *stone*, a sure H3368
39: 2 the house of his p things, the silver, H5238
2 the spices, and the p ointment, and all H2896
43: 4 Since thou wast p in my sight, thou H3365
Jer 15:19 take forth the p from the vile, thou H3368
20: 5 and all the p things thereof, and H3366
Lam 4: 2 The p sons of Zion, comparable to fine H3368
Ezk 22:25 the treasure and p things; they have H3366
27:20 Dedan *was* thy merchant in p clothes H2667
22 spices, and with all p stones, and gold. H3368
28:13 of God; every p stone *was* thy covering, H3368
Dan 11: 8 *and* with their p vessels of silver and H2532
38 and with p stones, and pleasant things. H3368
43 and over all the p things of Egypt: and H2530
Mt 26: 7 box of very p ointment, and poured G927
Mk 14: 3 of spikenard very p; and she brake the G4185
1Co 3:12 silver, p stones, wood, hay, stubble; G5093
Jas 5: 7 waiteth for the p fruit of the earth, and G5093
1Pt 1: 7 being much more p than of gold that G5093
19 But with the p blood of Christ, as of a G5093
2: 4 of men, but chosen of God, *and* p, G1784
6 stone, elect, p: and he that believeth G1784
7 believe *he is* p: but unto them which G5092
2Pt 1: 1 that have obtained like p faith with us G2472
4 great and p promises: that by these G5093
Rev 17: 4 with gold and p stones and pearls, G5093
18:12 and silver, and p stones, and of pearls, G5093
12 vessels of most p wood, and of brass, G5093
16 with gold, and p stones, and pearls! G5093
21:11 unto a stone most p, even like a jasper G5093
19 with all manner of p stones. The first G5093

PREDESTINATE
Ro 8:29 he also did **p** *to be* conformed to *G4309*
30 Moreover whom he did **p**, them he also *G4309*

PREDESTINATED
Eph 1: 5 Having **p** us unto the adoption of *G4309*
11 inheritance, being **p** according to the *G4309*

PREEMINENCE
Ecc 3:19 no **p** above a beast: for all *is* vanity. H4195
Col 1:18 that in all *things* he might have the **p**. *G4409*
3Jn 9 the **p** among them, receiveth us not. *G5383*

PREFER
Ps 137: 6 if I **p** not Jerusalem above my chief joy. H5927

PREFERRED
Est 2: 9 house: and he **p** her and her maids H8138
Dan 6: 3 Then this Daniel was **p** above the H5330
Jn 1:15 is **p** before me: for he was before me. *G1096*
27 He it is, who coming after me is **p** *G1096*
30 is **p** before me: for he was before me. *G1096*

PREFERRING
Ro 12:10 love; in honour **p** one another; *G4285*
1Ti 5:21 things without **p** one before another, *G4299*

PREMEDITATE
Mk 13:11 neither do ye **p**: but whatsoever shall *G3191*

PREPARATION
1Ch 22: 5 now make **p** for it. So David prepared H3559
Nah 2: 3 in the day of his **p**, and the fir trees shall H3559
Mt 27:62 the day of the **p**, the chief priests and *G3904*
Mk 15:42 **p**, that is, the day before the sabbath, *G3904*
Lk 23:54 And that day was the **p**, and the *G3904*
Jn 19:14 And it was the **p** of the passover, and *G3904*
31 because it was the **p**, that the bodies *G3904*
42 of the Jews' **p** *day*; for the sepulchre *G3904*
Eph 6:15 And your feet shod with the **p** of the *G2091*

PREPARATIONS
Prv 16: 1 The **p** of the heart in man, and the H4633

PREPARE
Ex 15: 2 my God, and I will **p** him an habitation;
16: 5 day they shall **p** *that* which they bring H3559
Nu 15: 5 offering shalt thou **p** with the burnt H6213
6 Or for a ram, thou shalt **p** *for* a meat H6213
12 that ye shall **p**, so shall ye do to every H6213
23: 1 **p** me here seven oxen and seven rams. H3559
29 here seven altars, and **p** me here seven H3559
Dt 19: 3 Thou shalt **p** thee a way, and divide the H3559
Jos 1:11 the people, saying, **P** you victuals; for H3559
22:26 Therefore we said, Let us now **p** to H6213
1Sa 7: 3 among you, and **p** your hearts unto the H3559
23:22 Go, I pray you, **p** yet, and know and see H3559
1Ki 18:44 up, say unto Ahab, **P** *thy chariot*, and get H631
1Ch 9:32 the shewbread, to **p** *it* every sabbath. H3559
29:18 thy people, and **p** their heart unto thee: H3559
2Ch 2: 9 Even to **p** me timber in abundance: for H3559
31:11 Then Hezekiah commanded to **p** H3559
35: 4 And **p** *yourselves* by the houses of your H3559
6 yourselves, and **p** your brethren, that H3559
Est 5: 8 that I shall **p** for them, and I will H6213
Job 8: 8 **p** thyself to the search of their fathers: H3559
11:13 If thou **p** thine heart, and stretch out H3559
27:16 as the dust, and **p** raiment as the clay; H3559
17 He may **p** *it*, but the just shall put *it* on, H3559
Ps 10:17 humble: thou wilt **p** their heart, thou H3559
59: 4 They run and **p** themselves without *my* H3559
61: 7 He shall abide before God for ever: O **p** H4487
107:36 that they may **p** a city for habitation; H3559
Prv 24:27 **P** thy work without, and make it fit for H3559
30:25 yet they **p** their meat in the summer; H3559
Isa 14:21 **P** slaughter for his children for the H3559
21: 5 **P** the table, watch in the watchtower, H6186
40: 3 in the wilderness, **P** ye the way of the H6437
20 workman to **p** a graven image, *that* H3559
57:14 And shall say, Cast ye up, cast ye up, **p** H6437
62:10 Go through, go through the gates; **p** ye H6437
65:11 mountain, that **p** a table for that troop, H6186
Jer 6: 4 **P** ye war against her; arise, and let us H6942
12: 3 and **p** them for the day of slaughter. H6942
22: 7 And I will **p** destroyers against thee, H6942
46:14 say ye, Stand fast, and **p** thee; for the H3559
51:12 up the watchmen, **p** the ambushes: for H3559
27 the nations, **p** the nations against H6942
28 **P** against her the nations with the H6942
Ezk 4:15 and thou shalt **p** thy bread therewith. H6213
12: 3 Therefore, thou son of man, **p** thee H6213
35: 6 Lord GOD, I will **p** thee unto blood, and H6213
38: 7 Be thou prepared, and **p** for thyself, H3559
43:25 Seven days shalt thou **p** every day a H6213
25 they shall also **p** a young bullock, and H6213
45:17 of Israel: he shall **p** the sin offering, H6213
22 And upon that day shall the prince **p** H6213
23 And seven days of the feast he shall **p** a H6213
24 And he shall **p** a meat offering of an H6213
46: 2 the priests shall **p** his burnt offering H6213
7 And he shall **p** a meat offering, an H6213
12 Now when the prince shall **p** a H6213
12 east, and he shall **p** his burnt offering H6213
13 Thou shalt daily **p** a burnt offering H6213
13 blemish: thou shalt **p** it every morning. H6213
14 And thou shalt **p** a meat offering for it H6213
15 Thus shall they **p** the lamb, and the H6942
Joel 3: 9 Proclaim ye this among the Gentiles; **P** H6942
Am 4:12 unto thee, **p** to meet thy God, O Israel. H3559
Mic 3: 5 mouths, they even **p** war against him. H6942
Mal 3: 1 and he shall **p** the way before me: H6437
Mt 3: 3 in the wilderness, **P** ye the way of the *G2090*
11:10 face, which shall **p** thy way before thee. *G2680*
26:17 that we **p** for thee to eat the passover? *G2090*
Mk 1: 2 face, which shall **p** thy way before thee. *G2680*
3 in the wilderness, **P** ye the way of the *G2090*
14:12 **p** that thou mayest eat the passover? *G2090*
Lk 1:76 the face of the Lord to **p** his ways; *G2090*
3: 4 in the wilderness, **P** ye the way of the *G2090*
7:27 face, which shall **p** thy way before thee. *G2680*
22: 8 and **p** us the passover, that we may eat. *G2090*
9 unto him, Where wilt thou that we **p**? *G2090*
Jn 14: 2 have told you. I go to **p** a place for you. *G2090*
3 And if I go and **p** a place for you, I will *G2090*
1Co 14: 8 who shall **p** himself to the battle? *G3903*
Phlm 22 But withal **p** me also a lodging: for I *G2090*

PREPARED
Gen 24:31 **p** the house, and room for the camels. H6437
27:17 had **p**, into the hand of her son Jacob. H6213
Ex 12:39 had they **p** for themselves any victual. H6213
23:20 bring thee into the place which I have **p**. H3559
Nu 21:27 let the city of Sihon be built and **p**: H3559
23: 4 unto him, I have **p** seven altars, and I H6186
Jos 4: 4 men, whom he had **p** of the children of H3559
13 About forty thousand **p** for war passed H2502
2Sa 15: 1 this, that Absalom **p** him chariots and H6213
1Ki 1: 5 will be king: and he **p** him chariots and H6213
5:18 **p** timber and stones to build the house. H3559
6:19 And the oracle he **p** in the house H3559
2Ki 6:23 And he **p** great provision for them: and H3739
1Ch 12:39 for their brethren had **p** for them. H3559
15: 1 city of David, and **p** a place for the ark H3559
3 unto his place, which he had **p** for it. H3559
12 unto *the place that* I have **p** for it. H3559
22: 3 And David **p** iron in abundance for the H3559
5 David **p** abundantly before his death. H3559
14 Now, behold, in my trouble I have **p** for H3559
14 have I **p**; and thou mayest add thereto. H3559
29: 2 Now I have **p** with all my might for the H3559
3 all that I have **p** for the holy house, H3559
16 store that we have **p** to build thee an H3559
2Ch 1: 4 *which* David had **p** for it: for he had H3559
3: 1 that David had **p** in the threshingfloor H3559
8:16 Now all the work of Solomon was **p** H3559
12:14 And he did evil, because he **p** not his H3559
16:14 kinds *of spices* **p** by the apothecaries' H7543
17:18 thousand ready **p** for the war. H2502
19: 3 and hast **p** thine heart to seek God. H3559
20:33 people had not **p** their hearts unto the H3559
26:14 And Uzziah **p** for them throughout all H3559
27: 6 he **p** his ways before the LORD his God. H3559
29:19 have we **p** and sanctified, and, H3559
36 that God had **p** the people: for the thing H3559
31:11 house of the LORD; and they **p** *them*, H3559
35:10 So the service was **p**, and the priests H3559
14 the Levites **p** for themselves, and H3559
15 their brethren the Levites **p** for them. H3559
16 So all the service of the LORD was **p** the H3559
20 After all this, when Josiah had **p** the H3559
Ezr 7:10 For Ezra had **p** his heart to seek the law H3559
Neh 5:18 Now *that* which was **p** *for me* daily *was* H6213
18 also fowls were **p** for me, and once in H6213
8:10 whom nothing is **p**: for *this* day *is* holy H3559
13: 5 And he had **p** for him a great chamber, H6213
Est 5: 4 unto the banquet that I have **p** for him. H6213
5 came to the banquet that Esther had **p**. H6213
12 that she had **p** but myself; and to H6213
Est 6: 4 on the gallows that he had **p** for him. H3559
14 unto the banquet that Esther had **p**. H6213
7:10 that he had **p** for Mordecai. Then H3559
Job 28:27 Then did he see it, and declare it; he **p** H3559
29: 7 the city, *when* I **p** my seat in the street! H3559
Ps 7:13 He hath also **p** for him the instruments H3559
9: 7 he hath **p** his throne for judgment. H3559
57: 6 They have **p** a net for my steps; my soul H3559
68:10 hast **p** of thy goodness for the poor. H3559
74:16 thine: thou hast **p** the light and the sun. H3559
103:19 The LORD hath **p** his throne in the H3559
Prv 8:27 When he **p** the heavens, I *was* there: H3559
19:29 Judgments are **p** for scorners, and H3559
21:31 The horse *is* **p** against the day of battle: H3559
Isa 30:33 for the king it is **p**; he hath made *it* deep H3559
64: 4 he hath **p** for him that waiteth for him. H6213
Ezk 23:41 bed, and a table **p** before it, whereupon H6186
28:13 of thy pipes was **p** in thee in the day H3559
38: 7 Be thou **p**, and prepare for thyself, thou, H3559
Dan 2: 9 for you: for ye have **p** lying and corrupt H2164
Hos 2: 8 silver and gold, *which* they **p** for Baal. H6213
6: 3 his going forth is **p** as the morning; and H3559
Jna 1:17 Now the LORD had **p** a great fish to H4487
4: 6 And the LORD God **p** a gourd, and H4487
7 But God **p** a worm when the morning H4487
8 did arise, that God **p** a vehement east H4487
Nah 2: 5 wall thereof, and the defence shall be **p**. H3559
Zep 1: 7 **p** a sacrifice, he hath bid his guests. H3559
Mt 20:23 *to them* for whom it is **p** of my Father. *G2090*
22: 4 Behold, I have **p** my dinner: my oxen *G2090*
25:34 inherit the kingdom **p** for you from the *G2090*
41 fire, **p** for the devil and his angels: *G2090*
Mk 10:40 *shall be given to them* for whom it is **p**. *G2090*
14:15 *and* **p**: there make ready for us. *G2092*
Lk 1:17 to make ready a people **p** for the Lord. *G2680*
2:31 Which thou hast **p** before the face of all *G2090*
12:47 knew his lord's will, and **p** not *himself*, *G2090*
23:56 And they returned, and **p** spices and *G2090*
24: 1 had **p**, and certain *others* with them. *G2090*
Ro 9:23 which he had afore **p** unto glory, *G4282*
1Co 2: 9 God hath **p** for them that love him. *G2090*
2Ti 2:21 use, *and* **p** unto every good work. *G2090*
Heb 10: 5 not, but a body hast thou **p** me: *G2675*
11: 7 moved with fear, **p** an ark to the saving *G2680*
16 their God: for he hath **p** for them a city. *G2090*
Rev 8: 6 seven trumpets **p** themselves to sound. *G2090*
9: 7 like unto horses **p** unto battle; and on *G2090*
15 which were **p** for an hour, and a day, *G2090*
12: 6 she hath a place **p** of God, that they *G2090*
16:12 way of the kings of the east might be **p**. *G2090*
21: 2 **p** as a bride adorned for her husband. *G2090*

PREPAREDST
Ps 80: 9 Thou **p** *room* before it, and didst cause H6437

PREPAREST
Nu 15: 8 And when thou **p** a bullock *for* a burnt H6213
Ps 23: 5 Thou **p** a table before me in the H6186
65: 9 is full of water: thou **p** them corn, when H3559

PREPARETH
2Ch 30:19 *That* **p** his heart to seek God, the LORD H3559
Job 15:35 forth vanity, and their belly **p** deceit. H3559
Ps 147: 8 with clouds, who **p** rain for the earth, H3559

PREPARING
Neh 13: 7 did for Tobiah, in **p** him a chamber in H6213
1Pt 3:20 the ark was a **p**, wherein few, that is, *G2680*

PRESBYTERY
1Ti 4:14 with the laying on of the hands of the **p**. *G4244*

PRESCRIBED
Isa 10: 1 write grievousness *which* they have **p**; H3789

PRESCRIBING
Ezr 7:22 of oil, and salt without **p** *how much*. H3792

PRESENCE
Gen 3: 8 from the **p** of the LORD God amongst H6440
4:16 And Cain went out from the **p** of the H6440
16:12 shall dwell in the **p** of all his brethren. H6440
23:11 I give it thee; in the **p** of the sons of my H5869
18 a possession in the **p** of the children of H5869
25:18 *and* he died in the **p** of all his brethren. H6440
27:30 gone out from the **p** of Isaac his father, H6440
41:46 went out from the **p** of Pharaoh, and H6440
45: 3 him; for they were troubled at his **p**. H6440
47:15 we die in thy **p**? for the money faileth. H5048

Ex 10:11 they were driven out from Pharaoh's **p**. H6440
33:14 And he said, My **p** shall go *with thee,* H6440
15 And he said unto him, If thy **p** go not H6440
35:20 of Israel departed from the **p** of Moses. H6440
Lev 22: 3 be cut off from my **p**: I *am* the LORD. H6440
Nu 20: 6 And Moses and Aaron went from the **p** H6440
Dt 25: 9 unto him in the **p** of the elders, and H5869
Jos 4:11 and the priests, in the **p** of the people. H6440
8:32 wrote in the **p** of the children of Israel. H6440
1Sa 18:11 And David avoided out of his **p** twice. H6440
19: 7 and he was in his **p**, as in times past. H6440
10 away out of Saul's **p**, and he smote the H6440
21:15 **p**? shall this *fellow* come into my house? H6440
2Sa 16:19 *I* not *serve* in the **p** of his son? as I have H6440
19 father's **p**, so will I be in thy presence. H6440
19 father's presence, so will I be in thy **p**. H6440
24: 4 host went out from the **p** of the king, to H6440
1Ki 1:28 the king's **p**, and stood before the king. H6440
8:22 altar of the LORD in the **p** of all the H5048
12: 2 was fled from the **p** of king Solomon, H6440
21:13 Naboth, in the **p** of the people, saying, H5048
2Ki 3:14 that I regard the **p** of Jehoshaphat the H6440
5:27 out from his **p** a leper *as white* as snow. H6440
13:23 neither cast he them from his **p** as yet. H6440
24:20 cast them out from his **p**, that Zedekiah H6440
25:19 were in the king's **p**, which were found H6440
1Ch 16:27 Glory and honour *are* in his **p**; strength H6440
33 sing out at the **p** of the LORD, because H6440
24:31 of Aaron in the **p** of David the king, H6440
2Ch 6:12 altar of the LORD in the **p** of all the H5048
9:23 earth sought the **p** of Solomon, to hear H6440
10: 2 he had fled from the **p** of Solomon the H6440
20: 9 house, and in thy **p**, (for thy name *is* in H6440
34: 4 of Baalim in his **p**; and the images, that H6440
Neh 2: 1 I had not been *beforetime* sad in his **p**. H6440
Est 1:10 served in the **p** of Ahasuerus the king, H6440
8:15 And Mordecai went out from the **p** of H6440
Job 1:12 went forth from the **p** of the LORD. H6440
2: 7 So went Satan forth from the **p** of the H6440
23:15 Therefore am I troubled at his **p**: when I H6440
Ps 9: 3 back, they shall fall and perish at thy **p**. H6440
16:11 path of life: in thy **p** *is* fulness of joy; at H6440
17: 2 Let my sentence come forth from thy **p**; H6440
23: 5 before me in the **p** of mine enemies: H5048
31:20 in the secret of thy **p** from the pride of H6440
51:11 Cast me not away from thy **p**; and take H6440
68: 2 *so* let the wicked perish at the **p** of God. H6440
8 dropped at the **p** of God: *even* Sinai H6440
8 at the **p** of God, the God of Israel. H6440
95: 2 Let us come before his **p** with H6440
97: 5 The hills melted like wax at the **p** of the H6440
5 at the **p** of the Lord of the whole earth. H6440
100: 2 come before his **p** with singing. H6440
114: 7 Tremble, thou earth, at the **p** of the H6440
7 the Lord, at the **p** of the God of Jacob; H6440
116:14 LORD now in the **p** of all his people. H5048
18 LORD now in the **p** of all his people, H6440
139: 7 spirit? or whither shall I flee from thy **p**? H6440
140:13 name: the upright shall dwell in thy **p**. H6440
Prv 14: 7 Go from the **p** of a foolish man, when H5048
17:18 becometh surety in the **p** of his friend. H6440
25: 6 Put not forth thyself in the **p** of the H6440
7 put lower in the **p** of the prince whom H6440
Isa 1: 7 devour it in your **p**, and *it is* desolate, as H5048
19: 1 shall be moved at his **p**, and the heart of H6440
63: 9 the angel of his **p** saved them: in his H6440
64: 1 mountains might flow down at thy **p**, H6440
2 *that* the nations may tremble at thy **p**! H6440
3 the mountains flowed down at thy **p**. H6440
Jer 4:26 **p** of the LORD, *and* by his fierce anger. H6440
5:22 not tremble at my **p**, which have placed H6440
23:39 your fathers, *and cast you* out of my **p**: H6440
28: 1 the LORD, in the **p** of the priests and of H5869
5 Hananiah in the **p** of the priests, and in H5869
5 priests, and in the **p** of all the people H5869
11 And Hananiah spake in the **p** of all the H5869
32:12 *son,* and in the **p** of the witnesses that H5869
52: 3 cast them out from his **p**, that Zedekiah H6440
Ezk 38:20 shall shake at my **p**, and the mountains H6440
Dan 2:27 Daniel answered in the **p** of the king, H6925
Jna 1: 3 Tarshish from the **p** of the LORD, and H6440
3 unto Tarshish from the **p** of the LORD. H6440
10 that he fled from the **p** of the LORD, H6440
Nah 1: 5 is burned at his **p**, yea, the world, and H6440
Zep 1: 7 Hold thy peace at the **p** of the Lord H6440
Lk 1:19 that stand in the **p** of God; and am sent *G1799*
13:26 **p**, and thou hast taught in our streets. *G1799*
14:10 the **p** of them that sit at meat with thee. *G1799*
15:10 there is joy in the **p** of the angels of God *G1799*
Jn 20:30 truly did Jesus in the **p** of his disciples, *G1799*
Act 3:13 denied him in the **p** of Pilate, when he *G4383*
16 this perfect soundness in the **p** of you all. *G561*
19 shall come from the **p** of the Lord; *G4383*
5:41 And they departed from the **p** of the *G4383*
27:35 thanks to God in **p** of them all: and *G1799*
1Co 1:29 That no flesh should glory in his **p**. *G1799*
2Co 10: 1 of Christ, who in **p** *am* base among *G4383*
10 but *his* bodily **p** *is* weak, and *his* speech *G3952*
Php 2:12 not as in my **p** only, but now much *G3952*
1Th 2:17 you for a short time in **p**, not in heart, *G4383*
19 not even ye in the **p** of our Lord Jesus *G1715*
2Th 1: 9 from the **p** of the Lord, and from *G4383*
Heb 9:24 now to appear in the **p** of God for us: *G4383*
Jude 24 the **p** of his glory with exceeding joy, *G2714*
Rev 14:10 brimstone in the **p** of the holy angels, *G1799*
10 holy angels, and in the **p** of the Lamb: *G1799*

PRESENT

Gen 32:13 to his hand a **p** for Esau his brother; H4503
18 Jacob's; it *is* a **p** sent unto my lord H4503
20 him with the **p** that goeth before me, H4503
21 So went the **p** over before him: and H4503
33:10 then receive my **p** at my hand: for H4503
43:11 down the man a **p**, a little balm, and a H4503
15 And the men took that **p**, and they took H4503
25 And they made ready the **p** against H4503
26 brought him the **p** which *was* in their H4503
Ex 34: 2 mount Sinai, and **p** thyself there to me H5324
Lev 14:11 *him* clean shall **p** the man that is to be H5975
16: 7 And he shall take the two goats, and **p** H5975
27: 8 then he shall **p** himself before the H5975
11 he shall **p** the beast before the priest: H5975
Nu 3: 6 Bring the tribe of Levi near, and **p** H5975
Dt 31:14 die: call Joshua, and **p** yourselves in the H3320
Jdg 3:15 sent a **p** unto Eglon the king of Moab. H4503
17 And he brought the **p** unto Eglon king H4503
18 an end to offer the **p**, he sent away the H4503
18 he sent away the people that bare the **p**. H4503
6:18 bring forth my **p**, and set *it* before thee. H4503
1Sa 9: 7 and *there is* not a **p** to bring to the man H8670
10:19 us. Now therefore **p** yourselves before H3320
13:15 **p** with him, about six hundred men. H4672
16 people *that were* **p** with them, abode in H4672
21: 3 bread in mine hand, or what there is **p**. H4672
30:26 saying, Behold a **p** for you of the spoil H1293
2Sa 20: 4 within three days, and be thou here **p**. H5975
1Ki 9:16 a **p** unto his daughter, Solomon's wife. H7964
10:25 And they brought every man his **p**, H4503
15:19 sent unto thee a **p** of silver and gold; H7810
20:27 and were all **p**, and went against them: H3557
2Ki 8: 8 Hazael, Take a **p** in thine hand, and go, H4503
9 him, and took a **p** with him, even of H4503
16: 8 sent *it for* a **p** to the king of Assyria. H7810
17: 4 Egypt, and brought no **p** to the king of H4503
18:31 with me by a **p**, and come out to me, H1293
20:12 sent letters and a **p** unto Hezekiah: for H4503
1Ch 29:17 are **p** here, to offer willingly unto thee. H4672
2Ch 5:11 priests *that were* **p** were sanctified, *and* H4672
9:24 And they brought every man his **p**, H4503
29:29 and all that were **p** with him bowed H4672
30:21 And the children of Israel that were **p** H4672
31: 1 Israel that were **p** went out to the cities H4672
34:32 And he caused all that were **p** in H4672
33 all that were **p** in Israel to serve, *even* H4672
35: 7 for all that were **p**, to the number of H4672
17 And the children of Israel that were **p** H4672
18 **p**, and the inhabitants of Jerusalem. H4672
Ezr 8:25 and all Israel *there* **p**, had offered: H4672
Est 1: 5 the people that were **p** in Shushan the H4672
4:16 all the Jews that are **p** in Shushan, and H4672
Job 1: 6 of God came to **p** themselves before the H3320
2: 1 of God came to **p** themselves before the H3320
1 them to **p** himself before the LORD. H3320
Ps 46: 1 and strength, a very **p** help in trouble. H4672
Isa 18: 7 In that time shall the **p** be brought unto H7862
36:16 with me *by* a **p**, and come out to me: H1293
39: 1 sent letters and a **p** to Hezekiah: for he H4503
Jer 36: 7 It may be they will **p** their supplication H5307
42: 9 me to **p** your supplication before him; H5307
Ezk 27:15 thee *for* a **p** horns of ivory and ebony. H814
Dan 9:18 for we do not **p** our supplications H5307
Hos 10: 6 unto Assyria *for* a **p** to king Jareb: H4503
Lk 2:22 him to Jerusalem, to **p** *him* to the Lord; *G3936*
5:17 power of the Lord was **p** to heal them.
13: 1 There were **p** at that season some that *G3918*
18:30 more in this **p** time, and in the world
Jn 14:25 spoken unto you, being *yet* **p** with you. *G3306*
Act 10:33 are we all here **p** before God, to hear *G3918*
21:18 unto James; and all the elders were **p**. *G3854*
25:24 which are here **p** with us, ye see this *G4840*
28: 2 of the **p** rain, and because of the cold. *G2186*
Ro 7:18 thing: for to will is **p** with me; but *how* *G3873*
21 I would do good, evil is **p** with me. *G3873*
8:18 sufferings of this **p** time *are* not worthy *G3568*
38 nor things **p**, nor things to come, *G1764*
11: 5 Even so then at this **p** time also there is *G3568*
12: 1 of God, that ye **p** your bodies a living *G3936*
1Co 3:22 **p**, or things to come; all are yours; *G1764*
4:11 Even unto this **p** hour we both hunger, *G737*
5: 3 For I verily, as absent in body, but **p** in *G3918*
3 as though I were **p**, *concerning* him that *G3918*
7:26 this is good for the **p** distress, *I say,* *G1764*
15: 6 unto this **p**, but some are fallen asleep. *G737*
2Co 4:14 also by Jesus, and shall **p** *us* with you. *G3936*
5: 8 the body, and to be **p** with the Lord. *G1736*
9 Wherefore we labour, that, whether **p** *G1736*
10: 2 not be bold when I am **p** with that *G3918*
11 *will we be* also in deed when we are **p**. *G3918*
11: 2 may **p** *you as* a chaste virgin to Christ. *G3936*
9 And when I was **p** with you, and *G3918*
13: 2 you, as if I were **p**, the second time; and *G3918*
10 being absent, lest being **p** I should use *G3918*
Gal 1: 4 us from this **p** evil world, according *G1764*
4:18 and not only when I am **p** with you. *G3918*
20 I desire to be **p** with you now, and to *G3918*
Eph 5:27 That he might **p** it to himself a glorious *G3936*
Col 1:22 flesh through death, to **p** you holy and *G3936*
28 **p** every man perfect in Christ Jesus: *G3936*
2Ti 4:10 me, having loved this **p** world, and is *G3568*
Tit 2:12 righteously, and godly, in this **p** world; *G3568*
Heb 9: 9 Which *was* a figure for the time then **p**, *G1764*
12:11 Now no chastening for the **p** seemeth *G3918*
2Pt 1:12 *them,* and be established in the **p** truth. *G3918*
Jude 24 falling, and to **p** *you* faultless before *G2476*

PRESENTED

Gen 46:29 to Goshen, and **p** himself unto him; H7200
47: 2 five men, and **p** them unto Pharaoh. H3322
Lev 2: 8 and when it is **p** unto the priest, he H7126
7:35 in the day *when* he **p** them to minister H7126
9:12 and Aaron's sons **p** unto him the H4672
13 And they **p** the burnt offering unto H4672
18 and Aaron's sons **p** unto him the H4672
16:10 shall be **p** alive before the LORD, H5975
Dt 31:14 Joshua went, and **p** themselves in the H3320
Jos 24: 1 and they **p** themselves before God. H3320
Jdg 6:19 *it* out unto him under the oak, and **p** *it.* H5066
20: 2 the tribes of Israel, **p** themselves in the H3320
1Sa 17:16 and evening, and **p** himself forty days. H3320
Jer 38:26 Then thou shalt say unto them, I **p** my H5307
Ezk 20:28 and there they **p** the provocation of H5414
Mt 2:11 treasures, they **p** unto him gifts; gold, *G4374*
Act 9:41 the saints and widows, **p** her alive. *G3936*
23:33 to the governor, **p** Paul also before him. *G3936*

PRESENTING

Dan 9:20 people Israel, and **p** my supplication H5307

PRESENTLY

1Sa 2:16 fail to burn the fat **p**, and *then* take *as* H3117
Prv 12:16 A fool's wrath is **p** known: but a H3117
Mt 21:19 ever. And **p** the fig tree withered away. *G3916*
26:53 and he shall **p** give me more than *G3936*
Php 2:23 Him therefore I hope to send **p**, so soon *G1824*

PRESENTS

1Sa 10:27 him no **p**. But he held his peace. H4503
1Ki 4:21 they brought **p**, and served Solomon H4503
2Ki 17: 3 became his servant, and gave him **p**. H4503
2Ch 17: 5 to Jehoshaphat **p**; and he had riches H4503
11 Jehoshaphat **p**, and tribute silver; and H4503
32:23 to Jerusalem, and **p** to Hezekiah king of H4030
Ps 68:29 shall kings bring **p** unto thee. H7862
72:10 isles shall bring **p**: the kings of Sheba H4503
76:11 **p** unto him that ought to be feared. H7862
Mic 1:14 Therefore shalt thou give **p** to H7964

PRESERVE

Gen 19:32 him, that we may **p** seed of our father. H2421
34 him, that we may **p** seed of our father. H2421
45: 5 God did send me before you to **p** life. H4241
7 And God sent me before you to **p** you a H7760
Dt 6:24 he might **p** us alive, as *it is* at this day. H2421
Ps 12: 7 **p** them from this generation for ever. H5341
16: 1 **P** me, O God: for in thee do I put my H8104
25:21 Let integrity and uprightness **p** me; for H5341
32: 7 Thou *art* my hiding place; thou shalt **p** H5341

P

Ps 40:11 and thy truth continually **p** me. H5341
41: 2 The LORD will **p** him, and keep him H8104
61: 7 mercy and truth, *which* may **p** him. H5341
64: 1 Hear my voice, O God, in my prayer: **p** H5341
79:11 **p** thou those that are appointed to die; H3498
86: 2 **P** my soul; for I *am* holy: O thou my H8104
121: 7 The LORD shall **p** thee from all evil: he H8104
7 thee from all evil: he shall **p** thy soul. H8104
8 The LORD shall **p** thy going out and H8104
140: 1 evil man: **p** me from the violent man; H5341
4 of the wicked; **p** me from the violent H5341
Prv 2:11 Discretion shall **p** thee, understanding H8104
4: 6 Forsake her not, and she shall **p** thee: H8104
14: 3 but the lips of the wise shall **p** them. H8104
20:28 Mercy and truth **p** the king: and his H5341
22:12 The eyes of the LORD **p** knowledge, H5341
Isa 31: 5 deliver *it; and* passing over he will **p** it. H4422
49: 8 thee: and I will **p** thee, and give thee H5341
Jer 49:11 Leave thy fatherless children, I will **p** H2421
Lk 17:33 whosoever shall lose his life shall **p** it. *G2225*
2Ti 4:18 every evil work, and will **p** *me* unto his *G4982*

PRESERVED
Gen 32:30 seen God face to face, and my life is **p**. H5337
Jos 24:17 in our sight, and **p** us in all the way H8104
1Sa 30:23 us, who hath **p** us, and delivered the H8104
2Sa 8: 6 LORD **p** David whithersoever he went. H3467
14 LORD **p** David whithersoever he went. H3467
1Ch 18: 6 LORD **p** David whithersoever he went. H3467
13 LORD **p** David whithersoever he went. H3467
Job 10:12 and thy visitation hath **p** my spirit. H8104
29: 2 past, as *in* the days *when* God **p** me; H8104
Ps 37:28 saints; they are **p** for ever: but the seed H8104
Isa 49: 6 and to restore the **p** of Israel: I will also H5336
Hos 12:13 of Egypt, and by a prophet was he **p**. H8104
Mt 9:17 wine into new bottles, and both are **p**. *G4933*
Lk 5:38 be put into new bottles; and both are **p**. *G4933*
1Th 5:23 soul and body be **p** blameless unto the *G5083*
Jude 1 and **p** in Jesus Christ, *and* called: *G5083*

PRESERVER
Job 7:20 unto thee, O thou **p** of men? why hast H5341

PRESERVEST
Neh 9: 6 *is* therein, and thou **p** them all; and the H2421
Ps 36: 6 deep: O LORD, thou **p** man and beast. H3467

PRESERVETH
Job 36: 6 He **p** not the life of the wicked: but H2421
Ps 31:23 saints: *for* the LORD **p** the faithful, and H5341
97:10 Ye that love the LORD, hate evil: he **p** H8104
116: 6 The LORD **p** the simple: I was brought H8104
145:20 The LORD **p** all them that love him: but H8104
146: 9 The LORD **p** the strangers; he relieveth H8104
Prv 2: 8 judgment, and **p** the way of his saints. H8104
16:17 evil: he that keepeth his way **p** his soul. H8104

PRESIDENTS
Dan 6: 2 And over these three **p**; of whom Daniel H5632
3 above the **p** and princes, because H5632
4 Then the **p** and princes sought to find H5632
6 Then these **p** and princes assembled H5632
7 All the **p** of the kingdom, the H5632

PRESS
Joel 3:13 get you down; for the **p** is full, the fats H1660
Hag 2:16 out of the **p**, there were *but* twenty. H6333
Mk 2: 4 unto him for the **p**, they uncovered the *G3793*
5:27 the **p** behind, and touched his garment. *G3793*
30 **p**, and said, Who touched my clothes? *G3793*
Lk 8:19 and could not come at him for the **p**. *G3793*
45 throng thee and **p** *thee*, and sayest thou, *G598*
19: 3 the **p**, because he was little of stature. *G3793*
Php 3:14 I **p** toward the mark for the prize of the *G1377*

PRESSED
Gen 19: 3 And he **p** upon them greatly; and they H6484
9 them. And they **p** sore upon the man, H6484
40:11 the grapes, and **p** them into Pharaoh's H7818
Jdg 16:16 And it came to pass, when she **p** him H6693
2Sa 13:25 unto thee. And he **p** him: howbeit he H6555
27 But Absalom **p** him, that he let Amnon H6555
Est 8:14 being hastened and **p** on by the king's H1765
Ezk 23: 3 were their breasts **p**, and there they H4600
Am 2:13 Behold, I am **p** under you, as a cart is H5781
13 you, as a cart is **p** *that is* full of sheaves. H5781
Mk 3:10 that they **p** upon him for to touch *G1968*
Lk 5: 1 that, as the people **p** upon him to hear *G1945*
6:38 good measure, **p** down, and shaken *G4085*
Act 18: 5 Paul was **p** in the spirit, and testified *G4912*
2Co 1: 8 in Asia, that we were **p** out of measure, *G916*

PRESSES
Neh 13:15 treading wine **p** on the sabbath, and H1660
Prv 3:10 thy **p** shall burst out with new wine. H3342
Isa 16:10 no wine in *their* **p**; I have made *their* H3342

PRESSETH
Ps 38: 2 fast in me, and thy hand **p** me sore. H5181
Lk 16:16 is preached, and every man **p** into it. *G971*

PRESSFAT
Hag 2:16 *one* came to the **p** for to draw out fifty H3342

PRESUME
Dt 18:20 But the prophet, which shall **p** to speak H2102
Est 7: 5 is he, that durst **p** in his heart to do so? H4390

PRESUMED
Nu 14:44 But they **p** to go up unto the hill top: H6075

PRESUMPTUOUS
Ps 19:13 Keep back thy servant also from **p** *sins*; H2086
2Pt 2:10 government. **P** *are they*, selfwilled, *G5113*

PRESUMPTUOUSLY
Ex 21:14 But if a man come **p** upon his H2102
Nu 15:30 But the soul that doeth *ought* **p**, H3027
Dt 1:43 the LORD, and went **p** up into the hill. H2102
17:12 And the man that will do **p**, and will not H2087
13 shall hear, and fear, and do no more **p**. H2102
18:22 it **p**: thou shalt not be afraid of him. H2087

PRETENCE
Mt 23:14 houses, and for a **p** make long prayer: *G4392*
Mk 12:40 houses, and for a **p** make long prayers: *G4392*
Php 1:18 way, whether in **p**, or in truth, Christ is *G4392*

PRETORIUM See PRAETORIUM.

PREVAIL
Gen 7:20 Fifteen cubits upward did the waters **p**; H1396
Nu 22: 6 I shall **p**, *that* we may smite them, H3201
Jdg 16: 5 *means* we may **p** against him, that we H3201
1Sa 2: 9 for by strength shall no man **p**. H1396
17: 9 servants: but if I **p** against him, and kill H3201
26:25 and also shalt still **p**. So David went on H3201
1Ki 22:22 *him,* and **p** also: go forth, and do so. H3201
2Ch 14:11 *art* our God; let not man **p** against thee. H6113
18:21 shalt also **p**: go out, and do *even* so. H3201
Est 6:13 fall, thou shalt not **p** against him, but H3201
Job 15:24 afraid; they shall **p** against him, as a H8630
18: 9 *and* the robber shall **p** against him. H2388
Ps 9:19 Arise, O LORD; let not man **p**: let the H5810
12: 4 our tongue will we **p**; our lips *are* our H1396
65: 3 Iniquities **p** against me: *as for* our H1396
Ecc 4:12 And if one **p** against him, two shall H8630
Isa 7: 1 against it, but could not **p** against it. H3898
16:12 sanctuary to pray; but he shall not **p**. H3201
42:13 roar; he shall **p** against his enemies. H1396
47:12 be able to profit, if so be thou mayest **p**. H6206
Jer 1:19 but they shall not **p** against thee; for I H3201
5:22 yet can they not **p**; though they roar, yet H3201
15:20 but they shall not **p** against thee: for I H3201
20:10 and we shall **p** against him, and we H3201
11 and they shall not **p**: they shall be H3201
Dan 11: 7 shall deal against them, and shall **p**: H2388
Mt 16:18 the gates of hell shall not **p** against it. *G2720*
27:24 When Pilate saw that he could **p** *G5623*
Jn 12:19 ye how ye **p** nothing? behold, the *G5623*

PREVAILED
Gen 7:18 And the waters **p**, and were increased H1396
19 And the waters **p** exceedingly upon the H1396
24 And the waters **p** upon the earth an H1396
30: 8 **p**: and she called his name Naphtali. H3201
32:25 And when he saw that he **p** not against H3201
28 with God and with men, and hast **p**. H3201
47:20 the famine **p** over them: so the land H2388
49:26 The blessings of thy father have **p** H1396
Ex 17:11 his hand, that Israel **p**: and when he let H1396
11 when he let down his hand, Amalek **p**. H1396
Jdg 1:35 **p**, so that they became tributaries. H3513
3:10 hand **p** against Chushan-rishathaim. H5810
4:24 prospered, and **p** against Jabin the H7186
6: 2 And the hand of Midian **p** against H5810
1Sa 17:50 So David **p** over the Philistine with a H2388
2Sa 11:23 Surely the men **p** against us, and came H1396
2Sa 24: 4 Notwithstanding the king's word **p** H2388
1Ki 16:22 But the people that followed Omri **p** H2388
2Ki 25: 3 month the famine **p** in the city, and H2388
1Ch 5: 2 For Judah **p** above his brethren, and of H1396
21: 4 Nevertheless the king's word **p** against H2388
2Ch 8: 3 to Hamath-zobah, and **p** against it. H2388
13:18 children of Judah **p**, because they relied H553
27: 5 Ammonites, and **p** against them. And H2388
Ps 13: 4 Lest mine enemy say, I have **p** against H3201
129: 2 youth: yet they have not **p** against me. H3201
Jer 20: 7 than I, and hast **p**: I am in derision H3201
38:22 thee on, and have **p** against thee: thy H3201
Lam 1:16 are desolate, because the enemy **p**. H1396
Dan 7:21 with the saints, and **p** against them; H3202
Hos 12: 4 the angel, and **p**: he wept, and made H3201
Oba 7 deceived thee, *and* **p** against thee; *they* H3201
Lk 23:23 of them and of the chief priests **p**. *G2729*
Act 19:16 them, and **p** against them, so that *G2480*
20 mightily grew the word of God and **p**. *G2480*
Rev 5: 5 of David, hath **p** to open the book, and *G3528*
12: 8 And **p** not; neither was their place *G2480*

PREVAILEST
Job 14:20 Thou **p** for ever against him, and he H8630

PREVAILETH
Lam 1:13 my bones, and it **p** against them: he H7287

PREVENT
Job 3:12 Why did the knees **p** me? or why the H6923
Ps 59:10 The God of my mercy shall **p** me: God H6923
79: 8 **p** us: for we are brought very low. H6923
88:13 in the morning shall my prayer **p** thee. H6923
119:148 Mine eyes **p** the *night* watches, that I H6923
Am 9:10 The evil shall not overtake nor **p** us. H6923
1Th 4:15 Lord shall not **p** them which are asleep. *G5348*

PREVENTED
2Sa 22: 6 me about; the snares of death **p** me; H6923
19 They **p** me in the day of my calamity: H6923
Job 30:27 rested not: the days of affliction **p** me. H6923
41:11 Who hath **p** me, that I should repay H6923
Ps 18: 5 me about: the snares of death **p** me. H6923
18 They **p** me in the day of my calamity: H6923
119:147 I **p** the dawning of the morning, and H6923
Isa 21:14 they **p** with their bread him that fled. H6923
Mt 17:25 the house, Jesus **p** him, saying, What *G4399*

PREVENTEST
Ps 21: 3 For thou **p** him with the blessings of H6923

PREY
Gen 49: 9 Judah *is* a lion's whelp: from the **p**, my H2964
27 **p**, and at night he shall divide the spoil. H5706
Nu 14: 3 should be a **p**? were it not better for H957
31 ye said should be a **p**, them will I bring H957
23:24 the **p**, and drink the blood of the slain. H2964
31:11 and all the **p**, *both* of men and of beasts. H4455
12 captives, and the **p**, and the spoil, unto H4455
26 Take the sum of the **p** that was taken, H4455
27 And divide the **p** into two parts; H4455
32 And the booty, *being* the rest of the **p** H957
Dt 1:39 ye said should be a **p**, and your children, H957
2:35 Only the cattle we took for a **p** unto H962
3: 7 of the cities, we took for a **p** to ourselves. H962
Jos 8: 2 shall ye take for a **p** unto yourselves: lay H962
27 city Israel took for a **p** unto themselves, H962
11:14 of Israel took for a **p** unto themselves; H962
Jdg 5:30 they *not* divided the **p**; to every man a H7998
30 *or* two; to Sisera a **p** of divers colours, a H7998
30 divers colours, a **p** of divers colours of H7998
8:24 man the earrings of his **p**. (For they had H7998
25 therein every man the earrings of his **p**. H7998
2Ki 21:14 a **p** and a spoil to all their enemies; H957
Neh 4: 4 give them for a **p** in the land of captivity: H961
Est 3:13 and *to take* the spoil of them for a **p**. H962
8:11 and *to take* the spoil of them for a **p**, H962
9:15 but on the **p** they laid not their hand. H961
16 but they laid not their hands on the **p**, H961
Job 4:11 The old lion perisheth for lack of **p**, and H2964
9:26 ships: as the eagle *that* hasteth to the **p**. H400
24: 5 betimes for a **p**: the wilderness *yieldeth* H2964
38:39 Wilt thou hunt the **p** for the lion? or fill H2964
39:29 From thence she seeketh the **p**, *and* her H400
Ps 17:12 Like as a lion *that* is greedy of his **p**, H2963
76: 4 *and* excellent than the mountains of **p**. H2964
104:21 The young lions roar after their **p**, and H2964
124: 6 hath not given us *as* a **p** to their teeth. H2964
Prv 23:28 She also lieth in wait as *for* a **p**, and H2863

Isa 5:29 lay hold of the p, and shall carry it away H2964
10: 2 p, and that they may rob the fatherless! H7998
6 and to take the p, and to tread them H957
31: 4 roaring on his p, when a multitude of H2964
33:23 the sail: then is the p of a great spoil H5706
23 a great spoil divided; the lame take the p. H957
42:22 they are for a p, and none delivereth; H957
49:24 Shall the p be taken from the mighty, H4455
25 away, and the p of the terrible shall H4455
59:15 maketh himself a p: and the LORD saw H7997
Jer 21: 9 and his life shall be unto him for a p. H7998
30:16 all that p upon thee will I give for a prey. H962
16 all that prey upon thee will I give for a p. H957
38: 2 shall have his life for a p, and shall live. H7998
39:18 life shall be for a p unto thee: because H7998
45: 5 for a p in all places whither thou goest. H7998
Ezk 7:21 the strangers for a p, and to the wicked of H957
19: 3 learned to catch the p; it devoured men. H2964
6 to catch the p, and devoured men. H2964
22:25 lion ravening the p; they have devoured H2964
27 ravening the p, to shed blood, and to H2964
26:12 thy riches, and make a p of thy H962
29:19 p; and it shall be the wages for his army. H957
34: 8 my flock became a p, and my flock H957
22 shall no more be a p; and I will judge H957
28 And they shall no more be a p to the H957
36: 4 which became a p and derision to the H957
5 despiteful minds, to cast it out for a p. H957
38:12 To take a spoil, and to take a p; to turn H957
13 company to take a p? to carry away silver H957
Dan 11:24 among them the p, and spoil, and riches: H961
Am 3: 4 when he hath no p? will a young lion cry H2964
Nah 2:12 holes with p, and his dens with ravin. H2964
13 I will cut off thy p from the earth, and H2964
3: 1 lies and robbery; the p departeth not; H2964
Zep 3: 8 I rise up to the p: for my determination H5706

PRICE
Lev 25:16 thou shalt increase the p thereof, and H4736
16 shalt diminish the p of it: for according H4736
50 of jubile: and the p of his sale shall be H3701
51 shall give again the p of his redemption
52 give him again the p of his redemption.
Dt 23:18 of a whore, or the p of a dog, into the H4242
2Sa 24:24 buy it of thee at a p: neither will I offer H4242
1Ki 10:28 received the linen yarn at a p. H4242
1Ch 21:22 it me for the full p: that the plague may H3701
24 buy it for the full p: for I will not take H3701
2Ch 1:16 received the linen yarn at a p. H4242
Job 28:13 Man knoweth not the p thereof; neither H6187
15 silver be weighed for the p thereof. H4242
18 for the p of wisdom is above rubies. H4901
Ps 44:12 dost not increase thy wealth by their p. H4242
Prv 17:16 Wherefore is there a p in the hand of a H4242
27:26 and the goats are the p of the field. H4242
31:10 woman? for her p is far above rubies. H4377
Isa 45:13 p nor reward, saith the LORD of hosts. H4242
55: 1 and milk without money and without p. H4242
Jer 15:13 the spoil without p, and that for all thy H4242
Zec 11:12 good, give me my p; and if not, forbear. H7939
12 weighed for my p thirty pieces of silver. H7939
13 potter: a goodly p that I was prised at H3366
Mt 13:46 one pearl of great p, went and sold all G4186
27: 6 treasury, because it is the p of blood. G5092
9 of silver, the p of him that was valued, G5092
Act 5: 2 And kept back part of the p, his wife G5092
3 to keep back part of the p of the land? G5092
19:19 they counted the p of them, and found G5092
1Co 6:20 For ye are bought with a p: therefore G5092
7:23 Ye are bought with a p; be not ye the G5092
1Pt 3: 4 which is in the sight of God of great p. G4185

PRICED See PRISED.

PRICES
Act 4:34 the p of the things that were sold, G5092

PRICKED
Ps 73:21 was grieved, and I was p in my reins. H8150
Act 2:37 Now when they heard this, they were p G2660

PRICKING
Ezk 28:24 And there shall be no more a p brier H3992

PRICKS
Nu 33:55 of them shall be p in your eyes, and H7899
Act 9: 5 it is hard for thee to kick against the p. G2759
26:14 it is hard for thee to kick against the p. G2759

PRIDE
Lev 26:19 And I will break the p of your power; H1347
1Sa 17:28 I know thy p, and the naughtiness H2087
2Ch 32:26 himself for the p of his heart, both he H1363
Job 33:17 his purpose, and hide p from man. H1466
35:12 answer, because of the p of evil men. H1347
41:15 His scales are his p, shut up together as H1346
34 he is a king over all the children of p. H7830
Ps 10: 2 The wicked in his p doth persecute the H1346
4 The wicked, through the p of his H1363
31:20 presence from the p of man: thou shalt H7407
36:11 Let not the foot of p come against me, H1346
59:12 be taken in their p: and for cursing and
73: 6 Therefore p compasseth them about as H1346
Prv 8:13 The fear of the LORD is to hate evil: p, H1344
11: 2 When p cometh, then cometh shame: H2087
13:10 Only by p cometh contention: but with H2087
14: 3 In the mouth of the foolish is a rod of p: H1346
16:18 P goeth before destruction, and an H1347
29:23 A man's p shall bring him low: but H1346
Isa 9: 9 that say in the p and stoutness of heart, H1346
16: 6 We have heard of the p of Moab; he is H1347
6 and his p, and his wrath: but his H1347
23: 9 it, to stain the p of all glory, and to H1347
25:11 bring down their p together with the H1346
28: 1 Woe to the crown of p, to the drunkards H1348
3 The crown of p, the drunkards of H1348
Jer 13: 9 will I mar the p of Judah, and the great H1347
9 of Judah, and the great p of Jerusalem. H1347
17 places for your p; and mine eye shall H1466
48:29 We have heard the p of Moab, (he is H1347
29 his p, and the haughtiness of his heart. H1346
49:16 thee, and the p of thine heart, O thou H2087
Ezk 7:10 rod hath blossomed, p hath budded. H2087
16:49 of thy sister Sodom, p, fulness of bread, H1347
56 by thy mouth in the day of thy p, H1347
30: 6 shall fall; and the p of her power shall H1347
Dan 4:37 those that walk in p he is able to abase. H1467
5:20 mind hardened in p, he was deposed H2103
Hos 5: 5 And the p of Israel doth testify to his H1347
7:10 And the p of Israel testifieth to his face: H1347
Oba 3 The p of thine heart hath deceived H2087
Zep 2:10 This shall they have for their p, because H1347
3:11 that rejoice in thy p, and thou shalt no H1346
Zec 9: 6 I will cut off the p of the Philistines. H1347
10:11 dry up: and the p of Assyria shall be H1347
11: 3 lions; for the p of Jordan is spoiled. H1347
Mk 7:22 an evil eye, blasphemy, p, foolishness: G5243
1Ti 3: 6 Not a novice, lest being lifted up with p G5187
1Jn 2:16 of the eyes, and the p of life, is not of the G212

PRIEST
Gen 14:18 and he was the p of the most high God. H3548
41:45 of Poti-pherah p of On. And Joseph H3548
50 of Poti-pherah p of On bare unto him. H3548
46:20 of Poti-pherah p of On bare unto him. H3548
Ex 2:16 Now the p of Midian had seven H3548
3: 1 father in law, the p of Midian: and he H3548
18: 1 When Jethro, the p of Midian, Moses' H3548
29:30 And that son that is p in his stead shall H3548
31:10 for Aaron the p, and the garments of H3548
35:19 for Aaron the p, and the garments of H3548
38:21 hand of Ithamar, son to Aaron the p. H3548
39:41 garments for Aaron the p, and his sons' H3548
Lev 1: 7 And the sons of Aaron the p shall put H3548
9 in water: and the p shall burn all on the H3548
12 and his fat: and the p shall lay them in H3548
13 water: and the p shall bring it all, and H3548
15 And the p shall bring it unto the altar, H3548
17 it asunder: and the p shall burn it upon H3548
2: 2 thereof; and the p shall burn the H3548
8 the p, he shall bring it unto the altar. H3548
9 And the p shall take from the meat H3548
16 And the p shall burn the memorial of H3548
3:11 And the p shall burn it upon the altar: H3548
16 And the p shall burn them upon the H3548
4: 3 If the p that is anointed do sin H3548
5 And the p that is anointed shall take of H3548
6 And the p shall dip his finger in the H3548
7 And the p shall put some of the blood H3548
10 offerings: and the p shall burn them H3548
16 And the p that is anointed shall bring H3548
17 And the p shall dip his finger in some H3548
20 do with this: and the p shall make an H3548
25 And the p shall take of the blood of the H3548
26 offerings: and the p shall make an H3548
30 And the p shall take of the blood H3548
31 offerings; and the p shall burn it upon H3548
31 the LORD; and the p shall make an H3548
Lev 4:34 And the p shall take of the blood of the H3548
35 offerings; and the p shall burn them H3548
35 the LORD; and the p shall make an H3548
5: 6 sin offering; and the p shall make an H3548
8 And he shall bring them unto the p, H3548
10 the manner: and the p shall make an H3548
12 Then shall he bring it to the p, and the H3548
12 to the priest, and the p shall take his H3548
13 And the p shall make an atonement for H3548
16 give it unto the p: and the priest shall H3548
16 the priest: and the p shall make an H3548
18 offering, unto the p: and the priest shall H3548
18 the priest: and the p shall make an H3548
6: 6 for a trespass offering, unto the p: H3548
7 And the p shall make an atonement for H3548
10 And the p shall put on his linen H3548
12 put out: and the p shall burn wood on H3548
22 And the p of his sons that is anointed H3548
23 For every meat offering for the p shall H3548
26 The p that offereth it for sin shall eat it: H3548
7: 5 And the p shall burn them upon the H3548
7 one law for them: the p that maketh H3548
8 And the p that offereth any man's H3548
8 burnt offering, even the p shall have to H3548
31 And the p shall burn the fat upon the H3548
32 ye give unto the p for an heave offering H3548
34 unto Aaron the p and unto his sons by H3548
12: 6 of the congregation, unto the p: H3548
8 sin offering: and the p shall make an H3548
13: 2 p, or unto one of his sons the priests: H3548
3 And the p shall look on the plague in H3548
3 of leprosy: and the p shall look on him, H3548
4 white; then the p shall shut up him that H3548
5 And the p shall look on him the H3548
5 p shall shut him up seven days more: H3548
6 And the p shall look on him again the H3548
6 in the skin, the p shall pronounce him H3548
7 been seen of the p for his cleansing, he H3548
7 he shall be seen of the p again: H3548
8 And if the p see that, behold, the scab H3548
8 in the skin, then the p shall pronounce H3548
9 then he shall be brought unto the p; H3548
10 And the p shall see him: and, behold, if H3548
11 of his flesh, and the p shall pronounce H3548
12 to his foot, wheresoever the p looketh; H3548
13 Then the p shall consider: and, behold, H3548
15 And the p shall see the raw flesh, and H3548
16 unto white, he shall come unto the p; H3548
17 And the p shall see him: and, behold, if H3548
17 white; then the p shall pronounce him H3548
19 reddish, and it be shewed to the p; H3548
20 And if, when the p seeth it, behold, it be H3548
20 be turned white; the p shall pronounce H3548
21 But if the p look on it, and, behold, H3548
21 the p shall shut him up seven days: H3548
22 in the skin, then the p shall pronounce H3548
23 and the p shall pronounce him clean. H3548
25 Then the p shall look upon it: and, H3548
25 wherefore the p shall pronounce him H3548
26 But if the p look on it, and, behold, H3548
26 the p shall shut him up seven days: H3548
27 And the p shall look upon him the H3548
27 in the skin, then the p shall pronounce H3548
28 the burning, and the p shall pronounce H3548
30 Then the p shall see the plague: and, H3548
30 thin hair; then the p shall pronounce H3548
31 And if the p look on the plague of the H3548
31 hair in it; then the p shall shut up him H3548
32 And in the seventh day the p shall look H3548
33 not shave; and the p shall shut up him H3548
34 And in the seventh day the p shall look H3548
34 the skin; then the p shall pronounce H3548
36 Then the p shall look on him: and, H3548
36 in the skin, the p shall not seek for H3548
37 and the p shall pronounce him clean. H3548
39 Then the p shall look: and, behold, if H3548
43 Then the p shall look upon it: and, H3548
44 he is unclean: the p shall pronounce H3548
49 leprosy, and shall be shewed unto the p: H3548
50 And the p shall look upon the plague, H3548
53 And if the p shall look, and, behold, the H3548
54 Then the p shall command that they H3548
55 And the p shall look on the plague, H3548
56 And if the p look, and, behold, the H3548
14: 2 He shall be brought unto the p: H3548
3 And the p shall go forth out of the H3548
3 of the camp; and the p shall look, and, H3548
4 Then shall the p command to take for H3548
5 And the p shall command that one of H3548

Lev 14:11 And the **p** that maketh *him* clean shall H3548
12 And the **p** shall take one he lamb, and H3548
14 And the **p** shall take *some* of the blood H3548
14 offering, and the **p** shall put *it* upon the H3548
15 And the **p** shall take *some* of the log of H3548
16 And the **p** shall dip his right finger in H3548
17 his hand shall the **p** put upon the tip of H3548
18 be cleansed: and the **p** shall make an H3548
19 And the **p** shall offer the sin offering, H3548
20 And the **p** shall offer the burnt offering H3548
20 upon the altar: and the **p** shall make an H3548
23 cleansing unto the **p**, unto the door of H3548
24 And the **p** shall take the lamb of the H3548
24 log of oil, and the **p** shall wave them *for* H3548
25 offering, and the **p** shall take *some* of H3548
26 And the **p** shall pour of the oil into the H3548
27 And the **p** shall sprinkle with his right H3548
28 And the **p** shall put of the oil that *is* in H3548
31 meat offering: and the **p** shall make an H3548
35 come and tell the **p**, saying, It seemeth H3548
36 Then the **p** shall command that they H3548
36 house, before the **p** go *into it* to see the H3548
36 the **p** shall go in to see the house: H3548
38 Then the **p** shall go out of the house to H3548
39 And the **p** shall come again the seventh H3548
40 Then the **p** shall command that they H3548
44 Then the **p** shall come and look, and, H3548
48 And if the **p** shall come in, and look H3548
48 then the **p** shall pronounce the H3548
15:14 congregation, and give them unto the **p**: H3548
15 And the **p** shall offer them, the one *for* H3548
15 burnt offering; and the **p** shall make an H3548
29 them unto the **p**, to the door of the H3548
30 And the **p** shall offer the one *for* a sin H3548
30 burnt offering; and the **p** shall make an H3548
16:30 For on that day shall *the p* make an
32 And the **p**, whom he shall anoint, and H3548
17: 5 unto the **p**, and offer them *for* peace H3548
6 And the **p** shall sprinkle the blood upon H3548
19:22 And the **p** shall make an atonement for H3548
21: 9 And the daughter of any **p**, if she H3548
10 And *he that is* the high **p** among his H3548
21 seed of Aaron the **p** shall come nigh to H3548
22:10 thing: a sojourner of the **p**, or an hired H3548
11 But if the **p** buy *any* soul with his H3548
14 give *it* unto the **p** with the holy thing. H3548
23:10 firstfruits of your harvest unto the **p**: H3548
11 after the sabbath the **p** shall wave it. H3548
20 And the **p** shall wave them with the H3548
20 they shall be holy to the LORD for the **p**. H3548
27: 8 himself before the **p**, and the priest H3548
8 the priest, and the **p** shall value him; H3548
8 that vowed shall the **p** value him. H3548
11 he shall present the beast before the **p**: H3548
12 And the **p** shall value it, whether it be H3548
12 valuest it, *who art* the **p**, so shall it be. H3548
14 the LORD, then the **p** shall estimate it, H3548
14 the **p** shall estimate it, so shall it stand. H3548
18 jubile, then the **p** shall reckon unto him H3548
23 Then the **p** shall reckon unto him the H3548
Nu 3: 6 the **p**, that they may minister unto him. H3548
32 And Eleazar the son of Aaron the **p** H3548
4:16 son of Aaron the **p** *pertaineth* the oil H3548
28 hand of Ithamar the son of Aaron the **p**. H3548
33 hand of Ithamar the son of Aaron the **p**. H3548
5: 8 LORD, *even* to the **p**; beside the ram of H3548
9 they bring unto the **p**, shall be his. H3548
10 any man giveth the **p**, it shall be his. H3548
15 his wife unto the **p**, and he shall bring H3548
16 And the **p** shall bring her near, and set H3548
17 And the **p** shall take holy water in an H3548
17 **p** shall take, and put *it* into the water: H3548
18 And the **p** shall set the woman before H3548
18 offering: and the **p** shall have in his H3548
19 And the **p** shall charge her by an oath, H3548
21 Then the **p** shall charge the woman H3548
21 of cursing, and the **p** shall say unto the H3548
23 And the **p** shall write these curses in a H3548
25 Then the **p** shall take the jealousy H3548
26 And the **p** shall take an handful of the H3548
30 **p** shall execute upon her all this law. H3548
6:10 pigeons, to the **p**, to the door of the H3548
11 And the **p** shall offer the one for a sin H3548
16 And the **p** shall bring *them* before the H3548
17 bread: the **p** shall offer also his meat H3548
19 And the **p** shall take the sodden H3548
20 And the **p** shall wave them *for* a wave H3548
20 this *is* holy for the **p**, with the wave H3548
7: 8 hand of Ithamar the son of Aaron the **p**. H3548

Nu 15:25 And the **p** shall make an atonement for H3548
28 And the **p** shall make an atonement for H3548
16:37 son of Aaron the **p**, that he take up the H3548
39 And Eleazar the **p** took the brasen H3548
18:28 LORD'S heave offering to Aaron the **p**. H3548
19: 3 unto Eleazar the **p**, that he may bring H3548
4 And Eleazar the **p** shall take of her H3548
6 And the **p** shall take cedar wood, and H3548
7 Then the **p** shall wash his clothes, and H3548
7 the **p** shall be unclean until the even. H3548
25: 7 son of Aaron the **p**, saw *it*, he rose up H3548
11 the son of Aaron the **p**, hath turned my H3548
26: 1 Eleazar the son of Aaron the **p**, saying, H3548
3 And Moses and Eleazar the **p** spake H3548
63 and Eleazar the **p**, who numbered the H3548
64 and Aaron the **p** numbered, when they H3548
27: 2 and before Eleazar the **p**, and before the H3548
19 And set him before Eleazar the **p**, and H3548
21 And he shall stand before Eleazar the **p**, H3548
22 the **p**, and before all the congregation: H3548
31: 6 son of Eleazar the **p**, to the war, with H3548
12 Moses, and Eleazar the **p**, and unto the H3548
13 And Moses, and Eleazar the **p**, and all H3548
21 And Eleazar the **p** said unto the men of H3548
26 and Eleazar the **p**, and the chief fathers H3548
29 **p**, *for* an heave offering of the LORD. H3548
31 And Moses and Eleazar the **p** did as the H3548
41 the **p**, as the LORD commanded Moses. H3548
51 And Moses and Eleazar the **p** took the H3548
54 And Moses and Eleazar the **p** took the H3548
32: 2 and to Eleazar the **p**, and unto the H3548
28 Eleazar the **p**, and Joshua the son H3548
33:38 And Aaron the **p** went up into mount H3548
34:17 the **p**, and Joshua the son of Nun. H3548
35:25 **p**, which was anointed with the holy oil. H3548
28 death of the high **p**: but after the death H3548
28 the death of the high **p** the slayer shall H3548
32 in the land, until the death of the **p**. H3548
Dt 17:12 not hearken unto the **p** that standeth to H3548
18: 3 shall give unto the **p** the shoulder, and H3548
20: 2 the battle, that the **p** shall approach H3548
26: 3 And thou shalt go unto the **p** that shall H3548
4 And the **p** shall take the basket out of H3548
Jos 14: 1 which Eleazar the **p**, and Joshua the son H3548
17: 4 before Eleazar the **p**, and before Joshua H3548
19:51 which Eleazar the **p**, and Joshua the son H3548
20: 6 the death of the high **p** that shall be in H3548
21: 1 unto Eleazar the **p**, and unto Joshua the H3548
4 of Aaron the **p**, *which were* of the H3548
13 of Aaron the **p** Hebron with her H3548
22:13 Phinehas the son of Eleazar the **p**, H3548
30 And when Phinehas the **p**, and the H3548
31 And Phinehas the son of Eleazar the **p** H3548
32 And Phinehas the son of Eleazar the **p**, H3548
Jdg 17: 5 one of his sons, who became his **p**. H3548
10 me a father and a **p**, and I will give thee H3548
12 his **p**, and was in the house of Micah. H3548
13 me good, seeing I have a Levite to *my* **p**. H3548
18: 4 me, and hath hired me, and I am his **p**. H3548
6 And the **p** said unto them, Go in peace: H3548
17 image: and the **p** stood in the entering H3548
18 said the **p** unto them, What do ye? H3548
19 us a father and a **p**: *is it* better for thee H3548
19 for thee to be a **p** unto the house of one H3548
19 a **p** unto a tribe and a family in Israel? H3548
24 I made, and the **p**, and ye are gone H3548
27 made, and the **p** which he had, and H3548
1Sa 1: 9 Now Eli the **p** sat upon a seat by a H3548
2:11 unto the LORD before Eli the **p**. H3548
14 brought up the **p** took for himself. So H3548
15 to roast for the **p**; for he will not have H3548
28 of Israel *to be* my **p**, to offer upon mine H3548
35 And I will raise me up a faithful **p**, *that* H3548
14: 3 of Eli, the LORD'S **p** in Shiloh, wearing H3548
19 talked unto the **p**, that the noise that H3548
19 said unto the **p**, Withdraw thine hand. H3548
36 the **p**, Let us draw near hither unto God. H3548
21: 1 to Ahimelech the **p**: and Ahimelech was H3548
2 And David said unto Ahimelech the **p**, H3548
4 And the **p** answered David, and said, H3548
5 And David answered the **p**, and said H3548
6 So the **p** gave him hallowed *bread*: for H3548
9 And the **p** said, The sword of Goliath H3548
22:11 call Ahimelech the **p**, the son of Ahitub, H3548
23: 9 Abiathar the **p**, Bring hither the ephod. H3548
30: 7 And David said to Abiathar the **p**, H3548
2Sa 15:27 The king said also unto Zadok the **p**, H3548
1Ki 1: 7 with Abiathar the **p**: and they following H3548
8 But Zadok the **p**, and Benaiah the son H3548

1Ki 1:19 king, and Abiathar the **p**, and Joab the H3548
25 and Abiathar the **p**; and, behold, they H3548
26 and Zadok the **p**, and Benaiah the son H3548
32 Call me Zadok the **p**, and Nathan the H3548
34 And let Zadok the **p** and Nathan the H3548
38 So Zadok the **p**, and Nathan the H3548
39 And Zadok the **p** took an horn of oil H3548
42 of Abiathar the **p** came: and Adonijah H3548
44 with him Zadok the **p**, and Nathan the H3548
45 And Zadok the **p** and Nathan the H3548
2:22 the **p**, and for Joab the son of Zeruiah. H3548
26 And unto Abiathar the **p** said the king, H3548
27 from being **p** unto the LORD; that H3548
35 and Zadok the **p** did the king put in the H3548
4: 2 he had; Azariah the son of Zadok the **p**, H3548
2Ki 11: 9 that Jehoiada the **p** commanded: and H3548
9 sabbath, and came to Jehoiada the **p**. H3548
10 hundreds did the **p** give king David's H3548
15 But Jehoiada the **p** commanded the H3548
15 the sword. For the **p** had said, Let her H3548
18 slew Mattan the **p** of Baal before the H3548
18 the altars. And the **p** appointed officers H3548
12: 2 wherein Jehoiada the **p** instructed him. H3548
7 called for Jehoiada the **p**, and the *other* H3548
9 But Jehoiada the **p** took a chest, and H3548
10 and the high **p** came up, and they put H3548
16:10 sent to Urijah the **p** the fashion of the H3548
11 And Urijah the **p** built an altar H3548
11 so Urijah the **p** made *it* against king H3548
15 Urijah the **p**, saying, Upon the great H3548
16 Thus did Urijah the **p**, according to all H3548
22: 4 Go up to Hilkiah the high **p**, that he H3548
8 And Hilkiah the high **p** said unto H3548
10 Hilkiah the **p** hath delivered me a H3548
12 Hilkiah the **p**, and Ahikam the son H3548
14 So Hilkiah the **p**, and Ahikam, and H3548
23: 4 Hilkiah the high **p**, and the priests of H3548
24 the **p** found in the house of the LORD. H3548
25:18 Seraiah the chief **p**, and Zephaniah the H3548
18 **p**, and the three keepers of the door: H3548
1Ch 16:39 And Zadok the **p**, and his brethren the H3548
24: 6 and Zadok the **p**, and Ahimelech the H3548
27: 5 of Jehoiada, a chief **p**: and in his course H3548
29:22 the chief governor, and Zadok *to be* **p**. H3548
2Ch 13: 9 may be a **p** of *them that are* no gods. H3548
15: 3 without a teaching **p**, and without law. H3548
19:11 And, behold, Amariah the chief **p** *is* H3548
22:11 of Jehoiada the **p**, (for she was the sister H3548
23: 8 that Jehoiada the **p** had commanded, H3548
8 the **p** dismissed not the courses. H3548
9 Moreover Jehoiada the **p** delivered to H3548
14 Then Jehoiada the **p** brought out the H3548
14 the sword. For the **p** said, Slay her not H3548
17 Mattan the **p** of Baal before the altars. H3548
24: 2 the LORD all the days of Jehoiada the **p**. H3548
20 of Jehoiada the **p**, which stood above H3548
25 of Jehoiada the **p**, and slew him on his H3548
26:17 And Azariah the **p** went in after him, H3548
20 And Azariah the chief **p**, and all the H3548
31:10 And Azariah the chief **p** of the house of H3548
34: 9 to Hilkiah the high **p**, they delivered the H3548
14 LORD, Hilkiah the **p** found a book of H3548
18 Hilkiah the **p** hath given me a book. H3548
Ezr 2:63 up a **p** with Urim and with Thummim. H3548
7: 5 of Eleazar, the son of Aaron the chief **p**: H3548
11 gave unto Ezra the **p**, the scribe, *even* a H3548
12 unto Ezra the **p**, a scribe of the law of H3549
21 Ezra the **p**, the scribe of the law H3549
8:33 son of Uriah the **p**; and with him *was* H3548
10:10 And Ezra the **p** stood up, and said unto H3548
16 so. And Ezra the **p**, *with* certain chief of H3548
Neh 3: 1 Then Eliashib the high **p** rose up with H3548
20 door of the house of Eliashib the high **p**. H3548
7:65 *up* a **p** with Urim and Thummim. H3548
8: 2 And Ezra the **p** brought the law before H3548
9 and Ezra the **p** the scribe, and the H3548
10:38 And the **p** the son of Aaron shall be H3548
12:26 governor, and of Ezra the **p**, the scribe. H3548
13: 4 And before this, Eliashib the **p**, having H3548
13 Shelemiah the **p**, and Zadok the scribe, H3548
28 of Eliashib the high **p**, *was* son in law to H3548
Ps 110: 4 repent, Thou *art* a **p** for ever after the H3548
Isa 8: 2 record, Uriah the **p**, and Zechariah the H3548
24: 2 so with the **p**; as with the servant, H3548
28: 7 out of the way; the **p** and the prophet H3548
Jer 6:13 unto the **p** every one dealeth falsely. H3548
8:10 unto the **p** every one dealeth falsely. H3548
14:18 prophet and the **p** go about into a land H3548
18:18 perish from the **p**, nor counsel from the H3548

Jer 20: 1 Now Pashur the son of Immer the **p**, H3548
21: 1 the son of Maaseiah the **p**, saying, H3548
23:11 For both prophet and **p** are profane; H3548
33 or the prophet, or a **p**, shall ask thee, H3548
34 And *as for* the prophet, and the **p**, and H3548
29:25 the **p**, and to all the priests, saying, H3548
26 The LORD hath made thee **p** in the H3548
26 of Jehoiada the **p**, that ye should be H3548
29 And Zephaniah the **p** read this letter in H3548
37: 3 son of Maaseiah the **p** to the prophet H3548
52:24 Seraiah the chief **p**, and Zephaniah the H3548
24 **p**, and the three keepers of the door: H3548
Lam 2: 6 of his anger the king and the **p**. H3548
20 long? shall the **p** and the prophet be H3548
Ezk 1: 3 unto Ezekiel the **p**, the son of Buzi, in H3548
7:26 the **p**, and counsel from the ancients. H3548
44:13 to do the office of a **p** unto me, nor to H3547
21 Neither shall any **p** drink wine, when H3548
22 Israel, or a widow that had a **p** before. H3548
30 also give unto the **p** the first of your H3548
45:19 And the **p** shall take of the blood of the H3548
Hos 4: 4 people *are* as they that strive with the **p**. H3548
6 thou shalt be no **p** to me: seeing thou H3547
9 And there shall be, like people, like **p**: H3548
Am 7:10 Then Amaziah the **p** of Beth-el sent to H3548
Hag 1: 1 the son of Josedech, the high **p**, saying, H3548
12 of Josedech, the high **p**, with all the H3548
14 of Josedech, the high **p**, and the spirit of H3548
2: 2 Josedech, the high **p**, and to the residue H3548
4 Josedech, the high **p**; and be strong, all H3548
Zec 3: 1 And he shewed me Joshua the high **p** H3548
8 Hear now, O Joshua the high **p**, thou, H3548
6:11 Joshua the son of Josedech, the high **p**; H3548
13 and he shall be a **p** upon his throne: H3548
Mt 8: 4 shew thyself to the **p**, and offer the gift G2409
26: 3 of the high **p**, who was called Caiaphas, G749
57 to Caiaphas the high **p**, where the scribes G749
62 And the high **p** arose, and said unto G749
63 But Jesus held his peace. And the high **p** G749
65 Then the high **p** rent his clothes, saying, G749
Mk 1:44 shew thyself to the **p**, and offer for thy G2409
2:26 of Abiathar the high **p**, and did eat the G749
14:47 servant of the high **p**, and cut off his ear. G749
53 And they led Jesus away to the high **p**: G749
54 palace of the high **p**: and he sat with the G749
60 And the high **p** stood up in the midst, G749
61 Again the high **p** asked him, and said G749
63 Then the high **p** rent his clothes, and G749
66 cometh one of the maids of the high **p**: G749
Lk 1: 5 Judaea, a certain **p** named Zacharias, G2409
5:14 shew thyself to the **p**, and offer for thy G2409
10:31 down a certain **p** that way: and when G2409
22:50 of the high **p**, and cut off his right ear. G749
Jn 11:49 being the high **p** that same year, said G749
51 himself: but being high **p** that year, he G749
18:13 which was the high **p** that same year. G749
15 unto the high **p**, and went in with Jesus G749
15 with Jesus into the palace of the high **p**. G749
16 unto the high **p**, and spake unto her G749
19 The high **p** then asked Jesus of his G749
22 saying, Answerest thou the high **p** so? G749
24 him bound unto Caiaphas the high **p**. G749
26 One of the servants of the high **p**, being G749
Act 4: 6 And Annas the high **p**, and Caiaphas, G749
6 **p**, were gathered together at Jerusalem. G748
5:17 Then the high **p** rose up, and all they G749
21 But the high **p** came, and they that G749
24 Now when the high **p** and the captain G2409
27 the council: and the high **p** asked them, G749
7: 1 Then said the high **p**, Are these things so? G749
9: 1 of the Lord, went unto the high **p**, G749
14:13 Then the **p** of Jupiter, which was before G2409
22: 5 As also the high **p** doth bear me witness, G749
23: 2 And the high **p** Ananias commanded G749
4 stood by said, Revilest thou God's high **p**? G749
5 he was the high **p**: for it is written, Thou G749
24: 1 And after five days Ananias the high **p** G749
25: 2 Then the high **p** and the chief of the Jews G749
Heb 2:17 and faithful high **p** in things *pertaining* G749
3: 1 High **P** of our profession, Christ Jesus; G749
4:14 Seeing then that we have a great high **p**, G749
15 For we have not an high **p** which cannot G749
5: 1 For every high **p** taken from among men G749
5 to be made an high **p**; but he that said G749
6 *place*, Thou *art* a **p** for ever after the G2409
10 Called of God an high **p** after the order of G749
6:20 **p** for ever after the order of Melchisedec. G749
7: 1 For this Melchisedec, king of Salem, **p** G2409
3 Son of God; abideth a **p** continually. G2409
Heb 7:11 *there* that another **p** should rise after G2409
15 of Melchisedec there ariseth another **p**, G2409
17 For he testifieth, Thou *art* a **p** for ever G2409
20 as not without an oath *he was made* **p**: G2409
21 repent, Thou *art* a **p** for ever after the G2409
26 For such an high **p** became us, *who is* G749
8: 1 have such an high **p**, who is set on the G749
3 For every high **p** is ordained to offer gifts G749
4 he should not be a **p**, seeing that there G2409
9: 7 But into the second *went* the high **p** G749
11 But Christ being come an high **p** of good G749
25 often, as the high **p** entereth into the G749
10:11 And every **p** standeth daily ministering G2409
21 And *having* an high **p** over the house of G2409
13:11 **p** for sin, are burned without the camp. G749

PRIESTHOOD

Ex 40:15 **p** throughout their generations. H3550
Nu 16:10 Levi with thee: and seek ye the **p** also? H3550
18: 1 thee shall bear the iniquity of your **p**. H3550
25:13 of an everlasting **p**; because he was H3550
Jos 18: 7 you; for the **p** of the LORD *is* their H3550
Ezr 2:62 were they, as polluted, put from the **p**. H3550
Neh 7:64 were they, as polluted, put from the **p**. H3550
13:29 have defiled the **p**, and the covenant of H3550
29 covenant of the **p**, and of the Levites. H3550
Heb 7: 5 receive the office of the **p**, have a G2405
11 were by the Levitical **p**, (for under it the G2420
12 For the **p** being changed, there is made G2420
14 Moses spake nothing concerning **p**. G2420
24 ever, hath an unchangeable **p**. G2420
1Pt 2: 5 house, an holy **p**, to offer up spiritual G2406
9 a royal **p**, an holy nation, a peculiar G2406

PRIESTS

Gen 47:22 Only the land of the **p** bought he not; H3548
22 he not; for the **p** had a portion *assigned* H3548
26 **p** only, *which* became not Pharaoh's. H3548
Ex 19: 6 me a kingdom of **p**, and an holy nation. H3548
22 And let the **p** also, which come near to H3548
24 but let not the **p** and the people break H3548
Lev 1: 5 the LORD: and the **p**, Aaron's sons, H3548
8 And the **p**, Aaron's sons, shall lay the H3548
11 the LORD: and the **p**, Aaron's sons, H3548
2: 2 to Aaron's sons the **p**: and he shall take H3548
3: 2 Aaron's sons the **p** shall sprinkle the H3548
6:29 All the males among the **p** shall eat H3548
7: 6 Every male among the **p** shall eat H3548
13: 2 the priest, or unto one of his sons the **p**: H3548
16:33 an atonement for the **p**, and for all the H3548
21: 1 Speak unto the **p** the sons of Aaron, H3548
Nu 3: 3 the sons of Aaron, the **p** which were H3548
10: 8 And the sons of Aaron, the **p**, shall blow H3548
Dt 17: 9 And thou shalt come unto the **p** the H3548
18 *that which is* before the **p** the Levites: H3548
18: 1 The **p** the Levites, *and* all the tribe of H3548
19:17 the LORD, before the **p** and the judges, H3548
21: 5 And the **p** the sons of Levi shall come H3548
24: 8 to all that the **p** the Levites shall teach H3548
27: 9 And Moses and the **p** the Levites spake H3548
31: 9 it unto the **p** the sons of Levi, which H3548
Jos 3: 3 your God, and the **p** the Levites bearing H3548
6 And Joshua spake unto the **p**, saying, H3548
8 And thou shalt command the **p** that H3548
13 of the feet of the **p** that bear the ark of H3548
14 Jordan, and the **p** bearing the ark of H3548
15 and the feet of the **p** that bare the ark H3548
17 And the **p** that bare the ark of the H3548
4: 9 the feet of the **p** which bare the ark H3548
10 For the **p** which bare the ark stood in H3548
11 and the **p**, in the presence of the people. H3548
16 Command the **p** that bear the ark of H3548
17 Joshua therefore commanded the **p**, H3548
18 And it came to pass, when the **p** that H3548
6: 4 And seven **p** shall bear before the ark H3548
4 and the **p** shall blow with the trumpets. H3548
6 And Joshua the son of Nun called the **p**, H3548
6 and let seven **p** bear seven trumpets H3548
8 that the seven **p** bearing the seven H3548
9 And the armed men went before the **p** H3548
9 came after the ark, *the* **p** going on, and H3548
12 and the **p** took up the ark of the LORD. H3548
13 And seven **p** bearing seven trumpets of H3548
13 ark of the LORD, *the* **p** going on, and
16 seventh time, when the **p** blew with the H3548
20 So the people shouted when *the* **p** blew H8628
8:33 side before the **p** the Levites, which H3548
21:19 of Aaron, the **p**, *were* thirteen cities H3548
Jdg 18:30 and his sons were **p** to the tribe of Dan H3548
1Sa 1: 3 the **p** of the LORD, *were* there. H3548
5: 5 Therefore neither the **p** of Dagon, nor H3548
6: 2 And the Philistines called for the **p** and H3548
22:11 father's house, the **p** that *were* in Nob: H3548
17 him, Turn, and slay the **p** of the LORD; H3548
17 hand to fall upon the **p** of the LORD. H3548
18 thou, and fall upon the **p**. And Doeg the H3548
18 he fell upon the **p**, and slew on that day H3548
19 And Nob, the city of the **p**, smote he H3548
21 David that Saul had slain the LORD'S **p**. H3548
2Sa 8:17 *were* the **p**; and Seraiah *was* the scribe; H3548
15:35 and Abiathar the **p**? therefore it shall be, H3548
35 tell *it* to Zadok and Abiathar the **p**. H3548
17:15 to Abiathar the **p**, Thus and thus did H3548
19:11 to Abiathar the **p**, saying, Speak unto H3548
20:25 and Zadok and Abiathar *were* the **p**: H3548
1Ki 4: 4 and Zadok and Abiathar *were* the **p**: H3548
8: 3 Israel came, and the **p** took up the ark. H3548
4 did the **p** and the Levites bring up. H3548
6 And the **p** brought in the ark of the H3548
10 And it came to pass, when the **p** were H3548
11 So that the **p** could not stand to H3548
12:31 places, and made **p** of the lowest of the H3548
32 in Beth-el the **p** of the high places H3548
13: 2 shall he offer the **p** of the high places H3548
33 of the people **p** of the high places: H3548
33 became *one* of the **p** of the high places. H3548
2Ki 10:11 his **p**, until he left him none remaining. H3548
19 and all his **p**; let none be wanting: H3548
12: 4 And Jehoash said to the **p**, All the H3548
5 Let the **p** take *it* to them, every man of H3548
6 of king Jehoash the **p** had not repaired H3548
7 and the *other* **p**, and said unto them, H3548
8 And the **p** consented to receive no H3548
9 the LORD: and the **p** that kept the door H3548
17:27 thither one of the **p** whom ye brought H3548
28 Then one of the **p** whom they had H3548
32 the lowest of them **p** of the high places, H3548
19: 2 and the elders of the **p**, covered with H3548
23: 2 with him, and the **p**, and the prophets, H3548
4 priest, and the **p** of the second order, H3548
5 And he put down the idolatrous **p**, H3649
8 And he brought all the **p** out of the H3548
8 places where the **p** had burned incense, H3548
9 Nevertheless the **p** of the high places H3548
20 And he slew all the **p** of the high places H3548
1Ch 9: 2 the **p**, Levites, and the Nethinims. H3548
10 And of the **p**; Jedaiah, and Jehoiarib, H3548
30 And *some* of the sons of the **p** made the H3548
13: 2 them *also* to the **p** and Levites *which* H3548
15:11 and Abiathar the **p**, and for the Levites, H3548
14 So the **p** and the Levites sanctified H3548
24 and Eliezer, the **p**, did blow with the H3548
16: 6 Benaiah also and Jahaziel the **p** with H3548
39 his brethren the **p**, before the tabernacle H3548
18:16 *were* the **p**; and Shavsha was scribe; H3548
23: 2 of Israel, with the **p** and the Levites. H3548
24: 6 of the fathers of the **p** and Levites: one H3548
31 of the fathers of the **p** and Levites, even H3548
28:13 Also for the courses of the **p** and the H3548
21 And, behold, the courses of the **p** and H3548
2Ch 4: 6 but the sea *was* for the **p** to wash in. H3548
9 the court of the **p**, and the great court, H3548
5: 5 did the **p** *and* the Levites bring up. H3548
7 And the **p** brought in the ark of the H3548
11 And it came to pass, when the **p** were H3548
11 *place*: (for all the **p** *that were* present H3548
12 and twenty **p** sounding with trumpets:) H3548
14 So that the **p** could not stand to H3548
6:41 thy strength: let thy **p**, O LORD God, be H3548
7: 2 And the **p** could not enter into the H3548
6 And the **p** waited on their offices: the H3548
6 ministry; and the **p** sounded trumpets H3548
8:14 the courses of the **p** to their service, H3548
14 before the **p**, as the duty of every H3548
15 of the king unto the **p** and Levites H3548
11:13 And the **p** and the Levites that *were* in H3548
15 And he ordained him **p** for the high H3548
13: 9 Have ye not cast out the **p** of the LORD, H3548
9 have made you **p** after the manner of H3548
10 him; and the **p**, which minister unto H3548
12 *our* captain, and his **p** with sounding H3548
14 and the **p** sounded with the trumpets. H3548
17: 8 with them Elishama and Jehoram, **p**. H3548
19: 8 Levites, and *of* the **p**, and of the chief of H3548
23: 4 the sabbath, of the **p** and of the Levites, H3548
6 the LORD, save the **p**, and they that H3548
18 by the hand of the **p** the Levites, whom H3548
24: 5 And he gathered together the **p** and the H3548

2Ch 26:17 **p** of the LORD, *that were* valiant men: H3548
18 LORD, but to the **p** the sons of Aaron, H3548
19 wroth with the **p**, the leprosy even rose H3548
19 before the **p** in the house of the LORD, H3548
20 priest, and all the **p**, looked upon him, H3548
29: 4 And he brought in the **p** and the H3548
16 And the **p** went into the inner part of H3548
21 commanded the **p** the sons of Aaron to H3548
22 So they killed the bullocks, and the **p** H3548
24 And the **p** killed them, and they made H3548
26 of David, and the **p** with the trumpets. H3548
34 But the **p** were too few, so that they H3548
34 and until the *other* **p** had sanctified H3548
34 heart to sanctify themselves than the **p**. H3548
30: 3 time, because the **p** had not sanctified H3548
15 month: and the **p** and the Levites were H3548
16 man of God: the **p** sprinkled the blood, H3548
21 the Levites and the **p** praised the LORD H3548
24 number of **p** sanctified themselves. H3548
25 of Judah, with the **p** and the Levites, H3548
27 Then the **p** the Levites arose and H3548
31: 2 the courses of the **p** and the Levites H3548
2 to his service, the **p** and Levites for H3548
4 the portion of the **p** and the Levites, H3548
9 Then Hezekiah questioned with the **p** H3548
15 in the cities of the **p**, in *their* set office, H3548
17 Both to the genealogy of the **p** by the H3548
19 Also of the sons of Aaron the **p**, *which* H3548
19 males among the **p**, and to all that were H3548
34: 5 And he burnt the bones of the **p** upon H3548
30 and the **p**, and the Levites, and H3548
35: 2 And he set the **p** in their charges, and H3548
8 the people, to the **p**, and to the Levites: H3548
8 God, gave unto the **p** for the passover H3548
10 So the service was prepared, and the **p** H3548
11 And they killed the passover, and the **p** H3548
14 and for the **p**: because the priests H3548
14 because the **p** the sons of Aaron *were* H3548
14 and for the **p** the sons of Aaron. H3548
18 kept, and the **p**, and the Levites, and H3548
36:14 Moreover all the chief of the **p**, and the H3548
Ezr 1: 5 Benjamin, and the **p**, and the Levites, H3548
2:36 The **p**: the children of Jedaiah, of the H3548
61 And of the children of the **p**: the H3548
70 So the **p**, and the Levites, and *some* of H3548
3: 2 his brethren the **p**, and Zerubbabel the H3548
8 of their brethren the **p** and the Levites, H3548
10 they set the **p** in their apparel with H3548
12 But many of the **p** and Levites and H3548
6: 9 of the **p** which *are* at Jerusalem, H3549
16 And the children of Israel, the **p**, and H3549
18 And they set the **p** in their divisions, H3549
20 For the **p** and the Levites were purified H3548
20 brethren the **p**, and for themselves. H3548
7: 7 of Israel, and of the **p**, and the Levites, H3548
13 Israel, and *of* his **p** and Levites, in my H3549
16 people, and of the **p**, offering willingly H3549
24 any of the **p** and Levites, singers, H3549
8:15 people, and the **p**, and found there none H3548
24 twelve of the chief of the **p**, Sherebiah, H3548
29 the chief of the **p** and the Levites, and H3548
30 So took the **p** and the Levites the H3548
9: 1 of Israel, and the **p**, and the Levites, H3548
7 we, our kings, *and* our **p**, been delivered H3548
10: 5 Then arose Ezra, and made the chief **p**, H3548
18 And among the sons of the **p** there H3548
Neh 2:16 Jews, nor to the **p**, nor to the nobles, nor H3548
3: 1 his brethren the **p**, and they builded the H3548
22 And after him repaired the **p**, the men H3548
28 the **p**, every one over against his house. H3548
5:12 Then I called the **p**, and took an oath of H3548
7:39 The **p**: the children of Jedaiah, of the H3548
63 And of the **p**: the children of Habaiah, H3548
73 So the **p**, and the Levites, and the H3548
8:13 of all the people, the **p**, and the Levites, H3548
9:32 and on our **p**, and on our prophets, H3548
34 our princes, our **p**, nor our fathers, kept H3548
38 our princes, Levites, *and* **p**, seal *unto it*. H3548
10: 8 Bilgai, Shemaiah: these *were* the **p**. H3548
28 And the rest of the people, the **p**, the H3548
34 And we cast the lots among the **p**, the H3548
36 **p** that minister in the house of our God: H3548
37 of oil, unto the **p**, to the chambers of H3548
39 and the **p** that minister, and the H3548
11: 3 *to wit*, Israel, the **p**, and the Levites, and H3548
10 Of the **p**: Jedaiah the son of Joiarib, H3548
20 And the residue of Israel, of the **p**, *and* H3548
12: 1 Now these *are* the **p** and the Levites H3548
7 the chief of the **p** and of their brethren H3548

Neh 12:12 And in the days of Joiakim were **p**, the H3548
22 the **p**, to the reign of Darius the Persian. H3548
30 And the **p** and the Levites purified H3548
41 And the **p**; Eliakim, Maaseiah, H3548
44 of the law for the **p** and Levites: for H3548
44 the **p** and for the Levites that waited. H3548
13: 5 the porters; and the offerings of the **p**. H3548
30 the wards of the **p** and the Levites, H3548
Ps 78:64 Their **p** fell by the sword; and their H3548
99: 6 Moses and Aaron among his **p**, and H3548
132: 9 Let thy **p** be clothed with H3548
16 I will also clothe her **p** with salvation: H3548
Isa 37: 2 and the elders of the **p** covered with H3548
61: 6 But ye shall be named the **P** of the H3548
66:21 And I will also take of them for **p** *and* H3548
Jer 1: 1 son of Hilkiah, of the **p** that *were* in H3548
18 against the **p** thereof, and against H3548
2: 8 The **p** said not, Where *is* the LORD? H3548
26 princes, and their **p**, and their prophets, H3548
4: 9 princes; and the **p** shall be astonished, H3548
5:31 falsely, and the **p** bear rule by their H3548
8: 1 the bones of the **p**, and the bones of the H3548
13:13 throne, and the **p**, and the prophets, H3548
19: 1 the people, and of the ancients of the **p**; H3548
26: 7 So the **p** and the prophets and all the H3548
8 people, that the **p** and the prophets and H3548
11 Then spake the **p** and the prophets H3548
16 people unto the **p** and to the prophets; H3548
27:16 Also I spake to the **p** and to all this H3548
28: 1 of the **p** and of all the people, saying, H3548
5 presence of the **p**, and in the presence H3548
29: 1 and to the **p**, and to the prophets, H3548
25 the priest, and to all the **p**, saying, H3548
31:14 And I will satiate the soul of the **p** with H3548
32:32 princes, their **p**, and their prophets, H3548
33:18 Neither shall the **p** the Levites want a H3548
21 with the Levites the **p**, my ministers. H3548
34:19 eunuchs, and the **p**, and all the people H3548
48: 7 *with* his **p** and his princes together. H3548
49: 3 *and* his **p** and his princes together. H3548
Lam 1: 4 are desolate: her **p** sigh, her virgins are H3548
19 deceived me: my **p** and mine elders H3548
4:13 iniquities of her **p**, that have shed the H3548
16 of the **p**, they favoured not the elders. H3548
Ezk 22:26 Her **p** have violated my law, and have H3548
40:45 the south, *is* for the **p**, the keepers of the H3548
46 the north *is* for the **p**, the keepers of the H3548
42:13 where the **p** that approach unto H3548
14 When the **p** enter therein, then shall H3548
43:19 And thou shalt give to the **p** the Levites H3548
24 the LORD, and the **p** shall cast salt H3548
27 and *so* forward, the **p** shall make your H3548
44:15 But the **p** the Levites, the sons of H3548
31 The **p** shall not eat of any thing that is H3548
45: 4 shall be for the **p** the ministers of the H3548
46: 2 of the gate, and the **p** shall prepare his H3548
19 holy chambers of the **p**, which looked H3548
20 the place where the **p** shall boil the H3548
48:10 And for them, *even* for the **p**, shall be H3548
11 *It shall be* for the **p** that are sanctified H3548
13 And over against the border of the **p** H3548
Hos 5: 1 Hear ye this, O **p**; and hearken, ye H3548
6: 9 *so* the company of **p** murder in the way H3548
10: 5 over it, and the **p** thereof *that* rejoiced H3649
Joel 1: 9 the **p**, the LORD'S ministers, mourn. H3548
13 Gird yourselves, and lament, ye **p**: howl, H3548
2:17 Let the **p**, the ministers of the LORD, H3548
Mic 3:11 for reward, and the **p** thereof teach for H3548
Zep 1: 4 the name of the Chemarims with the **p**; H3548
3: 4 persons: her **p** have polluted the H3548
Hag 2:11 now the **p** *concerning* the law, saying, H3548
12 And the **p** answered and said, No. H3548
13 unclean? And the **p** answered and said, H3548
Zec 7: 3 *And* to speak unto the **p** which *were* in H3548
5 the land, and to the **p**, saying, When ye H3548
Mal 1: 6 of hosts unto you, O **p**, that despise my H3548
2: 1 And now, O ye **p**, this commandment *is* H3548
Mt 2: 4 And when he had gathered all the chief **p** *G749*
12: 4 which were with him, but only for the **p**? *G2409*
5 the sabbath days the **p** in the temple *G2409*
16:21 elders and chief **p** and scribes, and be *G749*
20:18 unto the chief **p** and unto the scribes, *G749*
21:15 And when the chief **p** and scribes saw *G749*
23 temple, the chief **p** and the elders of the *G749*
45 And when the chief **p** and Pharisees had *G749*
26: 3 Then assembled together the chief **p**, and *G749*
14 Judas Iscariot, went unto the chief **p**, *G749*
47 from the chief **p** and elders of the people. *G749*
59 Now the chief **p**, and elders, and all the *G749*

Mt 27: 1 come, all the chief **p** and elders of the *G749*
3 pieces of silver to the chief **p** and elders, *G749*
6 And the chief **p** took the silver pieces, *G749*
12 And when he was accused of the chief **p** *G749*
20 But the chief **p** and elders persuaded the *G749*
41 Likewise also the chief **p** mocking *him*, *G749*
62 the chief **p** and Pharisees came *G749*
28:11 the chief **p** all the things that were done. *G749*
Mk 2:26 to eat but for the **p**, and gave also to *G2409*
8:31 and *of* the chief **p**, and scribes, and be *G749*
10:33 unto the chief **p**, and unto the scribes; *G749*
11:18 And the scribes and chief **p** heard *it*, and *G749*
27 chief **p**, and the scribes, and the elders, *G749*
14: 1 and the chief **p** and the scribes sought *G749*
10 the chief **p**, to betray him unto them. *G749*
43 chief **p** and the scribes and the elders. *G749*
53 chief **p** and the elders and the scribes. *G749*
55 And the chief **p** and all the council *G749*
15: 1 morning the chief **p** held a consultation *G749*
3 And the chief **p** accused him of many *G749*
10 For he knew that the chief **p** had *G749*
11 But the chief **p** moved the people, that he *G749*
31 Likewise also the chief **p** mocking said *G749*
Lk 3: 2 Annas and Caiaphas being the high **p**, *G749*
6: 4 is not lawful to eat but for the **p** alone? *G2409*
9:22 elders and chief **p** and scribes, and be *G749*
17:14 unto the **p**. And it came to pass, *G2409*
19:47 But the chief **p** and the scribes and *G749*
20: 1 gospel, the chief **p** and the scribes came *G749*
19 And the chief **p** and the scribes the same *G749*
22: 2 And the chief **p** and scribes sought how *G749*
4 with the chief **p** and captains, how he *G749*
52 Then Jesus said unto the chief **p**, and *G749*
66 and the chief **p** and the scribes came *G749*
23: 4 Then said Pilate to the chief **p** and *to* the *G749*
10 And the chief **p** and scribes stood and *G749*
13 the chief **p** and the rulers and the people, *G749*
23 of them and of the chief **p** prevailed. *G749*
24:20 And how the chief **p** and our rulers *G749*
Jn 1:19 when the Jews sent **p** and Levites from *G2409*
7:32 and the chief **p** sent officers to take him. *G749*
45 Then came the officers to the chief **p** and *G749*
11:47 Then gathered the chief **p** and the *G749*
57 Now both the chief **p** and the Pharisees *G749*
12:10 But the chief **p** consulted that they might *G749*
18: 3 from the chief **p** and Pharisees, cometh *G749*
35 and the chief **p** have delivered thee *G749*
19: 6 When the chief **p** therefore and officers *G749*
15 King? The chief **p** answered, We have *G749*
21 Then said the chief **p** of the Jews to *G749*
Act 4: 1 the people, the **p**, and the captain of the *G2409*
23 chief **p** and elders had said unto them. *G749*
5:24 and the chief **p** heard these things, they *G749*
6: 7 of the **p** were obedient to the faith. *G2409*
9:14 chief **p** to bind all that call on thy name. *G749*
21 might bring them bound unto the chief **p**? *G749*
19:14 a Jew, *and* chief of the **p**, which did so. *G749*
22:30 the chief **p** and all their council *G749*
23:14 And they came to the chief **p** and elders, *G749*
25:15 the chief **p** and the elders of the *G749*
26:10 from the chief **p**; and when they were *G749*
12 and commission from the chief **p**, *G749*
Heb 7:21 (For those **p** were made without an *G2409*
23 And they truly were many **p**, because *G2409*
27 Who needeth not daily, as those high **p**, *G749*
28 For the law maketh men high **p** which *G749*
8: 4 **p** that offer gifts according to the law: *G2409*
9: 6 thus ordained, the **p** went always into *G2409*
Rev 1: 6 And hath made us kings and **p** unto *G2409*
5:10 and **p**: and we shall reign on the earth. *G2409*
20: 6 but they shall be **p** of God and of *G2409*

PRIEST'S

Ex 28: 1 unto me in the **p** office, *even* Aaron, H3547
3 may minister unto me in the **p** office. H3547
4 may minister unto me in the **p** office. H3547
41 may minister unto me in the **p** office. H3547
29: 1 unto me in the **p** office: Take one H3547
9 on them: and the **p** office shall be theirs H3550
44 sons, to minister to me in the **p** office. H3547
30:30 may minister unto me in the **p** office. H3547
31:10 of his sons, to minister in the **p** office, H3547
35:19 of his sons, to minister in the **p** office. H3547
39:41 garments, to minister in the **p** office. H3547
40:13 may minister unto me in the **p** office. H3547
15 unto me in the **p** office: for their H3547
Lev 5:13 shall be the **p**, as a meat offering. H3548
7: 9 the pan, shall be the **p** that offereth it. H3548
14 *and* it shall be the **p** that sprinkleth the H3548

Lev 7:35 minister unto the LORD in the **p** office; H3547
14:13 sin offering *is* the **p**, *so is* the trespass H3548
18 oil that *is* in the **p** hand he shall pour H3548
29 And the rest of the oil that *is* in the **p** H3548
16:32 to minister in the **p** office in his H3547
22:12 If the **p** daughter also be *married* unto H3548
13 But if the **p** daughter be a widow, or H3548
27:21 the possession thereof shall be the **p**. H3548
Nu 3: 3 consecrated to minister in the **p** office. H3547
4 ministered in the **p** office in the sight of H3547
10 shall wait on their **p** office: and the H3550
18: 7 shall keep your **p** office for every thing H3550
7 I have given your **p** office *unto you* as a H3550
Dt 10: 6 ministered in the **p** office in his stead. H3547
18: 3 And this shall be the **p** due from the H3548
Jdg 18:20 And the **p** heart was glad, and he took H3548
1Sa 2:13 sacrifice, the **p** servant came, while H3548
15 Also before they burnt the fat, the **p** H3548
1Ch 6:10 that executed the **p** office in the temple H3547
24: 2 and Ithamar executed the **p** office. H3547
2Ch 11:14 executing the **p** office unto the LORD: H3547
24:11 scribe and the high **p** officer came and H3548
Ezk 44:30 shall be the **p**: ye shall also give unto H3548
Mal 2: 7 For the **p** lips should keep knowledge, H3548
Mt 26:51 of the high **p**, and smote off his ear. *G749*
58 off unto the high **p** palace, and went in, *G749*
Lk 1: 8 he executed the **p** office before God in *G2407*
9 According to the custom of the **p** office, *G2405*
22:54 **p** house. And Peter followed afar off. *G749*
Jn 18:10 it, and smote the high **p** servant, and cut *G749*

PRIESTS'

Jos 4: 3 the place where the **p** feet stood firm, H3548
18 *and* the soles of the **p** feet were lifted up H3548
1Sa 2:13 And the **p** custom with the people *was*, H3548
36 **p** offices, that I may eat a piece of bread.
2Ki 12:16 the house of the LORD: it was the **p**. H3548
Ezr 2:69 of silver, and one hundred **p** garments. H3548
Neh 7:70 five hundred and thirty **p** garments. H3548
72 and threescore and seven **p** garments. H3548
12:35 And *certain* of the **p** sons with H3548

PRINCE

Gen 23: 6 Hear us, my lord: thou *art* a mighty **p** H5387
32:28 but Israel: for as a **p** hast thou power
34: 2 of Hamor the Hivite, **p** of the country, H5387
Ex 2:14 And he said, Who made thee a **p** and a H8269
Nu 7:11 their offering, each **p** on his day, for the H5387
18 son of Zuar, **p** of Issachar, did offer: H5387
24 **p** of the children of Zebulun, *did offer*: H5387
30 **p** of the children of Reuben, *did offer*: H5387
36 **p** of the children of Simeon, *did offer*: H5387
42 Deuel, **p** of the children of Gad, *offered*: H5387
48 **p** of the children of Ephraim, *offered*: H5387
54 **p** of the children of Manasseh: H5387
60 **p** of the children of Benjamin, *offered*: H5387
66 **p** of the children of Dan, *offered*: H5387
72 **p** of the children of Asher, *offered*: H5387
78 **p** of the children of Naphtali, *offered*: H5387
16:13 make thyself altogether a **p** over us? H8323
17: 6 rod apiece, for each **p** one, according to H5387
25:14 the son of Salu, a **p** of a chief house H5387
18 the daughter of a **p** of Midian, their H5387
34:18 And ye shall take one **p** of every tribe, H5387
22 And the **p** of the tribe of the children of H5387
23 The **p** of the children of Joseph, for the H5387
24 And the **p** of the tribe of the children of H5387
25 And the **p** of the tribe of the children of H5387
26 And the **p** of the tribe of the children of H5387
27 And the **p** of the tribe of the children of H5387
28 And the **p** of the tribe of the children of H5387
Jos 22:14 each chief house a **p** throughout all the H5387
2Sa 3:38 ye not that there is a **p** and a great man H8269
1Ki 11:34 I will make him **p** all the days of his life H5387
14: 7 and made thee **p** over my people Israel, H5057
16: 2 and made thee **p** over my people Israel; H5057
1Ch 2:10 Nahshon, **p** of the children of Judah; H5387
5: 6 *captive*: he *was* **p** of the Reubenites. H5387
Ezr 1: 8 them unto Sheshbazzar, the **p** of Judah. H5387
Job 21:28 For ye say, Where *is* the house of the **p**? H5081
31:37 steps; as a **p** would I go near unto him. H5057
Prv 14:28 of people *is* the destruction of the **p**. H7333
17: 7 not a fool: much less do lying lips a **p**. H5081
19: 6 Many will entreat the favour of the **p**: H5081
25: 7 of the **p** whom thine eyes have seen. H5081
15 By long forbearing is a **p** persuaded, H7101
28:16 The **p** that wanteth understanding *is* H5057
Isa 9: 6 The everlasting Father, The **P** of Peace. H8269
Jer 51:59 reign. And *this* Seraiah *was* a quiet **p**. H8269

Ezk 7:27 The king shall mourn, and the **p** shall H5387
12:10 *concerneth* the **p** in Jerusalem, and all H5387
12 And the **p** that *is* among them shall H5387
21:25 And thou, profane wicked **p** of Israel, H5387
28: 2 Son of man, say unto the **p** of Tyrus, H5057
30:13 shall be no more a **p** of the land of H5387
34:24 servant David a **p** among them; I the H5387
37:25 servant David *shall be* their **p** for ever. H5387
38: 2 of Magog, the chief **p** of Meshech and H5387
3 Gog, the chief **p** of Meshech and Tubal: H5387
39: 1 Gog, the chief **p** of Meshech and Tubal: H5387
44: 3 *It is* for the **p**; the prince, he shall sit in H5387
3 *It is* for the prince; the **p**, he shall sit in H5387
45: 7 And a *portion shall be* for the **p** on the H5387
16 give this oblation for the **p** in Israel. H5387
22 And upon that day shall the **p** prepare H5387
46: 2 And the **p** shall enter by the way of the H5387
4 And the burnt offering that the **p** shall H5387
8 And when the **p** shall enter, he shall go H5387
10 And the **p** in the midst of them, when H5387
12 Now when the **p** shall prepare a H5387
16 Thus saith the Lord GOD; If the **p** give H5387
17 shall return to the **p**: but his inheritance H5387
18 Moreover the **p** shall not take of the H5387
48:21 And the residue *shall be* for the **p**, on H5387
21 the portions for the **p**: and it shall be the H5387
22 border of Benjamin, shall be for the **p**. H5387
Dan 1: 7 Unto whom the **p** of the eunuchs gave H8269
8 requested of the **p** of the eunuchs that H8269
9 tender love with the **p** of the eunuchs. H8269
10 And the **p** of the eunuchs said unto H8269
11 Melzar, whom the **p** of the eunuchs had H8269
18 them in, then the **p** of the eunuchs H8269
8:11 Yea, he magnified *himself* even to the **p** H8269
25 up against the **P** of princes; but he shall H8269
9:25 the Messiah the **P** *shall be* seven weeks, H5057
26 and the people of the **p** that shall come H5057
10:13 But the **p** of the kingdom of Persia H8269
20 to fight with the **p** of Persia: and when H8269
20 forth, lo, the **p** of Grecia shall come. H8269
21 me in these things, but Michael your **p**. H8269
11:18 take many: but a **p** for his own behalf H7101
22 broken; yea, also the **p** of the covenant. H5057
12: 1 up, the great **p** which standeth for H8269
Hos 3: 4 king, and without a **p**, and without a H8269
Mic 7: 3 earnestly, the **p** asketh, and the judge H8269
Mt 9:34 out devils through the **p** of the devils. *G758*
12:24 but by Beelzebub the **p** of the devils. *G758*
Mk 3:22 the **p** of the devils casteth he out devils. *G758*
Jn 12:31 now shall the **p** of this world be cast out. *G758*
14:30 with you: for the **p** of this world cometh, *G758*
16:11 Of judgment, because the **p** of this world *G758*
Act 3:15 And killed the **P** of life, whom God hath *G747*
5:31 right hand *to be* a **P** and a Saviour, for to *G747*
Eph 2: 2 according to the **p** of the power of the *G758*
Rev 1: 5 of the dead, and the **p** of the kings of the *G758*

PRINCES

Gen 12:15 The **p** also of Pharaoh saw her, and H8269
17:20 twelve **p** shall he beget, and H5387
25:16 twelve **p** according to their nations. H5387
Nu 1:16 of the congregation, **p** of the tribes of H5387
44 and the **p** of Israel, *being* twelve H5387
7: 2 That the **p** of Israel, heads of the house H5387
2 who *were* the **p** of the tribes, and were H5387
3 for two of the **p**, and for each one an H5387
10 And the **p** offered for dedicating of the H5387
10 **p** offered their offering before the altar. H5387
84 was anointed, by the **p** of Israel: twelve H5387
10: 4 *trumpet*, then the **p**, *which are* heads of H5387
16: 2 hundred and fifty **p** of the assembly, H5387
17: 2 fathers, of all their **p** according to the H5387
6 and every one of their **p** gave him a rod H5387
21:18 The **p** digged the well, the nobles of the H8269
22: 8 and the **p** of Moab abode with Balaam. H8269
13 and said unto the **p** of Balak, Get you H8269
14 And the **p** of Moab rose up, and they H8269
15 And Balak sent yet again **p**, more, and H8269
21 his ass, and went with the **p** of Moab. H8269
35 So Balaam went with the **p** of Balak. H8269
40 and to the **p** that *were* with him. H8269
23: 6 sacrifice, he, and all the **p** of Moab. H8269
17 offering, and the **p** of Moab with him. H8269
27: 2 priest, and before the **p** and all the H5387
31:13 the priest, and all the **p** of the H5387
32: 2 unto the **p** of the congregation, saying, H5387
36: 1 and before the **p**, the chief fathers of H5387
Jos 9:15 **p** of the congregation sware unto them. H5387
18 not, because the **p** of the congregation H5387

Jos 9:18 congregation murmured against the **p**. H5387
19 But all the **p** said unto all the H5387
21 And the **p** said unto them, Let them H5387
21 as the **p** had promised them. H5387
13:21 smote with the **p** of Midian, Evi, and H5387
17: 4 and before the **p**, saying, The LORD H5387
22:14 And with him ten **p**, of each chief house H5387
30 Phinehas the priest, and the **p** of the H5387
32 the priest, and the **p**, returned from the H5387
Jdg 5: 3 Hear, O ye kings; give ear, O ye **p**; I, H7336
15 And the **p** of Issachar *were* with H8269
7:25 And they took two **p** of the Midianites, H8269
8: 3 your hands the **p** of Midian, Oreb and H8269
6 And the **p** of Succoth said, *Are* the H8269
14 unto him the **p** of Succoth, and the H8269
10:18 And the people *and* **p** of Gilead said H8269
1Sa 2: 8 to set *them* among **p**, and to make them H5081
18:30 Then the **p** of the Philistines went forth: H8269
29: 3 Then said the **p** of the Philistines, What H8269
3 said unto the **p** of the Philistines, *Is* H8269
4 And the **p** of the Philistines were wroth H8269
4 with him; and the **p** of the Philistines H8269
9 the **p** of the Philistines have H8269
2Sa 10: 3 And the **p** of the children of Ammon H8269
19: 6 regardest neither **p** nor servants: for H8269
1Ki 4: 2 And these *were* the **p** which he had; H8269
9:22 servants, and his **p**, and his captains, H8269
20:14 young men of the **p** of the provinces. H8269
15 young men of the **p** of the provinces, H8269
17 And the young men of the **p** of the H8269
19 So these young men of the **p** of the H8269
2Ki 11:14 *was*, and the **p** and the trumpeters H8269
24:12 his servants, and his **p**, and his officers: H8269
14 and all the **p**, and all the mighty men H8269
1Ch 4:38 by *their* names *were* **p** in their families: H5387
7:40 valour, chief of the **p**. And the number H5387
19: 3 But the **p** of the children of Ammon H8269
22:17 David also commanded all the **p** of H8269
23: 2 And he gathered together all the **p** of H8269
24: 6 the king, and the **p**, and Zadok the H8269
27:22 These *were* the **p** of the tribes of Israel. H8269
28: 1 And David assembled all the **p** of H8269
1 of Israel, the **p** of the tribes, and the H8269
21 of service: also the **p** and all the people H8269
29: 6 Then the chief of the fathers and **p** of H8269
24 And all the **p**, and the mighty men, and H8269
2Ch 12: 5 and *to* the **p** of Judah, that were H8269
6 Whereupon the **p** of Israel and the king H8269
17: 7 he sent to his **p**, *even* to Ben-hail, and H8269
21: 4 and *divers* also of the **p** of Israel. H8269
9 Then Jehoram went forth with his **p**, H8269
22: 8 and found the **p** of Judah, and the sons H8269
23:13 in, and the **p** and the trumpets by H8269
24:10 And all the **p** and all the people H8269
17 of Jehoiada came the **p** of Judah, and H8269
23 destroyed all the **p** of the people from H8269
28:14 before the **p** and all the congregation. H8269
21 king, and of the **p**, and gave *it* unto the H8269
29:30 Moreover Hezekiah the king and the **p** H8269
30: 2 taken counsel, and his **p**, and all the H8269
6 the king and his **p** throughout all Israel H8269
12 and of the **p**, by the word of the LORD. H8269
24 thousand sheep; and the **p** gave to the H8269
31: 8 And when Hezekiah and the **p** came H8269
32: 3 He took counsel with his **p** and his H8269
31 of the **p** of Babylon, who sent H8269
35: 8 And his **p** gave willingly unto the H8269
36:18 his **p**; all *these* he brought to Babylon. H8269
Ezr 7:28 all the king's mighty **p**. And I was H8269
8:20 David and the **p** had appointed for the H8269
9: 1 were done, the **p** came to me, saying, H8269
2 the hand of the **p** and rulers hath been H8269
10: 8 the counsel of the **p** and the elders, all H8269
Neh 9:32 our kings, on our **p**, and on our priests, H8269
34 Neither have our kings, our **p**, our H8269
38 our **p**, Levites, *and* priests, seal *unto it*. H8269
12:31 Then I brought up the **p** of Judah upon H8269
32 Hoshaiah, and half of the **p** of Judah, H8269
Est 1: 3 a feast unto all his **p** and his servants; H8269
3 **p** of the provinces, *being* before him: H8269
11 the people and the **p** her beauty: for she H8269
14 the seven **p** of Persia and Media, H8269
16 the king and the **p**, Vashti the queen H8269
16 only, but also to all the **p**, and to all the H8269
18 unto all the king's **p**, which have heard H8269
21 the king and the **p**; and the king did H8269
2:18 feast unto all his **p** and his servants, H8269
3: 1 seat above all the **p** that *were* with him. H8269
5:11 above the **p** and servants of the king. H8269

P

Est 6: 9 the king's most noble **p**, that they may H8269
Job 3:15 Or with **p** that had gold, who filled their H8269
12:19 He leadeth **p** away spoiled, and H3548
21 He poureth contempt upon **p**, and H5081
29: 9 The **p** refrained talking, and laid *their* H8269
34:18 *art* wicked? *and* to **p**, *Ye are* ungodly? H5081
19 not the persons of **p**, nor regardeth the H8269
Ps 45:16 thou mayest make **p** in all the earth. H8269
47: 9 The **p** of the people are gathered H5081
68:27 their ruler, the **p** of Judah *and* their H8269
27 their council, the **p** of Zebulun, *and* the H8269
27 of Zebulun, *and* the **p** of Naphtali. H8269
31 **P** shall come out of Egypt; Ethiopia H2831
76:12 He shall cut off the spirit of **p**: *he is* H5057
82: 7 die like men, and fall like one of the **p**. H8269
83:11 all their **p** as Zebah, and as Zalmunna: H5257
105:22 To bind his **p** at his pleasure; and teach H8269
107:40 He poureth contempt upon **p**, and H5081
113: 8 That he may set *him* with **p**, *even* with H5081
8 princes, *even* with the **p** of his people. H5081
118: 9 the LORD than to put confidence in **p**. H5081
119:23 **P** also did sit *and* speak against me: H8269
161 **P** have persecuted me without a cause: H8269
146: 3 Put not your trust in **p**, *nor* in the son of H5081
148:11 Kings of the earth, and all people; **p**, H8269
Prv 8:15 By me kings reign, and **p** decree justice. H7336
16 By me **p** rule, and nobles, *even* all the H8269
17:26 *is* not good, *nor* to strike **p** for equity. H5081
19:10 less for a servant to have rule over **p**. H8269
28: 2 a land many *are* the **p** thereof: but by a H8269
31: 4 to drink wine; nor for **p** strong drink: H7336
Ecc 10: 7 **p** walking as servants upon the earth. H8269
16 *is* a child, and thy **p** eat in the morning! H8269
17 of nobles, and thy **p** eat in due season, H8269
Isa 1:23 Thy **p** *are* rebellious, and companions H8269
3: 4 And I will give children *to be* their **p**, H8269
14 people, and the **p** thereof: for ye have H8269
10: 8 For he saith, *Are* not my **p** altogether H8269
19:11 Surely the **p** of Zoan *are* fools, the H8269
13 The **p** of Zoan are become fools, the H8269
13 are become fools, the **p** of Noph are H8269
21: 5 drink: arise, ye **p**, *and* anoint the shield. H8269
23: 8 merchants *are* **p**, whose traffickers *are* H8269
30: 4 For his **p** were at Zoan, and his H8269
31: 9 for fear, and his **p** shall be afraid of the H8269
32: 1 and **p** shall rule in judgment. H8269
34:12 *be* there, and all her **p** shall be nothing. H8269
40:23 That bringeth the **p** to nothing; he H7336
41:25 shall come upon **p** as *upon* morter, and H5461
43:28 Therefore I have profaned the **p** of the H8269
49: 7 see and arise, **p** also shall worship, H8269
Jer 1:18 of Judah, against the **p** thereof, against H8269
2:26 **p**, and their priests, and their prophets, H8269
4: 9 the heart of the **p**; and the priests shall H8269
8: 1 the bones of his **p**, and the bones of the H8269
17:25 of this city kings and **p** sitting upon the H8269
25 they, and their **p**, the men of Judah, and H8269
24: 1 of Judah, and the **p** of Judah, with the H8269
8 of Judah, and his **p**, and the residue of H8269
25:18 thereof, and the **p** thereof, to make H8269
19 servants, and his **p**, and all his people; H8269
26:10 When the **p** of Judah heard these H8269
11 the prophets unto the **p** and to all the H8269
12 Then spake Jeremiah unto all the **p** and H8269
16 Then said the **p** and all the people unto H8269
21 men, and all the **p**, heard his words, the H8269
29: 2 and the eunuchs, the **p** of Judah and H8269
32:32 their kings, their **p**, their priests, and H8269
34:10 Now when all the **p**, and all the people, H8269
19 The **p** of Judah, and the princes of H8269
19 The princes of Judah, and the **p** of H8269
21 And Zedekiah king of Judah and his **p** H8269
35: 4 chamber of the **p**, which *was* above the H8269
36:12 and, lo, all the **p** sat there, *even* H8269
12 the son of Hananiah, and all the **p**. H8269
14 Therefore all the **p** sent Jehudi the son H8269
19 Then said the **p** unto Baruch, Go, hide H8269
21 of all the **p** which stood beside the king. H8269
37:14 Jeremiah, and brought him to the **p**. H8269
15 Wherefore the **p** were wroth with H8269
38: 4 Therefore the **p** said unto the king, We H8269
17 king of Babylon's **p**, then thy soul shall H8269
18 king of Babylon's **p**, then shall this city H8269
22 king of Babylon's **p**, and those *women* H8269
25 But if the **p** hear that I have talked with H8269
27 Then came all the **p** unto Jeremiah, H8269
39: 3 And all the **p** of the king of Babylon H8269
3 residue of the **p** of the king of Babylon. H8269
13 and all the king of Babylon's **p**; H7227
Jer 41: 1 royal, and the **p** of the king, even ten H7227
44:17 our kings, and our **p**, in the cities of H8269
21 kings, and your **p**, and the people of the H8269
48: 7 *with* his priests and his **p** together. H8269
49: 3 *and* his priests and his **p** together. H8269
38 the king and the **p**, saith the LORD. H8269
50:35 upon her **p**, and upon her wise *men*. H8269
51:57 And I will make drunk her **p**, and her H8269
52:10 slew also all the **p** of Judah in Riblah. H8269
Lam 1: 6 is departed: her **p** are become like harts H8269
2: 2 the kingdom and the **p** thereof. H8269
9 bars: her king and her **p** *are* among the H8269
5:12 **P** are hanged up by their hand: the H8269
Ezk 11: 1 the son of Benaiah, **p** of the people. H8269
17:12 king thereof, and the **p** thereof, and led H8269
19: 1 up a lamentation for the **p** of Israel, H5387
21:12 *be* upon all the **p** of Israel: terrors by H5387
22: 6 Behold, the **p** of Israel, every one were H5387
27 Her **p** in the midst thereof *are* like H8269
23:15 heads, all of them **p** to look to, after the H7991
26:16 Then all the **p** of the sea shall come H5387
27:21 Arabia, and all the **p** of Kedar, they H5387
32:29 There *is* Edom, her kings, and all her **p**, H5387
30 There *be* the **p** of the north, all of them, H5257
39:18 the blood of the **p** of the earth, of rams, H5387
45: 8 in Israel: and my **p** shall no more H5387
9 Let it suffice you, O **p** of Israel: remove H5387
Dan 1: 3 and of the king's seed, and of the **p**; H6579
3: 2 gather together the **p**, the governors, and H324
3 Then the **p**, the governors, and captains, H324
27 And the **p**, governors, and captains, and H324
5: 2 the king, and his **p**, his wives, and his H7261
3 the king, and his **p**, his wives, and his H7261
6: 1 and twenty **p**, which should be over H324
2 *was* first: that the **p** might give accounts H324
3 above the presidents and **p**, because an H324
4 Then the presidents and **p** sought to find H324
6 Then these presidents and **p** assembled H324
7 the governors, and the **p**, the counsellors, H324
8:25 **p**; but he shall be broken without hand. H8269
9: 6 to our kings, our **p**, and our fathers, H8269
8 our kings, to our **p**, and to our fathers, H8269
10:13 one of the chief **p**, came to help me; and H8269
11: 5 and *one* of his **p**; and he shall be strong H8269
8 their gods, with their **p**, *and* with their H5257
Hos 5:10 The **p** of Judah were like them that H8269
7: 3 wickedness, and the **p** with their lies. H8269
5 In the day of our king the **p** have made H8269
16 bow: their **p** shall fall by the sword H8269
8: 4 they have made **p**, and I knew *it* not: of H7786
10 a little for the burden of the king of **p**. H8269
9:15 them no more: all their **p** *are* revolters. H8269
13:10 thou saidst, Give me a king and **p**? H8269
Am 1:15 he and his **p** together, saith the LORD. H8269
2: 3 the **p** thereof with him, saith the LORD. H8269
Mic 3: 1 heads of Jacob, and ye **p** of the house of H7101
9 of Jacob, and **p** of the house of Israel, H7101
Hab 1:10 at the kings, and the **p** shall be a scorn H7336
Zep 1: 8 that I will punish the **p**, and the king's H8269
3: 3 Her **p** within her *are* roaring lions; her H8269
Mt 2: 6 least among the **p** of Juda: for out of *G2232*
20:25 said, Ye know that the **p** of the Gentiles *G758*
1Co 2: 6 the **p** of this world, that come to nought: *G758*
8 Which none of the **p** of this world knew: *G758*

PRINCE'S

Song 7: 1 thy feet with shoes, O **p** daughter! the H5081
Ezk 45:17 And it shall be the **p** part *to give* burnt H5387
48:22 *that* which is the **p**, between the border H5387

PRINCESS

Lam 1: 1 among the nations, *and* **p** among the H8282

PRINCESSES

1Ki 11: 3 And he had seven hundred wives, **p**, H8282

PRINCIPAL

Ex 30:23 Take thou also unto thee **p** spices, of H7218
Lev 6: 5 restore it in the **p**, and shall add the H7218
Nu 5: 7 his trespass with the **p** thereof, and add H7218
1Ki 4: 5 *was* **p** officer, *and* the king's friend: H3548
2Ki 25:19 in the city, and the **p** scribe of the host, H8269
1Ch 24: 6 and Levites: one **p** household being H1
31 Levites, even the **p** fathers over against H7218
Neh 11:17 son of Asaph, *was* the **p** to begin the H7218
Prv 4: 7 Wisdom *is* the **p** thing; *therefore* get H7225
Isa 16: 8 broken down the **p** plants thereof, they H8291
28:25 and cast in the **p** wheat and the H7795
Jer 25:34 *in the ashes*, ye **p** of the flock: for the H117
Jer 25:35 to flee, nor the **p** of the flock to escape. H117
36 an howling of the **p** of the flock, *shall be* H117
52:25 in the city; and the **p** scribe of the host, H8269
Mic 5: 5 him seven shepherds, and eight **p** men. H5257
Act 25:23 chief captains, and **p** men of the city, at *G1851*

PRINCIPALITIES

Jer 13:18 sit down: for your **p** shall come down, H4761
Ro 8:38 nor angels, nor **p**, nor powers, nor things *G746*
Eph 3:10 To the intent that now unto the **p** and *G746*
6:12 and blood, but against **p**, against powers, *G746*
Col 1:16 or dominions, or **p**, or powers: all things *G746*
2:15 *And* having spoiled **p** and powers, he *G746*
Tit 3: 1 Put them in mind to be subject to **p** and *G746*

PRINCIPALITY

Eph 1:21 Far above all **p**, and power, and might, *G746*
Col 2:10 which is the head of all **p** and power: *G746*

PRINCIPLES

Heb 5:12 which *be* the first **p** of the oracles of *G4747*
6: 1 Therefore leaving the **p** of the doctrine of *G746*

PRINT

Lev 19:28 **p** any marks upon you: I *am* the LORD. H5414
Job 13:27 settest a **p** upon the heels of my feet. H2707
Jn 20:25 in his hands the **p** of the nails, and put *G5179*
25 my finger into the **p** of the nails, and *G5179*

PRINTED

Job 19:23 written! oh that they were **p** in a book! H2710

PRISCA

2Ti 4:19 Salute **P** and Aquila, and the *G4251*

PRISCILLA

Act 18: 2 Italy, with his wife **P**; (because that *G4252*
18 and with him **P** and Aquila; having *G4252*
26 when Aquila and **P** had heard, they *G4252*
Ro 16: 3 Greet **P** and Aquila my helpers in *G4252*
1Co 16:19 you. Aquila and **P** salute you much in *G4252*

PRISED

Zec 11:13 price that I was **p** at of them. And I H3365

PRISON

Gen 39:20 him into the **p**, a place where H1004+H5470
20 and he was there in the **p**. H1104+H5470
21 the sight of the keeper of the **p**. H1004+H5470
22 And the keeper of the **p** H1004+H5470
22 *were* in the **p**; and whatsoever H1004+H5470
23 The keeper of the **p** looked not H1004+H5470
40: 3 into the **p**, the place where H1004+H5470
5 which *were* bound in the **p**. H1004+H5470
42:16 and ye shall be kept in **p**, that your words
19 in the house of your **p**: go ye, carry corn H4929
Jdg 16:21 of brass; and he did grind in the **p** house. H631
25 Samson out of the **p** house; and he made H631
1Ki 22:27 *fellow* in the **p**, and feed him H1004+H3608
2Ki 17: 4 him up, and bound him in **p**. H1004+H3608
25:27 king of Judah out of **p**; H1004+H3608
29 And changed his **p** garments: and he H3608
2Ch 16:10 and put him in a **p** house; for *he was* in H4115
18:26 *fellow* in the **p**, and feed him H1004+H3608
Neh 3:25 **p**. After him Pedaiah the son of Parosh. H4307
12:39 gate: and they stood still in the **p** gate. H4307
Ps 142: 7 Bring my soul out of **p**, that I may H4525
Ecc 4:14 For out of **p** he cometh to reign; H631+H1004
Isa 24:22 be shut up in the **p**, and after many H4525
42: 7 from the **p**, *and* them that sit in H4525
7 that sit in darkness out of the **p** house. H3608
22 they are hid in **p** houses: they are for H3608
53: 8 He was taken from **p** and from H6115
61: 1 of the **p** to *them that are* bound; H6495
Jer 29:26 put him in **p**, and in the stocks. H4115
32: 2 in the court of the **p**, which *was* in the H4307
8 in the court of the **p** according to the H4307
12 all the Jews that sat in the court of the **p**. H4307
33: 1 yet shut up in the court of the **p**, saying, H4307
37: 4 for they had not put him into **p**. H1004+H3628
15 and put him in **p** in the house of H612+H1004
15 for they had made that the **p**. H1004+H3628
18 that ye have put me in **p**? H1004+H3608
21 the court of the **p**, and that they should H4307
21 remained in the court of the **p**. H4307
38: 6 in the court of the **p**: and they let down H4307
13 remained in the court of the **p**. H4307
28 So Jeremiah abode in the court of the **p** H4307
39:14 out of the court of the **p**, and committed H4307

Jer 39:15 shut up in the court of the **p**, saying, H4307
52:11 in **p** till the day of his death. H1004+H6486
31 and brought him forth out of **p**, H1004+H3628
33 And changed his **p** garments: and he H3608
Mt 4:12 cast into **p**, he departed into Galilee; G3860
5:25 to the officer, and thou be cast into **p**. G5438
11: 2 Now when John had heard in the **p** the G1201
14: 3 and put *him* in **p** for Herodias' sake, G5438
10 he sent, and beheaded John in the **p**. G5438
18:30 him into **p**, till he should pay the debt. G5438
25:36 me: I was in **p**, and ye came unto me. G5438
39 Or when saw we thee sick, or in **p**, and G5438
43 sick, and in **p**, and ye visited me not. G5438
44 or in **p**, and did not minister unto thee? G5438
Mk 1:14 Now after that John was put in **p**, Jesus G3860
6:17 and bound him in **p** for Herodias' sake, G5438
27 he went and beheaded him in the **p**, G5438
Lk 3:20 this above all, that he shut up John in **p**. G5438
12:58 officer, and the officer cast thee into **p**. G5438
22:33 go with thee, both into **p**, and to death. G5438
23:19 city, and for murder, was cast into **p**.) G5438
25 was cast into **p**, whom they had desired; G5438
Jn 3:24 For John was not yet cast into **p**. G5438
Act 5:18 and put them in the common **p**. G5084
19 night opened the **p** doors, and brought G5438
21 and sent to the **p** to have them brought. G1201
22 not in the **p**, they returned, and told, G5438
23 Saying, The **p** truly found we shut with G1201
25 whom ye put in **p** are standing in the G5438
8: 3 men and women committed *them* to **p**. G5438
12: 4 he put *him* in **p**, and delivered *him* to G5438
5 Peter therefore was kept in **p**: but G5438
6 the keepers before the door kept the **p**. G5438
7 a light shined in the **p**: and he smote G3612
17 him out of the **p**. And he said, Go shew G5438
16:23 cast *them* into **p**, charging the jailor to G5438
24 **p**, and made their feet fast in the stocks. G5438
26 foundations of the **p** were shaken: and G1201
27 And the keeper of the **p** awaking out of G1200
27 and seeing the **p** doors open, he drew G5438
36 And the keeper of the **p** told this saying G1200
37 have cast *us* into **p**; and now do they G5438
40 And they went out of the **p**, and entered G5438
26:10 did I shut up in **p**, having received G5438
1Pt 3:19 went and preached unto the spirits in **p**; G5438
Rev 2:10 cast *some* of you into **p**, that ye may be G5438
20: 7 Satan shall be loosed out of his **p**, G5438

PRISONER
Ps 79:11 Let the sighing of the **p** come before H615
102:20 To hear the groaning of the **p**; to loose H615
Mt 27:15 unto the people a **p**, whom they would. G1198
16 And they had then a notable **p**, called G1198
Mk 15: 6 them one **p**, whomsoever they desired. G1198
Act 23:18 and said, Paul the **p** called me unto G1198
25:27 to send a **p**, and not withal to signify G1198
28:17 was I delivered **p** from Jerusalem into G1198
Eph 3: 1 For this cause I Paul, the **p** of Jesus G1198
4: 1 I therefore, the **p** of the Lord, beseech G1198
2Ti 1: 8 nor of me his **p**: but be thou partaker G1198
Phlm 1 Paul, a **p** of Jesus Christ, and Timothy G1198
9 aged, and now also a **p** of Jesus Christ. G1198

PRISONERS
Gen 39:20 where the king's **p** *were* bound: and he H615
22 hand all the **p** that *were* in the prison; H615
Nu 21: 1 Israel, and took *some* of them **p**. H7628
Job 3:18 *There* the **p** rest together; they hear not H615
Ps 69:33 the poor, and despiseth not his **p**. H615
146: 7 to the hungry. The LORD looseth the **p**: H631
Isa 10: 4 bow down under the **p**, and they shall fall H616
14:17 *that* opened not the house of his **p**? H615
20: 4 the Egyptians **p**, and the Ethiopians H7628
24:22 And they shall be gathered together, *as* **p** H616
42: 7 to bring out the **p** from the prison, *and* H616
49: 9 That thou mayest say to the **p**, Go forth; H631
Lam 3:34 To crush under his feet all the **p** of the H615
Zec 9:11 thy **p** out of the pit wherein *is* no water. H615
12 Turn you to the strong hold, ye **p** of H615
Act 16:25 unto God: and the **p** heard them. G1198
27 supposing that the **p** had been fled. G1198
27: 1 and certain other **p** unto *one* named G1202
42 was to kill the **p**, lest any of them should G1202
28:16 delivered the **p** to the captain of the G1198

PRISON-HOUSE See PRISON and HOUSE.

PRISONS
Lk 21:12 and into **p**, being brought before G5438
Act 22: 4 into **p** both men and women. G5438
2Co 11:23 in **p** more frequent, in deaths oft. G5438

PRIVATE
2Pt 1:20 the scripture is of any **p** interpretation. G2398

PRIVATELY
Mt 24: 3 came unto him **p**, saying, Tell us, when G2596
Mk 6:32 departed into a desert place by ship **p**. G2596
9:28 him **p**, Why could not we cast him out? G2596
13: 3 and John and Andrew asked him **p**, G2596
Lk 9:10 and went aside **p** into a desert place G2596
10:23 *his* disciples, and said **p**, Blessed *are* the G2596
Act 23:19 *with him* aside **p**, and asked *him*, What G2596
Gal 2: 2 the Gentiles, but **p** to them which were G2596

PRIVILY
Jdg 9:31 unto Abimelech **p**, saying, Behold, Gaal H8649
1Sa 24: 4 and cut off the skirt of Saul's robe **p**. H3909
Ps 10: 8 his eyes are **p** set against the poor. H6845
11: 2 they may **p** shoot at the upright in heart. H652
31: 4 laid **p** for me: for thou *art* my strength. H2934
64: 5 snares **p**; they say, Who shall see them? H2934
101: 5 Whoso **p** slandereth his neighbour, H5643
142: 3 walked have they **p** laid a snare for me. H2934
Prv 1:11 lurk **p** for the innocent without cause: H6845
18 blood; they lurk **p** for their *own* lives. H6845
Mt 1:19 was minded to put her away **p**. G2977
2: 7 Then Herod, when he had **p** called the G2977
Act 16:37 they thrust us out **p**? nay verily; but let G2977
Gal 2: 4 in, who came in **p** to spy out our liberty G3922
2Pt 2: 1 among you, who **p** shall bring in G3918

PRIVY
Dt 23: 1 stones, or hath his **p** member cut off, H8212
1Ki 2:44 thine heart is **p** to, that thou didst to H3045
Ezk 21:14 which entereth into their **p** chambers. H2314
Act 5: 2 his wife also being **p** *to it*, and brought G4894

PRIZE
1Co 9:24 the **p**? So run, that ye may obtain. G1017
Php 3:14 I press toward the mark for the **p** of the G1017

PROBATE See REPROBATE.

PROCEED
Ex 25:35 branches that **p** out of the candlestick. H3318
Jos 6:10 shall *any* word **p** out of your mouth, H3318
2Sa 7:12 thee, which shall **p** out of thy bowels, H3318
Job 40: 5 yea, twice; but I will **p** no further.
Isa 29:14 Therefore, behold, I will **p** to do a H3254
51: 4 for a law shall **p** from me, and I will H3318
Jer 9: 3 the earth; for they **p** from evil to evil, H3318
30:19 And out of them shall **p** thanksgiving H3318
21 governor shall **p** from the midst of H3318
Hab 1: 7 and their dignity shall **p** of themselves. H3318
Mt 15:18 But those things which **p** out of the G1607
19 For out of the heart **p** evil thoughts, G1831
Mk 7:21 of the heart of men, **p** evil thoughts, G1607
Eph 4:29 Let no corrupt communication **p** out of G1607
2Ti 3: 9 But they shall **p** no further: for their G4298

PROCEEDED
Nu 30:12 *them; then* whatsoever **p** out of her lips H4161
32:24 that which hath **p** out of your mouth. H3318
Jdg 11:36 to that which hath **p** out of thy mouth; H3318
Job 36: 1 Elihu also **p**, and said, H3254
Lk 4:22 words which **p** out of his mouth. And G1607
Jn 8:42 love me: for I **p** forth and came from G1831
Act 12: 3 the Jews, he **p** further to take Peter G4369
Rev 4: 5 And out of the throne **p** lightnings and G1607
19:21 which *sword* **p** out of his mouth: and G1607

PROCEEDETH
Gen 24:50 said, The thing **p** from the LORD: we H3318
Nu 30: 2 to all that **p** out of his mouth. H3318
Dt 8: 3 every *word* that **p** out of the mouth of H4161
1Sa 24:13 Wickedness **p** from the wicked: but H3318
Ecc 10: 5 sun, as an error *which* **p** from the ruler: H3318
Lam 3:38 Out of the mouth of the most High **p** H3318
Hab 1: 4 righteous; therefore wrong judgment **p**. H3318
Mt 4: 4 word that **p** out of the mouth of God. G1607
Jn 15:26 of truth, which **p** from the Father, he G1607
Jas 3:10 Out of the same mouth **p** blessing and G1831
Rev 11: 5 And if any man will hurt them, fire **p** G1607

PROCEEDING
Rev 22: 1 clear as crystal, **p** out of the throne of G1607

PROCESS
Gen 4: 3 And in **p** of time it came to pass, that H7093
38:12 And in **p** of time the daughter of Shuah H7235
Ex 2:23 And it came to pass in **p** of time, that H7227
Jdg 11: 4 And it came to pass in **p** of time, that the
2Ch 21:19 And it came to pass, that in **p** of time,

PROCHORUS
Act 6: 5 and Philip, and **P**, and Nicanor, and G4402

PROCLAIM
Ex 33:19 thee, and I will **p** the name of the LORD H7121
Lev 23: 2 LORD, which ye shall **p** *to be* holy H7121
4 which ye shall **p** in their seasons. H7121
21 And ye shall **p** on the selfsame day, H7121
37 LORD, which ye shall **p** *to be* holy H7121
25:10 fiftieth year, and **p** liberty throughout H7121
Dt 20:10 to fight against it, then **p** peace unto it. H7121
Jdg 7: 3 Now therefore go to, **p** in the ears of the H7121
1Ki 21: 9 And she wrote in the letters, saying, **P** a H7121
2Ki 10:20 And Jehu said, **P** a solemn assembly H6942
Neh 8:15 And that they should publish and **p** in H5674
Est 6: 9 of the city, and **p** before him, Thus H7121
Prv 20: 6 Most men will **p** every one his own H7121
Isa 61: 1 the brokenhearted, to **p** liberty to the H7121
2 To **p** the acceptable year of the LORD, H7121
Jer 3:12 Go and **p** these words toward the H7121
7: 2 house, and **p** there this word, and H7121
11: 6 Then the LORD said unto me, **P** all H7121
19: 2 **p** there the words that I shall tell thee, H7121
34: 8 at Jerusalem, to **p** liberty unto them; H7121
17 behold, I **p** a liberty for you, saith H7121
Joel 3: 9 **P** ye this among the Gentiles; Prepare H7121
Am 4: 5 with leaven, and **p** *and* publish the free H7121

PROCLAIMED
Ex 34: 5 there, and **p** the name of the LORD. H7121
6 by before him, and **p**, The LORD, The H7121
36: 6 caused it to be **p** throughout the camp, H6963
1Ki 21:12 They **p** a fast, and set Naboth on high H7121
2Ki 10:20 assembly for Baal. And they **p** *it*. H7121
23:16 of God **p**, who proclaimed these words. H7121
16 of God proclaimed, who **p** these words. H7121
17 from Judah, and **p** these things that H7121
2Ch 20: 3 and **p** a fast throughout all Judah. H7121
Ezr 8:21 Then I **p** a fast there, at the river of H7121
Est 6:11 of the city, and **p** before him, Thus H7121
Isa 62:11 Behold, the LORD hath **p** unto the end H8085
Jer 36: 9 month, *that* they **p** a fast before the H7121
Jna 3: 5 believed God, and **p** a fast, and put on H7121
7 And he caused *it* to be **p** and published H2199
Lk 12: 3 closets shall be **p** upon the housetops. G2784

PROCLAIMETH
Prv 12:23 but the heart of fools **p** foolishness. H7121

PROCLAIMING
Jer 34:15 in my sight, in **p** liberty every man to H7121
17 unto me, in **p** liberty, every one to H7121
Rev 5: 2 And I saw a strong angel **p** with a loud G2784

PROCLAMATION
Ex 32: 5 it; and Aaron made **p**, and said, To H7121
1Ki 15:22 Then king Asa made a **p** throughout all H8085
22:36 And there went a **p** throughout the host H7440
2Ch 24: 9 And they made a **p** through Judah and H6963
30: 5 to make **p** throughout all H5674+H6963
36:22 he made a **p** throughout all H5674+H6963
Ezr 1: 1 he made a **p** throughout all H5674+H6963
10: 7 And they made **p** throughout H5674+H6963
Dan 5:29 neck, and made a **p** concerning him, H3745

PROCURE
Jer 26:19 might we **p** great evil against our souls. H6213
33: 9 for all the prosperity that I **p** unto it. H6213

PROCURED
Jer 2:17 Hast thou not **p** this unto thyself, in H6213
4:18 Thy way and thy doings have **p** these H6213

PROCURETH
Prv 11:27 He that diligently seeketh good **p** H1245

PRODUCE
Isa 41:21 **P** your cause, saith the LORD; bring H7126

PROFANE
Lev 18:21 **p** the name of thy God: I *am* the LORD. H2490
19:12 **p** the name of thy God: I *am* the LORD. H2490

Lev 20: 3 my sanctuary, and to **p** my holy name. H2490
21: 4 man among his people, to **p** himself. H2490
6 their God, and not **p** the name of their H2490
7 *that is* a whore, or **p**; neither shall they H2491
9 And the daughter of any priest, if she **p** H2490
12 of the sanctuary, nor **p** the sanctuary of H2490
14 A widow, or a divorced woman, or **p**, *or* H2491
15 Neither shall he **p** his seed among his H2490
23 hath a blemish; that he **p** not my H2490
22: 2 and that they **p** not my holy name *in* H2490
9 they **p** it: I the LORD do sanctify them. H2490
15 And they shall not **p** the holy things of H2490
32 Neither shall ye **p** my holy name; but I H2490
Neh 13:17 this that ye do, and **p** the sabbath day? H2490
Jer 23:11 For both prophet and priest are **p**; yea, H2610
Ezk 21:25 And thou, **p** wicked prince of Israel, H2491
22:26 the holy and **p**, neither have they H2455
23:39 my sanctuary to **p** it; and, lo, thus have H2490
24:21 Behold, I will **p** my sanctuary, the H2490
28:16 I will cast thee as **p** out of the mountain H2490
42:20 between the sanctuary and the **p** place. H2455
44:23 the holy and **p**, and cause them to H2455
48:15 shall be a **p** *place* for the city, for H2455
Am 2: 7 the *same* maid, to **p** my holy name: H2490
Mt 12: 5 **p** the sabbath, and are blameless? G953
Act 24: 6 Who also hath gone about to **p** the G953
1Ti 1: 9 for unholy and **p**, for murderers of G952
4: 7 But refuse **p** and old wives' fables, and G952
6:20 thy trust, avoiding **p** *and* vain babblings, G952
2Ti 2:16 But shun **p** *and* vain babblings: for they G952
Heb 12:16 Lest there *be* any fornicator, or **p** person, G952

PROFANED

Lev 19: 8 because he hath **p** the hallowed thing H2490
Ps 89:39 **p** his crown *by casting it* to the ground. H2490
Isa 43:28 Therefore I have **p** the princes of the H2490
Ezk 22: 8 holy things, and hast **p** my sabbaths. H2490
26 my law, and have **p** mine holy things: H2490
26 my sabbaths, and I am **p** among them. H2490
23:38 the same day, and have **p** my sabbaths. H2490
25: 3 when it was **p**; and against the land H2490
36:20 they went, they **p** my holy name, when H2490
21 of Israel had **p** among the heathen, H2490
22 **p** among the heathen, whither ye went. H2490
23 great name, which was **p** among the H2490
23 which ye have **p** in the midst of them; H2490
Mal 1:12 But ye have **p** it, in that ye say, The H2490
2:11 for Judah hath **p** the holiness of the H2490

PROFANENESS

Jer 23:15 is **p** gone forth into all the land. H2613

PROFANETH

Lev 21: 9 the whore, she **p** her father: she shall H2490

PROFANING

Neh 13:18 wrath upon Israel by **p** the sabbath. H2490
Mal 2:10 by **p** the covenant of our fathers? H2490

PROFESS

Dt 26: 3 and say unto him, I **p** this day unto the H5046
Mt 7:23 And then will I **p** unto them, I never G3670
Tit 1:16 They **p** that they know God; but in G3670

PROFESSED

2Co 9:13 God for your **p** subjection unto the G3671
1Ti 6:12 called, and hast **p** a good profession G3670

PROFESSING

Ro 1:22 **P** themselves to be wise, they became G5335
1Ti 2:10 But (which becometh women **p** G1861
6:21 Which some **p** have erred concerning G1861

PROFESSION

1Ti 6:12 a good **p** before many witnesses. G3671
Heb 3: 1 and High Priest of our **p**, Christ Jesus; G3671
4:14 the Son of God, let us hold fast *our* **p**. G3671
10:23 Let us hold fast the **p** of *our* faith G3671

PROFIT

Gen 25:32 what **p** shall this birthright do to me?
37:26 his brethren, What **p** *is it* if we slay our H1215
1Sa 12:21 cannot **p** nor deliver; for they *are* vain. H3276
Est 3: 8 it *is* not for the king's **p** to suffer them. H7737
Job 21:15 **p** should we have, if we pray unto him? H3276
30: 2 **p** me, in whom old age was perished?
35: 3 thee? *and*, What **p** shall I have, *if I be* H3276
8 thy righteousness *may* **p** the son of man.
Ps 30: 9 What **p** *is there* in my blood, when I go H1215
Prv 10: 2 Treasures of wickedness **p** nothing: but H3276
11: 4 Riches **p** not in the day of wrath: but H3276
14:23 In all labour there is **p**: but the talk of H4195
Ecc 1: 3 What **p** hath a man of all his labour H3504
2:11 and *there was* no **p** under the sun. H3504
3: 9 What **p** hath he that worketh in that H3504
5: 9 Moreover the **p** of the earth is for all: H3504
16 he go: and what **p** hath he that hath H3504
7:11 *by it there is* **p** to them that see the sun. H3148
Isa 30: 5 *that* could not **p** them, nor be an help H3276
5 **p**, but a shame, and also a reproach. H3276
6 to a people *that* shall not **p** *them*. H3276
44: 9 things shall not **p**; and they *are* their H3276
47:12 able to **p**, if so be thou mayest prevail. H3276
48:17 teacheth thee to **p**, which leadeth thee H3276
57:12 thy works; for they shall not **p** thee. H3276
Jer 2: 8 and walked after *things that* do not **p**. H3276
11 their glory for *that which* doth not **p**. H3276
7: 8 ye trust in lying words, that cannot **p**. H3276
12:13 pain, *but* shall not **p**: and they shall be H3276
16:19 and *things* wherein *there is* no **p**. H3276
23:32 not **p** this people at all, saith the LORD. H3276
Mal 3:14 God: and what **p** *is it* that we have kept H1215
Mk 8:36 For what shall it **p** a man, if he shall G5623
Ro 3: 1 Jew? or what **p** *is there* of circumcision? G5622
1Co 7:35 And this I speak for your own **p**; not G4851
10:33 seeking mine own **p**, but the *profit* of G4851
33 the *p* of many, that they may be saved. G4851
12: 7 Spirit is given to every man to **p** withal. G4851
14: 6 what shall I **p** you, except I shall speak G5623
Gal 5: 2 Christ shall **p** you nothing. G5623
2Ti 2:14 **p**, *but* to the subverting of the hearers. G5539
Heb 4: 2 preached did not **p** them, not being G5623
12:10 but he for *our* **p**, that *we* might be G4851
Jas 2:14 What *doth it* **p**, my brethren, though a G3786
16 are needful to the body; what *doth it* **p**? G3786

PROFITABLE

Job 22: 2 Can a man be **p** unto God, as he that is H5532
2 he that is wise may be **p** unto himself? H5532
Ecc 10:10 strength: but wisdom *is* **p** to direct. H3504
Isa 44:10 a graven image *that* is **p** for nothing? H3276
Jer 13: 7 was marred, it was **p** for nothing. H6743
Mt 5:29 from thee: for it is **p** for thee that one of G4851
30 from thee: for it is **p** for thee that one of G4851
Act 20:20 nothing that was **p** *unto you*, but have G4851
1Ti 4: 8 little: but godliness is **p** unto all things, G5624
2Ti 3:16 of God, and *is* **p** for doctrine, for G5624
4:11 thee: for he is **p** to me for the ministry. G2173
Tit 3: 8 These things are good and **p** unto men. G5624
Phlm 11 but now **p** to thee and to me: G2173

PROFITED

Job 33:27 *that which was* right, and it **p** me not; H7737
Mt 15: 5 whatsoever thou mightest be **p** by me; G5623
16:26 For what is a man **p**, if he shall gain the G5623
Mk 7:11 mightest be **p** by me; *he shall be free.* G5623
Gal 1:14 And **p** in the Jews' religion above many G4298
Heb 13: 9 which have not **p** them that have been G5623

PROFITETH

Job 34: 9 For he hath said, It **p** a man nothing H5532
Hab 2:18 What **p** the graven image that the H3276
Jn 6:63 the flesh **p** nothing: the words G5623
Ro 2:25 For circumcision verily **p**, if thou keep G5623
1Co 13: 3 and have not charity, it **p** me nothing. G5623
1Ti 4: 8 For bodily exercise **p** little: but G2076

PROFITING

1Ti 4:15 to them; that thy **p** may appear to all. G4297

PROFOUND

Hos 5: 2 And the revolters are **p** to make H6009

PROGENITORS

Gen 49:26 the blessings of my **p** unto the utmost H2029

PROGNOSTICATORS

Isa 47:13 the monthly **p**, stand up, and save H3045

PROLONG

Dt 4:26 it; ye shall not **p** *your* days upon it, but H748
40 that thou mayest **p** *thy* days upon the H748
5:33 and *that* ye may **p** *your* days in the land H748
11: 9 And that ye may **p** *your* days in the land, H748
17:20 the end that he may **p** *his* days in his H748
22: 7 thee, and *that* thou mayest **p** *thy* days. H748
30:18 *that* ye shall not **p** *your* days upon the H748
32:47 this thing ye shall **p** *your* days in the H748
Job 6:11 *is* mine end, that I should **p** my life? H748
15:29 **p** the perfection thereof upon the earth. H5186
Ps 61: 6 Thou wilt **p** the king's life: *and* his H3254
Prv 28:16 hateth covetousness shall **p** *his* days. H748
Ecc 8:13 neither shall he **p** *his* days, *which are* as H748
Isa 53:10 see *his* seed, he shall **p** *his* days, and the H748

PROLONGED

Dt 5:16 thy days may be **p**, and that it may go H748
6: 2 of thy life; and that thy days may be **p**. H748
Prv 28: 2 knowledge the state *thereof* shall be **p**. H748
Ecc 8:12 and his *days* be **p**, yet surely I know that H748
Isa 13:22 to come, and her days shall not be **p**. H4900
Ezk 12:22 The days are **p**, and every vision faileth? H748
25 shall be no more **p**: for in your days, O H4900
28 of my words be **p** any more, but the H4900
Dan 7:12 their lives were **p** for a season and time. H754

PROLONGETH

Prv 10:27 The fear of the LORD **p** days: but the H3254
Ecc 7:15 *man* that **p** *his life* in his wickedness. H748

PROMISE

Nu 14:34 and ye shall know my breach of **p**. H8569
1Ki 8:56 of all his good **p**, which he promised H1697
2Ch 1: 9 Now, O LORD God, let thy **p** unto H1697
Neh 5:12 that they should do according to this **p**. H1697
13 not this **p**, even thus be he shaken H1697
13 And the people did according to this **p**. H1697
Ps 77: 8 for ever? doth *his* **p** fail for evermore? H562
105:42 For he remembered his holy **p**, *and* H1697
Lk 24:49 And, behold, I send the **p** of my Father G1860
Act 1: 4 but wait for the **p** of the Father, which, G1860
2:33 of the Father the **p** of the Holy Ghost, G1860
39 For the **p** is unto you, and to your G1860
7:17 But when the time of the **p** drew nigh, G1860
13:23 **p** raised unto Israel a Saviour, Jesus: G1860
32 the **p** which was made unto the fathers, G1860
23:21 they ready, looking for a **p** from thee. G1860
26: 6 of the **p** made of God unto our fathers: G1860
7 Unto which *p* our twelve tribes, instantly
Ro 4:13 For the **p**, that he should be the heir of G1860
14 void, and the **p** made of none effect: G1860
16 to the end the **p** might be sure to all G1860
20 He staggered not at the **p** of God G1860
9: 8 of the **p** are counted for the seed. G1860
9 For this *is* the word of **p**, At this time G1860
Gal 3:14 receive the **p** of the Spirit through faith. G1860
17 it should make the **p** of none effect. G1860
18 *it is* no more of **p**: but God gave *it* to G1860
18 but God gave *it* to Abraham by **p**. G1860
19 come to whom the **p** was made; *and it* G1861
22 under sin, that the **p** by faith of Jesus G1860
29 seed, and heirs according to the **p**. G1860
4:23 flesh; but he of the freewoman *was* by **p**. G1860
28 as Isaac was, are the children of **p**. G1860
Eph 1:13 ye were sealed with that holy Spirit of **p**, G1860
2:12 the covenants of **p**, having no hope, and G1860
3: 6 of his **p** in Christ by the gospel: G1860
6: 2 which is the first commandment with **p**; G1860
1Ti 4: 8 all things, having **p** of the life that now G1860
2Ti 1: 1 to the **p** of life which is in Christ Jesus, G1860
Heb 4: 1 Let us therefore fear, lest, a **p** being left G1860
6:13 For when God made **p** to Abraham, G1861
15 patiently endured, he obtained the **p**. G1860
17 unto the heirs of **p** the immutability of G1860
9:15 receive the **p** of eternal inheritance. G1860
10:36 the will of God, ye might receive the **p**. G1860
11: 9 By faith he sojourned in the land of **p**, G1860
9 Jacob, the heirs with him of the same **p**: G1860
39 report through faith, received not the **p**: G1860
2Pt 2:19 While they **p** them liberty, they G1861
3: 4 And saying, Where is the **p** of his G1860
9 The Lord is not slack concerning his **p**, G1860
13 Nevertheless we, according to his **p**, G1862
1Jn 2:25 And this is the **p** that he hath promised G1860

PROMISED

Ex 12:25 hath **p**, that ye shall keep this service. H1696
Nu 14:40 the LORD hath **p**: for we have sinned. H559
Dt 1:11 *are*, and bless you, as he hath **p** you!) H1696
6: 3 of thy fathers hath **p** thee, in the land H1696
9:28 the land which he **p** them, and because H1696
10: 9 according as the LORD thy God **p** him. H1696
12:20 thy border, as he hath **p** thee, and thou H1696
15: 6 thee, as he **p** thee: and thou shalt H1696
19: 8 which he **p** to give unto thy fathers; H1696
23:23 which thou hast **p** with thy mouth. H1696
26:18 people, as he hath **p** thee, and that *thou* H1696

Dt 27: 3 LORD God of thy fathers hath **p** thee. H1696
Jos 9:21 as the princes had **p** them. H1696
22: 4 brethren, as he **p** them: therefore now H1696
23: 5 as the LORD your God hath **p** unto you. H1696
10 that fighteth for you, as he hath **p** you. H1696
15 the LORD your God **p** you; so shall the H1696
2Sa 7:28 hast **p** this goodness unto thy servant: H1696
1Ki 2:24 an house, as he **p**, Adonijah shall be put H1696
5:12 wisdom, as he **p** him: and there was H1696
8:20 as the LORD **p**, and have built an house H1696
56 to all that he **p**: there hath not failed H1696
56 he **p** by the hand of Moses his servant. H1696
9: 5 for ever, as I **p** to David thy father, H1696
2Ki 8:19 sake, as he **p** him to give him alway H559
1Ch 17:26 hast **p** this goodness unto thy servant: H1696
2Ch 6:10 as the LORD **p**, and have built the H1696
15 which thou hast **p** him; and spakest H1696
16 which thou hast **p** him, saying, There H1696
21: 7 David, and as he **p** to give a light to him H559
Neh 9:23 which thou hadst **p** to their fathers, that H559
Est 4: 7 that Haman had **p** to pay to the king's H559
Jer 32:42 them all the good that I have **p** them. H1696
33:14 thing which I have **p** unto the house of H1696
Mt 14: 7 Whereupon he **p** with an oath to give *G3670*
Mk 14:11 were glad, and **p** to give him money. *G1861*
Lk 1:72 To perform the mercy *p* to our fathers,
22: 6 And he **p**, and sought opportunity to *G1843*
Act 7: 5 his foot on: yet he **p** that he would give *G1861*
Ro 1: 2 (Which he had **p** afore by his prophets *G4279*
4:21 he had **p**, he was able also to perform. *G1861*
Tit 1: 2 cannot lie, **p** before the world began; *G1861*
Heb 10:23 wavering; (for he *is* faithful that **p**;) *G1861*
11:11 she judged him faithful who had **p**. *G1861*
12:26 but now he hath **p**, saying, Yet once *G1861*
Jas 1:12 the Lord hath **p** to them that love him. *G1861*
2: 5 which he hath **p** to them that love him? *G1861*
1Jn 2:25 And this is the promise that he hath **p** *G1861*

PROMISEDST
1Ki 8:24 father that thou **p** him: thou spakest H1696
25 father that thou **p** him, saying, There H1696
Neh 9:15 for their thirst, and **p** them that they H559

PROMISES
Ro 9: 4 law, and the service *of God*, and the **p**; *G1860*
15: 8 to confirm the **p** *made* unto the fathers: *G1860*
2Co 1:20 For all the **p** of God in him *are* yea, and *G1860*
7: 1 Having therefore these **p**, dearly *G1860*
Gal 3:16 his seed were the **p** made. He saith not, *G1860*
21 *Is* the law then against the **p** of God? *G1860*
Heb 6:12 faith and patience inherit the **p**. *G1860*
7: 6 and blessed him that had the **p**. *G1860*
8: 6 which was established upon better **p**. *G1860*
11:13 received the **p**, but having seen them *G1860*
17 the **p** offered up his only begotten *son*, *G1860*
33 **p**, stopped the mouths of lions, *G1860*
2Pt 1: 4 and precious **p**: that by these ye might *G1862*

PROMISING
Ezk 13:22 from his wicked way, by **p** him life: H2421

PROMOTE
Nu 22:17 For I will **p** thee unto very great H3513
37 I not able indeed to **p** thee to honour? H3513
24:11 thy place: I thought to **p** thee unto great H3513
Est 3: 1 king Ahasuerus **p** Haman the son of H1431
Prv 4: 8 Exalt her, and she shall **p** thee: she H7311

PROMOTED
Jdg 9: 9 and man, and go to be **p** over the trees? H5128
11 fruit, and go to be **p** over the trees? H5128
13 and man, and go to be **p** over the trees? H5128
Est 5:11 the king had **p** him, and how he had H1431
Dan 3:30 Then the king **p** Shadrach, Meshach, H6744

PROMOTION
Ps 75: 6 For **p** *cometh* neither from the east, nor H7311
Prv 3:35 glory: but shame shall be the **p** of fools. H7311

PRONOUNCE
Lev 5: 4 *be* that a man shall **p** with an oath, and H981
13: 3 shall look on him, and **p** him unclean. H981
6 the priest shall **p** him clean: it *is but* a
8 shall **p** him unclean: it *is* a leprosy.
11 and the priest shall **p** him unclean, and
13 his flesh, he shall **p** *him* clean *that hath*
15 the raw flesh, and **p** him to be unclean:
17 the priest shall **p** *him* clean *that hath*
20 the priest shall **p** him unclean: it *is* a
Lev 13:22 priest shall **p** him unclean: it *is* a plague.
23 boil; and the priest shall **p** him clean.
25 the priest shall **p** him unclean: it *is* the
27 the priest shall **p** him unclean: it *is* the
28 and the priest shall **p** him clean: for it *is*
30 the priest shall **p** him unclean: it *is* a dry
34 the priest shall **p** him clean: and he shall
37 *is* clean: and the priest shall **p** him clean.
44 the priest shall **p** him utterly unclean;
59 to **p** it clean, or to pronounce it unclean.
59 to pronounce it clean, or to **p** it unclean.
14: 7 times, and shall **p** him clean, and shall
48 then the priest shall **p** the house clean,
Jdg 12: 6 could not frame to **p** *it* right. Then they H1696

PRONOUNCED
Neh 6:12 sent him; but that he **p** this prophecy H1696
Jer 11:17 planted thee, hath **p** evil against thee, H1696
16:10 hath the LORD **p** all this great evil H1696
18: 8 If that nation, against whom I have **p**, H1696
19:15 the evil that I have **p** against it, because H1696
25:13 which I have **p** against it, *even* all that H1696
26:13 of the evil that he hath **p** against you. H1696
19 evil which he had **p** against them? Thus H1696
34: 5 for I have **p** the word, saith the LORD. H1696
35:17 all the evil that I have **p** against them: H1696
36: 7 the LORD hath **p** against this people. H1696
18 Then Baruch answered them, He **p** all H7121
31 the evil that I have **p** against them; but H1696
40: 2 God hath **p** this evil upon this place. H1696

PRONOUNCING
Lev 5: 4 Or if a soul swear, **p** with *his* lips to do H981

PROOF
2Co 2: 9 I might know the **p** of you, whether ye *G1382*
8:24 the churches, the **p** of your love, and of *G1732*
13: 3 Since ye seek a **p** of Christ speaking in *G1382*
Php 2:22 But ye know the **p** of him, that, as a son *G1382*
2Ti 4: 5 evangelist, make full **p** of thy ministry. *G4135*

PROOFS
Act 1: 3 by many infallible **p**, being seen of them *G5039*

PROPER
1Ch 29: 3 I have of mine own **p** good, of gold and H5089
Act 1:19 is called in their **p** tongue, Aceldama, *G2398*
1Co 7: 7 man hath his **p** gift of God, one after *G2398*
Heb 11:23 they saw *he was* a **p** child; and they were *G791*

PROPHECIES
1Co 13: 8 but whether *there be* **p**, they shall fail; *G4394*
1Ti 1:18 according to the **p** which went before *G4394*

PROPHECY
2Ch 9:29 and in the **p** of Ahijah the Shilonite, H5016
15: 8 words, and the **p** of Oded the prophet, H5016
Neh 6:12 he pronounced this **p** against me: for H5016
Prv 30: 1 son of Jakeh, *even* the **p**: the man spake H4853
31: 1 The words of king Lemuel, the **p** that H4853
Dan 9:24 and **p**, and to anoint the most Holy. H5030
Mt 13:14 And in them is fulfilled the **p** of Esaias, *G4394*
Ro 12: 6 given to us, whether **p**, *let us prophesy* *G4394*
1Co 12:10 to another **p**; to another discerning *G4394*
13: 2 And though I have *the gift of* **p**, and *G4394*
1Ti 4:14 was given thee by **p**, with the laying on *G4394*
2Pt 1:19 We have also a more sure word of **p**; *G4397*
20 Knowing this first, that no **p** of the *G4394*
21 For the **p** came not in old time by the *G4394*
Rev 1: 3 hear the words of this **p**, and keep those *G4394*
11: 6 the days of their **p**: and have power over *G4394*
19:10 the testimony of Jesus is the spirit of **p**. *G4394*
22: 7 the sayings of the **p** of this book. *G4394*
10 **p** of this book: for the time is at hand. *G4394*
18 the words of the **p** of this book, If any *G4394*
19 of the book of this **p**, God shall take *G4394*

PROPHESIED
Nu 11:25 upon them, they **p**, and did not cease. H5012
26 the tabernacle: and they **p** in the camp. H5012
1Sa 10:10 came upon him, and he **p** among them. H5012
11 that, behold, he **p** among the prophets, H5012
18:10 upon Saul, and he **p** in the midst of the H5012
19:20 the messengers of Saul, and they also **p**. H5012
21 and they **p** likewise. And Saul sent H5012
21 again the third time, and they **p** also. H5012
23 **p**, until he came to Naioth in Ramah. H5012
24 clothes also, and **p** before Samuel in H5012
1Ki 18:29 past, and they **p** until the *time* of the H5012
1Ki 22:10 and all the prophets **p** before them. H5012
12 And all the prophets **p** so, saying, Go H5012
1Ch 25: 2 **p** according to the order of the king. H5012
3 Jeduthun, who **p** with a harp, to give H5012
2Ch 18: 7 him; for he never **p** good unto me, but H5012
9 and all the prophets **p** before them. H5012
11 And all the prophets **p** so, saying, Go H5012
20:37 of Mareshah **p** against Jehoshaphat, H5012
Ezr 5: 1 the son of Iddo, **p** unto the Jews that H5013
Jer 2: 8 me, and the prophets **p** by Baal, and H5012
20: 1 heard that Jeremiah **p** these things. H5012
6 thy friends, to whom thou hast **p** lies. H5012
23:13 of Samaria; they **p** in Baal, and caused H5012
21 I have not spoken to them, yet they **p**. H5012
25:13 hath **p** against all the nations. H5012
26: 9 Why hast thou **p** in the name of the H5012
11 to die; for he hath **p** against this city, as H5012
18 Micah the Morasthite **p** in the days of H5012
20 And there was also a man that **p** in the H5012
20 who **p** against this city and H5012
28: 6 which thou hast **p**, to bring again the H5012
8 before thee of old **p** both against many H5012
29:31 Shemaiah hath **p** unto you, and I sent H5012
37:19 Where *are* now your prophets which **p** H5012
Ezk 11:13 And it came to pass, when I **p**, that H5012
37: 7 So I **p** as I was commanded: and as I H5012
7 and as I **p**, there was a noise, and H5012
10 So I **p** as he commanded me, and the H5012
38:17 of Israel, which **p** in those days *many* H5012
Zec 13: 4 when he hath **p**; neither shall they wear H5012
Mt 7:22 Lord, have we not **p** in thy name? and *G4395*
11:13 For all the prophets and the law **p** until *G4395*
Mk 7: 6 Well hath Esaias **p** of you hypocrites, *G4395*
Lk 1:67 with the Holy Ghost, and **p**, saying, *G4395*
Jn 11:51 **p** that Jesus should die for that nation; *G4395*
Act 19: 6 and they spake with tongues, and **p**. *G4395*
1Co 14: 5 but rather that ye **p**: for greater *is* he *G4395*
1Pt 1:10 diligently, who **p** of the grace *that* *G4395*
Jude 14 from Adam, **p** of these, saying, Behold, *G4395*

PROPHESIETH
Jer 28: 9 The prophet which **p** of peace, when H5012
Ezk 12:27 and he **p** of the times *that are* far off. H5012
Zec 13: 3 shall thrust him through when he **p**. H5012
1Co 11: 5 But every woman that prayeth or **p** *G4395*
14: 3 But he that **p** speaketh unto men *to* *G4395*
4 but he that **p** edifieth the church. *G4395*
5 for greater *is* he that **p** than he that *G4395*

PROPHESY
Nu 11:27 Eldad and Medad do **p** in the camp. H5012
1Sa 10: 5 a harp, before them; and they shall **p**: H5012
6 and thou shalt **p** with them, and shalt H5012
1Ki 22: 8 for he doth not **p** good concerning me, H5012
18 **p** no good concerning me, but evil? H5012
1Ch 25: 1 who should **p** with harps, with H5012
2Ch 18:17 he would not **p** good unto me, but evil? H5012
Isa 30:10 and to the prophets, **P** not unto us right H2372
10 speak unto us smooth things, **p** deceits: H2372
Jer 5:31 The prophets **p** falsely, and the priests H5012
11:21 thy life, saying, **P** not in the name of H5012
14:14 me, The prophets **p** lies in my name: I H5012
14 unto them: they **p** unto you a false H5012
15 the prophets that **p** in my name, and I H5012
16 And the people to whom they **p** shall be H5012
19:14 had sent him to **p**; and he stood in the H5012
23:16 of the prophets that **p** unto you: they H5012
25 said, that **p** lies in my name, saying, H5012
26 of the prophets that **p** lies? yea, *they are* H5012
32 Behold, I *am* against them that **p** false H5012
25:30 Therefore **p** thou against them all these H5012
26:12 LORD sent me to **p** against this house H5012
27:10 For they **p** a lie unto you, to remove H5012
14 of Babylon: for they **p** a lie unto you. H5012
15 LORD, yet they **p** a lie in my name; that H5012
15 ye, and the prophets that **p** unto you. H5012
16 your prophets that **p** unto you, saying, H5012
16 from Babylon: for they **p** a lie unto you. H5012
29: 9 For they **p** falsely unto you in my H5012
21 Maaseiah, which **p** a lie unto you in my H5012
32: 3 dost thou **p**, and say, Thus saith H5012
Ezk 4: 7 uncovered, and thou shalt **p** against it. H5012
6: 2 of Israel, and **p** against them, H5012
11: 4 Therefore **p** against them, prophesy, O H5012
4 Therefore prophesy against them, **p**, O H5012
13: 2 Son of man, **p** against the prophets of H5012
2 of Israel that **p**, and say thou unto them H5012
2 thou unto them that **p** out of their own H5030
16 *To wit*, the prophets of Israel which **p** H5012

Ezk 13:17 of thy people, which **p** out of their own H5012
17 own heart; and **p** thou against them, H5012
20:46 **p** against the forest of the south field; H5012
21: 2 places, and **p** against the land of Israel, H5012
9 Son of man, **p**, and say, Thus saith the H5012
14 Thou therefore, son of man, **p**, and H5012
28 And thou, son of man, **p** and say, Thus H5012
25: 2 the Ammonites, and **p** against them; H5012
28:21 face against Zidon, and **p** against it, H5012
29: 2 **p** against him, and against all Egypt: H5012
30: 2 Son of man, **p** and say, Thus saith the H5012
34: 2 Son of man, **p** against the shepherds of H5012
2 of Israel, **p**, and say unto them, H5012
35: 2 against mount Seir, and **p** against it, H5012
36: 1 Also, thou son of man, **p** unto the H5012
3 Therefore **p** and say, Thus saith the H5012
6 **P** therefore concerning the land of H5012
37: 4 Again he said unto me, **P** upon these H5012
9 Then said he unto me, **P** unto the wind, H5012
9 unto the wind, **p**, son of man, and say H5012
12 Therefore **p** and say unto them, Thus H5012
38: 2 and Tubal, and **p** against him, H5012
14 Therefore, son of man, **p** and say unto H5012
39: 1 Therefore, thou son of man, **p** against H5012
Joel 2:28 daughters shall **p**, your old men shall H5012
Am 2:12 the prophets, saying, **P** not. H5012
3: 8 Lord GOD hath spoken, who can but **p**? H5012
7:12 and there eat bread, and **p** there: H5012
13 But **p** not again any more at Beth-el: H5012
15 unto me, Go, **p** unto my people Israel. H5012
16 Thou sayest, **P** not against Israel, and H5012
Mic 2: 6 **P** ye not, *say they to them that* H5197
6 *say they to them that* **p**: they shall not H5197
6 they shall not **p** to them, *that* they shall H5197
11 do lie, *saying*, I will **p** unto thee of wine H5197
Zec 13: 3 when any shall yet **p**, then his father H5012
Mt 15: 7 Ye hypocrites, well did Esaias **p** of you, *G4395*
26:68 Saying, **P** unto us, thou Christ, Who is *G4395*
Mk 14:65 to say unto him, **P**: and the servants did *G4395*
Lk 22:64 saying, **P**, who is it that smote thee? *G4395*
Act 2:17 daughters shall **p**, and your young men *G4395*
18 days of my Spirit; and they shall **p**: *G4395*
21: 9 four daughters, virgins, which did **p**. *G4395*
Ro 12: 6 *p* according to the proportion of faith; *G4394*
1Co 13: 9 For we know in part, and we **p** in part. *G4395*
14: 1 spiritual *gifts*, but rather that ye may **p**. *G4395*
24 But if all **p**, and there come in one that *G4395*
31 For ye may all **p** one by one, that all *G4395*
39 Wherefore, brethren, covet to **p**, and *G4395*
Rev 10:11 And he said unto me, Thou must **p** *G4395*
11: 3 and they shall **p** a thousand two *G4395*

PROPHESYING
1Sa 10:13 And when he had made an end of **p**, he H5012
19:20 of the prophets **p**, and Samuel standing H5012
Ezr 6:14 through the **p** of Haggai the prophet H5017
1Co 11: 4 Every man praying or **p**, having *his* *G4395*
14: 6 by knowledge, or by **p**, or by doctrine? *G4394*
22 believe not: but **p** *serveth* not for them *G4394*

PROPHESYINGS
1Th 5:20 Despise not **p**. *G4394*

PROPHET
Gen 20: 7 wife; for he *is* a **p**, and he shall pray for H5030
Ex 7: 1 and Aaron thy brother shall be thy **p**. H5030
Nu 12: 6 If there be a **p** among you, *I* the LORD H5030
Dt 13: 1 If there arise among you a **p**, or a H5030
3 the words of that **p**, or that dreamer of H5030
5 And that **p**, or that dreamer of dreams, H5030
18:15 up unto thee a **P** from the midst of H5030
18 I will raise them up a **P** from among H5030
20 But the **p**, which shall presume to speak H5030
20 of other gods, even that **p** shall die. H5030
22 When a **p** speaketh in the name of the H5030
22 not spoken, *but* the **p** hath spoken it H5030
34:10 And there arose not a **p** since in Israel H5030
Jdg 6: 8 That the LORD sent a **p** unto the H5030
1Sa 3:20 *was* established *to be* a **p** of the LORD. H5030
9: 9 a **P** was beforetime called a Seer.) H5030
22: 5 And the **p** Gad said unto David, Abide H5030
2Sa 7: 2 That the king said unto Nathan the **p**, H5030
12:25 of Nathan the **p**; and he called his name H5030
24:11 unto the **p** Gad, David's seer, saying, H5030
1Ki 1: 8 and Nathan the **p**, and Shimei, and Rei, H5030
10 But Nathan the **p**, and Benaiah, and the H5030
22 the king, Nathan the **p** also came in. H5030
23 Nathan the **p**. And when he was come H5030
32 and Nathan the **p**, and Benaiah the son H5030
1Ki 1:34 and Nathan the **p** anoint him there H5030
38 So Zadok the priest, and Nathan the **p**, H5030
44 and Nathan the **p**, and Benaiah the son H5030
45 And Zadok the priest and Nathan the **p** H5030
11:29 that the **p** Ahijah the Shilonite H5030
13:11 Now there dwelt an old **p** in Beth-el; H5030
18 He said unto him, I *am* a **p** also as thou H5030
20 unto the **p** that brought him back: H5030
23 for the **p** whom he had brought back. H5030
25 told *it* in the city where the old **p** dwelt. H5030
26 And when the **p** that brought him back H5030
29 And the **p** took up the carcase of the H5030
29 back: and the old **p** came to the city, to H5030
14: 2 there *is* Ahijah the **p**, which told me that H5030
18 by the hand of his servant Ahijah the **p**. H5030
16: 7 And also by the hand of the **p** Jehu the H5030
12 he spake against Baasha by Jehu the **p**, H5030
18:22 I only, remain a **p** of the LORD; but H5030
36 that Elijah the **p** came near, and said, H5030
19:16 shalt thou anoint *to be* **p** in thy room. H5030
20:13 And, behold, there came a **p** unto Ahab H5030
22 And the **p** came to the king of Israel, H5030
38 So the **p** departed, and waited for the H5030
22: 7 said, *Is there* not here a **p** of the LORD H5030
2Ki 3:11 *Is there* not here a **p** of the LORD, that H5030
5: 3 lord *were* with the **p** that *is* in Samaria! H5030
8 he shall know that there is a **p** in Israel. H5030
13 said, My father, *if* the **p** had bid thee *do* H5030
6:12 but Elisha, the **p** that *is* in Israel, telleth H5030
9: 1 And Elisha the **p** called one of the H5030
4 man the **p**, went to Ramoth-gilead. H5030
14:25 the **p**, which *was* of Gath-hepher. H5030
19: 2 to Isaiah the **p** the son of Amoz. H5030
20: 1 unto death. And the **p** Isaiah the son of H5030
11 And Isaiah the **p** cried unto the LORD: H5030
14 Then came Isaiah the **p** unto king H5030
23:18 of the **p** that came out of Samaria. H5030
1Ch 17: 1 said to Nathan the **p**, Lo, I dwell in an H5030
29:29 the **p**, and in the book of Gad the seer, H5030
2Ch 9:29 of Nathan the **p**, and in the prophecy H5030
12: 5 Then came Shemaiah the **p** to H5030
15 of Shemaiah the **p**, and of Iddo the seer H5030
13:22 *are* written in the story of the **p** Iddo. H5030
15: 8 of Oded the **p**, he took courage, and H5030
18: 6 said, *Is there* not here a **p** of the LORD H5030
21:12 from Elijah the **p**, saying, Thus saith the H5030
25:15 sent unto him a **p**, which said unto him, H5030
16 smitten? Then the **p** forbare, and said, I H5030
26:22 did Isaiah the **p**, the son of Amoz, write. H5030
28: 9 But a **p** of the LORD was there, whose H5030
29:25 seer, and Nathan the **p**: for *so was* the H5030
32:20 the king, and the **p** Isaiah the son of H5030
32 of Isaiah the **p**, the son of Amoz, *and* H5030
35:18 days of Samuel the **p**; neither did all the H5030
36:12 Jeremiah the **p** *speaking* from the H5030
Ezr 5: 1 Then the prophets, Haggai the **p**, and H5029
6:14 of Haggai the **p** and Zechariah the son H5029
Ps 51:ttl when Nathan the **p** came unto him, H5030
74: 9 *there is* no more any **p**: neither *is there* H5030
Isa 3: 2 the **p**, and the prudent, and the ancient, H5030
9:15 the **p** that teacheth lies, he *is* the tail. H5030
28: 7 the priest and the **p** have erred through H5030
37: 2 unto Isaiah the **p** the son of Amoz. H5030
38: 1 And Isaiah the **p** the son of Amoz came H5030
39: 3 Then came Isaiah the **p** unto king H5030
Jer 1: 5 I ordained thee a **p** unto the nations. H5030
6:13 and from the **p** even unto the priest H5030
8:10 from the **p** even unto the priest H5030
14:18 yea, both the **p** and the priest go about H5030
18:18 the word from the **p**. Come, and let us H5030
20: 2 Then Pashur smote Jeremiah the **p**, and H5030
23:11 For both **p** and priest are profane; yea, H5030
28 The **p** that hath a dream, let him tell a H5030
33 And when this people, or the **p**, or a H5030
34 And *as for* the **p**, and the priest, and the H5030
37 Thus shalt thou say to the **p**, What hath H5030
25: 2 The which Jeremiah the **p** spake unto H5030
28: 1 son of Azur the **p**, which *was* of Gibeon, H5030
5 Then the **p** Jeremiah said unto the H5030
5 said unto the **p** Hananiah in the H5030
6 Even the **p** Jeremiah said, Amen: the H5030
9 The **p** which prophesieth of peace, H5030
9 the word of the **p** shall come to pass, H5030
9 *then* shall the **p** be known, that the H5030
10 Then Hananiah the **p** took the yoke H5030
10 off the **p** Jeremiah's neck, and brake it. H5030
11 And the **p** Jeremiah went his way. H5030
12 came unto Jeremiah *the p*, after that H5030
12 that Hananiah the **p** had broken the H5030
Jer 28:12 off the neck of the **p** Jeremiah, saying, H5030
15 Then said the **p** Jeremiah unto H5030
15 Hananiah the **p**, Hear now, Hananiah; H5030
17 So Hananiah the **p** died the same year H5030
29: 1 letter that Jeremiah the **p** sent from H5030
26 maketh himself a **p**, that thou shouldest H5012
27 which maketh himself a **p** to you? H5012
29 this letter in the ears of Jeremiah the **p**. H5030
32: 2 and Jeremiah the **p** was shut up in the H5030
34: 6 Then Jeremiah the **p** spake all these H5030
36: 8 that Jeremiah the **p** commanded him, H5030
26 Jeremiah the **p**: but the LORD hid them. H5030
37: 2 which he spake by the **p** Jeremiah. H5030
3 the priest to the **p** Jeremiah, saying, H5030
6 the LORD unto the **p** Jeremiah, saying, H5030
13 he took Jeremiah the **p**, saying, Thou H5030
38: 9 to Jeremiah the **p**, whom they have cast H5030
10 the **p** out of the dungeon, before he die. H5030
14 took Jeremiah the **p** unto him into the H5030
42: 2 And said unto Jeremiah the **p**, Let, we H5030
4 Then Jeremiah the **p** said unto them, I H5030
43: 6 the **p**, and Baruch the son of Neriah. H5030
45: 1 The word that Jeremiah the **p** spake H5030
46: 1 to Jeremiah the **p** against the Gentiles; H5030
13 to Jeremiah the **p**, how Nebuchadrezzar H5030
47: 1 came to Jeremiah the **p** against the H5030
49:34 to Jeremiah the **p** against Elam in the H5030
50: 1 of the Chaldeans by Jeremiah the **p**. H5030
51:59 The word which Jeremiah the **p** H5030
Lam 2:20 **p** be slain in the sanctuary of the Lord? H5030
Ezk 2: 5 that there hath been a **p** among them. H5030
7:26 seek a vision of the **p**; but the law shall H5030
14: 4 and cometh to the **p**; I the LORD will H5030
7 and cometh to a **p** to inquire of him H5030
9 And if the **p** be deceived when he hath H5030
9 deceived that **p**, and I will stretch out H5030
10 punishment of the **p** shall be even as H5030
33:33 know that a **p** hath been among them. H5030
Dan 9: 2 came to Jeremiah the **p**, that he would H5030
Hos 4: 5 in the day, and the **p** also shall fall with H5030
9: 7 Israel shall know *it*: the **p** *is* a fool, the H5030
8 my God: *but* the **p** *is* a snare of a fowler H5030
12:13 And by a **p** the LORD brought Israel H5030
13 of Egypt, and by a **p** was he preserved. H5030
Am 7:14 I *was* no **p**, neither *was* I a prophet's H5030
Mic 2:11 he shall even be the **p** of this people. H5197
Hab 1: 1 The burden which Habakkuk the **p** did H5030
3: 1 A prayer of Habakkuk the **p** upon H5030
Hag 1: 1 by Haggai the **p** unto Zerubbabel the H5030
3 of the LORD by Haggai the **p**, saying, H5030
12 of Haggai the **p**, as the LORD their God H5030
2: 1 of the LORD by the **p** Haggai, saying, H5030
10 of the LORD by Haggai the **p**, saying, H5030
Zec 1: 1 Berechiah, the son of Iddo the **p**, saying, H5030
7 Berechiah, the son of Iddo the **p**, saying, H5030
13: 5 But he shall say, I *am* no **p**, I *am* an H5030
Mal 4: 5 Behold, I will send you Elijah the **p** H5030
Mt 1:22 was spoken of the Lord by the **p**, saying, *G4396*
2: 5 of Judaea: for thus it is written by the **p**, *G4396*
15 of the Lord by the **p**, saying, Out of *G4396*
17 was spoken by Jeremy the **p**, saying, *G4396*
3: 3 spoken of by the **p** Esaias, saying, The *G4396*
4:14 was spoken by Esaias the **p**, saying, *G4396*
8:17 by Esaias the **p**, saying, Himself took *G4396*
10:41 He that receiveth a **p** in the name of a *G4396*
41 in the name of a **p** shall receive a *G4396*
11: 9 But what went ye out for to see? A **p**? *G4396*
9 yea, I say unto you, and more than a **p**. *G4396*
12:17 was spoken by Esaias the **p**, saying, *G4396*
39 given to it, but the sign of the **p** Jonas: *G4396*
13:35 was spoken by the **p**, saying, I will open *G4396*
57 said unto them, A **p** is not without *G4396*
14: 5 because they counted him as a **p**. *G4396*
16: 4 but the sign of the **p** Jonas. And he left *G4396*
21: 4 which was spoken by the **p**, saying, *G4396*
11 is Jesus the **p** of Nazareth of Galilee. *G4396*
26 fear the people; for all hold John as a **p**. *G4396*
46 because they took him for a **p**. *G4396*
24:15 of by Daniel the **p**, stand in the holy *G4396*
27: 9 by Jeremy the **p**, saying, And they took *G4396*
35 was spoken by the **p**, They parted my *G4396*
Mk 6: 4 But Jesus said unto them, A **p** is not *G4396*
15 That it is a **p**, or as one of the prophets. *G4396*
11:32 counted John, that he was a **p** indeed. *G4396*
13:14 of by Daniel the **p**, standing where it *G4396*
Lk 1:76 And thou, child, shalt be called the **p** of *G4396*
3: 4 of Esaias the **p**, saying, The voice of *G4396*
4:17 the book of the **p** Esaias. And when he *G4396*
24 No **p** is accepted in his own country. *G4396*

Lk 4:27 time of Eliseus the p; and none of them G4396
7:16 That a great p is risen up among us; G4396
26 But what went ye out for to see? A p? G4396
26 say unto you, and much more than a p. G4396
28 is not a greater p than John the Baptist: G4396
39 man, if he were a p, would have known G4396
11:29 be given it, but the sign of Jonas the p. G4396
13:33 be that a p perish out of Jerusalem. G4396
20: 6 they be persuaded that John was a p. G4396
24:19 which was a p mighty in deed and G4396
Jn 1:21 Art thou that p? And he answered, No. G4396
23 way of the Lord, as said the p Esaias. G4396
25 not that Christ, nor Elias, neither that p? G4396
4:19 him, Sir, I perceive that thou art a p. G4396
44 For Jesus himself testified, that a p G4396
6:14 that p that should come into the world. G4396
7:40 this saying, said, Of a truth this is the P. G4396
52 and look: for out of Galilee ariseth no p. G4396
9:17 opened thine eyes? He said, He is a p. G4396
12:38 That the saying of Esaias the p might G4396
Act 2:16 is that which was spoken by the p Joel; G4396
30 Therefore being a p, and knowing that G4396
3:22 the fathers, A p shall the Lord your G4396
23 will not hear that p, shall be destroyed G4396
7:37 of Israel, A p shall the Lord your G4396
48 made with hands; as saith the p, G4396
8:28 sitting in his chariot read Esaias the p. G4396
30 heard him read the p Esaias, and said, G4396
34 speaketh the p this? of himself, or of G4396
13: 6 p, a Jew, whose name *was* Barjesus: G5578
20 and fifty years, until Samuel the p. G4396
21:10 Judaea a certain p, named Agabus. G4396
28:25 Ghost by Esaias the p unto our fathers, G4396
1Co 14:37 If any man think himself to be a p, or G4396
Tit 1:12 One of themselves, *even* a p of their G4396
2Pt 2:16 voice forbad the madness of the p. G4396
Rev 16:13 and out of the mouth of the false p. G5578
19:20 and with him the false p that wrought G5578
20:10 beast and the false p *are*, and shall be G5578

PROPHETESS
Ex 15:20 And Miriam the p, the sister of Aaron, H5031
Jdg 4: 4 And Deborah, a p, the wife of Lapidoth, H5031
2Ki 22:14 unto Huldah the p, the wife of Shallum H5031
2Ch 34:22 to Huldah the p, the wife of Shallum H5031
Neh 6:14 works, and on the p Noadiah, and the H5031
Isa 8: 3 And I went unto the p; and she H5031
Lk 2:36 And there was one Anna, a p, the G4398
Rev 2:20 calleth herself a p, to teach and to G4398

PROPHETS
Nu 11:29 people were p, *and* that the LORD H5030
1Sa 10: 5 a company of p coming down from H5030
10 a company of p met him; and the spirit H5030
11 among the p, then the people said H5030
11 son of Kish? *Is* Saul also among the p? H5030
12 a proverb, *Is* Saul also among the p? H5030
19:20 the company of the p prophesying, and H5030
24 they say, *Is* Saul also among the p? H5030
28: 6 by dreams, nor by Urim, nor by p. H5030
15 no more, neither by p, nor by dreams: H5030
1Ki 18: 4 For it was *so*, when Jezebel cut off the p H5030
4 took an hundred p, and hid them by H5030
13 Jezebel slew the p of the LORD, how I H5030
13 of the LORD'S p by fifty in a cave, and H5030
19 Carmel, and the p of Baal four hundred H5030
19 and fifty, and the p of the groves four H5030
20 the p together unto mount Carmel. H5030
22 p *are* four hundred and fifty men. H5030
25 And Elijah said unto the p of Baal, H5030
40 And Elijah said unto them, Take the p H5030
19: 1 he had slain all the p with the sword. H5030
10 and slain thy p with the sword; and H5030
14 and slain thy p with the sword; and H5030
20:35 And a certain man of the sons of the p H5030
41 discerned him that he *was* of the p. H5030
22: 6 Then the king of Israel gathered the p H5030
10 and all the p prophesied before them. H5030
12 And all the p prophesied so, saying, Go H5030
13 the words of the p *declare* good unto H5030
22 mouth of all his p. And he said, Thou H5030
23 of all these thy p, and the LORD hath H5030
2Ki 2: 3 And the sons of the p that *were* at H5030
5 And the sons of the p that *were* at H5030
7 And fifty men of the sons of the p went, H5030
15 And when the sons of the p which *were* H5030
3:13 get thee to the p of thy father, and to H5030
13 father, and to the p of thy mother. And H5030
4: 1 of the sons of the p unto Elisha, saying, H5030

2Ki 4:38 the sons of the p *were* sitting before H5030
38 and seethe pottage for the sons of the p. H5030
5:22 of the sons of the p: give them, I pray H5030
6: 1 And the sons of the p said unto Elisha, H5030
9: 1 of the children of the p, and said unto H5030
7 of my servants the p, and the blood of H5030
10:19 Now therefore call unto me all the p of H5030
17:13 Judah, by all the p, *and by* all the seers, H5030
13 I sent to you by my servants the p. H5030
23 his servants the p. So was Israel carried H5030
21:10 spake by his servants the p, saying, H5030
23: 2 priests, and the p, and all the people, H5030
24: 2 which he spake by his servants the p. H5030
1Ch 16:22 mine anointed, and do my p no harm. H5030
2Ch 18: 5 together of p four hundred men, H5030
9 and all the p prophesied before them. H5030
11 And all the p prophesied so, saying, Go H5030
12 the words of the p *declare* good to the H5030
21 mouth of all his p. And *the LORD* said, H5030
22 of these thy p, and the LORD hath H5030
20:20 believe his p, so shall ye prosper. H5030
24:19 Yet he sent p to them, to bring them H5030
29:25 commandment of the LORD by his p. H5030
36:16 and misused his p, until the wrath of H5030
Ezr 5: 1 Then the p, Haggai the prophet, and H5029
2 them *were* the p of God helping them. H5029
9:11 by thy servants the p, saying, The land, H5030
Neh 6: 7 And thou hast also appointed p to H5030
14 of the p, that would have put me in fear. H5030
9:26 and slew thy p which testified against H5030
30 by thy spirit in thy p: yet would they not H5030
32 and on our p, and on our fathers, H5030
Ps 105:15 mine anointed, and do my p no harm. H5030
Isa 29:10 your eyes: the p and your rulers, the H5030
30:10 See not; and to the p, Prophesy not unto H2374
Jer 2: 8 me, and the p prophesied by Baal, H5030
26 princes, and their priests, and their p, H5030
30 devoured your p, like a destroying lion. H5030
4: 9 be astonished, and the p shall wonder. H5030
5:13 And the p shall become wind, and the H5030
31 The p prophesy falsely, and the priests H5030
7:25 my servants the p, daily rising up early H5030
8: 1 the bones of the p, and the bones of the H5030
13:13 the priests, and the p, and all the H5030
14:13 GOD! behold, the p say unto them, Ye H5030
14 Then the LORD said unto me, The p H5030
15 concerning the p that prophesy in my H5030
15 and famine shall those p be consumed. H5030
23: 9 because of the p; all my bones shake; H5030
13 And I have seen folly in the p of H5030
14 I have seen also in the p of Jerusalem H5030
15 concerning the p; Behold, I will feed H5030
15 of gall: for from the p of Jerusalem is H5030
16 the words of the p that prophesy unto H5030
21 I have not sent these p, yet they ran: I H5030
25 I have heard what the p said, that H5030
26 in the heart of the p that prophesy lies? H5030
26 *are* p of the deceit of their own heart; H5030
30 Therefore, behold, I *am* against the p, H5030
31 Behold, I *am* against the p, saith the H5030
25: 4 all his servants the p, rising early and H5030
26: 5 of my servants the p, whom I sent unto H5030
7 So the priests and the p and all the H5030
8 the priests and the p and all the people H5030
11 Then spake the priests and the p unto H5030
16 the priests and to the p; This man *is* not H5030
27: 9 Therefore hearken not ye to your p, nor H5030
14 the words of the p that speak unto you, H5030
15 ye, and the p that prophesy unto you. H5030
16 the words of your p that prophesy unto H5030
18 But if they *be* p, and if the word of the H5030
28: 8 The p that have been before me and H5030
29: 1 the priests, and to the p, and to all the H5030
8 Let not your p and your diviners, that H5030
15 LORD hath raised us up p in Babylon; H5030
19 my servants the p, rising up early and H5030
32:32 priests, and their p, and the men of H5030
35:15 my servants the p, rising up early and H5030
37:19 Where *are* now your p which H5030
44: 4 all my servants the p, rising early and H5030
Lam 2: 9 p also find no vision from the LORD. H5030
14 Thy p have seen vain and foolish H5030
4:13 For the sins of her p, *and* the iniquities H5030
Ezk 13: 2 Son of man, prophesy against the p of H5030
3 unto the foolish p, that follow their own H5030
4 O Israel, thy p are like the foxes in the H5030
9 And mine hand shall be upon the p H5030
16 *To wit*, the p of Israel which prophesy H5030
22:25 *There is* a conspiracy of her p in the H5030

Ezk 22:28 And her p have daubed them with H5030
38:17 by my servants the p of Israel, which H5030
Dan 9: 6 thy servants the p, which spake in thy H5030
10 he set before us by his servants the p. H5030
Hos 6: 5 Therefore have I hewed *them* by the p; I H5030
12:10 I have also spoken by the p, and I have H5030
10 similitudes, by the ministry of the p. H5030
Am 2:11 And I raised up of your sons for p, and H5030
12 the p, saying, Prophesy not. H5030
3: 7 his secret unto his servants the p. H5030
Mic 3: 5 Thus saith the LORD concerning the p H5030
6 p, and the day shall be dark over them. H5030
11 for hire, and the p thereof divine for H5030
Zep 3: 4 Her p *are* light *and* treacherous H5030
Zec 1: 4 whom the former p have cried, saying, H5030
5 Your fathers, where *are* they? and the p, H5030
6 my servants the p, did they not take H5030
7: 3 of hosts, and to the p, saying, Should I H5030
7 by the former p, when Jerusalem was H5030
12 by the former p: therefore came a great H5030
8: 9 by the mouth of the p, which *were* in the H5030
13: 2 I will cause the p and the unclean spirit H5030
4 that day, *that* the p shall be ashamed H5030
Mt 2:23 by the p, He shall be called a Nazarene. G4396
5:12 they the p which were before you. G4396
17 the law, or the p: I am not come to G4396
7:12 so to them: for this is the law and the p. G4396
15 Beware of false p, which come to you in G5578
11:13 For all the p and the law prophesied G4396
13:17 For verily I say unto you, That many p G4396
16:14 and others, Jeremias, or one of the p. G4396
22:40 hang all the law and the p. G4396
23:29 the tombs of the p, and garnish the G4396
30 with them in the blood of the p. G4396
31 the children of them which killed the p. G4396
34 Wherefore, behold, I send unto you p, G4396
37 *thou* that killest the p, and stonest them G4396
24:11 And many false p shall rise, and shall G5578
24 Christs, and false p, and shall shew G5578
26:56 scriptures of the p might be fulfilled. G4396
Mk 1: 2 As it is written in the p, Behold, I send G4396
6:15 That it is a prophet, or as one of the p. G4396
8:28 *say*, Elias; and others, One of the p. G4396
13:22 For false Christs and false p shall rise, G5578
Lk 1:70 As he spake by the mouth of his holy p, G4396
6:23 manner did their fathers unto the p. G4396
26 for so did their fathers to the false p. G5578
9: 8 that one of the old p was risen again. G4396
19 *say*, that one of the old p is risen again. G4396
10:24 For I tell you, that many p and kings G4396
11:47 of the p, and your fathers killed them. G4396
49 I will send them p and apostles, and G4396
50 That the blood of all the p, which was G4396
13:28 Jacob, and all the p, in the kingdom of G4396
34 which killest the p, and stonest them G4396
16:16 The law and the p *were* until John: G4396
29 Moses and the p; let them hear them. G4396
31 not Moses and the p, neither will they G4396
18:31 are written by the p concerning the Son G4396
24:25 to believe all that the p have spoken: G4396
27 And beginning at Moses and all the p, G4396
44 p, and *in* the psalms, concerning me. G4396
Jn 1:45 in the law, and the p, did write, Jesus of G4396
6:45 It is written in the p, And they shall be G4396
8:52 is dead, and the p; and thou sayest, If a G4396
53 p are dead: whom makest thou thyself? G4396
Act 3:18 mouth of all his p, that Christ should G4396
21 of all his holy p since the world began. G4396
24 Yea, and all the p from Samuel and G4396
25 Ye are the children of the p, and of the G4396
7:42 in the book of the p, O ye house of G4396
52 Which of the p have not your fathers G4396
10:43 To him give all the p witness, that G4396
11:27 And in these days came p from G4396
13: 1 at Antioch certain p and teachers; as G4396
15 of the law and the p the rulers of the G4396
27 the voices of the p which are read every G4396
40 upon you, which is spoken of in the p; G4396
15:15 And to this agree the words of the p; as G4396
32 And Judas and Silas, being p also G4396
24:14 are written in the law and in the p: G4396
26:22 the p and Moses did say should come: G4396
27 King Agrippa, believest thou the p? I G4396
28:23 *out of* the p, from morning till evening. G4396
Ro 1: 2 (Which he had promised afore by his p G4396
3:21 being witnessed by the law and the p; G4396
11: 3 Lord, they have killed thy p, and digged G4396
16:26 the scriptures of the p, according to the G4397
1Co 12:28 secondarily p, thirdly teachers, after G4396

1Co 12:29 *Are* all apostles? *are* all **p**? *are* all G4396
14:29 Let the **p** speak two or three, and let the G4396
32 And the spirits of the **p** are subject to G4396
32 of the prophets are subject to the **p**. G4396
Eph 2:20 the apostles and **p**, Jesus Christ himself G4396
3: 5 his holy apostles and **p** by the Spirit; G4396
4:11 and some, **p**; and some, evangelists; G4396
1Th 2:15 and their own **p**, and have persecuted G4396
Heb 1: 1 in time past unto the fathers by the **p**, G4396
11:32 *of* David also, and Samuel, and *of* the **p**: G4396
Jas 5:10 Take, my brethren, the **p**, who have G4396
1Pt 1:10 Of which salvation the **p** have inquired G4396
2Pt 2: 1 But there were false **p** also among the G5578
3: 2 spoken before by the holy **p**, and of the G4396
1Jn 4: 1 false **p** are gone out into the world. G5578
Rev 10: 7 he hath declared to his servants the **p**. G4396
11:10 because these two **p** tormented them G4396
18 thy servants the **p**, and to the saints, G4396
16: 6 of saints and **p**, and thou hast given G4396
18:20 **p**; for God hath avenged you on her. G4396
24 And in her was found the blood of **p**, G4396
22: 6 God of the holy **p** sent his angel to shew G4396
9 thy brethren the **p**, and of them which G4396

PROPHET'S
Am 7:14 neither *was* I a **p** son; but I *was* an H5030
Mt 10:41 shall receive a **p** reward; and he that G4396

PROPITIATION
Ro 3:25 Whom God hath set forth *to be* a **p** G2435
1Jn 2: 2 And he is the **p** for our sins: and not for G2434
4:10 sent his Son *to be* the **p** for our sins. G2434

PROPORTION
1Ki 7:36 according to the **p** of every one, and H4626
Job 41:12 parts, nor his power, nor his comely **p**. H6187
Ro 12: 6 *us prophesy* according to the **p** of faith; G356

PROSELYTE
Mt 23:15 and land to make one **p**, and when he is G4339
Act 6: 5 Parmenas, and Nicolas a **p** of Antioch: G4339

PROSELYTES
Act 2:10 and strangers of Rome, Jews and **p**, G4339
13:43 Jews and religious **p** followed Paul and G4339

PROSPECT
Ezk 40:44 gate; and their **p** *was* toward the south: H6440
44 gate *having* the **p** toward the north. H6440
45 chamber, whose **p** *is* toward the south, H6440
46 And the chamber whose **p** *is* toward H6440
42:15 the gate whose **p** *is* toward the east, H6440
43: 4 of the gate whose **p** *is* toward the east. H6440

PROSPER
Gen 24:40 with thee, and **p** thy way; and thou H6743
42 if now thou do **p** my way which I go: H6743
39: 3 made all that he did to **p** in his hand. H6743
23 which he did, the LORD made *it* to **p**. H6743
Nu 14:41 of the LORD? but it shall not **p**. H6743
Dt 28:29 and thou shalt not **p** in thy ways: and H6743
29: 9 them, that ye may **p** in all that ye do. H7919
Jos 1: 7 mayest **p** whithersoever thou goest. H7919
1Ki 2: 3 that thou mayest **p** in all that thou H7919
22:12 and **p**: for the LORD shall H6743
15 him, Go, and **p**: for the LORD shall H6743
1Ch 22:11 be with thee; and **p** thou, and build the H6743
13 Then shalt thou **p**, if thou takest heed to H6743
2Ch 13:12 God of your fathers; for ye shall not **p**. H6743
18:11 and **p**: for the LORD shall H6743
14 said, Go ye up, and **p**, and they shall be H6743
20:20 believe his prophets, so shall ye **p**. H6743
24:20 that ye cannot **p**? because ye have H6743
26: 5 sought the LORD, God made him to **p**. H6743
Neh 1:11 fear thy name: and **p**, I pray thee, thy H6743
2:20 of heaven, he will **p** us; therefore we his H6743
Job 12: 6 The tabernacles of robbers **p**, and they H7951
Ps 1: 3 and whatsoever he doeth shall **p**. H6743
73:12 Behold, these *are* the ungodly, who **p** in H7961
122: 6 Jerusalem: they shall **p** that love thee. H7951
Prv 28:13 He that covereth his sins shall not **p**: H6743
Ecc 11: 6 not whether shall **p**, either this or that, H3787
Isa 53:10 of the LORD shall **p** in his hand. H6743
54:17 against thee shall **p**; and every tongue H6743
55:11 it shall **p** *in the thing* whereto I sent it. H6743
Jer 2:37 and thou shalt not **p** in them. H6743
5:28 yet they **p**; and the right of the H6743
10:21 **p**, and all their flocks shall be scattered. H7919
12: 1 way of the wicked **p**? *wherefore* are all H6743
Jer 20:11 for they shall not **p**: *their* everlasting H7919
22:30 man *that* shall not **p** in his days: for no H6743
30 man of his seed shall **p**, sitting upon the H6743
23: 5 shall reign and **p**, and shall execute H7919
32: 5 fight with the Chaldeans, ye shall not **p**. H6743
Lam 1: 5 chief, her enemies **p**; for the LORD hath H7951
Ezk 16:13 and thou didst **p** into a kingdom. H6743
17: 9 Lord GOD; Shall it **p**? shall he not pull H6743
10 Yea, behold, *being* planted, shall it **p**? H6743
15 people. Shall he **p**? shall he escape that H6743
Dan 8:24 and shall **p**, and practise, and shall H6743
25 cause craft to **p** in his hand; and he H6743
11:27 but it shall not **p**: for yet the end *shall* H6743
36 of gods, and shall **p** till the indignation H6743
3Jn 2 that thou mayest **p** and be in health, G2137

PROSPERED
Gen 24:56 the LORD hath **p** my way; send me H6743
Jdg 4:24 And the hand of the children of Israel **p**, H1980
2Sa 11: 7 how the people did, and how the war **p**. H7965
2Ki 18: 7 And the LORD was with him; *and* he **p** H7919
1Ch 29:23 father, and **p**; and all Israel obeyed him. H6743
2Ch 14: 7 rest on every side. So they built and **p**. H6743
31:21 God, he did *it* with all his heart, and **p**. H6743
32:30 And Hezekiah **p** in all his works. H6743
Ezr 6:14 Jews builded, and they **p** through the H6744
Job 9: 4 *himself* against him, and hath **p**? H7999
Dan 6:28 So this Daniel **p** in the reign of Darius, H6744
8:12 to the ground; and it practised, and **p**. H6743
1Co 16: 2 store, as *God* hath **p** him, that there be G2137

PROSPERETH
Ezr 5: 8 goeth fast on, and **p** in their hands. H6744
Ps 37: 7 of him who **p** in his way, because H6743
Prv 17: 8 hath it: whithersoever it turneth, it **p**. H7919
3Jn 2 and be in health, even as thy soul **p**. G2137

PROSPERITY
Dt 23: 6 peace nor their **p** all thy days for ever. H2896
1Sa 25: 6 to him that liveth *in p*, Peace *be* both to
1Ki 10: 7 **p** exceedeth the fame which I heard. H2896
Job 15:21 A dreadful sound *is* in his ears: in **p** the H7965
36:11 days in **p**, and their years in pleasures. H2896
Ps 30: 6 And in my **p** I said, I shall never be H7959
35:27 hath pleasure in the **p** of his servant. H7965
73: 3 foolish, *when* I saw the **p** of the wicked. H7965
118:25 O LORD, I beseech thee, send now **p**. H6743
122: 7 Peace be within thy walls, *and* **p** within H7962
Prv 1:32 and the **p** of fools shall destroy them. H7962
Ecc 7:14 In the day of **p** be joyful, but in the day H2896
Jer 22:21 I spake unto thee in thy **p**; *but* thou H7962
33: 9 and for all the **p** that I procure unto it. H7965
Lam 3:17 my soul far off from peace: I forgat **p**. H2896
Zec 1:17 My cities through **p** shall yet be spread H2896
7: 7 was inhabited and in **p**, and the cities H7961

PROSPEROUS
Gen 24:21 LORD had made his journey **p** or not. H6743
39: 2 and he was a **p** man; and he was in H6743
Jos 1: 8 make thy way **p**, and then thou shalt H6743
Jdg 18: 5 our way which we go shall be **p**. H6743
Job 8: 6 the habitation of thy righteousness **p**. H7999
Isa 48:15 him, and he shall make his way **p**. H6743
Zec 8:12 For the seed *shall be* **p**; the vine shall H7965
Ro 1:10 I might have a **p** journey by the will of G2137

PROSPEROUSLY
2Ch 7:11 and in his own house, he **p** effected. H6743
Ps 45: 4 And in thy majesty ride **p** because of H6743

PROSTITUTE
Lev 19:29 Do not **p** thy daughter, to cause her to H2490

PROTECTION
Dt 32:38 rise up and help you, *and* be your **p**. H5643

PROTEST
Gen 43: 3 man did solemnly **p** unto us, saying, Ye H5749
1Sa 8: 9 voice: howbeit yet **p** solemnly unto H5749
1Co 15:31 I **p** by your rejoicing which I have in G3513

PROTESTED
1Ki 2:42 by the LORD, and **p** unto thee, saying, H5749
Jer 11: 7 For I earnestly **p** unto your fathers in H5749
Zec 3: 6 And the angel of the LORD **p** unto H5749

PROTESTING
Jer 11: 7 early and **p**, saying, Obey my voice. H5749

PROUD
Job 9:13 the **p** helpers do stoop under him. H7293
26:12 he smiteth through the **p**. H7293
38:11 and here shall thy **p** waves be stayed? H1347
40:11 every one *that is* **p**, and abase him. H1343
12 Look on every one *that is* **p**, *and* bring H1343
Ps 12: 3 *and* the tongue that speaketh **p** things: H1419
31:23 and plentifully rewardeth the **p** doer. H1346
40: 4 not the **p**, nor such as turn aside to lies. H7295
86:14 O God, the **p** are risen against me, and H2086
94: 2 of the earth: render a reward to the **p**. H1343
101: 5 look and a **p** heart will not I suffer. H7342
119:21 Thou hast rebuked the **p** *that are* H2086
51 The **p** have had me greatly in derision: H2086
69 The **p** have forged a lie against me: *but* H2086
78 Let the **p** be ashamed; for they dealt H2086
85 The **p** have digged pits for me, which H2086
122 for good: let not the **p** oppress me. H2086
123: 4 at ease, *and* with the contempt of the **p**. H1349
124: 5 Then the **p** waters had gone over our H2121
138: 6 lowly: but the **p** he knoweth afar off. H1364
140: 5 The **p** have hid a snare for me, and H1343
Prv 6:17 A **p** look, a lying tongue, and hands H7311
15:25 the house of the **p**: but he will establish H1343
16: 5 Every one *that is* **p** in heart *is* an H1362
19 than to divide the spoil with the **p**. H1343
21: 4 An high look, and a **p** heart, *and* the H7342
24 **P** *and* haughty scorner *is* his name, H2086
24 *is* his name, who dealeth in **p** wrath. H2087
28:25 He that is of a **p** heart stirreth up strife: H7342
Ecc 7: 8 in spirit *is* better than the **p** in spirit. H1362
Isa 2:12 every *one that is* **p** and lofty, and upon H1343
13:11 arrogancy of the **p** to cease, and will H2086
16: 6 of Moab; *he is* very **p**: *even* of his H1341
Jer 13:15 Hear ye, and give ear; be not **p**: for the H1361
43: 2 Kareah, and all the **p** men, saying unto H2086
48:29 (he is exceeding **p**) his loftiness, and his H1343
50:29 for she hath been **p** against the LORD, H2102
31 thee, *O thou* most **p**, saith the Lord GOD H2087
32 And the most **p** shall stumble and fall, H2087
Hab 2: 5 by wine, *he is* a **p** man, neither keepeth H3093
Mal 3:15 And now we call the **p** happy; yea, they H2086
4: 1 oven; and all the **p**, yea, and all that do H2086
Lk 1:51 the **p** in the imagination of their hearts. G5244
Ro 1:30 Backbiters, haters of God, despiteful, **p**, G5244
1Ti 6: 4 He is **p**, knowing nothing, but doting G5187
2Ti 3: 2 boasters, **p**, blasphemers, disobedient G5244
Jas 4: 6 the **p**, but giveth grace unto the humble. G5244
1Pt 5: 5 the **p**, and giveth grace to the humble. G5244

PROUDLY
Ex 18:11 they dealt **p** *he was* above them. H2102
1Sa 2: 3 Talk no more so exceeding **p**; let *not* H1364
Neh 9:10 that they dealt **p** against them. So didst H2102
16 But they and our fathers dealt **p**, and H2102
29 law: yet they dealt **p**, and hearkened not H2102
Ps 17:10 own fat: with their mouth they speak **p**. H1348
31:18 grievous things **p** and contemptuously H1346
Isa 3: 5 behave himself **p** against the ancient, H7292
Oba 12 have spoken **p** in the day of distress. H1431

PROVE
Ex 16: 4 day, that I may **p** them, whether they H5254
20:20 for God is come to **p** you, and that his H5254
Dt 8: 2 thee, *and* to **p** thee, to know what H5254
16 and that he might **p** thee, to do thee H5254
33: 8 whom thou didst **p** at Massah, *and* H5254
Jdg 2:22 That through them I may **p** Israel, H5254
3: 1 the LORD left, to **p** Israel by them, *even* H5254
4 And they were to **p** Israel by them, to H5254
6:39 this once: let me **p**, I pray thee, but this H5254
1Ki 10: 1 she came to **p** him with hard questions. H5254
2Ch 9: 1 she came to **p** Solomon with hard H5254
Job 9:20 I *am* perfect, it shall also **p** me perverse.
Ps 26: 2 Examine me, O LORD, and **p** me; try H5254
Ecc 2: 1 I said in mine heart, Go to now, I will **p** H5254
Dan 1:12 **P** thy servants, I beseech thee, ten days; H5254
Mal 3:10 in mine house, and **p** me now herewith, H974
Lk 14:19 **p** them: I pray thee have me excused. G1381
Jn 6: 6 And this he said to **p** him: for he G3985
Act 24:13 Neither can they **p** the things whereof G3936
25: 7 against Paul, which they could not **p**. G584
Ro 12: 2 mind, that ye may **p** what *is* that good, G1381
2Co 8: 8 and to **p** the sincerity of your love. G1381
13: 5 ye be in the faith; **p** your own selves. G1381
Gal 6: 4 But let every man **p** his own work, and G1381
1Th 5:21 **P** all things; hold fast that which is G1381

PROVED
Gen 42:15 Hereby ye shall be p: By the life of H974
16 your words may be p, whether *there be* H974
Ex 15:25 an ordinance, and there he p them, H5254
1Sa 17:39 go; for he had not p *it*. And David said H5254
39 p *them*. And David put them off him. H5254
Ps 17: 3 Thou hast p mine heart; thou hast H974
66:10 For thou, O God, hast p us: thou hast H974
81: 7 I p thee at the waters of Meribah. Selah. H974
95: 9 When your fathers tempted me, p me, H974
Ecc 7:23 All this have I p by wisdom: I said, I H5254
Dan 1:14 in this matter, and p them ten days. H5254
Ro 3: 9 for we have before p both Jews and G4256
2Co 8:22 we have oftentimes p diligent in many G1381
1Ti 3:10 And let these also first be p; then let G1381
Heb 3: 9 When your fathers tempted me, p me, G1381

PROVENDER
Gen 24:25 and p enough, and room to lodge in. H4554
32 gave straw and p for the camels, and H4554
42:27 to give his ass p in the inn, he espied H4554
43:24 their feet; and he gave their asses p. H4554
Jdg 19:19 Yet there is both straw and p for our H4554
21 house, and gave p unto the asses: and H1101
Isa 30:24 shall eat clean p, which hath been H1098

PROVERB
Dt 28:37 an astonishment, a p, and a byword, H4912
1Sa 10:12 a p, *Is* Saul also among the prophets? H4912
24:13 As saith the p of the ancients, H4912
1Ki 9: 7 be a p and a byword among all people: H4912
2Ch 7:20 a p and a byword among all nations. H4912
Ps 69:11 my garment; and I became a p to them. H4912
Prv 1: 6 To understand a p, and the H4912
Isa 14: 4 That thou shalt take up this p against H4912
Jer 24: 9 a reproach and a p, a taunt and a curse, H4912
Ezk 12:22 Son of man, what *is* that p *that* ye have H4912
23 I will make this p to cease, and they H4912
23 no more use it as a p in Israel; but say H4911
14: 8 him a sign and a p, and I will cut him H4912
16:44 shall use *this* p against thee, saying, H4911
18: 2 What mean ye, that ye use this p H4912
3 any more to use this p in Israel. H4912
Hab 2: 6 and a taunting p against him, and say, H2420
Lk 4:23 say unto me this p, Physician, heal G3850
Jn 16:29 thou plainly, and speakest no p. G3942
2Pt 2:22 to the true p, The dog *is* turned to G3942

PROVERBS
Nu 21:27 Wherefore they that speak in p say, H4911
1Ki 4:32 And he spake three thousand p: and his H4912
Prv 1: 1 The p of Solomon the son of David, H4912
10: 1 The p of Solomon. A wise son maketh a H4912
25: 1 These *are* also p of Solomon, which the H4912
Ecc 12: 9 sought out, *and* set in order many p. H4912
Ezk 16:44 Behold, every one that useth p shall use H4911
Jn 16:25 unto you in p: but the time cometh, G3942
25 speak unto you in p, but I shall shew G3942

PROVETH
Dt 13: 3 the LORD your God p you, to know H5254

PROVIDE
Gen 22: 8 And Abraham said, My son, God will p H7200
30:30 shall I p for mine own house also? H6213
Ex 18:21 Moreover thou shalt p out of all the H2372
1Sa 16:17 And Saul said unto his servants, P me H7200
2Ch 2: 7 whom David my father did p. H3559
Ps 78:20 also? can he p flesh for his people? H3559
Mt 10: 9 P neither gold, nor silver, nor brass in G2932
Lk 12:33 Sell that ye have, and give alms; p G4160
Act 23:24 And p *them* beasts, that they may set G3936
Ro 12:17 Recompense to no man evil for evil. P G4306
1Ti 5: 8 But if any p not for his own, and G4306

PROVIDED
Dt 33:21 And he p the first part for himself, H7200
1Sa 16: 1 for I have p me a king among his sons. H7200
2Sa 19:32 old: and he had p the king of sustenance
1Ki 4: 7 all Israel, which p victuals for the king
27 And those officers p victual for king
2Ch 32:29 Moreover he p him cities, and H6213
Ps 65: 9 them corn, when thou hast so p for it. H3559
Lk 12:20 shall those things be, which thou hast p? G2090
Heb 11:40 God having p some better thing for us, G4265

PROVIDENCE
Act 24: 2 are done unto this nation by thy p, G4307

PROVIDETH
Job 38:41 Who p for the raven his food? when his H3559
Prv 6: 8 P her meat in the summer, *and* H3559

PROVIDING
2Co 8:21 P for honest things, not only in the G4306

PROVINCE
Ezr 2: 1 Now these *are* the children of the p that H4082
5: 8 that we went into the p of Judea, to the H4083
6: 2 that *is* in the p of the Medes, a roll, H4083
7:16 find in all the p of Babylon, with the H4083
Neh 1: 3 there in the p *are* in great affliction H4082
7: 6 These *are* the children of the p, that H4082
11: 3 Now these *are* the chief of the p that H4082
Est 1:22 into every p according to the writing H4082
3:12 *were* over every p, and to the rulers of H4082
12 people of every p according to the H4082
14 be given in every p was published unto H4082
4: 3 And in every p, whithersoever the king's H4082
8: 9 unto every p according to the writing H4082
11 of the people and p that would assault H4082
13 be given in every p *was* published unto H4082
17 And in every p, and in every city, H4082
9:28 family, every p, and every city; and H4082
Ecc 5: 8 and justice in a p, marvel not at the H4082
Dan 2:48 over the whole p of Babylon, and chief H4083
49 over the affairs of the p of Babylon: but H4083
3: 1 the plain of Dura, in the p of Babylon. H4083
12 over the affairs of the p of Babylon, H4083
30 and Abed-nego, in the p of Babylon. H4083
8: 2 which *is* in the p of Elam; and I saw H4082
11:24 places of the p; and he shall do *that* H4082
Act 23:34 he asked of what p he was. And when G1885
25: 1 Now when Festus was come into the p, G1885

PROVINCES
1Ki 20:14 the princes of the p. Then he said, Who H4082
15 the princes of the p, and they were two H4082
17 the princes of the p went out first; and H4082
19 of the princes of the p came out of the H4082
Ezr 4:15 unto kings and p, and that they have H4083
Est 1: 1 an hundred and seven and twenty p:) H4082
3 and princes of the p, *being* before him: H4082
16 *are* in all the p of the king Ahasuerus. H4082
22 For he sent letters into all the king's p, H4082
2: 3 officers in all the p of his kingdom, that H4082
18 made a release to the p, and gave gifts, H4082
3: 8 people in all the p of thy kingdom; and H4082
13 into all the king's p, to destroy, to kill, H4082
4:11 people of the king's p, do know, that H4082
8: 5 the Jews which *are* in all the king's p: H4082
9 and rulers of the p which *are* from H4082
9 twenty and seven p, unto every H4082
12 Upon one day in all the p of king H4082
9: 2 cities throughout all the p of the king H4082
3 And all the rulers of the p, and the H4082
4 out throughout all the p: for this man H4082
12 the rest of the king's p? now what *is* thy H4082
16 that *were* in the king's p gathered H4082
20 *were* in all the p of the king Ahasuerus, H4082
30 twenty and seven p of the kingdom of H4082
Ecc 2: 8 of kings and of the p: I gat me men H4082
Lam 1: 1 the p, *how* is she become tributary! H4082
Ezk 19: 8 side from the p, and spread their net H4082
Dan 3: 2 all the rulers of the p, to come to the H4083
3 all the rulers of the p, were gathered H4083

PROVING
Act 9:22 at Damascus, p that this is very Christ. G4822
Eph 5:10 P what is acceptable unto the Lord. G1381

PROVISION
Gen 42:25 and to give them p for the way: and H6720
45:21 Pharaoh, and gave them p for the way. H6720
Jos 9: 5 bread of their p was dry *and* mouldy. H6718
12 This our bread we took hot *for* our p H6679
1Ki 4: 7 each man his month in a year made p. H3557
22 And Solomon's p for one day was thirty H3899
2Ki 6:23 And he prepared great p for them: and H3740
1Ch 29:19 the palace, *for* the which I have made p. H3559
Ps 132:15 I will abundantly bless her p: I will H6718
Dan 1: 5 And the king appointed them a daily p H1697
Ro 13:14 p for the flesh, to *fulfil* the lusts *thereof*. G4307

PROVOCATION
1Ki 15:30 made Israel sin, by his p wherewith he H3708
21:22 son of Ahijah, for the p wherewith thou H3708
Job 17: 2 doth not mine eye continue in their p? H4784
Ps 95: 8 Harden not your heart, as in the p, *and* H4808
Jer 32:31 For this city hath been to me *as* a p of
Ezk 20:28 they presented the p of their offering: H3708
Heb 3: 8 Harden not your hearts, as in the p, in G3894
15 harden not your hearts, as in the p. G3894

PROVOCATIONS
2Ki 23:26 because of all the p that Manasseh had H3708
Neh 9:18 out of Egypt, and had wrought great p; H5007
26 them to thee, and they wrought great p. H5007

PROVOKE
Ex 23:21 Beware of him, and obey his voice, p H4843
Nu 14:11 will this people p me? and how long H5006
Dt 4:25 of the LORD thy God, to p him to anger:
9:18 the sight of the LORD, to p him to anger.
31:20 and p me, and break my covenant. H5006
29 of the LORD, to p him to anger through
32:21 p them to anger with a foolish nation.
1Ki 14: 9 molten images, to p me to anger, and
16: 2 to sin, to p me to anger with their sins;
26 Israel to sin, to p the LORD God of Israel
33 Ahab did more to p the LORD God of
2Ki 17:11 wicked things to p the LORD to anger:
17 the sight of the LORD, to p him to anger.
21: 6 the sight of the LORD, to p *him* to anger.
22:17 that they might p me to anger with all
23:19 Israel had made to p *the LORD* to anger,
2Ch 33: 6 the sight of the LORD, to p him to anger.
34:25 that they might p me to anger with all
Job 12: 6 and they that p God are secure; into H7264
Ps 78:40 How oft did they p him in the H4784
Isa 3: 8 the LORD, to p the eyes of his glory. H4784
Jer 7:18 other gods, that they may p me to anger.
19 Do they p me to anger? saith the LORD:
19 LORD: *do they* not p themselves to the
11:17 themselves to p me to anger in offering
25: 6 to worship them, and p me not to anger
7 that ye might p me to anger with the
32:29 unto other gods, to p me to anger.
32 they have done to p me to anger, they,
44: 3 have committed to p me to anger, in that
8 In that ye p me unto wrath with the
Ezk 8:17 have returned to p me to anger: and, lo,
16:26 thy whoredoms, to p me to anger.
Lk 11:53 and to p him to speak of many things: G653
Ro 10:19 Moses saith, I will p you to jealousy by G3863
11:11 the Gentiles, for to p them to jealousy. G3863
14 If by any means I may p to emulation G4863
1Co 10:22 Do we p the Lord to jealousy? are we G3863
Eph 6: 4 And, ye fathers, p not your children to G3949
Col 3:21 Fathers, p not your children to *anger*, G2042
Heb 3:16 For some, when they had heard, did p: G3893
10:24 And let us consider one another to p G3948

PROVOKED
Nu 14:23 shall any of them that p me see it: H5006
16:30 that these men have p the LORD. H5006
Dt 9: 8 Also in Horeb ye p the LORD to wrath, H7107
22 ye p the LORD to wrath.
32:16 They p him to jealousy with strange H3707
16 with abominations p they him to anger.
21 *is* not God; they have p me to anger with
Jdg 2:12 unto them, and p the LORD to anger.
1Sa 1: 6 And her adversary also p her sore, for H3707
7 of the LORD, so she p her; therefore she H3707
1Ki 14:22 LORD, and they p him to jealousy with
15:30 he p the LORD God of Israel to anger.
21:22 p *me* to anger, and made Israel to sin.
22:53 him, and p to anger the LORD God
2Ki 21:15 my sight, and have p me to anger, since
23:26 that Manasseh had p him withal. H3707
1Ch 21: 1 Israel, and p David to number Israel. H5496
2Ch 28:25 p to anger the LORD God of his fathers.
Ezr 5:12 But after that our fathers had p the H7265
Neh 4: 5 have p *thee* to anger before the builders.
Ps 78:56 Yet they tempted and p the most high H4784
58 For they p him to anger with their high
106: 7 p *him* at the sea, *even* at the Red sea. H4784
29 Thus they p *him* to anger with their
33 Because they p his spirit, so that he H4784
43 deliver them; but they p *him* with their H4784
Isa 1: 4 the LORD, they have p the Holy One of H5006
Jer 8:19 Why have they p me to anger with their
32:30 of Israel have only p me to anger with
Hos 12:14 Ephraim p *him* to anger most bitterly:
Zec 8:14 when your fathers p me to wrath, saith
1Co 13: 5 own, is not easily p, thinketh no evil; G3947
2Co 9: 2 ago; and your zeal hath p very many. G2042

P

PROVOKEDST
Dt 9: 7 Remember, *and* forget not, how thou **p**

PROVOKETH
Prv 20: 2 of a lion: *whoso* **p** him to anger sinneth H5674
Isa 65: 3 A people that **p** me to anger continually
Ezk 8: 3 image of jealousy, which **p** to jealousy.

PROVOKING
Dt 32:19 the **p** of his sons, and of his daughters. H3708
1Ki 14:15 made their groves, **p** the LORD to anger.
16: 7 of the LORD, in **p** him to anger with the
13 Israel to sin, in **p** the LORD God of Israel
Ps 78:17 by **p** the most High in the wilderness. H4784
Gal 5:26 Let us not be desirous of vain glory, **p** *G4292*

PRUDENCE
2Ch 2:12 son, endued with **p** and understanding, H7922
Prv 8:12 I wisdom dwell with **p**, and find out H6195
Eph 1: 8 toward us in all wisdom and **p**; *G5428*

PRUDENT
1Sa 16:18 a man of war, and **p** in matters, and a H995
Prv 12:16 known: but a **p** *man* covereth shame. H6175
23 A **p** man concealeth knowledge: but the H6175
13:16 Every **p** *man* dealeth with knowledge: H6175
14: 8 The wisdom of the **p** *is* to understand H6175
15 but the **p** *man* looketh well to his going. H6175
18 The simple inherit folly: but the **p** are H6175
15: 5 but he that regardeth reproof is **p**. H6191
16:21 The wise in heart shall be called **p**: and H995
18:15 The heart of the **p** getteth knowledge; H995
19:14 fathers: and a **p** wife *is* from the LORD. H7919
22: 3 A **p** *man* foreseeth the evil, and hideth H6175
27:12 A **p** *man* foreseeth the evil, *and* hideth H6175
Isa 3: 2 the prophet, and the **p**, and the ancient, H7080
5:21 their own eyes, and **p** in their own sight! H995
10:13 wisdom; for I am **p**: and I have removed H995
29:14 of their **p** *men* shall be hid. H995
Jer 49: 7 from the **p**? is their wisdom vanished? H995
Hos 14: 9 these *things*? **p**, and he shall know them? H995
Am 5:13 Therefore the **p** shall keep silence in H7919
Mt 11:25 **p**, and hast revealed them unto babes. *G4908*
Lk 10:21 from the wise and **p**, and hast revealed *G4908*
Act 13: 7 Sergius Paulus, a **p** man; who called for *G4908*
1Co 1:19 to nothing the understanding of the **p**. *G4908*

PRUDENTLY
Isa 52:13 Behold, my servant shall deal **p**, he H7919

PRUNE
Lev 25: 3 six years thou shalt **p** thy vineyard, and H2168
4 sow thy field, nor **p** thy vineyard. H2168

PRUNED
Isa 5: 6 And I will lay it waste: it shall not be **p**, H2168

PRUNING
Isa 18: 5 off the sprigs with **p** hooks, and take H4211

PRUNINGHOOKS
Isa 2: 4 their spears into **p**: nation shall not lift H4211
Joel 3:10 swords, and your **p** into spears: let the H4211
Mic 4: 3 their spears into **p**: nation shall not lift H4211

PSALM
1Ch 16: 7 delivered first *this* **p** to thank the LORD
Ps 3:ttl A **P** of David, when he fled from H4210
4:ttl To the chief Musician on Neginoth, A **P** H4210
5:ttl Musician upon Nehiloth, A **P** of David. H4210
6:ttl upon Sheminith, A **P** of David. H4210
8:ttl To the chief Musician upon Gittith, A **P** H4210
9:ttl upon Muth-labben, A **P** of David. H4210
11:ttl To the chief Musician, *A P* of David.
12:ttl upon Sheminith, A **P** of David. H4210
13:ttl To the chief Musician, A **P** of David. H4210
14:ttl To the chief Musician, *A P* of David.
15:ttl A **P** of David. H4210
18:ttl To the chief Musician, *A P* of David, H4210
19:ttl To the chief Musician, A **P** of David. H4210
20:ttl To the chief Musician, A **P** of David. H4210
21:ttl To the chief Musician, A **P** of David. H4210
22:ttl upon Aijeleth Shahar, A **P** of David. H4210
23:ttl A **P** of David. H4210
24:ttl A **P** of David.
25:ttl *A P* of David.
26:ttl *A P* of David.
27:ttl *A P* of David.
28:ttl *A P* of David.
Ps 29:ttl A **P** of David. H4210
30:ttl A **P** *and* Song *at* the dedication of the H4210
31:ttl To the chief Musician, A **P** of David. H4210
32:ttl *A P* of David, Maschil.
34:ttl *A P* of David, when he changed his
35:ttl *A P* of David.
36:ttl To the chief Musician, *A P* of David the
37:ttl *A P* of David.
38:ttl A **P** of David, to bring to remembrance. H4210
39:ttl *even* to Jeduthun, A **P** of David. H4210
40:ttl To the chief Musician, A **P** of David. H4210
41:ttl To the chief Musician, A **P** of David. H4210
47:ttl To the chief Musician, A **P** for the sons H4210
48:ttl A Song *and* **P** for the sons of Korah. H4210
49:ttl To the chief Musician, A **P** for the sons H4210
50:ttl A **P** of Asaph. H4210
51:ttl To the chief Musician, A **P** of David, H4210
52:ttl To the chief Musician, Maschil, *A P* of
53:ttl upon Mahalath, Maschil, *A P* of David.
54:ttl Maschil, *A P* of David, when the Ziphims
55:ttl on Neginoth, Maschil, *A P* of David.
61:ttl Musician upon Neginah, *A P* of David.
62:ttl To the chief Musician, to Jeduthun, A **P** H4210
63:ttl A **P** of David, when he was in the H4210
64:ttl To the chief Musician, A **P** of David. H4210
65:ttl To the chief Musician, A **P** *and* Song of H4210
66:ttl To the chief Musician, A Song *or* **P**. H4210
67:ttl To the chief Musician on Neginoth, A **P** H4210
68:ttl To the chief Musician, A **P** *or* Song of H4210
69:ttl upon Shoshannim, *A P* of David.
70:ttl To the chief Musician, *A P* of David, to
72:ttl *A P* for Solomon. H4210
73:ttl A **P** of Asaph. H4210
75:ttl To the chief Musician, Al-taschith, A **P** H4210
76:ttl To the chief Musician on Neginoth, A **P** H4210
77:ttl To the chief Musician, to Jeduthun, A **P** H4210
79:ttl A **P** of Asaph. H4210
80:ttl upon Shoshannim-Eduth, A **P** of Asaph.
81: 2 Take a **p**, and bring hither the timbrel, H2172
ttl To the chief Musician upon Gittith, *A P* H4210
82:ttl A **P** of Asaph. H4210
83:ttl A Song *or* **P** of Asaph. H4210
84:ttl To the chief Musician upon Gittith, A **P** H4210
85:ttl To the chief Musician, A **P** for the sons H4210
87:ttl A **P** *or* Song for the sons of Korah. H4210
88:ttl A Song or **P** for the sons of Korah, to H4210
92:ttl A **P** *or* Song for the sabbath day. H4210
98: 5 with the harp, and the voice of a **p**. H2172
ttl A **P**. H4210
100:ttl A **P** of praise. H4210
101:ttl A **P** of David. H4210
103:ttl *A P* of David.
108:ttl A Song *or* **P** of David. H4210
109:ttl To the chief Musician, A **P** of David. H4210
110:ttl A **P** of David. H4210
138:ttl *A P* of David.
139:ttl To the chief Musician, A **P** of David. H4210
140:ttl To the chief Musician, A **P** of David. H4210
141:ttl A **P** of David. H4210
143:ttl A **P** of David. H4210
144:ttl *A P* of David.
145:ttl David's *P* of praise.
Act 13:33 in the second **p**, Thou art my Son, this *G5568*
35 Wherefore he saith also in another *p*,
1Co 14:26 one of you hath a **p**, hath a doctrine, *G5568*

PSALMIST
2Sa 23: 1 Jacob, and the sweet **p** of Israel, said, H2158

PSALMS
1Ch 16: 9 Sing unto him, sing **p** unto him, talk ye H2167
Ps 95: 2 make a joyful noise unto him with **p**. H2158
105: 2 Sing unto him, sing **p** unto him: talk ye H2167
Lk 20:42 saith in the book of P, The *G5568*
24:44 prophets, and *in* the **p**, concerning me. *G5568*
Act 1:20 For it is written in the book of **P**, Let his *G5568*
Eph 5:19 Speaking to yourselves in **p** and hymns *G5568*
Col 3:16 one another in **p** and hymns and *G5568*
Jas 5:13 him pray. Is any merry? let him sing **p**. *G5567*

PSALTERIES
2Sa 6: 5 on harps, and on **p**, and on timbrels, H5035
1Ki 10:12 harps also and **p** for singers: there H5035
1Ch 13: 8 harps, and with **p**, and with timbrels, H5035
15:16 of musick, **p** and harps and cymbals, H5035
20 and Benaiah, with **p** on Alamoth; H5035
28 making a noise with **p** and harps. H5035
16: 5 and Jeiel with **p** and with harps; but H5035
25: 1 with harps, with **p**, and with cymbals: H5035
1Ch 25: 6 with cymbals, **p**, and harps, for the H5035
2Ch 5:12 cymbals and **p** and harps, stood at H5035
9:11 and harps and **p** for singers: and there H5035
20:28 And they came to Jerusalem with **p** and H5035
29:25 with cymbals, with **p**, and with harps, H5035
Neh 12:27 *with* cymbals, **p**, and with harps. H5035

PSALTERY
1Sa 10: 5 high place with a **p**, and a tabret, and a H5035
Ps 33: 2 the **p** *and* an instrument of ten strings. H5035
57: 8 Awake up, my glory; awake, **p** and H5035
71:22 I will also praise thee with the **p**, *even* H5627
81: 2 timbrel, the pleasant harp with the **p**. H5035
92: 3 **p**; upon the harp with a solemn sound. H5035
108: 2 Awake, **p** and harp: I *myself* will awake H5035
144: 9 O God: upon a **p** *and* an instrument H5035
150: 3 praise him with the **p** and harp. H5035
Dan 3: 5 harp, sackbut, **p**, dulcimer, and all H6460
7 flute, harp, sackbut, **p**, and all kinds of H6460
10 harp, sackbut, **p**, and dulcimer, and all H6460
15 harp, sackbut, **p**, and dulcimer, and all H6460

PTOLEMAIS
Act 21: 7 Tyre, we came to **P**, and saluted the *G4424*

PUA
Nu 26:23 Tolaites: of **P**, the family of the Punites: H6312

PUAH
Ex 1:15 Shiphrah, and the name of the other **P**: H6326
Jdg 10: 1 Tola the son of **P**, the son of Dodo, a H6312
1Ch 7: 1 Tola, and **P**, Jashub, and Shimron, four. H6312

PUBLIC
See PUBLICK.

PUBLICAN
Mt 10: 3 and Matthew the **p**; James *the son* of *G5057*
18:17 unto thee as an heathen man and a **p**. *G5057*
Lk 5:27 forth, and saw a **p**, named Levi, sitting *G5057*
18:10 the one a Pharisee, and the other a **p**. *G5057*
11 unjust, adulterers, or even as this **p**. *G5057*
13 And the **p**, standing afar off, would not *G5057*

PUBLICANS
Mt 5:46 have ye? do not even the **p** the same? *G5057*
47 more *than others*? do not even the **p** so? *G5057*
9:10 behold, many **p** and sinners came and *G5057*
11 eateth your Master with **p** and sinners? *G5057*
11:19 a friend of **p** and sinners. But wisdom *G5057*
21:31 unto you, That the **p** and the harlots go *G5057*
32 him not: but the **p** and the harlots *G5057*
Mk 2:15 his house, many **p** and sinners sat also *G5057*
16 saw him eat with **p** and sinners, they *G5057*
16 and drinketh with **p** and sinners? *G5057*
Lk 3:12 Then came also **p** to be baptized, and *G5057*
5:29 great company of **p** and of others that *G5057*
30 do ye eat and drink with **p** and sinners? *G5057*
7:29 *him*, and the **p**, justified God, being *G5057*
34 a winebibber, a friend of **p** and sinners! *G5057*
15: 1 Then drew near unto him all the **p** and *G5057*
19: 2 the chief among the **p**, and he was rich. *G754*

PUBLICK
Mt 1:19 to make her a **p** example, was minded *G3856*

PUBLICKLY
Act 18:28 the Jews, *and that* **p**, shewing by the *G1219*
20:20 taught you **p**, and from house to house, *G1219*

PUBLISH
Dt 32: 3 Because I will **p** the name of the LORD: H7121
1Sa 31: 9 round about, to **p** *it in* the house of H1319
2Sa 1:20 Tell *it* not in Gath, **p** *it* not in the streets H1319
Neh 8:15 And that they should **p** and proclaim H8085
Ps 26: 7 That I may **p** with the voice of H8085
Jer 4: 5 Declare ye in Judah, and **p** in H8085
16 nations; behold, **p** against Jerusalem, H8085
5:20 of Jacob, and **p** it in Judah, saying, H8085
31: 7 of the nations: **p** ye, praise ye, and say, H8085
46:14 Declare ye in Egypt, and **p** in Migdol, H8085
14 in Migdol, and **p** in Noph and in H8085
50: 2 Declare ye among the nations, and **p**, H8085
2 set up a standard; **p**, *and* conceal not: H8085
Am 3: 9 **P** in the palaces at Ashdod, and in the H8085
4: 5 and proclaim *and* **p** the free offerings: H8085
Mk 1:45 But he went out, and began to **p** *it* *G2784*
5:20 And he departed, and began to **p** in *G2784*

PUBLISHED

Est 1:20 shall make shall be **p** throughout all his H8085
22 and that *it* should be **p** according to the H1696
3:14 province was **p** unto all people, that H1540
8:13 province *was* **p** unto all people, and H1540
Ps 68:11 *was* the company of those that **p** *it*. H1319
Jna 3: 7 And he caused *it* to be proclaimed and **p** H559
Mk 7:36 so much the more a great deal they **p** *it*; *G2784*
13:10 And the gospel must first be **p** among *G2784*
Lk 8:39 he went his way, and **p** throughout the *G2784*
Act 10:37 That word, *I say*, ye know, which was **p** *G1096*
13:49 And the word of the Lord was **p** *G1308*

PUBLISHETH

Isa 52: 7 good tidings, that **p** peace; that H8085
7 of good, that **p** salvation; that saith H8085
Jer 4:15 For a voice declareth from Dan, and **p** H8085
Nah 1:15 good tidings, that **p** peace! O Judah, H8085

PUBLIUS

Act 28: 7 whose name was **P**; who received us, *G4196*
8 that the father of **P** lay sick of a fever *G4196*

PUDENS

2Ti 4:21 greeteth thee, and **P**, and Linus, and *G4227*

PUFFED

1Co 4: 6 of you be **p** up for one against another. *G5448*
18 Now some are **p** up, as though I would *G5448*
19 of them which are **p** up, but the power. *G5448*
5: 2 And ye are **p** up, and have not rather *G5448*
13: 4 charity vaunteth not itself, is not **p** up, *G5448*
Col 2:18 seen, vainly **p** up by his fleshly mind, *G5448*

PUFFETH

Ps 10: 5 *as for* all his enemies, he **p** at them. H6315
12: 5 *him* in safety *from him that* **p** at him. H6315
1Co 8: 1 Knowledge **p** up, but charity edifieth. *G5448*

PUHITES

1Ch 2:53 the Ithrites, and the **P**, and the H6336

PUL

2Ki 15:19 *And* **P** the king of Assyria came against H6322
19 Menahem gave **P** a thousand talents H6322
1Ch 5:26 up the spirit of **P** king of Assyria, and H6322
Isa 66:19 *to* Tarshish, **P**, and Lud, that draw H6322

PULL

1Ki 13: 4 that he could not **p** it in again to him. H7725
Ps 31: 4 **P** me out of the net that they have laid H3318
Isa 22:19 from thy state shall he **p** thee down. H2040
Jer 1:10 to root out, and to **p** down, and to H5422
12: 3 heart toward thee: **p** them out like H5423
18: 7 up, and to **p** down, and to destroy *it*; H5422
24: 6 them, and not **p** *them* down; and I will H2040
42:10 I build you, and not **p** *you* down, and I H2040
Ezk 17: 9 shall he not **p** up the roots thereof, H5423
Mic 2: 8 as an enemy: ye **p** off the robe with the H6584
Mt 7: 4 brother, Let me **p** out the mote out of *G1544*
Lk 6:42 Brother, let me **p** out the mote that is *G1544*
42 thou see clearly to **p** out the mote that *G1544*
12:18 And he said, This will I do: I will **p** *G2507*
14: 5 **p** him out on the sabbath day? *G385*

PULLED

Gen 8: 9 her, and **p** her in unto him into the ark. H4026
19:10 But the men put forth their hand, and **p** H935
Ezr 6:11 let timber be **p** down from his house, H5253
Lam 3:11 He hath turned aside my ways, and **p** H6582
Am 9:15 shall no more be **p** up out of their land H5428
Zec 7:11 But they refused to hearken, and **p** H5414
Act 23:10 should have been **p** in pieces of them, *G1288*

PULLING

2Co 10: 4 God to the **p** down of strong holds;) *G2506*
Jude 23 And others save with fear, **p** *them* out of *G726*

PULPIT

Neh 8: 4 And Ezra the scribe stood upon a **p** of H4026

PULSE

2Sa 17:28 and beans, and lentiles, and parched *p*,
Dan 1:12 give us **p** to eat, and water to drink. H2235
16 they should drink; and gave them **p**. H2235

PUNISH

Lev 26:18 **p** you seven times more for your sins. H3256
24 will **p** you yet seven times for your sins. H5221
Prv 17:26 Also to **p** the just *is* not good, *nor* to H6064
Isa 10:12 Jerusalem, I will **p** the fruit of the stout H6485
13:11 And I will **p** the world for *their* evil, and H6485
24:21 the LORD shall **p** the host of the high H6485
26:21 out of his place to **p** the inhabitants of H6485
27: 1 and strong sword shall **p** leviathan the H6485
Jer 9:25 LORD, that I will **p** all *them which are* H6485
11:22 Behold, I will **p** them: the young men H6485
13:21 What wilt thou say when he shall **p** H6485
21:14 But I will **p** you according to the fruit of H6485
23:34 I will even **p** that man and his house. H6485
25:12 *that* I will **p** the king of Babylon, H6485
27: 8 that nation will I **p**, saith the LORD, H6485
29:32 LORD; Behold, I will **p** Shemaiah the H6485
30:20 me, and I will **p** all that oppress them. H6485
36:31 And I will **p** him and his seed and his H6485
44:13 For I will **p** them that dwell in the land H6485
29 LORD, that I will **p** you in this place, H6485
46:25 Behold, I will **p** the multitude of No, H6485
50:18 Behold, I will **p** the king of Babylon H6485
51:44 And I will **p** Bel in Babylon, and I will H6485
Hos 4: 9 priest: and I will **p** them for their ways, H6485
14 I will not **p** your daughters when they H6485
12: 2 Judah, and will **p** Jacob according to H6485
Am 3: 2 I will **p** you for all your iniquities. H6485
Zep 1: 8 that I will **p** the princes, and the H6485
9 In the same day also will I **p** all those H6485
12 with candles, and **p** the men that are H6485
Zec 8:14 hosts; As I thought to **p** you, when your H7489
Act 4:21 how they might **p** them, because of the *G2849*

PUNISHED

Ex 21:20 die under his hand; he shall be surely **p**. H5358
21 he shall not be **p**: for he *is* his money. H5358
22 he shall be surely **p**, according as the H6064
Ezr 9:13 thou our God hast **p** us less than our H2820
Job 31:11 it *is* an iniquity *to be* **p** *by* the judges.
28 This also *were* an iniquity *to be* **p** *by* the
Prv 21:11 When the scorner is **p**, the simple is H6064
22: 3 but the simple pass on, and are **p**. H6064
27:12 *but* the simple pass on, *and* are **p**. H6064
Jer 44:13 of Egypt, as I have **p** Jerusalem, by the H6485
50:18 land, as I have **p** the king of Assyria. H6485
Zep 3: 7 off, howsoever I **p** them: but they rose H6485
Zec 10: 3 shepherds, and I **p** the goats: for the H6485
Act 22: 5 there bound unto Jerusalem, for to be **p**. *G5097*
26:11 And I **p** them oft in every synagogue, *G5097*
2Th 1: 9 Who shall be **p** with everlasting *G1349*
2Pt 2: 9 unjust unto the day of judgment to be **p**: *G2849*

PUNISHMENT

Gen 4:13 And Cain said unto the LORD, My **p** *is* H5771
Lev 26:41 then accept of the **p** of their iniquity: H5771
43 shall accept of the **p** of their iniquity: H5771
1Sa 28:10 shall no **p** happen to thee for this thing. H5771
Job 31: 3 a strange *p* to the workers of iniquity?
Prv 19:19 A man of great wrath shall suffer **p**: for H6066
Lam 3:39 complain, a man for the **p** of his sins?
4: 6 For the **p** of the iniquity of the daughter H5771
6 people is greater than the **p** of the sin of H2403
22 The **p** of thine iniquity is H5771
Ezk 14:10 And they shall bear the **p** of their H5771
10 their iniquity: the **p** of the prophet shall H5771
10 as the **p** of him that seeketh *unto him*; H5771
Am 1: 3 will not turn away *the* **p** thereof; because
6 will not turn away *the* **p** thereof; because
9 will not turn away *the* **p** thereof; because
11 not turn away *the* **p** thereof; because he
13 will not turn away *the* **p** thereof; because
2: 1 not turn away *the* **p** thereof; because he
4 will not turn away *the* **p** thereof; because
6 will not turn away *the* **p** thereof; because
Zec 14:19 This shall be the **p** of Egypt, and the H2403
19 of Egypt, and the **p** of all nations that H2403
Mt 25:46 **p**: but the righteous into life eternal. *G2851*
2Co 2: 6 Sufficient to such a man *is* this **p**, which *G2009*
Heb 10:29 Of how much sorer **p**, suppose ye, shall *G5098*
1Pt 2:14 by him for the **p** of evildoers, and for *G1557*

PUNISHMENTS

Job 19:29 *bringeth* the **p** of the sword, that ye H5771
Ps 149: 7 the heathen, *and* **p** upon the people; H5771

PUNITES

Nu 26:23 the Tolaites: of Pua, the family of the **P**: H6324

PUNON

Nu 33:42 from Zalmonah, and pitched in **P**. H6325
43 And they departed from **P**, and pitched H6325

PUR

Est 3: 7 they cast **P**, that *is*, the lot, before H6332
9:24 them, and had cast **P**, that *is*, the lot, to H6332
26 after the name of **P**. Therefore for all H6332

PURCHASE

Gen 49:32 The **p** of the field and of the cave that *is* H4735
Lev 25:33 And if a man **p** of the Levites, then the H1350
Jer 32:11 So I took the evidence of the **p**, *both* H4736
12 And I gave the evidence of the **p** unto H4736
12 the book of the **p**, before all the Jews H4736
14 evidence of the **p**, both which is sealed, H4736
16 evidence of the **p** unto Baruch the son H4736
1Ti 3:13 of a deacon well **p** to themselves a good *G4046*

PURCHASED

Gen 25:10 The field which Abraham **p** of the sons H7069
Ex 15:16 the people pass over, *which* thou hast **p**. H7069
Ru 4:10 of Mahlon, have I **p** to be my wife, to H7069
Ps 74: 2 *which* thou hast **p** of old; the rod of H7069
78:54 mountain, *which* his right hand had **p**. H7069
Act 1:18 Now this man **p** a field with the reward *G2932*
8:20 the gift of God may be **p** with money. *G2932*
20:28 which he hath **p** with his own blood. *G4046*
Eph 1:14 redemption of the **p** possession, unto *G4047*

PURE

Ex 25:11 And thou shalt overlay it with **p** gold, H2889
17 And thou shalt make a mercy seat *of* **p** H2889
24 And thou shalt overlay it with **p** gold, H2889
29 withal: *of* **p** gold shalt thou make them. H2889
31 And thou shalt make a candlestick *of* **p** H2889
36 it *shall be* one beaten work *of* **p** gold. H2889
38 snuffdishes thereof, *shall be of* **p** gold. H2889
39 *Of* a talent of **p** gold shall he make it, H2889
27:20 they bring thee **p** oil olive beaten for H2134
28:14 And two chains *of* **p** gold at the ends; *of* H2889
22 at the ends *of* wreathen work *of* **p** gold. H2889
36 And thou shalt make a plate *of* **p** gold, H2889
30: 3 And thou shalt overlay it with **p** gold, H2889
23 spices, of **p** myrrh five hundred H1865
34 sweet spices with **p** frankincense: of H2134
35 tempered together, **p** *and* holy: H2889
31: 8 furniture, and the **p** candlestick with H2889
37: 2 And he overlaid it with **p** gold within H2889
6 And he made the mercy seat *of* **p** gold: H2889
11 And he overlaid it with **p** gold, and H2889
16 his covers to cover withal, *of* **p** gold. H2889
17 And he made the candlestick *of* **p** gold: H2889
22 all of it *was* one beaten work *of* **p** gold. H2889
23 snuffers, and his snuffdishes, *of* **p** gold. H2889
24 *Of* a talent of **p** gold made he it, and all H2889
26 And he overlaid it with **p** gold, *both* the H2889
29 oil, and the **p** incense of sweet spices, H2889
39:15 at the ends, *of* wreathen work *of* **p** gold. H2889
25 And they made bells *of* **p** gold, and put H2889
30 of the holy crown *of* **p** gold, and wrote H2889
37 The **p** candlestick, *with* the lamps H2889
Lev 24: 2 bring unto thee **p** oil olive beaten for H2134
4 He shall order the lamps upon the **p** H2889
6 row, upon the **p** table before the LORD. H2889
7 And thou shalt put **p** frankincense H2134
Dt 32:14 didst drink the **p** blood of the grape. H2561
2Sa 22:27 With the **p** thou wilt shew thyself pure; H1305
27 With the pure thou wilt shew thyself **p**; H1305
1Ki 5:11 measures of **p** oil: thus gave Solomon H3795
6:20 and he overlaid it with **p** gold; and *so* H5462
21 house within with **p** gold: and he made H5462
7:49 And the candlesticks of **p** gold, five on H5462
50 and the censers *of* **p** gold; and the H5462
10:21 Lebanon *were of* **p** gold; none *were of* H5462
1Ch 28:17 Also **p** gold for the fleshhooks, and the H2889
2Ch 3: 4 and he overlaid it within with **p** gold. H2889
4:20 the manner before the oracle, *of* **p** gold; H5462
22 the censers, *of* **p** gold: and the entry H5462
9:17 of ivory, and overlaid it with **p** gold. H2889
20 Lebanon *were of* **p** gold: none *were of* H5462
13:11 *they in order* upon the **p** table; and the H2889
Ezr 6:20 all of them *were* **p**, and killed the H2889
Job 4:17 shall a man be more **p** than his maker? H2891
8: 6 If thou *wert* **p** and upright; surely now H2134
11: 4 For thou hast said, My doctrine *is* **p**, H2134
16:17 in mine hands: also my prayer *is* **p**. H2134
25: 5 not; yea, the stars are not **p** in his sight. H2141
28:19 neither shall it be valued with **p** gold. H2889
Ps 12: 6 The words of the LORD *are* **p** words: *as* H2889
18:26 With the **p** thou wilt shew thyself pure; H1305
26 With the pure thou wilt shew thyself **p**; H1305
19: 8 of the LORD *is* **p**, enlightening the eyes. H1249

Ps 21: 3 settest a crown of **p** gold on his head. H6337
24: 4 He that hath clean hands, and a **p** H1249
119:140 Thy word *is* very **p**: therefore thy H6884
Prv 15:26 *the words* of the **p** *are* pleasant words. H2889
20: 9 my heart clean, I am **p** from my sin? H2891
11 his work *be* **p**, and whether *it be* right. H2134
21: 8 but *as for* the **p**, his work *is* right. H2134
30: 5 Every word of God *is* **p**: he *is* a shield H6884
12 *There is* a generation *that are* **p** in their H2889
Dan 7: 9 his head like the **p** wool: his throne *was* H5343
Mic 6:11 Shall I count *them* **p** with the wicked H2135
Zep 3: 9 For then will I turn to the people a **p** H1305
Mal 1:11 unto my name, and a **p** offering: for my H2889
Mt 5: 8 Blessed *are* the **p** in heart: for they shall G2513
Act 20:26 that I *am* **p** from the blood of all *men*. G2513
Ro 14:20 things indeed *are* **p**; but *it is* evil for that G2513
Php 4: 8 things *are* **p**, whatsoever things *are* G53
1Ti 1: 5 is charity out of a **p** heart, and *of* a G2513
3: 9 Holding the mystery of the faith in a **p** G2513
5:22 of other men's sins: keep thyself **p**. G53
2Ti 1: 3 *my* forefathers with **p** conscience, that G2513
2:22 that call on the Lord out of a **p** heart. G2513
Tit 1:15 Unto the **p** all things *are* pure: but unto G2513
15 Unto the pure all things *are* **p**: but unto G2513
15 *is* nothing **p**; but even their mind G2513
Heb 10:22 and our bodies washed with **p** water. G2513
Jas 1:27 **P** religion and undefiled before God G2513
3:17 is from above is first **p**, then peaceable, G53
1Pt 1:22 one another with a **p** heart fervently: G2513
2Pt 3: 1 your **p** minds by way of remembrance: G1506
1Jn 3: 3 in him purifieth himself, even as he is **p**. G53
Rev 15: 6 clothed in **p** and white linen, and G2513
21:18 city *was* **p** gold, like unto clear glass. G2513
21 **p** gold, as it were transparent glass. G2513
22: 1 And he shewed me a **p** river of water of G2513

PURELY
Isa 1:25 upon thee, and **p** purge away thy dross, H1253

PURENESS
Job 22:30 it is delivered by the **p** of thine hands. H1252
Prv 22:11 He that loveth **p** of heart, *for* the grace H2890
2Co 6: 6 By **p**, by knowledge, by longsuffering, by G54

PURER
Lam 4: 7 Her Nazarites were **p** than snow, they H2141
Hab 1:13 *Thou art* of **p** eyes than to behold evil, H2889

PURGE
2Ch 34: 3 twelfth year he began to **p** Judah and H2891
Ps 51: 7 **P** me with hyssop, and I shall be clean: H2398
65: 3 thou shalt **p** them away. H3722
79: 9 **p** away our sins, for thy name's sake. H3722
Isa 1:25 thee, and purely **p** away thy dross, and H6884
Ezk 20:38 And I will **p** out from among you the H1305
43:20 about: thus shalt thou cleanse and **p** it. H3722
26 Seven days shall they **p** the altar and H3722
Dan 11:35 to try them, and to **p**, and to make *them* H1305
Mal 3: 3 sons of Levi, and **p** them as gold and H2212
Mt 3:12 and he will throughly **p** his floor, and G1245
Lk 3:17 he will throughly **p** his floor, and will G1245
1Co 5: 7 **P** out therefore the old leaven, that ye G1571
2Ti 2:21 If a man therefore **p** himself from G1571
Heb 9:14 spot to God, **p** your conscience from G2511

PURGED
1Sa 3:14 be **p** with sacrifice nor offering for ever. H3722
2Ch 34: 8 when he had **p** the land, and the house, H2891
Prv 16: 6 By mercy and truth iniquity is **p**: and by H3722
Isa 4: 4 and shall have **p** the blood of Jerusalem H1740
6: 7 iniquity is taken away, and thy sin **p**. H3722
22:14 shall not be **p** from you till ye die, H3722
27: 9 of Jacob be **p**; and this *is* all the fruit H3722
Ezk 24:13 because I have **p** thee, and thou wast H2891
13 and thou wast not **p**, thou shalt not be H2891
13 thou shalt not be **p** from thy filthiness H2891
Heb 1: 3 he had by himself **p** our sins, sat down G4160
9:22 And almost all things are by the law **p** G2511
10: 2 worshippers once **p** should have had G2508
2Pt 1: 9 that he was **p** from his old sins. G2512

PURGETH
Jn 15: 2 **p** it, that it may bring forth more fruit. G2508

PURGING
Mk 7:19 goeth out into the draught, **p** all meats? G2511

PURIFICATION
Nu 19: 9 a water of separation: it *is* a **p** for sin. H2403
19:17 of the burnt heifer of **p** for sin, and H2403
2Ch 30:19 according to the **p** of the sanctuary. H2893
Neh 12:45 and the ward of the **p**, according to the H2893
Est 2: 3 and let their things for **p** be given *them*: H8562
9 her her things for **p**, with such things as H8562
Lk 2:22 And when the days of her **p** according G2512
Act 21:26 of the days of **p**, until that an offering G49

PURIFICATIONS
Est 2:12 the days of their **p** accomplished, *to* H4795

PURIFIED
Lev 8:15 his finger, and **p** the altar, and poured H2398
Nu 8:21 And the Levites were **p**, and they H2398
31:23 it shall be **p** with the water of H2398
2Sa 11: 4 with her; for she was **p** from her H6942
Ezr 6:20 For the priests and the Levites were **p** H2891
Neh 12:30 And the priests and the Levites **p** H2891
30 themselves, and **p** the people, and the H2891
Ps 12: 6 in a furnace of earth, **p** seven times. H2212
Dan 12:10 Many shall be **p**, and made white, and H1305
Act 24:18 Asia found me **p** in the temple, neither G48
Heb 9:23 heavens should be **p** with these; but the G2511
1Pt 1:22 Seeing ye have **p** your souls in obeying G48

PURIFIER
Mal 3: 3 And he shall sit *as* a refiner and **p** of H2891

PURIFIETH
Nu 19:13 that is dead, and **p** not himself, defileth H2398
1Jn 3: 3 in him **p** himself, even as he is pure. G48

PURIFY
Nu 19:12 He shall **p** himself with it on the third H2398
12 be clean: but if he **p** not himself the H2398
19 day he shall **p** himself, and wash his H2398
20 and shall not **p** himself, that soul shall H2398
31:19 touched any slain, **p** *both* yourselves H2398
20 And **p** all *your* raiment, and all that is H2398
Job 41:25 reason of breakings they **p** themselves. H2398
Isa 66:17 They that sanctify themselves, and **p** H2891
Ezk 43:26 purge the altar and **p** it; and they shall H2891
Mal 3: 3 and he shall **p** the sons of Levi, and H2891
Jn 11:55 before the passover, to **p** themselves. G48
Act 21:24 Them take, and **p** thyself with them, and G48
Tit 2:14 from all iniquity, and **p** unto himself a G2511
Jas 4: 8 and **p** *your* hearts, *ye* double minded. G48

PURIFYING
Lev 12: 4 in the blood of her **p** three and thirty H2893
4 until the days of her **p** be fulfilled. H2892
5 blood of her **p** threescore and six days. H2893
6 And when the days of her **p** are H2892
Nu 8: 7 Sprinkle water of **p** upon them, and let H2403
1Ch 23:28 and in the **p** of all holy things, and H2893
Est 2:12 *other* things for the **p** of the women;) H8562
Jn 2: 6 after the manner of the **p** of the Jews, G2512
3:25 of John's disciples and the Jews about **p**. G2512
Act 15: 9 us and them, **p** their hearts by faith. G2511
21:26 and the next day **p** himself with them G48
Heb 9:13 sanctifieth to the **p** of the flesh: G2514

PURIM
Est 9:26 Wherefore they called these days **P** H6332
28 and *that* these days of **P** should not fail H6332
29 to confirm this second letter of **P**. H6332
31 To confirm these days of **P** in their H6332
32 of **P**; and it was written in the book. H6332

PURITY
1Ti 4:12 in charity, in spirit, in faith, in **p**. G47
5: 2 the younger as sisters, with all **p**. G47

PURLOINING
Tit 2:10 Not **p**, but shewing all good fidelity; G3557

PURPLE
Ex 25: 4 And blue, and **p**, and scarlet, and fine H713
26: 1 linen, and blue, and **p**, and scarlet: *with* H713
31 a vail *of* blue, and **p**, and scarlet, and fine H713
36 tent, *of* blue, and **p**, and scarlet, and fine H713
27:16 cubits, *of* blue, and **p**, and scarlet, and H713
28: 5 And they shall take gold, and blue, and **p**, H713
6 gold, *of* blue, and *of* **p**, *of* scarlet, and fine H713
8 and **p**, and scarlet, and fine twined linen. H713
15 *of* blue, and *of* **p**, and *of* scarlet, and *of* H713
33 *of* blue, and *of* **p**, and *of* scarlet, round H713
35: 6 And blue, and **p**, and scarlet, and fine H713
23 found blue, and **p**, and scarlet, and fine H713
Ex 35:25 and of **p**, *and* of scarlet, and of fine linen. H713
35 in blue, and in **p**, in scarlet, and in fine H713
36: 8 linen, and blue, and **p**, and scarlet: *with* H713
35 And he made a vail *of* blue, and **p**, and H713
37 door *of* blue, and **p**, and scarlet, and fine H713
38:18 *of* blue, and **p**, and scarlet, and fine H713
23 and in **p**, and in scarlet, and fine linen. H713
39: 1 And of the blue, and **p**, and scarlet, they H713
2 and **p**, and scarlet, and fine twined linen. H713
3 the blue, and in the **p**, and in the scarlet, H713
5 *of* gold, blue, and **p**, and scarlet, and fine H713
8 and **p**, and scarlet, and fine twined linen. H713
24 and **p**, and scarlet, *and* twined *linen*. H713
29 linen, and blue, and **p**, and scarlet, *of* H713
Nu 4:13 the altar, and spread a **p** cloth thereon: H713
Jdg 8:26 and collars, and **p** raiment that *was* on H713
2Ch 2: 7 and in iron, and in **p**, and crimson, and H710
14 and in timber, in **p**, in blue, and in fine H713
3:14 And he made the vail *of* blue, and **p**, and H713
Est 1: 6 of fine linen and **p** to silver rings and H713
8:15 of fine linen and **p**: and the city of H713
Prv 31:22 of tapestry; her clothing *is* silk and **p**. H713
Song 3:10 the covering of it *of* **p**, the midst thereof H713
7: 5 like **p**; the king *is* held in the galleries. H713
Jer 10: 9 the founder: blue and **p** *is* their clothing: H713
Ezk 27: 7 be thy sail; blue and **p** from the isles of H713
16 with emeralds, **p**, and broidered work, H713
Mk 15:17 And they clothed him with **p**, and G4209
20 they took off the **p** from him, and put G4209
Lk 16:19 was clothed in **p** and fine linen, and G4209
Jn 19: 2 his head, and they put on him a **p** robe, G4210
5 of thorns, and the **p** robe. And *Pilate* G4210
Act 16:14 named Lydia, a seller of **p**, of the city of G4211
Rev 17: 4 And the woman was arrayed in **p** and G4209
18:12 fine linen, and **p**, and silk, and scarlet, G4209
16 in fine linen, and **p**, and scarlet, and G4210

PURPOSE
Ru 2:16 of the handfuls of **p** for her, and leave H7997
1Ki 5: 5 And, behold, I **p** to build an house unto H559
2Ch 28:10 And now ye **p** to keep under the children H559
Ezr 4: 5 to frustrate their **p**, all the days of Cyrus H6098
Neh 8: 4 had made for the **p**; and beside him H1697
Job 33:17 That he may withdraw man *from his* **p**, H4639
Prv 20:18 *Every* **p** is established by counsel: and H4284
Ecc 3: 1 a time to every **p** under the heaven: H2656
17 there for every **p** and for every work. H2656
8: 6 Because to every **p** there is time and H2656
Isa 1:11 To what **p** *is* the multitude of your H4100
14:26 This *is* the **p** that is purposed upon the H6098
30: 7 in vain, and to no **p**: therefore have I H7385
Jer 6:20 To what **p** cometh there to me incense
26: 3 of the evil, which I **p** to do unto them H2803
36: 3 all the evil which I **p** to do unto them; H2803
49:30 and hath conceived a **p** against you. H4284
51:29 sorrow: for every **p** of the LORD shall H4284
Dan 6:17 of his lords; that the **p** might not be H6640
Mt 26: 8 saying, To what **p** *is* this waste? G5101
Act 11:23 them all, that with **p** of heart they G4286
26:16 unto thee for this **p**, to make thee a G5124
27:13 obtained *their* **p**, loosing *thence*, they G4286
43 them from *their* **p**; and commanded G1013
Ro 8:28 who are the called according to *his* **p**. G4286
9:11 or evil, that the **p** of God according to G4286
17 Even for this same **p** have I raised thee G846
2Co 1:17 or the things that I **p**, do I purpose G1011
17 I purpose, do I **p** according to the flesh, G1011
Eph 1:11 according to the **p** of him who worketh G4286
3:11 According to the eternal **p** which he G4286
6:22 you for the same **p**, that ye might know G846
Col 4: 8 you for the same **p**, that he might know G846
2Ti 1: 9 to his own **p** and grace, which was G4286
3:10 manner of life, **p**, faith, longsuffering, G4286
1Jn 3: 8 For this **p** the Son of God was G5124

PURPOSED
2Ch 32: 2 he was **p** to fight against Jerusalem, H6440
Ps 17: 3 **p** *that* my mouth shall not transgress. H2161
140: 4 who have **p** to overthrow my goings. H2803
Isa 14:24 pass; and as I have **p**, *so* shall it stand: H3289
26 This *is* the purpose that is **p** upon the H3289
27 For the LORD of hosts hath **p**, and who H3289
19:12 the LORD of hosts hath **p** upon Egypt. H3289
23: 9 The LORD of hosts hath **p** it, to stain H3289
46:11 it to pass; I have **p** *it*, I will also do it. H3335
Jer 4:28 have spoken *it*, I have **p** *it*, and will not H2161
49:20 that he hath **p** against the inhabitants H2803
50:45 that he hath **p** against the land of H2803
Lam 2: 8 The LORD hath **p** to destroy the wall of H2803

Dan 1: 8 But Daniel p in his heart that he would H7760
Act 19:21 After these things were ended, Paul p G5087
20: 3 he p to return through Macedonia. G1096
Ro 1:13 that oftentimes I p to come unto you, G4388
Eph 1: 9 pleasure which he hath p in himself: G4388
3:11 which he p in Christ Jesus our Lord: G4160

PURPOSES
Job 17:11 My days are past, my p are broken off, H2154
Prv 15:22 Without counsel p are disappointed: H4284
Isa 19:10 And they shall be broken in the p H8356
Jer 49:20 Edom; and his p, that he hath purposed H4284
50:45 against Babylon; and his p, that he hath H4284

PURPOSETH
2Co 9: 7 Every man according as he p in his G4255

PURPOSING
Gen 27:42 thee, doth comfort himself, *p* to kill thee.

PURSE
Prv 1:14 thy lot among us; let us all have one p: H3599
Mk 6: 8 no scrip, no bread, no money in *their* p: G2223
Lk 10: 4 Carry neither p, nor scrip, nor shoes: and G905
22:35 I sent you without p, and scrip, and G905
36 now, he that hath a p, let him take *it*, and G905

PURSES
Mt 10: 9 gold, nor silver, nor brass in your p, G2223

PURSUE
Gen 35: 5 they did not p after the sons of Jacob. H7291
Ex 15: 9 The enemy said, I will p, I will overtake, H7291
Dt 19: 6 Lest the avenger of the blood p the H7291
28:22 and they shall p thee until thou perish. H7291
45 thee, and shall p thee, and overtake H7291
Jos 2: 5 went I wot not: p after them quickly; H7291
8:16 called together to p after them: and H7291
10:19 And *stay ye* not, *but* p after your H7291
20: 5 And if the avenger of blood p after him, H7291
1Sa 24:14 thou p? after a dead dog, after a flea. H7291
25:29 Yet a man is risen to p thee, and to H7291
26:18 doth my lord thus p after his servant? H7291
30: 8 saying, Shall I p after this troop? shall H7291
8 And he answered him, P: for thou shalt H7291
2Sa 17: 1 I will arise and p after David this night: H7291
20: 6 servants, and p after him, lest he get H7291
7 to p after Sheba the son of Bichri. H7291
13 Joab, to p after Sheba the son of Bichri. H7291
24:13 while they p thee? or that there be H7291
Job 13:25 fro? and wilt thou p the dry stubble? H7291
30:15 Terrors are turned upon me: they p my H7291
Ps 34:14 evil, and do good; seek peace, and p it. H7291
Isa 30:16 therefore shall they that p you be swift. H7291
Jer 48: 2 O Madmen; the sword shall p thee. H3212
Ezk 35: 6 and blood shall p thee: sith thou hast H7291
6 hated blood, even blood shall p thee. H7291
Hos 8: 3 *that is* good: the enemy shall p him. H7291
Am 1:11 because he did p his brother with the H7291
Nah 1: 8 and darkness shall p his enemies. H7291

PURSUED
Gen 14:14 and eighteen, and p *them* unto Dan. H7291
15 smote them, and p them unto Hobah, H7291
31:23 with him, and p after him seven days' H7291
36 sin, that thou hast so hotly p after me? H1814
Ex 14: 8 of Egypt, and he p after the children of H7291
9 But the Egyptians p after them, all the H7291
23 And the Egyptians p, and went in after H7291
Dt 11: 4 them as they p after you, and *how* H7291
Jos 2: 7 And the men p after them the way to H7291
7 as they which p after them were gone H7291
8:16 them: and they p after Joshua, and H7291
17 left the city open, and p after Israel. H7291
24: 6 and the Egyptians p after your fathers H7291
Jdg 1: 6 But Adoni-bezek fled; and they p after H7291
4:16 But Barak p after the chariots, and H7291
22 And, behold, as Barak p Sisera, Jael H7291
7:23 Manasseh, and p after the Midianites. H7291
25 of Zeeb, and p Midian, and brought H7291
8:12 Zalmunna fled, he p after them, and H7291
20:45 men; and p hard after them unto H1692
1Sa 7:11 of Mizpeh, and p the Philistines, and H7291
17:52 and shouted, and p the Philistines, H7291
23:25 Saul heard *that,* he p after David in the H7291
30:10 But David p, he and four hundred men: H7291
2Sa 2:19 And Asahel p after Abner; and in going H7291
24 Joab also and Abishai p after Abner: H7291
28 stood still, and p after Israel no more, H7291
2Sa 20:10 brother p after Sheba the son of Bichri. H7291
22:38 I have p mine enemies, and destroyed H7291
1Ki 20:20 fled; and Israel p them: and Ben-hadad H7291
2Ki 25: 5 And the army of the Chaldees p after H7291
2Ch 13:19 And Abijah p after Jeroboam, and took H7291
14:13 *were* with him p them unto Gerar: and H7291
Ps 18:37 I have p mine enemies, and overtaken H7291
Isa 41: 3 He p them, *and* passed safely; *even* by H7291
Jer 39: 5 But the Chaldeans' army p after them, H7291
52: 8 But the army of the Chaldeans p after H7291
Lam 4:19 of the heaven: they p us upon the H1814

PURSUER
Lam 1: 6 are gone without strength before the p. H7291

PURSUERS
Jos 2:16 the mountain, lest the p meet you; and H7291
16 three days, until the p be returned: and H7291
22 days, until the p were returned: and H7291
22 were returned: and the p sought *them* H7291
8:20 the wilderness turned back upon the p. H7291

PURSUETH
Lev 26:17 you; and ye shall flee when none p you. H7291
36 sword; and they shall fall when none p. H7291
37 sword, when none p: and ye shall have H7291
Prv 11:19 that p evil *pursueth it* to his own death. H7291
19 that pursueth evil *p it* to his own death.
13:21 Evil p sinners: but to the righteous H7291
19: 7 go far from him? he p *them with* words, H7291
28: 1 The wicked flee when no man p: but the H7291

PURSUING
Jdg 8: 4 that *were* with him, faint, yet p *them.* H7291
5 *be* faint, and I am p after Zebah and H7291
1Sa 23:28 Wherefore Saul returned from p after H7291
2Sa 3:22 Joab came from *p* a troop, and brought
18:16 returned from p after Israel: for Joab H7291
1Ki 18:27 he is talking, or he is p, or he is in a H7873
22:33 Israel, that they turned back from p him. H310
2Ch 18:32 they turned back again from p him. H310

PURTENANCE
Ex 12: 9 with his legs, and with the p thereof. H7130

PUSH
Ex 21:29 But if the ox were wont to p with his H5056
32 If the ox shall p a manservant or a H5055
36 ox hath used to p in time past, and his H5056
Dt 33:17 with them he shall p the people H5055
1Ki 22:11 these shalt thou p the Syrians, until H5055
2Ch 18:10 shalt p Syria until they be consumed. H5055
Job 30:12 the youth; they p away my feet, and H7971
Ps 44: 5 Through thee will we p down our H5055
Dan 11:40 king of the south p at him: and the king H5055

PUSHED
Ezk 34:21 shoulder, and p all the diseased with H5055

PUSHING
Dan 8: 4 I saw the ram p westward, and H5055

PUT
Gen 2: 8 he p the man whom he had formed. H7760
15 God took the man, and p him into the H3240
3:15 And I will p enmity between thee and H7896
22 and now, lest he p forth his hand, and H7971
8: 9 earth: then he p forth his hand, and H7971
19:10 But the men p forth their hand, and H7971
24: 2 P, I pray thee, thy hand under my thigh: H7760
9 And the servant p his hand under the H7760
47 unto him: and I p the earring upon her H7760
26:11 or his wife shall surely be p to death.
27:15 p them upon Jacob her younger son: H3847
16 And she p the skins of the kids of the H3847
28:11 stones of that place, and p *them for* his H7760
18 stone that he had p *for* his pillows, and H7760
20 me bread to eat, and raiment to p on, H3847
29: 3 the sheep, and p the stone again upon H7725
30:40 of Laban; and he p his own flocks by H7896
40 and p them not unto Laban's cattle. H7896
42 But when the cattle were feeble, he p H7760
31:34 the images, and p them in the camel's H7760
32:16 and p a space betwixt drove and drove. H7760
33: 2 And he p the handmaids and their H7760
35: 2 that *were* with him, P away the strange H5493
37:34 And Jacob rent his clothes, and p H7760
38:14 And she p her widow's garments off H5493
19 p on the garments of her widowhood. H3847
Gen 38:28 that *the one* p out *his* hand: and the H5414
39: 4 and all *that* he had he p into his hand. H5414
20 And Joseph's master took him, and p H5414
40: 3 And he p them in ward in the house of H5414
15 they should p me into the dungeon. H7760
41:10 his servants, and p me in ward in the H5414
42 his hand, and p it upon Joseph's hand, H5414
42 and p a gold chain about his neck; H7760
42:17 And he p them all together into ward H622
43:22 tell who p our money in our sacks. H7760
44: 1 can carry, and p every man's money H7760
2 And p my cup, the silver cup, in the H7760
46: 4 shall p his hand upon thine eyes. H7896
47:29 grace in thy sight, p, I pray thee, thy H7760
48:18 p thy right hand upon his head. H7760
50:26 him, and he was p in a coffin in Egypt. H3455
Ex 2: 3 with pitch, and p the child therein; and H7760
3: 5 And he said, Draw not nigh hither: p H5394
22 and ye shall p *them* upon your sons, H7760
4: 4 And the LORD said unto Moses, P H7971
4 it by the tail. And he p forth his hand, H7971
6 unto him, P now thine hand into H935
6 thy bosom. And he p his hand into his H935
7 And he said, P thine hand into thy H7725
7 again. And he p his hand into his H7725
15 And thou shalt speak unto him, and p H7760
21 which I have p in thine hand: but I H7760
5:21 to p a sword in their hand to slay us. H5414
8:23 And I will p a division between my H7760
11: 7 the LORD doth p a difference between
12:15 first day ye shall p away leaven out of H7673
15:26 all his statutes, I will p none of these H7760
16:33 Take a pot, and p an omer full of H5414
17:12 took a stone, and p *it* under him, and H7760
14 Joshua: for I will utterly p out the H4229
19:12 the mount shall be surely p to death:
21:12 so that he die, shall be surely p to death.
15 or his mother, shall be surely p to death.
16 in his hand, he shall surely be p to death.
17 or his mother, shall surely be p to death.
29 and his owner also shall be p to death.
22: 5 be eaten, and shall p in his beast, and H7971
8 p his hand unto his neighbour's goods. H7971
11 that he hath not p his hand unto his H7971
19 with a beast shall surely be p to death.
23: 1 Thou shalt not raise a false report: p H7896
24: 6 of the blood, and p *it* in basons; and H7760
25:12 of gold for it, and p *them* in the four H5414
14 And thou shalt p the staves into the H935
16 And thou shalt p into the ark the H5414
21 And thou shalt p the mercy seat above H5414
21 p the testimony that I shall give thee. H5414
26 rings of gold, and p the rings in the H5414
26:11 of brass, and p the taches into the loops, H935
34 And thou shalt p the mercy seat upon H5414
35 thou shalt p the table on the north side. H5414
27: 5 And thou shalt p it under the compass H5414
7 And the staves shall be p into the rings, H935
28:12 And thou shalt p the two stones upon H7760
23 of gold, and shalt p the two rings on H5414
24 And thou shalt p the two wreathen H5414
25 the two ouches, and p *them* on the H5414
26 and thou shalt p them upon the two H7760
27 make, and shalt p them on the two H5414
30 And thou shalt p in the breastplate of H5414
37 And thou shalt p it on a blue lace, that H7760
41 And thou shalt p them upon Aaron thy H3847
29: 3 And thou shalt p them into one basket, H5414
5 the garments, and p upon Aaron the H3847
6 And thou shalt p the mitre upon his H7760
6 and p the holy crown upon the mitre. H5414
8 And thou shalt bring his sons, and p H3847
9 and his sons, and p the bonnets on H2280
10 and his sons shall p their hands upon H5564
12 the bullock, and p *it* upon the horns of H5414
15 and his sons shall p their hands upon H5564
17 him, and his legs, and p *them* unto his H5414
19 and his sons shall p their hands upon H5564
20 of his blood, and p *it* upon the tip of the H5414
24 And thou shalt p all in the hands of H7760
30 in his stead shall p them on seven days, H3847
30: 6 And thou shalt p it before the vail that H5414
18 *withal:* and thou shalt p it between the H5414
18 altar, and thou shalt p water therein. H5414
36 of it very small, and p of it before the H5414
31: 6 hearted I have p wisdom, that they H5414
14 defileth it shall surely be p to death: for
15 day, he shall surely be p to death.
32:27 God of Israel, P every man his sword H7760

P

Ex 33: 4 no man did **p** on him his ornaments. H7896
5 therefore now **p** off thy ornaments H3381
22 by, that I will **p** thee in a clift of the H7760
34:33 with them, he **p** a vail on his face. H5414
35 shone: and Moses **p** the vail upon his H7725
35: 2 doeth work therein shall be **p** to death.
34 And he hath **p** in his heart that he may H5414
36: 1 in whom the LORD **p** wisdom and H5414
2 the LORD had **p** wisdom, *even* every H5414
37: 5 And he **p** the staves into the rings by the H935
13 rings of gold, and **p** the rings upon the H5414
38: 7 And he **p** the staves into the rings on the H935
39: 7 And he **p** them on the shoulders of the H7760
16 gold rings; and **p** the two rings in the H5414
17 And they **p** the two wreathen chains of H5414
18 the two ouches, and **p** them on the H5414
19 And they made two rings of gold, and **p** H7760
20 golden rings, and **p** them on the two H5414
25 *of* pure gold, and **p** the bells between H5414
40: 3 And thou shalt **p** therein the ark of the H7760
5 the testimony, and **p** the hanging of the H7760
7 the altar, and shalt **p** water therein. H5414
13 And thou shalt **p** upon Aaron the holy H3847
18 thereof, and **p** in the bars thereof, H5414
19 tabernacle, and **p** the covering of the H7760
20 And he took and **p** the testimony into H5414
20 **p** the mercy seat above upon the ark: H5414
22 And he **p** the table in the tent of the H5414
24 And he **p** the candlestick in the tent of H7760
26 And he **p** the golden altar in the tent of H7760
29 And he **p** the altar of burnt offering *by* H7760
30 and **p** water there, to wash *withal*. H5414
Lev 1: 4 And he shall **p** his hand upon the head H5564
7 the priest shall **p** fire upon the altar, H5414
2: 1 upon it, and **p** frankincense thereon: H5414
15 And thou shalt **p** oil upon it, and lay H5414
4: 7 And the priest shall **p** *some* of the H5414
18 And he shall **p** *some* of the blood upon H5414
25 his finger, and **p** *it* upon the horns of H5414
30 his finger, and **p** *it* upon the horns of H5414
34 his finger, and **p** *it* upon the horns of H5414
5:11 sin offering; he shall **p** no oil upon it, H7760
11 it, neither shall he **p** *any* frankincense H5414
6:10 And the priest shall **p** on his linen H3847
10 breeches shall he **p** upon his flesh, and H3847
10 and he shall **p** them beside the altar. H7760
11 And he shall **p** off his garments, and H6584
11 off his garments, and **p** on other H3847
12 in it; it shall not be **p** out: and the priest H3847
8: 7 And he **p** upon him the coat, and H5414
7 with the robe, and **p** the ephod upon H5414
8 And he **p** the breastplate upon him: H7760
8 upon him: also he **p** in the breastplate H5414
9 And he **p** the mitre upon his head; also H7760
9 forefront, did he **p** the golden plate, the H7760
13 Aaron's sons, and **p** coats upon them, H3847
13 with girdles, and **p** bonnets upon them; H2280
15 the blood, and **p** *it* upon the horns of H5414
23 the blood of it, and **p** *it* upon the tip of H5414
24 sons, and Moses **p** of the blood upon H5414
26 one wafer, and **p** *them* on the fat, and H7760
27 And he **p** all upon Aaron's hands, and H5414
9: 9 in the blood, and **p** *it* upon the horns of H5414
20 And they **p** the fat upon the breasts, H7760
10: 1 his censer, and **p** fire therein, and put H5414
1 fire therein, and **p** incense thereon, and H7760
10 And that ye may **p** difference between
11:32 is done, it must be **p** into water, and it H935
38 But if *any* water be **p** upon the seed, H5414
13:45 bare, and he shall **p** a covering upon his
14:14 the priest shall **p** *it* upon the tip of the H5414
17 shall the priest **p** upon the tip of the H5414
25 offering, and **p** *it* upon the tip of the H5414
28 And the priest shall **p** of the oil that *is* H5414
29 hand he shall **p** upon the head of him H5414
34 a possession, and I **p** the plague of H5414
42 And they shall take other stones, and **p** H935
15:19 blood, she shall be **p** apart seven days: H5079
16: 4 He shall **p** on the holy linen coat, and H3847
4 his flesh in water, and *so* **p** them on. H3847
13 And he shall **p** the incense upon the fire H5414
18 of the goat, and **p** *it* upon the horns of H5414
23 and shall **p** off the linen garments, H6584
23 which he **p** on when he went into H3847
24 holy place, and **p** on his garments, and H3847
32 and shall **p** on the linen clothes, H3847
18:19 as she is **p** apart for her uncleanness. H5079
19:14 Thou shalt not curse the deaf, nor **p** a H5414
20 be **p** to death, because she was not free.

Lev 20: 2 he shall surely be **p** to death: the people
9 shall be surely **p** to death: he hath cursed
10 the adulteress shall surely be **p** to death.
11 shall surely be **p** to death; their blood
12 shall surely be **p** to death: they have
13 they shall surely be **p** to death; their
15 be **p** to death: and ye shall slay the beast.
16 they shall surely be **p** to death; their
25 Ye shall therefore **p** difference between
27 shall surely be **p** to death: they shall
21: 7 they take a woman **p** away from her H1644
10 is consecrated to **p** on the garments, H3847
22:14 then he shall **p** the fifth *part* thereof H3254
24: 7 And thou shalt **p** pure frankincense H5414
12 And they **p** him in ward, that the mind H3240
16 he shall surely be **p** to death, *and* all the
16 name *of the LORD*, shall be **p** to death.
17 any man shall surely be **p** to death.
21 that killeth a man, he shall be **p** to death.
26: 8 of you shall **p** ten thousand to flight:
27:29 redeemed; *but* shall surely be **p** to death.
Nu 1:51 that cometh nigh shall be **p** to death.
3:10 that cometh nigh shall be **p** to death.
38 that cometh nigh shall be **p** to death.
4: 6 And shall **p** thereon the covering of H5414
6 blue, and shall **p** in the staves thereof. H7760
7 cloth of blue, and **p** thereon the dishes, H5414
8 skins, and shall **p** in the staves thereof. H7760
10 And they shall **p** it and all the vessels H5414
10 skins, and shall **p** *it* upon a bar. H5414
11 skins, and shall **p** to the staves thereof: H7760
12 the sanctuary, and **p** *them* in a cloth of H5414
12 skins, and shall **p** *them* on a bar: H5414
14 And they shall **p** upon it all the vessels H5414
14 badgers' skins, and **p** to the staves of it. H7760
5: 2 of Israel, that they **p** out of the camp H7971
3 Both male and female shall ye **p** out, H7971
3 the camp shall ye **p** them; that they H7971
4 And the children of Israel did so, and **p** H7971
15 pour no oil upon it, nor **p** frankincense H5414
17 shall take, and **p** *it* into the water: H5414
18 head, and **p** the offering of memorial H5414
6:18 separation, and **p** *it* in the fire which *is* H5414
19 wafer, and shall **p** *them* upon the H5414
27 And they shall **p** my name upon the H7760
8:10 shall **p** their hands upon the Levites: H5564
11:17 thee, and will **p** *it* upon them; and they H7760
29 LORD would **p** his spirit upon them! H5414
15:34 And they **p** him in ward, because it was H3240
35 man shall be surely **p** to death: all the
38 and that they **p** upon the fringe of the H5414
16: 7 And **p** fire therein, and put incense in H5414
7 And put fire therein, and **p** incense in H7760
14 wilt thou **p** out the eyes of these H5365
17 And take every man his censer, and **p** H5414
18 his censer, and **p** fire in them, and laid H5414
46 a censer, and **p** fire therein from off H5414
46 off the altar, and **p** on incense, and go H7760
47 the people: and he **p** on incense, and H5414
18: 7 that cometh nigh shall be **p** to death.
19:17 water shall be **p** thereto in a vessel: H5414
20:26 And strip Aaron of his garments, and **p** H3847
28 his garments, and **p** them upon Eleazar H3847
21: 9 of brass, and **p** it upon a pole, and H7760
23: 5 And the LORD **p** a word in Balaam's H7760
12 which the LORD hath **p** in my mouth? H7760
16 And the LORD met Balaam, and **p** a H7760
27:20 And thou shalt **p** *some* of thine honour H5414
35:16 the murderer shall surely be **p** to death.
17 the murderer shall surely be **p** to death.
18 the murderer shall surely be **p** to death.
21 *him* shall surely be **p** to death; *for* he *is* a
30 the murderer shall be **p** to death by the
31 death: but he shall be surely **p** to death.
36: 3 and shall be **p** to the inheritance of H3254
4 inheritance be **p** unto the inheritance H3254
Dt 2:25 This day will I begin to **p** the dread of H5414
7:15 all sickness, and will **p** none of the evil H7760
22 And the LORD thy God will **p** out those H5394
10: 2 and thou shalt **p** them in the ark. H7760
5 the mount, and **p** the tables in the ark H7760
11:29 it, that thou shalt **p** the blessing upon H5414
12: 5 all your tribes to **p** his name there, *even* H7760
7 in all that ye **p** your hand unto, ye H4916
21 hath chosen to **p** his name there be too H7760
13: 5 of dreams, shall be **p** to death; because
5 **p** the evil away from the midst of thee. H1197
9 be first upon him to **p** him to death, and
16: 9 beginnest *to* **p** the sickle to the corn.

Dt 17: 6 worthy of death be **p** to death; *but* at the
6 of one witness he shall not be **p** to death.
7 be first upon him to **p** him to death, and
7 shalt **p** the evil away from among you. H1197
12 thou shalt **p** away the evil from Israel. H1197
18:18 unto thee, and will **p** my words in his H5414
19:13 him, but thou shalt **p** away *the guilt of* H1197
19 thou **p** the evil away from among you. H1197
21: 9 So shalt thou **p** away the *guilt of* H1197
13 And she shall **p** the raiment of her H5493
21 he die: so shalt thou **p** evil away from H1197
22 **p** to death, and thou hang him on a tree:
22: 5 shall a man **p** on a woman's garment: H3847
19 he may not **p** her away all his days. H7971
21 thou **p** evil away from among you. H1197
22 so shalt thou **p** away evil from Israel. H1197
24 shalt **p** away evil from among you. H1197
29 he may not **p** her away all his days. H7971
23:24 but thou shalt not **p** *any* in thy vessel. H5414
24: 7 shalt **p** evil away from among you. H1197
16 The fathers shall not be **p** to death for
16 the children be **p** to death for the fathers:
16 man shall be **p** to death for his own sin.
25: 6 that his name be not **p** out of Israel. H4229
26: 2 thee, and shalt **p** *it* in a basket, and H7760
28:48 and he shall **p** a yoke of iron upon H5414
30: 7 And the LORD thy God will **p** all these H5414
31:19 children of Israel: **p** it in their mouths, H7760
26 Take this book of the law, and **p** it in H7760
32:30 a thousand, and two **p** ten thousand to
33:10 thy law: they shall **p** incense before H7760
14 precious things **p** forth by the moon, H1645
Jos 1:18 him, he shall be **p** to death: only be
6:24 and of iron, they **p** into the treasury of H5414
7: 6 of Israel, and **p** dust upon their heads. H5927
11 have **p** *it* even among their own stuff. H7760
10:24 him, Come near, **p** your feet upon the H7760
24 **p** their feet upon the necks of them. H7760
17:13 strong, that they **p** the Canaanites to H5414
24: 7 unto the LORD, he **p** darkness between H7760
14 and in truth: and **p** away the gods H5493
23 Now therefore **p** away, *said he*, the H5493
Jdg 1:28 strong, that they **p** the Canaanites to H7760
3:21 And Ehud **p** forth his left hand, and H7971
5:26 She **p** her hand to the nail, and her H7971
6:19 flour: the flesh he **p** in a basket, and he H7760
19 in a basket, and he **p** the broth in a pot, H7760
21 Then the angel of the LORD **p** forth the H7971
31 for him, let him be **p** to death whilst *it is*
37 Behold, I will **p** a fleece of wool in the H3322
7:16 and he **p** a trumpet in every man's H5414
8:27 thereof, and **p** it in his city, *even* in H3322
9:15 you, *then* come *and* **p** your trust in my
26 of Shechem **p** their confidence in him.
49 Abimelech, and **p** *them* to the hold, H7760
10:16 And they **p** away the strange gods from H5493
12: 3 *me* not, I **p** my life in my hands, H7760
14:12 them, I will now **p** forth a riddle unto H2330
13 **P** forth thy riddle, that we may hear it. H2330
16 me not: thou hast **p** forth a riddle unto H2330
15: 4 tail to tail, and **p** a firebrand in the H7760
15 of an ass, and **p** forth his hand, and H7971
16: 3 them, bar and all, and **p** *them* upon his H7760
21 But the Philistines took him, and **p** out H5365
18: 7 land, that might **p** *them* to shame in H3637
21 So they turned and departed, and **p** the H7760
20:13 that we may **p** them to death, and put
13 to death, and **p** away evil from Israel. H1197
20 the men of Israel **p** themselves in array
22 they **p** themselves in array the first day.
30 the third day, and **p** themselves in array
33 of their place, and **p** themselves in array
21: 5 saying, He shall surely be **p** to death.
Ru 3: 3 anoint thee, and **p** thy raiment upon H7760
1Sa 1:14 drunken? **p** away thy wine from thee. H5493
2:36 and shall say, **P** me, I pray thee, into H5596
4: 2 And the Philistines **p** themselves in
6: 8 upon the cart; and **p** the jewels of gold, H7760
15 of gold *were*, and **p** *them* on the great H7760
7: 3 your hearts, *then* **p** away the strange H5493
4 Then the children of Israel did **p** away H5493
8:16 your asses, and **p** *them* to his work. H6213
11:11 morrow, that Saul **p** the people in three H7760
12 the men, that we may **p** them to death.
13 shall not a man be **p** to death this day:
14:26 but no man **p** his hand to his mouth: H5381
27 wherefore he **p** forth the end of the H7971
27 an honeycomb, and **p** his hand to his H7725
17:21 For Israel and the Philistines had **p** the

1Sa 17:38 armour, and he **p** an helmet of brass H5414
39 *them.* And David **p** them off him. H5493
40 out of the brook, and **p** them in a H7760
49 And David **p** his hand in his bag, and H7971
54 but he **p** his armour in his tent. H7760
19: 5 For he did **p** his life in his hand, and H7760
13 *it* in the bed, and **p** a pillow of goats' H7760
21: 6 the LORD, to **p** hot bread in the day H7760
22:17 king would not **p** forth their hand to H7971
24:10 and I said, I will not **p** forth mine hand H7971
28: 3 city. And Saul had **p** away those that H5493
8 And Saul disguised himself, and **p** on H3847
21 voice, and I have **p** my life in my hand, H7760
31:10 And they **p** his armour in the house of H7760
2Sa 1:24 delights, who **p** on ornaments of gold H5927
3:34 nor thy feet **p** into fetters: as a man H5066
6: 6 Uzzah **p** forth *his hand* to the H7971
7:15 from Saul, whom I **p** away before thee. H5493
8: 2 measured he to **p** to death, and with one
6 Then David **p** garrisons in Syria of H7760
14 And he **p** garrisons in Edom; H7760
14 all Edom **p** he garrisons, and all H7760
10: 8 came out, and **p** the battle in array at
9 and **p** *them* in array against the Syrians:
10 that he might **p** *them* in array against
12:13 hath **p** away thy sin; thou shalt not die.
31 *were* therein, and **p** *them* under saws, H7760
13:17 him, and said, **P** now this *woman* out H7971
19 And Tamar **p** ashes on her head, and H3947
14: 2 be a mourner, and **p** on now mourning H3847
3 him. So Joab **p** the words in her mouth. H7760
19 he bade me, and he **p** all these words in H7760
15: 5 him obeisance, he **p** forth his hand, and
17:23 to his city, and **p** his household in order,
18:12 *yet* would I not **p** forth mine hand H7971
19:21 Shall not Shimei be **p** to death for this,
22 there any man be **p** to death this day in
20: 3 the house, and **p** them in ward, and fed H5414
8 that he had **p** on was girded unto him,
21: 9 together, and were **p** to death in the days
1Ki 2: 5 of war in peace, and **p** the blood of war H5414
8 I will not **p** thee to death with the sword.
24 Adonijah shall be **p** to death this day.
26 not at this time **p** thee to death, because
35 And the king **p** Benaiah the son of H5414
35 did the king **p** in the room of Abiathar. H5414
5: 3 **p** them under the soles of his feet. H5414
7:39 And he **p** five bases on the right side of H5414
51 and the vessels, did he **p** among the H5414
8: 9 which Moses **p** there at Horeb, when H3240
9: 3 thou hast built, to **p** my name there for H7760
10:17 and the king **p** them in the house of H5414
24 wisdom, which God had **p** in his heart. H5414
11:36 I have chosen me to **p** my name there. H7760
12: 4 yoke which he **p** upon us, lighter, and H5414
9 which thy father did **p** upon us lighter? H5414
29 in Beth-el, and the other **p** he in Dan. H5414
13: 4 in Beth-el, that he **p** forth his hand H7971
4 his hand, which he **p** forth against him, H7971
14:21 the tribes of Israel, to **p** his name there. H7760
18:23 *it* on wood, and **p** no fire *under:* and I H7760
23 lay *it* on wood, and **p** no fire *under:* H7760
25 name of your gods, but **p** no fire *under.* H7760
33 And he **p** the wood in order, and cut H6186
42 and **p** his face between his knees, H7760
20: 6 **p** *it* in their hand, and take *it* away. H7760
24 place, and **p** captains in their rooms: H7760
31 let us, I pray thee, **p** sackcloth on our H7760
32 on their loins, and **p** ropes on their
21:27 his clothes, and **p** sackcloth upon his H7760
22:10 his throne, having **p** on their robes, in a H3847
23 the LORD hath **p** a lying spirit in the H5414
27 And say, Thus saith the king, **P** this H7760
30 into the battle; but **p** thou on thy robes. H3847
2Ki 2:20 a new cruse, and **p** salt therein. And H7760
3: 2 his mother: for he **p** away the image of H5493
21 all that were able to **p** on armour, and H2296
4:34 the child, and **p** his mouth upon his H7760
6: 7 And he **p** out his hand, and took it. H7971
9:13 his garment, and **p** *it* under him on the H7760
10: 7 persons, and **p** their heads in baskets, H7760
11:12 king's son, and **p** the crown upon him, H5414
12: 9 that kept the door **p** therein all the H5414
10 came up, and they **p** up in bags, and H6695
13:16 And he said to the king of Israel, **P** H7392
16 the bow. And he **p** his hand *upon it:* H7392
16 **p** his hands upon the king's hands. H7760
14: 6 shall not be **p** to death for the children, H4191
6 nor the children be **p** to death for the H4191
2Ki 14: 6 man shall be **p** to death for his own sin. H4191
12 And Judah was **p** to the worse before
16:14 and **p** it on the north side of the altar. H5414
17 it, and **p** it upon a pavement of stones. H5414
17:29 of their own, and **p** *them* in the houses H3240
18:11 unto Assyria, and **p** them in Halah and H5148
24 servants, and **p** thy trust on Egypt for
19:28 therefore I will **p** my hook in thy nose, H7760
21: 4 said, In Jerusalem will I **p** my name. H7760
7 of Israel, will I **p** my name for ever: H7760
23: 5 And he **p** down the idolatrous priests, H7673
24 did Josiah **p** away, that he might H1197
33 And Pharaoh-nechoh **p** him in bands at
33 reign in Jerusalem; and **p** the land to a H5414
25: 7 before his eyes, and **p** out the eyes of H5786
1Ch 1: 8 Cush, and Mizraim, **P**, and Canaan. H6316
5:20 them; because they **p** their trust in him.
10:10 And they **p** his armour in the house of H7760
11:19 men that have **p** their lives in jeopardy?
12:15 banks; and they **p** to flight all *them* of H7760
13: 9 of Chidon, Uzza **p** forth his hand to H7971
10 him, because he **p** his hand to the ark: H7971
18: 6 Then David **p** *garrisons* in H7760
13 And he **p** garrisons in Edom; and all H7760
19: 9 came out, and **p** the battle in array
10 and **p** *them* in array against the Syrians.
16 saw that they were **p** to the worse before
17 So when David had **p** the battle in array
19 saw that they were **p** to the worse before
21:27 the angel; and he **p** up his sword again H7725
27:24 was the number **p** in the account of the H5927
2Ch 1: 5 had made, he **p** before the tabernacle H7760
2:14 device which shall be **p** to him, with thy H5414
3:16 in the oracle, and **p** *them* on the heads H5414
16 and **p** *them* on the chains. H5414
4: 6 He made also ten lavers, and **p** five on H5414
5: 1 all the instruments, **p** he among the H5414
10 which Moses **p** *therein* at Horeb, when H5414
6:11 And in it have I **p** the ark, wherein *is* H7760
20 that thou wouldest **p** thy name there; to H7760
24 And if thy people Israel be **p** to the worse
9:16 And the king **p** them in the house of H5414
23 wisdom, that God had **p** in his heart. H5414
10: 4 he **p** upon us, and we will serve thee. H5414
9 the yoke that thy father did **p** upon us? H5414
11 For whereas my father **p** a heavy yoke H6006
11 upon you, I will **p** more to your yoke: H3254
11:11 And he fortified the strong holds, and **p** H5414
12 And in every several city *he* **p** shields
12:13 the tribes of Israel, to **p** his name there. H7760
15: 8 he took courage, and **p** away the H5674
13 of Israel should be **p** to death, whether
16:10 with the seer, and **p** him in a prison H5414
17:19 whom the king **p** in the fenced cities H5414
18:22 the LORD hath **p** a lying spirit in the H5414
26 And say, Thus saith the king, **P** this H7760
29 to the battle; but **p** thou on thy robes. H3847
22:11 were slain, and **p** him and his nurse in H5414
23: 7 house, he shall be **p** to death: but be ye
11 king's son, and **p** upon him the crown, H5414
25:22 And Judah was **p** to the worse before
29: 7 of the porch, and **p** out the lamps, and H3518
33: 7 of Israel, will I **p** my name for ever: H7760
14 great height, and **p** captains of war in H7760
34:10 And they **p** *it* in the hand of the H5414
35: 3 unto the LORD, **P** the holy ark in the H5414
24 that chariot, and **p** him in the second H7392
36: 3 And the king of Egypt **p** him down at H5493
7 and **p** them in his temple at Babylon. H5414
22 and **p** *it* also in writing, saying,
Ezr 1: 1 and **p** *it* also in writing, saying,
7 had **p** them in the house of his gods; H5414
2:62 they, as polluted, **p** from the priesthood.
6:12 people, that shall **p** to their hand to H7972
7:27 which hath **p** *such a thing* as this H5414
10: 3 with our God to **p** away all the wives, H3318
19 that they would **p** away their wives; H3318
Neh 2:12 what my God had **p** in my heart to do H5414
3: 5 but their nobles **p** not their necks to the H935
4:23 me, none of us **p** off our clothes, *saving* H6584
23 *that* every one **p** them off for washing. H7973
6:14 prophets, that would have **p** me in fear.
19 *And* Tobiah sent letters to **p** me in fear.
7: 5 And my God **p** into mine heart to H5414
64 they, as polluted, **p** from the priesthood.
Est 4: 1 his clothes, and **p** on sackcloth with H3847
11 *there is* one law of his to **p** *him* to death,
5: 1 day, that Esther **p** on *her* royal *apparel,* H3847
8: 3 him with tears to **p** away the mischief H5674
Est 9: 1 drew near to be **p** in execution, in the
Job 1:11 But **p** forth thine hand now, and touch H7971
12 only upon himself **p** not forth thine H7971
2: 5 But **p** forth thine hand now, and touch H7971
4:18 Behold, he **p** no trust in his servants;
11:14 If iniquity *be* in thine hand, **p** it far
13:14 my teeth, and **p** my life in mine hand? H7760
17: 3 Lay down now, **p** me in a surety with
18: 5 Yea, the light of the wicked shall be **p** H1846
6 and his candle shall be **p** out with him. H1846
19:13 He hath **p** my brethren far from me, H7368
21:17 How oft is the candle of the wicked **p** H1846
22:23 built up, thou shalt **p** away iniquity far
23: 6 No; but he would **p** *strength* in me. H7760
27:17 He may prepare *it,* but the just shall **p** H3847
29:14 I **p** on righteousness, and it clothed me: H3847
38:36 Who hath **p** wisdom in the inward H7896
41: 2 Canst thou **p** an hook into his nose? or H7760
Ps 2:12 *are* all they that **p** their trust in him.
4: 5 and **p** your trust in the LORD. H5414
7 Thou hast **p** gladness in my heart, H5414
5:11 But let all those that **p** their trust in thee
7: 1 O LORD my God, in thee do I **p** my trust:
8: 6 thou hast **p** all *things* under his feet: H7896
9: 5 **p** out their name for ever and ever. H4229
10 And they that know thy name will **p**
20 **P** them in fear, O LORD: *that* the H7896
11: 1 In the LORD **p** I my trust: how say ye to
16: 1 Preserve me, O God: for in thee do I **p**
17: 7 hand them which **p** their trust *in thee*
18:22 I did not **p** away his statutes from me. H5493
25:20 not be ashamed; for I **p** my trust in thee.
27: 9 Hide not thy face *far* from me; **p** not H5186
30:11 thou hast **p** off my sackcloth, and H6605
31: 1 In thee, O LORD, do I **p** my trust; let me
18 Let the lying lips be **p** to silence; which
35: 4 Let them be confounded and **p** to shame
36: 7 children of men **p** their trust under the
40: 3 And he hath **p** a new song in my H5414
14 and **p** to shame that wish me evil.
44: 7 and hast **p** them to shame that hated us.
9 But thou hast cast off, and **p** us to
53: 5 *against* thee: thou hast **p** *them* to shame,
55:20 He hath **p** forth his hands against such H7971
56: 4 in God I have **p** my trust; I will not fear
8 Thou tellest my wanderings: **p** thou my H7760
11 In God have I **p** my trust: I will not be
70: 2 and **p** to confusion, that desire my hurt.
71: 1 In thee, O LORD, do I **p** my trust: let me
1 my trust: let me never be **p** to confusion.
73:28 to God: I have **p** my trust in the Lord H7896
78:66 he **p** them to a perpetual reproach. H5414
83:17 yea, let them be **p** to shame, and perish:
88: 8 Thou hast **p** away mine acquaintance H7368
18 Lover and friend hast thou **p** far from H7368
118: 8 *It is* better to trust in the LORD than to **p**
9 *It is* better to trust in the LORD than to **p**
119:31 O LORD, **p** me not to shame.
125: 3 **p** forth their hands unto iniquity. H7971
146: 3 **P** not your trust in princes, *nor* in the
Prv 4:24 **P** away from thee a froward mouth, H5493
24 and perverse lips **p** far from thee. H7368
8: 1 and understanding **p** forth her voice? H5414
13: 9 the lamp of the wicked shall be **p** out. H1846
20:20 shall be **p** out in obscure darkness. H1846
23: 2 And **p** a knife to thy throat, if thou *be* a H7760
24:20 the candle of the wicked shall be **p** out. H1846
25: 6 **P** not forth thyself in the presence of H1921
7 that thou shouldest be **p** lower in the
8 thy neighbour hath **p** thee to shame.
10 Lest he that heareth *it* **p** thee to shame,
30: 5 unto them that **p** their trust in him.
Ecc 3:14 nothing can be **p** to it, nor any thing H3254
10:10 then must he **p** to more strength: but H1396
11:10 thy heart, and **p** away evil from thy H5674
Song 5: 3 I have **p** off my coat; how shall I put it H6584
3 I have put off my coat; how shall I **p** it H3847
4 My beloved **p** in his hand by the hole *of* H7971
Isa 1:16 Wash you, make you clean; **p** away the H5493
5:20 good evil; that **p** darkness for light, and H7760
20 **p** bitter for sweet, and sweet for bitter! H7760
10:13 and I have **p** down the inhabitants H3381
11: 8 shall **p** his hand on the cockatrice' den. H1911
20: 2 off thy loins, and **p** off thy shoe from H2502
36: 9 servants, and **p** thy trust on Egypt for
37:29 therefore will I **p** my hook in thy nose, H7760
42: 1 soul delighteth; I have **p** my spirit upon H5414
43:26 **P** me in remembrance: let us plead
47:11 not be able to **p** it off: and desolation H3722

P

Isa 50: 1 whom I have **p** away? or which of my H7971
1 transgressions is your mother **p** away. H7971
51: 9 Awake, awake, **p** on strength, O arm of H3847
16 And I have **p** my words in thy mouth, H7760
23 But I will **p** it into the hand of them H7760
52: 1 Awake, awake; **p** on thy strength, O H3847
1 thy strength, O Zion; **p** on thy beautiful H3847
53:10 him; he hath **p** *him* to grief: when thou
54: 4 thou shalt not be **p** to shame: for thou
59:17 For he **p** on righteousness as a H3847
17 his head; and he **p** on the garments of H3847
21 which I have **p** in thy mouth, shall H7760
63:11 *is* he that **p** his holy Spirit within him? H7760
Jer 1: 9 Then the LORD **p** forth his hand, and H7971
9 I have **p** my words in thy mouth. H5414
3: 1 They say, If a man **p** away his wife, and H7971
8 adultery I had **p** her away, and given H7971
19 But I said, How shall I **p** thee among H7896
4: 1 me: and if thou wilt **p** away thine H5493
7:21 hosts, the God of Israel; **P** your burnt H5595
8:14 our God hath **p** us to silence, and given
12:13 thorns: they have **p** themselves to pain,
13: 1 a linen girdle, and **p** it upon thy loins, H7760
1 it upon thy loins, and **p** it not in water. H935
2 of the LORD, and **p** *it* on my loins. H7760
18:21 let their men be **p** to death; *let* their H2026
20: 2 the prophet, and **p** him in the stocks H5414
26:15 But know ye for certain, that if ye **p** me
19 and all Judah **p** him at all to death? did
21 the king sought to **p** him to death: but
24 the hand of the people to **p** him to death.
27: 2 and yokes, and **p** them upon thy neck, H5414
8 and that will not **p** their neck under the H5414
28:14 of Israel; I have **p** a yoke of iron upon H5414
29:26 **p** him in prison, and in the stocks. H5414
31:33 saith the LORD, I will **p** my law in their H5414
32:14 is open; and **p** them in an earthen H5414
40 them good; but I will **p** my fear in their H5414
37: 4 for they had not **p** him into prison. H5414
15 smote him, and **p** him in prison in the H5414
18 people, that ye have **p** me in prison? H5414
38: 4 let this man be **p** to death: for thus he
7 heard that they had **p** Jeremiah in the H5414
12 unto Jeremiah, **P** now *these* old cast H7760
15 thou not surely **p** me to death? and if I
16 us this soul, I will not **p** thee to death,
25 us, and we will not **p** thee to death; also
39: 7 Moreover he **p** out Zedekiah's eyes, H5786
18 hast **p** thy trust in me, saith the LORD.
40:10 and oil, and **p** *them* in your vessels, H7760
43: 3 that they might **p** us to death, and carry
46: 4 the spears, *and* **p** on the brigandines. H3847
47: 6 ere thou be quiet? **p** up thyself into thy H622
50:14 **P** yourselves in array against Babylon
42 horses, *every one* **p** in array, like a man
52:11 Then he **p** out the eyes of Zedekiah; H5786
11 **p** him in prison till the day of his death. H5414
27 smote them, and **p** them to death in
Ezk 3:25 behold, they shall **p** bands upon thee, H5414
4: 9 and fitches, and **p** them in one vessel, H5414
8: 3 And he **p** forth the form of an hand, H7971
17 and, lo, they **p** the branch to their nose. H7971
10: 7 took *thereof*, and **p** *it* into the hands of H5414
11:19 heart, and I will **p** a new spirit within H5414
14: 3 idols in their heart, and **p** the H5414
16:11 ornaments, and I **p** bracelets upon thy H5414
12 And I **p** a jewel on thy forehead, and H5414
14 I had **p** upon thee, saith the Lord GOD. H7760
17: 2 Son of man, **p** forth a riddle, and speak H2330
19: 9 And they **p** him in ward in chains, and H5414
22:26 holy things: they have **p** no difference
23:42 the wilderness, which **p** bracelets upon H5414
24:17 upon thee, and **p** on thy shoes upon thy H7760
26:16 their robes, and **p** off their broidered H6584
29: 4 But I will **p** hooks in thy jaws, and I will H5414
30:13 and I will **p** a fear in the land of Egypt. H5414
21 up to be healed, to **p** a roller to bind it, H7760
24 king of Babylon, and **p** my sword in his H5414
25 when I shall **p** my sword into the hand H5414
32: 7 And when I shall **p** thee out, I will cover H3518
25 is **p** in the midst of *them that be* slain. H5414
36:26 a new spirit will I **p** within you: and I H5414
27 And I will **p** my spirit within you, and H5414
37: 6 you with skin, and **p** breath in you, and H5414
14 And shall **p** my spirit in you, and ye H5414
19 fellows, and will **p** them with him, *even* H5414
38: 4 And I will turn thee back, and **p** hooks H5414
42:14 they *are* holy; and shall **p** on other H3847
43: 9 Now let them **p** away their whoredom, H7368

Ezk 43:20 the blood thereof, and **p** *it* on the four H5414
44:19 people, they shall **p** off their garments H6584
19 and they shall **p** on other garments; H3847
22 nor her that is **p** away: but they shall H1644
45:19 sin offering, and **p** *it* upon the posts of H5414
Dan 5:19 set up; and whom he would he **p** down. H1934
29 with scarlet, and *p* a chain of gold about
Hos 2: 2 husband: let her therefore **p** away her H5493
Joel 3:13 **P** ye in the sickle, for the harvest is H7971
Am 6: 3 Ye that **p** far away the evil day, and
Jna 3: 5 a fast, and **p** on sackcloth, from H3847
Mic 2:12 of Israel; I will **p** them together as the H7760
7: 5 Trust ye not in a friend, **p** ye not
Nah 3: 9 infinite; **P** and Lubim were thy helpers. H6316
Zep 3:19 land where they have been **p** to shame.
Hag 1: 6 wages *to* **p** *it* into a bag with holes.
Mt 1:19 was minded to **p** her away privily. G630
5:15 Neither do men light a candle, and **p** it G5087
31 It hath been said, Whosoever shall **p** G630
32 whosoever shall **p** away his wife, saving G630
6:25 what ye shall **p** on. Is not the life more G1749
8: 3 And Jesus **p** forth *his* hand, and G1614
9:16 for that which is **p** in to fill it up taketh
17 Neither do men **p** new wine into old G906
17 perish: but they **p** new wine into new G906
25 But when the people were **p** forth, he G1544
10:21 and cause them to be **p** to death. G2289
12:18 is well pleased: I will **p** my spirit upon G5087
13:24 Another parable **p** he forth unto them, G3908
31 Another parable **p** he forth unto them, G3908
14: 3 bound him, and **p** *him* in prison for G5087
5 And when he would have **p** him to G615
19: 3 man to **p** away his wife for every cause? G630
6 joined together, let not man **p** asunder. G5562
7 of divorcement, and to **p** her away? G630
8 suffered you to **p** away your wives: but G630
9 And I say unto you, Whosoever shall **p** G630
9 which is **p** away doth commit adultery. G630
13 that he should **p** *his* hands on them, G2007
21: 7 ass, and the colt, and **p** on them their G2007
22:34 heard that he had **p** the Sadducees to G5392
25:27 Thou oughtest therefore to have **p** my G906
26:52 Then said Jesus unto him, **P** up again G654
59 against Jesus, to **p** him to death; G2289
27: 1 against Jesus to **p** him to death: G2289
6 It is not lawful for to **p** them into the G906
28 And they stripped him, and **p** on him a G4060
29 of thorns, they **p** *it* upon his head, and G2007
31 off from him, and **p** his own raiment G1746
48 **p** *it* on a reed, and gave him to drink. G4060
Mk 1:14 Now after that John was **p** in prison, G3860
41 And Jesus, moved with compassion, **p** G1614
2:22 but new wine must be **p** into new bottles. G992
4:21 brought to be **p** under a bushel, or G5087
5:40 But when he had **p** them all out, he G1544
6: 9 But *be* shod with sandals; and not **p** on G1746
7:32 beseech him to **p** his hand upon him. G2007
33 the multitude, and **p** his fingers into his G906
8:23 on his eyes, and **p** his hands upon him, G2007
25 After that he **p** *his* hands again upon G2007
10: 2 a man to **p** away *his* wife? tempting him. G630
4 a bill of divorcement, and to **p** *her* away. G630
9 joined together, let not man **p** asunder. G5562
11 Whosoever shall **p** away his wife, and G630
12 And if a woman shall **p** away her G630
16 And he took them up in his arms, **p** *his* G5087
13:12 and shall cause them to be **p** to death. G2289
14: 1 take him by craft, and **p** *him* to death. G615
55 to **p** him to death; and found none. G2289
15:17 of thorns, and **p** it about his *head*, G4060
20 from him, and **p** his own clothes on G1746
36 of vinegar, and **p** *it* on a reed, and gave G4060
Lk 1:52 He hath **p** down the mighty from *their* G2507
5:13 And he **p** forth *his* hand, and touched G1614
38 But new wine must be **p** into new G992
8:54 And he **p** them all out, and took her by G1544
9:62 him, No man, having **p** his hand to the G1911
12:22 for the body, what ye shall **p** on. G1746
14: 7 And he **p** forth a parable to those G3004
15:22 the best robe, and **p** *it* on him; and put G1746
22 put *it* on him; and **p** a ring on his hand, G1325
16: 4 do, that, when I am **p** out of the G3179
18 her that is **p** away from *her* husband G630
18:33 And they shall scourge *him*, and **p** him G615
21:16 of you shall they cause to be **p** to death. G2289
23:32 led with him to be **p** to death. G337
Jn 5: 7 is troubled, to **p** me into the pool: but G906
9:15 unto them, He **p** clay upon mine eyes, G2007
22 he should be **p** out of the synagogue.

Jn 11:53 counsel together for to **p** him to death. G615
12: 6 the bag, and bare what was **p** therein. G906
10 that they might **p** Lazarus also to death; G615
42 they should be **p** out of the synagogue: G1096
13: 2 the devil having now **p** into the heart of G906
16: 2 They shall **p** you out of the synagogues: G4160
18:11 Then said Jesus unto Peter, **P** up thy G906
31 not lawful for us to **p** any man to death: G615
19: 2 of thorns, and **p** *it* on his head, and G2007
2 head, and they **p** on him a purple robe, G4016
19 And Pilate wrote a title, and **p** *it* on the G5087
29 with vinegar, and **p** *it* upon hyssop, G4060
29 *it* upon hyssop, and **p** *it* to his mouth. G4374
20:25 of the nails, and **p** my finger into the G906
Act 1: 7 the Father hath **p** in his own power. G5087
4: 3 And they laid hands on them, and **p** G5087
5:18 and **p** them in the common prison. G5087
25 the men whom ye **p** in prison are G5087
34 to **p** the apostles forth a little space; G4160
7:33 Then said the Lord to him, **P** off thy G3089
9:40 But Peter **p** them all forth, and kneeled G1544
12: 4 him, he **p** *him* in prison, and G5087
19 that *they* should be **p** to death. And he G520
13:46 to you: but seeing ye **p** it from you, and G683
15: 9 And **p** no difference between us and G1252
10 Now therefore why tempt ye God, to **p** G2007
26:10 when they were **p** to death, I gave my G337
27: 6 sailing into Italy; and he **p** us therein. G1688
Ro 13:12 and let us **p** on the armour of light. G1746
14 But **p** ye on the Lord Jesus Christ, and G1746
14:13 that no man **p** a stumblingblock or G5087
1Co 5:13 judgeth. Therefore **p** away from among G1808
7:11 and let not the husband **p** away *his* wife. G863
12 dwell with him, let him not **p** her away. G863
13:11 a man, I **p** away childish things. G2673
15:24 he shall have **p** down all rule and all G2673
25 For he must reign, till he hath **p** all G5087
27 For he hath **p** all things under his feet. G5293
27 he saith all things are **p** under *him, it is* G5293
27 which did **p** all things under him. G5293
28 unto him that **p** all things under him, G5293
53 For this corruptible must **p** on G1746
53 and this mortal *must* **p** on immortality. G1746
54 So when this corruptible shall have **p** G1746
54 mortal shall have **p** on immortality, G1746
2Co 3:13 And not as Moses, *which* **p** a veil over G5087
8:16 But thanks *be* to God, which **p** the G1325
Gal 3:27 baptized into Christ have **p** on Christ. G1746
Eph 1:22 And hath **p** all *things* under his feet, G5293
4:22 That ye **p** off concerning the former G659
24 And that ye **p** on the new man, which G1746
31 be **p** away from you, with all malice: G142
6:11 **P** on the whole armour of God, that ye G1746
Col 3: 8 But now ye also **p** off all these; anger, G659
9 ye have **p** off the old man with his deeds; G554
10 And have **p** on the new *man*, which is G1746
12 **P** on therefore, as the elect of God, holy G1746
14 And above all these things *p on* charity,
1Th 2: 4 But as we were allowed of God to be **p** G4160
1Ti 1:19 some having **p** away concerning faith G683
4: 6 If thou **p** the brethren in remembrance G5294
2Ti 1: 6 Wherefore I **p** thee in remembrance that G363
2:14 Of these things **p** *them* in G5279
Tit 3: 1 **P** them in mind to be subject to G5279
Phlm 18 *thee* ought, **p** that on mine account; G1677
Heb 2: 5 For unto the angels hath he not **p** in G5293
8 Thou hast **p** all things in subjection G5293
8 feet. For in that he **p** all in subjection G5293
8 left nothing *that is* not **p** under him. But G506
8 we see not yet all things **p** under him. G5293
13 And again, I will **p** my trust in him. G3982
6: 6 afresh, and **p** *him* to an open shame. G3856
8:10 the Lord; I will **p** my laws into their G1325
9:26 to **p** away sin by the sacrifice of himself. G115
10:16 the Lord, I will **p** my laws into their G1325
Jas 3: 3 Behold, we **p** bits in the horses' mouths, G906
1Pt 2:15 with well doing ye may **p** to silence the G5392
3:18 us to God, being **p** to death in the flesh, G2289
2Pt 1:12 Wherefore I will not be negligent to **p** G5279
14 Knowing that shortly I must **p** off *this* G595
Jude 5 I will therefore **p** you in remembrance, G5279
Rev 2:24 I will **p** upon you none other burden. G906
11: 9 their dead bodies to be **p** in graves. G5087
17:17 For God hath **p** in their hearts to fulfil G1325

PUTEOLI

Act 28:13 blew, and we came the next day to **P**: G4223

PUTIEL
Ex 6:25 the daughters of P to wife; and she bare H6317

PUTRIFYING
Isa 1: 6 and bruises, and p sores: they have not H2961

PUTTEST
Nu 24:21 and thou p thy nest in a rock. H7760
Dt 12:18 in all that thou p thine hands unto. H4916
15:10 and in all that thou p thine hand unto. H4916
2Ki 18:14 that which thou p on me will I bear. H5414
Job 13:27 Thou p my feet also in the stocks, and H7760
Ps119:119 Thou p away all the wicked of the earth H7673
Hab 2:15 drink, that p thy bottle to *him*, and H5596

PUTTETH
Ex 30:33 like it, or whosoever p *any* of it upon a H5414
Nu 22:38 God p in my mouth, that shall I speak. H7760
Dt 25:11 smiteth him, and p forth her hand, and H7971
27:15 craftsman, and p *it* in a secret *place*. H7760
1Ki 20:11 boast himself as he that p it off. H6605
Job 15:15 Behold, he p no trust in his saints; yea,
Job 28: 9 He p forth his hand upon the rock; he H7971
33:11 He p my feet in the stocks, he marketh H7760
Ps 15: 5 *He that* p not out his money to usury, H5414
75: 7 But God *is* the judge: he p down one, H8213
Prv 28:25 strife: but he that p his trust in the LORD
29:25 p his trust in the LORD shall be safe.
Song 2:13 The fig tree p forth her green figs, and H2590
Isa 57:13 *them*: but he that p his trust in me shall
Jer 43:12 as a shepherd p on his garment; and H5844
Lam 3:29 He p his mouth in the dust; if so be H5414
Ezk 14: 4 in his heart, and p the stumblingblock H7760
7 in his heart, and p the stumblingblock H7760
Mic 3: 5 cry, Peace; and he that p not into their H5414
Mt 9:16 No man p a piece of new cloth unto an G1911
24:32 is yet tender, and p forth leaves, ye G1631
Mk 2:22 And no man p new wine into old bottles: G906
4:29 immediately he p in the sickle, because G649
13:28 is yet tender, and p forth leaves, ye G1631
Lk 5:36 unto them; No man p a piece of a new G1911
37 And no man p new wine into old bottles; G906
8:16 it with a vessel, or p *it* under a bed; but G5087
11:33 lighted a candle, p *it* in a secret place, G5087
16:18 Whosoever p away his wife, and G630
Jn 10: 4 And when he p forth his own sheep, he G1544

PUTTING
Gen 21:14 *it* unto Hagar, p *it* on her shoulder, and H7760
Lev 16:21 in all their sins, p them upon the head H5414
Jdg 7: 6 And the number of them that lapped, p
Isa 58: 9 thee the yoke, the p forth of the finger, H7971
Mal 2:16 that he hateth p away: for *one* covereth H7971
Act 9:12 coming in, and p *his* hand on him, that G2007
17 into the house; and p his hands on him G2007
19:33 the Jews p him forward. And G4261
Ro 15:15 in some sort, as p you in mind, because G1878
Eph 4:25 Wherefore p away lying, speak every G659
Col 2:11 without hands, in p off the body of the G555
1Th 5: 8 the day, be sober, p on the breastplate G1746
1Ti 1:12 me faithful, p me into the ministry; G5087
2Ti 1: 6 is in thee by the p on of my hands. G1936
1Pt 3: 3 wearing of gold, or of p on of apparel; G1745
21 save us (not the p away of the filth of the G595
2Pt 1:13 stir you up by p *you* in remembrance; G5279

PYGARG
Dt 14: 5 the p, and the wild ox, and the chamois. H1788

Q

QUAILS
Ex 16:13 And it came to pass, that at even the q H7958
Nu 11:31 and brought q from the sea, and let H7958
32 they gathered the q: he that gathered H7958
Ps 105:40 *The people* asked, and he brought q, H7958

QUAKE
Joel 2:10 The earth shall q before them; the H7264
Nah 1: 5 The mountains q at him, and the hills H7493
Mt 27:51 and the earth did q, and the rocks rent; G4579
Heb 12:21 Moses said, I exceedingly fear and q:) G1790

QUAKED
Ex 19:18 and the whole mount q greatly. H2729
1Sa 14:15 q: so it was a very great trembling. H7264

QUAKING
Ezk 12:18 Son of man, eat thy bread with q, and H7494
Dan 10: 7 vision; but a great q fell upon them, so H2731

QUANTITY
Isa 22:24 all vessels of small q, from the vessels of

QUARREL
Lev 26:25 shall avenge the q of *my* covenant: and H5359
2Ki 5: 7 and see how he seeketh a q against me. H579
Mk 6:19 Therefore Herodias had a q against G1758
Col 3:13 if any man have a q against any: even G3437

QUARRIES
Jdg 3:19 But he himself turned again from the q H6456
26 beyond the q, and escaped unto Seirath. H6456

QUARTER
Gen 19: 4 and young, all the people from every q: H7097
Nu 34: 3 Then your south q shall be from the H6285
Jos 15: 5 in the north q *was* from the bay of H6285
18:14 children of Judah: this *was* the west q. H6285
15 And the south q *was* from the end of H6285
Isa 47:15 every one to his q; none shall save thee. H5676
56:11 way, every one for his gain, from his q. H7097
Mk 1:45 and they came to him from every q. G3836

QUARTERS
Ex 13: 7 be leaven seen with thee in all thy q. H1366
Dt 22:12 fringes upon the four q of thy vesture, H3671
1Ch 9:24 In four q were the porters, toward the H7307
Jer 49:36 from the four q of heaven, and will H7098
Ezk 38: 6 of the north q, and all his bands: *and* H3411
Act 9:32 throughout all *q*, he came down also to
16: 3 were in those q: for they knew all that G5117
28: 7 In the same q were possessions of the G4012
Rev 20: 8 are in the four q of the earth, Gog and G1137

QUARTUS
Ro 16:23 the city saluteth you, and Q a brother. G2890

QUATERNIONS
Act 12: 4 *him* to four q of soldiers to keep him; G5069

QUEEN
1Ki 10: 1 And when the q of Sheba heard of the H4436
4 And when the q of Sheba had seen all H4436
10 the q of Sheba gave to king Solomon. H4436
13 And king Solomon gave unto the q of H4436
11:19 own wife, the sister of Tahpenes the q. H1377
15:13 from *being* q, because she had made H1377
2Ki 10:13 of the king and the children of the q. H1377
2Ch 9: 1 And when the q of Sheba heard of the H4436
3 And when the q of Sheba had seen the H4436
9 as the q of Sheba gave king Solomon. H4436
12 And king Solomon gave to the q of H4436
15:16 her from *being* q, because she had H1377
Neh 2: 6 And the king said unto me, (the q also H7694
Est 1: 9 Also Vashti the q made a feast for the H4436
11 To bring Vashti the q before the king H4436
12 But the q Vashti refused to come at the H4436
15 What shall we do unto the q Vashti H4436
16 Vashti the q hath not done wrong H4436
17 For *this* deed of the q shall come H4436
17 Vashti the q to be brought in before H4436
18 of the deed of the q. Thus *shall there* H4436
2: 4 the king be q instead of Vashti. And H4427
17 and made her q instead of Vashti. H4427
22 *it* unto Esther the q; and Esther certified H4436
4: 4 *it* her. Then was the q exceedingly H4436
5: 2 saw Esther the q standing in the court, H4436
3 What wilt thou, q Esther? and what *is* H4436
12 Yea, Esther the q did let no man come H4436
7: 1 came to banquet with Esther the q. H4436
2 *is* thy petition, q Esther? and it shall H4436
3 Then Esther the q answered and said, H4436
5 unto Esther the q, Who is he, and where H4436
6 was afraid before the king and the q. H4436
7 life to Esther the q; for he saw that there H4436
8 Will he force the q also before me in H4436
8: 1 unto Esther the q. And Mordecai came H4436
7 unto Esther the q and to Mordecai the H4436
9:12 And the king said unto Esther the q, H4436
29 Then Esther the q, the daughter of H4436
31 and Esther the q had enjoined them, H4436
Ps 45: 9 hand did stand the q in gold of Ophir. H7694
Jer 7:18 make cakes to the q of heaven, and to H4446
13:18 Say unto the king and to the q, Humble H1377
29: 2 (After that Jeconiah the king, and the q, H1377
44:17 incense unto the q of heaven, and to H4446
18 incense to the q of heaven, and to pour H4446
19 And when we burned incense to the q H4446
25 incense to the q of heaven, and to pour H4446
Dan 5:10 *Now* the q, by reason of the words of the H4433
10 house: *and* the q spake and said, O H4433
Mt 12:42 The q of the south shall rise up in the G938
Lk 11:31 The q of the south shall rise up in the G938
Act 8:27 under Candace q of the Ethiopians, who G938
Rev 18: 7 in her heart, I sit a q, and am no widow, G938

QUEENS
Song 6: 8 There are threescore q, and fourscore H4436
9 her; *yea*, the q and the concubines, H4436
Isa 49:23 fathers, and their q thy nursing H8282

QUENCH
2Sa 14: 7 and so they shall q my coal which is H3518
21:17 that thou q not the light of Israel. H3518
Ps 104:11 of the field: the wild asses q their thirst. H7665
Song 8: 7 Many waters cannot q love, neither H3518
Isa 1:31 burn together, and none shall q *them*. H3518
42: 3 flax shall he not q: he shall bring forth H3518
Jer 4: 4 q *it*, because of the evil of your doings. H3518
21:12 q *it*, because of the evil of your doings. H3518
Am 5: 6 *it*, and *there be* none to q *it* in Beth-el. H3518
Mt 12:20 flax shall he not q, till he send forth G4570
Eph 6:16 to q all the fiery darts of the wicked. G4570
1Th 5:19 Q not the Spirit. G4570

QUENCHED
Nu 11: 2 prayed unto the LORD, the fire was q. H8257
2Ki 22:17 against this place, and shall not be q. H3518
2Ch 34:25 out upon this place, and shall not be q. H3518
Ps 118:12 about like bees; they are q as the fire of H1846
Isa 34:10 It shall not be q night nor day; the H3518
43:17 rise: they are extinct, they are q as tow. H3518
66:24 shall their fire be q; and they shall be an H3518
Jer 7:20 and it shall burn, and shall not be q. H3518
17:27 of Jerusalem, and it shall not be q. H3518
Ezk 20:47 flame shall not be q, and all faces from H3518
48 LORD have kindled it: it shall not be q. H3518
Mk 9:43 hell, into the fire that never shall be q: G762
44 worm dieth not, and the fire is not q. G4570
45 hell, into the fire that never shall be q: G762
46 worm dieth not, and the fire is not q. G4570
48 worm dieth not, and the fire is not q. G4570
Heb 11:34 Q the violence of fire, escaped the edge G4570

QUESTION
Mt 22:35 *him a q*, tempting him, and saying,
Mk 8:11 and began to q with him, seeking of G4802
9:16 And he asked the scribes, What q ye G4802
11:29 ask of you one q, and answer me, and G3056
12:34 no man after that durst ask him *any q*.
Lk 20:40 that they durst not ask him any *q at all*.
Jn 3:25 Then there arose a q between *some* of G2214
Act 15: 2 the apostles and elders about this q. G2213
18:15 But if it be a q of words and names, G2213
19:40 For we are in danger to be called in q G1458
23: 6 of the dead I am called in q. G2919
24:21 dead I am called in q by you this day. G2919
1Co 10:25 eat, asking no q for conscience sake: G350
27 eat, asking no q for conscience sake. G350

QUESTIONED
2Ch 31: 9 Then Hezekiah q with the priests and H1875
Mk 1:27 that they q among themselves, G4802
Lk 23: 9 Then he q with him in many words; G1905

QUESTIONING
Mk 9:10 with themselves, q one with another G4802
14 them, and the scribes q with them. G4802

QUESTIONS
1Ki 10: 1 she came to prove him with hard q. H2420
3 And Solomon told her all her q: there H1697
2Ch 9: 1 with hard q at Jerusalem, with a H2420
2 And Solomon told her all her q: and H1697
Mt 22:46 from that day forth ask him any more q.
Lk 2:46 both hearing them, and asking them q. G1905
Act 23:29 Whom I perceived to be accused of q of G2213
25:19 But had certain q against him of their G2213
20 of such manner of q, I asked *him* G2214
26: 3 in all customs and q which are among G2213
1Ti 1: 4 which minister q, rather than godly G2214
6: 4 but doting about q and strifes of G2214
2Ti 2:23 But foolish and unlearned q avoid, G2214
Tit 3: 9 But avoid foolish q, and genealogies, G2214

QUICK
Lev 13:10 and *there be* q raw flesh in the rising; H4241
24 burning, and the q *flesh* that burneth H4241
Nu 16:30 and they go down q into the pit; then H2416
Ps 55:15 *and* let them go down q into hell: for H2416
124: 3 Then they had swallowed us up q, when H2416
Isa 11: 3 And shall make him of q understanding
Act 10:42 of God *to be* the Judge of q and dead. G2198
2Ti 4: 1 shall judge the q and the dead at his G2198
Heb 4:12 For the word of God *is* q, and powerful, G2198
1Pt 4: 5 is ready to judge the q and the dead. G2198

QUICKEN
Ps 71:20 troubles, shalt q me again, and shalt H2421
80:18 So will not we go back from thee: q us, H2421
119:25 My soul cleaveth unto the dust: q thou H2421
37 vanity; *and* q thou me in thy way. H2421
40 precepts: q me in thy righteousness. H2421
88 Q me after thy lovingkindness; so shall H2421
107 I am afflicted very much: q me, O H2421
149 q me according to thy judgment. H2421
154 Plead my cause, and deliver me: q me H2421
156 q me according to thy judgments. H2421
159 Consider how I love thy precepts: q me, H2421
143:11 Q me, O LORD, for thy name's sake: for H2421
Ro 8:11 from the dead shall also q your mortal G2227

QUICKENED
Ps 119:50 my affliction: for thy word hath q me. H2421
93 precepts: for with them thou hast q me. H2421
1Co 15:36 thou sowest is not q, except it die: G2227
Eph 2: 1 And you *hath he q*, who were dead in
5 dead in sins, hath q us together with G4806
Col 2:13 your flesh, hath he q together with him, G4806
1Pt 3:18 to death in the flesh, but q by the Spirit: G2227

QUICKENETH
Jn 5:21 up the dead, and q *them*; even so the G2227
21 *them*; even so the Son q whom he will. G2227
6:63 It is the spirit that q; the flesh profiteth G2227
Ro 4:17 *even* God, who q the dead, and calleth G2227
1Ti 6:13 the sight of God, who q all things, and G2227

QUICKENING
1Co 15:45 the last Adam *was made* a q spirit. G2227

QUICKLY
Gen 18: 6 said, Make ready q three measures of H4116
27:20 hast found *it* so q, my son? And he said, H4116
Ex 32: 8 They have turned aside q out of the H4118
Nu 16:46 on incense, and go q unto the H4120
Dt 9: 3 q, as the LORD hath said unto thee. H4118
12 get thee down q from hence; for thy H4118
12 they are q turned aside out of H4118
16 ye had turned aside q out of the way H4118
11:17 and *lest* ye perish q from off the good H4120
28:20 and until thou perish q; because of the H4118
Jos 2: 5 after them q; for ye shall overtake them. H4118
8:19 And the ambush arose q out of their H4120
10: 6 come up to us q, and save us, and help H4120
23:16 ye shall perish q from off the good land H4120
Jdg 2:17 them: they turned q out of the way H4118
1Sa 20:19 shalt go down q, and come to the place H3966
2Sa 17:16 Now therefore send q, and tell David, H4120
18 of them away q, and came to a man's H4120
21 Arise, and pass q over the water: for H4120
2Ki 1:11 thus hath the king said, Come down q. H4120
2Ch 18: 8 said, Fetch q Micaiah the son of Imla. H4116
Ecc 4:12 and a threefold cord is not q broken. H4120
Mt 5:25 Agree with thine adversary q, whiles G5035
28: 7 And go q, and tell his disciples that he G5035
8 And they departed q from the G5035
Mk 16: 8 And they went out q, and fled from the G5035
Lk 14:21 servant, Go out q into the streets and G5030
16: 6 thy bill, and sit down q, and write fifty. G5030
Jn 11:29 As soon as she heard *that*, she arose q, G5035
13:27 Jesus unto him, That thou doest, do q. G5032
Act 12: 7 saying, Arise up q. And his chains fell G1722
22:18 and get thee q out of Jerusalem: for G1722
Rev 2: 5 come unto thee q, and will remove thy G5034
16 Repent; or else I will come unto thee q, G5035
3:11 Behold, I come q: hold that fast which G5035
11:14 *and*, behold, the third woe cometh q. G5035
22: 7 Behold, I come q: blessed *is* he that G5035
12 And, behold, I come q; and my reward G5035
20 q. Amen. Even so, come, Lord Jesus. G5035

QUICKSANDS
Act 27:17 the q, strake sail, and so were driven. G4950

QUIET
Jdg 16: 2 of the city, and were q all the night, H2790
18: 7 of the Zidonians, q and secure; and H8252
27 *that were* at q and secure: and they H8252
2Ki 11:20 and the city was in q: and they slew H8252
1Ch 4:40 *was* wide, and q, and peaceable; for H8252
2Ch 14: 1 In his days the land was q ten years. H8252
5 and the kingdom was q before him. H8252
20:30 So the realm of Jehoshaphat was q: for H8252
23:21 and the city was q, after that they had H8252
Job 3:13 have lain still and been q, I should have H8252
26 I rest, neither was I q; yet trouble came. H5117
21:23 strength, being wholly at ease and q. H7961
Ps 35:20 against *them that are* q in the land. H7282
107:30 Then are they glad because they be q; so H8367
Prv 1:33 safely, and shall be q from fear of evil. H7599
Ecc 9:17 The words of wise *men are* heard in q H5183
Isa 7: 4 And say unto him, Take heed, and be q; H8252
14: 7 The whole earth is at rest, *and* is q: they H8252
32:18 sure dwellings, and in q resting places; H7600
33:20 shall see Jerusalem a q habitation, a H7600
Jer 30:10 be q, and none shall make *him* afraid. H7599
47: 6 *it be* ere thou be q? put up thyself into H8252
7 How can it be q, seeing the LORD hath H8252
49:23 *is* sorrow on the sea; it cannot be q. H8252
51:59 reign. And *this* Seraiah *was* a q prince. H4496
Ezk 16:42 I will be q, and will be no more angry. H8252
Nah 1:12 Thus saith the LORD; Though *they be* q, H8003
Act 19:36 ought to be q, and to do nothing rashly. G2687
1Th 4:11 And that ye study to be q, and to do G2270
1Ti 2: 2 we may lead a q and peaceable life in G2263
1Pt 3: 4 of a meek and q spirit, which is in the G2272

QUIETED
Ps 131: 2 Surely I have behaved and q myself, as H1826
Zec 6: 8 have q my spirit in the north country. H5117

QUIETETH
Job 37:17 when he q the earth by the south *wind*? H8252

QUIETLY
2Sa 3:27 to speak with him q, and smote him H7987
Lam 3:26 q wait for the salvation of the LORD.

QUIETNESS
Jdg 8:28 in q forty years in the days of Gideon. H8252
1Ch 22: 9 peace and q unto Israel in his days. H8253
Job 20:20 Surely he shall not feel q in his belly, he H7961
34:29 When he giveth q, who then can make H8252
Prv 17: 1 Better *is* a dry morsel, and q therewith, H7962
Ecc 4: 6 Better *is* an handful *with* q, than both H5183
Isa 30:15 ye be saved; in q and in confidence H8252
32:17 q and assurance for ever. H8252
Act 24: 2 we enjoy great q, and that very worthy G1515
2Th 3:12 q they work, and eat their own bread. G2271

QUIT
Ex 21:19 that smote *him* be q: only he shall pay H5352
28 but the owner of the ox *shall be* q. H5355
Jos 2:20 then we will be q of thine oath which H5355
1Sa 4: 9 Be strong, and q yourselves like men, O H1961
9 you: q yourselves like men, and fight. H1961
1Co 16:13 Watch ye, stand fast in the faith, q you G407

QUITE
Gen 31:15 and hath q devoured also our money. H398
Ex 23:24 them, and q break down their images. H7665
Nu 17:10 rebels; and thou shalt q take away their H3615
33:52 and q pluck down all their high places:
2Sa 3:24 hast sent him away, and he is q gone? H1980
Job 6:13 me? and is wisdom driven q from me? H5080
Hab 3: 9 Thy bow was made q naked, *according* H6181

QUIVER
Gen 27: 3 thy weapons, thy q and thy bow, and H8522
Job 39:23 The q rattleth against him, the glittering H827
Ps 127: 5 Happy *is* the man that hath his q full of H827
Isa 22: 6 And Elam bare the q with chariots of H827
49: 2 a polished shaft; in his q hath he hid me; H827
Jer 5:16 Their q *is* as an open sepulchre, they *are* H827
Lam 3:13 He hath caused the arrows of his q to H827

QUIVERED
Hab 3:16 belly trembled; my lips q at the voice: H6750

R

RAAMAH
Gen 10: 7 and Sabtah, and R, and Sabtecha: and H7484
7 and the sons of R; Sheba, and Dedan. H7484
1Ch 1: 9 and Sabta, and R, and Sabtecha. And H7484
9 And the sons of R; Sheba, and Dedan. H7484
Ezk 27:22 The merchants of Sheba and R, they H7484

RAAMIAH
Neh 7: 7 Azariah, R, Nahamani, Mordecai, H7485

RAAMSES
Ex 1:11 Pharaoh treasure cities, Pithom and R. H7486

RABBAH
Jos 13:25 of Ammon, unto Aroer that *is* before R; H7237
15:60 and R; two cities with their villages: H7237
2Sa 11: 1 R. But David tarried still at Jerusalem. H7237
12:26 And Joab fought against R of the H7237
27 R, and have taken the city of waters. H7237
29 to R, and fought against it, and took it. H7237
17:27 son of Nahash of R of the children of H7237
1Ch 20: 1 and besieged R. But David tarried at H7237
1 And Joab smote R, and destroyed it. H7237
Jer 49: 2 war to be heard in R of the Ammonites; H7237
3 cry, ye daughters of R, gird you with H7237
Ezk 25: 5 And I will make R a stable for camels, H7237
Am 1:14 But I will kindle a fire in the wall of R, H7237

RABBATH
Dt 3:11 of iron; *is* it not in R of the children of H7237
Ezk 21:20 may come to R of the Ammonites, H7237

RABBI
Mt 23: 7 and to be called of men, R, Rabbi. G4461
7 and to be called of men, Rabbi, R. G4461
8 But be not ye called R: for one is your G4461
Jn 1:38 They said unto him, R, (which is to say, G4461
49 saith unto him, R, thou art the Son of G4461
3: 2 said unto him, R, we know that thou G4461
26 said unto him, R, he that was with thee G4461
6:25 unto him, R, when camest thou hither? G4461

RABBITH
Jos 19:20 And R, and Kishion, and Abez, H7245

RABBONI
Jn 20:16 unto him, R; which is to say, Master. G4462

RAB-MAG
Jer 39: 3 Nergal-sharezer, **R**, with all the residue H7248
13 **R**, and all the king of Babylon's princes; H7248

RABSARIS
2Ki 18:17 sent Tartan and **R** and Rab-shakeh H7249

RAB-SARIS
Jer 39: 3 Sarsechim, **R**, Nergal-sharezer, H7249
13 Nebushasban, **R**, and Nergal-sharezer, H7249

RAB-SHAKEH
2Ki 18:17 and Rabsaris and **R** from Lachish to H7262
19 And **R** said unto them, Speak ye now to H7262
26 and Joah, unto **R**, Speak, I pray thee, H7262
27 But **R** said unto them, Hath my master H7262
28 Then **R** stood and cried with a loud H7262
37 rent, and told him the words of **R**. H7262
19: 4 all the words of **R**, whom the king of H7262
8 So **R** returned, and found the king of H7262
Isa 36: 2 And the king of Assyria sent **R** from H7262
4 And **R** said unto them, Say ye now to H7262
11 and Joah unto **R**, Speak, I pray thee, H7262
12 But **R** said, Hath my master sent me to H7262
13 Then **R** stood, and cried with a loud H7262
22 rent, and told him the words of **R**. H7262
37: 4 hear the words of **R**, whom the king of H7262
8 So **R** returned, and found the king of H7262

RACA
Mt 5:22 say to his brother, **R**, shall be in danger *G4469*

RACE
Ps 19: 5 *and* rejoiceth as a strong man to run a **r**. H734
Ecc 9:11 the sun, that the **r** *is* not to the swift, H4793
1Co 9:24 Know ye not that they which run in a **r** *G4712*
Heb 12: 1 with patience the **r** that is set before us, *G73*

RACHAB
Mt 1: 5 And Salmon begat Booz of **R**; and Booz *G4477*

RACHAL
1Sa 30:29 And to *them* which *were* in **R**, and to H7403

RACHEL
Gen 29: 6 **R** his daughter cometh with the sheep. H7354
9 And while he yet spake with them, **R** H7354
10 And it came to pass, when Jacob saw **R** H7354
11 And Jacob kissed **R**, and lifted up his H7354
12 And Jacob told **R** that he *was* her H7354
16 and the name of the younger *was* **R**. H7354
17 Leah *was* tender eyed; but **R** was H7354
18 And Jacob loved **R**; and said, I will H7354
18 years for **R** thy younger daughter. H7354
20 And Jacob served seven years for **R**; H7354
25 I serve with thee for **R**? wherefore then H7354
28 gave him **R** his daughter to wife also. H7354
29 And Laban gave to **R** his daughter H7354
30 And he went in also unto **R**, and he H7354
30 and he loved also **R** more than Leah, H7354
31 opened her womb: but **R** *was* barren. H7354
30: 1 And when **R** saw that she bare Jacob H7354
1 Jacob no children, **R** envied her sister; H7354
2 kindled against **R**: and he said, *Am* I in H7354
6 And **R** said, God hath judged me, and H7354
8 And **R** said, With great wrestlings have H7354
14 Leah. Then **R** said to Leah, Give me, H7354
15 also? And **R** said, Therefore he shall H7354
22 And God remembered **R**, and God H7354
25 And it came to pass, when **R** had born H7354
31: 4 And Jacob sent and called **R** and Leah H7354
14 And **R** and Leah answered and said H7354
19 his sheep: and **R** had stolen the images H7354
32 Jacob knew not that **R** had stolen them. H7354
34 Now **R** had taken the images, and put H7354
33: 1 unto **R**, and unto the two handmaids. H7354
2 after, and **R** and Joseph hindermost. H7354
7 and **R**, and they bowed themselves. H7354
35:16 **R** travailed, and she had hard labour. H7354
19 And **R** died, and was buried in the way H7354
24 The sons of **R**; Joseph, and Benjamin: H7354
46:19 The sons of **R** Jacob's wife; Joseph, and H7354
22 These *are* the sons of **R**, which were H7354
25 Laban gave unto **R** his daughter, and H7354
48: 7 from Padan, **R** died by me in the land H7354
Ru 4:11 thine house like **R** and like Leah, which H7354
Mt 2:18 and great mourning, **R** weeping *for* her *G4478*

RACHEL'S
Gen 30: 7 And Bilhah **R** maid conceived again, H7354
31:33 of Leah's tent, and entered into **R** tent. H7354
35:20 *is* the pillar of **R** grave unto this day. H7354
25 And the sons of Bilhah, **R** handmaid; H7354
1Sa 10: 2 find two men by **R** sepulchre in the H7354

RADDAI
1Ch 2:14 Nethaneel the fourth, **R** the fifth, H7288

RAFTERS
Song 1:17 of our house *are* cedar, *and* our **r** of fir. H7351

RAG See RAGGED and RAGS.

RAGAU
Lk 3:35 was *the son* of **R**, which was *the son* of *G4466*

RAGE
2Ki 5:12 So he turned and went away in a **r**. H2534
19:27 thy coming in, and thy **r** against me. H7264
28 Because thy **r** against me and thy H7264
2Ch 16:10 for *he was* in a **r** with him because of H2197
28: 9 in a **r** *that* reacheth up unto heaven. H2197
Job 39:24 fierceness and **r**: neither believeth he H7267
40:11 Cast abroad the **r** of thy wrath: and H5678
Ps 2: 1 Why do the heathen **r**, and the people H7283
7: 6 because of the **r** of mine enemies: and H5678
Prv 6:34 For jealousy *is* the **r** of a man: therefore H2534
29: 9 whether he **r** or laugh, *there is* no rest. H7264
Isa 37:28 thy coming in, and thy **r** against me. H7264
29 Because thy **r** against me, and thy H7264
Jer 46: 9 Come up, ye horses; and **r**, ye chariots; H1984
Dan 3:13 Then Nebuchadnezzar in *his* **r** and fury H7266
Hos 7:16 the sword for the **r** of their tongue: this H2195
Nah 2: 4 The chariots shall **r** in the streets, they H1984
Act 4:25 **r**, and the people imagine vain things? *G5433*

RAGED
Ps 46: 6 The heathen **r**, the kingdoms were H1993

RAGETH
Prv 14:16 evil: but the fool **r**, and is confident. H5674

RAGGED
Isa 2:21 into the tops of the **r** rocks, for fear of the

RAGING
Ps 89: 9 Thou rulest the **r** of the sea: when the H1348
Prv 20: 1 Wine *is* a mocker, strong drink *is* **r**: and H1993
Jna 1:15 the sea: and the sea ceased from her **r**. H2197
Lk 8:24 the wind and the **r** of the water: and *G2830*
Jude 13 **R** waves of the sea, foaming out their *G66*

RAGS
Prv 23:21 drowsiness shall clothe *a man* with **r**. H7168
Isa 64: 6 *are* as filthy **r**; and we all do fade as H899
Jer 38:11 and old rotten **r**, and let them down by H4418
12 cast clouts and rotten **r** under thine H4418

RAGUEL
Nu 10:29 Hobab, the son of **R** the Midianite, H7467

RAHAB
Jos 2: 1 house, named **R**, and lodged there. H7343
3 And the king of Jericho sent unto **R**, H7343
6:17 to the LORD: only **R** the harlot shall H7343
23 and brought out **R**, and her father, and H7343
25 And Joshua saved **R** the harlot alive, H7343
Ps 87: 4 I will make mention of **R** and Babylon H7294
89:10 Thou hast broken **R** in pieces, as one H7294
Isa 51: 9 hath cut **R**, *and* wounded the dragon? H7294
Heb 11:31 By faith the harlot **R** perished not with *G4460*
Jas 2:25 Likewise also was not **R** the harlot *G4460*

RAHAM
1Ch 2:44 And Shema begat **R**, the father of H7357

RAHEL
Jer 31:15 *and* bitter weeping; **R** weeping for her H7354

RAIL
2Ch 32:17 He wrote also letters to **r** on the LORD H2778

RAILED
1Sa 25:14 to salute our master; and he **r** on them. H5860
Mk 15:29 And they that passed by **r** on him, *G987*
Lk 23:39 which were hanged **r** on him, saying, If *G987*

RAILER
1Co 5:11 or an idolater, or a **r**, or a drunkard, or *G3060*

RAILING
1Pt 3: 9 Not rendering evil for evil, or **r** for *G3059*
9 for evil, or railing for **r**: but contrariwise *G3059*
2Pt 2:11 might, bring not **r** accusation against *G989*
Jude 9 against him a **r** accusation, but said, *G988*

RAILINGS
1Ti 6: 4 cometh envy, strife, **r**, evil surmisings, *G988*

RAIMENT
Gen 24:53 jewels of gold, and **r**, and gave *them* to H899
27:15 And Rebekah took goodly **r** of her eldest H899
27 the smell of his **r**, and blessed him, and H899
28:20 give me bread to eat, and **r** to put on, H899
41:14 his **r**, and came in unto Pharaoh. H8071
45:22 man changes of **r**; but to Benjamin he H8071
22 *pieces* of silver, and five changes of **r**. H8071
Ex 3:22 jewels of gold, and **r**: and ye shall put H8071
12:35 of silver, and jewels of gold, and **r**: H8071
21:10 *wife;* her food, her **r**, and her duty of H3682
22: 9 ass, for sheep, for **r**, *or* for any manner H8008
26 If thou at all take thy neighbour's **r** to H8008
27 For that *is* his covering only, it *is* his **r** H8071
Lev 11:32 any vessel of wood, or **r**, or skin, or sack, H899
Nu 31:20 And purify all *your* **r**, and all that is H899
Dt 8: 4 Thy **r** waxed not old upon thee, neither H8071
10:18 the stranger, in giving him food and **r**. H8071
21:13 And she shall put the **r** of her captivity H8071
22: 3 thou do with his **r**; and with all lost H8071
24:13 sleep in his own **r**, and bless thee: and H8008
17 nor take a widow's **r** to pledge: H899
Jos 22: 8 with very much **r**: divide the spoil of H8008
Jdg 3:16 gird it under his **r** upon his right thigh. H4055
8:26 and collars, and purple **r** that *was* on the H899
Ru 3: 3 thee, and put thy **r** upon thee, and get H8071
1Sa 28: 8 and put on other **r**, and he went, and two H899
2Ki 5: 5 *pieces* of gold, and ten changes of **r**. H899
7: 8 and gold, and **r**, and went and hid *it;* H899
2Ch 9:24 of gold, and **r**, harness, and spices, H8008
Est 4: 4 and she sent **r** to clothe Mordecai, and H899
Job 27:16 as the dust, and prepare **r** as the clay; H4403
Ps 45:14 She shall be brought unto the king in **r** H7553
Isa 14:19 branch, *and as* the **r** of those that are H3830
63: 3 my garments, and I will stain all my **r**. H4403
Ezk 16:13 and silver; and thy **r** *was of* fine linen, H4403
Zec 3: 4 and I will clothe thee with change of **r**. H4254
Mt 3: 4 And the same John had his **r** of camel's *G1742*
6:25 more than meat, and the body than **r**? *G1742*
28 And why take ye thought for **r**? Consider *G1742*
11: 8 clothed in soft **r**? behold, they that wear *G2440*
17: 2 sun, and his **r** was white as the light. *G2440*
27:31 and put his own **r** on him, and led him *G2440*
28: 3 like lightning, and his **r** white as snow: *G1742*
Mk 9: 3 And his **r** became shining, exceeding *G2440*
Lk 7:25 clothed in soft **r**? Behold, they which *G2440*
9:29 and his **r** *was* white *and* glistering. *G2441*
10:30 stripped him of his **r**, and wounded *him,*
12:23 than meat, and the body *is more* than **r**. *G1742*
23:34 do. And they parted his **r**, and cast lots. *G2440*
Jn 19:24 They parted my **r** among them, and for *G2440*
Act 18: 6 he shook *his* **r**, and said unto them, *G2440*
22:20 and kept the **r** of them that slew him. *G2440*
1Ti 6: 8 And having food and **r** let us be *G4629*
Jas 2: 2 there come in also a poor man in vile **r**; *G2066*
Rev 3: 5 be clothed in white **r**; and I will not blot *G2440*
18 be rich; and white **r**, that thou mayest *G2440*
4: 4 clothed in white **r**; and they had on *G2440*

RAIN
Gen 2: 5 not caused it to **r** upon the earth, and H4305
7: 4 I will cause it to **r** upon the earth forty H4305
12 And the **r** was upon the earth forty H1653
8: 2 and the **r** from heaven was restrained; H1653
Ex 9:18 I will cause it to **r** a very grievous hail, H4305
33 the **r** was not poured upon the earth. H4306
34 And when Pharaoh saw that the **r** and H4306
16: 4 Behold, I will **r** bread from heaven H4305
Lev 26: 4 Then I will give you **r** in due season, H1653
Dt 11:11 *and* drinketh water of the **r** of heaven: H4306
14 That I will give *you* the **r** of your land H4306
14 season, the first **r** and the latter rain, H3138
14 rain and the latter **r**, that thou mayest H4456
17 that there be no **r**, and that the land H4306
28:12 heaven to give the **r** unto thy land in H4306
24 The LORD shall make the **r** of thy land H4306
32: 2 My doctrine shall drop as the **r**, my H4306

R

Dt 32: 2 the dew, as the small **r** upon the tender H8164
1Sa 12:17 shall send thunder and **r**; that ye may H4306
18 sent thunder and **r** that day: and all the H4306
2Sa 1:21 neither *let there be* **r**, upon you, nor H4306
23: 4 out of the earth by clear shining after **r**. H4306
1Ki 8:35 up, and there is no **r**, because they have H4306
36 walk, and give **r** upon thy land, which H4306
17: 1 shall not be dew nor **r** these years, but H4306
7 there had been no **r** in the land. H1653
14 the LORD sendeth **r** upon the earth. H1653
18: 1 Ahab; and I will send **r** upon the earth. H4306
41 for *there is* a sound of abundance of **r**. H1653
44 get thee down, that the **r** stop thee not. H1653
45 **r**. And Ahab rode, and went to Jezreel. H1653
2Ki 3:17 shall ye see **r**; yet that valley shall H1653
2Ch 6:26 up, and there is no **r**, because they have H4306
27 walk; and send **r** upon thy land, which H4306
7:13 If I shut up heaven that there be no **r**, or H4306
Ezr 10: 9 of *this* matter, and for the great **r**. H1653
13 *is* a time of much **r**, and we are not able H1653
Job 5:10 Who giveth **r** upon the earth, and H4306
20:23 shall **r** *it* upon him while he is eating. H4305
28:26 When he made a decree for the **r**, and a H4306
29:23 And they waited for me as for the **r**; and H4306
23 their mouth wide *as* for the latter **r**. H4456
36:27 **r** according to the vapour thereof: H4306
37: 6 **r**, and to the great rain of his strength. H1653
6 rain, and to the great **r** of his strength. H1653
38:26 To cause it to **r** on the earth, *where* no H4305
28 Hath the **r** a father? or who hath H4306
Ps 11: 6 Upon the wicked he shall **r** snares, fire H4305
68: 9 Thou, O God, didst send a plentiful **r**, H1653
72: 6 He shall come down like **r** upon the H4306
84: 6 it a well; the **r** also filleth the pools. H4175
105:32 He gave them hail for **r**, *and* flaming H1653
135: 7 lightnings for the **r**; he bringeth the H4306
147: 8 who prepareth **r** for the earth, who H4306
Prv 16:15 his favour *is* as a cloud of the latter **r**. H4456
25:14 gift *is like* clouds and wind without **r**. H1653
23 The north wind driveth away **r**: so *doth* H1653
26: 1 As snow in summer, and as **r** in H4306
28: 3 a sweeping **r** which leaveth no food. H4306
Ecc 11: 3 If the clouds be full of **r**, they empty H1653
12: 2 nor the clouds return after the **r**: H1653
Song 2:11 For, lo, the winter is past, the **r** is over H1653
Isa 4: 6 and for a covert from storm and from **r**. H4306
5: 6 the clouds that they **r** no rain upon it. H4305
6 the clouds that they rain no **r** upon it. H4306
30:23 Then shall he give the **r** of thy seed, H4306
44:14 an ash, and the **r** doth nourish *it*. H1653
55:10 For as the **r** cometh down, and the H1653
Jer 3: 3 hath been no latter **r**; and thou hadst a H4456
5:24 God, that giveth **r**, both the former and H1653
10:13 lightnings with **r**, and bringeth forth the H4306
14: 4 for there was no **r** in the earth, the H1653
22 that can cause **r**? or can the heavens H1652
51:16 lightnings with **r**, and bringeth forth the H4306
Ezk 1:28 the cloud in the day of **r**, so *was* the H1653
38:22 blood; and I will **r** upon him, and upon H4305
22 an overflowing **r**, and great hailstones, H1653
Hos 6: 3 come unto us as the **r**, as the latter *and* H1653
3 the latter *and* former **r** unto the earth. H3384
10:12 he come and **r** righteousness upon you. H3384
Joel 2:23 you the former **r** moderately, and he H4175
23 down for you the **r**, the former rain, and H1653
23 **r**, and the latter rain in the first *month*. H4175
23 rain, and the latter **r** in the first *month*. H4456
Am 4: 7 And also I have withholden the **r** from H1653
7 and I caused it to **r** upon one city, and H4305
7 caused it not to **r** upon another city: H4305
Zec 10: 1 Ask ye of the LORD **r** in the time of the H4306
1 time of the latter **r**; *so* the LORD shall H4456
1 of **r**, to every one grass in the field. H1653
14:17 of hosts, even upon them shall be no **r**. H1653
18 not, that *have* no **r**; there shall be the
Mt 5:45 sendeth **r** on the just and on the unjust. *G1026*
7:25 And the **r** descended, and the floods *G1028*
27 And the **r** descended, and the floods *G1028*
Act 14:17 good, and gave us **r** from heaven, and *G5205*
28: 2 the present **r**, and because of the cold. *G5205*
Heb 6: 7 For the earth which drinketh in the **r** *G5205*
Jas 5: 7 it, until he receive the early and latter **r**. *G5205*
17 that it might not **r**: and it rained not on *G1026*
18 **r**, and the earth brought forth her fruit. *G5205*
Rev 11: 6 heaven, that it **r** not in the days of their *G1026*

RAINBOW

Rev 4: 3 and *there was* a **r** round about the *G2463*
10: 1 a cloud: and a **r** *was* upon his head, *G2463*

RAINED

Gen 19:24 Then the LORD **r** upon Sodom and H4305
Ex 9:23 LORD **r** hail upon the land of Egypt. H4305
Ps 78:24 And had **r** down manna upon them to H4305
27 He **r** flesh also upon them as dust, and H4305
Ezk 22:24 nor **r** upon in the day of indignation. H1656
Am 4: 7 city: one piece was **r** upon, and the H4305
7 the piece whereupon it **r** not withered. H4305
Lk 17:29 out of Sodom it **r** fire and brimstone *G1026*
Jas 5:17 not rain: and it **r** not on the earth by *G1026*

RAINY

Prv 27:15 A continual dropping in a very **r** day H5464

RAISE

Gen 38: 8 her, and **r** up seed to thy brother. H6965
Ex 23: 1 Thou shalt not **r** a false report: put not H5375
Dt 18:15 The LORD thy God will **r** up unto thee a H6965
18 I will **r** them up a Prophet from among H6965
25: 7 refuseth to **r** up unto his brother H6965
Jos 8:29 of the city, and **r** thereon a great heap H6965
Ru 4: 5 of the dead, to **r** up the name of the H6965
10 to be my wife, to **r** up the name of the H6965
1Sa 2:35 And I will **r** me up a faithful priest, *that* H6965
2Sa 12:11 Thus saith the LORD, Behold, I will **r** H6965
17 *and went* to him, to **r** him up from the H6965
1Ki 14:14 Moreover the LORD shall **r** him up a H6965
1Ch 17:11 fathers, that I will **r** up thy seed after H6965
Job 3: 8 who are ready to **r** up their mourning. H5782
19:12 His troops come together, and **r** up H5549
30:12 my feet, and they **r** up against me the H5549
Ps 41:10 and **r** me up, that I may requite them. H6965
Isa 15: 5 they shall **r** up a cry of destruction. H5782
29: 3 a mount, and I will **r** forts against thee. H6965
44:26 I will **r** up the decayed places thereof: H6965
49: 6 be my servant to **r** up the tribes of H6965
58:12 places: thou shalt **r** up the foundations H6965
61: 4 old wastes, they shall **r** up the former H6965
Jer 23: 5 the LORD, that I will **r** unto David a H6965
30: 9 their king, whom I will **r** up unto them. H6965
50: 9 For, lo, I will **r** and cause to come up H5782
32 fall, and none shall **r** him up: and I will H6965
51: 1 Thus saith the LORD; Behold, I will **r** H5782
Ezk 23:22 Behold, I will **r** up thy lovers against H5782
34:29 And I will **r** up for them a plant of H6965
Hos 6: 2 **r** us up, and we shall live in his sight. H6965
Joel 3: 7 Behold, I will **r** them out of the place H5782
Am 5: 2 her land; *there is* none to **r** her up. H6965
6:14 But, behold, I will **r** up against you a H6965
9:11 In that day will I **r** up the tabernacle of H6965
11 thereof; and I will **r** up his ruins, and I H6965
Mic 5: 5 then shall we **r** against him seven H6965
Hab 1: 3 are *that* **r** up strife and contention. H5375
6 For, lo, I **r** up the Chaldeans, *that* bitter H6965
Zec 11:16 For, lo, I will **r** up a shepherd in the H6965
Mt 3: 9 stones to **r** up children unto Abraham. *G1453*
10: 8 Heal the sick, cleanse the lepers, **r** the *G1453*
22:24 his wife, and **r** up seed unto his brother. *G450*
Mk 12:19 wife, and **r** up seed unto his brother. *G1817*
Lk 3: 8 stones to **r** up children unto Abraham. *G1453*
20:28 wife, and **r** up seed unto his brother. *G1817*
Jn 2:19 temple, and in three days I will **r** it up. *G1453*
6:39 but should **r** it up again at the last day. *G450*
40 life: and I will **r** him up at the last day. *G450*
44 him: and I will **r** him up at the last day. *G450*
54 life; and I will **r** him up at the last day. *G450*
Act 2:30 he would **r** up Christ to sit on his throne; *G450*
3:22 the Lord your God **r** up unto you of your *G450*
7:37 the Lord your God **r** up unto you of your *G450*
26: 8 with you, that God should **r** the dead? *G1453*
1Co 6:14 and will also **r** up us by his own power. *G1825*
2Co 4:14 Lord Jesus shall **r** up us also by Jesus, *G1453*
Heb 11:19 Accounting that God *was* able to **r** *him* *G1453*
Jas 5:15 and the Lord shall **r** him up; and if he *G1453*

RAISED

Ex 9:16 And in very deed for this *cause* have I **r** H5975
Jos 5: 7 And their children, *whom* he **r** up in H6965
7:26 And they **r** over him a great heap of H6965
Jdg 2:16 Nevertheless the LORD **r** up judges, H6965
18 And when the LORD **r** them up judges, H6965
3: 9 LORD, the LORD **r** up a deliverer to the H6965
15 LORD, the LORD **r** them up a deliverer, H6965
2Sa 23: 1 and the man *who was* **r** up on high, the H6965
1Ki 5:13 And king Solomon **r** a levy out of all H5927
9:15 king Solomon **r**; for to build the house H5927
2Ch 32: 5 was broken, and **r** *it* up to the towers, H5927
33:14 about Ophel, and **r** it up a very great H1361
Ezr 1: 5 spirit God had **r**, to go up to build the H5782
Job 14:12 not awake, nor be **r** out of their sleep. H5782
Song 8: 5 her beloved? I **r** thee up under the apple H5782
Isa 14: 9 of the earth; it hath **r** up from their H6965
23:13 thereof, they **r** up the palaces thereof; H6209
41: 2 Who **r** up the righteous *man* from the H5782
25 I have **r** up *one* from the north, and he H5782
45:13 I have **r** him up in righteousness, and I H5782
Jer 6:22 shall be **r** from the sides of the earth. H5782
25:32 be **r** up from the coasts of the earth. H5782
29:15 Because ye have said, The LORD hath **r** H6965
50:41 be **r** up from the coasts of the earth. H5782
51:11 the LORD hath **r** up the spirit of the H5782
Dan 7: 5 to a bear, and it **r** up itself on one side, H6966
Am 2:11 And I **r** up of your sons for prophets, H6965
Zec 2:13 for he is **r** up out of his holy habitation. H5782
9:13 Ephraim, and **r** up thy sons, O Zion, H5782
Mt 1:24 Then Joseph being **r** from sleep did as *G1326*
11: 5 hear, the dead are **r** up, and the poor *G1453*
16:21 be killed, and be **r** again the third day. *G1453*
17:23 day he shall be **r** again. And they were *G1453*
Lk 1:69 And hath **r** up an horn of salvation for *G1453*
7:22 are **r**, to the poor the gospel is preached. *G1453*
9:22 and be slain, and be **r** the third day. *G1453*
20:37 Now that the dead are **r**, even Moses *G1453*
Jn 12: 1 been dead, whom he **r** from the dead. *G1453*
9 also, whom he had **r** from the dead. *G1453*
17 and **r** him from the dead, bare record. *G1453*
Act 2:24 Whom God hath **r** up, having loosed the *G450*
32 This Jesus hath God **r** up, whereof we all *G450*
3:15 life, whom God hath **r** from the dead; *G1453*
26 Unto you first God, having **r** up his Son *G450*
4:10 whom God **r** from the dead, *even* *G1453*
5:30 The God of our fathers **r** up Jesus, *G1453*
10:40 Him God **r** up the third day, and *G1453*
12: 7 on the side, and **r** him up, saying, Arise *G1453*
13:22 And when he had removed him, he **r** *G1453*
23 promise **r** unto Israel a Saviour, Jesus: *G1453*
30 But God **r** him from the dead: *G1453*
33 in that he hath **r** up Jesus again; as it *G450*
34 And as concerning that he **r** him up *G450*
37 But he, whom God **r** again, saw no *G1453*
50 of the city, and **r** persecution against *G1892*
17:31 in that he hath **r** him from the dead. *G450*
Ro 4:24 that **r** up Jesus our Lord from the dead; *G1453*
25 and was **r** again for our justification. *G1453*
6: 4 like as Christ was **r** up from the dead *G1453*
9 Knowing that Christ being **r** from the *G1453*
7: 4 *even* to him who is **r** from the dead, *G1453*
8:11 But if the Spirit of him that **r** up Jesus *G1453*
11 in you, he that **r** up Christ from the *G1453*
9:17 purpose have I **r** thee up, that I might *G1825*
10: 9 that God hath **r** him from the dead, *G1453*
1Co 6:14 And God hath both **r** up the Lord, and *G1453*
15:15 of God that he **r** up Christ: whom he *G1453*
15 **r** not up, if so be that the dead rise not. *G1453*
16 if the dead rise not, then is not Christ **r**: *G1453*
17 And if Christ be not **r**, your faith *is* vain; *G1453*
35 How are the dead **r** up? and with what *G1453*
42 in corruption; it is **r** in incorruption: *G1453*
43 It is sown in dishonour; it is **r** in glory: *G1453*
43 it is sown in weakness; it is **r** in power: *G1453*
44 It is sown a natural body; it is **r** a *G1453*
52 the dead shall be **r** incorruptible, and *G1453*
2Co 4:14 Knowing that he which **r** up the Lord *G1453*
Gal 1: 1 the Father, who **r** him from the dead;) *G1453*
Eph 1:20 Which he wrought in Christ, when he **r** *G1453*
2: 6 And hath **r** *us* up together, and made *G4891*
Col 2:12 of God, who hath **r** him from the dead. *G1453*
1Th 1:10 heaven, whom he **r** from the dead, *even* *G1453*
2Ti 2: 8 the seed of David was **r** from the dead *G1453*
Heb 11:35 Women received their dead **r** to life *G386*
1Pt 1:21 Who by him do believe in God, that **r** *G1453*

RAISER

Dan 11:20 Then shall stand up in his estate a **r** of H5674

RAISETH

1Sa 2: 8 He **r** up the poor out of the dust, *and* H6965
Job 41:25 When he **r** up himself, the mighty are H7613
Ps 107:25 For he commandeth, and **r** the stormy H5975
113: 7 He **r** up the poor out of the dust, *and* H6965
145:14 The LORD upholdeth all that fall, and **r** H2210
146: 8 blind: the LORD **r** them that are bowed H2210
Jn 5:21 For as the Father **r** up the dead, and *G1453*
2Co 1: 9 ourselves, but in God which **r** the dead: *G1453*

RAISING

Hos 7: 4 baker, *who* ceaseth from **r** after he hath H5782
Act 24:12 man, neither **r** up the people, *G4160+G1999*

RAISINS
1Sa 25:18 clusters of **r**, and two hundred cakes H6778
30:12 and two clusters of **r**: and when he had H6778
2Sa 16: 1 bunches of **r**, and an hundred of H6778
1Ch 12:40 and bunches of **r**, and wine, and oil, H6778

RAKEM
1Ch 7:16 Sheresh; and his sons *were* Ulam and **R**. H7552

RAKKATH
Jos 19:35 and Ham-math, **R**, and Chinnereth, H7557

RAKKON
Jos 19:46 And Me-jarkon, and **R**, with the border H7542

RAM
Gen 15: 9 years old, and a **r** of three years old, and H352
22:13 behind *him* a **r** caught in a thicket by H352
13 went and took the **r**, and offered him up H352
Ex 29:15 Thou shalt also take one **r**; and Aaron H352
15 put their hands upon the head of the **r**. H352
16 And thou shalt slay the **r**, and thou shalt H352
17 And thou shalt cut the **r** in pieces, and H352
18 And thou shalt burn the whole **r** upon H352
19 And thou shalt take the other **r**; and H352
19 put their hands upon the head of the **r**. H352
20 Then shalt thou kill the **r**, and take of his H352
22 Also thou shalt take of the **r** the fat and H352
22 shoulder; for it *is* a **r** of consecration: H352
26 And thou shalt take the breast of the **r** of H352
27 which is heaved up, of the **r** of the H352
31 And thou shalt take the **r** of the H352
32 eat the flesh of the **r**, and the bread that H352
Lev 5:15 unto the LORD a **r** without blemish out H352
16 for him with the **r** of the trespass H352
18 And he shall bring a **r** without blemish H352
6: 6 unto the LORD, a **r** without blemish out H352
8:18 And he brought the **r** for the burnt H352
18 laid their hands upon the head of the **r**. H352
20 And he cut the **r** into pieces; and Moses H352
21 burnt the whole **r** upon the altar: it *was* H352
22 And he brought the other **r**, the ram of H352
22 And he brought the other ram, the **r** of H352
22 laid their hands upon the head of the **r**. H352
29 LORD: *for* of the **r** of consecration it was H352
9: 2 sin offering, and a **r** for a burnt offering, H352
4 Also a bullock and a **r** for peace H352
18 He slew also the bullock and the **r** *for* a H352
19 And the fat of the bullock and of the **r**, H352
16: 3 sin offering, and a **r** for a burnt offering. H352
5 offering, and one **r** for a burnt offering. H352
19:21 *even* a **r** for a trespass offering. H352
22 for him with the **r** of the trespass H352
Nu 5: 8 the priest; beside the **r** of the atonement, H352
6:14 **r** without blemish for peace offerings, H352
17 And he shall offer the **r** *for* a sacrifice of H352
19 shoulder of the **r**, and one unleavened H352
7:15 One young bullock, one **r**, one lamb of H352
21 One young bullock, one **r**, one lamb of H352
27 One young bullock, one **r**, one lamb of H352
33 One young bullock, one **r**, one lamb of H352
39 One young bullock, one **r**, one lamb of H352
45 One young bullock, one **r**, one lamb of H352
51 One young bullock, one **r**, one lamb of H352
57 One young bullock, one **r**, one lamb of H352
63 One young bullock, one **r**, one lamb of H352
69 One young bullock, one **r**, one lamb of H352
75 One young bullock, one **r**, one lamb of H352
81 One young bullock, one **r**, one lamb of H352
15: 6 Or for a **r**, thou shalt prepare *for* a meat H352
11 or for one **r**, or for a lamb, or a kid. H352
23: 2 offered on *every* altar a bullock and a **r**. H352
4 upon *every* altar a bullock and a **r**. H352
14 offered a bullock and a **r** on *every* altar. H352
30 offered a bullock and a **r** on *every* altar. H352
28:11 bullocks, and one **r**, seven lambs of the H352
12 meat offering, mingled with oil, for one **r**; H352
14 of an hin unto a **r**, and a fourth *part* of H352
19 bullocks, and one **r**, and seven lambs of H352
20 for a bullock, and two tenth deals for a **r**; H352
27 one **r**, seven lambs of the first year; H352
28 one bullock, two tenth deals unto one **r**, H352
29: 2 young bullock, one **r**, *and* seven lambs of H352
3 for a bullock, *and* two tenth deals for a **r**, H352
8 young bullock, one **r**, *and* seven lambs of H352
9 to a bullock, *and* two tenth deals to one **r**, H352
14 tenth deals to each **r** of the two rams, H352
36 one bullock, one **r**, seven lambs of the H352
37 the bullock, for the **r**, and for the lambs, H352
Ru 4:19 And Hezron begat **R**, and Ram begat H7410
19 And Hezron begat Ram, and **R** begat H7410
1Ch 2: 9 him; Jerahmeel, and **R**, and Chelubai. H7410
10 And **R** begat Amminadab; and H7410
25 of Hezron were, **R** the firstborn, and H7410
27 And the sons of **R** the firstborn of H7410
Ezr 10:19 *offered* a **r** of the flock for their trespass. H352
Job 32: 2 of the kindred of **R**: against Job was his H7410
Ezk 43:23 and a **r** out of the flock without blemish. H352
25 and a **r** out of the flock, without blemish. H352
45:24 for a **r**, and an hin of oil for an ephah. H352
46: 4 blemish, and a **r** without blemish. H352
5 *shall be* an ephah for a **r**, and the meat H352
6 and a **r**: they shall be without blemish. H352
7 and an ephah for a **r**, and for the lambs H352
11 and an ephah to a **r**, and to the lambs as H352
Dan 8: 3 before the river a **r** which had *two* horns: H352
4 I saw the **r** pushing westward, and H352
6 And he came to the **r** that had *two* H352
7 And I saw him come close unto the **r**, and H352
7 him, and smote the **r**, and brake his two H352
7 no power in the **r** to stand before him, H352
7 that could deliver the **r** out of his hand. H352
20 The **r** which thou sawest having *two* H352

RAMA
Mt 2:18 In **R** was there a voice heard, G4471

RAMAH
Jos 18:25 Gibeon, and **R**, and Beeroth, H7414
19:29 And *then* the coast turneth to **R**, and to H7414
36 And Adamah, and **R**, and Hazor, H7414
Jdg 4: 5 of Deborah between **R** and Beth-el in H7414
19:13 to lodge all night, in Gibeah, or in **R**. H7414
1Sa 1:19 to their house to **R**: and Elkanah knew H7414
2:11 And Elkanah went to **R** to his house. H7414
7:17 And his return *was* to **R**; for there *was* H7414
8: 4 together, and came to Samuel unto **R**, H7414
15:34 Then Samuel went to **R**; and Saul went H7414
16:13 So Samuel rose up, and went to **R**. H7414
19:18 to Samuel to **R**, and told him all that H7414
19 saying, Behold, David *is* at Naioth in **R**. H7414
22 Then went he also to **R**, and came to a H7414
22 said, Behold, *they be* at Naioth in **R**. H7414
23 And he went thither to Naioth in **R**: and H7414
23 until he came to Naioth in **R**. H7414
20: 1 And David fled from Naioth in **R**, and H7414
22: 6 under a tree in **R**, having his spear in H7414
25: 1 in his house at **R**. And David arose, and H7414
28: 3 and buried him in **R**, even in his own H7414
1Ki 15:17 Judah, and built **R**, that he might not H7414
21 off building of **R**, and dwelt in Tirzah. H7414
22 away the stones of **R**, and the timber H7414
2Ki 8:29 had given him at **R**, when he fought H7414
2Ch 16: 1 Judah, and built **R**, to the intent that he H7414
5 off building of **R**, and let his work cease. H7414
6 away the stones of **R**, and the timber H7414
22: 6 were given him at **R**, when he fought H7414
Ezr 2:26 The children of **R** and Gaba, six H7414
Neh 7:30 The men of **R** and Geba, six hundred H7414
11:33 Hazor, **R**, Gittaim, H7414
Isa 10:29 Geba; **R** is afraid; Gibeah of Saul is fled. H7414
Jer 31:15 was heard in **R**, lamentation, *and* bitter H7414
40: 1 let him go from **R**, when he had taken H7414
Hos 5: 8 *and* the trumpet in **R**: cry aloud *at* H7414

RAMATH
Jos 19: 8 to Baalath-beer, **R** of the south. This *is* H7418

RAMATHAIM-ZOPHIM
1Sa 1: 1 Now there was a certain man of **R**, of H7436

RAMATHITE
1Ch 27:27 *was* Shimei the **R**: over the increase of H7435

RAMATH-LEHI
Jdg 15:17 out of his hand, and called that place **R**. H7437

RAMATH-MIZPEH
Jos 13:26 And from Heshbon unto **R**, and H7434

RAMESES
Gen 47:11 land of **R**, as Pharaoh had commanded. H7486
Ex 12:37 journeyed from **R** to Succoth, about six H7486
Nu 33: 3 And they departed from **R** in the first H7486
5 from **R**, and pitched in Succoth. H7486

RAMIAH
Ezr 10:25 the sons of Parosh; **R**, and Jeziah, and H7422

RAMOTH
Dt 4:43 the Reubenites; and **R** in Gilead, of the H7216
Jos 20: 8 of Reuben, and **R** in Gilead out of the H7216
21:38 And out of the tribe of Gad, **R** in Gilead H7433
1Sa 30:27 **R**, and to *them* which *were* in Jattir, H7418
1Ki 22: 3 Know ye that **R** in Gilead *is* ours, and H7433
1Ch 6:73 And **R** with her suburbs, and Anem H7216
80 And out of the tribe of Gad; **R** in Gilead H7216
Ezr 10:29 and Adaiah, Jashub, and Sheal, and **R**. H3406

RAMOTH-GILEAD
1Ki 4:13 The son of Geber, in **R**; to him H7433
22: 4 me to battle to **R**? And Jehoshaphat said H7433
6 Shall I go against **R** to battle, or shall I H7433
12 saying, Go up to **R**, and prosper: for the H7433
15 we go against **R** to battle, or shall we H7433
20 go up and fall at **R**? And one said on this H7433
29 the king of Judah went up to **R**. H7433
2Ki 8:28 in **R**; and the Syrians wounded Joram. H7433
9: 1 box of oil in thine hand, and go to **R**: H7433
4 the young man the prophet, went to **R**. H7433
14 Joram had kept **R**, he and all Israel, H7433
2Ch 18: 2 persuaded him to go up *with him* to **R**. H7433
3 go with me to **R**? And he answered him, H7433
5 Shall we go to **R** to battle, or shall I H7433
11 saying, Go up to **R**, and prosper: for the H7433
14 shall we go to **R** to battle, or shall I H7433
19 may go up and fall at **R**? And one spake H7433
28 the king of Judah went up to **R**. H7433
22: 5 at **R**: and the Syrians smote Joram. H7433

RAMPART
Lam 2: 8 he made the **r** and the wall to lament; H2426
Nah 3: 8 about it, whose **r** *was* the sea, *and* her H2426

RAMS
Gen 31:10 and, behold, the **r** which leaped upon H6260
12 and see, all the **r** which leap upon the H6260
38 and the **r** of thy flock have I not eaten. H352
32:14 goats, two hundred ewes, and twenty **r**, H352
Ex 29: 1 bullock, and two **r** without blemish, H352
3 basket, with the bullock and the two **r**. H352
35:23 of **r**, and badgers' skins, brought *them*. H352
Lev 8: 2 two **r**, and a basket of unleavened bread; H352
23:18 bullock, and two **r**: they shall be *for* a H352
Nu 7:17 two oxen, five **r**, five he goats, five lambs H352
23 two oxen, five **r**, five he goats, five lambs H352
29 two oxen, five **r**, five he goats, five lambs H352
35 two oxen, five **r**, five he goats, five lambs H352
41 two oxen, five **r**, five he goats, five lambs H352
47 two oxen, five **r**, five he goats, five lambs H352
53 two oxen, five **r**, five he goats, five lambs H352
59 two oxen, five **r**, five he goats, five lambs H352
65 two oxen, five **r**, five he goats, five lambs H352
71 two oxen, five **r**, five he goats, five lambs H352
77 two oxen, five **r**, five he goats, five lambs H352
83 two oxen, five **r**, five he goats, five lambs H352
87 bullocks, the **r** twelve, the lambs of H352
88 four bullocks, the **r** sixty, the he goats H352
23: 1 prepare me here seven oxen and seven **r**. H352
29 me here seven bullocks and seven **r**. H352
29:13 bullocks, two **r**, *and* fourteen lambs H352
14 two tenth deals to each ram of the two **r**, H352
17 bullocks, two **r**, fourteen lambs of the H352
18 the bullocks, for the **r**, and for the lambs, H352
20 bullocks, two **r**, fourteen lambs of the H352
21 the bullocks, for the **r**, and for the lambs, H352
23 ten bullocks, two **r**, *and* fourteen lambs H352
24 the bullocks, for the **r**, and for the lambs, H352
26 And on the fifth day nine bullocks, two **r**, H352
27 the bullocks, for the **r**, and for the lambs, H352
29 eight bullocks, two **r**, *and* fourteen lambs H352
30 the bullocks, for the **r**, and for the lambs, H352
32 day seven bullocks, two **r**, *and* fourteen H352
33 the bullocks, for the **r**, and for the lambs, H352
Dt 32:14 with fat of lambs, and **r** of the breed of H352
1Sa 15:22 sacrifice, *and* to hearken than the fat of **r**. H352
2Ki 3: 4 an hundred thousand **r**, with the wool. H352
1Ch 15:26 they offered seven bullocks and seven **r**. H352
29:21 a thousand **r**, *and* a thousand lambs, H352
2Ch 13: 9 bullock and seven **r**, *the same* may be a H352
17:11 and seven hundred **r**, and seven H352
29:21 and seven **r**, and seven lambs, and H352
22 they had killed the **r**, they sprinkled the H352
32 an hundred **r**, *and* two hundred lambs: H352
Ezr 6: 9 bullocks, and **r**, and lambs, for the H1798
17 two hundred **r**, four hundred lambs; H1798

Ezr 7:17 money bullocks, r, lambs, with their H1798
8:35 ninety and six r, seventy and seven H352
Job 42: 8 seven bullocks and seven r, and go to my H352
Ps 66:15 r; I will offer bullocks with goats. Selah. H352
114: 4 The mountains skipped like r, *and* the H352
6 Ye mountains, *that* ye skipped like r; *and* H352
Isa 1:11 the burnt offerings of r, and the fat of fed H352
34: 6 of the kidneys of r: for the LORD hath a H352
60: 7 unto thee, the r of Nebaioth shall H352
Jer 51:40 to the slaughter, like r with he goats. H352
Ezk 4: 2 set *battering* r against it round about. H3733
21:22 appoint *battering* r against the gates, H3733
27:21 thee in lambs, and r, and goats: in these H352
34:17 cattle, between the r and the he goats. H352
39:18 of the earth, of r, of lambs, and of goats, H352
45:23 bullocks and seven r without blemish H352
Mic 6: 7 pleased with thousands of r, *or* with ten H352

RAM'S
Jos 6: 5 long *blast* with the r horn, *and* when ye H3104

RAMS'
Ex 25: 5 And r skins dyed red, and badgers' H352
26:14 for the tent *of* r skins dyed red, and H352
35: 7 And r skins dyed red, and badgers' H352
36:19 And he made a covering for the tent *of* r H352
39:34 And the covering of r skins dyed red, H352
Jos 6: 4 ark seven trumpets of r horns: and the H3104
6 of r horns before the ark of the LORD. H3104
8 seven trumpets of r horns passed on H3104
13 seven trumpets of r horns before the H3104

RAN
Gen 18: 2 he saw *them*, he r to meet them from H7323
7 And Abraham r unto the herd, and H7323
24:17 And the servant r to meet her, and H7323
20 the trough, and r again unto the well H7323
28 And the damsel r, and told *them of* her H7323
29 r out unto the man, unto the well. H7323
29:12 son: and she r and told her father. H7323
13 sister's son, that he r to meet him, and H7323
33: 4 And Esau r to meet him, and embraced H7323
Ex 9:23 and hail, and the fire r along upon the H1980
Nu 11:27 And there r a young man, and told H7323
16:47 commanded, and r into the midst of H7323
Jos 7:22 So Joshua sent messengers, and they r H7323
8:19 place, and they r as soon as he had H7323
Jdg 7:21 and all the host r, and cried, and fled. H7323
9:21 And Jotham r away, and fled, and went H7323
44 *other* companies r upon all *the people* H6584
13:10 And the woman made haste, and r, and H7323
1Sa 3: 5 And he r unto Eli, and said, Here *am* I; H7323
4:12 And there r a man of Benjamin out of H7323
10:23 And they r and fetched him thence: H7323
17:22 the carriage, and r into the army, and H7323
48 David hasted, and r toward the army H7323
51 Therefore David r, and stood upon the H7323
20:36 the lad r, he shot an arrow beyond him. H7323
2Sa 18:21 Cushi bowed himself unto Joab, and r. H7323
23 Run. Then Ahimaaz r by the way of the H7323
1Ki 2:39 servants of Shimei r away unto Achish H1272
18:35 And the water r round about the altar; H7323
46 up his loins, and r before Ahab to the H7323
19:20 And he left the oxen, and r after Elijah, H7323
22:35 and the blood r out of the wound into H3332
2Ch 32: 4 and the brook that r through the midst H7857
Ps 77: 2 the Lord: my sore r in the night, and H5064
105:41 out; they r in the dry places *like* a river. H1980
133: 2 the head, that r down upon the beard, H3331
Jer 23:21 prophets, yet they r: I have not spoken H7323
Ezk 1:14 And the living creatures r and returned H7519
47: 2 there r out waters on the right side. H6379
Dan 8: 6 and r unto him in the fury of his power. H7323
Mt 8:32 herd of swine r violently down a steep G3729
27:48 And straightway one of them r, and G5143
Mk 5: 6 But when he saw Jesus afar off, he r G5143
13 and the herd r violently down a steep G3729
6:33 knew him, and r afoot thither out of G4936
55 And r through that whole region round G4063
15:36 And one r and filled a spunge full of G5143
Lk 8:33 and the herd r violently down a steep G3729
15:20 r, and fell on his neck, and kissed him. G5143
19: 4 And he r before, and climbed up into a G4390
24:12 Then arose Peter, and r unto the G5143
Jn 20: 4 So they r both together: and the other G5143
Act 3:11 all the people r together unto them G4936
7:57 ears, and r upon him with one accord, G3729
8:30 And Philip r thither to *him*, and heard G4370
12:14 for gladness, but r in, and told how G1532
14:14 and r in among the people, crying out, G1530
21:30 and the people r together: and they G4890
32 centurions, and r down unto them: and G2701
27:41 two seas met, they r the ship aground; G2027
Jude 11 the way of Cain, and r greedily after the G1632

RANG
1Sa 4: 5 a great shout, so that the earth r again. H1949
1Ki 1:45 so that the city r again. This *is* the H1949

RANGE
Job 39: 8 The r of the mountains *is* his pasture, H3491

RANGES
Lev 11:35 *it be* oven, or r for pots, they shall be H3600
2Ki 11: 8 cometh within the r, let him be slain: H7713
15 her forth without the r: and him that H7713
2Ch 23:14 her forth of the r: and whoso followeth H7713

RANGING
Prv 28:15 *As* a roaring lion, and a r bear; *so is* a H8264

RANK
Gen 41: 5 came up upon one stalk, r and good. H1277
7 the seven r and full ears. And Pharaoh H1277
Nu 2:16 And they shall set forth in the second r.
24 And they shall go forward in the third r.
1Ch 12:33 keep r: *they were* not of double heart. H5737
38 All these men of war, that could keep r, H4634

RANKS
1Ki 7: 4 and light *was* against light *in* three r. H6471
5 and light *was* against light *in* three r. H6471
Joel 2: 7 his ways, and they shall not break their r: H734
Mk 6:40 And they sat down in r, by hundreds, G4237

RANSOM
Ex 21:30 he shall give for the r of his life H6306
30:12 give every man a r for his soul unto the H3724
Job 33:24 going down to the pit: I have found a r. H3724
36:18 then a great r cannot deliver thee. H3724
Ps 49: 7 his brother, nor give to God a r for him: H3724
Prv 6:35 He will not regard any r; neither will he H3724
13: 8 The r of a man's life *are* his riches: but H3724
21:18 The wicked *shall be* a r for the H3724
Isa 43: 3 *for* thy r, Ethiopia and Seba for thee. H3724
Hos 13:14 I will r them from the power of the H6299
Mt 20:28 and to give his life a r for many. G3083
Mk 10:45 and to give his life a r for many. G3083
1Ti 2: 6 Who gave himself a r for all, to be G487

RANSOMED
Isa 35:10 And the r of the LORD shall return, H6299
51:10 of the sea a way for the r to pass over? H1350
Jer 31:11 Jacob, and r him from the hand H1350

RAPHA
1Ch 8: 2 Nohah the fourth, and R the fifth. H7498
37 And Moza begat Binea: R *was* his son, H7498

RAPHU
Nu 13: 9 the tribe of Benjamin, Palti the son of R. H7505

RARE
Dan 2:11 And *it is* a r thing that the king H3358

RASE
Ps 137: 7 who said, R *it*, rase *it*, *even* to the H6168
7 *it*, r *it*, *even* to the foundation thereof. H6168

RASH
Ecc 5: 2 Be not r with thy mouth, and let not H926
Isa 32: 4 The heart also of the r shall understand H4116

RASHLY
Act 19:36 ought to be quiet, and to do nothing r. G4312

RASOR See RAZOR.

RATE
Ex 16: 4 gather a certain r every day, that I may H1697
1Ki 10:25 horses, and mules, a r year by year. H1697
2Ki 25:30 r for every day, all the days of his life. H1697
2Ch 8:13 Even after a certain r every day, H1697
9:24 horses, and mules, a r year by year. H1697

RATHER
Jos 22:24 And if we have not r done it for fear of
2Sa 10: 3 hath not David r sent his servants unto
2Ki 5:13 done *it?* how much r then, when he saith
Job 7:15 strangling, *and* death r than my life.
32: 2 because he justified himself r than God.
36:21 this hast thou chosen r than affliction.
Ps 52: 3 r than to speak righteousness. Selah.
84:10 a thousand. I had r be a doorkeeper in H977
Prv 8:10 silver; and knowledge r than choice gold. H408
16:16 r to be chosen than silver!
17:12 meet a man, r than a fool in his folly. H408
22: 1 A *good* name *is* r to be chosen than great
1 *and* loving favour r than silver and gold.
Jer 8: 3 And death shall be chosen r than life by
Mt 10: 6 But go r to the lost sheep of the house G3123
28 to kill the soul: but r fear him which is G3123
18: 8 life halt or maimed, r than having two G2228
9 life with one eye, r than having two G2228
25: 9 and you: but go ye r to them that sell, G3123
27:24 nothing, but *that* r a tumult was made, G3123
Mk 5:26 nothing bettered, but r grew worse, G3123
15:11 should r release Barabbas unto them. G3123
Lk 10:20 unto you; but r rejoice, because your G3123
11:28 But he said, Yea r, blessed *are* they that G3304
41 But r give alms of such things as ye G4183
12:31 But r seek ye the kingdom of God; and G4138
51 on earth? I tell you, Nay; but r division: G2228
17: 8 And will not r say unto him, Make ready
18:14 his house justified r than the other: for
Jn 3:19 loved darkness r than light, because G3123
Act 5:29 We ought to obey God r than men. G3123
Ro 3: 8 And not r, (as we be slanderously
8:34 that died, yea r, that is risen again, who G3123
11:11 fall? God forbid: but r through their fall
12:19 not yourselves, but r give place unto
14:13 but judge this r, that no man put a G3123
1Co 5: 2 And ye are puffed up, and have not r G3123
6: 7 Why do ye not r take wrong? why do G3123
7 not r *suffer yourselves to* be defrauded? G3123
7:21 if thou mayest be made free, use *it* r. G3123
9:12 you, *are* not we r? Nevertheless we have G3123
14: 1 *gifts*, but r that ye may prophesy. G3123
5 with tongues, but r that ye prophesied: G3123
19 Yet in the church I had r speak five G2309
2Co 2: 7 So that contrariwise ye *ought* r to G3123
3: 8 ministration of the spirit be r glorious? G3123
5: 8 We are confident, *I say*, and willing r to G3123
12: 9 gladly therefore will I r glory in my G3123
Gal 4: 9 known God, or r are known of God, G3123
Eph 4:28 Let him that stole steal no more: but r G3123
5: 4 not convenient: but r giving of thanks. G3123
11 works of darkness, but r reprove *them*. G3123
Php 1:12 r unto the furtherance of the gospel; G3123
1Ti 1: 4 questions, r than godly edifying G3123
4: 7 and exercise thyself r unto godliness.
6: 2 are brethren; but r do *them* service, G3123
Phlm 9 Yet for love's sake I r beseech *thee*, G3123
Heb 11:25 Choosing r to suffer affliction with the G3123
12: 9 shall we not much r be in subjection G3123
13 out of the way; but let it r be healed. G3123
13:19 But I beseech *you* the r to do this, that I G4056
2Pt 1:10 Wherefore the r, brethren, give G3123

RATTLETH
Job 39:23 The quiver r against him, the glittering H7439

RATTLING
Nah 3: 2 the noise of the r of the wheels, and of H7494

RAVEN
Gen 8: 7 And he sent forth a r, which went forth H6158
Lev 11:15 Every r after his kind; H6158
Dt 14:14 And every r after his kind, H6158
Job 38:41 Who provideth for the r his food? when H6158
Song 5:11 his locks *are* bushy, *and* black as a r. H6158
Isa 34:11 owl also and the r shall dwell in it: and H6158

RAVENING
Ps 22:13 their mouths, *as* a r and a roaring lion. H2963
Ezk 22:25 like a roaring lion r the prey; they have H2963
27 *are* like wolves r the prey, to shed H2963
Mt 7:15 clothing, but inwardly they are r wolves. G727
Lk 11:39 inward part is full of r and wickedness. G724

RAVENOUS
Isa 35: 9 No lion shall be there, nor *any* r beast H6530
46:11 Calling a r bird from the east, the man H5861
Ezk 39: 4 give thee unto the r birds of every sort, H5861

RAVENS
1Ki 17: 4 commanded the r to feed thee there. H6158

1Ki 17: 6 And the r brought him bread and flesh H6158
Ps 147: 9 his food, *and* to the young r which cry. H6158
Prv 30:17 *his* mother, the r of the valley shall pick H6158
Lk 12:24 Consider the r: for they neither sow nor G2876

RAVIN
Gen 49:27 Benjamin shall r *as* a wolf: in the H2963
Nah 2:12 his holes with prey, and his dens with r. H2966

RAVISHED
Prv 5:19 and be thou r always with her love. H7686
20 And why wilt thou, my son, be r with a H7686
Song 4: 9 Thou hast r my heart, my sister, *my* H3823
9 spouse; thou hast r my heart with one H3823
Isa 13:16 shall be spoiled, and their wives r. H7693
Lam 5:11 They r the women in Zion, *and* the H6031
Zec 14: 2 and the women r; and half of the city H7693

RAW
Ex 12: 9 Eat not of it r, nor sodden at all with H4995
Lev 13:10 and *there be* quick r flesh in the rising; H2416
14 But when r flesh appeareth in him, he H2416
15 And the priest shall see the r flesh, and H2416
15 *for* the r flesh *is* unclean: it *is* a leprosy. H2416
16 Or if the r flesh turn again, and be H2416
1Sa 2:15 will not have sodden flesh of thee, but r. H2416

RAZE See RASE.

RAZOR
Nu 6: 5 there shall no r come upon his head: H8593
Jdg 13: 5 bear a son; and no r shall come on his H4177
16:17 hath not come a r upon mine head; for H4177
1Sa 1:11 there shall no r come upon his head. H4177
Ps 52: 2 like a sharp r, working deceitfully. H8593
Isa 7:20 the Lord shave with a r that is hired, H8593
Ezk 5: 1 thee a barber's r, and cause *it* to pass H8593

REACH
Gen 11: 4 whose top *may* r unto heaven; and let
Ex 26:28 of the boards shall r from end to end. H1272
28:42 loins even unto the thighs they shall r: H1961
Lev 26: 5 And your threshing shall r unto the H5381
5 and the vintage shall r unto the sowing H5381
Nu 34:11 descend, and shall r unto the side of H4229
35: 4 the Levites, *shall* r from the wall of the
Job 20: 6 and his head r unto the clouds; H5060
Isa 8: 8 go over, he shall r *even* to the neck; and H5060
30:28 stream, shall r to the midst of the neck, H5060
Jer 48:32 over the sea, they r *even* to the sea of H5060
Zec 14: 5 mountains shall r unto Azal: yea, ye H5060
Jn 20:27 Then saith he to Thomas, R hither thy G5342
27 my hands; and r hither thy hand, and G5342
2Co 10:13 to us, a measure to r even unto you. G2185

REACHED
Gen 28:12 earth, and the top of it r to heaven: and H5060
Jos 19:11 and Maralah, and r to Dabbasheth, H6293
11 r to the river that *is* before Jokneam; H6293
Ru 2:14 the reapers: and he r her parched *corn*, H6642
Dan 4:11 the height thereof r unto heaven, and H4291
20 whose height r unto the heaven, and H4291
2Co 10:14 as though we r not unto you: for we G2185
Rev 18: 5 For her sins have r unto heaven, and G190

REACHETH
Nu 21:30 unto Nophah, which *r* unto Medeba.
Jos 19:22 And the coast r to Tabor, and H6293
26 Amad, and Misheal; and r to Carmel H6293
27 Beth-dagon, and r to Zebulun, and to H6293
34 to Hukkok, and r to Zebulun on the H6293
34 south side, and r to Asher on the west H6293
2Ch 28: 9 them in a rage *that* r up unto heaven. H5060
Ps 36: 5 *and* thy faithfulness *r* unto the clouds.
108: 4 heavens: and thy truth *r* unto the clouds.
Prv 31:20 yea, she r forth her hands to the needy. H7971
Jer 4:10 whereas the sword r unto the soul. H5060
18 is bitter, because it r unto thine heart. H5060
51: 9 for her judgment r unto heaven, and is H5060
Dan 4:22 is grown, and r unto heaven, and thy H4291

REACHING
2Ch 3:11 *was* five cubits, r to the wall of the H5060
11 r to the wing of the other cherub. H5060
12 *was* five cubits, r to the wall of the H5060
Php 3:13 are behind, and r forth unto those G1901

READ
Ex 24: 7 the covenant, and r in the audience of H7121
Dt 17:19 And it shall be with him, and he shall r H7121
31:11 choose, thou shalt r this law before all H7121
Jos 8:34 And afterward he r all the words of the H7121
35 which Joshua r not before all the H7121
2Ki 5: 7 king of Israel had r the letter, that he H7121
19:14 the messengers, and r it: and Hezekiah H7121
22: 8 gave the book to Shaphan, and he r it. H7121
10 book. And Shaphan r it before the king. H7121
16 book which the king of Judah hath r: H7121
23: 2 and great: and he r in their ears all the H7121
2Ch 34:18 book. And Shaphan r it before the king. H7121
24 they have r before the king of Judah: H7121
30 and small: and he r in their ears all the H7121
Ezr 4:18 unto us hath been plainly r before me. H7123
23 letter *was* r before Rehum, and H7123
Neh 8: 3 And he r therein before the street that H7121
8 So they r in the book in the law of God H7121
18 the last day, he r in the book of the law H7121
9: 3 And they stood up in their place, and r H7121
13: 1 On that day they r in the book of Moses H7121
Est 6: 1 and they were r before the king. H7121
Isa 29:11 is learned, saying, R this, I pray thee: H7121
12 learned, saying, R this, I pray thee: and H7121
34:16 of the LORD, and r: no one of these H7121
37:14 the messengers, and r it: and Hezekiah H7121
Jer 29:29 And Zephaniah the priest r this letter H7121
36: 6 Therefore go thou, and r in the roll, H7121
6 also thou shalt r them in the ears of all H7121
10 Then r Baruch in the book the words of H7121
13 r the book in the ears of the people. H7121
14 wherein thou hast r in the ears of the H7121
15 Sit down now, and r it in our ears. So H7121
15 in our ears. So Baruch r *it* in their ears. H7121
21 And Jehudi r it in the ears of the king, H7121
23 when Jehudi had r three or four leaves, H7121
51:61 shalt see, and shalt r all these words; H7121
Dan 5: 7 Whosoever shall r this writing, and H7123
8 but they could not r the writing, nor H7123
15 me, that they should r this writing, and H7123
16 now if thou canst r the writing, and H7123
17 another; yet I will r the writing unto the H7123
Mt 12: 3 But he said unto them, Have ye not r G314
5 Or have ye not r in the law, how that on G314
19: 4 them, Have ye not r, that he which made G314
21:16 Yea; have ye never r, Out of the mouth of G314
42 Jesus saith unto them, Did ye never r in G314
22:31 the dead, have ye not r that which was G314
Mk 2:25 And he said unto them, Have ye never r G314
12:10 And have ye not r this scripture; The G314
26 rise: have ye not r in the book of Moses, G314
Lk 4:16 on the sabbath day, and stood up for to r. G314
6: 3 said, Have ye not r so much as this, what G314
Jn 19:20 This title then r many of the Jews: for the G314
Act 8:28 in his chariot r Esaias the prophet. G314
30 and heard him r the prophet Esaias, and G314
32 The place of the scripture which he r was G314
13:27 prophets which are r every sabbath day, G314
15:21 r in the synagogues every sabbath day. G314
31 *Which* when they had r, they rejoiced for G314
23:34 And when the governor had r *the letter*, G314
2Co 1:13 you, than what ye r or acknowledge; and G314
3: 2 in our hearts, known and r of all men: G314
15 But even unto this day, when Moses is r, G314
Eph 3: 4 Whereby, when ye r, ye may understand G314
Col 4:16 And when this epistle is r among you, G314
16 cause that it be r also in the church of G314
16 ye likewise r the *epistle* from Laodicea. G314
1Th 5:27 epistle be r unto all the holy brethren. G314
Rev 5: 4 to r the book, neither to look thereon. G314

READEST
Lk 10:26 What is written in the law? how r thou? G314
Act 8:30 said, Understandest thou what thou r? G314

READETH
Hab 2: 2 upon tables, that he may run that r it. H7121
Mt 24:15 place, (whoso r, let him understand:) G314
Mk 13:14 not, (let him that r understand,) then let G314
Rev 1: 3 Blessed *is* he that r, and they that hear G314

READINESS
Act 17:11 the word with all r of mind, and G4288
2Co 8:11 *it*; that as *there was* a r to will, so *there* G4288
10: 6 And having in a r to revenge all G2092

READING
Neh 8: 8 and caused *them* to understand the r. H4744
Jer 36: 8 commanded him, r in the book the H7121
51:63 made an end of r this book, *that* thou H7121
Act 13:15 And after the r of the law and the G320
2Co 3:14 away in the r of the old testament; G320
1Ti 4:13 Till I come, give attendance to r, to G320

READY
Gen 18: 6 Sarah, and said, Make r quickly three H4116
43:16 slay, and make r; for *these* men shall H3559
25 And they made r the present against H3559
46:29 And Joseph made r his chariot, and H631
Ex 14: 6 And he made r his chariot, and took his H631
17: 4 people? they be almost r to stone me. H5750
19:11 And be r against the third day: for the H3559
15 And he said unto the people, Be r H3559
34: 2 And be r in the morning, and come up H3559
Nu 32:17 But we ourselves will go r armed before H2363
Dt 1:41 of war, ye were r to go up into the hill. H1951
26: 5 thy God, A Syrian r to perish *was* my
Jos 8: 4 very far from the city, but be ye all r: H3559
Jdg 6:19 And Gideon went in, and made r a kid, H6213
13:15 we shall have made r a kid for thee. H6213
1Sa 25:18 wine, and five sheep r dressed, and five
2Sa 15:15 thy servants *are r to do* whatsoever my
18:22 son, seeing that thou hast no tidings r? H4672
1Ki 6: 7 of stone made r before it was brought H8003
2Ki 9:21 And Joram said, Make r. And his chariot H631
21 chariot was made r. And Joram king of H631
1Ch 12:23 bands *that were* r armed to the war, *and*
24 and eight hundred, r armed to the war.
28: 2 God, and had made r for the building: H3559
2Ch 17:18 thousand r prepared for the war.
35:14 And afterward they made r for H3559
Ezr 7: 6 and he *was* a r scribe in the law of H4106
Neh 9:17 but thou *art* a God r to pardon, gracious
Est 3:14 that they should be r against that day. H6264
8:13 the Jews should be r against that day to H6264
Job 3: 8 who are r to raise up their mourning. H6264
12: 5 He that is r to slip with *his* feet *is as* a H3559
15:23 the day of darkness is r at his hand. H3559
24 against him, as a king r to the battle. H6264
28 which are r to become heaps. H6257
17: 1 days are extinct, the graves *are r* for me.
18:12 and destruction *shall be* r at his side. H3559
29:13 The blessing of him that was r to perish
32:19 no vent; it is r to burst like new bottles.
Ps 7:12 he hath bent his bow, and made it r. H3559
11: 2 bow, they make r their arrow upon the H3559
21:12 thou shalt make r *thine arrows* upon H3559
38:17 For I *am* r to halt, and my sorrow *is* H3559
45: 1 king: my tongue *is* the pen of a r writer. H4106
86: 5 For thou, Lord, *art* good, and r to
88:15 I *am* afflicted and r to die from *my*
Prv 24:11 death, and *those that are* r to be slain; H4131
31: 6 Give strong drink unto him that is r to
Ecc 5: 1 of God, and be more r to hear, than to H7138
Isa 27:13 come which were r to perish in the land
30:13 to you as a breach r to fall, swelling out
32: 4 stammerers shall be r to speak plainly. H4116
38:20 The LORD *was* r to save me: therefore
41: 7 anvil, saying, It *is* r for the sodering: H2896
51:13 as if he were r to destroy? and where H3559
Ezk 7:14 even to make all r; but none goeth to H3559
Dan 3:15 Now if ye be r that at what time ye hear H6263
Hos 7: 6 For they have made r their heart like H7126
Mt 22: 4 things *are* r: come unto the marriage. G2092
8 The wedding is r, but they which were G2092
24:44 Therefore be ye also r: for in such an G2092
25:10 and they that were r went in with him G2092
26:19 them; and they made r the passover. G2090
Mk 14:15 *and* prepared: there make r for us. G2090
16 them: and they made r the passover. G2090
38 spirit truly *is* r, but the flesh *is* weak. G4289
Lk 1:17 make r a people prepared for the Lord. G2090
7: 2 dear unto him, was sick, and r to die. G3195
9:52 of the Samaritans, to make r for him. G2090
12:40 Be ye therefore r also: for the Son of G2092
14:17 bidden, Come; for all things are now r. G2092
17: 8 say unto him, Make r wherewith I may G2090
22:12 upper room furnished: there make r. G2090
13 them: and they made r the passover. G2090
33 And he said unto him, Lord, I am r to G2092
Jn 7: 6 not yet come: but your time is alway r. G2092
Act 10:10 while they made r, he fell into a trance, G3903
20: 7 unto them, r to depart on the morrow; G3195
21:13 heart? for I am r not to be bound only, G2093
23:15 or ever he come near, are r to kill him. G2092
21 they r, looking for a promise from thee. G2092
23 saying, Make r two hundred soldiers G2090
Ro 1:15 So, as much as in me is, I am r to G4289
2Co 8:19 Lord, and *declaration of* your r mind: G4288

2Co 9: 2 that Achaia was r a year ago; and your G3903
3 this behalf; that, as I said, ye may be r: G3903
5 that the same might be r, as *a matter of* G2092
10:16 line of things made r to our hand. G2092
12:14 Behold, the third time I am r to come G2093
1Ti 6:18 r to distribute, willing to communicate; G2130
2Ti 4: 6 For I am now r to be offered, and the G4689
Tit 3: 1 to be r to every good work, G2092
Heb 8:13 and waxeth old *is* r to vanish away. G1451
1Pt 1: 5 r to be revealed in the last time. G2092
3:15 your hearts: and *be* r always to *give* an G2092
4: 5 Who shall give account to him that is r G2093
5: 2 not for filthy lucre, but of a r mind; G4289
Rev 3: 2 remain, that are r to die: for I have not G3195
12: 4 woman which was r to be delivered, for G3195
19: 7 come, and his wife hath made herself r. G2090

REAIA
1Ch 5: 5 Micah his son, R his son, Baal his son, H7211

REAIAH
1Ch 4: 2 And R the son of Shobal begat Jahath; H7211
Ezr 2:47 the children of Gahar, the children of R, H7211
Neh 7:50 The children of R, the children of Rezin, H7211

REALM
2Ch 20:30 So the r of Jehoshaphat was quiet: for H4438
Ezr 7:13 and Levites, in my r, which are minded H4437
23 against the r of the king and his sons? H4437
Dan 1:20 *and* astrologers that *were* in all his r. H4438
6: 3 thought to set him over the whole r. H4437
9: 1 made king over the r of the Chaldeans; H4438
11: 2 shall stir up all against the r of Grecia. H4438

REAP
Lev 19: 9 And when ye r the harvest of your land, H7114
9 shalt not wholly r the corners of thy H7114
23:10 you, and shall r the harvest thereof, H7114
22 And when ye r the harvest of your land, H7114
25: 5 thou shalt not r, neither gather the H7114
11 not sow, neither r that which groweth H7114
Ru 2: 9 field that they do r, and go thou after H7114
1Sa 8:12 his ground, and to r his harvest, and to H7114
2Ki 19:29 year sow ye, and r, and plant vineyards, H7114
Job 4: 8 and sow wickedness, r the same. H7114
24: 6 They r *every one* his corn in the field: H7114
Ps 126: 5 They that sow in tears shall r in joy. H7114
Prv 22: 8 He that soweth iniquity shall r vanity: H7114
Ecc 11: 4 he that regardeth the clouds shall not r. H7114
Isa 37:30 year sow ye, and r, and plant vineyards, H7114
Jer 12:13 They have sown wheat, but shall r H7114
Hos 8: 7 and they shall r the whirlwind: it hath H7114
10:12 Sow to yourselves in righteousness, r in H7114
Mic 6:15 Thou shalt sow, but thou shalt not r; H7114
Mt 6:26 neither do they r, nor gather into barns; G2325
25:26 knewest that I r where I sowed not, G2325
Lk 12:24 neither sow nor r; which neither have G2325
Jn 4:38 I sent you to r that whereon ye G2325
1Co 9:11 thing if we shall r your carnal things? G2325
2Co 9: 6 sparingly shall r also sparingly; and G2325
6 bountifully shall r also bountifully. G2325
Gal 6: 7 a man soweth, that shall he also r. G2325
8 shall of the flesh r corruption; but he G2325
8 shall of the Spirit r life everlasting. G2325
9 in due season we shall r, if we faint not. G2325
Rev 14:15 in thy sickle, and r: for the time is come G2325
15 to r; for the harvest of the earth is ripe. G2325

REAPED
Hos 10:13 Ye have plowed wickedness, ye have r H7114
Jas 5: 4 who have r down your fields, which G270
4 them which have r are entered into the G2325
Rev 14:16 sickle on the earth; and the earth was r. G2325

REAPER
Am 9:13 shall overtake the r, and the treader of H7114

REAPERS
Ru 2: 3 the field after the r: and her hap was to H7114
4 and said unto the r, The LORD *be* with H7114
5 set over the r, Whose damsel *is* this? H7114
6 And the servant that was set over the r H7114
7 gather after the r among the sheaves: H7114
14 she sat beside the r: and he reached her H7114
2Ki 4:18 that he went out to his father to the r. H7114
Mt 13:30 I will say to the r, Gather ye together G2327
39 of the world; and the r are the angels. G2327

REAPEST
Lev 23:22 thy field when thou r, neither shalt thou H7114
Lk 19:21 down, and r that thou didst not sow. G2325

REAPETH
Isa 17: 5 the corn, and r the ears with his arm; H7114
Jn 4:36 And he that r receiveth wages, and G2325
36 and he that r may rejoice together. G2325
37 saying true, One soweth, and another r. G2325

REAPING
1Sa 6:13 And *they of* Beth-shemesh *were* r their H7114
Mt 25:24 art an hard man, r where thou hast not G2325
Lk 19:22 laid not down, and r that I did not sow: G2325

REAR
Ex 26:30 And thou shalt r up the tabernacle H6965
Lev 26: 1 image, neither r you up a standing H6965
2Sa 24:18 unto him, Go up, r an altar unto the H6965
Jn 2:20 and wilt thou r it up in three days? G1453

REARED
Ex 40:17 month, *that* the tabernacle was r up. H6965
18 And Moses r up the tabernacle, and H6965
18 in the bars thereof, and r up his pillars. H6965
33 And he r up the court round about the H6965
Nu 9:15 tabernacle was r up the cloud covered H6965
2Sa 18:18 had taken and r up for himself a pillar, H5324
1Ki 16:32 And he r up an altar for Baal in the H6965
2Ki 21: 3 destroyed; and he r up altars for Baal, H6965
2Ch 3:17 And he r up the pillars before the H6965
33: 3 down, and he r up altars for Baalim, H6965

REARWARD
Nu 10:25 *which was* the r of all the camps H622
Jos 6: 9 trumpets, and the r came after the ark, H622
13 them; but the r came after the ark of H622
1Sa 29: 2 his men passed on in the r with Achish. H314
Isa 52:12 you; and the God of Israel *will be* your r. H622
58: 8 thee; the glory of the LORD shall be thy r. H622

REASON
Gen 41:31 known in the land by r of that famine H6440
47:13 of Canaan fainted by r of the famine. H6440
Ex 2:23 of Israel sighed by r of the bondage, H4480
23 came up unto God by r of the bondage. H4480
3: 7 have heard their cry by r of their H6440
8:24 corrupted by r of the swarm *of flies*. H6440
Nu 9:10 shall be unclean by r of a dead body, or
18: 8 I given them by r of the anointing, and
32 And ye shall bear no sin by r of it, when H5921
Dt 5: 5 ye were afraid by r of the fire, and went H6440
23:10 that is not clean by r of uncleanness that
Jos 9:13 become old by r of the very long journey.
Jdg 2:18 of their groanings by r of them that
1Sa 12: 7 Now therefore stand still, that I may r H8199
1Ki 9:15 And this *is* the r of the levy which king H1697
14: 4 see; for his eyes were set by r of his age. H1697
2Ch 5:14 to minister by r of the cloud: for the H6440
20:15 afraid nor dismayed by r of this great H6440
21:15 fall out by r of the sickness day by day. H4480
19 bowels fell out by r of his sickness: so H5973
Job 6:16 Which are blackish by r of the ice, *and* H4480
9:14 *and* choose out my words *to* r with him?
13: 3 Almighty, and I desire to r with God. H3198
15: 3 Should he r with unprofitable talk? or H3198
17: 7 Mine eye also is dim by r of sorrow, and
31:23 by r of his highness I could not endure.
35: 9 By r of the multitude of oppressions they
9 cry out by r of the arm of the mighty.
37:19 order *our speech* by r of darkness. H6440
41:25 by r of breakings they purify themselves.
Ps 38: 8 by r of the disquietness of my heart.
44:16 by r of the enemy and avenger. H6440
78:65 a mighty man that shouteth by r of wine.
88: 9 Mine eye mourneth by r of affliction: H4480
90:10 and ten; and if by r of strength *they be*
102: 5 By r of the voice of my groaning my
Prv 20: 4 The sluggard will not plow by r of the
26:16 than seven men that can render a r. H2940
Ecc 7:25 out wisdom, and the r *of things*, and to H2808
Isa 1:18 Come now, and let us r together, saith H3198
49:19 be too narrow by r of the inhabitants,
Ezk 19:10 full of branches by r of many waters.
21:12 of Israel: terrors by r of the sword shall H413
26:10 By r of the abundance of his horses their
27:12 Tarshish *was* thy merchant by r of the
16 Syria *was* thy merchant by r of the
28:17 thy wisdom by r of thy brightness: I H5921
Dan 4:36 At the same time my r returned unto H4486
5:10 *Now* the queen, by r of the words of the H6903
8:12 daily *sacrifice* by r of transgression, and
Jna 2: 2 And said, I cried by r of mine affliction
Mic 2:12 great noise by r of *the multitude of* men.
Mt 16: 8 ye of little faith, why r ye among G1260
Mk 2: 8 Why r ye these things in your hearts? G1260
8:17 unto them, Why r ye, because ye have G1260
Lk 5:21 began to r, saying, Who is this G1260
22 unto them, What r ye in your hearts? G1260
Jn 6:18 And the sea arose by r of a great wind
12:11 Because that by r of him many of the G1223
Act 6: 2 and said, It is not r that we should leave G701
18:14 r would that I should bear with you: G3056
Ro 8:20 not willingly, but by r of him who hath G1223
2Co 3:10 respect, by r of the glory that excelleth. G1752
Heb 5: 3 And by r hereof he ought, as for the G1223
14 *even* those who by r of use have their G1223
7:23 not suffered to continue by r of death:
1Pt 3:15 that asketh you a r of the hope that is G3056
2Pt 2: 2 ways; by r of whom the way of G1223
Rev 8:13 of the earth by r of the other voices of G1537
9: 2 darkened by r of the smoke of the pit. G1537
18:19 ships in the sea by r of her costliness! G1537

REASONABLE
Ro 12: 1 unto God, *which is* your r service. G3050

REASONED
Mt 16: 7 And they r among themselves, saying, G1260
21:25 or of men? And they r with themselves, G1260
Mk 2: 8 spirit that they so r within themselves, G1260
8:16 And they r among themselves, saying, G1260
11:31 And they r with themselves, saying, If G3049
Lk 20: 5 And they r with themselves, saying, If G4817
14 saw him, they r among themselves, G1260
24:15 *together* and r, Jesus himself drew near, G4802
Act 17: 2 days r with them out of the scriptures, G1256
18: 4 And he r in the synagogue every G1256
19 the synagogue, and r with the Jews. G1256
24:25 And as he r of righteousness, G1256

REASONING
Job 13: 6 Hear now my r, and hearken to the H8433
Mk 2: 6 sitting there, and r in their hearts, G1260
12:28 heard them r together, and perceiving G4802
Lk 9:46 Then there arose a r among them, G1261
Act 28:29 and had great r among themselves. G4803

REASONS
Job 32:11 r, whilst ye searched out what to say. H8394
Isa 41:21 your strong r, saith the King of Jacob.

REBA
Nu 31: 8 and Zur, and Hur, and R, five kings of H7254
Jos 13:21 Zur, and Hur, and R, *which were* dukes H7254

REBECCA
Ro 9:10 And not only *this*; but when R also had G4479

REBEKAH
Gen 22:23 And Bethuel begat R: these eight Milcah H7259
24:15 that, behold, R came out, who was H7259
29 And R had a brother, and his name H7259
30 the words of R his sister, saying, Thus H7259
45 heart, behold, R came forth with her H7259
51 Behold, R *is* before thee, take *her*, and H7259
53 and gave *them* to R: he gave also to her H7259
58 And they called R, and said unto her, H7259
59 And they sent away R their sister, and H7259
60 And they blessed R, and said unto her, H7259
61 And R arose, and her damsels, and H7259
61 the servant took R, and went his way. H7259
64 And R lifted up her eyes, and when she H7259
67 tent, and took R, and she became his H7259
25:20 years old when he took R to wife, the H7259
21 of him, and R his wife conceived. H7259
28 eat of *his* venison: but R loved Jacob. H7259
26: 7 R; because she *was* fair to look upon. H7259
8 Isaac *was* sporting with R his wife. H7259
35 a grief of mind unto Isaac and to R. H7259
27: 5 And R heard when Isaac spake to Esau H7259
6 And R spake unto Jacob her son, H7259
11 And Jacob said to R his mother, H7259
15 And R took goodly raiment of her H7259
42 son were told to R: and she sent and H7259
46 And R said to Isaac, I am weary of my H7259
28: 5 of R, Jacob's and Esau's mother. H7259
49:31 R his wife; and there I buried Leah. H7259

REBEKAH'S
Gen 29:12 R son: and she ran and told her father. H7259
35: 8 But Deborah R nurse died, and she was H7259

REBEL
Nu 14: 9 Only r not ye against the LORD, neither H4775
Jos 1:18 Whosoever *he be* that doth r against H4784
22:16 ye might r this day against the LORD? H4775
18 it will be, *seeing* ye r to day against the H4775
19 among us: but r not against the LORD, H4775
19 the LORD, nor r against us, in building H4775
29 God forbid that we should r against the H4775
1Sa 12:14 obey his voice, and not r against the H4784
15 voice of the LORD, but r against the H4784
Neh 2:19 that ye do? will ye r against the king? H4775
6: 6 and the Jews think to r: for which cause H4775
Job 24:13 They are of those that r against the H4775
Isa 1:20 But if ye refuse and r, ye shall be H4784
Hos 7:14 corn and wine, *and* they r against me. H5493

REBELLED
Gen 14: 4 and in the thirteenth year they r. H4775
Nu 20:24 Israel, because ye r against my word at H4784
27:14 For ye r against my commandment in H4784
Dt 1:26 would not go up, but r against the H4784
43 would not hear, but r against the H4784
9:23 have given you; then ye r against the H4784
1Ki 12:19 So Israel r against the house of David H6586
2Ki 1: 1 Then Moab r against Israel after the H6586
3: 5 of Moab r against the king of Israel. H6586
7 king of Moab hath r against me: wilt H6586
18: 7 went forth: and he r against the king of H4775
24: 1 then he turned and r against him. H4775
20 Zedekiah r against the king of Babylon. H4775
2Ch 10:19 And Israel r against the house of David H6586
13: 6 is risen up, and hath r against his lord. H4775
36:13 And he also r against king H4775
Neh 9:26 disobedient, and r against thee, and H4775
Ps 5:10 for they have r against thee. H4784
105:28 dark; and they r not against his word. H4784
107:11 Because they r against the words of H4784
Isa 1: 2 children, and they have r against me. H6586
63:10 But they r, and vexed his holy Spirit: H4784
Jer 52: 3 Zedekiah r against the king of Babylon. H4775
Lam 1:18 The LORD is righteous; for I have r H4784
20 I have grievously r: abroad the sword H4784
3:42 We have transgressed and have r: thou H4784
Ezk 2: 3 nation that hath r against me: they and H4775
17:15 But he r against him in sending his H4775
20: 8 But they r against me, and would not H4784
13 But the house of Israel r against me in H4784
21 Notwithstanding the children r against H4784
Dan 9: 5 and have r, even by departing from H4775
9 though we have r against him; H4775
Hos 13:16 for she hath r against her God: they H4784

REBELLEST
2Ki 18:20 dost thou trust, that thou r against me? H4775
Isa 36: 5 dost thou trust, that thou r against me? H4775

REBELLION
Dt 31:27 For I know thy r, and thy stiff neck: H4805
Jos 22:22 know; if *it be* in r, or if in transgression H4777
1Sa 15:23 For r *is as* the sin of witchcraft, and H4805
Ezr 4:19 r and sedition have been made therein. H4776
Neh 9:17 their necks, and in their r appointed a H4805
Job 34:37 For he addeth r unto his sin, he H6588
Prv 17:11 An evil *man* seeketh only r: therefore a H4805
Jer 28:16 thou hast taught r against the LORD. H5627
29:32 he hath taught r against the LORD. H5627

REBELLIOUS
Dt 9: 7 ye have been r against the LORD. H4784
24 Ye have been r against the LORD from H4784
21:18 If a man have a stubborn and r son, H4784
20 *is* stubborn and r, he will not obey our H4784
31:27 day, ye have been r against the LORD; H4784
1Sa 20:30 of the perverse r *woman,* do not I know H4780
Ezr 4:12 building the r and the bad city, and H4779
15 that this city *is* a r city, and hurtful H4779
Ps 66: 7 let not the r exalt themselves. Selah. H5637
68: 6 chains: but the r dwell in a dry *land.* H5637
18 men; yea, *for* the r also, that the LORD H5637
78: 8 fathers, a stubborn and r generation; a H4784
Isa 1:23 Thy princes *are* r, and companions of H5637
30: 1 Woe to the r children, saith the LORD, H5637
9 That this *is* a r people, lying children, H4805
50: 5 I was not r, neither turned away back. H4784
65: 2 all the day unto a r people, which H5637
Jer 4:17 been r against me, saith the LORD. H4784
5:23 But this people hath a revolting and a r H4784
Ezk 2: 3 of Israel, to a r nation that hath H4775
5 (for they *are* a r house,) yet shall know H4805
6 at their looks, though they *be* a r house. H4805
7 they will forbear: for they *are* most r. H4805
8 thee; Be not thou r like that rebellious H4805
8 rebellious like that r house: open thy H4805
3: 9 at their looks, though they *be* a r house. H4805
26 them a reprover: for they *are* a r house. H4805
27 let him forbear: for they *are* a r house. H4805
12: 2 in the midst of a r house, which have H4805
2 and hear not: for they *are* a r house. H4805
3 will consider, though they *be* a r house. H4805
9 of Israel, the r house, said unto thee, H4805
25 for in your days, O r house, will I say H4805
17:12 Say now to the r house, Know ye not H4805
24: 3 And utter a parable unto the r house, H4805
44: 6 And thou shalt say to the r, *even* to the H4805

REBELS
Nu 17:10 token against the r; and thou shalt quite H4805
20:10 Hear now, ye r; must we fetch you water H4784
Ezk 20:38 from among you the r, and them that H4775

REBUKE
Lev 19:17 shalt in any wise r thy neighbour, and H3198
Dt 28:20 vexation, and r, in all that thou settest H4045
Ru 2:16 that she may glean *them,* and r her not. H1605
2Ki 19: 3 of trouble, and of r, and blasphemy: for H8433
1Ch 12:17 of our fathers look *thereon,* and r *it.* H3198
Ps 6: 1 O LORD, r me not in thine anger, H3198
18:15 were discovered at thy r, O LORD, at the H1606
38: 1 O LORD, r me not in thy wrath: neither H3198
68:30 R the company of spearmen, the H1605
76: 6 At thy r, O God of Jacob, both the H1606
80:16 they perish at the r of thy countenance. H1606
104: 7 At thy r they fled; at the voice of thy H1606
Prv 9: 8 r a wise man, and he will love thee. H3198
13: 1 instruction: but a scorner heareth not r. H1606
8 his riches: but the poor heareth not r. H1606
24:25 But to them that r *him* shall be delight, H3198
27: 5 Open r *is* better than secret love. H8433
Ecc 7: 5 *It is* better to hear the r of the wise, H1606
Isa 2: 4 nations, and shall r many people: and H3198
17:13 but *God* shall r them, and they shall H1605
25: 8 all faces; and the r of his people shall H2781
30:17 One thousand *shall flee* at the r of one; H1606
17 of one; at the r of five shall ye flee: H1606
37: 3 of trouble, and of r, and of blasphemy: H8433
50: 2 behold, at my r I dry up the sea, I make H1606
51:20 the fury of the LORD, the r of thy God. H1606
54: 9 not be wroth with thee, nor r thee. H1605
66:15 with fury, and his r with flames of fire. H1606
Jer 15:15 know that for thy sake I have suffered r. H2781
Hos 5: 9 in the day of r: among the tribes of H8433
Mic 4: 3 many people, and r strong nations afar H3198
Zec 3: 2 Satan, The LORD r thee, O Satan; even H1605
2 chosen Jerusalem r thee: *is* not this a H1605
Mal 3:11 And I will r the devourer for your H1605
Mt 16:22 Then Peter took him, and began to r G2008
Mk 8:32 Peter took him, and began to r him. G2008
Lk 17: 3 r him; and if he repent, forgive him. G2008
19:39 said unto him, Master, r thy disciples. G2008
Php 2:15 sons of God, without r, in the midst of a G298
1Ti 5: 1 R not an elder, but entreat *him* as a G1969
20 Them that sin r before all, that others G1651
2Ti 4: 2 of season; reprove, r, exhort with all G2008
Tit 1:13 This witness is true. Wherefore r them G1651
2:15 These things speak, and exhort, and r G1651
Jude 9 accusation, but said, The Lord r thee. G2008
Rev 3:19 As many as I love, I r and chasten: be G1651

REBUKED
Gen 31:42 of my hands, and r *thee* yesternight. H3198
37:10 and his father r him, and said unto H1605
Neh 5: 7 Then I consulted with myself, and I r H7378
Ps 9: 5 Thou hast r the heathen, thou hast H1605
106: 9 He r the Red sea also, and it was dried H1605
119:21 Thou hast r the proud *that are* cursed, H1605
Mt 8:26 he arose, and r the winds and the sea; G2008
17:18 And Jesus r the devil; and he departed G2008
19:13 and pray: and the disciples r them. G2008
20:31 And the multitude r them, because G2008
Mk 1:25 And Jesus r him, saying, Hold thy G2008
4:39 And he arose, and r the wind, and said G2008
8:33 on his disciples, he r Peter, saying, Get G2008
9:25 together, he r the foul spirit, saying G2008
10:13 *his* disciples r those that brought *them.* G2008
Lk 4:35 And Jesus r him, saying, Hold thy G2008
39 And he stood over her, and r the fever; G2008
8:24 he arose, and r the wind and the raging G2008
9:42 *him.* And Jesus r the unclean spirit, G2008
55 But he turned, and r them, and said, Ye G2008
18:15 when *his* disciples saw *it,* they r them. G2008
39 And they which went before r him, that G2008
23:40 But the other answering r him, saying, G2008
Heb 12: 5 Lord, nor faint when thou art r of him: G1651
2Pt 2:16 But was r for his iniquity: the dumb ass G1649

REBUKER
Hos 5: 2 though I *have been* a r of them all. H4148

REBUKES
Ps 39:11 When thou with r dost correct man for H8433
Ezk 5:15 in furious r. I the LORD have spoken *it.* H8433
25:17 them with furious r; and they shall H8433

REBUKETH
Prv 9: 7 r a wicked *man getteth* himself a blot. H3198
28:23 He that r a man afterwards shall find H3198
Am 5:10 They hate him that r in the gate, and H3198
Nah 1: 4 He r the sea, and maketh it dry, and H1605

REBUKING
2Sa 22:16 discovered, at the r of the LORD, at the H1606
Lk 4:41 of God. And he r *them* suffered them G2008

RECALL
Lam 3:21 This I r to my mind, therefore have I H7725

RECEIPT
Mt 9: 9 sitting at the r of custom: and he saith G5058
Mk 2:14 sitting at the r of custom, and said G5058
Lk 5:27 Levi, sitting at the r of custom: and he G5058

RECEIVE
Gen 4:11 to r thy brother's blood from thy hand; H3947
33:10 in thy sight, then r my present at my H3947
38:20 the Adullamite, to r *his* pledge from the H3947
Ex 27: 3 And thou shalt make his pans to r his H1878
29:25 And thou shalt r them of their hands, H3947
Nu 18:28 tithes, which ye r of the children of H3947
Dt 9: 9 into the mount to r the tables of stone, H3947
33: 3 thy feet; *every one* shall r of thy words. H5375
1Sa 10: 4 which thou shalt r of their hands. H3947
2Sa 18:12 Though I should r a thousand *shekels* H8254
1Ki 5: 9 and thou shalt r *them:* and thou shalt H5375
8:64 *was* too little to r the burnt offerings, H3557
2Ki 5:16 I stand, I will r none. And he urged H3947
26 *Is it* a time to r money, and to receive H3947
26 receive money, and to r garments, and H3947
12: 7 now therefore r no *more* money of your H3947
8 And the priests consented to r no *more* H3947
2Ch 7: 7 was not able to r the burnt offerings, H3557
Job 2:10 What? shall we r good at the hand of H6901
10 and shall we not r evil? In all this did H6901
22:22 R, I pray thee, the law from his mouth, H3947
27:13 *which* they shall r of the Almighty. H3947
Ps 6: 9 the LORD will r my prayer. H3947
24: 5 He shall r the blessing from the LORD, H5375
49:15 of the grave: for he shall r me. Selah. H3947
73:24 counsel, and afterward r me *to* glory. H3947
75: 2 When I shall r the congregation I will H3947
Prv 1: 3 To r the instruction of wisdom, justice, H3947
2: 1 My son, if thou wilt r my words, and H3947
4:10 Hear, O my son, and r my sayings; and H3947
8:10 R my instruction, and not silver; and H3947
10: 8 The wise in heart will r H3947
19:20 Hear counsel, and r instruction, that H6901
Isa 57: 6 offering. Should I r comfort in these? H5162
Jer 5: 3 have refused to r correction: they have H3947
9:20 and let your ear r the word of his H3947
17:23 they might not hear, nor r instruction. H3947
32:33 have not hearkened to r instruction. H3947
35:13 Will ye not r instruction to hearken H3947
Ezk 3:10 speak unto thee r in thine heart, and H3947
16:61 when thou shalt r thy sisters, thine H3947
36:30 field, that ye shall r no more reproach H3947
Dan 2: 6 thereof, ye shall r of me gifts and H6902
Hos 10: 6 Ephraim shall r shame, and Israel shall H3947
14: 2 all iniquity, and r *us* graciously: so will H3947
Mic 1:11 he shall r of you his standing. H3947
Zep 3: 7 fear me, thou wilt r instruction; so their H3947
Mal 3:10 *there shall* not *be room* enough *to* r *it.*
Mt 10:14 And whosoever shall not r you, nor G1209
41 of a prophet shall r a prophet's reward; G2983
41 man shall r a righteous man's reward. G2983

Mt 11: 5 The blind **r** their sight, and the lame G308
14 And if ye will **r** *it*, this is Elias, which G1209
18: 5 And whoso shall **r** one such little child G1209
19:11 All *men* cannot **r** this saying, save *they* G5562
12 He that is able to **r** *it*, let him receive *it*. G5562
12 He that is able to receive *it*, let him **r** *it*. G5562
29 name's sake, shall **r** an hundredfold, G2983
20: 7 and whatsoever is right, *that* shall ye **r**. G2983
21:22 shall ask in prayer, believing, ye shall **r**. G2983
34 that they might **r** the fruits of it. G2983
23:14 ye shall **r** the greater damnation. G2983
Mk 2: 2 there was no room to **r** *them*, no, not so G5562
4:16 word, immediately **r** it with gladness; G2983
20 the word, and **r** *it*, and bring forth fruit, G3858
6:11 And whosoever shall not **r** you, nor G1209
9:37 Whosoever shall **r** one of such children G1209
37 whosoever shall **r** me, receiveth not G1209
10:15 shall not **r** the kingdom of God G1209
30 But he shall **r** an hundredfold now in G2983
51 unto him, Lord, that I might **r** my sight. G308
11:24 that ye **r** *them*, and ye shall have *them*. G2983
12: 2 that he might **r** from the husbandmen G2983
40 these shall **r** greater damnation. G2983
Lk 6:34 whom ye hope to **r**, what thank have ye? G618
34 also lend to sinners, to **r** as much again. G618
8:13 when they hear, **r** the word with joy; G1209
9: 5 And whosoever will not **r** you, when ye G1209
48 And said unto them, Whosoever shall **r** G1209
48 whosoever shall **r** me receiveth him G1209
53 And they did not **r** him, because his G1209
10: 8 city ye enter, and they **r** you, eat such G1209
10 ye enter, and they **r** you not, go your G1209
16: 4 they may **r** me into their houses. G1209
9 may **r** you into everlasting habitations. G1209
18:17 shall not **r** the kingdom of God G1209
30 Who shall not **r** manifold more in this G618
41 And he said, Lord, that I may **r** my sight. G308
42 And Jesus said unto him, **R** thy sight: thy G308
19:12 **r** for himself a kingdom, and to return. G2983
20:47 the same shall **r** greater damnation. G2983
23:41 And we indeed justly; for we **r** the due G618
Jn 3:11 we have seen; and ye **r** not our witness. G2983
27 John answered and said, A man can **r** G2983
5:34 But I **r** not testimony from man: but G2983
41 I **r** not honour from men. G2983
43 name, and ye **r** me not: if another shall G2983
43 come in his own name, him ye will **r**. G2983
44 How can ye believe, which **r** honour G2983
7:23 If a man on the sabbath day **r** G2983
39 on him should **r**: for the Holy Ghost was G2983
14: 3 will come again, and **r** you unto myself; G3880
17 the world cannot **r**, because it seeth him G2983
16:14 He shall glorify me: for he shall **r** of G2983
24 and ye shall **r**, that your joy may be full. G2983
20:22 saith unto them, **R** ye the Holy Ghost: G2983
Act 1: 8 But ye shall **r** power, after that the Holy G2983
2:38 and ye shall **r** the gift of the Holy Ghost. G2983
3: 5 expecting to **r** something of them. G2983
21 Whom the heaven must **r** until the G1209
7:59 and saying, Lord Jesus, **r** my spirit. G1209
8:15 them, that they might **r** the Holy Ghost: G2983
19 I lay hands, he may **r** the Holy Ghost. G2983
9:12 hand on him, that he might **r** his sight. G308
17 that thou mightest **r** thy sight, and be G308
10:43 in him shall **r** remission of sins. G2983
16:21 to **r**, neither to observe, being Romans. G3858
18:27 the disciples to **r** him: who, when he was G588
20:35 said, It is more blessed to give than to **r**. G2983
22:13 me, Brother Saul, **r** thy sight. And the G308
18 will not **r** thy testimony concerning me. G3858
26:18 that they may **r** forgiveness of sins, G2983
Ro 5:17 more they which **r** abundance of grace G2983
13: 2 resist shall **r** to themselves damnation. G2983
14: 1 Him that is weak in the faith **r** ye, *but* G4355
15: 7 Wherefore **r** ye one another, as Christ G4355
16: 2 That ye **r** her in the Lord, as becometh G4327
1Co 3: 8 and every man shall **r** his own reward G2983
14 built thereupon, he shall **r** a reward. G2983
4: 7 that thou didst not **r**? now if thou didst G2983
7 now if thou didst **r** *it*, why dost thou G2983
14: 5 that the church may **r** edifying. G2983
2Co 5:10 every one may **r** the things *done* in *his* G2865
6: 1 that ye **r** not the grace of God in vain. G1209
17 not the unclean *thing*; and I will **r** you, G1523
7: 2 **R** us; we have wronged no man, we G5562
9 ye might **r** damage by us in nothing. G2210
8: 4 that we would **r** the gift, and *take upon* G1209
11: 4 not preached, or *if* ye **r** another spirit, G2983
16 **r** me, that I may boast myself a little. G1209
Gal 3:14 that we might **r** the promise of the G2983
4: 5 that we might **r** the adoption of sons. G618
Eph 6: 8 doeth, the same shall he **r** of the Lord, G2865
Php 2:29 **R** him therefore in the Lord with all G4327
Col 3:24 Knowing that of the Lord ye shall **r** the G618
25 But he that doeth wrong shall **r** for the G2865
4:10 if he come unto you, **r** him;) G1209
1Ti 5:19 Against an elder **r** not an accusation, G3858
Phlm 12 **r** him, that is, mine own bowels: G4355
15 that thou shouldest **r** him for ever; G568
17 If thou count me therefore a partner, **r** G4355
Heb 7: 5 the sons of Levi, who **r** the office of the G2983
8 And here men that die **r** tithes; but G2983
9:15 **r** the promise of eternal inheritance. G2983
10:36 the will of God, ye might **r** the promise. G2865
11: 8 he should after **r** for an inheritance, G2983
Jas 1: 7 that he shall **r** any thing of the Lord. G2983
12 he is tried, he shall **r** the crown of life, G2983
21 naughtiness, and **r** with meekness the G1209
3: 1 we shall **r** the greater condemnation. G2983
4: 3 Ye ask, and **r** not, because ye ask G2983
5: 7 it, until he **r** the early and latter rain. G2983
1Pt 5: 4 appear, ye shall **r** a crown of glory that G2865
2Pt 2:13 And shall **r** the reward of G2865
1Jn 3:22 And whatsoever we ask, we **r** of him, G2983
5: 9 If we **r** the witness of men, the witness G2983
2Jn 8 wrought, but that we **r** a full reward. G618
10 not this doctrine, **r** him not into *your* G2983
3Jn 8 We therefore ought to **r** such, that we G618
10 doth he himself **r** the brethren, and G1926
Rev 4:11 Thou art worthy, O Lord, to **r** glory and G2983
5:12 that was slain to **r** power, and riches, G2983
13:16 free and bond, to **r** a mark in their G1325
14: 9 and his image, and **r** *his* mark in his G2983
17:12 as yet; but **r** power as kings one G2983
18: 4 sins, and that ye **r** not of her plagues. G2983

RECEIVED

Gen 26:12 Then Isaac sowed in that land, and **r** in H4672
Ex 32: 4 And he **r** *them* at their hand, and H3947
36: 3 And they **r** of Moses all the offering, H3947
Nu 12:14 days, and after that let her be **r** in *again*. H622
23:20 Behold, I have **r** *commandment* to H3947
34:14 their fathers, have **r** *their inheritance*; H3947
14 of Manasseh have **r** their inheritance: H3947
15 The two tribes and the half tribe have **r** H3947
36: 3 they are **r**: so shall it be taken from H1961
4 they are **r**: so shall their inheritance H1961
Jos 13: 8 the Gadites have **r** their inheritance, H3947
18: 2 which had not yet **r** their inheritance. H2505
7 of Manasseh, have **r** their inheritance H3947
Jdg 13:23 he would not have **r** a burnt offering H3947
1Sa 12: 3 whose hand have I **r** *any* bribe to blind H3947
25:35 So David **r** of her hand *that* which she H3947
1Ki 10:28 merchants **r** the linen yarn at a price. H3947
2Ki 19:14 And Hezekiah **r** the letter of the hand H3947
1Ch 12:18 thee. Then David **r** them, and made H6901
2Ch 1:16 merchants **r** the linen yarn at a price. H3947
4: 5 *and* it **r** and held three thousand baths. H2388
29:22 and the priests **r** the blood, and H6901
30:16 *which they* **r** of the hand of the Levites. H6901
Est 4: 4 his sackcloth from him: but he **r** *it* not. H6901
Job 4:12 to me, and mine ear **r** a little thereof. H3947
Ps 68:18 captive: thou hast **r** gifts for men; yea, H3947
Prv 24:32 I looked upon *it, and* **r** instruction. H3947
Isa 37:14 And Hezekiah **r** the letter from the H3947
40: 2 for she hath **r** of the LORD'S hand H3947
Jer 2:30 children; they **r** no correction: your H3947
Ezk 18:17 *that* hath not **r** usury nor increase, H3947
Zep 3: 2 She obeyed not the voice; she **r** not H3947
Mt 10: 8 out devils: freely ye have **r**, freely give. G2983
13:19 This is he which **r** seed by the way side. G4687
20 But he that **r** the seed into stony places, G4687
22 He also that **r** seed among the thorns is G4687
23 But he that **r** seed into the good ground G4687
17:24 they that **r** tribute *money* came G2983
20: 9 hour, they **r** every man a penny. G2983
10 that they should have **r** more; and they G2983
10 and they likewise **r** every man a penny. G2983
11 And when they had **r** *it*, they G2983
34 their eyes **r** sight, and they followed him. G308
25:16 Then he that had **r** the five talents went G2983
17 And likewise he that *had r* two, he also
18 But he that had **r** one went and digged G2983
20 And so he that had **r** five talents came G2983
22 He also that had **r** two talents came G2983
24 Then he which had **r** the one talent G2983
27 I should have **r** mine own with usury. G2865
Mk 7: 4 be, which they have **r** to hold, *as* the G3880
10:52 immediately he **r** his sight, and followed G308
15:23 mingled with myrrh: but he **r** *it* not. G2983
16:19 unto them, he was **r** up into heaven, and G353
Lk 6:24 are rich! for ye have **r** your consolation. G568
8:40 **r** him: for they were all waiting for him. G588
9:11 him: and he **r** them, and spake unto G1209
51 that he should be **r** up, he stedfastly set G1209
10:38 named Martha **r** him into her house. G5264
15:27 because he hath **r** him safe and sound. G618
18:43 And immediately he **r** his sight, and
19: 6 and came down, and **r** him joyfully. G5264
15 returned, having **r** the kingdom, then G2983
Jn 1:11 He came unto his own, and his own **r** G3880
12 But as many as **r** him, to them gave he G2983
16 And of his fulness have all we **r**, and G2983
3:33 He that hath **r** his testimony hath set to G2983
4:45 the Galilaeans **r** him, having seen all G1209
6:21 Then they willingly **r** him into the ship: G2983
9:11 and I went and washed, and I **r** sight. G308
15 him how he had **r** his sight. He said unto G308
18 been blind, and **r** his sight, until they G308
18 the parents of him that had **r** his sight. G308
10:18 commandment have I **r** of my Father. G2983
13:30 He then having **r** the sop went G2983
17: 8 me; and they have **r** *them*, and have G2983
18: 3 Judas then, having **r** a band *of men* G2983
19:30 When Jesus therefore had **r** the G2983
Act 1: 9 up; and a cloud **r** him out of their sight. G5274
2:33 and having **r** of the Father the promise G2983
41 Then they that gladly **r** his word were G588
3: 7 his feet and ankle bones **r** strength. G4732
7:38 who **r** the lively oracles to give unto us: G1209
53 Who have **r** the law by the disposition G2983
8:14 that Samaria had **r** the word of God, G1209
17 on them, and they **r** the Holy Ghost. G2983
9:18 been scales: and he **r** sight forthwith, G308
19 And when he had **r** meat, he was G2983
10:16 the vessel was **r** up again into heaven. G353
47 have **r** the Holy Ghost as well as we? G2983
11: 1 the Gentiles had also **r** the word of God. G1209
15: 4 they were **r** of the church, and *of* G588
16:24 Who, having **r** such a charge, thrust G2983
17: 7 Whom Jason hath **r**: and these all do G5264
11 in that they **r** the word with all G1209
19: 2 He said unto them, Have ye **r** the Holy G2983
20:24 which I have **r** of the Lord Jesus, to G2983
21:17 to Jerusalem, the brethren **r** us gladly. G1209
22: 5 from whom also I **r** letters unto the G1209
26:10 in prison, having **r** authority from the G2983
28: 2 they kindled a fire, and **r** us every one, G4355
7 was Publius; who **r** us, and lodged us G324
21 And they said unto him, We neither **r** G1209
30 house, and **r** all that came in unto him, G588
Ro 1: 5 By whom we have **r** grace and G2983
4:11 And he **r** the sign of circumcision, a G2983
5:11 whom we have now **r** the atonement. G2983
8:15 For ye have not **r** the spirit of bondage G2983
15 to fear; but ye have **r** the Spirit of G2983
14: 3 him that eateth: for God hath **r** him. G4355
15: 7 as Christ also **r** us to the glory of God. G4355
1Co 2:12 Now we have **r**, not the spirit of the G2983
4: 7 thou glory, as if thou hadst not **r** *it*? G2983
11:23 For I have **r** of the Lord that which also G3880
15: 1 also ye have **r**, and wherein ye stand; G3880
3 that which I also **r**, how that Christ died G3880
2Co 4: 1 as we have **r** mercy, we faint not; G1653
7:15 how with fear and trembling ye **r** him. G1209
11: 4 which ye have not **r**, or another gospel, G2983
24 Of the Jews five times **r** I forty *stripes* G2983
Gal 1: 9 than that ye have **r**, let him be accursed. G3880
12 For I neither **r** it of man, neither was I G3880
3: 2 This only would I learn of you, **R** ye the G2983
4:14 nor rejected; but **r** me as an angel of G1209
Php 4: 9 both learned, and **r**, and heard, and G3880
18 I am full, having **r** of Epaphroditus the G1209
Col 2: 6 As ye have therefore **r** Christ Jesus the G3880
4:10 whom ye **r** commandments: if G2983
17 hast **r** in the Lord, that thou fulfil it. G3880
1Th 1: 6 of the Lord, having **r** the word in much G1209
2:13 because, when ye **r** the word of God G3880
13 ye heard of us, ye **r** *it* not *as* the word of G1209
4: 1 that as ye have **r** of us how ye ought to G3880
2Th 2:10 because they **r** not the love of the truth, G1209
3: 6 not after the tradition which he **r** of us. G3880
1Ti 3:16 believed on in the world, **r** up into glory. G353
4: 3 hath created to be **r** with thanksgiving G1519
4 be refused, if it be **r** with thanksgiving: G2983
Heb 2: 2 **r** a just recompence of reward; G2983
7: 6 from them **r** tithes of Abraham, G1183

Heb 7:11 it the people **r** the law,) what further G3549
10:26 after that we have **r** the knowledge of G2983
11:11 Through faith also Sara herself **r** G2983
13 These all died in faith, not having **r** the G2983
17 and he that had **r** the promises offered G324
19 from whence also he **r** him in a figure. G2865
31 when she had **r** the spies with peace. G1209
35 Women **r** their dead raised to life G2983
39 report through faith, **r** not the promise: G2865
Jas 2:25 when she had **r** the messengers, and G5264
1Pt 1:18 *r* by tradition from your fathers;
4:10 As every man hath **r** the gift, *even so* G2983
2Pt 1:17 For he **r** from God the Father honour G2983
1Jn 2:27 But the anointing which ye have **r** of G2983
2Jn 4 **r** a commandment from the Father. G2983
Rev 2:27 to shivers: even as I **r** of my Father. G2983
3: 3 Remember therefore how thou hast **r** G2983
17:12 kings, which have **r** no kingdom as yet; G2983
19:20 them that had **r** the mark of the beast, G2983
20: 4 neither had **r** *his* mark upon their G2983

RECEIVEDST
Lk 16:25 thou in thy lifetime **r** thy good things, G618

RECEIVER
Isa 33:18 **r**? where *is* he that counted the towers? H8254

RECEIVETH
Jdg 19:18 and there *is* no man that **r** me to house. H622
Job 35: 7 thou him? or what **r** he of thine hand? H3947
Prv 21:11 the wise is instructed, he **r** knowledge. H3947
29: 4 land: but he that **r** gifts overthroweth it.
Jer 7:28 their God, nor **r** correction: truth is H3947
Mal 2:13 or **r** *it* with good will at your hand. H3947
Mt 7: 8 For every one that asketh **r**; and he that G2983
10:40 He that **r** you receiveth me, and he that G1209
40 He that receiveth you **r** me, and he that G1209
40 that **r** me receiveth him that sent me. G1209
40 that receiveth me **r** him that sent me. G1209
41 He that **r** a prophet in the name of a G1209
41 and he that **r** a righteous man in G2983
13:20 the word, and anon with joy **r** it; G2983
18: 5 one such little child in my name **r** me. G1209
Mk 9:37 in my name, **r** me: and whosoever G1209
37 me, **r** not me, but him that sent me. G1209
Lk 9:48 child in my name **r** me: and whosoever G1209
48 shall receive me **r** him that sent me: for G1209
11:10 For every one that asketh **r**; and he that G2983
15: 2 man **r** sinners, and eateth with them. G4327
Jn 3:32 testifieth; and no man **r** his testimony. G2983
4:36 And he that reapeth **r** wages, and G2983
12:48 He that rejecteth me, and **r** not my G2983
13:20 Verily, verily, I say unto you, He that **r** G2983
20 I send **r** me; and he that receiveth G2983
20 that **r** me receiveth him that sent me. G2983
20 that receiveth me **r** him that sent me. G2983
1Co 2:14 But the natural man **r** not the things of G1209
9:24 **r** the prize? So run, that ye may obtain. G2983
Heb 6: 7 it is dressed, **r** blessing from God: G3335
7: 8 tithes; but there he **r** *them*, of whom it is
9 And as I may so say, Levi also, who **r** G2983
12: 6 and scourgeth every son whom he **r**. G3858
3Jn 9 the preeminence among them, **r** us not. G1926
Rev 2:17 no man knoweth saving he that **r** *it*. G2983
14:11 and whosoever **r** the mark of his name. G2983

RECEIVING
2Ki 5:20 this Syrian, in not **r** at his hands that H3947
Act 17:15 unto Athens: and **r** a commandment G2983
Ro 1:27 is unseemly, and **r** in themselves that G618
11:15 the **r** *of them be*, but life from the dead? G4356
Php 4:15 as concerning giving and **r**, but ye only. G3028
Heb 12:28 Wherefore we **r** a kingdom which G3880
1Pt 1: 9 **R** the end of your faith, *even* the G2865

RECHAB
2Sa 4: 2 the name of the other **R**, the sons of H7394
5 the Beerothite, **R** and Baanah, went, H7394
6 **R** and Baanah his brother escaped. H7394
9 And David answered **R** and Baanah his H7394
2Ki 10:15 the son of **R** *coming* to meet him: H7394
23 the son of **R**, into the house of Baal, H7394
1Ch 2:55 of Hemath, the father of the house of **R**. H7394
Neh 3:14 the son of **R**, the ruler of part of H7394
Jer 35: 6 the son of **R** our father commanded H7394
8 the son of **R** our father in all that H7394
14 The words of Jonadab the son of **R**, that H7394
16 the son of **R** have performed the H7394
19 the son of **R** shall not want a man H7394

RECHABITES
Jer 35: 2 Go unto the house of the **R**, and speak H7397
3 his sons, and the whole house of the **R**; H7397
5 of the house of the **R** pots full of wine, H7397
18 the house of the **R**, Thus saith the LORD H7397

RECHAH
1Ch 4:12 of Irnahash. These *are* the men of **R**. H7397

RECHOKIM See JONATH-ELEM-RECHOKIM.

RECKON
Lev 25:50 And he shall **r** with him that bought H2803
27:18 the priest shall **r** unto him the money H2803
23 Then the priest shall **r** unto him the H2803
Nu 4:32 by name ye shall **r** the instruments of H6485
Ezk 44:26 And after he is cleansed, they shall **r** H5608
Mt 18:24 And when he had begun to **r**, one was G4868
Ro 6:11 Likewise **r** ye also yourselves to be G3049
8:18 For I **r** that the sufferings of this G3049

RECKONED
Nu 18:27 And *this* your heave offering shall be **r** H2803
23: 9 and shall not be **r** among the nations. H2803
2Sa 4: 2 (for Beeroth also was **r** to Benjamin: H2803
2Ki 12:15 Moreover they **r** not with the men, into H2803
1Ch 5: 1 is not to be **r** after the birthright. H3187
7 **r**, *were* the chief, Jeiel, and Zechariah, H3187
17 All these were **r** by genealogies in the H3187
7: 5 valiant men of might, **r** in all by their H3187
7 valour; and were **r** by their genealogies H3187
9: 1 So all Israel were **r** by genealogies; and, H3187
22 twelve. These were **r** by their genealogy H3187
2Ch 31:19 **r** by genealogies among the Levites. H3187
Ezr 2:62 those that were **r** by genealogy, but H3187
8: 3 and with him were **r** by genealogy of H3187
Neh 7: 5 that they might be **r** by genealogy. And H3187
64 those that were **r** by genealogy, but it H3187
Ps 40: 5 they cannot be **r** up in order unto thee:
Isa 38:13 I **r** till morning, *that*, as a lion, so will H7737
Lk 22:37 in me, And he was **r** among the G3049
Ro 4: 4 is the reward not **r** of grace, but of debt. G3049
9 was **r** to Abraham for righteousness. G3049
10 How was it then **r**? when he was in G3049

RECKONETH
Mt 25:19 servants cometh, and **r** with them. G4868

RECKONING
2Ki 22: 7 Howbeit there was no **r** made with H2803
1Ch 23:11 one **r**, according to *their* father's house. H6486

RECOMMENDED
Act 14:26 they had been **r** to the grace of God G3860
15:40 **r** by the brethren unto the grace of God. G3860

RECOMPENCE
Dt 32:35 To me *belongeth* vengeance, and **r**; H8005
Job 15:31 trust in vanity: for vanity shall be his **r**. H8545
Prv 12:14 *his* mouth: and the **r** of a man's hands H1576
Isa 35: 4 *with* a **r**; he will come and save you. H1576
59:18 to his adversaries, **r** to his enemies; to H1576
18 enemies; to the islands he will repay **r**. H1576
66: 6 LORD that rendereth **r** to his enemies. H1576
Jer 51: 6 vengeance; he will render unto her a **r**. H1576
Lam 3:64 Render unto them a **r**, O LORD, H1576
Hos 9: 7 are come, the days of **r** are come; Israel H7966
Joel 3: 4 ye render me a **r**? and if ye recompense H1576
4 I return your **r** upon your own head; H1576
7 will return your **r** upon your own head: H1576
Lk 14:12 bid thee again, and a **r** be made thee. G468
Ro 1:27 that **r** of their error which was meet. G489
11: 9 a stumblingblock, and a **r** unto them: G468
2Co 6:13 Now for a **r** in the same, (I speak as unto G489
Heb 2: 2 received a just **r** of reward; G3405
10:35 which hath great **r** of reward. G3405
11:26 he had respect unto the **r** of the reward. G3405

RECOMPENCES
Isa 34: 8 year of **r** for the controversy of Zion. H7966
Jer 51:56 the LORD God of **r** shall surely requite. H1578

RECOMPENSE
Nu 5: 7 done: and he shall **r** his trespass with H7725
8 But if the man have no kinsman to **r** H7725
Ru 2:12 The LORD **r** thy work, and a full H7999
2Sa 19:36 the king **r** it me with such a reward? H1580
Job 34:33 to thy mind? he will **r** it, whether thou H7999
Prv 20:22 Say not thou, I will **r** evil; *but* wait on H7999
Isa 65: 6 **r**, even recompense into their bosom, H7999
6 recompense, even **r** into their bosom, H7999
Jer 16:18 And first I will **r** their iniquity and their H7999
25:14 also: and I will **r** them according to H7999
50:29 thereof escape: **r** her according to her H7999
Ezk 7: 3 **r** upon thee all thine abominations. H5414
4 pity: but I will **r** thy ways upon thee, H5414
8 will **r** thee for all thine abominations. H5414
9 I have pity: I will **r** thee according to H5414
9:10 *but* I will **r** their way upon their head. H5414
11:21 I will **r** their way upon their H5414
16:43 I also will **r** thy way upon *thine* H5414
17:19 even it will I **r** upon his own head. H5414
23:49 And they shall **r** your lewdness upon H5414
Hos 12: 2 according to his doings will he **r** him. H7725
Joel 3: 4 and if ye **r** me, swiftly *and* speedily H1580
Lk 14:14 for they cannot **r** thee: for thou shalt be G467
Ro 12:17 **R** to no man evil for evil. Provide things G591
2Th 1: 6 to **r** tribulation to them that trouble you; G467
Heb 10:30 unto me, I will **r**, saith the Lord. And G467

RECOMPENSED
Nu 5: 8 let the trespass be **r** unto the LORD, H7725
2Sa 22:21 cleanness of my hands hath he **r** me. H7725
25 Therefore the LORD hath **r** me H7725
Ps 18:20 cleanness of my hands hath he **r** me. H7725
24 Therefore hath the LORD **r** me H7725
Prv 11:31 Behold, the righteous shall be **r** in the H7999
Jer 18:20 Shall evil be **r** for good? for they have H7999
Ezk 22:31 own way have I **r** upon their heads, H5414
Lk 14:14 shalt be **r** at the resurrection of the just. G467
Ro 11:35 to him, and it shall be **r** unto him again? G467

RECOMPENSEST
Jer 32:18 thousands, and **r** the iniquity of the H7999

RECOMPENSING
2Ch 6:23 the wicked, by **r** his way upon his own H5414

RECONCILE
Lev 6:30 the congregation to **r** *withal* in the holy H3722
1Sa 29: 4 should he **r** himself unto his master? H7521
Ezk 45:20 *that is* simple: so shall ye **r** the house. H3722
Eph 2:16 And that he might **r** both unto God in G604
Col 1:20 of his cross, by him to **r** all things unto G604

RECONCILED
Mt 5:24 thy way; first be **r** to thy brother, and G1259
Ro 5:10 enemies, we were **r** to God by the death G2644
10 being **r**, we shall be saved by his life. G2644
1Co 7:11 unmarried, or be **r** to *her* husband: and G2644
2Co 5:18 And all things *are* of God, who hath **r** G2644
20 *you* in Christ's stead, be ye **r** to God. G2644
Col 1:21 by wicked works, yet now hath he **r** G604

RECONCILIATION
Lev 8:15 and sanctified it, to make **r** upon it. H3722
2Ch 29:24 and they made **r** with their blood upon H2398
Ezk 45:15 make **r** for them, saith the Lord GOD. H3722
17 to make **r** for the house of Israel. H3722
Dan 9:24 sins, and to make **r** for iniquity, and to H3722
2Co 5:18 and hath given to us the ministry of **r**; G2643
19 hath committed unto us the word of **r**. G2643
Heb 2:17 to make **r** for the sins of the people. G2433

RECONCILING
Lev 16:20 And when he hath made an end of **r** H3722
Ro 11:15 For if the casting away of them *be* the **r** G2643
2Co 5:19 To wit, that God was in Christ, **r** the G2644

RECORD
Ex 20:24 in all places where I **r** my name I will H2142
Dt 30:19 I call heaven and earth to **r** this day H5749
31:28 heaven and earth to **r** against them. H5749
1Ch 16: 4 of the LORD, and to **r**, and to thank and H2142
Ezr 6: 2 a roll, and therein *was* a **r** thus written: H1799
Job 16:19 *is* in heaven, and my **r** *is* on high. H7717
Isa 8: 2 witnesses to **r**, Uriah the priest, and H5749
Jn 1:19 And this is the **r** of John, when the Jews G3141
32 And John bare **r**, saying, I saw the Spirit G3140
34 And I saw, and bare **r** that this is the G3140
8:13 **r** of thyself; thy record is not true. G3140
13 record of thyself; thy **r** is not true. G3141
14 them, Though I bear **r** of myself, *yet* my G3140
14 of myself, *yet* my **r** is true: for I know G3141
12:17 and raised him from the dead, bare **r**. G3140
19:35 And he that saw *it* bare **r**, and his G3140
35 bare record, and his **r** is true: and he G3141
Act 20:26 Wherefore I take you to **r** this day, that G3143

Ro 10: 2 For I bear them **r** that they have a zeal *G3140*
2Co 1:23 Moreover I call God for a **r** upon my *G3144*
8: 3 For to *their* power, I bear **r**, yea, and *G3140*
Gal 4:15 of? for I bear you **r**, that, if *it had been* *G3140*
Php 1: 8 For God is my **r**, how greatly I long after *G3144*
Col 4:13 For I bear him **r**, that he hath a great *G3140*
1Jn 5: 7 For there are three that bear **r** in *G3140*
10 not the **r** that God gave of his Son. *G3141*
11 And this is the **r**, that God hath given to *G3141*
3Jn 12 **r**; and ye know that our record is true. *G3140*
12 record; and ye know that our **r** is true. *G3141*
Rev 1: 2 Who bare **r** of the word of God, and of *G3140*

RECORDED
Neh 12:22 and Jaddua, *were* **r** chief of the fathers: H3789

RECORDER
2Sa 8:16 Jehoshaphat the son of Ahilud *was* **r**; H2142
20:24 Jehoshaphat the son of Ahilud *was* **r**: H2142
1Ki 4: 3 Jehoshaphat the son of Ahilud, the **r**. H2142
2Ki 18:18 scribe, and Joah the son of Asaph the **r**. H2142
37 the son of Asaph the **r**, to Hezekiah with H2142
1Ch 18:15 and Jehoshaphat the son of Ahilud, **r**. H2142
2Ch 34: 8 son of Joahaz the **r**, to repair the house H2142
Isa 36: 3 the scribe, and Joah, Asaph's son, the **r**. H2142
22 son of Asaph, the **r**, to Hezekiah with H2142

RECORDS
Ezr 4:15 in the book of the **r** of thy fathers: so H1799
15 in the book of the **r**, and know that this H1799
Est 6: 1 to bring the book of **r** of the chronicles; H2146

RECOUNT
Nah 2: 5 He shall **r** his worthies: they shall H2142

RECOVER
Jdg 11:26 did ye not **r** *them* within that time? H5337
1Sa 30: 8 overtake *them*, and without fail **r** *all*. H5337
2Sa 8: 3 to **r** his border at the river Euphrates. H7725
2Ki 1: 2 Ekron whether I shall **r** of this disease. H2421
5: 3 for he would **r** him of his leprosy. H622
6 that thou mayest **r** him of his leprosy. H622
7 send unto me to **r** a man of his leprosy? H622
11 his hand over the place, and **r** the leper. H622
8: 8 by him, saying, Shall I **r** of this disease? H2421
9 to thee, saying, Shall I **r** of this disease? H2421
10 mayest certainly **r**: howbeit the LORD H2421
14 He told me *that* thou shouldest surely **r**. H2421
2Ch 13:20 Neither did Jeroboam **r** strength again H6113
14:13 they could not **r** themselves; for they H4241
Ps 39:13 O spare me, that I may **r** strength, H1082
Isa 11:11 the second time to **r** the remnant of his H7069
38:16 so wilt thou **r** me, and make me to live. H2492
21 a plaister upon the boil, and he shall **r**. H2421
Hos 2: 9 thereof, and will **r** my wool and my flax H5337
Mk 16:18 lay hands on the sick, and they shall **r**. *G2573*
2Ti 2:26 And *that* they may **r** themselves out of *G366*

RECOVERED
1Sa 30:18 And David **r** all that the Amalekites H5337
19 they had taken to them: David **r** all. H7725
22 spoil that we have **r**, save to every man H5337
2Ki 13:25 beat him, and **r** the cities of Israel. H7725
14:28 and how he **r** Damascus, and Hamath, H7725
16: 6 At that time Rezin king of Syria **r** Elath H7725
20: 7 took and laid *it* on the boil, and he **r**. H2421
Isa 38: 9 been sick, and was **r** of his sickness: H2421
39: 1 heard that he had been sick, and was **r**. H2388
Jer 8:22 health of the daughter of my people **r**? H5927
41:16 whom he had **r** from Ishmael the son H7725

RECOVERING
Lk 4:18 the captives, and **r** of sight to the blind, *G309*

RED
Gen 25:25 And the first came out **r**, all over like an H132
30 with that same **r** *pottage*; for I *am* faint: H122
49:12 His eyes *shall be* **r** with wine, and his H2447
Ex 10:19 and cast them into the **R** sea; there H5488
13:18 the wilderness of the **R** sea: and the H5488
15: 4 captains also are drowned in the **R** sea. H5488
22 So Moses brought Israel from the **R** H5488
23:31 And I will set thy bounds from the **R** H5488
25: 5 And rams' skins dyed **r**, and badgers' H119
26:14 **r**, and a covering above *of* badgers' skins. H119
35: 7 And rams' skins dyed **r**, and badgers' H119
23 and goats' *hair*, and **r** skins of rams, and H119
36:19 *of* rams' skins dyed **r**, and a covering *of* H119
39:34 And the covering of rams' skins dyed **r**, H119
Nu 14:25 the wilderness by the way of the **R** sea. H5488
19: 2 they bring thee a **r** heifer without spot, H122
21: 4 by the way of the **R** sea, to compass the H5488
14 the **R** sea, and in the brooks of Arnon, H5492
33:10 from Elim, and encamped by the **R** sea. H5488
11 And they removed from the **R** sea, and H5488
Dt 1: 1 over against the **R** *sea*, between Paran, H5489
40 the wilderness by the way of the **R** sea. H5488
2: 1 by the way of the **R** sea, as the LORD H5488
11: 4 the water of the **R** sea to overflow them H5488
Jos 2:10 the water of the **R** sea for you, when ye H5488
4:23 God did to the **R** sea, which he dried H5488
24: 6 chariots and horsemen unto the **R** sea. H5488
Jdg 11:16 unto the **R** sea, and came to Kadesh; H5488
1Ki 9:26 shore of the **R** sea, in the land of Edom. H5488
2Ki 3:22 the water on the other side *as* **r** as blood: H122
Neh 9: 9 and heardest their cry by the **R** sea; H5488
Est 1: 6 a pavement of **r**, and blue, and white, H923
Ps 75: 8 and the wine is **r**; it is full of mixture; H5488
106: 7 *him* at the sea, *even* at the **R** sea. H5488
9 He rebuked the **R** sea also, and it was H5488
22 Ham, *and* terrible things by the **R** sea. H5488
136:13 To him which divided the **R** sea into H5488
15 **R** sea: for his mercy *endureth* for ever. H5488
Prv 23:31 Look not thou upon the wine when it is **r**, H119
Isa 1:18 be **r** like crimson, they shall be as wool. H119
27: 2 sing ye unto her, A vineyard of **r** wine. H119
63: 2 Wherefore *art thou* **r** in thine apparel, H122
Jer 49:21 noise thereof was heard in the **R** sea. H5488
Nah 2: 3 The shield of his mighty men is made **r**, H119
Zec 1: 8 man riding upon a **r** horse, and he stood H122
8 *were there* **r** horses, speckled, and white. H122
6: 2 In the first chariot *were* **r** horses; and in H122
Mt 16: 2 *It will be* fair weather: for the sky is **r**. *G4449*
3 day: for the sky is **r** and lowring. O *ye* *G4449*
Act 7:36 of Egypt, and in the **R** sea, and in the *G2063*
Heb 11:29 By faith they passed through the **R** sea *G2063*
Rev 6: 4 horse *that was* **r**: and power was given *G4450*
12: 3 and behold a great **r** dragon, having *G4450*

REDDISH
Lev 13:19 **r**, and it be shewed to the priest; H125
24 white bright spot, somewhat **r**, or white; H125
42 forehead, a white **r** sore; it *is* a leprosy H125
43 of the sore *be* white **r** in his bald head, or H125
49 And if the plague be greenish or **r** in the H125
14:37 **r**, which in sight *are* lower than the wall; H125

REDEEM
Ex 6: 6 and I will **r** you with a stretched H1350
13:13 an ass thou shalt **r** with a lamb; and if H6299
13 and if thou wilt not **r** it, then thou shalt H6299
13 of man among thy children shalt thou **r**. H6299
15 but all the firstborn of my children I **r**. H6299
34:20 But the firstling of an ass thou shalt **r** H6299
20 lamb: and if thou **r** *him* not, then shalt H6299
20 thy sons thou shalt **r**. And none shall H6299
Lev 25:25 any of his kin come to **r** it, then shall he H1350
25 shall he **r** that which his brother sold. H1350
26 And if the man have none to **r** it, and H1350
26 to redeem it, and himself be able to **r** it; H4672
29 city, then he may **r** it within a whole H1353
29 it is sold; *within* a full year may he **r** it. H1353
32 may the Levites **r** at any time. H1353
48 again; one of his brethren may **r** him: H1350
49 uncle's son, may **r** him, or *any* that is H1350
49 him of his family may **r** him; or if he be H1350
49 him; or if he be able, he may **r** himself. H1350
27:13 But if he will at all **r** it, then he shall H1350
15 And if he that sanctified it will **r** his H1350
19 will in any wise **r** it, then he shall add H1350
20 And if he will not **r** the field, or if he H1350
27 then he shall **r** *it* according to thine H6299
31 And if a man will at all **r** *ought* of his H1350
Nu 18:15 shalt thou surely **r**, and the firstling of H6299
15 firstling of unclean beasts shalt thou **r**. H6299
16 old shalt thou **r**, according to thine H6299
17 thou shalt not **r**; they *are* holy: thou H6299
Ru 4: 4 If thou wilt **r** *it*, redeem *it*: but if thou H1350
4 wilt redeem *it*, **r** *it*: but if thou wilt not H1350
4 *it*: but if thou wilt not **r** *it*, *then* tell me, H1350
4 *there is* none to **r** *it* beside thee; and I H1350
4 I *am* after thee. And he said, I will **r** *it*. H1350
6 And the kinsman said, I cannot **r** *it* for H1350
6 own inheritance: **r** thou my right to H1350
6 my right to thyself; for I cannot **r** *it*. H1350
2Sa 7:23 God went to **r** for a people to himself, H6299
1Ch 17:21 God went to **r** *to be* his own people, H6299
Neh 5: 5 *it* in our power *to* **r** *them*; for other men
Job 5:20 In famine he shall **r** thee from death: H6299
6:23 or, **R** me from the hand of the mighty? H6299
Ps 25:22 **R** Israel, O God, out of all his troubles. H6299
26:11 **r** me, and be merciful unto me. H6299
44:26 Arise for our help, and **r** us for thy H6299
49: 7 None *of them* can by any means **r** his H6299
15 But God will **r** my soul from the power H6299
69:18 Draw nigh unto my soul, *and* **r** it: H1350
72:14 He shall **r** their soul from deceit and H1350
130: 8 And he shall **r** Israel from all his H6299
Isa 50: 2 all, that it cannot **r**? or have I no power H6304
Jer 15:21 **r** thee out of the hand of the terrible. H6299
Hos 13:14 of the grave; I will **r** them from death: O H1350
Mic 4:10 **r** thee from the hand of thine enemies. H1350
Gal 4: 5 To **r** them that were under the law, that *G1805*
Tit 2:14 us, that he might **r** us from all iniquity, *G3084*

REDEEMED
Gen 48:16 The Angel which **r** me from all evil, H1350
Ex 15:13 *which* thou hast **r**: thou hast guided H1350
21: 8 shall he let her be **r**: to sell her unto a H6299
Lev 19:20 and not at all **r**, nor freedom given her; H6299
25:30 And if it be not **r** within the space of a H1350
31 be **r**, and they shall go out in the jubile. H1353
48 After that he is sold he may be **r** again; H1353
54 And if he be not **r** in these *years*, then H1350
27:20 man, it shall not be **r** any more. H1350
27 or if it be not **r**, then it shall be sold H1350
28 shall be sold or **r**: every devoted thing H1350
29 be **r**; *but* shall surely be put to death. H6299
33 thereof shall be holy; it shall not be **r**. H1350
Nu 3:46 And for those that are to be **r** of the two H6302
48 is to be **r**, unto Aaron and to his sons. H6302
49 above them that were **r** by the Levites: H6302
51 of them that were **r** unto Aaron and to H6306
18:16 And those that are to be **r** from a H6299
Dt 7: 8 a mighty hand, and **r** you out of the H6299
9:26 which thou hast **r** through thy H6299
13: 5 the land of Egypt, and **r** you out of the H6299
15:15 the LORD thy God **r** thee: therefore I H6299
21: 8 whom thou hast **r**, and lay not innocent H6299
24:18 and the LORD thy God **r** thee thence: H6299
2Sa 4: 9 who hath **r** my soul out of all adversity, H6299
1Ki 1:29 that hath **r** my soul out of all distress, H6299
1Ch 17:21 people, whom thou hast **r** out of Egypt? H6299
Neh 1:10 whom thou hast **r** by thy great power, H6299
5: 8 after our ability have **r** our brethren the H7069
Ps 31: 5 thou hast **r** me, O LORD God of truth. H6299
71:23 thee; and my soul, which thou hast **r**. H6299
74: 2 *which* thou hast **r**; this mount Zion, H1350
77:15 Thou hast with *thine* arm **r** thy people, H1350
106:10 **r** them from the hand of the enemy. H1350
107: 2 Let the **r** of the LORD say *so*, whom he H1350
2 he hath **r** from the hand of the enemy; H1350
136:24 And hath **r** us from our enemies: for H6561
Isa 1:27 Zion shall be **r** with judgment, and her H6299
29:22 Therefore thus saith the LORD, who **r** H6299
35: 9 found there; but the **r** shall walk *there*: H1350
43: 1 not: for I have **r** thee, I have called *thee* H1350
44:22 sins: return unto me; for I have **r** thee. H1350
23 **r** Jacob, and glorified himself in Israel. H1350
48:20 ye, The LORD hath **r** his servant Jacob. H1350
51:11 Therefore the **r** of the LORD shall H6299
52: 3 and ye shall be **r** without money. H1350
9 his people, he hath **r** Jerusalem. H1350
62:12 holy people, The **r** of the LORD: and H1350
63: 4 heart, and the year of my **r** is come. H1350
9 and in his pity he **r** them; and he bare H1350
Jer 31:11 For the LORD hath **r** Jacob, and H6299
Lam 3:58 causes of my soul; thou hast **r** my life. H1350
Hos 7:13 me: though I have **r** them, yet they have H6299
Mic 6: 4 the land of Egypt, and **r** thee out of the H6299
Zec 10: 8 them; for I have **r** them: and they shall H6299
Lk 1:68 for he hath visited and **r** his people, *G4160*
24:21 which should have **r** Israel: and beside *G3084*
Gal 3:13 Christ hath **r** us from the curse of the *G1805*
1Pt 1:18 that ye were not **r** with corruptible *G3084*
Rev 5: 9 slain, and hast **r** us to God by thy blood *G59*
14: 3 thousand, which were **r** from the earth. *G59*
4 he goeth. These were **r** from among men, *G59*

REDEEMEDST
2Sa 7:23 which thou **r** to thee from Egypt, H6299

REDEEMER
Job 19:25 For I know *that* my **r** liveth, and *that* he H1350
Ps 19:14 sight, O LORD, my strength, and my **r**. H1350
78:35 *was* their rock, and the high God their **r**. H1350
Prv 23:11 For their **r** *is* mighty; he shall plead H1350

Isa 41:14 LORD, and thy **r**, the Holy One of Israel. H1350
43:14 Thus saith the LORD, your **r**, the Holy H1350
44: 6 of Israel, and his **r** the LORD of hosts; H1350
24 Thus saith the LORD, thy **r**, and he that H1350
47: 4 *As for* our **r**, the LORD of hosts *is* his H1350
48:17 Thus saith the LORD, thy **R**, the Holy H1350
49: 7 Thus saith the LORD, the **R** of Israel, H1350
26 and thy **R**, the mighty One of Jacob. H1350
54: 5 *is* his name; and thy **R** the Holy One of H1350
8 mercy on thee, saith the LORD thy **R**. H1350
59:20 And the **R** shall come to Zion, and unto H1350
60:16 and thy **R**, the mighty One of Jacob. H1350
63:16 our **r**; thy name *is* from everlasting. H1350
Jer 50:34 Their **R** *is* strong; the LORD of hosts *is* H1350

REDEEMETH
Ps 34:22 The LORD **r** the soul of his servants: H6299
103: 4 Who **r** thy life from destruction; who H1350

REDEEMING
Ru 4: 7 in Israel concerning **r** and concerning H1353
Eph 5:16 **R** the time, because the days are evil. *G1805*
Col 4: 5 them that are without, **r** the time. *G1805*

REDEMPTION
Lev 25:24 ye shall grant a **r** for the land. H1353
51 the price of his **r** out of the money that H1353
52 he give him again the price of his **r**. H1353
Nu 3:49 And Moses took the **r** money of them H6306
Ps 49: 8 (For the **r** of their soul *is* precious, and H6306
111: 9 He sent **r** unto his people: he hath H6304
130: 7 *is* mercy, and with him *is* plenteous **r**. H6304
Jer 32: 7 for the right of **r** *is* thine to buy *it*. H1353
8 *is* thine, and the **r** *is* thine; buy *it* for H1353
Lk 2:38 all them that looked for **r** in Jerusalem. *G3085*
21:28 up your heads; for your **r** draweth nigh. *G629*
Ro 3:24 through the **r** that is in Christ Jesus: *G629*
8:23 the adoption, *to wit*, the **r** of our body. *G629*
1Co 1:30 righteousness, and sanctification, and **r**: *G629*
Eph 1: 7 In whom we have **r** through his blood, *G629*
14 until the **r** of the purchased possession, *G629*
4:30 whereby ye are sealed unto the day of **r**. *G629*
Col 1:14 In whom we have **r** through his blood, *G629*
Heb 9:12 place, having obtained eternal **r** *for us*. *G3085*
15 of death, for the **r** of the transgressions *G629*

REDNESS
Prv 23:29 without cause? who hath **r** of eyes? H2448

REDOUND
2Co 4:15 of many **r** to the glory of God. *G4052*

RED-SEA See RED and SEA.

REED
1Ki 14:15 For the LORD shall smite Israel, as a **r** H7070
2Ki 18:21 of this bruised **r**, *even* upon Egypt, on H7070
Job 40:21 trees, in the covert of the **r**, and fens. H7070
Isa 36: 6 of this broken **r**, on Egypt; whereon if H7070
42: 3 A bruised **r** shall he not break, and the H7070
Ezk 29: 6 been a staff of **r** to the house of Israel. H7070
40: 3 a measuring **r**; and he stood in the gate. H7070
5 hand a measuring **r** of six cubits *long* H7070
5 one **r**; and the height, one reed. H7070
5 one reed; and the height, one **r**. H7070
6 *which was* one **r** broad; and the other H7070
6 *of the gate, which was* one **r** broad. H7070
7 And *every* little chamber *was* one **r** H7070
7 one reed long, and one **r** broad; and H7070
7 the porch of the gate within *was* one **r**. H7070
8 also the porch of the gate within, one **r**. H7070
41: 8 *were* a full **r** of six great cubits. H7070
42:16 the measuring **r**, five hundred reeds, H7070
16 with the measuring **r** round about. H7070
17 with the measuring **r** round about. H7070
18 hundred reeds, with the measuring **r**. H7070
19 hundred reeds with the measuring **r**. H7070
Mt 11: 7 to see? A **r** shaken with the wind? *G2563*
12:20 A bruised **r** shall he not break, and *G2563*
27:29 his head, and a **r** in his right hand: and *G2563*
30 And they spit upon him, and took the **r**, *G2563*
48 and put *it* on a **r**, and gave him to drink. *G2563*
Mk 15:19 on the head with a **r**, and did spit upon *G2563*
36 and put *it* on a **r**, and gave him to drink, *G2563*
Lk 7:24 for to see? A **r** shaken with the wind? *G2563*
Rev 11: 1 And there was given me a **r** like unto a *G2563*
21:15 me had a golden **r** to measure the city, *G2563*
16 the city with the **r**, twelve thousand *G2563*

REEDS
Isa 19: 6 dried up: the **r** and flags shall wither. H7070
7 The paper **r** by the brooks, by the H6169
35: 7 lay, *shall be* grass with **r** and rushes. H7070
Jer 51:32 are stopped, and the **r** they have burned H98
Ezk 42:16 reed, five hundred **r**, with the H7070
17 side, five hundred **r**, with the measuring H7070
18 hundred **r**, with the measuring reed. H7070
19 hundred **r** with the measuring reed. H7070
20 five hundred **r** long, and five hundred
45: 1 twenty thousand **r**, and the breadth *shall*
48: 8 twenty thousand **r** *in* breadth, and *in*

REEL
Ps 107:27 They **r** to and fro, and stagger like a H2287
Isa 24:20 The earth shall **r** to and fro like a H5128

REELAIAH
Ezr 2: 2 Seraiah, **R**, Mordecai, Bilshan, H7480

REFINE
Zec 13: 9 the fire, and will **r** them as silver is H6884

REFINED
1Ch 28:18 And for the altar of incense **r** gold by H2212
29: 4 talents of **r** silver, to overlay the H2212
Isa 25: 6 of marrow, of wines on the lees well **r**. H2212
48:10 Behold, I have **r** thee, but not with H6884
Zec 13: 9 them as silver is **r**, and will try them as H6884

REFINER
Mal 3: 3 And he shall sit *as* a **r** and purifier of H6884

REFINER'S
Mal 3: 2 he *is* like a **r** fire, and like fullers' soap: H6884

REFORMATION
Heb 9:10 imposed *on them* until the time of **r**. *G1357*

REFORMED
Lev 26:23 And if ye will not be **r** by me by these H3256

REFRAIN
Gen 45: 1 Then Joseph could not **r** himself before H662
Job 7:11 Therefore I will not **r** my mouth; I will H2820
Prv 1:15 with them; **r** thy foot from their path: H4513
Ecc 3: 5 and a time to **r** from embracing; H7368
Isa 48: 9 will I **r** for thee, that I cut thee not off. H2413
64:12 Wilt thou **r** thyself for these *things*, O H662
Jer 31:16 Thus saith the LORD; **R** thy voice from H4513
Act 5:38 And now I say unto you, **R** from these *G868*
1Pt 3:10 good days, let him **r** his tongue from *G3973*

REFRAINED
Gen 43:31 and **r** himself, and said, Set on bread. H662
Est 5:10 Nevertheless Haman **r** himself: and H662
Job 29: 9 The princes **r** talking, and laid *their* H6113
Ps 40: 9 not **r** my lips, O LORD, thou knowest. H3607
119:101 I have **r** my feet from every evil way, H3607
Isa 42:14 I have been still, *and* **r** myself: *now* will I H662
Jer 14:10 they have not **r** their feet, therefore H2820

REFRAINETH
Prv 10:19 not sin: but he that **r** his lips *is* wise. H2820

REFRESH
1Ki 13: 7 **r** thyself, and I will give thee a reward. H5582
Act 27: 3 unto his friends to **r** himself. *G1958+G5177*
Phlm 20 in the Lord: **r** my bowels in the Lord. *G373*

REFRESHED
Ex 23:12 handmaid, and the stranger, may be **r**. H5314
31:17 on the seventh day he rested, and was **r**. H5314
1Sa 16:23 hand: so Saul was **r**, and was well, and H7304
2Sa 16:14 came weary, and **r** themselves there. H5314
Job 32:20 I will speak, that I may be **r**: I will open H7304
Ro 15:32 the will of God, and may with you be **r**. *G4875*
1Co 16:18 For they have **r** my spirit and yours: *G373*
2Co 7:13 Titus, because his spirit was **r** by you all. *G373*
2Ti 1:16 **r** me, and was not ashamed of my chain: *G404*
Phlm 7 of the saints are **r** by thee, brother. *G373*

REFRESHETH
Prv 25:13 him: for he **r** the soul of his masters. H7725

REFRESHING
Isa 28:12 this *is* the **r**: yet they would not hear. H4774
Act 3:19 when the times of **r** shall come from the *G403*

REFUGE
Nu 35: 6 *be* six cities for **r**, which ye shall appoint H4733
11 to be cities of **r** for you; that the slayer H4733
12 And they shall be unto you cities for **r** H4733
13 shall give six cities shall ye have for **r**. H4733
14 of Canaan, *which* shall be cities of **r**. H4733
15 These six cities shall be a **r**, *both* for the H4733
25 to the city of his **r**, whither he was fled: H4733
26 of the city of his **r**, whither he was fled; H4733
27 of the city of his **r**, and the revenger of H4733
28 in the city of his **r** until the death of the H4733
32 to the city of his **r**, that he should come H4733
Dt 33:27 The eternal God *is thy* **r**, and H4585
Jos 20: 2 for you cities of **r**, whereof I spake unto H4733
3 be your **r** from the avenger of blood. H4733
21:13 *to be* a city of **r** for the slayer; and H4733
21 *to be* a city of **r** for the slayer; and H4733
27 *to be* a city of **r** for the slayer; and H4733
32 *to be* a city of **r** for the slayer; and H4733
38 *to be* a city of **r** for the slayer; and H4733
2Sa 22: 3 high tower, and my **r**, my saviour; thou H4498
1Ch 6:57 Hebron, *the city* of **r**, and Libnah with H4733
67 *of* the cities of **r**, Shechem in mount H4733
Ps 9: 9 The LORD also will be a **r** for the H4869
9 the oppressed, a **r** in times of trouble. H4869
14: 6 of the poor, because the LORD *is* his **r**. H4268
46: 1 God *is* our **r** and strength, a very H4268
7 with us; the God of Jacob *is* our **r**. Selah. H4869
11 with us; the God of Jacob *is* our **r**. Selah. H4869
48: 3 God is known in her palaces for a **r**. H4869
57: 1 my **r**, until *these* calamities be overpast. H2620
59:16 defence and **r** in the day of my trouble. H4498
62: 7 of my strength, *and* my **r**, *is* in God. H4268
8 before him: God *is* a **r** for us. Selah. H4268
71: 7 unto many; but thou *art* my strong **r**. H4268
91: 2 I will say of the LORD, *He is* my **r** and H4268
9 **r**, *even* the most High, thy habitation; H4268
94:22 and my God *is* the rock of my **r**. H4268
104:18 The high hills *are* a **r** for the wild goats; H4268
142: 4 **r** failed me; no man cared for my soul. H4498
5 I said, Thou *art* my **r** *and* my portion in H4268
Prv 14:26 and his children shall have a place of **r**. H4268
Isa 4: 6 and for a place of **r**, and for a covert H4268
25: 4 in his distress, a **r** from the storm, a H4268
28:15 made lies our **r**, and under falsehood H4268
17 sweep away the **r** of lies, and the waters H4268
Jer 16:19 my fortress, and my **r** in the day of H4498
Heb 6:18 who have fled for **r** to lay hold upon the *G2703*

REFUSE
Ex 4:23 me: and if thou **r** to let him go, behold, H3985
8: 2 And if thou **r** to let *them* go, behold, I H3986
9: 2 For if thou **r** to let *them* go, and wilt H3986
10: 3 How long wilt thou **r** to humble thyself H3985
4 Else, if thou **r** to let my people go, H3986
16:28 unto Moses, How long **r** ye to keep my H3985
22:17 If her father utterly **r** to give her unto H3985
1Sa 15: 9 vile and **r**, that they destroyed utterly. H4549
Job 34:33 it, whether thou **r**, or whether thou H3988
Prv 8:33 Hear instruction, and be wise, and **r** it H6544
21: 7 them; because they **r** to do judgment. H3985
25 killeth him; for his hands **r** to labour. H3985
Isa 1:20 But if ye **r** and rebel, ye shall be H3985
7:15 to **r** the evil, and choose the good. H3988
16 For before the child shall know to **r** the H3988
Jer 8: 5 they hold fast deceit, they **r** to return. H3985
9: 6 they **r** to know me, saith the LORD. H3985
13:10 This evil people, which **r** to hear my H3987
25:28 And it shall be, if they **r** to take the cup H3985
38:21 But if thou **r** to go forth, this *is* the H3986
Lam 3:45 and **r** in the midst of the people. H3973
Am 8: 6 shoes; *yea*, and sell the **r** of the wheat? H4651
Act 25:11 worthy of death, I **r** not to die: but if *G3868*
1Ti 4: 7 But **r** profane and old wives' fables, *G3868*
5:11 But the younger widows **r**: for when *G3868*
Heb 12:25 See that ye **r** not him that speaketh. For *G3868*

REFUSED
Gen 37:35 him; but he **r** to be comforted; and H3985
39: 8 But he **r**, and said unto his master's H3985
48:19 And his father **r**, and said, I know *it*, my H3985
Nu 20:21 Thus Edom **r** to give Israel passage H3985
1Sa 8:19 Nevertheless the people **r** to obey the H3985
16: 7 because I have **r** him: for *the LORD* H3988
28:23 But he **r**, and said, I will not eat. But his H3985
2Sa 2:23 Howbeit he **r** to turn aside: wherefore H3985
13: 9 before him; but he **r** to eat. And Amnon H3985
1Ki 20:35 pray thee. And the man **r** to smite him. H3985
21:15 which he **r** to give thee for money: H3985

2Ki 5:16 And he urged him to take *it;* but he **r**. H3985
Neh 9:17 And **r** to obey, neither were mindful of H3985
Est 1:12 But the queen Vashti **r** to come at the H3985
Job 6: 7 The things *that* my soul **r** to touch *are* H3985
Ps 77: 2 ceased not: my soul **r** to be comforted. H3985
78:10 of God, and **r** to walk in his law; H3985
67 Moreover he **r** the tabernacle of Joseph, H3988
118:22 The stone *which* the builders **r** is H3988
Prv 1:24 Because I have called, and ye **r**; I have H3985
Isa 54: 6 youth, when thou wast **r**, saith thy God. H3988
Jer 5: 3 *but* they have **r** to receive correction: H3985
3 than a rock; they have **r** to return. H3985
11:10 forefathers, which **r** to hear my words; H3985
31:15 for her children **r** to be comforted for H3985
50:33 held them fast; they **r** to let them go. H3985
Ezk 5: 6 her: for they have **r** my judgments and H3988
Hos 11: 5 be his king, because they **r** to return. H3985
Zec 7:11 But they **r** to hearken, and pulled away H3985
Act 7:35 This Moses whom they **r**, saying, Who *G720*
1Ti 4: 4 be **r**, if it be received with thanksgiving: *G579*
Heb 11:24 was come to years, **r** to be called the son *G720*
12:25 escaped not who **r** him that spake on *G3868*

REFUSEDST
Jer 3: 3 forehead, thou **r** to be ashamed. H3985

REFUSETH
Ex 7:14 *is* hardened, he **r** to let the people go. H3985
Nu 22:13 LORD **r** to give me leave to go with you. H3985
14 and said, Balaam **r** to come with us. H3985
Dt 25: 7 husband's brother **r** to raise up unto H3985
Prv 10:17 but he that **r** reproof erreth. H5800
13:18 *be to* him that **r** instruction: but he that H6544
15:32 He that **r** instruction despiseth his own H6544
Isa 8: 6 Forasmuch as this people **r** the waters H3988
Jer 15:18 incurable, *which* **r** to be healed? wilt H3985

REGARD
Gen 45:20 Also **r** not your stuff; for the good of all H2347
Ex 5: 9 therein; and let them not **r** vain words. H8159
Lev 19:31 **R** not them that have familiar spirits, H6437
Dt 28:50 which shall not **r** the person of the old, H5375
1Sa 4:20 she answered not, neither did she **r** *it.* H7896
25:25 Let not my lord, I pray thee, **r** this man H3820
2Sa 13:20 he *is* thy brother; **r** not this thing. So H3820
2Ki 3:14 were it not that I **r** the presence of H5375
Job 3: 4 Let that day be darkness; let not God **r** H1875
35:13 vanity, neither will the Almighty **r** it. H7789
36:21 Take heed, **r** not iniquity: for this hast H6437
Ps 28: 5 Because they **r** not the works of the H995
31: 6 I have hated them that **r** lying vanities: H8104
66:18 If I **r** iniquity in my heart, the Lord will H7200
94: 7 see, neither shall the God of Jacob **r** *it.* H995
102:17 He will **r** the prayer of the destitute, H6437
Prv 5: 2 That thou mayest **r** discretion, and *that* H8104
6:35 He will not **r** any ransom; H5375+H6440
Ecc 8: 2 and *that* in **r** of the oath of God. H1700
Isa 5:12 feasts: but they **r** not the work of the H5027
13:17 which shall not **r** silver; and *as for* gold, H2803
Lam 4:16 he will no more **r** them: they respected H5027
Dan 11:37 Neither shall he **r** the God of his fathers, H995
37 of women, nor **r** any god: for he shall H995
Am 5:22 **r** the peace offerings of your fat beasts. H5027
Hab 1: 5 Behold ye among the heathen, and **r**, H5027
Mal 1: 9 means: will he **r** your persons? saith H5375
Lk 18: 4 Though I fear not God, nor **r** man; *G1788*
Act 8:11 And to him they had **r**, because that of *G4337*
Ro 14: 6 Lord he doth not **r** *it.* He that eateth, *G5426*

REGARDED
Ex 9:21 And he that **r** not the word of the LORD H7760
1Ki 18:29 voice, nor any to answer, nor any that **r**. H7182
1Ch 17:17 to come, and hast **r** me according to H7200
Ps 106:44 Nevertheless he **r** their affliction, when H7200
Prv 1:24 stretched out my hand, and no man **r**; H7181
Dan 3:12 O king, have not **r** thee: they H7761+H2942
Lk 1:48 For he hath **r** the low estate of his *G1914*
18: 2 which feared not God, neither **r** man: *G1788*
Heb 8: 9 and I **r** them not, saith the Lord. *G272*

REGARDEST
2Sa 19: 6 this day, that thou **r** neither princes nor
Job 30:20 hear me: I stand up, and thou **r** me *not.* H995
Mt 22:16 *man:* for thou **r** not the person of men. *G991*
Mk 12:14 for no man: for thou **r** not the person of *G991*

REGARDETH
Dt 10:17 **r** not persons, nor taketh reward: H5375
Job 34:19 of princes, nor **r** the rich more than the H5234
Job 39: 7 neither **r** he the crying of the driver. H8085
Prv 12:10 A righteous *man* **r** the life of his beast: H3045
13:18 but he that **r** reproof shall be honoured. H8104
15: 5 but he that **r** reproof is prudent. H8104
29: 7 the poor: *but* the wicked **r** not to know *it.* H995
Ecc 5: 8 highest **r**; and *there be* higher than they. H8104
11: 4 and he that **r** the clouds shall not reap. H7200
Isa 33: 8 hath despised the cities, he **r** no man. H2803
Dan 6:13 of Judah, **r** not thee, O king, H7761+H2942
Mal 2:13 insomuch that he **r** not the offering any H6437
Ro 14: 6 He that **r** the day, regardeth *it* unto the *G5426*
6 He that regardeth the day, **r** *it* unto the *G5426*
6 Lord; and he that **r** not the day, to the *G5426*

REGARDING
Job 4:20 they perish for ever without any **r** *it.* H7760
Php 2:30 nigh unto death, not **r** his life, to supply *G3851*

REGEM
1Ch 2:47 And the sons of Jahdai; **R**, and Jotham, H7276

REGEMMELECH
Zec 7: 2 God Sherezer and **R**, and their men, to H7278

REGENERATION
Mt 19:28 me, in the **r** when the Son of man *G3824*
Tit 3: 5 of **r**, and renewing of the Holy Ghost; *G3824*

REGION
Dt 3: 4 cities, all the **r** of Argob, the kingdom H2256
13 of Manasseh; all the **r** of Argob, with all H2256
1Ki 4:11 The son of Abinadab, in all the **r** of H5299
13 *also pertained* the **r** of Argob, which *is* H2256
24 For he had dominion over all *the* **r** on
Mt 3: 5 and all the **r** round about Jordan, *G4066*
4:16 which sat in the **r** and shadow of death *G5561*
Mk 1:28 all the **r** round about Galilee. *G4066*
6:55 And ran through that whole **r** round *G4066*
Lk 3: 1 Ituraea and of the **r** of Trachonitis, and *G5561*
4:14 of him through all the **r** round about. *G4066*
7:17 and throughout all the **r** round about. *G4066*
Act 13:49 was published throughout all the **r**. *G5561*
14: 6 and unto the **r** that lieth round about: *G4066*
16: 6 Phrygia and the **r** of Galatia, and were *G5561*

REGIONS
Act 8: 1 abroad throughout the **r** of Judaea and *G5561*
2Co 10:16 To preach the gospel in the *r* beyond
11:10 me of this boasting in the **r** of Achaia. *G2824*
Gal 1:21 Afterwards I came into the **r** of Syria *G2824*

REGISTER
Ezr 2:62 These sought their **r** *among* those that H3791
Neh 7: 5 And I found a **r** of the genealogy of H5612
64 These sought their **r** *among* those that H3791

REHABIAH
1Ch 23:17 And the sons of Eliezer *were,* **R** the H7345
17 sons; but the sons of **R** were very many. H7345
24:21 Concerning **R**: of the sons of Rehabiah, H7345
21 Concerning Rehabiah: of the sons of **R**, H7345
26:25 And his brethren by Eliezer; **R** his son, H7345

REHEARSE
Ex 17:14 in a book, and **r** *it* in the ears of Joshua: H7760
Jdg 5:11 there shall they **r** the righteous acts of H8567

REHEARSED
1Sa 8:21 and he **r** them in the ears of the LORD. H1696
17:31 David spake, they **r** *them* before Saul: H5046
Act 11: 4 But Peter **r** *the matter* from the *G756*
14:27 together, they **r** all that God had done *G312*

REHOB
Nu 13:21 of Zin unto **R**, as men come to Hamath. H7340
Jos 19:28 And Hebron, and **R**, and Hammon, and H7340
30 Ummah also, and Aphek, and **R**: H7340
21:31 Helkath with her suburbs, and **R** with H7340
Jdg 1:31 nor of Helbah, nor of Aphik, nor of **R**: H7340
2Sa 8: 3 the son of **R**, king of Zobah, as he H7340
12 of Hadadezer, son of **R**, king of Zobah. H7340
10: 8 of Zoba, and of **R**, and Ish-tob, and H7340
1Ch 6:75 And Hukok with her suburbs, and **R** H7340
Neh 10:11 Micha, **R**, Hashabiah, H7340

REHOBOAM
1Ki 11:43 and **R** his son reigned in his stead. H7346
12: 1 And **R** went to Shechem: for all Israel H7346
3 Israel came, and spake unto **R**, saying, H7346
1Ki 12: 6 And king **R** consulted with the old H7346
12 people came to **R** the third day, as the H7346
17 cities of Judah, **R** reigned over them. H7346
18 Then king **R** sent Adoram, who *was* H7346
18 Therefore king **R** made speed to get H7346
21 And when **R** was come to Jerusalem, he H7346
21 again to **R** the son of Solomon. H7346
23 Speak unto **R**, the son of Solomon, king H7346
27 lord, *even* unto **R** king of Judah, and H7346
27 me, and go again to **R** king of Judah. H7346
14:21 And **R** the son of Solomon reigned in H7346
21 reigned in Judah. **R** *was* forty and one H7346
25 fifth year of king **R**, *that* Shishak king of H7346
27 And king **R** made in their stead brasen H7346
29 Now the rest of the acts of **R**, and all H7346
30 And there was war between **R** and H7346
31 And **R** slept with his fathers, and was H7346
15: 6 And there was war between **R** and H7346
1Ch 3:10 And Solomon's son *was* **R**, Abia his son, H7346
2Ch 9:31 and **R** his son reigned in his stead. H7346
10: 1 And **R** went to Shechem: for to H7346
3 all Israel came and spake to **R**, saying, H7346
6 And king **R** took counsel with the old H7346
12 people came to **R** on the third day, as H7346
13 **R** forsook the counsel of the old men, H7346
17 cities of Judah, **R** reigned over them. H7346
18 Then king **R** sent Hadoram that *was* H7346
18 he died. But king **R** made speed to get H7346
11: 1 And when **R** was come to Jerusalem, he H7346
1 he might bring the kingdom again to **R**. H7346
3 Speak unto **R** the son of Solomon, king H7346
5 And **R** dwelt in Jerusalem, and built H7346
17 Judah, and made **R** the son of Solomon H7346
18 And **R** took him Mahalath the H7346
21 And **R** loved Maachah the daughter of H7346
22 And **R** made Abijah the son of H7346
12: 1 And it came to pass, when **R** had H7346
2 the fifth year of king **R** Shishak king of H7346
5 Then came Shemaiah the prophet to **R**, H7346
10 Instead of which king **R** made shields H7346
13 So king **R** strengthened himself in H7346
13 and reigned: for **R** *was* one and forty H7346
15 Now the acts of **R**, first and last, *are* H7346
15 between **R** and Jeroboam continually. H7346
16 And **R** slept with his fathers, and was H7346
13: 7 against **R** the son of Solomon, H7346
7 of Solomon, when **R** was young and H7346

REHOBOTH
Gen 10:11 Nineveh, and the city **R**, and Calah, H7344
26:22 the name of it **R**; and he said, For now H7344
36:37 And Samlah died, and Saul of **R** *by* the H7344
1Ch 1:48 of **R** by the river reigned in his stead. H7344

REHUM
Ezr 2: 2 Mispar, Bigvai, **R**, Baanah. The number H7348
4: 8 **R** the chancellor and Shimshai the H7348
9 Then *wrote* **R** the chancellor, and H7348
17 *Then* sent the king an answer unto **R** H7348
23 *was* read before **R**, and Shimshai the H7348
Neh 3:17 After him repaired the Levites, **R** the H7348
10:25 **R**, Hashabnah, Maaseiah, H7348
12: 3 Shechaniah, **R**, Meremoth, H7348

REI
1Ki 1: 8 and Shimei, and **R**, and the mighty men H7472

REIGN
Gen 37: 8 Shalt thou indeed **r** over us? or shalt H4427
Ex 15:18 The LORD shall **r** for ever and ever. H4427
Lev 26:17 that hate you shall **r** over you; and ye H7287
Dt 15: 6 and thou shalt **r** over many nations, H4910
6 nations, but they shall not **r** over thee. H4910
Jdg 9: 2 and ten persons, **r** over you, or that one H4910
2 you, or that one **r** over you? remember H4910
8 said unto the olive tree, **R** thou over us. H4427
10 the fig tree, Come thou, *and* **r** over us. H4427
12 the vine, Come thou, *and* **r** over us. H4427
14 the bramble, Come thou, *and* **r** over us. H4427
1Sa 8: 7 me, that I should not **r** over them. H4427
9 of the king that shall **r** over them. H4427
11 of the king that shall **r** over you: He will H4427
9:17 of! this same shall **r** over my people. H6113
11:12 said, Shall Saul **r** over us? bring the H4427
12:12 but a king shall **r** over us: when the H4427
2Sa 2:10 old when he began to **r** over Israel, and H4427
3:21 that thou mayest **r** over all that thine H4427
5: 4 began to **r**, *and* he reigned forty years. H4427
1Ki 1:11 **r**, and David our lord knoweth *it* not? H4427

1Ki 1:13 thy son shall **r** after me, and he shall H4427
13 my throne? why then doth Adonijah **r**? H4427
17 thy son shall **r** after me, and he shall H4427
24 Adonijah shall **r** after me, and he shall H4427
30 thy son shall **r** after me, and he shall H4427
2:15 on me, that I should **r**: howbeit the H4427
6: 1 year of Solomon's **r** over Israel, in the H4427
11:37 And I will take thee, and thou shalt **r** H4427
14:21 old when he began to **r**, and he reigned H4427
15:25 began to **r** over Israel in the second H4427
33 the son of Ahijah to **r** over all Israel in H4427
16: 8 to **r** over Israel in Tirzah, two years. H4427
11 when he began to **r**, as soon as he sat on H4427
15 king of Judah did Zimri **r** seven days in H4427
23 began Omri to **r** over Israel, twelve H4427
29 the son of Omri to **r** over Israel: and H4427
22:41 son of Asa began to **r** over Judah in the H4427
42 old when he began to **r**; and he reigned H4427
51 Ahaziah the son of Ahab began to **r** H4427
2Ki 3: 1 son of Ahab began to **r** over Israel in H4427
8:16 Jehoshaphat king of Judah began to **r**. H4427
17 he when he began to **r**; and he reigned H4427
25 son of Jehoram king of Judah begin to **r**. H4427
26 when he began to **r**; and he reigned one H4427
9:29 Ahab began Ahaziah to **r** over Judah. H4427
11: 3 And Athaliah did **r** over the land. H4427
21 old *was* Jehoash when he began to **r**. H4427
12: 1 Jehu Jehoash began to **r**; and forty years H4427
13: 1 son of Jehu began to **r** over Israel in H4427
10 the son of Jehoahaz to **r** over Israel in H4427
14: 2 when he began to **r**, and reigned twenty H4427
23 of Israel began to **r** in Samaria, *and* H4427
15: 1 son of Amaziah king of Judah to **r**. H4427
2 when he began to **r**, and he reigned two H4427
8 **r** over Israel in Samaria six months. H4427
13 Shallum the son of Jabesh began to **r** in H4427
17 the son of Gadi to **r** over Israel, *and* H4427
23 began to **r** over Israel in Samaria, H4427
27 began to **r** over Israel in Samaria, H4427
32 the son of Uzziah king of Judah to **r**. H4427
33 he when he began to **r**, and he reigned H4427
16: 1 son of Jotham king of Judah began to **r**. H4427
2 when he began to **r**, and reigned sixteen H4427
17: 1 to **r** in Samaria over Israel nine years. H4427
18: 1 son of Ahaz king of Judah began to **r**. H4427
2 he when he began to **r**; and he reigned H4427
21: 1 when he began to **r**, and reigned fifty H4427
19 when he began to **r**, and he reigned two H4427
22: 1 old when he began to **r**, and he reigned H4427
23:31 old when he began to **r**; and he reigned H4427
33 that he might not **r** in Jerusalem; and H4427
36 old when he began to **r**; and he reigned H4427
24: 8 when he began to **r**, and he reigned in H4427
12 took him in the eighth year of his **r**. H4427
18 old when he began to **r**, and he reigned H4427
25: 1 ninth year of his **r**, in the tenth month, H4427
27 that he began to **r** did lift up the head H4427
1Ch 4:31 *were* their cities unto the **r** of David. H4427
26:31 fortieth year of the **r** of David they were H4438
29:30 With all his **r** and his might, and the H4438
2Ch 1: 8 and hast made me to **r** in his stead. H4427
3: 2 month, in the fourth year of his **r**. H4438
12:13 old when he began to **r**, and he reigned H4427
13: 1 began Abijah to **r** over Judah. H4427
15:10 in the fifteenth year of the **r** of Asa. H4438
19 five and thirtieth year of the **r** of Asa. H4438
16: 1 In the six and thirtieth year of the **r** of H4438
12 ninth year of his **r** was diseased in his H4438
13 in the one and fortieth year of his **r**. H4427
17: 7 Also in the third year of his **r** he sent to H4427
20:31 old when he began to **r**, and he reigned H4427
21: 5 old when he began to **r**, and he reigned H4427
20 when he began to **r**, and he reigned in H4427
22: 2 when he began to **r**, and he reigned one H4427
23: 3 the king's son shall **r**, as the LORD hath H4427
24: 1 old when he began to **r**, and he reigned H4427
25: 1 old *when* he began to **r**, and he reigned H4427
26: 3 when he began to **r**, and he reigned fifty H4427
27: 1 old when he began to **r**, and he reigned H4427
8 when he began to **r**, and reigned sixteen H4427
28: 1 old when he began to **r**, and he reigned H4427
29: 1 Hezekiah began to **r** *when he was* five H4427
3 He in the first year of his **r**, in the first H4427
19 king Ahaz in his **r** did cast away in his H4438
33: 1 when he began to **r**, and he reigned fifty H4427
21 **r**, and reigned two years in Jerusalem. H4427
34: 1 when he began to **r**, and he reigned in H4427
3 For in the eighth year of his **r**, while he H4427
8 Now in the eighteenth year of his **r**, H4427

2Ch 35:19 In the eighteenth year of the **r** of Josiah H4438
36: 2 old when he began to **r**, and he reigned H4427
5 old when he began to **r**, and he reigned H4427
9 old when he began to **r**, and he reigned H4427
11 when he began to **r**, and reigned eleven H4427
20 until the **r** of the kingdom of Persia: H4427
Ezr 4: 5 until the **r** of Darius king of Persia. H4438
6 And in the **r** of Ahasuerus, in the H4438
6 beginning of his **r**, wrote they *unto him* H4438
24 year of the **r** of Darius king of Persia. H4437
6:15 sixth year of the **r** of Darius the king. H4437
7: 1 Now after these things, in the **r** of H4438
8: 1 in the **r** of Artaxerxes the king. H4438
Neh 12:22 priests, to the **r** of Darius the Persian. H4438
Est 1: 3 In the third year of his **r**, he made a H4427
2:16 Tebeth, in the seventh year of his **r**. H4438
Job 34:30 That the hypocrite **r** not, lest the people H4427
Ps 146:10 The LORD shall **r** for ever, *even* thy H4427
Prv 8:15 By me kings **r**, and princes decree H4427
Ecc 4:14 For out of prison he cometh to **r**; H4427
Isa 24:23 of hosts shall **r** in mount Zion, and H4427
32: 1 Behold, a king shall **r** in righteousness, H4427
Jer 1: 2 of Judah, in the thirteenth year of his **r**. H4427
22:15 Shalt thou **r**, because thou closest H4427
23: 5 and a King shall **r** and prosper, and H4427
26: 1 In the beginning of the **r** of Jehoiakim H4468
27: 1 In the beginning of the **r** of Jehoiakim H4467
28: 1 beginning of the **r** of Zedekiah king of H4467
33:21 not have a son to **r** upon his throne; H4427
49:34 the **r** of Zedekiah king of Judah, saying, H4438
51:59 **r**. And *this* Seraiah *was* a quiet prince. H4427
52: 1 old when he began to **r**, and he reigned H4427
4 ninth year of his **r**, in the tenth month, H4427
31 the *first* year of his **r** lifted up the head H4438
Dan 1: 1 In the third year of the **r** of Jehoiakim H4438
2: 1 And in the second year of the **r** of H4438
6:28 So this Daniel prospered in the **r** of H4437
28 and in the **r** of Cyrus the Persian. H4437
8: 1 In the third year of the **r** of king H4438
9: 2 In the first year of his **r** I Daniel H4427
Mic 4: 7 the LORD shall **r** over them in mount H4427
Mt 2:22 But when he heard that Archelaus did **r** *G936*
Lk 1:33 And he shall **r** over the house of Jacob *G936*
3: 1 Now in the fifteenth year of the **r** of *G2231*
19:14 We will not have this *man* to **r** over us. *G936*
27 not that I should **r** over them, bring *G936*
Ro 5:17 shall **r** in life by one, Jesus Christ.) *G936*
21 so might grace **r** through righteousness *G936*
6:12 Let not sin therefore **r** in your mortal *G936*
15:12 he that shall rise to **r** over the Gentiles; *G757*
1Co 4: 8 did **r**, that we also might reign with you. *G936*
8 did reign, that we also might **r** with you. *G936*
15:25 For he must **r**, till he hath put all enemies *G936*
2Ti 2:12 If we suffer, we shall also **r** with *him*: if *G4821*
Rev 5:10 and priests: and we shall **r** on the earth. *G936*
11:15 Christ; and he shall **r** for ever and ever. *G936*
20: 6 and shall **r** with him a thousand years. *G936*
22: 5 light: and they shall **r** for ever and ever. *G936*

REIGNED

Gen 36:31 And these *are* the kings that **r** in the H4427
31 **r** any king over the children of Israel. H4427
32 And Bela the son of Beor **r** in Edom: H4427
33 son of Zerah of Bozrah **r** in his stead. H4427
34 of the land of Temani **r** in his stead. H4427
35 in the field of Moab, **r** in his stead: and H4427
36 and Samlah of Masrekah **r** in his stead. H4427
37 of Rehoboth *by* the river **r** in his stead. H4427
38 the son of Achbor **r** in his stead. H4427
39 died, and Hadar **r** in his stead: and the H4427
Jos 12: 5 And **r** in mount Hermon, and in H4910
13:10 Amorites, which **r** in Heshbon, unto H4427
12 in Bashan, which **r** in Ashtaroth and in H4427
21 Amorites, which **r** in Heshbon, whom H4427
Jdg 4: 2 of Canaan, that **r** in Hazor; the captain H4427
9:22 When Abimelech had **r** three years H7786
1Sa 13: 1 Saul **r** one year; and when he had H4427
1 when he had **r** two years over Israel, H4427
2Sa 2:10 over Israel, and **r** two years. But the H4427
5: 4 he began to reign, *and* he **r** forty years. H4427
5 In Hebron he **r** over Judah seven years H4427
5 in Jerusalem he **r** thirty and three years H4427
8:15 And David **r** over all Israel; and David H4427
10: 1 died, and Hanun his son **r** in his stead. H4427
16: 8 stead thou hast **r**; and the LORD hath H4427
1Ki 2:11 And the days that David **r** over Israel H4427
11 years: seven years **r** he in Hebron, and H4427
11 and three years **r** he in Jerusalem. H4427
4:21 And Solomon **r** over all kingdoms from H4910

1Ki 11:24 and dwelt therein, and **r** in Damascus. H4427
25 he abhorred Israel, and **r** over Syria. H4427
42 And the time that Solomon **r** in H4427
43 and Rehoboam his son **r** in his stead. H4427
12:17 cities of Judah, Rehoboam **r** over them. H4427
14:19 and how he **r**, behold, they *are* written H4427
20 And the days which Jeroboam **r** *were* H4427
20 and Nadab his son **r** in his stead. H4427
21 And Rehoboam the son of Solomon **r** H4427
21 to reign, and he **r** seventeen years in H4427
31 And Abijam his son **r** in his stead. H4427
15: 1 the son of Nebat **r** Abijam over Judah. H4427
2 Three years **r** he in Jerusalem. And his H4427
8 David: and Asa his son **r** in his stead. H4427
9 king of Israel **r** Asa over Judah. H4427
10 And forty and one years **r** he in H4427
24 and Jehoshaphat his son **r** in his stead. H4427
25 of Judah, and **r** over Israel two years. H4427
28 did Baasha slay him, and **r** in his stead. H4427
29 And it came to pass, when he **r**, *that* he H4427
16: 6 Tirzah: and Elah his son **r** in his stead. H4427
10 of Asa king of Judah, and **r** in his stead. H4427
22 of Ginath: so Tibni died, and Omri **r**. H4427
23 twelve years: six years **r** he in Tirzah. H4427
28 and Ahab his son **r** in his stead. H4427
29 Ahab the son of Omri **r** over Israel in H4427
22:40 and Ahaziah his son **r** in his stead. H4427
42 to reign; and he **r** twenty and five years H4427
50 and Jehoram his son **r** in his stead. H4427
51 of Judah, and **r** two years over Israel. H4427
2Ki 1:17 And Jehoram **r** in his stead in the H4427
3: 1 king of Judah, and **r** twelve years. H4427
27 son that should have **r** in his stead, and H4427
8:15 that he died: and Hazael **r** in his stead. H4427
17 and he **r** eight years in Jerusalem. H4427
24 and Ahaziah his son **r** in his stead. H4427
26 began to reign; and he **r** one year in H4427
10:35 And Jehoahaz his son **r** in his stead. H4427
36 And the time that Jehu **r** over Israel in H4427
12: 1 and forty years **r** he in Jerusalem. And H4427
21 and Amaziah his son **r** in his stead. H4427
13: 1 Israel in Samaria, *and* **r** seventeen years.
9 and Joash his son **r** in his stead. H4427
10 Israel in Samaria, *and* **r** sixteen years.
24 and Ben-hadad his son **r** in his stead. H4427
14: 1 king of Israel **r** Amaziah the son of H4427
2 to reign, and he **r** twenty and nine years H4427
16 and Jeroboam his son **r** in his stead. H4427
23 in Samaria, *and* **r** forty and one years.
29 and Zachariah his son **r** in his stead. H4427
15: 2 to reign, and he **r** two and fifty years in H4427
7 and Jotham his son **r** in his stead. H4427
10 and slew him, and **r** in his stead. H4427
13 and he **r** a full month in Samaria. H4427
14 and slew him, and **r** in his stead. H4427
17 over Israel, *and* **r** ten years in Samaria.
22 and Pekahiah his son **r** in his stead. H4427
23 over Israel in Samaria, *and* **r** two years.
25 and he killed him, and **r** in his room. H4427
27 Israel in Samaria, *and* **r** twenty years.
30 and slew him, and **r** in his stead, in the H4427
33 to reign, and he **r** sixteen years in H4427
38 father: and Ahaz his son **r** in his stead. H4427
16: 2 began to reign, and **r** sixteen years in H4427
20 and Hezekiah his son **r** in his stead. H4427
18: 2 to reign; and he **r** twenty and nine H4427
19:37 And Esar-haddon his son **r** in his stead. H4427
20:21 and Manasseh his son **r** in his stead. H4427
21: 1 to reign, and **r** fifty and five years in H4427
18 Uzza: and Amon his son **r** in his stead. H4427
19 began to reign, and he **r** two years in H4427
26 Uzza: and Josiah his son **r** in his stead. H4427
22: 1 to reign, and he **r** thirty and one years H4427
23:31 to reign; and he **r** three months in H4427
36 began to reign; and he **r** eleven years in H4427
24: 6 and Jehoiachin his son **r** in his stead. H4427
8 to reign, and he **r** in Jerusalem three H4427
18 began to reign, and he **r** eleven years in H4427
1Ch 1:43 Now these *are* the kings that **r** in the H4427
43 before *any* king **r** over the children of H4427
44 son of Zerah of Bozrah **r** in his stead. H4427
45 land of the Temanites **r** in his stead. H4427
46 in the field of Moab, **r** in his stead: and H4427
47 Samlah of Masrekah **r** in his stead. H4427
48 of Rehoboth by the river **r** in his stead. H4427
49 the son of Achbor **r** in his stead. H4427
50 was dead, Hadad **r** in his stead: and H4427
3: 4 and there he **r** seven years and six H4427
4 Jerusalem he **r** thirty and three years. H4427

R

1Ch 18:14 So David **r** over all Israel, and executed H4427
19: 1 died, and his son **r** in his stead. H4427
29:26 Thus David the son of Jesse **r** over all H4427
27 And the time that he **r** over Israel *was* H4427
27 years; seven years **r** he in Hebron, and H4427
27 and three *years* **r** he in Jerusalem. H4427
28 and Solomon his son **r** in his stead. H4427
2Ch 1:13 of the congregation, and **r** over Israel. H4427
9:26 And he **r** over all the kings from the H4910
30 And Solomon **r** in Jerusalem over all H4427
31 and Rehoboam his son **r** in his stead. H4427
10:17 cities of Judah, Rehoboam **r** over them. H4427
12:13 in Jerusalem, and **r**: for Rehoboam *was* H4427
13 to reign, and he **r** seventeen years in H4427
16 and Abijah his son **r** in his stead. H4427
13: 2 He **r** three years in Jerusalem. His H4427
14: 1 and Asa his son **r** in his stead. In his H4427
17: 1 And Jehoshaphat his son **r** in his stead, H4427
20:31 And Jehoshaphat **r** over Judah: *he was* H4427
31 to reign, and he **r** twenty and five years H4427
21: 1 And Jehoram his son **r** in his stead. H4427
5 and he **r** eight years in Jerusalem. H4427
20 to reign, and he **r** in Jerusalem eight H4427
22: 1 the son of Jehoram king of Judah **r**. H4427
2 began to reign, and he **r** one year in H4427
12 six years: and Athaliah **r** over the land. H4427
24: 1 began to reign, and he **r** forty years in H4427
27 And Amaziah his son **r** in his stead. H4427
25: 1 to reign, and he **r** twenty and nine H4427
26: 3 to reign, and he **r** fifty and two years in H4427
23 and Jotham his son **r** in his stead. H4427
27: 1 to reign, and he **r** sixteen years in H4427
8 reign, and **r** sixteen years in Jerusalem. H4427
9 David: and Ahaz his son **r** in his stead. H4427
28: 1 to reign, and he **r** sixteen years in H4427
27 and Hezekiah his son **r** in his stead. H4427
29: 1 years old, and he **r** nine and twenty H4427
32:33 And Manasseh his son **r** in his stead. H4427
33: 1 he **r** fifty and five years in Jerusalem: H4427
20 house: and Amon his son **r** in his stead. H4427
21 to reign, and **r** two years in Jerusalem. H4427
34: 1 he **r** in Jerusalem one and thirty years. H4427
36: 2 and he **r** three months in Jerusalem. H4427
5 began to reign, and he **r** eleven years in H4427
8 and Jehoiachin his son **r** in his stead. H4427
9 to reign, and he **r** three months and ten H4427
11 reign, and **r** eleven years in Jerusalem. H4427
Est 1: 1 *is* Ahasuerus which **r**, from India even H4427
Isa 37:38 and Esar-haddon his son **r** in his stead. H4427
Jer 22:11 of Judah, which **r** instead of Josiah his H4427
37: 1 And king Zedekiah the son of Josiah **r** H4427
52: 1 began to reign, and he **r** eleven years in H4427
Ro 5:14 Nevertheless death **r** from Adam to *G936*
17 For if by one man's offence death **r** by *G936*
21 That as sin hath **r** unto death, even so *G936*
1Co 4: 8 ye are rich, ye have **r** as kings without *G936*
Rev 11:17 taken to thee thy great power, and hast **r**. *G936*
20: 4 lived and **r** with Christ a thousand years. *G936*

REIGNEST
1Ch 29:12 of thee, and thou **r** over all; and in H4910

REIGNETH
1Sa 12:14 also the king that **r** over you continue H4427
2Sa 15:10 then ye shall say, Absalom **r** in Hebron. H4427
1Ki 1:18 And now, behold, Adonijah **r**; and now, H4427
1Ch 16:31 say among the nations, The LORD **r**. H4427
Ps 47: 8 God **r** over the heathen: God sitteth H4427
93: 1 The LORD **r**, he is clothed with majesty; H4427
96:10 *that* the LORD **r**: the world also shall H4427
97: 1 The LORD **r**; let the earth rejoice; let the H4427
99: 1 The LORD **r**; let the people tremble: he H4427
Prv 30:22 For a servant when he **r**; and a fool H4427
Isa 52: 7 that saith unto Zion, Thy God **r**! H4427
Rev 17:18 city, which **r** over the kings of the earth. *G2192*
19: 6 Alleluia: for the Lord God omnipotent **r**. *G936*

REIGNING
1Sa 16: 1 rejected him from **r** over Israel? fill H4427

REINS
Job 16:13 he cleaveth my **r** asunder, and doth not H3629
19:27 *though* my **r** be consumed within me. H3629
Ps 7: 9 righteous God trieth the hearts and **r**. H3629
16: 7 **r** also instruct me in the night seasons. H3629
26: 2 and prove me; try my **r** and my heart. H3629
73:21 was grieved, and I was pricked in my **r**. H3629
139:13 For thou hast possessed my **r**: thou hast H3629
Prv 23:16 Yea, my **r** shall rejoice, when thy lips H3629
Isa 11: 5 and faithfulness the girdle of his **r**. H2504
Jer 11:20 that triest the **r** and the heart, let me H3629
12: 2 in their mouth, and far from their **r**. H3629
17:10 I the LORD search the heart, *I* try the **r**, H3629
20:12 *and* seest the **r** and the heart, let me H3629
Lam 3:13 arrows of his quiver to enter into my **r**. H3629
Rev 2:23 searcheth the **r** and hearts: and I will *G3510*

REJECT
Hos 4: 6 I will also **r** thee, that thou shalt H3988
Mk 6:26 which sat with him, he would not **r** her. *G114*
7: 9 And he said unto them, Full well ye **r** the *G114*
Tit 3:10 after the first and second admonition **r**; *G3868*

REJECTED
1Sa 8: 7 for they have not **r** thee, but they have H3988
7 **r** me, that I should not reign over them. H3988
10:19 And ye have this day **r** your God, who H3988
15:23 Because thou hast **r** the word of the H3988
23 he hath also **r** thee from *being* king. H3988
26 thee: for thou hast **r** the word of the H3988
26 hath **r** thee from being king over Israel. H3988
16: 1 Saul, seeing I have **r** him from reigning H3988
2Ki 17:15 And they **r** his statutes, and his H3988
20 And the LORD **r** all the seed of Israel, H3988
Isa 53: 3 He is despised and **r** of men; a man of H2310
Jer 2:37 for the LORD hath **r** thy confidences, H3988
6:19 unto my words, nor to my law, but **r** it. H3988
30 them, because the LORD hath **r** them. H3988
7:29 for the LORD hath **r** and forsaken the H3988
8: 9 lo, they have **r** the word of the LORD; H3988
14:19 Hast thou utterly **r** Judah? hath thy H3988
Lam 5:22 But thou hast utterly **r** us; thou art very H3988
Hos 4: 6 because thou hast **r** knowledge, I will H3988
Mt 21:42 which the builders **r**, the same is become *G593*
Mk 8:31 things, and be **r** of the elders, and *of* *G593*
12:10 **r** is become the head of the corner: *G593*
Lk 7:30 But the Pharisees and lawyers **r** the *G114*
9:22 things, and be **r** of the elders and chief *G593*
17:25 many things, and be **r** of this generation. *G593*
20:17 which the builders **r**, the same is become *G593*
Gal 4:14 despised not, nor **r**; but received me as *G1609*
Heb 6: 8 and briers *is* **r**, and *is* nigh unto cursing; *G96*
12:17 blessing, he was **r**: for he found no place *G593*

REJECTETH
Jn 12:48 He that **r** me, and receiveth not my *G114*

REJOICE
Lev 23:40 and ye shall **r** before the LORD your H8055
Dt 12: 7 God, and ye shall **r** in all that ye put H8055
12 And ye shall **r** before the LORD your H8055
18 and thou shalt **r** before the LORD thy H8055
14:26 thou shalt **r**, thou, and thine household, H8055
16:11 And thou shalt **r** before the LORD thy H8055
14 And thou shalt **r** in thy feast, thou, and H8055
15 hands, therefore thou shalt surely **r**. H8056
26:11 And thou shalt **r** in every good *thing* H8055
27: 7 there, and **r** before the LORD thy God. H8055
28:63 so the LORD will **r** over you to destroy H7797
30: 9 LORD will again **r** over thee for good, H7797
32:43 **R**, O ye nations, *with* his people: for he H7442
33:18 And of Zebulun he said, **R**, Zebulun, in H8055
Jdg 9:19 this day, *then* **r** ye in Abimelech, and H8055
19 in Abimelech, and let him also **r** in you: H8055
16:23 their god, and to **r**: for they said, Our H8057
1Sa 2: 1 enemies; because I **r** in thy salvation. H8055
19: 5 *it*, and didst **r**: wherefore then wilt H8055
2Sa 1:20 of the Philistines **r**, lest the daughters of H8055
1Ch 16:10 the heart of them **r** that seek the LORD. H8055
31 and let the earth **r**: and let *men* say H1523
32 let the fields **r**, and all that *is* therein. H5970
2Ch 6:41 and let thy saints **r** in goodness. H8055
20:27 had made them to **r** over their enemies. H8055
Neh 12:43 had made them **r** with great joy: the H8055
Job 3:22 Which **r** exceedingly, *and* are glad, H8056
20:18 *be*, and he shall not **r** *therein*. H5965
21:12 They take the timbrel and harp, and **r** H8055
Ps 2:11 Serve the LORD with fear, and **r** with H1523
5:11 their trust in thee **r**: let them ever shout H8055
9: 2 I will be glad and **r** in thee: I will sing H5970
14 of Zion: I will **r** in thy salvation. H1523
13: 4 that trouble me **r** when I am moved. H1523
5 my heart shall **r** in thy salvation. H1523
14: 7 Jacob shall **r**, *and* Israel shall be glad. H1523
20: 5 We will **r** in thy salvation, and in the H7442
21: 1 in thy salvation how greatly shall he **r**! H1523
30: 1 hast not made my foes to **r** over me. H8055
31: 7 I will be glad and **r** in thy mercy: for H8055
32:11 Be glad in the LORD, and **r**, ye H1523
33: 1 **R** in the LORD, O ye righteous: *for* H7442
21 For our heart shall **r** in him, because H8055
35: 9 in the LORD: it shall **r** in his salvation. H7797
19 wrongfully **r** over me: *neither* let H8055
24 and let them not **r** over me. H8055
26 together that **r** at mine hurt: let them H8056
38:16 they should **r** over me: when my foot H8055
40:16 Let all those that seek thee **r** and be H7797
48:11 Let mount Zion **r**, let the daughters of H8055
51: 8 bones *which* thou hast broken may **r**. H1523
53: 6 Jacob shall **r**, *and* Israel shall be glad. H1523
58:10 The righteous shall **r** when he seeth the H8055
60: 6 God hath spoken in his holiness; I will **r**, H5937
63: 7 in the shadow of thy wings will I **r**. H7442
11 But the king shall **r** in God; every one H8055
65: 8 of the morning and evening to **r**. H7442
12 and the little hills **r** on every side. H1524
66: 6 the flood on foot: there did we **r** in him. H8055
68: 3 But let the righteous be glad; let them **r** H5970
3 before God: yea, let them exceedingly **r**. H7797
4 by his name JAH, and **r** before him. H5937
70: 4 Let all those that seek thee **r** and be H7797
71:23 My lips shall greatly **r** when I sing unto H7442
85: 6 us again: that thy people may **r** in thee? H8055
86: 4 **R** the soul of thy servant: for unto thee, H8055
89:12 Tabor and Hermon shall **r** in thy name. H7442
16 In thy name shall they **r** all the day: H1523
42 thou hast made all his enemies to **r**. H8055
90:14 that we may **r** and be glad all our days. H7442
96:11 Let the heavens **r**, and let the earth be H8055
12 then shall all the trees of the wood **r** H7442
97: 1 The LORD reigneth; let the earth **r**; let H1523
12 **R** in the LORD, ye righteous; and give H8055
98: 4 a loud noise, and **r**, and sing praise. H7442
104:31 for ever: the LORD shall **r** in his works. H8055
105: 3 the heart of them **r** that seek the LORD. H8055
106: 5 chosen, that I may **r** in the gladness of H8055
107:42 The righteous shall see *it*, and **r**: and all H8055
108: 7 God hath spoken in his holiness; I will **r**, H5937
109:28 them be ashamed; but let thy servant **r**. H8055
118:24 hath made; we will **r** and be glad in it. H1523
119:162 I **r** at thy word, as one that findeth H7797
149: 2 Let Israel **r** in him that made him: let H8055
Prv 2:14 Who **r** to do evil, *and* delight in the H8056
5:18 Let thy fountain be blessed: and **r** with H8055
23:15 be wise, my heart shall **r**, even mine. H8055
16 Yea, my reins shall **r**, when thy lips H5937
24 shall greatly **r**: and he that begetteth H1523
25 be glad, and she that bare thee shall **r**. H1523
24:17 **R** not when thine enemy falleth, and let H8055
27: 9 Ointment and perfume **r** the heart: so H8055
28:12 When righteous *men* do **r**, *there is* great H5970
29: 2 the people **r**: but when the wicked H8055
6 but the righteous doth sing and **r**. H8056
31:25 and she shall **r** in time to come. H7832
Ecc 3:12 *a man* to **r**, and to do good in his life. H8055
22 that a man should **r** in his own works; H8055
4:16 after shall not **r** in him. Surely this also H8055
5:19 to **r** in his labour; this *is* the gift of God. H8055
11: 8 But if a man live many years, *and* **r** in H8055
9 **R**, O young man, in thy youth; and let H8055
Song 1: 4 we will be glad and **r** in thee, we will H8055
Isa 8: 6 and **r** in Rezin and Remaliah's son; H4885
9: 3 as *men* **r** when they divide the spoil. H1523
13: 3 *even* them that **r** in my highness. H5947
14: 8 Yea, the fir trees **r** at thee, *and* the H8055
29 **R** not thou, whole Palestina, because H8055
23:12 And he said, Thou shalt no more **r**, O H5937
24: 8 **r** endeth, the joy of the harp ceaseth. H5947
25: 9 we will be glad and **r** in his salvation. H8055
29:19 men shall **r** in the Holy One of Israel. H1523
35: 1 desert shall **r**, and blossom as the rose. H1523
2 It shall blossom abundantly, and **r** H1523
41:16 and thou shalt **r** in the LORD, *and* shalt H1523
61: 7 they shall **r** in their portion: therefore H7442
10 I will greatly **r** in the LORD, my soul H7797
62: 5 the bride, *so* shall thy God **r** over thee. H7797
65:13 shall **r**, but ye shall be ashamed: H8055
18 But be ye glad and **r** for ever *in that* H1523
19 And I will **r** in Jerusalem, and joy in my H1523
66:10 **R** ye with Jerusalem, and be glad with H8055
10 ye that love her: **r** for joy with her, all H7797
14 And when ye see *this*, your heart shall **r**, H7797
Jer 31:13 Then shall the virgin **r** in the dance, H8055
13 and make them **r** from their sorrow. H8055
32:41 Yea, I will **r** over them to do them good, H7797
51:39 that they may **r**, and sleep a perpetual H5937
Lam 2:17 *thine* enemy to **r** over thee, he hath set H8055

Lam 4:21 **R** and be glad, O daughter of Edom, H7797
Ezk 7:12 let not the buyer **r**, nor the seller mourn: H8055
35:15 As thou didst **r** at the inheritance of the H8057
Hos 9: 1 **R** not, O Israel, for joy, as *other* people: H8055
Joel 2:21 Fear not, O land; be glad and **r**: for the H8055
23 Be glad then, ye children of Zion, and **r** H8055
Am 6:13 Ye which **r** in a thing of nought, which H8056
Mic 7: 8 **R** not against me, O mine enemy: when H8055
Hab 1:15 drag: therefore they **r** and are glad. H8055
3:18 Yet I will **r** in the LORD, I will joy in the H5937
Zep 3:11 of thee them that **r** in thy pride, and H5947
14 Israel; be glad and **r** with all the heart, H5937
17 will save, he will **r** over thee with joy; he H7797
Zec 2:10 Sing and **r**, O daughter of Zion: for, lo, I H8055
4:10 things? for they shall **r**, and shall see the H8055
9: 9 **R** greatly, O daughter of Zion; shout, O H1523
10: 7 their heart shall **r** as through wine: yea, H8055
7 be glad; their heart shall **r** in the LORD. H1523
Mt 5:12 **R**, and be exceeding glad: for great *is* G5463
Lk 1:14 gladness; and many shall **r** at his birth. G5463
6:23 **R** ye in that day, and leap for joy: for, G5463
10:20 Notwithstanding in this **r** not, that the G5463
20 you; but rather **r**, because your names G5463
15: 6 saying unto them, **R** with me; for I G4796
9 together, saying, **R** with me; for I have G4796
19:37 the disciples began to **r** and praise God G5463
Jn 4:36 and he that reapeth may **r** together. G5463
5:35 were willing for a season to **r** in his light. G21
14:28 me, ye would **r**, because I said, I go G5463
16:20 but the world shall **r**: and ye shall be G5463
22 your heart shall **r**, and your joy no man G5463
Act 2:26 Therefore did my heart **r**, and my G2165
Ro 5: 2 and **r** in hope of the glory of God. G2744
12:15 **R** with them that do rejoice, and weep G5463
15 Rejoice with them that do **r**, and weep G5463
15:10 And again he saith, **R**, ye Gentiles, with G2165
1Co 7:30 not; and they that **r**, as though they G5463
12:26 be honoured, all the members **r** with it. G4796
2Co 2: 3 whom I ought to **r**; having confidence in G5463
7: 9 Now I **r**, not that ye were made sorry, G5463
16 I **r** therefore that I have confidence in G5463
Gal 4:27 For it is written, **R**, *thou* barren that G2165
Php 1:18 and I therein do **r**, yea, and will rejoice. G5463
18 and I therein do rejoice, yea, and will **r**. G5463
2:16 of life; that I may **r** in the day of Christ, G2745
17 of your faith, I joy, and **r** with you all. G4796
18 cause also do ye joy, and **r** with me. G4796
28 **r**, and that I may be the less sorrowful. G5463
3: 1 Finally, my brethren, **r** in the Lord. To G5463
3 in the spirit, and **r** in Christ Jesus, and G2744
4: 4 **R** in the Lord alway: *and* again I say, G5463
4 in the Lord alway: *and* again I say, **R**. G5463
Col 1:24 Who now **r** in my sufferings for you, G5463
1Th 5:16 **R** evermore. G5463
Jas 1: 9 Let the brother of low degree **r** in that G2744
4:16 But now ye **r** in your boastings: all such G2744
1Pt 1: 6 Wherein ye greatly **r**, though now for a G21
8 **r** with joy unspeakable and full of glory: G21
4:13 But **r**, inasmuch as ye are partakers of G5463
Rev 11:10 the earth shall **r** over them, and make G5463
12:12 Therefore **r**, *ye* heavens, and ye that G2165
18:20 **R** over her, *thou* heaven, and *ye* holy G2165
19: 7 Let us be glad and **r**, and give honour to G21

REJOICED
Ex 18: 9 And Jethro **r** for all the goodness which H2302
Dt 28:63 *that* as the LORD **r** over you to do you H7797
30: 9 thee for good, as he **r** over thy fathers: H7797
Jdg 19: 3 the damsel saw him, he **r** to meet him. H8055
1Sa 6:13 eyes, and saw the ark, and **r** to see *it*. H8055
11:15 Saul and all the men of Israel **r** greatly. H8055
1Ki 1:40 with pipes, and **r** with great joy, so that H8056
5: 7 of Solomon, that he **r** greatly, and said, H8055
2Ki 11:14 the people of the land **r**, and blew with H8056
20 And all the people of the land **r**, and the H8055
1Ch 29: 9 Then the people **r**, for that they offered H8055
9 David the king also **r** with great joy. H8055
2Ch 15:15 And all Judah **r** at the oath: for they H8055
23:13 people of the land **r**, and sounded with H8056
21 And all the people of the land **r**: and the H8055
24:10 And all the princes and all the people **r**, H8055
29:36 And Hezekiah **r**, and all the people, that H8055
30:25 of Israel, and that dwelt in Judah, **r**. H8055
Neh 12:43 sacrifices, and **r**: for God had made H8055
43 and the children **r**: so that the joy of H8055
44 Levites: for Judah **r** for the priests and H8057
Est 8:15 and the city of Shushan **r** and was glad. H6670
Job 31:25 If I **r** because my wealth *was* great, and H8055
29 If I **r** at the destruction of him that H8055
Ps 35:15 But in mine adversity they **r**, and H8055
97: 8 **r** because of thy judgments, O LORD. H1523
119:14 I have **r** in the way of thy testimonies, H7797
Ecc 2:10 any joy; for my heart **r** in all my labour: H8056
Jer 15:17 the mockers, nor **r**; I sat alone because H5937
50:11 Because ye were glad, because ye **r**, O ye H5937
Ezk 25: 6 with the feet, and **r** in heart with all thy H8055
Hos 10: 5 priests thereof *that* **r** on it, for the glory H1523
Oba 12 thou have **r** over the children of H8055
Mt 2:10 When they saw the star, they **r** with G5463
Lk 1:47 And my spirit hath **r** in God my Saviour. G21
58 mercy upon her; and they **r** with her. G4796
10:21 In that hour Jesus **r** in spirit, and said, I G21
13:17 and all the people **r** for all the glorious G5463
Jn 8:56 Your father Abraham **r** to see my day: G21
Act 7:41 and **r** in the works of their own hands. G2165
15:31 *Which* when they had read, they **r** for G5463
16:34 and **r**, believing in God with all his house. G21
1Co 7:30 as though they **r** not; and they that buy, G5463
2Co 7: 7 mind toward me; so that I **r** the more. G5463
Php 4:10 But I **r** in the Lord greatly, that now at G5463
2Jn 4 I **r** greatly that I found of thy children G5463
3Jn 3 For I **r** greatly, when the brethren came G5463

REJOICEST
Jer 11:15 thee? when thou doest evil, then thou **r**. H5937

REJOICETH
1Sa 2: 1 said, My heart **r** in the LORD, mine H5970
Job 39:21 He paweth in the valley, and **r** in *his* H7797
Ps 16: 9 glory **r**: my flesh also shall rest in hope. H1523
19: 5 *and* **r** as a strong man to run a race. H7797
28: 7 **r**; and with my song will I praise him. H5937
Prv 11:10 the righteous, the city **r**: and when the H5970
13: 9 The light of the righteous **r**: but the H8055
15:30 The light of the eyes **r** the heart: *and* a H8055
29: 3 Whoso loveth wisdom **r** his father: but H8055
Isa 5:14 and he that **r**, shall descend into it. H5938
62: 5 *as* the bridegroom **r** over the bride, *so* H4885
64: 5 Thou meetest him that **r** and worketh H7797
Ezk 35:14 whole earth **r**, I will make thee desolate. H8055
Mt 18:13 I say unto you, he **r** more of that *sheep*, G5463
Jn 3:29 and heareth him, **r** greatly because of G5463
1Co 13: 6 **R** not in iniquity, but rejoiceth in the G5463
6 Rejoiceth not in iniquity, but **r** in the G4796
Jas 2:13 mercy; and mercy **r** against judgment. G2620

REJOICING
1Ki 1:45 up from thence **r**, so that the city rang H8056
2Ch 23:18 law of Moses, with **r** and with singing, H8057
Job 8:21 with laughing, and thy lips with **r**. H8643
Ps 19: 8 The statutes of the LORD *are* right, **r** H8055
45:15 With gladness and **r** shall they be H1524
107:22 and declare his works with **r**. H7440
118:15 The voice of **r** and salvation *is* in the H7440
119:111 for ever: for they *are* the **r** of my heart. H8342
126: 6 with **r**, bringing his sheaves *with him*. H7440
Prv 8:30 daily *his* delight, **r** always before him; H7832
31 **R** in the habitable part of his earth; and H7832
Isa 65:18 Jerusalem a **r**, and her people a joy. H1525
Jer 15:16 me the joy and **r** of mine heart: for I H8057
Hab 3:14 **r** *was* as to devour the poor secretly. H5951
Zep 2:15 This *is* the **r** city that dwelt carelessly, H5947
Lk 15: 5 found *it*, he layeth *it* on his shoulders, **r**. G5463
Act 5:41 of the council, **r** that they were counted G5463
8:39 him no more: and he went on his way **r**. G5463
Ro 12:12 **R** in hope; patient in tribulation; G5463
1Co 15:31 I protest by your **r** which I have in G2746
2Co 1:12 For our **r** is this, the testimony of our G2746
14 that we are your **r**, even as ye also *are* G2745
6:10 As sorrowful, yet alway **r**; as poor, yet G5463
Gal 6: 4 **r** in himself alone, and not in another. G2745
Php 1:26 That your **r** may be more abundant in G2745
1Th 2:19 or joy, or crown of **r**? *Are* not even ye in G2746
Heb 3: 6 and the **r** of the hope firm unto the end. G2745
Jas 4:16 in your boastings: all such **r** is evil. G2746

REKEM
Nu 31: 8 *namely*, Evi, and **R**, and Zur, and Hur, H7552
Jos 13:21 Midian, Evi, and **R**, and Zur, and Hur, H7552
18:27 And **R**, and Irpeel, and Taralah, H7552
1Ch 2:43 and Tappuah, and **R**, and Shema. H7552
44 of Jorkoam: and **R** begat Shammai. H7552

RELEASE
Dt 15: 1 *every* seven years thou shalt make a **r**. H8059
2 And this *is* the manner of the **r**: Every H8059
2 neighbour shall **r** *it*; he shall not exact H8058
2 because it is called the LORD'S **r**. H8059
Dt 15: 3 with thy brother thine hand shall **r**; H8058
9 year, the year of **r**, is at hand; and thine H8059
31:10 the year of **r**, in the feast of tabernacles, H8059
Est 2:18 and he made a **r** to the provinces, and H2010
Mt 27:15 was wont to **r** unto the people a G630
17 will ye that I **r** unto you? Barabbas, G630
21 that I **r** unto you? They said, Barabbas. G630
Mk 15: 9 ye that I **r** unto you the King of the Jews? G630
11 he should rather **r** Barabbas unto them. G630
Lk 23:16 I will therefore chastise him, and **r** *him*. G630
17 (For of necessity he must **r** one unto G630
18 with this *man*, and **r** unto us Barabbas: G630
20 Pilate therefore, willing to **r** Jesus, spake G630
Jn 18:39 But ye have a custom, that I should **r** G630
39 that I **r** unto you the King of the Jews? G630
19:10 crucify thee, and have power to **r** thee? G630
12 And from thenceforth Pilate sought to **r** G630

RELEASED
Mt 27:26 Then **r** he Barabbas unto them: and G630
Mk 15: 6 Now at *that* feast he **r** unto them one G630
15 to content the people, **r** Barabbas unto G630
Lk 23:25 And he **r** unto them him that for sedition G630

RELIED
2Ch 13:18 **r** upon the LORD God of their fathers. H8172
16: 7 him, Because thou hast **r** on the king of H8172
7 of Syria, and not **r** on the LORD thy H8172

RELIEF
Act 11:29 to send **r** unto the brethren which G1519

RELIEVE
Lev 25:35 then thou shalt **r** him: *yea, though he* H2388
Isa 1:17 Learn to do well; seek judgment, **r** the H833
Lam 1:11 things for meat to **r** the soul: see, O H7725
16 that should **r** my soul is far from H7725
19 they sought their meat to **r** their souls. H7725
1Ti 5:16 widows, let them **r** them, and let not G1884
16 it may **r** them that are widows indeed. G1884

RELIEVED
1Ti 5:10 feet, if she have **r** the afflicted, if she G1884

RELIEVETH
Ps 146: 9 the strangers; he **r** the fatherless and H5749

RELIGION
Act 26: 5 straitest sect of our **r** I lived a Pharisee. G2356
Gal 1:13 past in the Jews' **r**, how that beyond G2454
14 And profited in the Jews' **r** above many G2454
Jas 1:26 his own heart, this man's **r** *is* vain. G2356
27 Pure **r** and undefiled before God and G2356

RELIGIOUS
Act 13:43 of the Jews and **r** proselytes followed G4576
Jas 1:26 If any man among you seem to be **r**, G2357

RELY
2Ch 16: 8 thou didst **r** on the LORD, he delivered H8172

REMAIN
Gen 38:11 his daughter in law, **R** a widow at thy H3427
Ex 8: 9 *that* they may **r** in the river only? H7604
11 people; they shall **r** in the river only. H7604
12:10 And ye shall let nothing of it **r** until the H3498
23:18 fat of my sacrifice **r** until the morning. H3885
29:34 or of the bread, **r** unto the morning, H3498
Lev 19: 6 and if ought **r** until the third day, H3498
25:28 which is sold shall **r** in the hand of him H1961
52 And if there **r** but few years unto the H7604
27:18 to the years that **r**, even unto the year of H3498
Nu 33:55 those which ye let **r** of them *shall be* H3498
Dt 2:34 ones, of every city, we left none to **r**: H8300
16: 4 at even, **r** all night until the morning. H3885
19:20 And those which **r** shall hear, and fear, H7604
21:13 off her, and shall **r** in thine house, and H3427
23 His body shall not **r** all night upon the H3885
Jos 1:14 your cattle, shall **r** in the land which H3427
2:11 neither did there **r** any more courage in H6965
8:22 that they let none of them **r** or escape. H8300
10:27 mouth, *which* **r** until this very day.
28 he let none **r**: and he did to the king H8300
30 he let none **r** in it; but did unto the H8300
23: 4 lot these nations that **r**, to be an H7604
7 these nations, these that **r** among you; H7604
12 *even* these that **r** among you, and shall H7604
Jdg 5:17 and why did Dan **r** in ships? Asher H1481
21: 7 for them that **r**, seeing we have sworn H3498

R

Jdg 21:16 for them that **r**, seeing the women are H3498
1Sa 20:19 *in hand,* and shalt **r** by the stone Ezel. H3427
1Ki 11:16 (For six months did Joab **r** there with H3427
18:22 I, *even* I only, **r** a prophet of the LORD; H3498
2Ki 7:13 of the horses that **r**, which are left in the H7604
Ezr 9:15 righteous: for we **r** yet escaped, as *it is* H7604
Job 21:32 to the grave, and shall **r** in the tomb. H8245
27:15 Those that **r** of him shall be buried in H8300
37: 8 Then the beasts go into dens, and **r** in H7931
Ps 55: 7 Lo, *then* would I wander far off, *and* **r** H3885
Prv 2:21 in the land, and the perfect shall **r** in it. H3498
21:16 shall **r** in the congregation of the dead. H5117
Isa 10:32 As yet shall he **r** at Nob that day: he H5975
32:16 and righteousness **r** in the fruitful field. H3427
44:13 of a man; that it may **r** in the house. H3427
65: 4 Which **r** among the graves, and lodge H3427
66:22 I will make, shall **r** before me, saith the H5975
22 so shall your seed and your name **r**. H5975
Jer 8: 3 of them that **r** of this evil family, which H7604
3 this evil family, which **r** in all the places H7604
17:25 Jerusalem: and this city shall **r** for ever. H3427
24: 8 of Jerusalem, that **r** in this land, and H7604
27:11 those will I let **r** still in their own land, H3240
19 residue of the vessels that **r** in this city, H3498
21 the vessels that **r** *in* the house of the H3498
30:18 palace shall **r** after the manner thereof. H3427
38: 4 men of war that **r** in this city, and the H7604
42:17 none of them shall **r** or escape from the H8300
44: 7 out of Judah, to leave you none to **r**; H7611
14 there, shall escape or **r**, that they should H8300
51:62 that none shall **r** in it, neither man nor H3427
Ezk 7:11 none of them *shall* **r**, nor of their
17:21 and they that **r** shall be scattered H7604
31:13 of the heaven **r**, and all the beasts of H7931
32: 4 of the heaven to **r** upon thee, and I will H7931
39:14 those that **r** upon the face of the H3498
Am 6: 9 And it shall come to pass, if there **r** ten H3498
Oba 14 of his that did **r** in the day of distress. H8300
Zec 5: 4 name: and it shall **r** in the midst of his H3885
12:14 All the families that **r**, every family H7604
Lk 10: 7 And in the same house **r**, eating and G3306
Jn 6:12 fragments that **r**, that nothing be lost. G4052
15:11 that my joy might **r** in you, and *that* G3306
16 your fruit should **r**: that whatsoever ye G3306
19:31 bodies should not **r** upon the cross on G3306
1Co 7:11 But and if she depart, let her **r** G3306
15: 6 the greater part **r** unto this present, but G3306
1Th 4:15 are alive *and* **r** unto the coming of G4035
17 Then we which are alive *and* **r** shall be G4035
Heb 12:27 things which cannot be shaken may **r**. G3306
1Jn 2:24 beginning shall **r** in you, ye also shall G3306
Rev 3: 2 the things which **r**, that are ready to die: G3062

REMAINDER

Ex 29:34 shalt burn the **r** with fire: it shall not H3498
Lev 6:16 And the **r** thereof shall Aaron and his H3498
7:16 morrow also the **r** of it shall be eaten: H3498
17 But the **r** of the flesh of the sacrifice on H3498
2Sa 14: 7 *neither* name nor **r** upon the earth. H7611
Ps 76:10 thee: the **r** of wrath shalt thou restrain. H7611

REMAINED

Gen 7:23 and Noah only **r** *alive,* and they that H7604
14:10 and they that **r** fled to the mountain. H7604
Ex 8:31 and from his people; there **r** not one. H7604
10:15 hail had left: and there **r** not any green H3498
19 the Red sea; there **r** not one locust in all H7604
14:28 there **r** not so much as one of them. H7604
Nu 11:26 But there **r** two *of the* men in the camp, H7604
35:28 Because he should have **r** in the city of H3427
36:12 their inheritance **r** in the tribe of the H1961
Dt 3:11 For only Og king of Bashan **r** of the H7604
4:25 and ye shall have **r** long in the land, H3462
Jos 10:20 **r** of them entered into fenced cities. H8277
11:22 Gaza, in Gath, and in Ashdod, there **r**. H7604
13:12 and in Edrei, who **r** of the remnant of H7604
18: 2 And there **r** among the children of H3498
21:20 the Levites which **r** of the children of H3498
26 of the children of Kohath that **r**. H3498
Jdg 7: 3 thousand; and there **r** ten thousand. H7604
1Sa 11:11 that they which **r** were scattered, so H7604
23:14 in strong holds, and **r** in a mountain in H3427
24: 3 and his men **r** in the sides of the cave. H3427
2Sa 13:20 this thing. So Tamar **r** desolate in her H3427
1Ki 22:46 sodomites, which **r** in the days of his H7604
2Ki 10:11 So Jehu slew all that **r** of the house of H7604
17 he slew all that **r** unto Ahab in H7604
13: 6 and there **r** the grove also in Samaria.) H5975
24:14 and smiths: none **r**, save the poorest H7604
2Ki 25:22 And *as for* the people that **r** in the land H7604
1Ch 13:14 And the ark of God **r** with the family of H3427
Ecc 2: 9 Jerusalem: also my wisdom **r** with me. H5975
Jer 34: 7 defenced cities **r** of the cities of Judah. H7604
37:10 you, and there **r** *but* wounded men H7604
16 and Jeremiah had **r** there many days; H3427
21 Jeremiah **r** in the court of the prison. H3427
38:13 Jeremiah **r** in the court of the prison. H3427
39: 9 of the people that **r** in the city, and H7604
9 him, with the rest of the people that **r**. H7604
41:10 all the people that **r** in Mizpah, whom H7604
48:11 **r** in him, and his scent is not changed. H5975
51:30 to fight, they have **r** in *their* holds: their H3427
52:15 of the people that **r** in the city, and H7604
Lam 2:22 none escaped nor **r**: those that I have H8300
Ezk 3:15 they sat, and **r** there astonished among H3427
Dan 10: 8 vision, and there **r** no strength in me: H7604
13 and I **r** there with the kings of Persia. H3498
17 straightway there **r** no strength in me, H5975
Mt 11:23 Sodom, it would have **r** until this day. G3306
14:20 fragments that **r** twelve baskets full. G4052
Lk 1:22 beckoned unto them, and **r** speechless. G1265
9:17 that **r** to them twelve baskets. G4052
Jn 6:13 loaves, which **r** over and above unto G4052
Act 5: 4 Whiles it **r**, was it not thine own? and G3306
27:41 stuck fast, and **r** unmoveable, but the G3306

REMAINEST

Lam 5:19 Thou, O LORD, **r** for ever; thy throne H3427
Heb 1:11 They shall perish; but thou **r**; and they G1265

REMAINETH

Gen 8:22 While the earth **r**, seedtime and H3117
Ex 10: 5 is escaped, which **r** unto you from the H7604
12:10 and that which **r** of it until the morning H3498
16:23 and that which **r** over lay up for you H5736
26:12 And the remnant that **r** of the curtains H5736
12 half curtain that **r**, shall hang over the H5736
13 side of that which **r** in the length of the H5736
Lev 8:32 And that which **r** of the flesh and of the H3498
10:12 meat offering that **r** of the offerings of H3498
16:16 congregation, that **r** among them in the H7931
Nu 24:19 and shall destroy him that **r** of the city. H8300
Jos 8:29 heap of stones, *that* **r** unto this day.
13: 1 **r** yet very much land to be possessed. H7604
2 This *is* the land that yet **r**: all the H7604
Jdg 5:13 Then he made him that **r** have H8300
1Sa 6:18 LORD: *which stone* **r** unto this day in the
16:11 he said, There **r** yet the youngest, and, H7604
1Ch 17: 1 covenant of the LORD *r* under curtains.
Ezr 1: 4 And whosoever **r** in any place where he H7604
Job 19: 4 I have erred, mine error **r** with myself. H3885
21:34 in your answers there **r** falsehood? H7604
41:22 In his neck **r** strength, and sorrow is H3885
Isa 4: 3 Zion, and *he that* **r** in Jerusalem, shall H3498
Jer 38: 2 Thus saith the LORD, He that **r** in this H3427
47: 4 every helper that **r**: for the LORD will H8300
Ezk 6:12 sword; and he that **r** and is besieged H7604
Hag 2: 5 so my spirit **r** among you: fear ye not. H5975
Zec 9: 7 teeth: but he that **r**, even he, *shall be* for H7604
Jn 9:41 ye say, We see; therefore your sin **r**. G3306
1Co 7:29 the time *is* short: it **r**, that both they that G2076
2Co 3:11 much more that which **r** *is* glorious. G3306
14 for until this day **r** the same veil G3306
9: 9 the poor: his righteousness **r** for ever. G3306
Heb 4: 6 Seeing therefore it **r** that some must G620
9 There **r** therefore a rest to the people of G620
10:26 truth, there **r** no more sacrifice for sins, G620
1Jn 3: 9 sin; for his seed **r** in him: and he G3306

REMAINING

Nu 9:22 the tabernacle, **r** thereon, the children H7931
Dt 3: 3 smote him until none was left to him **r**. H8300
Jos 10:33 his people, until he had left him none **r**. H8300
37 he left none **r**, according to all that H8300
39 he left none **r**: as he had done to H8300
40 their kings: he left none **r**, but utterly H8300
11: 8 smote them, until they left them none **r**. H8300
21:40 which were **r** of the families of the H3498
2Sa 21: 5 from **r** in any of the coasts of Israel, H3320
2Ki 10:11 and his priests, until he left him none **r**. H8300
1Ch 9:33 of the Levites, *who* **r** in the chambers
Job 18:19 his people, nor any **r** in his dwellings. H8300
Oba 18 shall not be *any* **r** of the house of Esau; H8300
Jn 1:33 descending, and **r** on him, the same is G3306

REMALIAH

2Ki 15:25 But Pekah the son of **R**, a captain of his, H7425
27 Pekah the son of **R** began to reign over H7425
2Ki 15:30 Pekah the son of **R**, and smote him, and H7425
32 Pekah the son of **R** king of Israel began H7425
37 king of Syria, and Pekah the son of **R**. H7425
16: 1 of Pekah the son of **R** Ahaz the son of H7425
5 and Pekah son of **R** king of Israel came H7425
2Ch 28: 6 For Pekah the son of **R** slew in Judah H7425
Isa 7: 1 Pekah the son of **R**, king of Israel, went H7425
4 of Rezin with Syria, and of the son of **R**. H7425
5 and the son of **R**, have taken evil H7425

REMALIAH'S

Isa 7: 9 head of Samaria *is* **R** son. If ye will not H7425
8: 6 softly, and rejoice in Rezin and **R** son; H7425

REMEDY

2Ch 36:16 against his people, till *there was* no **r**. H4832
Prv 6:15 suddenly shall he be broken without **r**. H4832
29: 1 be destroyed, and that without **r**. H4832

REMEMBER

Gen 9:15 And I will **r** my covenant, which *is* H2142
16 upon it, that I may **r** the everlasting H2142
40:23 Yet did not the chief butler **r** Joseph, H2142
41: 9 saying, I do **r** my faults this day: H2142
Ex 13: 3 And Moses said unto the people, **R** this H2142
20: 8 **R** the sabbath day, to keep it holy. H2142
32:13 **R** Abraham, Isaac, and Israel, thy H2142
Lev 26:42 Then will I **r** my covenant with Jacob, H2142
42 will I **r**; and I will remember the land. H2142
42 will I remember; and I will **r** the land. H2142
45 But I will for their sakes **r** the covenant H2142
Nu 11: 5 We **r** the fish, which we did eat in H2142
15:39 may look upon it, and **r** all the H2142
40 That ye may **r**, and do all my H2142
Dt 5:15 And **r** that thou wast a servant in the H2142
7:18 *but* shalt well **r** what the LORD thy H2142
8: 2 And thou shalt **r** all the way which the H2142
18 But thou shalt **r** the LORD thy God: for H2142
9: 7 **R**, *and* forget not, how thou provokedst H2142
27 **R** thy servants, Abraham, Isaac, and H2142
15:15 And thou shalt **r** that thou wast a H2142
16: 3 that thou mayest **r** the day when thou H2142
12 And thou shalt **r** that thou wast a H2142
24: 9 **R** what the LORD thy God did unto H2142
18 But thou shalt **r** that thou wast a H2142
22 And thou shalt **r** that thou wast a H2142
25:17 **R** what Amalek did unto thee by the H2142
32: 7 **R** the days of old, consider the years of H2142
Jos 1:13 **R** the word which Moses the servant of H2142
Jdg 9: 2 reign over you? **r** also that I *am* your H2142
16:28 said, O Lord GOD, **r** me, I pray thee, H2142
1Sa 1:11 handmaid, and **r** me, and not forget H2142
15: 2 Thus saith the LORD of hosts, I **r** *that* H6485
25:31 with my lord, then **r** thine handmaid. H2142
2Sa 14:11 Then said she, I pray thee, let the king **r** H2142
19:19 me, neither do thou **r** that which thy H2142
2Ki 9:25 the Jezreelite: for **r** how that, when I H2142
20: 3 I beseech thee, O LORD, **r** now how I H2142
1Ch 16:12 **R** his marvellous works that he hath H2142
2Ch 6:42 **r** the mercies of David thy servant. H2142
Neh 1: 8 **R**, I beseech thee, the word that thou H2142
4:14 ye afraid of them: **r** the Lord, *which is* H2142
13:14 **R** me, O my God, concerning this, and H2142
22 the sabbath day. **R** me, O my God, H2142
29 **R** them, O my God, because they have H2142
31 firstfruits. **R** me, O my God, for good. H2142
Job 4: 7 **R**, I pray thee, who *ever* perished, being H2142
7: 7 O **r** that my life *is* wind: mine eye shall H2142
10: 9 **R**, I beseech thee, that thou hast made H2142
11:16 *and* **r** *it* as waters *that* pass away: H2142
14:13 appoint me a set time, and **r** me! H2142
21: 6 Even when I **r** I am afraid, and H2142
36:24 **R** that thou magnify his work, which H2142
41: 8 Lay thine hand upon him, **r** the battle, H2142
Ps 20: 3 **R** all thy offerings, and accept thy H2142
7 will **r** the name of the LORD our God. H2142
22:27 All the ends of the world shall **r** and H2142
25: 6 **R**, O LORD, thy tender mercies and thy H2142
7 **R** not the sins of my youth, nor my H2142
7 to thy mercy **r** thou me for thy H2142
42: 4 When I **r** these *things,* I pour out my H2142
6 therefore will I **r** thee from the land of H2142
63: 6 When I **r** thee upon my bed, *and* H2142
74: 2 **R** thy congregation, *which* thou hast H2142
18 **R** this, *that* the enemy hath H2142
22 Arise, O God, plead thine own cause: **r** H2142
77:10 *but I will* **r** the years of the right H2142
11 I will **r** the works of the LORD: surely I H2142
11 surely I will **r** thy wonders of old. H2142

Ps 79: 8 O r not against us former iniquities: let H2142
89:47 R how short my time is: wherefore hast H2142
50 R, Lord, the reproach of thy servants; H2142
103:18 that r his commandments to do them. H2142
105: 5 R his marvellous works that he hath H2142
106: 4 R me, O LORD, with the favour *that* H2142
119:49 R the word unto thy servant, upon H2142
132: 1 LORD, r David, *and* all his afflictions: H2142
137: 6 If I do not r thee, let my tongue cleave H2142
7 R, O LORD, the children of Edom in the H2142
143: 5 I r the days of old; I meditate on all thy H2142
Prv 31: 7 his poverty, and r his misery no more. H2142
Ecc 5:20 For he shall not much r the days of his H2142
11: 8 all; yet let him r the days of darkness; H2142
12: 1 R now thy Creator in the days of thy H2142
Song 1: 4 in thee, we will r thy love more than H2142
Isa 38: 3 And said, R now, O LORD, I beseech H2142
43:18 R ye not the former things, neither H2142
25 mine own sake, and will not r thy sins. H2142
44:21 R these, O Jacob and Israel; for thou H2142
46: 8 R this, and shew yourselves men: bring H2142
9 R the former things of old: for I *am* H2142
47: 7 neither didst r the latter end of it. H2142
54: 4 and shalt not r the reproach of thy H2142
64: 5 *those that* r thee in thy ways: behold, H2142
9 O LORD, neither r iniquity for ever: H2142
Jer 2: 2 saith the LORD; I r thee, the kindness H2142
3:16 neither shall they r it; neither shall they H2142
14:10 r their iniquity, and visit their sins. H2142
21 glory: r, break not thy covenant with us. H2142
15:15 O LORD, thou knowest: r me, and visit H2142
17: 2 Whilst their children r their altars and H2142
18:20 a pit for my soul. R that I stood before H2142
31:20 I do earnestly r him still: therefore my H2142
34 iniquity, and I will r their sin no more. H2142
44:21 r them, and came it *not* into his mind? H2142
51:50 stand not still: r the LORD afar off, and H2142
Lam 5: 1 R, O LORD, what is come upon us: H2142
Ezk 6: 9 And they that escape of you shall r me H2142
16:60 Nevertheless I will r my covenant with H2142
61 Then thou shalt r thy ways, and be H2142
63 That thou mayest r, and be H2142
20:43 And there shall ye r your ways, and all H2142
23:27 eyes unto them, nor r Egypt any more. H2142
36:31 Then shall ye r your own evil ways, and H2142
Hos 7: 2 in their hearts *that* I r all their H2142
8:13 not; now will he r their iniquity, and H2142
9: 9 r their iniquity, he will visit their sins. H2142
Mic 6: 5 O my people, r now what Balak king of H2142
Hab 3: 2 years make known; in wrath r mercy. H2142
Zec 10: 9 and they shall r me in far countries; H2142
Mal 4: 4 R ye the law of Moses my servant, H2142
Mt 16: 9 Do ye not yet understand, neither r the G3421
27:63 Saying, Sir, we r that that deceiver G3415
Mk 8:18 ears, hear ye not? and do ye not r? G3421
Lk 1:72 our fathers, and to r his holy covenant; G3415
16:25 But Abraham said, Son, r that thou in G3415
17:32 R Lot's wife. G3421
23:42 And he said unto Jesus, Lord, r me G3415
24: 6 He is not here, but is risen: r how he G3415
Jn 15:20 R the word that I said unto you, The G3421
16: 4 come, ye may r that I told you of them. G3421
Act 20:31 Therefore watch, and r, that by the G3421
35 the weak, and to r the words of the G3421
1Co 11: 2 Now I praise you, brethren, that ye r G3415
Gal 2:10 Only *they would* that we should r the G3421
Eph 2:11 Wherefore r, that ye *being* in time past G3421
Col 4:18 R my bonds. Grace *be* with you. Amen. G3421
1Th 2: 9 For ye r, brethren, our labour and G3421
2Th 2: 5 R ye not, that, when I was yet with you, G3421
2Ti 2: 8 R that Jesus Christ of the seed of David G3421
Heb 8:12 and their iniquities will I r no more. G3415
10:17 And their sins and iniquities will I r no G3415
13: 3 R them that are in bonds, as bound G3403
7 R them which have the rule over you, G3421
3Jn 10 Wherefore, if I come, I will r his deeds G5279
Jude 17 But, beloved, r ye the words which G3415
Rev 2: 5 R therefore from whence thou art G3421
3: 3 R therefore how thou hast received and G3421

REMEMBERED
Gen 8: 1 And God r Noah, and every living H2142
19:29 of the plain, that God r Abraham, and H2142
30:22 And God r Rachel, and God hearkened H2142
42: 9 And Joseph r the dreams which he H2142
Ex 2:24 and God r his covenant with Abraham, H2142
6: 5 in bondage; and I have r my covenant. H2142
Nu 10: 9 and ye shall be r before the LORD your H2142
Jdg 8:34 And the children of Israel r not the H2142
1Sa 1:19 Hannah his wife; and the LORD r her. H2142
2Ch 24:22 Thus Joash the king r not the kindness H2142
Est 2: 1 was appeased, he r Vashti, and what H2142
9:28 And *that* these days *should be* r and H2142
Job 24:20 he shall be no more r; and wickedness H2142
Ps 45:17 I will make thy name to be r in all H2142
77: 3 I r God, and was troubled: I H2142
78:35 And they r that God *was* their rock, H2142
39 For he r that they *were but* flesh; a H2142
42 They r not his hand, *nor* the day when H2142
98: 3 He hath r his mercy and his truth H2142
105: 8 He hath r his covenant for ever, the H2142
42 For he r his holy promise, *and* H2142
106: 7 in Egypt; they r not the multitude of H2142
45 And he r for them his covenant, and H2142
109:14 Let the iniquity of his fathers be r with H2142
16 Because that he r not to shew mercy, H2142
111: 4 works to be r: the LORD *is* gracious H2143
119:52 I r thy judgments of old, O LORD; and H2142
55 I have r thy name, O LORD, in the H2142
136:23 Who r us in our low estate: for his H2142
137: 1 down, yea, we wept, when we r Zion. H2142
Ecc 9:15 city; yet no man r that same poor man. H2142
Isa 23:16 sing many songs, that thou mayest be r. H2142
57:11 lied, and hast not r me, nor laid *it* to H2142
63:11 Then he r the days of old, Moses, *and* H2142
65:17 shall not be r, nor come into mind. H2142
Jer 11:19 living, that his name may be no more r. H2142
Lam 1: 7 Jerusalem r in the days of her affliction H2142
2: 1 of Israel, and r not his footstool in H2142
Ezk 3:20 done shall not be r; but his blood will I H2142
16:22 thou hast not r the days of thy youth, H2142
43 Because thou hast not r the days of thy H2142
21:24 made your iniquity to be r, in that your H2142
32 *more* r: for I the LORD have spoken *it*. H2142
25:10 may not be r among the nations. H2142
33:13 shall not be r; but for his iniquity that H2142
Hos 2:17 they shall no more be r by their name. H2142
Am 1: 9 and r not the brotherly covenant: H2142
Jna 2: 7 When my soul fainted within me I r the H2142
Zec 13: 2 shall no more be r: and also I will cause H2142
Mt 26:75 And Peter r the word of Jesus, which G3415
Lk 22:61 Peter. And Peter r the word of the Lord, G5279
24: 8 And they r his words, G3415
Jn 2:17 And his disciples r that it was written, G3415
22 dead, his disciples r that he had said G3415
12:16 was glorified, then r they that these G3415
Act 11:16 Then r I the word of the Lord, how that G3415
Rev 18: 5 heaven, and God hath r her iniquities. G3421

REMEMBEREST
Ps 88: 5 grave, whom thou r no more: and they H2142
Mt 5:23 altar, and there r that thy brother hath G3415

REMEMBERETH
Ps 9:12 for blood, he r them: he forgetteth H2142
103:14 For he knoweth our frame; he r that we H2142
Lam 1: 9 Her filthiness *is* in her skirts; she r not H2142
Jn 16:21 of the child, she r no more the anguish, G3421
2Co 7:15 you, whilst he r the obedience of you G363

REMEMBERING
Lam 3:19 R mine affliction and my misery, the H2142
1Th 1: 3 R without ceasing your work of faith, G3421

REMEMBRANCE
Ex 17:14 the r of Amalek from under heaven. H2143
Nu 5:15 of memorial, bringing iniquity to r. H2142
Dt 25:19 shalt blot out the r of Amalek from H2143
32:26 r of them to cease from among men: H2143
2Sa 18:18 to keep my name in r: and he called the H2142
1Ki 17:18 to call my sin to r, and to slay my son? H2142
Job 18:17 His r shall perish from the earth, and H2143
Ps 6: 5 For in death *there is* no r of thee: in the H2143
30: 4 and give thanks at the r of his holiness. H2143
34:16 to cut off the r of them from the earth. H2143
38:ttl A Psalm of David, to bring to r. H2142
70:ttl *A Psalm* of David, to bring to r. H2142
77: 6 I call to r my song in the night: I H2142
83: 4 the name of Israel may be no more in r. H2142
97:12 and give thanks at the r of his holiness. H2143
102:12 for ever; and thy r unto all generations. H2143
112: 6 the righteous shall be in everlasting r. H2143
Ecc 1:11 *There is* no r of former *things*; neither H2146
11 shall there be *any* r of *things* that are to H2146
2:16 For *there is* no r of the wise more than H2146
Isa 26: 8 soul *is* to thy name, and to the r of thee. H2143
43:26 Put me in r: let us plead together: H2142
57: 8 hast thou set up thy r: for thou hast H2146
Lam 3:20 My soul hath *them* still in r, and is H2142
Ezk 21:23 r the iniquity, that they may be taken. H2142
24 to r, ye shall be taken with the hand. H2142
23:19 in calling to r the days of her youth, H2142
21 Thus thou calledst to r the lewdness of H6485
29:16 *their* iniquity to r, when they shall look H2142
Mal 3:16 *it*, and a book of r was written before H2146
Mk 11:21 And Peter calling to r saith unto him, G363
Lk 1:54 He hath holpen his servant Israel, in r G3415
22:19 which is given for you: this do in r of me. G364
Jn 14:26 r, whatsoever I have said unto you. G5279
Act 10:31 alms are had in r in the sight of God. G3415
1Co 4:17 bring you into r of my ways which be G363
11:24 is broken for you: this do in r of me. G364
25 do ye, as oft as ye drink *it*, in r of me. G364
Php 1: 3 I thank my God upon every r of you, G3417
1Th 3: 6 and that ye have good r of us always, G3417
1Ti 4: 6 If thou put the brethren in r of these G5294
2Ti 1: 3 r of thee in my prayers night and day; G3417
5 When I call to r the unfeigned faith G5280
6 Wherefore I put thee in r that thou stir G363
2:14 Of these things put *them* in r, charging G5279
Heb 10: 3 But in those *sacrifices there is* a r again G364
32 But call to r the former days, in which, G363
2Pt 1:12 to put you always in r of these things, G5279
13 to stir you up by putting *you* in r; G5280
15 to have these things always in r. G3420
3: 1 I stir up your pure minds by way of r: G5280
Jude 5 I will therefore put you in r, though ye G5279
Rev 16:19 Babylon came in r before God, to give G3415

REMEMBRANCES
Job 13:12 Your r *are* like unto ashes, your bodies H2146

REMETH
Jos 19:21 And R, and En-gannim, and H7432

REMISSION
Mt 26:28 which is shed for many for the r of sins. G859
Mk 1: 4 baptism of repentance for the r of sins. G859
Lk 1:77 unto his people by the r of their sins, G859
3: 3 baptism of repentance for the r of sins; G859
24:47 And that repentance and r of sins should G859
Act 2:38 Jesus Christ for the r of sins, and ye shall G859
10:43 believeth in him shall receive r of sins. G859
Ro 3:25 for the r of sins that are past, G3929
Heb 9:22 and without shedding of blood is no r. G859
10:18 Now where r of these *is, there is* no more G859

REMIT
Jn 20:23 Whose soever sins ye r, they are remitted G863

REMITTED
Jn 20:23 Whose soever sins ye remit, they are r G863

REMMON
Jos 19: 7 Ain, R, and Ether, and Ashan; four H7417

REMMONMETHOAR
Jos 19:13 and goeth out to R to Neah; H7417

REMNANT
Ex 26:12 And the r that remaineth of the H5629
Lev 2: 3 And the r of the meat offering *shall be* H3498
5:13 *r* shall be the priest's, as a meat offering.
14:18 And the r of the oil that *is* in the priest's H3498
Dt 3:11 remained of the r of giants; behold, his H3499
28:54 r of his children which he shall leave: H3499
Jos 12: 4 *which was* of the r of the giants, that H3499
13:12 who remained of the r of the giants: for H3499
23:12 cleave unto the r of these nations, *even* H3499
2Sa 21: 2 Israel, but of the r of the Amorites; and H3499
1Ki 12:23 and to the r of the people, saying, H3499
14:10 and will take away the r of the house of H310
22:46 And the r of the sodomites, which H3499
2Ki 19: 4 lift up *thy* prayer for the r that are left. H7611
30 And the r that is escaped of the house H7604
31 For out of Jerusalem shall go forth a r, H7611
21:14 And I will forsake the r of mine H7611
25:11 of Babylon, with the r of the multitude, H3499
1Ch 6:70 family of the r of the sons of Kohath. H3498
2Ch 30: 6 he will return to the r of you, that are H7604
34: 9 and of all the r of Israel, and of all H7611
Ezr 3: 8 Jozadak, and the r of their brethren the H7605
9: 8 our God, to leave us a r to escape, and to
14 that *there should be* no r nor escaping? H7611
Neh 1: 3 And they said unto me, The r that are H7604
Job 22:20 but the r of them the fire consumeth. H3499
Isa 1: 9 us a very small r, we should have been H8300

Isa 10:20 that day, *that* the **r** of Israel, and such H7605
21 The **r** shall return, *even* the remnant of H7605
21 The remnant shall return, *even* the **r** of H7605
22 of the sea, *yet* a **r** of them shall return: H7605
11:11 to recover the **r** of his people, which H7605
16 And there shall be an highway for the **r** H7605
14:22 the name, and **r**, and son, and nephew, H7605
30 with famine, and he shall slay thy **r**. H7611
15: 9 of Moab, and upon the **r** of the land. H7611
16:14 the **r** *shall be* very small *and* feeble. H7605
17: 3 and the **r** of Syria: they shall be H7605
37: 4 lift up *thy* prayer for the **r** that is left. H7611
31 And the **r** that is escaped of the house H7604
32 For out of Jerusalem shall go forth a **r**, H7611
46: 3 of Jacob, and all the **r** of the house of H7611
Jer 6: 9 glean the **r** of Israel as a vine: turn H7611
11:23 And there shall be no **r** of them: for I H7611
15:11 be well with thy **r**; verily I will cause the H8293
23: 3 And I will gather the **r** of my flock out H7611
25:20 and Ekron, and the **r** of Ashdod, H7611
31: 7 LORD, save thy people, the **r** of Israel. H7611
39: 9 into Babylon the **r** of the people that H3499
40:11 Babylon had left a **r** of Judah, and that H7611
15 be scattered, and the **r** in Judah perish? H7611
41:16 with him, all the **r** of the people whom H7611
42: 2 *even* for all this **r**; (for we are left *but* a H7611
15 of the LORD, ye **r** of Judah; Thus saith H7611
19 you, O ye **r** of Judah; Go ye not H7611
43: 5 forces, took all the **r** of Judah, that were H7611
44:12 And I will take the **r** of Judah, that have H7611
14 So that none of the **r** of Judah, which H7611
28 Judah, and all the **r** of Judah, that are H7611
47: 4 the **r** of the country of Caphtor. H7611
5 is cut off *with* the **r** of their valley: how H7611
Ezk 5:10 **r** of thee will I scatter into all the winds. H7611
6: 8 Yet will I leave a **r**, that ye may have H3498
11:13 thou make a full end of the **r** of Israel? H7611
14:22 Yet, behold, therein shall be left a **r** that H6413
23:25 and thine ears; and thy **r** shall fall by the H319
25:16 and destroy the **r** of the sea coast. H7611
Joel 2:32 and in the **r** whom the LORD shall call. H8300
Am 1: 8 Ekron: and the **r** of the Philistines shall H7611
5:15 will be gracious unto the **r** of Joseph. H7611
9:12 That they may possess the **r** of Edom, H7611
Mic 2:12 surely gather the **r** of Israel; I will put H7611
4: 7 And I will make her that halted a **r**, and H7611
5: 3 forth: then the **r** of his brethren shall H3499
7 And the **r** of Jacob shall be in the midst H7611
8 And the **r** of Jacob shall be among the H7611
7:18 of the **r** of his heritage? he retaineth H7611
Hab 2: 8 nations, all the **r** of the people shall H3499
Zep 1: 4 and I will cut off the **r** of Baal from this H7605
2: 7 And the coast shall be for the **r** of the H7611
9 the **r** of my people shall possess them. H3499
3:13 The **r** of Israel shall not do iniquity, nor H7611
Hag 1:12 high priest, with all the **r** of the people, H7611
14 the spirit of all the **r** of the people; and H7611
Zec 8: 6 in the eyes of the **r** of this people in H7611
12 and I will cause the **r** of this people to H7611
Mt 22: 6 And the **r** took his servants, and *G3062*
Ro 9:27 the sand of the sea, a **r** shall be saved: *G2640*
11: 5 is a **r** according to the election of grace. *G3005*
Rev 11:13 thousand: and the **r** were affrighted, *G3062*
12:17 make war with the **r** of her seed, which *G3062*
19:21 And the **r** were slain with the sword of *G3062*

REMOVE
Gen 48:17 father's hand, to **r** it from Ephraim's H5493
Nu 36: 7 children of Israel **r** from tribe to tribe: H5437
9 Neither shall the inheritance **r** from H5437
Dt 19:14 Thou shalt not **r** thy neighbour's H5253
Jos 3: 3 shall **r** from your place, and go after it. H5265
Jdg 9:29 then would I **r** Abimelech. And he H5493
2Sa 6:10 So David would not **r** the ark of the H5493
2Ki 23:27 And the LORD said, I will **r** Judah also H5493
24: 3 upon Judah, to **r** *them* out of his sight, H5493
2Ch 33: 8 Neither will I any more **r** the foot of H5493
Job 24: 2 *Some* **r** the landmarks; they violently H5381
27: 5 die I will not **r** mine integrity from me. H5493
Ps 36:11 let not the hand of the wicked **r** me. H5110
39:10 **R** thy stroke away from me: I am H5493
119:22 **R** from me reproach and contempt; for H1556
29 **R** from me the way of lying: and grant H5493
Prv 4:27 nor to the left: **r** thy foot from evil. H5493
5: 8 **R** thy way far from her, and come not H7368
22:28 **R** not the ancient landmark, which thy H5253
23:10 **R** not the old landmark; and enter not H5253
30: 8 **R** far from me vanity and lies: give me H7368
Ecc 11:10 Therefore **r** sorrow from thy heart, and H5493
Isa 13:13 and the earth shall **r** out of her place, in H7493
46: 7 place shall he not **r**: yea, *one* shall cry H4185
Jer 4: 1 out of my sight, then shalt thou not **r**. H5110
27:10 For they prophesy a lie unto you, to **r** H7368
32:31 that I should **r** it from before my face, H5493
50: 3 therein: they shall **r**, they shall depart, H5110
8 **R** out of the midst of Babylon, and go H5110
Ezk 12: 3 for removing, and **r** by day in their H1540
3 and thou shalt **r** from thy place to H1540
11 them: they shall **r** *and* go into captivity. H1473
21:26 Thus saith the Lord GOD; **R** the H5493
45: 9 O princes of Israel: **r** violence and spoil, H5493
Hos 5:10 like them that **r** the bound: *therefore* H5253
Joel 2:20 But I will **r** far off from you the H7368
3: 6 ye might **r** them far from their border. H7368
Mic 2: 3 which ye shall not **r** your necks; neither H4185
Zec 3: 9 **r** the iniquity of that land in one day. H4185
14: 4 mountain shall **r** toward the north, and H4185
Mt 17:20 unto this mountain, **R** hence to yonder *G3327*
20 place; and it shall **r**; and nothing shall *G3327*
Lk 22:42 Saying, Father, if thou be willing, **r** this *G3911*
1Co 13: 2 so that I could **r** mountains, and have *G3179*
Rev 2: 5 quickly, and will **r** thy candlestick out *G2795*

REMOVED
Gen 8:13 earth: and Noah **r** the covering of the H5493
12: 8 And he **r** from thence unto a mountain H6275
13:18 Then Abram **r** *his* tent, and came and
26:22 And he **r** from thence, and digged H6275
30:35 And he **r** that day the he goats that H5493
47:21 And as for the people, he **r** them to H5674
Ex 8:31 of Moses; and he **r** the swarms *of flies* H5493
14:19 the camp of Israel, **r** and went behind H5265
20:18 people saw *it*, they **r**, and stood afar off. H5128
Nu 12:16 And afterward the people **r** from H5265
21:12 From thence they **r**, and pitched in the H5265
13 From thence they **r**, and pitched on the H5265
33: 5 And the children of Israel **r** from H5265
7 And they **r** from Etham, and turned H5265
9 And they **r** from Marah, and came H5265
10 And they **r** from Elim, and encamped H5265
11 And they **r** from the Red sea, and H5265
14 And they **r** from Alush, and encamped H5265
16 And they **r** from the desert of Sinai, H5265
21 And they **r** from Libnah, and pitched at H5265
24 And they **r** from mount Shapher, and H5265
25 And they **r** from Haradah, and pitched H5265
26 And they **r** from Makheloth, and H5265
28 And they **r** from Tarah, and pitched in H5265
32 And they **r** from Bene-jaakan, and H5265
34 And they **r** from Jotbathah, and H5265
36 And they **r** from Ezion-gaber, and H5265
37 And they **r** from Kadesh, and pitched H5265
46 And they **r** from Dibon-gad, and H5265
47 And they **r** from Almon-diblathaim, H5265
Dt 28:25 be **r** into all the kingdoms of the earth. H2189
Jos 3: 1 morning; and they **r** from Shittim, and H5265
14 And it came to pass, when the people **r** H5265
1Sa 6: 3 to you why his hand is not **r** from you. H5493
18:13 Therefore Saul **r** him from him, and H5493
2Sa 20:12 stood still, he **r** Amasa out of the H5437
13 When he was **r** out of the highway, all H3014
1Ki 15:12 of the land, and **r** all the idols that his H5493
13 even her he **r** from *being* queen, H5493
14 But the high places were not **r**: H5493
2Ki 15: 4 Save that the high places were not **r**: the H5493
35 Howbeit the high places were not **r**: the H5493
16:17 of the bases, and **r** the laver from off H5493
17:18 with Israel, and **r** them out of his sight: H5493
23 Until the LORD **r** Israel out of his sight, H5493
26 which thou hast **r**, and placed in the H1540
18: 4 He **r** the high places, and brake the H5493
23:27 of my sight, as I have **r** Israel, and will H5493
1Ch 8: 6 of Geba, and they **r** them to Manahath: H1540
7 **r** them, and begat Uzza, and Ahihud. H1540
2Ch 15:16 of Asa the king, he **r** her from *being* H5493
35:12 And they **r** the burnt offerings, that H5493
Job 14:18 and the rock is **r** out of his place. H6275
18: 4 and shall the rock be **r** out of his place? H6275
19:10 and mine hope hath he **r** like a tree. H5265
36:16 Even so would he have **r** thee out of the H5496
Ps 46: 2 though the earth be **r**, and though the H4171
81: 6 I **r** his shoulder from the burden: his H5493
103:12 hath he **r** our transgressions from us. H7368
104: 5 earth, *that* it should not be **r** for ever. H4131
125: 1 *which* cannot be **r**, *but* abideth for ever. H4131
Prv 10:30 The righteous shall never be **r**: but the H4131
Isa 6:12 And the LORD have **r** men far away, H7368
10:13 and I have **r** the bounds of the people, H5493
Isa 10:31 Madmenah is **r**; the inhabitants of H5074
22:25 in the sure place be **r**, and be cut down, H4185
24:20 and shall be **r** like a cottage; and the H5110
26:15 **r** *it* far *unto* all the ends of the earth. H7368
29:13 me, but have **r** their heart far from H7368
30:20 not thy teachers be **r** into a corner any H3670
33:20 shall ever be **r**, neither shall any of H5265
38:12 Mine age is departed, and is **r** from me H1540
54:10 and the hills be **r**; but my kindness shall H4131
10 of my peace be **r**, saith the LORD that H4131
Jer 15: 4 And I will cause them to be **r** into all H2189
24: 9 And I will deliver them to be **r** into all H2189
29:18 deliver them to be **r** to all the kingdoms H2189
34:17 make you to be **r** into all the kingdoms H2189
Lam 1: 8 therefore she is **r**: all that honoured her H5206
3:17 And thou hast **r** my soul far off from H2186
Ezk 7:19 and their gold shall be **r**: their silver and H5079
23:46 and will give them to be **r** and spoiled. H2189
36:17 me as the uncleanness of a **r** woman. H5079
Am 6: 7 that stretched themselves shall be **r**. H5493
Mic 2: 4 how hath he **r** *it* from me! turning H4185
7:11 *in* that day shall the decree be far **r**. H7368
Mt 21:21 mountain, Be thou **r**, and be thou cast *G142*
Mk 11:23 mountain, Be thou **r**, and be thou cast *G142*
Act 7: 4 was dead, he **r** him into this land, *G3351*
13:22 And when he had **r** him, he raised up *G3179*
Gal 1: 6 I marvel that ye are so soon **r** from him *G3346*

REMOVETH
Dt 27:17 Cursed *be* he that **r** his neighbour's H5253
Job 9: 5 Which **r** the mountains, and they know H6275
12:20 He **r** away the speech of the trusty, and H5493
Ecc 10: 9 Whoso **r** stones shall be hurt therewith; H5265
Dan 2:21 the seasons: he **r** kings, and setteth up H5709

REMOVING
Gen 30:32 thy flock to day, **r** from thence all the H5493
Isa 49:21 a captive, and **r** to and fro? and who H5493
Ezk 12: 3 thee stuff for **r**, and remove by day H1473
4 sight, as stuff for **r**: and thou shalt go H1473
Heb 12:27 signifieth the **r** of those things that *G3331*

REMPHAN
Act 7:43 the star of your god **R**, figures which ye *G4481*

REND
Ex 39:23 about the hole, that it should not **r**. H7167
Lev 10: 6 heads, neither **r** your clothes; lest ye H6533
13:56 of it; then he shall **r** it out of the H7167
21:10 not uncover his head, nor **r** his clothes; H6533
2Sa 3:31 *were* with him, **R** your clothes, and gird H7167
1Ki 11:11 thee, I will surely **r** the kingdom from H7167
12 *but* I will **r** it out of the hand of thy son. H7167
13 Howbeit I will not **r** away all the H7167
31 Behold, I will **r** the kingdom out of H7167
2Ch 34:27 me, and didst **r** thy clothes, and weep H7167
Ecc 3: 7 A time to **r**, and a time to sew; a time to H7167
Isa 64: 1 Oh that thou wouldest **r** the heavens, H7167
Ezk 13:11 shall fall; and a stormy wind shall **r** *it*. H1234
13 Lord GOD; I will even **r** *it* with a stormy H1234
29: 7 didst break, and **r** all their shoulder: H1234
Hos 13: 8 *her whelps*, and will **r** the caul of their H7167
Joel 2:13 And **r** your heart, and not your H7167
Mt 7: 6 their feet, and turn again and **r** you. *G4486*
Jn 19:24 Let us not **r** it, but cast lots for it, *G4977*

RENDER
Nu 18: 9 which they shall **r** unto me, *shall be* H7725
Dt 32:41 judgment; I will **r** vengeance to mine H7725
43 servants, and will **r** vengeance to his H7725
Jdg 9:57 Shechem did God **r** upon their heads: H7725
1Sa 26:23 The LORD **r** to every man his H7725
2Ch 6:30 and forgive, and **r** unto every man H5414
Job 33:26 he will **r** unto man his righteousness. H7725
34:11 For the work of a man shall he **r** unto H7999
Ps 28: 4 of their hands; **r** to them their desert. H7725
38:20 They also that **r** evil for good are mine H7999
56:12 Thy vows *are* upon me, O God: I will **r** H7999
79:12 And **r** unto our neighbours sevenfold H7725
94: 2 of the earth: **r** a reward to the proud. H7725
116:12 What shall I **r** unto the LORD *for* all his H7725
Prv 24:12 **r** to *every* man according to his works? H7725
29 will **r** to the man according to his work. H7725
26:16 than seven men that can **r** a reason. H7725
Isa 66:15 a whirlwind, to **r** his anger with fury, H7725
Jer 51: 6 he will **r** unto her a recompence. H7999
24 And I will **r** unto Babylon and to all the H7999
Lam 3:64 **R** unto them a recompence, O LORD, H7725
Hos 14: 2 so will we **r** the calves of our lips. H7999

Joel 3: 4 Palestine? will ye **r** me a recompence? H7999
Zec 9:12 I declare *that* I will **r** double unto thee; H7725
Mt 21:41 shall **r** him the fruits in their seasons. *G591*
22:21 he unto them, **R** therefore unto Caesar *G591*
Mk 12:17 And Jesus answering said unto them, **R** *G591*
Lk 20:25 And he said unto them, **R** therefore unto *G591*
Ro 2: 6 Who will **r** to every man according to his *G591*
13: 7 **R** therefore to all their dues: tribute to *G591*
1Co 7: 3 Let the husband **r** unto the wife due *G591*
1Th 3: 9 For what thanks can we **r** to God again *G467*
5:15 See that none **r** evil for evil unto any *G591*

RENDERED
Jdg 9:56 Thus God **r** the wickedness of H7725
2Ki 3: 4 a sheepmaster, and **r** unto the king of H7725
2Ch 32:25 But Hezekiah **r** not again according to H7725
Prv 12:14 of a man's hands shall be **r** unto him. H7725

RENDEREST
Ps 62:12 **r** to every man according to his work. H7999

RENDERETH
Isa 66: 6 that **r** recompence to his enemies. H7999

RENDERING
1Pt 3: 9 Not **r** evil for evil, or railing for railing: *G591*

RENDING
Ps 7: 2 Lest he tear my soul like a lion, **r** *it* in H6561

RENEW
1Sa 11:14 go to Gilgal, and **r** the kingdom there. H2318
Ps 51:10 O God; and **r** a right spirit within me. H2318
Isa 40:31 the LORD shall **r** *their* strength; they H2498
41: 1 and let the people **r** *their* strength: let H2498
Lam 5:21 we shall be turned; **r** our days as of old. H2318
Heb 6: 6 If they shall fall away, to **r** them again *G340*

RENEWED
2Ch 15: 8 Ephraim, and **r** the altar of the LORD, H2318
Job 29:20 in me, and my bow was **r** in my hand. H2498
Ps 103: 5 *so that* thy youth is **r** like the eagle's. H2318
2Co 4:16 yet the inward *man* is **r** day by day. *G341*
Eph 4:23 And be **r** in the spirit of your mind; *G365*
Col 3:10 new *man*, which is **r** in knowledge after *G341*

RENEWEST
Job 10:17 Thou **r** thy witnesses against me, and H2318
Ps 104:30 and thou **r** the face of the earth. H2318

RENEWING
Ro 12: 2 transformed by the **r** of your mind, that *G342*
Tit 3: 5 of regeneration, and **r** of the Holy Ghost; *G342*

RENOUNCED
2Co 4: 2 But have **r** the hidden things of *G550*

RENOWN
Gen 6: 4 men which *were* of old, men of **r**. H8034
Nu 16: 2 famous in the congregation, men of **r**: H8034
Ezk 16:14 And thy **r** went forth among the H8034
15 because of thy **r**, and pouredst out thy H8034
34:29 And I will raise up for them a plant of **r**, H8034
39:13 shall be to them a **r** the day that I shall H8034
Dan 9:15 hast gotten thee **r**, as at this day; we H8034

RENOWNED
Nu 1:16 These *were* the **r** of the congregation, H7148
Isa 14:20 the seed of evildoers shall never be **r**. H7121
Ezk 23:23 and **r**, all of them riding upon horses. H7121
26:17 of seafaring men, the **r** city, which wast H1984

RENT
Gen 37:29 *was* not in the pit; and he **r** his clothes. H7167
33 Joseph is without doubt **r** in pieces. H2963
34 And Jacob **r** his clothes, and put H7167
44:13 Then they **r** their clothes, and laded H7167
Ex 28:32 hole of an habergeon, that it be not **r**. H7167
Lev 13:45 his clothes shall be **r**, and his head bare, H6533
Nu 14: 6 that searched the land, **r** their clothes: H7167
Jos 7: 6 And Joshua **r** his clothes, and fell to the H7167
9: 4 wine bottles, old, and **r**, and bound up; H1234
13 and, behold, they be **r**: and these our H1234
Jdg 11:35 saw her, that he **r** his clothes, and said, H7167
14: 6 upon him, and he **r** him as he would H8156
6 as he would have **r** a kid, and *he had* H8156
1Sa 4:12 clothes **r**, and with earth upon his head. H7167
15:27 upon the skirt of his mantle, and it **r**. H7167
28 The LORD hath **r** the kingdom of Israel H7167
1Sa 28:17 for the LORD hath **r** the kingdom out of H7167
2Sa 1: 2 with his clothes **r**, and earth upon his H7167
11 hold on his clothes, and **r** them; and H7167
13:19 on her head, and **r** her garment of H7167
31 servants stood by with their clothes **r**. H7167
15:32 his coat **r**, and earth upon his head: H7167
1Ki 1:40 that the earth **r** with the sound of them. H1234
11:30 *was* on him, and **r** it *in* twelve pieces: H7167
13: 3 the altar shall be **r**, and the ashes that H7167
5 The altar also was **r**, and the ashes H7167
14: 8 And **r** the kingdom away from the H7167
19:11 and strong wind **r** the mountains, and H6561
21:27 words, that he **r** his clothes, and put H7167
2Ki 2:12 own clothes, and **r** them in two pieces. H7167
5: 7 the letter, that he **r** his clothes, and H7167
8 king of Israel had **r** his clothes, that he H7167
8 hast thou **r** thy clothes? let him H7167
6:30 woman, that he **r** his clothes; and he H7167
11:14 and Athaliah **r** her clothes, and cried, H7167
17:21 For he **r** Israel from the house of David; H7167
18:37 with *their* clothes **r**, and told him the H7167
19: 1 heard *it*, that he **r** his clothes, and H7167
22:11 book of the law, that he **r** his clothes. H7167
19 and a curse, and hast **r** thy clothes, and H7167
2Ch 23:13 Then Athaliah **r** her clothes, and said, H7167
34:19 words of the law, that he **r** his clothes. H7167
Ezr 9: 3 And when I heard this thing, I **r** my H7167
5 and having **r** my garment and my H7167
Est 4: 1 done, Mordecai **r** his clothes, and put H7167
Job 1:20 Then Job arose, and **r** his mantle, and H7167
2:12 wept; and they **r** every one his mantle, H7167
26: 8 and the cloud is not **r** under them. H1234
Isa 3:24 of a girdle a **r**; and instead of well H5364
36:22 with *their* clothes **r**, and told him the H7167
37: 1 heard *it*, that he **r** his clothes, and H7167
Jer 36:24 Yet they were not afraid, nor **r** their H7167
41: 5 and their clothes **r**, and having cut H7167
Ezk 30:16 and No shall be **r** asunder, and Noph H1234
Mt 9:16 the garment, and the **r** is made worse. *G4978*
26:65 Then the high priest **r** his clothes, *G1284*
27:51 of the temple was **r** in twain from the *G4977*
51 the earth did quake, and the rocks **r**; *G4977*
Mk 2:21 from the old, and the **r** is made worse. *G4978*
9:26 And *the spirit* cried, and **r** him sore, *G4682*
14:63 Then the high priest **r** his clothes, and *G1284*
15:38 And the veil of the temple was **r** in *G4977*
Lk 5:36 the new maketh a **r**, and the piece that *G4977*
23:45 veil of the temple was **r** in the midst. *G4977*
Act 14:14 heard *of*, they **r** their clothes, and ran *G1284*
16:22 the magistrates **r** off their clothes, and *G4048*

RENTEST
Jer 4:30 of gold, though thou **r** thy face with H7167

REPAID See REPAYED.

REPAIR
2Ki 12: 5 and let them **r** the breaches of the H2388
7 unto them, Why **r** ye not the breaches H2388
8 neither to **r** the breaches of the house. H2388
12 hewed stone to **r** the breaches of the H2388
12 that was laid out for the house to **r** *it*. H2394
22: 5 LORD, to **r** the breaches of the house, H2388
6 timber and hewn stone to **r** the house. H2388
2Ch 24: 4 minded to **r** the house of the LORD. H2318
5 all Israel money to **r** the house of your H2388
12 and carpenters to **r** the house of the H2318
34: 8 to **r** the house of the LORD his God. H2388
10 of the LORD, to **r** and amend the house: H918
Ezr 9: 9 of our God, and to **r** the desolations H5975
Isa 61: 4 and they shall **r** the waste cities, the H2318

REPAIRED
Jdg 21:23 and **r** the cities, and dwelt in them. H1129
1Ki 11:27 built Millo, *and* **r** the breaches of the H5462
18:30 near unto him. And he **r** the altar of the H7495
2Ki 12: 6 had not **r** the breaches of the house. H2388
14 and **r** therewith the house of the LORD. H2388
1Ch 11: 8 about: and Joab **r** the rest of the city. H2421
2Ch 29: 3 of the house of the LORD, and **r** them. H2388
32: 5 wall without, and **r** Millo *in* the city of H2388
33:16 And he **r** the altar of the LORD, and H1129
Neh 3: 4 And next unto them **r** Meremoth the H2388
4 next unto them **r** Meshullam the son H2388
4 unto them **r** Zadok the son of Baana. H2388
5 And next unto them the Tekoites **r**; but H2388
6 Moreover the old gate **r** Jehoiada the H2388
7 And next unto them **r** Melatiah the H2388
8 Next unto him **r** Uzziel the son of H2388
Neh 3: 8 unto him also **r** Hananiah the son of H2388
9 And next unto them **r** Rephaiah the H2388
10 And next unto them **r** Jedaiah the son H2388
10 him **r** Hattush the son of Hashabniah. H2388
11 of Pahath-moab, **r** the other piece, and H2388
12 And next unto him **r** Shallum the son H2388
13 The valley gate **r** Hanun, and the H2388
14 But the dung gate **r** Malchiah the son of H2388
15 But the gate of the fountain **r** Shallun H2388
16 After him **r** Nehemiah the son of H2388
17 After him **r** the Levites, Rehum the son H2388
17 Next unto him **r** Hashabiah, the ruler H2388
18 After him **r** their brethren, Bavai the H2388
19 And next to him **r** Ezer the son of H2388
20 of Zabbai earnestly **r** the other piece, H2388
21 After him **r** Meremoth the son of H2388
22 And after him **r** the priests, the men of H2388
23 After him **r** Benjamin and Hashub over H2388
23 house. After him **r** Azariah the son of H2388
24 After him **r** Binnui the son of Henadad H2388
27 After them the Tekoites **r** another H2388
28 From above the horse gate **r** the H2388
29 After them **r** Zadok the son of Immer H2388
29 house. After him **r** also Shemaiah the H2388
30 After him **r** Hananiah the son of H2388
30 piece. After him **r** Meshullam the son H2388
31 After him **r** Malchiah the goldsmith's H2388
32 **r** the goldsmiths and the merchants. H2388

REPAIRER
Isa 58:12 shalt be called, The **r** of the breach, The H1443

REPAIRING
2Ch 24:27 upon him, and the **r** of the house of H3247

REPAY
Dt 7:10 hateth him, he will **r** him to his face. H7999
Job 21:31 who shall **r** him *what* he hath done? H7999
41:11 me, that I should **r** *him? whatsoever is* H7999
Isa 59:18 he will **r**, fury to his adversaries, H7999
18 to the islands he will **r** recompence. H7999
Lk 10:35 more, when I come again, I will **r** thee. *G591*
Ro 12:19 *is* mine; I will **r**, saith the Lord. *G467*
Phlm 19 own hand, I will **r** *it*: albeit I do not say *G661*

REPAYED
Prv 13:21 but to the righteous good shall be **r**. H7999

REPAYETH
Dt 7:10 And **r** them that hate him to their face, H7999

REPEATETH
Prv 17: 9 that **r** a matter separateth *very* friends. H8138

REPENT
Ex 13:17 the people **r** when they see war, H5162
32:12 and **r** of this evil against thy people. H5162
Nu 23:19 that he should **r**: hath he said, and shall H5162
Dt 32:36 judge his people, and **r** himself for his H5162
1Sa 15:29 will not lie nor **r**: for he *is* not a man, H5162
29 for he *is* not a man, that he should **r**. H5162
1Ki 8:47 captives, and **r**, and make supplication H7725
Job 42: 6 Wherefore I abhor *myself*, and **r** in H5162
Ps 90:13 Return, O LORD, how long? and let it **r** H5162
110: 4 The LORD hath sworn, and will not **r**, H5162
135:14 will **r** himself concerning his servants. H5162
Jer 4:28 not **r**, neither will I turn back from it. H5162
18: 8 from their evil, I will **r** of the evil that I H5162
10 my voice, then I will **r** of the good, H5162
26: 3 way, that I may **r** me of the evil, which H5162
13 and the LORD will **r** him of the evil that H5162
42:10 pluck *you* up: for I **r** me of the evil that H5162
Ezk 14: 6 the Lord GOD; **R**, and turn *yourselves* H7725
18:30 the Lord GOD. **R**, and turn *yourselves* H7725
24:14 neither will I **r**; according to thy ways, H5162
Joel 2:14 Who knoweth *if* he will return and **r**, H5162
Jna 3: 9 Who can tell *if* God will turn and **r**, and H5162
Mt 3: 2 And saying, **R** ye: for the kingdom of *G3340*
4:17 and to say, **R**: for the kingdom of *G3340*
Mk 1:15 is at hand: **r** ye, and believe the gospel. *G3340*
6:12 out, and preached that men should **r**. *G3340*
Lk 13: 3 I tell you, Nay: but, except ye **r**, ye shall *G3340*
5 I tell you, Nay: but, except ye **r**, ye shall *G3340*
16:30 unto them from the dead, they will **r**. *G3340*
17: 3 rebuke him; and if he **r**, forgive him. *G3340*
4 thee, saying, I **r**; thou shalt forgive him. *G3340*
Act 2:38 Then Peter said unto them, **R**, and be *G3340*
3:19 **R** ye therefore, and be converted, that *G3340*
8:22 **R** therefore of this thy wickedness, and *G3340*

Act 17:30 commandeth all men every where to r: G3340
26:20 that they should r and turn to God, and G3340
2Co 7: 8 a letter, I do not r, though I did repent: G3338
8 though I did r: for I perceive that the G3338
Heb 7:21 sware and will not r, Thou *art* a priest G3338
Rev 2: 5 art fallen, and r, and do the first works; G3340
5 out of his place, except thou r. G3340
16 R; or else I will come unto thee quickly, G3340
21 And I gave her space to r of her G3340
22 tribulation, except they r of their deeds. G3340
3: 3 and hold fast, and r. If therefore thou G3340
19 chasten: be zealous therefore, and r. G3340

REPENTANCE
Hos 13:14 r shall be hid from mine eyes. H5164
Mt 3: 8 Bring forth therefore fruits meet for r: G3341
11 I indeed baptize you with water unto r: G3341
9:13 to call the righteous, but sinners to r. G3341
Mk 1: 4 baptism of r for the remission of sins. G3341
2:17 to call the righteous, but sinners to r. G3341
Lk 3: 3 baptism of r for the remission of sins; G3341
8 Bring forth therefore fruits worthy of r, G3341
5:32 to call the righteous, but sinners to r. G3341
15: 7 and nine just persons, which need no r. G3341
24:47 And that r and remission of sins G3341
Act 5:31 give r to Israel, and forgiveness of sins. G3341
11:18 also to the Gentiles granted r unto life. G3341
13:24 baptism of r to all the people of Israel. G3341
19: 4 with the baptism of r, saying unto the G3341
20:21 also to the Greeks, r toward God, and G3341
26:20 turn to God, and do works meet for r. G3341
Ro 2: 4 the goodness of God leadeth thee to r? G3341
11:29 the gifts and calling of God *are* without r. G278
2Co 7: 9 that ye sorrowed to r: for ye were made G3341
10 For godly sorrow worketh r to G3341
2Ti 2:25 r to the acknowledging of the truth; G3341
Heb 6: 1 the foundation of r from dead works, G3341
6 them again unto r; seeing they crucify G3341
12:17 found no place of r, though he sought it G3341
2Pt 3: 9 perish, but that all should come to r. G3341

REPENTED
Gen 6: 6 And it r the LORD that he had made H5162
Ex 32:14 And the LORD r of the evil which he H5162
Jdg 2:18 of the judge: for it r the LORD because H5162
21: 6 And the children of Israel r them for H5162
15 And the people r them for Benjamin, H5162
1Sa 15:35 and the LORD r that he had made Saul H5162
2Sa 24:16 it, the LORD r him of the evil, and H5162
1Ch 21:15 beheld, and he r him of the evil, and H5162
Ps 106:45 his covenant, and r according to the H5162
Jer 8: 6 not aright: no man r him of his H5162
20:16 overthrew, and r not: and let him hear H5162
26:19 and the LORD r him of the evil which H5162
31:19 Surely after that I was turned, I r; and H5162
Am 7: 3 The LORD r for this: It shall not be, H5162
6 The LORD r for this: This also shall not H5162
Jna 3:10 evil way; and God r of the evil, that he H5162
Zec 8:14 saith the LORD of hosts, and I r not: H5162
Mt 11:20 works were done, because they r not: G3340
21 have r long ago in sackcloth and ashes. G3340
12:41 it: because they r at the preaching of G3340
21:29 I will not: but afterward he r, and went. G3338
32 ye had seen *it*, r not afterward, that G3338
27: 3 he was condemned, r himself, and G3338
Lk 10:13 ago r, sitting in sackcloth and ashes. G3340
11:32 it: for they r at the preaching of G3340
2Co 7:10 salvation not to be r of: but the sorrow of G278
12:21 and have not r of the uncleanness and G3340
Rev 2:21 of her fornication; and she r not. G3340
9:20 these plagues yet r not of the works of G3340
21 Neither r they of their murders, nor of G3340
16: 9 and they r not to give him glory. G3340
11 their sores, and r not of their deeds. G3340

REPENTEST
Jna 4: 2 of great kindness, and r thee of the evil. H5162

REPENTETH
Gen 6: 7 air; for it r me that I have made them. H5162
1Sa 15:11 It r me that I have set up Saul *to be* H5162
Joel 2:13 of great kindness, and r him of the evil. H5162
Lk 15: 7 one sinner that r, more than over ninety G3340
10 the angels of God over one sinner that r. G3340

REPENTING
Jer 15: 6 and destroy thee; I am weary with r. H5162

REPENTINGS
Hos 11: 8 within me, my r are kindled together. H5150

REPETITIONS
Mt 6: 7 But when ye pray, use not vain r, as the G945

REPHAEL
1Ch 26: 7 The sons of Shemaiah; Othni, and R, H7501

REPHAH
1Ch 7:25 And R *was* his son, also Resheph, and H7506

REPHAIAH
1Ch 3:21 the sons of R, the sons of Arnan, the H7509
4:42 and R, and Uzziel, the sons of Ishi. H7509
7: 2 And the sons of Tola; Uzzi, and R, and H7509
9:43 And Moza begat Binea; and R his son, H7509
Neh 3: 9 And next unto them repaired R the son H7509

REPHAIM
2Sa 5:18 spread themselves in the valley of R. H7497
22 spread themselves in the valley of R. H7497
23:13 the Philistines pitched in the valley of R. H7497
1Ch 11:15 Philistines encamped in the valley of R. H7497
14: 9 spread themselves in the valley of R. H7497
Isa 17: 5 he that gathereth ears in the valley of R. H7497

REPHAIMS
Gen 14: 5 him, and smote the R in Ashteroth H7497
15:20 Hittites, and the Perizzites, and the R, H7497

REPHIDIM
Ex 17: 1 and pitched in R: and *there was* no H7508
8 Amalek, and fought with Israel in R. H7508
19: 2 For they were departed from R, and H7508
Nu 33:14 and encamped at R, where was no H7508
15 And they departed from R, and pitched H7508

REPLENISH
Gen 1:28 and multiply, and r the earth, and H4390
9: 1 fruitful, and multiply, and r the earth. H4390

REPLENISHED
Isa 2: 6 because they be r from the east, and H4390
23: 2 of Zidon, that pass over the sea, have r. H4390
Jer 31:25 soul, and I have r every sorrowful soul. H4390
Ezk 26: 2 me: I shall be r, *now* she is laid waste: H4390
27:25 and thou wast r, and made very H4390

REPLIEST
Ro 9:20 Nay but, O man, who art thou that r G470

REPORT
Gen 37: 2 brought unto his father their evil r. H1681
Ex 23: 1 Thou shalt not raise a false r: put not H8088
Nu 13:32 And they brought up an evil r of the H1681
14:37 bring up the evil r upon the land, died H1681
Dt 2:25 who shall hear r of thee, and shall H8088
1Sa 2:24 Nay, my sons; for *it is* no good r that I H8052
1Ki 10: 6 And she said to the king, It was a true r H1697
2Ch 9: 5 And she said to the king, *It was* a true r H1697
Neh 6:13 an evil r, that they might reproach me. H8034
Prv 15:30 *and* a good r maketh the bones fat. H8052
Isa 23: 5 As at the r concerning Egypt, *so* shall H8088
5 they be sorely pained at the r of Tyre. H8088
28:19 be a vexation only *to* understand the r. H8052
53: 1 Who hath believed our r? and to whom H8052
Jer 20:10 fear on every side. R, *say they*, and we H5046
10 *they*, and we will r it. All my familiars H5046
50:43 The king of Babylon hath heard the r of H8088
Jn 12:38 hath believed our r? and to whom hath G189
Act 6: 3 men of honest r, full of the Holy Ghost G3140
10:22 God, and of good r among all the G3140
22:12 r of all the Jews which dwelt *there*, G3140
Ro 10:16 saith, Lord, who hath believed our r? G189
1Co 14:25 God, and r that God is in you of a truth. G518
2Co 6: 8 By honour and dishonour, by evil r and G1426
8 and good r: as deceivers, and *yet* true; G2162
Php 4: 8 things *are* of good r; if *there be* any G2163
1Ti 3: 7 Moreover he must have a good r of G3141
Heb 11: 2 For by it the elders obtained a good r. G3140
39 And these all, having obtained a good r G3140
3Jn 12 Demetrius hath good r of all *men*, and G3140

REPORTED
Neh 6: 6 Wherein *was* written, It is r among the H8085
7 now shall it be r to the king according H8085
19 Also they r his good deeds before me, H559
Est 1:17 when it shall be r, The king Ahasuerus H559
Ezk 9:11 by his side, r the matter, saying, H7725
Mt 28:15 r among the Jews until this day. G1310
Act 4:23 own company, and r all that the chief G518
16: 2 Which was well r of by the brethren G3140
Ro 3: 8 And not *rather*, (as we be slanderously r, G987
1Co 5: 1 It is r commonly *that there is* fornication G191
1Ti 5:10 Well r of for good works; if she have G3140
1Pt 1:12 which are now r unto you by them that G312

REPROACH
Gen 30:23 and said, God hath taken away my r: H2781
34:14 for that *were* a r unto us: H2781
Jos 5: 9 I rolled away the r of Egypt from off H2781
Ru 2:15 even among the sheaves, and r her not: H3637
1Sa 11: 2 eyes, and lay it *for* a r upon all Israel. H2781
17:26 taketh away the r from Israel? for who H2781
25:39 the cause of my r from the hand of H2781
2Ki 19: 4 hath sent to r the living God; and H2778
16 hath sent him to r the living God. H2778
Neh 1: 3 affliction and r: the wall of Jerusalem H2781
2:17 of Jerusalem, that we be no more a r. H2781
4: 4 and turn their r upon their own head, H2781
5: 9 of the r of the heathen our enemies? H2781
6:13 for an evil report, that they might r me. H2778
Job 19: 5 against me, and plead against me my r: H2781
20: 3 I have heard the check of my r, and the H3639
27: 6 heart shall not r *me* so long as I live. H2778
Ps 15: 3 taketh up a r against his neighbour. H2781
22: 6 But I *am* a worm, and no man; a r of H2781
31:11 I was a r among all mine enemies, but H2781
39: 8 make me not the r of the foolish. H2781
42:10 mine enemies r me; while they say H2778
44:13 Thou makest us a r to our neighbours, H2781
57: 3 save me *from* the r of him that would H2778
69: 7 Because for thy sake I have borne r; H2781
10 my soul with fasting, that was to my r. H2781
19 Thou hast known my r, and my shame, H2781
20 R hath broken my heart; and I am full H2781
71:13 r and dishonour that seek my hurt. H2781
74:10 O God, how long shall the adversary r? H2778
78:66 parts: he put them to a perpetual r. H2781
79: 4 We are become a r to our neighbours, a H2781
12 into their bosom their r, wherewith they H2781
89:41 spoil him: he is a r to his neighbours. H2781
50 Remember, Lord, the r of thy servants; H2781
50 my bosom *the r of* all the mighty people;
102: 8 Mine enemies r me all the day; *and* H2778
109:25 I became also a r unto them: *when* they H2781
119:22 Remove from me r and contempt; for I H2781
39 Turn away my r which I fear: for thy H2781
Prv 6:33 get; and his r shall not be wiped away. H2781
14:34 a nation: but sin *is* a r to any people. H2617
18: 3 also contempt, and with ignominy r. H2781
19:26 son that causeth shame, and bringeth r. H2659
22:10 go out; yea, strife and r shall cease. H7036
Isa 4: 1 called by thy name, to take away our r. H2781
30: 5 nor profit, but a shame, and also a r. H2781
37: 4 hath sent to r the living God, and H2778
17 which hath sent to r the living God. H2778
51: 7 fear ye not the r of men, neither be ye H2781
54: 4 the r of thy widowhood any more. H2781
Jer 6:10 unto them a r; they have no delight in it. H2781
20: 8 a r unto me, and a derision, daily. H2781
23:40 And I will bring an everlasting r upon H2781
24: 9 for *their* hurt, *to be* a r and a proverb, a H2781
29:18 and an hissing, and a r, among all the H2781
31:19 because I did bear the r of my youth. H2781
42:18 a r; and ye shall see this place no more. H2781
44: 8 a r among all the nations of the earth? H2781
12 an astonishment, and a curse, and a r. H2781
49:13 a desolation, a r, a waste, and a curse; H2781
51:51 we have heard r: shame hath covered H2781
Lam 3:30 that smiteth him: he is filled full with r. H2781
61 Thou hast heard their r, O LORD, *and* H2781
5: 1 upon us: consider, and behold our r. H2781
Ezk 5:14 thee waste, and a r among the nations H2781
15 So it shall be a r and a taunt, an H2781
16:57 at the time of *thy* r of the daughters of H2781
21:28 concerning their r; even say thou, The H2781
22: 4 I made thee a r unto the heathen, and H2781
36:15 thou bear the r of the people any more, H2781
30 more r of famine among the heathen. H2781
Dan 9:16 *are become* a r to all *that are* about us. H2781
11:18 shall cause the r offered by him to H2781
18 r he shall cause *it* to turn upon him. H2781
Hos 12:14 his r shall his Lord return unto him. H2781
Joel 2:17 not thine heritage to r, that the heathen H2781
19 more make you a r among the heathen: H2781
Mic 6:16 ye shall bear the r of my people. H2781

Zep 2: 8 I have heard the **r** of Moab, and the H2781
3:18 thee, *to whom* the **r** of it *was* a burden. H2781
Lk 1:25 on *me*, to take away my **r** among men. *G3681*
6:22 and shall **r** *you*, and cast out your *G3679*
2Co 11:21 I speak as concerning **r**, as though we *G819*
1Ti 3: 7 he fall into **r** and the snare of the devil. *G3680*
4:10 labour and suffer **r**, because we trust in *G3679*
Heb 11:26 Esteeming the **r** of Christ greater riches *G3680*
13:13 him without the camp, bearing his **r**. *G3680*

REPROACHED
2Ki 19:22 Whom hast thou **r** and blasphemed? H2778
23 By thy messengers thou hast **r** the H2778
Job 19: 3 These ten times have ye **r** me: ye are H3637
Ps 55:12 For *it was* not an enemy *that* **r** me; then H2778
69: 9 of them that **r** thee are fallen upon me. H2778
74:18 Remember this, *that* the enemy hath **r**, H2778
79:12 wherewith they have **r** thee, O Lord. H2778
89:51 Wherewith thine enemies have **r**, O H2778
51 have **r** the footsteps of thine anointed. H2778
Isa 37:23 Whom hast thou **r** and blasphemed? H2778
24 By thy servants hast thou **r** the Lord, H2778
Zep 2: 8 whereby they have **r** my people, and H2778
10 because they have **r** and magnified H2778
Ro 15: 3 of them that **r** thee fell on me. *G3679*
1Pt 4:14 If ye be **r** for the name of Christ, happy *G3679*

REPROACHES
Ps 69: 9 eaten me up; and the **r** of them that H2781
Isa 43:28 given Jacob to the curse, and Israel to **r**. H1421
Ro 15: 3 as it is written, The **r** of them that *G3680*
2Co 12:10 in infirmities, in **r**, in necessities, in *G5196*
Heb 10:33 both by **r** and afflictions; and *G3680*

REPROACHEST
Lk 11:45 Master, thus saying thou **r** us also. *G5195*

REPROACHETH
Nu 15:30 a stranger, the same **r** the LORD; and H1442
Ps 44:16 For the voice of him that **r** and H2778
74:22 how the foolish man **r** thee daily. H2781
119:42 him that **r** me: for I trust in thy word. H2778
Prv 14:31 He that oppresseth the poor **r** his H2778
17: 5 Whoso mocketh the poor **r** his Maker: H2778
27:11 glad, that I may answer him that **r** me. H2778

REPROACHFULLY
Job 16:10 upon the cheek **r**; they have gathered H2781
1Ti 5:14 occasion to the adversary to speak **r**. *G3059*

REPROBATE
Jer 6:30 **R** silver shall *men* call them, because H3988
Ro 1:28 them over to a **r** mind, to do those things *G96*
2Ti 3: 8 of corrupt minds, **r** concerning the faith. *G96*
Tit 1:16 disobedient, and unto every good work **r**. *G96*

REPROBATES
2Co 13: 5 that Jesus Christ is in you, except ye be **r**? *G96*
6 trust that ye shall know that we are not **r**. *G96*
7 that which is honest, though we be as **r**. *G96*

REPROOF
Job 26:11 tremble and are astonished at his **r**. H1606
Prv 1:23 Turn you at my **r**: behold, I will pour H8433
25 all my counsel, and would none of my **r**: H8433
30 of my counsel: they despised all my **r**. H8433
5:12 instruction, and my heart despised **r**; H8433
10:17 but he that refuseth **r** erreth. H8433
12: 1 but he that hateth **r** *is* brutish. H8433
13:18 he that regardeth **r** shall be honoured. H8433
15: 5 but he that regardeth **r** is prudent. H8433
10 the way: *and* he that hateth **r** shall die. H8433
31 The ear that heareth the **r** of life H8433
32 that heareth **r** getteth understanding. H8433
17:10 A **r** entereth more into a wise man than H1606
29:15 The rod and **r** give wisdom: but a child H8433
2Ti 3:16 for doctrine, for **r**, for correction, for *G1650*

REPROOFS
Ps 38:14 not, and in whose mouth *are* no **r**. H8433
Prv 6:23 and **r** of instruction *are* the way of life: H8433

REPROVE
2Ki 19: 4 God; and will **r** the words which the H3198
Job 6:25 words! but what doth your arguing **r**? H3198
26 Do ye imagine to **r** words, and the H3198
13:10 He will surely **r** you, if ye do secretly H3198
22: 4 Will he **r** thee for fear of thee? will he H3198
Ps 50: 8 I will not **r** thee for thy sacrifices or thy H3198
50:21 thyself: *but* I will **r** thee, and set *them* H3198
141: 5 and let him **r** me; *it shall be* an H3198
Prv 9: 8 **R** not a scorner, lest he hate thee: H3198
19:25 simple will beware: and **r** one that hath H3198
30: 6 Add thou not unto his words, lest he **r** H3198
Isa 11: 3 neither **r** after the hearing of his ears: H3198
4 the poor, and **r** with equity for the H3198
37: 4 God, and will **r** the words which the H3198
Jer 2:19 thy backslidings shall **r** thee: know H3198
Hos 4: 4 Yet let no man strive, nor **r** another: for H3198
Jn 16: 8 And when he is come, he will **r** the *G1651*
Eph 5:11 works of darkness, but rather **r** *them*. *G1651*
2Ti 4: 2 out of season; **r**, rebuke, exhort with *G1651*

REPROVED
Gen 20:16 thee, and with all *other*: thus she was **r**. H3198
21:25 And Abraham **r** Abimelech because of H3198
1Ch 16:21 wrong: yea, he **r** kings for their sakes, H3198
Ps 105:14 wrong: yea, he **r** kings for their sakes; H3198
Prv 29: 1 He, that being often **r** hardeneth *his* H8433
Jer 29:27 Now therefore why hast thou not **r** H1605
Hab 2: 1 and what I shall answer when I am **r**. H8433
Lk 3:19 But Herod the tetrarch, being **r** by him *G1651*
Jn 3:20 to the light, lest his deeds should be **r**. *G1651*
Eph 5:13 But all things that are **r** are made *G1651*

REPROVER
Prv 25:12 *so is* a wise **r** upon an obedient ear. H3198
Ezk 3:26 a **r**: for they *are* a rebellious house. H3198

REPROVETH
Job 40: 2 *him*? he that **r** God, let him answer it. H3198
Prv 9: 7 He that **r** a scorner getteth to himself H3256
15:12 A scorner loveth not one that **r** him: H3198
Isa 29:21 a snare for him that **r** in the gate, and H3198

REPUTATION
Ecc 10: 1 that is in **r** for wisdom *and* honour. H3368
Act 5:34 of the law, had in **r** among all the *G5093*
Gal 2: 2 which were of **r**, lest by any means I *G1380*
Php 2: 7 But made himself of no **r**, and took *G2758*
29 with all gladness; and hold such in **r**: *G1784*

REPUTED
Job 18: 3 as beasts, *and* **r** vile in your sight?
Dan 4:35 of the earth *are* **r** as nothing: and he H2804

REQUEST
Jdg 8:24 I would desire a **r** of you, that ye would H7596
2Sa 14:15 will perform the **r** of his handmaid. H1697
22 king hath fulfilled the **r** of his servant. H1697
Ezr 7: 6 him all his **r**, according to the hand H1246
Neh 2: 4 **r**? So I prayed to the God of heaven. H1245
Est 4: 8 to make **r** before him for her people. H1245
5: 3 and what *is* thy **r**? it shall be even given H1246
6 and what *is* thy **r**? even to the half of the H1246
7 and said, My petition and my **r** *is*; H1246
8 and to perform my **r**, let the king and H1246
7: 2 thee: and what *is* thy **r**? and it shall be H1246
3 at my petition, and my people at my **r**: H1246
7 stood up to make **r** for his life to Esther H1245
9:12 *is* thy **r** further? and it shall be done. H1246
Job 6: 8 Oh that I might have my **r**; and that H7596
Ps 21: 2 not withholden the **r** of his lips. Selah. H782
106:15 And he gave them their **r**; but sent H7596
Ro 1:10 Making **r**, if by any means now at *G1189*
Php 1: 4 of mine for you all making **r** with joy, *G1162*

REQUESTED
Jdg 8:26 earrings that he **r** was a thousand and H7592
1Ki 19: 4 tree: and he **r** for himself that he might H7592
1Ch 4:10 And God granted him that which he **r**. H7592
Dan 1: 8 therefore he **r** of the prince of the H1245
2:49 Then Daniel **r** of the king, and he set H1156

REQUESTS
Php 4: 6 let your **r** be made known unto God. *G155*

REQUIRE
Gen 9: 5 of your lives will I **r**; at the hand of H1875
5 every beast will I **r** it, and at the hand H1875
5 man's brother will I **r** the life of man. H1875
31:39 hand didst thou **r** it, *whether* stolen by H1245
43: 9 hand shalt thou **r** him: if I bring him H1245
Dt 10:12 the LORD thy God **r** of thee, but to fear H7592
18:19 speak in my name, I will **r** *it* of him. H1875
23:21 **r** it of thee; and it would be sin in thee. H1875
Jos 22:23 thereon, let the LORD himself **r** *it*; H1245
1Sa 20:16 **r** *it* at the hand of David's enemies. H1245
2Sa 3:13 but one thing I **r** of thee, that is, Thou H7592
4:11 I not therefore now **r** his blood of your H1245
19:38 thou shalt **r** of me, *that* will I do for thee. H977
1Ki 8:59 Israel at all times, as the matter shall **r**: H3117
1Ch 21: 3 then doth my lord **r** this thing? why will H1245
2Ch 24:22 said, The LORD look upon *it*, and **r** *it*. H1875
Ezr 7:21 shall **r** of you, it be done speedily, H7593
8:22 For I was ashamed to **r** of the king a H7592
Neh 5:12 *them*, and will **r** nothing of them; so H1245
Ps 10:13 said in his heart, Thou wilt not **r** *it*. H1875
Ezk 3:18 but his blood will I **r** at thine hand. H1245
20 but his blood will I **r** at thine hand. H1245
20:40 and there will I **r** your offerings, and H1875
33: 6 blood will I **r** at the watchman's hand. H1875
8 but his blood will I **r** at thine hand. H1245
34:10 and I will **r** my flock at their hand, H1875
Mic 6: 8 what doth the LORD **r** of thee, but to do H1875
1Co 1:22 For the Jews **r** a sign, and the Greeks *G154*
7:36 age, and need so **r**, let him do what he *G1096*

REQUIRED
Gen 42:22 therefore, behold, also his blood is **r**. H1875
Ex 12:36 *as they* **r**. And they spoiled the Egyptians.
1Sa 21: 8 because the king's business **r** haste. H1961
2Sa 12:20 and when he **r**, they set bread before H7592
1Ch 16:37 ark continually, as every day's work **r**: H3117
2Ch 8:14 duty of every day **r**: the porters also by H3117
24: 6 Why hast thou not **r** of the Levites to H1875
Ezr 3: 4 the custom, as the duty of every day **r**; H3117
Neh 5:18 yet for all this **r** not I the bread of the H1245
Est 2:15 unto the king, she **r** nothing but what H1245
Ps 40: 6 and sin offering hast thou not **r**. H7592
137: 3 us away captive **r** of us a song; and H7592
3 they that wasted us **r** *of us* mirth, *saying*,
Prv 30: 7 Two *things* have I **r** of thee; deny me H7592
Isa 1:12 **r** this at your hand, to tread my courts? H1245
Lk 11:50 the world, may be **r** of this generation; *G1567*
51 you, It shall be **r** of this generation. *G1567*
12:20 thy soul shall be **r** of thee: then whose *G523*
48 him shall be much **r**: and to whom men *G2212*
19:23 I might have **r** mine own with usury? *G4238*
23:24 gave sentence that it should be as they **r**. *G155*
1Co 4: 2 Moreover it is **r** in stewards, that a *G2212*

REQUIREST
Ru 3:11 thee all that thou **r**: for all the city of my H559

REQUIRETH
Ecc 3:15 been; and God **r** that which is past. H1245
Dan 2:11 And *it is* a rare thing that the king **r**, H7593

REQUIRING
Lk 23:23 And they were instant with loud voices, **r** *G154*

REQUITE
Gen 50:15 **r** us all the evil which we did unto him. H7725
Dt 32: 6 Do ye thus **r** the LORD, O foolish H1580
2Sa 2: 6 you: and I also will **r** you this kindness, H6213
16:12 will **r** me good for his cursing this day. H7725
2Ki 9:26 the LORD; and I will **r** thee in this plat, H7999
Ps 10:14 and spite, to **r** *it* with thy hand: the H5414
41:10 and raise me up, that I may **r** them. H7999
Jer 51:56 God of recompences shall surely **r**. H7999
1Ti 5: 4 at home, and to **r** their parents: for that *G287*

REQUITED
Jdg 1: 7 have done, so God hath **r** me. And they H7999
1Sa 25:21 him: and he hath **r** me evil for good. H7725

REQUITING
2Ch 6:23 judge thy servants, by **r** the wicked, by H7725

REREWARD See REARWARD.

RESCUE
Dt 28:31 and thou shalt have none to **r** *them*. H3467
Ps 35:17 Lord, how long wilt thou look on? **r** my H7725
Hos 5:14 I will take away, and none shall **r** *him*. H5337

RESCUED
1Sa 14:45 the people **r** Jonathan, that he died not. H6299
30:18 away: and David **r** his two wives. H5337
Act 23:27 I with an army, and **r** him, having *G1807*

RESCUETH
Dan 6:27 He delivereth and **r**, and he worketh H5338

RESEMBLANCE
Zec 5: 6 This *is* their **r** through all the earth. H5869

RESEMBLE
Lk 13:18 of God like? and whereunto shall I **r** it? G3666

RESEMBLED
Jdg 8:18 they; each one **r** the children of a king. H8389

RESEN
Gen 10:12 And **R** between Nineveh and Calah: the H7449

RESERVE
Jer 3: 5 Will he **r** *his anger* for ever? will he H5201
50:20 found: for I will pardon them whom I **r**. H7604
2Pt 2: 9 and to **r** the unjust unto the G5083

RESERVED
Gen 27:36 said, Hast thou not **r** a blessing for me? H680
Nu 18: 9 most holy things, *r* from the fire: every
Jdg 21:22 sakes: because we **r** not to each man H3947
Ru 2:18 that she had **r** after she was sufficed. H3498
2Sa 8: 4 but **r** of them *for* an hundred chariots. H3498
1Ch 18: 4 but **r** of them an hundred chariots. H3498
Job 21:30 That the wicked is **r** to the day of H2820
38:23 Which I have **r** against the time of H2820
Act 25:21 But when Paul had appealed to be **r** G5083
Ro 11: 4 God unto him? I have **r** to myself seven G2641
1Pt 1: 4 fadeth not away, **r** in heaven for you, G5083
2Pt 2: 4 of darkness, to be **r** unto judgment; G5083
17 the mist of darkness is **r** for ever. G5083
3: 7 are kept in store, **r** unto fire against the G5083
Jude 6 he hath **r** in everlasting chains G5083
13 is **r** the blackness of darkness for ever. G5083

RESERVETH
Jer 5:24 latter, in his season: he **r** unto us the H8104
Nah 1: 2 and he **r** *wrath* for his enemies. H5201

RESHEPH
1Ch 7:25 And Rephah *was* his son, also **R**, and H7566

RESIDUE
Ex 10: 5 and they shall eat the **r** of that which is H3499
1Ch 6:66 And *the* **r** of the families of the sons of
Neh 11:20 And the **r** of Israel, of the priests, *and* H7605
Isa 21:17 And the **r** of the number of archers, the H7605
28: 5 of beauty, unto the **r** of his people, H7605
38:10 I am deprived of the **r** of my years. H3499
44:17 And the **r** thereof he maketh a god, H7611
19 and shall I make the **r** thereof an H3499
Jer 8: 3 rather than life by all the **r** of them that H7611
15: 9 and the **r** of them will I deliver H7611
24: 8 his princes, and the **r** of Jerusalem, that H7611
27:19 **r** of the vessels that remain in this city, H3499
29: 1 unto the **r** of the elders which H3499
39: 3 **r** of the princes of the king of Babylon. H7611
41:10 captive all the **r** of the people that *were* H7611
52:15 the people, and the **r** of the people that H3499
Ezk 9: 8 destroy all the **r** of Israel in thy pouring H7611
23:25 and thy **r** shall be devoured by the fire. H319
34:18 with your feet the **r** of your pastures? H3499
18 but ye must foul the **r** with your feet? H3498
36: 3 unto the **r** of the heathen, and H7611
4 **r** of the heathen that *are* round about; H7611
5 against the **r** of the heathen, and H7611
48:18 And the **r** in length over against the H3498
21 And the **r** *shall be* for the prince, on the H3498
Dan 7: 7 and stamped the **r** with the feet of it: H7606
19 pieces, and stamped the **r** with his feet; H7606
Zep 2: 9 desolation: the **r** of my people shall H7611
Hag 2: 2 and to the **r** of the people, saying, H7611
Zec 8:11 But now I *will* not *be* unto the **r** of this H7611
14: 2 captivity, and the **r** of the people shall H3499
Mal 2:15 one? Yet had he the **r** of the spirit. And H7605
Mk 16:13 And they went and told *it* unto the **r**: G3062
Act 15:17 That the **r** of men might seek after the G2645

RESIST
Zec 3: 1 standing at his right hand to **r** him. H7853
Mt 5:39 But I say unto you, That ye **r** not evil: but G436
Lk 21:15 shall not be able to gainsay nor **r**. G436
Act 6:10 And they were not able to **r** the wisdom G436
7:51 ears, ye do always **r** the Holy Ghost: as G496
Ro 13: 2 **r** shall receive to themselves damnation. G436
2Ti 3: 8 so do these also **r** the truth: men of G436
Jas 4: 7 Submit yourselves therefore to God. **R** G436
5: 6 killed the just; *and* he doth not **r** you. G498
1Pt 5: 9 Whom **r** stedfast in the faith, knowing G436

RESISTED
Ro 9:19 he yet find fault? For who hath **r** his will? G436
Heb 12: 4 Ye have not yet **r** unto blood, striving G478

RESISTETH
Ro 13: 2 Whosoever therefore **r** the power, G498
2 the power, **r** the ordinance of God: G436
Jas 4: 6 he saith, God **r** the proud, but giveth G498
1Pt 5: 5 humility: for God **r** the proud, and giveth G498

RESOLVED
Lk 16: 4 I am **r** what to do, that, when I am put G1097

RESORT
Neh 4:20 of the trumpet, **r** ye thither unto us: our H6908
Ps 71: 3 I may continually **r**: thou hast given H935
Mk 10: 1 and the people **r** unto him again; and, G4848
Jn 18:20 **r**; and in secret have I said nothing. G4905

RESORTED
2Ch 11:13 all Israel **r** to him out of all their coasts. H3320
Mk 2:13 **r** unto him, and he taught them. G2064
Jn 10:41 And many **r** unto him, and said, John G2064
18: 2 ofttimes **r** thither with his disciples. G4863
Act 16:13 spake unto the women which **r** *thither*. G4905

RESPECT
Gen 4: 4 had **r** unto Abel and to his offering: H8159
5 he had not **r**. And Cain was very H8159
Ex 2:25 of Israel, and God had **r** unto *them*. H3045
Lev 19:15 thou shalt not **r** the person of the poor, H5375
26: 9 For I will have **r** unto you, and make H6437
Nu 16:15 said unto the LORD, **R** not thou their H6437
Dt 1:17 Ye shall not **r** persons in judgment; *but* H5234
16:19 thou shalt not **r** persons, neither take H5234
2Sa 14:14 neither doth God **r** *any* person: yet doth H5375
1Ki 8:28 Yet have thou **r** unto the prayer of thy H6437
2Ki 13:23 on them, and had **r** unto them, because H6437
2Ch 6:19 Have **r** therefore to the prayer of thy H6437
19: 7 nor **r** of persons, nor taking of gifts. H4856
Ps 74:20 Have **r** unto the covenant: for the dark H5027
119: 6 I have **r** unto all thy commandments. H5027
15 thy precepts, and have **r** unto thy ways. H5027
117 have **r** unto thy statutes continually. H8159
138: 6 high, yet hath he **r** unto the lowly: but H7200
Prv 24:23 good to have **r** of persons in judgment. H5234
28:21 To have **r** of persons *is* not good: for for H5234
Isa 17: 7 shall have **r** to the Holy One of Israel. H7200
8 neither shall **r** *that* which his fingers H7200
22:11 **r** unto him that fashioned it long ago. H7200
Ro 2:11 For there is no **r** of persons with God. G4382
2Co 3:10 **r**, by reason of the glory that excelleth. G3313
Eph 6: 9 neither is there **r** of persons with him. G3382
Php 4:11 Not that I speak in **r** of want: for I have G2596
Col 2:16 or in drink, or in **r** of an holyday, or of G3313
3:25 hath done: and there is no **r** of persons. G4382
Heb 11:26 **r** unto the recompence of the reward. G578
Jas 2: 1 *the Lord* of glory, with **r** of persons. G4382
3 And ye have **r** to him that weareth the G1914
9 But if ye have **r** to persons, ye commit G4380
1Pt 1:17 Father, who without **r** of persons judgeth G678

RESPECTED
Lam 4:16 regard them: they **r** not the persons of H5375

RESPECTER
Act 10:34 I perceive that God is no **r** of persons: G4381

RESPECTETH
Job 37:24 Men do therefore fear him: he **r** not any H7200
Ps 40: 4 his trust, and **r** not the proud, nor such H6437

RESPITE
Ex 8:15 But when Pharaoh saw that there was **r**, H7309
1Sa 11: 3 Give us seven days' **r**, that we may send H7503

REST
Gen 8: 9 But the dove found no **r** for the sole of H4494
18: 4 feet, and **r** yourselves under the tree: H8172
30:36 and Jacob fed the **r** of Laban's flocks. H3498
49:15 And he saw that **r** *was* good, and the H4496
Ex 5: 5 ye make them **r** from their burdens. H7673
16:23 To morrow *is* the **r** of the holy sabbath H7677
23:11 But the seventh *year* thou shalt let it **r** H8058
12 day thou shalt **r**: that thine ox and thine H7673
12 and thine ass may **r**, and the son of thy H5117
28:10 six names of the **r** on the other stone, H3498
31:15 *is* the sabbath of **r**, holy to the LORD: H7677
33:14 shall go *with thee*, and I will give thee **r**. H5117
34:21 day thou shalt **r**: in earing time and in H7673
21 earing time and in harvest thou shalt **r**. H7673
35: 2 holy day, a sabbath of **r** to the LORD: H7677
Lev 5: 9 the altar; and the **r** of the blood shall be H7604
14:17 And of the **r** of the oil that *is* in his H3499
29 And the **r** of the oil that *is* in the priest's H3498
16:31 It *shall be* a sabbath of **r** unto you, and H7677
23: 3 *is* the sabbath of **r**, an holy convocation; H7677
32 It *shall be* unto you a sabbath of **r**, and H7677
25: 4 shall be a sabbath of **r** unto the land, a H7677
5 *for* it is a year of **r** unto the land. H7677
26:34 shall the land **r**, and enjoy her sabbaths. H7673
35 As long as it lieth desolate it shall **r**; H7673
35 because it did not **r** in your sabbaths, H7673
Nu 31: 8 Midian, beside the **r** of them that were H5921
32 And the booty, *being* the **r** of the prey H3499
Dt 3:13 And the **r** of Gilead, and all Bashan, H3499
20 Until the LORD have given **r** unto your H5117
5:14 thy maidservant may **r** as well as thou. H5117
12: 9 For ye are not as yet come to the **r** and H4496
10 he giveth you **r** from all your enemies H5117
25:19 God hath given thee **r** from all thine H5117
28:65 of thy foot have **r**: but the LORD shall H4494
Jos 1:13 you **r**, and hath given you this land. H5117
15 your brethren **r**, as *he hath given* you, H5117
3:13 of all the earth, shall **r** in the waters of H5117
10:20 that the **r** *which* remained of H8300
13:27 and Zaphon, the **r** of the kingdom of H3499
14:15 And the land had **r** from war. H8252
17: 2 There was also *a lot* for the **r** of the H3498
6 his sons: and the **r** of Manasseh's sons H3498
21: 5 And the **r** of the children of Kohath *had* H3498
34 of Merari, the **r** of the Levites, out of H3498
44 And the LORD gave them **r** round H5117
22: 4 God hath given **r** unto your brethren, H5117
23: 1 LORD had given **r** unto Israel from all H5117
Jdg 3:11 And the land had **r** forty years. And H8252
30 And the land had **r** fourscore years. H8252
5:31 might. And the land had **r** forty years. H8252
7: 6 men: but all the **r** of the people bowed H3499
8 and he sent all *the* **r** *of* Israel every man
Ru 1: 9 The LORD grant you that ye may find **r**, H4496
3: 1 **r** for thee, that it may be well with thee? H4494
18 the man will not be in **r**, until he have H8252
1Sa 13: 2 of Benjamin: and the **r** of the people he H3499
15:15 and the **r** we have utterly destroyed. H3498
2Sa 3:29 Let it **r** on the head of Joab, and on all H2342
7: 1 **r** round about from all his enemies; H5117
11 caused thee to **r** from all thine enemies. H5117
10:10 And the **r** of the people he delivered H3499
12:28 Now therefore gather the **r** of the H3499
21:10 birds of the air to **r** on them by day, nor H5117
1Ki 5: 4 hath given me **r** on every side, *so that* H5117
8:56 Blessed *be* the LORD, that hath given **r** H4496
11:41 And the **r** of the acts of Solomon, and H3499
14:19 And the **r** of the acts of Jeroboam, how H3499
29 Now the **r** of the acts of Rehoboam, H3499
15: 7 Now the **r** of the acts of Abijam, and all H3499
23 The **r** of all the acts of Asa, and all his H3499
31 Now the **r** of the acts of Nadab, and all H3499
16: 5 Now the **r** of the acts of Baasha, and H3499
14 Now the **r** of the acts of Elah, and all H3499
20 Now the **r** of the acts of Zimri, and his H3499
27 Now the **r** of the acts of Omri which he H3499
20:30 But the **r** fled to Aphek, into the city; H3498
22:39 Now the **r** of the acts of Ahab, and all H3499
45 Now the **r** of the acts of Jehoshaphat, H3499
2Ki 1:18 Now the **r** of the acts of Ahaziah which H3499
2:15 of Elijah doth **r** on Elisha. And they H5117
4: 7 and live thou and thy children of the **r**. H3498
8:23 And the **r** of the acts of Joram, and all H3499
10:34 Now the **r** of the acts of Jehu, and all H3499
12:19 And the **r** of the acts of Joash, and all H3499
13: 8 Now the **r** of the acts of Jehoahaz, and H3499
12 And the **r** of the acts of Joash, and all H3499
14:15 Now the **r** of the acts of Jehoash which H3499
18 And the **r** of the acts of Amaziah, *are* H3499
28 Now the **r** of the acts of Jeroboam, and H3499
15: 6 And the **r** of the acts of Azariah, and all H3499
11 And the **r** of the acts of Zachariah, H3499
15 And the **r** of the acts of Shallum, and H3499
21 And the **r** of the acts of Menahem, and H3499
26 And the **r** of the acts of Pekahiah, and H3499
31 And the **r** of the acts of Pekah, and all H3499
36 Now the **r** of the acts of Jotham, and all H3499
16:19 Now the **r** of the acts of Ahaz which he H3499
20:20 And the **r** of the acts of Hezekiah, and H3499
21:17 Now the **r** of the acts of Manasseh, and H3499
25 Now the **r** of the acts of Amon which he H3499
23:28 Now the **r** of the acts of Josiah, and all H3499
24: 5 Now the **r** of the acts of Jehoiakim, and H3499

2Ki 25:11 Now the r of the people *that were* left in H3499
1Ch 4:43 And they smote the r of the Amalekites H7611
6:31 of the LORD, after that the ark had r. H4494
77 Unto the r of the children of Merari H3498
11: 8 and Joab repaired the r of the city. H7605
12:38 Israel: and all the r also of Israel *were* H7611
16:41 Jeduthun, and the r that were chosen, H7605
19:11 And the r of the people he delivered H3499
22: 9 shall be a man of r; and I will give him H4496
9 rest; and I will give him r from all his H5117
18 he *not* given you r on every side? for he H5117
23:25 Israel hath given r unto his people, that H5117
24:20 And the r of the sons of Levi *were* H3498
28: 2 to build an house of r for the ark of the H4496
2Ch 9:29 Now the r of the acts of Solomon, first H7605
13:22 And the r of the acts of Abijah, and his H3499
14: 6 for the land had r, and he had no war in H8252
6 because the LORD had given him r. H5117
7 and he hath given us r on every side. So H5117
11 our God; for we r on thee, and in thy H8172
15:15 the LORD gave them r round about. H5117
20:30 for his God gave him r round about. H5117
34 Now the r of the acts of Jehoshaphat, H3499
24:14 they brought the r of the money before H7605
25:26 Now the r of the acts of Amaziah, first H3499
26:22 Now the r of the acts of Uzziah, first H3499
27: 7 Now the r of the acts of Jotham, and all H3499
28:26 Now the r of his acts and of all his H3499
32:32 Now the r of the acts of Hezekiah, and H3499
33:18 Now the r of the acts of Manasseh, and H3499
35:26 Now the r of the acts of Josiah, and his H3499
36: 8 Now the r of the acts of Jehoiakim, and H3499
Ezr 4: 3 But Zerubbabel, and Jeshua, and the r H7605
7 Tabeel, and the r of their companions, H7605
9 Shimshai the scribe, and the r of their H7606
10 And the r of the nations whom the H7606
10 Samaria, and the r *that are* on this side H7606
17 the scribe, and *to* the r of their H7606
17 and *unto* the r beyond the river, Peace, H7606
6:16 Levites, and the r of the children of the H7606
7:18 to do with the r of the silver and the H7606
Neh 2:16 rulers, nor to the r that did the work. H3499
4:14 rulers, and to the r of the people, Be not H3499
19 rulers, and to the r of the people, The H3499
6: 1 the Arabian, and the r of our enemies, H3499
14 Noadiah, and the r of the prophets, H3499
7:72 And *that* which the r of the people gave H7611
9:28 But after they had r, they did evil again H5117
10:28 And the r of the people, the priests, the H7605
11: 1 at Jerusalem: the r of the people also H7605
Est 9:12 have they done in the r of the king's H7605
16 lives, and had r from their enemies, H5118
Job 3:13 I should have slept: then had I been at r, H5117
17 troubling; and there the weary be at r. H5117
18 *There* the prisoners r together; they H7599
26 I was not in safety, neither had I r, H8252
11:18 *and* thou shalt take thy r in safety. H7901
14: 6 Turn from him, that he may r, till he H2308
17:16 pit, when *our* r together *is* in the dust. H5183
30:17 night season: and my sinews take no r. H7901
Ps 16: 9 rejoiceth: my flesh also shall r in hope. H7931
17:14 the r of their *substance* to their babes. H3499
37: 7 R in the LORD, and wait patiently for H1826
38: 3 *any* r in my bones because of my sin. H7965
55: 6 *for then* would I fly away, and be at r. H7931
94:13 That thou mayest give him r from the H8252
95:11 that they should not enter into my r. H4496
116: 7 Return unto thy r, O my soul; for the H4494
125: 3 For the rod of the wicked shall not r H5117
132: 8 Arise, O LORD, into thy r; thou, and the H4496
14 This *is* my r for ever: here will I dwell; H4496
Prv 6:35 r content, though thou givest many gifts.
29: 9 whether he rage or laugh, *there is* no r. H5183
17 Correct thy son, and he shall give thee r; H5117
Ecc 2:23 not r in the night. This is also vanity. H7901
6: 5 *thing*: this hath more r than the other. H5183
Song 1: 7 *thy flock* to r at noon: for why should H7257
Isa 7:19 And they shall come, and shall r all of H5117
10:19 And the r of the trees of his forest shall H7605
11: 2 And the spirit of the LORD shall r upon H5117
10 seek: and his r shall be glorious. H4496
14: 3 shall give thee r from thy sorrow, and H5117
7 The whole earth is at r, *and* is quiet: H5117
18: 4 me, I will take my r, and I will consider H8252
23:12 Chittim; there also shalt thou have no r. H5117
25:10 hand of the LORD r, and Moab shall be H5117
28:12 To whom he said, This *is* the r H4496
12 may cause the weary to r; and this *is* the H5117
30:15 In returning and r shall ye be saved; in H5183
Isa 34:14 owl also shall r there, and find for H7280
14 there, and find for herself a place of r. H4494
51: 4 judgment to r for a light of the people. H7280
57: 2 He shall enter into peace: they shall r in H5117
20 r, whose waters cast up mire and dirt. H8252
62: 1 sake I will not r, until the righteousness H8252
7 And give him no r, till he establish, and H1824
63:14 caused him to r: so didst thou lead thy H5117
66: 1 me? and where *is* the place of my r? H4496
Jer 6:16 and ye shall find r for your souls. But H4771
30:10 and shall be in r, and be quiet, and H8252
31: 2 Israel, when I went to cause him to r. H7280
39: 9 with the r of the people that remained. H3499
45: 3 I fainted in my sighing, and I find no r. H4496
46:27 return, and be in r and at ease, and H8252
47: 6 thyself into thy scabbard, r, and be still. H7280
50:34 that he may give r to the land, and H7280
52:15 of Babylon, and the r of the multitude. H3499
Lam 1: 3 she findeth no r: all her persecutors H4494
2:18 no r; let not the apple of thine eye cease. H6314
5: 5 persecution: we labour, *and* have no r. H5117
Ezk 5:13 cause my fury to r upon them, and I H5117
16:42 So will I make my fury toward thee to r, H5117
21:17 my fury to r: I the LORD have said *it*. H5117
24:13 I have caused my fury to r upon thee. H5117
38:11 to them that are at r, that dwell safely, H8252
44:30 cause the blessing to r in thine house. H5117
45: 8 my people; and *the r of* the land shall
48:23 As for the r of the tribes, from the east H3499
Dan 2:18 with the r of the wise *men* of Babylon. H7606
4: 4 I Nebuchadnezzar was at r in mine H7954
7:12 As concerning the r of the beasts, they H7606
12:13 *be*: for thou shalt r, and stand in thy lot H5117
Mic 2:10 for this *is* not *your* r: because it is H4496
Hab 3:16 that I might r in the day of trouble: H5117
Zep 3:17 with joy; he will r in his love, he will joy H2790
Zec 1:11 all the earth sitteth still, and is at r. H8252
9: 1 *shall be* the r thereof: when the eyes H4496
11: 9 the r eat every one the flesh of another. H7604
Mt 11:28 are heavy laden, and I will give you r. G373
29 and ye shall find r unto your souls. G372
12:43 dry places, seeking r, and findeth none. G372
26:45 now, and take *your* r: behold, the hour is G373
27:49 The r said, Let be, let us see whether G3062
Mk 6:31 a desert place, and r a while: for there G373
14:41 on now, and take *your* r: it is enough, the G373
Lk 10: 6 your peace shall r upon it: if not, it G1879
11:24 dry places, seeking r; and finding none, G372
12:26 is least, why take ye thought for the r? G3062
24: 9 things unto the eleven, and to all the r. G3062
Jn 11:13 he had spoken of taking of r in sleep. G2838
Act 2:26 moreover also my flesh shall r in hope: G2681
37 Peter and to the r of the apostles, Men G3062
5:13 And of the r durst no man join himself G3062
7:49 the Lord: or what *is* the place of my r? G2663
9:31 Then had the churches r throughout all G1515
27:44 And the r, some on boards, and some G3062
Ro 11: 7 obtained it, and the r were blinded G3062
1Co 7:12 But to the r speak I, not the Lord: If any G3062
11:34 the r will I set in order when I come. G3062
2Co 2:13 I had no r in my spirit, because I found G425
7: 5 our flesh had no r, but we were troubled G425
12: 9 the power of Christ may r upon me. G1981
2Th 1: 7 And to you who are troubled r with us, G425
Heb 3:11 wrath, They shall not enter into my r.) G2663
18 into his r, but to them that believed not? G2663
4: 1 of entering into his r, any of you should G2663
3 do enter into r, as he said, As I have G2663
3 enter into my r: although the works G2663
4 r the seventh day from all his works. G2664
5 again, If they shall enter into my r. G2663
8 For if Jesus had given them r, then G2664
9 There remaineth therefore a r to the G4520
10 For he that is entered into his r, he also G2663
11 to enter into that r, lest any man fall G2663
1Pt 4: 2 That he no longer should live the r of G1954
Rev 2:24 But unto you I say, and unto the r in G3062
4: 8 within: and they r not day and night, G372
6:11 that they should r yet for a little season, G373
9:20 And the r of the men which were not G3062
14:11 and they have no r day nor night, who G372
13 that they may r from their labours; and G373
20: 5 But the r of the dead lived not again G3062

RESTED

Gen 2: 2 had made; and he r on the seventh day H7673
3 that in it he had r from all his work H7673
8: 4 And the ark r in the seventh month, on H5117
Ex 10:14 land of Egypt, and r in all the coasts of H5117
Ex 16:30 So the people r on the seventh day. H7673
20:11 that in them *is*, and r the seventh day: H5117
31:17 the seventh day he r, and was refreshed. H7673
Nu 9:18 the tabernacle they r in their tents. H2583
23 of the LORD they r in the tents, and at H2583
10:12 the cloud r in the wilderness of Paran. H7931
36 And when it r, he said, Return, O LORD, H5117
11:25 *that*, when the spirit r upon them, they H5117
26 and the spirit r upon them; and they H5117
Jos 11:23 their tribes. And the land r from war. H8252
1Ki 6:10 they r on the house *with* timber of cedar. H270
2Ch 32: 8 And the people r themselves upon the H5564
Est 9:17 day of the same r they, and made it a H5118
18 of the same they r, and made it a day of H5118
22 As the days wherein the Jews r from H5117
Job 30:27 My bowels boiled, and r not: the days H1826
Lk 23:56 and ointments; and r the sabbath day G2270

RESTEST

Ro 2:17 Behold, thou art called a Jew, and r in G1879

RESTETH

Job 24:23 he r; yet his eyes *are* upon their ways. H8172
Prv 14:33 Wisdom r in the heart of him that hath H5117
Ecc 7: 9 for anger r in the bosom of fools. H5117
1Pt 4:14 of glory and of God r upon you: on their G373

RESTING

Nu 10:33 to search out a r place for them. H4496
2Ch 6:41 God, into thy r place, thou, and the H5118
Prv 24:15 of the righteous; spoil not his r place: H7258
Isa 32:18 in sure dwellings, and in quiet r places; H4496

RESTINGPLACE

Jer 50: 6 to hill, they have forgotten their r. H7258

RESTITUTION

Ex 22: 3 should make full r; if he have nothing, H7999
5 of his own vineyard, shall he make r. H7999
6 that kindled the fire shall surely make r. H7999
12 he shall make r unto the owner thereof. H7999
Job 20:18 r *be*, and he shall not rejoice *therein*. H8545
Act 3:21 until the times of r of all things, which G605

RESTORE

Gen 20: 7 Now therefore r the man *his* wife; for H7725
7 live: and if thou r *her* not, know thou H7725
40:13 thine head, and r thee unto thy place: H7725
42:25 with corn, and to r every man's money H7725
Ex 22: 1 or sell it; he shall r five oxen for an ox, H7999
4 ox, or ass, or sheep; he shall r double. H7999
Lev 6: 4 that he shall r that which he took H7725
5 he shall even r it in the principal, and H7999
24:21 And he that killeth a beast, he shall r it: H7999
25:27 sale thereof, and r the overplus unto H7725
28 But if he be not able to r *it* to him, then H4672
Nu 35:25 congregation shall r him to the city of H7725
Dt 22: 2 it, and thou shalt r it to him again. H7725
Jdg 11:13 r those *lands* again peaceably. H7725
17: 3 now therefore I will r it unto thee. H7725
1Sa 12: 3 mine eyes therewith? and I will r it you. H7725
2Sa 9: 7 sake, and will r thee all the land of Saul H7725
12: 6 And he shall r the lamb fourfold, H7999
16: 3 Israel r me the kingdom of my father. H7725
1Ki 20:34 thy father, I will r; and thou shalt make H7725
2Ki 8: 6 officer, saying, R all that *was* hers, and H7725
Neh 5:11 R, I pray you, to them, even this day, H7725
12 Then said they, We will r *them*, and H7725
Job 20:10 poor, and his hands shall r their goods. H7725
18 That which he laboured for shall he r, H7725
Ps 51:12 R unto me the joy of thy salvation; and H7725
Prv 6:31 But *if* he be found, he shall r sevenfold; H7999
Isa 1:26 And I will r thy judges as at the first, H7725
42:22 for a spoil, and none saith, R. H7725
49: 6 of Jacob, and to r the preserved of H7725
57:18 lead him also, and r comforts unto him H7999
Jer 27:22 them up, and r them to this place. H7725
30:17 For I will r health unto thee, and I will H5927
Ezk 33:15 *If* the wicked r the pledge, give again H7725
Dan 9:25 the commandment to r and to build H7725
Joel 2:25 And I will r to you the years that the H7999
Mt 17:11 truly shall first come, and r all things. G600
Lk 19: 8 by false accusation, I r *him* fourfold. G591
Act 1: 6 this time r again the kingdom to Israel? G600
Gal 6: 1 are spiritual, r such an one in the spirit G2675

RESTORED

Gen 20:14 Abraham, and r him Sarah his wife. H7725
40:21 And he r the chief butler unto his H7725

Gen 41:13 **r** unto mine office, and him he hanged. H7725
42:28 My money is **r**; and, lo, *it is* even in H7725
Dt 28:31 and shall not be **r** to thee: thy sheep H7725
Jdg 17: 3 And when he had **r** the eleven hundred H7725
4 Yet he **r** the money unto his mother; H7725
1Sa 7:14 from Israel were **r** to Israel, from Ekron H7725
1Ki 13: 6 my hand may be **r** me again. And the H7725
6 the king's hand was **r** him again, and H7725
2Ki 8: 1 whose son he had **r** to life, saying, H2421
5 king how he had **r** a dead body to life, H2421
5 whose son he had **r** to life, cried to the H2421
5 this *is* her son, whom Elisha **r** to life. H2421
14:22 He built Elath, and **r** it to Judah, after H7725
25 He **r** the coast of Israel from the H7725
2Ch 8: 2 That the cities which Huram had **r** to H5414
26: 2 He built Eloth, and **r** it to Judah, after H7725
Ezr 6: 5 unto Babylon, be **r**, and brought again H8421
Ps 69: 4 then I **r** *that* which I took not away. H7725
Ezk 18: 7 And hath not oppressed any, *but* hath **r** H7725
12 by violence, hath not **r** the pledge, and H7725
Mt 12:13 and it was **r** whole, like as the other. *G600*
Mk 3: 5 and his hand was **r** whole as the other. *G600*
8:25 and he was **r**, and saw every man clearly. *G600*
Lk 6:10 and his hand was **r** whole as the other. *G600*
Heb 13:19 this, that I may be **r** to you the sooner. *G600*

RESTORER
Ru 4:15 And he shall be unto thee a **r** of *thy* life, H7725
Isa 58:12 the breach, The **r** of paths to dwell in. H7725

RESTORETH
Ps 23: 3 He **r** my soul: he leadeth me in the H7725
Mk 9:12 cometh first, and **r** all things; and how it *G600*

RESTRAIN
Job 15: 8 and dost thou **r** wisdom to thyself? H1639
Ps 76:10 the remainder of wrath shalt thou **r**. H2296

RESTRAINED
Gen 8: 2 and the rain from heaven was **r**; H3607
11: 6 nothing will be **r** from them, which H1219
16: 2 the LORD hath **r** me from bearing: I H6113
Ex 36: 6 So the people were **r** from bringing. H3607
1Sa 3:13 themselves vile, and he **r** them not. H3543
Isa 63:15 and of thy mercies toward me? are they **r**? H662
Ezk 31:15 for him, and I **r** the floods thereof, and H4513
Act 14:18 And with these sayings scarce **r** they *G2664*

RESTRAINEST
Job 15: 4 Yea, thou castest off fear, and **r** prayer H1639

RESTRAINT
1Sa 14: 6 us: for *there is* no **r** to the LORD to save H4622

RESTS
1Ki 6: 6 made narrowed **r** round about, that *the* H4052

RESURRECTION
Mt 22:23 say that there is no **r**, and asked him, *G386*
28 Therefore in the **r** whose wife shall she *G386*
30 For in the **r** they neither marry, nor are *G386*
31 But as touching the **r** of the dead, have *G386*
27:53 And came out of the graves after his **r**, *G1454*
Mk 12:18 there is no **r**; and they asked him, saying, *G386*
23 In the **r** therefore, when they shall rise, *G386*
Lk 14:14 shalt be recompensed at the **r** of the just. *G386*
20:27 that there is any **r**; and they asked him, *G386*
33 Therefore in the **r** whose wife of them is *G386*
35 that world, and the **r** from the dead, *G386*
36 of God, being the children of the **r**. *G386*
Jn 5:29 good, unto the **r** of life; and they that *G386*
29 have done evil, unto the **r** of damnation. *G386*
11:24 shall rise again in the **r** at the last day. *G386*
25 Jesus said unto her, I am the **r**, and the *G386*
Act 1:22 ordained to be a witness with us of his **r**. *G386*
2:31 He seeing this before spake of the **r** of *G386*
4: 2 through Jesus the **r** from the dead. *G386*
33 witness of the **r** of the Lord Jesus: and *G386*
17:18 he preached unto them Jesus, and the **r**. *G386*
32 And when they heard of the **r** of the *G386*
23: 6 **r** of the dead I am called in question. *G386*
8 For the Sadducees say that there is no **r**, *G386*
24:15 **r** of the dead, both of the just and unjust. *G386*
21 Touching the **r** of the dead I am called *G386*
Ro 1: 4 spirit of holiness, by the **r** from the dead: *G386*
6: 5 we shall be also *in the likeness* of *his* **r**: *G386*
1Co 15:12 among you that there is no **r** of the dead? *G386*
13 But if there be no **r** of the dead, then is *G386*
21 by man *came* also the **r** of the dead. *G386*
1Co 15:42 So also *is* the **r** of the dead. It is sown in *G386*
Php 3:10 the power of his **r**, and the fellowship of *G386*
11 I might attain unto the **r** of the dead. *G1815*
2Ti 2:18 saying that the **r** is past already; and *G386*
Heb 6: 2 **r** of the dead, and of eternal judgment. *G386*
11:35 that they might obtain a better **r**: *G386*
1Pt 1: 3 by the **r** of Jesus Christ from the dead, *G386*
3:21 toward God,) by the **r** of Jesus Christ: *G386*
Rev 20: 5 years were finished. This *is* the first **r**. *G386*
6 part in the first **r**: on such the second *G386*

RETAIN
Job 2: 9 **r** thine integrity? curse God, and die. H2388
Prv 4: 4 Let thine heart **r** my words: keep my H8551
11:16 honour: and strong *men* **r** riches. H8551
Ecc 8: 8 over the spirit to **r** the spirit; neither H3607
Dan 11: 6 but she shall not **r** the power of the H6113
Jn 20:23 soever *sins* ye **r**, they are retained. *G2902*
Ro 1:28 And even as they did not like to **r** God *G2192*

RETAINED
Jdg 7: 8 man unto his tent, and **r** those three H2388
19: 4 damsel's father, **r** him; and he abode H2388
Dan 10: 8 into corruption, and I **r** no strength. H6113
16 upon me, and I have **r** no strength. H6113
Jn 20:23 whose soever *sins* ye retain, they are **r**. *G2902*
Phlm 13 Whom I would have **r** with me, that in *G2722*

RETAINETH
Prv 3:18 her: and happy *is every one* that **r** her. H8551
11:16 A gracious woman **r** honour: and H8551
Mic 7:18 of his heritage? he **r** not his anger for H2388

RETIRE
2Sa 11:15 hottest battle, and **r** ye from him, that H7725
Jer 4: 6 Set up the standard toward Zion: **r**, stay H5756

RETIRED
Jdg 20:39 And when the men of Israel **r** in the H2015
2Sa 20:22 trumpet, and they **r** from the city, every H6327

RETURN
Gen 3:19 eat bread, till thou **r** unto the ground; H7725
19 thou *art*, and unto dust shalt thou **r**. H7725
14:17 meet him after his **r** from the slaughter H7725
16: 9 said unto her, **R** to thy mistress, and H7725
18:10 And he said, I will certainly **r** unto thee H7725
14 appointed I will **r** unto thee, according H7725
31: 3 And the LORD said unto Jacob, **R** unto H7725
13 and **r** unto the land of thy kindred. H7725
32: 9 saidst unto me, **R** unto thy country, H7725
Ex 4:18 go, I pray thee, and **r** unto my brethren H7725
19 in Midian, Go, **r** into Egypt: for all the H7725
21 thou goest to **r** into Egypt, see that H7725
13:17 when they see war, and they **r** to Egypt: H7725
Lev 25:10 you; and ye shall **r** every man unto his H7725
10 ye shall **r** every man unto his family. H7725
13 In the year of this jubile ye shall **r** every H7725
27 it; that he may **r** unto his possession. H7725
28 out, and he shall **r** unto his possession. H7725
41 him, and shall **r** unto his own family, H7725
41 the possession of his fathers shall he **r**. H7725
27:24 In the year of the jubile the field shall **r** H7725
Nu 10:36 And when it rested, he said, **R**, O LORD, H7725
14: 3 were it not better for us to **r** into Egypt? H7725
4 make a captain, and let us **r** into Egypt. H7725
23: 5 mouth, and said, **R** unto Balak, and H7725
32:18 We will not **r** unto our houses, until the H7725
22 afterward ye shall **r**, and be guiltless H7725
35:28 shall **r** into the land of his possession. H7725
Dt 3:20 and *then* shall ye **r** every man unto his H7725
17:16 the people to **r** to Egypt, to the end H7725
16 Ye shall henceforth **r** no more that way. H7725
20: 5 it? let him go and **r** to his house, lest he H7725
6 him *also* go and **r** unto his house, lest H7725
7 let him go and **r** unto his house, lest H7725
8 let him go and **r** unto his house, lest H7725
30: 2 And shalt **r** unto the LORD thy God, H7725
3 thee, and will **r** and gather thee from H7725
8 And thou shalt **r** and obey the voice of H7725
Jos 1:15 then ye shall **r** unto the land of your H7725
20: 6 shall the slayer **r**, and come unto his H7725
22: 4 therefore now **r** ye, and get you unto H6437
8 And he spake unto them, saying, **R** H7725
Jdg 7: 3 and afraid, let him **r** and depart early H7725
11:31 to meet me, when I **r** in peace from the H7725
Ru 1: 6 that she might **r** from the country of H7725
7 on the way to **r** unto the land of Judah. H7725
8 in law, Go, **r** each to her mother's H7725
Ru 1:10 And they said unto her, Surely we will **r** H7725
15 her gods: **r** thou after thy sister in law. H7725
16 not to leave thee, *or* to **r** from following H7725
1Sa 6: 3 empty; but in any wise **r** him a trespass H7725
4 offering which we shall **r** to him? They H7725
8 of gold, which ye **r** him *for* a trespass H7725
7: 3 saying, If ye do **r** unto the LORD with H7725
17 And his **r** *was* to Ramah; for there *was* H8666
9: 5 Come, and let us **r**; lest my father leave H7725
15:26 And Samuel said unto Saul, I will not **r** H7725
26:21 Then said Saul, I have sinned: **r**, my son H7725
29: 4 Make this fellow **r**, that he may go again H7725
7 Wherefore now **r**, and go in peace, that H7725
11 in the morning, to **r** into the land of the H7725
2Sa 2:26 people **r** from following their brethren? H7725
3:16 unto him, Go, **r**. And he returned. H7725
10: 5 until your beards be grown, and *then* **r**. H7725
12:23 go to him, but he shall not **r** to me. H7725
15:19 thou also with us? **r** to thy place, and H7725
20 go whither I may, **r** thou, and take back H7725
27 *not* thou a seer? **r** into the city in peace, H7725
34 But if thou **r** to the city, and say unto H7725
19:14 the king, **R** thou, and all thy servants. H7725
24:13 answer I shall **r** to him that sent me. H7725
1Ki 2:32 And the LORD shall **r** his blood upon H7725
33 Their blood shall therefore **r** upon the H7725
44 **r** thy wickedness upon thine own head; H7725
8:48 And *so* **r** unto thee with all their heart, H7725
12:24 children of Israel: **r** every man to his H7725
26 the kingdom **r** to the house of David: H7725
13:16 And he said, I may not **r** with thee, nor H7725
19:15 And the LORD said unto him, Go, **r** on H7725
20:22 doest: for at the **r** of the year the king H8666
26 And it came to pass at the **r** of the year, H8666
22:17 **r** every man to his house in peace. H7725
28 And Micaiah said, If thou **r** at all in H7725
2Ki 18:14 I have offended; **r** from me: that which H7725
19: 7 a rumour, and shall **r** to his own land; H7725
33 the same shall he **r**, and shall not come H7725
20:10 let the shadow **r** backward ten degrees. H7725
1Ch 19: 5 until your beards be grown, and *then* **r**. H7725
2Ch 6:24 thee; and shall **r** and confess thy name, H7725
38 If they **r** to thee with all their heart and H7725
10: 6 give ye *me* to **r** answer to this people? H7725
9 ye that we may **r** answer to this people, H7725
11: 4 your brethren: **r** every man to his H7725
18:16 master; let them **r** *therefore* every man H7725
26 water of affliction, until I **r** in peace. H7725
27 And Micaiah said, If thou certainly **r** in H7725
30: 6 Israel, and he will **r** to the remnant of H7725
9 *his* face from you, if ye **r** unto him. H7725
Neh 2: 6 when wilt thou **r**? So it pleased the king H7725
4:12 ye shall **r** unto us *they will be upon you*. H7725
9:17 a captain to **r** to their bondage: but H7725
Est 4:15 Then Esther bade *them* **r** Mordecai *this* H7725
9:25 the Jews, should **r** upon his own head, H7725
Job 1:21 and naked shall I **r** thither: the LORD H7725
6:29 **R**, I pray you, let it not be iniquity; yea, H7725
29 yea, **r** again, my righteousness *is* in it. H7725
7:10 He shall **r** no more to his house, neither H7725
10:21 Before I go *whence* I shall not **r**, *even* to H7725
15:22 He believeth not that he shall **r** out of H7725
16:22 I shall go the way *whence* I shall not **r**. H7725
17:10 But as for you all, do ye **r**, and come H7725
22:23 If thou **r** to the Almighty, thou shalt be H7725
33:25 he shall **r** to the days of his youth: H7725
36:10 commandeth that they **r** from iniquity. H7725
39: 4 they go forth, and **r** not unto them. H7725
Ps 6: 4 **R**, O LORD, deliver my soul: oh save me H7725
10 let them **r** *and* be ashamed suddenly. H7725
7: 7 for their sakes therefore **r** thou on high. H7725
16 His mischief shall **r** upon his own head, H7725
59: 6 They **r** at evening: they make a noise H7725
14 And at evening let them **r**; *and* let them H7725
73:10 Therefore his people **r** hither: and H7725
74:21 O let not the oppressed **r** ashamed: let H7725
80:14 **R**, we beseech thee, O God of hosts: look H7725
90: 3 and sayest, **R**, ye children of men. H7725
13 **R**, O LORD, how long? and let it repent H7725
94:15 But judgment shall **r** unto H7725
104:29 breath, they die, and **r** to their dust. H7725
116: 7 **R** unto thy rest, O my soul; for the H7725
Prv 2:19 None that go unto her **r** again, neither H7725
26:27 that rolleth a stone, it will **r** upon him. H7725
Ecc 1: 7 the rivers come, thither they **r** again. H7725
5:15 naked shall he **r** to go as he came, and H7725
12: 2 nor the clouds **r** after the rain: H7725
7 Then shall the dust **r** to the earth as it H7725
7 the spirit shall **r** unto God who gave it. H7725

Song 6:13 **R**, return, O Shulamite; return, return, H7725
13 Return, **r**, O Shulamite; return, return, H7725
13 Return, return, O Shulamite; **r**, return, H7725
13 Return, return, O Shulamite; return, **r**, H7725
Isa 6:13 tenth, and *it* shall **r**, and shall be eaten: H7725
10:21 The remnant shall **r**, *even* the remnant H7725
22 of them shall **r**: the consumption H7725
19:22 *it*: and they shall **r** *even* to the LORD, H7725
21:12 if ye will inquire, inquire ye: **r**, come. H7725
35:10 And the ransomed of the LORD shall **r**, H7725
37: 7 a rumour, and **r** to his own land; and H7725
34 the same shall he **r**, and shall not come H7725
44:22 **r** unto me; for I have redeemed thee. H7725
45:23 and shall not **r**, That unto me every H7725
51:11 of the LORD shall **r**, and come with H7725
55: 7 and let him **r** unto the LORD, and H7725
11 mouth: it shall not **r** unto me void, but H7725
63:17 from thy fear? **R** for thy servants' sake, H7725
Jer 3: 1 man's, shall he **r** unto her again? shall H7725
1 yet **r** again to me, saith the LORD. H7725
12 the north, and say, **R**, thou backsliding H7725
22 **R**, ye backsliding children, *and* I will H7725
4: 1 If thou wilt **r**, O Israel, saith the LORD, H7725
1 saith the LORD, **r** unto me: and if thou H7725
5: 3 than a rock; they have refused to **r**. H7725
8: 4 not arise? shall he turn away, and not **r**? H7725
5 they hold fast deceit, they refuse to **r**. H7725
12:15 them out I will **r**, and have compassion H7725
15: 7 *since* they **r** not from their ways. H7725
19 the LORD, If thou **r**, then will I bring H7725
19 mouth: let them **r** unto thee; but return H7725
19 unto thee; but **r** not thou unto them. H7725
18:11 against you: **r** ye now every one from H7725
22:10 **r** no more, nor see his native country. H7725
11 place; He shall not **r** thither any more: H7725
27 desire to **r**, thither shall they not return. H7725
27 desire to return, thither shall they not **r**. H7725
23:14 that none doth **r** from his wickedness: H7725
20 The anger of the LORD shall not **r**, until H7725
24: 7 shall **r** unto me with their whole heart. H7725
29:10 you, in causing you to **r** to this place. H7725
30: 3 I will cause them to **r** to the land that I H7725
10 and Jacob shall **r**, and shall be in rest, H7725
24 LORD shall not **r**, until he have done *it*, H7725
31: 8 a great company shall **r** thither. H7725
32:44 their captivity to **r**, saith the LORD. H7725
33: 7 to **r**, and will build them, as at the first. H7725
11 For I will cause to **r** the captivity of the H7725
26 captivity to **r**, and have mercy on them. H7725
34:11 had let go free, to **r**, and brought them H7725
16 their pleasure, to **r**, and brought them H7725
22 and cause them to **r** to this city; and H7725
35:15 *them*, saying, **R** ye now every man H7725
36: 3 that they may **r** every man from his H7725
7 LORD, and will **r** every one from his H7725
37: 7 shall **r** to Egypt into their own land. H7725
20 thou cause me not to **r** to the house of H7725
38:26 to **r** to Jonathan's house, to die there. H7725
42:12 and cause you to **r** to your own land. H7725
44:14 that they should **r** into the land of H7725
14 have a desire to **r** to dwell there: for H7725
14 none shall **r** but such as shall escape. H7725
28 the sword shall **r** out of the land of H7725
46:27 and Jacob shall **r**, and be in rest and at H7725
50: 9 expert man; none shall **r** in vain. H7725
Ezk 7:13 For the seller shall not **r** to that which H7725
13 *which* shall not **r**; neither shall any H7725
13:22 that he should not **r** from his wicked H7725
16:55 her daughters, shall **r** to their former H7725
55 daughters shall **r** to their former estate, H7725
55 daughters shall **r** to your former estate. H7725
18:23 he should **r** from his ways, and live? H7725
21: 5 of his sheath: it shall not **r** any more. H7725
30 Shall I cause *it* to **r** into his sheath? I H7725
29:14 will cause them to **r** *into* the land of H7725
35: 9 thy cities shall not **r**: and ye shall know H3427
46: 9 gate: he shall not **r** by the way of the H7725
17 after it shall **r** to the prince: but his H7725
47: 6 caused me to **r** to the brink of the river. H7725
Dan 10:20 and now will I **r** to fight with the prince H7725
11: 9 kingdom, and shall **r** into his own land. H7725
10 **r**, and be stirred up, *even* to his fortress. H7725
13 For the king of the north shall **r**, and H7725
28 Then shall he **r** into his land with great H7725
28 shall do *exploits*, and **r** to his own land. H7725
29 At the time appointed he shall **r**, and H7725
30 be grieved, and **r**, and have indignation H7725
30 he do; he shall even **r**, and have H7725
Hos 2: 7 say, I will go and **r** to my first husband; H7725
Hos 2: 9 Therefore will I **r**, and take away my H7725
3: 5 Afterward shall the children of Israel **r**, H7725
5:15 I will go *and* **r** to my place, till they H7725
6: 1 Come, and let us **r** unto the LORD: for H7725
7:10 and they do not **r** to the LORD their H7725
16 They **r**, *but* not to the most High: they H7725
8:13 visit their sins: they shall **r** to Egypt. H7725
9: 3 but Ephraim shall **r** to Egypt, and they H7725
11: 5 He shall not **r** into the land of Egypt, H7725
5 be his king, because they refused to **r**. H7725
9 anger, I will not **r** to destroy Ephraim: H7725
12:14 his reproach shall his Lord **r** unto him. H7725
14: 1 O Israel, **r** unto the LORD thy God; for H7725
7 his shadow shall **r**; they shall revive *as* H7725
Joel 2:14 Who knoweth *if* he will **r** and repent, H7725
3: 4 *and* speedily will I **r** your recompence H7725
7 sold them, and will **r** your recompence H7725
Oba 15 reward shall **r** upon thine own head. H7725
Mic 1: 7 and they shall **r** to the hire of an harlot. H7725
5: 3 shall **r** unto the children of Israel. H7725
Mal 1: 4 but we will **r** and build the desolate H7725
3: 7 not kept *them*. **R** unto me, and I will H7725
7 me, and I will **r** unto you, saith the H7725
7 hosts. But ye said, Wherein shall we **r**? H7725
18 Then shall ye **r**, and discern between H7725
Mt 2:12 that they should not **r** to Herod, they G344
10:13 be not worthy, let your peace **r** to you. G1994
12:44 Then he saith, I will **r** into my house G1994
24:18 Neither let him which is in the field **r** G1994
Lk 8:39 **R** to thine own house, and shew how G5290
11:24 **r** unto my house whence I came out. G5290
12:36 lord, when he will **r** from the wedding; G360
17:31 in the field, let him likewise not **r** back. G1994
19:12 receive for himself a kingdom, and to **r**. G5290
Act 13:34 *now* no more to **r** to corruption, he said G5290
15:16 After this I will **r**, and will build again the G390
18:21 but I will **r** again unto you, if God G344
20: 3 he purposed to **r** through Macedonia. G5290

RETURNED

Gen 8: 3 And the waters **r** from off the earth H7725
9 of her foot, and she **r** unto him into the H7725
12 which **r** not again unto him any more. H7725
14: 7 And they **r**, and came to En-mishpat, H7725
18:33 and Abraham **r** unto his place. H7725
21:32 they **r** into the land of the Philistines. H7725
22:19 So Abraham **r** unto his young men, H7725
31:55 Laban departed, and **r** unto his place. H7725
32: 6 And the messengers **r** to Jacob, saying, H7725
33:16 So Esau **r** that day on his way unto H7725
37:29 And Reuben **r** unto the pit; and, H7725
30 And he **r** unto his brethren, and said, H7725
38:22 And he **r** to Judah, and said, I cannot H7725
42:24 and wept; and **r** to them again, and H7725
43:10 surely now we had **r** this second time. H7725
18 money that was **r** in our sacks at the H7725
44:13 every man his ass, and **r** to the city. H7725
50:14 And Joseph **r** into Egypt, he, and his H7725
Ex 4:18 And Moses went and **r** to Jethro his H7725
20 an ass, and he **r** to the land of Egypt: H7725
5:22 And Moses **r** unto the LORD, and said, H7725
14:27 sea, and the sea **r** to his strength when H7725
28 And the waters **r**, and covered the H7725
19: 8 will do. And Moses **r** the words of the H7725
32:31 And Moses **r** unto the LORD, and said, H7725
34:31 of the congregation **r** unto him: and H7725
Lev 22:13 have no child, and is **r** unto her father's H7725
Nu 13:25 And they **r** from searching of the land H7725
14:36 search the land, who **r**, and made all the H7725
16:50 And Aaron **r** unto Moses unto the door H7725
23: 6 And he **r** unto him, and, lo, he stood by H7725
24:25 And Balaam rose up, and went and **r** to H7725
Dt 1:45 And ye **r** and wept before the LORD; H7725
Jos 2:16 **r**: and afterward may ye go your way. H7725
22 the pursuers were **r**: and the pursuers H7725
23 So the two men **r**, and descended from H7725
4:18 waters of Jordan **r** unto their place, and H7725
6:14 **r** into the camp: so they did six days. H7725
7: 3 And they **r** to Joshua, and said unto H7725
8:24 all the Israelites **r** unto Ai, and smote H7725
10:15 And Joshua **r**, and all Israel with him, H7725
21 And all the people **r** to the camp to H7725
38 And Joshua **r**, and all Israel with him, H7725
43 And Joshua **r**, and all Israel with him, H7725
22: 9 tribe of Manasseh **r**, and departed from H7725
32 and the princes, **r** from the children of H7725
Jdg 2:19 was dead, *that* they **r**, and corrupted H7725
5:29 her, yea, she **r** answer to herself, H7725
7: 3 Gilead. And there **r** of the people H7725
Jdg 7:15 he worshipped, and **r** into the host of H7725
8:13 And Gideon the son of Joash **r** from H7725
11:39 months, that she **r** unto her father, who H7725
14: 8 And after a time he **r** to take her, and H7725
21:23 caught: and they went and **r** unto their H7725
Ru 1:22 So Naomi **r**, and Ruth the Moabitess, H7725
22 with her, which **r** out of the country of H7725
1Sa 1:19 the LORD, and **r**, and came to their H7725
6:16 seen *it*, they **r** to Ekron the same day. H7725
17 the Philistines **r** *for* a trespass offering H7725
17:15 But David went and **r** from Saul to feed H7725
53 And the children of Israel **r** from H7725
57 And as David **r** from the slaughter of H7725
18: 6 when David was **r** from the slaughter H7725
23:28 Wherefore Saul **r** from pursuing after H7725
24: 1 And it came to pass, when Saul was **r** H7725
25:39 for the LORD hath **r** the wickedness of H7725
26:25 on his way, and Saul **r** to his place. H7725
27: 9 the apparel, and **r**, and came to Achish. H7725
2Sa 1: 1 when David was **r** from the slaughter H7725
22 and the sword of Saul **r** not empty. H7725
2:30 And Joab **r** from following Abner: and H7725
3:16 Abner unto him, Go, return. And he **r**. H7725
27 And when Abner was **r** to Hebron, Joab H7725
6:20 Then David **r** to bless his household. H7725
8:13 And David gat *him* a name when he **r** H7725
10:14 the city. So Joab **r** from the children of H7725
11: 4 uncleanness: and she **r** unto her house. H7725
12:31 and all the people **r** unto Jerusalem. H7725
14:24 face. So Absalom **r** to his own house, H5437
16: 8 The LORD hath **r** upon thee all the H7725
17: 3 all **r**: *so* all the people shall be in peace. H7725
20 not find *them*, they **r** to Jerusalem. H7725
18:16 and the people **r** from pursuing after H7725
19:15 So the king **r**, and came to Jordan. And H7725
39 him; and he **r** unto his own place. H7725
20:22 And Joab **r** to Jerusalem unto the king. H7725
23:10 and the people **r** after him only to spoil. H7725
1Ki 12:24 word of the LORD, and **r** to depart, H7725
13:10 So he went another way, and **r** not by H7725
33 After this thing Jeroboam **r** not from H7725
19:21 And he **r** back from him, and took a H7725
2Ki 2:25 and from thence he **r** to Samaria. H7725
3:27 from him, and **r** to *their own* land. H7725
4:35 Then he **r**, and walked in the house to H7725
5:15 And he **r** to the man of God, he and all H7725
7:15 the messengers **r**, and told the king. H7725
8: 3 that the woman **r** out of the land of the H7725
9:15 But king Joram was **r** to be healed in H7725
14:14 house, and hostages, and **r** to Samaria. H7725
19: 8 So Rab-shakeh **r**, and found the king of H7725
36 and went and **r**, and dwelt at Nineveh. H7725
23:20 bones upon them, and **r** to Jerusalem. H7725
1Ch 16:43 house: and David **r** to bless his house. H5437
20: 3 and all the people **r** to Jerusalem. H7725
2Ch 10: 2 heard *it*, that Jeroboam **r** out of Egypt. H7725
11: 4 and **r** from going against Jeroboam. H7725
14:15 in abundance, and **r** to Jerusalem. H7725
19: 1 And Jehoshaphat the king of Judah **r** to H7725
8 when they **r** to Jerusalem. H7725
20:27 Then they **r**, every man of Judah and H7725
22: 6 And he **r** to be healed in Jezreel H7725
25:10 Judah, and they **r** home in great anger. H7725
24 the hostages also, and **r** to Samaria. H7725
28:15 their brethren: then they **r** to Samaria. H7725
31: 1 the children of Israel **r**, every man to his H7725
32:21 of Assyria. So he **r** with shame of face H7725
34: 7 all the land of Israel, he **r** to Jerusalem. H7725
9 and Benjamin; and they **r** to Jerusalem. H7725
Ezr 5: 5 and then they **r** answer by letter H8421
11 And thus they **r** us answer, saying, We H8421
Neh 2:15 by the gate of the valley, and *so* **r**. H7725
4:15 to nought, that we **r** all of us to the H7725
9:28 yet when they **r**, and cried unto thee, H7725
Est 2:14 the morrow she **r** into the second house H7725
7: 8 Then the king **r** out of the palace H7725
Ps 35:13 and my prayer **r** into mine own bosom. H7725
60:ttl when Joab **r**, and smote of Edom H7725
78:34 they **r** and inquired early after God. H7725
Ecc 4: 1 So I **r**, and considered all the H7725
7 Then I **r**, and I saw vanity under the H7725
9:11 I **r**, and saw under the sun, that the race H7725
Isa 37: 8 So Rabshakeh **r**, and found the king of H7725
37 and went and **r**, and dwelt at Nineveh. H7725
38: 8 So the sun **r** ten degrees, by which H7725
Jer 3: 7 thou unto me. But she **r** not. And her H7725
14: 3 no water; they **r** with their vessels H7725
40:12 Even all the Jews **r** out of all places H7725
41:14 cast about and **r**, and went unto H7725

Jer 43: 5 of Judah, that were **r** from all nations, H7725
Ezk 1:14 And the living creatures ran and **r** as H7725
8:17 violence, and have **r** to provoke me to H7725
47: 7 Now when I had **r**, behold, at the bank H7725
Dan 4:34 understanding **r** unto me, and I blessed H8421
36 At the same time my reason **r** unto me; H8421
36 and brightness **r** unto me; and my H8421
Hos 6:11 when I **r** the captivity of my people. H7725
Am 4: 6 have ye not **r** unto me, saith the LORD. H7725
8 have ye not **r** unto me, saith the LORD. H7725
9 have ye not **r** unto me, saith the LORD. H7725
10 have ye not **r** unto me, saith the LORD. H7725
11 have ye not **r** unto me, saith the LORD. H7725
Zec 1: 6 fathers? and they **r** and said, Like as H7725
16 Therefore thus saith the LORD; I am **r** H7725
7:14 through nor **r**: for they laid the pleasant H7725
8: 3 Thus saith the LORD; I am **r** unto Zion, H7725
Mt 21:18 Now in the morning as he **r** into the *G1877*
Mk 14:40 And when he **r**, he found them asleep *G5290*
Lk 1:56 three months, and **r** to her own house. *G5290*
2:20 And the shepherds **r**, glorifying and *G1994*
39 of the Lord, they **r** into Galilee, to their *G5290*
43 the days, as they **r**, the child Jesus *G5290*
4: 1 And Jesus being full of the Holy Ghost **r** *G5290*
14 And Jesus **r** in the power of the Spirit *G5290*
8:37 up into the ship, and **r** back again. *G5290*
40 when Jesus was **r**, the people *gladly* *G5290*
9:10 And the apostles, when they were **r**, told *G5290*
10:17 And the seventy **r** again with joy, *G5290*
17:18 There are not found that **r** to give glory *G5290*
19:15 that when he was **r**, having received the *G1880*
23:48 were done, smote their breasts, and **r**. *G5290*
56 And they **r**, and prepared spices and *G5290*
24: 9 And **r** from the sepulchre, and told all *G5290*
33 And they rose up the same hour, and **r** *G5290*
52 And they worshipped him, and **r** to *G5290*
Act 1:12 Then **r** they unto Jerusalem from the *G5290*
5:22 them not in the prison, they **r**, and told, *G390*
8:25 word of the Lord, **r** to Jerusalem, and *G5290*
12:25 And Barnabas and Saul **r** from *G5290*
13:13 departing from them **r** to Jerusalem. *G5290*
14:21 taught many, they **r** again to Lystra, *G5290*
21: 6 we took ship; and they **r** home again. *G5290*
23:32 to go with him, and **r** to the castle: *G5290*
Gal 1:17 Arabia, and **r** again unto Damascus. *G5290*
Heb 11:15 might have had opportunity to have **r**. *G344*
1Pt 2:25 but are now **r** unto the Shepherd and *G1994*

RETURNETH
Ps 146: 4 His breath goeth forth, he **r** to his H7725
Prv 26:11 As a dog **r** to his vomit, *so* a fool H7725
11 to his vomit, *so* a fool **r** to his folly. H8138
Ecc 1: 6 wind **r** again according to his circuits. H7725
Isa 55:10 from heaven, and **r** not thither, but H7725
Ezk 35: 7 it him that passeth out and him that **r**. H7725
Zec 9: 8 of him that **r**: and no oppressor shall H7725

RETURNING
Isa 30:15 One of Israel; In **r** and rest shall ye be H7729
Lk 7:10 And they that were sent, **r** to the house, *G5290*
Act 8:28 Was **r**, and sitting in his chariot read *G5290*
Heb 7: 1 met Abraham **r** from the slaughter of *G5290*

REU
Gen 11:18 Peleg lived thirty years, and begat **R**: H7466
19 And Peleg lived after he begat **R** two H7466
20 And **R** lived two and thirty years, and H7466
21 And **R** lived after he begat Serug two H7466
1Ch 1:25 Eber, Peleg, **R**, H7466

REUBEN
Gen 29:32 called his name **R**: for she said, Surely H7205
30:14 And **R** went in the days of wheat H7205
35:22 in that land, that **R** went and lay with H7205
23 The sons of Leah; **R**, Jacob's firstborn, H7205
37:21 And **R** heard *it*, and he delivered him H7205
22 And **R** said unto them, Shed no blood, H7205
29 And **R** returned unto the pit; and, H7205
42:22 And **R** answered them, saying, Spake I H7205
37 And **R** spake unto his father, saying, H7205
46: 8 Jacob and his sons: **R**, Jacob's firstborn. H7205
9 And the sons of **R**; Hanoch, and Phallu, H7205
48: 5 as **R** and Simeon, they shall be mine. H7205
49: 3 **R**, thou *art* my firstborn, my might, and H7205
Ex 1: 2 **R**, Simeon, Levi, and Judah, H7205
6:14 The sons of **R** the firstborn of Israel; H7205
14 and Carmi: these *be* the families of **R**. H7205
Nu 1: 5 *the tribe of* **R**; Elizur the son of Shedeur. H7205
20 And the children of **R**, Israel's eldest H7205
Nu 1:21 *even* of the tribe of **R**, *were* forty and six H7205
2:10 of the camp of **R** according to their H7205
10 of **R** *shall be* Elizur the son of Shedeur. H7205
16 in the camp of **R** *were* an hundred H7205
7:30 prince of the children of **R**, *did offer*: H7205
10:18 And the standard of the camp of **R** set H7205
13: 4 tribe of **R**, Shammua the son of Zaccur. H7205
16: 1 the son of Peleth, sons of **R**, took *men*: H7205
26: 5 **R**, the eldest son of Israel: the children H7205
5 the children of **R**; Hanoch, *of whom* H7205
32: 1 Now the children of **R** and the children H7205
2 the children of **R** came and spake unto H7205
6 to the children of **R**, Shall your brethren H7205
25 the children of **R** spake unto Moses, H7205
29 and the children of **R** will pass with you H7205
31 the children of **R** answered, saying, As H7205
33 to the children of **R**, and unto half the H7205
37 And the children of **R** built Heshbon, H7205
34:14 For the tribe of the children of **R** H7206
Dt 11: 6 of Eliab, the son of **R**: how the earth H7205
27:13 Ebal to curse; **R**, Gad, and Asher, and H7205
33: 6 Let **R** live, and not die; and let *not* his H7205
Jos 4:12 And the children of **R**, and the children H7205
13:15 tribe of the children of **R** *inheritance* H7205
23 And the border of the children of **R** was H7205
23 of the children of **R** after their families, H7205
15: 6 up to the stone of Bohan the son of **R**: H7205
18: 7 and Gad, and **R**, and half the tribe of H7205
17 to the stone of Bohan the son of **R**, H7205
20: 8 out of the tribe of **R**, and Ramoth in H7205
21: 7 out of the tribe of **R**, and out of the tribe H7205
36 And out of the tribe of **R**, Bezer with her H7205
22: 9 And the children of **R** and the children H7205
10 the children of **R** and the children of H7205
11 the children of **R** and the children of H7205
13 the children of **R**, and to the children H7205
15 And they came unto the children of **R**, H7205
21 Then the children of **R** and the children H7205
25 you, ye children of **R** and children of H7205
30 the children of **R** and the children of H7205
31 the children of **R**, and to the children H7205
32 the children of **R**, and from the children H7205
33 the children of **R** and Gad dwelt. H7205
34 And the children of **R** and the children H7205
Jdg 5:15 of **R** *there were* great thoughts of heart. H7205
16 **R** *there were* great searchings of heart. H7205
1Ch 2: 1 These *are* the sons of Israel; **R**, Simeon, H7205
5: 1 Now the sons of **R** the firstborn of H7205
3 The sons, *I say*, of **R** the firstborn of H7205
18 The sons of **R**, and the Gadites, and half H7205
6:63 out of the tribe of **R**, and out of the tribe H7205
78 *them* out of the tribe of **R**, Bezer in the H7205
Ezk 48: 6 even unto the west side, a *portion for* **R**. H7205
7 And by the border of **R**, from the east H7205
31 **R**, one gate of Judah, one gate of Levi. H7205
Rev 7: 5 Of the tribe of **R** *were* sealed twelve *G4502*

REUBENITE
1Ch 11:42 Adina the son of Shiza the **R**, a captain H7206

REUBENITES
Nu 26: 7 These *are* the families of the **R**: and they H7206
Dt 3:12 gave I unto the **R** and to the Gadites. H7206
16 And unto the **R** and unto the Gadites I H7206
4:43 plain country, of the **R**; and Ramoth in H7206
29: 8 unto the **R**, and to the Gadites, H7206
Jos 1:12 And to the **R**, and to the Gadites, and to H7206
12: 6 unto the **R**, and the Gadites, and H7206
13: 8 With whom the **R** and the Gadites have H7206
22: 1 Then Joshua called the **R**, and the H7206
2Ki 10:33 Gadites, and the **R**, and the Manassites, H7206
1Ch 5: 6 away *captive*: he *was* prince of the **R**. H7206
26 away, even the **R**, and the Gadites, and H7206
11:42 a captain of the **R**, and thirty with him, H7206
12:37 of Jordan, of the **R**, and the Gadites, H7206
26:32 rulers over the **R**, the Gadites, and the H7206
27:16 the ruler of the **R** *was* Eliezer the son H7206

REUEL
Gen 36: 4 Esau Eliphaz; and Bashemath bare **R**; H7467
10 Adah the wife of Esau, **R** the son of H7467
13 And these *are* the sons of **R**; Nahath, H7467
17 And these *are* the sons of **R** Esau's son; H7467
17 *that came* of **R** in the land of Edom; H7467
Ex 2:18 And when they came to **R** their father, H7467
Nu 2:14 of Gad *shall be* Eliasaph the son of **R**. H7467
1Ch 1:35 The sons of Esau; Eliphaz, **R**, and Jeush, H7467
37 The sons of **R**; Nahath, Zerah, H7467
9: 8 the son of **R**, the son of Ibnijah; H7467

REUMAH
Gen 22:24 And his concubine, whose name *was* **R**, H7208

REVEAL
Job 20:27 The heaven shall **r** his iniquity; and the H1540
Jer 33: 6 cure them, and will **r** unto them the H1540
Dan 2:47 seeing thou couldest **r** this secret. H1541
Mt 11:27 *he* to whomsoever the Son will **r** *him*. *G601*
Lk 10:22 Son, and *he* to whom the Son will **r** *him*. *G601*
Gal 1:16 To **r** his Son in me, that I might preach *G601*
Php 3:15 minded, God shall **r** even this unto you. *G601*

REVEALED
Dt 29:29 *things which are* **r** *belong* unto us and H1540
1Sa 3: 7 the word of the LORD yet **r** unto him. H1540
21 for the LORD **r** himself to Samuel in H1540
2Sa 7:27 God of Israel, hast **r** to thy servant, H1540
Isa 22:14 And it was **r** in mine ears by the LORD H1540
23: 1 from the land of Chittim it is **r** to them. H1540
40: 5 And the glory of the LORD shall be **r**, H1540
53: 1 and to whom is the arm of the LORD **r**? H1540
56: 1 to come, and my righteousness to be **r**. H1540
Jer 11:20 them: for unto thee have I **r** my cause. H1540
Dan 2:19 Then was the secret **r** unto Daniel in a H1541
30 But as for me, this secret is not **r** to me H1541
10: 1 of Persia a thing was **r** unto Daniel, H1540
Mt 10:26 be **r**; and hid, that shall not be known. *G601*
11:25 prudent, and hast **r** them unto babes. *G601*
16:17 and blood hath not **r** *it* unto thee, but my *G601*
Lk 2:26 And it was **r** unto him by the Holy *G5537*
35 the thoughts of many hearts may be **r**. *G601*
10:21 prudent, and hast **r** them unto babes: *G601*
12: 2 be **r**; neither hid, that shall not be known. *G601*
17:30 it be in the day when the Son of man is **r**. *G601*
Jn 12:38 to whom hath the arm of the Lord been **r**? *G601*
Ro 1:17 For therein is the righteousness of God **r** *G601*
18 For the wrath of God is **r** from heaven *G601*
8:18 with the glory which shall be **r** in us. *G601*
1Co 2:10 But God hath **r** *them* unto us by his *G601*
3:13 because it shall be **r** by fire; and the fire *G601*
14:30 If *any thing* be **r** to another that sitteth *G601*
Gal 3:23 the faith which should afterwards be **r**. *G601*
Eph 3: 5 sons of men, as it is now **r** unto his holy *G601*
2Th 1: 7 be **r** from heaven with his mighty angels, *G602*
2: 3 that man of sin be **r**, the son of perdition; *G601*
6 that he might be **r** in his time. *G601*
8 And then shall that Wicked be **r**, whom *G601*
1Pt 1: 5 salvation ready to be **r** in the last time. *G601*
12 Unto whom it was **r**, that not unto *G601*
4:13 **r**, ye may be glad also with exceeding joy. *G602*
5: 1 a partaker of the glory that shall be **r**: *G601*

REVEALER
Dan 2:47 of kings, and a **r** of secrets, seeing thou H1541

REVEALETH
Prv 11:13 A talebearer **r** secrets: but he that is of H1540
20:19 He that goeth about *as* a talebearer **r** H1540
Dan 2:22 He **r** the deep and secret things: he H1541
28 But there is a God in heaven that **r** H1541
29 and he that **r** secrets maketh known H1541
Am 3: 7 do nothing, but he **r** his secret unto his H1540

REVELATION
Ro 2: 5 and **r** of the righteous judgment of God; *G602*
16:25 according to the **r** of the mystery, which *G602*
1Co 14: 6 to you either by **r**, or by knowledge, or *G602*
26 hath a tongue, hath a **r**, hath an *G602*
Gal 1:12 I taught *it*, but by the **r** of Jesus Christ. *G602*
2: 2 And I went up by **r**, and communicated *G602*
Eph 1:17 wisdom and **r** in the knowledge of him: *G602*
3: 3 How that by **r** he made known unto me *G602*
1Pt 1:13 brought unto you at the **r** of Jesus Christ; *G602*
Rev 1: 1 The **R** of Jesus Christ, which God gave *G602*

REVELATIONS
2Co 12: 1 I will come to visions and **r** of the Lord. *G602*
7 abundance of the **r**, there was given to *G602*

REVELLINGS
Gal 5:21 Envyings, murders, drunkenness, **r**, *G2970*
1Pt 4: 3 excess of wine, **r**, banquetings, and *G2970*

REVENGE
Jer 15:15 me, and visit me, and **r** me of my H5358
20:10 him, and we shall take our **r** on him. H5360
Ezk 25:15 have dealt by **r**, and have taken H5360
2Co 7:11 zeal, yea, *what* **r**! In all *things* ye have *G1557*
10: 6 And having in a readiness to **r** all *G1556*

REVENGED
Ezk 25:12 offended, and **r** himself upon them; H5358

REVENGER
Nu 35:19 The **r** of blood himself shall slay the H1350
21 *is* a murderer: the **r** of blood shall slay H1350
24 the slayer and the **r** of blood according H1350
25 of the hand of the **r** of blood, and the H1350
27 And the **r** of blood find him without the H1350
27 of his refuge, and the **r** of blood kill the H1350
Ro 13: 4 minister of God, a **r** to *execute* wrath *G1558*

REVENGERS
2Sa 14:11 not suffer the **r** of blood to destroy any H1350

REVENGES
Dt 32:42 the beginning of **r** upon the enemy. H6546

REVENGETH
Nah 1: 2 God *is* jealous, and the LORD **r**; the H5358
2 the LORD **r**, and *is* furious; the LORD H5358

REVENGING
Ps 79:10 in our sight *by* the **r** of the blood of thy H5360

REVENUE
Ezr 4:13 thou shalt endamage the **r** of the kings. H674
Prv 8:19 fine gold; and my **r** than choice silver. H8393
Isa 23: 3 *is* her **r**; and she is a mart of nations. H8393

REVENUES
Prv 15: 6 but in the **r** of the wicked is trouble. H8393
16: 8 than great **r** without right. H8393
Jer 12:13 ashamed of your **r** because of the fierce H8393

REVERENCE
Lev 19:30 Ye shall keep my sabbaths, and **r** my H3372
26: 2 Ye shall keep my sabbaths, and **r** my H3372
2Sa 9: 6 on his face, and did **r**. And David said, H7812
1Ki 1:31 to the earth, and did **r** to the king, and H7812
Est 3: 2 But Mordecai bowed not, nor did *him* **r**. H7812
5 him **r**, then was Haman full of wrath. H7812
Ps 89: 7 had in **r** of all *them that are* about him. H3372
Mt 21:37 his son, saying, They will **r** my son. *G1788*
Mk 12: 6 unto them, saying, They will **r** my son. *G1788*
Lk 20:13 be they will **r** *him* when they see him. *G1788*
Eph 5:33 the wife *see* that she **r** *her* husband. *G5399*
Heb 12: 9 and we gave *them* **r**: shall we not much *G1788*
28 God acceptably with **r** and godly fear: *G127*

REVERENCED
Est 3: 2 gate, bowed, and **r** Haman: for the king H7812

REVEREND
Ps 111: 9 for ever: holy and **r** *is* his name. H3372

REVERSE
Nu 23:20 and he hath blessed; and I cannot **r** it. H7725
Est 8: 5 let it be written to **r** the letters devised H7725
8 with the king's ring, may no man **r**. H7725

REVILE
Ex 22:28 Thou shalt not **r** the gods, nor curse the H7043
Mt 5:11 Blessed are ye, when *men* shall **r** you, *G3679*

REVILED
Mt 27:39 And they that passed by **r** him, wagging *G987*
Mk 15:32 that were crucified with him **r** him. *G3679*
Jn 9:28 Then they **r** him, and said, Thou art his *G3058*
1Co 4:12 our own hands: being **r**, we bless; being *G3058*
1Pt 2:23 Who, when he was **r**, reviled not again; *G3058*
23 Who, when he was reviled, **r** not again; *G486*

REVILERS
1Co 6:10 nor drunkards, nor **r**, nor extortioners, *G3060*

REVILEST
Act 23: 4 And they that stood by said, **R** thou *G3058*

REVILINGS
Isa 51: 7 of men, neither be ye afraid of their **r**. H1421
Zep 2: 8 of Moab, and the **r** of the children of H1421

REVIVE
Neh 4: 2 in a day? will they **r** the stones out of H2421
Ps 85: 6 Wilt thou not **r** us again: that thy H2421
138: 7 of trouble, thou wilt **r** me: thou shalt H2421
Isa 57:15 and humble spirit, to **r** the spirit of the H2421
15 and to **r** the heart of the contrite ones. H2421
Hos 6: 2 After two days will he **r** us: in the third H2421
14: 7 return; they shall **r** *as* the corn, and H2421
Hab 3: 2 was afraid: O LORD, **r** thy work in the H2421

REVIVED
Gen 45:27 him, the spirit of Jacob their father **r**: H2421
Jdg 15:19 again, and he **r**: wherefore he called H2421
1Ki 17:22 the child came into him again, and he **r**. H2421
2Ki 13:21 of Elisha, he **r**, and stood up on his feet. H2421
Ro 7: 9 commandment came, sin **r**, and I died. *G326*
14: 9 died, and rose, and **r**, that he might be *G326*

REVIVING
Ezr 9: 8 and give us a little **r** in our bondage. H4241
9 Persia, to give us a **r**, to set up the house H4241

REVOLT
2Ch 21:10 *also* did Libnah **r** from under his hand; H6586
Isa 1: 5 any more? ye will **r** more and more: the H5627
59:13 oppression and **r**, conceiving and H5627

REVOLTED
2Ki 8:20 In his days Edom **r** from under the H6586
22 Yet Edom **r** from under the hand of H6586
22 day. Then Libnah **r** at the same time. H6586
2Ch 21: 8 In his days the Edomites **r** from under H6586
10 So the Edomites **r** from under the hand H6586
Isa 31: 6 the children of Israel have deeply **r**. H5627
Jer 5:23 a rebellious heart; they are **r** and gone. H5493

REVOLTERS
Jer 6:28 They *are* all grievous **r**, walking with H5637
Hos 5: 2 And the **r** are profound to make H7846
9:15 them no more: all their princes *are* **r**. H5637

REVOLTING
Jer 5:23 But this people hath a **r** and a H5637

REWARD
Gen 15: 1 thy shield, *and* thy exceeding great **r**. H7939
Nu 18:31 for it *is* your **r** for your service in the H7939
Dt 10:17 regardeth not persons, nor taketh **r**: H7810
27:25 Cursed *be* he that taketh **r** to slay an H7810
32:41 enemies, and will **r** them that hate me. H7999
Ru 2:12 work, and a full **r** be given thee of the H4909
1Sa 24:19 the LORD **r** thee good for that thou H7999
2Sa 3:39 me: the LORD shall **r** the doer of evil H7999
4:10 have given him a **r** for his tidings: H1309
19:36 king recompense it me with such a **r**? H1578
1Ki 13: 7 refresh thyself, and I will give thee a **r**. H4991
2Ch 20:11 Behold, *I say, how* they **r** us, to come to H1580
Job 6:22 Did I say, Bring unto me? or, Give a **r** H7809
7: 2 an hireling looketh for *the* **r** *of* his work:
Ps 15: 5 to usury, nor taketh **r** against the H7810
19:11 *and* in keeping of them *there is* great **r**. H6118
40:15 Let them be desolate for a **r** of their H6118
54: 5 He shall **r** evil unto mine enemies: cut H7725
58:11 say, Verily *there is* a **r** for the righteous: H6529
70: 3 Let them be turned back for a **r** of their H6118
91: 8 behold and see the **r** of the wicked. H8011
94: 2 of the earth: render a **r** to the proud. H1576
109:20 *Let* this *be* the **r** of mine adversaries H6468
127: 3 *and* the fruit of the womb *is his* **r**. H7939
Prv 11:18 soweth righteousness *shall be* a sure **r**. H7938
21:14 A gift in secret pacifieth anger: and a **r** H7810
24:14 there shall be a **r**, and thy expectation H319
20 For there shall be no **r** to the evil *man*; H319
25:22 his head, and the LORD shall **r** thee. H7999
Ecc 4: 9 they have a good **r** for their labour. H7939
9: 5 **r**; for the memory of them is forgotten. H7939
Isa 3:11 the **r** of his hands shall be given him. H1576
5:23 Which justify the wicked for **r**, and take H7810
40:10 **r** *is* with him, and his work before him. H7939
45:13 for price nor **r**, saith the LORD of hosts. H7810
62:11 **r** *is* with him, and his work before him. H7939
Jer 40: 5 him victuals and a **r**, and let him go. H4864
Ezk 16:34 in that thou givest a **r**, and no reward is H868
34 a reward, and no **r** is given unto thee, H868
Hos 4: 9 for their ways, and **r** them their doings. H7725
9: 1 thou hast loved a **r** upon every cornfloor. H868
Oba 15 thy **r** shall return upon thine own head. H1576
Mic 3:11 The heads thereof judge for **r**, and the H7810
7: 3 judge *asketh* for a **r**; and the great *man*, H7966
Mt 5:12 for great *is* your **r** in heaven: for so *G3408*
46 love you, what **r** have ye? do not even *G3408*
6: 1 no **r** of your Father which is in heaven. *G3408*
2 Verily I say unto you, They have their **r**. *G3408*
4 in secret himself shall **r** thee openly. *G591*
5 Verily I say unto you, They have their **r**. *G3408*
Mt 6: 6 which seeth in secret shall **r** thee openly. *G591*
16 Verily I say unto you, They have their **r**. *G3408*
18 which seeth in secret, shall **r** thee openly. *G591*
10:41 a prophet's **r**; and he that receiveth *G3408*
41 man shall receive a righteous man's **r**. *G3408*
42 unto you, he shall in no wise lose his **r**. *G3408*
16:27 **r** every man according to his works. *G591*
Mk 9:41 I say unto you, he shall not lose his **r**. *G3408*
Lk 6:23 for, behold, your **r** *is* great in heaven: *G3408*
35 again; and your **r** shall be great, and ye *G3408*
23:41 for we receive the due **r** of our deeds: but *G514*
Act 1:18 a field with the **r** of iniquity; and falling *G3408*
Ro 4: 4 Now to him that worketh is the **r** not *G3408*
1Co 3: 8 his own **r** according to his own labour. *G3408*
14 built thereupon, he shall receive a **r**. *G3408*
9:17 willingly, I have a **r**: but if against my *G3408*
18 What is my **r** then? *Verily* that, when I *G3408*
Col 2:18 Let no man beguile you of your **r** in a *G2603*
3:24 ye shall receive the **r** of the inheritance: *G469*
1Ti 5:18 And, The labourer *is* worthy of his **r**. *G3408*
2Ti 4:14 the Lord **r** him according to his works: *G591*
Heb 2: 2 received a just recompence of **r**; *G3405*
10:35 which hath great recompence of **r**. *G3405*
11:26 respect unto the recompence of the **r**. *G3405*
2Pt 2:13 And shall receive the **r** of *G3408*
2Jn 8 wrought, but that we receive a full **r**. *G3408*
Jude 11 of Balaam for **r**, and perished in the *G3408*
Rev 11:18 shouldest give **r** unto thy servants the *G3408*
18: 6 **R** her even as she rewarded you, and *G591*
22:12 And, behold, I come quickly; and my **r** *G3408*

REWARDED
Gen 44: 4 Wherefore have ye **r** evil for good? H7999
1Sa 24:17 I: for thou hast **r** me good, whereas I H1580
17 me good, whereas I have **r** thee evil. H1580
2Sa 22:21 The LORD **r** me according to my H1580
2Ch 15: 7 hands be weak: for your work shall be **r**. H7939
Ps 7: 4 If I have **r** evil unto him that was at H1580
18:20 The LORD **r** me according to my H1580
35:12 They **r** me evil for good *to* the spoiling H7999
103:10 nor **r** us according to our iniquities. H1580
109: 5 And they have **r** me evil for good, and H7760
Prv 13:13 feareth the commandment shall be **r**. H7999
Isa 3: 9 for they have **r** evil unto themselves. H1580
Jer 31:16 thy work shall be **r**, saith the LORD; and H7939
Rev 18: 6 Reward her even as she **r** you, and *G591*

REWARDER
Heb 11: 6 is a **r** of them that diligently seek him. *G3406*

REWARDETH
Job 21:19 he **r** him, and he shall know *it*. H7999
Ps 31:23 and plentifully **r** the proud doer. H7999
137: 8 *be*, that **r** thee as thou hast served us. H7999
Prv 17:13 Whoso **r** evil for good, evil shall not H7725
26:10 formed all *things* both **r** the fool, and H7936
10 the fool, and **r** transgressors. H7936

REWARDS
Nu 22: 7 departed with the **r** of divination in their
Isa 1:23 and followeth after **r**: they judge not the H8021
Dan 2: 6 of me gifts and **r** and great honour: H5023
5:17 and give thy **r** to another; yet I will H5023
Hos 2:12 said, These *are* my **r** that my lovers have H866

REZEPH
2Ki 19:12 and Haran, and **R**, and the children of H7530
Isa 37:12 and Haran, and **R**, and the children of H7530

REZIA
1Ch 7:39 sons of Ulla; Arah, and Haniel, and **R**. H7525

REZIN
2Ki 15:37 against Judah **R** the king of Syria, and H7526
16: 5 Then **R** king of Syria and Pekah son of H7526
6 At that time **R** king of Syria recovered H7526
9 *people of* it captive to Kir, and slew **R**. H7526
Ezr 2:48 The children of **R**, the children of H7526
Neh 7:50 children of **R**, the children of Nekoda, H7526
Isa 7: 1 of Judah, *that* **R** the king of Syria, and H7526
4 the fierce anger of **R** with Syria, and of H7526
8 head of Damascus *is* **R**; and within H7526
8: 6 and rejoice in **R** and Remaliah's son; H7526
9:11 the adversaries of **R** against him, and H7526

REZON
1Ki 11:23 adversary, **R** the son of Eliadah, H7331

RHEGIUM
Act 28:13 and came to **R**: and after one day the G4484

RHESA
Lk 3:27 was *the son* of **R**, which was *the son* of G4488

RHODA
Act 12:13 a damsel came to hearken, named **R**. G4498

RHODES
Act 21: 1 unto **R**, and from thence unto Patara: G4499

RIB
Gen 2:22 And the **r**, which the LORD God had H6763
2Sa 2:23 him under the fifth *r*, that the spear came
3:27 under the fifth *r*, that he died, for the
4: 6 him under the fifth *r*: and Rechab and
20:10 in the fifth *r*, and shed out his bowels

RIBAI
2Sa 23:29 Ittai the son of **R** out of Gibeah of the H7380
1Ch 11:31 Ithai the son of **R** of Gibeah, *that* H7380

RIBBAND
Nu 15:38 the fringe of the borders a **r** of blue: H6616

RIBBON See RIBBAND.

RIBLAH
Nu 34:11 from Shepham to **R**, on the east side of H7247
2Ki 23:33 put him in bands at **R** in the land of H7247
25: 6 **R**; and they gave judgment upon him. H7247
20 them to the king of Babylon to **R**: H7247
21 them, and slew them at **R** in the land of H7247
Jer 39: 5 king of Babylon to **R** in the land of H7247
6 of Zedekiah in **R** before his eyes: also H7247
52: 9 the king of Babylon to **R** in the land of H7247
10 slew also all the princes of Judah in **R**. H7247
26 them to the king of Babylon to **R**. H7247
27 put them to death in **R** in the land of H7247

RIBS
Gen 2:21 he took one of his **r**, and closed up the H6763
Dan 7: 5 and *it had* three **r** in the mouth of it H5967

RICH
Gen 13: 2 And Abram *was* very **r** in cattle, in H3513
14:23 shouldest say, I have made Abram **r**: H6238
Ex 30:15 The **r** shall not give more, and the poor H6223
Lev 25:47 And if a sojourner or stranger wax **r** by H3027
Ru 3:10 not young men, whether poor or **r**. H6223
1Sa 2: 7 The LORD maketh poor, and maketh **r**: H6238
2Sa 12: 1 one city; the one **r**, and the other poor. H6223
2 The **r** *man* had exceeding many flocks H6223
4 And there came a traveller unto the **r** H6223
Job 15:29 He shall not be **r**, neither shall his H6238
27:19 The **r** man shall lie down, but he shall H6223
34:19 nor regardeth the **r** more than the H7771
Ps 45:12 with a gift; *even* the **r** among the people H6223
49: 2 Both low and high, **r** and poor, H6223
16 Be not thou afraid when one is made **r**, H6238
Prv 10: 4 but the hand of the diligent maketh **r**. H6238
15 The **r** man's wealth *is* his strong city: H6223
22 The blessing of the LORD, it maketh **r**, H6238
13: 7 There is that maketh himself **r**, yet *hath* H6238
14:20 but the **r** *hath* many friends. H6223
18:11 The **r** man's wealth *is* his strong city, H6223
23 The poor useth entreaties; but the **r** H6223
21:17 that loveth wine and oil shall not be **r**. H6238
22: 2 The **r** and poor meet together: the H6223
7 The **r** ruleth over the poor, and the H6223
16 to the **r**, *shall* surely *come* to want. H6223
23: 4 Labour not to be **r**: cease from thine H6238
28: 6 *is* perverse *in his* ways, though he *be* **r**. H6223
11 The **r** man *is* wise in his own conceit; H6223
20 haste to be **r** shall not be innocent. H6238
22 He that hasteth to be **r** *hath* an evil eye, H1952
Ecc 5:12 of the **r** will not suffer him to sleep. H6223
10: 6 Folly is set in great dignity, and the **r** sit H6223
20 and curse not the **r** in thy bedchamber: H6223
Isa 53: 9 and with the **r** in his death; because H6223
Jer 5:27 they are become great, and waxen **r**. H6238
9:23 let not the **r** *man* glory in his riches: H6223
Ezk 27:24 and in chests of **r** apparel, bound with
Hos 12: 8 And Ephraim said, Yet I am become **r**, I H6238
Mic 6:12 For the **r** men thereof are full of H6223
Zec 11: 5 the LORD; for I am **r**: and their own H6238
Mt 19:23 say unto you, That a **r** man shall hardly G4146
24 a needle, than for a **r** man to enter into G4146
Mt 27:57 there came a **r** man of Arimathaea, G4145
Mk 10:25 a needle, than for a **r** man to enter into G4146
12:41 and many that were **r** cast in much. G4145
Lk 1:53 and the **r** he hath sent empty away. G4147
6:24 But woe unto you that are **r**! for ye have G4145
12:16 certain **r** man brought forth plentifully: G4145
21 for himself, and is not **r** toward God. G4147
14:12 thy kinsmen, nor *thy* **r** neighbours; lest G4145
16: 1 was a certain **r** man, which had a G4145
19 There was a certain **r** man, which was G4145
21 fell from the **r** man's table: moreover G4146
22 the **r** man also died, and was buried; G4146
18:23 was very sorrowful: for he was very **r**. G4145
25 eye, than for a **r** man to enter into the G4146
19: 2 among the publicans, and he was **r**. G4145
21: 1 And he looked up, and saw the **r** men G4146
Ro 10:12 over all is **r** unto all that call upon him. G4147
1Co 4: 8 Now ye are full, now ye are **r**, ye have G4147
2Co 6:10 yet making many **r**; as having nothing, G4148
8: 9 though he was **r**, yet for your sakes he G4145
9 that ye through his poverty might be **r**. G4147
Eph 2: 4 But God, who is **r** in mercy, for his G4145
1Ti 6: 9 But they that will be **r** fall into G4147
17 Charge them that are **r** in this world, G4145
18 That they do good, that they be **r** in G4147
Jas 1:10 But the **r**, in that he is made low: G4145
11 shall the **r** man fade away in his ways. G4146
2: 5 poor of this world **r** in faith, and heirs G4145
6 But ye have despised the poor. Do not **r** G4146
5: 1 Go to now, *ye* **r** men, weep and howl G4146
Rev 2: 9 poverty, (but thou art **r**) and *I know* the G4145
3:17 Because thou sayest, I am **r**, and G4145
18 thou mayest be **r**; and white raiment, G4147
6:15 great men, and the **r** men, and the chief G4146
13:16 small and great, **r** and poor, free and G4145
18: 3 the earth are waxed **r** through the G4147
15 which were made **r** by her, shall stand G4147
19 were made **r** all that had ships in G4147

RICHER
Dan 11: 2 fourth shall be far **r** than *they* all: and H6238

RICHES
Gen 31:16 For all the **r** which God hath taken H6239
36: 7 For their **r** were more than that they H7399
Jos 22: 8 Return with much **r** unto your tents, H5233
1Sa 17:25 him with great **r**, and will give him his H6239
1Ki 3:11 life; neither hast asked **r** for thyself, nor H6239
13 not asked, both **r**, and honour: so that H6239
10:23 kings of the earth for **r** and for wisdom. H6239
1Ch 29:12 Both **r** and honour *come* of thee, and H6239
28 old age, full of days, **r**, and honour: and H6239
2Ch 1:11 hast not asked **r**, wealth, or honour, nor H6239
12 and I will give thee **r**, and wealth, and H6239
9:22 the kings of the earth in **r** and wisdom. H6239
17: 5 he had **r** and honour in abundance. H6239
18: 1 Now Jehoshaphat had **r** and honour in H6239
20:25 in abundance both **r** with the dead H7399
32:27 And Hezekiah had exceeding much **r** H6239
Est 1: 4 When he shewed the **r** of his glorious H6239
5:11 of the glory of his **r**, and the multitude H6239
Job 20:15 He hath swallowed down **r**, and he shall H2428
36:19 Will he esteem thy **r**? *no*, not gold, nor H7769
Ps 37:16 *is* better than the **r** of many wicked. H1995
39: 6 he heapeth up *r*, and knoweth not who
49: 6 themselves in the multitude of their **r**; H6239
52: 7 abundance of his **r**, *and* strengthened H6239
62:10 vain in robbery: if **r** increase, set not H2428
73:12 prosper in the world; they increase *in* **r**. H2428
104:24 made them all: the earth is full of thy **r**. H7075
112: 3 Wealth and **r** *shall be* in his house: and H6239
119:14 of thy testimonies, as *much as* in all **r**. H1952
Prv 3:16 *and* in her left hand **r** and honour. H6239
8:18 **R** and honour *are* with me; *yea*, H6239
18 me; *yea*, durable **r** and righteousness. H1952
11: 4 **R** profit not in the day of wrath: but H1952
16 honour: and strong *men* retain **r**. H6239
28 He that trusteth in his **r** shall fall: but H6239
13: 7 maketh himself poor, yet *hath* great **r**. H1952
8 The ransom of a man's life *are* his **r**: but H6239
14:24 The crown of the wise *is* their **r**: *but* the H6239
19:14 House and **r** *are* the inheritance of H1952
22: 1 chosen than great **r**, *and* loving favour H6239
4 of the LORD *are* **r**, and honour, and life. H6239
16 to increase his *r*, *and* he that giveth to
23: 5 that which is not? for *r* certainly make
24: 4 filled with all precious and pleasant **r**. H1952
27:24 For **r** *are* not for ever: and doth the H2633
30: 8 **r**; feed me with food convenient for me: H6239
Ecc 4: 8 eye satisfied with **r**; neither *saith he*, For H6239
5:13 the sun, *namely*, **r** kept for the owners H6239
14 But those **r** perish by evil travail: and H6239
19 God hath given **r** and wealth, and hath H6239
6: 2 A man to whom God hath given **r**, H6239
9:11 to the wise, nor yet **r** to men of H6239
Isa 8: 4 my mother, the **r** of Damascus and the H2428
10:14 as a nest the **r** of the people: and as H2428
30: 6 will carry their **r** upon the shoulders H2428
45: 3 and hidden **r** of secret places, that H4301
61: 6 ye shall eat the **r** of the Gentiles, and H2428
Jer 9:23 let not the rich *man* glory in his **r**: H6239
17:11 *so* he that getteth **r**, and not by right, H6239
48:36 the **r** *that* he hath gotten are perished. H3502
Ezk 26:12 And they shall make a spoil of thy **r**, H2428
27:12 of all *kind of* **r**; with silver, iron, tin, H1952
18 multitude of all **r**; in the wine of Helbon, H1952
27 Thy **r**, and thy fairs, thy merchandise, H1952
33 of thy **r** and of thy merchandise. H1952
28: 4 hast gotten thee **r**, and hast gotten gold H2428
5 thou increased thy **r**, and thine heart is H2428
5 thine heart is lifted up because of thy **r**: H2428
Dan 11: 2 through his **r** he shall stir up all against H6239
13 with a great army and with much **r**. H7399
24 prey, and spoil, and **r**: *yea*, and he shall H7399
28 his land with great **r**; and his heart *shall* H7399
Mt 13:22 deceitfulness of **r**, choke the word, and G4149
Mk 4:19 deceitfulness of **r**, and the lusts of other G4149
10:23 have **r** enter into the kingdom of God! G5536
24 in **r** to enter into the kingdom of God! G5536
Lk 8:14 with cares and **r** and pleasures of *this* G4149
16:11 who will commit to your trust the true **r**?
18:24 have **r** enter into the kingdom of God! G5536
Ro 2: 4 Or despisest thou the **r** of his goodness G4149
9:23 And that he might make known the **r** of G4149
11:12 Now if the fall of them *be* the **r** of the G4149
12 of them the **r** of the Gentiles; how G4149
33 O the depth of the **r** both of the wisdom G4149
2Co 8: 2 abounded unto the **r** of their liberality. G4149
Eph 1: 7 of sins, according to the **r** of his grace; G4149
18 and what the **r** of the glory of his G4149
2: 7 shew the exceeding **r** of his grace in *his* G4149
3: 8 Gentiles the unsearchable **r** of Christ; G4149
16 according to the **r** of his glory, to be G4149
Php 4:19 to his **r** in glory by Christ Jesus. G4149
Col 1:27 known what *is* the **r** of the glory of this G4149
2: 2 in love, and unto all **r** of the full G4149
1Ti 6:17 nor trust in uncertain **r**, but in the living G4149
Heb 11:26 of Christ greater **r** than the treasures in G4149
Jas 5: 2 Your **r** are corrupted, and your G4149
Rev 5:12 receive power, and **r**, and wisdom, and G4149
18:17 For in one hour so great **r** is come to G4149

RICHLY
Col 3:16 Let the word of Christ dwell in you **r** in G4146
1Ti 6:17 God, who giveth us **r** all things to enjoy; G4146

RID
Gen 37:22 him; that he might **r** him out of their H5337
Ex 6: 6 and I will **r** you out of their bondage, H5337
Lev 26: 6 afraid: and I will **r** evil beasts out of the H7673
Ps 82: 4 Deliver the poor and needy: **r** *them* out H5337
144: 7 Send thine hand from above; **r** me, and H6475
11 **R** me, and deliver me from the hand of H6475

RIDDANCE
Lev 23:22 not make clean **r** of the corners of thy H3615
Zep 1:18 **r** of all them that dwell in the land. H3617

RIDDEN
Nu 22:30 which thou hast **r** ever since *I was* thine H7392

RIDDLE
Jdg 14:12 now put forth a **r** unto you: if ye can H2420
13 Put forth thy **r**, that we may hear it. H2420
14 could not in three days expound the **r**. H2420
15 unto us the **r**, lest we burn thee and H2420
16 hast put forth a **r** unto the children of H2420
17 told the **r** to the children of her people. H2420
18 my heifer, ye had not found out my **r**. H2420
19 expounded the **r**. And his anger was H2420
Ezk 17: 2 Son of man, put forth a **r**, and speak a H2420

RIDE
Gen 41:43 And he made him to **r** in the second H7392
Dt 32:13 He made him **r** on the high places of H7392
Jdg 5:10 Speak, ye that **r** on white asses, ye that H7392
2Sa 16: 2 household to **r** on; and the bread and H7392
19:26 an ass, that I may **r** thereon, and go to H7392

1Ki 1:33 my son to **r** upon mine own mule, H7392
38 Solomon to **r** upon king David's mule, H7392
44 caused him to **r** upon the king's mule: H7392
2Ki 10:16 So they made him **r** in his chariot. H7392
Job 30:22 **r** *upon it,* and dissolvest my substance. H7392
Ps 45: 4 And in thy majesty **r** prosperously H7392
66:12 Thou hast caused men to **r** over our H7392
Isa 30:16 ye flee: and, We will **r** upon the swift; H7392
58:14 and I will cause thee to **r** upon the high H7392
Jer 6:23 the sea; and they **r** upon horses, set in H7392
50:42 sea, and they shall **r** upon horses, *every* H7392
Hos 10:11 make Ephraim to **r**; Judah shall plow, H7392
14: 3 Asshur shall not save us; we will not **r** H7392
Hab 3: 8 that thou didst **r** upon thine horses *and* H7392
Hag 2:22 and those that **r** in them; and the H7392

RIDER
Gen 49:17 heels, so that his **r** shall fall backward. H7392
Ex 15: 1 and his **r** hath he thrown into the sea. H7392
21 and his **r** hath he thrown into the sea. H7392
Job 39:18 high, she scorneth the horse and his **r**. H7392
Jer 51:21 the horse and his **r**; and with thee will I H7392
21 I break in pieces the chariot and his **r**; H7392
Zec 12: 4 and his **r** with madness: and H7392

RIDERS
2Ki 18:23 be able on thy part to set **r** upon them. H7392
Est 8:10 on horseback, *and* **r** on mules, camels, H7392
Isa 36: 8 be able on thy part to set **r** upon them. H7392
Hag 2:22 the horses and their **r** shall come down, H7392
Zec 10: 5 the **r** on horses shall be confounded. H7392

RIDETH
Lev 15: 9 And what saddle soever he **r** upon that H7392
Dt 33:26 of Jeshurun, *who* **r** upon the heaven in H7392
Est 6: 8 that the king **r** upon, and the crown H7392
Ps 68: 4 extol him that **r** upon the heavens by H7392
33 To him that **r** upon the heavens of H7392
Isa 19: 1 Behold, the LORD **r** upon a swift cloud, H7392
Am 2:15 shall he that **r** the horse deliver himself. H7392

RIDGES
Ps 65:10 Thou waterest the **r** thereof H8525

RIDING
Nu 22:22 him. Now he was **r** upon his ass, and H7392
2Ki 4:24 slack not *thy* **r** for me, except I bid thee. H7392
Jer 17:25 throne of David, **r** in chariots and on H7392
22: 4 throne of David, **r** in chariots and on H7392
Ezk 23: 6 young men, horsemen **r** upon horses. H7392
12 horsemen **r** upon horses, all of them H7392
23 renowned, all of them **r** upon horses. H7392
38:15 thee, all of them **r** upon horses, a great H7392
Zec 1: 8 I saw by night, and behold a man **r** H7392
9: 9 lowly, and **r** upon an ass, and upon H7392

RIE
Ex 9:32 But the wheat and the **r** were not H3698
Isa 28:25 barley and the **r** in their place? H3698

RIFLED
Zec 14: 2 taken, and the houses **r**, and the women H8155

RIGHT
Gen 13: 9 I will go to the **r**; or if *thou depart* to H3231
9 to the **r** hand, then I will go to the left. H3225
18:25 Shall not the Judge of all the earth do **r**? H4941
24:48 had led me in the **r** way to take my H571
49 I may turn to the **r** hand, or to the left. H3225
48:13 Ephraim in his **r** hand toward Israel's H3225
13 toward Israel's **r** hand, and brought H3225
14 And Israel stretched out his **r** hand, H3225
17 that his father laid his **r** hand upon the H3225
18 put thy **r** hand upon his head. H3225
Ex 14:22 them on their **r** hand, and on their left. H3225
29 them on their **r** hand, and on their left. H3225
15: 6 Thy **r** hand, O LORD, is become H3225
6 in power: thy **r** hand, O LORD, hath H3225
12 Thou stretchedst out thy **r** hand, the H3225
26 do that which is **r** in his sight, and wilt H3477
29:20 *it* upon the tip of the **r** ear of Aaron, and
20 upon the tip of the **r** ear of his sons, H3233
20 the thumb of their **r** hand, and upon H3233
20 great toe of their **r** foot, and sprinkle H3233
22 them, and the **r** shoulder; for it *is* a H3225
Lev 7:32 And the **r** shoulder shall ye give unto H3225
33 shall have the **r** shoulder for *his* part. H3225
8:23 the tip of Aaron's **r** ear, and upon the H3233
23 the thumb of his **r** hand, and upon the H3233
Lev 8:23 and upon the great toe of his **r** foot. H3233
24 the tip of their **r** ear, and upon the H3233
24 thumbs of their **r** hands, and upon the H3233
24 the great toes of their **r** feet: and Moses H3233
25 and their fat, and the **r** shoulder: H3225
26 on the fat, and upon the **r** shoulder: H3225
9:21 And the breasts and the **r** shoulder H3225
14:14 *it* upon the tip of the **r** ear of him that is H3233
14 the thumb of his **r** hand, and upon the H3233
14 and upon the great toe of his **r** foot: H3233
16 And the priest shall dip his **r** finger in H3233
17 upon the tip of the **r** ear of him that is H3233
17 the thumb of his **r** hand, and upon the H3233
17 the great toe of his **r** foot, upon the H3233
25 *it* upon the tip of the **r** ear of him that is H3233
25 the thumb of his **r** hand, and upon the H3233
25 and upon the great toe of his **r** foot: H3233
27 And the priest shall sprinkle with his **r** H3233
28 upon the tip of the **r** ear of him that is H3233
28 the thumb of his **r** hand, and upon the H3233
28 the great toe of his **r** foot, upon the H3233
Nu 18:18 breast and as the **r** shoulder are thine. H3225
20:17 we will not turn to the **r** hand nor to the H3225
22:26 turn either to the **r** hand or to the left. H3225
27: 7 The daughters of Zelophehad speak **r**: H3651
Dt 2:27 turn unto the **r** hand nor to the left. H3225
5:32 turn aside to the **r** hand or to the left. H3225
6:18 And thou shalt do *that which is* **r** and H3477
12: 8 man whatsoever *is* **r** in his own eyes. H3477
25 *that which is* **r** in the sight of the LORD. H3477
28 and **r** in the sight of the LORD thy God. H3477
13:18 *is* **r** in the eyes of the LORD thy God. H3477
17:11 shew thee, *to* the **r** hand, nor *to* the left. H3225
20 *to* the **r** hand, or *to* the left: H3225
21: 9 *that which is* **r** in the sight of the LORD. H3477
17 strength; the **r** of the firstborn *is* his. H4941
28:14 this day, *to* the **r** hand, or *to* the left, H3225
32: 4 and without iniquity, just and **r** *is* he. H3477
33: 2 his **r** hand *went* a fiery law for them. H3225
Jos 1: 7 not from it *to* the **r** hand or *to* the left, H3225
3:16 the people passed over **r** against Jericho.
9:25 good and **r** unto thee to do unto us, do. H3477
17: 7 went along on the **r** hand unto the H3225
23: 6 therefrom *to* the **r** hand or *to* the left; H3225
Jdg 3:16 it under his raiment upon his **r** thigh. H3225
21 his **r** thigh, and thrust it into his belly: H3225
5:26 She put her hand to the nail, and her **r** H3225
7:20 the trumpets in their **r** hands to blow H3225
12: 6 to pronounce *it* **r**. Then they took him, H3651
16:29 **r** hand, and of the other with his left. H3225
17: 6 did *that which was* **r** in his own eyes. H3477
21:25 did *that which was* **r** in his own eyes. H3477
Ru 4: 6 my **r** to thyself; for I cannot redeem *it.* H1353
1Sa 6:12 not aside to the **r** hand or *to* the left; H3225
11: 2 thrust out all your **r** eyes, and lay it *for* H3225
12:23 I will teach you the good and the **r** way: H3477
2Sa 2:19 turned not to the **r** hand nor to the left H3225
21 thee aside to thy **r** hand or to thy left, H3225
14:19 can turn to the **r** hand or to the left H3231
15: 3 *are* good and **r**; but *there is* no man H5228
16: 6 men *were* on his **r** hand and on his left. H3225
19:28 own table. What **r** therefore have I yet H6666
43 we have also more **r** in David than ye:
20: 9 the beard with the **r** hand to kiss him. H3225
24: 5 in Aroer, on the **r** side of the city that H3225
1Ki 2:19 mother; and she sat on his **r** hand. H3225
6: 8 *was* in the **r** side of the house: and H3233
7:21 and he set up the **r** pillar, and called H3233
39 And he put five bases on the **r** side of H3225
39 he set the sea on the **r** side of the house H3233
49 gold, five on the **r** *side,* and five on the H3225
11:33 to do *that which is* **r** in mine eyes, and H3477
38 and do *that is* **r** in my sight, to keep H3477
14: 8 do *that* only *which was* **r** in mine eyes; H3477
15: 5 Because David did *that which was* **r** in H3477
11 And Asa did *that which was* **r** in the H3477
22:19 by him on his **r** hand and on his left. H3225
43 *that which was* **r** in the eyes of the H3477
2Ki 10:15 him, Is thine heart **r**, as my heart *is* with H3477
30 *that which is* **r** in mine eyes, *and* hast H3477
11:11 about the king, from the **r** corner of the H3233
12: 2 And Jehoash did *that which was* **r** in H3477
9 the altar, on the **r** side as one cometh H3225
14: 3 And he did *that which was* **r** in the H3477
15: 3 And he did *that which was* **r** in the H3477
34 And he did *that which was* **r** in the H3477
16: 2 not *that which was* **r** in the sight of the H3477
17: 9 that *were* not **r** against the LORD their H3651
18: 3 And he did *that which was* **r** in the H3477
2Ki 22: 2 And he did *that which was* **r** in the H3477
2 not aside to the **r** hand or to the left. H3225
23:13 which *were* on the **r** hand of the mount H3225
1Ch 6:39 who stood on his **r** hand, *even* Asaph H3225
12: 2 could use both the **r** hand and the left H3231
13: 4 thing was **r** in the eyes of all the people. H3474
2Ch 3:17 the temple, one on the **r** hand, and the H3225
17 of that on the **r** hand Jachin, and the H3227
4: 6 put five on the **r** hand, and five on the H3225
7 five on the **r** hand, and five on the left. H3225
8 temple, five on the **r** side, and five on H3225
10 And he set the sea on the **r** side of the H3233
14: 2 And Asa did *that which was* good and **r** H3477
18:18 standing on his **r** hand and *on* his left. H3225
20:32 *which was* **r** in the sight of the LORD. H3477
23:10 his hand, from the **r** side of the temple H3233
24: 2 And Joash did *that which was* **r** in the H3477
25: 2 And he did *that which was* **r** in the H3477
26: 4 And he did *that which was* **r** in the H3477
27: 2 And he did *that which was* **r** in the H3477
28: 1 not *that which was* **r** in the sight of the H3477
29: 2 And he did *that which was* **r** in the H3477
31:20 **r** and truth before the LORD his God. H3477
34: 2 And he did *that which was* **r** in the H3477
2 *neither* to the **r** hand, nor to the left. H3225
Ezr 8:21 to seek of him a **r** way for us, and for H3477
Neh 2:20 nor **r**, nor memorial, in Jerusalem. H6666
8: 4 Maaseiah, on his **r** hand; and on his H3225
9:13 and gavest them **r** judgments, and true H3477
33 hast done **r**, but we have done wickedly: H571
12:31 *one* went on the **r** hand upon the wall H3225
Est 8: 5 the thing *seem* **r** before the king, and H3787
Job 6:25 How forcible are **r** words! but what H3476
23: 9 on the **r** hand, that I cannot see *him:* H3225
30:12 Upon *my* **r** *hand* rise the youth; they H3225
33:27 *which was* **r**, and it profited me not; H3477
34: 6 Should I lie against my **r**? my wound *is* H4941
17 Shall even he that hateth **r** govern? and H4941
23 man more *than* **r**; that he should enter
35: 2 Thinkest thou this to be **r**, *that* thou H4941
36: 6 of the wicked: but giveth **r** to the poor. H4941
40:14 that thine own **r** hand can save thee. H3225
42: 7 *thing that is* **r**, as my servant Job *hath.* H3559
8 *thing which is* **r**, like my servant Job. H3559
Ps 9: 4 For thou hast maintained my **r** and my H4941
4 thou satest in the throne judging **r**. H6664
16: 8 *is* at my **r** hand, I shall not be moved. H3225
11 of joy; at thy **r** hand *there are* pleasures H3225
17: 1 Hear the **r**, O LORD, attend unto my H6664
7 that savest by thy **r** hand them which H3225
18:35 salvation: and thy **r** hand hath holden H3225
19: 8 The statutes of the LORD *are* **r**, H3477
20: 6 with the saving strength of his **r** hand. H3225
21: 8 thine enemies: thy **r** hand shall find out H3225
26:10 In whose hands *is* mischief, and their **r** H3225
33: 4 For the word of the LORD *is* **r**; and all H3477
44: 3 save them: but thy **r** hand, and thine H3225
45: 4 **r** hand shall teach thee terrible things. H3225
6 sceptre of thy kingdom *is* a **r** sceptre. H4334
9 women: upon thy **r** hand did stand the H3225
46: 5 God shall help her, *and that* **r** early. H6437
48:10 thy **r** hand is full of righteousness. H3225
51:10 O God; and renew a **r** spirit within me. H3559
60: 5 save *with* thy **r** hand, and hear me. H3225
63: 8 My soul followeth hard after thee: thy **r** H3225
73:23 thou hast holden *me* by my **r** hand. H3225
74:11 thy **r** hand? pluck *it* out of thy bosom. H3225
77:10 years of the **r** hand of the most High. H3225
78:37 For their heart was not **r** with him, H3559
54 *which* his **r** hand had purchased. H3225
80:15 And the vineyard which thy **r** hand H3225
17 Let thy hand be upon the man of thy **r** H3225
89:13 is thy hand, *and* high is thy **r** hand. H3225
25 in the sea, and his **r** hand in the rivers. H3225
42 Thou hast set up the **r** hand of his H3225
91: 7 **r** hand; *but* it shall not come nigh thee. H3225
98: 1 things: his **r** hand, and his holy arm, H3225
107: 7 And he led them forth by the **r** way, H3477
108: 6 save *with* thy **r** hand, and answer me. H3225
109: 6 him: and let Satan stand at his **r** hand. H3225
31 For he shall stand at the **r** hand of the H3225
110: 1 Sit thou at my **r** hand, until I make H3225
5 The Lord at thy **r** hand shall strike H3225
118:15 the **r** hand of the LORD doeth valiantly. H3225
16 The **r** hand of the LORD is exalted: the H3225
16 the **r** hand of the LORD doeth valiantly. H3225
119:75 thy judgments *are* **r**, and *that* thou in H6664
128 *to be* **r**; *and* I hate every false way. H3474
121: 5 LORD *is* thy shade upon thy **r** hand. H3225

Ps 137: 5 If I forget thee, O Jerusalem, let my **r** H3225
138: 7 enemies, and thy **r** hand shall save me. H3225
139:10 lead me, and thy **r** hand shall hold me. H3225
14 and *that* my soul knoweth **r** well. H3225
140:12 of the afflicted, *and* the **r** of the poor. H4941
142: 4 I looked on *my* **r** hand, and beheld, but H3225
144: 8 **r** hand *is* a right hand of falsehood. H3225
8 right hand *is* a **r** hand of falsehood. H3225
11 **r** hand *is* a right hand of falsehood: H3225
11 right hand *is* a **r** hand of falsehood: H3225
Prv 3:16 Length of days *is* in her **r** hand; *and* in H3225
4:11 of wisdom; I have led thee in **r** paths. H3476
25 Let thine eyes look **r** on, and let thine H5227
27 Turn not to the **r** hand nor to the left: H3225
8: 6 the opening of my lips *shall be* **r** things. H4339
9 and **r** to them that find knowledge. H3477
9:15 To call passengers who go **r** on their H3474
12: 5 The thoughts of the righteous *are* **r**: *but* H4941
15 The way of a fool *is* **r** in his own eyes: H3477
14:12 There is a way which seemeth **r** unto a H3477
16: 8 than great revenues without **r**. H4941
13 and they love him that speaketh **r**. H3477
25 There is a way that seemeth **r** unto a H3477
20:11 his work *be* pure, and whether *it be* **r**. H3477
21: 2 Every way of a man *is* **r** in his own H3477
8 but *as for* the pure, his work *is* **r**. H3477
23:16 rejoice, when thy lips speak **r** things. H4339
24:26 kiss *his* lips that giveth a **r** answer. H5228
27:16 of his **r** hand, *which* bewrayeth *itself*. H3225
Ecc 4: 4 travail, and every **r** work, that for this a H3788
10: 2 A wise man's heart *is* at his **r** hand; but H3225
Song 2: 6 head, and his **r** hand doth embrace me. H3225
8: 3 and his **r** hand should embrace me. H3225
Isa 9:20 And he shall snatch on the **r** hand, and H3225
10: 2 to take away the **r** from the poor of my H4941
30:10 not unto us **r** things, speak unto us H5229
21 the **r** hand, and when ye turn to the left. H541
32: 7 words, even when the needy speaketh **r**. H4941
41:10 with the **r** hand of my righteousness. H3225
13 For I the LORD thy God will hold thy **r** H3225
44:20 nor say, *Is there* not a lie in my **r** hand? H3225
45: 1 to Cyrus, whose **r** hand I have holden, H3225
19 I declare things that are **r**. H4339
48:13 the earth, and my **r** hand hath spanned H3225
54: 3 For thou shalt break forth on the **r** H3225
62: 8 The LORD hath sworn by his **r** hand, H3225
63:12 That led *them* by the **r** hand of Moses H3225
Jer 2:21 vine, wholly a **r** seed: how then art thou H571
5:28 the **r** of the needy do they not judge. H4941
17:11 riches, and not by **r**, shall leave them in H4941
16 came out of my lips was *r* before thee. H5227
22:24 **r** hand, yet would I pluck thee thence; H3225
23:10 course is evil, and their force *is* not **r**.
32: 7 the **r** of redemption *is* thine to buy *it*. H4941
8 of Benjamin: for the **r** of inheritance *is* H4941
34:15 turned, and had done **r** in my sight, in H3477
49: 5 out every man **r** forth; and none shall H6440
Lam 2: 3 drawn back his **r** hand from before the H3225
4 enemy: he stood with his **r** hand as an H3225
3:35 To turn aside the **r** of a man before the H4941
Ezk 1:10 of a lion, on the **r** side: and they four H3225
4: 6 lie again on thy **r** side, and thou shalt H3225
10: 3 Now the cherubims stood on the **r** side H3225
16:46 **r** hand, *is* Sodom and her daughters. H3225
18: 5 just, and do that which is lawful and **r**, H6666
19 is lawful and **r**, *and* hath kept all my H6666
21 **r**, he shall surely live, he shall not die. H6666
27 lawful and **r**, he shall save his soul alive. H6666
21:16 *either* on the **r** hand, *or* on the left, H3231
22 At his **r** hand was the divination for H3225
27 whose **r** it is; and I will give it *him*. H4941
33:14 sin, and do that which is lawful and **r**; H6666
16 is lawful and **r**; he shall surely live. H6666
19 is lawful and **r**, he shall live thereby. H6666
39: 3 thine arrows to fall out of thy **r** hand. H3225
47: 1 under from the **r** side of the house, at H3233
2 there ran out waters on the **r** side. H3233
Dan 12: 7 he held up his **r** hand and his left hand H3225
Hos 14: 9 of the LORD *are* **r**, and the just shall H3477
Am 3:10 For they know not to do **r**, saith the H5229
5:12 aside the poor in the gate *from their* **r**.
Jna 4:11 between their **r** hand and their left H3225
Hab 2:16 the cup of the LORD'S **r** hand shall be H3225
Zec 3: 1 standing at his **r** hand to resist him. H3225
4: 3 by it, one upon the **r** *side* of the bowl, H3225
11 trees upon the **r** *side* of the candlestick H3225
11:17 arm, and upon his **r** eye: his arm shall H3225
17 and his **r** eye shall be utterly darkened. H3225
12: 6 about, on the **r** hand and on the left: H3225
Mal 3: 5 the stranger *from his* **r**, and fear not me,
Mt 5:29 And if thy **r** eye offend thee, pluck it *G1188*
30 And if thy **r** hand offend thee, cut it off, *G1188*
39 thy **r** cheek, turn to him the other also. *G1188*
6: 3 left hand know what thy **r** hand doeth: *G1188*
20: 4 and whatsoever is **r** I will give you. And *G1342*
7 whatsoever is **r**, *that* shall ye receive. *G1342*
21 may sit, the one on thy **r** hand, and the *G1188*
23 but to sit on my **r** hand, and on my left, *G1188*
22:44 Sit thou on my **r** hand, till I make thine *G1188*
25:33 And he shall set the sheep on his **r** *G1188*
34 say unto them on his **r** hand, Come, ye *G1188*
26:64 of man sitting on the **r** hand of power, *G1188*
27:29 and a reed in his **r** hand: and they *G1188*
38 on the **r** hand, and another on the left. *G1188*
Mk 5:15 in his **r** mind: and they were afraid. *G4993*
10:37 sit, one on thy **r** hand, and the other *G1188*
40 But to sit on my **r** hand and on my left *G1188*
12:36 Sit thou on my **r** hand, till I make thine *G1188*
14:62 of man sitting on the **r** hand of power, *G1188*
15:27 on his **r** hand, and the other on his left. *G1188*
16: 5 man sitting on the **r** side, clothed in a *G1188*
19 heaven, and sat on the **r** hand of God. *G1188*
Lk 1:11 on the **r** side of the altar of incense. *G1188*
6: 6 was a man whose **r** hand was withered. *G1188*
8:35 in his **r** mind: and they were afraid. *G4993*
10:28 answered **r**: this do, and thou shalt live. *G3723*
12:57 of yourselves judge ye not what is **r**? *G1342*
20:42 unto my Lord, Sit thou on my **r** hand, *G1188*
22:50 of the high priest, and cut off his **r** ear. *G1188*
69 sit on the **r** hand of the power of God. *G1188*
23:33 on the **r** hand, and the other on the left. *G1188*
Jn 18:10 and cut off his **r** ear. The servant's *G1188*
21: 6 Cast the net on the **r** side of the ship, *G1188*
Act 2:25 my **r** hand, that I should not be moved: *G1188*
33 Therefore being by the **r** hand of God *G1188*
34 unto my Lord, Sit thou on my **r** hand, *G1188*
3: 7 And he took him by the **r** hand, and *G1188*
4:19 Whether it be **r** in the sight of God to *G1342*
5:31 Him hath God exalted with his **r** hand *G1188*
7:55 Jesus standing on the **r** hand of God, *G1188*
56 of man standing on the **r** hand of God. *G1188*
8:21 for thy heart is not **r** in the sight of God. *G2117*
13:10 cease to pervert the **r** ways of the Lord? *G2117*
Ro 8:34 who is even at the **r** hand of God, who *G1188*
2Co 6: 7 on the **r** hand and on the left, *G1188*
Gal 2: 9 me and Barnabas the **r** hands of *G1188*
Eph 1:20 his own **r** hand in the heavenly *places*, *G1188*
6: 1 your parents in the Lord: for this is **r**. *G1342*
Col 3: 1 Christ sitteth on the **r** hand of God. *G1188*
Heb 1: 3 on the **r** hand of the Majesty on high; *G1188*
13 time, Sit on my **r** hand, until I make *G1188*
8: 1 who is set on the **r** hand of the throne *G1188*
10:12 ever, sat down on the **r** hand of God; *G1188*
12: 2 at the **r** hand of the throne of God. *G1188*
13:10 no **r** to eat which serve the tabernacle. *G1849*
1Pt 3:22 and is on the **r** hand of God; angels *G1188*
2Pt 2:15 Which have forsaken the **r** way, and *G2117*
Rev 1:16 And he had in his **r** hand seven stars: *G1188*
17 And he laid his **r** hand upon me, saying *G1188*
20 thou sawest in my **r** hand, and the *G1188*
2: 1 seven stars in his **r** hand, who walketh *G1188*
5: 1 And I saw in the **r** hand of him that sat *G1188*
7 **r** hand of him that sat upon the throne. *G1188*
10: 2 and he set his **r** foot upon the sea, and *G1188*
13:16 in their **r** hand, or in their foreheads: *G1188*
22:14 they may have **r** to the tree of life, and *G1849*

RIGHTEOUS

Gen 7: 1 I seen **r** before me in this generation. H6662
18:23 thou also destroy the **r** with the wicked? H6662
24 Peradventure there be fifty **r** within the H6662
24 the place for the fifty **r** that *are* therein? H6662
25 to slay the **r** with the wicked: and H6662
25 and that the **r** should be as the wicked, H6662
26 in Sodom fifty **r** within the city, then H6662
28 five of the fifty **r**: wilt thou destroy all H6662
20: 4 Lord, wilt thou slay also a **r** nation? H6662
38:26 hath been more **r** than I; because that H6663
Ex 9:27 *is* **r**, and I and my people *are* wicked. H6662
23: 7 the innocent and **r** slay thou not: for I H6662
8 wise, and perverteth the words of the **r**. H6662
Nu 23:10 of the **r**, and let my last end be like his! H3477
Dt 4: 8 and judgments *so* **r** as all this law, H6662
16:19 the wise, and pervert the words of the **r**. H6662
25: 1 justify the **r**, and condemn the wicked. H6662
Jdg 5:11 they rehearse the **r** acts of the LORD, H6666
11 the LORD, *even* the **r** acts *toward the* H6666
1Sa 12: 7 the LORD of all the **r** acts of the LORD, H6666
1Sa 24:17 And he said to David, Thou *art* more **r** H6662
2Sa 4:11 men have slain a **r** person in his own H6662
1Ki 2:32 two men more **r** and better than he, H6662
8:32 head; and justifying the **r**, to give him H6662
2Ki 10: 9 the people, Ye *be* **r**: behold, I conspired H6662
2Ch 6:23 and by justifying the **r**, by giving him H6662
12: 6 and they said, The LORD *is* **r**. H6662
Ezr 9:15 O LORD God of Israel, thou *art* **r**: for we H6662
Neh 9: 8 performed thy words; for thou *art* **r**: H6662
Job 4: 7 innocent? or where were the **r** cut off? H3477
9:15 Whom, though I were **r**, *yet* would I not H6663
10:15 me; and *if* I be **r**, *yet* will I not lift up H6663
15:14 *is* born of a woman, that he should be **r**? H6663
17: 9 The **r** also shall hold on his way, and he H6662
22: 3 that thou art **r**? or *is it* gain *to him*, H6663
19 The **r** see *it*, and are glad: and the H6662
23: 7 There the **r** might dispute with him; so H3477
32: 1 Job, because he *was* **r** in his own eyes. H6662
34: 5 For Job hath said, I am **r**: and God hath H6663
35: 7 If thou be **r**, what givest thou him? or H6663
36: 7 He withdraweth not his eyes from the **r**: H6662
40: 8 condemn me, that thou mayest be **r**? H6663
Ps 1: 5 nor sinners in the congregation of the **r**. H6662
6 For the LORD knoweth the way of the **r**: H6662
5:12 For thou, LORD, wilt bless the **r**; with H6662
7: 9 the **r** God trieth the hearts and reins. H6662
11 God judgeth the **r**, and God is angry H6662
11: 3 be destroyed, what can the **r** do? H6662
5 The LORD trieth the **r**: but the wicked H6662
7 For the **r** LORD loveth righteousness; H6662
14: 5 for God *is* in the generation of the **r**. H6662
19: 9 of the LORD *are* true *and* **r** altogether. H6663
31:18 and contemptuously against the **r**. H6662
32:11 Be glad in the LORD, and rejoice, ye **r**: H6662
33: 1 Rejoice in the LORD, O ye **r**: *for* praise H6662
34:15 The eyes of the LORD *are* upon the **r**, H6662
17 *The* **r** cry, and the LORD heareth, and
19 Many *are* the afflictions of the **r**: but the H6662
21 they that hate the **r** shall be desolate. H6662
35:27 that favour my **r** cause: yea, let them H6664
37:16 A little that a **r** man hath *is* better than H6662
17 broken: but the LORD upholdeth the **r**. H6662
21 but the **r** sheweth mercy, and giveth. H6662
25 **r** forsaken, nor his seed begging bread. H6662
29 The **r** shall inherit the land, and dwell H6662
30 The mouth of the **r** speaketh wisdom, H6662
32 The wicked watcheth the **r**, and seeketh H6662
39 But the salvation of the **r** *is* of the H6662
52: 6 The **r** also shall see, and fear, and shall H6662
55:22 he shall never suffer the **r** to be moved. H6662
58:10 The **r** shall rejoice when he seeth the H6662
11 *is* a reward for the **r**: verily he is a God H6662
64:10 The **r** shall be glad in the LORD, and H6662
68: 3 But let the **r** be glad; let them rejoice H6662
69:28 the living, and not be written with the **r**. H6662
72: 7 In his days shall the **r** flourish; and H6662
75:10 *but* the horns of the **r** shall be exalted. H6662
92:12 The **r** shall flourish like the palm tree: H6662
94:21 the **r**, and condemn the innocent blood. H6662
97:11 Light is sown for the **r**, and gladness for H6662
12 Rejoice in the LORD, ye **r**; and give H6662
107:42 The **r** shall see *it*, and rejoice: and all H3477
112: 4 gracious, and full of compassion, and **r**. H6662
6 **r** shall be in everlasting remembrance. H6662
116: 5 Gracious *is* the LORD, and **r**; yea, our H6662
118:15 tabernacles of the **r**: the right hand of H6662
20 This gate of the LORD, into which the **r** H6662
119: 7 I shall have learned thy **r** judgments. H6664
62 unto thee because of thy **r** judgments. H6664
106 *it*, that I will keep thy **r** judgments. H6664
137 **R** *art* thou, O LORD, and upright *are* H6662
138 commanded *are* **r** and very faithful. H6664
160 of thy **r** judgments *endureth* for ever. H6664
164 praise thee because of thy **r** judgments. H6664
125: 3 upon the lot of the **r**; lest the righteous H6662
3 **r** put forth their hands unto iniquity. H6662
129: 4 The LORD *is* **r**: he hath cut asunder the H6662
140:13 Surely the **r** shall give thanks unto thy H6662
141: 5 Let the **r** smite me; *it shall be* a H6662
142: 7 thy name: the **r** shall compass me H6662
145:17 The LORD *is* **r** in all his ways, and holy H6662
146: 8 are bowed down: the LORD loveth the **r**: H6662
Prv 2: 7 He layeth up sound wisdom for the **r**: *he* H3477
20 good *men*, and keep the paths of the **r**. H6662
3:32 to the LORD: but his secret *is* with the **r**. H3477
10: 3 suffer the soul of the **r** to famish: but he H6662
11 The mouth of a **r** *man is* a well of life: H6662
16 The labour of the **r** *tendeth* to life: the H6662
21 The lips of the **r** feed many: but fools H6662

Prv 10:24 but the desire of the r shall be granted. H6662
25 but the r is an everlasting foundation. H6662
28 The hope of the r shall be gladness: but H6662
30 The r shall never be removed: but the H6662
32 The lips of the r know what is H6662
11: 8 The r is delivered out of trouble, and H6662
10 When it goeth well with the r, the city H6662
21 but the seed of the r shall be delivered. H6662
23 The desire of the r is only good: but the H6662
28 fall: but the r shall flourish as a branch. H6662
30 The fruit of the r is a tree of life; and he H6662
31 Behold, the r shall be recompensed in H6662
12: 3 but the root of the r shall not be moved. H6662
5 The thoughts of the r are right: but the H6662
7 not: but the house of the r shall stand. H6662
10 A r man regardeth the life of his beast: H6662
12 men: but the root of the r yieldeth fruit. H6662
26 The r is more excellent than his H6662
13: 5 A r man hateth lying: but a wicked H6662
9 The light of the r rejoiceth: but the H6662
21 Evil pursueth sinners: but to the r good H6662
25 The r eateth to the satisfying of his H6662
14: 9 at sin: but among the r there is favour. H3477
19 and the wicked at the gates of the r. H6662
32 but the r hath hope in his death. H6662
15: 6 In the house of the r is much treasure: H6662
19 but the way of the r is made plain. H3477
28 The heart of the r studieth to answer: H6662
29 but he heareth the prayer of the r. H6662
16:13 R lips are the delight of kings; and they H6664
18: 5 to overthrow the r in judgment. H6662
10 tower: the r runneth into it, and is safe. H6662
21:12 The r man wisely considereth the H6662
18 The wicked shall be a ransom for the r, H6662
26 long: but the r giveth and spareth not. H6662
23:24 The father of the r shall greatly rejoice: H6662
24:15 of the r; spoil not his resting place: H6662
24 wicked, Thou art r; him shall the people H6662
25:26 A r man falling down before the wicked H6662
28: 1 pursueth: but the r are bold as a lion. H6662
10 Whoso causeth the r to go astray in an H3477
12 When r men do rejoice, there is great H6662
28 but when they perish, the r increase. H6662
29: 2 When the r are in authority, the people H6662
6 a snare: but the r doth sing and rejoice. H6662
7 The r considereth the cause of the H6662
16 increaseth: but the r shall see their fall. H6662
Ecc 3:17 shall judge the r and the wicked: for H6662
7:16 Be not r over much; neither make H6662
8:14 of the r: I said that this also is vanity. H6662
9: 1 all this, that the r, and the wise, and H6662
2 is one event to the r, and to the wicked; H6662
Isa 3:10 Say ye to the r, that it shall be well with H6662
5:23 the righteousness of the r from him! H6662
24:16 songs, even glory to the r. But I said, My H6662
26: 2 Open ye the gates, that the r nation H6662
41: 2 Who raised up the r man from the east, H6664
26 we may say, He is r? yea, there is none H6662
53:11 shall my r servant justify many; H6662
57: 1 The r perisheth, and no man layeth it H6662
1 r is taken away from the evil to come. H6662
60:21 Thy people also shall be all r: they shall H6662
Jer 12: 1 R art thou, O LORD, when I plead with H6662
20:12 But, O LORD of hosts, that triest the r, H6662
23: 5 will raise unto David a r Branch, and a H6662
Lam 1:18 The LORD is r; for I have rebelled H6662
Ezk 3:20 Again, When a r man doth turn from H6662
21 Nevertheless if thou warn the r man, H6662
21 man, that the r sin not, and he doth H6662
13:22 the heart of the r sad, whom I have not H6662
16:52 they are more r than thou: yea, be thou H6663
18:20 of the r shall be upon him, and H6662
24 But when the r turneth away from his H6662
26 When a r man turneth away from his H6662
21: 3 cut off from thee the r and the wicked. H6662
4 cut off from thee the r and the wicked, H6662
23:45 And the r men, they shall judge them H6662
33:12 of the r shall not deliver him H6662
12 neither shall the r be able to live for his H6662
13 When I shall say to the r, that he shall H6662
18 When the r turneth from his H6662
Dan 9:14 the LORD our God is r in all his works H6662
Am 2: 6 they sold the r for silver, and the poor H6662
Hab 1: 4 about the r; therefore wrong judgment H6662
13 the man that is more r than he? H6662
Mal 3:18 between the r and the wicked, between H6662
Mt 9:13 to call the r, but sinners to repentance. G1342
10:41 he that receiveth a r man in the name G1342
41 in the name of a r man shall receive a G1342
Mt 10:41 man shall receive a r man's reward. G1342
13:17 prophets and r men have desired to G1342
43 Then shall the r shine forth as the sun G1342
23:28 Even so ye also outwardly appear r G1342
29 and garnish the sepulchres of the r, G1342
35 That upon you may come all the r G1342
35 from the blood of r Abel unto the blood G1342
25:37 Then shall the r answer him, saying, G1342
46 punishment: but the r into life eternal. G1342
Mk 2:17 to call the r, but sinners to repentance. G1342
Lk 1: 6 And they were both r before God, G1342
5:32 I came not to call the r, but sinners to G1342
18: 9 that they were r, and despised others: G1342
23:47 saying, Certainly this was a r man. G1342
Jn 7:24 the appearance, but judge r judgment. G1342
17:25 O r Father, the world hath not known G1342
Ro 2: 5 revelation of the r judgment of God; G1341
3:10 As it is written, There is none r, no, not G1342
5: 7 For scarcely for a r man will one die: G1342
19 obedience of one shall many be made r. G1342
2Th 1: 5 Which is a manifest token of the r G1342
6 Seeing it is a r thing with God to G1342
1Ti 1: 9 law is not made for a r man, but for the G1342
2Ti 4: 8 the Lord, the r judge, shall give me G1342
Heb 11: 4 that he was r, God testifying of his G1342
Jas 5:16 prayer of a r man availeth much. G1342
1Pt 3:12 For the eyes of the Lord are over the r, G1342
4:18 And if the r scarcely be saved, where G1342
2Pt 2: 8 (For that r man dwelling among them, G1342
8 hearing, vexed his r soul from day to G1342
1Jn 2: 1 with the Father, Jesus Christ the r: G1342
29 If ye know that he is r, ye know that G1342
3: 7 is r, even as he is righteous. G1342
7 is righteous, even as he is r. G1342
12 works were evil, and his brother's r. G1342
Rev 16: 5 say, Thou art r, O Lord, which art, and G1342
7 true and r are thy judgments. G1342
19: 2 For true and r are his judgments: for he G1342
22:11 filthy still: and he that is r, let him be G1342
11 let him be r still: and he that is holy, G1344

RIGHTEOUSLY

Dt 1:16 and judge r between every man H6664
Ps 67: 4 shalt judge the people r, and govern the H4334
96:10 be moved: he shall judge the people r. H4339
Prv 31: 9 Open thy mouth, judge r, and plead the H6664
Isa 33:15 He that walketh r, and speaketh H6666
Jer 11:20 But, O LORD of hosts, that judgest r, H6664
Tit 2:12 r, and godly, in this present world; G1346
1Pt 2:23 himself to him that judgeth r: G1346

RIGHTEOUSNESS

Gen 15: 6 LORD; and he counted it to him for r. H6666
30:33 So shall my r answer for me in time to H6666
Lev 19:15 but in r shalt thou judge thy neighbour. H6664
Dt 6:25 And it shall be our r, if we observe to do H6666
9: 4 thee, saying, For my r the LORD hath H6666
5 Not for thy r, or for the uprightness of H6666
6 thy r; for thou art a stiffnecked people. H6666
24:13 r unto thee before the LORD thy God. H6666
33:19 offer sacrifices of r: for they shall suck H6664
1Sa 26:23 The LORD render to every man his r H6666
2Sa 22:21 me according to my r: according to the H6666
25 me according to my r; according to my H6666
1Ki 3: 6 in truth, and in r, and in uprightness H6666
8:32 to give him according to his r. H6666
2Ch 6:23 by giving him according to his r. H6666
Job 6:29 iniquity; yea, return again, my r is in it. H6664
8: 6 the habitation of thy r prosperous. H6664
27: 6 My r I hold fast, and will not let it go: H6666
29:14 I put on r, and it clothed me: my H6664
33:26 joy: for he will render unto man his r. H6666
35: 2 thou saidst, My r is more than God's? H6664
8 and thy r may profit the son of man. H6666
36: 3 afar, and will ascribe r to my Maker. H6664
Ps 4: 1 Hear me when I call, O God of my r: H6664
5 Offer the sacrifices of r, and put your H6664
5: 8 Lead me, O LORD, in thy r because of H6666
7: 8 according to my r, and according to H6664
17 according to his r: and will sing praise H6664
9: 8 And he shall judge the world in r, he H6664
11: 7 For the righteous LORD loveth r; his H6666
15: 2 r, and speaketh the truth in his heart. H6664
17:15 As for me, I will behold thy face in r: I H6664
18:20 me according to my r; according to the H6664
24 me according to my r, according to the H6664
22:31 They shall come, and shall declare his r H6666
23: 3 in the paths of r for his name's sake. H6664
24: 5 and r from the God of his salvation. H6666
Ps 31: 1 never be ashamed: deliver me in thy r. H6666
33: 5 He loveth r and judgment: the earth is H6666
35:24 thy r; and let them not rejoice over me. H6664
28 And my tongue shall speak of thy r and H6664
36: 6 Thy r is like the great mountains; thy H6666
10 thee; and thy r to the upright in heart. H6666
37: 6 And he shall bring forth thy r as the H6664
40: 9 I have preached r in the great H6664
10 I have not hid thy r within my heart; I H6666
45: 4 and meekness and r; and thy right hand H6664
7 Thou lovest r, and hatest wickedness: H6664
48:10 of the earth: thy right hand is full of r. H6664
50: 6 And the heavens shall declare his r: for H6664
51:14 and my tongue shall sing aloud of thy r. H6666
19 the sacrifices of r, with burnt offering H6664
52: 3 and lying rather than to speak r. Selah. H6664
58: 1 Do ye indeed speak r, O congregation? H6664
65: 5 By terrible things in r wilt thou answer H6664
69:27 and let them not come into thy r. H6666
71: 2 Deliver me in thy r, and cause me to H6666
15 My mouth shall shew forth thy r and H6666
16 mention of thy r, even of thine only. H6666
19 Thy r also, O God, is very high, who H6666
24 My tongue also shall talk of thy r all the H6666
72: 1 O God, and thy r unto the king's son. H6666
2 He shall judge thy people with r, and H6664
3 to the people, and the little hills, by r. H6666
85:10 Mercy and truth are met together; r H6664
11 and r shall look down from heaven. H6664
13 R shall go before him; and shall set us H6664
88:12 and thy r in the land of forgetfulness? H6666
89:16 day: and in thy r shall they be exalted. H6666
94:15 But judgment shall return unto r: and H6664
96:13 with r, and the people with his truth. H6664
97: 2 round about him: r and judgment are H6664
6 The heavens declare his r, and all the H6664
98: 2 his salvation: his r hath he openly H6666
9 the earth: with r shall he judge the H6664
99: 4 executest judgment and r in Jacob. H6666
103: 6 The LORD executeth r and judgment H6666
17 him, and his r unto children's children; H6666
106: 3 and he that doeth r at all times. H6666
31 And that was counted unto him for r H6666
111: 3 glorious: and his r endureth for ever. H6666
112: 3 his house: and his r endureth for ever. H6666
9 to the poor; his r endureth for ever; his H6666
118:19 Open to me the gates of r: I will go into H6664
119:40 after thy precepts: quicken me in thy r. H6666
123 thy salvation, and for the word of thy r. H6664
142 Thy r is an everlasting righteousness, H6666
142 Thy righteousness is an everlasting r, H6664
144 The r of thy testimonies is everlasting: H6664
172 word: for all thy commandments are r. H6664
132: 9 Let thy priests be clothed with r; and let H6664
143: 1 faithfulness answer me, and in thy r. H6666
145: 7 great goodness, and shall sing of thy r. H6666
Prv 2: 9 Then shalt thou understand r, and H6664
8: 8 All the words of my mouth are in r; H6664
18 are with me; yea, durable riches and r. H6666
20 I lead in the way of r, in the midst of the H6666
10: 2 nothing: but r delivereth from death. H6666
11: 4 of wrath: but r delivereth from death. H6666
5 The r of the perfect shall direct his way: H6666
6 The r of the upright shall deliver them: H6666
18 that soweth r shall be a sure reward. H6666
19 As r tendeth to life: so he that pursueth H6666
12:17 He that speaketh truth sheweth forth r: H6664
28 In the way of r is life; and in the H6666
13: 6 R keepeth him that is upright in the H6666
14:34 R exalteth a nation: but sin is a H6666
15: 9 but he loveth him that followeth after r. H6666
16: 8 Better is a little with r than great H6666
12 for the throne is established by r. H6666
31 of glory, if it be found in the way of r. H6666
21:21 He that followeth after r and mercy H6666
21 and mercy findeth life, r, and honour. H6666
25: 5 and his throne shall be established in r. H6664
Ecc 3:16 the place of r, that iniquity was there. H6664
7:15 perisheth in his r, and there is a wicked H6664
Isa 1:21 r lodged in it; but now murderers. H6664
26 be called, The city of r, the faithful city. H6664
27 with judgment, and her converts with r. H6666
5: 7 oppression; for r, but behold a cry. H6666
16 God that is holy shall be sanctified in r. H6666
23 away the r of the righteous from him! H6666
10:22 decreed shall overflow with r. H6666
11: 4 But with r shall he judge the poor, and H6664
5 And r shall be the girdle of his loins, H6664
16: 5 and seeking judgment, and hasting r. H6664

Isa 26: 9 the inhabitants of the world will learn **r**. H6664
10 *yet* will he not learn **r**: in the land of H6664
28:17 I lay to the line, and **r** to the plummet: H6666
32: 1 Behold, a king shall reign in **r**, and H6664
16 and **r** remain in the fruitful field. H6666
17 And the work of **r** shall be peace; and H6666
17 of **r** quietness and assurance for ever. H6666
33: 5 he hath filled Zion with judgment and **r**. H6666
41:10 uphold thee with the right hand of my **r**. H6664
42: 6 I the LORD have called thee in **r**, and H6664
45: 8 skies pour down **r**: let the earth open, H6664
8 salvation, and let **r** spring up together; H6666
13 I have raised him up in **r**, and I will H6664
19 speak **r**, I declare things that are right. H6664
23 of my mouth *in* **r**, and shall not return, H6666
24 the LORD have I **r** and strength: *even* H6666
46:12 me, ye stouthearted, that *are* far from **r**: H6666
13 I bring near my **r**; it shall not be far off, H6666
48: 1 God of Israel, *but* not in truth, nor in **r**. H6666
18 river, and thy **r** as the waves of the sea: H6666
51: 1 Hearken to me, ye that follow after **r**, ye H6664
5 My **r** *is* near; my salvation is gone H6664
6 ever, and my **r** shall not be abolished. H6666
7 Hearken unto me, ye that know **r**, the H6664
8 like wool: but my **r** shall be for ever, H6666
54:14 In **r** shalt thou be established: thou H6666
17 and their **r** *is* of me, saith the LORD. H6666
56: 1 near to come, and my **r** to be revealed. H6666
57:12 I will declare thy **r**, and thy works; for H6666
58: 2 a nation that did **r**, and forsook not the H6666
8 speedily: and thy **r** shall go before thee; H6664
59:16 unto him; and his **r**, it sustained him. H6666
17 For he put on **r** as a breastplate, and an H6666
60:17 thy officers peace, and thine exactors **r**. H6666
61: 3 be called trees of **r**, the planting of the H6664
10 me with the robe of **r**, as a bridegroom H6666
11 GOD will cause **r** and praise to spring H6666
62: 1 not rest, until the **r** thereof go forth as H6664
2 And the Gentiles shall see thy **r**, and all H6664
63: 1 I that speak in **r**, mighty to save. H6666
64: 5 and worketh **r**, *those that* remember H6664
Jer 4: 2 in judgment, and in **r**; and the nations H6666
9:24 judgment, and **r**, in the earth: for in H6666
22: 3 ye judgment and **r**, and deliver the H6666
23: 6 he shall be called, THE LORD OUR **R**. H6664
33:15 the Branch of **r** to grow up unto David; H6666
15 execute judgment and **r** in the land. H6666
16 she shall be called, The LORD our **r**. H6664
51:10 The LORD hath brought forth our **r**: H6666
Ezk 3:20 *man* doth turn from his **r**, and commit H6664
20 in his sin, and his **r** which he hath done H6666
14:14 souls by their **r**, saith the Lord GOD. H6666
20 *but* deliver their own souls by their **r**. H6666
18:20 of the son: the **r** of the righteous shall H6666
22 in his **r** that he hath done he shall live. H6666
24 away from his **r**, and committeth H6666
24 he live? All his **r** that he hath done shall H6666
26 away from his **r**, and committeth H6666
33:12 of thy people, The **r** of the righteous H6666
12 live for his *r* in the day that he sinneth.
13 if he trust to his own **r**, and commit H6666
18 When the righteous turneth from his **r**, H6666
Dan 4:27 off thy sins by **r**, and thine iniquities H6665
9: 7 O Lord, **r** *belongeth* unto thee, but unto H6666
16 O Lord, according to all thy **r**, I beseech H6666
24 bring in everlasting **r**, and to seal up the H6664
12: 3 to **r** as the stars for ever and ever. H6663
Hos 2:19 thee unto me in **r**, and in judgment, and H6664
10:12 Sow to yourselves in **r**, reap in mercy; H6666
12 till he come and rain **r** upon you. H6664
Am 5: 7 and leave off **r** in the earth, H6666
24 as waters, and **r** as a mighty stream. H6666
6:12 gall, and the fruit of **r** into hemlock: H6666
Mic 6: 5 that ye may know the **r** of the LORD. H6666
7: 9 to the light, *and* I shall behold his **r**. H6666
Zep 2: 3 his judgment; seek **r**, seek meekness: it H6664
Zec 8: 8 and I will be their God, in truth and in **r**. H6666
Mal 3: 3 offer unto the LORD an offering in **r**. H6666
4: 2 shall the Sun of **r** arise with healing in H6666
Mt 3:15 us to fulfil all **r**. Then he suffered him. *G1343*
5: 6 and thirst after **r**: for they shall be filled. *G1343*
20 For I say unto you, That except your **r** *G1343*
20 shall exceed *the* **r** of the scribes and *G1343*
6:33 of God, and his **r**; and all these things *G1343*
21:32 For John came unto you in the way of **r**, *G1343*
Lk 1:75 In holiness and **r** before him, all the *G1343*
Jn 16: 8 world of sin, and of **r**, and of judgment: *G1343*
10 Of **r**, because I go to my Father, and ye *G1343*
Act 10:35 and worketh **r**, is accepted with him. *G1343*
Act 13:10 *thou* enemy of all **r**, wilt thou not cease *G1343*
17:31 judge the world in **r** by *that* man whom *G1343*
24:25 And as he reasoned of **r**, temperance, *G1343*
Ro 1:17 For therein is the **r** of God revealed *G1343*
2:26 keep the **r** of the law, shall not *G1345*
3: 5 commend the **r** of God, what shall we *G1343*
21 But now the **r** of God without the law is *G1343*
22 Even the **r** of God *which is* by faith of *G1343*
25 to declare his **r** for the remission of *G1343*
26 To declare, *I say*, at this time his **r**: that *G1343*
4: 3 God, and it was counted unto him for **r**. *G1343*
5 the ungodly, his faith is counted for **r**. *G1343*
6 whom God imputeth **r** without works, *G1343*
9 faith was reckoned to Abraham for **r**. *G1343*
11 a seal of the **r** of the faith which *he* *G1343*
11 **r** might be imputed unto them also: *G1343*
13 the law, but through the **r** of faith. *G1343*
22 therefore it was imputed to him for **r**. *G1343*
5:17 and of the gift of **r** shall reign in life by *G1343*
18 even so by the **r** of one *the free gift* *G1345*
21 reign through **r** unto eternal life by *G1343*
6:13 members *as* instruments of **r** unto God. *G1343*
16 sin unto death, or of obedience unto **r**? *G1343*
18 from sin, ye became the servants of **r**. *G1343*
19 members servants to **r** unto holiness. *G1343*
20 the servants of sin, ye were free from **r**. *G1343*
8: 4 That the **r** of the law might be fulfilled *G1345*
10 of sin; but the Spirit *is* life because of **r**. *G1343*
9:28 and cut *it* short in **r**: because a short *G1343*
30 followed not after **r**, have attained to *G1343*
30 have attained to **r**, even the *G1343*
30 even the **r** which is of faith. *G1343*
31 after the law of **r**, hath not attained to *G1343*
31 hath not attained to the law of **r**. *G1343*
10: 3 For they being ignorant of God's **r**, and *G1343*
3 their own **r**, have not submitted *G1343*
3 themselves unto the **r** of God. *G1343*
4 For Christ *is* the end of the law for **r** to *G1343*
5 For Moses describeth the **r** which is of *G1343*
6 But the **r** which is of faith speaketh on *G1343*
10 For with the heart man believeth unto **r**; *G1343*
14:17 **r**, and peace, and joy in the Holy Ghost. *G1343*
1Co 1:30 **r**, and sanctification, and redemption: *G1343*
15:34 Awake to **r**, and sin not; for some have *G1346*
2Co 3: 9 the ministration of **r** exceed in glory. *G1343*
5:21 we might be made the **r** of God in him. *G1343*
6: 7 of **r** on the right hand and on the left, *G1343*
14 what fellowship hath **r** wIth *G1343*
9: 9 to the poor: his **r** remaineth for ever. *G1343*
10 sown, and increase the fruits of your **r**;) *G1343*
11:15 as the ministers of **r**; whose end shall be *G1343*
Gal 2:21 grace of God: for if **r** *come* by the law, *G1343*
3: 6 God, and it was accounted to him for **r**. *G1343*
21 verily **r** should have been by the law. *G1343*
5: 5 Spirit wait for the hope of **r** by faith. *G1343*
Eph 4:24 God is created in **r** and true holiness. *G1343*
5: 9 *is* in all goodness and **r** and truth;) *G1343*
6:14 and having on the breastplate of **r**; *G1343*
Php 1:11 Being filled with the fruits of **r**, which *G1343*
3: 6 the **r** which is in the law, blameless. *G1343*
9 having mine own **r**, which is of the law, *G1343*
9 of Christ, the **r** which is of God by faith: *G1343*
1Ti 6:11 and follow after **r**, godliness, faith, love, *G1343*
2Ti 2:22 Flee also youthful lusts: but follow **r**, *G1343*
3:16 for correction, for instruction in **r**: *G1343*
4: 8 for me a crown of **r**, which the Lord, the *G1343*
Tit 3: 5 Not by works of **r** which we have done, *G1343*
Heb 1: 8 of **r** *is* the sceptre of thy kingdom. *G2118*
9 Thou hast loved **r**, and hated iniquity; *G1343*
5:13 in the word of **r**: for he is a babe. *G1343*
7: 2 King of **r**, and after that also King *G1343*
11: 7 became heir of the **r** which is by faith. *G1343*
33 wrought **r**, obtained promises, *G1343*
12:11 peaceable fruit of **r** unto them which *G1343*
Jas 1:20 For the wrath of man worketh not the **r** *G1343*
2:23 **r**: and he was called the Friend of God. *G1343*
3:18 And the fruit of **r** is sown in peace of *G1343*
1Pt 2:24 unto **r**: by whose stripes ye were healed. *G1343*
2Pt 1: 1 **r** of God and our Saviour Jesus Christ: *G1343*
2: 5 a preacher of **r**, bringing in the flood *G1343*
21 known the way of **r**, than, after they *G1343*
3:13 and a new earth, wherein dwelleth **r**. *G1343*
1Jn 2:29 every one that doeth **r** is born of him. *G1343*
3: 7 **r** is righteous, even as he is righteous. *G1343*
10 doeth not **r** is not of God, neither *G1343*
Rev 19: 8 for the fine linen is the **r** of saints. *G1345*
11 and in **r** he doth judge and make war. *G1343*

RIGHTEOUSNESS'
Ps 143:11 thy **r** sake bring my soul out of trouble. H6666
Isa 42:21 The LORD is well pleased for his **r** sake; H6664
Mt 5:10 are persecuted for **r** sake: for theirs is *G1343*
1Pt 3:14 But and if ye suffer for **r** sake, happy *G1343*

RIGHTEOUSNESSES
Isa 64: 6 *thing*, and all our **r** *are* as filthy rags; H6666
Ezk 33:13 commit iniquity, all his **r** shall not be H6666
Dan 9:18 thee for our **r**, but for thy great mercies. H6666

RIGHTLY
Gen 27:36 And he said, Is not he **r** named Jacob? H3588
Lk 7:43 he said unto him, Thou hast **r** judged. *G3723*
20:21 and teachest **r**, neither acceptest thou *G3723*
2Ti 2:15 ashamed, **r** dividing the word of truth.

RIGOUR
Ex 1:13 the children of Israel to serve with **r**: H6531
14 they made them serve, *was* with **r**. H6531
Lev 25:43 Thou shalt not rule over him with **r**; but H6531
46 shall not rule one over another with **r**. H6531
53 not rule with **r** over him in thy sight. H6531

RIMMON
Jos 15:32 and Ain, and **R**: all the cities *are* twenty H7417
Jdg 20:45 unto the rock of **R**: and they gleaned of H7417
47 unto the rock **R**, and abode in the rock H7417
47 and abode in the rock **R** four months. H7417
21:13 **R**, and to call peaceably unto them. H7417
2Sa 4: 2 the sons of **R** a Beerothite, of the H7417
5 And the sons of **R** the Beerothite, H7417
9 the sons of **R** the Beerothite, and H7417
2Ki 5:18 into the house of **R** to worship there, H7417
18 in the house of **R**: when I bow down H7417
18 in the house of **R**, the LORD pardon thy H7417
1Ch 4:32 **R**, and Tochen, and Ashan, five cities: H7417
6:77 tribe of Zebulun, **R** with her suburbs, H7417
Zec 14:10 from Geba to **R** south of Jerusalem: H7417

RIMMON-PAREZ
Nu 33:19 from Rithmah, and pitched at **R**. H7428
20 And they departed from **R**, and pitched H7428

RING
Gen 41:42 And Pharaoh took off his **r** from his H2885
Ex 26:24 of it unto one **r**: thus shall it be for them H2885
36:29 thereof, to one **r**: thus he did to both H2885
Est 3:10 And the king took his **r** from his hand, H2885
12 it written, and sealed with the king's **r**. H2885
8: 2 And the king took off his **r**, which he H2885
8 *it* with the king's **r**: for the writing which H2885
8 with the king's **r**, may no man reverse. H2885
10 *it* with the king's **r**, and sent letters by H2885
Lk 15:22 a **r** on his hand, and shoes on *his* feet: *G1146*
Jas 2: 2 a man with a gold **r**, in goodly apparel, *G5554*

RINGLEADER
Act 24: 5 and a **r** of the sect of the Nazarenes: *G4414*

RINGS
Ex 25:12 And thou shalt cast four **r** of gold for it, H2885
12 thereof; and two **r** *shall be* in the one H2885
12 of it, and two **r** in the other side of it. H2885
14 And thou shalt put the staves into the **r** H2885
15 The staves shall be in the **r** of the ark: H2885
26 And thou shalt make for it four **r** of H2885
26 gold, and put the **r** in the four corners H2885
27 Over against the border shall the **r** be H2885
26:29 and make their **r** *of* gold *for* places for H2885
27: 4 brasen **r** in the four corners thereof. H2885
7 And the staves shall be put into the **r**, H2885
28:23 breastplate two **r** of gold, and shalt put H2885
23 **r** on the two ends of the breastplate. H2885
24 of gold in the two **r** *which are* on the H2885
26 And thou shalt make two **r** of gold, and H2885
27 And two *other* **r** of gold thou shalt H2885
28 breastplate by the **r** thereof unto the H2885
28 thereof unto the **r** of the ephod with a H2885
30: 4 And two golden **r** shalt thou make to it H2885
35:22 and earrings, and **r**, and tablets, all H2885
36:34 and made their **r** *of* gold *to be* places H2885
37: 3 And he cast for it four **r** of gold, *to be* H2885
3 of it; even two **r** upon the one side of H2885
3 it, and two **r** upon the other side of it. H2885
5 And he put the staves into the **r** by the H2885
13 And he cast for it four **r** of gold, and H2885
13 of gold, and put the **r** upon the four H2885
14 Over against the border were the **r**, the H2885

Ex 37:27 And he made two **r** of gold for it under H2885
38: 5 And he cast four **r** for the four ends of H2885
7 And he put the staves into the **r** on the H2885
39:16 *of* gold, and two gold **r**; and put the two H2885
16 two **r** in the two ends of the breastplate. H2885
17 two **r** on the ends of the breastplate. H2885
19 And they made two **r** of gold, and put H2885
20 And they made two *other* golden **r**, and H2885
21 breastplate by his **r** unto the rings of H2885
21 his rings unto the **r** of the ephod with a H2885
Nu 31:50 and bracelets, **r**, earrings, and tablets, H2885
Est 1: 6 purple to silver **r** and pillars of marble: H1550
Song 5:14 His hands *are as* gold **r** set with the H1550
Isa 3:21 The **r**, and nose jewels, H2885
Ezk 1:18 As for their **r**, they were so high that H1354
18 and their **r** *were* full of eyes round H1354

RINGSTRAKED
Gen 30:35 he goats that were **r** and spotted, and H6124
39 forth cattle **r**, speckled, and spotted. H6124
40 flocks toward the **r**, and all the brown in H6124
31: 8 if he said thus, The **r** shall be thy hire; H6124
8 be thy hire; then bare all the cattle **r**. H6124
10 the cattle *were* **r**, speckled, and grisled. H6124
12 leap upon the cattle *are* **r**, speckled, and H6124

RINNAH
1Ch 4:20 Amnon, and **R**, Ben-hanan, and Tilon. H7441

RINSED
Lev 6:28 it shall be both scoured, and **r** in water. H7857
15:11 and hath not **r** his hands in water, H7857
12 every vessel of wood shall be **r** in water. H7857

RIOT
Tit 1: 6 children not accused of **r** or unruly. *G810*
1Pt 4: 4 the same excess of **r**, speaking evil of *you*: *G810*
2Pt 2:13 it pleasure to **r** in the day time. Spots *G5172*

RIOTING
Ro 13:13 in the day; not in **r** and drunkenness, *G2970*

RIOTOUS
Prv 23:20 Be not among winebibbers; among **r** H2151
28: 7 of **r** *men* shameth his father. H2151
Lk 15:13 there wasted his substance with **r** living. *G811*

RIP
2Ki 8:12 and **r** up their women with child. H1234

RIPE
Gen 40:10 clusters thereof brought forth **r** grapes: H1310
Ex 22:29 *to offer* the first of thy **r** fruits, and of thy
Nu 18:13 *And* whatsoever is first **r** in the land, H1061
Jer 24: 2 figs *that are* first **r**: and the other basket H1073
Joel 3:13 Put ye in the sickle, for the harvest is **r**: H1310
Rev 14:15 to reap; for the harvest of the earth is **r**. *G3583*
18 of the earth; for her grapes are fully **r**. *G187*

RIPENING
Isa 18: 5 and the sour grape is **r** in the flower, he H1580

RIPHATH
Gen 10: 3 Ashkenaz, and **R**, and Togarmah. H7384
1Ch 1: 6 Ashchenaz, and **R**, and Togarmah. H7384

RIPPED
2Ki 15:16 therein that were with child he **r** up. H1234
Hos 13:16 their women with child shall be **r** up. H1234
Am 1:13 because they have **r** up the women with H1234

RISE
Gen 19: 2 feet, and ye shall **r** up early, and go on H7925
31:35 lord that I cannot **r** up before thee; for H6965
Ex 8:20 And the LORD said unto Moses, **R** up H7925
9:13 And the LORD said unto Moses, **R** up H7925
12:31 night, and said, **R** up, *and* get you forth H6965
21:19 If he **r** again, and walk abroad upon H6965
Lev 19:32 Thou shalt **r** up before the hoary head, H6965
Nu 10:35 that Moses said, **R** up, LORD, and let H6965
22:20 come to call thee, **r** up, *and* go with H6965
23:18 his parable, and said, **R** up, Balak, and H6965
24 Behold, the people shall **r** up as a great H6965
24:17 a Sceptre shall **r** out of Israel, and shall H6965
Dt 2:13 Now **r** up, *said I*, and get you over the H6965
24 **R** ye up, take your journey, and pass H6965
19:11 in wait for him, and **r** up against him, H6965
15 One witness shall not **r** up against a H6965
16 If a false witness **r** up against any man H6965
Dt 28: 7 thine enemies that **r** up against thee to H6965
29:22 children that shall **r** up after you, and H6965
31:16 this people will **r** up, and go a whoring H6965
32:38 offerings? let them **r** up and help you, H6965
33:11 loins of them that **r** against him, and of H6965
11 that hate him, that they **r** not again. H6965
Jos 8: 7 Then ye shall **r** up from the ambush, H6965
18: 4 and they shall **r**, and go through the H6965
Jdg 8:21 Then Zebah and Zalmunna said, **R** H6965
9:33 is up, thou shalt **r** early, and set upon H7925
20:38 flame with smoke **r** up out of the city. H5927
1Sa 22:13 that he should **r** against me, to lie in H6965
24: 7 them not to **r** against Saul. But Saul H6965
29:10 Wherefore now **r** up early in the H7925
2Sa 12:21 was dead, thou didst **r** and eat bread. H6965
18:32 king, and all that **r** against thee to do H6965
2Ki 16: 7 king of Israel, which **r** up against me. H6965
Neh 2:18 they said, Let us **r** up and build. So they H6965
Job 20:27 and the earth shall **r** up against him. H6965
30:12 Upon *my* right *hand* **r** the youth; they H6965
Ps 3: 1 many *are* they that **r** up against me. H6965
17: 7 *thee* from those that **r** up *against them*. H6965
18:38 able to **r**: they are fallen under my feet. H6965
48 above those that **r** up against me: thou H6965
27: 3 **r** against me, in this *will* I *be* confident. H6965
35:11 False witnesses did **r** up; they laid to H6965
36:12 cast down, and shall not be able to **r**. H6965
41: 8 *now* that he lieth he shall **r** up no more. H6965
44: 5 tread them under that **r** up against us. H6965
59: 1 me from them that **r** up against me. H6965
74:23 tumult of those that **r** up against thee H6965
92:11 of the wicked that **r** up against me. H6965
94:16 Who will **r** up for me against the H6965
119:62 At midnight I will **r** to give thanks unto H6965
127: 2 *It is* vain for you to **r** up early, to sit up H6965
139:21 with those that **r** up against thee? H8618
140:10 into deep pits, that they **r** not up again. H6965
Prv 24:22 For their calamity shall **r** suddenly; H6965
28:12 but when the wicked **r**, a man is hidden. H6965
28 When the wicked **r**, men hide H6965
Ecc 10: 4 If the spirit of the ruler **r** up against H5927
12: 4 is low, and he shall **r** up at the voice of H6965
Song 2:10 My beloved spake, and said unto me, **R** H6965
3: 2 I will **r** now, and go about the city in H6965
Isa 5:11 Woe unto them that **r** up early in the H7925
14:21 that they do not **r**, nor possess the land, H6965
22 For I will **r** up against them, saith the H6965
24:20 it; and it shall fall, and not **r** again. H6965
26:14 they shall not **r**: therefore hast thou H6965
28:21 For the LORD shall **r** up as *in* mount H6965
32: 9 **R** up, ye women that are at ease; hear H6965
33:10 Now will I **r**, saith the LORD; now will I H6965
43:17 they shall not **r**: they are extinct, they H6965
54:17 every tongue *that* shall **r** against thee in H6965
58:10 then shall thy light **r** in obscurity, and H2224
Jer 25:27 spue, and fall, and **r** no more, because H6965
37:10 *yet* should they **r** up every man in his H6965
47: 2 Thus saith the LORD; Behold, waters **r** H5927
49:14 against her, and **r** up to the battle. H6965
51: 1 **r** up against me, a destroying wind; H6965
64 sink, and shall not **r** from the evil that I H6965
Lam 1:14 *from whom* I am not able to **r** up. H6965
Dan 7:24 and another shall **r** after them; and he H6966
Am 5: 2 she shall no more **r**: she is forsaken H6965
7: 9 waste; and I will **r** against the house of H6965
8: 8 and it shall **r** up wholly as a flood; H5927
14 they shall fall, and never **r** up again. H6965
9: 5 and it shall **r** up wholly like a flood; H5927
Oba 1 ye, and let us **r** up against her in battle. H6965
Nah 1: 9 shall not **r** up the second time. H6965
Hab 2: 7 Shall they not **r** up suddenly that shall H6965
Zep 3: 8 until the day that I **r** up to the prey: for H6965
Zec 14:13 **r** up against the hand of his neighbour. H5927
Mt 5:45 he maketh his sun to **r** on the evil and on *G393*
10:21 the children shall **r** up against *their* *G1881*
12:41 The men of Nineveh shall **r** in judgment *G450*
42 The queen of the south shall **r** up in the *G1453*
20:19 *him*: and the third day he shall **r** again. *G450*
24: 7 For nation shall **r** against nation, and *G1453*
11 And many false prophets shall **r**, and *G1453*
26:46 **R**, let us be going: behold, he is at hand *G1453*
27:63 yet alive, After three days I will **r** again. *G1453*
Mk 3:26 And if Satan **r** up against himself, and *G450*
4:27 And should sleep, and **r** night and day, *G1453*
8:31 be killed, and after three days **r** again. *G450*
9:31 that he is killed, he shall **r** the third day. *G450*
10:34 him: and the third day he shall **r** again. *G450*
49 Be of good comfort, **r**; he calleth thee. *G1453*
12:23 when they shall **r**, whose wife shall she *G450*
Mk 12:25 For when they shall **r** from the dead, *G450*
26 And as touching the dead, that they **r**: *G1453*
13: 8 For nation shall **r** against nation, and *G1453*
12 and children shall **r** up against *their* *G1881*
22 prophets shall **r**, and shall shew signs *G1453*
14:42 **R** up, let us go; lo, he that betrayeth me *G1453*
Lk 5:23 forgiven thee; or to say, **R** up and walk? *G1453*
6: 8 withered hand, **R** up, and stand forth *G1453*
11: 7 with me in bed; I cannot **r** and give thee. *G450*
8 I say unto you, Though he will not **r** and *G450*
8 **r** and give him as many as he needeth. *G450*
31 The queen of the south shall **r** up in the *G1453*
32 The men of Nineve shall **r** up in the *G450*
12:54 When ye see a cloud **r** out of the west, *G393*
18:33 death: and the third day he shall **r** again. *G450*
21:10 Then said he unto them, Nation shall **r** *G1453*
22:46 And said unto them, Why sleep ye? **r** and *G450*
24: 7 be crucified, and the third day **r** again. *G450*
46 and to **r** from the dead the third day: *G450*
Jn 5: 8 Jesus saith unto him, **R**, take up thy *G1453*
11:23 Jesus saith unto her, Thy brother shall **r** *G450*
24 I know that he shall **r** again in the *G450*
20: 9 that he must **r** again from the dead. *G450*
Act 3: 6 Jesus Christ of Nazareth **r** up and walk. *G1453*
10:13 And there came a voice to him, **R**, Peter; *G450*
26:16 But **r**, and stand upon thy feet: for I have *G450*
23 the first that should **r** from the dead, and *G386*
Ro 15:12 and he that shall **r** to reign over the *G450*
1Co 15:15 not up, if so be that the dead **r** not. *G1453*
16 For if the dead **r** not, then is not Christ *G1453*
29 dead, if the dead **r** not at all? why are *G1453*
32 it me, if the dead **r** not? let us eat and *G1453*
1Th 4:16 God: and the dead in Christ shall **r** first: *G450*
Heb 7:11 another priest should **r** after the order of *G450*
Rev 11: 1 angel stood, saying, **R**, and measure the *G1453*
13: 1 sea, and saw a beast **r** up out of the sea, *G305*

RISEN
Gen 19:23 The sun was **r** upon the earth when Lot H3318
Ex 22: 3 If the sun be **r** upon him, *there shall be* H2224
Nu 32:14 And, behold, ye are **r** up in your H6965
Jdg 9:18 And ye are **r** up against my father's H6965
Ru 2:15 And when she was **r** up to glean, Boaz H6965
1Sa 25:29 Yet a man is **r** to pursue thee, and to H6965
2Sa 14: 7 And, behold, the whole family is **r** H6965
1Ki 8:20 he spake, and I am **r** up in the room of H6965
2Ki 6:15 the man of God was **r** early, and gone H6965
2Ch 6:10 spoken: for I am **r** up in the room of H6965
13: 6 son of David, is **r** up, and hath rebelled H6965
21: 4 Now when Jehoram was **r** up to the H6965
Ps 20: 8 fallen: but we are **r**, and stand upright. H6965
27:12 for false witnesses are **r** up against me, H6965
54: 3 For strangers are **r** up against me, and H6965
86:14 O God, the proud are **r** against me, and H6965
Isa 60: 1 the glory of the LORD is **r** upon thee. H2224
Ezk 7:11 Violence is **r** up into a rod of H6965
47: 5 the waters were **r**, waters to swim in, a H1342
Mic 2: 8 Even of late my people is **r** up as an H6965
Mt 11:11 there hath not **r** a greater than John *G1453*
14: 2 the Baptist; he is **r** from the dead; and *G1453*
17: 9 the Son of man be **r** again from the dead. *G450*
26:32 But after I am **r** again, I will go before *G1453*
27:64 the people, He is **r** from the dead: so *G1453*
28: 6 He is not here: for he is **r**, as he said. *G1453*
7 his disciples that he is **r** from the dead; *G1453*
Mk 6:14 the Baptist was **r** from the dead, and *G1453*
16 I beheaded: he is **r** from the dead. *G1453*
9: 9 till the Son of man were **r** from the dead. *G450*
14:28 But after that I am **r**, I will go before *G1453*
16: 6 crucified: he is **r**; he is not here: behold *G1453*
9 Now when *Jesus* was **r** early the first *day* *G450*
14 which had seen him after he was **r**. *G1453*
Lk 7:16 a great prophet is **r** up among us; and, *G1453*
9: 7 of some, that John was **r** from the dead; *G1453*
8 that one of the old prophets was **r** again. *G450*
19 that one of the old prophets is **r** again. *G450*
13:25 When once the master of the house is **r** *G1453*
24: 6 He is not here, but is **r**: remember how *G1453*
34 Saying, The Lord is **r** indeed, and hath *G1453*
Jn 2:22 When therefore he was **r** from the *G1453*
21:14 after that he was **r** from the dead. *G1453*
Act 17: 3 have suffered, and **r** again from the *G450*
Ro 8:34 yea rather, that is **r** again, who is even *G1453*
1Co 15:13 of the dead, then is Christ not **r**: *G1453*
14 And if Christ be not **r**, then *is* our *G1453*
20 But now is Christ **r** from the dead, *and* *G1453*
Col 2:12 also ye are **r** with *him* through the *G4891*
3: 1 If ye then be **r** with Christ, seek those *G4891*
Jas 1:11 For the sun is no sooner **r** with a burning *G393*

RISEST

Dt 6: 7 thou liest down, and when thou **r** up. H6965
11:19 thou liest down, and when thou **r** up. H6965

RISETH

Dt 22:26 death: for as when a man **r** against his H6965
Jos 6:26 the LORD, that **r** up and buildeth this H6965
2Sa 23: 4 *when* the sun **r**, *even* a morning without H2224
Job 9: 7 Which commandeth the sun, and it **r** H2224
14:12 So man lieth down, and **r** not: till the H6965
24:22 he **r** up, and no *man* is sure of life. H6965
27: 7 **r** up against me as the unrighteous. H6965
31:14 What then shall I do when God **r** up? H6965
Prv 24:16 seven times, and **r** up again: but the H6965
31:15 She **r** also while it is yet night, and H6965
Isa 47:11 from whence it **r**: and mischief shall fall H7837
Jer 46: 8 Egypt **r** up like a flood, and *his* waters H5927
Mic 7: 6 the daughter **r** up against her mother, H6965
Jn 13: 4 He **r** from supper, and laid aside his *G1453*

RISING

Lev 13: 2 the skin of his flesh a **r**, a scab, or bright H7613
10 and, behold, *if* the **r** *be* white in the H7613
10 and *there be* quick raw flesh in the **r**; H7613
19 boil there be a white **r**, or a bright spot, H7613
28 dark; it *is* a **r** of the burning, and H7613
43 and, behold, *if* the **r** of the sore *be* white H7613
14:56 And for a **r**, and for a scab, and for a H7613
Nu 2: 3 And on the east side toward the **r** of the H4217
Jos 12: 1 Jordan toward the **r** of the sun, from H4217
2Ch 36:15 by his messengers, **r** up betimes, and H7925
Neh 4:21 **r** of the morning till the stars appeared. H5927
Job 16: 8 **r** up in me beareth witness to my face. H6965
24: 5 to their work; **r** betimes for a prey: the H7836
14 The murderer **r** with the light killeth H6965
Ps 50: 1 the earth from the **r** of the sun unto the H4217
113: 3 From the **r** of the sun unto the going H4217
Prv 27:14 friend with a loud voice, **r** early in the H7925
30:31 a king, against whom *there is* no **r** up. H510
Isa 41:25 come: from the **r** of the sun shall he call H4217
45: 6 That they may know from the **r** of the H4217
59:19 his glory from the **r** of the sun. When H4217
60: 3 and kings to the brightness of thy **r**. H2225
Jer 7:13 and I spake unto you, **r** up early and H7925
25 daily **r** up early and sending *them*: H7925
11: 7 unto this day, **r** early and protesting, H7925
25: 3 spoken unto you, **r** early and speaking; H7925
4 the prophets, **r** early and sending *them*; H7925
26: 5 unto you, both **r** up early, and sending H7925
29:19 the prophets, **r** up early and sending H7925
32:33 I taught them, **r** up early and teaching H7925
35:14 spoken unto you, **r** early and speaking; H7925
15 the prophets, **r** up early and sending H7925
44: 4 the prophets, **r** early and sending *them*, H7925
Lam 3:63 Behold their sitting down, and their **r** H7012
Mal 1:11 For from the **r** of the sun even unto the H4217
Mk 1:35 And in the morning, **r** up a great while *GH50*
9:10 what the **r** from the dead should mean. *G450*
16: 2 unto the sepulchre at the **r** of the sun. *G393*
Lk 2:34 is set for the fall and **r** again of many in *G386*

RISSAH

Nu 33:21 from Libnah, and pitched at **R**. H7446
22 And they journeyed from **R**, and H7446

RITES

Nu 9: 3 to all the **r** of it, and according H2708

RITHMAH

Nu 33:18 from Hazeroth, and pitched in **R**. H7575
19 And they departed from **R**, and pitched H7575

RIVER

Gen 2:10 And a **r** went out of Eden to water the H5104
13 And the name of the second **r** *is* Gihon: H5104
14 And the name of the third **r** *is* H5104
14 Assyria. And the fourth **r** *is* Euphrates. H5104
15:18 this land, from the **r** of Egypt unto the H5104
18 unto the great **r**, the river Euphrates: H5104
18 unto the great river, the **r** Euphrates: H5104
31:21 and passed over the **r**, and set his face H5104
36:37 Rehoboth *by* the **r** reigned in his stead. H5104
41: 1 and, behold, he stood by the **r**. H2975
2 And, behold, there came up out of the **r** H2975
3 after them out of the **r**, ill favoured and H2975
3 the *other* kine upon the brink of the **r**. H2975
17 behold, I stood upon the bank of the **r**: H2975
18 And, behold, there came up out of the **r** H2975
Ex 1:22 shall cast into the **r**, and every daughter H2975
Ex 2: 5 wash *herself* at the **r**; and her maidens H2975
4: 9 of the water of the **r**, and pour *it* upon H2975
9 takest out of the **r** shall become blood H2975
7:17 the **r**, and they shall be turned to blood. H2975
18 And the fish that *is* in the **r** shall die, H2975
18 shall die, and the **r** shall stink; and the H2975
18 shall lothe to drink of the water of the **r**. H2975
20 waters that *were* in the **r**, in the sight of H2975
20 that *were* in the **r** were turned to blood. H2975
21 And the fish that *was* in the **r** died; and H2975
21 the river died; and the **r** stank, and the H2975
21 of the water of the **r**; and there was H2975
24 round about the **r** for water to drink; H2975
24 could not drink of the water of the **r**. H2975
25 after that the LORD had smitten the **r**. H2975
8: 3 And the **r** shall bring forth frogs H2975
9 *that* they may remain in the **r** only? H2975
11 people; they shall remain in the **r** only. H2975
17: 5 the **r**, take in thine hand, and go. H2975
23:31 the desert unto the **r**: for I will deliver H5104
Nu 22: 5 which *is* by the **r** of the land of the H5104
34: 5 Azmon unto the **r** of Egypt, and the H5158
Dt 1: 7 unto the great **r**, the river Euphrates. H5104
7 unto the great river, the **r** Euphrates. H5104
2:24 and pass over the **r** Arnon: behold, I H5158
36 *is* by the brink of the **r** of Arnon, and H5158
36 city that *is* by the **r**, even unto Gilead, H5158
37 any place of the **r** Jabbok, nor unto the H5158
3: 8 the **r** of Arnon unto mount Hermon; H5158
12 which *is* by the **r** Arnon, and half H5158
16 even unto the **r** Arnon half the valley, H5158
16 even unto the **r** Jabbok, *which is* the H5158
4:48 by the bank of the **r** Arnon, even unto H5158
11:24 and Lebanon, from the **r**, the river H5104
24 from the river, the **r** Euphrates, even H5104
Jos 1: 4 unto the great **r**, the river Euphrates, H5104
4 the great river, the **r** Euphrates, all the H5104
12: 1 the sun, from the **r** Arnon unto mount H5158
2 the bank of the **r** Arnon, and from the H5158
2 from the middle of the **r**, and from half H5158
2 even unto the **r** Jabbok, *which is* the H5158
13: 9 the bank of the **r** Arnon, and the city H5158
9 in the midst of the **r**, and all the plain of H5158
16 on the bank of the **r** Arnon, and the city H5158
16 of the **r**, and all the plain by Medeba; H5158
15: 4 went out unto the **r** of Egypt; and the H5158
7 the south side of the **r**: and the border H5158
47 villages, unto the **r** of Egypt, and the H5158
16: 8 westward unto the **r** Kanah; and the H5158
17: 9 And the coast descended unto the **r** H5158
9 southward of the **r**: these cities of H5158
9 north side of the **r**, and the outgoings of H5158
19:11 reached to the **r** that *is* before Jokneam; H5158
Jdg 4: 7 And I will draw unto thee to the **r** H5158
13 of the Gentiles unto the **r** of Kishon. H5158
5:21 The **r** of Kishon swept them away, that H5158
21 away, that ancient **r**, the river Kishon. O H5158
21 ancient river, the **r** Kishon. O my soul, H5158
2Sa 8: 3 recover his border at the **r** Euphrates. H5104
10:16 *were* beyond the **r**: and they came to H5104
17:13 draw it into the **r**, until there be not one H5158
24: 5 of the **r** of Gad, and toward Jazer: H5158
1Ki 4:21 from the **r** unto the land of the H5104
24 on this side the **r**, from Tiphsah even H5104
24 on this side the **r**: and he had peace on H5104
8:65 Hamath unto the **r** of Egypt, before the H5158
14:15 them beyond the **r**, because they have H5104
2Ki 10:33 the **r** Arnon, even Gilead and Bashan. H5158
17: 6 in Habor *by* the **r** of Gozan, and in the H5104
18:11 in Habor *by* the **r** of Gozan, and in the H5104
23:29 of Assyria to the **r** Euphrates: and king H5104
24: 7 taken from the **r** of Egypt unto the river H5158
7 of Egypt unto the **r** Euphrates all that H5104
1Ch 1:48 Rehoboth by the **r** reigned in his stead. H5104
5: 9 from the **r** Euphrates: because H5104
26 and to the **r** Gozan, unto this day. H5104
18: 3 his dominion by the **r** Euphrates. H5104
19:16 *were* beyond the **r**: and Shophach the H5104
2Ch 7: 8 in of Hamath unto the **r** of Egypt. H5158
9:26 the kings from the **r** even unto the land H5104
Ezr 4:10 on this side the **r**, and at such a time. H5103
11 on this side the **r**, and at such a time. H5103
16 shalt have no portion on this side the **r**. H5103
17 beyond the **r**, Peace, and at such a time. H5103
20 beyond the **r**; and toll, tribute, and H5103
5: 3 on this side the **r**, and Shethar-boznai, H5103
6 on this side the **r**, and Shethar-boznai, H5103
6 side the **r**, sent unto Darius the king: H5103
6: 6 beyond the **r**, Shethar-boznai, and H5103
Ezr 6: 6 *are* beyond the **r**, be ye far from thence: H5103
8 tribute beyond the **r**, forthwith expenses H5103
13 on this side the **r**, Shethar-boznai, and H5103
7:21 *are* beyond the **r**, that whatsoever Ezra H5103
25 *are* beyond the **r**, all such as know the H5103
8:15 And I gathered them together to the **r** H5104
21 Then I proclaimed a fast there, at the **r** H5104
31 Then we departed from the **r** of Ahava H5104
36 on this side the **r**: and they furthered H5104
Neh 2: 7 beyond the **r**, that they may convey H5104
9 beyond the **r**, and gave them the king's H5104
3: 7 of the governor on this side the **r**. H5104
Job 40:23 Behold, he drinketh up a **r**, *and* hasteth H5104
Ps 36: 8 them drink of the **r** of thy pleasures. H5158
46: 4 *There is* a **r**, the streams whereof shall H5104
65: 9 it with the **r** of God, *which* is full H6388
72: 8 from the **r** unto the ends of the earth. H5104
80:11 the sea, and her branches unto the **r**. H5104
105:41 out; they ran in the dry places *like* a **r**. H5104
Isa 7:20 by them beyond the **r**, by the king of H5104
8: 7 the waters of the **r**, strong and many, H5104
11:15 his hand over the **r**, and shall smite it in H5104
19: 5 and the **r** shall be wasted and dried up. H5104
23: 3 the harvest of the **r**, *is* her revenue; and H2975
10 Pass through thy land as a **r**, O H2975
27:12 the channel of the **r** unto the stream of H5104
48:18 thy peace been as a **r**, and thy H5104
66:12 peace to her like a **r**, and the glory of the H5104
Jer 2:18 of Assyria, to drink the waters of the **r**? H5104
17: 8 out her roots by the **r**, and shall not see H3105
46: 2 Egypt, which was by the **r** Euphrates in H5104
6 toward the north by the **r** Euphrates. H5104
10 the north country by the **r** Euphrates. H5104
Lam 2:18 run down like a **r** day and night: give H5158
Ezk 1: 1 the captives by the **r** of Chebar, *that* the H5104
3 the Chaldeans by the **r** Chebar; and the H5104
3:15 that dwelt by the **r** of Chebar, and I sat H5104
23 the **r** of Chebar: and I fell on my face. H5104
10:15 creature that I saw by the **r** of Chebar. H5104
20 of Israel by the **r** of Chebar; and I knew H5104
22 which I saw by the **r** of Chebar, their H5104
29: 3 hath said, My **r** *is* mine own, and I H2975
9 said, The **r** *is* mine, and I have made *it*. H2975
43: 3 the **r** Chebar; and I fell upon my face. H5104
47: 5 *and it was* a **r** that I could not pass H5158
5 in, a **r** that could not be passed over. H5158
6 me to return to the brink of the **r**. H5158
7 at the bank of the **r** *were* very many H5158
9 thing shall live whither the **r** cometh. H5158
12 And by the **r** upon the bank thereof, on H5158
19 *in* Kadesh, the **r** to the great sea. And H5158
48:28 *and* to the **r** toward the great sea. H5158
Dan 8: 2 in a vision, and I was by the **r** of Ulai. H180
3 stood before the **r** a ram which had *two* H180
6 standing before the **r**, and ran unto him H180
10: 4 side of the great **r**, which *is* Hiddekel; H5104
12: 5 of the bank of the **r**, and the other on H2975
5 other on that side of the bank of the **r**. H2975
6 the waters of the **r**, How long *shall it be* H2975
7 the waters of the **r**, when he held up his H2975
Am 6:14 of Hemath unto the **r** of the wilderness. H5158
Mic 7:12 even to the **r**, and from sea to sea, H5104
Zec 9:10 from the **r** *even* to the ends of the earth. H5104
10:11 all the deeps of the **r** shall dry up: and H2975
Mk 1: 5 in the **r** of Jordan, confessing their sins. *G4215*
Act 16:13 out of the city by a **r** side, where prayer *G4215*
Rev 9:14 are bound in the great **r** Euphrates. *G4215*
16:12 upon the great **r** Euphrates; and the *G4215*
22: 1 And he shewed me a pure **r** of water of *G4215*
2 either side of the **r**, *was there* the tree of *G4215*

RIVERS

Ex 7:19 upon their **r**, and upon their ponds, H2975
8: 5 streams, over the **r**, and over the ponds, H2975
Lev 11: 9 the seas, and in the **r**, them shall ye eat. H5158
10 seas, and in the **r**, of all that move in the H5158
Dt 10: 7 to Jotbath, a land of **r** of waters. H5158
2Ki 5:12 *Are* not Abana and Pharpar, **r** of H5104
19:24 I dried up all the **r** of besieged places. H2975
Job 20:17 He shall not see the **r**, the floods, the H6390
28:10 He cutteth out **r** among the rocks; and H2975
29: 6 and the rock poured me out **r** of oil; H6388
Ps 1: 3 a tree planted by the **r** of water, that H6388
74:15 and the flood: thou driedst up mighty **r**. H5104
78:16 and caused waters to run down like **r**. H5104
44 And had turned their **r** into blood; and H2975
89:25 in the sea, and his right hand in the **r**. H5104
107:33 He turneth **r** into a wilderness, and the H5104
119:136 **R** of waters run down mine eyes, H6388

Ps 137: 1 By the **r** of Babylon, there we sat down, H5104
Prv 5:16 abroad, *and* **r** of waters in the streets. H6388
21: 1 the LORD, *as* the **r** of water: he turneth H6388
Ecc 1: 7 All the **r** run into the sea; yet the sea *is* H5158
7 the **r** come, thither they return again. H5158
Song 5:12 His eyes *are* as *the eyes* of doves by the **r** H650
Isa 7:18 part of the **r** of Egypt, and for the H2975
18: 1 which *is* beyond the **r** of Ethiopia: H5104
2 down, whose land the **r** have spoiled! H5104
7 whose land the **r** have spoiled, to the H5104
19: 6 And they shall turn the **r** far away; *and* H5104
30:25 every high hill, **r** *and* streams of waters H6388
32: 2 from the tempest; as **r** of water in a dry H6388
33:21 us a place of broad **r** *and* streams; H5104
37:25 dried up all the **r** of the besieged places. H2975
41:18 I will open **r** in high places, and H5104
42:15 **r** islands, and I will dry up the pools. H5104
43: 2 thee; and through the **r**, they shall not H5104
19 in the wilderness, *and* **r** in the desert. H5104
20 wilderness, *and* **r** in the desert, to give H5104
44:27 the deep, Be dry, and I will dry up thy **r**: H5104
47: 2 leg, uncover the thigh, pass over the **r**. H5104
50: 2 the sea, I make the **r** a wilderness: their H5104
Jer 31: 9 to walk by the **r** of waters in a straight H5158
46: 7 flood, whose waters are moved as the **r**? H5104
8 are moved like the **r**; and he saith, I will H5104
Lam 3:48 Mine eye runneth down with **r** of water H6388
Ezk 6: 3 to the hills, to the **r**, and to the valleys; H650
29: 3 in the midst of his **r**, which hath said, H2975
4 the fish of thy **r** to stick unto thy scales, H2975
4 of the midst of thy **r**, and all the fish of H2975
4 fish of thy **r** shall stick unto thy scales. H2975
5 all the fish of thy **r**: thou shalt fall upon H2975
10 and against thy **r**, and I will make the H2975
30:12 And I will make the **r** dry, and sell the H2975
31: 4 up on high with her **r** running round H5104
4 her little **r** unto all the trees of the field. H8585
12 broken by all the **r** of the land; and all H650
32: 2 forth with thy **r**, and troubledst the H5104
2 with thy feet, and fouledst their **r**. H5104
6 and the **r** shall be full of thee. H650
14 **r** to run like oil, saith the Lord GOD. H5104
34:13 of Israel by the **r**, and in all the inhabited H650
35: 8 and in all thy **r**, shall they fall that are H650
36: 4 to the hills, to the **r**, and to the valleys, to H650
6 to the hills, to the **r**, and to the valleys, H650
47: 9 whithersoever the **r** shall come, shall H5158
Joel 1:20 unto thee: for the **r** of waters are dried H650
3:18 milk, and all the **r** of Judah shall flow H650
Mic 6: 7 ten thousands of **r** of oil? shall I give H5158
Nah 1: 4 drieth up all the **r**: Bashan languisheth, H5104
2: 6 The gates of the **r** shall be opened, and H5104
3: 8 situate among the **r**, *that had* the waters H2975
Hab 3: 8 Was the LORD displeased against the **r**? H5104
8 thine anger against the **r**? *was* thy wrath H5104
9 Thou didst cleave the earth with **r**. H5104
Zep 3:10 From beyond the **r** of Ethiopia my H5104
Jn 7:38 of his belly shall flow **r** of living water. G4215
Rev 8:10 the **r**, and upon the fountains of waters; G4215
16: 4 out his vial upon the **r** and fountains of G4215

RIVER'S
Ex 2: 3 she laid *it* in the flags by the **r** brink. H2975
5 along by the **r** side; and when she H2975
7:15 shalt stand by the **r** brink against he H2975
Nu 24: 6 as gardens by the **r** side, as the trees of H5104

RIZPAH
2Sa 3: 7 whose name *was* **R**, the daughter of H7532
21: 8 But the king took the two sons of **R** the H7532
10 And **R** the daughter of Aiah took H7532
11 And it was told David what **R** the H7532

ROAD
1Sa 27:10 have ye made a **r** to day? And David H6584

ROAR
1Ch 16:32 Let the sea **r**, and the fulness thereof: let H7481
Ps 46: 3 *Though* the waters thereof **r** *and* be H1993
74: 4 Thine enemies **r** in the midst of thy H7580
96:11 let the sea **r**, and the fulness thereof. H7481
98: 7 Let the sea **r**, and the fulness thereof; H7481
104:21 The young lions **r** after their prey, and H7580
Isa 5:29 a lion, they shall **r** like young lions: yea, H7580
29 yea, they shall **r**, and lay hold of the H5098
30 And in that day they shall **r** against H5098
42:13 **r**; he shall prevail against his enemies. H6873
59:11 We **r** all like bears, and mourn sore like H1993
Jer 5:22 they **r**, yet can they not pass over it? H1993
25:30 The LORD shall **r** from on high, and H7580
30 he shall mightily **r** upon his habitation; H7580
31:35 **r**; The LORD of hosts *is* his name: H1993
50:42 their voice shall **r** like the sea, and they H1993
51:38 They shall **r** together like lions: they H7580
55 her waves do **r** like great waters, a H1993
Hos 11:10 the LORD: he shall **r** like a lion: when H7580
10 a lion: when he shall **r**, then the children H7580
Joel 3:16 The LORD also shall **r** out of Zion, and H7580
Am 1: 2 And he said, The LORD will **r** from H7580
3: 4 Will a lion **r** in the forest, when he hath H7580

ROARED
Jdg 14: 5 behold, a young lion **r** against him. H7580
Ps 38: 8 I am feeble and sore broken: I have **r** H7580
Isa 51:15 **r**: The LORD of hosts *is* his name. H1993
Jer 2:15 The young lions **r** upon him, *and* H7580
Am 3: 8 The lion hath **r**, who will not fear? the H7580

ROARETH
Job 37: 4 After it a voice **r**: he thundereth with the H7580
Jer 6:23 no mercy; their voice **r** like the sea; and H1993
Rev 10: 3 as *when* a lion **r**: and when he had G3455

ROARING
Job 4:10 The **r** of the lion, and the voice of the H7581
Ps 22: 1 me, *and from* the words of my **r**? H7581
13 mouths, *as* a ravening and a **r** lion. H7580
32: 3 old through my **r** all the day long. H7581
Prv 19:12 The king's wrath *is* as the **r** of a lion; H5099
20: 2 The fear of a king *is* as the **r** of a lion: H5099
28:15 *As* a **r** lion, and a ranging bear; *so is* a H5098
Isa 5:29 Their **r** *shall be* like a lion, they shall H7581
30 them like the **r** of the sea: and if *one* H5100
31: 4 and the young lion **r** on his prey, when H1897
Ezk 19: 7 the fulness thereof, by the noise of his **r**. H7581
22:25 thereof, like a **r** lion ravening the prey; H7580
Zep 3: 3 Her princes within her *are* **r** lions; her H7580
Zec 11: 3 a voice of the **r** of young lions; for the H7581
Lk 21:25 with perplexity; the sea and the waves **r**; G2278
1Pt 5: 8 the devil, as a **r** lion, walketh about, G5612

ROARINGS
Job 3:24 my **r** are poured out like the waters. H7581

ROAST
Ex 12: 8 the flesh in that night, **r** with fire, and H6748
9 all with water, but **r** *with* fire; his head H6748
Dt 16: 7 And thou shalt **r** and eat *it* in the place H1310
1Sa 2:15 Give flesh to **r** for the priest; for he H6740
Isa 44:16 flesh; he roasteth **r**, and is satisfied: yea, H6748

ROASTED
2Ch 35:13 And they **r** the passover with fire H1310
Isa 44:19 thereof; I have **r** flesh, and eaten *it*: and H6740
Jer 29:22 whom the king of Babylon **r** in the fire; H7033

ROASTETH
Prv 12:27 The slothful *man* **r** not that which he H2760
Isa 44:16 he eateth flesh; he **r** roast, and is H6740

ROB
Lev 19:13 neighbour, neither **r** *him*: the wages of H1497
26:22 you, which shall **r** you of your children, H7921
1Sa 23: 1 Keilah, and they **r** the threshingfloors. H8154
Prv 22:22 **R** not the poor, because he *is* poor: H1497
Isa 10: 2 prey, and *that* they may **r** the fatherless! H962
17:14 spoil us, and the lot of them that **r** us. H962
Ezk 39:10 spoiled them, and **r** those that robbed H962
Mal 3: 8 Will a man **r** God? Yet ye have robbed H6906

ROBBED
Jdg 9:25 and they **r** all that came along H1497
2Sa 17: 8 minds, as a bear **r** of her whelps in the H7909
Ps 119:61 The bands of the wicked have **r** me: *but* H5749
Prv 17:12 Let a bear **r** of her whelps meet a man, H7909
Isa 10:13 people, and have **r** their treasures, and H8154
42:22 But this *is* a people **r** and spoiled; *they* H962
Jer 50:37 *is* upon her treasures; and they shall be **r**. H962
Ezk 33:15 again that he had **r**, walk in the statutes H1500
39:10 those that **r** them, saith the Lord GOD. H962
Mal 3: 8 Will a man rob God? Yet ye have **r** me. H6906
8 have we **r** thee? In tithes and offerings. H6906
9 ye have **r** me, *even* this whole nation. H6906
2Co 11: 8 I **r** other churches, taking wages *of* G4813

ROBBER
Job 5: 5 the **r** swalloweth up their substance. H6782
18: 9 *and* the **r** shall prevail against him. H6782
Ezk 18:10 If he beget a son *that is* a **r**, a shedder of H6530
Jn 10: 1 other way, the same is a thief and a **r**. G3027
18:40 but Barabbas. Now Barabbas was a **r**. G3027

ROBBERS
Job 12: 6 The tabernacles of **r** prosper, and they H7703
Isa 42:24 and Israel to the **r**? did not the LORD, he H962
Jer 7:11 become a den of **r** in your eyes? Behold, H6530
Ezk 7:22 for the **r** shall enter into it, and defile it. H6530
Dan 11:14 the south: also the **r** of thy people shall H6530
Hos 6: 9 And as troops of **r** wait for a man, *so* the
7: 1 in, *and* the troop of **r** spoileth without.
Oba 5 If thieves came to thee, if **r** by night, H7703
Jn 10: 8 and **r**: but the sheep did not hear them. G3027
Act 19:37 which are neither **r** of churches, nor yet G2417
2Co 11:26 waters, *in* perils of **r**, *in* perils by *mine* G3027

ROBBERY
Ps 62:10 not vain in **r**: if riches increase, set H1498
Prv 21: 7 The **r** of the wicked shall destroy them; H7701
Isa 61: 8 For I the LORD love judgment, I hate **r** H1498
Ezk 22:29 and exercised **r**, and have vexed the H1498
Am 3:10 store up violence and **r** in their palaces. H7701
Nah 3: 1 full of lies *and* **r**; the prey departeth not; H6563
Php 2: 6 thought it not **r** to be equal with God: G725

ROBBETH
Prv 28:24 Whoso **r** his father or his mother, and H1497

ROBE
Ex 28: 4 and an ephod, and a **r**, and a broidered H4598
31 And thou shalt make the **r** of the ephod H4598
34 upon the hem of the **r** round about. H4598
29: 5 the coat, and the **r** of the ephod, and H4598
39:22 And he made the **r** of the ephod *of* H4598
23 in the midst of the **r**, as the hole of an H4598
24 And they made upon the hems of the **r** H4598
25 the hem of the **r**, round about between H4598
26 the hem of the **r** to minister *in*; as the H4598
Lev 8: 7 him with the **r**, and put the ephod upon H4598
1Sa 18: 4 And Jonathan stripped himself of the **r** H4598
24: 4 and cut off the skirt of Saul's **r** privily. H4598
11 see the skirt of thy **r** in my hand: for in H4598
11 off the skirt of thy **r**, and killed thee not, H4598
1Ch 15:27 And David *was* clothed with a **r** of fine H4598
Job 29:14 my judgment *was* as a **r** and a diadem. H4598
Isa 22:21 And I will clothe him with thy **r**, and H3801
61:10 me with the **r** of righteousness, as H4598
Jna 3: 6 and he laid his **r** from him, and covered H155
Mic 2: 8 ye pull off the **r** with the garment from H145
Mt 27:28 him, and put on him a scarlet **r**. G5511
31 him, they took the **r** off from him, and G5511
Lk 15:22 forth the best **r**, and put *it* on him; and G4749
23:11 **r**, and sent him again to Pilate. G2066
Jn 19: 2 head, and they put on him a purple **r**, G2440
5 and the purple **r**. And *Pilate* saith unto G2440

ROBES
2Sa 13:18 her: for with such **r** were the king's H4598
1Ki 22:10 having put on their **r**, in a void place in H899
30 but put thou on thy **r**. And the king of H899
2Ch 18: 9 clothed in *their* **r**, and they sat in a void H899
29 but put thou on thy **r**. So the king of H899
Ezk 26:16 and lay away their **r**, and put off their H4598
Lk 20:46 to walk in long **r**, and love greetings in G4749
Rev 6:11 And white **r** were given unto every one G4749
7: 9 with white **r**, and palms in their hands; G4749
13 in white **r**? and whence came they? G4749
14 have washed their **r**, and made them G4749

ROBOAM
Mt 1: 7 And Solomon begat **R**; and Roboam G4497
7 And Solomon begat Roboam; and **R** G4497

ROCK
Ex 17: 6 there upon the **r** in Horeb; and thou H6697
6 shalt smite the **r**, and there shall come H6697
33:21 by me, and thou shalt stand upon a **r**: H6697
22 in a clift of the **r**, and will cover thee H6697
Nu 20: 8 speak ye unto the **r** before their eyes; H5553
8 water out of the **r**: so thou shalt give the H5553
10 before the **r**, and he said unto them, H5553
10 must we fetch you water out of this **r**? H5553
11 rod he smote the **r** twice: and the water H5553
24:21 and thou puttest thy nest in a **r**. H5553
Dt 8:15 thee forth water out of the **r** of flint; H6697
32: 4 *He is* the **R**, his work *is* perfect: for all H6697
13 of the **r**, and oil out of the flinty rock; H5553
13 of the rock, and oil out of the flinty **r**; H6697

Dt 32:15 lightly esteemed the **R** of his salvation. H6697
18 Of the **R** *that* begat thee thou art H6697
30 to flight, except their **R** had sold them, H6697
31 For their **r** *is* not as our Rock, even our H6697
31 For their rock *is* not as our **R**, even our H6697
37 gods, *their* **r** in whom they trusted, H6697
Jdg 1:36 to Akrabbim, from the **r**, and upward. H5553
6:20 lay *them* upon this **r**, and pour out the H5553
21 up fire out of the **r**, and consumed the H6697
26 the top of this **r**, in the ordered place, H4581
7:25 Oreb upon the **r** Oreb, and Zeeb they H6697
13:19 offered *it* upon a **r** unto the LORD: and H6697
15: 8 and dwelt in the top of the **r** Etam. H5553
11 to the top of the **r** Etam, and said to H5553
13 cords, and brought him up from the **r**. H5553
20:45 unto the **r** of Rimmon: and they H5553
47 unto the **r** Rimmon, and abode H5553
47 abode in the **r** Rimmon four months. H5553
21:13 that *were* in the **r** Rimmon, and to call H5553
1Sa 2: 2 neither *is there* any **r** like our God. H6697
14: 4 *there was* a sharp **r** on the one side, H5553
4 side, and a sharp **r** on the other side: H5553
23:25 came down into a **r**, and abode in the H5553
2Sa 21:10 it for her upon the **r**, from the beginning H6697
22: 2 And he said, The LORD *is* my **r**, and my H5553
3 The God of my **r**; in him will I trust: *he* H6697
32 LORD? and who *is* a **r**, save our God? H6697
47 The LORD liveth; and blessed *be* my **r**; H6697
47 be the God of the **r** of my salvation. H6697
23: 3 The God of Israel said, the **R** of Israel H6697
1Ch 11:15 went down to the **r** to David, into the H6697
2Ch 25:12 unto the top of the **r**, and cast them H5553
12 **r**, that they all were broken in pieces. H5553
Neh 9:15 for them out of the **r** for their thirst, H5553
Job 14:18 and the **r** is removed out of his place. H6697
18: 4 shall the **r** be removed out of his place? H6697
19:24 an iron pen and lead in the **r** for ever! H6697
24: 8 and embrace the **r** for want of a shelter. H6697
28: 9 He putteth forth his hand upon the **r**; he H2496
29: 6 and the **r** poured me out rivers of oil; H6697
39: 1 wild goats of the **r** bring forth? *or* canst H5553
28 She dwelleth and abideth on the **r**, upon H5553
28 the crag of the **r**, and the strong place. H5553
Ps 18: 2 The LORD *is* my **r**, and my fortress, and H5553
31 the LORD? or who *is* a **r** save our God? H6697
46 The LORD liveth; and blessed *be* my **r**; H6697
27: 5 he hide me; he shall set me up upon a **r**. H6697
28: 1 Unto thee will I cry, O LORD my **r**; be H6697
31: 2 **r**, for an house of defence to save me. H6697
3 For thou *art* my **r** and my fortress; H5553
40: 2 upon a **r**, *and* established my goings. H5553
42: 9 I will say unto God my **r**, Why hast thou H5553
61: 2 lead me to the **r** *that* is higher than I. H6697
62: 2 He only *is* my **r** and my salvation; *he is* H6697
6 He only *is* my **r** and my salvation: *he is* H6697
7 and my glory: the **r** of my strength, *and* H6697
71: 3 me; for thou *art* my **r** and my fortress. H5553
78:16 He brought streams also out of the **r**, H5553
20 Behold, he smote the **r**, that the waters H6697
35 **r**, and the high God their redeemer. H6697
81:16 out of the **r** should I have satisfied thee. H6697
89:26 my God, and the **r** of my salvation. H6697
92:15 *is* upright: *he is* my **r**, and *there is* no H6697
94:22 and my God *is* the **r** of my refuge. H6697
95: 1 a joyful noise to the **r** of our salvation. H6697
105:41 He opened the **r**, and the waters gushed H6697
114: 8 Which turned the **r** *into* a standing H6697
Prv 30:19 a serpent upon a **r**; the way of a ship in H6697
Song 2:14 O my dove, *that art* in the clefts of the **r**, H5553
Isa 2:10 Enter into the **r**, and hide thee in the H6697
8:14 and for a **r** of offence to both the H6697
10:26 of Midian at the **r** of Oreb: and *as* his H6697
17:10 been mindful of the **r** of thy strength, H6697
22:16 graveth an habitation for himself in a **r**? H5553
32: 2 the shadow of a great **r** in a weary land. H5553
42:11 inhabitants of the **r** sing, let them shout H5553
48:21 to flow out of the **r** for them: he clave H6697
21 the **r** also, and the waters gushed out. H6697
51: 1 look unto the **r** *whence* ye are hewn, H6697
Jer 5: 3 than a **r**; they have refused to return. H5553
13: 4 and hide it there in a hole of the **r**. H5553
18:14 *cometh* from the **r** of the field? *or* shall H6697
21:13 of the valley, *and* **r** of the plain, saith H6697
23:29 hammer *that* breaketh the **r** in pieces? H5553
48:28 and dwell in the **r**, and be like the dove H5553
49:16 in the clefts of the **r**, that holdest the H5553
Ezk 24: 7 it upon the top of a **r**; she poured it not H5553
8 top of a **r**, that it should not be covered. H5553
26: 4 her, and make her like the top of a **r**. H5553
Ezk 26:14 And I will make thee like the top of a **r**: H5553
Am 6:12 Shall horses run upon the **r**? will *one* H5553
Oba 3 in the clefts of the **r**, whose habitation *is* H5553
Mt 7:24 man, which built his house upon a **r**: *G4073*
25 it fell not: for it was founded upon a **r**. *G4073*
16:18 and upon this **r** I will build my church; *G4073*
27:60 hewn out in the **r**: and he rolled a great *G4073*
Mk 15:46 was hewn out of a **r**, and rolled a stone *G4073*
Lk 6:48 foundation on a **r**: and when the flood *G4073*
48 shake it: for it was founded upon a **r**. *G4073*
8: 6 And some fell upon a **r**; and as soon as *G4073*
13 They on the **r** *are they*, which, when *G4073*
Ro 9:33 and **r** of offence: and whosoever *G4073*
1Co 10: 4 of that spiritual **R** that followed them: *G4073*
4 followed them: and that **R** was Christ. *G4073*
1Pt 2: 8 And a stone of stumbling, and a **r** of *G4073*

ROCKS
Nu 23: 9 For from the top of the **r** I see him, and H6697
1Sa 13: 6 and in **r**, and in high places, and in pits. H5553
24: 2 his men upon the **r** of the wild goats. H6697
1Ki 19:11 brake in pieces the **r** before the LORD; H5553
Job 28:10 He cutteth out rivers among the **r**; and H6697
30: 6 *in* caves of the earth, and *in* the **r**. H3710
Ps 78:15 He clave the **r** in the wilderness, and H6697
104:18 the wild goats; *and* the **r** for the conies. H5553
Prv 30:26 folk, yet make they their houses in the **r**; H5553
Isa 2:19 And they shall go into the holes of the **r**, H6697
21 To go into the clefts of the **r**, and into H6697
21 the tops of the ragged **r**, for fear of the H5553
7:19 and in the holes of the **r**, and upon all H5553
33:16 the munitions of **r**: bread shall be given H5553
57: 5 in the valleys under the clifts of the **r**? H5553
Jer 4:29 climb up upon the **r**: every city *shall be* H3710
16:16 every hill, and out of the holes of the **r**. H5553
51:25 **r**, and will make thee a burnt mountain. H5553
Nah 1: 6 fire, and the **r** are thrown down by him. H6697
Mt 27:51 and the earth did quake, and the **r** rent; *G4073*
Act 27:29 have fallen upon **r**, they cast four *G5138*
Rev 6:15 the dens and in the **r** of the mountains; *G4073*
16 And said to the mountains and **r**, Fall *G4073*

ROD
Ex 4: 2 *is* that in thine hand? And he said, A **r**. H4294
4 it, and it became a **r** in his hand: H4294
17 And thou shalt take this **r** in thine H4294
20 Moses took the **r** of God in his hand. H4294
7: 9 Aaron, Take thy **r**, and cast *it* before H4294
10 cast down his **r** before Pharaoh, and H4294
12 For they cast down every man his **r**, and H4294
12 but Aaron's **r** swallowed up their rods. H4294
15 he come; and the **r** which was turned to H4294
17 I will smite with the **r** that *is* in mine H4294
19 Aaron, Take thy **r**, and stretch out thine H4294
20 he lifted up the **r**, and smote the waters H4294
8: 5 hand with thy **r** over the streams, over H4294
16 Stretch out thy **r**, and smite the dust of H4294
17 his hand with his **r**, and smote the dust H4294
9:23 And Moses stretched forth his **r** toward H4294
10:13 And Moses stretched forth his **r** over H4294
14:16 But lift thou up thy **r**, and stretch out H4294
17: 5 of Israel; and thy **r**, wherewith thou H4294
9 the hill with the **r** of God in mine hand. H4294
21:20 his maid, with a **r**, and he die under his H7626
Lev 27:32 passeth under the **r**, the tenth shall be H7626
Nu 17: 2 one of them a **r** according to the house H4294
2 thou every man's name upon his **r**. H4294
3 name upon the **r** of Levi: for one rod H4294
3 of Levi: for one **r** *shall be* for the head H4294
5 *that* the man's **r**, whom I shall choose, H4294
6 gave him a **r** apiece, for each prince H4294
6 the **r** of Aaron *was* among their rods. H4294
8 and, behold, the **r** of Aaron for the H4294
9 they looked, and took every man his **r**. H4294
10 Bring Aaron's **r** again before the H4294
20: 8 Take the **r**, and gather thou the H4294
9 And Moses took the **r** from before the H4294
11 hand, and with his **r** he smote the rock H4294
1Sa 14:27 the end of the **r** that *was* in his hand, H4294
43 with the end of the **r** that *was* in mine H4294
2Sa 7:14 him with the **r** of men, and with the H7626
Job 9:34 Let him take his **r** away from me, and H7626
21: 9 fear, neither *is* the **r** of God upon them. H7626
Ps 2: 9 Thou shalt break them with a **r** of iron; H7626
23: 4 thy **r** and thy staff they comfort me. H7626
74: 2 of old; the **r** of thine inheritance, H7626
89:32 the **r**, and their iniquity with stripes. H7626
110: 2 The LORD shall send the **r** of thy H4294
125: 3 For the **r** of the wicked shall not rest H7626
Prv 10:13 is found: but a **r** *is* for the back of him H7626
13:24 He that spareth his **r** hateth his son: H7626
14: 3 In the mouth of the foolish *is* a **r** of H2415
22: 8 vanity: and the **r** of his anger shall fail. H7626
15 of a child; *but* the **r** of correction shall H7626
23:13 beatest him with the **r**, he shall not die. H7626
14 Thou shalt beat him with the **r**, and H7626
26: 3 for the ass, and a **r** for the fool's back. H7626
29:15 The **r** and reproof give wisdom: but a H7626
Isa 9: 4 his shoulder, the **r** of his oppressor, as H7626
10: 5 O Assyrian, the **r** of mine anger, and H7626
15 it? as if the **r** should shake *itself* against H7626
24 smite thee with a **r**, and shall lift up his H7626
26 of Oreb: and *as* his **r** *was* upon the sea, H4294
11: 1 And there shall come forth a **r** out of H2415
4 the earth with the **r** of his mouth, and H7626
14:29 because the **r** of him that smote thee H7626
28:27 with a staff, and the cummin with a **r**. H7626
30:31 be beaten down, *which* smote with a **r**. H7626
Jer 1:11 And I said, I see a **r** of an almond tree. H4731
10:16 and Israel *is* the **r** of his inheritance: H7626
48:17 strong staff broken, *and* the beautiful **r**! H4731
51:19 and *Israel is* the **r** of his inheritance: H7626
Lam 3: 1 seen affliction by the **r** of his wrath. H7626
Ezk 7:10 **r** hath blossomed, pride hath budded. H4294
11 Violence is risen up into a **r** of H4294
19:14 And fire is gone out of a **r** of her H4294
14 she hath no strong **r** *to be* a sceptre to H4294
20:37 And I will cause you to pass under the **r**, H7626
21:10 the **r** of my son, *as* every tree. H7626
13 contemn even the **r**? it shall be no *more*, H7626
Mic 5: 1 judge of Israel with a **r** upon the cheek. H7626
6: 9 ye the **r**, and who hath appointed it. H4294
7:14 Feed thy people with thy **r**, the flock of H7626
1Co 4:21 unto you with a **r**, or in love, and *in* the *G4464*
Heb 9: 4 and Aaron's **r** that budded, and the *G4464*
Rev 2:27 And he shall rule them with a **r** of iron; *G4464*
11: 1 me a reed like unto a **r**: and the angel *G4464*
12: 5 rule all nations with a **r** of iron: and her *G4464*
19:15 shall rule them with a **r** of iron: and he *G4464*

RODE
Gen 24:61 damsels, and they **r** upon the camels, H7392
Jdg 10: 4 And he had thirty sons that **r** on thirty H7392
12:14 nephews, that **r** on threescore and ten H7392
1Sa 25:20 And it was *so, as* she **r** on the ass, that H7392
42 And Abigail hasted, and arose, and **r** H7392
30:17 men, which **r** upon camels, and fled. H7392
2Sa 18: 9 And Absalom **r** upon a mule, and the H7392
22:11 And he **r** upon a cherub, and did fly: H7392
1Ki 13:13 saddled him the ass: and he **r** thereon, H7392
18:45 rain. And Ahab **r**, and went to Jezreel. H7392
2Ki 9:16 So Jehu **r** in a chariot, and went to H7392
25 when I and thou **r** together after Ahab H7392
Neh 2:12 with me, save the beast that I **r** upon. H7392
Est 8:14 *So* the posts that **r** upon mules *and* H7392
Ps 18:10 And he **r** upon a cherub, and did fly: H7392

RODS
Gen 30:37 And Jacob took him **r** of green poplar, H4731
37 the white appear which *was* in the **r**. H4731
38 And he set the **r** which he had pilled H4731
39 And the flocks conceived before the **r**, H4731
41 that Jacob laid the **r** before the eyes of H4731
41 that they might conceive among the **r**. H4731
Ex 7:12 but Aaron's rod swallowed up their **r**. H4294
Nu 17: 2 fathers twelve **r**: write thou every man's H4294
6 *even* twelve **r**: and the rod of Aaron H4294
6 the rod of Aaron *was* among their **r**. H4294
7 And Moses laid up the **r** before the H4294
9 And Moses brought out all the **r** from H4294
Ezk 19:11 And she had strong **r** for the sceptres of H4294
12 her fruit: her strong **r** were broken and H4294
2Co 11:25 Thrice was I beaten with **r**, once was I *G4463*

ROE
2Sa 2:18 Asahel *was as* light of foot as a wild **r**. H6643
Prv 5:19 hind and pleasant **r**; let her breasts H3280
6: 5 Deliver thyself as a **r** from the hand *of* H6643
Song 2: 9 My beloved is like a **r** or a young hart: H6643
17 and be thou like a **r** or a young hart H6643
8:14 be thou like to a **r** or to a young hart H6643
Isa 13:14 And it shall be as the chased **r**, and as a H6643

ROEBUCK
Dt 12:15 thereof, as of the **r**, and as of the hart. H6643
22 Even as the **r** and the hart is eaten, so H6643
14: 5 The hart, and the **r**, and the fallow deer, H6643
15:22 *eat it* alike, as the **r**, and as the hart. H6643

ROEBUCKS
1Ki 4:23 and **r**, and fallowdeer, and fatted fowl. H6643

ROES
1Ch 12: 8 as swift as the **r** upon the mountains; H6643
Song 2: 7 Jerusalem, by the **r**, and by the hinds of H6643
3: 5 Jerusalem, by the **r**, and by the hinds of H6643
4: 5 Thy two breasts *are* like two young **r** H6646
7: 3 Thy two breasts *are* like two young **r** H6646

ROGEL See EN-ROGEL.

ROGELIM
2Sa 17:27 and Barzillai the Gileadite of **R**, H7274
19:31 came down from **R**, and went over H7274

ROHGAH
1Ch 7:34 And the sons of Shamer; Ahi, and **R**, H7303

ROI See LAHAI-ROI.

ROLL
Gen 29: 8 and *till* they **r** the stone from the well's H1556
Jos 10:18 And Joshua said, **R** great stones upon H1556
1Sa 14:33 **r** a great stone unto me this day. H1556
Ezr 6: 2 of the Medes, a **r**, and therein *was* a H4040
Isa 8: 1 Take thee a great **r**, and write in it with H1549
Jer 36: 2 Take thee a **r** of a book, and write H4039
4 spoken unto him, upon a **r** of a book. H4039
6 Therefore go thou, and read in the **r**, H4039
14 in thine hand the **r** wherein thou hast H4039
14 the **r** in his hand, and came unto them. H4039
20 but they laid up the **r** in the chamber of H4039
21 So the king sent Jehudi to fetch the **r**: H4039
23 until all the **r** was consumed in the H4039
25 burn the **r**: but he would not hear them. H4039
27 had burned the **r**, and the words which H4039
28 Take thee again another **r**, and write in H4039
28 were in the first **r**, which Jehoiakim the H4039
29 hast burned this **r**, saying, Why hast H4039
32 Then took Jeremiah another **r**, and gave H4039
51:25 upon thee, and **r** thee down from the H1556
Ezk 2: 9 me; and, lo, a **r** of a book *was* therein; H4039
3: 1 **r**, and go speak unto the house of Israel. H4039
2 mouth, and he caused me to eat that **r**. H4039
3 bowels with this **r** that I give thee. Then H4039
Mic 1:10 house of Aphrah **r** thyself in the dust. H6428
Zec 5: 1 eyes, and looked, and behold a flying **r**. H4039
2 I see a flying **r**; the length thereof *is* H4039
Mk 16: 3 Who shall **r** us away the stone from *G617*

ROLLED
Gen 29: 3 gathered: and they **r** the stone from the H1556
10 went near, and **r** the stone from the H1556
Jos 5: 9 This day have I **r** away the reproach of H1556
Job 30:14 desolation they **r** themselves *upon me*. H1556
Isa 9: 5 and garments **r** in blood; but *this* shall H1556
34: 4 heavens shall be **r** together as a scroll: H1556
Mt 27:60 in the rock: and he **r** a great stone to *G4351*
28: 2 and came and **r** back the stone from *G617*
Mk 15:46 out of a rock, and **r** a stone unto the *G4351*
16: 4 stone was **r** away: for it was very great. *G617*
Lk 24: 2 And they found the stone **r** away from *G617*
Rev 6:14 a scroll when it is **r** together; and every *G1507*

ROLLER
Ezk 30:21 be healed, to put a **r** to bind it, to make H2848

ROLLETH
Prv 26:27 that **r** a stone, it will return upon him. H1556

ROLLING
Isa 17:13 and like a **r** thing before the whirlwind. H1534

ROLLS
Ezr 6: 1 made in the house of the **r**, where the H5609

ROMAMTI-EZER
1Ch 25: 4 Giddalti, and **R**, Joshbekashah, H7320
31 The four and twentieth to **R**, *he*, his H7320

ROMAN
Act 22:25 a man that is a **R**, and uncondemned? *G4514*
26 what thou doest: for this man is a **R**. *G4514*
27 him, Tell me, art thou a **R**? He said, Yea. *G4514*
29 a **R**, and because he had bound him. *G4514*
23:27 having understood that he was a **R**. *G4514*

ROMANS
Jn 11:48 on him: and the **R** shall come and take *G4514*
Act 16:21 to receive, neither to observe, being **R**. *G4514*
37 being **R**, and have cast *us* into *G4514*
38 when they heard that they were **R**. *G4514*
25:16 the manner of the **R** to deliver any man *G4514*
28:17 from Jerusalem into the hands of the **R**. *G4514*

ROME
Act 2:10 and strangers of **R**, Jews and proselytes, *G4514*
18: 2 to depart from **R**:) and came unto them. *G4516*
19:21 I have been there, I must also see **R**. *G4516*
23:11 so must thou bear witness also at **R**. *G4516*
28:14 seven days: and so we went toward **R**. *G4516*
16 And when we came to **R**, the centurion *G4516*
Ro 1: 7 To all that be in **R**, beloved of God, *G4516*
15 the gospel to you that are at **R** also. *G4516*
2Ti 1:17 But, when he was in **R**, he sought me *G4516*

ROOF
Gen 19: 8 came they under the shadow of my **r**. H6982
Dt 22: 8 battlement for thy **r**, that thou bring not H1406
Jos 2: 6 But she had brought them up to the **r** of H1406
6 which she had laid in order upon the **r**. H1406
8 she came up unto them upon the **r**; H1406
Jdg 16:27 *were* upon the **r** about three thousand H1406
2Sa 11: 2 walked upon the **r** of the king's house: H1406
2 house: and from the **r** he saw a woman H1406
18:24 went up to the **r** over the gate unto the H1406
Neh 8:16 one upon the **r** of his house, and in H1406
Job 29:10 tongue cleaved to the **r** of their mouth. H2441
Ps 137: 6 cleave to the **r** of my mouth; if I prefer H2441
Song 7: 9 And the **r** of thy mouth like the best H2441
Lam 4: 4 cleaveth to the **r** of his mouth for thirst: H2441
Ezk 3:26 cleave to the **r** of thy mouth, that thou H2441
40:13 He measured then the gate from the **r** H1406
13 little chamber to the **r** of another: the H1406
Mt 8: 8 come under my **r**: but speak the word *G4721*
Mk 2: 4 uncovered the **r** where he was: and *G4721*
Lk 7: 6 that thou shouldest enter under my **r**: *G4721*

ROOFS
Jer 19:13 houses upon whose **r** they have burned H1406
32:29 upon whose **r** they have offered incense H1406

ROOM
Gen 24:23 I pray thee: is there **r** *in* thy father's H4725
25 provender enough, and **r** to lodge in. H4725
31 the house, and **r** for the camels. H4725
26:22 LORD hath made **r** for us, and we shall H7337
2Sa 19:13 before me continually in the **r** of Joab. H8478
1Ki 2:35 of Jehoiada in his **r** over the host: and H8478
35 did the king put in the **r** of Abiathar. H8478
5: 1 him king in the **r** of his father: for H8478
5 thy throne in thy **r**, he shall build an H8478
8:20 I am risen up in the **r** of David my H8478
19:16 shalt thou anoint *to be* prophet in thy **r**. H8478
2Ki 15:25 and he killed him, and reigned in his **r**. H8478
23:34 Josiah king in the **r** of Josiah his father, H8478
2Ch 6:10 I am risen up in the **r** of David my H8478
26: 1 king in the **r** of his father Amaziah. H8478
Ps 31: 8 thou hast set my feet in a large **r**. H4800
80: 9 Thou preparedst **r** before it, and didst
Prv 18:16 A man's gift maketh **r** for him, and H7337
Mal 3:10 *there shall* not *be* **r** enough *to receive it*.
Mt 2:22 in Judaea in the **r** of his father Herod, *G473*
Mk 2: 2 that there was no **r** to receive *them*, no, *G5362*
14:15 And he will shew you a large upper **r** *G508*
Lk 2: 7 there was no **r** for them in the inn. *G5117*
12:17 I have no **r** where to bestow my fruits?
14: 8 in the highest **r**; lest a more honourable *G4411*
9 begin with shame to take the lowest **r**. *G5117*
10 in the lowest **r**; that when he that bade *G5117*
22 hast commanded, and yet there is **r**. *G5117*
22:12 And he shall shew you a large upper **r** *G508*
Act 1:13 up into an upper **r**, where abode both *G5253*
24:27 came into Felix' **r**: and Felix, willing to *G1240*
1Co 14:16 he that occupieth the **r** of the unlearned *G5117*

ROOMS
Gen 6:14 Make thee an ark of gopher wood; **r** H7064
1Ki 20:24 of his place, and put captains in their **r**: H8478
1Ch 4:41 and dwelt in their **r**: because *there was* H8478
Mt 23: 6 And love the uppermost **r** at feasts, and *G4411*
Mk 12:39 and the uppermost **r** at feasts: *G4411*
Lk 14: 7 chose out the chief **r**; saying unto them, *G4411*
20:46 synagogues, and the chief **r** at feasts; *G4411*

ROOT
Dt 29:18 a **r** that beareth gall and wormwood; H8328
Jdg 5:14 Out of Ephraim *was there* a **r** of them H8328
1Ki 14:15 and he shall **r** up Israel out of this H5428
2Ki 19:30 **r** downward, and bear fruit upward. H8328
Job 5: 3 I have seen the foolish taking **r**: but H8327
14: 8 Though the **r** thereof wax old in the H8328
19:28 the **r** of the matter is found in me? H8328
29:19 My **r** *was* spread out by the waters, and H8328
31:12 and would **r** out all mine increase. H8327
Ps 52: 5 place, and **r** thee out of the land H8327
80: 9 it to take deep **r**, and it filled the land. H8327
Prv 12: 3 **r** of the righteous shall not be moved. H8328
12 but the **r** of the righteous yieldeth *fruit*. H8328
Isa 5:24 the chaff, *so* their **r** shall be as H8328
11:10 And in that day there shall be a **r** of H8328
14:29 out of the serpent's **r** shall come forth a H8328
30 and I will kill thy **r** with famine, and he H8328
27: 6 of Jacob to take **r**: Israel shall blossom H8327
37:31 **r** downward, and bear fruit upward: H8328
40:24 shall not take **r** in the earth: and he H8327
53: 2 plant, and as a **r** out of a dry ground: H8328
Jer 1:10 over the kingdoms, to **r** out, and to pull H5428
12: 2 they have taken **r**: they grow, yea, they H8327
Ezk 31: 7 branches: for his **r** was by great waters. H8328
Hos 9:16 Ephraim is smitten, their **r** is dried up, H8328
Mal 4: 1 shall leave them neither **r** nor branch. H8328
Mt 3:10 And now also the axe is laid unto the **r** *G4491*
13: 6 they had no **r**, they withered away. *G4491*
21 Yet hath he not **r** in himself, but dureth *G4491*
29 tares, ye **r** up also the wheat with them. *G1610*
Mk 4: 6 because it had no **r**, it withered away. *G4491*
17 And have no **r** in themselves, and so *G4491*
Lk 3: 9 And now also the axe is laid unto the **r** *G4491*
8:13 and these have no **r**, which for a while *G4491*
17: 6 thou plucked up by the **r**, and be thou *G1610*
Ro 11:16 if the **r** *be* holy, so *are* the branches. *G4491*
17 of the **r** and fatness of the olive tree; *G4491*
18 thou bearest not the **r**, but the root thee. *G4491*
18 bearest not the root, but the **r** thee. *G4491*
15:12 There shall be a **r** of Jesse, and he that *G4491*
1Ti 6:10 For the love of money is the **r** of all evil: *G4491*
Heb 12:15 grace of God; lest any **r** of bitterness *G4491*
Rev 5: 5 the tribe of Juda, the **R** of David, hath *G4491*
22:16 churches. I am the **r** and the offspring *G4491*

ROOTED
Dt 29:28 And the LORD **r** them out of their land H5428
Job 18:14 His confidence shall be **r** out of his H5423
31: 8 eat; yea, let my offspring be **r** out. H8327
Prv 2:22 the transgressors shall be **r** out of it. H5255
Zep 2: 4 the noon day, and Ekron shall be **r** up. H6131
Mt 15:13 Father hath not planted, shall be **r** up. *G1610*
Eph 3:17 that ye, being **r** and grounded in love, *G4492*
Col 2: 7 **R** and built up in him, and stablished *G4492*

ROOTS
2Ch 7:20 Then will I pluck them up by the **r** out H5428
Job 8:17 His **r** are wrapped about the heap, *and* H8328
18:16 His **r** shall be dried up beneath, and H8328
28: 9 he overturneth the mountains by the **r**. H8328
30: 4 bushes, and juniper **r** *for* their meat. H8328
Isa 11: 1 and a Branch shall grow out of his **r**: H8328
Jer 17: 8 spreadeth out her **r** by the river, and H8328
Ezk 17: 6 him, and the **r** thereof were under H8328
7 vine did bend her **r** toward him, and H8328
9 he not pull up the **r** thereof, and cut off H8328
9 people to pluck it up by the **r** thereof. H8328
Dan 4:15 Nevertheless leave the stump of his **r** in H8330
23 the stump of the **r** thereof in the earth, H8330
26 stump of the tree **r**; thy kingdom shall H8330
7: 8 plucked up by the **r**: and, behold, in this H6132
11: 7 But out of a branch of her **r** shall *one* H8328
Hos 14: 5 lily, and cast forth his **r** as Lebanon. H8328
Am 2: 9 from above, and his **r** from beneath. H8328
Mk 11:20 saw the fig tree dried up from the **r**. *G4491*
Jude 12 fruit, twice dead, plucked up by the **r**; *G1610*

ROPE
Isa 5:18 vanity, and sin as it were with a cart **r**: H5688

ROPES
Jdg 16:11 me fast with new **r** that never were H5688
12 Delilah therefore took new **r**, and bound H5688
2Sa 17:13 all Israel bring **r** to that city, and we H2256
1Ki 20:31 on our loins, and **r** upon our heads, H2256
32 loins, and *put* **r** on their heads, and H2256
Act 27:32 Then the soldiers cut off the **r** of the *G4979*

R

ROSE
Gen 4: 8 in the field, that Cain **r** up against Abel H6965
18:16 And the men **r** up from thence, and H6965
19: 1 Lot seeing *them* **r** up to meet them; and H6965
20: 8 Therefore Abimelech **r** early in the H7925
21:14 And Abraham **r** up early in the H7925
32 then Abimelech **r** up, and Phichol the H6965
22: 3 And Abraham **r** up early in the H7925
3 offering, and **r** up, and went unto the H6965
19 men, and they **r** up and went together H6965
24:54 all night; and they **r** up in the morning, H6965
25:34 eat and drink, and **r** up, and went his H6965
26:31 And they **r** up betimes in the morning, H7925
28:18 And Jacob **r** up early in the morning, H7925
31:17 Then Jacob **r** up, and set his sons and H6965
21 So he fled with all that he had; and he **r** H6965
55 And early in the morning Laban **r** up, H7925
32:22 And he **r** up that night, and took his H6965
31 And as he passed over Penuel the sun **r** H2224
37:35 And all his sons and all his daughters **r** H6965
43:15 Benjamin; and **r** up, and went down H6965
46: 5 And Jacob **r** up from Beer-sheba: and H6965
Ex 10:23 They saw not one another, neither **r** H6965
12:30 And Pharaoh **r** up in the night, he, and H6965
15: 7 them that **r** up against thee: thou H6965
24: 4 of the LORD, and **r** up early in the H7925
13 And Moses **r** up, and his minister H6965
32: 6 And they **r** up early on the morrow, H7925
6 to eat and to drink, and **r** up to play. H6965
33: 8 *that* all the people **r** up, and stood H6965
10 door: and all the people **r** up and H6965
34: 4 the first; and Moses **r** up early in the H7925
Nu 14:40 And they **r** up early in the morning, H7925
16: 2 And they **r** up before Moses, with H6965
25 And Moses **r** up and went unto Dathan H6965
22:13 And Balaam **r** up in the morning, and H6965
14 And the princes of Moab **r** up, and they H6965
21 And Balaam **r** up in the morning, and H6965
24:25 And Balaam **r** up, and went and H6965
25: 7 priest, saw *it*, he **r** up from among the H6965
Dt 33: 2 from Sinai, and **r** up from Seir unto H2224
Jos 3: 1 And Joshua **r** early in the morning; and H7925
16 above stood *and* **r** up upon an heap H6965
6:12 And Joshua **r** early in the morning, and H7925
15 seventh day, that they **r** early about the H7925
7:16 So Joshua **r** up early in the morning, H7925
8:10 And Joshua **r** up early in the morning, H7925
14 that they hasted and **r** up early, and the H7925
Jdg 6:21 cakes; and there **r** up fire out of the H7925
38 And it was so: for he **r** up early on the H7925
7: 1 *were* with him, **r** up early, and pitched H7925
9:34 And Abimelech **r** up, and all the people H6965
35 and Abimelech **r** up, and the people H6965
43 he **r** up against them, and smote them. H6965
19: 5 morning, that he **r** up to depart: and H6965
7 And when the man **r** up to depart, his H6965
9 And when the man **r** up to depart, he, H6965
10 that night, but he **r** up and departed, H6965
27 And her lord **r** up in the morning, and H6965
28 man **r** up, and gat him unto his place. H6965
20: 5 And the men of Gibeah **r** against me, H6965
19 And the children of Israel **r** up in the H6965
33 And all the men of Israel **r** up out of H6965
21: 4 that the people **r** early, and built there H7925
Ru 3:14 morning: and she **r** up before one could H6965
1Sa 1: 9 So Hannah **r** up after they had eaten in H6965
19 And they **r** up in the morning early, H7925
15:12 And when Samuel **r** early to meet Saul H7925
16:13 So Samuel **r** up, and went to Ramah. H6965
17:20 And David **r** up early in the morning, H7925
24: 7 Saul. But Saul **r** up out of the cave, and H6965
28:25 they **r** up, and went away that night. H6965
29:11 So David and his men **r** up early to H7925
2Sa 15: 2 And Absalom **r** up early, and stood H7925
18:31 day of all them that **r** up against thee. H6965
22:40 battle: them that **r** up against me hast H6965
49 above them that **r** up against me: thou H6965
1Ki 1:49 and **r** up, and went every man his way. H6965
2:19 And the king **r** up to meet her, and H6965
3:21 And when I **r** in the morning to give my H6965
21:16 dead, that Ahab **r** up to go down to the H6965
2Ki 3:22 And they **r** up early in the morning, H7925
24 Israel, the Israelites **r** up and smote the H6965
7: 5 And they **r** up in the twilight, to go unto H6965
8:21 with him: and he **r** by night, and smote H6965
2Ch 20:20 And they **r** early in the morning, and H7925
21: 9 with him: and he **r** up by night, and H6965
26:19 the leprosy even **r** up in his forehead H2224
28:15 by name **r** up, and took the captives, H6965
2Ch 29:20 Then Hezekiah the king **r** early, and H7925
Ezr 1: 5 Then **r** up the chief of the fathers of H6965
5: 2 Then **r** up Zerubbabel the son of H6965
10: 6 Then Ezra **r** up from before the house H6965
Neh 3: 1 Then Eliashib the high priest **r** up with H6965
4:14 And I looked, and **r** up, and said unto H6965
Job 1: 5 them, and **r** up early in the morning, H7925
Ps 18:39 under me those that **r** up against me. H6965
124: 2 on our side, when men **r** up against us: H6965
Song 2: 1 I *am* the **r** of Sharon, *and* the lily of the H2261
5: 5 I **r** up to open to my beloved; and my H6965
Isa 35: 1 shall rejoice, and blossom as the **r**. H2261
Jer 26:17 Then **r** up certain of the elders of the H6965
Lam 3:62 The lips of those that **r** up against me, H6965
Dan 3:24 was astonied, and **r** up in haste, *and* H6965
8:27 days; afterward I **r** up, and did the H6965
Jna 1: 3 But Jonah **r** up to flee unto Tarshish H6965
4: 7 when the morning **r** the next day, and H5927
Zep 3: 7 **r** early, *and* corrupted all their doings. H7925
Mk 10:50 And he, casting away his garment, **r**, and G450
Lk 4:29 And **r** up, and thrust him out of the city, G450
5:25 And immediately he **r** up before them, G450
28 And he left all, **r** up, and followed him. G450
16:31 persuaded, though one **r** from the dead. G450
22:45 And when he **r** up from prayer, and was G450
24:33 And they **r** up the same hour, and G450
Jn 11:31 saw Mary, that she **r** up hastily and went G450
Act 5:17 Then the high priest **r** up, and all they G450
36 For before these days **r** up Theudas, G450
37 After this man **r** up Judas of Galilee in G450
10:41 drink with him after he **r** from the dead. G450
14:20 about him, he **r** up, and came into the G450
15: 5 But there **r** up certain of the sect of the G1817
7 disputing, Peter **r** up, and said unto G450
16:22 And the multitude **r** up together G4911
26:30 And when he had thus spoken, the king **r** G450
Ro 14: 9 For to this end Christ both died, and **r**, G450
1Co 10: 7 down to eat and drink, and **r** up to play. G450
15: 4 And that he was buried, and that he **r** G1453
12 Now if Christ be preached that he **r** G1453
2Co 5:15 him which died for them, and **r** again. G1453
1Th 4:14 For if we believe that Jesus died and **r** G450
Rev 19: 3 And her smoke **r** up for ever and ever. G305

ROSH
Gen 46:21 and **R**, Muppim, and Huppim, and Ard. H7220

ROT
Nu 5:21 thy thigh to **r**, and thy belly to swell; H5307
22 and *thy* thigh to **r**: And the woman shall H5307
27 her thigh shall **r**: and the woman shall H5307
Prv 10: 7 but the name of the wicked shall **r**. H7537
Isa 40:20 a tree *that* will not **r**; he seeketh unto H7537

ROTTEN
Job 13:28 And he, as a **r** thing, consumeth, as a H7538
41:27 iron as straw, *and* brass as **r** wood. H7539
Jer 38:11 cast clouts and old **r** rags, and let them H4418
12 old cast clouts and **r** rags under thine H4418
Joel 1:17 The seed is **r** under their clods, the H5685

ROTTENNESS
Prv 12: 4 maketh ashamed *is* as **r** in his bones. H7538
14:30 of the flesh: but envy the **r** of the bones. H7538
Isa 5:24 root shall be as **r**, and their blossom H4716
Hos 5:12 a moth, and to the house of Judah as **r**. H7538
Hab 3:16 at the voice: **r** entered into my bones, H7538

ROUGH
Dt 21: 4 down the heifer unto a **r** valley, which is H386
Isa 27: 8 his **r** wind in the day of the east wind. H7186
40: 4 made straight, and the **r** places plain: H7406
Jer 51:27 horses to come up as the **r** caterpillers. H5569
Dan 8:21 And the **r** goat *is* the king of Grecia: H8163
Zec 13: 4 shall they wear a **r** garment to deceive: H8181
Lk 3: 5 and the **r** ways *shall be* made smooth; G5138

ROUGHLY
Gen 42: 7 them, and spake **r** unto them; and he H7186
30 of the land, spake **r** to us, and took us H7186
1Sa 20:10 me? or what *if* thy father answer thee **r**? H7186
1Ki 12:13 And the king answered the people **r**, H7186
2Ch 10:13 And the king answered them **r**; and H7186
Prv 18:23 entreaties; but the rich answereth **r**. H5794

ROUND
Gen 19: 4 the house **r**, both old and young, H5437
23:17 all the borders **r** about, were made sure H5439
35: 5 cities that *were* **r** about them, and they H5439
Gen 37: 7 your sheaves stood **r** about, and made H5437
41:48 field, which *was* **r** about every city, laid H5439
Ex 7:24 And all the Egyptians digged **r** about H5439
16:13 morning the dew lay **r** about the host. H5439
14 *there lay* a small **r** thing, *as* small as H2636
19:12 unto the people **r** about, saying, Take H5439
25:11 make upon it a crown of gold **r** about. H5439
24 make thereto a crown of gold **r** about. H5439
25 of an hand breadth **r** about, and thou H5439
25 crown to the border thereof **r** about. H5439
27:17 All the pillars **r** about the court *shall be* H5439
28:32 of woven work **r** about the hole of it, H5439
33 and *of* scarlet, **r** about the hem thereof; H5439
33 and bells of gold between them **r** about: H5439
34 upon the hem of the robe **r** about. H5439
29:16 and sprinkle *it* **r** about upon the altar. H5439
20 the blood upon the altar **r** about. H5439
30: 3 the sides thereof **r** about, and the horns H5439
3 make unto it a crown of gold **r** about. H5439
37: 2 and made a crown of gold to it **r** about. H5439
11 thereunto a crown of gold **r** about. H5439
12 an handbreadth **r** about; and made a H5439
12 of gold for the border thereof **r** about. H5439
26 the sides thereof **r** about, and the horns H5439
26 made unto it a crown of gold **r** about. H5439
38:16 All the hangings of the court **r** about H5439
20 and of the court **r** about, *were of* brass. H5439
31 And the sockets of the court **r** about, H5439
31 and all the pins of the court **r** about. H5439
39:23 *with* a band **r** about the hole, that H5439
25 **r** about between the pomegranates; H5439
26 a pomegranate, **r** about the hem of the H5439
40: 8 And thou shalt set up the court **r** about, H5439
33 And he reared up the court **r** about the H5439
Lev 1: 5 sprinkle the blood **r** about upon the H5439
11 his blood **r** about upon the altar. H5439
3: 2 the blood upon the altar **r** about. H5439
8 blood thereof **r** about upon the altar. H5439
13 blood thereof upon the altar **r** about. H5439
7: 2 he sprinkle **r** about upon the altar. H5439
8:15 the horns of the altar **r** about with his H5439
19 the blood upon the altar **r** about. H5439
24 the blood upon the altar **r** about. H5439
9:12 he sprinkled **r** about upon the altar. H5439
18 he sprinkled upon the altar **r** about, H5439
14:41 to be scraped within **r** about, and they H5439
16:18 *it* upon the horns of the altar **r** about. H5439
19:27 Ye shall not **r** the corners of your H5362
25:31 have no wall **r** about them shall be H5439
44 heathen that are **r** about you; of them H5439
Nu 1:50 shall encamp **r** about the tabernacle. H5439
53 But the Levites shall pitch **r** about the H5439
3:26 and by the altar **r** about, and the cords H5439
37 And the pillars of the court **r** about, H5439
4:26 and by the altar **r** about, and their H5439
32 And the pillars of the court **r** about, H5439
11:24 and set them **r** about the tabernacle. H5439
31 on the other side, **r** about the camp, H5439
32 for themselves **r** about the camp. H5439
16:34 And all Israel that *were* **r** about them H5439
22: 4 lick up all *that are* **r** about us, as the ox H5439
32:33 *even* the cities of the country **r** about. H5439
34:12 land with the coasts thereof **r** about. H5439
35: 2 suburbs for the cities **r** about them. H5439
4 outward a thousand cubits **r** about. H5439
Dt 6:14 of the people which *are* **r** about you; H5439
12:10 **r** about, so that ye dwell in safety; H5439
13: 7 the people which *are* **r** about you, nigh H5439
21: 2 which *are* **r** about him that is slain: H5439
25:19 all thine enemies **r** about, in the land H5439
Jos 6: 3 of war, *and* go **r** about the city once. H5362
7: 9 shall environ us **r**, and cut off our name H5437
15:12 **r** about according to their families. H5439
18:20 **r** about, according to their families. H5439
19: 8 And all the villages that *were* **r** about H5439
21:11 with the suburbs thereof **r** about it. H5439
42 **r** about them: thus *were* all these cities. H5439
44 And the LORD gave them rest **r** about, H5439
23: 1 all their enemies **r** about, that Joshua H5439
Jdg 2:12 the people that *were* **r** about them, and H5439
14 of their enemies **r** about, so that they H5439
7:21 man in his place **r** about the camp: and H5439
19:22 beset the house **r** about, *and* beat at the H5437
20: 5 beset the house **r** about upon me by H5437
29 And Israel set liers in wait **r** about H5439
43 *Thus* they inclosed the Benjamites **r** H3803
1Sa 14:21 *from the country* **r** about, even they H5439
23:26 David and his men **r** about to take them.
26: 5 and the people pitched **r** about him. H5439

1Sa 26: 7 Abner and the people lay **r** about him. H5439
31: 9 of the Philistines **r** about, to publish *it* H5439
2Sa 5: 9 built **r** about from Millo and inward. H5439
7: 1 him rest **r** about from all his enemies; H5439
22:12 And he made darkness pavilions **r** H5439
1Ki 3: 1 and the wall of Jerusalem **r** about. H5439
4:24 he had peace on all sides **r** about him. H5439
31 his fame was in all nations **r** about. H5439
6: 5 he built chambers **r** about, *against* the H5439
5 walls of the house **r** about, *both* of the H5439
5 oracle: and he made chambers **r** about: H5439
6 narrowed rests **r** about, that *the beams* H5439
29 walls of the house **r** about with carved H4524
7:12 And the great court **r** about *was* with H5439
18 and two rows **r** about upon the one H5439
20 rows **r** about upon the other chapiter. H5439
23 to the other: *it was* **r** all about, and his H5696
23 of thirty cubits did compass it **r** about. H5439
24 And under the brim of it **r** about *there* H5439
24 the sea **r** about: the knops *were* H5439
31 thereof *was* **r** *after* the work of the H5696
31 with their borders, foursquare, not **r**. H5696
35 And in the top of the base *was there* a **r** H5696
36 of every one, and additions **r** about. H5439
10:19 of the throne *was* **r** behind: and *there* H5696
18:35 And the water ran **r** about the altar; H5439
2Ki 6:17 and chariots of fire **r** about Elisha. H5439
11: 8 And ye shall compass the king **r** about, H5439
11 in his hand, **r** about the king, from H5439
17:15 the heathen that *were* **r** about them, H5439
23: 5 and in the places **r** about Jerusalem; H4524
25: 1 and they built forts against it **r** about. H5439
4 against the city **r** about:) and *the king* H5439
10 down the walls of Jerusalem **r** about. H5439
17 upon the chapiter **r** about, all of brass: H5439
1Ch 4:33 And all their villages that *were* **r** about H5439
6:55 and the suburbs thereof **r** about it. H5439
9:27 And they lodged **r** about the house of H5439
10: 9 land of the Philistines **r** about, to carry H5439
11: 8 And he built the city **r** about, even from H5439
8 even from Millo **r** about: and Joab H5439
22: 9 all his enemies **r** about: for his name H5439
28:12 of all the chambers **r** about, of the H5439
2Ch 4: 2 brim to brim, **r** in compass, and five H5696
2 of thirty cubits did compass it **r** about. H5439
3 did compass it **r** about: ten in a cubit, H5439
3 the sea **r** about. Two rows of H5439
14:14 And they smote all the cities **r** about H5439
15:15 and the LORD gave them rest **r** about. H5439
17:10 lands that *were* **r** about Judah, so that H5439
20:30 for his God gave him rest **r** about. H5439
23: 7 compass the king **r** about, every man H5439
10 and the temple, by the king **r** about. H5439
34: 6 Naphtali, with their mattocks **r** about. H5439
Neh 12:28 of the plain country **r** about Jerusalem, H5439
29 them villages **r** about Jerusalem. H5439
Job 10: 8 **r** about; yet thou dost destroy me. H5439
16:13 His archers compass me **r** about, he H5437
19:12 and encamp **r** about my tabernacle. H5439
22:10 Therefore snares *are* **r** about thee, and H5439
37:12 And it is turned **r** about by his H4524
41:14 his face? his teeth *are* terrible **r** about. H5439
Ps 3: 6 set *themselves* against me **r** about. H5439
18:11 place; his pavilion **r** about him *were* H5439
22:12 strong *bulls* of Bashan have beset me **r**. H3803
27: 6 mine enemies **r** about me: therefore H5439
34: 7 The angel of the LORD encampeth **r** H5439
44:13 a derision to them that are **r** about us. H5439
48:12 Walk about Zion, and go **r** about her: H5362
50: 3 shall be very tempestuous **r** about him. H5439
59: 6 like a dog, and go **r** about the city. H5437
14 like a dog, and go **r** about the city. H5437
76:11 God: let all that be **r** about him bring H5439
78:28 their camp, **r** about their habitations. H5439
79: 3 Their blood have they shed like water **r** H5439
4 derision to them that are **r** about us. H5439
88:17 They came **r** about me daily like water; H5437
89: 8 or to thy faithfulness **r** about thee? H5439
97: 2 Clouds and darkness *are* **r** about him: H5439
3 and burneth up his enemies **r** about. H5439
125: 2 As the mountains *are* **r** about H5439
2 so the LORD *is* **r** about his people from H5439
128: 3 like olive plants **r** about thy table. H5439
Song 7: 2 Thy navel *is like* a **r** goblet, *which* H5469
Isa 3:18 cauls, and *their* **r** tires like the moon, H7720
15: 8 For the cry is gone **r** about the borders H5362
29: 3 And I will camp against thee **r** about, H1754
42:25 set him on fire **r** about, yet he knew H5439
49:18 Lift up thine eyes **r** about, and behold: H5439
Isa 60: 4 Lift up thine eyes **r** about, and see: all H5439
Jer 1:15 the walls thereof **r** about, and against H5439
4:17 they against her **r** about; because she H5439
6: 3 tents against her **r** about; they shall H5439
12: 9 bird, the birds **r** about *are* against her; H5439
21:14 and it shall devour all things **r** about it. H5439
25: 9 all these nations **r** about, and will H5439
46: 5 *for* fear *was* **r** about, saith the LORD. H5439
14 for the sword shall devour **r** about thee. H5439
50:14 against Babylon **r** about: all ye that H5439
15 Shout against her **r** about: she hath H5439
29 bow, camp against it **r** about; let none H5439
32 and it shall devour all **r** about him. H5439
51: 2 they shall be against her **r** about. H5439
52: 4 it, and built forts against it **r** about. H5439
7 *were* by the city **r** about:) and they H5439
14 all the walls of Jerusalem **r** about. H5439
22 the chapiters **r** about, all *of* brass. The H5439
23 the network *were* an hundred **r** about. H5439
Lam 1:17 *should be* **r** about him: Jerusalem H5439
2: 3 flaming fire, *which* devoureth **r** about. H5439
22 day my terrors **r** about, so that in the H5439
Ezk 1:18 *were* full of eyes **r** about them four. H5439
27 the appearance of fire **r** about within it, H5439
27 of fire, and it had brightness **r** about. H5439
28 of the brightness **r** about. This *was* the H5439
4: 2 set *battering* rams against it **r** about. H5439
5: 5 and countries *that are* **r** about her. H5439
6 countries that *are* **r** about her: for they H5439
7 nations that *are* **r** about you, *and* have H5439
7 of the nations that *are* **r** about you; H5439
12 fall by the sword **r** about thee; and I H5439
14 the nations that *are* **r** about thee, in the H5439
15 nations that *are* **r** about thee, when I H5439
6: 5 scatter your bones **r** about your altars. H5439
13 among their idols **r** about their altars, H5439
8:10 pourtrayed upon the wall **r** about. H5439
10:12 *were* full of eyes **r** about, *even* the H5439
11:12 of the heathen that *are* **r** about you. H5439
16:37 even gather them **r** about against thee, H5439
57 Syria, and all *that are* **r** about her, the H5439
57 Philistines, which despise thee **r** about. H5439
23:24 shield and helmet **r** about: and I will H5439
27:11 *were* upon thy walls **r** about, and the H5439
11 upon thy walls **r** about; they have made H5439
28:24 thorn of all *that are* **r** about them, that H5439
26 that despise them **r** about them; and H5439
31: 4 her rivers running **r** about his plants, H5439
32:23 her company is **r** about her grave: all H5439
24 There *is* Elam and all her multitude **r** H5439
25 her graves *are* **r** about him: all of them H5439
26 her graves *are* **r** about him: all of them H5439
34:26 And I will make them and the places **r** H5439
36: 4 residue of the heathen that *are* **r** about; H5439
36 Then the heathen that are left **r** about H5439
37: 2 And caused me to pass by them **r** H5439
40: 5 of the house **r** about, and in the man's H5439
14 the post of the court **r** about the gate. H5439
16 within the gate **r** about, and likewise H5439
16 and windows *were* **r** about inward: and H5439
17 made for the court **r** about: thirty H5439
25 in the arches thereof **r** about, like those H5439
29 the arches thereof **r** about: *it was* fifty H5439
30 And the arches **r** about *were* five and H5439
33 the arches thereof **r** about: *it was* fifty H5439
36 the windows to it **r** about: the length H5439
43 broad, fastened **r** about: and upon the H5439
41: 5 cubits, **r** about the house on every side. H5439
6 the side chambers **r** about, that they H5439
7 went still upward **r** about the house: H5439
8 I saw also the height of the house **r** H5439
10 cubits **r** about the house on every side. H5439
11 that was left *was* five cubits **r** about. H5439
12 five cubits thick **r** about, and the length H5439
16 and the galleries **r** about on their three H5439
16 cieled with wood **r** about, and from the H5439
17 and by all the wall **r** about within and H5439
19 made through all the house **r** about. H5439
42:15 the east, and measured it **r** about. H5439
16 reeds, with the measuring reed **r** about. H5439
17 reeds, with the measuring reed **r** about. H5439
20 four sides: it had a wall **r** about, five H5439
43:12 limit thereof **r** about *shall be* most H5439
13 by the edge thereof **r** about *shall be* a H5439
20 and upon the border **r** about: thus shalt H5439
45: 1 holy in all the borders thereof **r** about. H5439
2 *in breadth*, square **r** about; and fifty H5439
2 cubits **r** about for the suburbs thereof. H5439
46:23 And *there was* a row *of building* **r** H5439
Ezk 46:23 about in them, **r** about them four, and H5439
23 boiling places under the rows **r** about. H5439
48:35 *It was* **r** about eighteen thousand H5439
Joel 3:11 together **r** about: thither cause H5439
12 I sit to judge all the heathen **r** about. H5439
Am 3:11 *there shall be* even **r** about the land; H5439
Jna 2: 5 the depth closed me **r** about, the weeds H5437
Nah 3: 8 *that had* the waters **r** about it, whose H5439
Zec 2: 5 her a wall of fire **r** about, and will be H5439
7: 7 and the cities thereof **r** about her, when H5439
12: 2 unto all the people **r** about, when they H5439
6 all the people **r** about, on the right H5439
14:14 of all the heathen **r** about shall be H5439
Mt 3: 5 and all the region **r** about Jordan, *G4066*
14:35 all that country **r** about, and brought *G4066*
21:33 and hedged it **r** about, and digged a
Mk 1:28 all the region **r** about Galilee. *G4066*
3: 5 And when he had looked **r** about on *G4017*
34 And he looked **r** about on them which *G2943*
5:32 And he looked **r** about to see her that *G4017*
6: 6 he went **r** about the villages, teaching. *G2943*
36 into the country **r** about, and into the *G2943*
55 And ran through that whole region **r** *G4066*
9: 8 And suddenly, when they had looked **r** *G4017*
10:23 And Jesus looked **r** about, and saith *G4017*
11:11 he had looked **r** about upon all things, *G4017*
Lk 1:65 And fear came on all that dwelt **r** about *G4039*
2: 9 of the Lord shone **r** about them: and *G4034*
4:14 of him through all the region **r** about. *G4066*
37 into every place of the country **r** about. *G4066*
6:10 And looking **r** about upon them all, he
7:17 and throughout all the region **r** about. *G4066*
8:37 of the Gadarenes **r** about besought him *G4066*
9:12 and country **r** about, and lodge, and *G2943*
19:43 thee **r**, and keep thee in on every side, *G4033*
Jn 10:24 Then came the Jews **r** about him, and *G2944*
Act 5:16 multitude *out* of the cities **r** about unto *G4038*
9: 3 **r** about him a light from heaven: *G4015*
14: 6 and unto the region that lieth **r** about: *G4066*
20 Howbeit, as the disciples stood **r** about *G2944*
22: 6 from heaven a great light **r** about me. *G4015*
25: 7 from Jerusalem stood **r** about, and laid *G4026*
26:13 of the sun, shining **r** about me and *G4034*
Ro 15:19 Jerusalem, and **r** about unto Illyricum, *G2943*
Heb 9: 4 covenant overlaid **r** about with gold, *G3840*
Rev 4: 3 *was* a rainbow **r** about the throne, in *G2943*
4 And **r** about the throne *were* four and *G2943*
6 of the throne, and **r** about the throne, *G2943*
5:11 of many angels **r** about the throne and *G2943*
7:11 And all the angels stood **r** about the *G2943*

ROUSE
Gen 49: 9 and as an old lion; who shall **r** him up? H6965

ROVERS
1Ch 12:21 the band *of the* **r**: for they *were* all mighty

ROW
Ex 28:17 of stones: *the first* **r** *shall be* a sardius, H2905
17 and a carbuncle: *this shall be* the first **r**. H2905
18 And the second **r** *shall be* an emerald, a H2905
19 And the third **r** a ligure, an agate, and H2905
20 And the fourth **r** a beryl, and an onyx, H2905
39:10 of stones: *the first* **r** *was* a sardius, a H2905
10 and a carbuncle: this *was* the first **r**. H2905
11 And the second **r**, an emerald, a H2905
12 And the third **r**, a ligure, an agate, and H2905
13 And the fourth **r**, a beryl, an onyx, and H2905
Lev 24: 6 **r**, upon the pure table before the LORD. H4635
7 upon *each* **r**, that it may be on the H4635
1Ki 6:36 hewed stone, and a **r** of cedar beams. H2905
7: 3 *lay* on forty five pillars, fifteen *in* a **r**. H2905
12 stones, and a **r** of cedar beams, both H2905
Ezr 6: 4 *With* three rows of great stones, and a **r** H5073
Ezk 46:23 And *there was* a **r** *of building* round H2905

ROWED
Jna 1:13 Nevertheless the men **r** hard to bring *it* H2864
Jn 6:19 So when they had **r** about five and *G1643*

ROWERS
Ezk 27:26 Thy **r** have brought thee into great H7751

ROWING
Mk 6:48 And he saw them toiling in **r**; for the *G1643*

ROWS
Ex 28:17 of stones, *even* four **r** of stones: *the first* H2905
39:10 And they set in it four **r** of stones: *the* H2905

R

Lev 24: 6 And thou shalt set them in two r, six on H4634
1Ki 6:36 court with three r of hewed stone, and H2905
7: 2 cubits, upon four r of cedar pillars, H2905
4 And *there were* windows *in* three r, and H2905
12 *was* with three r of hewed stones, and H2905
18 And he made the pillars, and two r H2905
20 r round about upon the other chapiter. H2905
24 *were* cast in two r, when it was cast. H2905
42 *even* two r of pomegranates for H2905
2Ch 4: 3 r of oxen *were* cast, when it was cast. H2905
13 two wreaths; two r of pomegranates on H2905
Ezr 6: 4 *With* three r of great stones, and a row H5073
Song 1:10 Thy cheeks are comely with r *of jewels*, H8447
Ezk 46:23 boiling places under the r round about. H2918

ROYAL
Gen 49:20 *be* fat, and he shall yield r dainties. H4428
Jos 10: 2 city, as one of the r cities, and because H4467
1Sa 27: 5 servant dwell in the r city with thee? H4467
2Sa 12:26 of Ammon, and took the r city. H4410
1Ki 10:13 gave her of his r bounty. So she turned H4428
2Ki 11: 1 she arose and destroyed all the seed r. H4467
25:25 of the seed r, came, and ten men H4410
1Ch 29:25 upon him *such* r majesty as had not H4438
2Ch 22:10 all the seed r of the house of Judah. H4467
Est 1: 7 another,) and r wine in abundance, H4438
9 for the women *in* the r house which H4438
11 with the crown r, to shew the people H4438
19 If it please the king, let there go a r H4438
19 the king give her r estate unto another H4438
2:16 into his house r in the tenth month, H4438
17 so that he set the r crown upon her H4438
5: 1 Esther put on *her* r *apparel*, and stood H4438
1 king sat upon his r throne in the royal H4438
1 his royal throne in the r house, over H4438
6: 8 Let the r apparel be brought which the H4438
8 the crown r which is set upon his head: H4438
8:15 of the king in r apparel of blue and H4438
Isa 62: 3 and a r diadem in the hand of thy God. H4410
Jer 41: 1 of the seed r, and the princes of the H4410
43:10 shall spread his r pavilion over them. H8237
Dan 6: 7 to establish a r statute, and to make H4430
Act 12:21 And upon a set day Herod, arrayed in r G937
Jas 2: 8 If ye fulfil the r law according to the G937
1Pt 2: 9 But ye *are* a chosen generation, a r G934

RUBBING
Lk 6: 1 and did eat, r *them* in *their* hands. G5597

RUBBISH
Neh 4: 2 of the heaps of the r which are burned? H6083
10 and *there is* much r; so that we are not H6083

RUBIES
Job 28:18 for the price of wisdom *is* above r. H6443
Prv 3:15 She *is* more precious than r: and all the H6443
8:11 For wisdom *is* better than r; and all the H6443
20:15 There is gold, and a multitude of r: but H6443
31:10 woman? for her price *is* far above r. H6443
Lam 4: 7 than r, their polishing *was* of sapphire: H6443

RUDDER
Act 27:40 and loosed the r bands, and hoised up G4079

RUDDY
1Sa 16:12 him in. Now he *was* r, *and* withal of a H132
17:42 a youth, and r, and of a fair countenance. H132
Song 5:10 My beloved *is* white and r, the chiefest H122
Lam 4: 7 they were more r in body than rubies, H119

RUDE
2Co 11: 6 But though *I be* r in speech, yet not in G2399

RUDIMENTS
Col 2: 8 the r of the world, and not after Christ. G4747
20 Christ from the r of the world, why, as G4747

RUE
Lk 11:42 ye tithe mint and r and all manner of G4076

RUFUS
Mk 15:21 of Alexander and R, to bear his cross. G4504
Ro 16:13 Salute R chosen in the Lord, and his G4504

RUHAMAH
Hos 2: 1 brethren, Ammi; and to your sisters, R. H7355

RUIN
2Ch 28:23 they were the r of him, and of all Israel. H3782
Ps 89:40 thou hast brought his strong holds to r. H4288
Prv 24:22 and who knoweth the r of them both? H6365
26:28 by it; and a flattering mouth worketh r. H4072
Isa 3: 6 ruler, and *let* this r *be* under thy hand: H4384
23:13 palaces thereof; *and* he brought it to r. H4654
25: 2 a defenced city a r: a palace of strangers H4654
Ezk 18:30 so iniquity shall not be your r. H4383
27:27 the midst of the seas in the day of thy r. H4658
31:13 Upon his r shall all the fowls of the H4658
Lk 6:49 fell; and the r of that house was great. G4485

RUINED
Isa 3: 8 For Jerusalem is r, and Judah is fallen: H3782
Ezk 36:35 and desolate and r cities *are become* H2040
36 LORD build the r *places, and* plant that H2040

RUINOUS
2Ki 19:25 to lay waste fenced cities *into* r heaps. H5327
Isa 17: 1 *being* a city, and it shall be a r heap. H4654
37:26 lay waste defenced cities *into* r heaps. H5327

RUINS
Ezk 21:15 faint, and *their* r be multiplied: ah! *it* H4383
Am 9:11 I will raise up his r, and I will build it as H2034
Act 15:16 again the r thereof, and I will set it up: G2679

RULE
Gen 1:16 the greater light to r the day, and the H4475
16 to r the night: *he made* the stars also. H4475
18 And to r over the day and over the H4910
3:16 thy husband, and he shall r over thee. H4910
4: 7 his desire, and thou shalt r over him. H4910
Lev 25:43 Thou shalt not r over him with rigour; H7287
46 not r one over another with rigour. H7287
53 not r with rigour over him in thy sight. H7287
Jdg 8:22 said unto Gideon, R thou over us, both H4910
23 And Gideon said unto them, I will not r H4910
23 shall my son r over you: the LORD H4910
23 over you: the LORD shall r over you. H4910
1Ki 9:23 fifty, which bare r over the people that H7287
22:31 captains that had r over his chariots,
2Ch 8:10 and fifty, that bare r over the people. H7287
Neh 5:15 servants bare r over the people: but H7980
Est 1:22 man should bear r in his own house, H8323
9: 1 Jews had r over them that hated them;) H7980
Ps 110: 2 r thou in the midst of thine enemies. H7287
136: 8 The sun to r by day: for his mercy H4475
9 The moon and stars to r by night: for H4475
Prv 8:16 By me princes r, and nobles, *even* all H8323
12:24 The hand of the diligent shall bear r: H4910
17: 2 A wise servant shall have r over a son H4910
19:10 for a servant to have r over princes. H4910
25:28 He that *hath* no r over his own spirit *is* H4623
29: 2 the wicked beareth r, the people mourn. H4910
Ecc 2:19 yet shall he have r over all my labour H7980
Isa 3: 4 princes, and babes shall r over them. H4910
12 and women r over them. O my people, H4910
14: 2 and they shall r over their oppressors. H7287
19: 4 a fierce king shall r over them, saith the H4910
28:14 r this people which *is* in Jerusalem. H4910
32: 1 and princes shall r in judgment. H8323
40:10 and his arm shall r for him: behold, his H4910
41: 2 and made *him* r over kings? he gave H7287
44:13 The carpenter stretcheth out *his* r; he H6957
52: 5 for nought? they that r over them make H4910
63:19 We are *thine*: thou never barest r over H4910
Jer 5:31 the priests bear r by their means; and H7287
Ezk 19:11 of them that bare r, and her stature was H4910
14 rod *to be* a sceptre to r. This *is* a H4910
20:33 with fury poured out, will I r over you: H4427
29:15 they shall no more r over the nations. H7287
Dan 2:39 which shall bear r over all the earth. H7981
4:26 shalt have known that the heavens do r. H7990
11: 3 up, that shall r with great dominion, H4910
39 cause them to r over many, and shall H4910
Joel 2:17 heathen should r over them: wherefore H4910
Zec 6:13 and shall sit and r upon his throne; H4910
Mt 2: 6 Governor, that shall r my people Israel. G4165
Mk 10:42 are accounted to r over the Gentiles G757
1Co 15:24 down all r and all authority and power. G746
2Co 10:13 to the measure of the r which God hath G2583
15 by you according to our r abundantly, G2583
Gal 6:16 according to this r, peace *be* on them, G2583
Php 3:16 the same r, let us mind the same thing. G2583
Col 3:15 And let the peace of God r in your G1018
1Ti 3: 5 (For if a man know not how to r his G4291
5:17 Let the elders that r well be counted G4291
Heb 13: 7 Remember them which have the r over G2233
17 Obey them that have the r over you, G2233
Heb 13:24 Salute all them that have the r over G2233
Rev 2:27 And he shall r them with a rod of iron; G4165
12: 5 child, who was to r all nations with a G4165
19:15 and he shall r them with a rod of iron: G4165

RULED
Gen 24: 2 of his house, that r over all that he had, H4910
41:40 all my people be r: only in the throne H5401
Jos 12: 2 in Heshbon, *and* r from Aroer, which *is* H4910
Ru 1: 1 days when the judges r, that there was a H8199
1Ki 5:16 hundred, which r over the people that H7287
1Ch 26: 6 sons born, that r throughout the house H4474
Ezr 4:20 which have r over all *countries* beyond H7990
Ps 106:41 and they that hated them r over them. H4910
Isa 14: 6 stroke, he that r the nations in anger, H7287
Lam 5: 8 Servants have r over us: *there is* none H4910
Ezk 34: 4 force and with cruelty have ye r them. H7287
Dan 5:21 the most high God r in the kingdom of H7990
11: 4 which he r: for his kingdom shall H4910

RULER
Gen 41:43 he made him r over all the land of Egypt.
43:16 he said to the r of his house, H834+H5921
45: 8 a r throughout all the land of Egypt. H4910
Ex 22:28 the gods, nor curse the r of thy people. H5387
Lev 4:22 When a r hath sinned, and done H5387
Nu 13: 2 send a man, every one a r among them. H5387
Jdg 9:30 And when Zebul the r of the city heard H8269
1Sa 25:30 shall have appointed thee r over Israel; H5057
2Sa 6:21 to appoint me r over the people of the H5057
7: 8 to be r over my people, over Israel: H5057
20:26 And Ira also the Jairite was a chief r H3548
1Ki 1:35 him to be r over Israel and over Judah. H5057
11:28 he made him r over all the charge of H6485
2Ki 25:22 son of Ahikam, the son of Shaphan, r. H6485
1Ch 5: 2 chief r; but the birthright *was* Joseph's:) H5057
9:11 of Ahitub, the r of the house of God; H5057
20 of Eleazar was the r over them in time H5057
11: 2 thou shalt be r over my people Israel. H5057
17: 7 shouldest be r over my people Israel: H5057
26:24 son of Moses, *was* r of the treasures. H5057
27: 4 *was* Mikloth also the r: in his course H5057
16 tribes of Israel: the r of the Reubenites H5057
28: 4 Judah *to be* the r; and of the house of H5057
2Ch 6: 5 man to be a r over my people Israel: H5057
7:18 not fail thee a man *to be* r in Israel. H4910
11:22 the chief, *to be* r among his brethren: H5057
19:11 of Ishmael, the r of the house of Judah, H5057
26:11 and Maaseiah the r, under the hand of H7860
31:12 r, and Shimei his brother *was* the next. H5057
13 and Azariah the r of the house of God. H5057
Neh 3: 9 Hur, the r of the half part of Jerusalem. H8269
12 of Halohesh, the r of the half part of H8269
14 the son of Rechab, the r of part of H8269
15 of Col-hozeh, the r of part of Mizpah; H8269
16 son of Azbuk, the r of the half part of H8269
17 r of the half part of Keilah, in his part. H8269
18 the r of the half part of Keilah. H8269
19 son of Jeshua, the r of Mizpah, another H8269
7: 2 and Hananiah the r of the palace, H8269
11:11 Ahitub, *was* the r of the house of God. H5057
Ps 68:27 There *is* little Benjamin *with* their r, the H7287
105:20 the r of the people, and let him go free. H4910
21 He made him lord of his house, and r H4910
Prv 6: 7 Which having no guide, overseer, or r, H4910
23: 1 When thou sittest to eat with a r, H4910
28:15 *so is* a wicked r over the poor people. H4910
29:12 If a r hearken to lies, all his servants H4910
Ecc 10: 4 If the spirit of the r rise up against thee, H4910
5 an error *which* proceedeth from the r: H7989
Isa 3: 6 r, and *let* this ruin *be* under thy hand: H7101
7 make me not a r of the people. H7101
16: 1 Send ye the lamb to the r of the land H4910
Jer 51:46 violence in the land, r against ruler. H4910
46 and violence in the land, ruler against r. H4910
Dan 2:10 *is* no king, lord, nor r, *that* asked such H7990
38 hath made thee r over them all. Thou H7981
48 gifts, and made him r over the whole H7981
5: 7 and shall be the third r in the kingdom. H7981
16 and shalt be the third r in the kingdom. H7981
29 should be the third r in the kingdom. H7990
Mic 5: 2 unto me *that is* to be r in Israel; whose H4910
Hab 1:14 things, *that have* no r over them? H4910
Mt 9:18 came a certain r, and worshipped him, G758
24:45 lord hath made r over his household, G2525
47 he shall make him r over all his goods. G2525
25:21 I will make thee r over many things: G2525
23 I will make thee r over many things: G2525
Mk 5:35 there came from the r of the synagogue's G752

Mk 5:36 he saith unto the **r** of the synagogue, Be G752
38 And he cometh to the house of the **r** of G752
Lk 8:41 and he was a **r** of the synagogue: and G758
49 one from the **r** of the synagogue's *house*, G752
12:42 lord shall make **r** over his household, G2525
44 will make him **r** over all that he hath. G2525
13:14 And the **r** of the synagogue answered G752
18:18 And a certain **r** asked him, saying, Good G758
Jn 2: 9 When the **r** of the feast had tasted the G755
3: 1 named Nicodemus, a **r** of the Jews: G758
Act 7:27 Who made thee a **r** and a judge over us? G758
35 Who made thee a **r** and a judge? the G758
35 God send *to be* a **r** and a deliverer by the G758
18: 8 And Crispus, the chief **r** of the G752
17 the chief **r** of the synagogue, and G752
23: 5 not speak evil of the **r** of thy people. G758

RULERS
Gen 47: 6 them, then make them **r** over my cattle. H8269
Ex 16:22 *man:* and all the **r** of the congregation H5387
18:21 over them, *to be* **r** of thousands, *and* H8269
21 of thousands, *and* **r** of hundreds, rulers H8269
21 **r** of fifties, and rulers of tens: H8269
21 rulers of fifties, and **r** of tens: H8269
25 over the people, **r** of thousands, rulers H8269
25 of thousands, **r** of hundreds, rulers H8269
25 **r** of fifties, and rulers of tens. H8269
25 rulers of fifties, and **r** of tens. H8269
34:31 Aaron and all the **r** of the congregation H5387
35:27 And the **r** brought onyx stones, and H5387
Dt 1:13 tribes, and I will make them **r** over you. H7218
Jdg 15:11 the Philistines *are* **r** over us? what *is* H4910
2Sa 8:18 and David's sons were chief **r**. H3548
1Ki 9:22 **r** of his chariots, and his horsemen. H8269
2Ki 10: 1 to Samaria, unto the **r** of Jezreel, to the H8269
11: 4 and fetched the **r** over hundreds, with H8269
19 And he took the **r** over hundreds, and H8269
1Ch 21: 2 And David said to Joab and to the **r** of H8269
26:32 whom king David made **r** over the H6485
27:31 All these *were* the **r** of the substance H8269
29: 6 **r** of the king's work, offered willingly, H8269
2Ch 29:20 and gathered the **r** of the city, and went H8269
35: 8 and Jehiel, **r** of the house of God, H5057
Ezr 9: 2 and **r** hath been chief in this trespass. H5461
10:14 Let now our **r** of all the congregation H8269
Neh 2:16 And the **r** knew not whither I went, or H5461
16 the **r**, nor to the rest that did the work. H5461
4:14 nobles, and to the **r**, and to the rest of H5461
16 **r** *were* behind all the house of Judah. H8269
19 And I said unto the nobles, and to the **r**, H5461
5: 7 nobles, and the **r**, and said unto them, H5461
17 fifty of the Jews and **r**, beside those that H5461
7: 5 nobles, and the **r**, and the people, that H5461
11: 1 And the **r** of the people dwelt at H8269
12:40 and I, and the half of the **r** with me: H5461
13:11 Then contended I with the **r**, and said, H5461
Est 3:12 and to the **r** of every people of every H8269
8: 9 and the deputies and **r** of the provinces H8269
9: 3 And all the **r** of the provinces, and the H8269
Ps 2: 2 and the **r** take counsel together, H7336
Isa 1:10 Hear the word of the LORD, ye **r** of H7101
14: 5 of the wicked, *and* the sceptre of the **r**. H4910
22: 3 All thy **r** are fled together, they are H7101
29:10 and your **r**, the seers hath he covered. H7218
49: 7 to a servant of **r**, Kings shall see and H4910
Jer 33:26 *any* of his seed *to be* **r** over the seed of H4910
51:23 will I break in pieces captains and **r**. H5461
28 and all the **r** thereof, and all the H5461
57 her captains, and her **r**, and her mighty H5461
Ezk 23: 6 with blue, captains and **r**, all of them H5461
12 captains and **r** clothed most H5461
23 men, captains and **r**, great lords and H5461
Dan 3: 2 and all the **r** of the provinces, to H7984
3 and all the **r** of the provinces, were H7984
Hos 4:18 her **r** *with* shame do love, Give ye. H4043
Mk 5:22 And, behold, there cometh one of the **r** G752
13: 9 be brought before **r** and kings for my G2232
Lk 21:12 before kings and **r** for my name's sake. G2232
23:13 chief priests and the **r** and the people, G758
35 beholding. And the **r** also with them G758
24:20 And how the chief priests and our **r** G758
Jn 7:26 unto him. Do the **r** know indeed that this G758
48 Have any of the **r** or of the Pharisees G758
12:42 Nevertheless among the chief **r** also G758
Act 3:17 ignorance ye did *it*, as *did* also your **r**. G758
4: 5 that their **r**, and elders, and scribes, G758
8 Ye **r** of the people, and elders of Israel, G758
26 earth stood up, and the **r** were gathered G758
13:15 the prophets the **r** of the synagogue sent G752
13:27 and their **r**, because they knew him G758
14: 5 of the Jews with their **r**, to use *them* G758
16:19 *them* into the marketplace unto the **r**, G758
17: 6 brethren unto the **r** of the city, crying, G4173
8 And they troubled the people and the **r** G4173
Ro 13: 3 For **r** are not a terror to good works, but G758
Eph 6:12 against the **r** of the darkness of this G2888

RULER'S
Prv 29:26 Many seek the **r** favour; but *every* H4910
Mt 9:23 And when Jesus came into the **r** house, G758

RULEST
2Ch 20: 6 in heaven? and **r** *not* thou over all the H4910
Ps 89: 9 Thou **r** the raging of the sea: when the H4910

RULETH
2Sa 23: 3 to me, He that **r** over men *must be* just, H4910
Ps 59:13 know that God **r** in Jacob unto the ends H4910
66: 7 He **r** by his power for ever; his eyes H4910
103:19 heavens; and his kingdom **r** over all. H4910
Prv 16:32 **r** his spirit than he that taketh a city. H4910
22: 7 The rich **r** over the poor, and the H4910
Ecc 8: 9 man **r** over another to his own hurt. H7980
9:17 than the cry of him that **r** among fools. H4910
Dan 4:17 that the most High **r** in the kingdom of H7990
25 that the most High **r** in the kingdom of H7990
32 that the most High **r** in the kingdom of H7990
Hos 11:12 deceit: but Judah yet **r** with God, and is H7300
Ro 12: 8 simplicity; he that **r**, with diligence; he G4291
1Ti 3: 4 One that **r** well his own house, having G4291

RULING
2Sa 23: 3 men *must be* just, **r** in the fear of God. H4910
Jer 22:30 of David, and **r** any more in Judah. H4910
1Ti 3:12 of one wife, **r** their children and their G4291

RUMAH
2Ki 23:36 Zebudah, the daughter of Pedaiah of **R**. H7316

RUMBLING
Jer 47: 3 *and at* the **r** of his wheels, the fathers H1995

RUMOUR
2Ki 19: 7 he shall hear a **r**, and shall return to his H8052
Isa 37: 7 he shall hear a **r**, and return to his own H8052
Jer 49:14 I have heard a **r** from the LORD, and H8052
51:46 and ye fear for the **r** that shall be heard H8052
46 in the land; a **r** shall both come *one* H8052
46 year *shall come* a **r**, and violence in the H8052
Ezk 7:26 mischief, and **r** shall be upon rumour; H8052
26 shall be upon **r**; then shall they seek H8052
Oba 1 We have heard a **r** from the LORD, and H8052
Lk 7:17 And this **r** of him went forth G3056

RUMOURS
Mt 24: 6 And ye shall hear of wars and **r** of wars: G189
Mk 13: 7 And when ye shall hear of wars and **r** of G189

RUMP
Ex 29:22 the ram the fat and the **r**, and the fat that H451
Lev 3: 9 *and* the whole **r**, it shall he take off hard H451
7: 3 **r**, and the fat that covereth the inwards, H451
8:25 And he took the fat, and the **r**, and all the H451
9:19 and of the ram, the **r**, and that which H451

RUN
Gen 49:22 a well; *whose* branches **r** over the wall: H6805
Lev 15: 3 whether his flesh **r** with his issue, or his H7325
25 separation, or if it **r** beyond the time of H2100
Jdg 18:25 lest angry fellows **r** upon thee, and thou H6293
1Sa 8:11 and *some* shall **r** before his chariots. H7323
17:17 and **r** to the camp to thy brethren; H7323
20: 6 of me that he might **r** to Beth-lehem his H7323
36 And he said unto his lad, **R**, find out H7323
2Sa 15: 1 horses, and fifty men to **r** before him. H7323
18:19 Let me now **r**, and bear the king tidings, H7323
22 I pray thee, also **r** after Cushi. And Joab H7323
22 wilt thou **r**, my son, seeing that H7323
23 But howsoever, *said he,* let me **r**. And he H7323
23 he said unto him, **R**. Then Ahimaaz ran H7323
22:30 For by thee I have **r** through a troop: by H7323
1Ki 1: 5 and fifty men to **r** before him. H7323
2Ki 4:22 **r** to the man of God, and come again. H7323
26 **R** now, I pray thee, to meet her, and H7323
5:20 **r** after him, and take somewhat of him. H7323
2Ch 16: 9 For the eyes of the LORD **r** to and fro H7751
Ps 18:29 For by thee I have **r** through a troop; H7323
19: 5 rejoiceth as a strong man to **r** a race. H7323
58: 7 Let them melt away as waters *which* **r** H1980
59: 4 They **r** and prepare themselves without H7323
78:16 caused waters to **r** down like rivers. H3381
104:10 the valleys, *which* **r** among the hills. H1980
119:32 I will **r** the way of thy commandments, H7323
136 Rivers of waters **r** down mine eyes, H3381
Prv 1:16 For their feet **r** to evil, and make haste H7323
Ecc 1: 7 All the rivers **r** into the sea; yet the sea H1980
Song 1: 4 Draw me, we will **r** after thee: the king H7323
Isa 33: 4 and fro of locusts shall he **r** upon them. H8264
40:31 eagles; they shall **r**, and not be weary; H7323
55: 5 not thee shall **r** unto thee because of H7323
59: 7 Their feet **r** to evil, and they make H7323
Jer 5: 1 **R** ye to and fro through the streets of H7751
9:18 that our eyes may **r** down with tears, H3381
12: 5 If thou hast **r** with the footmen, and H7323
13:17 shall weep sore, and **r** down with tears, H3381
14:17 Let mine eyes **r** down with tears night H3381
49: 3 lament, and **r** to and fro by the hedges; H7751
19 make him **r** away from her: and H7323
50:44 them suddenly **r** away from her: and H7323
51:31 One post shall **r** to meet another, and H7323
Lam 2:18 of Zion, let tears **r** down like a river day H3381
Ezk 24:16 nor weep, neither shall thy tears **r** down. H935
32:14 rivers to **r** like oil, saith the Lord GOD. H3212
Dan 12: 4 the end: many shall **r** to and fro, and H7751
Joel 2: 4 and as horsemen, so shall they **r**. H7323
7 They shall **r** like mighty men; they shall H7323
9 They shall **r** to and fro in the city; they H8264
9 the city; they shall **r** upon the wall, they H7323
Am 5:24 But let judgment **r** down as waters, and H1556
6:12 Shall horses **r** upon the rock? will *one* H7323
8:12 the east, they shall **r** to and fro to seek H7751
Nah 2: 4 torches, they shall **r** like the lightnings. H7323
Hab 2: 2 tables, that he may **r** that readeth it. H7323
Hag 1: 9 ye **r** every man unto his own house. H7323
Zec 2: 4 And said unto him, **R**, speak to this H7323
4:10 **r** to and fro through the whole earth. H7751
Mt 28: 8 and did **r** to bring his disciples word. G5143
1Co 9:24 Know ye not that they which **r** in a race G5143
24 run in a race **r** all, but one receiveth G5143
24 the prize? So **r**, that ye may obtain. G5143
26 I therefore so **r**, not as uncertainly; so G5143
Gal 2: 2 means I should **r**, or had run, in vain. G5143
2 means I should run, or had **r**, in vain. G5143
5: 7 Ye did **r** well; who did hinder you that G5143
Php 2:16 not **r** in vain, neither laboured in vain. G5143
Heb 12: 1 *us*, and let us **r** with patience the race G5143
1Pt 4: 4 Wherein they think it strange that ye **r** G4936

RUNNER See FORERUNNER.

RUNNEST
Prv 4:12 when thou **r**, thou shalt not stumble. H7323

RUNNETH
Ezr 8:15 to the river that **r** to Ahava; and there H935
Job 15:26 He **r** upon him, *even* on *his* neck, upon H7323
16:14 upon breach, he **r** upon me like a giant. H7323
Ps 23: 5 my head with oil; my cup **r** over. H7310
147:15 *upon* earth: his word **r** very swiftly. H7323
Prv 18:10 the righteous **r** into it, and is safe. H7323
Lam 1:16 mine eye, mine eye **r** down with water, H3381
3:48 Mine eye **r** down with rivers of water H3381
Mt 9:17 and the wine **r** out, and the bottles G1632
Jn 20: 2 Then she **r**, and cometh to Simon Peter, G5143
Ro 9:16 that **r**, but of God that sheweth mercy. G5143

RUNNING
Lev 14: 5 killed in an earthen vessel over **r** water: H2416
6 bird *that was* killed over the **r** water: H2416
50 birds in an earthen vessel over **r** water: H2416
51 bird, and in the **r** water, and sprinkle H2416
52 bird, and with the **r** water, and with the H2416
15: 2 any man hath a **r** issue out of his flesh, H2100
13 his flesh in **r** water, and shall be clean. H2416
22: 4 *is* a leper, or hath a **r** issue; he shall not H2100
Nu 19:17 **r** water shall be put thereto in a vessel: H2416
2Sa 18:24 and looked, and behold a man **r** alone. H7323
26 And the watchman saw another man **r**: H7323
26 *another* man **r** alone. And the king H7323
27 Me thinketh the **r** of the foremost is like H4794
27 is like the **r** of Ahimaaz the son H4794
2Ki 5:21 when Naaman saw *him* **r** after him, he H7323
2Ch 23:12 noise of the people **r** and praising the H7323
Prv 5:15 and **r** waters out of thine own well. H5140
6:18 feet that be swift in **r** to mischief, H7323
Isa 33: 4 caterpiller: as the **r** to and fro of locusts H4944
Ezk 31: 4 high with her rivers **r** round about his H1980

R

Mk 9:15 amazed, and **r** to *him* saluted him. G4370
25 When Jesus saw that the people came **r** G1998
10:17 there came one **r**, and kneeled to him, G4370
Lk 6:38 together, and **r** over, shall men give G5240
Act 27:16 And **r** under a certain island which is G5295
Rev 9: 9 of chariots of many horses **r** to battle. G5143

RUSH
Job 8:11 Can the **r** grow up without mire? can H1573
Isa 9:14 head and tail, branch and **r**, in one day. H100
17:13 The nations shall **r** like the rushing of H7582
19:15 the head or tail, branch or **r**, may do. H100

RUSHED
Jdg 9:44 that *was* with him, **r** forward, and H6584
20:37 And the liers in wait hasted, and **r** H6584
Act 19:29 they **r** with one accord into the theatre. G3729

RUSHES
Isa 35: 7 lay, *shall be* grass with reeds and **r**. H1573

RUSHETH
Jer 8: 6 course, as the horse **r** into the battle. H7857

RUSHING
Isa 17:12 seas; and to the **r** of nations, *that* make H7588
12 a **r** like the rushing of mighty waters! H7582
12 a rushing like the **r** of mighty waters! H7588
13 The nations shall rush like the **r** of H7588
Jer 47: 3 *horses*, at the **r** of his chariots, *and* H7494
Ezk 3:12 a voice of a great **r**, *saying*, Blessed *be* H7494
13 against them, and a noise of a great **r**. H7494
Act 2: 2 heaven as of a **r** mighty wind, and it G5342

RUST
Mt 6:19 where moth and **r** doth corrupt, and G1035
20 neither moth nor **r** doth corrupt, and G1035

Jas 5: 3 cankered; and the **r** of them shall be a G2447

RUTH
Ru 1: 4 name of the other **R**: and they dwelled H7327
14 mother in law; but **R** clave unto her. H7327
16 And **R** said, Entreat me not to leave H7327
22 So Naomi returned, and **R** the H7327
2: 2 And **R** the Moabitess said unto Naomi, H7327
8 Then said Boaz unto **R**, Hearest thou H7327
21 And **R** the Moabitess said, He said H7327
22 And Naomi said unto **R** her daughter H7327
3: 9 she answered, I *am* **R** thine handmaid: H7327
4: 5 buy *it* also of **R** the Moabitess, the wife H7327
10 Moreover **R** the Moabitess, the wife of H7327
13 So Boaz took **R**, and she was his wife: H7327
Mt 1: 5 begat Obed of **R**; and Obed begat Jesse; G4503

RYE See RIE.

S

SABACHTHANI
Mt 27:46 Eli, Eli, lama **s**? that is to say, My God, G4518
Mk 15:34 Eloi, Eloi, lama **s**? which is, being G4518

SABAOTH
Ro 9:29 Except the Lord of **S** had left us a seed, G4519
Jas 5: 4 entered into the ears of the Lord of **s**. G4519

SABBATH
Ex 16:23 *is* the rest of the holy **s** unto the LORD: H7676
25 day; for to day *is* a **s** unto the LORD: to H7676
26 *which is* the **s**, in it there shall be none. H7676
29 hath given you the **s**, therefore he giveth H7676
20: 8 Remember the **s** day, to keep it holy. H7676
10 But the seventh day *is* the **s** of the H7676
11 blessed the **s** day, and hallowed it. H7676
31:14 Ye shall keep the **s** therefore; for it *is* H7676
15 the seventh *is* the **s** of rest, holy to the H7676
15 **s** day, he shall surely be put to death. H7676
16 shall keep the **s**, to observe the sabbath H7676
16 to observe the **s** throughout their H7676
35: 2 to you an holy day, a **s** of rest to the H7676
3 your habitations upon the **s** day. H7676
Lev 16:31 It *shall be* a **s** of rest unto you, and ye H7676
23: 3 the seventh day *is* the **s** of rest, an holy H7676
3 the **s** of the LORD in all your dwellings. H7676
11 after the **s** the priest shall wave it. H7676
15 morrow after the **s**, from the day that ye H7676
16 after the seventh **s** shall ye number fifty H7676
24 shall ye have a **s**, a memorial of blowing H7677
32 It *shall be* unto you a **s** of rest, and ye H7676
32 unto even, shall ye celebrate your **s**. H7676
39 first day *shall be* a **s**, and on the eighth H7677
39 and on the eighth day *shall be* a **s**. H7677
24: 8 Every **s** he shall set it in order before H7676
25: 2 shall the land keep a **s** unto the LORD. H7676
4 But in the seventh year shall be a **s** of H7676
4 unto the land, a **s** for the LORD: thou H7676
6 And the **s** of the land shall be meat for H7676
Nu 15:32 that gathered sticks upon the **s** day. H7676
28: 9 And on the **s** day two lambs of the first H7676
10 *This is* the burnt offering of every **s**, H7676
Dt 5:12 Keep the **s** day to sanctify it, as the H7676
14 But the seventh day *is* the **s** of the H7676
15 commanded thee to keep the **s** day. H7676
2Ki 4:23 nor **s**. And she said, *It shall be* well. H7676
11: 5 enter in on the **s** shall even be keepers H7676
7 go forth on the **s**, even they shall keep H7676
9 were to come in on the **s**, with them that H7676
9 the **s**, and came to Jehoiada the priest. H7676
16:18 And the covert for the **s** that they had H7676
1Ch 9:32 the shewbread, to prepare *it* every **s**. H7676
2Ch 23: 4 entering on the **s**, of the priests and of H7676
8 to come in on the **s**, with them that were H7676
8 were to go *out* on the **s**: for Jehoiada the H7676
36:21 kept **s**, to fulfil threescore and ten years. H7673
Neh 9:14 them thy holy **s**, and commandedst H7676
10:31 victuals on the **s** day to sell, *that* we H7676
31 it of them on the **s**, or on the holy day: H7676
13:15 wine presses on the **s**, and bringing in H7676
15 Jerusalem on the **s** day: and I testified H7676
16 and sold on the **s** unto the children of H7676
Neh 13:17 this that ye do, and profane the **s** day? H7676
18 wrath upon Israel by profaning the **s**. H7676
19 be dark before the **s**, I commanded that H7676
19 till after the **s**: and *some* of my servants H7676
19 no burden be brought in on the **s** day. H7676
21 time forth came they no *more* on the **s**. H7676
22 to sanctify the **s** day. Remember me, H7676
Ps 92:ttl A Psalm *or* Song for the **s** day. H7676
Isa 56: 2 it; that keepeth the **s** from polluting it, H7676
6 that keepeth the **s** from polluting it, H7676
58:13 If thou turn away thy foot from the **s**, H7676
13 day; and call the **s** a delight, the holy of H7676
66:23 and from one **s** to another, shall all H7676
Jer 17:21 no burden on the **s** day, nor bring *it* in H7676
22 houses on the **s** day, neither do ye any H7676
22 **s** day, as I commanded your fathers. H7676
24 of this city on the **s** day, but hallow the H7676
24 hallow the **s** day, to do no work therein; H7676
27 me to hallow the **s** day, and not to bear H7676
27 of Jerusalem on the **s** day; then will I H7676
Ezk 46: 1 but on the **s** it shall be opened, H7676+H3117
4 unto the LORD in the **s** day *shall be* six H7676
12 as he did on the **s** day: then he shall go H7676
Am 8: 5 sell corn? and the **s**, that we may set H7676
Mt 12: 1 At that time Jesus went on the **s** day G4521
2 is not lawful to do upon the **s** day. G4521
5 how that on the **s** days the priests in G4521
5 profane the **s**, and are blameless? G4521
8 Son of man is Lord even of the **s** day. G4521
10 the **s** days? that they might accuse him. G4521
11 into a pit on the **s** day, will he not lay G4521
12 it is lawful to do well on the **s** days. G4521
24:20 not in the winter, neither on the **s** day: G4521
28: 1 In the end of the **s**, as it began to dawn G4521
Mk 1:21 straightway on the **s** day he entered G4521
2:23 the corn fields on the **s** day; and his G4521
24 on the **s** day that which is not lawful? G4521
27 And he said unto them, The **s** was G4521
27 made for man, and not man for the **s**: G4521
28 the Son of man is Lord also of the **s**. G4521
3: 2 the **s** day; that they might accuse him. G4521
4 to do good on the **s** days, or to do evil? G4521
6: 2 And when the **s** day was come, he G4521
15:42 that is, the day before the **s**, G4315
16: 1 And when the **s** was past, Mary G4521
Lk 4:16 on the **s** day, and stood up for to read. G4521
31 Galilee, and taught them on the **s** days. G4521
6: 1 And it came to pass on the second **s** G4521
2 which is not lawful to do on the **s** days? G4521
5 the Son of man is Lord also of the **s**. G4521
6 And it came to pass also on another **s**, G4521
7 he would heal on the **s** day; that they G4521
9 Is it lawful on the **s** days to do good, or G4521
13:10 in one of the synagogues on the **s**. G4521
14 had healed on the **s** day, and said unto G4521
14 and be healed, and not on the **s** day. G4521
15 one of you on the **s** loose his ox or *his* G4521
16 be loosed from this bond on the **s** day? G4521
14: 1 on the **s** day, that they watched him. G4521
3 saying, Is it lawful to heal on the **s** day? G4521
5 straightway pull him out on the **s** day? G4521
23:54 the preparation, and the **s** drew on. G4521
56 **s** day according to the commandment. G4521
Jn 5: 9 walked: and on the same day was the **s**. G4521
10 cured, It is the **s** day: it is not lawful G4521
16 he had done these things on the **s** day. G4521
18 had broken the **s**, but said also that God G4521
7:22 and ye on the **s** day circumcise a man. G4521
23 If a man on the **s** day receive G4521
23 a man every whit whole on the **s** day? G4521
9:14 And it was the **s** day when Jesus made G4521
16 he keepeth not the **s** day. Others said, G4521
19:31 upon the cross on the **s** day, (for that G4521
31 day, (for that **s** day was an high day,) G4521
Act 1:12 is from Jerusalem a **s** day's journey. G4521
13:14 synagogue on the **s** day, and sat down. G4521
27 are read every **s** day, they have fulfilled G4521
42 might be preached to them the next **s**. G4521
44 And the next **s** day came almost the G4521
15:21 read in the synagogues every **s** day. G4521
16:13 And on the **s** we went out of the city by G4521
17: 2 them, and three **s** days reasoned with G4521
18: 4 synagogue every **s**, and persuaded the G4521
Col 2:16 or of the new moon, or of the **s** *days*: G4521

SABBATH-DAY See SABBATH and DAY.

SABBATHS
Ex 31:13 saying, Verily my **s** ye shall keep: for it H7676
Lev 19: 3 keep my **s**: I *am* the LORD your God. H7676
30 Ye shall keep my **s**, and reverence my H7676
23:15 offering; seven **s** shall be complete: H7676
38 Beside the **s** of the LORD, and beside H7676
25: 8 And thou shalt number seven **s** of H7676
8 space of the seven **s** of years shall be H7676
26: 2 Ye shall keep my **s**, and reverence my H7676
34 Then shall the land enjoy her **s**, as long H7676
34 then shall the land rest, and enjoy her **s**. H7676
35 rest in your **s**, when ye dwelt upon it. H7676
43 and shall enjoy her **s**, while she lieth H7676
1Ch 23:31 the LORD in the **s**, in the new moons, H7676
2Ch 2: 4 and evening, on the **s**, and on the new H7676
8:13 of Moses, on the **s**, and on the new H7676
31: 3 offerings for the **s**, and for the new H7676
36:21 had enjoyed her **s**: *for* as long as she lay H7676
Neh 10:33 offering, of the **s**, of the new moons, for H7676
Isa 1:13 the new moons and **s**, the calling of H7676
56: 4 that keep my **s**, and choose *the things* H7676
Lam 1: 7 saw her, *and* did mock at her **s**. H4868
2: 6 solemn feasts and **s** to be forgotten in H7676
Ezk 20:12 Moreover also I gave them my **s**, to be a H7676
13 live in them; and my **s** they greatly H7676
16 **s**: for their heart went after their idols. H7676
20 And hallow my **s**; and they shall be a H7676
21 they polluted my **s**: then I said, I would H7676
24 had polluted my **s**, and their eyes were H7676
22: 8 holy things, and hast profaned my **s**. H7676
26 my **s**, and I am profaned among them. H7676
23:38 the same day, and have profaned my **s**. H7676
44:24 assemblies; and they shall hallow my **s**. H7676
45:17 moons, and in the **s**, in all solemnities H7676
46: 3 LORD in the **s** and in the new moons. H7676
Hos 2:11 and her **s**, and all her solemn feasts. H7676

SABEANS
Job 1:15 And the **S** fell *upon them*, and took H7614

Isa 45:14 and of the S, men of stature, shall H5436
Ezk 23:42 common sort *were* brought S from the H5433
Joel 3: 8 sell them to the S, to a people far off: for H7615

SABTA
1Ch 1: 9 and Havilah, and S, and Raamah, and H5454

SABTAH
Gen 10: 7 and Havilah, and S, and Raamah, and H5454

SABTECHA
Gen 10: 7 and Raamah, and S: and the sons of H5455
1Ch 1: 9 and Raamah, and S. And the sons of H5455

SACAR
1Ch 11:35 Ahiam the son of S the Hararite, H7940
26: 4 S the fourth, and Nethaneel the fifth, H7940

SACK
Gen 42:25 money into his s, and to give them H8242
27 And as one of them opened his s to give H8242
28 and, lo, *it is* even in my s: and their heart H572
35 money *was* in his s: and when *both* they H8242
43:21 in the mouth of his s, our money in full H572
44:11 down every man his s to the ground, and H572
11 the ground, and opened every man his s. H572
12 and the cup was found in Benjamin's s. H572
Lev 11:32 or skin, or s, whatsoever vessel *it* H8242

SACKBUT
Dan 3: 5 the cornet, flute, harp, s, psaltery, H5443
7 cornet, flute, harp, s, psaltery, and all H5443
10 the cornet, flute, harp, s, psaltery, and H5443
15 the cornet, flute, harp, s, psaltery, and H5443

SACKCLOTH
Gen 37:34 And Jacob rent his clothes, and put s H8242
2Sa 3:31 and gird you with s, and mourn before H8242
21:10 of Aiah took s, and spread it for her H8242
1Ki 20:31 us, I pray thee, put s on our loins, and H8242
32 So they girded s on their loins, and *put* H8242
21:27 clothes, and put s upon his flesh, and H8242
27 fasted, and lay in s, and went softly. H8242
2Ki 6:30 behold, *he had* s within upon his flesh. H8242
19: 1 s, and went into the house of the LORD. H8242
2 covered with s, to Isaiah the prophet H8242
1Ch 21:16 *were* clothed in s, fell upon their faces. H8242
Est 4: 1 and put on s with ashes, and went H8242
2 enter into the king's gate clothed with s. H8242
3 wailing; and many lay in s and ashes. H8242
4 his s from him: but he received *it* not. H8242
Job 16:15 I have sewed s upon my skin, and H8242
Ps 30:11 off my s, and girded me with gladness; H8242
35:13 my clothing *was* s: I humbled my soul H8242
69:11 I made s also my garment; and I H8242
Isa 3:24 of s; *and* burning instead of beauty. H8242
15: 3 themselves with s: on the tops of their H8242
20: 2 Go and loose the s from off thy loins, H8242
22:12 and to baldness, and to girding with s: H8242
32:11 you bare, and gird *s* upon *your* loins.
37: 1 s, and went into the house of the LORD. H8242
2 covered with s, unto Isaiah the prophet H8242
50: 3 blackness, and I make s their covering. H8242
58: 5 and to spread s and ashes *under him*? H8242
Jer 4: 8 For this gird you with s, lament and H8242
6:26 gird *thee* with s, and wallow thyself in H8242
48:37 *shall be* cuttings, and upon the loins s. H8242
49: 3 gird you with s; lament, and run to H8242
Lam 2:10 girded themselves with s: the virgins of H8242
Ezk 7:18 They shall also gird *themselves* with s, H8242
27:31 gird them with s, and they shall weep H8242
Dan 9: 3 with fasting, and s, and ashes: H8242
Joel 1: 8 Lament like a virgin girded with s for H8242
13 lie all night in s, ye ministers of my God: H8242
Am 8:10 and I will bring up s upon all loins, and H8242
Jna 3: 5 a fast, and put on s, from the greatest of H8242
6 covered *him* with s, and sat in ashes. H8242
8 be covered with s, and cry mightily unto H8242
Mt 11:21 have repented long ago in s and ashes. *G4526*
Lk 10:13 ago repented, sitting in s and ashes. *G4526*
Rev 6:12 sun became black as s of hair, and the *G4526*
11: 3 *and* threescore days, clothed in s. *G4526*

SACKCLOTHES
Neh 9: 1 and with s, and earth upon them. H8242

SACKS
Gen 42:25 Then Joseph commanded to fill their s H3627
35 they emptied their s, that, behold, every H8242
43:12 in the mouth of your s, carry *it* again in H572
18 returned in our s at the first time are we H572
21 that we opened our s, and, behold, *every* H572
22 cannot tell who put our money in our s. H572
23 you treasure in your s: I had your money. H572
44: 1 Fill the men's s *with* food, as much as H572
Jos 9: 4 and took old s upon their asses, and H8242

SACK'S
Gen 42:27 for, behold, it *was* in his s mouth. H572
44: 1 put every man's money in his s mouth. H572
2 And put my cup, the silver cup, in the s H572

SACKS'
Gen 44: 8 we found in our s mouths, we brought H572

SACRIFICE
Gen 31:54 Then Jacob offered s upon the mount, H2077
Ex 3:18 that we may s to the LORD our God. H2076
5: 3 the desert, and s unto the LORD our H2076
8 cry, saying, Let us go *and* s to our God. H2076
17 ye say, Let us go *and* do s to the LORD. H2076
8: 8 go, that they may do s unto the LORD. H2076
25 said, Go ye, s to your God in the land. H2076
26 to do; for we shall s the abomination of H2076
26 God: lo, shall we s the abomination of H2076
27 wilderness, and s to the LORD our God, H2076
28 you go, that ye may s to the LORD your H2076
29 letting the people go to s to the LORD. H2076
10:25 that we may s unto the LORD our God. H6213
12:27 That ye shall say, It *is* the s of the H2077
13:15 beast: therefore I s to the LORD all that H2076
20:24 unto me, and shalt s thereon thy burnt H2076
23:18 Thou shalt not offer the blood of my s H2077
18 fat of my s remain until the morning. H2282
29:28 children of Israel of the s of their peace H2077
30: 9 thereon, nor burnt s, nor meat offering; H5930
34:15 their gods, and do s unto their gods, H2076
15 and *one* call thee, and thou eat of his s; H2077
25 Thou shalt not offer the blood of my s H2077
25 neither shall the s of the feast of the H2077
Lev 1: 3 If his offering *be* a burnt s of the herd, H5930
9 *to be* a burnt s, an offering made by H5930
10 goats, for a burnt s; he shall bring it a H5930
13 altar: it *is* a burnt s, an offering made H5930
14 And if the burnt s for his offering to the H5930
17 fire: it *is* a burnt s, an offering made by H5930
3: 1 And if his oblation *be* a s of peace H2077
3 And he shall offer of the s of the peace H2077
5 upon the burnt s, which *is* upon the H5930
6 And if his offering for a s of peace H2077
9 And he shall offer of the s of the peace H2077
4:10 the bullock of the s of peace offerings: H2077
26 as the fat of the s of peace offerings: H2077
31 away from off the s of peace offerings; H2077
35 away from the s of the peace offerings; H2077
7:11 And this *is* the law of the s of peace H2077
12 he shall offer with the s of thanksgiving H2077
13 s of thanksgiving of his peace offerings. H2077
15 And the flesh of the s of his peace H2077
16 But if the s of his offering *be* a vow, or a H2077
16 he offereth his s: and on the morrow H2077
17 But the remainder of the flesh of the s H2077
18 And if *any* of the flesh of the s of his H2077
20 *of* the flesh of the s of peace offerings, H2077
21 of the flesh of the s of peace offerings, H2077
29 that offereth the s of his peace offerings H2077
29 LORD of the s of his peace offerings. H2077
37 and of the s of the peace offerings; H2077
8:21 it *was* a burnt s for a sweet savour, H5930
9: 4 peace offerings, to s before the LORD; H2076
17 beside the burnt s of the morning. H5930
18 and the ram *for* a s of peace offerings, H2077
17: 8 you, that offereth a burnt offering or s, H2077
19: 5 And if ye offer a s of peace offerings H2077
22:21 And whosoever offereth a s of peace H2077
29 And when ye will offer a s of H2077
23:19 Then ye shall s one kid of the goats for H6213
19 the first year for a s of peace offerings. H2077
37 and a meat offering, a s, and drink H2077
27:11 they do not offer a s unto the LORD, H7133
Nu 6:17 And he shall offer the ram *for* a s of H2077
18 *is* under the s of the peace offerings. H2077
7:17 And for a s of peace offerings, two H2077
23 And for a s of peace offerings, two H2077
29 And for a s of peace offerings, two H2077
35 And for a s of peace offerings, two H2077
41 And for a s of peace offerings, two H2077
47 And for a s of peace offerings, two H2077
Nu 7:53 And for a s of peace offerings, two H2077
59 And for a s of peace offerings, two H2077
65 And for a s of peace offerings, two H2077
71 And for a s of peace offerings, two H2077
77 And for a s of peace offerings, two H2077
83 And for a s of peace offerings, two H2077
88 And all the oxen for the s of the peace H2077
15: 3 offering, or a s in performing a vow, H2077
5 the burnt offering or s, for one lamb. H2077
8 offering, or *for* a s in performing a vow, H2077
25 their offering, a s made by fire unto the
23: 6 burnt s, he, and all the princes of Moab. H5930
28: 6 savour, a s made by fire unto the LORD.
8 shalt offer *it*, a s made by fire, of a sweet
13 savour, a s made by fire unto the LORD.
19 But ye shall offer a s made by fire *for* a
24 the meat of the s made by fire, of a sweet
29: 6 savour, a s made by fire unto the LORD.
13 And ye shall offer a burnt offering, a s
36 But ye shall offer a burnt offering, a s
Dt 15:21 shalt not s it unto the LORD thy God. H2076
16: 2 Thou shalt therefore s the passover H2076
5 Thou mayest not s the passover within H2076
6 there thou shalt s the passover at even, H2076
17: 1 Thou shalt not s unto the LORD thy H2076
18: 3 them that offer a s, whether *it be* ox or H2077
33:10 thee, and whole burnt s upon thine altar.
Jos 22:26 altar, not for burnt offering, nor for s: H2077
Jdg 6:26 and offer a burnt s with the wood of the H5930
16:23 for to offer a great s unto Dagon their H2077
1Sa 1: 3 to worship and to s unto the LORD of H2076
21 the LORD the yearly s, and his vow. H2077
2:13 any man offered s, the priest's servant H2077
19 with her husband to offer the yearly s. H2077
29 Wherefore kick ye at my s and at mine H2077
3:14 be purged with s nor offering for ever. H2077
9:12 s of the people to day in the high place: H2077
13 he doth bless the s; *and* afterwards they H2077
10: 8 offerings, *and* to s sacrifices of peace H2076
15:15 and of the oxen, to s unto the LORD thy H2076
21 to s unto the LORD thy God in Gilgal. H2076
22 s, *and* to hearken than the fat of rams. H2077
16: 2 and say, I am come to s to the LORD. H2076
3 And call Jesse to the s, and I will shew H2077
5 And he said, Peaceably: I am come to s H2076
5 with me to the s. And he sanctified Jesse H2077
5 and his sons, and called them to the s. H2077
20: 6 *is* a yearly s there for all the family. H2077
29 our family hath a s in the city; and my H2077
2Sa 24:22 *here be* oxen for burnt s, and threshing
1Ki 3: 4 And the king went to Gibeon to s there; H2076
8:62 with him, offered s before the LORD. H2077
63 And Solomon offered a s of peace H2077
12:27 If this people go up to do s in the house H2077
18:29 of the *evening* s, that *there was* neither H4503
33 pour *it* on the burnt s, and on the wood. H5930
36 of the *evening* s, that Elijah the prophet H4503
38 the burnt s, and the wood, and the H5930
2Ki 5:17 s unto other gods, but unto the LORD. H2077
10:19 for I have a great s *to do* to Baal; H2077
14: 4 s and burnt incense on the high places. H2076
16:15 and the king's burnt s, and his meat H5930
15 all the blood of the s: and the brasen H2077
17:35 to them, nor serve them, nor s to them: H2076
36 ye worship, and to him shall ye do s. H2076
2Ch 2: 6 house, save only to burn s before him? H6999
7: 5 And king Solomon offered a s of twenty H2077
12 this place to myself for an house of s. H2077
11:16 s unto the LORD God of their fathers. H2076
28:23 *therefore* will I s to them, that they may H2076
33:17 Nevertheless the people did s still in the H2076
Ezr 4: 2 ye *do*; and we do s unto him since the H2076
9: 4 and I sat astonied until the evening s. H4503
5 And at the evening s I arose up from H4503
Neh 4: 2 will they s? will they make an end H2076
Ps 20: 3 offerings, and accept thy burnt s; Selah.
40: 6 S and offering thou didst not desire; H2077
50: 5 have made a covenant with me by s. H2077
51:16 For thou desirest not s; else would I give H2077
54: 6 I will freely s unto thee: I will praise thy H2076
107:22 And let them s the sacrifices of H2076
116:17 I will offer to thee the s of thanksgiving, H2077
118:27 us light: bind the s with cords, *even* H2282
141: 2 lifting up of my hands *as* the evening s. H4503
Prv 15: 8 The s of the wicked *is* an abomination H2077
21: 3 *is* more acceptable to the LORD than s. H2077
27 The s of the wicked *is* abomination: H2077
Ecc 5: 1 hear, than to give the s of fools: for they H2077
Isa 19:21 day, and shall do s and oblation; yea, H2077

S

Isa 34: 6 for the LORD hath a s in Bozrah, and a H2077
57: 7 even thither wentest thou up to offer s. H2077
Jer 33:11 that shall bring the s of praise into the
18 meat offerings, and to do s continually. H2077
46:10 of hosts hath a s in the north country H2077
Ezk 39:17 every side to my s that I do sacrifice for H2077
17 my sacrifice that I do s for you, *even* a H2076
17 you, *even* a great s upon the mountains H2077
19 of my s which I have sacrificed for you. H2077
40:42 they slew the burnt offering and the s. H2077
44:11 offering and the s for the people, and H2077
46:24 the house shall boil the s of the people. H2077
Dan 8:11 by him the daily *s* was taken away, and
12 *him* against the daily *s* by reason of
13 the daily *s*, and the transgression
9:27 he shall cause the s and the oblation to H2077
11:31 shall take away the daily *s*, and they shall
12:11 And from the time *that* the daily *s* shall
Hos 3: 4 and without a s, and without an image, H2077
4:13 They s upon the tops of the mountains, H2076
14 with whores, and they s with harlots: H2076
6: 6 For I desired mercy, and not s; and the H2077
8:13 They s flesh *for* the sacrifices of mine H2076
12:11 are vanity: they s bullocks in Gilgal; H2076
13: 2 Let the men that s kiss the calves. H2076
Am 4: 5 And offer a s of thanksgiving with
Jna 1:16 a s unto the LORD, and made vows. H2077
2: 9 But I will s unto thee with the voice of H2076
Hab 1:16 Therefore they s unto their net, and H2076
Zep 1: 7 prepared a s, he hath bid his guests. H2077
8 day of the LORD'S s, that I will punish H2077
Zec 14:21 and all they that s shall come and take H2076
Mal 1: 8 And if ye offer the blind for s, *is it* not H2076
Mt 9:13 mercy, and not s: for I am not come to G2378
12: 7 mercy, and not s, ye would not have G2378
Mk 9:49 and every s shall be salted with salt. G2378
Lk 2:24 And to offer a s according to that G2378
Act 7:41 days, and offered s unto the idol, and G2378
14:13 and would have done s with the people. G2380
18 that they had not done s unto them. G2380
Ro 12: 1 bodies a living s, holy, acceptable unto G2378
1Co 8: 4 that are offered in s unto idols, we G1494
10:19 is offered in s to idols is any thing? G1494
20 which the Gentiles s, they sacrifice to G2380
20 sacrifice, they s to devils, and not to G2380
28 This is offered in s unto idols, eat not G1494
Eph 5: 2 a s to God for a sweetsmelling savour. G2378
Php 2:17 Yea, and if I be offered upon the s and G2378
4:18 a s acceptable, wellpleasing to God. G2378
Heb 7:27 priests, to offer up s, first for his own G2378
9:26 to put away sin by the s of himself. G2378
10: 5 the world, he saith, S and offering thou G2378
8 Above when he said, S and offering G2378
12 But this man, after he had offered one s G2378
26 there remaineth no more s for sins, G2378
11: 4 a more excellent s than Cain, by which G2378
13:15 By him therefore let us offer the s of G2378

SACRIFICED
Ex 24: 5 offerings, and s peace offerings of oxen H2076
32: 8 it, and have s thereunto, and said, H2076
Dt 32:17 They s unto devils, not to God; to gods H2076
Jos 8:31 unto the LORD, and s peace offerings. H2076
Jdg 2: 5 and they s there unto the LORD. H2076
1Sa 2:15 to the man that s, Give flesh to roast for H2076
6:15 offerings and s sacrifices the same H2076
11:15 and there they s sacrifices of peace H2076
2Sa 6:13 gone six paces, he s oxen and fatlings. H2076
1Ki 3: 2 Only the people s in high places, H2076
3 he s and burnt incense in high places. H2076
11: 8 burnt incense and s unto their gods. H2076
2Ki 12: 3 s and burnt incense in the high places. H2076
15: 4 the people s and burnt incense still H2076
35 the people s and burned incense H2076
16: 4 And he s and burnt incense in the high H2076
17:32 the high places, which s for them in the H6213
1Ch 21:28 of Ornan the Jebusite, then he s there. H2076
29:21 And they s sacrifices unto the LORD, H2076
2Ch 5: 6 before the ark, s sheep and oxen, which H2076
28: 4 He s also and burnt incense in the high H2076
23 For he s unto the gods of Damascus, H2076
33:16 altar of the LORD, and s thereon peace H2076
22 father: for Amon s unto all the carved H2076
34: 4 graves of them that had s unto them. H2076
Ps 106:37 Yea, they s their sons and their H2076
38 whom they s unto the idols of Canaan: H2076
Ezk 16:20 and these hast thou s unto them to be H2076
39:19 of my sacrifice which I have s for you. H2076
Hos 11: 2 from them: they s unto Baalim, and H2076
1Co 5: 7 For even Christ our passover is s for us: G2380
Rev 2:14 Israel, to eat things s unto idols, and to G1494
20 and to eat things s unto idols. G1494

SACRIFICEDST
Dt 16: 4 flesh, which thou s the first day at even, H2076

SACRIFICES
Gen 46: 1 s unto the God of his father Isaac. H2077
Ex 10:25 must give us also s and burnt offerings, H2077
18:12 a burnt offering and s for God: and H2077
Lev 7:32 of the s of your peace offerings. H2077
34 of Israel from off the s of their peace H2077
10:13 sons' due, of the s of the LORD made by H801
14 given out of the s of peace offerings of H2077
17: 5 may bring their s, which they offer in H2077
7 And they shall no more offer their s H2077
Nu 10:10 and over the s of your peace offerings; H2077
25: 2 And they called the people unto the s of H2077
28: 2 my bread for my s made by fire, *for* a
Dt 12: 6 and your s, and your tithes, and H2077
11 and your s, your tithes, and the H2077
27 the blood of thy s shall be poured out H2077
32:38 Which did eat the fat of their s, *and* H2077
33:19 they shall offer s of righteousness: for H2077
Jos 13:14 inheritance; the s of the LORD God of H801
22:27 and with our s, and with our peace H2077
28 offerings, nor for s; but it *is* a witness H2077
29 offerings, or for s, beside the altar of the H2077
1Sa 6:15 s the same day unto the LORD. H2077
10: 8 *and* to sacrifice s of peace offerings: H2077
11:15 they sacrificed s of peace offerings H2077
15:22 offerings and s, as in obeying the voice H2077
2Sa 15:12 while he offered s. And the conspiracy H2077
2Ki 10:24 And when they went in to offer s and H2077
1Ch 16: 1 burnt s and peace offerings before God. H5930
23:31 And to offer all burnt s unto the LORD H5930
29:21 And they sacrificed s unto the LORD, H2077
21 and s in abundance for all Israel: H2077
2Ch 7: 1 offering and the s; and the glory of the H2077
4 the people offered s before the LORD. H2077
13:11 evening burnt s and sweet incense: H5930
29:31 near and bring s and thank offerings H2077
31 brought in s and thank offerings; H2077
Ezr 6: 3 place where they offered s, and let the H1685
10 That they may offer s of sweet savours
Neh 12:43 Also that day they offered great s, and H2077
Ps 4: 5 Offer the s of righteousness, and put H2077
27: 6 in his tabernacle s of joy; I will sing, H2077
50: 8 I will not reprove thee for thy s or thy H2077
51:17 The s of God *are* a broken spirit: a H2077
19 Then shalt thou be pleased with the s H2077
66:15 I will offer unto thee burnt s of fatlings,
106:28 Baal-peor, and ate the s of the dead. H2077
107:22 And let them sacrifice the s of H2077
Prv 17: 1 than an house full of s *with* strife. H2077
Isa 1:11 multitude of your s unto me? saith the H2077
29: 1 add ye year to year; let them kill s. H2282
43:23 me with thy s. I have not caused thee H2077
24 with the fat of thy s: but thou hast made H2077
56: 7 offerings and their s *shall be* accepted H2077
Jer 6:20 acceptable, nor your s sweet unto me. H2077
7:21 offerings unto your s, and eat flesh. H2077
22 Egypt, concerning burnt offerings or s: H2077
17:26 offerings, and s, and meat offerings, H2077
26 s of praise, unto the house of the LORD.
Ezk 20:28 they offered there their s, and there they H2077
40:41 eight tables, whereupon they slew *their s*.
Hos 4:19 shall be ashamed because of their s. H2077
8:13 They sacrifice flesh *for* the s of mine H2077
9: 4 unto him: their s *shall be* unto them as H2077
Am 4: 4 and bring your s every morning, *and* H2077
5:25 Have ye offered unto me s and H2077
Mk 12:33 than all whole burnt offerings and s. G2378
Lk 13: 1 blood Pilate had mingled with their s. G2378
Act 7:42 slain beasts and s *by the space of* forty G2378
1Co 10:18 eat of the s partakers of the altar? G2378
Heb 5: 1 he may offer both gifts and s for sins: G2378
8: 3 to offer gifts and s: wherefore *it is* of G2378
9: 9 both gifts and s, that could not make G2378
23 themselves with better s than these. G2378
10: 1 never with those s which they offered G2378
3 But in those *s there is* a remembrance
6 In burnt offerings and *s* for sin thou hast
11 s, which can never take away sins: G2378
13:16 not: for with such s God is well pleased. G2378
1Pt 2: 5 s, acceptable to God by Jesus Christ. G2378

SACRIFICETH
Ex 22:20 He that s unto *any* god, save unto the H2076
Ecc 9: 2 unclean; to him that s, and to him that H2076
2 and to him that s not: as *is* the good, so H2076
Isa 65: 3 to my face; that s in gardens, and H2076
66: 3 a man; he that s a lamb, *as if* he cut H2076
Mal 1:14 and voweth, and s unto the Lord a H2076

SACRIFICING
1Ki 8: 5 before the ark, s sheep and oxen, that H2076
12:32 did he in Beth-el, s unto the calves that H2076

SACRILEGE
Ro 2:22 abhorrest idols, dost thou commit s? G2416

SAD
Gen 40: 6 upon them, and, behold, they *were* s. H2196
1Sa 1:18 eat, and her countenance was no more *s*.
1Ki 21: 5 spirit so s, that thou eatest no bread? H5620
Neh 2: 1 not been *beforetime* s in his presence. H7451
2 thy countenance s, seeing thou *art* not H7451
3 my countenance be s, when the city, the H3415
Ezk 13:22 of the righteous s, whom I have not H3512
22 I have not made s; and strengthened H3510
Mt 6:16 hypocrites, of a s countenance: for they G4659
Mk 10:22 And he was s at that saying, and went G4768
Lk 24:17 one to another, as ye walk, and are s? G4659

SADDLE
Lev 15: 9 And what s soever he rideth upon that H4817
2Sa 19:26 servant said, I will s me an ass, that I H2280
1Ki 13:13 And he said unto his sons, S me the H2280
27 And he spake to his sons, saying, S me H2280

SADDLED
Gen 22: 3 in the morning, and s his ass, and took H2280
Nu 22:21 in the morning, and s his ass, and went H2280
Jdg 19:10 s, his concubine also *was* with him. H2280
2Sa 16: 1 a couple of asses s, and upon them two H2280
17:23 not followed, he s *his* ass, and arose, H2280
1Ki 2:40 And Shimei arose, and s his ass, and H2280
13:13 s him the ass: and he rode thereon, H2280
23 had drunk, that he s for him the ass, *to* H2280
27 Saddle me the ass. And they s *him*. H2280
2Ki 4:24 Then she s an ass, and said to her H2280

SADDUCEES
Mt 3: 7 of the Pharisees and S come to his G4523
16: 1 The Pharisees also with the S came, G4523
6 the leaven of the Pharisees and of the S. G4523
11 the leaven of the Pharisees and of the S? G4523
12 doctrine of the Pharisees and of the S. G4523
22:23 The same day came to him the S, which G4523
34 he had put the S to silence, they were G4523
Mk 12:18 Then come unto him the S, which say G4523
Lk 20:27 Then came to *him* certain of the S, G4523
Act 4: 1 the temple, and the S, came upon them, G4523
5:17 the S,) and were filled with indignation, G4523
23: 6 that the one part were S, and the other G4523
7 the S: and the multitude was divided. G4523
8 For the S say that there is no G4523

SADLY
Gen 40: 7 saying, Wherefore look ye *so* s to day? H7451

SADNESS
Ecc 7: 3 for by the s of the countenance H7455

SADOC
Mt 1:14 And Azor begat S; and Sadoc begat G4524
14 And Azor begat Sadoc; and S begat G4524

SAFE
1Sa 12:11 enemies on every side, and ye dwelled s. H983
2Sa 18:29 young man Absalom s? And Ahimaaz H7965
32 man Absalom s? And Cushi answered, H7965
Job 21: 9 Their houses *are* s from fear, neither *is* H7965
Ps119:117 Hold thou me up, and I shall be s: and I H3467
Prv 18:10 the righteous runneth into it, and is s. H7682
29:25 putteth his trust in the LORD shall be s. H7682
Isa 5:29 *it* away s, and none shall deliver *it*. H6403
Ezk 34:27 and they shall be s in their land, and H983
Lk 15:27 he hath received him s and sound. G5198
Act 23:24 bring *him* s unto Felix the governor. G1295
27:44 to pass, that they escaped all s to land. G1295
Php 3: 1 indeed *is* not grievous, but for you *it is* s. G804

SAFEGUARD
1Sa 22:23 thy life: but with me thou *shalt be* in s. H4931

SAFELY
Lev 26: 5 to the full, and dwell in your land s. H983
1Ki 4:25 And Judah and Israel dwelt s, every man H983
Ps 78:53 And he led them on s, so that they feared H983
Prv 1:33 s, and shall be quiet from fear of evil. H983
3:23 Then shalt thou walk in thy way s, and H983
31:11 The heart of her husband doth s trust in
Isa 41: 3 He pursued them, and passed s; even by H7965
Jer 23: 6 Israel shall dwell s: and this is his name H983
32:37 place, and I will cause them to dwell s: H983
33:16 shall dwell s: and this is the name H983
Ezk 28:26 And they shall dwell s therein, and shall H983
34:25 they shall dwell s in the wilderness, and H983
28 s, and none shall make them afraid. H983
38: 8 and they shall dwell s all of them. H983
11 at rest, that dwell s, all of them dwelling H983
14 Israel dwelleth s, shalt thou not know it? H983
39:26 me, when they dwelt s in their land, and H983
Hos 2:18 earth, and will make them to lie down s. H983
Zec 14:11 but Jerusalem shall be s inhabited. H983
Mk 14:44 is he; take him, and lead him away s. G806
Act 16:23 charging the jailor to keep them s: G806

SAFETY
Lev 25:18 them; and ye shall dwell in the land in s. H983
19 shall eat your fill, and dwell therein in s. H983
Dt 12:10 round about, so that ye dwell in s; H983
33:12 shall dwell in s by him; and the LORD H983
28 Israel then shall dwell in s alone: the H983
Job 3:26 I was not in s, neither had I rest, neither H7951
5: 4 His children are far from s, and they are H3468
11 those which mourn may be exalted to s. H3468
11:18 thee, and thou shalt take thy rest in s. H983
24:23 Though it be given him to be in s, H983
Ps 4: 8 thou, LORD, only makest me dwell in s. H983
12: 5 him in s from him that puffeth at him. H3468
33:17 An horse is a vain thing for s: neither H8668
Prv 11:14 the multitude of counsellors there is s. H8668
21:31 the day of battle: but s is of the LORD. H8668
24: 6 in multitude of counsellors there is s. H8668
Isa 14:30 shall lie down in s: and I will kill thy root H983
Act 5:23 found we shut with all s, and the keepers G803
1Th 5: 3 For when they shall say, Peace and s; G803

SAFFRON
Song 4:14 Spikenard and s; calamus and H3750

SAID
Gen 1: 3 And God s, Let there be light: and there H559
6 And God s, Let there be a firmament in H559
9 And God s, Let the waters under the H559
11 And God s, Let the earth bring forth H559
14 And God s, Let there be lights in the H559
20 And God s, Let the waters bring forth H559
24 And God s, Let the earth bring forth the H559
26 And God s, Let us make man in our H559
28 And God blessed them, and God s unto H559
29 And God s, Behold, I have given you H559
2:18 And the LORD God s, It is not good that H559
23 And Adam s, This is now bone of my H559
3: 1 had made. And he s unto the woman, H559
1 Yea, hath God s, Ye shall not eat of every H559
2 And the woman s unto the serpent, We H559
3 garden, God hath s, Ye shall not eat of it, H559
4 And the serpent s unto the woman, Ye H559
9 Adam, and s unto him, Where art thou? H559
10 And he s, I heard thy voice in the garden, H559
11 And he s, Who told thee that thou wast H559
12 And the man s, The woman whom thou H559
13 And the LORD God s unto the woman, H559
13 s, The serpent beguiled me, and I did eat. H559
14 And the LORD God s unto the serpent, H559
16 Unto the woman he s, I will greatly H559
17 And unto Adam he s, Because thou hast H559
22 And the LORD God s, Behold, the man is H559
4: 1 s, I have gotten a man from the LORD. H559
6 And the LORD s unto Cain, Why art H559
9 And the LORD s unto Cain, Where is H559
9 s, I know not: Am I my brother's keeper? H559
10 And he s, What hast thou done? the voice H559
13 And Cain s unto the LORD, My H559
15 And the LORD s unto him, Therefore H559
23 And Lamech s unto his wives, Adah and H559
25 Seth: For God, s she, hath appointed
6: 3 And the LORD s, My spirit shall not H559
7 And the LORD s, I will destroy man H559
13 And God s unto Noah, The end of all H559
7: 1 And the LORD s unto Noah, Come thou H559
8:21 and the LORD s in his heart, I will not H559
Gen 9: 1 Noah and his sons, and s unto them, Be H559
12 And God s, This is the token of the H559
17 And God s unto Noah, This is the token H559
25 And he s, Cursed be Canaan; a servant of H559
26 And he s, Blessed be the LORD God of H559
10: 9 wherefore it is s, Even as Nimrod the H559
11: 3 And they s one to another, Go to, let us H559
4 And they s, Go to, let us build us a city H559
6 And the LORD s, Behold, the people is H559
12: 1 Now the LORD had s unto Abram, Get H559
7 unto Abram, and s, Unto thy seed will I H559
11 into Egypt, that he s unto Sarai his wife, H559
18 And Pharaoh called Abram, and s, What H559
13: 8 And Abram s unto Lot, Let there be no H559
14 And the LORD s unto Abram, after that H559
14:19 And he blessed him, and s, Blessed be H559
21 And the king of Sodom s unto Abram, H559
22 And Abram s to the king of Sodom, I H559
15: 2 And Abram s, Lord GOD, what wilt thou H559
3 And Abram s, Behold, to me thou hast H559
5 And he brought him forth abroad, and s, H559
5 and he s unto him, So shall thy seed be. H559
7 And he s unto him, I am the LORD that H559
8 And he s, Lord GOD, whereby shall I H559
9 And he s unto him, Take me an heifer of H559
13 And he s unto Abram, Know of a surety H559
16: 2 And Sarai s unto Abram, Behold now, H559
5 And Sarai s unto Abram, My wrong be H559
6 But Abram s unto Sarai, Behold, thy H559
8 And he s, Hagar, Sarai's maid, whence H559
8 thou go? And she s, I flee from the face of H559
9 And the angel of the LORD s unto her, H559
10 And the angel of the LORD s unto her, I H559
11 And the angel of the LORD s unto her, H559
13 God seest me: for she s, Have I also here H559
17: 1 to Abram, and s unto him, I am the H559
9 And God s unto Abraham, Thou shalt H559
15 And God s unto Abraham, As for Sarai H559
17 and laughed, and s in his heart, Shall a H559
18 And Abraham s unto God, O that H559
19 And God s, Sarah thy wife shall bear thee H559
23 selfsame day, as God had s unto him. H1696
18: 3 And s, My Lord, if now I have found H559
5 And they s, So do, as thou hast said. H559
5 And they said, So do, as thou hast s. H1696
6 unto Sarah, and s, Make ready quickly H559
9 And they s unto him, Where is Sarah thy H559
9 thy wife? And he s, Behold, in the tent. H559
10 And he s, I will certainly return unto thee H559
13 And the LORD s unto Abraham, H559
15 And he s, Nay; but thou didst laugh. H559
17 And the LORD s, Shall I hide from H559
20 And the LORD s, Because the cry of H559
23 And Abraham drew near, and s, Wilt H559
26 And the LORD s, If I find in Sodom fifty H559
27 And Abraham answered and s, Behold H559
28 lack of five? And he s, If I find there forty H559
29 And he spake unto him yet again, and s, H559
29 And he s, I will not do it for forty's sake. H559
30 And he s unto him, Oh let not the Lord H559
30 he s, I will not do it, if I find thirty there. H559
31 And he s, Behold now, I have taken upon H559
31 s, I will not destroy it for twenty's sake. H559
32 And he s, Oh let not the Lord be angry, H559
32 he s, I will not destroy it for ten's sake. H559
19: 2 And he s, Behold now, my lords, turn in, H559
2 ways. And they s, Nay; but we will abide H559
5 And they called unto Lot, and s unto H559
7 And s, I pray you, brethren, do not so H559
9 And they s, Stand back. And they said H559
9 And they said, Stand back. And they s H559
12 And the men s unto Lot, Hast thou here H559
14 his daughters, and s, Up, get you out of H559
17 abroad, that he s, Escape for thy life; look H559
18 And Lot s unto them, Oh, not so, my H559
21 And he s unto him, See, I have accepted H559
31 And the firstborn s unto the younger, H559
34 that the firstborn s unto the younger, H559
20: 2 And Abraham s of Sarah his wife, She is H559
3 by night, and s to him, Behold, thou H559
4 near her: and he s, Lord, wilt thou slay H559
5 S he not unto me, She is my sister? and H559
5 even she herself s, He is my brother: in H559
6 And God s unto him in a dream, Yea, I H559
9 Then Abimelech called Abraham, and s H559
10 And Abimelech s unto Abraham, What H559
11 And Abraham s, Because I thought, H559
13 house, that I s unto her, This is thy H559
15 And Abimelech s, Behold, my land is H559
Gen 20:16 And unto Sarah he s, Behold, I have H559
21: 1 And the LORD visited Sarah as he had s, H559
6 And Sarah s, God hath made me to H559
7 And she s, Who would have said unto H559
7 And she said, Who would have s unto H4448
10 Wherefore she s unto Abraham, Cast out H559
12 And God s unto Abraham, Let it not be H559
12 all that Sarah hath s unto thee, hearken H559
16 a bowshot: for she s, Let me not see the H559
17 out of heaven, and s unto her, What H559
24 And Abraham s, I will swear. H559
26 And Abimelech s, I wot not who hath H559
29 And Abimelech s unto Abraham, What H559
30 And he s, For these seven ewe lambs H559
22: 1 Abraham, and s unto him, Abraham: H559
1 Abraham: and he s, Behold, here I am. H559
2 And he s, Take now thy son, thine only H559
5 And Abraham s unto his young men, H559
7 his father, and s, My father: and he said, H559
7 My father: and he s, Here am I, my son. H559
7 I, my son. And he s, Behold the fire and H559
8 And Abraham s, My son, God will H559
11 him out of heaven, and s, Abraham, H559
11 Abraham: and he s, Here am I. H559
12 And he s, Lay not thine hand upon the H559
14 as it is s to this day, In the mount H559
16 And s, By myself have I sworn, saith the H559
24: 2 And Abraham s unto his eldest servant H559
5 And the servant s unto him, H559
6 And Abraham s unto him, Beware thou H559
12 And he s, O LORD God of my master H559
17 And the servant ran to meet her, and s, H559
18 And she s, Drink, my lord: and she H559
19 him drink, she s, I will draw water for H559
23 And s, Whose daughter art thou? tell me, H559
24 And she s unto him, I am the daughter H559
25 She s moreover unto him, We have both H559
27 And he s, Blessed be the LORD God of my H559
31 And he s, Come in, thou blessed of the H559
33 him to eat: but he s, I will not eat, until I H559
33 told mine errand. And he s, Speak on. H559
34 And he s, I am Abraham's servant. H559
39 And I s unto my master, Peradventure H559
40 And he s unto me, The LORD, before H559
42 And I came this day unto the well, and s, H559
45 I s unto her, Let me drink, I pray thee. H559
46 her shoulder, and s, Drink, and I will give H559
47 And I asked her, and s, Whose daughter H559
47 art thou? And she s, The daughter of H559
50 Then Laban and Bethuel answered and s, H559
54 and he s, Send me away unto my master. H559
55 And her brother and her mother s, Let H559
56 And he s unto them, Hinder me not, H559
57 And they s, We will call the damsel, and H559
58 And they called Rebekah, and s unto H559
58 go with this man? And she s, I will go. H559
60 And they blessed Rebekah, and s unto H559
65 For she had s unto the servant, What H559
65 And the servant had s, It is my master: H559
25:22 within her; and she s, If it be so, why am H559
23 And the LORD s unto her, Two nations H559
30 And Esau s to Jacob, Feed me, I pray H559
31 And Jacob s, Sell me this day thy H559
32 And Esau s, Behold, I am at the point to H559
33 And Jacob s, Swear to me this day; and H559
26: 2 unto him, and s, Go not down into Egypt; H559
7 of his wife; and he s, She is my sister: for H559
7 She is my wife; lest, s he, the men of the H559
9 And Abimelech called Isaac, and s, H559
9 sister? And Isaac s unto him, Because I H559
9 unto him, Because I s, Lest I die for her. H559
10 And Abimelech s, What is this thou hast H559
16 And Abimelech s unto Isaac, Go from H559
22 it Rehoboth; and he s, For now the LORD H559
24 the same night, and s, I am the God of H559
27 And Isaac s unto them, Wherefore come H559
28 And they s, We saw certainly that the H559
28 with thee: and we s, Let there be now an H559
32 and s unto him, We have found water. H559
27: 1 his eldest son, and s unto him, My son: H559
1 and he s unto him, Behold, here am I. H559
2 And he s, Behold now, I am old, I know H559
11 And Jacob s to Rebekah his mother, H559
13 And his mother s unto him, Upon me be H559
18 And he came unto his father, and s, My H559
18 he s, Here am I; who art thou, my son? H559
19 And Jacob s unto his father, I am Esau H559
20 And Isaac s unto his son, How is it that H559
20 my son? And he s, Because the LORD thy H559

S

Gen 27:21 And Isaac s unto Jacob, Come near, I H559
22 he felt him, and s, The voice *is* Jacob's H559
24 And he s, *Art* thou my very son Esau? H559
24 thou my very son Esau? And he s, I *am*. H559
25 And he s, Bring *it* near to me, and I will H559
26 And his father Isaac s unto him, Come H559
27 blessed him, and s, See, the smell of my H559
31 his father, and s unto his father, Let my H559
32 And Isaac his father s unto him, Who H559
32 he s, I *am* thy son, thy firstborn Esau. H559
33 exceedingly, and s, Who? where *is* he that H559
34 bitter cry, and s unto his father, Bless H559
35 And he s, Thy brother came with subtilty, H559
36 And he s, Is not he rightly named Jacob? H559
36 my blessing. And he s, Hast thou not H559
37 And Isaac answered and s unto Esau, H559
38 And Esau s unto his father, Hast thou H559
39 And Isaac his father answered and s H559
41 him: and Esau s in his heart, The days H559
42 younger son, and s unto him, Behold, H559
46 And Rebekah s to Isaac, I am weary of H559
28: 1 charged him, and s unto him, Thou shalt H559
13 stood above it, and s, I *am* the LORD God H559
16 of his sleep, and he s, Surely the LORD is H559
17 And he was afraid, and s, How dreadful H559
29: 4 And Jacob s unto them, My brethren, H559
4 *be* ye? And they s, Of Haran *are* we. H559
5 And he s unto them, Know ye Laban the H559
5 son of Nahor? And they s, We know *him*. H559
6 And he s unto them, *Is* he well? And they H559
6 *Is* he well? And they s, *He is* well: and, H559
7 And he s, Lo, *it is* yet high day, neither *is* H559
8 And they s, We cannot, until all the H559
14 And Laban s to him, Surely thou *art* my H559
15 And Laban s unto Jacob, Because thou H559
18 And Jacob loved Rachel; and s, I will H559
19 And Laban s, *It is* better that I give her to H559
21 And Jacob s unto Laban, Give *me* my H559
25 it *was* Leah: and he s to Laban, What *is* H559
26 And Laban s, It must not be so done in H559
32 Reuben: for she s, Surely the LORD hath H559
33 and bare a son; and s, Because the LORD H559
34 bare a son; and s, Now this time will my H559
35 bare a son: and she s, Now will I praise H559
30: 1 her sister; and s unto Jacob, Give me H559
2 Rachel: and he s, *Am* I in God's stead, H559
3 And she s, Behold my maid Bilhah, go in H559
6 And Rachel s, God hath judged me, and H559
8 And Rachel s, With great wrestlings have H559
11 And Leah s, A troop cometh: and she H559
13 And Leah s, Happy am I, for the H559
14 Leah. Then Rachel s to Leah, Give me, I H559
15 And she s unto her, *Is it* a small matter H559
15 also? And Rachel s, Therefore he shall lie H559
16 to meet him, and s, Thou must come in H559
18 And Leah s, God hath given me my hire, H559
20 And Leah s, God hath endued me *with* a H559
23 s, God hath taken away my reproach: H559
24 And she called his name Joseph; and s, H559
25 Joseph, that Jacob s unto Laban, Send H559
27 And Laban s unto him, I pray thee, if I H559
28 And he s, Appoint me thy wages, and I H559
29 And he s unto him, Thou knowest how I H559
31 And he s, What shall I give thee? And H559
31 thee? And Jacob s, Thou shalt not give H559
34 And Laban s, Behold, I would it might be H559
31: 3 And the LORD s unto Jacob, Return unto H559
5 And s unto them, I see your father's H559
8 If he s thus, The speckled shall be thy H559
8 bare speckled: and if he s thus, The H559
11 dream, *saying*, Jacob: And I s, Here *am* I. H559
12 And he s, Lift up now thine eyes, and see, H559
14 And Rachel and Leah answered and s H559
16 whatsoever God hath s unto thee, do. H559
24 by night, and s unto him, Take heed H559
26 And Laban s to Jacob, What hast thou H559
31 And Jacob answered and s to Laban, H559
31 I was afraid: for I s, Peradventure thou H559
35 And she s to her father, Let it not H559
36 answered and s to Laban, What *is* my H559
43 And Laban answered and s unto Jacob, H559
46 And Jacob s unto his brethren, Gather H559
48 And Laban s, This heap *is* a witness H559
49 And Mizpah; for he s, The LORD watch H559
51 And Laban s to Jacob, Behold this heap, H559
32: 2 And when Jacob saw them, he s, This *is* H559
8 And s, If Esau come to the one company, H559
9 And Jacob s, O God of my father H559
16 by themselves; and s unto his servants, H559

Gen 32:20 *is* behind us. For he s, I will appease him H559
26 And he s, Let me go, for the day H559
26 breaketh. And he s, I will not let thee go, H559
27 And he s unto him, What *is* thy name? H559
27 him, What *is* thy name? And he s, Jacob. H559
28 And he s, Thy name shall be called no H559
29 And Jacob asked *him*, and s, Tell *me*, I H559
29 thy name. And he s, Wherefore *is* it *that* H559
33: 5 the children; and s, Who *are* those with H559
5 with thee? And he s, The children which H559
8 And he s, What *meanest* thou by all this H559
8 I met? And he s, *These are* to find grace H559
9 And Esau s, I have enough, my brother; H559
10 And Jacob s, Nay, I pray thee, if now I H559
12 And he s, Let us take our journey, and let H559
13 And he s unto him, My lord knoweth H559
15 And Esau s, Let me now leave with thee H559
15 with me. And he s, What needeth it? let H559
34:11 And Shechem s unto her father and unto H559
13 father deceitfully, and s, because he had H1696
14 And they s unto them, We cannot do H559
30 And Jacob s to Simeon and Levi, Ye have H559
31 And they s, Should he deal with our sister H559
35: 1 And God s unto Jacob, Arise, go up to H559
2 Then Jacob s unto his household, and to H559
10 And God s unto him, Thy name *is* Jacob: H559
11 And God s unto him, I *am* God H559
17 that the midwife s unto her, Fear not; H559
37: 6 And he s unto them, Hear, I pray you, H559
8 And his brethren s to him, Shalt thou H559
9 told it his brethren, and s, Behold, I have H559
10 rebuked him, and s unto him, What *is* H559
13 And Israel s unto Joseph, Do not thy H559
13 unto them. And he s to him, Here *am* I. H559
14 And he s to him, Go, I pray thee, see H559
16 And he s, I seek my brethren: tell me, I H559
17 And the man s, They are departed hence; H559
19 And they s one to another, Behold, this H559
21 of their hands; and s, Let us not kill him. H559
22 And Reuben s unto them, Shed no H559
26 And Judah s unto his brethren, What H559
30 his brethren, and s, The child *is* not; and H559
32 *it* to their father; and s, This have we H559
33 And he knew it, and s, *It is* my son's coat; H559
35 comforted; and he s, For I will go down H559
38: 8 And Judah s unto Onan, Go in unto thy H559
11 Then s Judah to Tamar his daughter in H559
11 be grown: for he s, Lest peradventure he H559
16 by the way, and s, Go to, I pray thee, let H559
16 in law.) And she s, What wilt thou give H559
17 And he s, I will send *thee* a kid from the H559
17 the flock. And she s, Wilt thou give *me* a H559
18 And he s, What pledge shall I give thee? H559
18 give thee? And she s, Thy signet, and thy H559
21 they s, There was no harlot in this *place*. H559
22 And he returned to Judah, and s, I H559
22 s, *that* there was no harlot in this *place*. H559
23 And Judah s, Let her take *it* to her, lest H559
24 s, Bring her forth, and let her be burnt. H559
25 I with child: and she s, Discern, I pray H559
26 And Judah acknowledged *them*, and s, H559
29 came out: and she s, How hast thou H559
39: 7 eyes upon Joseph; and she s, Lie with me. H559
8 But he refused, and s unto his master's H559
40: 8 And they s unto him, We have dreamed H559
8 of it. And Joseph s unto them, *Do* not H559
9 to Joseph, and s to him, In my dream, H559
12 And Joseph s unto him, This *is* the H559
16 was good, he s unto Joseph, I also *was* H559
18 And Joseph answered and s, This *is* the H559
41:15 And Pharaoh s unto Joseph, I have H559
17 And Pharaoh s unto Joseph, In my H1696
25 And Joseph s unto Pharaoh, The dream H559
38 And Pharaoh s unto his servants, Can H559
39 And Pharaoh s unto Joseph, Forasmuch H559
41 And Pharaoh s unto Joseph, See, I have H559
44 And Pharaoh s unto Joseph, I *am* H559
51 For God, *s he*, hath made me forget
54 as Joseph had s: and the dearth was in H559
55 and Pharaoh s unto all the Egyptians, H559
42: 1 in Egypt, Jacob s unto his sons, Why do H559
2 And he s, Behold, I have heard that there H559
4 s, Lest peradventure mischief befall him. H559
7 unto them; and he s unto them, Whence H559
7 s, From the land of Canaan to buy food. H559
9 of them, and s unto them, Ye *are* spies; H559
10 And they s unto him, Nay, my lord, but H559
12 And he s unto them, Nay, but to see the H559
13 And they s, Thy servants *are* twelve H559

Gen 42:14 And Joseph s unto them, That *is it* that I H559
18 And Joseph s unto them the third day, H559
21 And they s one to another, We *are* verily H559
28 And he s unto his brethren, My money is H559
31 And we s unto him, We *are* true *men*; we H559
33 And the man, the lord of the country, s H559
36 And Jacob their father s unto them, Me H559
38 And he s, My son shall not go down with H559
43: 2 of Egypt, their father s unto them, Go H559
5 go down: for the man s unto us, Ye shall H559
6 And Israel s, Wherefore dealt ye *so* ill H559
7 And they s, The man asked us straitly of H559
8 And Judah s unto Israel his father, Send H559
11 And their father Israel s unto them, If *it* H559
16 with them, he s to the ruler of his house, H559
18 house; and they s, Because of the money H559
20 And s, O sir, we came indeed down at the H559
23 And he s, Peace *be* to you, fear not: your H559
27 *their* welfare, and s, *Is* your father well, H559
29 mother's son, and s, *Is* this your younger H559
29 he s, God be gracious unto thee, my son. H559
31 refrained himself, and s, Set on bread. H559
44: 4 not *yet* far off, Joseph s unto his steward, H559
7 And they s unto him, Wherefore saith H559
10 And he s, Now also *let* it *be* according H559
15 And Joseph s unto them, What deed *is* H559
16 And Judah s, What shall we say unto my H559
17 And he s, God forbid that I should do so: H559
18 Then Judah came near unto him, and s, H559
20 And we s unto my lord, We have a H559
22 And we s unto my lord, The lad cannot H559
25 And our father s, Go again, *and* buy us a H559
26 And we s, We cannot go down: if our H559
27 And thy servant my father s unto us, Ye H559
28 And the one went out from me, and I s, H559
45: 3 And Joseph s unto his brethren, I *am* H559
4 And Joseph s unto his brethren, Come H559
4 came near. And he s, I *am* Joseph your H559
17 And Pharaoh s unto Joseph, Say unto H559
24 departed: and he s unto them, See that H559
27 which he had s unto them: and when H1696
28 And Israel s, *It is* enough; Joseph my son H559
46: 2 s, Jacob, Jacob. And he said, Here *am* I. H559
2 said, Jacob, Jacob. And he s, Here *am* I. H559
3 And he s, I *am* God, the God of thy father: H559
30 And Israel s unto Joseph, Now let me H559
31 And Joseph s unto his brethren, and H559
47: 1 told Pharaoh, and s, My father and my H559
3 And Pharaoh s unto his brethren, What H559
3 And they s unto Pharaoh, Thy servants H559
4 They s moreover unto Pharaoh, For to H559
8 And Pharaoh s unto Jacob, How old *art* H559
9 And Jacob s unto Pharaoh, The days of H559
15 unto Joseph, and s, Give us bread: for H559
16 And Joseph s, Give your cattle; and I will H559
18 second year, and s unto him, We will not H559
23 Then Joseph s unto the people, Behold, I H559
25 And they s, Thou hast saved our lives: let H559
29 his son Joseph, and s unto him, If now I H559
30 And he s, I will do as thou hast said. H559
30 And he said, I will do as thou hast s. H1697
31 And he s, Swear unto me. And he sware H559
48: 2 And *one* told Jacob, and s, Behold, thy H559
3 And Jacob s unto Joseph, God Almighty H559
4 And s unto me, Behold, I will make thee H559
8 And Israel beheld Joseph's sons, and s, H559
9 And Joseph s unto his father, They *are* H559
9 in this *place*. And he s, Bring them, I pray H559
11 And Israel s unto Joseph, I had not H559
15 And he blessed Joseph, and s, God, H559
18 And Joseph s unto his father, Not so, my H559
19 And his father refused, and s, I know *it*, H559
21 And Israel s unto Joseph, Behold, I die: H559
49: 1 And Jacob called unto his sons, and s, H559
29 And he charged them, and s unto them, H559
50: 6 And Pharaoh s, Go up, and bury thy H559
11 floor of Atad, they s, This *is* a grievous H559
15 father was dead, they s, Joseph will H559
18 and they s, Behold, we *be* thy servants. H559
19 And Joseph s unto them, Fear not: for H559
24 And Joseph s unto his brethren, I die: H559
Ex 1: 9 And he s unto his people, Behold, the H559
16 And he s, When ye do the office of a H559
18 for the midwives, and s unto them, Why H559
19 And the midwives s unto Pharaoh, H559
2: 6 s, This *is one* of the Hebrews' children. H559
7 Then s his sister to Pharaoh's daughter, H559
8 And Pharaoh's daughter s to her, Go. H559
9 And Pharaoh's daughter s unto her, H559

Ex 2:10 s, Because I drew him out of the water. H559
13 together: and he s to him that did the H559
14 And he s, Who made thee a prince and a H559
14 feared, and s, Surely this thing is known. H559
18 their father, he s, How *is it that* ye are H559
19 And they s, An Egyptian delivered us out H559
20 And he s unto his daughters, And where H559
22 Gershom: for he s, I have been a stranger H559
3: 3 And Moses s, I will now turn aside, and H559
4 s, Moses, Moses. And he said, Here *am* I. H559
4 said, Moses, Moses. And he s, Here *am* I. H559
5 And he s, Draw not nigh hither: put off H559
6 Moreover he s, I *am* the God of thy H559
7 And the LORD s, I have surely seen the H559
11 And Moses s unto God, Who *am* I, that I H559
12 And he s, Certainly I will be with thee; H559
13 And Moses s unto God, Behold, *when* I H559
14 And God s unto Moses, I AM THAT I H559
14 I AM: and he s, Thus shalt thou say H559
15 And God s moreover unto Moses, Thus H559
17 And I have s, I will bring you up out of H559
4: 1 And Moses answered and s, But, behold, H559
2 And the LORD s unto him, What *is* that H559
2 *is* that in thine hand? And he s, A rod. H559
3 And he s, Cast it on the ground. And he H559
4 And the LORD s unto Moses, Put forth H559
6 And the LORD s furthermore unto him, H559
7 And he s, Put thine hand into thy bosom H559
10 And Moses s unto the LORD, O my Lord, H559
11 And the LORD s unto him, Who hath H559
13 And he s, O my Lord, send, I pray thee, H559
14 Moses, and he s, *Is* not Aaron the Levite H559
18 father in law, and s unto him, Let me go, H559
18 And Jethro s to Moses, Go in peace. H559
19 And the LORD s unto Moses in Midian, H559
21 And the LORD s unto Moses, When thou H559
25 cast *it* at his feet, and s, Surely a bloody H559
26 So he let him go: then she s, A bloody H559
27 And the LORD s to Aaron, Go into the H559
5: 2 And Pharaoh s, Who *is* the LORD, that I H559
3 And they s, The God of the Hebrews hath H559
4 And the king of Egypt s unto them, H559
5 And Pharaoh s, Behold, the people of the H559
17 But he s, Ye *are* idle, *ye are* idle: therefore H559
19 *case,* after it was s, Ye shall not minish H559
21 And they s unto them, The LORD look H559
22 the LORD, and s, Lord, wherefore hast H559
6: 1 Then the LORD s unto Moses, Now shalt H559
2 And God spake unto Moses, and s unto H559
26 to whom the LORD s, Bring out the H559
30 And Moses s before the LORD, Behold, I H559
7: 1 And the LORD s unto Moses, See, I have H559
13 not unto them; as the LORD had s. H1696
14 And the LORD s unto Moses, Pharaoh's H559
22 hearken unto them; as the LORD had s. H1696
8: 8 and Aaron, and s, Entreat the LORD, that H559
9 And Moses s unto Pharaoh, Glory over H559
10 And he s, To morrow. And he said, *Be it* H559
10 And he said, To morrow. And he s, *Be it* H559
15 not unto them; as the LORD had s. H1696
16 And the LORD s unto Moses, Say unto H559
19 Then the magicians s unto Pharaoh, H559
19 not unto them; as the LORD had s. H1696
20 And the LORD s unto Moses, Rise up H559
25 s, Go ye, sacrifice to your God in the land. H559
26 And Moses s, It is not meet so to do; for H559
28 And Pharaoh s, I will let you go, that ye H559
29 And Moses s, Behold, I go out from thee, H559
9: 1 Then the LORD s unto Moses, Go in unto H559
8 And the LORD s unto Moses and unto H559
13 And the LORD s unto Moses, Rise up H559
22 And the LORD s unto Moses, Stretch H559
27 and Aaron, and s unto them, I have H559
29 And Moses s unto him, As soon as I am H559
10: 1 And the LORD s unto Moses, Go in unto H559
3 in unto Pharaoh, and s unto him, Thus H559
7 And Pharaoh's servants s unto him, H559
8 Pharaoh: and he s unto them, Go, serve H559
9 And Moses s, We will go with our young H559
10 And he s unto them, Let the LORD be so H559
12 And the LORD s unto Moses, Stretch out H559
16 in haste; and he s, I have sinned against H559
21 And the LORD s unto Moses, Stretch out H559
24 And Pharaoh called unto Moses, and s, H559
25 And Moses s, Thou must give us also H559
28 And Pharaoh s unto him, Get thee from H559
29 And Moses s, Thou hast spoken well, I H559
11: 1 And the LORD s unto Moses, Yet will I H559
4 And Moses s, Thus saith the LORD, H559

Ex 11: 9 And the LORD s unto Moses, Pharaoh H559
12:21 of Israel, and s unto them, Draw out H559
31 by night, and s, Rise up, *and* get you H559
31 and go, serve the LORD, as ye have s. H1696
32 have s, and be gone; and bless me also. H1696
33 in haste; for they s, We *be* all dead *men.* H559
43 And the LORD s unto Moses and Aaron, H559
13: 3 And Moses s unto the people, H559
17 *was* near; for God s, Lest peradventure H559
14: 5 people, and they s, Why have we done H559
11 And they s unto Moses, Because *there* H559
13 And Moses s unto the people, Fear ye H559
15 And the LORD s unto Moses, Wherefore H559
25 that the Egyptians s, Let us flee from the H559
26 And the LORD s unto Moses, Stretch out H559
15: 9 The enemy s, I will pursue, I will H559
26 And s, If thou wilt diligently hearken to H559
16: 3 And the children of Israel s unto them, H559
4 Then s the LORD unto Moses, Behold, I H559
6 And Moses and Aaron s unto all the H559
8 And Moses s, *This shall be,* when the H559
15 Israel saw *it,* they s one to another, It *is* H559
15 it *was.* And Moses s unto them, This *is* H559
19 And Moses s, Let no man leave of it till H559
23 And he s unto them, This *is that* which H559
23 the LORD hath s, To morrow *is* the rest H1696
25 And Moses s, Eat that to day; for to day H559
28 And the LORD s unto Moses, How long H559
32 And Moses s, This *is* the thing which the H559
33 And Moses s unto Aaron, Take a pot, H559
17: 2 with Moses, and s, Give us water that we H559
2 drink. And Moses s unto them, Why H559
3 against Moses, and s, Wherefore *is* this H559
5 And the LORD s unto Moses, Go on H559
9 And Moses s unto Joshua, Choose us out H559
10 So Joshua did as Moses had s to him, H559
14 And the LORD s unto Moses, Write this H559
16 For he s, Because the LORD hath sworn H559
18: 3 s, I have been an alien in a strange land: H559
4 God of my father, *s he, was* mine help,
6 And he s unto Moses, I thy father in law H559
10 And Jethro s, Blessed *be* the LORD, who H559
14 to the people, he s, What *is* this thing that H559
15 And Moses s unto his father in law, H559
17 And Moses' father in law s unto him, H559
24 father in law, and did all that he had s. H559
19: 8 together, and s, All that the LORD hath H559
9 And the LORD s unto Moses, Lo, I come H559
10 And the LORD s unto Moses, Go unto H559
15 And he s unto the people, Be ready H559
21 And the LORD s unto Moses, Go down, H559
23 And Moses s unto the LORD, The people H559
24 And the LORD s unto him, Away, get H559
20:19 And they s unto Moses, Speak thou with H559
20 And Moses s unto the people, Fear not: H559
22 And the LORD s unto Moses, Thus thou H559
23:13 And in all *things* that I have s unto you H559
24: 1 And he s unto Moses, Come up unto the H559
3 with one voice, and s, All the words H559
3 which the LORD hath s will we do. H1696
7 the people: and they s, All that the LORD H559
7 hath s will we do, and be obedient. H1696
8 on the people, and s, Behold the blood of H559
12 And the LORD s unto Moses, Come up to H559
14 And he s unto the elders, Tarry ye here H559
30:34 And the LORD s unto Moses, Take unto H559
32: 1 unto Aaron, and s unto him, Up, make H559
2 And Aaron s unto them, Break off the H559
4 calf: and they s, These *be* thy gods, O H559
5 and s, To morrow *is* a feast to the LORD. H559
7 And the LORD s unto Moses, Go, get H1696
8 thereunto, and s, These *be* thy gods, O H559
9 And the LORD s unto Moses, I have seen H559
11 LORD his God, and s, LORD, why doth H559
17 as they shouted, he s unto Moses, *There* H559
18 And he s, *It is* not the voice of *them that* H559
21 And Moses s unto Aaron, What did this H559
22 And Aaron s, Let not the anger of my H559
23 For they s unto me, Make us gods, which H559
24 And I s unto them, Whosoever hath any H559
26 gate of the camp, and s, Who *is* on the H559
27 And he s unto them, Thus saith the H559
29 For Moses had s, Consecrate yourselves H559
30 that Moses s unto the people, Ye have H559
31 the LORD, and s, Oh, this people have H559
33 And the LORD s unto Moses, Whosoever H559
33: 1 And the LORD s unto Moses, Depart, H1696
5 For the LORD had s unto Moses, Say H559
12 And Moses s unto the LORD, See, thou H559

Ex 33:12 with me. Yet thou hast s, I know thee by H559
14 And he s, My presence shall go *with thee,* H559
15 And he s unto him, If thy presence go H559
17 And the LORD s unto Moses, I will do H559
18 And he s, I beseech thee, shew me thy H559
19 And he s, I will make all my goodness H559
20 And he s, Thou canst not see my face: for H559
21 And the LORD s, Behold, *there is* a place H559
34: 1 And the LORD s unto Moses, Hew thee H559
9 And he s, If now I have found grace in H559
10 And he s, Behold, I make a covenant: H559
27 And the LORD s unto Moses, Write thou H559
35: 1 together, and s unto them, These *are* H559
30 And Moses s unto the children of Israel, H559
Lev 8: 5 And Moses s unto the congregation, H559
31 And Moses s unto Aaron and to his H559
9: 2 And he s unto Aaron, Take thee a young H559
6 And Moses s, This *is* the thing which the H559
7 And Moses s unto Aaron, Go unto the H559
10: 3 Then Moses s unto Aaron, This *is it* that H559
4 of Aaron, and s unto them, Come near, H559
5 coats out of the camp; as Moses had s. H1696
6 And Moses s unto Aaron, and unto H559
19 And Aaron s unto Moses, Behold, this H1696
16: 2 And the LORD s unto Moses, Speak unto H559
17:12 Therefore I s unto the children of Israel, H559
14 thereof: therefore I s unto the children of H559
20:24 But I have s unto you, Ye shall inherit H559
21: 1 And the LORD s unto Moses, Speak unto H559
Nu 3:40 And the LORD s unto Moses, Number all H559
7:11 And the LORD s unto Moses, They shall H559
9: 7 And those men s unto him, We *are* H559
8 And Moses s unto them, Stand still, and H559
10:29 And Moses s unto Hobab, the son of H559
29 of which the LORD s, I will give it you: H559
30 And he s unto him, I will not go; but I H559
31 And he s, Leave us not, I pray thee; H559
35 that Moses s, Rise up, LORD, and H559
36 And when it rested, he s, Return, O H559
11: 4 and s, Who shall give us flesh to eat? H559
11 And Moses s unto the LORD, Wherefore H559
16 And the LORD s unto Moses, Gather H559
21 And Moses s, The people, among whom I H559
21 and thou hast s, I will give them flesh, H559
23 And the LORD s unto Moses, Is the H559
27 told Moses, and s, Eldad and Medad do H559
28 and s, My lord Moses, forbid them. H559
29 And Moses s unto him, Enviest thou for H559
12: 2 And they s, Hath the LORD indeed H559
6 And he s, Hear now my words: If there be H559
11 And Aaron s unto Moses, Alas, my lord, H559
14 And the LORD s unto Moses, If her H559
13:17 of Canaan, and s unto them, Get you up H559
27 And they told him, and s, We came unto H559
30 before Moses, and s, Let us go up at once, H559
31 But the men that went up with him s, We H559
14: 2 congregation s unto them, Would God H559
4 And they s one to another, Let us make a H559
11 And the LORD s unto Moses, How long H559
13 And Moses s unto the LORD, Then the H559
20 And the LORD s, I have pardoned H559
31 But your little ones, which ye s should be H559
35 I the LORD have s, I will surely do it H1696
41 And Moses s, Wherefore now do ye H559
15:35 And the LORD s unto Moses, The man H559
16: 3 against Aaron, and s unto them, *Ye take* H559
8 And Moses s unto Korah, Hear, I pray H559
12 of Eliab: which s, We will not come up: H559
15 And Moses was very wroth, and s unto H559
16 And Moses s unto Korah, Be thou and H559
22 And they fell upon their faces, and s, O H559
28 And Moses s, Hereby ye shall know that H559
34 they s, Lest the earth swallow us up *also.* H559
40 LORD s to him by the hand of Moses. H1696
46 And Moses s unto Aaron, Take a censer, H559
17:10 And the LORD s unto Moses, Bring H559
18: 1 And the LORD s unto Aaron, Thou and H559
24 therefore I have s unto them, Among the H559
20:10 the rock, and he s unto them, Hear now, H559
18 And Edom s unto him, Thou shalt not H559
19 And the children of Israel s unto him, H559
20 And he s, Thou shalt not go through. And H559
21: 2 unto the LORD, and s, If thou wilt indeed H559
7 to Moses, and s, We have sinned, for H559
8 And the LORD s unto Moses, Make thee H559
14 Wherefore it is s in the book of the wars H559
34 And the LORD s unto Moses, Fear him H559
22: 4 And Moab s unto the elders of Midian, H559
8 And he s unto them, Lodge here this H559

S

Nu 22: 9 And God came unto Balaam, and **s**, H559
10 And Balaam **s** unto God, Balak the son H559
12 And God **s** unto Balaam, Thou shalt not H559
13 in the morning, and **s** unto the princes of H559
14 and **s**, Balaam refuseth to come with us. H559
16 And they came to Balaam, and **s** to him, H559
18 And Balaam answered and **s** unto the H559
20 at night, and **s** unto him, If the men H559
28 of the ass, and she **s** unto Balaam, What H559
29 And Balaam **s** unto the ass, Because H559
30 And the ass **s** unto Balaam, *Am* not I H559
30 wont to do so unto thee? And he **s**, Nay. H559
32 And the angel of the LORD **s** unto him, H559
34 And Balaam **s** unto the angel of the H559
35 And the angel of the LORD **s** unto H559
37 And Balak **s** unto Balaam, Did I not H559
38 And Balaam **s** unto Balak, Lo, I am H559
23: 1 And Balaam **s** unto Balak, Build me here H559
3 And Balaam **s** unto Balak, Stand by thy H559
4 And God met Balaam: and he **s** unto H559
5 mouth, and **s**, Return unto Balak, and H559
7 And he took up his parable, and **s**, Balak H559
11 And Balak **s** unto Balaam, What hast H559
12 And he answered and **s**, Must I not take H559
13 And Balak **s** unto him, Come, I pray H559
15 And he **s** unto Balak, Stand here by thy H559
16 **s**, Go again unto Balak, and say thus. H559
17 him. And Balak **s** unto him, What hath H559
18 And he took up his parable, and **s**, Rise H559
19 repent: hath he **s**, and shall he not do *it?* H559
23 to this time it shall be **s** of Jacob and of H559
25 And Balak **s** unto Balaam, Neither curse H559
26 But Balaam answered and **s** unto Balak, H559
27 And Balak **s** unto Balaam, Come, I pray H559
29 And Balaam **s** unto Balak, Build me here H559
30 And Balak did as Balaam had **s**, and H559
24: 3 And he took up his parable, and **s**, H559
3 son of Beor hath **s**, and the man whose H5002
3 the man whose eyes are open hath **s**: H5002
4 He hath **s**, which heard the words of H5002
10 and Balak **s** unto Balaam, I called H559
12 And Balaam **s** unto Balak, Spake I not H559
15 And he took up his parable, and **s**, H559
15 son of Beor hath **s**, and the man whose H5002
15 the man whose eyes are open hath **s**: H5002
16 He hath **s**, which heard the words of H5002
20 up his parable, and **s**, Amalek *was* the H559
21 took up his parable, and **s**, Strong is thy H559
23 And he took up his parable, and **s**, Alas, H559
25: 4 And the LORD **s** unto Moses, Take all H559
5 And Moses **s** unto the judges of Israel, H559
26:65 For the LORD had **s** of them, They shall H559
27:12 And the LORD **s** unto Moses, Get thee up H559
18 And the LORD **s** unto Moses, Take thee H559
31:15 And Moses **s** unto them, Have ye saved H559
21 And Eleazar the priest **s** unto the men of H559
49 And they **s** unto Moses, Thy servants H559
32: 5 Wherefore, **s** they, if we have found H559
6 And Moses **s** unto the children of Gad H559
16 And they came near unto him, and **s**, We H559
20 And Moses **s** unto them, If ye will do this H559
29 And Moses **s** unto them, If the children H559
31 hath **s** unto thy servants, so will we do. H1696
36: 2 And they **s**, The LORD commanded my H559
5 tribe of the sons of Joseph hath **s** well. H1696
Dt 1:14 And ye answered me, and **s**, The thing H559
20 And I **s** unto you, Ye are come unto the H559
21 of thy fathers hath **s** unto thee; fear H1696
22 one of you, and **s**, We will send men H559
25 us word again, and **s**, *It is* a good land H559
27 And ye murmured in your tents, and **s**, H559
29 Then I **s** unto you, Dread not, neither be H559
39 Moreover your little ones, which ye **s** H559
41 Then ye answered and **s** unto me, We H559
42 And the LORD **s** unto me, Say unto H559
2: 9 And the LORD **s** unto me, Distress not H559
13 Now rise up, *s I*, and get you over the
31 And the LORD **s** unto me, Behold, I have H559
3: 2 And the LORD **s** unto me, Fear him not: H559
26 hear me: and the LORD **s** unto me, Let it H559
4:10 when the LORD **s** unto me, Gather me H559
5: 1 And Moses called all Israel, and **s** unto H559
24 And ye **s**, Behold, the LORD our God hath H559
28 me; and the LORD **s** unto me, I have H559
28 have well **s** all that they have spoken.
9: 3 quickly, as the LORD hath **s** unto thee. H1696
12 And the LORD **s** unto me, Arise, get thee H559
25 the LORD had **s** he would destroy you. H559
26 I prayed therefore unto the LORD, and **s**, H559

Dt 10: 1 At that time the LORD **s** unto me, Hew H559
11 And the LORD **s** unto me, Arise, take *thy* H559
11:25 shall tread upon, as he hath **s** unto you. H1696
17:16 as the LORD hath **s** unto you, Ye shall H559
18: 2 inheritance, as he hath **s** unto them. H1696
17 And the LORD **s** unto me, They have H559
29: 2 And Moses called unto all Israel, and **s** H559
13 a God, as he hath **s** unto thee, and as he H1696
31: 2 And he **s** unto them, I *am* an hundred H559
2 the LORD hath **s** unto me, Thou shalt H559
3 go over before thee, as the LORD hath **s**. H1696
7 And Moses called unto Joshua, and **s** H559
14 And the LORD **s** unto Moses, Behold, thy H559
16 And the LORD **s** unto Moses, Behold, H559
23 Nun a charge, and **s**, Be strong and of a H559
32:20 And he **s**, I will hide my face from them, I H559
26 I **s**, I would scatter them into corners, I H559
46 And he **s** unto them, Set your hearts H559
33: 2 And he **s**, The LORD came from Sinai, H559
7 of Judah: and he **s**, Hear, LORD, the voice H559
8 And of Levi he **s**, *Let* thy Thummim and H559
9 Who **s** unto his father and to his mother, H559
12 *And* of Benjamin he **s**, The beloved of the H559
13 And of Joseph he **s**, Blessed of the LORD H559
18 And of Zebulun he **s**, Rejoice, Zebulun, in H559
20 And of Gad he **s**, Blessed *be* he that H559
22 And of Dan he **s**, Dan *is* a lion's whelp: he H559
23 And of Naphtali he **s**, O Naphtali, H559
24 And of Asher he **s**, *Let* Asher *be* blessed H559
34: 4 And the LORD **s** unto him, This *is* the H559
Jos 1: 3 I given unto you, as I **s** unto Moses. H1696
2: 4 and hid them, and **s** thus, There came H559
9 And she **s** unto the men, I know that the H559
16 And she **s** unto them, Get you to the H559
17 And the men **s** unto her, We *will be* H559
21 And she **s**, According unto your words, H559
24 And they **s** unto Joshua, Truly the LORD H559
3: 5 And Joshua **s** unto the people, Sanctify H559
7 And the LORD **s** unto Joshua, This day H559
9 And Joshua **s** unto the children of Israel, H559
10 And Joshua **s**, Hereby ye shall know that H559
4: 5 And Joshua **s** unto them, Pass over H559
5: 2 At that time the LORD **s** unto Joshua, H559
9 And the LORD **s** unto Joshua, This day H559
13 unto him, and **s** unto him, *Art* thou for H559
14 And he **s**, Nay; but *as* captain of the host H559
14 did worship, and **s** unto him, What saith H559
15 And the captain of the LORD'S host **s** H559
6: 2 And the LORD **s** unto Joshua, See, I have H559
6 the priests, and **s** unto them, Take up H559
7 And he **s** unto the people, Pass on, and H559
16 the trumpets, Joshua **s** unto the people, H559
22 But Joshua had **s** unto the two men that H559
7: 3 And they returned to Joshua, and **s** unto H559
7 And Joshua **s**, Alas, O Lord GOD, H559
10 And the LORD **s** unto Joshua, Get thee H559
19 And Joshua **s** unto Achan, My son, give, H559
20 And Achan answered Joshua, and **s**, H559
25 And Joshua **s**, Why hast thou troubled H559
8: 1 And the LORD **s** unto Joshua, Fear not, H559
18 And the LORD **s** unto Joshua, Stretch out H559
9: 6 at Gilgal, and **s** unto him, and to the H559
7 And the men of Israel **s** unto the Hivites, H559
8 And they **s** unto Joshua, We *are* thy H559
8 And Joshua **s** unto them, Who *are* H559
9 And they **s** unto him, From a very far H559
19 But all the princes **s** unto all the H559
21 And the princes **s** unto them, Let them H559
24 And they answered Joshua, and **s**, H559
10: 8 And the LORD **s** unto Joshua, Fear them H559
12 of Israel, and he **s** in the sight of Israel, H559
18 And Joshua **s**, Roll great stones upon the H559
22 Then **s** Joshua, Open the mouth of the H559
24 men of Israel, and **s** unto the captains of H559
25 And Joshua **s** unto them, Fear not, nor H559
11: 6 And the LORD **s** unto Joshua, Be not H559
23 to all that the LORD **s** unto Moses; and H1696
13: 1 and the LORD **s** unto him, Thou art old H559
14 their inheritance, as he **s** unto them. H1696
33 their inheritance, as he **s** unto them. H1696
14: 6 the Kenezite **s** unto him, Thou knowest H559
6 that the LORD **s** unto Moses the man H1696
10 me alive, as he **s**, these forty and five H1696
12 able to drive them out, as the LORD **s**. H1696
15:16 And Caleb **s**, He that smiteth H559
18 Caleb **s** unto her, What wouldest thou? H559
17:16 And the children of Joseph **s**, The hill is H559
18: 3 And Joshua **s** unto the children of Israel, H559
22: 2 And **s** unto them, Ye have kept all that H559

Jos 22:21 answered, and **s** unto the heads of the H1696
26 Therefore we **s**, Let us now prepare to H559
28 Therefore **s** we, that it shall be, when H559
31 Eleazar the priest **s** unto the children of H559
23: 2 their officers, and **s** unto them, I am old H559
24: 2 And Joshua **s** unto all the people, Thus H559
16 And the people answered and **s**, God H559
19 And Joshua **s** unto the people, Ye cannot H559
21 And the people **s** unto Joshua, Nay; but H559
22 And Joshua **s** unto the people, Ye *are* H559
22 serve him. And they **s**, *We are* witnesses. H559
23 Now therefore put away, *s he,* the
24 And the people **s** unto Joshua, The H559
27 And Joshua **s** unto all the people, H559
Jdg 1: 2 And the LORD **s**, Judah shall go up: H559
3 And Judah **s** unto Simeon his brother, H559
7 And Adoni-bezek **s**, Threescore and ten H559
12 And Caleb **s**, He that smiteth H559
14 and Caleb **s** unto her, What wilt thou? H559
15 And she **s** unto him, Give me a blessing: H559
20 unto Caleb, as Moses **s**: and he expelled H1696
24 of the city, and they **s** unto him, Shew us, H559
2: 1 to Bochim, and **s**, I made you to go up H559
1 your fathers; and I **s**, I will never break H559
3 Wherefore I also **s**, I will not drive them H559
15 as the LORD had **s**, and as the LORD H1696
20 Israel; and he **s**, Because that this people H559
3:19 that *were* by Gilgal, and **s**, I have a secret H559
19 thee, O king: who **s**, Keep silence. And all H559
20 alone. And Ehud **s**, I have a message H559
24 *were* locked, they **s**, Surely he covereth H559
28 And he **s** unto them, Follow after me: for H559
4: 6 and **s** unto him, Hath not the H559
8 And Barak **s** unto her, If thou wilt go H559
9 And she **s**, I will surely go with thee: H559
14 And Deborah **s** unto Barak, Up; for this H559
18 And Jael went out to meet Sisera, and **s** H559
19 And he **s** unto her, Give me, I pray thee, H559
20 Again he **s** unto her, Stand in the door of H559
22 to meet him, and **s** unto him, Come, and H559
5:23 Curse ye Meroz, **s** the angel of the LORD, H559
6: 8 of Israel, which **s** unto them, Thus saith H559
10 And I **s** unto you, I *am* the LORD your H559
12 unto him, and **s** unto him, The LORD H559
13 And Gideon **s** unto him, Oh my Lord, if H559
14 And the LORD looked upon him, and **s**, H559
15 And he **s** unto him, Oh my Lord, H559
16 And the LORD **s** unto him, Surely I will H559
17 And he **s** unto him, If now I have found H559
18 he **s**, I will tarry until thou come again. H559
20 And the angel of God **s** unto him, Take H559
22 the LORD, Gideon **s**, Alas, O Lord GOD! H559
23 And the LORD **s** unto him, Peace *be* H559
25 that the LORD **s** unto him, Take thy H559
27 as the LORD had **s** unto him: and *so* it H1696
29 And they **s** one to another, Who hath H559
29 and asked, they **s**, Gideon the son of H559
30 Then the men of the city **s** unto Joash, H559
31 And Joash **s** unto all that stood against H559
36 And Gideon **s** unto God, If thou wilt save H559
36 Israel by mine hand, as thou hast **s**, H1696
37 Israel by mine hand, as thou hast **s**. H1696
39 And Gideon **s** unto God, Let not thine H559
7: 2 And the LORD **s** unto Gideon, The H559
4 And the LORD **s** unto Gideon, The H559
5 and the LORD **s** unto Gideon, Every one H559
7 And the LORD **s** unto Gideon, By the H559
9 that the LORD **s** unto him, Arise, get H559
13 his fellow, and **s**, Behold, I dreamed a H559
14 And his fellow answered and **s**, This *is* H559
15 host of Israel, and **s**, Arise; for the LORD H559
17 And he **s** unto them, Look on me, and do H559
8: 1 And the men of Ephraim **s** unto him, H559
2 And he **s** unto them, What have I done H559
3 toward him, when he had **s** that. H1696
5 And he **s** unto the men of Succoth, Give, H559
6 And the princes of Succoth **s**, *Are* the H559
7 And Gideon **s**, Therefore when the LORD H559
15 men of Succoth, and **s**, Behold Zebah and H559
18 Then **s** he unto Zebah and Zalmunna, H559
19 And he **s**, They *were* my brethren, *even* H559
20 And he **s** unto Jether his firstborn, Up, H559
21 Then Zebah and Zalmunna **s**, Rise thou, H559
22 Then the men of Israel **s** unto Gideon, H559
23 And Gideon **s** unto them, I will not rule H559
24 And Gideon **s** unto them, I would desire H559
9: 3 Abimelech; for they **s**, He *is* our brother. H559
7 and cried, and **s** unto them, Hearken H559
8 **s** unto the olive tree, Reign thou over us. H559

Jdg 9: 9 But the olive tree **s** unto them, Should I H559
10 And the trees **s** to the fig tree, Come H559
11 But the fig tree **s** unto them, Should I H559
12 Then **s** the trees unto the vine, Come H559
13 And the vine **s** unto them, Should I leave H559
14 Then **s** all the trees unto the bramble, H559
15 And the bramble **s** unto the trees, If in H559
28 And Gaal the son of Ebed **s**, Who *is* H559
29 Abimelech. And he **s** to Abimelech, H559
36 And when Gaal saw the people, he **s** to H559
36 And Zebul **s** unto him, Thou seest H559
37 And Gaal spake again and **s**, See there H559
38 Then **s** Zebul unto him, Where *is* now H559
48 his shoulder, and **s** unto the people that H559
54 his armourbearer, and **s** unto him, Draw H559
10:11 And the LORD **s** unto the children of H559
15 And the children of Israel **s** unto the H559
18 And the people *and* princes of Gilead **s** H559
11: 2 out Jephthah, and **s** unto him, Thou H559
6 And they **s** unto Jephthah, Come, and be H559
7 And Jephthah **s** unto the elders of H559
8 And the elders of Gilead **s** unto H559
9 And Jephthah **s** unto the elders of H559
10 And the elders of Gilead **s** unto H559
15 And **s** unto him, Thus saith Jephthah, H559
19 and Israel **s** unto him, Let us pass, H559
30 the LORD, and **s**, If thou shalt without H559
35 his clothes, and **s**, Alas, my daughter! H559
36 And she **s** unto him, My father, *if* thou H559
37 And she **s** unto her father, Let this thing H559
38 And he **s**, Go. And he sent her away *for* H559
12: 1 went northward, and **s** unto Jephthah, H559
2 And Jephthah **s** unto them, I and my H559
4 because they **s**, Ye Gileadites *are* fugitives H559
5 were escaped **s**, Let me go over; that H559
5 the men of Gilead **s** unto him, *Art* thou H559
5 *Art* thou an Ephraimite? If he **s**, Nay; H559
6 Then **s** they unto him, Say now H559
6 Shibboleth: and he **s** Sibboleth: for he H559
13: 3 the woman, and **s** unto her, Behold now, H559
7 But he **s** unto me, Behold, thou shalt H559
8 Then Manoah entreated the LORD, and **s**, H559
10 her husband, and **s** unto him, Behold, H559
11 to the man, and **s** unto him, *Art* thou the H559
11 spakest unto the woman? And he **s**, I *am*. H559
12 And Manoah **s**, Now let thy words come H559
13 And the angel of the LORD **s** unto H559
13 that I **s** unto the woman let her beware. H559
15 And Manoah **s** unto the angel of the H559
16 And the angel of the LORD **s** unto H559
17 And Manoah **s** unto the angel of the H559
18 And the angel of the LORD **s** unto him, H559
22 And Manoah **s** unto his wife, We shall H559
23 But his wife **s** unto him, If the LORD H559
14: 2 his mother, and **s**, I have seen a woman H559
3 Then his father and his mother **s** unto H559
3 And Samson **s** unto his father, Get her H559
12 And Samson **s** unto them, I will now put H559
13 And they **s** unto him, Put forth thy H559
14 And he **s** unto them, Out of the eater H559
15 day, that they **s** unto Samson's wife, H559
16 before him, and **s**, Thou dost but hate H559
16 told *it* me. And he **s** unto her, Behold, I H559
18 And the men of the city **s** unto him on H559
18 than a lion? And he **s** unto them, If ye H559
15: 1 with a kid; and he **s**, I will go in to my H559
2 And her father **s**, I verily thought that H559
3 And Samson **s** concerning them, Now H559
6 Then the Philistines **s**, Who hath done H559
7 And Samson **s** unto them, Though ye H559
10 And the men of Judah **s**, Why are ye H559
11 of the rock Etam, and **s** to Samson, H559
11 unto us? And he **s** unto them, As they did H559
12 And they **s** unto him, We are come down H559
12 And Samson **s** unto them, Swear unto H559
16 And Samson **s**, With the jawbone of an H559
18 on the LORD, and **s**, Thou hast given this H559
16: 5 up unto her, and **s** unto her, Entice him, H559
6 And Delilah **s** to Samson, Tell me, I pray H559
7 And Samson **s** unto her, If they bind me H559
9 the chamber. And she **s** unto him, The H559
10 And Delilah **s** unto Samson, Behold, H559
11 And he **s** unto her, If they bind me fast H559
12 him therewith, and **s** unto him, The H559
13 And Delilah **s** unto Samson, Hitherto H559
13 be bound. And he **s** unto her, If thou H559
14 And she fastened *it* with the pin, and **s** H559
15 And she **s** unto him, How canst thou say, H559
17 That he told her all his heart, and **s** unto H559

Jdg 16:20 And she **s**, The Philistines *be* upon thee, H559
20 out of his sleep, and **s**, I will go out as at H559
23 and to rejoice: for they **s**, Our god hath H559
24 their god: for they **s**, Our god hath H559
25 merry, that they **s**, Call for Samson, that H559
26 And Samson **s** unto the lad that held H559
28 the LORD, and **s**, O Lord GOD, remember H559
30 And Samson **s**, Let me die with the H559
17: 2 And he **s** unto his mother, The eleven H559
2 **s**, Blessed *be thou* of the LORD, my son. H559
3 his mother, his mother **s**, I had wholly H559
9 And Micah **s** unto him, Whence comest H559
9 thou? And he **s** unto him, I *am* a Levite H559
10 And Micah **s** unto him, Dwell with me, H559
13 Then **s** Micah, Now know I that the H559
18: 2 to search it; and they **s** unto them, Go, H559
3 in thither, and **s** unto him, Who brought H559
4 And he **s** unto them, Thus and thus H559
5 And they **s** unto him, Ask counsel, we H559
6 And the priest **s** unto them, Go in peace: H559
8 their brethren **s** unto them, What *say* ye? H559
9 And they **s**, Arise, that we may go up H559
14 of Laish, and **s** unto their brethren, H559
18 **s** the priest unto them, What do ye? H559
19 And they **s** unto him, Hold thy peace, lay H559
23 their faces, and **s** unto Micah, What H559
24 And he **s**, Ye have taken away my gods H559
25 And the children of Dan **s** unto him, Let H559
19: 5 the damsel's father **s** unto his son in law, H559
6 father had **s** unto the man, Be content, H559
8 and the damsel's father **s**, Comfort thine H559
9 damsel's father, **s** unto him, Behold, now H559
11 spent; and the servant **s** unto his master, H559
12 And his master **s** unto him, We will not H559
13 And he **s** unto his servant, Come, and let H559
17 and the old man **s**, Whither goest thou? H559
18 And he **s** unto him, We *are* passing from H559
20 And the old man **s**, Peace *be* with thee; H559
23 out unto them, and **s** unto them, Nay, H559
28 And he **s** unto her, Up, and let us be H559
30 And it was so, that all that saw it **s**, There H559
20: 3 to Mizpeh.) Then **s** the children of Israel, H559
4 answered and **s**, I came into Gibeah that H559
18 of God, and **s**, Which of us shall go H559
18 And the LORD **s**, Judah *shall go up* first. H559
23 And the LORD **s**, Go up against him.) H559
28 And the LORD **s**, Go up; for to morrow H559
32 And the children of Benjamin **s**, They *are* H559
32 children of Israel **s**, Let us flee, and draw H559
39 thirty persons: for they **s**, Surely they are H559
21: 3 And **s**, O LORD God of Israel, why is this H559
5 And the children of Israel **s**, Who *is there* H559
6 their brother, and **s**, There is one tribe H559
8 And they **s**, What one *is there* of the H559
16 Then the elders of the congregation **s**, H559
17 And they **s**, *There must be* an inheritance H559
19 Then they **s**, Behold, *there is* a feast of the H559
Ru 1: 8 And Naomi **s** unto her two daughters in H559
10 And they **s** unto her, Surely we will H559
11 And Naomi **s**, Turn again, my daughters: H559
15 And she **s**, Behold, thy sister in law is H559
16 And Ruth **s**, Entreat me not to leave thee, H559
19 about them, and they **s**, *Is* this Naomi? H559
20 And she **s** unto them, Call me not H559
2: 2 And Ruth the Moabitess **s** unto Naomi, H559
2 And she **s** unto her, Go, my daughter. H559
4 Beth-lehem, and **s** unto the reapers, The H559
5 Then **s** Boaz unto his servant that was H559
6 answered and **s**, It *is* the Moabitish H559
7 And she **s**, I pray you, let me glean and H559
8 Then **s** Boaz unto Ruth, Hearest thou H559
10 to the ground, and **s** unto him, Why H559
11 And Boaz answered and **s** unto her, It H559
13 Then she **s**, Let me find favour in thy H559
14 And Boaz **s** unto her, At mealtime come H559
19 And her mother in law **s** unto her, H559
19 she had wrought, and **s**, The man's name H559
20 And Naomi **s** unto her daughter in law, H559
20 dead. And Naomi **s** unto her, The man *is* H559
21 And Ruth the Moabitess **s**, He said unto H559
21 And Ruth the Moabitess said, He **s** unto H559
22 And Naomi **s** unto Ruth her daughter in H559
3: 1 Then Naomi her mother in law **s** unto H559
5 And she **s** unto her, All that thou sayest H559
9 And he **s**, Who *art* thou? And she H559
10 And he **s**, Blessed *be* thou of the LORD, H559
14 another. And he **s**, Let it not be known H559
15 Also he **s**, Bring the vail that *thou hast* H559
16 mother in law, she **s**, Who *art* thou, my H559

Ru 3:17 And she **s**, These six *measures* of barley H559
17 gave he me; for he **s** to me, Go not empty H559
18 Then **s** she, Sit still, my daughter, until H559
4: 1 by; unto whom he **s**, Ho, such a one! turn H559
2 **s**, Sit ye down here. And they sat down. H559
3 And he **s** unto the kinsman, Naomi, that H559
4 I *am* after thee. And he **s**, I will redeem *it*. H559
5 Then **s** Boaz, What day thou buyest the H559
6 And the kinsman **s**, I cannot redeem *it* H559
8 Therefore the kinsman **s** unto Boaz, Buy H559
9 And Boaz **s** unto the elders, and *unto* all H559
11 and the elders, **s**, *We are* witnesses. The H559
14 And the women **s** unto Naomi, Blessed H559
1Sa 1: 8 Then **s** Elkanah her husband to her, H559
11 And she vowed a vow, and **s**, O LORD of H559
14 And Eli **s** unto her, How long wilt thou H559
15 And Hannah answered and **s**, No, my H559
17 Then Eli answered and **s**, Go in peace: H559
18 And she **s**, Let thine handmaid find grace H559
22 But Hannah went not up; for she **s** unto H559
23 And Elkanah her husband **s** unto her, H559
26 And she **s**, Oh my lord, *as* thy soul liveth, H559
2: 1 And Hannah prayed, and **s**, My heart H559
15 servant came, and **s** to the man that H559
16 And *if* any man **s** unto him, Let them not H559
20 and his wife, and **s**, The LORD give thee H559
23 And he **s** unto them, Why do ye such H559
27 God unto Eli, and **s** unto him, Thus saith H559
30 of Israel saith, I **s** indeed *that* thy house, H559
3: 5 And he ran unto Eli, and **s**, Here *am* I; for H559
5 me. And he **s**, I called not; lie down H559
6 went to Eli, and **s**, Here *am* I; for thou H559
8 went to Eli, and **s**, Here *am* I; for thou H559
9 Therefore Eli **s** unto Samuel, Go, lie H559
11 And the LORD **s** to Samuel, Behold, I H559
16 Then Eli called Samuel, and **s**, Samuel, H559
17 And he **s**, What *is* the thing that *the* H559
17 *the LORD* hath **s** unto thee? I pray thee H1696
17 me of all the things that he **s** unto thee. H1696
18 from him. And he **s**, It *is* the LORD: let H559
4: 3 the elders of Israel **s**, Wherefore hath the H559
6 of the shout, they **s**, What *meaneth* the H559
7 afraid, for they **s**, God is come into the H559
7 camp. And they **s**, Woe unto us! for there H559
14 of the crying, he **s**, What *meaneth* the H559
16 And the man **s** unto Eli, I *am* he that H559
16 And he **s**, What is there done, my son? H559
17 And the messenger answered and **s**, H559
20 that stood by her **s** unto her, Fear not; H1696
22 And she **s**, The glory is departed from H559
5: 7 that *it was* so, they **s**, The ark of the God H559
8 unto them, and **s**, What shall we do with H559
11 the Philistines, and **s**, Send away the ark H559
6: 3 And they **s**, If ye send away the ark of the H559
4 Then **s** they, What *shall be* the trespass H559
20 And the men of Beth-shemesh **s**, Who is H559
7: 5 And Samuel **s**, Gather all Israel to H559
6 on that day, and **s** there, We have sinned H559
8 And the children of Israel **s** to Samuel, H559
8: 5 And **s** unto him, Behold, thou art old, H559
6 Samuel, when they **s**, Give us a king to H559
7 And the LORD **s** unto Samuel, Hearken H559
11 And he **s**, This will be the manner of the H559
19 **s**, Nay; but we will have a king over us; H559
22 And the LORD **s** to Samuel, Hearken H559
22 a king. And Samuel **s** unto the men of H559
9: 3 lost. And Kish **s** to Saul his son, Take H559
5 land of Zuph, Saul **s** to his servant that H559
6 And he **s** unto him, Behold now, *there is* H559
7 Then **s** Saul to his servant, But, behold, *if* H559
8 Saul again, and **s**, Behold, I have here at H559
10 Then **s** Saul to his servant, Well said; H559
10 Then said Saul to his servant, Well **s**; H1697
11 water, and **s** unto them, Is the seer here? H559
12 And they answered them, and **s**, He is; H559
17 Saul, the LORD **s** unto him, Behold the H6030
18 in the gate, and **s**, Tell me, I pray thee, H559
19 And Samuel answered Saul, and **s**, I *am* H559
21 And Saul answered and **s**, *Am* not I a H559
23 And Samuel **s** unto the cook, Bring the H559
23 of which I **s** unto thee, Set it by thee. H559
24 Saul. And *Samuel* **s**, Behold that which is H559
24 kept for thee since I **s**, I have invited the H559
27 end of the city, Samuel **s** to Saul, Bid the H559
10: 1 kissed him, and **s**, *Is it* not because the H559
11 then the people **s** one to another, What H559
12 answered and **s**, But who *is* their father? H559
14 And Saul's uncle **s** unto him and to his H559
14 went ye? And he **s**, To seek the asses: and H559

1Sa 10:15 And Saul's uncle s, Tell me, I pray thee, H559
15 me, I pray thee, what Samuel s unto you. H559
16 And Saul s unto his uncle, He told us H559
18 And s unto the children of Israel, Thus H559
19 and ye have s unto him, *Nay*, but set H559
24 And Samuel s to all the people, See ye H559
24 people shouted, and s, God save the king. H559
27 But the children of Belial s, How shall H559
11: 1 the men of Jabesh s unto Nahash, Make H559
3 And the elders of Jabesh s unto him, H559
5 of the field; and Saul s, What *aileth* the H559
9 And they s unto the messengers that H559
10 Therefore the men of Jabesh s, To H559
12 And the people s unto Samuel, Who *is* H559
12 Who *is* he that s, Shall Saul reign over H559
13 And Saul s, There shall not a man be put H559
14 Then s Samuel to the people, Come, and H559
12: 1 And Samuel s unto all Israel, Behold, I H559
1 voice in all that ye s unto me, and have H559
4 And they s, Thou hast not defrauded us, H559
5 And he s unto them, The LORD *is* H559
6 And Samuel s unto the people, *It is* the H559
10 And they cried unto the LORD, and s, We H559
12 against you, ye s unto me, Nay; but a H559
19 And all the people s unto Samuel, Pray H559
20 And Samuel s unto the people, Fear not: H559
13: 9 And Saul s, Bring hither a burnt offering H559
11 And Samuel s, What hast thou done? H559
11 done? And Saul s, Because I saw that the H559
12 Therefore s I, The Philistines will come H559
13 And Samuel s to Saul, Thou hast done H559
19 for the Philistines s, Lest the Hebrews H559
14: 1 the son of Saul s unto the young man H559
6 And Jonathan s to the young man that H559
7 And his armourbearer s unto him, Do all H559
8 Then s Jonathan, Behold, we will pass H559
11 and the Philistines s, Behold, the H559
12 armourbearer, and s, Come up to us, and H559
12 And Jonathan s unto his armourbearer, H559
17 Then s Saul unto the people that *were* H559
18 And Saul s unto Ahiah, Bring hither the H559
19 s unto the priest, Withdraw thine hand. H559
28 Then answered one of the people, and s, H559
29 Then s Jonathan, My father hath H559
33 with the blood. And he s, Ye have H559
34 And Saul s, Disperse yourselves among H559
36 And Saul s, Let us go down after the H559
36 man of them. And they s, Do whatsoever H559
36 unto thee. Then s the priest, Let us draw H559
38 And Saul s, Draw ye near hither, all the H559
40 Then s he unto all Israel, Be ye on one H559
40 And the people s unto Saul, Do what H559
41 Therefore Saul s unto the LORD God of H559
42 And Saul s, Cast *lots* between me and H559
43 Then Saul s to Jonathan, Tell me what H559
43 told him, and s, I did but taste a little H559
45 And the people s unto Saul, Shall H559
15: 1 Samuel also s unto Saul, The LORD sent H559
6 And Saul s unto the Kenites, Go, depart, H559
13 And Samuel came to Saul: and Saul s H559
14 And Samuel s, What *meaneth* then this H559
15 And Saul s, They have brought them H559
16 Then Samuel s unto Saul, Stay, and I will H559
16 the LORD hath s to me this night. And H1696
16 this night. And he s unto him, Say on. H559
17 And Samuel s, When thou *wast* little in H559
18 thee on a journey, and s, Go and utterly H559
20 And Saul s unto Samuel, Yea, I have H559
22 And Samuel s, Hath the LORD *as great* H559
24 And Saul s unto Samuel, I have sinned: H559
26 And Samuel s unto Saul, I will not return H559
28 And Samuel s unto him, The LORD hath H559
30 Then he s, I have sinned: *yet* honour me H559
32 Then s Samuel, Bring ye hither to me H559
32 s, Surely the bitterness of death is past. H559
33 And Samuel s, As thy sword hath made H559
16: 1 And the LORD s unto Samuel, How long H559
2 And Samuel s, How can I go? if Saul hear H559
2 me. And the LORD s, Take an heifer with H559
4 coming, and s, Comest thou peaceably? H559
5 And he s, Peaceably: I am come to H559
6 on Eliab, and s, Surely the LORD'S H559
7 But the LORD s unto Samuel, Look not H559
8 he s, Neither hath the LORD chosen this. H559
9 he s, Neither hath the LORD chosen this. H559
10 And Samuel s unto Jesse, The LORD H559
11 And Samuel s unto Jesse, Are here all *thy* H559
11 children? And he s, There remaineth yet H559
11 sheep. And Samuel s unto Jesse, Send H559

1Sa 16:12 LORD s, Arise, anoint him: for this *is* he. H559
15 And Saul's servants s unto him, Behold H559
17 And Saul s unto his servants, Provide H559
18 the servants, and s, Behold, I have seen a H559
19 unto Jesse, and s, Send me David thy son, H559
17: 8 of Israel, and s unto them, Why are H559
10 And the Philistine s, I defy the armies of H559
17 And Jesse s unto David his son, Take H559
25 And the men of Israel s, Have ye seen H559
28 David, and he s, Why camest thou down H559
29 And David s, What have I now done? *Is* H559
32 And David s to Saul, Let no man's heart H559
33 And Saul s to David, Thou art not able to H559
34 And David s unto Saul, Thy servant kept H559
37 David s moreover, The LORD that H559
37 And Saul s unto David, Go, and H559
39 *it*. And David s unto Saul, I cannot go H559
43 And the Philistine s unto David, *Am* I a H559
44 And the Philistine s to David, Come to H559
45 Then s David to the Philistine, Thou H559
55 the Philistine, he s unto Abner, the H559
55 s, *As* thy soul liveth, O king, I cannot tell. H559
56 And the king s, Inquire thou whose son H559
58 And Saul s to him, Whose son *art* thou, H559
18: 7 as they played, and s, Saul hath slain his H559
8 him; and he s, They have ascribed unto H559
11 And Saul cast the javelin; for he s, I will H559
17 And Saul s to David, Behold my elder H559
17 battles. For Saul s, Let not mine hand be H559
18 And David s unto Saul, Who *am* I? and H559
21 And Saul s, I will give him her, that she H559
21 Wherefore Saul s to David, Thou shalt H559
23 David. And David s, Seemeth it to you *a* H559
25 And Saul s, Thus shall ye say to David, H559
19: 4 his father, and s unto him, Let not the H559
14 to take David, she s, He *is* sick. H559
17 And Saul s unto Michal, Why hast thou H559
17 answered Saul, He s unto me, Let me go; H559
22 and he asked and s, Where *are* Samuel H559
22 s, Behold, *they be* at Naioth in Ramah. H559
20: 1 and came and s before Jonathan, What H559
2 And he s unto him, God forbid; thou H559
3 And David sware moreover, and s, Thy H559
4 Then s Jonathan unto David, H559
5 And David s unto Jonathan, Behold, to H559
9 And Jonathan s, Far be it from thee: for if H559
10 Then s David to Jonathan, Who shall tell H559
11 And Jonathan s unto David, Come, and H559
12 And Jonathan s unto David, O LORD H559
18 Then Jonathan s to David, To morrow *is* H559
27 was empty: and Saul s unto Jonathan his H559
29 And he s, Let me go, I pray thee; for our H559
30 Jonathan, and he s unto him, Thou son H559
32 his father, and s unto him, Wherefore H559
36 And he s unto his lad, Run, find out now H559
37 lad, and s, *Is* not the arrow beyond thee? H559
40 s unto him, Go, carry *them* to the city. H559
42 And Jonathan s to David, Go in peace, H559
21: 1 of David, and s unto him, Why *art* thou H559
2 And David s unto Ahimelech the priest, H559
2 a business, and hath s unto me, Let no H559
4 And the priest answered David, and s, H559
5 And David answered the priest, and s H559
8 And David s unto Ahimelech, And is H559
9 And the priest s, The sword of Goliath H559
9 s, *There is* none like that; give it me. H559
11 And the servants of Achish s unto him, H559
14 Then s Achish unto his servants, Lo, ye H559
22: 3 of Moab: and he s unto the king of H559
5 And the prophet Gad s unto David, H559
7 Then Saul s unto his servants that stood H559
9 of Saul, and s, I saw the son of Jesse H559
12 And Saul s, Hear now, thou son of H559
13 And Saul s unto him, Why have ye H559
14 the king, and s, And who *is so* faithful H559
16 And the king s, Thou shalt surely die, H559
17 And the king s unto the footmen that H559
18 And the king s to Doeg, Turn thou, and H559
22 And David s unto Abiathar, I knew *it* H559
23: 2 And the LORD s unto David, Go, and H559
3 And David's men s unto him, Behold, we H559
4 answered him and s, Arise, go down to H559
7 to Keilah. And Saul s, God hath delivered H559
9 him; and he s to Abiathar the priest, H559
10 Then s David, O LORD God of Israel, thy H559
11 And the LORD s, He will come down. H559
12 Then s David, Will the men of Keilah H559
12 the LORD s, They will deliver *thee* up. H559
17 And he s unto him, Fear not: for the H559

1Sa 23:21 And Saul s, Blessed *be* ye of the LORD; H559
24: 4 And the men of David s unto him, H559
4 of which the LORD s unto thee, Behold, I H559
6 And he s unto his men, The LORD forbid H559
9 And David s to Saul, Wherefore hearest H559
10 spared thee; and I s, I will not put forth H559
16 Saul, that Saul s, *Is* this thy voice, my H559
17 And he s to David, Thou *art* more H559
25: 5 men, and David s unto the young men, H559
10 servants, and s, Who *is* David? and who H559
13 And David s unto his men, Gird ye on H559
19 And she s unto her servants, Go on H559
21 Now David had s, Surely in vain have I H559
24 And fell at his feet, and s, Upon me, my H559
32 And David s to Abigail, Blessed *be* the H559
35 brought him, and s unto her, Go up in H559
39 was dead, he s, Blessed *be* the LORD, H559
41 face to the earth, and s, Behold, *let* thine H559
26: 6 Then answered David and s to H559
6 And Abishai s, I will go down with thee. H559
8 Then s Abishai to David, God hath H559
9 And David s to Abishai, Destroy him H559
10 David s furthermore, *As* the LORD H559
14 s, Who *art* thou *that* criest to the king? H559
15 And David s to Abner, *Art* not thou a H559
17 And Saul knew David's voice, and s, *Is* H559
17 David s, *It is* my voice, my lord, O king. H559
18 And he s, Wherefore doth my lord thus H559
21 Then s Saul, I have sinned: return, my H559
22 And David answered and s, Behold the H559
25 Then Saul s to David, Blessed *be* thou, H559
27: 1 And David s in his heart, I shall now H559
5 And David s unto Achish, If I have now H559
10 And Achish s, Whither have ye made a H559
10 to day? And David s, Against the south of H559
28: 1 Israel. And Achish s unto David, Know H559
2 And David s to Achish, Surely thou shalt H559
2 do. And Achish s to David, Therefore H559
7 Then s Saul unto his servants, Seek me a H559
7 And his servants s to him, Behold, *there* H559
8 by night: and he s, I pray thee, divine H559
9 And the woman s unto him, Behold, H559
11 Then s the woman, Whom shall I bring H559
11 thee? And he s, Bring me up Samuel. H559
13 And the king s unto her, Be not afraid: H559
13 And the woman s unto Saul, I saw gods H559
14 And he s unto her, What form *is* he of? H559
14 *is* he of? And she s, An old man cometh H559
15 And Samuel s to Saul, Why hast thou H559
16 Then s Samuel, Wherefore then dost H559
21 sore troubled, and s unto him, Behold, H559
23 But he refused, and s, I will not eat. But H559
29: 3 Then s the princes of the Philistines, H559
3 *here?* And Achish s unto the princes of H559
4 of the Philistines s unto him, Make this H559
6 Then Achish called David, and s unto H559
8 And David s unto Achish, But what have H559
9 And Achish answered and s to David, I H559
9 s, He shall not go up with us to the battle. H559
30: 7 And David s to Abiathar the priest, H559
13 And David s unto him, To whom H559
13 *art* thou? And he s, I *am* a young man of H559
15 And David s to him, Canst thou bring H559
15 company? And he s, Swear unto me by H559
20 *other* cattle, and s, This *is* David's spoil. H559
22 with David, and s, Because they went not H559
23 Then s David, Ye shall not do so, my H559
31: 4 Then s Saul unto his armourbearer, H559
2Sa 1: 3 And David s unto him, From whence H559
3 thou? And he s unto him, Out of the H559
4 And David s unto him, How went the H559
5 And David s unto the young man that H559
6 And the young man that told him s, As I H559
8 And he s unto me, Who *art* thou? And I H559
9 He s unto me again, Stand, I pray thee, H559
13 And David s unto the young man that H559
14 And David s unto him, How wast thou H559
15 young men, and s, Go near, *and* fall upon H559
16 And David s unto him, Thy blood *be* H559
2: 1 And the LORD s unto him, Go up. And H559
1 Go up. And David s, Whither shall I go H559
1 shall I go up? And he s, Unto Hebron. H559
5 Jabesh-gilead, and s unto them, Blessed H559
14 And Abner s to Joab, Let the young men H559
14 before us. And Joab s, Let them arise. H559
20 Then Abner looked behind him, and s, H559
21 And Abner s to him, Turn thee aside to H559
22 And Abner s again to Asahel, Turn thee H559
26 Then Abner called to Joab, and s, Shall H559

2Sa 2:27 And Joab s, *As* God liveth, unless thou H559
3: 7 and *Ish-bosheth* s to Abner, Wherefore H559
8 Ish-bosheth, and s, *Am* I a dog's head, H559
13 And he s, Well; I will make a league with H559
16 to Bahurim. Then s Abner unto him, Go, H559
21 And Abner s unto David, I will arise and H559
24 Then Joab came to the king, and s, What H559
28 And afterward when David heard *it*, he s, H559
31 And David s to Joab, and to all the H559
33 Abner, and s, Died Abner as a fool dieth? H559
38 And the king s unto his servants, Know H559
4: 8 to Hebron, and s to the king, Behold the H559
9 the Beerothite, and s unto them, *As* the H559
5: 2 and the LORD s to thee, Thou shalt feed H559
8 And David s on that day, Whosoever H559
8 Wherefore they s, The blind and the lame H559
19 And the LORD s unto David, Go up: for H559
20 smote them there, and s, The LORD hath H559
23 of the LORD, he s, Thou shalt not go up; H559
6: 9 that day, and s, How shall the ark of H559
20 to meet David, and s, How glorious was H559
21 And David s unto Michal, *It was* before H559
7: 2 That the king s unto Nathan the H559
3 And Nathan s to the king, Go, do all that H559
18 the LORD, and he s, Who *am* I, O Lord H559
25 *it* for ever, and do as thou hast s. H1696
9: 1 And David s, Is there yet any that is left H559
2 David, the king s unto him, *Art* thou H559
2 thou Ziba? And he s, Thy servant *is he*. H559
3 And the king s, *Is* there not yet any of the H559
3 him? And Ziba s unto the king, Jonathan H559
4 And the king s unto him, Where *is* he? H559
4 *is* he? And Ziba s unto the king, Behold, H559
6 And David s, Mephibosheth. And H559
7 And David s unto him, Fear not: for I H559
8 And he bowed himself, and s, What *is* H559
9 Saul's servant, and s unto him, I have H559
11 Then s Ziba unto the king, According to H559
11 As for Mephibosheth, *s the king*, he shall
10: 2 Then s David, I will shew kindness unto H559
3 of Ammon s unto Hanun their lord, H559
5 and the king s, Tarry at Jericho until H559
11 And he s, If the Syrians be too strong for H559
11: 3 the woman. And *one* s, *Is* not this H559
5 and told David, and s, I *am* with child. H559
8 And David s to Uriah, Go down to thy H559
10 his house, David s unto Uriah, Camest H559
11 And Uriah s unto David, The ark, and H559
12 And David s to Uriah, Tarry here to day H559
23 And the messenger s unto David, Surely H559
25 Then David s unto the messenger, Thus H559
12: 1 unto him, and s unto him, There were H559
5 the man; and he s to Nathan, *As* the H559
7 And Nathan s to David, Thou *art* the H559
13 And David s unto Nathan, I have sinned H559
13 And Nathan s unto David, The LORD H559
18 was dead: for they s, Behold, while the H559
19 therefore David s unto his servants, Is H559
19 Is the child dead? And they s, He is dead. H559
21 Then s his servants unto him, What H559
22 And he s, While the child was yet alive, I H559
22 and wept: for I s, Who can tell *whether* H559
27 to David, and s, I have fought against H559
13: 4 And he s unto him, Why *art* thou, *being* H559
4 tell me? And Amnon s unto him, I love H559
5 And Jonadab s unto him, Lay thee down H559
6 to see him, Amnon s unto the king, I H559
9 to eat. And Amnon s, Have out all men H559
10 And Amnon s unto Tamar, Bring the H559
11 s unto her, Come lie with me, my sister. H559
15 And Amnon s unto her, Arise, be gone. H559
16 And she s unto him, *There is* no cause: H559
17 unto him, and s, Put now this *woman* H559
20 And Absalom her brother s unto her, H559
24 And Absalom came to the king, and s, H559
25 And the king s to Absalom, Nay, my son, H559
26 Then s Absalom, If not, I pray thee, let H559
26 s unto him, Why should he go with thee? H559
32 answered and s, Let not my lord suppose H559
35 And Jonadab s unto the king, Behold, H559
35 sons come: as thy servant s, so it is. H1697
14: 2 a wise woman, and s unto her, I pray H559
4 and did obeisance, and s, Help, O king. H559
5 And the king s unto her, What aileth H559
7 and they s, Deliver him that smote H559
8 And the king s unto the woman, Go to H559
9 And the woman of Tekoah s unto the H559
10 And the king s, Whosoever saith *ought* H559
11 Then s she, I pray thee, let the king H559

2Sa 14:11 my son. And he s, *As* the LORD liveth, H559
12 Then the woman s, Let thine handmaid, I H559
12 unto my lord the king. And he s, Say on. H559
13 And the woman s, Wherefore then hast H559
15 and thy handmaid s, I will now speak H559
17 Then thine handmaid s, The word of my H559
18 Then the king answered and s unto the H559
18 s, Let my lord the king now speak. H559
19 And the king s, *Is not* the hand of Joab H559
19 answered and s, *As* thy soul liveth, my H559
21 And the king s unto Joab, Behold now, I H559
22 the king: and Joab s, To day thy servant H559
24 And the king s, Let him turn to his own H559
30 Therefore he s unto his servants, See, H559
31 *his* house, and s unto him, Wherefore H559
15: 2 unto him, and s, Of what city *art* thou? H559
2 *art* thou? And he s, Thy servant *is* of one H559
3 And Absalom s unto him, See, thy H559
4 Absalom s moreover, Oh that I were H559
7 that Absalom s unto the king, I pray H559
9 And the king s unto him, Go in peace. So H559
14 And David s unto all his servants that H559
15 And the king's servants s unto the king, H559
19 Then s the king to Ittai the Gittite, H559
21 And Ittai answered the king, and s, *As* H559
22 And David s to Ittai, Go and pass over. H559
25 And the king s unto Zadok, Carry back H559
27 The king s also unto Zadok the priest, H559
31 And David s, O LORD, I pray thee, H559
33 Unto whom David s, If thou passest on H559
16: 2 And the king s unto Ziba, What meanest H559
2 by these? And Ziba s, The asses *be* for the H559
3 And the king s, And where *is* thy master's H559
3 son? And Ziba s unto the king, Behold, H559
3 at Jerusalem: for he s, To day shall the H559
4 Then s the king to Ziba, Behold, thine H559
4 And Ziba s, I humbly beseech thee H559
7 And thus s Shimei when he cursed, H559
9 Then s Abishai the son of Zeruiah unto H559
10 And the king s, What have I to do with H559
10 the LORD hath s unto him, Curse David. H559
11 And David s to Abishai, and to all his H559
16 that Hushai s unto Absalom, God H559
17 And Absalom s to Hushai, *Is* this thy H559
18 And Hushai s unto Absalom, Nay; but H559
20 Then s Absalom to Ahithophel, Give H559
21 And Ahithophel s unto Absalom, Go in H559
17: 1 Moreover Ahithophel s unto Absalom, H559
5 Then s Absalom, Call now Hushai the H559
7 And Hushai s unto Absalom, The H559
8 For, s Hushai, thou knowest thy father H559
14 And Absalom and all the men of Israel s, H559
15 Then s Hushai unto Zadok and to H559
20 to the house, they s, Where *is* Ahimaaz H559
20 And the woman s unto them, They be H559
21 king David, and s unto David, Arise, and H559
29 to eat: for they s, The people *is* hungry, H559
18: 2 And the king s unto the people, I will H559
4 And the king s unto them, What H559
10 *it*, and told Joab, and s, Behold, I saw H559
11 And Joab s unto the man that told him, H559
12 And the man s unto Joab, Though I H559
14 Then s Joab, I may not tarry thus with H559
18 king's dale: for he s, I have no son to keep H559
19 Then s Ahimaaz the son of Zadok, Let H559
20 And Joab s unto him, Thou shalt not H559
21 Then s Joab to Cushi, Go tell the king H559
22 Then s Ahimaaz the son of Zadok yet H559
22 Cushi. And Joab s, Wherefore wilt thou H559
23 But howsoever, *s he*, let me run. And he
23 *he*, let me run. And he s unto him, Run. H559
25 king. And the king s, If he *be* alone, *there* H559
26 the porter, and s, Behold *another* man H559
26 And the king s, He also bringeth tidings. H559
27 And the watchman s, Me thinketh the H559
27 And the king s, He *is* a good man, and H559
28 And Ahimaaz called, and s unto the H559
28 the king, and s, Blessed *be* the LORD H559
29 And the king s, Is the young man H559
30 And the king s *unto him*, Turn aside, H559
31 And, behold, Cushi came; and Cushi s, H559
32 And the king s unto Cushi, Is the young H559
33 as he went, thus he s, O my son Absalom, H559
19: 5 to the king, and s, Thou hast shamed this H559
19 And s unto the king, Let not my lord H559
21 answered and s, Shall not Shimei be put H559
22 And David s, What have I to do with you, H559
23 Therefore the king s unto Shimei, Thou H559
25 the king, that the king s unto him, H559

2Sa 19:26 me: for thy servant s, I will saddle me an H559
29 And the king s unto him, Why speakest H559
29 I have s, Thou and Ziba divide the land. H559
30 And Mephibosheth s unto the king, Yea, H559
33 And the king s unto Barzillai, Come thou H559
34 And Barzillai s unto the king, How long H559
41 to the king, and s unto the king, Why H559
43 men of Judah, and s, We have ten parts H559
20: 1 a trumpet, and s, We have no part in H559
4 Then s the king to Amasa, Assemble me H559
6 And David s to Abishai, Now shall H559
9 And Joab s to Amasa, *Art* thou in health, H559
11 stood by him, and s, He that favoureth H559
17 her, the woman s, *Art* thou Joab? And he H559
17 I *am he*. Then she s unto him, Hear the H559
20 And Joab answered and s, Far be it, far H559
21 And the woman s unto Joab, Behold, his H559
21: 2 And the king called the Gibeonites, and s H559
3 Wherefore David s unto the Gibeonites, H559
4 And the Gibeonites s unto him, We will H559
4 in Israel. And he s, What ye shall say, H559
6 choose. And the king s, I will give *them*. H559
22: 2 And he s, The LORD *is* my rock, and my H559
23: 1 the son of Jesse s, and the man *who was* H5002
1 and the sweet psalmist of Israel, s, H5002
3 The God of Israel s, the Rock of Israel H559
15 And David longed, and s, Oh that one H559
17 And he s, Be it far from me, O LORD, that H559
24: 2 For the king s to Joab the captain of the H559
3 And Joab s unto the king, Now the LORD H559
10 people. And David s unto the LORD, I H559
13 and told him, and s unto him, Shall H559
14 And David s unto Gad, I am in a great H559
16 him of the evil, and s to the angel that H559
17 the people, and s, Lo, I have sinned, and H559
18 And Gad came that day to David, and s H559
21 And Araunah s, Wherefore is my lord the H559
21 And David s, To buy the threshingfloor H559
22 And Araunah s unto David, Let my lord H559
23 king. And Araunah s unto the king, The H559
24 And the king s unto Araunah, Nay; but I H559
1Ki 1: 2 Wherefore his servants s unto him, Let H559
16 And the king s, What wouldest thou? H559
17 And she s unto him, My lord, thou H559
24 And Nathan s, My lord, O king, hast thou H559
24 O king, hast thou s, Adonijah shall reign H559
28 Then king David answered and s, Call H559
29 And the king sware, and s, *As* the LORD H559
31 s, Let my lord king David live for ever. H559
32 And king David s, Call me Zadok the H559
33 The king also s unto them, Take with H559
36 the king, and s, Amen: the LORD God H559
39 all the people s, God save king Solomon. H559
41 of the trumpet, he s, Wherefore *is this* H559
42 and Adonijah s unto him, Come in; for H559
43 And Jonathan answered and s to H559
48 And also thus s the king, Blessed *be* the H559
52 And Solomon s, If he will shew himself a H559
53 Solomon s unto him, Go to thine house. H559
2: 4 thee (s he) a man on the throne of Israel. H559
13 of Solomon. And she s, Comest thou H559
13 thou peaceably? And he s, Peaceably. H559
14 He s moreover, I have somewhat to say H559
14 to say unto thee. And she s, Say on. H559
15 And he s, Thou knowest that the H559
16 me not. And she s unto him, Say on. H559
17 And he s, Speak, I pray thee, unto H559
18 And Bath-sheba s, Well; I will speak for H559
20 Then she s, I desire one small petition of H559
20 nay. And the king s unto her, Ask on, my H559
21 And she s, Let Abishag the Shunammite H559
22 And king Solomon answered and s unto H559
26 And unto Abiathar the priest s the king, H559
30 of the LORD, and s unto him, Thus saith H559
30 forth. And he s, Nay; but I will die here. H559
30 Thus s Joab, and thus he answered me. H1696
31 And the king s unto him, Do as he hath H559
31 Do as he hath s, and fall upon him, and H1696
36 for Shimei, and s unto him, Build thee H559
38 And Shimei s unto the king, The saying H559
38 lord the king hath s, so will thy servant H1696
42 for Shimei, and s unto him, Did I not H559
44 The king s moreover to Shimei, Thou H559
3: 5 and God s, Ask what I shall give thee. H559
6 And Solomon s, Thou hast shewed unto H559
11 And God s unto him, Because thou hast H559
17 And the one woman s, O my lord, I and H559
22 And the other woman s, Nay; but the H559
22 *is* thy son. And this s, No; but the dead *is* H559

1Ki 3:23 Then s the king, The one saith, This *is* H559
24 And the king s, Bring me a sword. And H559
25 And the king s, Divide the living child in H559
26 her son, and she s, O my lord, give her H559
26 it. But the other s, Let it be neither mine H559
27 Then the king answered and s, Give her H559
5: 7 greatly, and s, Blessed *be* the LORD H559
8:12 Then spake Solomon, The LORD s that H559
15 And he s, Blessed *be* the LORD God of H559
18 And the LORD s unto David my father, H559
23 And he s, LORD God of Israel, *there is* no H559
29 of which thou hast s, My name shall be H559
9: 3 And the LORD s unto him, I have heard H559
13 And he s, What cities *are* these which H559
10: 6 And she s to the king, It was a true H559
11: 2 which the LORD s unto the children of H559
11 Wherefore the LORD s unto Solomon, H559
21 was dead, Hadad s to Pharaoh, Let me H559
22 Then Pharaoh s unto him, But what hast H559
31 And he s to Jeroboam, Take thee ten H559
12: 5 And he s unto them, Depart yet *for* three H559
6 he yet lived, and s, How do ye advise that H559
9 And he s unto them, What counsel give H559
26 And Jeroboam s in his heart, Now shall H559
28 calves *of* gold, and s unto them, It is too H559
13: 2 of the LORD, and s, O altar, altar, thus H559
6 And the king answered and s unto the H559
7 And the king s unto the man of God, H1696
8 And the man of God s unto the king, If H559
12 And their father s unto them, What H1696
13 And he s unto his sons, Saddle me the H559
14 an oak: and he s unto him, *Art* thou the H559
14 that camest from Judah? And he s, I *am.* H559
15 Then he s unto him, Come home with H559
16 And he s, I may not return with thee, nor H559
17 For it was s to me by the word of the H1697
18 He s unto him, I *am* a prophet also as H559
26 heard *thereof,* he s, It *is* the man of God, H559
14: 2 And Jeroboam s to his wife, Arise, I pray H559
5 And the LORD s unto Ahijah, Behold, H559
6 at the door, that he s, Come in, thou wife H559
17: 1 of Gilead, s unto Ahab, *As* the LORD H559
10 he called to her, and s, Fetch me, I pray H559
11 he called to her, and s, Bring me, I pray H559
12 And she s, *As* the LORD thy God liveth, I H559
13 And Elijah s unto her, Fear not; go *and* H559
13 do as thou hast s: but make me thereof H1697
18 And she s unto Elijah, What have I to do H559
19 And he s unto her, Give me thy son. And H559
20 And he cried unto the LORD, and s, O H559
21 the LORD, and s, O LORD my God, I pray H559
23 mother: and Elijah s, See, thy son liveth. H559
24 And the woman s to Elijah, Now by this I H559
18: 5 And Ahab s unto Obadiah, Go into the H559
7 face, and s, *Art* thou that my lord Elijah? H559
9 And he s, What have I sinned, that thou H559
10 and when they s, *He is* not *there;* he took H559
15 And Elijah s, *As* the LORD of hosts liveth, H559
17 Elijah, that Ahab s unto him, *Art* thou he H559
21 all the people, and s, How long halt ye H559
22 Then s Elijah unto the people, I, *even* I H559
24 people answered and s, It is well spoken. H559
25 And Elijah s unto the prophets of Baal, H559
27 mocked them, and s, Cry aloud: for he *is* H559
30 And Elijah s unto all the people, Come H559
33 on the wood, and s, Fill four barrels with H559
34 And he s, Do *it* the second time. And they H559
34 time. And he s, Do *it* the third time. H559
36 prophet came near, and s, LORD God of H559
39 faces: and they s, The LORD, he *is* the H559
40 And Elijah s unto them, Take the H559
41 And Elijah s unto Ahab, Get thee up, eat H559
43 And s to his servant, Go up now, look H559
43 and looked, and s, *There is* nothing. And H559
43 nothing. And he s, Go again seven times. H559
44 time, that he s, Behold, there ariseth H559
44 hand. And he s, Go up, say unto Ahab, H559
19: 4 he might die; and s, It is enough; now, O H559
5 him, and s unto him, Arise *and* eat. H559
7 and touched him, and s, Arise *and* eat; H559
9 to him, and he s unto him, What doest H559
10 And he s, I have been very jealous for the H559
11 And he s, Go forth, and stand upon the H559
13 him, and s, What doest thou here, Elijah? H559
14 And he s, I have been very jealous for the H559
15 And the LORD s unto him, Go, return on H559
20 after Elijah, and s, Let me, I pray thee, H559
20 follow thee. And he s unto him, Go back H559
20: 2 and s unto him, Thus saith Ben-hadad, H559

1Ki 20: 4 And the king of Israel answered and s, H559
5 And the messengers came again, and s, H559
7 of the land, and s, Mark, I pray you, and H559
8 And all the elders and all the people s H559
9 Wherefore he s unto the messengers of H559
10 And Ben-hadad sent unto him, and s, H559
11 And the king of Israel answered and s, H559
12 pavilions, that he s unto his servants, Set H559
14 And Ahab s, By whom? And he said, H559
14 And Ahab said, By whom? And he s, H559
14 provinces. Then he s, Who shall order H559
18 And he s, Whether they be come out for H559
22 the king of Israel, and s unto him, Go, H559
23 And the servants of the king of Syria s H559
28 the king of Israel, and s, Thus saith the H559
28 the Syrians have s, The LORD *is* God of H559
31 And his servants s unto him, Behold H559
32 the king of Israel, and s, Thy servant H559
32 he s, *Is* he yet alive? he *is* my brother. H559
33 hastily catch *it:* and they s, Thy brother H559
33 Then he s, Go ye, bring him. Then H559
34 And *Ben-hadad* s unto him, The cities, H559
34 in Samaria. Then *s Ahab,* I will send
35 of the prophets s unto his neighbour in H559
36 Then s he unto him, Because thou hast H559
37 Then he found another man, and s, H559
39 the king: and he s, Thy servant went out H559
39 man unto me, and s, Keep this man: if by H559
40 the king of Israel s unto him, So *shall* thy H559
42 And he s unto him, Thus saith the H559
21: 3 And Naboth s to Ahab, The LORD forbid H559
4 to him: for he had s, I will not give thee H559
5 But Jezebel his wife came to him, and s H1696
6 And he s unto her, Because I spake H1696
6 the Jezreelite, and s unto him, Give me H559
7 And Jezebel his wife s unto him, Dost H559
15 dead, that Jezebel s to Ahab, Arise, take H559
20 And Ahab s to Elijah, Hast thou found H559
22: 3 And the king of Israel s unto his H559
4 And he s unto Jehoshaphat, Wilt thou go H559
4 And Jehoshaphat s to the king of Israel, H559
5 And Jehoshaphat s unto the king of H559
6 hundred men, and s unto them, Shall I H559
6 I forbear? And they s, Go up; for the Lord H559
7 And Jehoshaphat s, *Is there* not here a H559
8 And the king of Israel s unto H559
8 Jehoshaphat s, Let not the king say so. H559
9 an officer, and s, Hasten *hither* Micaiah H559
11 of iron: and he s, Thus saith the LORD, H559
14 And Micaiah s, *As* the LORD liveth, what H559
15 So he came to the king. And the king s H559
16 And the king s unto him, How many H559
17 And he s, I saw all Israel scattered upon H559
17 and the LORD s, These have no master: H559
18 And the king of Israel s unto H559
19 And he s, Hear thou therefore the word H559
20 And the LORD s, Who shall persuade H559
20 And one s on this manner, and H559
20 manner, and another s on that manner. H559
21 the LORD, and s, I will persuade him. H559
22 And the LORD s unto him, Wherewith? H559
22 And he s, I will go forth, and I H559
22 prophets. And he s, Thou shalt persuade H559
24 on the cheek, and s, Which way went the H559
25 And Micaiah s, Behold, thou shalt see in H559
26 And the king of Israel s, Take Micaiah, H559
28 And Micaiah s, If thou return at all in H559
28 s, Hearken, O people, every one of you. H559
30 And the king of Israel s unto H559
32 that they s, Surely it *is* the king of H559
34 wherefore he s unto the driver of his H559
49 Then s Ahaziah the son of Ahab unto H559
2Ki 1: 2 sent messengers, and s unto them, Go, H559
3 But the angel of the LORD s to Elijah H1696
5 back unto him, he s unto them, Why are H559
6 And they s unto him, There came a man H559
6 up to meet us, and s unto us, Go, turn H559
7 And he s unto them, What manner of H1696
8 loins. And he s, It *is* Elijah the Tishbite. H559
9 of God, the king hath s, Come down. H1696
10 And Elijah answered and s to the H1696
11 he answered and s unto him, O man of H1696
11 thus hath the king s, Come down quickly. H559
12 And Elijah answered and s unto them, H1696
13 him, and s unto him, O man of H1696
15 And the angel of the LORD s unto H1696
16 And he s unto him, Thus saith the H1696
2: 2 And Elijah s unto Elisha, Tarry here, I H559
2 to Beth-el. And Elisha s *unto him, As* the H559

2Ki 2: 3 forth to Elisha, and s unto him, Knowest H559
3 he s, Yea, I know *it;* hold ye your peace. H559
4 And Elijah s unto him, Elisha, tarry H559
4 to Jericho. And he s, *As* the LORD liveth, H559
5 to Elisha, and s unto him, Knowest thou H559
6 And Elijah s unto him, Tarry, I pray H559
6 to Jordan. And he s, *As* the LORD liveth, H559
9 over, that Elijah s unto Elisha, Ask what H559
9 from thee. And Elisha s, I pray thee, let a H559
10 And he s, Thou hast asked a hard thing: H559
14 the waters, and s, Where *is* the LORD H559
15 saw him, they s, The spirit of Elijah doth H559
16 And they s unto him, Behold now, there H559
16 some valley. And he s, Ye shall not send. H559
17 he was ashamed, he s, Send. They sent H559
18 at Jericho,) he s unto them, Did I not H559
19 And the men of the city s unto Elisha, H559
20 And he s, Bring me a new cruse, and put H559
21 salt in there, and s, Thus saith the LORD, H559
23 mocked him, and s unto him, Go up, H559
3: 7 to battle? And he s, I will go up: I *am* as H559
8 And he s, Which way shall we go up? And H559
10 And the king of Israel s, Alas! that the H559
11 But Jehoshaphat s, *Is there* not here a H559
11 answered and s, Here *is* Elisha the son H559
12 And Jehoshaphat s, The word of the H559
13 And Elisha s unto the king of Israel, H559
13 the king of Israel s unto him, Nay: for H559
14 And Elisha s, *As* the LORD of hosts H559
16 And he s, Thus saith the LORD, Make H559
23 And they s, This *is* blood: the kings are H559
4: 2 And Elisha s unto her, What shall I do H559
2 in the house? And she s, Thine handmaid H559
3 Then he s, Go, borrow thee vessels H559
6 were full, that she s unto her son, Bring H559
6 a vessel. And he s unto her, *There is* not H559
7 of God. And he s, Go, sell the oil, and pay H559
9 And she s unto her husband, Behold H559
12 And he s to Gehazi his servant, Call this H559
13 And he s unto him, Say now unto her, H559
14 And he s, What then *is* to be done for H559
15 And he s, Call her. And when he had H559
16 And he s, About this season, according to H559
16 a son. And she s, Nay, my lord, *thou* man H559
17 s unto her, according to the time of life. H1696
19 And he s unto his father, My head, my H559
19 he s to a lad, Carry him to his mother. H559
22 And she called unto her husband, and s, H559
23 And he s, Wherefore wilt thou go to him H559
23 nor sabbath. And she s, *It shall be* well. H559
24 Then she saddled an ass, and s to her H559
25 saw her afar off, that he s to Gehazi his H559
27 the man of God s, Let her alone; for her H559
28 Then she s, Did I desire a son of my lord? H559
29 Then he s to Gehazi, Gird up thy loins, H559
30 And the mother of the child s, *As* the H559
36 And he called Gehazi, and s, Call this H559
36 come in unto him, he s, Take up thy son. H559
38 before him: and he s unto his servant, H559
40 they cried out, and s, O *thou* man of God, H559
41 But he s, Then bring meal. And he cast *it* H559
41 the pot; and he s, Pour out for the people, H559
42 thereof. And he s, Give unto the people, H559
43 And his servitor s, What, should I set this H559
43 an hundred men? He s again, Give the H559
5: 3 And she s unto her mistress, Would God H559
4 s the maid that *is* of the land of Israel. H1696
5 And the king of Syria s, Go to, go, and I H559
7 his clothes, and s, *Am* I God, to kill and H559
11 went away, and s, Behold, I thought, He H559
13 unto him, and s, My father, *if* the prophet H559
15 before him: and he s, Behold, now I know H559
16 But he s, *As* the LORD liveth, before H559
17 And Naaman s, Shall there not then, I H559
19 And he s unto him, Go in peace. So he H559
20 the man of God, s, Behold, my master H559
21 the chariot to meet him, and s, *Is* all well? H559
22 And he s, All *is* well. My master hath sent H559
23 And Naaman s, Be content, take two H559
25 master. And Elisha s unto him, Whence H559
25 And he s, Thy servant went no whither. H559
26 And he s unto him, Went not mine heart H559
6: 1 And the sons of the prophets s unto H559
3 And one s, Be content, I pray thee, and H559
5 and s, Alas, master! for it was borrowed. H559
6 And the man of God s, Where fell it? And H559
7 Therefore s he, Take *it* up to thee. And H559
11 his servants, and s unto them, Will ye H559
12 And one of his servants s, None, my lord, H559

2Ki 6:13 And he s, Go and spy where he *is*, that I H559
15 And his servant s unto him, Alas, my H559
17 And Elisha prayed, and s, LORD, I pray H559
18 the LORD, and s, Smite this people, I H559
19 And Elisha s unto them, This *is* not the H559
20 that Elisha s, LORD, open the eyes H559
21 And the king of Israel s unto Elisha, H559
27 And he s, If the LORD do not help thee, H559
28 And the king s unto her, What aileth H559
28 This woman s unto me, Give thy son, H559
29 did eat him: and I s unto her on the next H559
31 Then he s, God do so and more also to H559
32 came to him, he s to the elders, See ye H559
33 unto him: and he s, Behold, this evil *is* of H559
7: 1 Then Elisha s, Hear ye the word of the H559
2 man of God, and s, Behold, *if* the LORD H559
2 thing be? And he s, Behold, thou shalt see H559
3 the gate: and they s one to another, Why H559
6 host: and they s one to another, Lo, the H559
9 Then they s one to another, We do not H559
12 And the king arose in the night, and s H559
13 And one of his servants answered and s, H559
17 man of God had s, who spake when the H1696
19 man of God, and s, Now, behold, *if* the H559
19 a thing be? And he s, Behold, thou shalt H559
8: 5 land. And Gehazi s, My lord, O king, this H559
8 And the king s unto Hazael, Take a H559
9 before him, and s, Thy son Ben-hadad H559
10 And Elisha s unto him, Go, say unto H559
12 And Hazael s, Why weepeth my lord? H559
13 And Hazael s, But what, *is* thy servant a H559
14 to his master; who s to him, What said H559
14 said to him, What s Elisha to thee? And H559
9: 1 of the prophets, and s unto him, Gird up H559
5 *were* sitting; and he s, I have an errand to H559
5 O captain. And Jehu s, Unto which of all H559
5 of all us? And he s, To thee, O captain. H559
6 on his head, and s unto him, Thus saith H559
11 of his lord: and *one* s unto him, *Is* all H559
11 to thee? And he s unto them, Ye know H559
12 And they s, *It is* false; tell us now. And he H559
12 tell us now. And he s, Thus and thus H559
15 of Syria.) And Jehu s, If it be your minds, H559
17 as he came, and s, I see a company. And H559
17 And Joram s, Take an horseman, H559
18 to meet him, and s, Thus saith the king, H559
18 *it* peace? And Jehu s, What hast thou to H559
19 came to them, and s, Thus saith the king, H559
21 And Joram s, Make ready. And his H559
22 saw Jehu, that he s, *Is it* peace, Jehu? And H559
23 and fled, and s to Ahaziah, *There is* H559
25 Then s *Jehu* to Bidkar his captain, Take H559
27 after him, and s, Smite him also in the H559
31 And as Jehu entered in at the gate, she s, H559
32 to the window, and s, Who *is* on my side? H559
33 And he s, Throw her down. So they threw H559
34 did eat and drink, and s, Go, see now this H559
36 told him. And he s, This *is* the word of H559
10: 4 But they were exceedingly afraid, and s, H559
8 king's sons. And he s, Lay ye them in two H559
9 and stood, and s to all the people, Ye H559
13 king of Judah, and s, Who *are* ye? And H559
14 And he s, Take them alive. And they took H559
15 saluted him, and s to him, Is thine heart H559
16 And he s, Come with me, and see my zeal H559
18 together, and s unto them, Ahab served H559
20 And Jehu s, Proclaim a solemn assembly H559
22 And he s unto him that *was* over the H559
23 the house of Baal, and s unto the H559
24 men without, and s, *If* any of the men H559
25 offering, that Jehu s to the guard and to H559
30 And the LORD s unto Jehu, Because H559
11:12 their hands, and s, God save the king. H559
15 of the host, and s unto them, Have her H559
15 For the priest had s, Let her not be slain H559
12: 4 And Jehoash s to the priests, All the H559
7 the *other* priests, and s unto them, Why H559
13:14 over his face, and s, O my father, my H559
15 And Elisha s unto him, Take bow and H559
16 And he s to the king of Israel, Put thine H559
17 And he s, Open the window eastward. H559
17 *it*. Then Elisha s, Shoot. And he shot. H559
17 And he shot. And he s, The arrow of the H559
18 And he s, Take the arrows. And he took H559
18 he took *them*. And he s unto the king of H559
19 with him, and s, Thou shouldest have H559
14:27 And the LORD s not that he would blot H1696
17:12 s unto them, Ye shall not do this thing. H559
23 sight, as he had s by all his servants the H1696

2Ki 18:19 And Rab-shakeh s unto them, Speak ye H559
22 taken away, and hath s to Judah and H559
25 it? The LORD s to me, Go up against H559
26 Then s Eliakim the son of Hilkiah, and H559
27 But Rab-shakeh s unto them, Hath my H559
19: 3 And they s unto him, Thus saith H559
6 And Isaiah s unto them, Thus shall ye H559
15 the LORD, and s, O LORD God of Israel, H559
23 the Lord, and hast s, With the multitude H559
20: 1 came to him, and s unto him, Thus saith H559
7 And Isaiah s, Take a lump of figs. And H559
8 And Hezekiah s unto Isaiah, What *shall* H559
9 And Isaiah s, This sign shalt thou have of H559
14 king Hezekiah, and s unto him, What H559
14 unto him, What s these men? and from H559
14 And Hezekiah s, They are come from H559
15 And he s, What have they seen in thine H559
16 And Isaiah s unto Hezekiah, Hear the H559
19 Then s Hezekiah unto Isaiah, Good *is* H559
19 spoken. And he s, *Is it* not *good*, if peace H559
21: 4 s, In Jerusalem will I put my name. H559
7 of which the LORD s to David, and to H559
22: 8 And Hilkiah the high priest s unto H559
9 word again, and s, Thy servants have H559
15 And she s unto them, Thus saith the H559
23:17 Then he s, What title *is* that that I see? H559
18 And he s, Let him alone; let no man H559
27 And the LORD s, I will remove Judah also H559
27 of which I s, My name shall be there. H559
24:13 temple of the LORD, as the LORD had s. H1696
25:24 to their men, and s unto them, Fear not H559
1Ch 10: 4 Then s Saul to his armourbearer, Draw H559
11: 2 and the LORD thy God s unto thee, Thou H559
5 And the inhabitants of Jebus s to David, H559
6 And David s, Whosoever smiteth the H559
17 And David longed, and s, Oh that one H559
19 And s, My God forbid it me, that I should H559
12:17 and answered and s unto them, If ye be H559
18 captains, *and he s*, Thine *are we*, David,
13: 2 And David s unto all the congregation of H559
4 And all the congregation s that they H559
14:10 And the LORD s unto him, Go up; for H559
11 there. Then David s, God hath broken in H559
14 of God; and God s unto him, Go not up H559
15: 2 Then David s, None ought to carry the H559
12 And s unto them, Ye *are* the chief of the H559
16:36 people s, Amen, and praised the LORD. H559
17: 1 his house, that David s to Nathan the H559
2 Then Nathan s unto David, Do all that *is* H559
16 the LORD, and s, Who *am* I, O LORD H559
23 for ever, and do as thou hast s. H1696
19: 2 And David s, I will shew kindness unto H559
3 of Ammon s to Hanun, Thinkest H559
5 And the king s, Tarry at Jericho until H559
12 And he s, If the Syrians be too strong for H559
21: 2 And David s to Joab and to the rulers of H559
8 And David s unto God, I have sinned H559
11 So Gad came to David, and s unto him, H559
13 And David s unto Gad, I am in a great H559
15 him of the evil, and s to the angel that H559
17 And David s unto God, *Is it* not I *that* H559
22 Then David s to Ornan, Grant me the H559
23 And Ornan s unto David, Take *it* to thee, H559
24 And king David s to Ornan, Nay; but I H559
22: 1 Then David s, This *is* the house of the H559
5 And David s, Solomon my son *is* young H559
7 And David s to Solomon, My son, as for H559
11 the LORD thy God, as he hath s of thee. H1696
23: 5 I made, *s David*, to praise *therewith*.
25 For David s, The LORD God of Israel H559
27:23 the LORD had s he would increase Israel H559
28: 2 up upon his feet, and s, Hear me, my H559
3 But God s unto me, Thou shalt not build H559
6 And he s unto me, Solomon thy son, he H559
19 All *this, s David*, the LORD made me
20 And David s to Solomon his son, Be H559
29: 1 Furthermore David the king s unto all H559
10 and David s, Blessed *be* thou, LORD H559
20 And David s to all the congregation, H559
2Ch 1: 7 s unto him, Ask what I shall give thee. H559
8 And Solomon s unto God, Thou hast H559
11 And God s to Solomon, Because this was H559
2:12 Huram s moreover, Blessed *be* the H559
6: 1 Then s Solomon, The LORD hath said H559
1 Then said Solomon, The LORD hath s H559
4 And he s, Blessed *be* the LORD God of H559
8 But the LORD s to David my father, H559
14 And s, O LORD God of Israel, *there is* no H559
20 whereof thou hast s that thou wouldest H559

2Ch 7:12 by night, and s unto him, I have heard H559
8:11 built for her: for he s, My wife shall not H559
9: 5 And she s to the king, *It was* a true H559
10: 5 And he s unto them, Come again unto H559
9 And he s unto them, What advice give ye H559
12: 5 of Shishak, and s unto them, Thus saith H559
6 and they s, The LORD *is* righteous. H559
13: 4 mount Ephraim, and s, Hear me, thou H559
14: 7 Therefore he s unto Judah, Let us build H559
11 LORD his God, and s, LORD, *it is* nothing H559
15: 2 And he went out to meet Asa, and s unto H559
16: 7 king of Judah, and s unto him, Because H559
18: 3 And Ahab king of Israel s unto H559
4 And Jehoshaphat s unto the king of H559
5 hundred men, and s unto them, Shall we H559
5 I forbear? And they s, Go up; for God will H559
6 But Jehoshaphat s, *Is there* not here a H559
7 And the king of Israel s unto H559
7 Jehoshaphat s, Let not the king say so. H559
8 s, Fetch quickly Micaiah the son of Imla. H559
10 him horns of iron, and s, Thus saith the H559
13 And Micaiah s, *As* the LORD liveth, even H559
14 the king, the king s unto him, Micaiah, H559
14 shall I forbear? And he s, Go ye up, and H559
15 And the king s to him, How many times H559
16 Then he s, I did see all Israel scattered H559
16 and the LORD s, These have no master; H559
17 And the king of Israel s to Jehoshaphat, H559
18 Again he s, Therefore hear the word of H559
19 And the LORD s, Who shall entice Ahab H559
20 the LORD, and s, I will entice him. And H559
20 And the LORD s unto him, Wherewith? H559
21 And he s, I will go out, and be a lying H559
21 And *the LORD* s, Thou shalt entice *him*, H559
23 the cheek, and s, Which way went the H559
24 And Micaiah s, Behold, thou shalt see on H559
25 Then the king of Israel s, Take ye H559
27 And Micaiah s, If thou certainly return in H559
27 by me. And he s, Hearken, all ye people. H559
29 And the king of Israel s unto H559
31 that they s, It *is* the king of Israel. H559
33 therefore he s to his chariot man, Turn H559
19: 2 to meet him, and s to king Jehoshaphat, H559
6 And s to the judges, Take heed what ye H559
20: 6 And s, O LORD God of our fathers, *art* H559
15 And he s, Hearken ye, all Judah, and ye H559
20 stood and s, Hear me, O Judah, and H559
22: 9 him: Because, s they, he *is* the son of H559
23: 3 of God. And he s unto them, Behold, the H559
3 the LORD hath s of the sons of David. H1696
11 anointed him, and s, God save the king. H559
13 her clothes, and s, Treason, Treason. H559
14 over the host, and s unto them, Have her H559
14 s, Slay her not in the house of the LORD. H559
24: 5 the Levites, and s to them, Go out unto H559
6 the chief, and s unto him, Why hast H559
20 the people, and s unto them, Thus saith H559
22 s, The LORD look upon *it*, and require *it*. H559
25: 9 And Amaziah s to the man of God, But H559
15 a prophet, which s unto him, Why hast H559
16 him, that *the king* s unto him, Art thou H559
16 forbare, and s, I know that God hath H559
26:18 the king, and s unto him, *It appertaineth* H559
23 to the kings; for they s, He *is* a leper: and H559
28: 9 to Samaria, and s unto them, Behold, H559
13 And s unto them, Ye shall not bring in H559
23 smote him: and he s, Because the gods of H559
29: 5 And s unto them, Hear me, ye Levites, H559
18 the king, and s, We have cleansed all H559
31 Then Hezekiah answered and s, Now ye H559
31:10 answered him, and s, Since *the people* H559
33: 4 the LORD had s, In Jerusalem shall my H559
7 God, of which God had s to David and to H559
34:15 And Hilkiah answered and s to Shaphan H559
35: 3 And s unto the Levites that taught all H559
23 and the king s to his servants, Have H559
Ezr 2:63 And the Tirshatha s unto them, that they H559
4: 2 of the fathers, and s unto them, Let us H559
3 fathers of Israel, s unto them, Ye have H559
5: 3 companions, and s thus unto them, Who H560
4 Then s we unto them after this manner, H560
9 Then asked we those elders, *and* s unto H560
15 And s unto him, Take these vessels, go, H560
8:28 And I s unto them, Ye *are* holy unto the H559
9: 6 And s, O my God, I am ashamed and H559
10: 2 answered and s unto Ezra, We have H559
10 And Ezra the priest stood up, and s unto H559
12 answered and s with a loud voice, As H559
12 voice, As thou hast s, so must we do. H1697

Neh 1: 3 And they s unto me, The remnant that H559
5 And s, I beseech thee, O LORD God of H559
2: 2 Wherefore the king s unto me, Why *is* H559
3 And s unto the king, Let the king live for H559
4 Then the king s unto me, For what dost H559
5 And I s unto the king, If it please the H559
6 And the king s unto me, (the queen also H559
7 Moreover I s unto the king, If it please H559
17 Then s I unto them, Ye see the distress H559
18 unto me. And they s, Let us rise up and H559
19 despised us, and s, What *is* this thing H559
20 Then answered I them, and s unto them, H559
4: 2 of Samaria, and s, What do these feeble H559
3 *was* by him, and he s, Even that which H559
10 And Judah s, The strength of the bearers H559
11 And our adversaries s, They shall not H559
12 by them came, they s unto us ten times, H559
14 And I looked, and rose up, and s unto H559
19 And I s unto the nobles, and to the H559
22 Likewise at the same time s I unto the H559
5: 2 For there were that s, We, our sons, and H559
3 *Some* also there were that s, We have H559
4 There were also that s, We have H559
7 and the rulers, and s unto them, Ye H559
8 And I s unto them, We after our ability H559
9 Also I s, It *is* not good that ye do: ought H559
12 Then s they, We will restore *them*, and H559
13 Also I shook my lap, and s, So God shake H559
13 the congregation s, Amen, and praised H559
6:10 shut up; and he s, Let us meet together H559
11 And I s, Should such a man as I flee? and H559
7: 3 And I s unto them, Let not the gates of H559
65 And the Tirshatha s unto them, that they H559
8: 9 taught the people, s unto all the people, H559
10 Then he s unto them, Go your way, eat H559
9: 5 *and* Pethahiah, s, Stand up *and* bless the H559
18 a molten calf, and s, This *is* thy God that H559
13:11 Then contended I with the rulers, and s, H559
17 of Judah, and s unto them, What evil H559
21 Then I testified against them, and s unto H559
Est 1:13 Then the king s to the wise men, which H559
2: 2 Then s the king's servants that H559
3: 3 in the king's gate, s unto Mordecai, Why H559
8 And Haman s unto king Ahasuerus, H559
11 And the king s unto Haman, The silver H559
5: 3 Then s the king unto her, What wilt H559
5 Then the king s, Cause Haman to make H559
5 do as Esther hath s. So the king and H1697
6 And the king s unto Esther at the H559
7 Then answered Esther, and s, My H559
8 I will do to morrow as the king hath s. H1697
12 Haman s moreover, Yea, Esther the H559
14 Then s Zeresh his wife and all his friends H559
6: 3 And the king s, What honour and dignity H559
3 for this? Then s the king's servants that H559
4 And the king s, Who *is* in the court? Now H559
5 And the king's servants s unto him, H559
5 court. And the king s, Let him come in. H559
6 So Haman came in. And the king s unto H559
10 Then the king s to Haman, Make haste, H559
10 horse, as thou hast s, and do even so to H1696
13 befallen him. Then s his wise men and H559
7: 2 And the king s again unto Esther on the H559
3 Then Esther the queen answered and s, If H559
5 answered and s unto Esther the queen, H559
6 And Esther s, The adversary and enemy H559
8 Esther *was*. Then s the king, Will he H559
9 of the chamberlains, s before the king, H559
9 Then the king s, Hang him thereon. H559
8: 5 And s, If it please the king, and if I have H559
7 Then the king Ahasuerus s unto Esther H559
9:12 And the king s unto Esther the queen, H559
13 Then s Esther, If it please the king, let it H559
Job 1: 5 of them all: for Job s, It may be that my H559
7 And the LORD s unto Satan, Whence H559
7 the LORD, and s, From going to and fro H559
8 And the LORD s unto Satan, Hast thou H559
9 Then Satan answered the LORD, and s, H559
12 And the LORD s unto Satan, Behold, all H559
14 unto Job, and s, The oxen were plowing, H559
16 also another, and s, The fire of God is H559
17 also another, and s, The Chaldeans made H559
18 also another, and s, Thy sons and thy H559
21 And s, Naked came I out of my mother's H559
2: 2 And the LORD s unto Satan, From H559
2 the LORD, and s, From going to and fro H559
3 And the LORD s unto Satan, Hast thou H559
4 And Satan answered the LORD, and s, H559
6 And the LORD s unto Satan, Behold, he H559

Job 2: 9 Then s his wife unto him, Dost thou still H559
10 But he s unto her, Thou speakest as one H559
3: 2 And Job spake, and s, H559
3 it was s, There is a man child conceived. H559
4: 1 Eliphaz the Temanite answered and s, H559
6: 1 But Job answered and s, H559
8: 1 answered Bildad the Shuhite, and s, H559
9: 1 Then Job answered and s, H559
22 This *is* one *thing*, therefore I s *it*, He H559
11: 1 answered Zophar the Naamathite, and s, H559
4 For thou hast s, My doctrine *is* pure, and H559
12: 1 And Job answered and s, H559
15: 1 answered Eliphaz the Temanite, and s, H559
16: 1 Then Job answered and s, H559
17:14 I have s to corruption, Thou *art* my H7121
18: 1 answered Bildad the Shuhite, and s, H559
19: 1 Then Job answered and s, H559
20: 1 answered Zophar the Naamathite, and s, H559
21: 1 But Job answered and s, H559
22: 1 Eliphaz the Temanite answered and s, H559
17 Which s unto God, Depart from us: and H559
23: 1 Then Job answered and s, H559
25: 1 answered Bildad the Shuhite, and s, H559
26: 1 But Job answered and s, H559
27: 1 Job continued his parable, and s, H559
28:28 And unto man he s, Behold, the fear of H559
29: 1 Job continued his parable, and s, H559
18 Then I s, I shall die in my nest, and I H559
31:24 If I have made gold my hope, or have s H559
31 If the men of my tabernacle s not, Oh H559
32: 6 answered and s, I *am* young, and ye *are* H559
7 I s, Days should speak, and multitude of H559
10 Therefore I s, Hearken to me; I also will H559
17 *I s*, I will answer also my part, I also will
34: 1 Furthermore Elihu answered and s, H559
5 For Job hath s, I am righteous: and God H559
9 For he hath s, It profiteth a man nothing H559
31 Surely it is meet to be s unto God, I have H559
35: 1 Elihu spake moreover, and s, H559
36: 1 Elihu also proceeded, and s, H559
38: 1 Job out of the whirlwind, and s, H559
11 And s, Hitherto shalt thou come, but no H559
40: 1 Moreover the LORD answered Job, and s, H559
3 Then Job answered the LORD, and s, H559
6 unto Job out of the whirlwind, and s, H559
42: 1 Then Job answered the LORD, and s, H559
7 unto Job, the LORD s to Eliphaz the H559
Ps 2: 7 the LORD hath s unto me, Thou *art* my H559
10: 6 He hath s in his heart, I shall not be H559
11 He hath s in his heart, God hath H559
13 s in his heart, Thou wilt not require *it*. H559
12: 4 Who have s, With our tongue will we H559
14: 1 The fool hath s in his heart, *There is* no H559
16: 2 *O my soul*, thou hast s unto the LORD, H559
18:ttl and from the hand of Saul: And he s, H559
27: 8 s unto thee, Thy face, LORD, will I seek. H559
30: 6 And in my prosperity I s, I shall never be H559
31:14 But I trusted in thee, O LORD: I s, Thou H559
22 For I s in my haste, I am cut off from H559
32: 5 have I not hid. I s, I will confess my H559
35:21 me, *and* s, Aha, aha, our eye hath seen *it*. H559
38:16 For I s, *Hear me*, lest *otherwise* they H559
39: 1 I s, I will take heed to my ways, that I sin H559
40: 7 Then s I, Lo, I come: in the volume of the H559
41: 4 I s, LORD, be merciful unto me: heal my H559
52:ttl and told Saul, and s unto him, David is H559
53: 1 The fool hath s in his heart, *There is* no H559
54:ttl Ziphims came and s to Saul, Doth not H559
55: 6 And I s, Oh that I had wings like a dove! H559
68:22 The Lord s, I will bring again from H559
74: 8 They s in their hearts, Let us destroy H559
75: 4 I s unto the fools, Deal not foolishly: and H559
77:10 And I s, This *is* my infirmity: *but I will* H559
78:19 Yea, they spake against God; they s, Can H559
82: 6 I have s, Ye *are* gods; and all of you *are* H559
83: 4 They have s, Come, and let us cut them H559
12 Who s, Let us take to ourselves the H559
87: 5 And of Zion it shall be s, This and that H559
89: 2 For I have s, Mercy shall be built up for H559
94:18 When I s, My foot slippeth; thy mercy, O H559
95:10 generation, and s, It *is* a people that do H559
102:24 I s, O my God, take me not away in the H559
106:23 Therefore he s that he would destroy H559
110: 1 The LORD s unto my Lord, Sit thou at H5002
116:11 I s in my haste, All men *are* liars. H559
119:57 *Thou art* my portion, O LORD: I have s H559
122: 1 I was glad when they s unto me, Let us H559
126: 2 with singing: then s they among the H559
137: 7 of Jerusalem; who s, Rase *it*, rase *it*, *even* H559

Ps 140: 6 I s unto the LORD, Thou *art* my God: H559
142: 5 I cried unto thee, O LORD: I s, Thou *art* H559
Prv 4: 4 He taught me also, and s unto me, Let H559
7:13 *and* with an impudent face s unto him, H559
25: 7 For better *it is* that it be s unto thee, H559
Ecc 1:10 Is there *any* thing whereof it may be s, H559
2: 1 I s in mine heart, Go to now, I will prove H559
2 I s of laughter, *It is* mad: and of mirth, H559
15 Then s I in my heart, As it happeneth to H559
15 I s in my heart, that this also *is* vanity. H1696
3:17 I s in mine heart, God shall judge the H559
18 I s in mine heart concerning the estate of H559
7:23 All this have I proved by wisdom: I s, I H559
8:14 the righteous: I s that this also *is* vanity. H559
9:16 Then s I, Wisdom *is* better than H559
Song 2:10 My beloved spake, and s unto me, Rise H559
3: 3 *I s*, Saw ye him whom my soul loveth?
7: 8 I s, I will go up to the palm tree, I will H559
Isa 5: 9 In mine ears *s* the LORD of hosts, Of a
6: 3 And one cried unto another, and s, Holy, H559
5 Then s I, Woe *is* me! for I am undone; H559
7 And he laid *it* upon my mouth, and s, Lo, H559
8 go for us? Then s I, Here *am* I; send me. H559
9 And he s, Go, and tell this people, Hear H559
11 Then s I, Lord, how long? And he H559
7: 3 Then s the LORD unto Isaiah, Go forth H559
12 But Ahaz s, I will not ask, neither will I H559
13 And he s, Hear ye now, O house of David; H559
8: 1 Moreover the LORD s unto me, Take H559
3 bare a son. Then s the LORD to me, Call H559
14:13 For thou hast s in thine heart, I will H559
18: 4 For so the LORD s unto me, I will take H559
20: 3 And the LORD s, Like as my servant H559
21: 6 For thus hath the Lord s unto me, Go, set H559
9 he answered and s, Babylon is fallen, is H559
12 The watchman s, The morning cometh, H559
16 For thus hath the Lord s unto me, H559
22: 4 Therefore s I, Look away from me; I will H559
23:12 And he s, Thou shalt no more rejoice, O H559
24:16 to the righteous. But I s, My leanness, my H559
25: 9 And it shall be s in that day, Lo, this *is* H559
28:12 To whom he s, This *is* the rest *wherewith* H559
15 Because ye have s, We have made a H559
29:13 Wherefore the Lord s, Forasmuch as this H559
30:16 But ye s, No; for we will flee upon horses; H559
32: 5 liberal, nor the churl s *to be* bountiful. H559
36: 4 And Rabshakeh s unto them, Say ye now H559
7 hath taken away, and s to Judah and to H559
10 it? the LORD s unto me, Go up against H559
11 Then s Eliakim and Shebna and Joah H559
12 But Rabshakeh s, Hath my master sent H559
13 language, and s, Hear ye the words of H559
37: 3 And they s unto him, Thus saith H559
6 And Isaiah s unto them, Thus shall ye H559
24 the Lord, and hast s, By the multitude of H559
38: 1 unto him, and s unto him, Thus saith H559
3 And s, Remember now, O LORD, I H559
10 I s in the cutting off of my days, I shall H559
11 I s, I shall not see the LORD, *even* the H559
21 For Isaiah had s, Let them take a lump of H559
22 Hezekiah also had s, What *is* the sign H559
39: 3 king Hezekiah, and s unto him, What H559
3 unto him, What s these men? and from H559
3 And Hezekiah s, They are come from H559
4 Then s he, What have they seen in thine H559
5 Then s Isaiah to Hezekiah, Hear the H559
8 Then s Hezekiah to Isaiah, Good *is* the H559
8 hast spoken. He s moreover, For there H559
40: 6 The voice s, Cry. And he said, What shall H559
6 The voice said, Cry. And he s, What shall H559
41: 6 *one* s to his brother, Be of good courage. H559
9 men thereof, and s unto thee, Thou *art* H559
45:19 place of the earth: I s not unto the seed H559
47:10 thou hast s, None seeth me. Thy H559
10 thee; and thou hast s in thine heart, I H559
49: 3 And s unto me, Thou *art* my servant, O H559
4 Then I s, I have laboured in vain, I have H559
6 And he s, It is a light thing that thou H559
14 But Zion s, The LORD hath forsaken me, H559
51:23 thee; which have s to thy soul, Bow H559
63: 8 For he s, Surely they *are* my people, H559
65: 1 sought me not: I s, Behold me, behold H559
66: 5 for my name's sake, s, Let the LORD be H559
Jer 1: 6 Then s I, Ah, Lord GOD! behold, I H559
7 But the LORD s unto me, Say not, I *am* a H559
9 And the LORD s unto me, Behold, I have H559
11 And I s, I see a rod of an almond tree. H559
12 Then s the LORD unto me, Thou hast H559
13 seest thou? And I s, I see a seething pot; H559

Jer 1:14 Then the LORD s unto me, Out of the H559
2: 6 Neither s they, Where *is* the LORD that H559
8 The priests s not, Where *is* the LORD? H559
3: 6 The LORD s also unto me in the days of H559
7 And I s after she had done all these H559
11 And the LORD s unto me, The H559
19 But I s, How shall I put thee among the H559
19 of nations? and I s, Thou shalt call me, H559
4:10 Then s I, Ah, Lord GOD! surely thou hast H559
11 At that time shall it be s to this people H559
27 For thus hath the LORD s, The whole H559
5: 4 Therefore I s, Surely these *are* poor; they H559
12 They have belied the LORD, and s, *It is* H559
6: 6 For thus hath the LORD of hosts s, Hew H559
16 But they s, We will not walk *therein*. H559
17 trumpet. But they s, We will not hearken. H559
10:19 s, Truly this *is* a grief, and I must bear it. H559
11: 5 answered I, and s, So be it, O LORD. H559
6 Then the LORD s unto me, Proclaim all H559
9 And the LORD s unto me, A conspiracy H559
12: 4 they s, He shall not see our last end. H559
13: 6 that the LORD s unto me, Arise, go to H559
14:11 Then s the LORD unto me, Pray not for H559
13 Then s I, Ah, Lord GOD! behold, the H559
14 Then the LORD s unto me, The prophets H559
15: 1 Then s the LORD unto me, Though H559
11 The LORD s, Verily it shall be well with H559
16:14 it shall no more be s, The LORD liveth, H559
17:19 Thus s the LORD unto me; Go and stand H559
18:10 wherewith I s I would benefit them. H559
12 And they s, There is no hope: but we will H559
18 Then s they, Come, and let us devise H559
19:14 LORD'S house; and s to all the people, H559
20: 3 of the stocks. Then s Jeremiah unto him, H559
9 Then I s, I will not make mention of him, H559
21: 3 Then s Jeremiah unto them, Thus shall H559
23:17 The LORD hath s, Ye shall have peace; H1696
25 I have heard what the prophets s, that H559
24: 3 Then s the LORD unto me, What seest H559
3 Jeremiah? And I s, Figs; the good figs, H559
25: 5 They s, Turn ye again now every one H559
26:16 Then s the princes and all the people H559
28: 5 Then the prophet Jeremiah s unto the H559
6 Even the prophet Jeremiah s, Amen: the H559
15 Then s the prophet Jeremiah unto H559
29:15 Because ye have s, The LORD hath raised H559
32: 6 And Jeremiah s, The word of the LORD H559
8 of the LORD, and s unto me, Buy my H559
25 And thou hast s unto me, O Lord GOD, H559
35: 5 cups, and I s unto them, Drink ye wine. H559
6 But they s, We will drink no wine: for H559
11 the land, that we s, Come, and let us go H559
18 And Jeremiah s unto the house of the H559
36:15 And they s unto him, Sit down now, and H559
16 one and other, and s unto Baruch, We H559
19 Then s the princes unto Baruch, Go, hide H559
37:14 Then s Jeremiah, *It is* false; I fall not H559
17 in his house, and s, Is there *any* word H559
17 And Jeremiah s, There is: for, said he, H559
17 said, There is: for, s he, thou shalt be H559
18 Moreover Jeremiah s unto king H559
38: 4 Therefore the princes s unto the king, H559
5 Then Zedekiah the king s, Behold, he *is* H559
12 And Ebed-melech the Ethiopian s unto H559
14 and the king s unto Jeremiah, I will H559
15 Then Jeremiah s unto Zedekiah, If I H559
17 Then s Jeremiah unto Zedekiah, Thus H559
19 And Zedekiah the king s unto Jeremiah, H559
20 But Jeremiah s, They shall not deliver H559
24 Then s Zedekiah unto Jeremiah, Let no H559
25 what thou hast s unto the king, hide H1696
25 death; also what the king s unto thee: H1696
40: 2 took Jeremiah, and s unto him, The H559
3 as he hath s: because ye have sinned H1696
5 not yet gone back, *he s*, Go back also to
14 And s unto him, Dost thou certainly H559
16 But Gedaliah the son of Ahikam s unto H559
41: 6 as he met them, he s unto them, Come to H559
8 among them that s unto Ishmael, Slay H559
42: 2 And s unto Jeremiah the prophet, Let, H559
4 Then Jeremiah the prophet s unto them, H559
5 Then they s to Jeremiah, The LORD be a H559
9 And s unto them, Thus saith the LORD, H559
19 The LORD hath s concerning you, O ye H1696
44:20 Then Jeremiah s unto all the people, to H559
24 Moreover Jeremiah s unto all the people, H559
46:16 another: and they s, Arise, and let us go H559
50: 7 and their adversaries s, We offend not, H559
51:61 And Jeremiah s to Seraiah, When thou H559

Lam 3:18 And I s, My strength and my hope is H559
54 Waters flowed over mine head; *then* I s, I H559
4:15 wandered, they s among the heathen, H559
20 pits, of whom we s, Under his shadow we H559
Ezk 2: 1 And he s unto me, Son of man, stand H559
3 And he s unto me, Son of man, I send H559
3: 1 Moreover he s unto me, Son of man, eat H559
3 And he s unto me, Son of man, cause thy H559
4 And he s unto me, Son of man, go, get H559
10 Moreover he s unto me, Son of man, all H559
22 upon me; and he s unto me, Arise, go H559
24 with me, and s unto me, Go, shut thyself H559
4:13 And the LORD s, Even thus shall the H559
14 Then s I, Ah Lord GOD! behold, my soul H559
15 Then he s unto me, Lo, I have given thee H559
16 Moreover he s unto me, Son of man, H559
6:10 *that* I have not s in vain that I would H1696
8: 5 Then s he unto me, Son of man, lift up H559
6 He s furthermore unto me, Son of man, H559
8 Then s he unto me, Son of man, dig now H559
9 And he s unto me, Go in, and behold the H559
12 Then s he unto me, Son of man, hast H559
13 He s also unto me, Turn thee yet again, H559
15 Then s he unto me, Hast thou seen *this*, H559
17 Then he s unto me, Hast thou seen *this*, H559
9: 4 And the LORD s unto him, Go through H559
5 And to the others he s in mine hearing, H559
7 And he s unto them, Defile the house, H559
8 and cried, and s, Ah Lord GOD! wilt thou H559
9 Then s he unto me, The iniquity of the H559
10: 2 with linen, and s, Go in between the H559
11: 2 Then s he unto me, Son of man, these H559
5 fell upon me, and s unto me, Speak; H559
5 Thus have ye s, O house of Israel: for H559
13 a loud voice, and s, Ah Lord GOD! wilt H559
15 of Jerusalem have s, Get you far from the H559
12: 9 house, s unto thee, What doest thou? H559
13:12 shall it not be s unto you, Where *is* the H559
16: 6 thine own blood, I s unto thee *when thou* H559
6 blood, Live; yea, I s unto thee *when thou* H559
20: 7 Then s I unto them, Cast ye away every H559
8 of Egypt: then I s, I will pour out my fury H559
13 polluted: then I s, I would pour out my H559
18 But I s unto their children in the H559
21 sabbaths: then I s, I would pour out my H559
29 Then I s unto them, What *is* the high H559
49 Then s I, Ah Lord GOD! they say of me, H559
21:17 my fury to rest: I the LORD have s *it*. H1696
23:36 The LORD s moreover unto me; Son of H559
43 Then s I unto *her that was* old in H559
24:19 And the people s unto me, Wilt thou not H559
26: 2 Son of man, because that Tyrus hath s H559
27: 3 thou hast s, I *am* of perfect beauty. H559
28: 2 up, and thou hast s, I *am* a God, I sit *in* H559
29: 3 his rivers, which hath s, My river *is* mine H559
9 s, The river *is* mine, and I have made *it*. H559
35:10 Because thou hast s, These two nations H559
36: 2 the enemy hath s against you, Aha, even H559
20 name, when they s to them, These *are* H559
37: 3 And he s unto me, Son of man, can these H559
4 Again he s unto me, Prophesy upon H559
9 Then s he unto me, Prophesy unto the H559
11 Then he s unto me, Son of man, these H559
40: 4 And the man s unto me, Son of man, H1696
45 And he s unto me, This chamber, H1696
41: 4 s unto me, This *is* the most holy *place*. H559
22 of wood: and he s unto me, This *is* the H1696
42:13 Then s he unto me, The north chambers H559
43: 7 And he s unto me, Son of man, the place H559
18 And he s unto me, Son of man, thus H559
44: 2 Then s the LORD unto me; This gate H559
5 And the LORD s unto me, Son of man, H559
46:20 Then s he unto me, This *is* the place H559
24 Then s he unto me, These *are* the places H559
47: 6 And he s unto me, Son of man, hast thou H559
8 Then s he unto me, These waters issue H559
Dan 1:10 And the prince of the eunuchs s unto H559
11 Then s Daniel to Melzar, whom the H559
18 that the king had s he should bring them H559
2: 3 And the king s unto them, I have H559
5 The king answered and s to the H560
7 They answered again and s, Let the king H560
8 The king answered and s, I know of H560
10 the king, and s, There is not a man upon H560
15 He answered and s to Arioch the king's H560
20 Daniel answered and s, Blessed be the H560
24 he went and s thus unto him; Destroy H560
25 the king in haste, and s thus unto him, I H560
26 The king answered and s to Daniel, H560

Dan 2:27 of the king, and s, The secret which the H560
47 The king answered unto Daniel, and s, Of H560
3: 9 They spake and s to the king H560
14 Nebuchadnezzar spake and s unto them, H560
16 answered and s to the king, O H560
24 *and* spake, and s unto his counsellors, H560
24 and s unto the king, True, O king. H560
25 He answered and s, Lo, I see four men H560
26 *and* spake, and s, Shadrach, Meshach, H560
28 *Then* Nebuchadnezzar spake, and s, H560
4:14 He cried aloud, and s thus, Hew down H560
19 king spake, and s, Belteshazzar, let not H560
19 answered and s, My lord, the dream *be* H560
30 The king spake, and s, Is not this great H560
5: 7 the king spake, and s to the wise *men* of H560
10 queen spake and s, O king, live for ever: H560
13 the king spake and s unto Daniel, *Art* H560
17 Then Daniel answered and s before the H560
6: 5 Then s these men, We shall not find any H560
6 to the king, and s thus unto him, King H560
12 king answered and s, The thing *is* true, H560
13 Then answered they and s before the H560
15 unto the king, and s unto the king, H560
16 the king spake and s unto Daniel, Thy H560
20 the king spake and s to Daniel, O Daniel, H560
21 Then s Daniel unto the king, O king, H4449
7: 2 Daniel spake and s, I saw in my vision by H560
5 s thus unto it, Arise, devour much flesh. H560
23 Thus he s, The fourth beast shall be the H560
8:13 and another saint s unto that certain H559
14 And he s unto me, Unto two thousand H559
16 which called, and s, Gabriel, make this H559
17 my face: but he s unto me, Understand, H559
19 And he s, Behold, I will make thee know H559
9: 4 confession, and s, O Lord, the great and H559
22 with me, and s, O Daniel, I am now come H559
10:11 And he s unto me, O Daniel, a man H559
12 Then s he unto me, Fear not, Daniel: for H559
16 and spake, and s unto him that stood H559
19 And s, O man greatly beloved, fear not: H559
19 strengthened, and s, Let my lord speak; H559
20 Then s he, Knowest thou wherefore I H559
12: 6 And *one* s to the man clothed in linen, H559
8 not: then s I, O my Lord, what *shall* H559
9 And he s, Go thy way, Daniel: for the H559
Hos 1: 2 And the LORD s to Hosea, Go, take unto H559
4 And the LORD s unto him, Call his name H559
6 daughter. And *God* s unto him, Call her H559
9 Then s *God*, Call his name Lo-ammi: for H559
10 place where it was s unto them, Ye *are* H559
10 *there* it shall be s unto them, *Ye are* the H559
2: 5 shamefully: for she s, I will go after my H559
12 trees, whereof she hath s, These *are* my H559
3: 1 Then s the LORD unto me, Go yet, love a H559
3 And I s unto her, Thou shalt abide for H559
12: 8 And Ephraim s, Yet I am become rich, I H559
Joel 2:32 as the LORD hath s, and in the remnant H559
Am 1: 2 And he s, The LORD will roar from Zion, H559
7: 2 of the land, then I s, O Lord GOD, forgive, H559
5 Then s I, O Lord GOD, cease, I beseech H559
8 And the LORD s unto me, Amos, what H559
8 seest thou? And I s, A plumbline. Then H559
8 A plumbline. Then s the Lord, Behold, I H559
12 Also Amaziah s unto Amos, O thou seer, H559
14 Then answered Amos, and s to H559
15 and the LORD s unto me, Go, prophesy H559
8: 2 And he s, Amos, what seest thou? And I H559
2 seest thou? And I s, A basket of summer H559
2 fruit. Then s the LORD unto me, The H559
9: 1 the altar: and he s, Smite the lintel of the H559
Jna 1: 6 So the shipmaster came to him, and s H559
7 And they s every one to his fellow, Come, H559
8 Then s they unto him, Tell us, we pray H559
9 And he s unto them, I *am* an Hebrew; H559
10 afraid, and s unto him, Why hast H559
11 Then s they unto him, What shall we do H559
12 And he s unto them, Take me up, and H559
14 the LORD, and s, We beseech thee, O H559
2: 2 And s, I cried by reason of mine affliction H559
4 Then I s, I am cast out of thy sight; yet I H559
3: 4 and he cried, and s, Yet forty days, and H559
10 the evil, that he had s that he would do H1696
4: 2 And he prayed unto the LORD, and s, I H559
4 Then s the LORD, Doest thou well to be H559
8 s, *It is* better for me to die than to live. H559
9 And God s to Jonah, Doest thou well to H559
9 s, I do well to be angry, *even* unto death. H559
10 Then s the LORD, Thou hast had pity on H559
Mic 3: 1 And I s, Hear, I pray you, O heads of H559

Mic 7:10 cover her which s unto me, Where is the H559
Hab 2: 2 And the LORD answered me, and s, H559
Zep 2:15 carelessly, that s in her heart, I *am*, and H559
3: 7 I s, Surely thou wilt fear me, thou wilt H559
16 In that day it shall be s to Jerusalem, H559
Hag 2:12 And the priests answered and s, No. H559
13 Then s Haggai, If *one that is* unclean by H559
13 answered and s, It shall be unclean. H559
14 Then answered Haggai, and s, So *is* this H559
Zec 1: 6 they returned and s, Like as the LORD of H559
9 Then s I, O my lord, what *are* these? And H559
9 talked with me s unto me, I will shew H559
10 answered and s, These *are they* whom H559
11 myrtle trees, and s, We have walked to H559
12 answered and s, O LORD of hosts, how H559
14 So the angel that communed with me s H559
19 And I s unto the angel that talked with H559
21 Then s I, What come these to do? And he H559
2: 2 Then s I, Whither goest thou? And he H559
2 goest thou? And he s unto me, To H559
4 And s unto him, Run, speak to this H559
3: 2 And the LORD s unto Satan, The LORD H559
4 And unto him he s, Behold, I have caused H559
5 And I s, Let them set a fair mitre upon H559
4: 2 And s unto me, What seest thou? And I H559
2 seest thou? And I s, I have looked, and H559
5 me answered and s unto me, Knowest H559
5 not what these be? And I s, No, my lord. H559
11 Then answered I, and s unto him, What H559
12 And I answered again, and s unto him, H559
13 And he answered me and s, Knowest H559
13 not what these *be*? And I s, No, my lord. H559
14 Then s he, These *are* the two anointed H559
5: 2 And he s unto me, What seest thou? And H559
3 Then s he unto me, This *is* the curse that H559
5 me went forth, and s unto me, Lift up H559
6 And I s, What *is* it? And he said, This *is* H559
6 And I said, What *is* it? And he s, This *is* H559
6 goeth forth. He s moreover, This *is* their H559
8 And he s, This *is* wickedness. And he cast H559
10 Then s I to the angel that talked with me, H559
11 And he s unto me, To build it an house H559
6: 4 Then I answered and s unto the angel H559
5 And the angel answered and s unto me, H559
7 the earth: and he s, Get you hence, walk H559
11: 9 Then s I, I will not feed you: that that H559
12 And I s unto them, If ye think good, give H559
13 And the LORD s unto me, Cast it unto H559
15 And the LORD s unto me, Take unto H559
Mal 1:13 Ye s also, Behold, what a weariness *is it*! H559
3: 7 hosts. But ye s, Wherein shall we return? H559
14 Ye have s, It *is* vain to serve God: and H559
Mt 2: 5 And they s unto him, In Bethlehem of G2036
8 And he sent them to Bethlehem, and s, G2036
3: 7 come to his baptism, he s unto them, O G2036
15 And Jesus answering s unto him, Suffer G2036
4: 3 came to him, he s, If thou be the Son of G2036
4 But he answered and s, It is written, G2036
7 Jesus s unto him, It is written again, G5346
5:21 Ye have heard that it was s by them of G4483
27 Ye have heard that it was s by them of G4483
31 It hath been s, Whosoever shall put G4483
33 that it hath been s by them of old time, G4483
38 Ye have heard that it hath been s, An G4483
43 Ye have heard that it hath been s, Thou G4483
8: 8 The centurion answered and s, Lord, I G5346
10 *it*, he marvelled, and s to them that G2036
13 And Jesus s unto the centurion, Go thy G2036
19 And a certain scribe came, and s unto G2036
21 And another of his disciples s unto G2036
22 But Jesus s unto him, Follow me; and G2036
32 And he s unto them, Go. And when G2036
9: 2 seeing their faith s unto the sick of the G2036
3 And, behold, certain of the scribes s G2036
4 And Jesus knowing their thoughts s, G2036
11 And when the Pharisees saw *it*, they s G2036
12 But when Jesus heard *that*, he s unto G2036
15 And Jesus s unto them, Can the G2036
21 For she s within herself, If I may but G3004
22 he saw her, he s, Daughter, be of good G2036
24 He s unto them, Give place: for the G3004
28 to do this? They s unto him, Yea, Lord. G3004
34 But the Pharisees s, He casteth out G3004
11: 3 And s unto him, Art thou he that G2036
4 Jesus answered and s unto them, Go G2036
25 At that time Jesus answered and s, I G2036
12: 2 But when the Pharisees saw *it*, they s G2036
3 But he s unto them, Have ye not read G2036
11 And he s unto them, What man shall G2036

Mt 12:23 And all the people were amazed, and s, G3004
24 But when the Pharisees heard *it*, they s, G2036
25 And Jesus knew their thoughts, and s G2036
39 But he answered and s unto them, An G2036
47 Then one s unto him, Behold, thy G2036
48 But he answered and s unto him that G2036
49 s, Behold my mother and my brethren! G2036
13:10 And the disciples came, and s unto G2036
11 He answered and s unto them, Because G2036
27 came and s unto him, Sir, didst G2036
28 He s unto them, An enemy hath done G5346
28 this. The servants s unto him, Wilt G2036
29 But he s, Nay; lest while ye gather up G5346
37 He answered and s unto them, He that G2036
52 Then s he unto them, Therefore every G2036
54 astonished, and s, Whence hath this G3004
57 in him. But Jesus s unto them, A G2036
14: 2 And s unto his servants, This is John G2036
4 For John s unto him, It is not lawful for G3004
8 of her mother, s, Give me here John G5346
16 But Jesus s unto them, They need not G2036
18 He s, Bring them hither to me. G2036
28 And Peter answered him and s, Lord, if G2036
29 And he s, Come. And when Peter was G2036
31 caught him, and s unto him, O thou of G3004
15: 3 But he answered and s unto them, Why G2036
10 And he called the multitude, and s G2036
12 Then came his disciples, and s unto G2036
13 But he answered and s, Every plant, G2036
15 Then answered Peter and s unto him, G2036
16 And Jesus s, Are ye also yet without G2036
24 But he answered and s, I am not sent G2036
26 But he answered and s, It is not meet to G2036
27 And she s, Truth, Lord: yet the dogs eat G2036
28 Then Jesus answered and s unto her, O G2036
32 *unto him*, and s, I have compassion G2036
34 they s, Seven, and a few little fishes. G2036
16: 2 He answered and s unto them, When it G2036
6 Then Jesus s unto them, Take heed and G2036
8 *Which* when Jesus perceived, he s unto G2036
14 And they s, Some *say that thou art* John G2036
16 And Simon Peter answered and s, Thou G2036
17 And Jesus answered and s unto him, G2036
23 But he turned, and s unto Peter, Get G2036
24 Then s Jesus unto his disciples, If any G2036
17: 4 Then answered Peter, and s unto Jesus, G2036
5 the cloud, which s, This is my beloved G3004
7 them, and s, Arise, and be not afraid. G2036
11 And Jesus answered and s unto them, G2036
17 Then Jesus answered and s, O faithless G2036
19 and s, Why could not we cast him out? G2036
20 And Jesus s unto them, Because of your G2036
22 in Galilee, Jesus s unto them, The Son G2036
24 s, Doth not your master pay tribute? G2036
18: 3 And s, Verily I say unto you, Except ye G2036
21 Then came Peter to him, and s, Lord, G2036
32 he had called him, s unto him, O thou G3004
19: 4 And he answered and s unto them, G2036
5 And s, For this cause shall a man leave G2036
11 But he s unto them, All *men* cannot G2036
14 But Jesus s, Suffer little children, and G2036
16 And, behold, one came and s unto him, G2036
17 And he s unto him, Why callest thou G2036
18 He saith unto him, Which? Jesus s, G2036
21 Jesus s unto him, If thou wilt be G5346
23 Then s Jesus unto his disciples, Verily I G2036
26 But Jesus beheld *them*, and s unto G2036
27 Then answered Peter and s unto him, G2036
28 And Jesus s unto them, Verily I say G2036
20: 4 And s unto them; Go ye also into the G2036
13 But he answered one of them, and s, G2036
17 apart in the way, and s unto them, G2036
21 And he s unto her, What wilt thou? She G2036
22 But Jesus answered and s, Ye know not G2036
25 But Jesus called them *unto him*, and s, G2036
32 s, What will ye that I shall do unto you? G2036
21:11 And the multitude s, This is Jesus the G3004
13 And s unto them, It is written, My G3004
16 And s unto him, Hearest thou what G2036
19 leaves only, and s unto it, Let no fruit G3004
21 Jesus answered and s unto them, G2036
23 was teaching, and s, By what authority G3004
24 And Jesus answered and s unto them, I G2036
27 And they answered Jesus, and s, We G2036
27 tell. And he s unto them, Neither G5346
28 s, Son, go work to day in my vineyard. G2036
29 He answered and s, I will not: but G2036
30 And he came to the second, and s G2036
30 answered and s, I *go*, sir: and went not. G2036

Mt 21:38 saw the son, they s among themselves, G2036
22: 1 unto them again by parables, and s, G3004
13 Then s the king to the servants, Bind G2036
18 and s, Why tempt ye me, *ye* hypocrites? G2036
24 Saying, Master, Moses s, If a man die, G2036
29 Jesus answered and s unto them, Ye do G2036
37 Jesus s unto him, Thou shalt love the G2036
44 The LORD s unto my G2036
24: 2 And Jesus s unto them, See ye not all G2036
4 And Jesus answered and s unto them, G2036
25: 8 And the foolish s unto the wise, Give us G2036
12 But he answered and s, Verily I say G2036
21 His lord s unto him, Well done, *thou* G5346
22 two talents came and s, Lord, thou G2036
23 His lord s unto him, Well done, good G5346
24 talent came and s, Lord, I knew thee G2036
26 His lord answered and s unto him, G2036
26: 1 these sayings, he s unto his disciples, G2036
5 But they s, Not on the feast *day*, lest G3004
10 When Jesus understood *it*, he s unto G2036
15 And s *unto them*, What will ye give me, G2036
18 And he s, Go into the city to such a G2036
21 And as they did eat, he s, Verily I say G2036
23 And he answered and s, He that G2036
25 answered and s, Master, is it I? He said G2036
25 is it I? He s unto him, Thou hast said. G3004
25 is it I? He said unto him, Thou hast s. G2036
26 and s, Take, eat; this is my body. G2036
33 Peter answered and s unto him, G2036
34 Jesus s unto him, Verily I say unto G5346
35 Peter s unto him, Though I should die G3004
35 thee. Likewise also s all the disciples. G2036
49 And forthwith he came to Jesus, and s, G2036
50 And Jesus s unto him, Friend, G2036
52 Then s Jesus unto him, Put up again G3004
55 In that same hour s Jesus to the G2036
61 And s, This *fellow* said, I am able to G2036
61 And said, This *fellow* s, I am able to G5346
62 And the high priest arose, and s unto G2036
63 answered and s unto him, I adjure thee G2036
64 Jesus saith unto him, Thou hast s: G2036
66 What think ye? They answered and s, G2036
71 saw him, and s unto them that were G3004
73 that stood by, and s to Peter, Surely G2036
75 of Jesus, which s unto him, Before the G2046
27: 4 s, What *is that* to us? see thou *to that*. G2036
6 silver pieces, and s, It is not lawful for G2036
11 And Jesus s unto him, Thou sayest. G5346
13 Then s Pilate unto him, Hearest thou G3004
17 together, Pilate s unto them, Whom G2036
21 The governor answered and s unto G2036
21 I release unto you? They s, Barabbas. G2036
23 And the governor s, Why, what evil G5346
25 Then answered all the people, and s, G2036
41 *him*, with the scribes and elders, s, G3004
43 have him: for he s, I am the Son of God. G2036
47 heard *that*, s, This *man* calleth for Elias. G3004
49 The rest s, Let be, let us see whether G3004
63 that that deceiver s, while he was yet G2036
65 Pilate s unto them, Ye have a watch: go G5346
28: 5 And the angel answered and s unto the G2036
6 He is not here: for he is risen, as he s. G2036
10 Then s Jesus unto them, Be not afraid: G3004
Mk 1:17 And Jesus s unto them, Come ye after G2036
37 And when they had found him, they s G3004
38 And he s unto them, Let us go into the G3004
2: 5 When Jesus saw their faith, he s unto G3004
8 themselves, he s unto them, Why G2036
14 of custom, and s unto him, Follow me. G3004
16 and sinners, they s unto his disciples, G3004
19 And Jesus s unto them, Can the G2036
24 And the Pharisees s unto him, Behold, G3004
25 And he s unto them, Have ye never G3004
27 And he s unto them, The sabbath was G3004
3:21 on him: for they s, He is beside himself. G3004
22 from Jerusalem s, He hath Beelzebub, G3004
23 And he called them *unto him*, and s G3004
30 Because they s, He hath an unclean G3004
32 him, and they s unto him, Behold, thy G2036
34 s, Behold my mother and my brethren! G3004
4: 2 and s unto them in his doctrine, G3004
9 And he s unto them, He that hath ears G3004
11 And he s unto them, Unto you it is G3004
13 And he s unto them, Know ye not this G3004
21 And he s unto them, Is a candle G3004
24 And he s unto them, Take heed what ye G3004
26 And he s, So is the kingdom of God, as G3004
30 And he s, Whereunto shall we liken the G3004
39 the wind, and s unto the sea, Peace, G2036

Mk 4:40 And he **s** unto them, Why are ye so G2036
41 And they feared exceedingly, and **s** one G3004
5: 7 And cried with a loud voice, and **s**, G2036
8 For he **s** unto him, Come out of the G3004
28 For she **s**, If I may touch but his clothes, G3004
30 press, and **s**, Who touched my clothes? G3004
31 And his disciples **s** unto him, Thou G3004
34 And he **s** unto her, Daughter, thy faith G2036
35 *certain* which **s**, Thy daughter is dead: G3004
41 by the hand, and **s** unto her, Talitha G3004
6: 4 But Jesus **s** unto them, A prophet is not G3004
10 And he **s** unto them, In what place G3004
14 spread abroad:) and he **s**, That John the G3004
15 Others **s**, That it is Elias. And others G3004
15 Elias. And others **s**, That it is a prophet, G3004
16 But when Herod heard *thereof*, he **s**, It G2036
18 For John had **s** unto Herod, It is not G3004
22 And when the daughter of the **s** G846
22 with him, the king **s** unto the damsel, G2036
24 And she went forth, and **s** unto her G2036
24 And she **s**, The head of John the Baptist. G2036
31 And he **s** unto them, Come ye G2036
35 unto him, and **s**, This is a desert place, G3004
37 He answered and **s** unto them, Give ye G2036
7: 6 He answered and **s** unto them, Well G2036
9 And he **s** unto them, Full well ye reject G3004
10 For Moses **s**, Honour thy father and thy G2036
14 *unto him*, he **s** unto them, Hearken G3004
20 And he **s**, That which cometh out of the G3004
27 But Jesus **s** unto her, Let the children G2036
28 And she answered and **s** unto him, Yes, G3004
29 And he **s** unto her, For this saying go G2036
8: 5 loaves have ye? And they **s**, Seven. G2036
20 took ye up? And they **s**, Seven. G2036
21 And he **s** unto them, How is it that ye G3004
24 And he looked up, and **s**, I see men as G3004
34 his disciples also, he **s** unto them, G2036
9: 1 And he **s** unto them, Verily I say unto G3004
5 And Peter answered and **s** to Jesus, G3004
17 answered and **s**, Master, I have brought G2036
21 came unto him? And he **s**, Of a child. G2036
23 Jesus **s** unto him, If thou canst believe, G2036
24 child cried out, and **s** with tears, Lord, I G3004
26 insomuch that many **s**, He is dead. G3004
29 And he **s** unto them, This kind can G2036
31 For he taught his disciples, and **s** unto G3004
36 taken him in his arms, he **s** unto them, G2036
39 But Jesus **s**, Forbid him not: for there is G2036
10: 3 And he answered and **s** unto them, G2036
4 And they **s**, Moses suffered to write a G2036
5 And Jesus answered and **s** unto them, G2036
14 displeased, and **s** unto them, Suffer the G2036
18 And Jesus **s** unto him, Why callest thou G2036
20 And he answered and **s** unto him, G2036
21 loved him, and **s** unto him, One thing G2036
29 And Jesus answered and **s**, Verily I say G2036
36 And he **s** unto them, What would ye G2036
37 They **s** unto him, Grant unto us that we G2036
38 But Jesus **s** unto them, Ye know not G2036
39 And they **s** unto him, We can. And G2036
39 We can. And Jesus **s** unto them, Ye G2036
51 And Jesus answered and **s** unto him, G3004
51 The blind man **s** unto him, Lord, that G2036
52 And Jesus **s** unto him, Go thy way; thy G2036
11: 5 And certain of them that stood there **s** G3004
6 And they **s** unto them even as Jesus G2036
14 And Jesus answered and **s** unto it, No G2036
29 And Jesus answered and **s** unto them, I G2036
33 And they answered and **s** unto Jesus, G3004
12: 7 But those husbandmen **s** among G2036
15 their hypocrisy, **s** unto them, Why G2036
16 And they **s** unto him, Caesar's. G2036
17 And Jesus answering **s** unto them, G2036
24 And Jesus answering **s** unto them, Do G2036
32 And the scribe **s** unto him, Well, G2036
32 Master, thou hast **s** the truth: for there G2036
34 discreetly, he **s** unto him, Thou art G2036
35 And Jesus answered and **s**, while he G3004
36 For David himself **s** by the Holy Ghost, G2036
36 **s** to my Lord, Sit thou G2036
38 And he **s** unto them in his doctrine, G3004
13: 2 And Jesus answering **s** unto him, Seest G2036
14: 2 But they **s**, Not on the feast *day*, lest G3004
4 themselves, and **s**, Why was this waste G3004
6 And Jesus **s**, Let her alone; why trouble G2036
12 his disciples **s** unto him, Where wilt G3004
16 found as he had **s** unto them: and they G2036
18 And as they sat and did eat, Jesus **s**, G2036
19 one by one, *Is* it I? and another *s*, *Is* it I?

Mk 14:20 And he answered and **s** unto them, *It is* G2036
22 them, and **s**, Take, eat: this is my body. G2036
24 And he **s** unto them, This is my blood G2036
29 But Peter **s** unto him, Although all shall G5346
31 in any wise. Likewise also **s** they all. G3004
36 And he **s**, Abba, Father, all things *are* G3004
48 And Jesus answered and **s** unto them, G2036
61 asked him, and **s** unto him, Art thou G3004
62 And Jesus **s**, I am: and ye shall see the G2036
67 upon him, and **s**, And thou also wast G3004
70 they that stood by **s** again to Peter, G3004
72 word that Jesus **s** unto him, Before the G2036
15: 2 answering **s** unto him, Thou sayest *it*. G2036
12 And Pilate answered and **s** again unto G2036
14 Then Pilate **s** unto them, Why, what G3004
31 priests mocking **s** among themselves G3004
35 they heard *it*, **s**, Behold, he calleth Elias. G3004
39 **s**, Truly this man was the Son of God. G2036
16: 3 And they **s** among themselves, Who G3004
7 there shall ye see him, as he **s** unto you. G2036
8 amazed: neither **s** they any thing to any G2036
15 And he **s** unto them, Go ye into all the G2036
Lk 1:13 But the angel **s** unto him, Fear not, G2036
18 And Zacharias **s** unto the angel, G2036
19 And the angel answering **s** unto him, I G2036
28 And the angel came in unto her, and **s**, G2036
30 And the angel **s** unto her, Fear not, G2036
34 Then **s** Mary unto the angel, How shall G2036
35 And the angel answered and **s** unto G2036
38 And Mary **s**, Behold the handmaid of G2036
42 a loud voice, and **s**, Blessed *art* thou G2036
46 And Mary **s**, My soul doth magnify the G2036
60 And his mother answered and **s**, Not *so*; G2036
61 And they **s** unto her, There is none of G2036
2:10 And the angel **s** unto them, Fear not: G2036
15 the shepherds **s** one to another, Let G2036
24 to that which is **s** in the law of the Lord, G2046
28 up in his arms, and blessed God, and **s**, G2036
34 And Simeon blessed them, and **s** unto G2036
48 and his mother **s** unto him, Son, why G2036
49 And he **s** unto them, How is it that ye G2036
3: 7 Then **s** he to the multitude that came G3004
12 **s** unto him, Master, what shall we do? G2036
13 And he **s** unto them, Exact no more G2036
14 shall we do? And he **s** unto them, Do G2036
22 heaven, which **s**, Thou art my beloved G3004
4: 3 And the devil **s** unto him, If thou be the G2036
6 And the devil **s** unto him, All this G2036
8 And Jesus answered and **s** unto him, G2036
9 of the temple, and **s** unto him, If thou G2036
12 And Jesus answering **s** unto him, It is G2036
12 unto him, It is **s**, Thou shalt not tempt G2046
22 And they **s**, Is not this Joseph's son? G3004
23 And he **s** unto them, Ye will surely say G2036
24 And he **s**, Verily I say unto you, No G2036
43 And he **s** unto them, I must preach the G2036
5: 4 Now when he had left speaking, he **s** G2036
5 And Simon answering **s** unto him, G2036
10 Simon. And Jesus **s** unto Simon, Fear G2036
20 And when he saw their faith, he **s** unto G2036
22 he answering **s** unto them, What G2036
24 to forgive sins, (he **s** unto the sick of G2036
27 custom: and he **s** unto him, Follow me. G2036
31 And Jesus answering **s** unto them, G2036
33 And they **s** unto him, Why do the G2036
34 And he **s** unto them, Can ye make the G2036
6: 2 And certain of the Pharisees **s** unto G2036
3 And Jesus answering them **s**, Have ye G2036
5 And he **s** unto them, That the Son of G3004
8 But he knew their thoughts, and **s** to G2036
9 Then **s** Jesus unto them, I will ask you G2036
10 upon them all, he **s** unto the man, G2036
20 his disciples, and **s**, Blessed *be ye* poor: G3004
7: 9 him about, and **s** unto the people that G2036
13 on her, and **s** unto her, Weep not. G2036
14 he **s**, Young man, I say unto thee, Arise. G2036
20 unto him, they **s**, John Baptist hath sent G2036
22 Then Jesus answering **s** unto them, Go G2036
31 And the Lord **s**, Whereunto then shall I G2036
40 And Jesus answering **s** unto him, G2036
43 Simon answered and **s**, I suppose that G2036
43 **s** unto him, Thou hast rightly judged. G2036
44 And he turned to the woman, and **s** G5346
48 And he **s** unto her, Thy sins are G2036
50 And he **s** to the woman, Thy faith hath G2036
8: 8 And when he had **s** these things, he G3004
10 And he **s**, Unto you it is given to know G2036
20 And it was told him *by certain* which **s**, G3004
21 And he answered and **s** unto them, My G2036

Lk 8:22 disciples: and he **s** unto them, Let us go G2036
25 And he **s** unto them, Where is your G2036
28 with a loud voice **s**, What have I to do G2036
30 is thy name? And he **s**, Legion: because G2036
45 And Jesus **s**, Who touched me? When G2036
45 were with him **s**, Master, the multitude G2036
46 And Jesus **s**, Somebody hath touched G2036
48 And he **s** unto her, Daughter, be of G2036
52 her: but he **s**, Weep not; she is not G2036
9: 3 And he **s** unto them, Take nothing for G2036
7 that it was **s** of some, that John was G3004
9 And Herod **s**, John have I beheaded: but G2036
12 the twelve, and **s** unto him, Send the G2036
13 But he **s** unto them, Give ye them to G2036
13 to eat. And they **s**, We have no more but G2036
14 men. And he **s** to his disciples, Make G2036
19 They answering **s**, John the Baptist; but G2036
20 He **s** unto them, But whom say ye that I G2036
20 Peter answering **s**, The Christ of God. G2036
23 And he **s** to *them* all, If any *man* will G3004
33 from him, Peter **s** unto Jesus, Master, G2036
33 one for Elias: not knowing what he **s**. G3004
41 And Jesus answering **s**, O faithless and G2036
43 which Jesus did, he **s** unto his disciples, G2036
48 And **s** unto them, Whosoever shall G2036
49 And John answered and **s**, Master, we G2036
50 And Jesus **s** unto him, Forbid *him* not: G2036
54 saw *this*, they **s**, Lord, wilt thou that G2036
55 them, and **s**, Ye know not what manner G2036
57 a certain *man* **s** unto him, Lord, I will G2036
58 And Jesus **s** unto him, Foxes have G2036
59 And he **s** unto another, Follow me. But G2036
59 Follow me. But he **s**, Lord, suffer me G2036
60 Jesus **s** unto him, Let the dead bury G2036
61 And another also **s**, Lord, I will follow G2036
62 And Jesus **s** unto him, No man, having G2036
10: 2 Therefore **s** he unto them, The harvest G3004
18 And he **s** unto them, I beheld Satan as G2036
21 in spirit, and **s**, I thank thee, O Father, G2036
23 *his* disciples, and **s** privately, Blessed G2036
26 He **s** unto him, What is written in the G2036
27 And he answering **s**, Thou shalt love the G2036
28 And he **s** unto him, Thou hast G2036
29 But he, willing to justify himself, **s** unto G2036
30 And Jesus answering **s**, A certain *man* G2036
35 to the host, and **s** unto him, Take care G2036
37 And he **s**, He that shewed mercy on G2036
37 on him. Then **s** Jesus unto him, Go, G2036
40 came to him, and **s**, Lord, dost thou not G2036
41 And Jesus answered and **s** unto her, G2036
11: 1 of his disciples **s** unto him, Lord, teach G2036
2 And he **s** unto them, When ye pray, G2036
5 And he **s** unto them, Which of you shall G2036
15 But some of them **s**, He casteth out G2036
17 But he, knowing their thoughts, **s** unto G2036
27 up her voice, and **s** unto him, Blessed *is* G2036
28 But he **s**, Yea rather, blessed *are* they G2036
39 And the Lord **s** unto him, Now do ye G2036
45 of the lawyers, and **s** unto him, Master, G3004
46 And he **s**, Woe unto you also, *ye* G2036
49 Therefore also **s** the wisdom of God, I G2036
53 And as he **s** these things unto them, the G3004
12:13 And one of the company **s** unto him, G2036
14 And he **s** unto him, Man, who made G2036
15 And he **s** unto them, Take heed, and G2036
18 And he **s**, This will I do: I will pull down G2036
20 But God **s** unto him, *Thou* fool, this G2036
22 And he **s** unto his disciples, Therefore I G2036
41 Then Peter **s** unto him, Lord, speakest G2036
42 And the Lord **s**, Who then is that G2036
54 And he **s** also to the people, When ye G3004
13: 2 And Jesus answering **s** unto them, G2036
7 Then **s** he unto the dresser of his G2036
8 And he answering **s** unto him, Lord, let G3004
12 *her to him*, and **s** unto her, Woman, G2036
14 the sabbath day, and **s** unto the people, G3004
15 The Lord then answered him, and **s**, G2036
17 And when he had **s** these things, all his G3004
18 Then **s** he, Unto what is the kingdom of G3004
20 And again he **s**, Whereunto shall I liken G2036
23 Then **s** one unto him, Lord, are there G2036
23 few that be saved? And he **s** unto them, G2036
32 And he **s** unto them, Go ye, and tell G2036
14:12 Then **s** he also to him that bade him, G3004
15 these things, he **s** unto him, Blessed *is* G2036
16 Then **s** he unto him, A certain man G2036
18 excuse. The first **s** unto him, I have G2036
19 And another **s**, I have bought five yoke G2036
20 And another **s**, I have married a wife, G2036

Lk 14:21 house being angry s to his servant, Go G2036
22 And the servant s, Lord, it is done as G2036
23 And the lord s unto the servant, Go out G2036
25 him: and he turned, and s unto them, G2036
15:11 And he s, A certain man had two sons: G2036
12 And the younger of them s to *his* G2036
17 And when he came to himself, he s, G2036
21 And the son s unto him, Father, I have G2036
22 But the father s to his servants, Bring G2036
27 And he s unto him, Thy brother is G2036
29 And he answering s to *his* father, Lo, G2036
31 And he s unto him, Son, thou art ever G2036
16: 1 And he s also unto his disciples, There G3004
2 And he called him, and s unto him, G2036
3 Then the steward s within himself, G2036
5 *unto him*, and s unto the first, How G3004
6 And he s, An hundred measures of oil. G2036
6 of oil. And he s unto him, Take thy G2036
7 Then s he to another, And how much G2036
7 thou? And he s, An hundred measures G2036
7 of wheat. And he s unto him, Take thy G3004
15 And he s unto them, Ye are they which G2036
24 And he cried and s, Father Abraham, G2036
25 But Abraham s, Son, remember that G2036
27 Then he s, I pray thee therefore, father, G2036
30 And he s, Nay, father Abraham: but if G2036
31 And he s unto him, If they hear not G2036
17: 1 Then s he unto the disciples, It is G2036
5 And the apostles s unto the Lord, G2036
6 And the Lord s, If ye had faith as a G2036
13 And they lifted up *their* voices, and s, G3004
14 And when he saw *them*, he s unto G2036
17 And Jesus answering s, Were there not G2036
19 And he s unto him, Arise, go thy way: G2036
20 them and s, The kingdom of God G2036
22 And he s unto the disciples, The days G2036
37 And they answered and s unto him, G3004
37 Where, Lord? And he s unto them, G2036
18: 4 but afterward he s within himself, G2036
6 And the Lord s, Hear what the unjust G2036
16 But Jesus called them *unto him*, and s, G2036
19 And Jesus s unto him, Why callest thou G2036
21 And he s, All these have I kept from my G2036
22 these things, he s unto him, Yet lackest G2036
24 very sorrowful, he s, How hardly shall G2036
26 And they that heard *it* s, Who then can G2036
27 And he s, The things which are G2036
28 Then Peter s, Lo, we have left all, and G2036
29 And he s unto them, Verily I say unto G2036
31 the twelve, and s unto them, Behold, G2036
41 he s, Lord, that I may receive my sight. G2036
42 And Jesus s unto him, Receive thy G2036
19: 5 up, and saw him, and s unto him, G2036
8 And Zacchaeus stood, and s unto the G2036
9 And Jesus s unto him, This day is G2036
12 He s therefore, A certain nobleman G2036
13 and s unto them, Occupy till I come. G2036
17 And he s unto him, Well, thou good G2036
19 And he s likewise to him, Be thou also G2036
24 And he s unto them that stood by, Take G2036
25 (And they s unto him, Lord, he hath G2036
32 and found even as he had s unto them. G2036
33 s unto them, Why loose ye the colt? G2036
34 And they s, The Lord hath need of him. G2036
39 the multitude s unto him, Master, G2036
40 And he answered and s unto them, I G2036
20: 3 And he answered and s unto them, I G2036
8 And Jesus s unto them, Neither tell I G2036
13 Then s the lord of the vineyard, What G2036
16 when they heard *it*, they s, God forbid. G2036
17 And he beheld them, and s, What is this G2036
23 But he perceived their craftiness, and s G2036
24 hath it? They answered and s, Caesar's. G2036
25 And he s unto them, Render therefore G2036
34 And Jesus answering s unto them, The G2036
39 Then certain of the scribes answering s, G2036
39 said, Master, thou hast well s. G2036
41 And he s unto them, How say they that G2036
42 s unto my Lord, Sit thou G2036
45 of all the people he s unto his disciples, G2036
21: 3 And he s, Of a truth I say unto you, that G2036
5 with goodly stones and gifts, he s, G2036
8 And he s, Take heed that ye be not G2036
10 Then s he unto them, Nation shall rise G3004
22: 9 And they s unto him, Where wilt thou G2036
10 And he s unto them, Behold, when ye G2036
13 And they went, and found as he had s G2046
15 And he s unto them, With desire I have G2036
17 and gave thanks, and s, Take this, and G2036

Lk 22:25 And he s unto them, The kings of the G2036
31 And the Lord s, Simon, Simon, behold, G2036
33 And he s unto him, Lord, I am ready to G2036
34 And he s, I tell thee, Peter, the cock shall G2036
35 And he s unto them, When I sent you G2036
35 ye any thing? And they s, Nothing. G2036
36 Then s he unto them, But now, he that G2036
38 And they s, Lord, behold, here *are* two G2036
38 And he s unto them, It is enough. G2036
40 And when he was at the place, he s G2036
46 And s unto them, Why sleep ye? rise G2036
48 But Jesus s unto him, Judas, betrayest G2036
49 would follow, they s unto him, Lord, G2036
51 And Jesus answered and s, Suffer ye G2036
52 Then Jesus s unto the chief priests, and G2036
56 and s, This man was also with him. G2036
58 saw him, and s, Thou art also of them. G5346
58 of them. And Peter s, Man, I am not. G2036
60 And Peter s, Man, I know not what thou G2036
61 Lord, how he had s unto him, Before G2036
67 Art thou the Christ? tell us. And he s G2036
70 Then s they all, Art thou then the Son G2036
70 And he s unto them, Ye say that I am. G5346
71 And they s, What need we any further G2036
23: 3 he answered him and s, Thou sayest *it*. G5346
4 Then s Pilate to the chief priests and *to* G2036
14 S unto them, Ye have brought this man G2036
22 And he s unto them the third time, G2036
28 But Jesus turning unto them s, G2036
34 Then s Jesus, Father, forgive them; for G3004
42 And he s unto Jesus, Lord, remember G3004
43 And Jesus s unto him, Verily I say unto G2036
46 with a loud voice, he s, Father, into thy G2036
46 having s thus, he gave up the ghost. G2036
24: 5 to the earth, they s unto them, Why G2036
17 And he s unto them, What manner of G2036
18 answering s unto him, Art thou G2036
19 And he s unto them, What things? And G2036
19 What things? And they s unto him, G2036
23 of angels, which s that he was alive. G3004
24 the women had s: but him they saw not. G2036
25 Then he s unto them, O fools, and slow G2036
32 And they s one to another, Did not our G2036
38 And he s unto them, Why are ye G2036
41 s unto them, Have ye here any meat? G2036
44 And he s unto them, These *are* the G2036
46 And s unto them, Thus it is written, G2036
Jn 1:22 Then s they unto him, Who art thou? G2036
23 He s, I *am* the voice of one crying in the G5346
23 of the Lord, as s the prophet Esaias. G2036
25 And they asked him, and s unto him, G2036
30 This is he of whom I s, After me cometh G2036
33 with water, the same s unto me, Upon G2036
38 What seek ye? They s unto him, Rabbi, G2036
42 beheld him, he s, Thou art Simon the G2036
46 And Nathanael s unto him, Can there G2036
48 answered and s unto him, Before that G2036
50 Jesus answered and s unto him, G2036
50 him, Because I s unto thee, I saw thee G2036
2:16 And s unto them that sold doves, Take G2036
18 Then answered the Jews and s unto G2036
19 Jesus answered and s unto them, G2036
20 Then s the Jews, Forty and six years G2036
22 that he had s this unto them; and G3004
22 and the word which Jesus had s. G2036
3: 2 The same came to Jesus by night, and s G2036
3 Jesus answered and s unto him, Verily, G2036
7 Marvel not that I s unto thee, Ye must G2036
9 Nicodemus answered and s unto him, G2036
10 Jesus answered and s unto him, Art G2036
26 And they came unto John, and s unto G2036
27 John answered and s, A man can G2036
28 Ye yourselves bear me witness, that I s, G2036
4:10 Jesus answered and s unto her, If thou G2036
13 Jesus answered and s unto her, G2036
17 The woman answered and s, I have no G2036
17 no husband. Jesus s unto her, Thou G3004
17 Thou hast well s, I have no husband: G2036
27 yet no man s, What seekest thou? G2036
32 But he s unto them, I have meat to eat G2036
33 Therefore s the disciples one to G3004
42 And s unto the woman, Now we G3004
48 Then s Jesus unto him, Except ye see G2036
52 to amend. And they s unto him, G2036
53 in the which Jesus s unto him, Thy son G2036
5:10 The Jews therefore s unto him that was G3004
11 s unto me, Take up thy bed, and walk. G2036
12 s unto thee, Take up thy bed, and walk? G2036
14 in the temple, and s unto him, Behold, G2036

Jn 5:18 the sabbath, but s also that God was G3004
19 Then answered Jesus and s unto them, G2036
6: 6 And this he s to prove him: for he G3004
10 And Jesus s, Make the men sit down. G2036
12 When they were filled, he s unto his G3004
14 that Jesus did, s, This is of a truth that G3004
25 side of the sea, they s unto him, Rabbi, G2036
26 Jesus answered them and s, Verily, G2036
28 Then s they unto him, What shall we G2036
29 Jesus answered and s unto them, This G2036
30 They s therefore unto him, What sign G2036
32 Then Jesus s unto them, Verily, verily, I G2036
34 Then s they unto him, Lord, evermore G2036
35 And Jesus s unto them, I am the bread G2036
36 But I s unto you, That ye also have seen G2036
41 at him, because he s, I am the bread G2036
42 And they s, Is not this Jesus, the son of G3004
43 Jesus therefore answered and s unto G2036
53 Then Jesus s unto them, Verily, verily, I G2036
59 These things s he in the synagogue, as G2036
60 they had heard *this*, s, This is an hard G2036
61 he s unto them, Doth this offend you? G2036
65 And he s, Therefore said I unto you, G3004
65 And he said, Therefore s I unto you, G2046
67 Then s Jesus unto the twelve, Will ye G2036
7: 3 His brethren therefore s unto him, G2036
6 Then Jesus s unto them, My time is not G3004
9 When he had s these words unto them, G2036
11 him at the feast, and s, Where is he? G3004
12 him: for some s, He is a good man: G3004
12 s, Nay; but he deceiveth the people. G3004
16 Jesus answered them, and s, My G2036
20 The people answered and s, Thou hast G2036
21 Jesus answered and s unto them, I G2036
25 Then s some of them of Jerusalem, Is G3004
31 on him, and s, When Christ cometh, G3004
33 Then s Jesus unto them, Yet a little G2036
35 Then s the Jews among themselves, G2036
36 What *manner of* saying is this that he s, G2036
38 as the scripture hath s, out of his belly G2036
40 saying, s, Of a truth this is the Prophet. G3004
41 Others s, This is the Christ. But some G3004
41 s, Shall Christ come out of Galilee? G3004
42 Hath not the scripture s, That Christ G2036
45 and they s unto them, Why have G2036
52 They answered and s unto him, Art G2036
8: 6 This they s, tempting him, that they G3004
7 up himself, and s unto them, He that G2036
10 but the woman, he s unto her, Woman, G2036
11 She s, No man, Lord. And Jesus said G2036
11 She said, No man, Lord. And Jesus s G2036
13 The Pharisees therefore s unto him, G2036
14 Jesus answered and s unto them, G2036
19 Then s they unto him, Where is thy G3004
21 Then s Jesus again unto them, I go my G2036
22 Then s the Jews, Will he kill himself? G3004
23 And he s unto them, Ye are from G2036
24 I s therefore unto you, that ye shall die G2036
25 Then s they unto him, Who art thou? G3004
25 that I s unto you from the beginning. G2980
28 Then s Jesus unto them, When ye have G2036
31 Then s Jesus to those Jews which G3004
39 They answered and s unto him, G2036
41 Ye do the deeds of your father. Then s G2036
42 Jesus s unto them, If God were your G2036
48 Then answered the Jews, and s unto G2036
52 Then s the Jews unto him, Now we G2036
57 Then s the Jews unto him, Thou art not G2036
58 Jesus s unto them, Verily, verily, I say G2036
9: 7 And s unto him, Go, wash in the pool G2036
8 s, Is not this he that sat and begged? G3004
9 Some s, This is he: others *said*, He is G3004
9 Some said, This is he: others *s*, He is like
9 *said*, He is like him: *but* he s, I am *he*. G3004
10 Therefore s they unto him, How were G3004
11 He answered and s, A man that is called G2036
11 mine eyes, and s unto me, Go to the G2036
12 Then s they unto him, Where is he? He G2036
12 him, Where is he? He s, I know not. G3004
15 his sight. He s unto them, He put clay G2036
16 Therefore s some of the Pharisees, This G3004
16 day. Others s, How can a man that G3004
17 thine eyes? He s, He is a prophet. G2036
20 His parents answered them and s, We G2036
23 Therefore s his parents, He is of age; G2036
24 was blind, and s unto him, Give God G2036
25 He answered and s, Whether he be a G2036
26 Then s they to him again, What did he G2036
28 Then they reviled him, and s, Thou art G2036

Jn 9:30 The man answered and s unto them, G2036
34 They answered and s unto him, Thou G2036
35 he had found him, he s unto him, Dost G2036
36 He answered and s, Who is he, Lord, G2036
37 And Jesus s unto him, Thou hast both G2036
38 And he s, Lord, I believe. And he G5346
39 And Jesus s, For judgment I am come G2036
40 and s unto him, Are we blind also? G2036
41 Jesus s unto them, If ye were blind, ye G2036
10: 7 Then s Jesus unto them again, Verily, G2036
20 And many of them s, He hath a devil, G3004
21 Others s, These are not the words of G3004
24 about him, and s unto him, How long G3004
26 ye are not of my sheep, as I s unto you. G2036
34 not written in your law, I s, Ye are gods? G2036
36 because I s, I am the Son of God? G2036
41 And many resorted unto him, and s, G3004
11: 4 When Jesus heard *that*, he s, This G2036
11 These things s he: and after that he G2036
12 Then s his disciples, Lord, if he sleep, G2036
14 Then s Jesus unto them plainly, G2036
16 Then s Thomas, which is called G2036
21 Then s Martha unto Jesus, Lord, if thou G2036
25 Jesus s unto her, I am the resurrection, G2036
28 And when she had so s, she went her G2036
34 And s, Where have ye laid him? They G2036
34 They s unto him, Lord, come and see. G3004
36 Then s the Jews, Behold how he loved G3004
37 And some of them s, Could not this G2036
39 Jesus s, Take ye away the stone. G3004
40 Jesus saith unto her, S I not unto thee, G2036
41 up *his* eyes, and s, Father, I thank thee G2036
42 which stand by I s *it*, that they may G2036
47 a council, and s, What do we? for this G3004
49 s unto them, Ye know nothing at all, G2036
12: 6 This he s, not that he cared for the poor; G2036
7 Then s Jesus, Let her alone: against the G2036
19 The Pharisees therefore s among G2036
29 by, and heard *it*, s that it thundered: G3004
29 others s, An angel spake to him. G3004
30 Jesus answered and s, This voice came G2036
33 This he s, signifying what death he G3004
35 Then Jesus s unto them, Yet a little G2036
39 believe, because that Esaias s again, G2036
41 These things s Esaias, when he saw his G2036
44 Jesus cried and s, He that believeth on G2036
50 as the Father s unto me, so I speak. G2046
13: 7 Jesus answered and s unto him, What I G2036
11 therefore s he, Ye are not all clean. G2036
12 set down again, he s unto them, Know G2036
21 When Jesus had thus s, he was troubled G2036
21 and testified, and s, Verily, verily, I say G2036
27 into him. Then s Jesus unto him, That G3004
29 that Jesus had s unto him, Buy *those* G3004
31 was gone out, Jesus s, Now is the Son of G3004
33 shall seek me: and as I s unto the Jews, G2036
36 Simon Peter s unto him, Lord, whither G3004
37 Peter s unto him, Lord, why cannot I G3004
14:23 Jesus answered and s unto him, If a G2036
26 whatsoever I have s unto you. G2036
28 Ye have heard how I s unto you, I go G2036
28 would rejoice, because I s, I go unto the G2036
15:20 Remember the word that I s unto you, G2036
16: 4 And these things I s not unto you at the G2036
6 But because I have s these things unto G2980
15 mine: therefore s I, that he shall take G2036
17 Then s *some* of his disciples among G2036
18 They s therefore, What is this that he G3004
19 to ask him, and s unto them, Do ye G2036
19 of that I s, A little while, and ye G2036
29 His disciples s unto him, Lo, now G3004
17: 1 to heaven, and s, Father, the hour is G2036
18: 4 forth, and s unto them, Whom seek ye? G2036
6 As soon then as he had s unto them, I G2036
7 seek ye? And they s, Jesus of Nazareth. G2036
11 Then s Jesus unto Peter, Put up thy G2036
20 resort; and in secret have I s nothing. G2980
21 me, what I have s unto them: behold, G2980
21 unto them: behold, they know what I s. G2036
25 himself. They s therefore unto him, G2036
25 disciples? He denied *it*, and s, I am not. G2036
29 Pilate then went out unto them, and s, G2036
30 They answered and s unto him, If he G2036
31 Then s Pilate unto them, Take ye him, G2036
31 The Jews therefore s unto him, It is not G2036
33 called Jesus, and s unto him, Art thou G2036
37 Pilate therefore s unto him, Art thou a G2036
38 And when he had s this, he went out G2036
19: 3 And s, Hail, King of the Jews! and they G3004

Jn 19:21 Then s the chief priests of the Jews to G3004
21 but that he s, I am King of the Jews. G2036
24 They s therefore among themselves, G2036
30 the vinegar, he s, It is finished: and he G2036
20:14 And when she had thus s, she turned G2036
20 And when he had so s, he shewed unto G2036
21 Then s Jesus to them again, Peace *be* G2036
22 And when he had s this, he breathed on G2036
25 The other disciples therefore s unto G3004
25 the Lord. But he s unto them, Except I G2036
26 in the midst, and s, Peace *be* unto you. G2036
28 And Thomas answered and s unto G2036
21: 6 And he s unto them, Cast the net on the G2036
17 because he s unto him the third time, G2036
17 thou me? And he s unto him, Lord, G2036
20 s, Lord, which is he that betrayeth thee? G2036
23 not die: yet Jesus s not unto him, He G2036
Act 1: 7 And he s unto them, It is not for you to G2036
11 Which also s, Ye men of Galilee, why G2036
15 of the disciples, and s, (the number of G2036
24 And they prayed, and s, Thou, Lord, G2036
2:13 Others mocking s, These men are full of G3004
14 up his voice, and s unto them, Ye men of G669
34 s unto my Lord, Sit thou G2036
37 in their heart, and s unto Peter and to G2036
38 Then Peter s unto them, Repent, and G5346
3: 4 eyes upon him with John, s, Look on us. G2036
6 Then Peter s, Silver and gold have I G2036
22 For Moses truly s unto the fathers, A G2036
4: 8 the Holy Ghost, s unto them, Ye rulers G2036
19 But Peter and John answered and s G2036
23 priests and elders had s unto them. G2036
24 one accord, and s, Lord, thou *art* God, G2036
25 David hast s, Why did the heathen G2036
32 of one soul: neither s any *of them* that G3004
5: 3 But Peter s, Ananias, why hath Satan G2036
8 so much? And she s, Yea, for so much. G2036
9 Then Peter s unto her, How is it that ye G2036
19 doors, and brought them forth, and s, G2036
29 answered and s, We ought to obey God G2036
35 And s unto them, Ye men of Israel, G2036
6: 2 *unto them*, and s, It is not reason that G2036
11 Then they suborned men, which s, We G3004
13 And set up false witnesses, which s, G3004
7: 1 Then s the high priest, Are these things G2036
2 And he s, Men, brethren, and fathers, G5346
3 And s unto him, Get thee out of thy G2036
7 will I judge, s God: and after that G2036
33 Then s the Lord to him, Put off thy G2036
37 This is that Moses, which s unto the G2036
56 And s, Behold, I see the heavens G2036
60 And when he had s this, he fell asleep. G2036
8:20 But Peter s unto him, Thy money G2036
24 Then answered Simon, and s, Pray ye to G2036
29 Then the Spirit s unto Philip, Go near, G2036
30 Esaias, and s, Understandest thou G2036
31 And he s, How can I, except some man G2036
34 And the eunuch answered Philip, and s, G2036
36 and the eunuch s, See, *here is* water; G5346
37 And Philip s, If thou believest with all G2036
37 he answered and s, I believe that Jesus G2036
9: 5 And he s, Who art thou, Lord? And the G2036
5 And the Lord s, I am Jesus whom thou G2036
6 And he trembling and astonished s, G2036
6 to do? And the Lord s unto him, Arise, G2036
10 and to him s the Lord in a vision, G2036
10 And he s, Behold, I *am here*, Lord. G2036
11 And the Lord s unto him, Arise, and go
15 But the Lord s unto him, Go thy way: G2036
17 his hands on him s, Brother Saul, the G2036
21 were amazed, and s; Is not this he that G3004
34 And Peter s unto him, Aeneas, Jesus G2036
40 *him* to the body s, Tabitha, arise. And G2036
10: 4 he was afraid, and s, What is it, Lord? G2036
4 is it, Lord? And he s unto him, Thy G2036
14 But Peter s, Not so, Lord; for I have G2036
19 vision, the Spirit s unto him, Behold, G2036
21 Cornelius; and s, Behold, I am he whom G2036
22 And they s, Cornelius the centurion, a G2036
28 And he s unto them, Ye know how that G5346
30 And Cornelius s, Four days ago I was G5346
31 And s, Cornelius, thy prayer is heard, G5346
34 Then Peter opened *his* mouth, and s, Of G2036
11: 8 But I s, Not so, Lord: for nothing G2036
13 which stood and s unto him, Send men G2036
16 the Lord, how that he s, John indeed G3004
12: 8 And the angel s unto him, Gird thyself, G2036
11 to himself, he s, Now I know of a surety, G2036
15 And they s unto her, Thou art mad. But G2036

Act 12:15 even so. Then s they, It is his angel. G3004
17 of the prison. And he s, Go shew these G2036
13: 2 fasted, the Holy Ghost s, Separate me G2036
10 And s, O full of all subtilty and all G2036
16 with *his* hand s, Men of Israel, and ye G2036
22 testimony, and s, I have found David G2036
25 And as John fulfilled his course, he s, G3004
34 to corruption, he s on this wise, I will G2046
46 waxed bold, and s, It was necessary G2036
14:10 S with a loud voice, Stand upright on G2036
15: 1 taught the brethren, *and s*, Except ye be
7 Peter rose up, and s unto them, Men G2036
36 And some days after Paul s unto G2036
16:18 turned and s to the spirit, I command G2036
30 And brought them out, and s, Sirs, what G5346
31 And they s, Believe on the Lord Jesus G2036
37 But Paul s unto them, They have G5346
17:18 him. And some s, What will this G3004
22 of Mars' hill, and s, *Ye* men of Athens, I G5346
28 have s, For we are also his offspring. G2046
32 and others s, We will hear thee again G2036
18: 6 *his* raiment, and s unto them, Your G2036
14 *his* mouth, Gallio s unto the Jews, If it G2036
19: 2 He s unto them, Have ye received the G2036
2 And they s unto him, We have G2036
3 And he s unto them, Unto what then G2036
3 And they s, Unto John's baptism. G2036
4 Then s Paul, John verily baptized with G2036
15 And the evil spirit answered and s, G2036
25 occupation, and s, Sirs, ye know that by G2036
35 the people, he s, *Ye* men of Ephesus, G5346
20:10 and embracing *him* s, Trouble not G2036
18 And when they were come to him, he s G2036
35 Jesus, how he s, It is more blessed to G2036
21: 4 seven days: who s to Paul through the G3004
11 and feet, and s, Thus saith the Holy G2036
20 the Lord, and s unto him, Thou seest, G2036
37 led into the castle, he s unto the chief G3004
37 thee? Who s, Canst thou speak Greek? G5346
39 But Paul s, I am a man *which am* a Jew G2036
22: 8 Lord? And he s unto me, I am Jesus G2036
10 And I s, What shall I do, Lord? And the G2036
10 And the Lord s unto me, Arise, and G2036
13 Came unto me, and stood, and s unto G2036
14 And he s, The God of our fathers hath G2036
19 And I s, Lord, they know that I G2036
21 And he s unto me, Depart: for I will G2036
22 up their voices, and s, Away with such a G3004
25 with thongs, Paul s unto the centurion G2036
27 Then the chief captain came, and s G2036
27 Tell me, art thou a Roman? He s, Yea. G5346
28 And Paul s, But I was *free* born. G5346
23: 1 the council, s, Men *and* brethren, G2036
3 Then s Paul unto him, God shall smite G2036
4 And they that stood by s, Revilest thou G2036
5 Then s Paul, I wist not, brethren, that G5346
7 And when he had so s, there arose a G2980
11 stood by him, and s, Be of good cheer, G2036
14 and elders, and s, We have bound G2036
17 unto *him*, and s, Bring this young man G5346
18 chief captain, and s, Paul the prisoner G5346
20 And he s, The Jews have agreed to G2036
35 I will hear thee, s he, when thine G5346
24:22 them, and s, When Lysias the chief G2036
25: 5 Let them therefore, s he, which among G5346
9 Paul, and s, Wilt thou go up to G2036
10 Then s Paul, I stand at Caesar's G2036
22 Then Agrippa s unto Festus, I would G5346
22 To morrow, s he, thou shalt hear him. G5346
24 And Festus s, King Agrippa, and all G5346
26: 1 Then Agrippa s unto Paul, Thou art G5346
15 And I s, Who art thou, Lord? And he G2036
15 he s, I am Jesus whom thou persecutest. G2036
24 for himself, Festus s with a loud voice, G5346
25 But he s, I am not mad, most noble G5346
28 Then Agrippa s unto Paul, Almost thou G5346
29 And Paul s, I would to God, that not G2036
32 Then s Agrippa unto Festus, This man G5346
27:10 And s unto them, Sirs, I perceive that G3004
21 of them, and s, Sirs, ye should have G2036
31 Paul s to the centurion and to the G2036
28: 4 on his hand, they s among themselves, G3004
6 their minds, and s that he was a god. G3004
17 come together, he s unto them, Men G3004
21 And they s unto him, We neither G2036
29 And when he had s these words, the G2036
Ro 7: 7 the law had s, Thou shalt not covet. G3004
9:12 It was s unto her, The elder shall serve G4483
26 place where it was s unto them, Ye *are* G4483

Ro 9:29 And as Esaias s before, Except the Lord G4280
1Co 11:24 he brake *it*, and s, Take, eat: this is my G2036
2Co 6:16 God; as God hath s, I will dwell in them, G2036
7: 3 *you*: for I have s before, that ye are in G4280
9: 3 this behalf; that, as I s, ye may be ready: G3004
12: 9 And he s unto me, My grace is G2046
Gal 1: 9 As we s before, so say I now again, If G4280
2:14 of the gospel, I s unto Peter before G2036
Tit 1:12 of their own, s, The Cretians *are* alway G2036
Heb 1: 5 For unto which of the angels s he at G2036
13 But to which of the angels s he at any G2046
3:10 generation, and s, They do alway err in G2036
15 While it is s, To day if ye will hear his G3004
4: 3 into rest, as he s, As I have sworn in my G2046
7 a time; as it is s, To day if ye will hear G2046
5: 5 priest; but he that s unto him, Thou art G2980
7:21 oath by him that s unto him, The Lord G3004
10: 7 Then s I, Lo, I come (in the volume of G2036
8 Above when he s, Sacrifice and offering G3004
9 Then s he, Lo, I come to do thy will, O G2046
15 to us: for after that he had s before, G4280
30 For we know him that hath s, G2036
11:18 Of whom it was s, That in Isaac shall G2980
12:21 Moses s, I exceedingly fear and quake:) G2036
13: 5 ye have: for he hath s, I will never leave G2046
Jas 2:11 For he that s, Do not commit adultery, G2036
11 commit adultery, s also, Do not kill. G2036
Jude 9 but s, The Lord rebuke thee. G2036
Rev 4: 1 with me; which s, Come up hither, and G3004
5:14 And the four beasts s, Amen. And the G3004
6:11 them; and it was s unto them, that they G4483
16 And s to the mountains and rocks, Fall G3004
7:14 And I s unto him, Sir, thou knowest. G2046
14 knowest. And he s to me, These are G2036
10: 8 me again, and s, Go *and* take the little G3004
9 And I went unto the angel, and s unto G3004
9 little book. And he s unto me, Take *it*, G3004
11 And he s unto me, Thou must prophesy G3004
17: 7 And the angel s unto me, Wherefore G2036
19: 3 And again they s, Alleluia. And her G2046
10 him. And he s unto me, See *thou do* G3004
21: 5 And he that sat upon the throne s, G2036
5 new. And he s unto me, Write: for G3004
6 And he s unto me, It is done. I am G2036
22: 6 And he s unto me, These sayings *are* G2036

SAIDST
Gen 12:19 Why s thou, She *is* my sister? so I might H559
26: 9 *is* thy wife: and how s thou, She *is* my H559
32: 9 the LORD which s unto me, Return unto H559
12 And thou s, I will surely do thee good, H559
44:21 And thou s unto thy servants, Bring him H559
23 And thou s unto thy servants, Except H559
Ex 32:13 thine own self, and s unto them, I will H1696
Jdg 9:38 wherewith thou s, Who *is* Abimelech, H559
1Ki 2:42 die? and thou s unto me, The word *that* H559
Job 35: 2 s, My righteousness *is* more than God's? H559
3 For thou s, What advantage will it be H559
Ps 27: 8 *When thou s*, Seek ye my face; my heart H559
89:19 thy holy one, and s, I have laid help upon H559
Isa 47: 7 And thou s, I shall be a lady for ever: *so* H559
57:10 of thy way; *yet* s thou not, There is no H559
Jer 2:20 bands; and thou s, I will not transgress; H559
25 thirst: but thou s, There is no hope: no; H559
22:21 *but* thou s, I will not hear. This H559
Lam 3:57 *that* I called upon thee: thou s, Fear not. H559
Ezk 25: 3 GOD; Because thou s, Aha, against my H559
Hos 13:10 thou s, Give me a king and princes? H559
Jn 4:18 is not thy husband: in that s thou truly. G2046

SAIL
Isa 33:23 not spread the s: then is the prey of a H5251
Ezk 27: 7 forth to be thy s; blue and purple from H5251
Act 20: 3 him, as he was about to s into Syria, he G321
16 For Paul had determined to s by G3896
27: 1 that we should s into Italy, they G636
2 meaning to s by the coasts of Asia; G4126
17 strake s, and so were driven. G5465
24 given thee all them that s with thee. G4126

SAILED
Lk 8:23 But as they s he fell asleep: and there G4126
Act 13: 4 and from thence they s to Cyprus. G636
14:26 And thence s to Antioch, from whence G636
15:39 took Mark, and s unto Cyprus; G1602
18:18 the brethren, and s thence into Syria, G1602
21 you, if God will. And he s from Ephesus. G321
20: 6 And we s away from Philippi after the G1602
13 And we went before to ship, and s unto G321
Act 20:15 And we s thence, and came the next *day* G636
21: 3 on the left hand, and s into Syria, and G4126
27: 4 from thence, we s under Cyprus, G5284
5 And when we had s over the sea of G1277
7 And when we had s slowly many days, G1020
7 s under Crete, over against Salmone; G5284
13 loosing *thence*, they s close by Crete. G3881

SAILING
Act 21: 2 And finding a ship s over unto G1276
27: 6 s into Italy; and he put us therein. G4126
9 spent, and when s was now dangerous, G4144

SAILORS
Rev 18:17 in ships, and s, and as many as trade G3492

SAINT
Ps 106:16 camp, *and* Aaron the s of the LORD. H6918
Dan 8:13 Then I heard one s speaking, and H6918
13 and another s said unto that certain H6918
13 unto that certain *s* which spake, How H6918
Php 4:21 Salute every s in Christ Jesus. The G40

SAINTS
Dt 33: 2 ten thousands of s: from his right hand H6944
3 Yea, he loved the people; all his s *are* in H6918
1Sa 2: 9 He will keep the feet of his s, and the H2623
2Ch 6:41 and let thy s rejoice in goodness. H2623
Job 5: 1 and to which of the s wilt thou turn? H6918
15:15 Behold, he putteth no trust in his s; yea, H6918
Ps 16: 3 *But* to the s that *are* in the earth, and *to* H6918
30: 4 Sing unto the LORD, O ye s of his, and H2623
31:23 O love the LORD, all ye his s: *for* the H2623
34: 9 O fear the LORD, ye his s: for *there is* no H6918
37:28 forsaketh not his s; they are preserved H2623
50: 5 Gather my s together unto me; those H2623
52: 9 on thy name; for *it is* good before thy s. H2623
79: 2 of thy s unto the beasts of the earth. H2623
85: 8 s: but let them not turn again to folly. H2623
89: 5 also in the congregation of the s. H6918
7 the assembly of the s, and to be had in H6918
97:10 the souls of his s; he delivereth them out H2623
116:15 sight of the LORD *is* the death of his s. H2623
132: 9 and let thy s shout for joy. H2623
16 and her s shall shout aloud for joy. H2623
145:10 O LORD; and thy s shall bless thee. H2623
148:14 praise of all his s; *even* of the children H2623
149: 1 *and* his praise in the congregation of s. H2623
5 Let the s be joyful in glory: let them H2623
9 have all his s. Praise ye the LORD. H2623
Prv 2: 8 and preserveth the way of his s. H2623
Dan 7:18 But the s of the most High shall take H6922
21 with the s, and prevailed against them; H6922
22 was given to the s of the most High; H6922
22 that the s possessed the kingdom. H6922
25 shall wear out the s of the most High, H6922
27 to the people of the s of the most High, H6922
Hos 11:12 with God, and is faithful with the s. H6918
Zec 14: 5 God shall come, *and* all the s with thee. H6918
Mt 27:52 many bodies of the s which slept arose, G40
Act 9:13 evil he hath done to thy s at Jerusalem: G40
32 down also to the s which dwelt at Lydda. G40
41 the s and widows, presented her alive. G40
26:10 and many of the s did I shut up in G40
Ro 1: 7 of God, called *to be* s: Grace to you and G40
8:27 for the s according to *the will of* God. G40
12:13 Distributing to the necessity of s; given to G40
15:25 go unto Jerusalem to minister unto the s. G40
26 for the poor s which are at Jerusalem. G40
31 for Jerusalem may be accepted of the s; G40
16: 2 Lord, as becometh s, and that ye assist G40
15 and all the s which are with them. G40
1Co 1: 2 Jesus, called *to be* s, with all that in every G40
6: 1 before the unjust, and not before the s? G40
2 Do ye not know that the s shall judge the G40
14:33 but of peace, as in all churches of the s. G40
16: 1 Now concerning the collection for the s, G40
15 themselves to the ministry of the s,) G40
2Co 1: 1 with all the s which are in all Achaia: G40
8: 4 the fellowship of the ministering to the s. G40
9: 1 For as touching the ministering to the s, G40
12 the want of the s, but is abundant also G40
13:13 All the s salute you. G40
Eph 1: 1 the will of God, to the s which are at G40
15 in the Lord Jesus, and love unto all the s, G40
18 of the glory of his inheritance in the s, G40
2:19 with the s, and of the household of God; G40
3: 8 than the least of all s, is this grace given, G40
18 May be able to comprehend with all s G40
Eph 4:12 For the perfecting of the s, for the work of G40
5: 3 once named among you, as becometh s; G40
6:18 perseverance and supplication for all s; G40
Php 1: 1 Christ, to all the s in Christ Jesus which G40
4:22 All the s salute you, chiefly they that are G40
Col 1: 2 To the s and faithful brethren in Christ G40
4 and of the love *which ye have* to all the s, G40
12 of the inheritance of the s in light: G40
26 but now is made manifest to his s: G40
1Th 3:13 of our Lord Jesus Christ with all his s. G40
2Th 1:10 be glorified in his s, and to be admired in G40
Phlm 5 toward the Lord Jesus, and toward all s; G40
7 of the s are refreshed by thee, brother. G40
Heb 6:10 ministered to the s, and do minister. G40
13:24 and all the s. They of Italy salute you. G40
Jude 3 which was once delivered unto the s. G40
14 Lord cometh with ten thousands of his s, G40
Rev 5: 8 full of odours, which are the prayers of s. G40
8: 3 the prayers of all s upon the golden altar G40
4 the prayers of the s, ascended up before G40
11:18 and to the s, and them that fear thy G40
13: 7 to make war with the s, and to overcome G40
10 Here is the patience and the faith of the s. G40
14:12 Here is the patience of the s: here *are* G40
15: 3 and true *are* thy ways, thou King of s. G40
16: 6 For they have shed the blood of s and G40
17: 6 the blood of the s, and with the blood of G40
18:24 of prophets, and of s, and of all that were G40
19: 8 for the fine linen is the righteousness of s. G40
20: 9 the camp of the s about, and the beloved G40

SAINTS'
1Ti 5:10 she have washed the s feet, if she have G40

SAITH
Gen 22:16 And said, By myself have I sworn, s the H5002
32: 4 Esau; Thy servant Jacob s thus, I have H559
41:55 Go unto Joseph; what he s to you, do. H559
44: 7 And they said unto him, Wherefore s H1696
45: 9 say unto him, Thus s thy son Joseph, H559
Ex 4:22 And thou shalt say unto Pharaoh, Thus s H559
5: 1 told Pharaoh, Thus s the LORD God of H559
10 s Pharaoh, I will not give you straw. H559
7:17 Thus s the LORD, In this thou shalt H559
8: 1 say unto him, Thus s the LORD, Let my H559
20 say unto him, Thus s the LORD, Let my H559
9: 1 and tell him, Thus s the LORD God of H559
13 say unto him, Thus s the LORD God of H559
10: 3 unto him, Thus s the LORD God of the H559
11: 4 And Moses said, Thus s the LORD, H559
32:27 And he said unto them, Thus s the H559
Nu 14:28 Say unto them, *As truly as* I live, s the H5002
20:14 of Edom, Thus s thy brother Israel, Thou H559
22:16 and said to him, Thus s Balak the son of H559
24:13 *but* what the LORD s, that will I speak? H1696
32:27 before the LORD to battle, as my lord s. H1696
Jos 5:14 him, What s my lord unto his servant? H1696
7:13 to morrow: for thus s the LORD God of H559
22:16 Thus s the whole congregation of the H559
24: 2 all the people, Thus s the LORD God of H559
Jdg 6: 8 said unto them, Thus s the LORD God of H559
11:15 And said unto him, Thus s Jephthah, H559
1Sa 2:27 said unto him, Thus s the LORD, Did I H559
30 Wherefore the LORD God of Israel s, I H5002
30 but now the LORD s, Be it far from me; H5002
9: 6 man; all that he s cometh surely to H1696
10:18 of Israel, Thus s the LORD God of Israel, H559
15: 2 Thus s the LORD of hosts, I remember H559
20: 3 in thine eyes; and he s, Let not Jonathan H559
24:13 As s the proverb of the ancients, H559
2Sa 7: 5 Go and tell my servant David, Thus s the H559
8 David, Thus s the LORD of hosts, I H559
12: 7 *art* the man. Thus s the LORD God of H559
11 Thus s the LORD, Behold, I will raise up H559
14:10 And the king said, Whosoever s *ought* H1696
17: 5 also, and let us hear likewise what he s. H6310
24:12 Go and say unto David, Thus s the H559
1Ki 2:30 unto him, Thus s the king, Come forth. H559
3:23 Then said the king, The one s, This *is* my H559
23 and the other s, Nay; but thy son *is* the H559
11:31 ten pieces: for thus s the LORD, the God H559
12:24 Thus s the LORD, Ye shall not go up, nor H559
13: 2 O altar, altar, thus s the LORD; Behold, a H559
21 saying, Thus s the LORD, Forasmuch H559
14: 7 Go, tell Jeroboam, Thus s the LORD God H559
17:14 For thus s the LORD God of Israel, The H559
20: 2 and said unto him, Thus s Ben-hadad, H559
13 saying, Thus s the LORD, Hast thou H559
14 And he said, Thus s the LORD, *Even* by H559

1Ki 20:28 and said, Thus s the LORD, Because the H559
32 servant Ben-hadad s, I pray thee, let me H559
42 And he said unto him, Thus s the LORD, H559
21:19 him, saying, Thus s the LORD, Hast thou H559
19 him, saying, Thus s the LORD, In the H559
22:11 and he said, Thus s the LORD, With H559
14 the LORD s unto me, that will I speak. H559
27 And say, Thus s the king, Put this *fellow* H559
2Ki 1: 4 Now therefore thus s the LORD, Thou H559
6 say unto him, Thus s the LORD, *Is it* not H559
16 And he said unto him, Thus s the LORD, H559
2:21 there, and said, Thus s the LORD, I have H559
3:16 And he said, Thus s the LORD, Make H559
17 For thus s the LORD, Ye shall not see H559
4:43 may eat: for thus s the LORD, They shall H559
5:13 when he s to thee, Wash, and be clean? H559
7: 1 word of the LORD; Thus s the LORD, To H559
9: 3 head, and say, Thus s the LORD, I have H559
6 said unto him, Thus s the LORD God of H559
12 to me, saying, Thus s the LORD, I have H559
18 and said, Thus s the king, *Is it* peace? H559
19 and said, Thus s the king, *Is it* peace? H559
26 the blood of his sons, s the LORD; and I H5002
26 thee in this plat, s the LORD. Now H5002
18:19 to Hezekiah, Thus s the great king, the H559
29 Thus s the king, Let not Hezekiah H559
31 Hearken not to Hezekiah: for thus s the H559
19: 3 And they said unto him, Thus s H559
6 to your master, Thus s the LORD, Be not H559
20 saying, Thus s the LORD God of Israel, H559
32 Therefore thus s the LORD concerning H559
33 not come into this city, s the LORD. H5002
20: 1 unto him, Thus s the LORD, Set thine H559
5 of my people, Thus s the LORD, the God H559
17 nothing shall be left, s the LORD. H559
21:12 Therefore thus s the LORD God of Israel, H559
22:15 And she said unto them, Thus s the H559
16 Thus s the LORD, Behold, I will bring H559
18 ye say to him, Thus s the LORD God of H559
19 me; I also have heard *thee*, s the LORD. H5002
1Ch 17: 4 Go and tell David my servant, Thus s the H559
7 David, Thus s the LORD of hosts, I H559
21:10 Go and tell David, saying, Thus s the H559
11 unto him, Thus s the LORD, Choose thee H559
2Ch 11: 4 Thus s the LORD, Ye shall not go up, nor H559
12: 5 unto them, Thus s the LORD, Ye have H559
18:10 and said, Thus s the LORD, With these H559
13 even what my God s, that will I speak. H559
26 And say, Thus s the king, Put this *fellow* H559
20:15 Jehoshaphat, Thus s the LORD unto you, H559
21:12 saying, Thus s the LORD God of David H559
24:20 unto them, Thus s God, Why transgress H559
32:10 Thus s Sennacherib king of Assyria, H559
34:23 And she answered them, Thus s the H559
24 Thus s the LORD, Behold, I will bring H559
26 say unto him, Thus s the LORD God of H559
27 have even heard *thee* also, s the LORD. H5002
36:23 Thus s Cyrus king of Persia, All the H559
Ezr 1: 2 Thus s Cyrus king of Persia, The LORD H559
Neh 6: 6 and Gashmu s *it, that* thou and the H559
Job 28:14 The depth s, It *is* not in me: and the sea H559
14 in me: and the sea s, *It is* not with me. H559
33:24 Then he is gracious unto him, and s, H559
35:10 But none s, Where *is* God my maker, who H559
37: 6 For he s to the snow, Be thou *on* the H559
39:25 He s among the trumpets, Ha, ha; and H559
Ps 12: 5 now will I arise, s the LORD; I will set H559
36: 1 The transgression of the wicked s H5002
50:16 But unto the wicked God s, What hast H559
Prv 9: 4 wanteth understanding, she s to him, H559
16 wanteth understanding, she s to him, H559
20:14 *It is* naught, *it is* naught, s the buyer: but H559
22:13 The slothful *man* s, *There is* a lion H559
23: 7 *is* he: Eat and drink, s he to thee; but his H559
24:24 He that s unto the wicked, Thou *art* H559
26:13 The slothful *man* s, *There is* a lion in the H559
19 his neighbour, and s, Am not I in sport? H559
28:24 father or his mother, and s, *It is* no H559
30:16 and the fire *that* s not, *It is* enough. H559
20 and s, I have done no wickedness. H559
Ecc 1: 2 Vanity of vanities, s the Preacher, vanity H559
4: 8 with riches; neither *s he*, For whom do I
7:27 Behold, this have I found, s the H559
10: 3 and he s to every one *that* he *is* a fool. H559
12: 8 Vanity of vanities, s the preacher; all *is* H559
Isa 1:11 sacrifices unto me? s the LORD: I am full H559
18 Come now, and let us reason together, s H559
24 Therefore s the Lord, the LORD of H5002
3:15 of the poor? s the Lord GOD of hosts. H5002
Isa 3:16 Moreover the LORD s, Because the H559
7: 7 Thus s the Lord GOD, It shall not stand, H559
10: 8 For he s, *Are* not my princes altogether H559
13 For he s, By the strength of my hand I H559
24 Therefore thus s the Lord GOD of hosts, H559
14:22 For I will rise up against them, s the H5002
22 and son, and nephew, s the LORD. H5002
23 of destruction, s the LORD of hosts. H5002
17: 3 children of Israel, s the LORD of hosts. H5002
6 thereof, s the LORD God of Israel. H5002
19: 4 them, s the Lord, the LORD of hosts. H5002
22:14 you till ye die, s the Lord GOD of hosts. H559
15 Thus s the Lord GOD of hosts, Go, get H559
25 In that day, s the LORD of hosts, shall H5002
28:16 Therefore thus s the Lord GOD, Behold, I H559
29:11 thee: and he s, I cannot; for it *is* sealed: H559
12 I pray thee: and he s, I am not learned. H559
22 Therefore thus s the LORD, who H559
30: 1 Woe to the rebellious children, s the H5002
12 Wherefore thus s the Holy One of Israel, H559
15 For thus s the Lord GOD, the Holy One of H559
31: 9 of the ensign, s the LORD, whose fire H5002
33:10 Now will I rise, s the LORD; now will I be H559
36: 4 to Hezekiah, Thus s the great king, the H559
14 Thus s the king, Let not Hezekiah H559
16 Hearken not to Hezekiah: for thus s the H559
37: 3 And they said unto him, Thus s H559
6 your master, Thus s the LORD, Be not H559
21 saying, Thus s the LORD God of Israel, H559
33 Therefore thus s the LORD concerning H559
34 not come into this city, s the LORD. H5002
38: 1 unto him, Thus s the LORD, Set thine H559
5 Go, and say to Hezekiah, Thus s the H559
39: 6 nothing shall be left, s the LORD. H559
40: 1 Comfort ye, comfort ye my people, s H559
25 me, or shall I be equal? s the Holy One. H559
41:14 I will help thee, s the LORD, and thy H5002
21 Produce your cause, s the LORD; bring H559
21 your strong *reasons*, s the King of Jacob. H559
42: 5 Thus s God the LORD, he that created H559
22 for a spoil, and none s, Restore. H559
43: 1 But now thus s the LORD that created H559
10 Ye *are* my witnesses, s the LORD, and H5002
12 witnesses, s the LORD, that I *am* God. H5002
14 Thus s the LORD, your redeemer, the H559
16 Thus s the LORD, which maketh a way H559
44: 2 Thus s the LORD that made thee, and H559
6 Thus s the LORD the King of Israel, and H559
16 s, Aha, I am warm, I have seen the fire: H559
17 it, and s, Deliver me; for thou *art* my god. H559
24 Thus s the LORD, thy redeemer, and he H559
26 messengers; that s to Jerusalem, Thou H559
27 That s to the deep, Be dry, and I will dry H559
28 That s of Cyrus, *He is* my shepherd, and H559
45: 1 Thus s the LORD to his anointed, to H559
10 Woe unto him that s unto *his* father, H559
11 Thus s the LORD, the Holy One of Israel, H559
13 price nor reward, s the LORD of hosts. H559
14 Thus s the LORD, The labour of Egypt, H559
18 For thus s the LORD that created the H559
48:17 Thus s the LORD, thy Redeemer, the H559
22 *There is* no peace, s the LORD, unto the H559
49: 5 And now, s the LORD that formed me H559
7 Thus s the LORD, the Redeemer of H559
8 Thus s the LORD, In an acceptable time H559
18 to thee. *As* I live, s the LORD, thou H5002
22 Thus s the Lord GOD, Behold, I will lift H559
25 But thus s the LORD, Even the captives H559
50: 1 Thus s the LORD, Where *is* the bill of H559
51:22 Thus s thy Lord the LORD, and thy God H559
52: 3 For thus s the LORD, Ye have sold H559
4 For thus s the Lord GOD, My people H559
5 Now therefore, what have I here, s the H5002
5 them to howl, s the LORD; and my H5002
7 that s unto Zion, Thy God reigneth! H559
54: 1 of the married wife, s the LORD. H559
6 when thou wast refused, s thy God. H559
8 on thee, s the LORD thy Redeemer. H559
10 s the LORD that hath mercy on thee. H559
17 righteousness *is* of me, s the LORD. H5002
55: 8 *are* your ways my ways, s the LORD. H5002
56: 1 Thus s the LORD, Keep ye judgment, H559
4 For thus s the LORD unto the eunuchs H559
8 the outcasts of Israel s, Yet will I gather H5002
57:15 For thus s the high and lofty One that H559
19 *is* near, s the LORD; and I will heal him. H559
21 *There is* no peace, s my God, to the H559
59:20 transgression in Jacob, s the LORD. H5002
21 with them, s the LORD; My spirit H559
Isa 59:21 of thy seed's seed, s the LORD, from H559
65: 7 fathers together, s the LORD, which have H559
8 Thus s the LORD, As the new wine is H559
8 cluster, and *one* s, Destroy it not; for a H559
13 Therefore thus s the Lord GOD, Behold, H559
25 in all my holy mountain, s the LORD. H559
66: 1 Thus s the LORD, The heaven *is* my H559
2 *things* have been, s the LORD: but to H5002
9 to bring forth? s the LORD: shall I cause H559
9 forth, and shut *the womb*? s thy God. H559
12 For thus s the LORD, Behold, I will H559
17 be consumed together, s the LORD. H5002
20 Jerusalem, s the LORD, as the children H559
21 for priests *and* for Levites, s the LORD. H559
22 remain before me, s the LORD, so shall H5002
23 come to worship before me, s the LORD. H559
Jer 1: 8 with thee to deliver thee, s the LORD. H5002
15 of the north, s the LORD; and they H5002
19 with thee, s the LORD, to deliver thee. H5002
2: 2 saying, Thus s the LORD; I remember H559
3 evil shall come upon them, s the LORD. H5002
5 Thus s the LORD, What iniquity have H559
9 Wherefore I will yet plead with you, s H5002
12 afraid, be ye very desolate, s the LORD. H5002
19 *is* not in thee, s the Lord GOD of hosts. H5002
22 is marked before me, s the Lord GOD. H5002
29 transgressed against me, s the LORD. H5002
3: 1 yet return again to me, s the LORD. H5002
10 whole heart, but feignedly, s the LORD. H5002
12 backsliding Israel, s the LORD; *and* I H5002
12 for I *am* merciful, s the LORD, *and* I H5002
13 have not obeyed my voice, s the LORD. H5002
14 Turn, O backsliding children, s the H5002
16 in those days, s the LORD, they shall H5002
20 with me, O house of Israel, s the LORD. H5002
4: 1 If thou wilt return, O Israel, s the H5002
3 For thus s the LORD to the men of Judah H559
9 And it shall come to pass at that day, s H5002
17 rebellious against me, s the LORD. H5002
5: 9 Shall I not visit for these *things*? s the H5002
11 treacherously against me, s the LORD. H5002
14 Wherefore thus s the LORD God of H559
15 O house of Israel, s the LORD: it *is* a H5002
18 Nevertheless in those days, s the H5002
22 Fear ye not me? s the LORD: will ye not H5002
29 Shall I not visit for these *things*? s the H5002
6: 9 Thus s the LORD of hosts, They shall H559
12 inhabitants of the land, s the LORD. H5002
15 they shall be cast down, s the LORD. H559
16 Thus s the LORD, Stand ye in the ways, H559
21 Therefore thus s the LORD, Behold, I will H559
22 Thus s the LORD, Behold, a people H559
7: 3 Thus s the LORD of hosts, the God of H559
11 even I have seen *it*, s the LORD. H5002
13 done all these works, s the LORD, and I H5002
19 Do they provoke me to anger? s the H5002
20 Therefore thus s the Lord GOD; Behold, H559
21 Thus s the LORD of hosts, the God of H559
30 evil in my sight, s the LORD: they have H5002
32 Therefore, behold, the days come, s the H5002
8: 1 At that time, s the LORD, they shall H5002
3 have driven them, s the LORD of hosts. H5002
4 unto them, Thus s the LORD; Shall they H559
12 they shall be cast down, s the LORD. H559
13 I will surely consume them, s the H5002
17 and they shall bite you, s the LORD. H5002
9: 3 and they know not me, s the LORD. H5002
6 they refuse to know me, s the LORD. H5002
7 Therefore thus s the LORD of hosts, H559
9 Shall I not visit them for these *things*? s H5002
13 And the LORD s, Because they have H559
15 Therefore thus s the LORD of hosts, the H559
17 Thus s the LORD of hosts, Consider ye, H559
22 Speak, Thus s the LORD, Even the H5002
23 Thus s the LORD, Let not the wise *man* H559
24 in these *things* I delight, s the LORD. H5002
25 Behold, the days come, s the LORD, H5002
10: 2 Thus s the LORD, Learn not the way of H559
18 For thus s the LORD, Behold, I will sling H559
11: 3 And say thou unto them, Thus s the H559
11 Therefore thus s the LORD, Behold, I will H559
21 Therefore thus s the LORD of the men of H559
22 Therefore thus s the LORD of hosts, H559
12:14 Thus s the LORD against all mine evil H559
17 and destroy that nation, s the LORD. H5002
13: 1 Thus s the LORD unto me, Go and get H559
9 Thus s the LORD, After this manner will H559
11 house of Judah, s the LORD; that they H5002
12 them this word; Thus s the LORD God of H559

S

Jer 13:13 Then shalt thou say unto them, Thus s H559
14 the sons together, s the LORD: I will H5002
25 from me, s the LORD; because H5002
14:10 Thus s the LORD unto this people, Thus H559
15 Therefore thus s the LORD concerning H559
15: 2 tell them, Thus s the LORD; Such as *are* H559
3 over them four kinds, s the LORD: the H5002
6 Thou hast forsaken me, s the LORD, H5002
9 before their enemies, s the LORD. H5002
19 Therefore thus s the LORD, If thou H559
20 thee and to deliver thee, s the LORD. H5002
16: 3 For thus s the LORD concerning the sons H559
5 For thus s the LORD, Enter not into the H559
5 from this people, s the LORD, *even* H5002
9 For thus s the LORD of hosts, the God of H559
11 have forsaken me, s the LORD, and H5002
14 Therefore, behold, the days come, s the H5002
16 Behold, I will send for many fishers, s H5002
17: 5 Thus s the LORD; Cursed *be* the man H559
21 Thus s the LORD; Take heed to H559
24 hearken unto me, s the LORD, to bring H5002
18: 6 you as this potter? s the LORD. Behold, H5002
11 saying, Thus s the LORD; Behold, I H559
13 Therefore thus s the LORD; Ask ye now H559
19: 1 Thus s the LORD, Go and get a potter's H559
3 of Jerusalem; Thus s the LORD of hosts, H559
6 Therefore, behold, the days come, s the H5002
11 And shalt say unto them, Thus s the H559
12 Thus will I do unto this place, s the H5002
15 Thus s the LORD of hosts, the God of H559
20: 4 For thus s the LORD, Behold, I will make H559
21: 4 Thus s the LORD God of Israel; Behold, I H559
7 And afterward, s the LORD, I will H5002
8 shalt say, Thus s the LORD; Behold, I H559
10 and not for good, s the LORD: it shall H5002
12 O house of David, thus s the LORD; H559
13 rock of the plain, s the LORD; which H5002
14 of your doings, s the LORD: and I will H5002
22: 1 Thus s the LORD; Go down to the house H559
3 Thus s the LORD; Execute ye judgment H559
5 I swear by myself, s the LORD, that this H5002
6 For thus s the LORD unto the king's H559
11 For thus s the LORD touching Shallum H559
14 That s, I will build me a wide house and H559
16 *was* not this to know me? s the LORD. H5002
18 Therefore thus s the LORD concerning H559
24 *As* I live, s the LORD, though Coniah H5002
30 Thus s the LORD, Write ye this man H559
23: 1 the sheep of my pasture! s the LORD. H5002
2 Therefore thus s the LORD God of Israel H559
2 you the evil of your doings, s the LORD. H5002
4 shall they be lacking, s the LORD. H5002
5 Behold, the days come, s the LORD, H5002
7 Therefore, behold, the days come, s the H5002
11 I found their wickedness, s the LORD. H5002
12 the year of their visitation, s the LORD. H5002
15 Therefore thus s the LORD of hosts H559
16 Thus s the LORD of hosts, Hearken not H559
23 *Am* I a God at hand, s the LORD, and H5002
24 shall not see him? s the LORD. Do not I H5002
24 not I fill heaven and earth? s the LORD. H5002
28 *is* the chaff to the wheat? s the LORD. H5002
29 *Is* not my word like as a fire? s the H5002
30 the prophets, s the LORD, that steal H5002
31 Behold, I *am* against the prophets, s H5002
31 that use their tongues, and say, He s. H5002
32 false dreams, s the LORD, and do tell H5002
32 profit this people at all, s the LORD. H5002
33 I will even forsake you, s the LORD. H5002
38 therefore thus s the LORD; Because ye H559
24: 5 Thus s the LORD, the God of Israel; Like H559
8 so evil; surely thus s the LORD, So will I H559
25: 7 Yet ye have not hearkened unto me, s H5002
8 Therefore thus s the LORD of hosts; H559
9 families of the north, s the LORD, and H5002
12 and that nation, s the LORD, for their H5002
15 For thus s the LORD God of Israel unto H559
27 unto them, Thus s the LORD of hosts, H559
28 unto them, Thus s the LORD of hosts; Ye H559
29 of the earth, s the LORD of hosts. H5002
31 *are* wicked to the sword, s the LORD. H5002
32 Thus s the LORD of hosts, Behold, evil H559
26: 2 Thus s the LORD; Stand in the court of H559
4 And thou shalt say unto them, Thus s H559
18 saying, Thus s the LORD of hosts; Zion H559
27: 2 Thus s the LORD to me; Make thee H559
4 masters, Thus s the LORD of hosts, the H559
8 will I punish, s the LORD, with the H5002
11 still in their own land, s the LORD; and H5002

Jer 27:15 For I have not sent them, s the LORD, H5002
16 saying, Thus s the LORD; Hearken H559
19 For thus s the LORD of hosts concerning H559
21 Yea, thus s the LORD of hosts, the God H559
22 that I visit them, s the LORD; then will H5002
28: 4 into Babylon, s the LORD: for I will H5002
11 saying, Thus s the LORD; Even so will H559
13 Go and tell Hananiah, saying, Thus s the H559
14 For thus s the LORD of hosts, the God of H559
16 Therefore thus s the LORD; Behold, I will H559
29: 4 Thus s the LORD of hosts, the God of H559
8 For thus s the LORD of hosts, the God of H559
9 I have not sent them, s the LORD. H5002
10 For thus s the LORD, That after seventy H559
11 I think toward you, s the LORD, H5002
14 And I will be found of you, s the LORD: H5002
14 I have driven you, s the LORD; and I H5002
16 *Know* that thus s the LORD of the king H559
17 Thus s the LORD of hosts; Behold, I will H559
19 to my words, s the LORD, which I sent H5002
19 but ye would not hear, s the LORD. H5002
21 Thus s the LORD of hosts, the God of H559
23 I know, and *am* a witness, s the LORD. H5002
31 saying, Thus s the LORD concerning H559
32 Therefore thus s the LORD; Behold, I will H559
32 do for my people, s the LORD; because H5002
30: 3 For, lo, the days come, s the LORD, H5002
3 Israel and Judah, s the LORD: and I will H559
5 For thus s the LORD; We have heard a H559
8 For it shall come to pass in that day, s H5002
10 my servant Jacob, s the LORD; neither H5002
11 For I *am* with thee, s the LORD, to save H5002
12 For thus s the LORD, Thy bruise *is* H559
17 of thy wounds, s the LORD; because H5002
18 Thus s the LORD; Behold, I will bring H559
21 to approach unto me? s the LORD. H5002
31: 1 At the same time, s the LORD, will I be H5002
2 Thus s the LORD, The people *which* H559
7 For thus s the LORD; Sing with gladness H559
14 with my goodness, s the LORD. H5002
15 Thus s the LORD; A voice was heard in H559
16 Thus s the LORD; Refrain thy voice from H559
16 shall be rewarded, s the LORD; and H5002
17 And there is hope in thine end, s the H5002
20 have mercy upon him, s the LORD. H5002
23 Thus s the LORD of hosts, the God of H559
27 Behold, the days come, s the LORD, H5002
28 to build, and to plant, s the LORD. H5002
31 Behold, the days come, s the LORD, H5002
32 an husband unto them, s the LORD: H5002
33 After those days, s the LORD, I will put H5002
34 greatest of them, s the LORD: for I will H5002
35 Thus s the LORD, which giveth the sun H559
36 from before me, s the LORD, *then* the H5002
37 Thus s the LORD; If heaven above can H559
37 for all that they have done, s the LORD. H5002
38 Behold, the days come, s the LORD, H5002
32: 3 and say, Thus s the LORD, Behold, I H559
5 until I visit him, s the LORD: though ye H5002
14 Thus s the LORD of hosts, the God of H559
15 For thus s the LORD of hosts, the God of H559
28 Therefore thus s the LORD; Behold, I will H559
30 the work of their hands, s the LORD. H5002
36 And now therefore thus s the LORD, the H559
42 For thus s the LORD; Like as I have H559
44 their captivity to return, s the LORD. H5002
33: 2 Thus s the LORD the maker thereof, the H559
4 For thus s the LORD, the God of Israel, H559
10 Thus s the LORD; Again there shall be H559
11 of the land, as at the first, s the LORD. H559
12 Thus s the LORD of hosts; Again in this H559
13 of him that telleth *them*, s the LORD. H559
14 Behold, the days come, s the LORD, H5002
17 For thus s the LORD; David shall never H559
20 Thus s the LORD; If ye can break my H559
25 Thus s the LORD; If my covenant *be* not H559
34: 2 Thus s the LORD, the God of Israel; Go H559
2 and tell him, Thus s the LORD; Behold, I H559
4 of Judah; Thus s the LORD of thee, Thou H559
5 pronounced the word, s the LORD. H5002
13 Thus s the LORD, the God of Israel; I H559
17 Therefore thus s the LORD; Ye have not H559
17 a liberty for you, s the LORD, to the H5002
22 Behold, I will command, s the LORD, H5002
35:13 Thus s the LORD of hosts, the God of H559
13 to hearken to my words? s the LORD. H5002
17 Therefore thus s the LORD God of hosts, H559
18 Rechabites, Thus s the LORD of hosts, H559
19 Therefore thus s the LORD of hosts, the H559

Jer 36:29 of Judah, Thus s the LORD; Thou hast H559
30 Therefore thus s the LORD of Jehoiakim H559
37: 7 Thus s the LORD, the God of Israel; Thus H559
9 Thus s the LORD; Deceive not H559
38: 2 Thus s the LORD, He that remaineth in H559
3 Thus s the LORD, This city shall surely H559
17 Zedekiah, Thus s the LORD, the God of H559
39:16 saying, Thus s the LORD of hosts, the H559
17 But I will deliver thee in that day, s the H5002
18 hast put thy trust in me, s the LORD. H5002
42: 9 And said unto them, Thus s the LORD, H559
11 not afraid of him, s the LORD: for I *am* H5002
15 of Judah; Thus s the LORD of hosts, the H559
18 For thus s the LORD of hosts, the God of H559
43:10 And say unto them, Thus s the LORD of H559
44: 2 Thus s the LORD of hosts, the God of H559
7 Therefore now thus s the LORD, the God H559
11 Therefore thus s the LORD of hosts, the H559
25 Thus s the LORD of hosts, the God of H559
26 by my great name, s the LORD, that my H559
29 And this *shall be* a sign unto you, s the H5002
30 Thus s the LORD; Behold, I will give H559
45: 2 Thus s the LORD, the God of Israel, unto H559
4 unto him, The LORD s thus; Behold, *that* H559
5 evil upon all flesh, s the LORD: but thy H5002
46: 5 *for* fear *was* round about, s the LORD. H5002
8 the rivers; and he s, I will go up, *and* will H559
18 *As* I live, s the King, whose name *is* the H5002
23 They shall cut down her forest, s the H5002
25 The LORD of hosts, the God of Israel, s; H559
26 as in the days of old, s the LORD. H5002
28 Fear thou not, O Jacob my servant, s H5002
47: 2 Thus s the LORD; Behold, waters rise up H559
48: 1 Against Moab thus s the LORD of hosts, H559
12 Therefore, behold, the days come, s the H5002
15 to the slaughter, s the King, whose H5002
25 off, and his arm is broken, s the LORD. H5002
30 I know his wrath, s the LORD; but *it* H5002
35 to cease in Moab, s the LORD, him that H5002
38 wherein *is* no pleasure, s the LORD. H5002
40 For thus s the LORD; Behold, he shall fly H559
43 O inhabitant of Moab, s the LORD. H5002
44 the year of their visitation, s the LORD. H5002
47 in the latter days, s the LORD. Thus far H5002
49: 1 Concerning the Ammonites, thus s the H559
2 Therefore, behold, the days come, s the H5002
2 them that were his heirs, s the LORD. H559
5 Behold, I will bring a fear upon thee, s H5002
6 of the children of Ammon, s the LORD. H5002
7 Concerning Edom, thus s the LORD of H559
12 For thus s the LORD; Behold, they whose H559
13 For I have sworn by myself, s the H5002
16 thee down from thence, s the LORD. H5002
18 *cities* thereof, s the LORD, no man shall H559
26 cut off in that day, s the LORD of hosts. H5002
28 shall smite, thus s the LORD; Arise ye, H559
30 inhabitants of Hazor, s the LORD; for H5002
31 without care, s the LORD, which have H5002
32 from all sides thereof, s the LORD. H5002
35 Thus s the LORD of hosts; Behold, I will H559
37 my fierce anger, s the LORD; and I will H5002
38 the king and the princes, s the LORD. H5002
39 the captivity of Elam, s the LORD. H5002
50: 4 In those days, and in that time, s the H5002
10 spoil her shall be satisfied, s the LORD. H5002
18 Therefore thus s the LORD of hosts, the H559
20 In those days, and in that time, s the H5002
21 destroy after them, s the LORD, and do H5002
30 shall be cut off in that day, s the LORD. H5002
31 *O thou* most proud, s the Lord GOD of H5002
33 Thus s the LORD of hosts; The children H559
35 A sword *is* upon the Chaldeans, s the H5002
40 *cities* thereof, s the LORD; *so* shall no H5002
51: 1 Thus s the LORD; Behold, I will raise up H559
24 done in Zion in your sight, s the LORD. H5002
25 mountain, s the LORD, which H5002
26 shalt be desolate for ever, s the LORD. H5002
33 For thus s the LORD of hosts, the God of H559
36 Therefore thus s the LORD; Behold, I will H559
39 sleep, and not wake, s the LORD. H5002
48 unto her from the north, s the LORD. H5002
52 Wherefore, behold, the days come, s H5002
53 spoilers come unto her, s the LORD. H5002
57 and not wake, s the King, whose name H5002
58 Thus s the LORD of hosts; The broad H559
Lam 3:24 The LORD *is* my portion, s my soul; H559
37 Who *is* he *that* s, and it cometh to pass, H559
Ezk 2: 4 say unto them, Thus s the Lord GOD. H559
3:11 tell them, Thus s the Lord GOD; whether H559

Ezk 3:27 say unto them, Thus **s** the Lord GOD; He H559
5: 5 Thus **s** the Lord GOD; This *is* Jerusalem: H559
7 Therefore thus **s** the Lord GOD; Because H559
8 Therefore thus **s** the Lord GOD; Behold, H559
11 Wherefore, *as* I live, **s** the Lord GOD; H5002
6: 3 Lord GOD; Thus **s** the Lord GOD to the H559
11 Thus **s** the Lord GOD; Smite with thine H559
7: 2 Also, thou son of man, thus **s** the Lord H559
5 Thus **s** the Lord GOD; An evil, an only H559
11: 5 me, Speak; Thus **s** the LORD; Thus have H559
7 Therefore thus **s** the Lord GOD; Your H559
8 a sword upon you, **s** the Lord GOD. H5002
16 Therefore say, Thus **s** the Lord GOD; H559
17 Therefore say, Thus **s** the Lord GOD; I H559
21 upon their own heads, **s** the Lord GOD. H5002
12:10 Say thou unto them, Thus **s** the Lord H559
19 of the land, Thus **s** the Lord GOD of the H559
23 Tell them therefore, Thus **s** the Lord H559
25 and will perform it, **s** the Lord GOD. H5002
28 Therefore say unto them, Thus **s** the H559
28 spoken shall be done, **s** the Lord GOD. H5002
13: 3 Thus **s** the Lord GOD; Woe unto the H559
6 saying, The LORD **s**: and the LORD H5002
7 LORD **s** *it*; albeit I have not spoken? H5002
8 Therefore thus **s** the Lord GOD; Because H559
8 I *am* against you, **s** the Lord GOD. H5002
13 Therefore thus **s** the Lord GOD; I will H559
16 and *there is* no peace, **s** the Lord GOD. H5002
18 And say, Thus **s** the Lord GOD; Woe to H559
20 Wherefore thus **s** the Lord GOD; Behold, H559
14: 4 unto them, Thus **s** the Lord GOD; Every H559
6 of Israel, Thus **s** the Lord GOD; Repent, H559
11 I may be their God, **s** the Lord GOD. H5002
14 by their righteousness, **s** the Lord GOD. H5002
16 *were* in it, *as* I live, **s** the Lord GOD, H5002
18 *were* in it, *as* I live, **s** the Lord GOD, H5002
20 *were* in it, *as* I live, **s** the Lord GOD, H5002
21 For thus **s** the Lord GOD; How much H559
23 that I have done in it, **s** the Lord GOD. H5002
15: 6 Therefore thus **s** the Lord GOD; As the H559
8 committed a trespass, **s** the Lord GOD. H5002
16: 3 And say, Thus **s** the Lord GOD unto H559
8 with thee, **s** the Lord GOD, and H5002
14 I had put upon thee, **s** the Lord GOD. H5002
19 and *thus* it was, **s** the Lord GOD. H5002
23 (woe, woe unto thee! **s** the Lord GOD;) H5002
30 How weak is thine heart, **s** the Lord H5002
36 Thus **s** the Lord GOD; Because thy H559
43 upon *thine* head, **s** the Lord GOD: and H5002
48 *As* I live, **s** the Lord GOD, Sodom thy H5002
58 and thine abominations, **s** the LORD. H5002
59 For thus **s** the Lord GOD; I will even deal H559
63 that thou hast done, **s** the Lord GOD. H5002
17: 3 And say, Thus **s** the Lord GOD; A great H559
9 Say thou, Thus **s** the Lord GOD; Shall it H559
16 *As* I live, **s** the Lord GOD, surely in the H5002
19 Therefore thus **s** the Lord GOD; *As* I live, H559
22 Thus **s** the Lord GOD; I will also take of H559
18: 3 *As* I live, **s** the Lord GOD, ye shall not H5002
9 he shall surely live, **s** the Lord GOD. H5002
23 should die? **s** the Lord GOD: *and* H5002
29 Yet **s** the house of Israel, The way of the H559
30 to his ways, **s** the Lord GOD. Repent, H5002
32 of him that dieth, **s** the Lord GOD: H5002
20: 3 unto them, Thus **s** the Lord GOD; Are ye H559
3 of me? *As* I live, **s** the Lord GOD, I will H5002
5 And say unto them, Thus **s** the Lord H559
27 unto them, Thus **s** the Lord GOD; Yet in H559
30 of Israel, Thus **s** the Lord GOD; Are ye H559
31 of Israel? *As* I live, **s** the Lord GOD, I H5002
33 *As* I live, **s** the Lord GOD, surely with a H5002
36 will I plead with you, **s** the Lord GOD. H5002
39 As for you, O house of Israel, thus **s** the H559
40 height of Israel, **s** the Lord GOD, there H5002
44 O ye house of Israel, **s** the Lord GOD. H5002
47 word of the LORD; Thus **s** the Lord GOD; H559
21: 3 And say to the land of Israel, Thus **s** the H559
7 be brought to pass, **s** the Lord GOD. H5002
9 Son of man, prophesy, and say, Thus **s** H559
13 it shall be no *more*, **s** the Lord GOD. H5002
24 Therefore thus **s** the Lord GOD; Because H559
26 Thus **s** the Lord GOD; Remove the H559
28 prophesy and say, Thus **s** the Lord GOD H559
22: 3 Then say thou, Thus **s** the Lord GOD, H559
12 and hast forgotten me, **s** the Lord GOD. H5002
19 Therefore thus **s** the Lord GOD; Because H559
28 unto them, saying, Thus **s** the Lord GOD, H559
31 upon their heads, **s** the Lord GOD. H5002
23:22 Therefore, O Aholibah, thus **s** the Lord H559

Ezk 23:28 For thus **s** the Lord GOD; Behold, I will H559
32 Thus **s** the Lord GOD; Thou shalt drink H559
34 for I have spoken *it*, **s** the Lord GOD. H5002
35 Therefore thus **s** the Lord GOD; Because H559
46 For thus **s** the Lord GOD; I will bring up H559
24: 3 unto them, Thus **s** the Lord GOD; Set on H559
6 Wherefore thus **s** the Lord GOD; Woe to H559
9 Therefore thus **s** the Lord GOD; Woe to H559
14 shall they judge thee, **s** the Lord GOD. H5002
21 Speak unto the house of Israel, Thus **s** H559
25: 3 the Lord GOD; Thus **s** the Lord GOD; H559
6 For thus **s** the Lord GOD; Because thou H559
8 Thus **s** the Lord GOD; Because that H559
12 Thus **s** the Lord GOD; Because that H559
13 Therefore thus **s** the Lord GOD; I will H559
14 know my vengeance, **s** the Lord GOD. H5002
15 Thus **s** the Lord GOD; Because the H559
16 Therefore thus **s** the Lord GOD; Behold, I H559
26: 3 Therefore thus **s** the Lord GOD; Behold, I H559
5 I have spoken *it*, **s** the Lord GOD: and H5002
7 For thus **s** the Lord GOD; Behold, I will H559
14 LORD have spoken *it*, **s** the Lord GOD. H5002
15 Thus **s** the Lord GOD to Tyrus; Shall not H559
19 For thus **s** the Lord GOD; When I shall H559
21 never be found again, **s** the Lord GOD. H5002
27: 3 for many isles, Thus **s** the Lord GOD; O H559
28: 2 of Tyrus, Thus **s** the Lord GOD; Because H559
6 Therefore thus **s** the Lord GOD; Because H559
10 for I have spoken *it*, **s** the Lord GOD. H5002
12 and say unto him, Thus **s** the Lord GOD; H559
22 And say, Thus **s** the Lord GOD; Behold, I H559
25 Thus **s** the Lord GOD; When I shall have H559
29: 3 Speak, and say, Thus **s** the Lord GOD; H559
8 Therefore thus **s** the Lord GOD; Behold, I H559
13 Yet thus **s** the Lord GOD; At the end of H559
19 Therefore thus **s** the Lord GOD; Behold, I H559
20 they wrought for me, **s** the Lord GOD. H5002
30: 2 Son of man, prophesy and say, Thus **s** H559
6 Thus **s** the LORD; They also that uphold H559
6 fall in it by the sword, **s** the Lord GOD. H5002
10 Thus **s** the Lord GOD; I will also make H559
13 Thus **s** the Lord GOD; I will also destroy H559
22 Therefore thus **s** the Lord GOD; Behold, I H559
31:10 Therefore thus **s** the Lord GOD; Because H559
15 Thus **s** the Lord GOD; In the day when H559
18 and all his multitude, **s** the Lord GOD. H5002
32: 3 Thus **s** the Lord GOD; I will therefore H559
8 upon thy land, **s** the Lord GOD. H5002
11 For thus **s** the Lord GOD; The sword of H559
14 rivers to run like oil, **s** the Lord GOD. H5002
16 for all her multitude, **s** the Lord GOD. H5002
31 slain by the sword, **s** the Lord GOD. H5002
32 and all his multitude, **s** the Lord GOD. H5002
33:11 Say unto them, *As* I live, **s** the Lord H5002
25 Wherefore say unto them, Thus **s** the H559
27 Say thou thus unto them, Thus **s** the H559
34: 2 unto them, Thus **s** the Lord GOD unto H559
8 *As* I live, **s** the Lord GOD, surely H5002
10 Thus **s** the Lord GOD; Behold, I *am* H559
11 For thus **s** the Lord GOD; Behold, I, *even* H559
15 them to lie down, **s** the Lord GOD. H5002
17 And *as for* you, O my flock, thus **s** the H559
20 Therefore thus **s** the Lord GOD unto H559
30 Israel, *are* my people, **s** the Lord GOD. H5002
31 *and* I *am* your God, **s** the Lord GOD. H5002
35: 3 And say unto it, Thus **s** the Lord GOD; H559
6 Therefore, *as* I live, **s** the Lord GOD, I H5002
11 Therefore, *as* I live, **s** the Lord GOD, I H5002
14 Thus **s** the Lord GOD; When the whole H559
36: 2 Thus **s** the Lord GOD; Because the H559
3 Therefore prophesy and say, Thus **s** the H559
4 Lord GOD; Thus **s** the Lord GOD to the H559
5 Therefore thus **s** the Lord GOD; Surely in H559
6 and to the valleys, Thus **s** the Lord GOD; H559
7 Therefore thus **s** the Lord GOD; I have H559
13 Thus **s** the Lord GOD; Because they say H559
14 thy nations any more, **s** the Lord GOD. H5002
15 to fall any more, **s** the Lord GOD. H5002
22 of Israel, Thus **s** the Lord GOD; I do not H559
23 I *am* the LORD, **s** the Lord GOD, when H5002
32 Not for your sakes do I *this*, **s** the Lord H5002
33 Thus **s** the Lord GOD; In the day that I H559
37 Thus **s** the Lord GOD; I will yet *for* this H559
37: 5 Thus **s** the Lord GOD unto these bones; H559
9 to the wind, Thus **s** the Lord GOD; Come H559
12 say unto them, Thus **s** the Lord GOD; H559
14 *it*, and performed *it*, **s** the LORD. H5002
19 Say unto them, Thus **s** the Lord GOD; H559
21 And say unto them, Thus **s** the Lord H559

Ezk 38: 3 And say, Thus **s** the Lord GOD; Behold, I H559
10 Thus **s** the Lord GOD; It shall also come H559
14 say unto Gog, Thus **s** the Lord GOD; In H559
17 Thus **s** the Lord GOD; *Art* thou he of H559
18 the land of Israel, **s** the Lord GOD, *that* H5002
21 all my mountains, **s** the Lord GOD: H5002
39: 1 Gog, and say, Thus **s** the Lord GOD; H559
5 for I have spoken *it*, **s** the Lord GOD. H5002
8 Behold, it is come, and it is done, **s** the H5002
10 that robbed them, **s** the Lord GOD. H5002
13 I shall be glorified, **s** the Lord GOD. H5002
17 And, thou son of man, thus **s** the Lord H559
20 with all men of war, **s** the Lord GOD. H5002
25 Therefore thus **s** the Lord GOD; Now will H559
29 the house of Israel, **s** the Lord GOD. H5002
43:18 And he said unto me, Son of man, thus **s** H559
19 to minister unto me, **s** the Lord GOD, a H5002
27 and I will accept you, **s** the Lord GOD. H5002
44: 6 of Israel, Thus **s** the Lord GOD; O ye H559
9 Thus **s** the Lord GOD; No stranger, H559
12 against them, **s** the Lord GOD, and H5002
15 the fat and the blood, **s** the Lord GOD: H5002
27 offer his sin offering, **s** the Lord GOD. H5002
45: 9 Thus **s** the Lord GOD; Let it suffice you, H559
9 from my people, **s** the Lord GOD. H5002
15 for them, **s** the Lord GOD. H5002
18 Thus **s** the Lord GOD; In the first *month*, H559
46: 1 Thus **s** the Lord GOD; The gate of the H559
16 Thus **s** the Lord GOD; If the prince give a H559
47:13 Thus **s** the Lord GOD; This *shall be* the H559
23 *him* his inheritance, **s** the Lord GOD. H5002
48:29 *are* their portions, **s** the Lord GOD. H5002
Hos 2:13 her lovers, and forgat me, **s** the LORD. H5002
16 And it shall be at that day, **s** the LORD, H5002
21 day, I will hear, **s** the LORD, I will hear H5002
11:11 place them in their houses, **s** the LORD. H5002
Joel 2:12 Therefore also now, **s** the LORD, turn H5002
Am 1: 3 Thus **s** the LORD; For three H559
5 go into captivity unto Kir, **s** the LORD. H559
6 Thus **s** the LORD; For three H559
8 Philistines shall perish, **s** the Lord GOD. H559
9 Thus **s** the LORD; For three H559
11 Thus **s** the LORD; For three H559
13 Thus **s** the LORD; For three H559
15 he and his princes together, **s** the LORD. H559
2: 1 Thus **s** the LORD; For three H559
3 princes thereof with him, **s** the LORD. H559
4 Thus **s** the LORD; For three H559
6 Thus **s** the LORD; For three H559
11 O ye children of Israel? **s** the LORD. H5002
16 away naked in that day, **s** the LORD. H5002
3:10 For they know not to do right, **s** the H5002
11 Therefore thus **s** the Lord GOD; An H559
12 Thus **s** the LORD; As the shepherd H559
13 **s** the Lord GOD, the God of hosts, H5002
15 houses shall have an end, **s** the LORD. H5002
4: 3 cast *them* into the palace, **s** the LORD. H5002
5 O ye children of Israel, **s** the Lord GOD. H5002
6 ye not returned unto me, **s** the LORD. H5002
8 ye not returned unto me, **s** the LORD. H5002
9 ye not returned unto me, **s** the LORD. H5002
10 ye not returned unto me, **s** the LORD. H5002
11 ye not returned unto me, **s** the LORD. H5002
5: 3 For thus **s** the Lord GOD; The city that H559
4 For thus **s** the LORD unto the house of H559
16 of hosts, the Lord, **s** thus; Wailing *shall* H559
17 for I will pass through thee, **s** the LORD. H559
27 beyond Damascus, **s** the LORD, whose H559
6: 8 The Lord GOD hath sworn by himself, **s** H5002
14 O house of Israel, **s** the LORD the God H5002
7: 3 for this: It shall not be, **s** the LORD. H559
6 This also shall not be, **s** the Lord GOD. H559
11 For thus Amos **s**, Jeroboam shall die by H559
17 Therefore thus **s** the LORD; Thy wife H559
8: 3 in that day, **s** the Lord GOD: *there* H5002
9 And it shall come to pass in that day, **s** H5002
11 Behold, the days come, **s** the Lord H5002
9: 7 O children of Israel? **s** the LORD. Have H5002
8 destroy the house of Jacob, **s** the LORD. H5002
12 my name, **s** the LORD that doeth this. H5002
13 Behold, the days come, **s** the LORD, H5002
15 I have given them, **s** the LORD thy God. H559
Oba 1 The vision of Obadiah. Thus **s** the Lord H559
3 *is* high; that **s** in his heart, Who shall H559
4 will I bring thee down, **s** the LORD. H5002
8 Shall I not in that day, **s** the LORD, H5002
Mic 2: 3 Therefore thus **s** the LORD; Behold, H559
3: 5 Thus **s** the LORD concerning the H559
4: 6 In that day, **s** the LORD, will I assemble H5002

Mic 5:10 And it shall come to pass in that day, s H5002
6: 1 Hear ye now what the LORD s; Arise, H559
Nah 1:12 Thus s the LORD; Though *they be* quiet, H559
2:13 Behold, I *am* against thee, s the LORD H5002
3: 5 Behold, I *am* against thee, s the LORD H5002
Hab 2:19 Woe unto him that s to the wood, H559
Zep 1: 2 *things* from off the land, s the LORD. H5002
3 off man from off the land, s the LORD. H5002
10 And it shall come to pass in that day, s H5002
2: 9 Therefore *as* I live, s the LORD of hosts, H5002
3: 8 Therefore wait ye upon me, s the H5002
20 captivity before your eyes, s the LORD. H559
Hag 1: 5 Now therefore thus s the LORD of hosts; H559
7 Thus s the LORD of hosts; Consider your H559
8 in it, and I will be glorified, s the LORD. H559
9 upon it. Why? s the LORD of hosts. H5002
13 saying, I *am* with you, s the LORD. H5002
2: 4 Yet now be strong, O Zerubbabel, s the H5002
4 ye people of the land, s the LORD, and H5002
4 for I *am* with you, s the LORD of hosts: H5002
6 For thus s the LORD of hosts; Yet once, it H559
7 house with glory, s the LORD of hosts. H559
8 the gold *is* mine, s the LORD of hosts. H5002
9 of the former, s the LORD of hosts: H559
9 will I give peace, s the LORD of hosts. H5002
11 Thus s the LORD of hosts; Ask now the H559
14 nation before me, s the LORD; and so H5002
17 yet ye *turned* not to me, s the LORD. H5002
23 In that day, s the LORD of hosts, will I H5002
23 son of Shealtiel, s the LORD, and will H5002
23 have chosen thee, s the LORD of hosts. H5002
Zec 1: 3 Therefore say thou unto them, Thus s H559
3 Turn ye unto me, s the LORD of hosts, H5002
3 I will turn unto you, s the LORD of hosts. H559
4 cried, saying, Thus s the LORD of hosts; H559
4 nor hearken unto me, s the LORD. H5002
14 thou, saying, Thus s the LORD of hosts; I H559
16 Therefore thus s the LORD; I am H559
16 shall be built in it, s the LORD of hosts, H5002
17 Cry yet, saying, Thus s the LORD of H559
2: 5 For I, s the LORD, will be unto her a H5002
6 the land of the north, s the LORD: for I H5002
6 four winds of the heaven, s the LORD. H5002
8 For thus s the LORD of hosts; After the H559
10 dwell in the midst of thee, s the LORD. H5002
3: 7 Thus s the LORD of hosts; If thou wilt H559
9 graving thereof, s the LORD of hosts, H5002
10 In that day, s the LORD of hosts, shall H5002
4: 6 but by my spirit, s the LORD of hosts. H559
5: 4 I will bring it forth, s the LORD of H5002
7:13 I would not hear, s the LORD of hosts: H559
8: 2 Thus s the LORD of hosts; I was jealous H559
3 Thus s the LORD; I am returned unto H559
4 Thus s the LORD of hosts; There shall H559
6 Thus s the LORD of hosts; If it be H559
6 in mine eyes? s the LORD of hosts. H5002
7 Thus s the LORD of hosts; Behold, I will H559
9 Thus s the LORD of hosts; Let your H559
11 the former days, s the LORD of hosts. H5002
14 For thus s the LORD of hosts; As I H559
14 s the LORD of hosts, and I repented not: H559
17 *are things* that I hate, s the LORD. H5002
19 Thus s the LORD of hosts; The fast of the H559
20 Thus s the LORD of hosts; *It shall* yet H559
23 Thus s the LORD of hosts; In those days H559
10:12 up and down in his name, s the LORD. H5002
11: 4 Thus s the LORD my God; Feed the flock H559
6 of the land, s the LORD: but, lo, I H5002
12: 1 the LORD for Israel, s the LORD, which H5002
4 In that day, s the LORD, I will smite H5002
13: 2 And it shall come to pass in that day, s H5002
7 *that is* my fellow, s the LORD of hosts: H5002
8 in all the land, s the LORD, two parts H5002
Mal 1: 2 I have loved you, s the LORD. Yet ye say, H559
2 brother? s the LORD: yet I loved Jacob, H5002
4 Whereas Edom s, We are impoverished, H559
4 places; thus s the LORD of hosts, They H559
6 where *is* my fear? s the LORD of hosts H559
8 accept thy person? s the LORD of hosts. H559
9 your persons? s the LORD of hosts. H559
10 no pleasure in you, s the LORD of hosts, H559
11 among the heathen, s the LORD of hosts. H559
13 have snuffed at it, s the LORD of hosts; H559
13 I accept this of your hand? s the LORD. H559
14 I *am* a great King, s the LORD of hosts, H559
2: 2 unto my name, s the LORD of hosts, I H559
4 might be with Levi, s the LORD of hosts. H559
8 covenant of Levi, s the LORD of hosts. H559
16 For the LORD, the God of Israel, s that H559
Mal 2:16 with his garment, s the LORD of hosts: H559
3: 1 he shall come, s the LORD of hosts. H559
5 and fear not me, s the LORD of hosts. H559
7 return unto you, s the LORD of hosts. H559
10 me now herewith, s the LORD of hosts, if H559
11 the time in the field, s the LORD of hosts. H559
12 a delightsome land, s the LORD of hosts. H559
13 stout against me, s the LORD. Yet ye say, H559
17 And they shall be mine, s the LORD of H559
4: 1 burn them up, s the LORD of hosts, that H559
3 that I shall do *this*, s the LORD of hosts. H559
Mt 4: 6 And s unto him, If thou be the Son of G3004
9 And s unto him, All these things will I G3004
10 Then s Jesus unto him, Get thee hence, G3004
19 And he s unto them, Follow me, and I G3004
7:21 Not every one that s unto me, Lord, G3004
8: 4 And Jesus s unto him, See thou tell no G3004
7 And Jesus s unto him, I will come and G3004
20 And Jesus s unto him, The foxes have G3004
26 And he s unto them, Why are ye G3004
9: 6 forgive sins, (then s he to the sick of the G3004
9 of custom: and he s unto him, Follow G3004
28 to him: and Jesus s unto them, Believe G3004
37 Then s he unto his disciples, The G3004
12:13 Then s he to the man, Stretch forth G3004
44 Then he s, I will return into my house G3004
13:14 of Esaias, which s, By hearing ye shall G3004
51 Jesus s unto them, Have ye understood G3004
15:34 And Jesus s unto them, How many G3004
16:15 He s unto them, But whom say ye that I G3004
17:25 He s, Yes. And when he was come into G3004
26 Peter s unto him, Of strangers. Jesus G3004
26 s unto him, Then are the children free. G5346
18:22 Jesus s unto him, I say not unto thee, G3004
19: 8 He s unto them, Moses because of the G3004
18 He s unto him, Which? Jesus said, G3004
20 The young man s unto him, All these G3004
20: 6 standing idle, and s unto them, Why G3004
7 hath hired us. He s unto them, Go ye G3004
8 of the vineyard s unto his steward, Call G3004
21 wilt thou? She s unto him, Grant that G3004
23 And he s unto them, Ye shall drink G3004
21:16 say? And Jesus s unto them, Yea; have G3004
31 The first. Jesus s unto them, Verily I G3004
42 Jesus s unto them, Did ye never read in G3004
22: 8 Then s he to his servants, The wedding G3004
12 And he s unto him, Friend, how camest G3004
20 And he s unto them, Whose *is* this G3004
21 They say unto him, Caesar's. Then s he G3004
43 He s unto them, How then doth David G3004
26:18 him, The Master s, My time is at hand; G3004
31 Then s Jesus unto them, All ye shall be G3004
36 Gethsemane, and s unto the disciples, G3004
38 Then s he unto them, My soul is G3004
40 them asleep, and s unto Peter, What, G3004
45 Then cometh he to his disciples, and s G3004
64 Jesus s unto him, Thou hast said: G3004
27:22 Pilate s unto them, What shall I do G3004
Mk 1:41 and s unto him, I will; be thou clean. G3004
44 And s unto him, See thou say nothing G3004
2:10 sins, (he s to the sick of the palsy,) G3004
17 When Jesus heard *it*, he s unto them, G3004
3: 3 And he s unto the man which had the G3004
4 And he s unto them, Is it lawful to do G3004
5 of their hearts, he s unto the man, G3004
4:35 even was come, he s unto them, Let us G3004
5:19 Howbeit Jesus suffered him not, but s G3004
36 was spoken, he s unto the ruler of the G3004
39 And when he was come in, he s unto G3004
6:38 He s unto them, How many loaves G3004
50 with them, and s unto them, Be of good G3004
7:18 And he s unto them, Are ye so without G3004
34 he sighed, and s unto him, Ephphatha, G3004
8: 1 disciples *unto him*, and s unto them, G3004
12 in his spirit, and s, Why doth this G3004
17 And when Jesus knew *it*, he s unto G3004
29 And he s unto them, But whom say ye G3004
29 and s unto him, Thou art the Christ. G3004
9:19 He answereth him, and s, O faithless G3004
35 the twelve, and s unto them, If any G3004
10:11 And he s unto them, Whosoever shall G3004
23 And Jesus looked round about, and s G3004
24 again, and s unto them, Children, G3004
27 And Jesus looking upon them s, With G3004
42 But Jesus called them *to him*, and s G3004
11: 2 And s unto them, Go your way into the G3004
21 And Peter calling to remembrance s G3004
22 And Jesus answering s unto them, G3004
23 things which he s shall come to pass; G3004
Mk 11:23 to pass; he shall have whatsoever he s. G2036
33 Jesus answering s unto them, Neither G3004
12:16 And they brought *it*. And he s unto G3004
43 his disciples, and s unto them, Verily I G3004
13: 1 of his disciples s unto him, Master, see G3004
14:13 of his disciples, and s unto them, Go ye G3004
14 the house, The Master s, Where is the G3004
27 And Jesus s unto them, All ye shall be G3004
30 And Jesus s unto him, Verily I say unto G3004
32 and he s to his disciples, Sit ye G3004
34 And s unto them, My soul is exceeding G3004
37 sleeping, and s unto Peter, Simon, G3004
41 And he cometh the third time, and s G3004
45 and s, Master, master; and kissed him. G3004
63 s, What need we any further witnesses? G3004
15:28 And the scripture was fulfilled, which s, G3004
16: 6 And he s unto them, Be not affrighted: G3004
Lk 3:11 He answereth and s unto them, He that G3004
5:39 desireth new: for he s, The old is better. G3004
7:40 say unto thee. And he s, Master, say on. G5346
11:24 finding none, he s, I will return unto my G3004
16:29 Abraham s unto him, They have Moses G3004
18: 6 Lord said, Hear what the unjust judge s. G3004
19:22 And he s unto him, Out of thine own G3004
20:42 And David himself s in the book of G3004
22:11 house, The Master s unto thee, Where G3004
24:36 and s unto them, Peace *be* unto you. G3004
Jn 1:21 thou Elias? And he s, I am not. Art thou G3004
29 unto him, and s, Behold the Lamb of G3004
36 walked, he s, Behold the Lamb of God! G3004
38 following, and s unto them, What seek G3004
39 He s unto them, Come and see. They G3004
41 Simon, and s unto him, We have G3004
43 Philip, and s unto him, Follow me. G3004
45 Philip findeth Nathanael, and s unto G3004
46 Philip s unto him, Come and see. G3004
47 to him, and s of him, Behold an G3004
48 Nathanael s unto him, Whence G3004
49 Nathanael answered and s unto him, G3004
51 And he s unto him, Verily, verily, I say G3004
2: 3 of Jesus s unto him, They have no wine. G3004
4 Jesus s unto her, Woman, what have I G3004
5 His mother s unto the servants, G3004
5 Whatsoever he s unto you, do *it*. G3004
7 Jesus s unto them, Fill the waterpots G3004
8 And he s unto them, Draw out now, G3004
10 And s unto him, Every man at the G3004
3: 4 Nicodemus s unto him, How can a G3004
4: 7 Jesus s unto her, Give me to drink. G3004
9 Then s the woman of Samaria unto G3004
10 and who it is that s to thee, Give me to G3004
11 The woman s unto him, Sir, thou hast G3004
15 The woman s unto him, Sir, give me G3004
16 Jesus s unto her, Go, call thy husband, G3004
19 The woman s unto him, Sir, I perceive G3004
21 Jesus s unto her, Woman, believe me, G3004
25 The woman s unto him, I know that G3004
26 Jesus s unto her, I that speak unto thee G3004
28 her way into the city, and s to the men, G3004
34 Jesus s unto them, My meat is to do the G3004
49 The nobleman s unto him, Sir, come G3004
50 Jesus s unto him, Go thy way; thy son G3004
5: 6 s unto him, Wilt thou be made whole? G3004
8 Jesus s unto him, Rise, take up thy bed, G3004
6: 5 come unto him, he s unto Philip, G3004
8 Simon Peter's brother, s unto him, G3004
20 But he s unto them, It is I; be not G3004
42 that he s, I came down from heaven? G3004
7:50 Nicodemus s unto them, (he that came G3004
8:22 he s, Whither I go, ye cannot come. G3004
25 thou? And Jesus s unto them, Even *the* G2036
39 is our father. Jesus s unto them, If ye G3004
11: 7 Then after that s he to *his* disciples, Let G3004
11 he: and after that he s unto them, Our G3004
23 Jesus s unto her, Thy brother shall rise G3004
24 Martha s unto him, I know that he G3004
27 She s unto him, Yea, Lord: I believe G3004
39 that was dead, s unto him, Lord, by G3004
40 Jesus s unto her, Said I not unto thee, G3004
44 a napkin. Jesus s unto them, Loose G3004
12: 4 Then s one of his disciples, Judas G3004
13: 6 Peter: and Peter s unto him, Lord, dost G3004
8 Peter s unto him, Thou shalt never G3004
9 Simon Peter s unto him, Lord, not my G3004
10 Jesus s to him, He that is washed G3004
25 He then lying on Jesus' breast s unto G3004
14: 5 Thomas s unto him, Lord, we know not G3004
6 Jesus s unto him, I am the way, the G3004
8 Philip s unto him, Lord, shew us the G3004

Jn 14: 9 Jesus s unto him, Have I been so long G3004
22 Judas s unto him, not Iscariot, Lord, G3004
16:17 is this that he s unto us, A little while, G3004
18 What is this that he s, A little while? we G3004
18 A little while? we cannot tell what he s. G2980
18: 5 of Nazareth. Jesus s unto them, I am G3004
17 Then s the damsel that kept the door G3004
17 of this man's disciples? He s, I am not. G3004
26 ear Peter cut off, s, Did not I see thee in G3004
38 Pilate s unto him, What is truth? And G3004
38 unto the Jews, and s unto them, I find G3004
19: 4 Pilate therefore went forth again, and s G3004
5 *Pilate* s unto them, Behold the man! G3004
6 crucify *him*. Pilate s unto them, Take G3004
9 hall, and s unto Jesus, Whence G3004
10 Then s Pilate unto him, Speakest thou G3004
14 he s unto the Jews, Behold your King! G3004
15 crucify him. Pilate s unto them, Shall I G3004
24 be fulfilled, which s, They parted my G3004
26 whom he loved, he s unto his mother, G3004
27 Then s he to the disciple, Behold thy G3004
28 scripture might be fulfilled, s, I thirst. G3004
35 that he s true, that ye might believe. G3004
37 And again another scripture s, They G3004
20: 2 Jesus loved, and s unto them, They G3004
13 why weepest thou? She s unto them, G3004
15 Jesus s unto her, Woman, why weepest G3004
15 be the gardener, s unto him, Sir, if thou G3004
16 Jesus s unto her, Mary. She turned G3004
16 herself, and s unto him, Rabboni; G3004
17 Jesus s unto her, Touch me not; for I G3004
19 and s unto them, Peace *be* unto you. G3004
22 s unto them, Receive ye the Holy Ghost: G3004
27 Then s he to Thomas, Reach hither thy G3004
29 Jesus s unto him, Thomas, because G3004
21: 3 Simon Peter s unto them, I go a fishing. G3004
5 Then Jesus s unto them, Children, have G3004
7 whom Jesus loved s unto Peter, It is the G3004
10 Jesus s unto them, Bring of the fish G3004
12 Jesus s unto them, Come *and* dine. And G3004
15 So when they had dined, Jesus s to G3004
15 than these? He s unto him, Yea, Lord; G3004
15 thee. He s unto him, Feed my lambs. G3004
16 He s to him again the second time, G3004
16 thou me? He s unto him, Yea, Lord; G3004
16 thee. He s unto him, Feed my sheep. G3004
17 He s unto him the third time, Simon, G3004
17 thee. Jesus s unto him, Feed my sheep. G3004
19 spoken this, he s unto him, Follow me. G3004
21 Peter seeing him s to Jesus, Lord, and G3004
22 Jesus s unto him, If I will that he tarry G3004
Act 1: 4 Father, which, *s he*, ye have heard of me.
2:17 in the last days, s God, I will pour out G3004
34 the heavens: but he s himself, The G3004
7:48 made with hands; as s the prophet, G3004
49 will ye build me? s the Lord: or what *is* G3004
12: 8 so he did. And he s unto him, Cast thy G3004
13:35 Wherefore he s also in another *psalm*, G3004
15:17 s the Lord, who doeth all these things. G3004
21:11 and said, Thus s the Holy Ghost, So G3004
22: 2 they kept the more silence: and he s,) G5346
Ro 3:19 soever the law s, it saith to them who G3004
19 the law saith, it s to them who are G2980
4: 3 For what s the scripture? Abraham G3004
9:15 For he s to Moses, I will have mercy on G3004
17 For the scripture s unto Pharaoh, Even G3004
25 As he s also in Osee, I will call them my G3004
10: 8 But what s it? The word is nigh thee, G3004
11 For the scripture s, Whosoever G3004
16 s, Lord, who hath believed our report? G3004
19 know? First Moses s, I will provoke you G3004
20 But Esaias is very bold, and s, I was G3004
21 But to Israel he s, All day long I have G3004
11: 2 what the scripture s of Elias? how he G3004
4 But what s the answer of God unto G3004
9 And David s, Let their table be made a G3004
12:19 *is* mine; I will repay, s the Lord. G3004
14:11 For it is written, *As* I live, s the Lord, G3004
15:10 And again he s, Rejoice, ye Gentiles, G3004
12 And again, Esaias s, There shall be a G3004
1Co 1:12 Now this I say, that every one of you s, I G3004
3: 4 For while one s, I am of Paul; and G3004
6:16 body? for two, s he, shall be one flesh. G5346
9: 8 Say I these things as a man? or s not G3004
10 Or s he *it* altogether for our sakes? For G3004
14:21 that will they not hear me, s the Lord. G3004
34 be under obedience, as also s the law. G3004
15:27 feet. But when he s all things are put G2036
2Co 6: 2 (For he s, I have heard thee in a time G3004

2Co 6:17 be ye separate, s the Lord, and touch G3004
18 and daughters, s the Lord Almighty. G3004
Gal 3:16 made. He s not, And to seeds, as G3004
4:30 Nevertheless what s the scripture? Cast G3004
Eph 4: 8 Wherefore he s, When he ascended up G3004
5:14 Wherefore he s, Awake thou that G3004
1Ti 5:18 For the scripture s, Thou shalt not G3004
Heb 1: 6 into the world, he s, And let all the G3004
7 And of the angels he s, Who maketh his G3004
8 But unto the Son *he s*, Thy throne, O God,
3: 7 Wherefore (as the Holy Ghost s, To day G3004
5: 6 As he s also in another *place*, Thou *art* G3004
8: 5 for, See, s he, *that* thou make G5346
8 For finding fault with them, he s, G3004
8 the days come, s the Lord, when I will G3004
9 and I regarded them not, s the Lord. G3004
10 after those days, s the Lord; I will put G3004
13 In that he s, A new *covenant*, he hath G3004
10: 5 into the world, he s, Sacrifice and G3004
16 after those days, s the Lord, I will put G3004
30 me, I will recompense, s the Lord. And G3004
Jas 2:23 And the scripture was fulfilled which s, G3004
4: 5 Do ye think that the scripture s in vain, G3004
6 grace. Wherefore he s, God resisteth the G3004
1Jn 2: 4 He that s, I know him, and keepeth not G3004
6 He that s he abideth in him ought G3004
9 He that s he is in the light, and hateth G3004
Rev 1: 8 and the ending, s the Lord, which is, G3004
2: 1 These things s he that holdeth the G3004
7 what the Spirit s unto the churches; To G3004
8 These things s the first and the last, G3004
11 what the Spirit s unto the churches; He G3004
12 These things s he which hath the sharp G3004
17 what the Spirit s unto the churches; To G3004
18 These things s the Son of God, who G3004
29 what the Spirit s unto the churches. G3004
3: 1 These things s he that hath the seven G3004
6 what the Spirit s unto the churches. G3004
7 These things s he that is holy, he that G3004
13 what the Spirit s unto the churches. G3004
14 These things s the Amen, the faithful G3004
22 what the Spirit s unto the churches. G3004
5: 5 And one of the elders s unto me, Weep G3004
14:13 henceforth: Yea, s the Spirit, that they G3004
17:15 And he s unto me, The waters which G3004
18: 7 give her: for she s in her heart, I sit a G3004
19: 9 And he s unto me, Write, Blessed *are* G3004
9 the Lamb. And he s unto me, These are G3004
22: 9 Then s he unto me, See *thou do it* not: G3004
10 And he s unto me, Seal not the sayings G3004
20 He which testifieth these things s, G3004

SAKE

Gen 3:17 *is* the ground for thy s; in sorrow shalt H5668
8:21 more for man's s; for the imagination H5668
12:13 with me for thy s; and my soul shall live H5668
16 And he entreated Abram well for her s: H5668
18:29 And he said, I will not do *it* for forty's s. H5668
31 said, I will not destroy *it* for twenty's s. H5668
32 he said, I will not destroy *it* for ten's s. H5668
20:11 and they will slay me for my wife's s. H1697
26:24 thy seed for my servant Abraham's s. H5668
30:27 the LORD hath blessed me for thy s. H1558
39: 5 house for Joseph's s; and the blessing of H1558
Ex 18: 8 for Israel's s, *and* all the travail that H182
21:26 he shall let him go free for his eye's s. H8478
27 he shall let him go free for his tooth's s. H8478
Nu 11:29 thou for my s? would God that all the
25:11 zealous for my s among them, that I H7068
18 in the day of the plague for Peor's s. H1697
1Sa 12:22 for his great name's s: because it hath H5668
23:10 to Keilah, to destroy the city for my s. H5668
2Sa 5:12 his kingdom for his people Israel's s. H5668
7:21 For thy word's s, and according to thine H5668
9: 1 shew him kindness for Jonathan's s? H5668
7 thy father's s, and will restore thee H5668
18: 5 *Deal* gently for my s with the young
1Ki 8:41 out of a far country for thy name's s; H4616
11:12 for David thy father's s: *but* I will rend it H4616
13 my servant's s, and for Jerusalem's H4616
13 for Jerusalem's s which I have chosen. H4616
32 servant David's s, and for Jerusalem's H4616
32 for Jerusalem's s, the city which I have H4616
34 my servant's s, whom I chose, because H4616
15: 4 Nevertheless for David's s did the H4616
2Ki 8:19 his servant's s, as he promised him H4616
19:34 own s, and for my servant David's sake. H4616
34 own sake, and for my servant David's s. H4616
20: 6 own s, and for my servant David's sake. H4616

2Ki 20: 6 own sake, and for my servant David's s. H4616
1Ch 17:19 O LORD, for thy servant's s, and H4616
2Ch 6:32 for thy great name's s, and thy mighty H4616
Neh 9:31 Nevertheless for thy great mercies' s
Job 19:17 for the children's s of mine own body.
Ps 6: 4 my soul: oh save me for thy mercies' s.
23: 3 paths of righteousness for his name's s. H4616
25: 7 thou me for thy goodness' s, O LORD. H4616
11 For thy name's s, O LORD, pardon mine H4616
31: 3 thy name's s lead me, and guide me. H4616
16 thy servant: save me for thy mercies' s.
44:22 Yea, for thy s are we killed all the day
26 help, and redeem us for thy mercies' s. H4616
69: 6 be ashamed for my s: let not those that
6 be confounded for my s, O God of Israel.
7 Because for thy s I have borne reproach;
79: 9 purge away our sins, for thy name's s.
106: 8 for his name's s, that he might make H4616
109:21 for thy name's s: because thy mercy *is* H4616
115: 1 glory, for thy mercy, *and* for thy truth's s.
132:10 For thy servant David's s turn not away H5668
143:11 Quicken me, O LORD, for thy name's s:
11 s bring my soul out of trouble.
Isa 37:35 own s, and for my servant David's sake.
35 own sake, and for my servant David's s. H4616
42:21 his righteousness' s; he will magnify the H4616
43:14 One of Israel; For your s I have sent to H4616
25 own s, and will not remember thy sins. H4616
45: 4 For Jacob my servant's s, and Israel H4616
48: 9 For my name's s will I defer mine H4616
11 For mine own s, *even* for mine own H4616
11 *even* for mine own s, will I do *it*: for how H4616
54:15 together against thee shall fall for thy s. H4616
62: 1 For Zion's s will I not hold my peace, H4616
1 for Jerusalem's s I will not rest, until H4616
63:17 s, the tribes of thine inheritance. H4616
66: 5 out for my name's s, said, Let the LORD H4616
Jer 14: 7 *it* for thy name's s: for our backslidings H4616
21 Do not abhor *us*, for thy name's s, do H4616
15:15 that for thy s I have suffered rebuke.
Ezk 20: 9 But I wrought for my name's s, that it H4616
14 But I wrought for my name's s, that it H4616
22 for my name's s, that it should not be
44 you for my name's s, not according to
36:22 for mine holy name's s, which ye have
Dan 9:17 that is desolate, for the Lord's s. H4616
19 not, for thine own s, O my God: for thy H4616
Jna 1:12 for my s this great tempest *is* upon you. H7945
Mic 3:12 Therefore shall Zion for your s be H1558
Mt 5:10 s: for theirs is the kingdom of heaven. G1752
11 of evil against you falsely, for my s. G1752
10:18 and kings for my s, for a testimony G1752
22 for my name's s: but he that endureth G1223
39 that loseth his life for my s shall find it. G1752
14: 3 Herodias' s, his brother Philip's wife. G1223
9 for the oath's s, and them which sat G1223
16:25 will lose his life for my s shall find it. G1752
19:12 of heaven's s. He that is able to receive G1223
29 lands, for my name's s, shall receive an G1752
24: 9 be hated of all nations for my name's s. G1223
22 elect's s those days shall be shortened. G1223
Mk 4:17 s, immediately they are offended. G1223
6:17 for Herodias' s, his brother Philip's G1223
26 *yet* for his oath's s, and for their sakes G1223
8:35 lose his life for my s and the gospel's, G1752
10:29 or lands, for my s, and the gospel's, G1752
13: 9 for my s, for a testimony against them. G1752
13 *men* for my name's s: but he that shall G1223
20 but for the elect's s, whom he hath G1223
Lk 6:22 name as evil, for the Son of man's s. G1752
9:24 his life for my s, the same shall save it. G1752
18:29 or children, for the kingdom of God's s, G1752
21:12 before kings and rulers for my name's s. G1752
17 be hated of all *men* for my name's s. G1223
Jn 12: 9 came not for Jesus' s only, but that they G1223
13:37 now? I will lay down my life for thy s. G5228
38 thy life for my s? Verily, verily, I say G5228
14:11 or else believe me for the very works' s. G1223
15:21 unto you for my name's s, because they G1223
Act 9:16 things he must suffer for my name's s. G5228
26: 7 For which hope's s, king Agrippa, I am G1680
Ro 4:23 Now it was not written for his s alone, G1223
8:36 As it is written, For thy s we are killed G1752
13: 5 for wrath, but also for conscience s. G1223
15:30 Lord Jesus Christ's s, and for the love of G1223
1Co 4:10 We *are* fools for Christ's s, but ye *are* G1223
9:23 And this I do for the gospel's s, that I G1223
10:25 asking no question for conscience s: G1223
27 asking no question for conscience s. G1223

1Co 10:28 eat not for his s that shewed it, and *G1223*
28 and for conscience s: for the earth *is* the
2Co 4: 5 and ourselves your servants for Jesus' s. *G1223*
11 death for Jesus' s, that the life also of *G1223*
12:10 for Christ's s: for when I am weak, *G5228*
Eph 4:32 as God for Christ's s hath forgiven you. *G1722*
Php 1:29 on him, but also to suffer for his s; *G5228*
Col 1:24 for his body's s, which is the church: *G5228*
3: 6 For which things' s the wrath of God *G1223*
1Th 1: 5 of men we were among you for your s. *G1223*
5:13 s. *And* be at peace among yourselves. *G1223*
1Ti 5:23 stomach's s and thine often infirmities. *G1223*
Tit 1:11 which they ought not, for filthy lucre's s. *G5484*
Phlm 9 Yet for love's s I rather beseech *thee*, *G1223*
1Pt 2:13 s: whether it be to the king, as supreme; *G1223*
3:14 But and if ye suffer for righteousness' s, *G1223*
1Jn 2:12 sins are forgiven you for his name's s. *G1223*
2Jn 2 For the truth's s, which dwelleth in us, *G1223*
3Jn 7 Because that for his name's s they went *G5228*
Rev 2: 3 s hast laboured, and hast not fainted. *G1223*

SAKES
Gen 18:26 then I will spare all the place for their s. H5668
Lev 26:45 But I will for their s remember the
Dt 1:37 with me for your s, saying, Thou also H1558
3:26 with me for your s, and would not hear H6616
4:21 with me for your s, and sware that I H1697
Jdg 21:22 unto them for our s: because we reserved
Ru 1:13 me much for your s that the hand of the
1Ch 16:21 yea, he reproved kings for their s, H5921
Ps 7: 7 their s therefore return thou on high. H5921
105:14 yea, he reproved kings for their s; H5921
106:32 so that it went ill with Moses for their s:
122: 8 For my brethren and companions' s, I H6616
Isa 65: 8 s, that I may not destroy them all. H6616
Ezk 36:22 do not *this* for your s, O house of Israel, H6616
32 Not for your s do I *this*, saith the Lord H6616
Dan 2:30 but for *their* s that shall make known H1701
Mal 3:11 And I will rebuke the devourer for your s,
Mk 6:26 sake, and for their s which sat with him,
Jn 11:15 And I am glad for your s that I was not *G1223*
12:30 came not because of me, but for your s. *G1223*
17:19 And for their s I sanctify myself, that *G5228*
Ro 11:28 enemies for your s: but as touching the *G1223*
28 *they are* beloved for the fathers' s. *G1223*
1Co 4: 6 Apollos for your s; that ye might learn *G1223*
9:10 Or saith he *it* altogether for our s? For *G1223*
10 our sakes? For our s, no doubt, *this* is *G1223*
2Co 2:10 s *forgave I it* in the person of Christ; *G1223*
4:15 For all things *are* for your s, that the *G1223*
8: 9 rich, yet for your s he became poor, *G1223*
1Th 3: 9 we joy for your s before our God; *G1223*
2Ti 2:10 for the elect's s, that they may also *G1223*

SALA
Lk 3:35 *son* of Heber, which was *the son* of S, *G4527*

SALAH
Gen 10:24 And Arphaxad begat S; and Salah begat H7974
24 And Arphaxad begat Salah; and S H7974
11:12 lived five and thirty years, and begat S: H7974
13 And Arphaxad lived after he begat S H7974
14 And S lived thirty years, and begat H7974
15 And S lived after he begat Eber four H7974

SALAMIS
Act 13: 5 And when they were at S, they preached *G4529*

SALATHIEL
1Ch 3:17 And the sons of Jeconiah; Assir, S his H7597
Mt 1:12 begat S; and Salathiel begat Zorobabel; *G4528*
12 begat Salathiel; and S begat Zorobabel; *G4528*
Lk 3:27 *the son* of S, which was *the son* of Neri, *G4528*

SALCAH
Jos 12: 5 Hermon, and in S, and in all Bashan, H5548
13:11 mount Hermon, and all Bashan unto S; H5548

SALCHAH
Dt 3:10 all Bashan, unto S and Edrei, cities of H5548
1Ch 5:11 them, in the land of Bashan unto S: H5548

SALE
Lev 25:27 Then let him count the years of the s H4465
50 and the price of his s shall be according H4465
Dt 18: 8 cometh of the s of his patrimony. H4465

SALEM
Gen 14:18 And Melchizedek king of S brought H8004
Ps 76: 2 In S also is his tabernacle, and his H8004
Heb 7: 1 For this Melchisedec, king of S, priest of *G4532*
2 also King of S, which is, King of peace; *G4532*

SALIM
Jn 3:23 in Aenon near to S, because there was *G4530*

SALLAI
Neh 11: 8 And after him Gabbai, S, nine hundred H5543
12:20 Of S, Kallai; of Amok, Eber; H5543

SALLU
1Ch 9: 7 And of the sons of Benjamin; S the son H5543
Neh 11: 7 And these *are* the sons of Benjamin; S H5543
12: 7 S, Amok, Hilkiah, Jedaiah. These *were* H5543

SALMA
1Ch 2:11 And Nahshon begat S, and Salma begat H8007
11 And Nahshon begat Salma, and S H8007
51 S the father of Beth-lehem, Hareph the H8007
54 The sons of S; Beth-lehem, and the H8007

SALMON
Ru 4:20 begat Nahshon, and Nahshon begat S, H8009
21 And S begat Boaz, and Boaz begat H8012
Ps 68:14 kings in it, it was *white* as snow in S. H6756
Mt 1: 4 begat Naasson; and Naasson begat S; *G4533*
5 And S begat Booz of Rachab; and Booz *G4533*
Lk 3:32 *son* of S, which was *the son* of Naasson, *G4533*

SALMONE
Act 27: 7 we sailed under Crete, over against S; *G4534*

SALOME
Mk 15:40 of James the less and of Joses, and S; *G4539*
16: 1 of James, and S, had bought sweet *G4539*

SALT
Gen 14: 3 the vale of Siddim, which is the s sea. H4417
19:26 him, and she became a pillar of s. H4417
Lev 2:13 thou season with s; neither shalt thou H4417
13 thou suffer the s of the covenant of thy H4417
13 all thine offerings thou shalt offer s. H4417
Nu 18:19 it *is* a covenant of s for ever before the H4417
34: 3 outmost coast of the s sea eastward: H4417
12 of it shall be at the s sea: this shall be H4417
Dt 3:17 s sea, under Ashdoth-pisgah eastward. H4417
29:23 *is* brimstone, and s, *and* burning, *that* it H4417
Jos 3:16 of the plain, *even* the s sea, failed, *and* H4417
12: 3 the plain, *even* the s sea on the east, the H4417
15: 2 the shore of the s sea, from the bay that H4417
5 And the east border *was* the s sea, *even* H4417
62 And Nibshan, and the city of S, and H5898
18:19 north bay of the s sea at the south end H4417
Jdg 9:45 beat down the city, and sowed it with s. H4417
2Sa 8:13 of s, *being* eighteen thousand *men*. H4417
2Ki 2:20 s therein. And they brought *it* to him. H4417
21 and cast the s in there, and said, Thus H4417
14: 7 He slew of Edom in the valley of s ten H4417
1Ch 18:12 in the valley of s eighteen thousand. H4417
2Ch 13: 5 him and to his sons by a covenant of s? H4417
25:11 went to the valley of s, and smote of the H4417
Ezr 6: 9 God of heaven, wheat, s, wine, and oil, H4416
7:22 and s without prescribing *how much*. H4416
Job 6: 6 be eaten without s? or is there *any* taste H4417
Ps 60: ttl in the valley of s twelve thousand. H4417
Jer 17: 6 *in* a s land and not inhabited. H4420
Ezk 43:24 priests shall cast s upon them, and they H4417
47:11 not be healed; they shall be given to s. H4417
Mt 5:13 Ye are the s of the earth: but if the salt *G217*
13 Ye are the salt of the earth: but if the s *G217*
Mk 9:49 and every sacrifice shall be salted with s. *G251*
50 S *is* good: but if the salt have lost his *G217*
50 Salt *is* good: but if the s have lost his *G217*
50 ye season it? Have s in yourselves, and *G217*
Lk 14:34 S *is* good: but if the salt have lost his *G217*
34 Salt *is* good: but if the s have lost his *G217*
Col 4: 6 seasoned with s, that ye may know how *G217*
Jas 3:12 no fountain both yield s water and fresh. *G252*

SALTED
Ezk 16: 4 wast not s at all, nor swaddled at all. H4414
Mt 5:13 shall it be s? it is thenceforth good *G233*
Mk 9:49 For every one shall be s with fire, and *G233*
49 and every sacrifice shall be s with salt. *G233*

SALTNESS
Mk 9:50 salt have lost his s, wherewith will ye *G1096*

SALTPITS
Zep 2: 9 of nettles, and s, and a perpetual H4417

SALT-SEA See SALT and SEA.

SALU
Nu 25:14 Zimri, the son of S, a prince of a chief H5543

SALUTATION
Lk 1:29 mind what manner of s this should be. *G783*
41 heard the s of Mary, the babe leaped *G783*
44 For, lo, as soon as the voice of thy s *G783*
1Co 16:21 The s of *me* Paul with mine own hand. *G783*
Col 4:18 The s by the hand of me Paul. *G783*
2Th 3:17 The s of Paul with mine own hand, *G783*

SALUTATIONS
Mk 12:38 clothing, and *love* s in the marketplaces, *G783*

SALUTE
1Sa 10: 4 And they will s thee, and give thee two H7965
13:10 out to meet him, that he might s him. H1288
25:14 to s our master; and he railed on them. H1288
2Sa 8:10 king David, to s him, and to H7592+H7965
2Ki 4:29 meet any man, s him not; and if any H1288
29 not; and if any s thee, answer him not H1288
10:13 and we go down to s the children of the H7965
Mt 5:47 And if ye s your brethren only, what do *G782*
10:12 And when ye come into an house, s it. *G782*
Mk 15:18 And began to s him, Hail, King of the *G782*
Lk 10: 4 nor shoes: and s no man by the way. *G782*
Act 25:13 Bernice came unto Caesarea to s Festus. *G782*
Ro 16: 5 that is in their house. S my well beloved *G782*
7 S Andronicus and Junia, my kinsmen, *G782*
9 S Urbane, our helper in Christ, and *G782*
10 S Apelles approved in Christ. Salute *G782*
10 Salute Apelles approved in Christ. S *G782*
11 S Herodion my kinsman. Greet them *G782*
12 S Tryphena and Tryphosa, who labour *G782*
12 labour in the Lord. S the beloved Persis, *G782*
13 S Rufus chosen in the Lord, and his *G782*
14 S Asyncritus, Phlegon, Hermas, *G782*
15 S Philologus, and Julia, Nereus, and his *G782*
16 S one another with an holy kiss. The *G782*
16 holy kiss. The churches of Christ s you. *G782*
21 and Sosipater, my kinsmen, s you. *G782*
22 I Tertius, who wrote *this* epistle, s you in *G782*
1Co 16:19 The churches of Asia s you. Aquila and *G782*
19 and Priscilla s you much in the Lord, *G782*
2Co 13:13 All the saints s you. *G782*
Php 4:21 S every saint in Christ Jesus. The *G782*
22 All the saints s you, chiefly they that are *G782*
Col 4:15 S the brethren which are in Laodicea, *G782*
2Ti 4:19 S Prisca and Aquila, and the household *G782*
Tit 3:15 All that are with me s thee. Greet them *G782*
Phlm 23 There s thee Epaphras, my *G782*
Heb 13:24 S all them that have the rule over you, *G782*
24 and all the saints. They of Italy s you. *G782*
3Jn 14 s thee. Greet the friends by name. *G782*

SALUTED
Jdg 18:15 the house of Micah, and s him. H7592+H7965
1Sa 17:22 and came and s his brethren. H7592+H7965
30:21 near to the people, he s them. H7592+H7965
2Ki 10:15 to meet him: and he s him, and said to H1288
Mk 9:15 amazed, and running to *him* s him. *G782*
Lk 1:40 the house of Zacharias, and s Elisabeth. *G782*
Act 18:22 s the church, he went down to Antioch. *G782*
21: 7 to Ptolemais, and s the brethren, and *G782*
19 And when he had s them, he declared *G782*

SALUTETH
Ro 16:23 of the whole church, s you. Erastus the *G782*
23 of the city s you, and Quartus a brother. *G782*
Col 4:10 Aristarchus my fellowprisoner s you, *G782*
12 you, a servant of Christ, s you, always *G782*
1Pt 5:13 *you*, s you; and *so doth* Marcus my son. *G782*

SALVATION
Gen 49:18 I have waited for thy s, O LORD. H3444
Ex 14:13 still, and see the s of the LORD, which H3444
15: 2 he is become my s: he *is* my God, and I H3444
Dt 32:15 and lightly esteemed the Rock of his s. H3444
1Sa 2: 1 enemies; because I rejoice in thy s. H3444
11:13 day the LORD hath wrought s in Israel. H8668
14:45 hath wrought this great s in Israel? God H3444
19: 5 wrought a great s for all Israel: thou H8668
2Sa 22: 3 the horn of my s, my high tower, and H3468
36 the shield of thy s: and thy gentleness H3468

2Sa 22:47 exalted be the God of the rock of my s. H3468
51 *He is* the tower of s for his king: and H3444
23: 5 for *this is* all my s, and all *my* desire, H3468
1Ch 16:23 earth; shew forth from day to day his s. H3444
35 And say ye, Save us, O God of our s, and H3468
2Ch 6:41 s, and let thy saints rejoice in goodness. H8668
20:17 ye *still*, and see the s of the LORD with H3444
Job 13:16 He also *shall be* my s: for an hypocrite H3444
Ps 3: 8 S *belongeth* unto the LORD: thy H3444
9:14 daughter of Zion: I will rejoice in thy s. H3444
13: 5 mercy; my heart shall rejoice in thy s. H3444
14: 7 Oh that the s of Israel *were come* out of H3444
18: 2 the horn of my s, *and* my high tower. H3468
35 the shield of thy s: and thy right hand H3468
46 and let the God of my s be exalted. H3468
20: 5 We will rejoice in thy s, and in the name H3444
21: 1 in thy s how greatly shall he rejoice! H3444
5 His glory *is* great in thy s: honour and H3444
24: 5 righteousness from the God of his s. H3468
25: 5 of my s; on thee do I wait all the day. H3468
27: 1 The LORD *is* my light and my s; whom H3468
9 not, neither forsake me, O God of my s. H3468
35: 3 me: say unto my soul, I *am* thy s. H3444
9 in the LORD: it shall rejoice in his s. H3444
37:39 But the s of the righteous *is* of the H8668
38:22 Make haste to help me, O Lord my s. H8668
40:10 and thy s: I have not concealed H8668
16 such as love thy s say continually, The H8668
50:23 *aright* will I shew the s of God. H3468
51:12 Restore unto me the joy of thy s; and H3468
14 thou God of my s: *and* my tongue shall H8668
53: 6 Oh that the s of Israel *were come* out of H3444
62: 1 upon God: from him *cometh* my s. H3444
2 He only *is* my rock and my s; *he is* my H3444
6 He only *is* my rock and my s: *he is* my H3444
7 In God *is* my s and my glory: the rock H3468
65: 5 answer us, O God of our s; *who art* the H3468
68:19 *benefits, even* the God of our s. Selah. H3444
20 *He that is* our God *is* the God of s; and H4190
69:13 thy mercy hear me, in the truth of thy s. H3468
29 But I *am* poor and sorrowful: let thy s, H3444
70: 4 such as love thy s say continually, Let H3444
71:15 *and* thy s all the day; for I know H8668
74:12 For God *is* my King of old, working s in H3444
78:22 not in God, and trusted not in his s: H3444
79: 9 Help us, O God of our s, for the glory of H3468
85: 4 Turn us, O God of our s, and cause H3468
7 thy mercy, O LORD, and grant us thy s. H3468
9 Surely his s *is* nigh them that fear him; H3468
88: 1 O LORD God of my s, I have cried day H3444
89:26 father, my God, and the rock of my s. H3444
91:16 will I satisfy him, and shew him my s. H3444
95: 1 make a joyful noise to the rock of our s. H3468
96: 2 shew forth his s from day to day. H3444
98: 2 The LORD hath made known his s: his H3444
3 of the earth have seen the s of our God. H3444
106: 4 *unto* thy people: O visit me with thy s; H3444
116:13 I will take the cup of s, and call upon H3444
118:14 strength and song, and is become my s. H3444
15 The voice of rejoicing and s *is* in the H3444
21 hast heard me, and art become my s. H3444
119:41 *even* thy s, according to thy word. H8668
81 My soul fainteth for thy s: *but* I hope in H8668
123 Mine eyes fail for thy s, and for the H3444
155 S *is* far from the wicked: for they seek H3444
166 LORD, I have hoped for thy s, and done H3444
174 I have longed for thy s, O LORD; and H3444
132:16 I will also clothe her priests with s: and H3468
140: 7 O GOD the Lord, the strength of my s, H3444
144:10 *It is he* that giveth s unto kings: who H8668
149: 4 people: he will beautify the meek with s. H3444
Isa 12: 2 Behold, God *is* my s; I will trust, and not H3444
2 and *my* song; he also is become my s. H3444
3 shall ye draw water out of the wells of s. H3444
17:10 the God of thy s, and hast not been H3468
25: 9 him, we will be glad and rejoice in his s. H3444
26: 1 have a strong city; s will *God* appoint H3444
33: 2 our s also in the time of trouble. H3444
6 s: the fear of the LORD *is* his treasure. H3444
45: 8 let them bring forth s, and let H3468
17 with an everlasting s: ye shall not be H8668
46:13 be far off, and my s shall not tarry: and H8668
13 will place s in Zion for Israel my glory. H8668
49: 6 be my s unto the end of the earth. H3444
8 and in a day of s have I helped thee: H3444
51: 5 My righteousness *is* near; my s is gone H3468
6 manner: but my s shall be for ever, and H3444
8 my s from generation to generation. H3444
52: 7 that publisheth s; that saith unto Zion, H3444

Isa 52:10 of the earth shall see the s of our God. H3444
56: 1 do justice: for my s *is* near to come, H3444
59:11 *is* none; for s, *but* it is far off from us. H3444
16 his arm brought s unto him; and his H3467
17 and an helmet of s upon his head; and H3444
60:18 call thy walls S, and thy gates Praise. H3444
61:10 the garments of s, he hath covered me H3468
62: 1 the s thereof as a lamp *that* burneth. H3444
11 Zion, Behold, thy s cometh; behold, his H3468
63: 5 s unto me; and my fury, it upheld me. H3467
Jer 3:23 Truly in vain *is s hoped for* from the
23 in the LORD our God *is* the s of Israel. H8668
Lam 3:26 and quietly wait for the s of the LORD. H8668
Jna 2: 9 that I have vowed. S *is* of the LORD. H3444
Mic 7: 7 the God of my s: my God will hear me. H3468
Hab 3: 8 upon thine horses *and* thy chariots of s? H3444
13 Thou wentest forth for the s of thy H3468
13 people, *even* for s with thine anointed; H3468
18 the LORD, I will joy in the God of my s. H3468
Zec 9: 9 *is* just, and having s; lowly, and riding H3467
Lk 1:69 And hath raised up an horn of s for us *G4991*
77 To give knowledge of s unto his people *G4991*
2:30 For mine eyes have seen thy s, *G4992*
3: 6 And all flesh shall see the s of God. *G4992*
19: 9 And Jesus said unto him, This day is s *G4991*
Jn 4:22 what we worship: for s is of the Jews. *G4991*
Act 4:12 Neither is there s in any other: for there *G4991*
13:26 God, to you is the word of this s sent. *G4991*
47 be for s unto the ends of the earth. *G4991*
16:17 God, which shew unto us the way of s. *G4991*
28:28 unto you, that the s of God is sent unto *G4992*
Ro 1:16 power of God unto s to every one that *G4991*
10:10 the mouth confession is made unto s. *G4991*
11:11 through their fall s *is come* unto the *G4991*
13:11 *is* our s nearer than when we believed. *G4991*
2Co 1: 6 consolation and s, which is effectual in *G4991*
6 *it is* for your consolation and s. *G4991*
6: 2 and in the day of s have I succoured *G4991*
2 time; behold, now *is* the day of s.) *G4991*
7:10 repentance to s not to be repented of: *G4991*
Eph 1:13 the gospel of your s: in whom also after *G4991*
6:17 And take the helmet of s, and the sword *G4992*
Php 1:19 For I know that this shall turn to my s *G4991*
28 but to you of s, and that of God. *G4991*
2:12 your own s with fear and trembling. *G4991*
1Th 5: 8 love; and for an helmet, the hope of s. *G4991*
9 to obtain s by our Lord Jesus Christ, *G4991*
2Th 2:13 chosen you to s through sanctification *G4991*
2Ti 2:10 may also obtain the s which is in Christ *G4991*
3:15 s through faith which is in Christ Jesus. *G4991*
Tit 2:11 For the grace of God that bringeth s *G4992*
Heb 1:14 for them who shall be heirs of s? *G4991*
2: 3 we neglect so great s; which at the first *G4991*
10 of their s perfect through sufferings. *G4991*
5: 9 eternal s unto all them that obey him; *G4991*
6: 9 accompany s, though we thus speak. *G4991*
9:28 the second time without sin unto s. *G4991*
1Pt 1: 5 s ready to be revealed in the last time. *G4991*
9 of your faith, *even* the s of *your* souls. *G4991*
10 Of which s the prophets have inquired *G4991*
2Pt 3:15 of our Lord *is* s; even as our beloved *G4991*
Jude 3 of the common s, it was needful for me *G4991*
Rev 7:10 And cried with a loud voice, saying, S *G4991*
12:10 Now is come s, and strength, and the *G4991*
19: 1 saying, Alleluia; S, and glory, and *G4991*

SAMARIA

1Ki 13:32 the cities of S, shall surely come to pass. H8111
16:24 And he bought the hill S of Shemer for H8111
24 name of Shemer, owner of the hill, S. H8111
28 and was buried in S: and Ahab his son H8111
29 over Israel in S twenty and two years. H8111
32 house of Baal, which he had built in S. H8111
18: 2 Ahab. And *there was* a sore famine in S. H8111
20: 1 and besieged S, and warred against it. H8111
10 also, if the dust of S shall suffice for H8111
17 saying, There are men come out of S. H8111
34 my father made in S. Then *said Ahab*, I H8111
43 heavy and displeased, and came to S. H8111
21: 1 hard by the palace of Ahab king of S. H8111
18 Israel, which *is* in S: behold, *he is* in the H8111
22:10 of the gate of S; and all the prophets H8111
37 So the king died, and was brought to S; H8111
37 Samaria; and they buried the king in S. H8111
38 in the pool of S; and the dogs licked H8111
51 over Israel in S the seventeenth year H8111
2Ki 1: 2 that *was* in S, and was sick: and he H8111
3 of the king of S, and say unto them, H8111
2:25 and from thence he returned to S. H8111

2Ki 3: 1 over Israel in S the eighteenth year H8111
6 And king Jehoram went out of S the H8111
5: 3 the prophet that *is* in S! for he would H8111
6:19 whom ye seek. But he led them to S. H8111
20 they were come into S, that Elisha said, H8111
20 and, behold, *they were* in the midst of S. H8111
24 his host, and went up, and besieged S. H8111
25 And there was a great famine in S: and, H8111
7: 1 of barley for a shekel, in the gate of S. H8111
18 morrow about this time in the gate of S: H8111
10: 1 And Ahab had seventy sons in S. And H8111
1 letters, and sent to S, unto the rulers of H8111
12 and came to S. *And* as he *was* at the H8111
17 And when he came to S, he slew all that H8111
17 unto Ahab in S, till he had destroyed H8111
35 they buried him in S. And Jehoahaz his H8111
36 Israel in S *was* twenty and eight years. H8111
13: 1 Israel in S, *and reigned* seventeen years. H8111
6 and there remained the grove also in S.) H8111
9 they buried him in S: and Joash his son H8111
10 Israel in S, *and reigned* sixteen years. H8111
13 was buried in S with the kings of Israel. H8111
14:14 house, and hostages, and returned to S. H8111
16 and was buried in S with the kings of H8111
23 in S, *and reigned* forty and one years. H8111
15: 8 reign over Israel in S six months. H8111
13 Judah; and he reigned a full month in S. H8111
14 and came to S, and smote Shallum H8111
14 son of Jabesh in S, and slew him, and H8111
17 over Israel, *and reigned* ten years in S. H8111
23 over Israel in S, *and reigned* two years. H8111
25 and smote him in S, in the palace of the H8111
27 Israel in S, *and reigned* twenty years. H8111
17: 1 to reign in S over Israel nine years. H8111
5 up to S, and besieged it three years. H8111
6 of Assyria took S, and carried Israel H8111
24 in the cities of S instead of the children H8111
24 S, and dwelt in the cities thereof. H8111
26 in the cities of S, know not the manner H8111
28 carried away from S came and dwelt in H8111
18: 9 came up against S, and besieged it. H8111
10 of Hoshea king of Israel, S was taken. H8111
34 they delivered S out of mine hand? H8111
21:13 the line of S, and the plummet of H8111
23:18 bones of the prophet that came out of S. H8111
19 in the cities of S, which the kings of H8111
2Ch 18: 2 down to Ahab to S. And Ahab killed H8111
9 in of the gate of S; and all the prophets H8111
22: 9 (for he was hid in S,) and brought him to H8111
25:13 of Judah, from S even unto Beth-horon, H8111
24 the hostages also, and returned to S. H8111
28: 8 from them, and brought the spoil to S. H8111
9 the host that came to S, and said unto H8111
15 their brethren: then they returned to S. H8111
Ezr 4:10 set in the cities of S, and the rest *that* H8115
17 that dwell in S, and *unto* the rest H8115
Neh 4: 2 and the army of S, and said, What do H8111
Isa 7: 9 And the head of Ephraim *is* S, and the H8111
9 and the head of S *is* Remaliah's son. If H8111
8: 4 and the spoil of S shall be taken away H8111
9: 9 the inhabitant of S, that say in the pride H8111
10: 9 as Arpad? *is* not S as Damascus? H8111
10 did excel them of Jerusalem and of S; H8111
11 Shall I not, as I have done unto S and H8111
36:19 have they delivered S out of my hand? H8111
Jer 23:13 in the prophets of S; they prophesied in H8111
31: 5 the mountains of S: the planters shall H8111
41: 5 Shiloh, and from S, *even* fourscore men, H8111
Ezk 16:46 And thine elder sister *is* S, she and her H8111
51 Neither hath S committed half of thy H8111
53 the captivity of S and her daughters, H8111
55 former estate, and S and her daughters H8111
23: 4 S *is* Aholah, and Jerusalem Aholibah. H8111
33 desolation, with the cup of thy sister S. H8111
Hos 7: 1 the wickedness of S: for they commit H8111
8: 5 Thy calf, O S, hath cast *thee* off; mine H8111
6 the calf of S shall be broken in pieces. H8111
10: 5 The inhabitants of S shall fear because H8111
7 *As for* S, her king is cut off as the foam H8111
13:16 S shall become desolate; for she hath H8111
Am 3: 9 the mountains of S, and behold the H8111
12 out that dwell in S in the corner of a H8111
4: 1 in the mountain of S, which oppress the H8111
6: 1 in the mountain of S, *which are* named H8111
8:14 They that swear by the sin of S, and say, H8111
Oba 19 S: and Benjamin *shall possess* Gilead. H8111
Mic 1: 1 he saw concerning S and Jerusalem. H8111
5 of Jacob? *is it* not S? and what *are* the H8111
6 Therefore I will make S as an heap of H8111

Lk 17:11 through the midst of S and Galilee. *G4540*
Jn 4: 4 And he must needs go through S. *G4540*
5 Then cometh he to a city of S, which is *G4540*
7 There cometh a woman of S to draw *G4540*
9 Then saith the woman of S unto him, *G4542*
9 am a woman of S? for the Jews have no *G4542*
Act 1: 8 in all Judaea, and in S, and unto the *G4540*
8: 1 of Judaea and S, except the apostles. *G4540*
5 Then Philip went down to the city of S, *G4540*
9 the people of S, giving out that himself *G4540*
14 heard that S had received the word *G4540*
9:31 and Galilee and S, and were edified; *G4540*
15: 3 Phenice and S, declaring the conversion *G4540*

SAMARITAN

Lk 10:33 But a certain S, as he journeyed, came *G4541*
17:16 feet, giving him thanks: and he was a S. *G4541*
Jn 8:48 well that thou art a S, and hast a devil? *G4541*

SAMARITANS

2Ki 17:29 places which the S had made, every H8118
Mt 10: 5 and into *any* city of the S enter ye not: *G4541*
Lk 9:52 village of the S, to make ready for him. *G4541*
Jn 4: 9 for the Jews have no dealings with the S. *G4541*
39 And many of the S of that city believed *G4541*
40 So when the S were come unto him, *G4541*
Act 8:25 the gospel in many villages of the S. *G4541*

SAME

Gen 2:13 second river *is* Gihon: the s *is* it that H1931
5:29 Noah, saying, This s shall comfort us
6: 4 to them, the s *became* mighty men H1992
7:11 day of the month, the s day were all the H2088
10:12 Nineveh and Calah: the s *is* a great city. H1931
14: 8 king of Bela (the s *is* Zoar;) and they H1931
15:18 In the s day the LORD made a H1931
19:37 name Moab: the s *is* the father of the H1931
38 Ben-ammi: the s *is* the father of the H1931
21: 8 feast the s day that Isaac was weaned.
23: 2 And Sarah died in Kirjath-arba; the s *is*
19 the s *is* Hebron in the land of Canaan.
24:14 drink also: *let the* s *be* she *that* thou hast
44 for thy camels: *let the* s *be* the woman
25:30 thee, with that s red *pottage;* for I *am* H122
26:12 received in the s year an hundredfold: H1931
24 unto him the s night, and said, I *am* H1931
32 And it came to pass the s day, that H1931
32:13 And he lodged there that s night; and
41:48 about every city, laid he up in the s. H8432
44: 6 and he spake unto them these s words. H428
48: 7 way of Ephrath; the s *is* Beth-lehem. H1931
Ex 5: 6 And Pharaoh commanded the s day H1931
12: 6 day of the s month: and the whole H2088
19: 1 land of Egypt, the s day came they *into*
25:31 knops, and his flowers, shall be of the s.
35 branches of the s, and a knop under two
35 branches of the s, and a knop under two
35 branches of the s, according to the six
36 shall be of the s: all it *shall be* one beaten
27: 2 s: and thou shalt overlay it with brass.
28: 8 it, shall be of the s, according to the work
30: 2 the horns thereof *shall be* of the s.
37:17 his knops, and his flowers, were of the s:
21 And a knop under two branches of the s,
21 branches of the s, and a knop under two
21 branches of the s, according to the six
22 were of the s: all of it *was* one beaten
25 of it; the horns thereof were of the s.
38: 2 of the s: and he overlaid it with brass.
39: 5 upon it, *was* of the s, according to the
Lev 7:15 shall be eaten the s day that it is offered;
16 it shall be eaten the s day that he
19: 6 It shall be eaten the s day ye offer it, H3117
22:30 On the s day it shall be eaten up; ye H1931
23: 6 And on the fifteenth day of the s month H2088
28 And ye shall do no work in that s day: H6106
29 be afflicted in that s day, he shall be cut H6106
30 any work in that s day, the same soul H6106
30 that same day, the s soul will I destroy H6106
Nu 4: 8 and cover the s with a covering of
6:11 and shall hallow his head that s day. H1931
9:13 passover, even the s soul shall be cut H1931
10:32 do unto us, the s will we do unto thee.
15:30 or a stranger, the s reproacheth the H1931
32:10 the s time, and he sware, saying, H1931
Dt 9:20 and I prayed for Aaron also the s time. H1931
14:28 thine increase the s year, and shalt lay H1931
27:11 And Moses charged the people the s H1931
31:22 Moses therefore wrote this song the s H1931

Jos 6:15 the city after the s manner seven times: H2088
11:16 of Israel, and the valley of the s;
15: 8 of the Jebusite; the s *is* Jerusalem: and H1931
Jdg 6:25 And it came to pass the s night, that H1931
7: 4 go with thee, the s shall go with thee; H1931
4 not go with thee, the s shall not go. H1931
9 And it came to pass the s night, that H1931
1Sa 4:12 and came to Shiloh the s day with his H1931
6:15 sacrifices the s day unto the LORD. H1931
16 *it*, they returned to Ekron the s day. H1931
9:17 of! this s shall reign over my people. H2008
10:12 And one of the s place answered and
14:35 unto the LORD: the s was the first altar
17:23 to the s words: and David heard *them.* H428
30 and spake after the s manner: and the H2008
31: 6 and all his men, that s day together. H1931
2Sa 2:23 and died in the s place: and it came to H8478
5: 7 hold of Zion: the s *is* the city of David. H1931
23: 7 be utterly burned with fire in the s place.
8 the captains; the s *was* Adino the H1931
1Ki 7:35 and the borders thereof *were* of the s.
8:64 The s day did the king hallow the H1931
13: 3 And he gave a sign the s day, saying, H1931
9 again by the s way that thou camest.
2Ki 3: 6 the s time, and numbered all Israel. H1931
8:22 Then Libnah revolted at the s time. H1931
19:29 springeth of the s; and in the third year
33 By the way that he came, by the s shall
1Ch 1:27 Abram; the s *is* Abraham. H1931
4:33 *were* round about the s cities, unto Baal.
16:17 And hath confirmed the s to Jacob for a
17: 3 And it came to pass the s night, that H1931
2Ch 7: 8 Also at the s time Solomon kept the H1931
13: 9 and seven rams, *the* s may be a priest of
15:11 And they offered unto the LORD the s H1931
16:10 *some* of the people the s time. H1931
18: 7 always evil: the s *is* Micaiah the son of H1931
20:26 the name of the s place was called, The H1931
21:10 unto this day. The s time *also* did H1931
27: 5 gave him the s year an hundred talents H1931
32:12 Hath not the s Hezekiah taken away H1931
30 This s Hezekiah also stopped the upper H1931
34:28 s. So they brought the king word again.
35:16 was prepared the s day, to keep the H1931
Ezr 4:15 within the s of old time: for which H1459
5: 3 At the s time came to them Tatnai,
13 king of Babylon *the* s king Cyrus made a
16 Then came the s Sheshbazzar, *and* laid H1791
6: 3 In the first year of Cyrus the king *the* s
10:23 Shimei, and Kelaiah, (the s *is* Kelita,) H1933
Neh 4:22 Likewise at the s time said I unto the H1931
6: 4 I answered them after the s manner. H2088
10:37 Levites, that the s Levites might have H1992
Est 9: 1 thirteenth day of the s, when the king's
17 day of the s rested they, and made
18 the fifteenth *day* of the s they rested, and
21 and the fifteenth day of the s, yearly,
Job 4: 8 iniquity, and sow wickedness, reap the s.
13: 2 What ye know, *the* s do I know also: I
Ps 68:23 *and* the tongue of thy dogs in the s.
75: 8 he poureth out of the s: but the dregs H2088
102:27 But thou *art* the s, and thy years shall H1931
105:10 And confirmed the s unto Jacob for a
113: 3 the s the LORD'S name *is* to be praised.
Prv 28:24 the s *is* the companion of a destroyer. H1931
Ecc 9:15 no man remembered that s poor man. H1931
Isa 7:20 In the s day shall the Lord shave with a H1931
20: 2 At the s time spake the LORD by Isaiah
37:30 springeth of the s: and in the third year
34 By the way that he came, by the s shall
Jer 27: 8 will not serve the s Nebuchadnezzar the
28: 1 And it came to pass the s year, in the H1931
17 So Hananiah the prophet died the s H1931
31: 1 At the s time, saith the LORD, will I be H1931
39:10 them vineyards and fields at the s time. H1931
Ezk 3:18 to save his life; the s wicked *man* shall H1931
10:16 the earth, the s wheels also turned not H1992
22 their faces *was* the s faces which I saw H1992
21:26 *shall* not *be* the s: exalt *him that is* low, H2063
23:38 s day, and have profaned my sabbaths. H1931
39 they came the s day into my sanctuary H1931
24: 2 the day, *even* of this s day: the king of H6106
2 himself against Jerusalem this s day. H6106
38:10 to pass, *that* at the s time shall things H1931
18 And it shall come to pass at the s time H1931
44: 3 gate, and shall go out by the way of the s.
Dan 3: 6 shall the s hour be cast into the
15 ye shall be cast the s hour into the midst
4:33 The s hour was the thing fulfilled upon

Dan 4:36 At the s time my reason returned unto
5: 5 In the s hour came forth fingers of a
12 were found in the s Daniel, whom the
7:21 I beheld, and the s horn made war with H1797
12: 1 *even* to that s time: and at that time H1931
Am 2: 7 the s maid, to profane my holy name:
Zep 1: 9 In the s day also will I punish all those H1931
Zec 6:10 and come thou the s day, and go into H1931
Mal 1:11 going down of the s my name *shall be*
Mt 3: 4 And the s John had his raiment of *G846*
5:19 teach *them*, the s shall be called great *G3778*
46 have ye? do not even the publicans the s? *G846*
10:19 you in that s hour what ye shall speak. *G1565*
12:50 s is my brother, and sister, and mother. *G846*
13: 1 The s day went Jesus out of the house, *G1565*
20 stony places, the s is he that heareth *G3778*
15:22 came out of the s coasts, and cried *G1565*
18: 1 At the s time came the disciples unto *G1565*
4 s is greatest in the kingdom of heaven. *G3778*
28 But the s servant went out, and found *G1565*
21:42 rejected, the s is become the head *G3778*
22:23 The s day came to him the Sadducees, *G1722*
24:13 unto the end, the s shall be saved. *G3778*
25:16 the s, and made *them* other five talents. *G846*
26:23 me in the dish, the s shall betray me. *G3778*
44 the third time, saying the s words. *G846*
48 I shall kiss, that s is he: hold him fast. *G846*
55 In that s hour said Jesus to the *G1565*
27:44 with him, cast the s in his teeth.
Mk 3:35 will of God, the s is my brother, and my *G3778*
4:35 And the s day, when the even was *G1565*
8:35 and the gospel's, the s shall save it. *G3778*
9:35 *s* shall be last of all, and servant of all.
10:10 asked him again of the s *matter.* *G846*
13:13 unto the end, the s shall be saved. *G3778*
14:39 and prayed, and spake the s words. *G846*
44 I shall kiss, that s is he; take him, and *G846*
Lk 2: 8 And there were in the s country *G846*
25 Simeon; and the s man *was* just and *G3778*
6:33 have ye? for sinners also do even the s. *G846*
38 For with the s measure that ye mete *G846*
7:21 And in that s hour he cured many of *G846*
47 whom little is forgiven, *the* s loveth little.
9:24 his life for my sake, the s shall save it. *G3778*
48 among you all, the s shall be great. *G3778*
10: 7 And in the s house remain, eating and *G846*
10 out into the streets of the s, and say, *G846*
12:12 you in the s hour what ye ought to say. *G846*
13:31 The s day there came certain of the *G846*
16: 1 a steward; and the s was accused unto *G3778*
17:29 But the s day that Lot went out of *G3739*
20:17 the s is become the head of the corner? *G3778*
19 and the scribes the s hour sought to lay *G846*
47 the s shall receive greater damnation. *G3778*
23:12 And the s day Pilate and Herod were *G846*
40 seeing thou art in the s condemnation? *G846*
51 (The s had not consented to the *G3778*
24:13 And, behold, two of them went that s *G846*
33 And they rose up the s hour, and *G846*
Jn 1: 2 The s was in the beginning with God. *G3778*
7 The s came for a witness, to bear *G3778*
33 with water, the s said unto me, Upon *G1565*
33 on him, the s is he which baptizeth *G3778*
3: 2 The s came to Jesus by night, and said *G3778*
26 s baptizeth, and all *men* come to him. *G3778*
4:53 So the father knew that *it was* at the s *G1565*
5: 9 and on the s day was the sabbath. *G1565*
11 me whole, the s said unto me, Take *G1565*
36 me to finish, the s works that I do, bear *G846*
7:18 that sent him, the s is true, and no *G3778*
8:25 them, Even *the* s that I said unto you
10: 1 other way, the s is a thief and a robber. *G1565*
11: 6 days still in the s place where he was. *G3739*
49 high priest that s year, said unto them, *G1565*
12:21 The s came therefore to Philip, which *G3778*
48 the s shall judge him in the last day. *G1565*
15: 5 and I in him, the s bringeth forth much *G3778*
18:13 which was the high priest that s year. *G1565*
20:19 Then the s day at evening, being the *G1565*
Act 1:11 up into heaven? this s Jesus, which is *G3778*
22 of John, unto that s day that he was
2:36 hath made that s Jesus, whom ye have *G5126*
41 were baptized: and the s day there were *G1565*
7:19 The s dealt subtilly with our kindred, *G3778*
35 and a judge? the s did God send *to be* a *G5126*
8: 9 beforetime in the s city used sorcery,
35 and began at the s scripture, and *G3778*
12: 6 him forth, the s night Peter was *G1565*
13:33 God hath fulfilled the s unto us their *G3778*

Act 14: 9 The s heard Paul speak: who stedfastly G3778
15:27 shall also tell you the s things by mouth.
16:17 The s followed Paul and us, and cried, G3778
18 out of her. And he came out the s hour. G846
33 And he took them the s hour of the G1565
18: 3 And because he was of the s craft, he G3673
19:23 And the s time there arose no small stir G2596
21: 9 And the s man had four daughters, G5129
22:13 And the s hour I looked up upon him. G846
24:20 Or else let these s here say, if they have G846
28: 7 In the s quarters were possessions of G1565
Ro 1:32 not only do the s, but have pleasure in G846
2: 1 for thou that judgest doest the s things. G846
3 and doest the s, that thou shalt escape G846
8:20 of him who hath subjected the s in hope,
9:17 Even for this s purpose have I raised G846
21 over the clay, of the s lump to make one G846
10:12 the Greek: for the s Lord over all is rich G846
12: 4 and all members have not the s office: G846
16 Be of the s mind one toward another. G846
13: 3 good, and thou shalt have praise of the s: G846
1Co 1:10 ye all speak the s thing, and that there G846
10 in the s mind and in the same judgment. G846
10 in the same mind and in the s judgment. G846
7:20 Let every man abide in the s calling G3588
8: 3 But if any man love God, the s is G3778
9: 8 a man? or saith not the law the s also? G5023
10: 3 And did all eat the s spiritual meat; G846
4 And did all drink the s spiritual drink: G846
11:23 the Lord Jesus the s night in which he G846
25 After the s manner also he took the G5615
12: 4 are diversities of gifts, but the s Spirit. G846
5 of administrations, but the s Lord. G846
6 it is the s God which worketh all in all. G846
8 the word of knowledge by the s Spirit; G846
9 To another faith by the s Spirit; to G846
9 the gifts of healing by the s Spirit; G846
25 should have the s care one for another. G846
15:39 All flesh is not the s flesh: but there is G846
2Co 1: 6 in the enduring of the s sufferings which G846
2: 2 but the s which is made sorry by me?
3 And I wrote this s unto you, lest, when I G846
3:14 day remaineth the s veil untaken away G846
18 changed into the s image from glory to G846
4:13 We having the s spirit of faith, according G846
6:13 Now for a recompence in the s, (I speak G846
7: 8 I perceive that the s epistle hath made G1565
8: 6 also finish in you the s grace also. G3778
16 But thanks be to God, which put the s G846
19 us to the glory of the s Lord, and G846
9: 4 ashamed in this s confident boasting. G3778
5 before, that the s might be ready, as a G3778
12:18 we not in the s spirit? walked we not G846
18 spirit? walked we not in the s steps? G846
Gal 2: 8 circumcision, the s was mighty in me G3588
10 the s which I also was forward to do. G846
3: 7 the s are the children of Abraham. G3778
Eph 3: 6 and of the s body, and partakers G4954
4:10 He that descended is the s also that G846
6: 8 man doeth, the s shall he receive of the G5124
9 And, ye masters, do the s things unto G3778
22 Whom I have sent unto you for the s G846
Php 1:30 Having the s conflict which ye saw in G846
2: 2 s love, being of one accord, of one mind. G846
18 For the s cause also do ye joy, and G846
3: 1 Lord. To write the s things to you, to me G846
16 by the s rule, let us mind the same thing. G846
16 by the same rule, let us mind the s thing. G846
4: 2 that they be of the s mind in the Lord. G846
Col 4: 2 Continue in prayer, and watch in the s G846
8 Whom I have sent unto you for the s G846
2Ti 2: 2 witnesses, the s commit thou to faithful G5023
Heb 1:12 art the s, and thy years shall not fail. G846
2:14 took part of the s; that through death he G846
4:11 man fall after the s example of unbelief. G846
6:11 of you do shew the s diligence to the full G846
10:11 oftentimes the s sacrifices, which can G846
11: 9 the heirs with him of the s promise: G846
13: 8 Jesus Christ the s yesterday, and to day, G846
Jas 3: 2 not in word, the s is a perfect man, and G3778
10 Out of the s mouth proceedeth blessing G846
11 Doth a fountain send forth at the s place G846
1Pt 2: 7 the s is made the head of the corner, G3778
4: 1 likewise with the s mind: for he that hath G846
4 the s excess of riot, speaking evil of you: G846
10 so minister the s one to another, as good G846
5: 9 faith, knowing that the s afflictions are G846
2Pt 2:19 of the s is he brought in bondage. G5129
3: 7 are now, by the s word are kept in store, G846
1Jn 2:23 Whosoever denieth the Son, the s hath G3761
27 you: but as the s anointing teacheth you G846
Rev 3: 5 He that overcometh, the s shall be G3778
11:13 And the s hour was there a great G1565
14:10 The s shall drink of the wine of the wrath G846

SAMGARNEBO

Jer 39: 3 even Nergal-sharezer, S, Sarsechim, H5562

SAMLAH

Gen 36:36 And Hadad died, and S of Masrekah H8072
37 And S died, and Saul of Rehoboth by H8072
1Ch 1:47 And when Hadad was dead, S of H8072
48 And when S was dead, Shaul of H8072

SAMOS

Act 20:15 next day we arrived at S, and tarried at G4544

SAMOTHRACIA

Act 16:11 to S, and the next day to Neapolis; G4543

SAMSON

Jdg 13:24 called his name S: and the child grew, H8123
14: 1 And S went down to Timnath, and saw H8123
3 Philistines? And S said unto his father, H8123
5 Then went S down, and his father and H8123
7 the woman; and she pleased S well. H8123
10 the woman: and S made there a feast; H8123
12 And S said unto them, I will now put H8123
15: 1 harvest, that S visited his wife with H8123
3 And S said concerning them, Now shall H8123
4 And S went and caught three hundred H8123
6 they answered, S, the son in law of the H8123
7 And S said unto them, Though ye have H8123
10 To bind S are we come up, to H8123
11 Etam, and said to S, Knowest thou not H8123
12 the Philistines. And S said unto them, H8123
16 And S said, With the jawbone of an H8123
16: 1 Then went S to Gaza, and saw there an H8123
2 And it was told the Gazites, saying, S is H8123
3 And S lay till midnight, and arose at H8123
6 And Delilah said to S, Tell me, I pray H8123
7 And S said unto her, If they bind me H8123
9 be upon thee, S. And he brake the withs, H8123
10 And Delilah said unto S, Behold, thou H8123
12 be upon thee, S. And there were liers H8123
13 And Delilah said unto S, Hitherto thou H8123
14 be upon thee, S. And he awaked out H8123
20 be upon thee, S. And he awoke out of H8123
23 delivered S our enemy into our hand. H8123
25 they said, Call for S, that he may make H8123
25 And they called for S out of the prison H8123
26 And S said unto the lad that held him H8123
27 that beheld while S made sport. H8123
28 And S called unto the LORD, and said, H8123
29 And S took hold of the two middle H8123
30 And S said, Let me die with the H8123
Heb 11:32 of Barak, and of S, and of Jephthae; of G4546

SAMSON'S

Jdg 14:15 that they said unto S wife, Entice thy H8123
16 And S wife wept before him, and said, H8123
20 But S wife was given to his companion, H8123

SAMUEL

1Sa 1:20 called his name S, saying, Because I H8050
2:18 But S ministered before the LORD, H8050
21 And the child S grew before the LORD. H8050
26 And the child S grew on, and was in H8050
3: 1 And the child S ministered unto the H8050
3 God was, and S was laid down to sleep; H8050
4 That the LORD called S: and he H8050
6 And the LORD called yet again, S. And H8050
6 Samuel. And S arose and went to Eli, H8050
7 Now S did not yet know the LORD, H8050
8 And the LORD called S again the third H8050
9 Therefore Eli said unto S, Go, lie down: H8050
9 So S went and lay down in his place. H8050
10 as at other times, S, Samuel. Then H8050
10 other times, Samuel, S. Then Samuel H8050
10 Samuel. Then S answered, Speak; for H8050
11 And the LORD said to S, Behold, I will H8050
15 And S lay until the morning, and H8050
15 And S feared to shew Eli the vision. H8050
16 Then Eli called S, and said, Samuel, my H8050
16 Then Eli called Samuel, and said, S, my H8050
18 And S told him every whit, and hid H8050
19 And S grew, and the LORD was with H8050
20 knew that S was established to be H8050
1Sa 3:21 to S in Shiloh by the word of the LORD. H8050
4: 1 And the word of S came to all Israel. H8050
7: 3 And S spake unto all the house of H8050
5 And S said, Gather all Israel to Mizpeh, H8050
6 the LORD. And S judged the children H8050
8 And the children of Israel said to S, H8050
9 And S took a sucking lamb, and offered H8050
9 the LORD: and S cried unto the LORD H8050
10 And as S was offering up the burnt H8050
12 Then S took a stone, and set it between H8050
13 against the Philistines all the days of S. H8050
15 And S judged Israel all the days of his H8050
8: 1 And it came to pass, when S was old, H8050
4 together, and came to S unto Ramah, H8050
6 But the thing displeased S, when they H8050
6 judge us. And S prayed unto the LORD. H8050
7 And the LORD said unto S, Hearken H8050
10 And S told all the words of the LORD H8050
19 obey the voice of S; and they said, Nay; H8050
21 And S heard all the words of the H8050
22 And the LORD said to S, Hearken unto H8050
22 them a king. And S said unto the men H8050
9:14 the city, behold, S came out against H8050
15 Now the LORD had told S in his ear a H8050
17 And when S saw Saul, the LORD said H8050
18 Then Saul drew near to S in the gate, H8050
19 And S answered Saul, and said, I am H8050
22 And S took Saul and his servant, and H8050
23 And S said unto the cook, Bring the H8050
24 it before Saul. And S said, Behold that
24 people. So Saul did eat with S that day. H8050
25 place into the city, S communed with
26 of the day, that S called Saul to the top H8050
26 out both of them, he and S, abroad. H8050
27 to the end of the city, S said to Saul, Bid H8050
10: 1 Then S took a vial of oil, and poured it H8050
9 his back to go from S, God gave him H8050
14 that they were no where, we came to S. H8050
15 me, I pray thee, what S said unto you. H8050
16 whereof S spake, he told him not. H8050
17 And S called the people together unto H8050
20 And when S had caused all the tribes of H8050
24 And S said to all the people, See ye him H8050
25 Then S told the people the manner of H8050
25 the LORD. And S sent all the people H8050
11: 7 Saul and after S, so shall it be done unto H8050
12 And the people said unto S, Who is he H8050
14 Then said S to the people, Come, and H8050
12: 1 And S said unto all Israel, Behold, I H8050
6 And S said unto the people, It is the H8050
11 Jephthah, and S, and delivered you out H8050
18 So S called unto the LORD; and the H8050
18 people greatly feared the LORD and S. H8050
19 And all the people said unto S, Pray for H8050
20 And S said unto the people, Fear not: H8050
13: 8 the set time that S had appointed: but H8050
8 appointed: but S came not to Gilgal; H8050
10 offering, behold, S came; and Saul H8050
11 And S said, What hast thou done? And H8050
13 And S said to Saul, Thou hast done H8050
15 And S arose, and gat him up from H8050
15: 1 S also said unto Saul, The LORD sent H8050
10 the word of the LORD unto S, saying, H8050
11 S; and he cried unto the LORD all night. H8050
12 And when S rose early to meet Saul in H8050
12 it was told S, saying, Saul came to H8050
13 And S came to Saul: and Saul said unto H8050
14 And S said, What meaneth then this H8050
16 Then S said unto Saul, Stay, and I will H8050
17 And S said, When thou wast little in H8050
20 And Saul said unto S, Yea, I have H8050
22 And S said, Hath the LORD as great H8050
24 And Saul said unto S, I have sinned: for H8050
26 And S said unto Saul, I will not return H8050
27 And as S turned about to go away, he H8050
28 And S said unto him, The LORD hath H8050
31 So S turned again after Saul; and Saul H8050
32 Then said S, Bring ye hither to me Agag H8050
33 And S said, As thy sword hath made H8050
33 women. And S hewed Agag in pieces H8050
34 Then S went to Ramah; and Saul went H8050
35 And S came no more to see Saul until H8050
35 nevertheless S mourned for Saul: and H8050
16: 1 And the LORD said unto S, How long H8050
2 And S said, How can I go? if Saul hear H8050
4 And S did that which the LORD spake, H8050
7 But the LORD said unto S, Look not on H8050
8 him pass before S. And he said, Neither H8050
10 to pass before S. And Samuel said unto H8050

1Sa 16:10 Samuel. And S said unto Jesse, The H8050
11 And S said unto Jesse, Are here all *thy* H8050
11 the sheep. And S said unto Jesse, Send H8050
13 Then S took the horn of oil, and H8050
13 So S rose up, and went to Ramah. H8050
19:18 and came to S to Ramah, and told H8050
18 he and S went and dwelt in Naioth. H8050
20 prophesying, and S standing *as* H8050
22 said, Where *are* S and David? And *one* H8050
24 prophesied before S in like manner, H8050
25: 1 And S died; and all the Israelites were H8050
28: 3 Now S was dead, and all Israel had H8050
11 unto thee? And he said, Bring me up S. H8050
12 And when the woman saw S, she cried H8050
14 that it *was* S, and he stooped with H8050
15 And S said to Saul, Why hast thou H8050
16 Then said S, Wherefore then dost thou H8050
20 of the words of S: and there was no H8050
1Ch 6:28 And the sons of S; the firstborn Vashni, H8050
9:22 S the seer did ordain in their set office. H8050
11: 3 according to the word of the LORD by S. H8050
26:28 And all that S the seer, and Saul the H8050
29:29 in the book of S the seer, and in the H8050
2Ch 35:18 from the days of S the prophet; neither H8050
Ps 99: 6 his priests, and S among them that call H8050
Jer 15: 1 Moses and S stood before me, *yet* H8050
Act 3:24 Yea, and all the prophets from S and G4545
13:20 and fifty years, until S the prophet. G4545
Heb 11:32 David also, and S, and *of* the prophets: G4545

SANBALLAT

Neh 2:10 When S the Horonite, and Tobiah the H5571
19 But when S the Horonite, and Tobiah H5571
4: 1 But it came to pass, that when S heard H5571
7 But it came to pass, *that* when S, and H5571
6: 1 Now it came to pass, when S, and H5571
2 That S and Geshem sent unto me, H5571
5 Then sent S his servant unto me in like H5571
12 me: for Tobiah and S had hired him. H5571
14 My God, think thou upon Tobiah and S H5571
13:28 *was* son in law to S the Horonite: H5571

SANCTIFICATION

1Co 1:30 righteousness, and s, and redemption: *G38*
1Th 4: 3 For this is the will of God, *even* your s, *G38*
4 to possess his vessel in s and honour; *G38*
2Th 2:13 s of the Spirit and belief of the truth: *G38*
1Pt 1: 2 the Father, through s of the Spirit, unto *G38*

SANCTIFIED

Gen 2: 3 seventh day, and s it: because that in it H6942
Ex 19:14 the people, and s the people; and they H6942
29:43 *the tabernacle* shall be s by my glory. H6942
Lev 8:10 and all that *was* therein, and s them. H6942
15 and s it, to make reconciliation upon it. H6942
30 with him; and s Aaron, *and* his H6942
10: 3 saying, I will be s in them that come H6942
27:15 And if he that s it will redeem his H6942
19 And if he that s the field will in any H6942
Nu 7: 1 had anointed it, and s it, and all the H6942
1 and had anointed them, and s them; H6942
8:17 in the land of Egypt I s them for myself. H6942
20:13 with the LORD, and he was s in them. H6942
Dt 32:51 of Zin; because ye s me not in the midst H6942
1Sa 7: 1 in the hill, and s Eleazar his son to keep H6942
16: 5 sacrifice. And he s Jesse and his sons, H6942
21: 5 though it were s this day in the vessel. H6942
1Ch 15:14 So the priests and the Levites s H6942
2Ch 5:11 were s, *and* did not *then* wait by course: H6942
7:16 For now have I chosen and s this H6942
20 which I have s for my name, will I H6942
29:15 brethren, and s themselves, and came, H6942
17 of the LORD: so they s the house of the H6942
19 we prepared and s, and, behold, they H6942
34 *other* priests had s themselves: for the H6942
30: 3 the priests had not s themselves H6942
8 which he hath s for ever: and serve the H6942
15 were ashamed, and s themselves, and H6942
17 that were not s: therefore the Levites H6942
24 a great number of priests s themselves. H6942
31:18 set office they s themselves in holiness: H6942
Neh 3: 1 the sheep gate; they s it, and set up the H6942
1 they s it, unto the tower of Hananeel. H6942
12:47 portion: and they s *holy things* unto the H6942
47 s *them* unto the children of Aaron. H6942
Job 1: 5 that Job sent and s them, and rose up H6942
Isa 5:16 that is holy shall be s in righteousness. H6942
13: 3 I have commanded my s ones, I have H6942
Jer 1: 5 forth out of the womb I s thee, *and* I H6942
Ezk 20:41 I will be s in you before the heathen. H6942
28:22 judgments in her, and shall be s in her. H6942
25 and shall be s in them in the sight H6942
36:23 I shall be s in you before their eyes. H6942
38:16 be s in thee, O Gog, before their eyes. H6942
39:27 s in them in the sight of many nations; H6942
48:11 *It shall be* for the priests that are s of H6942
Jn 10:36 Say ye of him, whom the Father hath s, *G37*
17:19 they also might be s through the truth. *G37*
Act 20:32 inheritance among all them which are s. *G37*
26:18 them which are s by faith that is in me. *G37*
Ro 15:16 be acceptable, being s by the Holy Ghost. *G37*
1Co 1: 2 to them that are s in Christ Jesus, called *G37*
6:11 washed, but ye are s, but ye are justified *G37*
7:14 For the unbelieving husband is s by the *G37*
14 the unbelieving wife is s by the husband: *G37*
1Ti 4: 5 For it is s by the word of God and prayer. *G37*
2Ti 2:21 unto honour, s, and meet for the master's *G37*
Heb 2:11 and they who are s *are* all of one: for *G37*
10:10 By the which will we are s through the *G37*
14 hath perfected for ever them that are s. *G37*
29 wherewith he was s, an unholy thing, and *G37*
Jude 1 to them that are s by God the Father, *G37*

SANCTIFIETH

Mt 23:17 the gold, or the temple that s the gold? *G37*
19 the gift, or the altar that s the gift? *G37*
Heb 2:11 For both he that s and they who are *G37*
9:13 unclean, s to the purifying of the flesh: *G37*

SANCTIFY

Ex 13: 2 S unto me all the firstborn, whatsoever H6942
19:10 the people, and s them to day and to H6942
22 near to the LORD, s themselves, lest H6942
23 Set bounds about the mount, and s it. H6942
28:41 them, and s them, that they may H6942
29:27 And thou shalt s the breast of the wave H6942
33 to consecrate *and* to s them: but a H6942
36 for it, and thou shalt anoint it, to s it. H6942
37 for the altar, and s it; and it shall be an H6942
44 And I will s the tabernacle of the H6942
44 the altar: I will s also both Aaron and H6942
30:29 And thou shalt s them, that they may H6942
31:13 that I *am* the LORD that doth s you. H6942
40:10 all his vessels, and s the altar: and it H6942
11 anoint the laver and his foot, and s it. H6942
13 anoint him, and s him; that he may H6942
Lev 8:11 both the laver and his foot, to s them. H6942
12 head, and anointed him, to s him. H6942
11:44 ye shall therefore s yourselves, and ye H6942
20: 7 S yourselves therefore, and be ye holy: H6942
8 do them: I *am* the LORD which s you. H6942
21: 8 Thou shalt s him therefore; for he H6942
8 for I the LORD, which s you, *am* holy. H6942
15 his people: for I the LORD do s him. H6942
23 sanctuaries: for I the LORD do s them. H6942
22: 9 they profane it: I the LORD do s them. H6942
16 holy things: for I the LORD do s them. H6942
27:14 And when a man shall s his house *to be* H6942
16 And if a man shall s unto the LORD H6942
17 If he s his field from the year of jubile, H6942
18 But if he s his field after the jubile, then H6942
22 And if *a man* s unto the LORD a field H6942
26 no man shall s it; whether *it be* ox, H6942
Nu 11:18 And say thou unto the people, S H6942
20:12 me not, to s me in the eyes of the H6942
27:14 the congregation, to s me at the water H6942
Dt 5:12 Keep the sabbath day to s it, as the H6942
15:19 flock thou shalt s unto the LORD thy H6942
Jos 3: 5 And Joshua said unto the people, S H6942
7:13 Up, s the people, and say, Sanctify H6942
13 Up, sanctify the people, and say, S H6942
1Sa 16: 5 unto the LORD: s yourselves, and come H6942
1Ch 15:12 of the Levites: s yourselves, *both* ye H6942
23:13 that he should s the most holy things, H6942
2Ch 29: 5 me, ye Levites, s now yourselves, and H6942
5 now yourselves, and s the house of the H6942
17 the first month to s, and on the eighth H6942
34 heart to s themselves than the priests. H6942
30:17 not clean, to s *them* unto the LORD. H6942
35: 6 So kill the passover, and s yourselves, H6942
Neh 13:22 keep the gates, to s the sabbath day. H6942
Isa 8:13 S the LORD of hosts himself; and *let* H6942
29:23 of him, they shall s my name, and H6942
23 my name, and s the Holy One of Jacob, H6942
66:17 They that s themselves, and purify H6942
Ezk 20:12 know that I *am* the LORD that s them. H6942
36:23 And I will s my great name, which was H6942
37:28 that I the LORD do s Israel, when my H6942
Ezk 38:23 Thus will I magnify myself, and s H6942
44:19 not s the people with their garments. H6942
46:20 out into the utter court, to s the people. H6942
Joel 1:14 S ye a fast, call a solemn assembly, H6942
2:15 Blow the trumpet in Zion, s a fast, call H6942
16 Gather the people, s the congregation, H6942
Jn 17:17 S them through thy truth: thy word is *G37*
19 And for their sakes I s myself, that they *G37*
Eph 5:26 That he might s and cleanse it with the *G37*
1Th 5:23 And the very God of peace s you wholly; *G37*
Heb 13:12 Wherefore Jesus also, that he might s the *G37*
1Pt 3:15 But s the Lord God in your hearts: and *G37*

SANCTUARIES

Lev 21:23 my s: for I the LORD do sanctify them. H4720
26:31 and bring your s unto desolation, and H4720
Jer 51:51 come into the s of the LORD'S house. H4720
Ezk 28:18 Thou hast defiled thy s by the H4720
Am 7: 9 be desolate, and the s of Israel shall be H4720

SANCTUARY

Ex 15:17 to dwell in, *in* the S, O Lord, *which* thy H4720
25: 8 And let them make me a s; that I may H4720
30:13 the shekel of the s: (a shekel *is* twenty H6944
24 shekel of the s, and of oil olive an hin: H6944
36: 1 the service of the s, according to all that H6944
3 of the service of the s, to make it *withal*. H6944
4 all the work of the s, came every man H6944
6 the offering of the s. So the people were H6944
38:24 thirty shekels, after the shekel of the s. H6944
25 fifteen shekels, after the shekel of the s: H6944
26 the shekel of the s, for every one that H6944
27 the sockets of the s, and the sockets of H6944
Lev 4: 6 the LORD, before the vail of the s. H6944
5:15 shekel of the s, for a trespass offering: H6944
10: 4 from before the s out of the camp. H6944
12: 4 nor come into the s, until the days of H4720
16:33 for the holy s, and he shall make an H4720
19:30 and reverence my s: I *am* the LORD. H4720
20: 3 my s, and to profane my holy name. H4720
21:12 Neither shall he go out of the s, nor H4720
12 nor profane the s of his God; for the H4720
26: 2 and reverence my s: I *am* the LORD. H4720
27: 3 of silver, after the shekel of the s. H6944
25 the s: twenty gerahs shall be the shekel. H6944
Nu 3:28 hundred, keeping the charge of the s. H6944
31 and the vessels of the s wherewith they H6944
32 of them that keep the charge of the s. H6944
38 the charge of the s for the charge of the H4720
47 the shekel of the s shalt thou take *them*: H6944
50 five *shekels*, after the shekel of the s: H6944
4:12 they minister in the s, and put *them* in a H6944
15 of covering the s, and all the vessels of H6944
15 the vessels of the s, as the camp is to set H6944
16 *is*, in the s, and in the vessels thereof. H6944
7: 9 the service of the s belonging unto H6944
13 the shekel of the s; both of them *were* H6944
19 the shekel of the s; both of them full of H6944
25 the shekel of the s; both of them full of H6944
31 the shekel of the s; both of them full of H6944
37 the shekel of the s; both of them full of H6944
43 the shekel of the s; both of them full of H6944
49 the shekel of the s; both of them full of H6944
55 the shekel of the s; both of them full of H6944
61 the shekel of the s; both of them full of H6944
67 the shekel of the s; both of them full of H6944
73 the shekel of the s; both of them full of H6944
79 the shekel of the s; both of them full of H6944
85 *shekels*, after the shekel of the s: H6944
86 the shekel of the s: all the gold of the H6944
8:19 children of Israel come nigh unto the s. H6944
10:21 bearing the s: and *the other* did set H4720
18: 1 the iniquity of the s: and thou and thy H4720
3 the vessels of the s and the altar, that H6944
5 And ye shall keep the charge of the s, H6944
16 shekel of the s, which *is* twenty gerahs. H6944
19:20 he hath defiled the s of the LORD: the H4720
Jos 24:26 an oak, that *was* by the s of the LORD. H4720
1Ch 9:29 instruments of the s, and the fine flour, H6944
22:19 and build ye the s of the LORD God, to H4720
24: 5 governors of the s, and governors *of the* H6944
28:10 an house for the s: be strong, and do *it*. H4720
2Ch 20: 8 thee a s therein for thy name, saying, H4720
26:18 go out of the s; for thou hast trespassed; H4720
29:21 and for the s, and for Judah. And H4720
30: 8 and enter into his s, which he hath H4720
19 according to the purification of the s. H6944
36:17 in the house of their s, and had no H4720
Neh 10:39 the vessels of the s, and the priests that H4720

Ps 20: 2 Send thee help from the **s**, and H6944
63: 2 thy glory, so *as* I have seen thee in the **s**. H6944
68:24 the goings of my God, my King, in the **s**. H6944
73:17 Until I went into the **s** of God; *then* H4720
74: 3 the enemy hath done wickedly in the **s**. H6944
7 They have cast fire into thy **s**, they have H4720
77:13 Thy way, O God, *is* in the **s**: who *is so* H6944
78:54 to the border of his **s**, *even to* this H6944
69 And he built his **s** like high *palaces*, like H4720
96: 6 him: strength and beauty *are* in his **s**. H4720
102:19 the height of his **s**; from heaven did the H6944
114: 2 Judah was his **s**, *and* Israel his H6944
134: 2 Lift up your hands *in* the **s**, and bless H6944
150: 1 Praise ye the LORD. Praise God in his **s**: H6944
Isa 8:14 And he shall be for a **s**; but for a stone H4720
16:12 to his **s** to pray; but he shall not prevail. H4720
43:28 the princes of the **s**, and have given H6944
60:13 the place of my **s**; and I will make the H4720
63:18 adversaries have trodden down thy **s**. H4720
Jer 17:12 from the beginning *is* the place of our **s**. H4720
Lam 1:10 entered into her **s**, whom thou didst H4720
2: 7 hath abhorred his **s**, he hath given up H4720
20 prophet be slain in the **s** of the Lord? H4720
4: 1 the stones of the **s** are poured out in the H6944
Ezk 5:11 hast defiled my **s** with all thy detestable H4720
8: 6 go far off from my **s**? but turn thee yet H4720
9: 6 and begin at my **s**. Then they began at H4720
11:16 be to them as a little **s** in the countries H4720
23:38 have defiled my **s** in the same day, and H4720
39 same day into my **s** to profane it; and, H4720
24:21 I will profane my **s**, the excellency of H4720
25: 3 saidst, Aha, against my **s**, when it was H4720
37:26 **s** in the midst of them for evermore. H4720
28 Israel, when my **s** shall be in the midst H4720
41:21 *and* the face of the **s**; the appearance *of* H6944
23 And the temple and the **s** had two H6944
42:20 between the **s** and the profane place. H6944
43:21 place of the house, without the **s**. H4720
44: 1 of the outward **s** which looketh toward H4720
5 house, with every going forth of the **s**. H4720
7 In that ye have brought *into my* **s**
7 in flesh, to be in my **s**, to pollute it, *even* H4720
8 of my charge in my **s** for yourselves. H4720
9 enter into my **s**, of any stranger that H4720
11 Yet they shall be ministers in my **s**, H4720
15 the charge of my **s** when the children of H4720
16 They shall enter into my **s**, and they H4720
27 And in the day that he goeth into the **s**, H6944
27 to minister in the **s**, he shall offer his sin H6944
45: 2 Of this there shall be for the **s** five H6944
3 shall be the **s** *and* the most holy *place*. H4720
4 the ministers of the **s**, which shall come H4720
4 houses, and an holy place for the **s**. H4720
18 without blemish, and cleanse the **s**: H4720
47:12 issued out of the **s**: and the fruit thereof H4720
48: 8 and the **s** shall be in the midst of it. H4720
10 in length: and the **s** of the LORD shall H4720
21 oblation; and the **s** of the house *shall* H4720
Dan 8:11 and the place of his **s** was cast down. H4720
13 to give both the **s** and the host to be H6944
14 days; then shall the **s** be cleansed. H6944
9:17 **s** that is desolate, for the Lord's sake. H4720
26 the city and the **s**; and the end thereof H6944
11:31 shall pollute the **s** of strength, and shall H4720
Zep 3: 4 **s**, they have done violence to the law. H6944
Heb 8: 2 A minister of the **s**, and of the true *G39*
9: 1 of divine service, and a worldly **s**. *G39*
2 and the shewbread; which is called the **s**. *G39*
13:11 is brought into the **s** by the high priest *G39*

SAND
Gen 22:17 heaven, and as the **s** which *is* upon the H2344
32:12 make thy seed as the **s** of the sea, which H2344
41:49 And Joseph gathered corn as the **s** of H2344
Ex 2:12 slew the Egyptian, and hid him in the **s**. H2344
Dt 33:19 of the seas, and *of* treasures hid in the **s**. H2344
Jos 11: 4 even as the **s** that *is* upon the sea H2344
Jdg 7:12 as the **s** by the sea side for multitude. H2344
1Sa 13: 5 and people as the **s** which *is* on the sea H2344
2Sa 17:11 Beer-sheba, as the **s** that *is* by the sea H2344
1Ki 4:20 Judah and Israel *were* many, as the **s** H2344
29 even as the **s** that *is* on the sea shore. H2344
Job 6: 3 For now it would be heavier than the **s** H2344
29:18 and I shall multiply *my* days as the **s**. H2344
Ps 78:27 feathered fowls like as the **s** of the sea: H2344
139:18 the **s**: when I awake, I am still with thee. H2344
Prv 27: 3 A stone *is* heavy, and the **s** weighty; but H2344
Isa 10:22 For though thy people Israel be as the **s** H2344
48:19 Thy seed also had been as the **s**, and the H2344
Jer 5:22 have placed the **s** *for* the bound of the H2344
15: 8 to me above the **s** of the seas: I have H2344
33:22 neither the **s** of the sea measured: H2344
Hos 1:10 Israel shall be as the **s** of the sea, which H2344
Hab 1: 9 they shall gather the captivity as the **s**. H2344
Mt 7:26 man, which built his house upon the **s**: *G285*
Ro 9:27 **s** of the sea, a remnant shall be saved: *G285*
Heb 11:12 **s** which is by the sea shore innumerable. *G285*
Rev 13: 1 And I stood upon the **s** of the sea, and *G285*
20: 8 number of whom *is* as the **s** of the sea. *G285*

SANDALS
Mk 6: 9 But *be* shod with **s**; and not put on two *G4547*
Act 12: 8 and bind on thy **s**. And so he did. And *G4547*

SANG
Ex 15: 1 Then **s** Moses and the children of Israel H7891
Nu 21:17 Then Israel **s** this song, Spring up, O H7891
Jdg 5: 1 Then **s** Deborah and Barak the son of H7891
1Sa 29: 5 *Is* not this David, of whom they **s** one H6030
2Ch 29:28 and the singers **s**, and the trumpeters H7891
30 Asaph the seer. And they **s** praises with
Ezr 3:11 And they **s** together by course in H6030
Neh 12:42 **s** loud, with Jezrahiah *their* overseer. H7891
Job 38: 7 When the morning stars **s** together, H7442
Ps 7:ttl Shiggaion of David, which he **s** unto H7891
106:12 Then believed they his words; they **s** his H7891
Act 16:25 Silas prayed, and **s** praises unto God: *G5214*

SANK
Ex 15: 5 The depths have covered them: they **s** H3381
10 they **s** as lead in the mighty waters. H6749

SANSANNAH
Jos 15:31 And Ziklag, and Madmannah, and **S**, H5578

SAP
Ps 104:16 The trees of the LORD are full *of* **s**; the

SAPH
2Sa 21:18 **S**, which *was* of the sons of the giant. H5593

SAPHIR
Mic 1:11 Pass ye away, thou inhabitant of **S**, H8208

SAPPHIRA
Act 5: 1 with **S** his wife, sold a possession, *G4551*

SAPPHIRE
Ex 24:10 a paved work of a **s** stone, and as it H5601
28:18 *be* an emerald, a **s**, and a diamond. H5601
39:11 And the second row, an emerald, a **s**, H5601
Job 28:16 Ophir, with the precious onyx, or the **s**. H5601
Lam 4: 7 than rubies, their polishing *was* of **s**: H5601
Ezk 1:26 appearance of a **s** stone: and upon the H5601
10: 1 over them as it were a **s** stone, as the H5601
28:13 and the jasper, the **s**, the emerald, and H5601
Rev 21:19 *was* jasper; the second, **s**; the third, a *G4552*

SAPPHIRES
Job 28: 6 The stones of it *are* the place of **s**: and it H5601
Song 5:14 belly *is as* bright ivory overlaid *with* **s**. H5601
Isa 54:11 colours, and lay thy foundations with **s**. H5601

SARA
Heb 11:11 Through faith also **S** herself received *G4564*
1Pt 3: 6 Even as **S** obeyed Abraham, calling *G4564*

SARAH
Gen 17:15 name Sarai, but **S** *shall* her name *be*. H8283
17 shall **S**, that is ninety years old, bear? H8283
19 And God said, **S** thy wife shall bear H8283
21 with Isaac, which **S** shall bear unto H8283
18: 6 into the tent unto **S**, and said, Make H8283
9 And they said unto him, Where *is* **S** thy H8283
10 of life; and, lo, **S** thy wife shall have a H8283
10 have a son. And **S** heard *it* in the tent H8283
11 Now Abraham and **S** *were* old *and* well H8283
11 be with **S** after the manner of women. H8283
12 Therefore **S** laughed within herself, H8283
13 Wherefore did **S** laugh, saying, Shall H8283
14 the time of life, and **S** shall have a son. H8283
15 Then **S** denied, saying, I laughed not; H8283
20: 2 And Abraham said of **S** his wife, She *is* H8283
2 king of Gerar sent, and took **S**. H8283
14 Abraham, and restored him **S** his wife. H8283
16 And unto **S** he said, Behold, I have H8283
18 because of **S** Abraham's wife. H8283
21: 1 And the LORD visited **S** as he had said, H8283
Gen 21: 1 the LORD did unto **S** as he had spoken. H8283
2 For **S** conceived, and bare Abraham a H8283
3 unto him, whom **S** bare to him, Isaac. H8283
6 And **S** said, God hath made me to H8283
7 Abraham, that **S** should have given H8283
9 And **S** saw the son of Hagar the H8283
12 in all that **S** hath said unto thee, H8283
23: 1 And **S** was an hundred and seven and H8283
1 old: *these were* the years of the life of **S**. H8283
2 And **S** died in Kirjath-arba; the same *is* H8283
2 to mourn for **S**, and to weep for her. H8283
19 And after this, Abraham buried **S** his H8283
24:36 And **S** my master's wife bare a son to H8283
25:10 was Abraham buried, and **S** his wife. H8283
49:31 There they buried Abraham and **S** his H8283
Nu 26:46 name of the daughter of Asher *was* **S**. H8294
Isa 51: 2 father, and unto **S** *that* bare you: for I H8283
Ro 9: 9 will I come, and **S** shall have a son. *G4564*

SARAH'S
Gen 24:67 her into his mother **S** tent, and took H8283
25:12 **S** handmaid, bare unto Abraham: H8283
Ro 4:19 neither yet the deadness of **S** womb: *G4564*

SARAI
Gen 11:29 of Abram's wife *was* **S**; and the name of H8297
30 But **S** was barren; she *had* no child. H8297
31 his son's son, and **S** his daughter in H8297
12: 5 And Abram took **S** his wife, and Lot his H8297
11 that he said unto **S** his wife, Behold H8297
17 plagues because of **S** Abram's wife. H8297
16: 1 Now **S** Abram's wife bare him no H8297
2 And **S** said unto Abram, Behold now, H8297
2 And Abram hearkened to the voice of **S**. H8297
3 And **S** Abram's wife took Hagar her H8297
5 And **S** said unto Abram, My wrong *be* H8297
6 But Abram said unto **S**, Behold, thy H8297
6 thee. And when **S** dealt hardly with her, H8297
8 I flee from the face of my mistress **S**. H8297
17:15 And God said unto Abraham, As for **S** H8297
15 name **S**, but Sarah *shall* her name *be*. H8297

SARAI'S
Gen 16: 8 And he said, Hagar, **S** maid, whence H8297

SARAPH
1Ch 4:22 Chozeba, and Joash, and **S**, who had the H8315

SARDINE
Rev 4: 3 like a jasper and a **s** stone: and *there* *G4555*

SARDIS
Rev 1:11 and unto **S**, and unto Philadelphia, *G4554*
3: 1 And unto the angel of the church in **S** *G4554*
4 Thou hast a few names even in **S** which *G4554*

SARDITES
Nu 26:26 the family of the **S**: of Elon, the family of H5625

SARDIUS
Ex 28:17 *the first* row *shall be* a **s**, a topaz, and a H124
39:10 *the first* row *was* a **s**, a topaz, and a H124
Ezk 28:13 *was* thy covering, the **s**, topaz, and the H124
Rev 21:20 The fifth, sardonyx; the sixth, **s**; the *G4556*

SARDONYX
Rev 21:20 The fifth, **s**; the sixth, sardius; the *G4557*

SAREPTA
Lk 4:26 sent, save unto **S**, *a city* of Sidon, unto *G4558*

SARGON
Isa 20: 1 Ashdod, (when **S** the king of Assyria H5623

SARID
Jos 19:10 border of their inheritance was unto **S**: H8301
12 And turned from **S** eastward toward H8301

SARON
Act 9:35 And all that dwelt at Lydda and **S** saw *G4565*

SARSECHIM
Jer 39: 3 Samgarnebo, **S**, Rab-saris, H8310

SARUCH
Lk 3:35 Which was *the son* of **S**, which was *the* *G4562*

SAT
Gen 18: 1 **s** in the tent door in the heat of the day; H3427

Gen 19: 1 at even; and Lot s in the gate of Sodom: H3427
21:16 And she went, and s her down over H3427
16 the child. And she s over against *him,* H3427
31:34 furniture, and s upon them. And H3427
37:25 And they s down to eat bread: and they H3427
38:14 herself, and s in an open place, which H3427
43:33 And they s before him, the firstborn H3427
48: 2 himself, and s upon the bed. H3427
Ex 2:15 of Midian: and he s down by a well. H3427
12:29 of Pharaoh that s on his throne unto H3427
16: 3 of Egypt, when we s by the flesh pots, H3427
17:12 *it* under him, and he s thereon; and H3427
18:13 that Moses s to judge the people: H3427
32: 6 and the people s down to eat and to H3427
Lev 15: 6 thing whereon he s that hath the issue H3427
22 any thing that she s upon shall wash H3427
Dt 33: 3 thy hand: and they s down at thy feet; H8497
Jdg 6:11 of the LORD, and s under an oak which H3427
13: 9 the woman as she s in the field: but H3427
19: 6 And they s down, and did eat and H3427
15 he went in, he s him down in a street H3427
20:26 and wept, and s there before the LORD, H3427
Ru 2:14 vinegar. And she s beside the reapers: H3427
4: 1 Then went Boaz up to the gate, and s H3427
1 here. And he turned aside, and s down. H3427
2 Sit ye down here. And they s down. H3427
1Sa 1: 9 Now Eli the priest s upon a seat by a H3427
4:13 And when he came, lo, Eli s upon a H3427
19: 9 upon Saul, as he s in his house with his H3427
20:24 come, the king s him down to eat meat. H3427
25 And the king s upon his seat, as at H3427
25 arose, and Abner s by Saul's side, and H3427
28:23 from the earth, and s upon the bed. H3427
2Sa 2:13 of Gibeon: and they s down, the one on H3427
7: 1 And it came to pass, when the king s in H3427
18 Then went king David in, and s before H3427
18:24 And David s between the two gates: H3427
19: 8 Then the king arose, and s in the gate. H3427
1Ki 2:12 Then s Solomon upon the throne of H3427
19 unto her, and s down on his throne, H3427
19 mother; and she s on his right hand. H3427
13:20 And it came to pass, as they s at the H3427
16:11 as soon as he s on his throne, *that* he H3427
19: 4 and came and s down under a juniper H3427
21:13 of Belial, and s before him: and the H3427
22:10 the king of Judah s each on his throne, H3427
2Ki 1: 9 and, behold, he s on the top of an hill. H3427
4:20 s on her knees till noon, and *then* died. H3427
6:32 But Elisha s in his house, and the H3427
32 and the elders s with him; and *the king* H3427
11:19 And he s on the throne of the kings. H3427
13:13 and Jeroboam s upon his throne: and H3427
1Ch 17: 1 Now it came to pass, as David s in his H3427
16 And David the king came and s before H3427
29:23 Then Solomon s on the throne of the H3427
2Ch 18: 9 king of Judah s either of them on his H3427
9 robes, and they s in a void place at the H3427
Ezr 9: 3 and of my beard, and s down astonied. H3427
4 I s astonied until the evening sacrifice. H3427
10: 9 and all the people s in the street of the H3427
16 separated, and s down in the first day H3427
Neh 1: 4 these words, that I s down and wept, H3427
8:17 made booths, and s under the booths: H3427
Est 1: 2 king Ahasuerus s on the throne of his H3427
14 *and* which s the first in the kingdom;) H3427
2:19 then Mordecai s in the king's gate. H3427
21 In those days, while Mordecai s in the H3427
3:15 king and Haman s down to drink; but H3427
5: 1 and the king s upon his royal throne H3427
Job 2: 8 and he s down among the ashes. H3427
13 So they s down with him upon the H3427
29:25 I chose out their way, and s chief, and H3427
Ps 26: 4 I have not s with vain persons, neither H3427
137: 1 By the rivers of Babylon, there we s H3427
Song 2: 3 among the sons. I s down under his H3427
Jer 3: 2 the ways hast thou s for them, as the H3427
15:17 I s not in the assembly of the mockers, H3427
17 nor rejoiced; I s alone because of thy H3427
26:10 of the LORD, and s down in the entry H3427
32:12 Jews that s in the court of the prison. H3427
36:12 and, lo, all the princes s there, *even* H3427
22 Now the king s in the winterhouse in H3427
39: 3 came in, and s in the middle gate, *even* H3427
Ezk 3:15 of Chebar, and I s where they sat, and H3427
15 I sat where they s, and remained there H3427
8: 1 of the month, *as* I s in mine house, and H3427
1 elders of Judah s before me, that the H3427
14 there s women weeping for Tammuz. H3427
14: 1 of Israel unto me, and s before me. H3427
Ezk 20: 1 inquire of the LORD, and s before me. H3427
Dan 2:49 but Daniel *s* in the gate of the king.
Jna 3: 6 *him* with sackcloth, and s in ashes. H3427
4: 5 So Jonah went out of the city, and s on H3427
5 him a booth, and s under it in the H3427
Mt 4:16 The people which s in darkness saw G2521
16 and to them which s in the region and G2521
9:10 And it came to pass, as Jesus s at meat G345
10 and s down with him and his disciples. G4873
13: 1 out of the house, and s by the sea side. G2521
2 went into a ship, and s; and the whole G2521
48 they drew to shore, and s down, and G2523
14: 9 and them which s with him at meat, he G4873
15:29 up into a mountain, and s down there. G2521
24: 3 And as he s upon the mount of Olives, G2521
26: 7 poured it on his head, as he s *at meat.* G345
20 Now when the even was come, he s G345
55 staves for to take me? I s daily with you G2516
58 and s with the servants, to see the end. G2521
69 Now Peter s without in the palace: and G2521
28: 2 the stone from the door, and s upon it. G2521
Mk 2:15 And it came to pass, that, as Jesus s at G2621
15 and sinners s also together with Jesus G4873
3:32 And the multitude s about him, and G2521
34 on them which s about him, and said, G2521
4: 1 into a ship, and s in the sea; and the G2521
6:22 and them that s with him, the king said G4873
26 s with him, he would not reject her. G4873
40 And they s down in ranks, by hundreds, G377
9:35 And he s down, and called the twelve, G2523
10:46 s by the highway side begging. G2521
11: 2 never man s; loose him, and bring *him.* G2523
7 garments on him; and he s upon him. G2523
12:41 And Jesus s over against the treasury, G2523
13: 3 And as he s upon the mount of Olives G2521
14: 3 the leper, as he s at meat, there came G2621
18 And as they s and did eat, Jesus said, G345
54 high priest: and he s with the servants, G2258
16:14 unto the eleven as they s at meat, and G345
19 heaven, and s on the right hand of God. G2523
Lk 4:20 the minister, and s down. And the eyes G2523
5: 3 the land. And he s down, and taught G2523
29 and of others that s down with them. G2621
7:15 And he that was dead s up, and began to G339
36 Pharisee's house, and s down to meat. G347
37 she knew that *Jesus* s at meat in the G345
49 And they that s at meat with him G4873
10:39 s at Jesus' feet, and heard his word. G3869
11:37 and he went in, and s down to meat. G377
14:15 And when one of them that s at meat G4873
18:35 blind man s by the way side begging: G2521
19:30 man s: loose him, and bring *him hither.* G2523
22:14 And when the hour was come, he s G377
55 together, Peter s down among them. G2521
56 But a certain maid beheld him as he s G2521
24:30 And it came to pass, as he s at meat G2625
Jn 4: 6 with *his* journey, s thus on the well: G2516
6: 3 and there he s with his disciples. G2521
10 s down, in number about five thousand. G377
8: 2 him; and he s down, and taught them. G2523
9: 8 said, Is not this he that s and begged? G2521
11:20 met him: but Mary s *still* in the house. G2516
12: 2 of them that s at the table with him. G4873
14 a young ass, s thereon; as it is written, G2523
19:13 brought Jesus forth, and s down in the G2523
Act 2: 3 as of fire, and it s upon each of them. G2523
3:10 And they knew that it was he which s G2521
6:15 And all that s in the council, looking G2516
9:40 eyes: and when she saw Peter, she s up. G339
12:21 in royal apparel, s upon his throne, G2523
13:14 on the sabbath day, and s down. G2523
14: 8 And there s a certain man at Lystra, G2521
16:13 to be made; and we s down, and spake G2523
20: 9 And there s in a window a certain G2521
25:17 on the morrow I s on the judgment G2523
26:30 and Bernice, and they that s with them: G4775
1Co 10: 7 The people s down to eat and drink, G2523
Heb 1: 3 purged our sins, s down on the right G2523
10:12 ever, s down on the right hand of God; G2523
Rev 4: 2 set in heaven, and *one* s on the throne. G2521
3 And he that s was to look upon like a G2521
9 and thanks to him that s on the throne, G2521
10 before him that s on the throne, and G2521
5: 1 hand of him that s on the throne a G2521
7 hand of him that s upon the throne. G2521
6: 2 horse: and he that s on him had a bow; G2521
4 was given to him that s thereon to take G2521
5 horse; and he that s on him had a pair G2521
8 and his name that s on him was Death, G2521
Rev 9:17 and them that s on them, having G2521
11:16 elders, which s before God on their G2521
14:14 the cloud *one* s like unto the Son of G2521
15 voice to him that s on the cloud, Thrust G2521
16 And he that s on the cloud thrust in his G2521
19: 4 s on the throne, saying, Amen; Alleluia. G2521
11 horse; and he that s upon him *was* G2521
19 s on the horse, and against his army. G2521
21 the sword of him that s upon the horse, G2521
20: 4 And I saw thrones, and they s upon G2523
11 and him that s on it, from whose face G2521
21: 5 And he that s upon the throne said, G2521

SATAN

1Ch 21: 1 And S stood up against Israel, and H7854
Job 1: 6 LORD, and S came also among them. H7854
7 And the LORD said unto S, Whence H7854
7 thou? Then S answered the LORD, H7854
8 And the LORD said unto S, Hast thou H7854
9 Then S answered the LORD, and said, H7854
12 And the LORD said unto S, Behold, all H7854
12 thine hand. So S went forth from the H7854
2: 1 the LORD, and S came also among H7854
2 And the LORD said unto S, From H7854
2 comest thou? And S answered the H7854
3 And the LORD said unto S, Hast thou H7854
4 And S answered the LORD, and said, H7854
6 And the LORD said unto S, Behold, he H7854
7 So went S forth from the presence of H7854
Ps 109: 6 him: and let S stand at his right hand. H7854
Zec 3: 1 of the LORD, and S standing at his H7854
2 And the LORD said unto S, The LORD H7854
2 rebuke thee, O S; even the LORD that H7854
Mt 4:10 Get thee hence, S: for it is written, Thou G4567
12:26 And if S cast out Satan, he is divided G4567
26 And if Satan cast out S, he is divided G4567
16:23 thee behind me, S: thou art an offence G4567
Mk 1:13 days, tempted of S; and was with the G4567
3:23 in parables, How can S cast out Satan? G4567
23 in parables, How can Satan cast out S? G4567
26 And if S rise up against himself, and be G4567
4:15 when they have heard, S cometh G4567
8:33 thee behind me, S: for thou savourest G4567
Lk 4: 8 Get thee behind me, S: for it is written, G4567
10:18 And he said unto them, I beheld S as G4567
11:18 If S also be divided against himself, G4567
13:16 of Abraham, whom S hath bound, lo, G4567
22: 3 Then entered S into Judas surnamed G4567
31 Simon, behold, S hath desired *to have* G4567
Jn 13:27 And after the sop S entered into him. G4567
Act 5: 3 But Peter said, Ananias, why hath S G4567
26:18 and *from* the power of S unto God, that G4567
Ro 16:20 And the God of peace shall bruise S G4567
1Co 5: 5 To deliver such an one unto S for the G4567
7: 5 S tempt you not for your incontinency. G4567
2Co 2:11 Lest S should get an advantage of us: G4567
11:14 And no marvel; for S himself is G4567
12: 7 the messenger of S to buffet me, lest I G4566
1Th 2:18 once and again; but S hindered us. G4567
2Th 2: 9 the working of S with all power and G4567
1Ti 1:20 delivered unto S, that they may learn G4567
5:15 some are already turned aside after S. G4567
Rev 2: 9 and are not, but *are* the synagogue of S. G4567
13 slain among you, where S dwelleth. G4567
24 the depths of S, as they speak; I will G4567
3: 9 the synagogue of S, which say they are G4567
12: 9 the Devil, and S, which deceiveth the G4567
20: 2 S, and bound him a thousand years, G4567
7 S shall be loosed out of his prison, G4567

SATAN'S

Rev 2:13 *even* where S seat *is*: and thou holdest G4567

SATEST

Ps 9: 4 thou s in the throne judging right. H3427
Ezk 23:41 And s upon a stately bed, and a table H3427

SATIATE

Jer 31:14 And I will s the soul of the priests with H7301
46:10 and it shall be s and made drunk with H7646

SATIATED

Jer 31:25 For I have s the weary soul, and I have H7301

SATISFACTION

Nu 35:31 Moreover ye shall take no s for the life H3724
32 And ye shall take no s for him that is H3724

SATISFIED
Ex 15: 9 my lust shall be s upon them; I will H4390
Lev 26:26 weight: and ye shall eat, and not be s. H7646
Dt 14:29 shall eat and be s; that the LORD thy H7646
33:23 And of Naphtali he said, O Naphtali, s H7649
Job 19:22 as God, and are not s with my flesh? H7646
27:14 his offspring shall not be s with bread. H7646
31:31 that we had of his flesh! we cannot be s. H7646
Ps 17:15 be s, when I awake, with thy likeness. H7646
22:26 The meek shall eat and be s: they shall H7646
36: 8 They shall be abundantly s with the H7301
37:19 in the days of famine they shall be s. H7646
59:15 for meat, and grudge if they be not s. H7646
63: 5 My soul shall be s as *with* marrow and H7646
65: 4 courts: we shall be s with the goodness H7646
81:16 out of the rock should I have s thee. H7646
104:13 earth is s with the fruit of thy works. H7646
105:40 and s them with the bread of heaven. H7646
Prv 12:11 He that tilleth his land shall be s with H7646
14 A man shall be s with good by the fruit H7646
14:14 and a good man *shall be* s from himself.
18:20 A man's belly shall be s with the fruit of H7646
19:23 abide s; he shall not be visited with evil. H7649
20:13 eyes, *and* thou shalt be s with bread. H7646
27:20 full; so the eyes of man are never s. H7646
30:15 s, *yea*, four *things* say not, *It is* enough: H7646
Ecc 1: 8 *it*: the eye is not s with seeing, nor the H7646
4: 8 neither is his eye s with riches; neither H7646
5:10 He that loveth silver shall not be s with H7646
Isa 9:20 they shall not be s: they shall eat every H7646
44:16 roast, and is s: yea, he warmeth H7646
53:11 soul, *and* shall be s: by his knowledge H7646
66:11 That ye may suck, and be s with the H7646
Jer 31:14 s with my goodness, saith the LORD. H7646
50:10 that spoil her shall be s, saith the LORD. H7646
19 be s upon mount Ephraim and Gilead. H7646
Lam 5: 6 *to* the Assyrians, to be s with bread. H7646
Ezk 16:28 with them, and yet couldest not be s. H7654
29 and yet thou wast not s herewith. H7646
Joel 2:19 oil, and ye shall be s therewith: and I H7646
26 And ye shall eat in plenty, and be s, and H7646
Am 4: 8 but they were not s: yet have ye not H7646
Mic 6:14 Thou shalt eat, but not be s; and thy H7646
Hab 2: 5 and cannot be s, but gathereth unto H7646

SATISFIEST
Ps 145:16 Thou openest thine hand, and s the H7646

SATISFIETH
Ps 103: 5 Who s thy mouth with good *things; so* H7646
107: 9 For he s the longing soul, and filleth the H7646
Isa 55: 2 for *that which* s not? hearken diligently H7654

SATISFY
Job 38:27 To s the desolate and waste *ground*; H7646
Ps 90:14 O s us early with thy mercy; that we H7646
91:16 With long life will I s him, and shew H7646
132:15 provision: I will s her poor with bread. H7646
Prv 5:19 roe; let her breasts s thee at all times; H7301
6:30 he steal to s his soul when he is hungry; H4390
Isa 58:10 to the hungry, and s the afflicted soul; H7646
11 continually, and s thy soul in drought, H7646
Ezk 7:19 they shall not s their souls, neither H7646
Mk 8: 4 whence can a man s these *men* with *G5526*

SATISFYING
Prv 13:25 The righteous eateth to the s of his H7648
Col 2:23 not in any honour to the s of the flesh. *G4140*

SATYR
Isa 34:14 of the island, and the s shall cry to his H8163

SATYRS
Isa 13:21 dwell there, and s shall dance there. H8163

SAUL
Gen 36:37 And Samlah died, and S of Rehoboth H7586
38 And S died, and Baal-hanan the son of H7586
1Sa 9: 2 And he had a son, whose name *was* S, a H7586
3 And Kish said to S his son, Take now H7586
5 the land of Zuph, S said to his servant H7586
7 Then said S to his servant, But, behold, H7586
8 And the servant answered S again, and H7586
10 Then said S to his servant, Well said; H7586
15 in his ear a day before S came, saying, H7586
17 And when Samuel saw S, the LORD H7586
18 Then S drew near to Samuel in the H7586
19 And Samuel answered S, and said, I *am* H7586
21 And S answered and said, *Am* not I a H7586
1Sa 9:22 And Samuel took S and his servant, H7586
24 it, and set *it* before S. And *Samuel* said, H7586
24 So S did eat with Samuel that day. H7586
25 with S upon the top of the house. H7586
26 that Samuel called S to the top of the H7586
26 thee away. And S arose, and they went H7586
27 Samuel said to S, Bid the servant pass H7586
10:11 of Kish? *Is* S also among the prophets? H7586
12 proverb, *Is* S also among the prophets? H7586
16 And S said unto his uncle, He told us H7586
21 was taken, and S the son of Kish was H7586
26 And S also went home to Gibeah; and H7586
11: 4 to Gibeah of S, and told the tidings H7586
5 And, behold, S came after the herd out H7586
5 of the field; and S said, What *aileth* the H7586
6 And the spirit of God came upon S H7586
7 not forth after S and after Samuel, so H7586
11 And it was *so* on the morrow, that S H7586
12 *is* he that said, Shall S reign over us? H7586
13 And S said, There shall not a man be H7586
15 and there they made S king before the H7586
15 LORD; and there S and all the men of H7586
13: 1 S reigned one year; and when he had H7586
2 S chose him three thousand *men* of H7586
2 were with S in Michmash and in H7586
3 heard *of it*. And S blew the trumpet H7586
4 And all Israel heard say *that* S had H7586
4 were called together after S to Gilgal. H7586
7 Gad and Gilead. As for S, he *was* yet in H7586
9 And S said, Bring hither a burnt H7586
10 Samuel came; and S went out to meet H7586
11 thou done? And S said, Because I saw H7586
13 And Samuel said to S, Thou hast done H7586
15 of Benjamin. And S numbered the H7586
16 And S, and Jonathan his son, and the H7586
22 that *were* with S and Jonathan: but H7586
22 but with S and with Jonathan H7586
14: 1 the son of S said unto the young H7586
2 And S tarried in the uttermost part of H7586
16 And the watchmen of S in Gibeah of H7586
17 Then said S unto the people that *were* H7586
18 And S said unto Ahiah, Bring hither H7586
19 And it came to pass, while S talked H7586
19 increased: and S said unto the priest, H7586
20 And S and all the people that *were* with H7586
21 that *were* with S and Jonathan. H7586
24 that day: for S had adjured the people, H7586
33 Then they told S, saying, Behold, the H7586
34 And S said, Disperse yourselves among H7586
35 And S built an altar unto the LORD: the H7586
36 And S said, Let us go down after the H7586
37 And S asked counsel of God, Shall I go H7586
38 And S said, Draw ye near hither, all the H7586
40 S, Do what seemeth good unto thee. H7586
41 Therefore S said unto the LORD God of H7586
41 a perfect *lot*. And S and Jonathan were H7586
42 And S said, Cast *lots* between me and H7586
43 Then S said to Jonathan, Tell me what H7586
44 And S answered, God do so and more H7586
45 And the people said unto S, Shall H7586
46 Then S went up from following the H7586
47 So S took the kingdom over Israel, and H7586
49 Now the sons of S were Jonathan, and H7586
51 And Kish *was* the father of S; and Ner H7586
52 all the days of S: and when Saul saw H7586
52 of Saul: and when S saw any strong H7586
15: 1 Samuel also said unto S, The LORD H7586
4 And S gathered the people together, H7586
5 And S came to a city of Amalek, and H7586
6 And S said unto the Kenites, Go, H7586
7 And S smote the Amalekites from H7586
9 But S and the people spared Agag, and H7586
11 It repenteth me that I have set up S *to* H7586
12 And when Samuel rose early to meet S H7586
12 told Samuel, saying, S came to Carmel, H7586
13 And Samuel came to S: and Saul said H7586
13 And Samuel came to Saul: and S said H7586
15 And S said, They have brought them H7586
16 Then Samuel said unto S, Stay, and I H7586
20 And S said unto Samuel, Yea, I have H7586
24 And S said unto Samuel, I have sinned: H7586
26 And Samuel said unto S, I will not H7586
31 So Samuel turned again after S; and H7586
31 Saul; and S worshipped the LORD. H7586
34 Then Samuel went to Ramah; and S H7586
34 went up to his house to Gibeah of S. H7586
35 And Samuel came no more to see S H7586
35 mourned for S: and the LORD repented H7586
35 that he had made S king over Israel. H7586
1Sa 16: 1 thou mourn for S, seeing I have rejected H7586
2 And Samuel said, How can I go? if S H7586
14 departed from S, and an evil spirit from H7586
17 And S said unto his servants, Provide H7586
19 Wherefore S sent messengers unto H7586
20 and sent *them* by David his son unto S. H7586
21 And David came to S, and stood before H7586
22 And S sent to Jesse, saying, Let David, I H7586
23 God was upon S, that David took an H7586
23 with his hand: so S was refreshed, and H7586
17: 2 And S and the men of Israel were H7586
8 and ye servants to S? choose you a man H7586
11 When S and all Israel heard those H7586
12 men *for* an old man in the days of S. H7586
13 went *and* followed S to the battle: and H7586
14 and the three eldest followed S. H7586
15 But David went and returned from S to H7586
19 Now S, and they, and all the men of H7586
31 *them* before S: and he sent for him. H7586
32 And David said to S, Let no man's heart H7586
33 And S said to David, Thou art not able H7586
34 And David said unto S, Thy servant H7586
37 Philistine. And S said unto David, Go, H7586
38 And S armed David with his armour, H7586
39 And David said unto S, I cannot go with H7586
55 And when S saw David go forth against H7586
57 him before S with the head of the H7586
58 And S said to him, Whose son *art* thou, H7586
18: 1 end of speaking unto S, that the soul of H7586
2 And S took him that day, and would let H7586
5 And David went out whithersoever S H7586
5 wisely: and S set him over the men H7586
6 to meet king S, with tabrets, with joy, H7586
7 they played, and said, S hath slain his H7586
8 And S was very wroth, and the saying H7586
9 And S eyed David from that day and H7586
10 God came upon S, and he prophesied in H7586
11 And S cast the javelin; for he said, I will H7586
12 And S was afraid of David, because the H7586
12 with him, and was departed from S. H7586
13 Therefore S removed him from him, H7586
15 Wherefore when S saw that he behaved H7586
17 And S said to David, Behold my elder H7586
17 battles. For S said, Let not mine hand H7586
18 And David said unto S, Who *am* I? and H7586
20 they told S, and the thing pleased him. H7586
21 And S said, I will give him her, that she H7586
21 him. Wherefore S said to David, Thou H7586
22 And S commanded his servants, H7586
24 And the servants of S told him, saying, H7586
25 And S said, Thus shall ye say to David, H7586
25 enemies. But S thought to make David H7586
27 S gave him Michal his daughter to wife. H7586
28 And S saw and knew that the LORD H7586
29 And S was yet the more afraid of H7586
29 S became David's enemy continually. H7586
30 of S; so that his name was much set by. H7586
19: 1 And S spake to Jonathan his son, and H7586
2 David, saying, S my father seeketh to H7586
4 of David unto S his father, and said H7586
6 And S hearkened unto the voice of H7586
6 of Jonathan: and S sware, *As* the LORD H7586
7 brought David to S, and he was in his H7586
9 the LORD was upon S, as he sat in his H7586
10 And S sought to smite David even to H7586
11 S also sent messengers unto David's H7586
14 And when S sent messengers to take H7586
15 And S sent the messengers *again* to see H7586
17 And S said unto Michal, Why hast thou H7586
17 Michal answered S, He said unto me, H7586
18 told him all that S had done to him. H7586
19 And it was told S, saying, Behold, David H7586
20 And S sent messengers to take David: H7586
20 of S, and they also prophesied. H7586
21 And when it was told S, he sent other H7586
21 likewise. And S sent messengers again H7586
24 they say, *Is* S also among the prophets? H7586
20:26 Nevertheless S spake not any thing that H7586
27 was empty: and S said unto Jonathan H7586
28 And Jonathan answered S, David H7586
32 And Jonathan answered S his father, H7586
33 And S cast a javelin at him to smite H7586
21: 7 Now a certain man of the servants of S H7586
7 of the herdmen that *belonged* to S. H7586
10 S, and went to Achish the king of Gath. H7586
11 him in dances, saying, S hath slain his H7586
22: 6 When S heard that David was H7586

1Sa 22: 6 *were* with him, (now S abode in Gibeah H7586
7 Then S said unto his servants that H7586
9 the servants of S, and said, I saw the H7586
12 And S said, Hear now, thou son of H7586
13 And S said unto him, Why have ye H7586
21 And Abiathar shewed David that S had H7586
22 would surely tell S: I have occasioned H7586
23: 7 And it was told S that David was come H7586
7 come to Keilah. And S said, God hath H7586
8 And S called all the people together to H7586
9 And David knew that S secretly H7586
10 heard that S seeketh to come to Keilah, H7586
11 into his hand? will S come down, as thy H7586
12 into the hand of S? And the LORD said, H7586
13 go. And it was told S that David was H7586
14 of Ziph. And S sought him every day, H7586
15 And David saw that S was come out to H7586
17 for the hand of S my father shall not H7586
17 and that also S my father knoweth. H7586
19 Then came up the Ziphites to S to H7586
21 And S said, Blessed *be* ye of the LORD; H7586
24 to Ziph before S: but David and his men H7586
25 S also and his men went to seek *him*. H7586
25 of Maon. And when S heard *that*, he H7586
26 And S went on this side of the H7586
26 away for fear of S; for Saul and his men H7586
26 for fear of Saul; for S and his men H7586
27 But there came a messenger unto S, H7586
28 Wherefore S returned from pursuing H7586
24: 1 And it came to pass, when S was H7586
2 Then S took three thousand chosen H7586
3 *was* a cave; and S went in to cover his H7586
7 not to rise against S. But Saul rose up H7586
7 against Saul. But S rose up out of the H7586
8 and cried after S, saying, My lord the H7586
8 king. And when S looked behind him, H7586
9 And David said to S, Wherefore hearest H7586
16 these words unto S, that Saul said, *Is* H7586
16 unto Saul, that S said, *Is* this thy voice, H7586
16 And S lifted up his voice, and wept. H7586
22 And David sware unto S. And Saul went H7586
22 And David sware unto Saul. And S H7586
25:44 But S had given Michal his daughter, H7586
26: 1 And the Ziphites came unto S to H7586
2 Then S arose, and went down to the H7586
3 And S pitched in the hill of Hachilah, H7586
3 S came after him into the wilderness. H7586
4 that S was come in very deed. H7586
5 to the place where S had pitched: and H7586
5 the place where S lay, and Abner the H7586
5 of his host: and S lay in the trench, and H7586
6 go down with me to S to the camp? And H7586
7 and, behold, S lay sleeping within H7586
17 And S knew David's voice, and said, *Is* H7586
21 Then said S, I have sinned: return, my H7586
25 Then S said to David, Blessed *be* thou, H7586
25 on his way, and S returned to his place. H7586
27: 1 day by the hand of S: *there is* nothing H7586
1 Philistines; and S shall despair of me, H7586
4 And it was told S that David was fled to H7586
28: 3 his own city. And S had put away those H7586
4 in Shunem: and S gathered all Israel H7586
5 And when S saw the host of the H7586
6 And when S inquired of the LORD, the H7586
7 Then said S unto his servants, Seek me H7586
8 And S disguised himself, and put on H7586
9 knowest what S hath done, how he H7586
10 And S sware to her by the LORD, H7586
12 woman spake to S, saying, Why hast H7586
12 hast thou deceived me? for thou *art* S. H7586
13 S, I saw gods ascending out of the earth. H7586
14 a mantle. And S perceived that it *was* H7586
15 And Samuel said to S, Why hast thou H7586
15 to bring me up? And S answered, I am H7586
20 Then S fell straightway all along on the H7586
21 And the woman came unto S, and saw H7586
25 And she brought *it* before S, and before H7586
29: 3 the servant of S the king of Israel, H7586
5 another in dances, saying, S slew his H7586
31: 2 hard upon S and upon his sons; H7586
3 And the battle went sore against S, and H7586
4 Then said S unto his armourbearer, H7586
4 S took a sword, and fell upon it. H7586
5 And when his armourbearer saw that S H7586
6 So S died, and his three sons, and his H7586
7 fled, and that S and his sons were H7586
8 that they found S and his three sons H7586
11 which the Philistines had done to S; H7586
12 took the body of S and the bodies of his H7586

2Sa 1: 1 after the death of S, when David was H7586
2 out of the camp from S with his clothes H7586
4 S and Jonathan his son are dead also. H7586
5 that S and Jonathan his son be dead? H7586
6 Gilboa, behold, S leaned upon his H7586
12 until even, for S, and for Jonathan his H7586
17 over S and over Jonathan his son: H7586
21 the shield of S, *as though he had* not H7586
22 and the sword of S returned not empty. H7586
23 S and Jonathan *were* lovely and H7586
24 Ye daughters of Israel, weep over S, H7586
2: 4 Jabesh-gilead *were they* that buried S. H7586
5 lord, *even* unto S, and have buried him. H7586
7 for your master S is dead, and also the H7586
8 S, and brought him over to Mahanaim; H7586
12 S, went out from Mahanaim to Gibeon. H7586
15 S, and twelve of the servants of David. H7586
3: 1 the house of S and the house of David: H7586
1 house of S waxed weaker and weaker. H7586
6 the house of S and the house of David, H7586
6 made himself strong for the house of S. H7586
7 And S had a concubine, whose name H7586
8 unto the house of S thy father, to his H7586
10 from the house of S, and to set up the H7586
4: 4 tidings came of S and Jonathan out of H7586
8 the son of S thine enemy, which H7586
8 the king this day of S, and of his seed. H7586
10 When one told me, saying, Behold, S is H7586
5: 2 Also in time past, when S was king H7586
6:20 the daughter of S came out to meet H7586
23 Therefore Michal the daughter of S had H7586
7:15 *it* from S, whom I put away before thee. H7586
9: 1 is left of the house of S, that I may shew H7586
2 And *there was* of the house of S a H7586
3 of the house of S, that I may shew the H7586
6 the son of S, was come unto David, H7586
7 thee all the land of S thy father; and H7586
9 that pertained to S and to all his house. H7586
12: 7 I delivered thee out of the hand of S; H7586
16: 5 of the house of S, whose name *was* H7586
8 of the house of S, in whose stead thou H7586
19:17 of the house of S, and his fifteen sons H7586
24 And Mephibosheth the son of S came H7586
21: 1 answered, *It is* for S, and for *his* bloody H7586
2 unto them: and S sought to slay them H7586
4 no silver nor gold of S, nor of his house; H7586
6 in Gibeah of S, *whom* the LORD did H7586
7 the son of S, because of the LORD'S H7586
7 David and Jonathan the son of S. H7586
8 whom she bare unto S, Armoni and H7586
8 the daughter of S, whom she brought H7586
11 of Aiah, the concubine of S, had done. H7586
12 took the bones of S and the bones of H7586
12 the Philistines had slain S in Gilboa: H7586
13 thence the bones of S and the bones of H7586
14 And the bones of S and Jonathan his H7586
22: 1 his enemies, and out of the hand of S: H7586
1Ch 5:10 And in the days of S they made war H7586
8:33 And Ner begat Kish, and Kish begat S, H7586
33 begat Saul, and S begat Jonathan, and H7586
9:39 And Ner begat Kish; and Kish begat S; H7586
39 begat Saul; and S begat Jonathan, and H7586
10: 2 hard after S, and after his sons; and H7586
2 and Malchishua, the sons of S. H7586
3 And the battle went sore against S, and H7586
4 Then said S to his armourbearer, Draw H7586
4 So S took a sword, and fell upon it. H7586
5 And when his armourbearer saw that S H7586
6 So S died, and his three sons, and all H7586
7 they fled, and that S and his sons were H7586
8 S and his sons fallen in mount Gilboa. H7586
11 all that the Philistines had done to S, H7586
12 away the body of S, and the bodies of H7586
13 So S died for his transgression which H7586
11: 2 past, even when S was king, thou *wast* H7586
12: 1 close because of S the son of Kish: and H7586
19 Philistines against S to battle: but they H7586
19 master S to *the jeopardy of* our heads. H7586
23 the kingdom of S to him, according to H7586
29 the kindred of S, three thousand: for H7586
29 had kept the ward of the house of S. H7586
13: 3 for we inquired not at it in the days of S. H7586
15:29 the daughter of S looking out at a H7586
26:28 And all that Samuel the seer, and S the H7586
Ps 18:ttl and from the hand of S: And he said, H7586
52:ttl came and told S, and said unto him, H7586
54:ttl S, Doth not David hide himself with us? H7586
57:ttl David, when he fled from S in the cave. H7586
59:ttl of David; when S sent, and they H7586

Isa 10:29 Ramah is afraid; Gibeah of S is fled. H7586
Act 7:58 a young man's feet, whose name was S. G4569
8: 1 And S was consenting unto his death. G4569
3 As for S, he made havock of the church, G4569
9: 1 And S, yet breathing out threatenings G4569
4 him, S, Saul, why persecutest thou me? G4549
4 him, Saul, S, why persecutest thou me? G4549
8 And S arose from the earth; and when G4569
11 S, of Tarsus: for, behold, he prayeth, G4569
17 on him said, Brother S, the Lord, *even* G4549
19 Then was S certain days with the G4569
22 But S increased the more in strength, G4569
24 But their laying await was known of S. G4569
26 And when S was come to Jerusalem, he G4569
11:25 Barnabas to Tarsus, for to seek S: G4569
30 elders by the hands of Barnabas and S. G4569
12:25 And Barnabas and S returned from G4569
13: 1 up with Herod the tetrarch, and S. G4569
2 me Barnabas and S for the work G4569
7 S, and desired to hear the word of God. G4569
9 Then S, (who also *is called* Paul,) filled G4569
21 gave unto them S the son of Cis, a man G4549
22: 7 me, S, Saul, why persecutest thou me? G4549
7 me, Saul, S, why persecutest thou me? G4549
13 unto me, Brother S, receive thy sight. G4549
26:14 the Hebrew tongue, S, Saul, why G4549
14 tongue, Saul, S, why persecutest thou G4549

SAUL'S

1Sa 9: 3 And the asses of Kish S father were H7586
10:14 And S uncle said unto him and to his H7586
15 And S uncle said, Tell me, I pray thee, H7586
14:50 And the name of S wife *was* Ahinoam, H7586
50 *was* Abner, the son of Ner, S uncle. H7586
16:15 And S servants said unto him, Behold H7586
18: 5 and also in the sight of S servants. H7586
10 and *there was* a javelin in S hand. H7586
19 time when Merab S daughter should H7586
20 And Michal S daughter loved David: H7586
23 And S servants spake those words in H7586
28 and *that* Michal S daughter loved him. H7586
19: 2 But Jonathan S son delighted much in H7586
10 away out of S presence, and he smote H7586
20:25 S side, and David's place was empty. H7586
30 Then S anger was kindled against H7586
23:16 And Jonathan S son arose, and went to H7586
24: 4 and cut off the skirt of S robe privily. H7586
5 him, because he had cut off S skirt. H7586
26:12 of water from S bolster; and they gat H7586
31: 2 Abinadab, and Malchishua, S sons. H7586
2Sa 2: 8 But Abner the son of Ner, captain of S H7586
10 Ish-bosheth S son *was* forty years old H7586
3:13 first bring Michal S daughter, when H7586
14 to Ish-bosheth S son, saying, Deliver H7586
4: 1 And when S son heard that Abner was H7586
2 And S son had two men *that were* H7586
4 And Jonathan, S son, had a son *that* H7586
6:16 of David, Michal S daughter looked H7586
9: 9 Then the king called to Ziba, S servant, H7586
1Ch 12: 2 a bow, *even* of S brethren of Benjamin. H7586

SAVE

Gen 12:12 will kill me, but they will s thee alive. H2421
14:24 S only that which the young men have H1107
39: 6 ought he had, s the bread which H3588+H518
45: 7 to s your lives by a great deliverance. H2421
50:20 as *it is* this day, to s much people alive. H2421
Ex 1:22 and every daughter ye shall s alive. H2421
12:16 be done in them, s *that* which every man H389
22:20 He that sacrificeth unto *any* god, s H1115
Nu 14:30 dwell therein, s Caleb the son of H3588+H518
26:65 a man of them, s Caleb the son H3588+H518
32:12 S Caleb the son of Jephunneh H3588+H518
Dt 1:36 S Caleb the son of Jephunneh; he shall H2108
15: 4 S when there shall be no poor among H657
20: 4 for you against your enemies, to s you. H3467
16 shalt s alive nothing that breatheth: H2421
22:27 cried, and *there was* none to s her. H3467
28:29 evermore, and no man shall s *thee*. H3467
Jos 2:13 And *that* ye will s alive my father, and H2421
10: 6 to us quickly, and s us, and help us: for H3467
11:13 s Hazor only; *that* did Joshua burn. H2108
19 the children of Israel, s the Hivites the H1115
14: 4 in the land, s cities to dwell *in*, H3588+H518
22:22 against the LORD, (s us not this day,) H3467
Jdg 6:14 and thou shalt s Israel from the hand H3467
15 wherewith shall I s Israel? behold, my H3467
31 for Baal? will ye s him? he that will H3467
36 God, If thou wilt s Israel by mine hand, H3467

Jdg 6:37 that thou wilt s Israel by mine hand, H3467
7: 7 that lapped will I s you, and deliver the H3467
14 *is* nothing else s the sword of H1115+H518
1Sa 4: 3 s us out of the hand of our enemies. H3467
7: 8 s us out of the hand of the Philistines. H3467
9:16 that he may s my people out of the H3467
10:24 shouted, and said, God s the king. H2421
27 shall this man s us? And they despised H3467
11: 3 man to s us, we will come out to thee. H3467
14: 6 to the LORD to s by many or by few. H3467
19:11 saying, If thou s not thy life to night, H4422
21: 9 *there is* no other s that here. And David H2108
23: 2 and smite the Philistines, and s Keilah. H3467
30:17 a man of them, s four hundred H3588+H518
22 recovered, s to every man his H3588+H518
2Sa 3:18 David I will s my people Israel out H3467
12: 3 had nothing, s one little ewe H3588+H518
16:16 God s the king, God save the king. H2421
16 God save the king, God s the king. H2421
22:28 And the afflicted people thou wilt s: but H3467
32 For who *is* God, s the LORD? and who H1107
32 LORD? and who *is* a rock, s our God? H1107
42 They looked, but *there was* none to s; H3467
1Ki 1:12 that thou mayest s thine own life, and H4422
25 him, and say, God s king Adonijah. H2421
34 trumpet, and say, God s king Solomon. H2421
39 the people said, God s king Solomon. H2421
3:18 us in the house, s we two in the house. H2108
8: 9 *There was* nothing in the ark s the two H7535
15: 5 s only in the matter of Uriah the Hittite.
18: 5 we may find grass to s the horses and H2421
20:31 of Israel: peradventure he will s thy life. H2421
22:31 s only with the king of Israel. H3588+H518
2Ki 4: 2 any thing in the house, s a pot of oil. H2421
7: 4 the Syrians: if they s us alive, we shall H2421
11:12 their hands, and said, God s the king. H2421
15: 4 S that the high places were not H7535
16: 7 son: come up, and s me out of the hand H3467
19:19 God, I beseech thee, s thou us out of his H3467
34 For I will defend this city, to s it, for H3467
24:14 none remained, s the poorest sort of H2108
1Ch 16:35 And say ye, S us, O God of our H3467
2Ch 2: 6 s only to burn sacrifice before him? H518
5:10 *There was* nothing in the ark s the two H7535
18:30 s only with the king of Israel. H3588+H518
21:17 s Jehoahaz, the youngest of his sons.
23: 6 of the LORD, s the priests, and H3588+H518
11 anointed him, and said, God s the king. H2421
Neh 2:12 me, s the beast that I rode upon. H3588+H518
6:11 the temple to s his life? I will not go in. H2425
Job 2: 6 he *is* in thine hand; but s his life. H8104
20:20 he shall not s of that which he desired. H4422
22:29 up; and he shall s the humble person. H3467
40:14 that thine own right hand can s thee. H3467
Ps 3: 7 Arise, O LORD; s me, O my God: for H3467
6: 4 Return, O LORD, deliver my soul: oh s H3467
7: 1 do I put my trust: s me from all them H3467
18:27 For thou wilt s the afflicted people; but H3467
31 For who *is* God s the LORD? or who *is* a H1107
31 the LORD? or who *is* a rock s our God? H2108
41 They cried, but *there was* none to s H3467
20: 9 S, LORD: let the king hear us when we H3467
22:21 S me from the lion's mouth: for thou H3467
28: 9 S thy people, and bless thine H3467
31: 2 rock, for an house of defence to s me. H3467
16 thy servant: s me for thy mercies' sake. H3467
37:40 and s them, because they trust in him. H3467
44: 3 did their own arm s them: but thy right H3467
6 my bow, neither shall my sword s me. H3467
54: 1 S me, O God, by thy name, and judge H3467
55:16 upon God; and the LORD shall s me. H3467
57: 3 He shall send from heaven, and s me H3467
59: 2 of iniquity, and s me from bloody men. H3467
60: 5 That thy beloved may be delivered; s H3467
69: 1 S me, O God; for the waters are come in H3467
35 For God will s Zion, and will build the H3467
71: 2 incline thine ear unto me, and s me. H3467
3 commandment to s me; for thou *art* H3467
72: 4 the people, he shall s the children of the H3467
13 and shall s the souls of the needy. H3467
76: 9 When God arose to judgment, to s all H3467
80: 2 up thy strength, and come *and* s us. H3444
86: 2 God, s thy servant that trusteth in thee. H3467
16 and s the son of thine handmaid. H3467
106:47 S us, O LORD our God, and gather us H3467
108: 6 That thy beloved may be delivered: s H3467
109:26 Help me, O LORD my God: O s me H3467
31 of the poor, to s *him* from those that H3467
118:25 S now, I beseech thee, O LORD: O H3467
Ps 119:94 I *am* thine, s me; for I have sought thy H3467
146 I cried unto thee; s me, and I shall keep H3467
138: 7 enemies, and thy right hand shall s me. H3467
145:19 also will hear their cry, and will s them. H3467
Prv 20:22 wait on the LORD, and he shall s thee. H3467
Isa 25: 9 him, and he will s us: this *is* the LORD; H3467
33:22 the LORD *is* our king; he will s us. H3467
35: 4 a recompence; he will come and s you. H3467
37:20 Now therefore, O LORD our God, s us H3467
35 For I will defend this city to s it for H3467
38:20 The LORD *was ready* to s me: therefore H3467
45:20 and pray unto a god *that* cannot s. H3467
46: 7 answer, nor s him out of his trouble. H3467
47:13 stand up, and s thee from *these things* H3467
15 one to his quarter; none shall s thee. H3467
49:25 with thee, and I will s thy children. H3467
59: 1 that it cannot s; neither his ear heavy, H3467
63: 1 speak in righteousness, mighty to s. H3467
Jer 2:27 trouble they will say, Arise, and s us. H3467
28 arise, if they can s thee in the time of H3467
11:12 but they shall not s them at all in the H3467
14: 9 man *that* cannot s? yet thou, O LORD, H3467
15:20 I *am* with thee to s thee and to deliver H3467
17:14 I shall be healed; s me, and I shall be H3467
30:10 for, lo, I will s thee from afar, and H3467
11 saith the LORD, to s thee: though I H3467
31: 7 s thy people, the remnant of Israel. H3467
42:11 I *am* with you to s you, and to deliver H3467
46:27 for, behold, I will s thee from afar off, H3467
48: 6 Flee, s your lives, and be like the heath H4422
Lam 4:17 for a nation *that* could not s *us*. H3467
Ezk 3:18 his wicked way, to s his life; the same H2421
13:18 ye s the souls alive *that come* unto you? H2421
19 not die, and to s the souls alive that H2421
18:27 and right, he shall s his soul alive. H2421
34:22 Therefore will I s my flock, and they H3467
36:29 I will also s you from all your H3467
37:23 but I will s them out of all their H3467
Dan 6: 7 for thirty days, s of thee, O king, he H3861
12 within thirty days, s of thee, O king, H3861
Hos 1: 7 of Judah, and will s them by the LORD H3467
7 God, and will not s them by bow, nor H3467
13:10 *other* that may s thee in all thy cities? H3467
14: 3 Asshur shall not s us; we will not ride H3467
Hab 1: 2 thee *of* violence, and thou wilt not s! H3467
Zep 3:17 *is* mighty; he will s, he will rejoice over H3467
19 thee: and I will s her that halteth, and H3467
Zec 8: 7 Behold, I will s my people from the H3467
13 of Israel; so will I s you, and ye shall be H3467
9:16 And the LORD their God shall s them H3467
10: 6 Judah, and I will s the house of Joseph, H3467
12: 7 The LORD also shall s the tents of H3467
Mt 1:21 for he shall s his people from their sins. G4982
8:25 him, saying, Lord, s us: we perish. G4982
11:27 man the Father, s the Son, and *he* to G1508
13:57 without honour, s in his own country, G1508
14:30 to sink, he cried, saying, Lord, s me. G4982
16:25 For whosoever will s his life shall lose G4982
17: 8 eyes, they saw no man, s Jesus only. G1508
18:11 For the Son of man is come to s that G4982
19:11 this saying, s *they* to whom it is given. G235
27:40 *it* in three days, s thyself. If thou be the G4982
42 He saved others; himself he cannot s. If G4982
49 us see whether Elias will come to s him. G4982
Mk 3: 4 or to do evil? to s life, or to kill? But G4982
5:37 to follow him, s Peter, and James, and G1508
6: 5 do no mighty work, s that he laid his G1508
8 for *their* journey, s a staff only; no G1508
8:35 For whosoever will s his life shall lose G4982
35 and the gospel's, the same shall s it. G4982
9: 8 any more, s Jesus only with themselves. G235
15:30 S thyself, and come down from the G4982
31 He saved others; himself he cannot s. G4982
Lk 4:26 But unto none of them was Elias sent, s G1508
6: 9 or to do evil? to s life, or to destroy *it*? G4982
8:51 no man to go in, s Peter, and James, G1508
9:24 For whosoever will s his life shall lose G4982
24 his life for my sake, the same shall s it. G4982
56 men's lives, but to s *them*. And they G4982
17:18 to give glory to God, s this stranger. G1508
33 Whosoever shall seek to s his life shall G4982
18:19 good? none *is* good, s one, *that is*, God. G1508
19:10 to seek and to s that which was lost. G4982
23:35 saved others; let him s himself, if he be G4982
37 If thou be the king of the Jews, s thyself. G4982
39 If thou be Christ, s thyself and us. G4982
Jn 6:22 other boat there, s that one whereinto G1508
46 seen the Father, s he which is of God, G1508
12:27 shall I say? Father, s me from this hour: G4982
Jn 12:47 to judge the world, but to s the world. G4982
13:10 needeth not s to wash *his* feet, but G2228
Act 2:40 exhort, saying, S yourselves from this G4982
20:23 S that the Holy Ghost witnesseth in G4133
21:25 no such thing, s only that they keep G1508
27:43 But the centurion, willing to s Paul, G1295
Ro 11:14 my flesh, and might s some of them. G4982
1Co 1:21 of preaching to s them that believe. G4982
2: 2 you, s Jesus Christ, and him crucified. G1508
11 the things of a man, s the spirit of man G1508
7:16 thou shalt s *thy* husband? or how G4982
16 O man, whether thou shalt s *thy* wife? G4982
9:22 *men*, that I might by all means s some. G4982
2Co 11:24 five times received I forty *stripes* s one. G3844
Gal 1:19 But other of the apostles saw I none, s G1508
6:14 But God forbid that I should glory, s in G1508
1Ti 1:15 world to s sinners; of whom I am chief. G4982
4:16 both s thyself, and them that hear thee. G4982
Heb 5: 7 that was able to s him from death, and G4982
7:25 Wherefore he is able also to s them to G4982
Jas 1:21 word, which is able to s your souls. G4982
2:14 and have not works? can faith s him? G4982
4:12 There is one lawgiver, who is able to s G4982
5:15 And the prayer of faith shall s the sick, G4982
20 of his way shall s a soul from death, G4982
1Pt 3:21 doth also now s us (not the putting G4982
Jude 23 And others s with fear, pulling *them* G4982
Rev 13:17 And that no man might buy or sell, s he G1508

SAVED

Gen 47:25 And they said, Thou hast s our lives: let
Ex 1:17 them, but s the men children alive. H2425
18 and have s the men children alive? H2425
14:30 Thus the LORD s Israel that day out of H3467
Nu 10: 9 and ye shall be s from your enemies. H3467
22:33 also I had slain thee, and s her alive. H2421
31:15 And Moses said unto them, Have ye s H2421
Dt 33:29 unto thee, O people s by the LORD, the H3467
Jos 6:25 And Joshua s Rahab the harlot alive, H2421
Jdg 7: 2 me, saying, Mine own hand hath s me. H3467
8:19 had s them alive, I would not slay you. H2421
21:14 which they had s alive of the women H2421
1Sa 10:19 God, who himself s you out of all your H3467
14:23 So the LORD s Israel that day: and the H3467
23: 5 So David s the inhabitants of Keilah. H3467
27:11 And David s neither man nor woman H2421
2Sa 19: 5 this day have s thy life, and the lives H4422
9 saying, The king s us out of the hand of H5337
22: 4 so shall I be s from mine enemies. H3467
2Ki 6:10 and s himself there, not once nor twice. H8104
14:27 heaven: but he s them by the hand of H3467
1Ch 11:14 LORD s *them* by a great deliverance. H3467
2Ch 32:22 Thus the LORD s Hezekiah and the H3467
Neh 9:27 saviours, who s them out of the hand H3467
Ps 18: 3 so shall I be s from mine enemies. H3467
33:16 There is no king s by the multitude of H3467
34: 6 *him*, and s him out of all his troubles. H3467
44: 7 But thou hast s us from our enemies, H3467
80: 3 thy face to shine; and we shall be s. H3467
7 thy face to shine; and we shall be s. H3467
19 thy face to shine; and we shall be s. H3467
106: 8 Nevertheless he s them for his name's H3467
10 And he s them from the hand of him H3467
107:13 *and* he s them out of their distresses. H3467
Prv 28:18 Whoso walketh uprightly shall be s: but H3467
Isa 30:15 rest shall ye be s; in quietness and in H3467
43:12 I have declared, and have s, and I have H3467
45:17 *But* Israel shall be s in the LORD with H3467
22 Look unto me, and be ye s, all the ends H3467
63: 9 of his presence s them: in his love and H3467
64: 5 those is continuance, and we shall be s. H3467
Jer 4:14 thou mayest be s. How long shall thy H3467
8:20 the summer is ended, and we are not s. H3467
17:14 and I shall be s: for thou *art* my praise. H3467
23: 6 In his days Judah shall be s, and Israel H3467
30: 7 trouble; but he shall be s out of it. H3467
33:16 In those days shall Judah be s, and H3467
Mt 10:22 he that endureth to the end shall be s. G4982
19:25 amazed, saying, Who then can be s? G4982
24:13 unto the end, the same shall be s. G4982
22 should no flesh be s: but for the elect's G4982
27:42 He s others; himself he cannot save. G4982
Mk 10:26 among themselves, Who then can be s? G4982
13:13 unto the end, the same shall be s. G4982
20 no flesh should be s: but for the elect's G4982
15:31 He s others; himself he cannot save. G4982
16:16 baptized shall be s; but he that believeth G4982
Lk 1:71 That we should be s from our enemies, G4991
7:50 Thy faith hath s thee; go in peace. G4982

Lk 8:12 hearts, lest they should believe and be s. G4982
13:23 few that be s? And he said unto them, G4982
18:26 that heard *it* said, Who then can be s? G4982
42 Receive thy sight: thy faith hath s thee. G4982
23:35 *him*, saying, He s others; let him save G4982
Jn 3:17 that the world through him might be s. G4982
5:34 these things I say, that ye might be s. G4982
10: 9 in, he shall be s, and shall go in and G4982
Act 2:21 call on the name of the Lord shall be s. G4982
47 to the church daily such as should be s. G4982
4:12 among men, whereby we must be s. G4982
11:14 thou and all thy house shall be s. G4982
15: 1 the manner of Moses, ye cannot be s. G4982
11 Jesus Christ we shall be s, even as they. G4982
16:30 and said, Sirs, what must I do to be s? G4982
31 and thou shalt be s, and thy house. G4982
27:20 we should be s was then taken away. G4982
31 these abide in the ship, ye cannot be s. G4982
Ro 5: 9 we shall be s from wrath through him. G4982
10 reconciled, we shall be s by his life. G4982
8:24 For we are s by hope: but hope that is G4982
9:27 sand of the sea, a remnant shall be s: G4982
10: 1 to God for Israel is, that they might be s. G4991
9 him from the dead, thou shalt be s. G4982
13 upon the name of the Lord shall be s. G4982
11:26 And so all Israel shall be s: as it is G4982
1Co 1:18 us which are s it is the power of God. G4982
3:15 he himself shall be s; yet so as by fire. G4982
5: 5 may be s in the day of the Lord Jesus. G4982
10:33 the *profit* of many, that they may be s. G4982
15: 2 By which also ye are s, if ye keep in G4982
2Co 2:15 that are s, and in them that perish: G4982
Eph 2: 5 together with Christ, (by grace ye are s;) G4982
8 For by grace are ye s through faith; and G4982
1Th 2:16 that they might be s, to fill up their sins G4982
2Th 2:10 love of the truth, that they might be s. G4982
1Ti 2: 4 Who will have all men to be s, and to G4982
15 Notwithstanding she shall be s in G4982
2Ti 1: 9 Who hath s us, and called *us* with an G4982
Tit 3: 5 to his mercy he s us, by the washing of G4982
1Pt 3:20 few, that is, eight souls were s by water. G1295
4:18 And if the righteous scarcely be s, G4982
2Pt 2: 5 And spared not the old world, but s G5442
Jude 5 the Lord, having s the people out of the G4982
Rev 21:24 And the nations of them which are s G4982

SAVEST
2Sa 22: 3 my saviour; thou s me from violence. H3467
Job 26: 2 s thou the arm *that hath* no strength? H3467
Ps 17: 7 O thou that s by thy right hand them H3467

SAVETH
1Sa 14:39 For, *as* the LORD liveth, which s Israel, H3467
17:47 that the LORD s not with sword and H3467
Job 5:15 But he s the poor from the sword, from H3467
Ps 7:10 My defence *is* of God, which s the H3467
20: 6 Now know I that the LORD s his H3467
34:18 and s such as be of a contrite spirit. H3467
107:19 *and* he s them out of their distresses. H3467

SAVING
Gen 19:19 unto me in s my life; and I cannot H2421
Neh 4:23 put off our clothes, *s that* every one put
Ps 20: 6 with the s strength of his right hand. H3468
28: 8 and he *is* the s strength of his anointed. H3444
67: 2 earth, thy s health among all nations. H3444
Ecc 5:11 s the beholding *of them* with their eyes? H518
Am 9: 8 face of the earth; s that I will not utterly H657
Mt 5:32 put away his wife, s for the cause of G3924
Lk 4:27 was cleansed, s Naaman the Syrian. G1508
Heb 10:39 of them that believe to the s of the soul. G4047
11: 7 an ark to the s of his house; by the G1519
Rev 2:17 no man knoweth s he that receiveth *it*. G1508

SAVIOUR
2Sa 22: 3 my s; thou savest me from violence. H3467
2Ki 13: 5 (And the LORD gave Israel a s, so that H3467
Ps 106:21 They forgat God their s, which had H3467
Isa 19:20 he shall send them a s, and a great one, H3467
43: 3 One of Israel, thy S: I gave Egypt *for* thy H3467
11 the LORD; and beside me *there is* no s. H3467
45:15 hidest thyself, O God of Israel, the S. H3467
21 God and a S; *there is* none beside me. H3467
49:26 the LORD *am* thy S and thy Redeemer, H3467
60:16 the LORD *am* thy S and thy Redeemer, H3467
63: 8 *that* will not lie: so he was their S. H3467
Jer 14: 8 O the hope of Israel, the s thereof in H3467
Hos 13: 4 god but me: for *there is* no s beside me. H3467
Lk 1:47 my spirit hath rejoiced in God my S. G4990
2:11 of David a S, which is Christ the Lord. G4990
Jn 4:42 is indeed the Christ, the S of the world. G4990
Act 5:31 *to be* a Prince and a S, for to give G4990
13:23 promise raised unto Israel a S, Jesus: G4990
Eph 5:23 the church: and he is the s of the body. G4990
Php 3:20 we look for the S, the Lord Jesus Christ: G4990
1Ti 1: 1 of God our S, and Lord Jesus Christ, G4990
2: 3 acceptable in the sight of God our S; G4990
4:10 God, who is the S of all men, specially G4990
2Ti 1:10 appearing of our S Jesus Christ, who G4990
Tit 1: 3 to the commandment of God our S; G4990
4 Father and the Lord Jesus Christ our S. G4990
2:10 the doctrine of God our S in all things. G4990
13 of the great God and our S Jesus Christ; G4990
3: 4 of God our S toward man appeared, G4990
6 abundantly through Jesus Christ our S; G4990
2Pt 1: 1 of God and our S Jesus Christ: G4990
11 of our Lord and S Jesus Christ. G4990
2:20 of the Lord and S Jesus Christ, they are G4990
3: 2 of us the apostles of the Lord and S: G4990
18 of our Lord and S Jesus Christ. To him G4990
1Jn 4:14 sent the Son *to be* the S of the world. G4990
Jude 25 To the only wise God our S, *be* glory G4990

SAVIOURS
Neh 9:27 thou gavest them s, who saved them out H3467
Oba 21 And s shall come up on mount Zion to H3467

SAVOUR
Gen 8:21 And the LORD smelled a sweet s; and H7381
Ex 5:21 ye have made our s to be abhorred in H7381
29:18 it *is* a sweet s, an offering made by H7381
25 for a sweet s before the LORD: it H7381
41 for a sweet s, an offering made by H7381
Lev 1: 9 by fire, of a sweet s unto the LORD. H7381
13 by fire, of a sweet s unto the LORD. H7381
17 by fire, of a sweet s unto the LORD. H7381
2: 2 by fire, of a sweet s unto the LORD: H7381
9 by fire, of a sweet s unto the LORD. H7381
12 not be burnt on the altar for a sweet s. H7381
3: 5 by fire, of a sweet s unto the LORD. H7381
16 for a sweet s: all the fat *is* the LORD'S. H7381
4:31 altar for a sweet s unto the LORD; and H7381
6:15 altar *for* a sweet s, *even* the memorial H7381
21 thou offer *for* a sweet s unto the LORD. H7381
8:21 for a sweet s, *and* an offering made H7381
28 for a sweet s: it *is* an offering made H7381
17: 6 the fat for a sweet s unto the LORD. H7381
23:13 the LORD *for* a sweet s: and the drink H7381
18 by fire, of sweet s unto the LORD. H7381
26:31 not smell the s of your sweet odours. H7381
Nu 15: 3 to make a sweet s unto the LORD, of H7381
7 of wine, *for* a sweet s unto the LORD. H7381
10 by fire, of a sweet s unto the LORD. H7381
13 by fire, of a sweet s unto the LORD. H7381
14 by fire, of a sweet s unto the LORD; as H7381
24 for a sweet s unto the LORD, with H7381
18:17 by fire, for a sweet s unto the LORD. H7381
28: 2 by fire, *for* a sweet s unto me, shall ye H7381
6 Sinai for a sweet s, a sacrifice made by H7381
8 by fire, of a sweet s unto the LORD. H7381
13 offering of a sweet s, a sacrifice made H7381
24 by fire, of a sweet s unto the LORD: it H7381
27 for a sweet s unto the LORD; two H7381
29: 2 for a sweet s unto the LORD; one H7381
6 for a sweet s, a sacrifice made by H7381
8 LORD *for* a sweet s; one young bullock, H7381
13 by fire, of a sweet s unto the LORD; H7381
36 by fire, of a sweet s unto the LORD: one H7381
Ecc 10: 1 forth a stinking s: *so doth* a little folly H887
Song 1: 3 Because of the s of thy good ointments H7381
Ezk 6:13 they did offer sweet s to all their idols. H7381
16:19 s: and *thus* it was, saith the Lord GOD. H7381
20:28 they made their sweet s, and poured out H7381
41 I will accept you with your sweet s, H7381
Joel 2:20 up, and his ill s shall come up, because H6709
Mt 5:13 salt have lost his s, wherewith shall it be G3471
Lk 14:34 his s, wherewith shall it be seasoned? G3471
2Co 2:14 s of his knowledge by us in every place. G3744
15 For we are unto God a sweet s of G2175
16 To the one *we are* the s of death unto G3744
16 to the other the s of life unto life. And G3744
Eph 5: 2 a sacrifice to God for a sweetsmelling s. G3744

SAVOUREST
Mt 16:23 unto me: for thou s not the things that G5426
Mk 8:33 Satan: for thou s not the things that be G5426

SAVOURS
Ezr 6:10 sacrifices of sweet s unto the God of H5208

SAVOURY
Gen 27: 4 And make me s meat, such as I love, H4303
7 Bring me venison, and make me s H4303
9 s meat for thy father, such as he loveth: H4303
14 made s meat, such as his father loved. H4303
17 And she gave the s meat and the bread, H4303
31 And he also had made s meat, and H4303

SAW
Gen 1: 4 And God s the light, that *it was* good: H7200
10 he Seas: and God s that *it was* good. H7200
12 his kind: and God s that *it was* good. H7200
18 darkness: and God s that *it was* good. H7200
21 his kind: and God s that *it was* good. H7200
25 his kind: and God s that *it was* good. H7200
31 And God s every thing that he had H7200
3: 6 And when the woman s that the tree H7200
6: 2 That the sons of God s the daughters of H7200
5 And GOD s that the wickedness of man H7200
9:22 And Ham, the father of Canaan, s the H7200
23 and they s not their father's nakedness. H7200
12:15 The princes also of Pharaoh s her, and H7200
16: 4 and when she s that she had conceived, H7200
5 and when she s that she had conceived, H7200
18: 2 by him: and when he s *them*, he ran to H7200
21: 9 And Sarah s the son of Hagar the H7200
19 And God opened her eyes, and she s a H7200
22: 4 up his eyes, and s the place afar off. H7200
24:30 And it came to pass, when he s the H7200
63 s, and, behold, the camels *were* coming. H7200
64 she s Isaac, she lighted off the camel. H7200
26: 8 at a window, and s, and, behold, Isaac H7200
28 And they said, We s certainly that the H7200
28: 6 When Esau s that Isaac had blessed H7200
29:10 And it came to pass, when Jacob s H7200
31 And when the LORD s that Leah *was* H7200
30: 1 And when Rachel s that she bare Jacob H7200
9 When Leah s that she had left bearing, H7200
31:10 up mine eyes, and s in a dream, and, H7200
32: 2 And when Jacob s them, he said, This H7200
25 And when he s that he prevailed not H7200
33: 5 And he lifted up his eyes, and s the H7200
34: 2 of the country, s her, he took her, and H7200
37: 4 And when his brethren s that their H7200
18 And when they s him afar off, even H7200
38: 2 And Judah s there a daughter of a H7200
14 to Timnath; for she s that Shelah was H7200
15 When Judah s her, he thought her *to be* H7200
39: 3 And his master s that the LORD *was* H7200
13 And it came to pass, when she s that he H7200
40:16 When the chief baker s that the H7200
41:19 s in all the land of Egypt for badness: H7200
22 And I s in my dream, and, behold, H7200
42: 1 Now when Jacob s that there was corn H7200
7 And Joseph s his brethren, and he H7200
21 brother, in that we s the anguish of his H7200
35 they and their father s the bundles of H7200
43:16 And when Joseph s Benjamin with H7200
29 And he lifted up his eyes, and s his H7200
44:28 is torn in pieces; and I s him not since: H7200
45:27 them: and when he s the wagons which H7200
48:17 And when Joseph s that his father laid H7200
49:15 And he s that rest *was* good, and the H7200
50:11 the Canaanites, s the mourning in the H7200
15 And when Joseph's brethren s that H7200
23 And Joseph s Ephraim's children of the H7200
Ex 2: 2 son: and when she s him that he *was a* H7200
5 side; and when she s the ark among the H7200
6 And when she had opened *it*, she s the H7200
12 way, and when he s that *there was* no H7200
3: 4 And when the LORD s that he turned H7200
8:15 But when Pharaoh s that there was H7200
9:34 And when Pharaoh s that the rain and H7200
10:23 They s not one another, neither rose H7200
14:30 and Israel s the Egyptians dead H7200
31 And Israel s that great work which the H7200
16:15 And when the children of Israel s *it*, H7200
18:14 And when Moses' father in law s all H7200
20:18 And all the people s the thunderings, H7200
18 s *it*, they removed, and stood afar off. H7200
24:10 And they s the God of Israel: and *there* H7200
11 also they s God, and did eat and drink. H2372
32: 1 And when the people s that Moses H7200
5 And when Aaron s *it*, he built an altar H7200
19 the camp, that he s the calf, and the H7200
25 And when Moses s that the people *were* H7200

Ex 33:10 And all the people s the cloudy pillar H7200
34:30 children of Israel s Moses, behold, the H7200
35 And the children of Israel s the face of H7200
Lev 9:24 s, they shouted, and fell on their faces. H7200
Nu 13:28 we s the children of Anak there. H7200
32 we s in it *are* men of a great stature. H7200
33 And there we s the giants, the sons of H7200
20:29 And when all the congregation s that H7200
22: 2 And Balak the son of Zippor s all that H7200
23 And the ass s the angel of the LORD H7200
25 And when the ass s the angel of the H7200
27 And when the ass s the angel of the H7200
31 of Balaam, and he s the angel of the H7200
33 And the ass s me, and turned from me H7200
24: 1 And when Balaam s that it pleased the H7200
2 And Balaam lifted up his eyes, and he s H7200
4 words of God, which s the vision of the H2372
16 the most High, *which* s the vision of the H2372
25: 7 Aaron the priest, s *it,* he rose up from H7200
32: 1 and when they s the land of Jazer, and H7200
9 valley of Eshcol, and s the land, they H7200
Dt 1:19 which ye s by the way of the mountain H7200
4:12 s no similitude; only *ye heard* a voice. H7200
15 unto yourselves; for ye s no manner of H7200
7:19 which thine eyes s, and the signs, and H7200
32:19 And when the LORD s *it,* he abhorred H7200
Jos 7:21 When I s among the spoils a goodly H7200
8:14 the king of Ai s *it,* that they hasted and H7200
20 behind them, they s, and, behold, the H7200
21 And when Joshua and all Israel s that H7200
Jdg 1:24 And the spies s a man come forth out H7200
3:24 and when they s that, behold, the doors H7200
9:36 And when Gaal s the people, he said to H7200
55 And when the men of Israel s that H7200
11:35 And it came to pass, when he s her, H7200
12: 3 And when I s that ye delivered *me* not, H7200
14: 1 down to Timnath, and s a woman in H7200
11 And it came to pass, when they s him, H7200
16: 1 Then went Samson to Gaza, and s H7200
18 And when Delilah s that he had told H7200
24 And when the people s him, they H7200
18: 7 to Laish, and s the people that *were* H7200
26 and when Micah s that they *were* too H7200
19: 3 damsel s him, he rejoiced to meet him. H7200
17 up his eyes, he s a wayfaring man in H7200
30 And it was so, that all that s it said, H7200
20:36 So the children of Benjamin s that they H7200
41 they s that evil was come upon them. H7200
Ru 1:18 When she s that she was stedfastly H7200
2:18 and her mother in law s what she had H7200
1Sa 5: 7 And when the men of Ashdod s that *it* H7200
6:13 and s the ark, and rejoiced to see *it.* H7200
9:17 And when Samuel s Saul, the LORD H7200
10:11 knew him beforetime s that, behold, he H7200
14 asses: and when we s that *they were* no H7200
12:12 And when ye s that Nahash the king of H7200
13: 6 When the men of Israel s that they H7200
11 said, Because I s that the people were H7200
14:52 and when Saul s any strong man, or H7200
17:24 And all the men of Israel, when they s H7200
42 looked about, and s David, he H7200
51 s their champion was dead, they fled. H7200
55 And when Saul s David go forth H7200
18:15 Wherefore when Saul s that he H7200
28 And Saul s and knew that the LORD H7200
19:20 and when they s the company of the H7200
22: 9 of Saul, and said, I s the son of Jesse H7200
23:15 And David s that Saul was come out to H7200
25:23 And when Abigail s David, she hasted, H7200
25 I thine handmaid s not the young men H7200
26: 3 the wilderness, and he s that Saul came H7200
12 away, and no man s *it,* nor knew *it,* H7200
28: 5 And when Saul s the host of the H7200
12 And when the woman s Samuel, she H7200
13 I s gods ascending out of the earth. H7200
21 And the woman came unto Saul, and s H7200
31: 5 And when his armourbearer s that H7200
7 the other side Jordan, s that the men of H7200
2Sa 1: 7 And when he looked behind him, he s H7200
6:16 a window, and s king David leaping H7200
10: 6 And when the children of Ammon s H7200
9 When Joab s that the front of the battle H7200
14 And when the children of Ammon s H7200
15 And when the Syrians s that they were H7200
19 to Hadarezer s that they were smitten H7200
11: 2 from the roof he s a woman washing H7200
12:19 But when David s that his servants H7200
14:24 own house, and s not the king's face. H7200
28 in Jerusalem, and s not the king's face. H7200
2Sa 17:18 Nevertheless a lad s them, and told H7200
23 And when Ahithophel s that his H7200
18:10 And a certain man s *it,* and told Joab, H7200
10 Behold, I s Absalom hanged in an oak. H7200
26 And the watchman s another man H7200
29 *me* thy servant, I s a great tumult, but H7200
20:12 And when the man s that all the people H7200
12 him, when he s that every one that H7200
24:17 the LORD when he s the angel that H7200
20 And Araunah looked, and s the king H7200
1Ki 3:28 the king: for they s that the wisdom of H7200
12:16 So when all Israel s that the king H7200
13:25 And, behold, men passed by, and s the H7200
16:18 And it came to pass, when Zimri s that H7200
18:17 And it came to pass, when Ahab s H7200
39 And when all the people s *it,* they fell H7200
19: 3 And when he s *that,* he arose, and went H7200
22:17 And he said, I s all Israel scattered H7200
19 of the LORD: I s the LORD sitting on H7200
32 of the chariots s Jehoshaphat, that they H7200
2Ki 2:12 And Elisha s *it,* and he cried, My H7200
12 thereof. And he s him no more: and he H7200
15 to view at Jericho s him, they said, The H7200
3:22 and the Moabites s the water on the H7200
26 And when the king of Moab s that the H7200
4:25 the man of God s her afar off, that he H7200
5:21 when Naaman s *him* running after H7200
6:17 young man; and he s: and, behold, the H7200
20 eyes, and they s; and, behold, *they were* H7200
21 Elisha, when he s them, My father, H7200
9:22 And it came to pass, when Joram s H7200
27 But when Ahaziah the king of Judah s H7200
11: 1 of Ahaziah s that her son was dead, H7200
12:10 And it was *so,* when they s that *there* H7200
13: 4 unto him: for he s the oppression of H7200
14:26 For the LORD s the affliction of Israel, H7200
16:10 of Assyria, and s an altar that *was* at H7200
12 the king s the altar: and the king H7200
1Ch 10: 5 And when his armourbearer s that H7200
7 *were* in the valley s that they fled, and H7200
15:29 out at a window s king David dancing H7200
19: 6 And when the children of Ammon s H7200
10 Now when Joab s that the battle was H7200
15 And when the children of Ammon s H7200
16 And when the Syrians s that they were H7200
19 And when the servants of Hadarezer s H7200
21:16 And David lifted up his eyes, and s the H7200
20 And Ornan turned back, and s the H7200
21 Ornan looked and s David, and went H7200
28 At that time when David s that the H7200
2Ch 7: 3 And when all the children of Israel s H7200
10:16 And when all Israel *s* that the king H7200
12: 7 And when the LORD s that they H7200
15: 9 s that the LORD his God *was* with him. H7200
18:18 of the LORD; I s the LORD sitting upon H7200
31 of the chariots s Jehoshaphat, that they H7200
22:10 of Ahaziah s that her son was dead, H7200
24:11 and when they s that *there was* much H7200
25:21 went up; and they s one another in the H7200
31: 8 the princes came and s the heaps, they H7200
32: 2 And when Hezekiah s that Sennacherib H7200
Neh 6:16 that *were* about us s *these things,* they H7200
13:15 In those days s I in Judah *some* H7200
23 In those days also s I Jews *that* had H7200
Est 1:14 and Media, which s the king's face, *and* H7200
3: 5 And when Haman s that Mordecai H7200
5: 2 And it was so, when the king s Esther H7200
9 but when Haman s Mordecai in the H7200
7: 7 the queen; for he s that there was evil H7200
Job 2:13 for they s that *his* grief was very great. H7200
3:16 been; as infants *which* never s light. H7200
20: 9 The eye also *which* s him shall *see him* H7805
29: 8 The young men s me, and hid H7200
11 the eye s *me,* it gave witness to me: H7200
31:21 fatherless, when I s my help in the gate: H7200
32: 5 When Elihu s that *there was* no answer H7200
42:16 and forty years, and s his sons, and his H7200
Ps 48: 5 They s *it, and* so they marvelled; they H7200
73: 3 *when* I s the prosperity of the wicked. H7200
77:16 The waters s thee, O God, the waters H7200
16 O God, the waters s thee; they were H7200
95: 9 me, proved me, and s my work. H7200
97: 4 the world: the earth s, and trembled. H7200
114: 3 The sea s *it,* and fled: Jordan was H7200
Prv 24:32 Then I s, *and* considered *it* well: I H2372
Ecc 2:13 Then I s that wisdom excelleth folly, as H7200
24 I s, that it *was* from the hand of God. H7200
3:16 And moreover I s under the sun the H7200
4: 7 Then I returned, and I s vanity under H7200
Ecc 8:10 And so I s the wicked buried, who had H7200
9:11 I returned, and s under the sun, that H7200
Song 3: 3 *I said,* S ye him whom my soul loveth? H7200
6: 9 The daughters s her, and blessed her; H7200
Isa 1: 1 of Amoz, which he s concerning Judah H2372
2: 1 The word that Isaiah the son of Amoz s H2372
6: 1 In the year that king Uzziah died I s H7200
10:15 *or* shall the s magnify itself against H4883
21: 7 And he s a chariot *with* a couple of H7200
41: 5 The isles s *it,* and feared; the ends of H7200
59:15 and the LORD s *it,* and it displeased H7200
16 And he s that *there was* no man, and H7200
Jer 3: 7 And her treacherous sister Judah s *it.* H7200
8 And I s, when for all the causes whereby H7200
39: 4 the king of Judah s them, and all the H7200
41:13 *were* with Ishmael s Johanan the son of H7200
44:17 victuals, and were well, and s no evil. H7200
Lam 1: 7 s her, *and* did mock at her sabbaths. H7200
Ezk 1: 1 were opened, and I s visions of God. H7200
27 And I s as the colour of amber, as the H7200
27 loins even downward, I s as it were the H7200
28 And when I s *it,* I fell upon my face, H7200
3:23 as the glory which I s by the river of H7200
8: 4 to the vision that I s in the plain. H7200
10 So I went in and s; and behold every H7200
10:15 creature that I s by the river of Chebar. H7200
20 This *is* the living creature that I s under H7200
22 faces which I s by the river of Chebar, H7200
11: 1 among whom I s Jaazaniah the son of H7200
16: 6 And when I passed by thee, and s thee H7200
50 therefore I took them away as I s *good.* H7200
19: 5 Now when she s that she had waited, H7200
20:28 to them, then they s every high hill, and H7200
23:11 And when her sister Aholibah s *this,* H7200
13 Then I s that she was defiled, *that* they H7200
14 for when she s men pourtrayed upon H7200
16 And as soon as she s them with her H4758
41: 8 I s also the height of the house round H7200
43: 3 the vision which I s, *even* according to H7200
3 to the vision that I s when I came to H7200
3 the vision that I s by the river Chebar; H7200
Dan 3:27 gathered together, s these men, upon H2370
4: 5 I s a dream which made me afraid, and H2370
10 head in my bed; I s, and behold a tree in H2370
13 I s in the visions of my head upon my H2370
23 And whereas the king s a watcher and H2370
5: 5 king s the part of the hand that wrote. H2370
7: 2 Daniel spake and said, I s in my vision H2370
7 After this I s in the night visions, and H1934
13 I s in the night visions, and, behold, H1934
8: 2 And I s in a vision; and it came to pass, H7200
2 to pass, when I s, that I *was* at Shushan H7200
2 of Elam; and I s in a vision, and I was H7200
3 Then I lifted up mine eyes, and s, and, H7200
4 I s the ram pushing westward, and H7200
7 And I s him come close unto the ram, H7200
10: 7 And I Daniel alone s the vision: for the H7200
7 that were with me s not the vision; but H7200
8 Therefore I was left alone, and s this H7200
Hos 5:13 When Ephraim s his sickness, and H7200
13 and Judah *s* his wound, then went
9:10 the wilderness; I s your fathers as the H7200
13 Ephraim, as I s Tyrus, *is* planted in a H7200
Am 1: 1 Tekoa, which he s concerning Israel in H2372
9: 1 I s the Lord standing upon the altar: H7200
Jna 3:10 And God s their works, that they H7200
Mic 1: 1 s concerning Samaria and Jerusalem. H2372
Hab 3: 7 I s the tents of Cushan in affliction: *and* H7200
10 The mountains s thee, *and* they H7200
Hag 2: 3 Who *is* left among you that s this house H7200
Zec 1: 8 I s by night, and behold a man riding H7200
18 Then lifted I up mine eyes, and s, and H7200
Mt 2: 9 the star, which they s in the east, went G1492
10 When they s the star, they rejoiced with G1492
11 the house, they s the young child with G2147
16 Then Herod, when he s that he was G1492
3: 7 But when he s many of the Pharisees G1492
16 unto him, and he s the Spirit of God G1492
4:16 The people which sat in darkness s G1492
18 by the sea of Galilee, s two brethren, G1492
21 And going on from thence, he s other G1492
8:14 Peter's house, he s his wife's mother G1492
18 Now when Jesus s great multitudes G1492
34 and when they s him, they besought G1492
9: 8 But when the multitudes s *it,* they G1492
9 forth from thence, he s a man, named G1492
11 And when the Pharisees s *it,* they said G1492
22 and when he s her, he said, Daughter, G1492
23 ruler's house, and s the minstrels and G1492

S

Mt 9:36 But when he **s** the multitudes, he was *G1492*
12: 2 But when the Pharisees **s** *it*, they said *G1492*
22 the blind and dumb both spake and **s**. *G991*
14:14 And Jesus went forth, and **s** a great *G1492*
26 And when the disciples **s** him walking *G1492*
30 But when he **s** the wind boisterous, he *G991*
15:31 when they **s** the dumb to speak, the *G991*
17: 8 eyes, they **s** no man, save Jesus only. *G1492*
18:31 So when his fellowservants **s** what was *G1492*
20: 3 third hour, and **s** others standing idle *G1492*
21:15 priests and scribes **s** the wonderful *G1492*
19 And when he **s** a fig tree in the way, he *G1492*
20 And when the disciples **s** *it*, they *G1492*
38 But when the husbandmen **s** the son, *G1492*
22:11 see the guests, he **s** there a man which *G1492*
25:37 Lord, when **s** we thee an hungred, *G1492*
38 When **s** we thee a stranger, and took *G1492*
39 Or when **s** we thee sick, or in prison, *G1492*
44 Lord, when **s** we thee an hungred, *G1492*
26: 8 But when his disciples **s** *it*, they had *G1492*
71 another *maid* **s** him, and said unto *G1492*
27: 3 betrayed him, when he **s** that he was *G1492*
24 When Pilate **s** that he could prevail *G1492*
54 watching Jesus, **s** the earthquake, and *G1492*
28:17 And when they **s** him, they worshipped *G1492*
Mk 1:10 of the water, he **s** the heavens opened, *G1492*
16 sea of Galilee, he **s** Simon and Andrew *G1492*
19 farther thence, he **s** James the *son* of *G1492*
2: 5 When Jesus **s** their faith, he said unto *G1492*
12 saying, We never **s** it on this fashion. *G1492*
14 And as he passed by, he **s** Levi the *son* *G1492*
16 And when the scribes and Pharisees **s** *G1492*
3:11 And unclean spirits, when they **s** him, *G2334*
5: 6 But when he **s** Jesus afar off, he ran *G1492*
16 And they that **s** *it* told them how it *G1492*
22 and when he **s** him, he fell at his feet, *G1492*
6:33 And the people **s** them departing, and *G1492*
34 And Jesus, when he came out, **s** much *G1492*
48 And he **s** them toiling in rowing; for the *G1492*
49 But when they **s** him walking upon the *G1492*
50 For they all **s** him, and were troubled. *G1492*
7: 2 And when they **s** some of his disciples *G1492*
8:23 upon him, he asked him if he **s** ought. *G991*
25 was restored, and **s** every man clearly. *G1689*
9: 8 round about, they **s** no man any more, *G1492*
14 And when he came to *his* disciples, he **s** *G1492*
20 him: and when he **s** him, straightway *G1492*
25 When Jesus **s** that the people came *G1492*
38 saying, Master, we **s** one casting out *G1492*
10:14 But when Jesus **s** *it*, he was much *G1492*
11:20 **s** the fig tree dried up from the roots. *G1492*
12:34 And when Jesus **s** that he answered *G1492*
14:67 And when she **s** Peter warming *G1492*
69 And a maid **s** him again, and began to *G1492*
15:39 over against him, **s** that he so cried out, *G1492*
16: 4 And when they looked, they **s** that the *G2334*
5 And entering into the sepulchre, they **s** *G1492*
Lk 1:12 And when Zacharias **s** *him*, he was *G1492*
29 And when she **s** *him*, she was troubled *G1492*
2:48 And when they **s** him, they were *G1492*
5: 2 And **s** two ships standing by the lake: *G1492*
8 When Simon Peter **s** *it*, he fell down at *G1492*
20 And when he **s** their faith, he said unto *G1492*
27 he went forth, and **s** a publican, named *G2300*
7:13 And when the Lord **s** her, he had *G1492*
39 had bidden him **s** *it*, he spake within *G1492*
8:28 When he **s** Jesus, he cried out, and fell *G1492*
34 When they that fed *them* **s** what was *G1492*
36 They also which **s** *it* told them by what *G1492*
47 And when the woman **s** that she was *G1492*
9:32 were awake, they **s** his glory, and the *G1492*
49 and said, Master, we **s** one casting out *G1492*
54 James and John **s** *this*, they said, Lord, *G1492*
10:31 **s** him, he passed by on the other side. *G1492*
33 he **s** him, he had compassion *on him*, *G1492*
11:38 And when the Pharisee **s** *it*, he *G1492*
13:12 And when Jesus **s** her, he called *her to* *G1492*
15:20 great way off, his father **s** him, and had *G1492*
17:14 And when he **s** *them*, he said unto *G1492*
15 And one of them, when he **s** that he *G1492*
18:15 *his* disciples **s** *it*, they rebuked them. *G1492*
24 And when Jesus **s** that he was very *G1492*
43 when they **s** *it*, gave praise unto God. *G1492*
19: 5 he looked up, and **s** him, and said unto *G1492*
7 And when they **s** *it*, they all murmured, *G1492*
20:14 But when the husbandmen **s** him, they *G1492*
21: 1 And he looked up, and **s** the rich men *G1492*
2 And he **s** also a certain poor widow *G1492*
22:49 When they which were about him **s** *G1492*
Lk 22:58 And after a little while another **s** him, *G1492*
23: 8 And when Herod **s** Jesus, he was *G1492*
47 Now when the centurion **s** what was *G1492*
24:24 women had said: but him they **s** not. *G1492*
Jn 1:32 And John bare record, saying, I **s** the *G2300*
34 And I **s**, and bare record that this is the *G3708*
38 Then Jesus turned, and **s** them *G2300*
39 They came and **s** where he dwelt, and *G1492*
47 Jesus **s** Nathanael coming to him, and *G1492*
48 thou wast under the fig tree, I **s** thee. *G1492*
50 I said unto thee, I **s** thee under the fig *G1492*
2:23 when they **s** the miracles which he did. *G2334*
5: 6 When Jesus **s** him lie, and knew that he *G1492*
6: 2 him, because they **s** his miracles which *G3708*
5 up *his* eyes, and **s** a great company *G2300*
22 side of the sea **s** that there was none *G1492*
24 When the people therefore **s** that Jesus *G1492*
26 me, not because ye **s** the miracles, but *G1492*
8:10 up himself, and **s** none but the woman, *G2300*
56 see my day: and he **s** *it*, and was glad. *G1492*
9: 1 And as *Jesus* passed by, he **s** a man *G1492*
11:31 her, when they **s** Mary, that she rose *G1492*
32 Jesus was, and **s** him, she fell down at *G1492*
33 When Jesus therefore **s** her weeping, *G1492*
12:41 These things said Esaias, when he **s** his *G1492*
19: 6 and officers **s** him, they cried out, *G1492*
26 When Jesus therefore **s** his mother, and *G1492*
33 But when they came to Jesus, and **s** *G1492*
35 And he that **s** *it* bare record, and his *G3708*
20: 5 And he stooping down, *and looking in*, **s** *G991*
8 to the sepulchre, and he **s**, and believed. *G1492*
14 herself back, and **s** Jesus standing, and *G2334*
20 disciples glad, when they **s** the Lord. *G1492*
21: 9 come to land, they **s** a fire of coals there, *G991*
Act 3: 9 And all the people **s** him walking and *G1492*
12 And when Peter **s** *it*, he answered unto *G1492*
4:13 Now when they **s** the boldness of Peter *G2334*
6:15 stedfastly on him, **s** his face as it had *G1492*
7:31 When Moses **s** *it*, he wondered at the *G1492*
55 into heaven, and **s** the glory of God, *G1492*
8:18 And when Simon **s** that through laying *G2300*
39 that the eunuch **s** him no more: and he *G1492*
9: 8 were opened, he **s** no man: but they led *G991*
35 Saron **s** him, and turned to the Lord. *G1492*
40 eyes: and when she **s** Peter, she sat up. *G1492*
10: 3 He **s** in a vision evidently about the *G1492*
11 And **s** heaven opened, and a certain *G2334*
11: 5 and in a trance I **s** a vision, A certain *G1492*
6 I considered, and **s** fourfooted beasts of *G1492*
12: 3 And because he **s** it pleased the Jews, *G1492*
9 by the angel; but thought he **s** a vision. *G991*
16 *door*, and **s** him, they were astonished. *G1492*
13:12 Then the deputy, when he **s** what was *G1492*
36 laid unto his fathers, and **s** corruption: *G1492*
37 But he, whom God raised again, **s** no *G1492*
45 But when the Jews **s** the multitudes, *G1492*
14:11 And when the people **s** what Paul had *G1492*
16:19 And when her masters **s** that the hope *G1492*
17:16 he **s** the city wholly given to idolatry. *G2334*
21:27 of Asia, when they **s** him in the temple, *G2300*
32 and when they **s** the chief captain and *G1492*
22: 9 And they that were with me **s** indeed *G2300*
18 And **s** him saying unto me, Make *G1492*
26:13 At midday, O king, I **s** in the way a light *G1492*
28: 4 And when the barbarians **s** the *G1492*
6 a great while, and **s** no harm come to *G2334*
15 **s**, he thanked God, and took courage. *G1492*
Gal 1:19 But other of the apostles **s** I none, save *G1492*
2: 7 But contrariwise, when they **s** that the *G1492*
14 But when I **s** that they walked not *G1492*
Php 1:30 Having the same conflict which ye **s** in *G1492*
Heb 3: 9 proved me, and **s** my works forty years. *G1492*
11:23 because they **s** *he was* a proper child; *G1492*
Rev 1: 2 Jesus Christ, and of all things that he **s**. *G1492*
12 turned, I **s** seven golden candlesticks; *G1492*
17 And when I **s** him, I fell at his feet as *G1492*
4: 4 and upon the seats I **s** four and twenty *G1492*
5: 1 And I **s** in the right hand of him that *G1492*
2 And I **s** a strong angel proclaiming *G1492*
6: 1 And I **s** when the Lamb opened one of *G1492*
2 And I **s**, and behold a white horse: and *G1492*
9 the fifth seal, I **s** under the altar the *G1492*
7: 1 And after these things I **s** four angels *G1492*
2 And I **s** another angel ascending from *G1492*
8: 2 And I **s** the seven angels which stood *G1492*
9: 1 And the fifth angel sounded, and I **s** a *G1492*
17 And thus I **s** the horses in the vision, *G1492*
10: 1 And I **s** another mighty angel come *G1492*
5 And the angel which I **s** stand upon the *G1492*
Rev 11:11 great fear fell upon them which **s** them. *G2334*
12:13 And when the dragon **s** that he was *G1492*
13: 1 of the sea, and **s** a beast rise up out of *G1492*
2 And the beast which I **s** was like unto a *G1492*
3 And I **s** one of his heads as it were *G1492*
14: 6 And I **s** another angel fly in the midst *G1492*
15: 1 And I **s** another sign in heaven, great *G1492*
2 And I **s** as it were a sea of glass *G1492*
16:13 And I **s** three unclean spirits like frogs *G1492*
17: 3 wilderness: and I **s** a woman sit upon a *G1492*
6 And I **s** the woman drunken with the *G1492*
6 of Jesus: and when I **s** her, I wondered *G1492*
18: 1 And after these things I **s** another angel *G1492*
18 And cried when they **s** the smoke of her *G3708*
19:11 And I **s** heaven opened, and behold a *G1492*
17 And I **s** an angel standing in the sun; *G1492*
19 And I **s** the beast, and the kings of the *G1492*
20: 1 And I **s** an angel come down from *G1492*
4 And I **s** thrones, and they sat upon *G1492*
4 unto them: and *I* **s** the souls of them that
11 And I **s** a great white throne, and him *G1492*
12 And I **s** the dead, small and great, *G1492*
21: 1 And I **s** a new heaven and a new earth: *G1492*
2 And I John **s** the holy city, new *G1492*
22 And I **s** no temple therein: for the Lord *G1492*
22: 8 And I John **s** these things, and heard *G991*

SAWED

1Ki 7: 9 of hewed stones, **s** with saws, within H1641

SAWEST

Gen 20:10 **s** thou, that thou hast done this thing? H7200
1Sa 19: 5 for all Israel: thou **s** *it*, and didst H7200
28:13 not afraid: for what **s** thou? And the H7200
2Sa 18:11 And, behold, thou **s** *him*, and why didst H7200
Ps 50:18 When thou **s** a thief, then thou H7200
Isa 57: 8 thou lovedst their bed where thou **s** *it*. H2372
Dan 2:31 Thou, O king, **s**, and behold a great H2370
34 Thou **s** till that a stone was cut out H2370
41 And whereas thou **s** the feet and toes, H2370
41 thou **s** the iron mixed with miry clay. H2370
43 And whereas thou **s** iron mixed with H2370
45 Forasmuch as thou **s** that the stone H2370
4:20 The tree that thou **s**, which grew, and H2370
8:20 The ram which thou **s** having *two* H7200
Rev 1:20 stars which thou **s** in my right hand, *G1492*
20 which thou **s** are the seven churches. *G1492*
17: 8 The beast that thou **s** was, and is not; *G1492*
12 And the ten horns which thou **s** are ten *G1492*
15 waters which thou **s**, where the whore *G1492*
16 And the ten horns which thou **s** upon *G1492*
18 And the woman which thou **s** is that *G1492*

SAWN

Heb 11:37 They were stoned, they were **s** asunder, *G4249*

SAWS

2Sa 12:31 put *them* under **s**, and under harrows H4050
1Ki 7: 9 sawed with **s**, within and without, H4050
1Ch 20: 3 and cut *them* with **s**, and with harrows H4050

SAY

Gen 12:12 that they shall **s**, This *is* his wife: and H559
13 **S**, I pray thee, thou *art* my sister: that it H559
14:23 shouldest **s**, I have made Abram rich: H559
20:13 we shall come, **s** of me, He *is* my brother. H559
24:14 to whom I shall **s**, Let down thy pitcher, H559
14 and she shall **s**, Drink, and I will give H559
43 to draw *water*, and I **s** to her, Give me, I H559
44 And she **s** to me, Both drink thou, and I H559
26: 7 for he feared to **s**, *She is* my wife; lest, H559
32:18 Then thou shalt **s**, *They be* thy servant H559
20 And **s** ye moreover, Behold, thy servant H559
34:11 and what ye shall **s** unto me I will give. H559
12 as ye shall **s** unto me: but give me H559
37:17 for I heard them **s**, Let us go to Dothan. H559
20 pit, and we will **s**, Some evil beast hath H559
41:15 it: and I have heard **s** of thee, *that* thou H559
43: 7 he would **s**, Bring your brother down? H559
44: 4 overtake them, **s** unto them, Wherefore H559
16 And Judah said, What shall we **s** unto H559
45: 9 Haste ye, and go up to my father, and **s** H559
17 And Pharaoh said unto Joseph, **S** unto H559
46:31 and shew Pharaoh, and **s** unto him, My H559
33 and shall **s**, What *is* your occupation? H559
34 That ye shall **s**, Thy servants' trade hath H559
50:17 So shall ye **s** unto Joseph, Forgive, I pray H559
Ex 3:13 of Israel, and shall **s** unto them, The God H559
13 you; and they shall **s** to me, What *is* his H559

Ex 3:13 *is* his name? what shall I **s** unto them? H559
14 Thus shalt thou **s** unto the children of H559
15 Thus shalt thou **s** unto the children of H559
16 together, and **s** unto them, The LORD H559
18 of Egypt, and ye shall **s** unto him, The H559
4: 1 voice: for they will **s**, The LORD hath not H559
12 and teach thee what thou shalt **s**. H1696
22 And thou shalt **s** unto Pharaoh, Thus H559
23 And I **s** unto thee, Let my son go, that he H559
5:16 servants, and they **s** to us, Make brick: H559
17 **s**, Let us go *and* do sacrifice to the LORD. H559
6: 6 Wherefore **s** unto the children of Israel, I H559
29 king of Egypt all that I **s** unto thee. H1696
7: 9 then thou shalt **s** unto Aaron, Take thy H559
16 And thou shalt **s** unto him, The LORD H559
19 And the LORD spake unto Moses, **S** unto H559
8: 1 Go unto Pharaoh, and **s** unto him, Thus H559
5 And the LORD spake unto Moses, **S** unto H559
16 And the LORD said unto Moses, **S** unto H559
20 to the water; and **s** unto him, Thus saith H559
9:13 Pharaoh, and **s** unto him, Thus saith H559
12:26 your children shall **s** unto you, What H559
27 That ye shall **s**, It *is* the sacrifice of the H559
13:14 that thou shalt **s** unto him, By strength H559
14: 3 For Pharaoh will **s** of the children of H559
16: 9 And Moses spake unto Aaron, **S** unto all H559
19: 3 Thus shalt thou **s** to the house of Jacob, H559
20:22 Thus thou shalt **s** unto the children of H559
21: 5 And if the servant shall plainly **s**, I love H559
32:12 speak, and **s**, For mischief did he bring H559
33: 5 For the LORD had said unto Moses, **S** H559
Lev 1: 2 Speak unto the children of Israel, and **s** H559
15: 2 Speak unto the children of Israel, and **s** H559
17: 2 of Israel, and **s** unto them; This *is* the H559
8 And thou shalt **s** unto them, Whatsoever H559
18: 2 Speak unto the children of Israel, and **s** H559
19: 2 of Israel, and **s** unto them, Ye shall be H559
20: 2 Again, thou shalt **s** to the children of H559
21: 1 sons of Aaron, and **s** unto them, There H559
22: 3 **S** unto them, Whosoever *he be* of all H559
18 of Israel, and **s** unto them, Whatsoever H559
23: 2 Speak unto the children of Israel, and **s** H559
10 Speak unto the children of Israel, and **s** H559
25: 2 Speak unto the children of Israel, and **s** H559
20 And if ye shall **s**, What shall we eat the H559
27: 2 Speak unto the children of Israel, and **s** H559
Nu 5:12 Speak unto the children of Israel, and **s** H559
19 by an oath, and **s** unto the woman, If no H559
21 and the priest shall **s** unto the woman, H559
22 And the woman shall **s**, Amen, amen. H559
6: 2 Speak unto the children of Israel, and **s** H559
8: 2 Speak unto Aaron, and **s** unto him, H559
11:12 that thou shouldest **s** unto me, Carry H559
18 And **s** thou unto the people, Sanctify H559
14:28 **S** unto them, *As truly as* I live, saith the H559
15: 2 Speak unto the children of Israel, and **s** H559
18 Speak unto the children of Israel, and **s** H559
18:26 Thus speak unto the Levites, and **s** unto H559
30 Therefore thou shalt **s** unto them, When H559
21:27 Wherefore they that speak in proverbs **s**, H559
22:19 what the LORD will **s** unto me more. H1696
20 I shall **s** unto thee, that shalt thou do. H1696
38 now any power at all to **s** any thing? the H1696
23:16 said, Go again unto Balak, and **s** thus. H1696
25:12 Wherefore **s**, Behold, I give unto him my H559
28: 2 Command the children of Israel, and **s** H559
3 And thou shalt **s** unto them, This *is* the H559
33:51 Speak unto the children of Israel, and **s** H559
34: 2 Command the children of Israel, and **s** H559
35:10 Speak unto the children of Israel, and **s** H559
Dt 1:42 And the LORD said unto me, **S** unto H559
4: 6 all these statutes, and **s**, Surely this great H559
5:27 our God shall **s**: and speak thou unto H559
30 Go **s** to them, Get you into your tents H559
6:21 Then thou shalt **s** unto thy son, We were H559
7:17 If thou shalt **s** in thine heart, These H559
8:17 And thou **s** in thine heart, My power and H559
9: 2 thou hast heard *s*, Who can stand before
28 broughtest us out **s**, Because the LORD H559
12:20 and thou shalt **s**, I will eat flesh, because H559
13:12 If thou shalt hear *s* in one of thy cities,
15:16 And it shall be, if he **s** unto thee, I will H559
17:14 therein, and shalt **s**, I will set a king over H559
18:21 And if thou **s** in thine heart, How shall H559
20: 3 And shall **s** unto them, Hear, O Israel, ye H559
8 and they shall **s**, What man *is there that* H559
21: 7 And they shall answer and **s**, Our hands H559
20 And they shall **s** unto the elders of his H559
22:14 upon her, and **s**, I took this woman, and H559

Dt 22:16 And the damsel's father shall **s** unto the H559
25: 7 the elders, and **s**, My husband's brother H559
8 he stand *to it*, and **s**, I like not to take her; H559
9 shall answer and **s**, So shall it be done H559
26: 3 in those days, and **s** unto him, I profess H559
5 And thou shalt speak and **s** before the H559
13 Then thou shalt **s** before the LORD thy H559
27:14 And the Levites shall speak, and **s** unto H559
15 all the people shall answer and **s**, Amen. H559
16 mother. And all the people shall **s**, Amen. H559
17 And all the people shall **s**, Amen. H559
18 way. And all the people shall **s**, Amen. H559
19 widow. And all the people shall **s**, Amen. H559
20 skirt. And all the people shall **s**, Amen. H559
21 beast. And all the people shall **s**, Amen. H559
22 mother. And all the people shall **s**, Amen. H559
23 in law. And all the people shall **s**, Amen. H559
24 And all the people shall **s**, Amen. H559
25 person. And all the people shall **s**, Amen. H559
26 them. And all the people shall **s**, Amen. H559
28:67 In the morning thou shalt **s**, Would God H559
67 at even thou shalt **s**, Would God it were H559
29:22 from a far land, shall **s**, when they see the H559
24 Even all nations shall **s**, Wherefore hath H559
25 Then men shall **s**, Because they have H559
30:12 It *is* not in heaven, that thou shouldest **s**, H559
13 that thou shouldest **s**, Who shall go over H559
31:17 so that they will **s** in that day, Are not H559
32:27 lest they should **s**, Our hand *is* high, and H559
37 And he shall **s**, Where *are* their gods, H559
40 For I lift up my hand to heaven, and **s**, I H559
33:27 before thee; and shall **s**, Destroy *them*. H559
Jos 7: 8 O Lord, what shall I **s**, when Israel H559
13 Up, sanctify the people, and **s**, Sanctify H559
8: 6 city; for they will **s**, They flee before us, as H559
9:11 to meet them, and **s** unto them, We *are* H559
22:11 And the children of Israel heard **s**, H559
27 children may not **s** to our children in H559
28 when they should *so* **s** to us or to our H559
28 come, that we may **s** *again*, Behold the H559
Jdg 4:20 of thee, and **s**, Is there any man here? H559
20 any man here? that thou shalt **s**, No. H559
7: 4 be, *that* of whom I **s** unto thee, This shall H559
4 of whomsoever I **s** unto thee, This shall H559
11 And thou shalt hear what they **s**; and H1696
18 **s**, *The sword* of the LORD, and of Gideon. H559
9:54 slay me, that men **s** not of me, A woman H559
12: 6 Then said they unto him, **S** now H559
16:15 How canst thou **s**, I love thee, when thine H559
18: 8 brethren said unto them, What *s* ye? H559
24 this *that* ye **s** unto me, What aileth thee? H559
21:22 that we will **s** unto them, Be favourable H559
Ru 1:12 If I should **s**, I have hope, *if* I should H559
1Sa 2:36 of bread, and shall **s**, Put me, I pray thee, H559
3: 9 that thou shalt **s**, Speak, LORD; for thy H559
8: 7 in all that they **s** unto thee: for they have H559
10: 2 and they will **s** unto thee, The asses H559
11: 9 came, Thus shall ye **s** unto the men of H559
13: 4 And all Israel heard **s** *that* Saul had H559
14: 9 If they **s** thus unto us, Tarry until we H559
10 But if they **s** thus, Come up unto us; then H559
34 the people, and **s** unto them, Bring me H559
15:16 this night. And he said unto him, **S** on. H1696
16: 2 **s**, I am come to sacrifice to the LORD. H559
18:22 David secretly, and **s**, Behold, the king H559
25 And Saul said, Thus shall ye **s** to David, H559
19:24 they **s**, *Is* Saul also among the prophets? H559
20: 6 If thy father at all miss me, then **s**, David H559
7 If he **s** thus, *It is* well; thy servant shall H559
21 If I expressly **s** unto the lad, Behold, H559
22 But if I **s** thus unto the young man, H559
25: 6 And thus shall ye **s** to him that liveth *in* H559
2Sa 7: 8 Now therefore so shalt thou **s** unto my H559
20 And what can David **s** more unto thee? H1696
11:20 king's wrath arise, and he **s** unto thee, H559
21 nigh the wall? then **s** thou, Thy servant H559
25 Thus shalt thou **s** unto Joab, Let not this H559
13: 5 cometh to see thee, **s** unto him, I pray H559
28 with wine, and when I **s** unto you, Smite H559
14:12 my lord the king. And he said, **S** on. H1696
32 thee to the king, to **s**, Wherefore am I H559
15:10 ye shall **s**, Absalom reigneth in Hebron. H559
26 But if he thus **s**, I have no delight in thee; H559
34 But if thou return to the city, and **s** unto H559
16:10 then **s**, Wherefore hast thou done so? H559
17: 9 heareth it will **s**, There is a slaughter H559
19: 2 the people heard **s** that day how the king H559
13 And **s** ye to Amasa, *Art* thou not of my H559
20:16 city, Hear, hear; **s**, I pray you, unto Joab, H559

2Sa 21: 4 What ye shall **s**, *that* will I do for you. H559
24: 1 them to **s**, Go, number Israel and Judah. H559
12 Go and **s** unto David, Thus saith the H1696
1Ki 1:13 king David, and **s** unto him, Didst not H559
25 him, and **s**, God save king Adonijah. H559
34 trumpet, and **s**, God save king Solomon. H559
36 LORD God of my lord the king **s** so *too*. H559
2:14 to **s** unto thee. And she said, Say on. H1697
14 to say unto thee. And she said, **S** on. H1696
16 me not. And she said unto him, **S** on. H1696
17 (for he will not **s** thee nay,) that he give H7725
20 thee; *I pray thee*, **s** me not nay. And the H7725
20 on, my mother: for I will not **s** thee nay. H7725
9: 8 shall hiss; and they shall **s**, Why hath the H559
12:10 us; thus shalt thou **s** unto them, My H1696
13:22 *the LORD* did **s** to thee, Eat no bread, H1696
14: 5 thus shalt thou **s** unto her: for it shall H1696
16:16 encamped heard **s**, Zimri hath conspired, H559
18:44 he said, Go up, **s** unto Ahab, Prepare H559
22: 8 Jehoshaphat said, Let not the king **s** so. H559
27 And **s**, Thus saith the king, Put this H559
2Ki 1: 3 of Samaria, and **s** unto them, *Is it* not H1696
6 that sent you, and **s** unto him, Thus H1696
2:18 unto them, Did I not **s** unto you, Go not? H559
4:13 And he said unto him, **S** now unto her, H559
26 Run now, I pray thee, to meet her, and **s** H559
28 my lord? did I not **s**, Do not deceive me? H559
7: 4 If we **s**, We will enter into the city, then H559
13 left in it: behold, *I s*, they *are* even as all
8:10 And Elisha said unto him, Go, **s** unto H559
9: 3 pour *it* on his head, and **s**, Thus saith the H559
17 to meet them, and let him **s**, *Is it* peace? H559
37 *so* that they shall not **s**, This *is* Jezebel. H559
18:22 But if ye **s** unto me, We trust in the H559
19: 6 Thus shall ye **s** to your master, Thus H559
9 And when he heard **s** of Tirhakah king H559
22:18 thus shall ye **s** to him, Thus saith the H559
1Ch 5: 3 The sons, *I s*, of Reuben the firstborn of
16:31 and let *men* **s** among the nations, H559
35 And **s** ye, Save us, O God of our H559
17: 7 Now therefore thus shalt thou **s** unto my H559
21:18 Gad to **s** to David, that David H559
2Ch 7:21 it; so that he shall **s**, Why hath the LORD H559
10:10 us; thus shalt thou **s** unto them, My little H559
18: 7 Jehoshaphat said, Let not the king **s** so. H559
15 thee that thou **s** nothing but the truth H1696
26 And **s**, Thus saith the king, Put this H559
20:11 Behold, *I s*, *how* they reward us, to come
21 the army, and to **s**, Praise the LORD; for H559
34:26 LORD, so shall ye **s** unto him, Thus saith H559
Ezr 8:17 what they should **s** unto Iddo, *and* to H1696
9:10 And now, O our God, what shall we **s** H559
Neh 7: 7 The number, *I s*, of the men of the people
9: 8 to give *it*, *I s*, to his seed, and hast
Est 1:18 Persia and Media **s** this day unto all the H559
Job 6:22 Did I **s**, Bring unto me? or, Give a reward H559
7: 4 When I lie down, I **s**, When shall I arise, H559
13 When I **s**, My bed shall comfort me, my H559
9:12 who will **s** unto him, What doest thou? H559
20 condemn me: *if* I **s**, I *am* perfect, it shall
27 If I **s**, I will forget my complaint, I will H559
10: 2 I will **s** unto God, Do not condemn me; H559
19:28 But ye should **s**, Why persecute we him, H559
20: 7 which have seen him shall **s**, Where *is* he? H559
21:14 Therefore they **s** unto God, Depart from H559
28 For ye **s**, Where *is* the house of the H559
22:29 then thou shalt **s**, *There is* lifting up; and H559
23: 5 understand what he would **s** unto me. H559
28:22 Destruction and death **s**, We have heard H559
32:11 whilst ye searched out what to **s**. H4405
13 Lest ye should **s**, We have found out H559
33:27 He looketh upon men, and *if any* **s**, I H559
32 If thou hast any thing to **s**, answer me: H4405
34:18 *Is it fit* to **s** to a king, *Thou art* wicked? H559
36:23 who can **s**, Thou hast wrought iniquity? H559
37:19 Teach us what we shall **s** unto him; *for* H559
38:35 may go, and **s** unto thee, Here we *are*? H559
Ps 3: 2 Many *there be* which **s** of my soul, *There* H559
4: 6 *There be* many that **s**, Who will shew us H559
11: 1 In the LORD put I my trust: how **s** ye to H559
13: 4 Lest mine enemy **s**, I have prevailed H559
27:14 thine heart: wait, I **s**, on the LORD.
35: 3 me: **s** unto my soul, I *am* thy salvation. H559
10 All my bones shall **s**, LORD, who *is* like H559
25 Let them not **s** in their hearts, Ah, so H559
25 them not **s**, We have swallowed him up. H559
27 yea, let them **s** continually, Let the LORD H559
40:15 of their shame that **s** unto me, Aha, aha. H559
16 **s** continually, The LORD be magnified. H559

Ps 41: 8 An evil disease, *s they,* cleaveth fast unto
42: 3 s unto me, Where *is* thy God? H559
9 I will s unto God my rock, Why hast H559
10 they s daily unto me, Where *is* thy God? H559
58:11 So that a man shall s, Verily *there is* a H559
59: 7 in their lips: for who, *s they,* doth hear?
64: 5 privily; they s, Who shall see them? H559
66: 3 S unto God, How terrible *art thou in* thy H559
70: 3 a reward of their shame that s, Aha, aha. H559
4 s continually, Let God be magnified. H559
73:11 And they s, How doth God know? and is H559
15 If I s, I will speak thus; behold, I should H559
79:10 Wherefore should the heathen s, Where H559
91: 2 I will s of the LORD, *He is* my refuge and H559
94: 7 Yet they s, The LORD shall not see, H559
96:10 S among the heathen *that* the LORD H559
106:48 the people s, Amen. Praise ye the LORD. H559
107: 2 Let the redeemed of the LORD s *so,* H559
115: 2 Wherefore should the heathen s, Where H559
118: 2 Let Israel now s, that his mercy *endureth* H559
3 Let the house of Aaron now s, that his H559
4 Let them now that fear the LORD s, that H559
122: 8 I will now s, Peace *be* within thee. H1696
124: 1 who was on our side, now may Israel s; H559
129: 1 me from my youth, may Israel now s: H559
8 Neither do they which go by s, The H559
130: 6 for the morning: *I s, more than* they that
139:11 If I s, Surely the darkness shall cover me; H559
Prv 1:11 If they s, Come with us, let us lay wait for H559
3:28 S not unto thy neighbour, Go, and come H559
5:12 And s, How have I hated instruction, and H559
7: 4 S unto wisdom, Thou *art* my sister; and H559
20: 9 Who can s, I have made my heart clean, I H559
22 S not thou, I will recompense evil; *but* H559
23:35 They have stricken me, *shalt thou s, and*
24:29 S not, I will do so to him as he hath done H559
30: 9 Lest I be full, and deny *thee,* and s, Who H559
15 *yea,* four *things* s not, *It is* enough: H559
Ecc 5: 6 thy flesh to sin; neither s thou before the H559
6: 3 he have no burial; I s, *that* an untimely H559
7:10 S not thou, What is *the cause* that the H559
8: 4 who may s unto him, What dost thou? H559
12: 1 thou shalt s, I have no pleasure in them; H559
Isa 2: 3 And many people shall go and s, Come H559
3:10 S ye to the righteous, that *it shall be* well H559
5:19 That s, Let him make speed, *and* hasten H559
7: 4 And s unto him, Take heed, and be H559
8:12 S ye not, A confederacy, to all *them to* H559
12 whom this people shall s, A confederacy; H559
19 And when they shall s unto you, Seek H559
9: 9 s in the pride and stoutness of heart, H559
12: 1 And in that day thou shalt s, O LORD, I H559
4 And in that day shall ye s, Praise the H559
14: 4 king of Babylon, and s, How hath the H559
10 All they shall speak and s unto thee, Art H559
19:11 brutish: how s ye unto Pharaoh, I *am* H559
20: 6 And the inhabitant of this isle shall s in H559
22:15 Shebna, which *is* over the house, *and s,* H559
29:15 s, Who seeth us? and who knoweth us? H559
16 for shall the work s of him that made it, H559
16 the thing framed s of him that framed it, H559
30:10 Which s to the seers, See not; and to the H559
22 thou shalt s unto it, Get thee hence. H559
33:24 And the inhabitant shall not s, I am sick: H559
35: 4 S to them *that are* of a fearful heart, Be H559
36: 4 And Rabshakeh said unto them, S ye H559
5 I s, *sayest thou,* (but *they are but* vain H559
7 But if thou s to me, We trust in the H559
37: 6 Thus shall ye s unto your master, Thus H559
9 And he heard s concerning Tirhakah H559
38: 5 Go, and s to Hezekiah, Thus saith the H559
15 What shall I s? he hath both spoken H1696
40: 9 *it* up, be not afraid; s unto the cities of H559
41:26 that we may s, *He is* righteous? yea, H559
27 The first *shall* s to Zion, Behold, behold
42:17 s to the molten images, Ye *are* our gods. H559
43: 6 I will s to the north, Give up; and to the H559
9 or let them hear, and s, *It is* truth. H559
44: 5 One shall s, I *am* the LORD'S; and H559
19 understanding to s, I have burned part of H559
20 nor s, *Is there* not a lie in my right hand? H559
45: 9 Shall the clay s to him that fashioneth H559
24 Surely, shall *one* s, in the LORD have I H559
48: 5 lest thou shouldest s, Mine idol hath H559
7 thou shouldest s, Behold, I knew them. H559
20 end of the earth; s ye, The LORD hath H559
49: 9 That thou mayest s to the prisoners, Go H559
20 lost the other, shall s again in thine ears, H559
21 Then shalt thou s in thine heart, Who H559

Isa 51:16 and s unto Zion, Thou *art* my people. H559
56: 3 let the eunuch s, Behold, I *am* a dry tree. H559
12 Come ye, *s they,* I will fetch wine, and we
57:14 And shall s, Cast ye up, cast ye up, H559
58: 3 Wherefore have we fasted, *s they,* and
9 cry, and he shall s, Here I *am.* If thou H559
62:11 end of the world, S ye to the daughter of H559
65: 5 Which s, Stand by thyself, come not near H559
Jer 1: 7 But the LORD said unto me, S not, I *am* H559
2:23 How canst thou s, I am not polluted, I H559
27 trouble they will s, Arise, and save us. H559
31 wherefore s my people, We are lords; H559
3: 1 They s, If a man put away his wife, and H559
12 toward the north, and s, Return, thou H559
16 LORD, they shall s no more, The ark of H559
4: 5 in Jerusalem; and s, Blow ye the trumpet H559
5 together, and s, Assemble yourselves, H559
5: 2 And though they s, The LORD liveth; H559
15 not, neither understandest what they s. H1696
19 to pass, when ye shall s, Wherefore doeth H559
24 Neither s they in their heart, Let us now H559
7: 2 this word, and s, Hear the word of the H559
10 by my name, and s, We are delivered to H559
28 But thou shalt s unto them, This *is* a H559
8: 4 Moreover thou shalt s unto them, Thus H559
8 How do ye s, We *are* wise, and the law of H559
10:11 Thus shall ye s unto them, The gods that H560
11: 3 And s thou unto them, Thus saith the H559
13:12 and they shall s unto thee, Do we not H559
13 Then shalt thou s unto them, Thus saith H559
18 S unto the king and to the queen, H559
21 What wilt thou s when he shall punish H559
22 And if thou s in thine heart, Wherefore H559
14:13 the prophets s unto them, Ye shall not H559
15 them not, yet they s, Sword and famine H559
17 Therefore thou shalt s this word unto H559
15: 2 And it shall come to pass, if they s unto H559
16:10 and they shall s unto thee, Wherefore H559
11 Then shalt thou s unto them, Because H559
19 the earth, and shall s, Surely our fathers H559
17:15 Behold, they s unto me, Where *is* the H559
20 And s unto them, Hear ye the word of H559
19: 3 And s, Hear ye the word of the LORD, O H559
11 And shalt s unto them, Thus saith the H559
20:10 on every side. Report, *s they,* and we will
21: 3 unto them, Thus shall ye s to Zedekiah: H559
8 And unto this people thou shalt s, Thus H559
11 Judah, *s,* Hear ye the word of the LORD;
13 saith the LORD; which s, Who shall come H559
22: 2 And s, Hear the word of the LORD, O H559
8 city, and they shall s every man to his H559
23: 7 they shall no more s, The LORD liveth, H559
17 They s still unto them that despise me, H559
17 peace; and they s unto every one that H559
31 that use their tongues, and s, He saith. H5001
33 thou shalt then s unto them, What H559
34 the people, that shall s, The burden of the H559
35 Thus shall ye s every one to his H559
37 Thus shalt thou s to the prophet, What H559
38 But since ye s, The burden of the LORD; H559
38 the LORD; Because ye s this word, The H559
38 Ye shall not s, The burden of the LORD; H559
25:27 Therefore thou shalt s unto them, Thus H559
28 then shalt thou s unto them, Thus saith H559
30 all these words, and s unto them, The H559
26: 4 And thou shalt s unto them, Thus saith H559
27: 4 And command them to s unto their H559
4 Thus shall ye s unto your masters; H559
31: 7 ye, praise ye, and s, O LORD, save thy H559
10 the isles afar off, and s, He that scattered H559
29 In those days they shall s no more, The H559
32: 3 prophesy, and s, Thus saith the LORD, H559
36 city, whereof ye s, It shall be delivered H559
43 land, whereof ye s, *It is* desolate without H559
33:10 this place, which ye s *shall be* desolate H559
11 of them that shall s, Praise the LORD of H559
36:29 And thou shalt s to Jehoiakim king of H559
37: 7 Thus shall ye s to the king of Judah, H559
38:22 those *women* shall s, Thy friends have set H559
25 unto thee, and s unto thee, Declare unto H559
26 Then thou shalt s unto them, I presented H559
39:12 unto him even as he shall s unto thee. H1696
42:13 But if ye s, We will not dwell in this land, H559
20 s, so declare unto us, and we will do *it.* H559
43: 2 to s, Go not into Egypt to sojourn there: H559
10 And s unto them, Thus saith the LORD H559
45: 3 Thou didst s, Woe is me now! for the H559
4 Thus shalt thou s unto him, The LORD H559
46:14 and in Tahpanhes: s ye, Stand fast, and H559

Jer 48:14 How s ye, We *are* mighty and strong H559
17 know his name, s, How is the strong staff H559
19 her that escapeth, *and* s, What is done? H559
50: 2 *and* conceal not: s, Babylon is taken, Bel H559
51:35 inhabitant of Zion s; and my blood upon H559
35 of Chaldea, shall Jerusalem s. H559
62 Then shalt thou s, O LORD, thou hast H559
64 And thou shalt s, Thus shall Babylon H559
Lam 2:12 They s to their mothers, Where *is* corn H559
16 the teeth: they s, We have swallowed H559
Ezk 2: 4 s unto them, Thus saith the Lord GOD. H559
8 But thou, son of man, hear what I s H1696
3:18 When I s unto the wicked, Thou shalt H559
27 and thou shalt s unto them, Thus saith H559
6: 3 And s, Ye mountains of Israel, hear the H559
11 with thy foot, and s, Alas for all the evil H559
8:12 imagery? for they s, The LORD seeth us H559
9: 9 for they s, The LORD hath forsaken H559
11: 3 Which s, *It is* not near; let us build H559
16 Therefore s, Thus saith the Lord GOD; H559
17 Therefore s, Thus saith the Lord GOD; I H559
12:10 S thou unto them, Thus saith the Lord H559
11 S, I *am* your sign: like as I have done, so H559
19 And s unto the people of the land, Thus H559
23 in Israel; but s unto them, The days H1696
25 house, will I s the word, and will H1696
27 *of* the house of Israel s, The vision that he H559
28 Therefore s unto them, Thus saith the H559
13: 2 that prophesy, and s thou unto them H559
7 whereas ye s, The LORD saith *it;* albeit H559
11 S unto them which daub *it* with H559
15 *morter,* and will s unto you, The wall *is* H559
18 And s, Thus saith the Lord GOD; Woe to H559
14: 4 Therefore speak unto them, and s unto H559
6 Therefore s unto the house of Israel, H559
17 that land, and s, Sword, go through the H559
16: 3 And s, Thus saith the Lord GOD unto H559
17: 3 And s, Thus saith the Lord GOD; A great H559
9 S thou, Thus saith the Lord GOD; Shall it H559
12 S now to the rebellious house, Know ye H559
18:19 Yet s ye, Why? doth not the son bear the H559
25 Yet ye s, The way of the Lord is not equal. H559
19: 2 And s, What *is* thy mother? A lioness: she H559
20: 3 of Israel, and s unto them, Thus saith H559
5 And s unto them, Thus saith the Lord H559
27 of Israel, and s unto them, Thus saith H559
30 Wherefore s unto the house of Israel, H559
32 not be at all, that ye s, We will be as the H559
47 And s to the forest of the south, Hear the H559
49 Then said I, Ah Lord GOD! they s of me, H559
21: 3 And s to the land of Israel, Thus saith H559
7 And it shall be, when they s unto thee, H559
9 Son of man, prophesy, and s, Thus saith H559
9 saith the LORD; S, A sword, a sword is H559
24 appear; because, *I s,* that ye are come to
28 And thou, son of man, prophesy and s, H559
28 reproach; even s thou, The sword, the H559
22: 3 Then s thou, Thus saith the Lord GOD, H559
24 Son of man, s unto her, Thou *art* the H559
24: 3 house, and s unto them, Thus saith H559
25: 3 And s unto the Ammonites, Hear the H559
8 Moab and Seir do s, Behold, the house of H559
26:17 for thee, and s to thee, How art thou H559
27: 3 And s unto Tyrus, O thou that art situate H559
28: 2 Son of man, s unto the prince of Tyrus, H559
9 Wilt thou yet s before him that slayeth H559
12 the king of Tyrus, and s unto him, Thus H559
22 And s, Thus saith the Lord GOD; Behold, H559
29: 3 Speak, and s, Thus saith the Lord GOD; H559
30: 2 Son of man, prophesy and s, Thus saith H559
32: 2 king of Egypt, and s unto him, Thou art H559
33: 2 of thy people, and s unto them, When I H559
8 When I s unto the wicked, O wicked H559
11 S unto them, *As* I live, saith the Lord H559
12 Therefore, thou son of man, s unto the H559
13 When I shall s to the righteous, *that* he H559
14 Again, when I s unto the wicked, Thou H559
17 Yet the children of thy people s, The way H559
20 Yet ye s, The way of the Lord is not equal. H559
25 Wherefore s unto them, Thus saith the H559
27 S thou thus unto them, Thus saith the H559
34: 2 prophesy, and s unto them, Thus saith H559
35: 3 And s unto it, Thus saith the Lord GOD; H559
36: 1 of Israel, and s, Ye mountains of Israel, H559
3 Therefore prophesy and s, Thus saith the H559
6 land of Israel, and s unto the mountains, H559
13 Thus saith the Lord GOD; Because they s H559
22 Therefore s unto the house of Israel, H559
35 And they shall s, This land that was H559

Ezk 37: 4 these bones, and s unto them, O ye dry H559
9 son of man, and s to the wind, Thus H559
11 of Israel: behold, they s, Our bones are H559
12 Therefore prophesy and s unto them, H559
19 S unto them, Thus saith the Lord GOD; H1696
21 And s unto them, Thus saith the Lord H1696
38: 3 And s, Thus saith the Lord GOD; Behold, H559
11 And thou shalt s, I will go up to the land H559
13 lions thereof, shall s unto thee, Art thou H559
14 Therefore, son of man, prophesy and s H559
39: 1 against Gog, and s, Thus saith the Lord H559
44: 5 ears all that I s unto thee concerning H1696
6 And thou shalt s to the rebellious, *even* H559
Dan 4:35 hand, or s unto him, What dost thou? H560
5:11 thy father, the king, *I s*, thy father, made
Hos 2: 1 S ye unto your brethren, Ammi; and to H559
7 then shall she s, I will go and return to H559
23 mercy; and I will s to *them which were* H559
23 and they shall s, *Thou art* my God. H559
10: 3 For now they shall s, We have no king, H559
8 and they shall s to the mountains, Cover H559
13: 2 of the craftsmen: they s of them, Let the H559
14: 2 and turn to the LORD: s unto him, Take H559
3 neither will we s any more to the work H559
8 Ephraim *shall s*, What have I to do any
Joel 2:17 altar, and let them s, Spare thy people, O H559
17 s among the people, Where *is* their God? H559
19 Yea, the LORD will answer and s unto H559
3:10 into spears: let the weak s, I *am* strong. H559
Am 3: 9 the land of Egypt, and s, Assemble H559
4: 1 the needy, which s to their masters, H559
5:16 and they shall s in all the highways, H559
6:10 house, and shall s unto him that *is* by H559
10 thee? and he shall s, No. Then shall he H559
10 No. Then shall he s, Hold thy tongue: for H559
13 of nought, which s, Have we not taken to H559
8:14 sin of Samaria, and s, Thy god, O Dan, H559
9:10 by the sword, which s, The evil shall not H559
Mic 2: 4 doleful lamentation, *and* s, We be utterly H559
6 Prophesy ye not, *s they to them that*
3:11 the LORD, and s, *Is* not the LORD among H559
4: 2 And many nations shall come, and s, H559
11 against thee, that s, Let her be defiled, H559
Nah 3: 7 flee from thee, and s, Nineveh is laid H559
Hab 2: 1 to see what he will s unto me, and what H1696
6 against him, and s, Woe to him that H559
Zep 1:12 on their lees: that s in their heart, The H559
Hag 1: 2 saying, This people s, The time is not H559
Zec 1: 3 Therefore s thou unto them, Thus saith H559
11: 5 and they that sell them s, Blessed *be* the H559
12: 5 And the governors of Judah shall s in H559
13: 3 begat him shall s unto him, Thou shalt H559
5 But he shall s, I *am* no prophet, I *am* an H559
6 And *one* shall s unto him, What *are* H559
9 hear them: I will s, It *is* my people: and H559
9 and they shall s, The LORD *is* my God. H559
Mal 1: 2 the LORD. Yet ye s, Wherein hast thou H559
5 And your eyes shall see, and ye shall s, H559
6 s, Wherein have we despised thy name? H559
7 mine altar; and ye s, Wherein have we H559
7 s, The table of the LORD *is* contemptible. H559
12 But ye have profaned it, in that ye s, The H559
2:14 Yet ye s, Wherefore? Because the LORD H559
17 your words. Yet ye s, Wherein have we H559
17 *him*? When ye s, Every one that doeth H559
3: 8 robbed me. But ye s, Wherein have we H559
13 saith the LORD. Yet ye s, What have we H559
Mt 3: 9 And think not to s within yourselves, *G3004*
9 to *our* father: for I s unto you, that God *G3004*
4:17 to preach, and to s, Repent: for the *G3004*
5:11 *you*, and shall s all manner of evil *G2036*
18 For verily I s unto you, Till heaven and *G3004*
20 For I s unto you, That except your *G3004*
22 But I s unto you, That whosoever is *G3004*
22 whosoever shall s to his brother, Raca, *G2036*
22 whosoever shall s, Thou fool, shall be in *G2036*
26 Verily I s unto thee, Thou shalt by no *G3004*
28 But I s unto you, That whosoever *G3004*
32 But I s unto you, That whosoever shall *G3004*
34 But I s unto you, Swear not at all; *G3004*
39 But I s unto you, That ye resist not evil: *G3004*
44 But I s unto you, Love your enemies, *G3004*
6: 2 I s unto you, They have their reward. *G3004*
5 I s unto you, They have their reward. *G3004*
16 I s unto you, They have their reward. *G3004*
25 Therefore I s unto you, Take no *G3004*
29 And yet I s unto you, That even *G3004*
7: 4 Or how wilt thou s to thy brother, Let *G2046*
22 Many will s to me in that day, Lord, *G2046*

Mt 8: 9 under me: and I s to this *man*, Go, and *G3004*
10 followed, Verily I s unto you, I have not *G3004*
11 And I s unto you, That many shall *G3004*
9: 5 For whether is easier, to s, *Thy* sins be *G2036*
5 forgiven thee; or to s, Arise, and walk? *G2036*
10:15 Verily I s unto you, It shall be more *G3004*
23 for verily I s unto you, Ye shall not *G3004*
42 a disciple, verily I s unto you, he shall *G3004*
11: 7 And as they departed, Jesus began to s *G3004*
9 I s unto you, and more than a prophet. *G3004*
11 Verily I s unto you, Among them that *G3004*
18 drinking, and they s, He hath a devil. *G3004*
19 and drinking, and they s, Behold a man *G3004*
22 But I s unto you, It shall be more *G3004*
24 But I s unto you, That it shall be more *G3004*
12: 6 But I s unto you, That in this place is *G3004*
31 Wherefore I s unto you, All manner of *G3004*
36 But I s unto you, That every idle word *G3004*
13:17 For verily I s unto you, That many *G3004*
30 of harvest I will s to the reapers, Gather *G2046*
51 things? They s unto him, Yea, Lord. *G3004*
14:17 And they s unto him, We have here but *G3004*
15: 5 But ye s, Whosoever shall say to *his* *G3004*
5 But ye say, Whosoever shall s to *his* *G2036*
33 And his disciples s unto him, Whence *G3004*
16: 2 it is evening, ye s, *It will be* fair weather: *G3004*
13 do men s that I the Son of man am? *G3004*
14 And they said, Some *s that thou art* John
15 He saith unto them, But whom s ye *G3004*
18 And I s also unto thee, That thou art *G3004*
28 Verily I s unto you, There be some *G3004*
17:10 s the scribes that Elias must first come? *G3004*
12 But I s unto you, That Elias is come *G3004*
20 for verily I s unto you, If ye have *G3004*
20 seed, ye shall s unto this mountain, *G2046*
18: 3 And said, Verily I s unto you, Except ye *G3004*
10 little ones; for I s unto you, That in *G3004*
13 And if so be that he find it, verily I s *G3004*
18 Verily I s unto you, Whatsoever ye *G3004*
19 Again I s unto you, That if two of you *G3004*
22 Jesus saith unto him, I s not unto thee, *G3004*
19: 7 They s unto him, Why did Moses then *G3004*
9 And I s unto you, Whosoever shall put *G3004*
10 His disciples s unto him, If the case of *G3004*
23 his disciples, Verily I s unto you, That a *G3004*
24 And again I s unto you, It is easier for a *G3004*
28 And Jesus said unto them, Verily I s *G3004*
20: 7 They s unto him, Because no man hath *G3004*
22 with? They s unto him, We are able. *G3004*
33 They s unto him, Lord, that our eyes *G3004*
21: 3 And if any *man* s ought unto you, ye *G2036*
3 unto you, ye shall s, The Lord hath need *G2046*
16 thou what these s? And Jesus saith unto *G3004*
21 them, Verily I s unto you, If ye have *G3004*
21 tree, but also if ye shall s unto this *G2036*
25 saying, If we shall s, From heaven; he *G2036*
25 heaven; he will s unto us, Why did ye *G2046*
26 But if we shall s, Of men; we fear the *G2036*
31 will of *his* father? They s unto him, The *G3004*
31 them, Verily I s unto you, That the *G3004*
41 They s unto him, He will miserably *G3004*
43 Therefore s I unto you, The kingdom of *G3004*
22:21 They s unto him, Caesar's. Then saith *G3004*
23 the Sadducees, which s that there is no *G3004*
42 he? They s unto him, *The son* of David. *G3004*
23: 3 after their works: for they s, and do not. *G3004*
16 Woe unto you, *ye* blind guides, which s, *G3004*
30 And s, If we had been in the days of our *G3004*
36 Verily I s unto you, All these things *G3004*
39 For I s unto you, Ye shall not see me *G3004*
39 till ye shall s, Blessed *is* he that cometh *G2036*
24: 2 things? verily I s unto you, There shall *G3004*
23 Then if any man shall s unto you, Lo, *G2036*
26 Wherefore if they shall s unto you, *G2036*
34 Verily I s unto you, This generation *G3004*
47 Verily I s unto you, That he shall make *G3004*
48 But and if that evil servant shall s in his *G2036*
25:12 But he answered and said, Verily I s *G3004*
34 Then shall the King s unto them on his *G2046*
40 And the King shall answer and s unto *G2046*
40 them, Verily I s unto you, Inasmuch *G3004*
41 Then shall he s also unto them on the *G2046*
45 saying, Verily I s unto you, Inasmuch *G3004*
26:13 Verily I s unto you, Wheresoever this *G3004*
18 to such a man, and s unto him, The *G2036*
21 And as they did eat, he said, Verily I s *G3004*
22 one of them to s unto him, Lord, is it I? *G3004*
29 But I s unto you, I will not drink *G3004*
34 Jesus said unto him, Verily I s unto *G3004*

Mt 26:64 nevertheless I s unto you, Hereafter *G3004*
27:22 all s unto him, Let him be crucified. *G3004*
33 Golgotha, that is to s, a place of a skull, *G3004*
46 that is to s, My God, my God, why *G2076*
64 him away, and s unto the people, He *G2036*
28:13 Saying, S ye, His disciples came by *G2036*
Mk 1:44 And saith unto him, See thou s nothing *G2036*
2: 9 Whether is it easier to s to the sick of *G2036*
9 s, Arise, and take up thy bed, and walk? *G2036*
11 I s unto thee, Arise, and take up thy *G3004*
18 they come and s unto him, Why do the *G3004*
3:28 Verily I s unto you, All sins shall be *G3004*
4:38 awake him, and s unto him, Master, *G3004*
5:41 Damsel, I s unto thee, arise. *G3004*
6:11 them. Verily I s unto you, It shall be *G3004*
37 to eat. And they s unto him, Shall we go *G3004*
38 they knew, they s, Five, and two fishes. *G3004*
7: 2 defiled, that is to s, with unwashen, *G5123*
11 But ye s, If a man shall say to his father *G3004*
11 But ye say, If a man shall s to his father *G2036*
11 *is* Corban, that is to s, a gift, by *G2076*
8:12 a sign? verily I s unto you, There shall *G3004*
19 took ye up? They s unto him, Twelve. *G3004*
27 unto them, Whom do men s that I am? *G3004*
28 *s*, Elias; and others, One of the prophets.
29 And he saith unto them, But whom s ye *G3004*
9: 1 And he said unto them, Verily I s unto *G3004*
6 For he wist not what to s; for they were *G2980*
11 And they asked him, saying, Why s the *G3004*
13 But I s unto you, That Elias is indeed *G3004*
41 s unto you, he shall not lose his reward. *G3004*
10:15 Verily I s unto you, Whosoever shall *G3004*
28 Then Peter began to s unto him, Lo, we *G3004*
29 And Jesus answered and said, Verily I s *G3004*
47 to cry out, and s, Jesus, *thou* son of *G3004*
11: 3 And if any man s unto you, Why do ye *G2036*
3 Why do ye this? s ye that the Lord hath *G2036*
23 For verily I s unto you, That whosoever *G3004*
23 whosoever shall s unto this mountain, *G2036*
24 Therefore I s unto you, What things *G3004*
28 And s unto him, By what authority *G3004*
31 saying, If we shall s, From heaven; he *G2036*
31 will s, Why then did ye not believe him? *G2046*
32 But if we shall s, Of men; they feared the *G2036*
12:14 And when they were come, they s unto *G3004*
18 the Sadducees, which s there is no *G3004*
35 in the temple, How s the scribes that *G3004*
43 them, Verily I s unto you, That this *G3004*
13: 5 And Jesus answering them began to s, *G3004*
21 And then if any man shall s to you, Lo, *G2036*
30 Verily I s unto you, that this generation *G3004*
37 And what I s unto you I say unto all, *G3004*
37 And what I say unto you I s unto all, *G3004*
14: 9 Verily I s unto you, Wheresoever this *G3004*
14 And wheresoever he shall go in, s ye to *G2036*
18 Jesus said, Verily I s unto you, One of *G3004*
19 be sorrowful, and to s unto him one by *G3004*
25 Verily I s unto you, I will drink no *G3004*
30 And Jesus saith unto him, Verily I s *G3004*
58 We heard him s, I will destroy this *G3004*
65 to buffet him, and to s unto him, *G3004*
69 and began to s to them that stood by, *G3004*
Lk 3: 8 and begin not to s within yourselves, *G3004*
8 to *our* father: for I s unto you, That *G3004*
4:21 And he began to s unto them, This day *G3004*
23 And he said unto them, Ye will surely s *G2046*
24 And he said, Verily I s unto you, No *G3004*
5:23 Whether is easier, to s, Thy sins be *G2036*
23 forgiven thee; or to s, Rise up and walk? *G2036*
24 of the palsy,) I s unto thee, Arise, and *G3004*
6:27 But I s unto you which hear, Love your *G3004*
42 Either how canst thou s to thy brother, *G3004*
46 Lord, and do not the things which I s? *G3004*
7: 7 unto thee: but s in a word, and my *G2036*
8 me soldiers, and I s unto one, Go, and *G3004*
9 followed him, I s unto you, I have not *G3004*
14 said, Young man, I s unto thee, Arise. *G3004*
26 A prophet? Yea, I s unto you, and much *G3004*
28 For I s unto you, Among those that are *G3004*
33 wine; and ye s, He hath a devil. *G3004*
34 drinking; and ye s, Behold a gluttonous *G3004*
40 I have somewhat to s unto thee. And he *G2036*
40 unto thee. And he saith, Master, s on. *G2036*
47 Wherefore I s unto thee, Her sins, *G3004*
49 with him began to s within themselves, *G3004*
9:18 saying, Whom s the people that I am? *G3004*
19 Baptist; but some *s*, Elias; and others *G2036*
19 Elias; and others *s*, that one of the old
20 He said unto them, But whom s ye that *G3004*

S

Lk 10: 5 ye enter, first s, Peace *be* to this house. G3004
9 that are therein, and s unto them, The G3004
10 out into the streets of the same, and s, G2036
12 But I s unto you, that it shall be more G3004
11: 2 When ye pray, s, Our Father which art G3004
5 at midnight, and s unto him, Friend, G2036
7 And he from within shall answer and s, G2036
8 I s unto you, Though he will not rise G3004
9 And I s unto you, Ask, and it shall be G3004
18 stand? because ye s that I cast out G3004
29 he began to s, This is an evil generation: G3004
51 the temple: verily I s unto you, It shall G3004
12: 1 he began to s unto his disciples first G3004
4 And I s unto you my friends, Be not G3004
5 into hell; yea, I s unto you, Fear him. G3004
8 Also I s unto you, Whosoever shall G3004
11 ye shall answer, or what ye shall s: G2036
12 in the same hour what ye ought to s. G2036
19 And I will s to my soul, Soul, thou hast G2046
22 Therefore I s unto you, Take no G3004
27 they spin not; and yet I s unto you, that G3004
37 watching: verily I s unto you, that he G3004
44 Of a truth I s unto you, that he will G3004
45 But and if that servant s in his heart, G2036
54 s, There cometh a shower; and so it is. G3004
55 wind blow, ye s, There will be heat; and G3004
13:24 gate: for many, I s unto you, will seek G3004
25 he shall answer and s unto you, I know G2046
26 Then shall ye begin to s, We have eaten G3004
27 But he shall s, I tell you, I know you not G2046
35 and verily I s unto you, Ye shall not G3004
35 come when ye shall s, Blessed *is* he that G2036
14: 9 him come and s to thee, Give this man G2046
10 cometh, he may s unto thee, Friend, go G2036
17 at supper time to s to them that were G2036
24 For I s unto you, That none of those G3004
15: 7 I s unto you, that likewise joy shall be G3004
10 Likewise, I s unto you, there is joy in G3004
18 father, and will s unto him, Father, I G2046
16: 9 And I s unto you, Make to yourselves G3004
17: 6 seed, ye might s unto this sycamine G3004
7 feeding cattle, will s unto him by and G2046
8 And will not rather s unto him, Make G2046
10 are commanded you, s, We are G3004
21 Neither shall they s, Lo here! or, lo G2046
23 And they shall s to you, See here; or, G2046
18:17 Verily I s unto you, Whosoever shall G3004
29 And he said unto them, Verily I s unto G3004
19:26 For I s unto you, That unto every one G3004
31 *him*? thus shall ye s unto him, Because G2046
20: 5 saying, If we shall s, From heaven; he G2036
5 he will s, Why then believed ye him not? G2046
6 But and if we s, Of men; all the people G2036
41 And he said unto them, How s they G3004
21: 3 And he said, Of a truth I s unto you, G3004
32 Verily I s unto you, This generation G3004
22:11 And ye shall s unto the goodman of the G2046
16 For I s unto you, I will not any more eat G3004
18 For I s unto you, I will not drink of the G3004
37 For I s unto you, that this that is G3004
70 And he said unto them, Ye s that I am. G3004
23:29 the which they shall s, Blessed *are* the G2046
30 Then shall they begin to s to the G3004
43 And Jesus said unto him, Verily I s G3004
Jn 1:38 Rabbi, (which is to s, being interpreted, G3004
51 Verily, verily, I s unto you, Hereafter G3004
3: 3 Verily, verily, I s unto thee, Except a G3004
5 Jesus answered, Verily, verily, I s unto G3004
11 Verily, verily, I s unto thee, We speak G3004
4:20 mountain; and ye s, that in Jerusalem is G3004
35 S not ye, There are yet four months, G3004
35 harvest? behold, I s unto you, Lift up G3004
5:19 Verily, verily, I s unto you, The Son can G3004
24 Verily, verily, I s unto you, He that G3004
25 Verily, verily, I s unto you, The hour is G3004
34 these things I s, that ye might be saved. G3004
6:26 Verily, verily, I s unto you, Ye seek me, G3004
32 Verily, verily, I s unto you, Moses gave G3004
47 Verily, verily, I s unto you, He that G3004
53 Verily, verily, I s unto you, Except ye G3004
7:26 But, lo, he speaketh boldly, and they s G3004
8: 4 They s unto him, Master, this woman G3004
26 I have many things to s and to judge of G2980
34 Jesus answered them, Verily, verily, I s G3004
46 I s the truth, why do ye not believe me? G3004
48 said unto him, S we not well that thou G3004
51 Verily, verily, I s unto you, If a man G3004
54 me; of whom ye s, that he is your God: G3004
55 and if I should s, I know him not, I shall G2036

Jn 8:58 Jesus said unto them, Verily, verily, I s G3004
9:17 They s unto the blind man again, What G3004
19 this your son, who ye s was born blind? G3004
41 s, We see; therefore your sin remaineth. G3004
10: 1 Verily, verily, I s unto you, He that G3004
7 s unto you, I am the door of the sheep. G3004
36 S ye of him, whom the Father hath G3004
11: 8 *His* disciples s unto him, Master, the G3004
12:24 Verily, verily, I s unto you, Except a G3004
27 and what shall I s? Father, save me from G2036
49 I should s, and what I should speak. G2036
13:13 Ye call me Master and Lord: and ye s G3004
16 Verily, verily, I s unto you, The servant G3004
20 Verily, verily, I s unto you, He that G3004
21 Verily, verily, I s unto you, that one of G3004
33 I go, ye cannot come; so now I s to you. G3004
38 Verily, verily, I s unto thee, The cock G3004
14:12 Verily, verily, I s unto you, He that G3004
16:12 I have yet many things to s unto you, G3004
20 Verily, verily, I s unto you, That ye G3004
23 Verily, verily, I s unto you, Whatsoever G3004
26 in my name: and I s not unto you, that G3004
20:13 And they s unto her, Woman, why G3004
16 him, Rabboni; which is to s, Master. G3004
17 my brethren, and s unto them, I ascend G2036
21: 3 I go a fishing. They s unto him, We also G3004
18 Verily, verily, I s unto thee, When thou G3004
Act 1:19 Aceldama, that is to s, The field of blood.
3:22 things whatsoever he shall s unto you. G2980
4:14 them, they could s nothing against it. G471
5:38 And now I s unto you, Refrain from G3004
6:14 For we have heard him s, that this Jesus G3004
10:37 That word, *I s*, ye know, which was
13:15 of exhortation for the people, s on. G3004
17:18 What will this babbler s? other some, He G3004
21:23 Do therefore this that we s to thee: We G3004
23: 8 For the Sadducees s that there is no G3004
18 who hath something to s unto thee. G2980
30 accusers also to s before thee what *they* G3004
24:20 Or else let these same *here* s, if they G2036
26:22 and Moses did s should come: G2980
28:26 Saying, Go unto this people, and s, G2036
Ro 3: 5 what shall we s? *Is* God unrighteous G2046
8 affirm that we s,) Let us do evil, that G3004
26 To declare, *I s*, at this time his
4: 1 What shall we s then that Abraham G2046
9 also? for we s that faith was reckoned G3004
6: 1 What shall we s then? Shall we G2046
7: 7 What shall we s then? *Is* the law sin? G2046
8:31 What shall we then s to these things? If G2046
9: 1 I s the truth in Christ, I lie not, my G3004
14 What shall we s then? *Is there* G2046
19 Thou wilt s then unto me, Why doth he G2046
20 the thing formed s to him that formed G2046
30 What shall we s then? That the G2046
10: 6 on this wise, S not in thine heart, Who G2036
18 But I s, Have they not heard? Yes verily, G3004
19 But I s, Did not Israel know? First G3004
11: 1 I s then, Hath God cast away his G3004
11 I s then, Have they stumbled that they G3004
19 Thou wilt s then, The branches were G2046
12: 3 For I s, through the grace given unto G3004
15: 8 Now I s that Jesus Christ was a G3004
1Co 1:12 Now this I s, that every one of you saith, G3004
15 Lest any should s that I had baptized in G2036
7: 8 I s therefore to the unmarried and G3004
26 *I s*, that *it is* good for a man so to be.
29 But this I s, brethren, the time *is* short: G5346
9: 8 S I these things as a man? or saith not G2980
10:15 speak as to wise men; judge ye what I s. G5346
19 What s I then? that the idol is any G5346
20 But *I s*, that the things which the Gentiles
28 But if any man s unto you, This is G2036
29 Conscience, I s, not thine own, but of G3004
11:22 have not? What shall I s to you? shall I G2036
12: 3 and *that* no man can s that Jesus is the G2036
15 If the foot shall s, Because I am not the G2036
16 And if the ear shall s, Because I am not G2036
21 And the eye cannot s unto the hand, I G2036
14:16 of the unlearned s Amen at thy giving G2046
23 will they not s that ye are mad? G2046
15:12 the dead, how s some among you that G3004
35 But some *man* will s, How are the dead G2046
50 Now this I s, brethren, that flesh and G5346
2Co 5: 8 We are confident, *I s*, and willing rather
9: 4 we (that we s not, ye) should be G3004
6 But this *I s*, He which soweth sparingly
10:10 For *his* letters, s they, *are* weighty and G5346
11:16 I s again, Let no man think me a fool; if G3004

2Co 12: 6 be a fool; for I will s the truth: but *now* G2046
Gal 1: 9 As we said before, so s I now again, If G3004
3:17 And this I s, *that* the covenant, that was G3004
4: 1 Now I s, *That* the heir, as long as he is a G3004
5: 2 Behold, I Paul s unto you, that if ye be G3004
16 *This* I s then, Walk in the Spirit, and ye G3004
Eph 4:17 This I s therefore, and testify in the G3004
Php 4: 4 Rejoice in the Lord alway: *and* again I s, G2046
Col 1:20 unto himself; by him, *I s*, whether *they be*
2: 4 And this I s, lest any man should G3004
4:17 And s to Archippus, Take heed to the G2036
1Th 4:15 For this we s unto you by the word of G3004
5: 3 For when they shall s, Peace and safety; G3004
1Ti 1: 7 what they s, nor whereof they affirm. G3004
2Ti 2: 7 Consider what I s; and the Lord give G3004
Tit 2: 8 having no evil thing to s of you. G3004
Phlm 19 *it*: albeit I do not s to thee how thou G3004
21 that thou wilt also do more than I s. G3004
Heb 5:11 Of whom we have many things to s, and G4183
7: 9 And as I may so s, Levi also, who G2031
9:11 hands, that is to s, not of this building; G5123
10:20 through the veil, that is to s, his flesh; G5123
11:14 For they that s such things declare G3004
32 And what shall I more s? for the time G3004
13: 6 So that we may boldly s, The Lord *is* my G3004
Jas 1:13 Let no man s when he is tempted, I am G3004
2: 3 gay clothing, and s unto him, Sit thou G2036
3 a good place; and s to the poor, Stand G2036
14 though a man s he hath faith, and have G3004
16 And one of you s unto them, Depart in G2036
18 Yea, a man may s, Thou hast faith, and G2046
4:13 Go to now, ye that s, To day or to G3004
15 For that ye *ought* to s, If the Lord will, G3004
1Jn 1: 6 If we s that we have fellowship with G2036
8 If we s that we have no sin, we deceive G2036
10 If we s that we have not sinned, we G2036
4:20 If a man s, I love God, and hateth his G2036
5:16 I do not s that he shall pray for it. G3004
Rev 2: 2 tried them which s they are apostles, G5335
9 of them which s they are Jews, and are G3004
24 But unto you I s, and unto the rest in G3004
3: 9 of Satan, which s they are Jews, and G3004
6: 3 the second beast s, Come and see. G3004
5 the third beast s, Come and see. And G3004
6 of the four beasts s, A measure of wheat G3004
7 of the fourth beast s, Come and see. G3004
16: 5 And I heard the angel of the waters s, G3004
7 And I heard another out of the altar s, G3004
22:17 And the Spirit and the bride s, Come. G3004
17 him that heareth s, Come. And let him G2036

SAYERS See GAINSAYERS and SOOTHSAYERS.

SAYEST
Ex 33:12 the LORD, See, thou s unto me, Bring up H559
Nu 22:17 do whatsoever thou s unto me: come H559
Ru 3: 5 And she said unto her, All that thou s H559
1Ki 18:11 And now thou s, Go, tell thy lord, Behold, H559
14 And now thou s, Go, tell thy lord, Behold, H559
2Ki 18:20 Thou s, (but *they are but* vain words,) *I* H559
2Ch 25:19 Thou s, Lo, thou hast smitten the H559
Neh 5:12 so will we do as thou s. Then I called the H559
6: 8 done as thou s, but thou feignest them H559
Job 22:13 And thou s, How doth God know? can he H559
35:14 Although thou s thou shalt not see him, H559
Ps 90: 3 Thou turnest man to destruction; and s, H559
Prv 24:12 If thou s, Behold, we knew it not; doth H559
Isa 36: 5 I say, *s thou*, (but *they are but* vain
40:27 Why s thou, O Jacob, and speakest, O H559
47: 8 carelessly, that s in thine heart, I *am*, H559
Jer 2:35 Yet thou s, Because I am innocent, surely H559
35 thee, because thou s, I have not sinned. H559
Am 7:16 word of the LORD: Thou s, Prophesy not H559
Mt 26:70 all, saying, I know not what thou s. G3004
27:11 Jews? And Jesus said unto him, Thou s. G3004
Mk 5:31 thee, and s thou, Who touched me? G3004
14:68 I what thou s. And he went out into G3004
15: 2 he answering said unto him, Thou s *it*. G3004
Lk 8:45 *thee*, and s thou, Who touched me? G3004
20:21 we know that thou s and teachest G3004
22:60 not what thou s. And immediately, G3004
23: 3 he answered him and said, Thou s *it*. G3004
Jn 1:22 that sent us. What s thou of thyself? G3004
8: 5 should be stoned: but what s thou? G3004
33 how s thou, Ye shall be made free? G3004
52 and thou s, If a man keep my saying, G3004
9:17 man again, What s thou of him, that he G3004
12:34 for ever: and how s thou, The Son of G3004
14: 9 how s thou *then*, Shew us the Father? G3004

Jn 18:34 Jesus answered him, S thou this thing G3004
37 answered, Thou s that I am a king. To G3004
Ro 2:22 Thou that s a man should not commit G3004
1Co 14:16 he understandeth not what thou s? G3004
Rev 3:17 Because thou s, I am rich, and G3004

SAYING
Gen 1:22 And God blessed them, s, Be fruitful, and H559
2:16 the man, s, Of every tree of the garden H559
3:17 I commanded thee, s, Thou shalt not eat H559
5:29 And he called his name Noah, s, This H559
8:15 And God spake unto Noah, s, H559
9: 8 unto Noah, and to his sons with him, s, H559
15: 1 Abram in a vision, s, Fear not, Abram: I H559
4 *came* unto him, s, This shall not be thine H559
18 with Abram, s, Unto thy seed have I H559
17: 3 on his face: and God talked with him, s, H559
18:12 within herself, s, After I am waxed old H559
13 did Sarah laugh, s, Shall I of a surety H559
15 Then Sarah denied, s, I laughed not; for H559
19:15 hastened Lot, s, Arise, take thy wife, H559
21:22 s, God *is* with thee in all that thou doest: H559
22:20 it was told Abraham, s, Behold, Milcah, H559
23: 3 dead, and spake unto the sons of Heth, s, H559
5 of Heth answered Abraham, s unto him, H559
8 And he communed with them, s, If it be H559
10 of all that went in at the gate of his city, s, H559
13 people of the land, s, But if thou *wilt give* H559
14 And Ephron answered Abraham, s unto H559
24: 7 sware unto me, s, Unto thy seed will I H559
30 of Rebekah his sister, s, Thus spake the H559
37 And my master made me swear, s, Thou H559
26:11 And Abimelech charged all *his* people, s, H559
20 Isaac's herdmen, s, The water *is* ours: H559
27: 6 unto Jacob her son, s, Behold, I heard thy H559
6 thy father speak unto Esau thy brother, s, H559
28: 6 gave him a charge, s, Thou shalt not take H559
20 And Jacob vowed a vow, s, If God will be H559
31: 1 of Laban's sons, s, Jacob hath taken H559
11 a dream, s, Jacob: And I said, Here *am* I.
29 me yesternight, s, Take thou heed that H559
32: 4 And he commanded them, s, Thus shall H559
6 And the messengers returned to Jacob, s, H559
17 And he commanded the foremost, s, H559
17 and asketh thee, s, Whose *art* thou? and H559
19 the droves, s, On this manner shall H559
34: 4 Hamor, s, Get me this damsel to wife. H559
8 And Hamor communed with them, s, H559
20 communed with the men of their city, s, H559
37:11 him; but his father observed the s. H1697
15 man asked him, s, What seekest thou? H559
38:13 And it was told Tamar, s, Behold thy H559
21 Then he asked the men of that place, s, H559
24 it was told Judah, s, Tamar thy daughter H559
25 to her father in law, s, By the man, whose H559
28 a scarlet thread, s, This came out first. H559
39:12 And she caught him by his garment, s, H559
14 spake unto them, s, See, he hath brought H559
17 to these words, s, The Hebrew servant, H559
19 spake unto him, s, After this manner did H559
40: 7 s, Wherefore look ye *so* sadly to day? H559
41: 9 s, I do remember my faults this day: H559
16 And Joseph answered Pharaoh, s, *It is* H559
42:14 *is it* that I spake unto you, s, Ye *are* spies: H559
22 And Reuben answered them, s, Spake I H559
22 I not unto you, s, Do not sin against the H559
28 they were afraid, s one to another, What H559
29 and told him all that befell unto them; s, H559
37 And Reuben spake unto his father, s, H559
43: 3 And Judah spake unto him, s, The man H559
3 protest unto us, s, Ye shall not see my H559
7 of our kindred, s, *Is* your father yet alive? H559
44: 1 of his house, s, Fill the men's sacks *with* H559
19 My lord asked his servants, s, Have ye a H559
32 lad unto my father, s, If I bring him not H559
45:16 Pharaoh's house, s, Joseph's brethren are H559
26 And told him, s, Joseph *is* yet alive, and H559
47: 5 And Pharaoh spake unto Joseph, s, Thy H559
48:20 And he blessed them that day, s, In thee H559
20 shall Israel bless, s, God make thee as H559
50: 4 house of Pharaoh, s, If now I have found H559
4 I pray you, in the ears of Pharaoh, s, H559
5 My father made me swear, s, Lo, I die: in H559
16 unto Joseph, s, Thy father did command H559
16 father did command before he died, s, H559
25 children of Israel, s, God will surely visit H559
Ex 1:22 And Pharaoh charged all his people, s, H559
3:16 Jacob, appeared unto me, s, I have surely H559
5: 6 of the people, and their officers, s, H559

Ex 5: 8 cry, s, Let us go *and* sacrifice to our God. H559
10 to the people, s, Thus saith Pharaoh, H559
13 And the taskmasters hasted *them*, s, H559
15 unto Pharaoh, s, Wherefore dealest thou H559
6:10 And the LORD spake unto Moses, s, H559
12 And Moses spake before the LORD, s, H559
29 That the LORD spake unto Moses, s, I H559
7: 8 spake unto Moses and unto Aaron, s, H559
9 When Pharaoh shall speak unto you, s, H559
16 sent me unto thee, s, Let my people go, H559
9: 5 And the LORD appointed a set time, s, H559
11: 8 unto me, s, Get thee out, and all H559
12: 1 Moses and Aaron in the land of Egypt, s, H559
3 of Israel, s, In the tenth *day* of this H559
13: 1 And the LORD spake unto Moses, s, H559
8 shew thy son in that day, s, *This is done* H559
14 thee in time to come, s, What *is* this? that H559
19 children of Israel, s, God will surely visit H559
14: 1 And the LORD spake unto Moses, s, H559
12 tell thee in Egypt, s, Let us alone, that we H559
15: 1 LORD, and spake, s, I will sing unto the H559
24 against Moses, s, What shall we drink? H559
16:11 And the LORD spake unto Moses, s, H559
12 speak unto them, s, At even ye shall eat H559
17: 4 And Moses cried unto the LORD, s, What H559
7 LORD, s, Is the LORD among us, or not? H559
19: 3 of the mountain, s, Thus shalt thou say H559
12 round about, s, Take heed to yourselves, H559
23 thou chargedst us, s, Set bounds about H559
20: 1 And God spake all these words, s, H559
25: 1 And the LORD spake unto Moses, s, H559
30:11 And the LORD spake unto Moses, s, H559
17 And the LORD spake unto Moses, s, H559
22 Moreover the LORD spake unto Moses, s, H559
31 children of Israel, s, This shall be an holy H559
31: 1 And the LORD spake unto Moses, s, H559
12 And the LORD spake unto Moses, s, H559
13 children of Israel, s, Verily my sabbaths H559
33: 1 to Jacob, s, Unto thy seed will I give it: H559
35: 4 the children of Israel, s, This *is* the thing H559
4 thing which the LORD commanded, s, H559
36: 5 And they spake unto Moses, s, The H559
6 the camp, s, Let neither man nor H559
40: 1 And the LORD spake unto Moses, s, H559
Lev 1: 1 of the tabernacle of the congregation, s, H559
4: 1 And the LORD spake unto Moses, s, H559
2 Speak unto the children of Israel, s, If a H559
5:14 And the LORD spake unto Moses, s, H559
6: 1 And the LORD spake unto Moses, s, H559
8 And the LORD spake unto Moses, s, H559
9 Command Aaron and his sons, s, This *is* H559
19 And the LORD spake unto Moses, s, H559
24 And the LORD spake unto Moses, s, H559
25 Speak unto Aaron and to his sons, s, This H559
7:22 And the LORD spake unto Moses, s, H559
23 Speak unto the children of Israel, s, Ye H559
28 And the LORD spake unto Moses, s, H559
29 Speak unto the children of Israel, s, He H559
8: 1 And the LORD spake unto Moses, s, H559
31 s, Aaron and his sons shall eat it. H559
9: 3 thou shalt speak, s, Take ye a kid of the H559
10: 3 the LORD spake, s, I will be sanctified in H559
8 And the LORD spake unto Aaron, s, H559
16 the sons of Aaron *which were* left *alive*, s, H559
11: 1 unto Moses and to Aaron, s unto them, H559
2 Speak unto the children of Israel, s, H559
12: 1 And the LORD spake unto Moses, s, H559
2 Speak unto the children of Israel, s, If a H559
13: 1 LORD spake unto Moses and Aaron, s, H559
14: 1 And the LORD spake unto Moses, s, H559
33 spake unto Moses and unto Aaron, s, H559
35 and tell the priest, s, It seemeth to me H559
15: 1 LORD spake unto Moses and to Aaron, s, H559
17: 1 And the LORD spake unto Moses, s, H559
2 which the LORD hath commanded, s, H559
18: 1 And the LORD spake unto Moses, s, H559
19: 1 And the LORD spake unto Moses, s, H559
20: 1 And the LORD spake unto Moses, s, H559
21:16 And the LORD spake unto Moses, s, H559
17 Speak unto Aaron, s, Whosoever *he be* of H559
22: 1 And the LORD spake unto Moses, s, H559
17 And the LORD spake unto Moses, s, H559
26 And the LORD spake unto Moses, s, H559
23: 1 And the LORD spake unto Moses, s, H559
9 And the LORD spake unto Moses, s, H559
23 And the LORD spake unto Moses, s, H559
24 Speak unto the children of Israel, s, In H559
26 And the LORD spake unto Moses, s, H559
33 And the LORD spake unto Moses, s, H559

Lev 23:34 Speak unto the children of Israel, s, The H559
24: 1 And the LORD spake unto Moses, s, H559
13 And the LORD spake unto Moses, s, H559
15 children of Israel, s, Whosoever curseth H559
25: 1 spake unto Moses in mount Sinai, s, H559
27: 1 And the LORD spake unto Moses, s, H559
Nu 1: 1 were come out of the land of Egypt, s, H559
48 For the LORD had spoken unto Moses, s, H559
2: 1 spake unto Moses and unto Aaron, s, H559
3: 5 And the LORD spake unto Moses, s, H559
11 And the LORD spake unto Moses, s, H559
14 unto Moses in the wilderness of Sinai, s, H559
44 And the LORD spake unto Moses, s, H559
4: 1 spake unto Moses and unto Aaron, s, H559
17 spake unto Moses and unto Aaron, s, H559
21 And the LORD spake unto Moses, s, H559
5: 1 And the LORD spake unto Moses, s, H559
5 And the LORD spake unto Moses, s, H559
11 And the LORD spake unto Moses, s, H559
6: 1 And the LORD spake unto Moses, s, H559
22 And the LORD spake unto Moses, s, H559
23 Speak unto Aaron and unto his sons, s, H559
23 bless the children of Israel, s unto them, H559
7: 4 And the LORD spake unto Moses, s, H559
8: 1 And the LORD spake unto Moses, s, H559
5 And the LORD spake unto Moses, s, H559
23 And the LORD spake unto Moses, s, H559
9: 1 were come out of the land of Egypt, s, H559
9 And the LORD spake unto Moses, s, H559
10 Speak unto the children of Israel, s, If H559
10: 1 And the LORD spake unto Moses, s, H559
11:13 me, s, Give us flesh, that we may eat. H559
18 ears of the LORD, s, Who shall give us H559
20 him, s, Why came we forth out of Egypt? H559
12:13 And Moses cried unto the LORD, s, Heal H559
13: 1 And the LORD spake unto Moses, s, H559
32 children of Israel, s, The land, through H559
14: 7 children of Israel, s, The land, which we H559
15 have heard the fame of thee will speak, s, H559
17 great, according as thou hast spoken, s, H559
26 spake unto Moses and unto Aaron, s, H559
40 of the mountain, s, Lo, we *be here*, and H559
15: 1 And the LORD spake unto Moses, s, H559
17 And the LORD spake unto Moses, s, H559
37 And the LORD spake unto Moses, s, H559
16: 5 all his company, s, Even to morrow the H559
20 spake unto Moses and unto Aaron, s, H559
23 And the LORD spake unto Moses, s, H559
24 Speak unto the congregation, s, Get you H559
26 And he spake unto the congregation, s, H559
36 And the LORD spake unto Moses, s, H559
41 s, Ye have killed the people of the LORD. H559
44 And the LORD spake unto Moses, s, H559
17: 1 And the LORD spake unto Moses, s, H559
12 spake unto Moses, s, Behold, we die, we H559
18:25 And the LORD spake unto Moses, s, H559
19: 1 spake unto Moses and unto Aaron, s, H559
2 hath commanded, s, Speak unto the H559
20: 3 Moses, and spake, s, Would God that we H559
7 And the LORD spake unto Moses, s, H559
23 Hor, by the coast of the land of Edom, s, H559
21:21 unto Sihon king of the Amorites, s, H559
22: 5 people, to call him, s, Behold, there is a H559
10 king of Moab, hath sent unto me, *s*,
23: 7 of the east, s, Come, curse me Jacob,
26 Told not I thee, s, All that the LORD H559
24:12 which thou sentest unto me, s, H559
25:10 And the LORD spake unto Moses, s, H559
16 And the LORD spake unto Moses, s, H559
26: 1 Eleazar the son of Aaron the priest, s, H559
3 plains of Moab by Jordan *near* Jericho, s, H559
52 And the LORD spake unto Moses, s, H559
27: 2 of the tabernacle of the congregation, s, H559
6 And the LORD spake unto Moses, s, H559
8 the children of Israel, s, If a man die, and H559
15 And Moses spake unto the LORD, s, H559
28: 1 And the LORD spake unto Moses, s, H559
30: 1 the children of Israel, s, This *is* the thing H559
31: 1 And the LORD spake unto Moses, s, H559
3 And Moses spake unto the people, s, Arm H559
25 And the LORD spake unto Moses, s, H559
32: 2 unto the princes of the congregation, s, H559
10 kindled the same time, and he sware, s, H559
25 spake unto Moses, s, Thy servants will do H559
31 Reuben answered, s, As the LORD hath H559
33:50 plains of Moab by Jordan *near* Jericho, s, H559
34: 1 And the LORD spake unto Moses, s, H559
13 the children of Israel, s, This *is* the land H559
16 And the LORD spake unto Moses, s, H559

Nu 35: 1 plains of Moab by Jordan *near* Jericho, s, H559
9 And the LORD spake unto Moses, s, H559
36: 5 the word of the LORD, s, The tribe of the H559
6 of Zelophehad, s, Let them marry to H559
Dt 1: 5 began Moses to declare this law, s, H559
6 unto us in Horeb, s, Ye have dwelt long H559
9 And I spake unto you at that time, s, I H559
16 And I charged your judges at that time, s, H559
23 And the s pleased me well: and I took H1697
28 our heart, s, The people *is* greater H559
34 words, and was wroth, and sware, s, H559
37 s, Thou also shalt not go in thither. H559
2: 2 And the LORD spake unto me, s, H559
4 And command thou the people, s, Ye *are* H559
17 That the LORD spake unto me, s, H559
26 king of Heshbon with words of peace, s, H559
3:18 And I commanded you at that time, s, H559
21 And I commanded Joshua at that time, s, H559
23 And I besought the LORD at that time, s, H559
5: 5 fire, and went not up into the mount;) s, H559
6:20 thee in time to come, s, What *mean* the H559
9: 4 from before thee, s, For my righteousness H559
13 Furthermore the LORD spake unto me, s, H559
23 Kadesh-barnea, s, Go up and possess the H559
12:30 after their gods, s, How did these nations H559
13: 2 he spake unto thee, s, Let us go after H559
6 thee secretly, s, Let us go and serve other H559
12 thy God hath given thee to dwell there, s, H559
13 of their city, s, Let us go and serve other H559
15: 9 thy wicked heart, s, The seventh year, the H559
11 I command thee, s, Thou shalt open H559
18:16 of the assembly, s, Let me not hear again H559
19: 7 Wherefore I command thee, s, Thou H559
20: 5 unto the people, s, What man *is there* H559
22:17 of speech *against her,* s, I found not thy H559
27: 1 commanded the people, s, Keep all the H559
9 spake unto all Israel, s, Take heed, and H559
11 charged the people the same day, s, H559
29:19 in his heart, s, I shall have peace, though H559
31:10 And Moses commanded them, s, At the H559
25 the ark of the covenant of the LORD, s, H559
32:48 spake unto Moses that selfsame day, s, H559
34: 4 and unto Jacob, s, I will give it unto thy H559
Jos 1: 1 the son of Nun, Moses' minister, s, H559
10 commanded the officers of the people, s, H559
11 the people, s, Prepare you victuals; H559
12 the tribe of Manasseh, spake Joshua, s, H559
13 commanded you, s, The LORD your God H559
16 And they answered Joshua, s, All that H559
2: 1 to spy secretly, s, Go view the land, even H559
2 And it was told the king of Jericho, s, H559
3 sent unto Rahab, s, Bring forth the men H559
3: 3 And they commanded the people, s, H559
6 And Joshua spake unto the priests, s, H559
8 of the covenant, s, When ye are come to H559
4: 1 that the LORD spake unto Joshua, s, H559
3 And command ye them, s, Take you H559
6 come, s, What *mean* ye by these stones? H559
15 And the LORD spake unto Joshua, s, H559
17 the priests, s, Come ye up out of Jordan. H559
21 children of Israel, s, When your children H559
21 to come, s, What *mean* these stones? H559
22 Then ye shall let your children know, s, H559
6:10 the people, s, Ye shall not shout, nor H559
26 And Joshua adjured *them* at that time, s, H559
7: 2 spake unto them, s, Go up and view the H559
8: 4 And he commanded them, s, Behold, ye H559
9:11 spake to us, s, Take victuals with you H559
22 spake unto them, s, Wherefore have ye H559
22 ye beguiled us, s, We *are* very far from H559
10: 3 Lachish, and unto Debir king of Eglon, s, H559
6 the camp to Gilgal, s, Slack not thy hand H559
17 And it was told Joshua, s, The five kings H559
14: 9 And Moses sware on that day, s, Surely H559
17: 4 and before the princes, s, The LORD H559
14 spake unto Joshua, s, Why hast thou H559
17 and to Manasseh, s, Thou *art* a great H559
18: 8 to describe the land, s, Go and walk H559
20: 1 The LORD also spake unto Joshua, s, H559
2 Speak to the children of Israel, s, Appoint H559
21: 2 the land of Canaan, s, The LORD H559
22: 8 And he spake unto them, s, Return with H559
15 of Gilead, and they spake with them, s, H559
24 fear of *this* thing, s, In time to come your H559
24 unto our children, s, What have ye to do H559
Jdg 1: 1 asked the LORD, s, Who shall go up for H559
4: 6 commanded, s, Go and draw toward
5: 1 Barak the son of Abinoam on that day, s, H559
6:13 fathers told us of, s, Did not the LORD H559
Jdg 6:32 him Jerubbaal, s, Let Baal plead against H559
7: 2 me, s, Mine own hand hath saved me. H559
3 the ears of the people, s, Whosoever *is* H559
24 mount Ephraim, s, Come down against H559
8: 9 the men of Penuel, s, When I come again H559
15 ye did upbraid me, s, *Are* the hands of H559
9: 1 of the house of his mother's father, s, H559
31 Abimelech privily, s, Behold, Gaal the H559
10:10 cried unto the LORD, s, We have sinned H559
11:12 of Ammon, s, What hast thou to do H559
17 the king of Edom, s, Let me, I pray thee, H559
13: 6 told her husband, s, A man of God came H559
15:13 And they spake unto him, s, No; but we H559
16: 2 *And it was told* the Gazites, s, Samson is H559
2 quiet all the night, s, In the morning, H559
18 of the Philistines, s, Come up this once, H559
19:22 the old man, s, Bring forth the man H559
20: 8 And all the people arose as one man, s, H559
12 tribe of Benjamin, s, What wickedness *is* H559
23 of the LORD, s, Shall I go up again to H559
28 it in those days,) s, Shall I yet again go H559
21: 1 sworn in Mizpeh, s, There shall not any H559
5 s, He shall surely be put to death. H559
10 commanded them, s, Go and smite the H559
18 of Israel have sworn, s, Cursed *be* he that H559
20 s, Go and lie in wait in the vineyards; H559
Ru 2:15 his young men, s, Let her glean even H559
4: 4 And I thought to advertise thee, s, Buy *it* H559
17 gave it a name, s, There is a son born to H559
1Sa 1:20 s, Because I have asked him of the LORD.
4:21 And she named the child Ichabod, s, The H559
5:10 cried out, s, They have brought about H559
6: 2 and the diviners, s, What shall we do to H559
21 of Kir-jath-jearim, s, The Philistines have H559
7: 3 the house of Israel, s, If ye do return unto H559
12 s, Hitherto hath the LORD helped us. H559
9:15 in his ear a day before Saul came, s, H559
26 top of the house, s, Up, that I may send H559
10: 2 for you, s, What shall I do for my son? H559
11: 7 of messengers, s, Whosoever cometh not H559
13: 3 all the land, s, Let the Hebrews hear. H559
14:24 adjured the people, s, Cursed *be* the man H559
28 with an oath, s, Cursed *be* the man that H559
33 Then they told Saul, s, Behold, the people H559
15:10 the word of the LORD unto Samuel, s, H559
12 it was told Samuel, s, Saul came to H559
16:22 And Saul sent to Jesse, s, Let David, I H559
17:26 that stood by him, s, What shall be done H559
27 after this manner, s, So shall it be done to H559
18: 8 And Saul was very wroth, and the s H1697
22 And Saul commanded his servants, *s,*
24 And the servants of Saul told him, s, On H559
19: 2 told David, s, Saul my father seeketh H559
11 wife told him, s, If thou save not thy life H559
15 *again* to see David, s, Bring him up to me H559
19 And it was told Saul, s, Behold, David *is* H559
20:16 the house of David, *s,* Let the LORD even
21 And, behold, I will send a lad, *s,* Go, find
42 the name of the LORD, s, The LORD be H559
21:11 of him in dances, s, Saul hath slain his H559
23: 1 Then they told David, s, Behold, the H559
2 Therefore David inquired of the LORD, s, H559
19 to Saul to Gibeah, s, Doth not David hide H559
27 But there came a messenger unto Saul, s, H559
24: 1 it was told him, s, Behold, David *is* in the H559
8 cried after Saul, s, My lord the king. And H559
9 words, s, Behold, David seeketh thy hurt? H559
25:14 Nabal's wife, s, Behold, David sent H559
40 spake unto her, s, David sent us unto H559
26: 1 Saul to Gibeah, s, Doth not David hide H559
6 brother to Joab, s, Who will go down with H559
14 the son of Ner, s, Answerest thou not, H559
19 of the LORD, s, Go, serve other gods. H559
27:11 *tidings* to Gath, s, Lest they should tell H559
11 should tell on us, s, So did David, and so H559
12 And Achish believed David, s, He hath H559
28:10 And Saul sware to her by the LORD, s, *As* H559
12 spake to Saul, s, Why hast thou deceived H559
29: 5 to another in dances, s, Saul slew his H559
30: 8 And David inquired at the LORD, s, Shall H559
26 *even* to his friends, s, Behold a present H559
2Sa 1:16 thee, s, I have slain the LORD'S anointed. H559
2: 1 of the LORD, s, Shall I go up into any H559
4 And they told David, s, *That* the men of H559
3:12 David on his behalf, s, Whose *is* the land? H559
12 Whose *is* the land? s *also,* Make thy H559
14 Saul's son, s, Deliver *me* my wife Michal, H559
17 with the elders of Israel, s, Ye sought for H559
18 spoken of David, s, By the hand of my H559
2Sa 3:23 they told Joab, s, Abner the son of Ner H559
35 yet day, David sware, s, So do God to me, H559
4:10 When one told me, s, Behold, Saul is H559
5: 1 s, Behold, we *are* thy bone and thy flesh. H559
6 spake unto David, s, Except thou take H559
19 And David inquired of the LORD, s, Shall H559
6:12 And it was told king David, s, The LORD H559
7: 4 word of the LORD came unto Nathan, s, H559
7 my people Israel, s, Why build ye not me H559
26 magnified for ever, s, The LORD of hosts H559
27 to thy servant, s, I will build thee an H559
11: 6 And David sent to Joab, *s,* Send me Uriah H559
10 And when they had told David, s, Uriah H559
15 And he wrote in the letter, s, Set ye Uriah H559
19 And charged the messenger, s, When H559
13: 7 Then David sent home to Tamar, s, Go H559
28 his servants, s, Mark ye now when H559
30 came to David, s, Absalom hath slain H559
14:32 I sent unto thee, s, Come hither, that I H559
15: 8 at Geshur in Syria, s, If the LORD shall H559
10 the tribes of Israel, s, As soon as ye hear H559
13 And there came a messenger to David, s, H559
31 And *one* told David, s, Ahithophel *is* H559
17: 4 And the s pleased Absalom well, and H1697
6 spake unto him, s, Ahithophel hath H559
6 we do *after* his s? if not; speak thou. H1697
16 and tell David, s, Lodge not this night H559
18: 5 Abishai and Ittai, s, *Deal* gently for my H559
12 Abishai and Ittai, s, Beware that none H559
19: 8 unto all the people, s, Behold, the king H559
9 the tribes of Israel, s, The king saved us H559
11 the priests, s, Speak unto the elders H559
11 the elders of Judah, s, Why are ye the last H559
20:18 Then she spake, s, They were wont to H559
18 speak in old time, s, They shall surely ask H559
21:17 sware unto him, s, Thou shalt go no H559
24:11 unto the prophet Gad, David's seer, s, H559
19 And David, according to the s of Gad, H1697
1Ki 1: 5 exalted himself, s, I will be king: and he H559
6 him at any time in s, Why hast thou done H559
11 of Solomon, s, Hast thou not heard H559
13 thine handmaid, s, Assuredly Solomon H559
17 thine handmaid, *s,* Assuredly Solomon
23 And they told the king, s, Behold Nathan H559
30 God of Israel, s, Assuredly Solomon H559
47 lord king David, s, God make the name H559
51 And it was told Solomon, s, Behold, H559
51 horns of the altar, s, Let king Solomon H559
2: 1 die; and he charged Solomon his son, s, H559
4 concerning me, s, If thy children take H559
8 him by the LORD, s, I will not put thee to H559
23 by the LORD, s, God do so to me, and H559
29 the son of Jehoiada, s, Go, fall upon him. H559
30 king word again, s, Thus said Joab, and H559
38 And Shimei said unto the king, The s *is* H1697
39 s, Behold, thy servants *be* in Gath. H559
42 unto thee, s, Know for a certain, on H559
5: 2 And Solomon sent to Hiram, s, H559
5 David my father, s, Thy son, whom I will H559
8 And Hiram sent to Solomon, s, I have H559
6:11 word of the LORD came to Solomon, s, H559
8:15 and hath with his hand fulfilled *it,* s, H559
25 promisedst him, s, There shall not fail H559
47 them captives, s, We have sinned, and H559
55 of Israel with a loud voice, s, H559
9: 5 to David thy father, s, There shall not fail H559
12: 3 came, and spake unto Rehoboam, s, H559
7 And they spake unto him, s, If thou wilt H559
9 who have spoken to me, s, Make the yoke H559
10 spake unto him, s, Thus shalt thou speak H559
10 spake unto thee, s, Thy father made our H559
12 s, Come to me again the third day. H559
14 of the young men, s, My father made H559
15 might perform his s, which the LORD H1697
16 answered the king, s, What portion have H559
22 came unto Shemaiah the man of God, s, H559
23 and to the remnant of the people, s, H559
13: 3 And he gave a sign the same day, s, This H559
4 heard the s of the man of God, which H1697
4 from the altar, s, Lay hold on him. And H559
9 word of the LORD, s, Eat no bread, nor H559
18 the word of the LORD, s, Bring him back H559
21 that came from Judah, s, Thus saith the H559
27 And he spake to his sons, s, Saddle me H559
30 mourned over him, *s,* Alas, my brother!
31 he spake to his sons, s, When I am dead, H559
32 For the s which he cried by the word of H1697
15:18 king of Syria, that dwelt at Damascus, s, H559
29 unto the s of the LORD, which H1697

1Ki 16: 1 the son of Hanani against Baasha, **s**, H559
17: 2 the word of the LORD came unto him, **s**, H559
8 the word of the LORD came unto him, **s**, H559
15 according to the **s** of Elijah: and she, H1697
18: 1 in the third year, **s**, Go, shew thyself unto H559
26 even until noon, **s**, O Baal, hear us. But H559
31 LORD came, **s**, Israel shall be thy name: H559
19: 2 unto Elijah, **s**, So let the gods do *to* H559
20: 4 to thy **s**, I *am* thine, and all that I have. H1697
5 Ben-hadad, **s**, Although I have sent H559
5 sent unto thee, **s**, Thou shalt deliver me H559
13 king of Israel, **s**, Thus saith the LORD, H559
17 **s**, There are men come out of Samaria. H559
21: 2 And Ahab spake unto Naboth, **s**, Give me H559
9 And she wrote in the letters, **s**, Proclaim H559
10 against him, **s**, Thou didst blaspheme H559
13 of the people, **s**, Naboth did blaspheme H559
14 Then they sent to Jezebel, **s**, Naboth is H559
17 the LORD came to Elijah the Tishbite, **s**, H559
19 And thou shalt speak unto him, **s**, Thus H559
19 speak unto him, **s**, Thus saith the LORD, H559
23 And of Jezebel also spake the LORD, **s**, H559
28 the LORD came to Elijah the Tishbite, **s**, H559
22:12 And all the prophets prophesied so, **s**, Go H559
13 spake unto him, **s**, Behold now, the H559
31 over his chariots, **s**, Fight neither with H559
36 down of the sun, **s**, Every man to his city, H559
2Ki 2:22 to the **s** of Elisha which he spake. H1697
3: 7 the king of Judah, **s**, The king of Moab H559
4: 1 unto Elisha, **s**, Thy servant my husband H559
31 and told him, **s**, The child is not awaked. H559
5: 4 And *one* went in, and told his lord, **s**, H559
6 the king of Israel, **s**, Now when this letter H559
8 he sent to the king, **s**, Wherefore hast H559
10 And Elisha sent a messenger unto him, **s**, H559
14 according to the **s** of the man of God: H1697
22 hath sent me, **s**, Behold, even now there H559
6: 8 with his servants, **s**, In such and such a H559
9 the king of Israel, **s**, Beware that thou H559
13 was told him, **s**, Behold, *he is* in Dothan. H559
26 unto him, **s**, Help, my lord, O king. H559
7:10 they told them, **s**, We came to the camp H559
12 in the field, **s**, When they come out H559
14 the host of the Syrians, **s**, Go and see. H559
18 spoken to the king, **s**, Two measures of H559
8: 1 restored to life, **s**, Arise, and go thou and H559
2 and did after the **s** of the man of God: H1697
4 of the man of God, **s**, Tell me, I pray thee, H559
6 a certain officer, **s**, Restore all that *was* H559
7 him, **s**, The man of God is come hither. H559
8 by him, **s**, Shall I recover of this disease? H559
9 to thee, **s**, Shall I recover of this disease? H559
9:12 spake he to me, **s**, Thus saith the LORD, H559
13 and blew with trumpets, **s**, Jehu is king. H559
18 watchman told, **s**, The messenger came H559
20 And the watchman told, **s**, He came even H559
36 Elijah the Tishbite, **s**, In the portion of H559
10: 1 them that brought up Ahab's *children*, **s**, H559
5 sent to Jehu, **s**, We *are* thy servants, H559
6 time to them, **s**, If ye *be* mine, and *if* H559
8 and told him, **s**, They have brought the H559
17 according to the **s** of the LORD, which H1697
11: 5 And he commanded them, **s**, This *is* the H559
14: 6 commanded, **s**, The fathers shall not H559
8 king of Israel, **s**, Come, let us look one H559
9 king of Judah, **s**, The thistle that *was* H559
9 *was* in Lebanon, **s**, Give thy daughter to H559
15:12 spake unto Jehu, **s**, Thy sons shall sit on H559
16: 7 king of Assyria, **s**, I *am* thy servant and H559
15 Urijah the priest, **s**, Upon the great altar H559
17:13 *by* all the seers, **s**, Turn ye from your evil H559
26 the king of Assyria, **s**, The nations which H559
27 Then the king of Assyria commanded, **s**, H559
35 and charged them, **s**, Ye shall not fear H559
18:14 of Assyria to Lachish, **s**, I have offended; H559
28 and spake, **s**, Hear the word of the H559
30 you trust in the LORD, **s**, The LORD will H559
32 you, **s**, The LORD will deliver us. H559
36 commandment was, **s**, Answer him not. H559
19: 9 sent messengers again unto Hezekiah, **s**, H559
10 king of Judah, **s**, Let not thy God in H559
10 deceive thee, **s**, Jerusalem shall not be H559
20 sent to Hezekiah, **s**, Thus saith the LORD H559
20: 2 to the wall, and prayed unto the LORD, **s**, H559
4 the word of the LORD came to him, **s**, H559
21:10 spake by his servants the prophets, **s**, H559
22: 3 the scribe, to the house of the LORD, **s**, H559
10 shewed the king, **s**, Hilkiah the priest H559
12 and Asahiah a servant of the king's, **s**, H559

2Ki 23:21 all the people, **s**, Keep the passover unto H559
1Ch 4: 9 Jabez, **s**, Because I bare him with sorrow. H559
10 And Jabez called on the God of Israel, **s**, H559
11: 1 **s**, Behold, we *are* thy bone and thy flesh. H559
12:19 sent him away, **s**, He will fall to his H559
13:12 And David was afraid of God that day, **s**, H559
14:10 And David inquired of God, **s**, Shall I go H559
16:18 **S**, Unto thee will I give the land of H559
22 **S**, Touch not mine anointed, and do my
17: 3 that the word of God came to Nathan, **s**, H559
6 to feed my people, **s**, Why have ye not H559
24 magnified for ever, **s**, The LORD of hosts H559
21: 9 LORD spake unto Gad, David's seer, **s**, H559
10 Go and tell David, **s**, Thus saith the H559
19 And David went up at the **s** of Gad, H1697
22: 8 But the word of the LORD came to me, **s**, H559
17 of Israel to help Solomon his son, **s**,
2Ch 2: 3 the king of Tyre, **s**, As thou didst deal H559
5:13 praised the LORD, **s**, For *he is* good; for
6: 4 with his mouth to my father David, **s**, H559
16 promised him, **s**, There shall not fail thee H559
37 of their captivity, **s**, We have sinned, we H559
7: 3 praised the LORD, **s**, For *he is* good; for
18 David thy father, **s**, There shall not fail H559
10: 3 Israel came and spake to Rehoboam, **s**, H559
6 while he yet lived, **s**, What counsel give H559
7 And they spake unto him, **s**, If thou be H559
9 have spoken to me, **s**, Ease somewhat the H559
10 him spake unto him, **s**, Thus shalt thou H559
10 spake unto thee, **s**, Thy father made our H559
12 **s**, Come again to me on the third day. H559
14 of the young men, **s**, My father made H559
16 answered the king, **s**, What portion have H559
11: 2 came to Shemaiah the man of God, **s**, H559
3 to all Israel in Judah and Benjamin, **s**, H559
12: 7 LORD came to Shemaiah, **s**, They have H559
16: 2 king of Syria, that dwelt at Damascus, **s**, H559
18:11 And all the prophets prophesied so, **s**, Go H559
12 spake to him, **s**, Behold, the words of H559
19 And one spake **s** after this manner, and H559
19 and another **s** after that manner. H559
30 *were* with him, **s**, Fight ye not with small H559
19: 9 And he charged them, **s**, Thus shall ye do H559
20: 2 that told Jehoshaphat, **s**, There cometh a H559
8 thee a sanctuary therein for thy name, **s**, H559
37 Jehoshaphat, **s**, Because thou hast joined H559
21:12 from Elijah the prophet, **s**, Thus saith the H559
25: 4 commanded, **s**, The fathers shall not H559
7 But there came a man of God to him, **s**, O H559
17 king of Israel, **s**, Come, let us see one H559
18 king of Judah, **s**, The thistle that *was* H559
18 *was* in Lebanon, **s**, Give thy daughter to H559
30: 6 of the king, **s**, Ye children of Israel, H559
18 **s**, The good LORD pardon every one H559
32: 4 the midst of the land, **s**, Why should the H559
6 city, and spake comfortably to them, **s**, H559
9 unto all Judah that *were* at Jerusalem, **s**, H559
11 and by thirst, **s**, The LORD our God shall H559
12 and Jerusalem, **s**, Ye shall worship before H559
17 speak against him, **s**, As the gods of the H559
34:16 king word back again, **s**, All that was H559
18 Then Shaphan the scribe told the king, **s**, H559
20 and Asaiah a servant of the king's, **s**, H559
35:21 But he sent ambassadors to him, **s**, What H559
36:22 his kingdom, and *put it* also in writing, **s**, H559
Ezr 1: 1 his kingdom, and *put it* also in writing, **s**, H559
5:11 And thus they returned us answer, **s**, We H560
8:22 unto the king, **s**, The hand of our God H559
9: 1 came to me, **s**, The people of Israel, H559
11 the prophets, **s**, The land, unto which H559
Neh 1: 8 thy servant Moses, **s**, *If* ye transgress, I H559
6: 2 sent unto me, **s**, Come, let us meet H559
3 And I sent messengers unto them, **s**, I *am* H559
7 of thee at Jerusalem, **s**, *There is* a king in H559
8 Then I sent unto him, **s**, There are no H559
9 For they all made us afraid, **s**, Their H559
8:11 So the Levites stilled all the people, **s**, H559
15 and in Jerusalem, **s**, Go forth unto the H559
13:25 swear by God, **s**, Ye shall not give your
Est 1:21 And the **s** pleased the king and the H1697
Job 4:16 *there was* silence, and I heard a voice, **s**,
8:18 *it* shall deny him, **s**, I have not seen thee. H559
15:23 He wandereth abroad for bread, **s**,
24:15 for the twilight, **s**, No eye shall see me: H559
33: 8 I have heard the voice of *thy* words, **s**,
Ps 2: 2 the LORD, and against his anointed, **s**,
22: 7 shoot out the lip, they shake the head, **s**,
49: 4 I will open my dark **s** upon the harp. H2420
71:11 **S**, God hath forsaken him: persecute and H559

Ps 105:11 **S**, Unto thee will I give the land of H559
15 **S**, Touch not mine anointed, and do my
119:82 Mine eyes fail for thy word, **s**, When wilt H559
137: 3 mirth, **s**, Sing us *one* of the songs of Zion.
Prv 1:21 in the city she uttereth her words, **s**,
Ecc 1:16 I communed with mine own heart, **s**, Lo, H559
Song 5: 2 that knocketh, **s**, Open to me, my sister,
Isa 3: 6 house of his father, **s**, Thou hast clothing,
7 In that day shall he swear, **s**, I will not be H559
4: 1 hold of one man, **s**, We will eat our own H559
6: 8 Also I heard the voice of the Lord, **s**, H559
7: 2 And it was told the house of David, **s**, H559
5 have taken evil counsel against thee, **s**, H559
10 the LORD spake again unto Ahaz, **s**, H559
8: 5 The LORD spake also unto me again, **s**, H559
11 not walk in the way of this people, **s**, H559
14: 8 cedars of Lebanon, **s**, Since thou art laid
16 *and* consider thee, **s**, *Is* this the man that
24 The LORD of hosts hath sworn, **s**, Surely H559
16:14 But now the LORD hath spoken, **s**, H559
18: 2 bulrushes upon the waters, **s**, Go, ye swift
19:25 Whom the LORD of hosts shall bless, **s**, H559
20: 2 the son of Amoz, **s**, Go and loose the H559
23: 4 strength of the sea, **s**, I travail not, nor H559
29:11 to one that is learned, **s**, Read this, I pray H559
12 that is not learned, **s**, Read this, I pray H559
30:21 a word behind thee, **s**, This *is* the way, H559
36:15 you trust in the LORD, **s**, The LORD will H559
18 *Beware* lest Hezekiah persuade you, **s**, H559
21 commandment was, **s**, Answer him not. H559
37: 9 *it*, he sent messengers to Hezekiah, **s**, H559
10 king of Judah, **s**, Let not thy God, in H559
10 deceive thee, **s**, Jerusalem shall not be H559
15 And Hezekiah prayed unto the LORD, **s**, H559
21 unto Hezekiah, **s**, Thus saith the LORD H559
38: 4 came the word of the LORD to Isaiah, **s**, H559
41: 7 that smote the anvil, **s**, It *is* ready for the H559
13 **s** unto thee, Fear not; I will help thee. H559
44:28 my pleasure: even **s** to Jerusalem, Thou H559
45:14 unto thee, **s**, Surely God *is* in thee;
46:10 that are not *yet* done, **s**, My counsel shall H559
56: 3 to the LORD, speak, **s**, The LORD hath H559
63:11 *and* his people, **s**, Where *is* he that
Jer 1: 4 the word of the LORD came unto me, **s**, H559
11 came unto me, **s**, Jeremiah, what seest H559
13 the second time, **s**, What seest thou? And H559
2: 1 the word of the LORD came to me, **s**, H559
2 Go and cry in the ears of Jerusalem, **s**, H559
27 **S** to a stock, Thou *art* my father; and to a H559
4:10 and Jerusalem, **s**, Ye shall have peace; H559
31 her hands, **s**, Woe *is* me now! for my
5:20 of Jacob, and publish it in Judah, **s**, H559
6:14 **s**, Peace, peace; when *there is* no peace. H559
17 Also I set watchmen over you, **s**, Hearken
7: 1 that came to Jeremiah from the LORD, **s**, H559
4 Trust ye not in lying words, **s**, The temple H559
23 But this thing commanded I them, **s**, H559
8: 6 of his wickedness, **s**, What have I done? H559
11 **s**, Peace, peace; when *there is* no peace. H559
11: 1 that came to Jeremiah from the LORD, **s**, H559
4 the iron furnace, **s**, Obey my voice, and H559
6 of Jerusalem, **s**, Hear ye the words of H559
7 early and protesting, **s**, Obey my voice. H559
19 against me, **s**, Let us destroy the tree
21 that seek thy life, **s**, Prophesy not in the H559
13: 3 LORD came unto me the second time, **s**, H559
8 the word of the LORD came unto me, **s**, H559
16: 1 word of the LORD came also unto me, **s**, H559
18: 1 came to Jeremiah from the LORD, **s**, H559
5 the word of the LORD came to me, **s**, H559
11 of Jerusalem, **s**, Thus saith the LORD; H559
20:10 for my halting, **s**, Peradventure he will
15 to my father, **s**, A man child is born H559
21: 1 the son of Maaseiah the priest, **s**, H559
22:18 lament for him, **s**, Ah my brother! or, Ah
18 for him, **s**, Ah lord! or, Ah his glory!
23:25 **s**, I have dreamed, I have dreamed. H559
33 shall ask thee, **s**, What *is* the burden of H559
38 sent unto you, **s**, Ye shall not say, The H559
24: 4 the word of the LORD came unto me, **s**, H559
25: 2 and to all the inhabitants of Jerusalem, **s**, H559
26: 1 Judah came this word from the LORD, **s**, H559
8 people took him, **s**, Thou shalt surely die. H559
9 name of the LORD, **s**, This house shall be H559
11 to all the people, **s**, This man *is* worthy to H559
12 to all the people, **s**, The LORD sent me to H559
17 spake to all the assembly of the people, **s**, H559
18 people of Judah, **s**, Thus saith the LORD H559
27: 1 word unto Jeremiah from the LORD, **s**, H559

Jer 27: 9 s, Ye shall not serve the king of Babylon: H559
12 to all these words, s, Bring your necks H559
14 speak unto you, s, Ye shall not serve the H559
16 to all this people, s, Thus saith the LORD; H559
16 prophesy unto you, s, Behold, the vessels H559
28: 1 of the priests and of all the people, s, H559
2 the God of Israel, s, I have broken the H559
11 of all the people, s, Thus saith the LORD; H559
12 off the neck of the prophet Jeremiah, s, H559
13 Go and tell Hananiah, s, Thus saith the H559
29: 3 to Nebuchadnezzar king of Babylon) s, H559
22 *are* in Babylon, s, The LORD make thee H559
24 speak to Shemaiah the Nehelamite, s, H559
25 the God of Israel, s, Because thou hast H559
25 the priest, and to all the priests, s, H559
28 us *in* Babylon, s, This *captivity is* long: H559
30 the word of the LORD unto Jeremiah, s, H559
31 Send to all them of the captivity, s, Thus H559
30: 1 that came to Jeremiah from the LORD, s, H559
2 Thus speaketh the LORD God of Israel, s, H559
17 thee an Outcast, *s*, This *is* Zion, whom no
31: 3 of old unto me, *s*, Yea, I have loved thee
34 man his brother, s, Know the LORD: for H559
32: 3 had shut him up, s, Wherefore dost thou H559
6 The word of the LORD came unto me, s, H559
7 come unto thee, s, Buy thee my field that H559
13 And I charged Baruch before them, s, H559
16 son of Neriah, I prayed unto the LORD, s, H559
26 the word of the LORD unto Jeremiah, s, H559
33: 1 yet shut up in the court of the prison, s, H559
19 of the LORD came unto Jeremiah, s, H559
23 word of the LORD came to Jeremiah, s, H559
24 have spoken, s, The two families which H559
34: 1 and against all the cities thereof, s, H559
5 will lament thee, *s*, Ah lord! for I have
12 came to Jeremiah from the LORD, s, H559
13 of Egypt, out of the house of bondmen, s, H559
35: 1 the son of Josiah king of Judah, s, H559
6 commanded us, s, Ye shall drink no H559
12 the word of the LORD unto Jeremiah, s, H559
15 early and sending *them*, s, Return ye now H559
36: 1 came unto Jeremiah from the LORD, s, H559
5 And Jeremiah commanded Baruch, s, I H559
14 unto Baruch, s, Take in thine hand the H559
17 And they asked Baruch, s, Tell us now, H559
27 wrote at the mouth of Jeremiah, s, H559
29 burned this roll, s, Why hast thou written H559
29 written therein, s, The king of Babylon H559
37: 3 prophet Jeremiah, s, Pray now unto the H559
6 the LORD unto the prophet Jeremiah, s, H559
9 not yourselves, s, The Chaldeans shall H559
13 s, Thou fallest away to the Chaldeans. H559
19 unto you, s, The king of Babylon H559
38: 1 had spoken unto all the people, s, H559
8 the king's house, and spake to the king, s, H559
10 the Ethiopian, s, Take from hence thirty H559
16 unto Jeremiah, s, *As* the LORD liveth, H559
39:11 the captain of the guard, s, H559
15 was shut up in the court of the prison, s, H559
16 the Ethiopian, s, Thus saith the LORD H559
40: 9 and to their men, s, Fear not to serve the H559
15 in Mizpah secretly, s, Let me go, I pray H559
42:14 S, No; but we will go into the land of H559
20 LORD your God, s, Pray for us unto the H559
43: 2 and all the proud men, s unto Jeremiah, H559
8 LORD unto Jeremiah in Tahpanhes, s, H559
44: 1 at Noph, and in the country of Pathros, s, H559
4 and sending *them*, s, Oh, do not this H559
15 Egypt, in Pathros, answered Jeremiah, s, H559
20 which had given him *that* answer, s, H559
25 the God of Israel, s; Ye and your wives H559
25 fulfilled with your hand, s, We will surely H559
26 land of Egypt, s, The Lord GOD liveth. H559
45: 1 the son of Josiah king of Judah, s, H559
48:39 They shall howl, *s*, How is it broken
49: 4 treasures, *s*, Who shall come unto me?
14 unto the heathen, *s*, Gather ye together,
34 of the reign of Zedekiah king of Judah, s, H559
50: 5 faces thitherward, *s*, Come, and let us
51:14 sworn by himself, *s*, Surely I will fill thee
Lam 2:15 of Jerusalem, *s*, *Is* this the city that *men*
Ezk 3:12 of a great rushing, *s*, Blessed *be* the glory
16 the word of the LORD came unto me, s, H559
6: 1 the word of the LORD came unto me, s, H559
7: 1 the word of the LORD came unto me, s, H559
9: 1 ears with a loud voice, s, Cause them that H559
11 the matter, s, I have done as thou H559
10: 6 man clothed with linen, s, Take fire from H559
11:14 the word of the LORD came unto me, s, H559

Ezk 12: 1 word of the LORD also came unto me, s, H559
8 came the word of the LORD unto me, s, H559
17 the word of the LORD came to me, s, H559
21 the word of the LORD came unto me, s, H559
22 in the land of Israel, s, The days are H559
26 the word of the LORD came to me, s, H559
13: 1 the word of the LORD came unto me, s, H559
6 lying divination, s, The LORD saith: and H559
10 my people, s, Peace; and *there was* H559
14: 2 the word of the LORD came unto me, s, H559
12 word of the LORD came again to me, s, H559
15: 1 the word of the LORD came unto me, s, H559
16: 1 the word of the LORD came unto me, s, H559
44 s, As *is* the mother, *so is* her daughter. H559
17: 1 the word of the LORD came unto me, s, H559
11 the word of the LORD came unto me, s, H559
18: 1 of the LORD came unto me again, s, H559
2 the land of Israel, s, The fathers have H559
20: 2 came the word of the LORD unto me, s, H559
5 unto them, s, I *am* the LORD your God; H559
45 the word of the LORD came unto me, s, H559
21: 1 the word of the LORD came unto me, s, H559
8 the word of the LORD came unto me, s, H559
18 of the LORD came unto me again, s, H559
22: 1 the word of the LORD came unto me, s, H559
17 the word of the LORD came unto me, s, H559
23 the word of the LORD came unto me, s, H559
28 lies unto them, s, Thus saith the Lord H559
23: 1 of the LORD came again unto me, s, H559
24: 1 the word of the LORD came unto me, s, H559
15 the word of the LORD came unto me, s, H559
20 The word of the LORD came unto me, s, H559
25: 1 of the LORD came again unto me, s, H559
26: 1 the word of the LORD came unto me, s, H559
27: 1 of the LORD came again unto me, s, H559
32 and lament over thee, *s*, What *city is* like
28: 1 of the LORD came again unto me, s, H559
11 the word of the LORD came unto me, s, H559
20 the word of the LORD came unto me, s, H559
29: 1 the word of the LORD came unto me, s, H559
17 the word of the LORD came unto me, s, H559
30: 1 of the LORD came again unto me, s, H559
20 the word of the LORD came unto me, s, H559
31: 1 the word of the LORD came unto me, s, H559
32: 1 the word of the LORD came unto me, s, H559
17 the word of the LORD came unto me, s, H559
33: 1 the word of the LORD came unto me, s, H559
10 Thus ye speak, s, If our transgressions H559
21 came unto me, s, The city is smitten. H559
23 the word of the LORD came unto me, s, H559
24 of Israel speak, s, Abraham was one, and H559
30 one to his brother, s, Come, I pray you, H559
34: 1 the word of the LORD came unto me, s, H559
35: 1 the word of the LORD came unto me, s, H559
12 of Israel, s, They are laid desolate, H559
36:16 the word of the LORD came unto me, s, H559
37:15 of the LORD came again unto me, s, H559
18 speak unto thee, s, Wilt thou not shew us H559
38: 1 the word of the LORD came unto me, s, H559
Dan 4: 8 gods: and before him I told the dream, *s*,
23 from heaven, and s, Hew the tree down, H560
31 a voice from heaven, *s*, O king
Am 2:12 the prophets, s, Prophesy not. H559
3: 1 I brought up from the land of Egypt, s,
7:10 king of Israel, s, Amos hath conspired H559
8: 5 S, When will the new moon be gone, that H559
Jna 1: 1 came unto Jonah the son of Amittai, s, H559
3: 1 came unto Jonah the second time, s, H559
7 and his nobles, s, Let neither man nor H559
4: 2 *was* not this my s, when I was yet in my H1697
Mic 2:11 falsehood do lie, *s*, I will prophesy unto
Hag 1: 1 the son of Josedech, the high priest, s, H559
2 Thus speaketh the LORD of hosts, s, This H559
3 of the LORD by Haggai the prophet, s, H559
13 people, s, I *am* with you, saith the LORD. H559
2: 1 of the LORD by the prophet Haggai, s, H559
2 priest, and to the residue of the people, s, H559
10 of the LORD by Haggai the prophet, s, H559
11 now the priests *concerning* the law, s, H559
20 four and twentieth *day* of the month, s, H559
21 s, I will shake the heavens and the earth; H559
Zec 1: 1 Berechiah, the son of Iddo the prophet, s, H559
4 have cried, s, Thus saith the LORD H559
7 Berechiah, the son of Iddo the prophet, s, H559
14 said unto me, Cry thou, s, Thus saith the H559
17 Cry yet, s, Thus saith the LORD of hosts; H559
21 do? And he spake, s, These *are* the horns H559
2: 4 to this young man, s, Jerusalem shall be H559
3: 4 stood before him, s, Take away the filthy H559

Zec 3: 6 of the LORD protested unto Joshua, s, H559
4: 4 with me, s, What *are* these, my lord? H559
6 Then he answered and spake unto me, s, H559
6 unto Zerubbabel, s, Not by might, nor by H559
8 the word of the LORD came unto me, s, H559
6: 8 spake unto me, s, Behold, these that go H559
9 the word of the LORD came unto me, s, H559
12 And speak unto him, s, Thus speaketh H559
12 the LORD of hosts, s, Behold the man H559
7: 3 to the prophets, s, Should I weep in the H559
4 word of the LORD of hosts unto me, s, H559
5 and to the priests, s, When ye fasted and H559
8 of the LORD came unto Zechariah, s, H559
9 Thus speaketh the LORD of hosts, s, H559
8: 1 word of the LORD of hosts came *to me*, s, H559
18 of the LORD of hosts came unto me, s, H559
21 shall go to another, s, Let us go speedily H559
23 him that is a Jew, s, We will go with you: H559
Mt 1:20 him in a dream, s, Joseph, thou son of *G3004*
22 spoken of the Lord by the prophet, s, *G3004*
2: 2 S, Where is he that is born King of the *G3004*
13 in a dream, s, Arise, and take the *G3004*
15 s, Out of Egypt have I called my son. *G3004*
17 was spoken by Jeremy the prophet, s, *G3004*
20 S, Arise, and take the young child and *G3004*
3: 2 And s, Repent ye: for the kingdom of *G3004*
3 the prophet Esaias, s, The voice of one *G3004*
14 But John forbad him, s, I have need to *G3004*
17 And lo a voice from heaven, s, This is *G3004*
4:14 was spoken by Esaias the prophet, s, *G3004*
5: 2 opened his mouth, and taught them, s, *G3004*
6:31 Therefore take no thought, s, What *G3004*
8: 2 worshipped him, s, Lord, if thou wilt, *G3004*
3 and touched him, s, I will; be thou *G3004*
6 And s, Lord, my servant lieth at home *G3004*
17 Esaias the prophet, s, Himself took our *G3004*
25 awoke him, s, Lord, save us: we perish. *G3004*
27 But the men marvelled, s, What *G3004*
29 And, behold, they cried out, s, What *G3004*
31 So the devils besought him, s, If thou *G3004*
9:14 disciples of John, s, Why do we and the *G3004*
18 worshipped him, s, My daughter is even *G3004*
27 s, *Thou* son of David, have mercy on us. *G3004*
29 Then touched he their eyes, s, *G3004*
30 them, s, See *that* no man know *it*. *G3004*
33 s, It was never so seen in Israel. *G3004*
10: 5 them, s, Go not into the way *G3004*
7 And as ye go, preach, s, The kingdom of *G3004*
11:17 And s, We have piped unto you, and ye *G3004*
12:10 they asked him, s, Is it lawful to heal on *G3004*
17 was spoken by Esaias the prophet, s, *G3004*
38 answered, s, Master, we would see *G3004*
13: 3 s, Behold, a sower went forth to sow; *G3004*
24 he forth unto them, s, The kingdom of *G3004*
31 he forth unto them, s, The kingdom of *G3004*
35 by the prophet, s, I will open my mouth *G3004*
36 came unto him, s, Declare unto us the *G3004*
14:15 came to him, s, This is a desert place, *G3004*
26 were troubled, s, It is a spirit; and they *G3004*
27 s, Be of good cheer; it is I; be not afraid. *G3004*
30 to sink, he cried, s, Lord, save me. *G3004*
33 s, Of a truth thou art the Son of God. *G3004*
15: 1 Pharisees, which were of Jerusalem, s, *G3004*
4 For God commanded, s, Honour thy *G3004*
7 well did Esaias prophesy of you, s, *G3004*
12 were offended, after they heard this s? *G3056*
22 cried unto him, s, Have mercy on me, *G3004*
23 s, Send her away; for she crieth after us. *G3004*
25 Then came she and worshipped him, s, *G3004*
16: 7 s, *It is* because we have taken no bread. *G3004*
13 his disciples, s, Whom do men say *G3004*
22 to rebuke him, s, Be it far from thee, *G3004*
17: 9 charged them, s, Tell the vision to no *G3004*
10 And his disciples asked him, s, Why *G3004*
14 man, kneeling down to him, and s, *G3004*
25 prevented him, s, What thinkest thou, *G3004*
18: 1 unto Jesus, s, Who is the greatest *G3004*
26 worshipped him, s, Lord, have patience *G3004*
28 the throat, s, Pay me that thou owest. *G3004*
29 besought him, s, Have patience with *G3004*
19: 3 him, and s unto him, Is it lawful *G3004*
11 this s, save *they* to whom it is given. *G3056*
22 But when the young man heard that s, *G3056*
25 amazed, s, Who then can be saved? *G3004*
20:12 S, These last have wrought *but* one *G3004*
30 by, cried out, s, Have mercy on us, O *G3004*
31 cried the more, s, Have mercy on us, O *G3004*
21: 2 S unto them, Go into the village over *G3004*
4 which was spoken by the prophet, s, *G3004*

Mt 21: 9 followed, cried, s, Hosanna to the son G3004
10 all the city was moved, s, Who is this? G3004
15 in the temple, and s, Hosanna to the G3004
20 *it*, they marvelled, s, How soon is the fig G3004
25 with themselves, s, If we shall say, From G3004
37 his son, s, They will reverence my son. G3004
22: 4 Again, he sent forth other servants, s, G3004
16 the Herodians, s, Master, we know that G3004
24 S, Master, Moses said, If a man die, G3004
31 which was spoken unto you by God, s, G3004
35 *him a question*, tempting him, and s, G3004
42 S, What think ye of Christ? whose son is G3004
43 doth David in spirit call him Lord, s, G3004
23: 2 S, The scribes and the Pharisees sit in G3004
24: 3 him privately, s, Tell us, when shall G3004
5 For many shall come in my name, s, I G3004
25: 9 But the wise answered, s, *Not so*; lest G3004
11 other virgins, s, Lord, Lord, open to us. G3004
20 brought other five talents, s, Lord, thou G3004
37 Then shall the righteous answer him, s, G3004
44 Then shall they also answer him, s, G3004
45 Then shall he answer them, s, Verily I G3004
26: 8 s, To what purpose *is* this waste? G3004
17 came to Jesus, s unto him, Where wilt G3004
27 and gave *it* to them, s, Drink ye all of it; G3004
39 face, and prayed, s, O my Father, if it be G3004
42 time, and prayed, s, O my Father, if this G3004
44 the third time, s the same words. G2036
48 gave them a sign, s, Whomsoever I shall G3004
65 Then the high priest rent his clothes, s, G3004
68 S, Prophesy unto us, thou Christ, Who G3004
69 s, Thou also wast with Jesus of Galilee. G3004
70 But he denied before *them* all, s, I know G3004
74 Then began he to curse and to swear, s, I
27: 4 S, I have sinned in that I have betrayed G3004
9 the prophet, s, And they took the thirty G3004
11 asked him, s, Art thou the King of G3004
19 sent unto him, s, Have thou nothing G3004
23 out the more, s, Let him be crucified. G3004
24 the multitude, s, I am innocent of the G3004
29 mocked him, s, Hail, King of the Jews! G3004
40 And s, Thou that destroyest the temple, G3004
46 cried with a loud voice, s, Eli, Eli, lama G3004
54 s, Truly this was the Son of God. G3004
63 S, Sir, we remember that that deceiver G3004
28: 9 Jesus met them, s, All hail. And they G3004
13 S, Say ye, His disciples came by night, G3004
15 were taught: and this s is commonly G3056
18 spake unto them, s, All power is given G3004
Mk 1: 7 And preached, s, There cometh one G3004
11 And there came a voice from heaven, s,
15 And s, The time is fulfilled, and the G3004
24 S, Let *us* alone; what have we to do with G3004
25 And Jesus rebuked him, s, Hold thy G3004
27 themselves, s, What thing is this? what G3004
40 down to him, and s unto him, If thou G3004
2:12 God, s, We never saw it on this fashion. G3004
3:11 and cried, s, Thou art the Son of God. G3004
33 And he answered them, s, Who is my G3004
5: 9 s, My name *is* Legion: for we are many. G3004
12 And all the devils besought him, s, Send G3004
23 And besought him greatly, s, My little G3004
6: 2 were astonished, s, From whence hath G3004
25 king, and asked, s, I will that thou give G3004
7:29 And he said unto her, For this s go thy G3056
37 astonished, s, He hath done all things G3004
8:15 And he charged them, s, Take heed, G3004
16 s, *It is* because we have no bread. G3004
26 And he sent him away to his house, s, G3004
27 his disciples, s unto them, Whom do G3004
32 And he spake that s openly. And Peter G3056
33 he rebuked Peter, s, Get thee behind G3004
9: 7 s, This is my beloved Son: hear him. G3004
10 And they kept that s with themselves, G3056
11 And they asked him, s, Why say the G3004
25 the foul spirit, s unto him, *Thou* dumb G3004
32 But they understood not that s, and G4487
38 And John answered him, s, Master, we G3004
10:22 And he was sad at that s, and went G3056
26 out of measure, s among themselves, G3004
33 S, Behold, we go up to Jerusalem; and the
35 come unto him, s, Master, we would G3004
49 the blind man, s unto him, Be of good G3004
11: 9 followed, cried, s, Hosanna; Blessed *is* G3004
17 And he taught, s unto them, Is it not G3004
31 And they reasoned with themselves, s, G3004
12: 6 them, s, They will reverence my son. G3004
18 no resurrection; and they asked him, s, G3004
26 God spake unto him, s, I *am* the God of G3004

Mk 13: 6 For many shall come in my name, s, I G3004
14:44 them a token, s, Whomsoever I shall G3004
57 and bare false witness against him, s, G3004
60 and asked Jesus, s, Answerest thou G3004
68 But he denied, s, I know not, neither G3004
71 But he began to curse and to swear, s, I
15: 4 And Pilate asked him again, s, G3004
9 But Pilate answered them, s, Will ye G3004
29 their heads, and s, Ah, thou that G3004
34 with a loud voice, s, Eloi, Eloi, lama G3004
36 gave him to drink, s, Let alone; let us G3004
Lk 1:24 and hid herself five months, s, G3004
29 troubled at his s, and cast in her mind G3056
63 table, and wrote, s, His name is John. G3004
66 up in their hearts, s, What manner of G3004
67 with the Holy Ghost, and prophesied, s, G3004
2:13 the heavenly host praising God, and s, G3004
17 known abroad the s which was told G4487
50 And they understood not the s which G4487
3: 4 the prophet, s, The voice of one crying G3004
10 And the people asked him, s, What G3004
14 demanded of him, s, And what shall we G3004
16 John answered, s unto *them* all, I G3004
4: 4 And Jesus answered him, s, It is G3004
34 S, Let *us* alone; what have we to do with G3004
35 And Jesus rebuked him, s, Hold thy G3004
36 themselves, s, What a word *is* this! G3004
41 crying out, and s, Thou art Christ the G3004
5: 8 at Jesus' knees, s, Depart from me; for G3004
12 besought him, s, Lord, if thou wilt, thou G3004
13 and touched him, s, I will: be thou G2036
21 began to reason, s, Who is this which G3004
26 s, We have seen strange things to day. G3004
30 his disciples, s, Why do ye eat and G3004
7: 4 him instantly, s, That he was worthy G3004
6 sent friends to him, s unto him, Lord, G3004
16 and they glorified God, s, That a great G3004
19 *them* to Jesus, s, Art thou he that should G3004
20 sent us unto thee, s, Art thou he that G3004
32 to another, and s, We have piped unto G3004
39 within himself, s, This man, if he were G3004
8: 9 And his disciples asked him, s, What G3004
24 and awoke him, s, Master, master, we G3004
25 afraid wondered, s one to another, G3004
30 And Jesus asked him, s, What is thy G3004
38 be with him: but Jesus sent him away, s, G3004
49 *house*, s to him, Thy daughter G3004
50 *it*, he answered him, s, Fear not: believe G3004
54 by the hand, and called, s, Maid, arise. G3004
9:18 s, Whom say the people that I am? G3004
22 S, The Son of man must suffer many G2036
35 s, This is my beloved Son: hear him. G3004
38 cried out, s, Master, I beseech thee, G3004
45 But they understood not this s, and it G4487
45 and they feared to ask him of that s. G4487
10:17 again with joy, s, Lord, even the devils G3004
25 and tempted him, s, Master, what shall G3004
11:45 thus s thou reproachest us also. G3004
12:16 And he spake a parable unto them, s, G3004
17 And he thought within himself, s, What G3004
13:25 knock at the door, s, Lord, Lord, open G3004
31 of the Pharisees, s unto him, Get thee G3004
14: 3 and Pharisees, s, Is it lawful to heal on G3004
5 And answered them, s, Which of you G2036
7 chose out the chief rooms; s unto them, G3004
30 S, This man began to build, and was G3004
15: 2 murmured, s, This man receiveth G3004
3 And he spake this parable unto them, s, G3004
6 and neighbours, s unto them, Rejoice G3004
9 together, s, Rejoice with me; for G3004
17: 4 thee, s, I repent; thou shalt forgive him. G3004
18: 2 S, There was in a city a judge, which G3004
3 him, s, Avenge me of mine adversary. G3004
13 s, God be merciful to me a sinner. G3004
18 And a certain ruler asked him, s, Good G3004
34 things: and this s was hid from them, G4487
38 And he cried, s, Jesus, *thou* son of G3004
41 S, What wilt thou that I shall do unto G3004
19: 7 all murmured, s, That he was gone to G3004
14 after him, s, We will not have this G3004
16 Then came the first, s, Lord, thy pound G3004
18 And the second came, s, Lord, thy G3004
20 And another came, s, Lord, behold, G3004
30 S, Go ye into the village over against G2036
38 S, Blessed *be* the King that cometh in G3004
42 S, If thou hadst known, even thou, at G3004
46 S unto them, It is written, My house is G3004
20: 2 And spake unto him, s, Tell us, by what G3004
5 And they reasoned with themselves, s, G3004

Lk 20:14 themselves, s, This is the heir: come, G3004
21 And they asked him, s, Master, we G3004
28 S, Master, Moses wrote unto us, If any G3004
21: 7 And they asked him, s, Master, but G3004
8 come in my name, s, I am *Christ*; and G3004
22: 8 And he sent Peter and John, s, Go and G2036
19 and gave unto them, s, This is my body G3004
20 Likewise also the cup after supper, s, G3004
42 S, Father, if thou be willing, remove this G3004
57 And he denied him, s, Woman, I know G3004
59 affirmed, s, Of a truth this *fellow* G3004
64 s, Prophesy, who is it that smote thee? G3004
66 and led him into their council, s, G3004
23: 2 And they began to accuse him, s, We G3004
2 s that he himself is Christ a King. G3004
3 And Pilate asked him, s, Art thou the G3004
5 And they were the more fierce, s, He G3004
18 And they cried out all at once, s, Away G3004
21 But they cried, s, Crucify *him*, crucify G3004
35 them derided *him*, s, He saved others; G3004
37 And s, If thou be the king of the Jews, G3004
39 s, If thou be Christ, save thyself and us. G3004
40 rebuked him, s, Dost not thou fear God, G3004
47 s, Certainly this was a righteous man. G3004
24: 7 S, The Son of man must be delivered G3004
23 body, they came, s, that they had also G3004
29 But they constrained him, s, Abide with G3004
34 S, The Lord is risen indeed, and hath G3004
Jn 1:15 John bare witness of him, and cried, s, G3004
26 John answered them, s, I baptize with G3004
32 And John bare record, s, I saw the Spirit G3004
4:31 his disciples prayed him, s, Master, eat. G3004
37 And herein is that s true, One soweth, G3056
39 on him for the s of the woman, which G3056
42 not because of thy s: for we have heard G2981
51 him, and told *him*, s, Thy son liveth. G3004
6:52 themselves, s, How can this man give G3004
60 said, This is an hard s; who can hear it? G3056
7:15 And the Jews marvelled, s, How G3004
28 as he taught, s, Ye both know me, and G3004
36 What *manner of* s is this that he said, G3056
37 stood and cried, s, If any man thirst, let G3004
40 s, said, Of a truth this is the Prophet. G3056
8:12 Then spake Jesus again unto them, s, I G3004
51 keep my s, he shall never see death. G3056
52 keep my s, he shall never taste of death. G3056
55 you: but I know him, and keep his s. G3056
9: 2 And his disciples asked him, s, Master, G3004
19 And they asked them, s, Is this your G3004
10:33 The Jews answered him, s, For a good G3004
11: 3 Therefore his sisters sent unto him, s, G3004
28 her sister secretly, s, The Master is G2036
31 out, followed her, s, She goeth unto the G3004
32 down at his feet, s unto him, Lord, if G3004
12:21 desired him, s, Sir, we would see Jesus. G3004
23 And Jesus answered them, s, The hour G3004
28 a voice from heaven, s, I have both
38 That the s of Esaias the prophet might G3056
15:20 kept my s, they will keep yours also. G3056
18: 9 That the s might be fulfilled, which he G3056
22 s, Answerest thou the high priest so? G2036
32 That the s of Jesus might be fulfilled, G3056
40 Then cried they all again, s, Not this G3004
19: 6 they cried out, s, Crucify *him*, crucify G3004
8 When Pilate therefore heard that s, he G3056
12 but the Jews cried out, s, If thou let this G3004
13 When Pilate therefore heard that s, he G3056
21:23 Then went this s abroad among the G3056
Act 1: 6 they asked of him, s, Lord, wilt thou at G3004
2: 7 and marvelled, s one to another, G3004
12 s one to another, What meaneth this? G3004
40 he testify and exhort, s, Save yourselves G3004
3:25 with our fathers, s unto Abraham, And G3004
4:16 S, What shall we do to these men? for G3004
5:23 S, The prison truly found we shut with G3004
25 Then came one and told them, s, G3004
28 S, Did not we straitly command you G3004
6: 5 And the s pleased the whole multitude: G3056
7:26 set them at one again, s, Sirs, ye are G2036
27 thrust him away, s, Who made thee a G2036
29 Then fled Moses at this s, and was a G3056
32 S, I *am* the God of thy fathers, the God of
35 This Moses whom they refused, s, Who G2036
40 S unto Aaron, Make us gods to go G2036
59 and s, Lord Jesus, receive my spirit. G3004
8:10 s, This man is the great power of God. G3004
19 S, Give me also this power, that on G3004
26 Lord spake unto Philip, s, Arise, and go G3004
9: 4 and heard a voice s unto him, Saul, G3004

S

Act 10: 3 in to him, and s unto him, Cornelius. G2036
26 But Peter took him up, s, Stand up; I G3004
11: 3 S, Thou wentest in to men G3004
4 expounded it by order unto them, s, G3004
7 And I heard a voice s unto me, Arise, G3004
18 and glorified God, s, Then hath God G3004
12: 7 raised him up, s, Arise up quickly. And G3004
22 And the people gave a shout, s, It is the
13:15 sent unto them, s, Ye men and G3004
47 For so hath the Lord commanded us, s, I
14:11 lifted up their voices, s in the speech of G3004
15 And s, Sirs, why do ye these things? We G3004
15: 5 which believed, s, That it was needful G3004
13 s, Men and brethren, hearken unto me: G3004
24 your souls, s, Ye must be circumcised, G3004
16: 9 and prayed him, s, Come over into G3004
15 she besought us, s, If ye have judged me G3004
17 and us, and cried, s, These men are the G3004
20 And brought them to the magistrates, s, G2036
28 But Paul cried with a loud voice, s, Do G3004
35 sent the serjeants, s, Let those men go. G3004
36 And the keeper of the prison told this s G3056
17: 7 s that there is another king, one Jesus. G3004
19 unto Areopagus, s, May we know what G3004
18:13 S, This fellow persuadeth men to G3004
21 But bade them farewell, s, I must by all G2036
19: 4 of repentance, s unto the people, that G3004
13 of the Lord Jesus, s, We adjure you by G3004
21 to go to Jerusalem, s, After I have been G2036
26 much people, s that they be no gods, G3004
28 out, s, Great is Diana of the Ephesians. G3004
20:23 s that bonds and afflictions abide me. G3004
21:14 ceased, s, The will of the Lord be done. G2036
21 to forsake Moses, s that they ought not G3004
40 unto them in the Hebrew tongue, s, G3004
22: 7 and heard a voice s unto me, Saul, G3004
18 And saw him s unto me, Make haste, G3004
26 the chief captain, s, Take heed what G3004
23: 9 arose, and strove, s, We find no evil in G3004
12 under a curse, s that they would G3004
23 him two centurions, s, Make ready two G2036
24: 2 to accuse him, s, Seeing that by thee G3004
9 And the Jews also assented, s that these G5335
25:14 unto the king, s, There is a certain man G3004
26:14 unto me, and s in the Hebrew tongue, G3004
22 to small and great, s none other things G3004
31 themselves, s, This man doeth nothing G3004
27:24 S, Fear not, Paul; thou must be brought G3004
33 them all to take meat, s, This day is the G3004
28:26 S, Go unto this people, and say, Hearing G3004
Ro 4: 7 S, Blessed are they whose iniquities are
11: 2 intercession to God against Israel, s, G3004
13: 9 in this s, namely, Thou shalt G3056
1Co 11:25 he had supped, s, This cup is the new G3004
15:54 to pass the s that is written, Death G3056
Gal 3: 8 s, In thee shall all nations be blessed.
1Ti 1:15 This is a faithful s, and worthy of all G3056
3: 1 This is a true s, If a man desire the G3056
4: 9 This is a faithful s and worthy of all G3056
2Ti 2:11 It is a faithful s: For if we be dead with G3056
18 Who concerning the truth have erred, s G3004
Tit 3: 8 This is a faithful s, and these things I G3056
Heb 2: 6 But one in a certain place testified, s, G3004
12 S, I will declare thy name unto my G3004
4: 7 Again, he limiteth a certain day, s in G3004
6:14 S, Surely blessing I will bless thee, and G3004
8:11 man his brother, s, Know the Lord: for G3004
9:20 S, This is the blood of the testament G3004
12:26 he hath promised, s, Yet once more I G3004
2Pt 3: 4 And s, Where is the promise of his G3004
Jude 14 of these, s, Behold, the Lord cometh G3004
Rev 1:11 S, I am Alpha and Omega, the first and G3004
17 hand upon me, s unto me, Fear not; I G3004
4: 8 not day and night, s, Holy, holy, holy, G3004
10 cast their crowns before the throne, s, G3004
5: 9 And they sung a new song, s, Thou art G3004
12 S with a loud voice, Worthy is the G3004
13 are in them, heard I s, Blessing, and G3004
6: 1 one of the four beasts s, Come and see. G3004
10 And they cried with a loud voice, s, G3004
7: 3 S, Hurt not the earth, neither the sea, G3004
10 And cried with a loud voice, s, G3004
12 S, Amen: Blessing, and glory, and G3004
13 And one of the elders answered, s unto G3004
8:13 midst of heaven, s with a loud voice, G3004
9:14 S to the sixth angel which had the G3004
10: 4 a voice from heaven s unto me, Seal up G3004
11: 1 the angel stood, s, Rise, and measure G3004
12 voice from heaven s unto them, Come G3004
Rev 11:15 voices in heaven, s, The kingdoms of G3004
17 S, We give thee thanks, O Lord God G3004
12:10 And I heard a loud voice s in heaven, G3004
13: 4 the beast, s, Who is like unto the G3004
14 sight of the beast; s to them that dwell G3004
14: 7 S with a loud voice, Fear God, and give G3004
8 And there followed another angel, s, G3004
9 And the third angel followed them, s G3004
13 And I heard a voice from heaven s unto G3004
18 the sharp sickle, s, Thrust in thy sharp G3004
15: 3 the song of the Lamb, s, Great and G3004
16: 1 out of the temple s to the seven angels, G3004
17 of heaven, from the throne, s, It is done. G3004
17: 1 and talked with me, s unto me, Come G3004
18: 2 a strong voice, s, Babylon the great is G3004
4 from heaven, s, Come out of her, my G3004
10 of her torment, s, Alas, alas that great G3004
16 And s, Alas, alas, that great city, that G3004
18 s, What city is like unto this great city! G3004
19 and wailing, s, Alas, alas, that great G3004
21 and cast it into the sea, s, Thus with G3004
19: 1 people in heaven, s, Alleluia; Salvation, G3004
4 sat on the throne, s, Amen; Alleluia. G3004
5 And a voice came out of the throne, s, G3004
6 thunderings, s, Alleluia: for the Lord G3004
17 with a loud voice, s to all the fowls that G3004
21: 3 out of heaven s, Behold, the tabernacle G3004
9 talked with me, s, Come hither, I will G3004

SAYINGS
Nu 14:39 And Moses told these s unto all the H1697
Jdg 13:17 s come to pass we may do thee honour? H1697
1Sa 25:12 and came and told him all those s. H1697
2Ch 13:22 his ways, and his s, are written in the H1697
33:19 are written among the s of the seers. H1697
Ps 49:13 their posterity approve their s. Selah. H6310
78: 2 in a parable: I will utter dark s of old: H2420
Prv 1: 6 the words of the wise, and their dark s. H2420
4:10 Hear, O my son, and receive my s; and H561
20 to my words; incline thine ear unto my s. H561
Mt 7:24 Therefore whosoever heareth these s of G3056
26 And every one that heareth these s of G3056
28 had ended these s, the people were G3056
19: 1 had finished these s, he departed from G3056
26: 1 all these s, he said unto his disciples, G3056
Lk 1:65 and all these s were noised abroad G4487
2:51 his mother kept all these s in her heart. G4487
6:47 and heareth my s, and doeth them, I G3056
7: 1 Now when he had ended all his s in the G4487
9:28 days after these s, he took Peter and G3056
44 Let these s sink down into your ears: G3056
Jn 10:19 again among the Jews for these s. G3056
14:24 He that loveth me not keepeth not my s: G3056
Act 14:18 And with these s scarce restrained they G3004
19:28 And when they heard these s, they were
Ro 3: 4 be justified in thy s, and mightest G3056
Rev 19: 9 unto me, These are the true s of God. G3056
22: 6 And he said unto me, These s are G3056
7 the s of the prophecy of this book. G3056
9 keep the s of this book: worship God. G3056
10 And he saith unto me, Seal not the s of G3056

SCAB
Lev 13: 2 his flesh a rising, a s, or bright spot, and H5597
6 clean: it is but a s: and he shall wash his H4556
7 But if the s spread much abroad in the H4556
8 And if the priest see that, behold, the s H4556
14:56 And for a rising, and for a s, and for a H5597
Dt 28:27 and with the s, and with the itch, H1618
Isa 3:17 Therefore the Lord will smite with a s H5596

SCABBARD
Jer 47: 6 up thyself into thy s, rest, and be still. H8593

SCABBED
Lev 21:20 scurvy, or s, or hath his stones broken; H3217
22:22 a wen, or scurvy, or s, ye shall not offer H3217

SCAFFOLD
2Ch 6:13 For Solomon had made a brasen s, of H3595

SCALES
Lev 11: 9 hath fins and s in the waters, in the H7193
10 And all that have not fins and s in the H7193
12 Whatsoever hath no fins nor s in the H7193
Dt 14: 9 all that have fins and s shall ye eat: H7193
10 And whatsoever hath not fins and s ye H7193
Job 41:15 His s are his pride, shut up H4043+H650
Isa 40:12 in s, and the hills in a balance? H6425
Ezk 29: 4 to stick unto thy s, and I will bring thee H7193
4 fish of thy rivers shall stick unto thy s. H7193
Act 9:18 eyes as it had been s: and he received G3013

SCALETH
Prv 21:22 A wise man s the city of the mighty, H5927

SCALL
Lev 13:30 him unclean: it is a dry s, even a leprosy H5424
31 on the plague of the s, and, behold, it be H5424
31 hath the plague of the s seven days: H5424
32 and, behold, if the s spread not, and H5424
32 s be not in sight deeper than the skin; H5424
33 He shall be shaven, but the s shall he H5424
33 him that hath the s seven days more: H5424
34 shall look on the s: and, behold, if the H5424
34 and, behold, if the s be not spread in H5424
35 But if the s spread much in the skin H5424
36 and, behold, if the s be spread in the H5424
37 But if the s be in his sight at a stay, and H5424
37 up therein; the s is healed, he is clean: H5424
14:54 all manner of plague of leprosy, and s, H5424

SCALP
Ps 68:21 and the hairy s of such an one as goeth H6936

SCANT
Mic 6:10 and the s measure that is abominable? H7332

SCAPEGOAT
Lev 16: 8 the LORD, and the other lot for the s. H5799
10 the lot fell to be the s, shall be presented H5799
10 to let him go for a s into the wilderness. H5799
26 And he that let go the goat for the s H5799

SCARCE
Gen 27:30 and Jacob was yet s gone out from the H3318
Act 14:18 And with these sayings s restrained G3433
27: 7 many days, and s were come over G3433

SCARCELY
Ro 5: 7 For s for a righteous man will one die: G3433
1Pt 4:18 And if the righteous s be saved, where G3433

SCARCENESS
Dt 8: 9 eat bread without s, thou shalt not lack H4544

SCAREST
Job 7:14 Then thou s me with dreams, and H2865

SCARLET
Gen 38:28 a s thread, saying, This came out first. H8144
30 that had the s thread upon his hand: H8144
Ex 25: 4 And blue, and purple, and s, H8438+H8144
26: 1 purple, and s: with cherubims H8438+H8144
31 purple, and s, and fine twined H8438+H8144
36 purple, and s, and fine twined H8438+H8144
27:16 purple, and s, and fine twined H8438+H8144
28: 5 purple, and s, and fine linen. H8438+H8144
6 of purple, of s, and fine twined H8438+H8144
8 and s, and fine twined linen. H8438+H8144
15 of purple, and of s, and of fine H8438+H8144
33 purple, and of s, round about H8438+H8144
35: 6 And blue, and purple, and s, H8438+H8144
23 purple, and s, and fine linen, H8438+H8144
25 and of s, and of fine linen. H8438+H8144
35 and in purple, in s, and in fine H8438+H8144
36: 8 purple, and s: with cherubims H8438+H8144
35 purple, and s, and fine twined H8438+H8144
37 purple, and s, and fine twined H8438+H8144
38:18 purple, and s, and fine twined H8438+H8144
23 purple, and in s, and fine linen. H8438+H8144
39: 1 purple, and s, they made cloths H8438+H8144
2 and s, and fine twined linen. H8438+H8144
3 and in the s, and in the fine H8438+H8144
5 purple, and s, and fine twined H8438+H8144
8 and s, and fine twined linen. H8438+H8144
24 and s, and twined linen. H8438+H8144
29 purple, and s, of needlework; H8438+H8144
Lev 14: 4 cedar wood, and s, and hyssop: H8438+H8144
6 cedar wood, and the s, and the H8438+H8144
49 cedar wood, and s, and hyssop: H8438+H8144
51 and the s, and the living bird, H8438+H8144
52 with the hyssop, and with the s: H8438+H8144
Nu 4: 8 a cloth of s, and cover the same H8438+H8144
19: 6 hyssop, and s, and cast it into H8438+H8144
Jos 2:18 bind this line of s thread in the window H8144
21 she bound the s line in the window. H8144
2Sa 1:24 clothed you in s, with other delights, H8144

Prv 31:21 for all her household *are* clothed with s. H8144
Song 4: 3 Thy lips *are* like a thread of s, and thy H8144
Isa 1:18 your sins be as s, they shall be as white H8144
Lam 4: 5 brought up in s embrace dunghills. H8438
Dan 5: 7 be clothed with s, and *have* a chain of H711
16 be clothed with s, and *have* a chain of H711
29 Daniel with s, and *put* a chain of gold H711
Nah 2: 3 valiant men *are* in s: the chariots *shall* H8529
Mt 27:28 stripped him, and put on him a s robe. *G2847*
Heb 9:19 with water, and s wool, and hyssop, *G2847*
Rev 17: 3 woman sit upon a s coloured beast, full *G2847*
4 in purple and s colour, and decked *G2847*
18:12 and silk, and s, and all thyine wood, *G2847*
16 and purple, and s, and decked with *G2847*

SCARLET-COLOURED See SCARLET and COLOURED.

SCATTER
Gen 11: 9 did the LORD s them abroad upon H6327
49: 7 them in Jacob, and s them in Israel. H6327
Lev 26:33 And I will s you among the heathen, H2219
Nu 16:37 the burning, and s thou the fire yonder; H2219
Dt 4:27 And the LORD shall s you among the H6327
28:64 And the LORD shall s thee among all H6327
32:26 I said, I would s them into corners, I H6284
1Ki 14:15 fathers, and shall s them beyond the H2219
Neh 1: 8 I will s you abroad among the nations: H6327
Ps 59:11 Slay them not, lest my people forget: s H5128
68:30 s thou the people *that* delight in war. H967
106:27 the nations, and to s them in the lands. H2219
144: 6 Cast forth lightning, and s them: shoot H6327
Isa 28:25 the fitches, and s the cummin, and cast H2236
41:16 whirlwind shall s them: and thou shalt H6327
Jer 9:16 I will s them also among the heathen, H6327
13:24 Therefore will I s them as the stubble H6327
18:17 I will s them as with an east wind H6327
23: 1 that destroy and s the sheep of my H6327
49:32 a spoil: and I will s into all winds them H2219
36 of heaven, and will s them toward all H2219
Ezk 5: 2 part thou shalt s in the wind; and I will H2219
10 of thee will I s into all the winds. H2219
12 thee; and I will s a third part into all H2219
6: 5 s your bones round about your altars. H2219
10: 2 cherubims, and s *them* over the city. H2236
12:14 And I will s toward every wind all that H2219
15 when I shall s them among the nations, H6327
20:23 that I would s them among the H6327
22:15 And I will s thee among the heathen, H6327
29:12 years: and I will s the Egyptians among H6327
30:23 And I will s the Egyptians among the H6327
26 And I will s the Egyptians among the H6327
Dan 4:14 off his leaves, and s his fruit: let the H921
11:24 fathers; he shall s among them the prey, H967
12: 7 accomplished to s the power of the holy H5310
Hab 3:14 as a whirlwind to s me: their rejoicing H6327
Zec 1:21 *their* horn over the land of Judah to s it. H2219

SCATTERED
Gen 11: 4 a name, lest we be s abroad upon the H6327
8 So the LORD s them abroad from H6327
Ex 5:12 So the people were s abroad H6327
Nu 10:35 let thine enemies be s; and let them that H6327
Dt 30: 3 whither the LORD thy God hath s thee. H6327
1Sa 11:11 remained were s, so that two of them H6327
13: 8 Gilgal; and the people were s from him. H6327
11 the people were s from me, and *that* H5310
2Sa 18: 8 For the battle was there s over the face H6327
22:15 And he sent out arrows, and s them; H6327
1Ki 22:17 And he said, I saw all Israel s upon the H6327
2Ki 25: 5 and all his army were s from him. H6327
2Ch 18:16 Then he said, I did see all Israel s upon H6327
Est 3: 8 There is a certain people s abroad and H6340
Job 4:11 the stout lion's whelps are s abroad. H6504
18:15 shall be s upon his habitation. H2219
Ps 18:14 Yea, he sent out his arrows, and s H6327
44:11 and hast s us among the heathen. H2219
53: 5 was: for God hath s the bones of him H6340
60: 1 us off, thou hast s us, thou hast been H6555
68: 1 Let God arise, let his enemies be s: let H6327
14 When the Almighty s kings in it, it was H6566
89:10 s thine enemies with thy strong arm. H6340
92: 9 all the workers of iniquity shall be s. H6504
141: 7 Our bones are s at the grave's mouth, H6340
Isa 18: 2 to a nation s and peeled, to a people H4900
7 of hosts of a people s and peeled, and H4900
33: 3 lifting up of thyself the nations were s. H5310
Jer 3:13 thy God, and hast s thy ways to the H6340
10:21 prosper, and all their flocks shall be s. H6327
23: 2 people; Ye have s my flock, and driven H6327
Jer 30:11 whither I have s thee, yet will I not H6327
31:10 off, and say, He that s Israel will gather H2219
40:15 be s, and the remnant in Judah perish? H6327
50:17 Israel *is* a s sheep; the lions have driven H6340
52: 8 and all his army was s from him. H6327
Ezk 6: 8 ye shall be s through the countries. H2219
11:16 and although I have s them among the H6327
17 s, and I will give you the land of Israel. H6327
17:21 remain shall be s toward all winds: and H6566
20:34 wherein ye are s, with a mighty hand, H6327
41 ye have been s; and I will be sanctified H6327
28:25 whom they are s, and shall be sanctified H6327
29:13 from the people whither they were s: H6327
34: 5 And they were s, because *there is* no H6327
5 the beasts of the field, when they were s. H6327
6 yea, my flock was s upon all the face of H6327
12 his sheep *that are* s; so will I seek out H6567
12 been s in the cloudy and dark day. H6327
21 your horns, till ye have s them abroad; H6327
36:19 And I s them among the heathen, and H6327
46:18 not s every man from his possession. H6327
Joel 3: 2 whom they have s among the nations, H6340
Nah 3:18 *the dust*: thy people is s upon the H6335
Hab 3: 6 mountains were s, the perpetual hills H6327
Zec 1:19 have s Judah, Israel, and Jerusalem. H2219
21 horns which have s Judah, so that no H2219
7:14 But I s them with a whirlwind among all
13: 7 and the sheep shall be s: and I will turn H6327
Mt 9:36 s abroad, as sheep having no shepherd. *G4496*
26:31 the sheep of the flock shall be s abroad. *G1287*
Mk 14:27 the shepherd, and the sheep shall be s. *G1287*
Lk 1:51 with his arm; he hath s the proud in the *G1287*
Jn 11:52 the children of God that were s abroad. *G1287*
16:32 that ye shall be s, every man to his own, *G4650*
Act 5:36 him, were s, and brought to nought. *G1262*
8: 1 and they were all s abroad throughout *G1289*
4 Therefore they that were s abroad went *G1289*
11:19 Now they which were s abroad upon *G1289*
Jas 1: 1 tribes which are s abroad, greeting. *G1290*
1Pt 1: 1 to the strangers s throughout Pontus, *G1290*

SCATTERETH
Job 37:11 the thick cloud: he s his bright cloud: H6327
38:24 *which* s the east wind upon the earth? H6327
Ps 147:16 He giveth snow like wool: he s the H6340
Prv 11:24 There is that s, and yet increaseth; and H6340
20: 8 judgment s away all evil with his eyes. H2219
26 A wise king s the wicked, and bringeth H2219
Isa 24: 1 and s abroad the inhabitants thereof. H6327
Mt 12:30 that gathereth not with me s abroad. *G4650*
Lk 11:23 and he that gathereth not with me s. *G4650*
Jn 10:12 wolf catcheth them, and s the sheep. *G4650*

SCATTERING
Isa 30:30 *with* s, and tempest, and hailstones. H5311

SCENT
Job 14: 9 *Yet* through the s of water it will bud, H7381
Jer 48:11 in him, and his s is not changed. H7381
Hos 14: 7 as the vine: the s thereof *shall be* as the H2143

SCEPTRE
Gen 49:10 The s shall not depart from Judah, nor H7626
Nu 24:17 of Jacob, and a S shall rise out of Israel, H7626
Est 4:11 out the golden s, that he may live: but H8275
5: 2 to Esther the golden s that *was* in his H8275
2 drew near, and touched the top of the s. H8275
8: 4 Then the king held out the golden s H8275
Ps 45: 6 the s of thy kingdom *is* a right sceptre. H7626
6 the sceptre of thy kingdom *is* a right s. H7626
Isa 14: 5 of the wicked, *and* the s of the rulers. H7626
Ezk 19:14 no strong rod *to be* a s to rule. This *is* a H7626
Am 1: 5 that holdeth the s from the house of H7626
8 that holdeth the s from Ashkelon, and H7626
Zec 10:11 and the s of Egypt shall depart away. H7626
Heb 1: 8 ever and ever: a s of righteousness *is* *G4464*
8 righteousness *is* the s of thy kingdom. *G4464*

SCEPTRES
Ezk 19:11 And she had strong rods for the s of H7626

SCEVA
Act 19:14 And there were seven sons of *one* S, a *G4630*

SCHISM
1Co 12:25 That there should be no s in the body; *G4978*

SCHOLAR
1Ch 25: 8 small as the great, the teacher as the s. H8527
Mal 2:12 master and the s, out of the tabernacles H6030

SCHOOL
Act 19: 9 daily in the s of one Tyrannus. *G4981*

SCHOOLMASTER
Gal 3:24 Wherefore the law was our s *to bring* *G3807*
25 is come, we are no longer under a s. *G3807*

SCIENCE
Dan 1: 4 and understanding s, and such as *had* H4093
1Ti 6:20 and oppositions of s falsely so called: *G1108*

SCOFF
Hab 1:10 And they shall s at the kings, and the H7046

SCOFFERS
2Pt 3: 3 days s, walking after their own lusts, *G1703*

SCORCH
Rev 16: 8 was given unto him to s men with fire. *G2739*

SCORCHED
Mt 13: 6 And when the sun was up, they were s; *G2739*
Mk 4: 6 But when the sun was up, it was s; and *G2739*
Rev 16: 9 And men were s with great heat, and *G2739*

SCORN
2Ki 19:21 *and* laughed thee to s; the daughter of H3932
2Ch 30:10 laughed them to s, and mocked them. H7832
Neh 2:19 they laughed us to s, and despised us, H3932
Est 3: 6 And he thought s to lay hands on H959
Job 12: 4 the just upright *man is* laughed to s. H7814
16:20 My friends s me: *but* mine eye poureth H3887
22:19 glad: and the innocent laugh them to s. H3932
Ps 22: 7 All they that see me laugh me to s: they H3932
44:13 to our neighbours, a s and a derision to H3933
79: 4 to our neighbours, a s and derision to H3933
Isa 37:22 *and* laughed thee to s; the daughter of H3932
Ezk 23:32 be laughed to s and had in derision; H6712
Hab 1:10 the princes shall be a s unto them: they H4890
Mt 9:24 sleepeth. And they laughed him to s. *G2606*
Mk 5:40 And they laughed him to s. But when he *G2606*
Lk 8:53 And they laughed him to s, knowing *G2606*

SCORNER
Prv 9: 7 He that reproveth a s getteth to himself H3887
8 Reprove not a s, lest he hate thee: H3887
13: 1 instruction: but a s heareth not rebuke. H3887
14: 6 A s seeketh wisdom, and *findeth it* not: H3887
15:12 A s loveth not one that reproveth him: H3887
19:25 Smite a s, and the simple will beware: H3887
21:11 When the s is punished, the simple is H3887
24 Proud *and* haughty s *is* his name, who H3887
22:10 Cast out the s, and contention shall go H3887
24: 9 and the s *is* an abomination to men. H3887
Isa 29:20 to nought, and the s is consumed, and H3887

SCORNERS
Prv 1:22 and the s delight in their scorning, H3887
3:34 Surely he scorneth the s: but he giveth H3887
19:29 Judgments are prepared for s, and H3887
Hos 7: 5 wine; he stretched out his hand with s. H3945

SCORNEST
Prv 9:12 but *if* thou s, thou alone shalt bear *it*. H3887
Ezk 16:31 been as an harlot, in that thou s hire; H7046

SCORNETH
Job 39: 7 He s the multitude of the city, neither H7832
18 on high, she s the horse and his rider. H7832
Prv 3:34 Surely he s the scorners: but he giveth H3887
19:28 An ungodly witness s judgment: and H3887

SCORNFUL
Ps 1: 1 sinners, nor sitteth in the seat of the s. H3887
Prv 29: 8 S men bring a city into a snare: but H3944
Isa 28:14 of the LORD, ye s men, that rule this H3944

SCORNING
Job 34: 7 like Job, *who* drinketh up s like water? H3933
Ps 123: 4 Our soul is exceedingly filled with the s H3933
Prv 1:22 in their s, and fools hate knowledge? H3944

SCORPION
Lk 11:12 he shall ask an egg, will he offer him a s? *G4651*
Rev 9: 5 torment of a s, when he striketh a man. *G4651*

SCORPIONS
Dt 8:15 *were* fiery serpents, and s, and drought, H6137
1Ki 12:11 whips, but I will chastise you with s. H6137
14 whips, but I will chastise you with s. H6137
2Ch 10:11 whips, but I *will chastise you* with s. H6137
14 whips, but I *will chastise you* with s. H6137
Ezk 2: 6 dost dwell among s: be not afraid of H6137
Lk 10:19 tread on serpents and s, and over all the G4651
Rev 9: 3 as the s of the earth have power. G4651
10 And they had tails like unto s, and there G4651

SCOURED
Lev 6:28 it shall be both s, and rinsed in water. H4838

SCOURGE
Job 5:21 Thou shalt be hid from the s of the H7752
9:23 If the s slay suddenly, he will laugh at H7752
Isa 10:26 And the LORD of hosts shall stir up a s H7752
28:15 the overflowing s shall pass through, H7752
18 the overflowing s shall pass through, H7752
Mt 10:17 and they will s you in their synagogues; G3146
20:19 to mock, and to s, and to crucify *him*: G3146
23:34 of them shall ye s in your synagogues, G3146
Mk 10:34 And they shall mock him, and shall s G3146
Lk 18:33 And they shall s *him*, and put him to G3146
Jn 2:15 And when he had made a s of small G5416
Act 22:25 Is it lawful for you to s a man that is a G3147

SCOURGED
Lev 19:20 her; she shall be s; they shall not be put H1244
Mt 27:26 and when he had s Jesus, he delivered G5417
Mk 15:15 when he had s *him*, to be crucified. G5417
Jn 19: 1 Then Pilate therefore took Jesus, and s G3146

SCOURGES
Jos 23:13 unto you, and s in your sides, and H7850

SCOURGETH
Heb 12: 6 and s every son whom he receiveth. G3146

SCOURGING
Act 22:24 be examined by s; that he might know G3148

SCOURGINGS
Heb 11:36 *cruel* mockings and s, yea, moreover of G3148

SCRABBLED
1Sa 21:13 their hands, and s on the doors of the H8427

SCRAPE
Lev 14:41 the dust that they s off without the city H7096
Job 2: 8 And he took him a potsherd to s H1623
Ezk 26: 4 towers: I will also s her dust from her, H5500

SCRAPED
Lev 14:41 And he shall cause the house to be s H7106
43 s the house, and after it is plaistered; H7096

SCREECH
Isa 34:14 to his fellow; the s owl also shall rest H3917

SCRIBE
2Sa 8:17 *were* the priests; and Seraiah *was* the s; H5608
20:25 And Sheva *was* s: and Zadok and H5608
2Ki 12:10 that the king's s and the high priest H5608
18:18 and Shebna the s, and Joah the son of H5608
37 and Shebna the s, and Joah the son of H5608
19: 2 and Shebna the s, and the elders of the H5608
22: 3 the s, to the house of the LORD, saying, H5608
8 unto Shaphan the s, I have found the H5608
9 And Shaphan the s came to the king, H5608
10 And Shaphan the s shewed the king, H5608
12 and Shaphan the s, and Asahiah a H5608
25:19 and the principal s of the host, which H5608
1Ch 18:16 *were* the priests; and Shavsha was s; H5608
24: 6 of Nethaneel the s, *one* of the Levites, H5608
27:32 a wise man, and a s: and Jehiel the son H5608
2Ch 24:11 much money, the king's s and the high H5608
26:11 hand of Jeiel the s and Maaseiah the H5608
34:15 to Shaphan the s, I have found the book H5608
18 Then Shaphan the s told the king, H5608
20 and Shaphan the s, and Asaiah a H5608
Ezr 4: 8 and Shimshai the s wrote a letter H5613
9 and Shimshai the s, and the rest of their H5613
17 and *to* Shimshai the s, and *to* the rest of H5613
23 Rehum, and Shimshai the s, and their H5613
7: 6 he *was* a ready s in the law of Moses, H5608
11 the priest, the s, *even* a scribe of the H5608
11 the scribe, *even* a s of the words of the H5608
Ezr 7:12 Ezra the priest, a s of the law of the H5613
21 the priest, the s of the law of the God H5613
Neh 8: 1 unto Ezra the s to bring the book of H5608
4 And Ezra the s stood upon a pulpit of H5608
9 Ezra the priest the s, and the Levites H5608
13 unto Ezra the s, even to understand H5608
12:26 governor, and of Ezra the priest, the s. H5608
36 of God, and Ezra the s before them. H5608
13:13 and Zadok the s, and of the Levites, H5608
Isa 33:18 Where *is* the s? where *is* the receiver? H5608
36: 3 s, and Joah, Asaph's son, the recorder. H5608
22 and Shebna the s, and Joah, the son of H5608
37: 2 and Shebna the s, and the elders of the H5608
Jer 36:10 of Shaphan the s, in the higher court, H5608
12 *even* Elishama the s, and Delaiah the H5608
20 of Elishama the s, and told all the H5608
26 to take Baruch the s and Jeremiah the H5608
32 it to Baruch the s, the son of Neriah; H5608
37:15 the s: for they had made that the prison. H5608
20 house of Jonathan the s, lest I die there. H5608
52:25 and the principal s of the host, who H5608
Mt 8:19 And a certain s came, and said unto G1122
13:52 Therefore every s *which is* instructed G1122
Mk 12:32 And the s said unto him, Well, Master, G1122
1Co 1:20 Where *is* the wise? where *is* the s? where G1122

SCRIBES
1Ki 4: 3 the sons of Shisha, s; Jehoshaphat the H5608
1Ch 2:55 And the families of the s which dwelt at H5608
2Ch 34:13 *there were* s, and officers, and porters. H5608
Est 3:12 Then were the king's s called on the H5608
8: 9 Then were the king's s called at that H5608
Jer 8: 8 made he *it*; the pen of the s *is* in vain. H5608
Mt 2: 4 the chief priests and s of the people G1122
5:20 of the s and Pharisees, ye shall G1122
7:29 *one* having authority, and not as the s. G1122
9: 3 And, behold, certain of the s said G1122
12:38 Then certain of the s and of the G1122
15: 1 Then came to Jesus s and Pharisees, G1122
16:21 chief priests and s, and be killed, and be G1122
17:10 say the s that Elias must first come? G1122
20:18 s, and they shall condemn him to death, G1122
21:15 And when the chief priests and s saw G1122
23: 2 Saying, The s and the Pharisees sit in G1122
13 But woe unto you, s and Pharisees, G1122
14 Woe unto you, s and Pharisees, G1122
15 Woe unto you, s and Pharisees, G1122
23 Woe unto you, s and Pharisees, G1122
25 Woe unto you, s and Pharisees, G1122
27 Woe unto you, s and Pharisees, G1122
29 Woe unto you, s and Pharisees, G1122
34 wise men, and s: and *some* of them ye G1122
26: 3 priests, and the s, and the elders of the G1122
57 the s and the elders were assembled. G1122
27:41 *him*, with the s and elders, said, G1122
Mk 1:22 one that had authority, and not as the s. G1122
2: 6 But there were certain of the s sitting G1122
16 And when the s and Pharisees saw him G1122
3:22 And the s which came down from G1122
7: 1 of the s, which came from Jerusalem. G1122
5 Then the Pharisees and s asked him, G1122
8:31 chief priests, and s, and be killed, and G1122
9:11 say the s that Elias must first come? G1122
14 them, and the s questioning with them. G1122
16 And he asked the s, What question ye G1122
10:33 and unto the s; and they shall condemn G1122
11:18 And the s and chief priests heard *it*, G1122
27 chief priests, and the s, and the elders, G1122
12:28 And one of the s came, and having G1122
35 the s that Christ is the son of David? G1122
38 Beware of the s, which love to go in long G1122
14: 1 chief priests and the s sought how they G1122
43 chief priests and the s and the elders. G1122
53 chief priests and the elders and the s. G1122
15: 1 the elders and s and the whole council, G1122
31 with the s, He saved others; himself G1122
Lk 5:21 And the s and the Pharisees began to G1122
30 But their s and Pharisees murmured G1122
6: 7 And the s and Pharisees watched him, G1122
9:22 chief priests and s, and be slain, and be G1122
11:44 Woe unto you, s and Pharisees, G1122
53 unto them, the s and the Pharisees G1122
15: 2 And the Pharisees and s murmured, G1122
19:47 priests and the s and the chief of the G1122
20: 1 the s came upon *him* with the elders, G1122
19 And the chief priests and the s the G1122
39 Then certain of the s answering said, G1122
46 Beware of the s, which desire to walk in G1122
22: 2 And the chief priests and s sought how G1122
Lk 22:66 priests and the s came together, and G1122
23:10 And the chief priests and s stood and G1122
Jn 8: 3 And the s and Pharisees brought unto G1122
Act 4: 5 that their rulers, and elders, and s, G1122
6:12 the elders, and the s, and came upon G1122
23: 9 And there arose a great cry: and the s G1122

SCRIBE'S
Jer 36:12 house, into the s chamber: and, lo, all H5608
21 of Elishama the s chamber. And Jehudi H5608

SCRIP
1Sa 17:40 he had, even in a s; and his sling *was* in H3219
Mt 10:10 Nor s for *your* journey, neither two G4082
Mk 6: 8 no s, no bread, no money in *their* purse: G4082
Lk 9: 3 neither staves, nor s, neither bread, G4082
10: 4 Carry neither purse, nor s, nor shoes: G4082
22:35 purse, and s, and shoes, lacked ye G4082
36 *it*, and likewise *his* s: and he that hath G4082

SCRIPTURE
Dan 10:21 is noted in the s of truth: and *there is* H3791
Mk 12:10 And have ye not read this s; The stone G1124
15:28 And the s was fulfilled, which saith, G1124
Lk 4:21 This day is this s fulfilled in your ears. G1124
Jn 2:22 s, and the word which Jesus had said. G1124
7:38 He that believeth on me, as the s hath G1124
42 Hath not the s said, That Christ cometh G1124
10:35 God came, and the s cannot be broken; G1124
13:18 but that the s may be fulfilled, He G1124
17:12 perdition; that the s might be fulfilled. G1124
19:24 it shall be: that the s might be fulfilled, G1124
28 the s might be fulfilled, saith, I thirst. G1124
36 For these things were done, that the s G1124
37 And again another s saith, They shall G1124
20: 9 For as yet they knew not the s, that he G1124
Act 1:16 Men *and* brethren, this s must needs G1124
8:32 The place of the s which he read was G1124
35 same s, and preached unto him Jesus. G1124
Ro 4: 3 For what saith the s? Abraham believed G1124
9:17 For the s saith unto Pharaoh, Even for G1124
10:11 For the s saith, Whosoever believeth on G1124
11: 2 ye not what the s saith of Elias? how he G1124
Gal 3: 8 And the s, foreseeing that God would G1124
22 But the s hath concluded all under sin, G1124
4:30 Nevertheless what saith the s? Cast out G1124
1Ti 5:18 For the s saith, Thou shalt not muzzle G1124
2Ti 3:16 All s *is* given by inspiration of God, and G1124
Jas 2: 8 according to the s, Thou shalt love thy G1124
23 And the s was fulfilled which saith, G1124
4: 5 Do ye think that the s saith in vain, The G1124
1Pt 2: 6 Wherefore also it is contained in the s, G1124
2Pt 1:20 of the s is of any private interpretation. G1124

SCRIPTURES
Mt 21:42 never read in the s, The stone which the G1124
22:29 knowing the s, nor the power of God. G1124
26:54 But how then shall the s be fulfilled, G1124
56 But all this was done, that the s of the G1124
Mk 12:24 not the s, neither the power of God? G1124
14:49 took me not: but the s must be fulfilled. G1124
Lk 24:27 all the s the things concerning himself. G1124
32 way, and while he opened to us the s? G1124
45 that they might understand the s, G1124
Jn 5:39 Search the s; for in them ye think ye G1124
Act 17: 2 days reasoned with them out of the s, G1124
11 s daily, whether those things were so. G1124
18:24 *and* mighty in the s, came to Ephesus. G1124
28 shewing by the s that Jesus was Christ. G1124
Ro 1: 2 afore by his prophets in the holy s,) G1124
15: 4 and comfort of the s might have hope. G1124
16:26 But now is made manifest, and by the s G1124
1Co 15: 3 died for our sins according to the s; G1124
4 again the third day according to the s: G1124
2Ti 3:15 hast known the holy s, which are able to G1121
2Pt 3:16 the other s, unto their own destruction. G1124

SCROLL
Isa 34: 4 together as a s: and all their host shall H5612
Rev 6:14 And the heaven departed as a s when it G975

SCULL See SKULL.

SCUM
Ezk 24: 6 city, to the pot whose s *is* therein, and H2457
6 and whose s is not gone out of it! H2457
11 in it, *that* the s of it may be consumed. H2457
12 lies, and her great s went not forth out H2457
12 out of her: her s *shall be* in the fire. H2457

SCURVY
Lev 21:20 in his eye, or be s, or scabbed, or hath H1618
22:22 having a wen, or s, or scabbed, ye shall H1618

SCYTHIAN
Col 3:11 Barbarian, S, bond *nor* free: but Christ *G4658*

SEA
Gen 1:26 over the fish of the s, and over the fowl H3220
28 over the fish of the s, and over the fowl H3220
9: 2 the s; into your hand are they delivered. H3220
14: 3 in the vale of Siddim, which is the salt s. H3220
22:17 which *is* upon the s shore; and thy seed H3220
32:12 as the sand of the s, which cannot be H3220
41:49 as the sand of the s, very much, until he H3220
49:13 at the haven of the s; and he *shall be* for H3220
Ex 10:19 them into the Red s; there remained not H3220
13:18 of the Red s: and the children of H3220
14: 2 between Migdol and the s, over against H3220
2 before it shall ye encamp by the s. H3220
9 them encamping by the s, beside H3220
16 hand over the s, and divide it: and the H3220
16 dry *ground* through the midst of the s. H3220
21 out his hand over the s; and the LORD H3220
21 the LORD caused the s to go *back* by a H3220
21 night, and made the s dry *land*, and the H3220
22 the midst of the s upon the dry *ground*: H3220
23 to the midst of the s, *even* all Pharaoh's H3220
26 hand over the s, that the waters may H3220
27 forth his hand over the s, and the sea H3220
27 over the sea, and the s returned to his H3220
27 the Egyptians in the midst of the s. H3220
28 that came into the s after them; there H3220
29 in the midst of the s; and the waters H3220
30 the Egyptians dead upon the s shore. H3220
15: 1 and his rider hath he thrown into the s. H3220
4 he cast into the s: his chosen captains H3220
4 captains also are drowned in the Red s. H3220
8 were congealed in the heart of the s. H3220
10 Thou didst blow with thy wind, the s H3220
19 his horsemen into the s, and the LORD H3220
19 the waters of the s upon them; but the H3220
19 went on dry *land* in the midst of the s. H3220
21 and his rider hath he thrown into the s. H3220
22 So Moses brought Israel from the Red s, H3220
20:11 and earth, the s, and all that in them H3220
23:31 from the Red s even unto the sea of H3220
31 sea even unto the s of the Philistines, H3220
Nu 11:22 all the fish of the s be gathered together H3220
31 quails from the s, and let *them* fall by H3220
13:29 by the s, and by the coast of Jordan. H3220
14:25 the wilderness by the way of the Red s. H3220
21: 4 by the way of the Red s, to compass the H3220
14 the Red s, and in the brooks of Arnon, H5492
33: 8 the midst of the s into the wilderness, H3220
10 from Elim, and encamped by the Red s. H3220
11 And they removed from the Red s, and H3220
34: 3 outmost coast of the salt s eastward: H3220
5 and the goings out of it shall be at the s. H3220
6 have the great s for a border: this shall H3220
7 s ye shall point out for you mount Hor: H3220
11 side of the s of Chinnereth eastward: H3220
12 it shall be at the salt s: this shall be your H3220
Dt 1: 1 against the Red *s*, between Paran, and
7 south, and by the s side, to the land of H3220
40 the wilderness by the way of the Red s. H3220
2: 1 the way of the Red s, as the LORD spake H3220
3:17 even unto the s of the plain, *even* the H3220
17 salt s, under Ashdoth-pisgah eastward. H3220
4:49 even unto the s of the plain, under the H3220
11: 4 water of the Red s to overflow them as H3220
24 the uttermost s shall your coast be. H3220
30:13 Neither *is* it beyond the s, that thou H3220
13 shall go over the s for us, and bring it H3220
34: 2 all the land of Judah, unto the utmost s, H3220
Jos 1: 4 and unto the great s toward the going H3220
2:10 the water of the Red s for you, when ye H3220
3:16 down toward the s of the plain, *even* H3220
16 *even* the salt s, failed, *and* were cut H3220
4:23 God did to the Red s, which he dried up H3220
5: 1 which *were* by the s, heard that the H3220
9: 1 the coasts of the great s over against H3220
11: 4 that *is* upon the s shore in multitude, H3220
12: 3 And from the plain to the s of H3220
3 east, and unto the s of the plain, *even* H3220
3 *even* the salt s on the east, the way H3220
13:27 the edge of the s of Chinnereth on the H3220
15: 2 s, from the bay that looketh southward: H3220
4 at the s: this shall be your south coast. H3220
Jos 15: 5 And the east border *was* the salt s, *even* H3220
5 of the s at the uttermost part of Jordan: H3220
11 goings out of the border were at the s. H3220
12 And the west border *was* to the great s, H3220
46 From Ekron even unto the s, all that *lay* H3220
47 and the great s, and the border *thereof*: H3220
16: 3 and the goings out thereof are at the s. H3220
6 And the border went out toward the s H3220
8 out thereof were at the s. This *is* the H3220
17: 9 and the outgoings of it were at the s: H3220
10 and the s is his border; and they H3220
18:14 the corner of the s southward, from the H3220
19 bay of the salt s at the south end of H3220
19:11 And their border went up toward the s, H3220
29 are at the s from the coast to Achzib: H3220
23: 4 cut off, even unto the great s westward. H3220
24: 6 ye came unto the s; and the Egyptians H3220
6 chariots and horsemen unto the Red s. H3220
7 and brought the s upon them, and H3220
Jdg 5:17 the s shore, and abode in his breaches. H3220
7:12 as the sand by the s side for multitude. H3220
11:16 unto the Red s, and came to Kadesh; H3220
1Sa 13: 5 which *is* on the s shore in multitude: H3220
2Sa 17:11 sand that *is* by the s for multitude; and H3220
22:16 And the channels of the s appeared, the H3220
1Ki 4:20 which *is* by the s in multitude, eating H3220
29 even as the sand that *is* on the s shore. H3220
5: 9 Lebanon unto the s: and I will convey H3220
9 will convey them by s in floats unto the H3220
7:23 And he made a molten s, ten cubits H3220
24 compassing the s round about: the H3220
25 the east: and the s *was set* above upon H3220
39 and he set the s on the right side of the H3220
44 And one s, and twelve oxen under the H3220
44 one sea, and twelve oxen under the s; H3220
9:26 shore of the Red s, in the land of Edom. H3220
27 of the s, with the servants of Solomon. H3220
10:22 For the king had at s a navy of H3220
18:43 look toward the s. And he went up, and H3220
44 cloud out of the s, like a man's hand. H3220
2Ki 14:25 of Hamath unto the s of the plain, H3220
16:17 took down the s from off the brasen H3220
25:13 and the brasen s that *was* in the house H3220
16 The two pillars, one s, and the bases H3220
1Ch 16:32 Let the s roar, and the fulness thereof: H3220
18: 8 made the brasen s, and the pillars, and H3220
2Ch 2:16 to thee in floats by s to Joppa; and thou H3220
4: 2 Also he made a molten s of ten cubits H3220
3 compassing the s round about. Two H3220
4 the east: and the s *was set* above upon H3220
6 but the s *was* for the priests to wash in. H3220
10 And he set the s on the right side of the H3220
15 One s, and twelve oxen under it. H3220
8:17 Eloth, at the s side in the land of Edom. H3220
18 knowledge of the s; and they went with H3220
20: 2 from beyond the s on this side Syria; H3220
Ezr 3: 7 Lebanon to the s of Joppa, according H3220
Neh 9: 9 and heardest their cry by the Red s; H3220
11 And thou didst divide the s before H3220
11 the midst of the s on the dry land; and H3220
Est 10: 1 the land, and *upon* the isles of the s. H3220
Job 6: 3 the sand of the s: therefore my words H3220
7:12 *Am* I a s, or a whale, that thou settest a H3220
9: 8 and treadeth upon the waves of the s. H3220
11: 9 than the earth, and broader than the s. H3220
12: 8 fishes of the s shall declare unto thee. H3220
14:11 *As* the waters fail from the s, and the H3220
26:12 He divideth the s with his power, and H3220
28:14 in me: and the s saith, *It is* not with me. H3220
36:30 it, and covereth the bottom of the s. H3220
38: 8 Or *who* shut up the s with doors, when H3220
16 the springs of the s? or hast thou walked H3220
41:31 he maketh the s like a pot of ointment. H3220
Ps 8: 8 The fowl of the air, and the fish of the s, H3220
33: 7 He gathereth the waters of the s H3220
46: 2 be carried into the midst of the s; H3220
65: 5 and of them that are afar off *upon* the s: H3220
66: 6 He turned the s into dry *land*: they H3220
68:22 *people* again from the depths of the s: H3220
72: 8 He shall have dominion also from s to H3220
8 also from sea to s, and from the river H3220
74:13 Thou didst divide the s by thy strength: H3220
77:19 Thy way *is* in the s, and thy path in the H3220
78:13 He divided the s, and caused them to H3220
27 feathered fowls like as the sand of the s: H3220
53 but the s overwhelmed their enemies. H3220
80:11 She sent out her boughs unto the s, and H3220
89: 9 Thou rulest the raging of the s: when H3220
25 I will set his hand also in the s, and his H3220
Ps 93: 4 *yea, than* the mighty waves of the s. H3220
95: 5 The s *is* his, and he made it: and his H3220
96:11 let the s roar, and the fulness thereof. H3220
98: 7 Let the s roar, and the fulness thereof; H3220
104:25 *So is* this great and wide s, wherein *are* H3220
106: 7 *him* at the s, *even* at the Red sea. H3220
7 *him* at the sea, *even* at the Red s. H3220
9 He rebuked the Red s also, and it was H3220
22 Ham, *and* terrible things by the Red s. H3220
107:23 They that go down to the s in ships, H3220
114: 3 The s saw *it*, and fled: Jordan was H3220
5 What *ailed* thee, O thou s, that thou H3220
136:13 To him which divided the Red s into H3220
15 Red s: for his mercy *endureth* for ever. H3220
139: 9 dwell in the uttermost parts of the s; H3220
146: 6 Which made heaven, and earth, the s, H3220
Prv 8:29 When he gave to the s his decree, that H3220
23:34 in the midst of the s, or as he that lieth H3220
30:19 s; and the way of a man with a maid. H3220
Ecc 1: 7 All the rivers run into the s; yet the sea H3220
7 All the rivers run into the sea; yet the s H3220
Isa 5:30 like the roaring of the s: and if *one* look H3220
9: 1 *by* the way of the s, beyond Jordan, in H3220
10:22 be as the sand of the s, *yet* a remnant of H3220
26 rod *was* upon the s, so shall he lift it up H3220
11: 9 of the LORD, as the waters cover the s. H3220
11 Hamath, and from the islands of the s. H3220
15 of the Egyptian s; and with his mighty H3220
16: 8 stretched out, they are gone over the s. H3220
18: 2 That sendeth ambassadors by the s, H3220
19: 5 And the waters shall fail from the s, and H3220
21: 1 The burden of the desert of the s. As H3220
23: 2 that pass over the s, have replenished. H3220
4 Be thou ashamed, O Zidon: for the s H3220
4 the strength of the s, saying, I travail H3220
11 He stretched out his hand over the s, he H3220
24:14 LORD, they shall cry aloud from the s. H3220
15 LORD God of Israel in the isles of the s. H3220
27: 1 he shall slay the dragon that *is* in the s. H3220
42:10 go down to the s, and all that is therein; H3220
43:16 the s, and a path in the mighty waters; H3220
48:18 thy righteousness as the waves of the s: H3220
50: 2 I dry up the s, I make the rivers a H3220
51:10 *Art* thou not it which hath dried the s, H3220
10 s a way for the ransomed to pass over? H3220
15 that divided the s, whose waves roared: H3220
57:20 But the wicked *are* like the troubled s, H3220
60: 5 abundance of the s shall be converted H3220
63:11 them up out of the s with the shepherd H3220
Jer 5:22 *for* the bound of the s by a perpetual H3220
6:23 roareth like the s; and they ride upon H3220
25:22 of the isles which *are* beyond the s, H3220
27:19 concerning the s, and concerning the H3220
31:35 which divideth the s when the waves H3220
33:22 the sand of the s measured: so will I H3220
46:18 as Carmel by the s, *so* shall he come. H3220
47: 7 the s shore? there hath he appointed it. H3220
48:32 are gone over the s, they reach *even* to H3220
32 reach *even* to the s of Jazer: the spoiler H3220
49:21 noise thereof was heard in the Red s. H3220
23 *is* sorrow on the s; it cannot be quiet. H3220
50:42 shall roar like the s, and they shall ride H3220
51:36 dry up her s, and make her springs dry. H3220
42 The s is come up upon Babylon: she is H3220
52:17 and the brasen s that *was* in the house H3220
20 The two pillars, one s, and twelve H3220
Lam 2:13 *is* great like the s: who can heal thee? H3220
4: 3 Even the s monsters draw out the breast,
Ezk 25:16 and destroy the remnant of the s coast. H3220
26: 3 as the s causeth his waves to come up. H3220
5 in the midst of the s: for I have spoken H3220
16 Then all the princes of the s shall come H3220
17 which wast strong in the s, she and her H3220
18 the s shall be troubled at thy departure. H3220
27: 3 situate at the entry of the s, *which art* a H3220
9 calkers: all the ships of the s with their H3220
29 all the pilots of the s, shall come down H3220
32 like the destroyed in the midst of the s? H3220
38:20 So that the fishes of the s, and the fowls H3220
39:11 on the east of the s: and it shall stop the H3220
47: 8 and go into the s: *which being* brought H3220
8 into the s, the waters shall be healed. H3220
10 the fish of the great s, exceeding many. H3220
15 from the great s, the way of Hethlon, H3220
17 And the border from the s shall be H3220
18 unto the east s. And *this is* the east side. H3220
19 s. And *this is* the south side southward. H3220
20 The west side also *shall be* the great s H3220
48:28 *and* to the river toward the great s. H3220

Dan 7: 2 of the heaven strove upon the great s. H3221
3 from the s, diverse one from another. H3221
Hos 1:10 be as the sand of the s, which cannot be H3220
4: 3 fishes of the s also shall be taken away. H3220
Joel 2:20 toward the east s, and his hinder part H3220
20 toward the utmost s, and his stink shall H3220
Am 5: 8 the waters of the s, and poureth them H3220
8:12 And they shall wander from s to sea, H3220
12 And they shall wander from sea to s, H3220
9: 3 in the bottom of the s, thence will I H3220
6 the waters of the s, and poureth them H3220
Jna 1: 4 wind into the s, and there was a mighty H3220
4 s, so that the ship was like to be broken. H3220
5 the ship into the s, to lighten *it* of them. H3220
9 hath made the s and the dry *land*. H3220
11 unto thee, that the s may be calm unto H3220
11 the s wrought, and was tempestuous. H3220
12 me forth into the s; so shall the sea be H3220
12 sea; so shall the s be calm unto you: for H3220
13 could not: for the s wrought, and was H3220
15 s: and the sea ceased from her raging. H3220
15 sea: and the s ceased from her raging. H3220
Mic 7:12 the river, and from s to sea, and *from* H3220
12 to s, and *from* mountain to mountain. H3220
19 all their sins into the depths of the s. H3220
Nah 1: 4 He rebuketh the s, and maketh it dry, H3220
3: 8 the s, *and* her wall *was* from the sea? H3220
8 the sea, *and* her wall *was* from the s? H3220
Hab 1:14 And makest men as the fishes of the s, H3220
2:14 of the LORD, as the waters cover the s. H3220
3: 8 wrath against the s, that thou didst ride H3220
15 Thou didst walk through the s with H3220
Zep 1: 3 and the fishes of the s, and the H3220
2: 5 Woe unto the inhabitants of the s H3220
6 And the s coast shall be dwellings *and* H3220
Hag 2: 6 the earth, and the s, and the dry *land*; H3220
Zec 9: 4 s; and she shall be devoured with fire. H3220
10 *shall be* from s *even* to sea, and from H3220
10 from sea *even* to s, and from the river H3220
10:11 And he shall pass through the s with H3220
11 the waves in the s, and all the deeps of H3220
14: 8 toward the former s, and half of them H3220
8 s: in summer and in winter shall it be. H3220
Mt 4:13 which is upon the s coast, in the G3864
15 *by* the way of the s, beyond Jordan, G2281
18 And Jesus, walking by the s of Galilee, G2281
18 a net into the s: for they were fishers. G2281
8:24 tempest in the s, insomuch that the ship G2281
26 and the s; and there was a great calm. G2281
27 even the winds and the s obey him! G2281
32 into the s, and perished in the waters. G2281
13: 1 out of the house, and sat by the s side. G2281
47 into the s, and gathered of every kind: G2281
14:24 in the midst of the s, tossed with waves: G2281
25 Jesus went unto them, walking on the s. G2281
26 walking on the s, they were troubled, G2281
15:29 nigh unto the s of Galilee; and went G2281
17:27 go thou to the s, and cast an hook, and G2281
18: 6 he were drowned in the depth of the s. G2281
21:21 be thou cast into the s; it shall be done. G2281
23:15 for ye compass s and land to make one G2281
Mk 1:16 Now as he walked by the s of Galilee, G2281
16 a net into the s: for they were fishers. G2281
2:13 And he went forth again by the s side; G2281
3: 7 with his disciples to the s: and a great G2281
4: 1 And he began again to teach by the s G2281
1 ship, and sat in the s; and the whole G2281
1 multitude was by the s on the land. G2281
39 and said unto the s, Peace, be still. And G2281
41 that even the wind and the s obey him? G2281
5: 1 the s, into the country of the Gadarenes. G2281
13 place into the s, (they were about two G2281
13 thousand;) and were choked in the s. G2281
21 unto him: and he was nigh unto the s. G2281
6:47 midst of the s, and he alone on the land. G2281
48 the s, and would have passed by them. G2281
49 walking upon the s, they supposed it G2281
7:31 he came unto the s of Galilee, through G2281
9:42 his neck, and he were cast into the s. G2281
11:23 thou cast into the s; and shall not doubt G2281
Lk 6:17 and from the s coast of Tyre and Sidon, G3882
17: 2 he cast into the s, than that he should G2281
6 planted in the s; and it should obey you. G2281
21:25 perplexity; the s and the waves roaring; G2281
Jn 6: 1 After these things Jesus went over the s G2281
1 of Galilee, which is *the* s of Tiberias. G2281
16 his disciples went down unto the s, G2281
17 ship, and went over the s toward G2281
18 And the s arose by reason of a great G2281
Jn 6:19 walking on the s, and drawing nigh G2281
22 other side of the s saw that there was G2281
25 other side of the s, they said unto him, G2281
21: 1 to the disciples at the s of Tiberias; and G2281
7 naked,) and did cast himself into the s. G2281
Act 4:24 earth, and the s, and all that in them is: G2281
7:36 Red s, and in the wilderness forty years. G2281
10: 6 house is by the s side: he shall tell thee G2281
32 a tanner by the s side: who, when he G2281
14:15 the s, and all things that are therein: G2281
17:14 to go as it were to the s: but Silas and G2281
27: 5 And when we had sailed over the s of G3989
30 the boat into the s, under colour as G2281
38 ship, and cast out the wheat into the s. G2281
40 unto the s, and loosed the rudder G2281
43 first *into the s*, and get to land:
28: 4 s, yet vengeance suffereth not to live. G2281
Ro 9:27 sand of the s, a remnant shall be saved: G2281
1Co 10: 1 the cloud, and all passed through the s; G2281
2 unto Moses in the cloud and in the s; G2281
2Co 11:26 in the s, *in* perils among false brethren; G2281
Heb 11:12 which is by the s shore innumerable. G2281
29 By faith they passed through the Red s G2281
Jas 1: 6 the s driven with the wind and tossed. G2281
3: 7 of things in the s, is tamed, and hath G1724
Jude 13 Raging waves of the s, foaming out G2281
Rev 4: 6 And before the throne *there was* a s of G2281
5:13 such as are in the s, and all that are in G2281
7: 1 the earth, nor on the s, nor on any tree. G2281
2 it was given to hurt the earth and the s, G2281
3 earth, neither the s, nor the trees, till we G2281
8: 8 was cast into the s: and the third part of G2281
8 the third part of the s became blood; G2281
9 which were in the s, and had life, died; G2281
10: 2 the s, and *his* left *foot* on the earth, G2281
5 stand upon the s and upon the earth G2281
6 are, and the s, and the things which G2281
8 upon the s and upon the earth. G2281
12:12 earth and of the s! for the devil is come G2281
13: 1 And I stood upon the sand of the s, and G2281
1 rise up out of the s, having seven heads G2281
14: 7 and the s, and the fountains of waters. G2281
15: 2 And I saw as it were a s of glass G2281
2 the s of glass, having the harps of God. G2281
16: 3 his vial upon the s; and it became as the G2281
3 *man*: and every living soul died in the s. G2281
18:17 as many as trade by s, stood afar off, G2281
19 that had ships in the s by reason of her G2281
21 and cast *it* into the s, saying, Thus with G2281
20: 8 number of whom *is* as the sand of the s. G2281
13 And the s gave up the dead which were G2281
21: 1 passed away; and there was no more s. G2281

SEAFARING
Ezk 26:17 *wast* inhabited of s men, the renowned H3220

SEAL
1Ki 21: 8 *them* with his s, and sent the letters H2368
Neh 9:38 princes, Levites, *and* priests, s *unto it*. H2856
Est 8: 8 the king's name, and s *it* with the king's H2856
Job 38:14 It is turned as clay *to* the s; and they H2368
41:15 pride, shut up together *as with* a close s. H2368
Song 8: 6 Set me as a s upon thine heart, as a H2368
6 thine heart, as a s upon thine arm: for H2368
Isa 8:16 Bind up the testimony, s the law H2856
Jer 32:44 evidences, and s *them*, and take H2856
Dan 9:24 and to s up the vision and prophecy, H2856
12: 4 up the words, and s the book, *even* to H2856
Jn 3:33 hath set to his s that God is true. G4972
Ro 4:11 sign of circumcision, a s of the G4973
1Co 9: 2 I am to you: for the s of mine G4973
2Ti 2:19 sure, having this s, The Lord knoweth G4973
Rev 6: 3 And when he had opened the second s, G4973
5 And when he had opened the third s, I G4973
7 And when he had opened the fourth s, I G4973
9 And when he had opened the fifth s, I G4973
12 opened the sixth s, and, lo, there was a G4973
7: 2 east, having the s of the living God: and G4973
8: 1 And when he had opened the seventh s, G4973
9: 4 not the s of God in their foreheads. G4973
10: 4 saying unto me, S up those things G4972
20: 3 him up, and set a s upon him, that he G4972
22:10 And he saith unto me, S not the G4972

SEALED
Dt 32:34 me, *and* s up among my treasures? H2856
1Ki 21: 8 Ahab's name, and s *them* with his seal, H2856
Neh 10: 1 Now those that s *were*, Nehemiah, the H2856
Est 3:12 it written, and s with the king's ring. H2856
Est 8: 8 king's name, and s with the king's ring, H2856
10 name, and s *it* with the king's ring, H2856
Job 14:17 My transgression *is* s up in a bag, and H2856
Song 4:12 spouse; a spring shut up, a fountain s. H2856
Isa 29:11 of a book that is s, which *men* deliver to H2856
11 thee: and he saith, I cannot; for it *is* s: H2856
Jer 32:10 And I subscribed the evidence, and s *it*, H2856
11 that which was s *according* to the law H2856
14 both which is s, and this evidence which H2856
Dan 6:17 the den; and the king s it with his own H2857
12: 9 closed up and s till the time of the end. H2856
Jn 6:27 you: for him hath God the Father s. G4972
Ro 15:28 this, and have s to them this fruit, I G4972
2Co 1:22 Who hath also s us, and given the G4972
Eph 1:13 were s with that holy Spirit of promise, G4972
4:30 ye are s unto the day of redemption. G4972
Rev 5: 1 and on the backside, s with seven seals. G2696
7: 3 trees, till we have s the servants of our G4972
4 of them which were s: *and there were* G4972
4 *and there were* s an hundred *and* forty G4972
5 Of the tribe of Juda *were* s twelve G4972
5 of Reuben *were* s twelve thousand. Of G4972
5 tribe of Gad *were* s twelve thousand. G4972
6 Of the tribe of Aser *were* s twelve G4972
6 of Nepthalim *were* s twelve thousand. G4972
6 of Manasses *were* s twelve thousand. G4972
7 Of the tribe of Simeon *were* s twelve G4972
7 tribe of Levi *were* s twelve thousand. Of G4972
7 of Issachar *were* s twelve thousand. G4972
8 Of the tribe of Zabulon *were* s twelve G4972
8 of Joseph *were* s twelve thousand. Of G4972
8 of Benjamin *were* s twelve thousand. G4972

SEALEST
Ezk 28:12 Lord GOD; Thou s up the sum, full of H2856

SEALETH
Job 9: 7 and it riseth not; and s up the stars. H2856
33:16 Then he openeth the ears of men, and s H2856
37: 7 He s up the hand of every man; that all H2856

SEALING
Mt 27:66 sure, s the stone, and setting a watch. G4972

SEALS
Rev 5: 1 on the backside, sealed with seven s. G4973
2 the book, and to loose the s thereof? G4973
5 book, and to loose the seven s thereof. G4973
9 and to open the s thereof: for thou wast G4973
6: 1 opened one of the s, and I heard, as it G4973

SEAM
Jn 19:23 s, woven from the top throughout. G729

SEARCH
Lev 27:33 He shall not s whether it be good or H1239
Nu 10:33 to s out a resting place for them. H8446
13: 2 Send thou men, that they may s the H8446
32 we have gone to s it, *is* a land that H8446
14: 7 to s it, *is* an exceeding good land. H8446
36 And the men, which Moses sent to s the H8446
38 men that went to s the land, lived *still*. H8446
Dt 1:22 us, and they shall s us out the land, and H2658
33 Who went in the way before you, to s H8446
13:14 Then shalt thou inquire, and make s, H2713
Jos 2: 2 children of Israel to s out the country. H2658
3 they be come to s out all the country. H2658
Jdg 18: 2 the land, and to s it; and they said unto H2713
2 unto them, Go, s the land: who when H2713
1Sa 23:23 land, that I will s him out throughout H2664
2Sa 10: 3 unto thee, to s the city, and to spy H2713
1Ki 20: 6 and they shall s thine house, and the H2664
2Ki 10:23 of Baal, S, and look that there H2664
1Ch 19: 3 unto thee for to s, and to overthrow, H2713
Ezr 4:15 That s may be made in the book of the H1240
19 And I commanded, and s hath been H1240
5:17 king, let there be s made in the king's H1240
6: 1 a decree, and s was made in the house H1240
Job 8: 8 prepare thyself to the s of their fathers: H2714
13: 9 Is it good that he should s you out? or H2713
38:16 hast thou walked in the s of the depth? H2714
Ps 44:21 Shall not God s this out? for he H2713
64: 6 They s out iniquities; they accomplish H2664
6 a diligent s: both the inward *thought* H2665
77: 6 heart: and my spirit made diligent s. H2664
139:23 S me, O God, and know my heart: try H2713
Prv 25: 2 the honour of kings *is* to s out a matter. H2713
27 *men* to s their own glory *is not* glory. H2714
Ecc 1:13 And I gave my heart to seek and s out H8446

Ecc 7:25 I applied mine heart to know, and to s, H8446
Jer 2:34 found it by secret s, but upon all these. H4290
17:10 I the LORD s the heart, *I* try the reins, H2713
29:13 ye shall s for me with all your heart. H1875
Lam 3:40 Let us s and try our ways, and turn H2664
Ezk 34: 6 and none did s or seek *after them.* H1875
8 did my shepherds s for my flock, but H1875
11 both s my sheep, and seek them out. H1875
39:14 the end of seven months shall they s. H2713
Am 9: 3 of Carmel, I will s and take them out H2664
Zep 1:12 that time, *that* I will s Jerusalem with H2664
Mt 2: 8 and said, Go and s diligently for the *G1833*
Jn 5:39 S the scriptures; for in them ye think ye *G2045*
7:52 also of Galilee? S, and look: for out of *G2045*

SEARCHED
Gen 31:34 s all the tent, but found *them* not. H4959
35 me. And he s, but found not the images. H2664
37 Whereas thou hast s all my stuff, what H4959
44:12 And he s, *and* began at the eldest, and H2664
Nu 13:21 So they went up, and s the land from H8446
32 which they had s unto the children of H8446
14: 6 them that s the land, rent their clothes: H8446
34 days in which ye s the land, *even* forty H8446
Dt 1:24 unto the valley of Eshcol, and s it out. H7270
Job 5:27 Lo this, we have s it, so it *is;* hear it, H2713
28:27 it; he prepared it, yea, and s it out. H2713
29:16 and the cause *which* I knew not I s out. H2713
32:11 reasons, whilst ye s out what to say. H2713
36:26 can the number of his years be s out. H2714
Ps 139: 1 O LORD, thou hast s me, and known H2713
Jer 31:37 of the earth s out beneath, I will also H2713
46:23 it cannot be s; because they are more H2713
Oba 6 How are *the things* of Esau s out! *how* H2664
Act 17:11 of mind, and s the scriptures daily, *G350*
1Pt 1:10 have inquired and s diligently, who *G1830*

SEARCHEST
Job 10: 6 after mine iniquity, and s after my sin? H1875
Prv 2: 4 If thou seekest her as silver, and s for H2664

SEARCHETH
1Ch 28: 9 mind: for the LORD s all hearts, and H1875
Job 28: 3 He setteth an end to darkness, and s H2713
39: 8 and he s after every green thing. H1875
Prv 18:17 but his neighbour cometh and s him. H2713
28:11 that hath understanding s him out. H2713
Ro 8:27 And he that s the hearts knoweth what *G2045*
1Co 2:10 for the Spirit s all things, yea, the deep *G2045*
Rev 2:23 I am he which s the reins and hearts: *G2045*

SEARCHING
Nu 13:25 And they returned from s of the land H8446
Job 11: 7 Canst thou by s find out God? canst H2714
Prv 20:27 s all the inward parts of the belly. H2664
Isa 40:28 *there is* no s of his understanding. H2714
1Pt 1:11 S what, or what manner of time the *G2045*

SEARCHINGS
Jdg 5:16 of Reuben *there were* great s of heart. H2714

SEARED
1Ti 4: 2 their conscience s with a hot iron; *G2743*

SEAS
Gen 1:10 he S: and God saw that *it was* good. H3220
22 the s, and let fowl multiply in the earth. H3220
Lev 11: 9 s, and in the rivers, them shall ye eat. H3220
10 and scales in the s, and in the rivers, of H3220
Dt 33:19 the s, and *of* treasures hid in the sand. H3220
Neh 9: 6 *are* therein, the s, and all that *is* therein, H3220
Ps 8: 8 passeth through the paths of the s. H3220
24: 2 For he hath founded it upon the s, and H3220
65: 7 Which stilleth the noise of the s, the H3220
69:34 s, and every thing that moveth therein. H3220
135: 6 in earth, in the s, and all deep places. H3220
Isa 17:12 the noise of the s; and to the rushing of H3220
Jer 15: 8 the sand of the s: I have brought upon H3220
Ezk 27: 4 Thy borders *are* in the midst of the s, H3220
25 made very glorious in the midst of the s. H3220
26 hath broken thee in the midst of the s. H3220
27 the midst of the s in the day of thy ruin. H3220
33 When thy wares went forth out of the s, H3220
34 be broken by the s in the depths of the H3220
28: 2 in the midst of the s; yet thou *art* a man, H3220
8 *them that are* slain in the midst of the s. H3220
32: 2 *art* as a whale in the s: and thou camest H3220
Dan 11:45 between the s in the glorious holy H3220
Jna 2: 3 in the midst of the s; and the floods H3220

Act 27:41 And falling into a place where two s *G1337*

SEA-SHORE See SEA and SHORE.

SEA-SIDE See SEA and SIDE.

SEASON
Gen 40: 4 them: and they continued a s in ward. H3117
Ex 13:10 ordinance in his s from year to year. H4150
Lev 2:13 offering shalt thou s with salt; neither H4414
26: 4 Then I will give you rain in due s, and H6256
Nu 9: 2 keep the passover at his appointed s. H4150
3 it in his appointed s: according to all H4150
7 s among the children of Israel? H4150
13 s, that man shall bear his sin. H4150
28: 2 observe to offer unto me in their due s. H4150
Dt 11:14 land in his due s, the first rain and the H6256
16: 6 s that thou camest forth out of Egypt. H4150
28:12 thy land in his s, and to bless all the H6256
Jos 24: 7 and ye dwelt in the wilderness a long s. H3117
2Ki 4:16 And he said, About this s, according to H4150
17 and bare a son at that s that Elisha had H4150
1Ch 21:29 at that s in the high place at Gibeon. H6256
2Ch 15: 3 Now for a long s Israel *hath been* H3117
Job 5:26 as a shock of corn cometh in in his s. H6256
30:17 the night s: and my sinews take no rest. H3915
38:32 Mazzaroth in his s? or canst thou guide H6256
Ps 1: 3 his fruit in his s; his leaf also shall not H6256
22: 2 not; and in the night s, and am not silent.
104:27 mayest give *them* their meat in due s. H6256
145:15 thou givest them their meat in due s. H6256
Prv 15:23 a word *spoken* in due s, how good *is it!* H6256
Ecc 3: 1 To every *thing there is* a s, and a time to H2165
10:17 princes eat in due s, for strength, and H6256
Isa 50: 4 how to speak a word in s to *him that is*
Jer 5:24 the latter, in his s: he reserveth unto us H6256
33:20 should not be day and night in their s; H6256
Ezk 34:26 his s; there shall be showers of blessing. H6256
Dan 7:12 lives were prolonged for a s and time. H2166
Hos 2: 9 and my wine in the s thereof, and will H4150
Mt 24:45 household, to give them meat in due s? *G2540*
Mk 9:50 wherewith will ye s it? Have salt in *G741*
12: 2 And at the s he sent to the *G2540*
Lk 1:20 words, which shall be fulfilled in their s. *G2540*
4:13 he departed from him for a s. *G891*
12:42 *them their* portion of meat in due s? *G2540*
13: 1 There were present at that s some that *G2540*
20:10 And at the s he sent a servant to the *G2540*
23: 8 to see him of a long s, because he had
Jn 5: 4 For an angel went down at a certain s *G2540*
35 willing for a s to rejoice in his light. *G5610*
Act 13:11 the sun for a s. And immediately there *G2540*
19:22 but he himself stayed in Asia for a s. *G5550*
24:25 I have a convenient s, I will call for thee. *G2540*
2Co 7: 8 you sorry, though *it were* but for a s. *G5610*
Gal 6: 9 in due s we shall reap, if we faint not. *G2540*
2Ti 4: 2 Preach the word; be instant in s, out of *G2122*
2 in season, out of s; reprove, rebuke, *G171*
Phlm 15 departed for a s, that thou shouldest *G5610*
Heb 11:25 to enjoy the pleasures of sin for a s; *G4340*
1Pt 1: 6 though now for a s, if need be, ye are in *G3641*
Rev 6:11 should rest yet for a little s, until their *G5550*
20: 3 after that he must be loosed a little s. *G5550*

SEASONED
Lk 14:34 lost his savour, wherewith shall it be s? *G741*
Col 4: 6 Let your speech *be* alway with grace, s *G741*

SEASONS
Gen 1:14 and for s, and for days, and years: H4150
Ex 18:22 And let them judge the people at all s: H6256
26 And they judged the people at all s: the H6256
Lev 23: 4 which ye shall proclaim in their s. H4150
Ps 16: 7 my reins also instruct me in the night s. H3915
104:19 He appointed the moon for s: the sun H4150
Dan 2:21 And he changeth the times and the s: he H2166
Mt 21:41 shall render him the fruits in their s. *G2540*
Act 1: 7 the times or the s, which the Father *G2540*
14:17 and fruitful s, filling our hearts with *G2540*
20:18 manner I have been with you at all s, *G5550*
1Th 5: 1 But of the times and the s, brethren, ye *G2540*

SEAT
Ex 25:17 And thou shalt make a mercy s *of* pure H3727
18 them, in the two ends of the mercy s. H3727
19 *even* of the mercy s shall ye make the H3727
20 the mercy s with their wings, and H3727
20 s shall the faces of the cherubims be. H3727
21 And thou shalt put the mercy s above H3727
Ex 25:22 above the mercy s, from between the H3727
26:34 And thou shalt put the mercy s upon H3727
30: 6 before the mercy s that *is* over the H3727
31: 7 and the mercy s that *is* thereupon, and H3727
35:12 mercy s, and the vail of the covering, H3727
37: 6 And he made the mercy s *of* pure gold: H3727
7 he them, on the two ends of the mercy s; H3727
8 side: out of the mercy s made he the H3727
9 over the mercy s, with their faces one H3727
39:35 and the staves thereof, and the mercy s, H3727
40:20 put the mercy s above upon the ark: H3727
Lev 16: 2 before the mercy s, which *is* upon the H3727
2 appear in the cloud upon the mercy s. H3727
13 may cover the mercy s that *is* upon the H3727
14 upon the mercy s eastward; and before H3727
14 before the mercy s shall he sprinkle of H3727
15 the mercy s, and before the mercy seat: H3727
15 the mercy seat, and before the mercy s: H3727
Nu 7:89 from off the mercy s that *was* upon the H3727
Jdg 3:20 unto thee. And he arose out of *his* s. H3678
1Sa 1: 9 a s by a post of the temple of the LORD. H3678
4:13 And when he came, lo, Eli sat upon a s H3678
18 he fell from off the s backward by the H3678
20:18 be missed, because thy s will be empty. H4186
25 And the king sat upon his s, as at other H4186
25 times, *even* upon a s by the wall: and H4186
2Sa 23: 8 that sat in the s, chief among the H7674
1Ki 2:19 and caused a s to be set for the king's H3678
10:19 s, and two lions stood beside the stays. H7675
1Ch 28:11 thereof, and of the place of the mercy s, H3727
Est 3: 1 him, and set his s above all the princes H3678
Job 23: 3 him! *that* I might come *even* to his s! H8499
29: 7 *when* I prepared my s in the street! H4186
Ps 1: 1 nor sitteth in the s of the scornful. H4186
Prv 9:14 on a s in the high places of the city, H3678
Ezk 8: 3 north; where *was* the s of the image of H4186
28: 2 a God, I sit *in* the s of God, in the midst H4186
Am 6: 3 cause the s of violence to come near; H7675
Mt 23: 2 and the Pharisees sit in Moses' s: *G2515*
27:19 on the judgment s, his wife sent unto *G968*
Jn 19:13 in the judgment s in a place that is called *G968*
Act 18:12 Paul, and brought him to the judgment s, *G968*
16 And he drave them from the judgment s. *G968*
17 the judgment s. And Gallio cared for *G968*
25: 6 s commanded Paul to be brought. *G968*
10 Caesar's judgment s, where I ought to be *G968*
17 on the judgment s, and commanded the *G968*
Ro 14:10 all stand before the judgment s of Christ. *G968*
2Co 5:10 the judgment s of Christ; that every *G968*
Rev 2:13 where Satan's s *is:* and thou holdest *G2362*
13: 2 power, and his s, and great authority. *G2362*
16:10 his vial upon the s of the beast; and his *G2362*

SEATED
Dt 33:21 lawgiver, *was he* s; and he came with H5603

SEATS
Mt 21:12 and the s of them that sold doves, *G2515*
23: 6 and the chief s in the synagogues, *G4410*
Mk 11:15 and the s of them that sold doves; *G2515*
12:39 And the chief s in the synagogues, and *G4410*
Lk 1:52 *their* s, and exalted them of low degree. *G2362*
11:43 the uppermost s in the synagogues, *G4410*
20:46 and the highest s in the synagogues, *G4410*
Jas 2: 6 and draw you before the judgment s? *G2922*
Rev 4: 4 four and twenty s: and upon the seats *G2362*
4 and upon the s I saw four and twenty *G2362*
11:16 God on their s, fell upon their faces, *G2362*

SEATWARD
Ex 37: 9 s were the faces of the cherubims. H3727

SEBA
Gen 10: 7 And the sons of Cush; S, and Havilah, H5434
1Ch 1: 9 And the sons of Cush; S, and Havilah, H5434
Ps 72:10 kings of Sheba and S shall offer gifts. H5434
Isa 43: 3 thy ransom, Ethiopia and S for thee. H5434

SEBAT
Zec 1: 7 *is* the month S, in the second year of H7627

SECACAH
Jos 15:61 Beth-arabah, Middin, and S, H5527

SECHU
1Sa 19:22 well that *is* in S: and he asked and said, H7906

SECOND
Gen 1: 8 and the morning were the s day. H8145

Gen 2:13 And the name of the s river *is* Gihon: H8145
6:16 s, and third *stories* shalt thou make it. H8145
7:11 of Noah's life, in the s month, the H8145
8:14 And in the s month, on the seven and H8145
22:15 Abraham out of heaven the s time, H8145
30: 7 again, and bare Jacob a s son. H8145
12 And Zilpah Leah's maid bare Jacob a s H8145
32:19 And so commanded he the s, and the H8145
41: 5 And he slept and dreamed the s time: H8145
43 And he made him to ride in the s H4932
52 And the name of the s called he H8145
43:10 surely now we had returned this s time. H6471
47:18 unto him the s year, and said unto H8145
Ex 2:13 And when he went out the s day, H8145
16: 1 fifteenth day of the s month after their H8145
26: 4 curtain, in the coupling of the s. H8145
5 the coupling of the s; that the loops may H8145
10 of the curtain which coupleth the s. H8145
20 And for the s side of the tabernacle on H8145
28:18 And the s row *shall be* an emerald, a H8145
36:11 curtain, in the coupling of the s. H8145
12 s: the loops held one *curtain* to another. H8145
17 of the curtain which coupleth the s. H8145
39:11 And the s row, an emerald, a sapphire, H8145
40:17 first month in the s year, on the first H8145
Lev 5:10 And he shall offer the s *for* a burnt H8145
13:58 washed the s time, and shall be clean. H8145
Nu 1: 1 on the first *day* of the s month, in the H8145
1 month, in the s year after they were H8145
18 the first *day* of the s month, and they H8145
2:16 And they shall set forth in the s rank. H8145
7:18 On the s day Nethaneel the son of Zuar, H8145
9: 1 first month of the s year after they were H8145
11 The fourteenth day of the s month at H8145
10: 6 When ye blow an alarm the s time, H8145
11 *day* of the s month, in the second H8145
11 month, in the s year, that the cloud H8145
29:17 And on the s day *ye shall offer* twelve H8145
Jos 5: 2 again the children of Israel the s time. H8145
6:14 And the s day they compassed the city H8145
10:32 took it on the s day, and smote it with H8145
19: 1 And the s lot came forth to Simeon, H8145
Jdg 6:25 bullock, even the s bullock of seven H8145
26 and take the s bullock, and offer a H8145
28 *was* by it, and the s bullock was offered H8145
20:24 the children of Benjamin the s day. H8145
25 out of Gibeah the s day, and destroyed H8145
1Sa 8: 2 and the name of his s, Abiah: *they were* H4932
20:27 *which was* the s *day* of the month, that H8145
34 eat no meat the s day of the month: for H8145
26: 8 and I will not *smite* him the s time. H8138
2Sa 3: 3 And his s, Chileab, of Abigail the wife of H4932
14:29 again the s time, he would not come. H8145
1Ki 6: 1 Zif, which *is* the s month, that he began H8145
9: 2 to Solomon the s time, as he had H8145
15:25 over Israel in the s year of Asa king of H8147
18:34 And he said, Do *it* the s time. And they H8138
34 And they did *it* the s time. And he said, H8138
19: 7 came again the s time, and touched H8145
2Ki 1:17 in his stead in the s year of Jehoram the H8147
9:19 Then he sent out a s on horseback, H8145
10: 6 Then he wrote a letter the s time to H8145
14: 1 In the s year of Joash son of Jehoahaz H8147
15:32 In the s year of Pekah the son of H8147
19:29 and in the s year that which springeth H8145
23: 4 and the priests of the s order, and the H4932
25:17 had the s pillar with wreathen work. H8145
18 Zephaniah the s priest, and the three H4932
1Ch 2:13 Abinadab the s, and Shimma the third, H8145
3: 1 the s Daniel, of Abigail the Carmelitess: H8145
15 Johanan, the s Jehoiakim, the third H8145
7:15 the name of the s *was* Zelophehad: and H8145
8: 1 Ashbel the s, and Aharah the third, H8145
39 Jehush the s, and Eliphelet the third. H8145
12: 9 Ezer the first, Obadiah the s, Eliab the H8145
15:18 And with them their brethren of the s H4932
23:11 and Zizah the s: but Jeush and Beriah H8145
19 first, Amariah the s, Jahaziel the third, H8145
20 Michah the first, and Jesiah the s. H8145
24: 7 forth to Jehoiarib, the s to Jedaiah, H8145
23 *first*, Amariah the s, Jahaziel the third, H8145
25: 9 to Joseph: the s to Gedaliah, who with H8145
26: 2 Jediael the s, Zebadiah the third, H8145
4 Jehozabad the s, Joah the third, and H8145
11 Hilkiah the s, Tebaliah the third, H8145
27: 4 And over the course of the s month *was* H8145
29:22 of David king the s time, and anointed H8145
2Ch 3: 2 And he began to build in the s *day* of H8145
2 s month, in the fourth year of his reign. H8145
2Ch 27: 5 him, both the s year, and the third. H8145
30: 2 to keep the passover in the s month. H8145
13 the s month, a very great congregation. H8145
15 *day* of the s month: and the priests H8145
35:24 and put him in the s chariot that he H4932
Ezr 1:10 silver basons of a s *sort* four hundred H4932
3: 8 Now in the s year of their coming unto H8145
8 at Jerusalem, in the s month, began H8145
4:24 it ceased unto the s year of the reign of H8648
Neh 8:13 And on the s day were gathered H8145
11: 9 the son of Senuah *was* s over the city. H4932
17 Bakbukiah the s among his brethren, H4932
Est 2:14 she returned into the s house of the H8145
19 together the s time, then Mordecai H8145
7: 2 unto Esther on the s day at the banquet H8145
9:29 to confirm this s letter of Purim. H8145
Job 42:14 the name of the s, Kezia; and the name H8145
Ecc 4: 8 There is one *alone*, and *there is* not a s; H8145
15 s child that shall stand up in his stead. H8145
Isa 11:11 his hand again the s time to recover the H8145
37:30 of itself; and the s year that which H8145
Jer 1:13 came unto me the s time, saying, What H8145
13: 3 came unto me the s time, saying, H8145
33: 1 unto Jeremiah the s time, while he was H8145
41: 4 And it came to pass the s day after he H8145
52:22 all *of* brass. The s pillar also and the H8145
24 Zephaniah the s priest, and the three H4932
Ezk 10:14 a cherub, and the s face *was* the face of H8145
43:22 And on the s day thou shalt offer a kid H8145
Dan 2: 1 And in the s year of the reign of H8147
7: 5 And behold another beast, a s, like to a H8578
Jna 3: 1 came unto Jonah the s time, saying, H8145
Nah 1: 9 affliction shall not rise up the s time.
Zep 1:10 s, and a great crashing from the hills. H4932
Hag 1: 1 In the s year of Darius the king, in the H8147
15 month, in the s year of Darius the king. H8147
2:10 *month*, in the s year of Darius, came H8147
Zec 1: 1 In the eighth month, in the s year of H8147
7 Sebat, in the s year of Darius, came H8147
6: 2 and in the s chariot black horses; H8145
Mt 21:30 And he came to the s, and said likewise. *G1208*
22:26 Likewise the s also, and the third, unto *G1208*
39 And the s *is* like unto it, Thou shalt *G1208*
26:42 He went away again the s time, and *G1208*
Mk 12:21 And the s took her, and died, neither *G1208*
31 And the s *is* like, *namely* this, Thou *G1208*
14:72 And the s time the cock crew. And *G1208*
Lk 6: 1 And it came to pass on the s sabbath *G1207*
12:38 And if he shall come in the s watch, or *G1208*
19:18 And the s came, saying, Lord, thy *G1208*
20:30 And the s took her to wife, and he died *G1208*
Jn 3: 4 old? can he enter the s time into his *G1208*
4:54 This *is* again the s miracle *that* Jesus *G1208*
21:16 He saith to him again the s time, *G1208*
Act 7:13 And at the s *time* Joseph was made *G1208*
10:15 him again the s time, What God hath *G1208*
12:10 When they were past the first and the s *G1208*
13:33 is also written in the s psalm, Thou art *G1208*
1Co 15:47 the s man *is* the Lord from heaven. *G1208*
2Co 1:15 before, that ye might have a s benefit; *G1208*
13: 2 if I were present, the s time; and being *G1208*
Tit 3:10 after the first and s admonition reject; *G1208*
Heb 8: 7 no place have been sought for the s. *G1208*
9: 3 And after the s veil, the tabernacle *G1208*
7 But into the s *went* the high priest *G1208*
28 the s time without sin unto salvation. *G1208*
10: 9 the first, that he may establish the s. *G1208*
2Pt 3: 1 This s epistle, beloved, I now write *G1208*
Rev 2:11 shall not be hurt of the s death. *G1208*
4: 7 like a lion, and the s beast like a calf, *G1208*
6: 3 And when he had opened the s seal, I *G1208*
3 I heard the s beast say, Come and see. *G1208*
8: 8 And the s angel sounded, and as it *G1208*
11:14 The s woe is past; *and*, behold, the *G1208*
16: 3 And the s angel poured out his vial *G1208*
20: 6 on such the s death hath no power, *G1208*
14 into the lake of fire. This is the s death. *G1208*
21: 8 and brimstone: which is the s death. *G1208*
19 *was* jasper; the s, sapphire; the third, *G1208*

SECONDARILY

1Co 12:28 first apostles, s prophets, thirdly *G1208*

SECRET

Gen 49: 6 O my soul, come not thou into their s; H5475
Dt 27:15 and putteth *it* in *a* s *place*. And all the H5643
29:29 The s *things belong* unto the LORD our H5641
Jdg 3:19 and said, I have a s errand unto thee, O H5643
13:18 thou thus after my name, seeing it *is* s? H6383
1Sa 5: 9 and they had emerods in their s parts. H8368
19: 2 and abide in a s *place*, and hide thyself: H5643
Job 14:13 wouldest keep me s, until thy wrath be H5641
15: 8 Hast thou heard the s of God? and dost H5475
11 with thee? is there any s thing with thee? H328
20:26 All darkness *shall be* hid in his s H6845
29: 4 the s of God *was* upon my tabernacle; H5475
40:13 dust together; *and* bind their faces in s. H2934
Ps 10: 8 of the villages: in the s places doth he H5465
17:12 it were a young lion lurking in s places. H5465
18:11 He made darkness his s place; his H5643
19:12 errors? cleanse thou me from s *faults*. H5641
25:14 The s of the LORD *is* with them that H5475
27: 5 his pavilion: in the s of his tabernacle H5643
31:20 Thou shalt hide them in the s of thy H5643
64: 2 Hide me from the s counsel of the H5475
4 That they may shoot in s at the perfect: H4565
81: 7 thee in the s place of thunder: I proved H5643
90: 8 s *sins* in the light of thy countenance. H5956
91: 1 He that dwelleth in the s place of the H5643
139:15 I was made in s, *and* curiously wrought H5643
Prv 3:32 LORD: but his s *is* with the righteous. H5475
9:17 sweet, and bread *eaten* in s is pleasant. H5643
21:14 A gift in s pacifieth anger: and a H5643
25: 9 and discover not a s to another: H5475
27: 5 Open rebuke *is* better than s love. H5641
Ecc 12:14 with every s thing, whether *it be* H5956
Song 2:14 of the rock, in the s *places* of the stairs, H5643
Isa 3:17 the LORD will discover their s parts. H6596
45: 3 and hidden riches of s places, that thou H4565
19 I have not spoken in s, in a dark place H5643
48:16 not spoken in s from the beginning; H5643
Jer 2:34 found it by s search, but upon all these.
13:17 my soul shall weep in s places for *your* H4565
23:24 Can any hide himself in s places that I H4565
49:10 uncovered his s places, and he shall H4565
Lam 3:10 lying in wait, *and as* a lion in s places. H4565
Ezk 7:22 shall pollute my s *place*: for the robbers H6845
28: 3 is no s that they can hide from thee: H5640
Dan 2:18 concerning this s; that Daniel and his H7328
19 Then was the s revealed unto Daniel in H7328
22 He revealeth the deep and s things: he H5642
27 and said, The s which the king hath H7328
30 But as for me, this s is not revealed to H7328
47 seeing thou couldest reveal this s. H7328
4: 9 *is* in thee, and no s troubleth thee, tell H7328
Am 3: 7 his s unto his servants the prophets. H5475
Mt 6: 4 That thine alms may be in s: and thy *G2927*
4 in s himself shall reward thee openly. *G2927*
6 thy Father which is in s; and thy Father *G2927*
6 seeth in s shall reward thee openly. *G2927*
18 thy Father which is in s: and thy Father, *G2927*
18 seeth in s, shall reward thee openly. *G2927*
13:35 s from the foundation of the world. *G2928*
24:26 *he is* in the s chambers; believe *it* not. *G5009*
Mk 4:22 kept s, but that it should come abroad. *G614*
Lk 8:17 For nothing is s, that shall not be made *G2927*
11:33 putteth *it* in a s place, neither under *G2926*
Jn 7: 4 doeth any thing in s, and he himself *G2927*
10 the feast, not openly, but as it were in s. *G2927*
18:20 resort; and in s have I said nothing. *G2927*
Ro 16:25 was kept s since the world began, *G4601*
Eph 5:12 things which are done of them in s. *G2931*

SECRETLY

Gen 31:27 Wherefore didst thou flee away s, and H2244
Dt 13: 6 soul, entice thee s, saying, Let us go and H5643
27:24 s. And all the people shall say, Amen. H5643
28:57 for want of all *things* s in the siege and H5643
Jos 2: 1 two men to spy s, saying, Go view the H2791
1Sa 18:22 with David s, and say, Behold, the H3909
23: 9 And David knew that Saul s practised H2790
2Sa 12:12 For thou didst *it* s: but I will do this H5643
2Ki 17: 9 And the children of Israel did s *those* H2644
Job 4:12 Now a thing was s brought to me, and H1589
13:10 He will surely reprove you, if ye do s H5643
31:27 And my heart hath been s enticed, or H5643
Ps 10: 9 He lieth in wait s as a lion in his den: H4565
31:20 shalt keep them s in a pavilion from H6845
Jer 37:17 the king asked him s in his house, and H5643
38:16 So Zedekiah the king sware s unto H5643
40:15 in Mizpah s, saying, Let me go, I H5643
Hab 3:14 rejoicing *was* as to devour the poor s. H4565
Jn 11:28 Mary her sister s, saying, The Master *G2977*
19:38 of Jesus, but s for fear of the Jews, *G2928*

SECRETS

Dt 25:11 forth her hand, and taketh him by the s: H4016
Job 11: 6 And that he would shew thee the s of H8587

Ps 44:21 out? for he knoweth the **s** of the heart. H8587
Prv 11:13 A talebearer revealeth **s**: but he that is H5475
20:19 revealeth **s**: therefore meddle not H5475
Dan 2:28 that revealeth **s**, and maketh known H7328
29 he that revealeth **s** maketh known to H7328
47 and a revealer of **s**, seeing thou couldest H7328
Ro 2:16 In the day when God shall judge the **s** *G2927*
1Co 14:25 And thus are the **s** of his heart made *G2927*

SECT
Act 5:17 him, (which is the **s** of the Sadducees,) *G139*
15: 5 But there rose up certain of the **s** of the *G139*
24: 5 a ringleader of the **s** of the Nazarenes: *G139*
26: 5 **s** of our religion I lived a Pharisee. *G139*
28:22 as concerning this **s**, we know that every *G139*

SECUNDUS
Act 20: 4 Aristarchus and **S**; and Gaius of Derbe, *G4580*

SECURE
Jdg 8:11 and smote the host: for the host was **s**. H983
18: 7 quiet and **s**; and *there was* no magistrate H982
10 unto a people **s**, and to a large land: for H982
27 *were* at quiet and **s**: and they smote them H982
Job 11:18 And thou shalt be **s**, because there is H982
12: 6 provoke God are **s**; into whose hand God H987
Mt 28:14 ears, we will persuade him, and **s** you. *G275*

SECURELY
Prv 3:29 neighbour, seeing he dwelleth **s** by thee. H983
Mic 2: 8 that pass by **s** as men averse from war. H983

SECURITY
Act 17: 9 And when they had taken **s** of Jason, *G2425*

SEDITION
Ezr 4:15 they have moved **s** within the same of H849
19 rebellion and **s** have been made therein. H849
Lk 23:19 (Who for a certain **s** made in the city, *G4714*
25 them him that for **s** and murder was *G4714*
Act 24: 5 and a mover of **s** among all the Jews *G4714*

SEDITIONS
Gal 5:20 emulations, wrath, strife, **s**, heresies, *G1370*

SEDUCE
Mk 13:22 to **s**, if *it were* possible, even the elect. *G635*
1Jn 2:26 unto you concerning them that **s** you. *G4105*
Rev 2:20 to teach and to **s** my servants to *G4105*

SEDUCED
2Ki 21: 9 and Manasseh **s** them to do more evil H8582
Isa 19:13 they have also **s** Egypt, *even they that* H8582
Ezk 13:10 Because, even because they have **s** my H2937

SEDUCERS
2Ti 3:13 But evil men and **s** shall wax worse and *G1114*

SEDUCETH
Prv 12:26 but the way of the wicked **s** them. H8582

SEDUCING
1Ti 4: 1 to **s** spirits, and doctrines of devils; *G4108*

SEE
Gen 2:19 unto Adam to **s** what he would call H7200
8: 8 Also he sent forth a dove from him, to **s** H7200
11: 5 And the LORD came down to **s** the city H7200
12:12 Egyptians shall **s** thee, that they shall H7200
18:21 I will go down now, and **s** whether they H7200
19:21 And he said unto him, **S**, I have H2009
21:16 she said, Let me not **s** the death of the H7200
27: 1 that he could not **s**, he called Esau his H7200
27 him, and said, **S**, the smell of my son H7200
31: 5 And said unto them, I **s** your father's H7200
12 thine eyes, and **s**, all the rams which H7200
50 **s**, God *is* witness betwixt me and thee. H7200
32:20 and afterward I will **s** his face; H7200
34: 1 went out to **s** the daughters of the land. H7200
37:14 And he said to him, Go, I pray thee, **s** H7200
20 shall **s** what will become of his dreams. H7200
39:14 them, saying, **S**, he hath brought in H7200
41:41 And Pharaoh said unto Joseph, **S**, I H7200
42: 9 Ye *are* spies; to **s** the nakedness of the H7200
12 And he said unto them, Nay, but to **s** H7200
43: 3 Ye shall not **s** my face, except your H7200
5 us, Ye shall not **s** my face, except your H7200
44:23 with you, ye shall **s** my face no more. H7200
26 for we may not **s** the man's face, except H7200
Gen 44:34 **s** the evil that shall come on my father. H7200
45:12 And, behold, your eyes **s**, and the eyes H7200
24 them, **S** that ye fall not out by the way.
28 alive: I will go and **s** him before I die. H7200
48:10 *so that* he could not **s**. And he brought H7200
11 I had not thought to **s** thy face: and, lo, H7200
Ex 1:16 women, and **s** *them* upon the stools; H7200
3: 3 turn aside, and **s** this great sight, why H7200
4 he turned aside to **s**, God called unto H7200
4:18 *are* in Egypt, and **s** whether they be yet H7200
21 to return into Egypt, **s** that thou do all H7200
5:19 of Israel did **s** *that* they *were* in evil H7200
6: 1 Now shalt thou **s** what I will do to H7200
7: 1 And the LORD said unto Moses, **S**, I H7200
10: 5 cannot be able to **s** the earth: and they H7200
28 heed to thyself, **s** my face no more; for H7200
29 well, I will **s** thy face again no more. H7200
12:13 ye *are*: and when I **s** the blood, I will H7200
13:17 they **s** war, and they return to Egypt: H7200
14:13 stand still, and **s** the salvation of the H7200
13 ye shall **s** them again no more for ever. H7200
16: 7 And in the morning, then ye shall **s** the H7200
29 **S**, for that the LORD hath given you the H7200
32 that they may **s** the bread wherewith H7200
22: 8 unto the judges, *to* **s** whether he have put
23: 5 If thou **s** the ass of him that hateth thee H7200
31: 2 **S**, I have called by name Bezaleel the H7200
33:12 And Moses said unto the LORD, **S**, thou H7200
20 And he said, Thou canst not **s** my face: H7200
20 for there shall no man **s** me, and live. H7200
23 and thou shalt **s** my back parts: but H7200
34:10 thou *art* shall **s** the work of the LORD: H7200
35:30 the children of Israel, **S**, the LORD hath H7200
Lev 13: 8 And *if* the priest **s** that, behold, the H7200
10 And the priest shall **s** *him*: and, behold, H7200
15 And the priest shall **s** the raw flesh, and H7200
17 And the priest shall **s** him: and, behold, H7200
30 Then the priest shall **s** the plague: and, H7200
14:36 priest go *into it* to **s** the plague, that all H7200
36 the priest shall go in to **s** the house: H7200
20:17 daughter, and **s** her nakedness, and H7200
17 and she **s** his nakedness; it *is* H7200
Nu 4:20 But they shall not go in to **s** when the H7200
11:15 and let me not **s** my wretchedness. H7200
23 short? thou shalt **s** now whether my H7200
13:18 And **s** the land, what it *is*; and the H7200
14:23 Surely they shall not **s** the land which I H7200
23 any of them that provoked me **s** it: H7200
22:41 might **s** the utmost *part* of the people. H7200
23: 9 For from the top of the rocks I **s** him, H7200
13 thou mayest **s** them: thou shalt see H7200
13 them: thou shalt **s** but the utmost part H7200
13 and shalt not **s** them all: and curse H7200
24:17 I shall **s** him, but not now: I shall H7200
27:12 Abarim, and **s** the land which I have H7200
32: 8 them from Kadesh-barnea to **s** the land. H7200
11 and upward, shall **s** the land which I H7200
Dt 1:35 evil generation **s** that good land, which H7200
36 he shall **s** it, and to him will I H7200
3:25 I pray thee, let me go over, and **s** the H7200
28 to inherit the land which thou shalt **s**. H7200
4:28 neither **s**, nor hear, nor eat, nor smell. H7200
18:16 God, neither let me **s** this great fire any H7200
22: 1 Thou shalt not **s** thy brother's ox or his H7200
4 Thou shalt not **s** thy brother's ass or his H7200
23:14 be holy: that he **s** no unclean thing in H7200
28:10 And all people of the earth shall **s** that H7200
34 sight of thine eyes which thou shalt **s**. H7200
67 sight of thine eyes which thou shalt **s**. H7200
68 thee, Thou shalt **s** it no more again: H7200
29: 4 to **s**, and ears to hear, unto this day. H7200
22 say, when they **s** the plagues of that H7200
30:15 **S**, I have set before thee this day life and H7200
32:20 from them, I will **s** what their end *shall* H7200
39 **S** now that I, *even I*, *am* he, and *there is* H7200
52 Yet thou shalt **s** the land before *thee*; H7200
34: 4 caused thee to **s** *it* with thine eyes, but H7200
Jos 3: 3 saying, When ye **s** the ark of the H7200
6: 2 And the LORD said unto Joshua, **S**, I H7200
8: 1 arise, go up to Ai: **s**, I have given into H7200
8 shall ye do. **S**, I have commanded you. H7200
22:10 an altar by Jordan, a great altar to **s** to. H4758
Jdg 9:37 And Gaal spake again and said, **S** there H2009
14: 8 he turned aside to **s** the carcase of the H7200
16: 5 Entice him, and **s** wherein his great H7200
21:21 And **s**, and, behold, if the daughters of H7200
1Sa 2:32 And thou shalt **s** an enemy *in my* H5027
3: 2 began to wax dim, *that* he could not **s**; H7200
4:15 his eyes were dim, that he could not **s**. H7200
1Sa 6: 9 And **s**, if it goeth up by the way of his H7200
13 and saw the ark, and rejoiced to **s** *it*. H7200
10:24 And Samuel said to all the people, **S** ye H7200
12:16 Now therefore stand and **s** this great H7200
17 ye may perceive and **s** that your H7200
14:17 Number now, and **s** who is gone from H7200
29 troubled the land: **s**, I pray you, how H7200
38 **s** wherein this sin hath been this day. H7200
15:35 And Samuel came no more to **s** Saul H7200
17:28 down that thou mightest **s** the battle. H7200
19: 3 of thee; and what I **s**, that I will tell thee. H7200
15 *again* to **s** David, saying, Bring H7200
20:29 away, I pray thee, and **s** my brethren. H7200
21:14 his servants, Lo, ye **s** the man is mad: H7200
23:22 yet, and know and **s** his place where his H7200
23 **S** therefore, and take knowledge of all H7200
24:11 Moreover, my father, **s**, yea, see the H7200
11 Moreover, my father, see, yea, **s** the H7200
11 know thou and **s** that *there is* neither H7200
15 me and thee, and **s**, and plead my H7200
25:35 to thine house; **s**, I have hearkened to H7200
26:16 And now **s** where the king's spear H7200
2Sa 3:13 is, Thou shalt not **s** my face, except H7200
13 when thou comest to **s** my face. H7200
7: 2 the prophet, **S** now, I dwell in an house H7200
13: 5 father cometh to **s** thee, say unto him, H7200
5 that I may **s** *it*, and eat *it* at her hand. H7200
6 king was come to **s** him, Amnon said H7200
14:24 and let him not **s** my face. So Absalom H7200
30 Therefore he said unto his servants, **S**, H7200
32 therefore let me **s** the king's face; and H7200
15: 3 And Absalom said unto him, **S**, thy H7200
28 **S**, I will tarry in the plain of the H7200
24: 3 lord the king may **s** *it*: but why doth my H7200
13 now advise, and **s** what answer I shall H7200
1Ki 9:12 And Hiram came out from Tyre to **s** H7200
12:16 O Israel: now **s** to thine own house, H7200
14: 4 Ahijah could not **s**; for his eyes were set H7200
17:23 and Elijah said, **S**, thy son liveth. H7200
20: 7 I pray you, and **s** how this *man* seeketh H7200
22 and mark, and **s** what thou doest: for H7200
22:25 And Micaiah said, Behold, thou shalt **s** H7200
2Ki 2:10 if thou **s** me *when I am* taken H7200
3:14 would not look toward thee, nor **s** thee. H7200
17 For thus saith the LORD, Ye shall not **s** H7200
17 neither shall ye **s** rain; yet that valley H7200
5: 7 **s** how he seeketh a quarrel against me. H7200
6:17 his eyes, that he may **s**. And the LORD H7200
20 that they may **s**. And the LORD opened H7200
32 said to the elders, **S** ye how this son of a H7200
7: 2 Behold, thou shalt **s** *it* with thine eyes, H7200
13 are consumed:) and let us send and **s**. H7200
14 host of the Syrians, saying, Go and **s**. H7200
19 Behold, thou shalt **s** it with thine eyes, H7200
8:29 went down to **s** Joram the son of Ahab H7200
9:16 of Judah was come down to **s** Joram. H7200
17 he came, and said, I **s** a company. And H7200
34 and said, Go, **s** now this cursed *woman*,
10:16 And he said, Come with me, and **s** my H7200
19:16 thine eyes, and **s**: and hear the words H7200
22:20 eyes shall not **s** all the evil which I will H7200
23:17 Then he said, What title *is* that that I **s**? H7200
2Ch 10:16 *and* now, David, **s** to thine own house. H7200
18:16 Then he said, I did **s** all Israel scattered H7200
24 And Micaiah said, Behold, thou shalt **s** H7200
20:17 stand ye *still*, and **s** the salvation of the H7200
22: 6 went down to **s** Jehoram the son of H7200
24: 5 year to year, and **s** that ye hasten the
25:17 Come, let us **s** one another in the face. H7200
29: 8 and to hissing, as ye **s** with your eyes. H7200
30: 7 gave them up to desolation, as ye **s**. H7200
34:28 shall thine eyes **s** all the evil that I will H7200
Ezr 4:14 was not meet for us to **s** the king's H2370
Neh 2:17 Then said I unto them, Ye **s** the distress H7200
4:11 not know, neither **s**, till we come in the H7200
9: 9 And didst **s** the affliction of our fathers H7200
Est 3: 4 told Haman, to **s** whether Mordecai's H7200
5:13 so long as I **s** Mordecai the Jew sitting H7200
8: 6 For how can I endure to **s** the evil that H7200
6 to **s** the destruction of my kindred? H7200
Job 3: 9 neither let it **s** the dawning of the day: H7200
6:21 For now ye are nothing; ye **s** *my* H7200
7: 7 *is* wind: mine eye shall no more **s** good. H7200
8 hath seen me shall **s** me no *more*: thine H7789
9:11 Lo, he goeth by me, and I **s** *him* not: he H7200
25 a post: they flee away, they **s** no good. H7200
10:15 therefore **s** thou mine affliction; H7202
17:15 hope? as for my hope, who shall **s** it? H7789
19:26 this *body*, yet in my flesh shall I **s** God: H2372

Job 19:27 Whom I shall s for myself, and mine H2372
20: 9 The eye also *which* saw him shall s *him*
17 He shall not s the rivers, the floods, the H7200
21:20 His eyes shall s his destruction, and he H7200
22:11 Or darkness, *that* thou canst not s; and H7200
19 The righteous s *it*, and are glad: and H7200
23: 9 on the right hand, that I cannot s *him*: H7200
24: 1 do they that know him not s his days? H2372
15 eye shall s me: and disguiseth *his* face. H7789
28:27 Then did he s it, and declare it; he H7200
31: 4 Doth not he s my ways, and count all H7200
33:26 him: and he shall s his face with joy: H7200
28 into the pit, and his life shall s the light. H7200
34:32 *That which* I s not teach thou me: if I H2372
35: 5 Look unto the heavens, and s; and H7200
14 Although thou sayest thou shalt not s H7789
36:25 Every man may s it; man may behold *it* H2372
37:21 And now *men* s not the bright light H7200
Ps 10:11 he hideth his face; he will never s *it*. H7200
14: 2 of men, to s if there were any that H7200
16:10 suffer thine Holy One to s corruption. H7200
22: 7 All they that s me laugh me to scorn: H7200
27:13 *I had fainted*, unless I had believed to s H7200
31:11 that did s me without fled from me. H7200
34: 8 O taste and s that the LORD *is* good: H7200
12 loveth *many* days, that he may s good? H7200
36: 9 of life: in thy light shall we s light. H7200
37:34 the wicked are cut off, thou shalt s *it*. H7200
40: 3 our God: many shall s *it*, and fear, and H7200
41: 6 And if he come to s *me*, he speaketh H7200
49: 9 still live for ever, *and* not s corruption. H7200
19 of his fathers; they shall never s light. H7200
52: 6 The righteous also shall s, and fear, and H7200
53: 2 of men, to s if there were *any* that H7200
58: 8 a woman, *that* they may not s the sun. H2372
59:10 let me s *my desire* upon mine enemies. H7200
63: 2 To s thy power and thy glory, so *as* I H7200
64: 5 privily; they say, Who shall s them? H7200
8 all that s them shall flee away. H7200
66: 5 Come and s the works of God: *he is* H7200
69:23 Let their eyes be darkened, that they s H7200
32 The humble shall s *this, and* be glad: H7200
74: 9 We s not our signs: *there is* no more H7200
86:17 hate me may s *it*, and be ashamed: H7200
89:48 and shall not s death? shall he deliver H7200
91: 8 behold and s the reward of the wicked. H7200
92:11 Mine eye also shall s *my desire* on H5027
94: 7 Yet they say, The LORD shall not s, H7200
9 he that formed the eye, shall he not s? H5027
97: 6 and all the people s his glory. H7200
106: 5 That I may s the good of thy chosen, H7200
107:24 These s the works of the LORD, and his H7200
42 The righteous shall s *it*, and rejoice: H7200
112: 8 until he s *his desire* upon his enemies. H7200
10 The wicked shall s *it*, and be grieved; H7200
115: 5 not: eyes have they, but they s not: H7200
118: 7 I s *my desire* upon them that hate me. H7200
119:74 be glad when they s me; because I have H7200
128: 5 and thou shalt s the good of Jerusalem H7200
6 Yea, thou shalt s thy children's H7200
135:16 not; eyes have they, but they s not; H7200
139:16 Thine eyes did s my substance, yet H7200
24 And s if *there be any* wicked way in H7200
Prv 24:18 Lest the LORD s *it*, and it displease H7200
29:16 but the righteous shall s their fall. H7200
Ecc 1:10 it may be said, S, this *is* new? it hath H7200
2: 3 folly, till I might s what *was* that good H7200
3:18 s that they themselves are beasts. H7200
22 bring him to s what shall be after him? H7200
7:11 *it there is* profit to them that s the sun. H7200
8:16 wisdom, and to s the business that is H7200
Song 2:14 the stairs, let me s thy countenance, let H7200
6:11 the garden of nuts to s the fruits of the H7200
11 of the valley, *and* to s whether the vine H7200
13 thee. What will ye s in the Shulamite? H2372
7:12 vineyards; let us s if the vine flourish, H7200
Isa 5:19 his work, that we may s *it*: and let the H7200
6: 9 not; and s ye indeed, but perceive not. H7200
10 eyes; lest they s with their eyes, and H7200
13: 1 which Isaiah the son of Amoz did s. H2372
14:16 They that s thee shall narrowly look H7200
18: 3 on the earth, s ye, when he lifteth up H7200
26:11 up, they will not s: *but* they shall see, H2372
11 see: *but* they shall s, and be ashamed H2372
29:18 s out of obscurity, and out of darkness. H7200
30:10 Which say to the seers, S not; and to H7200
20 but thine eyes shall s thy teachers: H7200
32: 3 And the eyes of them that s shall not be H7200
33:17 Thine eyes shall s the king in his H2372

Isa 33:19 Thou shalt not s a fierce people, a H7200
20 thine eyes shall s Jerusalem a quiet H7200
35: 2 and Sharon, they shall s the glory of the H7200
37:17 O LORD, and s: and hear all the words H7200
38:11 I said, I shall not s the LORD, *even* the H7200
40: 5 and all flesh shall s *it* together: for the H7200
41:20 That they may s, and know, and H7200
42:18 deaf; and look, ye blind, that ye may s. H7200
44: 9 witnesses; they s not, nor know; that H7200
18 that they cannot s; *and* their hearts, H7200
48: 6 Thou hast heard, s all this; and will not H2372
49: 7 rulers, Kings shall s and arise, princes H7200
52: 8 sing: for they shall s eye to eye, when H7200
10 earth shall s the salvation of our God. H7200
15 them shall they s; and *that* which they H7200
53: 2 and when we shall s him, *there is* no H7200
10 for sin, he shall s *his* seed, he shall H7200
11 He shall s of the travail of his soul, *and* H7200
60: 4 Lift up thine eyes round about, and s: H7200
5 Then thou shalt s, and flow together, H7200
61: 9 among the people: all that s them shall H7200
62: 2 And the Gentiles shall s thy H7200
64: 9 for ever: behold, s, we beseech thee, we H5027
66:14 And when ye s *this*, your heart shall H7200
18 and they shall come, and s my glory. H7200
Jer 1:10 S, I have this day set thee over the H7200
11 And I said, I s a rod of an almond tree. H7200
13 thou? And I said, I s a seething pot; and H7200
2:10 For pass over the isles of Chittim, and s; H7200
10 and s if there be such a thing. H7200
19 therefore and s that *it is* an evil *thing* H7200
23 not gone after Baalim? s thy way in the H7200
31 O generation, s ye the word of the H7200
3: 2 high places, and s where thou hast not H7200
4:21 How long shall I s the standard, *and* H7200
5: 1 of Jerusalem, and s now, and know, H7200
12 neither shall we s sword nor famine: H7200
21 s not; which have ears, and hear not: H7200
6:16 in the ways, and s, and ask for the old H7200
7:12 at the first, and s what I did to it for the H7200
11:20 the heart, let me s thy vengeance on H7200
12: 4 they said, He shall not s our last end. H7200
14:13 them, Ye shall not s the sword, neither H7200
17: 6 and shall not s when good cometh; H7200
8 and shall not s when heat cometh, H7200
20:12 the heart, let me s thy vengeance on H7200
18 of the womb to s labour and sorrow, H7200
22:10 no more, nor s his native country. H7200
12 captive, and shall s this land no more. H7200
23:24 that I shall not s him? saith the LORD. H7200
30: 6 Ask ye now, and s whether a man doth H7200
6 wherefore do I s every man with his H7200
42:14 where we shall s no war, nor hear the H7200
18 and ye shall s this place no more. H7200
51:61 shalt s, and shalt read all these words; H7200
Lam 1:11 meat to relieve the soul: s, O LORD, and H7200
12 pass by? behold, and s if there be any H7200
Ezk 8: 6 *and* thou shalt s greater abominations. H7200
13 s greater abominations that they do. H7200
15 s greater abominations than these. H7200
12: 2 which have eyes to s, and see not; they H7200
2 eyes to see, and s not; they have ears H7200
6 thy face, that thou s not the ground: for H7200
12 that he s not the ground with *his* eyes. H7200
13 he not s it, though he shall die there. H7200
13: 9 the prophets that s vanity, and that H2374
16 and which s visions of peace for H2374
23 Therefore ye shall s no more vanity, H2372
14:22 you, and ye shall s their way and their H7200
23 And they shall comfort you, when ye s H7200
16:37 that they may s all thy nakedness. H7200
20:48 And all flesh shall s that I the LORD H7200
21:29 Whiles they s vanity unto thee, whiles H2372
32:31 Pharaoh shall s them, and shall be H7200
33: 6 But if the watchman s the sword come, H7200
39:21 the heathen shall s my judgment that I H7200
Dan 1:10 for why should he s your faces worse H7200
2: 8 because ye s the thing is gone from me. H2370
3:25 He answered and said, Lo, I s four men H2370
5:23 and stone, which s not, nor hear, nor H2370
Joel 2:28 your young men shall s visions: H7200
Am 6: 2 Pass ye unto Calneh, and s; and from H7200
Jna 4: 5 might s what would become of the city. H7200
Mic 6: 9 *of* wisdom shall s thy name: hear ye the H7200
7:10 Then *she that is* mine enemy shall s *it*, H7200
16 The nations shall s and be confounded H7200
Hab 1: 1 which Habakkuk the prophet did s. H2372
2: 1 and will watch to s what he will say H7200
Zep 3:15 of thee: thou shalt not s evil any more. H7200

Hag 2: 3 and how do ye s it now? *is it* not in your H7200
Zec 2: 2 Jerusalem, to s what *is* the breadth H7200
4:10 rejoice, and shall s the plummet in the H7200
5: 2 And I answered, I s a flying roll; the H7200
5 and s what *is* this that goeth forth. H7200
9: 5 Ashkelon shall s *it*, and fear; Gaza also H7200
5 fear; Gaza also *shall s it*, and be very
10: 7 children shall s *it*, and be glad; their H7200
Mal 1: 5 And your eyes shall s, and ye shall say, H7200
Mt 5: 8 the pure in heart: for they shall s God. G3700
16 that they may s your good works, and G1492
7: 5 then shalt thou s clearly to cast out the G1227
8: 4 And Jesus saith unto him, S thou tell G3708
9:30 them, saying, S *that* no man know *it*. G3708
11: 4 those things which ye do hear and s: G991
7 to s? A reed shaken with the wind? G2300
8 But what went ye out for to s? A man G1492
9 But what went ye out for to s? A G1492
12:38 Master, we would s a sign from thee. G1492
13:13 they seeing s not; and hearing they G991
14 seeing ye shall s, and shall not perceive: G991
15 time they should s with *their* eyes, and G1492
16 But blessed *are* your eyes, for they s: and G991
17 have desired to s *those things* which G1492
17 *things* which ye s, and have not seen G991
15:31 to s: and they glorified the God of Israel. G991
16:28 taste of death, till they s the Son of man G1492
22:11 And when the king came in to s the G2300
23:39 For I say unto you, Ye shall not s me G1492
24: 2 And Jesus said unto them, S ye not all G991
6 and rumours of wars: s that ye be not G3708
15 When ye therefore shall s the G1492
30 and they shall s the Son of man coming G3700
33 So likewise ye, when ye shall s all these G1492
26:58 and sat with the servants, to s the end. G1492
64 Hereafter shall ye s the Son of man G3700
27: 4 said, What *is that* to us? s thou *to that*. G3700
24 the blood of this just person: s ye *to it*. G3700
49 The rest said, Let be, let us s whether G1492
28: 1 and the other Mary to s the sepulchre. G2334
6 Come, s the place where the Lord lay. G1492
7 there shall ye s him: lo, I have told you. G3700
10 into Galilee, and there shall they s me. G3700
Mk 1:44 And saith unto him, S thou say nothing G3708
4:12 That seeing they may s, and not perceive; G991
5:14 out to s what it was that was done. G1492
15 And they come to Jesus, and s him that G2334
32 And he looked round about to s her G1492
6:38 have ye? go and s. And when they knew, G1492
8:18 Having eyes, s ye not? and having ears, G991
24 And he looked up, and said, I s men as G991
12:15 me? bring me a penny, that I may s *it*. G1492
13: 1 unto him, Master, s what manner of G2396
14 But when ye shall s the abomination of G1492
26 And then shall they s the Son of man G3700
29 So ye in like manner, when ye shall s G1492
14:62 And Jesus said, I am: and ye shall s the G3700
15:32 cross, that we may s and believe. And G1492
36 Let alone; let us s whether Elias will G1492
16: 7 shall ye s him, as he said unto you. G3700
Lk 2:15 Bethlehem, and s this thing which is G1492
26 that he should not s death, before he G1492
3: 6 And all flesh shall s the salvation of G3700
6:42 then shalt thou s clearly to pull out the G1227
7:22 how that the blind s, the lame walk, the G308
24 for to s? A reed shaken with the wind? G2300
25 But what went ye out for to s? A man G1492
26 But what went ye out for to s? A G1492
8:10 they might not s, and hearing they might G991
16 that they which enter in may s the light. G991
20 stand without, desiring to s thee. G1492
35 Then they went out to s what was done; G1492
9: 9 such things? And he desired to s him. G1492
27 of death, till they s the kingdom of God. G1492
10:23 the eyes which s the things that ye see: G991
23 the eyes which see the things that ye s: G991
24 have desired to s those things which G1492
24 things which ye s, and have not seen G991
11:33 that they which come in may s the light. G991
12:54 people, When ye s a cloud rise out of G1492
55 And when *ye s* the south wind blow, ye
13:28 when ye shall s Abraham, and Isaac, G3700
35 you, Ye shall not s me, until *the time* G1492
14:18 and s it: I pray thee have me excused. G1492
17:22 ye shall desire to s one of the days of G1492
22 of the Son of man, and ye shall not s *it*. G3700
23 And they shall say to you, S here; or, G2400
23 to you, See here; or, s there: go not after G2400
19: 3 And he sought to s Jesus who he was; G1492

Lk 19: 4 to s him: for he was to pass that *way*. G1492
20:13 will reverence *him* when they s him. G1492
21:20 And when ye shall s Jerusalem G1492
27 And then shall they s the Son of man G3700
30 When they now shoot forth, ye s and G991
31 So likewise ye, when ye s these things G1492
23: 8 for he was desirous to s him of a long G1492
24:39 handle me, and s; for a spirit hath not G1492
39 not flesh and bones, as ye s me have. G2334
Jn 1:33 Upon whom thou shalt s the Spirit G1492
39 He saith unto them, Come and s. They G1492
46 Philip saith unto him, Come and s. G1492
50 thou shalt s greater things than these. G3700
51 Hereafter ye shall s heaven open, and G3700
3: 3 again, he cannot s the kingdom of God. G1492
36 the Son shall not s life; but the wrath of G3700
4:29 Come, s a man, which told me all G1492
48 Then said Jesus unto him, Except ye s G1492
6:19 furlongs, they s Jesus walking on the G2334
30 then, that we may s, and believe thee? G1492
62 *What* and if ye shall s the Son of man G2334
7: 3 also may s the works that thou doest. G2334
8:51 keep my saying, he shall never s death. G2334
56 Your father Abraham rejoiced to s my G1492
9:15 upon mine eyes, and I washed, and do s. G991
19 was born blind? how then doth he now s? G991
25 know, that, whereas I was blind, now I s. G991
39 that they which s not might see; and that G991
39 see not might s; and that they which G991
39 that they which s might be made blind. G991
41 say, We s; therefore your sin remaineth. G991
11:34 They said unto him, Lord, come and s. G1492
40 thou shouldest s the glory of God? G3700
12: 9 that they might s Lazarus also, whom G1492
21 him, saying, Sir, we would s Jesus. G1492
40 they should not s with *their* eyes, nor G1492
14:19 s me: because I live, ye shall live also. G2334
16:10 go to my Father, and ye s me no more; G2334
16 A little while, and ye shall not s me: G2334
16 shall s me, because I go to the Father. G3700
17 and ye shall not s me: and again, a G2334
17 s me: and, Because I go to the Father? G3700
19 and ye shall not s me: and again, a G2334
19 again, a little while, and ye shall s me? G3700
22 sorrow: but I will s you again, and your G3700
18:26 Did not I s thee in the garden with him? G1492
20:25 Except I shall s in his hands the print G1492
Act 2:17 young men shall s visions, and your G3700
27 suffer thine Holy One to s corruption. G1492
31 hell, neither his flesh did s corruption. G1492
33 shed forth this, which ye now s and hear. G991
3:16 strong, whom ye s and know: yea, the G2334
7:56 And said, Behold, I s the heavens G2334
8:36 the eunuch said, S, *here is* water; what G2400
13:35 suffer thine Holy One to s corruption. G1492
15:36 the word of the Lord, *and* s how they do.
19:21 I have been there, I must also s Rome. G1492
26 Moreover ye s and hear, that not alone G2334
20:25 of God, shall s my face no more. G3700
38 that they should s his face no more. G2334
22:11 And when I could not s for the glory of G1689
14 know his will, and s that Just One, and G1492
23:22 and charged *him, S thou* tell no man
25:24 present with us, ye s this man, about G2334
28:20 I called for you, to s *you*, and to speak G1492
26 and seeing ye shall s, and not perceive: G991
27 lest they should s with *their* eyes, and G1492
Ro 1:11 For I long to s you, that I may impart G1492
7:23 But I s another law in my members, G991
8:25 But if we hope for that we s not, *then* do G991
11: 8 that they should not s, and ears that they G991
10 not s, and bow down their back alway. G991
15:21 of, they shall s: and they that have not G3700
24 you: for I trust to s you in my journey, G2300
1Co 1:26 For ye s your calling, brethren, how that G991
8:10 For if any man s thee which hast G1492
13:12 For now we s through a glass, darkly; G991
16: 7 For I will not s you now by the way; but G1492
10 Now if Timotheus come, s that he may G991
2Co 8: 7 to us, *s* that ye abound in this grace also.
Gal 1:18 up to Jerusalem to s Peter, and abode G2477
6:11 Ye s how large a letter I have written G1492
Eph 3: 9 And to make all *men* s what *is* the G5461
5:15 S then that ye walk circumspectly, not as G991
33 wife *s* that she reverence *her* husband.
Php 1:27 I come and s you, or else be absent, G1492
2:23 soon as I shall s how it will go with me. G302
28 that, when ye s him again, ye may G1492
1Th 2:17 to s your face with great desire. G1492
1Th 3: 6 greatly to s us, as we also *to see* you: G1492
6 greatly to see us, as we also *to s* you:
10 that we might s your face, and might G1492
5:15 S that none render evil for evil unto G3708
1Ti 6:16 man hath seen, nor can s: to whom *be* G1492
2Ti 1: 4 Greatly desiring to s thee, being G1492
Heb 2: 8 we s not yet all things put under him. G3708
9 But we s Jesus, who was made a little G991
3:19 So we s that they could not enter in G991
8: 5 tabernacle: for, S, saith he, *that* thou G3708
10:25 the more, as ye s the day approaching. G991
11: 5 that he should not s death; and was not G1492
12:14 without which no man shall s the Lord: G3700
25 S that ye refuse not him that speaketh. G991
13:23 whom, if he come shortly, I will s you. G3700
Jas 2:24 Ye s then how that by works a man is G3708
1Pt 1: 8 though now ye s *him* not, yet believing, G3708
22 love of the brethren, *s that ye* love one
3:10 For he that will love life, and s good G1492
2Pt 1: 9 blind, and cannot s afar off, and hath G3467
1Jn 3: 2 be like him; for we shall s him as he is. G3700
5:16 If any man s his brother sin a sin *which* G1492
3Jn 14 But I trust I shall shortly s thee, and we G1492
Rev 1: 7 every eye shall s him, and they *also* G3700
12 And I turned to s the voice that spake G991
3:18 eyes with eyesalve, that thou mayest s. G991
6: 1 of the four beasts saying, Come and s. G991
3 heard the second beast say, Come and s. G991
5 say, Come and s. And I beheld, and lo G991
6 and *s* thou hurt not the oil and the wine.
7 voice of the fourth beast say, Come and s. G991
9:20 which neither can s, nor hear, nor walk: G991
11: 9 and nations shall s their dead bodies G991
16:15 he walk naked, and they s his shame. G991
18: 7 am no widow, and shall s no sorrow. G1492
9 they shall s the smoke of her burning, G991
19:10 he said unto me, S *thou do it* not: I am G3708
22: 4 And they shall s his face; and his name G3700
9 Then saith he unto me, S *thou do it* G3708

SEED

Gen 1:11 the herb yielding s, *and* the fruit tree H2233
11 his kind, whose s *is* in itself, upon the H2233
12 *and* herb yielding s after his kind, and H2233
12 fruit, whose s *was* in itself, after his H2233
29 herb bearing s, which *is* upon the face H2233
29 yielding s; to you it shall be for meat. H2233
3:15 and between thy s and her seed; it shall H2233
15 thy seed and her s; it shall bruise thy H2233
4:25 s instead of Abel, whom Cain slew. H2233
7: 3 s alive upon the face of all the earth. H2233
9: 9 with you, and with your s after you; H2233
12: 7 and said, Unto thy s will I give this H2233
13:15 thee will I give it, and to thy s for ever. H2233
16 And I will make thy s as the dust of the H2233
16 *then* shall thy s also be numbered. H2233
15: 3 thou hast given no s: and, lo, one born H2233
5 and he said unto him, So shall thy s be. H2233
13 a surety that thy s shall be a stranger in H2233
18 saying, Unto thy s have I given this H2233
16:10 I will multiply thy s exceedingly, that it H2233
17: 7 and thee and thy s after thee in their H2233
7 a God unto thee, and to thy s after thee. H2233
8 And I will give unto thee, and to thy s H2233
9 thy s after thee in their generations. H2233
10 me and you and thy s after thee; Every H2233
12 of any stranger, which *is* not of thy s. H2233
19 covenant, *and* with his s after him. H2233
19:32 that we may preserve s of our father. H2233
34 that we may preserve s of our father. H2233
21:12 voice; for in Isaac shall thy s be called. H2233
13 I make a nation, because he *is* thy s. H2233
22:17 I will multiply thy s as the stars of the H2233
17 s shall possess the gate of his enemies; H2233
18 And in thy s shall all the nations of the H2233
24: 7 saying, Unto thy s will I give this land; H2233
60 and let thy s possess the gate of those H2233
26: 3 thee, and unto thy s, I will give all these H2233
4 And I will make thy s to multiply as the H2233
4 will give unto thy s all these countries; H2233
4 and in thy s shall all the nations H2233
24 thy s for my servant Abraham's sake. H2233
28: 4 to thee, and to thy s with thee; that H2233
13 liest, to thee will I give it, and to thy s; H2233
14 And thy s shall be as the dust of the H2233
14 and in thee and in thy s shall all the H2233
32:12 and make thy s as the sand of the sea, H2233
35:12 to thy s after thee will I give the land. H2233
38: 8 her, and raise up s to thy brother. H2233
Gen 38: 9 And Onan knew that the s should not H2233
9 lest that he should give s to his brother. H2233
46: 6 Egypt, Jacob, and all his s with him: H2233
7 his s brought he with him into Egypt. H2233
47:19 and give *us* s, that we may live, and H2233
23 *is* s for you, and ye shall sow the land. H2233
24 be your own, for s of the field, and for H2233
48: 4 give this land to thy s after thee *for* an H2233
11 and, lo, God hath shewed me also thy s. H2233
19 s shall become a multitude of nations. H2233
Ex 16:31 it *was* like coriander s, white; and the H2233
28:43 for ever unto him and his s after him. H2233
30:21 to his s throughout their generations. H2233
32:13 I will multiply your s as the stars of H2233
13 your s, and they shall inherit *it* for ever. H2233
33: 1 Jacob, saying, Unto thy s will I give it: H2233
Lev 11:37 s which is to be sown, it *shall be* clean. H2233
38 But if *any* water be put upon the s, and H2233
12: 2 have conceived s, and born a man H2232
15:16 And if any man's s of copulation go out H2233
17 whereon is the s of copulation, shall H2233
18 man shall lie *with* s of copulation, they H2233
32 and *of him* whose s goeth from him, H2233
18:21 And thou shalt not let any of thy s pass H2233
19:19 thy field with mingled s: neither shall a H3610
20: 2 that giveth *any* of his s unto Molech; he H2233
3 he hath given of his s unto Molech, to H2233
4 of his s unto Molech, and kill him not: H2233
21:15 Neither shall he profane his s among H2233
17 *he be* of thy s in their generations H2233
21 No man that hath a blemish of the s of H2233
22: 3 *he be* of all your s among your H2233
4 What man soever of the s of Aaron *is* a H2233
4 or a man whose s goeth from him; H2233
26:16 s in vain, for your enemies shall eat it. H2233
27:16 according to the s thereof: an homer of H2233
16 an homer of barley s *shall be valued* at H2233
30 *whether* of the s of the land, *or* of the H2233
Nu 5:28 she shall be free, and shall conceive s. H2233
11: 7 And the manna *was* as coriander s, and H2233
14:24 he went; and his s shall possess it. H2233
16:40 which *is* not of the s of Aaron, come H2233
18:19 LORD unto thee and to thy s with thee. H2233
20: 5 it *is* no place of s, or of figs, or of vines, H2233
24: 7 his buckets, and his s *shall be* in many H2233
25:13 And he shall have it, and his s after H2233
Dt 1: 8 unto them and to their s after them. H2233
4:37 he chose their s after them, and H2233
10:15 and he chose their s after them, *even* H2233
11: 9 them and to their s, a land that floweth H2233
10 thou sowedst thy s, and wateredst *it* H2233
14:22 all the increase of thy s, that the field H2233
22: 9 lest the fruit of thy s which thou hast H2233
28:38 Thou shalt carry much s out into the H2233
46 for a wonder, and upon thy s for ever. H2233
59 the plagues of thy s, *even* great plagues, H2233
30: 6 the heart of thy s, to love the LORD thy H2233
19 life, that both thou and thy s may live: H2233
31:21 the mouths of their s: for I know their H2233
34: 4 give it unto thy s: I have caused thee to H2233
Jos 24: 3 multiplied his s, and gave him Isaac. H2233
Ru 4:12 unto Judah, of the s which the LORD H2233
1Sa 2:20 LORD give thee s of this woman for the H2233
8:15 And he will take the tenth of your s, and H2233
20:42 and between my s and thy seed for H2233
42 my seed and thy s for ever. And he H2233
24:21 wilt not cut off my s after me, and that H2233
2Sa 4: 8 the king this day of Saul, and of his s. H2233
7:12 I will set up thy s after thee, which shall H2233
22:51 unto David, and to his s for evermore. H2233
1Ki 2:33 the head of his s for ever: but upon H2233
33 and upon his s, and upon his house, H2233
11:14 he *was* of the king's s in Edom. H2233
39 And I will for this afflict the s of David, H2233
18:32 as would contain two measures of s. H2233
2Ki 5:27 thee, and unto thy s for ever. And he H2233
11: 1 she arose and destroyed all the s royal. H2233
17:20 And the LORD rejected all the s of H2233
25:25 Elishama, of the s royal, came, and ten H2233
1Ch 16:13 O ye s of Israel his servant, ye children H2233
17:11 I will raise up thy s after thee, which H2233
2Ch 20: 7 to the s of Abraham thy friend for ever? H2233
22:10 all the s royal of the house of Judah. H2233
Ezr 2:59 and their s, whether they *were* of Israel: H2233
9: 2 sons: so that the holy s have mingled H2233
Neh 7:61 nor their s, whether they *were* of Israel. H2233
9: 2 And the s of Israel separated H2233
8 to give *it, I say,* to his s, and hast H2233
Est 6:13 Mordecai *be* of the s of the Jews, before H2233

Est 9:27 and upon their s, and upon all such as H2233
28 memorial of them perish from their s. H2233
31 and for their s, the matters of the H2233
10: 3 people, and speaking peace to all his s. H2233
Job 5:25 Thou shalt know also that thy s *shall* H2233
21: 8 Their s is established in their sight with H2233
39:12 home thy s, and gather *it into* thy barn? H2233
Ps 18:50 to David, and to his s for evermore. H2233
21:10 s from among the children of men. H2233
22:23 him; all ye the s of Jacob, glorify him; H2233
23 him; and fear him, all ye the s of Israel. H2233
30 A s shall serve him; it shall be H2233
25:13 His soul shall dwell at ease; and his s H2233
37:25 forsaken, nor his s begging bread. H2233
26 and lendeth; and his s *is* blessed. H2233
28 but the s of the wicked shall be cut off. H2233
69:36 The s also of his servants shall inherit H2233
89: 4 Thy s will I establish for ever, and build H2233
29 His s also will I make *to endure* for H2233
36 His s shall endure for ever, and his H2233
102:28 their s shall be established before thee. H2233
105: 6 O ye s of Abraham his servant, ye H2233
106:27 To overthrow their s also among the H2233
112: 2 His s shall be mighty upon earth: the H2233
126: 6 bearing precious s, shall doubtless H2233
Prv 11:21 the s of the righteous shall be delivered. H2233
Ecc 11: 6 In the morning sow thy s, and in the H2233
Isa 1: 4 with iniquity, a s of evildoers, children H2233
5:10 the s of an homer shall yield an ephah. H2233
6:13 holy s *shall be* the substance thereof. H2233
14:20 s of evildoers shall never be renowned. H2233
17:11 thou make thy s to flourish: *but* the H2233
23: 3 And by great waters the s of Sihor, the H2233
30:23 Then shall he give the rain of thy s, that H2233
41: 8 chosen, the s of Abraham my friend. H2233
43: 5 I will bring thy s from the east, and H2233
44: 3 my spirit upon thy s, and my blessing H2233
45:19 I said not unto the s of Jacob, Seek ye H2233
25 In the LORD shall all the s of Israel be H2233
48:19 Thy s also had been as the sand, and H2233
53:10 he shall see *his* s, he shall prolong *his* H2233
54: 3 on the left; and thy s shall inherit the H2233
55:10 s to the sower, and bread to the eater: H2233
57: 3 the s of the adulterer and the whore. H2233
4 of transgression, a s of falsehood, H2233
59:21 the mouth of thy s, nor out of the mouth H2233
21 of thy seed's s, saith the LORD, from H2233
61: 9 And their s shall be known among the H2233
9 *are* the s *which* the LORD hath blessed. H2233
65: 9 And I will bring forth a s out of Jacob, H2233
23 for they *are* the s of the blessed of the H2233
66:22 so shall your s and your name remain. H2233
Jer 2:21 vine, wholly a right s: how then art thou H2233
7:15 brethren, *even* the whole s of Ephraim. H2233
22:28 out, he and his s, and are cast into a H2233
30 days: for no man of his s shall prosper, H2233
23: 8 up and which led the s of the house of H2233
29:32 and his s: he shall not have a man H2233
30:10 from afar, and thy s from the land of H2233
31:27 s of man, and with the seed of beast. H2233
27 seed of man, and with the s of beast. H2233
36 the LORD, *then* the s of Israel also shall H2233
37 will also cast off all the s of Israel for all H2233
33:22 so will I multiply the s of David my H2233
26 Then will I cast away the s of Jacob, H2233
26 not take *any* of his s *to be* rulers over H2233
26 *be* rulers over the s of Abraham, Isaac, H2233
35: 7 Neither shall ye build house, nor sow s, H2233
9 have we vineyard, nor field, nor s: H2233
36:31 And I will punish him and his s and his H2233
41: 1 of Elishama, of the s royal, and the H2233
46:27 afar off, and thy s from the land of H2233
49:10 to hide himself: his s is spoiled, and his H2233
Ezk 17: 5 He took also of the s of the land, and H2233
13 And hath taken of the king's s, and H2233
20: 5 hand unto the s of the house of Jacob, H2233
43:19 Levites that be of the s of Zadok, which H2233
44:22 maidens of the s of the house of Israel, H2233
Dan 1: 3 and of the king's s, and of the princes; H2233
2:43 with the s of men: but they shall H2234
9: 1 of Ahasuerus, of the s of the Medes, H2233
Joel 1:17 The s is rotten under their clods, the H6507
Am 9:13 him that soweth s; and the mountains H2233
Hag 2:19 Is the s yet in the barn? yea, as yet the H2233
Zec 8:12 For the s *shall be* prosperous; the vine H2233
Mal 2: 3 Behold, I will corrupt your s, and H2233
15 he might seek a godly s. Therefore take H2233
Mt 13:19 is he which received s by the way side. G4687
20 But he that received the s into stony G4687

Mt 13:22 He also that received s among the G4687
23 But he that received s into the good G4687
24 a man which sowed good s in his field: G4690
27 not thou sow good s in thy field? from G4690
31 a grain of mustard s, which a man took, G4615
37 soweth the good s is the Son of man; G4690
38 The field is the world; the good s are G4690
17:20 a grain of mustard s, ye shall say unto G4615
22:24 wife, and raise up s unto his brother. G4690
Mk 4:26 if a man should cast s into the ground; G4703
27 and day, and the s should spring and G4703
31 *It is* like a grain of mustard s, which, G4615
12:19 wife, and raise up s unto his brother. G4690
20 the first took a wife, and dying left no s. G4690
21 left he any s: and the third likewise. G4690
22 And the seven had her, and left no s: G4690
Lk 1:55 to Abraham, and to his s for ever. G4690
8: 5 A sower went out to sow his s: and as he G4703
11 Now the parable is this: The s is the G4703
13:19 It is like a grain of mustard s, which a G4615
17: 6 a grain of mustard s, ye might say unto G4615
20:28 wife, and raise up s unto his brother. G4690
Jn 7:42 cometh of the s of David, and out of G4690
8:33 We be Abraham's s, and were never in G4690
37 I know that ye are Abraham's s; but ye G4690
Act 3:25 And in thy s shall all the kindreds G4690
7: 5 and to his s after him, when *as yet* G4690
6 And God spake on this wise, That his s G4690
13:23 Of this man's s hath God according to G4690
Ro 1: 3 of the s of David according to the flesh; G4690
4:13 or to his s, through the law, but G4690
16 be sure to all the s; not to that only G4690
18 which was spoken, So shall thy s be. G4690
9: 7 Neither, because they are the s of G4690
7 but, In Isaac shall thy s be called. G4690
8 of the promise are counted for the s. G4690
29 had left us a s, we had been as Sodoma, G4690
11: 1 s of Abraham, *of* the tribe of Benjamin. G4690
1Co 15:38 him, and to every s his own body. G4690
2Co 9:10 Now he that ministereth s to the sower G4690
10 and multiply your s sown, and increase G4703
11:22 I. Are they the s of Abraham? so *am* I. G4690
Gal 3:16 Now to Abraham and his s were the G4690
16 as of one, And to thy s, which is Christ. G4690
19 till the s should come to whom G4690
29 s, and heirs according to the promise. G4690
2Ti 2: 8 Remember that Jesus Christ of the s of G4690
Heb 2:16 but he took on *him* the s of Abraham. G4690
11:11 to conceive s, and was delivered of G4690
18 said, That in Isaac shall thy s be called: G4690
1Pt 1:23 Being born again, not of corruptible s, G4701
1Jn 3: 9 sin; for his s remaineth in him: and G4690
Rev 12:17 the remnant of her s, which keep the G4690

SEEDS
Dt 22: 9 with divers s: lest the fruit of thy seed H3610
Mt 13: 4 And when he sowed, some *s* fell by the
32 Which indeed is the least of all s: but G4690
Mk 4:31 is less than all the s that be in the earth: G4690
Gal 3:16 saith not, And to s, as of many; but as G4690

SEED'S
Isa 59:21 of the mouth of thy s seed, saith the H2233

SEEDTIME
Gen 8:22 While the earth remaineth, s and H2233

SEEING
Gen 15: 2 wilt thou give me, s I go childless, and
18:18 S that Abraham shall surely become a
19: 1 of Sodom: and Lot s *them* rose up to H7200
22:12 that thou fearest God, s thou hast not
24:56 And he said unto them, Hinder me not, s
26:27 come ye to me, s ye hate me, and have
28: 8 And Esau s that the daughters of H7200
44:30 s that his life is bound up in the lad's life;
Ex 4:11 the s, or the blind? have not I the LORD? H6493
21: 8 s he hath dealt deceitfully with her.
22:10 or be hurt, or driven away, no man s *it*: H7200
23: 9 of a stranger, s ye were strangers in H3588
Lev 10:17 in the holy place, s it *is* most holy, and H3588
Nu 15:26 s all the people *were* in ignorance. H3588
16: 3 much upon you, s all the congregation H3588
35:23 a man may die, s *him* not, and cast *it* H7200
Jos 17:14 portion to inherit, s I *am* a great people,
22:18 and it will be, *s* ye rebel to day against
Jdg 13:18 thou thus after my name, s it *is* secret?
17:13 me good, s I have a Levite to *my* priest. H3588
19:23 do not *so* wickedly; s that this man is H310

Jdg 21: 7 them that remain, s we have sworn by
16 for them that remain, s the women are H3588
Ru 1:21 *then* call ye me Naomi, s the LORD hath
2:10 take knowledge of me, s I *am* a stranger?
1Sa 16: 1 mourn for Saul, s I have rejected him
17:36 be as one of them, s he hath defied the H3588
18:23 be a king's son in law, s that I *am* a poor
24: 6 him, s he *is* the anointed of the LORD.
25:26 and *as* thy soul liveth, s the LORD hath
28:16 thou ask of me, s the LORD is departed
2Sa 13:39 concerning Amnon, s he was dead.
15:20 and down with us? s I go whither I may,
18:22 son, s that thou hast no tidings ready?
19:11 back to his house? s the speech of all
1Ki 1:48 my throne this day, mine eyes even s *it*. H7200
11:28 and Solomon s the young man that H7200
2Ki 10: 2 cometh to you, s your master's sons *are*
1Ch 12:17 to mine enemies, s *there is* no wrong in
2Ch 2: 6 But who is able to build him an house, s
Ezr 9:13 our great trespass, s that thou our God H3588
Neh 2: 2 thy countenance sad, s thou *art* not sick?
Job 14: 5 S his days *are* determined, the number H518
19:28 s the root of the matter is found in me?
21:22 Shall *any* teach God knowledge? s he
34 How then comfort ye me in vain, s in
24: 1 Why, s times are not hidden from the
28:21 S it is hid from the eyes of all living, and
Ps 22: 8 him deliver him, s he delighted in him.
50:17 S thou hatest instruction, and castest my
Prv 3:29 Devise not evil against thy neighbour, s
17:16 to get wisdom, s *he hath* no heart *to it*?
20:12 The hearing ear, and the s eye, the H7200
Ecc 1: 8 with s, nor the ear filled with hearing. H7200
2:16 of the fool for ever; s that which now *is*
6:11 S there be many things that increase H3588
Isa 21: 3 *of it*; I was dismayed at the s *of it*. H7200
33:15 and shutteth his eyes from s evil; H7200
42:20 S many things, but thou observest not; H7200
49:21 hath begotten me these, s I have lost my
Jer 11:15 to do in mine house, *s* she hath wrought
47: 7 How can it be quiet, s the LORD hath
Ezk 16:30 the Lord GOD, s thou doest all these
17:18 S he despised the oath by breaking the
21: 4 S then that I will cut off from thee the H3282
22:28 *morter*, s vanity, and divining
Dan 2:47 s thou couldest reveal this secret. H1768
Hos 4: 6 be no priest to me: s thou hast forgotten
Mt 5: 1 And s the multitudes, he went up into a G1492
9: 2 a bed: and Jesus s their faith said unto G1492
13:13 because they s see not; and hearing G991
14 and s ye shall see, and shall not perceive: G991
Mk 4:12 That s they may see, and not perceive; G991
11:13 And s a fig tree afar off having leaves, G1492
Lk 1:34 How shall this be, s I know not a man? G1893
5:12 of leprosy: who s Jesus fell on *his* face, G1492
8:10 in parables; that s they might not see, G991
23:40 s thou art in the same condemnation? G3754
Jn 2:18 unto us, s that thou doest these things?
9: 7 way therefore, and washed, and came s. G991
21:21 Peter s him saith to Jesus, Lord, and G1492
Act 2:15 s it is *but* the third hour of the day. G1063
31 He s this before spake of the G4275
3: 3 Who s Peter and John about to go into G1492
7:24 And s one *of them* suffer wrong, he G1492
8: 6 hearing and s the miracles which he did. G991
9: 7 hearing a voice, but s no man. G2334
13:11 shalt be blind, not s the sun for a season. G991
46 spoken to you: but s ye put it from you, G1894
16:27 out of his sleep, and s the prison doors G1492
17:24 all things therein, s that he is Lord of
25 needed any thing, s he giveth to all life,
19:36 S then that these things cannot be
24: 2 *him*, saying, S that by thee we enjoy
28:26 and s ye shall see, and not perceive: G991
Ro 3:30 S *it is* one God, which shall justify the G1897
1Co 14:16 giving of thanks, s he understandeth G1894
2Co 3:12 S then that we have such hope, we use
4: 1 Therefore s we have this ministry, as we
11:18 S that many glory after the flesh, I will G1893
19 For ye suffer fools gladly, s ye *yourselves*
Col 3: 9 Lie not one to another, s that ye have put
2Th 1: 6 S *it is* a righteous thing with God to G1512
Heb 4: 6 S therefore it remaineth that some G1893
14 S then that we have a great high priest,
5:11 to be uttered, s ye are dull of hearing. G1893
6: 6 again unto repentance; s they crucify to
7:25 unto God by him, s he ever liveth to
8: 4 not be a priest, s that there are priests
11:27 he endured, as s him who is invisible. G3708

Heb 12: 1 Wherefore s we also are compassed
1Pt 1:22 S ye have purified your souls in obeying
2Pt 2: 8 among them, in s and hearing, vexed *his* G990
3:11 S then *that* all these things shall be
14 Wherefore, beloved, s that ye look for
17 Ye therefore, beloved, s ye know *these*

SEEK
Gen 37:16 And he said, I s my brethren: tell me, I H1245
43:18 in; that he may s occasion against us, H1556
Lev 13:36 not s for yellow hair; he *is* unclean. H1239
19:31 spirits, neither s after wizards, to be H1245
Nu 15:39 them; and that ye s not after your own H8446
16:10 with thee: and s ye the priesthood also? H1245
24: 1 at other times, to s for enchantments, H7125
Dt 4:29 But if from thence thou shalt s the H1245
29 find *him*, if thou s him with all thy H1875
12: 5 shall ye s, and thither thou shalt come: H1875
22: 2 until thy brother s after it, and thou H1875
23: 6 Thou shalt not s their peace nor their H1875
Ru 3: 1 shall I not s rest for thee, that it H1245
1Sa 9: 3 with thee, and arise, go s the asses. H1245
10: 2 thou wentest to s are found: and, lo, H1245
14 And he said, To s the asses: and when H1245
16:16 *are* before thee, to s out a man, *who is* H1245
23:15 was come out to s his life: and David H1245
25 Saul also and his men went to s *him*. H1245
24: 2 all Israel, and went to s David and his H1245
25:26 they that s evil to my lord, be as Nabal. H1245
29 thee, and to s thy soul: but the soul H1245
26: 2 to s David in the wilderness of Ziph. H1245
20 is come out to s a flea, as when one H1245
27: 1 despair of me, to s me any more in any H1245
28: 7 Then said Saul unto his servants, S me H1245
2Sa 5:17 came up to s David; and David heard H1245
1Ki 2:40 to Gath to Achish to s his servants: and H1245
18:10 hath not sent to s thee: and when they H1245
19:10 left; and they s my life, to take it away. H1245
14 left; and they s my life, to take it away. H1245
2Ki 2:16 go, we pray thee, and s thy master: lest H1245
6:19 whom ye s. But he led them to Samaria. H1245
1Ch 4:39 the valley, to s pasture for their flocks. H1245
14: 8 went up to s David. And David heard H1245
16:10 heart of them rejoice that s the LORD. H1245
11 S the LORD and his strength, seek his H1875
11 Seek the LORD and his strength, s his H1245
22:19 Now set your heart and your soul to s H1875
28: 8 of our God, keep and s for all the H1875
9 the thoughts: if thou s him, he will be H1875
2Ch 7:14 and pray, and s my face, and turn from H1245
11:16 as set their hearts to s the LORD God of H1245
12:14 prepared not his heart to s the LORD. H1875
14: 4 And commanded Judah to s the LORD H1875
15: 2 him; and if ye s him, he will be found H1875
12 And they entered into a covenant to s H1875
13 That whosoever would not s the LORD H1875
19: 3 and hast prepared thine heart to s God. H1875
20: 3 and set himself to s the LORD, and H1875
4 of Judah they came to s the LORD. H1245
30:19 *That* prepareth his heart to s God, the H1875
31:21 to s his God, he did *it* with H1875
34: 3 he began to s after the God of David H1875
Ezr 4: 2 with you: for we s your God, as ye *do*; H1875
6:21 to s the LORD God of Israel, did eat, H1875
7:10 For Ezra had prepared his heart to s H1875
8:21 before our God, to s of him a right way H1245
22 all them for good that s him; but his H1245
9:12 your sons, nor s their peace or their H1875
Neh 2:10 to s the welfare of the children of Israel. H1245
Job 5: 8 I would s unto God, and unto God H1875
7:21 s me in the morning, but I *shall* not *be*. H7836
8: 5 If thou wouldest s unto God betimes, H7836
20:10 His children shall s to please the poor,
Ps 4: 2 love vanity, *and* s after leasing? Selah. H1245
9:10 hast not forsaken them that s thee. H1875
10: 4 will not s *after God*: God *is* not H1875
15 and the evil *man*: s out his wickedness H1875
14: 2 any that did understand, *and* s God. H1875
22:26 s him: your heart shall live for ever. H1875
24: 6 This *is* the generation of them that s H1875
6 him, that s thy face, O Jacob. Selah. H1245
27: 4 the LORD, that will I s after; that I may H1245
8 *When thou saidst*, S ye my face; my H1245
8 said unto thee, Thy face, LORD, will I s. H1245
34:10 but they that s the LORD shall not H1875
14 Depart from evil, and do good; s peace, H1245
35: 4 put to shame that s after my soul: let H1245
38:12 They also that s after my life lay snares H1245
12 *for me*: and they that s my hurt speak H1875
Ps 40:14 together that s after my soul to destroy H1245
16 Let all those that s thee rejoice and be H1245
53: 2 that did understand, that did s God. H1875
54: 3 and oppressors s after my soul: they H1245
63: 1 O God, thou *art* my God; early will I s H7836
9 But those *that* s my soul, to destroy *it*, H1245
69: 6 let not those that s thee be confounded H1245
32 and your heart shall live that s God. H1875
70: 2 confounded that s after my soul: let H1245
4 Let all those that s thee rejoice and be H1245
71:13 and dishonour that s my hurt. H1245
24 brought unto shame, that s my hurt. H1245
83:16 that they may s thy name, O LORD. H1245
104:21 their prey, and s their meat from God. H1245
105: 3 heart of them rejoice that s the LORD. H1245
4 S the LORD, and his strength: seek his H1875
4 Seek the LORD, and his strength: s his H1245
109:10 and beg: let them s *their bread* also out H1875
119: 2 *and that* s him with the whole heart. H1875
45 And I will walk at liberty: for I s thy H1875
155 the wicked: for they s not thy statutes. H1875
176 I have gone astray like a lost sheep; s H1245
122: 9 of the LORD our God I will s thy good. H1245
Prv 1:28 s me early, but they shall not find me: H7836
7:15 to s thy face, and I have found thee. H7836
8:17 and those that s me early shall find me. H7836
21: 6 tossed to and fro of them that s death. H1245
23:30 the wine; they that go to s mixed wine. H2713
35 when shall I awake? I will s it yet again. H1245
28: 5 that s the LORD understand all *things*. H1245
29:10 hate the upright: but the just s his soul. H1245
26 Many s the ruler's favour; but *every* H1245
Ecc 1:13 And I gave my heart to s and search H1875
7:25 to search, and to s out wisdom, and the H1245
8:17 a man labour to s *it* out, yet he shall H1245
Song 3: 2 broad ways I will s him whom my soul H1245
6: 1 aside? that we may s him with thee. H1245
Isa 1:17 Learn to do well; s judgment, relieve H1875
8:19 And when they shall say unto you, S H1875
19 not a people s unto their God? for H1875
9:13 neither do they s the LORD of hosts. H1875
11:10 Gentiles s: and his rest shall be glorious. H1875
19: 3 and they shall s to the idols, and to the H1875
26: 9 within me will I s thee early: for when H7836
29:15 Woe unto them that s deep to hide their
31: 1 Holy One of Israel, neither s the LORD! H1875
34:16 S ye out of the book of the LORD, and H1875
41:12 Thou shalt s them, and shalt not find H1245
17 *When* the poor and needy s water, and H1245
45:19 the seed of Jacob, S ye me in vain: I the H1245
51: 1 ye that s the LORD: look unto H1245
55: 6 S ye the LORD while he may be found, H1875
58: 2 Yet they s me daily, and delight to H1875
Jer 2:24 away? all they that s her will not weary H1245
33 Why trimmest thou thy way to s love? H1245
4:30 will despise thee, they will s thy life. H1245
5: 1 and know, and s in the broad places H1245
11:21 of Anathoth, that s thy life, saying, H1245
19: 7 of them that s their lives: and their H1245
9 that s their lives, shall straiten them. H1245
21: 7 hand of those that s their life: and he H1245
22:25 hand of them that s thy life, and into H1245
29: 7 And s the peace of the city whither I H1875
13 And ye shall s me, and find *me*, when H1245
30:14 thee; they s thee not; for I have H1875
34:20 hand of them that s their life: and their H1245
21 hand of them that s their life, and into H1245
38:16 the hand of these men that s thy life. H1245
44:30 hand of them that s his life; as I gave H1245
45: 5 great things for thyself? s *them* not: for, H1245
46:26 the hand of those that s their lives, and H1245
49:37 before them that s their life: and I will H1245
50: 4 shall go, and s the LORD their God. H1245
Lam 1:11 All her people sigh, they s bread; they H1245
Ezk 7:25 Destruction cometh; and they shall s H1245
26 then shall they s a vision of the H1245
34: 6 and none did search or s *after them*. H1245
11 both search my sheep, and s them out. H1239
12 scattered; so will I s out my sheep, and H1239
16 I will s that which was lost, and bring H1245
Dan 9: 3 unto the Lord God, to s by prayer and H1245
Hos 2: 7 and she shall s them, but shall not H1245
3: 5 of Israel return, and s the LORD their H1245
5: 6 and with their herds to s the LORD; but H1245
15 their offence, and s my face: in their H1245
15 in their affliction they will s me early. H7836
7:10 LORD their God, nor s him for all this. H1245
10:12 for *it is* time to s the LORD, till he come H1875
Am 5: 4 of Israel, S ye me, and ye shall live: H1875
Am 5: 5 But s not Beth-el, nor enter into Gilgal, H1875
6 S the LORD, and ye shall live; lest he H1875
8 S *him* that maketh the seven stars and
14 S good, and not evil, that ye may live: H1875
8:12 shall run to and fro to s the word of the H1245
Nah 3: 7 whence shall I s comforters for thee? H1245
11 shalt s strength because of the enemy. H1245
Zep 2: 3 S ye the LORD, all ye meek of the earth, H1245
3 his judgment; s righteousness, seek H1245
3 righteousness, s meekness: it may be H1245
Zec 8:21 to s the LORD of hosts: I will go also. H1245
22 shall come to s the LORD of hosts in H1245
11:16 off, neither shall s the young one, nor H1245
12: 9 that day, *that* I will s to destroy all the H1245
Mal 2: 7 and they should s the law at his mouth: H1245
15 That he might s a godly seed. Therefore H1245
3: 1 the Lord, whom ye s, shall suddenly H1245
Mt 2:13 will s the young child to destroy him. G2212
6:32 do the Gentiles s:) for your heavenly G1934
33 But s ye first the kingdom of God, and G2212
7: 7 Ask, and it shall be given you; s, and ye G2212
28: 5 that ye s Jesus, which was crucified. G2212
Mk 1:37 they said unto him, All *men* s for thee. G2212
3:32 and thy brethren without s for thee. G2212
8:12 this generation s after a sign? verily I G2212
16: 6 not affrighted: Ye s Jesus of Nazareth, G2212
Lk 11: 9 shall be given you; s, and ye shall find; G2212
29 evil generation: they s a sign; and there G1934
12:29 And s not ye what ye shall eat, or what G2212
30 of the world s after: and your Father G1934
31 But rather s ye the kingdom of God; G2212
13:24 will s to enter in, and shall not be able. G2212
15: 8 house, and s diligently till she find *it*? G2212
17:33 Whosoever shall s to save his life shall G2212
19:10 For the Son of man is come to s and to G2212
24: 5 Why s ye the living among the dead? G2212
Jn 1:38 unto them, What s ye? They said unto G2212
5:30 is just; because I s not mine own will, G2212
44 of another, and s not the honour that G2212
6:26 I say unto you, Ye s me, not because ye G2212
7:25 Is not this he, whom they s to kill? G2212
34 Ye shall s me, and shall not find *me*: G2212
36 he said, Ye shall s me, and shall not G2212
8:21 way, and ye shall s me, and shall die in G2212
37 seed; but ye s to kill me, because my G2212
40 But now ye s to kill me, a man that G2212
50 And I s not mine own glory: there is G2212
13:33 with you. Ye shall s me: and as I said G2212
18: 4 forth, and said unto them, Whom s ye? G2212
7 Then asked he them again, Whom s G2212
8 ye s me, let these go their way: G2212
Act 10:19 unto him, Behold, three men s thee. G2212
21 I am he whom ye s: what *is* the cause G2212
11:25 Barnabas to Tarsus, for to s Saul: G327
15:17 That the residue of men might s after G1567
17:27 That they should s the Lord, if haply G2212
Ro 2: 7 in well doing s for glory and honour G2212
11: 3 and I am left alone, and they s my life. G2212
1Co 1:22 a sign, and the Greeks s after wisdom: G2212
7:27 Art thou bound unto a wife? s not to be G2212
27 thou loosed from a wife? s not a wife. G2212
10:24 Let no man s his own, but every man G2212
14:12 of spiritual *gifts*, s that ye may excel to G2212
2Co 12:14 to you: for I s not yours, but you: G2212
13: 3 Since ye s a proof of Christ speaking in G2212
Gal 1:10 or God? or do I s to please men? for if G2212
2:17 But if, while we s to be justified by G2212
Php 2:21 For all s their own, not the things G2212
Col 3: 1 If ye then be risen with Christ, s those G2212
Heb 11: 6 rewarder of them that diligently s him. G1567
14 declare plainly that they s a country. G1934
13:14 continuing city, but we s one to come. G1934
1Pt 3:11 do good; let him s peace, and ensue it. G2212
Rev 9: 6 And in those days shall men s death, G2212

SEEKEST
Gen 37:15 man asked him, saying, What s thou? H1245
Jdg 4:22 man whom thou s. And when he came H1245
2Sa 17: 3 man whom thou s *is* as if all returned: H1245
20:19 in Israel: thou s to destroy a city and H1245
1Ki 11:22 that, behold, thou s to go to thine own H1245
Prv 2: 4 If thou s her as silver, and searchest for H1245
Jer 45: 5 And s thou great things for thyself? H1245
Jn 4:27 s thou? or, Why talkest thou with her? G2212
20:15 thou? whom s thou? She, supposing G2212

SEEKETH
1Sa 19: 2 Saul my father s to kill thee: now H1245
20: 1 sin before thy father, that he s my life? H1245

1Sa 22:23 not: for he that s my life seeketh thy H1245
23 seeketh my life s thy life: but with me H1245
23:10 heard that Saul s to come to Keilah, to H1245
24: 9 saying, Behold, David s thy hurt? H1245
2Sa 16:11 of my bowels, s my life: how much H1245
1Ki 20: 7 and see how this *man* s mischief: for he H1245
2Ki 5: 7 and see how he s a quarrel against me. H579
Job 39:29 From thence she s the prey, *and* her H2658
Ps 37:32 the righteous, and s to slay him. H1245
Prv 11:27 He that diligently s good procureth H7836
27 that s mischief, it shall come unto him. H1875
14: 6 A scorner s wisdom, and *findeth it* not: H1245
15:14 understanding s knowledge: but the H1245
17: 9 He that covereth a transgression s love; H1245
11 An evil *man* s only rebellion: therefore H1245
19 he that exalteth his gate s destruction. H1245
18: 1 s *and* intermeddleth with all wisdom. H1245
15 and the ear of the wise s knowledge. H1245
31:13 She s wool, and flax, and worketh H1875
Ecc 7:28 Which yet my soul s, but I find not: one H1245
Isa 40:20 will not rot; he s unto him a cunning H1245
Jer 5: 1 that s the truth; and I will pardon it. H1245
30:17 This *is* Zion, whom no man s after. H1875
38: 4 them: for this man s not the welfare of H1875
Lam 3:25 wait for him, to the soul *that* s him. H1875
Ezk 14:10 the punishment of him that s *unto him*; H1875
34:12 As a shepherd s out his flock in the day H1243
Mt 7: 8 and he that s findeth; and to him *G2212*
12:39 generation s after a sign; and there *G1934*
16: 4 A wicked and adulterous generation s *G1934*
18:12 and s that which is gone astray? *G2212*
Lk 11:10 and he that s findeth; and to him *G2212*
Jn 4:23 for the Father s such to worship him. *G2212*
7: 4 and he himself s to be known openly. *G2212*
18 He that speaketh of himself s his own *G2212*
18 glory: but he that s his glory that sent *G2212*
8:50 glory: there is one that s and judgeth. *G2212*
Ro 3:11 there is none that s after God. *G1567*
11: 7 that which he s for; but the election *G1934*
1Co 13: 5 Doth not behave itself unseemly, s not *G2212*

SEEKING
Est 10: 3 of his brethren, s the wealth of his H1875
Isa 16: 5 s judgment, and hasting righteousness. H1875
Mt 12:43 dry places, s rest, and findeth none. *G2212*
13:45 unto a merchant man, s goodly pearls: *G2212*
Mk 8:11 with him, s of him a sign from heaven, *G2212*
Lk 2:45 turned back again to Jerusalem, s him. *G2212*
11:24 dry places, s rest; and finding none, *G2212*
54 Laying wait for him, and s to catch *G2212*
13: 7 three years I come s fruit on this fig *G2212*
Jn 6:24 and came to Capernaum, s for Jesus. *G2212*
Act 13: 8 withstood them, s to turn away the *G2212*
11 about s some to lead him by the hand. *G2212*
1Co 10:33 in all *things*, not s mine own profit, but *G2212*
1Pt 5: 8 walketh about, s whom he may devour: *G2212*

SEEM
Gen 27:12 me, and I shall s to him as a H1961+H5869
Dt 15:18 It shall not s hard unto thee, when thou H7185
25: 3 thy brother should s vile unto thee. H7034
Jos 24:15 And if it s evil unto you to H1961+H5869
1Sa 24: 4 to him as it shall s good unto H1961+H5869
2Sa 19:37 what shall s good unto thee. H1961+H5869
38 which shall s good unto thee: H1961+H5869
1Ki 21: 2 than it; *or*, if it s good to thee, I H1961+H5869
1Ch 13: 2 of Israel, If *it s* good unto you, and
Ezr 5:17 Now therefore, if *it s* good to the king, let
7:18 And whatsoever shall s good to thee, H3191
Neh 9:32 not all the trouble s little before thee, H4591
Est 5: 4 And Esther answered, If *it s* good unto
8: 5 his sight, and the thing *s* right before the
Jer 40: 4 thine hand. If it s good unto thee to H5869
4 well unto thee: but if it s ill unto thee to H5869
Nah 2: 4 ways: they shall s like torches, they H4758
1Co 11:16 But if any man s to be contentious, we *G1380*
12:22 s to be more feeble, are necessary: *G1380*
2Co 10: 9 That I may not s as if I would terrify *G1380*
Heb 4: 1 any of you should s to come short of it. *G1380*
Jas 1:26 If any man among you s to be *G1380*

SEEMED
Gen 19:14 this city. But he s as one that H1961+H5869
29:20 and they s unto him *but* a H1961+H5869
2Sa 3:19 in Hebron all that s good to Israel, and H5869
19 s good to the whole house of Benjamin. H5869
Ecc 9:13 under the sun, and it *s* great unto me:
Jer 18: 4 as s good to the potter to make *it*. H5869
27: 5 given it unto whom it s meet unto me. H5869
Mt 11:26 Even so, Father: for so it s *G1096+G2107*
Lk 1: 3 It s good to me also, having had perfect *G1380*
10:21 for so it s good in thy sight. *G1096+G2107*
24:11 And their words s to them as idle tales, *G5316*
Act 15:25 It s good unto us, being assembled with *G1380*
28 For it s good to the Holy Ghost, and to *G1380*
Gal 2: 6 But of these who s to be somewhat, *G1380*
6 for they who s *to be somewhat* in *G1380*
9 and John, who s to be pillars, perceived *G1380*

SEEMETH
Lev 14:35 priest, saying, It s to me *there is* as it H7200
Nu 16: 9 *S it but* a small thing unto you, that the
Jos 9:25 thine hand: as it s good and right unto H5869
Jdg 10:15 us whatsoever s good unto thee; deliver H5869
19:24 with them what s good unto you: but H5869
1Sa 1:23 unto her, Do what s thee good; tarry H5869
3:18 the LORD: let him do what s him good. H5869
11:10 do with us all that s good unto you. H5869
14:36 Do whatsoever s good unto thee. Then H5869
40 unto Saul, Do what s good unto thee. H5869
18:23 And David said, S it to you *a* light *thing* H5869
2Sa 10:12 the LORD do that which s him good. H5869
15:26 I, let him do to me as s good unto him. H5869
18: 4 And the king said unto them, What s H5869
24:22 and offer up what *s* good unto him: H5869
Est 3:11 to do with them as it s good to thee. H5869
Prv 14:12 There is a way which s right unto a H6440
16:25 There is a way that s right unto a man, H6440
18:17 *He that is* first in his own cause *s* just;
Jer 26:14 with me as s good and meet unto you. H5869
40: 4 thee: whither it s good and convenient H5869
5 or go wheresoever it s convenient unto H5869
Ezk 34:18 *S it* a small thing unto you to have eaten
Lk 8:18 be taken even that which he s to have. *G1380*
Act 17:18 other some, He s to be a setter forth of *G1380*
25:27 For it s to me unreasonable to send a *G1380*
1Co 3:18 any man among you s to be wise in this *G1380*
Heb 12:11 Now no chastening for the present s to *G1380*

SEEMLY
Prv 19:10 Delight is not s for a fool; much less for H5000
26: 1 in harvest, so honour is not s for a fool. H5000

SEEN
Gen 7: 1 for thee have I s righteous before me H7200
8: 5 were the tops of the mountains s. H7200
9:14 that the bow shall be s in the cloud: H7200
22:14 In the mount of the LORD it shall be s. H7200
31:12 I have s all that Laban doeth unto thee. H7200
42 empty. God hath s mine affliction and H7200
32:30 Peniel: for I have s God face to face, H7200
33:10 therefore I have s thy face, as though H7200
10 as though I had s the face of God, and H7200
45:13 of all that ye have s; and ye shall haste H7200
46:30 s thy face, because thou *art* yet alive. H7200
Ex 3: 7 And the LORD said, I have surely s the H7200
9 me: and I have also s the oppression H7200
16 and *s* that which is done to you in Egypt:
10: 6 fathers have s, since the day that they H7200
13: 7 leavened bread be s with thee, neither H7200
7 leaven s with thee in all thy quarters. H7200
14:13 whom ye have s to day, ye shall see H7200
19: 4 Ye have s what I did unto the H7200
20:22 of Israel, Ye have s that I have talked H7200
32: 9 unto Moses, I have s this people, and, H7200
33:23 back parts: but my face shall not be s. H7200
34: 3 let any man be s throughout all the H7200
Lev 5: 1 whether he hath s or known *of it;* if he H7200
13: 7 that he hath been s of the priest for his H7200
7 he shall be s of the priest again: H7200
Nu 14:14 thou LORD art s face to face, and *that* H7200
22 Because all those men which have s my H7200
23:21 neither hath he s perverseness in H7200
27:13 And when thou hast s it, thou also H7200
Dt 1:28 have s the sons of the Anakims there. H7200
31 where thou hast s how that the LORD H7200
3:21 Thine eyes have s all that the LORD H7200
4: 3 Your eyes have s what the LORD did H7200
9 thine eyes have s, and lest they depart H7200
5:24 of the fire: we have s this day that God H7200
9:13 me, saying, I have s this people, and, H7200
10:21 terrible things, which thine eyes have s. H7200
11: 2 which have not s the chastisement of H7200
7 But your eyes have s all the great acts H7200
16: 4 And there shall be no leavened bread s H7200
21: 7 this blood, neither have our eyes s *it*. H7200
29: 2 them, Ye have s all that the LORD did H7200
3 s, the signs, and those great miracles: H7200
Dt 29:17 And ye have s their abominations, and H7200
33: 9 mother, I have not s him; neither did H7200
Jos 23: 3 And ye have s all that the LORD your H7200
24: 7 your eyes have s what I have done in H7200
Jdg 2: 7 Joshua, who had s all the great works H7200
5: 8 s among forty thousand in Israel? H7200
6:22 s an angel of the LORD face to face. H7200
9:48 What ye have s me do, make haste, H7200
13:22 surely die, because we have s God. H7200
14: 2 and said, I have s a woman in Timnath H7200
18: 9 them: for we have s the land, and, H7200
19:30 deed done nor s from the day that the H7200
1Sa 6:16 the Philistines had s *it*, they returned to H7200
16:18 said, Behold, I have s a son of Jesse the H7200
17:25 And the men of Israel said, Have ye s H7200
23:22 is, *and* who hath s him there: for it is H7200
24:10 Behold, this day thine eyes have s how H7200
2Sa 17:17 for they might not be s to come into the H7200
18:21 what thou hast s. And Cushi bowed H7200
22:11 he was s upon the wings of the wind. H7200
1Ki 6:18 all *was* cedar; there was no stone s. H7200
8: 8 ends of the staves were s out in the holy H7200
8 and they were not s without: and there H7200
10: 4 And when the queen of Sheba had s all H7200
7 mine eyes had s *it:* and, behold, the H7200
12 almug trees, nor were s unto this day. H7200
13:12 For his sons had s what way the man of H7200
20:13 the LORD, Hast thou s all this great H7200
2Ki 9:26 Surely I have s yesterday the blood of H7200
20: 5 thy prayer, I have s thy tears: behold, I H7200
15 And he said, What have they s in thine H7200
15 house have they s: there is nothing H7200
23:29 him at Megiddo, when he had s him. H7200
1Ch 29:17 and now have I s with joy thy people, H7200
2Ch 5: 9 of the staves were s from the ark before H7200
9 s without. And there it is unto this day. H7200
9: 3 And when the queen of Sheba had s the H7200
6 mine eyes had s *it:* and, behold, the H7200
11 such s before in the land of Judah. H7200
Ezr 3:12 men, that had s the first house, when H7200
Est 9:26 *that* which they had s concerning this H7200
Job 4: 8 Even as I have s, they that plow H7200
5: 3 I have s the foolish taking root: but H7200
7: 8 The eye of him that hath s me shall see H7210
8:18 deny him, *saying*, I have not s thee. H7200
10:18 up the ghost, and no eye had s me! H7200
13: 1 Lo, mine eye hath s all *this*, mine ear H7200
15:17 and that *which* I have s I will declare; H2372
20: 7 have s him shall say, Where *is* he? H7200
27:12 Behold, all ye yourselves have s *it*; why H2372
28: 7 and which the vulture's eye hath not s: H7805
31:19 If I have s any perish for want of H7200
33:21 that it cannot be s; and his bones *that* H7210
21 and his bones *that* were not s stick out. H7200
38:17 s the doors of the shadow of death? H7200
22 or hast thou s the treasures of the hail, H7200
Ps 10:14 Thou hast s *it*; for thou beholdest H7200
18:15 Then the channels of waters were s, and H7200
35:21 *and* said, Aha, aha, our eye hath s *it*. H7200
22 *This* thou hast s, O LORD: keep not H7200
37:25 am old; yet have I not s the righteous H7200
35 I have s the wicked in great power, and H7200
48: 8 As we have heard, so have we s in the H7200
54: 7 hath s *his desire* upon mine enemies. H7200
55: 9 I have s violence and strife in the city. H7200
63: 2 so *as* I have s thee in the sanctuary. H2372
68:24 They have s thy goings, O God; *even* H7200
90:15 *and* the years *wherein* we have s evil. H7200
98: 3 earth have s the salvation of our God. H7200
119:96 I have s an end of all perfection: *but* H7200
Prv 25: 7 of the prince whom thine eyes have s. H7200
Ecc 1:14 I have s all the works that are done H7200
3:10 I have s the travail, which God hath H7200
4: 3 who hath not s the evil work that is H7200
5:13 There is a sore evil *which* I have s H7200
18 Behold *that* which I have s: *it is* good H7200
6: 1 There is an evil which I have s under H7200
5 Moreover he hath not s the sun, nor H7200
6 he s no good: do not all go to one place? H7200
7:15 All *things* have I s in the days of my H7200
8: 9 All this have I s, and applied my heart H7200
9:13 This wisdom have I s also under the H7200
10: 5 There is an evil *which* I have s under H7200
7 I have s servants upon horses, and H7200
Isa 6: 5 have s the King, the LORD of hosts. H7200
9: 2 in darkness have s a great light: they H7200
16:12 And it shall come to pass, when it is s H7200
22: 9 Ye have s also the breaches of the city H7200
38: 5 thy prayer, I have s thy tears: behold, I H7200

Isa 39: 4 Then said he, What have they s in thine H7200
4 house have they s: there is nothing H7200
44:16 Aha, I am warm, I have s the fire: H7200
47: 3 yea, thy shame shall be s: I will take H7200
57:18 I have s his ways, and will heal him: I H7200
60: 2 thee, and his glory shall be s upon thee. H7200
64: 4 hath the eye s, O God, beside thee, H7200
66: 8 a thing? who hath s such things? Shall H7200
19 fame, neither have s my glory; and they H7200
Jer 1:12 Thou hast well s: for I will hasten my H7200
3: 6 the king, Hast thou s *that* which H7200
7:11 even I have s *it*, saith the LORD. H7200
12: 3 me: thou hast s me, and tried mine H7200
13:27 I have s thine adulteries, and thy H7200
23:13 And I have s folly in the prophets of H7200
14 I have s also in the prophets of H7200
44: 2 of Israel; Ye have s all the evil that I H7200
46: 5 Wherefore have I s them dismayed *and* H7200
Lam 1: 8 because they have s her nakedness: H7200
10 for she hath s *that* the heathen entered H7200
2:14 Thy prophets have s vain and foolish H2372
14 thy captivity; but have s for thee false H2372
16 looked for; we have found, we have s *it*. H7200
3: 1 I *am* the man *that* hath s affliction by H7200
59 O LORD, thou hast s my wrong: judge H7200
60 Thou hast s all their vengeance *and* all H7200
Ezk 8:12 of man, hast thou s what the ancients H7200
15 Then said he unto me, Hast thou s *this*, H7200
17 Then he said unto me, Hast thou s *this*, H7200
11:24 vision that I had s went up from me. H7200
13: 3 their own spirit, and have s nothing! H7200
6 They have s vanity and lying H2372
7 Have ye not s a vain vision, and have H2372
8 vanity, and s lies, therefore, behold, H2372
47: 6 Son of man, hast thou s *this*? Then he H7200
Dan 2:26 I have s, and the interpretation thereof? H2370
4: 9 I have s, and the interpretation thereof. H2370
18 have s. Now thou, O Belteshazzar, H2370
8: 6 which I had s standing before the H7200
15 I, *even* I Daniel, had s the vision, and H7200
9:21 whom I had s in the vision at the H7200
Hos 6:10 I have s an horrible thing in the house H7200
Zec 9: 8 more: for now have I s with mine eyes. H7200
14 And the LORD shall be s over them, H7200
10: 2 the diviners have s a lie, and have told H2372
Mt 2: 2 Jews? for we have s his star in the east, G1492
6: 1 before men, to be s of them: otherwise G2300
5 that they may be s of men. Verily I say G5316
9:33 saying, It was never so s in Israel. G5316
13:17 see, and have not s *them*; and to hear G1492
21:32 and ye, when ye had s *it*, repented not G1492
23: 5 But all their works they do for to be s of G2300
Mk 9: 1 till they have s the kingdom of God G1492
9 things they had s, till the Son of man G1492
16:11 and had been s of her, believed not. G2300
14 which had s him after he was risen. G2300
Lk 1:22 that he had s a vision in the temple: G3708
2:17 And when they had s *it*, they made G1492
20 heard and s, as it was told unto them. G1492
26 before he had s the Lord's Christ. G1492
30 For mine eyes have s thy salvation, G1492
5:26 We have s strange things to day. G1492
7:22 things ye have s and heard; how that G1492
9:36 any of those things which they had s. G3708
10:24 see, and have not s *them*; and to hear G1492
19:37 for all the mighty works that they had s; G1492
23: 8 to have s some miracle done by him. G1492
24:23 that they had also s a vision of angels, G3708
37 and supposed that they had s a spirit. G2334
Jn 1:18 No man hath s God at any time; the G3708
3:11 have s; and ye receive not our witness. G3708
32 And what he hath s and heard, that he G3708
4:45 him, having s all the things that he G3708
5:37 his voice at any time, nor s his shape. G3708
6:14 Then those men, when they had s the G1492
36 But I said unto you, That ye also have s G3708
46 Not that any man hath s the Father, G3708
46 which is of God, he hath s the Father. G3708
8:38 I speak that which I have s with my G3708
38 that which ye have s with your father. G3708
57 years old, and hast thou s Abraham? G3708
9: 8 which before had s him that he was G2334
37 Thou hast both s him, and it is he that G3708
11:45 to Mary, and had s the things which G2300
14: 7 ye know him, and have s him. G3708
9 he that hath s me hath seen the Father; G3708
9 hath seen me hath s the Father; and G3708
15:24 s and hated both me and my Father. G3708
20:18 that she had s the Lord, and *that* he G3708
Jn 20:25 him, We have s the Lord. But he said G3708
29 because thou hast s me, thou hast G3708
29 that have not s, and *yet* have believed. G1492
Act 1: 3 proofs, being s of them forty days, G3700
11 as ye have s him go into heaven. G2300
4:20 the things which we have s and heard. G1492
7:34 I have s, I have seen the affliction of my G1492
34 I have seen, I have s the affliction of my G1492
44 according to the fashion that he had s. G3708
9:12 And hath s in a vision a man named G1492
27 them how he had s the Lord in the way, G1492
10:17 which he had s should mean, behold, G1492
11:13 And he shewed us how he had s an G1492
23 Who, when he came, and had s the G1492
13:31 And he was s many days of them which G3700
16:10 And after he had s the vision, G1492
40 and when they had s the brethren, they G1492
21:29 (For they had s before with him in the G4308
22:15 all men of what thou hast s and heard. G3708
26:16 which thou hast s, and of those things G1492
Ro 1:20 world are clearly s, being understood by G2529
8:24 but hope that is s is not hope: for what G991
1Co 2: 9 But as it is written, Eye hath not s, nor G1492
9: 1 free? have I not s Jesus Christ our Lord? G3708
15: 5 And that he was s of Cephas, then of G3700
6 After that, he was s of above five G3700
7 After that, he was s of James; then of G3700
8 And last of all he was s of me also, as of G3700
2Co 4:18 the things which are s, but at the things G991
18 which are not s: for the things which G991
18 things which are s *are* temporal; but the G991
18 the things which are not s *are* eternal. G991
Php 4: 9 and heard, and s in me, do: and the G1492
Col 2: 1 as have not s my face in the flesh; G3708
18 s, vainly puffed up by his fleshly mind, G3708
1Ti 3:16 in the Spirit, s of angels, preached G3700
6:16 no man hath s, nor can see: to whom G1492
Heb 11: 1 hoped for, the evidence of things not s. G991
3 that things which are s were not made of G991
7 of God of things not s as yet, moved with G991
13 but having s them afar off, and were G1492
Jas 5:11 of Job, and have s the end of the Lord; G1492
1Pt 1: 8 Whom having not s, ye love; in whom, G1492
1Jn 1: 1 which we have s with our eyes, which G3708
2 and we have s *it*, and bear witness, G3708
3 That which we have s and heard G3708
3: 6 hath not s him, neither known him. G3708
4:12 No man hath s God at any time. If we G2300
14 And we have s and do testify that the G2300
20 whom he hath s, how can he love God G3708
20 can he love God whom he hath not s? G3708
3Jn 11 but he that doeth evil hath not s God. G3708
Rev 1:19 Write the things which thou hast s, and G1492
11:19 and there was s in his temple the ark G3700
22: 8 I had heard and s, I fell down to worship G991

SEER

1Sa 9: 9 and let us go to the s: for *he that is* now H7200
9 a Prophet was beforetime called a S.) H7200
11 and said unto them, Is the s here? H7200
19 and said, I *am* the s: go up before me H7200
2Sa 15:27 *Art not* thou a s? return into the city H7200
24:11 unto the prophet Gad, David's s, saying, H2374
1Ch 9:22 the s did ordain in their set office. H7200
21: 9 spake unto Gad, David's s, saying, H2374
25: 5 of Heman the king's s in the words of H2374
26:28 And all that Samuel the s, and Saul the H7200
29:29 book of Samuel the s, and in the book of H7200
29 prophet, and in the book of Gad the s, H2374
2Ch 9:29 s against Jeroboam the son of Nebat? H2374
12:15 prophet, and of Iddo the s concerning H2374
16: 7 And at that time Hanani the s came to H7200
10 Then Asa was wroth with the s, and put H7200
19: 2 And Jehu the son of Hanani the s went H2374
29:25 and of Gad the king's s, and Nathan the H2374
30 and of Asaph the s. And they sang H2374
35:15 the king's s; and the porters *waited* H2374
Am 7:12 Amos, O thou s, go, flee thee away into H2374

SEERS

2Ki 17:13 *and by* all the s, saying, Turn ye from H2374
2Ch 33:18 the words of the s that spake to him in H2374
19 *are* written among the sayings of the s. H2374
Isa 29:10 and your rulers, the s hath he covered. H2374
30:10 Which say to the s, See not; and to the H7200
Mic 3: 7 Then shall the s be ashamed, and the H2374

SEER'S

1Sa 9:18 me, I pray thee, where the s house *is*. H7200

SEEST

Gen 13:15 For all the land which thou s, to thee H7200
16:13 her, Thou God s me: for she said, Have H7210
31:43 and all that thou s *is* mine: and what H7200
Ex 10:28 *that* day thou s my face thou shalt die. H7200
Dt 4:19 and when thou s the sun, and the H7200
12:13 offerings in every place that thou s: H7200
20: 1 enemies, and s horses, and chariots, H7200
21:11 And s among the captives a beautiful H7200
Jdg 9:36 unto him, Thou s the shadow of the H7200
1Ki 21:29 S thou how Ahab humbleth himself H7200
Job 10: 4 Hast thou eyes of flesh? or s thou as H7200
Prv 22:29 S thou a man diligent in his business? H2372
26:12 S thou a man wise in his own conceit? H7200
29:20 S thou a man *that is* hasty in his H2372
Ecc 5: 8 If thou s the oppression of the poor, H7200
Isa 58: 3 *say they*, and thou s not? *wherefore* H7200
7 thy house? when thou s the naked, that H7200
Jer 1:11 Jeremiah, what s thou? And I said, I see H7200
13 saying, What s thou? And I said, I see H7200
7:17 S thou not what they do in the cities of H7200
20:12 the righteous, *and* s the reins and the H7200
24: 3 Then said the LORD unto me, What s H7200
32:24 is come to pass; and, behold, thou s *it*. H7200
Ezk 8: 6 me, Son of man, s thou what they do? H7200
40: 4 all that thou s to the house of Israel. H7200
Dan 1:13 and as thou s, deal with thy servants. H7200
Am 7: 8 me, Amos, what s thou? And I said, A H7200
8: 2 And he said, Amos, what s thou? And I H7200
Zec 4: 2 And said unto me, What s thou? And I H7200
5: 2 And he said unto me, What s thou? H7200
Mk 5:31 And his disciples said unto him, Thou s G991
13: 2 And Jesus answering said unto him, S G991
Lk 7:44 said unto Simon, S thou this woman? I G991
Act 21:20 unto him, Thou s, brother, how many G2334
Jas 2:22 S thou how faith wrought with his G991
Rev 1:11 and, What thou s, write in a book, and G991

SEETH

Gen 16:13 I also here looked after him that s me? H7210
44:31 It shall come to pass, when he s that H7200
Ex 4:14 he s thee, he will be glad in his heart. H7200
12:23 and when he s the blood upon the H7200
Lev 13:20 And if, when the priest s it, behold, it H7200
Dt 32:36 servants, when he s that *their* power is H7200
1Sa 16: 7 him: for *the LORD* s not as man seeth;
7 *seeth* not as man s; for man looketh on H7200
2Ki 2:19 as my lord s: but the water *is* naught, H7200
Job 8:17 the heap, *and* s the place of stones. H2372
10: 4 eyes of flesh? or seest thou as man s? H7200
11:11 For he knoweth vain men: he s H7200
22:14 to him, that he s not; and he walketh H7200
28:10 and his eye s every precious thing. H7200
24 earth, *and* s under the whole heaven; H7200
34:21 ways of man, and he s all his goings. H7200
42: 5 of the ear: but now mine eye s thee. H7200
Ps 37:13 The Lord shall laugh at him: for he s H7200
49:10 For he s *that* wise men die, likewise the H7200
58:10 The righteous shall rejoice when he s H2372
Ecc 8:16 day nor night s sleep with his eyes:) H7200
Isa 21: 6 a watchman, let him declare what he s. H7200
28: 4 looketh upon it s, while it is yet in his H7200
29:15 say, Who s us? and who knoweth us? H7200
23 But when he s his children, the work of H7200
47:10 hast said, None s me. Thy wisdom and H7200
Ezk 8:12 say, The LORD s us not; the LORD hath H7200
9: 9 the earth, and the LORD s not. H7200
12:27 The vision that he s *is* for many days *to* H2372
18:14 Now, lo, *if* he beget a son, that s all his H7200
33: 3 If when he s the sword come upon the H7200
39:15 land, when *any* s a man's bone, then H7200
Mt 6: 4 thy Father which s in secret himself shall G991
6 s in secret shall reward thee openly. G991
18 s in secret, shall reward thee openly. G991
Mk 5:38 synagogue, and s the tumult, and them G2334
Lk 16:23 in torments, and s Abraham afar off, G3708
Jn 1:29 The next day John s Jesus coming unto G991
5:19 but what he s the Father do: for what G991
6:40 that every one which s the Son, and G2334
9:21 But by what means he now s, we know G991
10:12 the sheep are not, s the wolf coming, G2334
11: 9 not, because he s the light of this world. G991
12:45 And he that s me seeth him that sent G2334
45 And he that seeth me s him that sent G2334
14:17 receive, because it s him not, neither G2334
19 Yet a little while, and the world s me no G2334
20: 1 the sepulchre, and s the stone taken G991
6 sepulchre, and s the linen clothes lie, G2334
12 And s two angels in white sitting, the G2334

Jn 21:20 Then Peter, turning about, s the disciple *G991*
Ro 8:24 what a man s, why doth he yet hope for? *G991*
2Co 12: 6 he s me *to be*, or *that* he heareth of me. *G991*
1Jn 3:17 world's good, and s his brother have *G2334*

SEETHE
Ex 16:23 bake *to day*, and s that ye will seethe; H1310
23 and seethe that ye will s; and that which H1310
23:19 shalt not s a kid in his mother's milk. H1310
29:31 and s his flesh in the holy place. H1310
34:26 shalt not s a kid in his mother's milk. H1310
Dt 14:21 shalt not s a kid in his mother's milk. H1310
2Ki 4:38 s pottage for the sons of the prophets. H1310
Ezk 24: 5 and let them s the bones of it therein. H1310
Zec 14:21 take of them, and s therein: and in that H1310

SEETHED See SOD.

SEETHING
1Sa 2:13 the flesh was in s, with a fleshhook of H1310
Job 41:20 smoke, as *out* of a s pot or caldron. H5301
Jer 1:13 And I said, I see a s pot; and the face H5301

SEGUB
1Ki 16:34 in his youngest *son* S, according to the H7687
1Ch 2:21 years old; and she bare him S. H7687
22 And S begat Jair, who had three and H7687

SEIR
Gen 14: 6 And the Horites in their mount S, unto H8165
32: 3 unto the land of S, the country of Edom. H8165
33:14 until I come unto my lord unto S. H8165
16 returned that day on his way unto S. H8165
36: 8 Thus dwelt Esau in mount S: Esau *is* H8165
9 the father of the Edomites in mount S: H8165
20 These *are* the sons of S the Horite, who H8165
21 the children of S in the land of Edom. H8165
30 among their dukes in the land of S. H8165
Nu 24:18 And Edom shall be a possession, S also H8165
Dt 1: 2 way of mount S unto Kadesh-barnea.) H8165
44 destroyed you in S, *even* unto Hormah. H8165
2: 1 we compassed mount S many days. H8165
4 which dwell in S; and they shall be H8165
5 mount S unto Esau *for* a possession. H8165
8 which dwelt in S, through the way of H8165
12 The Horims also dwelt in S beforetime; H8165
22 which dwelt in S, when he destroyed H8165
29 which dwell in S, and the Moabites H8165
33: 2 and rose up from S unto them; he H8165
Jos 11:17 that goeth up to S, even unto Baal-gad H8165
12: 7 that goeth up to S; which Joshua gave H8165
15:10 unto mount S, and passed along unto H8165
24: 4 unto Esau mount S, to possess it; but H8165
Jdg 5: 4 LORD, when thou wentest out of S, H8165
1Ch 1:38 And the sons of S; Lotan, and Shobal, H8165
4:42 men, went to mount S, having for their H8165
2Ch 20:10 and Moab and mount S, whom thou H8165
22 Moab, and mount S, which were come H8165
23 of mount S, utterly to slay and destroy H8165
23 S, every one helped to destroy another. H8165
25:11 of the children of S ten thousand. H8165
14 of the children of S, and set them up *to* H8165
Isa 21:11 to me out of S, Watchman, what of H8165
Ezk 25: 8 that Moab and S do say, Behold, the H8165
35: 2 mount S, and prophesy against it, H8165
3 Behold, O mount S, I *am* against thee, H8165
7 Thus will I make mount S most H8165
15 be desolate, O mount S, and all Idumea, H8165

SEIRATH
Jdg 3:26 the quarries, and escaped unto S. H8167

SEIZE
Jos 8: 7 the ambush, and s upon the city: for H3423
Job 3: 6 As *for* that night, let darkness s upon H3947
Ps 55:15 Let death s upon them, *and* let them go H3451
Mt 21:38 kill him, and let us s on his inheritance. *G2722*

SEIZED
Jer 49:24 to flee, and fear hath s on *her*: anguish H2388

SELA
Isa 16: 1 of the land from S to the wilderness, H5554

SELAH
2Ki 14: 7 and took S by war, and called the H5554
Ps 3: 2 soul, *There is* no help for him in God. S. H5542
4 and he heard me out of his holy hill. S. H5542
8 thy blessing *is* upon thy people. S. H5542
Ps 4: 2 ye love vanity, *and* seek after leasing? S. H5542
4 heart upon your bed, and be still. S. H5542
7: 5 and lay mine honour in the dust. S. H5542
9:16 the work of his own hands. Higgaion. S. H5542
20 may know themselves *to be but* men. S. H5542
20: 3 and accept thy burnt sacrifice; S. H5542
21: 2 not withholden the request of his lips. S. H5542
24: 6 seek him, that seek thy face, O Jacob. S. H5542
10 of hosts, he *is* the King of glory. S. H5542
32: 4 turned into the drought of summer. S. H5542
5 thou forgavest the iniquity of my sin. S. H5542
7 me about with songs of deliverance. S. H5542
39: 5 at his best state *is* altogether vanity. S. H5542
11 a moth: surely every man *is* vanity. S. H5542
44: 8 long, and praise thy name for ever. S. H5542
46: 3 shake with the swelling thereof. S. H5542
7 us; the God of Jacob *is* our refuge. S. H5542
11 us; the God of Jacob *is* our refuge. S. H5542
47: 4 excellency of Jacob whom he loved. S. H5542
48: 8 God: God will establish it for ever. S. H5542
49:13 their posterity approve their sayings. S. H5542
15 of the grave: for he shall receive me. S. H5542
50: 6 for God *is* judge himself. S. H5542
52: 3 rather than to speak righteousness. S. H5542
5 root thee out of the land of the living. S. H5542
54: 3 they have not set God before them. S. H5542
55: 7 far off, *and* remain in the wilderness. S. H5542
19 abideth of old. S. Because they have no H5542
57: 3 swallow me up. S. God shall send forth H5542
6 whereof they are fallen *themselves*. S. H5542
59: 5 merciful to any wicked transgressors. S. H5542
13 in Jacob unto the ends of the earth. S. H5542
60: 4 be displayed because of the truth. S. H5542
61: 4 I will trust in the covert of thy wings. S. H5542
62: 4 their mouth, but they curse inwardly. S. H5542
8 before him: God *is* a refuge for us. S. H5542
66: 4 thee; they shall sing *to* thy name. S. H5542
7 not the rebellious exalt themselves. S. H5542
15 rams; I will offer bullocks with goats. S. H5542
67: 1 *and* cause his face to shine upon us; S. H5542
4 and govern the nations upon earth. S. H5542
68: 7 didst march through the wilderness; S: H5542
19 *even* the God of our salvation. S. H5542
32 earth; O sing praises unto the Lord; S: H5542
75: 3 dissolved: I bear up the pillars of it. S. H5542
76: 3 shield, and the sword, and the battle. S. H5542
9 to save all the meek of the earth. S. H5542
77: 3 and my spirit was overwhelmed. S. H5542
9 in anger shut up his tender mercies? S. H5542
15 people, the sons of Jacob and Joseph. S. H5542
81: 7 proved thee at the waters of Meribah. S. H5542
82: 2 and accept the persons of the wicked? S. H5542
83: 8 they have holpen the children of Lot. S. H5542
84: 4 house: they will be still praising thee. S. H5542
8 my prayer: give ear, O God of Jacob. S. H5542
85: 2 thou hast covered all their sin. S. H5542
87: 3 are spoken of thee, O city of God. S. H5542
6 people, *that* this *man* was born there. S. H5542
88: 7 hast afflicted *me* with all thy waves. S. H5542
10 shall the dead arise *and* praise thee? S. H5542
89: 4 up thy throne to all generations. S. H5542
37 and *as* a faithful witness in heaven. S. H5542
45 thou hast covered him with shame. S. H5542
48 his soul from the hand of the grave? S. H5542
140: 3 adders' poison *is* under their lips. S. H5542
5 wayside; they have set gins for me. S. H5542
8 device; *lest* they exalt themselves. S. H5542
143: 6 *thirsteth* after thee, as a thirsty land. S. H5542
Hab 3: 3 mount Paran. S. His glory covered the H5542
9 *even thy* word. S. Thou didst cleave the H5542
13 the foundation unto the neck. S. H5542

SELA-HAMMAHLEKOTH
1Sa 23:28 therefore they called that place S.

SELED
1Ch 2:30 And the sons of Nadab; S, and Appaim: H5540
30 Appaim: but S died without children. H5540

SELEUCIA
Act 13: 4 departed unto S; and from thence they *G4581*

SELF
Ex 32:13 by thine own s, and saidst unto them,
Jn 5:30 I can of mine own s do nothing: as I *G1683*
17: 5 me with thine own s with the glory *G4572*
1Co 4: 3 judgment: yea, I judge not mine own s. *G1683*
Phlm 19 unto me even thine own s besides. *G4572*
1Pt 2:24 Who his own s bare our sins in his own *G846*

SELFSAME
Gen 7:13 In the s day entered Noah, and H6106+H2088
17:23 foreskin in the s day, as God H6106+H2088
26 In the s day was Abraham H6106+H2088
Ex 12:17 for in this s day have I brought H6106+H2088
41 even the s day it came to pass, H6106+H2088
51 And it came to pass the s day, H6106+H2088
Lev 23:14 ears, until the s day that ye H6106+H2088
21 And ye shall proclaim on the s H6106+H2088
Dt 32:48 unto Moses that s day, saying, H6106+H2088
Jos 5:11 and parched *corn* in the s day. H6106+H2088
Ezk 40: 1 smitten, in the s day the hand H6106+H2088
Mt 8:13 his servant was healed in the s hour. *G1565*
1Co 12:11 But all these worketh that one and the s *G846*
2Co 5: 5 us for the s thing *is* God, who *G846+G5124*
7:11 For behold this s thing, that ye sorrowed *G846*

SELFWILL
Gen 49: 6 and in their s they digged down a wall. H7522

SELFWILLED
Tit 1: 7 of God; not s, not soon angry, not *G829*
2Pt 2:10 *are they*, s, they are not afraid to *G829*

SELL
Gen 25:31 And Jacob said, S me this day thy H4376
37:27 Come, and let us s him to the H4376
Ex 21: 7 And if a man s his daughter to be a H4376
8 be redeemed: to s her unto a strange H4376
35 then they shall s the live ox, and divide H4376
22: 1 and kill it, or s it; he shall restore five H4376
Lev 25:14 And if thou s ought unto thy H4376
15 years of the fruits he shall s unto thee: H4376
16 *years* of the fruits doth he s unto thee. H4376
29 And if a man s a dwelling house in a H4376
47 him wax poor, and s himself unto the H4376
Dt 2:28 Thou shalt s me meat for money, that I H7666
14:21 it; or thou mayest s it unto an alien: for H4376
21:14 will; but thou shalt not s her at all for H4376
Jdg 4: 9 for the LORD shall s Sisera into the H4376
1Ki 21:25 unto Ahab, which did s himself to work H4376
2Ki 4: 7 And he said, Go, s the oil, and pay thy H4376
Neh 5: 8 and will ye even s your brethren? or H4376
10:31 the sabbath day to s, *that* we would not H4376
Prv 23:23 Buy the truth, and s *it* not; *also* H4376
Ezk 30:12 And I will make the rivers dry, and s H4376
48:14 And they shall not s of it, neither H4376
Joel 3: 8 And I will s your sons and your H4376
8 and they shall s them to the Sabeans, H4376
Am 8: 5 be gone, that we may s corn? and the H7666
6 *yea*, and s the refuse of the wheat? H7666
Zec 11: 5 and they that s them say, Blessed *be* H4376
Mt 19:21 be perfect, go *and* s that thou hast, and *G4453*
25: 9 to them that s, and buy for yourselves. *G4453*
Mk 10:21 go thy way, s whatsoever thou hast, *G4453*
Lk 12:33 S that ye have, and give alms; provide *G4453*
18:22 thou one thing: s all that thou hast, and *G4453*
22:36 let him s his garment, and buy one. *G4453*
Jas 4:13 a year, and buy and s, and get gain: *G1710*
Rev 13:17 And that no man might buy or s, save *G4453*

SELLER
Isa 24: 2 buyer, so with the s; as with the lender, H4376
Ezk 7:12 rejoice, nor the s mourn: for wrath *is* H4376
13 For the s shall not return to that which H4376
Act 16:14 And a certain woman named Lydia, a s *G4211*

SELLERS
Neh 13:20 So the merchants and s of all kind of H4376

SELLEST
Ps 44:12 Thou s thy people for nought, and dost H4376

SELLETH
Ex 21:16 And he that stealeth a man, and s him, H4376
Dt 24: 7 of him, or s him; then that thief H4376
Ru 4: 3 the country of Moab, s a parcel of land, H4376
Prv 11:26 *shall be* upon the head of him that s *it*. H7666
31:24 She maketh fine linen, and s *it*; and H4376
Nah 3: 4 witchcrafts, that s nations through her H4376
Mt 13:44 s all that he hath, and buyeth that field. *G4453*

SELVEDGE
Ex 26: 4 curtain from the s in the coupling; and H7098
36:11 one curtain from the s in the coupling: H7098

SELVES
Lk 21:30 s that summer is now nigh at hand. *G1438*
Act 20:30 Also of your own s shall men arise, *G846*

2Co 8: 5 gave their own s to the Lord, and unto *G1438*
13: 5 prove your own s. Know ye not your *G1438*
5 ye not your own s, how that Jesus Christ *G1438*
2Ti 3: 2 For men shall be lovers of their own s, *G5367*
Jas 1:22 not hearers only, deceiving your own s. *G1438*

SEM
Lk 3:36 was *the son* of S, which was *the son* of *G4590*

SEMACHIAH
1Ch 26: 7 brethren *were* strong men, Elihu, and S. H5565

SEMBLANCE See RESEMBLANCE.

SEMEI
Lk 3:26 was *the son* of S, which was *the son* of *G4584*

SENAAH
Ezr 2:35 The children of S, three thousand and H5570
Neh 7:38 The children of S, three thousand nine H5570

SENATE
Act 5:21 and all the s of the children of Israel, *G1087*

SENATORS
Ps 105:22 his pleasure; and teach his s wisdom. H2205

SEND
Gen 24: 7 this land; he shall s his angel before H7971
12 I pray thee, s me good speed this H7136
40 whom I walk, will s his angel with thee, H7971
54 he said, S me away unto my master. H7971
56 s me away that I may go to my master. H7971
27:45 to him: then I will s, and fetch thee from H7971
30:25 said unto Laban, S me away, that I H7971
37:13 come, and I will s thee unto them. And H7971
38:17 And he said, I will s *thee* a kid from the H7971
17 thou give *me* a pledge, till thou s *it*? H7971
42:16 S one of you, and let him fetch your H7971
43: 4 If thou wilt s our brother with us, we H7971
5 But if thou wilt not s *him*, we will not H7971
8 And Judah said unto Israel his father, S H7971
14 man, that he may s away your other H7971
45: 5 did s me before you to preserve life. H7971
Ex 3:10 Come now therefore, and I will s thee H7971
4:13 And he said, O my Lord, s, I pray thee, H7971
13 by the hand *of him whom* thou wilt s. H7971
7: 2 s the children of Israel out of his land. H7971
8:21 go, behold, I will s swarms *of flies* upon H7971
9:14 For I will at this time s all my plagues H7971
19 S therefore now, *and* gather thy cattle, H7971
12:33 that they might s them out of the land H7971
23:20 Behold, I s an Angel before thee, to H7971
27 I will s my fear before thee, and will H7971
28 And I will s hornets before thee, which H7971
33: 2 And I will s an angel before thee; and I H7971
12 whom thou wilt s with me. Yet thou H7971
Lev 16:21 of the goat, and shall s *him* away by the H7971
26:22 I will also s wild beasts among you, H7971
25 within your cities, I will s the pestilence H7971
36 *alive* of you I will s a faintness into their H935
Nu 13: 2 S thou men, that they may search the H7971
2 fathers shall ye s a man, every one a H7971
22:37 Did I not earnestly s unto thee to call H7971
31: 4 tribes of Israel, shall ye s to the war. H7971
Dt 1:22 and said, We will s men before us, and H7971
7:20 Moreover the LORD thy God will s the H7971
11:15 And I will s grass in thy fields for thy H5414
19:12 Then the elders of his city shall s and H7971
24: 1 in her hand, and s her out of his house. H7971
28:20 The LORD shall s upon thee cursing, H7971
48 which the LORD shall s against thee, in H7971
32:24 I will also s the teeth of beasts upon H7971
Jos 18: 4 tribe: and I will s them, and they shall H7971
Jdg 13: 8 which thou didst s come again unto us, H7971
1Sa 5:11 and said, S away the ark of the H7971
6: 2 us wherewith we shall s it to his place. H7971
3 And they said, If ye s away the ark of H7971
3 the God of Israel, s it not empty; but in H7971
8 thereof; and s it away, that it may go. H7971
9:16 To morrow about this time I will s thee H7971
26 Up, that I may s thee away. And Saul H7971
11: 3 that we may s messengers unto all H7971
12:17 and he shall s thunder and rain; that H5414
16: 1 oil, and go, I will s thee to Jesse the H7971
11 said unto Jesse, S and fetch him: for we H7971
19 Jesse, and said, S me David thy son, H7971
20:12 I then s not unto thee, and shew it thee; H7971
13 shew it thee, and s thee away, that thou H7971
1Sa 20:21 And, behold, I will s a lad, *saying*, Go, H7971
31 Wherefore now s and fetch him unto H7971
21: 2 whereabout I s thee, and what I have H7971
25:25 men of my lord, whom thou didst s. H7971
2Sa 11: 6 And David sent to Joab, *saying*, S me H7971
14:32 hither, that I may s thee to the king, to H7971
15:36 s unto me every thing that ye can hear. H7971
17:16 Now therefore s quickly, and tell H7971
1Ki 8:44 thou shalt s them, and shall pray H7971
18: 1 Ahab; and I will s rain upon the earth. H5414
19 Now therefore s, *and* gather to me all H7971
20: 6 Yet I will s my servants unto thee to H7971
9 All that thou didst s for to thy servant H7971
34 *said Ahab*, I will s thee away with this H7971
2Ki 2:16 some valley. And he said, Ye shall not s. H7971
17 was ashamed, he said, S. They sent H7971
4:22 and said, S me, I pray thee, one H7971
5: 5 to, go, and I will s a letter unto the king H7971
7 alive, that this man doth s unto me to H7971
6:13 he *is*, that I may s and fetch him. And H7971
7:13 are consumed:) and let us s and see. H7971
9:17 an horseman, and s to meet them, and H7971
15:37 In those days the LORD began to s H7971
19: 7 Behold, I will s a blast upon him, and H5414
1Ch 13: 2 our God, let us s abroad unto our H7971
2Ch 2: 3 father, and didst s him cedars to build H7971
7 S me now therefore a man cunning to H7971
8 S me also cedar trees, fir trees, and H7971
15 spoken of, let him s unto his servants: H7971
6:27 should walk; and s rain upon thy land, H5414
34 that thou shalt s them, and they pray H7971
7:13 or if I s pestilence among my people; H7971
28:16 At that time did king Ahaz s unto the H7971
32: 9 king of Assyria s his servants to H7971
Ezr 5:17 and let the king s his pleasure to us H7972
Neh 2: 5 thou wouldest s me unto Judah, unto H7971
6 the king to s me; and I set him a time. H7971
8:10 the sweet, and s portions unto them H7971
12 and to drink, and to s portions, and to H7971
Job 21:11 They s forth their little ones like a flock, H7971
38:35 Canst thou s lightnings, that they may H7971
Ps 20: 2 S thee help from the sanctuary, and H7971
43: 3 O s out thy light and thy truth: let them H7971
57: 3 He shall s from heaven, and save me H7971
3 shall s forth his mercy and his truth. H7971
68: 9 Thou, O God, didst s a plentiful rain, H5130
33 s out his voice, *and that* a mighty voice. H5414
110: 2 The LORD shall s the rod of thy H7971
118:25 LORD, I beseech thee, s now prosperity.
144: 7 S thine hand from above; rid me, and H7971
Prv 10:26 so *is* the sluggard to them that s him. H7971
22:21 words of truth to them that s unto thee? H7971
25:13 to them that s him: for he refresheth H7971
Ecc 10: 1 of the apothecary to s forth a stinking H5042
Isa 6: 8 Whom shall I s, and who will go for H7971
8 go for us? Then said I, Here *am* I; s me. H7971
10: 6 I will s him against an hypocritical H7971
16 the Lord of hosts, s among his fat ones H7971
16: 1 S ye the lamb to the ruler of the land H7971
19:20 and he shall s them a saviour, and H7971
32:20 all waters, that s forth *thither* the feet H7971
37: 7 Behold, I will s a blast upon him, and H5414
57: 9 and didst s thy messengers far H7971
66:19 them, and I will s those that escape of H7971
Jer 1: 7 go to all that I shall s thee, and H7971
2:10 and see; and s unto Kedar, and H7971
8:17 For, behold, I will s serpents, H7971
9:16 known: and I will s a sword after them, H7971
17 may come; and s for cunning *women*, H7971
16:16 Behold, I will s for many fishers, saith H7971
16 and after will I s for many hunters, and H7971
24:10 And I will s the sword, the famine, and H7971
25: 9 Behold, I will s and take all the families H7971
15 nations, to whom I s thee, to drink it. H7971
16 of the sword that I will s among them. H7971
27 of the sword which I will s among you. H7971
27: 3 And s them to the king of Edom, and to H7971
29:17 Behold, I will s upon them the sword, H7971
31 S to all them of the captivity, saying, H7971
42: 5 the LORD thy God shall s thee to us. H7971
6 God, to whom we s thee; that it may be H7971
43:10 Israel; Behold, I will s and take H7971
48:12 the LORD, that I will s unto him H7971
49:37 the LORD; and I will s the sword after H7971
51: 2 And will s unto Babylon fanners, that H7971
Ezk 2: 3 And he said unto me, Son of man, I s H7971
4 stiffhearted. I do s thee unto them; and H7971
5:16 When I shall s upon them the evil H7971
16 *and* which I will s to destroy you: and H7971
Ezk 5:17 So will I s upon you famine and evil H7971
7: 3 thee, and I will s mine anger upon thee, H7971
14:13 thereof, and will s famine upon it, and H7971
19 Or *if* I s a pestilence into that land, and H7971
21 more when I s my four sore judgments H7971
28:23 For I will s into her pestilence, and H7971
39: 6 And I will s a fire on Magog, and H7971
Hos 8:14 cities: but I will s a fire upon his cities, H7971
Joel 2:19 Behold, I will s you corn, and wine, H7971
Am 1: 4 But I will s a fire into the house of H7971
7 But I will s a fire on the wall of Gaza, H7971
10 But I will s a fire on the wall of Tyrus, H7971
12 But I will s a fire upon Teman, which H7971
2: 2 But I will s a fire upon Moab, and it H7971
5 But I will s a fire upon Judah, and it H7971
8:11 GOD, that I will s a famine in the land, H7971
Mal 2: 2 of hosts, I will even s a curse upon you, H7971
3: 1 Behold, I will s my messenger, and he H7971
4: 5 Behold, I will s you Elijah the prophet H7971
Mt 9:38 will s forth labourers into his harvest. *G1544*
10:16 Behold, I s you forth as sheep in the *G649*
34 Think not that I am come to s peace on *G906*
34 I came not to s peace, but a sword. *G906*
11:10 written, Behold, I s my messenger before *G649*
12:20 till he s forth judgment unto victory. *G1544*
13:41 The Son of man shall s forth his angels, *G649*
14:15 time is now past; s the multitude away, *G630*
15:23 S her away; for she crieth after us. *G630*
32 eat: and I will not s them away fasting, *G630*
21: 3 of them; and straightway he will s them. *G649*
23:34 Wherefore, behold, I s unto you *G649*
24:31 And he shall s his angels with a great *G649*
Mk 1: 2 the prophets, Behold, I s my messenger *G649*
3:14 that he might s them forth to preach, *G649*
5:10 not s them away out of the country. *G649*
12 him, saying, S us into the swine, that *G3992*
6: 7 and began to s them forth by two and *G649*
36 S them away, that they may go into the *G630*
8: 3 And if I s them away fasting to their own *G630*
11: 3 and straightway he will s him hither. *G649*
12:13 And they s unto him certain of the *G649*
13:27 And then shall he s his angels, and shall *G649*
Lk 7:27 written, Behold, I s my messenger before *G649*
9:12 and said unto him, S the multitude *G630*
10: 2 s forth labourers into his harvest. *G1544*
3 Go your ways: behold, I s you forth as *G649*
11:49 of God, I will s them prophets and *G649*
12:49 I am come to s fire on the earth; and *G906*
16:24 mercy on me, and s Lazarus, that he *G3992*
27 wouldest s him to my father's house: *G3992*
20:13 shall I do? I will s my beloved son: it *G3992*
24:49 And, behold, I s the promise of my *G649*
Jn 13:20 whomsoever I s receiveth me; and he *G3992*
14:26 the Father will s in my name, he shall *G3992*
15:26 come, whom I will s unto you from the *G3992*
16: 7 but if I depart, I will s him unto you. *G3992*
17: 8 they have believed that thou didst s me. *G649*
20:21 Father hath sent me, even so s I you. *G3992*
Act 3:20 And he shall s Jesus Christ, which before *G649*
7:34 And now come, I will s thee into Egypt. *G649*
35 the same did God s *to be* a ruler and a *G649*
10: 5 And now s men to Joppa, and call for *G3992*
22 by an holy angel to s for thee into his *G3343*
32 S therefore to Joppa, and call hither *G3992*
11:13 and said unto him, S men to Joppa, and *G649*
29 determined to s relief unto the brethren *G3992*
15:22 whole church, to s chosen men of their *G3992*
23 elders and brethren *s* greeting unto the *G3992*
25 one accord, to s chosen men unto you *G3992*
22:21 I will s thee far hence unto the Gentiles. *G1821*
25: 3 that he would s for him to Jerusalem, *G3343*
21 to be kept till I might s him to Caesar. *G3992*
25 Augustus, I have determined to s him. *G3992*
27 For it seemeth to me unreasonable to s *G3992*
26:17 the Gentiles, unto whom now I s thee, *G649*
1Co 16: 3 *your* letters, them will I s to bring your *G3992*
Php 2:19 But I trust in the Lord Jesus to s *G3992*
23 Him therefore I hope to s presently, so *G3992*
25 Yet I supposed it necessary to s to you *G3992*
2Th 2:11 And for this cause God shall s them *G3992*
Tit 3:12 When I shall s Artemas unto thee, or *G3992*
Jas 3:11 Doth a fountain s forth at the same *G1032*
Rev 1:11 write in a book, and s *it* unto the seven *G3992*
11:10 merry, and shall s gifts one to another; *G3992*

SENDEST
Dt 15:13 And when thou s him out free from H7971
18 thee, when thou s him away free from H7971
Jos 1:16 whithersoever thou s us, we will go. H7971

S

2Ki 1: 6 God in Israel, *that* thou s to inquire of H7971
Job 14:20 his countenance, and s him away. H7971
Ps 104:30 Thou s forth thy spirit, they are H7971

SENDETH

Dt 24: 3 *it* in her hand, and s her out of his H7971
1Ki 17:14 *that* the LORD s rain upon the earth. H5414
Job 5:10 Who giveth rain upon the earth, and s H7971
12:15 dry up: also he s them out, and they H7971
Ps 104:10 He s the springs into the valleys, *which* H7971
147:15 He s forth his commandment *upon* H7971
18 He s out his word, and melteth them: H7971
Prv 26: 6 He that s a message by the hand of a H7971
Song 1:12 my spikenard s forth the smell thereof. H5414
Isa 18: 2 That s ambassadors by the sea, even in H7971
Mt 5:45 s rain on the just and on the unjust. *G1026*
Mk 11: 1 of Olives, he s forth two of his disciples, *G649*
14:13 And he s forth two of his disciples, and *G649*
Lk 14:32 a great way off, he s an ambassage, and *G649*
Act 23:26 most excellent governor Felix *s* greeting.

SENDING

2Sa 13:16 cause: this evil in s me away *is* greater H7971
2Ch 36:15 up betimes, and s; because he had H7971
Est 9:19 day, and of s portions one to another. H4916
22 and joy, and of s portions one to H4916
Ps 78:49 trouble, by s evil angels *among them*. H4917
Isa 7:25 it shall be for the s forth of oxen, and H4916
Jer 7:25 daily rising up early and s *them*: H7971
25: 4 rising early and s *them*; but ye have not H7971
26: 5 and s *them*, but ye have not hearkened; H7971
29:19 up early and s *them*; but ye would H7971
35:15 up early and s *them*, saying, Return H7971
44: 4 rising early and s *them*, saying, Oh, do H7971
Ezk 17:15 But he rebelled against him in s his H7971
Ro 8: 3 the flesh, God s his own Son in the *G3992*

SENEH

1Sa 14: 4 *was* Bozez, and the name of the other S. H5573

SENIR

1Ch 5:23 and S, and unto mount Hermon. H8149
Ezk 27: 5 of fir trees of S: they have taken cedars H8149

SENNACHERIB

2Ki 18:13 of king Hezekiah did S king of Assyria H5576
19:16 hear the words of S, which hath sent H5576
20 against S king of Assyria I have heard. H5576
36 So S king of Assyria departed, and H5576
2Ch 32: 1 thereof, S king of Assyria came, H5576
2 And when Hezekiah saw that S was H5576
9 After this did S king of Assyria send his H5576
10 Thus saith S king of Assyria, Whereon H5576
22 from the hand of S the king of Assyria, H5576
Isa 36: 1 Hezekiah, *that* S king of Assyria came H5576
37:17 all the words of S, which hath sent to H5576
21 prayed to me against S king of Assyria: H5576
37 So S king of Assyria departed, and H5576

SENSE

Neh 8: 8 and gave the s, and caused *them* to H7922

SENSES

Heb 5:14 of use have their s exercised to discern *G145*

SENSUAL

Jas 3:15 from above, but *is* earthly, s, devilish. *G5591*
Jude 19 themselves, s, having not the Spirit. *G5591*

SENT

Gen 3:23 Therefore the LORD God s him forth H7971
8: 7 And he s forth a raven, which went H7971
8 Also he s forth a dove from him, to see H7971
10 again he s forth the dove out of the ark; H7971
12 seven days; and s forth the dove; which H7971
12:20 him: and they s him away, and his H7971
19:13 and the LORD hath s us to destroy it. H7971
29 Abraham, and s Lot out of the midst H7971
20: 2 king of Gerar s, and took Sarah. H7971
21:14 and the child, and s her away: and she H7971
24:59 And they s away Rebekah their sister, H7971
25: 6 gave gifts, and s them away from Isaac H7971
26:27 me, and have s me away from you? H7971
29 good, and have s thee away in peace: H7971
31 and Isaac s them away, and they H7971
27:42 to Rebekah: and she s and called Jacob H7971
28: 5 And Isaac s away Jacob: and he went H7971
6 had blessed Jacob, and s him away to H7971
31: 4 And Jacob s and called Rachel and H7971
Gen 31:27 me, that I might have s thee away with H7971
42 me, surely thou hadst s me away now H7971
32: 3 And Jacob s messengers before him to H7971
5 and I have s to tell my lord, that H7971
18 it *is* a present s unto my lord Esau: H7971
23 And he took them, and s them over the H5674
23 over the brook, and s over that he had. H5674
37:14 word again. So he s him out of the vale H7971
32 And they s the coat of *many* colours, H7971
38:20 And Judah s the kid by the hand of his H7971
23 s this kid, and thou hast not found her. H7971
25 When she *was* brought forth, she s to H7971
41: 8 troubled; and he s and called for all the H7971
14 Then Pharaoh s and called Joseph, and H7971
42: 4 brother, Jacob s not with his brethren; H7971
43:34 And he took *and s* messes unto them H7971
44: 3 men were s away, they and their asses. H7971
45: 7 And God s me before you to preserve H7971
8 So now *it was* not you *that* s me hither, H7971
23 And to his father he s after this H7971
24 So he s his brethren away, and they H7971
27 which Joseph had s to carry him, the H7971
46: 5 which Pharaoh had s to carry him. H7971
28 And he s Judah before him unto H7971
50:16 And they s a messenger unto Joseph,
Ex 2: 5 the flags, she s her maid to fetch it. H7971
3:12 thee, that I have s thee: When thou H7971
13 your fathers hath s me unto you; and H7971
14 of Israel, I AM hath s me unto you. H7971
15 God of Jacob, hath s me unto you: this H7971
4:28 LORD who had s him, and all the signs H7971
5:22 people? why *is* it *that* thou hast s me? H7971
7:16 of the Hebrews hath s me unto thee, H7971
9: 7 And Pharaoh s, and, behold, there was H7971
23 and the LORD s thunder and hail, and H5414
27 And Pharaoh s, and called for Moses H7971
18: 2 Moses' wife, after he had s her back, H7964
24: 5 And he s young men of the children of H7971
Nu 13: 3 of the LORD s them from the H7971
16 men which Moses s to spy out the land. H7971
17 And Moses s them to spy out the land H7971
14:36 And the men, which Moses s to search H7971
16:12 And Moses s to call Dathan and H7971
28 that the LORD hath s me to do all these H7971
29 all men; *then* the LORD hath not s me. H7971
20:14 And Moses s messengers from Kadesh H7971
16 our voice, and s an angel, and hath H7971
21: 6 And the LORD s fiery serpents among H7971
21 And Israel s messengers unto Sihon H7971
32 And Moses s to spy out Jaazer, and H7971
22: 5 He s messengers therefore unto H7971
10 king of Moab, hath s unto me, *saying*, H7971
15 And Balak s yet again princes, more, H7971
40 and sheep, and s to Balaam, and to the H7971
31: 6 And Moses s them to the war, a H7971
32: 8 Thus did your fathers, when I s them H7971
Dt 2:26 And I s messengers out of the H7971
9:23 Likewise when the LORD s you from H7971
24: 4 Her former husband, which s her H7971
34:11 which the LORD s him to do in the land H7971
Jos 2: 1 And Joshua the son of Nun s out of H7971
3 And the king of Jericho s unto Rahab, H7971
21 so *be* it. And she s them away, and they H7971
6:17 she hid the messengers that we s. H7971
25 which Joshua s to spy out Jericho. H7971
7: 2 And Joshua s men from Jericho to Ai, H7971
22 So Joshua s messengers, and they ran H7971
8: 3 of valour, and s them away by night. H7971
9 Joshua therefore s them forth: and they H7971
10: 3 king of Jerusalem s unto Hoham king H7971
6 And the men of Gibeon s unto Joshua H7971
11: 1 *those things*, that he s to Jobab king of H7971
14: 7 of the LORD s me from Kadesh-barnea H7971
11 day that Moses s me: as my strength H7971
22: 6 So Joshua blessed them, and s them H7971
7 And when Joshua s them away also H7971
13 And the children of Israel s unto the H7971
24: 5 I s Moses also and Aaron, and I H7971
9 against Israel, and s and called Balaam H7971
12 And I s the hornet before you, which H7971
Jdg 1:23 And the house of Joseph s to descry
3:15 the children of Israel s a present unto H7971
18 the present, he s away the people that H7971
4: 6 And she s and called Barak the son of H7971
5:15 also Barak: he was s on foot into the H7971
6: 8 That the LORD s a prophet unto the H7971
14 of the Midianites: have not I s thee? H7971
35 And he s messengers throughout all H7971
35 after him: and he s messengers unto H7971
Jdg 7: 8 trumpets: and he s all *the rest of* Israel H7971
24 And Gideon s messengers throughout H7971
9:23 Then God s an evil spirit between H7971
31 And he s messengers unto Abimelech H7971
11:12 And Jephthah s messengers unto the H7971
14 And Jephthah s messengers again unto H7971
17 Then Israel s messengers unto the king H7971
17 in like manner they s unto the king of H7971
19 And Israel s messengers unto Sihon H7971
28 the words of Jephthah which he s him. H7971
38 And he said, Go. And he s her away *for* H7971
12: 9 *whom* he s abroad, and took in H7971
16:18 all his heart, she s and called for the H7971
18: 2 And the children of Dan s of their H7971
19:29 and s her into all the coasts of Israel. H7971
20: 6 her in pieces, and s her throughout all H7971
12 And the tribes of Israel s men through H7971
21:10 And the congregation s thither twelve H7971
13 And the whole congregation s *some* to H7971
1Sa 4: 4 So the people s to Shiloh, that they H7971
5: 8 They s therefore and gathered all the H7971
10 Therefore they s the ark of God to H7971
11 So they s and gathered together all the H7971
6:21 And they s messengers to the H7971
10:25 And Samuel s all the people away, H7971
11: 7 in pieces, and s *them* throughout all H7971
12: 8 then the LORD s Moses and Aaron, H7971
11 And the LORD s Jerubbaal, and Bedan, H7971
18 and the LORD s thunder and rain that H5414
13: 2 of the people he s every man to his tent. H7971
15: 1 Saul, The LORD s me to anoint thee *to* H7971
18 And the LORD s thee on a journey, and H7971
20 way which the LORD s me, and have H7971
16:12 And he s, and brought him in. Now he H7971
19 Wherefore Saul s messengers unto H7971
20 and s *them* by David his son unto Saul. H7971
22 And Saul s to Jesse, saying, Let David, I H7971
17:31 *them* before Saul: and he s for him. H3947
18: 5 Saul s him, *and* behaved himself H7971
19:11 Saul also s messengers unto David's H7971
14 And when Saul s messengers to take H7971
15 And Saul s the messengers *again* to see H7971
17 me so, and s away mine enemy, H7971
20 And Saul s messengers to take David: H7971
21 And when it was told Saul, he s other H7971
21 likewise. And Saul s messengers again H7971
20:22 way: for the LORD hath s thee away. H7971
22:11 Then the king s to call Ahimelech the H7971
25: 5 And David s out ten young men, and H7971
14 Behold, David s messengers out of the H7971
32 which s thee this day to meet me: H7971
39 head. And David s and communed H7971
40 her, saying, David s us unto thee, to H7971
26: 4 David therefore s out spies, and H7971
30:26 And when David came to Ziklag, he s H7971
31: 9 his armour, and s into the land of the H7971
2Sa 2: 5 And David s messengers unto the men H7971
3:12 And Abner s messengers to David on H7971
14 And David s messengers to H7971
15 And Ish-bosheth s, and took her from H7971
21 s Abner away; and he went in peace. H7971
22 s him away, and he was gone in peace. H7971
23 s him away, and he is gone in peace. H7971
24 hast s him away, and he is quite gone? H7971
26 out from David, he s messengers after H7971
5:11 And Hiram king of Tyre s messengers H7971
8:10 Then Toi s Joram his son unto king H7971
9: 5 Then king David s, and fetched him out H7971
10: 2 me. And David s to comfort him by the H7971
3 that he hath s comforters unto thee? H7971
3 not David *rather* s his servants unto H7971
4 to their buttocks, and s them away. H7971
5 When they told *it* unto David, he s to H7971
6 of Ammon s and hired the Syrians H7971
7 And when David heard of *it*, he s Joab, H7971
16 And Hadarezer s, and brought out the H7971
11: 1 *to battle*, that David s Joab, and his H7971
3 And David s and inquired after the H7971
4 And David s messengers, and took her; H7971
5 And the woman conceived, and s and H7971
6 And David s to Joab, *saying*, Send me H7971
6 the Hittite. And Joab s Uriah to David. H7971
14 to Joab, and s *it* by the hand of Uriah. H7971
18 Then Joab s and told David all the H7971
22 David all that Joab had s him for. H7971
27 was past, David s and fetched her to H7971
12: 1 And the LORD s Nathan unto David. H7971
25 And he s by the hand of Nathan the H7971
27 And Joab s messengers to David, and H7971

2Sa 13: 7 Then David s home to Tamar, saying, H7971
14: 2 And Joab s to Tekoah, and fetched H7971
29 Therefore Absalom s for Joab, to have H7971
29 for Joab, to have s him to the king; but H7971
29 to him: and when he s again the second H7971
32 Joab, Behold, I s unto thee, saying, H7971
15:10 But Absalom s spies throughout all the H7971
12 And Absalom s for Ahithophel the H7971
18: 2 And David s forth a third part of the H7971
29 When Joab s the king's servant, and H7971
19:11 And king David s to Zadok and to H7971
14 man; so that they s *this word* unto the H7971
22:15 And he s out arrows, and scattered H7971
17 He s from above, he took me; he drew H7971
24:13 answer I shall return to him that s me. H7971
15 So the LORD s a pestilence upon Israel H5414
1Ki 1:44 And the king hath s with him Zadok H7971
53 So king Solomon s, and they brought H7971
2:25 And king Solomon s by the hand of H7971
29 Then Solomon s Benaiah the son of H7971
36 And the king s and called for Shimei, H7971
42 And the king s and called for Shimei, H7971
5: 1 And Hiram king of Tyre s his servants H7971
2 And Solomon s to Hiram, saying, H7971
8 And Hiram s to Solomon, saying, I H7971
14 And he s them to Lebanon, ten H7971
7:13 And king Solomon s and fetched H7971
8:66 On the eighth day he s the people away: H7971
9:14 And Hiram s to the king sixscore H7971
27 And Hiram s in the navy his servants, H7971
12: 3 That they s and called him. And H7971
18 Then king Rehoboam s Adoram, who H7971
20 again, that they s and called him unto H7971
14: 6 for I *am* s to thee *with* heavy *tidings*. H7971
15:18 and king Asa s them to Ben-hadad, H7971
19 behold, I have s unto thee a present H7971
20 king Asa, and s the captains of the H7971
18:10 my lord hath not s to seek thee: and H7971
20 So Ahab s unto all the children of H7971
19: 2 Then Jezebel s a messenger unto Elijah, H7971
20: 2 And he s messengers to Ahab king of H7971
5 Although I have s unto thee, saying, H7971
7 mischief: for he s unto me for my H7971
10 And Ben-hadad s unto him, and said, H7971
17 and Ben-hadad s out, and they told H7971
34 a covenant with him, and s him away. H7971
21: 8 with his seal, and s the letters unto the H7971
11 did as Jezebel had s unto them, *and* as H7971
11 the letters which she had s unto them. H7971
14 Then they s to Jezebel, saying, Naboth H7971
2Ki 1: 2 was sick: and he s messengers, and H7971
6 unto the king that s you, and say unto H7971
9 Then the king s unto him a captain of H7971
11 Again also he s unto him another H7971
13 And he s again a captain of the third H7971
16 as thou hast s messengers to inquire H7971
2: 2 for the LORD hath s me to Beth-el. And H7971
4 for the LORD hath s me to Jericho. And H7971
6 for the LORD hath s me to Jordan. And H7971
17 said, Send. They s therefore fifty men; H7971
3: 7 And he went and s to Jehoshaphat the H7971
5: 6 I have *therewith* s Naaman my servant H7971
8 rent his clothes, that he s to the king, H7971
10 And Elisha s a messenger unto him, H7971
22 My master hath s me, saying, Behold, H7971
6: 9 And the man of God s unto the king of H7971
10 And the king of Israel s to the place H7971
14 Therefore s he thither horses, and H7971
23 and drunk, he s them away, and they H7971
32 him; and *the king* s a man from before H7971
32 of a murderer hath s to take away mine H7971
7:14 and the king s after the host of the H7971
8: 9 king of Syria hath s me to thee, saying, H7971
9:19 Then he s out a second on horseback, H7971
10: 1 wrote letters, and s to Samaria, unto H7971
5 up *of the children*, s to Jehu, saying, H7971
7 in baskets, and s him *them* to Jezreel. H7971
21 And Jehu s through all Israel: and all H7971
11: 4 And the seventh year Jehoiada s and H7971
12:18 king's house, and s *it* to Hazael king of H7971
14: 8 Then Amaziah s messengers to H7971
9 And Jehoash the king of Israel s to H7971
9 *was* in Lebanon s to the cedar that *was* H7971
19 to Lachish; but they s after him to H7971
16: 7 So Ahaz s messengers to H7971
8 s *it for* a present to the king of Assyria. H7971
10 and king Ahaz s to Urijah the priest H7971
11 king Ahaz had s from Damascus: so H7971
17: 4 for he had s messengers to So king H7971

2Ki 17:13 I s to you by my servants the prophets. H7971
25 the LORD s lions among them, H7971
26 therefore he hath s lions among them, H7971
18:14 And Hezekiah king of Judah s to the H7971
17 And the king of Assyria s Tartan and H7971
27 Hath my master s me to thy master, H7971
27 words? *hath he* not s *me* to the men
19: 2 And he s Eliakim, which *was* over the H7971
4 his master hath s to reproach the living H7971
9 against thee: he s messengers again H7971
16 hath s him to reproach the living God. H7971
20 Then Isaiah the son of Amoz s to H7971
20:12 king of Babylon, s letters and a present H7971
22: 3 *that* the king s Shaphan the son of H7971
15 of Israel, Tell the man that s you to me, H7971
18 But to the king of Judah which s you to H7971
23: 1 And the king s, and they gathered unto H7971
16 in the mount, and s, and took the bones H7971
24: 2 And the LORD s against him bands of H7971
2 of Ammon, and s them against Judah H7971
1Ch 8: 8 after he had s them away; Hushim H7971
10: 9 his armour, and s into the land of the H7971
12:19 upon advisement s him away, saying, H7971
14: 1 Now Hiram king of Tyre s messengers H7971
18:10 He s Hadoram his son to king David, to H7971
19: 2 to me. And David s messengers to H7971
3 that he hath s comforters unto thee? H7971
4 by their buttocks, and s them away. H7971
5 served. And he s to meet them: for the H7971
6 of Ammon s a thousand talents of H7971
8 And when David heard *of it*, he s Joab, H7971
16 before Israel, they s messengers, and H7971
21:12 I shall bring again to him that s me. H7971
14 So the LORD s pestilence upon Israel: H5414
15 And God s an angel unto Jerusalem to H7971
2Ch 2: 3 And Solomon s to Huram the king of H7971
11 in writing, which he s to Solomon, H7971
13 And now I have s a cunning man, H7971
7:10 seventh month he s the people away H7971
8:18 And Huram s him by the hands of his H7971
10: 3 And they s and called him. So H7971
18 Then king Rehoboam s Hadoram that H7971
16: 2 king's house, and s to Ben-hadad king H7971
3 behold, I have s thee silver and gold; H7971
4 unto king Asa, and s the captains of his H7971
17: 7 Also in the third year of his reign he s H7971
8 And with them *he* s Levites, *even*
24:19 Yet he s prophets to them, to bring H7971
23 the people, and s all the spoil of them H7971
25:13 army which Amaziah s back, that they H7725
15 Amaziah, and he s unto him a prophet, H7971
17 took advice, and s to Joash, the son of H7971
18 And Joash king of Israel s to Amaziah H7971
18 *was* in Lebanon s to the cedar that *was* H7971
27 to Lachish: but they s to Lachish after H7971
30: 1 And Hezekiah s to all Israel and Judah, H7971
32:21 And the LORD s an angel, which cut off H7971
31 of Babylon, who s unto him to inquire H7971
34: 8 and the house, he s Shaphan the son of H7971
23 Israel, Tell ye the man that s you to me, H7971
26 And as for the king of Judah, who s you H7971
29 Then the king s and gathered together H7971
35:21 But he s ambassadors to him, saying, H7971
36:10 Nebuchadnezzar s, and brought him to H7971
15 And the LORD God of their fathers s to H7971
Ezr 4:11 This *is* the copy of the letter that they s H7972
14 have we s and certified the king; H7972
17 *Then* s the king an answer unto Rehum H7972
18 The letter which ye s unto us hath been H7972
5: 6 side the river, s unto Darius the king: H7972
7 They s a letter unto him, wherein was H7972
6:13 the king had s, so they did speedily. H7972
7:14 Forasmuch as thou art s of the king, H7972
8:16 Then s I for Eliezer, for Ariel, for H7971
17 And I s them with commandment unto H6680
Neh 2: 9 Now the king had s captains of the H7971
6: 2 That Sanballat and Geshem s unto me, H7971
3 And I s messengers unto them, saying, H7971
4 Yet they s unto me four times after this H7971
5 Then s Sanballat his servant unto me H7971
8 Then I s unto him, saying, There are no H7971
12 And, lo, I perceived that God had not s H7971
17 the nobles of Judah s many letters unto H1980
19 *And* Tobiah s letters to put me in fear. H7971
Est 1:22 For he s letters into all the king's H7971
3:13 And the letters were s by posts into all H7971
4: 4 grieved; and she s raiment to clothe H7971
5:10 he came home, he s and called for his H7971
8:10 the king's ring, and s letters by posts on H7971

Est 9:20 these things, and s letters unto all the H7971
30 And he s the letters unto all the Jews, to H7971
Job 1: 4 one his day; and s and called for their H7971
5 about, that Job s and sanctified them, H7971
22: 9 Thou hast s widows away empty, and H7971
39: 5 Who hath s out the wild ass free? or H7971
Ps 18:14 Yea, he s out his arrows, and scattered H7971
16 He s from above, he took me, he drew H7971
59:ttl David; when Saul s, and they watched H7971
77:17 water: the skies s out a sound: thine H5414
78:25 Man did eat angels' food: he s them H7971
45 He s divers sorts of flies among them, H7971
80:11 She s out her boughs unto the sea, and H7971
105:17 He s a man before them, *even* Joseph, H7971
20 The king s and loosed him; *even* the H7971
26 He s Moses his servant; *and* Aaron H7971
28 He s darkness, and made it dark; and H7971
106:15 And he gave them their request; but s H7971
107:20 He s his word, and healed them, and H7971
111: 9 He s redemption unto his people: he H7971
135: 9 *Who* s tokens and wonders into the H7971
Prv 9: 3 She hath s forth her maidens: she H7971
17:11 cruel messenger shall be s against him. H7971
Isa 9: 8 The Lord s a word into Jacob, and it H7971
20: 1 the king of Assyria s him,) and fought H7971
36: 2 And the king of Assyria s Rabshakeh H7971
12 But Rabshakeh said, Hath my master s H7971
12 words? *hath he* not s *me* to the men that
37: 2 And he s Eliakim, who *was* over the H7971
4 his master hath s to reproach the living H7971
9 *it*, he s messengers to Hezekiah, saying, H7971
17 hath s to reproach the living God. H7971
21 Then Isaiah the son of Amoz s unto H7971
39: 1 king of Babylon, s letters and a present H7971
42:19 messenger *that* I s? *who is* blind as *he* H7971
43:14 For your sake I have s to Babylon, and H7971
48:16 Lord GOD, and his Spirit, hath s me. H7971
55:11 shall prosper *in the thing* whereto I s it. H7971
61: 1 the meek; he hath s me to bind up the H7971
Jer 7:25 this day I have even s unto you all my H7971
14: 3 And their nobles have s their little ones H7971
14 lies in my name: I s them not, neither H7971
15 in my name, and I s them not, yet they H7971
19:14 the LORD had s him to prophesy; and H7971
21: 1 king Zedekiah s unto him Pashur the H7971
23:21 I have not s these prophets, yet they H7971
32 their lightness; yet I s them not, nor H7971
38 LORD, and I have s unto you, saying, H7971
24: 5 whom I have s out of this place into H7971
25: 4 And the LORD hath s unto you all his H7971
17 drink, unto whom the LORD had s me: H7971
26: 5 the prophets, whom I s unto you, both H7971
12 saying, The LORD s me to prophesy H7971
15 the LORD hath s me unto you to speak H7971
22 And Jehoiakim the king s men into H7971
27:15 For I have not s them, saith the LORD, H7971
28: 9 that the LORD hath truly s him. H7971
15 LORD hath not s thee; but thou makest H7971
29: 1 the prophet s from Jerusalem unto H7971
3 king of Judah s unto Babylon to H7971
9 I have not s them, saith the LORD. H7971
19 the LORD, which I s unto them by my H7971
20 I have s from Jerusalem to Babylon: H7971
25 Because thou hast s letters in thy name H7971
28 For therefore he s unto us *in* Babylon, H7971
31 unto you, and I s him not, and he H7971
35:15 I have s also unto you all my servants H7971
36:14 Therefore all the princes s Jehudi the H7971
21 So the king s Jehudi to fetch the roll: H7971
37: 3 And Zedekiah the king s Jehucal the H7971
7 king of Judah, that s you unto me to H7971
17 Then Zedekiah the king s, and took him H7971
38:14 Then Zedekiah the king s, and took H7971
39:13 of the guard s, and Nebushasban, H7971
14 Even they s, and took Jeremiah out of H7971
40:14 Ammonites hath s Ishmael the son of H7971
42: 9 unto whom ye s me to present your H7971
20 hearts, when ye s me unto the LORD H7971
21 for the which he hath s me unto you. H7971
43: 1 s him to them, *even* all these words, H7971
2 our God hath not s thee to say, Go not H7971
44: 4 Howbeit I s unto you all my servants H7971
49:14 an ambassador is s unto the heathen, H7971
Lam 1:13 From above hath he s fire into my H7971
Ezk 2: 9 an hand *was* s unto me; and, lo, a H7971
3: 5 For thou *art* not s to a people of a H7971
6 Surely, had I s thee to them, they would H7971
13: 6 LORD hath not s them: and they have H7971
23:16 s messengers unto them into Chaldea. H7971

Ezk 23:40 And furthermore, that ye have s for H7971
40 a messenger *was* s; and, lo, they came: H7971
31: 4 his plants, and s out her little rivers H7971
Dan 3: 2 Then Nebuchadnezzar the king s to H7972
28 who hath s his angel, and delivered H7972
5:24 Then was the part of the hand s from H7972
6:22 My God hath s his angel, and hath shut H7972
10:11 unto thee am I now s. And when he had H7971
Hos 5:13 to the Assyrian, and s to king Jareb: yet H7971
Joel 2:25 my great army which I s among you. H7971
Am 4:10 I have s among you the pestilence after H7971
7:10 Then Amaziah the priest of Beth-el s to H7971
Oba 1 and an ambassador is s among the H7971
Jna 1: 4 But the LORD s out a great wind into H2904
Mic 6: 4 of servants; and I s before thee Moses, H7971
Hag 1:12 their God had s him, and the people H7971
Zec 1:10 s to walk to and fro through the earth. H7971
2: 8 the glory hath he s me unto the nations H7971
9 that the LORD of hosts hath s me. H7971
11 the LORD of hosts hath s me unto thee. H7971
4: 9 the LORD of hosts hath s me unto you. H7971
6:15 of hosts hath s me unto you. And *this* H7971
7: 2 When they had s unto the house of God H7971
12 of hosts hath s in his spirit by the H7971
9:11 covenant I have s forth thy prisoners H7971
Mal 2: 4 And ye shall know that I have s this H7971
Mt 2: 8 And he s them to Bethlehem, and said, G3992
16 wroth, and s forth, and slew all the G649
10: 5 These twelve Jesus s forth, and G649
40 receiveth me receiveth him that s me. G649
11: 2 of Christ, he s two of his disciples, G3992
13:36 Then Jesus s the multitude away, and G863
14:10 And he s, and beheaded John in the G3992
22 side, while he s the multitudes away. G630
23 And when he had s the multitudes away, G630
35 of him, they s out into all that country G649
15:24 But he answered and said, I am not s G649
39 And he s away the multitude, and took G630
20: 2 a day, he s them into his vineyard. G649
21: 1 of Olives, then s Jesus two disciples, G649
34 fruit drew near, he s his servants to the G649
36 Again, he s other servants more than the G649
37 But last of all he s unto them his son, G649
22: 3 And s forth his servants to call them that G649
4 Again, he s forth other servants, saying, G649
7 was wroth: and he s forth his armies, G3992
16 And they s out unto him their disciples G649
23:37 them which are s unto thee, how often G649
27:19 seat, his wife s unto him, saying, Have G649
Mk 1:43 him, and forthwith s him away; G1544
3:31 without, s unto him, calling him. G649
4:36 And when they had s away the G863
6:17 For Herod himself had s forth and laid G649
27 And immediately the king s an G649
45 Bethsaida, while he s away the people. G628
46 And when he had s them away, he G657
8: 9 four thousand: and he s them away. G630
26 And he s him away to his house, saying, G649
9:37 me, receiveth not me, but him that s me. G649
12: 2 And at the season he s to the G649
3 and beat him, and s *him* away empty. G649
4 And again he s unto them another G649
4 and s *him* away shamefully handled. G649
5 And again he s another; and him they G649
6 his wellbeloved, he s him also last unto G649
Lk 1:19 of God; and am s to speak unto thee, G649
26 angel Gabriel was s from God unto a city G649
53 and the rich he hath s empty away. G1821
4:18 to the poor; he hath s me to heal the G649
26 But unto none of them was Elias s, save G3992
43 to other cities also: for therefore am I s. G649
7: 3 And when he heard of Jesus, he s unto G649
6 the centurion s friends to him, saying G3992
10 And they that were s, returning to the G3992
19 of his disciples s *them* to Jesus, saying, G3992
20 John Baptist hath s us unto thee, saying, G649
8:38 with him: but Jesus s him away, saying, G630
9: 2 And he s them to preach the kingdom of G649
48 me receiveth him that s me: for he that is G649
52 And s messengers before his face: and G649
10: 1 seventy also, and s them two and two G649
16 despiseth me despiseth him that s me. G649
13:34 them that are s unto thee; how often G649
14:17 And s his servant at supper time to say G649
15:15 he s him into his fields to feed swine. G3992
19:14 But his citizens hated him, and s a G649
29 of Olives, he s two of his disciples, G649
32 And they that were s went their way, and G649
20:10 And at the season he s a servant to the G649

Lk 20:10 beat him, and s *him* away empty. G1821
11 And again he s another servant: and G3992
11 shamefully, and s *him* away empty. G1821
12 And again he s a third: and they G3992
20 And they watched *him*, and s forth spies, G649
22: 8 And he s Peter and John, saying, Go and G649
35 And he said unto them, When I s you G649
23: 7 jurisdiction, he s him to Herod, who G375
11 robe, and s him again to Pilate. G375
15 No, nor yet Herod: for I s you to him; G375
Jn 1: 6 There was a man s from God, whose G649
8 He was not that Light, but *was s* to bear
19 when the Jews s priests and Levites from G649
22 that s us. What sayest thou of thyself? G3992
24 And they which were s were of the G649
33 And I knew him not: but he that s me G3992
3:17 For God s not his Son into the world to G649
28 the Christ, but that I am s before him. G649
34 For he whom God hath s speaketh the G649
4:34 him that s me, and to finish his work. G3992
38 I s you to reap that whereon ye bestowed G649
5:23 not the Father which hath s him. G3992
24 on him that s me, hath everlasting G3992
30 the will of the Father which hath s me. G3992
33 Ye s unto John, and he bare witness unto G649
36 witness of me, that the Father hath s me. G649
37 And the Father himself, which hath s G3992
38 for whom he hath s, him ye believe not. G649
6:29 that ye believe on him whom he hath s. G649
38 own will, but the will of him that s me. G3992
39 will which hath s me, that of all which G3992
40 And this is the will of him that s me, G3992
44 Father which hath s me draw him: and G3992
57 As the living Father hath s me, and I live G649
7:16 doctrine is not mine, but his that s me. G3992
18 his glory that s him, the same is true, G3992
28 that s me is true, whom ye know not. G3992
29 for I am from him, and he hath s me. G649
32 the chief priests s officers to take him. G649
33 you, and *then* I go unto him that s me. G3992
8:16 alone, but I and the Father that s me. G3992
18 Father that s me beareth witness of me. G3992
26 of you: but he that s me is true; and I G3992
29 And he that s me is with me: the Father G3992
42 neither came I of myself, but he s me. G649
9: 4 I must work the works of him that s G3992
7 is by interpretation, S.) He went his way G649
10:36 sanctified, and s into the world, Thou G649
11: 3 Therefore his sisters s unto him, saying, G649
42 they may believe that thou hast s me. G649
12:44 not on me, but on him that s me. G3992
45 And he that seeth me seeth him that s G3992
49 the Father which s me, he gave me a G3992
13:16 that is s greater than he that sent him. G652
16 that is sent greater than he that s him. G3992
20 receiveth me receiveth him that s me. G3992
14:24 not mine, but the Father's which s me. G3992
15:21 because they know not him that s me. G3992
16: 5 But now I go my way to him that s me; G3992
17: 3 God, and Jesus Christ, whom thou hast s. G649
18 As thou hast s me into the world, even so G649
18 so have I also s them into the world. G649
21 world may believe that thou hast s me. G649
23 that thou hast s me, and hast loved G649
25 these have known that thou hast s me. G649
18:24 Now Annas had s him bound unto G649
20:21 *my* Father hath s me, even so send I you. G649
Act 3:26 up his Son Jesus, s him to bless you, in G649
5:21 s to the prison to have them brought. G649
7:12 corn in Egypt, he s out our fathers first. G1821
14 Then s Joseph, and called his father G649
8:14 of God, they s unto them Peter and John: G649
9:17 as thou camest, hath s me, that thou G649
30 to Caesarea, and s him forth to Tarsus. G1821
38 was there, they s unto him two men, G649
10: 8 things unto them, he s them to Joppa. G649
17 men which were s from Cornelius had G649
20 doubting nothing: for I have s them. G649
21 the men which were s unto him from G649
29 as soon as I was s for: I ask therefore G3343
29 for what intent ye have s for me? G3343
33 Immediately therefore I s to thee; and G3992
36 The word which *God* s unto the children G649
11:11 where I was, s from Caesarea unto me. G649
22 and they s forth Barnabas, that G1821
30 Which also they did, and s it to the G649
12:11 that the Lord hath s his angel, and hath G1821
13: 3 *their* hands on them, they s *them* away. G630
4 So they, being s forth by the Holy G1599

Act 13:15 of the synagogue s unto them, saying, *Ye* G649
26 to you is the word of this salvation s. G649
15:27 We have s therefore Judas and Silas, G649
16:35 And when it was day, the magistrates s G649
36 magistrates have s to let you go: now G649
17:10 And the brethren immediately s away G1599
14 And then immediately the brethren s G1821
19:22 So he s into Macedonia two of them that G649
31 were his friends, s unto him, desiring G3992
20:17 And from Miletus he s to Ephesus, and G3992
23:30 wait for the man, I s straightway to G3992
24:24 was a Jewess, he s for Paul, and heard G3343
26 loose him: wherefore he s for him the G3343
28:28 salvation of God is s unto the Gentiles, G649
Ro 10:15 except they be s? as it is written, How G649
1Co 1:17 For Christ s me not to baptize, but to G649
4:17 For this cause have I s unto you G3992
2Co 8:18 And we have s with him the brother, G4842
22 And we have s with them our brother, G4842
9: 3 Yet have I s the brethren, lest our G3992
12:17 you by any of them whom I s unto you? G649
18 I desired Titus, and with *him* I s a G4882
Gal 4: 4 was come, God s forth his Son, made G1821
6 And because ye are sons, God hath s G1821
Eph 6:22 Whom I have s unto you for the same G3992
Php 2:28 I s him therefore the more carefully, G3992
4:16 For even in Thessalonica ye s once and G3992
18 things *which were* s from you, an odour
Col 4: 8 Whom I have s unto you for the same G3992
1Th 3: 2 And s Timotheus, our brother, and G3992
5 longer forbear, I s to know your faith, G3992
2Ti 4:12 And Tychicus have I s to Ephesus. G649
Phlm 12 Whom I have s again: thou therefore G628
Heb 1:14 Are they not all ministering spirits, s G649
Jas 2:25 and had s *them* out another way? G1524
1Pt 1:12 the Holy Ghost s down from heaven; G649
2:14 unto them that are s by him for the G3992
1Jn 4: 9 because that God s his only begotten Son G649
10 that he loved us, and s his Son *to be* the G649
14 s the Son *to be* the Saviour of the world. G649
Rev 1: 1 to pass; and he s and signified *it* by his G649
5: 6 Spirits of God s forth into all the earth. G649
22: 6 of the holy prophets s his angel to shew G649
16 I Jesus have s mine angel to testify unto G3992

SENTENCE

Dt 17: 9 they shall shew thee the s of judgment: H1697
10 And thou shalt do according to the s, H1697
11 According to the s of the law which H6310
11 not decline from the s which they shall H1697
Ps 17: 2 Let my s come forth from thy presence; H4941
Prv 16:10 A divine s *is* in the lips of the king: his H7081
Ecc 8:11 Because s against an evil work is not H6599
Jer 4:12 me: now also will I give s against them. H4941
Lk 23:24 And Pilate gave s that it should be as G1948
Act 15:19 Wherefore my s is, that we trouble not G2919
2Co 1: 9 But we had the s of death in ourselves, G610

SENTENCES

Dan 5:12 and shewing of hard s, and dissolving of H280
8:23 understanding dark s, shall stand up. H2420

SENTEST

Ex 15: 7 up against thee: thou s forth thy wrath, H7971
Nu 13:27 land whither thou s us, and surely it H7971
24:12 which thou s unto me, saying, H7971
1Ki 5: 8 the things which thou s to me for: *and* I H7971

SENUAH

Neh 11: 9 the son of S *was* second over the city. H5574

SEORIM

1Ch 24: 8 The third to Harim, the fourth to S, H8188

SEPARATE

Gen 13: 9 *Is* not the whole land before thee? s H6504
30:40 And Jacob did s the lambs, and set the H6504
49:26 of him that was s from his brethren. H5139
Lev 15:31 Thus shall ye s the children of Israel H5144
22: 2 to his sons, that they s themselves from H5144
Nu 6: 2 or woman shall s *themselves* to vow a H6381
2 to s *themselves* unto the LORD: H5144
3 He shall s *himself* from wine and H5144
8:14 Thus shalt thou s the Levites from H914
16:21 S yourselves from among this H914
Dt 19: 2 Thou shalt s three cities for thee in the H914
7 saying, Thou shalt s three cities for thee. H914
29:21 And the LORD shall s him unto evil out H914
Jos 16: 9 And the s cities for the children of H3995

1Ki 8:53 For thou didst s them from among all H914
Ezr 10:11 his pleasure: and s yourselves from the H914
Jer 37:12 of Benjamin, to s himself thence in the H2505
Ezk 41:12 Now the building that *was* before the s H1508
13 long; and the s place, and the building, H1508
14 house, and of the s place toward the H1508
15 over against the s place which *was* H1508
42: 1 over against the s place, and which *was* H1508
10 s place, and over against the building. H1508
13 *are* before the s place, they *be* holy H1508
Mt 25:32 and he shall s them one from another, G873
Lk 6:22 and when they shall s you *from their* G873
Act 13: 2 the Holy Ghost said, S me Barnabas and G873
Ro 8:35 Who shall s us from the love of Christ? G5563
39 shall be able to s us from the love of G5563
2Co 6:17 them, and be ye s, saith the Lord, and G873
Heb 7:26 undefiled, s from sinners, and made G5563
Jude 19 These be they who s themselves, sensual, G592

SEPARATED

Gen 13:11 s themselves the one from the other. H6504
14 after that Lot was s from him, Lift up H6504
25:23 of people shall be s from thy bowels; H6504
Ex 33:16 us? so shall we be s, I and thy people, H6395
Lev 20:24 which have s you from *other* people. H914
25 which I have s from you as unclean. H914
Nu 16: 9 the God of Israel hath s you from the H914
Dt 10: 8 At that time the LORD s the tribe of Levi, H914
32: 8 when he s the sons of Adam, he H6504
33:16 of him *that was* s from his brethren. H5139
1Ch 12: 8 And of the Gadites there s themselves H914
23:13 and Aaron was s, that he should sanctify H914
25: 1 of the host s to the service of the sons H914
2Ch 25:10 Then Amaziah s them, *to wit,* the army H914
Ezr 6:21 and all such as had s themselves unto H914
8:24 Then I s twelve of the chief of the priests, H914
9: 1 Levites, have not s themselves from the H914
10: 8 and himself s from the congregation H914
16 *their* names, were s, and sat down in the H914
Neh 4:19 s upon the wall, one far from another. H6504
9: 2 And the seed of Israel s themselves from H914
10:28 all they that had s themselves from the H914
13: 3 s from Israel all the mixed multitude. H914
Prv 18: 1 Through desire a man, having s H6504
19: 4 but the poor is s from his neighbour. H6504
Isa 56: 3 LORD hath utterly s me from his people: H914
59: 2 But your iniquities have s between you H914
Hos 4:14 for themselves are s with whores, and H6504
9:10 to Baal-peor, and s themselves unto H5144
Act 19: 9 from them, and s the disciples, disputing G873
Ro 1: 1 *be* an apostle, s unto the gospel of God, G873
Gal 1:15 But when it pleased God, who s me from G873
2:12 he withdrew and s himself, fearing them G873

SEPARATETH

Nu 6: 5 in the which he s *himself* unto the H5144
6 All the days that he s *himself* unto the H5144
Prv 16:28 strife: and a whisperer s chief friends. H6504
17: 9 that repeateth a matter s *very* friends. H6504
Ezk 14: 7 in Israel, which s himself from me, and H5144

SEPARATING

Zec 7: 3 in the fifth month, s myself, as I have H5144

SEPARATION

Lev 12: 2 s for her infirmity shall she be unclean. H5079
5 two weeks, as in her s: and she shall H5079
15:20 she lieth upon in her s shall be unclean: H5079
25 of the time of her s, or if it run beyond H5079
25 the time of her s; all the days of the H5079
25 the days of her s: she *shall be* unclean. H5079
26 as the bed of her s: and whatsoever she H5079
26 be unclean, as the uncleanness of her s. H5079
Nu 6: 4 All the days of his s shall he eat nothing H5145
5 All the days of the vow of his s there H5145
8 All the days of his s he *is* holy unto the H5145
12 the days of his s, and shall bring a lamb H5145
12 shall be lost, because his s was defiled. H5145
13 the days of his s are fulfilled: he shall H5145
18 the head of his s *at* the door of the H5145
18 of the head of his s, and put *it* in the fire H5145
19 after *the hair of* his s is shaven: H5145
21 the LORD for his s, beside *that* that his H5145
21 so he must do after the law of his s. H5145
19: 9 a water of s: it *is* a purification for sin. H5079
13 the water of s was not sprinkled upon H5079
20 the water of s hath not been sprinkled H5079
21 the water of s shall wash his clothes; H5079
21 water of s shall be unclean until even. H5079

Nu 31:23 with the water of s: and all that abideth H5079
Ezk 42:20 hundred broad, to make a s between the H914

SEPHAR

Gen 10:30 thou goest unto S a mount of the east. H5611

SEPHARAD

Oba 20 S, shall possess the cities of the south. H5614

SEPHARVAIM

2Ki 17:24 and from S, and placed *them* in H5617
31 and Anammelech, the gods of S. H5617
18:34 *are* the gods of S, Hena, and Ivah? have H5617
19:13 king of the city of S, of Hena, and Ivah? H5617
Isa 36:19 where *are* the gods of S? and have they H5617
37:13 king of the city of S, Hena, and Ivah? H5617

SEPHARVITES

2Ki 17:31 Tartak, and the S burnt their children H5616

SEPULCHRE

Gen 23: 6 s, but that thou mayest bury thy dead. H6913
Dt 34: 6 no man knoweth of his s unto this day. H6900
Jdg 8:32 was buried in the s of Joash his father, H6913
1Sa 10: 2 two men by Rachel's s in the border of H6900
2Sa 2:32 buried him in the s of his father, which H6913
4:12 buried *it* in the s of Abner in Hebron. H6913
17:23 and was buried in the s of his father. H6913
21:14 in Zelah, in the s of Kish his father: and H6913
1Ki 13:22 shall not come unto the s of thy fathers. H6913
31 bury me in the s wherein the man of H6913
2Ki 9:28 s with his fathers in the city of David. H6900
13:21 the man into the s of Elisha: and when H6913
21:26 And he was buried in his s in the H6900
23:17 told him, *It is* the s of the man of God, H6913
30 him in his own s. And the people of the H6900
Ps 5: 9 an open s; they flatter with their tongue. H6913
Isa 22:16 hast hewed thee out a s here, *as* he that H6913
16 heweth him out a s on high, *and* that H6913
Jer 5:16 Their quiver *is* as an open s, they *are* all H6913
Mt 27:60 stone to the door of the s, and departed. G3419
61 other Mary, sitting over against the s. G5028
64 Command therefore that the s be made G5028
66 So they went, and made the s sure, G5028
28: 1 and the other Mary to see the s. G5028
8 And they departed quickly from the s G3419
Mk 15:46 and laid him in a s which was hewn G3419
46 rolled a stone unto the door of the s. G3419
16: 2 came unto the s at the rising of the sun. G3419
3 away the stone from the door of the s? G3419
5 And entering into the s, they saw a G3419
8 and fled from the s; for they trembled G3419
Lk 23:53 and laid it in a s that was hewn in G3418
55 the s, and how his body was laid. G3419
24: 1 came unto the s, bringing the spices G3418
2 found the stone rolled away from the s. G3419
9 And returned from the s, and told all G3419
12 Then arose Peter, and ran unto the s; G3419
22 astonished, which were early at the s; G3419
24 us went to the s, and found *it* even so G3419
Jn 19:41 new s, wherein was never man yet laid. G3419
42 *day*; for the s was nigh at hand. G3419
20: 1 yet dark, unto the s, and seeth the stone G3419
1 seeth the stone taken away from the s. G3419
2 the Lord out of the s, and we know not G3419
3 that other disciple, and came to the s. G3419
4 outrun Peter, and came first to the s. G3419
6 the s, and seeth the linen clothes lie, G3419
8 first to the s, and he saw, and believed. G3419
11 But Mary stood without at the s G3419
11 stooped down, *and looked* into the s, G3419
Act 2:29 and his s is with us unto this day. G3418
7:16 and laid in the s that Abraham bought G3418
13:29 down from the tree, and laid *him* in a s. G3419
Ro 3:13 Their throat *is* an open s; with their G5028

SEPULCHRES

Gen 23: 6 the choice of our s bury thy dead; none H6913
2Ki 23:16 he spied the s that *were* there in the H6913
16 the bones out of the s, and burned *them* H6913
2Ch 16:14 And they buried him in his own s, H6913
21:20 of David, but not in the s of the kings. H6913
24:25 buried him not in the s of the kings. H6913
28:27 him not into the s of the kings of Israel: H6913
32:33 in the chiefest of the s of the sons of H6913
35:24 in *one of* the s of his fathers. And all H6913
Neh 2: 3 of my fathers' s, *lieth* waste, and the H6913
5 city of my fathers' s, that I may build it. H6913
3:16 over against the s of David, and to the H6913

Mt 23:27 like unto whited s, which indeed appear G5028
29 and garnish the s of the righteous, G3419
Lk 11:47 Woe unto you! for ye build the s of the G3419
48 indeed killed them, and ye build their s. G3419

SERAH

Gen 46:17 and Beriah, and S their sister: and the H8294
1Ch 7:30 Ishuai, and Beriah, and S their sister. H8294

SERAIAH

2Sa 8:17 *were* the priests; and S *was* the scribe; H8304
2Ki 25:18 And the captain of the guard took S the H8304
23 of Careah, and S the son of Tanhumeth H8304
1Ch 4:13 And the sons of Kenaz; Othniel, and S: H8304
14 And Meonothai begat Ophrah: and S H8304
35 Josibiah, the son of S, the son of Asiel, H8304
6:14 And Azariah begat S, and Seraiah begat H8304
14 And Azariah begat Seraiah, and S H8304
Ezr 2: 2 Nehemiah, S, Reelaiah, Mordecai, H8304
7: 1 Ezra the son of S, the son of Azariah, H8304
Neh 10: 2 S, Azariah, Jeremiah, H8304
11:11 S the son of Hilkiah, the son of H8304
12: 1 Shealtiel, and Jeshua: S, Jeremiah, Ezra, H8304
12 of S, Meraiah; of Jeremiah, Hananiah; H8304
Jer 36:26 of Hammelech, and S the son of Azriel, H8304
40: 8 sons of Kareah, and S the son of H8304
51:59 commanded S the son of Neriah, the H8304
59 his reign. And *this* S *was* a quiet prince. H8304
61 And Jeremiah said to S, When thou H8304
52:24 And the captain of the guard took S the H8304

SERAPHIMS

Isa 6: 2 Above it stood the s: each one had six H8314
6 Then flew one of the s unto me, having H8314

SERED

Gen 46:14 And the sons of Zebulun; S, and Elon, H5624
Nu 26:26 their families: of S, the family of the H5624

SERGIUS

Act 13: 7 of the country, S Paulus, a prudent G4588

SERJEANTS

Act 16:35 sent the s, saying, Let those men go. G4465
38 And the s told these words unto the G4465

SERPENT

Gen 3: 1 Now the s was more subtil than any H5175
2 And the woman said unto the s, We H5175
4 And the s said unto the woman, Ye H5175
13 said, The s beguiled me, and I did eat. H5175
14 And the LORD God said unto the s, H5175
49:17 Dan shall be a s by the way, an adder H5175
Ex 4: 3 a s; and Moses fled from before it. H5175
7: 9 before Pharaoh, *and* it shall become a s. H8577
10 before his servants, and it became a s. H8577
15 to a s shalt thou take in thine hand. H5175
Nu 21: 8 Make thee a fiery s, and set it upon a H8314
9 And Moses made a s of brass, and put H5175
9 to pass, that if a s had bitten any man, H5175
9 when he beheld the s of brass, he lived. H5175
2Ki 18: 4 in pieces the brasen s that Moses had H5175
Job 26:13 his hand hath formed the crooked s. H5175
Ps 58: 4 Their poison *is* like the poison of a s: H5175
140: 3 tongues like a s; adders' poison *is* under H5175
Prv 23:32 At the last it biteth like a s, and stingeth H5175
30:19 air; the way of a s upon a rock; the way H5175
Ecc 10: 8 breaketh an hedge, a s shall bite him. H5175
11 Surely the s will bite without H5175
Isa 14:29 and his fruit *shall be* a fiery flying s. H8314
27: 1 the piercing s, even leviathan that H5175
1 that crooked s; and he shall slay the H5175
30: 6 and fiery flying s, they will carry their H8314
Jer 46:22 The voice thereof shall go like a s; for H5175
Am 5:19 his hand on the wall, and a s bit him. H5175
9: 3 command the s, and he shall bite them: H5175
Mic 7:17 They shall lick the dust like a s, they H5175
Mt 7:10 Or if he ask a fish, will he give him a s? G3789
Lk 11:11 *ask* a fish, will he for a fish give him a s? G3789
Jn 3:14 And as Moses lifted up the s in the G3789
2Co 11: 3 But I fear, lest by any means, as the s G3789
Rev 12: 9 cast out, that old s, called the Devil, and G3789
14 and half a time, from the face of the s. G3789
15 And the s cast out of his mouth water G3789
20: 2 dragon, that old s, which is the Devil, G3789

SERPENTS

Ex 7:12 rod, and they became s: but Aaron's rod H8577
Nu 21: 6 And the LORD sent fiery s among the H5175

S

Nu 21: 7 he take away the s from us. And Moses H5175
Dt 8:15 *wherein were* fiery s, and scorpions, H5175
32:24 them, with the poison of s of the dust. H2119
Jer 8:17 For, behold, I will send s, cockatrices, H5175
Mt 10:16 wise as s, and harmless as doves. G3789
23:33 *Ye* s, *ye* generation of vipers, how can G3789
Mk 16:18 They shall take up s; and if they drink G3789
Lk 10:19 power to tread on s and scorpions, and G3789
1Co 10: 9 also tempted, and were destroyed of s. G3789
Jas 3: 7 of birds, and of s, and of things in the G2062
Rev 9:19 *were* like unto s, and had heads, and G3789

SERPENT'S

Isa 14:29 for out of the s root shall come forth H5175
65:25 dust *shall be* the s meat. They shall not H5175

SERUG

Gen 11:20 lived two and thirty years, and begat S: H8286
21 And Reu lived after he begat S two H8286
22 And S lived thirty years, and begat H8286
23 And S lived after he begat Nahor two H8286
1Ch 1:26 S, Nahor, Terah, H8286

SERVANT

Gen 9:25 And he said, Cursed *be* Canaan; a s of H5650
26 God of Shem; and Canaan shall be his s. H5650
27 of Shem; and Canaan shall be his s. H5650
18: 3 pass not away, I pray thee, from thy s: H5650
5 ye come to your s. And they said, So do, H5650
19:19 Behold now, thy s hath found grace in H5650
24: 2 And Abraham said unto his eldest s of H5650
5 And the s said unto him, Peradventure H5650
9 And the s put his hand under the thigh H5650
10 And the s took ten camels of the camels H5650
14 appointed for thy s Isaac; and thereby H5650
17 And the s ran to meet her, and said, Let H5650
34 And he said, I *am* Abraham's s. H5650
52 when Abraham's s heard their words, H5650
53 And the s brought forth jewels of silver, H5650
59 nurse, and Abraham's s, and his men. H5650
61 the s took Rebekah, and went his way. H5650
65 For she *had* said unto the s, What man H5650
65 to meet us? And the s *had* said, It *is* my H5650
66 And the s told Isaac all things that he H5650
26:24 thy seed for my s Abraham's sake. H5650
32: 4 my lord Esau; Thy s Jacob saith thus, I H5650
10 shewed unto thy s; for with my staff I H5650
18 Then thou shalt say, *They be* thy s H5650
20 And say ye moreover, Behold, thy s H5650
33: 5 which God hath graciously given thy s. H5650
14 pass over before his s: and I will lead on H5650
39:17 The Hebrew s, which thou hast brought H5650
19 thy s to me; that his wrath was kindled. H5650
41:12 man, an Hebrew, s to the captain of the H5650
43:28 And they answered, Thy s our father *is* H5650
44:10 shall be my s; and ye shall be blameless. H5650
17 he shall be my s; and as for you, get you H5650
18 Oh my lord, let thy s, I pray thee, speak H5650
18 thy s: for thou *art* even as Pharaoh. H5650
24 came up unto thy s my father, we told H5650
27 And thy s my father said unto us, Ye H5650
30 Now therefore when I come to thy s my H5650
31 s our father with sorrow to the grave. H5650
32 For thy s became surety for the lad H5650
33 Now therefore, I pray thee, let thy s H5650
49:15 to bear, and became a s unto tribute. H5647
Ex 4:10 hast spoken unto thy s: but I *am* slow of H5650
12:44 But every man's s that is bought for H5650
45 A foreigner and an hired s shall not eat H7916
14:31 believed the LORD, and his s Moses. H5650
21: 2 If thou buy an Hebrew s, six years he H5650
5 And if the s shall plainly say, I love my H5650
20 And if a man smite his s, or his maid, H5650
26 And if a man smite the eye of his s, or H5650
33:11 the camp: but his s Joshua, the son of H8334
Lev 22:10 hired s, shall not eat *of* the holy thing. H7916
25: 6 for thee, and for thy s, and for thy maid, H5650
6 and for thy hired s, and for thy stranger H7916
40 *But* as an hired s, *and* as a sojourner, he H7916
50 time of an hired s shall it be with him. H7916
53 *And* as a yearly hired s shall he be with H7916
Nu 11:11 thou afflicted thy s? and wherefore have H5650
28 And Joshua the son of Nun, the s of H8334
12: 7 My s Moses *is* not so, who *is* faithful in H5650
8 afraid to speak against my s Moses? H5650
14:24 But my s Caleb, because he had H5650
Dt 3:24 begun to shew thy s thy greatness, and H5650
5:15 And remember that thou wast a s in H5650
15:17 he shall be thy s for ever. And also unto H5650
Dt 15:18 a double hired s *to thee*, in serving thee H7916
23:15 his master the s which is escaped from H5650
24:14 Thou shalt not oppress an hired s *that* H7916
34: 5 So Moses the s of the LORD died there H5650
Jos 1: 1 Now after the death of Moses the s of H5650
2 Moses my s is dead; now therefore H5650
7 which Moses my s commanded thee: H5650
13 Remember the word which Moses the s H5650
15 Moses the LORD'S s gave you on this H5650
5:14 him, What saith my lord unto his s? H5650
8:31 As Moses the s of the LORD H5650
33 Ebal; as Moses the s of the LORD had H5650
9:24 commanded his s Moses to give you all H5650
11:12 Moses the s of the LORD commanded. H5650
15 As the LORD commanded Moses his s, H5650
12: 6 Them did Moses the s of the LORD and H5650
6 and Moses the s of the LORD gave it H5650
13: 8 as Moses the s of the LORD gave them; H5650
14: 7 Forty years old *was* I when Moses the s H5650
18: 7 Moses the s of the LORD gave them. H5650
22: 2 kept all that Moses the s of the LORD H5650
4 which Moses the s of the LORD gave H5650
5 law, which Moses the s of the LORD H5650
24:29 the son of Nun, the s of the LORD, died, H5650
Jdg 2: 8 And Joshua the son of Nun, the s of the H5650
7:10 with Phurah thy s down to the host: H5288
11 with Phurah his s unto the outside of H5288
15:18 the hand of thy s: and now shall I die H5650
19: 3 her again, having his s with him, and a H5288
9 and his s, his father in law, the H5288
11 was far spent; and the s said unto his H5288
13 And he said unto his s, Come, and let us H5288
Ru 2: 5 Then said Boaz unto his s that was set H5288
6 And the s that was set over the reapers H5288
1Sa 2:13 the priest's s came, while the flesh H5288
15 the fat, the priest's s came, and said to H5288
3: 9 LORD; for thy s heareth. So Samuel H5650
10 answered, Speak; for thy s heareth. H5650
9: 5 Saul said to his s that *was* with him, H5288
7 Then said Saul to his s, But, behold, *if* H5288
8 And the s answered Saul again, and H5288
10 Then said Saul to his s, Well said; come, H5288
22 And Samuel took Saul and his s, and H5288
27 to Saul, Bid the s pass on before us, H5288
10:14 him and to his s, Whither went ye? And H5288
17:32 s will go and fight with this Philistine. H5650
34 And David said unto Saul, Thy s kept H5650
36 Thy s slew both the lion and the bear: H5650
58 the son of thy s Jesse the Beth-lehemite. H5650
19: 4 king sin against his s, against David; H5650
20: 7 If he say thus, *It is* well; thy s shall have H5650
8 kindly with thy s; for thou hast brought H5650
8 hast brought thy s into a covenant of H5650
22: 8 hath stirred up my s against me, to lie H5650
15 *any* thing unto his s, *nor* to all the house H5650
15 s knew nothing of all this, less or more. H5650
23:10 God of Israel, thy s hath certainly H5650
11 come down, as thy s hath heard? O H5650
11 thee, tell thy s. And the LORD said, H5650
25:39 and hath kept his s from evil: for the H5650
41 handmaid *be* a s to wash the feet of the H8198
26:18 pursue after his s? for what have I done? H5650
19 the words of his s. If the LORD have H5650
27: 5 thy s dwell in the royal city with thee? H5650
12 him; therefore he shall be my s for ever. H5650
28: 2 know what thy s can do. And Achish H5650
29: 3 not this David, the s of Saul the king of H5650
8 thou found in thy s so long as I have H5650
30:13 man of Egypt, s to an Amalekite; and H5650
2Sa 3:18 By the hand of my s David I will save H5650
7: 5 Go and tell my s David, Thus saith the H5650
8 thou say unto my s David, Thus saith H5650
20 for thou, Lord GOD, knowest thy s. H5650
21 great things, to make thy s know *them*. H5650
25 concerning thy s, and concerning his H5650
26 thy s David be established before thee. H5650
27 revealed to thy s, saying, I will build H5650
27 therefore hath thy s found in his heart H5650
28 hast promised this goodness unto thy s: H5650
29 the house of thy s, that it may continue H5650
29 the house of thy s be blessed for ever. H5650
9: 2 And *there was* of the house of Saul a s H5650
2 *Art* thou Ziba? And he said, Thy s *is he*. H5650
6 And he answered, Behold thy s! H5650
8 said, What *is* thy s, that thou shouldest H5650
9 Then the king called to Ziba, Saul's s, H5288
11 commanded his s, so shall thy servant H5650
11 so shall thy s do. As for Mephibosheth, H5650
11:21 Thy s Uriah the Hittite is dead also. H5650
2Sa 11:24 and thy s Uriah the Hittite is dead also. H5650
13:17 Then he called his s that ministered H5288
18 Then his s brought her out, and H8334
24 Behold now, thy s hath sheepshearers; H5650
24 thee, and his servants go with thy s. H5650
35 king's sons come: as thy s said, so it is. H5650
14:19 spoken: for thy s Joab, he bade me, and H5650
20 of speech hath thy s Joab done this H5650
22 said, To day thy s knoweth that I have H5650
22 king hath fulfilled the request of his s. H5650
15: 2 Thy s *is* of one of the tribes of Israel. H5650
8 For thy s vowed a vow while I abode at H5650
21 or life, even there also will thy s be. H5650
34 I will be thy s, O king; *as I have been* H5650
34 *been* thy father's s hitherto, so *will* I H5650
34 I now also *be* thy s: then mayest thou H5650
16: 1 behold, Ziba the s of Mephibosheth H5288
18:29 sent the king's s, and *me* thy servant, H5650
29 and *me* thy s, I saw a great tumult, H5650
19:17 with him, and Ziba the s of the house of H5288
19 that which thy s did perversely the day H5650
20 For thy s doth know that I have sinned: H5650
26 lord, O king, my s deceived me: for thy H5650
26 me: for thy s said, I will saddle me H5650
26 go to the king; because thy s *is* lame. H5650
27 And he hath slandered thy s unto my H5650
28 didst thou set thy s among them that H5650
35 and evil? can thy s taste what I eat or H5650
35 then should thy s be yet a burden unto H5650
36 Thy s will go a little way over Jordan H5650
37 Let thy s, I pray thee, turn back again, H5650
37 But behold thy s Chimham; let him go H5650
24:10 of thy s; for I have done very foolishly. H5650
21 king come to his s? And David said, To H5650
1Ki 1:19 but Solomon thy s hath he not called. H5650
26 But me, *even* me thy s, and Zadok the H5650
26 and thy s Solomon, hath he not called. H5650
27 shewed *it* unto thy s, who should sit on H5650
51 he will not slay his s with the sword. H5650
2:38 said, so will thy s do. And Shimei dwelt H5650
3: 6 shewed unto thy s David my father H5650
7 hast made thy s king instead of David H5650
8 And thy s *is* in the midst of thy people H5650
9 Give therefore thy s an understanding H5650
8:24 Who hast kept with thy s David my H5650
25 keep with thy s David my father that H5650
26 spakest unto thy s David my father. H5650
28 unto the prayer of thy s, and to his H5650
28 which thy s prayeth before thee to day: H5650
29 thy s shall make toward this place. H5650
30 of thy s, and of thy people Israel, H5650
52 of thy s, and unto the supplication H5650
53 the hand of Moses thy s, when thou H5650
56 he promised by the hand of Moses his s. H5650
59 the cause of his s, and the cause of his H5650
66 David his s, and for Israel his people. H5650
11:11 from thee, and will give it to thy s. H5650
26 of Zereda, Solomon's s, whose mother's H5650
32 (But he shall have one tribe for my s H5650
36 that David my s may have a light alway H5650
38 as David my s did; that I will be with H5650
12: 7 If thou wilt be a s unto this people this H5650
14: 8 not been as my s David, who kept my H5650
18 by the hand of his s Ahijah the prophet. H5650
15:29 he spake by his s Ahijah the Shilonite: H5650
16: 9 And his s Zimri, captain of half *his* H5650
18: 9 thy s into the hand of Ahab, to slay me? H5650
12 I thy s fear the LORD from my youth. H5650
36 and *that* I *am* thy s, and *that* I have H5650
43 And said to his s, Go up now, look H5288
19: 3 *belongeth* to Judah, and left his s there. H5288
20: 9 send for to thy s at the first I will do: H5650
32 and said, Thy s Ben-hadad saith, I H5650
39 and he said, Thy s went out into the H5650
40 And as thy s was busy here and there, H5650
2Ki 4: 1 saying, Thy s my husband is dead; H5650
1 knowest that thy s did fear the LORD: H5650
12 And he said to Gehazi his s, Call this H5288
24 ass, and said to her s, Drive, and go H5288
25 s, Behold, *yonder is* that Shunammite: H5288
38 he said unto his s, Set on the great pot, H5288
5: 6 sent Naaman my s to thee, that thou H5650
15 I pray thee, take a blessing of thy s. H5650
17 be given to thy s two mules' burden of H5650
17 of earth? for thy s will henceforth offer H5650
18 In this thing the LORD pardon thy s, H5650
18 the LORD pardon thy s in this thing. H5650
20 But Gehazi, the s of Elisha the man of H5288
25 And he said, Thy s went no whither. H5650

2Ki 6:15 And when the **s** of the man of God was H8334
15 chariots. And his **s** said unto him, Alas, H5288
8: 4 And the king talked with Gehazi the **s** H5288
13 And Hazael said, But what, *is* thy **s** a H5650
9:36 he spake by his **s** Elijah the Tishbite, H5650
10:10 *that* which he spake by his **s** Elijah. H5650
14:25 by the hand of his **s** Jonah, the son of H5650
16: 7 saying, I *am* thy **s** and thy son: come H5650
17: 3 became his **s**, and gave him presents. H5650
18:12 *and* all that Moses the **s** of the LORD H5650
19:34 own sake, and for my **s** David's sake. H5650
20: 6 own sake, and for my **s** David's sake. H5650
21: 8 that my **s** Moses commanded them. H5650
22:12 and Asahiah a **s** of the king's, saying, H5650
24: 1 became his **s** three years: then he H5650
25: 8 of the guard, a **s** of the king of Babylon, H5650
1Ch 2:34 **s**, an Egyptian, whose name *was* Jarha. H5650
35 his **s** to wife; and she bare him Attai. H5650
6:49 Moses the **s** of God had commanded. H5650
16:13 O ye seed of Israel his **s**, ye children of H5650
17: 4 Go and tell David my **s**, Thus saith the H5650
7 thou say unto my **s** David, Thus saith H5650
18 of thy **s**? for thou knowest thy servant. H5650
18 of thy servant? for thou knowest thy **s**. H5650
23 concerning thy **s** and concerning his H5650
24 David thy **s** *be* established before thee. H5650
25 For thou, O my God, hast told thy **s** H5650
25 therefore thy **s** hath found *in his heart* H5650
26 hast promised this goodness unto thy **s**: H5650
27 the house of thy **s**, that it may be before H5650
21: 8 of thy **s**; for I have done very foolishly. H5650
2Ch 1: 3 which Moses the **s** of the LORD had H5650
6:15 Thou which hast kept with thy **s** David H5650
16 keep with thy **s** David my father that H5650
17 thou hast spoken unto thy **s** David. H5650
19 to the prayer of thy **s**, and to his H5650
19 prayer which thy **s** prayeth before thee: H5650
20 which thy **s** prayeth toward this place. H5650
21 of thy **s**, and of thy people Israel, H5650
42 remember the mercies of David thy **s**. H5650
13: 6 Yet Jeroboam the son of Nebat, the **s** of H5650
24: 6 of Moses the **s** of the LORD, and of H5650
9 *that* Moses the **s** of God *laid* upon H5650
32:16 LORD God, and against his **s** Hezekiah. H5650
34:20 and Asaiah a **s** of the king's, saying, H5650
Neh 1: 6 the prayer of thy **s**, which I pray before H5650
7 which thou commandedst thy **s** Moses. H5650
8 commandedst thy **s** Moses, saying, *If* H5650
11 the prayer of thy **s**, and to the prayer of H5650
11 I pray thee, thy **s** this day, and grant H5650
2: 5 king, and if thy **s** have found favour in H5650
10 and Tobiah the **s**, the Ammonite, heard H5650
19 and Tobiah the **s**, the Ammonite, and H5650
4:22 Let every one with his **s** lodge within H5288
6: 5 Then sent Sanballat his **s** unto me in H5288
9:14 and laws, by the hand of Moses thy **s**: H5650
10:29 by Moses the **s** of God, and to observe H5650
Job 1: 8 considered my **s** Job, that *there is* none H5650
2: 3 considered my **s** Job, that *there is* none H5650
3:19 there; and the **s** *is* free from his master. H5650
7: 2 As a **s** earnestly desireth the shadow, H5650
19:16 I called my **s**, and he gave *me* no H5650
41: 4 wilt thou take him for a **s** for ever? H5650
42: 7 *the thing that is* right, as my **s** Job *hath*. H5650
8 and go to my **s** Job, and offer up for H5650
8 offering; and my **s** Job shall pray for H5650
8 *the thing which is* right, like my **s** Job. H5650
Ps 18:ttl of David, the **s** of the LORD, who spake H5650
19:11 Moreover by them is thy **s** warned: *and* H5650
13 Keep back thy **s** also from H5650
27: 9 me; put not thy **s** away in anger: thou H5650
31:16 Make thy face to shine upon thy **s**: save H5650
35:27 hath pleasure in the prosperity of his **s**. H5650
36:ttl *A Psalm* of David the **s** of the LORD. H5650
69:17 And hide not thy face from thy **s**; for I H5650
78:70 He chose David also his **s**, and took him H5650
86: 2 God, save thy **s** that trusteth in thee. H5650
4 Rejoice the soul of thy **s**: for unto thee, H5650
16 **s**, and save the son of thine handmaid. H5650
89: 3 chosen, I have sworn unto David my **s**, H5650
20 I have found David my **s**; with my holy H5650
39 covenant of thy **s**: thou hast profaned H5650
105: 6 O ye seed of Abraham his **s**, ye children H5650
17 *even* Joseph, *who* was sold for a **s**: H5650
26 He sent Moses his **s**; *and* Aaron whom H5650
42 his holy promise, *and* Abraham his **s**. H5650
109:28 them be ashamed; but let thy **s** rejoice. H5650
116:16 O LORD, truly I *am* thy **s**; I *am* thy H5650
16 servant; I *am* thy **s**, *and* the son of thine H5650

Ps 119:17 Deal bountifully with thy **s**, *that* I may H5650
23 *but* thy **s** did meditate in thy statutes. H5650
38 Stablish thy word unto thy **s**, who *is* H5650
49 Remember the word unto thy **s**, upon H5650
65 Thou hast dealt well with thy **s**, O H5650
76 according to thy word unto thy **s**. H5650
84 How many *are* the days of thy **s**? when H5650
122 Be surety for thy **s** for good: let not the H5650
124 Deal with thy **s** according unto thy H5650
125 I *am* thy **s**; give me understanding, that H5650
135 Make thy face to shine upon thy **s**; and H5650
140 Thy word *is* very pure: therefore thy **s** H5650
176 sheep; seek thy **s**; for I do not forget thy H5650
132:10 For thy **s** David's sake turn not away H5650
136:22 *Even* an heritage unto Israel his **s**: for H5650
143: 2 And enter not into judgment with thy **s**: H5650
12 them that afflict my soul: for I *am* thy **s**. H5650
144:10 David his **s** from the hurtful sword. H5650
Prv 11:29 the fool *shall be* **s** to the wise of heart. H5650
12: 9 *He that is* despised, and hath a **s**, *is* H5650
14:35 The king's favour *is* toward a wise **s**: but H5650
17: 2 A wise **s** shall have rule over a son that H5650
19:10 less for a **s** to have rule over princes. H5650
22: 7 and the borrower *is* **s** to the lender. H5650
29:19 A **s** will not be corrected by words: for H5650
21 He that delicately bringeth up his **s** H5650
30:10 Accuse not a **s** unto his master, lest he H5650
22 For a **s** when he reigneth; and a fool H5650
Ecc 7:21 spoken; lest thou hear thy **s** curse thee: H5650
Isa 20: 3 And the LORD said, Like as my **s** H5650
22:20 call my **s** Eliakim the son of Hilkiah: H5650
24: 2 priest; as with the **s**, so with his master; H5650
37:35 own sake, and for my **s** David's sake. H5650
41: 8 But thou, Israel, *art* my **s**, Jacob whom I H5650
9 thee, Thou *art* my **s**; I have chosen thee, H5650
42: 1 Behold my **s**, whom I uphold; mine H5650
19 Who *is* blind, but my **s**? or deaf, as my H5650
19 *is* perfect, and blind as the LORD'S **s**? H5650
43:10 saith the LORD, and my **s** whom I have H5650
44: 1 Yet now hear, O Jacob my **s**; and Israel, H5650
2 not, O Jacob, my **s**; and thou, Jesurun, H5650
21 for thou *art* my **s**: I have formed thee; H5650
21 thee; thou *art* my **s**: O Israel, thou shalt H5650
26 That confirmeth the word of his **s**, and H5650
48:20 The LORD hath redeemed his **s** Jacob. H5650
49: 3 And said unto me, Thou *art* my **s**, O H5650
5 womb *to be* his **s**, to bring Jacob again H5650
6 shouldest be my **s** to raise up the tribes H5650
7 abhorreth, to a **s** of rulers, Kings shall H5650
50:10 the voice of his **s**, that walketh *in* H5650
52:13 Behold, my **s** shall deal prudently, he H5650
53:11 shall my righteous **s** justify many; for H5650
Jer 2:14 *Is* Israel a **s**? *is* he a homeborn *slave*? H5650
25: 9 of Babylon, my **s**, and will bring them H5650
27: 6 of Babylon, my **s**; and the beasts of the H5650
30:10 Therefore fear thou not, O my **s** Jacob, H5650
33:21 with David my **s**, that he should not H5650
22 seed of David my **s**, and the Levites that H5650
26 and David my **s**, *so* that I will not take H5650
34:16 every man his **s**, and every man his H5650
43:10 of Babylon, my **s**, and will set his throne H5650
46:27 But fear not thou, O my **s** Jacob, and be H5650
28 Fear thou not, O Jacob my **s**, saith the H5650
Ezk 28:25 land that I have given to my **s** Jacob. H5650
34:23 them, *even* my **s** David; he shall feed H5650
24 be their God, and my **s** David a prince H5650
37:24 And David my **s** *shall be* king over H5650
25 unto Jacob my **s**, wherein your fathers H5650
25 **s** David *shall be* their prince for ever. H5650
Dan 6:20 Daniel, O Daniel, **s** of the living God, is H5649
9:11 law of Moses the **s** of God, because we H5650
17 hear the prayer of thy **s**, and his H5650
10:17 For how can the **s** of this my lord talk H5650
Hag 2:23 O Zerubbabel, my **s**, the son of Shealtiel, H5650
Zec 3: 8 I will bring forth my **s** the BRANCH. H5650
Mal 1: 6 A son honoureth *his* father, and a **s** his H5650
4: 4 Remember ye the law of Moses my **s**, H5650
Mt 8: 6 And saying, Lord, my **s** lieth at home *G3816*
8 word only, and my **s** shall be healed. *G3816*
9 and to my **s**, Do this, and he doeth *it*. *G1401*
13 his **s** was healed in the selfsame hour. *G3816*
10:24 *his* master, nor the **s** above his lord. *G1401*
25 his master, and the **s** as his lord. If they *G1401*
12:18 Behold my **s**, whom I have chosen; my *G3816*
18:26 The **s** therefore fell down, and *G1401*
27 Then the lord of that **s** was moved with *G1401*
28 But the same **s** went out, and found *G1401*
32 O thou wicked **s**, I forgave thee all that *G1401*
20:27 be chief among you, let him be your **s**: *G1401*

Mt 23:11 is greatest among you shall be your **s**. *G1249*
24:45 Who then is a faithful and wise **s**, whom *G1401*
46 Blessed *is* that **s**, whom his lord when *G1401*
48 But and if that evil **s** shall say in his *G1401*
50 The lord of that **s** shall come in a day *G1401*
25:21 *thou* good and faithful **s**: thou hast been *G1401*
23 good and faithful **s**; thou hast been *G1401*
26 and slothful **s**, thou knewest that I *G1401*
30 And cast ye the unprofitable **s** into *G1401*
26:51 and struck a **s** of the high priest's, *G1401*
Mk 9:35 *same* shall be last of all, and **s** of all. *G1249*
10:44 you will be the chiefest, shall be **s** of all. *G1401*
12: 2 husbandmen a **s**, that he might receive *G1401*
4 And again he sent unto them another **s**; *G1401*
14:47 **s** of the high priest, and cut off his ear. *G1401*
Lk 1:54 He hath holpen his **s** Israel, in *G3816*
69 for us in the house of his **s** David; *G3816*
2:29 Lord, now lettest thou thy **s** depart in *G1401*
7: 2 And a certain centurion's **s**, who was *G1401*
3 him that he would come and heal his **s**. *G1401*
7 in a word, and my **s** shall be healed. *G3816*
8 and to my **s**, Do this, and he doeth *it*. *G1401*
10 found the **s** whole that had been sick. *G1401*
12:43 Blessed *is* that **s**, whom his lord when *G1401*
45 But and if that **s** say in his heart, My *G1401*
46 The lord of that **s** will come in a day *G1401*
47 And that **s**, which knew his lord's will, *G1401*
14:17 And sent his **s** at supper time to say to *G1401*
21 So that **s** came, and shewed his lord *G1401*
21 angry said to his **s**, Go out quickly into *G1401*
22 And the **s** said, Lord, it is done as thou *G1401*
23 And the lord said unto the **s**, Go out into *G1401*
16:13 No **s** can serve two masters: for either *G3610*
17: 7 But which of you, having a **s** plowing or *G1401*
9 Doth he thank that **s** because he did the *G1401*
19:17 Well, thou good **s**: because thou hast *G1401*
22 thee, *thou* wicked **s**. Thou knewest that *G1401*
20:10 And at the season he sent a **s** to the *G1401*
11 And again he sent another **s**: and they *G1401*
22:50 And one of them smote the **s** of the *G1401*
Jn 8:34 committeth sin is the **s** of sin. *G1401*
35 And the **s** abideth not in the house for *G1401*
12:26 shall also my **s** be: if any man serve *G1249*
13:16 Verily, verily, I say unto you, The **s** is *G1401*
15:15 servants; for the **s** knoweth not what *G1401*
20 said unto you, The **s** is not greater than *G1401*
18:10 the high priest's **s**, and cut off his right *G1401*
Act 4:25 Who by the mouth of thy **s** David hast *G3816*
Ro 1: 1 Paul, a **s** of Jesus Christ, called *to be* an *G1401*
14: 4 another man's **s**? to his own master he *G3610*
16: 1 a **s** of the church which is at Cenchrea: *G1249*
1Co 7:21 Art thou called *being* a **s**? care not for it: *G1401*
22 in the Lord, *being* a **s**, is the Lord's *G1401*
22 he that is called, *being* free, is Christ's **s**. *G1401*
9:19 **s** unto all, that I might gain the more. *G1402*
Gal 1:10 men, I should not be the **s** of Christ. *G1401*
4: 1 from a **s**, though he be lord of all; *G1401*
7 Wherefore thou art no more a **s**, but a *G1401*
Php 2: 7 **s**, and was made in the likeness of men: *G1401*
Col 4:12 Epaphras, who is *one* of you, a **s** of *G1401*
2Ti 2:24 And the **s** of the Lord must not strive; *G1401*
Tit 1: 1 Paul, a **s** of God, and an apostle of *G1401*
Phlm 16 Not now as a **s**, but above a servant, a *G1401*
16 Not now as a servant, but above a **s**, a *G1401*
Heb 3: 5 all his house, as a **s**, for a testimony of *G2324*
Jas 1: 1 James, a **s** of God and of the Lord Jesus *G1401*
2Pt 1: 1 Simon Peter, a **s** and an apostle of *G1401*
Jude 1 Jude, the **s** of Jesus Christ, and brother *G1401*
Rev 1: 1 signified *it* by his angel unto his **s** John: *G1401*
15: 3 And they sing the song of Moses the **s** *G1401*

SERVANTS

Gen 9:25 of **s** shall he be unto his brethren. H5650
14:14 he armed his trained **s**, born in his own
15 them, he and his **s**, by night, and smote H5650
20: 8 and called all his **s**, and told all these H5650
21:25 **s** had violently taken away. H5650
26:14 of **s**: and the Philistines envied him. H5657
15 For all the wells which his father's **s** H5650
19 And Isaac's **s** digged in the valley, and H5650
25 there: and there Isaac's **s** digged a well. H5650
32 day, that Isaac's **s** came, and told him H5650
27:37 I given to him for **s**; and with corn and H5650
32:16 into the hand of his **s**, every drove by H5650
16 and said unto his **s**, Pass over before H5650
40:20 a feast unto all his **s**: and he lifted up H5650
20 and of the chief baker among his **s**. H5650
41:10 Pharaoh was wroth with his **s**, and put H5650
37 of Pharaoh, and in the eyes of all his **s**. H5650

S

Gen 41:38 And Pharaoh said unto his **s**, Can we H5650
42:10 lord, but to buy food are thy **s** come. H5650
11 we *are* true *men*, thy **s** are no spies. H5650
13 And they said, Thy **s** *are* twelve H5650
44: 7 thy **s** should do according to this thing: H5650
9 With whomsoever of thy **s** it be found, H5650
16 the iniquity of thy **s**: behold, we *are* my H5650
16 we *are* my lord's **s**, both we, and *he* also H5650
19 My lord asked his **s**, saying, Have ye a H5650
21 And thou saidst unto thy **s**, Bring him H5650
23 And thou saidst unto thy **s**, Except your H5650
31 will die: and thy **s** shall bring down the H5650
45:16 and it pleased Pharaoh well, and his **s**. H5650
47: 3 Pharaoh, Thy **s** *are* shepherds, both H5650
4 we come; for thy **s** have no pasture for H5650
4 let thy **s** dwell in the land of Goshen. H5650
19 our land will be **s** unto Pharaoh: and H5650
25 of my lord, and we will be Pharaoh's **s**. H5650
50: 2 And Joseph commanded his **s** the H5650
7 went up all the **s** of Pharaoh, the elders H5650
17 the trespass of the **s** of the God of thy H5650
18 face; and they said, Behold, we *be* thy **s**. H5650
Ex 5:15 Wherefore dealest thou thus with thy **s**? H5650
16 There is no straw given unto thy **s**, and H5650
16 and, behold, thy **s** *are* beaten; but the H5650
21 in the eyes of his **s**, to put a sword in H5650
7:10 before his **s**, and it became a serpent. H5650
20 in the sight of his **s**; and all the waters H5650
8: 3 the house of thy **s**, and upon thy people, H5650
4 upon thy people, and upon all thy **s**. H5650
9 thee, and for thy **s**, and for thy people, H5650
11 and from thy **s**, and from thy people; H5650
21 and upon thy **s**, and upon thy people, H5650
29 from Pharaoh, from his **s**, and from his H5650
31 from Pharaoh, from his **s**, and from his H5650
9:14 and upon thy **s**, and upon thy people; H5650
20 LORD among the **s** of Pharaoh made H5650
20 his **s** and his cattle flee into the houses: H5650
21 left his **s** and his cattle in the field. H5650
30 But as for thee and thy **s**, I know that ye H5650
34 and hardened his heart, he and his **s**. H5650
10: 1 and the heart of his **s**, that I might shew H5650
6 houses of all thy **s**, and the houses of all H5650
7 And Pharaoh's **s** said unto him, How H5650
11: 3 **s**, and in the sight of the people. H5650
8 And all these thy **s** shall come down H5650
12:30 he, and all his **s**, and all the Egyptians; H5650
14: 5 and of his **s** was turned against H5650
32:13 and Israel, thy **s**, to whom thou swarest H5650
Lev 25:42 For they *are* my **s**, which I brought forth H5650
55 For unto me the children of Israel *are* **s**; H5650
55 they *are* my **s** whom I brought forth H5650
Nu 22:18 and said unto the **s** of Balak, If Balak H5650
22 his ass, and his two **s** *were* with him. H5288
31:49 And they said unto Moses, Thy **s** have H5650
32: 4 a land for cattle, and thy **s** have cattle: H5650
5 be given unto thy **s** for a possession, H5650
25 Thy **s** will do as my lord commandeth. H5650
27 But thy **s** will pass over, every man H5650
31 hath said unto thy **s**, so will we do. H5650
Dt 9:27 Remember thy **s**, Abraham, Isaac, and H5650
29: 2 and unto all his **s**, and unto all his land; H5650
32:36 himself for his **s**, when he seeth that H5650
43 the blood of his **s**, and will render H5650
34:11 and to all his **s**, and to all his land, H5650
Jos 9: 8 We *are* thy **s**. And Joshua said unto H5650
9 far country thy **s** are come because of H5650
11 them, We *are* your **s**: therefore now H5650
24 certainly told thy **s**, how that the LORD H5650
10: 6 not thy hand from thy **s**; come up to us H5650
Jdg 3:24 When he was gone out, his **s** came; and H5650
6:27 Then Gideon took ten men of his **s**, and H5650
19:19 with thy **s**: *there is* no want of any thing. H5650
1Sa 4: 9 that ye be not **s** unto the Hebrews, as H5647
8:14 the best *of them*, and give *them* to his **s**. H5650
15 and give to his officers, and to his **s**. H5650
17 of your sheep: and ye shall be his **s**. H5650
9: 3 now one of the **s** with thee, and arise, H5288
12:19 Pray for thy **s** unto the LORD thy H5650
16:15 And Saul's **s** said unto him, Behold H5650
16 Let our lord now command thy **s**, *which* H5650
17 And Saul said unto his **s**, Provide me H5650
18 Then answered one of the **s**, and said, H5288
17: 8 Philistine, and ye **s** to Saul? choose you H5650
9 will we be your **s**: but if I prevail against H5650
9 then shall ye be our **s**, and serve us. H5650
18: 5 people, and also in the sight of Saul's **s**. H5650
22 And Saul commanded his **s**, *saying*, H5650
22 in thee, and all his **s** love thee: now H5650
1Sa 18:23 And Saul's **s** spake those words in the H5650
24 And the **s** of Saul told him, saying, On H5650
26 And when his **s** told David these words, H5650
30 wisely than all the **s** of Saul; so that his H5650
19: 1 to all his **s**, that they should kill David. H5650
21: 2 *my* **s** to such and such a place. H5288
7 Now a certain man of the **s** of Saul *was* H5650
11 And the **s** of Achish said unto him, *Is* H5650
14 Then said Achish unto his **s**, Lo, ye see H5650
22: 6 and all his **s** *were* standing about him;) H5650
7 Then Saul said unto his **s** that stood H5650
9 was set over the **s** of Saul, and said, I H5650
14 among all thy **s** as David, which is the H5650
17 it to me. But the **s** of the king would not H5650
24: 7 So David stayed his **s** with these words, H582
25: 8 hand unto thy **s**, and to thy son David. H5650
10 And Nabal answered David's **s**, and H5650
10 there be many **s** now a days that break H5650
19 And she said unto her **s**, Go on before H5288
40 And when the **s** of David were come to H5650
41 to wash the feet of the **s** of my lord. H5650
28: 7 Then said Saul unto his **s**, Seek me a H5650
7 of her. And his **s** said to him, Behold, H5650
23 will not eat. But his **s**, together with the H5650
25 and before his **s**; and they did eat. Then H5650
29:10 with thy master's **s** that are come with H5650
2Sa 2:12 And Abner the son of Ner, and the **s** of H5650
13 And Joab the son of Zeruiah, and the **s** H5650
15 of Saul, and twelve of the **s** of David. H5650
17 the men of Israel, before the **s** of David. H5650
30 of David's **s** nineteen men and Asahel. H5650
31 But the **s** of David had smitten of H5650
3:22 And, behold, the **s** of David and Joab H5650
38 And the king said unto his **s**, Know ye H5650
6:20 handmaids of his **s**, as one of the vain H5650
8: 2 became David's **s**, *and* brought gifts. H5650
6 the Syrians became **s** to David, *and* H5650
7 that were on the **s** of Hadadezer, and H5650
14 Edom became David's **s**. And the LORD H5650
9:10 Thou therefore, and thy sons, and thy **s**, H5650
10 Now Ziba had fifteen sons and twenty **s**. H5650
12 of Ziba *were* **s** unto Mephibosheth. H5650
10: 2 by the hand of his **s** for his father. And H5650
2 And David's **s** came into the land of H5650
3 *rather* sent his **s** unto thee, to search H5650
4 Wherefore Hanun took David's **s**, and H5650
19 And when all the kings *that were* **s** to H5650
11: 1 sent Joab, and his **s** with him, and all H5650
9 house with all the **s** of his lord, and H5650
11 my lord Joab, and the **s** of my lord, are H5650
13 his bed with the **s** of his lord, but went H5650
17 the people of the **s** of David; and Uriah H5650
24 off the wall upon thy **s**; and *some* of the H5650
24 *some* of the king's **s** be dead, and thy H5650
12:18 died. And the **s** of David feared to tell H5650
19 But when David saw that his **s** H5650
19 said unto his **s**, Is the child dead? And H5650
21 Then said his **s** unto him, What thing *is* H5650
13:24 thee, and his **s** go with thy servant. H5650
28 Now Absalom had commanded his **s**, H5288
29 And the **s** of Absalom did unto Amnon H5288
31 his **s** stood by with their clothes rent. H5650
36 king also and all his **s** wept very sore. H5650
14:30 Therefore he said unto his **s**, See, Joab's H5650
30 And Absalom's **s** set the field on fire. H5650
31 have thy **s** set my field on fire? H5650
15:14 And David said unto all his **s** that *were* H5650
15 And the king's **s** said unto the king, H5650
15 the king, Behold, thy **s** *are ready to do* H5650
18 And all his **s** passed on beside him; and H5650
16: 6 and at all the **s** of king David: and all H5650
11 and to all his **s**, Behold, my son, which H5650
17:20 And when Absalom's **s** came to the H5650
18: 7 slain before the **s** of David, and there H5650
9 And Absalom met the **s** of David. And H5650
19: 5 day the faces of all thy **s**, which this day H5650
6 princes nor **s**: for this day I perceive, H5650
7 unto thy **s**: for I swear by the LORD, H5650
14 the king, Return thou, and all thy **s**. H5650
17 and his twenty **s** with him; and they H5650
20: 6 thou thy lord's **s**, and pursue after him, H5650
21:15 down, and his **s** with him, and fought H5650
22 hand of David, and by the hand of his **s**. H5650
24:20 the king and his **s** coming on toward H5650
1Ki 1: 2 Wherefore his **s** said unto him, Let H5650
9 and all the men of Judah the king's **s**: H5650
33 Take with you the **s** of your lord, and H5650
47 And moreover the king's **s** came to H5650
2:39 that two of the **s** of Shimei ran away H5650
1Ki 2:39 saying, Behold, thy **s** *be* in Gath. H5650
40 Achish to seek his **s**: and Shimei went, H5650
40 went, and brought his **s** from Gath. H5650
3:15 offerings, and made a feast to all his **s**. H5650
5: 1 And Hiram king of Tyre sent his **s** unto H5650
6 of Lebanon; and my **s** shall be with thy H5650
6 shall be with thy **s**: and unto thee will I H5650
6 I give hire for thy **s** according to all that H5650
9 My **s** shall bring *them* down from H5650
8:23 mercy with thy **s** that walk before thee H5650
32 do, and judge thy **s**, condemning the H5650
36 the sin of thy **s**, and of thy people Israel, H5650
9:22 of war, and his **s**, and his princes, and H5650
27 And Hiram sent in the navy his **s**, H5650
27 of the sea, with the **s** of Solomon. H5650
10: 5 the sitting of his **s**, and the attendance H5650
8 *are* these thy **s**, which stand continually H5650
13 went to her own country, she and her **s**. H5650
11:17 of his father's **s** with him, to go into H5650
12: 7 to them, then they will be thy **s** for ever. H5650
15:18 into the hand of his **s**: and king Asa sent H5650
20: 6 Yet I will send my **s** unto thee to H5650
6 the houses of thy **s**; and it shall be, *that* H5650
12 that he said unto his **s**, Set *yourselves in* H5650
23 And the **s** of the king of Syria said unto H5650
31 And his **s** said unto him, Behold now, H5650
22: 3 And the king of Israel said unto his **s**, H5650
49 Let my **s** go with thy servants H5650
49 servants go with thy **s** in the ships. But H5650
2Ki 1:13 these fifty thy **s**, be precious in thy sight. H5650
2:16 there be with thy **s** fifty strong men; let H5650
3:11 of the king of Israel's **s** answered and H5650
5:13 And his **s** came near, and spake unto H5650
23 of his **s**; and they bare *them* before him. H5288
6: 3 with thy **s**. And he answered, I will go. H5650
8 counsel with his **s**, saying, In such and H5650
11 and he called his **s**, and said unto them, H5650
12 And one of his **s** said, None, my lord, O H5650
7:12 and said unto his **s**, I will now shew you H5650
13 And one of his **s** answered and said, H5650
9: 7 the blood of my **s** the prophets, and the H5650
7 **s** of the LORD, at the hand of Jezebel. H5650
11 Then Jehu came forth to the **s** of his H5650
28 And his **s** carried him in a chariot to H5650
10: 5 saying, We *are* thy **s**, and will do all that H5650
19 of Baal, all his **s**, and all his priests; let H5647
23 you none of the **s** of the LORD, but the H5650
12:20 And his **s** arose, and made a H5650
21 son of Shomer, his **s**, smote him, and he H5650
14: 5 **s** which had slain the king his father. H5650
17:13 I sent to you by my **s** the prophets. H5650
23 he had said by all his **s** the prophets. So H5650
18:24 of my master's **s**, and put thy trust on H5650
26 I pray thee, to thy **s** in the Syrian H5650
19: 5 So the **s** of king Hezekiah came to H5650
6 with which the **s** of the king of Assyria H5288
21:10 And the LORD spake by his **s** the H5650
23 And the **s** of Amon conspired against H5650
22: 9 and said, Thy **s** have gathered the H5650
23:30 And his **s** carried him in a chariot dead H5650
24: 2 which he spake by his **s** the prophets. H5650
10 At that time the **s** of Nebuchadnezzar H5650
11 the city, and his **s** did besiege it. H5650
12 mother, and his **s**, and his princes, and H5650
25:24 Fear not to be the **s** of the Chaldees: H5650
1Ch 18: 2 became David's **s**, *and* brought gifts. H5650
6 became David's **s**, *and* brought gifts. H5650
7 that were on the **s** of Hadarezer, and H5650
13 became David's **s**. Thus the LORD H5650
19: 2 his father. So the **s** of David came into H5650
3 thee? are not his **s** come unto thee for H5650
4 Wherefore Hanun took David's **s**, and H5650
19 And when the **s** of Hadarezer saw that H5650
19 and became his **s**: neither would the H5647
20: 8 hand of David, and by the hand of his **s**. H5650
21: 3 not all my lord's **s**? why then doth my H5650
2Ch 2: 8 for I know that thy **s** can skill to cut H5650
8 behold, my **s** *shall be* with thy servants, H5650
8 behold, my servants *shall be* with thy **s**, H5650
10 And, behold, I will give to thy **s**, the H5650
15 hath spoken of, let him send unto his **s**: H5650
6:14 mercy unto thy **s**, that walk before thee H5650
23 do, and judge thy **s**, by requiting the H5650
27 the sin of thy **s**, and of thy people Israel, H5650
8: 9 Solomon make no **s** for his work; but H5650
18 the hands of his **s** ships, and servants H5650
18 ships, and **s** that had knowledge H5650
18 and they went with the **s** of Solomon to H5650
9: 4 the sitting of his **s**, and the attendance H5650

2Ch 9: 7 *are* these thy **s**, which stand continually H5650
10 And the **s** also of Huram, and the H5650
10 of Huram, and the **s** of Solomon, which H5650
12 away to her own land, she and her **s**. H5650
21 to Tarshish with the **s** of Huram: every H5650
10: 7 to them, they will be thy **s** for ever. H5650
12: 8 Nevertheless they shall be his **s**; that H5650
24:25 diseases,) his own **s** conspired against H5650
25: 3 his **s** that had killed the king his father. H5650
32: 9 Assyria send his **s** to Jerusalem, (but he H5650
16 And his **s** spake yet *more* against the H5650
33:24 And his **s** conspired against him, and H5650
34:16 that was committed to thy **s**, they do *it*. H5650
35:23 king said to his **s**, Have me away; for H5650
24 His **s** therefore took him out of that H5650
36:20 where they were **s** to him and his sons H5650
Ezr 2:55 The children of Solomon's **s**: the H5650
58 **s**, *were* three hundred ninety and two. H5650
65 Beside their **s** and their maids, of H5650
4:11 the king; Thy **s** the men on this side H5649
5:11 saying, We are the **s** of the God of H5649
9:11 Which thou hast commanded by thy **s** H5650
Neh 1: 6 of Israel thy **s**, and confess the sins H5650
10 Now these *are* thy **s** and thy people, H5650
11 to the prayer of thy **s**, who desire to fear H5650
2:20 therefore we his **s** will arise and build: H5650
4:16 *that* the half of my **s** wrought in the H5288
23 So neither I, nor my brethren, nor my **s**, H5288
5: 5 our daughters to be **s**, and *some* of our H5650
10 I likewise, *and* my brethren, and my **s**, H5288
15 yea, even their **s** bare rule over the H5288
16 **s** *were* gathered thither unto the work. H5288
7:57 The children of Solomon's **s**: the H5650
60 **s**, *were* three hundred ninety and two. H5650
9:10 and on all his **s**, and on all the people H5650
36 Behold, we *are* **s** this day, and *for* the H5650
36 the good thereof, behold, we *are* **s** in it: H5650
11: 3 and the children of Solomon's **s**. H5650
13:19 and *some* of my **s** set I at the gates, *that* H5288
Est 1: 3 princes and his **s**; the power of Persia H5650
2: 2 Then said the king's **s** that ministered H5288
18 princes and his **s**, *even* Esther's feast; H5650
3: 2 And all the king's **s**, that *were* in the H5650
3 Then the king's **s**, which *were* in the H5650
4:11 All the king's **s**, and the people of the H5650
5:11 above the princes and **s** of the king. H5650
6: 3 said the king's **s** that ministered unto H5288
5 And the king's **s** said unto him, Behold, H5288
Job 1:15 they have slain the **s** with the edge of H5288
16 up the sheep, and the **s**, and consumed H5288
17 yea, and slain the **s** with the edge of the H5288
4:18 Behold, he put no trust in his **s**; and his H5650
Ps 34:22 The LORD redeemeth the soul of his **s**: H5650
69:36 The seed also of his **s** shall inherit it: H5650
79: 2 The dead bodies of thy **s** have they H5650
10 of the blood of thy **s** *which is* shed. H5650
89:50 Remember, Lord, the reproach of thy **s**; H5650
90:13 and let it repent thee concerning thy **s**. H5650
16 Let thy work appear unto thy **s**, and thy H5650
102:14 For thy **s** take pleasure in her stones, H5650
28 The children of thy **s** shall continue, H5650
105:25 his people, to deal subtilly with his **s**. H5650
113: 1 Praise ye the LORD. Praise, O ye **s** of H5650
119:91 to thine ordinances: for all *are* thy **s**. H5650
123: 2 Behold, as the eyes of **s** *look* unto the H5650
134: 1 Behold, bless ye the LORD, all *ye* **s** of H5650
135: 1 LORD; praise *him*, O ye **s** of the LORD. H5650
9 upon Pharaoh, and upon all his **s**. H5650
14 he will repent himself concerning his **s**. H5650
Prv 29:12 If a ruler hearken to lies, all his **s** *are* H8334
Ecc 2: 7 I got *me* **s** and maidens, and had H5650
7 maidens, and had **s** born in my house;
10: 7 I have seen **s** upon horses, and princes H5650
7 princes walking as **s** upon the earth. H5650
Isa 14: 2 of the LORD for **s** and handmaids: and H5650
36: 9 of my master's **s**, and put thy trust on H5650
11 thee, unto thy **s** in the Syrian language; H5650
37: 5 So the **s** of king Hezekiah came to H5650
6 wherewith the **s** of the king of Assyria H5288
24 By thy **s** hast thou reproached the H5650
54:17 the heritage of the **s** of the LORD, and H5650
56: 6 the LORD, to be his **s**, every one that H5650
65: 9 inherit it, and my **s** shall dwell there. H5650
13 GOD, Behold, my **s** shall eat, but ye H5650
13 behold, my **s** shall drink, but ye shall H5650
13 **s** shall rejoice, but ye shall be ashamed: H5650
14 Behold, my **s** shall sing for joy of heart, H5650
15 thee, and call his **s** by another name: H5650
66:14 be known toward his **s**, and *his* H5650

Jer 7:25 unto you all my **s** the prophets, daily H5650
21: 7 of Judah, and his **s**, and the people, and H5650
22: 2 thou, and thy **s**, and thy people that H5650
4 on horses, he, and his **s**, and his people. H5650
25: 4 unto you all his **s** the prophets, rising H5650
19 Pharaoh king of Egypt, and his **s**, and H5650
26: 5 To hearken to the words of my **s** the H5650
29:19 unto them by my **s** the prophets, rising H5650
34:11 and caused the **s** and the handmaids, H5650
11 subjection for **s** and for handmaids. H5650
16 be unto you for **s** and for handmaids. H5650
35:15 I have sent also unto you all my **s** the H5650
36:24 any of his **s** that heard all these words. H5650
31 his seed and his **s** for their iniquity; H5650
37: 2 But neither he, nor his **s**, nor the people H5650
18 or against thy **s**, or against this people, H5650
44: 4 Howbeit I sent unto you all my **s** the H5650
46:26 the hand of his **s**: and afterward it shall H5650
Lam 5: 8 **S** have ruled over us: *there is* none that H5650
Ezk 38:17 in old time by my **s** the prophets of H5650
46:17 to one of his **s**, then it shall be his to H5650
Dan 1:12 Prove thy **s**, I beseech thee, ten days; H5650
13 meat: and as thou seest, deal with thy **s**. H5650
2: 4 for ever: tell thy **s** the dream, and we H5649
7 the king tell his **s** the dream, and we H5649
3:26 Abed-nego, ye **s** of the most high God, H5649
28 and delivered his **s** that trusted in him, H5649
9: 6 Neither have we hearkened unto thy **s** H5650
10 he set before us by his **s** the prophets. H5650
Joel 2:29 And also upon the **s** and upon the H5650
Am 3: 7 his secret unto his **s** the prophets. H5650
Mic 6: 4 out of the house of **s**; and I sent before H5650
Zec 1: 6 I commanded my **s** the prophets, did H5650
2: 9 be a spoil to their **s**: and ye shall know H5647
Mt 13:27 So the **s** of the householder came and *G1401*
28 done this. The **s** said unto him, Wilt *G1401*
14: 2 And said unto his **s**, This is John the *G3816*
18:23 king, which would take account of his **s**. *G1401*
21:34 near, he sent his **s** to the husbandmen, *G1401*
35 And the husbandmen took his **s**, and *G1401*
36 Again, he sent other **s** more than the *G1401*
22: 3 And sent forth his **s** to call them that *G1401*
4 Again, he sent forth other **s**, saying, Tell *G1401*
6 And the remnant took his **s**, and *G1401*
8 Then saith he to his **s**, The wedding is *G1401*
10 So those **s** went out into the highways, *G1401*
13 Then said the king to the **s**, Bind him *G1249*
25:14 **s**, and delivered unto them his goods. *G1401*
19 After a long time the lord of those **s** *G1401*
26:58 in, and sat with the **s**, to see the end. *G5257*
Mk 1:20 with the hired **s**, and went after him. *G3411*
13:34 authority to his **s**, and to every man his *G1401*
14:54 the **s**, and warmed himself at the fire. *G5257*
65 Prophesy: and the **s** did strike him with *G5257*
Lk 12:37 Blessed *are* those **s**, whom the lord *G1401*
38 and find *them* so, blessed are those **s**. *G1401*
15:17 How many hired **s** of my father's have *G3407*
19 thy son: make me as one of thy hired **s**. *G3407*
22 But the father said to his **s**, Bring forth *G1401*
26 And he called one of the **s**, and asked *G3816*
17:10 are unprofitable **s**: we have done that *G1401*
19:13 And he called his ten **s**, and delivered *G1401*
15 commanded these **s** to be called unto *G1401*
Jn 2: 5 His mother saith unto the **s**, *G1249*
9 it was: (but the **s** which drew the water *G1249*
4:51 And as he was now going down, his **s** *G1401*
15:15 Henceforth I call you not **s**; for the *G1401*
18:18 And the **s** and officers stood there, who *G1401*
26 One of the **s** of the high priest, being *his* *G1401*
36 then would my **s** fight, that I should not *G5257*
Act 2:18 And on my **s** and on my handmaidens *G1401*
4:29 grant unto thy **s**, that with all boldness *G1401*
10: 7 of his household **s**, and a devout soldier *G3610*
16:17 These men are the **s** of the most high *G1401*
Ro 6:16 whom ye yield yourselves **s** to obey, his *G1401*
16 to obey, his **s** ye are to whom ye obey; *G1401*
17 But God be thanked, that ye were the **s** *G1401*
18 sin, ye became the **s** of righteousness. *G1402*
19 your members **s** to uncleanness and *G1401*
19 **s** to righteousness unto holiness. *G1401*
20 For when ye were the **s** of sin, ye were *G1401*
22 sin, and become **s** to God, ye have your *G1402*
1Co 7:23 with a price; be not ye the **s** of men. *G1401*
2Co 4: 5 and ourselves your **s** for Jesus' sake. *G1401*
Eph 6: 5 **S**, be obedient to them that are *your* *G1401*
6 but as the **s** of Christ, doing the *G1401*
Php 1: 1 Paul and Timotheus, the **s** of Jesus *G1401*
Col 3:22 **S**, obey in all things *your* masters *G1401*
4: 1 Masters, give unto *your* **s** that which is *G1401*

1Ti 6: 1 Let as many **s** as are under the yoke *G1401*
Tit 2: 9 *Exhort* **s** to be obedient unto their own *G1401*
1Pt 2:16 of maliciousness, but as the **s** of God. *G1401*
18 **S**, *be* subject to *your* masters with all *G3610*
2Pt 2:19 themselves are the **s** of corruption: for *G1401*
Rev 1: 1 to shew unto his **s** things which must *G1401*
2:20 teach and to seduce my **s** to commit *G1401*
7: 3 the **s** of our God in their foreheads. *G1401*
10: 7 he hath declared to his **s** the prophets. *G1401*
11:18 reward unto thy **s** the prophets, and to *G1401*
19: 2 avenged the blood of his **s** at her hand. *G1401*
5 our God, all ye his **s**, and ye that fear *G1401*
22: 3 shall be in it; and his **s** shall serve him: *G1401*
6 to shew unto his **s** the things which *G1401*

SERVANT'S

Gen 19: 2 you, into your **s** house, and tarry all H5650
2Sa 7:19 spoken also of thy **s** house for a great H5650
1Ki 11:13 thy son for David my **s** sake, and for H5650
34 life for David my **s** sake, whom I chose, H5650
2Ki 8:19 for David his **s** sake, as he promised H5650
1Ch 17:17 *also* spoken of thy **s** house for a great H5650
19 O LORD, for thy **s** sake, and according H5650
Isa 45: 4 For Jacob my **s** sake, and Israel mine H5650
Jn 18:10 his right ear. The **s** name was Malchus. *G1401*

SERVANTS'

Gen 46:34 That ye shall say, Thy **s** trade hath H5650
Ex 8:24 and *into* his **s** houses, and into all H5650
Isa 63:17 **s** sake, the tribes of thine inheritance. H5650
65: 8 so will I do for my **s** sakes, that I may H5650

SERVE

Gen 15:13 theirs, and shall **s** them; and they shall H5647
14 whom they shall **s**, will I judge: and H5647
25:23 and the elder shall **s** the younger. H5647
27:29 Let people **s** thee, and nations bow H5647
40 live, and shalt **s** thy brother; and it H5647
29:15 thou therefore **s** me for nought? tell me, H5647
18 and said, I will **s** thee seven years for H5647
25 done unto me? did not I **s** with thee for H5647
27 shalt **s** with me yet seven other years. H5647
Ex 1:13 the children of Israel to **s** with rigour: H5647
14 they made them **s**, *was* with rigour. H5647
3:12 ye shall **s** God upon this mountain. H5647
4:23 go, that he may **s** me: and if thou refuse H5647
7:16 people go, that they may **s** me in the H5647
8: 1 Let my people go, that they may **s** me. H5647
20 Let my people go, that they may **s** me. H5647
9: 1 Let my people go, that they may **s** me. H5647
13 Let my people go, that they may **s** me. H5647
10: 3 let my people go, that they may **s** me. H5647
7 go, that they may **s** the LORD their H5647
8 unto them, Go, **s** the LORD your God: H5647
11 Not so: go now ye *that are* men, and **s** H5647
24 and said, Go ye, **s** the LORD; only let H5647
26 must we take to **s** the LORD our God; H5647
26 **s** the LORD, until we come thither. H5647
12:31 and go, **s** the LORD, as ye have said. H5647
14:12 that we may **s** the Egyptians? For *it* H5647
12 better for us to **s** the Egyptians, than H5647
20: 5 to them, nor **s** them: for I the LORD H5647
21: 2 six years he shall **s**: and in the seventh H5647
6 with an aul; and he shall **s** him for ever. H5647
23:24 to their gods, nor **s** them, nor do after H5647
25 And ye shall **s** the LORD your God, and H5647
33 me: for if thou **s** their gods, it will H5647
Lev 25:39 not compel him to **s** as a bondservant: H5656
40 *and* shall **s** thee unto the year of jubile: H5647
Nu 4:24 the Gershonites, to **s**, and for burdens: H5647
26 that is made for them: so shall they **s**. H5647
8:25 service *thereof*, and shall **s** no more: H5647
18: 7 vail; and ye shall **s**: I have given your H5647
21 service which they **s**, *even* the service of H5647
Dt 4:19 them, and **s** them, which the LORD H5647
28 And there ye shall **s** gods, the work of H5647
5: 9 unto them, nor **s** them: for I the LORD H5647
6:13 **s** him, and shalt swear by his name. H5647
7: 4 me, that they may **s** other gods: so will H5647
16 neither shalt thou **s** their gods; for that H5647
8:19 other gods, and **s** them, and worship H5647
10:12 to love him, and to **s** the LORD thy God H5647
20 him shalt thou **s**, and to him shalt thou H5647
11:13 your God, and to **s** him with all your H5647
16 and **s** other gods, and worship them; H5647
12:30 **s** their gods? even so will I do likewise. H5647
13: 2 thou hast not known, and let us **s** them; H5647
4 ye shall **s** him, and cleave unto him. H5647
6 Let us go and **s** other gods, which thou H5647

S

Dt 13:13 s other gods, which ye have not known; H5647
15:12 unto thee, and s thee six years; then H5647
20:11 unto thee, and they shall s thee. H5647
28:14 left, to go after other gods to s them. H5647
36 thou s other gods, wood and stone. H5647
48 Therefore shalt thou s thine enemies H5647
64 there thou shalt s other gods, which H5647
29:18 our God, to go *and* s the gods of these H5647
30:17 and worship other gods, and s them; H5647
31:20 other gods, and s them, and provoke H5647
Jos 16:10 unto this day, and s under tribute. H5647
22: 5 unto him, and to s him with all your H5647
23: 7 s them, nor bow yourselves unto them: H5647
24:14 Now therefore fear the LORD, and s H5647
14 flood, and in Egypt; and s ye the LORD. H5647
15 And if it seem evil unto you to s the H5647
15 day whom ye will s; whether the gods H5647
15 me and my house, we will s the LORD. H5647
16 forsake the LORD, to s other gods; H5647
18 we also s the LORD; for he *is* our God. H5647
19 people, Ye cannot s the LORD: for he *is* H5647
20 If ye forsake the LORD, and s strange H5647
21 Joshua, Nay; but we will s the LORD. H5647
22 you the LORD, to s him. And they said, H5647
24 will we s, and his voice will we obey. H5647
Jdg 2:19 other gods to s them, and to bow down H5647
9:28 that we should s him? *is* not *he* the son H5647
28 Zebul his officer? s the men of Hamor H5647
28 of Shechem: for why should we s him? H5647
38 that we should s him? *is* not this the H5647
1Sa 7: 3 the LORD, and s him only: and he will H5647
10: 7 as occasion s thee; for God *is* with thee. H5647
11: 1 a covenant with us, and we will s thee. H5647
12:10 of our enemies, and we will s thee. H5647
14 If ye will fear the LORD, and s him, and H5647
20 but s the LORD with all your heart; H5647
24 Only fear the LORD, and s him in truth H5647
17: 9 then shall ye be our servants, and s us. H5647
26:19 of the LORD, saying, Go, s other gods. H5647
2Sa 15: 8 to Jerusalem, then I will s the LORD. H5647
16:19 And again, whom should I s? *should I* H5647
19 serve? *should I* not s in the presence of H5647
22:44 a people *which* I knew not shall s me. H5647
1Ki 9: 6 and s other gods, and worship them: H5647
12: 4 put upon us, lighter, and we will s thee. H5647
7 this day, and wilt s them, and answer H5647
2Ki 10:18 Baal a little; *but* Jehu shall s him much. H5647
17:35 nor s them, nor sacrifice to them: H5647
25:24 in the land, and s the king of Babylon; H5647
1Ch 28: 9 of thy father, and s him with a perfect H5647
2Ch 7:19 and s other gods, and worship them; H5647
10: 4 that he put upon us, and we will s thee. H5647
29:11 stand before him, to s him, and that ye H8334
30: 8 for ever: and s the LORD your God, H5647
33:16 Judah to s the LORD God of Israel. H5647
34:33 in Israel to s, *even* to serve the LORD H5647
33 to serve, *even* to s the LORD their God. H5647
35: 3 *your* shoulders: s now the LORD your H5647
Job 21:15 What *is* the Almighty, that we should s H5647
36:11 If they obey and s *him*, they shall spend H5647
39: 9 Will the unicorn be willing to s thee, or H5647
Ps 2:11 S the LORD with fear, and rejoice with H5647
18:43 *whom* I have not known shall s me. H5647
22:30 A seed shall s him; it shall be H5647
72:11 before him: all nations shall s him. H5647
97: 7 Confounded be all they that s graven H5647
100: 2 S the LORD with gladness: come before H5647
101: 6 walketh in a perfect way, he shall s me. H8334
102:22 and the kingdoms, to s the LORD. H5647
Isa 14: 3 bondage wherein thou wast made to s, H5647
19:23 Egyptians shall s with the Assyrians. H5647
43:23 not caused thee to s with an offering, H5647
24 hast made me to s with thy sins, thou H5647
56: 6 to the LORD, to s him, and to love the H8334
60:12 that will not s thee shall perish; yea, H5647
Jer 5:19 s strangers in a land *that is* not yours. H5647
11:10 after other gods to s them: the house of H5647
13:10 other gods, to s them, and to worship H5647
16:13 and there shall ye s other gods day and H5647
17: 4 I will cause thee to s thine enemies in H5647
25: 6 And go not after other gods to s them, H5647
11 s the king of Babylon seventy years. H5647
14 great kings shall s themselves of them H5647
27: 6 the field have I given him also to s him. H5647
7 And all nations shall s him, and his H5647
7 great kings shall s themselves of him. H5647
8 kingdom which will not s the same H5647
9 Ye shall not s the king of Babylon: H5647
11 of Babylon, and s him, those will I let H5647
Jer 27:12 and s him and his people, and live. H5647
13 that will not s the king of Babylon? H5647
14 Ye shall not s the king of Babylon: H5647
17 Hearken not unto them; s the king of H5647
28:14 that they may s Nebuchadnezzar king H5647
14 and they shall s him: and I have given H5647
30: 8 shall no more s themselves of him: H5647
9 But they shall s the LORD their God, H5647
34: 9 that none should s himself of them, *to* H5647
10 that none should s themselves of them H5647
35:15 after other gods to s them, and ye shall H5647
40: 9 saying, Fear not to s the Chaldeans: H5647
9 in the land, and s the king of Babylon, H5647
10 dwell at Mizpah to s the Chaldeans, H5975
44: 3 incense, *and* to s other gods, whom H5647
Ezk 20:32 of the countries, to s wood and stone. H8334
39 the Lord GOD; Go ye, s ye every one his H5647
40 of them in the land, s me: there will I H5647
29:18 his army to s a great service against H5647
48:18 be for food unto them that s the city. H5647
19 And they that s the city shall serve it H5647
19 And they that serve the city shall s it H5647
Dan 3:12 thee: they s not thy gods, nor worship H6399
14 do not ye s my gods, nor worship H6399
17 If it be *so*, our God whom we s is able H6399
18 that we will not s thy gods, nor worship H6399
28 they might not s nor worship any god, H6399
7:14 languages, should s him: his dominion H6399
27 all dominions shall s and obey him. H6399
Zep 3: 9 the LORD, to s him with one consent. H5647
Mal 3:14 Ye have said, It *is* vain to s God: and H5647
Mt 4:10 thy God, and him only shalt thou s. *G3000*
6:24 No man can s two masters: for either *G1398*
24 other. Ye cannot s God and mammon. *G1398*
Lk 1:74 our enemies might s him without fear, *G3000*
4: 8 thy God, and him only shalt thou s. *G3000*
10:40 sister hath left me to s alone? bid her *G1247*
12:37 meat, and will come forth and s them. *G1247*
15:29 these many years do I s thee, neither *G1398*
16:13 No servant can s two masters: for *G1398*
13 other. Ye cannot s God and mammon. *G1398*
17: 8 gird thyself, and s me, till I have eaten *G1247*
22:26 and he that is chief, as he that doth s. *G1247*
Jn 12:26 If any man s me, let him follow me; *G1247*
26 man s me, him will *my* Father honour. *G1247*
Act 6: 2 leave the word of God, and s tables. *G1247*
7: 7 they come forth, and s me in this place. *G3000*
27:23 of God, whose I am, and whom I s, *G3000*
Ro 1: 9 For God is my witness, whom I s with *G3000*
6: 6 that henceforth we should not s sin. *G1398*
7: 6 that we should s in newness of spirit, *G1398*
25 the mind I myself s the law of God; but *G1398*
9:12 It was said unto her, The elder shall s *G1398*
16:18 For they that are such s not our Lord *G1398*
Gal 5:13 to the flesh, but by love s one another. *G1398*
Col 3:24 inheritance: for ye s the Lord Christ. *G1398*
1Th 1: 9 from idols to s the living and true God; *G1398*
2Ti 1: 3 I thank God, whom I s from *my* *G3000*
Heb 8: 5 Who s unto the example and shadow *G3000*
9:14 from dead works to s the living God? *G3000*
12:28 whereby we may s God acceptably with *G3000*
13:10 no right to eat which s the tabernacle. *G3000*
Rev 7:15 of God, and s him day and night in *G3000*
22: 3 be in it; and his servants shall s him: *G3000*

SERVED

Gen 14: 4 Twelve years they s Chedorlaomer, and H5647
29:20 And Jacob s seven years for Rachel; H5647
30 and s with him yet seven other years. H5647
30:26 for whom I have s thee, and let me go: H5647
29 s thee, and how thy cattle was with me. H5647
31: 6 with all my power I have s your father. H5647
41 in thy house; I s thee fourteen years H5647
39: 4 in his sight, and he s him: and he made H8334
40: 4 with them, and he s them: and they H8334
Dt 12: 2 ye shall possess s their gods, upon the H5647
17: 3 And hath gone and s other gods, and H5647
29:26 For they went and s other gods, and H5647
Jos 23:16 have gone and s other gods, and bowed H5647
24: 2 of Nachor: and they s other gods. H5647
14 your fathers s on the other side of H5647
15 your fathers s that *were* on the other H5647
31 And Israel s the LORD all the days of H5647
Jdg 2: 7 And the people s the LORD all the days H5647
11 in the sight of the LORD, and s Baalim: H5647
13 And they forsook the LORD, and s Baal H5647
3: 6 to their sons, and s their gods. H5647
7 God, and s Baalim and the groves. H5647
8 s Chushan-rishathaim eight years. H5647
Jdg 3:14 So the children of Israel s Eglon the H5647
8: 1 Why hast thou s us thus, that thou H6213
10: 6 sight of the LORD, and s Baalim, and H5647
6 and forsook the LORD, and s not him. H5647
10 forsaken our God, and also s Baalim. H5647
13 Yet ye have forsaken me, and s other H5647
16 among them, and s the LORD: and his H5647
1Sa 7: 4 and Ashtaroth, and s the LORD only. H5647
8: 8 s other gods, so do they also unto thee. H5647
12:10 the LORD, and have s Baalim and H5647
2Sa 10:19 with Israel, and s them. So the Syrians H5647
16:19 of his son? as I have s in thy father's H5647
1Ki 4:21 and s Solomon all the days of his life. H5647
9: 9 them, and s them: therefore hath H5647
16:31 went and s Baal, and worshipped him. H5647
22:53 For he s Baal, and worshipped him, H5647
2Ki 10:18 unto them, Ahab s Baal a little; *but* H5647
17:12 For they s idols, whereof the LORD had H5647
16 all the host of heaven, and s Baal. H5647
33 They feared the LORD, and s their own H5647
41 the LORD, and s their graven images, H5647
18: 7 the king of Assyria, and s him not. H5647
21: 3 all the host of heaven, and s them. H5647
21 walked in, and s the idols that his H5647
21 that his father s, and worshipped them: H5647
1Ch 19: 5 how the men were s. And he sent to H5647
27: 1 and their officers that s the king in any H8334
2Ch 7:22 them, and s them: therefore hath H5647
24:18 of their fathers, and s groves and idols: H5647
33: 3 all the host of heaven, and s them. H5647
22 his father had made, and s them; H5647
Neh 9:35 For they have not s thee in their H5647
Est 1:10 chamberlains that s in the presence of H8334
Ps 106:36 And they s their idols: which were a H5647
137: 8 that rewardeth thee as thou hast s us. H1580
Ecc 5: 9 for all: the king *himself* is s by the field. H5647
Jer 5:19 forsaken me, and s strange gods in H5647
8: 2 whom they have s, and after whom they H5647
16:11 other gods, and have s them, and have H5647
22: 9 worshipped other gods, and s them. H5647
34:14 and when he hath s thee six years, thou H5647
52:12 the guard, *which* s the king of H5975+H6440
Ezk 29:18 for the service that he had s against it: H5647
20 wherewith he s against it, because they H5647
34:27 of those that s themselves of them. H5647
Hos 12:12 Syria, and Israel s for a wife, and for a H5647
Lk 2:37 the temple, but s *God* with fastings and *G3000*
Jn 12: 2 and Martha s: but Lazarus was one *G1247*
Act 13:36 For David, after he had s his own *G5256*
Ro 1:25 worshipped and s the creature more *G3000*
Php 2:22 father, he hath s with me in the gospel. *G1398*

SERVEDST

Dt 28:47 Because thou s not the LORD thy God H5647

SERVEST

Dan 6:16 thou s continually, he will deliver thee. H6399
20 God, whom thou s continually, able to H6399

SERVETH

Nu 3:36 vessels thereof, and all that s thereto, H5656
Mal 3:17 a man spareth his own son that s him. H5647
18 s God and him that serveth him not. H5647
18 serveth God and him that s him not. H5647
Lk 22:27 at meat, or he that s? *is* not he that *G1247*
27 meat? but I am among you as he that s. *G1247*
Ro 14:18 For he that in these things s Christ *is* *G1398*
1Co 14:22 not: but prophesying *s* not for them that
Gal 3:19 Wherefore then *s* the law? It was added

SERVICE

Gen 29:27 thee this also for the s which thou shalt H5656
30:26 knowest my s which I have done thee. H5656
Ex 1:14 in all manner of s in the field: all their H5656
14 the field: all their s, wherein they made H5656
12:25 hath promised, that ye shall keep this s. H5656
26 say unto you, What mean ye by this s? H5656
13: 5 thou shalt keep this s in this month. H5656
27:19 in all the s thereof, and all the H5656
30:16 appoint it for the s of the tabernacle of H5656
31:10 And the cloths of s, and the holy H8278
35:19 The cloths of s, to do service in the holy H8278
19 The cloths of service, to do s in the holy H8334
21 for all his s, and for the holy garments. H5656
24 wood for any work of the s, brought *it*. H5656
36: 1 of work for the s of the sanctuary, H5656
3 for the work of the s of the sanctuary, H5656
5 enough for the s of the work, which the H5656
38:21 of Moses, *for* the s of the Levites, by the H5656

Ex 39: 1 made cloths of s, to do service in the H8278
1 of service, to do s in the holy *place,* and H8334
40 all the vessels of the s of the tabernacle, H5656
41 The cloths of s to do service in the holy H8278
41 The cloths of service to do s in the holy H8334
Nu 3: 7 to do the s of the tabernacle. H5656
8 of Israel, to do the s of the tabernacle. H5656
26 and the cords of it for all the s thereof. H5656
31 and the hanging, and all the s thereof. H5656
4: 4 This *shall be* the s of the sons of H5656
19 every one to his s and to his burden: H5656
23 in to perform the s, to do the work in H6635
24 This *is* the s of the families of the H5656
26 of their s, and all that is made H5656
27 sons shall be all the s of the sons of the H5656
27 and in all their s: and ye shall appoint H5656
28 This *is* the s of the families of the sons H5656
30 entereth into the s, to do the work of the H6635
31 to all their s in the tabernacle of H5656
32 and with all their s: and by name ye H5656
33 This *is* the s of the families of the sons H5656
33 to all their s, in the tabernacle of H5656
35 entereth into the s, for the work in the H6635
37 all that might do s in the tabernacle of H5647
39 entereth into the s, for the work in the H6635
41 all that might do s in the tabernacle of H5647
43 entereth into the s, for the work in the H6635
47 came to do the s of the ministry, and H5656
47 ministry, and the s of the burden in the H5656
49 according to his s, and according to his H5656
7: 5 may be to do the s of the tabernacle of H5656
5 Levites, to every man according to his s. H5656
7 sons of Gershon, according to their s: H5656
8 unto their s, under the hand of Ithamar H5656
9 none: because the s of the sanctuary H5656
8:11 they may execute the s of the LORD. H5656
15 go in to do the s of the tabernacle of H5647
19 of Israel, to do the s of the children of H5656
22 in to do their s in the tabernacle of H5656
24 s of the tabernacle of the congregation: H6635
25 the s *thereof,* and shall serve no more: H5656
26 and shall do no s. Thus shalt thou do H5656
16: 9 himself to do the s of the tabernacle of H5656
18: 4 for all the s of the tabernacle: and H5656
6 s of the tabernacle of the congregation. H5656
7 *unto you* as a s of gift: and the stranger H5656
21 for their s which they serve, *even* H5656
21 s of the tabernacle of the congregation. H5656
23 But the Levites shall do the s of the H5656
31 s in the tabernacle of the congregation. H5656
Jos 22:27 we might do the s of the LORD before H5656
1Ki 12: 4 thou the grievous s of thy father, and H5656
1Ch 6:31 David set over the s of song in the H3027
48 s of the tabernacle of the house of God. H5656
9:13 the work of the s of the house of God. H5656
19 the work of the s, keepers of the gates H5656
23:24 the work for the s of the house of the H5656
26 nor any vessels of it for the s thereof. H5656
28 of Aaron for the s of the house of the H5656
28 the work of the s of the house of God; H5656
32 in the s of the house of the LORD. H5656
24: 3 according to their offices in their s. H5656
19 of them in their s to come into the H5656
25: 1 separated to the s of the sons of Asaph, H5656
1 the workmen according to their s was: H5656
6 and harps, for the s of the house of H5656
26: 8 strength for the s, *were* threescore and H5656
30 of the LORD, and in the s of the king. H5656
28:13 all the work of the s of the house of the H5656
13 vessels of s in the house of the LORD. H5656
14 of all manner of s; *silver also* for all H5656
14 for all instruments of every kind of s: H5656
20 for the s of the house of the LORD. H5656
21 *thee* for all the s of the house of God: H5656
21 for any manner of s: also the princes H5656
29: 5 his s this day unto the LORD? H3027
7 And gave for the s of the house of God H5656
2Ch 8:14 the priests to their s, and the Levites to H5656
12: 8 may know my s, and the service of the H5656
8 the s of the kingdoms of the countries. H5656
24:12 did the work of the s of the house of the H5656
29:35 offering. So the s of the house of the H5656
31: 2 man according to his s, the priests and H5656
16 daily portion for their s in their charges H5656
21 he began in the s of the house of God, H5656
34:13 in any manner of s: and of the Levites H5656
35: 2 them to the s of the house of the LORD, H5656
10 So the s was prepared, and the priests H5656
15 depart from their s; for their brethren H5656
2Ch 35:16 So all the s of the LORD was prepared H5656
Ezr 6:18 courses, for the s of God, which *is* at H5673
7:19 given thee for the s of the house of thy H6402
8:20 appointed for the s of the Levites, two H5656
Neh 10:32 shekel for the s of the house of our God; H5656
Ps 104:14 and herb for the s of man: that he may H5656
Jer 22:13 his neighbour's s without wages, and H5647
Ezk 29:18 to serve a great s against Tyrus: every H5656
18 for the s that he had served against it: H5656
44:14 house, for all the s thereof, and for all H5656
Jn 16: 2 you will think that he doeth God s. *G2999*
Ro 9: 4 and the s *of God,* and the promises; *G2999*
12: 1 unto God, *which is* your reasonable s. *G2999*
15:31 Judaea; and that my s which *I have* for *G1248*
2Co 9:12 For the administration of this s not *G3009*
11: 8 taking wages *of them,* to do you s. *G1248*
Gal 4: 8 not God, ye did s unto them which by *G1398*
Eph 6: 7 With good will doing s, as to the Lord, *G1398*
Php 2:17 the sacrifice and s of your faith, I joy, *G3009*
30 life, to supply your lack of s toward me. *G3009*
1Ti 6: 2 but rather do *them* s, because they are *G1398*
Heb 9: 1 of divine s, and a worldly sanctuary. *G2999*
6 tabernacle, accomplishing the s *of God.* *G2999*
9 make him that did the s perfect, as *G3000*
Rev 2:19 I know thy works, and charity, and s, *G1248*

SERVILE
Lev 23: 7 ye shall do no s work therein. H5656
8 ye shall do no s work *therein.* H5656
21 you: ye shall do no s work *therein: it* H5656
25 Ye shall do no s work *therein*: but ye H5656
35 ye shall do no s work *therein.* H5656
36 *and* ye shall do no s work *therein.* H5656
Nu 28:18 shall do no manner of s work *therein*: H5656
25 convocation; ye shall do no s work. H5656
26 convocation; ye shall do no s work: H5656
29: 1 ye shall do no s work: it is a day of H5656
12 ye shall do no s work, and ye shall keep H5656
35 ye shall do no s work *therein*: H5656

SERVING
Ex 14: 5 that we have let Israel go from s us? H5647
Dt 15:18 servant *to thee,* in s thee six years: and H5647
Lk 10:40 about much s, and came to him, and *G1248*
Act 20:19 S the Lord with all humility of mind, *G1398*
26: 7 tribes, instantly s *God* day and night, *G3000*
Ro 12:11 business; fervent in spirit; s the Lord; *G1398*
Tit 3: 3 deceived, s divers lusts and pleasures, *G1398*

SERVITOR
2Ki 4:43 And his s said, What, should I set this H8334

SERVITUDE
2Ch 10: 4 the grievous s of thy father, and his H5656
Lam 1: 3 because of great s: she dwelleth among H5656

SET
Gen 1:17 And God s them in the firmament of H5414
4:15 And the LORD s a mark upon Cain, H7760
6:16 the ark shalt thou s in the side thereof; H7760
9:13 I do s my bow in the cloud, and it shall H5414
17:21 thee at this s time in the next year. H4150
18: 8 had dressed, and s *it* before them; and H5414
19:16 him forth, and s him without the city. H3240
21: 2 his old age, at the s time of which God H4150
28 And Abraham s seven ewe lambs of the H5324
29 which thou hast s by themselves? H5324
24:33 And there was s *meat* before him to H7760
28:11 the sun was s; and he took of the stones H935
12 And he dreamed, and behold a ladder s H5324
18 his pillows, and s it up *for* a pillar, and H7760
22 And this stone, which I have s *for* a H7760
30:36 And he s three days' journey betwixt H7760
38 And he s the rods which he had pilled H3322
40 the lambs, and s the faces of the flocks H5414
31:17 Then Jacob rose up, and s his sons and H5375
21 s his face *toward* the mount Gilead. H7760
37 thy household stuff? s *it* here before my H7760
45 And Jacob took a stone, and s it up *for* H7311
35:14 And Jacob s up a pillar in the place H5324
20 And Jacob s a pillar upon her grave: H5324
41:33 wise, and s him over the land of Egypt. H7896
41 I have s thee over all the land of Egypt. H5414
43: 9 not unto thee, and s him before thee, H3322
31 himself, and said, S on bread. H7760
32 And they s on for him by himself, and H7760
44:21 me, that I may s mine eyes upon him. H7760
47: 7 his father, and s him before Pharaoh: H5975
48:20 and he s Ephraim before Manasseh. H7760
Ex 1:11 Therefore they did s over them H7760
4:20 and his sons, and s them upon an ass, H7392
5:14 taskmasters had s over them, were H7760
7:23 neither did he s his heart to this also. H7896
9: 5 And the LORD appointed a s time, H4150
13:12 That thou shalt s apart unto the LORD
19:12 And thou shalt s bounds unto the people
23 us, saying, S bounds about the mount,
21: 1 which thou shalt s before them. H7760
23:31 And I will s thy bounds from the Red H7896
25: 7 Onyx stones, and stones to be s in the H4394
30 And thou shalt s upon the table H5414
26:17 *be* in one board, s in order one against H7947
35 And thou shalt s the table without the H7760
28:11 make them to be s in ouches of gold. H4142
17 And thou shalt s in it settings of stones, H4390
20 shall be s in gold in their inclosings. H7660
31: 5 And in cutting of stones, to s *them,* and H4390
32:22 the people, that they *are* s on mischief.
35: 9 And onyx stones, and stones to be s for H4394
27 s, for the ephod, and for the breastplate; H4394
33 And in the cutting of stones, to s *them,* H4390
37: 3 rings of gold, *to be* s by the four corners
39:10 And they s in it four rows of stones: *the* H4390
37 the lamps to be s in order, and all the
40: 2 month shalt thou s up the tabernacle of H6965
4 And thou shalt bring in the table, and s
4 that are to be s in order upon it; and
5 And thou shalt s the altar of gold for H5414
6 And thou shalt s the altar of the burnt H5414
7 And thou shalt s the laver between the H5414
8 And thou shalt s up the court round H7760
18 his sockets, and s up the boards H7760
20 into the ark, and s the staves on the H7760
21 the tabernacle, and s up the vail of the H7760
23 And he s the bread in order upon it H6187
28 And he s up the hanging *at* the door of H7760
30 And he s the laver between the tent of H7760
33 and the altar, and s up the hanging of H5414
Lev 17:10 blood; I will even s my face against that H5414
20: 3 And I will s my face against that man, H5414
5 Then I will s my face against that man, H7760
6 them, I will even s my face against that H5414
24: 6 And thou shalt s them in two rows, six H7760
8 Every sabbath he shall s it in order
26: 1 neither shall ye s up *any* image of stone H5414
11 And I will s my tabernacle among you: H5414
17 And I will s my face against you, and H5414
Nu 1:51 the Levites shall s it up: and the H6965
2: 9 their armies. These shall first s forth. H5265
16 they shall s forth in the second rank. H5265
17 congregation shall s forward with the H5265
17 so shall they s forward, every man H5265
34 and so they s forward, every one H5265
4:15 as the camp is to s forward; after that, H5265
5:16 her near, and s her before the LORD: H5975
18 And the priest shall s the woman H5975
30 his wife, and shall s the woman before H5975
7: 1 Moses had fully s up the tabernacle, H6965
8:13 And thou shalt s the Levites before H5975
10:17 s forward, bearing the tabernacle. H5265
18 camp of Reuben s forward according H5265
21 And the Kohathites s forward, bearing H5265
21 s up the tabernacle against they came. H6965
22 of Ephraim s forward according to H5265
25 children of Dan s forward, *which was* H5265
28 to their armies, when they s forward. H5265
35 And it came to pass, when the ark s H5265
11:24 s them round about the tabernacle. H5975
21: 8 fiery serpent, and s it upon a pole: and H7760
10 And the children of Israel s forward, H5265
22: 1 And the children of Israel s forward, H5265
24: 1 but he s his face toward the wilderness. H7896
27:16 flesh, s a man over the congregation, H6485
19 And s him before Eleazar the priest, H5975
22 took Joshua, and s him before Eleazar H5975
29:39 the LORD in your s feasts, beside your H4150
Dt 1: 8 Behold, I have s the land before you: go H5414
21 Behold, the LORD thy God hath s the H5414
4: 8 this law, which I s before you this day? H5414
44 And this *is* the law which Moses s H7760
7: 7 The LORD did not s his love upon you,
11:26 Behold, I s before you this day a H5414
32 which I s before you this day. H5414
14:24 shall choose to s his name there, when H7760
16:22 Neither shalt thou s thee up *any* image; H6965
17:14 shalt say, I will s a king over me, like H7760
15 Thou shalt in any wise s *him* king over H7760
15 shalt thou s king over thee: thou H7760

Dt 17:15 thou mayest not s a stranger over thee, H5414
19:14 of old time have s in thine inheritance, H1379
26: 4 of thine hand, and s it down before the H3240
10 And thou shalt s it before the LORD thy H3240
27: 2 that thou shalt s thee up great stones, H6965
4 *that* ye shall s up these stones, which H6965
28: 1 the LORD thy God will s thee on high H5414
36 which thou shalt s over thee, unto a H6965
56 not adventure to s the sole of her foot H3322
30: 1 which I have s before thee, and thou H5414
15 See, I have s before thee this day life H5414
19 you, *that* I have s before you life and H5414
32: 8 sons of Adam, he s the bounds of the H5324
22 with her increase, and s on fire the
46 And he said unto them, S your hearts H7760
Jos 4: 9 And Joshua s up twelve stones in the H6965
6:26 *son* shall he s up the gates of it. H5324
8: 8 the city, *that* ye shall s the city on fire: H3341
12 men, and s them to lie in ambush H7760
13 And when they had s the people, *even* H7760
19 it, and hasted and s the city on fire. H3341
10:18 cave, and s men by it for to keep them: H6485
18: 1 at Shiloh, and s up the tabernacle of H7931
24:25 that day, and s them a statute and H7760
26 a great stone, and s it up there under H6965
Jdg 1: 8 of the sword, and s the city on fire. H7971
6:18 my present, and s *it* before thee. And H3240
7: 5 him shalt thou s by himself; likewise H3322
19 had but newly s the watch: and they H6965
22 and the LORD s every man's sword H7760
9:25 And the men of Shechem s liers in wait H7760
33 rise early, and s upon the city: and, H6584
49 to the hold, and s the hold on fire upon H3341
15: 5 And when he had s the brands on fire, H1197
16:25 and they s him between the pillars. H5975
18:30 And the children of Dan s up the H6965
31 And they s them up Micah's graven H7760
20:22 themselves, and s their battle again in
29 And Israel s liers in wait round about H7760
36 in wait which they had s beside Gibeah. H7760
48 s on fire all the cities that they came to. H7971
Ru 2: 5 his servant that was s over the reapers, H5324
6 And the servant that was s over the H5324
1Sa 2: 8 the dunghill, to s *them* among princes, H3427
8 and he hath s the world upon them. H7896
5: 2 the house of Dagon, and s it by Dagon. H3322
3 Dagon, and s him in his place again. H7725
6:18 whereon they s down the ark of the H3240
7:12 Then Samuel took a stone, and s *it* H7760
8:12 over fifties; and *will* s *them* to ear his H7760
9:20 lost three days ago, s not thy mind on H7760
23 of which I said unto thee, S it by thee. H7760
24 *was* upon it, and s *it* before Saul. And H7760
24 that which is left! s *it* before thee, *and* H7760
10:19 him, *Nay,* but s a king over us. Now H7760
12:13 the LORD hath s a king over you. H5414
13: 8 according to the s time that Samuel H4150
15:11 It repenteth me that I have s up Saul *to* H4427
12 and, behold, he s him up a place, and H5324
17: 2 valley of Elah, and s the battle in array
8 are ye come out to s *your* battle in array?
18: 5 wisely: and Saul s him over the men of H7760
30 Saul; so that his name was much s by. H3335
22: 9 which was s over the servants of H5324
26:24 And, behold, as thy life was much s by H1431
24 my life be much s by in the eyes of the H1431
28:22 and let me s a morsel of bread before H7760
2Sa 3:10 of Saul, and to s up the throne of David H6975
6: 3 And they s the ark of God upon a new H7392
17 of the LORD, and s it in his place, in H3322
7:12 thy fathers, I will s up thy seed after H3322
10:17 And the Syrians s themselves in array H6965
11:15 And he wrote in the letter, saying, S ye H3051
12:20 s bread before him, and he did eat. H7760
30 stones: and it was *s* on David's head.
14:30 there; go and s it on fire. And Absalom's
30 Absalom's servants s the field on fire. H3341
31 have thy servants s my field on fire? H3341
15:24 of God: and they s down the ark of H3332
18: 1 with him, and s captains of thousands H7760
13 wouldest have s thyself against *me.* H3320
19:28 yet didst thou s thy servant among H7896
20: 5 s time which he had appointed him. H4150
23:23 three. And David s him over his guard. H7760
1Ki 2:15 and *that* all Israel s their faces on me, H7760
19 a seat to be s for the king's mother; H7760
24 me, and s me on the throne of H3427
5: 5 son, whom I will s upon thy throne in H5414
6:19 house within, to s there the ark of the H5414

1Ki 6:27 And he s the cherubims within the H5414
7:16 *of* molten brass, to s upon the tops of H5414
21 And he s up the pillars in the porch of H6965
21 the temple: and he s up the right pillar, H6965
21 Jachin: and he s up the left pillar, and H6965
25 and the sea *was* s above upon them, and
39 the house: and he s the sea on the right H5414
8:21 And I have s there a place for the ark, H7760
9: 6 which I have s before you, but go and H5414
10: 9 in thee, to s thee on the throne of H5414
12:29 And he s the one in Beth-el, and the H7760
14: 4 for his eyes were s by reason of his age. H6965
15: 4 in Jerusalem, to s up his son after him, H6965
16:34 his firstborn, and s up the gates thereof H5324
20:12 said unto his servants, S *yourselves in* H7760
12 s *themselves in array* against the city. H7760
21: 9 s Naboth on high among the people: H3427
10 And s two men, sons of Belial, before H3427
12 They proclaimed a fast, and s Naboth H3427
2Ki 4: 4 thou shalt s aside that which is full. H5265
10 on the wall; and let us s for him there a H7760
38 unto his servant, S on the great pot, H8239
43 And his servitor said, What, should I s H5414
44 So he s *it* before them, and they did eat, H5414
6:22 and with thy bow? s bread and water H7760
8:12 holds wilt thou s on fire, and their H7971
10: 3 master's sons, and s *him* on his father's H7760
12: 4 that every man is s at, *and* all the H6187
9 in the lid of it, and s it beside the altar, H5414
17 Hazael s his face to go up to Jerusalem. H7760
17:10 And they s them up images and groves H5324
18:23 able on thy part to s riders upon them. H5414
20: 1 saith the LORD, S thine house in order;
H7760
21: 7 And he s a graven image of the grove H7760
25:19 an officer that was s over the men of H6496
28 And he spake kindly to him, and s his H5414
1Ch 6:31 And these *are they* whom David s over H5975
9:22 the seer did ordain in their s office. H530
26 were in *their* s office, and were over H530
31 Korahite, had the s office over the things H530
11:14 And they s themselves in the midst of H3320
25 three: and David s him over his guard. H7760
16: 1 So they brought the ark of God, and s it H3322
19:10 Now when Joab saw that the battle was s
11 brother, and they s *themselves* in array
17 upon them, and s *the battle* in array
20: 2 in it; and it was s upon David's head:
21:18 should go up, and s up an altar unto H6965
22: 2 land of Israel; and he s masons to hew H5975
19 Now s your heart and your soul to seek H5414
23: 4 thousand *were* to s forward the work of H5329
31 moons, and on the s feasts, by number, H4150
29: 2 and *stones* to be s, glistering stones, H4394
3 Moreover, because I have s my affection
2Ch 2:18 And he s threescore and ten thousand H6213
18 overseers to s the people a work. H5647
3: 5 and s thereon palm trees and chains. H5927
4: 4 and the sea *was* s above upon them, and
7 to their form, and s *them* in the temple, H5414
10 And he s the sea on the right side of the H5414
19 the tables whereon the shewbread *was* s;
6:10 my father, and am s on the throne of H3427
13 high, and had s it in the midst of the H5414
7:19 which I have s before you, and shall H5414
9: 8 in thee to s thee on his throne, *to* H5414
11:16 of Israel such as s their hearts to seek H5414
13: 3 And Abijah s the battle in array with an H631
3 men: Jeroboam also s the battle in array
11 the shewbread also s *they in order* upon
14:10 him, and they s the battle in array in
17: 2 of Judah, and s garrisons in the land H5414
19: 5 And he s judges in the land throughout H5975
8 did Jehoshaphat s of the Levites, and *of* H5975
20: 3 And Jehoshaphat feared, and s himself H5414
17 fight in this *battle:* s yourselves, stand H3320
22 to praise, the LORD s ambushments H5414
23:10 And he s all the people, every man H5975
14 that were s over the host, and said H6485
19 And he s the porters at the gates of the H5975
20 king's house, and s the king upon the H3427
24: 8 made a chest, and s it without at the H5414
13 by them, and they s the house of God in H5975
25:14 of Seir, and s them up *to be* his gods, H5975
29:25 And he s the Levites in the house of the H5975
35 the house of the LORD was s in order. H3559
31: 3 and for the s feasts, as *it is* written H4150
15 of the priests, in *their* s office, to give to H530
18 for in their s office they sanctified H530
32: 6 And he s captains of war over the H5414

2Ch 33: 7 And he s a carved image, the idol H7760
19 built high places, and s up groves and H5975
34:12 of the Kohathites, to s *it* forward; and H5329
35: 2 And he s the priests in their charges, H5975
Ezr 2:68 the house of God to s it up in his place: H5975
3: 3 And they s the altar upon his bases; for H3559
5 and of all the s feasts of the LORD that H4150
8 and upward, to s forward the work of H5329
9 of Judah, together, to s forward the H5329
10 of the LORD, they s the priests in their H5975
4:10 brought over, and s in the cities of H3488
12 the bad city, and have s up the walls H3635
13 and the walls s up *again, then* will they H3635
16 the walls thereof s up, by this means H3635
5:11 a great king of Israel builded and s up. H3635
6:11 his house, and being s up, let him be H2211
18 And they s the priests in their H6966
7:25 that *is* in thine hand, s magistrates and H4483
9: 9 us a reviving, to s up the house of our H7311
Neh 1: 9 that I have chosen to s my name there. H7931
2: 6 the king to send me; and I s him a time. H5414
3: 1 sanctified it, and s up the doors of it; H5975
3 thereof, and s up the doors thereof, H5975
6 thereof, and s up the doors thereof, H5975
13 they built it, and s up the doors thereof, H5975
14 he built it, and s up the doors thereof, H5975
15 covered it, and s up the doors thereof, H5975
4: 9 unto our God, and s a watch against H5975
13 Therefore s I in the lower places behind H5975
13 places, I even s the people after their H5975
5: 7 And I s a great assembly against them. H5414
6: 1 had not s up the doors upon the gates;) H5975
7: 1 built, and I had s up the doors, and the H5975
9:37 whom thou hast s over us because of H5414
10:33 moons, for the s feasts, and for the holy H4150
13:11 together, and s them in their place. H5975
19 of my servants s I at the gates, *that* H5975
Est 2:17 the virgins; so that he s the royal crown H7760
3: 1 him, and s his seat above all the H7760
6: 8 crown royal which is s upon his head: H5414
8: 2 s Mordecai over the house of Haman. H7760
Job 5:11 To s up on high those that be low; that H7760
6: 4 do s themselves in array against me.
7:17 thou shouldest s thine heart upon him? H7896
20 why hast thou s me as a mark against H7760
9:19 who shall s me a time *to plead*? H3259
14:13 me a s time, and remember me! H2706
16:12 me to pieces, and s me up for his mark. H6965
19: 8 and he hath s darkness in my paths. H7760
30: 1 to have s with the dogs of my flock. H7896
13 They mar my path, they s forward my
33: 5 If thou canst answer me, s *thy words* in
34:14 If he s his heart upon man, *if* he gather H7760
24 number, and s others in their stead. H5975
36:16 s on thy table *should be* full of fatness. H5183
38:10 decreed *place,* and s bars and doors, H7760
33 s the dominion thereof in the earth? H7760
Ps 2: 2 The kings of the earth s themselves, H3320
6 Yet have I s my king upon my holy hill H5258
3: 6 s *themselves* against me round about. H7896
4: 3 But know that the LORD hath s apart H6395
8: 1 hast s thy glory above the heavens. H5414
10: 8 his eyes are privily s against the poor. H6845
12: 5 the LORD; I will s *him* in safety *from* H7896
16: 8 I have s the LORD always before me: H7737
17:11 s their eyes bowing down to the earth; H7896
19: 4 hath he s a tabernacle for the sun, H7760
20: 5 of our God we will s up *our* banners: the
27: 5 hide me; he shall s me up upon a rock. H7311
31: 8 thou hast s my feet in a large room. H5975
40: 2 of the miry clay, and s my feet upon a H6965
50:21 and s *them* in order before thine eyes.
54: 3 they have not s God before them. Selah. H7760
57: 4 them that are s on fire, *even* the sons
62:10 increase, s not your heart *upon them.* H7896
69:29 thy salvation, O God, s me up on high.
73: 9 They s their mouth against the H8371
18 Surely thou didst s them in slippery H7896
74: 4 they s up their ensigns *for* signs. H7760
17 Thou hast s all the borders of the earth: H5324
78: 7 That they might s their hope in God, H7760
8 a generation *that* s not their heart H3559
85:13 and shall s *us* in the way of his steps. H7760
86:14 soul; and have not s thee before them. H7760
89:25 I will s his hand also in the sea, and his H7760
42 Thou hast s up the right hand of his H7311
90: 8 Thou hast s our iniquities before thee, H7896
91:14 Because he hath s his love upon me,
14 will I deliver him: I will s him on high,

Ps 101: 3 I will s no wicked thing before mine H7896
102:13 to favour her, yea, the s time, is come.
104: 9 Thou hast s a bound that they may not H7760
109: 6 S thou a wicked man over him: and let H6485
113: 8 That he may s *him* with princes, *even* H3427
118: 5 answered me, *and s me* in a large place.
122: 5 For there are s thrones of judgment, H3427
132:11 of thy body will I s upon thy throne. H7896
140: 5 wayside; they have s gins for me. Selah. H7896
141: 2 Let my prayer be s forth before thee *as* H3559
3 S a watch, O LORD, before my mouth; H7896
Prv 1:25 But ye have s at nought all my counsel,
8:23 I was s up from everlasting, from the H5258
27 s a compass upon the face of the depth: H2710
22:28 landmark, which thy fathers have s. H6213
23: 5 Wilt thou s thine eyes upon that which H5774
Ecc 3:11 time: also he hath s the world in their H5414
7:14 God also hath s the one over against H6213
8:11 sons of men is fully s in them to do evil. H4390
10: 6 Folly is s in great dignity, and the rich H5414
12: 9 out, *and* s in order many proverbs.
Song 5:12 of waters, washed with milk, *and* fitly s. H3427
14 His hands *are as* gold rings s with the H4390
15 His legs *are as* pillars of marble, s upon H3245
7: 2 an heap of wheat s about with lilies. H5473
8: 6 S me as a seal upon thine heart, as a H7760
Isa 3:24 and instead of well s hair baldness; and
7: 6 therein for us, and s a king in the midst H4427
9:11 Therefore the LORD shall s up the H7682
11:11 *that* the Lord shall s his hand again the H3254
12 And he shall s up an ensign for the H5375
14: 1 choose Israel, and s them in their own H3240
17:10 plants, and shalt s it with strange slips: H2232
19: 2 And I will s the Egyptians against the H5526
21: 6 said unto me, Go, s a watchman, let H5975
8 and I am s in my ward whole nights: H5324
22: 7 shall s themselves in array at the gate. H7896
23:13 the wilderness: they s up the towers H6965
27: 4 Fury *is* not in me: who would s the H5414
11 women come, *and* s them on fire: for it *is*
36: 8 able on thy part to s riders upon them. H5414
38: 1 saith the LORD, S thine house in order:
41:19 the oil tree; I will s in the desert the fir H7760
42: 4 till he have s judgment in the earth: H7760
25 battle: and it hath s him on fire round H7760
44: 7 declare it, and s it in order for me, since
45:20 no knowledge that s up the wood of H5375
46: 7 carry him, and s him in his place, and H3240
49:22 the Gentiles, and s up my standard to H7311
50: 7 therefore have I s my face like a flint, H7760
57: 7 hast thou s thy bed: even thither H7760
8 posts hast thou s up thy remembrance: H7760
62: 6 I have s watchmen upon thy walls, O H6485
66:19 And I will s a sign among them, and I H7760
Jer 1:10 See, I have this day s thee over the H6485
15 and they shall s every one his throne H5414
4: 6 S up the standard toward Zion: retire, H5375
5:26 snares; they s a trap, they catch men. H5324
6: 1 in Tekoa, and s up a sign of fire in H5375
17 Also I s watchmen over you, *saying,* H6965
23 ride upon horses, s in array as men for
27 I have s thee *for* a tower *and* a fortress H5414
7:12 in Shiloh, where I s my name at the H7931
30 LORD: they have s their abominations H7760
9:13 my law which I s before them, and H5414
10:20 tent any more, and to s up my curtains. H6965
11:13 of Jerusalem have ye s up altars to *that* H7760
21: 8 LORD; Behold, I s before you the way H5414
10 For I have s my face against this city H7760
23: 4 And I will s up shepherds over them H6965
24: 1 of figs *were* s before the temple of H3259
6 For I will s mine eyes upon them for H7760
26: 4 in my law, which I have s before you, H5414
31:21 S thee up waymarks, make thee high H5324
21 thee high heaps: s thine heart toward H7896
29 and the children's teeth are s on edge.
30 sour grape, his teeth shall be s on edge.
32:20 Which hast s signs and wonders in the H7760
29 shall come and s fire on this city, and H3341
34 But they s their abominations in the H7760
34:16 whom ye had s at liberty at their H7971
35: 5 And I s before the sons of the house of H5414
38:22 Thy friends have s thee on, and have H5496
40:11 and that he had s over them Gedaliah H6485
42:15 Israel; If ye wholly s your faces to enter H7760
17 So shall it be with all the men that s H7760
43:10 my servant, and will s his throne upon H7760
44:10 I s before you and before your fathers. H5414
11 Behold, I will s my face against you H7760
Jer 44:12 Judah, that have s their faces to go into H7760
49:38 And I will s my throne in Elam, and H7760
50: 2 and publish, and s up a standard; H5375
9 and they shall s themselves in array
51:12 S up the standard upon the walls of H5375
12 the watch strong, s up the watchmen, H6965
27 S ye up a standard in the land, blow the H5375
52:32 And spake kindly unto him, and s his H5414
Lam 2:17 hath s up the horn of thine adversaries. H7311
3: 6 He hath s me in dark places, as *they* H3427
12 He hath bent his bow, and s me as a H5324
Ezk 2: 2 unto me, and s me upon my feet, that H5975
3:24 Then the spirit entered into me, and s H5975
4: 2 a mount against it; s the camp also H5414
2 against it, and s *battering* rams against H7760
3 an iron pan, and s it *for* a wall of iron H5414
3 and the city: and s thy face against it, H3559
7 Therefore thou shalt s thy face toward H3559
5: 5 *is* Jerusalem: I have s it in the midst of H7760
6: 2 Son of man, s thy face toward the H7760
7:20 As for the beauty of his ornament, he s H7760
20 therefore have I s it far from them. H5414
9: 4 of Jerusalem, and s a mark upon the H8427
12: 6 ground: for I have s thee *for* a sign unto H5414
13:17 Likewise, thou son of man, s thy face H7760
14: 3 Son of man, these men have s up their H5927
8 And I will s my face against that man, H5414
15: 7 And I will s my face against them; they H5414
7 LORD, when I s my face against them. H7760
16:18 and thou hast s mine oil and mine H5414
19 thou hast even s it before them for a H5414
17: 4 traffick; he s it in a city of merchants. H7760
5 great waters, *and* s it *as* a willow tree. H7760
22 cedar, and will s *it;* I will crop off from H5414
18: 2 and the children's teeth are s on edge?
19: 8 Then the nations s against him on H5414
20:46 Son of man, s thy face toward the H7760
21: 2 Son of man, s thy face toward H7760
15 I have s the point of the sword against H5414
16 on the left, whithersoever thy face *is* s. H3259
22: 7 In thee have they s light by father and
10 her that was s apart for pollution. H5079
23:24 *which* shall s against thee buckler H7760
24 about: and I will s judgment before H5414
25 And I will s my jealousy against thee, H5414
41 thou hast s mine incense and mine oil. H7760
24: 2 the king of Babylon s himself against H5564
3 the Lord GOD; S on a pot, set *it* on, and H8239
3 pot, s *it* on, and also pour water into it: H7760
7 midst of her; she s it upon the top of a H7760
8 vengeance; I have s her blood upon the H5414
11 Then s it empty upon the coals thereof, H5975
25 whereupon they s their minds, their H4853
25: 2 Son of man, s thy face against the H7760
4 and they shall s their palaces in thee, H3427
26: 9 And he shall s engines of war against H5414
20 of old time, and shall s thee in the low H3427
20 I shall s glory in the land of the living; H5414
27:10 in thee; they s forth thy comeliness. H5414
28: 2 thou s thine heart as the heart of God: H5414
6 hast s thine heart as the heart of God; H5414
14 and I have s thee *so:* thou wast upon H5414
21 Son of man, s thy face against Zidon, H7760
29: 2 Son of man, s thy face against Pharaoh H7760
30: 8 when I have s a fire in Egypt, and H5414
14 desolate, and will s fire in Zoan, and H5414
16 And I will s fire in Egypt: Sin shall have H5414
31: 4 The waters made him great, the deep s H7311
32: 8 over thee, and s darkness upon thy H5414
23 Whose graves are s in the sides of the H5414
25 They have s her a bed in the midst of H5414
33: 2 coasts, and s him for their watchman: H5414
7 So thou, O son of man, I have s thee a H5414
34:23 And I will s up one shepherd over H6965
35: 2 Son of man, s thy face against mount H7760
37: 1 of the LORD, and s me down in the H5117
26 them, and will s my sanctuary in the H5414
38: 2 Son of man, s thy face against Gog, the H7760
39: 9 go forth, and shall s on fire and burn H1197
15 then shall he s up a sign by it, till the H1129
21 And I will s my glory among the H5414
40: 2 the land of Israel, and s me upon a very H5117
4 thine ears, and s thine heart upon all H7760
44: 8 but ye have s keepers of my charge H7760
Dan 1:11 of the eunuchs had s over Daniel, H4487
2:44 the God of heaven s up a kingdom, H6966
49 of the king, and he s Shadrach, H4483
3: 1 six cubits: he s it up in the plain of H6966
2 Nebuchadnezzar the king had s up. H6966
Dan 3: 3 the king had s up; and they stood H6966
3 image that Nebuchadnezzar had s up. H6966
5 Nebuchadnezzar the king hath s up: H6966
7 Nebuchadnezzar the king had s up. H6966
12 whom thou hast s over the affairs of H4483
12 the golden image which thou hast s up. H6966
14 the golden image which I have s up? H6966
18 the golden image which thou hast s up. H6966
5:19 s up; and whom he would he put down. H1934
6: 1 It pleased Darius to s over the kingdom H6966
3 thought to s him over the whole realm. H6966
14 with himself, and s *his* heart on Daniel H7761
7:10 was s, and the books were opened. H3488
8:18 but he touched me, and s me upright. H5975
9: 3 And I s my face unto the Lord God, to H5414
10 in his laws, which he s before us by his H5414
10:10 me, which s me upon my knees H5128
12 day that thou didst s thine heart to H5414
15 words unto me, I s my face toward the H5414
11:11 and he shall s forth a great multitude; H5975
13 return, and shall s forth a multitude H5975
17 He shall also s his face to enter with the H7760
12:11 maketh desolate s up, *there shall be* a H5414
Hos 2: 3 Lest I strip her naked, and s her as in H3322
3 a wilderness, and s her like a dry land, H7896
4: 8 and they s their heart on their iniquity. H5375
6:11 Also, O Judah, he hath s an harvest for H7896
8: 1 *S* the trumpet to thy mouth. *He shall*
4 They have s up kings, but not by me:
11: 8 *how* shall I s thee as Zeboim? mine H7760
Joel 2: 5 as a strong people s in battle array.
Am 7: 8 Lord, Behold, I will s a plumbline in the H7760
8: 5 that we may s forth wheat, making H6605
9: 4 them: and I will s mine eyes upon them H7760
Oba 4 and though thou s thy nest among the H7760
Nah 3: 6 vile, and will s thee as a gazing-stock. H7760
13 of thy land shall be s wide open unto
Hab 2: 1 I will stand upon my watch, and s me H3320
9 that he may s his nest on high, that H7760
Zec 3: 5 And I said, Let them s a fair mitre H7760
5 his head. So they s a fair mitre upon H7760
5:11 and s there upon her own base. H3240
6:11 make crowns, and s *them* upon the H7760
8:10 the affliction: for I s all men every one H7971
Mal 3:15 wickedness are s up; yea, *they that* H1129
Mt 5: 1 he was s, his disciples came unto him: G2523
14 A city that is s on an hill cannot be hid. G2749
10:35 For I am come to s a man at variance G1369
18: 2 him, and s him in the midst of them, G2476
21: 7 their clothes, and they s *him* thereon. G1940
25:33 And he shall s the sheep on his right G2476
27:19 When he was s down on the judgment G2521
37 And s up over his head his accusation G2007
Mk 1:32 And at even, when the sun did s, they G1416
4:21 a bed? and not to be s on a candlestick? G2007
6:41 to his disciples to s before them; and G3908
8: 6 to his disciples to s before *them;* and G3908
6 and they did s *them* before the people. G3908
7 to s them also before *them.* G3908
9:12 suffer many things, and be s at nought. G1847
36 And he took a child, and s him in the G2476
12: 1 a vineyard, and s an hedge about *it,* G4060
Lk 1: 1 have taken in hand to s forth in order a G392
2:34 this *child* is s for the fall and rising G2749
4: 9 to Jerusalem, and s him on a pinnacle G2476
18 to s at liberty them that are bruised, G649
7: 8 For I also am a man s under authority, G5021
9:16 the disciples to s before the multitude. G3908
47 heart, took a child, and s him by him, G2476
51 stedfastly s his face to go to Jerusalem, G4741
10: 8 eat such things as are s before you: G3908
34 in oil and wine, and s him on his own G1913
11: 6 and I have nothing to s before him? G3908
19:35 upon the colt, and they s Jesus thereon. G1913
22:55 of the hall, and were s down together, G4776
23:11 And Herod with his men of war s him G1848
Jn 2: 6 And there were s there six waterpots of G2749
10 beginning doth s forth good wine; and G5087
3:33 hath s to his seal that God is true. G4972
6:11 to them that were s down; and likewise G345
8: 3 and when they had s her in the midst, G2476
13:12 his garments, and was s down again, he G377
19:29 Now there was s a vessel full of G2749
Act 4: 7 And when they had s them in the G2476
11 This is the stone which was s at nought G1848
5:27 them, they s *them* before the council: G2476
6: 6 Whom they s before the apostles: and G2476
13 And s up false witnesses, which said, G2476
7: 5 not *so much as* to s his foot on: yet he G968

Act 7:26 and would have **s** them at one again, *G4900*
12:21 And upon a **s** day Herod, arrayed in *G5002*
13: 9 with the Holy Ghost, **s** his eyes on him, *G816*
47 us, *saying*, I have **s** thee to be a light of *G5087*
15:16 again the ruins thereof, and I will **s** it up: *G461*
16:34 into his house, he **s** meat before them, *G3908*
17: 5 a company, and **s** all the city on an *G2350*
18:10 For I am with thee, and no man shall **s** *G2007*
19:27 is in danger to be **s** at nought; but also *G2064*
21: 2 Phenicia, we went aboard, and **s** forth. *G321*
22:30 Paul down, and **s** him before them. *G2476*
23:24 that they may **s** Paul on, and bring *him* *G1913*
26:32 might have been **s** at liberty, if he had *G630*
Ro 3:25 Whom God hath **s** forth *to be* a *G4388*
14:10 or why dost thou **s** at nought thy *G1848*
1Co 4: 9 For I think that God hath **s** forth us the *G584*
6: 4 to this life, **s** them to judge who are *G2523*
10:27 to go; whatsoever is **s** before you, eat, *G3908*
11:34 the rest will I **s** in order when I come. *G1299*
12:18 But now hath God **s** the members every *G5087*
28 And God hath **s** some in the church, *G5087*
Gal 3: 1 evidently **s** forth, crucified among you? *G4270*
Eph 1:20 the dead, and **s** *him* at his own right *G2523*
Php 1:17 I am **s** for the defence of the gospel. *G2749*
Col 3: 2 **S** your affection on things above, not *G5426*
Tit 1: 5 thou shouldest **s** in order the things *G1930*
Heb 2: 7 **s** him over the works of thy hands: *G2525*
6:18 to lay hold upon the hope **s** before us: *G4295*
8: 1 high priest, who is **s** on the right hand *G2523*
12: 1 patience the race that is **s** before us, *G4295*
2 the joy that was **s** before him endured *G4295*
2 the shame, and is **s** down at the right *G2523*
13:23 Know ye that *our* brother Timothy is **s** at *G630*
Jas 3: 6 of nature; and it is **s** on fire of hell. *G5394*
Jude 7 after strange flesh, are **s** forth for an *G4295*
Rev 3: 8 I know thy works: behold, I have **s** *G1325*
21 **s** down with my Father in his throne. *G2523*
4: 2 **s** in heaven, and *one* sat on the throne. *G2749*
10: 2 book open: and he **s** his right foot upon *G5087*
20: 3 shut him up, and **s** a seal upon him, *G4972*

SETH
Gen 4:25 called his name **S**: For God, *said she*, H8352
26 And to **S**, to him also there was born a H8352
5: 3 after his image; and called his name **S**: H8352
4 he had begotten **S** were eight hundred H8352
6 And **S** lived an hundred and five years, H8352
7 And **S** lived after he begat Enos eight H8352
8 And all the days of **S** were nine H8352
Lk 3:38 was *the son* of **S**, which was *the son* of *G4589*

SETHUR
Nu 13:13 Of the tribe of Asher, **S** the son of H5639

SETTER
Act 17:18 seemeth to be a **s** forth of strange gods: *G2604*

SETTEST
Dt 23:20 in all that thou **s** thine hand to in the H4916
28: 8 in all that thou **s** thine hand unto; and H4916
20 in all that thou **s** thine hand unto for H4916
Job 7:12 *Am* I a sea, or a whale, that thou **s** a H7760
13:27 thou **s** a print upon the heels of my feet.
Ps 21: 3 **s** a crown of pure gold on his head. H7896
41:12 and **s** me before thy face for ever. H5324

SETTETH
Nu 1:51 And when the tabernacle **s** forward, the H5265
4: 5 And when the camp **s** forward, Aaron H5265
Dt 24:15 for he *is* poor, and **s** his heart upon it: H5375
27:16 Cursed *be* he that **s** light by his father H7034
2Sa 22:34 *feet*: and **s** me upon my high places. H5975
Job 28: 3 He **s** an end to darkness, and searcheth H7760
Ps 18:33 *feet*, and **s** me upon my high places. H5975
36: 4 He deviseth mischief upon his bed; he **s** H3320
65: 6 Which by his strength **s** fast the H3559
68: 6 God **s** the solitary in families: he H3427
75: 7 he putteth down one, and **s** up another. H3427
83:14 as the flame **s** the mountains on fire; H3857
107:41 Yet **s** he the poor on high from affliction,
Jer 5:26 lay wait, as he that **s** snares; they set a H7918
43: 3 But Baruch the son of Neriah **s** thee on H5496
Ezk 14: 4 of Israel that **s** up his idols in his heart, H5927
7 from me, and **s** up his idols in his H5927
Dan 2:21 kings, and **s** up kings: he giveth H6966
4:17 will, and **s** up over it the basest of men. H6966
Mt 4: 5 and **s** him on a pinnacle of the temple, *G2476*
Lk 8:16 *it* under a bed; but **s** *it* on a candlestick, *G2007*
Jas 3: 6 whole body, and **s** on fire the course of *G5394*

SETTING
Ezk 43: 8 In their **s** of their threshold by my H5414
Mt 27:66 sure, sealing the stone, and **s** a watch. *G3326*
Lk 4:40 Now when the sun was **s**, all they that *G1416*

SETTINGS
Ex 28:17 And thou shalt set in it **s** of stones, H4396

SETTLE
1Ch 17:14 But I will **s** him in mine house and in H5975
Ezk 36:11 fruit: and I will **s** you after your old H3427
43:14 *even* to the lower **s** *shall be* two cubits, H5835
14 from the lesser **s** *even* to the greater H5835
14 settle *even* to the greater **s** *shall be* four H5835
17 And the **s** *shall be* fourteen *cubits* long H5835
20 the four corners of the **s**, and upon the H5835
45:19 four corners of the **s** of the altar, and H5835
Lk 21:14 **S** *it* therefore in your hearts, not to *G5087*
1Pt 5:10 you perfect, stablish, strengthen, **s** *you*. *G2311*

SETTLED
1Ki 8:13 a **s** place for thee to abide in for ever. H4349
2Ki 8:11 And he **s** his countenance stedfastly, H5975
Ps 119:89 For ever, O LORD, thy word is **s** in H5324
Prv 8:25 Before the mountains were **s**, before the H2883
Jer 48:11 and he hath **s** on his lees, and hath H8252
Zep 1:12 the men that are **s** on their lees: that H7087
Col 1:23 faith grounded and **s**, and *be* not moved *G1476*

SETTLEST
Ps 65:10 abundantly: thou **s** the furrows thereof: H5181

SEVEN
Gen 5: 7 **s** years, and begat sons and daughters: H7651
25 eighty and **s** years, and begat Lamech: H7651
26 he begat Lamech **s** hundred eighty and H7651
31 And all the days of Lamech were **s** H7651
31 seventy and **s** years: and he died. H7651
7: 4 For yet **s** days, and I will cause it to H7651
10 And it came to pass after **s** days, that H7651
8:10 And he stayed yet other **s** days; and H7651
12 And he stayed yet other **s** days; and H7651
14 And in the second month, on the **s** and H7651
11:21 **s** years, and begat sons and daughters. H7651
21:28 And Abraham set **s** ewe lambs of the H7651
29 What *mean* these **s** ewe lambs which H7651
30 And he said, For *these* **s** ewe lambs H7651
23: 1 And Sarah was an hundred and **s** and H7651
25:17 and thirty and **s** years: and he gave up H7651
29:18 I will serve thee **s** years for Rachel thy H7651
20 And Jacob served **s** years for Rachel; H7651
27 shalt serve with me yet **s** other years. H7651
30 and served with him yet **s** other years. H7651
31:23 pursued after him **s** days' journey; and H7651
33: 3 to the ground **s** times, until he came H7651
41: 2 up out of the river **s** well favoured kine H7651
3 And, behold, **s** other kine came up after H7651
4 kine did eat up the **s** well favoured and H7651
5 time: and, behold, **s** ears of corn came H7651
6 And, behold, **s** thin ears and blasted H7651
7 And the **s** thin ears devoured the seven
7 And the seven thin ears devoured the **s** H7651
18 up out of the river **s** kine, fatfleshed H7651
19 And, behold, **s** other kine came up after H7651
20 kine did eat up the first **s** fat kine: H7651
22 And I saw in my dream, and, behold, **s** H7651
23 And, behold, **s** ears, withered, thin, *and* H7651
24 And the thin ears devoured the **s** good H7651
26 The **s** good kine *are* seven years; and H7651
26 The seven good kine *are* **s** years; and H7651
26 years; and the **s** good ears *are* seven H7651
26 good ears *are* **s** years: the dream *is* one. H7651
27 And the **s** thin and ill favoured kine H7651
27 came up after them *are* **s** years; and the H7651
27 years; and the **s** empty ears blasted H7651
27 east wind shall be **s** years of famine. H7651
29 Behold, there come **s** years of great H7651
30 And there shall arise after them **s** years H7651
34 land of Egypt in the **s** plenteous years. H7651
36 the land against the **s** years of famine, H7651
47 And in the **s** plenteous years the earth H7651
48 And he gathered up all the food of the **s** H7651
53 And the **s** years of plenteousness, that H7651
54 And the **s** years of dearth began to H7651
46:25 these unto Jacob: all the souls *were* **s**. H7651
47:28 was an hundred forty and **s** years. H7651
50:10 made a mourning for his father **s** days. H7651
Ex 2:16 Now the priest of Midian had **s** H7651
6:16 *were* an hundred thirty and **s** years. H7651
Ex 6:20 an hundred and thirty and **s** years. H7651
7:25 And **s** days were fulfilled, after that the H7651
12:15 **S** days shall ye eat unleavened bread; H7651
19 **S** days shall there be no leaven found H7651
13: 6 **S** days thou shalt eat unleavened H7651
7 Unleavened bread shall be eaten **s** H7651
22:30 with thy sheep: **s** days it shall be with H7651
23:15 eat unleavened bread **s** days, as I H7651
25:37 And thou shalt make the **s** lamps H7651
29:30 shall put them on **s** days, when he H7651
35 **s** days shalt thou consecrate them. H7651
37 **S** days thou shalt make an atonement H7651
34:18 shalt thou keep. **S** days thou shalt eat H7651
37:23 And he made his **s** lamps, and his H7651
38:24 nine talents, and **s** hundred and thirty H7651
25 talents, and a thousand **s** hundred and H7651
28 And of the thousand **s** hundred seventy H7651
Lev 4: 6 of the blood **s** times before the LORD, H7651
17 and sprinkle *it* **s** times before the H7651
8:11 upon the altar **s** times, and anointed H7651
33 congregation *in* **s** days, until the days H7651
33 end: for **s** days shall he consecrate you. H7651
35 day and night **s** days, and keep the H7651
12: 2 shall be unclean **s** days; according to H7651
13: 4 up *him that hath* the plague **s** days: H7651
5 priest shall shut him up **s** days more: H7651
21 the priest shall shut him up **s** days: H7651
26 the priest shall shut him up **s** days: H7651
31 *that hath* the plague of the scall **s** days: H7651
33 up *him that hath* the scall **s** days more: H7651
50 shut up *it that hath* the plague **s** days: H7651
54 *is*, and he shall shut it up **s** days more: H7651
14: 7 from the leprosy **s** times, and shall H7651
8 tarry abroad out of his tent **s** days. H7651
16 his finger **s** times before the LORD: H7651
27 his left hand **s** times before the LORD: H7651
38 house, and shut up the house **s** days: H7651
51 water, and sprinkle the house **s** times: H7651
15:13 shall number to himself **s** days for his H7651
19 she shall be put apart **s** days: and H7651
24 shall be unclean **s** days; and all the bed H7651
28 number to herself **s** days, and after that H7651
16:14 of the blood with his finger **s** times. H7651
19 it with his finger **s** times, and cleanse H7651
22:27 then it shall be **s** days under the dam; H7651
23: 6 **s** days ye must eat unleavened bread. H7651
8 unto the LORD **s** days: in the seventh H7651
15 offering; **s** sabbaths shall be complete: H7651
18 And ye shall offer with the bread **s** H7651
34 tabernacles *for* **s** days unto the LORD. H7651
36 **S** days ye shall offer an offering made H7651
39 unto the LORD **s** days: on the first day H7651
40 before the LORD your God **s** days. H7651
41 unto the LORD **s** days in the year. *It* H7651
42 Ye shall dwell in booths **s** days; all that H7651
25: 8 And thou shalt number **s** sabbaths of H7651
8 of years unto thee, **s** times seven years; H7651
8 thee, seven times **s** years; and the space H7651
8 and the space of the **s** sabbaths of years H7651
26:18 punish you **s** times more for your sins. H7651
21 me; I will bring **s** times more plagues H7651
24 punish you yet **s** times for your sins. H7651
28 will chastise you **s** times for your sins. H7651
Nu 1:31 fifty and **s** thousand and four hundred. H7651
39 and two thousand and **s** hundred. H7651
2: 8 fifty and **s** thousand and four hundred. H7651
26 and two thousand and **s** hundred. H7651
31 and fifty and **s** thousand and six H7651
3:22 *were* **s** thousand and five hundred. H7651
4:36 were two thousand **s** hundred and fifty. H7651
8: 2 the lamps, the **s** lamps shall give light H7651
12:14 not be ashamed **s** days? let her be shut H7651
14 out from the camp **s** days, and after H7651
15 shut out from the camp **s** days: and the H7651
13:22 built **s** years before Zoan in Egypt.) H7651
16:49 thousand and **s** hundred, beside them H7651
19: 4 tabernacle of the congregation **s** times: H7651
11 of any man shall be unclean **s** days. H7651
14 *is* in the tent, shall be unclean **s** days. H7651
16 or a grave, shall be unclean **s** days. H7651
23: 1 Build me here **s** altars, and prepare H7651
1 me here **s** oxen and seven rams. H7651
1 me here seven oxen and **s** rams. H7651
4 I have prepared **s** altars, and I have H7651
14 Pisgah, and built **s** altars, and offered a H7651
29 Build me here **s** altars, and prepare H7651
29 me here **s** bullocks and seven rams. H7651
29 me here seven bullocks and **s** rams. H7651
26: 7 thousand and **s** hundred and thirty. H7651

Nu 26:34 fifty and two thousand and **s** hundred. H7651
51 and a thousand **s** hundred and thirty. H7651
28:11 **s** lambs of the first year without spot; H7651
17 this month *is* the feast: **s** days shall H7651
19 and one ram, and **s** lambs of the first H7651
21 every lamb, throughout the **s** lambs: H7651
24 throughout the **s** days, the meat of the H7651
27 one ram, **s** lambs of the first year; H7651
29 one lamb, throughout the **s** lambs; H7651
29: 2 one ram, *and* **s** lambs of the first year H7651
4 for one lamb, throughout the **s** lambs: H7651
8 one ram, *and* **s** lambs of the first year; H7651
10 for one lamb, throughout the **s** lambs: H7651
12 keep a feast unto the LORD **s** days: H7651
32 And on the seventh day **s** bullocks, two H7651
36 bullock, one ram, **s** lambs of the first H7651
31:19 And do ye abide without the camp **s** H7651
36 thousand and **s** and thirty thousand H7651
43 **s** thousand and five hundred sheep, H7651
52 thousand **s** hundred and fifty shekels. H7651
Dt 7: 1 and the Jebusites, **s** nations greater H7651
15: 1 At the end of *every* **s** years thou shalt H7651
16: 3 bread with it; **s** days shalt thou eat H7651
4 in all thy coast **s** days; neither shall H7651
9 **S** weeks shalt thou number unto thee: H7651
9 to number the **s** weeks from *such time* H7651
13 of tabernacles **s** days, after that thou H7651
15 **S** days shalt thou keep a solemn feast H7651
28: 7 one way, and flee before thee **s** ways. H7651
25 them, and flee **s** ways before them: and H7651
31:10 At the end of *every* **s** years, in the H7651
Jos 6: 4 And **s** priests shall bear before the ark H7651
4 bear before the ark **s** trumpets of rams' H7651
4 shall compass the city **s** times, and the H7651
6 covenant, and let **s** priests bear seven H7651
6 seven priests bear **s** trumpets of rams' H7651
8 people, that the **s** priests bearing the H7651
8 priests bearing the **s** trumpets of rams' H7651
13 And **s** priests bearing seven trumpets H7651
13 And seven priests bearing **s** trumpets H7651
15 the same manner **s** times: only on that H7651
15 day they compassed the city **s** times. H7651
18: 2 children of Israel **s** tribes, which had H7651
5 And they shall divide it into **s** parts: H7651
6 the land *into* **s** parts, and bring *the* H7651
9 it by cities into **s** parts in a book, and H7651
Jdg 6: 1 them into the hand of Midian **s** years. H7651
25 the second bullock of **s** years old, and H7651
8:26 a thousand and **s** hundred *shekels* of H7651
12: 9 his sons. And he judged Israel **s** years. H7651
14:12 it me within the **s** days of the feast, and H7651
17 And she wept before him the **s** days, H7651
16: 7 If they bind me with **s** green withs that H7651
8 brought up to her **s** green withs which H7651
13 the **s** locks of my head with the web. H7651
19 to shave off the **s** locks of his head; and H7651
20:15 numbered **s** hundred chosen men. H7651
16 Among all this people *there were* **s** H7651
Ru 4:15 to thee than **s** sons, hath born him. H7651
1Sa 2: 5 barren hath born **s**; and she that hath H7651
6: 1 the country of the Philistines **s** months. H7651
10: 8 of peace offerings: **s** days shalt thou H7651
11: 3 unto him, Give us **s** days' respite, that H7651
13: 8 And he tarried **s** days, according to the H7651
16:10 Again, Jesse made **s** of his sons to pass H7651
31:13 a tree at Jabesh, and fasted **s** days. H7651
2Sa 2:11 of Judah was **s** years and six months. H7651
5: 5 In Hebron he reigned over Judah **s** H7651
8: 4 *chariots*, and **s** hundred horsemen, H7651
10:18 slew *the men of* **s** hundred chariots of H7651
21: 6 Let **s** men of his sons be delivered unto H7651
9 and they fell *all* **s** together, and were H7651
23:39 Uriah the Hittite: thirty and **s** in all. H7651
24:13 unto him, Shall **s** years of famine come H7651
1Ki 2:11 *were* forty years: **s** years reigned he in H7651
6: 6 and the third *was* **s** cubits broad: for H7651
38 of it. So was he **s** years in building it. H7651
7:17 top of the pillars; **s** for the one chapiter, H7651
17 chapiter, and **s** for the other chapiter. H7651
8:65 LORD our God, **s** days and seven days, H7651
65 days and **s** days, *even* fourteen days. H7651
11: 3 And he had **s** hundred wives, H7651
16:15 did Zimri reign **s** days in Tirzah. And H7651
18:43 nothing. And he said, Go again **s** times. H7651
19:18 Yet I have left *me* **s** thousand in Israel, H7651
20:15 children of Israel, *being* **s** thousand. H7651
29 against the other **s** days. And *so* it was, H7651
30 fell upon twenty and **s** thousand of the H7651
2Ki 3: 9 a compass of **s** days' journey: and there H7651

2Ki 3:26 he took with him **s** hundred men that H7651
4:35 **s** times, and the child opened his eyes. H7651
5:10 wash in Jordan **s** times, and thy flesh H7651
14 and dipped himself **s** times in Jordan, H7651
8: 1 shall also come upon the land **s** years. H7651
2 in the land of the Philistines **s** years. H7651
3 And it came to pass at the **s** years' end, H7651
11:21 **S** years old *was* Jehoash when he began H7651
24:16 And all the men of might, *even* **s** H7651
25:27 And it came to pass in the **s** and H7651
27 month, on the **s** and twentieth *day* of H7651
1Ch 3: 4 and there he reigned **s** years and six H7651
24 Johanan, and Dalaiah, and Anani, **s**. H7651
5:13 and Jachan, and Zia, and Heber, **s**. H7651
18 and forty thousand **s** hundred and H7651
7: 5 genealogies fourscore and **s** thousand. H7651
9:13 fathers, a thousand and **s** hundred and H7651
25 **s** days from time to time with them. H7651
10:12 the oak in Jabesh, and fasted **s** days. H7651
12:25 the war, **s** thousand and one hundred. H7651
27 *were* three thousand and **s** hundred; H7651
34 shield and spear thirty and **s** thousand. H7651
15:26 they offered **s** bullocks and seven rams. H7651
26 they offered seven bullocks and **s** rams. H7651
18: 4 chariots, and **s** thousand horsemen, H7651
19:18 slew of the Syrians **s** thousand *men* H7651
26:30 a thousand and **s** hundred, *were* H7651
32 two thousand and **s** hundred chief H7651
29: 4 gold of Ophir, and **s** thousand talents H7651
27 *was* forty years; **s** years reigned he in H7651
2Ch 7: 8 kept the feast **s** days, and all Israel H7651
9 altar **s** days, and the feast seven days. H7651
9 altar seven days, and the feast **s** days. H7651
13: 9 a young bullock and **s** rams, *the same* H7651
15:11 they had brought, **s** hundred oxen and H7651
11 hundred oxen and **s** thousand sheep. H7651
17:11 him flocks, **s** thousand and seven H7651
11 thousand and **s** hundred rams, and H7651
11 rams, and **s** thousand and seven H7651
11 thousand and **s** hundred he goats. H7651
24: 1 Joash *was* **s** years old when he began to H7651
26:13 thousand and **s** thousand and five H7651
29:21 And they brought **s** bullocks, and seven H7651
21 And they brought seven bullocks, and **s** H7651
21 seven rams, and **s** lambs, and seven he H7651
21 seven lambs, and **s** he goats, for a sin H7651
30:21 of unleavened bread **s** days with great H7651
22 the feast **s** days, offering peace H7651
23 to keep other **s** days: and they kept H7651
23 they kept *other* **s** days with gladness. H7651
24 bullocks and **s** thousand sheep; and H7651
35:17 the feast of unleavened bread **s** days. H7651
Ezr 2: 5 The children of Arah, **s** hundred H7651
9 The children of Zaccai, **s** hundred and H7651
25 **s** hundred and forty and three. H7651
33 The children of Lod, Hadid, and Ono, **s** H7651
38 a thousand two hundred forty and **s**. H7651
65 of whom *there were* **s** thousand three H7651
65 thirty and **s**: and *there were* among H7651
66 Their horses *were* **s** hundred thirty and H7651
67 six thousand **s** hundred and twenty. H7651
6:22 unleavened bread **s** days with joy: for H7651
7:14 the king, and of his **s** counsellors, to H7655
8:35 rams, seventy and **s** lambs, twelve he H7651
Neh 7:14 The children of Zaccai, **s** hundred and H7651
18 six hundred threescore and **s**. H7651
19 Bigvai, two thousand threescore and **s**. H7651
29 Beeroth, **s** hundred forty and three. H7651
37 The children of Lod, Hadid, and Ono, **s** H7651
41 a thousand two hundred forty and **s**. H7651
67 of whom *there were* **s** thousand three H7651
67 thirty and **s**: and they had two hundred H7651
68 Their horses, **s** hundred thirty and six: H7651
69 thousand **s** hundred and twenty asses. H7651
72 and threescore and **s** priests' garments. H7651
8:18 they kept the feast **s** days; and on the H7651
Est 1: 1 hundred and **s** and twenty provinces:) H7651
5 great and small, **s** days, in the court of H7651
10 and Carcas, the **s** chamberlains that H7651
14 Memucan, the **s** princes of Persia and H7651
2: 9 to her, and **s** maidens, *which were* H7651
8: 9 twenty and **s** provinces, unto every H7651
9:30 twenty and **s** provinces of the kingdom H7651
Job 1: 2 And there were born unto him **s** sons H7651
3 His substance also was **s** thousand H7651
2:13 him upon the ground **s** days and seven H7651
13 seven days and **s** nights, and none H7651
5:19 yea, in **s** there shall no evil touch thee. H7651
42: 8 Therefore take unto you now **s** bullocks H7651

Job 42: 8 bullocks and **s** rams, and go to my H7651
13 He had also **s** sons and three H7658
Ps 12: 6 in a furnace of earth, purified **s** times. H7659
119:164 **S** times a day do I praise thee because H7651
Prv 6:16 yea, **s** *are* an abomination unto him: H7651
9: 1 house, she hath hewn out her **s** pillars: H7651
24:16 For a just *man* falleth **s** times, and H7651
26:16 than **s** men that can render a reason. H7651
25 *there are* **s** abominations in his heart. H7651
Ecc 11: 2 Give a portion to **s**, and also to eight; for H7651
Isa 4: 1 And in that day **s** women shall take H7651
11:15 smite it in the **s** streams, and make H7651
30:26 as the light of **s** days, in the day that H7651
Jer 15: 9 She that hath borne **s** languisheth: she H7651
34:14 At the end of **s** years let ye go every H7651
52:25 the men of war; and **s** men of them that H7651
30 captive of the Jews **s** hundred forty and H7651
31 And it came to pass in the **s** and H7651
Ezk 3:15 there astonished among them **s** days. H7651
16 And it came to pass at the end of **s** H7651
29:17 And it came to pass in the **s** and H7651
39: 9 they shall burn them with fire **s** years: H7651
12 And **s** months shall the house of Israel H7651
14 the end of **s** months shall they search. H7651
40:22 they went up unto it by **s** steps; and the H7651
26 And *there were* **s** steps to go up to it, H7651
41: 3 and the breadth of the door, **s** cubits. H7651
43:25 **S** days shalt thou prepare every day a H7651
26 **S** days shall they purge the altar and H7651
44:26 they shall reckon unto him **s** days. H7651
45:21 a feast of **s** days; unleavened bread H7620
23 And **s** days of the feast he shall prepare H7651
23 to the LORD, **s** bullocks and seven H7651
23 bullocks and **s** rams without blemish H7651
23 blemish daily the **s** days; and a kid of H7651
25 in the feast of the **s** days, according to H7651
Dan 3:19 the furnace one **s** times more than it H7655
4:16 him; and let **s** times pass over him. H7655
23 of the field, till **s** times pass over him; H7655
25 of heaven, and **s** times shall pass over H7655
32 grass as oxen, and **s** times shall pass H7655
9:25 the Prince *shall be* **s** weeks, and H7651
Am 5: 8 *Seek him* that maketh the **s** stars and H3598
Mic 5: 5 **s** shepherds, and eight principal men. H7651
Zec 3: 9 one stone *shall be* **s** eyes: behold, I will H7651
4: 2 top of it, and his **s** lamps thereon, and H7651
2 lamps thereon, and **s** pipes to the seven H7651
2 seven pipes to the **s** lamps, which *are* H7651
10 *with* those **s**; they *are* the eyes of H7651
Mt 12:45 taketh with himself **s** other spirits more *G2033*
15:34 And they said, **S**, and a few little fishes. *G2033*
36 And he took the **s** loaves and the fishes, *G2033*
37 *meat* that was left **s** baskets full. *G2033*
16:10 Neither the **s** loaves of the four *G2033*
18:21 me, and I forgive him? till **s** times? *G2034*
22 **s** times: but, Until seventy times seven. *G2034*
22 seven times: but, Until seventy times **s**. *G2033*
22:25 Now there were with us **s** brethren: and *G2033*
28 shall she be of the **s**? for they all had her. *G2033*
Mk 8: 5 many loaves have ye? And they said, **S**. *G2033*
6 and he took the **s** loaves, and gave *G2033*
8 the broken *meat* that was left **s** baskets. *G2033*
20 And when the **s** among four thousand, *G2033*
20 fragments took ye up? And they said, **S**. *G2033*
12:20 Now there were **s** brethren: and the *G2033*
22 And the **s** had her, and left no seed: last *G2033*
23 be of them? for the **s** had her to wife. *G2033*
16: 9 out of whom he had cast **s** devils. *G2033*
Lk 2:36 an husband **s** years from her virginity; *G2033*
8: 2 Magdalene, out of whom went **s** devils, *G2033*
11:26 Then goeth he, and taketh *to him* **s** *G2033*
17: 4 And if he trespass against thee **s** times *G2034*
4 in a day, and **s** times in a day turn *G2034*
20:29 There were therefore **s** brethren: and *G2033*
31 in like manner the **s** also: and they left *G2033*
33 of them is she? for **s** had her to wife. *G2033*
Act 6: 3 look ye out among you **s** men of honest *G2033*
13:19 And when he had destroyed **s** nations *G2033*
19:14 And there were **s** sons of *one* Sceva, a *G2033*
20: 6 in five days; where we abode **s** days. *G2033*
21: 4 we tarried there **s** days: who said to *G2033*
8 was *one* of the **s**; and abode with him. *G2033*
27 And when the **s** days were almost *G2033*
28:14 **s** days: and so we went toward Rome. *G2033*
Ro 11: 4 reserved to myself **s** thousand men, *G2035*
Heb 11:30 they were compassed about **s** days. *G2033*
Rev 1: 4 John to the **s** churches which are in *G2033*
4 **s** Spirits which are before his throne; *G2033*
11 send *it* unto the **s** churches which are *G2033*

Rev 1:12 turned, I saw s golden candlesticks; *G2033*
13 And in the midst of the s candlesticks *G2033*
16 And he had in his right hand s stars: *G2033*
20 The mystery of the s stars which thou *G2033*
20 hand, and the s golden candlesticks. *G2033*
20 candlesticks. The s stars are the angels *G2033*
20 the angels of the s churches: and the *G2033*
20 churches: and the s candlesticks which *G2033*
20 which thou sawest are the s churches. *G2033*
2: 1 he that holdeth the s stars in his right *G2033*
1 the midst of the s golden candlesticks; *G2033*
3: 1 he that hath the s Spirits of God, and *G2033*
1 of God, and the s stars; I know thy *G2033*
4: 5 and *there were* s lamps of fire burning *G2033*
5 throne, which are the s Spirits of God. *G2033*
5: 1 on the backside, sealed with s seals. *G2033*
5 book, and to loose the s seals thereof. *G2033*
6 been slain, having s horns and seven *G2033*
6 seven horns and s eyes, which are the *G2033*
6 which are the s Spirits of God sent forth *G2033*
8: 2 And I saw the s angels which stood *G2033*
2 and to them were given s trumpets. *G2033*
6 And the s angels which had the seven *G2033*
6 And the seven angels which had the s *G2033*
10: 3 cried, s thunders uttered their voices. *G2033*
4 And when the s thunders had uttered *G2033*
4 s thunders uttered, and write them not. *G2033*
11:13 were slain of men s thousand: and the *G2033*
12: 3 dragon, having s heads and ten horns, *G2033*
3 horns, and s crowns upon his heads. *G2033*
13: 1 out of the sea, having s heads and ten *G2033*
15: 1 and marvellous, s angels having the *G2033*
1 angels having the s last plagues; for in *G2033*
6 And the s angels came out of the *G2033*
6 temple, having the s plagues, clothed in *G2033*
7 gave unto the s angels seven golden *G2033*
7 the seven angels s golden vials full of *G2033*
8 into the temple, till the s plagues of the *G2033*
8 plagues of the s angels were fulfilled. *G2033*
16: 1 saying to the s angels, Go your ways, *G2033*
17: 1 And there came one of the s angels *G2033*
1 which had the s vials, and talked with *G2033*
3 having s heads and ten horns. *G2033*
7 which hath the s heads and ten horns. *G2033*
9 hath wisdom. The s heads are seven *G2033*
9 seven heads are s mountains, on which *G2033*
10 And there are s kings: five are fallen, *G2033*
11 and is of the s, and goeth into perdition. *G2033*
21: 9 And there came unto me one of the s *G2033*
9 which had the s vials full of the seven *G2033*
9 vials full of the s last plagues, and *G2033*

SEVENFOLD
Gen 4:15 be taken on him s. And the LORD set a H7659
24 If Cain shall be avenged s, truly Lamech H7659
24 sevenfold, truly Lamech seventy and s. H7651
Ps 79:12 And render unto our neighbours s into H7659
Prv 6:31 But *if* he be found, he shall restore s; he H7659
Isa 30:26 light of the sun shall be s, as the light of H7659

SEVEN-HUNDRED See SEVEN and HUNDRED.

SEVENS
Gen 7: 2 shalt take to thee by s, the male and his H7651
3 Of fowls also of the air by s, the male H7651

SEVENTEEN
Gen 37: 2 Joseph, *being* s years old, was H7651+H6240
47:28 land of Egypt s years: so the H7651+H6240
Jdg 8:14 *even* threescore and s men. H7657+H7651
1Ki 14:21 and he reigned s years in H7651+H6240
2Ki 13: 1 Samaria, *and reigned* s years. H7651+H6240
1Ch 7:11 of valour, *were* s thousand and H7651+H6240
2Ch 12:13 and he reigned s years in H7651+H6240
Ezr 2:39 of Harim, a thousand and s. H7651+H6240
Neh 7:42 of Harim, a thousand and s. H7651+H6240
Jer 32: 9 money, *even* s shekels of silver. H7651+H6235

SEVENTEENTH
Gen 7:11 month, the s day of the month, H7651+H6240
8: 4 month, on the s day of the H7651+H6240
1Ki 22:51 in Samaria the s year of H7651+H6240
2Ki 16: 1 In the s year of Pekah the son H7651+H6240
1Ch 24:15 The s to Hezir, the eighteenth H7651+H6240
25:24 The s to Joshbekashah, *he*, his H7651+H6240

SEVENTH
Gen 2: 2 And on the s day God ended his work H7637
2 he rested on the s day from all his work H7637
3 And God blessed the s day, and H7637
8: 4 And the ark rested in the s month, on H7637
Ex 12:15 first day until the s day, that soul shall H7637
16 and in the s day there shall be an H7637
13: 6 the s day *shall be* a feast to the LORD. H7637
16:26 Six days ye shall gather it; but on the s H7637
27 of the people on the s day for to gather, H7637
29 man go out of his place on the s day. H7637
30 So the people rested on the s day. H7637
20:10 But the s day *is* the sabbath of the H7637
11 *is*, and rested the s day: wherefore the H7637
21: 2 in the s he shall go out free for nothing. H7637
23:11 But the s *year* thou shalt let it rest and H7637
12 work, and on the s day thou shalt rest: H7637
24:16 it six days: and the s day he called unto H7637
31:15 be done; but in the s *is* the sabbath of H7637
17 the s day he rested, and was refreshed. H7637
34:21 Six days thou shalt work, but on the s H7637
35: 2 done, but on the s day there shall be to H7637
Lev 13: 5 And the priest shall look on him the s H7637
6 on him again the s day: and, behold, *if* H7637
27 look upon him the s day: *and* if it be H7637
32 And in the s day the priest shall look on H7637
34 And in the s day the priest shall look on H7637
51 the plague on the s day: if the plague be H7637
14: 9 But it shall be on the s day, that he H7637
39 And the priest shall come again the s H7637
16:29 you: *that* in the s month, on the tenth H7637
23: 3 Six days shall work be done: but the s H7637
8 seven days: in the s day *is* an holy H7637
16 Even unto the morrow after the s H7637
24 saying, In the s month, in the first *day* H7637
27 Also on the tenth *day* of this s month H7637
34 day of this s month *shall be* the feast H7637
39 Also in the fifteenth day of the s month, H7637
41 ye shall celebrate it in the s month. H7637
25: 4 But in the s year shall be a sabbath of H7637
9 tenth *day* of the s month, in the day of H7637
20 shall we eat the s year? behold, we shall H7637
Nu 6: 9 on the s day shall he shave it. H7637
7:48 On the s day Elishama the son of H7637
19:12 day, and on the s day he shall be clean: H7637
12 then the s day he shall not be clean. H7637
19 third day, and on the s day: and on the H7637
19 day: and on the s day he shall purify H7637
28:25 And on the s day ye shall have an holy H7637
29: 1 And in the s month, on the first *day* of H7637
7 the tenth *day* of this s month an holy H7637
12 And on the fifteenth day of the s month H7637
32 And on the s day seven bullocks, two H7637
31:19 on the third day, and on the s day. H7637
24 And ye shall wash your clothes on the s H7637
Dt 5:14 But the s day *is* the sabbath of the H7637
15: 9 heart, saying, The s year, the year of H7651
12 years; then in the s year thou shalt let H7637
16: 8 bread: and on the s day *shall be* a H7637
Jos 6: 4 horns: and the s day ye shall compass H7637
15 And it came to pass on the s day, that H7637
16 And it came to pass at the s time, when H7637
19:40 *And* the s lot came out for the tribe of H7637
Jdg 14:15 And it came to pass on the s day, that H7637
17 to pass on the s day, that he told her, H7637
18 unto him on the s day before the sun H7637
2Sa 12:18 And it came to pass on the s day, that H7637
1Ki 8: 2 month Ethanim, which *is* the s month. H7637
16:10 in the twenty and s year of Asa king of H7651
15 In the twenty and s year of Asa king of H7651
18:44 And it came to pass at the s time, that H7637
20:29 it was, that in the s day the battle was H7637
2Ki 11: 4 And the s year Jehoiada sent and H7637
12: 1 In the s year of Jehu Jehoash began to H7651
13:10 In the thirty and s year of Joash king of H7651
15: 1 In the twenty and s year of Jeroboam H7651
18: 9 which *was* the s year of Hoshea son H7637
25: 8 And in the fifth month, on the s *day* of H7651
25 But it came to pass in the s month, that H7637
1Ch 2:15 Ozem the sixth, David the s: H7637
12:11 Attai the sixth, Eliel the s, H7637
24:10 The s to Hakkoz, the eighth to Abijah, H7637
25:14 The s to Jesharelah, *he*, his sons, and H7637
26: 3 Jehohanan the sixth, Elioenai the s. H7637
5 Ammiel the sixth, Issachar the s, H7637
27:10 The s *captain* for the seventh month H7637
10 The seventh *captain* for the s month H7637
2Ch 5: 3 in the feast which *was* in the s month. H7637
7:10 day of the s month he sent the people H7637
23: 1 And in the s year Jehoiada H7637
31: 7 and finished *them* in the s month. H7637
Ezr 3: 1 And when the s month was come, and H7637
6 From the first day of the s month H7637
7: 7 in the s year of Artaxerxes the king. H7651
8 which *was* in the s year of the king. H7637
Neh 7:73 cities; and when the s month came, the H7637
8: 2 upon the first day of the s month. H7637
14 in booths in the feast of the s month: H7637
10:31 s year, and the exaction of every debt. H7637
Est 1:10 On the s day, when the heart of the H7637
2:16 Tebeth, in the s year of his reign. H7651
Jer 28:17 died the same year in the s month. H7637
41: 1 Now it came to pass in the s month, H7637
52:28 captive: in the s year three thousand H7651
Ezk 20: 1 And it came to pass in the s year, in the H7637
30:20 first *month*, in the s *day* of the month, H7651
45:20 And so thou shalt do the s *day* of the H7651
25 In the s *month*, in the fifteenth day of H7637
Hag 2: 1 In the s *month*, in the one and H7637
Zec 7: 5 in the fifth and s *month*, even those H7637
8:19 and the fast of the s, and the fast of the H7637
Mt 22:26 second also, and the third, unto the s. *G2033*
Jn 4:52 at the s hour the fever left him. *G1442*
Heb 4: 4 For he spake in a certain place of the s *G1442*
4 did rest the s day from all his works. *G1442*
Jude 14 And Enoch also, the s from Adam, *G1442*
Rev 8: 1 And when he had opened the s seal, *G1442*
10: 7 But in the days of the voice of the s *G1442*
11:15 And the s angel sounded; and there *G1442*
16:17 And the s angel poured out his vial into *G1442*
21:20 the sixth, sardius; the s, chrysolyte; the *G1442*

SEVEN-THOUSAND See SEVEN and THOUSAND.

SEVENTY
Gen 4:24 truly Lamech s and sevenfold. H7657
5:12 And Cainan lived s years, and begat H7657
31 s and seven years: and he died. H7657
11:26 And Terah lived s years, and begat H7657
12: 4 and Abram *was* s and five years old H7657
Ex 1: 5 of Jacob were s souls: for Joseph was H7657
24: 1 and Abihu, and s of the elders of Israel; H7657
9 and Abihu, and s of the elders of Israel: H7657
38:28 And of the thousand seven hundred s H7657
29 And the brass of the offering *was* s H7657
Nu 7:13 one silver bowl of s shekels, after the H7657
19 one silver bowl of s shekels, after the H7657
25 one silver bowl of s shekels, after the H7657
31 one silver bowl of s shekels, after the H7657
37 one silver bowl of s shekels, after the H7657
43 a silver bowl of s shekels, after the H7657
49 one silver bowl of s shekels, after the H7657
55 one silver bowl of s shekels, after the H7657
61 one silver bowl of s shekels, after the H7657
67 one silver bowl of s shekels, after the H7657
73 one silver bowl of s shekels, after the H7657
79 one silver bowl of s shekels, after the H7657
85 thirty *shekels*, each bowl s: all the silver H7657
11:16 Gather unto me s men of the elders of H7657
24 and gathered the s men of the elders of H7657
25 gave *it* unto the s elders: and it came H7657
31:32 s thousand and five thousand sheep, H7657
Jdg 9:56 his father, in slaying his s brethren: H7657
2Sa 24:15 even to Beer-sheba s thousand men. H7657
2Ki 10: 1 And Ahab had s sons in Samaria. And H7657
6 king's sons, *being* s persons, *were* with H7657
7 sons, and slew s persons, and put their H7657
1Ch 21:14 and there fell of Israel s thousand men. H7657
Ezr 2: 3 two thousand an hundred s and two. H7657
4 Shephatiah, three hundred s and two. H7657
5 The children of Arah, seven hundred s H7657
36 of Jeshua, nine hundred s and three. H7657
40 of the children of Hodaviah, s and four. H7657
8: 7 son of Athaliah, and with him s males. H7657
14 and Zabbud, and with them s males. H7657
35 and six rams, s and seven lambs, H7657
Neh 7: 8 two thousand an hundred s and two. H7657
9 Shephatiah, three hundred s and two. H7657
39 of Jeshua, nine hundred s and three. H7657
43 of the children of Hodevah, s and four. H7657
11:19 the gates, *were* an hundred s and two. H7657
Est 9:16 slew of their foes s and five thousand, H7657
Isa 23:15 shall be forgotten s years, according to H7657
15 of s years shall Tyre sing as an harlot. H7657
17 after the end of s years, that the LORD H7657
Jer 25:11 shall serve the king of Babylon s years. H7657
12 And it shall come to pass, when s years H7657
29:10 For thus saith the LORD, That after s H7657
Ezk 8:11 And there stood before them s men of H7657
41:12 the west *was* s cubits broad; and the H7657
Dan 9: 2 s years in the desolations of Jerusalem. H7657

Dan 9:24 S weeks are determined upon thy H7657
Zec 7: 5 *month*, even those s years, did ye at all H7657
Mt 18:22 seven times: but, Until s times seven. G1441
Lk 10: 1 appointed other s also, and sent them G1440
17 And the s returned again with joy, G1440

SEVENTY-THOUSAND See SEVENTY and THOUSAND.

SEVER
Ex 8:22 And I will s in that day the land of H6395
9: 4 And the LORD shall s between the H6395
Ezk 39:14 And they shall s out men of continual H914
Mt 13:49 and s the wicked from among the just, G873

SEVERAL
Nu 28:13 And a s tenth deal of flour mingled with
21 A s tenth deal shalt thou offer for every
29 A s tenth deal unto one lamb,
29:10 A s tenth deal for one lamb, throughout
15 And a s tenth deal to each lamb of the
2Ki 15: 5 and dwelt in a s house. And Jotham H2669
2Ch 11:12 And in every s city *he put* shields and
26:21 and dwelt in a s house, *being* a leper; H2669
28:25 And in every s city of Judah he made
31:19 cities, in every s city, the men that were
Mt 25:15 man according to his s ability; and G2398
Rev 21:21 pearls; every s gate was of one G303+G1520

SEVERALLY
1Co 12:11 dividing to every man s as he will. G2398

SEVERED
Lev 20:26 *am* holy, and have s you from *other* H914
Dt 4:41 Then Moses s three cities on this side H914
Jdg 4:11 in law of Moses, had s himself from the H6504

SEVERITY
Ro 11:22 Behold therefore the goodness and s of G663
22 on them which fell, s; but toward thee, G663

SEW
Ecc 3: 7 A time to rend, and a time to s; a time H8609
Ezk 13:18 Woe to the *women* that s pillows to all H8609

SEWED
Gen 3: 7 naked; and they s fig leaves together, H8609
Job 16:15 I have s sackcloth upon my skin, and H8609

SEWEST
Job 14:17 in a bag, and thou s up mine iniquity. H2950

SEWETH
Mk 2:21 No man also s a piece of new cloth on G1976

SHAALABBIN
Jos 19:42 And S, and Ajalon, and Jethlah, H8169

SHAALBIM
Jdg 1:35 in Aijalon, and in S: yet the hand of the H8169
1Ki 4: 9 The son of Dekar, in Makaz, and in S, H8169

SHAALBONITE
2Sa 23:32 Eliahba the S, of the sons of Jashen, H8170
1Ch 11:33 the Baharumite, Eliahba the S, H8170

SHAAPH
1Ch 2:47 Ge-shan, and Pelet, and Ephah, and S. H8174
49 She bare also S the father of H8174

SHAARAIM
1Sa 17:52 to S, even unto Gath, and unto Ekron. H8189
1Ch 4:31 at Beth-birei, and at S. These *were* their H8189

SHAASHGAZ
Est 2:14 women, to the custody of S, the king's H8190

SHABBETHAI
Ezr 10:15 and S the Levite helped them. H7678
Neh 8: 7 Jamin, Akkub, S, Hodijah, Maaseiah, H7678
11:16 And S and Jozabad, of the chief of the H7678

SHACHIA
1Ch 8:10 And Jeuz, and S, and Mirma. These H7634

SHADE
Ps 121: 5 the LORD *is* thy s upon thy right hand. H6738

SHADOW
Gen 19: 8 came they under the s of my roof. H6738
Jdg 9:15 put your trust in my s: and if not, let fire H6738
36 s of the mountains as *if they were* men. H6738
2Ki 20: 9 hath spoken: shall the s go forward ten H6738
10 a light thing for the s to go down ten H6738
10 let the s return backward ten degrees. H6738
11 he brought the s ten degrees backward, H6738
1Ch 29:15 *are* as a s, and *there is* none abiding. H6738
Job 3: 5 Let darkness and the s of death stain it; H6757
7: 2 As a servant earnestly desireth the s, H6738
8: 9 because our days upon earth *are* a s:) H6738
10:21 the land of darkness and the s of death; H6757
22 *itself; and* of the s of death, without H6757
12:22 and bringeth out to light the s of death. H6757
14: 2 fleeth also as a s, and continueth not. H6738
16:16 and on my eyelids *is* the s of death; H6757
17: 7 sorrow, and all my members *are* as a s. H6738
24:17 to them even as the s of death: if *one* H6757
17 *they are in* the terrors of the s of death. H6757
28: 3 stones of darkness, and the s of death. H6757
34:22 *There is* no darkness, nor s of death, H6757
38:17 thou seen the doors of the s of death? H6757
40:22 The shady trees cover him *with* their s; H6752
Ps 17: 8 eye, hide me under the s of thy wings, H6738
23: 4 the valley of the s of death, I will fear H6757
36: 7 put their trust under the s of thy wings. H6738
44:19 and covered us with the s of death. H6757
57: 1 in thee: yea, in the s of thy wings will I H6738
63: 7 in the s of thy wings will I rejoice. H6738
80:10 The hills were covered with the s of it, H6738
91: 1 shall abide under the s of the Almighty. H6738
102:11 My days *are* like a s that declineth; and H6738
107:10 Such as sit in darkness and in the s of H6757
14 darkness and the s of death, and brake H6757
109:23 I am gone like the s when it declineth: I H6738
144: 4 his days *are* as a s that passeth away. H6738
Ecc 6:12 he spendeth as a s? for who can tell a H6738
8:13 a s; because he feareth not before God. H6738
Song 2: 3 sat down under his s with great delight, H6738
Isa 4: 6 And there shall be a tabernacle for a s H6738
9: 2 in the land of the s of death, upon them H6757
16: 3 make thy s as the night in the midst H6738
25: 4 from the storm, a s from the heat, H6738
5 *even* the heat with the s of a cloud: the H6738
30: 2 Pharaoh, and to trust in the s of Egypt! H6738
3 trust in the s of Egypt *your* confusion. H6738
32: 2 as the s of a great rock in a weary land. H6738
34:15 and gather under her s: there shall the H6738
38: 8 Behold, I will bring again the s of the H6738
49: 2 sword; in the s of his hand hath he H6738
51:16 thee in the s of mine hand, that I H6738
Jer 2: 6 and of the s of death, through a H6757
13:16 s of death, *and* make *it* gross darkness. H6757
48:45 They that fled stood under the s of H6738
Lam 4:20 his s we shall live among the heathen. H6738
Ezk 17:23 of every wing; in the s of the branches H6738
31: 6 and under his s dwelt all great nations. H6738
12 down from his s, and have left him. H6738
17 under his s in the midst of the heathen. H6738
Dan 4:12 of the field had s under it, and the H2927
Hos 4:13 and elms, because the s thereof *is* good: H6738
14: 7 They that dwell under his s shall H6738
Am 5: 8 and turneth the s of death into the H6757
Jna 4: 5 sat under it in the s, till he might see H6738
6 that it might be a s over his head, to H6738
Mt 4:16 and s of death light is sprung up. G4639
Mk 4:32 of the air may lodge under the s of it. G4639
Lk 1:79 and *in* the s of death, to guide our G4639
Act 5:15 at the least the s of Peter passing by G4639
Col 2:17 Which are a s of things to come; but G4639
Heb 8: 5 Who serve unto the example and s of G4639
10: 1 For the law having a s of good things to G4639
Jas 1:17 is no variableness, neither s of turning. G644

SHADOWING
Isa 18: 1 Woe to the land s with wings, which *is* H6767
Ezk 31: 3 and with a s shroud, and of an high H6751
Heb 9: 5 And over it the cherubims of glory s the G2683

SHADOWS
Song 2:17 Until the day break, and the s flee H6752
4: 6 Until the day break, and the s flee H6752
Jer 6: 4 the s of the evening are stretched out. H6752

SHADRACH
Dan 1: 7 to Hananiah, of S; and to Mishael, of H7714
2:49 the king, and he set S, Meshach, and H7715
3:12 province of Babylon, S, Meshach, and H7715
13 to bring S, Meshach, and Abed-nego. H7715
14 unto them, *Is it* true, O S, Meshach, and H7715
Dan 3:16 S, Meshach, and Abed-nego, answered H7715
19 was changed against S, Meshach, and H7715
20 in his army to bind S, Meshach, and H7715
22 took up S, Meshach, and Abed-nego. H7715
23 And these three men, S, Meshach, and H7715
26 *and* spake, and said, S, Meshach, and H7715
26 and come *hither.* Then S, Meshach, and H7715
28 Blessed *be* the God of S, Meshach, and H7715
29 against the God of S, Meshach, and H7715
30 Then the king promoted S, Meshach, H7715

SHADY
Job 40:21 He lieth under the s trees, in the covert H6628
22 The s trees cover him *with* their H6628

SHAFT
Ex 25:31 be made: his s, and his branches, his H3409
37:17 candlestick; his s, and his branch, his H3409
Nu 8: 4 gold, unto the s thereof, unto the H3409
Isa 49: 2 polished s; in his quiver hath he hid me; H2671

SHAGE
1Ch 11:34 Jonathan the son of S the Hararite, H7681

SHAHAR
Ps 22:ttl To the chief Musician upon Aijeleth S, H7837

SHAHARAIM
1Ch 8: 8 And S begat *children* in the country of H7842

SHAHAZIMAH
Jos 19:22 And the coast reacheth to Tabor, and S, H7831

SHAKE
Jdg 16:20 times before, and s myself. And he wist H5287
Neh 5:13 Also I shook my lap, and said, So God s H5287
Job 4:14 which made all my bones to s. H6342
15:33 He shall s off his unripe grape as the H2554
16: 4 against you, and s mine head at you. H5128
Ps 22: 7 out the lip, they s the head, *saying,* H5128
46: 3 s with the swelling thereof. Selah. H7493
69:23 and make their loins continually to s. H4571
72:16 fruit thereof shall s like Lebanon: and H7493
Isa 2:19 when he ariseth to s terribly the earth. H6206
21 when he ariseth to s terribly the earth. H6206
10:15 if the rod should s *itself* against them H5130
32 that day: he shall s his hand *against* H5130
11:15 wind shall he s his hand over the river, H5130
13: 2 voice unto them, s the hand, that they H5130
13 Therefore I will s the heavens, and the H7264
14:16 earth to tremble, that did s kingdoms; H7493
24:18 and the foundations of the earth do s. H7493
33: 9 Bashan and Carmel s off *their fruits.* H5287
52: 2 S thyself from the dust; arise, *and* sit H5287
Jer 23: 9 all my bones s; I am like a drunken H7363
Ezk 26:10 thee: thy walls shall s at the noise of the H7493
15 Shall not the isles s at the sound of thy H7493
27:28 The suburbs shall s at the sound of the H7493
31:16 I made the nations to s at the sound of H7493
38:20 of the earth, shall s at my presence, H7493
Dan 4:14 off his branches, s off his leaves, and H5426
Joel 3:16 the earth shall s: but the LORD *will be* H7493
Am 9: 1 that the posts may s: and cut them in H7493
Hag 2: 6 while, and I will s the heavens, and the H7493
7 And I will s all nations, and the desire H7493
21 I will s the heavens and the earth; H7493
Zec 2: 9 For, behold, I will s mine hand upon H5130
Mt 10:14 house or city, s off the dust of your feet. G1621
28: 4 And for fear of him the keepers did s, G4579
Mk 6:11 ye depart thence, s off the dust under G1621
Lk 6:48 not s it: for it was founded upon a rock. G4531
9: 5 ye go out of that city, s off the very dust G660
Heb 12:26 I s not the earth only, but also heaven. G4579

SHAKED
Ps 109:25 looked upon me they s their heads. H5128

SHAKEH See RAB-SHAKEH.

SHAKEN
Lev 26:36 and the sound of a s leaf shall chase H5086
1Ki 14:15 Israel, as a reed is s in the water, and H5110
2Ki 19:21 of Jerusalem hath s her head at thee. H5128
Neh 5:13 even thus be he s out, and emptied. H5287
Job 16:12 by my neck, and s me to pieces, and set H6327
38:13 that the wicked might be s out of it? H5287
Ps 18: 7 and were s, because he was wroth. H1607
Isa 37:22 of Jerusalem hath s her head at thee. H5128
Nah 2: 3 and the fir trees shall be terribly s. H7477

Nah 3:12 figs: if they be s, they shall even fall into H5128
Mt 11: 7 to see? A reed s with the wind? G4531
24:29 the powers of the heavens shall be s: G4531
Mk 13:25 the powers that are in heaven shall be s. G4531
Lk 6:38 down, and s together, and running G4531
7:24 for to see? A reed s with the wind? G4531
21:26 for the powers of heaven shall be s. G4531
Act 4:31 the place was s where they were G4531
16:26 of the prison were s: and immediately G4531
2Th 2: 2 That ye be not soon s in mind, or be G4531
Heb 12:27 things that are s, as of things that are G4531
27 things which cannot be s may remain. G4531
Rev 6:13 figs, when she is s of a mighty wind. G4579

SHAKETH
Job 9: 6 Which s the earth out of her place, and H7264
Ps 29: 8 The voice of the LORD s the wilderness; H2342
8 the LORD s the wilderness of Kadesh. H2342
60: 2 it: heal the breaches thereof; for it s. H4131
Isa 10:15 itself against him that s it? as if the rod H5130
19:16 the LORD of hosts, which he s over it. H5130
33:15 of oppressions, that s his hands from H5287

SHAKING
Job 41:29 stubble: he laugheth at the s of a spear. H7494
Ps 44:14 a s of the head among the people. H4493
Isa 17: 6 be left in it, as the s of an olive tree, two H5363
19:16 fear because of the s of the hand of the H8573
24:13 *shall be* as the s of an olive tree, *and* H5363
30:32 and in battles of s will he fight with it. H8573
Ezk 37: 7 and behold a s, and the bones came H7494
38:19 shall be a great s in the land of Israel; H7494

SHALAL See MAHER-SHALAL-HASH-BAZ.

SHALEM
Gen 33:18 And Jacob came to S, a city of Shechem, H8004

SHALIM
1Sa 9: 4 the land of S, and *there they were* H8171

SHALISHA
1Sa 9: 4 the land of S, but they found *them* H8031

SHALL See the Appendix.

SHALLECHETH
1Ch 26:16 with the gate S, by the causeway of H7996

SHALLUM
2Ki 15:10 And S the son of Jabesh conspired H7967
13 S the son of Jabesh began to reign in H7967
14 and smote S the son of Jabesh in H7967
15 And the rest of the acts of S, and his H7967
22:14 the wife of S the son of Tikvah, the H7967
1Ch 2:40 begat Sisamai, and Sisamai begat S, H7967
41 And S begat Jekamiah, and Jekamiah H7967
3:15 the third Zedekiah, the fourth S. H7967
4:25 S his son, Mibsam his son, Mishma his H7967
6:12 begat Zadok, and Zadok begat S, H7967
13 And S begat Hilkiah, and Hilkiah begat H7967
7:13 and Jezer, and S, the sons of Bilhah. H7967
9:17 And the porters *were*, S, and Akkub, H7967
17 and their brethren: S *was* the chief; H7967
19 And S the son of Kore, the son of H7967
31 the firstborn of S the Korahite, had the H7967
2Ch 28:12 the son of S, and Amasa the son H7967
34:22 the wife of S the son of Tikvath, H7967
Ezr 2:42 the children of S, the children of Ater, H7967
7: 2 The son of S, the son of Zadok, the son H7967
10:24 of the porters; S, and Telem, and Uri. H7967
42 S, Amariah, *and* Joseph. H7967
Neh 3:12 And next unto him repaired S the son H7967
7:45 The porters: the children of S, the H7967
Jer 22:11 For thus saith the LORD touching S the H7967
32: 7 Behold, Hanameel the son of S thine H7967
35: 4 the son of S, the keeper of the door: H7967

SHALLUN
Neh 3:15 But the gate of the fountain repaired S H7968

SHALMAI
Ezr 2:46 the children of S, the children of Hanan, H8073
Neh 7:48 children of Hagaba, the children of S, H8014

SHALMAN
Hos 10:14 be spoiled, as S spoiled Beth-arbel in H8020

SHALMANESER
2Ki 17: 3 Against him came up S king of Assyria; H8022
18: 9 king of Israel, *that* S king of Assyria H8022

SHALOM See JEHOVAH-SHALOM.

SHALT See the Appendix.

SHAMA
1Ch 11:44 Uzzia the Ashterathite, S and Jehiel the H8091

SHAMARIAH
2Ch 11:19 Which bare him children; Jeush, and S, H8114

SHAMBLES
1Co 10:25 Whatsoever is sold in the s, *that* eat, G3111

SHAME
Ex 32:25 unto *their* s among their enemies:) H8103
Jdg 18: 7 might put *them* to s in *any* thing; and H3637
1Sa 20:34 because his father had done him s. H3637
2Sa 13:13 And I, whither shall I cause my s to go? H2781
2Ch 32:21 So he returned with s of face to his own H1322
Job 8:22 shall be clothed with s; and the dwelling H1322
Ps 4: 2 *ye turn* my glory into s? *how long* will ye H3639
35: 4 Let them be confounded and put to s H3637
26 be clothed with s and dishonour that H1322
40:14 and put to s that wish me evil. H3637
15 of their s that say unto me, Aha, aha. H1322
44: 7 and hast put them to s that hated us. H954
9 But thou hast cast off, and put us to s; H3637
15 and the s of my face hath covered me, H1322
53: 5 to s, because God hath despised them. H954
69: 7 reproach; s hath covered my face. H3639
19 reproach, and my s, and my dishonour: H1322
70: 3 a reward of their s that say, Aha, aha. H1322
71:24 are brought unto s, that seek my hurt. H2659
83:16 Fill their faces with s; that they may H7036
17 yea, let them be put to s, and perish: H2659
89:45 thou hast covered him with s. Selah. H955
109:29 Let mine adversaries be clothed with s, H3639
119:31 testimonies: O LORD, put me not to s. H954
132:18 His enemies will I clothe with s: but H1322
Prv 3:35 The wise shall inherit glory: but s shall H7036
9: 7 scorner getteth to himself s: and he that H7036
10: 5 in harvest *is* a son that causeth s. H954
11: 2 *When* pride cometh, then cometh s: but H7036
12:16 known: but a prudent *man* covereth s. H7036
13: 5 *man* is loathsome, and cometh to s. H2659
18 Poverty and s *shall be to* him that H7036
14:35 his wrath is *against* him that causeth s. H954
17: 2 a son that causeth s, and shall have part H954
18:13 he heareth *it*, it *is* folly and s unto him. H3639
19:26 that causeth s, and bringeth reproach. H954
25: 8 when thy neighbour hath put thee to s. H3637
10 Lest he that heareth *it* put thee to s, and H2616
29:15 left *to himself* bringeth his mother to s. H954
Isa 20: 4 buttocks uncovered, to the s of Egypt. H6172
22:18 glory *shall be* the s of thy lord's house. H7036
30: 3 Pharaoh be your s, and the trust in the H1322
5 nor profit, but a s, and also a reproach. H1322
47: 3 yea, thy s shall be seen: I will H2781
50: 6 I hid not my face from s and spitting. H3639
54: 4 thou shalt not be put to s: for thou shalt H2659
4 thou shalt forget the s of thy youth, and H1322
61: 7 For your s *ye shall have* double; and *for* H1322
Jer 3:24 For s hath devoured the labour of our H1322
25 We lie down in our s, and our confusion H1322
13:26 upon thy face, that thy s may appear. H7036
20:18 my days should be consumed with s? H1322
23:40 s, which shall not be forgotten. H3640
46:12 The nations have heard of thy s, and H7036
48:39 the back with s! so shall Moab be a H954
51:51 heard reproach: s hath covered our H3639
Ezk 7:18 shall cover them; and s *shall be* upon all H955
16:52 bear thine own s for thy sins that thou H3639
52 s, in that thou hast justified thy sisters. H3639
54 That thou mayest bear thine own s, and H3639
63 because of thy s, when I am pacified H3639
32:24 s with them that go down to the pit. H3639
25 they borne their s with them that go H3639
30 s with them that go down to the pit. H3639
34:29 bear the s of the heathen any more. H3639
36: 6 ye have borne the s of the heathen: H3639
7 *are* about you, they shall bear their s. H3639
15 to hear in thee the s of the heathen any H3639
39:26 After that they have borne their s, and H3639
44:13 they shall bear their s, and their H3639
Dan 12: 2 some to s *and* everlasting contempt. H2781
Hos 4: 7 *therefore* will I change their glory into s. H7036
18 her rulers *with* s do love, Give ye. H7036
9:10 unto *that* s; and *their* abominations H1322
10: 6 shall receive s, and Israel shall be H1317
Oba 10 thy brother Jacob s shall cover thee, and H955
Mic 1:11 of Saphir, having thy s naked: the H1322
2: 6 to them, *that* they shall not take s. H3639
7:10 shall see *it*, and s shall cover her which H955
Nah 3: 5 thy nakedness, and the kingdoms thy s. H7036
Hab 2:10 Thou hast consulted s to thy house by H1322
16 Thou art filled with s for glory: drink H7036
Zep 3: 5 faileth not; but the unjust knoweth no s. H1322
19 land where they have been put to s. H1322
Lk 14: 9 begin with s to take the lowest room. G152
Act 5:41 counted worthy to suffer s for his name. G818
1Co 4:14 I write not these things to s you, but as G1788
6: 5 I speak to your s. Is it so, that there is G1791
11: 6 shorn: but if it be a s for a woman to be G149
14 a man have long hair, it is a s unto him? G819
22 of God, and s them that have not? G2617
14:35 is a s for women to speak in the church. G149
15:34 of God: I speak *this* to your s. G1791
Eph 5:12 For it is a s even to speak of those things G149
Php 3:19 *is* in their s, who mind earthly things.) G152
Heb 6: 6 God afresh, and put *him* to an open s. G3856
12: 2 despising the s, and is set down at the G152
Jude 13 out their own s; wandering stars, to G152
Rev 3:18 and *that* the s of thy nakedness do G152
16:15 lest he walk naked, and they see his s. G808

SHAMED
Gen 38:23 *it* to her, lest we be s: behold, I sent this H937
2Sa 19: 5 said, Thou hast s this day the faces of H3001
1Ch 8:12 and Misham, and S, who built Ono, and H8106
Ps 14: 6 Ye have s the counsel of the poor, H954

SHAMEFACEDNESS
1Ti 2: 9 apparel, with s and sobriety; not with G127

SHAMEFUL
Jer 11:13 up altars to *that* s thing, *even* altars to H1322
Hab 2:16 and s spewing *shall be* on thy glory. H7022

SHAMEFULLY
Hos 2: 5 them hath done s: for she said, I will go H3001
Mk 12: 4 the head, and sent *him* away s handled. G821
Lk 20:11 *him* s, and sent *him* away empty. G818
1Th 2: 2 before, and were s entreated, as ye G5195

SHAMELESSLY
2Sa 6:20 the vain fellows s uncovereth himself! H1540

SHAMER
1Ch 6:46 of Amzi, the son of Bani, the son of S, H8106
7:34 And the sons of S; Ahi, and Rohgah, H8106

SHAMETH
Prv 28: 7 companion of riotous *men* s his father. H3637

SHAMGAR
Jdg 3:31 And after him was S the son of Anath, H8044
5: 6 In the days of S the son of Anath, in the H8044

SHAMHUTH
1Ch 27: 8 fifth month *was* S the Izrahite: and in H8049

SHAMIR
Jos 15:48 And in the mountains, S, and Jattir, H8069
Jdg 10: 1 and he dwelt in S in mount Ephraim. H8069
2 years, and died, and was buried in S. H8069
1Ch 24:24 Michah: of the sons of Michah; S. H8053

SHAMMA
1Ch 7:37 Bezer, and Hod, and S, and Shilshah, H8037

SHAMMAH
Gen 36:13 and Zerah, S, and Mizzah: these were H8048
17 duke Zerah, duke S, duke Mizzah: these H8048
1Sa 16: 9 Then Jesse made S to pass by. And he H8048
17:13 unto him Abinadab, and the third S. H8048
2Sa 23:11 And after him *was* S the son of Agee H8048
25 S the Harodite, Elika the Harodite, H8048
33 S the Hararite, Ahiam the son of H8048
1Ch 1:37 The sons of Reuel; Nahath, Zerah, S, H8048

SHAMMAI
1Ch 2:28 And the sons of Onam were, S, and H8060
28 And the sons of S; Nadab, and Abishur. H8060
32 And the sons of Jada the brother of S; H8060

1Ch 2:44 father of Jorkoam: and Rekem begat **S**. H8060
45 And the son of **S** *was* Maon: and Maon H8060
4:17 **S**, and Ishbah the father of Eshtemoa. H8060

SHAMMOTH
1Ch 11:27 **S** the Harorite, Helez the Pelonite, H8054

SHAMMUA
Nu 13: 4 tribe of Reuben, **S** the son of Zaccur. H8051
2Sa 5:14 him in Jerusalem; **S**, and Shobab, and H8051
1Ch 14: 4 **S**, and Shobab, Nathan, and Solomon, H8051
Neh 11:17 **S**, the son of Galal, the son of Jeduthun. H8051
12:18 Of Bilgah, **S**; of Shemaiah, Jehonathan; H8051

SHAMSHERAI
1Ch 8:26 And **S**, and Sheheriah, and Athaliah, H8125

SHAN See BETH-SHAN.

SHAPE
Lk 3:22 in a bodily **s** like a dove upon him, *G1491*
Jn 5:37 his voice at any time, nor seen his **s**. *G1491*

SHAPEN
Ps 51: 5 Behold, I was **s** in iniquity; and in sin H2342

SHAPES
Rev 9: 7 And the **s** of the locusts *were* like unto *G3667*

SHAPHAM
1Ch 5:12 Joel the chief, and **S** the next, and H8223

SHAPHAN
2Ki 22: 3 *that* the king sent **S** the son of Azaliah, H8227
8 And Hilkiah the high priest said unto **S** H8227
8 gave the book to **S**, and he read it. H8227
9 And **S** the scribe came to the king, and H8227
10 And **S** the scribe shewed the king, H8227
10 a book. And **S** read it before the king. H8227
12 Ahikam the son of **S**, and Achbor the H8227
12 son of Michaiah, and **S** the scribe, and H8227
14 and Achbor, and **S**, and Asahiah, went H8227
25:22 the son of Ahikam, the son of **S**, ruler. H8227
2Ch 34: 8 the house, he sent **S** the son of Azaliah, H8227
15 And Hilkiah answered and said to **S** H8227
15 And Hilkiah delivered the book to **S**. H8227
16 And **S** carried the book to the king, and H8227
18 Then **S** the scribe told the king, saying, H8227
18 a book. And **S** read it before the king. H8227
20 Ahikam the son of **S**, and Abdon the H8227
20 the son of Micah, and **S** the scribe, and H8227
Jer 26:24 of Ahikam the son of **S** was with H8227
29: 3 By the hand of Elasah the son of **S**, and H8227
36:10 the son of **S** the scribe, in the higher H8227
11 the son of **S**, had heard out of the H8227
12 the son of **S**, and Zedekiah the son H8227
39:14 of Ahikam the son of **S**, that he should H8227
40: 5 Ahikam the son of **S**, whom the king of H8227
9 Ahikam the son of **S** sware unto them H8227
11 the son of Ahikam the son of **S**; H8227
41: 2 of Ahikam the son of **S** with the sword, H8227
43: 6 Ahikam the son of **S**, and Jeremiah the H8227
Ezk 8:11 the son of **S**, with every man his H8227

SHAPHAT
Nu 13: 5 Of the tribe of Simeon, **S** the son of H8202
1Ki 19:16 Elisha the son of **S** of Abel-meholah H8202
19 Elisha the son of **S**, who *was* plowing H8202
2Ki 3:11 Elisha the son of **S**, which poured water H8202
6:31 son of **S** shall stand on him this day. H8202
1Ch 3:22 and Bariah, and Neariah, and **S**, six. H8202
5:12 the next, and Jaanai, and **S** in Bashan. H8202
27:29 in the valleys *was* **S** the son of Adlai: H8202

SHAPHER
Nu 33:23 Kehelathah, and pitched in mount **S**. H8234
24 And they removed from mount **S**, and H8234

SHARAI
Ezr 10:40 Machnadebai, Shashai, **S**, H8298

SHARAIM
Jos 15:36 And **S**, and Adithaim, and Gederah, H8189

SHARAR
2Sa 23:33 Ahiam the son of **S** the Hararite, H8325

SHARE
1Sa 13:20 every man his **s**, and his coulter, and H4282

SHAREZER
2Ki 19:37 and **S** his sons smote him H8272
Isa 37:38 and **S** his sons smote him H8272

SHARON
1Ch 5:16 all the suburbs of **S**, upon their borders. H8289
27:29 And over the herds that fed in **S** *was* H8289
Song 2: 1 I *am* the rose of **S**, *and* the lily of the H8289
Isa 33: 9 *and* hewn down: **S** is like a wilderness; H8289
35: 2 of Carmel and **S**, they shall see the glory H8289
65:10 And **S** shall be a fold of flocks, and the H8289

SHARONITE
1Ch 27:29 *was* Shitrai the **S**: and over the herds H8290

SHARP
Ex 4:25 Then Zipporah took a **s** stone, and cut H6864
Jos 5: 2 unto Joshua, Make thee **s** knives, and H6697
3 And Joshua made him **s** knives, and H6697
1Sa 14: 4 *there was* a **s** rock on the one side, H8127
4 one side, and a **s** rock on the other side: H8127
Job 41:30 **S** stones *are* under him: he spreadeth H2303
30 **s** pointed things upon the mire. H2742
Ps 45: 5 Thine arrows *are* **s** in the heart of the H8150
52: 2 Thy tongue deviseth mischiefs; like a **s** H3913
57: 4 arrows, and their tongue a **s** sword. H2299
120: 4 **S** arrows of the mighty, with coals of H8150
Prv 5: 4 But her end is bitter as wormwood, **s** as H2299
25:18 *is* a maul, and a sword, and a **s** arrow. H8150
Isa 5:28 Whose arrows *are* **s**, and all their bows H8150
41:15 Behold, I will make thee a new **s** H2742
49: 2 And he hath made my mouth like a **s** H2299
Ezk 5: 1 And thou, son of man, take thee a **s** H2299
Act 15:39 And the contention was so **s** between
Rev 1:16 of his mouth went a **s** twoedged sword: *G3691*
2:12 which hath the **s** sword with two edges; *G3691*
14:14 crown, and in his hand a **s** sickle. *G3691*
17 is in heaven, he also having a **s** sickle. *G3691*
18 to him that had the **s** sickle, saying, *G3691*
18 Thrust in thy **s** sickle, and gather the *G3691*
19:15 And out of his mouth goeth a **s** sword, *G3691*

SHARPEN
1Sa 13:20 to the Philistines, to **s** every man his H3913
21 and for the axes, and to **s** the goads. H5324

SHARPENED
Ps 140: 3 They have **s** their tongues like a H8150
Ezk 21: 9 sword, a sword is **s**, and also furbished: H2300
10 It is **s** to make a sore slaughter; it is H2300
11 this sword is **s**, and it is furbished, H2300

SHARPENETH
Job 16: 9 teeth; mine enemy **s** his eyes upon me. H3913
Prv 27:17 Iron **s** iron; so a man sharpeneth the H2300
17 Iron sharpeneth iron; so a man **s** the H2300

SHARPER
Mic 7: 4 the most upright *is* **s** than a thorn hedge:
Heb 4:12 quick, and powerful, and **s** than any *G5114*

SHARPLY
Jdg 8: 1 And they did chide with him **s**. H2394
Tit 1:13 **s**, that they may be sound in the faith; *G664*

SHARPNESS
2Co 13:10 I should use **s**, according to the power *G664*

SHARUHEN
Jos 19: 6 And Beth-lebaoth, and **S**; thirteen cities H8287

SHASHAI
Ezr 10:40 Machnadebai, **S**, Sharai, H8343

SHASHAK
1Ch 8:14 And Ahio, **S**, and Jeremoth, H8349
25 Iphedeiah, and Penuel, the sons of **S**; H8349

SHAUL
Gen 46:10 and **S** the son of a Canaanitish woman. H7586
Ex 6:15 Jachin, and Zohar, and **S** the son of a H7586
Nu 26:13 of **S**, the family of the Shaulites. H7586
1Ch 1:48 And when Samlah was dead, **S** of H7586
49 And when **S** was dead, Baal-hanan the H7586
4:24 Nemuel, and Jamin, Jarib, Zerah, *and* **S**: H7586
6:24 his son, Uzziah his son, and **S** his son. H7586

SHAULITES
Nu 26:13 Zarhites: of Shaul, the family of the **S**. H7587

SHAVE
Lev 13:33 scall shall he not **s**; and the priest shall H1548
14: 8 his clothes, and **s** off all his hair, and H1548
9 day, that he shall **s** all his hair off his H1548
9 all his hair he shall **s** off: and he shall H1548
21: 5 neither shall they **s** off the corner of H1548
Nu 6: 9 then he shall **s** his head in the day H1548
9 on the seventh day shall he **s** it. H1548
18 And the Nazarite shall **s** the head of his H1548
8: 7 and let them **s** all their flesh, H8593+H5674
Dt 21:12 she shall **s** her head, and pare her nails; H1548
Jdg 16:19 she caused him to **s** off the seven locks H1548
Isa 7:20 In the same day shall the Lord **s** with a H1548
Ezk 44:20 Neither shall they **s** their heads, nor H1548
Act 21:24 that they may **s** *their* heads: and all *G3587*

SHAVED
Gen 41:14 the dungeon: and he **s** *himself*, and H1548
2Sa 10: 4 servants, and **s** off the one half of their H1548
1Ch 19: 4 servants, and **s** them, and cut off their H1548
Job 1:20 rent his mantle, and **s** his head, and fell H1494

SHAVEH
Gen 14: 5 Ham, and the Emims in **S** Kiriathaim, H7741
17 the valley of **S**, which *is* the king's dale. H7740

SHAVEH-KIRIATHAIM See SHAVEH and KIRIATHAIM.

SHAVEN
Lev 13:33 He shall be **s**, but the scall shall he not H1548
Nu 6:19 after *the hair of* his separation is **s**: H1548
Jdg 16:17 womb: if I be **s**, then my strength will H1548
22 began to grow again after he was **s**. H1548
Jer 41: 5 their beards **s**, and their clothes rent, H1548
1Co 11: 5 for that is even all one as if she were **s**. *G3587*
6 to be shorn or **s**, let her be covered. *G3587*

SHAVSHA
1Ch 18:16 *were* the priests; and **S** was scribe; H7798

SHE See the Appendix.

SHEAF
Gen 37: 7 field, and, lo, my **s** arose, and also stood H485
7 about, and made obeisance to my **s**. H485
Lev 23:10 ye shall bring a **s** of the firstfruits of H6016
11 And he shall wave the **s** before the H6016
12 when ye wave the **s** an he lamb without H6016
15 ye brought the **s** of the wave offering; H6016
Dt 24:19 and hast forgot a **s** in the field, thou H6016
Job 24:10 they take away the **s** *from* the hungry; H6016
Zec 12: 6 like a torch of fire in a **s**; and they shall H5995

SHEAL
Ezr 10:29 Adaiah, Jashub, and **S**, and Ramoth. H7594

SHEALTIEL
Ezr 3: 2 the son of **S**, and his brethren, and H7597
8 the son of **S**, and Jeshua the son H7597
5: 2 Then rose up Zerubbabel the son of **S**, H7598
Neh 12: 1 **S**, and Jeshua: Seraiah, Jeremiah, Ezra, H7597
Hag 1: 1 the son of **S**, governor of Judah, H7597
12 Then Zerubbabel the son of **S**, and H7597
14 the son of **S**, governor of Judah, H7597
2: 2 Speak now to Zerubbabel the son of **S**, H7597
23 servant, the son of **S**, saith the LORD, H7597

SHEAN See BETH-SHEAN.

SHEAR
Gen 31:19 And Laban went to **s** his sheep: and H1494
38:13 law goeth up to Timnath to **s** his sheep. H1494
Dt 15:19 bullock, nor **s** the firstling of thy sheep. H1494
1Sa 25: 4 wilderness that Nabal did **s** his sheep. H1494

SHEARER
Act 8:32 his **s**, so opened he not his mouth: *G2751*

SHEARERS
1Sa 25: 7 And now I have heard that thou hast **s**: H1494
11 I have killed for my **s**, and give *it* unto H1494
Isa 53: 7 as a sheep before her **s** is dumb, so he H1494

SHEARIAH
1Ch 8:38 and Ishmael, and **S**, and Obadiah, and H8187
9:44 and Ishmael, and **S**, and Obadiah, and H8187

SHEARING
1Sa 25: 2 and he was **s** his sheep in Carmel. H1494

2Ki 10:12 *was* at the **s** house in the way, H1044+H7462
14 at the pit of the **s** house, *even* two and H1044

SHEARING-HOUSE See SHEARING and HOUSE.

SHEAR-JASHUB
Isa 7: 3 Ahaz, thou, and **S** thy son, at the end of H7610

SHEATH
1Sa 17:51 drew it out of the **s** thereof, and slew H8593
2Sa 20: 8 his loins in the **s** thereof; and as he H8593
1Ch 21:27 up his sword again into the **s** thereof. H5084
Ezk 21: 3 sword out of his **s**, and will cut off from H8593
4 go forth out of his **s** against all flesh H8593
5 of his **s**: it shall not return any more. H8593
30 Shall I cause *it* to return into his **s**? I will H8593
Jn 18:11 thy sword into the s: the cup which my *G2336*

SHEAVES
Gen 37: 7 For, behold, we *were* binding **s** in the H485
7 and, behold, your **s** stood round about, H485
Ru 2: 7 among the **s**: so she came, and hath H6016
15 among the **s**, and reproach her not: H6016
Neh 13:15 and bringing in **s**, and lading asses; as H6194
Ps 126: 6 with rejoicing, bringing his **s** *with him*. H485
129: 7 hand; nor he that bindeth **s** his bosom.
Am 2:13 you, as a cart is pressed *that is* full of **s**. H5995
Mic 4:12 gather them as the **s** into the floor. H5995

SHEBA
Gen 10: 7 and the sons of Raamah; **S**, and Dedan. H7614
28 And Obal, and Abimael, and **S**, H7614
25: 3 And Jokshan begat **S**, and Dedan. And H7614
Jos 19: 2 Beer-sheba, or **S**, and Moladah, H7652
2Sa 20: 1 whose name *was* **S**, the son of Bichri, a H7652
2 *and* followed **S** the son of Bichri: but H7652
6 And David said to Abishai, Now shall **S** H7652
7 to pursue after **S** the son of Bichri. H7652
10 pursued after **S** the son of Bichri. H7652
13 to pursue after **S** the son of Bichri. H7652
21 mount Ephraim, **S** the son of Bichri by H7652
22 cut off the head of **S** the son of Bichri, H7652
1Ki 10: 1 And when the queen of **S** heard of the H7614
4 And when the queen of **S** had seen all H7614
10 the queen of **S** gave to king Solomon. H7614
13 gave unto the queen of **S** all her desire, H7614
1Ch 1: 9 And the sons of Raamah; **S**, and Dedan. H7614
22 And Ebal, and Abimael, and **S**, H7614
32 And the sons of Jokshan; **S**, and Dedan. H7614
5:13 and Meshullam, and **S**, and Jorai, and H7652
2Ch 9: 1 And when the queen of **S** heard of the H7614
3 And when the queen of **S** had seen the H7614
9 as the queen of **S** gave king Solomon. H7614
12 gave to the queen of **S** all her desire, H7614
Job 6:19 the companies of **S** waited for them. H7614
Ps 72:10 the kings of **S** and Seba shall offer gifts. H7614
15 of the gold of **S**: prayer also shall be H7614
Isa 60: 6 all they from **S** shall come: they shall H7614
Jer 6:20 me incense from **S**, and the sweet cane H7614
Ezk 27:22 The merchants of **S** and Raamah, they H7614
23 Eden, the merchants of **S**, Asshur, *and* H7614
38:13 **S**, and Dedan, and the merchants of H7614

SHEBAH
Gen 26:33 And he called it **S**: therefore the name of H7656

SHEBAM
Nu 32: 3 Elealeh, and **S**, and Nebo, and Beon, H7643

SHEBANIAH
1Ch 15:24 And **S**, and Jehoshaphat, and H7645
Neh 9: 4 Bani, Kadmiel, **S**, Bunni, Sherebiah, H7645
5 Hodijah, **S**, *and* Pethahiah, said, H7645
10: 4 Hattush, **S**, Malluch, H7645
10 And their brethren, **S**, Hodijah, Kelita, H7645
12 Zaccur, Sherebiah, **S**, H7645
12:14 Of Melicu, Jonathan; of **S**, Joseph; H7645

SHEBARIM
Jos 7: 5 the gate *even* unto **S**, and smote them in H7671

SHEBER
1Ch 2:48 Maachah, Caleb's concubine, bare **S**, H7669

SHEBNA
2Ki 18:18 household, and **S** the scribe, and Joah H7644
26 son of Hilkiah, and **S**, and Joah, unto H7644
37 household, and **S** the scribe, and Joah H7644
19: 2 household, and **S** the scribe, and the H7644
Isa 22:15 **S**, which *is* over the house, *and say*, H7644
36: 3 the house, and **S** the scribe, and Joah, H7644
11 Then said Eliakim and **S** and Joah unto H7644
22 household, and **S** the scribe, and Joah, H7644
37: 2 household, and **S** the scribe, and the H7644

SHEBUEL
1Ch 23:16 Of the sons of Gershom, **S** *was* the H7619
25: 4 Mattaniah, Uzziel, **S**, and Jerimoth, H7619
26:24 And **S** the son of Gershom, the son of H7619

SHECANIAH
1Ch 24:11 The ninth to Jeshua, the tenth to **S**, H7935
2Ch 31:15 Amariah, and **S**, in the cities of the H7935

SHECHANIAH
1Ch 3:21 the sons of Obadiah, the sons of **S**. H7935
22 And the sons of **S**; Shemaiah: and the H7935
Ezr 8: 3 Of the sons of **S**, of the sons of Pharosh; H7935
5 Of the sons of **S**; the son of Jahaziel, and H7935
10: 2 And **S** the son of Jehiel, *one* of the sons H7935
Neh 3:29 the son of **S**, the keeper of the east gate. H7935
6:18 the son in law of **S** the son of Arah; and H7935
12: 3 **S**, Rehum, Meremoth, H7935

SHECHEM
Gen 33:18 And Jacob came to Shalem, a city of **S**, H7927
34: 2 And when **S** the son of Hamor the H7928
4 And **S** spake unto his father Hamor, H7928
6 And Hamor the father of **S** went out H7928
8 The soul of my son **S** longeth for your H7928
11 And **S** said unto her father and unto H7928
13 And the sons of Jacob answered **S** and H7928
18 And their words pleased Hamor, and **S** H7928
20 And Hamor and **S** his son came unto H7928
24 And unto Hamor and unto **S** his son H7928
26 And they slew Hamor and **S** his son H7928
35: 4 hid them under the oak which *was* by **S**. H7927
37:12 went to feed their father's flock in **S**. H7927
13 feed *the flock* in **S**? come, and I will send H7927
14 of the vale of Hebron, and he came to **S**. H7927
Nu 26:31 and *of* **S**, the family of the Shechemites: H7928
Jos 17: 2 and for the children of **S**, and for the H7928
7 that *lieth* before **S**; and the border went H7927
20: 7 Naphtali, and **S** in mount Ephraim, H7927
21:21 For they gave them **S** with her suburbs H7927
24: 1 tribes of Israel to **S**, and called for the H7927
25 them a statute and an ordinance in **S**. H7927
32 buried they in **S**, in a parcel of ground H7927
32 the father of **S** for an hundred pieces H7927
Jdg 8:31 And his concubine that *was* in **S**, she H7927
9: 1 Jerubbaal went to **S** unto his mother's H7927
2 of all the men of **S**, Whether *is* better for H7927
3 of all the men of **S** all these words: and H7927
6 And all the men of **S** gathered together, H7927
6 by the plain of the pillar that *was* in **S**. H7927
7 of **S**, that God may hearken unto you. H7927
18 men of **S**, because he *is* your brother;) H7927
20 devour the men of **S**, and the house of H7927
20 from the men of **S**, and from the house H7927
23 and the men of **S**; and the men of H7927
23 **S** dealt treacherously with Abimelech: H7927
24 upon the men of **S**, which aided him in H7927
25 And the men of **S** set liers in wait for H7927
26 and went over to **S**: and the men of H7927
26 men of **S** put their confidence in him. H7927
28 and who *is* **S**, that we should serve H7927
28 of **S**: for why should we serve him? H7927
31 be come to **S**; and, behold, they fortify H7927
34 laid wait against **S** in four companies. H7927
39 And Gaal went out before the men of **S**, H7927
41 that they should not dwell in **S**. H7927
46 And when all the men of the tower of **S** H7927
47 the tower of **S** were gathered together. H7927
49 men of the tower of **S** died also, about a H7927
57 And all the evil of the men of **S** did God H7927
21:19 to **S**, and on the south of Lebonah. H7927
1Ki 12: 1 And Rehoboam went to **S**: for all Israel H7927
1 were come to **S** to make him king. H7927
25 Then Jeroboam built **S** in mount H7927
1Ch 6:67 cities of refuge, **S** in mount Ephraim H7927
7:19 Ahian, and **S**, and Likhi, and Aniam. H7928
28 the towns thereof; **S** also and the towns H7927
2Ch 10: 1 And Rehoboam went to **S**: for to H7927
1 to Shechem: for to **S** were all Israel H7927
Ps 60: 6 **S**, and mete out the valley of Succoth. H7927
108: 7 **S**, and mete out the valley of Succoth. H7927
Jer 41: 5 That there came certain from **S**, from H7927

SHECHEMITES
Nu 26:31 and *of* Shechem, the family of the **S**: H7930

SHECHEM'S
Gen 33:19 of Hamor, **S** father, for an hundred H7928
34:26 Dinah out of **S** house, and went out. H7928

SHED
Gen 9: 6 **s**: for in the image of God made he man. H8210
37:22 And Reuben said unto them, **S** no H8210
Ex 22: 2 he die, *there shall* no blood *be* **s** for him.
3 *shall be* blood **s** for him; *for* he should
Lev 17: 4 that man; he hath **s** blood; and that H8210
Nu 35:33 of the blood that is **s** therein, but by the H8210
33 but by the blood of him that **s** it. H8210
Dt 19:10 That innocent blood be not **s** in thy H8210
21: 7 hands have not **s** this blood, neither H8210
1Sa 25:26 thee from coming to *s* blood, and from
31 that thou hast **s** blood causeless, or H8210
33 day from coming to *s* blood, and from
2Sa 20:10 the fifth *rib*, and **s** out his bowels to the H8210
1Ki 2: 5 he slew, and **s** the blood of war in H7760
31 blood, which Joab **s**, from me, and from H8210
2Ki 21:16 Moreover Manasseh **s** innocent blood H8210
24: 4 blood that he **s**: for he filled Jerusalem H8210
1Ch 22: 8 saying, Thou hast **s** blood abundantly, H8210
8 because thou hast **s** much blood upon H8210
28: 3 *been* a man of war, and hast **s** blood. H8210
Ps 79: 3 Their blood have they **s** like water H8210
10 of the blood of thy servants *which is* **s**. H8210
106:38 And **s** innocent blood, *even* the blood H8210
Prv 1:16 run to evil, and make haste to **s** blood. H8210
6:17 and hands that **s** innocent blood, H8210
Isa 59: 7 make haste to **s** innocent blood: their H8210
Jer 7: 6 the widow, and **s** not innocent blood H8210
22: 3 neither **s** innocent blood in this place. H8210
17 and for to **s** innocent blood, and H8210
Lam 4:13 priests, that have **s** the blood of the just H8210
Ezk 16:38 wedlock and **s** blood are judged; and H8210
22: 4 that thou hast **s**; and hast defiled thyself H8210
6 were in thee to their power to **s** blood. H8210
9 In thee are men that carry tales to **s** H8210
12 In thee have they taken gifts to **s** blood; H8210
27 the prey, to **s** blood, *and* to destroy H8210
23:45 of women that **s** blood; because they H8210
33:25 **s** blood: and shall ye possess the land? H8210
35: 5 hatred, and hast **s** *the blood of* the H5064
36:18 that they had **s** upon the land, and H8210
Joel 3:19 have **s** innocent blood in their land. H8210
Mt 23:35 righteous blood s upon the earth, from *G1632*
26:28 is s for many for the remission of sins. *G1632*
Mk 14:24 new testament, which is s for many. *G1632*
Lk 11:50 which was s from the foundation *G1632*
22:20 in my blood, which is s for you. *G1632*
Act 2:33 **s** forth this, which ye now see and hear. *G1632*
22:20 Stephen was **s**, I also was standing *G1632*
Ro 3:15 Their feet *are* swift to **s** blood: *G1632*
5: 5 the love of God is **s** abroad in our *G1632*
Tit 3: 6 Which he **s** on us abundantly through *G1632*
Rev 16: 6 For they have **s** the blood of saints and *G1632*

SHEDDER
Ezk 18:10 If he beget a son *that is* a robber, a **s** of H8210

SHEDDETH
Gen 9: 6 Whoso **s** man's blood, by man shall his H8210
Ezk 22: 3 GOD, The city **s** blood in the midst of H8210

SHEDDING
Heb 9:22 and without **s** of blood is no remission. *G130*

SHEDEUR
Nu 1: 5 *the tribe of* Reuben; Elizur the son of **S**. H7707
2:10 of Reuben *shall be* Elizur the son of **S**. H7707
7:30 On the fourth day Elizur the son of **S**, H7707
35 *was* the offering of Elizur the son of **S**. H7707
10:18 over his host *was* Elizur the son of **S**. H7707

SHEEP
Gen 4: 2 of **s**, but Cain was a tiller of the ground. H6629
12:16 sake: and he had **s**, and oxen, and he H6629
20:14 And Abimelech took **s**, and oxen, and H6629
21:27 And Abraham took **s** and oxen, and H6629
29: 2 three flocks of **s** lying by it; for out of H6629
3 and watered the **s**, and put the stone H6629
6 Rachel his daughter cometh with the **s**. H6629
7 water ye the **s**, and go *and* feed *them*. H6629
8 the well's mouth; then we water the **s**. H6629
9 with her father's **s**: for she kept them. H6629

Gen 29:10 brother, and the **s** of Laban his H6629
30:32 cattle among the **s**, and the spotted and H3775
33 **s**, that shall be counted stolen with me. H3775
35 brown among the **s**, and gave *them* into H3775
31:19 And Laban went to shear his **s**: and H6629
34:28 They took their **s**, and their oxen, and H6629
38:13 law goeth up to Timnath to shear his **s**. H6629
Ex 9: 3 and upon the **s**: *there shall be* a very H6629
12: 5 take *it* out from the **s**, or from the goats: H3532
20:24 offerings, thy **s**, and thine oxen: in all H6629
22: 1 If a man shall steal an ox, or a **s**, and H7716
1 oxen for an ox, and four **s** for a sheep. H6629
1 oxen for an ox, and four sheep for a **s**. H7716
4 ox, or ass, or **s**; he shall restore double. H7716
9 for ox, for ass, for **s**, for raiment, *or* for H7716
10 an ass, or an ox, or a **s**, or any beast, to H7716
30 oxen, *and* with thy **s**: seven days it shall H6629
34:19 thy cattle, *whether* ox or **s**, *that is male*. H7716
Lev 1:10 *namely*, of the **s**, or of the goats, for a H3775
7:23 manner of fat, of ox, or of **s**, or of goat. H3775
22:19 of the beeves, of the **s**, or of the goats. H3775
21 in beeves or **s**, it shall be perfect to H6629
27 When a bullock, or a **s**, or a goat, is H3775
27:26 whether *it be* ox, or **s**: it *is* the LORD'S. H7716
Nu 18:17 or the firstling of a **s**, or the firstling of a H3775
22:40 And Balak offered oxen and **s**, and sent H6629
27:17 be not as **s** which have no shepherd. H6629
31:28 beeves, and of the asses, and of the **s**: H6629
32 seventy thousand and five thousand **s**, H6629
36 and thirty thousand and five hundred **s**: H6629
37 And the LORD'S tribute of the **s** was six H6629
43 *and* seven thousand and five hundred **s**, H6629
32:24 and folds for your **s**; and do that which H6792
36 fenced cities: and folds for **s**. H6629
Dt 7:13 the flocks of thy **s**, in the land which he H6629
14: 4 ye shall eat: the ox, the **s**, and the goat, H3775
26 for oxen, or for **s**, or for wine, or for H6629
15:19 bullock, nor shear the firstling of thy **s**. H6629
17: 1 *any* bullock, or **s**, wherein is blemish, H7716
18: 3 whether *it be* ox or **s**; and they shall give H7716
4 the fleece of thy **s**, shalt thou give him. H6629
22: 1 brother's ox or his **s** go astray, and hide H7716
28: 4 of thy kine, and the flocks of thy **s**. H6629
18 of thy kine, and the flocks of thy **s**. H6629
31 to thee: thy **s** *shall be* given unto H6629
51 of thy **s**, until he have destroyed thee. H6629
32:14 Butter of kine, and milk of **s**, with fat of H6629
Jos 6:21 **s**, and ass, with the edge of the sword. H7716
7:24 his asses, and his **s**, and his tent, and all H6629
Jdg 6: 4 for Israel, neither **s**, nor ox, nor ass. H7716
1Sa 8:17 He will take the tenth of your **s**: and ye H6629
14:32 the spoil, and took **s**, and oxen, and H6629
34 ox, and every man his **s**, and slay *them* H7716
15: 3 and suckling, ox and **s**, camel and ass. H7716
9 and the best of the **s**, and of the oxen, H6629
14 this bleating of the **s** in mine ears, and H6629
15 the best of the **s** and of the oxen, to H6629
21 But the people took of the spoil, **s** and H6629
16:11 he keepeth the **s**. And Samuel said unto H6629
19 me David thy son, which *is* with the **s**. H6629
17:15 to feed his father's **s** at Beth-lehem. H6629
20 and left the **s** with a keeper, and took, H6629
28 thou left those few **s** in the wilderness? H6629
34 kept his father's **s**, and there came a H6629
22:19 asses, and **s**, with the edge of the sword. H7716
25: 2 had three thousand **s**, and a thousand H6629
2 and he was shearing his **s** in Carmel. H6629
4 wilderness that Nabal did shear his **s**. H6629
16 while we were with them keeping the **s**. H6629
18 of wine, and five **s** ready dressed, and H6629
27: 9 and took away the **s**, and the oxen, and H6629
2Sa 7: 8 from following the **s**, to be ruler over my H6629
17:29 And honey, and butter, and **s**, and H6629
24:17 but these **s**, what have they done? H6629
1Ki 1: 9 And Adonijah slew **s** and oxen and fat H6629
19 and fat cattle and **s** in abundance, and H6629
25 and fat cattle and **s** in abundance, and H6629
4:23 and an hundred **s**, beside harts, and H6629
8: 5 ark, sacrificing **s** and oxen, that could H6629
63 twenty thousand **s**. So the king and all H6629
22:17 upon the hills, as **s** that have not a H6629
2Ki 5:26 and vineyards, and **s**, and oxen, and H6629
1Ch 5:21 thousand, and of **s** two hundred and H6629
12:40 oil, and oxen, and **s** abundantly: for H6629
17: 7 *even* from following the **s**, that thou H6629
21:17 but *as for* these **s**, what have they done? H6629
2Ch 5: 6 the ark, sacrificed **s** and oxen, which H6629
7: 5 twenty thousand **s**: so the king and all H6629
14:15 and carried away **s** and camels in H6629
2Ch 15:11 hundred oxen and seven thousand **s**. H6629
18: 2 And Ahab killed **s** and oxen for him in H6629
16 upon the mountains, as **s** that have no H6629
29:33 six hundred oxen and three thousand **s**. H6629
30:24 seven thousand **s**; and the princes gave H6629
24 and ten thousand **s**: and a great H6629
31: 6 tithe of oxen and **s**, and the tithe of holy H6629
Neh 3: 1 they builded the **s** gate; they sanctified H6629
32 the corner unto the **s** gate repaired the H6629
5:18 one ox *and* six choice **s**; also fowls were H6629
12:39 even unto the **s** gate: and they stood H6629
Job 1: 3 seven thousand **s**, and three thousand H6629
16 burned up the **s**, and the servants, and H6629
31:20 *not* warmed with the fleece of my **s**; H3532
42:12 fourteen thousand **s**, and six thousand H6629
Ps 8: 7 All **s** and oxen, yea, and the beasts of H6792
44:11 Thou hast given us like **s** *appointed* for H6629
22 we are counted as **s** for the slaughter. H6629
49:14 Like **s** they are laid in the grave; death H6629
74: 1 smoke against the **s** of thy pasture? H6629
78:52 to go forth like **s**, and guided them in H6629
79:13 So we thy people and **s** of thy pasture H6629
95: 7 pasture, and the **s** of his hand. To day H6629
100: 3 *are* his people, and the **s** of his pasture. H6629
119:176 I have gone astray like a lost **s**; seek thy H7716
144:13 of store: *that* our **s** may bring forth H6629
Song 4: 2 Thy teeth *are* like a flock *of* **s** *that are* H7353
6: 6 Thy teeth *are* as a flock of **s** which go H7353
Isa 7:21 shall nourish a young cow, and two **s**; H6629
13:14 roe, and as a **s** that no man taketh H6629
22:13 oxen, and killing **s**, eating flesh, and H6629
53: 6 All we like **s** have gone astray; we have H6629
7 and as a **s** before her shearers H7353
Jer 12: 3 pull them out like **s** for the slaughter, H6629
23: 1 the **s** of my pasture! saith the LORD. H6629
50: 6 My people hath been lost **s**: their H6629
17 Israel *is* a scattered **s**; the lions have H7716
Ezk 34: 6 My **s** wandered through all the H6629
11 both search my **s**, and seek them out. H6629
12 he is among his **s** *that are* scattered; so H6629
12 so will I seek out my **s**, and will deliver H6629
Hos 12:12 served for a wife, and for a wife he kept **s**.
Joel 1:18 yea, the flocks of **s** are made desolate. H6629
Mic 2:12 together as the **s** of Bozrah, as the flock H6629
5: 8 the flocks of **s**: who, if he go through, H6629
Zec 13: 7 shepherd, and the **s** shall be scattered: H6629
Mt 9:36 abroad, as **s** having no shepherd. *G4263*
10: 6 But go rather to the lost **s** of the house *G4263*
16 Behold, I send you forth as **s** in the *G4263*
12:11 shall have one **s**, and if it fall into a pit *G4263*
12 a man better than a **s**? Wherefore it is *G4263*
15:24 unto the lost **s** of the house of Israel. *G4263*
18:12 have an hundred **s**, and one of them be *G4263*
13 more of that **s**, than of the ninety and
25:32 shepherd divideth *his* **s** from the goats: *G4263*
33 And he shall set the **s** on his right hand, *G4263*
26:31 **s** of the flock shall be scattered abroad. *G4263*
Mk 6:34 they were as **s** not having a shepherd: *G4263*
14:27 shepherd, and the **s** shall be scattered. *G4263*
Lk 15: 4 What man of you, having an hundred **s**, *G4263*
6 for I have found my **s** which was lost. *G4263*
Jn 2:14 that sold oxen and **s** and doves, and *G4263*
15 the temple, and the **s**, and the oxen; and *G4263*
5: 2 Now there is at Jerusalem by the **s** *G4262*
10: 2 in by the door is the shepherd of the **s**. *G4263*
3 To him the porter openeth; and the **s** *G4263*
3 own **s** by name, and leadeth them out. *G4263*
4 And when he putteth forth his own **s**, he *G4263*
4 **s** follow him: for they know his voice. *G4263*
7 I say unto you, I am the door of the **s**. *G4263*
8 robbers: but the **s** did not hear them. *G4263*
11 good shepherd giveth his life for the **s**. *G4263*
12 whose own the **s** are not, seeth the wolf *G4263*
12 and leaveth the **s**, and fleeth: and the *G4263*
12 catcheth them, and scattereth the **s**. *G4263*
13 is an hireling, and careth not for the **s**. *G4263*
14 I am the good shepherd, and know my **s**,
15 Father: and I lay down my life for the **s**. *G4263*
16 And other **s** I have, which are not of *G4263*
26 ye are not of my **s**, as I said unto you. *G4263*
27 My **s** hear my voice, and I know them, *G4263*
21:16 love thee. He saith unto him, Feed my **s**. *G4263*
17 thee. Jesus saith unto him, Feed my **s**. *G4263*
Act 8:32 He was led as a **s** to the slaughter; and *G4263*
Ro 8:36 we are accounted as **s** for the slaughter. *G4263*
Heb 13:20 shepherd of the **s**, through the blood of *G4263*
1Pt 2:25 For ye were as **s** going astray; but are *G4263*
Rev 18:13 and beasts, and **s**, and horses, and *G4263*

SHEEPCOTE
2Sa 7: 8 took thee from the **s**, from following the H5116
1Ch 17: 7 I took thee from the **s**, *even* from H5116

SHEEPCOTES
1Sa 24: 3 And he came to the **s** by the H1448+H6629

SHEEPFOLD
Jn 10: 1 door into the **s**, but climbeth up *G833+G4263*

SHEEPFOLDS
Nu 32:16 We will build **s** here for our H1448+H6629
Jdg 5:16 Why abodest thou among the **s**, to hear H4942
Ps 78:70 and took him from the **s**: H4356+H6629

SHEEP-GATE See SHEEP and GATE.

SHEEP-MARKET See SHEEP and MARKET.

SHEEPMASTER
2Ki 3: 4 And Mesha king of Moab was a **s**, and H5349

SHEEP'S
Mt 7:15 come to you in **s** clothing, but inwardly *G4263*

SHEEPSHEARERS
Gen 38:12 up unto his **s** to Timnath, he H1494+H6629
2Sa 13:23 that Absalom had **s** in Baal-hazor, H1494
24 now, thy servant hath **s**; let the king, I H1494

SHEEPSKINS
Heb 11:37 about in **s** and goatskins; being *G3374*

SHEET
Act 10:11 as it had been a great **s** knit at the four *G3607*
11: 5 as it had been a great **s**, let down from *G3607*

SHEETS
Jdg 14:12 thirty **s** and thirty change of garments: H5466
13 ye give me thirty **s** and thirty change of H5466

SHEHARIAH
1Ch 8:26 And Shamsherai, and **S**, and Athaliah, H7841

SHEKEL
Gen 24:22 earring of half a **s** weight, and two H1235
Ex 30:13 numbered, half a **s** after the shekel of H8255
13 a shekel after the **s** of the sanctuary: (a H8255
13 of the sanctuary: (a **s** *is* twenty gerahs:) H8255
13 half **s** *shall be* the offering of the LORD. H8255
15 less than half a **s**, when *they* give an H8255
24 *shekels*, after the **s** of the sanctuary, H8255
38:24 shekels, after the **s** of the sanctuary. H8255
25 shekels, after the **s** of the sanctuary: H8255
26 A bekah for every man, *that is*, half a **s**, H8255
26 a shekel, after the **s** of the sanctuary, H8255
Lev 5:15 of silver, after the **s** of the sanctuary, H8255
27: 3 of silver, after the **s** of the sanctuary. H8255
25 be according to the **s** of the sanctuary: H8255
25 sanctuary: twenty gerahs shall be the **s**. H8255
Nu 3:47 by the poll, after the **s** of the sanctuary H8255
47 take *them*: (the **s** *is* twenty gerahs:) H8255
50 *shekels*, after the **s** of the sanctuary: H8255
7:13 shekels, after the **s** of the sanctuary; H8255
19 shekels, after the **s** of the sanctuary; H8255
25 shekels, after the **s** of the sanctuary; H8255
31 shekels, after the **s** of the sanctuary; H8255
37 shekels, after the **s** of the sanctuary; H8255
43 shekels, after the **s** of the sanctuary; H8255
49 shekels, after the **s** of the sanctuary; H8255
55 shekels, after the **s** of the sanctuary; H8255
61 shekels, after the **s** of the sanctuary; H8255
67 shekels, after the **s** of the sanctuary; H8255
73 shekels, after the **s** of the sanctuary; H8255
79 shekels, after the **s** of the sanctuary; H8255
85 *shekels*, after the **s** of the sanctuary: H8255
86 apiece, after the **s** of the sanctuary: all H8255
18:16 shekels, after the **s** of the sanctuary, H8255
1Sa 9: 8 fourth part of a **s** of silver: *that* will I H8255
2Ki 7: 1 flour *be sold* for a **s**, and two measures H8255
1 of barley for a **s**, in the gate of Samaria. H8255
16 was *sold* for a **s**, and two measures of H8255
16 a **s**, according to the word of the LORD. H8255
18 of barley for a **s**, and a measure of fine H8255
18 of fine flour for a **s**, shall be to morrow H8255
Neh 10:32 the third part of a **s** for the service of H8255
Ezk 45:12 And the **s** *shall be* twenty gerahs: H8255
Am 8: 5 small, and the **s** great, and falsifying H8255

S

SHEKELS
Gen 23:15 four hundred *s* of silver; what *is* that H8255
16 four hundred **s** of silver, current *money* H8255
24:22 for her hands of ten *s* weight of gold; H8255
Ex 21:32 **s** of silver, and the ox shall be stoned. H8255
30:23 five hundred *s*, and of sweet cinnamon
23 two hundred and fifty *s*, and of sweet
23 sweet calamus two hundred and fifty *s*,
24 And of cassia five hundred *s*, after the
38:24 **s**, after the shekel of the sanctuary. H8255
25 **s**, after the shekel of the sanctuary: H8255
28 seventy and five **s** he made hooks for the
29 and two thousand and four hundred **s**. H8255
Lev 5:15 thy estimation by **s** of silver, after the H8255
27: 3 shall be fifty **s** of silver, after the shekel H8255
4 then thy estimation shall be thirty **s**. H8255
5 twenty **s**, and for the female ten shekels. H8255
5 twenty shekels, and for the female ten **s**. H8255
6 be of the male five **s** of silver, and for H8255
6 thy estimation *shall be* three **s** of silver. H8255
7 fifteen **s**, and for the female ten shekels. H8255
7 fifteen shekels, and for the female ten **s**. H8255
16 seed *shall be valued* at fifty **s** of silver. H8255
Nu 3:47 Thou shalt even take five **s** apiece by H8255
50 five *s*, after the shekel of the sanctuary:
7:13 hundred and thirty *s*, one silver bowl of H259
13 bowl of seventy **s**, after the shekel of the H8255
14 One spoon of ten *s* of gold, full of
19 hundred and thirty *s*, one silver bowl of
19 bowl of seventy **s**, after the shekel of the H8255
20 One spoon of gold of ten *s*, full of H4392
25 hundred and thirty *s*, one silver bowl of H259
25 bowl of seventy **s**, after the shekel of the H8255
26 One golden spoon of ten *s*, full of H4392
31 hundred and thirty *s*, one silver bowl of H259
31 bowl of seventy **s**, after the shekel of the H8255
32 One golden spoon of ten *s*, full of H4392
37 hundred and thirty *s*, one silver bowl of H259
37 bowl of seventy **s**, after the shekel of the H8255
38 One golden spoon of ten *s*, full of H4392
43 an hundred and thirty *s*, a silver bowl of
43 bowl of seventy **s**, after the shekel of the H8255
44 One golden spoon of ten *s*, full of H4392
49 hundred and thirty *s*, one silver bowl of H259
49 bowl of seventy **s**, after the shekel of the H8255
50 One golden spoon of ten *s*, full of H4392
55 hundred and thirty *s*, one silver bowl of H259
55 bowl of seventy **s**, after the shekel of the H8255
56 One golden spoon of ten *s*, full of H4392
61 hundred and thirty *s*, one silver bowl of H259
61 bowl of seventy **s**, after the shekel of the H8255
62 One golden spoon of ten *s*, full of H4392
67 hundred and thirty *s*, one silver bowl of H259
67 bowl of seventy **s**, after the shekel of the H8255
68 One golden spoon of ten *s*, full of H4392
73 hundred and thirty *s*, one silver bowl of H259
73 bowl of seventy **s**, after the shekel of the H8255
74 One golden spoon of ten *s*, full of H4392
79 hundred and thirty *s*, one silver bowl of H259
79 bowl of seventy **s**, after the shekel of the H8255
80 One golden spoon of ten *s*, full of H4392
85 hundred and thirty *s*, each bowl seventy: H259
85 *s*, after the shekel of the sanctuary:
86 *weighing* ten *s* apiece, after the shekel
86 the spoons *was* an hundred and twenty *s*.
18:16 the money of five **s**, after the shekel of H8255
31:52 thousand seven hundred and fifty **s**. H8255
Dt 22:19 him in an hundred *s* of silver, and give
29 father fifty *s* of silver, and she shall
Jos 7:21 and two hundred **s** of silver, and a H8255
21 of gold of fifty **s** weight, then I coveted H8255
Jdg 8:26 and seven hundred *s* of gold; beside
17: 2 The eleven hundred *s* of silver that were
3 the eleven hundred *s* of silver to his
4 took two hundred *s* of silver, and gave
10 I will give thee ten *s* of silver by the year,
1Sa 17: 5 the coat *was* five thousand **s** of brass. H8255
7 six hundred **s** of iron: and one bearing H8255
2Sa 14:26 two hundred **s** after the king's weight. H8255
18:11 given thee ten *s* of silver, and a girdle.
12 receive a thousand *s* of silver in mine
21:16 three hundred *s* of brass in weight, he
24:24 and the oxen for fifty **s** of silver. H8255
1Ki 10:16 six hundred *s* of gold went to one target.
29 for six hundred *s* of silver, and an horse
2Ki 15:20 of each man fifty **s** of silver, to give to H8255
1Ch 21:25 place six hundred **s** of gold by weight. H8255
2Ch 1:17 for six hundred *s* of silver, and an horse
3: 9 And the weight of the nails *was* fifty **s** H8255
2Ch 9:15 *s* of beaten gold went to one target.
16 gold: three hundred *s* of gold went to one
Neh 5:15 wine, beside forty **s** of silver; yea, even H8255
Jer 32: 9 the money, *even* seventeen **s** of silver. H8255
Ezk 4:10 by weight, twenty **s** a day: from time to H8255
45:12 twenty gerahs: twenty **s**, five and twenty H8255
12 **s**, fifteen shekels, shall be your maneh. H8255
12 shekels, fifteen **s**, shall be your maneh. H8255

SHELAH
Gen 38: 5 and called his name **S**: and he was at H7956
11 father's house, till **S** my son be grown: H7956
14 for she saw that **S** was grown, and she H7956
26 that I gave her not to **S** my son. And he H7956
46:12 Er, and Onan, and **S**, and Pharez, and H7956
Nu 26:20 families were; of **S**, the family of the H7956
1Ch 1:18 And Arphaxad begat **S**, and Shelah H7974
18 And Arphaxad begat Shelah, and **S** H7974
24 Shem, Arphaxad, **S**, H7974
2: 3 The sons of Judah; Er, and Onan, and **S**: H7956
4:21 The sons of **S** the son of Judah *were*, Er H7956

SHELANITES
Nu 26:20 the family of the **S**: of Pharez, the family H8024

SHELEMIAH
1Ch 26:14 And the lot eastward fell to **S**. Then for H8018
Ezr 10:39 And **S**, and Nathan, and Adaiah, H8018
41 Azareel, and **S**, Shemariah, H8018
Neh 3:30 the son of **S**, and Hanun the sixth H8018
13:13 the treasuries, **S** the priest, and Zadok H8018
Jer 36:14 the son of **S**, the son of Cushi, unto H8018
26 son of Azriel, and **S** the son of Abdeel, H8018
37: 3 Jehucal the son of **S** and Zephaniah the H8018
13 *was* Irijah, the son of **S**, the son of H8018
38: 1 Jucal the son of **S**, and Pashur the son H8018

SHELEPH
Gen 10:26 And Joktan begat Almodad, and **S**, and H8026
1Ch 1:20 And Joktan begat Almodad, and **S**, and H8026

SHELESH
1Ch 7:35 Zophah, and Imna, and **S**, and Amal. H8028

SHELOMI
Nu 34:27 children of Asher, Ahihud the son of **S**. H8015

SHELOMITH
Lev 24:11 name *was* **S**, the daughter of Dibri, H8019
1Ch 3:19 and Hananiah, and **S** their sister: H8019
23: 9 The sons of Shimei; **S**, and Haziel, and H8013
18 Of the sons of Izhar; **S** the chief. H8019
26:25 son, and Zichri his son, and **S** his son. H8013
26 Which **S** and his brethren *were* over all H8013
28 the hand of **S**, and of his brethren. H8019
2Ch 11:20 him Abijah, and Attai, and Ziza, and **S**. H8019
Ezr 8:10 And of the sons of **S**; the son of H8019

SHELOMOTH
1Ch 24:22 Of the Izharites; **S**: of the sons of H8013
22 Shelomoth: of the sons of **S**; Jahath. H8013

SHELTER
Job 24: 8 and embrace the rock for want of a **s**. H4268
Ps 61: 3 For thou hast been a **s** for me, *and* a H4268

SHELUMIEL
Nu 1: 6 Of Simeon; **S** the son of Zurishaddai. H8017
2:12 *shall be* **S** the son of Zurishaddai. H8017
7:36 On the fifth day **S** the son of H8017
41 offering of **S** the son of Zurishaddai. H8017
10:19 Simeon *was* **S** the son of Zurishaddai. H8017

SHEM
Gen 5:32 and Noah begat **S**, Ham, and Japheth. H8035
6:10 And Noah begat three sons, **S**, Ham, H8035
7:13 Noah, and **S**, and Ham, and Japheth, H8035
9:18 forth of the ark, were **S**, and Ham, and H8035
23 And **S** and Japheth took a garment, H8035
26 of **S**; and Canaan shall be his servant. H8035
27 of **S**; and Canaan shall be his servant. H8035
10: 1 the sons of Noah, **S**, Ham, and Japheth: H8035
21 Unto **S** also, the father of all the H8035
22 The children of **S**; Elam, and Asshur, H8035
31 These *are* the sons of **S**, after their H8035
11:10 These *are* the generations of **S**: Shem H8035
10 These *are* the generations of Shem: **S** H8035
11 And **S** lived after he begat Arphaxad H8035
1Ch 1: 4 Noah, **S**, Ham, and Japheth. H8035
1Ch 1:17 The sons of **S**; Elam, and Asshur, and H8035
24 **S**, Arphaxad, Shelah, H8035

SHEMA
Jos 15:26 Amam, and **S**, and Moladah, H8090
1Ch 2:43 and Tappuah, and Rekem, and **S**. H8087
44 And **S** begat Raham, the father of H8087
5: 8 And Bela the son of Azaz, the son of **S**, H8087
8:13 Beriah also, and **S**, who *were* heads of H8087
Neh 8: 4 Mattithiah, and **S**, and Anaiah, and H8087

SHEMAAH
1Ch 12: 3 Joash, the sons of **S** the Gibeathite; and H8094

SHEMAIAH
1Ki 12:22 But the word of God came unto **S** the H8098
1Ch 3:22 And the sons of Shechaniah; **S**: and the H8098
22 and the sons of **S**; Hattush, and Igeal, H8098
4:37 Jedaiah, the son of Shimri, the son of **S**; H8098
5: 4 The sons of Joel; **S** his son, Gog his son, H8098
9:14 And of the Levites; **S** the son of H8098
16 And Obadiah the son of **S**, the son of H8098
15: 8 Of the sons of Elizaphan; **S** the chief, H8098
11 and Joel, **S**, and Eliel, and Amminadab, H8098
24: 6 And **S** the son of Nethaneel the scribe, H8098
26: 4 of Obed-edom *were*, **S** the firstborn, H8098
6 Also unto **S** his son were sons born, H8098
7 The sons of **S**; Othni, and Rephael, and H8098
2Ch 11: 2 But the word of the LORD came to **S** H8098
12: 5 Then came **S** the prophet to H8098
7 the LORD came to **S**, saying, They have H8098
15 in the book of **S** the prophet, and of H8098
17: 8 And with them *he sent* Levites, *even* **S**, H8098
29:14 of the sons of Jeduthun; **S**, and Uzziel. H8098
31:15 and Jeshua, and **S**, Amariah, and H8098
35: 9 Conaniah also, and **S** and Nethaneel, H8098
Ezr 8:13 and **S**, and with them threescore males. H8098
16 Then sent I for Eliezer, for Ariel, for **S**, H8098
10:21 Elijah, and **S**, and Jehiel, and Uzziah. H8098
31 Eliezer, Ishijah, Malchiah, **S**, Shimeon, H8098
Neh 3:29 After him repaired also **S** the son of H8098
6:10 Afterward I came unto the house of **S** H8098
10: 8 Maaziah, Bilgai, **S**: these *were* the H8098
11:15 Also of the Levites: **S** the son of H8098
12: 6 **S**, and Joiarib, Jedaiah, H8098
18 Of Bilgah, Shammua; of **S**, Jehonathan; H8098
34 Judah, and Benjamin, and **S**, and H8098
35 the son of **S**, the son of Mattaniah, H8098
36 And his brethren; **S**, and Azarael, H8098
42 And Maaseiah, and **S**, and Eleazar, and H8098
Jer 26:20 Urijah the son of **S** of Kirjathjearim, H8098
29:24 *Thus* shalt thou also speak to **S** the H8098
31 LORD concerning **S** the Nehelamite; H8098
31 Because that **S** hath prophesied unto H8098
32 I will punish **S** the Nehelamite, and H8098
36:12 Delaiah the son of **S**, and Elnathan the H8098

SHEMARIAH
1Ch 12: 5 and **S**, and Shephatiah the Haruphite, H8114
Ezr 10:32 Benjamin, Malluch, *and* **S**. H8114
41 Azareel, and Shelemiah, **S**, H8114

SHEMEBER
Gen 14: 2 of Admah, and **S** king of Zeboiim, and H8038

SHEMER
1Ki 16:24 And he bought the hill Samaria of **S** for H8106
24 name of **S**, owner of the hill, Samaria. H8106

SHEMIDA
Nu 26:32 And *of* **S**, the family of the Shemidaites: H8061
Jos 17: 2 and for the children of **S**: these *were* the H8061
1Ch 7:19 And the sons of **S** were, Ahian, and H8061

SHEMIDAITES
Nu 26:32 And *of* Shemida, the family of the **S**: H8062

SHEMINITH
1Ch 15:21 Azaziah, with harps on the **S** to excel. H8067
Ps 6:ttl on Neginoth upon **S**, A Psalm of David. H8067
12:ttl To the chief Musician upon **S**, A Psalm H8067

SHEMIRAMOTH
1Ch 15:18 Ben, and Jaaziel, and **S**, and Jehiel, and H8070
20 And Zechariah, and Aziel, and **S**, and H8070
16: 5 Jeiel, and **S**, and Jehiel, and Mattithiah, H8070
2Ch 17: 8 and Asahel, and **S**, and Jehonathan, H8070

SHEMITE See BETH-SHEMITE.

SHEMUEL
Nu 34:20 of Simeon, S the son of Ammihud. H8050
1Ch 6:33 a singer, the son of Joel, the son of S, H8050
7: 2 and Jibsam, and S, heads of their H8050

SHEN
1Sa 7:12 Mizpeh and S, and called the name H8129

SHENAZAR
1Ch 3:18 Malchiram also, and Pedaiah, and S, H8137

SHENIR
Dt 3: 9 call Sirion; and the Amorites call it S;) H8149
Song 4: 8 from the top of S and Hermon, from H8149

SHEPHAM
Nu 34:10 your east border from Hazar-enan to S: H8221
11 And the coast shall go down from S to H8221

SHEPHATHIAH
1Ch 9: 8 S, the son of Reuel, the son of Ibnijah; H8203

SHEPHATIAH
2Sa 3: 4 and the fifth, S the son of Abital; H8203
1Ch 3: 3 The fifth, S of Abital: the sixth, Ithream H8203
12: 5 and Shemariah, and S the Haruphite, H8203
27:16 the Simeonites, S the son of Maachah: H8203
2Ch 21: 2 and Michael, and S: all these *were* the H8203
Ezr 2: 4 The children of S, three hundred H8203
57 The children of S, the children of Hattil, H8203
8: 8 And of the sons of S; Zebadiah the son H8203
Neh 7: 9 The children of S, three hundred H8203
59 The children of S, the children of Hattil, H8203
11: 4 the son of S, the son of Mahalaleel, H8203
Jer 38: 1 Then S the son of Mattan, and H8203

SHEPHERD
Gen 46:34 for every s *is* an abomination H7462+H6629
49:24 thence *is* the s, the stone of Israel:) H7462
Nu 27:17 LORD be not as sheep which have no s. H7462
1Ki 22:17 that have not a s: and the LORD said, H7462
2Ch 18:16 that have no s: and the LORD said, H7462
Ps 23: 1 The LORD *is* my s; I shall not want. H7462
80: 1 Give ear, O S of Israel, thou that leadest H7462
Ecc 12:11 assemblies, *which* are given from one s. H7462
Isa 40:11 He shall feed his flock like a s: he shall H7462
44:28 That saith of Cyrus, *He is* my s, and H7462
63:11 of the sea with the s of his flock? where H7462
Jer 31:10 and keep him, as a s *doth* his flock. H7462
43:12 the land of Egypt, as a s putteth on his H7462
49:19 who *is* that s that will stand before me? H7462
50:44 who *is* that s that will stand before me? H7462
51:23 with thee the s and his flock; and with H7462
Ezk 34: 5 *there is* no s: and they became meat H7462
8 because *there was* no s, neither did my H7462
12 As a s seeketh out his flock in the day H7462
23 And I will set up one s over them, and H7462
23 shall feed them, and he shall be their s. H7462
37:24 all shall have one s: they shall also walk H7462
Am 3:12 Thus saith the LORD; As the s taketh H7462
Zec 10: 2 were troubled, because *there was* no s. H7462
11:15 thee yet the instruments of a foolish s. H7462
16 For, lo, I will raise up a s in the land, H7462
17 Woe to the idol s that leaveth the flock! H7473
13: 7 Awake, O sword, against my s, and H7462
7 of hosts: smite the s, and the sheep shall H7462
Mt 9:36 scattered abroad, as sheep having no s. G4166
25:32 a s divideth *his* sheep from the goats: G4166
26:31 I will smite the s, and the sheep of the G4166
Mk 6:34 not having a s: and he began to teach G4166
14:27 the s, and the sheep shall be scattered. G4166
Jn 10: 2 in by the door is the s of the sheep. G4166
11 I am the good s: the good shepherd G4166
11 I am the good shepherd: the good s G4166
12 But he that is an hireling, and not the s, G4166
14 I am the good s, and know my *sheep*, G4166
16 and there shall be one fold, *and* one s. G4166
Heb 13:20 Jesus, that great s of the sheep, through G4166
1Pt 2:25 unto the S and Bishop of your souls. G4166
5: 4 And when the chief S shall appear, ye G750

SHEPHERDS
Gen 46:32 And the men *are* s, for their H7462+H6629
47: 3 servants *are* s, both we, *and* H7462+H6629
Ex 2:17 And the s came and drove them away: H7462
19 out of the hand of the s, and also drew H7462
1Sa 25: 7 shearers: now thy s which were with H7462
Isa 13:20 shall the s make their fold there. H7462
31: 4 a multitude of s is called forth against H7462
56:11 and they *are* s *that* cannot understand: H7462
Jer 6: 3 The s with their flocks shall come unto H7462
23: 4 And I will set up s over them which H7462
25:34 Howl, ye s, and cry; and wallow H7462
35 And the s shall have no way to flee, nor H7462
36 A voice of the cry of the s, and an H7462
33:12 of s causing *their* flocks to lie down. H7462
50: 6 My people hath been lost sheep: their s H7462
Ezk 34: 2 Son of man, prophesy against the s of H7462
2 Lord GOD unto the s; Woe *be* to the H7462
2 Woe *be* to the s of Israel that do feed H7462
2 should not the s feed the flocks? H7462
7 Therefore, ye s, hear the word of the H7462
8 neither did my s search for my flock, H7462
8 s fed themselves, and fed not my flock; H7462
9 Therefore, O ye s, hear the word of the H7462
10 I *am* against the s; and I will require my H7462
10 neither shall the s feed themselves any H7462
Am 1: 2 habitations of the s shall mourn, and H7462
Mic 5: 5 him seven s, and eight principal men. H7462
Nah 3:18 Thy s slumber, O king of Assyria: thy H7462
Zep 2: 6 *and* cottages for s, and folds for flocks. H7462
Zec 10: 3 Mine anger was kindled against the s, H7462
11: 3 *There is* a voice of the howling of the s; H7462
5 am rich: and their own s pity them not. H7462
8 Three s also I cut off in one month; and H7462
Lk 2: 8 And there were in the same country s G4166
15 into heaven, the s said one to another, G4166
18 things which were told them by the s. G4166
20 And the s returned, glorifying and G4166

SHEPHERD'S
1Sa 17:40 and put them in a s bag which he had, H7462
Isa 38:12 from me as a s tent: I have cut off like H7473

SHEPHERDS'
Song 1: 8 and feed thy kids beside the s tents. H7462

SHEPHI
1Ch 1:40 and Ebal, S, and Onam. And the H8195

SHEPHO
Gen 36:23 and Manahath, and Ebal, S, and Onam. H8195

SHEPHUPHAN
1Ch 8: 5 And Gera, and S, and Huram. H8197

SHERAH
1Ch 7:24 (And his daughter *was* S, who built H7609

SHERD
Isa 30:14 in the bursting of it a s to take fire from H2789

SHERDS
Ezk 23:34 shalt break the s thereof, and pluck off H2789

SHEREBIAH
Ezr 8:18 son of Israel; and S, with his sons and H8274
24 of the priests, S, Hashabiah, and ten H8274
Neh 8: 7 Also Jeshua, and Bani, and S, Jamin, H8274
9: 4 Shebaniah, Bunni, S, Bani, *and* H8274
5 Hashabniah, S, Hodijah, Shebaniah, H8274
10:12 Zaccur, S, Shebaniah, H8274
12: 8 Jeshua, Binnui, Kadmiel, S, Judah, *and* H8274
24 Hashabiah, S, and Jeshua the son H8274

SHERESH
1Ch 7:16 S; and his sons *were* Ulam and Rakem. H8329

SHEREZER
Zec 7: 2 the house of God S and Regemmelech, H8272

SHERIFFS
Dan 3: 2 counsellors, the s, and all the rulers of H8614
3 counsellors, the s, and all the rulers of H8614

SHESHACH
Jer 25:26 the king of S shall drink after them. H8347
51:41 How is S taken! and how is the praise H8347

SHESHAI
Nu 13:22 where Ahiman, S, and Talmai, the H8344
Jos 15:14 three sons of Anak, S, and Ahiman, and H8344
Jdg 1:10 they slew S, and Ahiman, and Talmai. H8344

SHESHAN
1Ch 2:31 S. And the children of Sheshan; Ahlai. H8348
31 Sheshan. And the children of S; Ahlai. H8348
34 Now S had no sons, but daughters. H8348
1Ch 2:34 but daughters. And S had a servant, an H8348
35 And S gave his daughter to Jarha his H8348

SHESHBAZZAR
Ezr 1: 8 them unto S, the prince of Judah. H8339
11 All *these* did S bring up with *them* H8339
5:14 *was* S, whom he had made governor; H8340
16 Then came the same S, *and* laid the H8340

SHETH
Nu 24:17 Moab, and destroy all the children of S. H8352
1Ch 1: 1 Adam, S, Enosh, H8352

SHETHAR
Est 1:14 And the next unto him *was* Carshena, S, H8369

SHETHAR-BOZNAI
Ezr 5: 3 this side the river, and S, and their H8370
6 this side the river, and S, and his H8370
6: 6 governor beyond the river, S, and your H8370
13 on this side the river, S, and their H8370

SHEVA
2Sa 20:25 And S *was* scribe: and Zadok and H7724
1Ch 2:49 father of Madmannah, S the father of H7724

SHEW
Gen 12: 1 house, unto a land that I will s thee: H7200
20:13 which thou shalt s unto me; at every H6213
24:12 s kindness unto my master Abraham. H6213
40:14 with thee, and s kindness, I pray thee, H6213
46:31 I will go up, and s Pharaoh, and say H5046
Ex 7: 9 unto you, saying, S a miracle for you: H5414
9:16 thee up, for to s *in* thee my power; and H7200
10: 1 I might s these my signs before him: H7896
13: 8 And thou shalt s thy son in that day, H5046
14:13 which he will s to you to day: for the H6213
18:20 laws, and shalt s them the way wherein H3045
25: 9 According to all that I s thee, *after* the H7200
33:13 grace in thy sight, s me now thy way, H3045
18 And he said, I beseech thee, s me thy H7200
19 will s mercy on whom I will shew mercy.
19 will shew mercy on whom I will s mercy.
Nu 16: 5 the LORD will s who *are* his, and *who* H3045
Dt 1:33 in fire by night, to s you by what way ye H7200
3:24 O Lord GOD, thou hast begun to s thy H7200
5: 5 at that time, to s you the word of the H5046
7: 2 with them, nor s mercy unto them:
13:17 of his anger, and s thee mercy, and H5414
17: 9 shall s thee the sentence of judgment: H5046
10 shall choose shall s thee; and thou shalt H5046
11 s thee, *to* the right hand, nor *to* the left. H5046
28:50 of the old, nor s favour to the young:
32: 7 father, and he will s thee; thy elders, H5046
Jos 2:12 that ye will also s kindness unto my H6213
5: 6 that he would not s them the land, H7200
Jdg 1:24 said unto him, S us, we pray thee, the H7200
24 into the city, and we will s thee mercy. H6213
4:22 Come, and I will s thee the man whom H7200
6:17 s me a sign that thou talkest with me. H6213
1Sa 3:15 And Samuel feared to s Eli the vision. H5046
8: 9 unto them, and s them the manner of H5046
9: 6 he can s us our way that we should go. H5046
27 that I may s thee the word of God. H8085
10: 8 to thee, and s thee what thou shalt do. H3045
14:12 up to us, and we will s you a thing. And H3045
16: 3 and I will s thee what thou shalt H3045
20: 2 but that he will s it me: and why should H1540
12 I then send not unto thee, and s it thee; H1540
13 evil, then I will s it thee, and send thee H1540
14 while yet I live s me the kindness of H6213
22:17 he fled, and did not s it to me. But the H1540
25: 8 Ask thy young men, and they will s H5046
2Sa 2: 6 And now the LORD s kindness and H6213
3: 8 against Judah do s kindness this day H6213
9: 1 s him kindness for Jonathan's sake? H6213
3 of Saul, that I may s the kindness of H6213
7 not: for I will surely s thee kindness for H6213
10: 2 Then said David, I will s kindness unto H6213
15:25 and s me *both* it, and his habitation: H7200
22:26 With the merciful thou wilt s thyself
26 upright man thou wilt s thyself upright.
27 With the pure thou wilt s thyself pure;
27 froward thou wilt s thyself unsavoury.
1Ki 1:52 And Solomon said, If he will s himself a
2: 2 strong therefore, and s thyself a man;
7 But s kindness unto the sons of H6213
18: 1 year, saying, Go, s thyself unto Ahab; H7200
2 And Elijah went to s himself unto H7200

S

1Ki 18:15 I will surely s myself unto him to day. H7200
2Ki 6:11 them, Will ye not s me which of us *is* H5046
7:12 I will now s you what the Syrians H5046
1Ch 16:23 Sing unto the LORD, all the earth; s H1319
19: 2 And David said, I will s kindness unto H6213
2Ch 16: 9 the whole earth, to s himself strong in
Ezr 2:59 but they could not s their father's H5046
Neh 7:61 but they could not s their father's H5046
9:19 of fire by night, to s them light, and the
Est 1:11 the crown royal, to s the people and the H7200
2:10 charged her that she should not s *it*. H5046
4: 8 destroy them, to s *it* unto Esther, and H7200
Job 10: 2 not condemn me; s me wherefore thou H3045
11: 6 And that he would s thee the secrets of H5046
15:17 I will s thee, hear me; and that *which* I H2331
32: 6 and durst not s you mine opinion. H2331
10 to me; I also will s mine opinion. H2331
17 my part, I also will s mine opinion. H2331
33:23 to s unto man his uprightness: H5046
36: 2 Suffer me a little, and I will s thee that *I* H2331
Ps 4: 6 *There be* many that say, Who will s us H7200
9: 1 I will s forth all thy marvellous works. H5608
14 That I may s forth all thy praise in the H5608
16:11 Thou wilt s me the path of life: in thy H3045
17: 7 S thy marvellous lovingkindness, O thou
18:25 With the merciful thou wilt s thyself
25 upright man thou wilt s thyself upright;
26 With the pure thou wilt s thyself pure;
26 the froward thou wilt s thyself froward.
25: 4 S me thy ways, O LORD; teach me thy H3045
14 him; and he will s them his covenant. H3045
39: 6 Surely every man walketh in a vain s: H6754
50:23 *aright* will I s the salvation of God. H7200
51:15 and my mouth shall s forth thy praise. H5046
71:15 My mouth shall s forth thy H5608
79:13 s forth thy praise to all generations. H5608
85: 7 S us thy mercy, O LORD, and grant us H7200
86:17 S me a token for good; that they which H6213
88:10 Wilt thou s wonders to the dead? shall H6213
91:16 With long life will I satisfy him, and s H7200
92: 2 To s forth thy lovingkindness in the h5046
15 To s that the LORD *is* upright: *he is* my H5046
94: 1 whom vengeance belongeth, s thyself. H3313
96: 2 Sing unto the LORD, bless his name; s H1319
106: 2 LORD? *who* can s forth all his praise? H8085
109:16 Because that he remembered not to s H6213
Prv 18:24 A man *that hath* friends must s himself
Isa 3: 9 The s of their countenance doth H1971
27:11 that formed them will s them no favour.
30:30 heard, and shall s the lighting down of H7200
41:22 Let them bring *them* forth, and s us H5046
22 happen: let them s the former things, H5046
23 S the things that are to come hereafter, H5046
43: 9 declare this, and s us former things? let H8085
21 for myself; they shall s forth my praise. H5608
44: 7 and shall come, let them s unto them. H5046
46: 8 Remember this, and s yourselves men:
47: 6 hand: thou didst s them no mercy; H7760
49: 9 *are* in darkness, S yourselves. They H1540
58: 1 like a trumpet, and s my people their H5046
60: 6 shall s forth the praises of the LORD. H1319
Jer 16:10 when thou shalt s this people all these H5046
13 night; where I will not s you favour. H5414
18:17 the enemy; I will s them the back, and H7200
33: 3 will answer thee, and s thee great and H5046
42: 3 That the LORD thy God may s us the H5046
12 And I will s mercies unto you, that he H5414
50:42 cruel, and will not s mercy: their voice
51:31 meet another, to s the king of Babylon H5046
Ezk 22: 2 thou shalt s her all her abominations. H3045
33:31 their mouth they s much love, *but* their H6213
37:18 not s us what thou *meanest* by these? H5046
40: 4 all that I shall s thee; for to the intent H7200
4 intent that I might s *them* unto thee *art* H7200
43:10 Thou son of man, s the house to the H5046
11 they have done, s them the form of the H3045
Dan 2: 2 the Chaldeans, for to s the king his H5046
4 and we will s the interpretation. H2324
6 But if ye s the dream, and the H2324
6 honour: therefore s me the dream, and H2324
7 and we will s the interpretation of it. H2324
9 ye can s me the interpretation thereof. H2324
10 the earth that can s the king's matter: H2324
11 none other that can s it before the king, H2324
16 he would s the king the interpretation. H2324
24 I will s unto the king the interpretation. H2324
27 the soothsayers, s unto the king; H2324
4: 2 I thought it good to s the signs and H2324
5: 7 read this writing, and s me the H2324
Dan 5:12 called, and he will s the interpretation. H2324
15 not s the interpretation of the thing: H2324
9:23 and I am come to s *thee*; for thou *art* H5046
10:21 But I will s thee that which is noted in H5046
11: 2 And now will I s thee the truth. Behold, H5046
Joel 2:30 And I will s wonders in the heavens H5414
Mic 7:15 will I s unto him marvellous *things*. H7200
Nah 3: 5 thy face, and I will s the nations thy H7200
Hab 1: 3 Why dost thou s me iniquity, and H7200
Zec 1: 9 unto me, I will s thee what these *be*. H7200
7: 9 true judgment, and s mercy and H6213
Mt 8: 4 but go thy way, s thyself to the priest, G1166
11: 4 unto them, Go and s John again those G518
12:18 and he shall s judgment to the Gentiles. G518
14: 2 works do s forth themselves in him. G1754
16: 1 he would s them a sign from heaven. G1925
21 From that time forth began Jesus to s G1166
22:19 S me the tribute money. And they G1925
24: 1 for to s him the buildings of the temple. G1925
24 and shall s great signs and wonders; G1325
Mk 1:44 but go thy way, s thyself to the priest, G1166
6:14 works do s forth themselves in him. G1754
13:22 rise, and shall s signs and wonders, G1325
14:15 And he will s you a large upper room G1166
Lk 1:19 thee, and to s thee these glad tidings. G2097
5:14 man: but go, and s thyself to the priest, G1166
6:47 them, I will s you to whom he is like: G5263
8:39 Return to thine own house, and s how G1334
17:14 unto them, Go s yourselves unto the G1925
20:24 S me a penny. Whose image and G1925
47 houses, and for a s make long prayers: G4392
22:12 And he shall s you a large upper room G1166
Jn 5:20 doeth: and he will s him greater works G1166
7: 4 do these things, s thyself to the world. G5319
11:57 should s *it*, that they might take him. G3377
14: 8 Philip saith unto him, Lord, s us the G1166
9 how sayest thou *then*, S us the Father? G1166
16:13 speak: and he will s you things to come. G312
14 receive of mine, and shall s *it* unto you. G312
15 take of mine, and shall s *it* unto you. G312
25 but I shall s you plainly of the Father. G312
Act 1:24 s whether of these two thou hast chosen, G322
2:19 And I will s wonders in heaven above, G1325
7: 3 come into the land which I shall s thee. G1166
9:16 For I will s him how great things he G5263
12:17 And he said, Go s these things unto G518
16:17 which s unto us the way of salvation. G2605
24:27 s the Jews a pleasure, left Paul bound. G2698
26:23 the dead, and should s light unto the G2605
Ro 2:15 Which s the work of the law written in G1731
9:17 up, that I might s my power in thee, G1731
22 *What* if God, willing to s *his* wrath, and G1731
1Co 11:26 ye do s the Lord's death till he come. G2605
12:31 yet s I unto you a more excellent way. G1166
15:51 Behold, I s you a mystery; We shall not G3004
2Co 8:24 Wherefore s ye to them, and before the G1731
Gal 6:12 As many as desire to make a fair s in G2146
Eph 2: 7 That in the ages to come he might s the G1731
Col 2:15 powers, he made a s of them openly, G1165
23 Which things have indeed a s of G3056
1Th 1: 9 For they themselves s of us what manner G518
1Ti 1:16 first Jesus Christ might s forth all G1731
5: 4 them learn first to s piety at home, and G2151
6:15 Which in his times he shall s, *who is* the G1166
2Ti 2:15 Study to s thyself approved unto God, a G3936
Heb 6:11 one of you do s the same diligence to G1731
17 more abundantly to s unto the heirs of G1925
Jas 2:18 faith, and I have works: s me thy faith G1166
18 and I will s thee my faith by my works. G1166
3:13 among you? let him s out of a good G1166
1Pt 2: 9 that ye should s forth the praises of G1804
1Jn 1: 2 bear witness, and s unto you that eternal G518
Rev 1: 1 gave unto him, to s unto his servants G1166
4: 1 s thee things which must be hereafter. G1166
17: 1 me, Come hither; I will s unto thee the G1166
21: 9 I will s thee the bride, the Lamb's wife. G1166
22: 6 sent his angel to s unto his servants the G1166

SHEWBREAD

Ex 25:30 the table s before me alway. H3899+H6440
35:13 and all his vessels, and the s, H3899+H6440
39:36 the vessels thereof, and the s, H3899+H6440
Nu 4: 7 And upon the table of s they shall H6440
1Sa 21: 6 there but the s, that was taken H3899+H6440
1Ki 7:48 of gold, whereupon the s *was*, H3899+H6440
1Ch 9:32 s, to prepare *it* every sabbath. H3899+H4635
23:29 Both for the s, and for the fine H3899+H4635
28:16 for the tables of s, for every table; and H4635
2Ch 2: 4 for the continual s, and for the burnt H4635
2Ch 4:19 tables whereon the s *was set*; H3899+H6440
13:11 incense: the s also *set they in* H3899+H4635
29:18 the s table, with all the vessels thereof. H4635
Neh 10:33 For the s, and for the continual H3899+H4635
Mt 12: 4 and did eat the s, which was not G740+G4286
Mk 2:26 and did eat the s, which is not G740+G4286
Lk 6: 4 and eat the s, and gave also to G740+G4286
Heb 9: 2 s; which is called the sanctuary. G4286+G740

SHEWED

Gen 19:19 which thou hast s unto me in saving H6213
24:14 thou hast s kindness unto my master. H6213
32:10 which thou hast s unto thy servant; for H6213
39:21 But the LORD was with Joseph, and s H5186
41:25 hath s Pharaoh what he *is* about to do. H5046
39 as God hath s thee all this, *there is* H3045
48:11 and, lo, God hath s me also thy seed. H7200
Ex 15:25 and the LORD s him a tree, *which* H3384
25:40 pattern, which was s thee in the mount. H7200
26:30 thereof which was s thee in the mount. H7200
27: 8 make it: as it was s thee in the mount, H7200
Lev 13:19 reddish, and it be s to the priest; H7200
49 leprosy, and shall be s unto the priest: H7200
24:12 the mind of the LORD might be s them. H6567
Nu 8: 4 s Moses, so he made the candlestick. H7200
13:26 and s them the fruit of the land. H7200
14:11 the signs which I have s among them? H6213
Dt 4:35 Unto thee it was s, that thou mightest H7200
36 and upon earth he s thee his great fire; H7200
5:24 our God hath s us his glory and his H7200
6:22 And the LORD s signs and wonders, H5414
34: 1 s him all the land of Gilead, unto Dan, H7200
12 which Moses s in the sight of all Israel. H6213
Jos 2:12 since I have s you kindness, that ye H6213
Jdg 1:25 And when he s them the entrance into H7200
4:12 And they s Sisera that Barak the son of H5046
8:35 Neither s they kindness to the house of H6213
35 goodness which he had s unto Israel. H6213
13:10 and ran, and s her husband, and said H5046
23 would he have s us all these *things*, nor H7200
16:18 this once, for he hath s me all his heart. H5046
Ru 2:11 It hath fully been s me, all that thou H5046
19 of thee. And she s her mother in law H5046
3:10 *for* thou hast s more kindness in the H3190
1Sa 11: 9 came and s *it* to the men of Jabesh; H5046
15: 6 with them: for ye s kindness to all the H6213
19: 7 and Jonathan s him all those things. H5046
22:21 And Abiathar s David that Saul had H5046
24:18 And thou hast s this day how that thou H5046
2Sa 2: 5 that ye have s this kindness unto your H6213
10: 2 as his father s kindness unto me. And H6213
11:22 s David all that Joab had sent him for. H5046
1Ki 1:27 and thou hast not s *it* unto thy servant, H3045
3: 6 And Solomon said, Thou hast s unto H6213
16:27 his might that he s, *are* they not written H6213
22:45 his might that he s, and how he warred, H6213
2Ki 6: 6 fell it? And he s him the place. And H7200
8:10 hath s me that he shall surely die. H7200
13 s me that thou *shalt be* king over Syria. H7200
11: 4 of the LORD, and s them the king's son. H7200
20:13 unto them, and s them all the house of H7200
13 dominion, that Hezekiah s them not. H7200
15 my treasures that I have not s them. H7200
22:10 And Shaphan the scribe s the king, H5046
1Ch 19: 2 because his father s kindness to me. H6213
2Ch 1: 8 God, Thou hast s great mercy unto H6213
7:10 the LORD had s unto David, and to H6213
Ezr 9: 8 grace hath been *s* from the LORD our
Est 1: 4 When he s the riches of his glorious H7200
2:10 Esther had not s her people nor her H5046
20 Esther had not *yet* s her kindred nor H5046
3: 6 alone; for they had s him the people of H5046
Job 6:14 To him that is afflicted pity *should be* s
Ps 31:21 Blessed *be* the LORD: for he hath s me
60: 3 Thou hast s thy people hard things: H7200
71:18 me not; until I have s thy strength unto H5046
20 *Thou*, which hast s me great and sore H7200
78:11 and his wonders that he had s them. H7200
98: 2 he openly s in the sight of the heathen. H1540
105:27 They s his signs among them, and H7760
111: 6 He hath s his people the power of his H5046
118:27 God *is* the LORD, which hath s us light:
142: 2 before him; I s before him my trouble. H5046
Prv 26:26 be s before the *whole* congregation. H1540
Ecc 2:19 and wherein I have s myself wise under
Isa 26:10 Let favour be s to the wicked, *yet* will H2603
39: 2 And Hezekiah was glad of them, and s H7200
2 dominion, that Hezekiah s them not. H7200
4 my treasures that I have not s them. H7200

Isa 40:14 s to him the way of understanding? H3045
43:12 saved, and I have s, when *there was* no H8085
48: 3 of my mouth, and I s them; I did *them* H8085
5 it came to pass I s *it* thee: lest thou H8085
6 ye declare *it*? I have s thee new things H8085
Jer 24: 1 The LORD s me, and, behold, two H7200
38:21 *is* the word that the LORD hath s me: H7200
Ezk 11:25 all the things that the LORD had s me. H7200
20:11 And I gave them my statutes, and s H3045
22:26 neither have they s *difference* between H3045
Am 7: 1 Thus hath the Lord GOD s unto me; H7200
4 Thus hath the Lord GOD s unto me: H7200
7 Thus he s me: and, behold, the Lord H7200
8: 1 Thus hath the Lord GOD s unto me: H7200
Mic 6: 8 He hath s thee, O man, what *is* good; H5046
Zec 1:20 And the LORD s me four carpenters. H7200
3: 1 And he s me Joshua the high priest H7200
Mt 28:11 into the city, and s unto the chief priests G518
Lk 1:51 He hath s strength with his arm; he G4160
58 how the Lord had s great mercy upon G3170
4: 5 an high mountain, s unto him all the G1166
7:18 And the disciples of John s him of all G518
10:37 And he said, He that s mercy on him. G4160
14:21 So that servant came, and s his lord G518
20:37 even Moses s at the bush, when he G3377
24:40 And when he had thus spoken, he s G1925
Jn 10:32 good works have I s you from my G1166
20:20 And when he had so said, he s unto G1166
21: 1 After these things Jesus s himself again G5319
1 Tiberias; and on this wise s he *himself*. G5319
14 This is now the third time that Jesus s G5319
Act 1: 3 To whom also he s himself alive after G3936
3:18 God before had s by the mouth of all G4293
4:22 on whom this miracle of healing was s. G1096
7:26 And the next day he s himself unto G3700
36 after that he had s wonders and signs G4160
52 have slain them which s before of the G4293
10:28 but God hath s me that I should not G1166
40 day, and s him openly; G1325+G1717+1096
11:13 And he s us how he had seen an angel in G518
19:18 came, and confessed, and s their deeds. G312
20:20 *unto you*, but have s you, and have G312
35 I have s you all things, how that so G5263
23:22 that thou hast s these things to me. G1718
26:20 But s first unto them of Damascus, and G518
28: 2 And the barbarous people s us no little G3930
21 that came s or spake any harm of thee. G518
Ro 1:19 in them; for God hath s *it* unto them. G5319
1Co 10:28 for his sake that s it, and for conscience G3377
Heb 6:10 which ye have s toward his name, in G1731
8: 5 to the pattern s to thee in the mount. G1166
Jas 2:13 mercy, that hath s no mercy; and G4160
2Pt 1:14 as our Lord Jesus Christ hath s me. G1213
Rev 21:10 mountain, and s me that great city, the G1166
22: 1 And he s me a pure river of water of G1166
8 of the angel which s me these things. G1166

SHEWEDST
Neh 9:10 And s signs and wonders upon H5414
Jer 11:18 I know *it*: then thou s me their doings. H7200

SHEWEST
2Ch 6:14 keepest covenant, and *s* mercy unto thy
Job 10:16 thou s thyself marvellous upon me.
Jer 32:18 Thou s lovingkindness unto thousands, H6213
Jn 2:18 him, What sign s thou unto us, seeing G1166
6:30 him, What sign s thou then, that we G4160

SHEWETH
Gen 41:28 God *is* about to do he s unto Pharaoh. H7200
Nu 23: 3 whatsoever he s me I will tell thee. And H7200
1Sa 22: 8 *there is* none that s me that my son H1540
8 is sorry for me, or s unto me that my H1540
2Sa 22:51 for his king: and s mercy to his H6213
Job 36: 9 Then he s them their work, and their H5046
33 The noise thereof s concerning it, the H5046
Ps 18:50 giveth he to his king; and s mercy to his H6213
19: 1 and the firmament s his handywork. H5046
2 and night unto night s knowledge. H2331
37:21 but the righteous s mercy, and giveth.
112: 5 A good man s favour, and lendeth: he
147:19 He s his word unto Jacob, his statutes H5046
Prv 12:17 *He that* speaketh truth s forth H5046
27:25 the tender grass s itself, and herbs of H7200
Isa 41:26 *there is* none that s, yea, *there is* none H5046
Mt 4: 8 mountain, and s him all the kingdoms G1166
Jn 5:20 For the Father loveth the Son, and s G1166
Ro 9:16 that runneth, but of God that s mercy. G1653
12: 8 he that s mercy, with cheerfulness. G1653

SHEWING
Ex 20: 6 And s mercy unto thousands of them H6213
Dt 5:10 And s mercy unto thousands of them H6213
Ps 78: 4 their children, s to the generation to H5608
Song 2: 9 windows, s himself through the lattice. H6692
Dan 4:27 thine iniquities by s mercy to the poor; if
5:12 of dreams, and s of hard sentences, and H263
Lk 1:80 deserts till the day of his s unto Israel. G323
8: 1 preaching and s the glad tidings of the
Act 9:39 by him weeping, and s the coats and G1925
18:28 *that* publickly, s by the scriptures that G1925
2Th 2: 4 temple of God, s himself that he is God. G584
Tit 2: 7 In all things s thyself a pattern of good G3930
7 *s* uncorruptness, gravity, sincerity,
10 Not purloining, but s all good fidelity; G1731
3: 2 *but* gentle, s all meekness unto all men. G1731

SHIBBOLETH
Jdg 12: 6 Then said they unto him, Say now S: H7641

SHIBMAH
Nu 32:38 changed,) and S: and gave other names H7643

SHICRON
Jos 15:11 was drawn to S, and passed along to H7942

SHIELD
Gen 15: 1 thy s, *and* thy exceeding great reward. H4043
Dt 33:29 by the LORD, the s of thy help, and H4043
Jdg 5: 8 the gates: was there a s or spear seen H4043
1Sa 17: 7 and one bearing a s went before him. H6793
41 man that bare the s *went* before him. H6793
45 a spear, and with a s: but I come to thee H3591
2Sa 1:21 for there the s of the mighty is vilely H4043
21 cast away, the s of Saul, *as though he* H4043
22: 3 I trust: *he is* my s, and the horn of my H4043
36 Thou hast also given me the s of thy H4043
1Ki 10:17 of gold went to one s: and the king put H4043
2Ki 19:32 it with s, nor cast a bank against it. H4043
1Ch 12: 8 that could handle s and buckler, whose H6793
24 The children of Judah that bare s and H6793
34 s and spear thirty and seven thousand. H6793
2Ch 9:16 of gold went to one s. And the king put H4043
17:17 with bow and s two hundred thousand. H4043
25: 5 to war, that could handle spear and s. H6793
Job 39:23 him, the glittering spear and the s. H3591
Ps 3: 3 But thou, O LORD, *art* a s for me; my H4043
5:12 wilt thou compass him as *with* a s. H6793
18:35 Thou hast also given me the s of thy H4043
28: 7 The LORD *is* my strength and my s; my H4043
33:20 for the LORD: he *is* our help and our s. H4043
35: 2 Take hold of s and buckler, and stand H4043
59:11 and bring them down, O Lord our s. H4043
76: 3 s, and the sword, and the battle. Selah. H4043
84: 9 Behold, O God our s, and look upon the H4043
11 For the LORD God *is* a sun and s: the H4043
91: 4 his truth *shall be thy* s and buckler. H6793
115: 9 in the LORD: he *is* their help and their s. H4043
10 in the LORD: he *is* their help and their s. H4043
11 in the LORD: he *is* their help and their s. H4043
119:114 Thou *art* my hiding place and my s: I H4043
144: 2 my deliverer; my s, and *he* in whom I H4043
Prv 30: 5 Every word of God *is* pure: he *is* a s H4043
Isa 21: 5 arise, ye princes, *and* anoint the s. H4043
22: 6 *and* horsemen, and Kir uncovered the s. H4043
Jer 46: 3 Order ye the buckler and s, and draw H6793
9 that handle the s; and the Lydians, that H4043
Ezk 23:24 thee buckler and s and helmet round H4043
27:10 they hanged the s and helmet in thee; H4043
38: 5 them; all of them with s and helmet: H4043
Nah 2: 3 The s of his mighty men is made red, H4043
Eph 6:16 Above all, taking the s of faith, G2375

SHIELDS
2Sa 8: 7 And David took the s of gold that were H7982
1Ki 10:17 And *he made* three hundred s *of* H4043
14:26 the s of gold which Solomon had made. H4043
27 in their stead brasen s, and committed H4043
2Ki 11:10 s, that *were* in the temple of the LORD. H7982
1Ch 18: 7 And David took the s of gold that were H7982
2Ch 9:16 And three hundred s *made he of* H4043
11:12 And in every several city *he put* s and H6793
12: 9 the s of gold which Solomon had made. H4043
10 king Rehoboam made s of brass, and H4043
14: 8 that bare s and drew bows, two H4043
23: 9 and bucklers, and s, that *had been* king H7982
26:14 all the host s, and spears, and helmets, H4043
32: 5 and made darts and s in abundance. H4043
27 s, and for all manner of pleasant jewels; H4043
Neh 4:16 the spears, the s, and the bows, and the H4043
Ps 47: 9 Abraham: for the s of the earth *belong* H4043
Song 4: 4 thousand bucklers, all s of mighty men. H7982
Isa 37:33 it with s, nor cast a bank against it. H4043
Jer 51:11 Make bright the arrows; gather the s: H7982
Ezk 27:11 they hanged their s upon thy walls H7982
38: 4 and s, all of them handling swords: H4043
39: 9 weapons, both the s and the bucklers, H4043

SHIGGAION
Ps 7:ttl S of David, which he sang unto the H7692

SHIGIONOTH
Hab 3: 1 of Habakkuk the prophet upon S. H7692

SHIHOR
1Ch 13: 5 together, from S of Egypt even unto H7883

SHIHOR-LIBNATH
Jos 19:26 reacheth to Carmel westward, and to S; H7884

SHILHI
1Ki 22:42 name *was* Azubah the daughter of S. H7977
2Ch 20:31 name *was* Azubah the daughter of S. H7977

SHILHIM
Jos 15:32 And Lebaoth, and S, and Ain, and H7978

SHILLEM
Gen 46:24 Jahzeel, and Guni, and Jezer, and S. H8006
Nu 26:49 Of Jezer, the family of the Jezerites: of S, H8006

SHILLEMITES
Nu 26:49 Jezerites: of Shillem, the family of the S. H8016

SHILOAH
Isa 8: 6 the waters of S that go softly, and H7975

SHILOH
Gen 49:10 his feet, until S come; and unto him H7886
Jos 18: 1 together at S, and set up the tabernacle H7887
8 cast lots for you before the LORD in S. H7887
9 came *again* to Joshua to the host at S. H7887
10 And Joshua cast lots for them in S H7887
19:51 by lot in S before the LORD, at H7887
21: 2 And they spake unto them at S in the H7887
22: 9 of Israel out of S, which *is* in the land H7887
12 at S, to go up to war against them. H7887
Jdg 18:31 the time that the house of God was in S. H7887
21:12 to S, which *is* in the land of Canaan. H7887
19 feast of the LORD in S yearly *in a place* H7887
21 if the daughters of S come out to dance H7887
21 of S, and go to the land of Benjamin. H7887
1Sa 1: 3 LORD of hosts in S. And the two sons of H7887
9 they had eaten in S, and after they had H7887
24 LORD in S: and the child *was* young. H7887
2:14 So they did in S unto all the Israelites H7887
3:21 And the LORD appeared again in S: for H7887
21 Samuel in S by the word of the LORD. H7887
4: 3 the LORD out of S unto us, that, when H7887
4 So the people sent to S, that they might H7887
12 and came to S the same day with his H7887
14: 3 LORD'S priest in S, wearing an ephod. H7887
1Ki 2:27 spake concerning the house of Eli in S. H7887
14: 2 and get thee to S: behold, there *is* H7887
4 arose, and went to S, and came to the H7887
Ps 78:60 So that he forsook the tabernacle of S, H7887
Jer 7:12 which *was* in S, where I set my name H7887
14 and to your fathers, as I have done to S. H7887
26: 6 Then will I make this house like S, and H7887
9 house shall be like S, and this city shall H7887
41: 5 Shechem, from S, and from Samaria, H7887

SHILONI
Neh 11: 5 the son of Zechariah, the son of S. H8023

SHILONITE
1Ki 11:29 Ahijah the S found him in the way; H7888
12:15 the S unto Jeroboam the son of Nebat. H7888
15:29 he spake by his servant Ahijah the S: H7888
2Ch 9:29 of Ahijah the S, and in the visions of H7888
10:15 the S to Jeroboam the son of Nebat. H7888

SHILONITES
1Ch 9: 5 And of the S; Asaiah the firstborn, and H7888

SHILSHAH
1Ch 7:37 Bezer, and Hod, and Shamma, and S, H8030

SHIMEA
2Sa 21:21 son of S the brother of David slew him. H8092
1Ch 3: 5 him in Jerusalem; S, and Shobab, and H8092
6:30 S his son, Haggiah his son, Asaiah his H8092
39 the son of Berachiah, the son of S, H8092
20: 7 the son of S David's brother slew him. H8092

SHIMEAH
2Sa 13: 3 the son of S David's brother: and H8093
32 And Jonadab, the son of S David's H8093
1Ch 8:32 And Mikloth begat S. And these also H8039

SHIMEAM
1Ch 9:38 And Mikloth begat S. And they also H8043

SHIMEATH
2Ki 12:21 For Jozachar the son of S, and H8100
2Ch 24:26 Zabad the son of S an Ammonitess, H8100

SHIMEATHITES
1Ch 2:55 the Tirathites, the S, *and* Suchathites. H8101

SHIMEI
Nu 3:18 Gershon by their families; Libni, and S. H8096
2Sa 16: 5 whose name *was* S, the son of Gera: he H8096
7 And thus said S when he cursed, Come H8096
13 went by the way, S went along on the H8096
19:16 And S the son of Gera, a Benjamite, H8096
18 good. And S the son of Gera fell H8096
21 and said, Shall not S be put to death for H8096
23 Therefore the king said unto S, Thou H8096
1Ki 1: 8 the prophet, and S, and Rei, and the H8096
2: 8 And, behold, *thou hast* with thee S the H8096
36 And the king sent and called for S, and H8096
38 And S said unto the king, The saying *is* H8096
38 And S dwelt in Jerusalem many days. H8096
39 two of the servants of S ran away unto H8096
39 And they told S, saying, Behold, thy H8096
40 And S arose, and saddled his ass, and H8096
40 his servants: and S went, and brought H8096
41 And it was told Solomon that S had H8096
42 And the king sent and called for S, and H8096
44 The king said moreover to S, Thou H8096
4:18 S the son of Elah, in Benjamin: H8096
1Ch 3:19 Zerubbabel, and S: and the sons of H8096
4:26 his son, Zacchur his son, S his son. H8096
27 And S had sixteen sons and six H8096
5: 4 his son, Gog his son, S his son, H8096
6:17 of the sons of Gershom; Libni, and S. H8096
29 Libni his son, S his son, Uzza his son, H8096
42 Ethan, the son of Zimmah, the son of S, H8096
23: 7 Of the Gershonites *were*, Laadan, and S. H8096
9 The sons of S; Shelomith, and Haziel, H8096
10 And the sons of S *were*, Jahath, Zina, H8096
10 Beriah. These four *were* the sons of S. H8096
25:17 The tenth to S, *he*, his sons, and his H8096
27:27 And over the vineyards *was* S the H8096
2Ch 29:14 Heman; Jehiel, and S: and of the sons of H8096
31:12 ruler, and S his brother *was* the next. H8096
13 of Cononiah and S his brother, at the H8096
Ezr 10:23 Also of the Levites; Jozabad, and S, and H8096
33 Eliphelet, Jeremai, Manasseh, *and* S. H8096
38 And Bani, and Binnui, S, H8096
Est 2: 5 son of S, the son of Kish, a Benjamite; H8096
Zec 12:13 of S apart, and their wives apart; H8097

SHIMEON
Ezr 10:31 Eliezer, Ishijah, Malchiah, Shemaiah, S, H8095

SHIMHI
1Ch 8:21 Beraiah, and Shimrath, the sons of S; H8096

SHIMI
Ex 6:17 The sons of Gershon; Libni, and S, H8096

SHIMITES
Nu 3:21 and the family of the S: these *are* the H8097

SHIMMA
1Ch 2:13 Abinadab the second, and S the third, H8092

SHIMON
1Ch 4:20 And the sons of S *were*, Amnon, and H7889

SHIMRATH
1Ch 8:21 And Adaiah, and Beraiah, and S, the H8119

SHIMRI
1Ch 4:37 the son of S, the son of Shemaiah; H8113
1Ch 11:45 Jediael the son of S, and Joha his H8113
2Ch 29:13 And of the sons of Elizaphan; S, and H8113

SHIMRITH
2Ch 24:26 Jehozabad the son of S a Moabitess. H8116

SHIMRON
Gen 46:13 Tola, and Phuvah, and Job, and S. H8110
Nu 26:24 of S, the family of the Shimronites. H8110
Jos 11: 1 king of S, and to the king of Achshaph, H8110
19:15 And Kattath, and Nahallal, and S, and H8110
1Ch 7: 1 Tola, and Puah, Jashub, and S, four. H8110

SHIMRONITES
Nu 26:24 of Shimron, the family of the S. H8117

SHIMRON-MERON
Jos 12:20 The king of S, one; the king of H8112

SHIMSHAI
Ezr 4: 8 Rehum the chancellor and S the scribe H8124
9 chancellor, and S the scribe, and the H8124
17 chancellor, and *to* S the scribe, and *to* H8124
23 Rehum, and S the scribe, and their H8124

SHINAB
Gen 14: 2 king of Gomorrah, S king of Admah, H8134

SHINAR
Gen 10:10 and Accad, and Calneh, in the land of S. H8152
11: 2 in the land of S; and they dwelt there. H8152
14: 1 of Amraphel king of S, Arioch king of H8152
9 Amraphel king of S, and Arioch king of H8152
Isa 11:11 Elam, and from S, and from Hamath, H8152
Dan 1: 2 into the land of S to the house of his H8152
Zec 5:11 house in the land of S: and it shall be H8152

SHINE
Nu 6:25 The LORD make his face s upon thee, H215
Job 3: 4 above, neither let the light s upon it. H3313
10: 3 and s upon the counsel of the wicked? H3313
11:17 s forth, thou shalt be as the morning. H5774
18: 5 out, and the spark of his fire shall not s. H5050
22:28 and the light shall s upon thy ways. H5050
36:32 *to* s by *the cloud* that cometh betwixt.
37:15 and caused the light of his cloud to s? H3313
41:18 By his neesings a light doth s, and his H1984
32 He maketh a path to s after him; *one* H215
Ps 31:16 Make thy face to s upon thy servant: H215
67: 1 *and* cause his face to s upon us; Selah. H215
80: 1 *between* the cherubims, s forth. H3313
3 thy face to s; and we shall be saved. H215
7 thy face to s; and we shall be saved. H215
19 thy face to s; and we shall be saved. H215
104:15 to make *his* face to s, and bread *which* H6670
119:135 Make thy face to s upon thy servant; and H215
Ecc 8: 1 maketh his face to s, and the boldness of H215
Isa 13:10 the moon shall not cause her light to s. H5050
60: 1 Arise, s; for thy light is come, and the H215
Jer 5:28 They are waxen fat, they s: yea, they H6245
Dan 9:17 cause thy face to s upon thy sanctuary H215
12: 3 And they that be wise shall s as the H2094
Mt 5:16 Let your light so s before men, that G2989
13:43 Then shall the righteous s forth as the G1584
17: 2 and his face did s as the sun, and his G2989
2Co 4: 4 is the image of God, should s unto them. G826
6 the light to s out of darkness, hath G2989
Php 2:15 whom ye s as lights in the world; G5316
Rev 18:23 And the light of a candle shall s no G5316
21:23 of the moon, to s in it: for the glory of G5316

SHINED
Dt 33: 2 Seir unto them; he s forth from mount H3313
Job 29: 3 When his candle s upon my head, *and* H1984
31:26 If I beheld the sun when it s, or the H1984
Ps 50: 2 the perfection of beauty, God hath s. H3313
Isa 9: 2 of death, upon them hath the light s. H5050
Ezk 43: 2 waters: and the earth s with his glory. H215
Act 9: 3 s round about him a light from heaven: G4015
12: 7 *him*, and a light s in the prison: and he G2989
2Co 4: 6 out of darkness, hath s in our hearts, to G2989

SHINETH
Job 25: 5 Behold even to the moon, and it s not; H166
Ps 139:12 from thee; but the night s as the day: the H215
Prv 4:18 s more and more unto the perfect day. H215
Mt 24:27 of the east, and s even unto the west; G5316
Lk 17:24 under heaven, s unto the other *part* G2989
Jn 1: 5 And the light s in darkness; and the G5316
2Pt 1:19 unto a light that s in a dark place, until G5316
1Jn 2: 8 is past, and the true light now s. G5316
Rev 1:16 *was* as the sun s in his strength. G5316

SHINING
2Sa 23: 4 out of the earth by clear s after rain. H5051
Prv 4:18 But the path of the just *is* as the s light, H5051
Isa 4: 5 by day, and the s of a flaming fire by H5051
Joel 2:10 and the stars shall withdraw their s: H5051
3:15 and the stars shall withdraw their s. H5051
Hab 3:11 *and* at the s of thy glittering spear. H5051
Mk 9: 3 And his raiment became s, exceeding G4744
Lk 11:36 bright s of a candle doth give thee light. G796
24: 4 two men stood by them in s garments: G797
Jn 5:35 He was a burning and a s light: and ye G5316
Act 26:13 of the sun, s round about me and G4034

SHION
Jos 19:19 And Hapharaim, and S, and H7866

SHIP
Prv 30:19 a rock; the way of a s in the midst of the H591
Isa 33:21 neither shall gallant s pass thereby. H6716
Ezk 27: 5 They have made all thy *s* boards of fir
Jna 1: 3 and he found a s going to Tarshish: so H591
4 sea, so that the s was like to be broken. H591
5 that *were* in the s into the sea, to lighten H591
5 of the s; and he lay, and was fast asleep. H5600
Mt 4:21 his brother, in a s with Zebedee their G4143
22 And they immediately left the s and G4143
8:23 And when he was entered into a s, his G4143
24 insomuch that the s was covered with G4143
9: 1 And he entered into a s, and passed G4143
13: 2 that he went into a s, and sat; and the G4143
14:13 thence by s into a desert place apart: G4143
22 to get into a s, and to go before him G4143
24 But the s was now in the midst of the G4143
29 down out of the s, he walked on the G4143
32 And when they were come into the s, G4143
33 Then they that were in the s came and G4143
15:39 s, and came into the coasts of Magdala. G4143
Mk 1:19 also were in the s mending their nets. G4143
20 father Zebedee in the s with the hired G4143
3: 9 that a small s should wait on him G4142
4: 1 he entered into a s, and sat in the sea; G4143
36 as he was in the s. And there were also G4143
37 beat into the s, so that it was now full. G4143
38 And he was in the hinder part of the s, G4403
5: 2 And when he was come out of the s, G4143
18 And when he was come into the s, he G4143
21 over again by s unto the other side, G4143
6:32 into a desert place by s privately. G4143
45 to get into the s, and to go to the other G4143
47 And when even was come, the s was in G4143
51 And he went up unto them into the s; G4143
54 And when they were come out of the s, G4143
8:10 And straightway he entered into a s G4143
13 the s again departed to the other side. G4143
14 in the s with them more than one loaf. G4143
Lk 5: 3 and taught the people out of the s. G4143
7 were in the other s, that they should G4143
8:22 that he went into a s with his disciples: G4143
37 up into the s, and returned back again. G4143
Jn 6:17 And entered into a s, and went over the G4143
19 nigh unto the s: and they were afraid. G4143
21 him into the s: and immediately the G4143
21 s was at the land whither they went. G4143
21: 3 and entered into a s immediately; and G4143
6 the right side of the s, and ye shall find. G4143
8 came in a little s; (for they were not far G4142
Act 20:13 And we went before to s, and sailed G4143
38 And they accompanied him unto the s. G4143
21: 2 And finding a s sailing over unto G4143
3 there the s was to unlade her burden. G4143
6 took s; and they returned home again. G4143
27: 2 And entering into a s of Adramyttium, G4143
6 And there the centurion found a s of G4143
10 of the lading and s, but also of our lives. G4143
11 and the owner of the s, more than those G3490
15 And when the s was caught, and could G4143
17 undergirding the s; and, fearing lest G4143
18 the next *day* they lightened the s; G1546
19 our own hands the tackling of the s. G4143
22 *any man's* life among you, but of the s. G4143
30 to flee out of the s, when they had let G4143
31 these abide in the s, ye cannot be saved. G4143
37 And we were in all in the s two G4143
38 s, and cast out the wheat into the sea. G4143
39 if it were possible, to thrust in the s. G4143

Act 27:41 met, they ran the s aground; and the G3491
44 *pieces* of the s. And so it came to pass, G4143
28:11 we departed in a s of Alexandria, G4143

SHIPHI
1Ch 4:37 And Ziza the son of S, the son of Allon, H8230

SHIPHMITE
1Ch 27:27 for the wine cellars *was* Zabdi the S: H8225

SHIPHRAH
Ex 1:15 *was* S, and the name of the other Puah: H8236

SHIPHTAN
Nu 34:24 of Ephraim, Kemuel the son of S. H8204

SHIPMASTER
Jna 1: 6 So the s came to him, and said H7227+H2259
Rev 18:17 to nought. And every s, and all the G2942

SHIPMEN
1Ki 9:27 navy his servants, s that had H582+H591
Act 27:27 midnight the s deemed that they drew G3492
30 And as the s were about to flee out of G3492

SHIPPING
Jn 6:24 disciples, they also took s, and came to G4143

SHIPS
Gen 49:13 of s; and his border *shall be* unto Zidon. H591
Nu 24:24 And s *shall come* from the coast of H6716
Dt 28:68 Egypt again with s, by the way whereof I H591
Jdg 5:17 did Dan remain in s? Asher continued on H591
1Ki 9:26 And king Solomon made a navy of s in H590
22:48 Jehoshaphat made s of Tharshish to go H591
48 for the s were broken at Ezion-geber. H591
49 in the s. But Jehoshaphat would not. H591
2Ch 8:18 of his servants s, and servants that had H591
9:21 For the king's s went to Tarshish with H591
21 once came the s of Tarshish bringing H591
20:36 with him to make s to go to Tarshish: H591
36 and they made the s in Ezion-geber. H591
37 thy works. And the s were broken, that H591
Job 9:26 They are passed away as the swift s: as H591
Ps 48: 7 Thou breakest the s of Tarshish with an H591
104:26 There go the s: *there is* that leviathan, H591
107:23 They that go down to the sea in s, that do H591
Prv 31:14 She is like the merchants' s; she bringeth H591
Isa 2:16 And upon all the s of Tarshish, and H591
23: 1 The burden of Tyre. Howl, ye s of H591
14 Howl, ye s of Tarshish: for your strength H591
43:14 and the Chaldeans, whose cry *is* in the s. H591
60: 9 for me, and the s of Tarshish first, to H591
Ezk 27: 9 thy calkers: all the s of the sea with their H591
25 The s of Tarshish did sing of thee in thy H591
29 their s, they shall stand upon the land; H591
30: 9 forth from me in s to make the careless H6716
Dan 11:30 For the s of Chittim shall come against H6716
40 and with many s; and he shall enter into H591
Mk 4:36 there were also with him other little s. G4142
Lk 5: 2 And saw two s standing by the lake: G4143
3 And he entered into one of the s, which G4143
7 both the s, so that they began to sink. G4143
11 And when they had brought their s to G4143
Jas 3: 4 Behold also the s, which though *they be* G4143
Rev 8: 9 the third part of the s were destroyed. G4143
18:17 all the company in s, and sailors, and G4143
19 rich all that had s in the sea by reason G4143

SHIPWRECK
2Co 11:25 thrice I suffered s, a night and a day I G3489
1Ti 1:19 put away concerning faith have made s: G3489

SHISHA
1Ki 4: 3 Elihoreph and Ahiah, the sons of S, H7894

SHISHAK
1Ki 11:40 into Egypt, unto S king of Egypt, and H7895
14:25 Rehoboam, *that* S king of Egypt came H7895
2Ch 12: 2 year of king Rehoboam S king of Egypt H7895
5 because of S, and said unto them, H7895
5 have I also left you in the hand of S. H7895
7 out upon Jerusalem by the hand of S. H7895
9 So S king of Egypt came up against H7895

SHITRAI
1Ch 27:29 fed in Sharon *was* S the Sharonite: and H7861

SHITTAH
Isa 41:19 the cedar, the s tree, and the myrtle, H7848

SHITTAH-TREE See SHITTAH and TREE.

SHITTIM
Ex 25: 5 red, and badgers' skins, and s wood, H7848
10 And they shall make an ark *of* s wood: H7848
13 And thou shalt make staves *of* s wood, H7848
23 Thou shalt also make a table *of* s wood: H7848
28 And thou shalt make the staves *of* s H7848
26:15 the tabernacle *of* s wood standing up. H7848
26 And thou shalt make bars *of* s wood; H7848
32 four pillars of s *wood* overlaid with H7848
37 five pillars *of* s *wood*, and overlay them H7848
27: 1 And thou shalt make an altar *of* s H7848
6 s wood, and overlay them with brass. H7848
30: 1 upon: *of* s wood shalt thou make it. H7848
5 And thou shalt make the staves *of* s H7848
35: 7 red, and badgers' skins, and s wood, H7848
24 whom was found s wood for any work H7848
36:20 the tabernacle *of* s wood, standing up. H7848
31 And he made bars of s wood; five for H7848
36 And he made thereunto four pillars *of* s H7848
37: 1 And Bezaleel made the ark *of* s wood: H7848
4 And he made staves *of* s wood, and H7848
10 And he made the table *of* s wood: two H7848
15 And he made the staves *of* s wood, and H7848
25 And he made the incense altar *of* s H7848
28 And he made the staves *of* s wood, and H7848
38: 1 of burnt offering *of* s wood: five cubits H7848
6 And he made the staves *of* s wood, and H7848
Nu 25: 1 And Israel abode in S, and the people H7851
Dt 10: 3 And I made an ark *of* s wood, and H7848
Jos 2: 1 son of Nun sent out of S two men to spy H7851
3: 1 removed from S, and came to Jordan, H7851
Joel 3:18 LORD, and shall water the valley of S. H7851
Mic 6: 5 him from S unto Gilgal; that ye H7851

SHITTIM-WOOD See SHITTIM and WOOD.

SHIVERS
Rev 2:27 to s: even as I received of my Father. G4937

SHIZA
1Ch 11:42 Adina the son of S the Reubenite, a H7877

SHOA
Ezk 23:23 Pekod, and S, and Koa, *and* all the H7772

SHOBAB
2Sa 5:14 and S, and Nathan, and Solomon, H7727
1Ch 2:18 *are* these; Jesher, and S, and Ardon. H7727
3: 5 Shimea, and S, and Nathan, and H7727
14: 4 and S, Nathan, and Solomon, H7727

SHOBACH
2Sa 10:16 to Helam; and S the captain of the host H7731
18 and smote S the captain of their H7731

SHOBAI
Ezr 2:42 of S, *in* all an hundred thirty and nine. H7630
Neh 7:45 of S, an hundred thirty and eight. H7630

SHOBAL
Gen 36:20 Lotan, and S, and Zibeon, and Anah, H7732
23 And the children of S *were* these; H7732
29 duke S, duke Zibeon, duke Anah, H7732
1Ch 1:38 And the sons of Seir; Lotan, and S, and H7732
40 The sons of S; Alian, and Manahath, H7732
2:50 S the father of Kirjath-jearim, H7732
52 And S the father of Kirjath-jearim had H7732
4: 1 Hezron, and Carmi, and Hur, and S. H7732
2 And Reaiah the son of S begat Jahath; H7732

SHOBEK
Neh 10:24 Hallohesh, Pileha, S, H7733

SHOBI
2Sa 17:27 Mahanaim, that S the son of Nahash of H7629

SHOCHO
2Ch 28:18 and Gederoth, and S with the villages H7755

SHOCHOH
1Sa 17: 1 together at S, which *belongeth* to H7755
1 S and Azekah, in Ephes-dammim. H7755

SHOCK
Job 5:26 as a s of corn cometh in in his season. H1430

SHOCKS
Jdg 15: 5 and burnt up both the s, and also the H1430

SHOCO
2Ch 11: 7 And Beth-zur, and S, and Adullam, H7755

SHOD
2Ch 28:15 arrayed them, and s them, and gave H5274
Ezk 16:10 work, and s thee with badgers' skin, H5274
Mk 6: 9 But *be* s with sandals; and not put on G5265
Eph 6:15 And your feet s with the preparation of G5265

SHOE
Dt 25: 9 and loose his s from off his foot, and H5275
10 house of him that hath his s loosed. H5275
29: 5 thy s is not waxen old upon thy foot. H5275
Jos 5:15 Joshua, Loose thy s from off thy foot; H5275
Ru 4: 7 man plucked off his s, and gave *it* to his H5275
8 Buy *it* for thee. So he drew off his s. H5275
Ps 60: 8 will I cast out my s: Philistia, triumph H5275
108: 9 out my s; over Philistia will I triumph. H5275
Isa 20: 2 and put off thy s from thy foot. And he H5275

SHOE-LATCHET
Gen 14:23 even to a s, and that I will not H8288+H5275

SHOES
Ex 3: 5 hither: put off thy s from off thy feet, H5275
12:11 loins girded, your s on your feet, and H5275
Dt 33:25 Thy s *shall be* iron and brass; and as H4515
Jos 9: 5 And old s and clouted upon their feet, H5275
13 garments and our s are become old by H5275
1Ki 2: 5 loins, and in his s that *were* on his feet. H5275
Song 7: 1 How beautiful are thy feet with s, O H5275
Isa 5:27 nor the latchet of their s be broken: H5275
Ezk 24:17 and put on thy s upon thy feet, and H5275
23 heads, and your s upon your feet: ye H5275
Am 2: 6 for silver, and the poor for a pair of s; H5275
8: 6 s; *yea*, and sell the refuse of the wheat? H5275
Mt 3:11 than I, whose s I am not worthy to G5266
10:10 two coats, neither s, nor yet staves: for G5266
Mk 1: 7 latchet of whose s I am not worthy to G5266
Lk 3:16 latchet of whose s I am not worthy to G5266
10: 4 Carry neither purse, nor scrip, nor s: G5266
15:22 a ring on his hand, and s on *his* feet: G5266
22:35 and scrip, and s, lacked ye any thing? G5266
Act 7:33 Then said the Lord to him, Put off thy s G5266
13:25 s of *his* feet I am not worthy to loose. G5266

SHOE'S
Jn 1:27 s latchet I am not worthy to unloose. G5266

SHOHAM
1Ch 24:27 Beno, and S, and Zaccur, and Ibri. H7719

SHOMER
2Ki 12:21 the son of S, his servants, smote H7763
1Ch 7:32 And Heber begat Japhlet, and S, and H7763

S

SHONE
Ex 34:29 of his face s while he talked with him. H7160
30 the skin of his face s; and they were H7160
35 of Moses' face s: and Moses put the vail H7160
2Ki 3:22 and the sun s upon the water, and H2224
Lk 2: 9 glory of the Lord s round about them: G4034
Act 22: 6 suddenly there s from heaven a great G4015
Rev 8:12 and the day s not for a third part G5316

SHOOK
2Sa 6: 6 and took hold of it; for the oxen s *it*. H8058
22: 8 Then the earth s and trembled; the H1607
8 moved and s, because he was wroth. H1607
Neh 5:13 Also I s my lap, and said, So God shake H5287
Ps 18: 7 Then the earth s and trembled; the H1607
68: 8 The earth s, the heavens also dropped H7493
77:18 the world: the earth trembled and s. H7493
Isa 23:11 over the sea, he s the kingdoms: the H7264
Act 13:51 But they s off the dust of their feet G1621
18: 6 blasphemed, he s *his* raiment, and said G1621
28: 5 And he s off the beast into the fire, and G660
Heb 12:26 Whose voice then s the earth: but now G4531

SHOOT
Ex 36:33 And he made the middle bar to s H1272
1Sa 20:20 And I will s three arrows on the side H3384
36 the arrows which I s. *And* as the lad H3384

2Sa 11:20 ye not that they would s from the wall? H3384
2Ki 13:17 Then Elisha said, S. And he shot. And H3384
19:32 into this city, nor s an arrow there, nor H3384
1Ch 5:18 and sword, and to s with bow, and H1869
2Ch 26:15 the bulwarks, to s arrows and great H3384
Ps 11: 2 may privily s at the upright in heart. H3384
22: 7 me to scorn: they s out the lip, they H6362
58: 7 *s* his arrows, let them be as cut in pieces.
64: 3 *to s* their arrows, *even* bitter words:
4 That they may s in secret at the perfect: H3384
4 do they s at him, and fear not. H3384
7 But God shall s at them *with* an arrow; H3384
144: 6 s out thine arrows, and destroy them. H7971
Isa 37:33 into this city, nor s an arrow there, nor H3384
Jer 50:14 ye that bend the bow, s at her, spare no H3034
Ezk 31:14 height, neither s up their top among H5414
36: 8 But ye, O mountains of Israel, ye shall s H5414
Lk 21:30 When they now s forth, ye see and *G4261*

SHOOTERS
2Sa 11:24 And the s shot from off the wall upon H3384

SHOOTETH
Job 8:16 and his branch s forth in his garden. H3318
Isa 27: 8 In measure, when it s forth, thou wilt H7971
Mk 4:32 all herbs, and s out great branches; *G4160*

SHOOTING
1Ch 12: 2 in *hurling* stones and *s* arrows out of a
Am 7: 1 the beginning of the s up of the latter H5927

SHOPHACH
1Ch 19:16 the river: and S the captain of the host H7780
18 and killed S the captain of the host. H7780

SHOPHAN
Nu 32:35 And Atroth, S, and Jaazer, and H5855

SHORE
Gen 22:17 *is* upon the sea s; and thy seed shall H8193
Ex 14:30 saw the Egyptians dead upon the sea s. H8193
Jos 11: 4 *is* upon the sea s in multitude, with H8193
15: 2 And their south border was from the s H7097
Jdg 5:17 on the sea s, and abode in his breaches. H2348
1Sa 13: 5 *is* on the sea s in multitude: and they H8193
1Ki 4:29 even as the sand that *is* on the sea s. H8193
9:26 s of the Red sea, in the land of Edom. H8193
Jer 47: 7 the sea s? there hath he appointed it. H2348
Mt 13: 2 and the whole multitude stood on the s. *G123*
48 Which, when it was full, they drew to s, *G123*
Mk 6:53 land of Gennesaret, and drew to the s. *G4358*
Jn 21: 4 Jesus stood on the s: but the disciples *G123*
Act 21: 5 we kneeled down on the s, and prayed. *G123*
27:39 creek with a s, into the which they were *G123*
40 to the wind, and made toward s. *G123*
Heb 11:12 which is by the sea s innumerable. *G5491*

SHORN
Song 4: 2 *that are even* s, which came up from H7094
Act 18:18 Aquila; having s *his* head in Cenchrea: *G2751*
1Co 11: 6 let her also be s: but if it be a shame *G2751*
6 to be s or shaven, let her be covered. *G2751*

SHORT
Nu 11:23 hand waxed s? thou shalt see now H7114
2Ki 10:32 began to cut Israel s: and Hazael smote H7096
Job 17:12 day: the light *is* s because of darkness. H7138
20: 5 That the triumphing of the wicked *is* s, H7138
Ps 89:47 Remember how s my time is: H2465
Ro 3:23 For all have sinned, and come s of the *G5302*
9:28 For he will finish the work, and cut *it* s *G4932*
28 because a s work will the Lord make *G4932*
1Co 7:29 But this I say, brethren, the time *is* s: it *G4958*
1Th 2:17 from you for a s time in presence, not *G5610*
Heb 4: 1 any of you should seem to come s of it. *G5302*
Rev 12:12 he knoweth that he hath but a s time. *G3641*
17:10 he cometh, he must continue a s space. *G3641*

SHORTENED
Ps 89:45 The days of his youth hast thou s: thou H7114
102:23 my strength in the way; he s my days. H7114
Prv 10:27 but the years of the wicked shall be s. H7114
Isa 50: 2 Is my hand s at all, that it cannot H7114
59: 1 Behold, the LORD'S hand is not s, that H7114
Mt 24:22 And except those days should be s, *G2856*
22 for the elect's sake those days shall be s. *G2856*
Mk 13:20 And except that the Lord had s those *G2856*
20 he hath chosen, he hath s the days. *G2856*

SHORTER
Isa 28:20 For the bed is s than that *a man* can H7114
Ezk 42: 5 Now the upper chambers *were* s: for the H7114

SHORTLY
Gen 41:32 by God, and God will s bring it to pass. H4116
Jer 27:16 house shall now s be brought again H4120
Ezk 7: 8 Now will I s pour out my fury upon H7138
Act 25: 4 himself would depart s *thither.* *G1722+G5034*
Ro 16:20 your feet s. The grace of our *G1722+G5034*
1Co 4:19 But I will come to you s, if the Lord will, *G5030*
Php 2:19 to send Timotheus s unto you, that I *G5030*
24 the Lord that I also myself shall come s. *G5030*
1Ti 3:14 I unto thee, hoping to come unto thee s: *G5032*
2Ti 4: 9 Do thy diligence to come s unto me: *G5030*
Heb 13:23 with whom, if he come s, I will see you. *G5032*
2Pt 1:14 Knowing that s I must put off *this* my *G5031*
3Jn 14 But I trust I shall s see thee, and we *G2112*
Rev 1: 1 which must s come to pass; *G1722+G5034*
22: 6 things which must s be done. *G1722+G5034*

SHOSHANNIM
Ps 45:ttl To the chief Musician upon S, for the H7799
69:ttl To the chief Musician upon S, *A Psalm* H7799

SHOSHANNIM-EDUTH
Ps 80:ttl To the chief Musician upon S, A Psalm H7802

SHOT
Gen 40:10 *and* her blossoms s forth; and the H5927
49:23 him, and s *at him,* and hated him: H7232
Ex 19:13 be stoned, or s through; whether *it* H3384
Nu 21:30 We have s at them; Heshbon is H3384
1Sa 20:20 side *thereof,* as though I s at a mark. H7971
36 the lad ran, he s an arrow beyond him. H3384
37 Jonathan had s, Jonathan cried after H3384
2Sa 11:24 And the shooters s from off the wall H3384
2Ki 13:17 said, Shoot. And he s. And he said, The H3384
2Ch 35:23 And the archers s at king Josiah; and H3384
Ps 18:14 s out lightnings, and discomfited them. H7332
Jer 9: 8 Their tongue *is as* an arrow s out; it H7819
Ezk 17: 6 forth branches, and s forth sprigs. H7971
7 toward him, and s forth her branches H7971
31: 5 multitude of waters, when he s forth. H7971
10 and he hath s up his top among the H7971

SHOULD See the Appendix.

SHOULDER
Gen 21:14 putting *it* on her s, and the child, and H7926
24:15 brother, with her pitcher upon her s. H7926
45 her pitcher on her s; and she went down H7926
46 pitcher from her *s,* and said, Drink, and H7926
49:15 and bowed his s to bear, and became H7926
Ex 29:22 right s; for it *is* a ram of consecration: H7785
27 wave offering, and the s of the heave H7785
Lev 7:32 And the right s shall ye give unto the H7785
33 fat, shall have the right s for *his* part. H7785
34 For the wave breast and the heave s H7785
8:25 kidneys, and their fat, and the right s: H7785
26 *them* on the fat, and upon the right s: H7785
9:21 And the breasts and the right s Aaron H7785
10:14 And the wave breast and heave s shall H7785
15 The heave s and the wave breast shall H7785
Nu 6:19 And the priest shall take the sodden s H2220
20 breast and heave s: and after that the H7785
18:18 breast and as the right s are thine. H7785
Dt 18: 3 the s, and the two cheeks, and the maw. H2220
Jos 4: 5 a stone upon his s, according unto the H7926
Jdg 9:48 it, and laid *it* on his s, and said unto the H7926
1Sa 9:24 And the cook took up the s, and *that* H7785
Neh 9:29 and withdrew the s, and hardened their H3802
Job 31:22 *Then* let mine arm fall from my s H7929
36 Surely I would take it upon my s, *and* H7926
Ps 81: 6 I removed his s from the burden: his H7926
Isa 9: 4 and the staff of his s, the rod of his H7926
6 shall be upon his s: and his name shall H7926
10:27 away from off thy s, and his yoke from H7926
22:22 will I lay upon his s; so he shall open, H7926
46: 7 They bear him upon the s, they carry H3802
Ezk 12: 7 *and* I bare *it* upon *my* s in their sight. H3802
12 bear upon *his* s in the twilight, and H3802
24: 4 and the s; fill *it* with the choice bones. H3802
29: 7 and rend all their s: and when they H3802
18 bald, and every s *was* peeled: yet had H3802
34:21 with side and with s, and pushed all the H3802
Zec 7:11 pulled away the s, and stopped their H3802

SHOULDER-BLADE See SHOULDER and BLADE.

SHOULDERPIECES
Ex 28: 7 It shall have the two s thereof joined at H3802
25 *them* on the s of the ephod before it. H3802
39: 4 They made s for it, to couple *it* H3802
18 them on the s of the ephod, before it. H3802

SHOULDERS
Gen 9:23 laid *it* upon both their s, and went H7926
Ex 12:34 bound up in their clothes upon their s. H7926
28:12 two stones upon the s of the ephod *for* H3802
12 LORD upon his two s for a memorial. H3802
39: 7 And he put them on the s of the ephod, H3802
Nu 7: 9 *was that* they should bear upon their s. H3802
Dt 33:12 long, and he shall dwell between his s. H3802
Jdg 16: 3 put *them* upon his s, and carried them H3802
1Sa 9: 2 than he: from his s and upward *he was* H7926
10:23 of the people from his s and upward. H7926
17: 6 legs, and a target of brass between his s. H3802
1Ch 15:15 ark of God upon their s with the staves H3802
2Ch 35: 3 a burden upon *your* s: serve now the H3802
Isa 11:14 But they shall fly upon the s of the H3802
14:25 and his burden depart from off their s. H7926
30: 6 riches upon the s of young asses, and H3802
49:22 daughters shall be carried upon *their* s. H3802
Ezk 12: 6 bear *it* upon *thy* s, *and* carry *it* forth in H3802
Mt 23: 4 and lay *them* on men's s; but they *G5606*
Lk 15: 5 found *it,* he layeth *it* on his s, rejoicing. *G5606*

SHOULDEST See the Appendix.

SHOUT
Ex 32:18 the voice of *them that* s for mastery, H6030
Nu 23:21 and the s of a king *is* among them. H8643
Jos 6: 5 all the people shall s with a great shout; H7321
5 shout with a great s; and the wall of the H8643
10 Ye shall not s, nor make any noise H7321
10 the day I bid you s; then shall ye shout. H7321
10 the day I bid you shout; then shall ye s. H7321
16 S; for the LORD hath given you the city. H7321
20 with a great s, that the wall fell down H8643
1Sa 4: 5 a great s, so that the earth rang again. H8643
6 heard the noise of the s, they said, What H8643
6 noise of this great s in the camp of the H8643
2Ch 13:15 Then the men of Judah gave a s: and as H7321
Ezr 3:11 with a great s, when they praised the H8643
13 the noise of the s of joy from the noise H8643
13 loud s, and the noise was heard afar off. H8643
Ps 5:11 let them ever s for joy, because thou H7442
32:11 ye righteous: and s for joy, all *ye that* H7442
35:27 Let them s for joy, and be glad, that H7442
47: 1 O clap your hands, all ye people; s unto H7321
5 God is gone up with a s, the LORD with H8643
65:13 with corn; they s for joy, they also sing. H7321
132: 9 and let thy saints s for joy. H7442
16 and her saints shall s aloud for joy. H7442
Isa 12: 6 Cry out and s, thou inhabitant of Zion: H7442
42:11 them s from the top of the mountains. H6681
44:23 hath done *it:* s, ye lower parts of the H7321
Jer 25:30 he shall give a s, as they that tread *the* H1959
31: 7 for Jacob, and s among the chief of the H6670
50:15 S against her round about: she hath H7321
51:14 and they shall lift up a s against thee. H1959
Lam 3: 8 Also when I cry and s, he shutteth out H7768
Zep 3:14 Sing, O daughter of Zion; s, O Israel; be H7321
Zec 9: 9 Rejoice greatly, O daughter of Zion; s, O H7321
Act 12:22 And the people gave a s, *saying, It is* the *G2019*
1Th 4:16 heaven with a s, with the voice of the *G2752*

SHOUTED
Ex 32:17 of the people as they s, he said unto H7452
Lev 9:24 saw, they s, and fell on their faces. H7442
Jos 6:20 So the people s when *the priests* blew H7321
20 and the people s with a great shout, H7321
Jdg 15:14 the Philistines s against him: and the H7321
1Sa 4: 5 camp, all Israel s with a great shout, so H7321
10:24 people s, and said, God save the king. H7321
17:20 forth to the fight, and s for the battle. H7321
52 of Judah arose, and s, and pursued the H7321
2Ch 13:15 the men of Judah s, it came to pass, that H7321
Ezr 3:11 And all the people s with a great shout, H7321
12 a loud voice; and many s aloud for joy: H8643
13 for the people s with a loud shout, and H7321
Job 38: 7 and all the sons of God s for joy? H7321

SHOUTETH
Ps 78:65 a mighty man that s by reason of wine. H7442

SHOUTING
2Sa 6:15 s, and with the sound of the trumpet. H8643

1Ch 15:28 of the LORD with s, and with sound of H8643
2Ch 15:14 s, and with trumpets, and with cornets. H8643
Job 39:25 the thunder of the captains, and the s. H8643
Prv 11:10 and when the wicked perish, *there is* s. H7440
Isa 16: 9 Elealeh: for the s for thy summer fruits H1959
10 shall there be s: the treaders shall tread H7321
10 I have made *their vintage* s to cease. H1959
Jer 20:16 in the morning, and the s at noontide; H8643
48:33 s; *their* shouting *shall be* no shouting. H1959
33 shouting; *their* s *shall be* no shouting. H1959
33 shouting; *their* shouting *shall be* no s. H1959
Ezk 21:22 up the voice with s, to appoint *battering* H8643
Am 1:14 thereof, with s in the day of battle, H8643
2: 2 s, *and* with the sound of the trumpet: H8643

SHOUTINGS
Zec 4: 7 *with* s, *crying*, Grace, grace unto it. H8663

SHOVEL
Isa 30:24 winnowed with the s and with the fan. H7371

SHOVELS
Ex 27: 3 his ashes, and his s, and his basons, H3257
38: 3 the pots, and the s, and the basons, *and* H3257
Nu 4:14 and the s, and the basons, all H3257
1Ki 7:40 And Hiram made the lavers, and the s, H3257
45 And the pots, and the s, and the basons: H3257
2Ki 25:14 And the pots, and the s, and the H3257
2Ch 4:11 And Huram made the pots, and the s, H3257
16 The pots also, and the s, and the H3257
Jer 52:18 The caldrons also, and the s, and the H3257

SHOW See SHEW.

SHOWER
Ezk 13:11 be an overflowing s; and ye, O great H1653
13 be an overflowing s in mine anger, and H1653
34:26 I will cause the s to come down in his H1653
Lk 12:54 ye say, There cometh a s; and so it is. G3655

SHOWERS
Dt 32: 2 herb, and as the s upon the grass: H7241
Job 24: 8 They are wet with the s of the H2230
Ps 65:10 s: thou blessest the springing thereof. H7241
72: 6 mown grass: as s *that* water the earth. H7241
Jer 3: 3 Therefore the s have been withholden, H7241
14:22 the heavens give s? *art* not thou he, O H7241
Ezk 34:26 his season; there shall be s of blessing. H1653
Mic 5: 7 the LORD, as the s upon the grass, that H7241
Zec 10: 1 s of rain, to every one grass in the field. H4306

SHRANK
Gen 32:32 *of* the sinew which s, which *is* upon the H5384
32 of Jacob's thigh in the sinew that s. H5384

SHRED
2Ki 4:39 full, and came and s *them* into the pot H6398

SHRINES
Act 19:24 which made silver s for Diana, brought G3485

SHRINK See SHRANK.

SHROUD
Ezk 31: 3 and with a shadowing s, and of an high H2793

SHRUBS
Gen 21:15 she cast the child under one of the s. H7880

SHUA
1Ch 2: 3 of the daughter of S the Canaanitess. H7770
7:32 and Hotham, and S their sister. H7774

SHUAH
Gen 25: 2 Medan, and Midian, and Ishbak, and S. H7744
38: 2 whose name *was* S; and he took her, H7770
12 the daughter of S Judah's wife died; H7770
1Ch 1:32 and Ishbak, and S. And the sons of H7744
4:11 And Chelub the brother of S begat H7746

SHUAL
1Sa 13:17 *leadeth to* Ophrah, unto the land of S: H7777
1Ch 7:36 Harnepher, and S, and Beri, and Imrah, H7777

SHUBAEL
1Ch 24:20 S: of the sons of Shubael; Jehdeiah. H7619
20 Shubael: of the sons of S; Jehdeiah. H7619
25:20 The thirteenth to S, *he*, his sons, and his H7619

SHUHAM
Nu 26:42 their families: of S, the family of the H7748

SHUHAMITES
Nu 26:42 the family of the S. These *are* the H7749
43 All the families of the S, according to H7749

SHUHITE
Job 2:11 and Bildad the S, and Zophar the H7747
8: 1 Then answered Bildad the S, and said, H7747
18: 1 Then answered Bildad the S, and said, H7747
25: 1 Then answered Bildad the S, and said, H7747
42: 9 and Bildad the S *and* Zophar the H7747

SHULAMITE
Song 6:13 Return, return, O S; return, return, that H7759
13 What will ye see in the S? As it were the H7759

SHUMATHITES
1Ch 2:53 Puhites, and the S, and the Mishraites; H8126

SHUN
2Ti 2:16 But s profane *and* vain babblings: for G4026

SHUNAMMITE
1Ki 1: 3 a S, and brought her to the king. H7767
15 the S ministered unto the king. H7767
2:17 that he give me Abishag the S to wife. H7767
21 And she said, Let Abishag the S be H7767
22 ask Abishag the S for Adonijah? ask for H7767
2Ki 4:12 servant, Call this S. And when he had H7767
25 his servant, Behold, *yonder is* that S: H7767
36 and said, Call this S. So he called her. H7767

SHUNEM
Jos 19:18 toward Jezreel, and Chesulloth, and S, H7766
1Sa 28: 4 and pitched in S: and Saul gathered all H7766
2Ki 4: 8 Elisha passed to S, where *was* a great H7766

SHUNI
Gen 46:16 S, and Ezbon, Eri, and Arodi, and Areli. H7764
Nu 26:15 of S, the family of the Shunites: H7764

SHUNITES
Nu 26:15 Haggites: of Shuni, the family of the S: H7765

SHUNNED
Act 20:27 For I have not s to declare unto you all G5288

SHUPHAM
Nu 26:39 Of S, the family of the Shuphamites: of H8197

SHUPHAMITES
Nu 26:39 Of Shupham, the family of the S: of H7781

SHUPPIM
1Ch 7:12 S also, and Huppim, the children of Ir, H8206
15 of Huppim and S, whose sister's name H8206
26:16 To S and Hosah *the lot came forth* H8206

SHUR
Gen 16: 7 by the fountain in the way to S. H7793
20: 1 Kadesh and S, and sojourned in Gerar. H7793
25:18 And they dwelt from Havilah unto S, H7793
Ex 15:22 the wilderness of S; and they went three H7793
1Sa 15: 7 comest to S, that *is* over against Egypt. H7793
27: 8 goest to S, even unto the land of Egypt. H7793

SHUSHAN
Neh 1: 1 twentieth year, as I was in S the palace, H7800
Est 1: 2 kingdom, which *was* in S the palace, H7800
5 were present in S the palace, both unto H7800
2: 3 virgins unto S the palace, to the house H7800
5 *Now* in S the palace there was a certain H7800
8 together unto S the palace, to the H7800
3:15 was given in S the palace. And the H7800
15 to drink; but the city S was perplexed. H7800
4: 8 that was given at S to destroy them, to H7800
16 that are present in S, and fast ye for me, H7800
8:14 the decree was given at S the palace. H7800
15 and the city of S rejoiced and was glad. H7800
9: 6 And in S the palace the Jews slew and H7800
11 that were slain in S the palace was H7800
12 hundred men in S the palace, and the H7800
13 Jews which *are* in S to do to morrow H7800
14 S; and they hanged Haman's ten sons. H7800
15 For the Jews that *were* in S gathered H7800
15 hundred men at S; but on the prey they H7800
18 But the Jews that *were* at S assembled H7800
Dan 8: 2 I saw, that I *was* at S *in* the palace, H7800

SHUSHAN-EDUTH
Ps 60:ttl To the chief Musician upon S, Michtam H7802

SHUT
Gen 7:16 him: and the LORD s him in. H5462
19: 6 unto them, and s the door after him, H5462
10 the house to them, and s to the door. H5462
Ex 14: 3 the land, the wilderness hath s them in. H5462
Lev 13: 4 the priest shall s up *him that hath* the H5462
5 priest shall s him up seven days more: H5462
11 shall not s him up: for he *is* unclean. H5462
21 the priest shall s him up seven days: H5462
26 the priest shall s him up seven days: H5462
31 the priest shall s up *him that hath* the H5462
33 the priest shall s up *him that hath* the H5462
50 s up *it that hath* the plague seven days: H5462
54 *is*, and he shall s it up seven days more: H5462
14:38 house, and s up the house seven days: H5462
46 is s up shall be unclean until the even. H5462
Nu 12:14 days? let her be s out from the camp H5462
15 And Miriam was s out from the camp H5462
Dt 11:17 you, and he s up the heaven, that H6113
15: 7 s thine hand from thy poor brother: H7092
32:30 them, and the LORD had s them up? H5462
36 is gone, and *there is* none s up, or left. H6113
Jos 2: 7 them were gone out, they s the gate. H5462
6: 1 Now Jericho was straitly s up because H5462
Jdg 3:23 the porch, and s the doors of the H5462
9:51 of the city, and s *it* to them, and gat H5462
1Sa 1: 5 but the LORD had s up her womb. H5462
6 because the LORD had s up her womb. H5462
6:10 the cart, and s up their calves at home: H3607
23: 7 hand; for he is s in, by entering into H5462
2Sa 20: 3 So they were s up unto the day of their H6887
1Ki 8:35 When heaven is s up, and there is no H6113
14:10 *and* him that is s up and left in Israel, H6113
21:21 and him that is s up and left in Israel, H6113
2Ki 4: 4 in, thou shalt s the door upon thee H5462
5 So she went from him, and s the door H5462
21 s *the door* upon him, and went out. H5462
33 He went in therefore, and s the door H5462
6:32 cometh, s the door, and hold him H5462
9: 8 and him that is s up and left in Israel: H6113
14:26 for *there was* not any s up, nor any left, H6113
17: 4 s him up, and bound him in prison. H6113
2Ch 6:26 When the heaven is s up, and there is H6113
7:13 If I s up heaven that there be no rain, H6113
28:24 house of God, and s up the doors of the H5462
29: 7 Also they have s up the doors of the H5462
Neh 6:10 who *was* s up; and he said, Let H1479
10 the temple, and let us s the doors of the H5462
7: 3 stand by, let them s the doors, and bar H1479
13:19 gates should be s, and charged that they H5462
Job 3:10 Because it s not up the doors of my H5462
11:10 If he cut off, and s up, or gather H5462
38: 8 Or *who* s up the sea with doors, when it H5526
41:15 *His* scales *are his* pride, s up together H5462
Ps 31: 8 And hast not s me up into the hand of H5462
69:15 and let not the pit s her mouth upon me. H332
77: 9 in anger s up his tender mercies? Selah. H7092
88: 8 *I am* s up, and I cannot come forth. H3607
Ecc 12: 4 And the doors shall be s in the streets, H5462
Song 4:12 a spring s up, a fountain sealed. H5274
Isa 6:10 ears heavy, and s their eyes; lest they H8173
22:22 and none shall s; and he shall shut, and H5462
22 and he shall s, and none shall open. H5462
24:10 is s up, that no man may come in. H5462
22 pit, and shall be s up in the prison, and H5462
26:20 thy chambers, and s thy doors about H5462
44:18 for he hath s their eyes, that they H2902
45: 1 gates; and the gates shall not be s; H5462
52:15 the kings shall s their mouths at him: H7092
60:11 they shall not be s day nor night; that H5462
66: 9 forth, and s *the womb*? saith thy God. H6113
Jer 13:19 The cities of the south shall be s up, H5462
20: 9 as a burning fire s up in my bones, and H6113
32: 2 the prophet was s up in the court of the H3607
3 For Zedekiah king of Judah had s him H3607
33: 1 s up in the court of the prison, saying, H6113
36: 5 saying, I *am* s up; I cannot go into H6113
39:15 s up in the court of the prison, saying, H6113
Ezk 3:24 me, Go, s thyself within thine house. H5462
44: 1 looketh toward the east; and it *was* s. H5462
2 me; This gate shall be s, it shall not be H5462
2 entered in by it, therefore it shall be s. H5462
46: 1 the east shall be s the six working days; H5462
2 the gate shall not be s until the evening. H5462

Ezk 46:12 his going forth *one* shall **s** the gate. H5462
Dan 6:22 My God hath sent his angel, and hath **s** H5463
8:26 *is* true: wherefore **s** thou up the vision; H5640
12: 4 But thou, O Daniel, **s** up the words, and H5640
Mal 1:10 you that would **s** the doors *for nought*? H5462
Mt 6: 6 when thou hast **s** thy door, pray to thy G2808
23:13 hypocrites! for ye **s** up the kingdom of G2808
25:10 to the marriage: and the door was **s**. G2808
Lk 3:20 Added yet this above all, that he **s** up G2623
4:25 the heaven was **s** up three years and six G2808
11: 7 the door is now **s**, and my children are G2808
13:25 risen up, and hath **s** to the door, and ye G608
Jn 20:19 the doors were **s** where the disciples G2808
26 the doors being **s**, and stood in the G2808
Act 5:23 Saying, The prison truly found we **s** G2808
21:30 temple: and forthwith the doors were **s**. G2808
26:10 many of the saints did I **s** up in prison, G2623
Gal 3:23 kept under the law, **s** up unto the faith G4788
Rev 3: 8 and no man can **s** it: for thou hast a G2808
11: 6 These have power to **s** heaven, that it G2808
20: 3 pit, and **s** him up, and set a seal G2808
21:25 And the gates of it shall not be **s** at all G2808

SHUTHALHITES
Nu 26:35 the family of the **S**: of Becher, the family H8364

SHUTHELAH
Nu 26:35 their families: of **S**, the family of the H7803
36 And these *are* the sons of **S**: of Eran, the H7803
1Ch 7:20 And the sons of Ephraim; **S**, and Bered H7803
21 And Zabad his son, and **S** his son, and H7803

SHUTTETH
Job 12:14 be built again: he **s** up a man, and H5462
Prv 16:30 He **s** his eyes to devise froward things: H6095
17:28 wise: *and* he that **s** his lips *is esteemed* a H331
Isa 33:15 blood, and **s** his eyes from seeing evil; H6105
Lam 3: 8 Also when I cry and shout, he **s** out my H5640
1Jn 3:17 have need, and **s** up his bowels *of* G2808
Rev 3: 7 **s**; and shutteth, and no man openeth; G2808
7 shutteth; and **s**, and no man openeth; G2808

SHUTTING
Jos 2: 5 And it came to pass *about the time* of **s** H5462

SHUTTLE
Job 7: 6 My days are swifter than a weaver's **s**, H708

SIA
Neh 7:47 The children of Keros, the children of **S**, H5517

SIAHA
Ezr 2:44 The children of Keros, the children of **S**, H5517

SIBBECAI
1Ch 11:29 **S** the Hushathite, Ilai the Ahohite, H5444
27:11 eighth month *was* **S** the Hushathite, of H5444

SIBBECHAI
2Sa 21:18 at Gob: then **S** the Hushathite slew H5444
1Ch 20: 4 at which time **S** the Hushathite slew H5444

SIBBOLETH
Jdg 12: 6 and he said **S**: for he could not frame H5451

SIBMAH
Jos 13:19 And Kirjathaim, and **S**, and H7643
Isa 16: 8 *and* the vine of **S**: the lords of the H7643
9 of Jazer the vine of **S**: I will water thee H7643
Jer 48:32 O vine of **S**, I will weep for thee with the H7643

SIBRAIM
Ezk 47:16 Hamath, Berothah, **S**, which *is* between H5453

SICHEM
Gen 12: 6 unto the place of **S**, unto the plain of H7927

SICK
Gen 48: 1 thy father *is* **s**: and he took with him H2470
Lev 15:33 And of her that is **s** of her flowers, and H1739
1Sa 19:14 to take David, she said, He *is* **s**. H2470
30:13 me, because three days agone I fell **s**. H2470
2Sa 12:15 wife bare unto David, and it was very **s**. H605
13: 2 And Amnon was so vexed, that he fell **s** H2470
5 and make thyself **s**: and when thy father H2470
6 and made himself **s**: and when the king H2470
1Ki 14: 1 time Abijah the son of Jeroboam fell **s**. H2470
5 her son; for he *is* **s**: thus and thus shalt H2470
17:17 of the house, fell **s**; and his sickness was H2470
2Ki 1: 2 in Samaria, and was **s**: and he sent H2470
8: 7 king of Syria was **s**; and it was told him, H2470
29 of Ahab in Jezreel, because he was **s**. H2470
13:14 Now Elisha was fallen **s** of his sickness H2470
20: 1 In those days was Hezekiah **s** unto H2470
12 he had heard that Hezekiah had been **s**. H2470
2Ch 22: 6 of Ahab at Jezreel, because he was **s**. H2470
32:24 In those days Hezekiah was **s** to the H2470
Neh 2: 2 thou *art* not **s**? this *is* nothing *else* but H2470
Ps 35:13 But as for me, when they were **s**, my H2470
Prv 13:12 Hope deferred maketh the heart **s**: but H2470
23:35 *say, and* I was not **s**; they have beaten H2470
Song 2: 5 me with apples: for I *am* **s** of love. H2470
5: 8 that ye tell him, that I *am* **s** of love. H2470
Isa 1: 5 head is **s**, and the whole heart faint. H2483
33:24 shall not say, I am **s**: the people that H2470
38: 1 In those days was Hezekiah **s** unto H2470
9 **s**, and was recovered of his sickness: H2470
39: 1 that he had been **s**, and was recovered. H2470
Jer 14:18 them that are **s** with famine! yea, both H8463
Ezk 34: 4 that which was **s**, neither have ye bound H2470
16 that which was **s**: but I will destroy the H2470
Dan 8:27 And I Daniel fainted, and was **s** *certain* H2470
Hos 7: 5 have made *him* **s** with bottles of wine; H2470
Mic 6:13 Therefore also will I make *thee* **s** in H2470
Mal 1: 8 offer the lame and **s**, *is it* not evil? offer H2470
13 the lame, and the **s**; thus ye brought an H2470
Mt 4:24 unto him all **s** people that were G2560+G2192
8: 6 **s** of the palsy, grievously tormented. G3885
14 his wife's mother laid, and **s** of a fever. G4445
16 and healed all that were **s**: G2192+G2560
9: 2 to him a man **s** of the palsy, lying on G3885
2 faith said unto the **s** of the palsy; Son, G3885
6 saith he to the **s** of the palsy,) Arise, G3885
12 not a physician, but they that are **s**. G2560
10: 8 Heal the **s**, cleanse the lepers, raise the G770
14:14 toward them, and he healed their **s**. G732
25:36 Naked, and ye clothed me: I was **s**, and G770
39 Or when saw we thee **s**, or in prison, and G772
43 **s**, and in prison, and ye visited me not. G772
44 or naked, or **s**, or in prison, and did G772
Mk 1:30 But Simon's wife's mother lay **s** of a G4445
34 that were **s** of divers diseases, G2192+G2560
2: 3 **s** of the palsy, which was borne of four. G3885
4 the bed wherein the **s** of the palsy lay. G3885
5 he said unto the **s** of the palsy, Son, thy G3885
9 Whether is it easier to say to the **s** of G3885
10 sins, (he saith to the **s** of the palsy,) G3885
17 they that are **s**: I came not to G2192+G2560
6: 5 upon a few **s** folk, and healed *them*. G732
13 oil many that were **s**, and healed *them*. G732
55 **s**, where they heard he was. G2192+G2560
56 they laid the **s** in the streets, and G770
16:18 hands on the **s**, and they shall recover. G732
Lk 4:40 they that had any **s** with divers diseases G770
5:24 (he said unto the **s** of the palsy,) I say G3885
31 a physician; but they that are **s**. G2192+G2560
7: 2 him, was **s**, and ready to die. G2192+G2560
10 found the servant whole that had been **s**. G770
9: 2 the kingdom of God, and to heal the **s**. G770
10: 9 And heal the **s** that are therein, and say G772
Jn 4:46 whose son was **s** at Capernaum. G770
11: 1 Now a certain *man* was **s**, *named* G770
2 her hair, whose brother Lazarus was **s**.) G770
3 Lord, behold, he whom thou lovest is **s**. G770
6 that he was **s**, he abode two days still G770
Act 5:15 Insomuch that they brought forth the **s** G772
16 bringing **s** folks, and them which G772
9:33 bed eight years, and was **s** of the palsy. G3885
37 days, that she was **s**, and died: whom G770
19:12 brought unto the **s** handkerchiefs or G770
28: 8 father of Publius lay **s** of a fever and of a
Php 2:26 that ye had heard that he had been **s**. G770
27 For indeed he was **s** nigh unto death: but G770
2Ti 4:20 but Trophimus have I left at Miletum **s**. G770
Jas 5:14 Is any **s** among you? let him call for the G770
15 And the prayer of faith shall save the **s**, G2577

SICKLE
Dt 16: 9 thou beginnest *to put* the **s** to the corn. H2770
23:25 a **s** unto thy neighbour's standing corn. H2770
Jer 50:16 him that handleth the **s** in the time of H4038
Joel 3:13 Put ye in the **s**, for the harvest is ripe: H4038
Mk 4:29 in the **s**, because the harvest is come. G1407
Rev 14:14 crown, and in his hand a sharp **s**. G1407
15 Thrust in thy **s**, and reap: for the time G1407
16 cloud thrust in his **s** on the earth; and G1407
17 is in heaven, he also having a sharp **s**. G1407
18 that had the sharp **s**, saying, Thrust in G1407
Rev 14:18 in thy sharp **s**, and gather the clusters G1407
19 And the angel thrust in his **s** into the G1407

SICKLY
1Co 11:30 For this cause many *are* weak and **s** G732

SICKNESS
Ex 23:25 will take **s** away from the midst of thee. H4245
Lev 20:18 having her **s**, and shall uncover her H1739
Dt 7:15 away from thee all **s**, and will put none H2483
28:61 Also every **s**, and every plague, which *is* H2483
1Ki 8:37 plague, whatsoever **s** *there be;* H4245
17:17 fell sick; and his **s** was so sore, that H2483
2Ki 13:14 Now Elisha was fallen sick of his **s** H2483
2Ch 6:28 sore or whatsoever **s** *there be:* H4245
21:15 And thou *shalt have* great **s** by disease H2483
15 fall out by reason of the **s** day by day. H2483
19 out by reason of his **s**: so he died of sore H2483
Ps 41: 3 thou wilt make all his bed in his **s**. H2483
Ecc 5:17 *hath* much sorrow and wrath with his **s**. H2483
Isa 38: 9 been sick, and was recovered of his **s**: H2483
12 me off with pining **s**: from day *even* to H1803
Hos 5:13 When Ephraim saw his **s**, and Judah H2483
Mt 4:23 all manner of **s** and all manner of G3554
9:35 **s** and every disease among the people. G3554
10: 1 manner of **s** and all manner of disease. G3554
Jn 11: 4 When Jesus heard *that*, he said, This **s** is G769

SICKNESSES
Dt 28:59 and sore **s**, and of long continuance. H2483
29:22 the **s** which the LORD hath laid upon it; H8463
Mt 8:17 took our infirmities, and bare *our* **s**. G3554
Mk 3:15 And to have power to heal **s**, and to cast G3554

SIDDIM
Gen 14: 3 in the vale of **S**, which is the salt sea. H7708
8 joined battle with them in the vale of **S**; H7708
10 And the vale of **S** *was full of* slimepits; H7708

SIDE
Gen 6:16 thou set in the **s** thereof; *with* lower, H6654
38:21 *was* openly by the way **s**? And they said, H1870
Ex 2: 5 by the river's **s**; and when she saw the H3027
12: 7 strike *it* on the two **s** posts and on the
22 lintel and the two **s** posts with the blood
23 and on the two **s** posts, the LORD will
17:12 the one on the one **s**, and the other on the
12 other on the other **s**; and his hands were
25:12 *shall be* in the one **s** of it, and two rings H6763
12 of it, and two rings in the other **s** of it. H6763
32 out of the one **s**, and three branches H6654
32 of the candlestick out of the other **s**: H6654
26:13 And a cubit on the one **s**, and a cubit on H2088
13 a cubit on the other **s** of that which
13 on this **s** and on that side, to cover it. H2088
13 on this side and on that **s**, to cover it.
18 boards on the south **s** southward. H6285
20 And for the second **s** of the tabernacle H6763
20 north **s** *there shall be* twenty boards: H6285
26 boards of the one **s** of the tabernacle, H6763
27 of the other **s** of the tabernacle, and H6763
27 the boards of the **s** of the tabernacle, H6763
35 the table on the **s** of the tabernacle H6763
35 thou shalt put the table on the north **s**. H6763
27: 9 for the south **s** southward *there shall* H6285
9 of an hundred cubits long for one **s**: H6285
11 And likewise for the north **s** in length H6285
12 court on the west **s** *shall be* hangings of H6285
13 the east **s** eastward *shall be* fifty cubits. H6285
14 The hangings of one **s** *of the gate shall* H3802
15 And on the other **s** *shall be* hangings H3802
28:26 which *is* in the **s** of the ephod inward. H5676
32:15 one **s** and on the other *were* they written.
26 *is* on the LORD'S **s**? *let him come* unto
27 his sword by his **s**, *and* go in and out H3409
36:11 in the uttermost **s** of *another* curtain, H8193
23 boards for the south **s** southward: H6285
25 And for the other **s** of the tabernacle, H6763
31 boards of the one **s** of the tabernacle, H6763
32 of the other **s** of the tabernacle, and H6763
37: 3 two rings upon the one **s** of it, and two H6763
3 it, and two rings upon the other **s** of it. H6763
8 One cherub on the end on this **s**, and
8 *other* end on that **s**: out of the mercy seat
18 out of the one **s** thereof, and three H6654
18 candlestick out of the other **s** thereof: H6654
38: 9 And he made the court: on the south **s** H6285
11 And for the north **s** *the hangings were* H6285
12 And for the west **s** *were* hangings of H6285

Ex 38:13 And for the east s eastward fifty cubits. H6285
14 The hangings of the one s *of the gate* H3802
15 And for the other s of the court gate, on H3802
39:19 *was* on the s of the ephod inward. H5676
40:22 upon the s of the tabernacle H3409
24 on the s of the tabernacle southward. H3409
Lev 1:11 And he shall kill it on the s of the altar H3409
15 shall be wrung out at the s of the altar: H7023
5: 9 offering upon the s of the altar; and the H7023
Nu 2: 3 And on the east s toward the rising of H6924
10 On the south s *shall be* the standard of H8486
18 On the west s *shall be* the standard of H3220
25 *be* on the north s by their armies: and
3:29 on the s of the tabernacle southward. H3409
35 on the s of the tabernacle northward. H3409
10: 6 that lie on the south s shall take their H8486
11:31 journey on this s, and as it were a day's H3541
31 on the other s, round about the camp, H3541
16:27 Abiram, on every s: and Dathan and H5439
21:13 on the other s of Arnon, which *is* in H5676
22: 1 of Moab on this s Jordan *by* Jericho. H5676
24 *being* on this s, and a wall on that side.
24 *being* on this side, and a wall on that s.
24: 6 by the river's s, as the trees of lign aloes
32:19 them on yonder s Jordan, or forward; H5676
19 fallen to us on this s Jordan eastward. H5676
32 on this s Jordan *may be* ours. H5676
34:11 to Riblah, on the east s of Ain; and the H6924
11 the s of the sea of Chinnereth eastward: H3802
15 on this s Jordan *near* Jericho H5676
35: 5 the city on the east s two thousand H6285
5 and on the south s two thousand H6285
5 and on the west s two thousand cubits, H6285
5 and on the north s two thousand H6285
14 Ye shall give three cities on this s H5676
Dt 1: 1 unto all Israel on this s Jordan in the H5676
5 On this s Jordan, in the land of Moab, H5676
7 and by the sea s, to the land of the H2348
3: 8 that *was* on this s Jordan, from the H5676
4:32 *ask* from the one s of heaven unto the H7097
41 on this s Jordan toward the sunrising; H5676
46 On this s Jordan, in the valley over H5676
47 on this s Jordan toward the sunrising; H5676
49 And all the plain on this s Jordan H5676
11:30 *Are* they not on the other s Jordan, by H5676
31:26 law, and put it in the s of the ark of the H6654
Jos 1:14 gave you on this s Jordan; but ye shall H5676
15 on this s Jordan toward the sunrising. H5676
2:10 *were* on the other s Jordan, Sihon and H5676
5: 1 which *were* on the s of Jordan H5676
7: 2 on the east s of Beth-el, and spake H6924
7 and dwelt on the other s Jordan! H5676
8: 9 and Ai, on the west s of Ai: but Joshua H3220
11 on the north s of Ai: now *there was*
12 Beth-el and Ai, on the west s of the city. H3220
22 some on this s, and some on that side:
22 side, and some on that s: and they smote
33 stood on this s the ark and on that side
33 the ark and on that s before the priests
9: 1 *were* on this s Jordan, in the hills, H5676
12: 1 land on the other s Jordan toward the H5676
7 smote on this s Jordan on the west, H5676
13:27 on the other s Jordan eastward. H5676
32 other s Jordan, by Jericho, eastward. H5676
14: 3 tribe on the other s Jordan: but unto H5676
15: 3 And it went out to the south s to H5045
3 up on the south s unto Kadesh-barnea, H5045
7 *is* on the south s of the river: and the H5045
8 unto the south s of the Jebusite; the H3802
10 along unto the s of mount Jearim, H3802
10 on the north s, and went down to
11 And the border went out unto the s of H3802
16: 5 on the east s was Ataroth-addar, H4217
6 on the north s; and the border went
17: 5 which *were* on the other s Jordan; H5676
9 *was* on the north s of the river, and the
18:12 And their border on the north s was H6285
12 went up to the s of Jericho on the north H3802
12 on the north s, and went up through
13 toward Luz, to the s of Luz, which *is* H3802
13 the south s of the nether Beth-horon. H5045
16 of Hinnom, to the s of Jebusi on the H3802
18 And passed along toward the s over H3802
19 And the border passed along to the s of H3802
20 border of it on the east s. This *was* the H6285
19:14 it on the north s to Hannathon: and the
27 toward the north s of Beth-emek, and
34 on the south s, and reacheth to Asher H5045
34 Asher on the west s, and to Judah upon H3220

Jos 20: 8 And on the other s Jordan by Jericho H5676
22: 4 LORD gave you on the other s Jordan. H5676
7 brethren on this s Jordan westward. H5676
24: 2 dwelt on the other s of the flood in old H5676
3 from the other s of the flood, and led H5676
8 dwelt on the other s Jordan; and they H5676
14 on the other s of the flood, and in H5676
15 *were* on the other s of the flood, or the H5676
30 on the north s of the hill of Gaash.
Jdg 2: 9 on the north s of the hill Gaash.
7: 1 were on the north s of them, by the hill
12 as the sand by the sea s for multitude. H8193
18 also on every s of all the camp, and H5439
25 Zeeb to Gideon on the other s Jordan. H5676
8:34 hands of all their enemies on every s: H5439
10: 8 *were* on the other s Jordan in the land H5676
11:18 came by the east s of the land of Moab,
18 on the other s of Arnon, but came H5676
19: 1 sojourning on the s of mount Ephraim, H3411
18 toward the s of mount Ephraim; H3411
21:19 *is* on the north s of Beth-el, on the east
19 Beth-el, on the east s of the highway that
1Sa 4:18 backward by the s of the gate, and his H3027
6: 8 in a coffer by the s thereof; and send it H6654
12:11 enemies on every s, and ye dwelled safe. H5439
14: 1 the other s. But he told not his father. H5676
4 rock on the one s, and a sharp rock on H5676
4 rock on the other s: and the name of the H5676
40 Be ye on one s, and I and Jonathan H5676
40 be on the other s. And the people said H5676
47 enemies on every s, against Moab, and H5439
17: 3 on the one s, and Israel stood on a
3 s: and *there was* a valley between them.
20:20 And I will shoot three arrows on the s H6654
21 arrows *are* on this s of thee, take them; H6654
25 Saul's s, and David's place was empty. H6654
23:26 And Saul went on this s of the H6654
26 his men on that s of the mountain: and H6654
26:13 Then David went over to the other s, H5676
31: 7 *were* on the other s of the valley, and H5676
7 *were* on the other s Jordan, saw that H5676
2Sa 2:13 the one on the one s of the pool, and the
13 and the other on the other s of the pool.
16 sword in his fellow's s; so they fell down H6654
13:34 by the way of the hill s behind him. H6654
16:13 along on the hill's s over against him, H6763
18: 4 stood by the gate s, and all the people H3027
24: 5 in Aroer, on the right s of the city that H3225
1Ki 4:24 all *the region* on this s the river, from H5676
24 the kings on this s the river: and he had H5676
5: 3 him on every s, until the LORD put H5437
4 given me rest on every s, *so that there is* H5439
6: 8 *was* in the right s of the house: and H3802
31 *and* s posts *were* a fifth part *of the wall.*
7: 7 from one s of the floor to the other.
30 molten, at the s of every addition. H5676
39 And he put five bases on the right s of H3802
39 and five on the left s of the house: and H3802
39 sea on the right s of the house eastward H3802
49 five on the right s, and five on the left,
10:19 stays on either s on the place of the seat,
20 And twelve lions stood there on the one s
2Ki 3:22 water on the other s *as* red as blood: H5048
9:32 said, Who *is* on my s? who? And there
12: 9 altar, on the right s as one cometh into H3225
16:14 and put it on the north s of the altar. H3409
1Ch 4:39 *even* unto the east s of the valley, to H4217
6:78 And on the other s Jordan by Jericho, H5676
78 on the east s of Jordan, *were given* H4217
12:18 David, and on thy s, thou son of Jesse:
37 And on the other s of Jordan, of the H5676
22:18 you rest on every s? for he hath given H5439
26:30 of Israel on this s Jordan westward in H5676
2Ch 4: 8 five on the right s, and five on the left. H3225
10 And he set the sea on the right s of the H3802
8:17 Eloth, at the sea s in the land of Edom. H8193
9:18 and stays on each s of the sitting place,
19 And twelve lions stood there on the one s
11:12 having Judah and Benjamin on his s.
14: 7 on every s. So they built and prospered. H5439
20: 2 the sea on this s Syria; and, behold, they
23:10 from the right s of the temple to the H3802
10 temple to the left s of the temple, along H3802
32:22 all *other,* and guided them on every s. H5439
30 down to the west s of the city of David. H4628
33:14 of David, on the west s of Gihon, in the H4628
Ezr 4:10 on this s the river, and at such a time. H5675
11 on this s the river, and at such a time. H5675
16 have no portion on this s the river. H5675

Ezr 5: 3 governor on this s the river, and H5675
6 governor on this s the river, and H5675
6 s the river, sent unto Darius the king: H5675
6:13 Then Tatnai, governor on this s the H5675
8:36 governors on this s the river: and they H5676
Neh 3: 7 of the governor on this s the river. H5676
4:18 girded by his s, and *so* builded. And H4975
Job 1:10 he hath on every s? thou hast blessed H5439
18:11 every s, and shall drive him to his feet. H5439
12 and destruction *shall be* ready at his s. H6763
19:10 He hath destroyed me on every s, and I H5439
Ps 12: 8 The wicked walk on every s, when the H5439
31:13 fear *was* on every s: while they took H5439
65:12 and the little hills rejoice on every s. H2296
71:21 greatness, and comfort me on every s. H5437
91: 7 A thousand shall fall at thy s, and ten H6654
118: 6 The LORD *is* on my s; I will not fear:
124: 1 who was on our s, now may Israel say;
2 on our s, when men rose up against us:
Ecc 4: 1 and on the s of their oppressors H3027
Isa 60: 4 thy daughters shall be nursed at *thy* s. H6654
Jer 6:25 of the enemy *and* fear *is* on every s. H5439
20:10 fear on every s. Report, *say they,* and H5439
49:29 shall cry unto them, Fear *is* on every s. H5439
52:23 on a s; *and* all the pomegranates H7307
Ezk 1:10 a lion, on the right s: and they four had H3225
10 of an ox on the left s; they four also had H8040
23 covered on this s, and every one had H2007
23 which covered on that s, their bodies. H2007
4: 4 Lie thou also upon thy left s, and lay the H6654
6 lie again on thy right s, and thou shalt H6654
8 thee from one s to another, till thou H6654
9 shalt lie upon thy s, three hundred and H6654
9: 2 inkhorn by his s: and they went in, and H4975
3 which *had* the writer's inkhorn by his s; H4975
11 *had* the inkhorn by his s, reported the H4975
10: 3 Now the cherubims stood on the right s H3225
11:23 which *is* on the east s of the city. H6924
16:33 unto thee on every s for thy whoredom. H5439
19: 8 him on every s from the provinces, H5439
23:22 will bring them against thee on every s; H5439
25: 9 Therefore, behold, I will open the s of H3802
28:23 upon her on every s; and they shall H5439
34:21 Because ye have thrust with s and with H6654
36: 3 you up on every s, that ye might be a H5439
37:21 s, and bring them into their own land: H5439
39:17 on every s to my sacrifice that H5439
40:10 *were* three on this s, and three on that H6311
10 and three on that s; they three *were* of H6311
10 one measure on this s and on that side.
10 one measure on this side and on that s.
12 one cubit *on this* s, and the space *was*
12 *was* one cubit on that s: and the little
12 on this s, and six cubits on that side.
12 on this side, and six cubits on that s.
18 And the pavement by the s of the gates H3802
21 *were* three on this s and three on that
21 and three on that s; and the posts thereof
26 trees, one on this s, and another on that
26 another on that s, upon the posts thereof.
34 thereof, on this s, and on that side: and
34 s: and the going up to it *had* eight steps.
37 thereof, on this s, and on that side: and
37 s: and the going up to it *had* eight steps.
39 two tables on this s, and two tables on
39 two tables on that s, to slay thereon the
40 And at the s without, as one goeth up H3802
40 and on the other s, which *was* at the H3802
41 Four tables *were* on this s, and four H3802
41 four tables on that s, by the side of the H3802
41 on that side, by the s of the gate; eight H3802
44 which *was* at the s of the north gate; H3802
44 the south: one at the s of the east gate H3802
48 five cubits on this s, and five cubits on
48 five cubits on that s: and the breadth of
48 on this s, and three cubits on that side.
48 on this side, and three cubits on that s.
49 one on this s, and another on that side.
49 one on this side, and another on that s.
41: 1 broad on the one s, and six cubits H6311
1 broad on the other s, *which was* the H6311
2 cubits on the one s, and five cubits on the
2 cubits on the other s: and he measured
5 the breadth of *every* s chamber, four H6763
5 round about the house on every s. H5439
6 And the s chambers *were* three, one H6763
6 of the house for the s chambers round H6763
7 still upward to the s chambers: for the H6763
8 foundations of the s chambers *were* a H6763

Ezk 41: 9 which *was* for the s chamber without, H6763
9 of the s chambers that *were* within. H6763
10 round about the house on every s. H5439
11 And the doors of the s chambers *were* H6763
15 thereof on the one s and on the other
15 and on the other s, an hundred cubits,
19 tree on the one s, and the face of a young
19 tree on the other s: *it was* made through
26 trees on the one s and on the other side,
26 and on the other s, on the sides of the
26 and *upon* the s chambers of the house, H6763
42: 9 the entry on the east s, as one goeth into H6921
16 He measured the east s with the H7307
17 He measured the north s, five hundred H7307
18 He measured the south s, five hundred H7307
19 He turned about to the west s, *and* H7307
45: 7 prince on the one s and on the other side
7 and on the other s of the oblation of the
7 the city, from the west s westward, and H6285
7 and from the east s eastward: and the H6285
46:19 which *was* at the s of the gate, into the H3802
47: 1 from the right s of the house, at the H3802
1 of the house, at the south *s* of the altar.
2 there ran out waters on the right s. H3802
7 trees on the one s and on the other.
12 thereof, on this s and on that side, shall
12 side and on that s, shall grow all trees for
15 toward the north s, from the great sea, H6285
17 of Hamath. And *this is* the north s. H6285
18 And the east s ye shall measure from H6285
18 unto the east sea. And *this is* the east s. H6285
19 And the south s southward, from H6285
19 sea. And *this is* the south s southward. H6285
20 The west s also *shall be* the great sea H6285
20 over against Hamath. This *is* the west s. H6285
48: 2 Dan, from the east s unto the west side, H6285
2 unto the west s, a *portion for* Asher. H6285
3 from the east s even unto the west side, H6285
3 unto the west s, a *portion for* Naphtali. H6285
4 from the east s unto the west side, a H6285
4 the west s, a *portion for* Manasseh. H6285
5 from the east s unto the west side, a H6285
5 unto the west s, a *portion for* Ephraim. H6285
6 from the east s even unto the west side, H6285
6 unto the west s, a *portion for* Reuben. H6285
7 from the east s unto the west side, a H6285
7 unto the west s, a *portion for* Judah. H6285
8 from the east s unto the west side, shall H6285
8 east side unto the west s, shall be the H6285
8 from the east s unto the west side: and H6285
8 side unto the west s: and the sanctuary H6285
16 thereof; the north s four thousand and H6285
16 and the south s four thousand and H6285
16 and on the east s four thousand and H6285
16 west s four thousand and five hundred. H6285
21 prince, on the one s and on the other of H6285
23 from the east s unto the west side, H6285
23 west s, Benjamin *shall have* a *portion*. H6285
24 from the east s unto the west side, H6285
24 the west s, Simeon *shall have* a *portion*. H6285
25 from the east s unto the west side, H6285
25 side unto the west s, Issachar a *portion*. H6285
26 s unto the west side, Zebulun a *portion*. H6285
26 side unto the west s, Zebulun a *portion*. H6285
27 s unto the west side, Gad a *portion*. H6285
27 east side unto the west s, Gad a *portion*. H6285
28 of Gad, at the south s southward, the H6285
30 city on the north s, four thousand and H6285
32 And at the east s four thousand and H6285
33 And at the south s four thousand and H6285
34 At the west s four thousand and five H6285
Dan 7: 5 up itself on one s, and *it had* three ribs H7859
10: 4 s of the great river, which *is* Hiddekel; H3027
11:17 not stand *on his s*, neither be for him.
12: 5 two, the one on this s of the bank of the H2008
5 other on that s of the bank of the river. H2008
Oba 11 on the other s, in the day that the H5048
Jna 4: 5 sat on the east s of the city, and there H6924
Zec 4: 3 one upon the right *s* of the bowl, and the
3 and the other upon the left *s* thereof.
11 upon the right *s* of the candlestick and
11 candlestick and upon the left *s* thereof?
5: 3 be cut off *as* on this s according to it;
3 be cut off *as* on that s according to it.
Mt 8:18 to depart unto the other s. *G4008*
28 And when he was come to the other s *G4008*
13: 1 out of the house, and sat by the sea s. *G2281*
4 fell by the way s, and the fowls came *G3598*
19 is he which received seed by the way s. *G3598*
Mt 14:22 s, while he sent the multitudes away. *G4008*
16: 5 s, they had forgotten to take bread. *G4008*
20:30 sitting by the way s, when they heard *G3844*
Mk 2:13 And he went forth again by the sea s; *G2281*
4: 1 to teach by the sea s: and there was *G2281*
4 fell by the way s, and the fowls of the *G3598*
15 And these are they by the way s, where *G3598*
35 them, Let us pass over unto the other s. *G4008*
5: 1 And they came over unto the other s of *G4008*
21 unto the other s, much people gathered *G4008*
6:45 and to go to the other s before unto *G4008*
8:13 the ship again departed to the other s. *G4008*
10: 1 by the farther s of Jordan: and the *G4008*
46 Timaeus, sat by the highway s begging. *G3598*
16: 5 sitting on the right s, clothed in a long *G1188*
Lk 1:11 on the right s of the altar of incense. *G1188*
8: 5 fell by the way s; and it was trodden *G3598*
12 Those by the way s are they that hear; *G3598*
22 s of the lake. And they launched forth. *G4008*
10:31 he saw him, he passed by on the other s. *G492*
32 *on him*, and passed by on the other s. *G492*
18:35 blind man sat by the way s begging: *G3598*
19:43 thee round, and keep thee in on every s, *G3840*
Jn 6:22 stood on the other s of the sea saw that *G4008*
25 him on the other s of the sea, they said *G4008*
19:18 on either s one, and Jesus in the midst. *G1782*
34 spear pierced his s, and forthwith came *G4125*
20:20 *his* hands and his s. Then were the *G4125*
25 my hand into his s, I will not believe. *G4125*
27 s: and be not faithless, but believing. *G4125*
21: 6 the net on the right s of the ship, and ye *G3313*
Act 10: 6 house is by the sea s: he shall tell thee *G2281*
32 a tanner by the sea s: who, when he *G2281*
12: 7 he smote Peter on the s, and raised him *G4125*
16:13 the city by a river s, where prayer was *G4215*
2Co 4: 8 *We are* troubled on every s, yet not *G3956*
7: 5 were troubled on every s; without *were* *G3956*
Rev 22: 2 of it, and on either s of the river, *was* *G1782*

SIDE-CHAMBER See SIDE and CHAMBER.

SIDE-POSTS See SIDE and POSTS.

SIDES
Ex 25:14 the rings by the s of the ark, that the H6763
32 come out of the s of it; three branches H6654
26:13 hang over the s of the tabernacle on H6654
22 And for the s of the tabernacle H3411
23 corners of the tabernacle in the two s. H3411
27 the tabernacle, for the two s westward. H3411
27: 7 upon the two s of the altar, to bear it. H6763
28:27 put them on the two s of the ephod H3802
30: 3 thereof, and the s thereof round about, H7023
4 upon the two s of it shalt thou make H6654
32:15 on both their s; on the one side and H5676
36:27 And for the s of the tabernacle H3411
28 corners of the tabernacle in the two s. H3411
32 of the tabernacle for the s westward. H3411
37: 5 by the s of the ark, to bear the ark. H6763
18 And six branches going out of the s H6654
26 top of it, and the s thereof round about, H7023
27 of it, upon the two s thereof, to be H6654
38: 7 the rings on the s of the altar, to bear H6763
39:20 put them on the two s of the ephod H3802
Nu 33:55 thorns in your s, and shall vex you in H6654
Jos 23:13 scourges in your s, and thorns in your H6654
Jdg 2: 3 *as thorns* in your s, and their gods shall H6654
5:30 on both s, *meet* for the necks of
1Sa 24: 3 his men remained in the s of the cave. H3411
1Ki 4:24 he had peace on all s round about him. H5676
6:16 And he built twenty cubits on the s of H3411
2Ki 19:23 mountains, to the s of Lebanon, and H3411
Ps 48: 2 Zion, *on* the s of the north, the city H3411
128: 3 fruitful vine by the s of thine house: thy H3411
Isa 14:13 the congregation, in the s of the north: H3411
15 brought down to hell, to the s of the pit. H3411
37:24 mountains, to the s of Lebanon; and I H3411
66:12 *her* s, and be dandled upon *her* knees. H6654
Jer 6:22 shall be raised from the s of the earth. H3411
48:28 her nest in the s of the hole's mouth. H5676
49:32 from all s thereof, saith the LORD. H5676
Ezk 1: 8 on their four s; and they four had their H7253
17 s: *and* they turned not when they went. H7253
10:11 upon their four s; they turned not as H7253
32:23 Whose graves are set in the s of the pit, H3411
41: 2 ten cubits; and the s of the door *were* H3802
26 other side, on the s of the porch, and H3802
42:20 He measured it by the four s: it had a H7307
46:19 *was* a place on the two s westward. H3411
Ezk 48: 1 his s east *and* west; a *portion for* Dan. H6285
Am 6:10 him that *is* by the s of the house, *Is* H3411
Jna 1: 5 down into the s of the ship; and he lay, H3411

SIDON
Gen 10:15 And Canaan begat S his firstborn, and H6721
19 was from S, as thou comest to Gerar, H6721
Mt 11:21 done in Tyre and S, they would have *G4605*
22 S at the day of judgment, than for you. *G4605*
15:21 departed into the coasts of Tyre and S. *G4605*
Mk 3: 8 about Tyre and S, a great multitude, *G4605*
7:24 of Tyre and S, and entered into an *G4605*
31 coasts of Tyre and S, he came unto the *G4605*
Lk 4:26 of S, unto a woman *that was* a widow. *G4605*
6:17 coast of Tyre and S, which came to hear *G4605*
10:13 done in Tyre and S, which have been *G4605*
14 and S at the judgment, than for you. *G4605*
Act 12:20 them of Tyre and S: but they came with *G4606*
27: 3 And the next *day* we touched at S. And *G4605*

SIDONIANS
Dt 3: 9 (*Which* Hermon the S call Sirion; and H6722
Jos 13: 4 that *is* beside the S, unto Aphek, to the H6722
6 *and* all the S, them will I drive out H6722
Jdg 3: 3 and the S, and the Hivites that H6722
1Ki 5: 6 can skill to hew timber like unto the S. H6722

SIEGE
Dt 20:19 *is* man's *life*) to employ *them* in the s: H4692
28:53 hath given thee, in the s, and in the H4692
55 left him in the s, and in the straitness, H4692
57 *things* secretly in the s and straitness, H4692
1Ki 15:27 and all Israel laid s to Gibbethon. H6696
2Ch 32: 9 he *himself laid* s against Lachish, and
10 that ye abide in the s in Jerusalem? H4692
Isa 29: 3 about, and will lay s against thee with H6696
Jer 19: 9 of his friend in the s and straitness, H4692
Ezk 4: 2 And lay s against it, and build a fort H4692
3 and thou shalt lay s against it. This H6696
7 thy face toward the s of Jerusalem, and H4692
8 till thou hast ended the days of thy s. H4692
5: 2 the days of the s are fulfilled: and thou H4692
Mic 5: 1 he hath laid s against us: they shall H4692
Nah 3:14 Draw thee waters for the s, fortify thy H4692
Zec 12: 2 when they shall be in the s both against H4692

SIEVE
Isa 30:28 nations with the s of vanity: and *there* H5299
Am 9: 9 as *corn* is sifted in a s, yet shall not the H3531

SIFT
Isa 30:28 of the neck, to s the nations with the H5130
Am 9: 9 For, lo, I will command, and I will s the H5128
Lk 22:31 *have* you, that he may s *you* as wheat: *G4617*

SIFTED
Am 9: 9 like as *corn* is s in a sieve, yet shall not H5128

SIGH
Isa 24: 7 languisheth, all the merryhearted do s. H584
Lam 1: 4 her priests s, her virgins are afflicted, H584
11 All her people s, they seek bread; they H584
21 They have heard that I s: *there is* none to H584
Ezk 9: 4 of the men that s and that cry for all the H584
21: 6 S therefore, thou son of man, with the H584
6 and with bitterness s before their eyes. H584

SIGHED
Ex 2:23 the children of Israel s by reason of the H584
Mk 7:34 And looking up to heaven, he s, and *G4727*
8:12 And he s deeply in his spirit, and saith, *G389*

SIGHEST
Ezk 21: 7 thee, Wherefore s thou? that thou shalt H584

SIGHETH
Lam 1: 8 yea, she s, and turneth backward. H584

SIGHING
Job 3:24 For my s cometh before I eat, and my H585
Ps 12: 5 For the oppression of the poor, for the s H603
31:10 and my years with s: my strength faileth H585
79:11 Let the s of the prisoner come before H603
Isa 21: 2 all the s thereof have I made to cease. H585
35:10 and sorrow and s shall flee away. H585
Jer 45: 3 I fainted in my s, and I find no rest. H585

SIGHS
Lam 1:22 for my s *are* many, and my heart *is* faint. H585

SIGHT

Gen 2: 9 is pleasant to the s, and good for food; H4758
18: 3 favour in thy s, pass not away, I pray H5869
19:19 hath found grace in thy s, and thou hast H5869
21:11 in Abraham's s because of his son. H5869
12 be grievous in thy s because of the lad, H5869
23: 4 that I may bury my dead out of my s. H6440
8 dead out of my s; hear me, and entreat H6440
32: 5 my lord, that I may find grace in thy s. H5869
33: 8 *are* to find grace in the s of my lord. H5869
10 found grace in thy s, then receive my H5869
15 it? let me find grace in the s of my lord. H5869
38: 7 s of the LORD; and the LORD slew him. H5869
39: 4 And Joseph found grace in his s, and he H5869
21 in the s of the keeper of the prison. H5869
47:18 ought left in the s of my lord, but our H6440
25 find grace in the s of my lord, and we H5869
29 found grace in thy s, put, I pray thee, H5869
Ex 3: 3 this great s, why the bush is not burnt. H4758
21 favour in the s of the Egyptians: and H5869
4:30 and did the signs in the s of the people. H5869
7:20 in the river, in the s of Pharaoh, and in H5869
20 and in the s of his servants; and H5869
9: 8 toward the heaven in the s of Pharaoh. H5869
11: 3 people favour in the s of the Egyptians. H5869
3 of Egypt, in the s of Pharaoh's servants, H5869
3 servants, and in the s of the people. H5869
12:36 favour in the s of the Egyptians, so H5869
15:26 is right in his s, and wilt give ear to H5869
17: 6 did so in the s of the elders of Israel. H5869
19:11 s of all the people upon mount Sinai. H5869
24:17 And the s of the glory of the LORD *was* H4758
33:12 and thou hast also found grace in my s. H5869
13 found grace in thy s, shew me now thy H5869
13 find grace in thy s: and consider that H5869
16 found grace in thy s? *is it* not in that H5869
17 in my s, and I know thee by name. H5869
34: 9 found grace in thy s, O Lord, let my H5869
40:38 it by night, in the s of all the house of H5869
Lev 10:19 been accepted in the s of the LORD? H5869
13: 3 and the plague in s *be* deeper than the H4758
4 of his flesh, and in s *be* not deeper than H4758
5 *if* the plague in his s be at a stay, *and* H5869
20 it, behold, it *be* in s lower than the skin, H4758
25 white, and it *be in* s deeper than the H4758
30 behold, if it *be* in s deeper than the H4758
31 it *be* not in s deeper than the skin, H4758
32 scall *be* not in s deeper than the skin; H4758
34 in the skin, nor *be* in s deeper than the H4758
37 But if the scall be in his s at a stay, and H5869
14:37 which in s *are* lower than the wall; H4758
20:17 be cut off in the s of their people: he H5869
25:53 not rule with rigour over him in thy s. H5869
26:45 of Egypt in the s of the heathen, that H5869
Nu 3: 4 office in the s of Aaron their father. H6440
11:11 favour in thy s, that thou layest the H5869
15 s; and let me not see my wretchedness. H5869
13:33 were in our own s as grasshoppers, and H5869
33 grasshoppers, and so we were in their s. H5869
19: 5 And *one* shall burn the heifer in his s; H5869
20:27 Hor in the s of all the congregation. H5869
25: 6 woman in the s of Moses, and in the H5869
6 of Moses, and in the s of all the H5869
27:19 and give him a charge in their s. H5869
32: 5 found grace in thy s, let this land be H5869
13 in the s of the LORD, was consumed. H5869
33: 3 high hand in the s of all the Egyptians. H5869
Dt 4: 6 in the s of the nations, which H5869
25 shall do evil in the s of the LORD thy H5869
37 s with his mighty power out of Egypt; H6440
6:18 and good in the s of the LORD: that it H5869
9:18 doing wickedly in the s of the LORD, to H5869
12:25 *that which is* right in the s of the LORD. H5869
28 and right in the s of the LORD thy God. H5869
17: 2 wickedness in the s of the LORD thy H5869
21: 9 *that which is* right in the s of the LORD. H5869
28:34 So that thou shalt be mad for the s of H4758
67 the s of thine eyes which thou shalt see. H4758
31: 7 unto him in the s of all Israel, Be strong H5869
29 ye will do evil in the s of the LORD, to H5869
34:12 Moses shewed in the s of all Israel. H5869
Jos 3: 7 thee in the s of all Israel, that they H5869
4:14 Joshua in the s of all Israel; and they H5869
10:12 and he said in the s of Israel, Sun, H5869
23: 5 from out of your s; and ye shall possess H6440
24:17 great signs in our s, and preserved us in H5869
Jdg 2:11 the s of the LORD, and served Baalim: H5869
3: 7 Israel did evil in the s of the LORD, and H5869
12 evil again in the s of the LORD: and the H5869
Jdg 3:12 they had done evil in the s of the LORD. H5869
4: 1 s of the LORD, when Ehud was dead. H5869
6: 1 did evil in the s of the LORD: and the H5869
17 found grace in thy s, then shew me a H5869
21 angel of the LORD departed out of his s. H5869
10: 6 did evil again in the s of the LORD, and H5869
13: 1 evil again in the s of the LORD; and the H5869
Ru 2: 2 after *him* in whose s I shall find grace. H5869
13 find favour in thy s, my lord; for that H5869
1Sa 1:18 find grace in thy s. So the woman went H5869
12:17 the s of the LORD, in asking you a king. H5869
15:17 *wast* little in thine own s, *wast* thou not H5869
19 and didst evil in the s of the LORD? H5869
16:22 me; for he hath found favour in my s. H5869
18: 5 accepted in the s of all the people, and H5869
5 and also in the s of Saul's servants. H5869
29: 6 the host *is* good in my s: for I have not H5869
9 *art* good in my s, as an angel of God: H5869
2Sa 6:22 be base in mine own s: and of the H5869
7: 9 enemies out of thy s, and have made H6440
19 And this was yet a small thing in thy s, H5869
12: 9 to do evil in his s? thou hast killed Uriah H5869
11 lie with thy wives in the s of this sun. H5869
13: 5 the meat in my s, that I may see *it*, and H5869
6 in my s, that I may eat at her hand. H5869
8 cakes in his s, and did bake the cakes. H5869
14:22 found grace in thy s, my lord, O king, in H5869
16: 4 may find grace in thy s, my lord, O king. H5869
22 concubines in the s of all Israel. H5869
22:25 according to my cleanness in his eye s. H5869
1Ki 8:25 thee a man in my s to sit on the throne H6440
9: 7 I cast out of my s; and Israel shall be a H6440
11: 6 And Solomon did evil in the s of the H5869
19 And Hadad found great favour in the s H5869
38 *that is* right in my s, to keep my statutes H5869
14:22 And Judah did evil in the s of the H5869
15:26 And he did evil in the s of the LORD, H5869
34 And he did evil in the s of the LORD, H5869
16: 7 evil that he did in the s of the LORD, in H5869
19 in doing evil in the s of the LORD, in H5869
30 did evil in the s of the LORD above H5869
21:20 to work evil in the s of the LORD, H5869
25 work wickedness in the s of the LORD, H5869
22:52 And he did evil in the s of the LORD, H5869
2Ki 1:13 fifty thy servants, be precious in thy s. H5869
14 let my life now be precious in thy s. H5869
3: 2 And he wrought evil in the s of the H5869
18 And this is *but* a light thing in the s of H5869
8:18 and he did evil in the s of the LORD. H5869
27 and did evil in the s of the LORD, as H5869
12: 2 *was* right in the s of the LORD all his H5869
13: 2 And he did *that which was* evil in the s H5869
11 And he did *that which was* evil in the s H5869
14: 3 *was* right in the s of the LORD, yet not H5869
24 And he did *that which was* evil in the s H5869
15: 3 *which was* right in the s of the LORD, H5869
9 And he did *that which was* evil in the s H5869
18 And he did *that which was* evil in the s H5869
24 And he did *that which was* evil in the s H5869
28 And he did *that which was* evil in the s H5869
34 *was* right in the s of the LORD: he did H5869
16: 2 *was* right in the s of the LORD his God, H5869
17: 2 And he did *that which was* evil in the s H5869
17 to do evil in the s of the LORD, to H5869
18 them out of his s: there was none left H6440
20 until he had cast them out of his s. H6440
23 Israel out of his s, as he had said by all H6440
18: 3 *which was* right in the s of the LORD, H5869
20: 3 good in thy s. And Hezekiah wept sore. H5869
21: 2 And he did *that which was* evil in the s H5869
6 wickedness in the s of the LORD, to H5869
15 *was* evil in my s, and have provoked H5869
16 *which was* evil in the s of the LORD. H5869
20 And he did *that which was* evil in the s H5869
22: 2 *was* right in the s of the LORD, and H5869
23:27 also out of my s, as I have removed H6440
32 And he did *that which was* evil in the s H5869
37 And he did *that which was* evil in the s H5869
24: 3 remove *them* out of his s, for the sins of H6440
9 And he did *that which was* evil in the s H5869
19 And he did *that which was* evil in the s H5869
1Ch 2: 3 in the s of the LORD; and he slew him. H5869
19:13 the LORD do *that which is* good in his s. H5869
22: 8 much blood upon the earth in my s. H6440
28: 8 Now therefore in the s of all Israel the H5869
29:25 exceedingly in the s of all Israel, and H5869
2Ch 6:16 fail thee a man in my s to sit upon the H6440
7:20 I cast out of my s, and will make it *to be* H6440
20:32 *which was* right in the s of the LORD. H5869
2Ch 22: 4 Wherefore he did evil in the s of the H5869
24: 2 *was* right in the s of the LORD all the H5869
25: 2 *was* right in the s of the LORD, but not H5869
26: 4 *which was* right in the s of the LORD, H5869
27: 2 *which was* right in the s of the LORD, H5869
28: 1 s of the LORD, like David his father: H5869
29: 2 *which was* right in the s of the LORD, H5869
32:23 in the s of all nations from thenceforth. H5869
33: 2 But did *that which was* evil in the s of H5869
6 much evil in the s of the LORD, to H5869
22 But he did *that which was* evil in the s H5869
34: 2 *was* right in the s of the LORD, and H5869
36: 5 *was* evil in the s of the LORD his God. H5869
9 *which was* evil in the s of the LORD. H5869
12 And he did *that which was* evil in the s H5869
Ezr 9: 9 unto us in the s of the kings of Persia, H6440
Neh 1:11 him mercy in the s of this man. For I H6440
2: 5 favour in thy s, that thou wouldest H6440
8: 5 And Ezra opened the book in the s of H5869
Est 2:15 the s of all them that looked upon her. H5869
17 and favour in his s more than all the H6440
5: 2 favour in his s: and the king held out H5869
8 If I have found favour in the s of the H5869
7: 3 favour in thy s, O king, and if it please H5869
8: 5 favour in his s, and the thing *seem* H6440
Job 15:15 yea, the heavens are not clean in his s. H5869
18: 3 as beasts, *and* reputed vile in your s? H5869
19:15 for a stranger: I am an alien in their s. H5869
21: 8 Their seed is established in their s with H6440
25: 5 not; yea, the stars are not pure in his s. H5869
34:26 as wicked men in the open s of others; H7200
41: 9 *one* be cast down even at the s of him? H4758
Ps 5: 5 The foolish shall not stand in thy s: H5869
9:19 let the heathen be judged in thy s. H6440
10: 5 above out of his s: *as for* all his enemies, H5048
19:14 be acceptable in thy s, O LORD, my H6440
51: 4 *this* evil in thy s: that thou mightest be H5869
72:14 precious shall their blood be in his s. H5869
76: 7 in thy s when once thou art angry? H6440
78:12 Marvellous things did he in the s of H5048
79:10 the heathen in our s *by* the revenging of H5869
90: 4 For a thousand years in thy s *are but* as H5869
98: 2 openly shewed in the s of the heathen. H5869
101: 7 that telleth lies shall not tarry in my s. H5869
116:15 Precious in the s of the LORD *is* the H5869
143: 2 in thy s shall no man living be justified. H6440
Prv 1:17 Surely in vain the net is spread in the s H5869
3: 4 in the s of God and man. H5869
4: 3 only *beloved* in the s of my mother. H6440
Ecc 2:26 man that *is* good in his s wisdom, and H6440
6: 9 Better *is* the s of the eyes than the H4758
8: 3 Be not hasty to go out of his s: stand not H6440
11: 9 heart, and in the s of thine eyes: but H4758
Isa 5:21 own eyes, and prudent in their own s! H6440
11: 3 not judge after the s of his eyes, neither H4758
26:17 so have we been in thy s, O LORD. H6440
38: 3 good in thy s. And Hezekiah wept sore. H5869
43: 4 Since thou wast precious in my s, thou H5869
Jer 4: 1 out of my s, then shalt thou not remove. H6440
7:15 And I will cast you out of my s, as I H6440
30 done evil in my s, saith the LORD: they H5869
15: 1 *them* out of my s, and let them go forth. H6440
18:10 If it do evil in my s, that it obey not my H5869
23 out their sin from thy s, but let them be H6440
19:10 in the s of the men that go with thee, H5869
32:12 Maaseiah, in the s of Hanameel mine H5869
34:15 had done right in my s, in proclaiming H5869
43: 9 in the s of the men of Judah; H5869
51:24 done in Zion in your s, saith the LORD. H5869
Ezk 4:12 dung that cometh out of man, in their s. H5869
5: 8 the midst of thee in the s of the nations. H5869
14 about thee, in the s of all that pass by. H5869
10: 2 over the city. And he went in in my s. H5869
19 the earth in my s: when they went out, H5869
12: 3 by day in their s; and thou shalt remove H5869
3 place in their s: it may be they will H5869
4 by day in their s, as stuff for removing: H5869
4 s, as they that go forth into captivity. H5869
5 Dig thou through the wall in their s, and H5869
6 In their s shalt thou bear *it* upon *thy* H5869
7 I bare *it* upon *my* shoulder in their s. H5869
16:41 upon thee in the s of many women: H5869
20: 9 *were*, in whose s I made myself known H5869
14 in whose s I brought them out. H5869
22 be polluted in the s of the heathen, in H5869
22 in whose s I brought them forth. H5869
43 in your own s for all your evils that H6440
21:23 divination in their s, to them that have H5869
22:16 in thyself in the s of the heathen, and H5869

Ezk 28:18 in the s of all them that behold thee. H5869
25 in them in the s of the heathen, then H5869
36:31 in your own s for your iniquities and H6440
34 desolate in the s of all that passed by. H5869
39:27 in them in the s of many nations; H5869
43:11 write *it* in their s, that they may keep H5869
Dan 4:11 the s thereof to the end of all the earth: H2379
20 and the s thereof to all the earth; H2379
Hos 2: 2 out of her s, and her adulteries from H6440
10 her lewdness in the s of her lovers, and H5869
6: 2 raise us up, and we shall live in his s. H6440
Am 9: 3 be hid from my s in the bottom of the H5869
Jna 2: 4 Then I said, I am cast out of thy s; yet I H5869
Mal 2:17 evil *is* good in the s of the LORD, and H5869
Mt 11: 5 The blind receive their s, and the lame G308
26 Father: for so it seemed good in thy s. G1715
20:34 eyes received s, and they followed him. G308
Mk 10:51 him, Lord, that I might receive my s. G308
52 his s, and followed Jesus in the way. G308
Lk 1:15 For he shall be great in the s of the G1799
4:18 and recovering of s to the blind, to set at G309
7:21 and unto many *that were* blind he gave s. G991
10:21 Father; for so it seemed good in thy s. G1715
15:21 heaven, and in thy s, and am no more G1799
16:15 men is abomination in the s of God. G1799
18:41 he said, Lord, that I may receive my s. G308
42 And Jesus said unto him, Receive thy s: G308
43 And immediately he received his s, and G308
23:48 together to that s, beholding the things G2335
24:31 knew him; and he vanished out of their s. G575
Jn 9:11 and I went and washed, and I received s. G308
15 he had received his s. He said unto them, G308
18 and received his s, until they called the G308
18 parents of him that had received his s. G308
Act 1: 9 and a cloud received him out of their s. G3788
4:19 it be right in the s of God to hearken G1799
7:10 and wisdom in the s of Pharaoh king of G1726
31 wondered at the s: and as he drew near G3705
8:21 for thy heart is not right in the s of God. G1799
9: 9 And he was three days without s, and G991
12 hand on him, that he might receive his s. G308
17 thy s, and be filled with the Holy Ghost. G308
18 and he received s forthwith, and arose, G308
10:31 had in remembrance in the s of God. G1799
22:13 Saul, receive thy s. And the same hour I G308
Ro 3:20 s: for by the law *is* the knowledge of sin. G1799
12:17 things honest in the s of all men. G1799
2Co 2:17 God, in the s of God speak we in Christ. G2714
4: 2 every man's conscience in the s of God. G1799
5: 7 (For we walk by faith, not by s:) G1491
7:12 in the s of God might appear unto you. G1799
8:21 not only in the s of the Lord, but also G1799
21 of the Lord, but also in the s of men. G1799
Gal 3:11 by the law in the s of God, *it is* evident: G3844
Col 1:22 and unreproveable in his s: G2714
1Th 1: 3 Christ, in the s of God and our Father; G1715
1Ti 2: 3 For this *is* good and acceptable in the s G1799
6:13 I give thee charge in the s of God, who G1799
Heb 4:13 not manifest in his s: but all things *are* G1799
12:21 And so terrible was the s, *that* Moses G5324
13:21 is wellpleasing in his s, through Jesus G1799
Jas 4:10 Humble yourselves in the s of the Lord, G1799
1Pt 3: 4 which is in the s of God of great price. G1799
1Jn 3:22 those things that are pleasing in his s. G1799
Rev 4: 3 the throne, in s like unto an emerald. G3706
13:13 heaven on the earth in the s of men, G1799
14 power to do in the s of the beast; saying G1799

SIGHTS
Lk 21:11 and fearful s and great signs shall G5400

SIGN
Ex 4: 8 voice of the first s, that they will believe H226
8 they will believe the voice of the latter s. H226
8:23 thy people: to morrow shall this s be. H226
13: 9 And it shall be for a s unto thee upon H226
31:13 keep: for it *is* a s between me and you H226
17 It *is* a s between me and the children of H226
Nu 16:38 shall be a s unto the children of Israel. H226
26:10 and fifty men: and they became a s. H5251
Dt 6: 8 And thou shalt bind them for a s upon H226
11:18 bind them for a s upon your hand, that H226
13: 1 dreams, and giveth thee a s or a wonder, H226
2 And the s or the wonder come to pass, H226
28:46 And they shall be upon thee for a s and H226
Jos 4: 6 That this may be a s among you, *that* H226
Jdg 6:17 shew me a s that thou talkest with me. H226
20:38 Now there was an appointed s between H4150
1Sa 2:34 And this *shall be* a s unto thee, that shall H226
1Sa 14:10 our hand: and this *shall be* a s unto us. H226
1Ki 13: 3 And he gave a s the same day, saying, H4159
3 saying, This *is* the s which the LORD H4159
5 according to the s which the man of H4159
2Ki 19:29 And this *shall be* a s unto thee, Ye shall H226
20: 8 What *shall be* the s that the LORD will H226
9 And Isaiah said, This s shalt thou have H226
2Ch 32:24 he spake unto him, and he gave him a s. H4159
Isa 7:11 Ask thee a s of the LORD thy God; ask it H226
14 shall give you a s; Behold, a virgin shall H226
19:20 And it shall be for a s and for a witness H226
20: 3 three years *for* a s and wonder upon H226
37:30 And this *shall be* a s unto thee, Ye shall H226
38: 7 And this *shall be* a s unto thee from the H226
22 Hezekiah also had said, What *is* the s H226
55:13 an everlasting s *that* shall not be cut off. H226
66:19 And I will set a s among them, and I will H226
Jer 6: 1 and set up a s of fire in Beth-haccerem: H4864
44:29 And this *shall be* a s unto you, saith the H226
Ezk 4: 3 it. This *shall be* a s to the house of Israel. H226
12: 6 set thee *for* a s unto the house of Israel. H4159
11 Say, I *am* your s: like as I have done, so H4159
14: 8 will make him a s and a proverb, and I H226
20:12 my sabbaths, to be a s between me and H226
20 and they shall be a s between me and H226
24:24 Thus Ezekiel is unto you a s: according H4159
27 thou shalt be a s unto them; and they H4159
39:15 shall he set up a s by it, till the buriers H6725
Dan 6: 8 the decree, and s the writing, that it be H7560
Mt 12:38 Master, we would see a s from thee. G4592
39 seeketh after a s; and there shall no sign G4592
39 and there shall no s be given to it, but G4592
39 to it, but the s of the prophet Jonas: G4592
16: 1 he would shew them a s from heaven. G4592
4 seeketh after a s; and there shall no sign G4592
4 and there shall no s be given unto it, G4592
4 unto it, but the s of the prophet Jonas. G4592
24: 3 what *shall be* the s of thy coming, and G4592
30 And then shall appear the s of the Son G4592
26:48 betrayed him gave them a s, saying, G4592
Mk 8:11 of him a s from heaven, tempting him. G4592
12 seek after a s? verily I say unto you, G4592
12 no s be given unto this generation. G4592
13: 4 and what *shall be* the s when all these G4592
Lk 2:12 And this *shall be* a s unto you; Ye shall G4592
34 for a s which shall be spoken against; G4592
11:16 *him*, sought of him a s from heaven. G4592
29 they seek a s; and there shall no sign G4592
29 and there shall no s be given it, but the G4592
29 given it, but the s of Jonas the prophet. G4592
30 For as Jonas was a s unto the G4592
21: 7 be? and what s *will there be* when these G4592
Jn 2:18 unto him, What s shewest thou unto G4592
6:30 They said therefore unto him, What s G4592
Act 28:11 isle, whose s was Castor and Pollux. G3902
Ro 4:11 And he received the s of circumcision, G4592
1Co 1:22 For the Jews require a s, and the Greeks G4592
14:22 Wherefore tongues are for a s, not to G4592
Rev 15: 1 And I saw another s in heaven, great G4592

SIGNED
Dan 6: 9 Wherefore king Darius s the writing H7560
10 that the writing was s, he went into his H7560
12 Hast thou not s a decree, that every H7560
13 decree that thou hast s, but maketh his H7560

SIGNET
Gen 38:18 And she said, Thy s, and thy bracelets, H2368
25 *are* these, the s, and bracelets, and staff. H2858
Ex 28:11 engravings of a s, shalt thou engrave H2368
21 the engravings of a s; every one with his H2368
36 of a s, HOLINESS TO THE LORD. H2368
39:14 the engravings of a s, every one with his H2368
30 of a s, HOLINESS TO THE LORD. H2368
Jer 22:24 king of Judah were the s upon my right H2368
Dan 6:17 it with his own s, and with the signet H5824
17 and with the s of his lords; that the H5824
Hag 2:23 make thee as a s: for I have chosen thee, H2368

SIGNETS
Ex 39: 6 of gold, graven, as s are graven, with H2368

SIGNIFICATION
1Co 14:10 the world, and none of them *is* without s. G880

SIGNIFIED
Act 11:28 Agabus, and s by the Spirit that there G4591
Rev 1: 1 s *it* by his angel unto his servant John: G4591

SIGNIFIETH
Heb 12:27 And this *word*, Yet once more, s the G1213

SIGNIFY
Act 21:26 entered into the temple, to s the G1229
23:15 Now therefore ye with the council s to G1718
25:27 withal to s the crimes *laid* against him. G4591
1Pt 1:11 was in them did s, when it testified G1213

SIGNIFYING
Jn 12:33 This he said, s what death he should G4591
18:32 he spake, s what death he should die. G4591
21:19 This spake he, s by what death he G4591
Heb 9: 8 The Holy Ghost this s, that the way into G1213

SIGNS
Gen 1:14 and let them be for s, and for seasons, H226
Ex 4: 9 also these two s, neither hearken unto H226
17 in thine hand, wherewith thou shalt do s. H226
28 all the s which he had commanded him. H226
30 and did the s in the sight of the people. H226
7: 3 s and my wonders in the land of Egypt. H226
10: 1 that I might shew these my s before him: H226
2 in Egypt, and my s which I have done H226
Nu 14:11 the s which I have shewed among them? H226
Dt 4:34 by temptations, by s, and by wonders, H226
6:22 And the LORD shewed s and wonders, H226
7:19 eyes saw, and the s, and the wonders, H226
26: 8 and with s, and with wonders: H226
29: 3 seen, the s, and those great miracles: H226
34:11 In all the s and the wonders, which the H226
Jos 24:17 which did those great s in our sight, and H226
1Sa 10: 7 And let it be, when these s are come unto H226
9 and all those s came to pass that day. H226
Neh 9:10 And shewedst s and wonders upon H226
Ps 74: 4 they set up their ensigns *for* s. H226
9 We see not our s: *there is* no more any H226
78:43 How he had wrought his s in Egypt, and H226
105:27 They shewed his s among them, H226+H1697
Isa 8:18 given me *are* for s and for wonders in H226
Jer 10: 2 not dismayed at the s of heaven; for the H226
32:20 Which hast set s and wonders in the H226
21 land of Egypt with s, and with wonders, H226
Dan 4: 2 I thought it good to shew the s and H852
3 How great *are* his s! and how mighty *are* H852
6:27 and he worketh s and wonders in H852
Mt 16: 3 can ye not *discern* the s of the times? G4592
24:24 and shall shew great s and wonders; G4592
Mk 13:22 rise, and shall shew s and wonders, to G4592
16:17 And these s shall follow them that G4592
20 the word with s following. Amen. G4592
Lk 1:62 And they made s to his father, how he G1770
21:11 and great s shall there be from heaven. G4592
25 And there shall be s in the sun, and in G4592
Jn 4:48 see s and wonders, ye will not believe. G4592
20:30 And many other s truly did Jesus in the G4592
Act 2:19 above, and s in the earth beneath; G4592
22 and wonders and s, which God did by G4592
43 and s were done by the apostles. G4592
4:30 to heal; and that s and wonders may be G4592
5:12 were many s and wonders wrought G4592
7:36 wonders and s in the land of Egypt, G4592
8:13 the miracles and s which were done. G4592
14: 3 and granted s and wonders to be done G4592
Ro 15:19 Through mighty s and wonders, by the G4592
2Co 12:12 Truly the s of an apostle were wrought G4592
12 in s, and wonders, and mighty deeds. G4592
2Th 2: 9 all power and s and lying wonders, G4592
Heb 2: 4 witness, both with s and wonders, and G4592

SIHON
Nu 21:21 And Israel sent messengers unto S king H5511
23 And S would not suffer Israel to pass H5511
23 his border: but S gathered all his H5511
26 For Heshbon *was* the city of S the king H5511
27 let the city of S be built and prepared: H5511
28 from the city of S: it hath consumed Ar H5511
29 captivity unto S king of the Amorites. H5511
34 him as thou didst unto S king of the H5511
32:33 the kingdom of S king of the Amorites, H5511
Dt 1: 4 After he had slain S the king of the H5511
2:24 into thine hand S the Amorite, king of H5511
26 of Kedemoth unto S king of Heshbon H5511
30 But S king of Heshbon would not let us H5511
31 begun to give S and his land before H5511
32 Then S came out against us, he and all H5511
3: 2 him as thou didst unto S king of the H5511
6 as we did unto S king of Heshbon, H5511
4:46 in the land of S king of the Amorites, H5511

Dt 29: 7 And when ye came unto this place, S H5511
31: 4 them as he did to S and to Og, kings of H5511
Jos 2:10 S and Og, whom ye utterly destroyed. H5511
9:10 beyond Jordan, to S king of Heshbon, H5511
12: 2 S king of the Amorites, who dwelt in H5511
5 the border of S king of Heshbon. H5511
13:10 And all the cities of S king of the H5511
21 and all the kingdom of S king of the H5511
21 dukes of S, dwelling in the country. H5511
27 of the kingdom of S king of Heshbon, H5511
Jdg 11:19 And Israel sent messengers unto S king H5511
20 But S trusted not Israel to pass through H5511
20 his coast: but S gathered all his people H5511
21 of Israel delivered S and all his people H5511
1Ki 4:19 Gilead, *in* the country of S king of the H5511
Neh 9:22 the land of S, and the land of the H5511
Ps 135:11 S king of the Amorites, and Og king of H5511
136:19 S king of the Amorites: for his mercy H5511
Jer 48:45 from the midst of S, and shall devour H5511

SIHOR
Jos 13: 3 From S, which *is* before Egypt, even H7883
Isa 23: 3 And by great waters the seed of S, the H7883
Jer 2:18 the waters of S? or what hast thou to H7883

SILAS
Act 15:22 and S, chief men among the brethren: G4609
27 We have sent therefore Judas and S, G4609
32 And Judas and S, being prophets also G4609
34 Notwithstanding it pleased S to abide G4609
40 And Paul chose S, and departed, being G4609
16:19 caught Paul and S, and drew *them* into G4609
25 And at midnight Paul and S prayed, G4609
29 and fell down before Paul and S, G4609
17: 4 with Paul and S; and of the devout G4609
10 away Paul and S by night unto Berea: G4609
14 but S and Timotheus abode there still. G4609
15 unto S and Timotheus for G4609
18: 5 And when S and Timotheus were come G4609

SILENCE
Jdg 3:19 who said, Keep s. And all that stood by H2013
Job 4:16 *there was* s, and I heard a voice, *saying*, H1827
29:21 and waited, and kept s at my counsel. H1826
31:34 I kept s, *and* went not out of the door? H1826
Ps 31:18 Let the lying lips be put to s; which speak H481
32: 3 When I kept s, my bones waxed old H2790
35:22 keep not s: O Lord, be not far from me. H2790
39: 2 I was dumb with s, I held my peace, H1747
50: 3 and shall not keep s: a fire shall devour H2790
21 done, and I kept s; thou thoughtest that H2790
83: 1 Keep not thou s, O God: hold not thy H1824
94:17 my help, my soul had almost dwelt in s. H1745
115:17 LORD, neither any that go down into s. H1745
Ecc 3: 7 a time to keep s, and a time to speak; H2814
Isa 15: 1 *and* brought to s; because in the night H1820
1 of Moab is laid waste, *and* brought to s; H1820
41: 1 Keep s before me, O islands; and let the H2790
62: 6 make mention of the LORD, keep not s, H1824
65: 6 before me: I will not keep s, but will H2814
Jer 8:14 our God hath put us to s, and given us H1826
Lam 2:10 ground, *and* keep s: they have cast up H1826
3:28 He sitteth alone and keepeth s, because H1826
Am 5:13 Therefore the prudent shall keep s in H1826
8: 3 place; they shall cast *them* forth with s. H2013
Hab 2:20 let all the earth keep s before him. H2013
Mt 22:34 to s, they were gathered together. G5392
Act 15:12 Then all the multitude kept s, and gave G4601
21:40 was made a great s, he spake unto *them* G4602
22: 2 they kept the more s: and he saith,) G2271
1Co 14:28 let him keep s in the church; and let G4601
34 Let your women keep s in the churches: G4601
1Ti 2:11 Let the woman learn in s with all G2271
12 authority over the man, but to be in s. G2271
1Pt 2:15 put to s the ignorance of foolish men: G5392
Rev 8: 1 seal, there was s in heaven about the G4602

SILENT
1Sa 2: 9 wicked shall be s in darkness; for by H1826
Ps 22: 2 and in the night season, and am not s. H1747
28: 1 my rock; be not s to me: lest, *if* thou be H2790
1 to me: lest, *if* thou be s to me, I become H2814
30:12 to thee, and not be s. O LORD my God, I H1826
31:17 *and* let them be s in the grave. H1826
Isa 47: 5 Sit thou s, and get thee into darkness, O H1748
Jer 8:14 and let us be s there: for the LORD H1826
Zec 2:13 Be s, O all flesh, before the LORD: for he H2013

SILK
Prv 31:22 tapestry; her clothing *is* s and purple. H8336
Ezk 16:10 fine linen, and I covered thee with s. H4897
13 *was of* fine linen, and s, and broidered H4897
Rev 18:12 and purple, and s, and scarlet, and all G4596

SILLA
2Ki 12:20 house of Millo, which goeth down to S. H5538

SILLY
Job 5: 2 man, and envy slayeth the s one. H6601
Hos 7:11 Ephraim also is like a s dove without H6601
2Ti 3: 6 and lead captive s women laden with G1133

SILOAH
Neh 3:15 the wall of the pool of S by the king's H7975

SILOAM
Lk 13: 4 the tower in S fell, and slew them, G4611
Jn 9: 7 wash in the pool of S, (which is by G4611
11 me, Go to the pool of S, and wash: and I G4611

SILVANUS
2Co 1:19 *even* by me and S and Timotheus, was G4610
1Th 1: 1 Paul, and S, and Timotheus, unto the G4610
2Th 1: 1 Paul, and S, and Timotheus, unto the G4610
1Pt 5:12 By S, a faithful brother unto you, as I G4610

SILVER
Gen 13: 2 And Abram *was* very rich in cattle, in s, H3701
20:16 *pieces* of s: behold, he *is* to thee H3701
23:15 shekels of s; what *is* that betwixt H3701
16 to Ephron the s, which he had named H3701
16 of s, current *money* with the merchant. H3701
24:35 flocks, and herds, and s, and gold, and H3701
53 forth jewels of s, and jewels of gold, and H3701
37:28 s: and they brought Joseph into Egypt. H3701
44: 2 And put my cup, the s cup, in the H3701
8 steal out of thy lord's house s or gold? H3701
45:22 *pieces* of s, and five changes of raiment. H3701
Ex 3:22 house, jewels of s, and jewels of gold, H3701
11: 2 jewels of s, and jewels of gold. H3701
12:35 of s, and jewels of gold, and raiment: H3701
20:23 Ye shall not make with me gods of s, H3701
21:32 shekels of s, and the ox shall be stoned. H3701
25: 3 take of them; gold, and s, and brass, H3701
26:19 And thou shalt make forty sockets of s H3701
21 And their forty sockets *of* s; two sockets H3701
25 their sockets *of* s, sixteen sockets; two H3701
32 *be of* gold, upon the four sockets of s. H3701
27:10 the pillars and their fillets *shall be of* s. H3701
11 hooks of the pillars and their fillets *of* s. H3701
17 *be* filleted with s; their hooks *shall be* H3701
17 *shall be of* s, and their sockets *of* brass. H3701
31: 4 to work in gold, and in s, and in brass, H3701
35: 5 of the LORD; gold, and s, and brass, H3701
24 Every one that did offer an offering of s H3701
32 to work in gold, and in s, and in brass, H3701
36:24 And forty sockets of s he made under H3701
26 And their forty sockets of s; two sockets H3701
30 of s, under every board two sockets. H3701
36 and he cast for them four sockets of s. H3701
38:10 of the pillars and their fillets *were of* s. H3701
11 hooks of the pillars and their fillets *of* s. H3701
12 hooks of the pillars and their fillets *of* s. H3701
17 and their fillets *of* s; and the overlaying H3701
17 their chapiters *of* s; and all the pillars of H3701
17 pillars of the court *were* filleted with s. H3701
19 their hooks *of* s, and the overlaying of H3701
19 of their chapiters and their fillets *of* s. H3701
25 And the s of them that were numbered H3701
27 And of the hundred talents of s were H3701
Lev 5:15 by shekels of s, after the shekel of the H3701
27: 3 of s, after the shekel of the sanctuary. H3701
6 five shekels of s, and for the female thy H3701
6 estimation *shall be* three shekels of s. H3701
16 seed *shall be valued* at fifty shekels of s. H3701
Nu 7:13 And his offering *was* one s charger, the H3701
13 thirty *shekels*, one s bowl of seventy H3701
19 He offered *for* his offering one s H3701
19 thirty *shekels*, one s bowl of seventy H3701
25 His offering *was* one s charger, the H3701
25 thirty *shekels*, one s bowl of seventy H3701
31 His offering *was* one s charger of the H3701
31 thirty *shekels*, one s bowl of seventy H3701
37 His offering *was* one s charger, the H3701
37 thirty *shekels*, one s bowl of seventy H3701
43 His offering *was* one s charger of the H3701
43 and thirty *shekels*, a s bowl of seventy H3701
Nu 7:49 His offering *was* one s charger, the H3701
49 thirty *shekels*, one s bowl of seventy H3701
55 His offering *was* one s charger of the H3701
55 thirty *shekels*, one s bowl of seventy H3701
61 His offering *was* one s charger, the H3701
61 thirty *shekels*, one s bowl of seventy H3701
67 His offering *was* one s charger, the H3701
67 thirty *shekels*, one s bowl of seventy H3701
73 His offering *was* one s charger, the H3701
73 thirty *shekels*, one s bowl of seventy H3701
79 His offering *was* one s charger, the H3701
79 thirty *shekels*, one s bowl of seventy H3701
84 Israel: twelve chargers of s, twelve silver H3701
84 twelve s bowls, twelve spoons of gold: H3701
85 Each charger of s *weighing* an hundred H3701
85 seventy: all the s vessels *weighed* two H3701
10: 2 Make thee two trumpets of s; of a whole H3701
22:18 his house full of s and gold, I cannot go H3701
24:13 his house full of s and gold, I cannot go H3701
31:22 Only the gold, and the s, the brass, the H3701
Dt 7:25 not desire the s or gold *that is* on them, H3701
8:13 multiply, and thy s and thy gold is H3701
17:17 greatly multiply to himself s and gold. H3701
22:19 *shekels* of s, and give *them* unto H3701
29 fifty *shekels* of s, and she shall be his H3701
29:17 s and gold, which *were* among them:) H3701
Jos 6:19 But all the s, and gold, and vessels of H3701
24 therein: only the s, and the gold, and H3701
7:21 shekels of s, and a wedge of gold H3701
21 midst of my tent, and the s under it. H3701
22 *was* hid in his tent, and the s under it. H3701
24 of Zerah, and the s, and the garment, H3701
22: 8 much cattle, with s, and with gold, and H3701
24:32 hundred pieces of s: and it became the H7192
Jdg 9: 4 and ten *pieces* of s out of the house of H3701
16: 5 one of us eleven hundred *pieces* of s. H3701
17: 2 *shekels* of s that were taken from H3701
2 ears, behold, the s *is* with me; I took it. H3701
3 *shekels* of s to his mother, his mother H3701
3 dedicated the s unto the LORD from H3701
4 *shekels* of s, and gave them to the H3701
10 thee ten *shekels* of s by the year, and a H3701
1Sa 2:36 to him for a piece of s and a morsel of H3701
9: 8 part of a shekel of s: *that* will I give to H3701
2Sa 8:10 him vessels of s, and vessels of gold, H3701
11 LORD, with the s and gold that he had H3701
18:11 given thee ten *shekels* of s, and a girdle. H3701
12 *shekels* of s in mine hand, *yet* would H3701
21: 4 We will have no s nor gold of Saul, nor H3701
24:24 and the oxen for fifty shekels of s. H3701
1Ki 7:51 *even* the s, and the gold, and the H3701
10:21 gold; none *were of* s: it was nothing H3701
22 and s, ivory, and apes, and peacocks. H3701
25 present, vessels of s, and vessels of gold, H3701
27 And the king made s *to be* in Jerusalem H3701
29 *shekels* of s, and an horse for an H3701
15:15 of the LORD, s, and gold, and vessels. H3701
18 Then Asa took all the s and the gold H3701
19 thee a present of s and gold; come and H3701
16:24 for two talents of s, and built on the hill, H3701
20: 3 Thy s and thy gold *is* mine; thy wives H3701
5 deliver me thy s, and thy gold, and thy H3701
7 and for my s, and for my gold; and H3701
39 life, or else thou shalt pay a talent of s. H3701
2Ki 5: 5 him ten talents of s, and six thousand H3701
22 of s, and two changes of garments. H3701
23 two talents of s in two bags, with two H3701
6:25 for fourscore *pieces* of s, and the fourth H3701
25 a cab of dove's dung for five *pieces* of s. H3701
7: 8 carried thence s, and gold, and raiment, H3701
12:13 the LORD bowls of s, snuffers, basons, H3701
13 gold, or vessels of s, of the money *that* H3701
14:14 And he took all the gold and s, and all H3701
15:19 talents of s, that his hand might H3701
20 fifty shekels of s, to give to the king of H3701
16: 8 And Ahaz took the s and gold that was H3701
18:14 talents of s and thirty talents of gold. H3701
15 And Hezekiah gave *him* all the s that H3701
20:13 things, the s, and the gold, and the H3701
22: 4 he may sum the s which is brought into H3701
23:33 talents of s, and a talent of gold. H3701
35 And Jehoiakim gave the s and the gold H3701
35 he exacted the s and the gold of the H3701
25:15 *in* gold, and of s, *in* silver, the captain H3701
15 s, the captain of the guard took away. H3701
1Ch 18:10 of vessels of gold and s and brass. H3701
11 LORD, with the s and the gold that he H3701
19: 6 talents of s to hire them chariots H3701
22:14 talents of s; and of brass and iron H3701

S

1Ch 22:16 Of the gold, the s, and the brass, and the H3701
28:14 all manner of service; *s also* for all
14 all instruments of s by weight, for all H3701
15 the candlesticks of s by weight, *both* for H3701
16 and *likewise* s for the tables of silver: H3701
16 and *likewise* silver for the tables of s: H3701
17 *s* by weight for every bason of silver:
17 *silver* by weight for every bason of s: H3701
29: 2 of gold, and the s for *things* of silver, H3701
2 silver for *things* of s, and the brass for H3701
3 good, of gold and s, *which* I have given H3701
4 talents of refined s, to overlay the walls H3701
5 The gold for *things* of gold, and the s H3701
5 silver for *things* of s, and for all manner H3701
7 drams, and of s ten thousand talents, H3701
2Ch 1:15 And the king made s and gold at H3701
17 *shekels* of s, and an horse for an H3701
2: 7 in gold, and in s, and in brass, and in H3701
14 in gold, and in s, in brass, in iron, in H3701
5: 1 dedicated; and the s, and the gold, and H3701
9:14 brought gold and s to Solomon. H3701
20 gold: none *were of* s; it was *not* any H3701
21 and s, ivory, and apes, and peacocks. H3701
24 present, vessels of s, and vessels of gold, H3701
27 And the king made s in Jerusalem as H3701
15:18 had dedicated, s, and gold, and vessels. H3701
16: 2 Then Asa brought out s and gold out of H3701
3 I have sent thee s and gold; go, break H3701
17:11 and tribute s; and the Arabians brought H3701
21: 3 them great gifts of s, and of gold, and of H3701
24:14 vessels of gold and s. And they offered H3701
25: 6 out of Israel for an hundred talents of s. H3701
24 And *he took* all the gold and the s, and H3701
27: 5 hundred talents of s, and ten thousand H3701
32:27 treasuries for s, and for gold, and for H3701
36: 3 talents of s and a talent of gold. H3701
Ezr 1: 4 help him with s, and with gold, and H3701
6 with vessels of s, with gold, with goods, H3701
9 chargers of s, nine and twenty knives, H3701
10 Thirty basons of gold, s basons of a H3701
11 All the vessels of gold and of s *were* five H3701
2:69 s, and one hundred priests' garments. H3701
5:14 And the vessels also of gold and s of the H3702
6: 5 And also let the golden and s vessels of H3702
7:15 And to carry the s and gold, which the H3702
16 And all the s and gold that thou canst H3702
18 with the rest of the s and the gold, that H3702
22 Unto an hundred talents of s, and to an H3702
8:25 And weighed unto them the s, and the H3701
26 and fifty talents of s, and silver vessels H3701
26 of silver, and s vessels an hundred H3701
28 holy also; and the s and the gold *are* a H3701
30 the weight of the s, and the gold, and H3701
33 Now on the fourth day was the s and H3701
Neh 5:15 beside forty shekels of s; yea, even their H3701
7:71 thousand and two hundred pound of s. H3701
72 pound of s, and threescore and H3701
Est 1: 6 and purple to s rings and pillars of H3701
6 *were of* gold and s, upon a pavement of H3701
3: 9 talents of s to the hands of those H3701
11 And the king said unto Haman, The s H3701
Job 3:15 had gold, who filled their houses with s: H3701
22:25 defence, and thou shalt have plenty of s. H3701
27:16 Though he heap up s as the dust, and H3701
17 on, and the innocent shall divide the s. H3701
28: 1 Surely there is a vein for the s, and a H3701
15 shall s be weighed *for* the price thereof. H3701
Ps 12: 6 *are* pure words: *as* s tried in a furnace H3701
66:10 us: thou hast tried us, as s is tried. H3701
68:13 s, and her feathers with yellow gold. H3701
30 with pieces of s: scatter thou the people H3701
105:37 He brought them forth also with s and H3701
115: 4 Their idols *are* s and gold, the work of H3701
119:72 unto me than thousands of gold and s. H3701
135:15 The idols of the heathen *are* s and gold, H3701
Prv 2: 4 If thou seekest her as s, and searchest H3701
3:14 of s, and the gain thereof than fine gold. H3701
8:10 Receive my instruction, and not s; and H3701
19 gold; and my revenue than choice s. H3701
10:20 The tongue of the just *is as* choice s: the H3701
16:16 rather to be chosen than s! H3701
17: 3 The fining pot *is* for s, and the furnace H3701
22: 1 loving favour rather than s and gold. H3701
25: 4 Take away the dross from the s, and H3701
11 *is like* apples of gold in pictures of s. H3701
26:23 *like* a potsherd covered with s dross. H3701
27:21 *As* the fining pot for s, and the furnace H3701
Ecc 2: 8 I gathered me also s and gold, and the H3701
5:10 He that loveth s shall not be satisfied H3701
Ecc 5:10 be satisfied with s; nor he that loveth H3701
12: 6 Or ever the s cord be loosed, or the H3701
Song 1:11 thee borders of gold with studs of s. H3701
3:10 He made the pillars thereof *of* s, the H3701
8: 9 her a palace of s: and if she *be* a door, H3701
11 was to bring a thousand *pieces* of s. H3701
Isa 1:22 Thy s is become dross, thy wine mixed H3701
2: 7 Their land also is full of s and gold, H3701
20 cast his idols of s, and his idols of gold, H3701
13:17 shall not regard s; and *as for* gold, they H3701
30:22 graven images of s, and the ornament H3701
31: 7 cast away his idols of s, and his idols of H3701
39: 2 things, the s, and the gold, and the H3701
40:19 it over with gold, and casteth s chains. H3701
46: 6 bag, and weigh s in the balance, *and* H3701
48:10 thee, but not with s; I have chosen thee H3701
60: 9 from far, their s and their gold with H3701
17 iron I will bring s, and for wood brass, H3701
Jer 6:30 Reprobate s shall *men* call them, H3701
10: 4 They deck it with s and with gold; they H3701
9 S spread into plates is brought from H3701
32: 9 the money, *even* seventeen shekels of s. H3701
52:19 *that* which *was* of s *in* silver, took the H3701
19 s, took the captain of the guard away. H3701
Ezk 7:19 They shall cast their s in the streets, H3701
19 be removed: their s and their gold shall H3701
16:13 Thus wast thou decked with gold and s; H3701
17 my gold and of my s, which I had given H3701
22:18 the furnace; they are *even* the dross of s. H3701
20 *As* they gather s, and brass, and iron, H3701
22 As s is melted in the midst of the H3701
27:12 *of* riches; with s, iron, tin, and lead, H3701
28: 4 gotten gold and s into thy treasures: H3701
38:13 to carry away s and gold, to take away H3701
Dan 2:32 of s, his belly and his thighs of brass, H3702
35 the clay, the brass, the s, and the gold, H3702
45 brass, the clay, the s, and the gold; the H3702
5: 2 the golden and s vessels which his H3702
4 of gold, and of s, of brass, of iron, of H3702
23 the gods of s, and gold, of brass, iron, H3702
11: 8 precious vessels of s and of gold; and H3701
38 with gold, and s, and with precious H3701
43 of gold and of s, and over all the H3701
Hos 2: 8 and multiplied her s and gold, *which* H3701
3: 2 fifteen *pieces* of s, and *for* an homer of H3701
8: 4 *it* not: of their s and their gold have H3701
9: 6 *places* for their s, nettles shall possess H3701
13: 2 images of their s, *and* idols according H3701
Joel 3: 5 Because ye have taken my s and my H3701
Am 2: 6 for s, and the poor for a pair of shoes; H3701
8: 6 That we may buy the poor for s, and the H3701
Nah 2: 9 Take ye the spoil of s, take the spoil of H3701
Hab 2:19 over with gold and s, and *there is* no H3701
Zep 1:11 down; all they that bear s are cut off. H3701
18 Neither their s nor their gold shall be H3701
Hag 2: 8 The s *is* mine, and the gold *is* mine, H3701
Zec 6:11 Then take s and gold, and make H3701
9: 3 and heaped up s as the dust, and fine H3701
11:12 weighed for my price thirty *pieces* of s. H3701
13 the thirty *pieces* of s, and cast them to H3701
13: 9 will refine them as s is refined, and will H3701
14:14 and s, and apparel, in great abundance. H3701
Mal 3: 3 and purifier of s: and he shall purify H3701
3 them as gold and s, that they may offer H3701
Mt 10: 9 Provide neither gold, nor s, nor brass in *G696*
26:15 with him for thirty pieces of s. *G694*
27: 3 pieces of s to the chief priests and elders, *G694*
5 And he cast down the pieces of s in the *G694*
6 And the chief priests took the s pieces, *G694*
9 the thirty pieces of s, the price of him *G694*
Lk 15: 8 ten pieces of s, if she lose one piece, *G1406*
Act 3: 6 Then Peter said, S and gold have I none; *G694*
17:29 is like unto gold, or s, or stone, graven by *G696*
19:19 and found *it* fifty thousand *pieces* of s. *G694*
24 which made s shrines for Diana, *G693*
20:33 I have coveted no man's s, or gold, or *G694*
1Co 3:12 s, precious stones, wood, hay, stubble; *G696*
2Ti 2:20 of gold and of s, but also of wood and *G693*
Jas 5: 3 Your gold and s is cankered; and the *G696*
1Pt 1:18 things, *as* s and gold, from your *G694*
Rev 9:20 idols of gold, and s, and brass, and stone, *G693*
18:12 The merchandise of gold, and s, and *G696*

SILVERLINGS
Isa 7:23 s, it shall *even* be for briers and thorns. H3701

SILVERSMITH
Act 19:24 For a certain *man* named Demetrius, a s, *G695*

SIMEON
Gen 29:33 this *son* also: and she called his name S. H8095
34:25 the sons of Jacob, S and Levi, Dinah's H8095
30 And Jacob said to S and Levi, Ye have H8095
35:23 firstborn, and S, and Levi, and Judah, H8095
42:24 S, and bound him before their eyes. H8095
36 Joseph *is* not, and S *is* not, and ye will H8095
43:23 And he brought S out unto them. H8095
46:10 And the sons of S; Jemuel, and Jamin, H8095
48: 5 as Reuben and S, they shall be mine. H8095
49: 5 S and Levi *are* brethren; instruments of H8095
Ex 1: 2 Reuben, S, Levi, and Judah, H8095
6:15 And the sons of S; Jemuel, and Jamin, H8095
15 woman: these *are* the families of S. H8095
Nu 1: 6 Of S; Shelumiel the son of Zurishaddai. H8095
22 Of the children of S, by their H8095
23 *even* of the tribe of S, *were* fifty and H8095
2:12 *be* the tribe of S: and the captain of the H8095
12 of the children of S *shall be* Shelumiel H8095
7:36 prince of the children of S, *did offer*: H8095
10:19 of the children of S *was* Shelumiel the H8095
13: 5 Of the tribe of S, Shaphat the son of H8095
26:12 The sons of S after their families: of H8095
34:20 And of the tribe of the children of S, H8095
Dt 27:12 are come over Jordan; S, and Levi, and H8095
Jos 19: 1 And the second lot came forth to S, H8095
1 of the children of S according to their H8095
8 of S according to their families. H8095
9 of the children of S: for the part of the H8095
9 the children of S had their inheritance H8095
21: 4 out of the tribe of S, and out of the tribe H8099
9 of the children of S, these cities which H8095
Jdg 1: 3 And Judah said unto S his brother, H8095
3 thee into thy lot. So S went with him. H8095
17 And Judah went with S his brother, H8095
1Ch 2: 1 These *are* the sons of Israel; Reuben, S, H8095
4:24 The sons of S *were*, Nemuel, and H8095
42 *even* of the sons of S, five hundred men, H8095
6:65 of the children of S, and out of the tribe H8095
12:25 Of the children of S, mighty men of H8095
2Ch 15: 9 and out of S: for they fell to him out H8095
34: 6 and Ephraim, and S, even unto H8095
Ezk 48:24 the west side, S *shall have a portion*. H8095
25 And by the border of S, from the east H8095
33 three gates; one gate of S, one gate of H8095
Lk 2:25 whose name *was* S; and the same man *G4826*
34 And S blessed them, and said unto *G4826*
3:30 Which was *the son* of S, which was *the* *G4826*
Act 13: 1 as Barnabas, and S that was called *G4826*
15:14 S hath declared how God at the first *G4826*
Rev 7: 7 Of the tribe of S *were* sealed twelve *G4826*

SIMEONITES
Nu 25:14 a prince of a chief house among the S. H8099
26:14 These *are* the families of the S, twenty H8099
1Ch 27:16 the S, Shephatiah the son of Maachah: H8099

SIMILITUDE
Nu 12: 8 speeches; and the s of the LORD shall H8544
Dt 4:12 but saw no s; only *ye heard* a voice. H8544
15 saw no manner of s on the day *that* the H8544
16 a graven image, the s of any figure, the H8544
2Ch 4: 3 And under it *was* the s of oxen, which H1823
Ps 106:20 into the s of an ox that eateth grass. H8403
144:12 stones, polished *after* the s of a palace: H8403
Dan 10:16 And, behold, *one* like the s of the sons H1823
Ro 5:14 not sinned after the s of Adam's *G3667*
Heb 7:15 for that after the s of Melchisedec there *G3665*
Jas 3: 9 which are made after the s of God. *G3669*

SIMILITUDES
Hos 12:10 used s, by the ministry of the prophets. H1819

SIMON
Mt 4:18 saw two brethren, S called Peter, and *G4613*
10: 2 these; The first, S, who is called Peter, *G4613*
4 S the Canaanite, and Judas Iscariot, *G4613*
13:55 James, and Joses, and S, and Judas? *G4613*
16:16 And S Peter answered and said, Thou *G4613*
17 Blessed art thou, S Barjona: for flesh *G4613*
17:25 thinkest thou, S? of whom do the kings *G4613*
26: 6 in Bethany, in the house of S the leper, *G4613*
27:32 a man of Cyrene, S by name: him they *G4613*
Mk 1:16 sea of Galilee, he saw S and Andrew his *G4613*
29 of S and Andrew, with James and John. *G4613*
36 And S and they that were with him *G4613*
3:16 And S he surnamed Peter; *G4613*
18 and Thaddaeus, and S the Canaanite, *G4613*
6: 3 and of Juda, and S? and are not his *G4613*

Mk 14: 3 And being in Bethany in the house of S G4613
37 and saith unto Peter, S, sleepest thou? G4613
15:21 And they compel one S a Cyrenian, G4613
Lk 5: 4 he said unto S, Launch out into the G4613
5 And S answering said unto him, G4613
8 When S Peter saw *it*, he fell down at G4613
10 partners with S. And Jesus said unto G4613
10 And Jesus said unto S, Fear not; from G4613
6:14 S, (whom he also named Peter,) and G4613
15 *son* of Alphaeus, and S called Zelotes, G4613
7:40 And Jesus answering said unto him, S, I G4613
43 S answered and said, I suppose that *he*, G4613
44 woman, and said unto S, Seest thou this G4613
22:31 And the Lord said, S, Simon, behold, G4613
31 And the Lord said, Simon, S, behold, G4613
23:26 hold upon one S, a Cyrenian, coming G4613
24:34 is risen indeed, and hath appeared to S. G4613
Jn 1:40 him, was Andrew, S Peter's brother. G4613
41 He first findeth his own brother S, and G4613
42 he said, Thou art S the son of Jona: G4613
6: 8 One of his disciples, Andrew, S Peter's G4613
68 Then S Peter answered him, Lord, to G4613
71 He spake of Judas Iscariot *the son* of S: G4613
13: 6 Then cometh he to S Peter: and Peter G4613
9 S Peter saith unto him, Lord, not my G4613
24 S Peter therefore beckoned to him, that G4613
26 he gave *it* to Judas Iscariot, *the son* of S. G4613
36 S Peter said unto him, Lord, whither G4613
18:10 Then S Peter having a sword drew it, G4613
15 And S Peter followed Jesus, and *so did* G4613
25 And S Peter stood and warmed G4613
20: 2 Then she runneth, and cometh to S G4613
6 Then cometh S Peter following him, G4613
21: 2 There were together S Peter, and G4613
3 S Peter saith unto them, I go a fishing. G4613
7 Lord. Now when S Peter heard that it G4613
11 S Peter went up, and drew the net to G4613
15 Jesus saith to S Peter, Simon, *son* of G4613
15 to Simon Peter, S, *son* of Jonas, lovest G4613
16 the second time, S, *son* of Jonas, lovest G4613
17 He saith unto him the third time, S, *son* G4613
Act 1:13 of Alphaeus, and S Zelotes, and Judas G4613
8: 9 But there was a certain man, called S, G4613
13 Then S himself believed also: and when G4613
18 And when S saw that through laying on G4613
24 Then answered S, and said, Pray ye to G4613
9:43 days in Joppa with one S a tanner. G4613
10: 5 call for *one* S, whose surname is Peter: G4613
6 He lodgeth with one S a tanner, whose G4613
18 And called, and asked whether S, which G4613
32 and call hither S, whose surname is G4613
32 the house of *one* S a tanner by the sea G4613
11:13 and call for S, whose surname is Peter; G4613
2Pt 1: 1 S Peter, a servant and an apostle of G4826

SIMON'S

Mk 1:30 But S wife's mother lay sick of a fever, G4613
Lk 4:38 and entered into S house. And Simon's G4613
38 house. And S wife's mother was taken G4613
5: 3 the ships, which was S, and prayed him G4613
Jn 12: 4 S *son*, which should betray him, G4613
13: 2 of Judas Iscariot, S *son*, to betray him; G4613
Act 10:17 for S house, and stood before the gate, G4613

SIMPLE

Ps 19: 7 of the LORD *is* sure, making wise the s. H6612
116: 6 The LORD preserveth the s: I was H6612
119:130 it giveth understanding unto the s. H6612
Prv 1: 4 To give subtilty to the s, to the young H6612
22 How long, ye s ones, will ye love H6612
32 For the turning away of the s shall slay H6612
7: 7 And beheld among the s ones, I H6612
8: 5 O ye s, understand wisdom: and, ye H6612
9: 4 Whoso *is* s, let him turn in hither: *as for* H6612
13 A foolish woman *is* clamorous: *she is* s, H6615
16 Whoso *is* s, let him turn in hither: and H6612
14:15 The s believeth every word: but the H6612
18 The s inherit folly: but the prudent are H6612
19:25 Smite a scorner, and the s will beware: H6612
21:11 When the scorner is punished, the s is H6612
22: 3 but the s pass on, and are punished. H6612
27:12 *but* the s pass on, *and* are punished. H6612
Ezk 45:20 *that is* s: so shall ye reconcile the house. H6612
Ro 16:18 fair speeches deceive the hearts of the s. G172
19 which is good, and s concerning evil. G185

SIMPLICITY

2Sa 15:11 in their s, and they knew not any thing. H8537
Prv 1:22 How long, ye simple ones, will ye love s? H6612
Ro 12: 8 *let him do it* with s; he that ruleth, with G572
2Co 1:12 conscience, that in s and godly sincerity, G572
11: 3 be corrupted from the s that is in Christ. G572

SIMRI

1Ch 26:10 of Merari, had sons; S the chief, (for H8113

SIN

Gen 4: 7 doest not well, s lieth at the door. And H2403
18:20 and because their s is very grievous; H2403
20: 9 my kingdom a great s? thou hast done H2401
31:36 what *is* my s, that thou hast so hotly H2403
39: 9 great wickedness, and s against God? H2398
42:22 saying, Do not s against the child; and H2398
50:17 and their s; for they did unto thee H2403
Ex 10:17 I pray thee, my s only this once, and H2403
16: 1 the wilderness of S, which *is* between H5512
17: 1 the wilderness of S, after their journeys, H5512
20:20 may be before your faces, that ye s not. H2398
23:33 they make thee s against me: for if thou H2398
29:14 fire without the camp: it *is* a s offering. H2403
36 every day a bullock *for* a s offering for H2403
30:10 with the blood of the s offering of H2403
32:21 hast brought so great a s upon them? H2401
30 sinned a great s: and now I will go up H2401
30 I shall make an atonement for your s. H2403
31 s, and have made them gods of gold. H2401
34 I visit I will visit their s upon them. H2403
34: 7 transgression and s, and that will by no H2403
9 our s, and take us for thine inheritance. H2403
Lev 4: 2 If a soul shall s through ignorance H2398
3 If the priest that is anointed do s H2398
3 according to the s of the people; then let H819
3 let him bring for his s, which he hath H2403
3 blemish unto the LORD for a s offering. H2403
8 of the bullock for the s offering; the fat H2403
13 of Israel s through ignorance, H7686
14 When the s, which they have sinned H2403
14 bullock for the s, and bring him before H2403
20 the bullock for a s offering, so shall he H2403
21 it *is* a s offering for the congregation. H2403
23 Or if his s, wherein he hath sinned, H2403
24 before the LORD: it *is* a s offering. H2403
25 of the blood of the s offering with his H2403
26 his s, and it shall be forgiven him. H2403
27 And if any one of the common people s H2398
28 Or if his s, which he hath sinned, come H2403
28 for his s which he hath sinned. H2403
29 the head of the s offering, and slay the H2403
29 and slay the s offering in the place H2403
32 And if he bring a lamb for a s offering, H2403
33 the head of the s offering, and slay it H2403
33 and slay it for a s offering in the place H2403
34 of the blood of the s offering with his H2403
35 an atonement for his s that he hath H2403
5: 1 And if a soul s, and hear the voice of H2398
6 unto the LORD for his s which he hath H2403
6 of the goats, for a s offering; and the H2403
6 an atonement for him concerning his s. H2403
7 the LORD; one for a s offering, and the H2403
8 which *is* for the s offering first, and H2403
9 of the blood of the s offering upon the H2403
9 bottom of the altar: it *is* a s offering. H2403
10 for him for his s which he hath sinned, H2403
11 of fine flour for a s offering; he shall H2403
11 thereon: for it *is* a s offering. H2403
12 by fire unto the LORD: it *is* a s offering. H2403
13 as touching his s that he hath sinned H2403
15 If a soul commit a trespass, and s H2398
17 And if a soul s, and commit any of these H2398
6: 2 If a soul s, and commit a trespass H2398
17 s offering, and as the trespass offering. H2403
25 *is* the law of the s offering: In the place H2403
25 is killed shall the s offering be killed H2403
26 The priest that offereth it for s shall eat H2398
30 And no s offering, whereof *any* of the H2403
7: 7 As the s offering *is*, so *is* the trespass H2403
37 and of the s offering, and of the H2403
8: 2 a bullock for the s offering, and two H2403
14 And he brought the bullock for the s H2403
14 head of the bullock for the s offering. H2403
9: 2 a young calf for a s offering, and a ram H2403
3 of the goats for a s offering; and a calf H2403
7 and offer thy s offering, and thy burnt H2403
8 of the s offering, which *was* for himself. H2403
10 the liver of the s offering, he burnt H2403
15 which *was* the s offering for the people, H2403
15 slew it, and offered it for s, as the first. H2398
22 offering of the s offering, and the burnt H2403
Lev 10:16 the goat of the s offering, and, behold, H2403
17 Wherefore have ye not eaten the s H2403
19 they offered their s offering and their H2403
19 and *if* I had eaten the s offering to day, H2403
12: 6 a turtledove, for a s offering, unto the H2403
8 and the other for a s offering: and the H2403
14:13 he shall kill the s offering and the burnt H2403
13 holy place: for as the s offering *is* the H2403
19 And the priest shall offer the s offering, H2403
22 the one shall be a s offering, and the H2403
31 to get, the one *for* a s offering, and the H2403
15:15 the one *for* a s offering, and the other H2403
30 And the priest shall offer the one *for* a s H2403
16: 3 bullock for a s offering, and a ram H2403
5 of the goats for a s offering, and one H2403
6 his bullock of the s offering, which *is* H2403
9 lot fell, and offer him *for* a s offering. H2403
11 the bullock of the s offering, which *is* H2403
11 of the s offering which *is* for himself: H2403
15 Then shall he kill the goat of the s H2403
25 And the fat of the s offering shall he H2403
27 And the bullock *for* the s offering, and H2403
27 the goat *for* the s offering, whose blood H2403
19:17 neighbour, and not suffer s upon him. H2399
22 the LORD for his s which he hath done: H2403
22 done: and the s which he hath done H2403
20:20 bear their s; they shall die childless. H2399
22: 9 lest they bear s for it, and die therefore, H2399
23:19 of the goats for a s offering, and two H2403
24:15 curseth his God shall bear his s. H2399
Nu 5: 6 shall commit any s that men commit, H2403
7 Then they shall confess their s which H2403
6:11 And the priest shall offer the one for a s H2403
14 blemish for a s offering, and one ram H2403
16 his s offering, and his burnt offering: H2403
7:16 One kid of the goats for a s offering: H2403
22 One kid of the goats for a s offering: H2403
28 One kid of the goats for a s offering: H2403
34 One kid of the goats for a s offering: H2403
40 One kid of the goats for a s offering: H2403
46 One kid of the goats for a s offering: H2403
52 One kid of the goats for a s offering: H2403
58 One kid of the goats for a s offering: H2403
64 One kid of the goats for a s offering: H2403
70 One kid of the goats for a s offering: H2403
76 One kid of the goats for a s offering: H2403
82 One kid of the goats for a s offering: H2403
87 kids of the goats for s offering twelve. H2403
8: 8 bullock shalt thou take for a s offering. H2403
12 offer the one *for* a s offering, and the H2403
9:13 season, that man shall bear his s. H2399
12:11 thee, lay not the s upon us, wherein we H2403
15:24 one kid of the goats for a s offering. H2403
25 LORD, and their s offering before the H2403
27 And if any soul s through ignorance, H2398
27 goat of the first year for a s offering. H2403
16:22 shall one man s, and wilt thou be wroth H2398
18: 9 of theirs, and every s offering of theirs, H2403
22 congregation, lest they bear s, and die. H2399
32 And ye shall bear no s by reason of it, H2399
19: 9 of separation: it *is* a purification for s. H2403
17 of purification for s, and running water H2403
27: 3 but died in his own s, and had no sons. H2399
28:15 And one kid of the goats for a s offering H2403
22 And one goat *for* a s offering, to make H2403
29: 5 And one kid of the goats *for* a s H2403
11 One kid of the goats *for* a s offering; H2403
11 beside the s offering of atonement, H2403
16 And one kid of the goats *for* a s H2403
19 And one kid of the goats *for* a s H2403
22 And one goat *for* a s offering; beside H2403
25 And one kid of the goats *for* a s H2403
28 And one goat *for* a s offering; beside H2403
31 And one goat *for* a s offering; beside H2403
34 And one goat *for* a s offering; beside H2403
38 And one goat *for* a s offering; beside H2403
32:23 and be sure your s will find you out. H2403
33:11 and encamped in the wilderness of S. H5512
12 of S, and encamped in Dophkah. H5512
Dt 9:21 And I took your s, the calf which ye had H2403
27 nor to their wickedness, nor to their s: H2403
15: 9 against thee, and it be s unto thee. H2399
19:15 or for any s, in any sin that he sinneth: H2403
15 for any sin, in any s that he sinneth: at H2399
20:18 ye s against the LORD your God. H2398
21:22 And if a man have committed a s H2399
22:26 in the damsel no s *worthy* of death: for H2399
23:21 it of thee; and it would be s in thee. H2399
22 forbear to vow, it shall be no s in thee. H2399

Dt 24: 4 cause the land to s, which the LORD thy H2398
15 unto the LORD, and it be s unto thee. H2399
16 man shall be put to death for his own s. H2399
1Sa 2:17 Wherefore the s of the young men was H2403
25 If one man s against another, the judge H2398
25 him: but if a man s against the LORD, H2398
12:23 that I should s against the LORD in H2398
14:33 Behold, the people s against the LORD, H2398
34 here, and eat; and s not against the H2398
38 see wherein this s hath been this day. H2403
15:23 For rebellion *is as* the s of witchcraft, H2403
25 thee, pardon my s, and turn again with H2403
19: 4 Let not the king s against his servant, H2398
5 then wilt thou s against innocent H2398
20: 1 and what *is* my s before thy father, that H2403
2Sa 12:13 hath put away thy s; thou shalt not die. H2403
1Ki 8:34 and forgive the s of thy people Israel, H2403
35 from their s, when thou afflictest them: H2403
36 and forgive the s of thy servants, and H2403
46 If they s against thee, (for *there is* no H2398
12:30 And this thing became a s: for the H2403
13:34 And this thing became s unto the house H2403
14:16 who did s, and who made Israel to sin. H2398
16 who did sin, and who made Israel to s. H2398
15:26 his s wherewith he made Israel to sin. H2403
26 his sin wherewith he made Israel to s. H2398
30 he made Israel s, by his provocation H2398
34 his s wherewith he made Israel to sin. H2403
34 his sin wherewith he made Israel to s. H2398
16: 2 my people Israel to s, to provoke me to H2398
13 they made Israel to s, in provoking the H2398
19 s which he did, to make Israel to sin. H2403
19 his sin which he did, to make Israel to s. H2398
26 Nebat, and in his s wherewith he made H2403
26 he made Israel to s, to provoke the H2398
17:18 s to remembrance, and to slay my son? H5771
21:22 *me* to anger, and made Israel to s. H2398
22:52 the son of Nebat, who made Israel to s: H2398
2Ki 3: 3 Israel to s; he departed not therefrom. H2398
10:29 who made Israel to s, Jehu departed not H2398
31 of Jeroboam, which made Israel to s. H2398
12:16 The trespass money and s money was H2403
13: 2 Israel to s; he departed not therefrom. H2398
6 who made Israel s, *but* walked therein: H2398
11 made Israel s: *but* he walked therein. H2398
14: 6 man shall be put to death for his own s. H2399
24 the son of Nebat, who made Israel to s. H2398
15: 9 the son of Nebat, who made Israel to s. H2398
18 the son of Nebat, who made Israel to s. H2398
24 the son of Nebat, who made Israel to s. H2398
28 the son of Nebat, who made Israel to s. H2398
17:21 LORD, and made them s a great sin. H2398
21 the LORD, and made them sin a great s. H2401
21:11 made Judah also to s with his idols: H2398
16 beside his s wherewith he made H2403
16 he made Judah to s, in doing *that which* H2398
17 he did, and his s that he sinned, *are* H2403
23:15 made Israel to s, had made, both that H2398
2Ch 6:22 If a man s against his neighbour, and H2398
25 and forgive the s of thy people Israel, H2403
26 their s, when thou dost afflict them; H2403
27 and forgive the s of thy servants, and H2403
36 If they s against thee, (for *there is* no H2398
7:14 forgive their s, and will heal their land. H2403
25: 4 but every man shall die for his own s. H2399
29:21 seven he goats, for a s offering for the H2403
23 he goats *for* the s offering before the H2403
24 s offering *should be made* for all Israel. H2403
33:19 of him, and all his s, and his trespass, H2403
Ezr 6:17 lambs; and for a s offering for all H2409
8:35 he goats *for* a s offering: all *this was* H2403
Neh 4: 5 and let not their s be blotted out from H2403
6:13 and do so, and s, and *that* they might H2398
10:33 *things*, and for the s offerings to make H2403
13:26 Did not Solomon king of Israel s by H2398
26 him did outlandish women cause to s. H2398
Job 2:10 In all this did not Job s with his lips. H2398
5:24 visit thy habitation, and shalt not s. H2398
10: 6 mine iniquity, and searchest after my s? H2403
14 If I s, then thou markest me, and thou H2398
13:23 me to know my transgression and my s. H2403
14:16 steps: dost thou not watch over my s? H2403
20:11 His bones are full *of the* s of his youth,
31:30 Neither have I suffered my mouth to s H2398
34:37 For he addeth rebellion unto his s, he H2403
35: 3 shall I have, *if I be cleansed* from my s? H2403
Ps 4: 4 Stand in awe, and s not: commune H2398
32: 1 *is* forgiven, *whose* s *is* covered. H2401
5 I acknowledged my s unto thee, and H2403

Ps 32: 5 forgavest the iniquity of my s. Selah. H2403
38: 3 *any* rest in my bones because of my s. H2403
18 mine iniquity; I will be sorry for my s. H2403
39: 1 heed to my ways, that I s not with my H2398
40: 6 and s offering hast thou not required. H2401
51: 2 iniquity, and cleanse me from my s. H2403
3 and my s *is* ever before me. H2403
5 and in s did my mother conceive me. H2399
59: 3 transgression, nor *for* my s, O LORD. H2403
12 *For* the s of their mouth *and* the words H2403
85: 2 thou hast covered all their s. Selah. H2403
109: 7 and let his prayer become s. H2401
14 not the s of his mother be blotted out. H2403
119:11 heart, that I might not s against thee. H2398
Prv 10:16 to life: the fruit of the wicked to s. H2403
19 s: but he that refraineth his lips *is* wise. H6588
14: 9 Fools make a mock at s: but among the H817
34 Righteousness exalteth a nation: but s H2403
20: 9 my heart clean, I am pure from my s? H2403
21: 4 *and* the plowing of the wicked, *is* s. H2403
24: 9 The thought of foolishness *is* s: and the H2403
Ecc 5: 6 to cause thy flesh to s; neither say thou H2398
Isa 3: 9 and they declare their s as Sodom, they H2403
5:18 and s as it were with a cart rope: H2403
6: 7 is taken away, and thy s purged. H2403
27: 9 to take away his s; when he maketh all H2403
30: 1 of my spirit, that they may add s to sin: H2403
1 of my spirit, that they may add sin to s: H2403
31: 7 own hands have made unto you *for* a s. H2399
53:10 his soul an offering for s, he shall see *his* H817
12 and he bare the s of many, and made H2399
Jer 16:10 iniquity? or what *is* our s that we have H2403
18 iniquity and their s double; because H2403
17: 1 The s of Judah *is* written with a pen of H2403
3 places for s, throughout all thy borders. H2403
18:23 blot out their s from thy sight, but let H2403
31:34 and I will remember their s no more. H2403
32:35 this abomination, to cause Judah to s. H2398
36: 3 I may forgive their iniquity and their s. H2403
51: 5 with s against the Holy One of Israel. H817
Lam 4: 6 punishment of the s of Sodom, that was
Ezk 3:20 warning, he shall die in his s, and his H2403
21 that the righteous s not, and he doth H2398
21 and he doth not s, he shall surely live, H2398
18:24 and in his s that he hath sinned, H2403
30:15 And I will pour my fury upon S, the H5512
16 And I will set fire in Egypt: S shall have H5512
33:14 s, and do that which is lawful and right; H2403
40:39 the s offering and the trespass offering. H2403
42:13 offering, and the s offering, and the H2403
43:19 GOD, a young bullock for a s offering. H2403
21 bullock also of the s offering, and he H2403
22 blemish for a s offering; and they shall H2403
25 day a goat *for* a s offering: they shall H2403
44:27 offer his s offering, saith the Lord GOD. H2403
29 offering, and the s offering, and the H2403
45:17 he shall prepare the s offering, and the H2403
19 of the blood of the s offering, and put *it* H2403
22 of the land a bullock *for* a s offering. H2403
23 a kid of the goats daily *for* a s offering. H2403
25 according to the s offering, according H2403
46:20 offering and the s offering, where they H2403
Dan 9:20 and confessing my s and the sin of my H2403
20 my sin and the s of my people Israel, H2403
Hos 4: 8 They eat up the s of my people, and H2403
8:11 to s, altars shall be unto him to sin. H2398
11 to sin, altars shall be unto him to s. H2398
10: 8 The high places also of Aven, the s of H2403
12: 8 find none iniquity in me that *were* s. H2399
13: 2 And now they s more and more, and H2398
12 of Ephraim *is* bound up; his s *is* hid. H2403
Am 8:14 They that swear by the s of Samaria, and H819
Mic 1:13 beginning of the s to the daughter of H2403
3: 8 his transgression, and to Israel his s. H2403
6: 7 fruit of my body *for* the s of my soul? H2403
Zec 13: 1 of Jerusalem for s and for uncleanness. H2403
Mt 12:31 you, All manner of s and blasphemy G266
18:21 oft shall my brother s against me, and I G264
Jn 1:29 which taketh away the s of the world. G266
5:14 art made whole: s no more, lest a worse G264
8: 7 He that is without s among you, let him G361
11 do I condemn thee: go, and s no more. G264
34 committeth s is the servant of sin. G266
34 committeth sin is the servant of s. G266
46 Which of you convinceth me of s? And if I G266
9: 2 Master, who did s, this man, or his G264
41 ye should have no s: but now ye say, We G266
41 say, We see; therefore your s remaineth. G266
15:22 they had not had s: but now they have no G266

Jn 15:22 but now they have no cloak for their s. G266
24 they had not had s: but now have they G266
16: 8 s, and of righteousness, and of judgment: G266
9 Of s, because they believe not on me; G266
19:11 me unto thee hath the greater s. G266
Act 7:60 Lord, lay not this s to their charge. And G266
Ro 3: 9 and Gentiles, that they are all under s; G266
20 sight: for by the law *is* the knowledge of s. G266
4: 8 man to whom the Lord will not impute s. G266
5:12 Wherefore, as by one man s entered into G266
12 and death by s; and so death passed G266
13 (For until the law s was in the world: but G266
13 s is not imputed when there is no law. G266
20 abound. But where s abounded, grace G266
21 That as s hath reigned unto death, even G266
6: 1 we continue in s, that grace may abound? G266
2 are dead to s, live any longer therein? G266
6 that the body of s might be destroyed, G266
6 that henceforth we should not serve s. G266
7 For he that is dead is freed from s. G266
10 For in that he died, he died unto s once: G266
11 dead indeed unto s, but alive unto God G266
12 Let not s therefore reign in your mortal G266
13 unto s: but yield yourselves G266
14 For s shall not have dominion over you: G266
15 What then? shall we s, because we are G264
16 ye obey; whether of s unto death, or of G266
17 the servants of s, but ye have obeyed G266
18 Being then made free from s, ye became G266
20 For when ye were the servants of s, ye G266
22 But now being made free from s, and G266
23 For the wages of s *is* death; but the gift of G266
7: 7 What shall we say then? *Is* the law s? God G266
7 I had not known s, but by the law: for I G266
8 But s, taking occasion by the G266
8 For without the law s *was* dead. G266
9 came, s revived, and I died. G266
11 For s, taking occasion by the G266
13 God forbid. But s, that it might appear G266
13 it might appear s, working death in me G266
13 that which is good; that s by the G266
14 is spiritual: but I am carnal, sold under s. G266
17 Now then it is no more I that do it, but s G266
20 I that do it, but s that dwelleth in me. G266
23 to the law of s which is in my members. G266
25 of God; but with the flesh the law of s. G266
8: 2 me free from the law of s and death. G266
3 and for s, condemned sin in the flesh: G266
3 and for sin, condemned s in the flesh: G266
10 *is* dead because of s; but the Spirit *is* life G266
14:23 of faith: for whatsoever *is* not of faith is s. G266
1Co 6:18 Flee fornication. Every s that a man G265
8:12 But when ye s so against the brethren, G264
12 weak conscience, ye s against Christ. G264
15:34 Awake to righteousness, and s not; for G264
56 The sting of death *is* s; and the strength G266
56 *is* sin; and the strength of s *is* the law. G266
2Co 5:21 For he hath made him *to be* s for us, who G266
21 for us, who knew no s; that we might be G266
Gal 2:17 Christ the minister of s? God forbid. G266
3:22 all under s, that the promise by G266
Eph 4:26 Be ye angry, and s not: let not the sun go G264
2Th 2: 3 of s be revealed, the son of perdition; G266
1Ti 5:20 Them that s rebuke before all, that G264
Heb 3:13 hardened through the deceitfulness of s. G266
4:15 tempted like as *we are, yet* without s. G266
9:26 to put away s by the sacrifice of himself. G266
28 second time without s unto salvation. G266
10: 6 In burnt offerings and *sacrifices* for s G266
8 and *offering* for s thou wouldest not, G266
18 of these *is, there is* no more offering for s. G266
26 For if we s wilfully after that we have G264
11:25 to enjoy the pleasures of s for a season; G266
12: 1 weight, and the s which doth so easily G266
4 resisted unto blood, striving against s. G266
13:11 for s, are burned without the camp. G266
Jas 1:15 it bringeth forth s: and sin, when it is G266
15 forth sin: and s, when it is finished, G266
2: 9 ye commit s, and are convinced of G266
4:17 do good, and doeth *it* not, to him it is s. G266
1Pt 2:22 Who did no s, neither was guile found in G266
4: 1 suffered in the flesh hath ceased from s; G266
2Pt 2:14 cannot cease from s; beguiling unstable G266
1Jn 1: 7 Christ his Son cleanseth us from all s. G266
8 If we say that we have no s, we deceive G266
2: 1 I unto you, that ye s not. And if any man G264
1 And if any man s, we have an advocate G264
3: 4 Whosoever committeth s transgresseth G266
4 law: for s is the transgression of the law. G266

1Jn 3: 5 to take away our sins; and in him is no s. G266
8 He that committeth s is of the devil; for G266
9 God doth not commit s; for his seed G266
9 he cannot s, because he is born of God. G264
5:16 If any man see his brother s a sin *which* G264
16 If any man see his brother sin a s *which* G266
16 life for them that s not unto death. There G264
16 death. There is a s unto death: I do not G266
17 All unrighteousness is s: and there is a G266
17 is sin: and there is a s not unto death. G266

SINA
Act 7:30 of mount S an angel of the Lord G4614
38 to him in the mount S, and *with* our G4614

SINAI
Ex 16: 1 *is* between Elim and S, on the fifteenth H5514
19: 1 day came they *into* the wilderness of S. H5514
2 *to* the desert of S, and had pitched in H5514
11 sight of all the people upon mount S. H5514
18 And mount S was altogether on a H5514
20 down upon mount S, on the top of the H5514
23 come up to mount S: for thou chargedst H5514
24:16 upon mount S, and the cloud covered H5514
31:18 with him upon mount S, two tables of H5514
34: 2 unto mount S, and present thyself H5514
4 up unto mount S, as the LORD had H5514
29 down from mount S with the two tables H5514
32 LORD had spoken with him in mount S. H5514
Lev 7:38 Moses in mount S, in the day that he H5514
38 unto the LORD, in the wilderness of S. H5514
25: 1 spake unto Moses in mount S, saying, H5514
26:46 in mount S by the hand of Moses. H5514
27:34 for the children of Israel in mount S. H5514
Nu 1: 1 the wilderness of S, in the tabernacle of H5514
19 numbered them in the wilderness of S. H5514
3: 1 LORD spake with Moses in mount S. H5514
4 in the wilderness of S, and they had no H5514
14 Moses in the wilderness of S, saying, H5514
9: 1 the wilderness of S, in the first month of H5514
5 the wilderness of S: according to all that H5514
10:12 of the wilderness of S; and the cloud H5514
26:64 children of Israel in the wilderness of S. H5514
28: 6 in mount S for a sweet savour, H5514
33:15 and pitched in the wilderness of S. H5514
16 And they removed from the desert of S, H5514
Dt 33: 2 And he said, The LORD came from S, H5514
Jdg 5: 5 S from before the LORD God of Israel. H5514
Neh 9:13 Thou camest down also upon mount S, H5514
Ps 68: 8 of God: *even* S itself *was moved* at H5514
17 among them, *as in* S, in the holy *place*. H5514
Gal 4:24 from the mount S, which gendereth to G4614
25 For this Agar is mount S in Arabia, and G4614

SINCE
Gen 30:30 hath blessed thee s my coming: and now
44:28 he is torn in pieces; and I saw him not s: H2008
46:30 Now let me die, s I have seen thy face, H310
Ex 4:10 heretofore, nor s thou hast spoken unto H227
5:23 For s I came to Pharaoh to speak in thy H4480
9:18 not been in Egypt s the foundation H4480
24 the land of Egypt s it became a nation. H4480
10: 6 fathers have seen, s the day that they H4480
Nu 22:30 hast ridden ever s *I was* thine unto this H5750
Dt 4:32 were before thee, s the day that God H4480
34:10 And there arose not a prophet s in H5750
Jos 2:12 me by the LORD, s I have shewed you H3588
14:10 five years, even s the LORD spake this H227
Ru 2:11 thy mother in law s the death of thine H310
1Sa 8: 8 they have done s the day that I brought
9:24 been kept for thee s I said, I have invited
21: 5 these three days, s I came out, and the
29: 3 in him s he fell *unto me* unto this day? H3117
6 not found evil in thee s the day of thy
2Sa 7: 6 Whereas I have not dwelt in *any* house s
11 And as s the time that I commanded H4480
1Ki 8:16 S the day that I brought forth my H4480
2Ki 8: 6 fruits of the field s the day that she left
21:15 me to anger, s the day their fathers H4480
1Ch 17: 5 For I have not dwelt in an house s the H4480
10 And s the time that I commanded judges
2Ch 6: 5 S the day that I brought forth my H4480
30:26 So there was great joy in Jerusalem: for s
31:10 him, and said, S *the people* began to
Ezr 4: 2 do sacrifice unto him s the days of
5:16 in Jerusalem: and s that time even until H4481
9: 7 S the days of our fathers *have we been* in
Neh 8:17 the booths: for s the days of Jeshua the
9:32 on all thy people, s the time of the kings

Job 20: 4 Knowest thou *not* this of old, s man H4480
38:12 Hast thou commanded the morning s
Isa 14: 8 Lebanon, *saying*, S thou art laid down, H227
16:13 spoken concerning Moab s that time.
43: 4 S thou wast precious in my sight, thou
44: 7 set it in order for me, s I appointed the
64: 4 For s the beginning of the world *men*
Jer 7:25 S the day that your fathers came forth H4480
15: 7 *s* they return not from their ways.
20: 8 For s I spake, I cried out, I cried H1767
23:38 But s ye say, The burden of the LORD; H518
31:20 a pleasant child? for s I spake against H1767
44:18 But s we left off to burn incense H4480+H227
48:27 thieves? for s thou spakest of him, H1767
Dan 12: 1 such as never was s there was a nation
Hag 2:16 S those *days* were, when *one* came to an
Mt 24:21 such as was not s the beginning of the G575
Mk 9:21 How long is it ago s this came unto G5613
Lk 1:70 which have been s the world began: G575
7:45 but this woman s the time I came in G575
16:16 *were* until John: s that time the kingdom G575
24:21 is the third day s these things were done. G575
Jn 9:32 S the world began was it not heard that G1537
Act 3:21 all his holy prophets s the world began. G575
19: 2 the Holy Ghost s ye believed? And they
24:11 s I went up to Jerusalem for to worship. G3739
Ro 16:25 which was kept secret s the world began,
1Co 15:21 For s by man *came* death, by man G1894
2Co 13: 3 S ye seek a proof of Christ speaking in G1893
Col 1: 4 S we heard of your faith in Christ Jesus,
6 *it doth* also in you, s the day ye heard *of* G575
9 For this cause we also, s the day we G575
Heb 7:28 oath, which was s the law, *maketh* the G3326
9:26 For then must he often have suffered s G575
2Pt 3: 4 his coming? for s the fathers fell G575+G3739
Rev 16:18 as was not s men were upon G575+G3739

SINCERE
Php 1:10 that ye may be s and without offence G1506
1Pt 2: 2 As newborn babes, desire the s milk of G97

SINCERELY
Jdg 9:16 done truly and s, in that ye have made H8549
19 If ye then have dealt truly and s with H8549
Php 1:16 of contention, not s, supposing to add G55

SINCERITY
Jos 24:14 and serve him in s and in truth: and H8549
1Co 5: 8 the unleavened *bread* of s and truth. G1505
2Co 1:12 and godly s, not with fleshly wisdom, G1505
2:17 of God: but as of s, but as of God, in the G1505
8: 8 others, and to prove the s of your love. G1103
Eph 6:24 love our Lord Jesus Christ in s. Amen. G861
Tit 2: 7 *shewing* uncorruptness, gravity, s, G861

SINEW
Gen 32:32 eat not *of* the s which shrank, which H1517
32 of Jacob's thigh in the s that shrank. H1517
Isa 48: 4 neck *is* an iron s, and thy brow brass; H1517

SINEWS
Job 10:11 and hast fenced me with bones and s. H1517
30:17 the night season: and my s take no rest. H6207
40:17 He moveth his tail like a cedar: the s of H1517
Ezk 37: 6 And I will lay s upon you, and will H1517
8 And when I beheld, lo, the s and the H1517

SINFUL
Nu 32:14 an increase of s men, to augment yet H2400
Isa 1: 4 Ah s nation, a people laden with H2398
Am 9: 8 GOD *are* upon the s kingdom, and I H2401
Mk 8:38 adulterous and s generation; of him also G268
Lk 5: 8 from me; for I am a s man, O Lord. G268
24: 7 into the hands of s men, and be G268
Ro 7:13 might become exceeding s. G268
8: 3 Son in the likeness of s flesh, and for sin, G266

SING
Ex 15: 1 saying, I will s unto the LORD, for H7891
21 And Miriam answered them, S ye to H7891
32:18 *but* the noise of *them that* s do I hear. H6031
Nu 21:17 song, Spring up, O well; s ye unto it: H6030
Jdg 5: 3 I, *even* I, will s unto the LORD; I will H7891
3 will s *praise* to the LORD God of Israel. H2167
1Sa 21:11 land? did they not s one to another of H6030
2Sa 22:50 and I will s praises unto thy name. H2167
1Ch 16: 9 S unto him, sing psalms unto him, talk H7891
9 Sing unto him, s psalms unto him, talk
23 S unto the LORD, all the earth; shew H7891

1Ch 16:33 Then shall the trees of the wood s out H7442
2Ch 20:22 And when they began to s and to H7440
23:13 and such as taught to s praise. Then H1984
29:30 the Levites to s praise unto the LORD H1984
Job 29:13 I caused the widow's heart to s for joy. H7442
Ps 7:17 and will s praise to the name of
9: 2 I will be glad and rejoice in thee: I will s
11 S praises to the LORD, which dwelleth in
13: 6 I will s unto the LORD, because he hath H7891
18:49 heathen, and s praises unto thy name.
21:13 *so* will we s and praise thy power. H7891
27: 6 of joy; I will s, yea, I will sing praises H7891
6 sing, yea, I will s praises unto the LORD.
30: 4 S unto the LORD, O ye saints of his, H2167
12 To the end that *my* glory may s praise to
33: 2 Praise the LORD with harp: s unto him H2167
3 S unto him a new song; play skilfully H7891
47: 6 S praises to God, sing praises: sing H2167
6 Sing praises to God, s praises: sing H2167
6 Sing praises to God, sing praises: s H2167
6 sing praises unto our King, s praises. H2167
7 For God *is* the King of all the earth: s ye H2167
51:14 shall s aloud of thy righteousness. H7442
57: 7 heart is fixed: I will s and give praise. H7891
9 I will s unto thee among the nations. H2167
59:16 But I will s of thy power; yea, I will sing H7891
16 But I will sing of thy power; yea, I will s H7442
17 Unto thee, O my strength, will I s: for H2167
61: 8 So will I s praise unto thy name for H2167
65:13 corn; they shout for joy, they also s. H7891
66: 2 S forth the honour of his name: make H2167
4 thee, and shall s unto thee; they shall H2167
4 thee; they shall s *to* thy name. Selah. H2167
67: 4 O let the nations be glad and s for joy: H7442
68: 4 S unto God, sing praises to his name: H7891
4 Sing unto God, s praises to his name: H2167
32 S unto God, ye kingdoms of the earth; H7891
32 earth; O s praises unto the Lord; Selah: H2167
71:22 unto thee will I s with the harp, O thou H2167
23 My lips shall greatly rejoice when I s H2167
75: 9 But I will declare for ever; I will s praises
81: 1 S aloud unto God our strength: make a H7442
89: 1 I will s of the mercies of the LORD for H7891
92: 1 s praises unto thy name, O most High: H2167
95: 1 O come, let us s unto the LORD: let us H7442
96: 1 O s unto the LORD a new song: sing H7891
1 O sing unto the LORD a new song: s H7891
2 S unto the LORD, bless his name; shew H7891
98: 1 O s unto the LORD a new song; for he H7891
4 a loud noise, and rejoice, and s praise. H2167
5 S unto the LORD with the harp; with H2167
101: 1 I will s of mercy and judgment: unto H7891
1 judgment: unto thee, O LORD, will I s. H2167
104:12 *which* s among the branches. H5414+H6963
33 I will s unto the LORD as long as I live: H7891
33 long as I live: I will s praise to my God H2167
105: 2 S unto him, sing psalms unto him: talk H7891
2 Sing unto him, s psalms unto him: talk H2167
108: 1 O God, my heart is fixed; I will s and H7891
3 s praises unto thee among the nations. H2167
135: 3 the LORD *is* good: s praises unto his H2167
137: 3 *saying*, S us *one* of the songs of Zion. H7891
4 How shall we s the LORD'S song in a H7891
138: 1 the gods will I s praise unto thee. H2167
5 Yea, they shall s in the ways of the H7891
144: 9 I will s a new song unto thee, O God: H7891
9 of ten strings will I s praises unto thee. H2167
145: 7 and shall s of thy righteousness. H7442
146: 2 the LORD: I will s praises unto my God H2167
147: 1 Praise ye the LORD: for *it is* good to s H2167
7 S unto the LORD with thanksgiving; H6030
7 s praise upon the harp unto our God: H2167
149: 1 Praise ye the LORD. S unto the LORD a H7891
3 dance: let them s praises unto him with H2167
5 glory: let them s aloud upon their beds. H7442
Prv 29: 6 but the righteous doth s and rejoice. H7442
Isa 5: 1 Now will I s to my wellbeloved a song H7891
12: 5 S unto the LORD; for he hath done H2167
23:15 seventy years shall Tyre s as an harlot. H7892
16 sweet melody, s many songs, that thou
24:14 voice, they shall s for the majesty of the H7442
26:19 they arise. Awake and s, ye that dwell in H7442
27: 2 In that day s ye unto her, A vineyard of H6031
35: 6 of the dumb s: for in the wilderness H7442
38:20 me: therefore we will s my songs to the
42:10 S unto the LORD a new song, *and* his H7891

Isa 42:11 of the rock **s**, let them shout from H7442
44:23 **S**, O ye heavens; for the LORD hath H7442
49:13 **S**, O heavens; and be joyful, O earth; H7442
52: 8 together shall they **s**: for they shall see H7442
9 Break forth into joy, **s** together, ye H7442
54: 1 **S**, O barren, thou *that* didst not bear; H7442
65:14 Behold, my servants shall **s** for joy of H7442
Jer 20:13 **S** unto the LORD, praise ye the LORD: H7891
31: 7 For thus saith the LORD; **S** with H7442
12 Therefore they shall come and **s** in the H7442
51:48 *is* therein, shall **s** for Babylon: for the H7442
Ezk 27:25 The ships of Tarshish did **s** of thee in H7788
Hos 2:15 and she shall **s** there, as in the days H6030
Zep 2:14 of it; *their* voice shall **s** in the windows; H7891
3:14 **S**, O daughter of Zion; shout, O Israel; H7442
Zec 2:10 **S** and rejoice, O daughter of Zion: for, H7442
Ro 15: 9 the Gentiles, and **s** unto thy name. *G5567*
1Co 14:15 also: I will **s** with the spirit, and *G5567*
15 I will **s** with the understanding also. *G5567*
Heb 2:12 of the church will I **s** praise unto thee. *G524*
Jas 5:13 pray. Is any merry? let him **s** psalms. *G5567*
Rev 15: 3 And they **s** the song of Moses the servant *G103*

SINGED
Dan 3:27 hair of their head **s**, neither were their H2761

SINGER
1Ch 6:33 a **s**, the son of Joel, the son of Shemuel, H7891
Hab 3:19 the chief **s** on my stringed instruments. H5329

SINGERS
1Ki 10:12 and psalteries for **s**: there came no such H7891
1Ch 9:33 And these *are* the **s**, chief of the fathers H7891
15:16 brethren *to be* the **s** with instruments H7891
19 So the **s**, Heman, Asaph, and Ethan, H7891
27 the ark, and the **s**, and Chenaniah the H7891
27 of the song with the **s**: David also *had* H7891
2Ch 5:12 Also the Levites *which were* the **s**, all of H7891
13 trumpeters and **s** *were* as one, to make H7891
9:11 and psalteries for **s**: and there were H7891
20:21 he appointed **s** unto the LORD, and H7891
23:13 trumpets, also the **s** with instruments H7891
29:28 and the **s** sang, and the trumpeters H7892
35:15 And the **s** the sons of Asaph *were* in H7891
Ezr 2:41 The **s**: the children of Asaph, an H7891
70 people, and the **s**, and the porters, and H7891
7: 7 Levites, and the **s**, and the porters, and H7891
24 and Levites, **s**, porters, Nethinims, H2171
10:24 Of the **s** also; Eliashib: and of the H7891
Neh 7: 1 the **s** and the Levites were appointed, H7891
44 The **s**: the children of Asaph, an H7891
73 the porters, and the **s**, and *some* of the H7891
10:28 the porters, the **s**, the Nethinims, and H7891
39 the porters, and the **s**: and we will not H7891
11:22 the sons of Asaph, the **s** *were* over the H7891
23 should be for the **s**, due for every day. H7891
12:28 And the sons of the **s** gathered H7891
29 Azmaveth: for the **s** had builded them H7891
42 and Ezer. And the **s** sang loud, with H7891
45 And both the **s** and the porters kept the H7891
46 *were* chief of the **s**, and songs of praise H7891
47 the portions of the **s** and the porters, H7891
13: 5 Levites, and the **s**, and the porters; and H7891
10 the Levites and the **s**, that did the work, H7891
Ps 68:25 The **s** went before, the players on H7891
87: 7 As well the **s** as the players on H7891
Ecc 2: 8 I gat me men **s** and women singers, H7891
8 and women **s**, and the delights of the H7891
Ezk 40:44 chambers of the **s** in the inner court, H7891

SINGETH
Prv 25:20 so *is* he that **s** songs to an heavy heart. H7891

SINGING
1Sa 18: 6 of all cities of Israel, **s** and dancing, to H7891
2Sa 19:35 more the voice of **s** men and singing H7891
35 singing men and **s** women? wherefore H7891
1Ch 6:32 congregation with **s**, until Solomon had H7892
13: 8 might, and with **s**, and with harps, and H7892
2Ch 23:18 and with **s**, *as it was ordained* by David. H7892
30:21 **s** with loud instruments unto the LORD.
35:25 for Josiah: and all the **s** men and the H7891
25 men and the **s** women spake of Josiah H7891
Ezr 2:65 hundred **s** men and singing women. H7891
65 hundred singing men and **s** women. H7891
Neh 7:67 and five **s** men and singing women. H7891
67 and five singing men and **s** women. H7891
12:27 and with **s**, *with* cymbals, psalteries, H7892
Ps 100: 2 come before his presence with **s**. H7445
Ps 126: 2 and our tongue with **s**: then said they H7440
Song 2:12 the time of the **s** *of birds* is come, and H2158
Isa 14: 7 *and* is quiet: they break forth into **s**. H7440
16:10 there shall be no **s**, neither shall there H7442
35: 2 rejoice even with joy and **s**: the glory of H7444
44:23 break forth into **s**, ye mountains, O H7440
48:20 with a voice of **s** declare ye, tell this, H7440
49:13 break forth into **s**, O mountains: for the H7440
51:11 return, and come with **s** unto Zion; and H7440
54: 1 break forth into **s**, and cry aloud, thou H7440
55:12 before you into **s**, and all the trees of the H7440
Zep 3:17 in his love, he will joy over thee with **s**. H7440
Eph 5:19 spiritual songs, **s** and making melody *G103*
Col 3:16 **s** with grace in your hearts to the Lord. *G103*

SINGLE
Mt 6:22 be **s**, thy whole body shall be full of light. *G573*
Lk 11:34 when thine eye is **s**, thy whole body also *G573*

SINGLENESS
Act 2:46 their meat with gladness and **s** of heart, *G858*
Eph 6: 5 in **s** of your heart, as unto Christ; *G572*
Col 3:22 but in **s** of heart, fearing God: *G572*

SINGULAR
Lev 27: 2 a man shall make a **s** vow, the persons H6381

SINIM
Isa 49:12 the west; and these from the land of **S**. H5515

SINITE
Gen 10:17 the Hivite, and the Arkite, and the **S**, H5513
1Ch 1:15 the Hivite, and the Arkite, and the **S**, H5513

SINK
Ps 69: 2 I **s** in deep mire, where *there is* no H2883
14 and let me not **s**: let me be delivered H2883
Jer 51:64 shall Babylon **s**, and shall not rise from H8257
Mt 14:30 to **s**, he cried, saying, Lord, save me. *G2670*
Lk 5: 7 both the ships, so that they began to **s**. *G1036*
9:44 Let these sayings **s** down into your *G5087*

SINNED
Ex 9:27 said unto them, I have **s** this time: the H2398
34 were ceased, he **s** yet more, and H2398
10:16 he said, I have **s** against the LORD your H2398
32:30 people, Ye have **s** a great sin: and now H2398
31 this people have **s** a great sin, and have H2398
33 Whosoever hath **s** against me, him will H2398
Lev 4: 3 sin, which he hath **s**, a young bullock H2398
14 When the sin, which they have **s** H2398
22 When a ruler hath **s**, and done H2398
23 Or if his sin, wherein he hath **s**, come to H2398
28 Or if his sin, which he hath **s**, come to H2398
28 blemish, for his sin which he hath **s**. H2398
5: 5 confess that he hath **s** in that *thing*: H2398
6 sin which he hath **s**, a female from the H2398
10 he hath **s**, and it shall be forgiven him. H2398
11 then he that **s** shall bring for his H2398
13 sin that he hath **s** in one of these, and H2398
6: 4 Then it shall be, because he hath **s**, and H2398
Nu 6:11 for him, for that he **s** by the dead, and H2398
12:11 done foolishly, and wherein we have **s**. H2398
14:40 the LORD hath promised: for we have **s**. H2398
21: 7 and said, We have **s**, for we have H2398
22:34 the LORD, I have **s**; for I knew not that H2398
32:23 so, behold, ye have **s** against the LORD: H2398
Dt 1:41 unto me, We have **s** against the LORD, H2398
9:16 And I looked, and, behold, ye had **s** H2398
18 your sins which ye **s**, in doing wickedly H2398
Jos 7:11 Israel hath **s**, and they have also H2398
20 Indeed I have **s** against the LORD God H2398
Jdg 10:10 saying, We have **s** against thee, both H2398
15 the LORD, We have **s**: do thou unto us H2398
11:27 Wherefore I have not **s** against thee, H2398
1Sa 7: 6 there, We have **s** against the LORD. H2398
12:10 and said, We have **s**, because we have H2398
15:24 And Saul said unto Samuel, I have **s**: for H2398
30 Then he said, I have **s**: *yet* honour me H2398
19: 4 he hath not **s** against thee, and because H2398
24:11 and I have not **s** against thee; yet thou H2398
26:21 Then said Saul, I have **s**: return, my son H2398
2Sa 12:13 And David said unto Nathan, I have **s** H2398
19:20 For thy servant doth know that I have **s**: H2398
24:10 the LORD, I have **s** greatly in that I H2398
17 and said, Lo, I have **s**, and I have done H2398
1Ki 8:33 because they have **s** against thee, and H2398
35 because they have **s** against thee; if H2398
47 saying, We have **s**, and have done H2398
1Ki 8:50 And forgive thy people that have **s** H2398
15:30 which he **s**, and which he made H2398
16:13 son, by which they **s**, and by which they H2398
19 For his sins which he **s** in doing evil in H2398
18: 9 And he said, What have I **s**, that thou H2398
2Ki 17: 7 of Israel had **s** against the LORD their H2398
21:17 did, and his sin that he **s**, *are* they not H2398
1Ch 21: 8 And David said unto God, I have **s** H2398
17 I it is that have **s** and done evil indeed; H2398
2Ch 6:24 because they have **s** against thee; and H2398
26 because they have **s** against thee; *yet* if H2398
37 saying, We have **s**, we have done amiss, H2398
39 thy people which have **s** against thee. H2398
Neh 1: 6 which we have **s** against thee: both I H2398
6 both I and my father's house have **s**. H2398
9:29 but **s** against thy judgments, H2398
Job 1: 5 that my sons have **s**, and cursed God in H2398
22 In all this Job **s** not, nor charged God H2398
7:20 I have **s**; what shall I do unto thee, O H2398
8: 4 If thy children have **s** against him, and H2398
24:19 *so doth* the grave *those which* have **s**. H2398
33:27 *if any* say, I have **s**, and perverted *that* H2398
Ps 41: 4 heal my soul; for I have **s** against thee. H2398
51: 4 Against thee, thee only, have I **s**, and H2398
78:17 And they **s** yet more against him by H2398
32 For all this they **s** still, and believed not H2398
106: 6 We have **s** with our fathers, we have H2398
Isa 42:24 whom we have **s**? for they would not H2398
43:27 Thy first father hath **s**, and thy teachers H2398
64: 5 art wroth; for we have **s**: in those is H2398
Jer 2:35 thee, because thou sayest, I have not **s**. H2398
3:25 us: for we have **s** against the LORD our H2398
8:14 because we have **s** against the LORD. H2398
14: 7 are many; we have **s** against thee. H2398
20 our fathers: for we have **s** against thee. H2398
33: 8 whereby they have **s** against me; and I H2398
8 whereby they have **s**, and whereby they H2398
40: 3 because ye have **s** against the LORD, H2398
44:23 because ye have **s** against the LORD, H2398
50: 7 because they have **s** against the LORD, H2398
14 for she hath **s** against the LORD. H2398
Lam 1: 8 Jerusalem hath grievously **s**; therefore H2398
5: 7 Our fathers have **s**, *and are* not; and we H2398
16 our head: woe unto us, that we have **s**! H2398
Ezk 18:24 sin that he hath **s**, in them shall he die. H2398
28:16 and thou hast **s**: therefore I will cast H2398
37:23 wherein they have **s**, and will cleanse H2398
Dan 9: 5 We have **s**, and have committed H2398
8 because we have **s** against thee. H2398
11 of God, because we have **s** against him. H2398
15 day; we have **s**, we have done wickedly. H2398
Hos 4: 7 As they were increased, so they **s** H2398
10: 9 O Israel, thou hast **s** from the days of H2398
Mic 7: 9 because I have **s** against him, until he H2398
Hab 2:10 people, and hast **s** *against* thy soul. H2398
Zep 1:17 because they have **s** against the LORD: H2398
Mt 27: 4 Saying, I have **s** in that I have betrayed *G264*
Lk 15:18 I have **s** against heaven, and before thee, *G264*
21 him, Father, I have **s** against heaven, *G264*
Jn 9: 3 Jesus answered, Neither hath this man **s**, *G264*
Ro 2:12 For as many as have **s** without law shall *G264*
12 **s** in the law shall be judged by the law; *G264*
3:23 For all have **s**, and come short of the *G264*
5:12 passed upon all men, for that all have **s**: *G264*
14 them that had not **s** after the similitude *G264*
16 And not as *it was* by one that **s**, *so is* the *G264*
1Co 7:28 But and if thou marry, thou hast not **s**; *G264*
28 she hath not **s**. Nevertheless such shall *G264*
2Co 12:21 many which have **s** already, and have *G4258*
13: 2 heretofore have **s**, and to all other, that, *G4258*
Heb 3:17 **s**, whose carcases fell in the wilderness? *G264*
2Pt 2: 4 For if God spared not the angels that **s**, *G264*
1Jn 1:10 If we say that we have not **s**, we make *G264*

SINNER
Prv 11:31 earth: much more the wicked and the **s**. H2398
13: 6 but wickedness overthroweth the **s**. H2403
22 wealth of the **s** *is* laid up for the just. H2398
Ecc 2:26 and joy: but to the **s** he giveth travail, H2398
7:26 her; but the **s** shall be taken by her. H2398
8:12 Though a **s** do evil an hundred times, H2398
9: 2 *is* the good, so *is* the **s**; *and* he that H2398
18 war: but one **s** destroyeth much good. H2398
Isa 65:20 years old; but the **s** *being* an hundred H2398
Lk 7:37 city, which was a **s**, when she knew that *G268*
39 *this is* that toucheth him: for she is a **s**. *G268*
15: 7 be in heaven over one **s** that repenteth, *G268*
10 angels of God over one **s** that repenteth. *G268*
18:13 breast, saying, God be merciful to me a **s**. *G268*

Lk 19: 7 gone to be guest with a man that is a s. G268
Jn 9:16 can a man that is a s do such miracles? G268
24 the praise: we know that this man is a s. G268
25 Whether he be a s *or no*, I know not: one G268
Ro 3: 7 his glory; why yet am I also judged as a s? G268
Jas 5:20 converteth the s from the error of his G268
1Pt 4:18 shall the ungodly and the s appear? G268

SINNERS
Gen 13:13 and s before the LORD exceedingly. H2400
Nu 16:38 The censers of these s against their H2400
1Sa 15:18 utterly destroy the s the Amalekites, H2400
Ps 1: 1 s, nor sitteth in the seat of the scornful. H2400
5 s in the congregation of the righteous. H2400
25: 8 therefore will he teach s in the way. H2400
26: 9 Gather not my soul with s, nor my life H2400
51:13 and s shall be converted unto thee. H2400
104:35 Let the s be consumed out of the earth, H2400
Prv 1:10 My son, if s entice thee, consent thou H2400
13:21 Evil pursueth s: but to the righteous H2400
23:17 Let not thine heart envy s: but *be thou* H2400
Isa 1:28 and of the s *shall be* together, and H2400
13: 9 he shall destroy the s thereof out of it. H2400
33:14 The s in Zion are afraid; fearfulness H2400
Am 9:10 All the s of my people shall die by the H2400
Mt 9:10 publicans and s came and sat down G268
11 eateth your Master with publicans and s? G268
13 to call the righteous, but s to repentance. G268
11:19 s. But wisdom is justified of her children. G268
26:45 of man is betrayed into the hands of s. G268
Mk 2:15 publicans and s sat also together with G268
16 with publicans and s, they said unto his G268
16 and drinketh with publicans and s? G268
17 to call the righteous, but s to repentance. G268
14:41 of man is betrayed into the hands of s. G268
Lk 5:30 do ye eat and drink with publicans and s? G268
32 I came not to call the righteous, but s to G268
6:32 ye? for s also love those that love them. G268
33 have ye? for s also do even the same. G268
34 thank have ye? for s also lend to sinners, G268
34 also lend to s, to receive as much again. G268
7:34 winebibber, a friend of publicans and s! G268
13: 2 these Galilaeans were s above all the G268
4 ye that they were s above all men that G3781
15: 1 all the publicans and s for to hear him. G268
2 man receiveth s, and eateth with them. G268
Jn 9:31 Now we know that God heareth not s: but G268
Ro 5: 8 while we were yet s, Christ died for us. G268
19 many were made s, so by the obedience G268
Gal 2:15 We *who are* Jews by nature, and not s of G268
17 also are found s, *is* therefore Christ the G268
1Ti 1: 9 the ungodly and for s, for unholy and G268
15 the world to save s; of whom I am chief. G268
Heb 7:26 s, and made higher than the heavens; G268
12: 3 contradiction of s against himself, lest G268
Jas 4: 8 *your* hands, *ye* s; and purify *your* hearts, G268
Jude 15 ungodly s have spoken against him. G268

SINNEST
Job 35: 6 If thou s, what doest thou against him? H2398

SINNETH
Nu 15:28 for the soul that s ignorantly, when he H7683
28 when he s by ignorance before H2398
29 Ye shall have one law for him that s H6213
Dt 19:15 in any sin that he s: at the mouth of two H2398
1Ki 8:46 *is* no man that s not,) and thou be H2398
2Ch 6:36 *is* no man which s not,) and thou be H2398
Prv 8:36 But he that s against me wrongeth his H2398
14:21 He that despiseth his neighbour s: but H2398
19: 2 and he that hasteth with *his* feet s. H2398
20: 2 him to anger s *against* his own soul. H2398
Ecc 7:20 upon earth, that doeth good, and s not. H2398
Ezk 14:13 Son of man, when the land s against H2398
18: 4 son is mine: the soul that s, it shall die. H2398
20 The soul that s, it shall die. The son H2398
33:12 his *righteousness* in the day that he s. H2398
1Co 6:18 fornication s against his own body. G264
7:36 do what he will, he s not: let them marry. G264
Tit 3:11 and s, being condemned of himself. G264
1Jn 3: 6 Whosoever abideth in him s not: G264
6 s hath not seen him, neither known him. G264
8 devil; for the devil s from the beginning. G264
5:18 is born of God s not; but he that is G264

SINNING
Gen 20: 6 thee from s against me: therefore H2398
Lev 6: 3 of all these that a man doeth, s therein: H2398

SIN-OFFERING See SIN and OFFERING.

SINS
Lev 16:16 in all their s: and so shall he do for H2403
21 in all their s, putting them upon H2403
30 clean from all your s before the LORD. H2403
34 Israel for all their s once a year. And he H2403
26:18 punish you seven times more for your s. H2403
21 plagues upon you according to your s. H2403
24 punish you yet seven times for your s. H2403
28 will chastise you seven times for your s. H2403
Nu 16:26 theirs, lest ye be consumed in all their s. H2403
Dt 9:18 because of all your s which ye sinned, H2403
Jos 24:19 forgive your transgressions nor your s. H2403
1Sa 12:19 unto all our s *this* evil, to ask us a king. H2403
1Ki 14:16 up because of the s of Jeroboam, who H2403
22 to jealousy with their s which they had H2403
15: 3 And he walked in all the s of his father, H2403
30 Because of the s of Jeroboam which he H2403
16: 2 sin, to provoke me to anger with their s; H2403
13 For all the s of Baasha, and the sins of H2403
13 For all the sins of Baasha, and the s of H2403
19 For his s which he sinned in doing evil H2403
31 him to walk in the s of Jeroboam the H2403
2Ki 3: 3 Nevertheless he cleaved unto the s of H2403
10:29 Howbeit *from* the s of Jeroboam the H2399
31 not from the s of Jeroboam, which H2403
13: 2 and followed the s of Jeroboam the son H2403
6 departed not from the s of the house of H2403
11 not from all the s of Jeroboam the son H2403
14:24 not from all the s of Jeroboam the son H2403
15: 9 not from the s of Jeroboam the son H2403
18 all his days from the s of Jeroboam the H2403
24 not from the s of Jeroboam the son H2403
28 not from the s of Jeroboam the son H2403
17:22 walked in all the s of Jeroboam which H2403
24: 3 out of his sight, for the s of Manasseh, H2403
2Ch 28:10 with you, s against the LORD your God? H819
13 to add *more* to our s and to our trespass:
Neh 1: 6 and confess the s of the children of H2403
9: 2 s, and the iniquities of their fathers. H2403
37 over us because of our s: also they have H2403
Job 13:23 How many *are* mine iniquities and s? H2403
Ps 19:13 from presumptuous *s*; let them not have
25: 7 Remember not the s of my youth, nor H2403
18 and my pain; and forgive all my s. H2403
51: 9 Hide thy face from my s, and blot out H2399
69: 5 and my s are not hid from thee. H819
79: 9 purge away our s, for thy name's sake. H2403
90: 8 secret *s* in the light of thy countenance.
103:10 He hath not dealt with us after our s; H2399
Prv 5:22 shall be holden with the cords of his s. H2403
10:12 up strifes: but love covereth all s. H6588
28:13 He that covereth his s shall not H6588
Isa 1:18 though your s be as scarlet, they shall H2399
38:17 hast cast all my s behind thy back. H2399
40: 2 of the LORD's hand double for all her s. H2403
43:24 to serve with thy s, thou hast wearied H2403
25 own sake, and will not remember thy s. H2403
44:22 as a cloud, thy s: return unto me; for H2403
58: 1 and the house of Jacob their s. H2403
59: 2 God, and your s have hid *his* face from H2403
12 thee, and our s testify against us: for H2403
Jer 5:25 *things*, and your s have withholden H2403
14:10 their iniquity, and visit their s. H2403
15:13 *that* for all thy s, even in all thy borders. H2403
30:14 iniquity; *because* thy s were increased. H2403
15 *because* thy s were increased, I have H2403
50:20 *be* none; and the s of Judah, and they H2403
Lam 3:39 a man for the punishment of his s? H2399
4:13 For the s of her prophets, *and* the H2403
22 of Edom; he will discover thy s. H2403
Ezk 16:51 half of thy s; but thou hast multiplied H2403
52 own shame for thy s that thou hast H2403
18:14 all his father's s which he hath done, H2403
21 But if the wicked will turn from all his s H2403
21:24 your doings your s do appear; because, H2403
23:49 ye shall bear the s of your idols: and ye H2399
33:10 and our s *be* upon us, and we H2403
16 None of his s that he hath committed H2403
Dan 4:27 and break off thy s by righteousness, H2408
9:16 because for our s, and for the iniquities H2399
24 and to make an end of s, and to make H2403
Hos 8:13 visit their s: they shall return to Egypt. H2403
9: 9 their iniquity, he will visit their s. H2403
Am 5:12 and your mighty s: they afflict the just, H2403
Mic 1: 5 this, and for the s of the house of Israel. H2403
6:13 making *thee* desolate because of thy s. H2403
7:19 all their s into the depths of the sea. H2403
Mt 1:21 for he shall save his people from their s. G266
3: 6 of him in Jordan, confessing their s. G266
9: 2 be of good cheer; thy s be forgiven thee. G266
5 For whether is easier, to say, *Thy* s be G266
6 on earth to forgive s, (then saith he to the G266
26:28 is shed for many for the remission of s. G266
Mk 1: 4 of repentance for the remission of s. G266
5 in the river of Jordan, confessing their s. G266
2: 5 of the palsy, Son, thy s be forgiven thee. G266
7 who can forgive s but God only? G266
9 of the palsy, *Thy* s be forgiven thee; or to G266
10 s, (he saith to the sick of the palsy,) G266
3:28 Verily I say unto you, All s shall be G265
4:12 and *their* s should be forgiven them. G265
Lk 1:77 his people by the remission of their s, G266
3: 3 of repentance for the remission of s; G266
5:20 unto him, Man, thy s are forgiven thee. G266
21 Who can forgive s, but God alone? G266
23 Whether is easier, to say, Thy s be G266
24 earth to forgive s, (he said unto the sick G266
7:47 Wherefore I say unto thee, Her s, which G266
48 And he said unto her, Thy s are forgiven. G266
49 Who is this that forgiveth s also? G266
11: 4 And forgive us our s; for we also forgive G266
24:47 And that repentance and remission of s G266
Jn 8:21 in your s: whither I go, ye cannot come. G266
24 ye shall die in your s: for if ye believe not G266
24 not that I am *he*, ye shall die in your s. G266
9:34 altogether born in s, and dost thou teach G266
20:23 Whose soever s ye remit, they are G266
23 soever *s* ye retain, they are retained.
Act 2:38 the remission of s, and ye shall receive G266
3:19 that your s may be blotted out, when G266
5:31 to Israel, and forgiveness of s. G266
10:43 in him shall receive remission of s. G266
13:38 is preached unto you the forgiveness of s: G266
22:16 thy s, calling on the name of the Lord. G266
26:18 forgiveness of s, and inheritance among G266
Ro 3:25 the remission of s that are past, through G265
4: 7 are forgiven, and whose s are covered. G266
7: 5 the motions of s, which were by the law, G266
11:27 them, when I shall take away their s. G266
1Co 15: 3 for our s according to the scriptures; G266
17 your faith *is* vain; ye are yet in your s. G266
Gal 1: 4 Who gave himself for our s, that he G266
Eph 1: 7 of s, according to the riches of his grace; G3900
2: 1 who were dead in trespasses and s; G266
5 Even when we were dead in s, hath G3900
Col 1:14 his blood, *even* the forgiveness of s: G266
2:11 off the body of the s of the flesh by the G266
13 And you, being dead in your s and the G3900
1Th 2:16 to fill up their s alway: for the wrath G266
1Ti 5:22 of other men's s: keep thyself pure. G266
24 Some men's s are open beforehand, G266
2Ti 3: 6 laden with s, led away with divers lusts, G266
Heb 1: 3 by himself purged our s, sat down on the G266
2:17 reconciliation for the s of the people. G266
5: 1 may offer both gifts and sacrifices for s: G266
3 people, so also for himself, to offer for s. G266
7:27 first for his own s, and then for the G266
8:12 and their s and their iniquities will G266
9:28 So Christ was once offered to bear the s G266
10: 2 should have had no more conscience of s. G266
3 again *made* of s every year. G266
4 of bulls and of goats should take away s. G266
11 sacrifices, which can never take away s: G266
12 one sacrifice for s for ever, sat down on G266
17 And their s and iniquities will I G266
26 there remaineth no more sacrifice for s, G266
Jas 5:15 committed s, they shall be forgiven him. G266
20 death, and shall hide a multitude of s. G266
1Pt 2:24 Who his own self bare our s in his own G266
24 that we, being dead to s, should live unto G266
3:18 For Christ also hath once suffered for s, G266
4: 8 for charity shall cover the multitude of s. G266
2Pt 1: 9 that he was purged from his old s. G266
1Jn 1: 9 If we confess our s, he is faithful and just G266
9 just to forgive us *our* s, and to cleanse us G266
2: 2 And he is the propitiation for our s: and G266
2 but also for *the s of* the whole world.
12 s are forgiven you for his name's sake. G266
3: 5 to take away our s; and in him is no sin. G266
4:10 his Son *to be* the propitiation for our s. G266
Rev 1: 5 washed us from our s in his own blood, G266
18: 4 s, and that ye receive not of her plagues. G266
5 For her s have reached unto heaven, and G266

SION
Dt 4:48 even unto mount S, which *is* Hermon, H7865

S

Ps 65: 1 Praise waiteth for thee, O God, in **S**: and H6726
Mt 21: 5 Tell ye the daughter of **S**, Behold, thy *G4622*
Jn 12:15 Fear not, daughter of **S**: behold, thy *G4622*
Ro 9:33 As it is written, Behold, I lay in **S** a *G4622*
11:26 shall come out of **S** the Deliverer, and *G4622*
Heb 12:22 But ye are come unto mount **S**, and *G4622*
1Pt 2: 6 Behold, I lay in **S** a chief corner stone, *G4622*
Rev 14: 1 stood on the mount **S**, and with him an *G4622*

SIPHMOTH
1Sa 30:28 which *were* in **S**, and to *them* which H8224

SIPPAI
1Ch 20: 4 the Hushathite slew **S**, *that was* of the H5598

SIR
Gen 43:20 And said, O **s**, we came indeed down at H113
Mt 13:27 said unto him, **S**, didst not thou sow *G2962*
21:30 and said, I *go*, **s**: and went not. *G2962*
27:63 Saying, **S**, we remember that that *G2962*
Jn 4:11 The woman saith unto him, **S**, thou *G2962*
15 The woman saith unto him, **S**, give me *G2962*
19 The woman saith unto him, **S**, I *G2962*
49 The nobleman saith unto him, **S**, come *G2962*
5: 7 The impotent man answered him, **S**, I *G2962*
12:21 him, saying, **S**, we would see Jesus. *G2962*
20:15 saith unto him, **S**, if thou have borne *G2962*
Rev 7:14 And I said unto him, **S**, thou knowest. *G2962*

SIRAH
2Sa 3:26 the well of **S**: but David knew *it* not. H5626

SIRION
Dt 3: 9 (*Which* Hermon the Sidonians call **S**; H8303
Ps 29: 6 Lebanon and **S** like a young unicorn. H8303

SIRS
Act 7:26 at one again, saying, **S**, ye are brethren; *G435*
14:15 And saying, **S**, why do ye these things? *G435*
16:30 And brought them out, and said, **S**, *G2962*
19:25 and said, **S**, ye know that by this *G435*
27:10 And said unto them, **S**, I perceive that *G435*
21 of them, and said, **S**, ye should have *G435*
25 Wherefore, **s**, be of good cheer: for I *G435*

SISAMAI
1Ch 2:40 And Eleasah begat **S**, and Sisamai H5581
40 And Eleasah begat Sisamai, and **S** H5581

SISERA
Jdg 4: 2 of whose host *was* **S**, which dwelt in H5516
7 to the river Kishon **S**, the captain of H5516
9 the LORD shall sell **S** into the hand of a H5516
12 And they shewed **S** that Barak the son H5516
13 And **S** gathered together all his H5516
14 hath delivered **S** into thine hand: is not H5516
15 And the LORD discomfited **S**, and all H5516
15 Barak; so that **S** lighted down off *his* H5516
16 and all the host of **S** fell upon the edge H5516
17 Howbeit **S** fled away on his feet to the H5516
18 And Jael went out to meet **S**, and said H5516
22 And, behold, as Barak pursued **S**, Jael H5516
22 her *tent*, behold, **S** lay dead, and the H5516
5:20 stars in their courses fought against **S**. H5516
26 she smote **S**, she smote off his head, H5516
28 The mother of **S** looked out at a H5516
30 a damsel *or* two; to **S** a prey of divers H5516
1Sa 12: 9 into the hand of **S**, captain of the host H5516
Ezr 2:53 children of **S**, the children of Thamah, H5516
Neh 7:55 children of **S**, the children of Tamah, H5516
Ps 83: 9 *to* **S**, as *to* Jabin, at the brook of Kison: H5516

SISTER
Gen 4:22 and the **s** of Tubal-cain *was* Naamah. H269
12:13 Say, I pray thee, thou *art* my **s**: that it H269
19 Why saidst thou, She *is* my **s**? so I might H269
20: 2 his wife, She *is* my **s**: and Abimelech king H269
5 Said he not unto me, She *is* my **s**? and H269
12 And yet indeed *she is* my **s**; she *is* the H269
24:30 of Rebekah his **s**, saying, Thus spake the H269
59 And they sent away Rebekah their **s**, and H269
60 her, Thou *art* our **s**, be thou *the mother* H269
25:20 Padan-aram, the **s** to Laban the Syrian. H269
26: 7 he said, She *is* my **s**: for he feared to say, H269
9 thou, She *is* my **s**? And Isaac said unto H269
28: 9 son, the **s** of Nebajoth, to be his wife. H269
30: 1 Rachel envied her **s**; and said unto Jacob, H269
8 have I wrestled with my **s**, and I have H269
34:13 because he had defiled Dinah their **s**: H269
Gen 34:14 this thing, to give our **s** to one that is H269
27 the city, because they had defiled their **s**. H269
31 And they said, Should he deal with our **s** H269
36: 3 And Bashemath Ishmael's daughter, **s** of H269
22 and Hemam; and Lotan's **s** *was* Timna. H269
46:17 and Serah their **s**: and the sons of Beriah; H269
Ex 2: 4 And his **s** stood afar off, to wit what H269
7 Then said his **s** to Pharaoh's daughter, H269
6:20 his father's **s** to wife; and she bare H1733
23 of Amminadab, **s** of Naashon, to wife; H269
15:20 And Miriam the prophetess, the **s** of H269
Lev 18: 9 The nakedness of thy **s**, the daughter of H269
11 **s**, thou shalt not uncover her nakedness. H269
12 **s**: she *is* thy father's near kinswoman. H269
13 of thy mother's **s**: for she *is* thy mother's H269
18 Neither shalt thou take a wife to her **s**, to H269
20:17 And if a man shall take his **s**, his father's H269
19 of thy mother's **s**, nor of thy father's H269
19 nor of thy father's **s**: for he uncovereth H269
21: 3 And for his **s** a virgin, that is nigh unto H269
Nu 6: 7 his brother, or for his **s**, when they die: H269
25:18 of Midian, their **s**, which was slain in the H269
26:59 Aaron and Moses, and Miriam their **s**. H269
Dt 27:22 Cursed *be* he that lieth with his **s**, the H269
Jdg 15: 2 *is* not her younger **s** fairer than she? take H269
Ru 1:15 And she said, Behold, thy **s** in law is H2994
15 her gods: return thou after thy **s** in law. H2994
2Sa 13: 1 of David had a fair **s**, whose name *was* H269
2 he fell sick for his **s** Tamar; for she *was* a H269
4 I love Tamar, my brother Absalom's **s**. H269
5 I pray thee, let my **s** Tamar come, and H269
6 thee, let Tamar my **s** come, and make H269
11 said unto her, Come lie with me, my **s**. H269
20 now thy peace, my **s**: he *is* thy brother; H269
22 because he had forced his **s** Tamar. H269
32 from the day that he forced his **s** Tamar. H269
17:25 of Nahash, **s** to Zeruiah Joab's mother. H269
1Ki 11:19 him to wife the **s** of his own wife, the H269
19 own wife, the **s** of Tahpenes the queen. H269
20 And the **s** of Tahpenes bare him H269
2Ki 11: 2 of king Joram, **s** of Ahaziah, took Joash H269
1Ch 1:39 and Homam: and Timna *was* Lotan's **s**. H269
3: 9 of the concubines, and Tamar their **s**. H269
19 and Hananiah, and Shelomith their **s**: H269
4: 3 and the name of their **s** *was* Hazelelponi: H269
19 And the sons of *his* wife Hodiah the **s** of H269
7:15 And Machir took to wife *the* **s** of H269
18 And his **s** Hammoleketh bare Ishod, and H269
30 Ishuai, and Beriah, and Serah their **s**. H269
32 Shomer, and Hotham, and Shua their **s**. H269
2Ch 22:11 (for she was the **s** of Ahaziah,) hid him H269
Job 17:14 worm, *Thou art* my mother, and my **s**. H269
Prv 7: 4 Say unto wisdom, Thou *art* my **s**; and H269
Song 4: 9 Thou hast ravished my heart, my **s**, *my* H269
10 How fair is thy love, my **s**, *my* spouse! H269
12 A garden inclosed *is* my **s**, *my* spouse; a H269
5: 1 I am come into my garden, my **s**, *my* H269
2 Open to me, my **s**, my love, my dove, my H269
8: 8 We have a little **s**, and she hath no H269
8 shall we do for our **s** in the day when she H269
Jer 3: 7 not. And her treacherous **s** Judah saw *it*. H269
8 yet her treacherous **s** Judah feared not, H269
10 And yet for all this her treacherous **s** H269
22:18 Ah my brother! or, Ah **s**! they shall not H269
Ezk 16:45 and thou *art* the **s** of thy sisters, which H269
46 And thine elder **s** *is* Samaria, she and H269
46 and thy younger **s**, that dwelleth at thy H269
48 GOD, Sodom thy **s** hath not done, she H269
49 Behold, this was the iniquity of thy **s** H269
56 For thy **s** Sodom was not mentioned by H269
22:11 humbled his **s**, his father's daughter. H269
23: 4 and Aholibah her **s**: and they were mine, H269
11 And when her **s** Aholibah saw *this*, she H269
11 more than her **s** in *her* whoredoms. H269
18 as my mind was alienated from her **s**. H269
31 Thou hast walked in the way of thy **s**; H269
33 with the cup of thy **s** Samaria. H269
44:25 for brother, or for **s** that hath had no H269
Mt 12:50 same is my brother, and **s**, and mother. *G79*
Mk 3:35 is my brother, and my **s**, and mother. *G79*
Lk 10:39 And she had a **s** called Mary, which also *G79*
40 not care that my **s** hath left me to serve *G79*
Jn 11: 1 the town of Mary and her **s** Martha. *G79*
5 Now Jesus loved Martha, and her **s**, and *G79*
28 called Mary her **s** secretly, saying, The *G79*
39 the stone. Martha, the **s** of him that was *G79*
19:25 and his mother's **s**, Mary the *wife* of *G79*
Ro 16: 1 I commend unto you Phebe our **s**, which *G79*
15 Nereus, and his **s**, and Olympas, and all *G79*
1Co 7:15 A brother or a **s** is not under bondage *G79*
9: 5 Have we not power to lead about a **s**, a *G79*
Jas 2:15 If a brother or **s** be naked, and destitute *G79*
2Jn 13 The children of thy elect **s** greet thee. *G79*

SISTER-IN-LAW See SISTER and LAW.

SISTERS
Jos 2:13 my brethren, and my **s**, and all that they H269
1Ch 2:16 Whose **s** *were* Zeruiah, and Abigail. And H269
Job 1: 4 three **s** to eat and to drink with them. H269
42:11 and all his **s**, and all they that had H269
Ezk 16:45 *art* the sister of thy **s**, which lothed their H269
51 and hast justified thy **s** in all thine H269
52 Thou also, which hast judged thy **s**, bear H269
52 shame, in that thou hast justified thy **s**. H269
55 When thy **s**, Sodom and her daughters, H269
61 shalt receive thy **s**, thine elder and thy H269
Hos 2: 1 Ammi; and to your **s**, Ruhamah. H269
Mt 13:56 And his **s**, are they not all with us? *G79*
19:29 or brethren, or **s**, or father, or mother, *G79*
Mk 6: 3 and are not his **s** here with us? And they *G79*
10:29 or brethren, or **s**, or father, or mother, *G79*
30 and brethren, and **s**, and mothers, and *G79*
Lk 14:26 and brethren, and **s**, yea, and his own life *G79*
Jn 11: 3 Therefore his **s** sent unto him, saying, *G79*
1Ti 5: 2 the younger as **s**, with all purity. *G79*

SISTER'S
Gen 24:30 bracelets upon his **s** hands, and when he H269
29:13 tidings of Jacob his **s** son, that he ran to H269
Lev 20:17 **s** nakedness; he shall bear his iniquity. H269
1Ch 7:15 Shuppim, whose **s** name *was* Maachah;) H269
Ezk 23:32 shalt drink of thy **s** cup deep and large: H269
Act 23:16 And when Paul's **s** son heard of their *G79*
Col 4:10 you, and Marcus, **s** son to Barnabas, *G431*

SIT
Gen 27:19 me: arise, I pray thee, **s** and eat of my H3427
Nu 32: 6 brethren go to war, and shall ye **s** here? H3427
Jdg 5:10 **s** in judgment, and walk by the way. H3427
Ru 3:18 Then said she, **S** still, my daughter, H3427
4: 1 a one! turn aside, **s** down here. And he H3427
2 **S** ye down here. And they sat down. H3427
1Sa 9:22 and made them **s** in the chiefest place H5414
16:11 we will not **s** down till he come hither. H5437
20: 5 I should not fail to **s** with the king at H3427
2Sa 19: 8 the king doth **s** in the gate. And all H3427
1Ki 1:13 me, and he shall **s** upon my throne? H3427
17 me, and he shall **s** upon my throne. H3427
20 them who shall **s** on the throne of my H3427
24 me, and he shall **s** upon my throne? H3427
27 who should **s** on the throne of my H3427
30 me, and he shall **s** upon my throne in H3427
35 he may come and **s** upon my throne; H3427
48 hath given *one* to **s** on my throne this H3427
3: 6 son to **s** on his throne, as *it is* this day. H3427
8:20 David my father, and **s** on the throne of H3427
25 in my sight to **s** on the throne of Israel; H3427
2Ki 7: 3 to another, Why **s** we here until we die? H3427
4 there: and if we **s** still here, we die also. H3427
10:30 shall **s** on the throne of Israel. H3427
15:12 Thy sons shall **s** on the throne of Israel H3427
18:27 *me* to the men which **s** on the wall, that H3427
1Ch 28: 5 my son to **s** upon the throne of the H3427
2Ch 6:16 in my sight to **s** upon the throne of H3427
Ps 26: 5 doers; and will not **s** with the wicked. H3427
69:12 They that **s** in the gate speak against H3427
107:10 Such as **s** in darkness and in the H3427
110: 1 The LORD said unto my Lord, **S** thou H3427
119:23 Princes also did **s** *and* speak against H3427
127: 2 *It is* vain for you to rise up early, to **s** H3427
132:12 also **s** upon thy throne for evermore. H3427
Ecc 10: 6 dignity, and the rich **s** in low place. H3427
Isa 3:26 *being* desolate shall **s** upon the ground. H3427
14:13 the stars of God: I will **s** also upon the H3427
16: 5 and he shall **s** upon it in truth in the H3427
30: 7 this, Their strength *is* to **s** still. H3427
36:12 to the men that **s** upon the wall, that H3427
42: 7 **s** in darkness out of the prison house. H3427
47: 1 Come down, and **s** in the dust, O virgin H3427
1 of Babylon, **s** on the ground: *there* H3427
5 **S** thou silent, and get thee into H3427
8 me; I shall not **s** *as* a widow, neither H3427
14 coal to warm at, *nor* fire to **s** before it. H3427
52: 2 dust; arise, *and* **s** down, O Jerusalem: H3427
Jer 8:14 Why do we **s** still? assemble yourselves, H3427
13:13 the kings that **s** upon David's throne, H3427
18 Humble yourselves, **s** down: for your H3427

Jer 16: 8 to s with them to eat and to drink. H3427
33:17 want a man to s upon the throne of the H3427
36:15 And they said unto him, S down now, H3427
30 shall have none to s upon the throne of H3427
48:18 *thy* glory, and s in thirst; for the spoiler H3427
Lam 1: 1 How doth the city s solitary, *that was* H3427
2:10 The elders of the daughter of Zion s H3427
Ezk 26:16 they shall s upon the ground, and H3427
28: 2 said, I *am* a God, I s *in* the seat of God, H3427
33:31 cometh, and they s before thee *as* my H3427
44: 3 *It is* for the prince; the prince, he shall s H3427
Dan 7: 9 of days did s, whose garment *was* H3488
26 But the judgment shall s, and they shall H3488
Joel 3:12 s to judge all the heathen round about. H3427
Mic 4: 4 But they shall s every man under his H3427
7: 8 I shall arise; when I s in darkness, the H3427
Zec 3: 8 thy fellows that s before thee: for they H3427
6:13 the glory, and shall s and rule upon his H3427
Mal 3: 3 And he shall s *as* a refiner and purifier H3427
Mt 8:11 east and west, and shall s down with G347
14:19 And he commanded the multitude to s G347
15:35 And he commanded the multitude to s G377
19:28 Son of man shall s in the throne of his G2523
28 his glory, ye also shall s upon twelve G2523
20:21 my two sons may s, the one on thy right G2523
23 with: but to s on my right hand, and G2523
22:44 said unto my Lord, S thou on my right G2521
23: 2 Saying, The scribes and the Pharisees s G2523
25:31 shall he s upon the throne of his glory: G2523
26:36 S ye here, while I go and pray yonder. G2523
Mk 6:39 And he commanded them to make all s G347
8: 6 And he commanded the people to s G377
10:37 us that we may s, one on thy right hand, G2523
40 But to s on my right hand and on my G2523
12:36 said to my Lord, S thou on my right G2521
14:32 disciples, S ye here, while I shall pray. G2523
Lk 1:79 To give light to them that s in darkness G2521
9:14 them s down by fifties in a company. G2625
15 And they did so, and made them all s G347
12:37 and make them to s down to meat, and G347
13:29 and shall s down in the kingdom of God. G347
14: 8 *man* to a wedding, s not down in the G2625
10 But when thou art bidden, go and s G377
10 of them that s at meat with thee. G4873
16: 6 and s down quickly, and write fifty. G2523
17: 7 from the field, Go and s down to meat? G377
20:42 my Lord, S thou on my right hand, G2521
22:30 my kingdom, and s on thrones judging G2523
69 Hereafter shall the Son of man s on the G2521
Jn 6:10 And Jesus said, Make the men s down. G377
Act 2:30 raise up Christ to s on his throne; G2523
34 my Lord, S thou on my right hand, G2521
8:31 that he would come up and s with him. G2523
1Co 8:10 hast knowledge s at meat in the idol's G2621
Eph 2: 6 and made *us* s together in heavenly G4776
Heb 1:13 he at any time, S on my right hand, G2521
Jas 2: 3 and say unto him, S thou here in a G2521
3 there, or s here under my footstool: G2521
Rev 3:21 will I grant to s with me in my throne, G2523
17: 3 and I saw a woman s upon a scarlet G2521
18: 7 in her heart, I s a queen, and am no G2521
19:18 and of them that s on them, and the G2521

SITH
Ezk 35: 6 shall pursue thee: s thou hast not hated H518

SITNAH
Gen 26:21 that also: and he called the name of it S. H7856

SITTEST
Ex 18:14 to the people? why s thou thyself alone, H3427
Dt 6: 7 them when thou s in thine house, and H3427
11:19 them when thou s in thine house, and H3427
Ps 50:20 Thou s *and* speakest against thy H3427
Prv 23: 1 When thou s to eat with a ruler, H3427
Jer 22: 2 king of Judah, that s upon the throne of H3427
Act 23: 3 whited wall: for s thou to judge me G2521

SITTETH
Ex 11: 5 of Pharaoh that s upon his throne, H3427
Lev 15: 4 thing, whereon he s, shall be unclean. H3427
6 And he that s on *any* thing whereon he H3427
20 also that she s upon shall be unclean. H3427
23 thing whereon she s, when he toucheth H3427
26 and whatsoever she s upon shall be H3427
Dt 17:18 And it shall be, when he s upon the H3427
1Ki 1:46 And also Solomon s on the throne of H3427
Est 6:10 the Jew, that s at the king's gate: let H3427
Ps 1: 1 nor s in the seat of the scornful. H3427
Ps 2: 4 He that s in the heavens shall laugh: H3427
10: 8 He s in the lurking places of the H3427
29:10 The LORD s upon the flood; yea, the H3427
10 flood; yea, the LORD s King for ever. H3427
47: 8 God reigneth over the heathen: God s H3427
99: 1 the people tremble: he s *between* the H3427
Prv 9:14 For she s at the door of her house, on a H3427
20: 8 A king that s in the throne of judgment H3427
31:23 when he s among the elders of the land. H3427
Song 1:12 While the king *s* at his table, my
Isa 28: 6 to him that s in judgment, and for H3427
40:22 *It is* he that s upon the circle of the H3427
Jer 17:11 *As* the partridge s *on eggs*, and H1716
29:16 of the king that s upon the throne of H3427
Lam 3:28 He s alone and keepeth silence, H3427
Zec 1:11 all the earth s still, and is at rest. H3427
5: 7 that s in the midst of the ephah. H3427
Mt 23:22 of God, and by him that s thereon. G2521
Lk 14:28 to build a tower, s not down first, and G2523
31 another king, s not down first, and G2523
22:27 For whether *is* greater, he that s at meat, G345
27 *is* not he that s at meat? but I am among G345
1Co 14:30 that s by, let the first hold his peace. G2521
Col 3: 1 Christ s on the right hand of God. G2076
2Th 2: 4 so that he as God s in the temple of G2523
Rev 5:13 *be* unto him that s upon the throne, G2521
6:16 face of him that s on the throne, and G2521
7:10 s upon the throne, and unto the Lamb. G2521
15 and he that s on the throne shall G2521
17: 1 great whore that s upon many waters: G2521
9 mountains, on which the woman s. G2521
15 where the whore s, are peoples, and G2521

SITTING
Dt 22: 6 eggs, and the dam s upon the young, or H7257
Jdg 3:20 unto him; and he was s in a summer H3427
1Ki 10: 5 And the meat of his table, and the s of H4186
13:14 and found him s under an oak: and he H3427
22:19 I saw the LORD s on his throne, and all H3427
2Ki 4:38 the prophets *were* s before him: and he H3427
9: 5 of the host *were* s; and he said, I have H3427
2Ch 9: 4 And the meat of his table, and the s of H4186
18 on each side of the s place, and two H3427
18:18 I saw the LORD s upon his throne, and H3427
Neh 2: 6 me, (the queen also s by him,) For how H3427
Est 5:13 Mordecai the Jew s at the king's gate. H3427
Isa 6: 1 I saw also the Lord s upon a throne, high H3427
Jer 17:25 kings and princes s upon the throne of H3427
22: 4 of this house kings s upon the throne of H3427
30 seed shall prosper, s upon the throne of H3427
38: 7 the king then s in the gate of Benjamin; H3427
Lam 3:63 Behold their s down, and their rising H3427
Mt 9: 9 named Matthew, s at the receipt of G2521
11:16 like unto children s in the markets, and G2521
20:30 And, behold, two blind men s by the G2521
21: 5 thee, meek, and s upon an ass, and a G1910
26:64 the Son of man s on the right hand of G2521
27:36 And s down they watched him there; G2521
61 Mary, s over against the sepulchre. G2521
Mk 2: 6 But there were certain of the scribes s G2521
14 the *son* of Alphaeus s at the receipt of G2521
5:15 had the legion, s, and clothed, and in G2521
14:62 the Son of man s on the right hand of G2521
16: 5 saw a young man s on the right side, G2521
Lk 2:46 him in the temple, s in the midst of the G2516
5:17 and doctors of the law s by, which were G2521
27 named Levi, s at the receipt of custom: G2521
7:32 They are like unto children s in the G2521
8:35 were departed, s at the feet of Jesus, G2521
10:13 ago repented, s in sackcloth and ashes. G2521
Jn 2:14 doves, and the changers of money s: G2521
12:15 thy King cometh, s on an ass's colt. G2521
20:12 And seeth two angels in white s, the one G2516
Act 2: 2 it filled all the house where they were s. G2521
8:28 Was returning, and s in his chariot G2521
25: 6 and the next day s on the judgment G2523
Rev 4: 4 and twenty elders s, clothed in white G2521

SITTING-PLACE See SITTING and PLACE.

SITUATE
1Sa 14: 5 The forefront of the one *was* s H4690
Ezk 27: 3 And say unto Tyrus, O thou that art s H3427
Nah 3: 8 No, that was s among the rivers, *that* H3427

SITUATION
2Ki 2:19 I pray thee, the s of this city *is* pleasant, H4186
Ps 48: 2 Beautiful for s, the joy of the whole H5131

SIVAN
Est 8: 9 that *is*, the month S, on the three and H5510

SIX
Gen 7: 6 And Noah *was* s hundred years old H8337
11 In the s hundredth year of Noah's life, H8337
8:13 And it came to pass in the s hundredth H8337
16:16 And Abram *was* fourscore and s years H8337
30:20 I have born him s sons: and she called H8337
31:41 daughters, and s years for thy cattle: H8337
46:26 all the souls *were* threescore and s; H8337
Ex 12:37 to Succoth, about s hundred thousand H8337
14: 7 And he took s hundred chosen H8337
16:26 S days ye shall gather it; but on the H8337
20: 9 S days shalt thou labour, and do all thy H8337
11 For *in* s days the LORD made heaven H8337
21: 2 If thou buy an Hebrew servant, s years H8337
23:10 And s years thou shalt sow thy land, H8337
12 S days thou shalt do thy work, and on H8337
24:16 the cloud covered it s days: and the H8337
25:32 And s branches shall come out of the H8337
33 a flower: so in the s branches that come H8337
35 same, according to the s branches that H8337
26: 9 by themselves, and s curtains by H8337
22 westward thou shalt make s boards. H8337
28:10 S of their names on one stone, and *the* H8337
10 and *the other* s names of the rest on H8337
31:15 S days may work be done; but in the H8337
17 for ever: for *in* s days the LORD made H8337
34:21 S days thou shalt work, but on the H8337
35: 2 S days shall work be done, but on the H8337
36:16 and s curtains by themselves. H8337
27 westward he made s boards. H8337
37:18 And s branches going out of the sides H8337
19 s branches going out of the candlestick. H8337
21 to the s branches going out of it. H8337
38:26 and upward, for s hundred thousand H8337
Lev 12: 5 of her purifying threescore and s days. H8337
23: 3 S days shall work be done: but the H8337
24: 6 And thou shalt set them in two rows, s H8337
25: 3 S years thou shalt sow thy field, and six H8337
3 Six years thou shalt sow thy field, and s H8337
Nu 1:21 forty and s thousand and five hundred. H8337
25 and five thousand s hundred and fifty. H8337
27 and fourteen thousand and s hundred. H8337
46 numbered were s hundred thousand H8337
2: 4 and fourteen thousand and s hundred. H8337
9 thousand and s thousand and four H8337
11 forty and s thousand and five hundred. H8337
15 five thousand and s hundred and fifty. H8337
31 thousand and s hundred. They shall H8337
32 their hosts *were* s hundred thousand H8337
3:28 thousand and s hundred, keeping the H8337
34 *were* s thousand and two hundred. H8337
4:40 thousand and s hundred and thirty. H8337
7: 3 before the LORD, s covered wagons, H8337
11:21 whom I *am*, *are* s hundred thousand H8337
26:41 forty and five thousand and s hundred. H8337
51 children of Israel, s hundred thousand H8337
31:32 had caught, was s hundred thousand H8337
37 s hundred and threescore and fifteen. H8337
38 And the beeves *were* thirty and s H8337
44 And thirty and s thousand beeves, H8337
35: 6 *there shall be* s cities for refuge, which H8337
13 And of these cities which ye shall give s H8337
15 These s cities shall be a refuge, *both* for H8337
Dt 5:13 S days thou shalt labour, and do all thy H8337
15:12 thee, and serve thee s years; then in the H8337
18 in serving thee s years: and the LORD H8337
16: 8 S days thou shalt eat unleavened H8337
Jos 6: 3 city once. Thus shalt thou do s days. H8337
14 into the camp: so they did s days. H8337
7: 5 about thirty and s men: for they chased H8337
15:59 and Eltekon; s cities with their villages: H8337
62 and En-gedi; s cities with their villages. H8337
Jdg 3:31 of the Philistines s hundred men with H8337
12: 7 And Jephthah judged Israel s years. H8337
18:11 and out of Eshtaol, s hundred men H8337
16 And the s hundred men appointed with H8337
17 of the gate with the s hundred men *that* H8337
20:15 cities twenty and s thousand men that H8337
47 But s hundred men turned and fled to H8337
Ru 3:15 it, he measured s *measures* of barley, H8337
17 And she said, These s *measures* of H8337
1Sa 13: 5 chariots, and s thousand horsemen, H8337
15 with him, about s hundred men. H8337
14: 2 with him *were* about s hundred men; H8337
17: 4 whose height *was* s cubits and a span. H8337
7 head *weighed* s hundred shekels of H8337

1Sa 23:13 *which were* about s hundred, arose and H8337
27: 2 over with the s hundred men that *were* H8337
30: 9 So David went, he and the s hundred H8337
2Sa 2:11 Judah was seven years and s months. H8337
5: 5 seven years and s months: and in H8337
6:13 s paces, he sacrificed oxen and fatlings. H8337
15:18 all the Gittites, s hundred men which H8337
21:20 had on every hand s fingers, and on H8337
20 and on every foot s toes, four and H8337
1Ki 6: 6 the middle *was* s cubits broad, and the H8337
10:14 in one year was s hundred threescore H8337
14 threescore and s talents of gold, H8337
16 *of* beaten gold: s hundred *shekels* of H8337
19 The throne had s steps, and the top of H8337
20 on the other upon the s steps: there was H8337
29 out of Egypt for s hundred *shekels* of H8337
11:16 (For s months did Joab remain there H8337
16:23 years: s years reigned he in Tirzah. H8337
2Ki 5: 5 of silver, and s thousand *pieces* of H8337
11: 3 of the LORD s years. And Athaliah H8337
13:19 smitten five or s times; then hadst thou H8337
15: 8 reign over Israel in Samaria s months. H8337
1Ch 3: 4 *These* s were born unto him in Hebron; H8337
4 seven years and s months: and in H8337
22 Bariah, and Neariah, and Shaphat, s. H8337
4:27 And Shimei had sixteen sons and s H8337
7: 2 and twenty thousand and s hundred. H8337
4 soldiers for war, s and thirty thousand H8337
40 battle *was* twenty and s thousand men. H8337
8:38 And Azel had s sons, whose names *are* H8337
9: 6 their brethren, s hundred and ninety. H8337
9 and fifty and s. All these men *were* H8337
44 And Azel had s sons, whose names *are* H8337
12:24 and spear *were* s thousand and eight H8337
26 of Levi four thousand and s hundred. H8337
35 and eight thousand and s hundred. H8337
20: 6 four and twenty, s *on each hand,* and H8337
6 *on each hand,* and s *on each foot:* and H8337
21:25 So David gave to Ornan for the place s H8337
23: 4 s thousand *were* officers and judges: H8337
25: 3 and Mattithiah, s, under the hands of H8337
26:17 Eastward *were* s Levites, northward H8337
2Ch 1:17 Egypt a chariot for s hundred *shekels* H8337
2: 2 and s hundred to oversee them. H8337
17 and three thousand and s hundred. H8337
18 thousand and s hundred overseers to H8337
3: 8 gold, *amounting* to s hundred talents. H8337
9:13 in one year was s hundred and H8337
13 and threescore and s talents of gold; H8337
15 *of* beaten gold: s hundred *shekels* of H8337
18 And *there were* s steps to the throne, H8337
19 the other upon the s steps. There was H8337
16: 1 In the s and thirtieth year of the reign H8337
22:12 the house of God s years: and Athaliah H8337
26:12 *were* two thousand and s hundred. H8337
29:33 And the consecrated things *were* s H8337
35: 8 two thousand and s hundred *small* H8337
Ezr 2:10 The children of Bani, s hundred forty H8337
11 The children of Bebai, s hundred H8337
13 The children of Adonikam, s hundred H8337
13 of Adonikam, six hundred sixty and s. H8337
14 of Bigvai, two thousand fifty and s. H8337
22 The men of Netophah, fifty and s. H8337
26 The children of Ramah and Gaba, s H8337
30 of Magbish, an hundred fifty and s. H8337
35 thousand and s hundred and thirty. H8337
60 of Nekoda, s hundred fifty and two. H8337
66 thirty and s; their mules, two hundred H8337
67 s thousand seven hundred and twenty. H8337
8:26 I even weighed unto their hand s H8337
35 Israel, ninety and s rams, seventy and H8337
Neh 5:18 *was* one ox *and* s choice sheep; also H8337
7:10 The children of Arah, s hundred fifty H8337
15 The children of Binnui, s hundred forty H8337
16 The children of Bebai, s hundred H8337
18 The children of Adonikam, s hundred H8337
20 The children of Adin, s hundred fifty H8337
30 The men of Ramah and Geba, s H8337
62 of Nekoda, s hundred forty and two. H8337
68 thirty and s: their mules, two hundred H8337
69 thirty and five: s thousand seven H8337
Est 2:12 *to wit,* s months with oil of myrrh, H8337
12 oil of myrrh, and s months with sweet H8337
Job 5:19 He shall deliver thee in s troubles: yea, H8337
42:12 sheep, and s thousand camels, and H8337
Prv 6:16 These s *things* doth the LORD hate: H8337
Isa 6: 2 each one had s wings; with twain he H8337
Jer 34:14 hath served thee s years, thou shalt let H8337
52:23 And there were ninety and s H8337
Jer 52:30 *were* four thousand and s hundred. H8337
Ezk 9: 2 And, behold, s men came from the way H8337
40: 5 measuring reed of s cubits *long* by the H8337
12 chambers *were* s cubits on this side, H8337
12 on this side, and s cubits on that side. H8337
41: 1 the posts, s cubits broad on the H8337
1 the one side, and s cubits broad on the H8337
3 and the door, s cubits; and the breadth H8337
5 the wall of the house, s cubits; and the H8337
8 *were* a full reed of s great cubits. H8337
46: 1 shall be shut the s working days; but on H8337
4 day *shall be* s lambs without blemish, H8337
6 blemish, and s lambs, and a ram: they H8337
Dan 3: 1 breadth thereof s cubits: he set it up in H8353
Mt 17: 1 And after s days Jesus taketh Peter, G1803
Mk 9: 2 And after s days Jesus taketh *with him* G1803
Lk 4:25 up three years and s months, when G1803
13:14 people, There are s days in which men G1803
Jn 2: 6 And there were set there s waterpots of G1803
20 Then said the Jews, Forty and s years G1803
12: 1 Then Jesus s days before the passover G1803
Act 11:12 doubting. Moreover these s brethren G1803
18:11 And he continued *there* a year and s G1803
Jas 5:17 the space of three years and s months. G1803
Rev 4: 8 And the four beasts had each of them s G1803
13:18 *is* S hundred threescore *and* six. G1803
18 *is* Six hundred threescore *and* s. G1803
14:20 of a thousand *and* s hundred furlongs. G1812

SIX-HUNDRED See SIX and HUNDRED.

SIXSCORE
1Ki 9:14 And Hiram sent to the king s H3967+H6242
Jna 4:11 more than s thousand H8147+H6240+H7239

SIXTEEN
Gen 46:18 bare unto Jacob, *even* s souls. H8337+H6240
Ex 26:25 *of* silver, s sockets; two sockets H8337+H6240
36:30 their sockets *were* s sockets of H8337+H6240
Nu 26:22 s thousand and five hundred. H8337+H6240
31:40 And the persons *were* s H8337+H6240
46 And s thousand persons;) H8337+H6240
52 was s thousand seven H8337+H6240
Jos 15:41 s cities with their villages: H8337+H6240
19:22 s cities with their villages. H8337+H6240
2Ki 13:10 Samaria, *and reigned* s years. H8337+H6240
14:21 which *was* s years old, and H8337+H6240
15: 2 S years old was he when he H8337+H6240
33 and he reigned s years in H8337+H6240
16: 2 reign, and reigned s years in H8337+H6240
1Ch 4:27 And Shimei had s sons and six H8337+H6240
24: 4 *there were* s chief men of the H8337+H6240
2Ch 13:21 and two sons, and s daughters. H8337+H6240
26: 1 who *was* s years old, and made H8337+H6240
3 S years old *was* Uzziah when H8337+H6240
27: 1 and he reigned s years in H8337+H6240
8 reigned s years in Jerusalem. H8337+H6240
28: 1 and he reigned s years in H8337+H6240
Act 27:37 two hundred threescore and s souls. G1803

SIXTEENTH
1Ch 24:14 The fifteenth to Bilgah, the s to H8337+H6240
25:23 The s to Hananiah, *he,* his H8337+H6240
2Ch 29:17 and in the s day of the first H8337+H6240

SIXTH
Gen 1:31 and the morning were the s day. H8345
30:19 again, and bare Jacob the s son. H8345
Ex 16: 5 And it shall come to pass, that on the s H8345
22 And it came to pass, *that* on the s day H8345
29 he giveth you on the s day the bread of H8345
26: 9 and shalt double the s curtain in the H8345
Lev 25:21 upon you in the s year, and it shall H8345
Nu 7:42 On the s day Eliasaph the son of Deuel, H8345
29:29 And on the s day eight bullocks, two H8345
Jos 19:32 The s lot came out to the children of H8345
2Sa 3: 5 And the s, Ithream, by Eglah David's H8345
1Ki 16: 8 In the twenty and s year of Asa king of H8337
2Ki 18:10 took it: *even* in the s year of Hezekiah, H8337
1Ch 2:15 Ozem the s, David the seventh: H8345
3: 3 The fifth, Shephatiah of Abital: the s, H8345
12:11 Attai the s, Eliel the seventh, H8345
24: 9 The fifth to Malchijah, the s to H8345
25:13 The s to Bukkiah, *he,* his sons, and his H8345
26: 3 Elam the fifth, Jehohanan the s, H8345
5 Ammiel the s, Issachar the seventh, H8345
27: 9 The s *captain* for the sixth month *was* H8345
9 The sixth *captain* for the s month *was* H8345
Ezr 6:15 s year of the reign of Darius the king. H8353
Neh 3:30 and Hanun the s son of Zalaph, H8345
Ezk 4:11 by measure, the s part of an hin: from H8345
8: 1 And it came to pass in the s year, in the H8345
1 sixth year, in the s *month,* in the fifth H8345
39: 2 and leave but the s part of thee, and H8338
45:13 ye shall offer; the s part of an ephah of H8345
13 ye shall give the s part of an ephah of H8341
46:14 morning, the s part of an ephah, and H8345
Hag 1: 1 the king, in the s month, in the first day H8345
15 In the four and twentieth day of the s H8345
Mt 20: 5 Again he went out about the s and G1623
27:45 Now from the s hour there was G1623
Mk 15:33 And when the s hour was come, there G1623
Lk 1:26 And in the s month the angel Gabriel G1623
36 age: and this is the s month with her, G1623
23:44 And it was about the s hour, and there G1623
Jn 4: 6 the well: *and* it was about the s hour. G1623
19:14 and about the s hour: and he saith unto G1623
Act 10: 9 the housetop to pray about the s hour: G1623
Rev 6:12 And I beheld when he had opened the s G1623
9:13 And the s angel sounded, and I heard a G1623
14 Saying to the s angel which had the G1623
16:12 And the s angel poured out his vial G1623
21:20 The fifth, sardonyx; the s, sardius; the G1623

SIX-THOUSAND See SIX and THOUSAND.

SIXTY
Gen 5:15 And Mahalaleel lived s and five years, H8346
18 And Jared lived an hundred s and two H8346
20 hundred s and two years: and he died. H8346
21 And Enoch lived s and five years, and H8346
23 were three hundred s and five years: H8346
27 hundred s and nine years: and he died. H8346
Lev 27: 3 old even unto s years old, even thy H8346
7 And if *it be* from s years old and above; H8346
Nu 7:88 bullocks, the rams s, the he goats sixty, H8346
88 sixty, the he goats s, the lambs of the H8346
88 lambs of the first year s. This *was* the H8346
Ezr 2:13 of Adonikam, six hundred s and six. H8346
Mt 13:23 an hundredfold, some s, some thirty. G1835
Mk 4: 8 and some s, and some an hundred. G1835
20 some s, and some an hundred. G1835

SIXTYFOLD
Mt 13: 8 hundredfold, some s, some thirtyfold. G1835

SIZE
Ex 36: 9 cubits: the curtains *were* all of one s. H4060
15 the eleven curtains *were* of one s. H4060
1Ki 6:25 *were* of one measure and one s. H7095
7:37 one casting, one measure, *and* one s. H7095
1Ch 23:29 and for all manner of measure and s; H4060

SKIES
2Sa 22:12 dark waters, *and* thick clouds of the s. H7834
Ps 18:11 dark waters *and* thick clouds of the s. H7834
77:17 The clouds poured out water: the s sent H7834
Isa 45: 8 from above, and let the s pour down H7834
Jer 51: 9 heaven, and is lifted up *even* to the s. H7834

SKILFUL
1Ch 5:18 with bow, and s in war, *were* four and H3925
15:22 about the song, because he *was* s. H995
28:21 every willing s man, for any manner H2451
2Ch 2:14 a man of Tyre, s to work in gold, and H3045
Ezk 21:31 hand of brutish men, *and* s to destroy. H2796
Dan 1: 4 well favoured, and s in all wisdom, and H7919
Am 5:16 such as are s of lamentation to wailing. H3045

SKILFULLY
Ps 33: 3 Sing unto him a new song; play s with H3190

SKILFULNESS
Ps 78:72 and guided them by the s of his hands. H8394

SKILL
1Ki 5: 6 us any that can s to hew timber like H3045
2Ch 2: 7 blue, and that can s to grave with the H3045
8 that thy servants can s to cut timber in H3045
34:12 that could s of instruments of musick. H995
Ecc 9:11 favour to men of s; but time and chance H3045
Dan 1:17 knowledge and s in all learning and H7919
9:22 forth to give thee s and understanding. H7919

SKIN
Ex 22:27 *is* his raiment for his s: wherein shall he H5785
29:14 But the flesh of the bullock, and his s, H5785
34:29 wist not that the s of his face shone H5785

Ex 34:30 Moses, behold, the s of his face shone; H5785
35 face of Moses, that the s of Moses' face H5785
Lev 4:11 And the s of the bullock, and all his H5785
7: 8 to himself the s of the burnt offering H5785
11:32 or raiment, or s, or sack, whatsoever H5785
13: 2 When a man shall have in the s of his H5785
2 and it be in the s of his flesh *like* the H5785
3 on the plague in the s of the flesh: and H5785
3 *be* deeper than the s of his flesh, it *is* a H5785
4 If the bright spot *be* white in the s of his H5785
4 deeper than the s, and the hair thereof H5785
5 spread not in the s; then the priest shall H5785
6 spread not in the s, the priest shall H5785
7 abroad in the s, after that he hath been H5785
8 spreadeth in the s, then the priest shall H5785
10 *be* white in the s, and it have turned the H5785
11 It *is* an old leprosy in the s of his flesh, H5785
12 out abroad in the s, and the leprosy H5785
12 cover all the s of *him that hath* the H5785
18 The flesh also, in which, *even* in the s H5785
20 lower than the s, and the hair thereof H5785
21 not lower than the s, but *be* somewhat H5785
22 And if it spread much abroad in the s, H5785
24 Or if there be *any* flesh, in the s whereof H5785
25 deeper than the s; it *is* a leprosy broken H5785
26 than the *other* s, but *be* somewhat dark; H5785
27 abroad in the s, then the priest shall H5785
28 spread not in the s, but it *be* somewhat H5785
30 deeper than the s; *and there be* in it a H5785
31 deeper than the s, and *that there is* no H5785
32 scall *be* not in sight deeper than the s; H5785
34 be not spread in the s, nor *be* in sight H5785
34 deeper than the s; then the priest shall H5785
35 But if the scall spread much in the s H5785
36 be spread in the s, the priest shall not H5785
38 If a man also or a woman have in the s H5785
39 the bright spots in the s of their flesh *be* H5785
39 spot *that* groweth in the s; he *is* clean. H5785
43 leprosy appeareth in the s of the flesh; H5785
48 in a s, or in any thing made of skin; H5785
48 in a skin, or in any thing made of s; H5785
49 garment, or in the s, either in the warp, H5785
49 or in any thing of s; it *is* a plague of H5785
51 the woof, or in a s, *or* in any work that H5785
51 that is made of s; the plague *is* a fretting H5785
52 or any thing of s, wherein the plague H5785
53 or in the woof, or in any thing of s; H5785
56 s, or out of the warp, or out of the woof: H5785
57 or in any thing of s; it *is* a spreading H5785
58 thing of s *it be,* which thou shalt H5785
15:17 And every garment, and every s, H5785
Nu 19: 5 in his sight; her s, and her flesh, and her H5785
Job 2: 4 LORD, and said, S for skin, yea, all that H5785
4 and said, Skin for s, yea, all that a man H5785
7: 5 s is broken, and become loathsome. H5785
10:11 Thou hast clothed me with s and flesh, H5785
16:15 I have sewed sackcloth upon my s, and H1539
18:13 It shall devour the strength of his s: H5785
19:20 My bone cleaveth to my s and to my H5785
20 I am escaped with the s of my teeth. H5785
26 And *though* after my s *worms* destroy H5785
30:30 My s is black upon me, and my bones H5785
41: 7 Canst thou fill his s with barbed irons? H5785
Ps 102: 5 my groaning my bones cleave to my s. H1320
Jer 13:23 Can the Ethiopian change his s, or the H5785
Lam 3: 4 My flesh and my s hath he made old; H5785
4: 8 in the streets: their s cleaveth to their H5785
5:10 Our s was black like an oven because of H5785
Ezk 16:10 thee with badgers' s, and I girded thee
37: 6 cover you with s, and put breath in you, H5785
8 them, and the s covered them above: H5785
Mic 3: 2 pluck off their s from off them, and H5785
3 and flay their s from off them; and H5785
Mk 1: 6 with a girdle of a s about his loins; and *G1193*

SKINS

Gen 3:21 God make coats of s, and clothed them. H5785
27:16 And she put the s of the kids of the H5785
Ex 25: 5 And rams' s dyed red, and badgers' H5785
5 red, and badgers' s, and shittim wood, H5785
26:14 for the tent *of* rams' s dyed red, and a H5785
14 red, and a covering above *of* badgers' s. H5785
35: 7 And rams' s dyed red, and badgers' H5785
7 red, and badgers' s, and shittim wood, H5785
23 *hair,* and red s of rams, and badgers' H5785
23 of rams, and badgers' s, brought *them.* H5785
36:19 for the tent *of* rams' s dyed red, and a H5785
19 a covering *of* badgers' s above *that.* H5785
39:34 And the covering of rams' s dyed red, H5785
Ex 39:34 badgers' s, and the vail of the covering, H5785
Lev 13:59 or any thing of s, to pronounce it clean, H5785
16:27 their s, and their flesh, and their dung. H5785
Nu 4: 6 of badgers' s, and shall spread over H5785
8 s, and shall put in the staves thereof. H5785
10 badgers' s, and shall put *it* upon a bar. H5785
11 s, and shall put to the staves thereof: H5785
12 badgers' s, and shall put *them* on a bar: H5785
14 of badgers' s, and put to the staves of it. H5785
25 of the badgers' s that *is* above upon it,
31:20 all that is made of s, and all work of H5785

SKIP

Ps 29: 6 He maketh them also to s like a calf; H7540

SKIPPED

Ps 114: 4 The mountains s like rams, *and* the H7540
6 Ye mountains, *that* ye s like rams; *and* H7540

SKIPPEDST

Jer 48:27 thou spakest of him, thou s for joy. H5110

SKIPPING

Song 2: 8 upon the mountains, s upon the hills. H7092

SKIRT

Dt 22:30 father's wife, nor discover his father's s. H3671
27:20 s. And all the people shall say, Amen. H3671
Ru 3: 9 therefore thy s over thine handmaid; H3671
1Sa 15:27 upon the s of his mantle, and it rent. H3671
24: 4 and cut off the s of Saul's robe privily. H3671
5 him, because he had cut off Saul's s. H3671
11 Moreover, my father, see, yea, see the s H3671
11 in that I cut off the s of thy robe, and H3671
Ezk 16: 8 love; and I spread my s over thee, and H3671
Hag 2:12 If one bear holy flesh in the s of his H3671
12 and with his s do touch bread, or H3671
Zec 8:23 take hold of the s of him that is a Jew, H3671

SKIRTS

Ps 133: 2 went down to the s of his garments; H6310
Jer 2:34 Also in thy s is found the blood of the H3671
13:22 s discovered, *and* thy heels made bare. H7757
26 Therefore will I discover thy s upon thy H7757
Lam 1: 9 Her filthiness *is* in her s; she H7757
Ezk 5: 3 few in number, and bind them in thy s. H3671
Nah 3: 5 I will discover thy s upon thy face, and H7757

SKULL

Jdg 9:53 head, and all to brake his s. H1538
2Ki 9:35 of her than the s, and the feet, and the H1538
Mt 27:33 Golgotha, that is to say, a place of a s, *G2898*
Mk 15:22 is, being interpreted, The place of a s. *G2898*
Jn 19:17 *the place* of a s, which is called in the *G2898*

SKY

Dt 33:26 thy help, and in his excellency on the s. H7834
Job 37:18 Hast thou with him spread out the s, H7834
Mt 16: 2 *It will be* fair weather: for the s is red. *G3772*
3 to day: for the s is red and lowring. *G3772*
3 the face of the s; but can ye not *discern* *G3772*
Lk 12:56 the face of the s and of the earth; but *G3772*
Heb 11:12 as the stars of the s in multitude, and *G3772*

SLACK

Dt 7:10 he will not be s to him that hateth him, H309
23:21 God, thou shalt not s to pay it: for the H309
Jos 10: 6 to Gilgal, saying, S not thy hand from H7503
18: 3 How long *are* ye s to go to possess the H7503
2Ki 4:24 and go forward; s not *thy* riding for H6113
Prv 10: 4 He becometh poor that dealeth *with* a s H7423
Zep 3:16 *and to* Zion, Let not thine hands be s. H7503
2Pt 3: 9 The Lord is not s concerning his *G1019*

SLACKED

Hab 1: 4 Therefore the law is s, and judgment H6313

SLACKNESS

2Pt 3: 9 some men count s; but is longsuffering *G1022*

SLAIN

Gen 4:23 my speech: for I have s a man to my H2026
34:27 The sons of Jacob came upon the s, and H2491
Lev 14:51 in the blood of the s bird, and in the H7819
26:17 and ye shall be s before your enemies: H5062
Nu 11:22 Shall the flocks and the herds be s for H7819
14:16 he hath s them in the wilderness. H7819
19:16 And whosoever toucheth one that is s H2491
18 bone, or one s, or one dead, or a grave: H2491
Nu 22:33 also I had s thee, and saved her alive. H2026
23:24 *of* the prey, and drink the blood of the s. H2491
25:14 Israelite that was s, *even* that was slain H5221
14 *even* that was s with the Midianitish H5221
15 woman that was s *was* Cozbi, the H5221
18 sister, which was s in the day of the H5221
31: 8 of them that were s; *namely,* Evi, and H2491
19 hath touched any s, purify *both* H2491
Dt 1: 4 After he had s Sihon the king of the H5221
21: 1 If *one* be found s in the land which the H2491
1 *and* it be not known who hath s him: H5221
2 which *are* round about him that is s: H2491
3 *is* next unto the s man, even the elders H2491
6 *are* next unto the s *man,* shall wash H2491
28:31 Thine ox *shall be* s before thine eyes, H2873
32:42 the blood of the s and of the captives, H2491
Jos 11: 6 them up all s before Israel: thou shalt H2491
13:22 among them that were s by them. H2491
Jdg 9:18 house this day, and have s his sons, H2026
15:16 jaw of an ass have I s a thousand men. H5221
20: 4 woman that was s, answered and said, H7523
5 *and* thought to have s me: and my H2026
1Sa 4:11 of Eli, Hophni and Phinehas, were s. H4191
18: 7 said, Saul hath s his thousands, and H5221
19: 6 *As* the LORD liveth, he shall not be s. H4191
11 life to night, to morrow thou shalt be s. H4191
20:32 shall he be s? what hath he done? H4191
21:11 saying, Saul hath s his thousands, and H5221
22:21 that Saul had s the LORD'S priests. H2026
31: 1 and fell down s in mount Gilboa. H2491
8 came to strip the s, that they found Saul H2491
2Sa 1:16 saying, I have s the LORD'S anointed. H4191
19 The beauty of Israel is s upon thy high H2491
22 From the blood of the s, from the fat of H2491
25 *thou wast* s in thine high places. H2491
3:30 because he had s their brother Asahel H4191
4:11 wicked men have s a righteous person H2026
12: 9 thy wife, and hast s him with the sword H2026
13:30 Absalom hath s all the king's sons, and H5221
32 *that* they have s all the young men the H4191
18: 7 Where the people of Israel were s H5062
21:12 the Philistines had s Saul in Gilboa: H5221
16 a new *sword,* thought to have s David. H5221
1Ki 1:19 And he hath s oxen and fat cattle and H2076
25 this day, and hath s oxen and fat cattle H2076
9:16 it with fire, and s the Canaanites that H2026
11:15 up to bury the s, after he had smitten H2491
13:26 torn him, and s him, according to the H4191
16:16 and hath also s the king: wherefore H5221
19: 1 had s all the prophets with the sword. H2026
10 thine altars, and s thy prophets with H2026
14 thine altars, and s thy prophets with H2026
2Ki 3:23 the kings are surely s, and they have H2717
11: 2 sons *which were* s; and they hid him, H4191
2 from Athaliah, so that he was not s. H4191
8 ranges, let him be s: and be ye with the H4191
15 her not be s in the house of the LORD. H4191
16 the king's house: and there was she s. H4191
14: 5 which had s the king his father. H5221
1Ch 5:22 For there fell down many s, because the H2491
10: 1 and fell down s in mount Gilboa. H2491
8 came to strip the s, that they found Saul H2491
11:11 three hundred s *by him* at one time. H2491
2Ch 13:17 so there fell down s of Israel five H2491
21:13 and also hast s thy brethren of thy H2026
22: 1 to the camp had s all the eldest. So H2026
9 when they had s him, they buried him: H4191
11 sons that were s, and put him and his H4191
23:14 her, let him be s with the sword. For H4191
21 they had s Athaliah with the sword. H4191
28: 9 hand, and ye have s them in a rage *that* H2026
Est 7: 4 destroyed, to be s, and to perish. But if H2026
9:11 of those that were s in Shushan the H2026
12 The Jews have s and destroyed five H2026
Job 1:15 yea, they have s the servants with the H5221
17 away, yea, and s the servants with the H5221
39:30 blood: and where the s *are,* there *is* she. H2491
Ps 62: 3 a man? ye shall be s all of you: as a H7523
88: 5 Free among the dead, like the s that lie H2491
89:10 as one that is s; thou hast scattered H2491
Prv 7:26 many strong *men* have been s by her. H2026
22:13 lion without, I shall be s in the streets. H7523
24:11 death, and *those that are* ready to be s; H2027
Isa 10: 4 fall under the s. For all this his anger H2026
14:19 of those that are s, thrust through with H2026
20 thy land, *and* s thy people: the seed H2026
22: 2 a joyous city: thy s *men are* not slain H2491
2 s with the sword, nor dead in battle. H2491
26:21 blood, and shall no more cover her s. H2026

S

Isa 27: 7 smote him? *or* is he s according to the H2026
7 slaughter of them that are s by him? H2026
34: 3 Their s also shall be cast out, and their H2491
66:16 and the s of the LORD shall be many. H2491
Jer 9: 1 for the s of the daughter of my people! H2491
14:18 then behold the s with the sword! and H2491
18:21 young men *be* s by the sword in battle. H5221
25:33 And the s of the LORD shall be at that H2491
33: 5 men, whom I have s in mine anger and H5221
41: 4 had s Gedaliah, and no man knew *it*, H4191
9 whom he had s because of Gedaliah, H5221
9 filled it with *them that were* s. H2491
16 after *that* he had s Gedaliah the son of H5221
18 of Nethaniah had s Gedaliah the son of H5221
51: 4 Thus the s shall fall in the land of the H2491
47 all her s shall fall in the midst of her. H2491
49 As Babylon *hath caused* the s of Israel H2491
49 Babylon shall fall the s of all the earth. H2491
Lam 2:20 be s in the sanctuary of the Lord? H2026
21 sword; thou hast s *them* in the day of H2026
3:43 us: thou hast s, thou hast not pitied. H2026
4: 9 *They that be* s with the sword are H2491
9 than *they that be* s with hunger: for H2491
Ezk 6: 4 down your s *men* before your idols. H2491
7 And the s shall fall in the midst of you, H2491
13 the LORD, when their s *men* shall be H2491
9: 7 the courts with the s: go ye forth. And H2491
11: 6 Ye have multiplied your s in this city, H2491
6 have filled the streets thereof with the s. H2491
7 Lord GOD; Your s whom ye have laid H2491
16:21 That thou hast s my children, and H7819
21:14 the sword of the s: it *is* the sword of the H2491
14 the great *men that are* s, which entereth H2491
29 of *them that are* s, of the wicked, whose H2491
23:39 For when they had s their children to H7819
26: 6 in the field shall be s by the sword; and H2026
28: 8 *them that are* s in the midst of the seas. H2491
30: 4 when the s shall fall in Egypt, and H2491
11 Egypt, and fill the land with the s. H2491
31:17 unto *them that be* s with the sword; H2491
18 with *them that be* s by the sword. This H2491
32:20 of *them that are* s by the sword: she is H2491
21 they lie uncircumcised, s by the sword. H2491
22 him: all of them s, fallen by the sword: H2491
23 grave: all of them s, fallen by the sword, H2491
24 grave, all of them s, fallen by the sword, H2491
25 bed in the midst of the s with all her H2491
25 uncircumcised, s by the sword: though H2491
25 he is put in the midst of *them that be* s. H2491
26 uncircumcised, s by the sword, though H2490
28 lie with *them that are* s with the sword. H2491
29 by *them that were* s by the sword: they H2491
30 down with the s; with their terror they H2491
30 with *them that be* s by the sword, and H2491
31 s by the sword, saith the Lord GOD. H2491
32 with *them that are* s with the sword, H2491
35: 8 And I will fill his mountains with his s H2491
8 shall they fall that are s with the sword. H2491
37: 9 upon these s, that they may live. H2026
Dan 2:13 wise *men* should be s; and they sought H6992
13 sought Daniel and his fellows to be s. H6992
5:30 Belshazzar the king of the Chaldeans s. H6992
7:11 *even* till the beast was s, and his body H6992
11:26 overflow: and many shall fall down s. H2491
Hos 6: 5 prophets; I have s them by the words of H2026
Am 4:10 young men have I s with the sword, H2026
Nah 3: 3 *is* a multitude of s, and a great number H2491
Zep 2:12 Ye Ethiopians also, ye *shall be* s by my H2491
Lk 9:22 and be s, and be raised the third day. *G615*
Act 2:23 by wicked hands have crucified and s: *G337*
5:36 who was s; and all, as many as obeyed *G337*
7:42 ye offered to me s beasts and sacrifices *G4968*
52 and they have s them which shewed *G615*
13:28 desired they Pilate that he should be s. *G337*
23:14 we will eat nothing until we have s Paul. *G615*
Eph 2:16 the cross, having s the enmity thereby: *G615*
Heb 11:37 tempted, were s with the sword: they *G599*
Rev 2:13 was s among you, where Satan dwelleth. *G615*
5: 6 as it had been s, having seven horns *G4969*
9 for thou wast s, and hast redeemed *G4969*
12 the Lamb that was s to receive power, *G4969*
6: 9 of them that were s for the word of *G4969*
11:13 the earthquake were s of men seven *G615*
13: 8 s from the foundation of the world. *G4969*
18:24 and of all that were s upon the earth. *G4969*
19:21 And the remnant were s with the sword *G615*

SLANDER
Nu 14:36 him, by bringing up a s upon the land, H1681
Ps 31:13 For I have heard the s of many: fear H1681
Prv 10:18 lips, and he that uttereth a s, *is* a fool. H1681

SLANDERED
2Sa 19:27 And he hath s thy servant unto my lord H7270

SLANDERERS
1Ti 3:11 grave, not s, sober, faithful in all things. *G1228*

SLANDEREST
Ps 50:20 thou s thine own mother's son. H5414+H1848

SLANDERETH
Ps 101: 5 Whoso privily s his neighbour, him will H3960

SLANDEROUSLY
Ro 3: 8 And not *rather*, (as we be s reported, *G987*

SLANDERS
Jer 6:28 walking with s: *they are* brass and iron; H7400
9: 4 and every neighbour will walk with s. H7400

SLANG
1Sa 17:49 thence a stone, and s *it*, and smote the H7049

SLAUGHTER
Gen 14:17 his return from the s of Chedorlaomer, H5221
Jos 10:10 slew them with a great s at Gibeon, and H4347
20 them with a very great s, till they were H4347
Jdg 11:33 with a very great s. Thus the children of H4347
15: 8 thigh with a great s: and he went down H4347
1Sa 4:10 was a very great s; for there fell of Israel H4347
17 been also a great s among the people, H4046
6:19 *many* of the people with a great s. H4347
14:14 And that first s, which Jonathan and his H4347
30 much greater s among the Philistines? H4347
17:57 And as David returned from the s of H5221
18: 6 returned from the s of the Philistine, H5221
19: 8 with a great s; and they fled from him. H4347
23: 5 them with a great s. So David saved the H4347
2Sa 1: 1 returned from the s of the Amalekites, H5221
17: 9 will say, There is a s among the people H4046
18: 7 s that day of twenty thousand *men*. H4046
1Ki 20:21 and slew the Syrians with a great s. H4347
2Ch 13:17 them with a great s: so there fell down H4347
25:14 come from the s of the Edomites, that H5221
28: 5 of Israel, who smote him with a great s. H4347
Est 9: 5 of the sword, and s, and destruction, H2027
Ps 44:22 long; we are counted as sheep for the s. H2878
Prv 7:22 an ox goeth to the s, or as a fool to the H2874
Isa 10:26 according to the s of Midian at the rock H4347
14:21 Prepare s for his children for the H4293
27: 7 to the s of them that are slain by him? H2027
30:25 day of the great s, when the towers fall. H2027
34: 2 them, he hath delivered them to the s. H2874
6 and a great s in the land of Idumea. H2874
53: 7 as a lamb to the s, and as a sheep H2874
65:12 all bow down to the s: because when I H2874
Jer 7:32 but the valley of s: for they shall bury in H2028
11:19 is brought to the s; and I knew not that H2873
12: 3 like sheep for the s, and prepare them H2878
3 and prepare them for the day of s. H2028
19: 6 the son of Hinnom, but The valley of s. H2028
25:34 for the days of your s and of your H2873
48:15 are gone down to the s, saith the King, H2874
50:27 go down to the s: woe unto them! for H2874
51:40 lambs to the s, like rams with he goats. H2873
Ezk 9: 2 and every man a s weapon in his hand; H4660
21:10 It is sharpened to make a sore s; it is H2873
15 made bright, *it is* wrapped up for the s. H2874
22 the mouth in the s, to lift up the voice H7524
28 *is* drawn: for the s *it is* furbished, to H2874
26:15 the s is made in the midst of thee? H2027
Hos 5: 2 profound to make s, though I *have been* H7819
Oba 9 the mount of Esau may be cut off by s. H6993
Zec 11: 4 LORD my God; Feed the flock of the s; H2028
7 And I will feed the flock of s, *even* you, H2028
Act 8:32 led as a sheep to the s; and like a lamb *G4967*
9: 1 out threatenings and s against the *G5408*
Ro 8:36 we are accounted as sheep for the s. *G4967*
Heb 7: 1 the s of the kings, and blessed him; *G2871*
Jas 5: 5 nourished your hearts, as in a day of s. *G4967*

SLAVE
Jer 2:14 *Is* Israel a servant? *is* he a homeborn s?

SLAVES
Rev 18:13 and chariots, and s, and souls of men. *G4983*

SLAY
Gen 4:14 every one that findeth me shall s me. H2026
18:25 this manner, to s the righteous with the H4191
20: 4 wilt thou s also a righteous nation? H2026
11 and they will s me for my wife's sake. H2026
22:10 hand, and took the knife to s his son. H7819
27:41 at hand; then will I s my brother Jacob. H2026
34:30 against me, and s me; and I shall be H5221
37:18 they conspired against him to s him. H4191
20 Come now therefore, and let us s him, H2026
26 s our brother, and conceal his blood? H2026
42:37 his father, saying, S my two sons, if I H4191
43:16 men home, and s, and make ready; for H2875
Ex 2:15 thing, he sought to s Moses. But Moses H2026
4:23 I will s thy son, *even* thy firstborn. H2026
5:21 to put a sword in their hand to s us. H2026
21:14 his neighbour, to s him with guile; thou H2026
23: 7 and righteous s thou not: for I will not H2026
29:16 And thou shalt s the ram, and thou H7819
32:12 he bring them out, to s them in the H2026
27 the camp, and s every man his brother, H2026
Lev 4:29 sin offering, and s the sin offering in H7819
33 sin offering, and s it for a sin offering H7819
14:13 And he shall s the lamb in the place H7819
20:15 put to death: and ye shall s the beast. H2026
Nu 19: 3 and *one* shall s her before his face: H7819
25: 5 judges of Israel, S ye every one his men H2026
35:19 The revenger of blood himself shall s H4191
19 when he meeteth him, he shall s him. H4191
21 s the murderer, when he meeteth him. H4191
Dt 9:28 them out to s them in the wilderness. H4191
19: 6 way is long, and s him; whereas he *was* H5221
27:25 Cursed *be* he that taketh reward to s an H5221
Jos 13:22 the children of Israel s with the sword H2026
Jdg 8:19 saved them alive, I would not s you. H2026
20 his firstborn, Up, *and* s them. But the H2026
9:54 thy sword, and s me, that men say not H4191
1Sa 2:25 because the LORD would s them. H4191
5:10 of Israel to us, to s us and our people. H4191
11 his own place, that it s us not, and our H4191
14:34 his sheep, and s *them* here, and eat; H7819
15: 3 them not; but s both man and woman, H4191
19: 5 blood, to s David without a cause? H4191
11 to watch him, and to s him in the H4191
15 up to me in the bed, that I may s him. H4191
20: 8 be in me iniquity, s me thyself; for why H4191
33 determined of his father to s David. H4191
22:17 him, Turn, and s the priests of the H4191
2Sa 1: 9 thee, upon me, and s me: for anguish is H4191
3:37 of the king to s Abner the son of Ner. H4191
21: 2 and Saul sought to s them in his zeal to H5221
1Ki 1:51 he will not s his servant with the sword. H4191
3:26 and in no wise s it. But the other said, H4191
27 no wise s it: she *is* the mother thereof. H4191
15:28 Baasha s him, and reigned in his stead. H4191
17:18 sin to remembrance, and to s my son? H4191
18: 9 servant into the hand of Ahab, to s me? H4191
12 find thee, he shall s me: but I thy H2026
14 Elijah *is here:* and he shall s me. H2026
19:17 of Hazael shall Jehu s: and him that H4191
17 from the sword of Jehu shall Elisha s. H4191
20:36 me, a lion shall s thee. And as soon as H5221
2Ki 8:12 men wilt thou s with the sword, and H2026
10:25 Go in, *and* s them; let none come H5221
17:26 and, behold, they s them, because they H4191
2Ch 20:23 Seir, utterly to s and destroy *them:* and H2763
23:14 S her not in the house of the LORD. H4191
Neh 4:11 s them, and cause the work to cease. H2026
6:10 for they will come to s thee; yea, in the H2026
10 in the night will they come to s thee. H2026
Est 8:11 life, to destroy, to s, and to cause to H2026
Job 9:23 If the scourge s suddenly, he will laugh H4191
13:15 Though he s me, yet will I trust in him: H6991
20:16 of asps: the viper's tongue shall s him. H2026
Ps 34:21 Evil shall s the wicked: and they that H4191
37:14 to s such as be of upright conversation. H2873
32 the righteous, and seeketh to s him. H4191
59:11 S them not, lest my people forget: H2026
94: 6 They s the widow and the stranger, and H2026
109:16 he might even s the broken in heart. H4191
139:19 Surely thou wilt s the wicked, O God: H6991
Prv 1:32 of the simple shall s them, and the H2026
Isa 11: 4 breath of his lips shall he s the wicked. H4191
14:30 famine, and he shall s thy remnant. H2026
27: 1 he shall s the dragon that *is* in the sea. H2026
65:15 the Lord GOD shall s thee, and call his H4191
Jer 5: 6 of the forest shall s them, *and* a wolf of H5221
15: 3 the sword to s, and the dogs to tear, H2026
18:23 against me to s *me*: forgive not their H4194

Jer 20: 4 and shall s them with the sword. H5221
29:21 and he shall s them before your eyes; H5221
40:14 of Nethaniah to s thee? But Gedaliah H5221
15 thee, and I will s Ishmael the son of H5221
15 should he s thee, that all the Jews H5221
41: 8 unto Ishmael, S us not: for we have H4191
50:27 S all her bullocks; let them go down to H2717
Ezk 9: 6 S utterly old *and* young, both maids, H2026
13:19 for pieces of bread, to s the souls that H4191
23:47 swords; they shall s their sons and H2026
26: 8 He shall s with the sword thy daughters H2026
11 thy streets: he shall s thy people by the H2026
40:39 on that side, to s thereon the burnt H7819
44:11 house: they shall s the burnt offering H7819
Dan 2:14 forth to s the wise *men* of Babylon: H6992
Hos 2: 3 like a dry land, and s her with thirst. H4191
9:16 s *even* the beloved *fruit* of their womb. H4191
Am 2: 3 midst thereof, and will s all the princes H2026
9: 1 all of them; and I will s the last of them H2026
4 sword, and it shall s them: and I will H2026
Hab 1:17 not spare continually to s the nations? H2026
Zec 11: 5 Whose possessors s them, and hold H2026
Lk 11:49 *some* of them they shall s and persecute: G615
19:27 bring hither, and s *them* before me. G2695
Jn 5:16 and sought to s him, because he had G615
Act 5:33 *to the heart*, and took counsel to s them. G337
9:29 Grecians: but they went about to s him. G337
11: 7 saying unto me, Arise, Peter; s and eat. G2380
Rev 9:15 and a year, for to s the third part of men. G615

SLAYER
Nu 35:11 for you; that the s may flee thither, H7523
24 judge between the s and the revenger of H5221
25 shall deliver the s out of the hand of the H7523
26 But if the s shall at any time come H7523
27 kill the s; he shall not be guilty of blood: H7523
28 of the high priest the s shall return into H7523
Dt 4:42 That the s might flee thither, which H7523
19: 3 parts, that every s may flee thither. H7523
4 And this *is* the case of the s, which shall H7523
6 blood pursue the s, while his heart is H7523
Jos 20: 3 That the s that killeth *any* person H7523
5 shall not deliver the s up into his hand; H7523
6 then shall the s return, and come unto H7523
21:13 for the s; and Libnah with her suburbs, H7523
21 for the s; and Gezer with her suburbs, H7523
27 of refuge for the s; and Beesh-terah with H7523
32 of refuge for the s; and Hammoth-dor H7523
38 the s; and Mahanaim with her suburbs, H7523
Ezk 21:11 to give it into the hand of the s. H2026

SLAYETH
Gen 4:15 whosoever s Cain, vengeance shall H2026
Dt 22:26 s him, even so *is* this matter: H7523+H5315
Job 5: 2 foolish man, and envy s the silly one. H4191
Ezk 28: 9 Wilt thou yet say before him that s H2026
9 no God, in the hand of him that s thee. H2490

SLAYING
Jos 8:24 made an end of s all the inhabitants of H2026
10:20 had made an end of s them with a very H5221
Jdg 9:56 his father, in s his seventy brethren: H2026
1Ki 17:20 with whom I sojourn, by s her son? H4191
Isa 22:13 And behold joy and gladness, s oxen, H2026
57: 5 every green tree, s the children in the H7819
Ezk 9: 8 And it came to pass, while they were s H5221

SLEEP
Gen 2:21 And the LORD God caused a deep s to H8639
15:12 down, a deep s fell upon Abram; and, H8639
28:11 pillows, and lay down in that place to s. H7901
16 And Jacob awaked out of his s, and he H8142
31:40 and my s departed from mine eyes. H8142
Ex 22:27 wherein shall he s? and it shall come to H7901
Dt 24:12 poor, thou shalt not s with his pledge: H7901
13 goeth down, that he may s in his own H7901
31:16 Behold, thou shalt s with thy fathers; H7901
Jdg 16:14 he awaked out of his s, and went away H8142
19 And she made him s upon her knees; H3462
20 he awoke out of his s, and said, I will go H8142
1Sa 3: 3 God *was*, and Samuel was laid down *to s;*
26:12 because a deep s from the LORD was H8639
2Sa 7:12 and thou shalt s with thy fathers, I will H7901
1Ki 1:21 lord the king shall s with his fathers, H7901
Est 6: 1 On that night could not the king s, and H8142
Job 4:13 the night, when deep s falleth on men, H8639
7:21 for now shall I s in the dust; and thou H7901
14:12 not awake, nor be raised out of their s. H8142
33:15 night, when deep s falleth upon men, in H8639
Ps 4: 8 I will both lay me down in peace, and s: H3462
13: 3 mine eyes, lest I s the *sleep of* death; H3462
3 mine eyes, lest I sleep the *s of* death; H3462
76: 5 have slept their s: and none of the men H8142
6 chariot and horse are cast into a dead s. H7290
78:65 Then the Lord awaked as one out of s, H3463
90: 5 they are *as* a s: in the morning *they* H8142
121: 4 Israel shall neither slumber nor s. H3462
127: 2 sorrows: *for* so he giveth his beloved s. H8142
132: 4 I will not give s to mine eyes, *or* H8142
Prv 3:24 shalt lie down, and thy s shall be sweet. H8142
4:16 For they s not, except they have done H3462
16 and their s is taken away, unless H8142
6: 4 Give not s to thine eyes, nor slumber to H8142
9 How long wilt thou s, O sluggard? when H7901
9 when wilt thou arise out of thy s? H8142
10 *Yet* a little s, a little slumber, a little H8142
10 a little folding of the hands to s: H7901
19:15 Slothfulness casteth into a deep s; and H8639
20:13 Love not s, lest thou come to poverty; H8142
24:33 *Yet* a little s, a little slumber, a little H8142
33 a little folding of the hands to s: H7901
Ecc 5:12 The s of a labouring man *is* sweet, H8142
12 of the rich will not suffer him to s. H3462
8:16 day nor night seeth s with his eyes:) H8142
Song 5: 2 I s, but my heart waketh: *it is* the voice H3463
Isa 5:27 shall slumber nor s; neither shall the H3462
29:10 you the spirit of deep s, and hath closed H8639
Jer 31:26 beheld; and my s was sweet unto me. H8142
51:39 may rejoice, and s a perpetual sleep, H3462
39 s, and not wake, saith the LORD. H8142
57 and they shall s a perpetual sleep, and H3462
57 sleep a perpetual s, and not wake, saith H8142
Ezk 34:25 in the wilderness, and s in the woods. H3462
Dan 2: 1 troubled, and his s brake from him. H8142
6:18 before him: and his s went from him. H8139
8:18 I was in a deep s on my face toward the H7290
10: 9 was I in a deep s on my face, and my H7290
12: 2 And many of them that s in the dust of H3463
Zec 4: 1 as a man that is wakened out of his s, H8142
Mt 1:24 Then Joseph being raised from s did as G5258
26:45 saith unto them, S on now, and take G2518
Mk 4:27 And should s, and rise night and day, G2518
14:41 saith unto them, S on now, and take G2518
Lk 9:32 were heavy with s: and when they were G5258
22:46 And said unto them, Why s ye? rise G2518
Jn 11:11 but I go, that I may awake him out of s. G1852
12 Then said his disciples, Lord, if he s, he G2837
13 that he had spoken of taking of rest in s. G5258
Act 13:36 will of God, fell on s, and was laid unto G2837
16:27 awaking out of his s, and seeing the G1096
20: 9 fallen into a deep s: and as Paul was G5258
9 sunk down with s, and fell down from G5258
Ro 13:11 time to awake out of s: for now *is* our G5258
1Co 11:30 and sickly among you, and many s. G2837
15:51 not all s, but we shall all be changed, G2837
1Th 4:14 s in Jesus will God bring with him. G2837
5: 6 Therefore let us not s, as *do* others; but G2518
7 For they that s sleep in the night; and G2518
7 For they that sleep s in the night; and G2518
10 or s, we should live together with him. G2518

SLEEPER
Jna 1: 6 meanest thou, O s? arise, call upon thy H7290

SLEEPEST
Ps 44:23 Awake, why s thou, O Lord? arise, cast H3462
Prv 6:22 thee; when thou s, it shall keep thee; H7901
Mk 14:37 unto Peter, Simon, s thou? couldest not G2518
Eph 5:14 Wherefore he saith, Awake thou that s, G2518

SLEEPETH
1Ki 18:27 he s, and must be awaked. H3463
Prv 10: 5 son: *but* he that s in harvest *is* a son H7290
Hos 7: 6 wait: their baker s all the night; in the H3463
Mt 9:24 but s. And they laughed him to scorn. G2518
Mk 5:39 weep? the damsel is not dead, but s. G2518
Lk 8:52 said, Weep not; she is not dead, but s. G2518
Jn 11:11 friend Lazarus s; but I go, that I may G2837

SLEEPING
1Sa 26: 7 behold, Saul lay s within the trench, H3463
Isa 56:10 bark; s, lying down, loving to slumber. H1957
Mk 13:36 Lest coming suddenly he find you s. G2518
14:37 And he cometh, and findeth them s, G2518
Lk 22:45 disciples, he found them s for sorrow, G2837
Act 12: 6 night Peter was s between two soldiers, G2837

SLEIGHT
Eph 4:14 wind of doctrine, by the s of men, *and* G2940

SLEPT
Gen 2:21 Adam, and he s: and he took one of his H3462
41: 5 And he s and dreamed the second H3462
2Sa 11: 9 But Uriah s at the door of the king's H7901
1Ki 2:10 So David s with his fathers, and was H7901
3:20 thine handmaid s, and laid it in her H3463
11:21 in Egypt that David s with his fathers, H7901
43 And Solomon s with his fathers, and H7901
14:20 years: and he s with his fathers, and H7901
31 And Rehoboam s with his fathers, and H7901
15: 8 And Abijam s with his fathers; and H7901
24 And Asa s with his fathers, and was H7901
16: 6 So Baasha s with his fathers, and was H7901
28 So Omri s with his fathers, and was H7901
19: 5 And as he lay and s under a juniper H3462
22:40 So Ahab s with his fathers; and H7901
50 And Jehoshaphat s with his fathers, H7901
2Ki 8:24 And Joram s with his fathers, and was H7901
10:35 And Jehu s with his fathers: and they H7901
13: 9 And Jehoahaz s with his fathers; and H7901
13 And Joash s with his fathers; and H7901
14:16 And Jehoash s with his fathers, and H7901
22 after that the king s with his fathers. H7901
29 And Jeroboam s with his fathers, *even* H7901
15: 7 So Azariah s with his fathers; and they H7901
22 And Menahem s with his fathers; and H7901
38 And Jotham s with his fathers, and was H7901
16:20 And Ahaz s with his fathers, and was H7901
20:21 And Hezekiah s with his fathers: and H7901
21:18 And Manasseh s with his fathers, and H7901
24: 6 So Jehoiakim s with his fathers: and H7901
2Ch 9:31 And Solomon s with his fathers, and he H7901
12:16 And Rehoboam s with his fathers, and H7901
14: 1 So Abijah s with his fathers, and they H7901
16:13 And Asa s with his fathers, and died in H7901
21: 1 Now Jehoshaphat s with his fathers, H7901
26: 2 after that the king s with his fathers. H7901
23 So Uzziah s with his fathers, and they H7901
27: 9 And Jotham s with his fathers, and H7901
28:27 And Ahaz s with his fathers, and they H7901
32:33 And Hezekiah s with his fathers, and H7901
33:20 So Manasseh s with his fathers, and H7901
Job 3:13 I should have s: then had I been at rest, H3462
Ps 3: 5 I laid me down and s; I awaked; for the H3462
76: 5 are spoiled, they have s their sleep: and H5123
Mt 13:25 But while men s, his enemy came and G2518
25: 5 tarried, they all slumbered and s. G2518
27:52 bodies of the saints which s arose, G2837
28:13 night, and stole him *away* while we s. G2837
1Co 15:20 become the firstfruits of them that s. G2837

SLEW
Gen 4: 8 up against Abel his brother, and s him. H2026
25 seed instead of Abel, whom Cain s. H2026
34:25 the city boldly, and s all the males. H2026
26 And they s Hamor and Shechem his H2026
38: 7 of the LORD; and the LORD s him. H4191
10 the LORD: wherefore he s him also. H4191
49: 6 for in their anger they s a man, and in H2026
Ex 2:12 *was* no man, he s the Egyptian, and hid H5221
13:15 go, that the LORD s all the firstborn in H2026
Lev 8:15 And he s *it;* and Moses took the blood, H7819
23 And he s *it;* and Moses took of the H7819
9: 8 unto the altar, and s the calf of the sin H7819
12 And he s the burnt offering; and H7819
15 s it, and offered it for sin, as the first. H7819
18 He s also the bullock and the ram *for* a H7819
Nu 31: 7 Moses; and they s all the males. H2026
8 And they s the kings of Midian, beside H2026
8 the son of Beor they s with the sword. H2026
Jos 8:21 they turned again, and s the men of Ai. H5221
9:26 children of Israel, that they s them not. H2026
10:10 before Israel, and s them with a great H5221
11 the children of Israel s with the sword. H2026
26 smote them, and s them, and hanged H4191
11:17 he took, and smote them, and s them. H4191
Jdg 1: 4 s of them in Bezek ten thousand men. H5221
5 s the Canaanites and the Perizzites. H5221
10 s Sheshai, and Ahiman, and Talmai. H5221
17 brother, and they s the Canaanites that H5221
3:29 And they s of Moab at that time about H5221
31 of Anath, which s of the Philistines six H5221
7:25 Zeeb; and they s Oreb upon the rock H2026
25 and Zeeb they s at the winepress of H2026
8:17 of Penuel, and s the men of the city. H2026
18 *they* whom ye s at Tabor? And they H2026

S

Jdg 8:21 And Gideon arose, and s Zebah and H2026
9: 5 at Ophrah, and s his brethren the sons H2026
24 brother, which s them; and upon the H2026
44 that *were* in the fields, and s them. H5221
45 took the city, and s the people that *was* H2026
54 of me, A woman s him. And his young H2026
12: 6 took him, and s him at the passages H7819
14:19 to Ashkelon, and s thirty men of them, H5221
15:15 it, and s a thousand men therewith. H5221
16:24 of our country, which s many of us. H2491
30 the dead which he s at his death were H4191
30 more than *they* which he s in his life. H4191
20:45 and s two thousand men of them. H5221
1Sa 1:25 And they s a bullock, and brought the H7819
4: 2 and they s of the army in the field H5221
11:11 watch, and s the Ammonites until H5221
14:13 and his armourbearer s after him. H4191
32 and calves, and s *them* on the ground: H7819
34 with him that night, and s *them* there. H7819
17:35 his beard, and smote him, and s him. H4191
36 Thy servant s both the lion and the H5221
50 the Philistine, and s him; but *there was* H4191
51 thereof, and s him, and cut off his H4191
18:27 he and his men, and s of the Philistines H5221
19: 5 in his hand, and s the Philistine, and H5221
8 the Philistines, and s them with a great H5221
22:18 the priests, and s on that day fourscore H4191
29: 5 saying, Saul s his thousands, and H5221
30: 2 that *were* therein: they s not any, either H4191
31: 2 and the Philistines s Jonathan, and H5221
2Sa 1:10 So I stood upon him, and s him, H4191
3:30 So Joab and Abishai his brother s H2026
4: 7 smote him, and s him, and beheaded H4191
10 hold of him, and s him in Ziklag, who H2026
12 men, and they s them, and cut off their H2026
8: 5 of Zobah, David s of the Syrians two H5221
10:18 Israel; and David s *the men of* seven H2026
14: 6 but the one smote the other, and s him. H4191
7 brother whom he s; and we will destroy H2026
18:15 about and smote Absalom, and s him. H4191
21: 1 house, because he s the Gibeonites. H4191
18 the Hushathite s Saph, which *was* of H5221
19 a Beth-lehemite, s *the brother of* Goliath H5221
21 of Shimea the brother of David s him. H5221
23: 8 eight hundred, whom he s at one time. H2491
12 defended it, and s the Philistines: and H5221
18 hundred, *and* s *them*, and had the H2491
20 many acts, he s two lionlike men of H5221
20 down also and s a lion in the midst of H5221
21 And he s an Egyptian, a goodly man: H5221
21 hand, and s him with his own spear. H2026
1Ki 1: 9 And Adonijah s sheep and oxen and fat H2076
2: 5 Jether, whom he s, and shed the blood H2026
32 than he, and s them with the sword, H2026
34 fell upon him, and s him: and he was H4191
11:24 a band, when David s them *of Zobah:* H2026
13:24 by the way, and s him: and his carcase H4191
16:11 on his throne, *that* he s all the house of H5221
18:13 I did when Jezebel s the prophets of the H2026
40 to the brook Kishon, and s them there. H7819
19:21 a yoke of oxen, and s them, and boiled H2076
20:20 And they s every one his man: and the H5221
21 s the Syrians with a great slaughter. H5221
29 children of Israel s of the Syrians an H5221
36 from him, a lion found him, and s him. H5221
2Ki 9:31 *Had* Zimri peace, who s his master? H2026
10: 7 king's sons, and s seventy persons, and H7819
9 and s him: but who slew all these? H2026
9 and slew him: but who s all these? H5221
11 So Jehu s all that remained of the H5221
14 them alive, and s them at the pit of the H7819
17 And when he came to Samaria, he s all H5221
11:18 thoroughly, and s Mattan the priest of H2026
20 in quiet: and they s Athaliah with the H4191
12:20 a conspiracy, and s Joash in the house H5221
14: 5 his hand, that he s his servants which H5221
6 But the children of the murderers he s H4191
7 He s of Edom in the valley of salt ten H5221
19 after him to Lachish, and s him there. H4191
15:10 and s him, and reigned in his stead. H4191
14 and s him, and reigned in his stead. H4191
30 smote him, and s him, and reigned in H4191
16: 9 *people of* it captive to Kir, and s Rezin. H4191
17:25 among them, which s *some* of them. H2026
21:23 him, and s the king in his own house. H4191
24 And the people of the land s all them H5221
23:20 And he s all the priests of the high H2076
29 him; and he s him at Megiddo, when H4191
25: 7 And they s the sons of Zedekiah before H7819
2Ki 25:21 smote them, and s them at Riblah in H4191
1Ch 2: 3 in the sight of the LORD; and he s him. H4191
7:21 born in *that* land s, because they came H2026
10: 2 and the Philistines s Jonathan, and H5221
14 therefore he s him, and turned the H4191
11:14 delivered it, and s the Philistines; and H5221
20 three hundred, he s *them*, and had a H2491
22 many acts; he s two lionlike men of H5221
22 and s a lion in a pit in a snowy day. H5221
23 And he s an Egyptian, a man of *great* H5221
23 hand, and s him with his own spear. H2026
18: 5 of Zobah, David s of the Syrians two H5221
12 Moreover Abishai the son of Zeruiah s H5221
19:18 Israel; and David s of the Syrians seven H2026
20: 4 the Hushathite s Sippai, *that was* of the H5221
5 the son of Jair s Lahmi the brother of H5221
7 son of Shimea David's brother s him. H5221
2Ch 13:17 And Abijah and his people s them with H5221
21: 4 himself, and s all his brethren with H2026
22: 8 that ministered to Ahaziah, he s them. H2026
11 from Athaliah, so that she s him not. H4191
23:15 by the king's house, they s her there. H4191
17 in pieces, and s Mattan the priest of H2026
24:22 done to him, but s his son. And when H2026
25 the priest, and s him on his bed, and H2026
25: 3 to him, that he s his servants that had H2026
4 But he s not their children, but *did* as *it* H4191
27 to Lachish after him, and s him there. H4191
28: 6 For Pekah the son of Remaliah s in H2026
7 man of Ephraim, s Maaseiah the king's H2026
32:21 own bowels s him there with the sword. H5307
33:24 him, and s him in his own house. H4191
25 But the people of the land s all them H5221
36:17 of the Chaldees, who s their young men H2026
Neh 9:26 their backs, and s thy prophets which H2026
Est 9: 6 And in Shushan the palace the Jews s H2026
10 enemy of the Jews, s they; but on the H2026
15 month Adar, and s three hundred men H2026
16 from their enemies, and s of their foes H2026
Ps 78:31 upon them, and s the fattest of them, H2026
34 When he s them, then they sought him: H2026
105:29 their waters into blood, and s their fish. H4191
135:10 Who smote great nations, and s mighty H2026
136:18 And s famous kings: for his mercy H2026
Isa 66: 3 He that killeth an ox *is as if* he s a man; H5221
Jer 20:17 Because he s me not from the womb; or H4191
26:23 the king; who s him with the sword, H5221
39: 6 Then the king of Babylon s the sons of H7819
6 of Babylon s all the nobles of Judah. H7819
41: 2 the sword, and s him, whom the king H4191
3 Ishmael also s all the Jews that were H5221
7 the son of Nethaniah s them, *and cast* H7819
8 and s them not among their brethren. H4191
52:10 And the king of Babylon s the sons of H7819
10 before his eyes: he s also all the princes H7819
Lam 2: 4 as an adversary, and s all *that were* H2026
Ezk 9: 7 And they went forth, and s in the city. H5221
23:10 daughters, and s her with the sword: H2026
40:41 whereupon they s *their sacrifices*. H7819
42 s the burnt offering and the sacrifice. H7819
Dan 3:22 flame of the fire s those men that took H6992
5:19 he would he s; and whom he would H6992
Mt 2:16 and sent forth, and s all the children that G337
21:39 cast *him* out of the vineyard, and s *him*. G615
22: 6 entreated *them* spitefully, and s *them*. G615
23:35 ye s between the temple and the altar. G5407
Lk 13: 4 in Siloam fell, and s them, think ye that G615
Act 5:30 Jesus, whom ye s and hanged on a tree. G1315
10:39 whom they s and hanged on a tree: G337
22:20 and kept the raiment of them that s him. G337
Ro 7:11 deceived me, and by it s *me*. G615
1Jn 3:12 that wicked one, and s his brother. And G4969
12 And wherefore s he him? Because his G4969

SLEWEST
1Sa 21: 9 whom thou s in the valley of Elah, H5221

SLIDDEN
Jer 8: 5 Why *then* is this people of Jerusalem s H7725

SLIDE
Dt 32:35 their foot shall s in *due* time: for the H4131
Ps 26: 1 also in the LORD; *therefore* I shall not s. H4571
37:31 *is* in his heart; none of his steps shall s. H4571

SLIDETH
Hos 4:16 For Israel s back as a backsliding H5637

SLIGHT See SLEIGHT.

SLIGHTLY
Jer 6:14 of my people s, saying, Peace, peace; H7043
8:11 of my people s, saying, Peace, peace; H7043

SLIME
Gen 11: 3 for stone, and s had they for morter. H2564
Ex 2: 3 daubed it with s and with pitch, and H2564

SLIMEPITS
Gen 14:10 And the vale of Siddim *was full of* s; and H875

SLING
Jdg 20:16 every one could s stones at an hair H7049
1Sa 17:40 in a scrip; and his s *was* in his hand: H7050
50 the Philistine with a s and with a stone, H7050
25:29 he s out, *as out* of the middle of a sling. H7049
29 he sling out, *as out* of the middle of a s. H7050
Prv 26: 8 As he that bindeth a stone in a s, so *is* H4773
Jer 10:18 Behold, I will s out the inhabitants H7049
Zec 9:15 and subdue with s stones; and they H7050

SLINGERS
2Ki 3:25 the s went about *it*, and smote it. H7051

SLINGS
2Ch 26:14 and bows, and s *to cast* stones. H7050

SLINGSTONES
Job 41:28 make him flee: s are turned with H68+H7050

SLIP
2Sa 22:37 under me; so that my feet did not s. H4571
Job 12: 5 He that is ready to s with *his* feet *is as* a H4571
Ps 17: 5 in thy paths, *that* my footsteps s not. H4131
18:36 steps under me, that my feet did not s. H4571
Heb 2: 1 lest at any time we should let *them* s. G3901

SLIPPED
1Sa 19:10 the javelin; but he s away out of Saul's H6362
Ps 73: 2 almost gone; my steps had well nigh s. H8210

SLIPPERY
Ps 35: 6 Let their way be dark and s: and let the H2519
73:18 Surely thou didst set them in s places: H2513
Jer 23:12 shall be unto them as s *ways* in the H2519

SLIPPETH
Dt 19: 5 the tree, and the head s from the helve, H5394
Ps 38:16 s, they magnify *themselves* against me. H4131
94:18 When I said, My foot s; thy mercy, O H4131

SLIPS
Isa 17:10 plants, and shalt set it with strange s: H2156

SLOTHFUL
Jdg 18: 9 *are* ye still? be not s to go, *and* to enter H6101
Prv 12:24 rule: but the s shall be under tribute. H7423
27 The s *man* roasteth not that which he H7423
15:19 The way of the s *man is* as an hedge of H6102
18: 9 He also that is s in his work is brother H7503
19:24 A s *man* hideth his hand in *his* bosom, H6102
21:25 The desire of the s killeth him; for his H6102
22:13 The s *man* saith, *There is* a lion H6102
24:30 I went by the field of the s, and by the H6102
26:13 The s *man* saith, *There is* a lion in the H6102
14 his hinges, so *doth* the s upon his bed. H6102
15 The s hideth his hand in *his* bosom; it H6102
Mt 25:26 him, *Thou* wicked and s servant, thou G3636
Ro 12:11 Not s in business; fervent in spirit; G3636
Heb 6:12 That ye be not s, but followers of them G3576

SLOTHFULNESS
Prv 19:15 S casteth into a deep sleep; and an idle H6103
Ecc 10:18 By much s the building decayeth; and H6103

SLOW
Ex 4:10 I *am* s of speech, and of a slow tongue. H3515
10 I *am* slow of speech, and of a s tongue. H3515
Neh 9:17 and merciful, s to anger, and of great H750
Ps 103: 8 The LORD *is* merciful and gracious, s to H750
145: 8 s to anger, and of great mercy. H750
Prv 14:29 *He that is* s to wrath *is* of great H750
15:18 but *he that is* s to anger appeaseth strife. H750
16:32 *He that is* s to anger *is* better than the H750
Joel 2:13 and merciful, s to anger, and of great H750
Jna 4: 2 God, and merciful, s to anger, and of H750
Nah 1: 3 The LORD *is* s to anger, and great in H750
Lk 24:25 Then he said unto them, O fools, and s G1021
Tit 1:12 *are* alway liars, evil beasts, s bellies. G692

Jas 1:19 swift to hear, s to speak, slow to wrath: G1021
19 swift to hear, slow to speak, s to wrath: G1021

SLOWLY
Act 27: 7 And when we had sailed s many days, G1020

SLUGGARD
Prv 6: 6 Go to the ant, thou s; consider her ways, H6102
9 How long wilt thou sleep, O s? when wilt H6102
10:26 eyes, so *is* the s to them that send him. H6102
13: 4 The soul of the s desireth, and *hath* H6102
20: 4 The s will not plow by reason of the H6102
26:16 The s *is* wiser in his own conceit than H6102

SLUICES
Isa 19:10 all that make s *and* ponds for fish. H7938

SLUMBER
Ps 121: 3 moved: he that keepeth thee will not s. H5123
4 keepeth Israel shall neither s nor sleep. H5123
132: 4 I will not give sleep to mine eyes, *or* s to H8572
Prv 6: 4 Give not sleep to thine eyes, nor s to H8572
10 *Yet* a little sleep, a little s, a little folding H8572
24:33 *Yet* a little sleep, a little s, a little folding H8572
Isa 5:27 them; none shall s nor sleep; neither H5123
56:10 bark; sleeping, lying down, loving to s. H5123
Nah 3:18 Thy shepherds s, O king of Assyria: thy H5123
Ro 11: 8 given them the spirit of s, eyes that they G2659

SLUMBERED
Mt 25: 5 tarried, they all s and slept. G3573

SLUMBERETH
2Pt 2: 3 not, and their damnation s not. G3573

SLUMBERINGS
Job 33:15 falleth upon men, in s upon the bed; H8572

SMALL
Gen 19:11 blindness, both s and great: so that H6996
30:15 And she said unto her, *Is it* a s matter H4592
Ex 9: 9 And it shall become s dust in all the land
16:14 *there lay* a s round thing, *as* small H1851
14 *as* s as the hoar frost on the ground. H1851
18:22 unto thee, but every s matter they shall H6996
26 every s matter they judged themselves. H6996
30:36 And thou shalt beat *some* of it very s, H1854
Lev 16:12 beaten s, and bring *it* within the vail: H1851
Nu 16: 9 *Seemeth it but* a s thing unto you, that H4592
13 *Is it* a s thing that thou hast brought us H4592
32:41 went and took the s towns thereof, and
Dt 1:17 ye shall hear the s as well as the great; H6996
9:21 *and* ground *it* very s, *even* until it was H3190
21 until it was as s as dust: and I cast the H1854
25:13 thy bag divers weights, a great and a s. H6996
14 house divers measures, a great and a s. H6996
32: 2 as the dew, as the s rain upon the tender
1Sa 5: 9 of the city, both s and great, and they H6996
20: 2 either great or s, but that he will shew H6996
30: 2 any, either great or s, but carried *them* H6996
19 to them, neither s nor great, neither H6996
2Sa 7:19 And this was yet a s thing in thy sight, H6994
17:13 there be not one s stone found there. H1571
22:43 Then did I beat them as s as the dust of
1Ki 2:20 Then she said, I desire one s petition of H6996
19:12 the fire: and after the fire a still s voice. H1851
22:31 Fight neither with s nor great, save H6996
2Ki 19:26 Therefore their inhabitants were of s H7116
23: 2 all the people, both s and great: and he H6996
6 and stamped *it* s to powder, and cast H1854
15 *it* s to powder, and burned the grove. H1854
25:26 And all the people, both s and great, H6996
1Ch 17:17 And *yet* this was a s thing in thine eyes, H6994
25: 8 *ward*, as well the s as the great, the H6996
26:13 And they cast lots, as well the s as the H6996
2Ch 15:13 s or great, whether man or woman. H6996
18:30 Fight ye not with s or great, save only H6996
24:24 came with a s company of men, and H4705
31:15 courses, as well to the great as to the s: H6996
34:30 people, great and s: and he read in their H6996
35: 8 *s cattle*, and three hundred oxen.
9 *s cattle*, and five hundred oxen.
36:18 of God, great and s, and the treasures of H6996
Est 1: 5 unto great and s, seven days, in the H6996
20 husbands honour, both to great and s. H6996
Job 3:19 The s and great are there; and the H6996
8: 7 Though thy beginning was s, yet thy H4705
15:11 *Are* the consolations of God s with H4592
36:27 For he maketh s the drops of water: H1639
Job 37: 6 likewise to the s rain, and to the great H4306
Ps 18:42 Then did I beat them s as the dust before
104:25 innumerable, both s and great beasts. H6996
115:13 that fear the LORD, *both* s and great. H6996
119:141 I *am* s and despised: *yet* do not I forget H6810
Prv 24:10 in the day of adversity, thy strength *is* s. H6862
Ecc 2: 7 of great and s cattle above all that
Isa 1: 9 had left unto us a very s remnant, we H4592
7:13 of David; *Is it* a s thing for you to weary H4592
16:14 the remnant *shall be* very s *and* feeble. H4213
22:24 issue, all vessels of s quantity, from the H6996
29: 5 shall be like s dust, and the multitude H1851
37:27 Therefore their inhabitants *were* of s H7116
40:15 are counted as the s dust of the balance:
41:15 s, and shalt make the hills as chaff. H1854
43:23 Thou hast not brought me the s cattle of
54: 7 For a s moment have I forsaken thee; H6996
60:22 a thousand, and a s one a strong H6810
Jer 16: 6 Both the great and the s shall die in this H6996
30:19 glorify them, and they shall not be s. H6819
44:28 Yet a s number that escape the sword H4962
49:15 For, lo, I will make thee s among the H6996
Ezk 16:20 *Is this* of thy whoredoms a s matter, H4592
34:18 *Seemeth it* a s thing unto you to have H4592
Dan 11:23 shall become strong with a s people. H4592
Am 7: 2 by whom shall Jacob arise? for he *is* s. H6996
5 by whom shall Jacob arise? for he *is* s. H6996
8: 5 making the ephah s, and the shekel H6994
Oba 2 Behold, I have made thee s among the H6996
Zec 4:10 For who hath despised the day of s H6996
Mk 3: 9 And he spake to his disciples, that a s G4142
8: 7 And they had a few s fishes: and he G2485
Jn 2:15 And when he had made a scourge of s G4979
6: 9 loaves, and two s fishes: but what are G3795
Act 12:18 was day, there was no s stir among the G3641
15: 2 and Barnabas had no s dissension and G3641
19:23 And the same time there arose no s stir G3641
24 brought no s gain unto the craftsmen; G3641
26:22 witnessing both to s and great, saying G3398
27:20 appeared, and no s tempest lay on *us*, G3641
1Co 4: 3 But with me it is a very s thing that I G1646
Jas 3: 4 turned about with a very s helm, G1646
Rev 11:18 that fear thy name, s and great; and G3398
13:16 And he causeth all, both s and great, G3398
19: 5 and ye that fear him, both s and great. G3398
18 *both* free and bond, both s and great. G3398
20:12 And I saw the dead, s and great, stand G3398

SMALLEST
1Sa 9:21 a Benjamite, of the s of the tribes of H6996
1Co 6: 2 are ye unworthy to judge the s matters? G1646

SMART
Prv 11:15 a stranger shall s *for it*: and he H7321+H7451

SMELL
Gen 27:27 he smelled the s of his raiment, and H7381
27 and said, See, the s of my son *is* as the H7381
27 of my son *is* as the s of a field which the H7381
Ex 30:38 like unto that, to s thereto, shall even H7306
Lev 26:31 not s the savour of your sweet odours. H7306
Dt 4:28 neither see, nor hear, nor eat, nor s. H7306
Ps 45: 8 All thy garments *s* of myrrh, and aloes,
115: 6 not: noses have they, but they s not: H7306
Song 1:12 spikenard sendeth forth the s thereof. H7381
2:13 grape give a *good* s. Arise, my love, my H7381
4:10 the s of thine ointments than all spices! H7381
11 thy tongue; and the s of thy garments *is* H7381
11 thy garments *is* like the s of Lebanon. H7381
7: 8 vine, and the s of thy nose like apples; H7381
13 The mandrakes give a s, and at our H7381
Isa 3:24 instead of sweet s there shall be stink; H1314
Dan 3:27 nor the s of fire had passed on them. H7382
Hos 14: 6 as the olive tree, and his s as Lebanon. H7381
Am 5:21 I will not s in your solemn assemblies. H7306
Php 4:18 an odour of a sweet s, a sacrifice G2175

SMELLED
Gen 8:21 And the LORD s a sweet savour; and H7306
27:27 him: and he s the smell of his raiment, H7306

SMELLETH
Job 39:25 Ha, ha; and he s the battle afar off, the H7306

SMELLING
Song 5: 5 s myrrh, upon the handles of the lock. H5674
13 lips *like* lilies, dropping sweet s myrrh. H5674
1Co 12:17 whole *were* hearing, where *were* the s? G3750

SMITE
Gen 8:21 will I again s any more every thing H5221
32: 8 one company, and s it, then the other H5221
11 s me, *and* the mother with the children. H5221
Ex 3:20 And I will stretch out my hand, and s H5221
7:17 behold, I will s with the rod that *is* H5221
8: 2 I will s all thy borders with frogs: H5062
16 out thy rod, and s the dust of the land, H5221
9:15 hand, that I may s thee and thy people H5221
12:12 night, and will s all the firstborn in the H5221
13 destroy *you*, when I s the land of Egypt. H5221
23 For the LORD will pass through to s the H5062
23 to come in unto your houses to s *you*. H5062
17: 6 and thou shalt s the rock, and there H5221
21:18 And if men strive together, and one s H5221
20 And if a man s his servant, or his maid, H5221
26 And if a man s the eye of his servant, or H5221
27 And if he s out his manservant's tooth, H5307
Nu 14:12 I will s them with the pestilence, and H5221
22: 6 *that* we may s them, and *that* I may H5221
24:17 out of Israel, and shall s the corners of H4272
25:17 Vex the Midianites, and s them: H5221
35:16 And if he s him with an instrument of H5221
17 And if he s him with throwing a stone, H5221
18 Or *if* he s him with an hand weapon of H5221
21 Or in enmity s him with his hand, that H5221
Dt 7: 2 thee; thou shalt s them, *and* utterly H5221
13:15 Thou shalt surely s the inhabitants of H5221
19:11 against him, and s him mortally that H5221
20:13 hands, thou shalt s every male thereof H5221
28:22 The LORD shall s thee with a H5221
27 The LORD will s thee with the botch of H5221
28 The LORD shall s thee with madness, H5221
35 The LORD shall s thee in the knees, H5221
33:11 work of his hands: s through the loins H4272
Jos 7: 3 men go up and s Ai; *and* make not all H5221
10: 4 me, that we may s Gibeon: for it hath H5221
19 your enemies, and s the hindmost of
12: 6 the children of Israel s: and Moses the H5221
13:12 these did Moses s, and cast them out. H5221
Jdg 6:16 thou shalt s the Midianites as one man. H5221
20:31 and they began to s of the people, *and* H5221
39 began to s *and* kill of the men H5221
21:10 saying, Go and s the inhabitants of H5221
1Sa 15: 3 Now go and s Amalek, and utterly H5221
17:46 hand; and I will s thee, and take thine H5221
18:11 for he said, I will s David even to the H5221
19:10 And Saul sought to s David even to the H5221
20:33 And Saul cast a javelin at him to s him: H5221
23: 2 Shall I go and s these Philistines? And H5221
2 and s the Philistines, and save Keilah. H5221
26: 8 therefore let me s him, I pray thee, with H5221
8 and I will not *s* him the second time.
10 the LORD shall s him; or his day shall H5062
2Sa 2:22 should I s thee to the ground? H5221
5:24 thee, to s the host of the Philistines. H5221
13:28 I say unto you, S Amnon; then kill him, H5221
15:14 s the city with the edge of the sword. H5221
17: 2 shall flee; and I will s the king only: H5221
18:11 why didst thou not s him there to the H5221
1Ki 14:15 For the LORD shall s Israel, as a reed is H5221
20:35 of the LORD, S me, I pray thee. And H5221
35 thee. And the man refused to s him. H5221
37 man, and said, S me, I pray thee. And H5221
2Ki 3:19 And ye shall s every fenced city, and H5221
6:18 LORD, and said, S this people, I pray H5221
21 shall I s *them?* shall I smite *them?* H5221
21 shall I smite *them?* shall I s *them?* H5221
22 And he answered, Thou shalt not s H5221
22 wouldest thou s those whom thou hast H5221
9: 7 And thou shalt s the house of Ahab thy H5221
27 after him, and said, S him also in the H5221
13:17 for thou shalt s the Syrians in Aphek, H5221
18 the king of Israel, S upon the ground. H5221
19 now thou shalt s Syria *but* thrice. H5221
1Ch 14:15 thee to s the host of the Philistines. H5221
2Ch 21:14 will the LORD s thy people, and thy H5062
Ps 121: 6 The sun shall not s thee by day, nor the H5221
141: 5 Let the righteous s me; *it shall be* a H1986
Prv 19:25 S a scorner, and the simple will H5221
Isa 3:17 Therefore the Lord will s with a scab H5596
10:24 the Assyrian: he shall s thee with a rod, H5221
11: 4 earth: and he shall s the earth with the H5221
15 the river, and shall s it in the seven H5221
19:22 And the LORD shall s Egypt: he shall H5062
22 Egypt: he shall s and heal *it*: and they H5062
49:10 the heat nor sun s them: for he that H5221
58: 4 and debate, and to s with the fist of H5221
Jer 18:18 Come, and let us s him with the tongue, H5221

Jer 21: 6 And I will s the inhabitants of this city, H5221
7 life: and he shall s them with the edge H5221
43:11 And when he cometh, he shall s the H5221
46:13 should come *and* s the land of Egypt. H5221
49:28 of Babylon shall s, thus saith the LORD; H5221
Ezk 5: 2 a third part, *and* s about it with a knife: H5221
6:11 Thus saith the Lord GOD; S with thine H5221
9: 5 the city, and s: let not your eye spare, H5221
21:12 my people: s therefore upon *thy* thigh. H5606
14 prophesy, and s *thine* hands together, H5221
17 I will also s mine hands together, and I H5221
32:15 full, when I shall s all them that dwell H5221
39: 3 And I will s thy bow out of thy left H5221
Am 3:15 And I will s the winter house with the H5221
6:11 and he will s the great house with H5221
9: 1 the altar: and he said, S the lintel of the H5221
Mic 5: 1 us: they shall s the judge of Israel with H5221
Nah 2:10 and the knees s together, and much H6375
Zec 9: 4 out, and he will s her power in the sea; H5221
10:11 and shall s the waves in the sea, H5221
11: 6 and they shall s the land, and out of H3807
12: 4 In that day, saith the LORD, I will s H5221
4 of Judah, and will s every horse of the H5221
13: 7 LORD of hosts: s the shepherd, and the H5221
14:12 the LORD will s all the people that have H5062
18 the LORD will s the heathen that come H5062
Mal 4: 6 lest I come and s the earth with a curse. H5221
Mt 5:39 but whosoever shall s thee on thy right *G4474*
24:49 And shall begin to s *his* fellowservants, *G5180*
26:31 it is written, I will s the shepherd, and *G3960*
Mk 14:27 it is written, I will s the shepherd, and *G3960*
Lk 22:49 him, Lord, shall we s with the sword? *G3960*
Act 23: 2 stood by him to s him on the mouth. *G5180*
3 Then said Paul unto him, God shall s *G5180*
2Co 11:20 himself, if a man s you on the face. *G1194*
Rev 11: 6 to blood, and to s the earth with all *G3960*
19:15 with it he should s the nations: and he *G3960*

SMITERS
Isa 50: 6 I gave my back to the s, and my cheeks H5221

SMITEST
Ex 2:13 wrong, Wherefore s thou thy fellow? H5221
Jn 18:23 of the evil: but if well, why s thou me? *G1194*

SMITETH
Ex 21:12 He that s a man, so that he die, shall be H5221
15 And he that s his father, or his mother, H5221
Dt 25:11 hand of him that s him, and putteth H5221
27:24 Cursed *be* he that s his neighbour H5221
Jos 15:16 And Caleb said, He that s H5221
Jdg 1:12 And Caleb said, He that s H5221
2Sa 5: 8 to the gutter, and s the Jebusites, and H5221
1Ch 11: 6 And David said, Whosoever s the H5221
Job 26:12 he s through the proud. H4272
Isa 9:13 not unto him that s them, neither do H5221
Lam 3:30 He giveth *his* cheek to him that s him: H5221
Ezk 7: 9 shall know that I *am* the LORD that s. H5221
Lk 6:29 And unto him that s thee on the *one* *G5180*

SMITH
1Sa 13:19 Now there was no s found throughout H2796
Isa 44:12 The s with the tongs both H1270+H2796
54:16 Behold, I have created the s that H2796

SMITHS
2Ki 24:14 all the craftsmen and s: none remained, H4525
16 craftsmen and s a thousand, all *that* H4525
Jer 24: 1 carpenters and s, from Jerusalem, and H4525
29: 2 the s, were departed from Jerusalem;) H4525

SMITING
Ex 2:11 s an Hebrew, one of his brethren. H5221
2Sa 8:13 he returned from s of the Syrians in the H5221
1Ki 20:37 him, so that in s he wounded *him.* H5221
2Ki 3:24 s the Moabites, even in *their* country. H5221
Mic 6:13 Therefore also will I make *thee* sick in s H5221

SMITTEN
Ex 7:25 after that the LORD had s the river. H5221
9:31 And the flax and the barley was s: for H5221
32 But the wheat and the rie were not s: for H5221
22: 2 up, and be s that he die, *there shall* H5221
Nu 14:42 that ye be not s before your enemies. H5062
22:28 that thou hast s me these three times? H5221
32 hast thou s thine ass these three H5221
33: 4 the LORD had s among them: upon H5221
Dt 1:42 you; lest ye be s before your enemies. H5062
28: 7 up against thee to be s before thy face: H5062
Dt 28:25 The LORD shall cause thee to be s H5062
Jdg 1: 8 had taken it, and s it with the edge of H5221
20:32 said, They *are* s down before us, as at H5062
36 saw that they were s: for the men of H5062
39 s down before us, as *in* the first battle. H5062
1Sa 4: 2 joined battle, Israel was s before the H5062
3 hath the LORD s us to day before the H5062
10 and Israel was s, and they fled every H5062
5:12 And the men that died not were s with H5221
6:19 the LORD had s *many* of the people H5221
7:10 them; and they were s before Israel. H5062
13: 4 And all Israel heard say *that* Saul had s H5221
30: 1 and s Ziklag, and burned it with fire; H5221
2Sa 2:31 But the servants of David had s of H5221
8: 9 David had s all the host of Hadadezer, H5221
10 Hadadezer, and s him: for Hadadezer H5221
10:15 saw that they were s before Israel, they H5062
19 saw that they were s before Israel, they H5062
11:15 ye from him, that he may be s, and die. H5221
1Ki 8:33 When thy people Israel be s down H5062
11:15 after he had s every male in Edom; H5221
2Ki 2:14 when he also had s the waters, they H5221
3:23 and they have s one another: now H5221
13:19 shouldest have s five or six times; then H5221
19 then hadst thou s Syria till thou hadst H5221
14:10 Thou hast indeed s Edom, and thine H5221
1Ch 18: 9 heard how David had s all the host of H5221
10 Hadarezer, and s him; (for Hadarezer H5221
2Ch 20:22 come against Judah; and they were s. H5062
25:16 shouldest thou be s? Then the prophet H5221
19 Thou sayest, Lo, thou hast s the H5221
26:20 to go out, because the LORD had s him. H5060
28:17 s Judah, and carried away captives. H5221
Job 16:10 mouth; they have s me upon the cheek H5221
Ps 3: 7 God: for thou hast s all mine enemies H5221
69:26 whom thou hast s; and they talk to the H5221
102: 4 My heart is s, and withered like grass; H5221
143: 3 my soul; he hath s my life down to the H1792
Isa 5:25 them, and hath s them: and the hills H5221
24:12 and the gate is s with destruction. H3807
27: 7 Hath he s him, as he smote those that H5221
53: 4 him stricken, s of God, and afflicted. H5221
Jer 2:30 In vain have I s your children; they H5221
14:19 why hast thou s us, and *there is* no H5221
37:10 For though ye had s the whole army of H5221
Ezk 22:13 Behold, therefore I have s mine hand at H5221
33:21 came unto me, saying, The city is s. H5221
40: 1 that the city was s, in the selfsame day H5221
Hos 6: 1 us; he hath s, and he will bind us up. H5221
9:16 Ephraim is s, their root is dried up, they H5221
Am 4: 9 I have s you with blasting and mildew: H5221
Act 23: 3 me to be s contrary to the law? *G5180*
Rev 8:12 of the sun was s, and the third part of *G4141*

SMOKE
Gen 19:28 and, lo, the s of the country went H7008
28 country went up as the s of a furnace. H7008
Ex 19:18 And mount Sinai was altogether on a s, H6225
18 it in fire: and the s thereof ascended as H6227
18 ascended as the s of a furnace, and the H6227
Dt 29:20 his jealousy shall s against that man, H6225
Jos 8:20 and, behold, the s of the city ascended H6227
21 city, and that the s of the city ascended, H6227
Jdg 20:38 flame with s rise up out of the city. H6227
40 with a pillar of s, the Benjamites looked H6227
2Sa 22: 9 There went up a s out of his nostrils, H6227
Job 41:20 Out of his nostrils goeth s, as *out* of a H6227
Ps 18: 8 There went up a s out of his nostrils, H6227
37:20 into s shall they consume away. H6227
68: 2 As s is driven away, *so* drive *them* H6227
74: 1 s against the sheep of thy pasture? H6225
102: 3 For my days are consumed like s, and H6227
104:32 he toucheth the hills, and they s. H6225
119:83 For I am become like a bottle in the s; H7008
144: 5 touch the mountains, and they shall s. H6225
Prv 10:26 As vinegar to the teeth, and as s to the H6227
Song 3: 6 like pillars of s, perfumed with myrrh H6227
Isa 4: 5 a cloud and s by day, and the shining H6227
6: 4 cried, and the house was filled with s. H6227
9:18 shall mount up *like* the lifting up of s. H6227
14:31 from the north a s, and none *shall be* H6227
34:10 night nor day; the s thereof shall go up H6227
51: 6 vanish away like s, and the earth shall H6227
65: 5 thou. These *are* a s in my nose, a fire H6227
Hos 13: 3 floor, and as the s out of the chimney. H6227
Joel 2:30 earth, blood, and fire, and pillars of s. H6227
Nah 2:13 her chariots in the s, and the sword H6227
Act 2:19 blood, and fire, and vapour of s: *G2586*
Rev 8: 4 And the s of the incense, *which came* *G2586*
Rev 9: 2 and there arose a s out of the pit, as the *G2586*
2 of the pit, as the s of a great furnace; *G2586*
2 darkened by reason of the s of the pit. *G2586*
3 And there came out of the s locusts *G2586*
17 issued fire and s and brimstone. *G2586*
18 fire, and by the s, and by the brimstone, *G2586*
14:11 And the s of their torment ascendeth *G2586*
15: 8 And the temple was filled with s from *G2586*
18: 9 they shall see the s of her burning, *G2586*
18 And cried when they saw the s of her *G2586*
19: 3 And her s rose up for ever and ever. *G2586*

SMOKING
Gen 15:17 was dark, behold a s furnace, and a H6227
Ex 20:18 and the mountain s: and when the H6226
Isa 7: 4 two tails of these s firebrands, for the H6226
42: 3 he not break, and the s flax shall he not H3544
Mt 12:20 he not break, and s flax shall he not *G5188*

SMOOTH
Gen 27:11 *is* a hairy man, and I *am* a s man: H2509
16 his hands, and upon the s of his neck: H2513
1Sa 17:40 and chose him five s stones out of the H2512
Isa 30:10 unto us s things, prophesy deceits: H2513
57: 6 Among the s *stones* of the stream *is* thy H2511
Lk 3: 5 and the rough ways *shall be* made s; *G3006*

SMOOTHER
Ps 55:21 *The words* of his mouth were s than H2505
Prv 5: 3 and her mouth *is* s than oil: H2509

SMOOTHETH
Isa 41: 7 *and* he that s *with* the hammer him H2505

SMOTE
Gen 14: 5 *were* with him, and s the Rephaims in H5221
7 *is* Kadesh, and s all the country of the H5221
15 by night, and s them, and pursued H5221
19:11 And they s the men that *were* at the H5221
36:35 son of Bedad, who s Midian in the field H5221
Ex 7:20 up the rod, and s the waters that *were* H5221
8:17 hand with his rod, and s the dust of the H5221
9:25 And the hail s throughout all the land H5221
25 beast; and the hail s every herb of the H5221
12:27 in Egypt, when he s the Egyptians, and H5062
29 the LORD s all the firstborn in the H5221
21:19 then shall he that s *him* be quit: only he H5221
Nu 3:13 on the day that I s all the firstborn in H5221
8:17 on the day that I s every firstborn in H5221
11:33 s the people with a very great plague. H5221
14:45 dwelt in that hill, and s them, and H5221
20:11 with his rod he s the rock twice: and H5221
21:24 And Israel s him with the edge of the H5221
35 So they s him, and his sons, and all his H5221
22:23 s the ass, to turn her into the way. H5221
25 against the wall: and he s her again. H5221
27 kindled, and he s the ass with a staff. H5221
24:10 Balaam, and he s his hands together: H5606
32: 4 *Even* the country which the LORD s H5221
35:21 that he die: he that s *him* shall surely H5221
Dt 2:33 s him, and his sons, and all his people. H5221
3: 3 all his people: and we s him until none H5221
4:46 the children of Israel s, after they were H5221
25:18 How he met thee by the way, and s the
29: 7 against us unto battle, and we s them: H5221
Jos 7: 5 And the men of Ai s of them about H5221
5 Shebarim, and s them in the going H5221
8:22 that side: and they s them, so that they H5221
24 Ai, and s it with the edge of the sword. H5221
9:18 And the children of Israel s them not, H5221
10:10 s them to Azekah, and unto Makkedah. H5221
26 And afterward Joshua s them, and slew H5221
28 Makkedah, and s it with the edge of the H5221
30 of Israel; and he s it with the edge of H5221
32 second day, and s it with the edge of H5221
33 and Joshua s him and his people, H5221
35 And they took it on that day, and s it H5221
37 And they took it, and s it with the edge H5221
39 thereof; and they s them with the edge H5221
40 So Joshua s all the country of the hills, H5221
41 And Joshua s them from H5221
11: 8 of Israel, who s them, and chased them H5221
8 and they s them, until they left H5221
10 took Hazor, and s the king thereof with H5221
11 And they s all the souls that *were* H5221
12 Joshua take, and s them with the edge H5221
14 every man they s with the edge of the H5221
17 he took, and s them, and slew them. H5221
12: 1 children of Israel s, and possessed their H5221

Jos 12: 7 children of Israel s on this side Jordan H5221
13:21 whom Moses s with the princes of H5221
19:47 and took it, and s it with the edge of the H5221
20: 5 his hand; because he s his neighbour H5221
Jdg 1:25 into the city, they s the city with the H5221
3:13 and went and s Israel, and possessed H5221
4:21 softly unto him, and s the nail into his H8628
5:26 the hammer she s Sisera, she smote off H1986
26 smote Sisera, she s off his head, when H4277
7:13 unto a tent, and s it that it fell, and H5221
8:11 and s the host: for the host was secure. H5221
9:43 he rose up against them, and s them. H5221
11:21 of Israel, and they s them: so Israel H5221
33 And he s them from Aroer, even till H5221
12: 4 the men of Gilead s Ephraim, because H5221
15: 8 And he s them hip and thigh with a H5221
18:27 secure: and they s them with the edge H5221
20:35 And the LORD s Benjamin before H5062
37 s all the city with the edge of the sword. H5221
48 of Benjamin, and s them with the edge H5221
1Sa 4: 8 *are* the Gods that s the Egyptians with H5221
5: 6 them, and s them with emerods, H5221
9 and he s the men of the city, H5221
6: 9 not his hand *that* s us: it *was* a chance H5060
19 And he s the men of Beth-shemesh, H5221
19 the LORD, even he s of the people fifty H5221
7:11 Philistines, and s them, until *they came* H5221
13: 3 And Jonathan s the garrison of the H5221
14:31 And they s the Philistines that day H5221
48 And he gathered an host, and s the H5221
15: 7 And Saul s the Amalekites from H5221
17:35 And I went out after him, and s him, H5221
35 by his beard, and s him, and slew him. H5221
49 and slang *it*, and s the Philistine in his H5221
50 with a stone, and s the Philistine, and H5221
19:10 presence, and he s the javelin into the H5221
22:19 And Nob, the city of the priests, s he H5221
23: 5 their cattle, and s them with a great H5221
24: 5 that David's heart s him, because he H5221
25:38 that the LORD s Nabal, that he died. H5062
27: 9 And David s the land, and left neither H5221
30:17 And David s them from the twilight H5221
2Sa 1:15 upon him. And he s him that he died. H5221
2:23 end of the spear s him under the fifth H5221
3:27 him quietly, and s him there under the H5221
4: 6 wheat; and they s him under the fifth H5221
7 and they s him, and slew him, H5221
5:20 and David s them there, and said, H5221
25 him; and s the Philistines from H5221
6: 7 Uzzah; and God s him there for *his* H5221
8: 1 pass, that David s the Philistines, and H5221
2 And he s Moab, and measured them H5221
3 David s also Hadadezer, the son of H5221
10:18 horsemen, and s Shobach the captain H5221
11:21 Who s Abimelech the son of H5221
14: 6 but the one s the other, and slew him. H5221
7 Deliver him that s his brother, that we H5221
18:15 about and s Absalom, and slew him. H5221
20:10 in Joab's hand: so he s him therewith in H5221
21:17 him, and s the Philistine, and killed H5221
23:10 He arose, and s the Philistines until his H5221
24:10 And David's heart s him after that he H5221
17 he saw the angel that s the people, and H5221
1Ki 15:20 of Israel, and s Ijon, and Dan, and H5221
27 him; and Baasha s him at Gibbethon, H5221
29 he reigned, *that* he s all the house of H5221
16:10 And Zimri went in and s him, and H5221
20:21 And the king of Israel went out, and s H5221
37 thee. And the man s him, so that in H5221
22:24 went near, and s Micaiah on the cheek, H5221
34 at a venture, and s the king of Israel H5221
2Ki 2: 8 *it* together, and s the waters, and they H5221
14 fell from him, and s the waters, and H5221
3:24 rose up and s the Moabites, so that H5221
25 the slingers went about *it*, and s it. H5221
6:18 with blindness. And he s them with H5221
8:21 he rose by night, and s the Edomites H5221
9:24 full strength, and s Jehoram between H5221
10:25 forth. And they s them with the edge H5221
32 s them in all the coasts of Israel; H5221
12:21 his servants, s him, and he died; and H5221
13:18 ground. And he s thrice, and stayed. H5221
15: 5 And the LORD s the king, so that he H5060
10 against him, and s him before the H5221
14 to Samaria, and s Shallum the son of H5221
16 Then Menahem s Tiphsah, and all that H5221
16 *to him*, therefore he s *it; and* all the H5221
25 against him, and s him in Samaria, in H5221
30 of Remaliah, and s him, and slew him, H5221
2Ki 18: 8 He s the Philistines, *even* unto Gaza, H5221
19:35 went out, and s in the camp of the H5221
37 Sharezer his sons s him with the sword: H5221
25:21 And the king of Babylon s them, and H5221
25 with him, and s Gedaliah, that he died, H5221
1Ch 1:46 of Bedad, which s Midian in the field of H5221
4:41 king of Judah, and s their tents, and H5221
43 And they s the rest of the Amalekites H5221
13:10 Uzza, and he s him, because he put H5221
14:11 and David s them there. Then David H5221
16 him: and they s the host of the H5221
18: 1 pass, that David s the Philistines, and H5221
2 And he s Moab; and the Moabites H5221
3 And David s Hadarezer king of Zobah H5221
20: 1 And Joab s Rabbah, and destroyed it. H5221
21: 7 with this thing; therefore he s Israel. H5221
2Ch 13:15 to pass, that God s Jeroboam and all H5062
14:12 So the LORD s the Ethiopians before H5062
14 And they s all the cities round about H5221
15 They s also the tents of cattle, and H5221
16: 4 of Israel; and they s Ijon, and Dan, and H5221
18:23 came near, and s Micaiah upon the H5221
33 at a venture, and s the king of Israel H5221
21: 9 up by night, and s the Edomites which H5221
18 And after all this the LORD s him in his H5062
22: 5 and the Syrians s Joram. H5221
25:11 s of the children of Seir ten thousand. H5221
13 Beth-horon, and s three thousand of H5221
28: 5 of Syria; and they s him, and carried H5221
5 who s him with a great slaughter. H5221
23 Damascus, which s him: and he said, H5221
Neh 13:25 cursed them, and s certain of them, H5221
Est 9: 5 Thus the Jews s all their enemies with H5221
Job 1:19 wilderness, and s the four corners of H5060
2: 7 of the LORD, and s Job with sore boils H5221
Ps 60:ttl returned, and s of Edom in the valley H5221
78:20 Behold, he s the rock, that the waters H5221
31 and s down the chosen *men* of Israel. H3766
51 And s all the firstborn in Egypt; the H5221
66 And he s his enemies in the hinder H5221
105:33 He s their vines also and their fig trees; H5221
36 He s also all the firstborn in their land, H5221
135: 8 Who s the firstborn of Egypt, both of H5221
10 Who s great nations, and slew mighty H5221
136:10 To him that s Egypt in their firstborn: H5221
17 To him which s great kings: for his H5221
Song 5: 7 found me, they s me, they wounded H5221
Isa 10:20 upon him that s them; but shall stay H5221
14: 6 He who s the people in wrath with a H5221
29 rod of him that s thee is broken: for out H5221
27: 7 Hath he smitten him, as he s those that H4347
7 smote those that s him? *or* is he slain H5221
30:31 be beaten down, *which* s with a rod. H5221
37:36 went forth, and s in the camp of the H5221
38 Sharezer his sons s him with the sword; H5221
41: 7 hammer him that s the anvil, saying, It H1986
57:17 was I wroth, and s him: I hid me, and H5221
60:10 thee: for in my wrath I s thee, but in my H5221
Jer 20: 2 Then Pashur s Jeremiah the prophet, H5221
31:19 I was instructed, I s upon *my* thigh: I H5606
37:15 Jeremiah, and s him, and put him in H5221
41: 2 with him, and s Gedaliah the son of H5221
46: 2 king of Babylon s in the fourth year of H5221
47: 1 before that Pharaoh s Gaza. H5221
52:27 And the king of Babylon s them, and H5221
Dan 2:34 hands, which s the image upon his H4223
35 and the stone that s the image became H4223
5: 6 and his knees s one against another. H5368
8: 7 against him, and s the ram, and brake H5221
Jna 4: 7 day, and it s the gourd that it withered. H5221
Hag 2:17 I s you with blasting and with mildew H5221
Mt 26:51 of the high priest's, and s off his ear. G851
67 s *him* with the palms of their hands, G4474
68 us, thou Christ, Who is he that s thee? G3817
27:30 took the reed, and s him on the head. G5180
Mk 14:47 by drew a sword, and s a servant of the G3817
15:19 And they s him on the head with a G5180
Lk 18:13 unto heaven, but s upon his breast, G5180
22:50 And one of them s the servant of the G3960
63 that held Jesus mocked him, and s *him*. G1194
64 saying, Prophesy, who is it that s thee? G3817
23:48 done, s their breasts, and returned. G5180
Jn 18:10 drew it, and s the high priest's servant, G3817
19: 3 Jews! and they s him with their hands. G1325
Act 7:24 was oppressed, and s the Egyptian: G3960
12: 7 the prison: and he s Peter on the side, G3960
23 the angel of the Lord s him, because he G3960

SMOTEST
Ex 17: 5 s the river, take in thine hand, and go. H5221

SMYRNA
Rev 1:11 and unto S, and unto Pergamos, G4667
2: 8 And unto the angel of the church in S G4668

SNAIL
Lev 11:30 and the lizard, and the s, and the mole. H2546
Ps 58: 8 As a s *which* melteth, let *every one of* H7642

SNARE
Ex 10: 7 this man be a s unto us? let the men H4170
23:33 gods, it will surely be a s unto thee. H4170
34:12 lest it be for a s in the midst of thee: H4170
Dt 7:16 gods; for that *will be* a s unto thee. H4170
Jdg 2: 3 and their gods shall be a s unto you. H4170
8:27 a s unto Gideon, and to his house. H4170
1Sa 18:21 that she may be a s to him, and that H4170
28: 9 thou a s for my life, to cause me to die? H5367
Job 18: 8 his own feet, and he walketh upon a s. H7639
10 The s *is* laid for him in the ground, and H2256
Ps 69:22 Let their table become a s before them: H6341
91: 3 Surely he shall deliver thee from the s H6341
106:36 their idols: which were a s unto them. H4170
119:110 The wicked have laid a s for me: yet I H6341
124: 7 as a bird out of the s of the fowlers: the H6341
7 the s is broken, and we are escaped. H6341
140: 5 The proud have hid a s for me, and H6341
142: 3 have they privily laid a s for me. H6341
Prv 7:23 s, and knoweth not that it *is* for his life. H6341
18: 7 and his lips *are* the s of his soul. H4170
20:25 *It is* a s to the man *who* devoureth *that* H4170
22:25 Lest thou learn his ways, and get a s to H4170
29: 6 evil man *there is* a s: but the righteous H4170
8 Scornful men bring a city into a s: but H6315
25 The fear of man bringeth a s: but whoso H4170
Ecc 9:12 are caught in the s; so *are* the sons of H6341
Isa 8:14 for a s to the inhabitants of Jerusalem. H4170
24:17 Fear, and the pit, and the s, *are* upon H6341
18 be taken in the s: for the windows from H6341
29:21 for a word, and lay a s for him that H6983
Jer 48:43 Fear, and the pit, and the s, *shall be* H6341
44 be taken in the s: for I will bring upon H6341
50:24 I have laid a s for thee, and thou art H3369
Lam 3:47 Fear and a s is come upon us, H6354
Ezk 12:13 be taken in my s: and I will bring him H4686
17:20 be taken in my s, and I will bring him H4686
Hos 5: 1 ye have been a s on Mizpah, and a net H6341
9: 8 the prophet *is* a s of a fowler in all his H6341
Am 3: 5 Can a bird fall in a s upon the earth, H6341
5 *one* take up a s from the earth, and H6341
Lk 21:35 For as a s shall it come on all them that G3803
Ro 11: 9 table be made a s, and a trap, and a G3803
1Co 7:35 that I may cast a s upon you, but for G1029
1Ti 3: 7 fall into reproach and the s of the devil. G3803
6: 9 into temptation and a s, and *into* many G3803
2Ti 2:26 out of the s of the devil, who are G3803

SNARED
Dt 7:25 thee, lest thou be s therein: for it *is* an H3369
12:30 Take heed to thyself that thou be not s H5367
Ps 9:16 the wicked is s in the work of his own H5367
Prv 6: 2 Thou art s with the words of thy H3369
12:13 The wicked is s by the transgression of H4170
Ecc 9:12 the sons of men s in an evil time, when H3369
Isa 8:15 and be broken, and be s, and be taken. H3369
28:13 and be broken, and s, and taken. H3369
42:22 *are* all of them s in holes, and they are H6351

SNARES
Jos 23:13 but they shall be s and traps unto you, H6341
2Sa 22: 6 me about; the s of death prevented me; H4170
Job 22:10 Therefore s *are* round about thee, and H6341
40:24 his eyes: *his* nose pierceth through s. H4170
Ps 11: 6 Upon the wicked he shall rain s, fire H6341
18: 5 me about: the s of death prevented me. H4170
38:12 They also that seek after my life lay s H5367
64: 5 s privily; they say, Who shall see them? H4170
141: 9 Keep me from the s *which* they have H6341
Prv 13:14 of life, to depart from the s of death. H4170
14:27 of life, to depart from the s of death. H4170
22: 5 Thorns *and* s *are* in the way of the H6341
Ecc 7:26 whose heart *is* s and nets, *and* her H4685
Jer 5:26 s; they set a trap, they catch men. H3353
18:22 a pit to take me, and hid s for my feet. H6341

SNATCH
Isa 9:20 And he shall s on the right hand, and H1504

SNEEZED
2Ki 4:35 him: and the child s seven times, and H2237

SNORTING
Jer 8:16 The s of his horses was heard from H5170

SNOUT
Prv 11:22 *As* a jewel of gold in a swine's s, *so is* a H639

SNOW
Ex 4: 6 out, behold, his hand *was* leprous as s. H7950
Nu 12:10 leprous, *white* as s: and Aaron looked H7950
2Sa 23:20 a lion in the midst of a pit in time of s: H7950
2Ki 5:27 from his presence a leper *as white* as s. H7950
Job 6:16 of the ice, *and* wherein the s is hid: H7950
9:30 If I wash myself with s water, and H7950
24:19 Drought and heat consume the s H7950
37: 6 For he saith to the s, Be thou *on* the H7950
38:22 treasures of the s? or hast thou seen the H7950
Ps 51: 7 wash me, and I shall be whiter than s. H7950
68:14 kings in it, it was *white* as s in Salmon. H7949
147:16 He giveth s like wool: he scattereth the H7950
148: 8 Fire, and hail; s, and vapour; stormy H7950
Prv 25:13 As the cold of s in the time of harvest, H7950
26: 1 As s in summer, and as rain in harvest, H7950
31:21 She is not afraid of the s for her H7950
Isa 1:18 be as white as s; though they be red like H7950
55:10 For as the rain cometh down, and the s H7950
Jer 18:14 Will *a man* leave the s of Lebanon H7950
Lam 4: 7 Her Nazarites were purer than s, they H7950
Dan 7: 9 *was* white as s, and the hair of his head H8517
Mt 28: 3 lightning, and his raiment white as s: *G5510*
Mk 9: 3 white as s; so as no fuller on earth *G5510*
Rev 1:14 s; and his eyes *were* as a flame of fire; *G5510*

SNOWY
1Ch 11:22 down and slew a lion in a pit in a s day. H7950

SNUFFDISHES
Ex 25:38 And the tongs thereof, and the s H4289
37:23 and his snuffers, and his s, *of* pure gold. H4289
Nu 4: 9 and his tongs, and his s, and all the oil H4289

SNUFFED
Jer 14: 6 the high places, they s up the wind like H7602
Mal 1:13 *is it*! and ye have s at it, saith the LORD H5301

SNUFFERS
Ex 37:23 his s, and his snuffdishes, *of* pure gold. H4457
1Ki 7:50 And the bowls, and the s, and the H4212
2Ki 12:13 bowls of silver, s, basons, trumpets, any H4212
25:14 shovels, and the s, and the spoons, and H4212
2Ch 4:22 And the s, and the basons, and the H4212
Jer 52:18 shovels, and the s, and the bowls, and H4212

SNUFFETH
Jer 2:24 wilderness, *that* s up the wind at her H7602

SO See the Appendix.

SOAKED
Isa 34: 7 their land shall be s with blood, and H7301

SOAP
Jer 2:22 take thee much s, *yet* thine iniquity is H1287
Mal 3: 2 *is* like a refiner's fire, and like fullers' s: H1287

SOBER
2Co 5:13 or whether we be s, *it is* for your cause. *G4993*
1Th 5: 6 as *do* others; but let us watch and be s. *G3525*
8 But let us, who are of the day, be s, *G3525*
1Ti 3: 2 one wife, vigilant, s, of good behaviour, *G4998*
11 not slanderers, s, faithful in all things. *G3524*
Tit 1: 8 of good men, s, just, holy, temperate; *G4998*
2: 2 That the aged men be s, grave, *G3524*
4 women to be s, to love their husbands, *G4994*
6 Young men likewise exhort to be s *G4993*
1Pt 1:13 of your mind, be s, and hope to the end *G3525*
4: 7 ye therefore s, and watch unto prayer. *G4993*
5: 8 Be s, be vigilant; because your *G3525*

SOBERLY
Ro 12: 3 think; but to think s, according as God *G4993*
Tit 2:12 we should live s, righteously, and godly, *G4996*

SOBER-MINDED See SOBER and MINDED.

SOBERNESS
Act 26:25 speak forth the words of truth and s. *G4997*

SOBRIETY
1Ti 2: 9 and s; not with broided hair, *G4997*
15 in faith and charity and holiness with s. *G4997*

SOCHO
1Ch 4:18 the father of S, and Jekuthiel the father H7755

SOCHOH
1Ki 4:10 *pertained* S, and all the land of Hepher: H7755

SOCKET
Ex 38:27 of the hundred talents, a talent for a s. H134

SOCKETS
Ex 26:19 And thou shalt make forty s of silver H134
19 twenty boards; two s under one board H134
19 tenons, and two s under another board H134
21 And their forty s *of* silver; two sockets H134
21 And their forty sockets *of* silver; two s H134
21 board, and two s under another board. H134
25 boards, and their s *of* silver, sixteen H134
25 *of* silver, sixteen s; two sockets under one H134
25 sockets; two s under one board, and H134
25 board, and two s under another board. H134
32 *shall be of* gold, upon the four s of silver. H134
37 thou shalt cast five s of brass for them. H134
27:10 and their twenty s *shall be of* brass; the H134
11 and their twenty s *of* brass; the hooks of H134
12 cubits: their pillars ten, and their s ten. H134
14 their pillars three, and their s three. H134
15 their pillars three, and their s three. H134
16 pillars *shall be* four, and their s four. H134
17 *shall be of* silver, and their s *of* brass. H134
18 *of* fine twined linen, and their s *of* brass. H134
35:11 his boards, his bars, his pillars, and his s, H134
17 pillars, and their s, and the hanging for H134
36:24 And forty s of silver he made under the H134
24 twenty boards; two s under one board H134
24 tenons, and two s under another board H134
26 And their forty s of silver; two sockets H134
26 And their forty sockets of silver; two s H134
26 board, and two s under another board. H134
30 And there were eight boards; and their s H134
30 *were* sixteen s of silver, under every H134
30 of silver, under every board two s. H134
36 and he cast for them four s of silver. H134
38 with gold: but their five s *were of* brass. H134
38:10 and their brasen s twenty; the hooks of H134
11 twenty, and their s of brass twenty; the H134
12 ten, and their s ten; the hooks of the H134
14 their pillars three, and their s three. H134
15 their pillars three, and their s three. H134
17 And the s for the pillars *were of* brass; H134
19 And their pillars *were* four, and their s *of* H134
27 of silver were cast the s of the sanctuary, H134
27 the sanctuary, and the s of the vail; an H134
27 the vail; an hundred s of the hundred H134
30 And therewith he made the s to the door H134
31 And the s of the court round about, and H134
31 about, and the s of the court gate, and H134
39:33 his bars, and his pillars, and his s, H134
40 his pillars, and his s, and the hanging for H134
40:18 and fastened his s, and set up the boards H134
Nu 3:36 thereof, and the s thereof, and all the H134
37 their s, and their pins, and their cords. H134
4:31 and the pillars thereof, and s thereof, H134
32 about, and their s, and their pins, and H134
Song 5:15 of marble, set upon s of fine gold: his H134

SOCOH
Jos 15:35 Jarmuth, and Adullam, S, and Azekah, H7755
48 mountains, Shamir, and Jattir, and S, H7755

SOD
Gen 25:29 And Jacob s pottage: and Esau came H2102
2Ch 35:13 holy *offerings* s they in pots, and in H1310

SODDEN
Ex 12: 9 Eat not of it raw, nor s at all with H1310
Lev 6:28 But the earthen vessel wherein it is s H1310
28 and if it be s in a brasen pot, it shall H1310
Nu 6:19 And the priest shall take the s shoulder H1311
1Sa 2:15 he will not have s flesh of thee, but raw. H1310
Lam 4:10 The hands of the pitiful women have s H1310

SODERING
Isa 41: 7 It *is* ready for the s: and he fastened it H1694

SODI
Nu 13:10 tribe of Zebulun, Gaddiel the son of S. H5476

SODOM
Gen 10:19 thou goest, unto S, and Gomorrah, and H5467
13:10 the LORD destroyed S and Gomorrah, H5467
12 the plain, and pitched *his* tent toward S. H5467
13 But the men of S *were* wicked and H5467
14: 2 with Bera king of S, and with Birsha H5467
8 And there went out the king of S, and H5467
10 and the kings of S and Gomorrah fled, H5467
11 And they took all the goods of S and H5467
12 dwelt in S, and his goods, and departed. H5467
17 And the king of S went out to meet him H5467
21 And the king of S said unto Abram, H5467
22 And Abram said to the king of S, I have H5467
18:16 looked toward S: and Abraham went H5467
20 Because the cry of S and Gomorrah is H5467
22 and went toward S: but Abraham stood H5467
26 And the LORD said, If I find in S fifty H5467
19: 1 And there came two angels to S at H5467
1 sat in the gate of S: and Lot seeing *them* H5467
4 *even* the men of S, compassed the house H5467
24 Then the LORD rained upon S and H5467
28 And he looked toward S and H5467
Dt 29:23 like the overthrow of S, and Gomorrah, H5467
32:32 For their vine *is* of the vine of S, and of H5467
Isa 1: 9 have been as S, *and* we should have H5467
10 LORD, ye rulers of S; give ear unto the H5467
3: 9 their sin as S, they hide *it* not. Woe H5467
13:19 when God overthrew S and Gomorrah. H5467
Jer 23:14 them unto me as S, and the inhabitants H5467
49:18 As in the overthrow of S and Gomorrah H5467
50:40 As God overthrew S and Gomorrah H5467
Lam 4: 6 of the sin of S, that was overthrown H5467
Ezk 16:46 thy right hand, *is* S and her daughters. H5467
48 *As* I live, saith the Lord GOD, S thy H5467
49 of thy sister S, pride, fulness of bread, H5467
53 the captivity of S and her daughters, H5467
55 When thy sisters, S and her daughters, H5467
56 For thy sister S was not mentioned by H5467
Am 4:11 as God overthrew S and Gomorrah, H5467
Zep 2: 9 Moab shall be as S, and the children of H5467
Mt 10:15 for the land of S and Gomorrha in the *G4670*
11:23 thee, had been done in S, it would have *G4670*
24 S in the day of judgment, than for thee. *G4670*
Mk 6:11 more tolerable for S and Gomorrha in *G4670*
Lk 10:12 in that day for S, than for that city. *G4670*
17:29 But the same day that Lot went out of S *G4670*
2Pt 2: 6 And turning the cities of S and *G4670*
Jude 7 Even as S and Gomorrha, and the cities *G4670*
Rev 11: 8 is called S and Egypt, where also *G4670*

SODOMA
Ro 9:29 S, and been made like unto Gomorrha. *G4670*

SODOMITE
Dt 23:17 of Israel, nor a s of the sons of Israel. H6945

SODOMITES
1Ki 14:24 And there were also s in the land: *and* H6945
15:12 And he took away the s out of the land, H6945
22:46 And the remnant of the s, which H6945
2Ki 23: 7 And he brake down the houses of the s, H6945

SOEVER
Lev 15: 9 And what saddle s he rideth upon that H834
17: 3 What man s *there be* of the house of H376
22: 4 What man s of the seed of Aaron *is* a H376
Dt 12:32 What thing s I command you, observe to H834
2Sa 15:35 be, *that* what thing s thou shalt hear out H834
24: 3 the people, how many s they be, an
1Ki 8:38 What prayer and supplication s be *made* H834
2Ch 6:29 *Then* what prayer *or* what supplication s H834
19:10 And what cause s shall come to you of
Mk 3:28 s they shall blaspheme: *G3745+G302*
6:10 And he said unto them, In what place s *G1437*
11:24 What things s ye desire, when *G3745+G302*
Jn 5:19 do: for what things s he doeth, these also *G302*
20:23 Whose s sins ye remit, they are remitted *G302*
23 whose s *sins* ye retain, they are retained. *G302*
Ro 3:19 Now we know that what things s the *G1437*

SOFT
Job 23:16 For God maketh my heart s, and the H7401
41: 3 thee? will he speak s *words* unto thee? H7390
Ps 65:10 thou makest it s with showers: thou H4127
Prv 15: 1 A s answer turneth away wrath: but H7390
25:15 and a s tongue breaketh the bone. H7390

Mt 11: 8 A man clothed in s raiment? behold, G3120
8 wear s *clothing* are in kings' houses. G3120
Lk 7:25 A man clothed in s raiment? Behold, G3120

SOFTER
Ps 55:21 s than oil, yet *were* they drawn swords. H7401

SOFTLY
Gen 33:14 and I will lead on s, according as the H328
Jdg 4:21 hand, and went s unto him, and smote H3814
Ru 3: 7 and she came s, and uncovered his feet, H3909
1Ki 21:27 fasted, and lay in sackcloth, and went s. H328
Isa 8: 6 of Shiloah that go s, and rejoice in Rezin H328
38:15 done *it*: I shall go s all my years in the H1718
Act 27:13 And when the south wind blew s, G5285

SOIL
Ezk 17: 8 It was planted in a good s by great H7704

SOJOURN
Gen 12:10 into Egypt to s there; for the famine H1481
19: 9 *fellow* came in to s, and he will needs be H1481
26: 3 S in this land, and I will be with thee, H1481
47: 4 Pharaoh, For to s in the land are we H1481
Ex 12:48 And when a stranger shall s with thee, H1481
Lev 17: 8 the strangers which s among you, that H1481
10 of the strangers that s among you, that H1481
13 the strangers that s among you, which H1481
19:33 And if a stranger s with thee in your H1481
20: 2 of the strangers that s in Israel, that H1481
25:45 strangers that do s among you, of them H1481
Nu 9:14 And if a stranger shall s among you, H1481
15:14 And if a stranger s with you, or H1481
Jdg 17: 8 to s where he could find H1481
9 and I go to s where I may find *a place*. H1481
Ru 1: 1 went to s in the country of Moab, H1481
1Ki 17:20 with whom I s, by slaying her son? H1481
2Ki 8: 1 household, and s wheresoever thou H1481
1 thou canst s: for the LORD hath called H1481
Ps 120: 5 Woe is me, that I s in Mesech, *that* I H1481
Isa 23: 7 her own feet shall carry her afar off to s. H1481
52: 4 into Egypt to s there; and the Assyrian H1481
Jer 42:15 to enter into Egypt, and go to s there; H1481
17 to go into Egypt to s there; they shall H1481
22 place whither ye desire to go *and* to s. H1481
43: 2 to say, Go not into Egypt to s there: H1481
44:12 land of Egypt to s there, and they shall H1481
14 land of Egypt to s there, shall escape or H1481
28 the land of Egypt to s there, shall know H1481
Lam 4:15 heathen, They shall no more s *there*. H1481
Ezk 20:38 where they s, and they shall not enter H4033
47:22 the strangers that s among you, which H1481
Act 7: 6 his seed should s in a strange land; and G3941

SOJOURNED
Gen 20: 1 Kadesh and Shur, and s in Gerar. H1481
21:23 and to the land wherein thou hast s. H1481
34 And Abraham s in the Philistines' land H1481
32: 4 saith thus, I have s with Laban, and H1481
35:27 *is* Hebron, where Abraham and Isaac s. H1481
Dt 18: 6 Israel, where he s, and come with all the H1481
26: 5 into Egypt, and s there with a few, and H1481
Jdg 17: 7 who *was* a Levite, and he s there. H1481
19:16 Ephraim; and he s in Gibeah: but the H1481
2Ki 8: 2 her household, and s in the land of the H1481
Ps 105:23 Egypt; and Jacob s in the land of Ham. H1481
Heb 11: 9 By faith he s in the land of promise, as G3939

SOJOURNER
Gen 23: 4 I *am* a stranger and a s with you: give H8453
Lev 22:10 *of* the holy thing: a s of the priest, or an H8453
25:35 or a s; that he may live with thee. H8453
40 *But* as an hired servant, *and* as a s, he H8453
47 And if a s or stranger wax rich by thee, H1616
47 the stranger *or* s by thee, or to the stock H8453
Nu 35:15 and for the s among them: that every H8453
Ps 39:12 thee, *and* a s, as all my fathers *were*. H8453

SOJOURNERS
Lev 25:23 for ye *are* strangers and s with me. H8453
2Sa 4: 3 and were s there until this day.) H1481
1Ch 29:15 For we *are* strangers before thee, and s, H8453

SOJOURNETH
Ex 3:22 and of her that s in her house, jewels H1481
12:49 unto the stranger that s among you. H1481
Lev 16:29 or a stranger that s among you: H1481
17:12 stranger that s among you eat blood. H1481
18:26 nor any stranger that s among you: H1481
Lev 25: 6 and for thy stranger that s with thee, H1481
Nu 15:15 for the stranger that s *with you*, an H1481
16 and for the stranger that s with you. H1481
26 the stranger that s among them; seeing H1481
29 for the stranger that s among them. H1481
19:10 s among them, for a statute for ever. H1481
Jos 20: 9 the stranger that s among them, that H1481
Ezr 1: 4 any place where he s, let the men of his H1481
Ezk 14: 7 of the stranger that s in Israel, which H1481
47:23 tribe the stranger s, there shall ye give H1481

SOJOURNING
Ex 12:40 Now the s of the children of Israel, who H4186
Jdg 19: 1 a certain Levite s on the side of mount H1481
1Pt 1:17 pass the time of your s *here* in fear: G3940

SOLACE
Prv 7:18 morning: let us s ourselves with loves. H5965

SOLD
Gen 25:33 him: and he s his birthright unto Jacob. H4376
31:15 for he hath s us, and hath quite H4376
37:28 out of the pit, and s Joseph to the H4376
36 And the Midianites s him into Egypt H4376
41:56 storehouses, and s unto the Egyptians; H7666
42: 6 *and* he *it was* that s to all the people of H7666
45: 4 your brother, whom ye s into Egypt. H4376
5 yourselves, that ye s me hither: for God H4376
47:20 for the Egyptians s every man his field, H4376
22 them: wherefore they s not their lands. H4376
Ex 22: 3 nothing, then he shall be s for his theft. H4376
Lev 25:23 The land shall not be s for ever: for the H4376
25 poor, and hath s away *some* of his H4376
25 he redeem that which his brother s. H4465
27 the man to whom he s it; that he may H4376
28 then that which is s shall remain in the H4465
29 is s; *within* a full year may he redeem it. H4465
33 the house that was s, and the city of his H4465
34 be s; for it *is* their perpetual possession. H4376
39 poor, and be s unto thee; thou shalt H4376
42 Egypt: they shall not be s as bondmen. H4376
48 After that he is s he may be redeemed H4376
50 year that he was s to him unto the year H4376
27:20 field, or if he have s the field to another H4376
27 shall be s according to thy estimation. H4376
28 shall be s or redeemed: every H4376
Dt 15:12 woman, be s unto thee, and serve H4376
28:68 there ye shall be s unto your enemies H4376
32:30 their Rock had s them, and the LORD H4376
Jdg 2:14 them, and he s them into the hands H4376
3: 8 Israel, and he s them into the hand H4376
4: 2 And the LORD s them into the hand of H4376
10: 7 Israel, and he s them into the hands H4376
1Sa 12: 9 their God, he s them into the hand H4376
1Ki 21:20 because thou hast s thyself to work evil H4376
2Ki 6:25 an ass's head was *s* for fourscore *pieces*
7: 1 of fine flour *be s* for a shekel, and two
16 of fine flour was *s* for a shekel, and two
17:17 and s themselves to do evil H4376
Neh 5: 8 Jews, which were s unto the heathen; H4376
8 or shall they be s unto us? Then held H4376
13:15 in the day wherein they s victuals. H4376
16 of ware, and s on the sabbath unto H4376
Est 7: 4 For we are s, I and my people, to be H4376
4 But if we had been s for bondmen and H4376
Ps 105:17 *even* Joseph, *who* was s for a servant: H4376
Isa 50: 1 *is it* to whom I have s you? Behold, for H4376
1 iniquities have ye s yourselves, and for H4376
52: 3 For thus saith the LORD, Ye have s H4376
Jer 34:14 which hath been s unto thee; and when H4376
Lam 5: 4 water for money; our wood is s unto us. H935
Ezk 7:13 to that which is s, although they were H4465
Joel 3: 3 s a girl for wine, that they might drink. H4376
6 Jerusalem have ye s unto the Grecians, H4376
7 whither ye have s them, and will return H4376
Am 2: 6 because they s the righteous for silver, H4376
Mt 10:29 Are not two sparrows s for a farthing? G4453
13:46 and s all that he had, and bought it. G4097
18:25 him to be s, and his wife, and children, G4097
21:12 out all them that s and bought in the G4453
12 and the seats of them that s doves, G4453
26: 9 For this ointment might have been s G4097
Mk 11:15 cast out them that s and bought in the G4453
15 and the seats of them that s doves; G4453
14: 5 For it might have been s for more than G4097
Lk 12: 6 Are not five sparrows s for two G4453
17:28 they s, they planted, they builded; G4453
19:45 that s therein, and them that bought; G4453
Jn 2:14 And found in the temple those that s G4453
Jn 2:16 And said unto them that s doves, Take G4453
12: 5 Why was not this ointment s for three G4097
Act 2:45 And s their possessions and goods, and G4097
4:34 of lands or houses s them, and brought G4453
34 the prices of the things that were s, G4097
37 Having land, s *it*, and brought the G4453
5: 1 with Sapphira his wife, s a possession, G4453
4 and after it was s, was it not in thine G4097
8 her, Tell me whether ye s the land for so G591
7: 9 And the patriarchs, moved with envy, s G591
Ro 7:14 spiritual: but I am carnal, s under sin. G4097
1Co 10:25 Whatsoever is s in the shambles, *that* G4453
Heb 12:16 for one morsel of meat s his birthright. G591

SOLDERING See SODERING.

SOLDIER
Jn 19:23 parts, to every s a part; and also *his* G4757
Act 10: 7 and a devout s of them that waited G4757
28:16 dwell by himself with a s that kept him. G4757
2Ti 2: 3 hardness, as a good s of Jesus Christ. G4757
4 him who hath chosen him to be a s. G4758

SOLDIERS
1Ch 7: 4 *were* bands of s for war, six and thirty H6635
11 s, fit to go out for war *and* battle.
2Ch 25:13 But the s of the army which Amaziah H1121
Ezr 8:22 the king a band of s and horsemen to H2428
Isa 15: 4 the armed s of Moab shall cry out; H2502
Mt 8: 9 authority, having s under me: and I say G4757
27:27 Then the s of the governor took Jesus G4757
27 gathered unto him the whole band *of s*.
28:12 they gave large money unto the s, G4757
Mk 15:16 And the s led him away into the hall, G4757
Lk 3:14 And the s likewise demanded of him, G4754
7: 8 having under me s, and I say unto one, G4757
23:36 And the s also mocked him, coming to G4757
Jn 19: 2 And the s platted a crown of thorns, G4757
23 Then the s, when they had crucified G4757
24 lots. These things therefore the s did. G4757
32 Then came the s, and brake the legs of G4757
34 But one of the s with a spear pierced G4757
Act 12: 4 quaternions of s to keep him; intending G4757
6 between two s, bound with two chains: G4757
18 among the s, what was become of Peter. G4757
21:32 Who immediately took s and G4757
32 and the s, they left beating of Paul. G4757
35 of the s for the violence of the people. G4757
23:10 commanded the s to go down, and to G4753
23 two hundred s to go to Caesarea, and G4757
31 Then the s, as it was commanded them, G4757
27:31 Paul said to the centurion and to the s, G4757
32 Then the s cut off the ropes of the boat, G4757

SOLDIERS'
Act 27:42 And the s counsel was to kill the G4757

SOLE
Gen 8: 9 But the dove found no rest for the s of H3709
Dt 28:35 s of thy foot unto the top of thy head. H3709
56 to set the s of her foot upon the H3709
65 neither shall the s of thy foot have rest: H3709
Jos 1: 3 Every place that the s of your foot shall H3709
2Sa 14:25 beauty: from the s of his foot even to H3709
2Ki 19:24 and with the s of my feet have I dried H3709
Job 2: 7 from the s of his foot unto his crown. H3709
Isa 1: 6 From the s of the foot even unto the H3709
37:25 and with the s of my feet have I dried H3709
Ezk 1: 7 feet; and the s of their feet *was* like H3709
7 feet *was* like the s of a calf's foot: and H3709

S

SOLEMN
Lev 23:36 the LORD: it *is* a s assembly; *and* ye H6116
Nu 10:10 and in your s days, and in the H4150
15: 3 or in your s feasts, to make a sweet H4150
29:35 On the eighth day ye shall have a s H6116
Dt 16: 8 day *shall be* a s assembly to the LORD H6116
15 Seven days shalt thou keep a s feast H2287
2Ki 10:20 And Jehu said, Proclaim a s assembly H6116
2Ch 2: 4 moons, and on the s feasts of the LORD H4150
7: 9 And in the eighth day they made a s H6116
8:13 moons, and on the s feasts, three times H4150
Neh 8:18 eighth day *was* a s assembly, according H6116
Ps 81: 3 the time appointed, on our s feast day. H2282
92: 3 psaltery; upon the harp with a s sound.
Isa 1:13 with; *it is* iniquity, even the s meeting. H6116
Lam 1: 4 none come to the s feasts: all her gates H4150
2: 6 hath caused the s feasts and sabbaths H4150
7 of the LORD, as in the day of a s feast. H4150

Lam 2:22 Thou hast called as in a s day my H4150
Ezk 36:38 of Jerusalem in her s feasts; so shall the H4150
46: 9 before the LORD in the s feasts, he that H4150
Hos 2:11 and her sabbaths, and all her s feasts. H4150
9: 5 What will ye do in the s day, and in the H4150
12: 9 as in the days of the s feast. H4150
Joel 1:14 Sanctify ye a fast, call a s assembly, H6116
2:15 Zion, sanctify a fast, call a s assembly: H6116
Am 5:21 I will not smell in your s assemblies. H6116
Nah 1:15 O Judah, keep thy s feasts, perform thy H2282
Zep 3:18 sorrowful for the s assembly, *who* are H4150
Mal 2: 3 the dung of your s feasts; and *one* shall H2282

SOLEMNITIES
Isa 33:20 Look upon Zion, the city of our s: thine H4150
Ezk 45:17 sabbaths, in all s of the house of Israel: H4150
46:11 And in the feasts and in the s the meat H4150

SOLEMNITY
Dt 31:10 *every* seven years, in the s of the year of H4150
Isa 30:29 the night *when* a holy s is kept; and H2282

SOLEMNLY
Gen 43: 3 The man did s protest unto us, saying, H5749
1Sa 8: 9 yet protest s unto them, and shew H5749

SOLES
Dt 11:24 Every place whereon the s of your feet H3709
Jos 3:13 as soon as the s of the feet of the priests H3709
4:18 of Jordan, *and* the s of the priests' feet H3709
1Ki 5: 3 LORD put them under the s of his feet. H3709
Isa 60:14 down at the s of thy feet; and they H3709
Ezk 43: 7 the place of the s of my feet, where I H3709
Mal 4: 3 be ashes under the s of your feet in the H3709

SOLITARILY
Mic 7:14 which dwell s *in* the wood, in the midst H910

SOLITARY
Job 3: 7 Lo, let that night be s, let no joyful voice H1565
30: 3 For want and famine *they were* s; H1565
Ps 68: 6 God setteth the s in families: he H3173
107: 4 They wandered in the wilderness in a s H3452
Isa 35: 1 The wilderness and the s place shall be H6723
Lam 1: 1 How doth the city sit s, *that was* full of H910
Mk 1:35 into a s place, and there prayed. *G2048*

SOLOMON
2Sa 5:14 and Shobab, and Nathan, and S, H8010
12:24 his name S: and the LORD loved him. H8010
1Ki 1:10 men, and S his brother, he called not. H8010
11 the mother of S, saying, Hast thou not H8010
12 thine own life, and the life of thy son S. H8010
13 saying, Assuredly S thy son shall reign H8010
17 *saying,* Assuredly S thy son shall reign H8010
19 but S thy servant hath he not called. H8010
21 my son S shall be counted offenders. H8010
26 and thy servant S, hath he not called. H8010
30 saying, Assuredly S thy son shall reign H8010
33 lord, and cause S my son to ride upon H8010
34 the trumpet, and say, God save king S. H8010
37 even so be he with S, and make his H8010
38 down, and caused S to ride upon king H8010
39 and anointed S. And they blew the H8010
39 and all the people said, God save king S. H8010
43 our lord king David hath made S king. H8010
46 And also S sitteth on the throne of the H8010
47 make the name of S better than thy H8010
50 And Adonijah feared because of S, and H8010
51 And it was told S, saying, Behold, H8010
51 feareth king S: for, lo, he hath caught H8010
51 saying, Let king S swear unto me to H8010
52 And S said, If he will shew himself a H8010
53 So king S sent, and they brought him H8010
53 himself to king S: and Solomon said H8010
53 and S said unto him, Go to thine house. H8010
2: 1 die; and he charged S his son, saying, H8010
12 Then sat S upon the throne of David H8010
13 the mother of S. And she said, Comest H8010
17 And he said, Speak, I pray thee, unto S H8010
19 Bath-sheba therefore went unto king S, H8010
22 And king S answered and said unto his H8010
23 Then king S sware by the LORD, H8010
25 And king S sent by the hand of Benaiah H8010
27 So S thrust out Abiathar from being H8010
29 And it was told king S that Joab was H8010
29 *is* by the altar. Then S sent Benaiah the H8010
41 And it was told S that Shimei had gone H8010
45 And king S *shall be* blessed, and the H8010

1Ki 2:46 was established in the hand of S. H8010
3: 1 And S made affinity with Pharaoh king H8010
3 And S loved the LORD, walking in the H8010
4 offerings did S offer upon that altar. H8010
5 In Gibeon the LORD appeared to S in a H8010
6 And S said, Thou hast shewed unto thy H8010
10 And the speech pleased the Lord, that S H8010
15 And S awoke; and, behold, *it was* a H8010
4: 1 So king S was king over all Israel. H8010
7 And S had twelve officers over all H8010
11 had Taphath the daughter of S to wife: H8010
15 took Basmath the daughter of S to wife: H8010
21 And S reigned over all kingdoms from H8010
21 and served S all the days of his life. H8010
25 even to Beersheba, all the days of S. H8010
26 And S had forty thousand stalls of H8010
27 victual for king S, and for all that came H8010
29 And God gave S wisdom and H8010
34 the wisdom of S, from all kings of the H8010
5: 1 his servants unto S; for he had heard H8010
2 And S sent to Hiram, saying, H8010
7 the words of S, that he rejoiced greatly, H8010
8 And Hiram sent to S, saying, I have H8010
10 So Hiram gave S cedar trees and fir H8010
11 And S gave Hiram twenty thousand H8010
11 oil: thus gave S to Hiram year by year. H8010
12 And the LORD gave S wisdom, as he H8010
12 S; and they two made a league together. H8010
13 And king S raised a levy out of all H8010
15 And S had threescore and ten H8010
6: 2 And the house which king S built for H8010
11 And the word of the LORD came to S, H8010
14 So S built the house, and finished it. H8010
21 So S overlaid the house within with H8010
7: 1 But S was building his own house H8010
8 of the like work. S made also an house H8010
13 And king S sent and fetched Hiram out H8010
14 to king S, and wrought all his work. H8010
40 made king S for the house of the LORD: H8010
45 made to king S for the house of the H8010
47 And S left all the vessels *unweighed,* H8010
48 And S made all the vessels that H8010
51 So was ended all the work that king S H8010
51 of the LORD. And S brought in the H8010
8: 1 Then S assembled the elders of Israel, H8010
1 of Israel, unto king S in Jerusalem, that H8010
2 unto king S at the feast in the month H8010
5 And king S, and all the congregation of H8010
12 Then spake S, The LORD said that he H8010
22 And S stood before the altar of the H8010
54 And it was *so,* that when S had made H8010
63 And S offered a sacrifice of peace H8010
65 And at that time S held a feast, and all H8010
9: 1 And it came to pass, when S had H8010
2 That the LORD appeared to S the H8010
10 years, when S had built the two houses, H8010
11 had furnished S with cedar trees and H8010
11 that then king S gave Hiram twenty H8010
12 the cities which S had given him; and H8010
15 levy which king S raised; for to build H8010
17 And S built Gezer, and Beth-horon the H8010
19 And all the cities of store that S had, H8010
19 and that which S desired to build in H8010
21 upon those did S levy a tribute of H8010
22 But of the children of Israel did S make H8010
24 her house which *S* had built for her: then H8010
25 And three times in a year did S offer H8010
26 And king S made a navy of ships in H8010
27 of the sea, with the servants of S. H8010
28 twenty talents, and brought *it* to king S. H8010
10: 1 of the fame of S concerning the name H8010
2 she was come to S, she communed with H8010
3 And S told her all her questions: there H8010
10 the queen of Sheba gave to king S. H8010
13 And king S gave unto the queen of H8010
13 beside *that* which S gave her of his H8010
14 Now the weight of gold that came to S H8010
16 And king S made two hundred targets H8010
21 nothing accounted of in the days of S. H8010
23 So king S exceeded all the kings of the H8010
24 And all the earth sought to S, to hear his H8010
26 And S gathered together chariots and H8010
28 And S had horses brought out of Egypt, H8010
11: 1 But king S loved many strange women, H8010
2 their gods: S clave unto these in love. H8010
4 For it came to pass, when S was old, H8010
5 For S went after Ashtoreth the goddess H8010
6 And S did evil in the sight of the LORD, H8010
7 Then did S build an high place for H8010

1Ki 11: 9 And the LORD was angry with S, H8010
11 Wherefore the LORD said unto S, H8010
14 up an adversary unto S, Hadad the H8010
25 all the days of S, beside the mischief H8010
27 against the king: S built Millo, *and* H8010
28 of valour: and S seeing the young man H8010
31 of S, and will give ten tribes to thee: H8010
40 S sought therefore to kill Jeroboam. H8010
40 and was in Egypt until the death of S. H8010
41 And the rest of the acts of S, and all that H8010
41 not written in the book of the acts of S? H8010
42 And the time that S reigned in H8010
43 And S slept with his fathers, and was H8010
12: 2 king S, and Jeroboam dwelt in Egypt;) H8010
6 that stood before S his father while he H8010
21 again to Rehoboam the son of S. H8010
23 Speak unto Rehoboam, the son of S, H8010
14:21 And Rehoboam the son of S reigned in H8010
26 the shields of gold which S had made. H8010
2Ki 21: 7 said to David, and to S his son, In this H8010
23:13 corruption, which S the king of Israel H8010
24:13 of gold which S king of Israel had made H8010
25:16 the bases which S had made for the H8010
1Ch 3: 5 and Nathan, and S, four, of Bath-shua H8010
6:10 in the temple that S built in Jerusalem:) H8010
32 with singing, until S had built the H8010
14: 4 Shammua, and Shobab, Nathan, and S, H8010
18: 8 brass, wherewith S made the brasen H8010
22: 5 And David said, S my son *is* young and H8010
6 Then he called for S his son, and H8010
7 And David said to S, My son, as for me, H8010
9 for his name shall be S, and I will give H8010
17 of Israel to help S his son, *saying,* H8010
23: 1 he made S his son king over Israel. H8010
28: 5 he hath chosen S my son to sit upon H8010
6 And he said unto me, S thy son, he H8010
9 And thou, S my son, know thou the H8010
11 Then David gave to S his son the H8010
20 And David said to S his son, Be strong H8010
29: 1 all the congregation, S my son, whom H8010
19 And give unto S my son a perfect heart, H8010
22 And they made S the son of David king H8010
23 Then S sat on the throne of the LORD H8010
24 submitted themselves unto S the king. H8010
25 And the LORD magnified S exceedingly H8010
28 and S his son reigned in his stead. H8010
2Ch 1: 1 And S the son of David was H8010
2 Then S spake unto all Israel, to the H8010
3 So S, and all the congregation with him, H8010
5 S and the congregation sought unto it. H8010
6 And S went up thither to the brasen H8010
7 In that night did God appear unto S, H8010
8 And S said unto God, Thou hast H8010
11 And God said to S, Because this was in H8010
13 Then S came *from his journey* to the H8010
14 And S gathered chariots and H8010
16 And S had horses brought out of Egypt, H8010
2: 1 And S determined to build an house for H8010
2 And S told out threescore and ten H8010
3 And S sent to Huram the king of Tyre, H8010
11 which he sent to S, Because the LORD H8010
17 And S numbered all the strangers that H8010
3: 1 Then S began to build the house of the H8010
3 Now these *are the things wherein* S was H8010
4:11 make for king S for the house of God; H8010
16 make to king S for the house of the H8010
18 Thus S made all these vessels in great H8010
19 And S made all the vessels that *were* H8010
5: 1 Thus all the work that S made for the H8010
1 was finished: and S brought in *all* the H8010
2 Then S assembled the elders of Israel, H8010
6 Also king S, and all the congregation of H8010
6: 1 Then said S, The LORD hath said that H8010
13 For S had made a brasen scaffold, of H8010
7: 1 Now when S had made an end of H8010
5 And king S offered a sacrifice of twenty H8010
7 Moreover S hallowed the middle of the H8010
7 altar which S had made was not able H8010
8 Also at the same time S kept the feast H8010
10 and to S, and to Israel his people. H8010
11 Thus S finished the house of the LORD, H8010
12 And the LORD appeared to S by night, H8010
8: 1 years, wherein S had built the house H8010
2 had restored to S, Solomon built them, H8010
2 to Solomon, S built them, and caused H8010
3 And S went to Hamath-zobah, and H8010
6 the store cities that S had, and all the H8010
6 and all that S desired to build in H8010
8 S make to pay tribute until this day. H8010

2Ch 8: 9 But of the children of Israel did S make H8010
11 And S brought up the daughter of H8010
12 Then S offered burnt offerings unto the H8010
16 Now all the work of S was prepared H8010
17 Then went S to Ezion-geber, and to H8010
18 the servants of S to Ophir, and took H8010
18 of gold, and brought *them* to king S. H8010
9: 1 of the fame of S, she came to prove H8010
1 she came to prove S with hard H8010
1 she was come to S, she communed with H8010
2 And S told her all her questions: and H8010
2 hid from S which he told her not. H8010
3 of S, and the house that he had built, H8010
9 spice as the queen of Sheba gave king S. H8010
10 the servants of S, which brought gold H8010
12 And king S gave to the queen of Sheba H8010
13 Now the weight of gold that came to S H8010
14 country brought gold and silver to S. H8010
15 And king S made two hundred targets H8010
20 And all the drinking vessels of king S H8010
20 any thing accounted of in the days of S. H8010
22 And king S passed all the kings of the H8010
23 the presence of S, to hear his wisdom, H8010
25 And S had four thousand stalls for H8010
28 And they brought unto S horses out of H8010
29 Now the rest of the acts of S, first and H8010
30 And S reigned in Jerusalem over all H8010
31 And S slept with his fathers, and he H8010
10: 2 the presence of S the king, heard *it*, H8010
6 had stood before S his father while he H8010
11: 3 Speak unto Rehoboam the son of S, H8010
17 the son of S strong, three years: H8010
17 they walked in the way of David and S. H8010
12: 9 the shields of gold which S had made. H8010
13: 6 the servant of S the son of David, is H8010
7 the son of S, when Rehoboam was H8010
30:26 for since the time of S the son of David H8010
33: 7 said to David and to S his son, In this H8010
35: 3 in the house which S the son of David H8010
4 according to the writing of S his son. H8010
Neh 12:45 of David, *and* of S his son. H8010
13:26 Did not S king of Israel sin by these H8010
Ps 72:ttl *A Psalm* for S. H8010
127:ttl A Song of degrees for S. H8010
Prv 1: 1 The proverbs of S the son of David, H8010
10: 1 The proverbs of S. A wise son maketh a H8010
25: 1 These *are* also proverbs of S, which the H8010
Song 1: 5 the tents of Kedar, as the curtains of S. H8010
3: 9 King S made himself a chariot of the H8010
11 Zion, and behold king S with the crown H8010
8:11 S had a vineyard at Baal-hamon; he let H8010
12 *is* before me: thou, O S, *must have* a H8010
Jer 52:20 bases, which king S had made in the H8010
Mt 1: 6 S of her *that had been the wife* of Urias; *G4672*
7 And S begat Roboam; and Roboam *G4672*
6:29 And yet I say unto you, That even S in *G4672*
12:42 the wisdom of S; and, behold, a greater *G4672*
42 and, behold, a greater than S *is* here. *G4672*
Lk 11:31 the wisdom of S; and, behold, a greater *G4672*
31 and, behold, a greater than S *is* here. *G4672*
12:27 say unto you, that S in all his glory was *G4672*
Act 7:47 But S built him an house. *G4672*

SOLOMON'S

1Ki 4:22 And S provision for one day was thirty H8010
27 came unto king S table, every man in H8010
30 And S wisdom excelled the wisdom of H8010
5:16 Beside the chief of S officers which H8010
18 And S builders and Hiram's builders H8010
6: 1 the fourth year of S reign over Israel, in H8010
9: 1 all S desire which he was pleased to do, H8010
16 *for* a present unto his daughter, S wife. H8010
23 that *were* over S work, five hundred H8010
10: 4 Sheba had seen all S wisdom, and the H8010
21 And all king S drinking vessels *were of* H8010
11:26 of Zereda, S servant, whose mother's H8010
1Ch 3:10 And S son *was* Rehoboam, Abia his H8010
2Ch 7:11 all that came into S heart to make in H8010
8:10 And these *were* the chief of king S H8010
Ezr 2:55 The children of S servants: the children H8010
58 All the Nethinims, and the children of S H8010
Neh 7:57 The children of S servants: the children H8010
60 All the Nethinims, and the children of S H8010
11: 3 and the children of S servants. H8010
Song 1: 1 The song of songs, which *is* S. H8010
3: 7 Behold his bed, which *is* S; threescore H8010
Jn 10:23 And Jesus walked in the temple in S *G4672*
Act 3:11 that is called S, greatly wondering. *G4672*
5:12 were all with one accord in S porch. *G4672*

SOME

Gen 19:19 mountain, lest *s* evil take me, and I die:
27: 3 out to the field, and take me *s* venison;
30:35 every one that had *s* white in it, and all
33:15 leave with thee *s* of the folk that *are* with
37:20 and cast him into *s* pit, and we will say, H259
20 pit, and we will say, S evil beast hath
47: 2 And he took *s* of his brethren, *even* five H7097
Ex 16:17 did so, and gathered, *s* more, some less.
17 did so, and gathered, some more, *s* less.
20 unto Moses; but *s* of them left of it until H582
27 *that* there went out *s* of the people on the
30:36 And thou shalt beat *s* of it very small,
Lev 4: 7 And the priest shall put *s* of the blood
17 And the priest shall dip his finger *in s* of
18 And he shall put *s* of the blood upon the
14:14 And the priest shall take *s* of the blood of
15 And the priest shall take *s* of the log of
25 the priest shall take *s* of the blood of the
27 his right finger *s* of the oil that *is* in his
25:25 hath sold away *s* of his possession, and
27:16 unto the LORD *s part* of a field of his
Nu 5:20 be defiled, and *s* man have lain with thee
21: 1 Israel, and took *s* of them prisoners.
27:20 And thou shalt put *s* of thine honour
31: 3 saying, Arm *s* of yourselves unto the H582
Dt 24: 1 he hath found *s* uncleanness in her: H1697
Jos 8:22 in the midst of Israel, *s* on this side, and H428
22 on this side, and *s* on that side: and they H428
Jdg 21:13 And the whole congregation sent *s* to
Ru 2:16 And let fall also *s* of the handfuls of
1Sa 8:11 and *s* shall run before his chariots.
13: 7 And *s of* the Hebrews went over Jordan
24:10 in the cave: and *s* bade *me* kill thee: but
27: 5 give me a place in *s* town in the country, H259
2Sa 11:17 Joab: and there fell *s* of the people of the
24 thy servants; and *s* of the king's servants
17: 9 Behold, he is hid now in *s* pit, or in some H259
9 Behold, he is hid now in some pit, or in *s* H259
9 to pass, when *s* of them be overthrown
12 So shall we come upon him in *s* place H259
1Ki 14:13 him there is found *s* good thing toward
2Ki 2:16 and cast him upon *s* mountain, or into H259
16 *s* valley. And he said, Ye shall not send. H259
5:13 had bid thee *do s* great thing, wouldest
7: 9 the morning light, *s* mischief will come
13 and said, Let *s* take, I pray thee, five
9:33 threw her down: and *s* of her blood was
17:25 lions among them, which slew *s* of them.
1Ch 4:42 And *s* of them, *even* of the sons of
9:29 *S* of them also *were* appointed to oversee
30 And *s* of the sons of the priests made the
12:19 And there fell *s* of Manasseh to David,
2Ch 12: 7 I will grant them *s* deliverance; and my H4592
16:10 oppressed *s* of the people the same time.
17:11 Also *s* of the Philistines brought
20: 2 Then there came *s* that told
Ezr 2:68 And *s* of the chief of the fathers, when
70 So the priests, and the Levites, and *s* of
7: 7 And there went up *s* of the children of
10:44 All these had taken strange wives: and *s*
Neh 2:12 And I arose in the night, I and *s* few H4592
5: 3 *S* also there were that said, We have
5 to be servants, and *s* of our daughters
6: 2 us meet together in *s one of* the villages
7:70 And *s* of the chief of the fathers gave H7097
71 And *s* of the chief of the fathers gave to
73 the singers, and *s* of the people, and the
11:25 And for the villages, with their fields, *s*
12:44 And at that time were *s* appointed over H582
13:15 In those days saw I in Judah *s* treading
19 the sabbath: and *s* of my servants set I at
Job 24: 2 *S* remove the landmarks; they violently
Ps 20: 7 *S trust* in chariots, and some in horses: H428
7 Some *trust* in chariots, and *s* in horses: H428
69:20 and I looked *for s* to take pity, but *there*
Prv 4:16 is taken away, unless they cause *s* to fall.
Jer 49: 9 they not leave *s* gleaning grapes? if
Ezk 6: 8 that ye may have *s* that shall escape the
Dan 8:10 and it cast down *s* of the host and of the
11:35 And *s* of them of understanding shall
12: 2 earth shall awake, *s* to everlasting life, H428
2 *s* to shame *and* everlasting contempt. H428
Am 4:11 I have overthrown *s* of you, as God
Oba 5 to thee, would they not leave *s* grapes?
Mt 13: 4 And when he sowed, *s seeds* G3588+G3203
5 S fell upon stony places, where they had G243
7 And s fell among thorns; and the thorns G243
8 forth fruit, s an hundredfold, some G3303

Mt 13: 8 s sixtyfold, some thirtyfold. *G3739*
8 some sixtyfold, s thirtyfold. *G3739*
23 bringeth forth, s an hundredfold, some *G3303*
23 an hundredfold, s sixty, some thirty. *G3739*
23 an hundredfold, some sixty, s thirty. *G3739*
16:14 And they said, S *say that thou art* John *G3588*
14 *art* John the Baptist: s, Elias; and others, *G243*
28 Verily I say unto you, There be s *G5100*
19:12 For there are s eunuchs, which were so
12 and there are s eunuchs, which were
23:34 and scribes: and *s* of them ye shall kill
34 kill and crucify; and *s* of them shall ye
27:47 S of them that stood there, when they *G5100*
28:11 Now when they were going, behold, *s* of *G5100*
17 they worshipped him: but s doubted. *G3588*
Mk 2: 1 into Capernaum after *s* days; and it was
4: 4 as he sowed, s fell by the way *G3588+G3203*
5 And s fell on stony ground, where it had *G243*
7 And s fell among thorns, and the thorns *G243*
8 and brought forth, s thirty, and some *G1520*
8 and s sixty, and some an hundred. *G1520*
8 and some sixty, and s an hundred. *G1520*
20 and bring forth fruit, s thirtyfold, some *G1520*
20 s sixty, and some an hundred. *G1520*
20 some sixty, and s an hundred. *G1520*
7: 2 And when they saw s of his disciples *G5100*
8:28 the Baptist: but s *say*, Elias; and others, *G243*
9: 1 you, That there be s of them that stand *G5100*
12: 5 beating s, and killing some. *G3588+G3203*
5 others; beating some, and killing s. *G3588*
14: 4 And there were s that had indignation *G5100*
65 And s began to spit on him, and to *G5100*
15:35 And s of them that stood by, when they *G5100*
Lk 8: 5 as he sowed, s fell by the way *G3588+G3203*
6 And s fell upon a rock; and as soon as *G2087*
7 And s fell among thorns; and the *G2087*
9: 7 of s, that John was risen from the dead; *G5100*
8 And of s, that Elias had appeared; and *G5100*
19 the Baptist; but s *say*, Elias; and others *G243*
27 But I tell you of a truth, there be s *G5100*
11:15 But s of them said, He casteth out *G5100*
49 *s* of them they shall slay and persecute:
13: 1 There were present at that season s *G5100*
19:39 And s of the Pharisees from among the *G5100*
21: 5 And as s spake of the temple, how it *G5100*
16 and friends; and *s* of you shall they
23: 8 to have seen s miracle done by him. *G5100*
Jn 3:25 Then there arose a question between *s* of
6:64 But there are s of you that believe not. *G5100*
7:12 him: for s said, He is a good *G3588+G3203*
25 Then said s of them of Jerusalem, Is *G5100*
41 Others said, This is the Christ. But s *G243*
44 And s of them would have taken him; *G5100*
9: 9 S said, This is he: others *said*, He is like *G243*
16 Therefore said s of the Pharisees, This *G5100*
40 And *s* of the Pharisees which were with
10: 1 but climbeth up s other way, the same
11:37 And s of them said, Could not this *G5100*
46 But s of them went their ways to the *G5100*
13:29 For s *of them* thought, because Judas *G5100*
16:17 Then said *s* of his disciples among
Act 5:15 by might overshadow s of them. *G5100*
8: 9 giving out that himself was s great one: *G5100*
31 And he said, How can I, except *s* man
34 this? of himself, or of *s* other man?
11:20 And s of them were men of Cyprus and *G5100*
13:11 about seeking *s* to lead him by the hand.
15:36 And s days after Paul said unto *G5100*
17: 4 And s of them believed, and consorted *G5100*
18 him. And s said, What will this *G5100*
18 babbler say? other s, He seemeth to be a *G3588*
21 either to tell, or to hear s new thing.) *G5100*
32 of the dead, s mocked: and *G3588+G3203*
18:23 And after he had spent s time *there*, he *G5100*
19:32 S therefore cried one thing, and some *G243*
32 Some therefore cried one thing, and s *G243*
21:34 And s cried one thing, some another, *G243*
34 And some cried one thing, s another, *G243*
27:27 that they drew near to s country; *G5100*
34 Wherefore I pray you to take *s* meat: for
36 of good cheer, and they also took *s* meat.
44 And the rest, s on boards, and *G3588+G3203*
44 And the rest, some on boards, and s on *G1161*
28:24 And s believed the things *G3588+G3203*
24 which were spoken, and s believed not. *G3588*
Ro 1:11 impart unto you s spiritual gift, to the *G5100*
13 that I might have s fruit among you *G5100*
3: 3 For what if s did not believe? shall their *G5100*
8 reported, and as s affirm that we say,) *G5100*

Ro 5: 7 a good man s would even dare to die. G5100
11:14 *are* my flesh, and might save s of them. G5100
17 And if s of the branches be broken off, G5100
15:15 unto you in s sort, as putting G575+G3313
1Co 4:18 Now s are puffed up, as though I would G5100
6:11 And such were s of you: but ye are G5100
8: 7 knowledge: for s with conscience of the G5100
9:22 *men*, that I might by all means save s. G5100
10: 7 Neither be ye idolaters, as *were* s of G5100
8 Neither let us commit fornication, as s G5100
9 Neither let us tempt Christ, as s of G5100
10 Neither murmur ye, as s of them also G5100
12:28 And God hath set s in the G3588+G3208
15: 6 this present, but s are fallen asleep. G5100
12 the dead, how say s among you that G5100
34 and sin not; for s have not the G5100
35 But s *man* will say, How are the dead G5100
37 chance of wheat, or of s other *grain*: G5100
2Co 3: 1 or need we, as s *others*, epistles of G5100
10: 2 to be bold against s, which think of us G5100
12 ourselves with s that commend G5100
Gal 1: 7 Which is not another; but there be s G5100
Eph 4:11 And he gave s, apostles; and G3588+G3208
11 And he gave some, apostles; and s, G3588
11 prophets; and s, evangelists; and some, G3588
11 and s, pastors and teachers; G3588
Php 1:15 S indeed preach Christ even of envy G5100
15 envy and strife; and s also of good will: G5100
Col 3: 7 In the which ye also walked s time, when
1Th 3: 5 your faith, lest by s means the tempter
2Th 3:11 For we hear that there are s which walk G5100
1Ti 1: 3 s that they teach no other doctrine, G5100
6 From which s having swerved have G5100
19 conscience; which s having put away G5100
4: 1 in the latter times s shall depart from G5100
5:15 For s are already turned aside after G5100
24 S men's sins are open beforehand, G5100
24 judgment; and s *men* they follow after. G5100
25 Likewise also the good works *of* s are
6:10 evil: which while s coveted after, they G5100
21 Which s professing have erred G5100
2Ti 2:18 already; and overthrow the faith of s. G5100
20 of earth; and s to honour, and G3588+G3208
20 some to honour, and s to dishonour. G3739
Heb 3: 4 For every house is builded by s *man*; G5100
16 For s, when they had heard, did G5100
4: 6 Seeing therefore it remaineth that s G5100
10:25 as the manner of s *is*; but exhorting G5100
11:40 God having provided s better thing for G5100
13: 2 s have entertained angels unawares. G5100
1Pt 4:12 s strange thing happened unto you:
2Pt 3: 9 his promise, as s men count slackness; G5100
16 things; in which are s things hard to be G5100
Jude 22 And of s have compassion, G3588+G3208
Rev 2:10 the devil shall cast s of you into prison,

SOMEBODY
Lk 8:46 And Jesus said, S hath touched me: for G5100
Act 5:36 himself to be s; to whom a number G5100

SOMETHING
1Sa 20:26 for he thought, S hath befallen him, he H4745
Mk 5:43 that s should be given her to eat.
Lk 11:54 seeking to catch s out of his mouth, G5100
Jn 13:29 or, that he should give s to the poor. G5100
Act 3: 5 them, expecting to receive s of them. G5100
23:15 ye would inquire s more perfectly
18 unto thee, who hath s to say unto thee. G5100
Gal 6: 3 For if a man think himself to be s, when G5100

SOMETIME
Col 1:21 And you, that were s alienated and G4218
1Pt 3:20 Which s were disobedient, when once G4218

SOMETIMES
Eph 2:13 But now in Christ Jesus ye who s were
5: 8 For ye were s darkness, but now *are ye* G4218
Tit 3: 3 For we ourselves also were s foolish, G4218

SOMEWHAT
Lev 4:13 and they have done s *against* any of the
22 When a ruler hath sinned, and done s
27 while he doeth s *against* any of the
13: 6 *if* the plague *be* s dark, *and* the plague H3544
19 s reddish, and it be shewed to the priest;
21 the skin, but *be* s dark; then the priest H3544
24 a white bright spot, s reddish, or white;
26 the *other* skin, but *be* s dark; then the H3544
28 the skin, but it *be* s dark; it *is* a rising of H3544
Lev 13:56 the plague *be* s dark after the washing H3544
1Ki 2:14 He said moreover, I have s to say unto
2Ki 5:20 I will run after him, and take s of him. H3972
2Ch 10: 4 now therefore ease thou s the grievous
9 to me, saying, Ease s the yoke that thy
10 but make thou *it* s lighter for us; thus
Lk 7:40 Simon, I have s to say unto thee. And G5100
Act 23:20 would inquire s of him more perfectly. G5100
25:26 had, I might have s to write. G5100
Ro 15:24 I be s filled with your *company*. G575+G3313
2Co 5:12 that ye may have s to *answer* them
10: 8 For though I should boast s more of G5100
Gal 2: 6 But of these who seemed to be s, G5100
6 *be* s in conference added nothing to me:
Heb 8: 3 that this man have s also to offer. G5100
Rev 2: 4 Nevertheless I have s against thee,

SON
Gen 4:17 the city, after the name of his s, Enoch. H1121
25 and she bare a s, and called his name H1121
26 there was born a s; and he called his H1121
5: 3 years, and begat *a s* in his own likeness,
28 eighty and two years, and begat a s: H1121
9:24 what his younger s had done unto him. H1121
11:31 And Terah took Abram his s, and Lot H1121
31 son, and Lot the s of Haran his son's H1121
31 son of Haran his son's s, and Sarai his H1121
31 in law, his s Abram's wife; and they H1121
12: 5 and Lot his brother's s, and all their H1121
14:12 And they took Lot, Abram's brother's s, H1121
16:11 and shalt bear a s, and shalt call his H1121
15 And Hagar bare Abram a s: and Abram H1121
17:16 And I will bless her, and give thee a s H1121
19 shall bear thee a s indeed; and thou H1121
23 And Abraham took Ishmael his s, and H1121
25 And Ishmael his s *was* thirteen years H1121
26 circumcised, and Ishmael his s. H1121
18:10 wife shall have a s. And Sarah heard *it* H1121
14 time of life, and Sarah shall have a s. H1121
19:12 here any besides? s in law, and thy H1121
37 And the firstborn bare a s, and called H1121
38 And the younger, she also bare a s, and H1121
21: 2 bare Abraham a s in his old age, at the H1121
3 And Abraham called the name of his s H1121
4 And Abraham circumcised his s Isaac H1121
5 when his s Isaac was born unto him. H1121
7 for I have born *him* a s in his old age. H1121
9 And Sarah saw the s of Hagar the H1121
10 and her s: for the son of this H1121
10 her son: for the s of this bondwoman H1121
10 not be heir with my s, *even* with Isaac. H1121
11 in Abraham's sight because of his s. H1121
13 And also of the s of the bondwoman H1121
23 me, nor with my s, nor with my son's H5209
23 nor with my son's s: *but* according to H5220
22: 2 And he said, Take now thy s, thine only H1121
2 thy son, thine only *s* Isaac, whom thou H3173
3 with him, and Isaac his s, and clave the H1121
6 *it* upon Isaac his s; and he took the fire H1121
7 Here *am* I, my s. And he said, Behold H1121
8 And Abraham said, My s, God will H1121
9 bound Isaac his s, and laid him on the H1121
10 hand, and took the knife to slay his s. H1121
12 withheld thy s, thine only *son* from me. H1121
12 withheld thy son, thine only *s* from me. H3173
13 for a burnt offering in the stead of his s. H1121
16 hast not withheld thy s, thine only *son:* H1121
16 hast not withheld thy son, thine only *s:* H3173
23: 8 entreat for me to Ephron the s of Zohar, H1121
24: 3 a wife unto my s of the daughters of H1121
4 and take a wife unto my s Isaac. H1121
5 I needs bring thy s again unto the land H1121
6 that thou bring not my s thither again. H1121
7 take a wife unto my s from thence. H1121
8 oath: only bring not my s thither again. H1121
15 born to Bethuel, s of Milcah, the wife of H1121
24 of Bethuel the s of Milcah, which she H1121
36 And Sarah my master's wife bare a s to H1121
37 take a wife to my s of the daughters of H1121
38 my kindred, and take a wife unto my s. H1121
40 take a wife for my s of my kindred, and H1121
44 hath appointed out for my master's s. H1121
47 Bethuel, Nahor's s, whom Milcah bare H1121
48 master's brother's daughter unto his s. H1121
25: 6 from Isaac his s, while he yet lived, H1121
9 the field of Ephron the s of Zohar the H1121
11 that God blessed his s Isaac; and Isaac H1121
12 Ishmael, Abraham's s, whom Hagar the H1121
19 Abraham's s: Abraham begat Isaac: H1121
Gen 27: 1 Esau his eldest s, and said unto him, H1121
1 said unto him, My s: and he said unto H1121
5 spake to Esau his s. And Esau went to H1121
6 And Rebekah spake unto Jacob her s, H1121
8 Now therefore, my s, obey my voice H1121
13 *be* thy curse, my s: only obey my voice, H1121
15 of her eldest s Esau, which *were* with H1121
15 put them upon Jacob her younger s: H1121
17 prepared, into the hand of her s Jacob. H1121
18 he said, Here *am* I; who *art* thou, my s? H1121
20 And Isaac said unto his s, How *is it* that H1121
20 found *it* so quickly, my s? And he said, H1121
21 I may feel thee, my s, whether thou *be* H1121
21 whether thou *be* my very s Esau or not. H1121
24 And he said, *Art* thou my very s Esau? H1121
26 Come near now, and kiss me, my s. H1121
27 the smell of my s *is* as the smell of a H1121
32 he said, I *am* thy s, thy firstborn Esau. H1121
37 what shall I do now unto thee, my s? H1121
42 And these words of Esau her elder s H1121
42 Jacob her younger s, and said unto him, H1121
43 Now therefore, my s, obey my voice; H1121
28: 5 unto Laban, s of Bethuel the Syrian, H1121
9 s, the sister of Nebajoth, to be his wife. H1121
29: 5 ye Laban the s of Nahor? And they H1121
12 s: and she ran and told her father. H1121
13 Jacob his sister's s, that he ran to meet H1121
32 And Leah conceived, and bare a s, and H1121
33 And she conceived again, and bare a s; H1121
33 *s* also: and she called his name Simeon.
34 And she conceived again, and bare a s; H1121
35 And she conceived again, and bare a s: H1121
30: 5 Bilhah conceived, and bare Jacob a s. H1121
6 a s: therefore called she his name Dan. H1121
7 again, and bare Jacob a second s. H1121
10 And Zilpah Leah's maid bare Jacob a s. H1121
12 Leah's maid bare Jacob a second s. H1121
17 conceived, and bare Jacob the fifth s. H1121
19 again, and bare Jacob the sixth s. H1121
23 And she conceived, and bare a s; and H1121
24 The LORD shall add to me another s. H1121
34: 2 And when Shechem the s of Hamor the H1121
8 The soul of my s Shechem longeth for H1121
18 Hamor, and Shechem Hamor's s. H1121
20 And Hamor and Shechem his s came H1121
24 unto Shechem his s hearkened all that H1121
26 and Shechem his s with the edge of the H1121
35:17 Fear not; thou shalt have this s also. H1121
36:10 sons; Eliphaz the s of Adah the wife of H1121
10 the s of Bashemath the wife of Esau. H1121
12 to Eliphaz Esau's s; and she bare to H1121
15 the firstborn s of Esau; duke Teman, H1060
17 of Reuel Esau's s; duke Nahath, duke H1121
32 And Bela the s of Beor reigned in H1121
33 And Bela died, and Jobab the s of H1121
35 And Husham died, and Hadad the s of H1121
38 And Saul died, and Baal-hanan the s of H1121
39 And Baal-hanan the s of Achbor died, H1121
37: 3 he *was* the s of his old age: and he H1121
34 and mourned for his s many days. H1121
35 the grave unto my s mourning. Thus H1121
38: 3 And she conceived, and bare a s; and he H1121
4 And she conceived again, and bare a s; H1121
5 and bare a s; and called his name H1121
11 till Shelah my s be grown: for he said, H1121
26 my s. And he knew her again no more. H1121
42:38 And he said, My s shall not go down H1121
43:29 his mother's s, and said, *Is* this your H1121
29 said, God be gracious unto thee, my s. H1121
45: 9 him, Thus saith thy s Joseph, God hath H1121
28 Joseph my s *is* yet alive: I will go H1121
46:10 Shaul the s of a Canaanitish woman. H1121
47:29 and he called his s Joseph, and said H1121
48: 2 said, Behold, thy s Joseph cometh unto H1121
19 said, I know *it*, my s, I know *it:* he also H1121
49: 9 from the prey, my s, thou art gone up: H1121
50:23 also of Machir the s of Manasseh were H1121
Ex 1:16 the stools; if it *be* a s, then ye shall kill H1121
22 saying, Every s that is born ye shall H1121
2: 2 and bare a s: and when she saw him H1121
10 and he became her s. And she called his H1121
22 And she bare *him* a s, and he called his H1121
4:22 LORD, Israel *is* my s, *even* my firstborn: H1121
23 And I say unto thee, Let my s go, that H1121
23 I will slay thy s, *even* thy firstborn. H1121
25 the foreskin of her s, and cast *it* at his H1121
6:15 and Shaul the s of a Canaanitish H1121
25 And Eleazar Aaron's s took him *one* of H1121
10: 2 in the ears of thy s, and of thy son's son, H1121

Ex 10: 2 and of thy son's s, what things I have H1121
13: 8 And thou shalt shew thy s in that day, H1121
14 And it shall be when thy s asketh thee H1121
20:10 thou, nor thy s, nor thy daughter, thy H1121
21: 9 And if he have betrothed her unto his s, H1121
31 Whether he have gored a s, or have H1121
23:12 may rest, and the s of thy handmaid, H1121
29:30 *And* that s that is priest in his stead H1121
31: 2 name Bezaleel the s of Uri, the son of H1121
2 Uri, the s of Hur, of the tribe of Judah: H1121
6 him Aholiab, the s of Ahisamach, of H1121
32:29 man upon his s, and upon his brother; H1121
33:11 Joshua, the s of Nun, a young man, H1121
35:30 name Bezaleel the s of Uri, the son of H1121
30 Uri, the s of Hur, of the tribe of Judah; H1121
34 the s of Ahisamach, of the tribe of Dan. H1121
38:21 hand of Ithamar, s to Aaron the priest. H1121
22 And Bezaleel the s of Uri, the son of H1121
22 And Bezaleel the son of Uri, the s of H1121
23 And with him *was* Aholiab, s of H1121
Lev 12: 6 are fulfilled, for a s, or for a daughter, H1121
21: 2 his father, and for his s, and for his H1121
24:10 And the s of an Israelitish woman, H1121
10 of Israel: and this s of the Israelitish H1121
11 And the Israelitish woman's s H1121
25:49 Either his uncle, or his uncle's s, may H1121
Nu 1: 5 *of* Reuben; Elizur the s of Shedeur. H1121
6 Of Simeon; Shelumiel the s of H1121
7 Of Judah; Nahshon the s of H1121
8 Of Issachar; Nethaneel the s of Zuar. H1121
9 Of Zebulun; Eliab the s of Helon. H1121
10 Elishama the s of Ammihud: of H1121
10 Manasseh; Gamaliel the s of Pedahzur. H1121
11 Of Benjamin; Abidan the s of Gideoni. H1121
12 Of Dan; Ahiezer the s of Ammishaddai. H1121
13 Of Asher; Pagiel the s of Ocran. H1121
14 Of Gad; Eliasaph the s of Deuel. H1121
15 Of Naphtali; Ahira the s of Enan. H1121
20 Israel's eldest s, by their generations, H1060
2: 3 and Nahshon the s of Amminadab H1121
5 and Nethaneel the s of Zuar *shall be* H1121
7 and Eliab the s of Helon *shall be* H1121
10 Reuben *shall be* Elizur the s of Shedeur. H1121
12 *shall be* Shelumiel the s of Zurishaddai. H1121
14 of Gad *shall be* Eliasaph the s of Reuel. H1121
18 *shall be* Elishama the s of Ammihud. H1121
20 *shall be* Gamaliel the s of Pedahzur. H1121
22 *shall be* Abidan the s of Gideoni. H1121
25 *shall be* Ahiezer the s of Ammishaddai. H1121
27 of Asher *shall be* Pagiel the s of Ocran. H1121
29 Naphtali *shall be* Ahira the s of Enan. H1121
3:24 *shall be* Eliasaph the s of Lael. H1121
30 *shall be* Elizaphan the s of Uzziel. H1121
32 And Eleazar the s of Aaron the priest H1121
35 *was* Zuriel the s of Abihail: *these* shall H1121
4:16 And to the office of Eleazar the s of H1121
28 of Ithamar the s of Aaron the priest. H1121
33 of Ithamar the s of Aaron the priest. H1121
7: 8 of Ithamar the s of Aaron the priest. H1121
12 s of Amminadab, of the tribe of Judah: H1121
17 of Nahshon the s of Amminadab. H1121
18 On the second day Nethaneel the s of H1121
23 the offering of Nethaneel the s of Zuar. H1121
24 On the third day Eliab the s of Helon, H1121
29 *was* the offering of Eliab the s of Helon. H1121
30 On the fourth day Elizur the s of H1121
35 the offering of Elizur the s of Shedeur. H1121
36 On the fifth day Shelumiel the s of H1121
41 of Shelumiel the s of Zurishaddai. H1121
42 On the sixth day Eliasaph the s of H1121
47 the offering of Eliasaph the s of Deuel. H1121
48 On the seventh day Elishama the s of H1121
53 of Elishama the s of Ammihud. H1121
54 Gamaliel the s of Pedahzur, prince H1121
59 offering of Gamaliel the s of Pedahzur. H1121
60 On the ninth day Abidan the s of H1121
65 the offering of Abidan the s of Gideoni. H1121
66 On the tenth day Ahiezer the s of H1121
71 of Ahiezer the s of Ammishaddai. H1121
72 On the eleventh day Pagiel the s of H1121
77 the offering of Pagiel the s of Ocran. H1121
78 On the twelfth day Ahira the s of Enan, H1121
83 *was* the offering of Ahira the s of Enan. H1121
10:14 *was* Nahshon the s of Amminadab. H1121
15 Issachar *was* Nethaneel the s of Zuar. H1121
16 of Zebulun *was* Eliab the s of Helon. H1121
18 his host *was* Elizur the s of Shedeur. H1121
19 *was* Shelumiel the s of Zurishaddai. H1121
20 of Gad *was* Eliasaph the s of Deuel. H1121

Nu 10:22 host *was* Elishama the s of Ammihud. H1121
23 *was* Gamaliel the s of Pedahzur. H1121
24 Benjamin *was* Abidan the s of Gideoni. H1121
25 *was* Ahiezer the s of Ammishaddai. H1121
26 of Asher *was* Pagiel the s of Ocran. H1121
27 of Naphtali *was* Ahira the s of Enan. H1121
29 And Moses said unto Hobab, the s of H1121
11:28 And Joshua the s of Nun, the servant of H1121
13: 4 of Reuben, Shammua the s of Zaccur. H1121
5 Of the tribe of Simeon, Shaphat the s of H1121
6 Of the tribe of Judah, Caleb the s of H1121
7 Of the tribe of Issachar, Igal the s of H1121
8 Of the tribe of Ephraim, Oshea the s of H1121
9 Of the tribe of Benjamin, Palti the s of H1121
10 Of the tribe of Zebulun, Gaddiel the s of H1121
11 tribe of Manasseh, Gaddi the s of Susi. H1121
12 Of the tribe of Dan, Ammiel the s of H1121
13 Of the tribe of Asher, Sethur the s of H1121
14 Of the tribe of Naphtali, Nahbi the s of H1121
15 Of the tribe of Gad, Geuel the s of H1121
16 called Oshea the s of Nun Jehoshua. H1121
14: 6 And Joshua the s of Nun, and Caleb the H1121
6 and Caleb the s of Jephunneh, *which* H1121
30 save Caleb the s of Jephunneh, and H1121
30 of Jephunneh, and Joshua the s of Nun. H1121
38 But Joshua the s of Nun, and Caleb the H1121
38 and Caleb the s of Jephunneh, *which* H1121
16: 1 Now Korah, the s of Izhar, the son of H1121
1 Now Korah, the son of Izhar, the s of H1121
1 the son of Kohath, the s of Levi, and H1121
1 s of Peleth, sons of Reuben, took *men*: H1121
37 Speak unto Eleazar the s of Aaron the H1121
20:25 Take Aaron and Eleazar his s, and H1121
26 upon Eleazar his s: and Aaron shall be H1121
28 upon Eleazar his s; and Aaron died H1121
22: 2 And Balak the s of Zippor saw all that H1121
4 And Balak the s of Zippor *was* king H1121
5 unto Balaam the s of Beor to Pethor, H1121
10 And Balaam said unto God, Balak the s H1121
16 Thus saith Balak the s of Zippor, Let H1121
23:18 hearken unto me, thou s of Zippor: H1121
19 lie; neither the s of man, that he should H1121
24: 3 said, Balaam the s of Beor hath said, H1121
15 said, Balaam the s of Beor hath said, H1121
25: 7 And when Phinehas, the s of Eleazar, H1121
7 the son of Eleazar, the s of Aaron the H1121
11 Phinehas, the s of Eleazar, the son of H1121
11 Phinehas, the son of Eleazar, the s of H1121
14 *was* Zimri, the s of Salu, a prince of a H1121
26: 1 the s of Aaron the priest, saying, H1121
5 Reuben, the eldest s of Israel: the H1060
33 And Zelophehad the s of Hepher had H1121
65 save Caleb the s of Jephunneh, and H1121
65 of Jephunneh, and Joshua the s of Nun. H1121
27: 1 of Zelophehad, the s of Hepher, the son H1121
1 son of Hepher, the s of Gilead, the son H1121
1 son of Gilead, the s of Machir, the son H1121
1 son of Machir, the s of Manasseh, of H1121
1 of Manasseh the s of Joseph: and these H1121
4 he hath no s? Give unto us *therefore* H1121
8 die, and have no s, then ye shall cause H1121
18 thee Joshua the s of Nun, a man in H1121
31: 6 them and Phinehas the s of Eleazar the H1121
8 the s of Beor they slew with the sword. H1121
32:12 Save Caleb the s of Jephunneh the H1121
12 and Joshua the s of Nun: for they have H1121
28 and Joshua the s of Nun, and the chief H1121
33 tribe of Manasseh the s of Joseph, the H1121
39 And the children of Machir the s of H1121
40 s of Manasseh; and he dwelt therein. H1121
41 And Jair the s of Manasseh went and H1121
34:17 the priest, and Joshua the s of Nun. H1121
19 of Judah, Caleb the s of Jephunneh. H1121
20 of Simeon, Shemuel the s of Ammihud. H1121
21 Of the tribe of Benjamin, Elidad the s H1121
22 children of Dan, Bukki the s of Jogli. H1121
23 of Manasseh, Hanniel the s of Ephod. H1121
24 of Ephraim, Kemuel the s of Shiphtan. H1121
25 of Zebulun, Elizaphan the s of Parnach. H1121
26 of Issachar, Paltiel the s of Azzan. H1121
27 of Asher, Ahihud the s of Shelomi. H1121
28 Naphtali, Pedahel the s of Ammihud. H1121
36: 1 of Gilead, the s of Machir, the son of H1121
1 son of Machir, the s of Manasseh, of H1121
12 of Manasseh the s of Joseph, and their H1121
Dt 1:31 man doth bear his s, in all the way that H1121
36 Save Caleb the s of Jephunneh; he shall H1121
38 *But* Joshua the s of Nun, which H1121
3:14 Jair the s of Manasseh took all the H1121

Dt 5:14 thou, nor thy s, nor thy daughter, nor H1121
6: 2 thou, and thy s, and thy son's son, all H1121
2 son, and thy son's s, all the days of thy H1121
20 *And* when thy s asketh thee in time to H1121
21 Then thou shalt say unto thy s, We were H1121
7: 3 not give unto his s, nor his daughter H1121
3 his daughter shalt thou take unto thy s. H1121
4 For they will turn away thy s from H1121
8: 5 s, *so* the LORD thy God chasteneth thee. H1121
10: 6 and Eleazar his s ministered in the H1121
11: 6 sons of Eliab, the s of Reuben: how the H1121
12:18 thou, and thy s, and thy daughter, and H1121
13: 6 If thy brother, the s of thy mother, or H1121
6 thy mother, or thy s, or thy daughter, or H1121
16:11 God, thou, and thy s, and thy daughter, H1121
14 thou, and thy s, and thy daughter, and H1121
18:10 that maketh his s or his daughter to H1121
21:15 the firstborn s be hers that was hated: H1121
16 he may not make the s of the beloved H1121
16 before the s of the hated, *which* H1121
17 But he shall acknowledge the s of the H1121
18 and rebellious s, which will not obey H1121
20 of his city, This our s *is* stubborn and H1121
23: 4 thee Balaam the s of Beor of Pethor of H1121
28:56 toward her s, and toward her daughter, H1121
31:23 And he gave Joshua the s of Nun a H1121
32:44 people, he, and Hoshea the s of Nun. H1121
34: 9 And Joshua the s of Nun was full of the H1121
Jos 1: 1 the s of Nun, Moses' minister, saying, H1121
2: 1 And Joshua the s of Nun sent out of H1121
23 to Joshua the s of Nun, and told him H1121
6: 6 And Joshua the s of Nun called the H1121
26 youngest *s* shall he set up the gates of it.
7: 1 for Achan, the s of Carmi, the son of H1121
1 son of Carmi, the s of Zabdi, the son of H1121
1 son of Zabdi, the s of Zerah, of the tribe H1121
18 and Achan, the s of Carmi, the son of H1121
18 son of Carmi, the s of Zabdi, the son of H1121
18 son of Zabdi, the s of Zerah, of the tribe H1121
19 And Joshua said unto Achan, My s, H1121
24 took Achan the s of Zerah, and the H1121
13:22 Balaam also the s of Beor, the H1121
31 of Machir the s of Manasseh, *even* to H1121
14: 1 and Joshua the s of Nun, and the heads H1121
6 and Caleb the s of Jephunneh the H1121
13 unto Caleb the s of Jephunneh Hebron H1121
14 of Caleb the s of Jephunneh the H1121
15: 6 to the stone of Bohan the s of Reuben: H1121
8 by the valley of the s of Hinnom unto H1121
13 And unto Caleb the s of Jephunneh he H1121
17 And Othniel the s of Kenaz, the brother H1121
17: 2 the s of Joseph by their families. H1121
3 But Zelophehad, the s of Hepher, the H1121
3 son of Hepher, the s of Gilead, the son H1121
3 son of Gilead, the s of Machir, the son H1121
3 son of Machir, the s of Manasseh, had H1121
4 before Joshua the s of Nun, and before H1121
18:16 the valley of the s of Hinnom, *and* H1121
17 to the stone of Bohan the s of Reuben, H1121
19:49 to Joshua the s of Nun among them: H1121
51 and Joshua the s of Nun, and the heads H1121
21: 1 unto Joshua the s of Nun, and unto the H1121
12 the s of Jephunneh for his possession. H1121
22:13 Phinehas the s of Eleazar the priest, H1121
20 Did not Achan the s of Zerah commit a H1121
31 And Phinehas the s of Eleazar the H1121
32 And Phinehas the s of Eleazar the H1121
24: 9 Then Balak the s of Zippor, king of H1121
9 Balaam the s of Beor to curse you: H1121
29 that Joshua the s of Nun, the servant H1121
33 And Eleazar the s of Aaron died; and H1121
33 *to* Phinehas his s, which was given him H1121
Jdg 1:13 And Othniel the s of Kenaz, Caleb's H1121
2: 8 And Joshua the s of Nun, the servant of H1121
3: 9 s of Kenaz, Caleb's younger brother. H1121
11 years. And Othniel the s of Kenaz died. H1121
15 Ehud the s of Gera, a Benjamite, H1121
31 And after him was Shamgar the s of H1121
4: 6 And she sent and called Barak the s of H1121
12 that Barak the s of Abinoam was gone H1121
5: 1 Then sang Deborah and Barak the s of H1121
6 In the days of Shamgar the s of Anath, H1121
12 captivity captive, thou s of Abinoam. H1121
6:11 Abi-ezrite: and his s Gideon threshed H1121
29 the s of Joash hath done this thing. H1121
30 Joash, Bring out thy s, that he may die: H1121
7:14 of Gideon the s of Joash, a man of H1121
8:13 And Gideon the s of Joash returned H1121
22 both thou, and thy s, and thy son's son H1121

Jdg 8:22 son, and thy son's s also: for thou hast H1121
23 neither shall my s rule over you: the H1121
29 And Jerubbaal the s of Joash went and H1121
31 a s, whose name he called Abimelech. H1121
32 And Gideon the s of Joash died in a H1121
9: 1 And Abimelech the s of Jerubbaal went H1121
5 the youngest s of Jerubbaal was left; H1121
18 Abimelech, the s of his maidservant, H1121
26 And Gaal the s of Ebed came with his H1121
28 And Gaal the s of Ebed said, Who *is* H1121
28 him? *is* not *he* the s of Jerubbaal? and H1121
30 the s of Ebed, his anger was kindled. H1121
31 Behold, Gaal the s of Ebed and his H1121
35 And Gaal the s of Ebed went out, and H1121
57 the curse of Jotham the s of Jerubbaal. H1121
10: 1 Israel Tola the s of Puah, the son of H1121
1 son of Puah, the s of Dodo, a man of H1121
11: 1 and he *was* the s of an harlot: and H1121
2 for thou *art* the s of a strange woman. H1121
25 than Balak the s of Zippor, king of H1121
34 her he had neither s nor daughter. H1121
12:13 And after him Abdon the s of Hillel, a H1121
15 And Abdon the s of Hillel the H1121
13: 3 but thou shalt conceive, and bear a s. H1121
5 and bear a s; and no razor shall come H1121
7 and bear a s; and now drink no wine H1121
24 And the woman bare a s, and called his H1121
15: 6 Samson, the s in law of the Timnite, H2860
17: 2 Blessed *be thou* of the LORD, my s. H1121
3 my hand for my s, to make a graven H1121
18:30 and Jonathan, the s of Gershom, the H1121
30 of Gershom, the s of Manasseh, he and H1121
19: 5 said unto his s in law, Comfort thine H2860
20:28 And Phinehas, the s of Eleazar, the son H1121
28 And Phinehas, the son of Eleazar, the s H1121
Ru 4:13 gave her conception, and she bare a s. H1121
17 saying, There is a s born to Naomi; and H1121
1Sa 1: 1 *was* Elkanah, the s of Jeroham, the son H1121
1 of Jeroham, the s of Elihu, the son of H1121
1 son of Elihu, the s of Tohu, the son of H1121
1 of Tohu, the s of Zuph, an Ephrathite: H1121
20 that she bare a s, and called his name H1121
23 gave her s suck until she weaned him. H1121
3: 6 I called not, my s; lie down again. H1121
16 my s. And he answered, Here *am* I. H1121
4:16 And he said, What is there done, my s? H1121
20 thou hast born a s. But she answered H1121
7: 1 his s to keep the ark of the LORD. H1121
9: 1 *was* Kish, the s of Abiel, the son of H1121
1 son of Abiel, the s of Zeror, the son of H1121
1 the son of Zeror, the s of Bechorath, the H1121
1 son of Bechorath, the s of Aphiah, a H1121
2 And he had a s, whose name *was* Saul, H1121
3 said to Saul his s, Take now one of the H1121
10: 2 you, saying, What shall I do for my s? H1121
11 is come unto the s of Kish? *Is* Saul also H1121
21 and Saul the s of Kish was taken: and H1121
13:16 And Saul, and Jonathan his s, and the H1121
22 with Jonathan his s was there found. H1121
14: 1 that Jonathan the s of Saul said unto H1121
3 And Ahiah, the s of Ahitub, Ichabod's H1121
3 brother, the s of Phinehas, the son H1121
3 of Phinehas, the s of Eli, the LORD'S H1121
39 be in Jonathan my s, he shall surely die. H1121
40 and Jonathan my s will be on the other H1121
42 my s. And Jonathan was taken. H1121
50 *was* Abner, the s of Ner, Saul's uncle. H1121
51 the father of Abner *was* the s of Abiel. H1121
16:18 Behold, I have seen a s of Jesse the H1121
19 me David thy s, which *is* with the sheep. H1121
20 sent *them* by David his s unto Saul. H1121
17:12 Now David *was* the s of that Ephrathite H1121
17 And Jesse said unto David his s, Take H1121
55 host, Abner, whose s *is* this youth? And H1121
56 Inquire thou whose s the stripling *is*. H1121
58 And Saul said to him, Whose s *art* H1121
58 I *am* the s of thy servant Jesse H1121
18:18 that I should be s in law to the king? H2860
21 be my s in law in *the one of* the twain. H2859
22 now therefore be the king's s in law. H2859
23 to be a king's s in law, seeing that I H2859
26 s in law: and the days were not expired. H2859
27 be the king's s in law. And Saul gave H2859
19: 1 And Saul spake to Jonathan his s, and H1121
2 But Jonathan Saul's s delighted much H1121
20:27 unto Jonathan his s, Wherefore cometh H1121
27 cometh not the s of Jesse to meat, H1121
30 said unto him, Thou s of the perverse H1121
30 hast chosen the s of Jesse to thine own H1121
1Sa 20:31 For as long as the s of Jesse liveth upon H1121
22: 7 will the s of Jesse give every one H1121
8 me that my s hath made a league H1121
8 a league with the s of Jesse, and *there is* H1121
8 unto me that my s hath stirred up my H1121
9 and said, I saw the s of Jesse coming to H1121
9 to Nob, to Ahimelech the s of Ahitub. H1121
11 the priest, the s of Ahitub, and all his H1121
12 And Saul said, Hear now, thou s of H1121
13 me, thou and the s of Jesse, in that thou H1121
14 which is the king's s in law, and goeth H2860
20 And one of the sons of Ahimelech the s H1121
23: 6 when Abiathar the s of Ahimelech fled H1121
16 And Jonathan Saul's s arose, and went H1121
24:16 *Is* this thy voice, my s David? And Saul H1121
25: 8 unto thy servants, and to thy s David. H1121
10 and who *is* the s of Jesse? there be H1121
17 for he *is such* a s of Belial, that *a man* H1121
44 the s of Laish, which *was* of Gallim. H1121
26: 5 lay, and Abner the s of Ner, the captain H1121
6 Hittite, and to Abishai the s of Zeruiah, H1121
14 and to Abner the s of Ner, saying, H1121
17 this thy voice, my s David? And David H1121
21 sinned: return, my s David: for I will no H1121
25 *be* thou, my s David: thou shalt both H1121
27: 2 Achish, the s of Maoch, king of Gath. H1121
30: 7 Ahimelech's s, I pray thee, bring me H1121
2Sa 1: 4 Saul and Jonathan his s are dead also. H1121
5 that Saul and Jonathan his s be dead? H1121
12 for Jonathan his s, and for the people of H1121
13 I *am* the s of a stranger, an Amalekite. H1121
17 over Saul and over Jonathan his s: H1121
2: 8 But Abner the s of Ner, captain of H1121
8 Ish-bosheth the s of Saul, and brought H1121
10 Ish-bosheth Saul's s *was* forty years old H1121
12 And Abner the s of Ner, and the H1121
12 of Ish-bosheth the s of Saul, went out H1121
13 And Joab the s of Zeruiah, and the H1121
15 to Ish-bosheth the s of Saul, and twelve H1121
3: 3 Absalom the s of Maacah the daughter H1121
4 And the fourth, Adonijah the s of H1121
4 the fifth, Shephatiah the s of Abital; H1121
14 Ish-bosheth Saul's s, saying, Deliver *me* H1121
15 *even* from Phaltiel the s of Laish. H1121
23 saying, Abner the s of Ner came to the H1121
25 Thou knowest Abner the s of Ner, that H1121
28 from the blood of Abner the s of Ner: H1121
37 of the king to slay Abner the s of Ner. H1121
4: 1 And when Saul's s heard that Abner H1121
2 And Saul's s had two men *that were* H1121
4 And Jonathan, Saul's s, had a son *that* H1121
4 And Jonathan, Saul's son, had a s *that* H1121
8 Ish-bosheth the s of Saul thine enemy, H1121
7:14 I will be his father, and he shall be my s. H1121
8: 3 David smote also Hadadezer, the s of H1121
10 Then Toi sent Joram his s unto king H1121
12 Hadadezer, s of Rehob, king of Zobah. H1121
16 And Joab the s of Zeruiah *was* over the H1121
16 the s of Ahilud *was* recorder; H1121
17 And Zadok the s of Ahitub, and H1121
17 Ahimelech the s of Abiathar, *were* the H1121
18 And Benaiah the s of Jehoiada *was* H1121
9: 3 hath yet a s, *which is* lame on *his* feet. H1121
4 Machir, the s of Ammiel, in Lo-debar. H1121
5 the s of Ammiel, from Lo-debar. H1121
6 Now when Mephibosheth, the s of H1121
6 of Jonathan, the s of Saul, was come H1121
9 unto thy master's s all that pertained to H1121
10 that thy master's s may have food to H1121
10 thy master's s shall eat bread alway H1121
12 And Mephibosheth had a young s, H1121
10: 1 and Hanun his s reigned in his stead. H1121
2 unto Hanun the s of Nahash, as his H1121
11:21 Who smote Abimelech the s of H1121
27 and bare him a s. But the thing that H1121
12:24 her: and she bare a s, and he called his H1121
13: 1 that Absalom the s of David had a fair H1121
1 and Amnon the s of David loved her. H1121
3 *was* Jonadab, the s of Shimeah David's H1121
4 *being* the king's s, lean from day to day? H1121
25 Absalom, Nay, my s, let us not all now H1121
32 And Jonadab, the s of Shimeah David's H1121
37 to Talmai, the s of Ammihud, king of H1121
37 *David* mourned for his s every day. H1121
14: 1 Now Joab the s of Zeruiah perceived H1121
11 they destroy my s. And he said, *As* the H1121
11 not one hair of thy s fall to the earth. H1121
16 me and my s together out of the H1121
15:27 thy s, and Jonathan the son of Abiathar. H1121
2Sa 15:27 son, and Jonathan the s of Abiathar. H1121
36 sons, Ahimaaz Zadok's *s*, and Jonathan
36 Abiathar's *s*; and by them ye shall
16: 3 *is* thy master's s? And Ziba said unto H1121
5 *was* Shimei, the s of Gera: he came H1121
8 of Absalom thy s: and, behold, thou *art* H1121
9 Then said Abishai the s of Zeruiah H1121
11 Behold, my s, which came forth of H1121
19 the presence of his s? as I have served in H1121
17:25 *was* a man's s, whose name *was* Ithra H1121
27 that Shobi the s of Nahash of Rabbah H1121
27 and Machir the s of Ammiel of H1121
18: 2 hand of Abishai the s of Zeruiah, Joab's H1121
12 against the king's s: for in our hearing H1121
18 he said, I have no s to keep my name in H1121
19 Then said Ahimaaz the s of Zadok, Let H1121
20 no tidings, because the king's s is dead. H1121
22 Then said Ahimaaz the s of Zadok yet H1121
22 wilt thou run, my s, seeing that thou H1121
27 of Ahimaaz the s of Zadok. And the H1121
33 thus he said, O my s Absalom, my son, H1121
33 son Absalom, my s, my son Absalom! H1121
33 my son, my s Absalom! would God H1121
33 died for thee, O Absalom, my s, my son! H1121
33 died for thee, O Absalom, my son, my s! H1121
19: 2 day how the king was grieved for his s. H1121
4 with a loud voice, O my s Absalom, O H1121
4 Absalom, O Absalom, my s, my son! H1121
4 Absalom, O Absalom, my son, my s! H1121
16 And Shimei the s of Gera, a Benjamite, H1121
18 And Shimei the s of Gera fell down H1121
21 But Abishai the s of Zeruiah answered H1121
24 And Mephibosheth the s of Saul came H1121
20: 1 *was* Sheba, the s of Bichri, a Benjamite: H1121
1 inheritance in the s of Jesse: every man H1121
2 Sheba the s of Bichri: but the men H1121
6 shall Sheba the s of Bichri do us more H1121
7 to pursue after Sheba the s of Bichri. H1121
10 pursued after Sheba the s of Bichri. H1121
13 to pursue after Sheba the s of Bichri. H1121
21 Sheba the s of Bichri by name, hath H1121
22 head of Sheba the s of Bichri, and cast H1121
23 and Benaiah the s of Jehoiada *was* over H1121
24 the s of Ahilud *was* recorder: H1121
21: 7 the s of Jonathan the son H1121
7 of Jonathan the s of Saul, because of H1121
7 David and Jonathan the s of Saul. H1121
8 the s of Barzillai the Meholathite: H1121
12 of Jonathan his s from the men of H1121
13 of Jonathan his s; and they gathered the H1121
14 and Jonathan his s buried they in the H1121
17 But Abishai the s of Zeruiah succoured H1121
19 where Elhanan the s of Jaare-oregim, a H1121
21 Jonathan the s of Shimea the brother H1121
23: 1 of David. David the s of Jesse said, and H1121
9 And after him *was* Eleazar the s of H1121
11 And after him *was* Shammah the s of H1121
18 And Abishai, the brother of Joab, the s H1121
20 And Benaiah the s of Jehoiada, the son H1121
20 And Benaiah the son of Jehoiada, the s H1121
22 These *things* did Benaiah the s of H1121
24 Elhanan the s of Dodo of Beth-lehem, H1121
26 Helez the Paltite, Ira the s of Ikkesh the H1121
29 Heleb the s of Baanah, a Netophathite, H1121
29 Ittai the s of Ribai out of Gibeah H1121
33 Shammah the Hararite, Ahiam the s of H1121
34 Eliphelet the s of Ahasbai, the son of H1121
34 Eliphelet the son of Ahasbai, the s of H1121
34 Eliam the s of Ahithophel the Gilonite, H1121
36 Igal the s of Nathan of Zobah, Bani the H1121
37 armourbearer to Joab the s of Zeruiah, H1121
1Ki 1: 5 Then Adonijah the s of Haggith exalted H1121
7 And he conferred with Joab the s of H1121
8 and Benaiah the s of Jehoiada, and H1121
11 that Adonijah the s of Haggith doth H1121
12 own life, and the life of thy s Solomon. H1121
13 Solomon thy s shall reign after me, H1121
17 Solomon thy s shall reign after me, H1121
21 s Solomon shall be counted offenders. H1121
26 and Benaiah the s of Jehoiada, and thy H1121
30 Solomon thy s shall reign after me, H1121
32 and Benaiah the s of Jehoiada. And H1121
33 Solomon my s to ride upon mine own H1121
36 And Benaiah the s of Jehoiada H1121
38 and Benaiah the s of Jehoiada, and the H1121
42 Jonathan the s of Abiathar the priest H1121
44 and Benaiah the s of Jehoiada, and the H1121
2: 1 and he charged Solomon his s, saying, H1121
5 also what Joab the s of Zeruiah did to H1121

1Ki 2: 5 unto Abner the s of Ner, and unto H1121
5 unto Amasa the s of Jether, whom he H1121
8 thee Shimei the s of Gera, a Benjamite H1121
13 And Adonijah the s of Haggith came to H1121
22 priest, and for Joab the s of Zeruiah. H1121
25 of Benaiah the s of Jehoiada; and he H1121
29 sent Benaiah the s of Jehoiada, saying, H1121
32 *to wit,* Abner the s of Ner, captain of H1121
32 s of Jether, captain of the host of Judah. H1121
34 So Benaiah the s of Jehoiada went up, H1121
35 And the king put Benaiah the s of H1121
39 away unto Achish s of Maachah king of H1121
46 So the king commanded Benaiah the s H1121
3: 6 a s to sit on his throne, as *it is* this day. H1121
20 and took my s from beside me, while H1121
21 it was not my s, which I did bear. H1121
22 the living *is* my s, and the dead *is* thy H1121
22 the dead *is* thy s. And this said, No; but H1121
22 but the dead *is* thy s, and the living *is* H1121
22 my s. Thus they spake before the king. H1121
23 saith, This *is* my s that liveth, and thy H1121
23 liveth, and thy s *is* the dead: and the H1121
23 s *is* the dead, and my son *is* the living. H1121
23 son *is* the dead, and my s *is* the living. H1121
26 yearned upon her s, and she said, O my H1121
4: 2 had; Azariah the s of Zadok the priest, H1121
3 the s of Ahilud, the recorder. H1121
4 And Benaiah the s of Jehoiada *was* H1121
5 And Azariah the s of Nathan *was* over H1121
5 and Zabud the s of Nathan *was* H1121
6 the s of Abda *was* over the tribute. H1121
8 And these *are* their names: The s of H1133
9 The s of Dekar, in Makaz, and in H1128
10 The s of Hesed, in Aruboth; to him H1136
11 The s of Abinadab, in all the region of H1125
12 Baana the s of Ahilud; *to him* H1121
13 The s of Geber, in Ramoth-gilead; to H1127
13 towns of Jair the s of Manasseh, which H1121
14 Ahinadab the s of Iddo *had* H1121
16 Baanah the s of Hushai *was* in Asher H1121
17 Jehoshaphat the s of Paruah, in H1121
18 Shimei the s of Elah, in Benjamin: H1121
19 Geber the s of Uri *was* in the country of H1121
5: 5 saying, Thy s, whom I will set upon H1121
7 David a wise s over this great people. H1121
7:14 He *was* a widow's s of the tribe of H1121
8:19 the house; but thy s that shall come H1121
11:12 I will rend it out of the hand of thy s. H1121
13 give one tribe to thy s for David my H1121
20 him Genubath his s, whom Tahpenes H1121
23 Rezon the s of Eliadah, which fled H1121
26 And Jeroboam the s of Nebat, an H1121
36 And unto his s will I give one tribe, that H1121
43 Rehoboam his s reigned in his stead. H1121
12: 2 Jeroboam the s of Nebat, who was yet H1121
15 Shilonite unto Jeroboam the s of Nebat. H1121
16 *we* inheritance in the s of Jesse: to your H1121
21 again to Rehoboam the s of Solomon. H1121
23 Speak unto Rehoboam, the s of H1121
14: 1 At that time Abijah the s of Jeroboam H1121
5 of thee for her s; for he *is* sick: thus and H1121
20 and Nadab his s reigned in his stead. H1121
21 And Rehoboam the s of Solomon H1121
31 And Abijam his s reigned in his stead. H1121
15: 1 s of Nebat reigned Abijam over Judah. H1121
4 s after him, and to establish Jerusalem: H1121
8 and Asa his s reigned in his stead. H1121
18 to Ben-hadad, the s of Tabrimon, the H1121
18 of Tabrimon, the s of Hezion, king of H1121
24 Jehoshaphat his s reigned in his stead. H1121
25 And Nadab the s of Jeroboam began to H1121
27 And Baasha the s of Ahijah, of the H1121
33 began Baasha the s of Ahijah to reign H1121
16: 1 s of Hanani against Baasha, saying, H1121
3 the house of Jeroboam the s of Nebat. H1121
6 and Elah his s reigned in his stead. H1121
7 prophet Jehu the s of Hanani came the H1121
8 began Elah the s of Baasha to reign H1121
13 sins of Elah his s, by which they sinned, H1121
21 followed Tibni the s of Ginath, to make H1121
22 followed Tibni the s of Ginath: so Tibni H1121
26 of Jeroboam the s of Nebat, and in his H1121
28 and Ahab his s reigned in his stead. H1121
29 began Ahab the s of Omri to reign over H1121
29 and Ahab the s of Omri reigned over H1121
30 And Ahab the s of Omri did evil in the H1121
31 sins of Jeroboam the s of Nebat, that he H1121
34 in his youngest *s* Segub, according to
34 which he spake by Joshua the s of Nun. H1121

1Ki 17:12 and my s, that we may eat it, and die. H1121
13 and after make for thee and for thy s. H1121
17 things, *that* the s of the woman, the H1121
18 sin to remembrance, and to slay my s? H1121
19 And he said unto her, Give me thy s. H1121
20 with whom I sojourn, by slaying her s? H1121
23 and Elijah said, See, thy s liveth. H1121
19:16 And Jehu the s of Nimshi shalt thou H1121
16 Israel: and Elisha the s of Shaphat of H1121
19 found Elisha the s of Shaphat, who *was* H1121
21:22 of Jeroboam the s of Nebat, and like H1121
22 house of Baasha the s of Ahijah, for the H1121
22: 8 man, Micaiah the s of Imlah, by whom H1121
9 Hasten *hither* Micaiah the s of Imlah. H1121
11 And Zedekiah the s of Chenaanah H1121
24 But Zedekiah the s of Chenaanah went H1121
26 of the city, and to Joash the king's s; H1121
40 and Ahaziah his s reigned in his stead. H1121
41 And Jehoshaphat the s of Asa began to H1121
49 Then said Ahaziah the s of Ahab unto H1121
50 and Jehoram his s reigned in his stead. H1121
51 Ahaziah the s of Ahab began to reign H1121
52 the s of Nebat, who made Israel to sin: H1121
2Ki 1:17 of Jehoram the s of Jehoshaphat king H1121
17 king of Judah; because he had no s. H1121
3: 1 Now Jehoram the s of Ahab began to H1121
3 sins of Jeroboam the s of Nebat, which H1121
11 Here *is* Elisha the s of Shaphat, which H1121
27 Then he took his eldest s that should H1121
4: 6 that she said unto her s, Bring me yet a H1121
16 shalt embrace a s. And she said, Nay, H1121
17 and bare a s at that season that Elisha H1121
28 Then she said, Did I desire a s of my H1121
36 in unto him, he said, Take up thy s. H1121
37 and took up her s, and went out. H1121
6:28 unto me, Give thy s, that we may eat H1121
28 to day, and we will eat my s to morrow. H1121
29 So we boiled my s, and did eat him: and H1121
29 next day, Give thy s, that we may eat H1121
29 we may eat him: and she hath hid her s. H1121
31 head of Elisha the s of Shaphat shall H1121
32 See ye how this s of a murderer hath H1121
8: 1 the woman, whose s he had restored to H1121
5 the woman, whose s he had restored to H1121
5 *is* her s, whom Elisha restored to life. H1121
9 and said, Thy s Ben-hadad king of H1121
16 And in the fifth year of Joram the s of H1121
16 Jehoram the s of Jehoshaphat king H1121
24 and Ahaziah his s reigned in his stead. H1121
25 In the twelfth year of Joram the s of H1121
25 did Ahaziah the s of Jehoram king of H1121
27 *was* the s in law of the house of Ahab. H2860
28 And he went with Joram the s of Ahab H1121
29 And Ahaziah the s of Jehoram king of H1121
29 to see Joram the s of Ahab in Jezreel, H1121
9: 2 out there Jehu the s of Jehoshaphat the H1121
2 Jehoshaphat the s of Nimshi, and go in, H1121
9 of Jeroboam the s of Nebat, and like H1121
9 the house of Baasha the s of Ahijah: H1121
14 So Jehu the s of Jehoshaphat the son of H1121
14 So Jehu the son of Jehoshaphat the s of H1121
20 s of Nimshi; for he driveth furiously. H1121
29 And in the eleventh year of Joram the s H1121
10:15 on Jehonadab the s of Rechab *coming* H1121
23 And Jehu went, and Jehonadab the s of H1121
29 of Jeroboam the s of Nebat, who made H1121
35 Jehoahaz his s reigned in his stead. H1121
11: 1 saw that her s was dead, she arose H1121
2 took Joash the s of Ahaziah, and stole H1121
4 LORD, and shewed them the king's s. H1121
12 And he brought forth the king's s, and H1121
12:21 For Jozachar the s of Shimeath, and H1121
21 and Jehozabad the s of Shomer, his H1121
21 and Amaziah his s reigned in his stead. H1121
13: 1 year of Joash the s of Ahaziah king of H1121
1 Jehoahaz the s of Jehu began to reign H1121
2 sins of Jeroboam the s of Nebat, which H1121
3 the s of Hazael, all *their* days. H1121
9 and Joash his s reigned in his stead. H1121
10 began Jehoash the s of Jehoahaz to H1121
11 of Jeroboam the s of Nebat, who made H1121
24 Ben-hadad his s reigned in his stead. H1121
25 And Jehoash the s of Jehoahaz took H1121
25 of Ben-hadad the s of Hazael the cities, H1121
14: 1 In the second year of Joash s of H1121
1 Amaziah the s of Joash king of Judah. H1121
8 to Jehoash, the s of Jehoahaz son of H1121
8 the son of Jehoahaz s of Jehu, king of H1121
9 thy daughter to my s to wife: and there H1121

2Ki 14:13 king of Judah, the s of Jehoash the son H1121
13 the son of Jehoash the s of Ahaziah, at H1121
16 Jeroboam his s reigned in his stead. H1121
17 And Amaziah the s of Joash king of H1121
17 death of Jehoash s of Jehoahaz king of H1121
23 In the fifteenth year of Amaziah the s H1121
23 Jeroboam the s of Joash king of Israel H1121
24 the s of Nebat, who made Israel to sin. H1121
25 his servant Jonah, the s of Amittai, the H1121
27 by the hand of Jeroboam the s of Joash. H1121
29 Zachariah his s reigned in his stead. H1121
15: 1 s of Amaziah king of Judah to reign. H1121
5 Jotham the king's s *was* over the house, H1121
7 and Jotham his s reigned in his stead. H1121
8 did Zachariah the s of Jeroboam reign H1121
9 the s of Nebat, who made Israel to sin. H1121
10 And Shallum the s of Jabesh conspired H1121
13 Shallum the s of Jabesh began to reign H1121
14 For Menahem the s of Gadi went up H1121
14 and smote Shallum the s of Jabesh in H1121
17 Menahem the s of Gadi to reign over H1121
18 the s of Nebat, who made Israel to sin. H1121
22 Pekahiah his s reigned in his stead. H1121
23 Pekahiah the s of Menahem began H1121
24 the s of Nebat, who made Israel to sin. H1121
25 But Pekah the s of Remaliah, a captain H1121
27 Judah Pekah the s of Remaliah began H1121
28 the s of Nebat, who made Israel to sin. H1121
30 And Hoshea the s of Elah made a H1121
30 against Pekah the s of Remaliah, and H1121
30 year of Jotham the s of Uzziah. H1121
32 In the second year of Pekah the s of H1121
32 the s of Uzziah king of Judah to reign. H1121
37 of Syria, and Pekah the s of Remaliah. H1121
38 and Ahaz his s reigned in his stead. H1121
16: 1 In the seventeenth year of Pekah the s H1121
1 Ahaz the s of Jotham king of Judah H1121
3 yea, and made his s to pass through H1121
5 Then Rezin king of Syria and Pekah s H1121
7 servant and thy s: come up, and save H1121
20 Hezekiah his s reigned in his stead. H1121
17: 1 began Hoshea the s of Elah to reign in H1121
21 Jeroboam the s of Nebat king: and H1121
18: 1 year of Hoshea s of Elah king of Israel, H1121
1 s of Ahaz king of Judah began to reign. H1121
9 year of Hoshea s of Elah king of Israel, H1121
18 to them Eliakim the s of Hilkiah, which H1121
18 and Joah the s of Asaph the recorder. H1121
26 Then said Eliakim the s of Hilkiah, and H1121
37 Then came Eliakim the s of Hilkiah, H1121
37 and Joah the s of Asaph the recorder, H1121
19: 2 to Isaiah the prophet the s of Amoz. H1121
20 Then Isaiah the s of Amoz sent to H1121
37 Esar-haddon his s reigned in his stead. H1121
20: 1 prophet Isaiah the s of Amoz came to H1121
12 At that time Berodach-baladan, the s H1121
21 Manasseh his s reigned in his stead. H1121
21: 6 And he made his s pass through the H1121
7 to Solomon his s, In this house, and in H1121
18 and Amon his s reigned in his stead. H1121
24 made Josiah his s king in his stead. H1121
26 and Josiah his s reigned in his stead. H1121
22: 3 sent Shaphan the s of Azaliah, the son H1121
3 son of Azaliah, the s of Meshullam, the H1121
12 and Ahikam the s of Shaphan, and H1121
12 and Achbor the s of Michaiah, and H1121
14 of Shallum the s of Tikvah, the son of H1121
14 son of Tikvah, the s of Harhas, keeper H1121
23:10 might make his s or his daughter to H1121
15 Jeroboam the s of Nebat, who made H1121
30 land took Jehoahaz the s of Josiah, and H1121
34 made Eliakim the s of Josiah king in H1121
24: 6 Jehoiachin his s reigned in his stead. H1121
25:22 s of Ahikam, the son of Shaphan, ruler. H1121
22 son of Ahikam, the s of Shaphan, ruler. H1121
23 even Ishmael the s of Nethaniah, and H1121
23 and Johanan the s of Careah, and H1121
23 and Seraiah the s of Tanhumeth the H1121
23 s of a Maachathite, they and their men. H1121
25 that Ishmael the s of Nethaniah, the H1121
25 of Nethaniah, the s of Elishama, of the H1121
1Ch 1:43 of Israel; Bela the s of Beor: and the H1121
44 And when Bela was dead, Jobab the s H1121
46 was dead, Hadad the s of Bedad, which H1121
49 the s of Achbor reigned in his stead. H1121
2:18 And Caleb the s of Hezron begat H1121
45 And the s of Shammai *was* Maon: and H1121
50 These were the sons of Caleb the s of H1121
3: 2 The third, Absalom the s of Maachah H1121

1Ch 3: 2 the fourth, Adonijah the s of Haggith: H1121
10 And Solomon's s *was* Rehoboam, Abia H1121
10 his s, Asa his son, Jehoshaphat his son, H1121
10 his son, Asa his s, Jehoshaphat his son, H1121
10 his son, Asa his son, Jehoshaphat his s, H1121
11 Joram his s, Ahaziah his son, Joash his H1121
11 Joram his son, Ahaziah his s, Joash his H1121
11 his son, Ahaziah his son, Joash his s, H1121
12 Amaziah his s, Azariah his son, Jotham H1121
12 Amaziah his son, Azariah his s, Jotham H1121
12 his son, Azariah his son, Jotham his s, H1121
13 Ahaz his s, Hezekiah his son, Manasseh H1121
13 Ahaz his son, Hezekiah his s, Manasseh H1121
13 son, Hezekiah his son, Manasseh his s, H1121
14 Amon his s, Josiah his son. H1121
14 Amon his son, Josiah his s. H1121
16 Jeconiah his s, Zedekiah his son. H1121
16 Jeconiah his son, Zedekiah his s. H1121
17 sons of Jeconiah; Assir, Salathiel his s, H1121
4: 2 And Reaiah the s of Shobal begat H1121
8 the families of Aharhel the s of Harum. H1121
15 And the sons of Caleb the s of H1121
21 The sons of Shelah the s of Judah *were,* H1121
25 Shallum his s, Mibsam his son, Mishma H1121
25 Shallum his son, Mibsam his s, Mishma H1121
25 his son, Mibsam his son, Mishma his s. H1121
26 And the sons of Mishma; Hamuel his s, H1121
26 his son, Zacchur his s, Shimei his son. H1121
26 his son, Zacchur his son, Shimei his s. H1121
34 Jamlech, and Joshah the s of Amaziah, H1121
35 And Joel, and Jehu the s of Josibiah, the H1121
35 the s of Seraiah, the son of Asiel, H1121
35 the son of Seraiah, the s of Asiel, H1121
37 And Ziza the s of Shiphi, the son of H1121
37 And Ziza the son of Shiphi, the s of H1121
37 son of Allon, the s of Jedaiah, the son of H1121
37 the s of Shimri, the son of Shemaiah; H1121
37 the son of Shimri, the s of Shemaiah; H1121
5: 1 sons of Joseph the s of Israel: and the H1121
4 The sons of Joel; Shemaiah his s, Gog H1121
4 his son, Gog his s, Shimei his son, H1121
4 his son, Gog his son, Shimei his s, H1121
5 Micah his s, Reaia his son, Baal his son, H1121
5 Micah his son, Reaia his s, Baal his son, H1121
5 Micah his son, Reaia his son, Baal his s, H1121
6 Beerah his s, whom Tilgath-pilneser H1121
8 And Bela the s of Azaz, the son of H1121
8 And Bela the son of Azaz, the s of H1121
8 son of Shema, the s of Joel, who dwelt H1121
14 These *are* the children of Abihail the s H1121
14 son of Huri, the s of Jaroah, the son of H1121
14 son of Jaroah, the s of Gilead, the son H1121
14 son of Gilead, the s of Michael, the son H1121
14 of Michael, the s of Jeshishai, the son H1121
14 the s of Jahdo, the son of Buz; H1121
14 the son of Jahdo, the s of Buz; H1121
15 Ahi the s of Abdiel, the son of Guni, H1121
15 Ahi the son of Abdiel, the s of Guni, H1121
6:20 Of Gershom; Libni his s, Jahath his son, H1121
20 Of Gershom; Libni his son, Jahath his s, H1121
20 his son, Jahath his son, Zimmah his s, H1121
21 Joah his s, Iddo his son, Zerah his son, H1121
21 Joah his son, Iddo his s, Zerah his son, H1121
21 Joah his son, Iddo his son, Zerah his s, H1121
21 his son, Zerah his son, Jeaterai his s. H1121
22 The sons of Kohath; Amminadab his s, H1121
22 his son, Korah his s, Assir his son, H1121
22 his son, Korah his son, Assir his s, H1121
23 Elkanah his s, and Ebiasaph his son, H1121
23 Elkanah his son, and Ebiasaph his s, H1121
23 and Ebiasaph his son, and Assir his s, H1121
24 Tahath his s, Uriel his son, Uzziah his H1121
24 Tahath his son, Uriel his s, Uzziah his H1121
24 his son, Uzziah his s, and Shaul his son. H1121
24 his son, Uzziah his son, and Shaul his s. H1121
26 Zophai his s, and Nahath his son, H1121
26 Zophai his son, and Nahath his s, H1121
27 Eliab his s, Jeroham his son, Elkanah H1121
27 Eliab his son, Jeroham his s, Elkanah H1121
27 his son, Jeroham his son, Elkanah his s. H1121
29 The sons of Merari; Mahli, Libni his s, H1121
29 his son, Shimei his s, Uzza his son, H1121
29 his son, Shimei his son, Uzza his s, H1121
30 Shimea his s, Haggiah his son, Asaiah H1121
30 Shimea his son, Haggiah his s, Asaiah H1121
30 his son, Haggiah his son, Asaiah his s. H1121
33 singer, the s of Joel, the son of Shemuel, H1121
33 singer, the son of Joel, the s of Shemuel, H1121
34 The s of Elkanah, the son of Jeroham, H1121

1Ch 6:34 The son of Elkanah, the s of Jeroham, H1121
34 Jeroham, the s of Eliel, the son of Toah, H1121
34 Jeroham, the son of Eliel, the s of Toah, H1121
35 The s of Zuph, the son of Elkanah, the H1121
35 The son of Zuph, the s of Elkanah, the H1121
35 the s of Mahath, the son of Amasai, H1121
35 the son of Mahath, the s of Amasai, H1121
36 The s of Elkanah, the son of Joel, the H1121
36 The son of Elkanah, the s of Joel, the H1121
36 the s of Azariah, the son of Zephaniah, H1121
36 the son of Azariah, the s of Zephaniah, H1121
37 The s of Tahath, the son of Assir, the H1121
37 The son of Tahath, the s of Assir, the H1121
37 the s of Ebiasaph, the son of Korah, H1121
37 the son of Ebiasaph, the s of Korah, H1121
38 The s of Izhar, the son of Kohath, the H1121
38 The son of Izhar, the s of Kohath, the H1121
38 Kohath, the s of Levi, the son of Israel. H1121
38 Kohath, the son of Levi, the s of Israel. H1121
39 the s of Berachiah, the son of Shimea, H1121
39 the son of Berachiah, the s of Shimea, H1121
40 The s of Michael, the son of Baaseiah, H1121
40 The son of Michael, the s of Baaseiah, H1121
40 the son of Baaseiah, the s of Malchiah, H1121
41 The s of Ethni, the son of Zerah, the H1121
41 The son of Ethni, the s of Zerah, the H1121
41 the son of Zerah, the s of Adaiah, H1121
42 The s of Ethan, the son of Zimmah, the H1121
42 The son of Ethan, the s of Zimmah, the H1121
42 the son of Zimmah, the s of Shimei, H1121
43 The s of Jahath, the son of Gershom, H1121
43 The son of Jahath, the s of Gershom, H1121
43 the son of Gershom, the s of Levi. H1121
44 hand: Ethan the s of Kishi, the son of H1121
44 Kishi, the s of Abdi, the son of Malluch, H1121
44 Kishi, the son of Abdi, the s of Malluch, H1121
45 The s of Hashabiah, the son of H1121
45 The son of Hashabiah, the s of H1121
45 the son of Amaziah, the s of Hilkiah, H1121
46 The s of Amzi, the son of Bani, the son H1121
46 The son of Amzi, the s of Bani, the son H1121
46 The son of Amzi, the son of Bani, the s H1121
47 The s of Mahli, the son of Mushi, the H1121
47 The son of Mahli, the s of Mushi, the H1121
47 Mushi, the s of Merari, the son of Levi. H1121
47 Mushi, the son of Merari, the s of Levi. H1121
50 s, Phinehas his son, Abishua his son, H1121
50 son, Phinehas his s, Abishua his son, H1121
50 son, Phinehas his son, Abishua his s, H1121
51 Bukki his s, Uzzi his son, Zerahiah his H1121
51 Bukki his son, Uzzi his s, Zerahiah his H1121
51 his son, Uzzi his son, Zerahiah his s, H1121
52 Meraioth his s, Amariah his son, H1121
52 Meraioth his son, Amariah his s, H1121
52 his son, Amariah his son, Ahitub his s, H1121
53 Zadok his s, Ahimaaz his son. H1121
53 Zadok his son, Ahimaaz his s. H1121
56 they gave to Caleb the s of Jephunneh. H1121
7:16 of Machir bare a s, and she called his H1121
17 the s of Machir, the son of Manasseh. H1121
17 the son of Machir, the s of Manasseh. H1121
20 and Bered his s, and Tahath his son, H1121
20 and Tahath his s, and Eladah his son, H1121
20 and Eladah his s, and Tahath his son, H1121
20 and Eladah his son, and Tahath his s, H1121
21 And Zabad his s, and Shuthelah his H1121
21 son, and Shuthelah his s, and Ezer, and H1121
23 and bare a s, and he called his name H1121
25 And Rephah *was* his s, also Resheph, H1121
25 and Telah his s, and Tahan his son, H1121
25 and Telah his son, and Tahan his s, H1121
26 Laadan his s, Ammihud his son, H1121
26 Laadan his son, Ammihud his s, H1121
26 son, Ammihud his son, Elishama his s, H1121
27 Non his s, Jehoshua his son. H1121
27 Non his son, Jehoshua his s. H1121
29 the children of Joseph the s of Israel. H1121
8:30 And his firstborn s Abdon, and Zur, H1121
34 And the s of Jonathan *was* Merib-baal; H1121
37 *was* his s, Eleasah his son, Azel his son: H1121
37 *was* his son, Eleasah his s, Azel his son: H1121
37 *was* his son, Eleasah his son, Azel his s: H1121
9: 4 Uthai the s of Ammihud, the son of H1121
4 Uthai the son of Ammihud, the s of H1121
4 son of Omri, the s of Imri, the son of H1121
4 the son of Imri, the s of Bani, of the H1121
4 of the children of Pharez the s of Judah. H1121
7 Sallu the s of Meshullam, the son H1121
7 s of Hodaviah, the son of Hasenuah, H1121

1Ch 9: 7 son of Hodaviah, the s of Hasenuah, H1121
8 And Ibneiah the s of Jeroham, and H1121
8 and Elah the s of Uzzi, the son of H1121
8 the son of Uzzi, the s of Michri, and H1121
8 Meshullam the s of Shephathiah, the H1121
8 the s of Reuel, the son of Ibnijah; H1121
8 the son of Reuel, the s of Ibnijah; H1121
11 And Azariah the s of Hilkiah, the son of H1121
11 And Azariah the son of Hilkiah, the s of H1121
11 of Meshullam, the s of Zadok, the son H1121
11 the son of Zadok, the s of Meraioth, the H1121
11 of Meraioth, the s of Ahitub, the ruler H1121
12 And Adaiah the s of Jeroham, the son H1121
12 And Adaiah the son of Jeroham, the s H1121
12 son of Pashur, the s of Malchijah, and H1121
12 and Maasiai the s of Adiel, the son of H1121
12 son of Adiel, the s of Jahzerah, the son H1121
12 of Jahzerah, the s of Meshullam, the H1121
12 s of Meshillemith, the son of Immer; H1121
12 son of Meshillemith, the s of Immer; H1121
14 And of the Levites; Shemaiah the s of H1121
14 of Hasshub, the s of Azrikam, the son H1121
14 s of Hashabiah, of the sons of Merari; H1121
15 Mattaniah the s of Micah, the son of H1121
15 the s of Zichri, the son of Asaph; H1121
15 the son of Zichri, the s of Asaph; H1121
16 And Obadiah the s of Shemaiah, the H1121
16 of Shemaiah, the s of Galal, the son of H1121
16 the son of Galal, the s of Jeduthun, and H1121
16 and Berechiah the s of Asa, the son of H1121
16 the son of Asa, the s of Elkanah, that H1121
19 And Shallum the s of Kore, the son of H1121
19 And Shallum the son of Kore, the s of H1121
19 of Ebiasaph, the s of Korah, and his H1121
20 And Phinehas the s of Eleazar was the H1121
21 *And* Zechariah the s of Meshelemiah H1121
36 And his firstborn s Abdon, then Zur, H1121
40 And the s of Jonathan *was* Merib-baal: H1121
43 his s, Eleasah his son, Azel his son. H1121
43 his son, Eleasah his s, Azel his son. H1121
43 his son, Eleasah his son, Azel his s. H1121
10:14 the kingdom unto David the s of Jesse. H1121
11: 6 So Joab the s of Zeruiah went first H1121
12 And after him *was* Eleazar the s of H1121
22 Benaiah the s of Jehoiada, the son of a H1121
22 Benaiah the son of Jehoiada, the s of a H1121
24 These *things* did Benaiah the s of H1121
26 Elhanan the s of Dodo of Beth-lehem, H1121
28 Ira the s of Ikkesh the Tekoite, Abi-ezer H1121
30 Maharai the Netophathite, Heled the s H1121
31 Ithai the s of Ribai of Gibeah, *that* H1121
34 Jonathan the s of Shage the Hararite, H1121
35 Ahiam the s of Sacar the Hararite, H1121
35 Sacar the Hararite, Eliphal the s of Ur, H1121
37 Hezro the Carmelite, Naarai the s of H1121
38 of Nathan, Mibhar the s of Haggeri, H1121
39 armourbearer of Joab the s of Zeruiah, H1121
41 Uriah the Hittite, Zabad the s of Ahlai, H1121
42 Adina the s of Shiza the Reubenite, a H1121
43 Hanan the s of Maachah, and H1121
45 Jediael the s of Shimri, and Joha his H1121
12: 1 of Saul the s of Kish: and they *were* H1121
18 and on thy side, thou s of Jesse: peace, H1121
15:17 So the Levites appointed Heman the s H1121
17 Asaph the s of Berechiah; and of H1121
17 brethren, Ethan the s of Kushaiah; H1121
16:38 s of Jeduthun and Hosah *to be* porters: H1121
17:13 I will be his father, and he shall be my s: H1121
18:10 He sent Hadoram his s to king David, H1121
12 Moreover Abishai the s of Zeruiah slew H1121
15 And Joab the s of Zeruiah *was* over the H1121
15 Jehoshaphat the s of Ahilud, recorder. H1121
16 And Zadok the s of Ahitub, and H1121
16 Abimelech the s of Abiathar, *were* the H1121
17 And Benaiah the s of Jehoiada *was* H1121
19: 1 died, and his s reigned in his stead. H1121
2 unto Hanun the s of Nahash, because H1121
20: 5 and Elhanan the s of Jair slew Lahmi H1121
6 *foot:* and he also was the s of the giant. H3205
7 s of Shimea David's brother slew him. H1121
22: 5 And David said, Solomon my s *is* H1121
6 Then he called for Solomon his s, and H1121
7 And David said to Solomon, My s, as H1121
9 Behold, a s shall be born to thee, who H1121
10 and he shall be my s, and I *will be* his H1121
11 Now, my s, the LORD be with thee; and H1121
17 of Israel to help Solomon his s, *saying,* H1121
23: 1 made Solomon his s king over Israel. H1121
24: 6 And Shemaiah the s of Nethaneel the H1121

1Ch 24: 6 and Ahimelech the s of Abiathar, and H1121
29 Concerning Kish: the s of Kish *was* H1121
26: 1 the s of Kore, of the sons of Asaph. H1121
6 Also unto Shemaiah his s were sons H1121
14 for Zechariah his s, a wise counsellor, H1121
24 And Shebuel the s of Gershom, the son H1121
24 And Shebuel the son of Gershom, the s H1121
25 Rehabiah his s, and Jeshaiah his son, H1121
25 and Jeshaiah his s, and Joram his son, H1121
25 and Joram his s, and Zichri his son, and H1121
25 and Zichri his s, and Shelomith his son. H1121
25 and Zichri his son, and Shelomith his s. H1121
28 seer, and Saul the s of Kish, and Abner H1121
28 and Abner the s of Ner, and Joab the H1121
28 of Ner, and Joab the s of Zeruiah, had H1121
27: 2 Jashobeam the s of Zabdiel: and in his H1121
5 *was* Benaiah the s of Jehoiada, a chief H1121
6 in his course *was* Ammizabad his s. H1121
7 and Zebadiah his s after him: and in H1121
9 sixth month *was* Ira the s of Ikkesh the H1121
16 *was* Eliezer the s of Zichri: of the H1121
16 Shephatiah the s of Maachah: H1121
17 Of the Levites, Hashabiah the s of H1121
18 of Issachar, Omri the s of Michael: H1121
19 Of Zebulun, Ishmaiah the s of Obadiah: H1121
19 of Naphtali, Jerimoth the s of Azriel: H1121
20 Hoshea the s of Azaziah: of the half H1121
20 of Manasseh, Joel the s of Pedaiah: H1121
21 in Gilead, Iddo the s of Zechariah: of H1121
21 of Benjamin, Jaasiel the s of Abner: H1121
22 Of Dan, Azareel the s of Jeroham. H1121
24 Joab the s of Zeruiah began to number, H1121
25 *was* Azmaveth the s of Adiel: and over H1121
25 *was* Jehonathan the s of Uzziah: H1121
26 of the ground *was* Ezri the s of Chelub: H1121
29 the valleys *was* Shaphat the s of Adlai: H1121
32 and Jehiel the s of Hachmoni *was* with H1121
34 *was* Jehoiada the s of Benaiah, and H1121
28: 5 Solomon my s to sit upon the throne H1121
6 And he said unto me, Solomon thy s, he H1121
6 him *to be* my s, and I will be his father. H1121
9 And thou, Solomon my s, know thou H1121
11 Then David gave to Solomon his s the H1121
20 And David said to Solomon his s, Be H1121
29: 1 Solomon my s, whom alone God hath H1121
19 And give unto Solomon my s a perfect H1121
22 Solomon the s of David king the second H1121
26 Thus David the s of Jesse reigned over H1121
28 and Solomon his s reigned in his stead. H1121
2Ch 1: 1 And Solomon the s of David was H1121
5 that Bezaleel the s of Uri, the son of H1121
5 the son of Uri, the s of Hur, had made, H1121
2:12 the king a wise s, endued with prudence H1121
14 The s of a woman of the daughters of H1121
6: 9 the house; but thy s which shall come H1121
9:29 seer against Jeroboam the s of Nebat? H1121
31 Rehoboam his s reigned in his stead. H1121
10: 2 Jeroboam the s of Nebat, who *was* in H1121
15 Shilonite to Jeroboam the s of Nebat. H1121
16 inheritance in the s of Jesse: every man H1121
11: 3 Speak unto Rehoboam the s of H1121
17 Rehoboam the s of Solomon strong, H1121
18 of Jerimoth the s of David to wife, *and* H1121
18 the daughter of Eliab the s of Jesse; H1121
22 And Rehoboam made Abijah the s of H1121
12:16 and Abijah his s reigned in his stead. H1121
13: 6 Yet Jeroboam the s of Nebat, the H1121
6 of Solomon the s of David, is risen up, H1121
7 Rehoboam the s of Solomon, when H1121
14: 1 and Asa his s reigned in his stead. H1121
15: 1 God came upon Azariah the s of Oded: H1121
17: 1 And Jehoshaphat his s reigned in his H1121
16 And next him *was* Amasiah the s of H1121
18: 7 same *is* Micaiah the s of Imla. And H1121
8 Fetch quickly Micaiah the s of Imla. H1121
10 And Zedekiah the s of Chenaanah had H1121
23 Then Zedekiah the s of Chenaanah H1121
25 of the city, and to Joash the king's s; H1121
19: 2 And Jehu the s of Hanani the seer went H1121
11 and Zebadiah the s of Ishmael, the H1121
20:14 Then upon Jahaziel the s of Zechariah, H1121
14 of Zechariah, the s of Benaiah, the son H1121
14 son of Benaiah, the s of Jeiel, the son of H1121
14 son of Jeiel, the s of Mattaniah, a Levite H1121
34 book of Jehu the s of Hanani, who *is* H1121
37 Then Eliezer the s of Dodavah of H1121
21: 1 And Jehoram his s reigned in his stead. H1121
17 that there was never a s left him, save H1121
22: 1 his youngest s king in his stead: for H1121

2Ch 22: 1 the s of Jehoram king of Judah reigned. H1121
5 with Jehoram the s of Ahab king of H1121
6 And Azariah the s of Jehoram king of H1121
6 to see Jehoram the s of Ahab at Jezreel, H1121
7 against Jehu the s of Nimshi, whom the H1121
9 said they, he *is* the s of Jehoshaphat, H1121
10 saw that her s was dead, she arose H1121
11 took Joash the s of Ahaziah, and stole H1121
23: 1 Azariah the s of Jeroham, and Ishmael H1121
1 and Ishmael the s of Jehohanan, and H1121
1 and Azariah the s of Obed, and H1121
1 and Maaseiah the s of Adaiah, and H1121
1 the s of Zichri, into covenant with him. H1121
3 Behold, the king's s shall reign, as the H1121
11 Then they brought out the king's s, and H1121
24:20 Zechariah the s of Jehoiada the priest, H1121
22 him, but slew his s. And when he died, H1121
26 him; Zabad the s of Shimeath an H1121
26 the s of Shimrith a Moabitess. H1121
27 Amaziah his s reigned in his stead. H1121
25:17 sent to Joash, the s of Jehoahaz, the son H1121
17 son of Jehoahaz, the s of Jehu, king of H1121
18 thy daughter to my s to wife: and there H1121
23 king of Judah, the s of Joash, the son of H1121
23 the son of Joash, the s of Jehoahaz, at H1121
25 And Amaziah the s of Joash king of H1121
25 the death of Joash s of Jehoahaz king of H1121
26:21 and Jotham his s *was* over the king's H1121
22 the prophet, the s of Amoz, write. H1121
23 and Jotham his s reigned in his stead. H1121
27: 9 and Ahaz his s reigned in his stead. H1121
28: 3 in the valley of the s of Hinnom, and H1121
6 For Pekah the s of Remaliah slew in H1121
7 the king's s, and Azrikam the governor H1121
12 Azariah the s of Johanan, Berechiah H1121
12 Berechiah the s of Meshillemoth, and H1121
12 and Jehizkiah the s of Shallum, and H1121
12 and Amasa the s of Hadlai, stood up H1121
27 Hezekiah his s reigned in his stead. H1121
29:12 Then the Levites arose, Mahath the s of H1121
12 and Joel the s of Azariah, of the sons H1121
12 Merari, Kish the s of Abdi, and Azariah H1121
12 and Azariah the s of Jehalelel: and of H1121
12 s of Zimmah, and Eden the son of Joah: H1121
12 son of Zimmah, and Eden the s of Joah: H1121
30:26 of Solomon the s of David king of Israel H1121
31:14 And Kore the s of Imnah the Levite, the H1121
32:20 s of Amoz, prayed and cried to heaven. H1121
32 the prophet, the s of Amoz, *and* in the H1121
33 Manasseh his s reigned in his stead. H1121
33: 6 in the valley of the s of Hinnom: also he H1121
7 to Solomon his s, In this house, and in H1121
20 and Amon his s reigned in his stead. H1121
25 made Josiah his s king in his stead. H1121
34: 8 he sent Shaphan the s of Azaliah, and H1121
8 the city, and Joah the s of Joahaz the H1121
20 and Ahikam the s of Shaphan, and H1121
20 and Abdon the s of Micah, and H1121
22 of Shallum the s of Tikvath, the son H1121
22 of Tikvath, the s of Hasrah, keeper of H1121
35: 3 Solomon the s of David king of Israel H1121
4 to the writing of Solomon his s. H1121
36: 1 land took Jehoahaz the s of Josiah, and H1121
8 Jehoiachin his s reigned in his stead. H1121
Ezr 3: 2 Then stood up Jeshua the s of Jozadak, H1121
2 Zerubbabel the s of Shealtiel, and his H1121
8 Zerubbabel the s of Shealtiel, and H1121
8 and Jeshua the s of Jozadak, and the H1121
5: 1 prophet, and Zechariah the s of Iddo, H1247
2 Then rose up Zerubbabel the s of H1247
2 and Jeshua the s of Jozadak, and began H1247
6:14 and Zechariah the s of Iddo. And they H1247
7: 1 of Persia, Ezra the s of Seraiah, the son H1121
1 the s of Azariah, the son of Hilkiah, H1121
1 the son of Azariah, the s of Hilkiah, H1121
2 The s of Shallum, the son of Zadok, the H1121
2 The son of Shallum, the s of Zadok, the H1121
2 the son of Zadok, the s of Ahitub, H1121
3 The s of Amariah, the son of Azariah, H1121
3 The son of Amariah, the s of Azariah, H1121
3 the son of Azariah, the s of Meraioth, H1121
4 The s of Zerahiah, the son of Uzzi, the H1121
4 The son of Zerahiah, the s of Uzzi, the H1121
4 the son of Uzzi, the s of Bukki, H1121
5 The s of Abishua, the son of Phinehas, H1121
5 The son of Abishua, the s of Phinehas, H1121
5 of Phinehas, the s of Eleazar, the son of H1121
5 Eleazar, the s of Aaron the chief priest: H1121
8: 4 Elihoenai the s of Zerahiah, and with H1121

Ezr 8: 5 Of the sons of Shechaniah; the s of H1121
6 Of the sons also of Adin; Ebed the s of H1121
7 And of the sons of Elam; Jeshaiah the s H1121
8 Zebadiah the s of Michael, and with H1121
9 Of the sons of Joab; Obadiah the s of H1121
10 And of the sons of Shelomith; the s of H1121
11 Zechariah the s of Bebai, and with him H1121
12 Johanan the s of Hakkatan, and with H1121
18 sons of Mahli, the s of Levi, the son of H1121
18 the son of Levi, the s of Israel; and H1121
33 of Meremoth the s of Uriah the priest; H1121
33 him *was* Eleazar the s of Phinehas; and H1121
33 them *was* Jozabad the s of Jeshua, and H1121
33 and Noadiah the s of Binnui, Levites; H1121
10: 2 And Shechaniah the s of Jehiel, *one* of H1121
6 of Johanan the s of Eliashib: and *when* H1121
15 Only Jonathan the s of Asahel and H1121
15 and Jahaziah the s of Tikvah were H1121
18 sons of Jeshua the s of Jozadak, and his H1121
Neh 1: 1 The words of Nehemiah the s of H1121
3: 2 to them builded Zaccur the s of Imri. H1121
4 Meremoth the s of Urijah, the son of H1121
4 son of Urijah, the s of Koz. And next H1121
4 Meshullam the s of Berechiah, the son H1121
4 son of Berechiah, the s of Meshezabeel. H1121
4 them repaired Zadok the s of Baana. H1121
6 repaired Jehoiada the s of Paseah, and H1121
6 Meshullam the s of Besodeiah; they H1121
8 Next unto him repaired Uzziel the s of H1121
8 repaired Hananiah the s of *one of* the H1121
9 Rephaiah the s of Hur, the ruler of the H1121
10 Jedaiah the s of Harumaph, even H1121
10 repaired Hattush the s of Hashabniah. H1121
11 Malchijah the s of Harim, and Hashub H1121
11 and Hashub the s of Pahath-moab, H1121
12 Shallum the s of Halohesh, the ruler H1121
14 Malchiah the s of Rechab, the ruler H1121
15 Shallun the s of Col-hozeh, the ruler H1121
16 After him repaired Nehemiah the s of H1121
17 Rehum the s of Bani. Next unto him H1121
18 Bavai the s of Henadad, the ruler H1121
19 And next to him repaired Ezer the s of H1121
20 After him Baruch the s of Zabbai H1121
21 After him repaired Meremoth the s of H1121
21 the son of Urijah the s of Koz another H1121
23 Azariah the s of Maaseiah the son H1121
23 the s of Ananiah by his house. H1121
24 After him repaired Binnui the s of H1121
25 Palal the s of Uzai, over against the H1121
25 After him Pedaiah the s of Parosh. H1121
29 After them repaired Zadok the s of H1121
29 also Shemaiah the s of Shechaniah, the H1121
30 After him repaired Hananiah the s of H1121
30 Hanun the sixth s of Zalaph, another H1121
30 Meshullam the s of Berechiah over H1121
31 the goldsmith's s unto the place of the H1121
6:10 of Shemaiah the s of Delaiah the son of H1121
10 the son of Delaiah the s of Mehetabeel, H1121
18 he *was* the s in law of Shechaniah H2860
18 of Shechaniah the s of Arah; and his H1121
18 of Arah; and his s Johanan had taken H1121
18 of Meshullam the s of Berechiah. H1121
8:17 days of Jeshua the s of Nun unto that H1121
10: 1 the s of Hachaliah, and Zidkijah, H1121
9 And the Levites: both Jeshua the s of H1121
38 And the priest the s of Aaron shall be H1121
11: 4 Athaiah the s of Uzziah, the son of H1121
4 son of Uzziah, the s of Zechariah, the H1121
4 of Zechariah, the s of Amariah, the son H1121
4 of Amariah, the s of Shephatiah, the H1121
4 of Shephatiah, the s of Mahalaleel, of H1121
5 And Maaseiah the s of Baruch, the son H1121
5 And Maaseiah the son of Baruch, the s H1121
5 of Col-hozeh, the s of Hazaiah, the son H1121
5 of Hazaiah, the s of Adaiah, the son of H1121
5 son of Adaiah, the s of Joiarib, the son H1121
5 the s of Zechariah, the son of Shiloni. H1121
5 the son of Zechariah, the s of Shiloni. H1121
7 Sallu the s of Meshullam, the son H1121
7 of Meshullam, the s of Joed, the son of H1121
7 son of Joed, the s of Pedaiah, the son H1121
7 of Pedaiah, the s of Kolaiah, the son H1121
7 of Kolaiah, the s of Maaseiah, the son H1121
7 the s of Ithiel, the son of Jesaiah. H1121
7 the son of Ithiel, the s of Jesaiah. H1121
9 And Joel the s of Zichri *was* their H1121
9 s of Senuah *was* second over the city. H1121
10 Of the priests: Jedaiah the s of Joiarib, H1121
11 Seraiah the s of Hilkiah, the son of H1121

Neh 11:11 Seraiah the son of Hilkiah, the s of H1121
11 of Meshullam, the s of Zadok, the son H1121
11 the son of Zadok, the s of Meraioth, the H1121
11 of Meraioth, the s of Ahitub, *was* the H1121
12 and Adaiah the s of Jeroham, the son H1121
12 of Jeroham, the s of Pelaliah, the son H1121
12 of Pelaliah, the s of Amzi, the son of H1121
12 son of Amzi, the s of Zechariah, the son H1121
12 the s of Pashur, the son of Malchiah, H1121
12 the son of Pashur, the s of Malchiah, H1121
13 and Amashai the s of Azareel, the son H1121
13 son of Azareel, the s of Ahasai, the son H1121
13 s of Meshillemoth, the son of Immer, H1121
13 son of Meshillemoth, the s of Immer, H1121
14 Zabdiel, the s of *one of* the great men. H1121
15 Also of the Levites: Shemaiah the s of H1121
15 of Hashub, the s of Azrikam, the son H1121
15 the s of Hashabiah, the son of Bunni; H1121
15 the son of Hashabiah, the s of Bunni; H1121
17 And Mattaniah the s of Micha, the son H1121
17 And Mattaniah the son of Micha, the s H1121
17 son of Zabdi, the s of Asaph, *was* the H1121
17 and Abda the s of Shammua, the son H1121
17 the s of Galal, the son of Jeduthun. H1121
17 the son of Galal, the s of Jeduthun. H1121
22 *was* Uzzi the s of Bani, the son of H1121
22 the son of Bani, the s of Hashabiah, the H1121
22 of Hashabiah, the s of Mattaniah, the H1121
22 of Mattaniah, the s of Micha. Of the H1121
24 And Pethahiah the s of Meshezabeel, of H1121
24 of Zerah the s of Judah, *was* at the H1121
12: 1 with Zerubbabel the s of Shealtiel, and H1121
23 the days of Johanan the s of Eliashib. H1121
24 and Jeshua the s of Kadmiel, with their H1121
26 These *were* in the days of Joiakim the s H1121
26 son of Jeshua, the s of Jozadak, and in H1121
35 Zechariah the s of Jonathan, the son H1121
35 of Jonathan, the s of Shemaiah, the son H1121
35 of Shemaiah, the s of Mattaniah, the H1121
35 of Mattaniah, the s of Michaiah, the H1121
35 the s of Zaccur, the son of Asaph: H1121
35 the son of Zaccur, the s of Asaph: H1121
45 of David, *and* of Solomon his s. H1121
13:13 *was* Hanan the s of Zaccur, the son of H1121
13 son of Zaccur, the s of Mattaniah: for H1121
28 And *one* of the sons of Joiada, the s of H1121
28 high priest, *was* s in law to Sanballat H2860
Est 2: 5 *was* Mordecai, the s of Jair, the son of H1121
5 the son of Jair, the s of Shimei, the son H1121
5 of Shimei, the s of Kish, a Benjamite; H1121
3: 1 Haman the s of Hammedatha the H1121
10 it unto Haman the s of Hammedatha H1121
8: 5 by Haman the s of Hammedatha the H1121
9:10 The ten sons of Haman the s of H1121
24 Because Haman the s of Hammedatha, H1121
Job 18:19 He shall neither have s nor nephew H5209
25: 6 and the s of man, *which is* a worm? H1121
32: 2 the wrath of Elihu the s of Barachel the H1121
6 And Elihu the s of Barachel the Buzite H1121
35: 8 righteousness *may profit* the s of man. H1121
Ps 2: 7 *art* my S; this day have I begotten thee. H1121
12 Kiss the S, lest he be angry, and ye H1248
3:ttl when he fled from Absalom his s. H1121
8: 4 the s of man, that thou visitest him? H1121
50:20 thou slanderest thine own mother's s. H1121
72: 1 and thy righteousness unto the king's s. H1121
20 The prayers of David the s of Jesse are H1121
80:17 hand, upon the s of man *whom* thou H1121
86:16 and save the s of thine handmaid. H1121
89:22 nor the s of wickedness afflict him. H1121
116:16 servant, *and* the s of thine handmaid: H1121
144: 3 of him! *or* the s of man, that thou H1121
146: 3 the s of man, in whom *there is* no help. H1121
Prv 1: 1 The proverbs of Solomon the s of H1121
8 My s, hear the instruction of thy father, H1121
10 My s, if sinners entice thee, consent H1121
15 My s, walk not thou in the way with H1121
2: 1 My s, if thou wilt receive my words, and H1121
3: 1 My s, forget not my law; but let thine H1121
11 My s, despise not the chastening of the H1121
12 as a father the s *in whom* he delighteth. H1121
21 My s, let not them depart from thine H1121
4: 3 For I was my father's s, tender and only H1121
10 Hear, O my s, and receive my sayings; H1121
20 My s, attend to my words; incline thine H1121
5: 1 My s, attend unto my wisdom, *and* bow H1121
20 And why wilt thou, my s, be ravished H1121
6: 1 My s, if thou be surety for thy friend, *if* H1121
3 Do this now, my s, and deliver thyself, H1121

Prv 6:20 My s, keep thy father's commandment, H1121
7: 1 My s, keep my words, and lay up my H1121
10: 1 The proverbs of Solomon. A wise s H1121
1 foolish s *is* the heaviness of his mother. H1121
5 summer *is* a wise s: *but* he that sleepeth H1121
5 in harvest *is* a s that causeth shame. H1121
13: 1 A wise s *heareth* his father's H1121
24 He that spareth his rod hateth his s: but H1121
15:20 A wise s maketh a glad father: but a H1121
17: 2 A wise servant shall have rule over a s H1121
25 A foolish s *is* a grief to his father, and H1121
19:13 A foolish s *is* the calamity of his father: H1121
18 Chasten thy s while there is hope, and H1121
26 *his* mother, *is* a s that causeth shame, H1121
27 Cease, my s, to hear the instruction *that* H1121
23:15 My s, if thine heart be wise, my heart H1121
19 Hear thou, my s, and be wise, and guide H1121
26 My s, give me thine heart, and let thine H1121
24:13 My s, eat thou honey, because *it is* H1121
21 My s, fear thou the LORD and the king: H1121
27:11 My s, be wise, and make my heart glad, H1121
28: 7 Whoso keepeth the law *is* a wise s: but H1121
29:17 Correct thy s, and he shall give thee H1121
21 have him become *his* s at the length. H4497
30: 1 The words of Agur the s of Jakeh, *even* H1121
31: 2 What, my s? and what, the son of my H1248
2 What, my son? and what, the s of my H1248
2 my womb? and what, the s of my vows? H1248
Ecc 1: 1 The words of the Preacher, the s of H1121
5:14 a s, and *there is* nothing in his hand. H1121
10:17 thy king *is* the s of nobles, and thy H1121
12:12 And further, by these, my s, be H1121
Isa 1: 1 The vision of Isaiah the s of Amoz, H1121
2: 1 The word that Isaiah the s of Amoz H1121
7: 1 days of Ahaz the s of Jotham, the son of H1121
1 son of Jotham, the s of Uzziah, king of H1121
1 and Pekah the s of Remaliah, king of H1121
3 Shear-jashub thy s, at the end of the H1121
4 with Syria, and of the s of Remaliah. H1121
5 Because Syria, Ephraim, and the s of H1121
6 in the midst of it, *even* the s of Tabeal: H1121
9 *is* Remaliah's s. If ye will not believe, H1121
14 a s, and shall call his name Immanuel. H1121
8: 2 and Zechariah the s of Jeberechiah. H1121
3 and bare a s. Then said the LORD H1121
6 and rejoice in Rezin and Remaliah's s; H1121
9: 6 For unto us a child is born, unto us a s H1121
13: 1 which Isaiah the s of Amoz did see. H1121
14:12 heaven, O Lucifer, s of the morning! H1121
22 and s, and nephew, saith the LORD. H5209
19:11 s of the wise, the son of ancient kings? H1121
11 son of the wise, the s of ancient kings? H1121
20: 2 by Isaiah the s of Amoz, saying, Go H1121
22:20 my servant Eliakim the s of Hilkiah: H1121
36: 3 Eliakim, Hilkiah's s, which was over the H1121
3 and Joah, Asaph's s, the recorder. H1121
22 Then came Eliakim, the s of Hilkiah, H1121
22 and Joah, the s of Asaph, the recorder, H1121
37: 2 unto Isaiah the prophet the s of Amoz. H1121
21 Then Isaiah the s of Amoz sent unto H1121
38 Esar-haddon his s reigned in his stead. H1121
38: 1 the prophet the s of Amoz came unto H1121
39: 1 At that time Merodach-baladan, the s H1121
49:15 on the s of her womb? yea, they H1121
51:12 s of man *which* shall be made *as* grass; H1121
56: 2 doeth this, and the s of man *that* layeth H1121
3 Neither let the s of the stranger, that H1121
Jer 1: 1 The words of Jeremiah the s of Hilkiah, H1121
2 days of Josiah the s of Amon king of H1121
3 of Jehoiakim the s of Josiah king of H1121
3 year of Zedekiah the s of Josiah king of H1121
6:26 mourning, *as for* an only s, most bitter H3173
7:31 *is* in the valley of the s of Hinnom, to H1121
32 the valley of the s of Hinnom, but the H1121
15: 4 of Manasseh the s of Hezekiah king of H1121
19: 2 And go forth unto the valley of the s of H1121
6 The valley of the s of Hinnom, but The H1121
20: 1 Now Pashur the s of Immer the priest, H1121
21: 1 him Pashur the s of Melchiah, and H1121
1 the s of Maaseiah the priest, saying, H1121
22:11 Shallum the s of Josiah king of Judah, H1121
18 Jehoiakim the s of Josiah king of Judah; H1121
24 though Coniah the s of Jehoiakim king H1121
24: 1 Jeconiah the s of Jehoiakim king of H1121
25: 1 of Jehoiakim the s of Josiah king of H1121
3 From the thirteenth year of Josiah the s H1121
26: 1 of Jehoiakim the s of Josiah king of H1121
20 the LORD, Urijah the s of Shemaiah of H1121
22 Elnathan the s of Achbor, and *certain* H1121

Jer 26:24 Nevertheless the hand of Ahikam the s H1121
27: 1 of Jehoiakim the s of Josiah king of H1121
7 serve him, and his s, and his son's son, H1121
7 son, and his son's s, until the very time H1121
20 Jeconiah the s of Jehoiakim king of H1121
28: 1 month, *that* Hananiah the s of Azur the H1121
4 place Jeconiah the s of Jehoiakim king H1121
29: 3 By the hand of Elasah the s of H1121
3 and Gemariah the s of Hilkiah, (whom H1121
21 Israel, of Ahab the s of Kolaiah, and of H1121
21 of Zedekiah the s of Maaseiah, which H1121
25 to Zephaniah the s of Maaseiah the H1121
31:20 *Is* Ephraim my dear s? *is he* a pleasant H1121
32: 7 Behold, Hanameel the s of Shallum H1121
8 So Hanameel mine uncle's s came to H1121
9 my uncle's s, that *was* in Anathoth, H1121
12 unto Baruch the s of Neriah, the son of H1121
12 son of Neriah, the s of Maaseiah, in the H1121
12 mine uncle's *s*, and in the presence
16 unto Baruch the s of Neriah, I prayed H1121
35 *are* in the valley of the s of Hinnom, to H1121
33:21 should not have a s to reign upon his H1121
35: 1 the s of Josiah king of Judah, saying, H1121
3 Then I took Jaazaniah the s of H1121
3 of Jeremiah, the s of Habaziniah, and H1121
4 of Hanan, the s of Igdaliah, a man of H1121
4 s of Shallum, the keeper of the door: H1121
6 for Jonadab the s of Rechab our father H1121
8 of Jonadab the s of Rechab our father H1121
14 The words of Jonadab the s of Rechab, H1121
16 Because the sons of Jonadab the s of H1121
19 Jonadab the s of Rechab shall not H1121
36: 1 of Jehoiakim the s of Josiah king of H1121
4 Then Jeremiah called Baruch the s of H1121
8 And Baruch the s of Neriah did H1121
9 of Jehoiakim the s of Josiah king of H1121
10 of Gemariah the s of Shaphan the H1121
11 When Michaiah the s of Gemariah, the H1121
11 son of Gemariah, the s of Shaphan, had H1121
12 and Delaiah the s of Shemaiah, and H1121
12 and Elnathan the s of Achbor, and H1121
12 and Gemariah the s of Shaphan, and H1121
12 the s of Hananiah, and all the princes. H1121
14 sent Jehudi the s of Nethaniah, the son H1121
14 of Nethaniah, the s of Shelemiah, the H1121
14 son of Shelemiah, the s of Cushi, unto H1121
14 So Baruch the s of Neriah took the roll H1121
26 Jerahmeel the s of Hammelech, and H1121
26 son of Seraiah the s of Azriel, and H1121
26 and Shelemiah the s of Abdeel, to take H1121
32 the scribe, the s of Neriah; who wrote H1121
37: 1 And king Zedekiah the s of Josiah H1121
1 of Coniah the s of Jehoiakim, whom H1121
3 sent Jehucal the s of Shelemiah and H1121
3 Zephaniah the s of Maaseiah the priest H1121
13 *was* Irijah, the s of Shelemiah, the son H1121
13 of Shelemiah, the s of Hananiah; and H1121
38: 1 Then Shephatiah the s of Mattan, and H1121
1 and Gedaliah the s of Pashur, and Jucal H1121
1 and Jucal the s of Shelemiah, and H1121
1 and Pashur the s of Malchiah, heard H1121
6 of Malchiah the s of Hammelech, that H1121
39:14 unto Gedaliah the s of Ahikam the son H1121
14 son of Ahikam the s of Shaphan, that H1121
40: 5 to Gedaliah the s of Ahikam the son of H1121
5 son of Ahikam the s of Shaphan, whom H1121
6 unto Gedaliah the s of Ahikam to H1121
7 Gedaliah the s of Ahikam governor H1121
8 even Ishmael the s of Nethaniah, and H1121
8 and Seraiah the s of Tanhumeth, and H1121
8 s of a Maachathite, they and their men. H1121
9 And Gedaliah the s of Ahikam the son H1121
9 And Gedaliah the son of Ahikam the s H1121
11 the s of Ahikam the son of Shaphan; H1121
11 the son of Ahikam the s of Shaphan; H1121
13 Moreover Johanan the s of Kareah, H1121
14 sent Ishmael the s of Nethaniah to slay H1121
14 the s of Ahikam believed them not. H1121
15 Then Johanan the s of Kareah spake to H1121
15 slay Ishmael the s of Nethaniah, and H1121
16 But Gedaliah the s of Ahikam said unto H1121
16 unto Johanan the s of Kareah, Thou H1121
41: 1 *that* Ishmael the s of Nethaniah the son H1121
1 of Nethaniah the s of Elishama, of the H1121
1 came unto Gedaliah the s of Ahikam to H1121
2 Then arose Ishmael the s of Nethaniah, H1121
2 Gedaliah the s of Ahikam the son of H1121
2 son of Ahikam the s of Shaphan with H1121
6 And Ishmael the s of Nethaniah went H1121

Jer 41: 6 Come to Gedaliah the s of Ahikam. H1121
7 that Ishmael the s of Nethaniah slew H1121
9 *and* Ishmael the s of Nethaniah filled H1121
10 to Gedaliah the s of Ahikam: and H1121
10 and Ishmael the s of Nethaniah carried H1121
11 But when Johanan the s of Kareah, and H1121
11 Ishmael the s of Nethaniah had done, H1121
12 with Ishmael the s of Nethaniah, and H1121
13 saw Johanan the s of Kareah, and all H1121
14 went unto Johanan the s of Kareah. H1121
15 But Ishmael the s of Nethaniah H1121
16 Then took Johanan the s of Kareah, H1121
16 from Ishmael the s of Nethaniah, from H1121
16 slain Gedaliah the s of Ahikam, *even* H1121
18 Ishmael the s of Nethaniah had slain H1121
18 slain Gedaliah the s of Ahikam, whom H1121
42: 1 and Johanan the s of Kareah, and H1121
1 and Jezaniah the s of Hoshaiah, and all H1121
8 Then called he Johanan the s of H1121
43: 2 Then spake Azariah the s of Hoshaiah, H1121
2 and Johanan the s of Kareah, and all H1121
3 But Baruch the s of Neriah setteth thee H1121
4 So Johanan the s of Kareah, and all the H1121
5 But Johanan the s of Kareah, and all H1121
6 with Gedaliah the s of Ahikam the son H1121
6 son of Ahikam the s of Shaphan, and H1121
6 prophet, and Baruch the s of Neriah. H1121
45: 1 unto Baruch the s of Neriah, when he H1121
1 the s of Josiah king of Judah, saying, H1121
46: 2 Jehoiakim the s of Josiah king of Judah. H1121
49:18 neither shall a s of man dwell in it. H1121
33 there, nor *any* s of man dwell in it. H1121
50:40 shall any s of man dwell therein. H1121
51:43 doth *any* s of man pass thereby. H1121
59 Seraiah the s of Neriah, the son of H1121
59 son of Neriah, the s of Maaseiah, when H1121
Ezk 1: 3 the priest, the s of Buzi, in the land H1121
2: 1 And he said unto me, S of man, stand H1121
3 And he said unto me, S of man, I send H1121
6 And thou, s of man, be not afraid of H1121
8 But thou, s of man, hear what I say H1121
3: 1 Moreover he said unto me, S of man, H1121
3 And he said unto me, S of man, cause H1121
4 And he said unto me, S of man, go, get H1121
10 Moreover he said unto me, S of man, H1121
17 S of man, I have made thee a H1121
25 But thou, O s of man, behold, they shall H1121
4: 1 Thou also, s of man, take thee a tile, H1121
16 Moreover he said unto me, S of man, H1121
5: 1 And thou, s of man, take thee a sharp H1121
6: 2 S of man, set thy face toward the H1121
7: 2 Also, thou s of man, thus saith the Lord H1121
8: 5 Then said he unto me, S of man, lift up H1121
6 He said furthermore unto me, S of H1121
8 Then said he unto me, S of man, dig H1121
11 Jaazaniah the s of Shaphan, with every H1121
12 Then said he unto me, S of man, hast H1121
15 thou seen *this*, O s of man? turn thee H1121
17 thou seen *this*, O s of man? Is it a light H1121
11: 1 I saw Jaazaniah the s of Azur, and H1121
1 the s of Benaiah, princes of the people. H1121
2 Then said he unto me, S of man, these H1121
4 against them, prophesy, O s of man. H1121
13 that Pelatiah the s of Benaiah died. H1121
15 S of man, thy brethren, *even* thy H1121
12: 2 S of man, thou dwellest in the midst of H1121
3 Therefore, thou s of man, prepare thee H1121
9 S of man, hath not the house of Israel, H1121
18 S of man, eat thy bread with quaking, H1121
22 S of man, what *is* that proverb *that* ye H1121
27 S of man, behold, *they of* the house of H1121
13: 2 S of man, prophesy against the H1121
17 Likewise, thou s of man, set thy face H1121
14: 3 S of man, these men have set up their H1121
13 S of man, when the land sinneth H1121
20 deliver neither s nor daughter; they H1121
15: 2 S of man, What is the vine tree more H1121
16: 2 S of man, cause Jerusalem to know her H1121
17: 2 S of man, put forth a riddle, and speak H1121
18: 4 also the soul of the s is mine: the soul H1121
10 If he beget a s *that is* a robber, a H1121
14 Now, lo, *if* he beget a s, that seeth all his H1121
19 Yet say ye, Why? doth not the s bear H1121
19 the father? When the s hath done that H1121
20 The soul that sinneth, it shall die. The s H1121
20 the iniquity of the s: the righteousness H1121
20: 3 S of man, speak unto the elders of H1121
4 Wilt thou judge them, s of man, wilt H1121
27 Therefore, s of man, speak unto the H1121

Ezk 20:46 S of man, set thy face toward the south, H1121
21: 2 S of man, set thy face toward H1121
6 Sigh therefore, thou s of man, with the H1121
9 S of man, prophesy, and say, Thus H1121
10 the rod of my s, *as* every tree. H1121
12 Cry and howl, s of man: for it shall be H1121
14 Thou therefore, s of man, prophesy, H1121
19 Also, thou s of man, appoint thee two H1121
28 And thou, s of man, prophesy and say, H1121
22: 2 Now, thou s of man, wilt thou judge, H1121
18 S of man, the house of Israel is to me H1121
24 S of man, say unto her, Thou *art* the H1121
23: 2 S of man, there were two women, the H1121
36 The LORD said moreover unto me; S of H1121
24: 2 S of man, write thee the name of the H1121
16 S of man, behold, I take away from H1121
25 Also, thou s of man, *shall it* not *be* in H1121
25: 2 S of man, set thy face against the H1121
26: 2 S of man, because that Tyrus hath said H1121
27: 2 Now, thou s of man, take up a H1121
28: 2 S of man, say unto the prince of Tyrus, H1121
12 S of man, take up a lamentation upon H1121
21 S of man, set thy face against Zidon, H1121
29: 2 S of man, set thy face against Pharaoh H1121
18 S of man, Nebuchadrezzar king of H1121
30: 2 S of man, prophesy and say, Thus saith H1121
21 S of man, I have broken the arm of H1121
31: 2 S of man, speak unto Pharaoh king of H1121
32: 2 S of man, take up a lamentation for H1121
18 S of man, wail for the multitude of H1121
33: 2 S of man, speak to the children of thy H1121
7 So thou, O s of man, I have set thee a H1121
10 Therefore, O thou s of man, speak unto H1121
12 Therefore, thou s of man, say unto the H1121
24 S of man, they that inhabit those H1121
30 Also, thou s of man, the children of thy H1121
34: 2 S of man, prophesy against the H1121
35: 2 S of man, set thy face against mount H1121
36: 1 Also, thou s of man, prophesy unto the H1121
17 S of man, when the house of Israel H1121
37: 3 And he said unto me, S of man, can H1121
9 wind, prophesy, s of man, and say to H1121
11 Then he said unto me, S of man, these H1121
16 Moreover, thou s of man, take thee one H1121
38: 2 S of man, set thy face against Gog, the H1121
14 Therefore, s of man, prophesy and say H1121
39: 1 Therefore, thou s of man, prophesy H1121
17 And, thou s of man, thus saith the Lord H1121
40: 4 And the man said unto me, S of man, H1121
43: 7 And he said unto me, S of man, the H1121
10 Thou s of man, shew the house to the H1121
18 And he said unto me, S of man, thus H1121
44: 5 And the LORD said unto me, S of man, H1121
25 for mother, or for s, or for daughter, for H1121
47: 6 And he said unto me, S of man, hast H1121
Dan 3:25 form of the fourth is like the S of God. H1247
5:22 And thou his s, O Belshazzar, hast not H1247
7:13 *one* like the S of man came with the H1247
8:17 Understand, O s of man: for at the time H1121
9: 1 In the first year of Darius the s of H1121
Hos 1: 1 unto Hosea, the s of Beeri, in the days H1121
1 Jeroboam the s of Joash, king of Israel. H1121
3 which conceived, and bare him a s. H1121
8 she conceived, and bare a s. H1121
11: 1 him, and called my s out of Egypt. H1121
13:13 he *is* an unwise s; for he should not stay H1121
Joel 1: 1 that came to Joel the s of Pethuel. H1121
Am 1: 1 days of Jeroboam the s of Joash king of H1121
7:14 neither *was* I a prophet's s; but I *was* an H1121
8:10 s, and the end thereof as a bitter day.
Jna 1: 1 unto Jonah the s of Amittai, saying, H1121
Mic 6: 5 what Balaam the s of Beor answered H1121
7: 6 For the s dishonoureth the father, the H1121
Zep 1: 1 Zephaniah the s of Cushi, the son of H1121
1 son of Cushi, the s of Gedaliah, the son H1121
1 of Gedaliah, the s of Amariah, the son H1121
1 son of Amariah, the s of Hizkiah, in the H1121
1 of Josiah the s of Amon, king of Judah. H1121
Hag 1: 1 Zerubbabel the s of Shealtiel, governor H1121
1 s of Josedech, the high priest, saying, H1121
12 Then Zerubbabel the s of Shealtiel, and H1121
12 and Joshua the s of Josedech, the high H1121
14 spirit of Zerubbabel the s of Shealtiel, H1121
14 of Joshua the s of Josedech, the high H1121
2: 2 Speak now to Zerubbabel the s of H1121
2 and to Joshua the s of Josedech, the H1121
4 be strong, O Joshua, s of Josedech, the H1121
23 my servant, the s of Shealtiel, saith the H1121
Zec 1: 1 Zechariah, the s of Berechiah, the son H1121

Zec 1: 1 the s of Iddo the prophet, saying, H1121
7 Zechariah, the s of Berechiah, the son H1121
7 the s of Iddo the prophet, saying, H1121
6:10 the house of Josiah the s of Zephaniah; H1121
11 the s of Josedech, the high priest; H1121
14 and to Hen the s of Zephaniah, for a H1121
12:10 for *his* only s, and shall be in bitterness
Mal 1: 6 A s honoureth *his* father, and a servant H1121
3:17 spareth his own s that serveth him. H1121
Mt 1: 1 the s of David, the son of Abraham. G5207
1 the son of David, the s of Abraham. G5207
20 Joseph, thou s of David, fear not to G5207
21 And she shall bring forth a s, and thou G5207
23 shall bring forth a s, and they shall call G5207
25 s: and he called his name JESUS. G5207
2:15 saying, Out of Egypt have I called my s. G5207
3:17 beloved S, in whom I am well pleased. G5207
4: 3 If thou be the S of God, command that G5207
6 And saith unto him, If thou be the S of G5207
21 James *the* s of Zebedee, and John
7: 9 s ask bread, will he give him a stone? G5207
8:20 nests; but the S of man hath not where G5207
29 thee, Jesus, thou S of God? art thou G5207
9: 2 the sick of the palsy; S, be of good cheer; G5043
6 But that ye may know that the S of G5207
27 *Thou* s of David, have mercy on us. G5207
10: 2 *the* s of Zebedee, and John his brother;
3 James *the* s of Alphaeus, and Lebbaeus,
23 of Israel, till the S of man be come. G5207
37 and he that loveth s or daughter more G5207
11:19 The S of man came eating and G5207
27 no man knoweth the S, but the Father; G5207
27 the Father, save the S, and *he* to G5207
27 to whomsoever the S will reveal *him*. G5207
12: 8 For the S of man is Lord even of the G5207
23 and said, Is not this the s of David? G5207
32 a word against the S of man, it shall be G5207
40 belly; so shall the S of man be three G5207
13:37 soweth the good seed is the S of man; G5207
41 The S of man shall send forth his G5207
55 Is not this the carpenter's s? is not his G5207
14:33 saying, Of a truth thou art the S of God. G5207
15:22 on me, O Lord, *thou* s of David; my G5207
16:13 do men say that I the S of man am? G5207
16 art the Christ, the S of the living God. G5207
27 For the S of man shall come in the G5207
28 the S of man coming in his kingdom. G5207
17: 5 This is my beloved S, in whom I am well G5207
9 S of man be risen again from the dead. G5207
12 shall also the S of man suffer of them. G5207
15 Lord, have mercy on my s: for he is G5207
22 said unto them, The S of man shall be G5207
18:11 For the S of man is come to save that G5207
19:28 when the S of man shall sit in the G5207
20:18 and the S of man shall be betrayed G5207
28 Even as the S of man came not to be G5207
30 mercy on us, O Lord, *thou* s of David. G5207
31 mercy on us, O Lord, *thou* s of David. G5207
21: 9 Hosanna to the s of David: Blessed *is* G5207
15 s of David; they were sore displeased, G5207
28 said, S, go work to day in my vineyard. G5043
37 But last of all he sent unto them his s, G5207
37 son, saying, They will reverence my s. G5207
38 But when the husbandmen saw the s, G5207
22: 2 king, which made a marriage for his s, G5207
42 of Christ? whose s is he? They say unto G5207
42 is he? They say unto him, *The* s of David.
45 then call him Lord, how is he his s? G5207
23:35 of Zacharias s of Barachias, whom G5207
24:27 also the coming of the S of man be. G5207
30 And then shall appear the sign of the S G5207
30 they shall see the S of man coming in G5207
37 also the coming of the S of man be. G5207
39 also the coming of the S of man be. G5207
44 as ye think not the S of man cometh. G5207
25:13 the hour wherein the S of man cometh. G5207
31 When the S of man shall come in his G5207
26: 2 the S of man is betrayed to be crucified. G5207
24 The S of man goeth as it is written of G5207
24 that man by whom the S of man is G5207
45 at hand, and the S of man is betrayed G5207
63 thou be the Christ, the S of God. G5207
64 shall ye see the S of man sitting on the G5207
27:40 S of God, come down from the cross. G5207
43 him: for he said, I am the S of God. G5207
54 saying, Truly this was the S of God. G5207
28:19 and of the S, and of the Holy Ghost: G5207
Mk 1: 1 the gospel of Jesus Christ, the S of God; G5207
11 beloved S, in whom I am well pleased. G5207

Mk 1:19 he saw James the *s* of Zebedee, and John
2: 5 of the palsy, S, thy sins be forgiven thee. G5043
10 But that ye may know that the S of G5207
14 And as he passed by, he saw Levi the *s* of
28 Therefore the S of man is Lord also of G5207
3:11 cried, saying, Thou art the S of God. G5207
17 And James the *s* of Zebedee, and John
18 and James the *s* of Alphaeus, and
5: 7 thee, Jesus, *thou* S of the most high G5207
6: 3 Is not this the carpenter, the s of Mary, G5207
8:31 And he began to teach them, that the S G5207
38 of him also shall the S of man be G5207
9: 7 saying, This is my beloved S: hear him. G5207
9 the S of man were risen from the dead. G5207
12 it is written of the S of man, that he G5207
17 thee my s, which hath a dumb spirit; G5207
31 unto them, The S of man is delivered G5207
10:33 and the S of man shall be delivered G5207
45 For even the S of man came not to be G5207
46 Bartimaeus, the s of Timaeus, sat by G5207
47 *thou* s of David, have mercy on me. G5207
48 *Thou* s of David, have mercy on me. G5207
12: 6 Having yet therefore one s, his G5207
6 them, saying, They will reverence my s. G5207
35 the scribes that Christ is the s of David? G5207
37 is he *then* his s? And the common G5207
13:12 and the father the s; and children shall G5043
26 And then shall they see the S of man G5207
32 in heaven, neither the S, but the Father. G5207
34 *For the S of man is* as a man taking a far
14:21 The S of man indeed goeth, as it is G5207
21 that man by whom the S of man is G5207
41 come; behold, the S of man is betrayed G5207
61 thou the Christ, the S of the Blessed? G5207
62 ye shall see the S of man sitting on the G5207
15:39 said, Truly this man was the S of God. G5207
Lk 1:13 a s, and thou shalt call his name John. G5207
31 forth a s, and shalt call his name JESUS. G5207
32 shall be called the S of the Highest: and G5207
35 of thee shall be called the S of God. G5207
36 also conceived a s in her old age: and G5207
57 be delivered; and she brought forth a s. G5207
2: 7 And she brought forth her firstborn s, G5207
48 said unto him, S, why hast thou thus G5043
3: 2 the s of Zacharias in the wilderness. G5207
22 my beloved S; in thee I am well pleased. G5207
23 s of Joseph, which was *the son* of Heli, G5207
23 son of Joseph, which was *the s* of Heli,
24 Which was *the s* of Matthat, which was
24 which was *the s* of Levi, which was *the*
24 which was *the s* of Melchi, which was
24 *s* of Janna, which was *the son* of Joseph,
24 *son* of Janna, which was *the s* of Joseph,
25 Which was *the s* of Mattathias, which
25 which was *the s* of Amos, which was
25 which was *the s* of Naum, which was
25 *the s* of Esli, which was *the son* of Nagge,
25 *the son* of Esli, which was *the s* of Nagge,
26 Which was *the s* of Maath, which was
26 which was *the s* of Mattathias, which
26 which was *the s* of Semei, which was
26 *s* of Joseph, which was *the son* of Juda,
26 *son* of Joseph, which was *the s* of Juda,
27 Which was *the s* of Joanna, which was
27 which was *the s* of Rhesa, which was
27 which was *the s* of Zorobabel, which
27 *s* of Salathiel, which was *the son* of Neri,
27 *son* of Salathiel, which was *the s* of Neri,
28 Which was *the s* of Melchi, which was
28 which was *the s* of Addi, which was *the*
28 which was *the s* of Cosam, which was
28 *s* of Elmodam, which was *the son* of Er,
28 *son* of Elmodam, which was *the s* of Er,
29 Which was *the s* of Jose, which was *the*
29 which was *the s* of Eliezer, which was
29 which was *the s* of Jorim, which was
29 *s* of Matthat, which was *the son* of Levi,
29 *son* of Matthat, which was *the s* of Levi,
30 Which was *the s* of Simeon, which was
30 which was *the s* of Juda, which was *the*
30 which was *the s* of Joseph, which was
30 which was *the s* of Jonan, which was
30 of Jonan, which was *the s* of Eliakim,
31 Which was *the s* of Melea, which was *the*
31 which was *the s* of Menan, which was
31 which was *the s* of Mattatha, which was
31 *s* of Nathan, which was *the son* of David,
31 *son* of Nathan, which was *the s* of David,
32 Which was *the s* of Jesse, which was *the*

Lk 3:32 which was *the s* of Obed, which was *the*
32 which was *the s* of Booz, which was *the*
32 which was *the s* of Salmon, which was
32 of Salmon, which was *the s* of Naasson,
33 Which was *the s* of Aminadab, which
33 which was *the s* of Aram, which was
33 which was *the s* of Esrom, which was
33 *s* of Phares, which was *the son* of Juda,
33 *son* of Phares, which was *the s* of Juda,
34 Which was *the s* of Jacob, which was *the*
34 which was *the s* of Isaac, which was
34 which was *the s* of Abraham, which was
34 *s* of Thara, which was *the son* of Nachor,
34 *son* of Thara, which was *the s* of Nachor,
35 Which was *the s* of Saruch, which was
35 which was *the s* of Ragau, which was
35 which was *the s* of Phalec, which was
35 *s* of Heber, which was *the son* of Sala,
35 *son* of Heber, which was *the s* of Sala,
36 Which was *the s* of Cainan, which was
36 which was *the s* of Arphaxad, which
36 which was *the s* of Sem, which was *the*
36 *s* of Noe, which was *the son* of Lamech,
36 *son* of Noe, which was *the s* of Lamech,
37 Which was *the s* of Mathusala, which
37 which was *the s* of Enoch, which was
37 which was *the s* of Jared, which was
37 which was *the s* of Maleleel, which was
37 of Maleleel, which was *the s* of Cainan,
38 Which was *the s* of Enos, which was *the*
38 which was *the s* of Seth, which was *the*
38 *s* of Adam, which was *the son* of God.
38 *son* of Adam, which was *the s* of God.
4: 3 him, If thou be the S of God, command G5207
9 S of God, cast thyself down from hence: G5207
22 And they said, Is not this Joseph's s? G5207
41 Thou art Christ the S of God. And he G5207
5:24 But that ye may know that the S of G5207
6: 5 And he said unto them, That the S of G5207
15 Matthew and Thomas, James the *s* of
22 name as evil, for the S of man's sake. G5207
7:12 out, the only s of his mother, and she G5207
34 The S of man is come eating and G5207
8:28 thee, Jesus, *thou* S of God most high? I G5207
9:22 Saying, The S of man must suffer many G5207
26 of him shall the S of man be ashamed, G5207
35 saying, This is my beloved S: hear him. G5207
38 upon my s: for he is mine only child. G5207
41 you, and suffer you? Bring thy s hither. G5207
44 into your ears: for the S of man shall be G5207
56 For the S of man is not come to destroy G5207
58 nests; but the S of man hath not where G5207
10: 6 And if the s of peace be there, your G5207
22 knoweth who the S is, but the Father; G5207
22 Father is, but the S, and *he* to whom the G5207
22 and *he* to whom the S will reveal *him*. G5207
11:11 If a s shall ask bread of any of you that G5207
30 also the S of man be to this generation. G5207
12: 8 him shall the S of man also confess G5207
10 a word against the S of man, it shall be G5207
40 Be ye therefore ready also: for the S of G5207
53 against the s, and the son against G5207
53 the son, and the s against the father; G5207
15:13 And not many days after the younger s G5207
19 s: make me as one of thy hired servants. G5207
21 And the s said unto him, Father, I have G5207
21 am no more worthy to be called thy s. G5207
24 For this my s was dead, and is alive G5207
25 Now his elder s was in the field: and as G5207
30 But as soon as this thy s was come, G5207
31 And he said unto him, S, thou art ever G5043
16:25 But Abraham said, S, remember that G5043
17:22 of the S of man, and ye shall not see *it*. G5207
24 so shall also the S of man be in his day. G5207
26 it be also in the days of the S of man. G5207
30 the day when the S of man is revealed. G5207
18: 8 when the S of man cometh, shall G5207
31 the S of man shall be accomplished. G5207
38 And he cried, saying, Jesus, *thou* s of G5207
39 *Thou* s of David, have mercy on me. G5207
19: 9 as he also is a s of Abraham. G5207
10 For the S of man is come to seek and to G5207
20:13 send my beloved s: it may be they will G5207
41 How say they that Christ is David's s? G5207
44 calleth him Lord, how is he then his s? G5207
21:27 And then shall they see the S of man G5207
36 pass, and to stand before the S of man. G5207
22:22 And truly the S of man goeth, as it was G5207
48 thou the S of man with a kiss? G5207

Lk 22:69 Hereafter shall the S of man sit on the G5207
70 Then said they all, Art thou then the S G5207
24: 7 Saying, The S of man must be delivered G5207
Jn 1:18 the only begotten S, which is in the G5207
34 bare record that this is the S of God. G5207
42 art Simon the s of Jona: thou shalt be G5207
45 Jesus of Nazareth, the s of Joseph. G5207
49 S of God; thou art the King of Israel. G5207
51 and descending upon the S of man. G5207
3:13 *even* the S of man which is in heaven. G5207
14 even so must the S of man be lifted up: G5207
16 his only begotten S, that whosoever G5207
17 For God sent not his S into the world to G5207
18 the name of the only begotten S of God. G5207
35 The Father loveth the S, and hath given G5207
36 He that believeth on the S hath G5207
36 believeth not the S shall not see life; but G5207
4: 5 ground that Jacob gave to his s Joseph. G5207
46 whose s was sick at Capernaum. G5207
47 his s: for he was at the point of death. G5207
50 Jesus saith unto him, Go thy way; thy s G5207
51 him, and told *him*, saying, Thy s liveth. G3816
53 unto him, Thy s liveth: and himself G5207
5:19 I say unto you, The S can do nothing of G5207
19 doeth, these also doeth the S likewise. G5207
20 For the Father loveth the S, and G5207
21 even so the S quickeneth whom he will. G5207
22 committed all judgment unto the S: G5207
23 That all *men* should honour the S, even G5207
23 honoureth not the S honoureth not the G5207
25 S of God: and they that hear shall live. G5207
26 he given to the S to have life in himself; G5207
27 also, because he is the S of man. G5207
6:27 life, which the S of man shall give unto G5207
40 one which seeth the S, and believeth on G5207
42 And they said, Is not this Jesus, the s of G5207
53 eat the flesh of the S of man, and drink G5207
62 *What* and if ye shall see the S of man G5207
69 art that Christ, the S of the living God. G5207
71 He spake of Judas Iscariot *the s* of
8:28 have lifted up the S of man, then shall G5207
35 house for ever: *but* the S abideth ever. G5207
36 If the S therefore shall make you free, G5207
9:19 Is this your s, who ye say was born G5207
20 is our s, and that he was born blind: G5207
35 him, Dost thou believe on the S of God? G5207
10:36 because I said, I am the S of God? G5207
11: 4 the S of God might be glorified thereby. G5207
27 thou art the Christ, the S of God, which G5207
12: 4 Simon's *s*, which should betray him,
23 that the S of man should be glorified. G5207
34 how sayest thou, The S of man must be G5207
34 must be lifted up? who is this S of man? G5207
13: 2 Judas Iscariot, Simon's *s*, to betray him;
26 gave *it* to Judas Iscariot, *the s* of Simon.
31 said, Now is the S of man glorified, and G5207
14:13 the Father may be glorified in the S. G5207
17: 1 S, that thy Son also may glorify thee: G5207
1 Son, that thy S also may glorify thee: G5207
12 is lost, but the s of perdition; that the G5207
19: 7 because he made himself the S of God. G5207
26 unto his mother, Woman, behold thy s! G5207
20:31 is the Christ, the S of God; and that G5207
21:15 Peter, Simon, *s* of Jonas, lovest thou
16 time, Simon, *s* of Jonas, lovest thou
17 third time, Simon, *s* of Jonas, lovest thou
Act 1:13 James *the s* of Alphaeus, and Simon
3:13 hath glorified his S Jesus; whom ye G3816
26 raised up his S Jesus, sent him to bless G3816
4:36 interpreted, The s of consolation,) a G5207
7:21 up, and nourished him for her own s. G5207
56 opened, and the S of man standing on G5207
8:37 believe that Jesus Christ is the S of God. G5207
9:20 the synagogues, that he is the S of God. G5207
13:21 them Saul the s of Cis, a man of the G5207
22 found David the *s* of Jesse, a man after
33 art my S, this day have I begotten thee. G5207
16: 1 Timotheus, the s of a certain woman, G5207
23: 6 I am a Pharisee, the s of a Pharisee: of G5207
16 And when Paul's sister's s heard of G5207
Ro 1: 3 Concerning his S Jesus Christ our Lord, G5207
4 And declared *to be* the S of God with G5207
9 the gospel of his S, that without ceasing G5207
5:10 by the death of his S, much more, being G5207
8: 3 sending his own S in the likeness of G5207
29 to the image of his S, that he might be G5207
32 He that spared not his own S, but G5207
9: 9 will I come, and Sarah shall have a s. G5207
1Co 1: 9 of his S Jesus Christ our Lord. G5207

1Co 4:17 who is my beloved **s**, and faithful in the G5043
15:28 then shall the **S** also himself be subject G5207
2Co 1:19 For the **S** of God, Jesus Christ, who was G5207
Gal 1:16 To reveal his **S** in me, that I might G5207
2:20 by the faith of the **S** of God, who loved G5207
4: 4 God sent forth his **S**, made of a woman, G5207
6 the Spirit of his **S** into your hearts, G5207
7 a servant, but a **s**; and if a son, then an G5207
7 a **s**, then an heir of God through Christ. G5207
30 and her **s**: for the son of the G5207
30 her son: for the **s** of the bondwoman G5207
30 be heir with the **s** of the freewoman. G5207
Eph 4:13 the knowledge of the **S** of God, unto a G5207
Php 2:22 of him, that, as a **s** with the father, he G5043
Col 1:13 *us* into the kingdom of his dear **S**: G5207
4:10 and Marcus, sister's **s** to Barnabas, G431
1Th 1:10 And to wait for his **S** from heaven, G5207
2Th 2: 3 of sin be revealed, the **s** of perdition; G5207
1Ti 1: 2 Unto Timothy, *my* own **s** in the faith: G5043
18 This charge I commit unto thee, **s** G5043
2Ti 1: 2 To Timothy, *my* dearly beloved **s**: G5043
2: 1 Thou therefore, my **s**, be strong in the G5043
Tit 1: 4 To Titus, *mine* own **s** after the common G5043
Phlm 10 I beseech thee for my **s** Onesimus, G5043
Heb 1: 2 spoken unto us by *his* **S**, whom he hath G5207
5 any time, Thou art my **S**, this day have I G5207
5 him a Father, and he shall be to me a **S**? G5207
8 But unto the **S** *he saith*, Thy throne, O G5207
2: 6 or the **s** of man, that thou visitest him? G5207
3: 6 But Christ as a **s** over his own house; G5207
4:14 heavens, Jesus the **S** of God, let us hold G5207
5: 5 art my **S**, to day have I begotten thee. G5207
8 Though he were a **S**, yet learned he G5207
6: 6 to themselves the **S** of God afresh, and G5207
7: 3 **S** of God; abideth a priest continually. G5207
28 the **S**, who is consecrated for evermore. G5207
10:29 under foot the **S** of God, and hath G5207
11:17 promises offered up his only begotten **s**,
24 be called the **s** of Pharaoh's daughter; G5207
12: 5 as unto children, My **s**, despise not thou G5207
6 scourgeth every **s** whom he receiveth. G5207
7 **s** is he whom the father chasteneth not? G5207
Jas 2:21 had offered Isaac his **s** upon the altar? G5207
1Pt 5:13 saluteth you; and *so doth* Marcus my **s**. G5207
2Pt 1:17 beloved **S**, in whom I am well pleased. G5207
2:15 way of Balaam *the* **s** of Bosor, who loved
1Jn 1: 3 the Father, and with his **S** Jesus Christ. G5207
7 Christ his **S** cleanseth us from all sin. G5207
2:22 that denieth the Father and the **S**. G5207
23 Whosoever denieth the **S**, the same G5207
23 the **S** hath the Father also.
24 continue in the **S**, and in the Father. G5207
3: 8 For this purpose the **S** of God was G5207
23 on the name of his **S** Jesus Christ, and G5207
4: 9 his only begotten **S** into the world, that G5207
10 his **S** *to be* the propitiation for our sins. G5207
14 the **S** *to be* the Saviour of the world. G5207
15 that Jesus is the **S** of God, God dwelleth G5207
5: 5 believeth that Jesus is the **S** of God? G5207
9 of God which he hath testified of his **S**. G5207
10 He that believeth on the **S** of God hath G5207
10 not the record that God gave of his **S**. G5207
11 to us eternal life, and this life is in his **S**. G5207
12 He that hath the **S** hath life; *and* he that G5207
12 that hath not the **S** of God hath not life. G5207
13 the name of the **S** of God; that ye may G5207
13 believe on the name of the **S** of God. G5207
20 And we know that the **S** of God is G5207
20 is true, *even* in his **S** Jesus Christ. This G5207
2Jn 3 the **S** of the Father, in truth and love. G5207
9 he hath both the Father and the **S**. G5207
Rev 1:13 *one* like unto the **S** of man, clothed G5207
2:18 things saith the **S** of God, who hath his G5207
14:14 sat like unto the **S** of man, having on G5207
21: 7 I will be his God, and he shall be my **s**. G5207

SONG

Ex 15: 1 of Israel this **s** unto the LORD, and H7892
2 The LORD *is* my strength and **s**, and he H2176
Nu 21:17 Then Israel sang this **s**, Spring up, O H7892
Dt 31:19 Now therefore write ye this **s** for you, H7892
19 mouths, that this **s** may be a witness H7892
21 them, that this **s** shall testify against H7892
22 Moses therefore wrote this **s** the same H7892
30 words of this **s**, until they were ended. H7892
32:44 all the words of this **s** in the ears of the H7892
Jdg 5:12 awake, utter a **s**: arise, Barak, and lead H7892
2Sa 22: 1 the words of this **s** in the day *that* the H7892
1Ch 6:31 over the service of **s** in the house of the H7892
1Ch 15:22 Levites, *was* for **s**: he instructed about H4853
22 about the **s**, because he *was* skilful. H4853
27 the master of the **s** with the singers: H4853
25: 6 of their father for **s** *in* the house of the H7892
2Ch 29:27 began, the **s** of the LORD began H7892
Job 30: 9 And now am I their **s**, yea, I am their H5058
Ps 18:ttl the words of this **s** in the day *that* the H7892
28: 7 and with my **s** will I praise him. H7892
30:ttl A Psalm *and* **S** *at* the dedication of the H7892
33: 3 Sing unto him a new **s**; play skilfully H7892
40: 3 And he hath put a new **s** in my mouth, H7892
42: 8 in the night his **s** *shall be* with me, *and* H7892
45:ttl sons of Korah, Maschil, A **S** of loves. H7892
46:ttl the sons of Korah, A **S** upon Alamoth. H7892
48:ttl A **S** *and* Psalm for the sons of Korah. H7892
65:ttl To the chief Musician, A Psalm *and* **S** H7892
66:ttl To the chief Musician, A **S** *or* Psalm. H7892
67:ttl Musician on Neginoth, A Psalm *or* **S**. H7892
68:ttl To the chief Musician, A Psalm *or* **S** of H7892
69:12 me; and I *was* the **s** of the drunkards. H5058
30 I will praise the name of God with a **s**, H7892
75:ttl Al-taschith, A Psalm *or* **S** of Asaph. H7892
76:ttl on Neginoth, A Psalm *or* **S** of Asaph. H7892
77: 6 I call to remembrance my **s** in the H5058
83:ttl A **S** *or* Psalm of Asaph. H7892
87:ttl A Psalm *or* **S** for the sons of Korah. H7892
88:ttl A **S** or Psalm for the sons of Korah, to H7892
92:ttl A Psalm *or* **S** for the sabbath day. H7892
96: 1 O sing unto the LORD a new **s**: sing H7892
98: 1 O sing unto the LORD a new **s**; for he H7892
108:ttl A **S** *or* Psalm of David. H7892
118:14 The LORD *is* my strength and **s**, and is H2176
120:ttl A **S** of degrees. H7892
121:ttl A **S** of degrees. H7892
122:ttl A **S** of degrees of David. H7892
123:ttl A **S** of degrees. H7892
124:ttl A **S** of degrees of David. H7892
125:ttl A **S** of degrees. H7892
126:ttl A **S** of degrees. H7892
127:ttl A **S** of degrees for Solomon. H7892
128:ttl A **S** of degrees. H7892
129:ttl A **S** of degrees. H7892
130:ttl A **S** of degrees. H7892
131:ttl A **S** of degrees of David. H7892
132:ttl A **S** of degrees. H7892
133:ttl A **S** of degrees of David. H7892
134:ttl A **S** of degrees. H7892
137: 3 of us a **s**; and they that wasted H1697+H7892
4 How shall we sing the LORD'S **s** in a H7892
144: 9 I will sing a new **s** unto thee, O God: H7892
149: 1 the LORD a new **s**, *and* his praise in the H7892
Ecc 7: 5 than for a man to hear the **s** of fools. H7892
Song 1: 1 The **s** of songs, which *is* Solomon's. H7892
Isa 5: 1 Now will I sing to my wellbeloved a **s** of H7892
12: 2 *my* **s**; he also is become my salvation. H2176
24: 9 They shall not drink wine with a **s**; H7892
26: 1 In that day shall this **s** be sung in the H7892
30:29 Ye shall have a **s**, as in the night *when* a H7892
42:10 Sing unto the LORD a new **s**, *and* his H7892
Lam 3:14 to all my people; *and* their **s** all the day. H5058
Ezk 33:32 as a very lovely **s** of one that hath a H7892
Rev 5: 9 And they sung a new **s**, saying, Thou art G5603
14: 3 And they sung as it were a new **s** before G5603
3 could learn that **s** but the hundred *and* G5603
15: 3 And they sing the **s** of Moses the G5603
3 of God, and the **s** of the Lamb, saying, G5603

SONGS

Gen 31:27 and with **s**, with tabret, and with harp? H7892
1Ki 4:32 and his **s** were a thousand and five. H7892
1Ch 25: 7 instructed in the **s** of the LORD, *even* H7892
Neh 12:46 **s** of praise and thanksgiving unto God. H7892
Job 35:10 my maker, who giveth **s** in the night; H2158
Ps 32: 7 me about with **s** of deliverance. Selah. H7438
119:54 Thy statutes have been my **s** in the H2158
137: 3 *saying*, Sing us *one* of the **s** of Zion. H7892
Prv 25:20 *is* he that singeth **s** to an heavy heart. H7892
Song 1: 1 The song of **s**, which *is* Solomon's. H7892
Isa 23:16 **s**, that thou mayest be remembered. H7892
24:16 earth have we heard **s**, *even* glory to the H2158
35:10 come to Zion with **s** and everlasting joy H7440
38:20 we will sing my **s** to the stringed H5058
Ezk 26:13 And I will cause the noise of thy **s** to H7892
Am 5:23 the noise of thy **s**; for I will not hear the H7892
8: 3 And the **s** of the temple shall be H7892
10 and all your **s** into lamentation; and H7892
Eph 5:19 and spiritual **s**, singing and making G5603
Col 3:16 and spiritual **s**, singing with grace in G5603

SON-IN-LAW See SON and LAW.

SONS

Gen 5: 4 years: and he begat **s** and daughters: H1121
7 years, and begat **s** and daughters: H1121
10 years, and begat **s** and daughters: H1121
13 forty years, and begat **s** and daughters: H1121
16 years, and begat **s** and daughters: H1121
19 years, and begat **s** and daughters: H1121
22 years, and begat **s** and daughters: H1121
26 two years, and begat **s** and daughters: H1121
30 five years, and begat **s** and daughters: H1121
6: 2 That the **s** of God saw the daughters of H1121
4 that, when the **s** of God came in unto H1121
10 And Noah begat three **s**, Shem, Ham, H1121
18 ark, thou, and thy **s**, and thy wife, and H1121
7: 7 And Noah went in, and his **s**, and his H1121
13 and Japheth, the **s** of Noah, and Noah's H1121
13 wives of his **s** with them, into the ark; H1121
8:16 and thy **s**, and thy sons' wives with thee. H1121
18 And Noah went forth, and his **s**, and his H1121
9: 1 And God blessed Noah and his **s**, and H1121
8 And God spake unto Noah, and to his **s** H1121
18 And the **s** of Noah, that went forth of H1121
19 These *are* the three **s** of Noah: and of H1121
10: 1 Now these *are* the generations of the **s** H1121
1 unto them were **s** born after the flood. H1121
2 The **s** of Japheth; Gomer, and Magog, H1121
3 And the **s** of Gomer; Ashkenaz, and H1121
4 And the **s** of Javan; Elishah, and H1121
6 And the **s** of Ham; Cush, and Mizraim, H1121
7 And the **s** of Cush; Seba, and Havilah, H1121
7 the **s** of Raamah; Sheba, and Dedan. H1121
20 These *are* the **s** of Ham, after their H1121
25 And unto Eber were born two **s**: the H1121
29 Jobab: all these *were* the **s** of Joktan. H1121
31 These *are* the **s** of Shem, after their H1121
32 These *are* the families of the **s** of Noah, H1121
11:11 years, and begat **s** and daughters. H1121
13 three years, and begat **s** and daughters. H1121
15 three years, and begat **s** and daughters. H1121
17 years, and begat **s** and daughters. H1121
19 nine years, and begat **s** and daughters. H1121
21 years, and begat **s** and daughters. H1121
23 years, and begat **s** and daughters. H1121
25 years, and begat **s** and daughters. H1121
19:12 in law, and thy **s**, and thy daughters, H1121
14 And Lot went out, and spake unto his **s** H2860
14 as one that mocked unto his **s** in law. H2860
23: 3 and spake unto the **s** of Heth, saying, H1121
11 the presence of the **s** of my people give H1121
16 audience of the **s** of Heth, four hundred H1121
20 of a burying-place by the **s** of Heth. H1121
25: 3 and Dedan. And the **s** of Dedan were H1121
4 And the **s** of Midian; Ephah, and H1121
6 But unto the **s** of the concubines, which H1121
9 And his **s** Isaac and Ishmael buried H1121
10 purchased of the **s** of Heth: there was H1121
13 And these *are* the names of the **s** of H1121
16 These *are* the **s** of Ishmael, and these H1121
27:29 let thy mother's **s** bow down to thee: H1121
29:34 **s**: therefore was his name called Levi. H1121
30:20 six **s**: and she called his name Zebulun. H1121
35 and gave *them* into the hand of his **s**. H1121
31: 1 And he heard the words of Laban's **s**, H1121
17 Then Jacob rose up, and set his **s** and H1121
28 And hast not suffered me to kiss my **s** H1121
55 up, and kissed his **s** and his daughters, H1121
32:22 **s**, and passed over the ford Jabbok. H3206
34: 5 daughter: now his **s** were with his cattle H1121
7 And the **s** of Jacob came out of the field H1121
13 And the **s** of Jacob answered Shechem H1121
25 that two of the **s** of Jacob, Simeon and H1121
27 The **s** of Jacob came upon the slain, H1121
35: 5 they did not pursue after the **s** of Jacob. H1121
22 *it*. Now the **s** of Jacob were twelve: H1121
23 The **s** of Leah; Reuben, Jacob's H1121
24 The **s** of Rachel; Joseph, and Benjamin: H1121
25 And the **s** of Bilhah, Rachel's H1121
26 And the **s** of Zilpah, Leah's handmaid; H1121
26 these *are* the **s** of Jacob, which were H1121
29 and his **s** Esau and Jacob buried him. H1121
36: 5 these *are* the **s** of Esau, which were H1121
6 And Esau took his wives, and his **s**, and H1121
10 These *are* the names of Esau's **s**; H1121
11 And the **s** of Eliphaz were Teman, H1121
12 these *were* the **s** of Adah Esau's wife. H1121
13 And these *are* the **s** of Reuel; Nahath, H1121
13 were the **s** of Bashemath Esau's wife. H1121

Gen 36:14 And these were the s of Aholibamah, H1121
15 These *were* dukes of the s of Esau: the H1121
15 the sons of Esau: the s of Eliphaz the H1121
16 of Edom; these *were* the s of Adah. H1121
17 And these *are* the s of Reuel Esau's son; H1121
17 *are* the s of Bashemath Esau's wife. H1121
18 And these *are* the s of Aholibamah H1121
19 These *are* the s of Esau, who *is* Edom, H1121
20 These *are* the s of Seir the Horite, who H1121
37: 2 lad *was* with the s of Bilhah, and with H1121
2 and with the s of Zilpah, his father's H1121
35 And all his s and all his daughters rose H1121
41:50 And unto Joseph were born two s H1121
42: 1 s, Why do ye look one upon another? H1121
5 And the s of Israel came to buy *corn* H1121
11 We *are* all one man's s; we *are* true H1121
13 brethren, the s of one man in the land H1121
32 We *be* twelve brethren, s of our father; H1121
37 Slay my two s, if I bring him not to H1121
44:27 us, Ye know that my wife bare me two *s:*
46: 5 and the s of Israel carried Jacob H1121
7 His s, and his sons' sons with him, his H1121
7 His sons, and his sons' s with him, his H1121
8 and his s: Reuben, Jacob's firstborn. H1121
9 And the s of Reuben; Hanoch, and H1121
10 And the s of Simeon; Jemuel, and H1121
11 And the s of Levi; Gershon, Kohath, H1121
12 And the s of Judah; Er, and Onan, and H1121
12 s of Pharez were Hezron and Hamul. H1121
13 And the s of Issachar; Tola, and H1121
14 And the s of Zebulun; Sered, and Elon, H1121
15 These *be* the s of Leah, which she bare H1121
15 all the souls of his s and his daughters H1121
16 And the s of Gad; Ziphion, and Haggi, H1121
17 And the s of Asher; Jimnah, and H1121
17 the s of Beriah; Heber, and Malchiel. H1121
18 These *are* the s of Zilpah, whom Laban H1121
19 The s of Rachel Jacob's wife; Joseph, H1121
21 And the s of Benjamin *were* Belah, and H1121
22 These *are* the s of Rachel, which were H1121
23 And the s of Dan; Hushim. H1121
24 And the s of Naphtali; Jahzeel, and H1121
25 These *are* the s of Bilhah, which Laban H1121
27 And the s of Joseph, which were born H1121
48: 1 him his two s, Manasseh and Ephraim. H1121
5 And now thy two s, Ephraim and H1121
8 And Israel beheld Joseph's s, and said, H1121
9 They *are* my s, whom God hath given H1121
49: 1 And Jacob called unto his s, and said, H1121
2 and hear, ye s of Jacob; and hearken H1121
33 commanding his s, he gathered up his H1121
50:12 And his s did unto him according as he H1121
13 For his s carried him into the land of H1121
Ex 3:22 put *them* upon your s, and upon your H1121
4:20 And Moses took his wife and his s, and H1121
6:14 houses: The s of Reuben the firstborn H1121
15 And the s of Simeon; Jemuel, and H1121
16 And these *are* the names of the s of H1121
17 The s of Gershon; Libni, and Shimi, H1121
18 And the s of Kohath; Amram, and H1121
19 And the s of Merari; Mahali and H1121
21 And the s of Izhar; Korah, and Nepheg, H1121
22 And the s of Uzziel; Mishael, and H1121
24 And the s of Korah; Assir, and H1121
10: 9 with our old, with our s and with our H1121
12:24 ordinance to thee and to thy s for ever. H1121
18: 3 And her two s; of which the name of the H1121
5 law, came with his s and his wife unto H1121
6 and thy wife, and her two s with her. H1121
21: 4 she have born him s or daughters; the H1121
22:29 of thy s shalt thou give unto me. H1121
27:21 Aaron and his s shall order it from H1121
28: 1 thy brother, and his s with him, from H1121
1 Abihu, Eleazar and Ithamar, Aaron's s. H1121
4 brother, and his s, that he may minister H1121
40 And for Aaron's s thou shalt make H1121
41 brother, and his s with him; and shalt H1121
43 and upon his s, when they come in H1121
29: 4 And Aaron and his s thou shalt bring H1121
8 And thou shalt bring his s, and put H1121
9 Aaron and his s, and put the bonnets H1121
9 thou shalt consecrate Aaron and his s. H1121
10 and Aaron and his s shall put their H1121
15 and Aaron and his s shall put their H1121
19 and Aaron and his s shall put their H1121
20 of the right ear of his s, and upon the H1121
21 and upon his s, and upon the garments H1121
21 the garments of his s with him: and he H1121
21 his s, and his sons' garments with him. H1121

Ex 29:24 in the hands of his s; and shalt wave H1121
27 for Aaron, and of *that* which is for his s: H1121
32 And Aaron and his s shall eat the flesh H1121
35 Aaron, and to his s, according to all H1121
44 s, to minister to me in the priest's office. H1121
30:19 For Aaron and his s shall wash their H1121
30 And thou shalt anoint Aaron and his s, H1121
31:10 of his s, to minister in the priest's office, H1121
32: 2 wives, of your s, and of your daughters, H1121
26 unto me. And all the s of Levi gathered H1121
34:16 unto thy s, and their daughters H1121
16 thy s go a whoring after their gods. H1121
20 firstborn of thy s thou shalt redeem. H1121
35:19 of his s, to minister in the priest's office. H1121
39:27 *of* woven work for Aaron, and for his s, H1121
40:12 And thou shalt bring Aaron and his s H1121
14 And thou shalt bring his s, and clothe H1121
31 And Moses and Aaron and his s H1121
Lev 1: 5 priests, Aaron's s, shall bring the blood, H1121
7 And the s of Aaron the priest shall put H1121
8 And the priests, Aaron's s, shall lay the H1121
11 the priests, Aaron's s, shall sprinkle his H1121
2: 2 And he shall bring it to Aaron's s the H1121
3: 2 and Aaron's s the priests shall sprinkle H1121
5 And Aaron's s shall burn it on the altar H1121
8 and Aaron's s shall sprinkle the blood H1121
13 and the s of Aaron shall sprinkle H1121
6: 9 Command Aaron and his s, saying, H1121
14 meat offering: the s of Aaron shall offer H1121
16 Aaron and his s eat: with unleavened H1121
20 of Aaron and of his s, which they shall H1121
22 And the priest of his s that is anointed H1121
25 Speak unto Aaron and to his s, saying, H1121
7:10 dry, shall all the s of Aaron have, one H1121
33 He among the s of Aaron, that offereth H1121
34 and unto his s by a statute for ever H1121
35 anointing of his s, out of the offerings H1121
8: 2 Take Aaron and his s with him, and H1121
6 And Moses brought Aaron and his s, H1121
13 And Moses brought Aaron's s, and put H1121
14 and Aaron and his s laid their hands H1121
18 and Aaron and his s laid their hands H1121
22 and Aaron and his s laid their hands H1121
24 And he brought Aaron's s, and Moses H1121
30 and upon his s, and upon his sons' H1121
30 his s, and his sons' garments with him. H1121
31 Aaron and to his s, Boil the flesh *at* the H1121
31 saying, Aaron and his s shall eat it. H1121
36 So Aaron and his s did all things which H1121
9: 1 and his s, and the elders of Israel; H1121
9 And the s of Aaron brought the blood H1121
12 and Aaron's s presented unto him H1121
18 and Aaron's s presented unto him H1121
10: 1 And Nadab and Abihu, the s of Aaron, H1121
4 and Elzaphan, the s of Uzziel the uncle H1121
6 unto Ithamar, his s, Uncover not your H1121
9 thou, nor thy s with thee, when ye go H1121
12 unto Ithamar, his s that were left, Take H1121
14 thou, and thy s, and thy daughters with H1121
16 and Ithamar, the s of Aaron *which* H1121
13: 2 priest, or unto one of his s the priests: H1121
16: 1 death of the two s of Aaron, when they H1121
17: 2 Speak unto Aaron, and unto his s, and H1121
21: 1 the priests the s of Aaron, and say unto H1121
24 his s, and unto all the children of Israel. H1121
22: 2 Speak unto Aaron and to his s, that H1121
18 Speak unto Aaron, and to his s, and H1121
26:29 And ye shall eat the flesh of your s, and H1121
Nu 2:14 and the captain of the s of Gad *shall be* H1121
18 the captain of the s of Ephraim *shall be* H1121
22 the captain of the s of Benjamin *shall* H1121
3: 2 And these *are* the names of the s of H1121
3 These *are* the names of the s of Aaron, H1121
9 unto Aaron and to his s: they *are* wholly H1121
10 Aaron and his s, and they shall wait H1121
17 And these were the s of Levi by their H1121
18 And these *are* the names of the s of H1121
19 And the s of Kohath by their families; H1121
20 And the s of Merari by their families; H1121
25 And the charge of the s of Gershon in H1121
29 The families of the s of Kohath shall H1121
36 and charge of the s of Merari *shall be* H1121
38 and Aaron and his s, keeping the H1121
48 be redeemed, unto Aaron and to his s. H1121
51 Aaron and to his s, according to the H1121
4: 2 Take the sum of the s of Kohath from H1121
2 from among the s of Levi, after their H1121
4 This *shall be* the service of the s of H1121
5 come, and his s, and they shall take H1121

Nu 4:15 And when Aaron and his s have made H1121
15 after that, the s of Kohath shall come H1121
15 *are* the burden of the s of Kohath in the H1121
19 things: Aaron and his s shall go in, and H1121
22 Take also the sum of the s of Gershon, H1121
27 At the appointment of Aaron and his s H1121
27 the service of the s of the Gershonites, H1121
28 the families of the s of Gershon in the H1121
29 As for the s of Merari, thou shalt H1121
33 of the families of the s of Merari, H1121
34 numbered the s of the Kohathites after H1121
38 And those that were numbered of the s H1121
41 the families of the s of Gershon, of all H1121
42 of the families of the s of Merari, H1121
45 of the families of the s of Merari, whom H1121
6:23 Speak unto Aaron and unto his s, H1121
7: 7 oxen he gave unto the s of Gershon, H1121
8 he gave unto the s of Merari, according H1121
9 But unto the s of Kohath he gave none: H1121
8:13 and before his s, and offer them *for* an H1121
19 to Aaron and to his s from among the H1121
22 and before his s: as the LORD had H1121
10: 8 And the s of Aaron, the priests, shall H1121
17 down; and the s of Gershon and the H1121
17 of Gershon and the s of Merari set H1121
13:33 And there we saw the giants, the s of H1121
16: 1 and Abiram, the s of Eliab, and On, the H1121
1 son of Peleth, s of Reuben, took *men*: H1121
7 *take* too much upon you, ye s of Levi. H1121
8 Korah, Hear, I pray you, ye s of Levi: H1121
10 all thy brethren the s of Levi with thee: H1121
12 and Abiram, the s of Eliab: which said, H1121
27 and their s, and their little children. H1121
18: 1 Thou and thy s and thy father's house H1121
1 and thou and thy s with thee shall bear H1121
2 thee: but thou and thy s with thee *shall* H1121
7 Therefore thou and thy s with thee H1121
8 and to thy s, by an ordinance for ever. H1121
9 *shall be* most holy for thee and for thy s. H1121
11 thee, and to thy s and to thy daughters H1121
19 thee, and thy s and thy daughters with H1121
21:29 he hath given his s that escaped, and H1121
35 So they smote him, and his s, and all his H1121
26: 8 And the s of Pallu; Eliab. H1121
9 And the s of Eliab; Nemuel, and H1121
12 The s of Simeon after their families: of H1121
19 The s of Judah *were* Er and Onan: and H1121
20 And the s of Judah after their families H1121
21 And the s of Pharez were; of Hezron, H1121
23 *Of* the s of Issachar after their families: H1121
26 *Of* the s of Zebulun after their families: H1121
28 The s of Joseph after their families H1121
29 Of the s of Manasseh: of Machir, the H1121
30 These *are* the s of Gilead: *of* Jeezer, the H1121
33 of Hepher had no s, but daughters: and H1121
35 These *are* the s of Ephraim after their H1121
36 And these *are* the s of Shuthelah: of H1121
37 These *are* the families of the s of H1121
37 *are* the s of Joseph after their families. H1121
38 The s of Benjamin after their families: H1121
40 And the s of Bela were Ard and H1121
41 These *are* the s of Benjamin after their H1121
42 These *are* the s of Dan after their H1121
45 Of the s of Beriah: of Heber, the family H1121
47 These *are* the families of the s of Asher H1121
48 *Of* the s of Naphtali after their families: H1121
27: 3 but died in his own sin, and had no s. H1121
36: 1 of the families of the s of Joseph, came H1121
3 And if they be married to any of the s H1121
5 tribe of the s of Joseph hath said well. H1121
11 married unto their father's brothers' s: H1121
12 the families of the s of Manasseh the H1121
Dt 1:28 have seen the s of the Anakims there. H1121
2:33 smote him, and his s, and all his people. H1121
4: 9 teach them thy s, and thy sons' sons; H1121
9 teach them thy sons, and thy sons' s; H1121
11: 6 and Abiram, the s of Eliab, the son of H1121
12:12 your God, ye, and your s, and your H1121
31 for even their s and their daughters H1121
18: 5 of the LORD, him and his s for ever. H1121
21: 5 And the priests the s of Levi shall come H1121
16 Then it shall be, when he maketh his s H1121
23:17 Israel, nor a sodomite of the s of Israel. H1121
28:32 Thy s and thy daughters *shall be* given H1121
41 Thou shalt beget s and daughters, but H1121
53 the flesh of thy s and of thy daughters, H1121
31: 9 the priests the s of Levi, which bare H1121
32: 8 he separated the s of Adam, he set the H1121
19 of his s, and of his daughters. H1121

Jos 7:24 of gold, and his s, and his daughters, H1121
15:14 And Caleb drove thence the three s of H1121
17: 3 of Manasseh, had no s, but daughters: H1121
6 among his s: and the rest of Manasseh's H1121
6 of Manasseh's s had the land of Gilead. H1121
24:32 bought of the s of Hamor the father H1121
Jdg 1:20 he expelled thence the three s of Anak. H1121
3: 6 to their s, and served their gods. H1121
8:19 brethren, *even* the s of my mother: *as* H1121
30 And Gideon had threescore and ten s H1121
9: 2 either that all the s of Jerubbaal, *which* H1121
5 his brethren the s of Jerubbaal, *being* H1121
18 and have slain his s, threescore and ten H1121
24 threescore and ten s of Jerubbaal might H1121
10: 4 And he had thirty s that rode on thirty H1121
11: 2 And Gilead's wife bare him s; and his H1121
2 sons; and his wife's s grew up, and they H1121
12: 9 And he had thirty s, and thirty H1121
9 his s. And he judged Israel seven years. H1121
14 And he had forty s and thirty nephews, H1121
17: 5 one of his s, who became his priest. H1121
11 man was unto him as one of his s. H1121
18:30 he and his s were priests to the tribe H1121
19:22 of the city, certain s of Belial, beset the H1121
Ru 1: 1 of Moab, he, and his wife, and his two s. H1121
2 name of his two s Mahlon and Chilion, H1121
3 died; and she was left, and her two s. H1121
5 was left of her two s and her husband. H3206
11 yet *any more* s in my womb, that they H1121
12 also to night, and should also bear s; H1121
4:15 to thee than seven s, hath born him. H1121
1Sa 1: 3 And the two s of Eli, Hophni and H1121
4 all her s and her daughters, portions: H1121
8 *am* not I better to thee than ten s? H1121
2:12 Now the s of Eli *were* sons of Belial; H1121
12 Now the sons of Eli *were* s of Belial; H1121
21 and bare three s and two daughters. H1121
22 heard all that his s did unto all Israel; H1121
24 Nay, my s; for *it is* no good report that I H1121
29 and honourest thy s above me, to make H1121
34 come upon thy two s, on Hophni and H1121
3:13 because his s made themselves vile, H1121
4: 4 and the two s of Eli, Hophni and H1121
11 taken; and the two s of Eli, Hophni and H1121
17 people, and thy two s also, Hophni and H1121
8: 1 that he made his s judges over Israel. H1121
3 And his s walked not in his ways, but H1121
5 art old, and thy s walk not in thy ways: H1121
11 He will take your s, and appoint *them* H1121
12: 2 and, behold, my s *are* with you: and I H1121
14:49 Now the s of Saul were Jonathan, and H1121
16: 1 I have provided me a king among his s. H1121
5 his s, and called them to the sacrifice. H1121
10 Again, Jesse made seven of his s to H1121
17:12 and he had eight s: and the man went H1121
13 And the three eldest s of Jesse went *and* H1121
13 names of his three s that went to the H1121
22:20 And one of the s of Ahimelech the son H1121
28:19 *shalt* thou and thy s *be* with me: the H1121
30: 3 wives, and their s, and their daughters, H1121
6 grieved, every man for his s and for his H1121
19 nor great, neither s nor daughters, H1121
31: 2 Saul and upon his s; and the Philistines H1121
2 Abinadab, and Malchishua, Saul's s. H1121
6 So Saul died, and his three s, and his H1121
7 and that Saul and his s were dead, they H1121
8 and his three s fallen in mount Gilboa. H1121
12 and the bodies of his s from the wall of H1121
2Sa 2:18 And there were three s of Zeruiah H1121
3: 2 And unto David were s born in H1121
39 and these men the s of Zeruiah *be* too H1121
4: 2 the other Rechab, the s of Rimmon a H1121
5 And the s of Rimmon the Beerothite, H1121
9 his brother, the s of Rimmon the H1121
5:13 yet s and daughters born to David. H1121
6: 3 the s of Abinadab, drave the new cart. H1121
8:18 and David's s were chief rulers. H1121
9:10 Thou therefore, and thy s, and thy H1121
10 Ziba had fifteen s and twenty servants. H1121
11 eat at my table, as one of the king's s. H1121
13:23 and Absalom invited all the king's s. H1121
27 and all the king's s go with him. H1121
29 Then all the king's s arose, and every H1121
30 s, and there is not one of them left. H1121
32 men the king's s; for Amnon only is H1121
33 s are dead: for Amnon only is dead. H1121
35 s come: as thy servant said, so it is. H1121
36 behold, the king's s came, and lifted up H1121
14: 6 And thy handmaid had two s, and they H1121

2Sa 14:27 were born three s, and one daughter, H1121
15:27 and your two s with you, Ahimaaz H1121
36 them their two s, Ahimaaz Zadok's *son,* H1121
16:10 I to do with you, ye s of Zeruiah? so let H1121
19: 5 the lives of thy s and of thy daughters, H1121
17 Saul, and his fifteen s and his twenty H1121
22 I to do with you, ye s of Zeruiah, that ye H1121
21: 6 Let seven men of his s be delivered H1121
8 But the king took the two s of Rizpah H1121
8 and the five s of Michal the daughter H1121
16 And Ishbi-benob, which *was* of the s of H3211
18 Saph, which *was* of the s of the giant. H3211
23: 6 But *the* s of Belial *shall be* all of them as
32 Eliahba the Shaalbonite, of the s of H1121
1Ki 1: 9 the king's s, and all the men of Judah H1121
19 hath called all the s of the king, and H1121
25 all the king's s, and the captains of H1121
2: 7 But shew kindness unto the s of H1121
4: 3 Elihoreph and Ahiah, the s of Shisha, H1121
31 and Darda, the s of Mahol: and his H1121
11:20 household among the s of Pharaoh. H1121
12:31 people, which were not of the s of Levi. H1121
13:11 in Beth-el; and his s came and told him H1121
12 went he? For his s had seen what way H1121
13 And he said unto his s, Saddle me the H1121
27 And he spake to his s, saying, Saddle H1121
31 he spake to his s, saying, When I am H1121
18:31 of the tribes of the s of Jacob, unto H1121
20:35 And a certain man of the s of the H1121
21:10 And set two men, s of Belial, before H1121
2Ki 2: 3 And the s of the prophets that *were* at H1121
5 And the s of the prophets that *were* at H1121
7 And fifty men of the s of the prophets H1121
15 And when the s of the prophets which H1121
4: 1 of the wives of the s of the prophets H1121
1 unto him my two s to be bondmen. H3206
4 thee and upon thy s, and shalt pour out H1121
5 her and upon her s, who brought *the* H1121
38 the land; and the s of the prophets *were* H1121
38 seethe pottage for the s of the prophets. H1121
5:22 two young men of the s of the prophets: H1121
6: 1 And the s of the prophets said unto H1121
9:26 the blood of his s, saith the LORD; and H1121
10: 1 And Ahab had seventy s in Samaria. H1121
2 your master's s *are* with you, and *there* H1121
3 of your master's s, and set *him* on his H1121
6 men your master's s, and come to me to H1121
6 Now the king's s, *being* seventy persons, H1121
7 they took the king's s, and slew seventy H1121
8 heads of the king's s. And he said, Lay H1121
11: 2 among the king's s *which were* slain; H1121
15:12 unto Jehu, saying, Thy s shall sit on the H1121
17:17 And they caused their s and their H1121
19:37 and Sharezer his s smote him with the H1121
20:18 And of thy s that shall issue from thee, H1121
25: 7 And they slew the s of Zedekiah before H1121
1Ch 1: 5 The s of Japheth; Gomer, and Magog, H1121
6 And the s of Gomer; Ashchenaz, and H1121
7 And the s of Javan; Elishah, and H1121
8 The s of Ham; Cush, and Mizraim, Put, H1121
9 And the s of Cush; Seba, and Havilah, H1121
9 the s of Raamah; Sheba, and Dedan. H1121
17 The s of Shem; Elam, and Asshur, and H1121
19 And unto Eber were born two s: the H1121
23 Jobab. All these *were* the s of Joktan. H1121
28 The s of Abraham; Isaac, and Ishmael. H1121
31 Kedemah. These are the s of Ishmael. H1121
32 Now the s of Keturah, Abraham's H1121
32 the s of Jokshan; Sheba, and Dedan. H1121
33 And the s of Midian; Ephah, and H1121
33 Eldaah. All these *are* the s of Keturah. H1121
34 And Abraham begat Isaac. The s of H1121
35 The s of Esau; Eliphaz, Reuel, and H1121
36 The s of Eliphaz; Teman, and Omar, H1121
37 The s of Reuel; Nahath, Zerah, H1121
38 And the s of Seir; Lotan, and Shobal, H1121
39 And the s of Lotan; Hori, and Homam: H1121
40 The s of Shobal; Alian, and Manahath, H1121
40 And the s of Zibeon; Aiah, and Anah. H1121
41 The s of Anah; Dishon. And the sons of H1121
41 The sons of Anah; Dishon. And the s of H1121
42 The s of Ezer; Bilhan, and Zavan, *and* H1121
42 Jakan. The s of Dishan; Uz, and Aran. H1121
2: 1 These *are* the s of Israel; Reuben, H1121
3 The s of Judah; Er, and Onan, and H1121
4 and Zerah. All the s of Judah *were* five. H1121
5 The s of Pharez; Hezron, and Hamul. H1121
6 And the s of Zerah; Zimri, and Ethan, H1121
7 And the s of Carmi; Achar, the troubler H1121

1Ch 2: 8 And the s of Ethan; Azariah. H1121
9 The s also of Hezron, that were born H1121
16 Abigail. And the s of Zeruiah; Abishai, H1121
18 and of Jerioth: her s *are* these; Jesher, H1121
23 *to* the s of Machir the father of Gilead. H1121
25 And the s of Jerahmeel the firstborn of H1121
27 And the s of Ram the firstborn of H1121
28 And the s of Onam were, Shammai, H1121
28 s of Shammai; Nadab, and Abishur. H1121
30 And the s of Nadab; Seled, and H1121
31 And the s of Appaim; Ishi. And the H1121
31 Ishi. And the s of Ishi; Sheshan. And H1121
32 And the s of Jada the brother of H1121
33 And the s of Jonathan; Peleth, and H1121
33 Zaza. These were the s of Jerahmeel. H1121
34 Now Sheshan had no s, but daughters. H1121
42 Now the s of Caleb the brother of H1121
42 the s of Mareshah the father of Hebron. H1121
43 And the s of Hebron; Korah, and H1121
47 And the s of Jahdai; Regem, and H1121
50 These were the s of Caleb the son of H1121
52 had s; Haroeh, *and* half of H1121
54 The s of Salma; Beth-lehem, and the H1121
3: 1 Now these were the s of David, which H1121
9 *These were* all the s of David, beside H1121
9 David, beside the s of the concubines, H1121
15 And the s of Josiah *were,* the firstborn H1121
16 And the s of Jehoiakim: Jeconiah his H1121
17 And the s of Jeconiah; Assir, Salathiel H1121
19 And the s of Pedaiah *were,* Zerubbabel, H1121
19 and Shimei: and the s of Zerubbabel; H1121
21 And the s of Hananiah; Pelatiah, and H1121
21 and Jesaiah: the s of Rephaiah, the H1121
21 of Rephaiah, the s of Arnan, the sons of H1121
21 s of Obadiah, the sons of Shechaniah. H1121
21 sons of Obadiah, the s of Shechaniah. H1121
22 And the s of Shechaniah; Shemaiah: H1121
22 and the s of Shemaiah; Hattush, H1121
23 And the s of Neariah; Elioenai, and H1121
24 And the s of Elioenai *were,* Hodaiah, H1121
4: 1 The s of Judah; Pharez, Hezron, and H1121
4 These *are* the s of Hur, the firstborn H1121
6 These *were* the s of Naarah. H1121
7 And the s of Helah *were,* Zereth, and H1121
13 And the s of Kenaz; Othniel, and H1121
13 Seraiah: and the s of Othniel; Hathath. H1121
15 And the s of Caleb the son of H1121
15 Naam: and the s of Elah, even Kenaz. H1121
16 And the s of Jehaleleel; Ziph, and H1121
17 And the s of Ezra *were,* Jether, and H1121
18 And these *are* the s of Bithiah the H1121
19 And the s of *his* wife Hodiah the sister H1121
20 And the s of Shimon *were,* Amnon, and H1121
20 s of Ishi *were,* Zoheth, and Ben-zoheth. H1121
21 The s of Shelah the son of Judah *were,* H1121
24 The s of Simeon *were,* Nemuel, and H1121
26 And the s of Mishma; Hamuel his son, H1121
27 And Shimei had sixteen s and six H1121
42 And *some* of them, *even* of the s of H1121
42 and Rephaiah, and Uzziel, the s of Ishi. H1121
5: 1 Now the s of Reuben the firstborn of H1121
1 given unto the s of Joseph the son of H1121
3 The s, *I say,* of Reuben the firstborn of H1121
4 The s of Joel; Shemaiah his son, Gog H1121
18 The s of Reuben, and the Gadites, and H1121
6: 1 The s of Levi; Gershon, Kohath, and H1121
2 And the s of Kohath; Amram, Izhar, H1121
3 and Miriam. The s also of Aaron; H1121
16 The s of Levi; Gershom, Kohath, and H1121
17 And these *be* the names of the s of H1121
18 And the s of Kohath *were,* Amram, and H1121
19 The s of Merari; Mahli, and Mushi. H1121
22 The s of Kohath; Amminadab his son, H1121
25 And the s of Elkanah; Amasai, and H1121
26 *As for* Elkanah: the s of Elkanah; H1121
28 And the s of Samuel; the firstborn H1121
29 The s of Merari; Mahli, Libni his son, H1121
33 children. Of the s of the Kohathites: H1121
44 And their brethren the s of Merari H1121
49 But Aaron and his s offered upon the H1121
50 And these *are* the s of Aaron; Eleazar H1121
54 in their coasts, of the s of Aaron, of the H1121
57 And to the s of Aaron they gave the H1121
61 And unto the s of Kohath, *which were* H1121
62 And to the s of Gershom throughout H1121
63 Unto the s of Merari *were given* by lot, H1121
66 And *the residue* of the families of the s H1121
70 of the remnant of the s of Kohath. H1121
71 Unto the s of Gershom *were given* out H1121

1Ch 7: 1 Now the s of Issachar *were*, Tola, and H1121
2 And the s of Tola; Uzzi, and Rephaiah, H1121
3 And the s of Uzzi; Izrahiah: and the H1121
3 Uzzi; Izrahiah: and the s of Izrahiah; H1121
4 *men:* for they had many wives and s. H1121
6 *The* s of Benjamin; Bela, and Becher,
7 And the s of Bela; Ezbon, and Uzzi, and H1121
8 And the s of Becher; Zemira, and H1121
8 Alameth. All these *are* the s of Becher. H1121
10 The s also of Jediael; Bilhan: and the H1121
10 Bilhan: and the s of Bilhan; Jeush, and H1121
11 All these the s of Jediael, by the heads H1121
12 of Ir, *and* Hushim, the s of Aher. H1121
13 The s of Naphtali; Jahziel, and Guni, H1121
13 and Jezer, and Shallum, the s of Bilhah. H1121
14 The s of Manasseh; Ashriel, whom she H1121
16 and his s *were* Ulam and Rakem. H1121
17 And the s of Ulam; Bedan. These *were* H1121
17 These *were* the s of Gilead, the son of H1121
19 And the s of Shemida were, Ahian, and H1121
20 And the s of Ephraim; Shuthelah, and H1121
30 The s of Asher; Imnah, and Isuah, and H1121
31 And the s of Beriah; Heber, and H1121
33 And the s of Japhlet; Pasach, and H1121
34 And the s of Shamer; Ahi, and Rohgah, H1121
35 And the s of his brother Helem; H1121
36 The s of Zophah; Suah, and H1121
38 And the s of Jether; Jephunneh, and H1121
39 And the s of Ulla; Arah, and Haniel, H1121
8: 3 And the s of Bela were, Addar, and H1121
6 And these *are* the s of Ehud: these are H1121
10 These *were* his s, heads of the fathers. H1121
12 The s of Elpaal; Eber, and Misham, H1121
16 and Ispah, and Joha, the s of Beriah; H1121
18 and Jezliah, and Jobab, the s of Elpaal; H1121
21 and Shimrath, the s of Shimhi; H1121
25 And Iphedeiah, and Penuel, the s of H1121
27 and Eliah, and Zichri, the s of Jeroham. H1121
35 And the s of Micah *were*, Pithon, and H1121
38 And Azel had six s, whose names *are* H1121
38 Hanan. All these *were* the s of Azel. H1121
39 And the s of Eshek his brother *were*, H1121
40 And the s of Ulam were mighty men of H1121
40 and had many s, and sons' sons, an H1121
40 sons, and sons' s, an hundred and fifty. H1121
40 fifty. All these *are* of the s of Benjamin. H1121
9: 5 Asaiah the firstborn, and his s. H1121
6 And of the s of Zerah; Jeuel, and their H1121
7 And of the s of Benjamin; Sallu the son H1121
14 son of Hashabiah, of the s of Merari; H1121
30 And *some* of the s of the priests made H1121
32 And *other* of their brethren, of the s of H1121
41 And the s of Micah *were*, Pithon, and H1121
44 And Azel had six s, whose names *are* H1121
44 and Hanan: these *were* the s of Azel. H1121
10: 2 Saul, and after his s; and the Philistines H1121
2 and Malchishua, the s of Saul. H1121
6 So Saul died, and his three s, and all his H1121
7 and that Saul and his s were dead, then H1121
8 Saul and his s fallen in mount Gilboa. H1121
12 the bodies of his s, and brought them to H1121
11:34 The s of Hashem the Gizonite, H1121
44 and Jehiel the s of Hothan the Aroerite, H1121
46 s of Elnaam, and Ithmah the Moabite, H1121
12: 3 The chief *was* Ahiezer, then Joash, the s H1121
3 and Pelet, the s of Azmaveth; and H1121
7 And Joelah, and Zebadiah, the s of H1121
14 These *were* of the s of Gad, captains of H1121
14: 3 David begat more s and daughters. H1121
15: 5 Of the s of Kohath; Uriel the chief, and H1121
6 Of the s of Merari; Asaiah the chief, H1121
7 Of the s of Gershom; Joel the chief, and H1121
8 Of the s of Elizaphan; Shemaiah the H1121
9 Of the s of Hebron; Eliel the chief, and H1121
10 Of the s of Uzziel; Amminadab the H1121
17 and of the s of Merari their brethren, H1121
16:42 And the s of Jeduthun *were* porters. H1121
17:11 thy s; and I will establish his kingdom. H1121
18:17 s of David *were* chief about the king. H1121
21:20 and his four s with him hid themselves. H1121
23: 6 among the s of Levi, *namely*, Gershon, H1121
8 The s of Laadan; the chief *was* Jehiel, H1121
9 The s of Shimei; Shelomith, and Haziel, H1121
10 And the s of Shimei *were*, Jahath, Zina, H1121
10 These four *were* the s of Shimei. H1121
11 had not many s; therefore they were H1121
12 The s of Kohath; Amram, Izhar, H1121
13 The s of Amram; Aaron and Moses: H1121
13 things, he and his s for ever, to burn H1121

1Ch 23:14 his s were named of the tribe of Levi. H1121
15 The s of Moses *were*, Gershom, and H1121
16 Of the s of Gershom, Shebuel *was* the H1121
17 And the s of Eliezer *were*, Rehabiah the H1121
17 Eliezer had none other s; but the sons of H1121
17 but the s of Rehabiah were very many. H1121
18 Of the s of Izhar; Shelomith the chief. H1121
19 Of the s of Hebron; Jeriah the first, H1121
20 Of the s of Uzziel; Michah the first, and H1121
21 The s of Merari; Mahli, and Mushi. The H1121
21 The s of Mahli; Eleazar, and Kish. H1121
22 And Eleazar died, and had no s, but H1121
22 their brethren the s of Kish took them. H1121
23 The s of Mushi; Mahli, and Eder, and H1121
24 These *were* the s of Levi after the house H1121
28 *was* to wait on the s of Aaron for the H1121
32 and the charge of the s of Aaron their H1121
24: 1 Now *these are* the divisions of the s of H1121
1 of Aaron. The s of Aaron; Nadab, and H1121
3 both Zadok of the s of Eleazar, and H1121
3 and Ahimelech of the s of Ithamar, H1121
4 men found of the s of Eleazar than of H1121
4 than of the s of Ithamar; and *thus* H1121
4 Among the s of Eleazar *there were* H1121
4 and eight among the s of Ithamar H1121
5 of God, were of the s of Eleazar, and of H1121
5 of Eleazar, and of the s of Ithamar. H1121
20 And the rest of the s of Levi *were these:* H1121
20 Levi *were these:* Of the s of Amram; H1121
20 Shubael: of the s of Shubael; Jehdeiah. H1121
21 Concerning Rehabiah: of the s of H1121
22 Of the Izharites; Shelomoth: of the s of H1121
23 And the s *of Hebron;* Jeriah *the first*, H1121
24 *Of* the s of Uzziel; Michah: of the sons H1121
24 *Of* the sons of Uzziel; Michah: of the s H1121
25 Isshiah: of the s of Isshiah; Zechariah. H1121
26 The s of Merari *were* Mahli and Mushi: H1121
26 and Mushi: the s of Jaaziah; Beno. H1121
27 The s of Merari by Jaaziah; Beno, and H1121
28 Of Mahli *came* Eleazar, who had no s. H1121
30 The s also of Mushi; Mahli, and Eder, H1121
30 These *were* the s of the Levites after the H1121
31 their brethren the s of Aaron in the H1121
25: 1 to the service of the s of Asaph, and of H1121
2 Of the s of Asaph; Zaccur, and Joseph, H1121
2 and Asarelah, the s of Asaph under the H1121
3 Of Jeduthun: the s of Jeduthun; H1121
4 Of Heman: the s of Heman; Bukkiah, H1121
5 All these *were* the s of Heman the H1121
5 Heman fourteen s and three daughters. H1121
9 with his brethren and s *were* twelve: H1121
10 The third to Zaccur, *he*, his s, and his H1121
11 The fourth to Izri, *he*, his s, and his H1121
12 The fifth to Nethaniah, *he*, his s, and his H1121
13 The sixth to Bukkiah, *he*, his s, and his H1121
14 The seventh to Jesharelah, *he*, his s, and H1121
15 The eighth to Jeshaiah, *he*, his s, and his H1121
16 The ninth to Mattaniah, *he*, his s, and H1121
17 The tenth to Shimei, *he*, his s, and his H1121
18 The eleventh to Azareel, *he*, his s, and H1121
19 The twelfth to Hashabiah, *he*, his s, and H1121
20 The thirteenth to Shubael, *he*, his s, and H1121
21 The fourteenth to Mattithiah, *he*, his s, H1121
22 The fifteenth to Jeremoth, *he*, his s, and H1121
23 The sixteenth to Hananiah, *he*, his s, H1121
24 *he*, his s, and his brethren, *were* twelve: H1121
25 The eighteenth to Hanani, *he*, his s, and H1121
26 The nineteenth to Mallothi, *he*, his s, H1121
27 The twentieth to Eliathah, *he*, his s, and H1121
28 *he*, his s, and his brethren, *were* twelve: H1121
29 *he*, his s, and his brethren, *were* twelve: H1121
30 *he*, his s, and his brethren, *were* twelve: H1121
31 *he*, his s, and his brethren, *were* twelve. H1121
26: 1 the son of Kore, of the s of Asaph. H1121
2 And the s of Meshelemiah *were*, H1121
4 Moreover the s of Obed-edom *were*, H1121
6 Also unto Shemaiah his son were s H1121
7 The s of Shemaiah; Othni, and H1121
8 All these of the s of Obed-edom: they H1121
8 they and their s and their brethren, H1121
9 And Meshelemiah had s and brethren, H1121
10 of Merari, had s; Simri the chief, (for H1121
11 s and brethren of Hosah *were* thirteen. H1121
15 To Obed-edom southward; and to his s H1121
19 the porters among the s of Kore, and H1121
19 of Kore, and among the s of Merari. H1121
21 *As concerning* the s of Laadan; the H1121
21 sons of Laadan; the s of the Gershonite H1121
22 The s of Jehieli; Zetham, and Joel his H1121

1Ch 26:29 Of the Izharites, Chenaniah and his s H1121
27:32 son of Hachmoni *was* with the king's s: H1121
28: 1 king, and of his s, with the officers, and H1121
4 and among the s of my father he liked H1121
5 And of all my s, (for the LORD hath H1121
5 hath given me many s,) he hath chosen H1121
29:24 men, and all the s likewise of king H1121
2Ch 5:12 with their s and their brethren, H1121
11:14 Jeroboam and his s had cast them off H1121
21 and eight s, and threescore daughters.) H1121
13: 5 him and to his s by a covenant of salt? H1121
8 in the hand of the s of David; and ye *be* H1121
9 of the LORD, the s of Aaron, and the H1121
10 the LORD, *are* the s of Aaron, and the H1121
21 and two s, and sixteen daughters. H1121
20:14 a Levite of the s of Asaph, came the H1121
21: 2 And he had brethren the s of H1121
2 the s of Jehoshaphat king of Israel. H1121
7 give a light to him and to his s for ever. H1121
17 house, and his s also, and his wives; H1121
17 save Jehoahaz, the youngest of his s. H1121
22: 8 of Judah, and the s of the brethren of H1121
11 among the king's s that were slain, and H1121
23: 3 the LORD hath said of the s of David. H1121
11 Jehoiada and his s anointed him, and H1121
24: 3 wives; and he begat s and daughters. H1121
7 For the s of Athaliah, that wicked H1121
25 for the blood of the s of Jehoiada the H1121
27 Now *concerning* his s, and the H1121
26:18 to the priests the s of Aaron, that are H1121
28: 8 thousand, women, s, and daughters, H1121
29: 9 sword, and our s and our daughters H1121
11 My s, be not now negligent: for the H1121
12 of Azariah, of the s of the Kohathites: H1121
12 and of the s of Merari, Kish the H1121
13 And of the s of Elizaphan; Shimri, and H1121
13 s of Asaph; Zechariah, and Mattaniah: H1121
14 And of the s of Heman; Jehiel, and H1121
14 s of Jeduthun; Shemaiah, and Uzziel. H1121
21 the priests the s of Aaron to offer *them* H1121
31:18 wives, and their s, and their daughters, H1121
19 Also of the s of Aaron the priests, H1121
32:33 the sepulchres of the s of David: and all H1121
34:12 the Levites, of the s of Merari; and H1121
12 Meshullam, of the s of the Kohathites, H1121
35:14 the priests the s of Aaron *were busied* H1121
14 and for the priests the s of Aaron. H1121
15 And the singers the s of Asaph *were* in H1121
36:20 to him and his s until the reign of the H1121
Ezr 3: 9 Then stood Jeshua *with* his s and his H1121
9 Kadmiel and his s, the sons of Judah, H1121
9 and his sons, the s of Judah, together, H1121
9 house of God: the s of Henadad, *with* H1121
9 their s and their brethren the Levites. H1121
10 and the Levites the s of Asaph with H1121
6:10 pray for the life of the king, and of his s. H1123
7:23 against the realm of the king and his s? H1123
8: 2 Of the s of Phinehas; Gershom: of the H1121
2 Gershom: of the s of Ithamar; Daniel: H1121
2 Daniel: of the s of David; Hattush. H1121
3 Of the s of Shechaniah, of the sons of H1121
3 Of the sons of Shechaniah, of the s of H1121
4 Of the s of Pahath-moab; Elihoenai the H1121
5 Of the s of Shechaniah; the son of H1121
6 Of the s also of Adin; Ebed the son of H1121
7 And of the s of Elam; Jeshaiah the son H1121
8 And of the s of Shephatiah; Zebadiah H1121
9 Of the s of Joab; Obadiah the son of H1121
10 And of the s of Shelomith; the son of H1121
11 And of the s of Bebai; Zechariah the H1121
12 And of the s of Azgad; Johanan the son H1121
13 And of the last s of Adonikam, whose H1121
14 Of the s also of Bigvai; Uthai, and H1121
15 and found there none of the s of Levi. H1121
18 of the s of Mahli, the son of H1121
18 with his s and his brethren, eighteen; H1121
19 him Jeshaiah of the s of Merari, his H1121
19 his brethren and their s, twenty; H1121
9: 2 and for their s: so that the holy seed H1121
12 unto their s, neither take their H1121
12 unto your s, nor seek their peace H1121
10: 2 Jehiel, *one* of the s of Elam, answered H1121
18 And among the s of the priests there H1121
18 *namely*, of the s of Jeshua the son of H1121
20 And of the s of Immer; Hanani, and H1121
21 And of the s of Harim; Maaseiah, and H1121
22 And of the s of Pashur; Elioenai, H1121
25 Moreover of Israel: of the s of Parosh; H1121
26 And of the s of Elam; Mattaniah, H1121

Ezr 10:27 And of the s of Zattu; Elioenai, H1121
28 Of the s also of Bebai; Jehohanan, H1121
29 And of the s of Bani; Meshullam, H1121
30 And of the s of Pahath-moab; Adna, H1121
31 And *of* the s of Harim; Eliezer, Ishijah, H1121
33 Of the s of Hashum; Mattenai, H1121
34 Of the s of Bani; Maadai, Amram, and H1121
43 Of the s of Nebo; Jeiel, Mattithiah, H1121
Neh 3: 3 But the fish gate did the s of Hassenaah H1121
4:14 brethren, your s, and your daughters, H1121
5: 2 For there were that said, We, our s, and H1121
5 into bondage our s and our daughters H1121
10: 9 Binnui of the s of Henadad, Kadmiel; H1121
28 their wives, their s, and their daughters, H1121
30 land, nor take their daughters for our s: H1121
36 Also the firstborn of our s, and of our H1121
11: 6 All the s of Perez that dwelt at H1121
7 And these *are* the s of Benjamin; Sallu H1121
22 of Micha. Of the s of Asaph, the singers H1121
12:23 The s of Levi, the chief of the fathers, H1121
28 And the s of the singers gathered H1121
35 And *certain* of the priests' s with H1121
13:25 unto their s, nor take their daughters H1121
25 unto your s, or for yourselves. H1121
28 And *one* of the s of Joiada, the son of H1121
Est 9:10 The ten s of Haman the son of H1121
12 and the ten s of Haman; what have H1121
13 ten s be hanged upon the gallows. H1121
14 and they hanged Haman's ten s. H1121
25 his s should be hanged on the gallows. H1121
Job 1: 2 And there were born unto him seven s H1121
4 And his s went and feasted *in their* H1121
5 It may be that my s have sinned, and H1121
6 Now there was a day when the s of God H1121
13 And there was a day when his s and his H1121
18 and said, Thy s and thy daughters *were* H1121
2: 1 Again there was a day when the s of H1121
14:21 His s come to honour, and he knoweth H1121
38: 7 and all the s of God shouted for joy? H1121
32 or canst thou guide Arcturus with his s? H1121
42:13 He had also seven s and three H1121
16 years, and saw his s, and his sons' sons, H1121
16 and his sons' s, *even* four generations. H1121
Ps 4: 2 O ye s of men, how long *will ye turn* my H1121
31:19 that trust in thee before the s of men! H1121
33:13 heaven; he beholdeth all the s of men. H1121
42:ttl Musician, Maschil, for the s of Korah. H1121
44:ttl To the chief Musician for the s of H1121
45:ttl s of Korah, Maschil, A Song of loves. H1121
46:ttl To the chief Musician for the s of H1121
47:ttl Musician, A Psalm for the s of Korah. H1121
48:ttl A Song *and* Psalm for the s of Korah. H1121
49:ttl Musician, A Psalm for the s of Korah. H1121
57: 4 on fire, *even* the s of men, whose teeth H1121
58: 1 do ye judge uprightly, O ye s of men? H1121
77:15 the s of Jacob and Joseph. Selah. H1121
84:ttl Gittith, A Psalm for the s of Korah. H1121
85:ttl Musician, A Psalm for the s of Korah. H1121
87:ttl A Psalm *or* Song for the s of Korah. H1121
88:ttl A Song or Psalm for the s of Korah, to H1121
89: 6 *who* among the s of the mighty can be H1121
106:37 Yea, they sacrificed their s and their H1121
38 *even* the blood of their s and of their H1121
144:12 That our s *may be* as plants grown up H1121
145:12 To make known to the s of men his H1121
Prv 8: 4 I call; and my voice *is* to the s of man. H1121
31 my delights *were* with the s of men. H1121
Ecc 1:13 the s of man to be exercised therewith. H1121
2: 3 that good for the s of men, which they H1121
8 the delights of the s of men, *as* musical H1121
3:10 to the s of men to be exercised in it. H1121
18 the estate of the s of men, that God H1121
19 For that which befalleth the s of men H1121
8:11 s of men is fully set in them to do evil. H1121
9: 3 the heart of the s of men is full of evil, H1121
12 snare; so *are* the s of men snared in an H1121
Song 2: 3 among the s. I sat down under his H1121
Isa 37:38 and Sharezer his s smote him with the H1121
39: 7 And of thy s that shall issue from thee, H1121
43: 6 not back: bring my s from far, and my H1121
45:11 concerning my s, and concerning the H1121
49:22 shall bring thy s in *their* arms, and thy H1121
51:18 her among all the s *whom* she hath H1121
18 of all the s *that* she hath brought up. H1121
20 Thy s have fainted, they lie at the head H1121
52:14 and his form more than the s of men: H1121
56: 5 better than of s and of daughters: I H1121
6 Also the s of the stranger, that join H1121
57: 3 But draw near hither, ye s of the H1121
Isa 60: 4 come to thee: thy s shall come from far, H1121
9 first, to bring thy s from far, their silver H1121
10 And the s of strangers shall build up H1121
14 The s also of them that afflicted thee H1121
61: 5 flocks, and the s of the alien *shall be* H1121
62: 5 virgin, *so* shall thy s marry thee: and *as* H1121
8 enemies; and the s of the stranger shall H1121
Jer 3:24 their herds, their s and their daughters. H1121
5:17 bread, *which* thy s and thy daughters H1121
6:21 the fathers and the s together shall fall H1121
7:31 to burn their s and their daughters H1121
11:22 die by the sword; their s and their H1121
13:14 the fathers and the s together, saith the H1121
14:16 wives, nor their s, nor their daughters: H1121
16: 2 thou have s or daughters in this place. H1121
3 concerning the s and concerning the H1121
19: 5 Baal, to burn their s with fire *for* burnt H1121
9 the flesh of their s and the flesh of their H1121
29: 6 Take ye wives, and beget s and H1121
6 take wives for your s, and give your H1121
6 they may bear s and daughters; that H1121
32:19 all the ways of the s of men: to give H1121
35 to cause their s and their daughters H1121
35: 3 and all his s, and the whole house H1121
4 chamber of the s of Hanan, the son of H1121
5 And I set before the s of the house of H1121
6 no wine, *neither ye*, nor your s for ever: H1121
8 we, our wives, our s, nor our daughters; H1121
14 he commanded his s not to drink wine, H1121
16 Because the s of Jonadab the son of H1121
39: 6 Then the king of Babylon slew the s of H1121
40: 8 and Jonathan the s of Kareah, and H1121
8 and the s of Ephai the Netophathite, H1121
48:46 perisheth: for thy s are taken captives, H1121
49: 1 Hath Israel no s? hath he no heir? why H1121
52:10 And the king of Babylon slew the s of H1121
Lam 4: 2 The precious s of Zion, comparable to H1121
Ezk 5:10 Therefore the fathers shall eat the s in H1121
10 of thee, and the s shall eat their fathers; H1121
14:16 deliver neither s nor daughters; they H1121
18 deliver neither s nor daughters, but H1121
22 forth, *both* s and daughters: behold, H1121
16:20 Moreover thou hast taken thy s and thy H1121
20:31 ye make your s to pass through the H1121
23: 4 and they bare s and daughters. Thus H1121
10 they took her s and her daughters, H1121
25 they shall take thy s and thy daughters; H1121
37 also caused their s, whom they bare H1121
47 shall slay their s and their daughters, H1121
24:21 pitieth; and your s and your daughters H1121
25 minds, their s and their daughters, H1121
40:46 altar: these *are* the s of Zadok among H1121
46 of Zadok among the s of Levi, which H1121
44:15 But the priests the Levites, the s of H1121
46:16 gift unto any of his s, the inheritance H1121
18 he shall give his s inheritance out of his H1121
48:11 are sanctified of the s of Zadok; which H1121
Dan 5:21 And he was driven from the s of men; H1123
10:16 similitude of the s of men touched my H1121
11:10 But his s shall be stirred up, and shall H1121
Hos 1:10 them, *Ye are* the s of the living God. H1121
Joel 1:12 joy is withered away from the s of men. H1121
2:28 upon all flesh; and your s and your H1121
3: 8 And I will sell your s and your H1121
Am 2:11 And I raised up of your s for prophets, H1121
7:17 in the city, and thy s and thy daughters H1121
Mic 5: 7 for man, nor waiteth for the s of men. H1121
Zec 9:13 and raised up thy s, O Zion, against thy H1121
13 Zion, against thy s, O Greece, and made H1121
Mal 3: 3 he shall purify the s of Levi, and purge H1121
6 ye s of Jacob are not consumed. H1121
Mt 20:20 children with her s, worshipping *him*, G5207
21 that these my two s may sit, the one on G5207
21:28 man had two s; and he came to the G5043
26:37 Peter and the two s of Zebedee, and G5207
Mk 3:17 Boanerges, which is, The s of thunder: G5207
28 be forgiven unto the s of men, and G5207
10:35 And James and John, the s of Zebedee, G5207
Lk 5:10 And so *was* also James, and John, the s G5207
11:19 by whom do your s cast *them* out? G5207
15:11 And he said, A certain man had two s: G5207
Jn 1:12 to become the s of God, *even* to them G5043
21: 2 in Galilee, and the s of Zebedee, and two
Act 2:17 upon all flesh: and your s and your G5207
7:16 the s of Emmor *the father* of Sychem. G5207
29 land of Madian, where he begat two s. G5207
19:14 And there were seven s of *one* Sceva, a G5207
Ro 8:14 the Spirit of God, they are the s of God. G5207
19 for the manifestation of the s of God. G5207
1Co 4:14 you, but as my beloved s I warn *you*. G5043
2Co 6:18 and ye shall be my s and daughters, G5207
Gal 4: 5 that we might receive the adoption of s. G5206
6 And because ye are s, God hath sent G5207
22 that Abraham had two s, the one by a G5207
Eph 3: 5 known unto the s of men, as it is now G5207
Php 2:15 and harmless, the s of God, without G5043
Heb 2:10 in bringing many s unto glory, to make G5207
7: 5 And verily they that are of the s of Levi, G5207
11:21 dying, blessed both the s of Joseph; and G5207
12: 7 with you as with s; for what son is he G5207
8 then are ye bastards, and not s. G5207
1Jn 3: 1 be called the s of God: therefore the G5043
2 Beloved, now are we the s of God, and G5043

SON'S

Gen 11:31 son of Haran his s son, and Sarai his H1121
16:15 s name, which Hagar bare, Ishmael. H1121
21:23 son, nor with my s son: *but* according H5220
24:51 s wife, as the LORD hath spoken. H1121
27:25 I will eat of my s venison, that my soul H1121
31 s venison, that thy soul may bless me. H1121
30:14 me, I pray thee, of thy s mandrakes. H1121
15 take away my s mandrakes also? And H1121
15 with thee to night for thy s mandrakes. H1121
16 thee with my s mandrakes. And he H1121
37:32 now whether it *be* thy s coat or no. H1121
33 And he knew it, and said, *It is* my s H1121
Ex 10: 2 thy son, and of thy s son, what things I H1121
Lev 18:10 The nakedness of thy s daughter, or of H1121
15 in law: she *is* thy s wife; thou shalt not H1121
17 shalt thou take her s daughter, or her H1121
Dt 6: 2 thy son, and thy s son, all the days of H1121
Jdg 8:22 thy son, and thy s son also: for thou H1121
1Ki 11:35 But I will take the kingdom out of his s H1121
21:29 days: *but* in his s days will I bring the H1121
Prv 30: 4 what *is* his s name, if thou canst tell? H1121
Jer 27: 7 his son, and his s son, until the very H1121

SONS'

Gen 6:18 and thy wife, and thy s wives with thee. H1121
7: 7 his wife, and his s wives with him, into H1121
8:16 thy sons, and thy s wives with thee. H1121
18 and his wife, and his s wives with him: H1121
46: 7 His sons, and his s sons with him, his H1121
7 daughters, and his s daughters, and all H1121
26 besides Jacob's s wives, all the souls H1121
Ex 29:21 his sons, and his s garments with him. H1121
28 And it shall be Aaron's and his s by a H1121
29 of Aaron shall be his s after him, to be H1121
39:41 the priest, and his s garments, to H1121
Lev 2: 3 *be* Aaron's and his s: *it is* a thing most H1121
10 *be* Aaron's and his s: *it is* a thing most H1121
7:31 the breast shall be Aaron's and his s. H1121
8:27 and upon his s hands, and waved them H1121
30 and upon his s garments with him; H1121
30 his sons, and his s garments with him. H1121
10:13 it *is* thy due, and thy s due, of the H1121
14 thy due, and thy s due, *which* are given H1121
15 shall be thine, and thy s with thee, by a H1121
24: 9 And it shall be Aaron's and his s; and H1121
Dt 4: 9 teach them thy sons, and thy s sons; H1121
1Ch 8:40 many sons, and s sons, an hundred H1121
Job 42:16 and his s sons, *even* four generations. H1121
Ezk 46:16 thereof shall be his s; it *shall be* their H1121
17 his inheritance shall be his s for them. H1121

SOON

Gen 18:33 And the LORD went his way, as s as he H834
27:30 And it came to pass, as s as Isaac had H834
44: 3 As s as the morning was light, the men
Ex 2:18 How *is it that* ye are come so s to day? H4116
9:29 And Moses said unto him, As s as I am
32:19 And it came to pass, as s as he came H834
Dt 4:26 day, that ye shall s utterly perish from H4118
Jos 2: 7 unto the fords: and as s as they which H834
11 And as s as we had heard *these things*,
3:13 And it shall come to pass, as s as the
8:19 and they ran as s as he had stretched out
29 eventide: and as s as the sun was down,
Jdg 8:33 And it came to pass, as s as Gideon was H834
9:33 And it shall be, *that* in the morning, as s
1Sa 9:13 As s as ye be come into the city, ye shall
13:10 And it came to pass, that as s as he had
20:41 *And* as s as the lad was gone, David
29:10 with thee: and as s as ye be up early in
2Sa 6:18 And as s as David had made an end of
13:36 And it came to pass, as s as he had made
15:10 Israel, saying, As s as ye hear the sound

S

2Sa 22:45 unto me: as s as they hear, they shall
1Ki 16:11 he began to reign, as s as he sat on his
18:12 And it shall come to pass, *as s as* I am
20:36 LORD, behold, as s as thou art departed
36 slay thee. And as s as he was departed
2Ki 10: 2 Now as s as this letter cometh to you,
25 And it came to pass, as s as he had made
14: 5 And it came to pass, as s as the kingdom H834
2Ch 31: 5 And as s as the commandment came
Job 32:22 my maker would s take me away. H4592
Ps 18:44 As s as they hear of me, they shall obey
37: 2 For they shall s be cut down like the H4120
58: 3 as s as they be born, speaking lies.
68:31 shall s stretch out her hands unto God. H7323
81:14 I should s have subdued their enemies, H4592
90:10 for it is s cut off, and we fly away. H2440
106:13 They s forgat his works; they waited H4116
Prv 14:17 *He that is* s angry dealeth foolishly: H7116
Isa 66: 8 at once? for as s as Zion travailed, she H1571
Ezk 23:16 And as s as she saw them with her H4758
Mt 21:20 How s is the fig tree withered away! *G3916*
Mk 1:42 And as s as he had spoken, immediately
5:36 As s as Jesus heard the word that was *G2112*
11: 2 you: and as s as ye be entered into *G2112*
14:45 And as s as he was come, he goeth
Lk 1:23 And it came to pass, that, as s as the
44 For, lo, as s as the voice of thy salutation
8: 6 And some fell upon a rock; and as s as it
15:30 But as s as this thy son was come, *G3753*
22:66 And as s as it was day, the elders of the
23: 7 And as s as he knew that he belonged
Jn 11:20 Then Martha, as s as she heard that
29 As s as she heard *that*, she arose quickly,
16:21 is come: but as s as she is delivered of *G3752*
18: 6 As s then as he had said unto them, I am
21: 9 As s then as they were come to land,
Act 10:29 gainsaying, as s as I was sent for: I ask
12:18 Now as s as it was day, there was no *G1096*
Gal 1: 6 I marvel that ye are so s removed from *G5030*
Php 2:23 so s as I shall see how it will go with me.
2Th 2: 2 That ye be not s shaken in mind, or be *G5030*
Tit 1: 7 not selfwilled, not s angry, not given to *G3711*
Rev 10:10 s as I had eaten it, my belly was bitter. *G3753*
12: 4 to devour her child as s as it was born. *G3752*

SOONER
Heb 13:19 this, that I may be restored to you the s. *G5032*
Jas 1:11 For the sun is no s risen with a burning *G5032*

SOOTHSAYER
Jos 13:22 Balaam also the son of Beor, the s, did H7080

SOOTHSAYERS
Isa 2: 6 the east, and *are* s like the Philistines, H6049
Dan 2:27 magicians, the s, shew unto the king; H1505
4: 7 and the s: and I told the dream H1505
5: 7 and the s. *And* the king spake, H1505
11 astrologers, Chaldeans, *and* s; H1505
Mic 5:12 hand; and thou shalt have no *more* s: H6049

SOOTHSAYING
Act 16:16 brought her masters much gain by s: *G3132*

SOP
Jn 13:26 I shall give a s, when I have dipped *G5596*
26 he had dipped the s, he gave *it* to Judas *G5596*
27 And after the s Satan entered into him. *G5596*
30 He then having received the s went *G5596*

SOPATER
Act 20: 4 him into Asia S of Berea; and of the *G4986*

SOPHERETH
Ezr 2:55 children of S, the children of Peruda, H5618
Neh 7:57 the children of S, the children of Perida, H5618

SORCERER
Act 13: 6 found a certain s, a false prophet, a Jew, *G3097*
8 But Elymas the s (for so is his name by *G3097*

SORCERERS
Ex 7:11 wise men and the s: now the magicians H3784
Jer 27: 9 nor to your s, which speak unto you, H3786
Dan 2: 2 and the s, and the Chaldeans, H3784
Mal 3: 5 witness against the s, and against the H3784
Rev 21: 8 and s, and idolaters, and all *G5332*
22:15 For without *are* dogs, and s, and *G5333*

SORCERESS
Isa 57: 3 But draw near hither, ye sons of the s, H6049

SORCERIES
Isa 47: 9 the multitude of thy s, *and* for the great H3785
12 multitude of thy s, wherein thou hast H3785
Act 8:11 time he had bewitched them with s. *G3095*
Rev 9:21 nor of their s, nor of their fornication, *G5331*
18:23 for by thy s were all nations deceived. *G5331*

SORCERY
Act 8: 9 the same city used s, and bewitched the *G3096*

SORE
Gen 19: 9 And they pressed s upon the man, *even* H3966
20: 8 their ears: and the men were s afraid. H3966
31:30 gone, because thou s longedst after thy H3700
34:25 when they were s, that two of the sons H3510
41:56 famine waxed s in the land of Egypt. H2388
57 that the famine was *so* s in all lands. H2388
43: 1 And the famine *was* s in the land. H3515
47: 4 flocks; for the famine *is* s in the land of H3515
13 famine *was* very s, so that the land of H3515
50:10 a great and very s lamentation: and he H3515
Ex 14:10 them; and they were s afraid: and the H3966
Lev 13:42 a white reddish s; it *is* a leprosy sprung H5061
43 *if* the rising of the s *be* white reddish in H5061
Nu 22: 3 And Moab was s afraid of the people, H3966
Dt 6:22 great and s, upon Egypt, upon Pharaoh, H7451
28:35 in the legs, with a s botch that cannot H7451
59 s sicknesses, and of long continuance. H7451
Jos 9:24 therefore we were s afraid of our lives H3966
Jdg 10: 9 so that Israel was s distressed. H3966
14:17 because she lay s upon him: and she H6693
15:18 And he was s athirst, and called on the H3966
20:34 and the battle was s: but they knew not H3513
21: 2 and lifted up their voices, and wept s; H1419
1Sa 1: 6 And her adversary also provoked her s, H3708
10 and prayed unto the LORD, and wept s. H1058
5: 7 is s upon us, and upon Dagon our god. H7185
14:52 And there was s war against the H2389
17:24 man, fled from him, and were s afraid. H3966
21:12 was s afraid of Achish the king of Gath. H3966
28:15 answered, I am s distressed; for the H3966
20 the earth, and was s afraid, because of H3966
21 saw that he was s troubled, and said H3966
31: 3 And the battle went s against Saul, and H3513
3 and he was s wounded of the archers. H3966
4 not; for he was s afraid. Therefore Saul H3966
2Sa 2:17 And there was a very s battle that day; H7186
13:36 also and all his servants wept very s. H1419
1Ki 17:17 s, that there was no breath left in him. H2389
18: 2 And *there was a* s famine in Samaria. H2389
2Ki 3:26 the battle was too s for him, he took H2388
6:11 the king of Syria was s troubled for this
20: 3 good in thy sight. And Hezekiah wept s. H1419
1Ch 10: 3 And the battle went s against Saul, and H3513
4 not; for he was s afraid. So Saul took H3966
2Ch 6:28 s or whatsoever sickness *there be*: H5061
29 know his own s and his own grief, and H5061
21:19 so he died of s diseases. And his people H7451
28:19 and transgressed s against the LORD. H4604
35:23 Have me away; for I am s wounded. H3966
Ezr 10: 1 and children: for the people wept very s.
Neh 2: 2 of heart. Then I was very s afraid, H7235
13: 8 And it grieved me s: therefore I cast H3966
Job 2: 7 smote Job with s boils from the sole of H7451
5:18 For he maketh s, and bindeth up: he H3510
Ps 2: 5 and vex them in his s displeasure.
6: 3 My soul is also s vexed: but thou, O H3966
10 Let all mine enemies be ashamed and s H3966
38: 2 fast in me, and thy hand presseth me s. H5181
8 I am feeble and s broken: I have roared H3966
11 my s; and my kinsmen stand afar off. H5061
44:19 Though thou hast s broken us in the
55: 4 My heart is s pained within me: and the
71:20 me great and s troubles, shalt quicken H7451
77: 2 the Lord; my s ran in the night, and H3027
118:13 Thou hast thrust s at me that I might H1760
18 The LORD hath chastened me s: but he H3256
Ecc 1:13 under heaven: this s travail hath God H7451
4: 8 This *is* also vanity, yea, it *is* a s travail. H7451
5:13 There is a s evil *which* I have seen H2470
16 And this also *is* a s evil, *that* in all H2470
Isa 27: 1 In that day the LORD with his s and H7186
38: 3 good in thy sight. And Hezekiah wept s. H1419
59:11 We roar all like bears, and mourn s H1897
64: 9 Be not wroth very s, O LORD, neither H3966
12 hold thy peace, and afflict us very s? H3966
Jer 13:17 eye shall weep s, and run down with H1830
22:10 him: *but* weep s for him that goeth H1058
50:12 Your mother shall be s confounded; H3966
52: 6 the famine was s in the city, so that H2388
Lam 1: 2 She weepeth s in the night, and her H1058
3:52 Mine enemies chased me s, like a bird, H6679
Ezk 14:21 when I send my four s judgments upon H7451
21:10 It is sharpened to make a s slaughter; it H2874
27:35 kings shall be s afraid, they shall be H8178
Dan 6:14 *these* words, was s displeased with H7690
Mic 2:10 destroy *you*, even with a s destruction. H4834
Zec 1: 2 The LORD hath been s displeased with H7110
15 And I am very s displeased with the H7110
Mt 17: 6 fell on their face, and were s afraid. *G4970*
15 he is lunatick, and s vexed: for ofttimes *G2560*
21:15 the son of David; they were s displeased, *G23*
Mk 6:51 and they were s amazed in themselves *G3029*
9: 6 not what to say; for they were s afraid. *G1630*
26 And *the spirit* cried, and rent him s, *G4183*
14:33 to be s amazed, and to be very heavy; *G1568*
Lk 2: 9 about them: and they were s afraid. *G3173*
Act 20:37 And they all wept s, and fell on Paul's *G2425*
Rev 16: 2 and grievous s upon the men which *G1668*

SOREK
Jdg 16: 4 valley of S, whose name *was* Delilah. H7796

SORELY
Gen 49:23 The archers have s grieved him, and H4843
Isa 23: 5 they be s pained at the report of Tyre.

SORER
Heb 10:29 Of how much s punishment, suppose *G5501*

SORES
Isa 1: 6 and putrifying s: they have not been H4347
Lk 16:20 which was laid at his gate, full of s, *G1669*
21 the dogs came and licked his s. *G1668*
Rev 16:11 their s, and repented not of their deeds. *G1668*

SORROW
Gen 3:16 multiply thy s and thy conception; H6093
16 thy conception; in s thou shalt bring H6089
17 for thy sake; in s shalt thou eat *of* it all H6093
42:38 down my gray hairs with s to the grave. H3015
44:29 down my gray hairs with s to the grave. H7451
31 servant our father with s to the grave. H3015
Ex 15:14 The people shall hear, *and* be afraid: s H2427
Lev 26:16 eyes, and cause s of heart: and ye shall H1727
Dt 28:65 and failing of eyes, and s of mind: H1671
1Ch 4: 9 saying, Because I bare him with s. H6090
Neh 2: 2 s of heart. Then I was very sore afraid, H7455
Est 9:22 unto them from s to joy, and from H3015
Job 3:10 womb, nor hid s from mine eyes. H5999
6:10 harden myself in s: let him not spare; H2427
17: 7 Mine eye also is dim by reason of s, and H3708
41:22 In his neck remaineth strength, and s H1670
Ps 13: 2 in my soul, *having* s in my heart daily? H3015
38:17 For I *am* ready to halt, and my s *is* H4341
39: 2 *even* from good; and my s was stirred. H3511
55:10 also and s *are* in the midst of it. H5999
90:10 s; for it is soon cut off, and we fly away. H205
107:39 through oppression, affliction, and s. H3015
116: 3 hold upon me: I found trouble and s. H3015
Prv 10:10 He that winketh with the eye causeth s: H6094
22 rich, and he addeth no s with it. H6089
15:13 by s of the heart the spirit is broken. H6094
17:21 He that begetteth a fool *doeth it* to his s: H8424
23:29 Who hath woe? who hath s? who hath H17
Ecc 1:18 that increaseth knowledge increaseth s. H4341
5:17 much s and wrath with his sickness. H3707
7: 3 S *is* better than laughter: for by the H3708
11:10 Therefore remove s from thy heart, H3708
Isa 5:30 behold darkness *and* s, and the light is H6862
14: 3 thee rest from thy s, and from thy fear, H6090
17:11 in the day of grief and of desperate s. H3511
29: 2 and s: and it shall be unto me as Ariel. H592
35:10 and s and sighing shall flee away. H3015
50:11 of mine hand; ye shall lie down in s. H4620
51:11 *and* s and mourning shall flee away. H3015
65:14 but ye shall cry for s of heart, and shall H3511
Jer 8:18 *When* I would comfort myself against s, H3015
20:18 womb to see labour and s, that my days H3015
30:15 affliction? thy s *is* incurable for the H4341
31:12 and they shall not s any more at all. H1669
13 and make them rejoice from their s. H3015
45: 3 added grief to my s; I fainted in my H4341
49:23 *there is* s on the sea; it cannot be quiet. H1674
51:29 And the land shall tremble and s: for H2342

Lam 1:12 and see if there be any s like unto my H4341
12 like unto my s, which is done unto H4341
18 and behold my s: my virgins and my H4341
3:65 Give them s of heart, thy curse unto H4044
Ezk 23:33 with drunkenness and s, with the cup of H3015
Hos 8:10 and they shall s a little for the burden H2490
Lk 22:45 disciples, he found them sleeping for s, G3077
Jn 16: 6 unto you, s hath filled your heart. G3077
20 but your s shall be turned into joy. G3077
21 A woman when she is in travail hath s, G3077
22 And ye now therefore have s: but I will G3077
Ro 9: 2 heaviness and continual s in my heart. G3601
2Co 2: 3 I should have s from them of whom G3077
7 be swallowed up with overmuch s. G3077
7:10 For godly s worketh repentance to G3077
10 but the s of the world worketh death. G3077
Php 2:27 also, lest I should have s upon sorrow. G3077
27 also, lest I should have sorrow upon s. G3077
1Th 4:13 are asleep, that ye s not, even as others G3076
Rev 18: 7 torment and s give her: for she saith G3997
7 and am no widow, and shall see no s. G3997
21: 4 death, neither s, nor crying, neither G3997

SORROWED
2Co 7: 9 sorry, but that ye s to repentance: for G3076
11 thing, that ye s after a godly sort, what G3076

SORROWETH
1Sa 10: 2 care of the asses, and s for you, saying, H1672

SORROWFUL
1Sa 1:15 *am* a woman of a s spirit: I have drunk H7186
Job 6: 7 soul refused to touch *are* as my s meat. H1741
Ps 69:29 But I *am* poor and s: let thy salvation, O H3510
Prv 14:13 Even in laughter the heart is s; and the H3510
Jer 31:25 and I have replenished every s soul. H1669
Zep 3:18 I will gather *them that are* s for the H3013
Zec 9: 5 *see it*, and be very s, and Ekron; for her H2342
Mt 19:22 away s: for he had great possessions. G3076
26:22 And they were exceeding s, and began G3076
37 and began to be s and very heavy. G3076
38 My soul is exceeding s, even unto death: G4036
Mk 14:19 And they began to be s, and to say unto G3076
34 s unto death: tarry ye here, and watch. G4036
Lk 18:23 And when he heard this, he was very s: G4036
24 And when Jesus saw that he was very s, G4036
Jn 16:20 and ye shall be s, but your sorrow shall G3076
2Co 6:10 As s, yet alway rejoicing; as poor, yet G3076
Php 2:28 may rejoice, and that I may be the less s. G253

SORROWING
Lk 2:48 thy father and I have sought thee s. G3600
Act 20:38 S most of all for the words which he G3600

SORROWS
Ex 3: 7 of their taskmasters; for I know their s; H4341
2Sa 22: 6 The s of hell compassed me about; the H2256
Job 9:28 I am afraid of all my s, I know that thou H6094
21:17 them! *God* distributeth s in his anger. H2256
39: 3 their young ones, they cast out their s. H2256
Ps 16: 4 Their s shall be multiplied *that* hasten H6094
18: 4 The s of death compassed me, and the H2256
5 The s of hell compassed me about: the H2256
32:10 Many s *shall be* to the wicked: but he H4341
116: 3 The s of death compassed me, and the H2256
127: 2 of s: *for* so he giveth his beloved sleep. H6089
Ecc 2:23 For all his days *are* s, and his travail H4341
Isa 13: 8 And they shall be afraid: pangs and s H2256
53: 3 of men; a man of s, and acquainted H4341
4 and carried our s: yet we did esteem H4341
Jer 13:21 not s take thee, as a woman in travail? H2256
49:24 *her*: anguish and s have taken her, as a H2256
Dan 10:16 by the vision my s are turned upon me, H6735
Hos 13:13 The s of a travailing woman shall come H2256
Mt 24: 8 All these *are* the beginning of s. G5604
Mk 13: 8 troubles: these *are* the beginnings of s. G5604
1Ti 6:10 themselves through with many s. G3601

SORRY
1Sa 22: 8 none of you that is s for me, or sheweth H2470
Neh 8:10 neither be ye s; for the joy of the LORD H6087
Ps 38:18 mine iniquity; I will be s for my sin. H1672
Isa 51:19 unto thee; who shall be s for thee? H5110
Mt 14: 9 And the king was s: nevertheless for the G3076
17:23 again. And they were exceeding s. G3076
18:31 they were very s, and came and told G3076
Mk 6:26 And the king was exceeding s; *yet* for G4036
2Co 2: 2 For if I make you s, who is he then that G3076
2 but the same which is made s by me? G3076
2Co 7: 8 For though I made you s with a letter, I G3076
8 you s, though *it were* but for a season. G3076
9 Now I rejoice, not that ye were made s, G3076
9 for ye were made s after a godly G3076

SORT
Gen 6:19 flesh, two of every *s* shalt thou bring into
20 his kind, two of every *s* shall come unto
7:14 fowl after his kind, every bird of every s. H3671
2Ki 24:14 the poorest s of the people of the land. H1803
1Ch 24: 5 Thus were they divided by lot, one s with H428
29:14 willingly after this s? for all things *come*
2Ch 30: 5 of a long *time in such s* as it was written.
Ezr 1:10 basons of a second *s* four hundred and
4: 8 to Artaxerxes the king in this s: H3660
Neh 6: 4 times after this s; and I answered them H1697
Ezk 23:42 of the common s *were* brought Sabeans H120
39: 4 birds of every s, and *to* the beasts of H3671
44:30 of all, of every *s* of your oblations, shall
Dan 1:10 which *are* of your s? then shall ye make H1524
3:29 no other God that can deliver after this s.
Act 17: 5 fellows of the baser s, and gathered a
Ro 15:15 unto you in some s, as putting you in G3313
1Co 3:13 try every man's work of what s it is. G3697
2Co 7:11 after a godly s, what carefulness it G2596
2Ti 3: 6 For of this s are they which creep into G5130
3Jn 6 after a godly s, thou shalt do well: G516

SORTS
Dt 22:11 divers s, *as* of woollen and linen together.
Neh 5:18 days store of all s of wine: yet for all this
Ps 78:45 He sent divers s of flies among them,
105:31 He spake, and there came divers s of
Ecc 2: 8 musical instruments, and that of all s. H7705
Ezk 27:24 These *were* thy merchants in all s *of* H4360
38: 4 clothed with all s *of armour, even* a H4358

SOSIPATER
Ro 16:21 Jason, and S, my kinsmen, salute you. G4989

SOSTHENES
Act 18:17 Then all the Greeks took S, the chief G4988
1Co 1: 1 the will of God, and S *our* brother, G4988

SOTAI
Ezr 2:55 the children of S, the children of H5479
Neh 7:57 the children of S, the children of H5479

SOTTISH
Jer 4:22 me; they *are* s children, and they have H5530

SOUGHT
Gen 43:30 brother: and he s *where* to weep; and H1245
Ex 2:15 this thing, he s to slay Moses. But H1245
4:19 all the men are dead which s thy life. H1245
24 the LORD met him, and s to kill him. H1245
33: 7 every one which s the LORD went out H1245
Lev 10:16 And Moses diligently s the goat of the H1875
Nu 35:23 *was* not his enemy, neither s his harm: H1245
Dt 13:10 because he hath s to thrust thee away H1245
Jos 2:22 and the pursuers s *them* throughout all H1245
Jdg 14: 4 of the LORD, that he s an occasion H1245
18: 1 of the Danites s them an inheritance H1245
1Sa 10:21 they s him, he could not be found. H1245
13:14 the LORD hath s him a man after his H1245
14: 4 which Jonathan s to go over unto the H1245
19:10 And Saul s to smite David even to the H1245
23:14 of Ziph. And Saul s him every day, but H1245
27: 4 Gath: and he s no more again for him. H1245
2Sa 3:17 Israel, saying, Ye s for David in times H1245
4: 8 enemy, which s thy life; and the LORD H1245
17:20 when they had s and could not find H1245
21: 2 them: and Saul s to slay them in his H1245
1Ki 1: 2 him, Let there be s for my lord the king H1245
3 So they s for a fair damsel throughout H1245
10:24 And all the earth s to Solomon, to hear H1245
11:40 Solomon s therefore to kill Jeroboam. H1245
2Ki 2:17 they s three days, but found him not. H1245
1Ch 15:13 that we s him not after the due order. H1875
26:31 of David they were s for, and there H1875
2Ch 1: 5 and the congregation s unto it. H1875
9:23 And all the kings of the earth s the H1245
14: 7 because we have s the LORD our God, H1875
7 our God, we have s *him*, and he hath H1875
15: 4 and s him, he was found of them. H1245
15 all their heart, and s him with their H1245
16:12 in his disease he s not to the LORD, but H1875
17: 3 father David, and s not unto Baalim; H1875
4 But s to the *LORD* God of his father, H1875
2Ch 22: 9 And he s Ahaziah: and they caught H1245
9 Jehoshaphat, who s the LORD with all H1875
25:15 Why hast thou s after the gods of the H1875
20 because they s after the gods of Edom. H1875
26: 5 And he s God in the days of Zechariah, H1875
5 s the LORD, God made him to prosper. H1875
Ezr 2:62 These s their register *among* those that H1245
Neh 7:64 These s their register *among* those that H1245
12:27 of Jerusalem they s the Levites out of H1245
Est 2: 2 be fair young virgins s for the king: H1245
21 s to lay hand on the king Ahasuerus. H1245
3: 6 wherefore Haman s to destroy all the H1245
6: 2 s to lay hand on the king Ahasuerus. H1245
9: 2 hand on such as s their hurt: and no H1245
Ps 34: 4 I s the LORD, and he heard me, and H1875
37:36 yea, I s him, but he could not be found. H1245
77: 2 In the day of my trouble I s the Lord: H1875
78:34 When he slew them, then they s him: H1875
86:14 violent *men* have s after my soul; and H1245
111: 2 The works of the LORD *are* great, s out H1875
119:10 With my whole heart have I s thee: O H1875
94 I *am* thine, save me; for I have s thy H1875
Ecc 2: 3 I s in mine heart to give myself unto H8446
7:29 but they have s out many inventions. H1245
12: 9 s out, *and* set in order many proverbs. H2713
10 The preacher s to find out acceptable H1245
Song 3: 1 By night on my bed I s him whom my H1245
1 loveth: I s him, but I found him not. H1245
2 loveth: I s him, but I found him not. H1245
5: 6 when he spake: I s him, but I could not H1245
Isa 62:12 be called, S out, A city not forsaken. H1875
65: 1 I am s of *them that* asked not *for me*; I H1875
1 of *them that* s me not: I said, Behold H1245
10 down in, for my people that have s me. H1875
Jer 8: 2 whom they have s, and whom they have H1875
10:21 and have not s the LORD: therefore H1875
26:21 words, the king s to put him to death: H1245
44:30 Babylon, his enemy, and that s his life. H1245
50:20 of Israel shall be s for, and *there shall* H1245
Lam 1:19 they s their meat to relieve their souls. H1245
Ezk 22:30 And I s for a man among them, that H1245
26:21 though thou be s for, yet shalt thou H1245
34: 4 neither have ye s that which was lost; H1245
Dan 2:13 s Daniel and his fellows to be slain. H1158
4:36 and my lords s unto me; and I was H1158
6: 4 Then the presidents and princes s to H1158
8:15 the vision, and s for the meaning, then, H1245
Oba 6 out! *how* are his hidden things s up! H1156
Zep 1: 6 not s the LORD, nor inquired for him. H1245
Zec 6: 7 And the bay went forth, and s to go H1245
Mt 2:20 are dead which s the young child's life. G2212
21:46 But when they s to lay hands on him, G2212
26:16 And from that time he s opportunity to G2212
59 all the council, s false witness against G2212
Mk 11:18 heard *it*, and s how they might destroy G2212
12:12 And they s to lay hold on him, but G2212
14: 1 and the scribes s how they might take G2212
11 him money. And he s how he might G2212
55 and all the council s for witness against G2212
Lk 2:44 journey; and they s him among *their* G327
48 thy father and I have s thee sorrowing. G2212
49 How is it that ye s me? wist ye not that G2212
4:42 and the people s him, and came unto G2212
5:18 a palsy: and they s *means* to bring him G2212
6:19 And the whole multitude s to touch G2212
11:16 And others, tempting *him*, s of him a G2212
13: 6 and s fruit thereon, and found none. G2212
19: 3 And he s to see Jesus who he was; and G2212
47 the chief of the people s to destroy him, G2212
20:19 the same hour s to lay hands on him; G2212
22: 2 And the chief priests and scribes s how G2212
6 And he promised, and s opportunity to G2212
Jn 5:16 Jesus, and s to slay him, because G2212
18 Therefore the Jews s the more to kill G2212
7: 1 in Jewry, because the Jews s to kill him. G2212
11 Then the Jews s him at the feast, and G2212
30 Then they s to take him: but no man G2212
10:39 Therefore they s again to take him: but G2212
11: 8 the Jews of late s to stone thee; and G2212
56 Then s they for Jesus, and spake G2212
19:12 And from thenceforth Pilate s to G2212
Act 12:19 And when Herod had s for him, and G1934
17: 5 and s to bring them out to the people. G2212
Ro 9:32 Wherefore? Because *they s* it not by G2212
10:20 of them that s me not; I was made G2212
1Th 2: 6 Nor of men s we glory, neither of you, G2212
2Ti 1:17 But, when he was in Rome, he s me out G2212
Heb 8: 7 no place have been s for the second. G2212
12:17 though he s it carefully with tears. G1567

SOUL
Gen 2: 7 of life; and man became a living s. H5315
12:13 and my s shall live because of thee. H5315
17:14 not circumcised, that s shall be cut off H5315
19:20 it not a little one?) and my s shall live. H5315
27: 4 that my s may bless thee before I die. H5315
19 of my venison, that thy s may bless me. H5315
25 venison, that my s may bless thee. And H5315
31 son's venison, that thy s may bless me. H5315
34: 3 And his s clave unto Dinah the H5315
8 them, saying, The s of my son Shechem H5315
35:18 And it came to pass, as her s was in H5315
42:21 the anguish of his s, when he besought H5315
49: 6 O my s, come not thou into their secret; H5315
Ex 12:15 day, that s shall be cut off from Israel. H5315
19 even that s shall be cut off from H5315
30:12 man a ransom for his s unto the LORD, H5315
31:14 *any* work therein, that s shall be cut off H5315
Lev 4: 2 of Israel, saying, If a s shall sin through H5315
5: 1 And if a s sin, and hear the voice of H5315
2 Or if a s touch any unclean thing, H5315
4 Or if a s swear, pronouncing with *his* H5315
15 If a s commit a trespass, and sin H5315
17 And if a s sin, and commit any of these H5315
6: 2 If a s sin, and commit a trespass H5315
7:18 and the s that eateth of it shall H5315
20 But the s that eateth *of* the flesh of the H5315
20 that s shall be cut off from his people. H5315
21 Moreover the s that shall touch any H5315
21 that s shall be cut off from his people. H5315
25 LORD, even the s that eateth *it* shall be H5315
27 Whatsoever s *it be* that eateth any H5315
27 that s shall be cut off from his people. H5315
17:10 face against that s that eateth blood, H5315
11 *that* maketh an atonement for the s. H5315
12 of Israel, No s of you shall eat blood, H5315
15 And every s that eateth that which died H5315
19: 8 LORD: and that s shall be cut off from H5315
20: 6 And the s that turneth after such as H5315
6 face against that s, and will cut him off H5315
22: 3 upon him, that s shall be cut off from H5315
6 The s which hath touched any such H5315
11 But if the priest buy *any* s with his H5315
23:29 For whatsoever s *it be* that shall not be H5315
30 And whatsoever s *it be* that doeth any H5315
30 s will I destroy from among his people. H5315
26:11 you: and my s shall not abhor you. H5315
15 my statutes, or if your s abhor my H5315
30 of your idols, and my s shall abhor you. H5315
43 because their s abhorred my statutes. H5315
Nu 9:13 even the same s shall be cut off from H5315
11: 6 But now our s *is* dried away: *there is* H5315
15:27 And if any s sin through ignorance, H5315
28 an atonement for the s that sinneth H5315
30 But the s that doeth *ought* H5315
30 LORD; and that s shall be cut off from H5315
31 that s shall utterly be cut off; H5315
19:13 LORD; and that s shall be cut off from H5315
20 himself, that s shall be cut off from H5315
22 be unclean; and the s that toucheth *it* H5315
21: 4 of Edom: and the s of the people was H5315
5 and our s loatheth this light bread. H5315
30: 2 oath to bind his s with a bond; he shall H5315
4 hath bound her s, and her father shall H5315
4 she hath bound her s shall stand. H5315
5 hath bound her s, shall stand: and the H5315
6 of her lips, wherewith she bound her s; H5315
7 wherewith she bound her s shall stand. H5315
8 she bound her s, of none effect: and the H5315
10 or bound her s by a bond with an oath; H5315
11 wherewith she bound her s shall stand. H5315
12 the bond of her s, shall not stand: her H5315
13 oath to afflict the s, her husband may H5315
31:28 out to battle: one s of five hundred, H5315
Dt 4: 9 and keep thy s diligently, lest thou H5315
29 him with all thy heart and with all thy s. H5315
6: 5 with all thy s, and with all thy might. H5315
10:12 God with all thy heart and with all thy s, H5315
11:13 with all your heart and with all your s, H5315
18 heart and in your s, and bind them for a H5315
12:15 gates, whatsoever thy s lusteth after, H5315
20 flesh, because thy s longeth to eat flesh; H5315
20 eat flesh, whatsoever thy s lusteth after. H5315
21 gates whatsoever thy s lusteth after. H5315
13: 3 with all your heart and with all your s. H5315
6 *is* as thine own s, entice thee secretly, H5315
14:26 for whatsoever thy s lusteth after, for H5315
26 for whatsoever thy s desireth: and thou H5315
26:16 with all thine heart, and with all thy s. H5315
Dt 30: 2 with all thine heart, and with all thy s; H5315
6 and with all thy s, that thou mayest live. H5315
10 with all thine heart, and with all thy s. H5315
Jos 22: 5 with all your heart and with all your s. H5315
Jdg 5:21 my s, thou hast trodden down strength. H5315
10:16 s was grieved for the misery of Israel. H5315
16:16 *so* that his s was vexed unto death; H5315
1Sa 1:10 And she *was* in bitterness of s, and H5315
15 have poured out my s before the LORD. H5315
26 And she said, Oh my lord, *as* thy s H5315
2:16 take *as much* as thy s desireth; then he H5315
17:55 *As* thy s liveth, O king, I cannot tell. H5315
18: 1 unto Saul, that the s of Jonathan was H5315
1 was knit with the s of David, and H5315
1 and Jonathan loved him as his own s. H5315
3 because he loved him as his own s. H5315
20: 3 liveth, and *as* thy s liveth, *there is* but a H5315
4 thy s desireth, I will even do *it* for thee. H5315
17 for he loved him as he loved his own s. H5315
23:20 the desire of thy s to come down; and H5315
24:11 thee; yet thou huntest my s to take it. H5315
25:26 liveth, and *as* thy s liveth, seeing the H5315
29 and to seek thy s: but the soul of my H5315
29 thy soul: but the s of my lord shall be H5315
26:21 harm, because my s was precious in H5315
30: 6 him, because the s of all the people was H5315
2Sa 4: 9 redeemed my s out of all adversity, H5315
5: 8 hated of David's s, *he shall be chief and* H5315
11:11 *as* thy s liveth, I will not do this thing. H5315
13:39 And *the s of* king David longed to go
14:19 and said, *As* thy s liveth, my lord the H5315
1Ki 1:29 hath redeemed my s out of all distress, H5315
2: 4 and with all their s, there shall not fail H5315
8:48 and with all their s, in the land of their H5315
11:37 to all that thy s desireth, and shalt be H5315
17:21 let this child's s come into him again. H5315
22 of Elijah; and the s of the child came H5315
2Ki 2: 2 liveth, and *as* thy s liveth, I will not H5315
4 liveth, and *as* thy s liveth, I will not H5315
6 liveth, and *as* thy s liveth, I will not H5315
4:27 her alone; for her s *is* vexed within her: H5315
30 liveth, and *as* thy s liveth, I will not H5315
23: 3 heart and all *their* s, to perform the H5315
25 heart, and with all his s, and with all his H5315
1Ch 22:19 Now set your heart and your s to seek H5315
2Ch 6:38 and with all their s in the land of their H5315
15:12 with all their heart and with all their s; H5315
34:31 and with all his s, to perform the words H5315
Job 3:20 is in misery, and life unto the bitter *in* s; H5315
6: 7 The things *that* my s refused to touch H5315
7:11 I will complain in the bitterness of my s. H5315
15 So that my s chooseth strangling, *and* H5315
9:21 not know my s: I would despise my life. H5315
10: 1 My s is weary of my life; I will leave my H5315
1 I will speak in the bitterness of my s. H5315
12:10 In whose hand *is* the s of every living H5315
14:22 and his s within him shall mourn. H5315
16: 4 I also could speak as ye *do*: if your s H5315
19: 2 How long will ye vex my s, and break H5315
21:25 of his s, and never eateth with pleasure. H5315
23:13 *what* his s desireth, even *that* he doeth. H5315
24:12 of the city, and the s of the wounded H5315
27: 2 the Almighty, *who* hath vexed my s; H5315
8 gained, when God taketh away his s? H5315
30:15 they pursue my s as the wind: and my H5082
16 And now my s is poured out upon me; H5315
25 was *not* my s grieved for the poor? H5315
31:30 mouth to sin by wishing a curse to his s. H5315
33:18 He keepeth back his s from the pit, and H5315
20 bread, and his s dainty meat. H5315
22 Yea, his s draweth near unto the grave, H5315
28 He will deliver his s from going into the H5315
30 To bring back his s from the pit, to be H5315
Ps 3: 2 Many *there be* which say of my s, *There* H5315
6: 3 My s is also sore vexed: but thou, O H5315
4 Return, O LORD, deliver my s: oh save H5315
7: 2 Lest he tear my s like a lion, rending *it* H5315
5 Let the enemy persecute my s, and take H5315
11: 1 my s, Flee *as* a bird to your mountain? H5315
5 him that loveth violence his s hateth. H5315
13: 2 How long shall I take counsel in my s, H5315
16: 2 *O my s*, thou hast said unto the LORD,
10 For thou wilt not leave my s in hell; H5315
17:13 s from the wicked, *which is* thy sword: H5315
19: 7 converting the s: the testimony of the H5315
22:20 Deliver my s from the sword; my H5315
29 him: and none can keep alive his own s. H5315
23: 3 He restoreth my s: he leadeth me in the H5315
24: 4 s unto vanity, nor sworn deceitfully. H5315
Ps 25: 1 Unto thee, O LORD, do I lift up my s. H5315
13 His s shall dwell at ease; and his seed H5315
20 O keep my s, and deliver me: let me not H5315
26: 9 Gather not my s with sinners, nor my H5315
30: 3 O LORD, thou hast brought up my s H5315
31: 7 thou hast known my s in adversities; H5315
9 with grief, *yea*, my s and my belly. H5315
33:19 To deliver their s from death, and to H5315
20 Our s waiteth for the LORD: he *is* our H5315
34: 2 My s shall make her boast in the H5315
22 The LORD redeemeth the s of his H5315
35: 3 me: say unto my s, I *am* thy salvation. H5315
4 that seek after my s: let them be turned H5315
7 cause they have digged for my s. H5315
9 And my s shall be joyful in the LORD: it H5315
12 me evil for good *to* the spoiling of my s. H5315
13 I humbled my s with fasting; and my H5315
17 look on? rescue my s from their H5315
40:14 that seek after my s to destroy it; let H5315
41: 4 my s; for I have sinned against thee. H5315
42: 1 so panteth my s after thee, O God. H5315
2 My s thirsteth for God, for the living H5315
4 I pour out my s in me: for I had gone H5315
5 Why art thou cast down, O my s? and H5315
6 O my God, my s is cast down within H5315
11 Why art thou cast down, O my s? and H5315
43: 5 Why art thou cast down, O my s? and H5315
44:25 For our s is bowed down to the dust: H5315
49: 8 (For the redemption of their s *is* H5315
15 But God will redeem my s from the H5315
18 Though while he lived he blessed his s: H5315
54: 3 seek after my s: they have not set God H5315
4 the Lord *is* with them that uphold my s. H5315
55:18 He hath delivered my s in peace from H5315
56: 6 my steps, when they wait for my s. H5315
13 For thou hast delivered my s from H5315
57: 1 unto me: for my s trusteth in thee: yea, H5315
4 My s *is* among lions: *and* I lie *even* H5315
6 for my steps; my s is bowed down: they H5315
59: 3 For, lo, they lie in wait for my s: the H5315
62: 1 Truly my s waiteth upon God: from H5315
5 My s, wait thou only upon God; for my H5315
63: 1 I seek thee: my s thirsteth for thee, my H5315
5 My s shall be satisfied as *with* marrow H5315
8 My s followeth hard after thee: thy H5315
9 But those *that* seek my s, to destroy *it*, H5315
66: 9 Which holdeth our s in life, and H5315
16 will declare what he hath done for my s. H5315
69: 1 for the waters are come in unto *my* s. H5315
10 When I wept, *and chastened* my s with H5315
18 Draw nigh unto my s, *and* redeem it: H5315
70: 2 that seek after my s: let them be turned H5315
71:10 lay wait for my s take counsel together, H5315
13 adversaries to my s; let them be covered H5315
23 and my s, which thou hast redeemed. H5315
72:14 He shall redeem their s from deceit and H5315
74:19 O deliver not the s of thy turtledove H5315
77: 2 not: my s refused to be comforted. H5315
78:50 spared not their s from death, but gave H5315
84: 2 My s longeth, yea, even fainteth for the H5315
86: 2 Preserve my s; for I *am* holy: O thou my H5315
4 Rejoice the s of thy servant: for unto H5315
4 for unto thee, O Lord, do I lift up my s. H5315
13 delivered my s from the lowest hell. H5315
14 s; and have not set thee before them. H5315
88: 3 For my s is full of troubles: and my life H5315
14 LORD, why castest thou off my s? *why* H5315
89:48 his s from the hand of the grave? Selah. H5315
94:17 help, my s had almost dwelt in silence. H5315
19 within me thy comforts delight my s. H5315
21 against the s of the righteous, and H5315
103: 1 Bless the LORD, O my s: and all that is H5315
2 Bless the LORD, O my s, and forget not H5315
22 his dominion: bless the LORD, O my s. H5315
104: 1 Bless the LORD, O my s. O LORD my H5315
35 the LORD, O my s. Praise ye the LORD. H5315
106:15 request; but sent leanness into their s. H5315
107: 5 Hungry and thirsty, their s fainted in H5315
9 For he satisfieth the longing s, and H5315
9 and filleth the hungry s with goodness. H5315
18 Their s abhorreth all manner of meat; H5315
26 their s is melted because of trouble. H5315
109:20 of them that speak evil against my s. H5315
31 *him* from those that condemn his s. H5315
116: 4 O LORD, I beseech thee, deliver my s. H5315
7 Return unto thy rest, O my s; for the H5315
8 For thou hast delivered my s from H5315
119:20 My s breaketh for the longing *that it* H5315
25 My s cleaveth unto the dust: quicken H5315

Ps 119:28 My **s** melteth for heaviness: strengthen H5315
81 My **s** fainteth for thy salvation: *but* I H5315
109 My **s** *is* continually in my hand: yet do I H5315
129 therefore doth my **s** keep them. H5315
167 My **s** hath kept thy testimonies; and I H5315
175 Let my **s** live, and it shall praise thee; H5315
120: 2 Deliver my **s**, O LORD, from lying lips, H5315
6 My **s** hath long dwelt with him that H5315
121: 7 from all evil: he shall preserve thy **s**. H5315
123: 4 Our **s** is exceedingly filled with the H5315
124: 4 us, the stream had gone over our **s**: H5315
5 the proud waters had gone over our **s**. H5315
7 Our **s** is escaped as a bird out of the H5315
130: 5 I wait for the LORD, my **s** doth wait, H5315
6 My **s** *waiteth* for the Lord more than H5315
131: 2 mother: my **s** *is* even as a weaned child. H5315
138: 3 me *with* strength in my **s**. H5315
139:14 and *that* my **s** knoweth right well. H5315
141: 8 is my trust; leave not my **s** destitute. H5315
142: 4 failed me; no man cared for my **s**. H5315
7 Bring my **s** out of prison, that I may H5315
143: 3 For the enemy hath persecuted my **s**; he H5315
6 unto thee: my **s** *thirsteth* after thee, H5315
8 walk; for I lift up my **s** unto thee. H5315
11 sake bring my **s** out of trouble. H5315
12 that afflict my **s**: for I *am* thy servant. H5315
146: 1 ye the LORD. Praise the LORD, O my **s**. H5315
Prv 2:10 and knowledge is pleasant unto thy **s**; H5315
3:22 So shall they be life unto thy **s**, and H5315
6:30 steal to satisfy his **s** when he is hungry; H5315
32 he *that* doeth it destroyeth his own **s**. H5315
8:36 own **s**: all they that hate me love death. H5315
10: 3 The LORD will not suffer the **s** of the H5315
11:17 good to his own **s**: but *he that is* cruel H5315
25 The liberal **s** shall be made fat: and he H5315
13: 2 of *his* mouth: but the **s** of the H5315
4 The **s** of the sluggard desireth, and H5315
4 the **s** of the diligent shall be made fat. H5315
19 is sweet to the **s**: but *it is* abomination H5315
25 **s**: but the belly of the wicked shall want. H5315
15:32 despiseth his own **s**: but he that heareth H5315
16:17 that keepeth his way preserveth his **s**. H5315
24 sweet to the **s**, and health to the bones. H5315
18: 7 and his lips *are* the snare of his **s**. H5315
19: 2 Also, *that* the **s** *be* without knowledge, H5315
8 loveth his own **s**: he that keepeth H5315
15 sleep; and an idle **s** shall suffer hunger. H5315
16 keepeth his own **s**; *but* he that despiseth H5315
18 and let not thy **s** spare for his crying. H5315
20: 2 him to anger sinneth *against* his own **s**. H5315
21:10 The **s** of the wicked desireth evil: his H5315
23 his tongue keepeth his **s** from troubles. H5315
22: 5 doth keep his **s** shall be far from them. H5315
23 spoil the **s** of those that spoiled them. H5315
25 learn his ways, and get a snare to thy **s**. H5315
23:14 rod, and shalt deliver his **s** from hell. H5315
24:12 that keepeth thy **s**, doth *not* he know *it*? H5315
14 *be* unto thy **s**: when thou hast found H5315
25:13 for he refresheth the **s** of his masters. H5315
25 *As* cold waters to a thirsty **s**, so *is* good H5315
27: 7 The full **s** loatheth an honeycomb; but H5315
7 the hungry **s** every bitter thing is sweet. H5315
29:10 hate the upright: but the just seek his **s**. H5315
17 yea, he shall give delight unto thy **s**. H5315
24 hateth his own **s**: he heareth cursing, H5315
Ecc 2:24 he should make his **s** enjoy good in his H5315
4: 8 and bereave my **s** of good? This *is* also H5315
6: 2 nothing for his **s** of all that he desireth, H5315
3 be many, and his **s** be not filled with H5315
7:28 Which yet my **s** seeketh, but I find not: H5315
Song 1: 7 Tell me, O thou whom my **s** loveth, H5315
3: 1 him whom my **s** loveth: I sought him, H5315
2 him whom my **s** loveth: I sought him, H5315
3 *I said*, Saw ye him whom my **s** loveth? H5315
4 him whom my **s** loveth: I held him, and H5315
5: 6 *and* was gone: my **s** failed when he H5315
6:12 Or ever I was aware, my **s** made me H5315
Isa 1:14 feasts my **s** hateth: they are a trouble H5315
3: 9 not. Woe unto their **s**! for they have H5315
10:18 fruitful field, both **s** and body: and they H5315
26: 8 the desire of *our* **s** *is* to thy name, and H5315
9 With my **s** have I desired thee in the H5315
29: 8 he awaketh, and his **s** is empty: or as H5315
8 *he is* faint, and his **s** hath appetite: so H5315
32: 6 to make empty the **s** of the hungry, and H5315
38:15 all my years in the bitterness of my **s**. H5315
17 hast in love to my **s** *delivered it* from H5315
42: 1 elect, *in whom* my **s** delighteth; I have H5315
44:20 he cannot deliver his **s**, nor say, *Is there* H5315

Isa 51:23 have said to thy **s**, Bow down, that we H5315
53:10 shalt make his **s** an offering for sin, he H5315
11 He shall see of the travail of his **s**, *and* H5315
12 poured out his **s** unto death: and he H5315
55: 2 and let your **s** delight itself in fatness. H5315
3 hear, and your **s** shall live; and I will H5315
58: 3 we afflicted our **s**, and thou takest no H5315
5 a man to afflict his **s**? *is it* to bow down H5315
10 And *if* thou draw out thy **s** to the H5315
10 the afflicted **s**; then shall thy light rise H5315
11 and satisfy thy **s** in drought, and make H5315
61:10 I will greatly rejoice in the LORD, my **s** H5315
66: 3 **s** delighteth in their abominations. H5315
Jer 4:10 whereas the sword reacheth unto the **s**. H5315
19 hast heard, O my **s**, the sound of the H5315
31 my **s** is wearied because of murderers. H5315
5: 9 **s** be avenged on such a nation as this? H5315
29 **s** be avenged on such a nation as this? H5315
6: 8 Jerusalem, lest my **s** depart from thee; H5315
9: 9 **s** be avenged on such a nation as this? H5315
12: 7 of my **s** into the hand of her enemies. H5315
13:17 But if ye will not hear it, my **s** shall H5315
14:19 Judah? hath thy **s** lothed Zion? why H5315
18:20 a pit for my **s**. Remember that I stood H5315
20:13 he hath delivered the **s** of the poor from H5315
31:12 of the herd: and their **s** shall be as a H5315
14 And I will satiate the **s** of the priests H5315
25 For I have satiated the weary **s**, and I H5315
25 I have replenished every sorrowful **s**. H5315
32:41 my whole heart and with my whole **s**. H5315
38:16 that made us this **s**, I will not put thee H5315
17 princes, then thy **s** shall live, and this H5315
20 be well unto thee, and thy **s** shall live. H5315
50:19 and Bashan, and his **s** shall be satisfied H5315
51: 6 every man his **s**: be not cut off in her H5315
45 his **s** from the fierce anger of the LORD. H5315
Lam 1:11 meat to relieve the **s**: see, O LORD, and H5315
16 should relieve my **s** is far from me: my H5315
2:12 city, when their **s** was poured out into H5315
3:17 And thou hast removed my **s** far off H5315
20 My **s** hath *them* still in remembrance, H5315
24 The LORD *is* my portion, saith my **s**; H5315
25 wait for him, to the **s** *that* seeketh him. H5315
58 of my **s**; thou hast redeemed my life. H5315
Ezk 3:19 iniquity; but thou hast delivered thy **s**. H5315
21 warned; also thou hast delivered thy **s**. H5315
4:14 Lord GOD! behold, my **s** hath not been H5315
18: 4 Behold, all souls are mine; as the **s** of H5315
4 father, so also the **s** of the son is mine: H5315
4 is mine: the **s** that sinneth, it shall die. H5315
20 The **s** that sinneth, it shall die. The son H5315
27 and right, he shall save his **s** alive. H5315
24:21 and that which your **s** pitieth; and your H5315
33: 5 that taketh warning shall deliver his **s**. H5315
9 iniquity; but thou hast delivered thy **s**. H5315
Hos 9: 4 bread for their **s** shall not come into H5315
Jna 2: 5 about, *even* to the **s**: the depth closed H5315
7 When my **s** fainted within me I H5315
Mic 6: 7 the fruit of my body *for* the sin of my **s**? H5315
7: 1 to eat: my **s** desired the firstripe fruit. H5315
Hab 2: 4 Behold, his **s** *which* is lifted up is not H5315
10 people, and hast sinned *against* thy **s**. H5315
Zec 11: 8 one month; and my **s** lothed them, and H5315
8 them, and their **s** also abhorred me. H5315
Mt 10:28 not able to kill the **s**: but rather fear him G5590
28 able to destroy both **s** and body in hell. G5590
12:18 in whom my **s** is well pleased: I will G5590
16:26 and lose his own **s**? or what shall a man G5590
26 shall a man give in exchange for his **s**? G5590
22:37 with all thy **s**, and with all thy mind. G5590
26:38 Then saith he unto them, My **s** is G5590
Mk 8:36 the whole world, and lose his own **s**? G5590
37 shall a man give in exchange for his **s**? G5590
12:30 and with all thy **s**, and with all thy G5590
33 and with all the **s**, and with all the G5590
14:34 And saith unto them, My **s** is exceeding G5590
Lk 1:46 And Mary said, My **s** doth magnify the G5590
2:35 pierce through thy own **s** also,) that the G5590
10:27 and with all thy **s**, and with all thy G5590
12:19 And I will say to my **s**, Soul, thou hast G5590
19 And I will say to my soul, **S**, thou hast G5590
20 fool, this night thy **s** shall be required G5590
Jn 12:27 Now is my **s** troubled; and what shall I G5590
Act 2:27 Because thou wilt not leave my **s** in G5590
31 of Christ, that his **s** was not left in hell, G5590
43 And fear came upon every **s**: and many G5590
3:23 And it shall come to pass, *that* every **s**, G5590
4:32 heart and of one **s**: neither said any *of* G5590
Ro 2: 9 Tribulation and anguish, upon every **s** G5590

Ro 13: 1 Let every **s** be subject unto the higher G5590
1Co 15:45 was made a living **s**; the last Adam *was* G5590
2Co 1:23 a record upon my **s**, that to spare you I G5590
1Th 5:23 your whole spirit and **s** and body be G5590
Heb 4:12 asunder of **s** and spirit, and of the G5590
6:19 as an anchor of the **s**, both sure and G5590
10:38 my **s** shall have no pleasure in him. G5590
39 them that believe to the saving of the **s**. G5590
Jas 5:20 his way shall save a **s** from death, and G5590
1Pt 2:11 fleshly lusts, which war against the **s**; G5590
2Pt 2: 8 *his* righteous **s** from day to day with G5590
3Jn 2 be in health, even as thy **s** prospereth. G5590
Rev 16: 3 *man*: and every living **s** died in the sea. G5590
18:14 And the fruits that thy **s** lusted after are G5590

SOULS

Gen 12: 5 had gathered, and the **s** that they had H5315
46:15 Dinah: all the **s** of his sons and his H5315
18 she bare unto Jacob, *even* sixteen **s**. H5315
22 born to Jacob: all the **s** *were* fourteen. H5315
25 these unto Jacob: all the **s** *were* seven. H5315
26 All the **s** that came with Jacob into H5315
26 wives, all the **s** *were* threescore and six; H5315
27 in Egypt, *were* two **s**: all the souls of the H5315
27 *were* two souls: all the **s** of the house of H5315
Ex 1: 5 And all the **s** that came out of the loins H5315
5 **s**: for Joseph was in Egypt *already*. H5315
12: 4 to the number of the **s**; every man H5315
30:15 to make an atonement for your **s**. H5315
16 to make an atonement for your **s**. H5315
Lev 16:29 ye shall afflict your **s**, and do no work at H5315
31 shall afflict your **s**, by a statute for ever. H5315
17:11 for your **s**: for it *is* the blood *that* H5315
18:29 even the **s** that commit *them* shall H5315
20:25 not make your **s** abominable by beast, H5315
23:27 shall afflict your **s**, and offer an offering H5315
32 shall afflict your **s**: in the ninth *day* of H5315
Nu 16:38 against their own **s**, let them make H5315
29: 7 your **s**: ye shall not do any work *therein*: H5315
30: 9 bound their **s**, shall stand against her. H5315
31:50 atonement for our **s** before the LORD. H5315
Jos 10:28 them, and all the **s** that *were* therein; H5315
30 sword, and all the **s** that *were* therein; H5315
32 sword, and all the **s** that *were* therein, H5315
35 sword, and all the **s** that *were* therein H5315
37 and all the **s** that *were* therein; he H5315
37 utterly, and all the **s** that *were* therein. H5315
39 destroyed all the **s** that *were* therein; he H5315
11:11 And they smote all the **s** that *were* H5315
23:14 and in all your **s**, that not one thing H5315
1Sa 25:29 thy God; and the **s** of thine enemies, H5315
Ps 72:13 and shall save the **s** of the needy. H5315
97:10 evil: he preserveth the **s** of his saints; he H5315
Prv 11:30 of life; and he that winneth **s** *is* wise. H5315
14:25 A true witness delivereth **s**: but a H5315
Isa 57:16 me, and the **s** *which* I have made. H5397
Jer 2:34 found the blood of the **s** of the poor H5315
6:16 find rest for your **s**. But they said, We H5315
26:19 we procure great evil against our **s**. H5315
44: 7 evil against your **s**, to cut off from you H5315
Lam 1:19 they sought their meat to relieve their **s**. H5315
Ezk 7:19 shall not satisfy their **s**, neither fill their H5315
13:18 stature to hunt **s**! Will ye hunt the souls H5315
18 Will ye hunt the **s** of my people, and H5315
18 ye save the **s** alive *that come* unto you? H5315
19 bread, to slay the **s** that should not die, H5315
19 and to save the **s** alive that should not H5315
20 ye there hunt the **s** to make *them* fly, H5315
20 and will let the **s** go, *even* the souls that H5315
20 the **s** that ye hunt to make *them* fly. H5315
14:14 *but* their own **s** by their righteousness, H5315
20 their own **s** by their righteousness. H5315
18: 4 Behold, all **s** are mine; as the soul of H5315
22:25 have devoured **s**; they have taken the H5315
27 *and* to destroy **s**, to get dishonest gain. H5315
Mt 11:29 heart: and ye shall find rest unto your **s**. G5590
Lk 21:19 In your patience possess ye your **s**. G5590
Act 2:41 *unto them* about three thousand **s**. G5590
7:14 all his kindred, threescore and fifteen **s**. G5590
14:22 Confirming the **s** of the disciples, *and* G5590
15:24 subverting your **s**, saying, *Ye must* be G5590
27:37 two hundred threescore and sixteen **s**. G5590
1Th 2: 8 own **s**, because ye were dear unto us. G5590
Heb 13:17 watch for your **s**, as they that must give G5590
Jas 1:21 word, which is able to save your **s**. G5590
1Pt 1: 9 your faith, *even* the salvation of *your* **s**. G5590
22 Seeing ye have purified your **s** in G5590
2:25 the Shepherd and Bishop of your **s**. G5590
3:20 that is, eight **s** were saved by water. G5590

1Pt 4:19 keeping of their s *to him* in well doing, *G5590*
2Pt 2:14 beguiling unstable s: an heart they have *G5590*
Rev 6: 9 under the altar the s of them that were *G5590*
18:13 and chariots, and slaves, and s of men. *G5590*
20: 4 them: and *I saw* the s of them that were *G5590*

SOUL'S
Job 16: 4 soul were in my s stead, I could heap H5315

SOUND
Ex 28:35 minister: and his s shall be heard when H6963
Lev 25: 9 of the jubile to s on the tenth *day* of H5674
9 the trumpet s throughout all your land. H5674
26:36 enemies; and the s of a shaken leaf H6963
Nu 10: 7 shall blow, but ye shall not s an alarm. H7321
Jos 6: 5 when ye hear the s of the trumpet, all H6963
20 people heard the s of the trumpet, and H6963
2Sa 5:24 And let it be, when thou hearest the s of H6963
6:15 and with the s of the trumpet. H6963
15:10 as ye hear the s of the trumpet, then H6963
1Ki 1:40 that the earth rent with the s of them. H6963
41 Joab heard the s of the trumpet, he H6963
14: 6 And it was *so*, when Ahijah heard the s H6963
18:41 for *there is* a s of abundance of rain. H6963
2Ki 6:32 the s of his master's feet behind him? H6963
1Ch 14:15 thou shalt hear a s of going in the tops H6963
15:19 *appointed* to s with cymbals of brass; H8085
28 and with s of the cornet, and with H6963
16: 5 but Asaph made a s with cymbals; H8085
42 that should make a s, and with musical H8085
2Ch 5:13 as one, to make one s to be heard in H6963
Neh 4:20 In what place *therefore* ye hear the s of H6963
Job 15:21 A dreadful s *is* in his ears: in prosperity H6963
21:12 harp, and rejoice at the s of the organ. H6963
37: 2 and the s *that* goeth out of his mouth. H1899
39:24 he that *it is* the s of the trumpet. H6963
Ps 47: 5 the LORD with the s of a trumpet. H6963
77:17 out a s: thine arrows also went abroad. H6963
89:15 know the joyful s: they shall walk, O H8643
92: 3 upon the harp with a solemn s. H1902
98: 6 With trumpets and s of cornet make a H6963
119:80 Let my heart be s in thy statutes; that I H8549
150: 3 Praise him with the s of the trumpet: H8629
Prv 2: 7 He layeth up s wisdom for the H8454
3:21 eyes: keep s wisdom and discretion: H8454
8:14 Counsel *is* mine, and s wisdom: I *am* H8454
14:30 A s heart *is* the life of the flesh: but H4832
Ecc 12: 4 streets, when the s of the grinding is H6963
Isa 16:11 Wherefore my bowels shall s like an H1993
Jer 4:19 the s of the trumpet, the alarm of war. H6963
21 *and* hear the s of the trumpet? H6963
6:17 Hearken to the s of the trumpet. But H6963
8:16 trembled at the s of the neighing of his H6963
25:10 of the bride, the s of the millstones, and H6963
42:14 war, nor hear the s of the trumpet, nor H6963
48:36 Therefore mine heart shall s for Moab H1993
36 and mine heart shall s like pipes for the H1993
50:22 A s of battle *is* in the land, and of great H6963
51:54 A s of a cry *cometh* from Babylon, and H6963
Ezk 10: 5 And the s of the cherubims' wings was H6963
26:13 s of thy harps shall be no more heard. H6963
15 isles shake at the s of thy fall, when the H6963
27:28 The suburbs shall shake at the s of the H6963
31:16 I made the nations to shake at the s of H6963
33: 4 Then whosoever heareth the s of the H6963
5 He heard the s of the trumpet, and took H6963
Dan 3: 5 *That* at what time ye hear the s of the H7032
7 people heard the s of the cornet, flute, H7032
10 that shall hear the s of the cornet, flute, H7032
15 time ye hear the s of the cornet, flute, H7032
Joel 2: 1 Blow ye the trumpet in Zion, and s an H7321
Am 2: 2 *and* with the s of the trumpet: H6963
6: 5 That chant to the s of the viol, *and* H6310
Mt 6: 2 *thine* alms, do not s a trumpet before *G4537*
24:31 with a great s of a trumpet, and they *G5456*
Lk 15:27 he hath received him safe and s. *G5198*
Jn 3: 8 thou hearest the s thereof, but canst *G5456*
Act 2: 2 And suddenly there came a s from *G2279*
Ro 10:18 Yes verily, their s went into all the *G5353*
1Co 14: 7 And even things without life giving s, *G5456*
8 For if the trumpet give an uncertain s, *G5456*
15:52 the trumpet shall s, and the dead shall *G4537*
1Ti 1:10 thing that is contrary to s doctrine; *G5198*
2Ti 1: 7 of power, and of love, and of a s mind. *G4995*
13 Hold fast the form of s words, which *G5198*
4: 3 will not endure s doctrine; but after *G5198*
Tit 1: 9 he may be able by s doctrine both to *G5198*
13 sharply, that they may be s in the faith; *G5198*
2: 1 the things which become s doctrine: *G5198*
Tit 2: 2 s in faith, in charity, in patience. *G5198*
8 S speech, that cannot be condemned; *G5199*
Heb 12:19 And the s of a trumpet, and the voice of *G2279*
Rev 1:15 and his voice as the s of many waters. *G5456*
8: 6 trumpets prepared themselves to s. *G4537*
13 of the three angels, which are yet to s! *G4537*
9: 9 of iron; and the s of their wings *was* as *G5456*
9 wings *was* as the s of chariots of many *G5456*
10: 7 he shall begin to s, the mystery of God *G4537*
18:22 in thee; and the s of a millstone shall *G5456*

SOUNDED
Ex 19:19 And when the voice of the trumpet s H6963
1Sa 20:12 when I have s my father about to H2713
2Ch 7: 6 and the priests s trumpets before them, H2690
13:14 and the priests s with the trumpets. H2690
23:13 the land rejoiced, and s with trumpets, H8628
29:28 the trumpeters s: *and* all *this continued* H2690
Neh 4:18 And he that s the trumpet *was* by me. H8628
Lk 1:44 of thy salutation s in mine ears, the *G1096*
Act 27:28 And s, and found *it* twenty fathoms: *G1001*
28 s again, and found *it* fifteen fathoms. *G1001*
1Th 1: 8 For from you s out the word of the Lord *G1837*
Rev 8: 7 The first angel s, and there followed *G4537*
8 And the second angel s, and as it were a *G4537*
10 And the third angel s, and there fell a *G4537*
12 And the fourth angel s, and the third *G4537*
9: 1 And the fifth angel s, and I saw a star *G4537*
13 And the sixth angel s, and I heard a *G4537*
11:15 And the seventh angel s; and there were *G4537*

SOUNDETH
Ex 19:13 s long, they shall come up to the mount.

SOUNDING
1Ch 15:16 s, by lifting up the voice with joy. H8085
2Ch 5:12 and twenty priests s with trumpets:) H2690
13:12 his priests with s trumpets to cry alarm H8643
Ps 150: 5 praise him upon the high s cymbals. H8643
Isa 63:15 thy strength, the s of thy bowels and of H1995
Ezk 7: 7 and not the s again of the mountains. H1906
1Co 13: 1 *as* s brass, or a tinkling cymbal. *G2278*

SOUNDNESS
Ps 38: 3 *There is* no s in my flesh because of H4974
7 *disease*: and *there is* no s in my flesh. H4974
Isa 1: 6 the head *there is* no s in it; *but* wounds, H4974
Act 3:16 this perfect s in the presence of you all. *G3647*

SOUNDS
1Co 14: 7 a distinction in the s, how shall it be *G5353*

SOUR
Isa 18: 5 is perfect, and the s grape is ripening in H1155
Jer 31:29 have eaten a s grape, and the children's H1155
30 s grape, his teeth shall be set on edge. H1155
Ezk 18: 2 fathers have eaten s grapes, and the H5493
Hos 4:18 Their drink is s: they have committed H5493

SOUTH
Gen 12: 9 journeyed, going on still toward the s. H5045
13: 1 he had, and Lot with him, into the s. H5045
3 And he went on his journeys from the s H5045
20: 1 from thence toward the s country, and H5045
24:62 Lahai-roi; for he dwelt in the s country. H5045
28:14 north, and to the s: and in thee and in H5045
Ex 26:18 twenty boards on the s side southward. H5045
35 toward the s: and thou shalt put the H8486
27: 9 the tabernacle: for the s side southward H5045
36:23 boards for the s side southward: H5045
38: 9 And he made the court: on the s side H5045
Nu 2:10 On the s side *shall be* the standard of H8486
10: 6 that lie on the s side shall take their H8486
13:22 And they ascended by the s, and came H5045
29 in the land of the s: and the Hittites, H5045
21: 1 which dwelt in the s, heard tell that H5045
33:40 which dwelt in the s in the land of H5045
34: 3 Then your s quarter shall be from the H5045
3 of Edom, and your s border shall be the H5045
4 And your border shall turn from the s H5045
4 shall be from the s to Kadesh-barnea, H5045
35: 5 cubits, and on the s side two thousand H5045
Dt 1: 7 vale, and in the s, and by the sea side, H5045
33:23 LORD: possess thou the west and the s. H1864
34: 3 And the s, and the plain of the valley of H5045
Jos 10:40 hills, and of the s, and of the vale, and H5045
11: 2 and of the plains s of Chinneroth, and H5045
16 hills, and all the s country, and all the H5045
12: 3 and from the s, under Ashdoth-pisgah: H8486
Jos 12: 8 and in the s country; the Hittites, H5045
13: 4 From the s, all the land of the H8486
15: 1 *was* the uttermost part of the s coast. H5045
2 And their s border was from the shore H5045
3 And it went out to the s side to H5045
3 up on the s side unto Kadesh-barnea, H5045
4 at the sea: this shall be your s coast. H5045
7 which *is* on the s side of the river: and H5045
8 Hinnom unto the s side of the Jebusite; H5045
19 hast given me a s land; give me also H5045
18: 5 in their coast on the s, and the house of H5045
13 on the s side of the nether Beth-horon. H5045
15 And the s quarter *was* from the end of H5045
16 on the s, and descended to En-rogel, H5045
19 the salt sea at the s end of Jordan: this H5045
19 end of Jordan: this *was* the s coast. H5045
19: 8 Ramath of the s. This *is* the inheritance H5045
34 to Zebulun on the s side, and reacheth H5045
Jdg 1: 9 and in the s, and in the valley. H5045
15 hast given me a s land; give me also H5045
16 which *lieth* in the s of Arad; and they H5045
21:19 to Shechem, and on the s of Lebonah. H5045
1Sa 20:41 *a place* toward the s, and fell on his face H5045
23:19 which *is* on the s of Jeshimon? H3225
24 in the plain on the s of Jeshimon. H3225
27:10 David said, Against the s of Judah, and H5045
10 and against the s of the Jerahmeelites, H5045
10 and against the s of the Kenites. H5045
30: 1 had invaded the s, and Ziklag, and H5045
14 We made an invasion *upon* the s of the H5045
14 Judah, and upon the s of Caleb; and we H5045
27 which *were* in s Ramoth, and to *them* H5045
2Sa 24: 7 to the s of Judah, *even* to Beer-sheba. H5045
1Ki 7:25 toward the s, and three looking toward H5045
39 the house eastward over against the s. H5045
1Ch 9:24 toward the east, west, north, and s. H5045
2Ch 4: 4 toward the s, and three looking toward H5045
10 side of the east end, over against the s. H5045
28:18 and of the s of Judah, and had taken H5045
Job 9: 9 Pleiades, and the chambers of the s. H8486
37: 9 Out of the s cometh the whirlwind: and H2315
17 he quieteth the earth by the s *wind*? H1864
39:26 *and* stretch her wings toward the s? H8486
Ps 75: 6 east, nor from the west, nor from the s. H4057
78:26 by his power he brought in the s wind. H8486
89:12 The north and the s thou hast created H3225
107: 3 west, from the north, and from the s. H3220
126: 4 O LORD, as the streams in the s. H5045
Ecc 1: 6 The wind goeth toward the s, and H1864
11: 3 fall toward the s, or toward the north, H1864
Song 4:16 wind; and come, thou s; blow upon my H8486
Isa 21: 1 whirlwinds in the s pass through; *so* it H5045
30: 6 The burden of the beasts of the s: into H5045
43: 6 up; and to the s, Keep not back: bring H8486
Jer 13:19 The cities of the s shall be shut up, and H5045
17:26 and from the s, bringing burnt H5045
32:44 and in the cities of the s: for I will cause H5045
33:13 in the cities of the s, and in the land of H5045
Ezk 20:46 Son of man, set thy face toward the s, H8486
46 *thy word* toward the s, and prophesy H1864
46 against the forest of the s field; H5045
47 And say to the forest of the s, Hear the H5045
47 s to the north shall be burned therein. H5045
21: 4 against all flesh from the s to the north: H5045
40: 2 *was* as the frame of a city on the s. H5045
24 After that he brought me toward the s, H1864
24 a gate toward the s: and he measured H1864
27 court toward the s: and he measured H1864
27 to gate toward the s an hundred cubits. H1864
28 the inner court by the s gate: and he H1864
28 the s gate according to these measures; H1864
44 *was* toward the s: one at the side of the H1864
45 *is* toward the s, *is* for the priests, the H1864
41:11 door toward the s: and the breadth of H1864
42:12 *were* toward the s *was* a door in the H1864
13 chambers *and* the s chambers, which H1864
18 He measured the s side, five hundred H1864
46: 9 by the way of the s gate; and he that H5045
9 by the way of the s gate shall go forth H5045
47: 1 of the house, at the s *side* of the altar. H5045
19 And the s side southward, from Tamar H5045
19 sea. And *this is* the s side southward. H8486
48:10 and toward the s five and twenty H5045
16 hundred, and the s side four thousand H5045
17 and toward the s two hundred and H5045
28 And by the border of Gad, at the s side H5045
33 And at the s side four thousand and H5045
Dan 8: 9 great, toward the s, and toward the H5045
11: 5 And the king of the s shall be strong, H5045

Dan 11: 6 daughter of the s shall come to the king H5045
9 So the king of the s shall come into *his* H5045
11 And the king of the s shall be moved H5045
14 the king of the s: also the robbers of thy H5045
15 the arms of the s shall not withstand, H5045
25 the king of the s with a great army; and H5045
25 and the king of the s shall be stirred up H5045
29 come toward the s; but it shall not be as H5045
40 the king of the s push at him: and the H5045
Oba 19 And *they of* the s shall possess the H5045
20 shall possess the cities of the s. H5045
Zec 6: 6 grisled go forth toward the s country. H8486
7: 7 *men* inhabited the s and the plain? H5045
9:14 and shall go with whirlwinds of the s. H8486
14: 4 the north, and half of it toward the s. H5045
10 Geba to Rimmon s of Jerusalem: and it H5045
Mt 12:42 The queen of the s shall rise up in the *G3558*
Lk 11:31 The queen of the s shall rise up in the *G3558*
12:55 And when *ye see* the s wind blow, ye *G3558*
13:29 and *from* the s, and shall sit down in *G3558*
Act 8:26 and go toward the s unto the way that *G3314*
27:12 lieth toward the s west and north west. *G3047*
13 And when the s wind blew softly, *G3558*
28:13 after one day the s wind blew, and we *G3558*
Rev 21:13 three gates; on the s three gates; and on *G3558*

SOUTH-COUNTRY See SOUTH and COUNTRY.

SOUTH-QUARTER See SOUTH and QUARTER.

SOUTH-SIDE See SOUTH and SIDE.

SOUTHWARD
Gen 13:14 and s, and eastward, and westward: H5045
Ex 26:18 twenty boards on the south side s. H8486
27: 9 for the south side s *there shall be* H8486
36:23 twenty boards for the south side s: H8486
38: 9 on the south side s the hangings of the H8486
40:24 table, on the side of the tabernacle s. H5045
Nu 3:29 pitch on the side of the tabernacle s. H8486
13:17 *way* s, and go up into the mountain: H5045
Dt 3:27 northward, and s, and eastward, and H8486
Jos 15: 1 wilderness of Zin s *was* the uttermost H5045
2 the salt sea, from the bay that looketh s: H5045
21 s were Kabzeel, and Eder, and Jagur, H5045
17: 9 the river Kanah, s of the river: these H5045
10 S *it was* Ephraim's, and northward *it* H5045
18:13 Luz, which *is* Beth-el, s; and the border H5045
14 the corner of the sea s, from the hill that H5045
14 before Beth-horon s; and the goings out H5045
1Sa 14: 5 and the other s over against Gibeah. H5045
1Ch 26:15 To Obed-edom s; and to his sons the H5045
17 four a day, s four a day, and toward H5045
Ezk 47:19 And the south side s, from Tamar *even* H8486
19 great sea. And *this is* the south side s. H5045
48:28 at the south side s, the border shall be H8486
Dan 8: 4 and northward, and s; so that no beasts H5045

SOUTH-WEST See SOUTH and WEST.

SOUTH-WIND See SOUTH and WIND.

SOW
Gen 47:23 *is* seed for you, and ye shall s the land. H2232
Ex 23:10 And six years thou shalt s thy land, H2232
Lev 19:19 thou shalt not s thy field with mingled H2232
25: 3 Six years thou shalt s thy field, and six H2232
4 s thy field, nor prune thy vineyard. H2232
11 you: ye shall not s, neither reap that H2232
20 shall not s, nor gather in our increase: H2232
22 And ye shall s the eighth year, and eat H2232
26:16 heart: and ye shall s your seed in vain, H2232
Dt 22: 9 Thou shalt not s thy vineyard with H2232
2Ki 19:29 in the third year s ye, and reap, and H2232
Job 4: 8 and s wickedness, reap the same. H2232
31: 8 *Then* let me s, and let another eat; yea, H2232
Ps 107:37 And s the fields, and plant vineyards, H2232
126: 5 They that s in tears shall reap in joy. H2232
Ecc 11: 4 He that observeth the wind shall not s; H2232
6 In the morning s thy seed, and in the H2232
Isa 28:24 Doth the plowman plow all day to s? H2232
30:23 that thou shalt s the ground withal; H2232
32:20 Blessed *are* ye that s beside all waters, H2232
37:30 in the third year s ye, and reap, and H2232
Jer 4: 3 ground, and s not among thorns. H2232
31:27 LORD, that I will s the house of Israel H2232
35: 7 Neither shall ye build house, nor s H2232
Hos 2:23 And I will s her unto me in the earth; H2232
10:12 S to yourselves in righteousness, reap H2232
Mic 6:15 Thou shalt s, but thou shalt not reap; H2232
Zec 10: 9 And I will s them among the people: H2232
Mt 6:26 Behold the fowls of the air: for they s *G4687*
13: 3 saying, Behold, a sower went forth to s; *G4687*
27 Sir, didst not thou s good seed in thy *G4687*
Mk 4: 3 Behold, there went out a sower to s: *G4687*
Lk 8: 5 A sower went out to s his seed: and as *G4687*
12:24 Consider the ravens: for they neither s *G4687*
19:21 down, and reapest that thou didst not s. *G4687*
22 not down, and reaping that I did not s: *G4687*
2Pt 2:22 again; and the s that was washed to *G5300*

SOWED
Gen 26:12 Then Isaac s in that land, and received H2232
Jdg 9:45 beat down the city, and s it with salt. H2232
Mt 13: 4 And when he s, some *seeds* fell by the *G4687*
24 a man which s good seed in his field: *G4687*
25 his enemy came and s tares among the *G4687*
31 which a man took, and s in his field: *G4687*
39 The enemy that s them is the devil; the *G4687*
25:26 that I reap where I s not, and gather *G4687*
Mk 4: 4 And it came to pass, as he s, some fell *G4687*
Lk 8: 5 his seed: and as he s, some fell by the *G4687*

SOWEDST
Dt 11:10 came out, where thou s thy seed, and H2232

SOWER
Isa 55:10 seed to the s, and bread to the eater: H2232
Jer 50:16 Cut off the s from Babylon, and him H2232
Mt 13: 3 saying, Behold, a s went forth to sow; *G4687*
18 Hear ye therefore the parable of the s. *G4687*
Mk 4: 3 Hearken; Behold, there went out a s to *G4687*
14 The s soweth the word. *G4687*
Lk 8: 5 A s went out to sow his seed: and as he *G4687*
2Co 9:10 Now he that ministereth seed to the s *G4687*

SOWEST
1Co 15:36 *Thou* fool, that which thou s is not *G4687*
37 And that which thou s, thou sowest not *G4687*
37 And that which thou sowest, thou s not *G4687*

SOWETH
Prv 6:14 mischief continually; he s discord. H7971
19 and he that s discord among brethren. H7971
11:18 s righteousness *shall be* a sure reward. H2232
16:28 A froward man s strife: and a H7971
22: 8 He that s iniquity shall reap vanity: H2232
Am 9:13 of grapes him that s seed; and the H4900
Mt 13:37 that s the good seed is the Son of man; *G4687*
Mk 4:14 The sower s the word. *G4687*
Jn 4:36 that both he that s and he that reapeth *G4687*
37 And herein is that saying true, One s, *G4687*
2Co 9: 6 But this *I say*, He which s sparingly *G4687*
6 and he which s bountifully shall reap *G4687*
Gal 6: 7 a man s, that shall he also reap. *G4687*
8 For he that s to his flesh shall of the *G4687*
8 but he that s to the Spirit shall of *G4687*

SOWING
Lev 11:37 fall upon any s seed which is to be H2221
26: 5 reach unto the s time: and ye shall eat H2233

SOWING-TIME See SOWING and TIME.

SOWN
Ex 23:16 which thou hast s in the field: and the H2232
Lev 11:37 seed which is to be s, it *shall be* clean. H2232
Dt 21: 4 neither eared nor s, and shall strike off H2232
22: 9 which thou hast s, and the fruit of thy H2232
29:23 *that* it is not s, nor beareth, nor any H2232
Jdg 6: 3 And *so* it was, when Israel had s, that H2232
Ps 97:11 Light is s for the righteous, and H2232
Isa 19: 7 and every thing s by the brooks, shall H4218
40:24 they shall not be s: yea, their stock shall H2232
61:11 the things that are s in it to spring H2221
Jer 2: 2 the wilderness, in a land *that was* not s. H2232
12:13 They have s wheat, but shall reap H2232
Ezk 36: 9 unto you, and ye shall be tilled and s: H2232
Hos 8: 7 For they have s the wind, and they H2232
Nah 1:14 of thy name be s: out of the house of thy H2232
Hag 1: 6 Ye have s much, and bring in little; ye H2232
Mt 13:19 that which was s in his heart. This is *G4687*
25:24 thou hast not s, and gathering where *G4687*
Mk 4:15 where the word is s; but when they have *G4687*
15 the word that was s in their hearts. *G4687*
16 And these are they likewise which are s *G4687*
18 And these are they which are s among *G4687*
20 And these are they which are s on good *G4687*
Mk 4:31 which, when it is s in the earth, is less *G4687*
32 But when it is s, it groweth up, and *G4687*
1Co 9:11 If we have s unto you spiritual things, *G4687*
15:42 of the dead. It is s in corruption; it is *G4687*
43 It is s in dishonour; it is raised in glory: *G4687*
43 it is s in weakness; it is raised in power: *G4687*
44 It is s a natural body; it is raised a *G4687*
2Co 9:10 multiply your seed s, and increase the *G4703*
Jas 3:18 And the fruit of righteousness is s in *G4687*

SPACE
Gen 29:14 he abode with him the s of a month. H3117
32:16 and put a s betwixt drove and drove. H7305
Lev 25: 8 years; and the s of the seven sabbaths H3117
30 And if it be not redeemed within the s H4390
Dt 2:14 And the s in which we came from H3117
Jos 3: 4 Yet there shall be a s between you and H7350
1Sa 26:13 afar off; a great s *being* between them: H4725
Ezr 9: 8 And now for a little s grace hath been H7281
Jer 28:11 nations within the s of two full years. H5750
Ezk 40:12 The s also before the little chambers H1366
12 *on this side*, and the s *was* one cubit on H1366
Lk 22:59 And about the s of one hour after *G1339*
Act 5: 7 And it was about the s of three hours *G1292*
34 to put the apostles forth a little s; *G1024*
7:42 *by the s of* forty years in the wilderness?
13:20 judges about the s of four hundred and
21 tribe of Benjamin, by the s of forty years.
15:33 And after they had tarried *there* a s, *G5550*
19: 8 spake boldly for the s of three months, *G1909*
10 And this continued by the s of two *G1909*
34 voice about the s of two hours cried *G1909*
20:31 that by the s of three years I ceased *G4158*
Jas 5:17 by the s of three years and six months.
Rev 2:21 And I gave her s to repent of her *G5550*
8: 1 in heaven about the s of half an hour.
14:20 bridles, by the s of a thousand *and* six *G575*
17:10 he cometh, he must continue a short s. *G3641*

SPAIN
Ro 15:24 Whensoever I take my journey into S, I *G4681*
28 this fruit, I will come by you into S. *G4681*

SPAKE
Gen 8:15 And God s unto Noah, saying, H1696
9: 8 And God s unto Noah, and to his sons H559
16:13 of the LORD that s unto her, Thou God H1696
18:29 And he s unto him yet again, and said, H1696
19:14 And Lot went out, and s unto his sons H1696
21:22 captain of his host s unto Abraham, H559
22: 7 And Isaac s unto Abraham his father, H559
23: 3 and s unto the sons of Heth, saying, H1696
13 And he s unto Ephron in the audience H1696
24: 7 and which s unto me, and that sware H1696
30 saying, Thus s the man unto me; that H1696
27: 5 And Rebekah heard when Isaac s to H1696
6 And Rebekah s unto Jacob her son, H559
29: 9 And while he yet s with them, Rachel H1696
31:11 And the angel of God s unto me in a H559
29 the God of your father s unto me H559
34: 3 damsel, and s kindly unto the damsel. H1696
4 And Shechem s unto his father Hamor, H559
35:15 place where God s with him, Beth-el. H1696
39:10 And it came to pass, as she s to Joseph H1696
14 of her house, and s unto them, saying, H559
17 And she s unto him according to these H1696
19 his wife, which she s unto him, saying, H1696
41: 9 Then s the chief butler unto Pharaoh, H1696
42: 7 unto them, and s roughly unto them; H1696
14 that I s unto you, saying, Ye *are* spies: H1696
22 And Reuben answered them, saying, S I H559
23 for he s unto them by an interpreter.
30 The man, *who is* the lord of the land, s H1696
37 And Reuben s unto his father, saying, H559
43: 3 And Judah s unto him, saying, The man H559
27 the old man of whom ye s? *Is* he yet alive? H559
29 of whom ye s unto me? And he said, H559
44: 6 And he overtook them, and he s unto H1696
46: 2 And God s unto Israel in the visions of H559
47: 5 And Pharaoh s unto Joseph, saying, Thy H559
49:28 *is it* that their father s unto them, and H1696
50: 4 were past, Joseph s unto the house of H1696
17 Joseph wept when they s unto him. H1696
21 them, and s kindly unto them. H1696
Ex 1:15 And the king of Egypt s to the Hebrew H559
4:30 And Aaron s all the words which the H1696
5:10 officers, and they s to the people, saying, H559
6: 2 And God s unto Moses, and said unto H1696
9 And Moses s so unto the children of H1696

S

Ex 6:10 And the LORD s unto Moses, saying, H1696
12 And Moses s before the LORD, saying, H1696
13 And the LORD s unto Moses and unto H1696
27 These *are* they which s to Pharaoh king H1696
28 s unto Moses in the land of Egypt, H1696
29 That the LORD s unto Moses, saying, I H1696
7: 7 years old, when they s unto Pharaoh. H1696
8 And the LORD s unto Moses and unto H559
19 And the LORD s unto Moses, Say unto H559
8: 1 And the LORD s unto Moses, Go unto H559
5 And the LORD s unto Moses, Say unto H559
12: 1 And the LORD s unto Moses and Aaron H559
13: 1 And the LORD s unto Moses, saying, H1696
14: 1 And the LORD s unto Moses, saying, H1696
15: 1 the LORD, and s, saying, I will sing unto H559
16: 9 And Moses s unto Aaron, Say unto all H559
10 And it came to pass, as Aaron s unto H1696
11 And the LORD s unto Moses, saying, H1696
19:19 s, and God answered him by a voice. H1696
25 down unto the people, and s unto them. H559
20: 1 And God s all these words, saying, H1696
25: 1 And the LORD s unto Moses, saying, H1696
30:11 And the LORD s unto Moses, saying, H1696
17 And the LORD s unto Moses, saying, H1696
22 Moreover the LORD s unto Moses, H1696
31: 1 And the LORD s unto Moses, saying, H1696
12 And the LORD s unto Moses, saying, H559
33:11 And the LORD s unto Moses face to H1696
34:34 he came out, and s unto the children of H1696
35: 4 And Moses s unto all the congregation of H559
36: 5 And they s unto Moses, saying, The H559
40: 1 And the LORD s unto Moses, saying, H1696
Lev 1: 1 unto Moses, and s unto him out of the H1696
4: 1 And the LORD s unto Moses, saying, H1696
5:14 And the LORD s unto Moses, saying, H1696
6: 1 And the LORD s unto Moses, saying, H1696
8 And the LORD s unto Moses, saying, H1696
19 And the LORD s unto Moses, saying, H1696
24 And the LORD s unto Moses, saying, H1696
7:22 And the LORD s unto Moses, saying, H1696
28 And the LORD s unto Moses, saying, H1696
8: 1 And the LORD s unto Moses, saying, H1696
10: 3 *is it* that the LORD s, saying, I will be H1696
8 And the LORD s unto Aaron, saying, H1696
12 And Moses s unto Aaron, and unto H1696
11: 1 And the LORD s unto Moses and to H1696
12: 1 And the LORD s unto Moses, saying, H1696
13: 1 And the LORD s unto Moses and H1696
14: 1 And the LORD s unto Moses, saying, H1696
33 And the LORD s unto Moses and unto H1696
15: 1 And the LORD s unto Moses and to H1696
16: 1 And the LORD s unto Moses after the H1696
17: 1 And the LORD s unto Moses, saying, H1696
18: 1 And the LORD s unto Moses, saying, H1696
19: 1 And the LORD s unto Moses, saying, H1696
20: 1 And the LORD s unto Moses, saying, H1696
21:16 And the LORD s unto Moses, saying, H1696
22: 1 And the LORD s unto Moses, saying, H1696
17 And the LORD s unto Moses, saying, H1696
26 And the LORD s unto Moses, saying, H1696
23: 1 And the LORD s unto Moses, saying, H1696
9 And the LORD s unto Moses, saying, H1696
23 And the LORD s unto Moses, saying, H1696
26 And the LORD s unto Moses, saying, H1696
33 And the LORD s unto Moses, saying, H1696
24: 1 And the LORD s unto Moses, saying, H1696
13 And the LORD s unto Moses, saying, H1696
23 And Moses s to the children of Israel, H1696
25: 1 And the LORD s unto Moses in mount H1696
27: 1 And the LORD s unto Moses, saying, H1696
Nu 1: 1 And the LORD s unto Moses in the H1696
2: 1 And the LORD s unto Moses and unto H1696
3: 1 the LORD s with Moses in mount Sinai. H1696
5 And the LORD s unto Moses, saying, H1696
11 And the LORD s unto Moses, saying, H1696
14 And the LORD s unto Moses in the H1696
44 And the LORD s unto Moses, saying, H1696
4: 1 And the LORD s unto Moses and unto H1696
17 And the LORD s unto Moses and unto H1696
21 And the LORD s unto Moses, saying, H1696
5: 1 And the LORD s unto Moses, saying, H1696
4 as the LORD s unto Moses, so did H1696
5 And the LORD s unto Moses, saying, H1696
11 And the LORD s unto Moses, saying, H1696
6: 1 And the LORD s unto Moses, saying, H1696
22 And the LORD s unto Moses, saying, H1696
7: 4 And the LORD s unto Moses, saying, H559
89 the two cherubims: and he s unto him. H1696
8: 1 And the LORD s unto Moses, saying, H1696

Nu 8: 5 And the LORD s unto Moses, saying, H1696
23 And the LORD s unto Moses, saying, H1696
9: 1 And the LORD s unto Moses in the H1696
4 And Moses s unto the children of H1696
9 And the LORD s unto Moses, saying, H1696
10: 1 And the LORD s unto Moses, saying, H1696
11:25 in a cloud, and s unto him, and took H1696
12: 1 And Miriam and Aaron s against H1696
4 And the LORD s suddenly unto Moses, H559
13: 1 And the LORD s unto Moses, saying, H1696
14: 7 And they s unto all the company of the H559
26 And the LORD s unto Moses and unto H1696
15: 1 And the LORD s unto Moses, saying, H1696
17 And the LORD s unto Moses, saying, H1696
37 And the LORD s unto Moses, saying, H559
16: 5 And he s unto Korah and unto all his H1696
20 And the LORD s unto Moses and unto H1696
23 And the LORD s unto Moses, saying, H1696
26 And he s unto the congregation, H1696
36 And the LORD s unto Moses, saying, H1696
44 And the LORD s unto Moses, saying, H1696
17: 1 And the LORD s unto Moses, saying, H1696
6 And Moses s unto the children of H1696
12 And the children of Israel s unto Moses, H559
18: 8 And the LORD s unto Aaron, Behold, I H1696
20 And the LORD s unto Aaron, Thou shalt H559
25 And the LORD s unto Moses, saying, H1696
19: 1 And the LORD s unto Moses and unto H1696
20: 3 And the people chode with Moses, and s, H559
7 And the LORD s unto Moses, saying, H1696
12 And the LORD s unto Moses and Aaron, H559
23 And the LORD s unto Moses and Aaron H559
21: 5 And the people s against God, and H1696
16 whereof the LORD s unto Moses, Gather H559
22: 7 and s unto him the words of Balak. H1696
24:12 And Balaam said unto Balak, S I not H1696
25:10 And the LORD s unto Moses, saying, H1696
16 And the LORD s unto Moses, saying, H1696
26: 1 that the LORD s unto Moses and unto H559
3 And Moses and Eleazar the priest s H1696
52 And the LORD s unto Moses, saying, H1696
27: 6 And the LORD s unto Moses, saying, H559
15 And Moses s unto the LORD, saying, H1696
28: 1 And the LORD s unto Moses, saying, H1696
30: 1 And Moses s unto the heads of the H1696
31: 1 And the LORD s unto Moses, saying, H1696
3 And Moses s unto the people, saying, H1696
25 And the LORD s unto Moses, saying, H559
32: 2 Reuben came and s unto Moses, and to H559
25 the children of Reuben s unto Moses, H559
33:50 And the LORD s unto Moses in the H1696
34: 1 And the LORD s unto Moses, saying, H1696
16 And the LORD s unto Moses, saying, H1696
35: 1 And the LORD s unto Moses in the H1696
9 And the LORD s unto Moses, saying, H1696
36: 1 came near, and s before Moses, and H1696
Dt 1: 1 These *be* the words which Moses s unto H1696
3 *that* Moses s unto the children of H1696
6 The LORD our God s unto us in Horeb, H1696
9 And I s unto you at that time, saying, I H559
43 So I s unto you; and ye would not hear, H1696
2: 1 sea, as the LORD s unto me: and we H1696
2 And the LORD s unto me, saying, H559
17 That the LORD s unto me, saying, H1696
4:12 And the LORD s unto you out of the H1696
15 day *that* the LORD s unto you in Horeb H1696
45 which Moses s unto the children of H1696
5:22 These words the LORD s unto all your H1696
28 words, when ye s unto me; and the H1696
9:10 which the LORD s with you in the H1696
13 Furthermore the LORD s unto me, H559
10: 4 which the LORD s unto you in the H1696
13: 2 to pass, whereof he s unto thee, saying, H1696
27: 9 And Moses and the priests the Levites s H1696
28:68 by the way whereof I s unto thee, Thou H559
31: 1 And Moses went and s these words H1696
30 And Moses s in the ears of all the H1696
32:44 And Moses came and s all the words of H1696
48 And the LORD s unto Moses that H1696
Jos 1: 1 that the LORD s unto Joshua the son H559
12 the tribe of Manasseh, s Joshua, saying, H559
3: 6 And Joshua s unto the priests, saying, H559
4: 1 that the LORD s unto Joshua, saying, H559
8 as the LORD s unto Joshua, according H1696
12 of Israel, as Moses s unto them: H1696
15 And the LORD s unto Joshua, saying, H559
21 And he s unto the children of Israel, H559
7: 2 side of Beth-el, and s unto them, saying, H559
9:11 of our country s to us, saying, Take H559

Jos 9:22 And Joshua called for them, and he s H1696
10:12 Then s Joshua to the LORD in the day H1696
14:10 even since the LORD s this word unto H1696
12 whereof the LORD s in that day; for H1696
17:14 And the children of Joseph s unto H1696
17 And Joshua s unto the house of Joseph, H559
20: 1 The LORD also s unto Joshua, saying, H1696
2 I s unto you by the hand of Moses: H1696
21: 2 And they s unto them at Shiloh in the H1696
22: 8 And he s unto them, saying, Return with H559
15 of Gilead, and they s with them, saying, H1696
30 of Manasseh s, it pleased them. H1696
23:14 LORD your God s concerning you; all H1696
24:27 LORD which he s unto us: it shall be H1696
Jdg 2: 4 angel of the LORD s these words unto H1696
8: 8 And he went up thence to Penuel, and s H1696
9 And he s also unto the men of Penuel, H559
9: 3 And his mother's brethren s of him in H1696
37 And Gaal s again and said, See there H1696
15:13 And they s unto him, saying, No; but we H559
19:22 at the door, and s to the master of the H559
Ru 4: 1 of whom Boaz s came by; unto whom H1696
1Sa 1:13 Now Hannah, she s in her heart; only H1696
7: 3 And Samuel s unto all the house of H559
9: 9 of God, thus he s, Come, and let us go H559
17 the man whom I s to thee of! this same H559
10:16 whereof Samuel s, he told him not. H559
16: 4 And Samuel did that which the LORD s, H1696
17:23 the Philistines, and s according to the H1696
26 And David s to the men that stood by H559
28 heard when he s unto the men; and H1696
30 another, and s after the same manner: H559
31 which David s, they rehearsed *them* H1696
18:23 And Saul's servants s those words in H1696
24 him, saying, On this manner s David. H1696
19: 1 And Saul s to Jonathan his son, and to H1696
4 And Jonathan s good of David unto H1696
20:26 Nevertheless Saul s not any thing that H1696
25: 9 men came, they s to Nabal according H1696
40 to Carmel, they s unto her, saying, H1696
28:12 and the woman s to Saul, saying, Why H559
17 hath done to him, as he s by me: for the H1696
30: 6 for the people s of stoning him, because H559
2Sa 3:19 And Abner also s in the ears of H1696
5: 1 unto Hebron, and s, saying, Behold, we H559
6 of the land: which s unto David, saying, H559
7: 7 children of Israel s I a word with any of H1696
12:18 was yet alive, we s unto him, and he H1696
13:22 And Absalom s unto his brother H1696
14: 4 And when the woman of Tekoah s to the H559
17: 6 Absalom, Absalom s unto him, saying, H559
20:18 Then she s, saying, They were wont to H559
22: 1 And David s unto the LORD the words H1696
23: 2 The Spirit of the LORD s by me, and his H1696
3 said, the Rock of Israel s to me, He that H1696
24:17 And David s unto the LORD when he H559
1Ki 1:11 Wherefore Nathan s unto Bath-sheba H559
42 And while he yet s, behold, Jonathan H1696
2: 4 his word which he s concerning me, H1696
27 s concerning the house of Eli in Shiloh. H1696
3:22 *is* my son. Thus they s before the king. H1696
26 Then s the woman whose the living child H559
4:32 And he s three thousand proverbs: and H1696
33 And he s of trees, from the cedar tree H1696
33 out of the wall: he s also of beasts, and H1696
5: 5 my God, as the LORD s unto David my H1696
6:12 thee, which I s unto David thy father: H1696
8:12 Then s Solomon, The LORD said that he H559
15 of Israel, which s with his mouth unto H1696
20 his word that he s, and I am risen up in H1696
12: 3 came, and s unto Rehoboam, saying, H1696
7 And they s unto him, saying, If thou H1696
10 up with him s unto him, saying, Thus H1696
10 this people that s unto thee, saying, H1696
14 And s to them after the counsel of the H1696
15 which the LORD s by Ahijah the H1696
13:18 thou *art*; and an angel s unto me by the H1696
26 of the LORD, which he s unto him. H1696
27 And he s to his sons, saying, Saddle me H1696
31 buried him, that he s to his sons, saying, H559
14:18 LORD, which he s by the hand of his H1696
15:29 he s by his servant Ahijah the Shilonite: H1696
16:12 s against Baasha by Jehu the prophet, H1696
34 which he s by Joshua the son of Nun. H1696
17:16 of the LORD, which he s by Elijah. H1696
20:28 And there came a man of God, and s H559
21: 2 And Ahab s unto Naboth, saying, Give H1696
6 And he said unto her, Because I s unto H1696
23 And of Jezebel also s the LORD, saying, H1696

1Ki 22:13 to call Micaiah s unto him, saying, H1696
38 unto the word of the LORD which he s. H1696
2Ki 1: 9 top of an hill. And he s unto him, Thou H1696
2:22 to the saying of Elisha which he s. H1696
5:13 And his servants came near, and s H1696
7:17 s when the king came down to him. H1696
8: 1 Then s Elisha unto the woman, whose H1696
9:12 Thus and thus s he to me, saying, Thus H559
36 LORD, which he s by his servant Elijah H1696
10:10 which the LORD s concerning the H1696
10 *that* which he s by his servant Elijah. H1696
17 of the LORD, which he s to Elijah. H1696
14:25 of Israel, which he s by the hand of his H1696
15:12 the LORD which he s unto Jehu, saying, H1696
17:26 Wherefore they s to the king of Assyria, H559
18:28 language, and s, saying, Hear the word H1696
21:10 And the LORD s by his servants the H1696
22:19 heardest what I s against this place, H1696
24: 2 he s by his servants the prophets. H1696
25:28 And he s kindly to him, and set his H1696
1Ch 15:16 And David s to the chief of the Levites to H559
17: 6 with all Israel, s I a word to any of the H1696
21: 9 And the LORD s unto Gad, David's H1696
19 which he s in the name of the LORD. H1696
2Ch 1: 2 Then Solomon s unto all Israel, to the H559
6: 4 *that* which he s with his mouth to my H1696
10: 3 came and s to Rehoboam, saying, H1696
7 And they s unto him, saying, If thou be H1696
10 up with him s unto him, saying, Thus H1696
10 the people that s unto thee, saying, Thy H1696
15 word, which he s by the hand of Ahijah H1696
18:12 went to call Micaiah s to him, saying, H1696
19 And one s saying after this manner, H559
30:22 And Hezekiah s comfortably unto all H1696
32: 6 and s comfortably to them, saying, H1696
16 And his servants s yet *more* against the H1696
19 And they s against the God of H1696
24 he s unto him, and he gave him a sign. H559
33:10 And the LORD s to Manasseh, and to H1696
18 of the seers that s to him in the name H1696
34:22 college:) and they s to her to that *effect*. H1696
35:25 the singing women s of Josiah in their H559
Neh 4: 2 And he s before his brethren and the H559
8: 1 gate; and they s unto Ezra the scribe H559
13:24 And their children s half in the speech H1696
Est 3: 4 Now it came to pass, when they s daily H559
4:10 Again Esther s unto Hatach, and gave H559
8: 3 And Esther s yet again before the king, H1696
Job 2:13 nights, and none s a word unto him: H1696
3: 2 And Job s, and said, H6030
19:18 me; I arose, and they s against me. H1696
29:22 After my words they s not again; and my
32:16 When I had waited, (for they s not, but H1696
35: 1 Elihu s moreover, and said, H6030
Ps 18:ttl of the LORD, who s unto the LORD the H1696
33: 9 For he s, and it was *done*; he H559
39: 3 fire burned: *then* s I with my tongue, H1696
78:19 Yea, they s against God; they said, Can H1696
99: 7 He s unto them in the cloudy pillar: H1696
105:31 He s, and there came divers sorts of flies, H559
34 He s, and the locusts came, and H559
106:33 so that he s unadvisedly with his lips. H981
Prv 30: 1 s unto Ithiel, even unto Ithiel and Ucal, H5002
Song 2:10 My beloved s, and said unto me, Rise H6030
5: 6 failed when he s: I sought him, but I H1696
Isa 7:10 Moreover the LORD s again unto Ahaz, H1696
8: 5 The LORD s also unto me again, H1696
11 For the LORD s thus to me with a strong H559
20: 2 At the same time s the LORD by Isaiah H1696
65:12 answer; when I s, ye did not hear; but H1696
66: 4 answer; when I s, they did not hear: but H1696
Jer 7:13 the LORD, and I s unto you, rising up H1696
22 For I s not unto your fathers, nor H1696
8: 6 I hearkened and heard, *but* they s not H1696
14:14 them, neither s unto them: they H1696
19: 5 nor s *it*, neither came *it* into my mind: H1696
20: 8 For since I s, I cried out, I cried violence H1696
22:21 I s unto thee in thy prosperity; *but* thou H1696
25: 2 The which Jeremiah the prophet s unto H1696
26:11 Then s the priests and all the prophets unto H559
12 Then s Jeremiah unto all the princes and H559
17 of the land, and s to all the assembly of H559
18 king of Judah, and s to all the people of H559
27:12 I s also to Zedekiah king of Judah H1696
16 Also I s to the priests and to all this H1696
28: 1 *was* of Gibeon, s unto me in the house H559
11 And Hananiah s in the presence of all H559
30: 4 that the LORD s concerning Israel and H1696
31:20 child? for since I s against him, I do H1696
Jer 34: 6 Then Jeremiah the prophet s all these H1696
36: 2 from the day I s unto thee, from the H1696
37: 2 which he s by the prophet Jeremiah. H1696
38: 8 king's house, and s to the king, saying, H1696
40:15 Then Johanan the son of Kareah s to H559
43: 2 Then s Azariah the son of Hoshaiah, and H559
45: 1 The word that Jeremiah the prophet s H1696
46:13 The word that the LORD s to Jeremiah H1696
50: 1 The word that the LORD s against H1696
51:12 s against the inhabitants of Babylon. H1696
52:32 And s kindly unto him, and set his H1696
Ezk 1:28 face, and I heard a voice of one that s. H1696
2: 2 into me when he s unto me, and set me H1696
2 feet, that I heard him that s unto me. H1696
3:24 upon my feet, and s with me, and said H1696
10: 2 And he s unto the man clothed with H559
11:25 Then I s unto them of the captivity all H1696
24:18 So I s unto the people in the morning: H1696
Dan 1: 3 And the king s unto Ashpenaz the H559
2: 4 Then s the Chaldeans to the king in H1696
3: 9 They s and said to the king H6032
14 Nebuchadnezzar s and said unto them, H6032
19 *therefore* he s, and commanded that H6032
24 up in haste, *and* s, and said unto his H6032
26 burning fiery furnace, *and* s, and said, H6032
28 *Then* Nebuchadnezzar s, and said, H6032
4:19 him. The king s, and said, Belteshazzar, H6032
30 The king s, and said, Is not this great H6032
5: 7 *And* the king s, and said to the wise H6032
10 *and* the queen s and said, O king, live H6032
13 the king. *And* the king s and said unto H6032
6:12 Then they came near, and s before the H560
16 *Now* the king s and said unto Daniel, H6032
20 *and* the king s and said to Daniel, H6032
7: 2 Daniel s and said, I saw in my vision H6032
11 which the horn s: I beheld *even* till the H4449
20 and a mouth that s very great things, H4449
8:13 *saint* which s, How long *shall be* the H1696
9: 6 prophets, which s in thy name to our H1696
12 his words, which he s against us, and H1696
10:16 my mouth, and s, and said unto him H1696
Hos 12: 4 him *in* Beth-el, and there he s with us; H1696
13: 1 When Ephraim s trembling, he exalted H1696
Jna 2:10 And the LORD s unto the fish, and it H559
Hag 1:13 Then s Haggai the LORD'S messenger in H559
Zec 1:21 these to do? And he s, saying, These *are* H559
3: 4 And he answered and s unto those that H559
4: 4 So I answered and s to the angel that H559
6 Then he answered and s unto me, H559
6: 8 Then cried he upon me, and s unto me, H1696
Mal 3:16 Then they that feared the LORD s often H1696
Mt 9:18 While he s these things unto them, G2980
33 was cast out, the dumb s: and the G2980
12:22 the blind and dumb both s and saw. G2980
13: 3 And he s many things unto them in G2980
33 Another parable s he unto them; The G2980
34 All these things s Jesus unto the G2980
34 without a parable s he not unto them: G2980
14:27 But straightway Jesus s unto them, G2980
16:11 not understand that I s *it* not to you G2036
17: 5 While he yet s, behold, a bright cloud G2980
13 Then the disciples understood that he s G2036
21:45 they perceived that he s of them. G3004
22: 1 And Jesus answered and s unto them G2036
23: 1 Then s Jesus to the multitude, and to G2980
26:47 And while he yet s, lo, Judas, one of the G2980
28:18 And Jesus came and s unto them, G2980
Mk 3: 9 And he s to his disciples, that a small G2036
4:33 And with many such parables s he the G2980
34 But without a parable s he not unto G2980
5:35 While he yet s, there came from the G2980
7:35 his tongue was loosed, and he s plain. G2980
8:32 And he s that saying openly. And Peter G2980
9:18 away: and I s to thy disciples that G2036
12:26 in the bush God s unto him, saying, I G2036
14:31 But he s the more vehemently, If I G3004
39 and prayed, and s the same words. G2036
43 And immediately, while he yet s, G2980
Lk 1:42 And she s out with a loud voice, and G400
55 As he s to our fathers, to Abraham, and G2980
64 *loosed*, and he s, and praised God. G2980
70 As he s by the mouth of his holy G2980
2:38 the Lord, and s of him to all them that G2980
50 not the saying which he s unto them. G2980
4:36 And they were all amazed, and s G4814
5:36 And he s also a parable unto them; No G3004
6:39 And he s a parable unto them, Can the G2036
7:39 him saw *it*, he s within himself, saying, G2036
8: 4 him out of every city, he s by a parable: G2036
Lk 8:49 While he yet s, there cometh one from G2980
9:11 them, and s unto them of the kingdom G2980
31 Who appeared in glory, and s of his G3004
34 While he thus s, there came a cloud, G3004
11:14 the dumb s; and the people wondered. G2980
27 And it came to pass, as he s these G3004
37 And as he s, a certain Pharisee G2980
12:16 And he s a parable unto them, saying, G2036
13: 6 He s also this parable; A certain *man* G3004
14: 3 And Jesus answering s unto the G2036
15: 3 And he s this parable unto them, G2036
18: 1 And he s a parable unto them *to this* G3004
9 And he s this parable unto certain G2036
19:11 he added and s a parable, because he G2036
20: 2 And s unto him, saying, Tell us, by G2036
21: 5 And as some s of the temple, how it G3004
29 And he s to them a parable; Behold the G2036
22:47 And while he yet s, behold a multitude, G2980
60 while he yet s, the cock crew. G2980
65 blasphemously s they against him. G3004
23:20 to release Jesus, s again to them. G4377
24: 6 s unto you when he was yet in Galilee, G2980
36 And as they thus s, Jesus himself stood G2980
44 the words which I s unto you, while I G2980
Jn 1:15 was he of whom I s, He that cometh G2036
2:21 But he s of the temple of his body. G3004
6:71 He s of Judas Iscariot *the son* of Simon: G3004
7:13 Howbeit no man s openly of him for G2980
39 (But this s he of the Spirit, which they G2036
46 The officers answered, Never man s G2980
8:12 Then s Jesus again unto them, saying, I G2980
20 These words s Jesus in the treasury, as G2980
27 They understood not that he s to them G3004
30 As he s these words, many believed on G2980
9:22 These *words* s his parents, because G2036
29 We know that God s unto Moses: *as for* G2980
10: 6 This parable s Jesus unto them: but G2036
6 things they were which he s unto them. G2980
41 that John s of this man were true. G2036
11:13 Howbeit Jesus s of his death: but they G2046
51 And this s he not of himself: but being G2036
56 Then sought they for Jesus, and s G3004
12:29 others said, An angel s to him. G2980
36 of light. These things s Jesus, and G2980
38 be fulfilled, which he s, Lord, who hath G2036
41 when he saw his glory, and s of him. G2980
13:22 one on another, doubting of whom he s. G3004
24 ask who it should be of whom he s. G3004
28 for what intent he s this unto him. G2036
17: 1 These words s Jesus, and lifted up his G2980
18: 9 be fulfilled, which he s, Of them which G2036
16 high priest, and s unto her that kept G2036
20 Jesus answered him, I s openly to the G2980
32 s, signifying what death he should die. G2036
21:19 This s he, signifying by what death he G2036
Act 1:16 mouth of David s before concerning G4277
2:31 He seeing this before s of the G2980
4: 1 And as they s unto the people, the G2980
31 they s the word of God with boldness. G2980
6:10 wisdom and the spirit by which he s. G2980
7: 6 And God s on this wise, That his seed G2980
38 the angel which s to him in the mount G2980
8: 6 which Philip s, hearing and seeing G3004
26 And the angel of the Lord s unto Philip, G2980
9:29 And he s boldly in the name of the Lord G2980
10: 7 And when the angel which s unto G2980
15 And the voice *s* unto him again the
44 While Peter yet s these words, the Holy G2980
11:20 come to Antioch, s unto the Grecians, G2980
13:45 with envy, and s against those things G483
14: 1 of the Jews, and so s, that a great G2980
16:13 we sat down, and s unto the women G2980
32 And they s unto him the word of the G2980
18: 9 Then s the Lord to Paul in the night by G2036
25 in the spirit, he s and taught diligently G2980
19: 6 they s with tongues, and prophesied. G2980
8 And he went into the synagogue, and s
9 and believed not, but s evil of that way G2551
20:38 words which he s, that they should see G2046
21:40 a great silence, he s unto *them* in the G4377
22: 2 (And when they heard that he s in the G4377
9 heard not the voice of him that s to me. G2980
26:24 And as he thus s for himself, Festus said G626
28:19 But when the Jews s against *it*, I was G483
21 came shewed or s any harm of thee. G2980
25 one word, Well s the Holy Ghost by G2980
1Co 13:11 When I was a child, I s as a child, I G2980
14: 5 I would that ye all s with tongues, but G2980
2Co 7:14 but as we s all things to you in truth, G2980

Gal 4:15 Where is then the blessedness ye s of? for
Heb 1: 1 in divers manners s in time past unto G2980
4: 4 For he s in a certain place of the G2046
7:14 s nothing concerning priesthood. G2980
12:25 who refused him that s on earth, much G5537
2Pt 1:21 holy men of God s *as they were* moved G2980
Rev 1:12 And I turned to see the voice that s G2980
10: 8 from heaven s unto me again, and G2980
13:11 like a lamb, and he s as a dragon. G2980

SPAKEST
Jdg 13:11 s unto the woman? And he said, I *am*. H1696
17: 2 thou cursedst, and s of also in mine ears, H559
1Sa 28:21 unto thy words which thou s unto me. H1696
1Ki 8:24 him: thou s also with thy mouth, H1696
26 s unto thy servant David my father. H1696
53 as thou s by the hand of Moses H1696
2Ch 6:15 him; and s with thy mouth, and H1696
Neh 9:13 mount Sinai, and s with them from H1696
Ps 89:19 Then thou s in vision to thy holy one, H1696
Jer 48:27 thou s of him, thou skippedst for joy. H1697

SPAN
Ex 28:16 *being* doubled; a s *shall be* the length H2239
16 and a s *shall be* the breadth thereof. H2239
39: 9 double: a s *was* the length thereof, H2239
9 a s the breadth thereof, *being* doubled. H2239
1Sa 17: 4 whose height *was* six cubits and a s. H2239
Isa 40:12 heaven with the s, and comprehended H2239
Lam 2:20 fruit, *and* children of a s long? shall the H2949
Ezk 43:13 about *shall be* a s: and this *shall be* the H2239

SPANNED
Isa 48:13 right hand hath s the heavens: *when* I H2946

SPARE
Gen 18:24 destroy and not s the place for the fifty H5375
26 then I will s all the place for their sakes. H5375
Dt 13: 8 thou s, neither shalt thou conceal him: H2550
29:20 The LORD will not s him, but then the H5545
1Sa 15: 3 that they have, and s them not; but slay H2550
Neh 13:22 this also, and s me according to the H2347
Job 6:10 let him not s; for I have not concealed H2550
16:13 and doth not s; he poureth out my gall H2550
20:13 *Though* he s it, and forsake it not; but H2550
27:22 For *God* shall cast upon him, and not s: H2550
30:10 from me, and s not to spit in my face. H2820
Ps 39:13 O s me, that I may recover strength, H8159
72:13 He shall s the poor and needy, and H2347
Prv 6:34 he will not s in the day of vengeance. H2550
19:18 and let not thy soul s for his crying. H5375
Isa 9:19 of the fire: no man shall s his brother. H2550
13:18 womb; their eye shall not s children. H2347
30:14 he shall not s: so that there shall not H2550
54: 2 of thine habitations: s not, lengthen thy H2820
58: 1 Cry aloud, s not, lift up thy voice like a H2820
Jer 13:14 s, nor have mercy, but destroy them. H2347
21: 7 he shall not s them, neither have H2347
50:14 bow, shoot at her, s no arrows: for she H2550
51: 3 his brigandine: and s ye not her young H2550
Ezk 5:11 mine eye s, neither will I have any pity. H2347
7: 4 And mine eye shall not s thee, neither H2347
9 And mine eye shall not s, neither will I H2347
8:18 mine eye shall not s, neither will I have H2347
9: 5 let not your eye s, neither have ye pity: H2347
10 mine eye shall not s, neither will I have H2347
24:14 go back, neither will I s, neither will I H2347
Joel 2:17 altar, and let them say, S thy people, O H2347
Jna 4:11 And should not I s Nineveh, that great H2347
Hab 1:17 not s continually to slay the nations? H2550
Mal 3:17 my jewels; and I will s them, as a man H2550
Lk 15:17 and to s, and I perish with hunger! G4052
Ro 11:21 *take heed* lest he also s not thee. G5339
1Co 7:28 have trouble in the flesh: but I s you. G5339
2Co 1:23 to s you I came not as yet unto Corinth. G5339
13: 2 other, that, if I come again, I will not s: G5339

SPARED
1Sa 15: 9 But Saul and the people s Agag, and H2550
15 for the people s the best of the sheep H2550
24:10 thee: but *mine eye* s thee; and I said, I H2347
2Sa 12: 4 rich man, and he s to take of his own H2550
21: 7 But the king s Mephibosheth, the son H2550
2Ki 5:20 my master hath s Naaman this Syrian, H2820
Ps 78:50 He made a way to his anger; he s not H2820
Ezk 20:17 Nevertheless mine eye s them from H2347
Ro 8:32 He that s not his own Son, but G5339
11:21 For if God s not the natural branches, G5339
2Pt 2: 4 For if God s not the angels that sinned, G5339
2: 5 And s not the old world, but saved G5339

SPARETH
Prv 13:24 He that s his rod hateth his son: but he H2820
17:27 He that hath knowledge s his words: H2820
21:26 but the righteous giveth and s not. H2820
Mal 3:17 a man s his own son that serveth him. H2550

SPARING
Act 20:29 enter in among you, not s the flock. G5339

SPARINGLY
2Co 9: 6 But this *I say*, He which soweth s shall G5340
6 shall reap also s; and he which soweth G5340

SPARK
Job 18: 5 out, and the s of his fire shall not shine. H7632
Isa 1:31 maker of it as a s, and they shall both H5213

SPARKLED
Ezk 1: 7 s like the colour of burnished brass. H5340

SPARKS
Job 5: 7 trouble, as the s fly upward. H1121+H7565
41:19 burning lamps, *and* s of fire leap out. H3590
Isa 50:11 about with s: walk in the light of your H2131
11 fire, and in the s *that* ye have kindled. H2131

SPARROW
Ps 84: 3 Yea, the s hath found an house, and H6833
102: 7 I watch, and am as a s alone upon the H6833

SPARROWS
Mt 10:29 Are not two s sold for a farthing? and G4765
31 ye are of more value than many s. G4765
Lk 12: 6 Are not five s sold for two farthings, G4765
7 ye are of more value than many s. G4765

SPAT
Jn 9: 6 When he had thus spoken, he s on the G4429

SPEAK
Gen 18:27 have taken upon me to s unto the Lord, H1696
30 angry, and I will s: Peradventure there H1696
31 have taken upon me to s unto the Lord: H1696
32 be angry, and I will s yet but this once: H1696
24:33 told mine errand. And he said, S on. H1696
50 we cannot s unto thee bad or good. H1696
27: 6 father s unto Esau thy brother, saying, H1696
31:24 thou s not to Jacob either good or bad. H1696
29 thou s not to Jacob either good or bad. H1696
32: 4 Thus shall ye s unto my lord Esau; Thy H559
19 shall ye s unto Esau, when ye find him. H1696
37: 4 and could not s peaceably unto him. H1696
44:16 what shall we s? or how shall we clear H1696
18 I pray thee, s a word in my lord's H1696
50: 4 grace in your eyes, s, I pray you, in the H1696
Ex 4:14 I know that he can s well. And also, H1696
15 And thou shalt s unto him, and put H1696
5:23 For since I came to Pharaoh to s in thy H1696
6:11 Go in, s unto Pharaoh king of Egypt, H1696
29 I *am* the LORD: s thou unto Pharaoh H1696
7: 2 Thou shalt s all that I command thee: H1696
2 thy brother shall s unto Pharaoh, that H1696
9 When Pharaoh shall s unto you, H1696
11: 2 S now in the ears of the people, and let H1696
12: 3 S ye unto all the congregation of Israel, H1696
14: 2 S unto the children of Israel, that they H1696
15 thou unto me? s unto the children of H1696
16:12 children of Israel: s unto them, saying, H1696
19: 6 thou shalt s unto the children of Israel. H1696
9 may hear when I s with thee, and H1696
20:19 And they said unto Moses, S thou with H1696
19 but let not God s with us, lest we die. H1696
23: 2 evil; neither shalt thou s in a cause to H6030
22 and do all that I s; then I will be an H1696
25: 2 S unto the children of Israel, that they H1696
28: 3 And thou shalt s unto all *that are* wise H1696
29:42 I will meet you, to s there unto thee. H1696
30:31 And thou shalt s unto the children of H1696
31:13 S thou also unto the children of Israel, H1696
32:12 Wherefore should the Egyptians s, and H559
34:34 the LORD to s with him, he took the H1696
35 again, until he went in to s with him. H1696
Lev 1: 2 S unto the children of Israel, and say H1696
4: 2 S unto the children of Israel, saying, If H1696
6:25 S unto Aaron and to his sons, saying, H1696
7:23 S unto the children of Israel, saying, Ye H1696
29 S unto the children of Israel, saying, He H1696
Lev 9: 3 Israel thou shalt s, saying, Take ye a kid H1696
11: 2 S unto the children of Israel, saying, H1696
12: 2 S unto the children of Israel, saying, If H1696
15: 2 S unto the children of Israel, and say H1696
16: 2 And the LORD said unto Moses, S unto H1696
17: 2 S unto Aaron, and unto his sons, and H1696
18: 2 S unto the children of Israel, and say H1696
19: 2 S unto all the congregation of the H1696
21: 1 And the LORD said unto Moses, S unto H559
17 S unto Aaron, saying, Whosoever *he be* H1696
22: 2 S unto Aaron and to his sons, that they H1696
18 S unto Aaron, and to his sons, and H1696
23: 2 S unto the children of Israel, and say H1696
10 S unto the children of Israel, and say H1696
24 S unto the children of Israel, saying, In H1696
34 S unto the children of Israel, saying, H1696
24:15 And thou shalt s unto the children of H1696
25: 2 S unto the children of Israel, and say H1696
27: 2 S unto the children of Israel, and say H1696
Nu 5: 6 S unto the children of Israel, When a H1696
12 S unto the children of Israel, and say H1696
6: 2 S unto the children of Israel, and say H1696
23 S unto Aaron and unto his sons, H1696
7:89 the congregation to s with him, then he H1696
8: 2 S unto Aaron, and say unto him, When H1696
9:10 S unto the children of Israel, saying, If H1696
12: 6 vision, *and* will s unto him in a dream. H1696
8 With him will I s mouth to mouth, even H1696
8 afraid to s against my servant Moses? H1696
14:15 heard the fame of thee will s, saying, H559
15: 2 S unto the children of Israel, and say H1696
18 S unto the children of Israel, and say H1696
38 S unto the children of Israel, and bid H1696
16:24 S unto the congregation, saying, Get H1696
37 S unto Eleazar the son of Aaron the H559
17: 2 S unto the children of Israel, and take H1696
18:26 Thus s unto the Levites, and say unto H1696
19: 2 saying, S unto the children of H1696
20: 8 thy brother, and s ye unto the rock H1696
21:27 Wherefore they that s in proverbs say,
22: 8 as the LORD shall s unto me: and the H1696
35 word that I shall s unto thee, that thou H1696
35 that thou shalt s. So Balaam went with H1696
38 God putteth in my mouth, that shall I s. H1696
23: 5 unto Balak, and thus thou shalt s. H1696
12 I not take heed to s that which the H1696
24:13 *but* what the LORD saith, that will I s? H1696
27: 7 The daughters of Zelophehad s right: H1696
8 And thou shalt s unto the children of H1696
33:51 S unto the children of Israel, and say H1696
35:10 S unto the children of Israel, and say H1696
Dt 3:26 thee; s no more unto me of this matter. H1696
5: 1 judgments which I s in your ears this H1696
27 God shall say: and s thou unto us all H1696
27 our God shall s unto thee; and we will H1696
31 by me, and I will s unto thee all the H1696
9: 4 S not thou in thine heart, after that the H559
11: 2 And know ye this day: for *I s* not with
18:18 and he shall s unto them all that I H1696
19 s in my name, I will require *it* of him. H1696
20 shall presume to s a word in my name, H1696
20 him to s, or that shall speak in H1696
20 or that shall s in the name of other H1696
20: 2 shall approach and s unto the people, H1696
5 And the officers shall s unto the people, H1696
8 And the officers shall s further unto the H1696
25: 8 shall call him, and s unto him: and *if* H1696
26: 5 And thou shalt s and say before the H6030
27:14 And the Levites shall s, and say unto all H6030
31:28 that I may s these words in their H1696
32: 1 Give ear, O ye heavens, and I will s; and H1696
Jos 4:10 Joshua to s unto the people, according H1696
20: 2 S to the children of Israel, saying, H1696
22:24 your children might s unto our children, H559
Jdg 5:10 S, ye that ride on white asses, ye that sit H7878
6:39 me, and I will s but this once: let me H1696
9: 2 S, I pray you, in the ears of all the men H1696
19: 3 went after her, to s friendly unto her, H1696
30 of it, take advice, and s *your minds*. H1696
21:13 sent *some* to s to the children of H1696
1Sa 3: 9 thou shalt say, S, LORD; for thy servant H1696
10 answered, S; for thy servant heareth. H1696
25:17 of Belial, that *a man* cannot s to him. H1696
24 I pray thee, s in thine audience, and H1696
2Sa 3:19 went also to s in the ears of David H1696
27 in the gate to s with him quietly, and H1696
7:17 vision, so did Nathan s unto David. H1696
13:13 I pray thee, s unto the king; for he H1696
14: 3 And come to the king, and s on this H1696

2Sa 14:12 I pray thee, s *one* word unto my lord H1696
13 for the king doth s this thing as one H1696
15 Now therefore that I am come to s of H1696
15 said, I will now s unto the king; it may H1696
18 said, Let my lord the king now s. H1696
17: 6 we do *after* his saying? if not; s thou. H1696
19: 7 Now therefore arise, go forth, and s H1696
10 Now therefore why s ye not a word of H2790
11 the priests, saying, S unto the elders of H1696
20:16 near hither, that I may s with thee. H1696
18 They were wont to s in old time, H1696
1Ki 2:17 And he said, S, I pray thee, unto Solomon H559
18 And Bath-sheba said, Well; I will s for H1696
19 unto king Solomon, to s unto him for H1696
12: 7 and answer them, and s good words to H1696
10 Thus shalt thou s unto this people that H559
23 S unto Rehoboam, the son of Solomon, H559
21:19 And thou shalt s unto him, saying, H1696
19 And thou shalt s unto him, saying, H1696
22:13 one of them, and s *that which is* good. H1696
14 the LORD saith unto me, that will I s. H1696
24 of the LORD from me to s unto thee? H1696
2Ki 18:19 And Rab-shakeh said unto them, S ye H559
26 unto Rab-shakeh, S, I pray thee, to thy H1696
27 and to thee, to s these words? *hath he* H1696
19:10 Thus shall ye s to Hezekiah king of H559
1Ch 17:15 vision, so did Nathan s unto David. H1696
18 What can David *s* more to thee for the
2Ch 10: 7 and please them, and s good words to H1696
11: 3 S unto Rehoboam the son of Solomon, H559
18:12 be like one of theirs, and s thou good. H1696
13 even what my God saith, that will I s. H1696
23 of the LORD from me to s unto thee? H1696
32:17 of Israel, and to s against him, saying, H559
Neh 13:24 and could not s in the Jews' language, H1696
Est 5:14 and to morrow s thou unto the king that H559
6: 4 of the king's house, to s unto the king to H559
Job 7:11 my mouth; I will s in the anguish of my H1696
8: 2 How long wilt thou s these *things*? and H4448
9:19 If *I s* of strength, lo, *he is* strong: and if
35 *Then* would I s, and not fear him; but *it* H1696
10: 1 I will s in the bitterness of my soul. H1696
11: 5 But oh that God would s, and open his H1696
12: 8 Or s to the earth, and it shall teach H7878
13: 3 Surely I would s to the Almighty, and I H1696
7 Will ye s wickedly for God? and talk H1696
13 I may s, and let come on me what *will*. H1696
22 or let me s, and answer thou me. H1696
16: 4 I also could s as ye *do*: if your soul were H1696
6 Though I s, my grief is not asswaged: H1696
18: 2 words? mark, and afterwards we will s. H1696
21: 3 Suffer me that I may s; and after that I H1696
27: 4 My lips shall not s wickedness, nor my H1696
32: 7 I said, Days should s, and multitude of H1696
20 I will s, that I may be refreshed: I will H1696
33:31 unto me: hold thy peace, and I will s. H1696
32 answer me: s, for I desire to justify thee. H1696
34:33 not I: therefore s what thou knowest. H1696
36: 2 that *I have* yet to s on God's behalf. H4405
37:20 Shall it be told him that I s? if a man H1696
20 a man s, surely he shall be swallowed up. H559
41: 3 thee? will he s soft *words* unto thee? H1696
42: 4 Hear, I beseech thee, and I will s: I will H1696
Ps 2: 5 Then shall he s unto them in his wrath, H1696
5: 6 Thou shalt destroy them that s leasing: H1696
12: 2 They s vanity every one with his H1696
2 lips *and* with a double heart do they s. H1696
17:10 fat: with their mouth they s proudly. H1696
28: 3 of iniquity, which s peace to their H1696
29: 9 his temple doth every one s of *his* glory. H559
31:18 put to silence; which s grievous things H1696
35:20 For they s not peace: but they devise H1696
28 And my tongue shall s of thy H1897
38:12 they that seek my hurt s mischievous H1696
40: 5 I would declare and s *of them*, they are H1696
41: 5 Mine enemies s evil of me, When shall H559
45: 1 My heart is inditing a good matter: I s of H559
49: 3 My mouth shall s of wisdom; and the H1696
50: 7 Hear, O my people, and I will s; O H1696
52: 3 rather than to s righteousness. Selah. H1696
58: 1 Do ye indeed s righteousness, O H1696
59:12 and for cursing and lying *which* they s. H5608
63:11 of them that s lies shall be stopped. H1696
69:12 They that sit in the gate s against me; H7878
71:10 For mine enemies s against me; and H559
73: 8 They are corrupt, and s wickedly H1696
8 *concerning* oppression: they s loftily. H1696
15 If I say, I will s thus; behold, I should H5608
75: 5 Lift not up your horn on high: s *not* H1696
Ps 77: 4 I am so troubled that I cannot s. H1696
85: 8 I will hear what God the LORD will s: H1696
8 will speak: for he will s peace unto his H1696
94: 4 *How long* shall they utter *and* s hard H1696
109:20 and of them that s evil against my soul. H1696
115: 5 They have mouths, but they s not: eyes H1696
7 not: neither s they through their throat. H1897
119:23 Princes also did sit *and* s against me: H1696
46 I will s of thy testimonies also before H1696
172 My tongue shall s of thy word: for all H6030
120: 7 I *am for* peace: but when I s, they *are* H1696
127: 5 shall s with the enemies in the gate. H1696
135:16 They have mouths, but they s not; eyes H1696
139:20 For they s against thee wickedly, *and* H559
145: 5 I will s of the glorious honour of thy H7878
6 And *men* shall s of the might of thy H559
11 They shall s of the glory of thy kingdom, H559
21 My mouth shall s the praise of the H1696
Prv 8: 6 Hear; for I will s of excellent things; H1696
7 For my mouth shall s truth; and H1897
23: 9 S not in the ears of a fool: for he will H1696
16 rejoice, when thy lips s right things. H1696
Ecc 3: 7 a time to keep silence, and a time to s; H1696
Song 7: 9 the lips of those that are asleep to s. H1680
Isa 8:10 come to nought; s the word, and it shall H1696
20 To the law and to the testimony: if they s H559
14:10 All they shall s and say unto thee, Art H6030
19:18 in the land of Egypt s the language of H1696
28:11 another tongue will he s to this people. H1696
29: 4 down, *and* shalt s out of the ground, H1696
30:10 unto us right things, s unto us smooth H1696
32: 4 stammerers shall be ready to s plainly. H1696
6 For the vile person will s villany, and H1696
36:11 unto Rabshakeh, S, I pray thee, unto H1696
11 we understand *it*: and s not to us in the H1696
12 and to thee to s these words? *hath he* H1696
37:10 Thus shall ye s to Hezekiah king of H559
40: 2 S ye comfortably to Jerusalem, and cry H1696
41: 1 near; then let them s: let us come near H1696
45:19 in vain: I the LORD s righteousness, I H1696
50: 4 know how to s a word in season to H5790
52: 6 that I *am* he that doth s: behold, *it is* I. H1696
56: 3 to the LORD, s, saying, The LORD hath H559
59: 4 trust in vanity, and s lies; they conceive H1696
63: 1 that s in righteousness, mighty to save. H1696
Jer 1: 6 behold, I cannot s: for I *am* a child. H1696
7 I command thee thou shalt s. H1696
17 and arise, and s unto them all that I H1696
5: 5 men, and will s unto them; for they H1696
14 hosts, Because ye s this word, behold, I H1696
6:10 To whom shall I s, and give warning, H1696
7:27 Therefore thou shalt s all these words H1696
9: 5 and will not s the truth: they have H1696
5 taught their tongue to s lies, *and* weary H1696
22 S, Thus saith the LORD, Even the H1696
10: 5 They *are* upright as the palm tree, but s H1696
11: 2 of this covenant, and s unto the men of H1696
12: 6 not, though they s fair words unto thee. H1696
13:12 Therefore thou shalt s unto them this H559
18: 7 *At what* instant I shall s concerning a H1696
9 And *at what* instant I shall s H1696
11 Now therefore go to, s to the men of H559
20 before thee to s good for them, *and* H1696
20: 9 of him, nor s any more in his name. H1696
22: 1 king of Judah, and s there this word, H1696
23:16 you vain: they s a vision of their own H1696
28 my word, let him s my word faithfully. H1696
26: 2 house, and s unto all the cities of H1696
2 to s unto them; diminish not a word: H1696
8 *him* to s unto all the people, H1696
15 you to s all these words in your ears. H1696
27: 9 sorcerers, which s unto you, saying, Ye H559
14 the prophets that s unto you, saying, Ye H559
28: 7 this word that I s in thine ears, and in H1696
29:24 *Thus* shalt thou also s to Shemaiah the H559
32: 4 Babylon, and shall s with him mouth to H1696
34: 2 of Israel; Go and s to Zedekiah king of H559
3 and he shall s with thee mouth to H1696
35: 2 the Rechabites, and s unto them, and H1696
38:20 of the LORD, which I s unto thee: so it H1696
39:16 Go and s to Ebed-melech the Ethiopian, H559
Ezk 2: 1 upon thy feet, and I will s unto thee. H1696
7 And thou shalt s my words unto them, H1696
3: 1 roll, and go s unto the house of Israel. H1696
4 Israel, and s with my words unto them. H1696
10 words that I shall s unto thee receive in H1696
11 of thy people, and s unto them, and tell H1696
27 But when I s with thee, I will open thy H1696
11: 5 me, and said unto me, S; Thus saith the H559
Ezk 12:25 For I *am* the LORD: I will s, and the H1696
25 word that I shall s shall come to pass; H1696
14: 4 Therefore s unto them, and say unto H1696
17: 2 Son of man, put forth a riddle, and s a H4911
20: 3 Son of man, s unto the elders of Israel, H1696
27 Therefore, son of man, s unto the H1696
49 they say of me, Doth he not s parables? H4911
24:21 S unto the house of Israel, Thus saith the H559
27 and thou shalt s, and be no more dumb: H1696
29: 3 S, and say, Thus saith the Lord GOD; H1696
31: 2 Son of man, s unto Pharaoh king of H559
32:21 The strong among the mighty shall s to H1696
33: 2 Son of man, s to the children of thy H1696
8 if thou dost not s to warn the wicked H1696
10 Therefore, O thou son of man, s unto the H559
10 house of Israel; Thus ye s, saying, If our H559
24 of the land of Israel s, saying, Abraham H559
30 of the houses, and s one to another, H1696
37:18 of thy people shall s unto thee, saying, H559
39:17 the Lord GOD; S unto every feathered H559
Dan 2: 9 and corrupt words to s before me, till the H560
3:29 and language, which s any thing amiss H560
7:25 And he shall s *great* words against the H4449
10:11 the words that I s unto thee, and stand H1696
19 lord s; for thou hast strengthened me. H1696
11:27 and they shall s lies at one table; but H1696
36 god, and shall s marvellous things H1696
Hos 2:14 and s comfortably unto her. H1696
Hab 2: 3 at the end it shall s, and not lie: though H6315
Zep 3:13 do iniquity, nor s lies; neither shall a H1696
Hag 2: 2 S now to Zerubbabel the son of Shealtiel, H559
21 S to Zerubbabel, governor of Judah, H559
Zec 2: 4 And said unto him, Run, s to this H1696
6:12 And s unto him, saying, Thus speaketh H559
7: 3 *And* to s unto the priests which *were* in H559
5 S unto all the people of the land, and to H559
8:16 These *are* the things that ye shall do; S H1696
9:10 cut off: and he shall s peace unto the H1696
Mt 8: 8 my roof: but s the word only, and G2036
10:19 or what ye shall s: for it shall be given G2980
19 you in that same hour what ye shall s. G2980
20 For it is not ye that s, but the Spirit of G2980
27 What I tell you in darkness, *that* s ye in G2036
12:34 can ye, being evil, s good things? for G2980
36 that men shall s, they shall give account G2980
46 stood without, desiring to s with him. G2980
47 stand without, desiring to s with thee. G2980
13:13 Therefore s I to them in parables: G2980
15:31 saw the dumb to s, the maimed to be G2980
Mk 1:34 the devils to s, because they knew him. G2980
2: 7 Why doth this *man* thus s G2980
7:37 the deaf to hear, and the dumb to s. G2980
9:39 my name, that can lightly s evil of me. G2551
12: 1 And he began to s unto them by G3004
13:11 what ye shall s, neither do ye G2980
11 in that hour, that s ye: for it is not ye G2980
11 it is not ye that s, but the Holy Ghost. G2980
14:71 I know not this man of whom ye s. G3004
16:17 devils; they shall s with new tongues; G2980
Lk 1:19 God; and am sent to s unto thee, and to G2980
20 and not able to s, until the day that G2980
22 And when he came out, he could not s G2980
4:41 to s: for they knew that he was Christ. G2980
6:26 Woe unto you, when all men shall s G2036
7:15 s. And he delivered him to his mother. G2980
24 departed, he began to s unto the people G3004
11:53 and to provoke him to s of many things: G653
12:10 And whosoever shall s a word against G2046
13 unto him, Master, s to my brother, that G2036
20: 9 Then began he to s to the people this G3004
Jn 1:37 And the two disciples heard him s, and G2980
40 One of the two which heard John s, and
3:11 Verily, verily, I say unto thee, We s that G2980
4:26 Jesus saith unto her, I that s unto thee G2980
6:63 the words that I s unto you, *they* are G2980
7:17 it be of God, or *whether* I s of myself. G2980
8:26 me is true; and I s to the world those G3004
28 Father hath taught me, I s these things. G2980
38 I s that which I have seen with my G2980
9:21 of age; ask him: he shall s for himself. G2980
12:49 what I should say, and what I should s. G2980
50 whatsoever I s therefore, even as the G2980
50 even as the Father said unto me, so I s. G2980
13:18 I s not of you all: I know whom I have G3004
14:10 the words that I s unto you I speak not G2980
10 I speak unto you I s not of myself: but G2980
16:13 truth: for he shall not s of himself; but G2980
13 s: and he will shew you things to come. G2980
25 I shall no more s unto you in proverbs, G2980

Jn 17:13 and these things I s in the world, that G2980
Act 2: 4 and began to s with other tongues, G2980
6 man heard them s in his own language. G2980
7 are not all these which s Galilaeans? G2980
11 we do hear them s in our tongues the G2980
29 Men *and* brethren, let me freely s unto G2036
4:17 s henceforth to no man in this name. G2980
18 s at all nor teach in the name of Jesus. G5350
20 For we cannot but s the things which G2980
29 with all boldness they may s thy word, G2980
5:20 Go, stand and s in the temple to the G2980
40 s in the name of Jesus, and let them go. G2980
6:11 have heard him s blasphemous words G2980
13 ceaseth not to s blasphemous words G2980
10:32 when he cometh, shall s unto thee. G2980
46 For they heard them s with tongues, G2980
11:15 And as I began to s, the Holy Ghost fell G2980
14: 9 The same heard Paul s: who stedfastly G2980
18: 9 afraid, but s, and hold not thy peace: G2980
26 And he began to s boldly in the
21:37 captain, May I s unto thee? Who said, G2036
37 thee? Who said, Canst thou s Greek? G1097
39 thee, suffer me to s unto the people. G2980
23: 5 not s evil of the ruler of thy people. G2046
24:10 unto him to s, answered, Forasmuch G3004
26: 1 art permitted to s for thyself. Then Paul G3004
25 s forth the words of truth and soberness. G669
26 before whom also I s freely: for I am G2980
28:20 to see *you*, and to s with *you*: because G4354
Ro 3: 5 who taketh vengeance? (I s as a man) G3004
6:19 I s after the manner of men because of G3004
7: 1 Know ye not, brethren, (for I s to them G2980
11:13 For I s to you Gentiles, inasmuch as I G3004
15:18 For I will not dare to s of any of those G2980
1Co 1:10 Christ, that ye all s the same thing, and G3004
2: 6 Howbeit we s wisdom among them G2980
7 But we s the wisdom of God in a G2980
13 Which things also we s, not in the G2980
3: 1 And I, brethren, could not s unto you G2980
6: 5 I s to your shame. Is it so, that there is G3004
7: 6 But I s this by permission, *and* not of G3004
12 But to the rest s I, not the Lord: If any G3004
35 And this I s for your own profit; not G3004
10:15 I s as to wise men; judge ye what I say. G3004
12:30 Have all the gifts of healing? do all s G2980
13: 1 Though I s with the tongues of men G2980
14: 6 you, except I shall s to you either by G2980
9 is spoken? for ye shall s into the air. G2980
18 I thank my God, I s with tongues more G2980
19 Yet in the church I had rather s five G2980
21 other lips will I s unto this people; and G2980
23 one place, and all s with tongues, and G2980
27 If any man s in an *unknown* tongue, *let* G2980
28 and let him s to himself, and to God. G2980
29 Let the prophets s two or three, and let G2980
34 permitted unto them to s; but *they are* G2980
35 a shame for women to s in the church. G2980
39 and forbid not to s with tongues. G2980
15:34 of God: I s *this* to your shame. G3004
2Co 2:17 God, in the sight of God s we in Christ. G2980
4:13 spoken; we also believe, and therefore s; G2980
6:13 Now for a recompence in the same, (I s G3004
7: 3 I s not *this* to condemn *you*: for I have G3004
8: 8 I s not by commandment, but by G3004
11:17 That which I s, I speak *it* not after the G2980
17 That which I speak, I s *it* not after the G2980
21 I s as concerning reproach, as though G3004
21 is bold, (I s foolishly,) I am bold also. G3004
23 Are they ministers of Christ? (I s as a G2980
12:19 unto you? we s before God in Christ: G2980
Gal 3:15 Brethren, I s after the manner of men; G3004
Eph 4:25 Wherefore putting away lying, s every G2980
5:12 For it is a shame even to s of those G3004
32 This is a great mystery: but I s G3004
6:20 I may s boldly, as I ought to speak.
20 I may speak boldly, as I ought to s. G2980
Php 1:14 more bold to s the word without fear. G2980
4:11 Not that I s in respect of want: for I G3004
Col 4: 3 of utterance, to s the mystery of Christ, G2980
4 I may make it manifest, as I ought to s. G2980
1Th 1: 8 so that we need not to s any thing. G2980
2: 2 were bold in our God to s unto you the G2980
4 the gospel, even so we s; not as pleasing G2980
16 Forbidding us to s to the Gentiles that G2980
1Ti 2: 7 and an apostle, (I s the truth in Christ, G3004
5:14 to the adversary to s reproachfully.
Tit 2: 1 But s thou the things which become G2980
15 These things s, and exhort, and rebuke G2980
3: 2 To s evil of no man, to be no brawlers, G987

Heb 2: 5 the world to come, whereof we s. G2980
6: 9 accompany salvation, though we thus s. G2980
9: 5 of which we cannot now s particularly. G3004
Jas 1:19 swift to hear, slow to s, slow to wrath: G2980
2:12 So s ye, and so do, as they that shall be G2980
4:11 S not evil one of another, brethren. He G2635
1Pt 2:12 that, whereas they s against you as G2635
3:10 evil, and his lips that they s no guile: G2980
16 that, whereas they s evil of you, as of G2635
4:11 If any man s, *let him speak* as the G2980
11 If any man speak, *let him* s as the G2980
2Pt 2:10 they are not afraid to s evil of dignities. G987
12 and destroyed, s evil of the things that G987
18 For when they s great swelling *words* of G5350
1Jn 4: 5 They are of the world: therefore s they G2980
2Jn 12 s face to face, that our joy may be full. G2980
3Jn 14 thee, and we shall s face to face. Peace G2980
Jude 8 despise dominion, and s evil of dignities. G987
10 But these s evil of those things which G987
Rev 2:24 of Satan, as they s; I will put upon you G3004
13:15 beast should both s, and cause that as G2980

SPEAKER

Ps 140:11 Let not an evil s be established H376+H3956
Act 14:12 Mercurius, because he was the chief s. G3056

SPEAKEST

1Sa 9:21 wherefore then s thou so to me? H1696
2Sa 19:29 And the king said unto him, Why s H1696
2Ki 6:12 words that thou s in thy bedchamber. H1696
Job 2:10 But he said unto her, Thou s as one of H1696
Ps 50:20 Thou sittest *and* s against thy brother; H1696
51: 4 thou s, *and* be clear when thou judgest. H1696
Isa 40:27 Why sayest thou, O Jacob, and s, O H1696
Jer 40:16 this thing: for thou s falsely of Ishmael. H1696
43: 2 Jeremiah, Thou s falsely: the LORD our H1696
Ezk 3:18 not warning, nor s to warn the wicked H1696
Zec 13: 3 not live; for thou s lies in the name of H1696
Mt 13:10 Why s thou unto them in parables? G2980
Lk 12:41 Then Peter said unto him, Lord, s thou G3004
Jn 16:29 His disciples said unto him, Lo, now s G2980
29 thou plainly, and s no proverb. G3004
19:10 Then saith Pilate unto him, S thou not G2980
Act 17:19 this new doctrine, whereof thou s, *is*? G2980

SPEAKETH

Gen 45:12 that *it is* my mouth that s unto you. H1696
Ex 33:11 to face, as a man s unto his friend. And H1696
Nu 23:26 All that the LORD s, that I must do? H1696
Dt 18:22 When a prophet s in the name of the H1696
1Ki 20: 5 and said, Thus s Ben-hadad, saying, H559
Job 2:10 of the foolish women s. What? shall we H1696
17: 5 He that s flattery to *his* friends, even H5046
33:14 For God s once, yea twice, *yet man* H1696
Ps 12: 3 *and* the tongue that s proud things: H1696
15: 2 and s the truth in his heart. H1696
37:30 The mouth of the righteous s wisdom, H1897
41: 6 And if he come to see *me*, he s vanity: H1696
144: 8 Whose mouth s vanity, and their right H1696
11 whose mouth s vanity, and their right H1696
Prv 2:12 from the man that s froward things; H1696
6:13 He winketh with his eyes, he s with his H4448
19 A false witness *that* s lies, and he that H6315
10:32 the mouth of the wicked *s* frowardness.
12:17 *He that* s truth sheweth forth H6315
18 There is that s like the piercings of a H981
14:25 souls: but a deceitful *witness* s lies. H6315
16:13 of kings; and they love him that s right. H1696
19: 5 and *he that* s lies shall not escape. H6315
9 and *he that* s lies shall perish. H6315
21:28 but the man that heareth s constantly. H1696
26:25 When he s fair, believe him not: for H6963
Isa 9:17 and every mouth s folly. For all this his H1696
32: 7 words, even when the needy s right. H1696
33:15 He that walketh righteously, and s H1696
Jer 9: 8 an arrow shot out; it s deceit: *one* H1696
8 speaketh deceit: *one* s peaceably to his H1696
10: 1 Hear ye the word which the LORD s H1696
28: 2 Thus s the LORD of hosts, the God of H559
29:25 Thus s the LORD of hosts, the God of H559
30: 2 Thus s the LORD God of Israel, saying, H559
Ezk 10: 5 voice of the Almighty God when he s. H1696
Am 5:10 and they abhor him that s uprightly. H1696
Hag 1: 2 Thus s the LORD of hosts, saying, This H559
Zec 6:12 And speak unto him, saying, Thus s the H559
7: 9 Thus s the LORD of hosts, saying, H559
Mt 10:20 Spirit of your Father which s in you. G2980
12:32 And whosoever s a word against the G2036
32 him: but whosoever s against the Holy G2036

Mt 12:34 the abundance of the heart the mouth s. G2980
Lk 5:21 Who is this which s blasphemies? Who G2980
6:45 the abundance of the heart his mouth s. G2980
Jn 3:31 is earthly, and s of the earth: he that G2980
34 For he whom God hath sent s the G2980
7:18 He that s of himself seeketh his own G2980
26 But, lo, he s boldly, and they say G2980
8:44 in him. When he s a lie, he speaketh of G2980
44 speaketh a lie, he s of his own: for he is G2980
19:12 maketh himself a king s against Caesar. G488
Act 2:25 For David s concerning him, I foresaw G3004
8:34 thee, of whom s the prophet this? of G3004
Ro 10: 6 which is of faith s on this wise, Say not G3004
1Co 14: 2 For he that s in an *unknown* tongue G2980
2 *unknown* tongue s not unto men, but G2980
2 howbeit in the spirit he s mysteries. G2980
3 But he that prophesieth s unto men *to* G2980
4 He that s in an *unknown* tongue G2980
5 than he that s with tongues, except G2980
11 be unto him that s a barbarian, and he G2980
11 he that s *shall be* a barbarian unto me. G2980
13 Wherefore let him that s in an G2980
1Ti 4: 1 Now the Spirit s expressly, that in the G3004
Heb 11: 4 his gifts: and by it he being dead yet s. G2980
12: 5 exhortation which s unto you as unto G1256
24 that s better things than *that of* Abel. G2980
25 See that ye refuse not him that s. For if G2980
25 turn away from him that s from heaven:
Jas 4:11 brethren. He that s evil of *his* brother, G2635
11 his brother, s evil of the law, and G2635
Jude 16 lusts; and their mouth s great swelling G2980

SPEAKING

Gen 24:15 he had done s, that, behold, Rebekah H1696
45 And before I had done s in mine heart, H1696
Ex 34:33 And *till* Moses had done s with them, H1696
Nu 7:89 the voice of one s unto him from off the H1696
16:31 made an end of s all these words, that H1696
Dt 4:33 Did *ever* people hear the voice of God s H1696
5:26 of the living God s out of the midst of H1696
11:19 your children, s of them when thou H1696
20: 9 made an end of s unto the people, that H1696
32:45 And Moses made an end of s all these H1696
Jdg 15:17 made an end of s, that he cast away the H1696
Ru 1:18 to go with her, then she left s unto her. H1696
1Sa 18: 1 made an end of s unto Saul, that the H1696
24:16 had made an end of s these words unto H1696
2Sa 13:36 had made an end of s, that, behold, the H1696
2Ch 36:12 prophet *s* from the mouth of the LORD.
Est 10: 3 his people, and s peace to all his seed. H1696
Job 1:16 While he *was* yet s, there came also H1696
17 While he *was* yet s, there came also H1696
18 While he *was* yet s, there came also H1696
4: 2 but who can withhold himself from s? H4405
32:15 they answered no more: they left off s. H4405
Ps 34:13 from evil, and thy lips from s guile. H1696
58: 3 astray as soon as they be born, s lies. H1696
Isa 58: 9 forth of the finger, and s vanity; H1696
13 own pleasure, nor s *thine own* words: H1696
59:13 from our God, s oppression and revolt, H1696
65:24 and while they are yet s, I will hear. H1696
Jer 7:13 up early and s, but ye heard not; and H1696
25: 3 early and s; but ye have not hearkened. H1696
26: 7 heard Jeremiah s these words in the H1696
8 made an end of s all that the LORD had H1696
35:14 and s; but ye hearkened not unto me. H1696
38: 4 of all the people, in s such words unto H1696
27 So they left off s with him; for the H2790
43: 1 made an end of s unto all the people all H1696
Ezk 43: 6 And I heard *him* s unto me out of the H1696
Dan 7: 8 of man, and a mouth s great things. H4449
8:13 Then I heard one saint s, and another H1696
18 Now as he was s with me, I was in a H1696
9:20 And whiles I *was* s, and praying, and H1696
21 Yea, whiles I *was* s in prayer, even the H1696
Mt 6: 7 they shall be heard for their much s. G4180
Lk 5: 4 Now when he had left s, he said unto G2980
Act 1: 3 them forty days, and s of the things G3004
7:44 he had appointed, s unto Moses, that G2980
13:43 Barnabas: who, s to them, persuaded G4354
14: 3 Long time therefore abode they s boldly
20:30 shall men arise, s perverse things, to G2980
26:14 I heard a voice s unto me, and saying G2980
1Co 12: 3 that no man s by the Spirit of God G2980
14: 6 Now, brethren, if I come unto you s G2980
2Co 13: 3 Since ye seek a proof of Christ s in me, G2980
Eph 4:15 But s the truth in love, may grow up into G226
31 s, be put away from you, with all malice: G988
5:19 S to yourselves in psalms and hymns G2980

1Ti 4: 2 S lies in hypocrisy; having their G5573
5:13 s things which they ought not. G2980
1Pt 4: 4 to the same excess of riot, s evil of *you*: G987
2Pt 2:16 the dumb ass s with man's voice G5350
3:16 As also in all *his* epistles, s in them of G2980
Rev 13: 5 unto him a mouth s great things and G2980

SPEAKINGS
1Pt 2: 1 hypocrisies, and envies, and all evil s, G2636

SPEAR
Jos 8:18 Stretch out the s that *is* in thy hand H3591
18 stretched out the s that *he had* in his H3591
26 stretched out the s, until he had utterly H3591
Jdg 5: 8 s seen among forty thousand in Israel? H7420
1Sa 13:22 neither sword nor s found in the hand H2595
17: 7 And the staff of his s *was* like a H2595
45 sword, and with a s, and with a shield: H2595
47 with sword and s: for the battle *is* the H2595
21: 8 under thine hand s or sword? for I have H2595
22: 6 having his s in his hand, and all H2595
26: 7 within the trench, and his s stuck in the H2595
8 I pray thee, with the s even to the earth H2595
11 thee, take thou now the s that *is* at his H2595
12 So David took the s and the cruse of H2595
16 where the king's s *is*, and the cruse of H2595
22 Behold the king's s! and let one of the H2595
2Sa 1: 6 leaned upon his s; and, lo, the chariots H2595
2:23 hinder end of the s smote him under H2595
23 the fifth *rib*, that the s came out behind H2595
21:16 the weight of whose s *weighed* three H7013
19 of whose s *was* like a weaver's beam. H2595
23: 7 and the staff of a s; and they shall be H2595
8 *he lift up his s* against eight hundred,
18 And he lifted up his s against three H2595
21 Egyptian had a s in his hand; but he H2595
21 staff, and plucked the s out of the H2595
21 hand, and slew him with his own s. H2595
1Ch 11:11 he lifted up his s against three hundred H2595
20 three: for lifting up his s against three H2595
23 hand *was* a s like a weaver's beam; H2595
23 and plucked the s out of the Egyptian's H2595
23 hand, and slew him with his own s. H2595
12:24 bare shield and s *were* six thousand H7420
34 shield and s thirty and seven thousand. H2595
20: 5 whose s staff *was* like a weaver's beam. H2595
2Ch 25: 5 to war, that could handle s and shield. H7420
Job 39:23 him, the glittering s and the shield. H2595
41:26 hold: the s, the dart, nor the habergeon. H2595
29 he laugheth at the shaking of a s. H3591
Ps 35: 3 Draw out also the s, and stop *the way* H2595
46: 9 and cutteth the s in sunder; he burneth H2595
Jer 6:23 They shall lay hold on bow and s; they H3591
Nah 3: 3 and the glittering s: and *there is* a H2595
Hab 3:11 *and* at the shining of thy glittering s. H2595
Jn 19:34 But one of the soldiers with a s pierced G3057

SPEARMEN
Ps 68:30 Rebuke the company of s, the multitude H7070
Act 23:23 and ten, and s two hundred, at the G1187

SPEARS
1Sa 13:19 the Hebrews make *them* swords or s: H2595
2Ki 11:10 give king David's s and shields, that H2595
2Ch 11:12 *he put* shields and s, and made them H7420
14: 8 bare targets and s, out of Judah three H7420
23: 9 of hundreds s, and bucklers, and H2595
26:14 host shields, and s, and helmets, and H7420
Neh 4:13 their swords, their s, and their bows. H7420
16 held both the s, the shields, and the H7420
21 of them held the s from the rising of the H7420
Job 41: 7 barbed irons? or his head with fish s? H6767
Ps 57: 4 whose teeth *are* s and arrows, and their H2595
Isa 2: 4 and their s into pruninghooks: H2595
Jer 46: 4 the s, *and* put on the brigandines. H7420
Ezk 39: 9 and the s, and they shall burn H7420
Joel 3:10 into s: let the weak say, I *am* strong. H7420
Mic 4: 3 and their s into pruninghooks: H2595

SPEAR'S
1Sa 17: 7 beam; and his s head *weighed* six H2595

SPECIAL
Dt 7: 6 thee to be a s people unto himself, H5459
Act 19:11 And God wrought s miracles by the G3756

SPECIALLY
Dt 4:10 *S* the day that thou stoodest before the
Act 25:26 before you, and s before thee, O king G3122
1Ti 4:10 of all men, s of those that believe. G3122
5: 8 for his own, and s for those of his own G3122
Tit 1:10 deceivers, s they of the circumcision: G3122
Phlm 16 a brother beloved, s to me, but how G3122

SPECKLED
Gen 30:32 thence all the s and spotted cattle, and H5348
32 the spotted and s among the goats: and H5348
33 one that *is* not s and spotted among H5348
35 she goats that were s and spotted, *and* H5348
39 forth cattle ringstraked, s, and spotted. H5348
31: 8 If he said thus, The s shall be thy H5348
8 all the cattle bare s: and if he said thus, H5348
10 cattle *were* ringstraked, s, and grisled. H5348
12 *are* ringstraked, s, and grisled: for I H5348
Jer 12: 9 Mine heritage *is* unto me *as* a s bird, H6641
Zec 1: 8 him *were there* red horses, s, and white. H8320

SPECTACLE
1Co 4: 9 for we are made a s unto the world, G2302

SPED
Jdg 5:30 Have they not s? have they *not* divided H4672

SPEECH
Gen 4:23 hearken unto my s: for I have slain a H565
11: 1 earth was of one language, and of one s. H1697
7 may not understand one another's s. H8193
Ex 4:10 but I *am* slow of s, and of a slow tongue. H6310
Dt 22:14 And give occasions of s against her, H1697
17 And, lo, he hath given occasions of s H1697
32: 2 My doctrine shall drop as the rain, my s H565
2Sa 14:20 To fetch about this form of s hath thy H1697
19:11 house? seeing the s of all Israel is come H1697
1Ki 3:10 And the s pleased the Lord, that H1697
2Ch 32:18 voice in the Jews' s unto the people of H3066
Neh 13:24 And their children spake half in the s of H3066
Job 12:20 He removeth away the s of the trusty, H8193
13:17 Hear diligently my s, and my H4405
21: 2 Hear diligently my s, and let this be H4405
24:25 a liar, and make my s nothing worth? H4405
29:22 again; and my s dropped upon them. H4405
37:19 order *our* s by reason of darkness.
Ps 17: 6 incline thine ear unto me, *and hear* my s. H565
19: 2 Day unto day uttereth s, and night unto H562
3 *There is* no s nor language, *where* their H562
Prv 7:21 With her much fair s she caused him to H3948
17: 7 Excellent s becometh not a fool: much H8193
Song 4: 3 of scarlet, and thy s *is* comely: thy H4057
Isa 28:23 hear my voice; hearken, and hear my s. H565
29: 4 ground, and thy s shall be low out of the H565
4 and thy s shall whisper out of the dust. H565
32: 9 ye careless daughters; give ear unto my s. H565
33:19 a people of a deeper s than thou canst H8193
Jer 31:23 yet they shall use this s in the land of H1697
Ezk 1:24 the voice of s, as the noise of an host: H1999
3: 5 of a strange s and of an hard language, H8193
6 Not to many people of a strange s and H8193
Hab 3: 2 O LORD, I have heard thy s, *and* was H8088
Mt 26:73 *one* of them; for thy s bewrayeth thee. G2981
Mk 7:32 impediment in his s; and they beseech G3424
14:70 a Galilaean, and thy s agreeth *thereto*. G2981
Jn 8:43 Why do ye not understand my s? *even* G2981
Act 14:11 saying in the s of Lycaonia, The gods G3072
20: 7 and continued his s until midnight. G3056
1Co 2: 1 not with excellency of s or of wisdom, G3056
4 And my s and my preaching *was* not G3056
4:19 will know, not the s of them which are G3056
2Co 3:12 such hope, we use great plainness of s: G3954
7: 4 Great *is* my boldness of s toward you, G3954
10:10 *is* weak, and *his* s contemptible. G3056
11: 6 But though *I be* rude in s, yet not in G3056
Col 4: 6 Let your s *be* alway with grace, G3056
Tit 2: 8 Sound s, that cannot be condemned; G3056

SPEECHES
Nu 12: 8 and not in dark s; and the similitude of H2420
Job 6:26 words, and the s of one that is desperate, H561
15: 3 or with s wherewith he can do no good? H4405
32:14 neither will I answer him with your s. H561
33: 1 Wherefore, Job, I pray thee, hear my s, H4405
Ro 16:18 fair s deceive the hearts of the simple. G2129
Jude 15 of all their hard *s* which ungodly sinners

SPEECHLESS
Mt 22:12 a wedding garment? And he was s. G5392
Lk 1:22 beckoned unto them, and remained s. G2974
Act 9: 7 s, hearing a voice, but seeing no man. G1769

SPEED
Gen 24:12 send me good s this day, and shew H7136
1Sa 20:38 the lad, Make s, haste, stay not. And H4120
2Sa 15:14 Absalom: make s to depart, lest he H4116
1Ki 12:18 Rehoboam made s to get him up to his H553
2Ch 10:18 Rehoboam made s to get him up to *his* H553
Ezr 6:12 have made a decree; let it be done with s. H629
Isa 5:19 That say, Let him make s, *and* hasten H4116
26 behold, they shall come with s swiftly: H4120
Act 17:15 come to him with all s, they departed. G5613
2Jn 10 into *your* house, neither bid him God s: G5463
11 For he that biddeth him God s is G5463

SPEEDILY
Gen 44:11 Then they s took down every man his H4116
1Sa 27: 1 me than that I should s escape into the H4422
2Sa 17:16 the wilderness, but s pass over; lest the H5674
2Ch 35:13 divided *them* s among all the people. H7323
Ezr 6:13 Darius the king had sent, so they did s. H629
7:17 That thou mayest buy s with this money H629
21 heaven, shall require of you, it be done s, H629
26 be executed s upon him, whether *it* H629
Est 2: 9 of him; and he s gave her her things for H926
Ps 31: 2 Bow down thine ear to me; deliver me s: H4120
69:17 servant; for I am in trouble: hear me s. H4118
79: 8 thy tender mercies s prevent us: for we H4118
102: 2 me: in the day *when* I call answer me s. H4118
143: 7 Hear me s, O LORD: my spirit faileth: H4118
Ecc 8:11 is not executed s, therefore the heart of H4120
Isa 58: 8 health shall spring forth s: and thy H4120
Joel 3: 4 me, swiftly *and* s will I return your H4120
Zec 8:21 saying, Let us go s to pray before the H1980
Lk 18: 8 I tell you that he will avenge them s. G1722

SPEEDY
Zep 1:18 shall make even a s riddance of all them H926

SPEND
Dt 32:23 them; I will s mine arrows upon them. H3615
Job 21:13 They s their days in wealth, H3615+H1086
36:11 If they obey and serve *him*, they shall s H3615
Ps 90: 9 we s our years as a tale *that is told*. H3615
Isa 55: 2 Wherefore do ye s money for *that* H8254
Act 20:16 he would not s the time in Asia: for G5551
2Co 12:15 And I will very gladly s and be spent G1159

SPENDEST
Lk 10:35 whatsoever thou s more, when I come G4325

SPENDETH
Prv 21:20 of the wise; but a foolish man s it up. H1104
29: 3 company with harlots s *his* substance. H6
Ecc 6:12 vain life which he s as a shadow? for H6213

SPENT
Gen 21:15 And the water was s in the bottle, and H3615
47:18 that our money is s; my lord also hath H8552
Lev 26:20 And your strength shall be s in vain: H8552
Jdg 19:11 the day was far s; and the servant said H7286
1Sa 9: 7 for the bread is s in our vessels, and H235
Job 7: 6 shuttle, and are s without hope. H3615
Ps 31:10 For my life is s with grief, and my years H3615
Isa 49: 4 in vain, I have s my strength for H3615
Jer 37:21 bread in the city were s. Thus Jeremiah H8552
Mk 5:26 and had s all that she had, and G1159
6:35 And when the day was now far s, his G1096
Lk 8:43 years, which had s all her living upon G4321
15:14 And when he had s all, there arose a G1159
24:29 far s. And he went in to tarry with them. G2827
Act 17:21 which were there s their time in G2119
18:23 And after he had s some time *there*, he G4160
27: 9 Now when much time was s, and when G1230
Ro 13:12 The night is far s, the day is at hand: let G4298
2Co 12:15 And I will very gladly spend and be s G1550

SPEWING
Hab 2:16 and shameful s *shall be* on thy glory. H7022

SPICE
Ex 35:28 And s, and oil for the light, and for the H1314
1Ki 10:15 the traffick of the s merchants, and of H7402
2Ch 9: 9 there any such s as the queen of Sheba H1314
Song 5: 1 my myrrh with my s; I have eaten my H1313
Ezk 24:10 s it well, and let the bones be burned. H7543

SPICED
Song 8: 2 s wine of the juice of my pomegranate. H7544

S

SPICERY
Gen 37:25 camels bearing s and balm and myrrh, H5219

SPICES
Gen 43:11 s, and myrrh, nuts, and almonds: H5219
Ex 25: 6 Oil for the light, s for anointing oil, and H1314
30:23 Take thou also unto thee principal s, of H1314
34 unto thee sweet s, stacte, and onycha, H5561
34 *these* sweet s with pure frankincense: H5561
35: 8 And oil for the light, and s for H1314
37:29 incense of sweet s, according to the H5561
1Ki 10: 2 camels that bare s, and very much gold, H1314
10 of gold, and of s very great store, and H1314
10 such abundance of s as these which the H1314
25 and armour, and s, horses, and mules, H1314
2Ki 20:13 the gold, and the s, and the precious H1314
1Ch 9:29 the oil, and the frankincense, and the s. H1314
30 the priests made the ointment of the s. H1314
2Ch 9: 1 and camels that bare s, and gold in H1314
9 of gold, and of s great abundance, and H1314
24 harness, and s, horses, and mules, H1314
16:14 and divers kinds *of s* prepared by the
32:27 stones, and for s, and for shields, and H1314
Song 4:10 the smell of thine ointments than all s! H1314
14 myrrh and aloes, with all the chief s: H1314
16 garden, *that* the s thereof may flow out. H1314
5:13 His cheeks *are* as a bed of s, *as* sweet H1314
6: 2 to the beds of s, to feed in the gardens, H1314
8:14 a young hart upon the mountains of s. H1314
Isa 39: 2 the gold, and the s, and the precious H1314
Ezk 27:22 with chief of all s, and with all precious H1314
Mk 16: 1 s, that they might come and anoint him. *G759*
Lk 23:56 And they returned, and prepared s and *G759*
24: 1 bringing the s which they had prepared, *G759*
Jn 19:40 s, as the manner of the Jews is to bury. *G759*

SPIDER
Prv 30:28 The s taketh hold with her hands, and H8079

SPIDER'S
Job 8:14 off, and whose trust *shall be* a s web. H5908
Isa 59: 5 and weave the s web: he that eateth H5908

SPIED
Ex 2:11 burdens: and he s an Egyptian smiting H7200
Jos 6:22 two men that had s out the country, Go H7270
2Ki 9:17 in Jezreel, and he s the company of H7200
13:21 that, behold, they s a band *of men;* and H7200
23:16 And as Josiah turned himself, he s the H7200
24 that were s in the land of Judah H7200

SPIES
Gen 42: 9 said unto them, Ye *are* s; to see the H7270
11 we *are* true *men,* thy servants are no s. H7270
14 that I spake unto you, saying, Ye *are* s: H7270
16 by the life of Pharaoh surely ye *are* s. H7270
30 to us, and took us for s of the country. H7270
31 unto him, We *are* true *men;* we are no s: H7270
34 that ye *are* no s, but *that* ye *are* true H7270
Nu 21: 1 came by the way of the s; then he fought H871
Jos 6:23 And the young men that were s went H7270
Jdg 1:24 And the s saw a man come forth out of H8104
1Sa 26: 4 David therefore sent out s, and H7270
2Sa 15:10 But Absalom sent s throughout all the H7270
Lk 20:20 And they watched *him,* and sent forth s, *G1455*
Heb 11:31 she had received the s with peace. *G2685*

SPIKENARD
Song 1:12 While the king *sitteth* at his table, my s H5373
4:13 with pleasant fruits; camphire, with s, H5373
14 S and saffron; calamus and cinnamon, H5373
Mk 14: 3 box of ointment of s very precious; and *G3487*
Jn 12: 3 pound of ointment of s, very costly, and *G3487*

SPILLED
Gen 38: 9 wife, that he s *it* on the ground, lest H7843
Mk 2:22 and the wine is s, and the bottles will *G1632*
Lk 5:37 and be s, and the bottles shall perish. *G1632*

SPILT
2Sa 14:14 die, and *are* as water s on the ground, H5064

SPIN
Ex 35:25 wise hearted did s with their hands, H2901
Mt 6:28 grow; they toil not, neither do they s: *G3514*
Lk 12:27 they toil not, they s not; and yet I say *G3514*

SPINDLE
Prv 31:19 She layeth her hands to the s, and her H3601

SPIRIT
Gen 1: 2 of the deep. And the S of God moved H7307
6: 3 And the LORD said, My s shall not H7307
41: 8 morning that his s was troubled; and H7307
38 this *is,* a man in whom the s of God *is?* H7307
45:27 him, the s of Jacob their father revived: H7307
Ex 6: 9 for anguish of s, and for cruel bondage. H7307
28: 3 filled with the s of wisdom, that they H7307
31: 3 And I have filled him with the s of God, H7307
35:21 one whom his s made willing, *and* they H7307
31 And he hath filled him with the s of H7307
Lev 20:27 that hath a familiar s, or that is a wizard, H178
Nu 5:14 And the s of jealousy come upon him, H7307
14 be defiled: or if the s of jealousy come H7307
30 Or when the s of jealousy cometh upon H7307
11:17 I will take of the s which *is* upon thee, H7307
25 and took of the s that *was* upon him, H7307
25 *that,* when the s rested upon them, they H7307
26 Medad: and the s rested upon them; H7307
29 the LORD would put his s upon them! H7307
14:24 he had another s with him, and hath H7307
24: 2 and the s of God came upon him. H7307
27:18 *is* the s, and lay thine hand upon him; H7307
Dt 2:30 God hardened his s, and made his heart H7307
34: 9 was full of the s of wisdom; for Moses H7307
Jos 5: 1 neither was there s in them any more, H7307
Jdg 3:10 And the s of the LORD came upon him, H7307
6:34 But the s of the LORD came upon H7307
9:23 Then God sent an evil s between H7307
11:29 Then the s of the LORD came upon H7307
13:25 And the s of the LORD began to move H7307
14: 6 And the s of the LORD came mightily H7307
19 And the s of the LORD came upon him, H7307
15:14 him: and the s of the LORD came H7307
19 he had drunk, his s came again, and he H7307
1Sa 1:15 of a sorrowful s: I have drunk neither H7307
10: 6 And the s of the LORD will come upon H7307
10 met him; and the s of God came upon H7307
11: 6 And the s of God came upon Saul when H7307
16:13 brethren: and the s of the LORD came H7307
14 But the s of the LORD departed from H7307
14 an evil s from the LORD troubled him. H7307
15 now, an evil s from God troubleth thee. H7307
16 when the evil s from God is upon thee, H7307
23 And it came to pass, when the *evil* s H7307
23 well, and the evil s departed from him. H7307
18:10 that the evil s from God came upon H7307
19: 9 And the evil s from the LORD was H7307
20 over them, the s of God was upon the H7307
23 in Ramah: and the s of God was upon H7307
28: 7 hath a familiar s, that I may go to her, H178
7 woman that hath a familiar s at En-dor. H178
8 me by the familiar s, and bring me *him* H178
30:12 he had eaten, his s came again to him: H7307
2Sa 23: 2 The S of the LORD spake by me, and H7307
1Ki 10: 5 the LORD; there was no more s in her. H7307
18:12 from thee, that the s of the LORD shall H7307
21: 5 thy s so sad, that thou eatest no bread? H7307
22:21 And there came forth a s, and stood H7307
22 I will be a lying s in the mouth of all his H7307
23 hath put a lying s in the mouth of all H7307
24 way went the s of the LORD from me H7307
2Ki 2: 9 a double portion of thy s be upon me. H7307
15 they said, The s of Elijah doth rest on H7307
16 peradventure the s of the LORD hath H7307
1Ch 5:26 And the God of Israel stirred up the s of H7307
26 of Assyria, and the s of Tilgath-pilneser H7307
10:13 *one that had* a familiar s, to inquire *of it;* H178
12:18 Then the s came upon Amasai, *who* H7307
28:12 that he had by the s, of the courts of the H7307
2Ch 9: 4 the LORD; there was no more s in her. H7307
15: 1 And the s of God came upon Azariah H7307
18:20 Then there came out a s, and stood H7307
21 out, and be a lying s in the mouth of all H7307
22 hath put a lying s in the mouth of these H7307
23 way went the s of the LORD from me H7307
20:14 Asaph, came the s of the LORD in the H7307
21:16 Jehoram the s of the Philistines, and H7307
24:20 And the s of God came upon Zechariah H7307
33: 6 with a familiar s, and with wizards: he H178
36:22 stirred up the s of Cyrus king of Persia, H7307
Ezr 1: 1 stirred up the s of Cyrus king of Persia, H7307
5 all *them* whose s God had raised, to go H7307
Neh 9:20 Thou gavest also thy good s to instruct H7307
30 them by thy s in thy prophets: yet H7307
Job 4:15 Then a s passed before my face; the H7307
6: 4 drinketh up my s: the terrors of God do H7307
7:11 the anguish of my s; I will complain in H7307
10:12 and thy visitation hath preserved my s. H7307
15:13 That thou turnest thy s against God, H7307
20: 3 my reproach, and the s of my H7307
21: 4 *so,* why should not my s be troubled? H7307
26: 4 words? and whose s came from thee? H5397
13 By his s he hath garnished the heavens; H7307
27: 3 me, and the s of God *is* in my nostrils; H7307
32: 8 But *there is* a s in man: and the H7307
18 For I am full of matter, the s within me H7307
33: 4 The S of God hath made me, and the H7307
34:14 unto himself his s and his breath; H7307
Ps 31: 5 Into thine hand I commit my s: thou H7307
32: 2 and in whose s *there is* no guile. H7307
34:18 and saveth such as be of a contrite s. H7307
51:10 O God; and renew a right s within me. H7307
11 and take not thy holy s from me. H7307
12 and uphold me *with thy* free s. H7307
17 The sacrifices of God *are* a broken s: a H7307
76:12 He shall cut off the s of princes: *he is* H7307
77: 3 and my s was overwhelmed. Selah. H7307
6 heart: and my s made diligent search. H7307
78: 8 and whose s was not stedfast with God. H7307
104:30 Thou sendest forth thy s, they are H7307
106:33 Because they provoked his s, so that he H7307
139: 7 Whither shall I go from thy s? or H7307
142: 3 When my s was overwhelmed within H7307
143: 4 Therefore is my s overwhelmed within H7307
7 Hear me speedily, O LORD: my s H7307
10 *art* my God: thy s *is* good; lead me into H7307
Prv 1:23 I will pour out my s unto you, I will H7307
11:13 is of a faithful s concealeth the matter. H7307
14:29 but *he that is* hasty of s exalteth folly. H7307
15: 4 therein *is* a breach in the s. H7307
13 by sorrow of the heart the s is broken. H7307
16:18 and an haughty s before a fall. H7307
19 Better *it is to be* of an humble s with H7307
32 ruleth his s than he that taketh a city. H7307
17:22 but a broken s drieth the bones. H7307
27 of understanding is of an excellent s. H7307
18:14 The s of a man will sustain his H7307
14 but a wounded s who can bear? H7307
20:27 The s of man *is* the candle of the H5397
25:28 He that *hath* no rule over his own s *is* H7307
29:23 honour shall uphold the humble in s. H7307
Ecc 1:14 behold, all *is* vanity and vexation of s. H7307
17 perceived that this also is vexation of s. H7307
2:11 and vexation of s, and *there was* no H7307
17 me: for all *is* vanity and vexation of s. H7307
26 This also *is* vanity and vexation of s. H7307
3:21 Who knoweth the s of man that goeth H7307
21 upward, and the s of the beast that H7307
4: 4 This *is* also vanity and vexation of s. H7307
6 full *with* travail and vexation of s. H7307
16 this also *is* vanity and vexation of s. H7307
6: 9 this *is* also vanity and vexation of s. H7307
7: 8 in s *is* better than the proud in spirit. H7307
8 in spirit *is* better than the proud in s. H7307
9 Be not hasty in thy s to be angry: for H7307
8: 8 power over the s to retain the spirit; H7307
8 the spirit to retain the s; neither *hath he* H7307
10: 4 If the s of the ruler rise up against thee, H7307
11: 5 *is* the way of the s, *nor* how the bones H7307
12: 7 the s shall return unto God who gave it. H7307
Isa 4: 4 thereof by the s of judgment, and by H7307
4 of judgment, and by the s of burning. H7307
11: 2 And the s of the LORD shall rest upon H7307
2 rest upon him, the s of wisdom and H7307
2 the s of counsel and might, H7307
2 and might, the s of knowledge and of H7307
19: 3 And the s of Egypt shall fail in the H7307
14 The LORD hath mingled a perverse s in H7307
26: 9 yea, with my s within me will I seek H7307
28: 6 And for a s of judgment to him that H7307
29: 4 hath a familiar s, out of the ground, and H178
10 out upon you the s of deep sleep, and H7307
24 They also that erred in s shall come to H7307
30: 1 of my s, that they may add sin to sin: H7307
31: 3 flesh, and not s. When the LORD shall H7307
32:15 Until the s be poured upon us from on H7307
34:16 and his s it hath gathered them. H7307
38:16 *is* the life of my s: so wilt thou recover H7307
40: 7 because the s of the LORD bloweth H7307
13 Who hath directed the s of the LORD, H7307
42: 1 I have put my s upon him: he shall H7307
5 it, and s to them that walk therein: H7307
44: 3 I will pour my s upon thy seed, and H7307
48:16 the Lord GOD, and his S, hath sent me. H7307
54: 6 and grieved in s, and a wife of youth, H7307
57:15 and humble s, to revive the spirit of H7307
15 to revive the s of the humble, and H7307

Isa 57:16 wroth: for the s should fail before me, H7307
59:19 in like a flood, the S of the LORD shall H7307
21 the LORD; My s that *is* upon thee, and H7307
61: 1 The S of the Lord GOD *is* upon me; H7307
3 of praise for the s of heaviness; that H7307
63:10 But they rebelled, and vexed his holy S: H7307
11 *is* he that put his holy S within him? H7307
14 down into the valley, the S of the LORD H7307
65:14 heart, and shall howl for vexation of s. H7307
66: 2 a contrite s, and trembleth at my word. H7307
Jer 51:11 hath raised up the s of the kings of the H7307
Ezk 1:12 whither the s was to go, they went; H7307
20 Whithersoever the s was to go, they H7307
20 went, thither *was their* s to go; and the H7307
20 them: for the s of the living creature H7307
21 them: for the s of the living creature H7307
2: 2 And the s entered into me when he H7307
3:12 Then the s took me up, and I heard H7307
14 So the s lifted me up, and took me H7307
14 in the heat of my s; but the hand of the H7307
24 Then the s entered into me, and set me H7307
8: 3 head; and the s lifted me up between H7307
10:17 the s of the living creature *was* in them. H7307
11: 1 Moreover the s lifted me up, and H7307
5 And the S of the LORD fell upon me, H7307
19 I will put a new s within you; and I will H7307
24 Afterwards the s took me up, and H7307
24 me in a vision by the S of God into H7307
13: 3 their own s, and have seen nothing! H7307
18:31 s: for why will ye die, O house of Israel? H7307
21: 7 feeble, and every s shall faint, and all H7307
36:26 you, and a new s will I put within you: H7307
27 And I will put my s within you, and H7307
37: 1 me out in the s of the LORD, and set H7307
14 And shall put my s in you, and ye shall H7307
39:29 poured out my s upon the house of H7307
43: 5 So the s took me up, and brought me H7307
Dan 2: 1 wherewith his s was troubled, and his H7307
3 my s was troubled to know the dream. H7307
4: 8 in whom *is* the s of the holy gods: and H7308
9 I know that the s of the holy gods *is* in H7308
18 for the s of the holy gods *is* in thee. H7308
5:11 in whom *is* the s of the holy gods; and H7308
12 Forasmuch as an excellent s, and H7308
14 I have even heard of thee, that the s of H7308
6: 3 an excellent s *was* in him; and the H7308
7:15 I Daniel was grieved in my s in the H7308
Hos 4:12 unto them: for the s of whoredoms H7307
5: 4 their God: for the s of whoredoms *is* in H7307
Joel 2:28 I will pour out my s upon all flesh; and H7307
29 in those days will I pour out my s. H7307
Mic 2: 7 house of Jacob, is the s of the LORD H7307
11 If a man walking in the s and falsehood H7307
3: 8 But truly I am full of power by the s of H7307
Hag 1:14 And the LORD stirred up the s of H7307
14 of Judah, and the s of Joshua the son of H7307
14 priest, and the s of all the remnant of H7307
2: 5 s remaineth among you: fear ye not. H7307
Zec 4: 6 but by my s, saith the LORD of hosts. H7307
6: 8 have quieted my s in the north country. H7307
7:12 hosts hath sent in his s by the former H7307
12: 1 and formeth the s of man within him. H7307
10 of Jerusalem, the s of grace and of H7307
13: 2 the unclean s to pass out of the land. H7307
Mal 2:15 the residue of the s. And wherefore one? H7307
15 take heed to your s, and let none deal H7307
16 your s, that ye deal not treacherously. H7307
Mt 3:16 and he saw the S of God descending G4151
4: 1 Then was Jesus led up of the S into the G4151
5: 3 Blessed *are* the poor in s: for theirs is G4151
10:20 For it is not ye that speak, but the S of G4151
12:18 I will put my s upon him, and he shall G4151
28 But if I cast out devils by the S of God, G4151
43 When the unclean s is gone out of a G4151
14:26 It is a s; and they cried out for fear. G5326
22:43 doth David in s call him Lord, saying, G4151
26:41 temptation: the s indeed *is* willing, but G4151
Mk 1:10 the S like a dove descending upon him: G4151
12 And immediately the S driveth him G4151
23 with an unclean s; and he cried out, G4151
26 And when the unclean s had torn him, G4151
2: 8 perceived in his s that they so reasoned G4151
3:30 they said, He hath an unclean s. G4151
5: 2 of the tombs a man with an unclean s, G4151
8 Come out of the man, *thou* unclean s. G4151
6:49 supposed it had been a s, and cried out: G5326
7:25 had an unclean s, heard of him, and G4151
8:12 And he sighed deeply in his s, and saith, G4151
9:17 unto thee my son, which hath a dumb s; G4151

Mk 9:20 straightway the s tare him; and he fell G4151
25 he rebuked the foul s, saying unto him, G4151
25 dumb and deaf s, I charge thee, come G4151
26 And *the* s cried, and rent him sore, and
14:38 s truly *is* ready, but the flesh *is* weak. G4151
Lk 1:17 And he shall go before him in the s and G4151
47 And my s hath rejoiced in God my G4151
80 and waxed strong in s, and was in the G4151
2:27 And he came by the S into the temple: G4151
40 waxed strong in s, filled with wisdom: G4151
4: 1 was led by the S into the wilderness, G4151
14 in the power of the S into Galilee: and G4151
18 The S of the Lord *is* upon me, because G4151
33 a man, which had a s of an unclean G4151
8:29 (For he had commanded the unclean s G4151
55 And her s came again, and she arose G4151
9:39 And, lo, a s taketh him, and he G4151
42 the unclean s, and healed the child, G4151
55 know not what manner of s ye are of. G4151
10:21 In that hour Jesus rejoiced in s, and G4151
11:13 give the Holy S to them that ask him? G4151
24 When the unclean s is gone out of a G4151
13:11 which had a s of infirmity eighteen G4151
23:46 I commend my s: and having said thus, G4151
24:37 and supposed that they had seen a s. G4151
39 me, and see; for a s hath not flesh and G4151
Jn 1:32 saying, I saw the S descending from G4151
33 thou shalt see the S descending, and G4151
3: 5 water and *of* the S, he cannot enter into G4151
6 and that which is born of the S is spirit. G4151
6 and that which is born of the Spirit is s. G4151
8 so is every one that is born of the S. G4151
34 giveth not the S by measure *unto him*. G4151
4:23 the Father in s and in truth: for the G4151
24 God *is* a S: and they that worship him G4151
24 must worship *him* in s and in truth. G4151
6:63 It is the s that quickeneth; the flesh G4151
63 unto you, *they* are s, and *they* are life. G4151
7:39 (But this spake he of the S, which they G4151
11:33 he groaned in the s, and was troubled, G4151
13:21 he was troubled in s, and testified, and G4151
14:17 *Even* the S of truth; whom the world G4151
15:26 the Father, *even* the S of truth, which G4151
16:13 Howbeit when he, the S of truth, is G4151
Act 2: 4 tongues, as the S gave them utterance. G4151
17 pour out of my S upon all flesh: and G4151
18 days of my S; and they shall prophesy: G4151
5: 9 to tempt the S of the Lord? behold, G4151
6:10 wisdom and the s by which he spake. G4151
7:59 and saying, Lord Jesus, receive my s. G4151
8:29 Then the S said unto Philip, Go near, G4151
39 of the water, the S of the Lord caught G4151
10:19 on the vision, the S said unto him, G4151
11:12 And the S bade me go with them, G4151
28 signified by the S that there should be G4151
16: 7 Bithynia: but the S suffered them not. G4151
16 possessed with a s of divination met G4151
18 and said to the s, I command thee in G4151
17:16 at Athens, his s was stirred in him, G4151
18: 5 was pressed in the s, and testified to the G4151
25 fervent in the s, he spake and taught G4151
19:15 And the evil s answered and said, Jesus G4151
16 And the man in whom the evil s was G4151
21 purposed in the s, when he had passed G4151
20:22 And now, behold, I go bound in the s G4151
21: 4 Paul through the S, that he should not G4151
23: 8 nor s: but the Pharisees confess both. G4151
9 in this man: but if a s or an angel hath G4151
Ro 1: 4 according to the s of holiness, by the G4151
9 I serve with my s in the gospel of his G4151
2:29 *that* of the heart, in the s, *and* not in the G4151
7: 6 of s, and not *in* the oldness of the letter. G4151
8: 1 walk not after the flesh, but after the S. G4151
2 For the law of the S of life in Christ G4151
4 walk not after the flesh, but after the S. G4151
5 are after the S the things of the Spirit. G4151
5 are after the Spirit the things of the S. G4151
9 But ye are not in the flesh, but in the S, G4151
9 if so be that the S of God dwell in you. G4151
9 not the S of Christ, he is none of his. G4151
10 the S *is* life because of righteousness. G4151
11 But if the S of him that raised up Jesus G4151
11 bodies by his S that dwelleth in you. G4151
13 if ye through the S do mortify the deeds G4151
14 For as many as are led by the S of God, G4151
15 For ye have not received the s of G4151
15 ye have received the S of adoption, G4151
16 The S itself beareth witness with our G4151
16 our s, that we are the children of God: G4151

Ro 8:23 firstfruits of the S, even we ourselves G4151
26 Likewise the S also helpeth our G4151
26 as we ought: but the S itself maketh G4151
27 *is* the mind of the S, because he maketh G4151
11: 8 given them the s of slumber, eyes that G4151
12:11 Not slothful in business; fervent in s; G4151
15:19 the power of the S of God; so that from G4151
30 and for the love of the S, that ye strive G4151
1Co 2: 4 demonstration of the S and of power: G4151
10 unto us by his S: for the Spirit searcheth G4151
10 his Spirit: for the S searcheth all things, G4151
11 of a man, save the s of man which is in G4151
11 God knoweth no man, but the S of God. G4151
12 Now we have received, not the s of the G4151
12 of the world, but the s which is of God; G4151
14 the things of the S of God: for they are G4151
3:16 and *that* the S of God dwelleth in you? G4151
4:21 or in love, and *in* the s of meekness? G4151
5: 3 but present in s, have judged already, G4151
4 together, and my s, with the power of G4151
5 the flesh, that the s may be saved in the G4151
6:11 the Lord Jesus, and by the S of our God. G4151
17 he that is joined unto the Lord is one s. G4151
20 body, and in your s, which are God's. G4151
7:34 in body and in s: but she that is married G4151
40 I think also that I have the S of God. G4151
12: 3 speaking by the S of God calleth Jesus G4151
4 are diversities of gifts, but the same S. G4151
7 But the manifestation of the S is given G4151
8 For to one is given by the S the word of G4151
8 the word of knowledge by the same S; G4151
9 To another faith by the same S; to G4151
9 the gifts of healing by the same S; G4151
11 and the selfsame S, dividing to every G4151
13 For by one S are we all baptized into G4151
13 have been all made to drink into one S. G4151
14: 2 howbeit in the s he speaketh mysteries. G4151
14 *unknown* tongue, my s prayeth, but my G4151
15 What is it then? I will pray with the s, G4151
15 I will sing with the s, and I will sing with G4151
16 Else when thou shalt bless with the s, G4151
15:45 last Adam *was made* a quickening s. G4151
16:18 For they have refreshed my s and G4151
2Co 1:22 given the earnest of the S in our hearts. G4151
2:13 I had no rest in my s, because I found G4151
3: 3 ink, but with the S of the living God; G4151
6 letter, but of the s: for the letter killeth, G4151
6 the letter killeth, but the s giveth life. G4151
8 How shall not the ministration of the s G4151
17 Now the Lord is that S: and where the G4151
17 the S of the Lord *is*, there *is* liberty. G4151
18 to glory, *even* as by the S of the Lord. G4151
4:13 We having the same s of faith, G4151
5: 5 hath given unto us the earnest of the S. G4151
7: 1 s, perfecting holiness in the fear of God. G4151
13 because his s was refreshed by you all. G4151
11: 4 ye receive another s, which ye have not G4151
12:18 s? walked we not in the same steps? G4151
Gal 3: 2 Received ye the S by the works of the G4151
3 Are ye so foolish? having begun in the S, G4151
5 to you the S, and worketh miracles G4151
14 the promise of the S through faith. G4151
4: 6 hath sent forth the S of his Son into G4151
29 *was born* after the S, even so *it is* now. G4151
5: 5 For we through the S wait for the hope G4151
16 *This* I say then, Walk in the S, and ye G4151
17 For the flesh lusteth against the S, and G4151
17 the Spirit, and the S against the flesh: G4151
18 But if ye be led of the S, ye are not under G4151
22 But the fruit of the S is love, joy, peace, G4151
25 If we live in the S, let us also walk in the G4151
25 in the Spirit, let us also walk in the S. G4151
6: 1 such an one in the s of meekness; G4151
8 that soweth to the S shall of the Spirit G4151
8 shall of the S reap life everlasting. G4151
18 Lord Jesus Christ *be* with your s. Amen. G4151
Eph 1:13 sealed with that holy S of promise, G4151
17 may give unto you the s of wisdom and G4151
2: 2 of the air, the s that now worketh in G4151
18 have access by one S unto the Father. G4151
22 for an habitation of God through the S. G4151
3: 5 his holy apostles and prophets by the S; G4151
16 with might by his S in the inner man; G4151
4: 3 Endeavouring to keep the unity of the S G4151
4 *There is* one body, and one S, even as ye G4151
23 And be renewed in the s of your mind; G4151
30 And grieve not the holy S of God, G4151
5: 9 (For the fruit of the S *is* in all goodness G4151
18 is excess; but be filled with the S; G4151

Eph 6:17 of the S, which is the word of God: G4151
18 in the S, and watching thereunto G4151
Php 1:19 and the supply of the S of Jesus Christ, G4151
27 ye stand fast in one s, with one mind G4151
2: 1 of the S, if any bowels and mercies, G4151
3: 3 God in the s, and rejoice in Christ G4151
Col 1: 8 also declared unto us your love in the S. G4151
2: 5 am I with you in the s, joying and G4151
1Th 4: 8 who hath also given unto us his holy S. G4151
5:19 Quench not the S. G4151
23 *God* your whole s and soul and body be G4151
2Th 2: 2 neither by s, nor by word, nor by G4151
8 consume with the s of his mouth, and G4151
13 of the S and belief of the truth: G4151
1Ti 3:16 flesh, justified in the S, seen of angels, G4151
4: 1 Now the S speaketh expressly, that in G4151
12 in charity, in s, in faith, in purity. G4151
2Ti 1: 7 For God hath not given us the s of fear; G4151
4:22 The Lord Jesus Christ *be* with thy s. G4151
Phlm 25 Lord Jesus Christ *be* with your s. Amen. G4151
Heb 4:12 of soul and s, and of the joints and G4151
9:14 the eternal S offered himself without G4151
10:29 hath done despite unto the S of grace? G4151
Jas 2:26 For as the body without the s is dead, G4151
4: 5 s that dwelleth in us lusteth to envy? G4151
1Pt 1: 2 of the S, unto obedience and G4151
11 of time the S of Christ which was G4151
22 the truth through the S unto unfeigned G4151
3: 4 a meek and quiet s, which is in the sight G4151
18 in the flesh, but quickened by the S: G4151
4: 6 flesh, but live according to God in the s. G4151
14 *are ye*; for the s of glory and of God G4151
1Jn 3:24 in us, by the S which he hath given us. G4151
4: 1 Beloved, believe not every s, but try the G4151
2 Hereby know ye the S of God: Every G4151
2 of God: Every s that confesseth that G4151
3 And every s that confesseth not that G4151
3 and this is that *s* of antichrist, whereof G4151
6 we the s of truth, and the spirit of error. G4151
6 we the spirit of truth, and the s of error. G4151
13 in us, because he hath given us of his S. G4151
5: 6 And it is the S that beareth witness, G4151
6 beareth witness, because the S is truth. G4151
8 in earth, the S, and the water, and G4151
Jude 19 themselves, sensual, having not the S. G4151
Rev 1:10 I was in the S on the Lord's day, and G4151
2: 7 let him hear what the S saith unto the G4151
11 let him hear what the S saith unto the G4151
17 let him hear what the S saith unto the G4151
29 what the S saith unto the churches. G4151
3: 6 what the S saith unto the churches. G4151
13 what the S saith unto the churches. G4151
22 what the S saith unto the churches. G4151
4: 2 And immediately I was in the s: and, G4151
11:11 And after three days and an half the S G4151
14:13 Yea, saith the S, that they may rest from G4151
17: 3 So he carried me away in the s into the G4151
18: 2 hold of every foul s, and a cage of every G4151
19:10 testimony of Jesus is the s of prophecy. G4151
21:10 And he carried me away in the s to a G4151
22:17 And the S and the bride say, Come. G4151

SPIRITS

Lev 19:31 Regard not them that have familiar s, H178
20: 6 as have familiar s, and after wizards, to H178
Nu 16:22 the God of the s of all flesh, shall one H7307
27:16 Let the LORD, the God of the s of all H7307
Dt 18:11 s, or a wizard, or a necromancer. H178
1Sa 28: 3 s, and the wizards, out of the land. H178
9 that have familiar s, and the wizards, out H178
2Ki 21: 6 dealt with familiar s and wizards: he H178
23:24 Moreover the *workers with* familiar s, H178
Ps 104: 4 Who maketh his angels s; his ministers H7307
Prv 16: 2 own eyes; but the LORD weigheth the s. H7307
Isa 8:19 that have familiar s, and unto wizards H178
19: 3 that have familiar s, and to the wizards. H178
Zec 6: 5 me, These *are* the four s of the heavens, H7307
Mt 8:16 he cast out the s with *his* word, and G4151
10: 1 *against* unclean s, to cast them out, and G4151
12:45 seven other s more wicked than G4151
Mk 1:27 the unclean s, and they do obey him. G4151
3:11 And unclean s, when they saw him, fell G4151
5:13 leave. And the unclean s went out, and G4151
6: 7 and gave them power over unclean s; G4151
Lk 4:36 the unclean s, and they come out. G4151
6:18 with unclean s: and they were healed. G4151
7:21 and of evil s; and unto many *that* G4151
8: 2 been healed of evil s and infirmities, G4151
10:20 not, that the s are subject unto you; G4151
Lk 11:26 *to him* seven other s more wicked than G4151
Act 5:16 s: and they were healed every one. G4151
8: 7 For unclean s, crying with loud voice, G4151
19:12 them, and the evil s went out of them. G4151
13 which had evil s the name of the Lord G4151
1Co 12:10 discerning of s; to another *divers* kinds G4151
14:32 And the s of the prophets are subject to G4151
1Ti 4: 1 to seducing s, and doctrines of devils; G4151
Heb 1: 7 s, and his ministers a flame of fire. G4151
14 Are they not all ministering s, sent forth G4151
12: 9 unto the Father of s, and live? G4151
23 and to the s of just men made perfect, G4151
1Pt 3:19 and preached unto the s in prison; G4151
1Jn 4: 1 spirit, but try the s whether they are of G4151
Rev 1: 4 seven S which are before his throne; G4151
3: 1 hath the seven S of God, and the seven G4151
4: 5 throne, which are the seven S of God. G4151
5: 6 S of God sent forth into all the earth. G4151
16:13 And I saw three unclean s like frogs G4151
14 For they are the s of devils, working G4151

SPIRITUAL

Hos 9: 7 *is* a fool, the s man *is* mad, for the H7307
Ro 1:11 s gift, to the end ye may be established; G4152
7:14 For we know that the law is s: but I am G4152
15:27 partakers of their s things, their duty is G4152
1Co 2:13 comparing s things with spiritual. G4152
13 comparing spiritual things with s. G4152
15 But he that is s judgeth all things, yet G4152
3: 1 unto you as unto s, but as unto carnal, G4152
9:11 If we have sown unto you s things, *is it* G4152
10: 3 And did all eat the same s meat; G4152
4 And did all drink the same s drink: for G4152
4 they drank of that s Rock that followed G4152
12: 1 Now concerning s *gifts*, brethren, I G4152
14: 1 Follow after charity, and desire s *gifts*, G4152
12 as ye are zealous of s *gifts*, seek that ye G4151
37 himself to be a prophet, or s, let him G4152
15:44 body; it is raised a s body. There is a G4152
44 is a natural body, and there is a s body. G4152
46 Howbeit that *was* not first which is s, G4152
46 natural; and afterward that which is s. G4152
Gal 6: 1 a fault, ye which are s, restore such an G4152
Eph 1: 3 s blessings in heavenly *places* in Christ: G4152
5:19 and hymns and s songs, singing and G4152
6:12 against s wickedness in high *places*. G4152
Col 1: 9 in all wisdom and s understanding; G4152
3:16 and hymns and s songs, singing with G4152
1Pt 2: 5 Ye also, as lively stones, are built up a s G4152
5 to offer up s sacrifices, acceptable G4152

SPIRITUALLY

Ro 8: 6 but to be s minded *is* life and peace. G4151
1Co 2:14 *them*, because they are s discerned. G4153
Rev 11: 8 great city, which s is called Sodom and G4153

SPIT

Lev 15: 8 And if he that hath the issue s upon H7556
Nu 12:14 her father had but s in her face, should H3417
Dt 25: 9 off his foot, and s in his face, and shall H3417
Job 30:10 from me, and spare not to s in my face. H7536
Mt 26:67 Then did they s in his face, and G1716
27:30 And they s upon him, and took the G1716
Mk 7:33 ears, and he s, and touched his tongue; G4429
8:23 and when he had s on his eyes, and put G4429
10:34 him, and shall s upon him, and shall G1716
14:65 And some began to s on him, and to G1716
15:19 with a reed, and did s upon him, and G1716

SPITE

Ps 10:14 mischief and s, to requite *it* with thy H3708

SPITEFULLY

Mt 22: 6 and entreated *them* s, and slew *them*. G5195
Lk 18:32 and s entreated, and spitted on: G5195

SPITTED

Lk 18:32 and spitefully entreated, and s on: G1716

SPITTING

Isa 50: 6 I hid not my face from shame and s. H7536

SPITTLE

1Sa 21:13 and let his s fall down upon his beard. H7388
Job 7:19 let me alone till I swallow down my s? H7536
Jn 9: 6 made clay of the s, and he anointed the G4427

SPOIL

Gen 49:27 prey, and at night he shall divide the s. H7998
Ex 3:22 and ye shall s the Egyptians. H5337
15: 9 I will divide the s; my lust shall be H7998
Nu 31: 9 ones, and took the s of all their cattle, H962
11 And they took all the s, and all the prey, H7998
12 the prey, and the s, unto Moses, and H7998
53 (*For* the men of war had taken s, every H962
Dt 2:35 and the s of the cities which we took. H7998
3: 7 But all the cattle, and the s of the cities, H7998
13:16 And thou shalt gather all the s of it into H7998
16 city, and all the s thereof every whit, for H7998
20:14 city, *even* all the s thereof, shalt thou H7998
14 thou shalt eat the s of thine enemies, H7998
Jos 8: 2 her king: only the s thereof, and the H7998
27 Only the cattle and the s of that city H7998
11:14 And all the s of these cities, and the H7998
22: 8 s of your enemies with your brethren. H7998
Jdg 5:30 for the necks of *them that take* the s? H7998
14:19 and took their s, and gave change of H2488
1Sa 14:30 freely to day of the s of their enemies H7998
32 And the people flew upon the s, and H7998
36 by night, and s them until the morning H962
15:19 didst fly upon the s, and didst evil in the H7998
21 But the people took of the s, sheep and H7998
30:16 of all the great s that they had taken H7998
19 daughters, neither s, nor any *thing* that H7998
20 *other* cattle, and said, This *is* David's s. H7998
22 give them *ought* of the s that we have H7998
26 he sent of the s unto the elders of H7998
26 of the s of the enemies of the LORD; H7998
2Sa 3:22 and brought in a great s with them: but H7998
8:12 and of the s of Hadadezer, son of H7998
12:30 the s of the city in great abundance. H7998
23:10 the people returned after him only to s. H6584
2Ki 3:23 another: now therefore, Moab, to the s. H7998
21:14 a prey and a s to all their enemies; H4933
1Ch 20: 2 also exceeding much s out of the city. H7998
2Ch 14:13 and they carried away very much s. H7998
14 for there was exceeding much s in them. H961
15:11 the same time, of the s *which* they had H7998
20:25 to take away the s of them, they found H7998
25 in gathering of the s, it was so much. H7998
24:23 s of them unto the king of Damascus. H7998
25:13 thousand of them, and took much s. H961
28: 8 took also away much s from them, and H7998
8 them, and brought the s to Samaria. H7998
14 captives and the s before the princes and H961
15 and with the s clothed all that were H7998
Ezr 9: 7 captivity, and to a s, and to confusion of H961
Est 3:13 and *to take* the s of them for a prey. H7998
8:11 and *to take* the s of them for a prey, H7998
9:10 but on the s laid they not their hand. H961
Job 29:17 and plucked the s out of his teeth. H2964
Ps 44:10 they which hate us s for themselves. H8154
68:12 she that tarried at home divided the s. H7998
89:41 All that pass by the way s him: he is a H8155
109:11 hath; and let the strangers s his labour. H962
119:162 at thy word, as one that findeth great s. H7998
Prv 1:13 we shall fill our houses with s: H7998
16:19 than to divide the s with the proud. H7998
22:23 s the soul of those that spoiled them. H6906
24:15 of the righteous; s not his resting place: H7703
31:11 her, so that he shall have no need of s. H7998
Song 2:15 Take us the foxes, the little foxes, that s H2254
Isa 3:14 the s of the poor *is* in your houses. H1500
8: 4 Damascus and the s of Samaria shall H7998
9: 3 as *men* rejoice when they divide the s. H7998
10: 6 a charge, to take the s, and to take the H7998
11:14 the west; they shall s them of the east H962
17:14 s us, and the lot of them that rob us. H8154
33: 1 thou shalt cease to s, thou shalt be H7703
4 And your s shall be gathered *like* the H7998
23 great s divided; the lame take the prey. H7998
42:22 for a s, and none saith, Restore. H4933
24 Who gave Jacob for a s, and Israel to H4933
53:12 he shall divide the s with the strong; H7998
Jer 5: 6 of the evenings shall s them, a leopard H7703
6: 7 violence and s is heard in her; before H7701
15:13 will I give to the s without price, and *that* H957
17: 3 thy treasures to the s, *and* thy high places H957
20: 5 which shall s them, and take them, H962
8 I cried violence and s; because the word H7701
30:16 and they that s thee shall be a spoil, H7601
16 thee shall be a s, and all that prey upon H4933
47: 4 Because of the day that cometh to s all H7703
4 for the LORD will s the Philistines, the H7703
49:28 up to Kedar, and s the men of the east. H7703
32 of their cattle a s: and I will scatter into H7998
50:10 And Chaldea shall be a s: all that spoil H7998
10 And Chaldea shall be a spoil: all that s H7997

Ezk 7:21 earth for a s; and they shall pollute it. H7998
14:15 the land, and they s it, so that it be H7921
25: 7 deliver thee for a s to the heathen; and I H957
26: 5 and it shall become a s to the nations. H957
12 And they shall make a s of thy riches, H7997
29:19 and take her s, and take her prey; and H7998
32:12 and they shall s the pomp of Egypt, H7703
38:12 To take a s, and to take a prey; to turn H7998
13 come to take a s? hast thou gathered H7998
13 away cattle and goods, to take a great s? H7998
39:10 fire: and they shall s those that spoiled H7997
45: 9 violence and s, and execute judgment H7701
Dan 11:24 the prey, and s, and riches: *yea*, and H7998
33 flame, by captivity, and by s, *many* days. H961
Hos 10: 2 their altars, he shall s their images. H7703
13:15 s the treasure of all pleasant vessels. H8154
Nah 2: 9 Take ye the s of silver, take the spoil of H962
9 Take ye the spoil of silver, take the s of H962
Hab 2: 8 of the people shall s thee; because of H7997
17 thee, and the s of beasts, *which* made H7701
Zep 2: 9 of my people shall s them, and the H962
Zec 2: 9 and they shall be a s to their servants: H7998
14: 1 s shall be divided in the midst of thee. H7998
Mt 12:29 man's house, and s his goods, except G1283
29 man? and then he will s his house. G1283
Mk 3:27 man's house, and s his goods, except G1283
27 man; and then he will s his house. G1283
Col 2: 8 Beware lest any man s you through G4812

SPOILED

Gen 34:27 upon the slain, and s the city, because H962
29 and s even all that *was* in the house. H962
Ex 12:36 *required.* And they s the Egyptians. H5337
Dt 28:29 only oppressed and s evermore, and no H1497
Jdg 2:14 of spoilers that s them, and he sold H8155
16 out of the hand of those that s them. H8154
1Sa 14:48 out of the hands of them that s them. H8154
17:53 the Philistines, and they s their tents. H8155
2Ki 7:16 And the people went out, and s the tents H962
2Ch 14:14 them: and they s all the cities; for there H962
Job 12:17 He leadeth counsellors away s, and H7758
19 He leadeth princes away s, and H7758
Ps 76: 5 The stouthearted are s, they have slept H7997
Prv 22:23 and spoil the soul of those that s them. H6906
Isa 13:16 shall be s, and their wives ravished. H8155
18: 2 down, whose land the rivers have s! H958
7 the rivers have s, to the place of the name H958
24: 3 s: for the LORD hath spoken this word. H962
33: 1 and thou *wast* not s; and dealest H7703
1 thou shalt be s; *and* when thou shalt H7703
42:22 But this *is* a people robbed and s; *they* H8154
Jer 2:14 *is* he a homeborn *slave*? why is he s? H957
4:13 than eagles. Woe unto us! for we are s. H7703
20 for the whole land is s: suddenly are my H7703
20 tents s, *and* my curtains in a moment. H7703
30 And *when* thou *art* s, what wilt thou do? H7703
9:19 of Zion, How are we s! we are greatly H7703
10:20 My tabernacle is s, and all my cords are H7703
21:12 deliver *him that is* s out of the hand of H1497
22: 3 and deliver the s out of the hand of the H1497
25:36 for the LORD hath s their pasture. H7703
48: 1 unto Nebo! for it is s: Kiriathaim is H7703
15 Moab is s, and gone up *out of* her cities, H7703
20 cry; tell ye it in Arnon, that Moab is s, H7703
49: 3 Howl, O Heshbon, for Ai is s: cry, ye H7703
10 his seed is s, and his brethren, and H7703
51:55 Because the LORD hath s Babylon, and H7703
Ezk 18: 7 his pledge, hath s none by violence, H1497
12 and needy, hath s by violence, hath not H1497
16 neither hath s by violence, *but* hath H1497
18 he cruelly oppressed, s his brother by H1497
23:46 and will give them to be removed and s. H957
39:10 spoil those that s them, and rob those H7997
Hos 10:14 fortresses shall be s, as Shalman spoiled H7703
14 as Shalman s Beth-arbel in the day H7701
Am 3:11 from thee, and thy palaces shall be s. H962
5: 9 That strengtheneth the s against the H7701
9 the s shall come against the fortress. H7701
Mic 2: 4 say, We be utterly s: he hath changed H7703
Hab 2: 8 Because thou hast s many nations, all H7997
Zec 2: 8 the nations which s you: for he that H7997
11: 2 the mighty are s: howl, O ye oaks of H7703
3 for their glory is s: a voice of the roaring H7703
3 young lions; for the pride of Jordan is s. H7703
Col 2:15 *And* having s principalities and powers, G554

SPOILER

Isa 16: 4 the face of the s: for the extortioner is H7703
4 is at an end, the s ceaseth, the H7701
Isa 21: 2 and the s spoileth. Go up, O Elam: H7703
Jer 6:26 for the s shall suddenly come upon us. H7703
15: 8 the young men a s at noonday: I have H7703
48: 8 And the s shall come upon every city, H7703
18 and sit in thirst; for the s of Moab shall H7703
32 the sea of Jazer: the s is fallen upon thy H7703
51:56 Because the s is come upon her, *even* H7703

SPOILERS

Jdg 2:14 into the hands of s that spoiled them, H8154
1Sa 13:17 And the s came out of the camp of the H7843
14:15 garrison, and the s, they also trembled, H7843
2Ki 17:20 into the hand of s, until he had cast H8154
Jer 12:12 The s are come upon all high places H7703
51:48 Babylon: for the s shall come unto her H7703
53 shall s come unto her, saith the LORD. H7703

SPOILEST

Isa 33: 1 Woe to thee that s, and thou *wast* not H7703

SPOILETH

Ps 35:10 and the needy from him that s him? H1497
Isa 21: 2 and the spoiler s. Go up, O Elam: H7703
Hos 7: 1 in, *and* the troop of robbers s without. H6584
Nah 3:16 the cankerworm s, and flieth away. H6584

SPOILING

Ps 35:12 They rewarded me evil for good *to* the s H7908
Isa 22: 4 of the s of the daughter of my people. H7701
Jer 48: 3 Horonaim, s and great destruction. H7701
Hab 1: 3 grievance? for s and violence *are* before H7701
Heb 10:34 and took joyfully the s of your goods, G724

SPOILS

Jos 7:21 When I saw among the s a goodly H7998
1Ch 26:27 Out of the s won in battles did they H7998
Isa 25:11 pride together with the s of their hands. H698
Lk 11:22 wherein he trusted, and divideth his s. G4661
Heb 7: 4 Abraham gave the tenth of the s. G205

SPOKEN

Gen 12: 4 So Abram departed, as the LORD had s H1696
18:19 Abraham that which he hath s of him. H1696
19:21 this city, for the which thou hast s. H1696
21: 1 the LORD did unto Sarah as he had s. H1696
2 the set time of which God had s to him. H1696
24:51 master's son's wife, as the LORD hath s. H1696
28:15 done *that* which I have s to thee of. H1696
41:28 This *is* the thing which I have s unto H1696
44: 2 to the word that Joseph had s. H1696
Ex 4:10 since thou hast s unto thy servant: but H1696
30 the LORD had s unto Moses, and did H1696
9:12 them; as the LORD had s unto Moses. H1696
35 Israel go; as the LORD had s by Moses. H1696
10:29 And Moses said, Thou hast s well, I will H1696
19: 8 the LORD hath s we will do. And Moses H1696
32:13 land that I have s of will I give unto your H559
34 of which I have s unto thee: behold, H1696
33:17 thing also that thou hast s: for thou hast H1696
34:32 LORD had s with him in mount Sinai. H1696
Lev 10:11 hath s unto them by the hand of Moses. H1696
Nu 1:48 For the LORD had s unto Moses, H1696
10:29 LORD hath s good concerning Israel. H1696
12: 2 And they said, Hath the LORD indeed s H1696
2 s also by us? And the LORD heard *it*. H1696
14:17 great, according as thou hast s, saying, H1696
28 have s in mine ears, so will I do to you: H1696
15:22 which the LORD hath s unto Moses, H1696
21: 7 for we have s against the LORD, and H1696
23: 2 And Balak did as Balaam had s; and H1696
17 said unto him, What hath the LORD s? H1696
19 he s, and shall he not make it good? H1696
Dt 1:14 which thou hast s *is* good *for us* to do. H1696
5:28 which they have s unto thee: they have H1696
28 they have well said all that they have s. H1696
6:19 from before thee, as the LORD hath s. H1696
13: 5 because he hath s to turn *you* away H1696
18:17 have well *s that* which they have spoken.
17 well *spoken that* which they have s. H1696
21 the word which the LORD hath not s? H1696
22 LORD hath not s, *but* the prophet hath H1696
22 the prophet hath s it presumptuously: H1696
26:19 unto the LORD thy God, as he hath s. H1696
Jos 6: 8 And it came to pass, when Joshua had s H559
21:45 the LORD had s unto the house of H1696
Ru 2:13 for that thou hast s friendly unto thine H1696
1Sa 1:16 complaint and grief have I s hitherto. H1696
3:12 which I have s concerning his house: H1696
20:23 thou and I have s of, behold, the LORD H1696
25:30 good that he hath s concerning thee, H1696
2Sa 2:27 unless thou hadst s, surely then in the H1696
3:18 Now then do *it*: for the LORD hath s of H559
6:22 s of, of them shall I be had in honour. H559
7:19 but thou hast s also of thy servant's H1696
25 word that thou hast s concerning thy H1696
29 O Lord GOD, hast s *it*: and with thy H1696
14:19 my lord the king hath s: for thy servant H1696
17: 6 Ahithophel hath s after this manner: H1696
1Ki 2:23 not s this word against his own life. H1696
12: 9 this people, who have s to me, saying, H1696
13: 3 the LORD hath s; Behold, the altar shall H1696
11 which he had s unto the king, them H1696
14:11 of the air eat: for the LORD hath s *it*. H1696
18:24 people answered and said, It is well s. H1697
21: 4 the Jezreelite had s to him: for he had H1696
22:23 the LORD hath s evil concerning thee. H1696
28 LORD hath not s by me. And he said, H1696
2Ki 1:17 LORD which Elijah had s. And Jehoram H1696
4:13 wouldest thou be s for to the king, or to H1696
7:18 man of God had s to the king, saying, H1696
19:21 This *is* the word that the LORD hath s H1696
20: 9 thing that he hath s: shall the shadow H1696
19 which thou hast s. And he said, *Is it* not H1696
1Ch 17:17 for thou hast *also* s of thy servant's H1696
23 that thou hast s concerning thy servant H1696
2Ch 2:15 hath s of, let him send unto his servants: H559
6:10 word that he hath s: for I am risen up in H1696
17 thou hast s unto thy servant David. H1696
10: 9 which have s to me, saying, Ease H1696
18:22 and the LORD hath s evil against thee. H1696
27 not the LORD s by me. And he said, H1696
36:22 the word of the LORD *s* by the mouth of
Ezr 8:22 because we had s unto the king, saying, H559
Neh 2:18 words that he had s unto me. And they H559
Est 6:10 let nothing fail of all that thou hast s. H1696
7: 9 who had s good for the king, standeth H1696
Job 21: 3 speak; and after that I have s, mock on. H1696
32: 4 Now Elihu had waited till Job had s, H1697
33: 2 mouth, my tongue hath s in my mouth. H1696
8 Surely thou hast s in mine hearing, and I H559
34:35 Job hath s without knowledge, and his H1696
40: 5 Once have I s; but I will not answer: H1696
42: 7 the LORD had s these words unto Job, H1696
7 for ye have not s of me *the thing that* H1696
8 in that ye have not s of me *the thing* H1696
Ps 50: 1 the LORD, hath s, and called the earth H1696
60: 6 God hath s in his holiness; I will H1696
62:11 God hath s once; twice have I heard H1696
66:14 mouth hath s, when I was in trouble. H1696
87: 3 Glorious things are s of thee, O city of H1696
108: 7 God hath s in his holiness; I will H1696
109: 2 have s against me with a lying tongue. H1696
116:10 I believed, therefore have I s: I was H1696
Prv 15:23 a word *s* in due season, how good *is it*!
25:11 A word fitly s *is like* apples of gold in H1696
Ecc 7:21 s; lest thou hear thy servant curse thee: H1696
Song 8: 8 in the day when she shall be s for? H1696
Isa 1: 2 for the LORD hath s, I have nourished H1696
20 for the mouth of the LORD hath s *it*. H1696
16:13 This *is* the word that the LORD hath s H1696
14 But now the LORD hath s, saying, H1696
21:17 for the LORD God of Israel hath s *it*. H1696
22:25 shall be cut off: for the LORD hath s *it*. H1696
23: 4 for the sea hath s, *even* the strength of H559
24: 3 spoiled: for the LORD hath s this word. H1696
25: 8 off all the earth: for the LORD hath s *it*. H1696
31: 4 For thus hath the LORD s unto me, Like H559
37:22 the LORD hath s concerning him; The H1696
38: 7 LORD will do this thing that he hath s; H1696
15 What shall I say? he hath both s unto H559
39: 8 which thou hast s. He said moreover, H1696
40: 5 for the mouth of the LORD hath s *it*. H1696
45:19 I have not s in secret, in a dark place of H1696
46:11 yea, I have s *it*, I will also bring it H1696
48:15 I, *even* I, have s; yea, I have called him: H1696
16 ye this; I have not s in secret from the H1696
58:14 for the mouth of the LORD hath s *it*. H1696
59: 3 your lips have s lies, your tongue hath H1696
Jer 3: 5 s and done evil things as thou couldest. H1696
4:28 because I have s *it*, I have purposed H1696
9:12 of the LORD hath s, that he may declare H1696
13:15 ear; be not proud: for the LORD hath s. H1696
23:21 not s to them, yet they prophesied. H1696
35 answered? and, What hath the LORD s? H1696
37 thee? and, What hath the LORD s? H1696
25: 3 me, and I have s unto you, rising early H1696
26:16 to die: for he hath s to us in the name H1696
27:13 as the LORD hath s against the nation H1696

Jer 29:23 wives, and have s lying words in my H1696
30: 2 words that I have s unto thee in a book. H1696
32:24 what thou hast s is come to pass; and, H1696
33:24 this people have s, saying, The two H1696
35:14 I have s unto you, rising early H1696
17 because I have s unto them, but they H1696
36: 2 words that I have s unto thee against H1696
4 had s unto him, upon a roll of a book. H1696
38: 1 had s unto all the people, saying, H1696
44:16 *As for* the word that thou hast s unto H1696
25 wives have both s with your mouths, H1696
48: 8 shall be destroyed, as the LORD hath s. H559
51:62 LORD, thou hast s against this place, to H1696
Ezk 5:13 I the LORD have s *it* in my zeal, when H1696
15 furious rebukes. I the LORD have s *it*. H1696
17 sword upon thee. I the LORD have s *it*. H1696
12:28 s shall be done, saith the Lord GOD. H1696
13: 7 and have ye not s a lying divination, H559
7 The LORD saith *it*; albeit I have not s? H1696
8 Because ye have s vanity, and seen lies, H1696
14: 9 when he hath s a thing, I the LORD H1696
17:21 ye shall know that I the LORD have s *it*. H1696
24 I the LORD have s and have done *it*. H1696
21:32 remembered: for I the LORD have s *it*. H1696
22:14 I the LORD have s *it*, and will do *it*. H1696
28 Lord GOD, when the LORD hath not s. H1696
23:34 for I have s *it*, saith the Lord GOD. H1696
24:14 I the LORD have s *it*: it shall come to H1696
26: 5 of the sea: for I have s *it*, saith the Lord H1696
14 LORD have s *it*, saith the Lord GOD. H1696
28:10 for I have s *it*, saith the Lord GOD. H1696
30:12 hand of strangers: I the LORD have s *it*. H1696
34:24 among them; I the LORD have s *it*. H1696
35:12 which thou hast s against the mountains H559
36: 5 of my jealousy have I s against the H1696
6 Behold, I have s in my jealousy and H1696
36 I the LORD have s *it*, and I will do *it*. H1696
37:14 s *it*, and performed *it*, saith the LORD. H1696
38:17 he of whom I have s in old time by my H1696
19 of my wrath have I s, Surely in that day H1696
39: 5 for I have s *it*, saith the Lord GOD. H1696
8 GOD; this *is* the day whereof I have s. H1696
Dan 4:31 is s; The kingdom is departed from thee. H560
10:11 s this word unto me, I stood trembling. H1696
15 And when he had s such words unto H1696
19 And when he had s unto me, I was H1696
Hos 7:13 them, yet they have s lies against me. H1696
10: 4 They have s words, swearing falsely in H1696
12:10 I have also s by the prophets, and I H1696
Joel 3: 8 a people far off: for the LORD hath s *it*. H1696
Am 3: 1 Hear this word that the LORD hath s H1696
8 GOD hath s, who can but prophesy? H1696
5:14 of hosts, shall be with you, as ye have s. H559
Oba 12 have s proudly in the day of distress. H6310
18 house of Esau; for the LORD hath s *it*. H1696
Mic 4: 4 mouth of the LORD of hosts hath s *it*. H1696
6:12 thereof have s lies, and their tongue H1696
Zec 10: 2 For the idols have s vanity, and the H1696
Mal 3:13 What have we s *so much* against thee? H1696
Mt 1:22 s of the Lord by the prophet, saying, *G4483*
2:15 which was s of the Lord by the prophet, *G4483*
17 Then was fulfilled that which was s by *G4483*
23 which was s by the prophets, He *G4483*
3: 3 For this is he that was s of by the *G4483*
4:14 That it might be fulfilled which was s *G4483*
8:17 That it might be fulfilled which was s *G4483*
12:17 That it might be fulfilled which was s *G4483*
13:35 That it might be fulfilled which was s *G4483*
21: 4 which was s by the prophet, saying, *G4483*
22:31 which was s unto you by God, saying, *G4483*
24:15 of desolation, s of by Daniel the *G4483*
26:65 saying, He hath s blasphemy; what *G987*
27: 9 Then was fulfilled that which was s by *G4483*
35 which was s by the prophet, They *G4483*
Mk 1:42 And as soon as he had s, immediately *G2036*
5:36 the word that was s, he saith unto the *G2980*
12:12 knew that he had s the parable against *G2036*
13:14 of desolation, s of by Daniel the *G4488*
14: 9 shall be s of for a memorial of her. *G2980*
16:19 So then after the Lord had s unto them, *G2980*
Lk 2:33 at those things which were s of him. *G2980*
34 and for a sign which shall be s against; *G483*
12: 3 Therefore whatsoever ye have s in *G2036*
3 and that which ye have s in the ear in *G2980*
18:34 knew they the things which were s. *G3004*
19:28 And when he had thus s, he went *G2036*
20:19 he had s this parable against them. *G2036*
24:25 to believe all that the prophets have s: *G2980*
40 And when he had thus s, he shewed *G2036*
Jn 4:50 had s unto him, and he went his way. *G2036*
9: 6 When he had thus s, he spat on the *G2036*
11:13 that he had s of taking of rest in sleep. *G3004*
43 And when he thus had s, he cried with a *G2036*
12:48 word that I have s, the same shall judge *G2980*
49 For I have not s of myself; but the *G2980*
14:25 These things have I s unto you, being *G2980*
15: 3 the word which I have s unto you. *G2980*
11 These things have I s unto you, that my *G2980*
22 If I had not come and s unto them, they *G2980*
16: 1 These things have I s unto you, that ye *G2980*
25 These things have I s unto you in *G2980*
33 These things I have s unto you, that in *G2980*
18: 1 When Jesus had s these words, he went *G2036*
22 And when he had thus s, one of the *G2036*
23 Jesus answered him, If I have s evil, *G2980*
20:18 *that* he had s these things unto her. *G2036*
21:19 s this, he saith unto him, Follow me. *G2036*
Act 1: 9 And when he had s these things, while *G2036*
2:16 But this is that which was s by the *G2046*
3:21 which God hath s by the mouth of all *G2980*
24 s, have likewise foretold of these days. *G2980*
8:24 things which ye have s come upon me. *G2046*
9:27 and that he had s to him, and how he *G2980*
13:40 upon you, which is s of in the prophets; *G2046*
45 those things which were s by Paul, *G3004*
46 first have been s to you: but seeing ye *G2980*
16:14 unto the things which were s of Paul. *G2980*
19:36 Seeing then that these things cannot be s *G369*
41 And when he had thus s, he dismissed *G2036*
20:36 And when he had thus s, he kneeled *G2036*
23: 9 s to him, let us not fight against God. *G2980*
26:30 And when he had thus s, the king rose *G2036*
27:11 than those things which were s by Paul. *G3004*
35 And when he had thus s, he took bread, *G2036*
28:22 we know that every where it is s against. *G483*
24 which were s, and some believed not. *G3004*
25 that Paul had s one word, Well spake *G2036*
Ro 1: 8 is s of throughout the whole world. *G2605*
4:18 that which was s, So shall thy seed be. *G2046*
14:16 Let not then your good be evil s of: *G987*
15:21 To whom he was not s of, they shall see: *G312*
1Co 10:30 evil s of for that for which I give thanks? *G987*
14: 9 what is s? for ye shall speak into the air. *G2980*
2Co 4:13 I s; we also believe, and therefore speak; *G2980*
Heb 1: 2 Hath in these last days s unto us by *his* *G2980*
2: 2 For if the word s by angels was *G2980*
3 first began to be s by the Lord, and was *G2980*
3: 5 of those things which were to be s after; *G2980*
4: 8 he not afterward have s of another day. *G2980*
7:13 For he of whom these things are s *G3004*
8: 1 Now of the things which we have s *this* *G3004*
9:19 For when Moses had s every precept to *G2980*
12:19 should not be s to them any more: *G4369*
13: 7 you, who have s unto you the word of *G2980*
Jas 5:10 who have s in the name of the Lord, *G2980*
1Pt 4:14 evil s of, but on your part he is glorified. *G987*
2Pt 2: 2 whom the way of truth shall be evil s of. *G987*
3: 2 words which were s before by the holy *G4280*
Jude 15 ungodly sinners have s against him. *G2980*
17 the words which were s before of the *G4280*

SPOKES
1Ki 7:33 felloes, and their s, *were* all molten. H2840

SPOKESMAN
Ex 4:16 And he shall be thy s unto the people: H1696

SPONGE See SPUNGE.

SPOON
Nu 7:14 One s of ten *shekels* of gold, full of H3709
20 One s of gold of ten *shekels*, full of H3709
26 One golden s of ten *shekels*, full of H3709
32 One golden s of ten *shekels*, full of H3709
38 One golden s of ten *shekels*, full of H3709
44 One golden s of ten *shekels*, full of H3709
50 One golden s of ten *shekels*, full of H3709
56 One golden s of ten *shekels*, full of H3709
62 One golden s of ten *shekels*, full of H3709
68 One golden s of ten *shekels*, full of H3709
74 One golden s of ten *shekels*, full of H3709
80 One golden s of ten *shekels*, full of H3709

SPOONS
Ex 25:29 thereof, and s thereof, and covers H3709
37:16 his dishes, and his s, and his bowls, and H3709
Nu 4: 7 dishes, and the s, and the bowls, and H3709
7:84 twelve silver bowls, twelve s of gold: H3709
Nu 7:86 The golden s *were* twelve, full of H3709
86 s *was* an hundred and twenty *shekels*. H3709
1Ki 7:50 basons, and the s, and the censers *of* H3709
2Ki 25:14 snuffers, and the s, and all the vessels of H3709
2Ch 4:22 basons, and the s, and the censers, *of* H3709
24:14 offer *withal*, and s, and vessels of gold H3709
Jer 52:18 the bowls, and the s, and all the vessels H3709
19 and the s, and the cups; *that* which H3709

SPORT
Jdg 16:25 he may make us s. And they called for H7832
25 s: and they set him between the pillars. H6711
27 that beheld while Samson made s. H7832
Prv 10:23 *It is* as s to a fool to do mischief: but a H7814
26:19 his neighbour, and saith, Am not I in s? H7832
Isa 57: 4 Against whom do ye s yourselves? H6026

SPORTING
Gen 26: 8 Isaac *was* s with Rebekah his wife. H6711
2Pt 2:13 and blemishes, s themselves with their *G1792*

SPOT
Lev 13: 2 a scab, or bright s, and it be in the skin H934
4 If the bright s *be* white in the skin of his H934
19 white rising, or a bright s, white, and H934
23 But if the bright s stay in his place, *and* H934
24 bright s, somewhat reddish, or white; H934
25 hair in the bright s be turned white, and H934
26 hair in the bright s, and it *be* no lower H934
28 And if the bright s stay in his place, *and* H934
39 s *that* groweth in the skin; he *is* clean. H933
14:56 rising, and for a scab, and for a bright s: H934
Nu 19: 2 a red heifer without s, wherein *is* no H8549
28: 3 first year without s day by day, *for* a H8549
9 first year without s, and two tenth deals H8549
11 seven lambs of the first year without s; H8549
29:17 lambs of the first year without s: H8549
26 lambs of the first year without s: H8549
Dt 32: 5 themselves, their s *is* not *the spot* of his H3971
5 their spot *is* not *the* s of his children:
Job 11:15 up thy face without s; yea, thou shalt be H3971
Song 4: 7 Thou *art* all fair, my love; *there is* no s H3971
Eph 5:27 not having s, or wrinkle, or any such *G4696*
1Ti 6:14 without s, unrebukeable, until *G784*
Heb 9:14 himself without s to God, purge your *G299*
1Pt 1:19 of a lamb without blemish and without s: *G784*
2Pt 3:14 him in peace, without s, and blameless. *G784*

SPOTS
Lev 13:38 flesh bright s, *even* white bright spots; H934
38 flesh bright spots, *even* white bright s; H934
39 *if* the bright s in the skin of their flesh H934
Jer 13:23 or the leopard his s? *then* may ye also H2272
2Pt 2:13 riot in the day time. S *they are* and *G4696*
Jude 12 These are s in your feasts of charity, *G4694*

SPOTTED
Gen 30:32 all the speckled and s cattle, and all the H2921
32 the sheep, and the s and speckled H2921
33 *is* not speckled and s among the goats, H2921
35 ringstraked and s, and all the she goats H2921
35 were speckled and s, *and* every one that H2921
39 cattle ringstraked, speckled, and s. H2921
Jude 23 hating even the garment s by the flesh. *G4695*

SPOUSE
Song 4: 8 Come with me from Lebanon, *my* s, H3618
9 my sister, *my* s; thou hast ravished my H3618
10 How fair is thy love, my sister, *my* s! H3618
11 Thy lips, O *my* s, drop *as* the H3618
12 A garden inclosed *is* my sister, *my* s; a H3618
5: 1 my sister, *my* s: I have gathered my H3618

SPOUSES
Hos 4:13 and your s shall commit adultery. H3618
14 nor your s when they commit adultery: H3618

SPRANG
Mk 4: 5 s up, because it had no depth of earth: *G1816*
8 did yield fruit that s up and increased; *G305*
Lk 8: 7 the thorns s up with it, and choked it. *G4855*
8 And other fell on good ground, and s *G5453*
Act 16:29 Then he called for a light, and s in, and *G1530*
Heb 7:14 For *it is* evident that our Lord s out of *G393*
11:12 Therefore s there even of one, and him *G1080*

SPREAD
Gen 10:18 families of the Canaanites s abroad. H6327
28:14 and thou shalt s abroad to the west, H6555

Gen 33:19 where he had s his tent, at the hand H5186
35:21 And Israel journeyed, and s his tent H5186
Ex 9:29 of the city, I will s abroad my hands H6566
33 Pharaoh, and s abroad his hands unto H6566
37: 9 And the cherubims s out *their* wings on H6566
40:19 And he s abroad the tent over the H6566
Lev 13: 5 *and* the plague s not in the skin; then H6581
6 *and* the plague s not in the skin, the H6581
7 But if the scab s much abroad in the H6581
22 And if it s much abroad in the skin, H6581
23 in his place, *and* s not, it *is* a burning H6581
27 day: *and* if it be s much abroad in the H6581
28 in his place, *and* s not in the skin, but H6581
32 behold, *if* the scall s not, and there be H6581
34 *if* the scall be not s in the skin, nor *be* H6581
35 But if the scall s much in the skin after H6581
36 if the scall be s in the skin, the priest H6581
51 if the plague be s in the garment, either H6581
53 the plague be not s in the garment, H6581
55 the plague be not s; it *is* unclean; thou H6581
14:39 plague be s in the walls of the house; H6581
44 *if* the plague be s in the house, it *is* a H6581
48 plague hath not s in the house, after H6581
Nu 4: 6 skins, and shall s over *it* a cloth wholly H6566
7 they shall s a cloth of blue, and H6566
8 And they shall s upon them a cloth of H6566
11 And upon the golden altar they shall s H6566
13 the altar, and s a purple cloth thereon: H6566
14 and they shall s upon it a covering of H6566
11:32 homers: and they s *them* all abroad for H7849
24: 6 As the valleys are they s forth, as H5186
Dt 22:17 s the cloth before the elders of the city. H6566
Jdg 8:25 *them*. And they s a garment, and did H6566
15: 9 in Judah, and s themselves in Lehi. H5203
Ru 3: 9 thine handmaid: s therefore thy skirt H6566
1Sa 30:16 behold, *they were* s abroad upon all the H5203
2Sa 5:18 The Philistines also came and s H5203
22 s themselves in the valley of Rephaim. H5203
16:22 So they s Absalom a tent upon the top H5186
17:19 And the woman took and s a covering H6566
19 the well's mouth, and s ground corn H7849
21:10 sackcloth, and s it for her upon the H5186
22:43 of the street, *and* did s them abroad. H7554
1Ki 6:32 *them* with gold, and s gold upon the H7286
8: 7 For the cherubims s forth *their* two H6566
22 and s forth his hands toward heaven: H6566
38 s forth his hands toward this house: H6566
54 knees with his hands s up to heaven. H6566
2Ki 8:15 *it* in water, and s *it* on his face, so that H6566
19:14 of the LORD, and s it before the LORD. H6566
1Ch 14: 9 And the Philistines came and s H6584
13 And the Philistines yet again s H6584
28:18 cherubims, that s out *their wings,* and H6566
2Ch 3:13 The wings of these cherubims s H6566
5: 8 For the cherubims s forth *their* wings H6566
6:12 of Israel, and s forth his hands: H6566
13 and s forth his hands toward heaven, H6566
29 shall s forth his hands in this house: H6566
26: 8 and his name s abroad *even* to the H3212
15 And his name s far abroad; for he was H3318
Ezr 9: 5 my knees, and s out my hands unto H6566
Job 29:19 My root *was* s out by the waters, and H6605
37:18 Hast thou with him s out the sky, H7554
Ps 105:39 He s a cloud for a covering; and fire to H6566
140: 5 cords; they have s a net by the wayside; H6566
Prv 1:17 Surely in vain the net is s in the sight of H2219
Isa 1:15 And when ye s forth your hands, I will H6566
14:11 viols: the worm is s under thee, and the H3331
19: 8 s nets upon the waters shall languish. H6566
25: 7 and the vail that is s over all nations. H5259
11 And he shall s forth his hands in the H6566
33:23 they could not s the sail: then is the H6566
37:14 of the LORD, and s it before the LORD. H6566
42: 5 them out; he that s forth the earth, and H7554
58: 5 a bulrush, and to s sackcloth and ashes H3331
65: 2 I have s out my hands all the day unto H6566
Jer 8: 2 And they shall s them before the sun, H7849
10: 9 Silver s into plates is brought from H7554
43:10 he shall s his royal pavilion over them. H5186
48:40 eagle, and shall s his wings over Moab. H6566
49:22 fly as the eagle, and s his wings over H6566
Lam 1:10 The adversary hath s out his hand H6566
13 them: he hath s a net for my feet, he H6566
Ezk 2:10 And he s it before me; and it *was* H6566
12:13 My net also will I s upon him, and he H6566
16: 8 time of love; and I s my skirt over thee, H6566
17:20 And I will s my net upon him, and he H6566
19: 8 the provinces, and s their net over him: H6566
26:14 shalt be *a place* to s nets upon; thou H4894
Ezk 32: 3 I will therefore s out my net over thee H6566
47:10 shall be a *place* to s forth nets; their H4894
Hos 5: 1 on Mizpah, and a net s upon Tabor. H6566
7:12 When they shall go, I will s my net H6566
14: 6 His branches shall s, and his beauty H3212
Joel 2: 2 as the morning s upon the mountains: H6566
Hab 1: 8 horsemen shall s themselves, and their H6335
Zec 1:17 shall yet be s abroad; and the LORD H6327
2: 6 LORD: for I have s you abroad as the H6566
Mal 2: 3 Behold, I will corrupt your seed, and s H2219
Mt 9:31 But they, when they were departed, s G1810
21: 8 And a very great multitude s their G4766
Mk 1:28 And immediately his fame s abroad G1831
6:14 (for his name was s abroad:) and he
11: 8 And many s their garments in the way: G4766
Lk 19:36 And as he went, they s their clothes in G5291
Act 4:17 But that it s no further among the G1268
1Th 1: 8 to God-ward is s abroad; so that we G5318

SPREADEST
Ezk 27: 7 that which thou s forth to be thy sail; H4666

SPREADETH
Lev 13: 8 behold, the scab s in the skin, then the H6581
Dt 32:11 over her young, s abroad her wings, H6566
Job 9: 8 Which alone s out the heavens, and H5186
26: 9 of his throne, *and* s his cloud upon it. H6576
36:30 Behold, he s his light upon it, and H6566
41:30 Sharp stones *are* under him: he s sharp H7502
Prv 29: 5 A man that flattereth his neighbour s a H6566
Isa 25:11 he that swimmeth s forth *his hands* to H6566
40:19 and the goldsmith s it over with gold, H7554
22 and s them out as a tent to dwell in: H4969
44:24 that s abroad the earth by myself; H7554
Jer 4:31 herself, *that* s her hands, *saying,* Woe H6566
17: 8 waters, and *that* s out her roots by the H7971
Lam 1:17 Zion s forth her hands, *and there is* H6566

SPREADING
Lev 13:57 of skin; it *is* a s *plague*: thou shalt burn H6524
Ps 37:35 and s himself like a green bay tree. H6168
Ezk 17: 6 And it grew, and became a s vine of H5628
26: 5 It shall be *a place for* the s of nets in the H4894

SPREADINGS
Job 36:29 Also can *any* understand the s of the H4666

SPRIGS
Isa 18: 5 both cut off the s with pruning hooks, H2150
Ezk 17: 6 forth branches, and shot forth s. H6288

SPRING
Nu 21:17 Then Israel sang this song, S up, O H5927
Dt 8: 7 depths that s out of valleys and hills; H3318
Jdg 19:25 when the day began to s, they let her go. H5927
1Sa 9:26 to pass about the s of the day, that H5927
2Ki 2:21 And he went forth unto the s of the H4161
Job 5: 6 doth trouble s out of the ground; H6779
38:27 the bud of the tender herb to s forth? H6779
Ps 85:11 Truth shall s out of the earth; and H6779
92: 7 When the wicked s as the grass, and H6524
Prv 25:26 *as* a troubled fountain, and a corrupt s. H4726
Song 4:12 spouse; a s shut up, a fountain sealed. H1530
Isa 42: 9 before they s forth I tell you of them. H6779
43:19 thing; now it shall s forth; shall ye not H6779
44: 4 And they shall s up *as* among the grass, H6779
45: 8 let righteousness s up together; I the H6779
58: 8 thine health shall s forth speedily: and H6779
11 like a s of water, whose waters fail not. H4161
61:11 are sown in it to s forth; so the Lord H6779
11 praise to s forth before all the nations. H6779
Ezk 17: 9 the leaves of her s, even without great H6780
Hos 13:15 and his s shall become dry, and H4726
Joel 2:22 the wilderness do s, for the tree beareth H1876
Mk 4:27 s and grow up, he knoweth not how. G985

SPRINGETH
1Ki 4:33 the hyssop that s out of the wall: he H3318
2Ki 19:29 year that which s of the same; and in H7823
Isa 37:30 year that which s of the same: and in H7823
Hos 10: 4 thus judgment s up as hemlock in the H6524

SPRINGING
Gen 26:19 and found there a well of s water. H2416
2Sa 23: 4 *as* the tender grass s out of the earth by
Ps 65:10 showers: thou blessest the s thereof. H6780
Jn 4:14 a well of water s up into everlasting life. G242
Heb 12:15 root of bitterness s up trouble *you,* and G5453

SPRINGS
Dt 4:49 sea of the plain, under the s of Pisgah. H794
Jos 10:40 the vale, and of the s, and all their kings: H794
12: 8 the plains, and in the s, and in the H794
15:19 land; give me also s of water. And he H1543
19 her the upper s, and the nether springs. H1543
19 her the upper springs, and the nether s. H1543
Jdg 1:15 land; give me also s of water. And H1543
15 her the upper s and the nether springs. H1543
15 her the upper springs and the nether s. H1543
Job 38:16 Hast thou entered into the s of the sea? H5033
Ps 87: 7 *shall be there*: all my s *are* in thee. H4599
104:10 He sendeth the s into the valleys, *which* H4599
Isa 35: 7 and the thirsty land s of water: in the H4002
41:18 of water, and the dry land s of water. H4161
49:10 by the s of water shall he guide them. H4002
Jer 51:36 will dry up her sea, and make her s dry. H4726

SPRINKLE
Ex 9: 8 and let Moses s it toward the heaven H2236
29:16 and s *it* round about upon the altar. H2236
20 s the blood upon the altar round about. H2236
21 anointing oil, and s *it* upon Aaron, and H5137
Lev 1: 5 the blood, and s the blood round about H2236
11 s his blood round about upon the altar. H2236
3: 2 s the blood upon the altar round about. H2236
8 Aaron's sons shall s the blood thereof H2236
13 of Aaron shall s the blood thereof upon H2236
4: 6 in the blood, and s of the blood seven H5137
17 *some* of the blood, and s *it* seven times H5137
5: 9 And he shall s of the blood of the sin H5137
7: 2 shall he s round about upon the altar. H2236
14: 7 And he shall s upon him that is to be H5137
16 left hand, and shall s of the oil with his H5137
27 And the priest shall s with his right H5137
51 water, and s the house seven times: H5137
16:14 of the bullock, and s *it* with his finger H5137
14 seat shall he s of the blood with his H5137
15 of the bullock, and s it upon the mercy H5137
19 And he shall s of the blood upon it with H5137
17: 6 And the priest shall s the blood upon H2236
Nu 8: 7 to cleanse them: S water of purifying H5137
18:17 holy: thou shalt s their blood upon the H2236
19: 4 his finger, and s of her blood directly H5137
18 in the water, and s *it* upon the tent, and H5137
19 And the clean *person* shall s upon the H5137
2Ki 16:15 offerings; and s upon it all the blood H2236
Isa 52:15 So shall he s many nations; the kings H5137
Ezk 36:25 Then will I s clean water upon you, and H2236
43:18 thereon, and to s blood thereon. H2236

SPRINKLED
Ex 9:10 and Moses s it up toward heaven; H2236
24: 6 and half of the blood he s on the altar. H2236
8 And Moses took the blood, and s *it* on H2236
Lev 6:27 and when there is s of the blood thereof H5137
27 that whereon it was s in the holy place. H5137
8:11 And he s thereof upon the altar seven H5137
19 And he killed *it;* and Moses s the blood H2236
24 s the blood upon the altar round about. H2236
30 the altar, and s *it* upon Aaron, *and* H5137
9:12 which he s round about upon the altar. H2236
18 which he s upon the altar round about, H2236
Nu 19:13 was not s upon him, he shall be H2236
20 not been s upon him; he *is* unclean. H2236
2Ki 9:33 of her blood was s on the wall, and on H5137
16:13 offering, and s the blood of his peace H2236
2Ch 29:22 the blood, and s *it* on the altar: H2236
22 the rams, they s the blood upon the H2236
22 and they s the blood upon the altar. H2236
30:16 of God: the priests s the blood, *which* H2236
35:11 and the priests s *the blood* from their H2236
Job 2:12 s dust upon their heads toward heaven. H2236
Isa 63: 3 blood shall be s upon my garments, H5137
Heb 9:19 and s both the book, and all the people, G4472
21 Moreover he s with blood both the G4472
10:22 faith, having our hearts s from an evil G4472

SPRINKLETH
Lev 7:14 that s the blood of the peace offerings. H2236
Nu 19:21 unto them, that he that s the water of H5137

SPRINKLING
Heb 9:13 the ashes of an heifer s the unclean, G4472
11:28 the passover, and the s of blood, lest he G4378
12:24 to the blood of s, that speaketh better G4473
1Pt 1: 2 obedience and s of the blood of Jesus G4473

SPROUT
Job 14: 7 down, that it will s again, and that the H2498

SPRUNG
Gen 41: 6 with the east wind s up after them. H6779
23 with the east wind, s up after them: H6779
Lev 13:42 sore; it *is* a leprosy s up in his bald H6542
Mt 4:16 region and shadow of death light is s up. *G393*
13: 5 and forthwith they s up, because they *G1816*
7 and the thorns s up, and choked them: *G305*
26 But when the blade was s up, and *G985*
Lk 8: 6 and as soon as it was s up, it withered *G5453*

SPUE
Lev 18:28 That the land s not you out also, when H6958
20:22 you to dwell therein, s you not out. H6958
Jer 25:27 be drunken, and s, and fall, and rise no H7006
Rev 3:16 nor hot, I will s thee out of my mouth. *G1692*

SPUED
Lev 18:28 s out the nations that *were* before you. H6958

SPUN
Ex 35:25 which they had s, *both* of blue, and of H4299
26 them up in wisdom s goats' *hair*. H2901

SPUNGE
Mt 27:48 ran, and took a s, and filled *it* with *G4699*
Mk 15:36 And one ran and filled a s full of *G4699*
Jn 19:29 and they filled a s with vinegar, and *G4699*

SPY
Nu 13:16 Moses sent to s out the land. And H8446
17 And Moses sent them to s out the land H8446
21:32 And Moses sent to s out Jaazer, and H7270
Jos 2: 1 two men to s secretly, saying, Go H7270
6:25 which Joshua sent to s out Jericho. H7270
Jdg 18: 2 from Eshtaol, to s out the land, and to H7270
14 men that went to s out the country of H7270
17 And the five men that went to s out the H7270
2Sa 10: 3 and to s it out, and to overthrow it? H7270
2Ki 6:13 And he said, Go and s where he *is*, that H7200
1Ch 19: 3 to overthrow, and to s out the land? H7200
Gal 2: 4 who came in privily to s out our liberty *G2684*

SQUARE
1Ki 7: 5 And all the doors and posts *were* s, with H7251
Ezk 43:16 broad, s in the four squares thereof. H7251
45: 2 *in breadth*, s round about; and fifty H7251

SQUARED
Ezk 41:21 The posts of the temple *were* s, *and* the H7251

SQUARES
Ezk 43:16 broad, square in the four s thereof. H7253
17 broad in the four s thereof; and the H7253

STABILITY
Isa 33: 6 shall be the s of thy times, *and* strength H530

STABLE
1Ch 16:30 also shall be s, that it be not moved. H3559
Ezk 25: 5 And I will make Rabbah a s for camels, H5116

STABLISH
2Sa 7:13 s the throne of his kingdom for ever. H3559
1Ch 17:12 He shall build me an house, and I will s H3559
18: 3 s his dominion by the river Euphrates. H5324
2Ch 7:18 Then will I s the throne of thy H6965
Est 9:21 To s *this* among them, that they should H6965
Ps 119:38 S thy word unto thy servant, who *is* H6965
Ro 16:25 Now to him that is of power to s you *G4741*
1Th 3:13 To the end he may s your hearts *G4741*
2Th 2:17 Comfort your hearts, and s you in *G4741*
3: 3 But the Lord is faithful, who shall s *G4741*
Jas 5: 8 Be ye also patient; s your hearts: for the *G4741*
1Pt 5:10 you perfect, s, strengthen, settle *you*. *G4741*

STABLISHED
2Ch 17: 5 Therefore the LORD s the kingdom in H3559
Ps 93: 1 world also is s, that it cannot be moved. H3559
148: 6 He hath also s them for ever and ever: H5975
Col 2: 7 Rooted and built up in him, and s in the *G950*

STABLISHETH
Hab 2:12 with blood, and s a city by iniquity! H3559
2Co 1:21 Now he which s us with you in Christ, *G950*

STACHYS
Ro 16: 9 our helper in Christ, and S my beloved. *G4720*

STACKS
Ex 22: 6 in thorns, so that the s of corn, or the H1430

STACTE
Ex 30:34 thee sweet spices, s, and onycha, and H5198

STAFF
Gen 32:10 for with my s I passed over this Jordan; H4731
38:18 thy bracelets, and thy s that *is* in thine H4294
25 these, the signet, and bracelets, and s. H4294
Ex 12:11 feet, and your s in your hand; and ye H4731
21:19 abroad upon his s, then shall he that H4938
Lev 26:26 *And* when I have broken the s of your H4294
Nu 13:23 two upon a s; and *they brought* of H4132
22:27 kindled, and he smote the ass with a s. H4731
Jdg 6:21 the end of the s that *was* in his hand, H4938
1Sa 17: 7 And the s of his spear *was* like a H2671
40 And he took his s in his hand, and H4731
2Sa 3:29 that leaneth on a s, or that falleth on the H6418
21:19 the Gittite, the s of whose spear *was* H6086
23: 7 with iron and the s of a spear; and they H6086
21 to him with a s, and plucked the spear H7626
2Ki 4:29 loins, and take my s in thine hand, and H4938
29 and lay my s upon the face of the child. H4938
31 them, and laid the s upon the face of H4938
18:21 Now, behold, thou trustest upon the s H4938
1Ch 11:23 to him with a s, and plucked the spear H7626
20: 5 spear s *was* like a weaver's beam. H6086
Ps 23: 4 me; thy rod and thy s they comfort me. H4938
105:16 the land: he brake the whole s of bread. H4294
Isa 3: 1 the stay and the s, the whole stay of H4938
9: 4 burden, and the s of his shoulder, the H4294
10: 5 the s in their hand is mine indignation. H4294
15 it up, *or* as if the s should lift up *itself*, H4294
24 shall lift up his s against thee, after the H4294
14: 5 The LORD hath broken the s of the H4294
28:27 with a s, and the cummin with a rod. H4294
30:32 the grounded s shall pass, which the H4294
36: 6 Lo, thou trustest in the s of this broken H4938
Jer 48:17 strong s broken, *and* the beautiful rod! H4294
Ezk 4:16 I will break the s of bread in Jerusalem: H4294
5:16 you, and will break your s of bread: H4294
14:13 it, and will break the s of the bread H4294
29: 6 been a s of reed to the house of Israel. H4938
Hos 4:12 their stocks, and their s declareth unto H4731
Zec 8: 4 man with his s in his hand for very age. H4938
11:10 And I took my s, *even* Beauty, and cut it H4731
14 Then I cut asunder mine other s, *even* H4731
Mk 6: 8 journey, save a s only; no scrip, no *G4464*
Heb 11:21 *leaning* upon the top of his s. *G4464*

STAGGER
Job 12:25 maketh them to s like *a* drunken *man*. H8582
Ps 107:27 They reel to and fro, and s like a H5128
Isa 29: 9 wine; they s, but not with strong drink. H5128

STAGGERED
Ro 4:20 He s not at the promise of God through *G1252*

STAGGERETH
Isa 19:14 as a drunken *man* s in his vomit. H8582

STAID See STAYED.

STAIN
Job 3: 5 shadow of death s it; let a cloud dwell H1350
Isa 23: 9 purposed it, to s the pride of all glory, H2490
63: 3 garments, and I will s all my raiment. H1351

STAIRS
1Ki 6: 8 went up with winding s into the middle H3883
2Ki 9:13 him on the top of the s, and blew with H4609
Neh 3:15 s that go down from the city of David. H4609
9: 4 Then stood up upon the s, of the H4608
12:37 went up by the s of the city of David, H4609
Song 2:14 secret *places* of the s, let me see thy H4095
Ezk 40: 6 east, and went up the s thereof, and H4609
43:17 and his s shall look toward the east. H4609
Act 21:35 And when he came upon the s, so it was, *G304*
40 Paul stood on the s, and beckoned with *G304*

STAKES
Isa 33:20 not one of the s thereof shall ever be H3489
54: 2 thy cords, and strengthen thy s; H3489

STALK
Gen 41: 5 came up upon one s, rank and good. H7070
22 ears came up in one s, full and good: H7070
Hos 8: 7 it hath no s: the bud shall yield no H7054

STALKS
Jos 2: 6 hid them with the s of flax, which she H6086

STALL
Am 6: 4 and the calves out of the midst of the s; H4770
Mal 4: 2 go forth, and grow up as calves of the s. H4770
Lk 13:15 the s, and lead *him* away to watering? *G5336*

STALLED
Prv 15:17 love is, than a s ox and hatred therewith. H75

STALLS
1Ki 4:26 And Solomon had forty thousand s of H723
2Ch 9:25 And Solomon had four thousand s for H723
32:28 wine, and oil; and s for all manner of H723
Hab 3:17 fold, and *there shall be* no herd in the s: H7517

STAMMERERS
Isa 32: 4 of the s shall be ready to speak plainly. H5926

STAMMERING
Isa 28:11 For with s lips and another tongue will H3934
33:19 perceive; of a s tongue, *that thou canst* H3932

STAMP
2Sa 22:43 of the earth, I did s them as the mire of H1854
Ezk 6:11 thine hand, and s with thy foot, and H7554

STAMPED
Dt 9:21 it with fire, and s it, *and* ground *it* very H3807
2Ki 23: 6 brook Kidron, and s *it* small to powder, H1854
15 high place, *and* s *it* small to powder, H1854
2Ch 15:16 s *it*, and burnt *it* at the brook Kidron. H1854
Ezk 25: 6 *thine* hands, and s with the feet, and H7554
Dan 7: 7 in pieces, and s the residue with the H7512
19 pieces, and s the residue with his feet; H7512
8: 7 to the ground, and s upon him: and H7429
10 stars to the ground, and s upon them. H7429

STAMPING
Jer 47: 3 At the noise of the s of the hoofs of his H8161

STANCHED
Lk 8:44 and immediately her issue of blood s. *G2476*

STAND
Gen 19: 9 And they said, S back. And they said H5066
24:13 Behold, I s *here* by the well of water; H5324
43 Behold, I s by the well of water; and it H5324
Ex 7:15 and thou shalt s by the river's brink H5324
8:20 the morning, and s before Pharaoh; lo, H3320
9:11 And the magicians could not s before H5975
13 in the morning, and s before Pharaoh, H3320
14:13 people, Fear ye not, s still, and see the H3320
17: 6 Behold, I will s before thee there upon H5975
9 to morrow I will s on the top of the hill H5324
18:14 s by thee from morning unto even? H5324
33:10 the cloudy pillar s *at* the tabernacle H5975
21 by me, and thou shalt s upon a rock: H5324
Lev 18:23 shall any woman s before a beast to lie H5975
19:16 neither shalt thou s against the blood H5975
26:37 no power to s before your enemies. H8617
27:14 the priest shall estimate it, so shall it s. H6965
17 according to thy estimation it shall s. H6965
Nu 1: 5 of the men that shall s with you: of *the* H5975
9: 8 And Moses said unto them, S still, and H5975
11:16 that they may s there with thee. H3320
16: 9 of the LORD, and to s before the H5975
23: 3 And Balaam said unto Balak, S by thy H3320
15 And he said unto Balak, S here by thy H3320
27:21 And he shall s before Eleazar the H5975
30: 4 all her vows shall s, and every bond H6965
4 she hath bound her soul shall s. H6965
5 her soul, shall s: and the LORD shall H6965
7 then her vows shall s, and her bonds H6965
7 wherewith she bound her soul shall s. H6965
9 bound their souls, shall s against her. H6965
11 all her vows shall s, and every bond H6965
11 wherewith she bound her soul shall s. H6965
12 her soul, shall not s: her husband hath H6965
35:12 s before the congregation in judgment. H5975
Dt 5:31 But as for thee, s thou here by me, and H5975
7:24 no man be able to s before thee, until H3320
9: 2 Who can s before the children of Anak! H3320

Dt 10: 8 of the LORD, to s before the LORD to H5975
11:25 There shall no man be able to s before H3320
18: 5 of all thy tribes, to s to minister in the H5975
7 *do,* which s there before the LORD. H5975
19:17 *is,* shall s before the LORD, before H5975
24:11 Thou shalt s abroad, and the man to H5975
25: 8 he s *to it,* and say, I like not to take her; H5975
27:12 These shall s upon mount Gerizim to H5975
13 And these shall s upon mount Ebal to H5975
29:10 Ye s this day all of you before the H5324
Jos 1: 5 There shall not any man be able to s H3320
3: 8 of Jordan, ye shall s still in Jordan. H5975
13 above; and they shall s upon an heap. H5975
7:12 of Israel could not s before their H6965
13 thou canst not s before thine enemies, H6965
10: 8 shall not a man of them s before thee. H5975
12 of Israel, Sun, s thou still upon Gibeon; H1826
20: 4 those cities shall s at the entering of the H5975
6 in that city, until he s before the H5975
23: 9 been able to s before you unto this day. H5975
Jdg 2:14 not any longer s before their enemies. H5975
4:20 Again he said unto her, S in the door of H5975
1Sa 6:20 Who is able to s before this holy LORD H5975
9:27 he passed on,) but s thou still a while, H5975
12: 7 Now therefore s still, that I may reason H3320
16 Now therefore s and see this great H3320
14: 9 to you; then we will s still in our place, H5975
16:22 David, I pray thee, s before me; for he H5975
19: 3 And I will go out and s beside my H5975
2Sa 1: 9 He said unto me again, S, I pray thee, H5975
18:30 Turn aside, *and* s here. And he turned H3320
1Ki 1: 2 virgin: and let her s before the king, H5975
8:11 So that the priests could not s to H5975
10: 8 servants, which s continually before H5975
17: 1 before whom I s, there shall not be dew H5975
18:15 before whom I s, I will surely shew H5975
19:11 And he said, Go forth, and s upon the H5975
2Ki 3:14 before whom I s, surely, were it not that H5975
5:11 out to me, and s, and call on the name H5975
16 before whom I s, I will receive none. H5975
6:31 son of Shaphat shall s on him this day. H5975
10: 4 not before him: how then shall we s? H5975
1Ch 21:16 angel of the LORD s between the earth H5975
23:30 And to s every morning to thank and H5975
2Ch 5:14 So that the priests could not s to H5975
9: 7 servants, which s continually before H5975
20: 9 or famine, we s before this house, and H5975
17 set yourselves, s ye *still,* and see the H5975
29:11 chosen you to s before him, to serve H5975
34:32 and Benjamin to s *to it.* And the H5975
35: 5 And s in the holy *place* according to the H5975
Ezr 9:15 we cannot s before thee because of this. H5975
10:13 we are not able to s without, neither *is* H5975
14 all the congregation s, and let all them H5975
Neh 7: 3 and while they s by, let them shut the H5975
9: 5 *and* Pethahiah, said, S up *and* bless the H6965
Est 3: 4 matters would s: for he had told them H5975
8:11 together, and to s for their life, to H5975
Job 8:15 but it shall not s: he shall hold it fast, H5975
19:25 shall s at the latter *day* upon the earth: H6965
30:20 me: I s up, and thou regardest me *not.* H5975
33: 5 set *thy words* in order before me, s up. H3320
37:14 Hearken unto this, O Job: s still, and H5975
38:14 *to* the seal; and they s as a garment. H3320
41:10 up: who then is able to s before me? H3320
Ps 1: 5 Therefore the ungodly shall not s in the H6965
4: 4 S in awe, and sin not: commune with
5: 5 The foolish shall not s in thy sight: thou H3320
20: 8 fallen: but we are risen, and s upright. H5749
24: 3 LORD? or who shall s in his holy place? H6965
30: 7 my mountain to s strong: thou didst H5975
33: 8 of the world s in awe of him. H1481
35: 2 Take hold of shield and buckler, and s H6965
38:11 My lovers and my friends s aloof from H5975
11 my sore; and my kinsmen s afar off. H5975
45: 9 hand did s the queen in gold of Ophir. H5324
73: 7 Their eyes s out with fatness: they have H3318
76: 7 and who may s in thy sight when once H5975
78:13 he made the waters to s as an heap. H5324
89:28 and my covenant shall s fast with him. H539
43 hast not made him to s in the battle. H6965
94:16 *or* who will s up for me against the H3320
109: 6 him: and let Satan s at his right hand. H5975
31 For he shall s at the right hand of the H5975
111: 8 They s fast for ever and ever, *and are* H5564
122: 2 Our feet shall s within thy gates, O H5975
130: 3 mark iniquities, O Lord, who shall s? H5975
134: 1 by night s in the house of the LORD. H5975
135: 2 Ye that s in the house of the LORD, in H5975
Ps 147:17 like morsels: who can s before his cold? H5975
Prv 12: 7 but the house of the righteous shall s. H5975
19:21 the counsel of the LORD, that shall s. H6965
22:29 his business? he shall s before kings; he H3320
29 kings; he shall not s before mean *men.* H3320
25: 6 and s not in the place of great *men:* H5975
27: 4 but who *is* able to s before envy? H5975
Ecc 4:15 child that shall s up in his stead. H5975
8: 3 Be not hasty to go out of his sight: s not H5975
Isa 7: 7 Thus saith the Lord GOD, It shall not s, H6965
8:10 and it shall not s: for God *is* with us. H6965
11:10 Jesse, which shall s for an ensign of the H5975
14:24 and as I have purposed, *so* shall it s: H6965
21: 8 And he cried, A lion: My lord, I s H5975
27: 9 the groves and images shall not s up. H6965
28:18 with hell shall not s; when the H6965
32: 8 things; and by liberal things shall he s. H6965
40: 8 the word of our God shall s for ever. H6965
44:11 together, let them s up; *yet* they shall H5975
46:10 shall s, and I will do all my pleasure: H6965
47:12 S now with thine enchantments, and H5975
13 prognosticators, s up, and save thee H5975
48:13 I call unto them, they s up together. H5975
50: 8 with me? let us s together: who *is* mine H5975
51:17 Awake, awake, s up, O Jerusalem, H6965
61: 5 And strangers shall s and feed your H5975
65: 5 Which say, S by thyself, come not near H7126
Jer 6:16 Thus saith the LORD, S ye in the ways, H5975
7: 2 S in the gate of the LORD'S house, and H5975
10 And come and s before me in this H5975
14: 6 And the wild asses did s in the high H5975
15:19 *and* thou shalt s before me: and if thou H5975
17:19 Thus said the LORD unto me; Go and s H5975
26: 2 Thus saith the LORD; S in the court of H5975
35:19 not want a man to s before me for ever. H5975
44:28 whose words shall s, mine, or theirs. H6965
29 shall surely s against you for evil: H6965
46: 4 up, ye horsemen, and s forth with *your* H3320
14 say ye, S fast, and prepare thee; H3320
21 they did not s, because the day of their H5975
48:19 O inhabitant of Aroer, s by the way, H5975
49:19 *is* that shepherd that will s before me? H5975
50:44 *is* that shepherd that will s before me? H5975
51:50 sword, go away, s not still: remember H5975
Ezk 2: 1 And he said unto me, Son of man, s H5975
13: 5 s in the battle in the day of the LORD. H5975
17:14 by keeping of his covenant it might s. H5975
22:30 up the hedge, and s in the gap before H5975
27:29 their ships, they shall s upon the land; H5975
29: 7 and madest all their loins to be at a s. H5976
31:14 neither their trees s up in their height, H5975
33:26 Ye s upon your sword, ye work H5975
44:11 s before them to minister unto them. H5975
15 me, and they shall s before me to offer H5975
24 And in controversy they shall s in H5975
46: 2 without, and shall s by the post of the H5975
47:10 the fishers shall s upon it from En-gedi H5975
Dan 1: 4 ability in them to s in the king's palace, H5975
5 thereof they might s before the king. H5975
2:44 these kingdoms, and it shall s for ever. H6966
7: 4 earth, and made s upon the feet as a H6966
8: 4 no beasts might s before him, neither H5975
7 in the ram to s before him, but he cast H5975
22 kingdoms shall s up out of the nation, H5975
23 dark sentences, shall s up. H5975
25 he shall also s up against the Prince H5975
10:11 unto thee, and s upright: for unto thee H5975
11: 2 Behold, there shall s up yet three kings H5975
3 And a mighty king shall s up, that shall H5975
4 And when he shall s up, his kingdom H5975
6 neither shall he s, nor his arm: but she H5975
7 of her roots shall *one* s up in his estate, H5975
14 And in those times there shall many s H5975
16 and none shall s before him: and he H5975
16 him: and he shall s in the glorious land, H5975
17 not s *on his side,* neither be for him. H5975
20 Then shall s up in his estate a raiser of H5975
21 And in his estate shall s up a vile H5975
25 but he shall not s: for they shall forecast H5975
31 And arms shall s on his part, and they H5975
12: 1 And at that time shall Michael s up, the H5975
13 and s in thy lot at the end of the days. H5975
Am 2:15 Neither shall he s that handleth the H5975
Mic 5: 4 And he shall s and feed in the strength H5975
Nah 1: 6 Who can s before his indignation? and H5975
2: 8 shall flee away. S, stand, *shall they cry;* H5975
8 flee away. Stand, s, *shall they cry;* but H5975'
Hab 2: 1 I will s upon my watch, and set me H5975
Zec 3: 7 places to walk among these that s by. H5975
Zec 4:14 that s by the Lord of the whole earth. H5975
14: 4 And his feet shall s in that day upon H5975
12 away while they s upon their feet, and H5975
Mal 3: 2 and who shall s when he appeareth? H5975
Mt 12:25 house divided against itself shall not s: G2476
26 himself; how shall then his kingdom s? G2476
47 s without, desiring to speak with thee. G2476
20: 6 them, Why s ye here all the day idle? G2476
24:15 the prophet, s in the holy place, (whoso G2476
Mk 3: 3 which had the withered hand, S forth. G1453
24 against itself, that kingdom cannot s. G2476
25 against itself, that house cannot s. G2476
26 divided, he cannot s, but hath an end. G2476
9: 1 some of them that s here, which shall G2476
11:25 And when ye s praying, forgive, if ye G4739
Lk 1:19 I am Gabriel, that s in the presence of G3936
6: 8 Rise up, and s forth in the midst. And G2476
8:20 brethren s without, desiring to see thee. G2476
11:18 shall his kingdom s? because ye say that G2476
13:25 and ye begin to s without, and to knock G2476
21:36 to pass, and to s before the Son of man. G2476
Jn 11:42 of the people which s by I said *it,* that G4026
Act 1:11 men of Galilee, why s ye gazing up into G2476
4:10 doth this man s here before you whole. G3936
5:20 Go, s and speak in the temple to the G2476
8:38 And he commanded the chariot to s G2476
10:26 But Peter took him up, saying, S up; I G450
14:10 Said with a loud voice, S upright on thy G450
25:10 Then said Paul, I s at Caesar's G1510
26: 6 And now I s and am judged for the G2476
16 But rise, and s upon thy feet: for I have G2476
Ro 5: 2 grace wherein we s, and rejoice in hope G2476
9:11 s, not of works, but of him that calleth;) G3306
14: 4 up: for God is able to make him s. G2476
10 all s before the judgment seat of Christ. G3936
1Co 2: 5 That your faith should not s in the G5600
15: 1 also ye have received, and wherein ye s; G2476
30 And why s we in jeopardy every hour? G2793
16:13 Watch ye, s fast in the faith, quit you G4739
2Co 1:24 are helpers of your joy: for by faith ye s. G2476
Gal 4:20 change my voice; for I s in doubt of you. G639
5: 1 S fast therefore in the liberty wherewith G4739
Eph 6:11 able to s against the wiles of the devil. G2476
13 the evil day, and having done all, to s. G2476
14 S therefore, having your loins girt G2476
Php 1:27 affairs, that ye s fast in one spirit, with G4739
4: 1 s fast in the Lord, *my* dearly beloved. G4739
Col 4:12 that ye may s perfect and complete G2476
1Th 3: 8 For now we live, if ye s fast in the Lord. G4739
2Th 2:15 Therefore, brethren, s fast, and hold G4739
Jas 2: 3 say to the poor, S thou there, or sit here G2476
1Pt 5:12 is the true grace of God wherein ye s. G2476
Rev 3:20 Behold, I s at the door, and knock: if G2476
6:17 is come; and who shall be able to s? G2476
10: 5 And the angel which I saw s upon the G2476
15: 2 of his name, s on the sea of glass, G2476
18:15 rich by her, shall s afar off for the fear G2476
20:12 And I saw the dead, small and great, s G2476

S

STANDARD

Nu 1:52 by his own s, throughout their hosts. H1714
2: 2 pitch by his own s, with the ensign of H1714
3 shall they of the s of the camp of Judah H1714
10 On the south side *shall be* the s of the H1714
18 On the west side *shall be* the s of the H1714
25 The s of the camp of Dan *shall be* on H1714
10:14 In the first *place* went the s of the camp H1714
18 And the s of the camp of Reuben set H1714
22 And the s of the camp of the children of H1714
25 And the s of the camp of the children of H1714
Isa 49:22 and set up my s to the people: and they H5251
59:19 the LORD shall lift up a s against him. H5127
62:10 out the stones; lift up a s for the people. H5251
Jer 4: 6 Set up the s toward Zion: retire, stay H5251
21 How long shall I see the s, *and* hear the H5251
50: 2 and set up a s; publish, *and* conceal H5251
51:12 Set up the s upon the walls of Babylon, H5251
27 Set ye up a s in the land, blow the H5251

STANDARDBEARER

Isa 10:18 and they shall be as when a s fainteth. H5263

STANDARDS

Nu 2:17 every man in his place by their s. H1714
31 They shall go hindmost with their s. H1714
34 they pitched by their s, and so they set H1714

STANDEST

Gen 24:31 LORD; wherefore s thou without? for I H5975

Ex 3: 5 place whereon thou s *is* holy ground. H5975
Jos 5:15 thou s *is* holy. And Joshua did so. H5975
Ps 10: 1 Why s thou afar off, O LORD? *why* H5975
Act 7:33 the place where thou s is holy ground. G2476
Ro 11:20 s by faith. Be not highminded, but fear: G2476

STANDETH

Nu 14:14 and *that* thy cloud s over them, and H5975
Dt 1:38 *But* Joshua the son of Nun, which s H5975
17:12 unto the priest that s to minister there H5975
29:15 But with *him* that s here with us this H5975
Jdg 16:26 the house s, that I may lean upon them. H3559
Est 6: 5 Behold, Haman s in the court. And the H5975
7: 9 good for the king, s in the house of H5975
Ps 1: 1 of the ungodly, nor s in the way of H5975
26:12 My foot s in an even place: in the H5975
33:11 The counsel of the LORD s for ever, the H5975
82: 1 God s in the congregation of the H5324
119:161 but my heart s in awe of thy word.
Prv 8: 2 She s in the top of high places, by the H5324
Song 2: 9 hart: behold, he s behind our wall, he H5975
Isa 3:13 The LORD s up to plead, and standeth H5324
13 The LORD standeth up to plead, and s H5975
46: 7 his place, and he s; from his place shall H5975
59:14 and justice s afar off: for truth is H5975
Dan 12: 1 great prince which s for the children of H5975
Zec 11:16 nor feed that that s still: but he shall H5324
Jn 1:26 s one among you, whom ye know not; G2476
3:29 which s and heareth him, rejoiceth G2476
Ro 14: 4 his own master he s or falleth. Yea, he G4739
1Co 7:37 Nevertheless he that s stedfast in his G2476
8:13 s, lest I make my brother to offend. G1519
10:12 Wherefore let him that thinketh he s G2476
2Ti 2:19 Nevertheless the foundation of God s G2476
Heb 10:11 And every priest s daily ministering G2476
Jas 5: 9 behold, the judge s before the door. G2476
Rev 10: 8 s upon the sea and upon the earth. G2476

STANDING

Ex 22: 6 of corn, or the s corn, or the field, be H7054
26:15 for the tabernacle *of* shittim wood s up. H5975
36:20 the tabernacle *of* shittim wood, s up. H5975
Lev 26: 1 rear you up a s image, neither shall H4676
Nu 22:23 angel of the LORD s in the way, and his H5324
31 angel of the LORD s in the way, and his H5324
Dt 23:25 When thou comest into the s corn of H7054
25 a sickle unto thy neighbour's s corn. H7054
Jdg 15: 5 let *them* go into the s corn of the H7054
5 s corn, with the vineyards *and* olives. H7054
1Sa 19:20 and Samuel s *as* appointed over them, H5975
22: 6 and all his servants *were* s about him;) H5324
1Ki 13:25 way, and the lion s by the carcase: and H5975
28 ass and the lion s by the carcase: the H5975
22:19 the host of heaven s by him on his right H5975
2Ch 9:18 place, and two lions s by the stays: H5975
18:18 s on his right hand and *on* his left. H5975
Est 5: 2 Esther the queen s in the court, *that* she H5975
Ps 69: 2 I sink in deep mire, where *there is* no s: H4613
107:35 He turneth the wilderness into a s water, H98
114: 8 Which turned the rock *into* a s water, H98
Dan 8: 6 which I had seen s before the river, and H5975
Am 9: 1 I saw the Lord s upon the altar: and he H5324
Mic 1:11 Beth-ezel; he shall receive of you his s. H5979
5:13 I cut off, and thy s images out of the H4676
Zec 3: 1 the high priest s before the angel of the H5975
1 Satan s at his right hand to resist him. H5975
6: 5 from s before the Lord of all the earth. H3320
Mt 6: 5 they love to pray s in the synagogues G2476
16:28 Verily I say unto you, There be some s G2476
20: 3 saw others s idle in the marketplace, G2476
6 and found others s idle, and saith unto G2476
Mk 3:31 s without, sent unto him, calling him. G2476
13:14 the prophet, s where it ought not, G2476
Lk 1:11 angel of the Lord s on the right side of G2476
5: 2 And saw two ships s by the lake: but G2476
9:27 But I tell you of a truth, there be some s G2476
18:13 And the publican, s afar off, would not G2476
Jn 8: 9 alone, and the woman s in the midst. G2476
19:26 and the disciple s by, whom he loved, G3936
20:14 Jesus s, and knew not that it was Jesus. G2476
Act 2:14 But Peter, s up with the eleven, lifted G2476
4:14 which was healed s with them, they G2476
5:23 and the keepers s without before the G2476
25 put in prison are s in the temple, and G2476
7:55 and Jesus s on the right hand of God, G2476
56 Son of man s on the right hand of God. G2476
22:20 shed, I also was s by, and consenting G2186
24:21 one voice, that I cried s among them, G2476
Heb 9: 8 while as the first tabernacle was yet s: G4714
2Pt 3: 5 s out of the water and in the water: G4921
Rev 7: 1 I saw four angels s on the four corners G2476
11: 4 s before the God of the earth. G2476
18:10 S afar off for the fear of her torment, G2476
19:17 And I saw an angel s in the sun; and he G2476

STANK

Ex 7:21 died; and the river s, and the Egyptians H887
8:14 together upon heaps: and the land s. H887
16:20 and s: and Moses was wroth with them. H887
2Sa 10: 6 saw that they s before David, the H887

STAR

Nu 24:17 there shall come a S out of Jacob, and a H3556
Am 5:26 your images, the s of your god, which H3556
Mt 2: 2 we have seen his s in the east, and are G792
7 diligently what time the s appeared. G792
9 and, lo, the s, which they saw in the G792
10 When they saw the s, they rejoiced with G792
Act 7:43 of Moloch, and the s of your god G798
1Co 15:41 s differeth from *another* star in glory. G792
41 star differeth from *another* s in glory. G792
2Pt 1:19 and the day s arise in your hearts: G5459
Rev 2:28 And I will give him the morning s. G792
8:10 there fell a great s from heaven, burning G792
11 And the name of the s is called G792
9: 1 and I saw a s fall from heaven unto G792
22:16 of David, *and* the bright and morning s. G792

STARE

Ps 22:17 I may tell all my bones: they look *and* s H7200

STARGAZERS

Isa 47:13 astrologers, the s, the monthly H2374+H3556

STARS

Gen 1:16 to rule the night: *he made* the s also. H3556
15: 5 and tell the s, if thou be able to number H3556
22:17 thy seed as the s of the heaven, and as H3556
26: 4 to multiply as the s of heaven, and will H3556
37: 9 and the eleven s made obeisance to me. H3556
Ex 32:13 your seed as the s of heaven, and all H3556
Dt 1:10 day as the s of heaven for multitude. H3556
4:19 the moon, and the s, *even* all the host of H3556
10:22 thee as the s of heaven for multitude. H3556
28:62 whereas ye were as the s of heaven for H3556
Jdg 5:20 They fought from heaven; the s in their H3556
1Ch 27:23 Israel like to the s of the heavens. H3556
Neh 4:21 of the morning till the s appeared. H3556
9:23 thou as the s of heaven, and broughtest H3556
Job 3: 9 Let the s of the twilight thereof be dark; H3556
9: 7 and it riseth not; and sealeth up the s. H3556
22:12 the height of the s, how high they are! H3556
25: 5 not; yea, the s are not pure in his sight. H3556
38: 7 When the morning s sang together, H3556
Ps 8: 3 and the s, which thou hast ordained; H3556
136: 9 The moon and s to rule by night: for his H3556
147: 4 He telleth the number of the s; he H3556
148: 3 and moon: praise him, all ye s of light. H3556
Ecc 12: 2 or the moon, or the s, be not darkened, H3556
Isa 13:10 For the s of heaven and the H3556
14:13 throne above the s of God: I will sit also H3556
Jer 31:35 moon and of the s for a light by night, H3556
Ezk 32: 7 and make the s thereof dark; I will H3556
Dan 8:10 the host and of the s to the ground, and H3556
12: 3 as the s for ever and ever. H3556
Joel 2:10 and the s shall withdraw their shining: H3556
3:15 and the s shall withdraw their shining. H3556
Am 5: 8 *Seek him* that maketh the seven s and H3598
Oba 4 thy nest among the s, thence will I bring H3556
Nah 3:16 above the s of heaven: the cankerworm H3556
Mt 24:29 give her light, and the s shall fall from G792
Mk 13:25 And the s of heaven shall fall, and the G792
Lk 21:25 moon, and in the s; and upon the earth G798
Act 27:20 And when neither sun nor s in many G798
1Co 15:41 glory of the s: for *one* star differeth G792
Heb 11:12 *so many* as the s of the sky in multitude, G798
Jude 13 shame; wandering s, to whom is reserved G792
Rev 1:16 And he had in his right hand seven s: and G792
20 The mystery of the seven s which thou G792
20 The seven s are the angels of the G792
2: 1 holdeth the seven s in his right hand, G792
3: 1 God, and the seven s; I know thy works, G792
6:13 And the s of heaven fell unto the earth, G792
8:12 third part of the s; so as the third part of G792
12: 1 and upon her head a crown of twelve s: G792
4 And his tail drew the third part of the s G792

STATE

Gen 43: 7 us straitly of our s, and of our kindred,
2Ch 24:13 of God in his s, and strengthened it. H4971
Est 1: 7 according to the s of the king. H3027
2:18 gifts, according to the s of the king. H3027
Ps 39: 5 at his best s *is* altogether vanity. Selah. H5324
Prv 27:23 Be thou diligent to know the s of thy H6440
28: 2 the s *thereof* shall be prolonged. H3651
Isa 22:19 and from thy s shall he pull thee down. H4612
Mt 12:45 there: and the last s of that man is worse
Lk 11:26 last s of that man is worse than the first.
Php 2:19 comfort, when I know your s. G3588+G4012
20 will naturally care for your s. G3588+G4012
4:11 s I am, *therewith* to be content. G3739
Col 4: 7 All my s shall Tychicus declare G3588+G2596

STATELY

Ezk 23:41 And satest upon a s bed, and a table H3520

STATION

Isa 22:19 And I will drive thee from thy s, and H4673

STATURE

Nu 13:32 that we saw in it *are* men of a great s. H4060
1Sa 16: 7 on the height of his s; because I have H6967
2Sa 21:20 was a man of *great* s, that had on every H4055
1Ch 11:23 a man of *great* s, five cubits high; and H4060
20: 6 a man of *great* s, whose fingers and toes H4060
Song 7: 7 This thy s is like to a palm tree, and thy H6967
Isa 10:33 the high ones of s *shall be* hewn down, H6967
45:14 Sabeans, men of s, shall come over unto H4060
Ezk 13:18 the head of every s to hunt souls! Will H6967
17: 6 vine of low s, whose branches turned H6967
19:11 bare rule, and her s was exalted among H6967
31: 3 and of an high s; and his top was H6967
Mt 6:27 thought can add one cubit unto his s? G2244
Lk 2:52 And Jesus increased in wisdom and s, G2244
12:25 thought can add to his s one cubit? G2244
19: 3 for the press, because he was little of s. G2244
Eph 4:13 of the s of the fulness of Christ: G2244

STATUTE

Ex 15:25 made for them a s and an ordinance, H2706
27:21 LORD: *it shall be* a s for ever unto their H2708
28:43 die: *it shall be* a s for ever unto him H2708
29: 9 theirs for a perpetual s: and thou shalt H2708
28 and his sons' by a s for ever from the H2706
30:21 not: and it shall be a s for ever to them, H2706
Lev 3:17 *It shall be* a perpetual s for your H2708
6:18 eat of it. *It shall be* a s for ever in your H2706
22 shall offer it: *it is* a s for ever unto the H2706
7:34 and unto his sons by a s for ever from H2706
36 s for ever throughout their generations. H2708
10: 9 s for ever throughout your generations: H2708
15 with thee, by a s for ever; as the LORD H2706
16:29 And *this* shall be a s for ever unto you: H2708
31 shall afflict your souls, by a s for ever. H2708
34 And this shall be an everlasting s unto H2708
17: 7 This shall be a s for ever unto them H2708
23:14 God: *it shall be* a s for ever throughout H2708
21 *it shall be* a s for ever in all your H2708
31 work: *it shall be* a s for ever throughout H2708
41 the year. *It shall be* a s for ever in your H2708
24: 3 *be* a s for ever in your generations. H2708
9 the LORD made by fire by a perpetual s. H2706
Nu 18:11 with thee, by a s for ever: every one H2706
19 with thee, by a s for ever: it *is* a H2706
23 *it shall be* a s for ever throughout H2708
19:10 among them, for a s for ever. H2708
21 And it shall be a perpetual s unto them, H2708
27:11 of Israel a s of judgment, as the H2708
35:29 So these *things* shall be for a s of H2708
Jos 24:25 a s and an ordinance in Shechem. H2706
1Sa 30:25 that he made it a s and an ordinance H2706
Ps 81: 4 For this *was* a s for Israel, *and* a law of H2706
Dan 6: 7 establish a royal s, and to make a firm H7010
15 That no decree nor s which the king H7010

STATUTES

Gen 26: 5 commandments, my s, and my laws. H2708
Ex 15:26 and keep all his s, I will put none of H2706
18:16 *them* know the s of God, and his laws. H2706
Lev 10:11 of Israel all the s which the LORD hath H2706
18: 5 Ye shall therefore keep my s, and my H2708
26 Ye shall therefore keep my s and my H2708
19:19 Ye shall keep my s. Thou shalt not let H2708
37 Therefore shall ye observe all my s, and H2708
20: 8 And ye shall keep my s, and do them: I H2708
22 Ye shall therefore keep all my s, and all H2708

Lev 25:18 Wherefore ye shall do my **s**, and keep H2708
26: 3 If ye walk in my **s**, and keep my H2708
15 And if ye shall despise my **s**, or if your H2708
43 and because their soul abhorred my **s**. H2708
46 These *are* the **s** and judgments and H2706
Nu 30:16 These *are* the **s**, which the LORD H2706
Dt 4: 1 O Israel, unto the **s** and unto the H2706
5 Behold, I have taught you **s** and H2706
6 shall hear all these **s**, and say, Surely H2706
8 *so* great, that hath **s** and judgments *so* H2706
14 time to teach you **s** and judgments, H2706
40 Thou shalt keep therefore his **s**, and his H2706
45 These *are* the testimonies, and the **s**, H2706
5: 1 Hear, O Israel, the **s** and judgments H2706
31 and the **s**, and the judgments, H2706
6: 1 the **s**, and the judgments, H2706
2 God, to keep all his **s** and his H2708
17 his **s**, which he hath commanded thee. H2706
20 and the **s**, and the judgments, H2706
24 us to do all these **s**, to fear the LORD H2706
7:11 and the **s**, and the judgments, H2706
8:11 his **s**, which I command thee this day: H2708
10:13 the LORD, and his **s**, which I command H2708
11: 1 charge, and his **s**, and his judgments, H2708
32 And ye shall observe to do all the **s** and H2706
12: 1 These *are* the **s** and judgments, which H2706
16:12 and thou shalt observe and do these **s**. H2706
17:19 of this law and these **s**, to do them: H2706
26:16 thee to do these **s** and judgments: thou H2706
17 ways, and to keep his **s**, and his H2706
27:10 his **s**, which I command thee this day. H2706
28:15 and his **s** which I command thee H2708
45 and his **s** which he commanded thee: H2708
30:10 and his **s** which are written in H2708
16 and his **s** and his judgments, H2708
2Sa 22:23 *as for* his **s**, I did not depart from them. H2708
1Ki 2: 3 his ways, to keep his **s**, and his H2708
3: 3 walking in the **s** of David his father: H2708
14 my ways, to keep my **s** and my H2706
6:12 thou wilt walk in my **s**, and execute my H2708
8:58 and his **s**, and his judgments, H2706
61 God, to walk in his **s**, and to keep his H2706
9: 4 *and* wilt keep my **s** and my judgments: H2706
6 *and* my **s** which I have set before H2708
11:11 my covenant and my **s**, which I have H2708
33 and *to keep* my **s** and my judgments, H2708
34 he kept my commandments and my **s**: H2708
38 my sight, to keep my **s** and my H2708
2Ki 17: 8 And walked in the **s** of the heathen, H2708
13 *and* my **s**, according to all the H2708
15 And they rejected his **s**, and his H2706
19 in the **s** of Israel which they made. H2708
34 do they after their **s**, or after their H2708
37 And the **s**, and the ordinances, and the H2706
23: 3 and his **s** with all *their* heart and H2708
1Ch 22:13 heed to fulfil the **s** and judgments H2706
29:19 and thy **s**, and to do all *these things*, H2706
2Ch 7:17 shalt observe my **s** and my judgments; H2706
19 But if ye turn away, and forsake my **s** H2708
19:10 commandment, **s** and judgments, ye H2706
33: 8 the whole law and the **s** and the H2706
34:31 and his **s**, with all his heart, and H2706
Ezr 7:10 and to teach in Israel **s** and judgments. H2706
11 of the LORD, and of his **s** to Israel. H2706
Neh 1: 7 nor the **s**, nor the judgments, H2706
9:13 true laws, good **s** and commandments: H2706
14 them precepts, **s**, and laws, by the hand H2706
10:29 our Lord, and his judgments and his **s**; H2706
Ps 18:22 and I did not put away his **s** from me. H2708
19: 8 The **s** of the LORD *are* right, rejoicing H6490
50:16 to do to declare my **s**, or *that* thou H2706
89:31 If they break my **s**, and keep not my H2708
105:45 That they might observe his **s**, and keep H2706
119: 5 my ways were directed to keep thy **s**! H2706
8 I will keep thy **s**: O forsake me not H2706
12 *art* thou, O LORD: teach me thy **s**. H2706
16 I will delight myself in thy **s**: I will not H2708
23 *but* thy servant did meditate in thy **s**. H2706
26 and thou heardest me: teach me thy **s**. H2706
33 Teach me, O LORD, the way of thy **s**; H2706
48 have loved; and I will meditate in thy **s**. H2706
54 Thy **s** have been my songs in the house H2706
64 is full of thy mercy: teach me thy **s**. H2706
68 good, and doest good; teach me thy **s**. H2706
71 been afflicted; that I might learn thy **s**. H2706
80 Let my heart be sound in thy **s**; that I be H2706
83 in the smoke; *yet* do I not forget thy **s**. H2706
112 thy **s** alway, *even unto* the end. H2706
117 have respect unto thy **s** continually. H2706
Ps119:118 from thy **s**: for their deceit *is* falsehood. H2706
124 unto thy mercy, and teach me thy **s**. H2706
135 upon thy servant; and teach me thy **s**. H2706
145 hear me, O LORD: I will keep thy **s**. H2706
155 from the wicked: for they seek not thy **s**. H2706
171 praise, when thou hast taught me thy **s**. H2706
147:19 He sheweth his word unto Jacob, his **s** H2706
Jer 44:10 in my law, nor in my **s**, that I set before H2708
23 in his law, nor in his **s**, nor in his H2708
Ezk 5: 6 the nations, and my **s** more than the H2708
6 my **s**, they have not walked in them. H2708
7 not walked in my **s**, neither have kept H2708
11:12 not walked in my **s**, neither executed H2706
20 That they may walk in my **s**, and keep H2708
18: 9 Hath walked in my **s**, and hath kept my H2708
17 hath walked in my **s**; he shall not die for H2708
19 hath kept all my **s**, and hath done them, H2708
21 and keep all my **s**, and do that which is H2708
20:11 And I gave them my **s**, and shewed H2708
13 walked not in my **s**, and they despised H2708
16 walked not in my **s**, but polluted my H2708
18 Walk ye not in the **s** of your fathers, H2706
19 I *am* the LORD your God; walk in my **s**, H2708
21 walked not in my **s**, neither kept my H2708
24 had despised my **s**, and had polluted H2708
25 Wherefore I gave them also **s** *that were* H2706
33:15 robbed, walk in the **s** of life, without H2708
36:27 you to walk in my **s**, and ye shall keep H2706
37:24 and observe my **s**, and do them. H2708
44:24 keep my laws and my **s** in all mine H2708
Mic 6:16 For the **s** of Omri are kept, and all the H2708
Zec 1: 6 But my words and my **s**, which I H2706
Mal 4: 4 for all Israel, *with* the **s** and judgments. H2706

STAUNCHED See STANCHED.

STAVES
Ex 25:13 And thou shalt make **s** *of* shittim wood, H905
14 And thou shalt put the **s** into the rings by H905
15 The **s** shall be in the rings of the ark: H905
27 be for places of the **s** to bear the table. H905
28 And thou shalt make the **s** *of* shittim H905
27: 6 And thou shalt make **s** for the altar, H905
6 staves for the altar, **s** *of* shittim wood, H905
7 And the **s** shall be put into the rings, and H905
7 the rings, and the **s** shall be upon the two H905
30: 4 be for places for the **s** to bear it withal. H905
5 And thou shalt make the **s** *of* shittim H905
35:12 The ark, and the **s** thereof, *with* the H905
13 The table, and his **s**, and all his vessels, H905
15 And the incense altar, and his **s**, and the H905
16 brasen grate, his **s**, and all his vessels, the H905
37: 4 And he made **s** *of* shittim wood, and H905
5 And he put the **s** into the rings by the H905
14 the places for the **s** to bear the table. H905
15 And he made the **s** *of* shittim wood, and H905
27 to be places for the **s** to bear it withal. H905
28 And he made the **s** *of* shittim wood, and H905
38: 5 the grate of brass, *to be* places for the **s**. H905
6 And he made the **s** *of* shittim wood, and H905
7 And he put the **s** into the rings on the H905
39:35 The ark of the testimony, and the **s** H905
39 grate of brass, his **s**, and all his vessels, H905
40:20 the ark, and set the **s** on the ark, and put H905
Nu 4: 6 of blue, and shall put in the **s** thereof. H905
8 skins, and shall put in the **s** thereof. H905
11 skins, and shall put to the **s** thereof: H905
14 of badgers' skins, and put to the **s** of it. H905
21:18 with their **s**. And from the wilderness H4938
1Sa 17:43 comest to me with **s**? And the Philistine H4731
1Ki 8: 7 covered the ark and the **s** thereof above. H905
8 And they drew out the **s**, that the ends of H905
8 that the ends of the **s** were seen out in H905
1Ch 15:15 shoulders with the **s** thereon, as Moses H4133
2Ch 5: 8 covered the ark and the **s** thereof above. H905
9 And they drew out the **s** *of the ark*, that H905
9 that the ends of the **s** were seen from the H905
Hab 3:14 Thou didst strike through with his **s** the H4294
Zec 11: 7 I took unto me two **s**; the one I called H4731
Mt 10:10 shoes, nor yet **s**: for the workman is *G4464*
26:47 with swords and **s**, from the chief *G3586*
55 with swords and **s** for to take me? I sat *G3586*
Mk 14:43 with swords and **s**, from the chief *G3586*
48 with swords and *with* **s** to take me? *G3586*
Lk 9: 3 journey, neither **s**, nor scrip, neither *G4464*
22:52 as against a thief, with swords and **s**? *G3586*

STAY
Gen 19:17 thee, neither **s** thou in all the plain; H5975
Ex 9:28 will let you go, and ye shall **s** no longer. H5975
Lev 13: 5 in his sight be at a **s**, *and* the plague H5975
23 But if the bright spot **s** in his place, *and* H5975
28 And if the bright spot **s** in his place, H5975
37 But if the scall be in his sight at a **s**, and H5975
Jos 10:19 And **s** ye not, *but* pursue after your H5975
Ru 1:13 were grown? would ye **s** for them from H5702
1Sa 15:16 Then Samuel said unto Saul, **S**, and I H7503
20:38 speed, haste, **s** not. And Jonathan's H5975
2Sa 22:19 my calamity: but the LORD was my **s**. H4937
24:16 It is enough: **s** now thine hand. And H7503
1Ch 21:15 It is enough, **s** now thine hand. And H7503
Job 37: 4 will not **s** them when his voice is heard. H6117
38:37 or who can **s** the bottles of heaven, H7901
Ps 18:18 my calamity: but the LORD was my **s**. H4937
Prv 28:17 shall flee to the pit; let no man **s** him. H8551
Song 2: 5 **S** me with flagons, comfort me with H5564
Isa 3: 1 and from Judah the **s** and the staff, the H4937
1 **s** of bread, and the whole stay of water, H4937
1 stay of bread, and the whole **s** of water, H4937
10:20 no more again **s** upon him that smote H8172
20 them; but shall **s** upon the LORD, the H8172
19:13 *they that are* the **s** of the tribes thereof. H6438
29: 9 **S** yourselves, and wonder; cry ye out, H4102
30:12 and perverseness, and **s** thereon: H8172
31: 1 for help; and **s** on horses, and trust H8172
48: 2 of the holy city, and **s** themselves upon H5564
50:10 of the LORD, and **s** upon his God. H8172
Jer 4: 6 Zion: retire, **s** not: for I will bring H5975
20: 9 weary with forbearing, and I could not **s**.
Dan 4:35 and none can **s** his hand, or say unto H4223
Hos 13:13 for he should not **s** long in *the place of* H5975

STAYED
Gen 8:10 And he **s** yet other seven days; and H2342
12 And he **s** yet other seven days; and sent H3176
32: 4 with Laban, and **s** there until now: H309
Ex 10:24 **s**: let your little ones also go with you. H3322
17:12 Aaron and Hur **s** up his hands, the one H8551
Nu 16:48 and the living; and the plague was **s**. H6113
50 the congregation: and the plague was **s**. H6113
25: 8 was **s** from the children of Israel. H6113
Dt 10:10 And I **s** in the mount, according to the H5975
Jos 10:13 And the sun stood still, and the moon **s**, H5975
1Sa 20:19 And *when* thou hast **s** three days, *then*
24: 7 So David **s** his servants with these H8156
30: 9 where those that were left behind **s**. H5975
2Sa 17:17 Now Jonathan and Ahimaaz **s** by H5975
24:21 the plague may be **s** from the people. H6113
25 land, and the plague was **s** from Israel. H6113
1Ki 22:35 and the king was **s** up in his chariot H5975
2Ki 4: 6 *is* not a vessel more. And the oil **s**. H5975
13:18 the ground. And he smote thrice, and **s**. H5975
15:20 back, and **s** not there in the land. H5975
1Ch 21:22 the plague may be **s** from the people. H6113
2Ch 18:34 the king of Israel **s** *himself* up in *his* H5975
Job 38:11 and here shall thy proud waves be **s**? H7896
Ps 106:30 judgment: and *so* the plague was **s**. H6113
Isa 26: 3 **s** *on thee*: because he trusteth in thee. H5564
Lam 4: 6 in a moment, and no hands **s** on her. H2342
Ezk 31:15 the great waters were **s**: and I caused H3607
Hag 1:10 Therefore the heaven over you is **s** H3607
10 dew, and the earth is **s** *from* her fruit. H3607
Lk 4:42 unto him, and **s** him, that he should *G2722*
Act 19:22 but he himself **s** in Asia for a season. *G1907*

STAYETH
Isa 27: 8 debate with it: he **s** his rough wind in H1898

STAYS
1Ki 10:19 and *there were* **s** on either side on the H3027
19 seat, and two lions stood beside the **s**. H3027
2Ch 9:18 to the throne, and **s** on each side of the H3027
18 place, and two lions standing by the **s**: H3027

STEAD
Gen 22:13 for a burnt offering in the **s** of his son. H8478
30: 2 *Am* I in God's **s**, who hath withheld H8478
36:33 son of Zerah of Bozrah reigned in his **s**. H8478
34 of the land of Temani reigned in his **s**. H8478
35 **s**: and the name of his city *was* Avith. H8478
36 Samlah of Masrekah reigned in his **s**. H8478
37 Rehoboth *by* the river reigned in his **s**. H8478
38 the son of Achbor reigned in his **s**. H8478
39 reigned in his **s**: and the name of his H8478
Ex 29:30 *And* that son that is priest in his **s** shall H8478
Lev 6:22 is anointed in his **s** shall offer it: *it is* a H8478
16:32 office in his father's **s**, shall make the H8478
Nu 32:14 up in your fathers' **s**, an increase of H8478

Dt 2:12 and dwelt in their s; as Israel did unto H8478
21 succeeded them, and dwelt in their s: H8478
22 and dwelt in their s even unto this day: H8478
23 destroyed them, and dwelt in their s.) H8478
10: 6 ministered in the priest's office in his s. H8478
Jos 5: 7 he raised up in their s, them Joshua H8478
2Sa 10: 1 and Hanun his son reigned in his s. H8478
16: 8 of Saul, in whose s thou hast reigned; H8478
1Ki 1:30 s; even so will I certainly do this day. H8478
35 be king in my s: and I have appointed H8478
11:43 and Rehoboam his son reigned in his s. H8478
14:20 and Nadab his son reigned in his s. H8478
27 And king Rehoboam made in their s H8478
31 And Abijam his son reigned in his s. H8478
15: 8 David: and Asa his son reigned in his s. H8478
24 Jehoshaphat his son reigned in his s. H8478
28 Baasha slay him, and reigned in his s. H8478
16: 6 and Elah his son reigned in his s. H8478
10 Asa king of Judah, and reigned in his s. H8478
28 and Ahab his son reigned in his s. H8478
22:40 and Ahaziah his son reigned in his s. H8478
50 and Jehoram his son reigned in his s. H8478
2Ki 1:17 reigned in his s in the second year of H8478
3:27 reigned in his s, and offered him *for* H8478
8:15 he died: and Hazael reigned in his s. H8478
24 and Ahaziah his son reigned in his s. H8478
10:35 And Jehoahaz his son reigned in his s. H8478
12:21 and Amaziah his son reigned in his s. H8478
13: 9 and Joash his son reigned in his s. H8478
24 and Ben-hadad his son reigned in his s. H8478
14:16 and Jeroboam his son reigned in his s. H8478
29 and Zachariah his son reigned in his s. H8478
15: 7 and Jotham his son reigned in his s. H8478
10 and slew him, and reigned in his s. H8478
14 and slew him, and reigned in his s. H8478
22 and Pekahiah his son reigned in his s. H8478
30 and reigned in his s, in the twentieth H8478
38 and Ahaz his son reigned in his s. H8478
16:20 and Hezekiah his son reigned in his s. H8478
19:37 Esar-haddon his son reigned in his s. H8478
20:21 and Manasseh his son reigned in his s. H8478
21:18 and Amon his son reigned in his s. H8478
24 land made Josiah his son king in his s. H8478
26 and Josiah his son reigned in his s. H8478
23:30 and made him king in his father's s. H8478
24: 6 and Jehoiachin his son reigned in his s. H8478
17 s, and changed his name to Zedekiah. H8478
1Ch 1:44 son of Zerah of Bozrah reigned in his s. H8478
45 land of the Temanites reigned in his s. H8478
46 s: and the name of his city *was* Avith. H8478
47 Samlah of Masrekah reigned in his s. H8478
48 Rehoboth by the river reigned in his s. H8478
49 the son of Achbor reigned in his s. H8478
50 reigned in his s: and the name of his H8478
19: 1 died, and his son reigned in his s. H8478
29:28 and Solomon his son reigned in his s. H8478
2Ch 1: 8 and hast made me to reign in his s. H8478
9:31 and Rehoboam his son reigned in his s. H8478
12:16 and Abijah his son reigned in his s. H8478
14: 1 son reigned in his s. In his days the land H8478
17: 1 son reigned in his s, and strengthened H8478
21: 1 And Jehoram his son reigned in his s. H8478
22: 1 son king in his s: for the band of men H8478
24:27 And Amaziah his son reigned in his s. H8478
26:23 and Jotham his son reigned in his s. H8478
27: 9 and Ahaz his son reigned in his s. H8478
28:27 and Hezekiah his son reigned in his s. H8478
32:33 And Manasseh his son reigned in his s. H8478
33:20 and Amon his son reigned in his s. H8478
25 land made Josiah his son king in his s. H8478
36: 1 him king in his father's s in Jerusalem. H8478
8 and Jehoiachin his son reigned in his s. H8478
Job 16: 4 were in my soul's s, I could heap up H8478
33: 6 God's s: I also am formed out of the clay.
34:24 number, and set others in their s. H8478
Prv 11: 8 trouble, and the wicked cometh in his s. H8478
Ecc 4:15 second child that shall stand up in his s. H8478
Isa 37:38 Esar-haddon his son reigned in his s. H8478
Jer 29:26 thee priest in the s of Jehoiada the H8478
2Co 5:20 in Christ's s, be ye reconciled to God. *G5228*
Phlm 13 with me, that in thy s he might have *G5228*

STEADFAST See STEDFAST.

STEADS
1Ch 5:22 they dwelt in their s until the captivity. H8478

STEADY
Ex 17:12 were s until the going down of the sun. H530

STEAL
Gen 31:27 away secretly, and s away from me; H1589
44: 8 s out of thy lord's house silver or gold? H1589
Ex 20:15 Thou shalt not s. H1589
22: 1 If a man shall s an ox, or a sheep, and H1589
Lev 19:11 Ye shall not s, neither deal falsely, H1589
Dt 5:19 Neither shalt thou s. H1589
2Sa 19: 3 s away when they flee in battle. H1589
Prv 6:30 *Men* do not despise a thief, if he s to H1589
30: 9 s, and take the name of my God *in vain*. H1589
Jer 7: 9 Will ye s, murder, and commit H1589
23:30 the LORD, that s my words every one H1589
Mt 6:19 and where thieves break through and s: *G2813*
20 thieves do not break through nor s: *G2813*
19:18 not s, Thou shalt not bear false witness, *G2813*
27:64 by night, and s him away, and say *G2813*
Mk 10:19 Do not kill, Do not s, Do not bear false *G2813*
Lk 18:20 Do not kill, Do not s, Do not bear false *G2813*
Jn 10:10 The thief cometh not, but for to s, and *G2813*
Ro 2:21 a man should not s, dost thou steal? *G2813*
21 a man should not steal, dost thou s? *G2813*
13: 9 Thou shalt not s, Thou shalt not bear *G2813*
Eph 4:28 Let him that stole s no more: but rather *G2813*

STEALETH
Ex 21:16 And he that s a man, and selleth him, H1589
Job 27:20 a tempest s him away in the night. H1589
Zec 5: 3 for every one that s shall be cut off *as* H1589

STEALING
Dt 24: 7 If a man be found s any of his brethren H1589
Hos 4: 2 and killing, and s, and committing H1589

STEALTH
2Sa 19: 3 And the people gat them by s that day H1589

STEDFAST
Job 11:15 yea, thou shalt be s, and shalt not fear: H3332
Ps 78: 8 and whose spirit was not s with God. H539
37 him, neither were they s in his covenant. H539
Dan 6:26 the living God, and s for ever, and his H7011
1Co 7:37 Nevertheless he that standeth s in his *G1476*
15:58 Therefore, my beloved brethren, be ye s, *G1476*
2Co 1: 7 And our hope of you *is* s, knowing, that *G949*
Heb 2: 2 For if the word spoken by angels was s, *G949*
3:14 of our confidence s unto the end; *G949*
6:19 soul, both sure and s, and which entereth *G949*
1Pt 5: 9 Whom resist s in the faith, knowing *G4731*

STEDFASTLY
Ru 1:18 When she saw that she was s minded to H553
2Ki 8:11 And he settled his countenance s, until H7760
Lk 9:51 up, he s set his face to go to Jerusalem, *G4741*
Act 1:10 And while they looked s toward heaven *G2258*
2:42 And they continued s in the apostles' *G2258*
6:15 And all that sat in the council, looking s *G816*
7:55 Ghost, looked up s into heaven, and saw *G816*
14: 9 The same heard Paul speak: who s *G816*
2Co 3: 7 of Israel could not s behold the face of *G816*
13 of Israel could not s look to the end of *G816*

STEDFASTNESS
Col 2: 5 order, and the s of your faith in Christ. *G4733*
2Pt 3:17 of the wicked, fall from your own s. *G4740*

STEEL
2Sa 22:35 that a bow of s is broken by mine arms. H5154
Job 20:24 the bow of s shall strike him through. H5154
Ps 18:34 that a bow of s is broken by mine arms. H5154
Jer 15:12 iron break the northern iron and the s? H5178

STEEP
Ezk 38:20 down, and the s places shall fall, and H4095
Mic 1: 4 waters *that are* poured down a s place. H4174
Mt 8:32 violently down a s place into the sea, *G2911*
Mk 5:13 violently down a s place into the sea, *G2911*
Lk 8:33 s place into the lake, and were choked. *G2911*

STEM
Isa 11: 1 a rod out of the s of Jesse, and a Branch H1503

STEP
1Sa 20: 3 *there is* but a s between me and death. H6587
Job 31: 7 If my s hath turned out of the way, and H838

STEPHANAS
1Co 1:16 And I baptized also the household of S: *G4734*
16:15 (ye know the house of S, that it is the *G4734*
17 I am glad of the coming of S and *G4734*

STEPHEN
Act 6: 5 and they chose S, a man full of faith *G4736*
8 And S, full of faith and power, did great *G4736*
9 of Cilicia and of Asia, disputing with S. *G4736*
7:59 And they stoned S, calling upon *God*, *G4736*
8: 2 And devout men carried S *to his burial*, *G4736*
11:19 that arose about S travelled as far as *G4736*
22:20 And when the blood of thy martyr S *G4736*

STEPPED
Jn 5: 4 of the water s in was made whole *G1684*

STEPPETH
Jn 5: 7 am coming, another s down before me. *G2597*

STEPS
Ex 20:26 Neither shalt thou go up by s unto H4609
2Sa 22:37 Thou hast enlarged my s under me; so H6806
1Ki 10:19 The throne had six s, and the top of the H4609
20 other upon the six s: there was not the H4609
2Ch 9:18 And *there were* six s to the throne, with H4609
19 other upon the six s. There was not the H4609
Job 14:16 For now thou numberest my s: dost H6806
18: 7 The s of his strength shall be H6806
23:11 My foot hath held his s, his way have I H838
29: 6 When I washed my s with butter, and H1978
31: 4 not he see my ways, and count all my s? H6806
37 s; as a prince would I go near unto him. H6806
Ps 17:11 They have now compassed us in our s: H838
18:36 Thou hast enlarged my s under me, H6806
37:23 The s of a *good* man are ordered by the H4703
31 *is* in his heart; none of his s shall slide. H838
44:18 have our s declined from thy way; H838
56: 6 mark my s, when they wait for my soul. H6119
57: 6 They have prepared a net for my s; my H6471
73: 2 almost gone; my s had well nigh slipped. H838
85:13 him; and shall set *us* in the way of his s. H6471
119:133 Order my s in thy word: and let not any H6471
Prv 4:12 When thou goest, thy s shall not be H6806
5: 5 Her feet go down to death; her s take H6806
16: 9 his way: but the LORD directeth his s. H6806
Isa 26: 6 feet of the poor, *and* the s of the needy. H6471
Jer 10:23 not in man that walketh to direct his s. H6806
Lam 4:18 They hunt our s, that we cannot go in H6806
Ezk 40:22 up unto it by seven s; and the arches H4609
26 And *there were* seven s to go up to it, H4609
31 and the going up to it *had* eight s. H4609
34 side: and the going up to it *had* eight s. H4609
37 side: and the going up to it *had* eight s. H4609
49 *brought me* by the s whereby they went H4609
Dan 11:43 and the Ethiopians *shall be* at his s. H4703
Ro 4:12 also walk in the s of that faith of our *G2487*
2Co 12:18 spirit? *walked we* not in the same s? *G2487*
1Pt 2:21 an example, that ye should follow his s: *G2487*

STERN
Act 27:29 out of the s, and wished for the day. *G4403*

STEWARD
Gen 15: 2 and the s of my house *is* this H1121+H4943
43:19 near to the s of Joseph's H376+H834+H5921
44: 1 And he commanded the s of his H834+H5921
4 said unto his s, Up, follow after H834+H5921
1Ki 16: 9 of Arza s of *his* house in Tirzah. H834+H5921
Mt 20: 8 saith unto his s, Call the labourers, and *G2012*
Lk 8: 3 of Chuza Herod's s, and Susanna, and *G2012*
12:42 faithful and wise s, whom *his* lord shall *G3623*
16: 1 man, which had a s; and the same was *G3623*
2 for thou mayest be no longer s. *G3621*
3 Then the s said within himself, What *G3623*
8 And the lord commended the unjust s, *G3623*
Tit 1: 7 be blameless, as the s of God; not *G3623*

STEWARDS
1Ch 28: 1 the hundreds, and the s over all the H8269
1Co 4: 1 of Christ, and s of the mysteries of God. *G3623*
2 Moreover it is required in s, that a man *G3623*
1Pt 4:10 as good s of the manifold grace of God. *G3623*

STEWARDSHIP
Lk 16: 2 s; for thou mayest be no longer steward. *G3622*
3 s: I cannot dig; to beg I am ashamed. *G3622*
4 I am put out of the s, they may receive *G3622*

STICK
2Ki 6: 6 he cut down a s, and cast *it* in thither; H6086
Job 33:21 and his bones *that* were not seen s out. H8205
41:17 They are joined one to another, they s H3920
Ps 38: 2 For thine arrows s fast in me, and thy H5181

Lam 4: 8 it is withered, it is become like a **s**. H6086
Ezk 29: 4 of thy rivers to **s** unto thy scales, and H1692
4 fish of thy rivers shall **s** unto thy scales. H1692
37:16 take thee one **s**, and write upon it, For H6086
16 then take another **s**, and write upon it, H6086
16 it, For Joseph, the **s** of Ephraim, and H6086
17 to another into one **s**; and they shall H6086
19 I will take the **s** of Joseph, which *is* in H6086
19 with him, *even* with the **s** of Judah, and H6086
19 **s**, and they shall be one in mine hand. H6086

STICKETH

Prv 18:24 is a friend *that* **s** closer than a brother. H1695

STICKS

Nu 15:32 that gathered **s** upon the sabbath day. H6086
33 And they that found him gathering **s** H6086
1Ki 17:10 there gathering of **s**: and he called to H6086
12 I *am* gathering two **s**, that I may go in H6086
Ezk 37:20 And the **s** whereon thou writest shall be H6086
Act 28: 3 a bundle of **s**, and laid *them* on the *G5434*

STIFF

Dt 31:27 For I know thy rebellion, and thy **s** H7186
Ps 75: 5 horn on high: speak *not with* a **s** neck. H6277
Jer 17:23 made their neck **s**, that they might not H7185

STIFFENED

2Ch 36:13 swear by God: but he **s** his neck, and H7185

STIFFHEARTED

Ezk 2: 4 children and **s**. I do send thee H2389+H3820

STIFFNECKED

Ex 32: 9 and, behold, it *is* a **s** people: H7186+H6203
33: 3 for thou *art* a **s** people: lest I H7186+H6203
5 Ye *are* a **s** people: I will come H7186+H6203
34: 9 us; for it *is* a **s** people; and H7186+H6203
Dt 9: 6 for thou *art* a **s** people. H7186+H6203
13 and, behold, it *is* a **s** people: H7186+H6203
10:16 your heart, and be no more **s**. H7185+H6203
2Ch 30: 8 Now be ye not **s**, as your H7185+H6203
Act 7:51 Ye **s** and uncircumcised in heart and *G4644*

STILL

Gen 12: 9 And Abram journeyed, going on **s** H5265
41:21 but they *were* **s** ill favoured, as at the
Ex 9: 2 to let *them* go, and wilt hold them **s**,
14:13 people, Fear ye not, stand **s**, and see the H3320
15:16 they shall be *as* **s** as a stone; till thy H1826
23:11 let it rest and lie **s**; that the poor of thy H5203
Lev 13:57 And if it appear **s** in the garment, H5750
Nu 9: 8 And Moses said unto them, Stand **s**, H5975
14:38 men that went to search the land, lived *s*.
Jos 3: 8 of Jordan, ye shall stand **s** in Jordan. H5975
10:12 Sun, stand thou **s** upon Gibeon; and H1826
13 And the sun stood **s**, and the moon H1826
13 So the sun stood **s** in the midst of H5975
11:13 But *as for* the cities that stood **s** in their
24:10 **s**: so I delivered you out of his hand. H1288
Jdg 18: 9 good: and *are* ye **s**? be not slothful to go, H2814
Ru 3:18 Then said she, Sit **s**, my daughter, until H3427
1Sa 9:27 on,) but stand thou **s** a while, that I may
12: 7 Now therefore stand **s**, that I may H3320
25 But if ye shall **s** do wickedly, ye shall be H7489
14: 9 then we will stand **s** in our place, and H5975
26:25 and also shalt **s** prevail. So David went H3201
2Sa 2:23 Asahel fell down and died stood **s**. H5975
28 all the people stood **s**, and pursued after H5975
11: 1 But David tarried **s** at Jerusalem.
14:32 *to have been* there **s**: now therefore let
16: 5 he came forth, and cursed **s** as he came.
18:30 here. And he turned aside, and stood **s**. H5975
20:12 the people stood **s**, he removed Amasa H5975
12 every one that came by him stood **s**. H5975
1Ki 19:12 fire: and after the fire a **s** small voice. H1827
22: 3 *is* ours, and we *be* **s**, *and* take it not out H2814
2Ki 2:11 And it came to pass, as they **s** went on, H1980
7: 4 there: and if we sit **s** here, we die also. H3427
12: 3 away: the people **s** sacrificed and burnt
15: 4 and burnt incense **s** on the high places.
35 burned incense **s** in the high places. He
2Ch 20:17 stand ye *s*, and see the salvation
22: 9 had no power to keep **s** the kingdom.
33:17 Nevertheless the people did sacrifice **s** in
Neh 12:39 and they stood **s** in the prison gate. H5975
Job 2: 3 evil? and **s** he holdeth fast his integrity,
9 Then said his wife unto him, Dost thou **s**
3:13 For now should I have lain **s** and been H7901
Job 4:16 It stood **s**, but I could not discern the H5975
20:13 it not; but keep it **s** within his mouth:
32:16 but stood **s**, *and* answered no more;) H5975
37:14 Hearken unto this, O Job: stand **s**, and H5975
Ps 4: 4 heart upon your bed, and be **s**. Selah.
8: 2 mightest **s** the enemy and the avenger.
23: 2 he leadeth me beside the **s** waters. H4496
46:10 Be **s**, and know that I *am* God: I will be H7503
49: 9 That he should **s** live for ever, *and* not
68:21 an one as goeth on **s** in his trespasses. H1980
76: 8 heaven; the earth feared, and was **s**, H8252
78:32 For all this they sinned **s**, and believed
83: 1 hold not thy peace, and be not **s**, O God. H8252
84: 4 house: they will be **s** praising thee. Selah.
92:14 They shall **s** bring forth fruit in old age;
107:29 a calm, so that the waves thereof are **s**. H2814
139:18 sand: when I awake, I am **s** with thee. H5750
Ecc 12: 9 was wise, he **s** taught the people
Isa 5:25 away, but his hand *is* stretched out **s**.
9:12 away, but his hand *is* stretched out **s**.
17 away, but his hand *is* stretched out **s**.
21 away, but his hand *is* stretched out **s**.
10: 4 away, but his hand *is* stretched out **s**.
23: 2 Be **s**, ye inhabitants of the isle; thou H1826
30: 7 this, Their strength *is* to sit **s**. H7674
42:14 my peace; I have been **s**, *and* refrained H2790
Jer 8:14 Why do we sit **s**? assemble yourselves, H3427
23:17 They say **s** unto them that despise me, H559
27:11 will I let remain **s** in their own land,
31:20 remember him **s**: therefore my bowels
42:10 If ye will **s** abide in this land, then will I H7725
47: 6 thyself into thy scabbard, rest, and be **s**. H1826
51:50 away, stand not **s**: remember the LORD H5975
Lam 3:20 My soul hath *them* **s** in remembrance, H2142
Ezk 33:30 of thy people **s** are talking against thee
41: 7 a winding about **s** upward to the side
7 of the house went **s** upward round about
7 of the house *was* **s** upward, and so
Hab 3:11 The sun *and* moon stood **s** in their H5975
Zec 1:11 all the earth sitteth **s**, and is at rest. H3427
11:16 that that standeth **s**: but he shall eat the
Mt 20:32 And Jesus stood **s**, and called them, and *G2476*
Mk 4:39 unto the sea, Peace, be **s**. And the wind *G5392*
10:49 And Jesus stood **s**, and commanded *G2476*
Lk 7:14 bare *him* stood **s**. And he said, Young *G2476*
Jn 7: 9 words unto them, he abode *s* in Galilee.
11: 6 days **s** in the same place where he was. *G5119*
20 met him: but Mary sat *s* in the house.
Act 8:38 chariot to stand **s**: and they went down *G2476*
15:34 it pleased Silas to abide there **s**. *G1961*
17:14 but Silas and Timotheus abode there **s**. *G5278*
Ro 11:23 And they also, if they abide not **s** in *G1961*
1Ti 1: 3 As I besought thee to abide **s** at *G4357*
Rev 22:11 He that is unjust, let him be unjust **s**: *G2089*
11 filthy, let him be filthy **s**: and he that is *G2089*
11 him be righteous **s**: and he that is holy, *G2089*
11 and he that is holy, let him be holy **s**. *G2089*

STILLED

Nu 13:30 And Caleb **s** the people before Moses, H2013
Neh 8:11 So the Levites **s** all the people, saying, H2814

STILLEST

Ps 89: 9 the waves thereof arise, thou **s** them. H7623

STILLETH

Ps 65: 7 Which **s** the noise of the seas, the noise H7623

STING

1Co 15:55 O death, where *is* thy **s**? O grave, where *G2759*
56 The **s** of death *is* sin; and the strength *G2759*

STINGETH

Prv 23:32 At the last it biteth like a serpent, and **s** H6567

STINGS

Rev 9:10 and there were **s** in their tails: and their *G2759*

STINK

Gen 34:30 troubled me to make me to **s** among the H887
Ex 7:18 and the river shall **s**; and the Egyptians H887
16:24 **s**, neither was there any worm therein. H887
Ps 38: 5 My wounds **s** *and* are corrupt because of H887
Isa 3:24 there shall be **s**; and instead of a girdle H4716
34: 3 cast out, and their **s** shall come up out of H889
Joel 2:20 sea, and his **s** shall come up, and his H889
Am 4:10 I have made the **s** of your camps to come H889

STINKETH

Isa 50: 2 their fish **s**, because *there is* no water, H887
Jn 11:39 he **s**: for he hath been *dead* four days. *G3605*

STINKING

Ecc 10: 1 to send forth a **s** savour: *so doth* a little H887

STIR

Nu 24: 9 lion: who shall **s** him up? Blessed *is* he H6965
Job 17: 8 **s** up himself against the hypocrite. H5782
41:10 None *is so* fierce that dare **s** him up: H5782
Ps 35:23 **S** up thyself, and awake to my H5782
78:38 away, and did not **s** up all his wrath. H5782
80: 2 and Manasseh **s** up thy strength, and H5782
Prv 15: 1 wrath: but grievous words **s** up anger. H5927
Song 2: 7 of the field, that ye **s** not up, nor awake H5782
3: 5 of the field, that ye **s** not up, nor awake H5782
8: 4 Jerusalem, that ye **s** not up, nor awake H5782
Isa 10:26 And the LORD of hosts shall **s** up a H5782
13:17 Behold, I will **s** up the Medes against H5782
42:13 man, he shall **s** up jealousy like a man H5782
Dan 11: 2 **s** up all against the realm of Grecia. H5782
25 And he shall **s** up his power and his H5782
Act 12:18 was no small **s** among the soldiers, *G5017*
19:23 there arose no small **s** about that way. *G5017*
2Ti 1: 6 that thou **s** up the gift of God, which *G329*
2Pt 1:13 this tabernacle, to **s** you up by putting *G1326*
3: 1 in *both* which I **s** up your pure minds *G1326*

STIRRED

Ex 35:21 one whose heart **s** him up, and every H5375
26 And all the women whose heart **s** them H5375
36: 2 one whose heart **s** him up to come unto H5375
1Sa 22: 8 me that my son hath **s** up my servant H6965
26:19 If the LORD have **s** thee up against me, H5496
1Ki 11:14 And the LORD **s** up an adversary unto H6965
23 And God **s** him up *another* adversary, H6965
21:25 the LORD, whom Jezebel his wife **s** up. H5496
1Ch 5:26 And the God of Israel **s** up the spirit of H5782
2Ch 21:16 Moreover the LORD **s** up against H5782
36:22 the LORD **s** up the spirit of Cyrus H5782
Ezr 1: 1 be fulfilled, the LORD **s** up the spirit of H5782
Ps 39: 2 *even* from good; and my sorrow was **s**. H5916
Dan 11:10 But his sons shall be **s** up, and shall H1624
10 and be **s** up, *even* to his fortress. H1624
25 the south shall be **s** up to battle with a H1624
Hag 1:14 And the LORD **s** up the spirit of H5782
Act 6:12 And they **s** up the people, and the *G4787*
13:50 But the Jews **s** up the devout and *G3951*
14: 2 But the unbelieving Jews **s** up the *G1892*
17:13 came thither also, and **s** up the people. *G4531*
16 his spirit was **s** in him, when he saw *G3947*
21:27 him in the temple, **s** up all the people, *G4797*

STIRRETH

Dt 32:11 As an eagle **s** up her nest, fluttereth H5782
Prv 10:12 Hatred **s** up strifes: but love covereth H5782
15:18 A wrathful man **s** up strife: but *he that* H1624
28:25 He that is of a proud heart **s** up strife: H1624
29:22 An angry man **s** up strife, and a furious H1624
Isa 14: 9 at thy coming: it **s** up the dead for thee, H5782
64: 7 thy name, that **s** up himself to take H5782
Lk 23: 5 more fierce, saying, He **s** up the people, *G383*

STIRS

Isa 22: 2 Thou that art full of **s**, a tumultuous H8663

STOCK

Lev 25:47 thee, or to the **s** of the stranger's family: H6133
Job 14: 8 and the **s** thereof die in the ground; H1503
Isa 40:24 be sown: yea, their **s** shall not take root H1503
44:19 shall I fall down to the **s** of a tree? H944
Jer 2:27 Saying to a **s**, Thou *art* my father; and H6086
10: 8 foolish: the **s** *is* a doctrine of vanities. H6086
Act 13:26 Men *and* brethren, children of the **s** of *G1085*
Php 3: 5 Circumcised the eighth day, of the **s** of *G1085*

STOCKS

Job 13:27 Thou puttest my feet also in the **s**, and H5465
33:11 He putteth my feet in the **s**, he marketh H5465
Prv 7:22 or as a fool to the correction of the **s**; H5914
Jer 3: 9 adultery with stones and with **s**. H6086
20: 2 and put him in the **s** that *were* in the H4115
3 out of the **s**. Then said Jeremiah H4115
29:26 put him in prison, and in the **s**. H6729
Hos 4:12 My people ask counsel at their **s**, and H6086
Act 16:24 prison, and made their feet fast in the **s**. *G3586*

S

STOICKS
Act 17:18 and of the S, encountered him. And G4770

STOLE
Gen 31:20 And Jacob s away unawares to Laban H1589
2Sa 15: 6 s the hearts of the men of Israel. H1589
2Ki 11: 2 of Ahaziah, and s him from among the H1589
2Ch 22:11 of Ahaziah, and s him from among the H1589
Mt 28:13 night, and s him *away* while we slept. G2813
Eph 4:28 Let him that s steal no more: but rather G2813

STOLEN
Gen 30:33 sheep, that shall be counted s with me. H1589
31:19 had s the images that *were* her father's. H1589
26 that thou hast s away unawares to me, H1589
30 *yet* wherefore hast thou s my gods? H1589
32 knew not that Rachel had s them. H1589
39 it, *whether* s by day, or stolen by night. H1589
39 it, *whether* stolen by day, or s by night. H1589
40:15 For indeed I was s away out of the land H1589
Ex 22: 7 to keep, and it be s out of the man's H1589
12 And if it be s from him, he shall make H1589
Jos 7:11 and have also s, and dissembled also, H1589
2Sa 19:41 the men of Judah s thee away, and H1589
21:12 which had s them from the street H1589
Prv 9:17 S waters are sweet, and bread *eaten* in H1589
Oba 5 they not have s till they had enough? H1589

STOMACHER
Isa 3:24 and instead of a s a girding of H6614

STOMACH'S
1Ti 5:23 thy s sake and thine often infirmities. G4751

STONE
Gen 2:12 *is* good: there *is* bdellium and the onyx s. H68
11: 3 for s, and slime had they for morter. H68
28:18 and took the s that he had put *for* his H68
22 And this s, which I have set *for* a pillar, H68
29: 2 and a great s *was* upon the well's mouth. H68
3 and they rolled the s from the well's H68
3 the sheep, and put the s again upon the H68
8 *till* they roll the s from the well's mouth; H68
10 and rolled the s from the well's mouth, H68
31:45 And Jacob took a s, and set it up *for* a H68
35:14 *even* a pillar of s: and he poured a drink H68
49:24 thence *is* the shepherd, the s of Israel:) H68
Ex 4:25 Then Zipporah took a sharp s, and cut H6864
7:19 in *vessels of* wood, and in *vessels of* s. H68
8:26 their eyes, and will they not s us? H5619
15: 5 them: they sank into the bottom as a s. H68
16 shall be *as* still as a s; till thy people pass H68
17: 4 people? they be almost ready to s me. H5619
12 and they took a s, and put *it* under him, H68
20:25 And if thou wilt make me an altar of s, H68
25 build it of hewn s: for if thou lift up thy H1496
21:18 another with a s, or with *his* fist, and he H68
24:10 work of a sapphire s, and as it were the H68
12 will give thee tables of s, and a law, and H68
28:10 Six of their names on one s, and *the other* H68
10 on the other s, according to their birth. H68
11 With the work of an engraver in s, *like* H68
31:18 tables of s, written with the finger of God. H68
34: 1 thee two tables of s like unto the first: H68
4 And he hewed two tables of s like unto H68
4 and took in his hand the two tables of s. H68
Lev 20: 2 of the land shall s him with stones. H7275
27 to death: they shall s them with stones: H7275
24:14 and let all the congregation s him. H7275
16 shall certainly s him: as well the H7275
23 out of the camp, and s him with stones. H7275
26: 1 up *any* image of s in your land, to bow H68
Nu 14:10 But all the congregation bade s them H7275
15:35 s him with stones without the camp. H7275
35:17 And if he smite him with throwing a s, H68
23 Or with any s, wherewith a man may die, H68
Dt 4:13 and he wrote them upon two tables of s. H68
28 hands, wood and s, which neither see, H68
5:22 tables of s, and delivered them unto me. H68
9: 9 the tables of s, *even* the tables of the H68
10 me two tables of s written with the finger H68
11 of s, *even* the tables of the covenant. H68
10: 1 thee two tables of s like unto the first, H68
3 two tables of s like unto the first, and H68
13:10 And thou shalt s him with stones, that H5619
17: 5 shalt s them with stones, till they die. H5619
21:21 And all the men of his city shall s him H7275
22:21 of her city shall s her with stones that H5619
24 city, and ye shall s them with stones H5619
Dt 28:36 shalt thou serve other gods, wood and s. H68
64 fathers have known, *even* wood and s. H68
29:17 idols, wood and s, silver and gold, which H68
Jos 4: 5 every man of you a s upon his shoulder, H68
15: 6 up to the s of Bohan the son of Reuben: H68
18:17 to the s of Bohan the son of Reuben, H68
24:26 and took a great s, and set it up there H68
27 Behold, this s shall be a witness unto H68
Jdg 9: 5 persons, upon one s: notwithstanding yet H68
18 ten persons, upon one s, and have made H68
1Sa 6:14 *there was* a great s: and they clave the H68
15 put *them* on the great s: and the men of H68
18 even unto the great *s of* Abel, whereon
18 the LORD: *which s remaineth* unto this
7:12 Then Samuel took a s, and set *it* between H68
14:33 roll a great s unto me this day. H68
17:49 and took thence a s, and slang *it*, and H68
49 his forehead, that the s sunk into his H68
50 with a sling and with a s, and smote the H68
20:19 *in hand*, and shalt remain by the s Ezel. H68
25:37 died within him, and he became *as* a s. H68
2Sa 17:13 there be not one small s found there. H6872
20: 8 When they *were* at the great s which *is* in H68
1Ki 1: 9 fat cattle by the s of Zoheleth, which *is* H68
6: 7 was built of s made ready before it H68
18 all *was* cedar; there was no s seen. H68
36 of hewed s, and a row of cedar beams. H1496
8: 9 save the two tables of s, which Moses put H68
21:10 him out, and s him, that he may die. H5619
2Ki 3:25 cast every man his s, and filled it; and H68
12:12 And to masons, and hewers of s, and to H68
12 buy timber and hewed s to repair the H68
19:18 s: therefore they have destroyed them. H68
22: 6 timber and hewn s to repair the house. H68
1Ch 22:14 timber also and s have I prepared; and H68
15 and workers of s and timber, and all H68
2Ch 2:14 in brass, in iron, in s, and in timber, in H68
34:11 they *it*, to buy hewn s, and timber for H68
Neh 4: 3 he shall even break down their s wall. H68
9:11 the deeps, as a s into the mighty waters. H68
Job 28: 2 earth, and brass *is* molten *out of* the s. H68
38: 6 or who laid the corner s thereof; H68
30 The waters are hid as *with* a s, and the H68
41:24 His heart is as firm as a s; yea, as hard as H68
Ps 91:12 hands, lest thou dash thy foot against a s. H68
118:22 The s *which* the builders refused is H68
22 is become the head *s* of the corner.
Prv 17: 8 A gift *is as* a precious s in the eyes of him H68
24:31 and the s wall thereof was broken down. H68
26: 8 As he that bindeth a s in a sling, so *is* he H68
27 that rolleth a s, it will return upon him. H68
27: 3 A s *is* heavy, and the sand weighty; but a H68
Isa 8:14 but for a s of stumbling and for H68
28:16 Zion for a foundation a s, a tried stone, a H68
16 a stone, a tried s, a precious corner H68
16 a precious corner *s*, a sure foundation: he
37:19 s: therefore they have destroyed them. H68
Jer 2:27 my father; and to a s, Thou hast brought H68
51:26 And they shall not take of thee a s for a H68
26 for a corner, nor a s for foundations; but H68
63 thou shalt bind a s to it, and cast it into H68
Lam 3: 9 He hath inclosed my ways with hewn s, H1496
53 in the dungeon, and cast a s upon me. H68
Ezk 1:26 of a sapphire s: and upon the likeness H68
10: 1 it were a sapphire s, as the appearance of H68
9 the wheels *was* as the colour of a beryl s. H68
16:40 and they shall s thee with stones, and H7275
20:32 of the countries, to serve wood and s. H68
23:47 And the company shall s them with H7275
28:13 every precious s *was* thy covering, the H68
40:42 And the four tables *were* of hewn s for H68
Dan 2:34 Thou sawest till that a s was cut out H69
35 for them: and the s that smote the image H69
45 Forasmuch as thou sawest that the s was H69
5: 4 silver, of brass, of iron, of wood, and of s. H69
23 iron, wood, and s, which see not, nor H69
6:17 And a s was brought, and laid upon the H69
Am 5:11 houses of hewn s, but ye shall not dwell H1496
Hab 2:11 For the s shall cry out of the wall, and H68
19 to the dumb s, Arise, it shall teach! H68
Hag 2:15 from before a s was laid upon a stone H68
15 laid upon a s in the temple of the LORD: H68
Zec 3: 9 For behold the s that I have laid before H68
9 Joshua; upon one s *shall be* seven eyes: H68
7:12 *as* an adamant s, lest they should hear H8068
12: 3 a burdensome s for all people: all that H68
Mt 4: 6 any time thou dash thy foot against a s. G3037
7: 9 if his son ask bread, will he give him a s? G3037
21:42 the scriptures, The s which the builders G3037
Mt 21:44 And whosoever shall fall on this s shall G3037
24: 2 be left here one s upon another, that G3037
27:60 he rolled a great s to the door of the G3037
66 sure, sealing the s, and setting a watch. G3037
28: 2 the s from the door, and sat upon it. G3037
Mk 12:10 this scripture; The s which the builders G3037
13: 2 not be left one s upon another, that G3037
15:46 a s unto the door of the sepulchre. G3037
16: 3 the s from the door of the sepulchre? G3037
4 s was rolled away: for it was very great. G3037
Lk 4: 3 command this s that it be made bread. G3037
11 any time thou dash thy foot against a s. G3037
11:11 will he give him a s? or if *he ask* a fish, G3037
19:44 not leave in thee one s upon another; G3037
20: 6 men; all the people will s us: for they be G2642
17 is written, The s which the builders G3037
18 Whosoever shall fall upon that s shall G3037
21: 6 not be left one s upon another, that G3037
23:53 s, wherein never man before was laid. G2991
24: 2 And they found the s rolled away from G3037
Jn 1:42 Cephas, which is by interpretation, A s. G4074
2: 6 six waterpots of s, after the manner of G3035
8: 7 among you, let him first cast a s at her. G3037
10:31 Then the Jews took up stones again to s G3034
32 for which of those works do ye s me? G3034
33 For a good work we s thee not; but for G3034
11: 8 to s thee; and goest thou thither again? G3034
38 It was a cave, and a s lay upon it. G3037
39 Jesus said, Take ye away the s. Martha, G3037
41 Then they took away the s *from the* G3037
20: 1 the s taken away from the sepulchre. G3037
Act 4:11 This is the s which was set at nought of G3037
14: 5 to use *them* despitefully, and to s them, G3036
17:29 or s, graven by art and man's device. G3037
2Co 3: 3 of s, but in fleshy tables of the heart. G3035
Eph 2:20 Christ himself being the chief corner *s*;
1Pt 2: 4 To whom coming, *as unto* a living s, G3037
6 in Sion a chief corner s, elect, precious: G3037
7 be disobedient, the s which the builders G3037
8 And a s of stumbling, and a rock of G3037
Rev 2:17 give him a white s, and in the stone a G5586
17 stone, and in the s a new name written, G5586
4: 3 jasper and a sardine s: and *there was* a G3037
9:20 and brass, and s, and of wood: which G3035
16:21 of heaven, *every s* about the weight of a
18:21 And a mighty angel took up a s like a G3037
21:11 *was* like unto a s most precious, even G3037
11 even like a jasper s, clear as crystal; G3037

STONED
Ex 19:13 but he shall surely be s, or shot through; H5619
21:28 ox shall be surely s, and his flesh shall H5619
29 the ox shall be s, and his owner also H5619
32 shekels of silver, and the ox shall be s. H5619
Nu 15:36 the camp, and s him with stones, and H7275
Jos 7:25 day. And all Israel s him with stones, H7275
25 fire, after they had s them with stones. H5619
1Ki 12:18 and all Israel s him with stones, that H7275
21:13 and s him with stones, that he died. H5619
14 saying, Naboth is s, and is dead. H5619
15 that Naboth was s, and was dead, that H5619
2Ch 10:18 the children of Israel s him with stones, H7275
24:21 And they conspired against him, and s H7275
Mt 21:35 one, and killed another, and s another. G3036
Jn 8: 5 such should be s: but what sayest thou? G3036
Act 5:26 the people, lest they should have been s. G3034
7:58 And cast *him* out of the city, and s *him*: G3036
59 And they s Stephen, calling upon *God*, G3036
14:19 and, having s Paul, drew *him* out G3034
2Co 11:25 with rods, once was I s, thrice I suffered G3034
Heb 11:37 They were s, they were sawn asunder, G3034
12:20 shall be s, or thrust through with a dart: G3036

STONES
Gen 28:11 and he took of the s of that place, and H68
31:46 brethren, Gather s; and they took stones, H68
46 and they took s, and made an heap: and H68
Ex 25: 7 Onyx s, and stones to be set in the ephod, H68
7 Onyx stones, and s to be set in the H68
28: 9 And thou shalt take two onyx s, and H68
11 engrave the two s with the names of the H68
12 And thou shalt put the two s upon the H68
12 of the ephod *for* s of memorial unto the H68
17 And thou shalt set in it settings of s, *even* H68
17 *even* four rows of s: *the first* row *shall be* H68
21 And the s shall be with the names of the H68
31: 5 And in cutting of s, to set *them*, and in H68
35: 9 And onyx s, and stones to be set for the H68
9 And onyx stones, and s to be set for the H68

Ex 35:27 And the rulers brought onyx s, and H68
27 onyx stones, and s to be set, for the H68
33 And in the cutting of s, to set *them*, and H68
39: 6 And they wrought onyx s inclosed in H68
7 *that they should be* s for a memorial to H68
10 And they set in it four rows of s: *the first* H68
14 And the s *were* according to the names H68
Lev 14:40 they take away the s in which the plague H68
42 And they shall take other s, and put *them* H68
42 in the place of those s; and he shall take H68
43 hath taken away the s, and after he hath H68
45 And he shall break down the house, the s H68
20: 2 people of the land shall stone him with s. H68
27 with s: their blood *shall be* upon them. H68
21:20 scurvy, or scabbed, or hath his s broken; H810
24:23 and stone him with s. And the children of H68
Nu 14:10 stone them with s. And the glory of the H68
15:35 shall stone him with s without the camp. H68
36 stoned him with s, and he died; as the H68
Dt 8: 9 in it; a land whose s *are* iron, and out of H68
13:10 And thou shalt stone him with s, that he H68
17: 5 and shalt stone them with s, till they die. H68
21:21 stone him with s, that he die: so shalt H68
22:21 stone her with s that she die: because H68
24 shall stone them with s that they die; the H68
23: 1 He that is wounded in the s, or hath his
27: 2 great s, and plaister them with plaister: H68
4 ye shall set up these s, which I command H68
5 thy God, an altar of s: thou shalt not lift H68
6 thy God of whole s: and thou shalt offer H68
8 And thou shalt write upon the s all the H68
Jos 4: 3 stood firm, twelve s, and ye shall carry H68
6 come, saying, What *mean* ye by these s? H68
7 were cut off: and these s shall be for a H68
8 and took up twelve s out of the midst of H68
9 And Joshua set up twelve s in the midst H68
20 And those twelve s, which they took out H68
21 to come, saying, What *mean* these s? H68
7:25 stoned him with s, and burned them with H68
25 fire, after they had stoned them with s. H68
26 a great heap of s unto this day. So the H68
8:29 heap of s, *that remaineth* unto this day. H68
31 an altar of whole s, over which no man H68
32 And he wrote there upon the s a copy of H68
10:11 cast down great s from heaven upon H68
18 And Joshua said, Roll great s upon the H68
27 hid, and laid great s in the cave's mouth, H68
Jdg 20:16 sling s at an hair *breadth*, and not miss. H68
1Sa 17:40 him five smooth s out of the brook, and H68
2Sa 12:30 with the precious s: and it was *set* on H68
16: 6 And he cast s at David, and at all the H68
13 went, and threw s at him, and cast dust. H68
18:17 a very great heap of s upon him: and all H68
1Ki 5:17 they brought great s, costly stones, *and* H68
17 great stones, costly s, *and* hewed stones, H68
17 s, to lay the foundation of the house. H68
18 timber and s to build the house. H68
7: 9 All these *were of* costly s, according to H68
9 of hewed s, sawed with saws, within H1496
10 And the foundation *was of* costly s, even H68
10 stones, even great s, stones of ten cubits, H68
10 even great stones, s of ten cubits, and H68
10 of ten cubits, and s of eight cubits. H68
11 And above *were* costly s, after the H68
11 the measures of hewed s, and cedars. H1496
12 rows of hewed s, and a row of cedar H1496
10: 2 gold, and precious s: and when she was H68
10 store, and precious s: there came no H68
11 plenty of almug trees, and precious s. H68
27 *be* in Jerusalem as s, and cedars made he H68
12:18 Israel stoned him with s, that he died. H68
15:22 they took away the s of Ramah, and the H68
18:31 And Elijah took twelve s, according to the H68
32 And with the s he built an altar in the H68
38 the wood, and the s, and the dust, and H68
21:13 city, and stoned him with s, that he died. H68
2Ki 3:19 and mar every good piece of land with s. H68
25 left they the s thereof; howbeit the H68
16:17 it, and put it upon a pavement of s. H68
1Ch 12: 2 the left in *hurling* s and *shooting* arrows H68
20: 2 *were* precious s in it; and it was set upon H68
22: 2 hew wrought s to build the house of God. H68
29: 2 of wood; onyx s, and *stones* to be set, H68
2 onyx stones, and *s* to be set, glistering
2 *stones* to be set, glistering s, and of divers H68
2 s, and marble stones in abundance. H68
2 stones, and marble s in abundance. H68
8 And they with whom *precious* s were H68
2Ch 1:15 *as plenteous* as s, and cedar trees made H68
2Ch 3: 6 with precious s for beauty: and the gold H68
9: 1 and precious s: and when she was come H68
9 and precious s: neither was there any H68
10 brought algum trees and precious s. H68
27 in Jerusalem as s, and cedar trees made H68
10:18 stoned him with s, that he died. But king H68
16: 6 carried away the s of Ramah, and the H68
24:21 stoned him with s at the commandment H68
26:14 and bows, and slings *to cast* s. H68
15 arrows and great s withal. And his name H68
32:27 and for precious s, and for spices, and H68
Ezr 5: 8 builded with great s, and timber is laid in H69
6: 4 *With* three rows of great s, and a row of H69
Neh 4: 2 will they revive the s out of the heaps of H68
Job 5:23 For thou shalt be in league with the s of H68
6:12 *Is* my strength the strength of s? or *is* my H68
8:17 about the heap, *and* seeth the place of s. H68
14:19 The waters wear the s: thou washest H68
22:24 the *gold* of Ophir as the s of the brooks. H6697
28: 3 s of darkness, and the shadow of death. H68
6 The s of it *are* the place of sapphires: H68
40:17 sinews of his s are wrapped together. H6344
41:30 Sharp s *are* under him: he spreadeth H2789
Ps 18:12 clouds passed, hail *s* and coals of fire.
13 gave his voice; hail *s* and coals of fire.
102:14 For thy servants take pleasure in her s, H68
137: 9 dasheth thy little ones against the s. H5553
144:12 *may be* as corner s, polished *after* the H2106
Ecc 3: 5 A time to cast away s, and a time to H68
5 and a time to gather s together; a time to H68
10: 9 Whoso removeth s shall be hurt H68
Isa 5: 2 gathered out the s thereof, and planted H5619
9:10 build with hewn s: the sycomores are H1496
14:19 that go down to the s of the pit; as a H68
27: 9 when he maketh all the s of the altar as H68
34:11 line of confusion, and the s of emptiness. H68
54:11 I will lay thy s with fair colours, and H68
12 and all thy borders of pleasant s. H68
57: 6 Among the smooth *s* of the stream *is* thy
60:17 brass, and for s iron: I will also make H68
62:10 the s; lift up a standard for the people. H68
Jer 3: 9 adultery with s and with stocks. H68
43: 9 Take great s in thine hand, and hide H68
10 throne upon these s that I have hid; and H68
Lam 3:16 s, he hath covered me with ashes. H2687
4: 1 gold changed! the s of the sanctuary are H68
Ezk 16:40 shall stone thee with s, and thrust thee H68
23:47 stone them with s, and dispatch them H68
26:12 they shall lay thy s and thy timber and H68
27:22 spices, and with all precious s, and gold. H68
28:14 up and down in the midst of the s of fire. H68
16 cherub, from the midst of the s of fire. H68
Dan 11:38 and with precious s, and pleasant things. H68
Mic 1: 6 I will pour down the s thereof into the H68
Zec 5: 4 the timber thereof and the s thereof. H68
9:15 subdue with sling s; and they shall drink, H68
16 they *shall be as* the s of a crown, lifted H68
Mt 3: 9 s to raise up children unto Abraham. G3037
4: 3 command that these s be made bread. G3037
Mk 5: 5 crying, and cutting himself with s. G3037
12: 4 at him they cast s, and wounded *him* in G3036
13: 1 of s and what buildings *are here*! G3037
Lk 3: 8 s to raise up children unto Abraham. G3037
19:40 the s would immediately cry out. G3037
21: 5 with goodly s and gifts, he said, G3037
Jn 8:59 Then took they up s to cast at him: but G3037
10:31 Then the Jews took up s again to stone G3037
1Co 3:12 silver, precious s, wood, hay, stubble; G3037
2Co 3: 7 *and* engraven in s, was glorious, so that G3037
1Pt 2: 5 Ye also, as lively s, are built up a G3037
Rev 17: 4 gold and precious s and pearls, having G3037
18:12 and precious s, and of pearls, and fine G3037
16 with gold, and precious s, and pearls! G3037
21:19 of precious s. The first foundation G3037

STONE'S
Lk 22:41 s cast, and kneeled down, and prayed, G3037

STONESQUARERS
1Ki 5:18 hew *them*, and the s: so they prepared H1382

STONEST
Mt 23:37 the prophets, and s them which are G3036
Lk 13:34 the prophets, and s them that are sent G3036

STONING
1Sa 30: 6 people spake of s him, because the soul H5619

STONY
Ps 141: 6 When their judges are overthrown in s H5553
Ezk 11:19 and I will take the s heart out of their H68
36:26 I will take away the s heart out of your H68
Mt 13: 5 Some fell upon s places, where they G4075
20 But he that received the seed into s G4075
Mk 4: 5 And some fell on s ground, where it G4075
16 are sown on s ground; who, when G4075

STOOD
Gen 18: 2 and, lo, three men s by him: and when H5324
8 them; and he s by them under the tree, H5975
22 but Abraham s yet before the LORD. H5975
19:27 the place where he s before the LORD: H5975
23: 3 And Abraham s up from before his H6965
7 And Abraham s up, and bowed himself H6965
24:30 behold, he s by the camels at the well. H5975
28:13 And, behold, the LORD s above it, and H5324
37: 7 arose, and also s upright; and, behold, H5324
7 your sheaves s round about, and made
41: 1 and, behold, he s by the river. H5975
3 leanfleshed; and s by the *other* kine H5975
17 behold, I s upon the bank of the river: H5975
46 years old when he s before Pharaoh H5975
43:15 down to Egypt, and s before Joseph. H5975
45: 1 all them that s by him; and he cried, H5324
1 me. And there s no man with him, H5975
Ex 2: 4 And his sister s afar off, to wit what H3320
17 away: but Moses s up and helped them, H6965
5:20 And they met Moses and Aaron, who s H5324
9:10 the furnace, and s before Pharaoh; and H5975
14:19 before their face, and s behind them: H5975
15: 8 the floods s upright as an heap, H5324
18:13 and the people s by Moses from the H5975
19:17 they s at the nether part of the mount. H3320
20:18 saw *it*, they removed, and s afar off. H5975
21 And the people s afar off, and Moses H5975
32:26 Then Moses s in the gate of the camp, H5975
33: 8 rose up, and s every man *at* his tent H5324
9 descended, and s *at* the door of the H5975
34: 5 in the cloud, and s with him there, and H3320
Lev 9: 5 drew near and s before the LORD. H5975
Nu 11:32 And the people s up all that day, and H6965
12: 5 of the cloud, and s *in* the door of the H5975
16:18 thereon, and s in the door of the H5975
27 came out, and s in the door of their H5324
48 And he s between the dead and the H5975
22:22 angel of the LORD s in the way for an H3320
24 But the angel of the LORD s in a path H5975
26 went further, and s in a narrow place, H5975
23: 6 And he returned unto him, and, lo, he s H5324
17 And when he came to him, behold, he s H5324
27: 2 And they s before Moses, and before H5975
Dt 4:11 And ye came near and s under the H5975
5: 5 (I s between the LORD and you at that H5975
31:15 cloud s over the door of the tabernacle. H5975
Jos 3:16 down from above s *and* rose up upon H5975
17 of the LORD s firm on dry ground H5975
4: 3 the priests' feet s firm, twelve stones, H4673
9 s: and they are there unto this day. H4673
10 For the priests which bare the ark s in H5975
5:13 looked, and, behold, there s a man over H5975
8:33 and their judges, s on this side the ark H5975
10:13 And the sun s still, and the moon H1826
13 Jasher? So the sun s still in the midst of H5975
11:13 But *as for* the cities that s still in their H5975
20: 9 until he s before the congregation. H5975
21:44 fathers: and there s not a man of all H5975
Jdg 3:19 all that s by him went out from him. H5975
6:31 And Joash said unto all that s against H5975
7:21 And they s every man in his place. H5975
9: 7 he went and s in the top of mount H5975
35 went out, and s in the entering of the H5975
44 forward, and s in the entering of the H5975
16:29 which the house s, and on which it was H3559
18:16 of Dan, s by the entering of the gate. H5324
17 and the priest s in the entering of the H5324
20:28 the son of Aaron, s before it in those H5975
1Sa 1:26 s by thee here, praying unto the LORD. H5324
3:10 And the LORD came, and s, and called H3320
4:20 the women that s by her said unto her, H5324
6:14 a Bethshemite, and s there, where *there* H5975
10:23 and when he s among the people, he H3320
16:21 And David came to Saul, and s before H5975
17: 3 And the Philistines s on a mountain on H5975
3 side, and Israel s on a mountain on the H5975
8 And he s and cried unto the armies of H5975
26 And David spake to the men that s by H5975
51 Therefore David ran, and s upon the H5975

1Sa 22: 7 Then Saul said unto his servants that s H5324
17 the footmen that s about him, Turn, H5324
26:13 to the other side, and s on the top of an H5975
2Sa 1:10 So I s upon him, and slew him, because H5975
2:23 where Asahel fell down and died s still. H5975
25 one troop, and s on the top of an hill. H5975
28 and all the people s still, and pursued H5975
13:31 servants s by with their clothes rent. H5324
15: 2 And Absalom rose up early, and s beside
18: 4 do. And the king s by the gate side, and H5975
30 here. And he turned aside, and s still. H5975
20:11 And one of Joab's men s by him, and H5975
12 that all the people s still, he removed H5975
12 that every one that came by him s still. H5975
15 the city, and it s in the trench: and all H5975
23:12 But he s in the midst of the ground, H3320
1Ki 1:28 king's presence, and s before the king. H5975
3:15 to Jerusalem, and s before the ark of H5975
16 unto the king, and s before him. H5975
7:25 It s upon twelve oxen, three looking H5975
8:14 (and all the congregation of Israel s;) H5975
22 And Solomon s before the altar of the H5975
55 And he s, and blessed all the H5975
10:19 seat, and two lions s beside the stays. H5975
20 And twelve lions s there on the one side H5975
12: 6 the old men, that s before Solomon his H5975
8 up with him, *and* which s before him: H5975
13: 1 s by the altar to burn incense. H5975
24 way, and the ass s by it, the lion also H5975
24 by it, the lion also s by the carcase. H5975
19:13 and went out, and s in the entering in H5975
22:21 And there came forth a spirit, and s H5975
2Ki 2: 7 went, and s to view afar off: and H5975
7 view afar off: and they two s by Jordan. H5975
13 back, and s by the bank of Jordan; H5975
3:21 and upward, and s in the border. H5975
4:12 he had called her, she s before him. H5975
15 he had called her, she s in the door. H5975
5: 9 and s at the door of the house of Elisha. H5975
15 and came, and s before him: and he H5975
25 But he went in, and s before his H5975
8: 9 and came and s before him, and said, H5975
9:17 And there s a watchman on the tower H5975
10: 4 Behold, two kings s not before him: H5975
9 he went out, and s, and said to all the H5975
11:11 And the guard s, every man with his H5975
14 behold, the king s by a pillar, as the H5975
13:21 Elisha, he revived, and s up on his feet. H6965
18:17 up, they came and s by the conduit of H5975
28 Then Rab-shakeh s and cried with a H5975
23: 3 And the king s by a pillar, and made a H5975
3 And all the people s to the covenant. H5975
1Ch 6:39 And his brother Asaph, who s on his H5975
44 And their brethren the sons of Merari *s*
21: 1 And Satan s up against Israel, and H5975
15 the angel of the LORD s by the H5975
28: 2 Then David the king s up upon his feet, H6965
2Ch 3:13 cubits: and they s on their feet, and H5975
4: 4 It s upon twelve oxen, three looking H5975
5:12 and harps, s at the east end of the H5975
6: 3 and all the congregation of Israel s. H5975
12 And he s before the altar of the LORD H5975
13 and upon it he s, and kneeled down H5975
7: 6 trumpets before them, and all Israel s. H5975
9:19 And twelve lions s there on the one side H5975
10: 6 old men that had s before Solomon his H5975
8 up with him, that s before him. H5975
13: 4 And Abijah s up upon mount H6965
18:20 Then there came out a spirit, and s H5975
20: 5 And Jehoshaphat s in the congregation H5975
13 And all Judah s before the LORD, with H5975
19 of the Korhites, s up to praise the H6965
20 Jehoshaphat s and said, Hear me, H5975
23 and Moab s up against the inhabitants H5975
23:13 And she looked, and, behold, the king s H5975
24:20 the priest, which s above the people, H5975
28:12 the son of Hadlai, s up against them H6965
29:26 And the Levites s with the instruments H5975
30:16 And they s in their place after their H5975
34:31 And the king s in his place, and made a H5975
35:10 and the priests s in their place, and the H5975
Ezr 2:63 things, till there s up a priest with Urim H5975
3: 2 Then s up Jeshua the son of Jozadak, H6965
9 Then s Jeshua *with* his sons and his H5975
10:10 And Ezra the priest s up, and said unto H6965
Neh 7:65 things, till there s *up* a priest with Urim H5975
8: 4 And Ezra the scribe s upon a pulpit of H5975
4 and beside him s Mattithiah, and H5975
5 when he opened it, all the people s up: H5975

Neh 8: 7 the law: and the people *s* in their place.
9: 2 all strangers, and s and confessed their H5975
3 And they s up in their place, and read H6965
4 Then s up upon the stairs, of the H6965
12:39 gate: and they s still in the prison gate. H5975
40 So s the two *companies of them that* H5975
Est 5: 1 royal *apparel*, and s in the inner court H5975
9 gate, that he s not up, nor moved for H6965
7: 7 and Haman s up to make request H5975
8: 4 So Esther arose, and s before the king, H5975
9:16 together, and s for their lives, and had H5975
Job 4:15 my face; the hair of my flesh s up: H5568
16 It s still, but I could not discern the H5975
29: 8 and the aged arose, *and* s up. H5975
30:28 I went mourning without the sun: I s H6965
32:16 not, but s still, *and* answered no more;) H5978
Ps 33: 9 *done*; he commanded, and it s fast. H5978
104: 6 the waters s above the mountains. H5975
106:23 Moses his chosen s before him in the H5975
30 Then s up Phinehas, and executed H5975
Isa 6: 2 Above it s the seraphims: each one had H5975
36: 2 army. And he s by the conduit of the H5975
13 Then Rabshakeh s, and cried with a H5975
Jer 15: 1 and Samuel s before me, *yet* my mind H5975
18:20 Remember that I s before thee to speak H5975
19:14 prophesy; and he s in the court of the H5975
23:18 For who hath s in the counsel of the H5975
22 But if they had s in my counsel, and H5975
28: 5 people that s in the house of the LORD, H5975
36:21 all the princes which s beside the king. H5975
44:15 and all the women that s by, a great H5975
46:15 swept away? they s not, because the H5975
48:45 They that fled s under the shadow of H5975
Lam 2: 4 like an enemy: he s with his right hand H5324
Ezk 1:21 and when those s, *these* stood; and H5975
21 those stood, *these* s; and when those H5975
24 when they s, they let down their wings. H5975
25 they s, *and* had let down their wings. H5975
3:23 glory of the LORD s there, as the glory H5975
8:11 And there s before them seventy men H5975
11 the midst of them s Jaazaniah the son H5975
9: 2 went in, and s beside the brasen altar. H5975
10: 3 Now the cherubims s on the right side H5975
4 the cherub, *and s* over the threshold of
6 he went in, and s beside the wheels. H5975
17 When they s, *these* stood; and when H5975
17 When they stood, *these* s; and when H5975
18 of the house, and s over the cherubims. H5975
19 and *every one* s at the door of the east H5975
11:23 of the city, and s upon the mountain H5975
21:21 For the king of Babylon s at the parting H5975
37:10 they lived, and s up upon their feet, an H5975
40: 3 a measuring reed; and he s in the gate. H5975
43: 6 out of the house; and the man s by me. H5975
47: 1 of the house s *toward* the east, and
Dan 1:19 therefore s they before the king. H5975
2: 2 So they came and s before the king. H5975
31 *was* excellent, s before thee; and the H6966
3: 3 set up; and they s before the image that H6966
7:10 times ten thousand s before him: the H6966
16 I came near unto one of them that s by, H6966
8: 3 and, behold, there s before the river a H5975
15 then, behold, there s before me as the H5975
17 So he came near where I s: and when he H5977
22 Now that being broken, whereas four s H5975
10:11 this word unto me, I s trembling. H5975
16 said unto him that s before me, O my H5975
11: 1 I, s to confirm and to strengthen him. H5977
12: 5 and, behold, there s other two, the one H5975
Hos 10: 9 of Gibeah: there they s: the battle in H5975
Am 7: 7 behold, the Lord s upon a wall *made* by H5324
Oba 14 Neither shouldest thou have s in the H5975
Hab 3: 6 He s, and measured the earth: he H5975
11 The sun *and* moon s still in their H5975
Zec 1: 8 a red horse, and he s among the myrtle H5975
10 And the man that s among the myrtle H5975
11 of the LORD that s among the myrtle H5975
3: 3 filthy garments, and s before the angel. H5975
4 unto those that s before him, saying, H5975
5 And the angel of the LORD s by. H5975
Mt 2: 9 and s over where the young child was. G2476
12:46 s without, desiring to speak with him. G2476
13: 2 the whole multitude s on the shore. G2476
20:32 And Jesus s still, and called them, and G2476
26:73 unto *him* they that s by, and said to G2476
27:11 And Jesus s before the governor: and G2476
47 Some of them that s there, when they G2476
Mk 10:49 And Jesus s still, and commanded him G2476
11: 5 And certain of them that s there said G2476

Mk 14:47 And one of them that s by drew a G3936
60 And the high priest s up in the midst, G450
69 to them that s by, This is *one* of them. G3936
70 after, they that s by said again to Peter, G3936
15:35 And some of them that s by, when they G3936
39 And when the centurion, which s over G3936
Lk 4:16 on the sabbath day, and s up for to read. G450
39 And he s over her, and rebuked the G2186
5: 1 of God, he s by the lake of Gennesaret, G2258
6: 8 in the midst. And he arose and s forth. G2476
17 And he came down with them, and s in G2476
7:14 they that bare *him* s still. And he said, G2476
38 And s at his feet behind *him* weeping, G2476
9:32 glory, and the two men that s with him. G4921
10:25 And, behold, a certain lawyer s up, and G450
17:12 men that were lepers, which s afar off: G2476
18:11 The Pharisee s and prayed thus with G2476
40 And Jesus s, and commanded him to be G2476
19: 8 And Zacchaeus s, and said unto the G2476
24 And he said unto them that s by, Take G3936
23:10 And the chief priests and scribes s and G2476
35 And the people s beholding. And the G2476
49 s afar off, beholding these things. G2476
24: 4 men s by them in shining garments: G2186
36 And as they thus spake, Jesus himself s G2476
Jn 1:35 Again the next day after John s, and G2476
6:22 the people which s on the other side of G2476
7:37 of the feast, Jesus s and cried, saying, If G2476
11:56 as they s in the temple, What G2476
12:29 The people therefore, that s by, and G2476
18: 5 also, which betrayed him, s with them. G2476
16 But Peter s at the door without. Then G2476
18 And the servants and officers s there, G2476
18 s with them, and warmed himself. G2258
22 of the officers which s by struck Jesus G3936
25 And Simon Peter s and warmed G2258
19:25 Now there s by the cross of Jesus his G2476
20:11 But Mary s without at the sepulchre G2476
19 came Jesus and s in the midst, and G2476
26 being shut, and s in the midst, and G2476
21: 4 now come, Jesus s on the shore: but the G2476
Act 1:10 two men s by them in white apparel; G3936
15 And in those days Peter s up in the G450
3: 8 And he leaping up s, and walked, and G2476
4:26 The kings of the earth s up, and the G3936
5:34 Then s there up one in the council, a G450
9: 7 with him s speechless, hearing G2476
39 all the widows s by him weeping, and G3936
10:17 Simon's house, and s before the gate, G2186
30 a man s before me in bright clothing, G2476
11:13 his house, which s and said unto him, G2476
28 And there s up one of them named G450
12:14 and told how Peter s before the gate. G2476
13:16 Then Paul s up, and beckoning with *his* G450
14:20 Howbeit, as the disciples s round about G2944
16: 9 Paul in the night; There s a man of G2258
17:22 Then Paul s in the midst of Mars' hill, G2476
21:40 him licence, Paul s on the stairs, and G2476
22:13 Came unto me, and s, and said unto G2186
25 the centurion that s by, Is it lawful for G2476
23: 2 s by him to smite him on the mouth. G3936
4 And they that s by said, Revilest thou G3936
11 And the night following the Lord s by G2186
24:20 in me, while I s before the council, G2476
25: 7 from Jerusalem s round about, and G4026
18 Against whom when the accusers s up, G2476
27:21 But after long abstinence Paul s forth G2476
23 For there s by me this night the angel of G3936
2Ti 4:16 At my first answer no man s with me, G4836
17 Notwithstanding the Lord s with me, G3936
Heb 9:10 *Which* s only in meats and drinks, and
Rev 5: 6 of the elders, s a Lamb as it had been G2476
7: 9 and tongues, s before the throne, and G2476
11 And all the angels s round about the G2476
8: 2 And I saw the seven angels which s G2476
3 And another angel came and s at the G2476
11: 1 a rod: and the angel s, saying, Rise, and G2476
11 them, and they s upon their feet; and G2476
12: 4 and the dragon s before the woman G2476
13: 1 And I s upon the sand of the sea, and G2476
14: 1 And I looked, and, lo, a Lamb s on the G2476
18:17 and as many as trade by sea, s afar off, G2476

STOODEST

Nu 22:34 not that thou s in the way against me: H5324
Dt 4:10 *Specially* the day that thou s before the H5975
Oba 11 In the day that thou s on the other side, H5975

STOOL
2Ki 4:10 and a table, and a **s**, and a candlestick: H3678

STOOLS
Ex 1:16 see *them* upon the **s**; if it *be* a son, then ye H70

STOOP
Job 9:13 the proud helpers do **s** under him. H7817
Prv 12:25 it **s**: but a good word maketh it glad. H7812
Isa 46: 2 They **s**, they bow down together; they H7164
Mk 1: 7 am not worthy to **s** down and unloose. *G2955*

STOOPED
Gen 49: 9 art gone up: he **s** down, he couched as H3766
1Sa 24: 8 him, David **s** with his face to the H6915
28:14 Samuel, and he **s** with *his* face to the H6915
2Ch 36:17 old man, or him that **s** for age: he gave H3486
Jn 8: 6 him. But Jesus **s** down, and with *his* *G2955*
8 And again he **s** down, and wrote on the *G2955*
20:11 **s** down, *and looked* into the sepulchre, *G3879*

STOOPETH
Isa 46: 1 Bel boweth down, Nebo **s**, their idols H7164

STOOPING
Lk 24:12 the sepulchre; and **s** down, he beheld *G3879*
Jn 20: 5 And he **s** down, *and looking in*, saw the *G3879*

STOP
1Ki 18:44 get thee down, that the rain **s** thee not. H6113
2Ki 3:19 good tree, and **s** all wells of water, and H5640
2Ch 32: 3 his mighty men to **s** the waters of the H5640
Ps 35: 3 Draw out also the spear, and **s** *the way* H5462
107:42 and all iniquity shall **s** her mouth. H7092
Ezk 39:11 the sea: and it shall **s** the *noses* of the H2629
2Co 11:10 me, no man shall **s** me of this boasting *G4972*

STOPPED
Gen 8: 2 of heaven were **s**, and the rain from H5534
26:15 had **s** them, and filled them with earth. H5640
18 for the Philistines had **s** them after the H5640
Lev 15: 3 **s** from his issue, it *is* his uncleanness. H2856
2Ki 3:25 and filled it; and they **s** all the wells of H5640
2Ch 32: 4 together, who **s** all the fountains, and H5640
30 This same Hezekiah also **s** the upper H5640
Neh 4: 7 to be **s**, then they were very wroth, H5640
Ps 63:11 of them that speak lies shall be **s**. H5534
Jer 51:32 And that the passages are **s**, and the H8610
Zec 7:11 **s** their ears, that they should not hear. H3513
Act 7:57 a loud voice, and **s** their ears, and ran *G4912*
Ro 3:19 mouth may be **s**, and all the world may *G5420*
Tit 1:11 Whose mouths must be **s**, who subvert *G1993*
Heb 11:33 promises, **s** the mouths of lions, *G5420*

STOPPETH
Job 5:16 So the poor hath hope, and iniquity **s** H7092
Ps 58: 4 *are* like the deaf adder *that* **s** her ear; H331
Prv 21:13 Whoso **s** his ears at the cry of the poor, H331
Isa 33:15 of bribes, that **s** his ears from hearing H331

STORE
Gen 26:14 of herds, and great **s** of servants: and the
41:36 And that food shall be for **s** to the land H6487
Lev 25:22 her fruits come in ye shall eat *of* the old **s**.
26:10 And ye shall eat old **s**, and bring forth H3462
Dt 28: 5 Blessed *shall be* thy basket and thy **s**. H4863
17 Cursed *shall be* thy basket and thy **s**. H4863
32:34 *Is* not this laid up in **s** with me, *and* H3647
1Ki 9:19 And all the cities of **s** that Solomon H4543
10:10 spices very great **s**, and precious stones: H7235
2Ki 20:17 have laid up in **s** unto this day, shall be H686
1Ch 29:16 O LORD our God, all this **s** that we H1995
2Ch 8: 4 the **s** cities, which he built in Hamath. H4543
6 And Baalath, and all the **s** cities that H4543
11:11 and **s** of victual, and of oil and wine. H214
16: 4 and all the **s** cities of Naphtali. H4543
17:12 he built in Judah castles, and cities of **s**. H4543
31:10 and that which is left *is* this great **s**. H1995
Neh 5:18 once in ten days **s** of all sorts of wine: H7235
Ps 144:13 all manner of **s**: *that* our sheep may bring
Isa 39: 6 have laid up in **s** until this day, shall be H686
Am 3:10 saith the LORD, who **s** up violence and H686
Nah 2: 9 *is* none end of the **s** *and* glory out of all H8498
1Co 16: 2 of you lay by him in **s**, as *God* hath *G2343*
1Ti 6:19 Laying up in **s** for themselves a good *G597*
2Pt 3: 7 word are kept in **s**, reserved unto fire *G2343*

STOREHOUSE
Mal 3:10 Bring ye all the tithes into the **s**, that H214
Lk 12:24 neither have **s** nor barn; and God *G5009*

STOREHOUSES
Gen 41:56 Joseph opened all the **s**, and sold unto the H834
Dt 28: 8 upon thee in thy **s**, and in all that thou H618
1Ch 27:25 Adiel: and over the **s** in the fields, in the H214
2Ch 32:28 **S** also for the increase of corn, and H4543
Ps 33: 7 as an heap: he layeth up the depth in **s**. H214
Jer 50:26 border, open her **s**: cast her up as H3965

STORIES
Gen 6:16 second, and third *s* shalt thou make it.
Ezk 41:16 on their three **s**, over against the door,
42: 3 *was* gallery against gallery in three *s*.
6 For they *were* in three *s*, but had not
Am 9: 6 *It is* he that buildeth his **s** in the H4609

STORK
Lev 11:19 And the **s**, the heron after her kind, and H2624
Dt 14:18 And the **s**, and the heron after her kind, H2624
Ps 104:17 *as for* the **s**, the fir trees *are* her house. H2624
Jer 8: 7 Yea, the **s** in the heaven knoweth her H2624
Zec 5: 9 like the wings of a **s**: and they lifted up H2624

STORM
Job 21:18 and as chaff that the **s** carrieth away. H5492
27:21 and as a **s** hurleth him out of his place.
Ps 55: 8 escape from the windy **s** *and* tempest. H5584
83:15 and make them afraid with thy **s**. H5492
107:29 He maketh the **s** a calm, so that the H5591
Isa 4: 6 and for a covert from **s** and from rain. H2230
25: 4 a refuge from the **s**, a shadow from the H2230
4 terrible ones *is* as a **s** *against* the wall. H2230
28: 2 *and* a destroying **s**, as a flood of mighty H8178
29: 6 great noise, with **s** and tempest, and H5492
Ezk 38: 9 Thou shalt ascend and come like a **s**, H7722
Nah 1: 3 **s**, and the clouds *are* the dust of his feet. H8183
Mk 4:37 And there arose a great **s** of wind, and *G2978*
Lk 8:23 came down a **s** of wind on the lake; *G2978*

STORMY
Ps 107:25 For he commandeth, and raiseth the **s** H5591
148: 8 Fire, and hail; snow, and vapour; **s** H5591
Ezk 13:11 shall fall; and a **s** wind shall rend *it*. H5591
13 even rend *it* with a **s** wind in my fury; H5591

STORY
2Ch 13:22 *are* written in the **s** of the prophet Iddo. H4097
24:27 *are* written in the **s** of the book of the H4097

STOUT
Job 4:11 the **s** lion's whelps are scattered abroad.
Isa 10:12 the fruit of the **s** heart of the king of H1433
Dan 7:20 look *was* more **s** than his fellows. H7229
Mal 3:13 Your words have been **s** against me, H2388

STOUTHEARTED
Ps 76: 5 The **s** are spoiled, they have slept H47+H3820
Isa 46:12 Hearken unto me, ye **s**, that *are* H47+H3820

STOUTNESS
Isa 9: 9 that say in the pride and **s** of heart, H1433

STRAIGHT
Jos 6: 5 shall ascend up every man **s** before him.
20 **s** before him, and they took the city.
1Sa 6:12 And the kine took the **s** way to the way H3474
2Ch 32:30 and brought it **s** down to the west side H3474
Ps 5: 8 make thy way **s** before my face. H3474
Prv 4:25 and let thine eyelids look **s** before thee. H3474
Ecc 1:15 cannot be made **s**: and that which is H8626
7:13 *that* **s**, which he hath made crooked? H8626
Isa 40: 3 **s** in the desert a highway for our God. H3474
4 be made **s**, and the rough places plain: H4334
42:16 crooked things **s**. These things will I do H4334
45: 2 the crooked places **s**: I will break in H3474
Jer 31: 9 of waters in a **s** way, wherein they shall H3477
Ezk 1: 7 And their feet *were* **s** feet; and the sole H3477
9 went; they went every one **s** forward. H5676
12 And they went every one **s** forward: H5676
23 *were* their wings **s**, the one toward the H3477
10:22 they went every one **s** forward. H5676
Mt 3: 3 the way of the Lord, make his paths **s**. *G2117*
Mk 1: 3 the way of the Lord, make his paths **s**. *G2117*
Lk 3: 4 the way of the Lord, make his paths **s**. *G2117*
5 shall be made **s**, and the rough ways *G2117*
13:13 she was made **s**, and glorified God. *G461*
Jn 1:23 wilderness, Make **s** the way of the Lord, *G2116*
Act 9:11 which is called **S**, and inquire in the *G2117*
16:11 Troas, we came with a **s** course to *G2113*
21: 1 we came with a **s** course unto Coos, *G2113*
Heb 12:13 And make **s** paths for your feet, lest *G3717*

STRAIGHTLY See STRAITLY.

STRAIGHTWAY
1Sa 9:13 the city, ye shall **s** find him, before he H3651
28:20 Then Saul fell **s** all along on the earth, H4116
Prv 7:22 He goeth after her **s**, as an ox goeth to H6597
Dan 10:17 lord? for as for me, **s** there remained no H6258
Mt 3:16 baptized, went up **s** out of the water: *G2117*
4:20 And they **s** left *their* nets, and followed *G2112*
14:22 And **s** Jesus constrained his disciples to *G2112*
27 But **s** Jesus spake unto them, saying, Be *G2112*
21: 2 against you, and **s** ye shall find an ass *G2112*
3 need of them; and **s** he will send them. *G2112*
25:15 several ability; and **s** took his journey. *G2112*
27:48 And **s** one of them ran, and took a *G2112*
Mk 1:10 And **s** coming up out of the water, he *G2112*
18 And **s** they forsook their nets, and *G2112*
20 And **s** he called them: and they left *G2112*
21 And they went into Capernaum; and **s** *G2112*
2: 2 And **s** many were gathered together, *G2112*
3: 6 And the Pharisees went forth, and **s** *G2112*
5:29 And **s** the fountain of her blood was *G2112*
42 And **s** the damsel arose, and walked; *G2112*
6:25 And she came in **s** with haste unto the *G2112*
45 And **s** he constrained his disciples to *G2112*
54 come out of the ship, **s** they knew him, *G2112*
7:35 And **s** his ears were opened, and the *G2112*
8:10 And **s** he entered into a ship with his *G2112*
9:15 And **s** all the people, when they beheld *G2112*
20 when he saw him, **s** the spirit tare him; *G2112*
24 And **s** the father of the child cried out, *G2112*
11: 3 of him; and **s** he will send him hither. *G2112*
14:45 was come, he goeth **s** to him, and saith, *G2112*
15: 1 And **s** in the morning the chief priests *G2112*
Lk 5:39 No man also having drunk old *wine* **s** *G2112*
8:55 **s**: and he commanded to give her meat. *G3916*
12:54 out of the west, **s** ye say, There cometh *G2112*
14: 5 not **s** pull him out on the sabbath day? *G2112*
Jn 13:32 him in himself, and shall **s** glorify him. *G2117*
Act 5:10 Then fell she down **s** at his feet, and *G3916*
9:20 And **s** he preached Christ in the *G2112*
16:33 and was baptized, he and all his, **s**. *G3916*
22:29 Then **s** they departed from him which *G2112*
23:30 for the man, I sent **s** to thee, and gave *G1824*
Jas 1:24 goeth his way, and **s** forgetteth what *G2112*

STRAIN
Mt 23:24 *Ye* blind guides, which **s** at a gnat, and *G1368*

STRAIT
1Sa 13: 6 that they were in a **s**, (for the people H6887
2Sa 24:14 I am in a great **s**: let us fall now into the H6887
2Ki 6: 1 where we dwell with thee is too **s** for us. H6862
1Ch 21:13 I am in a great **s**: let me fall now into H6887
Job 36:16 thee out of the **s** *into* a broad place, H6862
Isa 49:20 The place *is* too **s** for me: give place to H6862
Mt 7:13 Enter ye in at the **s** gate: for wide *is* the *G4728*
14 Because **s** *is* the gate, and narrow *is* the *G4728*
Lk 13:24 Strive to enter in at the **s** gate: for *G4728*
Php 1:23 For I am in a **s** betwixt two, having a *G4912*

STRAITEN
Jer 19: 9 they that seek their lives, shall **s** them. H6693

STRAITENED
Job 18: 7 The steps of his strength shall be **s**, and H3334
37:10 and the breadth of the waters is **s**. H4164
Prv 4:12 thy steps shall not be **s**; and when thou H3334
Ezk 42: 6 *the building* was **s** more than the lowest H680
Mic 2: 7 the spirit of the LORD **s**? *are* these his H7114
Lk 12:50 and how am I **s** till it be accomplished! *G4912*
2Co 6:12 Ye are not **s** in us, but ye are straitened *G4729*
12 Ye are not straitened in us, but ye are **s** *G4729*

STRAITENETH
Job 12:23 the nations, and **s** them *again*. H5148

STRAITEST
Act 26: 5 **s** sect of our religion I lived a Pharisee. *G196*

STRAITLY
Gen 43: 7 And they said, The man asked us **s** of H7592
Ex 13:19 him: for he had **s** sworn the children H7650
Jos 6: 1 Now Jericho was **s** shut up because of H5462
1Sa 14:28 said, Thy father **s** charged the people H7650

S

Mt 9:30 And their eyes were opened; and Jesus s
Mk 1:43 And he s charged him, and forthwith
3:12 And he s charged them that they G4183
5:43 And he charged them s that no man G4183
Lk 9:21 And he s charged them, and
Act 4:17 the people, let us s threaten them, that G547
5:28 Saying, Did not we s command you that

STRAITNESS
Dt 28:53 the siege, and in the s, wherewith thine H4689
55 the siege, and in the s, wherewith thine H4689
57 in the siege and s, wherewith thine H4689
Job 36:16 where *there is* no s; and that which H4164
Jer 19: 9 in the siege and s, wherewith their H4689

STRAITS
Job 20:22 he shall be in s: every hand of the H3334
Lam 1: 3 persecutors overtook her between the s. H4712

STRAKE
Act 27:17 quicksands, s sail, and so were driven. G5465

STRAKES
Gen 30:37 and pilled white s in them, and made H6479
Lev 14:37 the house with hollow s, greenish or H8258

STRANGE
Gen 35: 2 with him, Put away the s gods that *are* H5236
4 And they gave unto Jacob all the s gods H5236
42: 7 but made himself s unto them, and H5234
Ex 2:22 said, I have been a stranger in a s land. H5237
18: 3 said, I have been an alien in a s land: H5237
21: 8 to sell her unto a s nation he shall have H5237
30: 9 Ye shall offer no s incense thereon, nor H2114
Lev 10: 1 and offered s fire before the LORD, H2114
Nu 3: 4 when they offered s fire before the H2114
26:61 they offered s fire before the LORD. H2114
Dt 32:12 him, and *there was* no s god with him. H5236
16 They provoked him to jealousy with s H2114
Jos 24:20 If ye forsake the LORD, and serve s H5236
23 Now therefore put away, *said he,* the s H5236
Jdg 10:16 And they put away the s gods from H5236
11: 2 house; for thou *art* the son of a s woman. H312
1Sa 7: 3 hearts, *then* put away the s gods and H5236
1Ki 11: 1 But king Solomon loved many s H5237
8 And likewise did he for all his s wives, H5237
2Ki 19:24 I have digged and drunk s waters, and H2114
2Ch 14: 3 For he took away the altars of the s H5236
33:15 And he took away the s gods, and the H5236
Ezr 10: 2 and have taken s wives of the people H5237
10 and have taken s wives, to increase the H5237
11 of the land, and from the s wives. H5237
14 which have taken s wives in our cities H5237
17 that had taken s wives by the first day H5237
18 that had taken s wives: *namely,* of the H5237
44 All these had taken s wives: and *some* H5237
Neh 13:27 against our God in marrying s wives? H5237
Job 19: 3 *that* ye make yourselves s to me. H1970
17 My breath is s to my wife, though I H2114
31: 3 the wicked? and a s *punishment* to the H5235
Ps 44:20 or stretched out our hands to a s god; H2114
81: 9 There shall no s god be in thee; neither H2114
9 neither shalt thou worship any s god. H5236
114: 1 of Jacob from a people of s language; H3937
137: 4 we sing the LORD'S song in a s land? H5236
144: 7 waters, from the hand of s children; H5236
11 me from the hand of s children, whose H5236
Prv 2:16 To deliver thee from the s woman, *even* H2114
5: 3 For the lips of a s woman drop *as* an H2114
20 son, be ravished with a s woman, and H2114
6:24 the flattery of the tongue of a s woman. H5237
7: 5 That they may keep thee from the s H2114
20:16 take a pledge of him for a s woman. H5237
21: 8 The way of man *is* froward and s: but *as* H2054
22:14 The mouth of s women *is* a deep pit: he H2054
23:27 For a whore *is* a deep ditch; and a s H5237
33 Thine eyes shall behold s women, and H2114
27:13 take a pledge of him for a s woman. H5237
Isa 17:10 plants, and shalt set it with s slips: H2114
28:21 do his work, his s work; and bring to H2114
21 and bring to pass his act, his s act. H5237
43:12 when *there was* no s *god* among you: H2114
Jer 2:21 degenerate plant of a s vine unto me? H5237
5:19 me, and served s gods in your land, so H5236
8:19 graven images, *and* with s vanities? H5236
Ezk 3: 5 For thou *art* not sent to a people of a s H6012
6 Not to many people of a s speech and H6012
Dan 11:39 holds with a s god, whom he shall H5236
Hos 5: 7 have begotten s children: now shall H2114
Hos 8:12 law, *but* they were counted as a s thing. H2114
Zep 1: 8 all such as are clothed with s apparel. H5237
Mal 2:11 hath married the daughter of a s god. H5236
Lk 5:26 saying, We have seen s things to day. G3861
Act 7: 6 should sojourn in a s land; and that they G245
17:18 be a setter forth of s gods: because he G3581
20 For thou bringest certain s things to G3579
26:11 I persecuted *them* even unto s cities. G1854
Heb 11: 9 of promise, as *in* a s country, dwelling in G245
13: 9 Be not carried about with divers and s G3581
1Pt 4: 4 Wherein they think it s that ye run not G3579
12 Beloved, think it not s concerning the G3579
12 some s thing happened unto you: G3579
Jude 7 and going after s flesh, are set forth for G2087

STRANGELY
Dt 32:27 themselves s, *and* lest they should H5234

STRANGER
Gen 15:13 thy seed shall be a s in a land *that is* H1616
17: 8 land wherein thou art a s, all the land of H4033
12 any s, which *is* not of thy seed. H1121+H5236
27 s, were circumcised with him. H1121+H5236
23: 4 I *am* a s and a sojourner with you: give H1616
28: 4 art a s, which God gave unto Abraham. H4033
37: 1 father was a s, in the land of Canaan. H4033
Ex 2:22 said, I have been a s in a strange land. H1616
12:19 whether he be a s, or born in the land. H1616
43 There shall no s eat thereof: H1121+H5236
48 And when a s shall sojourn with thee, H1616
49 unto the s that sojourneth among you. H1616
20:10 cattle, nor thy s that *is* within thy gates: H1616
22:21 Thou shalt neither vex a s, nor oppress H1616
23: 9 Also thou shalt not oppress a s: for ye H1616
9 know the heart of a s, seeing ye were H1616
12 handmaid, and the s, may be refreshed. H1616
29:33 them: but a s shall not eat *thereof,* H2114
30:33 s, shall even be cut off from his people. H2114
Lev 16:29 or a s that sojourneth among you: H1616
17:12 s that sojourneth among you eat blood. H1616
15 own country, or a s, he shall both wash H1616
18:26 nor any s that sojourneth among you: H1616
19:10 poor and s: I *am* the LORD your God. H1616
33 And if a s sojourn with thee in your H1616
34 *But* the s that dwelleth with you shall H1616
22:10 There shall no s eat *of* the holy thing: a H2114
12 be *married* unto a s, she may not H376+H2114
13 meat: but there shall no s eat thereof. H2114
23:22 and to the s: I *am* the LORD your God. H1616
24:16 him: as well the s, as he that is born in H1616
22 law, as well for the s, as for one of your H1616
25: 6 and for thy s that sojourneth with thee, H8453
35 *though he be* a s, or a sojourner; that H1616
47 And if a sojourner or s wax rich by H8453
47 himself unto the s *or* sojourner by thee, H1616
Nu 1:51 set it up: and the s that cometh nigh H2114
3:10 office: and the s that cometh nigh shall H2114
38 of Israel; and the s that cometh nigh H2114
9:14 And if a s shall sojourn among you, H1616
14 both for the s, and for him that was H1616
15:14 And if a s sojourn with you, or H1616
15 and also for the s that sojourneth *with* H1616
15 *are,* so shall the s be before the LORD. H1616
16 and for the s that sojourneth with you. H1616
26 of Israel, and the s that sojourneth H1616
29 for the s that sojourneth among them. H1616
30 born in the land, or a s, the same H1616
16:40 Israel, that no s, which *is* not of H376+H2114
18: 4 and a s shall not come nigh unto you. H2114
7 of gift: and the s that cometh nigh shall H2114
19:10 and unto the s that sojourneth among H1616
35:15 of Israel, and for the s, and for the H1616
Dt 1:16 his brother, and the s *that is* with him. H1616
5:14 of thy cattle, nor thy s that *is* within thy H1616
10:18 the s, in giving him food and raiment. H1616
19 Love ye therefore the s: for ye were H1616
14:21 give it unto the s that *is* in thy gates, H1616
29 thee,) and the s, and the fatherless, and H1616
16:11 thy gates, and the s, and the fatherless, H1616
14 and the Levite, the s, and the fatherless, H1616
17:15 not set a s over thee, which H376+H5237
23: 7 because thou wast a s in his land. H1616
20 Unto a s thou mayest lend upon usury; H5237
24:17 judgment of the s, *nor* of the fatherless; H1616
19 it: it shall be for the s, for the fatherless, H1616
20 s, for the fatherless, and for the widow. H1616
21 s, for the fatherless, and for the widow. H1616
25: 5 without unto a s: her husband's H376+H2114
26:11 the Levite, and the s that *is* among you. H1616
Dt 26:12 the Levite, the s, the fatherless, and the H1616
13 and unto the s, to the fatherless, and H1616
27:19 the judgment of the s, fatherless, and H1616
28:43 The s that *is* within thee shall get up H1616
29:11 Your little ones, your wives, and thy s H1616
22 up after you, and the s that shall come H5237
31:12 children, and thy s that *is* within thy H1616
Jos 8:33 LORD, as well the s, as he that was born H1616
20: 9 of Israel, and for the s that sojourneth H1616
Jdg 19:12 into the city of a s, that *is* not of the H5237
Ru 2:10 take knowledge of me, seeing I *am* a s? H5237
2Sa 1:13 *am* the son of a s, an Amalekite. H376+H1616
15:19 king: for thou *art* a s, and also an exile. H5237
1Ki 3:18 *there was* no s with us in the house, H2114
8:41 Moreover concerning a s, that *is* not of H5237
43 to all that the s calleth to thee for: that H5237
2Ch 6:32 Moreover concerning the s, which is not H5237
33 to all that the s calleth to thee for; that H5237
Job 15:19 given, and no s passed among them. H2114
19:15 me for a s: I am an alien in their sight. H2114
31:32 The s did not lodge in the street: *but* I H1616
Ps 39:12 my tears: for I *am* a s with thee, *and* a H1616
69: 8 I am become a s unto my brethren, and H2114
94: 6 They slay the widow and the s, and H1616
119:19 I *am* a s in the earth: hide not thy H1616
Prv 2:16 the s *which* flattereth with her words; H5237
5:10 and thy labours *be* in the house of a s; H5237
20 woman, and embrace the bosom of a s? H5237
6: 1 *if* thou hast stricken thy hand with a s, H2114
7: 5 the s *which* flattereth with her words. H5237
11:15 He that is surety for a s shall smart *for* H2114
14:10 a s doth not intermeddle with his joy. H2114
20:16 Take his garment that is surety *for* a s: H2114
27: 2 own mouth; a s, and not thine own lips. H5237
13 Take his garment that is surety for a s, H2114
Ecc 6: 2 thereof, but a s eateth it: this *is* H376+H5237
Isa 56: 3 Neither let the son of the s, that hath H5236
6 Also the sons of the s, that join H5236
62: 8 and the sons of the s shall not drink thy H5236
Jer 7: 6 *If* ye oppress not the s, the fatherless, H1616
14: 8 thou be as a s in the land, and as a H1616
22: 3 no violence to the s, the fatherless, nor H1616
Ezk 14: 7 of Israel, or of the s that sojourneth in H1616
22: 7 with the s: in thee have they vexed H1616
29 they have oppressed the s wrongfully. H1616
44: 9 Thus saith the Lord GOD; No s, H1121+H5236
9 of any s that *is* among the H1121+H5236
47:23 in what tribe the s sojourneth, there H1616
Oba 12 that he became a s; neither shouldest H5235
Zec 7:10 the fatherless, the s, nor the poor; and H1616
Mal 3: 5 that turn aside the s *from his right,* and H1616
Mt 25:35 me drink: I was a s, and ye took me in: G3581
38 When saw we thee a s, and took *thee* in? G3581
43 I was a s, and ye took me not in: naked, G3581
44 or athirst, or a s, or naked, or sick, or G3581
Lk 17:18 returned to give glory to God, save this s. G241
24:18 Art thou only a s in Jerusalem, and G3939
Jn 10: 5 And a s will they not follow, but will flee G245
Act 7:29 this saying, and was a s in the land of G3941

STRANGERS
Gen 31:15 Are we not counted of him s? for he hath H5237
36: 7 wherein they were s could not bear H4033
Ex 6: 4 their pilgrimage, wherein they were s. H1481
22:21 him: for ye were s in the land of Egypt. H1616
23: 9 seeing ye were s in the land of Egypt. H1616
Lev 17: 8 of Israel, or of the s which sojourn H1616
10 house of Israel, or of the s that sojourn H1616
13 of Israel, or of the s that sojourn H1616
19:34 for ye were s in the land of Egypt: H1616
20: 2 of Israel, or of the s that sojourn in H1616
22:18 of Israel, or of the s in Israel, that will H1616
25:23 for ye *are* s and sojourners with me. H1616
45 Moreover of the children of the s that H8453
Dt 10:19 for ye were s in the land of Egypt. H1616
24:14 s that *are* in thy land within thy gates: H1616
31:16 the gods of the s of the land, whither H5236
Jos 8:35 s that were conversant among them. H1616
2Sa 22:45 S shall submit themselves unto H1121+H5236
46 S shall fade away, and they H1121+H5236
1Ch 16:19 ye were but few, even a few, and s in it. H1481
22: 2 together the s that *were* in the land H1616
29:15 For we *are* s before thee, and H1616
2Ch 2:17 all the s that *were* in the H582+H1616
15: 9 Benjamin, and the s with them out of H1481
30:25 of Israel, and the s that came out of the H1616
Neh 9: 2 from all s, and stood and H1121+H5236
13:30 Thus cleansed I them from all s, and H5236
Ps 18:44 obey me: the s shall submit H1121+H5236

Ps 18:45 The s shall fade away, and be H1121+H5236
54: 3 For s are risen up against me, and H2114
105:12 in number; yea, very few, and s in it. H1481
109:11 he hath; and let the s spoil his labour. H2114
146: 9 The LORD preserveth the s; he relieveth H1616
Prv 5:10 Lest s be filled with thy wealth; and thy H2114
Isa 1: 7 with fire: your land, s devour it in your H2114
7 and *it is* desolate, as overthrown by s. H2114
2: 6 please themselves in the children of s. H5237
5:17 waste places of the fat ones shall s eat. H1481
14: 1 own land: and the s shall be joined H1616
25: 2 of s to be no city; it shall never be built. H2114
5 Thou shalt bring down the noise of s, as H2114
29: 5 Moreover the multitude of thy s shall H2114
60:10 And the sons of s shall build up thy H5236
61: 5 And s shall stand and feed your flocks, H2114
Jer 2:25 I have loved s, and after them will I go. H2114
3:13 thy ways to the s under every green H2114
5:19 ye serve s in a land *that is* not yours. H2114
30: 8 thy bonds, and s shall no more serve H2114
35: 7 many days in the land where ye *be* s. H1481
51:51 our faces: for s are come into the H2114
Lam 5: 2 Our inheritance is turned to s, our H2114
Ezk 7:21 And I will give it into the hands of the s H2114
11: 9 you into the hands of s, and will execute H2114
16:32 *which* taketh s instead of her husband! H2114
28: 7 Behold, therefore I will bring s upon H2114
10 by the hand of s: for I have spoken *it*, H2114
30:12 hand of s: I the LORD have spoken *it*. H2114
31:12 And s, the terrible of the nations, have H2114
44: 7 *my sanctuary* s, uncircumcised H1121+H5236
47:22 you, and to the s that sojourn among H1616
Hos 7: 9 S have devoured his strength, and he H2114
8: 7 so be it yield, the s shall swallow it up. H2114
Joel 3:17 shall no s pass through her any more. H2114
Oba 11 side, in the day that the s carried away H2114
Mt 17:25 or tribute? of their own children, or of s? G245
26 Peter saith unto him, Of s. Jesus saith G245
27: 7 them the potter's field, to bury s in. G3581
Jn 10: 5 him: for they know not the voice of s. G245
Act 2:10 and s of Rome, Jews and proselytes, G1927
13:17 they dwelt as s in the land of Egypt, G3940
17:21 (For all the Athenians and s which G3581
Eph 2:12 of Israel, and s from the covenants G3581
19 Now therefore ye are no more s and G3581
1Ti 5:10 if she have lodged s, if she have washed G3580
Heb 11:13 they were s and pilgrims on the earth. G3581
13: 2 Be not forgetful to entertain s: for G5381
1Pt 1: 1 of Jesus Christ, to the s scattered G3927
2:11 Dearly beloved, I beseech *you* as s and G3941
3Jn 5 thou doest to the brethren, and to s; G3581

STRANGER'S
Lev 22:25 Neither from a s hand shall ye H1121+H5236
25:47 by thee, or to the stock of the s family: H1616

STRANGERS'
Prv 5:17 Let them be only thine own, and not s H2114

STRANGLED
Nah 2:12 his whelps, and s for his lionesses, and H2614
Act 15:20 and *from* things s, and *from* blood. G4156
29 blood, and from things s, and from G4156
21:25 and from s, and from fornication. G4156

STRANGLING
Job 7:15 So that my soul chooseth s, *and* death H4267

STRAW
Gen 24:25 We have both s and provender enough, H8401
32 camels, and gave s and provender for H8401
Ex 5: 7 Ye shall no more give the people s to H8401
7 them go and gather s for themselves. H8401
10 saith Pharaoh, I will not give you s. H8401
11 Go ye, get you s where ye can find it: H8401
12 of Egypt to gather stubble instead of s. H8401
13 *your* daily tasks, as when there was s. H8401
16 There is no s given unto thy servants, H8401
18 for there shall no s be given you, yet H8401
Jdg 19:19 Yet there is both s and provender for H8401
1Ki 4:28 Barley also and s for the horses and H8401
Job 41:27 He esteemeth iron as s, *and* brass as H8401
Isa 11: 7 and the lion shall eat s like the ox. H8401
25:10 as s is trodden down for the dunghill. H4963
65:25 the lion shall eat s like the bullock: and H8401

STRAWED
Ex 32:20 *it* to powder, and s *it* upon the water, H2219
Mt 21: 8 from the trees, and s *them* in the way. G4766

Mt 25:24 and gathering where thou hast not s: G1287
26 not, and gather where I have not s: G1287
Mk 11: 8 off the trees, and s *them* in the way. G4766

STRAY See ASTRAY.

STREAKS See STRAKES.

STREAM
Nu 21:15 And at the s of the brooks that goeth H793
Job 6:15 *and* as the s of brooks they pass away; H650
Ps 124: 4 us, the s had gone over our soul: H5158
Isa 27:12 of the river unto the s of Egypt, and ye H5158
30:28 And his breath, as an overflowing s, H5158
33 like a s of brimstone, doth kindle it. H5158
57: 6 Among the smooth *stones* of the s *is* H5158
66:12 like a flowing s: then shall ye suck, ye H5158
Dan 7:10 A fiery s issued and came forth from H5103
Am 5:24 and righteousness as a mighty s. H5158
Lk 6:48 the flood arose, the s beat vehemently G4215
49 earth; against which the s did beat G4215

STREAMS
Ex 7:19 of Egypt, upon their s, upon their rivers, H5104
8: 5 thy rod over the s, over the rivers, and H5104
Ps 46: 4 *There is* a river, the s whereof shall H6388
78:16 He brought s also out of the rock, and H5140
20 out, and the s overflowed; can he H5158
126: 4 captivity, O LORD, as the s in the south. H650
Song 4:15 of living waters, and s from Lebanon. H5140
Isa 11:15 s, and make *men* go over dryshod. H5158
30:25 hill, rivers *and* s of waters in the day H2988
33:21 broad rivers *and* s; wherein shall go no H2975
34: 9 And the s thereof shall be turned into H5158
35: 6 waters break out, and s in the desert. H5158

STREET
Gen 19: 2 Nay; but we will abide in the s all night. H7339
Dt 13:16 the midst of the s thereof, and shalt H7339
Jos 2:19 thy house into the s, his blood *shall be* H2351
Jdg 19:15 he sat him down in a s of the city: for H7339
17 man in the s of the city: and the old H7339
20 *lie* upon me; only lodge not in the s. H7339
2Sa 21:12 them from the s of Beth-shan, where H7339
22:43 of the s, *and* did spread them abroad. H2351
2Ch 29: 4 gathered them together into the east s, H7339
32: 6 to him in the s of the gate of the city, H7339
Ezr 10: 9 people sat in the s of the house of God, H7339
Neh 8: 1 one man into the s that *was* before the H7339
3 And he read therein before the s that H7339
16 of God, and in the s of the water gate, H7339
16 and in the s of the gate of Ephraim. H7339
Est 4: 6 Mordecai unto the s of the city, which H7339
6: 9 through the s of the city, and proclaim H7339
11 through the s of the city, and H7339
Job 18:17 and he shall have no name in the s. H2351
29: 7 city, *when* I prepared my seat in the s! H7339
31:32 The stranger did not lodge in the s: *but* I H2351
Prv 7: 8 Passing through the s near her corner; H7784
Isa 42: 2 nor cause his voice to be heard in the s. H2351
51:23 and as the s, to them that went over. H2351
59:14 fallen in the s, and equity cannot enter. H7339
Jer 37:21 out of the bakers' s, until all the bread H2351
Lam 2:19 faint for hunger in the top of every s. H2351
4: 1 are poured out in the top of every s. H2351
Ezk 16:24 hast made thee an high place in every s. H7339
31 place in every s; and hast not been as H7339
Dan 9:25 two weeks: the s shall be built again, H7339
Act 9:11 Arise, and go into the s which is called G4505
12:10 on through one s; and forthwith the G4505
Rev 11: 8 And their dead bodies *shall lie* in the s G4113
21:21 of one pearl: and the s of the city *was* G4113
22: 2 In the midst of the s of it, and on either G4113

STREETS
2Sa 1:20 *it* not in the s of Askelon; lest the H2351
1Ki 20:34 and thou shalt make s for thee in H2351
Ps 18:42 I did cast them out as the dirt in the s. H2351
55:11 deceit and guile depart not from her s. H7339
144:13 thousands and ten thousands in our s: H2351
14 that *there be* no complaining in our s. H7339
Prv 1:20 without; she uttereth her voice in the s: H7339
5:16 abroad, *and* rivers of waters in the s. H7339
7:12 Now *is she* without, now in the s, and H7339
22:13 *is* a lion without, I shall be slain in the s. H7339
26:13 *is* a lion in the way; a lion *is* in the s. H7339
Ecc 12: 4 And the doors shall be shut in the s, H7784
5 home, and the mourners go about the s: H7784
Song 3: 2 the city in the s, and in the broad ways H7784

Isa 5:25 torn in the midst of the s. For all this his H2351
10: 6 tread them down like the mire of the s. H2351
15: 3 In their s they shall gird themselves H2351
3 and in their s, every one shall howl, H7339
24:11 *There is* a crying for wine in the s; all H2351
51:20 the head of all the s, as a wild bull in a H2351
Jer 5: 1 Run ye to and fro through the s of H2351
7:17 of Judah and in the s of Jerusalem? H2351
34 and from the s of Jerusalem, the voice H2351
9:21 without, *and* the young men from the s. H7339
11: 6 of Judah, and in the s of Jerusalem, H2351
13 the number of the s of Jerusalem have H2351
14:16 shall be cast out in the s of Jerusalem H2351
33:10 Judah, and in the s of Jerusalem, that H2351
44: 6 of Judah and in the s of Jerusalem; and H2351
9 of Judah, and in the s of Jerusalem? H2351
17 of Judah, and in the s of Jerusalem: for H2351
21 of Judah, and in the s of Jerusalem, ye, H2351
48:38 Moab, and in the s thereof: for I have H7339
49:26 shall fall in her s, and all the men of war H7339
50:30 men fall in the s, and all her men of war H7339
51: 4 *they that are* thrust through in her s. H2351
Lam 2:11 the sucklings swoon in the s of the city. H7339
12 wounded in the s of the city, when their H7339
21 the ground in the s: my virgins and my H2351
4: 5 are desolate in the s: they that were H2351
8 not known in the s: their skin cleaveth H2351
14 blind *men* in the s, they have polluted H2351
18 cannot go in our s: our end is near, our H7339
Ezk 7:19 They shall cast their silver in the s, and H2351
11: 6 have filled the s thereof with the slain. H2351
26:11 he tread down all thy s: he shall slay thy H2351
28:23 and blood into her s; and the wounded H2351
Am 5:16 *shall be* in all s; and they shall say in H7339
Mic 7:10 be trodden down as the mire of the s. H2351
Nah 2: 4 The chariots shall rage in the s, they H2351
3:10 at the top of all the s: and they cast lots H2351
Zep 3: 6 I made their s waste, that none passeth H2351
Zec 8: 4 dwell in the s of Jerusalem, and every H7339
5 And the s of the city shall be full of H7339
5 boys and girls playing in the s thereof. H7339
9: 3 dust, and fine gold as the mire of the s. H2351
10: 5 in the mire of the s in the battle: and H2351
Mt 6: 2 and in the s, that they may have G4505
5 in the corners of the s, that they may be G4113
12:19 shall any man hear his voice in the s. G4113
Mk 6:56 laid the sick in the s, and besought him G58
Lk 10:10 out into the s of the same, and say, G4113
13:26 presence, and thou hast taught in our s. G4113
14:21 quickly into the s and lanes of the city, G4113
Act 5:15 the sick into the s, and laid *them* on G4113

STRENGTH
Gen 4:12 yield unto thee her s; a fugitive and a H3581
49: 3 the beginning of my s, the excellency of H202
24 But his bow abode in s, and the arms of H386
Ex 13: 3 of bondage; for by s of hand the LORD H2392
14 say unto him, By s of hand the LORD H2392
16 thine eyes: for by s of hand the LORD H2392
14:27 sea returned to his s when the morning H386
15: 2 The LORD *is* my s and song, and he is H5797
13 *them* in thy s unto thy holy habitation. H5797
Lev 26:20 And your s shall be spent in vain: for H3581
Nu 23:22 he hath as it were the s of an unicorn. H8443
24: 8 hath as it were the s of an unicorn: he H8443
Dt 21:17 of his s; the right of the firstborn *is* his. H202
33:25 and as thy days, *so shall* thy s *be*. H1679
Jos 11:13 stood still in their s, Israel burned none H8510
14:11 sent me: as my s *was* then, even so *is* H3581
11 even so *is* my s now, for war, both to H3581
Jdg 5:21 O my soul, thou hast trodden down s. H5797
8:21 man *is, so is* his s. And Gideon arose, H1369
16: 5 wherein his great s *lieth*, and by what H3581
6 thee, wherein thy great s *lieth*, and H3581
9 the fire. So his s was not known. H3581
15 not told me wherein thy great s *lieth*. H3581
17 shaven, then my s will go from me, and H3581
19 to afflict him, and his s went from him. H3581
1Sa 2: 4 they that stumbled are girded with s. H2428
9 darkness; for by s shall no man prevail. H3581
10 and he shall give s unto his king, and H5797
15:29 And also the S of Israel will not lie nor H5331
28:20 and there was no s in him; for he had H3581
22 have s, when thou goest on thy way. H3581
2Sa 22:33 God *is* my s *and* power: and he maketh H4581
40 For thou hast girded me with s to H2428
1Ki 19: 8 and went in the s of that meat forty H3581
2Ki 9:24 And Jehu drew a bow with his full s, H3027
18:20 *have* counsel and s for the war. Now on H1369

S

2Ki 19: 3 birth, and *there is* not s to bring forth. H3581
1Ch 16:11 Seek the LORD and his s, seek his face H5797
27 Glory and honour *are* in his presence; s H5797
28 people, give unto the LORD glory and s. H5797
26: 8 able men for s for the service, *were* H3581
29:12 *is* to make great, and to give s unto all. H2388
2Ch 6:41 and the ark of thy s: let thy priests, O H5797
13:20 Neither did Jeroboam recover s again H3581
Neh 4:10 And Judah said, The s of the bearers of H3581
8:10 sorry; for the joy of the LORD is your s. H4581
Job 6:11 What *is* my s, that I should hope? and H3581
12 *Is* my s the strength of stones? or *is* my H3581
12 *Is* my strength the s of stones? or *is* my H3581
9: 4 *He is* wise in heart, and mighty in s: H3581
19 If *I speak* of s, lo, *he is* strong: and if of H3581
12:13 With him *is* wisdom and s, he hath H1369
16 With him *is* s and wisdom: the H5797
21 and weakeneth the s of the mighty. H4206
18: 7 The steps of his s shall be straitened, H202
12 His s shall be hunger-bitten, and H202
13 It shall devour the s of his skin: *even* the H905
13 the firstborn of death shall devour his s. H905
21:23 One dieth in his full s, being wholly at H6106
23: 6 power? No; but he would put *s* in me.
26: 2 *how* savest thou the arm *that hath* no s? H5797
30: 2 Yea, whereto *might* the s of their hands H3581
36: 5 not *any*: *he is* mighty in s *and* wisdom. H3581
19 *no*, not gold, nor all the forces of s. H3581
37: 6 small rain, and to the great rain of his s. H5797
39:11 Wilt thou trust him, because his s *is* H3581
19 Hast thou given the horse s? hast thou H1369
21 s: he goeth on to meet the armed men. H3581
40:16 Lo now, his s *is* in his loins, and his H3581
41:22 In his neck remaineth s, and sorrow is H5797
Ps 8: 2 hast thou ordained s because of thine H5797
18: 1 I will love thee, O LORD, my s. H2391
2 my God, my s, in whom I will trust; H6697
32 *It is* God that girdeth me with s, and H2428
39 For thou hast girded me with s unto the H2428
19:14 sight, O LORD, my s, and my redeemer. H6697
20: 6 with the saving s of his right hand. H1369
21: 1 The king shall joy in thy s, O LORD; and H5797
13 Be thou exalted, LORD, in thine own s: H5797
22:15 My s is dried up like a potsherd; and H3581
19 O LORD: O my s, haste thee to help me. H360
27: 1 s of my life; of whom shall I be afraid? H4581
28: 7 The LORD *is* my s and my shield; my H5797
8 The LORD *is* their s, and he *is* the H5797
8 and he *is* the saving s of his anointed. H4581
29: 1 mighty, give unto the LORD glory and s. H5797
11 The LORD will give s unto his people; H5797
31: 4 laid privily for me: for thou *art* my s. H4581
10 with sighing: my s faileth because of H3581
33:16 mighty man is not delivered by much s. H3581
17 shall he deliver *any* by his great s. H2428
37:39 *he is* their s in the time of trouble. H4581
38:10 My heart panteth, my s faileth me: as H3581
39:13 O spare me, that I may recover s, before H1082
43: 2 For thou *art* the God of my s: why dost H4581
46: 1 God *is* our refuge and s, a very present H5797
52: 7 made not God his s; but trusted in the H4581
54: 1 by thy name, and judge me by thy s. H1369
59: 9 *Because of* his s will I wait upon thee: H5797
17 Unto thee, O my s, will I sing: for God *is* H5797
60: 7 s of mine head; Judah *is* my lawgiver; H4581
62: 7 rock of my s, *and* my refuge, *is* in God. H5797
65: 6 Which by his s setteth fast the H3581
68:28 Thy God hath commanded thy s: H5797
34 Ascribe ye s unto God: his excellency *is* H5797
34 *is* over Israel, and his s *is* in the clouds. H5797
35 *is* he that giveth s and power unto *his* H5797
71: 9 age; forsake me not when my s faileth. H3581
16 I will go in the s of the Lord GOD: I will H1369
18 until I have shewed thy s unto *this* H2220
73: 4 bands in their death: but their s *is* firm. H193
26 s of my heart, and my portion for ever. H6697
74:13 Thou didst divide the sea by thy s: thou H5797
77:14 hast declared thy s among the people. H5797
78: 4 the LORD, and his s, and his wonderful H5807
51 of *their* s in the tabernacles of Ham: H202
61 And delivered his s into captivity, and H5797
80: 2 stir up thy s, and come *and* save us. H1369
81: 1 Sing aloud unto God our s: make a H5797
84: 5 Blessed *is* the man whose s *is* in thee; H5797
7 They go from s to strength, *every one* H2428
7 They go from strength to s, *every one of* H2428
86:16 upon me; give thy s unto thy servant, H5797
88: 4 into the pit: I am as a man *that hath* no s: H353
89:17 For thou *art* the glory of their s: and in H5797
Ps 90:10 and if by reason of s *they be* fourscore H1369
10 years, yet *is* their s labour and sorrow; H7296
93: 1 is clothed with s, *wherewith* he hath H5797
95: 4 of the earth: the s of the hills *is* his also. H8443
96: 6 Honour and majesty *are* before him: s H5797
7 people, give unto the LORD glory and s. H5797
99: 4 The king's s also loveth judgment; thou H5797
102:23 He weakened my s in the way; he H3581
103:20 angels, that excel in s, that do his H3581
105: 4 Seek the LORD, and his s: seek his face H5797
36 in their land, the chief of all their s. H202
108: 8 s of mine head; Judah *is* my lawgiver; H4581
110: 2 The LORD shall send the rod of thy s H5797
118:14 The LORD *is* my s and song, and is H5797
132: 8 into thy rest; thou, and the ark of thy s. H5797
138: 3 strengthenedst me *with* s in my soul. H5797
140: 7 O GOD the Lord, the s of my salvation, H5797
144: 1 Blessed *be* the LORD my s, which H6697
147:10 He delighteth not in the s of the horse: H1369
Prv 8:14 wisdom: I *am* understanding; I have s. H1369
10:29 The way of the LORD *is* s to the H4581
14: 4 but much increase *is* by the s of the ox. H3581
20:29 The glory of young men *is* their s: and H3581
21:22 down the s of the confidence thereof. H5797
24: 5 yea, a man of knowledge increaseth s. H3581
10 in the day of adversity, thy s *is* small. H3581
31: 3 Give not thy s unto women, nor thy H2428
17 She girdeth her loins with s, and H5797
25 S and honour *are* her clothing; and she H5797
Ecc 9:16 Then said I, Wisdom *is* better than s: H1369
10:10 s: but wisdom *is* profitable to direct. H2428
17 season, for s, and not for drunkenness! H1369
Isa 5:22 and men of s to mingle strong drink: H2428
10:13 For he saith, By the s of my hand I have H3581
12: 2 JEHOVAH *is* my s and *my* song; he H5797
17:10 of the rock of thy s, therefore shalt thou H4581
23: 4 spoken, *even* the s of the sea, saying, I H4581
10 of Tarshish: *there is* no more s. H4206
14 Howl, ye ships of Tarshish: for your s is H4581
25: 4 For thou hast been a s to the poor, a H4581
4 to the poor, a s to the needy in his H4581
26: 4 in the LORD JEHOVAH *is* everlasting s: H6697
27: 5 Or let him take hold of my s, *that* he H4581
28: 6 judgment, and for s to them that turn H1369
30: 2 themselves in the s of Pharaoh, and to H4581
3 Therefore shall the s of Pharaoh be H4581
7 concerning this, Their s *is* to sit still. H7294
15 shall be your s: and ye would not. H1369
33: 6 of thy times, *and* s of salvation: the fear H2633
36: 5 *I have* counsel and s for war: now on H1369
37: 3 birth, and *there is* not s to bring forth. H3581
40: 9 lift up thy voice with s; lift *it* up, be not H3581
29 *that have* no might he increaseth s. H6109
31 shall renew *their* s; they shall mount up H3581
41: 1 the people renew *their* s: let them come H3581
42:25 of his anger, and the s of battle: and it H5807
44:12 it with the s of his arms: yea, he H3581
12 is hungry, and his s faileth: he drinketh H3581
45:24 I righteousness and s: *even* to him shall H5797
49: 4 I have spent my s for nought, and in H3581
5 of the LORD, and my God shall be my s. H5797
51: 9 Awake, awake, put on s, O arm of the H5797
52: 1 Awake, awake; put on thy s, O Zion; put H5797
62: 8 and by the arm of his s, Surely I will no H5797
63: 1 the greatness of his s? I that speak in H3581
6 I will bring down their s to the earth. H5332
15 *is* thy zeal and thy s, the sounding of thy H1369
Jer 16:19 O LORD, my s, and my fortress, and my H5797
20: 5 Moreover I will deliver all the s of this H2633
51:53 the height of her s, *yet* from me shall H5797
Lam 1: 6 are gone without s before the pursuer. H3581
14 he hath made my s to fall, the Lord H3581
3:18 And I said, My s and my hope is H5331
Ezk 24:21 excellency of your s, the desire of your H5797
25 from them their s, the joy of their glory, H4581
30:15 And I will pour my fury upon Sin, the s H4581
18 the pomp of her s shall cease in her: as H5797
33:28 the pomp of her s shall cease; and the H5797
Dan 2:37 a kingdom, power, and s, and glory. H8632
41 there shall be in it of the s of the iron, H5326
10: 8 and there remained no s in me: for my H3581
8 me into corruption, and I retained no s. H3581
16 upon me, and I have retained no s. H3581
17 there remained no s in me, neither is H3581
11: 2 all: and by his s through his riches he H2393
15 *shall there be any* s to withstand. H3581
17 face to enter with the s of his whole H8633
31 the sanctuary of s, and shall take away H4581
Hos 7: 9 Strangers have devoured his s, and he H3581
Hos 12: 3 and by his s he had power with God: H202
Joel 2:22 the fig tree and the vine do yield their s. H2428
3:16 and the s of the children of Israel. H4581
Am 3:11 bring down thy s from thee, and thy H5797
6:13 we not taken to us horns by our own s? H2392
Mic 5: 4 And he shall stand and feed in the s of H5797
Nah 3: 9 Ethiopia and Egypt *were* her s, and *it* H6109
11 also shalt seek s because of the enemy. H4581
Hab 3:19 The LORD God *is* my s, and he will H2428
Hag 2:22 I will destroy the s of the kingdoms of H2392
Zec 12: 5 *be* my s in the LORD of hosts their God. H556
Mk 12:30 all thy s: this *is* the first commandment. G2479
33 soul, and with all the s, and to love *his* G2479
Lk 1:51 He hath shewed s with his arm; he hath G2904
10:27 soul, and with all thy s, and with all thy G2479
Act 3: 7 his feet and ankle bones received s. G4732
9:22 But Saul increased the more in s, and G1743
Ro 5: 6 For when we were yet without s, in due G772
1Co 15:56 The sting of death *is* sin; and the s of G1411
2Co 1: 8 of measure, above s, insomuch that we G1411
12: 9 for thee: for my s is made perfect in G1411
Heb 9:17 is of no s at all while the testator liveth. G2480
11:11 herself received s to conceive seed, and G1411
Rev 1:16 *was* as the sun shineth in his s. G1411
3: 8 for thou hast a little s, and hast kept my G1411
5:12 s, and honour, and glory, and blessing. G2479
12:10 salvation, and s, and the kingdom of G1411
17:13 give their power and s unto the beast. G1849

STRENGTHEN

Dt 3:28 him, and s him: for he shall go over H553
Jdg 16:28 I pray thee, and s me, I pray thee, only H2388
1Ki 20:22 said unto him, Go, s thyself, and mark, H2388
Ezr 6:22 unto them, to s their hands in the work H2388
Neh 6: 9 Now therefore, *O God*, s my hands. H2388
Job 16: 5 *But* I would s you with my mouth, and H553
Ps 20: 2 the sanctuary, and s thee out of Zion; H5582
27:14 s thine heart: wait, I say, on the LORD. H553
31:24 Be of good courage, and he shall s your H553
41: 3 The LORD will s him upon the bed of H5582
68:28 thy strength: s, O God, that which thou H5810
89:21 established: mine arm also shall s him. H553
119:28 My soul melteth for heaviness: s thou H6965
Isa 22:21 him with thy robe, and s him with thy H2388
30: 2 at my mouth; to s themselves in the H5810
33:23 could not well s their mast, they could H2388
35: 3 S ye the weak hands, and confirm the H2388
41:10 for I *am* thy God: I will s thee; yea, I will H553
54: 2 lengthen thy cords, and s thy stakes; H2388
Jer 23:14 walk in lies: they s also the hands of H2388
Ezk 7:13 any s himself in the iniquity of his life. H2388
16:49 she s the hand of the poor and needy. H2388
30:24 And I will s the arms of the king of H2388
25 But I will s the arms of the king of H2388
34:16 broken, and will s that which was sick: H2388
Dan 11: 1 *even* I, stood to confirm and to s him. H4581
Am 2:14 the strong shall not s his force, neither H553
Zec 10: 6 And I will s the house of Judah, and I H1396
12 And I will s them in the LORD; and H1396
Lk 22:32 thou art converted, s thy brethren. G4741
1Pt 5:10 make you perfect, stablish, s, settle *you*. G4599
Rev 3: 2 Be watchful, and s the things which G4741

STRENGTHENED

Gen 48: 2 Israel s himself, and sat upon the bed. H2388
Jdg 3:12 and the LORD s Eglon the king of H2388
7:11 thine hands be s to go down unto the H2388
1Sa 23:16 into the wood, and s his hand in God. H2388
2Sa 2: 7 Therefore now let your hands be s, and H2388
1Ch 11:10 David had, who s themselves with him H2388
2Ch 1: 1 And Solomon the son of David was s in H2388
11:17 So they s the kingdom of Judah, and H2388
12: 1 the kingdom, and had s himself, he H2393
13 So king Rehoboam s himself in H2388
13: 7 of Belial, and have s themselves against H553
17: 1 his stead, and s himself against Israel. H2388
21: 4 of his father, he s himself, and slew all H2388
23: 1 And in the seventh year Jehoiada s H2388
24:13 set the house of God in his state, and s it. H553
25:11 And Amaziah s himself, and led forth H2388
26: 8 of Egypt; for he s *himself* exceedingly. H2388
28:20 him, and distressed him, but s him not. H2388
32: 5 Also he s himself, and built up all the H2388
Ezr 1: 6 And all they that *were* about them s H2388
7:28 princes. And I was s as the hand of the H2388
Neh 2:18 they s their hands for *this* good *work*. H2388
Job 4: 3 many, and thou hast s the weak hands. H2388
4 falling, and thou hast s the feeble knees. H553
Ps 52: 7 riches, *and* s himself in his wickedness. H5810

Ps 147:13 For he hath s the bars of thy gates; he H2388
Prv 8:28 when he s the fountains of the deep: H5810
Ezk 13:22 not made sad; and s the hands of the H2388
34: 4 The diseased have ye not s, neither H2388
Dan 10:18 the appearance of a man, and he s me, H2388
19 unto me, I was s, and said, Let my lord H2388
19 Let my lord speak; for thou hast s me. H2388
11: 6 her, and he that s her in *these* times. H2388
12 thousands: but he shall not be s *by it.* H5810
Hos 7:15 Though I have bound *and* s their arms, H2388
Act 9:19 meat, he was s. Then was Saul certain *G1765*
Eph 3:16 of his glory, to be s with might by his *G2901*
Col 1:11 S with all might, according to his *G1412*
2Ti 4:17 with me, and s me; that by me the *G1743*

STRENGTHENEDST
Ps 138: 3 me, *and* s me *with* strength in my soul. H7292

STRENGTHENETH
Job 15:25 and s himself against the Almighty. H1396
Ps 104:15 shine, and bread *which* s man's heart. H5582
Prv 31:17 her loins with strength, and s her arms. H553
Ecc 7:19 Wisdom s the wise more than ten H5810
Isa 44:14 the oak, which he s for himself among H553
Am 5: 9 That s the spoiled against the strong, H1082
Php 4:13 all things through Christ which s me. *G1743*

STRENGTHENING
Lk 22:43 an angel unto him from heaven, s him. *G1765*
Act 18:23 Phrygia in order, s all the disciples. *G1991*

STRETCH
Ex 3:20 And I will s out my hand, and smite H7971
7: 5 the LORD, when I s forth mine hand H5186
19 Take thy rod, and s out thine hand H5186
8: 5 Say unto Aaron, S forth thine hand H5186
16 Say unto Aaron, S out thy rod, and H5186
9:15 For now I will s out my hand, that I H7971
22 And the LORD said unto Moses, S forth H5186
10:12 And the LORD said unto Moses, S out H5186
21 And the LORD said unto Moses, S out H5186
14:16 But lift thou up thy rod, and s out thine H5186
26 And the LORD said unto Moses, S out H5186
25:20 And the cherubims shall s forth *their* H6566
Jos 8:18 And the LORD said unto Joshua, S out H5186
1Sa 24: 6 anointed, to s forth mine hand against H7971
26: 9 him not: for who can s forth his hand H7971
11 The LORD forbid that I should s forth H7971
23 day, but I would not s forth mine hand H7971
2Sa 1:14 thou not afraid to s forth thine hand to H7971
2Ki 21:13 And I will s over Jerusalem the line of H5186
Job 11:13 If thou prepare thine heart, and s out H6566
30:24 Howbeit he will not s out *his* hand to H7971
39:26 Doth the hawk fly by thy wisdom, *and* s H6566
Ps 68:31 shall soon s out her hands unto God. H7323
138: 7 revive me: thou shalt s forth thine hand H7971
143: 6 I s forth my hands unto thee: my soul H6566
Isa 28:20 that *a man* can s himself *on it*: and the H8311
31: 3 the LORD shall s out his hand, both he H5186
34:11 in it: and he shall s out upon it the line H5186
54: 2 tent, and let them s forth the curtains H5186
Jer 6:12 together: for I will s out my hand upon H5186
10:20 not: *there is* none to s forth my tent any H5186
15: 6 therefore will I s out my hand against H5186
51:25 earth: and I will s out mine hand upon H5186
Ezk 6:14 So will I s out my hand upon them, and H5186
14: 9 prophet, and I will s out my hand upon H5186
13 then will I s out mine hand upon H5186
25: 7 Behold, therefore I will s out mine H5186
13 GOD; I will also s out mine hand upon H5186
16 Behold, I will s out mine hand upon H5186
30:25 he shall s it out upon the land of Egypt. H5186
35: 3 thee, and I will s out mine hand H5186
Dan 11:42 He shall s forth his hand also upon the H7971
Am 6: 4 That lie upon beds of ivory, and s H5628
Zep 1: 4 I will also s out mine hand upon Judah, H5186
2:13 And he will s out his hand against the H5186
Mt 12:13 Then saith he to the man, S forth thine *G1614*
Mk 3: 5 unto the man, S forth thine hand. And *G1614*
Lk 6:10 unto the man, S forth thy hand. And *G1614*
Jn 21:18 be old, thou shalt s forth thy hands, *G1614*
2Co 10:14 For we s not ourselves beyond *our* *G5239*

STRETCHED
Gen 22:10 And Abraham s forth his hand, and H7971
48:14 And Israel s out his right hand, and H7971
Ex 6: 6 a s out arm, and with great judgments: H5186
8: 6 And Aaron s out his hand over the H5186
17 And they did so; for Aaron s out his H5186
9:23 And Moses s forth his rod toward H5186
10:13 And Moses s forth his rod over the land H5186
22 And Moses s forth his hand toward H5186
14:21 And Moses s out his hand over the sea; H5186
27 And Moses s forth his hand over the H5186
Dt 4:34 hand, and by a s out arm, and by great H5186
5:15 hand and by a s out arm: therefore the H5186
7:19 hand, and the s out arm, whereby the H5186
9:29 thy mighty power and by thy s out arm. H5186
11: 2 his mighty hand, and his s out arm, H5186
Jos 8:18 hand. And Joshua s out the spear that H5186
19 as soon as he had s out his hand: and H5186
26 wherewith he s out the spear, until H5186
2Sa 24:16 And when the angel s out his hand H7971
1Ki 6:27 house: and they s forth the wings of the H6566
8:42 hand, and of thy s out arm;) when he H5186
17:21 And he s himself upon the child three H4058
2Ki 4:34 his hands: and he s himself upon the H1457
35 and went up, and s himself upon him: H1457
17:36 great power and a s out arm, him shall H5186
1Ch 21:16 drawn sword in his hand s out over H5186
2Ch 6:32 hand, and thy s out arm; if they come H5186
Job 38: 5 or who hath s the line upon it? H5186
Ps 44:20 or s out our hands to a strange god; H6566
88: 9 thee, I have s out my hands unto thee. H7849
136: 6 To him that s out the earth above the H7554
12 With a strong hand, and with a s out H5186
Prv 1:24 s out my hand, and no man regarded; H5186
Isa 3:16 and walk with s forth necks and H5186
5:25 and he hath s forth his hand against H5186
25 turned away, but his hand *is* s out still. H5186
9:12 turned away, but his hand *is* s out still. H5186
17 turned away, but his hand *is* s out still. H5186
21 turned away, but his hand *is* s out still. H5186
10: 4 turned away, but his hand *is* s out still. H5186
14:26 hand that is s out upon all the nations. H5186
27 *is* s out, and who shall turn it back? H5186
16: 8 are s out, they are gone over the sea. H5203
23:11 He s out his hand over the sea, he H5186
42: 5 the heavens, and s them out; he that H5186
45:12 my hands, have s out the heavens, and H5186
51:13 maker, that hath s forth the heavens, H5186
Jer 6: 4 the shadows of the evening are s out. H5186
10:12 s out the heavens by his discretion. H5186
32:17 great power and s out arm, *and* there H5186
21 with a s out arm, and with great terror; H5186
51:15 s out the heaven by his understanding. H5186
Lam 2: 8 of Zion: he hath s out a line, he hath H5186
Ezk 1:11 their wings *were* s upward; two *wings* H6504
22 crystal, s forth over their heads above. H5186
10: 7 And *one* cherub s forth his hand from H7971
16:27 Behold, therefore I have s out my hand H5186
20:33 hand, and with a s out arm, and with H5186
34 a s out arm, and with fury poured out. H5186
Hos 7: 5 wine; he s out his hand with scorners. H4900
Am 6: 7 that s themselves shall be removed. H5628
Zec 1:16 a line shall be s forth upon Jerusalem. H5186
Mt 12:13 hand. And he s *it* forth; and it was *G1614*
49 And he s forth his hand toward his *G1614*
14:31 And immediately Jesus s forth *his* *G1614*
26:51 were with Jesus s out *his* hand, and *G1614*
Mk 3: 5 hand. And he s *it* out: and his hand *G1614*
Lk 22:53 you in the temple, ye s forth no hands *G1614*
Act 12: 1 Now about that time Herod the king s *G1911*
26: 1 for thyself. Then Paul s forth the hand, *G1614*
Ro 10:21 All day long I have s forth my hands *G1600*

STRETCHEDST
Ex 15:12 Thou s out thy right hand, the earth H5186

STRETCHEST
Ps 104: 2 who s out the heavens like a curtain: H5186

STRETCHETH
Job 15:25 For he s out his hand against God, and H5186
26: 7 He s out the north over the empty H5186
Prv 31:20 She s out her hand to the poor; yea, she H6566
Isa 40:22 grasshoppers; that s out the heavens as H5186
44:13 The carpenter s out *his* rule; he H5186
24 all *things*; that s forth the heavens H5186
Zec 12: 1 the LORD, which s forth the heavens, H5186

STRETCHING
Isa 8: 8 to the neck; and the s out of his wings H4298
Act 4:30 By s forth thine hand to heal; and that *G1614*

STREWED See STRAWED.

STRICKEN
Gen 18:11 *were* old *and* well s in age; *and* it ceased H935
24: 1 And Abraham was old, *and* well s in age: H935
Jos 13: 1 Now Joshua was old *and* s in years; and H935
1 Thou art old *and* s in years, and there H935
23: 1 that Joshua waxed old *and* s in age. H935
2 said unto them, I am old *and* s in age: H935
Jdg 5:26 had pierced and s through his temples. H2498
1Ki 1: 1 Now king David was old *and* s in years; H935
Prv 6: 1 *if* thou hast s thy hand with a stranger, H8628
23:35 They have s me, *shalt thou say, and* I H5221
Isa 1: 5 Why should ye be s any more? ye will H5221
16: 7 shall ye mourn; surely *they are* s. H5218
53: 4 him s, smitten of God, and afflicted. H5060
8 transgression of my people was he s. H5061
Jer 5: 3 truth? thou hast s them, but they have H5221
Lam 4: 9 these pine away, s through for *want of* H1856
Lk 1: 7 and they both were *now* well s in years. *G4260*
18 old man, and my wife well s in years. *G4260*

STRIFE
Gen 13: 7 And there was a s between the H7379
8 Let there be no s, I pray thee, between H4808
Nu 27:14 of Zin, in the s of the congregation, H4808
Dt 1:12 and your burden, and your s? H7379
Jdg 12: 2 were at great s with the children of H7379
2Sa 19: 9 And all the people were at s throughout H1777
Ps 31:20 in a pavilion from the s of tongues. H7379
55: 9 I have seen violence and s in the city. H7379
80: 6 Thou makest us a s unto our H4066
106:32 at the waters of s, so that it went ill with H4808
Prv 15:18 A wrathful man stirreth up s: but *he* H4066
18 but *he that is* slow to anger appeaseth s. H7379
16:28 A froward man soweth s: and a H4066
17: 1 than an house full of sacrifices *with* s. H7379
14 The beginning of s *is as* when one H4066
19 He loveth transgression that loveth s: H4683
20: 3 from s: but every fool will be meddling. H7379
22:10 go out; yea, s and reproach shall cease. H1779
26:17 meddleth with s *belonging* not to him, H7379
20 *there is* no talebearer, the s ceaseth. H4066
21 fire; so *is* a contentious man to kindle s. H7379
28:25 He that is of a proud heart stirreth up s: H4066
29:22 An angry man stirreth up s, and a H4066
30:33 so the forcing of wrath bringeth forth s. H7379
Isa 58: 4 Behold, ye fast for s and debate, and to H7379
Jer 15:10 me a man of s and a man of contention H7379
Ezk 47:19 the waters of s *in* Kadesh, the H4808+H4809
48:28 the waters of s *in* Kadesh, *and* H4808+H4809
Hab 1: 3 are *that* raise up s and contention. H7379
Lk 22:24 And there was also a s among them, *G5379*
Ro 13:13 and wantonness, not in s and envying. *G2054*
1Co 3: 3 you envying, and s, and divisions, are *G2054*
Gal 5:20 wrath, s, seditions, heresies, *G2052*
Php 1:15 envy and s; and some also of good will: *G2054*
2: 3 *Let* nothing *be done* through s or *G2052*
1Ti 6: 4 envy, s, railings, evil surmisings, *G2054*
Heb 6:16 confirmation *is* to them an end of all s. *G485*
Jas 3:14 But if ye have bitter envying and s in *G2052*
16 For where envying and s *is*, there *is* *G2052*

STRIFES
Prv 10:12 Hatred stirreth up s: but love covereth H4090
2Co 12:20 envyings, wraths, s, backbitings, *G2052*
1Ti 6: 4 questions and s of words, whereof *G3055*
2Ti 2:23 avoid, knowing that they do gender s. *G3163*

STRIKE
Ex 12: 7 And they shall take of the blood, and s H5414
22 *is* in the bason, and s the lintel and the H5060
Dt 21: 4 s off the heifer's neck there in the valley:
2Ki 5:11 his God, and s his hand over the place, H5130
Job 17: 3 who *is* he *that* will s hands with me? H8628
20:24 the bow of steel shall s him through. H2498
Ps 110: 5 The Lord at thy right hand shall s H4272
Prv 7:23 Till a dart s through his liver; as a bird H6398
17:26 *is* not good, *nor* to s princes for equity. H5221
22:26 Be not thou *one* of them that s hands, H8628
Hab 3:14 Thou didst s through with his staves H5344
Mk 14:65 did s him with the palms of their hands. *G906*

STRIKER
1Ti 3: 3 Not given to wine, no s, not greedy of *G4131*
Tit 1: 7 to wine, no s, not given to filthy lucre; *G4131*

STRIKETH
Job 34:26 He s them as wicked men in the open H5606
Prv 17:18 A man void of understanding s hands, H8628
Rev 9: 5 of a scorpion, when he s a man. *G3817*

STRING
Ps 11: 2 arrow upon the s, that they may privily H3499
Mk 7:35 opened, and the s of his tongue was *G1199*

STRINGED
Ps 150: 4 him with s instruments and organs. H4482
Isa 38:20 my songs to the s instruments all the H5058
Hab 3:19 the chief singer on my s instruments. H5058

STRINGS
Ps 21:12 upon thy s against the face of them. H4340
33: 2 the psaltery *and* an instrument of ten s.
92: 3 Upon an instrument of ten s, and upon
144: 9 of ten s will I sing praises unto thee.

STRIP
Nu 20:26 And s Aaron of his garments, and put H6584
1Sa 31: 8 came to s the slain, that they found H6584
1Ch 10: 8 came to s the slain, that they found H6584
Isa 32:11 ye careless ones: s you, and make you H6584
Ezk 16:39 high places: they shall s thee also of thy H6584
23:26 They shall also s thee out of thy clothes, H6584
Hos 2: 3 Lest I s her naked, and set her as in the H6584

STRIPE
Ex 21:25 burning, wound for wound, s for stripe. H2250
25 burning, wound for wound, stripe for s. H2250

STRIPES
Dt 25: 3 Forty s he may give him, *and* not H5221
3 these with many s, then thy brother H4347
2Sa 7:14 and with the s of the children of men: H5061
Ps 89:32 with the rod, and their iniquity with s. H5061
Prv 17:10 man than an hundred s into a fool. H5221
19:29 for scorners, and s for the back of fools. H4112
20:30 so *do* s the inward parts of the belly. H4347
Isa 53: 5 him; and with his s we are healed. H2250
Lk 12:47 to his will, shall be beaten with many *s*.
48 things worthy of s, shall be beaten with *G4127*
48 shall be beaten with few *s*. For unto *G4127*
Act 16:23 And when they had laid many s upon *G4127*
33 and washed *their* s; and was baptized, *G4127*
2Co 6: 5 In s, in imprisonments, in tumults, in *G4127*
11:23 more abundant, in s above measure, in *G4127*
24 Of the Jews five times received I forty *s*
1Pt 2:24 by whose s ye were healed. *G3468*

STRIPLING
1Sa 17:56 said, Inquire thou whose son the s *is*. H5958

STRIPPED
Ex 33: 6 And the children of Israel s themselves H5337
Nu 20:28 And Moses s Aaron of his garments, H6584
1Sa 18: 4 And Jonathan s himself of the robe that H6584
19:24 And he s off his clothes also, and H6584
31: 9 And they cut off his head, and s off his H6584
1Ch 10: 9 And when they had s him, they took his H6584
2Ch 20:25 jewels, which they s off for themselves, H5337
Job 19: 9 He hath s me of my glory, and taken H6584
22: 6 and s the naked of their clothing. H6584
Mic 1: 8 and howl, I will go s and naked: I will H7758
Mt 27:28 And they s him, and put on him a *G1562*
Lk 10:30 thieves, which s him of his raiment, *G1562*

STRIPT
Gen 37:23 that they s Joseph out of his coat, H6584

STRIVE
Gen 6: 3 shall not always s with man, for that he H1777
26:20 And the herdmen of Gerar did s with H7378
Ex 21:18 And if men s together, and one smite H7378
22 If men s, and hurt a woman with child, H5327
Dt 25:11 When men s together one with H5327
33: 8 thou didst s at the waters of Meribah; H7378
Jdg 11:25 Moab? did he ever s against Israel, or H7378
Job 33:13 Why dost thou s against him? for he H7378
Ps 35: 1 with them that s with me: fight against H3401
Prv 3:30 S not with a man without cause, if he H7378
25: 8 Go not forth hastily to s, lest *thou know* H7378
Isa 41:11 and they that s with thee shall perish. H7379
45: 9 *Let* the potsherd s with the potsherds of
Hos 4: 4 Yet let no man s, nor reprove another: H7378
4 *are* as they that s with the priest. H7378
Mt 12:19 He shall not s, nor cry; neither shall any *G2051*
Lk 13:24 S to enter in at the strait gate: for many, *G75*
Ro 15:30 the Spirit, that ye s together with me in *G4865*
2Ti 2: 5 And if a man also s for masteries, *yet* is *G118*
5 is he not crowned, except he s lawfully. *G118*
14 the Lord that they s not about words to *G3054*
2Ti 2:24 And the servant of the Lord must not s; *G3164*

STRIVED
Ro 15:20 Yea, so have I s to preach the gospel, *G5389*

STRIVEN
Jer 50:24 because thou hast s against the LORD. H1624

STRIVETH
Isa 45: 9 Woe unto him that s with his Maker! H7378
1Co 9:25 And every man that s for the mastery is *G75*

STRIVING
Php 1:27 s together for the faith of the gospel; *G4866*
Col 1:29 Whereunto I also labour, s according to *G75*
Heb 12: 4 Ye have not yet resisted unto blood, s *G464*

STRIVINGS
2Sa 22:44 Thou also hast delivered me from the s H7379
Ps 18:43 Thou hast delivered me from the s of H7379
Tit 3: 9 contentions, and s about the law; for *G3163*

STROKE
Dt 17: 8 plea, and between s and stroke, *being* H5061
8 between stroke and s, *being* matters of H5061
19: 5 hand fetcheth a s with the axe to cut H5080
21: 5 every controversy and every s be *tried*: H5061
Est 9: 5 enemies with the s of the sword, and H4347
Job 23: 2 my s is heavier than my groaning. H3027
36:18 take thee away with *his* s: then a great H5607
Ps 39:10 Remove thy s away from me: I am H5061
Isa 14: 6 with a continual s, he that ruled the H4347
30:26 and healeth the s of their wound. H4273
Ezk 24:16 of thine eyes with a s: yet neither shalt H4046

STROKES
Prv 18: 6 and his mouth calleth for s. H4112

STRONG
Gen 49:14 Issachar *is* a s ass couching down H1634
24 hands were made s by the hands of the H6339
Ex 6: 1 for with a s hand shall he let them H2389
1 go, and with a s hand shall he drive H2389
10:19 And the LORD turned a mighty s west H2389
13: 9 thy mouth: for with a s hand hath the H2389
14:21 sea to go *back* by a s east wind all that H5794
Lev 10: 9 Do not drink wine nor s drink, thou, nor
Nu 6: 3 from wine and s drink, and shall drink H7941
3 wine, or vinegar of s drink, neither shall
13:18 they *be* s or weak, few or many; H2389
19 dwell in, whether in tents, or in s holds; H4013
28 Nevertheless the people *be* s that dwell H5794
20:20 with much people, and with a s hand. H2389
21:24 border of the children of Ammon *was* s. H5794
24:21 parable, and said, S is thy dwellingplace, H386
28: 7 thou cause the s wine to be poured H7941
Dt 2:36 not one city too s for us: the LORD our H7682
11: 8 that ye may be s, and go in and possess H2388
14:26 sheep, or for wine, or for s drink, or for H7941
29: 6 ye drunk wine or s drink: that ye might H7941
31: 6 Be s and of a good courage, fear not, H2388
7 sight of all Israel, Be s and of a good H2388
23 and said, Be s and of a good courage: H2388
Jos 1: 6 Be s and of a good courage: for unto H2388
7 Only be thou s and very courageous, H2388
9 Have not I commanded thee? Be s and H2388
18 death: only be s and of a good courage. H2388
10:25 be dismayed, be s and of good courage: H2388
14:11 As yet I *am as* s this day as *I was* in the H2389
17:13 of Israel were waxen s, that they put the H2388
18 iron chariots, *and* though they *be* s. H2389
19:29 Ramah, and to the s city Tyre; and the H4013
23: 9 great nations and s: but *as for* you, no H6099
Jdg 1:28 And it came to pass, when Israel was s, H2388
6: 2 the mountains, and caves, and s holds. H4679
9:51 But there was a s tower within the city, H5797
13: 4 s drink, and eat not any unclean *thing*: H7941
7 drink no wine nor s drink, neither eat H7941
14 her drink wine or s drink, nor eat any H7941
14:14 and out of the s came forth sweetness. H5794
18:26 that they *were* too s for him, he turned H2389
1Sa 1:15 drunk neither wine nor s drink, but have
4: 9 Be s, and quit yourselves like men, O ye H2388
14:52 Saul saw any s man, or any valiant H1368
23:14 And David abode in the wilderness in s H4679
19 himself with us in s holds in the wood, H4679
29 thence, and dwelt in s holds at En-gedi. H4679
2Sa 3: 6 made himself s for the house of Saul. H2388
5: 7 Nevertheless David took the s hold of H4686
2Sa 10:11 And he said, If the Syrians be too s for H2388
11 of Ammon be too s for thee, then I will H2388
11:25 thy battle more s against the city, and H2388
15:12 And the conspiracy was s; for the people H533
16:21 the hands of all that *are* with thee be s. H2388
22:18 He delivered me from my s enemy, *and* H5794
18 hated me: for they were too s for me. H553
24: 7 And came to the s hold of Tyre, and to H4013
1Ki 2: 2 I go the way of all the earth: be thou s H2388
8:42 name, and of thy s hand, and of thy H2389
19:11 by, and a great and s wind rent the H2389
2Ki 2:16 thy servants fifty s men; let them go, we H2428
8:12 of Israel: their s holds wilt thou set on H4013
24:16 all *that were* s *and* apt for war, even H1368
1Ch 19:12 And he said, If the Syrians be too s for H2388
12 be too s for thee, then I will help thee. H2388
22:13 Israel: be s, and of good courage; H2388
26: 7 *were* s men, Elihu, and Semachiah. H2428
9 sons and brethren, s men, eighteen. H2428
28:10 house for the sanctuary: be s, and do *it*. H2388
20 his son, Be s and of good courage, H2388
2Ch 11:11 And he fortified the s holds, and put H4694
12 them exceeding s, having Judah and H2388
17 the son of Solomon s, three years: for H553
15: 7 Be ye s therefore, and let not your H2388
16: 9 to shew himself s in the behalf of *them* H2388
25: 8 But if thou wilt go, do *it*, be s for the H2388
26:15 was marvellously helped, till he was s. H2388
16 But when he was s, his heart was lifted H2393
32: 7 Be s and courageous, be not afraid nor H2388
Ezr 9:12 that ye may be s, and eat the good of H2388
Neh 1:10 by thy great power, and by thy s hand. H2389
9:25 And they took s cities, and a fat land, H1219
Job 8: 2 words of thy mouth *be like* a s wind? H3524
9:19 If *I speak* of strength, lo, *he is* s: and if of H533
30:21 to me: with thy s hand thou opposest H6108
33:19 the multitude of his bones with s *pain*: H386
37:18 *is* s, *and* as a molten looking glass? H2389
39:28 the crag of the rock, and the s place. H4686
40:18 His bones *are as* s pieces of brass; his H650
Ps 10:10 that the poor may fall by his s ones. H6099
18:17 He delivered me from my s enemy, and H5794
17 hated me: for they were too s for me. H553
19: 5 *and* rejoiceth as a s man to run a race. H1368
22:12 Many bulls have compassed me: s *bulls* H47
24: 8 Who *is* this King of glory? The LORD s H5808
30: 7 mountain to stand s: thou didst hide H5797
31: 2 be thou my s rock, for an house of H4581
21 me his marvellous kindness in a s city. H4692
35:10 him that is too s for him, yea, the poor H2389
38:19 *and* they are s: and they that hate me H6105
60: 9 Who will bring me *into* the s city? who H4692
61: 3 for me, *and* a s tower from the enemy. H5797
71: 3 Be thou my s habitation, whereunto I H6697
7 unto many; but thou *art* my s refuge. H5797
80:15 branch *that* thou madest s for thyself. H553
17 of man *whom* thou madest s for thyself. H553
89: 8 O LORD God of hosts, who *is* a s LORD H2626
10 scattered thine enemies with thy s arm. H5797
13 Thou hast a mighty arm: s is thy hand, H5810
40 thou hast brought his s holds to ruin. H4013
108:10 Who will bring me into the s city? who H4013
136:12 With a s hand, and with a stretched H2389
144:14 *That* our oxen *may be* s to labour; *that*
Prv 7:26 many s *men* have been slain by her. H6099
10:15 The rich man's wealth *is* his s city: the H5797
11:16 honour: and s *men* retain riches. H6184
14:26 In the fear of the LORD *is* s confidence: H5797
18:10 The name of the LORD *is* a s tower: the H5797
11 The rich man's wealth *is* his s city, and H5797
19 *to be won* than a s city: and *their* H5797
20: 1 Wine *is* a mocker, s drink *is* raging: and
21:14 and a reward in the bosom s wrath. H5794
24: 5 A wise man *is* s; yea, a man of H5797
30:25 The ants *are* a people not s, yet they H5794
31: 4 to drink wine; nor for princes s drink:
6 Give s drink unto him that is ready to
Ecc 9:11 the battle to the s, neither yet bread to H1368
12: 3 shall tremble, and the s men shall bow H2428
Song 8: 6 arm: for love *is* s as death; jealousy *is* H5794
Isa 1:31 And the s shall be as tow, and the H2634
5:11 they may follow s drink; that continue
22 and men of strength to mingle s drink:
8: 7 of the river, s and many, *even* the H6099
11 spake thus to me with a s hand, and H2393
17: 9 In that day shall his s cities be as a H4581
23:11 *city*, to destroy the s holds thereof. H4581
24: 9 They shall not drink wine with a song; s
25: 3 Therefore shall the s people glorify H5794

Isa 26: 1 Judah; We have a s city; salvation will H5797
27: 1 and great and s sword shall punish H2389
28: 2 Behold, the Lord hath a mighty and s H533
7 wine, and through s drink are out of the
7 have erred through s drink, they are
7 of the way through s drink; they err in
22 bands be made s: for I have heard from H2388
29: 9 wine; they stagger, but not with s drink.
31: 1 they are very s; but they look not unto H6105
9 And he shall pass over to his s hold for H5553
35: 4 of a fearful heart, Be s, fear not: behold, H2388
40:10 Behold, the Lord GOD will come with s H2389
26 for that *he is* s in power; not one faileth. H533
41:21 your s *reasons*, saith the King of Jacob. H6110
53:12 the spoil with the s; because he hath H6099
56:12 will fill ourselves with s drink; and to
60:22 and a small one a s nation: I the LORD H6099
Jer 8:16 of the neighing of his s ones; for they are H47
21: 5 hand and with a s arm, even in anger, H2389
32:21 wonders, and with a s hand, and with a H2389
47: 3 of the hoofs of his s *horses*, at the H47
48:14 How say ye, We *are* mighty and s men H2428
17 s staff broken, *and* the beautiful rod! H5797
18 thee, *and* he shall destroy thy s holds. H4013
41 Kerioth is taken, and the s holds are H4679
49:19 habitation of the s: but I will suddenly H386
50:34 Their Redeemer *is* s; the LORD of hosts H2389
44 habitation of the s: but I will make them H386
51:12 make the watch s, set up the watchmen, H2388
Lam 2: 2 in his wrath the s holds of the daughter H4013
5 he hath destroyed his s holds, and hath H4013
Ezk 3: 8 Behold, I have made thy face s against H2389
8 thy forehead s against their foreheads. H2389
14 the hand of the LORD was s upon me. H2388
7:24 the pomp of the s to cease; and their H5794
19:11 And she had s rods for the sceptres of H5797
12 up her fruit: her s rods were broken H5797
14 that she hath no s rod *to be* a sceptre to H5797
22:14 thine hands be s, in the days that I shall H2388
26:11 the sword, and thy s garrisons shall go H5797
17 city, which wast s in the sea, she and H2389
30:21 bind it, to make it s to hold the sword. H2388
22 his arms, the s, and that which was H2389
32:21 The s among the mighty shall speak to H410
34:16 the s; I will feed them with judgment. H2389
Dan 2:40 And the fourth kingdom shall be s as H8624
42 shall be partly s, and partly broken. H8624
4:11 The tree grew, and was s, and the H8631
20 grew, and was s, whose height reached H8631
22 and become s: for thy greatness is H8631
7: 7 and terrible, and s exceedingly; and it H8624
8: 8 and when he was s, the great horn was H6105
10:19 *be* unto thee, be s, yea, be strong. And H2388
19 be strong, yea, be s. And when he had H2388
11: 5 And the king of the south shall be s, and H2388
5 and he shall be s above him, and have H2388
23 shall become s with a small people. H6105
24 against the s holds, even for a time. H4013
32 their God shall be s, and do *exploits*. H2388
39 Thus shall he do in the most s holds H4581
Joel 1: 6 come up upon my land, s, and without H6099
2: 2 a great people and a s; there hath not H6099
5 as a s people set in battle array. H6099
11 very great: for *he is* s that executeth his H6099
3:10 into spears: let the weak say, I *am* s. H1368
Am 2: 9 cedars, and he *was* s as the oaks; yet I H2634
14 the swift, and the s shall not strengthen H2389
5: 9 against the s, so that the spoiled shall H5794
Mic 2:11 of wine and of s drink; he shall even H7941
4: 3 and rebuke s nations afar off; and H6099
7 that was cast far off a s nation: and the H6099
8 And thou, O tower of the flock, the s H6076
5:11 land, and throw down all thy s holds: H4013
6: 2 and ye s foundations of the earth: H386
Nah 1: 7 The LORD *is* good, a s hold in the day H4581
2: 1 *thy* loins s, fortify *thy* power mightily. H2388
3:12 All thy s holds *shall be like* fig trees H4013
14 siege, fortify thy s holds: go into clay, H4013
14 tread the morter, make s the brickkiln. H2388
Hab 1:10 shall deride every s hold; for they shall H4013
Hag 2: 4 Yet now be s, O Zerubbabel, saith the H2388
4 the LORD; and be s, O Joshua, son of H2388
4 high priest; and be s, all ye people of the H2388
Zec 8: 9 Let your hands be s, ye that hear in H2388
13 fear not, *but* let your hands be s. H2388
22 Yea, many people and s nations shall H6099
9: 3 And Tyrus did build herself a s hold, H4692
12 Turn you to the s hold, ye prisoners of H1225
Mt 12:29 Or else how can one enter into a s G2478
Mt 12:29 s man? and then he will spoil his house. G2478
Mk 3:27 No man can enter into a s man's G2478
27 s man; and then he will spoil his house. G2478
Lk 1:15 neither wine nor s drink; and he shall G4608
80 And the child grew, and waxed s in G2901
2:40 And the child grew, and waxed s in G2901
11:21 When a s man armed keepeth his G2478
Act 3:16 hath made this man s, whom ye see and G4732
Ro 4:20 but was s in faith, giving glory to God; G1743
15: 1 We then that are s ought to bear the G1415
1Co 4:10 weak, but ye *are* s; ye *are* honourable, G2478
16:13 fast in the faith, quit you like men, be s. G2901
2Co 10: 4 God to the pulling down of s holds;) G3794
12:10 sake: for when I am weak, then am I s. G1415
13: 9 are weak, and ye are s: and this also we G1415
Eph 6:10 Finally, my brethren, be s in the Lord, G1743
2Th 2:11 shall send them s delusion, that they G1753
2Ti 2: 1 Thou therefore, my son, be s in the G1743
Heb 5: 7 supplications with s crying and tears G2478
12 have need of milk, and not of s meat. G4731
14 But s meat belongeth to them that are G4731
6:18 lie, we might have a s consolation, who G2478
11:34 were made s, waxed valiant in fight, G1743
1Jn 2:14 because ye are s, and the word of God G2478
Rev 5: 2 And I saw a s angel proclaiming with a G2478
18: 2 And he cried mightily with a s voice, G3173
8 for s *is* the Lord God who judgeth her. G2478

STRONGER

Gen 25:23 *the one* people shall be s than *the other* H553
30:41 And it came to pass, whensoever the s H7194
42 feebler were Laban's, and the s Jacob's. H7194
Nu 13:31 the people; for they *are* s than we. H2389
Jdg 14:18 and what *is* s than a lion? And he H5794
2Sa 1:23 than eagles, they were s than lions. H1396
3: 1 but David waxed s and stronger, and H1980
1 stronger and s, and the house of Saul H2390
13:14 s than she, forced her, and lay with her. H2388
1Ki 20:23 they were s than we; but let us fight H2388
23 and surely we shall be s than they. H2388
25 surely we shall be s than they. And he H2388
Job 17: 9 clean hands shall be s and stronger.
9 hath clean hands shall be stronger and s. H555
Ps 105:24 and made them s than their enemies. H6105
142: 6 my persecutors; for they are s than I. H553
Jer 20: 7 deceived: thou art s than I, and hast H2388
31:11 the hand of *him that was* s than he. H2389
Lk 11:22 But when a s than he shall come upon G2478
1Co 1:25 and the weakness of God is s than men. G2478
10:22 the Lord to jealousy? are we s than he? G2478

STRONGEST

Prv 30:30 A lion *which is* s among beasts, and H1368

STRONGLY

Ezr 6: 3 thereof be s laid; the height thereof

STROVE

Gen 26:20 the well Esek; because they s with him. H6229
21 And they digged another well, and s for H7378
22 and for that they s not: and he called H7378
Ex 2:13 of the Hebrews s together: and he said H5327
Lev 24:10 a man of Israel s together in the camp; H5327
Nu 20:13 children of Israel s with the LORD, and H7378
26: 9 congregation, who s against Moses and H5327
9 Korah, when they s against the LORD: H5327
2Sa 14: 6 two sons, and they two s together in the H5327
Ps 60: ttl David, to teach; when he s with H5327
Dan 7: 2 of the heaven s upon the great sea. H1519
Jn 6:52 The Jews therefore s among G3164
Act 7:26 unto them as they s, and would have set G3164
23: 9 part arose, and s, saying, We find no G1264

STROWED

2Ch 34: 4 dust *of them*, and s *it* upon the graves H2236

STRUCK

1Sa 2:14 And he s *it* into the pan, or kettle, or H5221
2Sa 12:15 And the LORD s the child that Uriah's H5062
20:10 to the ground, and s him not again; H8138
2Ch 13:20 and the LORD s him, and he died. H5062
Mt 26:51 his sword, and s a servant of the high G3960
Lk 22:64 him, they s him on the face, and G5180
Jn 18:22 which stood by s Jesus with the palm G1325

STRUGGLED

Gen 25:22 And the children s together within her; H7533

STUBBLE

Ex 5:12 of Egypt to gather s instead of straw. H7179
15: 7 thy wrath, *which* consumed them as s. H7179
Job 13:25 and fro? and wilt thou pursue the dry s? H7179
21:18 They are as s before the wind, and as H8401
41:28 slingstones are turned with him into s. H7179
29 Darts are counted as s: he laugheth at H7179
Ps 83:13 like a wheel; as the s before the wind. H7179
Isa 5:24 Therefore as the fire devoureth the s, H7179
33:11 s: your breath, *as* fire, shall devour you. H7179
40:24 whirlwind shall take them away as s. H7179
41: 2 his sword, *and* as driven s to his bow. H7179
47:14 Behold, they shall be as s; the fire shall H7179
Jer 13:24 Therefore will I scatter them as the s H7179
Joel 2: 5 s, as a strong people set in battle array. H7179
Oba 18 the house of Esau for s, and they shall H7179
Nah 1:10 they shall be devoured as s fully dry. H7179
Mal 4: 1 do wickedly, shall be s: and the day that H7179
1Co 3:12 silver, precious stones, wood, hay, s; G2562

STUBBORN

Dt 21:18 If a man have a s and rebellious son, H5637
20 This our son *is* s and rebellious, he will H5637
Jdg 2:19 their own doings, nor from their s way. H7186
Ps 78: 8 And might not be as their fathers, a s H5637
Prv 7:11 (She *is* loud and s; her feet abide not in H5637

STUBBORNNESS

Dt 9:27 look not unto the s of this people, nor H7190
1Sa 15:23 of witchcraft, and s *is as* iniquity and H6484

STUCK

1Sa 26: 7 and his spear s in the ground at his H4600
Ps 119:31 I have s unto thy testimonies: O LORD, H1692
Act 27:41 and the forepart s fast, and remained G2043

STUDIETH

Prv 15:28 The heart of the righteous s to answer: H1897
24: 2 For their heart s destruction, and their H1897

STUDS

Song 1:11 thee borders of gold with s of silver. H5351

STUDY

Ecc 12:12 and much s *is* a weariness of the flesh. H3854
1Th 4:11 And that ye s to be quiet, and to do G5389
2Ti 2:15 S to shew thyself approved unto God, a G4704

STUFF

Gen 31:37 Whereas thou hast searched all my s, H3627
37 of all thy household s? set *it* here before H3627
45:20 Also regard not your s; for the good of H3627
Ex 22: 7 money or s to keep, and it be stolen H3627
36: 7 For the s they had was sufficient for all H4399
Jos 7:11 have put *it* even among their own s. H3627
1Sa 10:22 he hath hid himself among the s. H3627
25:13 men; and two hundred abode by the s. H3627
30:24 tarrieth by the s: they shall part alike. H3627
Neh 13: 8 s of Tobiah out of the chamber. H3627
Ezk 12: 3 man, prepare thee s for removing, and H3627
4 Then shalt thou bring forth thy s by H3627
4 in their sight, as s for removing: and H3627
7 I brought forth my s by day, as stuff for H3627
7 stuff by day, as s for captivity, and in H3627
Lk 17:31 the housetop, and his s in the house, let G4632

STUMBLE

Prv 3:23 thy way safely, and thy foot shall not s. H5062
4:12 when thou runnest, thou shalt not s. H3782
19 darkness: they know not at what they s. H3782
Isa 5:27 None shall be weary nor s among H3782
8:15 And many among them shall s, and fall, H3782
28: 7 they err in vision, they s *in* judgment. H6328
59:10 *had* no eyes: we s at noonday as in the H3782
63:13 the wilderness, *that* they should not s? H3782
Jer 13:16 and before your feet s upon the dark H5062
18:15 caused them to s in their ways *from* the H3782
20:11 persecutors shall s, and they shall not H3782
31: 9 they shall not s: for I am a father to H3782
46: 6 escape; they shall s, and fall toward the H3782
50:32 And the most proud shall s and fall, H3782
Dan 11:19 he shall s and fall, and not be found. H3782
Nah 2: 5 they shall s in their walk; they shall H3782
3: 3 corpses; they s upon their corpses: H3782
Mal 2: 8 caused many to s at the law; ye have H3782
1Pt 2: 8 *to them* which s at the word, being G4350

STUMBLED

1Sa 2: 4 they that s are girded with strength. H3782

1Ch 13: 9 his hand to hold the ark; for the oxen **s**. H8058
Ps 27: 2 me to eat up my flesh, they **s** and fell. H3782
Jer 46:12 mighty man hath **s** against the mighty, H3782
Ro 9:32 law. For they **s** at that stumblingstone; *G4350*
11:11 I say then, Have they **s** that they should *G4417*

STUMBLETH
Prv 24:17 let not thine heart be glad when he **s**: H3782
Jn 11: 9 in the day, he **s** not, because he seeth *G4350*
10 But if a man walk in the night, he **s**, *G4350*
Ro 14:21 **s**, or is offended, or is made weak. *G4350*

STUMBLING
Isa 8:14 but for a stone of **s** and for a rock of H5063
1Pt 2: 8 And a stone of **s**, and a rock of offence, *G4348*
1Jn 2:10 and there is none occasion of **s** in him. *G4625*

STUMBLINGBLOCK
Lev 19:14 the deaf, nor put a **s** before the blind, H4383
Isa 57:14 up the **s** out of the way of my people. H4383
Ezk 3:20 and I lay a **s** before him, he shall H4383
7:19 because it is the **s** of their iniquity. H4383
14: 3 heart, and put the **s** of their iniquity H4383
4 and putteth the **s** of his iniquity before H4383
7 and putteth the **s** of his iniquity before H4383
Ro 11: 9 and a **s**, and a recompence unto them: *G4625*
14:13 that no man put a **s** or an occasion to *G4348*
1Co 1:23 a **s**, and unto the Greeks foolishness; *G4625*
8: 9 become a **s** to them that are weak. *G4348*
Rev 2:14 Balac to cast a **s** before the children *G4625*

STUMBLINGBLOCKS
Jer 6:21 Behold, I will lay **s** before this people, H4383
Zep 1: 3 of the sea, and the **s** with the wicked; H4384

STUMBLINGSTONE
Ro 9:32 of the law. For they stumbled at that **s**; *G3037*
33 As it is written, Behold, I lay in Sion a **s** *G3037*

STUMP
1Sa 5: 4 only *the* **s** *of* Dagon was left to him.
Dan 4:15 Nevertheless leave the **s** of his roots in H6136
23 it; yet leave the **s** of the roots thereof H6136
26 to leave the **s** of the tree roots; thy H6136

SUAH
1Ch 7:36 The sons of Zophah; **S**, and Harnepher, H5477

SUBDUE
Gen 1:28 the earth, and **s** it: and have dominion H3533
1Ch 17:10 Moreover I will **s** all thine enemies. H3665
Ps 47: 3 He shall **s** the people under us, and the H1696
Isa 45: 1 I have holden, to **s** nations before him; H7286
Dan 7:24 the first, and he shall **s** three kings. H8214
Mic 7:19 upon us; he will **s** our iniquities; and H3533
Zec 9:15 shall devour, and **s** with sling stones; H3533
Php 3:21 is able even to **s** all things unto himself. *G5293*

SUBDUED
Nu 32:22 And the land be **s** before the LORD: H3533
29 the land shall be **s** before you; then ye H3533
Dt 20:20 that maketh war with thee, until it be **s**. H3381
Jos 18: 1 there. And the land was **s** before them. H3533
Jdg 3:30 So Moab was **s** that day under the H3665
4:23 So God **s** on that day Jabin the king of H3665
8:28 Thus was Midian **s** before the children H3665
11:33 were **s** before the children of Israel. H3665
1Sa 7:13 So the Philistines were **s**, and they came H3665
2Sa 8: 1 Philistines, and **s** them: and David took H3665
11 had dedicated of all nations which he **s**; H3533
22:40 up against me hast thou **s** under me. H3766
1Ch 18: 1 Philistines, and **s** them, and took Gath H3665
20: 4 children of the giant: and they were **s**. H3665
22:18 and the land is **s** before the LORD, and H3533
Ps 18:39 battle: thou hast **s** under me those that H3766
81:14 I should soon have **s** their enemies, and H3665
1Co 15:28 And when all things shall be **s** unto *G5293*
Heb 11:33 Who through faith **s** kingdoms, *G2610*

SUBDUEDST
Neh 9:24 the land, and thou **s** before them the H3665

SUBDUETH
Ps 18:47 *It is* God that avengeth me, and **s** the H1696
144: 2 I trust; who **s** my people under me. H7286
Dan 2:40 in pieces and **s** all *things*: and as iron H2827

SUBJECT
Lk 2:51 and was **s** unto them: but his mother *G5293*
10:17 devils are **s** unto us through thy name. *G5293*
20 not, that the spirits are **s** unto you; but *G5293*
Ro 8: 7 God: for it is not **s** to the law of God, *G5293*
20 For the creature was made **s** to vanity, *G5293*
13: 1 Let every soul be **s** unto the higher *G5293*
5 Wherefore *ye* must needs be **s**, not only *G5293*
1Co 14:32 And the spirits of the prophets are **s** to *G5293*
15:28 also himself be **s** unto him that put all *G5293*
Eph 5:24 Therefore as the church is **s** unto *G5293*
Col 2:20 in the world, are ye **s** to ordinances, *G1379*
Tit 3: 1 Put them in mind to be **s** to *G5293*
Heb 2:15 were all their lifetime **s** to bondage. *G1777*
Jas 5:17 Elias was a man **s** to like passions as *G3663*
1Pt 2:18 Servants, *be* **s** to *your* masters with all *G5293*
3:22 and powers being made **s** unto him. *G5293*
5: 5 Yea, all *of you* be **s** one to another, and *G5293*

SUBJECTED
Ro 8:20 of him who hath **s** *the same* in hope, *G5293*

SUBJECTION
Ps 106:42 were brought into **s** under their hand. H3665
Jer 34:11 into **s** for servants and for handmaids. H3533
16 brought them into **s**, to be unto you for H3533
1Co 9:27 and bring *it* into **s**: lest that by any *G1396*
2Co 9:13 for your professed **s** unto the gospel of *G5292*
Gal 2: 5 To whom we gave place by **s**, no, not for *G5292*
1Ti 2:11 the woman learn in silence with all **s**. *G5292*
3: 4 his children in **s** with all gravity; *G5292*
Heb 2: 5 For unto the angels hath he not put in **s** *G5293*
8 Thou hast put all things in **s** under his *G5293*
8 in that he put all in **s** under him, he left *G5293*
12: 9 in **s** unto the Father of spirits, and live? *G5293*
1Pt 3: 1 Likewise, ye wives, *be* in **s** to your own *G5293*
5 being in **s** unto their own husbands: *G5293*

SUBMIT
Gen 16: 9 and **s** thyself under her hands. H6031
2Sa 22:45 Strangers shall **s** themselves unto me: H3584
Ps 18:44 strangers shall **s** themselves unto me. H3584
66: 3 thine enemies **s** themselves unto thee. H3584
68:30 *till every one* **s** himself with pieces H7511
1Co 16:16 That ye **s** yourselves unto such, and to *G5293*
Eph 5:22 Wives, **s** yourselves unto your own *G5293*
Col 3:18 Wives, **s** yourselves unto your own *G5293*
Heb 13:17 the rule over you, and **s** yourselves: for *G5226*
Jas 4: 7 **S** yourselves therefore to God. Resist *G5293*
1Pt 2:13 **S** yourselves to every ordinance of man *G5293*
5: 5 Likewise, ye younger, **s** yourselves unto *G5293*

SUBMITTED
1Ch 29:24 **s** themselves unto Solomon the king. H5414
Ps 81:15 The haters of the LORD should have **s** H3584
Ro 10: 3 have not **s** themselves unto the *G5293*

SUBMITTING
Eph 5:21 **S** yourselves one to another in the fear *G5293*

SUBORNED
Act 6:11 Then they **s** men, which said, We have *G5260*

SUBSCRIBE
Isa 44: 5 and another shall **s** *with* his hand unto H3789
Jer 32:44 Men shall buy fields for money, and **s** H3789

SUBSCRIBED
Jer 32:10 And I **s** the evidence, and sealed *it*, and H3789
12 of the witnesses that **s** the book of the H3789

SUBSTANCE
Gen 7: 4 and every living **s** that I have made will H3351
23 And every living **s** was destroyed which H3351
12: 5 son, and all their **s** that they had H7399
13: 6 together: for their **s** was great, so that H7399
15:14 shall they come out with great **s**. H7399
34:23 *Shall* not their cattle and their **s** and H7075
36: 6 beasts, and all his **s**, which he had got H7075
Dt 11: 6 tents, and all the **s** that *was* in their H3351
33:11 Bless, LORD, his **s**, and accept the work H2428
Jos 14: 4 suburbs for their cattle and for their **s**. H7075
1Ch 27:31 rulers of the **s** which *was* king David's. H7399
28: 1 over all the **s** and possession of the H7399
2Ch 21:17 away all the **s** that was found in the H7399
31: 3 portion of his **s** for the burnt offerings, H7399
32:29 for God had given him **s** very much. H7399
35: 7 bullocks: these *were* of the king's **s**. H7399
Ezr 8:21 and for our little ones, and for all our **s**. H7399
10: 8 the elders, all his **s** should be forfeited, H7399
Job 1: 3 His **s** also was seven thousand sheep, H4735
1:10 and his **s** is increased in the land. H4735
5: 5 and the robber swalloweth up their **s**. H2428
6:22 me? or, Give a reward for me of your **s**? H3581
15:29 He shall not be rich, neither shall his **s** H2428
20:18 according to *his* **s** *shall* the restitution H2428
22:20 Whereas our **s** is not cut down, but the H7009
30:22 me to ride *upon it*, and dissolvest my **s**. H7738
Ps 17:14 leave the rest of their *s* to their babes.
105:21 lord of his house, and ruler of all his **s**: H7075
139:15 My **s** was not hid from thee, when I H6108
16 Thine eyes did see my **s**, yet being H1564
Prv 1:13 We shall find all precious **s**, we shall fill H1952
3: 9 Honour the LORD with thy **s**, and with H1952
6:31 he shall give all the **s** of his house. H1952
8:21 inherit **s**; and I will fill their treasures. H3426
10: 3 but he casteth away the **s** of the wicked. H1942
12:27 but the **s** of a diligent man *is* precious. H1952
28: 8 increaseth his **s**, he shall gather it for H1952
29: 3 company with harlots spendeth *his* **s**. H1952
Song 8: 7 would give all the **s** of his house for H1952
Isa 6:13 as an oak, whose **s** *is* in them, when H4678
13 *so* the holy seed *shall be* the **s** thereof. H4678
Jer 15:13 Thy **s** and thy treasures will I give to H2428
17: 3 I will give thy **s** *and* all thy treasures H2428
Hos 12: 8 I have found me out **s**: *in* all my labours H202
Oba 13 on their **s** in the day of their calamity; H2428
Mic 4:13 **s** unto the Lord of the whole earth. H2428
Lk 8: 3 which ministered unto him of their **s**. *G5224*
15:13 there wasted his **s** with riotous living. *G3776*
Heb 10:34 in heaven a better and an enduring **s**. *G5223*
11: 1 Now faith is the **s** of things hoped for, *G5287*

SUBTIL
Gen 3: 1 Now the serpent was more **s** than any H6175
2Sa 13: 3 and Jonadab *was* a very **s** man. H2450
Prv 7:10 the attire of an harlot, and **s** of heart. H5341

SUBTILLY
1Sa 23:22 for it is told me *that* he dealeth very **s**. H6191
Ps 105:25 his people, to deal **s** with his servants. H5230
Act 7:19 The same dealt **s** with our kindred, and *G2686*

SUBTILTY
Gen 27:35 And he said, Thy brother came with **s**, H4820
2Ki 10:19 But Jehu did *it* in **s**, to the intent that he H6122
Prv 1: 4 To give **s** to the simple, to the young H6195
Mt 26: 4 they might take Jesus by **s**, and kill *him*. *G1388*
Act 13:10 And said, O full of all **s** and all *G1388*
2Co 11: 3 Eve through his **s**, so your minds should *G3834*

SUBTLE See SUBTIL.

SUBURBS
Lev 25:34 But the field of the **s** of their cities may H4054
Nu 35: 2 **s** for the cities round about them. H4054
3 dwell in; and the **s** of them shall be for H4054
4 And the **s** of the cities, which ye shall H4054
5 this shall be to them the **s** of the cities. H4054
7 cities: them *shall ye give* with their **s**. H4054
Jos 14: 4 *in*, with their **s** for their cattle and for H4054
21: 2 in, with the **s** thereof for our cattle. H4054
3 of the LORD, these cities and their **s**. H4054
8 these cities with their **s**, as the LORD H4054
11 with the **s** thereof round about it. H4054
13 Hebron with her **s**, *to be* a city of refuge H4054
13 for the slayer; and Libnah with her **s**, H4054
14 And Jattir with her **s**, and Eshtemoa H4054
14 her suburbs, and Eshtemoa with her **s**, H4054
15 And Holon with her **s**, and Debir with H4054
15 with her suburbs, and Debir with her **s**, H4054
16 And Ain with her **s**, and Juttah with her H4054
16 Juttah with her **s**, *and* Beth-shemesh H4054
16 her **s**; nine cities out of those two tribes. H4054
17 with her **s**, Geba with her suburbs, H4054
17 with her suburbs, Geba with her **s**, H4054
18 Anathoth with her **s**, and Almon with H4054
18 and Almon with her **s**; four cities. H4054
19 priests, *were* thirteen cities with their **s**. H4054
21 For they gave them Shechem with her **s** H4054
21 for the slayer; and Gezer with her **s**, H4054
22 And Kibzaim with her **s**, and H4054
22 and Beth-horon with her **s**; four cities. H4054
23 with her **s**, Gibbethon with her suburbs, H4054
23 with her suburbs, Gibbethon with her **s**, H4054
24 Aijalon with her **s**, Gath-rimmon with H4054
24 Gath-rimmon with her **s**; four cities. H4054
25 Tanach with her **s**, and Gath-rimmon H4054
25 and Gath-rimmon with her **s**; two cities. H4054
26 All the cities *were* ten with their **s** for H4054

Jos 21:27 Bashan with her s, to be a city of refuge H4054
27 and Beesh-terah with her s; two cities. H4054
28 with her s, Dabareh with her suburbs, H4054
28 with her suburbs, Dabareh with her s, H4054
29 Jarmuth with her s, En-gannim with H4054
29 En-gannim with her s; four cities. H4054
30 with her s, Abdon with her suburbs, H4054
30 with her suburbs, Abdon with her s, H4054
31 Helkath with her s, and Rehob with her H4054
31 and Rehob with her s; four cities. H4054
32 in Galilee with her s, to be a city of H4054
32 with her s, and Kartan with her H4054
32 and Kartan with her s; three cities. H4054
33 families were thirteen cities with their s. H4054
34 her s, and Kartah with her suburbs, H4054
34 her suburbs, and Kartah with her s, H4054
35 Dimnah with her s, Nahalal with her H4054
35 suburbs, Nahalal with her s; four cities. H4054
36 her s, and Jahazah with her suburbs,
36 her suburbs, and Jahazah with her s,
37 Kedemoth with her s, and Mephaath
37 and Mephaath with her s; four cities.
38 in Gilead with her s, to be a city of H4054
38 the slayer; and Mahanaim with her s, H4054
39 Heshbon with her s, Jazer with her H4054
39 Jazer with her s; four cities in all. H4054
41 were forty and eight cities with their s. H4054
42 These cities were every one with their s H4054
2Ki 23:11 which was in the s, and burned the H6503
1Ch 5:16 all the s of Sharon, upon their borders. H4054
6:55 and the s thereof round about it. H4054
57 and Libnah with her s, and Jattir, and H4054
57 and Jattir, and Eshtemoa, with their s, H4054
58 And Hilen with her s, Debir with her H4054
58 with her suburbs, Debir with her s, H4054
59 And Ashan with her s, and H4054
59 suburbs, and Beth-shemesh with her s: H4054
60 Geba with her s, and Alemeth with her H4054
60 Alemeth with her s, and Anathoth with H4054
60 and Anathoth with her s. All their cities H4054
64 to the Levites these cities with their s. H4054
67 Ephraim with her s; they gave also H4054
67 they gave also Gezer with her s, H4054
68 And Jokmeam with her s, and H4054
68 her suburbs, and Beth-horon with her s, H4054
69 And Aijalon with her s, and H4054
69 suburbs, and Gath-rimmon with her s: H4054
70 Aner with her s, and Bileam with her H4054
70 Bileam with her s, for the family of the H4054
71 her s, and Ashtaroth with her suburbs: H4054
71 her suburbs, and Ashtaroth with her s: H4054
72 with her s, Daberath with her suburbs, H4054
72 with her suburbs, Daberath with her s, H4054
73 And Ramoth with her s, and Anem with H4054
73 with her suburbs, and Anem with her s: H4054
74 her s, and Abdon with her suburbs, H4054
74 her suburbs, and Abdon with her s, H4054
75 And Hukok with her s, and Rehob with H4054
75 with her suburbs, and Rehob with her s: H4054
76 in Galilee with her s, and Hammon with H4054
76 her s, and Kirjathaim with her suburbs. H4054
76 her suburbs, and Kirjathaim with her s. H4054
77 with her s, Tabor with her suburbs: H4054
77 with her suburbs, Tabor with her s: H4054
78 her s, and Jahzah with her suburbs, H4054
78 her suburbs, and Jahzah with her s, H4054
79 Kedemoth also with her s, and H4054
79 her suburbs, and Mephaath with her s: H4054
80 her s, and Mahanaim with her suburbs, H4054
80 her suburbs, and Mahanaim with her s, H4054
81 And Heshbon with her s, and Jazer with H4054
81 with her suburbs, and Jazer with her s. H4054
13: 2 are in their cities and s, that they may H4054
2Ch 11:14 For the Levites left their s and their H4054
31:19 in the fields of the s of their cities, in H4054
Ezk 27:28 The s shall shake at the sound of the H4054
45: 2 cubits round about for the s thereof. H4054
48:15 dwelling, and for s: and the city shall be H4054
17 And the s of the city shall be toward the H4054

SUBVERT
Lam 3:36 To s a man in his cause, the Lord H5791
Tit 1:11 Whose mouths must be stopped, who s G396

SUBVERTED
Tit 3:11 Knowing that he that is such is s, and G1612

SUBVERTING
Act 15:24 you with words, s your souls, saying, Ye G384
2Ti 2:14 to no profit, but to the s of the hearers. G2692

SUCCEED
Dt 25: 6 she beareth shall s in the name of his H6965

SUCCEEDED
Dt 2:12 children of Esau s them, when they had H3423
21 they s them, and dwelt in their stead: H3423
22 them; and they s them, and dwelt in H3423

SUCCEEDEST
Dt 12:29 thou s them, and dwellest in their land; H3423
19: 1 thee, and thou s them, and dwellest H3423

SUCCESS
Jos 1: 8 and then thou shalt have good s. H7919

SUCCOR See SUCCOUR.

SUCCOTH
Gen 33:17 And Jacob journeyed to S, and built H5523
17 the name of the place is called S. H5523
Ex 12:37 from Rameses to S, about six hundred H5523
13:20 And they took their journey from S, and H5523
Nu 33: 5 from Rameses, and pitched in S. H5523
6 And they departed from S, and pitched H5523
Jos 13:27 Beth-nimrah, and S, and Zaphon, the H5523
Jdg 8: 5 And he said unto the men of S, Give, I H5523
6 And the princes of S said, Are the H5523
8 him as the men of S had answered him. H5523
14 man of the men of S, and inquired of H5523
14 him the princes of S, and the elders H5523
15 And he came unto the men of S, and H5523
16 and with them he taught the men of S. H5523
1Ki 7:46 clay ground between S and Zarthan. H5523
2Ch 4:17 ground between S and Zeredathah. H5523
Ps 60: 6 Shechem, and mete out the valley of S. H5523
108: 7 Shechem, and mete out the valley of S. H5523

SUCCOTH-BENOTH
2Ki 17:30 And the men of Babylon made S, and H5524

SUCCOUR
2Sa 8: 5 came to s Hadadezer king of Zobah, H5826
18: 3 it is better that thou s us out of the city. H5826
Heb 2:18 he is able to s them that are tempted. G997

SUCCOURED
2Sa 21:17 But Abishai the son of Zeruiah s him, H5826
2Co 6: 2 of salvation have I s thee: behold, now is G997

SUCCOURER
Ro 16: 2 been a s of many, and of myself also. G4368

SUCH
Gen 4:20 was the father of s as dwell in tents, and
20 as dwell in tents, and of s as have cattle.
21 of all s as handle the harp and organ.
27: 4 And make me savoury meat, s as I love,
9 meat for thy father, s as he loveth:
14 savoury meat, s as his father loved.
46 daughters of Heth, s as these which are
30:32 the goats: and of s shall be my hire.
41:19 and leanfleshed, s as I never saw in all H2007
38 Can we find s a one as this is, a man
44:15 that s a man as I can certainly divine?
Ex 9:18 very grievous hail, s as hath not been in
24 hail, very grievous, s as there was none
10:14 there were no s locusts as they, neither H3651
14 as they, neither after them shall be s.
11: 6 all the land of Egypt, s as there was none
12:36 lent unto them s things as they required.
18:21 people able men, s as fear God, men of
21 and place s over them, to be rulers
34:10 I will do marvels, s as have not been
Lev 10:19 the LORD; and s things have befallen H428
11:34 that on which s water cometh shall be
34 drunk in every s vessel shall be unclean.
14:22 two young pigeons, s as he is able to get;
30 or of the young pigeons, s as he can get;
31 Even s as he is able to get, the one for a
20: 6 And the soul that turneth after s as have
22: 6 The soul which hath touched any s shall
27: 9 giveth of s unto the LORD shall be holy.
Nu 8:16 of Israel; instead of s as open every
Dt 4:32 hath been any s thing as this great thing
5:29 O that there were s an heart in them, H2088
13:11 any s wickedness as this is among you. H1697
14 s abomination is wrought among you; H2063
Dt 16: 9 the seven weeks from s time as thou
17: 4 s abomination is wrought in Israel: H2063
19:20 commit no more any s evil among you. H1697
25:16 For all that do s things, and all that do H428
Jdg 3: 2 least s as before knew nothing thereof;
13:23 this time have told us s things as these.
18:23 that thou comest with s a company?
19:30 There was no s deed done nor seen H2063
Ru 4: 1 whom he said, Ho, s a one! turn aside, H6423
1Sa 2:23 And he said unto them, Why do ye s H428
4: 7 hath not been s a thing heretofore. H2063
21: 2 my servants to s and such a place. H6423
2 my servants to such and s a place. H492
25:17 for he is s a son of Belial, that a
2Sa 9: 8 look upon s a dead dog as I am?
12: 8 have given unto thee s and such things. H2007
8 have given unto thee such and s things. H2007
13:12 not force me; for no s thing ought to be H3651
18 upon her: for with s robes were the H3651
14:13 hast thou thought s a thing against the H2063
16: 2 and the wine, that s as be faint in the
19:36 recompense it me with s a reward? H2063
1Ki 10:10 came no more s abundance of spices H1931
12 there came no s almug trees, nor were H3651
2Ki 6: 8 s and such a place shall be my camp. H6423
8 In such and s a place shall be my camp. H492
9 that thou pass not s a place; for thither H2088
7:19 in heaven, might s a thing be? And he H2088
19:29 Ye shall eat this year s things as grow of
21:12 I am bringing s evil upon Jerusalem
23:22 Surely there was not holden s a H2088
25:15 And the firepans, and the bowls, and s
1Ch 12:33 Of Zebulun, s as went forth to battle,
36 And of Asher, s as went forth to battle,
29:25 upon him s royal majesty as had
2Ch 1:12 and honour, s as none of the kings H834
4: 6 to wash in them: s things as they offered
9: 9 was there any s spice as the queen of H1932
11 none s seen before in the land of Judah. H1992
11:16 the tribes of Israel s as set their hearts to
23:13 of musick, and s as taught to sing praise.
24:12 And the king and Jehoiada gave it to s as
12 LORD, and also s as wrought iron and
30: 5 of a long time in s sort as it was written.
35:18 the kings of Israel keep s a passover as
Ezr 4:10 on this side the river, and at s a time. H3706
11 on this side the river, and at s a time. H3706
17 the river, Peace, and at s a time. H3706
6:21 of captivity, and all s as had separated
7:12 heaven, perfect peace, and at s a time. H3706
25 the river, all s as know the laws of
27 which hath put s a thing as this in the
8:31 and of s as lay in wait by the way.
9:13 and hast given us s deliverance as this;
10: 3 all the wives, and s as are born of them,
Neh 6: 8 There are no s things done as thou H428
11 And I said, Should s a man as I flee? H3644
Est 2: 9 purification, with s things as belonged to
4:11 to death, except s to whom the king shall H834
14 come to the kingdom for s a time as this?
9: 2 to lay hand on s as sought their hurt:
27 their seed, and upon all s as joined
Job 12: 3 who knoweth not s things as these? H3644
14: 3 And dost thou open thine eyes upon s H2088
15:13 and lettest s words go out of thy mouth?
16: 2 I have heard many s things: miserable H428
18:21 Surely s are the dwellings of the wicked, H428
23:14 me: and many s things are with him. H2007
Ps 25:10 and truth unto s as keep his covenant
27:12 against me, and s as breathe out cruelty.
34:18 and saveth s as be of a contrite spirit.
37:14 to slay s as be of upright conversation.
22 For s as be blessed of him shall inherit
40: 4 not the proud, nor s as turn aside to lies.
16 be glad in thee: let s as love thy salvation
50:21 I was altogether s an one as thyself: but
55:20 He hath put forth his hands against s as
68:21 the hairy scalp of s an one as goeth on
70: 4 in thee: and let s as love thy salvation
73: 1 Truly God is good to Israel, even to s as
103:18 To s as keep his covenant, and to those
107:10 S as sit in darkness and in the shadow of
125: 5 As for s as turn aside unto their crooked
139: 6 S knowledge is too wonderful for me; it
144:15 Happy is that people, that is in s a case: H3602
Prv 11:20 to the LORD: but s as are upright in their
28: 4 but s as keep the law contend with them.
30:20 S is the way of an adulterous woman; H3651
31: 8 of all s as are appointed to destruction.

S

Ecc 4: 1 behold the tears of s *as were* oppressed,
Isa 9: 1 Nevertheless the dimness *shall* not *be* s
10:20 of Israel, and s as are escaped of the
20: 6 that day, Behold, s *is* our expectation, H3541
37:30 shall eat *this* year s as groweth of itself;
58: 5 Is it s a fast that I have chosen? a day H2088
66: 8 Who hath heard s a thing? who hath H2063
8 who hath seen s things? Shall the earth H428
Jer 2:10 diligently, and see if there be s a thing. H2063
5: 9 soul be avenged on s a nation as this? H834
29 soul be avenged on s a nation as this? H834
9: 9 soul be avenged on s a nation as this?
15: 2 saith the LORD; S as *are* for death, to
2 to death; and s as *are* for the sword,
2 to the sword; and s as *are* for the famine,
2 s as *are* for the captivity, to the captivity.
18:13 who hath heard s things: the virgin of H428
21: 7 the people, and s as are left in this city
38: 4 people, in speaking s words unto them: H428
43:11 Egypt, *and deliver* s *as are* for death to
11 to death; and s *as are* for captivity to
11 and s *as are* for the sword to the sword.
44:14 none shall return but s as shall escape.
Ezk 17:15 he escape that doeth s *things*? or shall he H428
18:14 and considereth, and doeth not s like, H2007
Dan 1: 4 science, and s as *had* ability in them
2:10 nor ruler, *that* asked s things at any H1836
10:15 And when he had spoken s words unto H428
11:32 And s as do wickedly against the
12: 1 be a time of trouble, s as never was since H834
Am 5:16 s as are skilful of lamentation to wailing.
Mic 5:15 the heathen, s as they have not heard.
Zep 1: 8 all s as are clothed with strange apparel.
Mt 9: 8 which had given s power unto men. *G5108*
18: 5 And whoso shall receive one s little *G5108*
19:14 me: for of s is the kingdom of heaven. *G5108*
24:21 For then shall be great tribulation, s as *G3634*
44 Therefore be ye also ready: for in s an
26:18 And he said, Go into the city to s a *G1170*
Mk 4:18 among thorns; s as hear the word, *G3778*
20 on good ground; s as hear the word, *G3748*
33 And with many s parables spake he the *G5108*
6: 2 unto him, that even s mighty works are *G5108*
7: 8 and many other s like things ye do. *G5108*
13 delivered: and many s like things do ye. *G5108*
9:37 Whosoever shall receive one of s *G5108*
10:14 not: for of s is the kingdom of God. *G5108*
13: 7 ye not troubled: for *s things* must needs
19 For *in* those days shall be affliction, s *G3634*
Lk 9: 9 s things? And he desired to see him. *G3634*
10: 7 and drinking s things as they give: for
8 you, eat s things as are set before you:
11:41 But rather give alms of s things as ye
13: 2 because they suffered s things? *G5108*
18:16 not: for of s is the kingdom of God. *G5108*
Jn 4:23 the Father seeketh s to worship him. *G5108*
7:32 people murmured s things concerning *G5023*
8: 5 us, that s should be stoned: but *G5108*
9:16 man that is a sinner do s miracles? And *G5108*
Act 2:47 to the church daily s as should be saved.
3: 6 have I none; but s as I have give I thee:
15:24 to whom we gave no *s* commandment:
16:24 Who, having received s a charge, *G5108*
18:15 *to it*; for I will be no judge of s *matters*. *G5130*
21:25 they observe no s thing, save only that *G5108*
22:22 and said, Away with s a *fellow* from the *G5108*
25:18 accusation of s things as I supposed:
20 And because I doubted of s manner of
26:29 s as I am, except these bonds. *G5108*
28:10 laded *us* with s things as were necessary.
Ro 1:32 which commit s things are worthy of *G5108*
2: 2 against them which commit s things. *G5108*
3 them which do s things, and doest the *G5108*
16:18 For they that are s serve not our Lord *G5108*
1Co 5: 1 among you, and s fornication as is not *G5108*
5 To deliver s an one unto Satan for the *G5108*
11 extortioner; with s an one no not to eat. *G5108*
6:11 And s were some of you: but ye are *G5023*
7:15 under bondage in s *cases*: but God hath *G5108*
28 Nevertheless s shall have trouble in *G5108*
10:13 taken you but s as is common to man:
11:16 s custom, neither the churches of God. *G5108*
15:48 As *is* the earthy, s *are* they also that are *G5108*
48 s *are* they also that are heavenly. *G5108*
16:16 That ye submit yourselves unto s, and *G5108*
18 acknowledge ye them that are s. *G5108*
2Co 2: 6 Sufficient to s a man *is* this *G5108*
7 *him*, lest perhaps s a one should be *G5108*
3: 4 And s trust have we through Christ to *G5108*
2Co 3:12 Seeing then that we have s hope, we *G5108*
10:11 Let s an one think this, that, such as we *G3634*
11 Let such an one think this, that, s as we *G5108*
11 we are absent, s *will we be* also in deed *G5108*
11:13 For s *are* false apostles, deceitful *G5108*
12: 2 s an one caught up to the third heaven. *G5108*
3 And I knew s a man, (whether in the *G5108*
5 Of s an one will I glory: yet of myself I *G5108*
20 I shall not find you s as I would, and *G3634*
20 be found unto you s as ye would not: *G3634*
Gal 5:21 revellings, and s like: of the which I tell *G5125*
21 that they which do s things shall not *G5108*
23 Meekness, temperance: against s there *G5108*
6: 1 spiritual, restore s an one in the spirit *G5108*
Eph 5:27 or wrinkle, or any s thing; but that it *G5108*
Php 2:29 all gladness; and hold s in reputation: *G5108*
1Th 4: 6 *is* the avenger of all s, as we also have *G5130*
2Th 3:12 Now them that are s we command and *G5108*
1Ti 6: 5 is godliness: from s withdraw thyself. *G5108*
2Ti 3: 5 the power thereof: from s turn away. *G5128*
Tit 3:11 Knowing that he that is s is subverted, *G5108*
Phlm 9 *thee*, being s an one as Paul the aged, *G5108*
Heb 5:12 and are become s as have need of milk,
7:26 For s an high priest became us, *who is* *G5108*
8: 1 the sum: We have s an high priest, who *G5108*
11:14 For they that say s things declare *G5108*
12: 3 For consider him that endured s *G5108*
13: 5 *be* content with s things as ye have: for *G3588*
16 for with s sacrifices God is well pleased. *G5108*
Jas 4:13 we will go into s a city, and continue *G3592*
16 in your boastings: all s rejoicing is evil. *G5108*
2Pt 1:17 when there came s a voice to him from *G5107*
3:14 that ye look for s things, be diligent *G5023*
3Jn 8 We therefore ought to receive s, that we *G5108*
Rev 5:13 the earth, and s as are in the sea, and
16:18 a great earthquake, s as was not since *G3634*
20: 6 resurrection: on s the second death *G5130*

SUCHATHITES
1Ch 2:55 the Shimeathites, *and* S. These *are* the H7756

SUCK
Gen 21: 7 given children s? for I have born *him* H3243
Dt 32:13 he made him to s honey out of the rock, H3243
33:19 for they shall s *of* the abundance of H3243
1Sa 1:23 gave her son s until she weaned him. H3243
1Ki 3:21 to give my child s, behold, it was dead: H3243
Job 3:12 me? or why the breasts that I should s? H3243
20:16 He shall s the poison of asps: the H3243
39:30 Her young ones also s up blood: and H5966
Isa 60:16 Thou shalt also s the milk of the H3243
16 the Gentiles, and shalt s the breast of H3243
66:11 That ye may s, and be satisfied with the H3243
12 then shall ye s, ye shall be borne upon H3243
Lam 4: 3 breast, they give s to their young ones: H3243
Ezk 23:34 Thou shalt even drink it and s *it* out, H4680
Joel 2:16 and those that s the breasts: let the H3243
Mt 24:19 and to them that give s in those days! *G2337*
Mk 13:17 and to them that give s in those days! *G2337*
Lk 21:23 to them that give s, in those days! for *G2337*
23:29 bare, and the paps which never gave s. *G2337*

SUCKED
Song 8: 1 O that thou *wert* as my brother, that s H3243
Lk 11:27 thee, and the paps which thou hast s. *G2337*

SUCKING
Nu 11:12 father beareth the s child, unto the H3243
1Sa 7: 9 And Samuel took a s lamb, and offered H2461
Isa 11: 8 And the s child shall play on the hole of H3243
49:15 Can a woman forget her s child, that H5764
Lam 4: 4 The tongue of the s child cleaveth to H3243

SUCKLING
Dt 32:25 the s *also* with the man of gray hairs. H3243
1Sa 15: 3 and s, ox and sheep, camel and ass. H3243
Jer 44: 7 woman, child and s, out of Judah, to H3243

SUCKLINGS
1Sa 22:19 children and s, and oxen, and asses, H3243
Ps 8: 2 Out of the mouth of babes and s hast H3243
Lam 2:11 the s swoon in the streets of the city. H3243
Mt 21:16 babes and s thou hast perfected praise? *G2337*

SUDDEN
Job 22:10 about thee, and s fear troubleth thee; H6597
Prv 3:25 Be not afraid of s fear, neither of the H6597
1Th 5: 3 and safety; then s destruction cometh *G160*

SUDDENLY
Nu 6: 9 And if any man die very s by him, and H6597
12: 4 And the LORD spake s unto Moses, H6597
35:22 But if he thrust him s without enmity, H6621
Dt 7: 4 kindled against you, and destroy thee s. H4118
Jos 10: 9 Joshua therefore came unto them s, *and* H6597
11: 7 of Merom s; and they fell upon them. H6597
2Sa 15:14 lest he overtake us s, and bring evil H4116
2Ch 29:36 the people: for the thing was *done* s. H6597
Job 5: 3 root: but s I cursed his habitation. H6597
9:23 If the scourge slay s, he will laugh at the H6597
Ps 6:10 let them return *and* be ashamed s. H7281
64: 4 s do they shoot at him, and fear not. H6597
7 an arrow; s shall they be wounded. H6597
Prv 6:15 Therefore shall his calamity come s; H6597
15 s shall he be broken without remedy. H6621
24:22 For their calamity shall rise s; and who H6597
29: 1 *his* neck, shall s be destroyed, and that H6621
Ecc 9:12 evil time, when it falleth s upon them. H6597
Isa 29: 5 away: yea, it shall be at an instant s. H6597
30:13 whose breaking cometh s at an instant. H6597
47:11 upon thee s, *which* thou shalt not know. H6597
48: 3 I did *them* s, and they came to pass. H6597
Jer 4:20 land is spoiled: s are my tents spoiled, H6597
6:26 for the spoiler shall s come upon us. H6597
15: 8 fall upon it s, and terrors upon the city. H6597
18:22 shalt bring a troop s upon them: for H6597
49:19 strong: but I will s make him run away H7280
50:44 I will make them s run away from her: H7280
51: 8 Babylon is s fallen and destroyed: howl H6597
Hab 2: 7 Shall they not rise up s that shall bite H6621
Mal 3: 1 ye seek, shall s come to his temple, H6597
Mk 9: 8 And s, when they had looked round *G1819*
13:36 Lest coming s he find you sleeping. *G1810*
Lk 2:13 And s there was with the angel a *G1810*
9:39 And, lo, a spirit taketh him, and he s *G1810*
Act 2: 2 And s there came a sound from heaven *G869*
9: 3 Damascus: and s there shined round *G1810*
16:26 And s there was a great earthquake, so *G869*
22: 6 about noon, s there shone from heaven *G1810*
28: 6 or fallen down dead s: but after they had *G869*
1Ti 5:22 Lay hands s on no man, neither be *G5030*

SUE
Mt 5:40 And if any man will s thee at the law, *G2919*

SUFFER
Ex 12:23 the door, and will not s the destroyer to H5414
22:18 Thou shalt not s a witch to live.
Lev 2:13 salt; neither shalt thou s the salt of the
19:17 thy neighbour, and not s sin upon him. H5375
22:16 Or s them to bear the iniquity of H5375
Nu 21:23 And Sihon would not s Israel to pass H5414
Jos 10:19 hindmost of them; s them not to enter H5414
Jdg 1:34 not s them to come down to the valley: H5414
15: 1 But her father would not s him to go in. H5414
16:26 him by the hand, S me that I may feel H3240
2Sa 14:11 that thou wouldest not s the revengers of
1Ki 15:17 that he might not s any to go out or H5414
Est 3: 8 it *is* not for the king's profit to s them. H3240
Job 9:18 He will not s me to take my breath, but H5414
21: 3 S me that I may speak; and after that I H5375
24:11 *and* tread *their* winepresses, and s thirst.
36: 2 S me a little, and I will shew thee that *I* H3803
Ps 9:13 my trouble *which I* s of them that hate
16:10 s thine Holy One to see corruption. H5414
34:10 The young lions do lack, and s hunger:
55:22 shall never s the righteous to be moved. H5414
88:15 *while* I s thy terrors I am distracted. H5375
89:33 from him, nor s my faithfulness to fail.
101: 5 high look and a proud heart will not I s. H3201
121: 3 He will not s thy foot to be moved: he H5414
Prv 10: 3 The LORD will not s the soul of the H7456
19:15 sleep; and an idle soul shall s hunger.
19 A man of great wrath shall s H5375
Ecc 5: 6 S not thy mouth to cause thy flesh to H5414
12 of the rich will not s him to sleep. H3240
Ezk 44:20 their heads, nor s their locks to grow
Mt 3:15 And Jesus answering said unto him, S *it* *G863*
8:21 s me first to go and bury my father. *G2010*
31 s us to go away into the herd of swine. *G2010*
16:21 Jerusalem, and s many things of the *G3958*
17:12 shall also the Son of man s of them. *G3958*
17 shall I s you? bring him hither to me. *G430*
19:14 But Jesus said, S little children, and *G863*
23:13 s ye them that are entering to go in. *G863*
Mk 7:12 And ye s him no more to do ought for his *G863*
8:31 Son of man must s many things, and *G3958*
9:12 s many things, and be set at nought. *G3958*

Mk 9:19 long shall I s you? bring him unto me. G430
10:14 said unto them, S the little children to G863
11:16 And would not s that any man should G863
Lk 8:32 him that he would s them to enter into G2010
9:22 Saying, The Son of man must s many G3958
41 you, and s you? Bring thy son hither. G430
59 s me first to go and bury my father. G2010
17:25 But first must he s many things, and be G3958
18:16 *him*, and said, S little children to come G863
22:15 to eat this passover with you before I s: G3958
51 And Jesus answered and said, S ye thus G1439
24:46 behoved Christ to s, and to rise from the G3958
Act 2:27 s thine Holy One to see corruption. G1325
3:18 that Christ should s, he hath so fulfilled. G3958
5:41 counted worthy to s shame for his name. G818
7:24 And seeing one *of them* s wrong, he
9:16 things he must s for my name's sake. G3958
13:35 not s thine Holy One to see corruption. G1325
21:39 thee, s me to speak unto the people. G2010
26:23 That Christ should s, *and* that he G3805
Ro 8:17 if so be that we s with *him*, that we may G4841
1Co 3:15 burned, he shall s loss: but he himself G2210
4:12 we bless; being persecuted, we s it: G430
6: 7 not rather s *yourselves to* be defrauded?
9:12 used this power; but s all things, lest we G4722
10:13 who will not s you to be tempted above G1439
12:26 And whether one member s, all the G3958
26 suffer, all the members s with it; or one G4841
2Co 1: 6 which we also s: or whether we be G3958
11:19 For ye s fools gladly, seeing ye G430
20 For ye s, if a man bring you into G430
Gal 5:11 why do I yet s persecution? then is G1377
6:12 s persecution for the cross of Christ. G1377
Php 1:29 on him, but also to s for his sake; G3958
4:12 hungry, both to abound and to s need. G5302
1Th 3: 4 that we should s tribulation; even as
2Th 1: 5 the kingdom of God, for which ye also s: G3958
1Ti 2:12 But I s not a woman to teach, nor to G2010
4:10 For therefore we both labour and s
2Ti 1:12 For the which cause I also s these G3958
2: 9 Wherein I s trouble, as an evil doer, G2553
12 If we s, we shall also reign with *him*: if G5278
3:12 in Christ Jesus shall s persecution. G1377
Heb 11:25 Choosing rather to s affliction with the G4778
13: 3 *and* them which s adversity, as being G2558
22 And I beseech you, brethren, s the word G430
1Pt 2:20 when ye do well, and s *for it*, ye take it G3958
3:14 But and if ye s for righteousness' sake, G3958
17 ye s for well doing, than for evil doing. G3958
4:15 But let none of you s as a murderer, or G3958
16 Yet if *any man s* as a Christian, let him
19 Wherefore let them that s according to G3958
Rev 2:10 which thou shalt s: behold, the devil G3958
11: 9 s their dead bodies to be put in graves. G863

SUFFERED
Gen 20: 6 me: therefore s I thee not to touch her. H5414
31: 7 times; but God s him not to hurt me. H5414
28 And hast not s me to kiss my sons and H5203
Dt 8: 3 And he humbled thee, and s thee to
18:14 LORD thy God hath not s thee so *to do*. H5414
Jdg 3:28 Moab, and s not a man to pass over. H5414
1Sa 24: 7 these words, and s them not to rise H5414
2Sa 21:10 out of heaven, and s neither the birds H5414
1Ch 16:21 He s no man to do them wrong: yea, he H3240
Job 31:30 Neither have I s my mouth to sin by H5414
Ps 105:14 He s no man to do them wrong: yea, he H3240
Jer 15:15 know that for thy sake I have s rebuke. H5375
Mt 3:15 to fulfil all righteousness. Then he s him. G863
19: 8 of your hearts s you to put away your G2010
24:43 not have s his house to be broken up. G1439
27:19 man: for I have s many things this day G3958
Mk 1:34 out many devils; and s not the devils to G863
5:19 Howbeit Jesus s him not, but saith unto G863
26 And had s many things of many G3958
37 And he s no man to follow him, save G863
10: 4 And they said, Moses s to write a bill of G2010
Lk 4:41 he rebuking *them* s them not to speak: G1439
8:32 to enter into them. And he s them. G2010
51 And when he came into the house, he s G863
12:39 have s his house to be broken through. G863
13: 2 Galilaeans, because they s such things? G3958
24:26 Ought not Christ to have s these things, G3958
Act 13:18 And about the time of forty years s he G5159
14:16 Who in times past s all nations to walk G1439
16: 7 into Bithynia: but the Spirit s them not. G1439
17: 3 must needs have s, and risen again G3958
19:30 the people, the disciples s him not. G1439
28:16 but Paul was s to dwell by himself G2010
2Co 7:12 for his cause that s wrong, but that our
11:25 I stoned, thrice I s shipwreck, a night
Gal 3: 4 Have ye s so many things in vain? if *it* G3958
Php 3: 8 for whom I have s the loss of all things, G2210
1Th 2: 2 But even after that we had s before, G4310
14 for ye also have s like things of your G3958
Heb 2:18 For in that he himself hath s being G3958
5: 8 he obedience by the things which he s; G3958
7:23 not s to continue by reason of death: G2967
9:26 For then must he often have s since the G3958
13:12 with his own blood, s without the gate. G3958
1Pt 2:21 Christ also s for us, leaving us an G3958
23 again; when he s, he threatened not; but G3958
3:18 For Christ also hath once s for sins, the G3958
4: 1 Forasmuch then as Christ hath s for us G3958
1 s in the flesh hath ceased from sin; G3958
5:10 after that ye have s a while, make you G3958

SUFFEREST
Rev 2:20 thee, because thou s that woman G1439

SUFFERETH
Ps 66: 9 Which holdeth our soul in life, and s H5414
107:38 and s not their cattle to decrease.
Mt 11:12 kingdom of heaven s violence, and the G971
Act 28: 4 the sea, yet vengeance s not to live. G1439
1Co 13: 4 Charity s long, *and* is kind; charity G3114

SUFFERING
Act 27: 7 the wind not s us, we sailed under G4330
Heb 2: 9 the angels for the s of death, crowned G3804
Jas 5:10 example of s affliction, and of patience. G2552
1Pt 2:19 toward God endure grief, s wrongfully. G3958
Jude 7 s the vengeance of eternal fire. G5254

SUFFERINGS
Ro 8:18 For I reckon that the s of this present G3804
2Co 1: 5 For as the s of Christ abound in us, so G3804
6 of the same s which we also suffer: G3804
7 s, so *shall ye be* also of the consolation. G3804
Php 3:10 the fellowship of his s, being made G3804
Col 1:24 Who now rejoice in my s for you, and G3804
Heb 2:10 of their salvation perfect through s. G3804
1Pt 1:11 beforehand the s of Christ, and the G3804
4:13 of Christ's s; that, when his glory G3804
5: 1 a witness of the s of Christ, and also a G3804

SUFFICE
Nu 11:22 be slain for them, to s them? or shall all H4672
22 gathered together for them, to s them? H4672
Dt 3:26 unto me, Let it s thee; speak no more H7227
1Ki 20:10 of Samaria shall s for handfuls for all H5606
Ezk 44: 6 let it s you of all your abominations, H7227
45: 9 Thus saith the Lord GOD; Let it s you, H7227
1Pt 4: 3 For the time past of *our* life may s us to G713

SUFFICED
Jdg 21:14 and yet so they s them not. H4672
Ru 2:14 and she did eat, and was s, and left. H7646
18 that she had reserved after she was s. H7648

SUFFICETH
Jn 14: 8 Lord, shew us the Father, and it s us. G714

SUFFICIENCY
Job 20:22 In the fulness of his s he shall be in H5607
2Co 3: 5 as of ourselves; but our s *is* of God; G2426
9: 8 ye, always having all s in all *things*, may G841

SUFFICIENT
Ex 36: 7 For the stuff they had was s for all the H1767
Dt 15: 8 surely lend him s for his need, *in that* H1767
33: 7 let his hands be s for him; and be thou H7227
Prv 25:16 eat so much as is s for thee, lest thou be H1767
Isa 40:16 And Lebanon *is* not s to burn, nor the H1767
16 beasts thereof s for a burnt offering. H1767
Mt 6:34 itself. S unto the day *is* the evil thereof. G713
Lk 14:28 the cost, whether he have s to finish *it*?
Jn 6: 7 of bread is not s for them, that every G714
2Co 2: 6 S to such a man *is* this punishment, G2425
16 unto life. And who *is* s for these things? G2425
3: 5 Not that we are s of ourselves to think G2425
12: 9 And he said unto me, My grace is s for G714

SUFFICIENTLY
2Ch 30: 3 themselves s, neither had the people H4078
Isa 23:18 to eat s, and for durable clothing. H7654

SUIT
Jdg 17:10 by the year, and a s of apparel, and thy H6187
2Sa 15: 4 which hath any s or cause might come H7379
Job 11:19 yea, many shall make s unto thee. H2470

SUITS
Isa 3:22 The changeable s of apparel, and the

SUKKIIMS
2Ch 12: 3 the Lubims, the S, and the Ethiopians. H5525

SUM
Ex 21:30 If there be laid on him a s of money, H3724
30:12 When thou takest the s of the children H7218
38:21 This is the s of the tabernacle, *even* of H6485
Nu 1: 2 Take ye the s of all the congregation of H7218
49 s of them among the children of Israel: H7218
4: 2 Take the s of the sons of Kohath from H7218
22 Take also the s of the sons of Gershon, H7218
26: 2 Take the s of all the congregation of the H7218
4 *Take the s of the people,* from twenty
31:26 Take the s of the prey that was taken, H7218
49 have taken the s of the men of war H7218
2Sa 24: 9 And Joab gave up the s of the number H4557
2Ki 22: 4 priest, that he may s the silver which is H8552
1Ch 21: 5 And Joab gave the s of the number of H4557
Est 4: 7 him, and of the s of the money that H6575
Ps 139:17 me, O God! how great is the s of them! H7218
Ezk 28:12 s, full of wisdom, and perfect in beauty. H8508
Dan 7: 1 dream, *and* told the s of the matters. H7217
Act 7:16 bought for a s of money of the sons G5092
22:28 With a great s obtained I this freedom. G2774
Heb 8: 1 spoken *this is* the s: We have such an G2774

SUMMER
Gen 8:22 cold and heat, and s and winter, and H7019
Jdg 3:20 he was sitting in a s parlour, which he H4747
24 he covereth his feet in his s chamber. H4747
2Sa 16: 1 of s fruits, and a bottle of wine. H7019
2 and the bread and s fruit for the young H7019
Ps 32: 4 is turned into the drought of s. Selah. H7019
74:17 the earth: thou hast made s and winter. H7019
Prv 6: 8 Provideth her meat in the s, *and* H7019
10: 5 He that gathereth in s *is* a wise son: *but* H7019
26: 1 As snow in s, and as rain in harvest, so H7019
30:25 yet they prepare their meat in the s; H7019
Isa 16: 9 thy s fruits and for thy harvest is fallen. H7019
18: 6 and the fowls shall s upon them, and H6972
28: 4 fruit before the s; which *when* he that H7019
Jer 8:20 The harvest is past, the s is ended, and H7019
40:10 ye wine, and s fruits, and oil, and put H7019
12 gathered wine and s fruits very much. H7019
48:32 upon thy s fruits and upon thy vintage. H7019
Dan 2:35 the chaff of the s threshingfloors; and H7007
Am 3:15 house with the s house; and the houses H7019
8: 1 unto me: and behold a basket of s fruit. H7019
2 I said, A basket of s fruit. Then said the H7019
Mic 7: 1 they have gathered the s fruits, as the H7019
Zec 14: 8 sea: in s and in winter shall it be. H7019
Mt 24:32 forth leaves, ye know that s *is* nigh: G2330
Mk 13:28 forth leaves, ye know that s is near: G2330
Lk 21:30 own selves that s is now nigh at hand. G2330

SUMPTUOUSLY
Lk 16:19 and fine linen, and fared s every day: G2988

SUN
Gen 15:12 And when the s was going down, a H8121
17 And it came to pass, that, when the s H8121
19:23 The s was risen upon the earth when H8121
28:11 all night, because the s was set; and he H8121
32:31 And as he passed over Penuel the s H8121
37: 9 and, behold, the s and the moon and H8121
Ex 16:21 and when the s waxed hot, it melted. H8121
17:12 steady until the going down of the s. H8121
22: 3 If the s be risen upon him, *there shall* H8121
26 it unto him by that the s goeth down: H8121
Lev 22: 7 And when the s is down, he shall be H8121
Nu 2: 3 the rising of the s shall they of the
25: 4 the LORD against the s, that the fierce H8121
Dt 4:19 thou seest the s, and the moon, and H8121
11:30 the way where the s goeth down, in the H8121
16: 6 going down of the s, at the season that H8121
17: 3 them, either the s, or moon, or any of H8121
23:11 and when the s is down, he shall come H8121
24:13 again when the s goeth down, that he H8121
15 neither shall the s go down upon it; for H8121
33:14 *forth* by the s, and for the precious H8121
Jos 1: 4 going down of the s, shall be your coast. H8121

S

Jos 8:29 and as soon as the s was down, Joshua H8121
10:12 in the sight of Israel, S, stand thou still H8121
13 And the s stood still, and the moon H8121
13 of Jasher? So the s stood still in the H8121
27 the going down of the s, *that* Joshua H8121
12: 1 the rising of the s, from the river Arnon H8121
Jdg 5:31 that love him *be* as the s when he goeth H8121
8:13 from battle before the s *was up*, H2775
9:33 as soon as the s is up, thou shalt rise H8121
14:18 day before the s went down, What *is* H2775
19:14 their way; and the s went down upon H8121
1Sa 11: 9 by *that time* the s be hot, ye shall have H8121
2Sa 2:24 Abner: and the s went down when they H8121
3:35 bread, or ought else, till the s be down. H8121
12:11 lie with thy wives in the sight of this s. H8121
12 thing before all Israel, and before the s. H8121
23: 4 *when* the s riseth, *even* a morning H8121
1Ki 22:36 going down of the s, saying, Every man H8121
2Ki 3:22 the morning, and the s shone upon the H8121
23: 5 unto Baal, to the s, and to the moon, H8121
11 had given to the s, at the entering in of H8121
11 burned the chariots of the s with fire. H8121
2Ch 18:34 the time of the s going down he died. H8121
Neh 7: 3 be opened until the s be hot; and while H8121
Job 8:16 He *is* green before the s, and his branch H8121
9: 7 Which commandeth the s, and it riseth H2775
30:28 I went mourning without the s: I stood H2535
31:26 If I beheld the s when it shined, or the H216
Ps 19: 4 them hath he set a tabernacle for the s, H8121
50: 1 of the s unto the going down thereof. H8121
58: 8 a woman, *that* they may not see the s. H8121
72: 5 They shall fear thee as long as the s H8121
17 as long as the s: and *men* shall be H8121
74:16 thou hast prepared the light and the s. H8121
84:11 For the LORD God *is* a s and shield: the H8121
89:36 ever, and his throne as the s before me. H8121
104:19 seasons: the s knoweth his going down. H8121
22 The s ariseth, they gather themselves H8121
113: 3 From the rising of the s unto the going H8121
121: 6 The s shall not smite thee by day, nor H8121
136: 8 The s to rule by day: for his mercy H8121
148: 3 Praise ye him, s and moon: praise him, H8121
Ecc 1: 3 his labour which he taketh under the s? H8121
5 The s also ariseth, and the sun goeth H8121
5 The sun also ariseth, and the s goeth H8121
9 and *there is* no new *thing* under the s. H8121
14 are done under the s; and, behold, all *is* H8121
2:11 and *there was* no profit under the s. H8121
17 is wrought under the s *is* grievous unto H8121
18 had taken under the s: because I should H8121
19 wise under the s. This *is* also vanity. H8121
20 all the labour which I took under the s. H8121
22 wherein he hath laboured under the s? H8121
3:16 And moreover I saw under the s the H8121
4: 1 done under the s: and behold the tears H8121
3 the evil work that is done under the s. H8121
7 returned, and I saw vanity under the s. H8121
15 walk under the s, with the second child H8121
5:13 seen under the s, *namely*, riches kept H8121
18 he taketh under the s all the days of his H8121
6: 1 the s, and it *is* common among men: H8121
5 Moreover he hath not seen the s, nor H8121
12 what shall be after him under the s? H8121
7:11 *it there is* profit to them that see the s. H8121
8: 9 that is done under the s: *there is* a time H8121
15 thing under the s, than to eat, and to H8121
15 life, which God giveth him under the s. H8121
17 is done under the s: because though a H8121
9: 3 done under the s, that *there is* one event H8121
6 in any *thing* that is done under the s. H8121
9 thee under the s, all the days of thy H8121
9 labour which thou takest under the s. H8121
11 I returned, and saw under the s, that H8121
13 the s, and it *seemed* great unto me: H8121
10: 5 seen under the s, as an error *which* H8121
11: 7 *thing it is* for the eyes to behold the s: H8121
12: 2 While the s, or the light, or the moon, or H8121
Song 1: 6 black, because the s hath looked upon H8121
6:10 moon, clear as the s, *and* terrible as *an* H2535
Isa 13:10 give their light: the s shall be darkened H8121
24:23 and the s ashamed, when the H2535
30:26 as the light of the s, and the light of the H2535
26 the light of the s shall be sevenfold, as H2535
38: 8 is gone down in the s dial of Ahaz, ten H8121
8 backward. So the s returned ten H8121
41:25 the rising of the s shall he call upon my H8121
45: 6 the rising of the s, and from the west, H8121
49:10 shall the heat nor s smite them: for he H8121
59:19 the rising of the s. When the enemy H8121
Isa 60:19 The s shall be no more thy light by day; H8121
20 Thy s shall no more go down; neither H8121
Jer 8: 2 them before the s, and the moon, and H8121
15: 9 up the ghost: her s is gone down while H8121
31:35 which giveth the s for a light by day, H8121
Ezk 8:16 they worshipped the s toward the east. H8121
32: 7 I will cover the s with a cloud, and the H8121
Dan 6:14 the going down of the s to deliver him. H8122
Joel 2:10 shall tremble: the s and the moon shall H8121
31 The s shall be turned into darkness, H8121
3:15 The s and the moon shall be darkened, H8121
Am 8: 9 I will cause the s to go down at noon, H8121
Jna 4: 8 And it came to pass, when the s did H8121
8 east wind; and the s beat upon the H8121
Mic 3: 6 divine; and the s shall go down over H8121
Nah 3:17 day, *but* when the s ariseth they flee H8121
Hab 3:11 The s *and* moon stood still in their H8121
Mal 1:11 For from the rising of the s even unto H8121
4: 2 my name shall the S of righteousness H8121
Mt 5:45 for he maketh his s to rise on the evil *G2246*
13: 6 And when the s was up, they were *G2246*
43 shine forth as the s in the kingdom of *G2246*
17: 2 did shine as the s, and his raiment was *G2246*
24:29 days shall the s be darkened, and the *G2246*
Mk 1:32 And at even, when the s did set, they *G2246*
4: 6 But when the s was up, it was scorched; *G2246*
13:24 tribulation, the s shall be darkened, *G2246*
16: 2 unto the sepulchre at the rising of the s. *G2246*
Lk 4:40 Now when the s was setting, all they *G2246*
21:25 And there shall be signs in the s, and in *G2246*
23:45 And the s was darkened, and the veil of *G2246*
Act 2:20 The s shall be turned into darkness, *G2246*
13:11 not seeing the s for a season. And *G2246*
26:13 brightness of the s, shining round about *G2246*
27:20 And when neither s nor stars in many *G2246*
1Co 15:41 *There is* one glory of the s, and another *G2246*
Eph 4:26 Be ye angry, and sin not: let not the s *G2246*
Jas 1:11 For the s is no sooner risen with a *G2246*
Rev 1:16 *was* as the s shineth in his strength. *G2246*
6:12 and the s became black as sackcloth *G2246*
7:16 shall the s light on them, nor any heat. *G2246*
8:12 third part of the s was smitten, and the *G2246*
9: 2 furnace; and the s and the air were *G2246*
10: 1 were the s, and his feet as pillars of fire: *G2246*
12: 1 clothed with the s, and the moon under *G2246*
16: 8 out his vial upon the s; and power was *G2246*
19:17 And I saw an angel standing in the s; *G2246*
21:23 And the city had no need of the s, *G2246*
22: 5 neither light of the s; for the Lord God *G2246*

SUNDER
Ps 46: 9 in s; he burneth the chariot in the fire. H7112
107:14 of death, and brake their bands in s.
16 of brass, and cut the bars of iron in s. H1438
Isa 27: 9 that are beaten in s, the groves and H5310
45: 2 of brass, and cut in s the bars of iron: H1438
Nah 1:13 off thee, and will burst thy bonds in s.
Lk 12:46 will cut him in s, and will appoint him *G1371*

SUNDERED
Job 41:17 stick together, that they cannot be s. H6504

SUNDRY
Heb 1: 1 God, who at s times and in divers *G4181*

SUNG
Isa 26: 1 In that day shall this song be s in the H7891
Mt 26:30 And when they had s an hymn, they *G5214*
Mk 14:26 And when they had s an hymn, they *G5214*
Rev 5: 9 And they s a new song, saying, Thou art *G103*
14: 3 And they s as it were a new song before *G103*

SUNK
1Sa 17:49 that the stone s into his forehead; and H2883
2Ki 9:24 his heart, and he s down in his chariot. H3766
Ps 9:15 The heathen are s down in the pit *that* H2883
Jer 38: 6 but mire: so Jeremiah s in the mire. H2883
22 thee: thy feet are s in the mire, *and* they H2883
Lam 2: 9 Her gates are s into the ground; he H2883
Act 20: 9 long preaching, he s down with sleep, *G2702*

SUNRISING
Nu 21:11 *is* before Moab, toward the s. H4217+H8121
34:15 *near* Jericho eastward, toward the s. H4217
Dt 4:41 this side Jordan toward the s; H4217+H8121
47 this side Jordan toward the s; H4217+H8121
Jos 1:15 this side Jordan toward the s. H4217+H8121
13: 5 toward the s, from Baal-gad H4217+H8121
19:12 toward the s unto the border H4217+H8121
Jos 19:27 And turneth toward the s to H4217+H8121
34 upon Jordan toward the s. H4217+H8121
Jdg 20:43 against Gibeah toward the s. H4217+H8121

SUP
Hab 1: 9 their faces shall s up *as* the east wind, H4041
Lk 17: 8 wherewith I may s, and gird thyself, *G1172*
Rev 3:20 and will s with him, and he with me. *G1172*

SUPERFLUITY
Jas 1:21 Wherefore lay apart all filthiness and s *G4050*

SUPERFLUOUS
Lev 21:18 he that hath a flat nose, or any thing s, H8311
22:23 hath any thing s or lacking in his parts, H8311
2Co 9: 1 the saints, it is s for me to write to you: *G4053*

SUPERSCRIPTION
Mt 22:20 unto them, Whose *is* this image and s? *G1923*
Mk 12:16 s? And they said unto him, Caesar's. *G1923*
15:26 And the s of his accusation was written *G1923*
Lk 20:24 Shew me a penny. Whose image and s *G1923*
23:38 And a s also was written over him in *G1923*

SUPERSTITION
Act 25:19 him of their own s, and of one Jesus, *G1175*

SUPERSTITIOUS
Act 17:22 I perceive that in all things ye are too s. *G1174*

SUPPED
1Co 11:25 cup, when he had s, saying, This cup is *G1172*

SUPPER
Mk 6:21 his birthday made a s to his lords, high *G1173*
Lk 14:12 a dinner or a s, call not thy friends, *G1173*
16 man made a great s, and bade many: *G1173*
17 And sent his servant at s time to say to *G1173*
24 which were bidden shall taste of my s. *G1173*
22:20 Likewise also the cup after s, saying, *G1172*
Jn 12: 2 There they made him a s; and Martha *G1173*
13: 2 And s being ended, the devil having *G1173*
4 He riseth from s, and laid aside his *G1173*
21:20 on his breast at s, and said, Lord, which *G1173*
1Co 11:20 one place, *this* is not to eat the Lord's s. *G1173*
21 *other* his own s: and one is hungry, and *G1173*
Rev 19: 9 unto the marriage s of the Lamb. And *G1173*
17 together unto the s of the great God; *G1173*

SUPPLANT
Jer 9: 4 will utterly s, and every neighbour H6117

SUPPLANTED
Gen 27:36 Jacob? for he hath s me these two H6117

SUPPLE
Ezk 16: 4 in water to s *thee*; thou wast not H4935

SUPPLIANTS
Zep 3:10 of Ethiopia my s, *even* the daughter of H6282

SUPPLICATION
1Sa 13:12 I have not made s unto the LORD: I H2470
1Ki 8:28 servant, and to his s, O LORD my God, H8467
30 And hearken thou to the s of thy H8467
33 and make s unto thee in this house: H2603
38 What prayer and s soever be *made* by H8467
45 and their s, and maintain their cause. H8467
47 repent, and make s unto thee in the H2603
49 Then hear thou their prayer and their s H8467
52 That thine eyes may be open unto the s H8467
52 and unto the s of thy people Israel, H8467
54 all this prayer and s unto the LORD, he H8467
59 I have made s before the LORD, be H2603
9: 3 thy prayer and thy s, that thou hast H8467
2Ch 6:19 servant, and to his s, O LORD my God, H8467
24 and make s before thee in this house; H2603
29 *Then* what prayer *or* what s soever H8467
35 and their s, and maintain their cause. H8467
33:13 and heard his s, and brought him again H8467
Est 4: 8 the king, to make s unto him, and to H2603
Job 8: 5 and make thy s to the Almighty; H2603
9:15 *but* I would make s to my judge. H2603
Ps 6: 9 The LORD hath heard my s; the LORD H8467
30: 8 O LORD; and unto the LORD I made s. H2603
55: 1 O God; and hide not thyself from my s. H8467
119:170 Let my s come before thee: deliver me H8467
142: 1 voice unto the LORD did I make my s. H2603
Isa 45:14 they shall make s unto thee, *saying*, H6419

Jer 36: 7 It may be they will present their s H8467
37:20 lord the king: let my s, I pray thee, be H8467
38:26 I presented my s before the king, that H8467
42: 2 beseech thee, our s be accepted before H8467
9 sent me to present your s before him; H8467
Dan 6:11 praying and making s before his God. H2604
9:20 presenting my s before the LORD my H8467
Hos 12: 4 wept, and made s unto him: he found H2603
Act 1:14 in prayer and s, with the women, and G1162
Eph 6:18 Praying always with all prayer and s in G1162
18 all perseverance and s for all saints; G1162
Php 4: 6 by prayer and s with thanksgiving let G1162

SUPPLICATIONS

2Ch 6:21 Hearken therefore unto the s of thy H8469
39 prayer and their s, and maintain their H8467
Job 41: 3 Will he make many s unto thee? will he H8469
Ps 28: 2 Hear the voice of my s, when I cry unto H8469
6 he hath heard the voice of my s. H8469
31:22 voice of my s when I cried unto thee. H8469
86: 6 prayer; and attend to the voice of my s. H8469
116: 1 he hath heard my voice *and* my s. H8469
130: 2 ears be attentive to the voice of my s. H8469
140: 6 God: hear the voice of my s, O LORD. H8469
143: 1 give ear to my s: in thy faithfulness H8469
Jer 3:21 weeping *and* s of the children of Israel: H8469
31: 9 weeping, and with s will I lead them: I H8469
Dan 9: 3 seek by prayer and s, with fasting, and H8469
17 servant, and his s, and cause thy face to H8469
18 do not present our s before thee for our H8469
23 At the beginning of thy s the H8469
Zec 12:10 of grace and of s: and they shall look H8469
1Ti 2: 1 I exhort therefore, that, first of all, s, G1162
5: 5 in s and prayers night and day. G1162
Heb 5: 7 up prayers and s with strong crying G2428

SUPPLIED

1Co 16:17 was lacking on your part they have s. G378
2Co 11: 9 from Macedonia s: and in all *things* I G4322

SUPPLIETH

2Co 9:12 this service not only s the want of the G2076
Eph 4:16 which every joint s, according to the G2024

SUPPLY

2Co 8:14 *may be a* s for their want, that their
14 also may be *a* s for your want: that there
Php 1:19 and the s of the Spirit of Jesus Christ, G2024
2:30 life, to s your lack of service toward me. G378
4:19 But my God shall s all your need G4137

SUPPORT

Act 20:35 ye ought to s the weak, and to remember G482
1Th 5:14 s the weak, be patient toward all *men*. G472

SUPPOSE

2Sa 13:32 Let not my lord s *that* they have slain H559
Lk 7:43 Simon answered and said, I s that *he*, G5274
12:51 S ye that I am come to give peace on G1380
13: 2 And Jesus answering said unto them, S G1380
Jn 21:25 every one, I s that even the world G3633
Act 2:15 For these are not drunken, as ye s, G5274
1Co 7:26 I s therefore that this is good for the G3543
2Co 11: 5 For I s I was not a whit behind the very G3049
Heb 10:29 Of how much sorer punishment, s ye, G1380
1Pt 5:12 unto you, as I s, I have written briefly, G3049

SUPPOSED

Mt 20:10 But when the first came, they s that G3543
Mk 6:49 s it had been a spirit, and cried out: G1380
Lk 3:23 age, being (as was s) the son of Joseph, G3543
24:37 and s that they had seen a spirit. G1380
Act 7:25 For he s his brethren would have G3543
21:29 whom they s that Paul had brought G3543
25:18 none accusation of such things as I s: G5282
Php 2:25 Yet I s it necessary to send to you G2233

SUPPOSING

Lk 2:44 But they, s him to have been in the G3543
Jn 20:15 seekest thou? She, s him to be the G1380
Act 14:19 *him* out of the city, s he had been dead. G3543
16:27 s that the prisoners had been fled. G3543
27:13 And when the south wind blew softly, s G1380
Php 1:16 s to add affliction to my bonds: G3633
1Ti 6: 5 of the truth, s that gain is godliness: G3543

SUPREME

1Pt 2:13 sake: whether it be to the king, as s; G5242

SUR

2Ki 11: 6 *be* at the gate of S; and a third part at H5495

SURE

Gen 23:17 the borders round about, were made s H6965
20 were made s unto Abraham for a H6965
Ex 3:19 And I am s that the king of Egypt will H3045
Nu 32:23 and be s your sin will find you out. H3045
Dt 12:23 Only be s that thou eat not the blood: H2388
1Sa 2:35 I will build him a s house; and he shall H539
20: 7 be s that evil is determined by him. H3045
25:28 make my lord a s house; because my H539
2Sa 1:10 because I was s that he could not live H3045
23: 5 in all *things*, and s: for *this is* all my H8104
1Ki 11:38 and build thee a s house, as I built for H539
Neh 9:38 And because of all this we make a s H548
Job 24:22 he riseth up, and no *man* is s of life. H539
Ps 19: 7 of the LORD *is* s, making wise the simple. H539
93: 5 Thy testimonies are very s: holiness H539
111: 7 judgment; all his commandments *are* s. H539
Prv 6: 3 humble thyself, and make s thy friend. H7292
11:15 *for it*: and he that hateth suretiship is s. H982
18 righteousness *shall be* a s reward. H571
Isa 22:23 And I will fasten him *as* a nail in a s H539
25 is fastened in the s place be removed, H539
28:16 corner *stone*, a s foundation: he that H3245
32:18 s dwellings, and in quiet resting places; H4009
33:16 shall be given him; his waters *shall be* s. H539
55: 3 with you, *even* the s mercies of David. H539
Dan 2:45 certain, and the interpretation thereof s. H540
4:26 kingdom shall be s unto thee, after that H7011
Mt 27:64 sepulchre be made s until the third day, G805
65 go your way, make *it* as s as ye can. G805
66 So they went, and made the sepulchre s, G805
Lk 10:11 be ye s of this, that the kingdom G1097
Jn 6:69 And we believe and are s that thou art G1097
16:30 Now are we s that thou knowest all G1492
Act 13:34 I will give you the s mercies of David. G4103
Ro 2: 2 But we are s that the judgment of God G1492
4:16 promise might be s to all the seed; not to G949
15:29 And I am s that, when I come unto you, G1492
2Ti 2:19 of God standeth s, having this seal, The G4731
Heb 6:19 of the soul, both s and stedfast, and G804
2Pt 1:10 and election s: for if ye do these things, G949
19 We have also a more s word of G949

SURELY

Gen 2:17 thou eatest thereof thou shalt s die. H4191
3: 4 unto the woman, Ye shall not s die: H4191
9: 5 And s your blood of your lives will I H389
18:18 Seeing that Abraham shall s become a
20: 7 shalt s die, thou, and all that *are* thine. H4191
11 Because I thought, S the fear of God *is* H7535
26:11 man or his wife shall s be put to death. H4191
28:16 sleep, and he said, S the LORD is in this H403
22 give me I will s give the tenth unto thee. H6237
29:14 And Laban said to him, S thou *art* my H389
32 for she said, S the LORD hath looked H3588
30:16 in unto me; for s I have hired thee with H7936
31:42 had been with me, s thou hadst sent H3588
32:12 And thou saidst, I will s do thee good, H3190
42:16 else by the life of Pharaoh s ye *are* spies.
43:10 For except we had lingered, s now we
44:28 me, and I said, S he is torn in pieces; H2963
46: 4 and I will also s bring thee up *again*: H5927
50:24 I die: and God will s visit you, and H6485
25 saying, God will s visit you, and ye H6485
Ex 2:14 feared, and said, S this thing is known. H403
3: 7 And the LORD said, I have s seen the H7200
16 me, saying, I have s visited you, and H6485
4:25 S a bloody husband *art* thou to me. H3588
11: 1 shall s thrust you out hence altogether. H1644
13:19 saying, God will s visit you; and ye H6485
18:18 Thou wilt s wear away, both thou, and H5034
19:12 the mount shall be s put to death: H4191
13 it, but he shall s be stoned, or shot H5619
21:12 so that he die, shall be s put to death. H4191
15 or his mother, shall be s put to death. H4191
16 in his hand, he shall s be put to death. H4191
17 or his mother, shall s be put to death. H4191
20 under his hand; he shall be s punished. H5358
22 mischief follow: he shall be s punished, H6064
28 the ox shall be s stoned, and his flesh H5619
36 him in; he shall s pay ox for ox; and the H7999
22: 6 the fire shall s make restitution. H7999
14 not with it, he shall s make *it* good. H7999
16 her, he shall s endow her to be his wife. H4117
19 Whosoever lieth with a beast shall s be H4191
23 at all unto me, I will s hear their cry; H8085
Ex 23: 4 thou shalt s bring it back to him again. H7725
5 to help him, thou shalt s help with him. H5800
33 gods, it will s be a snare unto thee. H3588
31:14 defileth it shall s be put to death: for H4191
15 sabbath day, he shall s be put to death. H4191
40:15 their anointing shall s be an everlasting
Lev 20: 2 Molech; he shall s be put to death: the H4191
9 mother shall be s put to death: he hath H4191
10 the adulteress shall s be put to death. H4191
11 both of them shall s be put to death; H4191
12 both of them shall s be put to death: H4191
13 they shall s be put to death; their H4191
15 And if a man lie with a beast, he shall s H4191
16 beast: they shall s be put to death; their H4191
27 is a wizard, shall s be put to death: they H4191
24:16 of the LORD, he shall s be put to death, H4191
17 And he that killeth any man shall s be H4191
27:29 redeemed; *but* shall s be put to death. H4191
Nu 13:27 sentest us, and s it floweth with milk
14:23 S they shall not see the land which I H518
35 I the LORD have said, I will s do it unto H518
15:35 The man shall be s put to death: all the H4191
18:15 of man shalt thou s redeem, and the H6299
22:33 turned from me, s now also I had slain H3588
23:23 S *there is* no enchantment against Jacob,
26:65 of them, They shall s die in the H4191
27: 7 speak right: thou shalt s give them a H5414
32:11 S none of the men that came up out of H518
35:16 the murderer shall s be put to death. H4191
17 the murderer shall s be put to death. H4191
18 the murderer shall s be put to death. H4191
21 smote *him* shall s be put to death; *for* H4191
31 of death: but he shall be s put to death. H4191
Dt 1:35 S there shall not one of these men of this H518
4: 6 statutes, and say, S this great nation *is* a
8:19 you this day that ye shall s perish. H6
13: 9 But thou shalt s kill him; thine hand H2026
15 Thou shalt s smite the inhabitants of H5221
15: 8 him, and shalt s lend him sufficient H5670
10 Thou shalt s give him, and thine heart H5414
16:15 hands, therefore thou shalt s rejoice. H389
22: 4 shalt s help him to lift *them* up again. H6965
23:21 LORD thy God will s require it of thee; H1875
30:18 day, that ye shall s perish, *and that* ye H6
31:18 And I will s hide my face in that day for H5641
Jos 14: 9 And Moses sware on that day, saying, S H518
Jdg 3:24 locked, they said, S he covereth his feet H389
4: 9 And she said, I will s go with thee: H1980
6:16 And the LORD said unto him, S I will H3588
11:31 of Ammon, shall s be the LORD'S, and
13:22 shall s die, because we have seen God. H4191
15:13 their hand: but s we will not kill thee. H4191
20:39 for they said, S they are smitten down H389
21: 5 saying, He shall s be put to death. H4191
Ru 1:10 And they said unto her, S we will H3588
1Sa 9: 6 he saith cometh s to pass: now let us go
14:39 my son, he shall s die. But *there was* H3588
44 also: for thou shalt s die, Jonathan. H4191
15:32 said, S the bitterness of death is past. H403
16: 6 S the LORD'S anointed *is* before him. H389
17:25 that is come up? s to defy Israel is he H3588
20:26 him, he *is* not clean; s he *is* not clean. H3588
31 and fetch him unto me, for he shall s die.
22:16 And the king said, Thou shalt s die, H4191
22 there, that he would s tell Saul: I have H5046
24:20 that thou shalt s be king, and that the H4427
25:21 Now David had said, S in vain have I H389
34 to meet me, s there had not H3588+H518
28: 2 And David said to Achish, S thou shalt H3651
29: 6 and said unto him, S, *as* the LORD liveth,
30: 8 for thou shalt s overtake *them*, and H5381
2Sa 2:27 hadst spoken, s then in the morning H3588
9: 7 Fear not: for I will s shew thee kindness H6213
11:23 And the messenger said unto David, S H3588
12: 5 that hath done this *thing* shall s die: H1121
14 also *that is* born unto thee shall s die. H4191
15:21 the king liveth, s in what place my lord H3588
18: 2 I will s go forth with you myself also. H3318
20:18 saying, They shall s ask *counsel* at H7592
24:24 Nay; but I will s buy *it* of thee at H3588+H518
1Ki 2:37 that thou shalt s die: thy blood shall H4191
42 that thou shalt s die? and thou saidst H4191
8:13 I have s built thee an house to dwell in, H1129
11: 2 in unto you: *for* s they will turn away H403
11 thee, I will s rend the kingdom from H7167
13:32 cities of Samaria, shall s come to pass. H3588
18:15 I will s shew myself unto him to day. H3588
20:23 and s we shall be stronger than they. H518
25 in the plain, *and* s we shall be stronger H518

1Ki 22:32 that they said, S it *is* the king of Israel. H389
2Ki 1: 4 but shalt s die. And Elijah departed. H4191
6 which thou art gone up, but shalt s die. H4191
16 which thou art gone up, but shalt s die. H4191
3:14 whom I stand, s, were it not that I regard
23 the kings are s slain, and they have H2717
5:11 I thought, He will s come out to me, H3318
8:10 hath shewed me that he shall s die. H4191
14 told me *that* thou shouldest s recover. H2421
9:26 S I have seen yesterday the blood of
18:30 The LORD will s deliver us, and this H5337
23:22 S there was not holden such a passover H3588
24: 3 S at the commandment of the LORD H389
Est 6:13 against him, but shalt s fall before him. H5307
Job 8: 6 If thou *wert* pure and upright; s now he H3588
13: 3 S I would speak to the Almighty, and I H199
10 He will s reprove you, if ye do secretly H3198
14:18 And s the mountain falling cometh to H199
18:21 S such *are* the dwellings of the wicked, H389
20:20 S he shall not feel quietness in his belly, H3588
28: 1 S there is a vein for the silver, and a H3588
31:36 S I would take it upon my H518+H3808
33: 8 S thou hast spoken in mine hearing, and H389
34:12 Yea, s God will not do wickedly, neither H551
31 S it is meet to be said unto God, I have H3588
35:13 S God will not hear vanity, neither will H389
37:20 man speak, s he shall be swallowed up. H3588
40:20 S the mountains bring him forth food, H3588
Ps 23: 6 S goodness and mercy shall follow me H389
32: 6 thou mayest be found: s in the floods of H7535
39: 6 S every man walketh in a vain shew: H389
6 in a vain shew: s they are disquieted in H389
11 like a moth: s every man *is* vanity. Selah. H389
62: 9 S men of low degree *are* vanity, *and* men H389
73:18 S thou didst set them in slippery places: H389
76:10 S the wrath of man shall praise thee: H3588
77:11 s I will remember thy wonders of old.
85: 9 S his salvation *is* nigh them that fear H389
91: 3 S he shall deliver thee from the snare of H3588
112: 6 S he shall not be moved for ever: the H3588
131: 2 S I have behaved and quieted myself, H3808
132: 3 S I will not come into the tabernacle of H518
139:11 If I say, S the darkness shall cover me; H389
19 S thou wilt slay the wicked, O God: H518
140:13 S the righteous shall give thanks unto
Prv 1:17 S in vain the net is spread in the sight H3588
3:34 S he scorneth the scorners: but he giveth H518
10: 9 He that walketh uprightly walketh s: but H983
22:16 giveth to the rich, *shall* s *come* to want. H389
23:18 For s there is an end; and thine
30: 2 S I *am* more brutish than *any* man, H3588
33 S the churning of milk bringeth forth H3588
Ecc 4:16 not rejoice in him. S this also *is* vanity H3588
7: 7 S oppression maketh a wise man mad; H3588
8:12 be prolonged, yet s I know that it shall H3588
10:11 S the serpent will bite without H518
Isa 7: 9 believe, s ye shall not be established. H3588
14:24 hath sworn, saying, S as I have H518+H3808
16: 7 shall ye mourn; s *they are* stricken. H389
19:11 S the princes of Zoan *are* fools, the H389
22:14 the LORD of hosts, S this iniquity shall H518
17 mighty captivity, and will s cover thee. H5844
18 He will s violently turn and toss thee H6801
29:16 S your turning of things upside down H518
36:15 The LORD will s deliver us: this city H5337
40: 7 bloweth upon it: s the people *is* grass. H403
45:14 unto thee, *saying*, S God *is* in thee; and H389
24 S, shall *one* say, in the LORD have I
49: 4 and in vain: *yet* s my judgment *is* with H403
18 the LORD, thou shalt s clothe thee with H3588
53: 4 S he hath borne our griefs, and carried H403
54:15 Behold, they shall s gather together, H1481
60: 9 S the isles shall wait for me, and the H3588
62: 8 of his strength, S I will no more give thy H518
63: 8 For he said, S they *are* my people, H389
Jer 2:35 I am innocent, s his anger shall turn H389
3:20 S *as* a wife treacherously departeth from H403
4:10 Then said I, Ah, Lord GOD! s thou hast H403
5: 2 And though they say, The LORD liveth; s H403
4 Therefore I said, S these *are* poor; they H389
8:13 I will s consume them, saith the LORD: H622
16:19 earth, and shall say, S our fathers have H389
22: 6 Lebanon: *yet* s I will make thee H518+H3808
22 go into captivity: s then shalt thou be H3588
24: 8 they are so evil; s thus saith the LORD, H3588
26: 8 took him, saying, Thou shalt s die. H4191
15 me to death, ye shall s bring innocent H3588
31:18 I have s heard Ephraim bemoaning H8085
19 S after that I was turned, I repented; H3588
Jer 31:20 for him; I will s have mercy upon him, H7355
32: 4 but shall s be delivered into the H5414
34: 3 of his hand, but shalt s be taken, and H8610
36:16 will s tell the king of all these words. H5046
37: 9 Chaldeans shall s depart from us: for H1980
38: 3 Thus saith the LORD, This city shall s H5414
15 thee, wilt thou not s put me to death? H4191
39:18 For I will s deliver thee, and thou shalt H4422
44:25 saying, We will s perform our vows H6213
25 unto her: ye will s accomplish your H6965
25 your vows, and s perform your vows. H6213
29 words shall s stand against you for evil: H6965
46:18 LORD of hosts, S as Tabor *is* among H3588
49:12 but thou shalt s drink *of it*. H8354
20 of Teman: S the least of the flock H518+H3808
20 them out: s he shall make their H518+H3808
50:45 the Chaldeans: S the least of the H518+H3808
45 them out: s he shall make *their* H518+H3808
51:14 *saying*, S I will fill thee with H3588+H518
56 God of recompences shall s requite. H7999
Lam 3: 3 S against me is he turned; he turneth his H389
Ezk 3: 6 understand. S, had I sent thee to H518+H3808
18 Thou shalt s die; and thou givest H4191
21 not sin, he shall s live, because he is H2421
5:11 the Lord GOD; S, because thou H518+H3808
17:16 *As* I live, saith the Lord GOD, s H518+H3808
19 GOD; *As* I live, s mine oath that H518+H3808
18: 9 just, he shall s live, saith the Lord GOD. H2421
13 shall s die; his blood shall be upon him. H4191
17 the iniquity of his father, he shall s live. H2421
19 and hath done them, he shall s live. H2421
21 right, he shall s live, he shall not die. H2421
28 he shall s live, he shall not die. H2421
20:33 *As* I live, saith the Lord GOD, s H518+H3808
31:11 the heathen; he shall s deal with him: I H6213
33: 8 *man*, thou shalt s die; if thou dost not H4191
13 *that* he shall s live; if he trust to his H2421
14 Thou shalt s die; if he turn from H4191
15 iniquity; he shall s live, he shall not die. H2421
16 is lawful and right; he shall s live. H2421
27 GOD; *As* I live, s they that *are* in H518+H3808
34: 8 *As* I live, saith the Lord GOD, s H518+H3808
36: 5 the Lord GOD; S in the fire of H518+H3808
7 up mine hand, S the heathen H518+H3808
38:19 have I spoken, S in that day H518+H3808
Hos 5: 9 I made known that which shall s be. H539
12:11 *Is there* iniquity *in* Gilead? s they are H389
Am 3: 7 S the Lord GOD will do nothing, but he H3588
5: 5 for Gilgal shall s go into captivity, and H1540
7:11 and Israel shall s be led away captive H1540
17 s go into captivity forth of his land. H1540
8: 7 S I will never forget any of their works.
Mic 2:12 I will s assemble, O Jacob, all of thee; I H622
12 all of thee; I will s gather the remnant H6908
Hab 2: 3 because it will s come, it will not tarry. H935
Zep 2: 9 the God of Israel, S Moab shall be as H3588
3: 7 I said, S thou wilt fear me, thou wilt
Mt 26:73 and said to Peter, S thou also art *one* of G230
Mk 14:70 by said again to Peter, S thou art *one* of G230
Lk 1: 1 which are most s believed among us, G4135
4:23 And he said unto them, Ye will s say G3843
Jn 17: 8 and have known s that I came out from G230
Heb 6:14 Saying, S blessing I will bless thee, and G2229
Rev 22:20 He which testifieth these things saith, S G3483

SURETIES
Prv 22:26 hands, *or* of them that are s for debts. H6148

SURETISHIP
Prv 11:15 *for it*: and he that hateth s is sure. H8628

SURETY
Gen 15:13 And he said unto Abram, Know of a s H3045
18:13 Shall I of a s bear a child, which am old? H552
26: 9 said, Behold, of a s she *is* thy wife: and H389
43: 9 I will be s for him; of my hand shalt H6148
44:32 For thy servant became s for the lad H6148
Job 17: 3 Lay down now, put me in a s with thee; H6148
Ps119:122 Be s for thy servant for good: let not the H6148
Prv 6: 1 My son, if thou be s for thy friend, *if* H6148
11:15 He that is s for a stranger shall smart H6148
17:18 s in the presence of his friend. H6161
20:16 Take his garment that is s *for* a H6148
27:13 Take his garment that is s for a H6148
Act 12:11 Now I know of a s, that the Lord hath G230
Heb 7:22 By so much was Jesus made a s of a G1450

SURFEITING
Lk 21:34 overcharged with s, and drunkenness, G2897

SURMISINGS
1Ti 6: 4 cometh envy, strife, railings, evil s, G5283

SURNAME
Isa 44: 5 and s *himself* by the name of Israel. H3655
Mt 10: 3 Lebbaeus, whose s was Thaddaeus; G1941
Act 10: 5 call for *one* Simon, whose s is Peter: G1941
32 Simon, whose s is Peter; he is lodged G1941
11:13 and call for Simon, whose s is Peter; G1941
12:12 of John, whose s was Mark; where G1941
25 with them John, whose s was Mark. G1941
15:37 with them John, whose s was Mark. G2564

SURNAMED
Isa 45: 4 by thy name: I have s thee, though thou H3655
Mk 3:16 And Simon he s Peter; G2007
17 of James; and he s them Boanerges, G2007
Lk 22: 3 Then entered Satan into Judas s G1941
Act 1:23 who was s Justus, and Matthias. G1941
4:36 And Joses, who by the apostles was s G1941
10:18 which was s Peter, were lodged there. G1941
15:22 *namely*, Judas s Barsabas, and Silas, G1941

SURPRISED
Isa 33:14 fearfulness hath s the hypocrites. Who H270
Jer 48:41 the strong holds are s, and the mighty H8610
51:41 of the whole earth s! how is Babylon H8610

SUSAH See HAZAR-SUSAH.

SUSANCHITES
Ezr 4: 9 the S, the Dehavites, *and* the Elamites, H7801

SUSANNA
Lk 8: 3 steward, and S, and many others, G4677

SUSI
Nu 13:11 tribe of Manasseh, Gaddi the son of S. H5485

SUSIM See HAZAR-SUSIM.

SUSTAIN
1Ki 17: 9 a widow woman there to s thee. H3557
Neh 9:21 Yea, forty years didst thou s them in H3557
Ps 55:22 and he shall s thee: he shall never H3557
Prv 18:14 The spirit of a man will s his infirmity; H3557

SUSTAINED
Gen 27:37 and wine have I s him: and what shall H5564
Ps 3: 5 slept; I awaked; for the LORD s me. H5564
Isa 59:16 him; and his righteousness, it s him. H5564

SUSTENANCE
Jdg 6: 4 Gaza, and left no s for Israel, neither H4241
2Sa 19:32 the king of s while he lay at Mahanaim; H3557
Act 7:11 affliction: and our fathers found no s. G5527

SWADDLED
Lam 2:22 those that I have s and brought up hath H2946
Ezk 16: 4 thou wast not salted at all, nor s at all. H2853

SWADDLING
Lk 2: 7 wrapped him in s clothes, and laid him G4683
12 in s clothes, lying in a manger. G4683

SWADDLINGBAND
Job 38: 9 thereof, and thick darkness a s for it, H2854

SWADDLING-CLOTHES See SWADDLING and CLOTHES.

SWALLOW
Nu 16:30 her mouth, and s them up, with all that H1104
34 they said, Lest the earth s us up *also*. H1104
2Sa 20:19 thou s up the inheritance of the LORD? H1104
20 from me, that I should s up or destroy. H1104
Job 7:19 let me alone till I s down my spittle? H1104
20:18 and shall not s *it* down: according H1104
Ps 21: 9 the LORD shall s them up in his wrath, H1104
56: 1 for man would s me up; he fighting H7602
2 Mine enemies would daily s *me* up: for H7602
57: 3 of him that would s me up. Selah. God H7602
69:15 let the deep s me up, and let not the H1104
84: 3 an house, and the s a nest for herself, H1866
Prv 1:12 Let us s them up alive as the grave; and H1104
26: 2 As the bird by wandering, as the s by H1866
Ecc 10:12 but the lips of a fool will s up himself. H1104
Isa 25: 8 He will s up death in victory; and the H1104
38:14 Like a crane *or* a s, so did I chatter: I H5693
Jer 8: 7 the crane and the s observe the time of H5693

Hos 8: 7 so be it yield, the strangers shall **s** it up. H1104
Am 8: 4 Hear this, O ye that **s** up the needy, H7602
Oba 16 and they shall **s** down, and they shall H3886
Jna 1:17 a great fish to **s** up Jonah. And Jonah H1104
Mt 23:24 which strain at a gnat, and **s** a camel. *G2666*

SWALLOWED
Ex 7:12 but Aaron's rod **s** up their rods. H1104
15:12 out thy right hand, the earth **s** them. H1104
Nu 16:32 And the earth opened her mouth, and **s** H1104
26:10 And the earth opened her mouth, and **s** H1104
Dt 11: 6 her mouth, and **s** them up, and their H1104
2Sa 17:16 lest the king be **s** up, and all the people H1104
Job 6: 3 of the sea: therefore my words are **s** up. H3886
20:15 He hath **s** down riches, and he shall H1104
37:20 if a man speak, surely he shall be **s** up. H1104
Ps 35:25 it: let them not say, We have **s** him up. H1104
106:17 The earth opened and **s** up Dathan, H1104
124: 3 Then they had **s** us up quick, when H1104
Isa 28: 7 drink, they are **s** up of wine, they are H1104
49:19 they that **s** thee up shall be far away. H1104
Jer 51:34 vessel, he hath **s** me up like a dragon, H1104
44 mouth that which he hath **s** up: and the H1105
Lam 2: 2 The Lord hath **s** up all the habitations H1104
5 The Lord was as an enemy: he hath **s** H1104
5 up Israel, he hath **s** up all her palaces: H1104
16 they say, We have **s** *her* up: certainly H1104
Ezk 36: 3 *you* desolate, and **s** you up on every H7602
Hos 8: 8 Israel is **s** up: now shall they be among H1104
1Co 15:54 that is written, Death is **s** up in victory. *G2666*
2Co 2: 7 should be **s** up with overmuch sorrow. *G2666*
5: 4 that mortality might be **s** up of life. *G2666*
Rev 12:16 her mouth, and **s** up the flood which *G2666*

SWALLOWETH
Job 5: 5 and the robber **s** up their substance. H7602
39:24 He **s** the ground with fierceness and H1572

SWAN
Lev 11:18 And the **s**, and the pelican, and the gier H8580
Dt 14:16 little owl, and the great owl, and the **s**, H8580

SWARE
Gen 21:31 because there they **s** both of them. H7650
24: 7 unto me, and that **s** unto me, saying, H7650
9 and **s** to him concerning that matter. H7650
25:33 me this day; and he **s** unto him: and he H7650
26: 3 which I **s** unto Abraham thy father; H7650
31 the morning, and **s** one to another: and H7650
31:53 Jacob **s** by the fear of his father Isaac. H7650
47:31 And he said, Swear unto me. And he **s** H7650
50:24 **s** to Abraham, to Isaac, and to Jacob. H7650
Ex 13: 5 which he **s** unto thy fathers to give H7650
11 Canaanites, as he **s** unto thee and to H7650
33: 1 the land which I **s** unto Abraham, to H7650
Nu 14:16 into the land which he **s** unto them, H7650
23 the land which I **s** unto their fathers, H7650
30 which I **s** to make you dwell H5375+H3027
32:10 kindled the same time, and he **s**, saying, H7650
11 the land which I **s** unto Abraham, unto H7650
Dt 1: 8 which the LORD **s** unto your fathers, H7650
34 words, and was wroth, and **s**, saying, H7650
35 which I **s** to give unto your fathers, H7650
2:14 the host, as the LORD **s** unto them. H7650
4:21 your sakes, and **s** that I should not go H7650
31 of thy fathers which he **s** unto them. H7650
6:10 the land which he **s** unto thy fathers, to H7650
18 which the LORD **s** unto thy fathers, H7650
23 us the land which he **s** unto our fathers. H7650
7:12 the mercy which he **s** unto thy fathers: H7650
13 which he **s** unto thy fathers to give thee. H7650
8: 1 which the LORD **s** unto your fathers. H7650
18 he **s** unto thy fathers, as *it is* this day. H7650
9: 5 which the LORD **s** unto thy fathers, H7650
10:11 I **s** unto their fathers to give unto them. H7650
11: 9 which the LORD **s** unto your fathers to H7650
21 which the LORD **s** unto your fathers to H7650
26: 3 LORD **s** unto our fathers for to give us. H7650
28:11 LORD **s** unto thy fathers to give thee. H7650
30:20 which the LORD **s** unto thy fathers, to H7650
31:20 the land which I **s** unto their fathers, H7650
21 brought them into the land which I **s**. H7650
23 I **s** unto them: and I will be with thee. H7650
34: 4 *is* the land which I **s** unto Abraham, H7650
Jos 1: 6 I **s** unto their fathers to give them. H7650
5: 6 whom the LORD **s** that he would not H7650
6 which the LORD **s** unto their fathers H7650
6:22 and all that she hath, as ye **s** unto her. H7650
9:15 of the congregation **s** unto them. H7650
Jos 9:20 of the oath which we **s** unto them. H7650
14: 9 And Moses **s** on that day, saying, H7650
21:43 the land which he **s** to give unto their H7650
44 to all that he **s** unto their fathers: and H7650
Jdg 2: 1 the land which I **s** unto your fathers; H7650
1Sa 19: 6 and Saul **s**, *As* the LORD liveth, H7650
20: 3 And David **s** moreover, and said, Thy H7650
24:22 And David **s** unto Saul. And Saul went H7650
28:10 And Saul **s** to her by the LORD, saying, H7650
2Sa 3:35 yet day, David **s**, saying, So do God to H7650
19:23 shalt not die. And the king **s** unto him. H7650
21:17 the men of David **s** unto him, saying, H7650
1Ki 1:29 And the king **s**, and said, *As* the LORD H7650
30 Even as I **s** unto thee by the LORD God H7650
2: 8 at Jordan, and I **s** to him by the LORD, H7650
23 Then king Solomon **s** by the LORD, H7650
2Ki 25:24 And Gedaliah **s** to them, and to their H7650
2Ch 15:14 And they **s** unto the LORD with a loud H7650
Ezr 10: 5 do according to this word. And they **s**. H7650
Ps 95:11 Unto whom I **s** in my wrath that they H7650
132: 2 How he **s** unto the LORD, *and* vowed H7650
Jer 38:16 So Zedekiah the king **s** secretly unto H7650
40: 9 the son of Shaphan **s** unto them and to H7650
Ezk 16: 8 thy nakedness: yea, I **s** unto thee, and H7650
Dan 12: 7 unto heaven, and **s** by him that liveth H7650
Mk 6:23 And he **s** unto her, Whatsoever thou *G3660*
Lk 1:73 The oath which he **s** to our father *G3660*
Heb 3:11 So I **s** in my wrath, They shall not enter *G3660*
18 And to whom **s** he that they should not *G3660*
6:13 swear by no greater, he **s** by himself, *G3660*
7:21 him, The Lord **s** and will not repent, *G3660*
Rev 10: 6 And **s** by him that liveth for ever and *G3660*

SWAREST
Ex 32:13 to whom thou **s** by thine own self, and H7650
Nu 11:12 land which thou **s** unto their fathers? H7650
Dt 26:15 given us, as thou **s** unto our fathers, a H7650
1Ki 1:17 And she said unto him, My lord, thou **s** H7650
Ps 89:49 *which* thou **s** unto David in thy truth? H7650

SWARM
Ex 8:24 there came a grievous **s** *of flies* into the H6157
24 corrupted by reason of the **s** *of flies*. H6157
Jdg 14: 8 *there was* a **s** of bees and honey in H5712

SWARMS
Ex 8:21 behold, I will send **s** *of flies* upon thee, H6157
21 shall be full of **s** *of flies*, and also the H6157
22 dwell, that no **s** *of flies* shall be there; H6157
29 the LORD that the **s** *of flies* may depart H6157
31 he removed the **s** *of flies* from Pharaoh, H6157

SWEAR
Gen 21:23 Now therefore **s** unto me here by God H7650
24 And Abraham said, I will **s**. H7650
24: 3 And I will make thee **s** by the LORD, H7650
37 And my master made me **s**, saying, H7650
25:33 And Jacob said, **S** to me this day; and H7650
47:31 And he said, **S** unto me. And he sware H7650
50: 5 My father made me **s**, saying, Lo, I die: H7650
6 thy father, according as he made thee **s**. H7650
Ex 6: 8 the which I did **s** to give it to Abraham, H3027
Lev 5: 4 Or if a soul **s**, pronouncing with *his* lips H7650
19:12 And ye shall not **s** by my name falsely, H7650
Nu 30: 2 unto the LORD, or **s** an oath to bind his H7650
Dt 6:13 serve him, and shalt **s** by his name. H7650
10:20 shalt thou cleave, and **s** by his name. H7650
Jos 2:12 Now therefore, I pray you, **s** unto me H7650
17 thine oath which thou hast made us **s**. H7650
20 oath which thou hast made us to **s**. H7650
23: 7 gods, nor cause to **s** *by them*, neither H7650
Jdg 15:12 said unto them, **S** unto me, that ye will H7650
1Sa 20:17 And Jonathan caused David to **s** again, H7650
24:21 **S** now therefore unto me by the LORD, H7650
30:15 And he said, **S** unto me by God, that H7650
2Sa 19: 7 thy servants: for I **s** by the LORD, if H7650
1Ki 1:13 thou, my lord, O king, **s** unto thine H7650
51 Let king Solomon **s** unto me to day that H7650
2:42 I not make thee to **s** by the LORD, and H7650
8:31 him to cause him to **s**, and the oath come H422
2Ch 6:22 him to make him **s**, and the oath come H422
36:13 who had made him **s** by God: but he H7650
Ezr 10: 5 and all Israel, to **s** that they should do H7650
Neh 13:25 and made them **s** by God, *saying*, Ye H7650
Isa 3: 7 In that day shall he **s**, saying, I will not H5375
19:18 of Canaan, and **s** to the LORD of hosts; H7650
45:23 knee shall bow, every tongue shall **s**. H7650
48: 1 of Judah, which **s** by the name of the H7650
65:16 in the earth shall **s** by the God of truth; H7650
Jer 4: 2 And thou shalt **s**, The LORD liveth, in H7650
5: 2 The LORD liveth; surely they **s** falsely. H7650
7: 9 adultery, and **s** falsely, and burn H7650
12:16 of my people, to **s** by my name, The H7650
16 my people to **s** by Baal; then shall they H7650
22: 5 But if ye will not hear these words, I **s** H7650
32:22 which thou didst **s** to their fathers to H7650
Hos 4:15 to Beth-aven, nor **s**, The LORD liveth. H7650
Am 8:14 They that **s** by the sin of Samaria, and H7650
Zep 1: 5 worship *and* that **s** by the LORD, and H7650
5 by the LORD, and that **s** by Malcham; H7650
Mt 5:34 But I say unto you, **S** not at all; neither *G3660*
36 Neither shalt thou **s** by thy head, *G3660*
23:16 Whosoever shall **s** by the temple, it is *G3660*
16 but whosoever shall **s** by the gold of the *G3660*
18 And, Whosoever shall **s** by the altar, it *G3660*
20 Whoso therefore shall **s** by the altar, *G3660*
21 And whoso shall **s** by the temple, *G3660*
22 And he that shall **s** by heaven, *G3660*
26:74 Then began he to curse and to **s**, *saying*, *G3660*
Mk 14:71 But he began to curse and to **s**, *saying*, I *G3660*
Heb 6:13 **s** by no greater, he sware by himself, *G3660*
16 For men verily **s** by the greater: and an *G3660*
Jas 5:12 But above all things, my brethren, **s** *G3660*

SWEARERS
Mal 3: 5 and against false **s**, and against those H7650

SWEARETH
Lev 6: 3 concerning it, and **s** falsely; in any of H7650
Ps 15: 4 **s** to *his own* hurt, and changeth not. H7650
63:11 every one that **s** by him shall glory: but H7650
Ecc 9: 2 he that **s**, as *he* that feareth an oath. H7650
Isa 65:16 of truth; and he that **s** in the earth shall H7650
Zec 5: 3 and every one that **s** shall be cut off *as* H7650
4 the house of him that **s** falsely by my H7650
Mt 23:18 **s** by the gift that is upon it, he is guilty. *G3660*
20 altar, **s** by it, and by all things thereon. *G3660*
21 And whoso shall swear by the temple, **s** *G3660*
22 And he that shall swear by heaven, **s** by *G3660*

SWEARING
Lev 5: 1 And if a soul sin, and hear the voice of **s**, H423
Jer 23:10 for because of **s** the land mourneth; the H423
Hos 4: 2 By **s**, and lying, and killing, and stealing, H422
10: 4 They have spoken words, **s** falsely in H422

SWEAT
Gen 3:19 In the **s** of thy face shalt thou eat bread, H2188
Ezk 44:18 with any thing that causeth **s**. H3154
Lk 22:44 earnestly: and his **s** was as it were great *G2402*

SWEEP
Isa 14:23 water: and I will **s** it with the besom of H2894
28:17 and the hail shall **s** away the refuge of H3261
Lk 15: 8 not light a candle, and **s** the house, and *G4563*

SWEEPING
Prv 28: 3 *is like* a **s** rain which leaveth no food. H5502

SWEET
Gen 8:21 And the LORD smelled a **s** savour; and H5207
Ex 15:25 waters were made **s**: there he made for H4985
25: 6 for anointing oil, and for **s** incense, H5561
29:18 the LORD: it *is* a **s** savour, an offering H5207
25 burnt offering, for a **s** savour before the H5207
41 thereof, for a **s** savour, an offering H5207
30: 7 And Aaron shall burn thereon **s** H5561
23 *shekels*, and of **s** cinnamon half so H1314
23 *shekels*, and of **s** calamus two hundred H1314
34 Take unto thee **s** spices, stacte, and H5561
34 and galbanum; *these* **s** spices with pure H5561
31:11 And the anointing oil, and **s** incense for H5561
35: 8 for anointing oil, and for the **s** incense, H5561
15 oil, and the **s** incense, and the hanging H5561
28 the anointing oil, and for the **s** incense. H5561
37:29 pure incense of **s** spices, according to H5561
39:38 oil, and the **s** incense, and the hanging H5561
40:27 And he burnt **s** incense thereon; as the H5561
Lev 1: 9 by fire, of a **s** savour unto the LORD. H5207
13 by fire, of a **s** savour unto the LORD. H5207
17 by fire, of a **s** savour unto the LORD. H5207
2: 2 by fire, of a **s** savour unto the LORD: H5207
9 by fire, of a **s** savour unto the LORD. H5207
12 not be burnt on the altar for a **s** savour. H5207
3: 5 by fire, of a **s** savour unto the LORD. H5207
16 for a **s** savour: all the fat *is* the LORD'S. H5207
4: 7 of the altar of **s** incense before the H5561
31 the altar for a **s** savour unto the LORD; H5207

Lev 6:15 upon the altar *for* a s savour, *even* the H5207
21 offer *for* a s savour unto the LORD. H5207
8:21 sacrifice for a s savour, *and* an offering H5207
28 for a s savour: it *is* an offering H5207
16:12 and his hands full of s incense beaten H5561
17: 6 the fat for a s savour unto the LORD. H5207
23:13 the LORD *for* a s savour: and the drink H5207
18 by fire, of s savour unto the LORD. H5207
26:31 not smell the savour of your s odours. H5207
Nu 4:16 for the light, and the s incense, and the H5561
15: 3 feasts, to make a s savour unto the H5207
7 of wine, *for* a s savour unto the LORD. H5207
10 by fire, of a s savour unto the LORD. H5207
13 by fire, of a s savour unto the LORD. H5207
14 made by fire, of a s savour unto the H5207
24 offering, for a s savour unto the LORD, H5207
18:17 by fire, for a s savour unto the LORD. H5207
28: 2 made by fire, *for* a s savour unto me, H5207
6 mount Sinai for a s savour, a sacrifice H5207
8 by fire, of a s savour unto the LORD. H5207
13 burnt offering of a s savour, a sacrifice H5207
24 made by fire, of a s savour unto the H5207
27 offering for a s savour unto the LORD; H5207
29: 2 offering for a s savour unto the LORD; H5207
6 their manner, for a s savour, a sacrifice H5207
8 the LORD *for* a s savour; one young H5207
13 made by fire, of a s savour unto the H5207
36 made by fire, of a s savour unto the H5207
2Sa 23: 1 and the s psalmist of Israel, said, H5273
2Ch 2: 4 burn before him s incense, and for the H5561
13:11 sacrifices and s incense: the shewbread H5561
16:14 was filled with s odours and divers H1314
Ezr 6:10 That they may offer sacrifices of s H5208
Neh 8:10 fat, and drink the s, and send portions H4477
Est 2:12 six months with s odours, and with H1314
Job 20:12 Though wickedness be s in his mouth, H4985
21:33 The clods of the valley shall be s unto H4985
38:31 Canst thou bind the s influences of H4575
Ps 55:14 We took s counsel together, *and* H4985
104:34 My meditation of him shall be s: I will H6149
119:103 How s are thy words unto my taste! H4452
141: 6 they shall hear my words; for they are s. H5276
Prv 3:24 shalt lie down, and thy sleep shall be s. H6149
9:17 Stolen waters are s, and bread *eaten* in H4985
13:19 The desire accomplished is s to the H6149
16:24 Pleasant words *are as* an honeycomb, s H4966
20:17 Bread of deceit *is* s to a man; but H6156
23: 8 thou vomit up, and lose thy s words. H5273
24:13 the honeycomb, *which is* s to thy taste: H4966
27: 7 the hungry soul every bitter thing is s. H4966
Ecc 5:12 The sleep of a labouring man *is* s, H4966
11: 7 Truly the light *is* s, and a pleasant *thing* H4966
Song 2: 3 delight, and his fruit *was* s to my taste. H4966
14 hear thy voice; for s *is* thy voice, and H6156
5: 5 my fingers *with* s smelling myrrh, upon H5674
13 His cheeks *are* as a bed of spices, *as* s H4840
13 *like* lilies, dropping s smelling myrrh. H5674
16 His mouth *is* most s: yea, he *is* H4477
Isa 3:24 *that* instead of s smell there shall be H1314
5:20 put bitter for s, and sweet for bitter! H4966
20 put bitter for sweet, and s for bitter! H4966
23:16 forgotten; make s melody, sing many H3190
43:24 Thou hast bought me no s cane with
49:26 own blood, as with s wine: and all flesh H6070
Jer 6:20 from Sheba, and the s cane from a far H2896
20 nor your sacrifices s unto me. H6149
31:26 beheld; and my sleep was s unto me. H6149
Ezk 6:13 they did offer s savour to all their idols. H5207
16:19 before them for a s savour: and *thus* it H5207
20:28 they made their s savour, and poured H5207
41 I will accept you with your s savour, H5207
Dan 2:46 an oblation and s odours unto him. H5208
Am 9:13 drop s wine, and all the hills shall melt. H6070
Mic 6:15 and s wine, but shalt not drink wine. H8492
Mk 16: 1 had bought s spices, that they might
2Co 2:15 For we are unto God a s savour of *G2175*
Php 4:18 you, an odour of a s smell, a sacrifice *G2175*
Jas 3:11 at the same place s *water* and bitter? *G1099*
Rev 10: 9 but it shall be in thy mouth s as honey. *G1099*
10 it was in my mouth s as honey: and as *G1099*

SWEETER
Jdg 14:18 down, What *is* s than honey? and what H4966
Ps 19:10 s also than honey and the honeycomb. H4966
119:103 taste! *yea, s* than honey to my mouth!

SWEETLY
Job 24:20 worm shall feed s on him; he shall be H4988
Song 7: 9 that goeth *down* s, causing the lips of H4339

SWEETNESS
Jdg 9:11 I forsake my s, and my good fruit, and H4987
14:14 strong came forth s. And they could not H4966
Prv 16:21 the s of the lips increaseth learning. H4986
27: 9 s of a man's friend by hearty counsel. H4986
Ezk 3: 3 and it was in my mouth as honey for s. H4966

SWEETSMELLING
Eph 5: 2 and a sacrifice to God for a s savour. *G2175*

SWELL
Nu 5:21 make thy thigh to rot, and thy belly to s; H6639
22 make *thy* belly to s, and *thy* thigh to rot: H6638
27 and her belly shall s, and her thigh shall H6638
Dt 8: 4 neither did thy foot s, these forty years. H1216

SWELLED
Neh 9:21 waxed not old, and their feet s not. H1216

SWELLING
Ps 46: 3 shake with the s thereof. Selah. H1346
Isa 30:13 ready to fall, s out in a high wall, whose H1158
Jer 12: 5 how wilt thou do in the s of Jordan? H1347
49:19 a lion from the s of Jordan against the H1347
50:44 like a lion from the s of Jordan unto the H1347
2Pt 2:18 For when they speak great s *words* of *G5246*
Jude 16 speaketh great s *words*, having men's *G5246*

SWELLINGS
2Co 12:20 backbitings, whisperings, s, tumults: *G5450*

SWEPT
Jdg 5:21 The river of Kishon s them away, that H1640
Jer 46:15 Why are thy valiant *men* s away? they H5502
Mt 12:44 he findeth *it* empty, s, and garnished. *G4563*
Lk 11:25 And when he cometh, he findeth *it* s *G4563*

SWERVED
1Ti 1: 6 From which some having s have turned *G795*

SWIFT
Dt 28:49 end of the earth, *as* s as the eagle flieth; a
1Ch 12: 8 as s as the roes upon the mountains; H4116
Job 9:26 They are passed away as the s ships: as H16
24:18 He *is* s as the waters; their portion is H7031
Prv 6:18 feet that be s in running to mischief, H4116
Ecc 9:11 race *is* not to the s, nor the battle to the H7031
Isa 18: 2 *saying*, Go, ye s messengers, to a H7031
19: 1 rideth upon a s cloud, and shall come H7031
30:16 will ride upon the s; therefore shall they H7031
16 shall they that pursue you be s. H7043
66:20 mules, and upon s beasts, to my holy H3753
Jer 2:23 *art* a s dromedary traversing her ways; H7031
46: 6 Let not the s flee away, nor the mighty H7031
Am 2:14 perish from the s, and the strong shall H7031
15 and *he that is* s of foot shall not deliver H7031
Mic 1:13 the chariot to the s beast: she *is* the H7409
Mal 3: 5 and I will be a s witness against the H4116
Ro 3:15 Their feet *are* s to shed blood: *G3691*
Jas 1:19 s to hear, slow to speak, slow to wrath: *G5036*
2Pt 2: 1 bring upon themselves s destruction. *G5031*

SWIFTER
2Sa 1:23 divided: they were s than eagles, they H7043
Job 7: 6 My days are s than a weaver's shuttle, H7043
9:25 Now my days are s than a post: they H7043
Jer 4:13 his horses are s than eagles. Woe unto H7043
Lam 4:19 Our persecutors are s than the eagles of H7031
Hab 1: 8 Their horses also are s than the H7043

SWIFTLY
Ps 147:15 *upon* earth: his word runneth very s. H4120
Isa 5:26 behold, they shall come with speed s: H7031
Dan 9:21 being caused to fly s, touched me about H3288
Joel 3: 4 ye recompense me, s *and* speedily will I H7031

SWIM
2Ki 6: 6 and cast *it* in thither; and the iron did s. H6687
Ps 6: 6 to s; I water my couch with my tears. H7811
Isa 25:11 forth *his hands* to s: and he shall bring H7811
Ezk 47: 5 risen, waters to s in, a river that could H7813
Act 27:42 any of them should s out, and escape. *G1579*
43 that they which could s should cast *G2860*

SWIMMEST
Ezk 32: 6 the land wherein thou s, *even* to the H6824

SWIMMETH
Isa 25:11 of them, as he that s spreadeth forth H7811

SWINE
Lev 11: 7 And the s, though he divide the hoof, H2386
Dt 14: 8 And the s, because it divideth the hoof, H2386
Mt 7: 6 your pearls before s, lest they trample *G5519*
8:30 from them an herd of many s feeding. *G5519*
31 suffer us to go away into the herd of s. *G5519*
32 went into the herd of s: and, behold, the *G5519*
32 the whole herd of s ran violently down *G5519*
Mk 5:11 mountains a great herd of s feeding. *G5519*
12 into the s, that we may enter into them. *G5519*
13 and entered into the s: and the herd ran *G5519*
14 And they that fed the s fled, and told *it* *G5519*
16 the devil, and *also* concerning the s. *G5519*
Lk 8:32 And there was there an herd of many s *G5519*
33 and entered into the s: and the herd ran *G5519*
15:15 and he sent him into his fields to feed s. *G5519*
16 s did eat: and no man gave unto him. *G5519*

SWINE'S
Prv 11:22 *As* a jewel of gold in a s snout, *so is* a H2386
Isa 65: 4 which eat s flesh, and broth of H2386
66: 3 *as if he offered* s blood; he that burneth H2386
17 in the midst, eating s flesh, and the H2386

SWOLLEN
Act 28: 6 he should have s, or fallen down dead *G4092*

SWOON
Lam 2:11 the sucklings s in the streets of the city. H5848

SWOONED
Lam 2:12 wine? when they s as the wounded in H5848

SWORD
Gen 3:24 and a flaming s which turned every H2719
27:40 And by thy s shalt thou live, and shalt H2719
31:26 daughters, as captives *taken* with the s? H2719
34:25 took each man his s, and came upon H2719
26 the edge of the s, and took Dinah out H2719
48:22 Amorite with my s and with my bow. H2719
Ex 5: 3 upon us with pestilence, or with the s. H2719
21 to put a s in their hand to slay us. H2719
15: 9 my s, my hand shall destroy them. H2719
17:13 and his people with the edge of the s. H2719
18: 4 delivered me from the s of Pharaoh: H2719
22:24 kill you with the s; and your wives shall H2719
32:27 Put every man his s by his side, *and* go H2719
Lev 26: 6 shall the s go through your land. H2719
7 and they shall fall before you by the s. H2719
8 enemies shall fall before you by the s. H2719
25 And I will bring a s upon you, that H2719
33 will draw out a s after you: and your H2719
36 as fleeing from a s; and they shall fall H2719
37 as it were before a s, when none H2719
Nu 14: 3 land, to fall by the s, that our wives and H2719
43 and ye shall fall by the s: because ye are H2719
19:16 that is slain with a s in the open fields, H2719
20:18 lest I come out against thee with the s. H2719
21:24 with the edge of the s, and possessed his H2719
22:23 the way, and his s drawn in his hand: H2719
29 there were a s in mine hand, for now H2719
31 the way, and his s drawn in his hand: H2719
31: 8 also the son of Beor they slew with the s. H2719
Dt 13:15 the edge of the s, destroying it utterly, H2719
15 the cattle thereof, with the edge of the s. H2719
20:13 male thereof with the edge of the s: H2719
28:22 and with the s, and with blasting, and H2719
32:25 The s without, and terror within, shall H2719
41 If I whet my glittering s, and mine hand H2719
42 blood, and my s shall devour flesh; *and* H2719
33:29 and who *is* the s of thy excellency! and H2719
Jos 5:13 him with his s drawn in his hand: H2719
6:21 sheep, and ass, with the edge of the s. H2719
8:24 on the edge of the s, until they were H2719
24 Ai, and smote it with the edge of the s. H2719
10:11 the children of Israel slew with the s. H2719
28 the edge of the s, and the king thereof H2719
30 the edge of the s, and all the souls that H2719
32 the edge of the s, and all the souls that H2719
35 the edge of the s, and all the souls that H2719
37 the edge of the s, and the king thereof, H2719
39 the edge of the s, and utterly destroyed H2719
11:10 thereof with the s: for Hazor beforetime H2719
11 with the edge of the s, utterly destroying H2719
12 with the edge of the s, *and* he utterly H2719
14 with the edge of the s, until they had H2719
13:22 s among them that were slain by them. H2719
19:47 the edge of the s, and possessed it, and H2719
24:12 *but* not with thy s, nor with thy bow. H2719

Jdg 1: 8 the edge of the s, and set the city on fire. H2719
25 the edge of the s; but they let go the man H2719
4:15 the edge of the s before Barak; so that H2719
16 of the s; *and* there was not a man left. H2719
7:14 else save the s of Gideon the son of H2719
18 say, *The* s of the LORD, and of Gideon.
20 The s of the LORD, and of Gideon. H2719
22 set every man's s against his fellow, H2719
8:10 and twenty thousand men that drew s. H2719
20 the youth drew not his s: for he feared, H2719
9:54 him, Draw thy s, and slay me, that men H2719
18:27 of the s, and burnt the city with fire. H2719
20: 2 hundred thousand footmen that drew s. H2719
15 men that drew s, beside the inhabitants H2719
17 that drew s: all these *were* men of war. H2719
25 thousand men; all these drew the s. H2719
35 an hundred men: all these drew the s. H2719
37 smote all the city with the edge of the s. H2719
46 drew the s; all these *were* men of valour. H2719
48 with the edge of the s, as well the men of H2719
21:10 the s, with the women and the children. H2719
1Sa 13:22 there was neither s nor spear found in H2719
14:20 every man's s was against his fellow, H2719
15: 8 all the people with the edge of the s. H2719
33 And Samuel said, As thy s hath made H2719
17:39 And David girded his s upon his H2719
45 to me with a s, and with a spear, and H2719
47 saveth not with s and spear: for the H2719
50 *there was* no s in the hand of David. H2719
51 and took his s, and drew it out of the H2719
18: 4 his s, and to his bow, and to his girdle. H2719
21: 8 thine hand spear or s? for I have neither H2719
8 brought my s nor my weapons with H2719
9 And the priest said, The s of Goliath H2719
22:10 gave him the s of Goliath the Philistine. H2719
13 him bread, and a s, and hast inquired H2719
19 the edge of the s, both men and women, H2719
19 asses, and sheep, with the edge of the s. H2719
25:13 on every man his s. And they girded on H2719
13 on every man his s; and David also H2719
13 also girded on his s: and there went up H2719
31: 4 Draw thy s, and thrust me through H2719
4 Therefore Saul took a s, and fell upon it. H2719
5 likewise upon his s, and died with him. H2719
2Sa 1:12 Israel; because they were fallen by the s. H2719
22 and the s of Saul returned not empty. H2719
2:16 and *thrust* his s in his fellow's side; H2719
26 and said, Shall the s devour for ever? H2719
3:29 falleth on the s, or that lacketh bread. H2719
11:25 thee, for the s devoureth one as well H2719
12: 9 the Hittite with the s, and hast taken his H2719
9 with the s of the children of Ammon. H2719
10 Now therefore the s shall never depart H2719
15:14 and smite the city with the edge of the s. H2719
18: 8 people that day than the s devoured. H2719
20: 8 it a girdle *with* a s fastened upon his H2719
10 But Amasa took no heed to the s that H2719
21:16 a new *s*, thought to have slain David.
23:10 clave unto the s: and the LORD wrought H2719
24: 9 men that drew the s; and the men of H2719
1Ki 1:51 he will not slay his servant with the s. H2719
2: 8 I will not put thee to death with the s. H2719
32 them with the s, my father David not H2719
3:24 And the king said, Bring me a s. And H2719
24 And they brought a s before the king. H2719
19: 1 he had slain all the prophets with the s. H2719
10 prophets with the s; and I, *even* I only, H2719
14 prophets with the s; and I, *even* I only, H2719
17 that escapeth the s of Hazael shall Jehu H2719
17 from the s of Jehu shall Elisha slay. H2719
2Ki 6:22 captive with thy s and with thy bow? H2719
8:12 thou slay with the s, and wilt dash their H2719
10:25 the edge of the s; and the guard and the H2719
11:15 her kill with the s. For the priest had H2719
20 with the s *beside* the king's house. H2719
19: 7 him to fall by the s in his own land. H2719
37 him with the s: and they escaped into H2719
1Ch 5:18 to bear buckler and s, and to shoot with H2719
10: 4 Draw thy s, and thrust me through H2719
4 afraid. So Saul took a s, and fell upon it. H2719
5 dead, he fell likewise on the s, and died. H2719
21: 5 men that drew s: and Judah *was* four H2719
5 and ten thousand men that drew s. H2719
12 foes, while that the s of thine enemies H2719
12 else three days the s of the LORD, even H2719
16 having a drawn s in his hand stretched H2719
27 up his s again into the sheath thereof. H2719
30 of the s of the angel of the LORD. H2719
2Ch 20: 9 If, *when* evil cometh upon us, *as* the s, H2719
2Ch 21: 4 brethren with the s, and *divers* also of H2719
23:14 be slain with the s. For the priest said, H2719
21 that they had slain Athaliah with the s. H2719
29: 9 For, lo, our fathers have fallen by the s, H2719
32:21 own bowels slew him there with the s. H2719
36:17 men with the s in the house of their H2719
20 And them that had escaped from the s H2719
Ezr 9: 7 of the lands, to the s, to captivity, and to H2719
Neh 4:18 For the builders, every one had his s H2719
Est 9: 5 the stroke of the s, and slaughter, and H2719
Job 1:15 the edge of the s; and I only am escaped H2719
17 the edge of the s; and I only am escaped H2719
5:15 But he saveth the poor from the s, from H2719
20 and in war from the power of the s. H2719
15:22 darkness, and he is waited for of the s. H2719
19:29 Be ye afraid of the s: for wrath *bringeth* H2719
29 of the s, that ye may know *there* H2719
20:25 yea, the glittering s cometh out of his H1300
27:14 *it is* for the s: and his offspring shall H2719
33:18 pit, and his life from perishing by the s. H7973
36:12 s, and they shall die without knowledge. H7973
39:22 neither turneth he back from the s. H2719
40:19 can make his s to approach *unto him*. H2719
41:26 The s of him that layeth at him cannot H2719
Ps 7:12 If he turn not, he will whet his s; he hath H2719
17:13 my soul from the wicked, *which is* thy s: H2719
22:20 Deliver my soul from the s; my darling H2719
37:14 The wicked have drawn out the s, and H2719
15 Their s shall enter into their own heart, H2719
42:10 *As* with a s in my bones, mine enemies H7524
44: 3 by their own s, neither did their own H2719
6 in my bow, neither shall my s save me. H2719
45: 3 Gird thy s upon *thy* thigh, O *most* H2719
57: 4 and arrows, and their tongue a sharp s. H2719
63:10 They shall fall by the s: they shall be a H2719
64: 3 Who whet their tongue like a s, *and* H2719
76: 3 shield, and the s, and the battle. Selah. H2719
78:62 He gave his people over also unto the s; H2719
64 Their priests fell by the s; and their H2719
89:43 Thou hast also turned the edge of his s, H2719
144:10 David his servant from the hurtful s. H2719
149: 6 mouth, and a twoedged s in their hand; H2719
Prv 5: 4 as wormwood, sharp as a twoedged s. H2719
12:18 a s: but the tongue of the wise *is* health. H2719
25:18 *is* a maul, and a s, and a sharp arrow. H2719
Song 3: 8 man *hath* his s upon his thigh because H2719
Isa 1:20 be devoured with the s: for the mouth of H2719
2: 4 shall not lift up s against nation, H2719
3:25 Thy men shall fall by the s, and thy H2719
13:15 is joined *unto them* shall fall by the s. H2719
14:19 through with a s, that go down to the H2719
21:15 from the drawn s, and from the bent H2719
22: 2 not slain with the s, nor dead in battle. H2719
27: 1 and great and strong s shall punish H2719
31: 8 Then shall the Assyrian fall with the s, H2719
8 man; and the s, not of a mean man, H2719
8 shall flee from the s, and his young men H2719
34: 5 For my s shall be bathed in heaven: H2719
6 The s of the LORD is filled with blood, H2719
37: 7 him to fall by the s in his own land. H2719
38 him with the s; and they escaped into H2719
41: 2 his s, *and* as driven stubble to his bow. H2719
49: 2 like a sharp s; in the shadow of his H2719
51:19 the s: by whom shall I comfort thee? H2719
65:12 Therefore will I number you to the s, H2719
66:16 For by fire and by his s will the LORD H2719
Jer 2:30 your own s hath devoured your H2719
4:10 whereas the s reacheth unto the soul. H2719
5:12 us; neither shall we see s nor famine: H2719
17 wherein thou trustedst, with the s. H2719
6:25 by the way; for the s of the enemy *and* H2719
9:16 and I will send a s after them, till I have H2719
11:22 shall die by the s; their sons and their H2719
12:12 wilderness: for the s of the LORD shall H2719
14:12 them by the s, and by the famine, H2719
13 shall not see the s, neither shall ye have H2719
15 not, yet they say, S and famine shall H2719
15 be in this land; By s and famine shall H2719
16 famine and the s; and they shall have H2719
18 the slain with the s! and if I enter into H2719
15: 2 such as *are* for the s, to the sword; and H2719
2 the sword, to the s; and such as *are* for H2719
3 the LORD: the s to slay, and the dogs H2719
9 s before their enemies, saith the LORD. H2719
16: 4 consumed by the s, and by famine; and H2719
18:21 by the force of the s; and let their wives H2719
21 young men *be* slain by the s in battle. H2719
19: 7 cause them to fall by the s before their H2719
20: 4 shall fall by the s of their enemies, and H2719
Jer 20: 4 Babylon, and shall slay them with the s. H2719
21: 7 from the s, and from the famine, H2719
7 with the edge of the s; he shall not spare H2719
9 shall die by the s, and by the famine, H2719
24:10 And I will send the s, the famine, and H2719
25:16 of the s that I will send among them. H2719
27 of the s which I will send among you. H2719
29 for I will call for a s upon all the H2719
31 *are* wicked to the s, saith the LORD. H2719
26:23 slew him with the s, and cast his dead H2719
27: 8 LORD, with the s, and with the famine, H2719
13 thy people, by the s, by the famine, and H2719
29:17 upon them the s, the famine, and the H2719
18 And I will persecute them with the s, H2719
31: 2 *were* left of the s found grace in the H2719
32:24 it, because of the s, and of the famine, H2719
36 of Babylon by the s, and by the famine, H2719
33: 4 down by the mounts, and by the s; H2719
34: 4 of thee, Thou shalt not die by the s: H2719
17 the LORD, to the s, to the pestilence, H2719
38: 2 shall die by the s, by the famine, and H2719
39:18 not fall by the s, but thy life shall be H2719
41: 2 of Shaphan with the s, and slew him, H2719
42:16 Then it shall come to pass, *that* the s, H2719
17 shall die by the s, by the famine, and H2719
22 ye shall die by the s, by the famine, and H2719
43:11 and such *as are* for the s to the sword. H2719
11 and such *as are* for the sword to the s. H2719
44:12 consumed by the s *and* by the famine: H2719
12 greatest, by the s and by the famine: H2719
13 s, by the famine, and by the pestilence: H2719
18 consumed by the s and by the famine. H2719
27 consumed by the s and by the famine, H2719
28 Yet a small number that escape the s H2719
46:10 and the s shall devour, and it H2719
14 for the s shall devour round about thee. H2719
16 of our nativity, from the oppressing s. H2719
47: 6 O thou s of the LORD, how long *will it* H2719
48: 2 O Madmen; the s shall pursue thee. H2719
10 he that keepeth back his s from blood. H2719
49:37 and I will send the s after them, till I H2719
50:16 fear of the oppressing s they shall turn H2719
35 A s *is* upon the Chaldeans, saith the H2719
36 A s *is* upon the liars; and they shall H2719
36 they shall dote: a s *is* upon her mighty H2719
37 A s *is* upon their horses, and upon their H2719
37 as women: a s *is* upon her treasures; H2719
51:50 Ye that have escaped the s, go away, H2719
Lam 1:20 s bereaveth, at home *there is* as death. H2719
2:21 are fallen by the s; thou hast slain *them* H2719
4: 9 *They that be* slain with the s are better H2719
5: 9 lives because of the s of the wilderness. H2719
Ezk 5: 2 and I will draw out a s after them. H2719
12 shall fall by the s round about thee; H2719
12 and I will draw out a s after them. H2719
17 s upon thee. I the LORD have spoken *it*. H2719
6: 3 I, *even* I, will bring a s upon you, and I H2719
8 shall escape the s among the nations, H2719
11 s, by the famine, and by the pestilence. H2719
12 near shall fall by the s; and he that H2719
7:15 The s *is* without, and the pestilence H2719
15 shall die with the s; and he that *is* in the H2719
11: 8 Ye have feared the s; and I will bring a H2719
8 a s upon you, saith the Lord GOD. H2719
10 Ye shall fall by the s; I will judge you in H2719
12:14 and I will draw out the s after them. H2719
16 of them from the s, from the famine, H2719
14:17 Or *if* I bring a s upon that land, and H2719
17 land, and say, S, go through the land; H2719
21 Jerusalem, the s, and the famine, and H2719
17:21 shall fall by the s, and they that remain H2719
21: 3 will draw forth my s out of his sheath, H2719
4 therefore shall my s go forth out of his H2719
5 drawn forth my s out of his sheath: it H2719
9 saith the LORD; Say, A s, a sword is H2719
9 a s is sharpened, and also furbished: H2719
11 be handled: this s is sharpened, and it H2719
12 by reason of the s shall be upon my H2719
13 Because *it is* a trial, and what if *the* s
14 and let the s be doubled the third H2719
14 the third time, the s of the slain: it *is* H2719
14 of the slain: it *is* the s of the great *men* H2719
15 I have set the point of the s against all H2719
19 thee two ways, that the s of the king of H2719
20 Appoint a way, that the s may come to H2719
28 even say thou, The s, the sword *is* H2719
28 thou, The sword, the s *is* drawn: for the H2719
23:10 and slew her with the s: and she became H2719
25 shall fall by the s: they shall take thy H2719

S

Ezk 24:21 whom ye have left shall fall by the s. H2719
25:13 and they of Dedan shall fall by the s. H2719
26: 6 be slain by the s; and they shall know H2719
8 He shall slay with the s thy daughters H2719
11 slay thy people by the s, and thy strong H2719
28:23 of her by the s upon her on every side; H2719
29: 8 I will bring a s upon thee, and cut off H2719
30: 4 And the s shall come upon Egypt, and H2719
5 in league, shall fall with them by the s. H2719
6 fall in it by the s, saith the Lord GOD. H2719
17 shall fall by the s: and these *cities* shall H2719
21 bind it, to make it strong to hold the s. H2719
22 I will cause the s to fall out of his hand. H2719
24 and put my s in his hand: but I will H2719
25 I shall put my s into the hand of the H2719
31:17 *be* slain with the s; and *they that were* H2719
18 *be* slain by the s. This *is* Pharaoh and H2719
32:10 I shall brandish my s before them; and H2719
11 For thus saith the Lord GOD; The s of H2719
20 *are* slain by the s: she is delivered to the H2719
20 the s: draw her and all her multitudes. H2719
21 they lie uncircumcised, slain by the s. H2719
22 him: all of them slain, fallen by the s: H2719
23 slain, fallen by the s, which caused H2719
24 slain, fallen by the s, which are gone H2719
25 slain by the s: though their terror H2719
26 slain by the s, though they caused H2719
28 lie with *them that are* slain with the s. H2719
29 *were* slain by the s: they shall lie with H2719
30 *be* slain by the s, and bear their shame H2719
31 army slain by the s, saith the Lord GOD. H2719
32 *are* slain with the s, *even* Pharaoh and H2719
33: 2 When I bring the s upon a land, if the H2719
3 If when he seeth the s come upon the H2719
4 not warning; if the s come, and take H2719
6 But if the watchman see the s come, H2719
6 not warned; if the s come, and take *any* H2719
26 Ye stand upon your s, ye work H2719
27 shall fall by the s, and him that *is* in the H2719
35: 5 by the force of the s in the time of their H2719
8 shall they fall that are slain with the s. H2719
38: 8 back from the s, *and is* gathered out H2719
21 And I will call for a s against him H2719
21 man's s shall be against his brother. H2719
39:23 of their enemies: so fell they all by the s. H2719
Dan 11:33 they shall fall by the s, and by flame, by H2719
Hos 1: 7 them by bow, nor by s, nor by battle, by H2719
2:18 the bow and the s and the battle out of H2719
7:16 shall fall by the s for the rage of their H2719
11: 6 And the s shall abide on his cities, and H2719
13:16 shall fall by the s: their infants shall be H2719
Joel 2: 8 upon the s, they shall not be wounded. H7973
Am 1:11 brother with the s, and did cast off all H2719
4:10 I slain with the s, and have taken away H2719
7: 9 the house of Jeroboam with the s. H2719
11 shall die by the s, and Israel shall surely H2719
17 shall fall by the s, and thy land shall be H2719
9: 1 last of them with the s: he that fleeth of H2719
4 I command the s, and it shall slay them: H2719
10 shall die by the s, which say, The evil H2719
Mic 4: 3 shall not lift up a s against nation, H2719
5: 6 of Assyria with the s, and the land of H2719
6:14 thou deliverest will I give up to the s. H2719
Nah 2:13 the smoke, and the s shall devour thy H2719
3: 3 up both the bright s and the glittering H2719
15 There shall the fire devour thee; the s H2719
Zep 2:12 also, ye *shall be* slain by my s. H2719
Hag 2:22 down, every one by the s of his brother. H2719
Zec 9:13 made thee as the s of a mighty man. H2719
11:17 the flock! the s *shall be* upon his arm, H2719
13: 7 Awake, O s, against my shepherd, and H2719
Mt 10:34 earth: I came not to send peace, but a s. G3162
26:51 and drew his s, and struck a servant G3162
52 Put up again thy s into his place: for all G3162
52 take the s shall perish with the sword. G3162
52 take the sword shall perish with the s. G3162
Mk 14:47 And one of them that stood by drew a s, G3162
Lk 2:35 (Yea, a s shall pierce through thy own G4501
21:24 And they shall fall by the edge of the s, G3162
22:36 s, let him sell his garment, and buy one. G3162
49 him, Lord, shall we smite with the s? G3162
Jn 18:10 Then Simon Peter having a s drew it, G3162
11 Peter, Put up thy s into the sheath: the G3162
Act 12: 2 James the brother of John with the s. G3162
16:27 he drew out his s, and would have killed G3162
Ro 8:35 or famine, or nakedness, or peril, or s? G3162
13: 4 he beareth not the s in vain: for he is G3162
Eph 6:17 salvation, and the s of the Spirit, which G3162
Heb 4:12 any twoedged s, piercing even to the G3162
Heb 11:34 the edge of the s, out of weakness were G3162
37 slain with the s: they wandered about G5408
Rev 1:16 went a sharp twoedged s: and his G4501
2:12 which hath the sharp s with two edges; G4501
16 against them with the s of my mouth. G4501
6: 4 and there was given unto him a great s. G3162
8 earth, to kill with s, and with hunger, G4501
13:10 killeth with the s must be killed with G3162
10 be killed with the s. Here is the patience G3162
14 had the wound by a s, and did live. G3162
19:15 And out of his mouth goeth a sharp s, G4501
21 And the remnant were slain with the s G4501
21 the horse, which *s* proceeded out of his

SWORDS
1Sa 13:19 the Hebrews make *them* s or spears: H2719
2Ki 3:26 men that drew s, to break through *even* H2719
Neh 4:13 their s, their spears, and their bows. H2719
Ps 55:21 softer than oil, yet *were* they drawn s. H6609
59: 7 with their mouth: s *are* in their lips: for H2719
Prv 30:14 whose teeth *are as* s, and their jaw teeth H2719
Song 3: 8 They all hold s, *being* expert in war: H2719
Isa 2: 4 shall beat their s into plowshares, and H2719
21:15 For they fled from the s, from the drawn H2719
Ezk 16:40 and thrust thee through with their s. H2719
23:47 them with their s; they shall slay their H2719
28: 7 shall draw their s against the beauty of H2719
30:11 shall draw their s against Egypt, and H2719
32:12 By the s of the mighty will I cause thy H2719
27 have laid their s under their heads, but H2719
38: 4 and shields, all of them handling s: H2719
Joel 3:10 Beat your plowshares into s, and your H2719
Mic 4: 3 shall beat their s into plowshares, and H2719
Mt 26:47 multitude with s and staves, from the G3162
55 a thief with s and staves for to take G3162
Mk 14:43 multitude with s and staves, from the G3162
48 with s and *with* staves to take me? G3162
Lk 22:38 s. And he said unto them, It is enough. G3162
52 as against a thief, with s and staves? G3162

SWORE See SWARE.

SWORN
Gen 22:16 And said, By myself have I s, saith the H7650
Ex 13:19 for he had straitly s the children of H7650
17:16 hath s *that* the LORD H3027+H5921+H3678
Lev 6: 5 Or all that about which he hath s H7650
Dt 7: 8 oath which he had s unto your fathers, H7650
13:17 thee, as he hath s unto thy fathers; H7650
19: 8 thy coast, as he hath s unto thy fathers, H7650
28: 9 as he hath s unto thee, if thou shalt H7650
29:13 and as he hath s unto thy fathers, to H7650
31: 7 the LORD hath s unto their fathers to H7650
Jos 9:18 congregation had s unto them by the H7650
19 We have s unto them by the LORD H7650
Jdg 2:15 as the LORD had s unto them: and they H7650
21: 1 Now the men of Israel had s in Mizpeh, H7650
7 seeing we have s by the LORD that we H7650
18 of Israel have s, saying, Cursed *be* he H7650
1Sa 3:14 And therefore I have s unto the house H7650
20:42 as we have s both of us in the name H7650
2Sa 3: 9 hath s to David, even so I do to him; H7650
21: 2 of Israel had s unto them: and Saul H7650
2Ch 15:15 oath: for they had s with all their heart, H7650
Neh 6:18 in Judah s unto him, because H1167+H7621
9:15 land which thou hadst s to give them. H3027
Ps 24: 4 his soul unto vanity, nor s deceitfully. H7650
89: 3 I have s unto David my servant, H7650
35 Once have I s by my holiness that I will H7650
102: 8 are mad against me are s against me. H7650
110: 4 The LORD hath s, and will not repent, H7650
119:106 I have s, and I will perform *it*, that I will H7650
132:11 The LORD hath s *in* truth unto David; H7650
Isa 14:24 The LORD of hosts hath s, saying, H7650
45:23 I have s by myself, the word is gone out H7650
54: 9 me: for *as* I have s that the waters of H7650
9 earth; so have I s that I would not be H7650
62: 8 The LORD hath s by his right hand, H7650
Jer 5: 7 forsaken me, and s by *them that are* no H7650
11: 5 oath which I have s unto your fathers, H7650
44:26 Behold, I have s by my great name, H7650
49:13 For I have s by myself, saith the LORD, H7650
51:14 The LORD of hosts hath s by himself, H7650
Ezk 21:23 to them that have s oaths: but he will H7650
Am 4: 2 The Lord GOD hath s by his holiness, H7650
6: 8 The Lord GOD hath s by himself, saith H7650
8: 7 The LORD hath s by the excellency of H7650
Mic 7:20 s unto our fathers from the days of old. H7650
Act 2:30 that God had s with an oath to him, G3660
Act 7:17 nigh, which God had s to Abraham, the G3660
Heb 4: 3 he said, As I have s in my wrath, if they G3660

SYCAMINE
Lk 17: 6 say unto this s tree, Be thou plucked G4807

SYCAMORE See SYCOMORE.

SYCHAR
Jn 4: 5 which is called S, near to the parcel of G4965

SYCHEM
Act 7:16 And were carried over into S, and laid G4966
16 of the sons of Emmor *the father* of S. G4966

SYCOMORE
1Ki 10:27 he *to be* as the s trees that *are* in the H8256
1Ch 27:28 And over the olive trees and the s trees H8256
2Ch 1:15 made he as the s trees that *are* in the H8256
9:27 made he as the s trees that *are* in the H8256
Ps 78:47 with hail, and their s trees with frost. H8256
Am 7:14 an herdman, and a gatherer of s fruit: H8256
Lk 19: 4 climbed up into a s tree to see him: for G4809

SYCOMORES
Isa 9:10 hewn stones: the s are cut down, but H8256

SYCOMORE-TREES See SYCOMORE and TREES.

SYENE
Ezk 29:10 of S even unto the border of Ethiopia. H5482
30: 6 from the tower of S shall they fall in it H5482

SYNAGOGUE
Mt 12: 9 departed thence, he went into their s: G4864
13:54 them in their s, insomuch that they G4864
Mk 1:21 day he entered into the s, and taught. G4864
23 And there was in their s a man with an G4864
29 come out of the s, they entered into the G4864
3: 1 And he entered again into the s; and G4864
5:22 of the rulers of the s, Jairus by name; and G752
36 ruler of the s, Be not afraid, only believe. G752
38 of the ruler of the s, and seeth the tumult, G752
6: 2 to teach in the s: and many hearing *him* G4864
Lk 4:16 he went into the s on the sabbath day, G4864
20 were in the s were fastened on him. G4864
28 And all they in the s, when they heard G4864
33 And in the s there was a man, which G4864
38 And he arose out of the s, and entered G4864
6: 6 he entered into the s and taught: and G4864
7: 5 our nation, and he hath built us a s. G4864
8:41 was a ruler of the s: and he fell down at G4864
13:14 And the ruler of the s answered with G752
Jn 6:59 These things said he in the s, as he G4864
9:22 was Christ, he should be put out of the s. G656
12:42 *him*, lest they should be put out of the s: G656
18:20 I ever taught in the s, and in the temple, G4864
Act 6: 9 Then there arose certain of the s, which G4864
9 which is called *the* s of the Libertines, G4864
13:14 s on the sabbath day, and sat down. G4864
15 the rulers of the s sent unto them, G752
42 gone out of the s, the Gentiles besought G4864
14: 1 together into the s of the Jews, and so G4864
17: 1 where was a s of the Jews: G4864
10 *thither* went into the s of the Jews. G4864
17 Therefore disputed he in the s with the G4864
18: 4 And he reasoned in the s every G4864
7 God, whose house joined hard to the s. G4864
8 And Crispus, the chief ruler of the s, G752
17 chief ruler of the s, and beat *him* before G752
19 into the s, and reasoned with the Jews. G4864
26 And he began to speak boldly in the s: G4864
19: 8 And he went into the s, and spake G4864
22:19 in every s them that believed on thee: G2596
26:11 And I punished them oft in every s, and G4864
Rev 2: 9 and are not, but *are* the s of Satan. G4864
3: 9 Behold, I will make them of the s of G4864

SYNAGOGUES
Ps 74: 8 burned up all the s of God in the land. H4150
Mt 4:23 teaching in their s, and preaching the G4864
6: 2 do in the s and in the streets, that G4864
5 standing in the s and in the corners of G4864
9:35 teaching in their s, and preaching the G4864
10:17 and they will scourge you in their s; G4864
23: 6 at feasts, and the chief seats in the s, G4864
34 s, and persecute *them* from city to city: G4864
Mk 1:39 And he preached in their s throughout G4864
12:39 And the chief seats in the s, and the G4864

Mk 13: 9 and in the **s** ye shall be beaten: and G4864
Lk 4:15 And he taught in their **s**, being glorified G4864
44 And he preached in the **s** of Galilee. G4864
11:43 in the **s**, and greetings in the markets. G4864
12:11 And when they bring you unto the **s**, G4864
13:10 And he was teaching in one of the **s** on G4864
20:46 in the **s**, and the chief rooms at feasts; G4864
21:12 *you* up to the **s**, and into prisons, being G4864
Jn 16: 2 They shall put you out of the **s**: yea, the G656
Act 9: 2 Damascus to the **s**, that if he found any G4864
20 Christ in the **s**, that he is the Son of God. G4864
13: 5 word of God in the **s** of the Jews: and G4864
15:21 being read in the **s** every sabbath day. G4864
24:12 people, neither in the **s**, nor in the city: G4864

SYNAGOGUE'S
Mk 5:35 the ruler of the **s** *house certain* which G752
Lk 8:49 the ruler of the **s** *house*, saying to him, G752

SYNTYCHE
Php 4: 2 I beseech Euodias, and beseech **S**, that G4941

SYRACUSE
Act 28:12 And landing at **S**, we tarried *there* three G4946

SYRIA
Jdg 10: 6 and the gods of **S**, and the gods of Zidon, H758
2Sa 8: 6 Then David put garrisons in **S** of H758
12 Of **S**, and of Moab, and of the children of H758
15: 8 abode at Geshur in **S**, saying, If the LORD H758
1Ki 10:29 for the kings of **S**, did they bring *them* H758
11:25 he abhorred Israel, and reigned over **S**. H758
15:18 of **S**, that dwelt at Damascus, saying, H758
19:15 comest, anoint Hazael *to be* king over **S**: H758
20: 1 And Ben-hadad the king of **S** gathered H758
20 the king of **S** escaped on an horse H758
22 the king of **S** will come up against thee. H758
23 And the servants of the king of **S** said H758
22: 1 years without war between **S** and Israel. H758
3 it not out of the hand of the king of **S**? H758
31 But the king of **S** commanded his thirty H758
2Ki 5: 1 the host of the king of **S**, was a great man H758
1 deliverance unto **S**: he was also a mighty H758
5 And the king of **S** said, Go to, go, and I H758
6: 8 Then the king of **S** warred against Israel, H758
11 Therefore the heart of the king of **S** was H758
23 **S** came no more into the land of Israel. H758
24 that Ben-hadad king of **S** gathered all his H758
7: 5 of **S**, behold, *there was* no man there. H758
8: 7 the king of **S** was sick; and it was H758
9 son Ben-hadad king of **S** hath sent me to H758
13 shewed me that thou *shalt be* king over **S**. H758
28 Hazael king of **S** in Ramoth-gilead; and H758
29 Hazael king of **S**. And Ahaziah the son H758
9:14 all Israel, because of Hazael king of **S**. H758
15 Hazael king of **S**.) And Jehu said, If it be H758
12:17 Then Hazael king of **S** went up, and H758
18 of **S**: and he went away from Jerusalem. H758
13: 3 of Hazael king of **S**, and into the hand of H758
4 because the king of **S** oppressed them. H758
7 for the king of **S** had destroyed them, H758
17 deliverance from **S**: for thou shalt smite H758
19 then hadst thou smitten **S** till thou hadst H758
19 now thou shalt smite **S** *but* thrice. H758
22 But Hazael king of **S** oppressed Israel all H758
2Ki 13:24 So Hazael king of **S** died; and Ben-hadad H758
15:37 of **S**, and Pekah the son of Remaliah. H758
16: 5 Then Rezin king of **S** and Pekah son of H758
6 At that time Rezin king of **S** recovered H758
6 recovered Elath to **S**, and drave the Jews H758
7 hand of the king of **S**, and out of the hand H758
2Ch 1:17 and for the kings of **S**, by their means. H758
16: 2 of **S**, that dwelt at Damascus, saying, H758
7 on the king of **S**, and not relied on the H758
7 the king of **S** escaped out of thine hand. H758
18:10 shalt push **S** until they be consumed. H758
30 Now the king of **S** had commanded the H758
20: 2 the sea on this side **S**; and, behold, they H758
22: 5 Hazael king of **S** at Ramoth-gilead: and H758
6 Hazael king of **S**. And Azariah the son H758
24:23 *that* the host of **S** came up against him: H758
28: 5 the hand of the king of **S**; and they smote H758
23 of the kings of **S** help them, *therefore* H758
Isa 7: 1 Rezin the king of **S**, and Pekah the son of H758
2 of David, saying, **S** is confederate with H758
4 Rezin with **S**, and of the son of Remaliah. H758
5 Because **S**, Ephraim, and the son of H758
8 For the head of **S** *is* Damascus, and the H758
17: 3 and the remnant of **S**: they shall be as the H758
Ezk 16:57 of the daughters of **S**, and all *that are* H758
27:16 **S** *was* thy merchant by reason of the H758
Hos 12:12 And Jacob fled into the country of **S**, and H758
Am 1: 5 Eden: and the people of **S** shall go into H758
Mt 4:24 And his fame went throughout all **S**: G4947
Lk 2: 2 made when Cyrenius was governor of **S**.) G4947
Act 15:23 Gentiles in Antioch and **S** and Cilicia: G4947
41 And he went through **S** and Cilicia, G4947
18:18 and sailed thence into **S**, and with him G4947
20: 3 was about to sail into **S**, he purposed to G4947
21: 3 and sailed into **S**, and landed at Tyre: G4947
Gal 1:21 Afterwards I came into the regions of **S** G4947

SYRIACK
Dan 2: 4 to the king in **S**, O king, live for ever: H762

SYRIA-DAMASCUS
1Ch 18: 6 Then David put *garrisons* in **S**; H758+H1834

SYRIA-MAACHAH
1Ch 19: 6 and out of **S**, and out of Zobah. H758+H4601

SYRIAN
Gen 25:20 of Bethuel the **S** of Padan-aram, the H761
20 of Padan-aram, the sister to Laban the **S**. H761
28: 5 son of Bethuel the **S**, the brother of H761
31:20 the **S**, in that he told him not that he fled. H761
24 And God came to Laban the **S** in a H761
Dt 26: 5 LORD thy God, A **S** ready to perish *was* H761
2Ki 5:20 Naaman this **S**, in not receiving at his H761
18:26 to thy servants in the **S** language; for we H762
Ezr 4: 7 letter *was* written in the **S** tongue, and H762
7 tongue, and interpreted in the **S** tongue. H762
Isa 36:11 thy servants in the **S** language; for we H762
Lk 4:27 was cleansed, saving Naaman the **S**. G4948

SYRIANS
2Sa 8: 5 And when the **S** of Damascus came to H758
5 of the **S** two and twenty thousand men. H758
6 Damascus: and the **S** became servants to H758
13 from smiting of the **S** in the valley of H758
2Sa 10: 6 sent and hired the **S** of Beth-rehob, and H758
6 and the **S** of Zoba, twenty thousand H758
8 in of the gate: and the **S** of Zoba, and of H758
9 and put *them* in array against the **S**: H758
11 And he said, If the **S** be too strong for H758
13 against the **S**: and they fled before him. H758
14 saw that the **S** were fled, then fled they H758
15 And when the **S** saw that they were H758
16 brought out the **S** that *were* beyond the H758
17 to Helam. And the **S** set themselves in H758
18 And the **S** fled before Israel; and David H758
18 chariots of the **S**, and forty thousand H758
19 served them. So the **S** feared to help the H758
1Ki 20:20 one his man: and the **S** fled; and Israel H758
21 and slew the **S** with a great slaughter. H758
26 numbered the **S**, and went up to Aphek, H758
27 of kids; but the **S** filled the country. H758
28 the LORD, Because the **S** have said, The H758
29 of Israel slew of the **S** an hundred H758
22:11 the **S**, until thou have consumed them. H758
35 chariot against the **S**, and died at even: H758
2Ki 5: 2 And the **S** had gone out by companies, H758
6: 9 a place; for thither the **S** are come down. H758
7: 4 the host of the **S**: if they save us alive, H758
5 the camp of the **S**: and when they were H758
6 For the Lord had made the host of the **S** H758
10 to the camp of the **S**, and, behold, *there* H758
12 shew you what the **S** have done to us. H758
14 after the host of the **S**, saying, Go and see. H758
15 vessels, which the **S** had cast away in H758
16 the tents of the **S**. So a measure of fine H758
8:28 and the **S** wounded Joram. H761
29 wounds which the **S** had given him at H761
9:15 the wounds which the **S** had given him, H761
13: 5 the hand of the **S**: and the children of H758
17 shalt smite the **S** in Aphek, till thou have H758
16: 6 from Elath: and the **S** came to Elath, and H758
24: 2 and bands of the **S**, and bands of the H758
1Ch 18: 5 And when the **S** of Damascus came to H758
5 of the **S** two and twenty thousand men. H758
6 and the **S** became David's servants, H758
19:10 and put *them* in array against the **S**. H758
12 And he said, If the **S** be too strong for H758
14 nigh before the **S** unto the battle; and H758
15 saw that the **S** were fled, they likewise H758
16 And when the **S** saw that they were put H758
16 and drew forth the **S** that *were* beyond H758
17 array against the **S**, they fought with him. H758
18 But the **S** fled before Israel; and David H758
18 David slew of the **S** seven thousand *men* H758
19 **S** help the children of Ammon any more. H758
2Ch 18:34 chariot against the **S** until the even: and H758
22: 5 Ramoth-gilead: and the **S** smote Joram. H761
24:24 For the army of the **S** came with a small H758
Isa 9:12 The **S** before, and the Philistines behind; H758
Jer 35:11 army of the **S**: so we dwell at Jerusalem. H758
Am 9: 7 from Caphtor, and the **S** from Kir? H758

SYROPHENICIAN
Mk 7:26 The woman was a Greek, a **S** by nation; G4949

T

TAANACH
Jos 12:21 The king of **T**, one; the king of Megiddo, H8590
17:11 the inhabitants of **T** and her towns, H8590
Jdg 1:27 her towns, nor **T** and her towns, nor H8590
5:19 kings of Canaan in **T** by the waters of H8590
1Ki 4:12 *to him pertained* **T** and Megiddo, and H8590
1Ch 7:29 and her towns, **T** and her towns, H8590

TAANATH-SHILOH
Jos 16: 6 eastward unto **T**, and passed by it on H8387

TABBAOTH
Ezr 2:43 children of Hasupha, the children of **T**, H2884
Neh 7:46 children of Hashupha, the children of **T**, H2884

TABBATH
Jdg 7:22 to the border of Abel-meholah, unto **T**. H2888

TABEAL
Isa 7: 6 in the midst of it, *even* the son of **T**: H2870

TABEEL
Ezr 4: 7 Mithredath, **T**, and the rest of their H2870

TABERAH
Nu 11: 3 And he called the name of the place **T**: H8404
Dt 9:22 And at **T**, and at Massah, and at H8404

TABERING
Nah 2: 7 the voice of doves, **t** upon their breasts. H8608

TABERNACLE
Ex 25: 9 the pattern of the **t**, and the pattern of H4908
26: 1 Moreover thou shalt make the **t** *with* H4908
6 with the taches: and it shall be one **t**. H4908
7 the **t**: eleven curtains shalt thou make. H4908
9 the sixth curtain in the forefront of the **t**. H168
12 shall hang over the backside of the **t**. H4908
13 the sides of the **t** on this side and on H4908
15 And thou shalt make boards for the **t** *of* H4908
17 thou make for all the boards of the **t**. H4908
18 the boards for the **t**, twenty boards on H4908
20 And for the second side of the **t** on the H4908
22 And for the sides of the **t** westward H4908
23 for the corners of the **t** in the two sides. H4908
26 for the boards of the one side of the **t**, H4908
27 other side of the **t**, and five bars for the H4908
27 side of the **t**, for the two sides westward. H4908

Ex 26:30 And thou shalt rear up the t according H4908
35 on the side of the t toward the south: H4908
27: 9 And thou shalt make the court of the t: H4908
19 All the vessels of the t in all the service H4908
21 In the t of the congregation without the H168
28:43 come in unto the t of the congregation, H168
29: 4 the door of the t of the congregation, H168
10 brought before the t of the congregation: H168
11 *by* the door of the t of the congregation. H168
30 he cometh into the t of the congregation H168
32 *by* the door of the t of the congregation. H168
42 *at* the door of the t of the congregation H168
43 and *the t* shall be sanctified by my glory.
44 And I will sanctify the t of the H168
30:16 the service of the t of the congregation; H168
18 put it between the t of the congregation H168
20 When they go into the t of the H168
26 And thou shalt anoint the t of the H168
36 testimony in the t of the congregation, H168
31: 7 The t of the congregation, and the ark of H168
7 thereupon, and all the furniture of the t, H168
33: 7 And Moses took the t, and pitched it H168
7 and called it the T of the congregation. H168
7 went out unto the t of the congregation, H168
8 went out unto the t, *that* all the people H168
8 after Moses, until he was gone into the t. H168
9 entered into the t, the cloudy pillar H168
9 the t, and *the LORD* talked with Moses. H168
10 pillar stand *at* the t door: and all the H168
11 a young man, departed not out of the t. H168
35:11 The t, his tent, and his covering, his H4908
15 for the door at the entering in of the t, H4908
18 The pins of the t, and the pins of the H4908
21 to the work of the t of the congregation, H168
36: 8 the work of the t made ten curtains *of* H4908
13 with the taches: so it became one t. H4908
14 the t: eleven curtains he made them. H4908
20 And he made boards for the t *of* H4908
22 did he make for all the boards of the t. H4908
23 And he made boards for the t; twenty H4908
25 And for the other side of the t, *which is* H4908
27 And for the sides of the t westward he H4908
28 for the corners of the t in the two sides. H4908
31 for the boards of the one side of the t, H4908
32 other side of the t, and five bars for the H4908
32 boards of the t for the sides westward. H4908
37 And he made an hanging for the t door H168
38: 8 *at* the door of the t of the congregation. H168
20 And all the pins of the t, and of the H4908
21 This is the sum of the t, *even* of the H4908
21 *even* of the t of testimony, as it was H4908
30 to the door of the t of the congregation, H168
31 all the pins of the t, and all the pins of H4908
39:32 Thus was all the work of the t of the H4908
33 And they brought the t unto Moses, the H4908
38 incense, and the hanging for the t door, H168
40 of the t, for the tent of the congregation, H4908
40: 2 up the t of the tent of the congregation. H4908
5 and put the hanging of the door to the t. H4908
6 of the t of the tent of the congregation. H4908
9 oil, and anoint the t, and all that *is* H4908
12 the door of the t of the congregation, H168
17 of the month, *that* the t was reared up. H4908
18 And Moses reared up the t, and H4908
19 the tent over the t, and put the covering H4908
21 And he brought the ark into the t, and H4908
22 of the t northward, without the vail. H4908
24 table, on the side of the t southward. H4908
28 set up the hanging *at* the door of the t. H4908
29 *by* the door of the t of the tent of the H4908
33 round about the t and the altar, and set H4908
34 and the glory of the LORD filled the t. H4908
35 and the glory of the LORD filled the t. H4908
36 up from over the t, the children of Israel H4908
38 *was* upon the t by day, and fire was H4908
Lev 1: 1 out of the t of the congregation, saying, H168
3 t of the congregation before the LORD. H168
5 *by* the door of the t of the congregation. H168
3: 2 kill it *at* the door of the t of the H168
8 kill it before the t of the congregation: H168
13 kill it before the t of the congregation: H168
4: 4 the door of the t of the congregation H168
5 and bring it to the t of the congregation: H168
7 which *is* in the t of the congregation; H168
7 *at* the door of the t of the congregation. H168
14 him before the t of the congregation. H168
16 blood to the t of the congregation: H168
18 that *is* in the t of the congregation, H168
18 *at* the door of the t of the congregation. H168
Lev 6:16 the t of the congregation they shall eat it. H168
26 in the court of the t of the congregation. H168
30 is brought into the t of the congregation H168
8: 3 the door of the t of the congregation. H168
4 the door of the t of the congregation. H168
10 oil, and anointed the t and all that *was* H4908
31 *at* the door of the t of the congregation: H168
33 of the door of the t of the congregation *in* H168
35 *at* the door of the t of the congregation H168
9: 5 before the t of the congregation: H168
23 And Moses and Aaron went into the t of H168
10: 7 the door of the t of the congregation, H168
9 thee, when ye go into the t of the H168
12: 6 the t of the congregation, unto the priest: H168
14:11 *at* the door of the t of the congregation: H168
23 t of the congregation, before the LORD. H168
15:14 the door of the t of the congregation, H168
29 to the door of the t of the congregation. H168
31 they defile my t that *is* among them. H4908
16: 7 *at* the door of the t of the congregation. H168
16 shall he do for the t of the congregation, H168
17 And there shall be no man in the t of the H168
20 holy *place*, and the t of the congregation, H168
23 And Aaron shall come into the t of the H168
33 atonement for the t of the congregation, H168
17: 4 And bringeth it not unto the door of the t H168
4 LORD before the t of the LORD; blood H4908
5 the door of the t of the congregation, H168
6 *at* the door of the t of the congregation, H168
9 And bringeth it not unto the door of the t H168
19:21 the door of the t of the congregation, H168
24: 3 testimony, in the t of the congregation, H168
26:11 And I will set my t among you: and my H4908
Nu 1: 1 of Sinai, in the t of the congregation, H168
50 the Levites over the t of testimony, and H4908
50 they shall bear the t, and all the vessels H4908
50 it, and shall encamp round about the t. H4908
51 And when the t setteth forward, the H4908
51 and when the t is to be pitched, the H4908
53 round about the t of testimony, that H4908
53 keep the charge of the t of testimony. H4908
2: 2 the t of the congregation shall they pitch. H168
17 Then the t of the congregation shall set H168
3: 7 before the t of the congregation, H168
7 congregation, to do the service of the t. H4908
8 instruments of the t of the congregation, H168
8 of Israel, to do the service of the t. H4908
23 shall pitch behind the t westward. H4908
25 of Gershon in the t of the congregation H168
25 *shall be* the t, and the tent, the covering H4908
25 for the door of the t of the congregation, H168
26 which *is* by the t, and by the altar round H4908
29 pitch on the side of the t southward. H4908
35 pitch on the side of the t northward. H4908
36 *be* the boards of the t, and the bars H4908
38 But those that encamp before the t H4908
38 *even* before the t of the congregation H168
4: 3 do the work in the t of the congregation. H168
4 of Kohath in the t of the congregation, H168
15 of Kohath in the t of the congregation. H168
16 the oversight of all the t, and of all that H4908
23 do the work in the t of the congregation. H168
25 And they shall bear the curtains of the t, H4908
25 the tabernacle, and the t of the H168
25 for the door of the t of the congregation, H168
26 which *is* by the t and by the altar round H4908
28 of Gershon in the t of the congregation: H168
30 do the work of the t of the congregation. H168
31 their service in the t of the congregation; H168
31 the boards of the t, and the bars H4908
33 all their service, in the t of the H168
35 for the work in the t of the congregation: H168
37 do service in the t of the congregation, H168
39 for the work in the t of the congregation, H168
41 do service in the t of the congregation, H168
43 for the work in the t of the congregation, H168
47 the burden in the t of the congregation, H168
5:17 in the floor of the t the priest shall take, H4908
6:10 to the door of the t of the congregation: H168
13 the door of the t of the congregation: H168
18 *at* the door of the t of the congregation, H168
7: 1 fully set up the t, and had anointed it, H4908
3 ox: and they brought them before the t. H4908
5 the service of the t of the congregation; H168
89 And when Moses was gone into the t of H168
8: 9 Levites before the t of the congregation: H168
15 the service of the t of the congregation: H168
19 of Israel in the t of the congregation, H168
22 their service in the t of the congregation H168
Nu 8:24 the service of the t of the congregation: H168
26 brethren in the t of the congregation, H168
9:15 And on the day that the t was reared H4908
15 cloud covered the t, *namely*, the tent of H4908
15 there was upon the t as it were the H4908
17 taken up from the t, then after that the H168
18 upon the t they rested in their tents. H4908
19 long upon the t many days, then the H4908
20 a few days upon the t; according to the H4908
22 tarried upon the t, remaining thereon, H4908
10: 3 at the door of the t of the congregation. H168
11 up from off the t of the testimony. H4908
17 And the t was taken down; and the H4908
17 of Merari set forward, bearing the t. H4908
21 did set up the t against they came. H4908
11:16 them unto the t of the congregation, H168
24 people, and set them round about the t. H168
26 the t: and they prophesied in the camp. H168
12: 4 ye three unto the t of the congregation. H168
5 *in* the door of the t, and called Aaron and H168
10 And the cloud departed from off the t; H168
14:10 appeared in the t of the congregation H168
16: 9 the service of the t of the LORD, and to H4908
18 in the door of the t of the congregation H168
19 the door of the t of the congregation: H168
24 the t of Korah, Dathan, and Abiram. H4908
27 So they gat up from the t of Korah, H4908
42 looked toward the t of the congregation: H168
43 And Moses and Aaron came before the t H168
50 the door of the t of the congregation: H168
17: 4 And thou shalt lay them up in the t of H168
7 rods before the LORD in the t of witness. H168
8 went into the t of witness; and, behold, H168
13 near unto the t of the LORD shall die: H4908
18: 2 *shall minister* before the t of witness. H168
3 the charge of all the t: only they shall not H168
4 the charge of the t of the congregation, H168
4 the service of the t: and a stranger shall H168
6 the service of the t of the congregation. H168
21 the service of the t of the congregation. H168
22 come nigh the t of the congregation, H168
23 the service of the t of the congregation, H168
31 your service in the t of the congregation. H168
19: 4 the t of the congregation seven times: H168
13 defileth the t of the LORD; and that H4908
20: 6 the door of the t of the congregation, H168
25: 6 the door of the t of the congregation. H168
27: 2 door of the t of the congregation, saying, H168
31:30 keep the charge of the t of the LORD. H4908
47 the charge of the t of the LORD; as the H4908
54 brought it into the t of the congregation, H168
Dt 31:14 yourselves in the t of the congregation, H168
14 themselves in the t of the congregation. H168
15 And the LORD appeared in the t in a H168
15 of the cloud stood over the door of the t. H168
Jos 18: 1 and set up the t of the congregation H168
19:51 at the door of the t of the congregation. H168
22:19 the LORD'S t dwelleth, and take H4908
29 of the LORD our God that *is* before his t. H4908
1Sa 2:22 *at* the door of the t of the congregation. H168
2Sa 6:17 in the midst of the t that David had H168
7: 6 but have walked in a tent and in a t. H4908
1Ki 1:39 of oil out of the t, and anointed Solomon. H168
2:28 Joab fled unto the t of the LORD, and H168
29 was fled unto the t of the LORD; and, H168
30 And Benaiah came to the t of the LORD, H168
8: 4 the LORD, and the t of the congregation, H168
4 that *were* in the t, even those did the H168
1Ch 6:32 place of the t of the congregation with H168
48 of service of the t of the house of God. H4908
9:19 of the gates of the t: and their fathers, H168
21 of the door of the t of the congregation. H168
23 *namely*, the house of the t, by wards. H168
16:39 priests, before the t of the LORD in the H4908
17: 5 tent to tent, and from *one* t *to another*. H4908
21:29 For the t of the LORD, which Moses H4908
23:26 no *more* carry the t, nor any vessels of it H4908
32 the charge of the t of the congregation, H168
2Ch 1: 3 for there was the t of the congregation of H168
5 he put before the t of the LORD: and H4908
6 which *was* at the t of the congregation, H168
13 from before the t of the congregation, H168
5: 5 And they brought up the ark, and the t H168
5 that *were* in the t, these did the priests H168
24: 6 of Israel, for the t of witness? H168
Job 5:24 And thou shalt know that thy t *shall be* H168
18: 6 The light shall be dark in his t, and his H168
14 be rooted out of his t, and it shall bring H168
15 It shall dwell in his t, because *it is* none of H168

Job 19:12 me, and encamp round about my **t**. H168
20:26 it shall go ill with him that is left in his **t**. H168
29: 4 when the secret of God *was* upon my **t**; H168
31:31 If the men of my **t** said not, Oh that we H168
36:29 of the clouds, *or* the noise of his **t**? H5521
Ps 15: 1 LORD, who shall abide in thy **t**? who shall H168
19: 4 In them hath he set a **t** for the sun, H168
27: 5 in the secret of his **t** shall he hide me; he H168
6 will I offer in his **t** sacrifices of joy; I will H168
61: 4 I will abide in thy **t** for ever: I will trust in H168
76: 2 In Salem also is his **t**, and his dwelling H5520
78:60 So that he forsook the **t** of Shiloh, the H4908
67 Moreover he refused the **t** of Joseph, and H168
132: 3 Surely I will not come into the **t** of my H168
Prv 14:11 but the **t** of the upright shall flourish. H168
Isa 4: 6 And there shall be a **t** for a shadow in H5521
16: 5 it in truth in the **t** of David, judging, and H168
33:20 a quiet habitation, a **t** *that* shall not be H168
Jer 10:20 My **t** is spoiled, and all my cords are H168
Lam 2: 4 to the eye in the **t** of the daughter of H168
6 And he hath violently taken away his **t**, H7900
Ezk 37:27 My **t** also shall be with them: yea, I will H4908
41: 1 side, *which was* the breadth of the **t**. H168
Am 5:26 But ye have borne the **t** of your Moloch H5522
9:11 In that day will I raise up the **t** of David H5521
Act 7:43 Yea, ye took up the **t** of Moloch, and *G4633*
44 Our fathers had the **t** of witness in the *G4633*
46 desired to find a **t** for the God of Jacob. *G4638*
15:16 will build again the **t** of David, which is *G4633*
2Co 5: 1 house of *this* **t** were dissolved, we have *G4636*
4 For we that are in *this* **t** do groan, being *G4636*
Heb 8: 2 **t**, which the Lord pitched, and not man. *G4633*
5 about to make the **t**: for, See, saith he, *G4633*
9: 2 For there was a **t** made; the first, *G4633*
3 And after the second veil, the **t** which is *G4633*
6 **t**, accomplishing the service *of God*. *G4633*
8 while as the first **t** was yet standing: *G4633*
11 and more perfect **t**, not made with *G4633*
21 the **t**, and all the vessels of the ministry. *G4633*
13:10 have no right to eat which serve the **t**. *G4633*
2Pt 1:13 long as I am in this **t**, to stir you up by *G4638*
14 put off *this* my **t**, even as our Lord Jesus *G4638*
Rev 13: 6 his **t**, and them that dwell in heaven. *G4633*
15: 5 the temple of the **t** of the testimony in *G4633*
21: 3 Behold, the **t** of God *is* with men, *G4633*

TABERNACLES

Lev 23:34 of **t** *for* seven days unto the LORD. H5521
Nu 24: 5 thy tents, O Jacob, *and* thy **t**, O Israel! H4908
Dt 16:13 Thou shalt observe the feast of **t** seven H5521
16 and in the feast of **t**: and they shall not H5521
31:10 of the year of release, in the feast of **t**, H5521
2Ch 8:13 the feast of weeks, and in the feast of **t**. H5521
Ezr 3: 4 They kept also the feast of **t**, as *it is* H5521
Job 11:14 and let not wickedness dwell in thy **t**. H168
12: 6 The **t** of robbers prosper, and they that H168
15:34 and fire shall consume the **t** of bribery. H168
22:23 shalt put away iniquity far from thy **t**. H168
Ps 43: 3 bring me unto thy holy hill, and to thy **t**. H4908
46: 4 the holy *place* of the **t** of the most High. H4908
78:51 chief of *their* strength in the **t** of Ham: H168
83: 6 The **t** of Edom, and the Ishmaelites; of H168
84: 1 How amiable *are* thy **t**, O LORD of H4908
118:15 salvation *is* in the **t** of the righteous: the H168
132: 7 We will go into his **t**: we will worship at H4908
Dan 11:45 And he shall plant the **t** of his palace H168
Hos 9: 6 possess them: thorns *shall be* in their **t**. H168
12: 9 in **t**, as in the days of the solemn feast. H168
Zec 14:16 of hosts, and to keep the feast of **t**. H5521
18 that come not up to keep the feast of **t**. H5521
19 that come not up to keep the feast of **t**. H5521
Mal 2:12 scholar, out of the **t** of Jacob, and him H168
Mt 17: 4 make here three **t**; one for thee, and one *G4633*
Mk 9: 5 let us make three **t**; one for thee, and *G4633*
Lk 9:33 let us make three **t**; one for thee, and *G4633*
Jn 7: 2 Now the Jews' feast of **t** was at hand. *G4634*
Heb 11: 9 dwelling in **t** with Isaac and Jacob, *G4633*

TABITHA

Act 9:36 certain disciple named **T**, which by *G5000*
40 *him* to the body said, **T**, arise. And she *G5000*

TABLE

Ex 25:23 Thou shalt also make a **t** *of* shittim H7979
27 be for places of the staves to bear the **t**. H7979
28 that the **t** may be borne with them. H7979
30 And thou shalt set upon the **t** H7979
26:35 And thou shalt set the **t** without the H7979
35 over against the **t** on the side of the H7979
Ex 26:35 thou shalt put the **t** on the north side. H7979
30:27 And the **t** and all his vessels, and the H7979
31: 8 And the **t** and his furniture, and the H7979
35:13 The **t**, and his staves, and all his vessels, H7979
37:10 And he made the **t** *of* shittim wood: two H7979
14 the places for the staves to bear the **t**. H7979
15 overlaid them with gold, to bear the **t**. H7979
16 *were* upon the **t**, his dishes, and his H7979
39:36 The **t**, *and* all the vessels thereof, and H7979
40: 4 And thou shalt bring in the **t**, and set in H7979
22 And he put the **t** in the tent of the H7979
24 over against the **t**, on the side of the H7979
Lev 24: 6 row, upon the pure **t** before the LORD. H7979
Nu 3:31 *shall be* the ark, and the **t**, and the H7979
4: 7 And upon the **t** of shewbread they shall H7979
Jdg 1: 7 *meat* under my **t**: as I have done, so H7979
1Sa 20:29 he cometh not unto the king's **t**. H7979
34 So Jonathan arose from the **t** in fierce H7979
2Sa 9: 7 shalt eat bread at my **t** continually. H7979
10 eat bread alway at my **t**. Now Ziba had H7979
11 eat at my **t**, as one of the king's sons. H7979
13 king's **t**; and was lame on both his feet. H7979
19:28 eat at thine own **t**. What right therefore H7979
1Ki 2: 7 that eat at thy **t**: for so they came to H7979
4:27 unto king Solomon's **t**, every man in his H7979
7:48 of gold, and the **t** of gold, whereupon H7979
10: 5 And the meat of his **t**, and the sitting of H7979
13:20 And it came to pass, as they sat at the **t**, H7979
18:19 four hundred, which eat at Jezebel's **t**. H7979
2Ki 4:10 there a bed, and a **t**, and a stool, and a H7979
1Ch 28:16 for every **t**; and *likewise* silver for H7979
2Ch 9: 4 And the meat of his **t**, and the sitting of H7979
13:11 upon the pure **t**; and the candlestick H7979
29:18 **t**, with all the vessels thereof. H7979
Neh 5:17 Moreover *there were* at my **t** an H7979
Job 36:16 be set on thy **t** *should be* full of fatness. H7979
Ps 23: 5 Thou preparest a **t** before me in the H7979
69:22 Let their **t** become a snare before them: H7979
78:19 Can God furnish a **t** in the wilderness? H7979
128: 3 like olive plants round about thy **t**. H7979
Prv 3: 3 write them upon the **t** of thine heart: H3871
7: 3 write them upon the **t** of thine heart. H3871
9: 2 her wine; she hath also furnished her **t**. H7979
Song 1:12 While the king *sitteth* at his **t**, my H4524
Isa 21: 5 Prepare the **t**, watch in the watchtower, H7979
30: 8 Now go, write it before them in a **t**, and H3871
65:11 that prepare a **t** for that troop, and that H7979
Jer 17: 1 *is* graven upon the **t** of their heart, and H3871
Ezk 23:41 And satest upon a stately bed, and a **t** H7979
39:20 Thus ye shall be filled at my **t** with H7979
41:22 This *is* the **t** that *is* before the LORD. H7979
44:16 come near to my **t**, to minister unto me, H7979
Dan 11:27 shall speak lies at one **t**; but it shall not H7979
Mal 1: 7 say, The **t** of the LORD *is* contemptible. H7979
12 it, in that ye say, The **t** of the LORD *is* H7979
Mt 15:27 crumbs which fall from their masters' **t**. *G5132*
Mk 7:28 the **t** eat of the children's crumbs. *G5132*
Lk 1:63 And he asked for a writing **t**, and wrote, *G4093*
16:21 the rich man's **t**: moreover the dogs *G5132*
22:21 that betrayeth me *is* with me on the **t**. *G5132*
30 That ye may eat and drink at my **t** in *G5132*
Jn 12: 2 one of them that sat at the **t** with him. *G4873*
13:28 Now no man at the **t** knew for what *G345*
Ro 11: 9 And David saith, Let their **t** be made a *G5132*
1Co 10:21 of the Lord's **t**, and of the table of devils. *G5132*
21 the Lord's table, and of the **t** of devils. *G5132*
Heb 9: 2 and the **t**, and the shewbread; *G5132*

TABLES

Ex 24:12 and I will give thee **t** of stone, and a H3871
31:18 mount Sinai, two **t** of testimony, tables H3871
18 of testimony, **t** of stone, written with H3871
32:15 and the two **t** of the testimony *were* H3871
15 in his hand: the **t** *were* written on both H3871
16 And the **t** *were* the work of God, and H3871
16 the writing of God, graven upon the **t**. H3871
19 and he cast the **t** out of his hands, and H3871
34: 1 Hew thee two **t** of stone like unto the H3871
1 write upon *these* **t** the words that were H3871
1 were in the first **t**, which thou brakest. H3871
4 And he hewed two **t** of stone like unto H3871
4 and took in his hand the two **t** of stone. H3871
28 he wrote upon the **t** the words of the H3871
29 Sinai with the two **t** of testimony in H3871
Dt 4:13 and he wrote them upon two **t** of stone. H3871
5:22 **t** of stone, and delivered them unto me. H3871
9: 9 to receive the **t** of stone, *even* the tables H3871
9 of stone, *even* the **t** of the covenant H3871
10 And the LORD delivered unto me two **t** H3871
Dt 9:11 gave me the two **t** of stone, *even* the H3871
11 of stone, *even* the **t** of the covenant. H3871
15 fire: and the two **t** of the covenant *were* H3871
17 And I took the two **t**, and cast them out H3871
10: 1 me, Hew thee two **t** of stone like unto H3871
2 And I will write on the **t** the words that H3871
2 were in the first **t** which thou brakest, H3871
3 and hewed two **t** of stone like unto the H3871
3 mount, having the two **t** in mine hand. H3871
4 And he wrote on the **t**, according to the H3871
5 and put the **t** in the ark which I had H3871
1Ki 8: 9 the ark save the two **t** of stone, which H3871
1Ch 28:16 And by weight *he gave* gold for the **t** of H7979
16 and *likewise* silver for the **t** of silver: H7979
2Ch 4: 8 He made also ten **t**, and placed *them* in H7979
19 the **t** whereon the shewbread *was set*; H7979
5:10 the ark save the two **t** which Moses put H3871
Isa 28: 8 For all **t** are full of vomit *and* filthiness, H7979
Ezk 40:39 And in the porch of the gate *were* two **t** H7979
39 this side, and two **t** on that side, to slay H7979
40 gate, *were* two **t**; and on the other side, H7979
40 *was* at the porch of the gate, *were* two **t**. H7979
41 Four **t** *were* on this side, and four H7979
41 this side, and four **t** on that side, by the H7979
41 **t**, whereupon they slew *their sacrifices*. H7979
42 And the four **t** *were* of hewn stone for H7979
43 upon the **t** *was* the flesh of the offering. H7979
Hab 2: 2 upon **t**, that he may run that readeth it. H3871
Mt 21:12 temple, and overthrew the **t** of the *G5132*
Mk 7: 4 cups, and pots, brasen vessels, and of **t**. *G2825*
11:15 temple, and overthrew the **t** of the *G5132*
Jn 2:15 changers' money, and overthrew the **t**; *G5132*
Act 6: 2 leave the word of God, and serve **t**. *G5132*
2Co 3: 3 the living God; not in **t** of stone, but in *G4109*
3 of stone, but in fleshy **t** of the heart. *G4109*
Heb 9: 4 that budded, and the **t** of the covenant; *G4109*

TABLETS

Ex 35:22 and rings, and **t**, all jewels of gold: and H3558
Nu 31:50 earrings, and **t**, to make an atonement H3558
Isa 3:20 and the **t**, and the earrings, H1004+H5315

TABOR

Jos 19:22 And the coast reacheth to **T**, and H8396
Jdg 4: 6 toward mount **T**, and take with thee ten H8396
12 of Abinoam was gone up to mount **T**. H8396
14 **T**, and ten thousand men after him. H8396
8:18 whom ye slew at **T**? And they answered, H8396
1Sa 10: 3 to the plain of **T**, and there shall meet H8396
1Ch 6:77 with her suburbs, **T** with her suburbs: H8396
Ps 89:12 hast created them: **T** and Hermon shall H8396
Jer 46:18 of hosts, Surely as **T** *is* among the H8396
Hos 5: 1 on Mizpah, and a net spread upon **T**. H8396

TABRET

Gen 31:27 and with songs, with **t**, and with harp? H8596
1Sa 10: 5 a psaltery, and a **t**, and a pipe, and a H8596
Job 17: 6 the people; and aforetime I was as a **t**. H8611
Isa 5:12 And the harp, and the viol, the **t**, and H8596

TABRETS

1Sa 18: 6 king Saul, with **t**, with joy, and with H8596
Isa 24: 8 The mirth of **t** ceaseth, the noise of H8596
30:32 him, *it* shall be with **t** and harps: and in H8596
Jer 31: 4 adorned with thy **t**, and shalt go forth in H8596
Ezk 28:13 of thy **t** and of thy pipes was H8596

TABRIMON

1Ki 15:18 the son of **T**, the son of Hezion, king H2886

TACHES

Ex 26: 6 And thou shalt make fifty **t** of gold, and H7165
6 the **t**: and it shall be one tabernacle. H7165
11 And thou shalt make fifty **t** of brass, H7165
11 brass, and put the **t** into the loops, and H7165
33 the vail under the **t**, that thou mayest H7165
35:11 his covering, his **t**, and his boards, his H7165
36:13 And he made fifty **t** of gold, and H7165
13 with the **t**: so it became one tabernacle. H7165
18 And he made fifty **t** *of* brass to couple H7165
39:33 his furniture, his **t**, his boards, his bars, H7165

TACHMONITE

2Sa 23: 8 David had: The **T** that sat in the seat, H8461

TACKLING

Act 27:19 with our own hands the **t** of the ship. *G4631*

TACKLINGS
Isa 33:23 Thy t are loosed; they could not well

TADMOR
1Ki 9:18 And Baalath, and T in the H8412+H8559
2Ch 8: 4 And he built T in the wilderness, and H8412

TAHAN
Nu 26:35 of T, the family of the Tahanites. H8465
1Ch 7:25 and Telah his son, and T his son, H8465

TAHANITES
Nu 26:35 Bachrites: of Tahan, the family of the T. H8470

TAHAPANES
Jer 2:16 Also the children of Noph and T have H8471

TAHATH
Nu 33:26 from Makheloth, and encamped at T. H8480
27 And they departed from T, and pitched H8480
1Ch 6:24 T his son, Uriel his son, Uzziah his son, H8480
37 The son of T, the son of Assir, the son of H8480
7:20 and Bered his son, and T his son, and H8480
20 son, and Eladah his son, and T his son, H8480

TAHPANHES
Jer 43: 7 of the LORD: thus came they *even* to T. H8471
8 of the LORD unto Jeremiah in T, saying, H8471
9 in T, in the sight of the men of Judah; H8471
44: 1 at Migdol, and at T, and at Noph, and H8471
46:14 in Noph and in T: say ye, Stand fast, H8471

TAHPENES
1Ki 11:19 his own wife, the sister of T the queen. H8472
20 And the sister of T bare him Genubath H8472
20 his son, whom T weaned in Pharaoh's H8472

TAHREA
1Ch 9:41 Pithon, and Melech, and T, *and Ahaz.* H8475

TAHTIMHODSHI
2Sa 24: 6 and to the land of T; and they came to H8483

TAIL
Ex 4: 4 and take it by the t. And he put forth his H2180
Dt 28:13 head, and not the t; and thou shalt be H2180
44 be the head, and thou shalt be the t. H2180
Jdg 15: 4 and turned t to tail, and put a H2180
4 and turned tail to t, and put a firebrand H2180
Job 40:17 He moveth his t like a cedar: the sinews H2180
Isa 9:14 and t, branch and rush, in one day. H2180
15 prophet that teacheth lies, he *is* the t. H2180
19:15 the head or t, branch or rush, may do. H2180
Rev 12: 4 And his t drew the third part of the *G3769*

TAILS
Jdg 15: 4 a firebrand in the midst between two t. H2180
Isa 7: 4 for the two t of these smoking H2180
Rev 9:10 And they had t like unto scorpions, and *G3769*
10 stings in their t: and their power *was* *G3769*
19 and in their t: for their tails *were* like *G3769*
19 in their tails: for their t *were* like unto

TAKE
Gen 3:22 his hand, and t also of the tree of life, H3947
6:21 And t thou unto thee of all food that is H3947
7: 2 Of every clean beast thou shalt t to thee H3947
12:19 behold thy wife, t *her*, and go thy way. H3947
13: 9 me: if *thou wilt* t the left hand, then I
14:21 the persons, and t the goods to thyself. H3947
23 That I will not *t* from a thread even to a
23 and that I will not t any thing that *is* H3947
24 and Mamre; let them t their portion. H3947
15: 9 And he said unto him, T me an heifer H3947
19:15 Lot, saying, Arise, t thy wife, and thy H3947
19 lest some evil t me, and I die: H1692
21:30 lambs shalt thou t of my hand, that H3947
22: 2 And he said, T now thy son, thine only H3947
23:13 for the field; t *it* of me, and I will bury H3947
24: 3 that thou shalt not t a wife unto my son H3947
4 and t a wife unto my son Isaac. H3947
7 shalt t a wife unto my son from thence. H3947
37 Thou shalt not t a wife to my son of the H3947
38 my kindred, and t a wife unto my son. H3947
40 and thou shalt t a wife for my son of H3947
48 me in the right way to t my master's H3947
51 Behold, Rebekah *is* before thee, t *her*, H3947
27: 3 Now therefore t, I pray thee, thy H5375
3 out to the field, and t me *some* venison; H6679
Gen 27:46 of Heth: if Jacob t a wife of the H3947
28: 1 not t a wife of the daughters of Canaan. H3947
2 father; and t thee a wife from thence H3947
6 to Padan-aram, to t him a wife from H3947
6 not t a wife of the daughters of Canaan; H3947
30:15 and wouldest thou t away my son's H3947
31:24 and said unto him, T heed that thou
29 saying, T thou heed that thou
31 t by force thy daughters from me.
32 with me, and t *it* to thee. For Jacob H3947
50 or if thou shalt t *other* wives beside my H3947
33:11 T, I pray thee, my blessing that is H3947
12 And he said, Let us t our journey, and let
34: 9 unto us, and t our daughters unto you. H3947
16 you, and we will t your daughters to us, H3947
17 we t our daughter, and we will be gone. H3947
21 for them; let us t their daughters to us H3947
38:23 And Judah said, Let her t *it* to her, lest H3947
41:34 over the land, and t up the fifth part of
42:33 *here* with me, and t *food for* the famine H3947
36 *is* not, and ye will t Benjamin *away*: all H3947
43:11 *be* so now, do this; t of the best fruits in H3947
12 And t double money in your hand; and H3947
13 T also your brother, and arise, go H3947
18 and t us for bondmen, and our asses. H3947
44:29 And if ye t this also from me, and H3947
45:18 And t your father and your households, H3947
19 Now thou art commanded, this do ye; t H3947
Ex 2: 9 said unto her, T this child away, and H3212
4: 4 thine hand, and t it by the tail. And he H270
9 that thou shalt t of the water of the H3947
17 And thou shalt t this rod in thine hand, H3947
6: 7 And I will t you to me for a people, and H3947
7: 9 say unto Aaron, T thy rod, and cast *it* H3947
15 to a serpent shalt thou t in thine hand. H3947
19 Say unto Aaron, T thy rod, and stretch H3947
8: 8 the LORD, that he may t away the frogs
9: 8 and unto Aaron, T to you handfuls of H3947
10:17 he may t away from me this death only.
26 for thereof must we t to serve the LORD H3947
28 Get thee from me, t heed to thyself, see
12: 3 month they shall t to them every man a H3947
4 unto his house t *it* according to the H3947
5 the first year: ye shall t *it* out from the H3947
7 And they shall t of the blood, and strike H3947
21 Draw out and t you a lamb according H3947
22 And ye shall t a bunch of hyssop, and H3947
32 Also t your flocks and your herds, as ye H3947
15:14 t hold on the inhabitants of Palestina.
15 trembling shall t hold upon them; all
16:16 of your persons; t ye every man for H3947
33 And Moses said unto Aaron, T a pot, H3947
17: 5 the people, and t with thee of the elders H3947
5 the river, t in thine hand, and go. H3947
19:12 about, saying, T heed to yourselves, *that*
20: 7 Thou shalt not t the name of the LORD H5375
21:10 If he t him another *wife*; her food, her H3947
14 t him from mine altar, that he may die. H3947
22:26 If thou at all t thy neighbour's raiment H2254
23: 8 And thou shalt t no gift: for the gift H3947
25 t sickness away from the midst of thee. H5493
25: 2 with his heart ye shall t my offering. H3947
3 And this *is* the offering which ye shall t H3947
26: 5 that the loops may t hold one of another.
28: 1 And t thou unto thee Aaron thy H7126
5 And they shall t gold, and blue, and H3947
9 And thou shalt t two onyx stones, and H3947
29: 1 the priest's office: T one young bullock, H3947
5 And thou shalt t the garments, and put H3947
7 Then shalt thou t the anointing oil, and H3947
12 And thou shalt t of the blood of the H3947
13 And thou shalt t all the fat that H3947
15 Thou shalt also t one ram; and Aaron H3947
16 and thou shalt t his blood, and sprinkle H3947
19 And thou shalt t the other ram; and H3947
20 Then shalt thou kill the ram, and t of H3947
21 And thou shalt t of the blood that *is* H3947
22 Also thou shalt t of the ram the fat and H3947
26 And thou shalt t the breast of the ram H3947
31 And thou shalt t the ram of the H3947
30:16 And thou shalt t the atonement money H3947
23 T thou also unto thee principal spices, H3947
34 And the LORD said unto Moses, T unto H3947
33:23 And I will t away mine hand, and thou
34: 9 our sin, and t us for thine inheritance.
12 T heed to thyself, lest thou make a
16 And thou t of their daughters unto thy H3947
35: 5 T ye from among you an offering unto H3947
40: 9 And thou shalt t the anointing oil, and H3947
Lev 2: 2 and he shall t thereout his handful H7061
9 And the priest shall t from the meat H7311
3: 4 liver, with the kidneys, it shall he t away.
9 whole rump, it shall he t off hard by the
10 liver, with the kidneys, it shall he t away.
15 liver, with the kidneys, it shall he t away.
4: 5 And the priest that is anointed shall t H3947
8 And he shall t off from it all the fat of the
9 liver, with the kidneys, it shall he t away,
19 And he shall t all his fat from him, and H7311
25 And the priest shall t of the blood of the H3947
30 And the priest shall t of the blood H3947
31 And he shall t away all the fat thereof, as
34 And the priest shall t of the blood of the H3947
35 And he shall t away all the fat thereof, as
5:12 the priest shall t his handful of it, *even* H7061
6:10 his flesh, and t up the ashes which H7311
15 And he shall t of it his handful, of the H7311
7: 4 liver, with the kidneys, it shall he t away:
8: 2 T Aaron and his sons with him, and H3947
9: 2 And he said unto Aaron, T thee a H3947
3 speak, saying, T ye a kid of the goats H3947
10:12 that were left, T the meat offering that H3947
14: 4 Then shall the priest command to t for H3947
6 As for the living bird, he shall t it, and H3947
10 And on the eighth day he shall t two he H3947
12 And the priest shall t one he lamb, and H3947
14 And the priest shall t *some* of the blood H3947
15 And the priest shall t *some* of the log of H3947
21 then he shall t one lamb *for* a trespass H3947
24 And the priest shall t the lamb of the H3947
25 the priest shall t *some* of the blood of H3947
40 that they t away the stones in which
42 And they shall t other stones, and put H3947
42 and he shall t other morter, and shall H3947
49 And he shall t to cleanse the house two H3947
51 And he shall t the cedar wood, and the H3947
15:14 And on the eighth day he shall t to him H3947
29 And on the eighth day she shall t unto H3947
16: 5 And he shall t of the congregation of H3947
7 And he shall t the two goats, and H3947
12 And he shall t a censer full of burning H3947
14 And he shall t of the blood of the H3947
18 for it; and shall t of the blood of the H3947
18:17 neither shalt thou t her son's daughter, H3947
18 Neither shalt thou t a wife to her sister, H3947
20:14 And if a man t a wife and her mother, H3947
17 And if a man shall t his sister, his H3947
21 And if a man shall t his brother's wife, H3947
21: 7 They shall not t a wife *that is* a whore, H3947
7 neither shall they t a woman put away H3947
13 And he shall t a wife in her virginity. H3947
14 these shall he not t: but he shall take a H3947
14 t a virgin of his own people to wife. H3947
22: 5 man of whom he may t uncleanness,
23:40 And ye shall t you on the first day the H3947
24: 5 And thou shalt t fine flour, and bake H3947
25:36 T thou no usury of him, or increase: H3947
46 And ye shall t them as an inheritance for
Nu 1: 2 T ye the sum of all the congregation of H5375
49 tribe of Levi, neither t the sum of them H5375
51 the Levites shall t it down: and when the
3:40 and t the number of their names. H5375
41 And thou shalt t the Levites for me (I H3947
45 T the Levites instead of all the firstborn H3947
47 Thou shalt even t five shekels apiece by H3947
47 t *them*: (the shekel *is* twenty gerahs:) H3947
4: 2 T the sum of the sons of Kohath from H5375
5 and they shall t down the covering vail, H3381
9 And they shall t a cloth of blue, and H3947
12 And they shall t all the instruments of H3947
13 And they shall t away the ashes from the
22 T also the sum of the sons of Gershon, H5375
5:17 And the priest shall t holy water in an H3947
17 priest shall t, and put *it* into the water: H3947
25 Then the priest shall t the jealousy H3947
26 And the priest shall t an handful of the
6:18 and shall t the hair of the head H3947
19 And the priest shall t the sodden H3947
7: 5 T *it* of them, that they may be to do the H3947
8: 6 T the Levites from among the children H3947
8 Then let them t a young bullock with H3947
8 bullock shalt thou t for a sin offering. H3947
10: 6 the south side shall t their journey: they
11:17 there: and I will t of the spirit which *is* H680
16: 3 said unto them, *Ye t* too much upon you,
6 This do; T you censers, Korah, and all H3947
7 *ye t* too much upon you, ye sons of Levi.
17 And t every man his censer, and put H3947

Nu 16:37 the priest, that he t up the censers out H7311
46 And Moses said unto Aaron, T a H3947
17: 2 Speak unto the children of Israel, and t H3947
10 and thou shalt quite t away their H3615
18:26 unto them, When ye t of the children of H3947
19: 4 And Eleazar the priest shall t of her H3947
6 And the priest shall t cedar wood, and H3947
17 And for an unclean *person* they shall t H3947
18 And a clean person shall t hyssop, and H3947
20: 8 T the rod, and gather thou the H3947
25 T Aaron and Eleazar his son, and bring H3947
21: 7 the LORD, that he t away the serpents H5493
23:12 And he answered and said, Must I not t
25: 4 And the LORD said unto Moses, T all H3947
26: 2 T the sum of all the congregation of the H5375
4 *T the sum of the people,* from twenty
27:18 And the LORD said unto Moses, T thee H3947
31:26 T the sum of the prey that was taken, H5375
29 T *it* of their half, and give it unto H3947
30 half, thou shalt t one portion of fifty, H3947
34:18 And ye shall t one prince of every tribe, H3947
35:31 Moreover ye shall t no satisfaction for H3947
32 And ye shall t no satisfaction for him H3947
Dt 1: 7 Turn you, and t your journey, and go to
13 T you wise men, and understanding, H3051
40 But *as for* you, turn you, and t your
2: 4 t ye good heed unto yourselves therefore:
24 Rise ye up, t your journey, and pass over
4: 9 Only t heed to thyself, and keep thy soul
15 T ye therefore good heed unto
23 T heed unto yourselves, lest ye forget the
34 Or hath God assayed to go *and* t him a H3947
5:11 Thou shalt not t the name of the LORD H5375
7: 3 his daughter shalt thou t unto thy son. H3947
15 And the LORD will t away from thee all H5493
25 *is* on them, nor t *it* unto thee, lest thou H3947
10:11 And the LORD said unto me, Arise, t H3212
11:16 T heed to yourselves, that your heart be
12:13 T heed to thyself that thou offer not thy
19 T heed to thyself that thou forsake not
26 thy vows, thou shalt t, and go unto the H5375
30 T heed to thyself that thou be not snared
15:17 Then thou shalt t an aul, and thrust *it* H3947
16:19 persons, neither t a gift: for a gift doth H3947
20: 7 in the battle, and another man t her. H3947
14 thereof, shalt thou t unto thyself; and H962
19 war against it to t it, thou shalt not H8610
21: 3 of that city shall t an heifer, which hath H3947
22: 6 shalt not t the dam with the young: H3947
7 let the dam go, and t the young to thee; H3947
13 If any man t a wife, and go in unto her, H3947
15 and her mother, t and bring forth *the* H3947
18 And the elders of that city shall t that H3947
30 A man shall not t his father's wife, nor H3947
24: 4 her away, may not t her again to be his H3947
6 No man shall t the nether or the upper H2254
8 T heed in the plague of leprosy, that
17 nor t a widow's raiment to pledge: H2254
25: 5 go in unto her, and t her to him to wife, H3947
7 And if the man like not to t his H3947
8 stand *to it,* and say, I like not to t her; H3947
26: 2 That thou shalt t of the first of all the H3947
4 And the priest shall t the basket out of H3947
27: 9 all Israel, saying, T heed, and hearken, H5535
31:26 T this book of the law, and put it in the H3947
32:41 and mine hand t hold on judgment; I H270
Jos 3: 6 the priests, saying, T up the ark of the H5375
12 Now therefore t you twelve men out of H3947
4: 2 T you twelve men out of the people, out H3947
3 And command ye them, saying, T you H5375
5 of Jordan, and t ye up every man of H7311
6: 6 and said unto them, T up the ark of the H5375
18 accursed, when ye t of the accursed H3947
7:13 enemies, until ye t away the accursed H5493
14 which the LORD shall t shall come by H3920
14 LORD shall t shall come man by man. H3920
8: 1 be thou dismayed: t all the people of H3947
2 cattle thereof, shall ye t for a prey unto
29 that they should t his carcase down H3381
9:11 to us, saying, T victuals with you for H3947
10:42 land did Joshua t at one time, because H3920
11:12 of them, did Joshua t, and smote them H3920
20: 4 of that city, they shall t him into the city H622
22: 5 But t diligent heed to do the
19 dwelleth, and t possession among us: H270
23:11 T good heed therefore unto yourselves,
Jdg 4: 6 mount Tabor, and t with thee ten H3947
5:30 for the necks of *them that* t the spoil?
6:20 And the angel of God said unto him, T H3947

Jdg 6:25 said unto him, T thy father's young H3947
26 the ordered place, and t the second H3947
7:24 the Midianites, and t before them the H3920
14: 3 people, that thou goest to t a wife of the H3947
8 And after a time he returned to t her, H3947
15 called us to t that we have? *is it* not *so?* H3423
15: 2 she? t her, I pray thee, instead of her. H1961
19:30 of it, t advice, and speak *your minds.* H5779
20:10 And we will t ten men of an hundred H3947
Ru 2:10 that thou shouldest t knowledge of me, H5234
19 be he that did t knowledge of thee. And
1Sa 2:16 and *then* t *as much* as thy soul H3947
16 *it me* now: and if not, I will t *it* by force. H3947
6: 7 Now therefore make a new cart, and t H3947
8 And t the ark of the LORD, and lay it H3947
8:11 reign over you: He will t your sons, and H3947
13 And he will t your daughters *to be* H3947
14 And he will t your fields, and your H3947
15 And he will t the tenth of your seed, and
16 And he will t your menservants, and H3947
17 He will t the tenth of your sheep: and ye
9: 3 said to Saul his son, T now one of the H3947
5 for the asses, and t thought for us.
16: 2 the LORD said, T an heifer with thee, H3947
17:17 And Jesse said unto David his son, T H3947
18 thy brethren fare, and t their pledge. H3947
46 smite thee, and t thine head from thee; H5493
19: 2 I pray thee, t heed to thyself until
14 And when Saul sent messengers to t H3947
20 And Saul sent messengers to t David: H3947
20:21 on this side of thee, t them; then come H3947
21: 9 the ephod: if thou wilt t that, take *it:* for H3947
9 wilt take that, t *it:* for *there is* no other H3947
23:23 See therefore, and t knowledge of all the
26 and his men round about to t them. H8610
24:11 thee; yet thou huntest my soul to t it. H3947
25:11 Shall I then t my bread, and my water, H3947
39 with Abigail, to t her to him to wife. H3947
40 us unto thee, to t thee to him to wife. H3947
26:11 but, I pray thee, t thou now the spear H3947
2Sa 2:21 young men, and t thee his armour. But H3947
4:11 hand, and t you away from the earth? H1197
5: 6 Except thou t away the blind and H5493
12: 4 and he spared to t of his own flock and H3947
11 own house, and I will t thy wives before H3947
28 the city, and t it: lest I take the city, H3920
28 and take it: lest I t the city, and it be H3920
13:33 Now therefore let not my lord the king t H7760
15:20 return thou, and t back thy brethren:
16: 9 go over, I pray thee, and t off his head. H5493
19:19 that the king should t it to his heart. H7760
30 king, Yea, let him t all, forasmuch as H3947
20: 6 than *did* Absalom: t thou thy lord's H3947
24:10 thee, O LORD, t away the iniquity of H5674
22 my lord the king t and offer up what H3947
1Ki 1:33 The king also said unto them, T with H3947
2: 4 If thy children t heed to their way, to
31 that thou mayest t away the innocent H5493
8:25 so that thy children t heed to their way,
11:31 And he said to Jeroboam, T thee ten H3947
34 Howbeit I will not t the whole kingdom H3947
35 But I will t the kingdom out of his son's H3947
37 And I will t thee, and thou shalt reign H3947
14: 3 And t with thee ten loaves, and H3947
10 in Israel, and will t away the remnant H1197
16: 3 Behold, I will t away the posterity of H1197
18:40 And Elijah said unto them, T the H8610
19: 4 now, O LORD, t away my life; for I *am* H3947
10 left; and they seek my life, to t it away. H3947
14 left; and they seek my life, to t it away. H3947
20: 6 shall put *it* in their hand, and t *it* away. H3947
18 out for peace, t them alive; or whether H8610
18 they be come out for war, t them alive. H8610
24 And do this thing, T the kings away, H5493
21:15 said to Ahab, Arise, t possession of the H3423
16 the Jezreelite, to t possession of it. H3423
21 thee, and will t away thy posterity, H1197
22: 3 we *be* still, *and* t it not out of the hand H3947
26 And the king of Israel said, T Micaiah, H3947
2Ki 2: 1 when the LORD would t up Elijah into H5927
3 that the LORD will t away thy master H3947
5 that the LORD will t away thy master H3947
4: 1 creditor is come to t unto him my two H3947
29 up thy loins, and t my staff in thine H3947
36 in unto him, he said, T up thy son. H5375
5:15 I pray thee, t a blessing of thy servant. H3947
16 he urged him to t *it;* but he refused. H3947
20 run after him, and t somewhat of him. H3947
23 And Naaman said, Be content, t two H3947

2Ki 6: 2 unto Jordan, and t thence every man a H3947
7 Therefore said he, T *it* up to thee. And H7311
32 hath sent to t away mine head? look, H5493
7:13 said, Let *some* t, I pray thee, five of the H3947
8: 8 And the king said unto Hazael, T a H3947
9: 1 up thy loins, and t this box of oil in H3947
3 Then t the box of oil, and pour *it* on his H3947
17 And Joram said, T an horseman, and H3947
25 Then said *Jehu* to Bidkar his captain, T H5375
26 Now therefore t *and* cast him into the H5375
10: 6 unto my voice, t ye the heads of the H3947
14 And he said, T them alive. And they H8610
12: 5 Let the priests t *it* to them, every man H3947
13:15 And Elisha said unto him, T bow and H3947
18 And he said, T the arrows. And he took H3947
18:32 Until I come and t you away to a land H3947
19:30 shall yet again t root downward, and H3947
20: 7 And Isaiah said, T a lump of figs. And H3947
18 beget, shall they t away; and they shall H3947
1Ch 7:21 they came down to t away their cattle. H3947
17:13 my son: and I will not t my mercy away H5493
21:23 And Ornan said unto David, T *it* to H3947
24 price: for I will not t *that* which *is* thine H5375
28:10 T heed now; for the LORD hath chosen H7200
2Ch 6:16 so that thy children t heed to their way
18:25 Then the king of Israel said, T ye H3947
19: 6 And said to the judges, T heed what ye H7200
7 be upon you; t heed and do *it:* for *there*
20:25 his people came to t away the spoil of H962
32:18 trouble them; that they might t the city. H3920
33: 8 so that they will t heed to do all that I
Ezr 4:22 T heed now that ye fail not to do this: H2095
5:14 did Cyrus the king t out of the temple H5312
15 And said unto him, T these vessels, go, H5376
9:12 their sons, neither t their daughters H5375
Neh 5: 2 therefore we t up corn *for them,* that H3947
6: 7 therefore, and let us t counsel together.
10:30 nor t their daughters for our sons: H3947
38 when the Levites t tithes: and the Levites
13:25 their sons, nor t their daughters unto H5375
Est 3:13 and *to* t the spoil of them for a prey.
4: 4 Mordecai, and to t away his sackcloth H5493
6:10 Make haste, *and* t the apparel and the H3947
8:11 and *to* t the spoil of them for a prey,
Job 7:21 my transgression, and t away mine H5674
9:18 He will not suffer me to t my breath, H7725
34 Let him t his rod away from me, and H5493
10:20 me alone, that I may t comfort a little,
11:18 *thee, and* thou shalt t thy rest in safety. H7901
13:14 Wherefore do I t my flesh in my teeth, H5375
18: 9 The gin shall t *him* by the heel, *and* the H270
21:12 They t the timbrel and harp, and H5375
23:10 But he knoweth the way that I t: *when* H5978
24: 2 t away flocks, and feed *thereof.* H1497
3 they t the widow's ox for a pledge. H2254
9 the breast, and t a pledge of the poor. H2254
10 they t away the sheaf *from* the hungry; H5375
27:20 Terrors t hold on him as waters, a H5381
30:17 night season: and my sinews t no rest. H7901
31:36 Surely I would t it upon my shoulder, H5375
32:22 my maker would soon t me away. H5375
36:17 judgment and justice t hold *on thee.* H8551
18 Because *there is* wrath, *beware* lest he t H5496
21 T heed, regard not iniquity: for this hast
38:13 That it might t hold of the ends of the H270
20 That thou shouldest t it to the bound H3947
41: 4 wilt thou t him for a servant for ever? H3947
42: 8 Therefore t unto you now seven H3947
Ps 2: 2 and the rulers t counsel together, against
7: 5 Let the enemy persecute my soul, and t H5381
13: 2 How long shall I t counsel in my soul, H7896
16: 4 offer, nor t up their names into my lips. H5375
27:10 forsake me, then the LORD will t me up. H622
31:13 me, they devised to t away my life. H3947
35: 2 T hold of shield and buckler, and stand H2388
39: 1 I said, I will t heed to my ways, that I sin
50: 9 I will t no bullock out of thy house, *nor* H3947
16 shouldest t my covenant in thy mouth? H5375
51:11 and t not thy holy spirit from me. H3947
52: 5 thee for ever, he shall t thee away, and H2846
58: 9 thorns, he shall t them away as with a H8157
69:20 I looked *for some* to t pity, but *there was*
24 let thy wrathful anger t hold of them. H5381
71:10 lay wait for my soul t counsel together,
11 t him; for *there is* none to deliver *him.* H8610
80: 9 it to t deep root, and it filled the land.
81: 2 T a psalm, and bring hither the H5375
83:12 Who said, Let us t to ourselves the
89:33 will I not utterly t from him, nor suffer H6331

Ps 102:14 For thy servants **t** pleasure in her stones,
24 I said, O my God, **t** me not away in the H5927
109: 8 Let his days be few; *and* let another **t** H3947
116:13 I will **t** the cup of salvation, and call H5375
119:43 And **t** not the word of truth utterly out H5337
139: 9 *If* I **t** the wings of the morning, *and* H5375
20 *and* thine enemies **t** *thy name* in vain. H5375
Prv 2:19 neither **t** they hold of the paths of life. H5381
4:13 **T** fast hold of instruction; let *her* not H2388
5: 5 Her feet go down to death; her steps **t** H8551
22 His own iniquities shall **t** the wicked H3920
6:25 neither let her **t** thee with her eyelids. H3947
27 Can a man **t** fire in his bosom, and his H2846
7:18 Come, let us **t** our fill of love until the
20:16 **T** his garment that is surety *for* a H3947
16 **t** a pledge of him for a strange woman. H3947
22:27 he **t** away thy bed from under thee? H2254
25: 4 **T** away the dross from the silver, and H3947
5 **T** away the wicked *from* before the H1898
27:13 **T** his garment that is surety for a H3947
13 **t** a pledge of him for a strange woman. H2254
30: 9 and **t** the name of my God *in vain*. H8610
Ecc 5:15 as he came, and shall **t** nothing of his H5375
19 eat thereof, and to **t** his portion, and to H5375
7:18 *It is* good that thou shouldest **t** hold of H270
21 Also **t** no heed unto all words that are H5414
Song 2:15 **T** us the foxes, the little foxes, that spoil H270
7: 8 the palm tree, I will **t** hold of the boughs H270
Isa 1:25 away thy dross, and **t** away all thy tin: H5493
3: 1 of hosts, doth **t** away from Jerusalem H5493
6 When a man shall **t** hold of his brother H8610
18 In that day the Lord will **t** away the H5493
4: 1 And in that day seven women shall **t** H2388
1 by thy name, to **t** away our reproach. H622
5: 5 to my vineyard: I will **t** away the hedge H5493
23 wicked for reward, and **t** away the H5493
7: 4 And say unto him, **T** heed, and be quiet;
8: 1 Moreover the LORD said unto me, **T** H3947
10 **T** counsel together, and it shall come to
10: 2 judgment, and to **t** away the right from H1497
6 him a charge, to **t** the spoil, and to take H7997
6 the spoil, and to **t** the prey, and to tread H962
13: 8 and sorrows shall **t** hold of them; they H270
14: 2 And the people shall **t** them, and bring H3947
2 and they shall **t** them captives, whose
4 That thou shalt **t** up this proverb H5375
16: 3 **T** counsel, execute judgment; make thy H935
18: 4 For so the LORD said unto me, I will **t**
5 and **t** away *and* cut down the branches. H5493
23:16 **T** an harp, go about the city, thou H3947
25: 8 his people shall he **t** away from off all H5493
27: 5 Or let him **t** hold of my strength, *that* H2388
6 that come of Jacob to **t** root: Israel shall H2388
9 *is* all the fruit to **t** away his sin; when H5493
28:19 it goeth forth it shall **t** you: for morning H3947
30: 1 the LORD, that **t** counsel, but not of H6213
14 of it a sherd to **t** fire from the hearth, H2846
14 or to **t** water *withal* out of the pit. H2834
33:23 a great spoil divided; the lame **t** the prey. H962
36:17 Until I come and **t** you away to a land H3947
37:31 **t** root downward, and bear fruit upward:
38:21 For Isaiah had said, Let them **t** a lump H5375
39: 7 beget, shall they **t** away; and they shall H3947
40:24 stock shall not **t** root in the earth: and H3947
24 shall **t** them away as stubble. H5375
44:15 to burn: for he will **t** thereof, and warm H3947
45:21 near; yea, let them **t** counsel together:
47: 2 **T** the millstones, and grind meal: H3947
3 shall be seen: I will **t** vengeance, and I H3947
56: 4 please me, and **t** hold of my covenant; H2388
57:13 away; vanity shall **t** *them*: but he that H3947
14 up, prepare the way, **t** up the H7311
58: 2 they **t** delight in approaching to God.
9 say, Here I *am*. If thou **t** away from the H5493
64: 7 up himself to **t** hold of thee: for thou H2388
66:21 And I will also **t** of them for priests *and* H3947
Jer 2:22 with nitre, and **t** thee much soap, *yet*
3:14 you: and I will **t** you one of a city, and H3947
4: 4 to the LORD, and **t** away the foreskins H5493
5:10 not a full end: **t** away her battlements; H5493
7:29 cast *it* away, and **t** up a lamentation on H5375
9: 4 **T** ye heed every one of his neighbour,
10 For the mountains will I **t** up a weeping H5375
18 And let them make haste, and **t** up a H5375
13: 4 **T** the girdle that thou hast got, which *is* H3947
6 go to Euphrates, and **t** the girdle from H3947
21 sorrows **t** thee, as a woman in travail? H270
15:15 of my persecutors; **t** me not away in thy H3947
19 me: and if thou **t** forth the precious H3318

Jer 16: 2 Thou shalt not **t** thee a wife, neither H3947
17:21 Thus saith the LORD; **T** heed to
18:22 pit to **t** me, and hid snares for my feet. H3920
19: 1 earthen bottle, and *t* of the ancients of
20: 5 **t** them, and carry them to Babylon. H3947
10 and we shall **t** our revenge on him. H3947
25: 9 Behold, I will send and **t** all the families H3947
10 Moreover I will **t** from them the voice of H6
15 of Israel unto me; **T** the wine cup of H3947
28 And it shall be, if they refuse to **t** the H3947
29: 6 **T** ye wives, and beget sons and H3947
6 daughters; and **t** wives for your sons, H3947
32: 3 of the king of Babylon, and he shall **t** it; H3920
14 the God of Israel; **T** these evidences, H3947
24 unto the city to **t** it; and the city is given H3920
25 for money, and **t** witnesses; for the city H5749
28 king of Babylon, and he shall **t** it: H3920
44 seal *them*, and **t** witnesses in the land H5749
33:26 *so* that I will not **t** *any* of his seed *to be* H3947
34:22 against it, and **t** it, and burn it with H3920
36: 2 **T** thee a roll of a book, and write H3947
14 Baruch, saying, **T** in thine hand the roll H3947
26 son of Abdeel, to **t** Baruch the scribe H3947
28 **T** thee again another roll, and write in H3947
37: 8 this city, and **t** it, and burn it with fire. H3920
38: 3 of Babylon's army, which shall **t** it. H3920
10 Ethiopian, saying, **T** from hence thirty H3947
10 men with thee, and **t** up Jeremiah the H3947
39:12 **T** him, and look well to him, and do H3947
43: 9 **T** great stones in thine hand, and hide H3947
10 I will send and **t** Nebuchadrezzar the H3947
44:12 And I will **t** the remnant of Judah, that H3947
46:11 Go up into Gilead, and **t** balm, O virgin, H3947
49:29 Their tents and their flocks shall they **t** H3947
29 away: they shall **t** to themselves their H5375
50:15 of the LORD: **t** vengeance upon her;
51: 8 howl for her; **t** balm for her pain, if H3947
26 And they shall not **t** of thee a stone for H3947
36 thy cause, and **t** vengeance for thee; and
Lam 2:13 What thing shall I **t** to witness for thee?
Ezk 4: 1 Thou also, son of man, **t** thee a tile, and H3947
3 Moreover **t** thou unto thee an iron pan, H3947
9 **T** thou also unto thee wheat, and H3947
5: 1 And thou, son of man, **t** thee a sharp H3947
1 thee a sharp knife, **t** thee a barber's H3947
1 upon thy beard: then **t** thee balances to H3947
2 and thou shalt **t** a third part, *and* smite H3947
3 Thou shalt also **t** thereof a few in H3947
4 Then **t** of them again, and cast them H3947
10: 6 with linen, saying, **T** fire from between H3947
11:18 and they shall **t** away all the detestable H5493
19 you; and I will **t** the stony heart out H5493
14: 5 That I may **t** the house of Israel in their H8610
15: 3 **t** a pin of it to hang any vessel thereon? H3947
16:16 And of thy garments thou didst **t**, and H3947
39 clothes, and shall **t** thy fair jewels, and H3947
17:22 Thus saith the Lord GOD; I will also **t** of H3947
19: 1 Moreover **t** thou up a lamentation for H5375
21:26 the diadem, and **t** off the crown: this H7311
22:16 And thou shalt **t** thine inheritance in
23:25 thee: they shall **t** away thy nose and H5493
25 the sword: they shall **t** thy sons and thy H3947
26 thy clothes, and **t** away thy fair jewels. H3947
29 and shall **t** away all thy labour, H3947
24: 5 **T** the choice of the flock, and burn also H3947
8 fury to come up to **t** vengeance; I have H5358
16 Son of man, behold, I **t** away from thee H3947
25 *be* in the day when I **t** from them their H3947
26:17 And they shall **t** up a lamentation for H5375
27: 2 Now, thou son of man, **t** up a H5375
32 And in their wailing they shall **t** up a H5375
28:12 Son of man, **t** up a lamentation upon H5375
29:19 and he shall **t** her multitude, and take H5375
19 her multitude, and **t** her spoil, and take H7997
19 and take her spoil, and **t** her prey; and it H962
30: 4 and they shall **t** away her multitude, H3947
32: 2 Son of man, **t** up a lamentation for H5375
33: 2 the people of the land **t** a man of their H3947
4 sword come, and **t** him away, his blood H3947
6 the sword come, and **t** *any* person from H3947
36:24 For I will **t** you from among the H3947
26 you: and I will **t** away the stony heart H5493
37:16 Moreover, thou son of man, **t** thee one H3947
16 companions: then **t** another stick, and H3947
19 Behold, I will **t** the stick of Joseph, H3947
21 Behold, I will **t** the children of Israel H3947
38:12 To **t** a spoil, and to take a prey; to turn H7997
12 To take a spoil, and to **t** a prey; to turn H962
13 Art thou come to **t** a spoil? hast thou H7997

Ezk 38:13 thy company to **t** a prey? to carry away H962
13 silver and gold, to **t** away cattle and H3947
13 cattle and goods, to **t** a great spoil? H7997
39:10 So that they shall **t** no wood out of the H5375
43:20 And thou shalt **t** of the blood thereof, H3947
21 Thou shalt **t** the bullock also of the sin H3947
44:22 Neither shall they **t** for their wives a H3947
22 but they shall **t** maidens of the seed H3947
45: 9 and justice, **t** away your exactions H7311
18 the month, thou shalt **t** a young bullock H3947
19 And the priest shall **t** of the blood of the H3947
46:18 Moreover the prince shall not **t** of the H3947
Dan 6:23 that they should **t** Daniel up out of the H5267
7:18 But the saints of the most High shall **t** H6902
26 sit, and they shall **t** away his dominion, H5709
11:15 cast up a mount, and **t** the most fenced H3920
18 the isles, and shall **t** many: but a prince H3920
31 of strength, and shall **t** away the daily H5493
Hos 1: 2 said to Hosea, Go, **t** unto thee a wife of H3947
6 of Israel; but I will utterly **t** them away. H5375
2: 9 Therefore will I return, and **t** away my H3947
17 For I will **t** away the names of Baalim H5493
4:10 they have left off to **t** heed to the LORD.
11 Whoredom and wine and new wine **t** H3947
5:14 will **t** away, and none shall rescue *him*. H5375
11: 4 them as they that **t** off the yoke on their H7311
14: 2 **T** with you words, and turn to the H3947
2 say unto him, **T** away all iniquity, and H5375
Am 3: 5 for him? shall *one* **t** up a snare from the H5927
4: 2 upon you, that he will **t** you away with H5375
5: 1 Hear ye this word which I **t** up against H5375
11 the poor, and ye **t** from him burdens of H3947
12 the just, they **t** a bribe, and they turn H3947
23 **T** thou away from me the noise of thy H5493
6:10 And a man's uncle shall **t** him up, and H5375
9: 2 shall mine hand **t** them; though they H3947
3 I will search and **t** them out thence; H3947
Jna 1:12 And he said unto them, **T** me up, and H5375
4: 3 Therefore now, O LORD, **t**, I beseech H3947
Mic 2: 2 And they covet fields, and **t** *them* by H5375
2 and houses, and **t** *them* away: so they H5375
4 In that day shall *one* **t** up a parable H5375
6 to them, *that* they shall not **t** shame. H5253
6:14 and thou shalt **t** hold, but shalt not H5253
Nah 1: 2 the LORD will **t** vengeance on his
2: 9 **T** ye the spoil of silver, take the spoil of H962
9 Take ye the spoil of silver, **t** the spoil of H962
Hab 1:10 hold; for they shall heap dust, and **t** it. H3920
15 They **t** up all of them with the angle, H5927
2: 6 Shall not all these **t** up a parable H5375
Zep 3:11 me: for then I will **t** away out of the H5493
Hag 1: 8 house; and I will **t** pleasure in it, and I
2:23 of hosts, will I **t** thee, O Zerubbabel, H3947
Zec 1: 6 did they not **t** hold of your fathers? H5381
3: 4 before him, saying, **T** away the filthy H5493
6:10 **T** of *them of* the captivity, *even* of H3947
11 Then **t** silver and gold, and make H3947
8:23 *pass*, that ten men shall **t** hold out of all H2388
23 nations, even shall **t** hold of the skirt of H2388
9: 7 And I will **t** away his blood out of his H5493
11:15 And the LORD said unto me, **T** unto H3947
14:21 shall come and **t** of them, and seethe H3947
Mal 2: 3 feasts; and *one* shall **t** you away with it. H5375
15 seed. Therefore **t** heed to your spirit, and
16 of hosts: therefore **t** heed to your spirit,
Mt 1:20 David, fear not to **t** unto thee Mary thy *G3880*
2:13 saying, Arise, and **t** the young child *G3880*
20 Saying, Arise, and **t** the young child *G3880*
5:40 at the law, and **t** away thy coat, let him *G2983*
6: 1 **T** heed that ye do not your alms before
25 Therefore I say unto you, **T** no thought *G3309*
28 And why **t** ye thought for raiment?
31 Therefore **t** no thought, saying, What *G3309*
34 **T** therefore no thought for the morrow: *G3309*
34 the morrow shall **t** thought for the things
9: 6 **t** up thy bed, and go unto thine house. *G142*
10:19 But when they deliver you up, **t** no *G3309*
11:12 violence, and the violent **t** it by force. *G726*
29 **T** my yoke upon you, and learn of me; *G142*
15:26 It is not meet to **t** the children's bread, *G2983*
16: 5 side, they had forgotten to **t** bread. *G2983*
6 Then Jesus said unto them, **T** heed and
24 and **t** up his cross, and follow me. *G142*
17:25 kings of the earth **t** custom or tribute? *G2983*
27 cast an hook, and **t** up the fish that first *G142*
27 **t**, and give unto them for me and thee. *G2983*
18:10 **T** heed that ye despise not one of these
16 But if he will not hear *thee, then* **t** with *G3880*
23 which would **t** account of his servants. *G4868*

Mt 20:14 T *that* thine *is,* and go thy way: I will G142
22:13 hand and foot, and t him away, and cast G142
24: 4 them, T heed that no man deceive you.
17 down to t any thing out of his house: G142
18 is in the field return back to t his clothes. G142
25:28 T therefore the talent from him, and give G142
26: 4 And consulted that they might t Jesus G2902
26 and said, T, eat; this is my body. G2983
45 Sleep on now, and t *your* rest: behold,
52 t the sword shall perish with the sword. G2983
55 and staves for to t me? I sat daily with G4815
Mk 2: 9 say, Arise, and t up thy bed, and walk? G142
11 I say unto thee, Arise, and t up thy bed, G142
4:24 And he said unto them, T heed what ye
6: 8 them that they should t nothing for *their* G142
7:27 it is not meet to t the children's bread, G2983
8:14 Now *the disciples* had forgotten to t G2983
15 And he charged them, saying, T heed,
34 and t up his cross, and follow me. G142
10:21 and come, t up the cross, and follow me. G142
12:19 his brother should t his wife, and raise G2983
13: 5 to say, T heed lest any *man* deceive you:
9 But t heed to yourselves: for they shall
11 and deliver you up, t no thought G4305
15 *therein,* to t any thing out of his house: G142
16 turn back again for to t up his garment. G142
23 But t ye heed: behold, I have foretold you G991
33 T ye heed, watch and pray: for ye know
14: 1 t him by craft, and put *him* to death. G2902
22 them, and said, T, eat: this is my body. G2983
36 *are* possible unto thee; t away this cup G3911
41 them, Sleep on now, and t *your* rest: it is
44 is he; t him, and lead *him* away safely. G2902
48 with swords and *with* staves to t me? G4815
15:24 upon them, what every man should t. G142
36 whether Elias will come to t him down. G2507
16:18 They shall t up serpents; and if they G142
Lk 1:25 *me,* to t away my reproach among men. G851
5:24 t up thy couch, and go into thine house. G142
6: 4 house of God, and did t and eat the G2983
29 thy cloak forbid not *to t thy* coat also.
8:18 T heed therefore how ye hear: for
9: 3 And he said unto them, T nothing for G142
23 and t up his cross daily, and follow me. G142
10:35 and said unto him, T care of him; and
11:35 T heed therefore that the light which is G4648
12:11 and powers, t ye no thought how or
15 And he said unto them, T heed, and
19 t thine ease, eat, drink, *and* be merry.
22 I say unto you, T no thought for your G3309
26 is least, why t ye thought for the rest?
14: 9 begin with shame to t the lowest room. G2722
16: 6 he said unto him, T thy bill, and sit G1209
7 him, T thy bill, and write fourscore. G1209
17: 3 T heed to yourselves: If thy brother
31 not come down to t it away: and he that G142
19:24 And he said unto them that stood by, T G142
20:20 that they might t hold of his words, G1949
26 And they could not t hold of his words G1949
28 his brother should t his wife, and raise G2983
21: 8 And he said, T heed that ye be not
34 And t heed to yourselves, lest at any
22:17 T this, and divide *it* among yourselves: G2983
36 a purse, let him t *it,* and likewise *his* G142
Jn 2:16 And said unto them that sold doves, T G142
5: 8 Jesus saith unto him, Rise, t up thy bed, G142
11 said unto me, T up thy bed, and walk. G142
12 said unto thee, T up thy bed, and walk? G142
6: 7 that every one of them may t a little. G2983
15 would come and t him by force, to make G726
7:30 Then they sought to t him: but no man G4084
32 the chief priests sent officers to t him. G4084
10:17 down my life, that I might t it again. G2983
18 and I have power to t it again. This G2983
39 Therefore they sought again to t him: G4084
11:39 Jesus said, T ye away the stone. Martha, G142
48 and t away both our place and nation. G142
57 should shew *it,* that they might t him. G4084
16:15 t of mine, and shall shew *it* unto you. G2983
17:15 I pray not that thou shouldest t them out G142
18:31 Then said Pilate unto them, T ye him, G2983
19: 6 saith unto them, T ye him, and crucify G2983
38 that he might t away the body of Jesus: G142
20:15 hast laid him, and I will t him away. G142
Act 1:20 and his bishoprick let another t. G2983
25 That he may t part of this ministry and G2983
5:35 And said unto them, Ye men of Israel, t
12: 3 further to t Peter also. (Then were G4815
15:14 to t out of them a people for his name. G2983
Act 15:37 And Barnabas determined to t with G4838
38 But Paul thought not good to t him G4838
20:13 there intending to t in Paul: for so had G353
26 Wherefore I t you to record this day, G3143
28 T heed therefore unto yourselves, and to
21:24 Them t, and purify thyself with them, G3880
22:26 captain, saying, T heed what thou doest:
23:10 to go down, and to t him by force from G726
24: 8 thyself mayest t knowledge of all these
27:33 *them* all to t meat, saying, This day G3335
34 Wherefore I pray you to t *some* meat: G4355
Ro 11:21 *t heed* lest he also spare not thee.
27 them, when I shall t away their sins. G851
15:24 Whensoever I t my journey into Spain, I
1Co 3:10 man t heed how he buildeth thereupon.
6: 7 do ye not rather t wrong? why do ye not
15 of Christ? shall I then t the members of G142
8: 9 But t heed lest by any means this liberty
9: 9 out the corn. Doth God t care for oxen?
10:12 thinketh he standeth t heed lest he fall.
11:24 he brake *it,* and said, T, eat: this is my G2983
2Co 8: 4 the gift, and *t upon us* the fellowship
11:20 *you,* if a man t *of you,* if a man exalt G2983
12:10 Therefore I t pleasure in infirmities, in
Gal 5:15 But if ye bite and devour one another, t
Eph 6:13 Wherefore t unto you the whole armour G353
17 And t the helmet of salvation, and the G1209
Col 4:17 And say to Archippus, T heed to the
1Ti 3: 5 shall he t care of the church of God?)
4:16 T heed unto thyself, and unto the
2Ti 4:11 Only Luke is with me. T Mark, and bring G353
Heb 3:12 T heed, brethren, lest there be in any of
7: 5 a commandment to t tithes of the people
10: 4 of bulls and of goats should t away sins. G851
11 sacrifices, which can never t away sins: G4014
Jas 5:10 T, my brethren, the prophets, who have G2983
1Pt 2:20 your faults, ye shall t it patiently? but if,
20 t it patiently, this *is* acceptable with God.
2Pt 1:19 ye do well that ye t heed, as unto a light
1Jn 3: 5 And ye know that he was manifested to t G142
Rev 3:11 thou hast, that no man t thy crown. G2983
5: 9 art worthy to t the book, and to open G2983
6: 4 that sat thereon to t peace from the G2983
10: 8 and said, Go *and* t the little book which G2983
9 he said unto me, T *it,* and eat it up; and G2983
22:17 will, let him t the water of life freely. G2983
19 And if any man shall t away from the G851
19 God shall t away his part out of G851

TAKEN

Gen 2:22 And the rib, which the LORD God had t H3947
23 Woman, because she was t out of Man. H3947
3:19 out of it wast thou t: for dust thou *art,* H3947
23 to till the ground from whence he was t. H3947
4:15 vengeance shall be t on him sevenfold.
12:15 the woman was t into Pharaoh's house. H3947
19 so I might have t her to me to wife: now H3947
14:14 his brother was t captive, he armed his H7617
18:27 now, I have t upon me to speak unto H2974
31 And he said, Behold now, I have t upon H2974
20: 3 thou hast t; for she *is* a man's wife. H3947
21:25 servants had violently t away. H1497
27:33 *is* he that hath t venison, and brought H6679
35 subtilty, and hath t away thy blessing. H3947
36 now he hath t away my blessing. And H3947
30:15 that thou hast t my husband? and H3947
23 and said, God hath t away my reproach: H622
31: 1 saying, Jacob hath t away all that *was* H3947
9 Thus God hath t away the cattle of your H5337
16 For all the riches which God hath t H5337
26 daughters, as captives *t* with the sword?
34 Now Rachel had t the images, and put H3947
Ex 14:11 Egypt, hast thou t us away to die in the H3947
25:15 of the ark: they shall not be t from it. H5493
40:36 And when the cloud was t up from over H5927
37 But if the cloud were not t up, then they H5927
37 not till the day that it was t up. H5927
Lev 4:10 As it was t off from the bullock of the H7311
31 thereof, as the fat is t away from off the H7311
35 the fat of the lamb is t away from the H7311
6: 2 or in a thing t away by violence, or H1497
7:34 shoulder have I t of the children of H3947
14:43 after that he hath t away the stones, H2502
24: 8 continually, *being t* from the children of
Nu 3:12 And I, behold, I have t the Levites from H3947
5:13 her, neither she be t *with the manner;* H8610
8:16 of Israel, have I t them unto me. H3947
18 And I have t the Levites for all the H3947
9:17 And when the cloud was t up from the H5927
Nu 9:21 *that* the cloud was t up in the morning, H5927
21 that the cloud was t up, they journeyed. H5927
22 but when it was t up, they journeyed. H5927
10:11 that the cloud was t up from off the H5927
17 And the tabernacle was t down; and H3381
16:15 I have not t one ass from them, H5375
18: 6 And I, behold, I have t your brethren H3947
21:26 king of Moab, and t all his land out of H3947
31:26 Take the sum of the prey that was t, H7628
49 Thy servants have t the sum of the men H5375
53 (*For* the men of war had t spoil, every H962
36: 3 inheritance be t from the inheritance H1639
3 it be t from the lot of our inheritance. H1639
4 their inheritance be t away from the H1639
Dt 4:20 But the LORD hath t you, and brought H3947
20: 7 wife, and hath not t her? let him go and H3947
21:10 hands, and thou hast t them captive, H7617
24: 1 When a man hath t a wife, and H3947
5 When a man hath t a new wife, he shall H3947
5 shall cheer up his wife which he hath t. H3947
26:14 neither have I t away *ought* thereof H1197
28:31 *shall be* violently t away from before H1497
Jos 7:11 for they have even t of the accursed H3947
15 And it shall be, *that* he that is t with the H3920
16 tribes; and the tribe of Judah was t: H3920
17 Zarhites man by man; and Zabdi was t: H3920
18 of Zerah, of the tribe of Judah, was t. H3920
8: 8 And it shall be, when ye have t the city, H8610
21 the ambush had t the city, and that the H3920
10: 1 how Joshua had t Ai, and had utterly H3920
Jdg 1: 8 and had t it, and smitten it with H3920
11:36 as the LORD hath t vengeance for thee H6213
14: 9 them that he had t the honey out of the H7287
15: 6 because he had t his wife, and given H3947
17: 2 of silver that were t from thee, about H3947
18:24 And he said, Ye have t away my gods H3947
1Sa 4:11 And the ark of God was t; and the two H3947
17 are dead, and the ark of God is t. H3947
19 the ark of God was t, and that her father H3947
21 the ark of God was t, and because of her H3947
22 from Israel: for the ark of God is t. H3947
7:14 the Philistines had t from Israel were H3947
10:20 come near, the tribe of Benjamin was t. H3920
21 of Matri was t, and Saul the son of H3920
21 son of Kish was t: and when they sought H3920
12: 3 whose ox have I t? or whose ass have I H3947
3 or whose ass have I t? or whom have I H3947
4 hast thou t ought of any man's hand. H3947
14:41 were t: but the people escaped. H3920
42 Jonathan my son. And Jonathan was t. H3920
21: 6 that was t from before the LORD, H5493
6 bread in the day when it was t away. H3947
30: 2 And had t the women captives, that *were*
3 and their daughters, were t captives.
5 And David's two wives were t captives,
16 spoil that they had t out of the land of H3947
19 they had t to them: David recovered all. H3947
2Sa 12: 9 the sword, and hast t his wife *to be* thy H3947
10 me, and hast t the wife of Uriah the H3947
27 Rabbah, and have t the city of waters. H3920
16: 8 and, behold, thou *art* t in thy mischief,
18: 9 the oak, and he was t up between the H5414
18 Now Absalom in his lifetime had t and H3947
23: 6 because they cannot be t with hands: H3947
1Ki 7: 8 he had t *to wife,* like unto this porch. H3947
9: 9 of Egypt, and have t hold upon other H2388
16 had gone up, and t Gezer, and burnt it H3920
16:18 that the city was t, that he went into the H3920
21:19 killed, and also t possession? And thou
22:43 places were not t away; *for* the people H5493
2Ki 2: 9 thee, before I be t away from thee. And H3947
10 see me *when I am* t from thee, it shall H3947
16 of the LORD hath t him up, and cast H5375
4:20 And when he had t him, and brought H5375
6:22 whom thou hast t captive with thy sword
12: 3 But the high places were not t away: H5493
13:25 cities, which he had t out of the hand of H3947
14: 4 Howbeit the high places were not t H5493
18:10 of Hoshea king of Israel, Samaria was t. H3920
22 Hezekiah hath t away, and hath said H5493
24: 7 king of Babylon had t from the river of H3947
1Ch 24: 6 t for Eleazar, and *one* taken for Ithamar. H270
6 taken for Eleazar, and *one* t for Ithamar. H270
2Ch 15: 8 which he had t from mount Ephraim, H3920
17 But the high places were not t away out H5493
17: 2 of Ephraim, which Asa his father had t. H3920
19: 3 in that thou hast t away the groves out H1197
20:33 Howbeit the high places were not t H5493
28:11 which ye have t captive of your brethren:

2Ch 28:18 of Judah, and had t Beth-shemesh, and H3920
30: 2 For the king had t counsel, and his
32:12 Hath not the same Hezekiah t away his H5493
Ezr 9: 2 For they have t of their daughters for H5375
10: 2 our God, and have t strange wives of H3427
10 and have t strange wives, to increase H3427
14 them which have t strange wives in our H3427
17 the men that had t strange wives by the H3427
18 were found that had t strange wives: H3427
44 All these had t strange wives: and *some* H5375
Neh 5:15 people, and had t of them bread and H3947
6:18 his son Johanan had t the daughter of H3947
Est 2:15 who had t her for his daughter, H3947
16 So Esther was t unto king Ahasuerus H3947
8: 2 ring, which he had t from Haman, and H5674
Job 1:21 the LORD hath t away; blessed be the H3947
16:12 he hath also t *me* by my neck, and H270
19: 9 He hath stripped me of my glory, and t H5493
20:19 t away an house which he builded not; H1497
22: 6 For thou hast t a pledge from thy H2254
24:24 low; they are t out of the way as all H7092
27: 2 *As* God liveth, *who* hath t away my H5493
28: 2 Iron is t out of the earth, and brass *is* H3947
30:16 days of affliction have t hold upon me. H270
34: 5 and God hath t away my judgment. H5493
20 mighty shall be t away without hand. H5493
Ps 9:15 net which they hid is their own foot t. H3920
10: 2 poor: let them be t in the devices that H8610
40:12 iniquities have t hold upon me, so that H5381
59:12 let them even be t in their pride: and H3920
83: 3 They have t crafty counsel against thy
85: 3 Thou hast t away all thy wrath: thou H5375
119:53 Horror hath t hold upon me because of H270
111 Thy testimonies have I t as an heritage
143 Trouble and anguish have t hold on H4672
Prv 3:26 and shall keep thy foot from being t. H3921
4:16 t away, unless they cause *some* to fall. H1497
6: 2 thou art t with the words of thy mouth. H3920
7:20 He hath t a bag of money with him, H3947
11: 6 shall be t in *their own* naughtiness. H3920
Ecc 2:18 which I had t under the sun: because H6001
3:14 to it, nor any thing t from it: and God H1639
7:26 her; but the sinner shall be t by her. H3920
9:12 the fishes that are t in an evil net, and as H270
Isa 6: 6 had t with the tongs from off the altar: H3947
7 iniquity is t away, and thy sin purged. H5493
7: 5 have t evil counsel against thee, saying,
8: 4 be t away before the king of Assyria. H5375
15 and be broken, and be snared, and be t. H3920
10:27 his burden shall be t away from off thy H5493
29 passage: they have t up their lodging at H3885
16:10 And gladness is t away, and joy out of H622
17: 1 Damascus is t away from *being* a city, H5493
21: 3 pain: pangs have t hold upon me, as the H270
23: 8 Who hath t this counsel against Tyre,
24:18 of the pit shall be t in the snare: for the H3920
28:13 and be broken, and snared, and t. H3920
33:20 *that* shall not be t down; not one of the H6813
36: 7 Hezekiah hath t away, and said to H5493
41: 9 *Thou* whom I have t from the ends of H2388
49:24 Shall the prey be t from the mighty, or H3947
25 mighty shall be t away, and the prey H3947
51:22 Behold, I have t out of thine hand the H3947
52: 5 that my people is t away for nought? H3947
53: 8 He was t from prison and from H3947
57: 1 and merciful men *are* t away, none H622
1 is t away from the evil *to come*. H622
64: 6 like the wind, have t us away. H5375
Jer 6:11 t, the aged with *him that is* full of days. H3920
24 anguish hath t hold of us, *and* pain, H2388
8: 9 they are dismayed and t: lo, they have H3920
21 black; astonishment hath t hold on me. H2388
12: 2 Thou hast planted them, yea, they have t
16: 5 them: for I have t away my peace from H622
29:22 And of them shall be t up a curse by all H3947
34: 3 but shalt surely be t, and delivered into H8610
38:23 hand, but shalt be t by the hand of the H8610
28 Jerusalem was t: and he was *there* when H3920
28 and he was *there* when Jerusalem was t. H3920
39: 5 when they had t him, they brought him H3947
40: 1 when he had t him being bound in H3947
10 and dwell in your cities that ye have t. H8610
48: 1 t: Misgab is confounded and dismayed. H3920
7 thou shalt also be t: and Chemosh shall H3920
33 And joy and gladness is t from the H622
41 Kerioth is t, and the strong holds are H3920
44 of the pit shall be t in the snare: for I H3920
46 t captives, and thy daughters captives. H3947
49:20 that he hath t against Edom; and H3289

Jer 49:24 have t her, as a woman in travail. H270
30 of Babylon hath t counsel against you,
50: 2 say, Babylon is t, Bel is confounded, H3920
9 thence she shall be t: their arrows *shall* H3920
24 and thou art also t, O Babylon, and H3920
45 that he hath t against Babylon; and H3289
51:31 of Babylon that his city is t at *one* end, H3920
41 How is Sheshach t! and how is the H3920
56 her mighty men are t, every one of their H3920
Lam 2: 6 And he hath violently t away his
4:20 of the LORD, was t in their pits, of H3920
Ezk 12:13 and he shall be t in my snare: and I will H8610
15: 3 Shall wood be t thereof to do any work? H3947
16:17 Thou hast also t thy fair jewels of my H3947
20 Moreover thou hast t thy sons and thy H3947
37 whom thou hast t pleasure, and all *them*
17:12 and hath t the king thereof, and H3947
13 And hath t of the king's seed, and H3947
13 with him, and hath t an oath of him: he H935
13 he hath also t the mighty of the land: H3947
20 and he shall be t in my snare, and I will H8610
18: 8 neither hath t any increase, *that* hath H3947
13 usury, and hath t increase: shall he H3947
17 *That* hath t off his hand from the poor, H7725
19: 4 The nations also heard of him; he was t H8610
8 their net over him: he was t in their pit. H8610
21:23 the iniquity, that they may be t. H8610
24 ye shall be t with the hand. H8610
22:12 In thee have they t gifts to shed blood; H3947
12 blood; thou hast t usury and increase, H3947
25 souls; they have t the treasure and H3947
25:15 revenge, and have t vengeance with a H5358
27: 5 trees of Senir: they have t cedars from H3947
33: 6 from among them, he is t away in his H3947
36: 3 and ye are t up in the lips of talkers, H5927
Dan 5: 2 had t out of the temple which H5312
3 vessels that were t out of the temple of H5312
6:23 So Daniel was t up out of the den, and H5267
7:12 their dominion t away: yet their lives H5709
8:11 the daily *sacrifice* was t away, and the H7311
11:12 *And* when he hath t away the H5375
12:11 daily *sacrifice* shall be t away, and the H5493
Hos 4: 3 the fishes of the sea also shall be t away. H622
Joel 3: 5 Because ye have t my silver and my H3947
Am 3: 4 cry out of his den, if he have t nothing? H3920
5 the earth, and have t nothing at all? H3920
12 of Israel be t out that dwell in Samaria H5337
4:10 sword, and have t away your horses; H7628
6:13 not t to us horns by our own strength? H3947
Mic 2: 9 have ye t away my glory for ever. H3947
4: 9 have t thee as a woman in travail. H2388
Zep 3:15 The LORD hath t away thy judgments, H5493
Zec 14: 2 the city shall be t, and the houses rifled, H3920
Mt 4:24 people that were t with divers diseases G4912
9:15 be t from them, and then shall they fast. G522
13:12 him shall be t away even that he hath. G142
16: 7 *It is* because we have t no bread. G2983
21:43 of God shall be t from you, and given G142
24:40 the one shall be t, and the other left. G3880
41 the one shall be t, and the other left. G3880
25:29 shall be t away even that which he hath. G142
27:59 And when Joseph had t the body, he G2983
28:12 the elders, and had t counsel, they gave G2983
Mk 2:20 shall be t away from them, and G522
4:25 him shall be t even that which he hath. G142
6:41 And when he had t the five loaves and G2983
9:36 t him in his arms, he said unto them, G1723
Lk 1: 1 Forasmuch as many have t in hand to G2021
4:38 wife's mother was t with a great fever; G4912
5: 5 night, and have t nothing: nevertheless G2983
9 draught of the fishes which they had t: G4815
18 bed a man which was t with a palsy: and
35 shall be t away from them, and G522
36 t out of the new agreeth not with the old.
8:18 be t even that which he seemeth to have. G142
37 for they were t with great fear: and G4912
9:17 and there was t up of fragments that G142
10:42 part, which shall not be t away from her. G851
11:52 Woe unto you, lawyers! for ye have t G142
17:34 shall be t, and the other shall be left. G3880
35 the one shall be t, and the other left. G3880
36 the one shall be t, and the other left. G3880
19: 8 poor; and if I have t any thing from any G4811
26 that he hath shall be t away from him. G142
Jn 7:44 And some of them would have t him; G4084
8: 3 him a woman t in adultery; and when G2638
4 was t in adultery, in the very act. G2638
13:12 their feet, and had t his garments, and G2983
19:31 broken, and *that* they might be t away. G142

Jn 20: 1 the stone t away from the sepulchre. G142
2 them, They have t away the Lord out of G142
13 Because they have t away my Lord, and G142
Act 1: 2 Until the day in which he was t up, after G353
9 they beheld, he was t up; and a cloud G1869
11 same Jesus, which is t up from you into G353
22 day that he was t up from us, must one G353
2:23 of God, ye have t, and by wicked hands G2983
8: 7 *them*: and many t with palsies, and that
33 In his humiliation his judgment was t G142
33 for his life is t from the earth. G142
17: 9 And when they had t security of Jason, G2983
20: 9 from the third loft, and was t up dead. G142
21: 6 And when we had t our leave one of G782
23:27 This man was t of the Jews, and should G4815
27:17 Which when they had t up, they used G142
20 we should be saved was then t away. G4014
33 continued fasting, having t nothing. G4355
40 And when they had t up the anchors, G4014
Ro 9: 6 Not as though the word of God hath t
1Co 5: 2 deed might be t away from among you. G1808
10:13 There hath no temptation t you but G2983
2Co 3:16 to the Lord, the veil shall be t away. G4014
1Th 2:17 But we, brethren, being t from you for a G642
2Th 2: 7 *will let*, until he be t out of the way. G1096
1Ti 5: 9 Let not a widow be t into the number G2639
2Ti 2:26 who are t captive by him at his will. G2221
Heb 5: 1 For every high priest t from among G2983
2Pt 2:12 beasts, made to be t and destroyed, G259
Rev 5: 8 And when he had t the book, the four G2983
11:17 because thou hast t to thee thy great G2983
19:20 And the beast was t, and with him the G4084

TAKER
Isa 24: 2 as with the t of usury, so with the

TAKEST
Ex 4: 9 water which thou t out of the river shall H3947
30:12 When thou t the sum of the children of H5375
Jdg 4: 9 the journey that thou t shall not be for H1980
1Ch 22:13 Then shalt thou prosper, if thou t heed H8104
Ps 104:29 are troubled: thou t away their breath, H622
144: 3 LORD, what *is* man, that thou t
Ecc 9: 9 thy labour which thou t under the sun. H6001
Isa 58: 3 our soul, and thou t no knowledge?
Lk 19:21 austere man: thou t up that thou layedst G142

TAKETH
Ex 20: 7 him guiltless that t his name in vain. H5375
Dt 5:11 *him* guiltless that t his name in vain. H5375
10:17 regardeth not persons, nor t reward: H3947
24: 6 pledge: for he t *a man's* life to pledge. H2254
25:11 her hand, and t him by the secrets: H2388
27:25 Cursed *be* he that t reward to slay an H3947
32:11 t them, beareth them on her wings: H3947
Jos 7:14 which the LORD t shall come according H3920
15:16 and t it, to him will I give H3920
Jdg 1:12 and t it, to him will I give H3920
1Sa 17:26 this Philistine, and t away the reproach H5493
1Ki 14:10 a man t away dung, till it be all gone. H1197
Job 5: 5 eateth up, and t it even out of the H3947
13 He t the wise in their own craftiness: H3920
9:12 Behold, he t away, who can hinder H2862
12:20 t away the understanding of the aged. H3947
24 He t away the heart of the chief of the H5493
21: 6 afraid, and trembling t hold on my flesh. H270
27: 8 hath gained, when God t away his soul? H7953
40:24 He t it with his eyes: *his* nose pierceth H3947
Ps 15: 3 t up a reproach against his neighbour. H5375
5 to usury, nor t reward against the H3947
118: 7 The LORD t my part with them that help
137: 9 Happy *shall he be*, that t and dasheth H270
147:10 he t not pleasure in the legs of a man.
11 The LORD t pleasure in them that fear
149: 4 For the LORD t pleasure in his people:
Prv 1:19 t away the life of the owners thereof. H3947
16:32 ruleth his spirit than he that t a city. H3920
17:23 A wicked *man* t a gift out of the bosom H3947
25:20 *As* he that t away a garment in cold H5710
26:17 him, *is like* one that t a dog by the ears. H2388
30:28 The spider t hold with her hands, and H8610
Ecc 1: 3 all his labour which he t under the sun? H5998
2:23 t not rest in the night. This is also vanity.
5:18 all his labour that he t under the sun all H5998
Isa 13:14 a sheep that no man t up: they shall H6908
40:15 he t up the isles as a very little thing. H5190
44:14 He heweth him down cedars, and t the H3947
51:18 *is there any* that t her by the hand of all H2388
56: 6 polluting it, and t hold of my covenant; H2388

Ezk 16:32 t strangers instead of her husband! H3947
33: 4 of the trumpet, and t not warning; if the
5 he that t warning shall deliver his soul.
Am 3:12 Thus saith the LORD; As the shepherd t H5337
Mt 4: 5 Then the devil t him up into the holy G3880
8 Again, the devil t him up into an G3880
9:16 is put in to fill it up t from the garment, G142
10:38 And he that t not his cross, and G2983
12:45 Then goeth he, and t with himself G3880
17: 1 And after six days Jesus t Peter, James, G3880
Mk 2:21 that filled it up t away from the old, and G142
4:15 immediately, and t away the word that G142
5:40 put them all out, he t the father and the G3880
9: 2 And after six days Jesus t *with him* G3880
18 And wheresoever he t him, he teareth G2638
14:33 And he t with him Peter and James and G3880
Lk 6:29 and him that t away thy cloak forbid G142
30 t away thy goods ask *them* not again. G142
8:12 the devil, and t away the word out of G142
9:39 And, lo, a spirit t him, and he suddenly G2983
11:22 and overcome him, he t from him all his G142
26 Then goeth he, and t *to him* seven G3880
16: 3 I do? for my lord t away from me the G851
Jn 1:29 God, which t away the sin of the world. G142
10:18 No man t it from me, but I lay it down of G142
15: 2 beareth not fruit he t away: and every G142
16:22 rejoice, and your joy no man t from you. G142
21:13 Jesus then cometh, and t bread, and G2983
Ro 3: 5 who t vengeance? (I speak as a man) G2018
1Co 3:19 He t the wise in their own craftiness. G1405
11:21 For in eating every one t before *other* G4301
Heb 5: 4 And no man t this honour unto G2983
10: 9 thy will, O God. He t away the first, that G337

TAKING

2Ch 19: 7 nor respect of persons, nor t of gifts. H4727
Job 5: 3 I have seen the foolish t root: but
Ps 119: 9 by t heed *thereto* according to thy word.
Jer 50:46 At the noise of the t of Babylon the H8610
Ezk 25:12 the house of Judah by t vengeance, and H5358
Hos 11: 3 I taught Ephraim also to go, t them by H3947
Mt 6:27 Which of you by t thought can add one
Mk 13:34 *For the Son of man is* as a man t a far
Lk 4: 5 And the devil, t him up into an high G321
12:25 And which of you with t thought can add
19:22 was an austere man, t up that I laid not G142
Jn 11:13 that he had spoken of t of rest in sleep.
Ro 7: 8 But sin, t occasion by the G2983
11 For sin, t occasion by the G2983
2Co 2:13 my brother: but t my leave of them, I
11: 8 I robbed other churches, t wages *of* G2983
Eph 6:16 Above all, t the shield of faith, G353
2Th 1: 8 In flaming fire t vengeance on them G1325
1Pt 5: 2 is among you, t the oversight *thereof,*
3Jn 7 went forth, t nothing of the Gentiles. G2983

TALE

Ex 5: 8 And the t of the bricks, which they did H4971
18 you, yet shall ye deliver the t of bricks. H8506
1Sa 18:27 gave them in full t to the king, that he
1Ch 9:28 they should bring them in and out by t. H4557
Ps 90: 9 we spend our years as a t *that is told.* H1899

TALEBEARER

Lev 19:16 Thou shalt not go up and down *as* a t H7400
Prv 11:13 A t revealeth secrets: but he H1980+H7400
18: 8 The words of a t *are* as wounds, and H5372
20:19 He that goeth about *as* a t revealeth H7400
26:20 so where *there is* no t, the strife ceaseth. H5372
22 The words of a t *are* as wounds, and H5372

TALENT

Ex 25:39 *Of* a t of pure gold shall he make it, H3603
37:24 *Of* a t of pure gold made he it, and all H3603
38:27 of the hundred talents, a t for a socket. H3603
2Sa 12:30 weight whereof *was* a t of gold with the H3603
1Ki 20:39 life, or else thou shalt pay a t of silver. H3603
2Ki 5:22 them, I pray thee, a t of silver, and two H3603
23:33 talents of silver, and a t of gold. H3603
1Ch 20: 2 found it to weigh a t of gold, and *there* H3603
2Ch 36: 3 talents of silver and a t of gold. H3603
Zec 5: 7 And, behold, there was lifted up a t of H3603
Mt 25:24 Then he which had received the one t G5007
25 and went and hid thy t in the earth: lo, G5007
28 Take therefore the t from him, and give G5007
Rev 16:21 the weight of a t: and men blasphemed G5006

TALENTS

Ex 38:24 twenty and nine t, and seven hundred H3603
25 *was* an hundred t, and a thousand H3603
27 And of the hundred t of silver were cast H3603
27 of the hundred t, a talent for a socket. H3603
29 *was* seventy t, and two thousand and H3603
1Ki 9:14 And Hiram sent to the king sixscore t H3603
28 t, and brought *it* to king Solomon. H3603
10:10 and twenty t of gold, and of spices H3603
14 hundred threescore and six t of gold, H3603
16:24 of Shemer for two t of silver, and built H3603
2Ki 5: 5 took with him ten t of silver, and six H3603
23 content, take two t. And he urged him, H3603
23 and bound two t of silver in two bags, H3603
15:19 Pul a thousand t of silver, that his hand H3603
18:14 t of silver and thirty talents of gold. H3603
14 talents of silver and thirty t of gold. H3603
23:33 t of silver, and a talent of gold. H3603
1Ch 19: 6 sent a thousand t of silver to hire them H3603
22:14 an hundred thousand t of gold, and a H3603
14 thousand t of silver; and of brass H3603
29: 4 *Even* three thousand t of gold, of the H3603
4 seven thousand t of refined silver, to H3603
7 gold five thousand t and ten thousand H3603
7 ten thousand t, and of brass eighteen H3603
7 eighteen thousand t, and one hundred H3603
7 and one hundred thousand t of iron. H3603
2Ch 3: 8 fine gold, *amounting* to six hundred t. H3603
8:18 four hundred and fifty t of gold, and H3603
9: 9 and twenty t of gold, and of spices H3603
13 and threescore and six t of gold; H3603
25: 6 out of Israel for an hundred t of silver. H3603
9 do for the hundred t which I have given H3603
27: 5 year an hundred t of silver, and ten H3603
36: 3 hundred t of silver and a talent of gold. H3603
Ezr 7:22 Unto an hundred t of silver, and to an H3604
8:26 hundred and fifty t of silver, and silver H3603
26 t, *and of* gold an hundred talents; H3603
26 talents, *and* of gold an hundred t; H3603
Est 3: 9 will pay ten thousand t of silver to the H3603
Mt 18:24 him, which owed him ten thousand t. G5007
25:15 And unto one he gave five t, to another G5007
16 Then he that had received the five t G5007
16 the same, and made *them* other five t. G5007
20 And so he that had received five t came G5007
20 brought other five t, saying, Lord, thou G5007
20 unto me five t: behold, I have gained G5007
20 I have gained beside them five t more. G5007
22 He also that had received two t came G5007
22 unto me two t: behold, I have gained G5007
22 I have gained two other t beside them. G5007
28 and give *it* unto him which hath ten t. G5007

TALES

Ezk 22: 9 In thee are men that carry t to shed H7400
Lk 24:11 as idle t, and they believed them not. G3026

TALITHA

Mk 5:41 and said unto her, T cumi; which is, G5008

TALK

Nu 11:17 And I will come down and t with thee H1696
Dt 5:24 God doth t with man, and he liveth. H1696
6: 7 and shalt t of them when thou sittest H1696
1Sa 2: 3 T no more so exceeding proudly; let H1696
2Ki 18:26 understand *it:* and t not with us in the H1696
1Ch 16: 9 Sing unto him, sing psalms unto him, t H7878
Job 11: 2 and should a man full of t be justified? H8193
13: 7 Will ye speak wickedly for God? and t H1696
15: 3 Should he reason with unprofitable t? or H1697
Ps 69:26 smitten; and they t to the grief of those H5608
71:24 My tongue also shall t of thy H1897
77:12 also of all thy work, and t of thy doings. H7878
105: 2 Sing unto him, sing psalms unto him: t H7878
119:27 so shall I t of thy wondrous works. H7878
145:11 of thy kingdom, and t of thy power; H1696
Prv 6:22 *when* thou awakest, it shall t with thee. H7878
14:23 In all labour there is profit: but the t of H1697
24: 2 destruction, and their lips t of mischief. H1696
Ecc 10:13 end of his t *is* mischievous madness. H6310
Jer 12: 1 with thee: yet let me t with thee of *thy* H1696
Ezk 3:22 the plain, and I will there t with thee. H1696
Dan 10:17 of this my lord t with this my lord? for H1696
Mt 22:15 how they might entangle him in *his* t. G3056
Jn 14:30 Hereafter I will not t much with you: G2980

TALKED

Gen 4: 8 And Cain t with Abel his brother: and it H559
17: 3 And Abram fell on his face: and God t H1696
35:13 him in the place where he t with him. H1696
14 in the place where he t with him, *even* a H1696
Gen 45:15 and after that his brethren t with him. H1696
Ex 20:22 that I have t with you from heaven. H1696
33: 9 and *the LORD* t with Moses. H1696
34:29 of his face shone while he t with him. H1696
31 unto him: and Moses t with them. H1696
Dt 5: 4 The LORD t with you face to face in the H1696
Jdg 14: 7 And he went down, and t with the H1696
1Sa 14:19 And it came to pass, while Saul t unto H1696
17:23 And as he t with them, behold, there H1696
1Ki 1:22 And, lo, while she yet t with the king, H1696
2Ki 2:11 still went on, and t, that, behold, *there* H1696
6:33 And while he yet t with them, behold, H1696
8: 4 And the king t with Gehazi the servant H1696
2Ch 25:16 And it came to pass, as he t with him, H1696
Jer 38:25 But if the princes hear that I have t H1696
Dan 9:22 And he informed *me,* and t with me, H1696
Zec 1: 9 And the angel that t with me said unto H1696
13 the angel that t with me *with* good H1696
19 And I said unto the angel that t with H1696
2: 3 And, behold, the angel that t with me H1696
4: 1 And the angel that t with me came H1696
4 to the angel that t with me, saying, H1696
5 Then the angel that t with me H1696
5: 5 Then the angel that t with me went H1696
10 Then said I to the angel that t with me, H1696
6: 4 t with me, What *are* these, my lord? H1696
Mt 12:46 While he yet t to the people, behold, *his* G2980
Mk 6:50 immediately he t with them, and saith G2980
Lk 9:30 And, behold, there t with him two men, G4814
24:14 And they t together of all these things G3656
32 within us, while he t with us by the G2980
Jn 4:27 marvelled that he t with the woman: G2980
Act 10:27 And as he t with him, he went in, and G4926
20:11 and eaten, and t a long while, even till G3656
26:31 And when they were gone aside, they t G2980
Rev 17: 1 seven vials, and t with me, saying unto G2980
21: 9 last plagues, and t with me, saying, G2980
15 And he that t with me had a golden G2980

TALKERS

Ezk 36: 3 of t, and *are* an infamy of the people: H3956
Tit 1:10 For there are many unruly and vain t G3151

TALKEST

Jdg 6:17 shew me a sign that thou t with me. H1696
1Ki 1:14 Behold, while thou yet t there with the H1696
Jn 4:27 seekest thou? or, Why t thou with her? G2980

TALKETH

Ps 37:30 wisdom, and his tongue t of judgment. H1696
Jn 9:37 seen him, and it is he that t with thee. G2980

TALKING

Gen 17:22 And he left off t with him, and God H1696
1Ki 18:27 *is* a god; either he is t, or he is pursuing, H7879
Est 6:14 And while they *were* yet t with him, H1696
Job 29: 9 The princes refrained t, and laid *their* H4405
Ezk 33:30 thy people still are t against thee by the H1696
Mt 17: 3 unto them Moses and Elias t with him. G4814
Mk 9: 4 with Moses: and they were t with Jesus. G4814
Eph 5: 4 Neither filthiness, nor foolish t, nor G3473
Rev 4: 1 it were of a trumpet t with me; which G2980

TALL

Dt 2:10 and many, and t, as the Anakims; H7311
21 A people great, and many, and t, as the H7311
9: 2 A people great and t, the children of the H7311
2Ki 19:23 will cut down the t cedar trees thereof, H6967
Isa 37:24 I will cut down the t cedars thereof, H6967

TALLER

Dt 1:28 *is* greater and t than we; the cities *are* H7311

TALMAI

Nu 13:22 Sheshai, and T, the children of Anak, H8526
Jos 15:14 Ahiman, and T, the children of Anak. H8526
Jdg 1:10 they slew Sheshai, and Ahiman, and T. H8526
2Sa 3: 3 the daughter of T king of Geshur; H8526
13:37 But Absalom fled, and went to T, the H8526
1Ch 3: 2 the daughter of T king of Geshur: the H8526

TALMON

1Ch 9:17 and Akkub, and T, and Ahiman, and H2929
Ezr 2:42 the children of T, the children of Akkub, H2929
Neh 7:45 the children of T, the children of Akkub, H2929
11:19 Moreover the porters, Akkub, T, and H2929
12:25 Meshullam, T, Akkub, *were* porters H2929

T

TAMAH
Neh 7:55 the children of Sisera, the children of T, H8547

TAMAR
Gen 38: 6 for Er his firstborn, whose name *was* T. H8559
11 Then said Judah to T his daughter in H8559
11 T went and dwelt in her father's house. H8559
13 And it was told T, saying, Behold thy H8559
24 Judah, saying, T thy daughter in law H8559
Ru 4:12 of Pharez, whom T bare unto Judah, of H8559
2Sa 13: 1 whose name *was* T; and Amnon the son H8559
2 sick for his sister T; for she *was* a virgin; H8559
4 I love T, my brother Absalom's sister. H8559
5 thee, let my sister T come, and give me H8559
6 I pray thee, let T my sister come, and H8559
7 Then David sent home to T, saying, Go H8559
8 So T went to her brother Amnon's H8559
10 And Amnon said unto T, Bring the H8559
10 of thine hand. And T took the cakes H8559
19 And T put ashes on her head, and rent H8559
20 not this thing. So T remained desolate H8559
22 because he had forced his sister T. H8559
32 from the day that he forced his sister T. H8559
14:27 whose name *was* T: she was a woman H8559
1Ch 2: 4 And T his daughter in law bare him H8559
3: 9 of the concubines, and T their sister. H8559
Ezk 47:19 And the south side southward, from T H8559
48:28 shall be even from T *unto* the waters of H8559

TAME
Mk 5: 4 in pieces: neither could any *man* t him. *G1150*
Jas 3: 8 But the tongue can no man t; *it is* an *G1150*

TAMED
Jas 3: 7 is t, and hath been tamed of mankind: *G1150*
7 is tamed, and hath been t of mankind: *G1150*

TAMMUZ
Ezk 8:14 behold, there sat women weeping for T. H8542

TANACH
Jos 21:25 of Manasseh, T with her suburbs, and H8590

TANGLE See ENTANGLE.

TANHUMETH
2Ki 25:23 Seraiah the son of T the Netophathite, H8576
Jer 40: 8 Seraiah the son of T, and the sons of H8576

TANNER
Act 9:43 many days in Joppa with one Simon a t. *G1038*
10: 6 He lodgeth with one Simon a t, whose *G1038*
32 of *one* Simon a t by the sea side: who, *G1038*

TAPESTRY
Prv 7:16 with coverings of t, with carved *works*, H4765
31:22 She maketh herself coverings of t; her H4765

TAPHATH
1Ki 4:11 had T the daughter of Solomon to wife: H2955

TAPPUAH
Jos 12:17 The king of T, one; the king of Hepher, H8599
15:34 And Zanoah, and En-gannim, T, and H8599
16: 8 The border went out from T westward H8599
17: 8 *Now* Manasseh had the land of T: but H8599
8 of Tappuah: but T on the border of H8599
1Ch 2:43 And the sons of Hebron; Korah, and T, H8599

TARAH
Nu 33:27 from Tahath, and pitched at T. H8646
28 And they removed from T, and pitched H8646

TARALAH
Jos 18:27 And Rekem, and Irpeel, and T, H8634

TARE
2Sa 13:31 Then the king arose, and t his H7167
2Ki 2:24 and t forty and two children of them. H1234
Mk 9:20 the spirit t him; and he fell on the *G4682*
Lk 9:42 threw him down, and t *him*. And Jesus *G4952*

TAREA
1Ch 8:35 Pithon, and Melech, and T, and Ahaz. H8390

TARES
Mt 13:25 t among the wheat, and went his way. *G2215*
26 forth fruit, then appeared the t also. *G2215*
27 in thy field? from whence then hath it t? *G2215*
29 t, ye root up also the wheat with them. *G2215*
30 ye together first the t, and bind them in *G2215*
36 unto us the parable of the t of the field. *G2215*
38 the t are the children of the wicked *one*; *G2215*
40 As therefore the t are gathered and *G2215*

TARGET
1Sa 17: 6 and a t of brass between his shoulders. H3591
1Ki 10:16 hundred *shekels* of gold went to one t. H6793
2Ch 9:15 *shekels* of beaten gold went to one t. H6793

TARGETS
1Ki 10:16 made two hundred t *of* beaten gold: six H6793
2Ch 9:15 made two hundred t *of* beaten gold: six H6793
14: 8 *of men* that bare t and spears, out of H6793

TARPELITES
Ezr 4: 9 the T, the Apharsites, the H2967

TARRIED
Gen 24:54 with him, and t all night; and they rose H3885
28:11 a certain place, and t there all night, H3885
31:54 eat bread, and t all night in the mount. H3885
Nu 9:19 And when the cloud t long upon the H748
22 a year, that the cloud t upon the H748
Jdg 3:25 And they t till they were ashamed: and, H2342
26 And Ehud escaped while they t, and H4102
19: 8 thee. And they t until afternoon, and H4102
Ru 2: 7 now, that she t a little in the house. H3427
1Sa 13: 8 And he t seven days, according to the H3176
14: 2 And Saul t in the uttermost part of H3427
2Sa 11: 1 Rabbah. But David t still at Jerusalem. H3427
15:17 him, and t in a place that was far off. H5975
29 again to Jerusalem: and they t there. H3427
20: 5 of Judah: but he t longer than the set H3186
2Ki 2:18 to him, (for he t at Jericho,) he said H3427
1Ch 20: 1 But David t at Jerusalem. And Joab H3427
Ps 68:12 she that t at home divided the spoil. H5116
Mt 25: 5 While the bridegroom t, they all *G5549*
Lk 1:21 that he t so long in the temple. *G5549*
2:43 the child Jesus t behind in Jerusalem; *G5278*
Jn 3:22 and there he t with them, and baptized. *G1304*
Act 9:43 And it came to pass, that he t many *G3306*
15:33 And after they had t *there* a space, they *G4160*
18:18 And Paul *after this* t *there* yet a good *G4357*
20: 5 These going before t for us at Troas. *G3306*
15 at Samos, and t at Trogyllium; and the *G3306*
21: 4 And finding disciples, we t there seven *G1961*
10 And as we t *there* many days, there *G1961*
25: 6 And when he had t among them more *G1304*
27:33 day that ye have t and continued *G4328*
28:12 And landing at Syracuse, we t *there* *G1961*

TARRIEST
Act 22:16 And now why t thou? arise, and be *G3195*

TARRIETH
1Sa 30:24 that t by the stuff: they shall part alike. H3427
Mic 5: 7 upon the grass, that t not for man, nor H6960

TARRY
Gen 19: 2 house, and t all night, and wash H3885
27:44 And t with him a few days, until thy H3427
30:27 in thine eyes, *t: for* I have learned by
45: 9 of all Egypt: come down unto me, t not: H5975
Ex 12:39 Egypt, and could not t, neither had they H4102
24:14 And he said unto the elders, T ye here H3427
Lev 14: 8 t abroad out of his tent seven days. H3427
Nu 22:19 Now therefore, I pray you, t ye also H3427
Jdg 5:28 coming? why t the wheels of his chariots? H309
6:18 he said, I will t until thou come again. H3427
19: 6 t all night, and let thine heart be merry. H3885
9 I pray you t all night: behold, the H3885
10 But the man would not t that night, but H3885
Ru 1:13 Would ye t for them till they were H7663
3:13 T this night, and it shall be in the H3885
1Sa 1:23 thee good; t until thou have weaned H3427
10: 8 days shalt thou t, till I come to thee, and H3176
14: 9 If they say thus unto us, T until we H1826
2Sa 10: 5 and the king said, T at Jericho until H3427
11:12 And David said to Uriah, T here to day H3427
15:28 See, I will t in the plain of the H4102
18:14 Then said Joab, I may not t thus with H3176
19: 7 there will not t one with thee this night: H3885
2Ki 2: 2 And Elijah said unto Elisha, T here, I H3427
4 And Elijah said unto him, Elisha, t H3427
6 And Elijah said unto him, T, I pray H3427
7: 9 our peace: if we t till the morning light, H2442
9: 3 open the door, and flee, and t not. H2442
14:10 up: glory *of this*, and t at home: for why H3427
1Ch 19: 5 And the king said, T at Jericho until H3427
Ps 101: 7 that telleth lies shall not t in my sight. H3559
Prv 23:30 They that t long at the wine; they that go H309
Isa 46:13 my salvation shall not t: and I will place H309
Jer 14: 8 man *that* turneth aside to t for a night? H3885
Hab 2: 3 not lie: though it t, wait for it; because H4102
3 because it will surely come, it will not t. H309
Mt 26:38 death: t ye here, and watch with me. *G3306*
Mk 14:34 unto death: t ye here, and watch. *G3306*
Lk 24:29 spent. And he went in to t with them. *G3306*
49 Father upon you: but t ye in the city of *G2523*
Jn 4:40 him that he would t with them: and he *G3306*
21:22 Jesus saith unto him, If I will that he t *G3306*
23 he t till I come, what *is that* to thee? *G3306*
Act 10:48 Then prayed they him to t certain days. *G1961*
18:20 When they desired *him* to t longer time *G3306*
28:14 were desired to t with them seven days: *G1961*
1Co 11:33 come together to eat, t one for another. *G1551*
16: 7 t a while with you, if the Lord permit. *G1961*
8 But I will t at Ephesus until Pentecost. *G1961*
1Ti 3:15 But if I t long, that thou mayest know *G1019*
Heb 10:37 shall come will come, and will not t. *G5549*

TARRYING
Ps 40:17 and my deliverer; make no t, O my God. H309
70: 5 and my deliverer; O LORD, make no t. H309

TARSHISH
Gen 10: 4 And the sons of Javan; Elishah, and T, H8659
1Ch 1: 7 And the sons of Javan; Elishah, and T, H8659
2Ch 9:21 For the king's ships went to T with the H8659
21 came the ships of T bringing gold, and H8659
20:36 ships to go to T: and they made the H8659
37 that they were not able to go to T. H8659
Est 1:14 Admatha, T, Meres, Marsena, *and* H8659
Ps 48: 7 Thou breakest the ships of T with an H8659
72:10 The kings of T and of the isles shall H8659
Isa 2:16 And upon all the ships of T, and upon H8659
23: 1 The burden of Tyre. Howl, ye ships of T; H8659
6 Pass ye over to T; howl, ye inhabitants H8659
10 of T: *there is* no more strength. H8659
14 Howl, ye ships of T: for your strength is H8659
60: 9 and the ships of T first, to bring thy H8659
66:19 the nations, *to* T, Pul, and Lud, that H8659
Jer 10: 9 plates is brought from T, and gold from H8659
Ezk 27:12 T *was* thy merchant by reason of the H8659
25 The ships of T did sing of thee in thy H8659
38:13 the merchants of T, with all the young H8659
Jna 1: 3 But Jonah rose up to flee unto T from H8659
3 a ship going to T: so he paid the fare H8659
3 unto T from the presence of the LORD. H8659
4: 2 I fled before unto T: for I knew that H8659

TARSUS
Act 9:11 Saul, of T: for, behold, he prayeth, *G5018*
30 to Caesarea, and sent him forth to T. *G5019*
11:25 Then departed Barnabas to T, for to *G5019*
21:39 *which am* a Jew of T, *a city* in Cilicia, a *G5018*
22: 3 *am* a Jew, born in T, *a city* in Cilicia, yet *G5019*

TARTAK
2Ki 17:31 And the Avites made Nibhaz and T, H8662

TARTAN
2Ki 18:17 And the king of Assyria sent T and H8661
Isa 20: 1 In the year that T came unto Ashdod, H8661

TASCHITH See AL-TASCHITH.

TASK
Ex 5:14 ye not fulfilled your t in making brick H2706
19 *ought* from your bricks of your daily t. H1697

TASKMASTERS
Ex 1:11 set over them t to afflict them H8269+H4522
3: 7 of their t; for I know their sorrows; H5065
5: 6 the same day the t of the people, and H5065
10 And the t of the people went out, and H5065
13 And the t hasted *them*, saying, Fulfil H5065
14 which Pharaoh's t had set over them, H5065

TASKS
Ex 5:13 *your* daily t, as when there was straw. H1697

TASTE
Ex 16:31 t of it *was* like wafers *made* with honey. H2940
Nu 11: 8 the t of it was as the taste of fresh oil. H2940
8 the taste of it was as the t of fresh oil. H2940

1Sa 14:43 and said, I did but **t** a little honey with H2938
2Sa 3:35 and more also, if I **t** bread, or ought H2938
19:35 can thy servant **t** what I eat or what I H2938
Job 6: 6 or is there *any* **t** in the white of an egg? H2940
30 cannot my **t** discern perverse things? H2441
12:11 try words? and the mouth **t** his meat? H2938
Ps 34: 8 O **t** and see that the LORD *is* good: H2938
119:103 How sweet are thy words unto my **t**! H2441
Prv 24:13 the honeycomb, *which is* sweet to thy **t**: H2441
Song 2: 3 delight, and his fruit *was* sweet to my **t**. H2441
Jer 48:11 therefore his **t** remained in him, and H2940
Jna 3: 7 herd nor flock, **t** any thing: let them H2938
Mt 16:28 which shall not **t** of death, till they see *G1089*
Mk 9: 1 which shall not **t** of death, till they have *G1089*
Lk 9:27 which shall not **t** of death, till they see *G1089*
14:24 were bidden shall **t** of my supper. *G1089*
Jn 8:52 my saying, he shall never **t** of death. *G1089*
Col 2:21 (Touch not; **t** not; handle not; *G1089*
Heb 2: 9 of God should **t** death for every man. *G1089*

TASTED
1Sa 14:24 So none of the people **t** *any* food. H2938
29 because I **t** a little of this honey. H2938
Dan 5: 2 Belshazzar, whiles he **t** the wine, H2942
Mt 27:34 he had **t** *thereof*, he would not drink. *G1089*
Jn 2: 9 When the ruler of the feast had **t** the *G1089*
Heb 6: 4 and have **t** of the heavenly gift, *G1089*
5 And have **t** the good word of God, and *G1089*
1Pt 2: 3 If so be ye have **t** that the Lord *is* *G1089*

TASTETH
Job 34: 3 For the ear trieth words, as the mouth **t** H2938

TATNAI
Ezr 5: 3 At the same time came to them **T**, H8674
6 The copy of the letter that **T**, governor H8674
6: 6 Now *therefore*, **T**, governor beyond the H8674
13 Then **T**, governor on this side the river, H8674

TATTLERS
1Ti 5:13 and not only idle, but **t** also and *G5397*

TAUGHT
Dt 4: 5 Behold, I have **t** you statutes and H3925
31:22 day, and **t** it the children of Israel. H3925
Jdg 8:16 and with them he **t** the men of Succoth. H3045
2Ki 17:28 **t** them how they should fear the LORD. H3384
2Ch 6:27 when thou hast **t** them the good way, H3384
17: 9 And they **t** in Judah, and *had* the book H3925
9 all the cities of Judah, and **t** the people. H3925
23:13 and such as **t** to sing praise. Then H3045
30:22 unto all the Levites that **t** the good H7919
35: 3 And said unto the Levites that **t** all H4000
Neh 8: 9 the Levites that **t** the people, said unto H995
Ps 71:17 O God, thou hast **t** me from my youth: H3925
119:102 from thy judgments: for thou hast **t** me. H3384
171 when thou hast **t** me thy statutes. H3925
Prv 4: 4 He **t** me also, and said unto me, Let H3384
11 I have **t** thee in the way of wisdom; I H3384
31: 1 the prophecy that his mother **t** him. H3256
Ecc 12: 9 preacher was wise, he still **t** the people H3925
Isa 29:13 toward me is **t** by the precept of men: H3925
40:13 or *being* his counsellor hath **t** him? H3045
14 him, and **t** him in the path of H3925
14 of judgment, and **t** him knowledge, and H3925
54:13 And all thy children *shall be* **t** of the H3928
Jer 2:33 thou also **t** the wicked ones thy ways. H3925
9: 5 truth: they have **t** their tongue to speak H3925
14 Baalim, which their fathers **t** them: H3925
12:16 liveth; as they **t** my people to swear H3925
13:21 punish thee? for thou hast **t** them *to be* H3925
28:16 thou hast **t** rebellion against the LORD. H1696
29:32 he hath **t** rebellion against the LORD. H1696
32:33 not the face: though I **t** them, rising up H3925
Ezk 23:48 may be **t** not to do after your lewdness. H3256
Hos 10:11 And Ephraim *is as* an heifer *that is* **t**, H3925
11: 3 I **t** Ephraim also to go, taking them by H7270
Zec 13: 5 man **t** me to keep cattle from my youth.
Mt 5: 2 And he opened his mouth, and **t** them, *G1321*
7:29 For he **t** them as *one* having authority, *G2258*
13:54 his own country, he **t** them in their *G1321*
28:15 did as they were **t**: and this saying is *G1321*
Mk 1:21 he entered into the synagogue, and **t**. *G1321*
22 doctrine: for he **t** them as one that had *G1321*
2:13 resorted unto him, and he **t** them. *G1321*
4: 2 And he **t** them many things by *G1321*
6:30 they had done, and what they had **t**. *G1321*
9:31 For he **t** his disciples, and said unto *G1321*
10: 1 and, as he was wont, he **t** them again. *G1321*
Mk 11:17 And he **t**, saying unto them, Is it not *G1321*
12:35 and said, while he **t** in the temple, How *G1321*
Lk 4:15 And he **t** in their synagogues, being *G1321*
31 and **t** them on the sabbath days. *G2258*
5: 3 down, and **t** the people out of the ship. *G1321*
6: 6 the synagogue and **t**: and there was a *G1321*
11: 1 us to pray, as John also **t** his disciples. *G1321*
13:26 presence, and thou hast **t** in our streets. *G1321*
19:47 And he **t** daily in the temple. But the *G2258*
20: 1 of those days, as he **t** the people in the *G1321*
Jn 6:45 they shall be all **t** of God. Every man *G1318*
59 the synagogue, as he **t** in Capernaum. *G1321*
7:14 Jesus went up into the temple, and **t**. *G1321*
28 Then cried Jesus in the temple as he **t**, *G1321*
8: 2 him; and he sat down, and **t** them. *G1321*
20 the treasury, as he **t** in the temple: and *G1321*
28 Father hath **t** me, I speak these things. *G1321*
18:20 to the world; I ever **t** in the synagogue, *G1321*
Act 4: 2 Being grieved that they **t** the people, *G1321*
5:21 the morning, and **t**. But the high priest *G1321*
11:26 the church, and **t** much people. And *G1321*
14:21 to that city, and had **t** many, they *G3100*
15: 1 down from Judaea **t** the brethren, *and* *G1321*
18:25 he spake and **t** diligently the things *G1321*
20:20 you, and have **t** you publickly, and *G1321*
22: 3 feet of Gamaliel, *and* **t** according to the *G3811*
Gal 1:12 of man, neither was I **t** *it*, but by the *G1321*
6: 6 Let him that is **t** in the word *G2727*
Eph 4:21 been **t** by him, as the truth is in Jesus: *G1321*
Col 2: 7 **t**, abounding therein with thanksgiving. *G1321*
1Th 4: 9 are **t** of God to love one another. *G2312*
2Th 2:15 been **t**, whether by word, or our epistle. *G1321*
Tit 1: 9 as he hath been **t**, that he may be able *G2596*
1Jn 2:27 as it hath **t** you, ye shall abide in him. *G1321*
Rev 2:14 of Balaam, who **t** Balac to cast a *G1321*

TAUNT
Jer 24: 9 and a proverb, a **t** and a curse, in all H8148
Ezk 5:15 So it shall be a reproach and a **t**, an H1422

TAUNTING
Hab 2: 6 against him, and a **t** proverb against H4426

TAVERNS
Act 28:15 and The three **t**: whom when Paul saw, *G4999*

TAXATION
2Ki 23:35 to his **t**, to give *it* unto Pharaoh-nechoh. H6187

TAXED
2Ki 23:35 to Pharaoh; but he **t** the land to give the H6186
Lk 2: 1 Augustus, that all the world should be **t**. *G583*
3 And all went to be **t**, every one into his *G583*
5 To be **t** with Mary his espoused wife, *G583*

TAXES
Dan 11:20 his estate a raiser of **t** *in* the glory of the H5065

TAXING
Lk 2: 2 (*And* this **t** was first made when *G582*
Act 5:37 in the days of the **t**, and drew away much *G582*

TEACH
Ex 4:12 mouth, and **t** thee what thou shalt say. H3384
15 mouth, and will **t** you what ye shall do. H3384
18:20 And thou shalt **t** them ordinances and H2094
24:12 have written; that thou mayest **t** them. H3384
35:34 his heart that he may **t**, *both* he, and H3384
Lev 10:11 And that ye may **t** the children of Israel H3384
14:57 To **t** when *it is* unclean, and when *it is* H3384
Dt 4: 1 which I **t** you, for to do *them*, H3925
9 but **t** them thy sons, and thy sons' sons; H3045
10 and *that* they may **t** their children. H3925
14 me at that time to **t** you statutes and H3925
5:31 which thou shalt **t** them, that they may H3925
6: 1 commanded to **t** you, that ye might do H3925
7 And thou shalt **t** them diligently unto H8150
11:19 And ye shall **t** them your children, H3925
17:11 which they shall **t** thee, and according H3384
20:18 That they **t** you not to do after all their H3925
24: 8 priests the Levites shall **t** you: as I H3384
31:19 song for you, and **t** it the children of H3925
33:10 They shall **t** Jacob thy judgments, and H3384
Jdg 3: 2 might know, to **t** them war, at the least H3925
13: 8 again unto us, and **t** us what we shall H3384
1Sa 12:23 I will **t** you the good and the right way: H3384
2Sa 1:18 (Also he bade them **t** the children of H3925
1Ki 8:36 Israel, that thou **t** them the good way H3384
2Ki 17:27 there, and let him **t** them the manner of H3384
2Ch 17: 7 to Michaiah, to **t** in the cities of Judah. H3925
Ezr 7:10 to **t** in Israel statutes and judgments. H3925
25 and **t** ye them that know *them* not. H3046
Job 6:24 **T** me, and I will hold my tongue: and H3384
8:10 Shall not they **t** thee, *and* tell thee, and H3384
12: 7 But ask now the beasts, and they shall **t** H3384
8 Or speak to the earth, and it shall **t** H3384
21:22 Shall *any* **t** God knowledge? seeing he H3925
27:11 I will **t** you by the hand of God: *that* H3384
32: 7 multitude of years should **t** wisdom. H3045
33:33 thy peace, and I shall **t** thee wisdom. H502
34:32 *That which* I see not **t** thou me: if I H3384
37:19 **T** us what we shall say unto him; *for* we H3045
Ps 25: 4 Shew me thy ways, O LORD; **t** me thy H3925
5 Lead me in thy truth, and **t** me: for H3925
8 therefore will he **t** sinners in the way. H3384
9 and the meek will he **t** his way. H3925
12 he **t** in the way *that* he shall choose. H3384
27:11 **T** me thy way, O LORD, and lead me in H3384
32: 8 I will instruct thee and **t** thee in the way H3384
34:11 me: I will **t** you the fear of the LORD. H3925
45: 4 right hand shall **t** thee terrible things. H3384
51:13 *Then* will I **t** transgressors thy ways; H3925
60:ttl of David, to **t**; when he strove with H3925
86:11 **T** me thy way, O LORD; I will walk in H3384
90:12 So **t** *us* to number our days, that we H3045
105:22 To bind his princes at his pleasure; and **t**
119:12 Blessed *art* thou, O LORD: **t** me thy H3925
26 thou heardest me: **t** me thy statutes. H3925
33 **T** me, O LORD, the way of thy statutes; H3384
64 is full of thy mercy: **t** me thy statutes. H3925
66 **T** me good judgment and knowledge: H3925
68 Thou *art* good, and doest good; **t** me H3925
108 O LORD, and **t** me thy judgments. H3925
124 unto thy mercy, and **t** me thy statutes. H3925
135 thy servant; and **t** me thy statutes. H3925
132:12 that I shall **t** them, their children H3925
143:10 **T** me to do thy will; for thou *art* my H3925
Prv 9: 9 will be yet wiser: **t** a just *man*, and he H3045
Isa 2: 3 Jacob; and he will **t** us of his ways, and H3384
28: 9 Whom shall he **t** knowledge? and H3384
26 him to discretion, *and* doth **t** him. H3384
Jer 9:20 of his mouth, and **t** your daughters H3925
31:34 And they shall **t** no more every man his H3925
Ezk 44:23 And they shall **t** my people *the* H3384
Dan 1: 4 whom they might **t** the learning and H3925
Mic 3:11 the priests thereof **t** for hire, and the H3384
4: 2 Jacob; and he will **t** us of his ways, and H3384
Hab 2:19 Arise, it shall **t**! Behold, it *is* laid over H3384
Mt 5:19 and shall **t** men so, he shall be *G1321*
19 shall do and **t** *them*, the same shall *G1321*
11: 1 thence to **t** and to preach in their cities. *G1321*
28:19 Go ye therefore, and **t** all nations, *G3100*
Mk 4: 1 And he began again to **t** by the sea side: *G1321*
6: 2 come, he began to **t** in the synagogue: *G1321*
34 and he began to **t** them many things. *G1321*
8:31 And he began to **t** them, that the Son of *G1321*
Lk 11: 1 unto him, Lord, **t** us to pray, as John *G1321*
12:12 For the Holy Ghost shall **t** you in the *G1321*
Jn 7:35 among the Gentiles, and **t** the Gentiles? *G1321*
9:34 dost thou **t** us? And they cast him out. *G1321*
14:26 my name, he shall **t** you all things, and *G1321*
Act 1: 1 of all that Jesus began both to do and **t**, *G1321*
4:18 speak at all nor **t** in the name of Jesus. *G1321*
5:28 that ye should not **t** in this name? and, *G1321*
42 ceased not to **t** and preach Jesus Christ. *G1321*
16:21 And **t** customs, which are not lawful *G2605*
1Co 4:17 as I **t** every where in every church. *G1321*
11:14 Doth not even nature itself **t** you, that, *G1321*
14:19 *my voice* I might **t** others also, than ten *G2727*
1Ti 1: 3 some that they **t** no other doctrine, *G2085*
2:12 But I suffer not a woman to **t**, nor to *G1321*
3: 2 behaviour, given to hospitality, apt to **t**; *G1317*
4:11 These things command and **t**. *G1321*
6: 2 the benefit. These things **t** and exhort. *G1321*
3 If any man **t** otherwise, and consent *G2085*
2Ti 2: 2 men, who shall be able to **t** others also. *G1321*
24 be gentle unto all *men*, apt to **t**, patient, *G1317*
Tit 2: 4 That they may **t** the young women to *G4994*
Heb 5:12 need that one **t** you again which *be* *G1321*
8:11 And they shall not **t** every man his *G1321*
1Jn 2:27 need not that any man **t** you: but as the *G1321*
Rev 2:20 a prophetess, to **t** and to seduce my *G1321*

TEACHER
1Ch 25: 8 small as the great, the **t** as the scholar. H995
Hab 2:18 image, and a **t** of lies, that the maker H3384
Jn 3: 2 that thou art a **t** come from God: for *G1320*
Ro 2:20 An instructor of the foolish, a **t** of *G1320*

1Ti 2: 7 a t of the Gentiles in faith and verity. *G1320*
2Ti 1:11 and an apostle, and a t of the Gentiles. *G1320*

TEACHERS
Ps 119:99 than all my t: for thy testimonies *are* H3925
Prv 5:13 And have not obeyed the voice of my t, H3384
Isa 30:20 yet shall not thy t be removed into a H3384
20 any more, but thine eyes shall see thy t: H3384
43:27 Thy first father hath sinned, and thy t H3887
Act 13: 1 prophets and t; as Barnabas, and *G1320*
1Co 12:28 prophets, thirdly t, after that miracles, *G1320*
29 *are* all t? *are* all workers of miracles? *G1320*
Eph 4:11 evangelists; and some, pastors and t; *G1320*
1Ti 1: 7 Desiring to be t of the law; *G2547*
2Ti 4: 3 to themselves t, having itching ears; *G1320*
Tit 2: 3 given to much wine, t of good things; *G3567*
Heb 5:12 For when for the time ye ought to be t, *G1320*
2Pt 2: 1 there shall be false t among you, who *G5572*

TEACHEST
Ps 94:12 O LORD, and t him out of thy law; H3925
Mt 22:16 thou art true, and t the way of God in *G1321*
Mk 12:14 of men, but t the way of God in truth: *G1321*
Lk 20:21 that thou sayest and t rightly, neither *G1321*
21 *of any*, but t the way of God truly: *G1321*
Act 21:21 of thee, that thou t all the Jews which *G1321*
Ro 2:21 Thou therefore which t another, *G1321*
21 teachest another, t thou not thyself? *G1321*

TEACHETH
2Sa 22:35 He t my hands to war; so that a bow of H3925
Job 35:11 Who t us more than the beasts of the H502
36:22 exalteth by his power: who t like him? H3384
Ps 18:34 He t my hands to war, so that a bow of H3925
94:10 t man knowledge, *shall not he know*? H3925
144: 1 strength, which t my hands to war, *and* H3925
Prv 6:13 with his feet, he t with his fingers; H3384
16:23 The heart of the wise t his mouth, and H7919
Isa 9:15 the prophet that t lies, he *is* the tail. H3384
48:17 thy God which t thee to profit, which H3925
Act 21:28 is the man, that t all *men* every where *G1321*
Ro 12: 7 ministering: or he that t, on teaching; *G1321*
1Co 2:13 man's wisdom t, but which the Holy *G1318*
13 the Holy Ghost t; comparing spiritual *G1318*
Gal 6: 6 unto him that t in all good things. *G2727*
1Jn 2:27 same anointing t you of all things, and *G1321*

TEACHING
2Ch 15: 3 without a t priest, and without law. H3384
Jer 32:33 up early and t *them*, yet they have H3925
Mt 4:23 And Jesus went about all Galilee, t in *G1321*
9:35 the cities and villages, t in their *G1321*
15: 9 But in vain they do worship me, t *for* *G1321*
21:23 unto him as he was t, and said, By what *G1321*
26:55 I sat daily with you t in the temple, and *G1321*
28:20 T them to observe all things *G1321*
Mk 6: 6 And he went round about the villages, t. *G1321*
7: 7 Howbeit in vain do they worship me, t *G1321*
14:49 I was daily with you in the temple t, and *G1321*
Lk 5:17 certain day, as he was t, that there were *G1321*
13:10 And he was t in one of the synagogues *G1321*
22 t, and journeying toward Jerusalem. *G1321*
21:37 And in the day time he was t in the *G1321*
23: 5 up the people, t throughout all Jewry, *G1321*
Act 5:25 in the temple, and t the people. *G1321*
15:35 in Antioch, t and preaching the word *G1321*
18:11 t the word of God among them. *G1321*
28:31 Preaching the kingdom of God, and t *G1321*
Ro 12: 7 ministering: or he that teacheth, on t; *G1319*
Col 1:28 every man, and t every man in all *G1321*
3:16 in all wisdom; t and admonishing one *G1321*
Tit 1:11 whole houses, t things which they *G1321*
2:12 T us that, denying ungodliness and *G3811*

TEAR
Jdg 8: 7 hand, then I will t your flesh with the H1758
Ps 7: 2 Lest he t my soul like a lion, rending *it* H2963
35:15 *it* not; they did t *me*, and ceased not: H7167
50:22 forget God, lest I t *you* in pieces, and H2963
Jer 15: 3 and the dogs to t, and the fowls of the H5498
16: 7 Neither shall *men* t *themselves* for H6536
Ezk 13:20 *them* fly, and I will t them from your H7167
21 Your kerchiefs also will I t, and deliver H7167
Hos 5:14 I, *even* I, will t and go away; I will take H2963
13: 8 like a lion: the wild beast shall t them. H1234
Am 1:11 and his anger did t perpetually, and he H2963
Nah 2:12 The lion did t in pieces enough for his H2963
Zec 11:16 of the fat, and t their claws in pieces. H6561

TEARETH
Dt 33:20 t the arm with the crown of the head. H2963
Job 16: 9 He t *me* in his wrath, who hateth me: H2963
18: 4 He t himself in his anger: shall the H2963
Mic 5: 8 and t in pieces, and none can deliver. H2963
Mk 9:18 And wheresoever he taketh him, he t *G4486*
Lk 9:39 crieth out; and it t him that he foameth *G4682*

TEARS
2Ki 20: 5 I have seen thy t: behold, I will heal H1832
Est 8: 3 besought him with t to put away the H1058
Job 16:20 *but* mine eye poureth out *t* unto God.
Ps 6: 6 to swim; I water my couch with my t. H1832
39:12 thy peace at my t: for I *am* a stranger H1832
42: 3 My t have been my meat day and H1832
56: 8 put thou my t into thy bottle: *are they* H1832
80: 5 Thou feedest them with the bread of t; H1832
5 givest them t to drink in great measure. H1832
116: 8 eyes from t, *and* my feet from falling. H1832
126: 5 They that sow in t shall reap in joy. H1832
Ecc 4: 1 sun: and behold the t of *such as were* H1832
Isa 16: 9 thee with my t, O Heshbon, and Elealeh: H1832
25: 8 will wipe away t from off all faces; and H1832
38: 5 I have seen thy t: behold, I will add unto H1832
Jer 9: 1 eyes a fountain of t, that I might weep H1832
18 t, and our eyelids gush out with waters. H1832
13:17 run down with t, because the LORD'S H1832
14:17 run down with t night and day, and H1832
31:16 thine eyes from t: for thy work shall be H1832
Lam 1: 2 She weepeth sore in the night, and her t H1832
2:11 Mine eyes do fail with t, my bowels are H1832
18 of Zion, let t run down like a river H1832
Ezk 24:16 nor weep, neither shall thy t run down. H1832
Mal 2:13 of the LORD with t, with weeping, and H1832
Mk 9:24 out, and said with t, Lord, I believe; *G1144*
Lk 7:38 wash his feet with t, and did wipe *them* *G1144*
44 my feet with t, and wiped *them* with *G1144*
Act 20:19 and with many t, and temptations, *G1144*
31 to warn every one night and day with t. *G1144*
2Co 2: 4 you with many t; not that ye should be *G1144*
2Ti 1: 4 of thy t, that I may be filled with joy; *G1144*
Heb 5: 7 strong crying and t unto him that was *G1144*
12:17 though he sought it carefully with t. *G1144*
Rev 7:17 shall wipe away all t from their eyes. *G1144*
21: 4 And God shall wipe away all t from *G1144*

TEATS
Isa 32:12 They shall lament for the t, for the H7699
Ezk 23: 3 they bruised the t of their virginity. H1717
21 in bruising thy t by the Egyptians for H1717

TEBAH
Gen 22:24 she bare also T, and Gaham, and H2875

TEBALIAH
1Ch 26:11 Hilkiah the second, T the third, H2882

TEBETH
Est 2:16 T, in the seventh year of his reign. H2887

TEDIOUS
Act 24: 4 Notwithstanding, that I be not further t *G1465*

TEETH
Gen 49:12 with wine, and his t white with milk. H8127
Nu 11:33 yet between their t, ere it was chewed, H8127
Dt 32:24 I will also send the t of beasts upon H8127
1Sa 2:13 with a fleshhook of three t in his hand; H8127
Job 4:10 the t of the young lions, are broken. H8127
13:14 Wherefore do I take my flesh in my t, H8127
16: 9 upon me with his t; mine enemy H8127
19:20 and I am escaped with the skin of my t. H8127
29:17 and plucked the spoil out of his t. H8127
41:14 his face? his t *are* terrible round about. H8127
Ps 3: 7 thou hast broken the t of the ungodly. H8127
35:16 they gnashed upon me with their t. H8127
37:12 just, and gnasheth upon him with his t. H8127
57: 4 of men, whose t *are* spears and arrows, H8127
58: 6 Break their t, O God, in their mouth: H8127
6 the great t of the young lions, O LORD. H4973
112:10 gnash with his t, and melt away: the H8127
124: 6 hath not given us *as* a prey to their t. H8127
Prv 10:26 As vinegar to the t, and as smoke to the H8127
30:14 *There is* a generation, whose t *are as* H8127
14 and their jaw t *as* knives, to devour H4973
Song 4: 2 Thy t *are* like a flock *of sheep that are* H8127
6: 6 Thy t *are* as a flock of sheep which go H8127
Isa 41:15 instrument having t: thou shalt thresh H6374
Jer 31:29 and the children's t are set on edge. H8127
31:30 sour grape, his t shall be set on edge. H8127
Lam 2:16 hiss and gnash the t: they say, We have H8127
3:16 He hath also broken my t with gravel H8127
Ezk 18: 2 and the children's t are set on edge? H8127
Dan 7: 5 of it between the t of it: and they said H8128
7 and it had great iron t: it devoured and H8128
19 dreadful, whose t *were of* iron, and his H8128
Joel 1: 6 number, whose t *are* the teeth of a lion, H8127
6 teeth *are* the t of a lion, and he hath H8127
6 and he hath the cheek t of a great lion. H4973
Am 4: 6 you cleanness of t in all your cities, and H8127
Mic 3: 5 that bite with their t, and cry, Peace; H8127
Zec 9: 7 from between his t: but he that H8127
Mt 8:12 shall be weeping and gnashing of t. *G3599*
13:42 there shall be wailing and gnashing of t. *G3599*
50 there shall be wailing and gnashing of t. *G3599*
22:13 shall be weeping and gnashing of t. *G3599*
24:51 shall be weeping and gnashing of t. *G3599*
25:30 shall be weeping and gnashing of t. *G3599*
27:44 with him, cast the same in his t. *G3679*
Mk 9:18 gnasheth with his t, and pineth away: *G3599*
Lk 13:28 and gnashing of t, when ye shall see *G3599*
Act 7:54 and they gnashed on him with *their* t. *G3599*
Rev 9: 8 and their t were as *the teeth* of lions. *G3599*
8 and their teeth were as *the* t of lions.

TEHAPHNEHES
Ezk 30:18 At T also the day shall be darkened, H8471

TEHINNAH
1Ch 4:12 and Paseah, and T the father of H8468

TEIL
Isa 6:13 shall be eaten: as a t tree, and as an oak, H424

TEKEL
Dan 5:25 written, MENE, MENE, T, UPHARSIN. H8625
27 T; Thou art weighed in the balances, H8625

TEKOA
1Ch 2:24 wife bare him Ashur the father of T. H8620
4: 5 And Ashur the father of T had two H8620
2Ch 11: 6 even Beth-lehem, and Etam, and T, H8620
20:20 the wilderness of T: and as they went H8620
Jer 6: 1 the trumpet in T, and set up a sign of H8620
Am 1: 1 among the herdmen of T, which he saw H8620

TEKOAH
2Sa 14: 2 And Joab sent to T, and fetched thence H8620
4 And when the woman of T spake to the H8621
9 And the woman of T said unto the H8621

TEKOITE
2Sa 23:26 the Paltite, Ira the son of Ikkesh the T, H8621
1Ch 11:28 Ira the son of Ikkesh the T, Abi-ezer the H8621
27: 9 son of Ikkesh the T: and in his course H8621

TEKOITES
Neh 3: 5 And next unto them the T repaired; but H8621
27 After them the T repaired another H8621

TEL-ABIB
Ezk 3:15 of the captivity at T, that dwelt by the H8512

TELAH
1Ch 7:25 and T his son, and Tahan his son, H8520

TELAIM
1Sa 15: 4 them in T, two hundred thousand H2923

TELASSAR
Isa 37:12 the children of Eden which *were* in T? H8515

TELEM
Jos 15:24 Ziph, and T, and Bealoth, H2928
Ezr 10:24 of the porters; Shallum, and T, and Uri. H2928

TEL-HARESHA
Neh 7:61 from Telmelah, T, Cherub, Addon, and H8521

TEL-HARSA
Ezr 2:59 from Telmelah, T, Cherub, Addan, *and* H8521

TELL
Gen 12:18 thou not t me that she *was* thy wife? H5046
15: 5 heaven, and t the stars, if thou be H5608
21:26 neither didst thou t me, neither yet H5046
22: 2 of the mountains which I will t thee of. H559
24:23 And said, Whose daughter *art* thou? t H5046

Gen 24:49 with my master, t me: and if not, tell H5046
49 tell me: and if not, t me; that I may H5046
26: 2 dwell in the land which I shall t thee of: H559
29:15 nought? t me, what shall thy wages be? H5046
31:27 me; and didst not t me, that I might H5046
32: 5 and I have sent to t my lord, that I may H5046
29 And Jacob asked him, and said, T me, I H5046
37:16 And he said, I seek my brethren: t me, I H5046
40: 8 belong to God? t me them, I pray you. H5608
43: 6 ill with me, as to t the man whether ye H5046
22 t who put our money in our sacks. H3045
45:13 And ye shall t my father of all my glory H5046
49: 1 that I may t you that which shall H5046
Ex 9: 1 Pharaoh, and t him, Thus saith the H1696
10: 2 And that thou mayest t in the ears of H5608
14:12 Is not this the word that we did t thee H1696
19: 3 of Jacob, and t the children of Israel; H5046
Lev 14:35 shall come and t the priest, saying, It H5046
Nu 14:14 And they will t it to the inhabitants of H559
21: 1 in the south, heard t that Israel came by
23: 3 t thee. And he went to an high place. H5046
Dt 17:11 which they shall t thee, thou shalt do: H559
32: 7 thee; thy elders, and they will t thee. H559
Jos 7:19 unto him; and t me now what thou H5046
Jdg 14:16 nor my mother, and shall I t it thee? H5046
16: 6 And Delilah said to Samson, T me, I H5046
10 and told me lies: now t me, I pray thee, H5046
13 and told me lies: t me wherewith thou H5046
20: 3 Israel, T us, how was this wickedness? H1696
Ru 3: 4 and he will t thee what thou shalt do. H5046
4: 4 redeem it, then t me, that I may know: H5046
1Sa 6: 2 the ark of the LORD? t us wherewith we H3045
9: 8 give to the man of God, to t us our way. H5046
18 in the gate, and said, T me, I pray thee, H5046
19 and will t thee all that is in thine heart. H5046
10:15 And Saul's uncle said, T me, I pray H5046
14:43 Then Saul said to Jonathan, T me what H5046
15:16 Stay, and I will t thee what the LORD H5046
17:55 As thy soul liveth, O king, I cannot t. H3045
19: 3 thee; and what I see, that I will t thee. H5046
20: 9 upon thee, then would not I t it thee? H5046
10 Who shall t me? or what if thy father H5046
22:22 that he would surely t Saul: I have H5046
23:11 I beseech thee, t thy servant. And the H5046
27:11 Lest they should t on us, saying, So did H5046
2Sa 1: 4 I pray thee, t me. And he answered, H5046
20 T it not in Gath, publish it not in the H5046
7: 5 Go and t my servant David, Thus saith H559
12:18 of David feared to t him that the child H5046
18 if we t him that the child is dead? H559
22 I said, Who can t whether GOD will be H3045
13: 4 to day? wilt thou not t me? And Amnon H5046
15:35 t it to Zadok and Abiathar the priests. H5046
17:16 Now therefore send quickly, and t H5046
18:21 Then said Joab to Cushi, Go t the king H5046
1Ki 1:20 thou shouldest t them who shall sit on H5046
14: 3 t thee what shall become of the child. H5046
7 Go, t Jeroboam, Thus saith the LORD H559
18: 8 And he answered him, I am: go, t thy H559
11 And now thou sayest, Go, t thy lord, H559
12 so when I come and t Ahab, and he H5046
14 And now thou sayest, Go, t thy lord, H559
20: 9 of Ben-hadad, T my lord the king, All H559
11 and said, T him, Let not him that H1696
22:16 thee that thou t me nothing but that H1696
18 Did I not t thee that he would prophesy H559
2Ki 4: 2 shall I do for thee? t me, what hast thou H5046
7: 9 we may go and t the king's household. H5046
8: 4 of God, saying, T me, I pray thee, all H5608
9:12 And they said, It is false; t us now. And H5046
15 out of the city to go to t it in Jezreel. H5046
20: 5 Turn again, and t Hezekiah the captain H559
22:15 of Israel, T the man that sent you to me, H559
1Ch 17: 4 Go and t David my servant, Thus saith H559
10 Furthermore I t thee that the LORD H5046
21:10 Go and t David, saying, Thus saith the H1696
2Ch 18:17 Did I not t thee that he would not H559
34:23 Israel, T ye the man that sent you to me, H559
Job 1:15 and I only am escaped alone to t thee. H5046
16 and I only am escaped alone to t thee. H5046
17 and I only am escaped alone to t thee. H5046
19 and I only am escaped alone to t thee. H5046
8:10 Shall not they teach thee, and t thee, and H559
12: 7 fowls of the air, and they shall t thee: H5046
34:34 Let men of understanding t me, and let a H559
Ps 22:17 I may t all my bones: they look and H5608
26: 7 and t of all thy wondrous works. H5608
48:12 round about her: t the towers thereof. H5608
13 ye may t it to the generation following. H5608
Ps 50:12 If I were hungry, I would not t thee: for H559
Prv 30: 4 what is his son's name, if thou canst t? H3045
Ecc 6:12 for who can t a man what shall be H5046
8: 7 be: for who can t him when it shall be? H5046
10:14 a man cannot t what shall be; and H3045
14 what shall be after him, who can t him? H5046
20 which hath wings shall t the matter. H5046
Song 1: 7 T me, O thou whom my soul loveth, H5046
5: 8 that ye t him, that I am sick of love. H5046
Isa 5: 5 And now go to; I will t you what I will H3045
6: 9 And he said, Go, and t this people, Hear H559
19:12 men? and let them t thee now, and let H5046
42: 9 before they spring forth I t you of them. H8085
45:21 T ye, and bring them near; yea, let H5046
48:20 singing declare ye, t this, utter it even H8085
Jer 15: 2 then thou shalt t them, Thus saith the H559
19: 2 there the words that I shall t thee, H1696
23:27 dreams which they t every man to his H5608
28 a dream, let him t a dream; and he that H5608
32 the LORD, and do t them, and cause H5608
28:13 Go and t Hananiah, saying, Thus saith H559
34: 2 king of Judah, and t him, Thus saith the H559
35:13 of Israel; Go and t the men of Judah and H559
36:16 will surely t the king of all these words. H5046
17 And they asked Baruch, saying, T us H5046
48:20 t ye it in Arnon, that Moab is spoiled, H5046
Ezk 3:11 unto them, and t them, Thus saith the H559
12:23 T them therefore, Thus saith the Lord H559
17:12 these things mean? t them, Behold, the H559
24:19 unto me, Wilt thou not t us what these H5046
Dan 2: 4 O king, live for ever: t thy servants the H560
7 and said, Let the king t his servants the H560
9 changed: therefore t me the dream, and H560
36 This is the dream; and we will t the H560
4: 9 troubleth thee, t me the visions of my H560
Joel 1: 3 T ye your children of it, and let your H5608
3 let your children t their children, and
Jna 1: 8 Then said they unto him, T us, we pray H5046
3: 9 Who can t if God will turn and repent, H3045
Mt 8: 4 And Jesus saith unto him, See thou t no G2036
10:27 What I t you in darkness, that speak ye G3004
16:20 t no man that he was Jesus the Christ. G2036
17: 9 them, saying, T the vision to no man, G2036
18:15 thee, go and t him his fault between G1651
17 And if he shall neglect to hear them, t it G2036
21: 5 T ye the daughter of Sion, Behold, thy G2036
24 thing, which if ye t me, I in like wise G2036
24 me, I in like wise will t you by what G2046
27 said, We cannot t. And he said unto G1492
27 them, Neither t I you by what authority G3004
22: 4 servants, saying, T them which are G2036
17 T us therefore, What thinkest thou? Is G2036
24: 3 him privately, saying, T us, when shall G2036
26:63 God, that thou t us whether thou be G2036
28: 7 And go quickly, and t his disciples that G2036
9 And as they went to t his disciples, G518
10 Be not afraid: go t my brethren that they G518
Mk 1:30 of a fever, and anon they t him of her. G3004
5:19 to thy friends, and t them how great G312
7:36 that they should t no man: but the G2036
8:26 the town, nor t it to any in the town. G2036
30 them that they should t no man of him. G3004
9: 9 that they should t no man what things G1334
10:32 and began to t them what things G3004
11:29 me, and I will t you by what authority G2046
33 unto Jesus, We cannot t. And Jesus G1492
33 unto them, Neither do I t you by what G3004
13: 4 T us, when shall these things be? and G2036
16: 7 But go your way, t his disciples and G2036
Lk 4:25 But I t you of a truth, many widows G3004
5:14 And he charged him to t no man: but G2036
7:22 Go your way, and t John what things ye G518
42 them both. T me therefore, which G2036
8:56 they should t no man what was done. G2036
9:21 them to t no man that thing; G2036
27 But I t you of a truth, there be some G3004
10:24 For I t you, that many prophets and G3004
12:51 earth? I t you, Nay; but rather division: G3004
59 I t thee, thou shalt not depart thence, G3004
13: 3 I t you, Nay: but, except ye repent, ye G3004
5 I t you, Nay: but, except ye repent, ye G3004
27 But he shall say, I t you, I know you not G3004
32 And he said unto them, Go ye, and t G2036
17:34 I t you, in that night there shall be two G3004
18: 8 I t you that he will avenge them G3004
14 I t you, this man went down to his G3004
19:40 said unto them, I t you that, if these G3004
20: 2 And spake unto him, saying, T us, by G2036
7 that they could not t whence it was. G1492
Lk 20: 8 And Jesus said unto them, Neither t I G3004
22:34 And he said, I t thee, Peter, the cock G3004
67 Art thou the Christ? t us. And he said G2036
67 them, If I t you, ye will not believe: G2036
Jn 3: 8 but canst not t whence it cometh, and G1492
12 ye believe, if I t you of heavenly things? G2036
4:25 when he is come, he will t us all things. G312
8:14 t whence I come, and whither I go. G1492
45 And because I t you the truth, ye G3004
10:24 If thou be the Christ, t us plainly. G2036
12:22 and again Andrew and Philip t Jesus. G3004
13:19 Now I t you before it come, that, when G3004
16: 7 Nevertheless I t you the truth; It is G3004
18 little while? we cannot t what he saith. G3756
18:34 of thyself, or did others t it thee of me? G2036
20:15 borne him hence, t me where thou hast G2036
Act 5: 8 And Peter answered unto her, T me G2036
10: 6 shall t thee what thou oughtest to do. G2980
11:14 Who shall t thee words, whereby thou G2980
15:27 also t you the same things by mouth. G518
17:21 either to t, or to hear some new thing.) G3004
22:27 T me, art thou a Roman? He said, Yea. G3004
23:17 for he hath a certain thing to t him. G518
19 him, What is that thou hast to t me? G518
22 him, See thou t no man that thou hast G1583
2Co 12: 2 the body, I cannot t; or whether out of G1492
2 of the body, I cannot t: God knoweth;) G1492
3 of the body, I cannot t: God knoweth;) G1492
Gal 4:16 your enemy, because I t you the truth? G226
21 T me, ye that desire to be under the G3004
5:21 like: of the which I t you before, as I G4302
Php 3:18 you often, and now t you even weeping, G3004
Heb 11:32 would fail me to t of Gedeon, and of G1334
Rev 17: 7 thou marvel? I will t thee the mystery of G2046

TELLEST

Ps 56: 8 Thou t my wanderings: put thou my H5608

TELLETH

2Sa 7:11 t thee that he will make thee an house. H5046
2Ki 6:12 that is in Israel, t the king of Israel the H5046
Ps 41: 6 to itself; when he goeth abroad, he t it. H1696
101: 7 he that t lies shall not tarry in my sight. H1696
147: 4 He t the number of the stars; he calleth H4487
Jer 33:13 of him that t them, saith the LORD. H4487
Jn 12:22 Philip cometh and t Andrew: and again G3004

TELLING

Jdg 7:15 And it was so, when Gideon heard the t H4557
2Sa 11:19 t the matters of the war unto the king, H1696
2Ki 8: 5 And it came to pass, as he was t the H5608

TELMELAH

Ezr 2:59 went up from T, Tel-harsa, Cherub, H8528
Neh 7:61 went up also from T, Tel-haresha, H8528

TEMA

Gen 25:15 Hadar, and T, Jetur, Naphish, and H8485
1Ch 1:30 and Dumah, Massa, Hadad, and T, H8485
Job 6:19 The troops of T looked, the companies H8485
Isa 21:14 The inhabitants of the land of T H8485
Jer 25:23 Dedan, and T, and Buz, and all that are H8485

TEMAN

Gen 36:11 And the sons of Eliphaz were T, Omar, H8487
15 son of Esau; duke T, duke Omar, duke H8487
42 Duke Kenaz, duke T, duke Mibzar, H8487
1Ch 1:36 The sons of Eliphaz; T, and Omar, H8487
53 Duke Kenaz, duke T, duke Mibzar, H8487
Jer 49: 7 no more in T? is counsel perished H8487
20 the inhabitants of T: Surely the least of H8487
Ezk 25:13 it desolate from T; and they of Dedan H8487
Am 1:12 But I will send a fire upon T, which H8487
Oba 9 And thy mighty men, O T, shall be H8487
Hab 3: 3 God came from T, and the Holy One H8487

TEMANI

Gen 36:34 of the land of T reigned in his stead. H8489

TEMANITE

Job 2:11 place; Eliphaz the T, and Bildad the H8489
4: 1 Then Eliphaz the T answered and said, H8489
15: 1 Then answered Eliphaz the T, and said, H8489
22: 1 Then Eliphaz the T answered and said, H8489
42: 7 to Eliphaz the T, My wrath is kindled H8489
9 So Eliphaz the T and Bildad the H8489

TEMANITES

1Ch 1:45 the land of the T reigned in his stead. H8489

TEMENI
1Ch 4: 6 and Hepher, and T, and Haahashtari. H8488

TEMPER
Ezk 46:14 of an hin of oil, to t with the fine flour; H7450

TEMPERANCE
Act 24:25 And as he reasoned of righteousness, t, G1466
Gal 5:23 Meekness, t: against such there is no G1466
2Pt 1: 6 And to knowledge t; and to temperance G1466
6 And to knowledge temperance; and to t G1466

TEMPERATE
1Co 9:25 for the mastery is t in all things. Now G1467
Tit 1: 8 a lover of good men, sober, just, holy, t; G1468
2: 2 That the aged men be sober, grave, t, G4998

TEMPERED
Ex 29: 2 cakes unleavened t with oil, and wafers H1101
30:35 apothecary, t together, pure *and* holy: H4414
1Co 12:24 need: but God hath t the body together, G4786

TEMPEST
Job 9:17 For he breaketh me with a t, and H8183
27:20 Terrors take hold on him as waters, a t H5492
Ps 11: 6 t: *this shall be* the portion of their cup. H7307
55: 8 my escape from the windy storm *and* t. H5591
83:15 So persecute them with thy t, and make H5591
Isa 28: 2 strong one, *which* as a t of hail *and* a H2230
29: 6 and t, and the flame of devouring fire. H5591
30:30 *with* scattering, and t, and hailstones. H2230
32: 2 a covert from the t; as rivers of water in H2230
54:11 O thou afflicted, tossed with t, *and* not H5590
Am 1:14 with a t in the day of the whirlwind: H5591
Jna 1: 4 was a mighty t in the sea, so that the H5591
12 for my sake this great t *is* upon you. H5591
Mt 8:24 And, behold, there arose a great t in G4578
Act 27:18 a t, the next *day* they lightened the ship; G5492
20 and no small t lay on *us*, all hope that G5494
Heb 12:18 unto blackness, and darkness, and t, G2366
2Pt 2:17 are carried with a t; to whom the mist G2978

TEMPESTUOUS
Ps 50: 3 and it shall be very t round about him. H8175
Jna 1:11 unto us? for the sea wrought, and was t. H5590
13 sea wrought, and was t against them. H5590
Act 27:14 against it a t wind, called Euroclydon. G5189

TEMPLE
1Sa 1: 9 a seat by a post of the t of the LORD. H1964
3: 3 went out in the t of the LORD, where H1964
2Sa 22: 7 his t, and my cry *did enter* into his ears. H1964
1Ki 6: 3 And the porch before the t of the house, H1964
5 about, *both* of the t and of the oracle: H1964
17 And the house, that *is*, the t before it, H1964
33 So also made he for the door of the t H1964
7:21 in the porch of the t: and he set up the H1964
50 the doors of the house, *to wit*, of the t. H1964
2Ki 11:10 shields, that *were* in the t of the LORD. H1004
11 right corner of the t to the left corner of H1004
11 the t, *along* by the altar and the temple. H1004
11 the temple, *along* by the altar and the t. H1004
13 to the people into the t of the LORD. H1004
18:16 the doors of the t of the LORD, and H1964
23: 4 forth out of the t of the LORD all the H1964
24:13 t of the LORD, as the LORD had said. H1964
1Ch 6:10 the t that Solomon built in Jerusalem:) H1004
10:10 fastened his head in the t of Dagon. H1004
2Ch 3:17 the pillars before the t, one on the right H1964
4: 7 set *them* in the t, five on the right hand, H1964
8 placed *them* in the t, five on the right H1964
22 doors of the house of the t, *were of* gold. H1964
23:10 right side of the t to the left side of the H1004
10 the left side of the t, along by the altar H1004
10 altar and the t, by the king round about. H1004
26:16 and went into the t of the LORD to H1964
27: 2 not into the t of the LORD. And the H1964
29:16 they found in the t of the LORD into the H1964
35:20 had prepared the t, Necho king of Egypt H1004
36: 7 and put them in his t at Babylon. H1964
Ezr 3: 6 of the t of the LORD was not *yet* laid. H1964
10 foundation of the t of the LORD, they H1964
4: 1 the t unto the LORD God of Israel; H1964
5:14 took out of the t that *was* in Jerusalem, H1965
14 them into the t of Babylon, those did H1965
14 take out of the t of Babylon, and they H1965
15 them into the t that *is* in Jerusalem, H1965
6: 5 forth out of the t which *is* at Jerusalem, H1965
5 again unto the t which *is* at Jerusalem, H1965
Neh 6:10 of God, within the t, and let us shut the H1964
10 the doors of the t: for they will come to H1964
11 the t to save his life? I will not go in. H1964
Ps 5: 7 fear will I worship toward thy holy t. H1964
11: 4 The LORD *is* in his holy t, the LORD'S H1964
18: 6 my voice out of his t, and my cry came H1964
27: 4 of the LORD, and to inquire in his t. H1964
29: 9 his t doth every one speak of *his* glory. H1964
48: 9 O God, in the midst of thy t. H1964
65: 4 of thy house, *even* of thy holy t. H1964
68:29 Because of thy t at Jerusalem shall H1964
79: 1 thy holy t have they defiled; they H1964
138: 2 I will worship toward thy holy t, and H1964
Isa 6: 1 and lifted up, and his train filled the t. H1964
44:28 to the t, Thy foundation shall be laid. H1964
66: 6 a voice from the t, a voice of the LORD H1964
Jer 7: 4 saying, The t of the LORD, The temple H1964
4 of the LORD, The t of the LORD, The H1964
4 LORD, The t of the LORD, *are* these. H1964
24: 1 *were* set before the t of the LORD, after H1964
50:28 LORD our God, the vengeance of his t. H1964
51:11 of the LORD, the vengeance of his t. H1964
Ezk 8:16 at the door of the t of the LORD, H1964
16 backs toward the t of the LORD, and H1964
41: 1 Afterward he brought me to the t, and H1964
4 cubits, before the t: and he said unto H1964
15 inner t, and the porches of the court; H1964
20 trees made, and *on* the wall of the t. H1964
21 The posts of the t *were* squared, *and* H1964
23 And the t and the sanctuary had two H1964
25 on the doors of the t, cherubims and H1964
42: 8 lo, before the t *were* an hundred cubits. H1964
Dan 5: 2 had taken out of the t which *was* in H1965
3 taken out of the t of the house of God H1965
Am 8: 3 And the songs of the t shall be howlings H1964
Jna 2: 4 yet I will look again toward thy holy t. H1964
7 came in unto thee, into thine holy t. H1964
Mic 1: 2 against you, the Lord from his holy t. H1964
Hab 2:20 But the LORD *is* in his holy t: let all the H1964
Hag 2:15 laid upon a stone in the t of the LORD: H1964
18 of the LORD'S t was laid, consider *it*. H1964
Zec 6:12 and he shall build the t of the LORD: H1964
13 Even he shall build the t of the LORD; H1964
14 for a memorial in the t of the LORD. H1964
15 and build in the t of the LORD, and ye H1964
8: 9 was laid, that the t might be built. H1964
Mal 3: 1 come to his t, even the messenger H1964
Mt 4: 5 and setteth him on a pinnacle of the t, G2411
12: 5 the priests in the t profane the sabbath, G2411
6 in this place is *one* greater than the t. G2411
21:12 And Jesus went into the t of God, and G2411
12 and bought in the t, and overthrew the G2411
14 to him in the t; and he healed them. G2411
15 crying in the t, and saying, Hosanna G2411
23 And when he was come into the t, the G2411
23:16 shall swear by the t, it is nothing; but G3485
16 by the gold of the t, he is a debtor! G3485
17 gold, or the t that sanctifieth the gold? G3485
21 And whoso shall swear by the t, G3485
35 ye slew between the t and the altar. G3485
24: 1 departed from the t: and his disciples G2411
1 for to shew him the buildings of the t. G2411
26:55 in the t, and ye laid no hold on me. G2411
61 t of God, and to build it in three days. G3485
27: 5 of silver in the t, and departed, and G3485
40 And saying, Thou that destroyest the t, G3485
51 And, behold, the veil of the t was rent G3485
Mk 11:11 and into the t: and when he had looked G2411
15 went into the t, and began to cast out G2411
15 and bought in the t, and overthrew the G2411
16 should carry *any* vessel through the t. G2411
27 was walking in the t, there come to him G2411
12:35 he taught in the t, How say the scribes G2411
13: 1 And as he went out of the t, one of his G2411
3 over against the t, Peter and James and G2411
14:49 I was daily with you in the t teaching, G2411
58 We heard him say, I will destroy this t G3485
15:29 the t, and buildest *it* in three days, G3485
38 And the veil of the t was rent in twain G3485
Lk 1: 9 when he went into the t of the Lord. G3485
21 that he tarried so long in the t. G3485
22 a vision in the t: for he beckoned unto G3485
2:27 And he came by the Spirit into the t: G2411
37 not from the t, but served *God* with G2411
46 found him in the t, sitting in the midst G2411
4: 9 a pinnacle of the t, and said unto him, G2411
11:51 the altar and the t: verily I say unto you, G3624
18:10 Two men went up into the t to pray; the G2411
19:45 And he went into the t, and began to G2411
Lk 19:47 And he taught daily in the t. But the G2411
20: 1 the people in the t, and preached the G2411
21: 5 And as some spake of the t, how it was G2411
37 teaching in the t; and at night he went G2411
38 to him in the t, for to hear him. G2411
22:52 captains of the t, and the elders, which G2411
53 When I was daily with you in the t, ye G2411
23:45 the veil of the t was rent in the midst. G3485
24:53 And were continually in the t, praising G2411
Jn 2:14 And found in the t those that sold oxen G2411
15 them all out of the t, and the sheep, and G2411
19 t, and in three days I will raise it up. G3485
20 six years was this t in building, and G3485
21 But he spake of the t of his body. G3485
5:14 Afterward Jesus findeth him in the t, G2411
7:14 Jesus went up into the t, and taught. G2411
28 Then cried Jesus in the t as he taught, G2411
8: 2 again into the t, and all the people came G2411
20 as he taught in the t: and no man laid G2411
59 and went out of the t, going through the G2411
10:23 And Jesus walked in the t in Solomon's G2411
11:56 they stood in the t, What think ye, that G2411
18:20 and in the t, whither the Jews always G2411
Act 2:46 one accord in the t, and breaking bread G2411
3: 1 up together into the t at the hour of G2411
2 daily at the gate of the t which is called G2411
2 ask alms of them that entered into the t; G2411
3 about to go into the t asked an alms. G2411
8 with them into the t, walking, and G2411
10 gate of the t: and they were filled G2411
4: 1 t, and the Sadducees, came upon them, G2411
5:20 Go, stand and speak in the t to the G2411
21 entered into the t early in the morning, G2411
24 and the captain of the t and the chief G2411
25 in the t, and teaching the people. G2411
42 And daily in the t, and in every house, G2411
19:27 but also that the t of the great goddess G2411
21:26 them entered into the t, to signify the G2411
27 they saw him in the t, stirred up all the G2411
28 the t, and hath polluted this holy place. G2411
29 that Paul had brought into the t.) G2411
30 t: and forthwith the doors were shut. G2411
22:17 while I prayed in the t, I was in a trance; G2411
24: 6 to profane the t: whom we took, and G2411
12 And they neither found me in the t G2411
18 found me purified in the t, neither with G2411
25: 8 neither against the t, nor yet against G2411
26:21 me in the t, and went about to kill *me*. G2411
1Co 3:16 Know ye not that ye are the t of God, G3485
17 If any man defile the t of God, him G3485
17 t of God is holy, which *temple* ye are. G3485
17 the temple of God is holy, which *t* ye are.
6:19 your body is the t of the Holy Ghost G3485
8:10 at meat in the idol's t, shall not the G1493
9:13 *of the things* of the t? and they which G2411
2Co 6:16 And what agreement hath the t of God G3485
16 for ye are the t of the living God; as G3485
Eph 2:21 groweth unto an holy t in the Lord: G3485
2Th 2: 4 as God sitteth in the t of God, shewing G3485
Rev 3:12 a pillar in the t of my God, and he shall G3485
7:15 and night in his t: and he that sitteth on G3485
11: 1 Rise, and measure the t of God, and the G3485
2 But the court which is without the t G3485
19 And the t of God was opened in G3485
19 there was seen in his t the ark of his G3485
14:15 And another angel came out of the t, G3485
17 And another angel came out of the t G3485
15: 5 and, behold, the t of the tabernacle of G3485
6 And the seven angels came out of the t, G3485
8 And the t was filled with smoke from G3485
8 to enter into the t, till the seven plagues G3485
16: 1 And I heard a great voice out of the t G3485
17 voice out of the t of heaven, from the G3485
21:22 And I saw no t therein: for the Lord G3485
22 Almighty and the Lamb are the t of it. G3485

TEMPLES
Jdg 4:21 the nail into his t, and fastened it into H7541
22 lay dead, and the nail *was* in his t. H7541
5:26 had pierced and stricken through his t. H7541
Song 4: 3 *is* comely: thy t *are* like a piece of a H7541
6: 7 As a piece of a pomegranate *are* thy t H7541
Hos 8:14 Maker, and buildeth t; and Judah hath H1964
Joel 3: 5 into your t my goodly pleasant things: H1964
Act 7:48 dwelleth not in t made with hands; as G3485
17:24 dwelleth not in t made with hands; G3485

TEMPORAL
2Co 4:18 which are seen *are* t; but the things G4340

TEMPT
Gen 22: 1 that God did **t** Abraham, and said H5254
Ex 17: 2 with me? wherefore do ye **t** the LORD? H5254
Dt 6:16 Ye shall not **t** the LORD your God, as ye H5254
Isa 7:12 I will not ask, neither will I **t** the LORD. H5254
Mal 3:15 yea, *they that* **t** God are even delivered. H974
Mt 4: 7 Thou shalt not **t** the Lord thy God. *G1598*
22:18 and said, Why **t** ye me, *ye* hypocrites? *G3985*
Mk 12:15 unto them, Why **t** ye me? bring me a *G3985*
Lk 4:12 said, Thou shalt not **t** the Lord thy God. *G1598*
20:23 and said unto them, Why **t** ye me? *G3985*
Act 5: 9 agreed together to **t** the Spirit of the *G3985*
15:10 Now therefore why **t** ye God, to put a *G3985*
1Co 7: 5 Satan **t** you not for your incontinency. *G3985*
10: 9 Neither let us **t** Christ, as some of them *G1598*

TEMPTATION
Ps 95: 8 *and* as *in* the day of **t** in the wilderness: H4531
Mt 6:13 And lead us not into **t**, but deliver us *G3986*
26:41 ye enter not into **t**: the spirit indeed *is* *G3986*
Mk 14:38 Watch ye and pray, lest ye enter into **t**. *G3986*
Lk 4:13 And when the devil had ended all the **t**, *G3986*
8:13 believe, and in time of **t** fall away. *G3986*
11: 4 us not into **t**; but deliver us from evil. *G3986*
22:40 unto them, Pray that ye enter not into **t**. *G3986*
46 ye? rise and pray, lest ye enter into **t**. *G3986*
1Co 10:13 There hath no **t** taken you but such as *G3986*
13 but will with the **t** also make a way to *G3986*
Gal 4:14 And my **t** which was in my flesh ye *G3986*
1Ti 6: 9 But they that will be rich fall into **t** and *G3986*
Heb 3: 8 in the day of **t** in the wilderness: *G3986*
Jas 1:12 Blessed *is* the man that endureth **t**: for *G3986*
Rev 3:10 from the hour of **t**, which shall come *G3986*

TEMPTATIONS
Dt 4:34 of *another* nation, by **t**, by signs, and by H4531
7:19 The great **t** which thine eyes saw, and H4531
29: 3 The great **t** which thine eyes have seen, H4531
Lk 22:28 which have continued with me in my **t**. *G3986*
Act 20:19 many tears, and **t**, which befell me by *G3986*
Jas 1: 2 count it all joy when ye fall into divers **t**; *G3986*
1Pt 1: 6 ye are in heaviness through manifold **t**: *G3986*
2Pt 2: 9 the godly out of **t**, and to reserve the *G3986*

TEMPTED
Ex 17: 7 and because they **t** the LORD, saying, H5254
Nu 14:22 and have **t** me now these ten times, H5254
Dt 6:16 LORD your God, as ye **t** *him* in Massah. H5254
Ps 78:18 And they **t** God in their heart by asking H5254
41 Yea, they turned back and **t** God, and H5254
56 Yet they **t** and provoked the most high H5254
95: 9 When your fathers **t** me, proved me, H5254
106:14 the wilderness, and **t** God in the desert. H5254
Mt 4: 1 into the wilderness to be **t** of the devil. *G3985*
Mk 1:13 forty days, **t** of Satan; and was with *G3985*
Lk 4: 2 Being forty days **t** of the devil. And in *G3985*
10:25 stood up, and **t** him, saying, Master, *G1598*
1Co 10: 9 also **t**, and were destroyed of serpents. *G3985*
13 not suffer you to be **t** above that ye are *G3985*
Gal 6: 1 considering thyself, lest thou also be **t**. *G3985*
1Th 3: 5 have **t** you, and our labour be in vain. *G3985*
Heb 2:18 suffered being **t**, he is able to succour *G3985*
18 he is able to succour them that are **t**. *G3985*
3: 9 When your fathers **t** me, proved me, *G3985*
4:15 points **t** like as *we are, yet* without sin. *G3985*
11:37 asunder, were **t**, were slain with the *G3985*
Jas 1:13 Let no man say when he is **t**, I am *G3985*
13 he is tempted, I am **t** of God: for God *G3985*
13 **t** with evil, neither tempteth he any man: *G551*
14 But every man is **t**, when he is drawn *G3985*

TEMPTER
Mt 4: 3 And when the **t** came to him, he said, If *G3985*
1Th 3: 5 some means the **t** have tempted you, *G3985*

TEMPTETH
Jas 1:13 with evil, neither **t** he any man: *G3985*

TEMPTING
Mt 16: 1 came, and **t** desired him that he *G3985*
19: 3 The Pharisees also came unto him, **t** *G3985*
22:35 *him a question*, **t** him, and saying, *G3985*
Mk 8:11 of him a sign from heaven, **t** him. *G3985*
10: 2 for a man to put away *his* wife? **t** him. *G3985*
Lk 11:16 And others, **t** *him*, sought of him a sign *G3985*
Jn 8: 6 This they said, **t** him, that they might *G3985*

TEN
Gen 5:14 nine hundred and **t** years: and he died. H6235
Gen 16: 3 Abram had dwelt **t** years in the land of H6235
18:32 Peradventure **t** shall be found there. H6235
24:10 And the servant took **t** camels of the H6235
22 her hands of **t** *shekels* weight of gold; H6235
55 at the least **t**; after that she shall go. H6218
31: 7 my wages **t** times; but God suffered H6235
41 thou hast changed my wages **t** times. H6235
32:15 **t** bulls, twenty she asses, and ten foals. H6235
15 ten bulls, twenty she asses, and **t** foals. H6235
42: 3 And Joseph's **t** brethren went down to H6235
45:23 after this *manner*; **t** asses laden with H6235
23 of Egypt, and **t** she asses laden with H6235
46:27 came into Egypt, *were* threescore and **t**. H7657
50: 3 for him threescore and **t** days. H7657
22 Joseph lived an hundred and **t** years. H6235
26 So Joseph died, *being* an hundred and **t** H6235
Ex 15:27 threescore and **t** palm trees: and they H7657
26: 1 the tabernacle *with* **t** curtains *of* fine H6235
16 **T** cubits *shall be* the length of a board, H6235
27:12 their pillars **t**, and their sockets ten. H6235
12 their pillars ten, and their sockets **t**. H6235
34:28 of the covenant, the **t** commandments. H6235
36: 8 the tabernacle made **t** curtains *of* fine H6235
21 The length of a board *was* **t** cubits, and H6235
38:12 their pillars **t**, and their sockets ten; H6235
12 ten, and their sockets **t**; the hooks of the H6235
Lev 26: 8 of you shall put **t** thousand to flight: H7233
26 of your bread, **t** women shall bake your H6235
27: 5 shekels, and for the female **t** shekels. H6235
7 shekels, and for the female **t** shekels. H6235
Nu 7:14 One spoon of **t** *shekels* of gold, full of H6235
20 One spoon of gold of **t** *shekels*, full of H6235
26 One golden spoon of **t** *shekels*, full of H6235
32 One golden spoon of **t** *shekels*, full of H6235
38 One golden spoon of **t** *shekels*, full of H6235
44 One golden spoon of **t** *shekels*, full of H6235
50 One golden spoon of **t** *shekels*, full of H6235
56 One golden spoon of **t** *shekels*, full of H6235
62 One golden spoon of **t** *shekels*, full of H6235
68 One golden spoon of **t** *shekels*, full of H6235
74 One golden spoon of **t** *shekels*, full of H6235
80 One golden spoon of **t** *shekels*, full of H6235
86 of incense, *weighing* **t** *shekels* apiece, H6235
11:19 days, neither **t** days, nor twenty days; H6235
32 least gathered **t** homers: and they H6235
14:22 me now these **t** times, and have not H6235
29:23 And on the fourth day **t** bullocks, two H6235
33: 9 **t** palm trees; and they pitched there. H7657
Dt 4:13 to perform, *even* **t** commandments; H6235
10: 4 the first writing, the **t** commandments, H6235
22 threescore and **t** persons; and now the H7657
32:30 and two put **t** thousand to flight, except H7233
33: 2 and he came with **t** thousands of H7233
17 earth: and they *are* the **t** thousands of H7233
Jos 15:57 Cain, Gibeah, and Timnah; **t** cities with H6235
17: 5 And there fell **t** portions to Manasseh, H6235
21: 5 of the half tribe of Manasseh, **t** cities. H6235
26 All the cities *were* **t** with their suburbs H6235
22:14 And with him **t** princes, of each chief H6235
24:29 died, *being* an hundred and **t** years old. H6235
Jdg 1: 4 slew of them in Bezek **t** thousand men. H6235
7 Threescore and **t** kings, having their H7657
2: 8 died, *being* an hundred and **t** years old. H6235
3:29 at that time about **t** thousand men, all H6235
4: 6 and take with thee **t** thousand men of H6235
10 he went up with **t** thousand men at his H6235
14 Tabor, and **t** thousand men after him. H6235
6:27 Then Gideon took **t** men of his H6235
7: 3 and there remained **t** thousand. H6235
8:30 And Gideon had threescore and **t** sons H7657
9: 2 *are* threescore and **t** persons, reign H7657
4 And they gave him threescore and **t** H7657
5 threescore and **t** persons, upon one H7657
18 threescore and **t** persons, upon one H7657
24 the threescore and **t** sons of Jerubbaal H7657
12:11 Israel; and he judged Israel **t** years. H6235
14 on threescore and **t** ass colts: and he H7657
17:10 and I will give thee **t** *shekels* of silver by H6235
20:10 And we will take **t** men of an hundred H6235
10 a thousand out of **t** thousand, to fetch H7233
34 And there came against Gibeah **t** H6235
Ru 1: 4 and they dwelled there about **t** years. H6235
4: 2 And he took **t** men of the elders of the H6235
1Sa 1: 8 *am* not I better to thee than **t** sons? H6235
6:19 threescore and **t** men: and the people H7657
15: 4 and **t** thousand men of Judah. H6235
17:17 *corn*, and these **t** loaves, and run to the H6235
18 And carry these **t** cheeses unto the H6235
18: 7 thousands, and David his **t** thousands. H7233
1Sa 18: 8 unto David **t** thousands, and to me H7233
21:11 thousands, and David his **t** thousands? H7233
25: 5 And David sent out **t** young men, and H6235
38 And it came to pass about **t** days *after*, H6235
29: 5 thousands, and David his **t** thousands? H7233
2Sa 15:16 And the king left **t** women, *which were* H6235
18: 3 now *thou art* worth **t** thousand of us: H6235
11 thee **t** *shekels* of silver, and a girdle. H6235
15 And **t** young men that bare Joab's H6235
19:43 and said, We have **t** parts in the king, H6235
20: 3 and the king took the **t** women *his* H6235
1Ki 4:23 **T** fat oxen, and twenty oxen out of the H6235
5:14 And he sent them to Lebanon, **t** H6235
15 And Solomon had threescore and **t** H7657
6: 3 of the house; *and* **t** cubits *was* the H6235
23 *of* olive tree, *each* **t** cubits high. H6235
24 part of the other *were* **t** cubits. H6235
25 And the other cherub *was* **t** cubits: both H6235
26 The height of the one cherub *was* **t** H6235
7:10 of **t** cubits, and stones of eight cubits. H6235
23 And he made a molten sea, **t** cubits H6235
24 compassing it, **t** in a cubit, compassing H6235
27 And he made **t** bases of brass; four H6235
37 After this *manner* he made the **t** bases: H6235
38 Then made he **t** lavers of brass: one H6235
38 upon every one of the **t** bases one laver. H6235
43 And the **t** bases, and ten lavers on the H6235
43 And the ten bases, and **t** lavers on the H6235
11:31 And he said to Jeroboam, Take thee **t** H6235
31 Solomon, and will give **t** tribes to thee: H6235
35 and will give it unto thee, *even* **t** tribes. H6235
14: 3 And take with thee **t** loaves, and H6235
2Ki 5: 5 and took with him **t** talents of silver, H6235
5 of gold, and **t** changes of raiment. H6235
13: 7 fifty horsemen, and **t** chariots, and ten H6235
7 ten chariots, and **t** thousand footmen; H6235
14: 7 He slew of Edom in the valley of salt **t** H6235
15:17 Israel, *and reigned* **t** years in Samaria. H6235
20: 9 **t** degrees, or go back ten degrees? H6235
9 ten degrees, or go back **t** degrees? H6235
10 to go down **t** degrees: nay, but let H6235
10 the shadow return backward **t** degrees. H6235
11 the shadow **t** degrees backward, by H6235
24:14 of valour, *even* **t** thousand captives, H6235
25:25 royal, came, and **t** men with him, and H6235
1Ch 6:61 half *tribe* of Manasseh, by lot, **t** cities. H6235
21: 5 and **t** thousand men that drew sword. H7657
29: 7 talents and **t** thousand drams, and H7239
7 and of silver **t** thousand talents, and H6235
2Ch 2: 2 And Solomon told out threescore and **t** H7657
18 And he set threescore and **t** thousand H7657
4: 1 thereof, and **t** cubits the height thereof. H6235
2 Also he made a molten sea of **t** cubits H6235
3 compass it round about: **t** in a cubit, H6235
6 He made also **t** lavers, and put five on H6235
7 And he made **t** candlesticks of gold H6235
8 He made also **t** tables, and placed *them* H6235
14: 1 In his days the land was quiet **t** years. H6235
25:11 of the children of Seir **t** thousand. H6235
12 And *other* **t** thousand *left* alive did the H6235
27: 5 of silver, and **t** thousand measures H6235
5 of wheat, and **t** thousand of barley. H6235
29:32 threescore and **t** bullocks, an hundred H7657
30:24 bullocks and **t** thousand sheep: and H6235
36: 9 three months and **t** days in Jerusalem: H6235
21 to fulfil threescore and **t** years. H7657
Ezr 1:10 and **t**, *and* other vessels a thousand. H6235
8:12 and with him an hundred and **t** males. H6235
24 and **t** of their brethren with them, H6235
Neh 4:12 they said unto us **t** times, From all H6235
5:18 me, and once in **t** days store of all sorts H6235
11: 1 to bring one of **t** to dwell in Jerusalem H6235
Est 3: 9 and I will pay **t** thousand talents of H6235
9:10 The **t** sons of Haman the son of H6235
12 palace, and the **t** sons of Haman; what H6235
13 **t** sons be hanged upon the gallows. H6235
14 and they hanged Haman's **t** sons. H6235
Job 19: 3 These **t** times have ye reproached me: H6235
Ps 3: 6 I will not be afraid of **t** thousands of H7233
33: 2 psaltery *and* an instrument of **t** strings. H6218
90:10 years and **t**; and if by reason of strength H7657
91: 7 A thousand shall fall at thy side, and **t** H7233
92: 3 Upon an instrument of **t** strings, and H6218
144: 9 of **t** strings will I sing praises unto thee. H6218
13 and **t** thousands in our streets: H7231
Ecc 7:19 **t** mighty *men* which are in the city. H6235
Song 5:10 ruddy, the chiefest among **t** thousand. H7233
Isa 5:10 Yea, **t** acres of vineyard shall yield one H6235
38: 8 sun dial of Ahaz, **t** degrees backward. H6235

Isa 38: 8 So the sun returned **t** degrees, by which H6235
Jer 41: 1 of the king, even **t** men with him, came H6235
2 and the **t** men that were with H6235
8 But **t** men were found among them H6235
42: 7 And it came to pass after **t** days, that H6235
Ezk 40:11 the entry of the gate, **t** cubits; *and* the H6235
41: 2 And the breadth of the door *was* **t** H6235
42: 4 *was* a walk of **t** cubits breadth inward, H6235
45: 1 breadth *shall be* **t** thousand. This *shall* H6235
3 and the breadth of **t** thousand: and in it H6235
5 of length, and the **t** thousand of H6235
14 of **t** baths; for ten baths *are* an homer: H6235
14 of ten baths; for **t** baths *are* an homer: H6235
48: 9 in length, and of **t** thousand in breadth. H6235
10 toward the west **t** thousand in breadth, H6235
10 toward the east **t** thousand in breadth, H6235
13 in length, and **t** thousand in breadth: H6235
13 thousand, and the breadth **t** thousand. H6235
18 *portion shall be* **t** thousand eastward, H6235
18 eastward, and **t** thousand westward: H6235
Dan 1:12 Prove thy servants, I beseech thee, **t** H6235
14 in this matter, and proved them **t** days. H6235
15 And at the end of **t** days their H6235
20 he found them **t** times better than all H6235
7: 7 that *were* before it; and it had **t** horns. H6236
10 unto him, and **t** thousand times ten H7240
10 ten thousand times **t** thousand stood H7240
20 And of the **t** horns that *were* in his H6236
24 And the **t** horns out of this kingdom H6236
24 of this kingdom *are* **t** kings *that* shall H6236
11:12 cast down *many* **t** thousands: but he H7239
Am 5: 3 shall leave **t**, to the house of Israel. H6235
6: 9 **t** men in one house, that they shall die. H6235
Mic 6: 7 of rams, *or* with **t** thousands of rivers H7233
Hag 2:16 there were *but* **t**: when *one* came to the H6235
Zec 1:12 these threescore and **t** years? H7657
5: 2 cubits, and the breadth thereof **t** cubits. H6235
8:23 *come to pass*, that **t** men shall take H6235
Mt 18:24 which owed him **t** thousand talents. *G3468*
20:24 And when the **t** heard *it*, they were *G1176*
25: 1 be likened unto **t** virgins, which took *G1176*
28 give *it* unto him which hath **t** talents. *G1176*
Mk 10:41 And when the **t** heard *it*, they began to *G1176*
Lk 14:31 he be able with **t** thousand to meet him *G1176*
15: 8 Either what woman having **t** pieces of *G1176*
17:12 there met him **t** men that were lepers, *G1176*
17 not **t** cleansed? but where *are* the nine? *G1176*
19:13 And he called his **t** servants, and *G1176*
13 delivered them **t** pounds, and said unto *G1176*
16 Lord, thy pound hath gained **t** pounds. *G1176*
17 little, have thou authority over **t** cities. *G1176*
24 and give *it* to him that hath **t** pounds. *G1176*
25 unto him, Lord, he hath **t** pounds.) *G1176*
Act 23:23 threescore and **t**, and spearmen two *G1440*
25: 6 them more than **t** days, he went down *G1176*
1Co 4:15 For though ye have **t** thousand *G3463*
14:19 others also, than **t** thousand words in *G3463*
Jude 14 cometh with **t** thousands of his saints, *G3461*
Rev 2:10 have tribulation **t** days: be thou faithful *G1176*
5:11 of them was **t** thousand times ten *G3461*
11 ten thousand times **t** thousand, and *G3461*
12: 3 seven heads and **t** horns, and seven *G1176*
13: 1 seven heads and **t** horns, and upon his *G1176*
1 upon his horns **t** crowns, and upon his *G1176*
17: 3 having seven heads and **t** horns. *G1176*
7 hath the seven heads and **t** horns. *G1176*
12 And the **t** horns which thou sawest are *G1176*
12 thou sawest are **t** kings, which have *G1176*
16 And the **t** horns which thou sawest *G1176*

TEND
Prv 21: 5 The thoughts of the diligent *t* only to

TENDER
Gen 18: 7 and fetcht a calf **t** and good, and gave H7390
29:17 Leah *was* **t** eyed; but Rachel was H7390
33:13 the children *are* **t**, and the flocks and H7390
Dt 28:54 *So that* the man *that is* **t** among you, H7390
56 The **t** and delicate woman among you, H7390
32: 2 rain upon the **t** herb, and as the showers
2Sa 23: 4 clouds; *as* the **t** grass *springing* out of
2Ki 22:19 Because thine heart was **t**, and thou H7401
1Ch 22: 5 son *is* young and **t**, and the house *that* H7390
29: 1 *is yet* young and **t**, and the work *is* H7390
2Ch 34:27 Because thine heart was **t**, and thou H7401
Job 14: 7 that the **t** branch thereof will not cease. H3127
38:27 the bud of the **t** herb to spring forth?
Ps 25: 6 Remember, O LORD, thy **t** mercies and
40:11 Withhold not thou thy **t** mercies from
Ps 51: 1 thy **t** mercies blot out my transgressions.
69:16 to the multitude of thy **t** mercies.
77: 9 he in anger shut up his **t** mercies? Selah.
79: 8 iniquities: let thy **t** mercies speedily
103: 4 thee with lovingkindness and **t** mercies;
119:77 Let thy **t** mercies come unto me, that I
156 Great *are* thy **t** mercies, O LORD:
145: 9 The LORD *is* good to all: and his **t**
Prv 4: 3 For I was my father's son, **t** and only H7390
12:10 but the **t** mercies of the wicked *are* cruel.
27:25 The hay appeareth, and the **t** grass
Song 2:13 the vines *with* the **t** grape give a *good*
15 the vines: for our vines *have* **t** grapes.
7:12 *whether* the **t** grape appear, *and* the
Isa 47: 1 shalt no more be called **t** and delicate. H7390
53: 2 For he shall grow up before him as a **t** H3126
Ezk 17:22 his young twigs a **t** one, and will plant H7390
Dan 1: 9 **t** love with the prince of the eunuchs.
4:15 and brass, in the **t** grass of the field; and
23 and brass, in the **t** grass of the field; and
Mt 24:32 his branch is yet **t**, and putteth forth *G527*
Mk 13:28 her branch is yet **t**, and putteth forth *G527*
Lk 1:78 Through the **t** mercy of our God; *G4698*
Jas 5:11 the Lord is very pitiful, and of **t** mercy. *G3629*

TENDER-EYED See TENDER and EYED.

TENDERHEARTED
2Ch 13: 7 was young and **t**, and could not H7390+H3824
Eph 4:32 And be ye kind one to another, **t**, *G2155*

TENDERNESS
Dt 28:56 delicateness and **t**, her eye shall be evil H7391

TENDETH
Prv 10:16 The labour of the righteous *t* to life: the
11:19 As righteousness *t* to life: so he that
24 more than is meet, but *it t* to poverty.
14:23 but the talk of the lips *t* only to penury.
19:23 The fear of the LORD *t* to life: and *he*

TENONS
Ex 26:17 Two **t** *shall there be* in one board, set in H3027
19 one board for his two **t**, and two sockets H3027
19 under another board for his two **t**. H3027
36:22 One board had two **t**, equally distant H3027
24 one board for his two **t**, and two sockets H3027
24 under another board for his two **t**. H3027

TENOR
Gen 43: 7 according to the **t** of these words: could H6310
Ex 34:27 for after the **t** of these words I have H6310

TENS
Ex 18:21 rulers of fifties, and rulers of **t**: H6235
25 rulers of fifties, and rulers of **t**. H6235
Dt 1:15 over **t**, and officers among your tribes. H6235

TEN'S
Gen 18:32 he said, I will not destroy *it* for **t** sake. H6235

TENT
Gen 9:21 and he was uncovered within his **t**. H168
12: 8 and pitched his **t**, *having* Beth-el on the H168
13: 3 the place where his **t** had been at the H168
12 plain, and pitched *his* **t** toward Sodom. H167
18 Then Abram removed *his* **t**, and came H167
18: 1 he sat in the **t** door in the heat of the day; H168
2 meet them from the **t** door, and bowed H168
6 And Abraham hastened into the **t** unto H168
9 thy wife? And he said, Behold, in the **t**. H168
10 *it* in the **t** door, which *was* behind him. H168
24:67 his mother Sarah's **t**, and took Rebekah, H168
26:17 **t** in the valley of Gerar, and dwelt there. H2583
25 and pitched his **t** there: and there Isaac's H168
31:25 had pitched his **t** in the mount: and H168
33 And Laban went into Jacob's **t**, and into H168
33 tent, and into Leah's **t**, and into the two H168
33 Leah's **t**, and entered into Rachel's tent. H168
33 Leah's tent, and entered into Rachel's **t**. H168
34 searched all the **t**, but found *them* not. H168
33:18 and pitched his **t** before the city. H2583
19 he had spread his **t**, at the hand of the H168
35:21 And Israel journeyed, and spread his **t** H168
Ex 18: 7 of *their* welfare; and they came into the **t**. H168
26:11 couple the **t** together, that it may be one. H168
12 the curtains of the **t**, the half curtain that H168
13 of the curtains of the **t**, it shall hang over H168
14 And thou shalt make a covering for the **t** H168
Ex 26:36 for the door of the **t**, *of* blue, and purple, H168
33: 8 every man *at* his **t** door, and looked after H168
10 worshipped, every man *in* his **t** door. H168
35:11 The tabernacle, his **t**, and his covering, H168
36:14 goats' *hair* for the **t** over the tabernacle: H168
18 the **t** together, that it might be one. H168
19 And he made a covering for the **t** *of* H168
39:32 tabernacle of the **t** of the congregation H168
33 unto Moses, the **t**, and all his furniture, H168
40 tabernacle, for the **t** of the congregation, H168
40: 2 tabernacle of the **t** of the congregation. H168
6 tabernacle of the **t** of the congregation. H168
7 laver between the **t** of the congregation H168
19 And he spread abroad the **t** over the H168
19 the covering of the **t** above upon it; as H168
22 And he put the table in the **t** of the H168
24 And he put the candlestick in the **t** of the H168
26 And he put the golden altar in the **t** of H168
29 tabernacle of the **t** of the congregation, H168
30 And he set the laver between the **t** of the H168
32 When they went into the **t** of the H168
34 Then a cloud covered the **t** of the H168
35 to enter into the **t** of the congregation, H168
Lev 14: 8 tarry abroad out of his **t** seven days. H168
Nu 3:25 the tabernacle, and the **t**, the covering H168
9:15 *namely*, the **t** of the testimony: and H168
11:10 in the door of his **t**: and the anger of the H168
19:14 This *is* the law, when a man dieth in a **t**: H168
14 that come into the **t**, and all that *is* in the H168
14 *is* in the **t**, shall be unclean seven days. H168
18 *it* upon the **t**, and upon all the vessels, H168
25: 8 of Israel into the **t**, and thrust both of H6898
Jos 7:21 the midst of my **t**, and the silver under it. H168
22 they ran unto the **t**; and, behold, *it was* H168
22 *it was* hid in his **t**, and the silver under it. H168
23 of the midst of the **t**, and brought them H168
24 his sheep, and his **t**, and all that he had: H168
Jdg 4:11 and pitched his **t** unto the plain of H168
17 on his feet to the **t** of Jael the wife of H168
18 into the **t**, she covered him with a mantle. H168
20 in the door of the **t**, and it shall be, when H168
21 took a nail of the **t**, and took an hammer H168
22 he came into her *t*, behold, Sisera lay
5:24 shall she be above women in the **t**. H168
7: 8 every man unto his **t**, and retained those H168
13 and came unto a **t**, and smote it that it H168
13 and overturned it, that the **t** lay along. H168
20: 8 any *of us* go to his **t**, neither will we any H168
1Sa 4:10 fled every man into his **t**: and there was a H168
13: 2 of the people he sent every man to his **t**. H168
17:54 Jerusalem; but he put his armour in his **t**. H168
2Sa 7: 6 have walked in a **t** and in a tabernacle. H168
16:22 So they spread Absalom a **t** upon the top H168
18:17 him: and all Israel fled every one to his **t**. H168
19: 8 for Israel had fled every man to his **t**. H168
20:22 every man to his **t**. And Joab returned to H168
2Ki 7: 8 they went into one **t**, and did eat and H168
8 into another **t**, and carried thence *also*, H168
1Ch 15: 1 for the ark of God, and pitched for it a **t**. H168
16: 1 it in the midst of the **t** that David had H168
17: 5 but have gone from **t** to tent, and from H168
5 to **t**, and from *one* tabernacle *to another*. H168
2Ch 1: 4 for he had pitched a **t** for it at Jerusalem. H168
25:22 Israel, and they fled every man to his **t**. H168
Ps 78:60 the **t** *which* he placed among men; H168
Isa 13:20 the Arabian pitch **t** there; neither shall H167
38:12 me as a shepherd's **t**: I have cut off like a H168
40:22 spreadeth them out as a **t** to dwell in: H168
54: 2 Enlarge the place of thy **t**, and let them H168
Jer 10:20 **t** any more, and to set up my curtains. H168
37:10 man in his **t**, and burn this city with fire. H168

TENT-DOOR See TENT and DOOR.

TENTH
Gen 8: 5 until the **t** month: in the tenth H6224
5 month: in the **t** *month*, on the first *day* H6224
28:22 me I will surely give the **t** unto thee. H6237
Ex 12: 3 saying, In the **t** *day* of this month they H6218
16:36 Now an omer *is* the **t** *part* of an ephah. H6224
29:40 And with the one lamb a **t** deal of flour H6241
Lev 5:11 for his offering the **t** part of an ephah of H6224
6:20 he is anointed; the **t** part of an ephah of H6224
14:10 blemish, and three **t** deals of fine flour H6241
21 for him, and one **t** deal of fine flour H6241
16:29 month, on the **t** *day* of the month, ye H6218
23:13 thereof *shall be* two **t** deals of fine flour H6241
17 wave loaves of two **t** deals: they shall be H6241
27 Also on the **t** *day* of this seventh month H6218

Lev 24: 5 two **t** deals shall be in one cake. H6241
25: 9 to sound on the **t** *day* of the seventh H6218
27:32 rod, the **t** shall be holy unto the LORD. H6224
Nu 5:15 for her, the **t** *part* of an ephah of H6224
7:66 On the **t** day Ahiezer the son of H6224
15: 4 a meat offering of a **t** deal of flour H6241
6 a meat offering two **t** deals of flour H6241
9 meat offering of three **t** deals of flour H6241
18:21 children of Levi all the **t** in Israel for an H4643
26 for the LORD, *even* a **t** *part* of the tithe. H4643
28: 5 And a **t** *part* of an ephah of flour for a H6224
9 spot, and two **t** deals of flour *for* a meat H6241
12 And three **t** deals of flour *for* a meat H6241
12 bullock; and two **t** deals of flour *for* a H6241
13 And a several **t** deal of flour mingled H6241
20 with oil: three **t** deals shall ye offer for H6241
20 for a bullock, and two **t** deals for a ram; H6241
21 A several **t** deal shalt thou offer for H6241
28 with oil, three **t** deals unto one bullock, H6241
28 one bullock, two **t** deals unto one ram, H6241
29 A several **t** deal unto one lamb, H6241
29: 3 with oil, three **t** deals for a bullock, H6241
3 for a bullock, *and* two **t** deals for a ram, H6241
4 And one **t** deal for one lamb, H6241
7 And ye shall have on the **t** *day* of this H6218
9 with oil, three **t** deals to a bullock, *and* H6241
9 a bullock, *and* two **t** deals to one ram, H6241
10 A several **t** deal for one lamb, H6241
14 with oil, three **t** deals unto every H6241
14 **t** deals to each ram of the two rams, H6241
15 And a several **t** deal to each lamb of the H6241
Dt 23: 2 LORD; even to his **t** generation shall he H6224
3 even to their **t** generation shall they H6224
Jos 4:19 out of Jordan on the **t** *day* of the first H6218
1Sa 8:15 And he will take the **t** of your seed, and H6237
17 He will take the **t** of your sheep: and ye H6237
2Ki 25: 1 of his reign, in the **t** month, in the tenth H6224
1 month, in the **t** *day* of the month, *that* H6218
1Ch 12:13 Jeremiah the **t**, Machbanai the eleventh. H6224
24:11 The ninth to Jeshua, the **t** to Shecaniah, H6224
25:17 The **t** to Shimei, *he,* his sons, and his H6224
27:13 The **t** *captain* for the tenth month *was* H6224
13 The tenth *captain* for the **t** month *was* H6224
Ezr 10:16 of the **t** month to examine the matter. H6224
Est 2:16 house royal in the **t** month, which *is* the H6224
Isa 6:13 But yet in it *shall be* a **t**, and *it* shall H6224
Jer 32: 1 the LORD in the **t** year of Zedekiah H6224
39: 1 king of Judah, in the **t** month, came H6224
52: 4 of his reign, in the **t** month, in the tenth H6224
4 month, in the **t** *day* of the month, *that* H6218
12 Now in the fifth month, in the **t** *day* of H6218
Ezk 20: 1 the fifth *month*, the **t** *day* of the month, H6218
24: 1 Again in the ninth year, in the **t** month, H6224
1 month, in the **t** *day* of the month, the H6218
29: 1 In the **t** year, in the tenth *month*, in the H6224
1 In the tenth year, in the **t** *month*, in the H6224
33:21 captivity, in the **t** *month*, in the fifth H6224
40: 1 of the year, in the **t** *day* of the month, H6218
45:11 may contain the **t** part of an homer, H4643
11 and the ephah the **t** part of an homer: H6224
14 *ye shall offer* the **t** part of a bath out of H4643
Zec 8:19 and the fast of the **t**, shall be to the H6224
Jn 1:39 that day: for it was about the **t** hour. G1182
Heb 7: 2 To whom also Abraham gave a **t** part G1181
4 Abraham gave the **t** of the spoils. G1181
Rev 11:13 and the **t** part of the city fell, and G1182
21:20 ninth, a topaz; the **t**, a chrysoprasus; G1182

TEN-THOUSAND See TEN and THOUSAND.

TENTMAKERS
Act 18: 3 for by their occupation they were **t**. G4635

TENTS
Gen 4:20 as dwell in **t**, and *of such as have* cattle. H168
9:27 shall dwell in the **t** of Shem; and Canaan H168
13: 5 Abram, had flocks, and herds, and **t**. H168
25:27 and Jacob *was* a plain man, dwelling in **t**. H168
31:33 two maidservants' **t**; but he found *them* H168
Ex 16:16 ye every man for *them* which *are* in his **t**. H168
Nu 1:52 shall pitch their **t**, every man by his own H2583
9:17 the children of Israel pitched their **t**. H2583
18 upon the tabernacle they rested in their **t**.
20 they abode in their **t**, and according to
22 abode in their **t**, and journeyed not: but
23 LORD they rested in the **t**, and at the
13:19 in, whether in **t**, or in strong holds; H4264
16:26 I pray you, from the **t** of these wicked H168
27 in the door of their **t**, and their wives, H168
Nu 24: 2 abiding *in his* **t** according to their tribes;
5 How goodly are thy **t**, O Jacob, *and* thy H168
Dt 1:27 And ye murmured in your **t**, and said, H168
33 place to pitch your **t** *in*, in fire by night, H2583
5:30 Go say to them, Get you into your **t** H168
11: 6 and their **t**, and all the substance H168
16: 7 turn in the morning, and go unto thy **t**. H168
33:18 in thy going out; and, Issachar, in thy **t**. H168
Jos 3:14 from their **t**, to pass over Jordan, H168
22: 4 get you unto your **t**, *and* unto the land of H168
6 them away: and they went unto their **t**. H168
7 also unto their **t**, then he blessed them, H168
8 riches unto your **t**, and with very much H168
Jdg 6: 5 their cattle and their **t**, and they came as H168
8:11 them that dwelt in **t** on the east of Nobah H168
1Sa 17:53 the Philistines, and they spoiled their **t**. H4264
2Sa 11:11 Judah, abide in **t**; and my lord Joab, H5521
20: 1 son of Jesse: every man to his **t**, O Israel. H168
1Ki 8:66 went unto their **t** joyful and glad of heart H168
12:16 of Jesse: to your **t**, O Israel: now see to H168
16 David. So Israel departed unto their **t**. H168
2Ki 7: 7 and left their **t**, and their horses, and H168
10 and asses tied, and the **t** as they *were*. H168
16 and spoiled the **t** of the Syrians. So a H4264
8:21 chariots: and the people fled into their **t**. H168
13: 5 of Israel dwelt in their **t**, as beforetime. H168
14:12 Israel; and they fled every man to their **t**. H168
1Ch 4:41 and smote their **t**, and the habitations H168
5:10 **t** throughout all the east *land* of Gilead. H168
2Ch 7:10 away into their **t**, glad and merry in heart H168
10:16 every man to your **t**, O Israel: *and* now, H168
16 own house. So all Israel went to their **t**. H168
14:15 They smote also the **t** of cattle, and H168
31: 2 praise in the gates of the **t** of the LORD. H4264
Ezr 8:15 there abode we in **t** three days: and I H2583
Ps 69:25 be desolate; *and* let none dwell in their **t**. H168
78:55 the tribes of Israel to dwell in their **t**. H168
84:10 than to dwell in the **t** of wickedness. H168
106:25 But murmured in their **t**, *and* hearkened H168
120: 5 in Mesech, *that* I dwell in the **t** of Kedar! H168
Song 1: 5 **t** of Kedar, as the curtains of Solomon. H168
8 feed thy kids beside the shepherds' **t**. H4908
Jer 4:20 **t** spoiled, *and* my curtains in a moment. H168
6: 3 they shall pitch *their* **t** against her round H168
30:18 captivity of Jacob's **t**, and have mercy on H168
35: 7 ye shall dwell in **t**; that ye may live many H168
10 But we have dwelt in **t**, and have obeyed, H168
49:29 Their **t** and their flocks shall they take H168
Hab 3: 7 I saw the **t** of Cushan in affliction: *and* H168
Zec 12: 7 The LORD also shall save the **t** of Judah H168
14:15 that shall be in these **t**, as this plague. H4264

TERAH
Gen 11:24 nine and twenty years, and begat **T**: H8646
25 And Nahor lived after he begat **T** an H8646
26 And **T** lived seventy years, and begat H8646
27 Now these *are* the generations of **T**: H8646
27 of Terah: **T** begat Abram, Nahor, H8646
28 And Haran died before his father **T** in H8646
31 And **T** took Abram his son, and Lot the H8646
32 And the days of **T** were two hundred H8646
32 and five years: and **T** died in Haran. H8646
Jos 24: 2 flood in old time, *even* **T**, the father of H8646
1Ch 1:26 Serug, Nahor, **T**, H8646

TERAPHIM
Jdg 17: 5 an ephod, and **t**, and consecrated one H8655
18:14 an ephod, and **t**, and a graven image, H8655
17 the ephod, and the **t**, and the molten H8655
18 the ephod, and the **t**, and the molten H8655
20 the ephod, and the **t**, and the graven H8655
Hos 3: 4 and without an ephod, and *without* **t**: H8655

TERESH
Est 2:21 Bigthan and **T**, of those which kept H8657
6: 2 told of Bigthana and **T**, two of the king's H8657

TERMED
Isa 62: 4 Thou shalt no more be **t** Forsaken; H559
4 land any more be **t** Desolate: but thou H559

TERRACES
2Ch 9:11 And the king made *of* the algum trees **t** H4546

TERRESTRIAL
1Co 15:40 bodies, and bodies **t**: but the glory of the G1919
40 *is* one, and the *glory* of the **t** *is* another. G1919

TERRIBLE
Ex 34:10 for it *is* a **t** thing that I will do with thee. H3372
Dt 1:19 all that great and **t** wilderness, which H3372
7:21 God *is* among you, a mighty God and **t**. H3372
8:15 Who led thee through that great and **t** H3372
10:17 a mighty, and a **t**, which regardeth not H3372
21 **t** things, which thine eyes have seen. H3372
Jdg 13: 6 angel of God, very **t**: but I asked him not H3372
2Sa 7:23 great things and **t**, for thy land, before H3372
Neh 1: 5 the great and **t** God, that keepeth H3372
4:14 *which is* great and **t**, and fight for your H3372
9:32 the mighty, and the **t** God, who keepest H3372
Job 37:22 out of the north: with God *is* **t** majesty. H3372
39:20 grasshopper? the glory of his nostrils *is* **t**. H367
41:14 of his face? his teeth *are* **t** round about. H367
Ps 45: 4 thy right hand shall teach thee **t** things. H3372
47: 2 For the LORD most high *is* **t**; *he is* a H3372
65: 5 *By* **t** things in righteousness wilt thou H3372
66: 3 Say unto God, How **t** *art thou in* thy H3372
5 Come and see the works of God: *he is* **t** H3372
68:35 O God, *thou art* **t** out of thy holy places: H3372
76:12 princes: *he is* **t** to the kings of the earth. H3372
99: 3 Let them praise thy great and **t** name; H3372
106:22 of Ham, *and* **t** things by the Red sea. H3372
145: 6 **t** acts: and I will declare thy greatness. H3372
Song 6: 4 as Jerusalem, **t** as *an army* with banners. H366
10 the sun, *and* **t** as *an army* with banners? H366
Isa 13:11 will lay low the haughtiness of the **t**. H6184
18: 2 and peeled, to a people **t** from their H3372
7 peeled, and from a people **t** from their H3372
21: 1 cometh from the desert, from a **t** land. H3372
25: 3 the city of the **t** nations shall fear thee. H6184
4 **t** ones *is* as a storm *against* the wall. H6184
5 of the **t** ones shall be brought low. H6184
29: 5 multitude of the **t** ones *shall be* as chaff H6184
20 For the **t** one is brought to nought, and H6184
49:25 and the prey of the **t** shall be delivered: H6184
64: 3 When thou didst **t** things *which* we H3372
Jer 15:21 redeem thee out of the hand of the **t**. H6184
20:11 But the LORD *is* with me as a mighty **t** H6184
Lam 5:10 like an oven because of the **t** famine. H2152
Ezk 1:22 as the colour of the **t** crystal, stretched H3372
28: 7 upon thee, the **t** of the nations: and H6184
30:11 He and his people with him, the **t** of the H6184
31:12 And strangers, the **t** of the nations, H6184
32:12 to fall, the **t** of the nations, all of H6184
Dan 2:31 before thee; and the form thereof *was* **t**. H1763
7: 7 fourth beast, dreadful and **t**, and strong H574
Joel 2:11 great and very **t**; and who can abide it? H3372
31 great and the **t** day of the LORD come. H3372
Hab 1: 7 They *are* **t** and dreadful: their judgment H366
Zep 2:11 The LORD *will be* **t** unto them: for he H3372
Heb 12:21 And so **t** was the sight, *that* Moses said, G5398

TERRIBLENESS
Dt 26: 8 **t**, and with signs, and with wonders: H4172
1Ch 17:21 name of greatness and **t**, by driving out H3372
Jer 49:16 Thy **t** hath deceived thee, *and* the pride H8606

TERRIBLY
Isa 2:19 when he ariseth to shake **t** the earth. H6206
21 when he ariseth to shake **t** the earth. H6206
Nah 2: 3 and the fir trees shall be **t** shaken.

TERRIFIED
Dt 20: 3 neither be ye **t** because of them; H6206
Lk 21: 9 be not **t**: for these things must G4422
24:37 But they were **t** and affrighted, and G4422
Php 1:28 And in nothing **t** by your adversaries: G4426

TERRIFIEST
Job 7:14 with dreams, and **t** me through visions: H1204

TERRIFY
Job 3: 5 upon it; let the blackness of the day **t** it. H1204
9:34 from me, and let not his fear **t** me: H1204
31:34 of families **t** me, that I kept silence, H2865
2Co 10: 9 That I may not seem as if I would **t** you G1629

TERROR
Gen 35: 5 And they journeyed: and the **t** of God H2847
Lev 26:16 appoint over you **t**, consumption, and H928
Dt 32:25 The sword without, and **t** within, shall H367
34:12 and in all the great **t** which Moses H4172
Jos 2: 9 land, and that your **t** is fallen upon us, H367
Job 31:23 For destruction *from* God *was* a **t** to H6343
33: 7 Behold, my **t** shall not make thee afraid, H367
Ps 91: 5 Thou shalt not be afraid for the **t** by H6343
Isa 10:33 lop the bough with **t**: and the high ones H4637

T

Isa 19:17 And the land of Judah shall be a **t** unto H2283
33:18 Thine heart shall meditate **t**. Where *is* the H367
54:14 from **t**; for it shall not come near thee. H4288
Jer 17:17 Be not a **t** unto me: thou *art* my hope in H4288
20: 4 I will make thee a **t** to thyself, and to all H4032
32:21 a stretched out arm, and with great **t**; H4172
Ezk 26:17 cause their **t** *to be* on all that haunt it! H2851
21 I will make thee a **t**, and thou *shalt be* H1091
27:36 be a **t**, and never *shalt be* any more. H1091
28:19 a **t**, and never *shalt* thou *be* any more. H1091
32:23 which caused **t** in the land of the living. H2851
24 caused their **t** in the land of the living; H2851
25 though their **t** was caused in the land H2851
26 caused their **t** in the land of the living. H2851
27 **t** of the mighty in the land of the living. H2851
30 slain; with their **t** they are ashamed of H2851
32 For I have caused my **t** in the land of H2851
Ro 13: 3 For rulers are not a **t** to good works, G5401
2Co 5:11 Knowing therefore the **t** of the Lord, we G5401
1Pt 3:14 not afraid of their **t**, neither be troubled; G5401

TERRORS
Dt 4:34 out arm, and by great **t**, according to all H4172
Job 6: 4 up my spirit: the **t** of God do set H1161
18:11 **T** shall make him afraid on every side, H1091
14 and it shall bring him to the king of **t**. H1091
20:25 cometh out of his gall: **t** *are* upon him. H367
24:17 *they are in* the **t** of the shadow of death. H1091
27:20 **T** take hold on him as waters, a H1091
30:15 **T** are turned upon me: they pursue my H1091
Ps 55: 4 and the **t** of death are fallen upon me. H367
73:19 they are utterly consumed with **t**. H1091
88:15 up: *while* I suffer thy **t** I am distracted. H367
16 Thy fierce wrath goeth over me; thy **t** H1161
Jer 15: 8 upon it suddenly, and **t** upon the city. H928
Lam 2:22 a solemn day my **t** round about, so that H4032
Ezk 21:12 the princes of Israel: **t** by reason of the H4048

TERTIUS
Ro 16:22 I **T**, who wrote *this* epistle, salute you in G5060

TERTULLUS
Act 24: 1 orator *named* **T**, who informed the G5061
2 And when he was called forth, **T** began G5061

TESTAMENT
Mt 26:28 For this is my blood of the new **t**, which G1242
Mk 14:24 of the new **t**, which is shed for many. G1242
Lk 22:20 **t** in my blood, which is shed for you. G1242
1Co 11:25 cup is the new **t** in my blood: this do G1242
2Co 3: 6 of the new **t**; not of the letter, but G1242
14 old **t**; which *veil* is done away in Christ. G1242
Heb 7:22 was Jesus made a surety of a better **t**. G1242
9:15 of the new **t**, that by means of death, G1242
15 under the first **t**, they which are called G1242
16 For where a **t** *is*, there must also of G1242
17 For a **t** *is* of force after men are dead: G1242
18 Whereupon neither the first *t* was
20 Saying, This *is* the blood of the **t** which G1242
Rev 11:19 temple the ark of his **t**: and there were G1242

TESTATOR
Heb 9:16 also of necessity be the death of the **t**. G1303
17 is of no strength at all while the **t** liveth. G1303

TESTIFIED
Ex 21:29 and it hath been **t** to his owner, and he H5749
Dt 19:18 *and* hath **t** falsely against his brother; H6030
Ru 1:21 the LORD hath **t** against me, and the H6030
2Sa 1:16 thy mouth hath **t** against thee, saying, H6030
2Ki 17:13 Yet the LORD **t** against Israel, and H5749
15 which he **t** against them; and they H5749
2Ch 24:19 the LORD; and they **t** against them: but H5749
Neh 9:26 prophets which **t** against them to turn H5749
13:15 sabbath day: and I **t** *against them* in H5749
21 Then I **t** against them, and said unto H5749
Jn 4:39 which **t**, He told me all that ever I did. G3140
44 For Jesus himself **t**, that a prophet hath G3140
13:21 in spirit, and **t**, and said, Verily, verily, G3140
Act 8:25 And they, when they had **t** and G1263
18: 5 and **t** to the Jews *that* Jesus *was* Christ. G1263
23:11 for as thou hast **t** of me in Jerusalem, G1263
28:23 he expounded and **t** the kingdom of G1263
1Co 15:15 because we have **t** of God that he raised G3140
1Th 4: 6 as we also have forewarned you and **t**. G1263
1Ti 2: 6 a ransom for all, to be **t** in due time. G3142
Heb 2: 6 But one in a certain place **t**, saying, G1263
1Pt 1:11 did signify, when it **t** beforehand the G4303
1Jn 5: 9 of God which he hath **t** of his Son. G3140
3Jn 3 came and **t** of the truth that is in G3140

TESTIFIEDST
Neh 9:29 And **t** against them, that thou mightest H5749
30 forbear them, and **t** against them by H5749

TESTIFIETH
Hos 7:10 And the pride of Israel **t** to his face: H6030
Jn 3:32 **t**; and no man receiveth his testimony. G3140
21:24 This is the disciple which **t** of these G3140
Heb 7:17 For he **t**, Thou *art* a priest for ever after G3140
Rev 22:20 He which **t** these things saith, Surely I G3140

TESTIFY
Nu 35:30 witness shall not **t** against any person H6030
Dt 8:19 worship them, I **t** against you this day H5749
19:16 to **t** against him *that which is* wrong; H6030
31:21 that this song shall **t** against them as a H6030
32:46 all the words which I **t** among you this H5749
Neh 9:34 wherewith thou didst **t** against them. H5749
Job 15: 6 not I: yea, thine own lips **t** against thee. H6030
Ps 50: 7 **t** against thee: I *am* God, *even* thy God. H5749
81: 8 Hear, O my people, and I will **t** unto H5749
Isa 59:12 thee, and our sins **t** against us: for our H6030
Jer 14: 7 O LORD, though our iniquities **t** H6030
Hos 5: 5 And the pride of Israel doth **t** to his H6030
Am 3:13 Hear ye, and **t** in the house of Jacob, H5749
Mic 6: 3 have I wearied thee? **t** against me. H6030
Lk 16:28 For I have five brethren; that he may **t** G1263
Jn 2:25 And needed not that any should **t** of G3140
3:11 we do know, and **t** that we have seen; G3140
5:39 life: and they are they which **t** of me. G3140
7: 7 I **t** of it, that the works thereof are evil. G3140
15:26 from the Father, he shall **t** of me: G3140
Act 2:40 And with many other words did he **t** G1263
10:42 the people, and to **t** that it is he which G1263
20:24 to **t** the gospel of the grace of God. G1263
26: 5 if they would **t**, that after the most G3140
Gal 5: 3 For I **t** again to every man that is G3143
Eph 4:17 This I say therefore, and **t** in the Lord, G3143
1Jn 4:14 And we have seen and do **t** that the G3140
Rev 22:16 I Jesus have sent mine angel to **t** unto G3140
18 For I **t** unto every man that heareth the G4828

TESTIFYING
Act 20:21 **T** both to the Jews, and also to the G1263
Heb 11: 4 righteous, God **t** of his gifts: and by it G3140
1Pt 5:12 exhorting, and **t** that this is the true G1957

TESTIMONIES
Dt 4:45 These *are* the **t**, and the statutes, and H5713
6:17 your God, and his **t**, and his statutes, H5713
20 What *mean* the **t**, and the statutes, and H5713
1Ki 2: 3 and his **t**, as it is written in the H5715
2Ki 17:15 fathers, and his **t** which he testified H5715
23: 3 and his **t** and his statutes with H5715
1Ch 29:19 thy **t**, and thy statutes, and H5715
2Ch 34:31 and his **t**, and his statutes, with H5715
Neh 9:34 and thy **t**, wherewith thou didst H5715
Ps 25:10 such as keep his covenant and his **t**. H5713
78:56 the most high God, and kept not his **t**: H5713
93: 5 Thy **t** are very sure: holiness becometh H5713
99: 7 **t**, and the ordinance *that* he gave them. H5713
119: 2 Blessed *are* they that keep his **t**, *and* H5713
14 I have rejoiced in the way of thy **t**, as H5715
22 and contempt; for I have kept thy **t**. H5713
24 Thy **t** also *are* my delight *and* my H5713
31 I have stuck unto thy **t**: O LORD, put me H5715
36 Incline my heart unto thy **t**, and not to H5715
46 I will speak of thy **t** also before kings, H5713
59 my ways, and turned my feet unto thy **t**. H5713
79 me, and those that have known thy **t**. H5713
95 to destroy me: *but* I will consider thy **t**. H5713
99 teachers: for thy **t** *are* my meditation. H5715
111 Thy **t** have I taken as an heritage for H5715
119 earth *like* dross: therefore I love thy **t**. H5713
125 understanding, that I may know thy **t**. H5713
129 Thy **t** *are* wonderful: therefore doth my H5715
138 Thy **t** *that* thou hast commanded *are* H5713
144 The righteousness of thy **t** *is* H5715
146 thee; save me, and I shall keep thy **t**. H5713
152 Concerning thy **t**, I have known of old H5713
157 enemies; *yet* do I not decline from thy **t**. H5715
167 My soul hath kept thy **t**; and I love them H5713
168 I have kept thy precepts and thy **t**: for H5713
Jer 44:23 statutes, nor in his **t**; therefore this evil H5715

TESTIMONY
Ex 16:34 Aaron laid it up before the **T**, to be kept. H5715
25:16 And thou shalt put into the ark the **t** H5715
21 shalt put the **t** that I shall give thee. H5715
22 the ark of the **t**, of all *things* which I H5715
26:33 vail the ark of the **t**: and the vail shall H5715
34 the ark of the **t** in the most holy *place*. H5715
27:21 which *is* before the **t**, Aaron and his H5715
30: 6 *is* by the ark of the **t**, before the mercy H5715
6 over the **t**, where I will meet with thee. H5715
26 therewith, and the ark of the **t**, H5715
36 put of it before the **t** in the tabernacle H5715
31: 7 and the ark of the **t**, and the mercy seat H5715
18 two tables of **t**, tables of stone, written H5715
32:15 two tables of the **t** *were* in his hand: the H5715
34:29 with the two tables of **t** in Moses' hand, H5715
38:21 of the tabernacle of **t**, as it was counted, H5715
39:35 The ark of the **t**, and the staves thereof, H5715
40: 3 of the **t**, and cover the ark with the vail. H5715
5 the ark of the **t**, and put the hanging H5715
20 And he took and put the **t** into the ark, H5715
21 the **t**; as the LORD commanded Moses. H5715
Lev 16:13 seat that *is* upon the **t**, that he die not: H5715
24: 3 Without the vail of the **t**, in the H5715
Nu 1:50 over the tabernacle of **t**, and over all the H5715
53 the tabernacle of **t**, that there be no H5715
53 keep the charge of the tabernacle of **t**. H5715
4: 5 vail, and cover the ark of **t** with it: H5715
7:89 upon the ark of **t**, from between the two H5715
9:15 the tent of the **t**: and at even there was H5715
10:11 up from off the tabernacle of the **t**. H5715
17: 4 before the **t**, where I will meet with you. H5715
10 again before the **t**, to be kept for a token H5715
Jos 4:16 the **t**, that they come up out of Jordan. H5715
Ru 4: 7 neighbour: and this *was* a **t** in Israel. H8584
2Ki 11:12 and *gave him* the **t**; and they made him H5715
2Ch 23:11 and *gave him* the **t**, and made him king. H5715
Ps 19: 7 the soul: the **t** of the LORD *is* sure, H5715
78: 5 For he established a **t** in Jacob, and H5715
81: 5 This he ordained in Joseph *for* a **t**, when H5715
119:88 so shall I keep the **t** of thy mouth. H5715
122: 4 the LORD, unto the **t** of Israel, to give H5715
132:12 covenant and my **t** that I shall teach H5713
Isa 8:16 Bind up the **t**, seal the law among my H8584
20 To the law and to the **t**: if they speak not H8584
Mt 8: 4 Moses commanded, for a **t** unto them. G3142
10:18 for a **t** against them and the Gentiles. G3142
Mk 1:44 Moses commanded, for a **t** unto them. G3142
6:11 your feet for a **t** against them. Verily G3142
13: 9 kings for my sake, for a **t** against them. G3142
Lk 5:14 Moses commanded, for a **t** unto them. G3142
9: 5 from your feet for a **t** against them. G3142
21:13 And it shall turn to you for a **t**. G3142
Jn 3:32 testifieth; and no man receiveth his **t**. G3141
33 He that hath received his **t** hath set to G3141
5:34 But I receive not **t** from man: but these G3141
8:17 It is also written in your law, that the **t** G3141
21:24 things: and we know that his **t** is true. G3141
Act 13:22 also he gave **t**, and said, I have found G3140
14: 3 Lord, which gave **t** unto the word of his G3140
22:18 will not receive thy **t** concerning me. G3141
1Co 1: 6 Even as the **t** of Christ was confirmed G3142
2: 1 declaring unto you the **t** of God. G3142
2Co 1:12 For our rejoicing is this, the **t** of our G3142
2Th 1:10 **t** among you was believed) in that day. G3142
2Ti 1: 8 Be not thou therefore ashamed of the **t** G3142
Heb 3: 5 as a servant, for a **t** of those things G3142
11: 5 he had this **t**, that he pleased God. G3140
Rev 1: 2 of God, and of the **t** of Jesus Christ, and G3141
9 of God, and for the **t** of Jesus Christ. G3141
6: 9 of God, and for the **t** which they held: G3141
11: 7 have finished their **t**, the beast that G3141
12:11 the word of their **t**; and they loved not G3141
17 of God, and have the **t** of Jesus Christ. G3141
15: 5 of the **t** in heaven was opened: G3142
19:10 that have the **t** of Jesus: worship God: G3141
10 the **t** of Jesus is the spirit of prophecy. G3141

TETRARCH
Mt 14: 1 At that time Herod the **t** heard of the G5076
Lk 3: 1 and Herod being **t** of Galilee, and his G5075
1 his brother Philip **t** of Ituraea and of G5075
1 and Lysanias the **t** of Abilene, G5075
19 But Herod the **t**, being reproved by him G5076
9: 7 Now Herod the **t** heard of all that was G5076
Act 13: 1 brought up with Herod the **t**, and Saul. G5076

THADDAEUS
Mt 10: 3 and Lebbaeus, whose surname was **T**; G2280
Mk 3:18 and **T**, and Simon the Canaanite, G2280

THAHASH
Gen 22:24 and Gaham, and T, and Maachah. H8477

THAMAH
Ezr 2:53 the children of Sisera, the children of T, H8547

THAMAR
Mt 1: 3 And Judas begat Phares and Zara of T; *G2283*

THAN See the Appendix.

THANK
1Ch 16: 4 to t and praise the LORD God of Israel: H3034
7 first *this psalm* to t the LORD into the H3034
23:30 And to stand every morning to t and H3034
29:13 Now therefore, our God, we t thee, and H3034
2Ch 29:31 sacrifices and t offerings into the house H8426
31 in sacrifices and t offerings; and as H8426
33:16 peace offerings and t offerings, and H8426
Dan 2:23 I t thee, and praise thee, O thou God of H3029
Mt 11:25 and said, I t thee, O Father, Lord *G1843*
Lk 6:32 love you, what t have ye? for sinners *G5485*
33 good to you, what t have ye? for sinners *G5485*
34 to receive, what t have ye? for sinners *G5485*
10:21 spirit, and said, I t thee, O Father, Lord *G1843*
17: 9 Doth he t that servant because he did *G5485*
18:11 himself, God, I t thee, that I am not as *G2168*
Jn 11:41 I t thee that thou hast heard me. *G2168*
Ro 1: 8 First, I t my God through Jesus Christ *G2168*
7:25 I t God through Jesus Christ our Lord. *G2168*
1Co 1: 4 I t my God always on your behalf, for *G2168*
14 I t God that I baptized none of you, but *G2168*
14:18 I t my God, I speak with tongues more *G2168*
Php 1: 3 I t my God upon every remembrance of *G2168*
1Th 2:13 For this cause also t we God without *G2168*
2Th 1: 3 We are bound to t God always for you, *G2168*
1Ti 1:12 And I t Christ Jesus our Lord, who hath *G2192*
2Ti 1: 3 I t God, whom I serve from *my* *G2192*
Phlm 4 I t my God, making mention of thee *G2168*

THANKED
2Sa 14:22 himself, and t the king: and Joab said, H1288
Act 28:15 Paul saw, he t God, and took courage. *G2168*
Ro 6:17 But God be t, that ye were the servants *G5485*

THANKFUL
Ps 100: 4 be t unto him, *and* bless his name. H3034
Ro 1:21 God, neither were t; but became vain in *G2168*
Col 3:15 ye are called in one body; and be ye t. *G2170*

THANKFULNESS
Act 24: 3 in all places, most noble Felix, with all t. *G2169*

THANKING
2Ch 5:13 in praising and t the LORD; and when H3034

THANKS
2Sa 22:50 Therefore I will give t unto thee, O H3034
1Ch 16: 8 Give t unto the LORD, call upon his H3034
34 O give t unto the LORD; for *he is* good; H3034
35 that we may give t to thy holy name, H3034
41 by name, to give t to the LORD, H3034
25: 3 harp, to give t and to praise the LORD. H3034
2Ch 31: 2 and to give t, and to praise in the H3034
Ezr 3:11 and giving t unto the LORD; because H3034
Neh 12:24 to praise *and* to give t, according to the H3034
31 *of them that gave* t, *whereof one* went H8426
38 *of them that gave* t went over against H8426
40 *of them that gave* t in the house of God, H8426
Ps 6: 5 thee: in the grave who shall give thee t? H3034
18:49 Therefore will I give t unto thee, O H3034
30: 4 t at the remembrance of his holiness. H3034
12 my God, I will give t unto thee for ever. H3034
35:18 I will give thee t in the great H3034
75: 1 Unto thee, O God, do we give t, *unto* H3034
1 *thee* do we give t: for *that* thy name is H3034
79:13 will give thee t for ever: we will shew H3034
92: 1 *It is a* good *thing* to give t unto the H3034
97:12 t at the remembrance of his holiness. H3034
105: 1 O give t unto the LORD; call upon his H3034
106: 1 Praise ye the LORD. O give t unto the H3034
47 heathen, to give t unto thy holy name, H3034
107: 1 O give t unto the LORD, for *he is* good: H3034
118: 1 O give t unto the LORD; for *he is* good: H3034
29 O give t unto the LORD; for *he is* good: H3034
119:62 At midnight I will rise to give t unto H3034
122: 4 to give t unto the name of the LORD. H3034
136: 1 O give t unto the LORD; for *he is* good: H3034
2 O give t unto the God of gods: for his H3034
Ps 136: 3 O give t to the Lord of lords: for his H3034
26 O give t unto the God of heaven: for his H3034
140:13 Surely the righteous shall give t unto H3034
Dan 6:10 t before his God, as he did aforetime. H3029
Mt 15:36 fishes, and gave t, and brake *them*, and *G2168*
26:27 And he took the cup, and gave t, and *G2168*
Mk 8: 6 loaves, and gave t, and brake, and gave *G2168*
14:23 when he had given t, he gave *it* to them: *G2168*
Lk 2:38 And she coming in that instant gave t *G437*
17:16 giving him t: and he was a Samaritan. *G2168*
22:17 And he took the cup, and gave t, and *G2168*
19 And he took bread, and gave t, and *G2168*
Jn 6:11 when he had given t, he distributed to *G2168*
23 bread, after that the Lord had given t:) *G2168*
Act 27:35 bread, and gave t to God in presence of *G2168*
Ro 14: 6 for he giveth God t; and he that eateth *G2168*
6 Lord he eateth not, and giveth God t. *G2168*
16: 4 whom not only I give t, but also all the *G2168*
1Co 10:30 evil spoken of for that for which I give t? *G2168*
11:24 And when he had given t, he brake *it*, *G2168*
14:16 Amen at thy giving of t, seeing he *G2169*
17 For thou verily givest t well, but the *G2168*
15:57 But t *be* to God, which giveth us the *G5485*
2Co 1:11 t may be given by many on our behalf. *G2168*
2:14 Now t *be* unto God, which always *G5485*
8:16 But t *be* to God, which put the same *G5485*
9:15 T *be* unto God for his unspeakable gift. *G5485*
Eph 1:16 Cease not to give t for you, making *G2168*
5: 4 not convenient: but rather giving of t. *G2169*
20 Giving t always for all things unto God *G2168*
Col 1: 3 We give t to God and the Father of our *G2168*
12 Giving t unto the Father, which hath *G2168*
3:17 giving t to God and the Father by him. *G2168*
1Th 1: 2 We give t to God always for you all, *G2168*
3: 9 For what t can we render to God again *G2169*
5:18 In every thing give t: for this is the will *G2168*
2Th 2:13 But we are bound to give t alway to *G2168*
1Ti 2: 1 *and* giving of t, be made for all men; *G2169*
Heb 13:15 fruit of *our* lips giving t to his name. *G3670*
Rev 4: 9 and honour and t to him that sat on *G2169*
11:17 Saying, We give thee t, O Lord God *G2168*

THANKSGIVING
Lev 7:12 If he offer it for a t, then he shall offer H8426
12 with the sacrifice of t unleavened cakes H8426
13 the sacrifice of t of his peace offerings. H8426
15 peace offerings for t shall be eaten the H8426
22:29 And when ye will offer a sacrifice of t H8426
Neh 11:17 to begin the t in prayer: and Bakbukiah H3034
12: 8 *was* over the t, he and his brethren. H1960
46 and songs of praise and t unto God. H3034
Ps 26: 7 That I may publish with the voice of t, H8426
50:14 Offer unto God t; and pay thy vows unto H8426
69:30 a song, and will magnify him with t. H8426
95: 2 Let us come before his presence with t, H8426
100: 4 Enter into his gates with t, *and* into his H8426
107:22 And let them sacrifice the sacrifices of t, H8426
116:17 I will offer to thee the sacrifice of t, and H8426
147: 7 Sing unto the LORD with t; sing praise H8426
Isa 51: 3 therein, t, and the voice of melody. H8426
Jer 30:19 And out of them shall proceed t and H8426
Am 4: 5 And offer a sacrifice of t with leaven, H8426
Jna 2: 9 with the voice of t; I will pay *that* that I H8426
2Co 4:15 t of many redound to the glory of God. *G2169*
9:11 which causeth through us t to God. *G2169*
Php 4: 6 supplication with t let your requests be *G2169*
Col 2: 7 been taught, abounding therein with t. *G2169*
4: 2 in prayer, and watch in the same with t; *G2169*
1Ti 4: 3 to be received with t of them which *G2169*
4 to be refused, if it be received with t: *G2169*
Rev 7:12 and wisdom, and t, and honour, and *G2169*

THANKSGIVINGS
Neh 12:27 both with t, and with singing, *with* H8426
2Co 9:12 is abundant also by many t unto God; *G2169*

THANKWORTHY
1Pt 2:19 For this *is* t, if a man for conscience *G5485*

THARA
Lk 3:34 *son* of T, which was *the son* of Nachor, *G2291*

THARSHISH
1Ki 10:22 For the king had at sea a navy of T with H8659
22 came the navy of T, bringing gold, and H8659
22:48 Jehoshaphat made ships of T to go to H8659
1Ch 7:10 and Zethan, and T, and Ahishahar. H8659

THAT See the Appendix.

THE See the Appendix.

THEATRE
Act 19:29 they rushed with one accord into the t. *G2302*
31 would not adventure himself into the t. *G2302*

THEBEZ
Jdg 9:50 Then went Abimelech to T, and H8405
50 and encamped against T, and took it. H8405
2Sa 11:21 that he died in T? why went ye nigh the H8405

THEE See the Appendix.

THEE-WARD
1Sa 19: 4 his works *have been* to t very good:

THEFT
Ex 22: 3 nothing, then he shall be sold for his t. H1591
4 If the t be certainly found in his hand H1591

THEFTS
Mt 15:19 t, false witness, blasphemies: *G2829*
Mk 7:22 T, covetousness, wickedness, deceit, *G2829*
Rev 9:21 nor of their fornication, nor of their t. *G2809*

THEIR See the Appendix.

THEIRS
Gen 15:13 in a land *that is* not t, and shall serve H1992
34:23 and every beast of t *be* ours? only let us
43:34 so much as any of t. And they drank, and
Ex 29: 9 office shall be t for a perpetual statute: H1992
Lev 18:10 uncover: for t *is* thine own nakedness. H2007
Nu 16:26 t, lest ye be consumed in all their sins. H1992
18: 9 every oblation of t, every meat offering of
9 meat offering of t, and every sin offering
9 every sin offering of t, and every trespass
9 trespass offering of t, which they shall
Jos 21:10 of Levi, had: for t was the first lot. H1992
1Ch 6:54 of the Kohathites: for t was the lot. H1992
2Ch 18:12 be like one of t, and speak thou good. H1992
Jer 44:28 whose words shall stand, mine, or t. H1992
Ezk 7:11 nor of any of t: neither *shall there be* H1992
44:29 dedicated thing in Israel shall be t. H1992
Hab 1: 6 possess the dwellingplaces *that are* not t.
Mt 5: 3 Blessed *are* the poor in spirit: for t is the *G846*
10 sake: for t is the kingdom of heaven. *G846*
1Co 1: 2 of Jesus Christ our Lord, both t and ours: *G846*
2Ti 3: 9 be manifest unto all *men*, as t also was. *G1565*

THELASAR
2Ki 19:12 the children of Eden which *were* in T? H8515

THEM See the Appendix.

THEMSELVES See the Appendix.

THEN See the Appendix.

THENCE
Gen 2:10 garden; and from t it was parted, and H8033
11: 8 them abroad from t upon the face of all H8033
9 earth: and from t did the LORD scatter H8033
12: 8 And he removed from t unto a H8033
18:16 And the men rose up from t, and looked H8033
22 And the men turned their faces from t, H8033
20: 1 And Abraham journeyed from t H8033
24: 7 shalt take a wife unto my son from t. H8033
26:17 And Isaac departed t, and pitched his H8033
22 And he removed from t, and digged H8033
23 And he went up from t to Beer-sheba. H8033
27: 9 and fetch me from t two good kids of H8033
45 and fetch thee from t: why should I be H8033
28: 2 thee a wife from t of the daughters of H8033
6 take him a wife from t; and that as he H8033
30:32 removing from t all the speckled and H8033
42: 2 us from t; that we may live, and not die. H8033
26 asses with the corn, and departed t. H8033
49:24 t *is* the shepherd, the stone of Israel:) H8033
Nu 13:23 and cut down from t a branch with one H8033
24 the children of Israel cut down from t. H8033
21:12 From t they removed, and pitched in H8033
13 From t they removed, and pitched on H8033
16 And from t *they went* to Beer: that *is* H8033
22:41 of Baal, that t he might see the utmost H8033
23:13 see them all: and curse me them from t. H8033
27 that thou mayest curse me them from t. H8033
Dt 4:29 But if from t thou shalt seek the LORD H8033
5:15 brought thee out t through a mighty H8033

Dt 6:23 And he brought us out from **t**, that he H8033
10: 7 From **t** they journeyed unto Gudgodah; H8033
19:12 and fetch him **t**, and deliver him into H8033
22: 8 upon thine house, if any man fall from **t**.
24:18 redeemed thee **t**: therefore I command H8033
30: 4 of heaven, from **t** will the LORD thy H8033
4 thee, and from **t** will he fetch thee: H8033
Jos 6:22 and bring out **t** the woman, and all H8033
15: 4 *From t* it passed toward Azmon, and
14 And Caleb drove **t** the three sons of H8033
15 And he went up **t** to the inhabitants of H8033
18:13 And the border went over from **t** H8033
14 And the border was drawn *t*, and
19:13 And from **t** passeth on along on the H8033
34 and goeth out from **t** to Hukkok, and H8033
Jdg 1:11 And from **t** he went against the H8033
20 he expelled **t** the three sons of Anak. H8033
8: 8 And he went up **t** to Penuel, and spake H8033
18:11 And there went from **t** of the family of H8033
13 And they passed **t** unto mount H8033
19:18 Ephraim; from **t** *am* I: and I went to H8033
21:24 And the children of Israel departed **t** at H8033
24 from **t** every man to his inheritance. H8033
1Sa 4: 4 they might bring from **t** the ark of the H8033
10: 3 Then shalt thou go on forward from **t**, H8033
23 And they ran and fetched him **t**: and H8033
17:49 his bag, and took **t** a stone, and slang H8033
22: 1 David therefore departed **t**, and H8033
3 And David went **t** to Mizpeh of Moab: H8033
23:29 And David went up from **t**, and dwelt in H8033
2Sa 6: 2 to bring up from **t** the ark of God, H8033
14: 2 And Joab sent to Tekoah, and fetched **t** H8033
16: 5 Bahurim, behold, **t** came out a man of H8033
21:13 And he brought up from **t** the bones of H8033
1Ki 1:45 are come up from **t** rejoicing, so that H8033
2:36 there, and go not forth **t** any whither. H8033
9:28 and fetched from **t** gold, four hundred H8033
12:25 and went out from **t**, and built Penuel. H8033
19:19 So he departed **t**, and found Elisha the H8033
2Ki 2:21 from **t** any more death or barren *land*. H8033
23 And he went up from **t** unto Beth-el: H8033
25 And he went from **t** to mount Carmel, H8033
25 and from **t** he returned to Samaria. H8033
6: 2 Jordan, and take **t** every man a beam, H8033
7: 8 drink, and carried **t** silver, and gold, H8033
8 and carried **t** *also*, and went and hid *it*. H8033
10:15 And when he was departed **t**, he lighted H8033
17:27 ye brought from **t**; and let them go and H8033
33 whom they carried away from **t**. H8033
23:12 *them* down from **t**, and cast the dust of H8033
24:13 And he carried out **t** all the treasures of H8033
1Ch 13: 6 Judah, to bring up **t** the ark of God the H8033
2Ch 8:18 to Ophir, and took **t** four hundred and H8033
26:20 him out from **t**; yea, himself hasted H8033
Ezr 6: 6 *are* beyond the river, be ye far from **t**: H8536
Neh 1: 9 gather them from **t**, and will bring them H8033
Job 39:29 From **t** she seeketh the prey, *and* her H8033
Isa 52:11 Depart ye, depart ye, go ye out from **t**, H8033
65:20 There shall be no more **t** an infant of H8033
Jer 5: 6 one that goeth out **t** shall be torn in H2007
13: 6 the girdle from **t**, which I commanded H8033
22:24 my right hand, yet would I pluck thee **t**;
36:29 cause to cease from **t** man and beast? H8033
37:12 himself **t** in the midst of the people. H8033
38:11 treasury, and took **t** old cast clouts and H8033
43:12 and he shall go forth from **t** in peace. H8033
49:16 thee down from **t**, saith the LORD. H8033
38 will destroy from **t** the king and the H8033
50: 9 against her; from **t** she shall be taken: H8033
Ezk 11:18 and all the abominations thereof from **t**.
Hos 2:15 And I will give her her vineyards from **t**, H8033
Am 6: 2 and see; and from **t** go ye to Hamath H8033
9: 2 Though they dig into hell, **t** shall mine H8033
2 up to heaven, **t** will I bring them down: H8033
3 and take them out **t**; and though they be H8033
3 bottom of the sea, **t** will I command the H8033
4 their enemies, **t** will I command the H8033
Oba 4 nest among the stars, **t** will I bring thee H8033
Mt 4:21 And going on from **t**, he saw other two *G1564*
5:26 no means come out **t**, till thou hast paid *G1564*
9: 9 And as Jesus passed forth from **t**, he *G1564*
27 And when Jesus departed **t**, two blind *G1564*
10:11 it is worthy; and there abide till ye go **t**. *G1831*
11: 1 **t** to teach and to preach in their cities. *G1564*
12: 9 And when he was departed **t**, he went *G1564*
15 himself from **t**: and great multitudes *G1564*
13:53 finished these parables, he departed **t**. *G1564*
14:13 When Jesus heard *of it*, he departed **t** *G1564*
15:21 Then Jesus went **t**, and departed into *G1564*
Mt 15:29 And Jesus departed from **t**, and came *G1564*
19:15 laid *his* hands on them, and departed **t**. *G1564*
Mk 1:19 And when he had gone a little farther **t**, *G1564*
6: 1 And he went out from **t**, and came into *G1564*
11 when ye depart **t**, shake off the dust *G1564*
7:24 And from **t** he arose, and went into the *G1564*
9:30 And they departed **t**, and passed *G1564*
10: 1 And he arose from **t**, and cometh into *G2547*
Lk 9: 4 ye enter into, there abide, and **t** depart. *G1564*
12:59 I tell thee, thou shalt not depart **t**, till *G1564*
16:26 they pass to us, that *would come* from **t**. *G1564*
Jn 4:43 Now after two days he departed **t**, and *G1564*
11:54 the Jews; but went **t** unto a country *G1564*
Act 7: 4 and from **t**, when his father was *G2547*
13: 4 and from **t** they sailed to Cyprus. *G1564*
14:26 And **t** sailed to Antioch, from whence *G2547*
16:12 And from **t** to Philippi, which is the *G1564*
18: 7 And he departed **t**, and entered into a *G1564*
18 and sailed **t** into Syria, and with *G1602*
20:15 And we sailed **t**, and came the next *day* *G2547*
21: 1 unto Rhodes, and from **t** unto Patara: *G2547*
27: 4 And when we had launched from **t**, we *G2547*
12 part advised to depart **t** also, if by any *G1564*
13 loosing *t*, they sailed close by Crete.
28:13 And from **t** we fetched a compass, and *G3606*
15 And from **t**, when the brethren heard of *G2547*
2Co 2:13 of them, I went from **t** into Macedonia. *G1831*

THENCEFORTH
Lev 22:27 from the eighth day and **t** it shall be H1973
2Ch 32:23 in the sight of all nations from **t**. H310
Mt 5:13 it be salted? it is **t** good for nothing, but *G2089*
Jn 19:12 And from **t** Pilate sought to release *G5127*

THEOPHILUS
Lk 1: 3 unto thee in order, most excellent **T**, *G2321*
Act 1: 1 The former treatise have I made, O **T**, of *G2321*

THERE See the Appendix.

THEREABOUT
Lk 24: 4 much perplexed **t**, behold, two men *G4012*

THEREAT
Ex 30:19 shall wash their hands and their feet **t**:
40:31 sons washed their hands and their feet **t**:
Mt 7:13 and many there be which go in **t**: *G1223+G846*

THEREBY
Gen 24:14 thy servant Isaac; and **t** shall I know that
Lev 11:43 with them, that ye should be defiled **t**.
Job 22:21 be at peace: **t** good shall come unto thee.
Prv 20: 1 and whosoever is deceived **t** is not wise.
Ecc 10: 9 that cleaveth wood shall be endangered **t**.
Isa 33:21 oars, neither shall gallant ship pass **t**.
Jer 18:16 one that passeth **t** shall be astonished, H5921
19: 8 one that passeth **t** shall be astonished H5921
51:43 neither doth *any* son of man pass **t**. H2004
Ezk 12: 5 the wall in their sight, and carry out **t**.
12 wall to carry out **t**: he shall cover his face,
33:12 he shall not fall **t** in the day that he
18 committeth iniquity, he shall even die **t**.
19 which is lawful and right, he shall live **t**.
Zec 9: 2 And Hamath also shall border **t**; Tyrus,
Jn 11: 4 Son of God might be glorified **t**. *G1223+G846*
Eph 2:16 cross, having slain the enmity **t**: *G1722+G846*
Heb 12:11 unto them which are exercised **t**. *G1223+G846*
15 *you*, and **t** many be defiled; *G1223+G3778*
13: 2 strangers: for **t** some have *G1223+G3778*
1Pt 2: 2 of the word, that ye may grow **t**: *G1722+G846*

THEREFORE See the Appendix.

THEREFROM
Jos 23: 6 aside **t** *to* the right hand or *to* the left;
2Ki 3: 3 made Israel to sin; he departed not **t**.
13: 2 made Israel to sin; he departed not **t**.

THEREIN
Gen 9: 7 abundantly in the earth, and multiply **t**.
18:24 place for the fifty righteous that *are* **t**? H7130
23:11 and the cave that *is* **t**, I give it thee; in the
17 the cave which *was* **t**, and all the trees
20 And the field, and the cave that *is* **t**, were
34:10 ye **t**, and get you possessions therein.
10 ye therein, and get you possessions **t**.
21 in the land, and trade **t**; for the land,
47:27 **t**, and grew, and multiplied exceedingly.
49:32 that *is* **t** *was* from the children of Heth.
Ex 2: 3 and put the child **t**; and she laid *it* in the
5: 9 **t**; and let them not regard vain words.
16:24 not stink, neither was there any worm **t**.
33 full of manna **t**, and lay it up before H8033
21:33 not cover it, and an ox or an ass fall **t**; H8033
29:29 **t**, and to be consecrated in them.
30:18 the altar, and thou shalt put water **t**. H8033
31:14 doeth *any* work **t**, that soul shall be cut
35: 2 doeth work **t** shall be put to death.
40: 3 And thou shalt put **t** the ark of the H8033
7 and the altar, and shalt put water **t**. H8033
9 and all that *is* **t**, and shalt hallow it, and
Lev 6: 3 of all these that a man doeth, sinning **t**: H2007
7 of all that he hath done in trespassing **t**.
8:10 and all that *was* **t**, and sanctified them.
10: 1 and put fire **t**, and put incense thereon, H2004
13:21 *be* no white hairs **t**, and *if it be* not lower
37 hair grown up **t**; the scall is healed, he
18: 4 to walk **t**: I *am* the LORD your God.
30 yourselves **t**: I *am* the LORD your God.
20:22 I bring you to dwell **t**, spue you not out.
22:21 be accepted; there shall be no blemish **t**.
23: 3 ye shall do no work *t*: it *is* the sabbath of
7 ye shall do no servile work **t**.
8 ye shall do no servile work *t*.
21 do no servile work *t*: *it shall be* a statute
25 Ye shall do no servile work *t*: but ye shall
35 ye shall do no servile work *t*.
36 *and* ye shall do no servile work *t*.
25:19 shall eat your fill, and dwell **t** in safety. H5921
26:32 which dwell **t** shall be astonished at it.
Nu 4:16 and of all that **t** *is*, in the sanctuary,
13:18 that dwelleth **t**, whether they *be* strong H5921
20 there be wood **t**, or not. And be ye of
14:30 to make you dwell **t**, save Caleb the son
16: 7 And put fire **t**, and put incense in them H2004
46 and put fire **t** from off the altar, and H5921
28:18 ye shall do no manner of servile work *t*:
29: 7 your souls: ye shall not do any work *t*:
35 assembly: ye shall do no servile work *t*:
32:40 the son of Manasseh; and he dwelt **t**.
33:53 the land, and dwell **t**: for I have given you
35:33 **t**, but by the blood of him that shed it.
Dt 2:10 The Emims dwelt **t** in times past, a
20 giants: giants dwelt **t** in old time; and the
7:25 thee, lest thou be snared **t**: for it *is* an
8:12 hast built goodly houses, and dwelt *t*;
10:14 thy God, the earth *also*, with all that **t** *is*.
11:31 you, and ye shall possess it, and dwell **t**.
13:15 and all that *is* **t**, and the cattle thereof,
15:21 And if there be *any* blemish **t**, *as if it be*
16: 8 LORD thy God: thou shalt do no work *t*.
17:14 it, and shalt dwell **t**, and shalt say, I will
19 and he shall read **t** all the days of his life:
20:11 *that is* found **t** shall be tributaries unto
26: 1 and possessest it, and dwellest **t**;
28:30 thou shalt not dwell **t**: thou shalt plant a
29:23 any grass groweth **t**, like the overthrow of
Jos 1: 8 shalt meditate **t** day and night, that thou
8 to all that is written **t**: for then thou shalt
6:17 it, and all that *are* **t**, to the LORD: only
24 and all that *was* **t**: only the silver, and the
10:28 the souls that *were* **t**; he let none remain:
30 the souls that *were* **t**; he let none remain
32 the souls that *were* **t**, according to all that
35 the souls that *were* **t** he utterly destroyed
37 all the souls that *were* **t**; he left none
37 it utterly, and all the souls that *were* **t**.
39 all the souls that *were* **t**; he left none
11:11 And they smote all the souls that *were* **t**
19:47 it, and dwelt **t**, and called Leshem, Dan,
50 and he built the city, and dwelt **t**.
21:43 and they possessed it, and dwelt **t**.
Jdg 2:22 walk **t**, as their fathers did keep *it*, or not.
8:25 **t** every man the earrings of his prey. H8033
9:45 the people that *was* **t**, and beat down the
16:30 people that *were* **t**. So the dead which he
18: 7 the people that *were* **t**, how they dwelt H7130
28 And they built a city, and dwelt **t**.
1Sa 30: 2 captives, that *were* **t**: they slew not any,
2Sa 12:31 people that *were* **t**, and put *them* under
1Ki 8:16 my name might be **t**; but I chose David H8033
11:24 and dwelt **t**, and reigned in Damascus.
12:25 and dwelt **t**; and went out from thence,
2Ki 2:20 put salt **t**. And they brought *it* to him. H8033
12: 9 kept the door put **t** all the money *that* H8033
13: 6 sin, *but* walked **t**: and there remained
11 who made Israel sin: *but* he walked **t**.
15:16 and all that *were* **t**, and the coasts thereof

2Ki 15:16 t that were with child he ripped up.
1Ch 16:32 let the fields rejoice, and all that is t.
21:22 I may build an altar t unto the LORD:
2Ch 2: 3 an house to dwell t, even so deal with me.
5:10 which Moses put t at Horeb, when the
20: 8 And they dwelt t, and have built thee a
8 thee a sanctuary t for thy name, saying,
Ezr 4:19 rebellion and sedition have been made t.
6: 2 a roll, and t was a record thus written: H1459
Neh 6: 1 was no breach left t; (though at that time
7: 4 few t, and the houses were not builded.
5 came up at the first, and found written t,
8: 3 And he read t before the street that was
9: 6 all things that are t, the seas, and all H5921
6 seas, and all that is t, and thou preservest
13: 1 of the people; and t was found written,
16 There dwelt men of Tyre also t, which
Job 3: 7 be solitary, let no joyful voice come t.
20:18 restitution be, and he shall not rejoice t.
Ps 24: 1 thereof; the world, and they that dwell t.
37:29 inherit the land, and dwell t for ever. H5921
68:10 Thy congregation hath dwelt t: thou, O
69:34 the seas, and every thing that moveth t.
36 and they that love his name shall dwell t.
96:12 Let the field be joyful, and all that is t:
98: 7 thereof; the world, and they that dwell t.
104:26 whom thou hast made to play t.
107:34 for the wickedness of them that dwell t.
111: 2 out of all them that have pleasure t.
119:35 of thy commandments; for t do I delight.
146: 6 all that t is: which keepeth truth for ever:
Prv 15: 4 perverseness t is a breach in the spirit.
22:14 that is abhorred of the LORD shall fall t. H8033
26:27 Whoso diggeth a pit shall fall t: and he
Ecc 2:21 hath not laboured t shall he leave it for
Isa 5: 2 made a winepress t: and he looked that H8432
7: 6 us make a breach t for us, and set a king
24: 6 earth, and they that dwell t are desolate:
33:24 dwell t shall be forgiven their iniquity.
34: 1 hear, and all that is t; the world, and all H4393
17 to generation shall they dwell t.
35: 8 men, though fools, shall not err t.
42: 5 upon it, and spirit to them that walk t:
10 t; the isles, and the inhabitants thereof. H4393
44:23 and every tree t: for the LORD hath
51: 3 t, thanksgiving, and the voice of melody.
6 and they that dwell t shall die in like
59: 8 whosoever goeth t shall not know peace.
Jer 4:29 be forsaken, and not a man dwell t. H2004
6:16 way, and walk t, and ye shall find rest
16 souls. But they said, We will not walk t.
8:16 is in it; the city, and those that dwell t.
9:13 not obeyed my voice, neither walked t;
12: 4 of them that dwell t? the beasts are
17:24 hallow the sabbath day, to do no work t;
23:12 driven on, and fall t: for I will bring evil
27:11 LORD; and they shall till it, and dwell t.
36: 2 Take thee a roll of a book, and write t all H413
29 hast thou written t, saying, The king of H5921
32 Neriah; who wrote t from the mouth of H5921
44: 2 are a desolation, and no man dwelleth t,
47: 2 and all that is t; the city, and them that H4393
2 them that dwell t: then the men shall cry,
48: 9 shall be desolate, without any to dwell t. H2004
50: 3 and none shall dwell t: they shall remove,
39 the owls shall dwell t: and it shall be no
40 neither shall any son of man dwell t.
51:48 and all that is t, shall sing for Babylon:
Ezk 2: 9 unto me; and, lo, a roll of a book was t;
10 t lamentations, and mourning, and woe. H413
7:20 t: therefore have I set it far from them.
12:19 from all that is t, because of the H4393
19 of the violence of all them that dwell t.
14:22 Yet, behold, t shall be left a remnant that
20:47 the south to the north shall be burned t.
24: 5 and let them seethe the bones of it t. H8432
6 pot whose scum is t, and whose scum is
28:26 And they shall dwell safely t, and shall H5921
30:12 waste, and all that is t, by the hand of H4393
32:15 all them that dwell t, then shall they
37:25 they shall dwell t, even they, and their
40:33 there were windows t and in the arches
42:14 When the priests enter t, then shall they
44:14 thereof, and for all that shall be done t.
Dan 5: 2 wives, and his concubines, might drink t.
Hos 4: 3 one that dwelleth t shall languish, with
14: 9 in them: but the transgressors shall fall t.
Am 6: 8 will I deliver up the city with all that is t. H4393
8: 8 that dwelleth t? and it shall rise up wholly
Am 9: 5 and all that dwell t shall mourn: and it
Mic 1: 2 earth, and all that t is: and let the Lord H4393
7:13 that dwell t, for the fruit of their doings.
Nah 1: 5 yea, the world, and all that dwell t.
Hab 2: 8 land, of the city, and of all that dwell t.
17 land, of the city, and of all that dwell t.
18 work trusteth t, to make dumb idols? H5921
Zec 2: 4 for the multitude of men and cattle t: H8432
6: 6 The black horses which are t go forth
13: 8 LORD, two parts t shall be cut off and
8 off and die; but the third shall be left t.
14:21 them, and seethe t: and in that day there
Mt 23:21 by it, and by him that dwelleth t. G846
Mk 10:15 a little child, he shall not enter t. G1519+G846
13:15 enter t, to take any thing out of his house:
Lk 10: 9 And heal the sick that are t, and G1722+G846
18:17 child shall in no wise enter t. G1519+G846
19:45 sold t, and them that bought; G1722+G846
Jn 12: 6 had the bag, and bare what was put t. G906
Act 1:20 let no man dwell t: and his G1722+G846
14:15 the sea, and all things that are t: G1722+G846
17:24 and all things t, seeing that he is G1722+G846
27: 6 sailing into Italy; and he put us t. G1519+G846
Ro 1:17 For t is the righteousness of God G1722+G846
6: 2 are dead to sin, live any longer t? G1722+G846
1Co 7:24 he is called, t abide with God. G1722+G5129
Eph 6:20 in bonds: that t I may speak G1722+G846
Php 1:18 and I t do rejoice, yea, G1722+G5129
Col 2: 7 abounding t with thanksgiving. G1722+G846
Heb 4: 6 must enter t, and they to whom G1519+G846
10: 8 pleasure t; which are offered by the law;
13: 9 that have been occupied t. G1722+G3639
Jas 1:25 and continueth t, he being not a forgetful
2Pt 2:20 again entangled t, and overcome, the G5125
3:10 that are t shall be burned up. G1722+G846
Rev 1: 3 written t: for the time is at hand. G1722+G846
10: 6 the things that t are, and the G1722+G846
6 the things that t are, and the G1722+G846
6 which are t, that there should G1722+G846
11: 1 altar, and them that worship t. G1722+G846
13:12 which dwell t to worship the G1722+G846
21:22 And I saw no temple t: for the G1722+G846

THEREINTO
Lk 21:21 that are in the countries enter t. G1519+G846

THEREOF See the Appendix.

THEREON
Gen 35:14 offering t, and he poured oil thereon. H5921
14 offering thereon, and he poured oil t. H5921
Ex 17:12 him, and he sat t; and Aaron and Hur H5921
20:24 me, and shalt sacrifice t thy burnt H5921
26 that thy nakedness be not discovered t. H5921
30: 7 And Aaron shall burn t sweet incense H5921
9 Ye shall offer no strange incense t, nor H5921
9 neither shall ye pour drink offering t. H5921
40:27 And he burnt sweet incense t; as the H5921
35 the cloud abode t, and the glory of the H5921
Lev 2: 1 pour oil upon it, and put frankincense t: H5921
6 and pour oil t: it is a meat offering. H5921
15 lay frankincense t: it is a meat offering. H5921
5:11 frankincense t: for it is a sin offering. H5921
6:12 burn t the fat of the peace offerings. H5921
10: 1 and put incense t, and offered strange H5921
11:38 fall t, it shall be unclean unto you. H5921
Nu 4: 6 And shall put t the covering of badgers' H5921
7 of blue, and put t the dishes, and the H5921
7 and the continual bread shall be t: H5921
13 the altar, and spread a purple cloth t: H5921
5:15 put frankincense t; for it is an offering H5921
9:22 remaining t, the children of Israel H5921
16:18 and laid incense t, and stood in the H5921
Dt 27: 6 offerings t unto the LORD thy God: H5921
Jos 8:29 of the city, and raise t a great heap of H5921
31 and they offered t burnt offerings unto H5921
22:23 or if to offer t burnt offering or meat H5921
23 t, let the LORD himself require it; H5921
2Sa 17:19 corn t; and the thing was not known. H5921
19:26 that I may ride t, and go to the king; H5921
1Ki 6:35 And he carved t cherubims and palm
13:13 they saddled him the ass: and he rode t, H5921
2Ki 16:12 approached to the altar, and offered t. H5921
1Ch 12:17 God of our fathers look t, and rebuke it.
15:15 with the staves t, as Moses commanded H5921
2Ch 3: 5 gold, and set t palm trees and chains. H5921
14 fine linen, and wrought cherubims t. H5921
33:16 and sacrificed t peace offerings and H5921
Ezr 3: 2 burnt offerings t, as it is written in the H5921
Ezr 3: 3 burnt offerings t unto the LORD, even H5921
6:11 let him be hanged t; and let his house be H5921
Est 5:14 may be hanged t: then go thou in H5921
7: 9 Then the king said, Hang him t. H5921
Isa 30:12 and perverseness, and stay t: H5921
35: 9 beast shall go up t, it shall not be found
Ezk 15: 3 take a pin of it to hang any vessel t? H5921
40:39 on that side, to slay t the burnt offering H5921
43:18 t, and to sprinkle blood thereon. H5921
18 thereon, and to sprinkle blood t. H5921
Zec 4: 2 his seven lamps t, and seven pipes to H5921
Mt 21: 7 their clothes, and they set him t. G1883+G846
19 found nothing t, but leaves only, G1722+G846
23:20 by it, and by all things t. G1883+G846
22 of God, and by him that sitteth t. G1883+G846
Mk 11:13 find any thing t: and when he G1722+G846
14:72 thrice. And when he thought t, he wept. G1911
Lk 13: 6 sought fruit t, and found none. G1722+G846
19:35 upon the colt, and they set Jesus t. G1913
Jn 12:14 a young ass, sat t; as it is written, G1909+G846
21: 9 coals there, and fish laid t, and bread. G1945
1Co 3:10 another buildeth t. But let every man G2026
Rev 5: 3 able to open the book, neither to look t. G846
4 and to read the book, neither to look t. G846
6: 4 to him that sat t to take peace G1909+G846
21:12 names written t, which are the names G1924

THEREOUT
Lev 2: 2 and he shall take t his handful of the H8033
Jdg 15:19 there came water t; and when he had H3318

THERETO
Ex 25:24 make t a crown of gold round about.
29:41 at even, and shalt do t according to the
30:38 t, shall even be cut off from his people.
Lev 5:16 add the fifth part t, and give it unto the H5921
6: 5 the fifth part more t, and give it unto H5921
18:23 a beast to lie down t: it is confusion.
20:16 beast, and lie down t, thou shalt kill the
27:27 add a fifth part of it t: or if it be not H5921
31 he shall add t the fifth part thereof. H5921
Nu 3:36 the vessels thereof, and all that serveth t,
19:17 running water shall be put t in a vessel: H5921
Dt 12:32 shalt not add t, nor diminish from it. H5921
Jdg 11:17 would not hearken t. And in like manner
1Ch 22:14 I prepared; and thou mayest add t. H5921
2Ch 10:14 but I will add t: my father chastised H5921
21:11 fornication, and compelled Judah t.
Ps 119: 9 by taking heed t according to thy word.
Isa 44:15 it a graven image, and falleth down t.
Mk 14:70 art a Galilaean, and thy speech agreeth t.
Gal 3:15 no man disannulleth, or addeth t. G1928

THEREUNTO
Ex 32: 8 and have sacrificed t, and said, These be
36:36 And he made t four pillars of shittim
37:11 made t a crown of gold round about.
12 Also he made t a border of an
Dt 1: 7 all the places nigh t, in the plain, in the
Eph 6:18 and watching t with all G1519+G846+G5124
1Th 3: 3 know that we are appointed t. G1519+G5124
Heb 10: 1 continually make the comers t perfect. G4334
1Pt 3: 9 that ye are t called, that ye G1519+G5124

THEREUPON
Ex 31: 7 t, and all the furniture of the tabernacle,
Ezk 16:16 playedst the harlot t: the like things shall
Zep 2: 7 Judah; they shall feed t: in the houses of
1Co 3:10 every man take heed how he buildeth t. G2026
14 hath built t, he shall receive a reward. G2026

THEREWITH
Ex 22: 6 field, be consumed t; he that kindled the
30:26 t, and the ark of the testimony,
38:30 And t he made the sockets to the door of
Lev 7: 7 that maketh atonement t shall have it.
8: 7 of the ephod, and bound it unto him t.
15:32 seed goeth from him, and is defiled t;
18:23 beast to defile thyself t: neither shall any
22: 8 eat to defile himself t: I am the LORD.
Dt 16: 3 unleavened bread t, even the bread of H5921
23:13 thou shalt dig t, and shalt turn back
Jdg 15:15 and took it, and slew a thousand men t.
16:12 and bound him t, and said unto him, The
1Sa 12: 3 mine eyes t? and I will restore it you.
17:51 and cut off his head t. And when the
31: 4 and thrust me through t; lest these
2Sa 20:10 so he smote him t in the fifth rib, and
2Ki 5: 6 thee, behold, I have t sent Naaman my

T

2Ki 12:14 and repaired t the house of the LORD.
1Ch 10: 4 and thrust me through t; lest these
23: 5 which I made, *said David*, to praise t.
2Ch 16: 6 and he built t Geba and Mizpah.
Prv 15:16 LORD than great treasure and trouble t.
17 love is, than a stalled ox and hatred t.
17: 1 Better *is* a dry morsel, and quietness t,
25:16 for thee, lest thou be filled t, and vomit it.
Ecc 1:13 to the sons of man to be exercised t.
2: 6 I made me pools of water, to water t the
10: 9 Whoso removeth stones shall be hurt t;
Isa 10:15 him that heweth t? *or* shall the saw
Ezk 4:15 and thou shalt prepare thy bread t. H5921
Joel 2:19 ye shall be satisfied t: and I will no more H854
Php 4:11 in whatsoever state I am, *t* to be content.
1Ti 6: 8 food and raiment let us be t content. G5125
Jas 3: 9 T bless we God, even the Father; G1722+G846
9 the Father; and t curse we men, G1722+G846
3Jn 10 not content t, neither doth he G1909+G5125

THESE See the Appendix.

THESSALONIANS
Act 20: 4 of Berea; and of the T, Aristarchus and G2331
1Th 1: 1 the church of the T *which is* in God the G2331
2Th 1: 1 the church of the T in God our Father G2331

THESSALONICA
Act 17: 1 T, where was a synagogue of the Jews: G2332
11 These were more noble than those in T, G2332
13 But when the Jews of T had knowledge G2332
27: 2 a Macedonian of T, being with us. G2331
Php 4:16 For even in T ye sent once and again G2332
2Ti 4:10 is departed unto T; Crescens to Galatia, G2332

THEUDAS
Act 5:36 For before these days rose up T, G2333

THEY See the Appendix.

THICK
Ex 10:22 and there was a t darkness in all the H653
19: 9 unto thee in a t cloud, that the people H5645
16 and lightnings, and a t cloud upon the H3515
20:21 near unto the t darkness where God *was*.
Lev 23:40 and the boughs of t trees, and willows H5687
Dt 4:11 with darkness, clouds, and t darkness. H6205
5:22 the cloud, and of the t darkness, with a H6205
32:15 thou art grown t, thou art covered *with* H5666
2Sa 18: 9 went under the t boughs of a great oak,
22:12 dark waters, *and* t clouds of the skies.
1Ki 7: 6 pillars and the t beam *were* before them.
26 And it *was* an hand breadth t, and the H5672
8:12 that he would dwell in the t darkness.
2Ki 8:15 that he took a t cloth, and dipped *it*
2Ch 6: 1 that he would dwell in the t darkness.
Neh 8:15 t trees, to make booths, as *it is* written. H5687
Job 15:26 neck, upon the t bosses of his bucklers: H5672
22:14 T clouds *are* a covering to him, that he
26: 8 He bindeth up the waters in his t clouds;
37:11 Also by watering he wearieth the t cloud:
38: 9 and t darkness a swaddlingband for it,
Ps 18:11 dark waters *and* t clouds of the skies.
12 *was* before him his t clouds passed, hail
74: 5 he had lifted up axes upon the t trees. H5442
Isa 44:22 I have blotted out, as a t cloud, thy
Ezk 6:13 and under every t oak, the place where H5687
8:11 hand; and a t cloud of incense went up. H6282
19:11 exalted among the t branches, and she H5688
20:28 hill, and all the t trees, and they offered H5687
31: 3 and his top was among the t boughs. H5688
10 up his top among the t boughs, and his H5688
14 top among the t boughs, neither their H5688
41:12 *was* five cubits t round about, and the H7341
25 and *there were* t planks upon the face H5646
26 chambers of the house, and t planks.
Joel 2: 2 day of clouds and of t darkness, as the
Hab 2: 6 to him that ladeth himself with t clay!
Zep 1:15 a day of clouds and t darkness,
Lk 11:29 And when the people were gathered t

THICKER
1Ki 12:10 *finger* shall be t than my father's loins. H5666
2Ch 10:10 *finger* shall be t than my father's loins. H5666

THICKET
Gen 22:13 a ram caught in a t by his horns: and H5442
Jer 4: 7 The lion is come up from his t, and the H5441

THICKETS
1Sa 13: 6 in caves, and in t, and in rocks, and in H2337
Isa 9:18 shall kindle in the t of the forest, and H5442
10:34 And he shall cut down the t of the H5442
Jer 4:29 they shall go into t, and climb up upon H5645

THICKNESS
2Ch 4: 5 And the t of it *was* an handbreadth, H5672
Jer 52:21 it; and the t thereof *was* four fingers: H5672
Ezk 41: 9 The t of the wall, which *was* for the side H7341
42:10 The chambers *were* in the t of the wall H7341

THIEF
Ex 22: 2 If a t be found breaking up, and be H1590
7 if the t be found, let him pay double. H1590
8 If the t be not found, then the master of H1590
Dt 24: 7 him; then that t shall die; and thou H1590
Job 24:14 and needy, and in the night is as a t. H1590
30: 5 *men*, (they cried after them as *after* a t;) H1590
Ps 50:18 When thou sawest a t, then thou H1590
Prv 6:30 *Men* do not despise a t, if he steal to H1590
29:24 Whoso is partner with a t hateth his H1590
Jer 2:26 As the t is ashamed when he is found, H1590
Hos 7: 1 falsehood; and the t cometh in, *and* the H1590
Joel 2: 9 shall enter in at the windows like a t. H1590
Zec 5: 4 the house of the t, and into the house of H1590
Mt 24:43 in what watch the t would come, he G2812
26:55 out as against a t with swords and G3027
Mk 14:48 out, as against a t, with swords and G3027
Lk 12:33 not, where no t approacheth, neither G2812
39 what hour the t would come, he would G2812
22:52 as against a t, with swords and staves? G3027
Jn 10: 1 other way, the same is a t and a robber. G2812
10 The t cometh not, but for to steal, and G2812
12: 6 because he was a t, and had the bag, G2812
1Th 5: 2 the Lord so cometh as a t in the night. G2812
4 that day should overtake you as a t. G2812
1Pt 4:15 murderer, or *as* a t, or *as* an evildoer, or G2812
2Pt 3:10 But the day of the Lord will come as a t G2812
Rev 3: 3 come on thee as a t, and thou shalt not G2812
16:15 Behold, I come as a t. Blessed *is* he that G2812

THIEVES
Isa 1:23 companions of t: every one loveth gifts, H1590
Jer 48:27 was he found among t? for since thou H1590
49: 9 gleaning grapes? if t by night, they will H1590
Oba 5 If t came to thee, if robbers by night, H1590
Mt 6:19 and where t break through and steal: G2812
20 where t do not break through nor steal: G2812
21:13 prayer; but ye have made it a den of t. G3027
27:38 Then were there two t crucified with G3027
44 The t also, which were crucified with G3027
Mk 11:17 prayer? but ye have made it a den of t. G3027
15:27 And with him they crucify two t; the one G3027
Lk 10:30 and fell among t, which stripped him G3027
36 unto him that fell among the t? G3027
19:46 prayer: but ye have made it a den of t. G3027
Jn 10: 8 All that ever came before me are t and G2812
1Co 6:10 Nor t, nor covetous, nor drunkards, nor G2812

THIGH
Gen 24: 2 Put, I pray thee, thy hand under my t: H3409
9 his hand under the t of Abraham his H3409
32:25 the hollow of his t; and the hollow of H3409
25 hollow of Jacob's t was out of joint, as H3409
31 upon him, and he halted upon his t. H3409
32 upon the hollow of the t, unto this day: H3409
32 of Jacob's t in the sinew that shrank. H3409
47:29 hand under my t, and deal kindly and H3409
Nu 5:21 make thy t to rot, and thy belly to swell; H3409
22 belly to swell, and *thy* t to rot: And the H3409
27 shall swell, and her t shall rot: and the H3409
Jdg 3:16 it under his raiment upon his right t. H3409
21 his right t, and thrust it into his belly: H3409
15: 8 And he smote them hip and t with a H3409
Ps 45: 3 Gird thy sword upon *thy* t, O *most* H3409
Song 3: 8 upon his t because of fear in the night. H3409
Isa 47: 2 leg, uncover the t, pass over the rivers. H7785
Jer 31:19 I smote upon *my* t: I was ashamed, yea, H3409
Ezk 21:12 my people: smite therefore upon *thy* t. H3409
24: 4 good piece, the t, and the shoulder; fill H3409
Rev 19:16 And he hath on *his* vesture and on his t G3382

THIGHS
Ex 28:42 loins even unto the t they shall reach: H3409
Song 7: 1 the joints of thy t *are* like jewels, the H3409
Dan 2:32 of silver, his belly and his t of brass, H3410

THIMNATHAH
Jos 19:43 And Elon, and T, and Ekron, H8553

THIN
Gen 41: 6 And, behold, seven t ears and blasted H1851
7 And the seven t ears devoured the H1851
23 And, behold, seven ears, withered, t, H1851
24 And the t ears devoured the seven good H1851
27 And the seven t and ill favoured kine H7534
Ex 39: 3 And they did beat the gold into t plates,
Lev 13:30 *be* in it a yellow t hair; then the priest H1851
1Ki 7:29 *were* certain additions made of t work. H4174
Isa 17: 4 shall be made t, and the fatness of his H1809

THINE See the Appendix.

THING
Gen 1:24 and creeping t, and beast of the earth H7431
25 kind, and every t that creepeth upon the
26 t that creepeth upon the earth. H7431
28 living t that moveth upon the earth. H2416
30 air, and to every t that creepeth upon the
31 And God saw every t that he had made,
6: 7 and the creeping t, and the fowls of the H7431
17 every t that *is* in the earth shall die. H3605
19 And of every living t of all flesh, two of H2416
20 of every creeping t of the earth after his H7431
7: 8 of every t that creepeth upon the earth,
14 every creeping t that creepeth upon H7431
21 of every creeping t that creepeth upon H8318
8: 1 and every living t, and all the cattle that H2416
17 Bring forth with thee every living t that H2416
17 of every creeping t that creepeth upon H7431
19 Every beast, every creeping t, and every H7431
21 any more every t living, as I have done. H2416
9: 3 Every moving t that liveth shall be H7431
14:23 I will not take any t that *is* thine, lest
18:14 Is any t too hard for the LORD? At the H1697
17 I hide from Abraham that t which I do; H834
19:21 concerning this t also, that I will not H1697
22 for I cannot do any t till thou be come H1697
20:10 sawest thou, that thou hast done this t? H1697
21:11 And the t was very grievous in H1697
26 hath done this t: neither didst thou tell H1697
22:12 do thou any t unto him: for now I H3972
16 hast done this t, and hast not withheld H1697
24:50 and said, The t proceedeth from the H1697
30:31 not give me any t: if thou wilt do this H3972
31 if thou wilt do this t for me, I will again H1697
34: 7 daughter; which t ought not to be done. H3651
14 We cannot do this t, to give our sister to H1697
19 not to do the t, because he had delight H1697
38:10 And the t which he did displeased the H834
39: 9 he kept back any t from me but thee, H3972
23 looked not to any t *that was* under his H3972
41:28 This *is* the t which I have spoken unto H1697
32 *it is* because the t *is* established by God, H1697
37 And the t was good in the eyes of H1697
44: 7 servants should do according to this t: H1697
Ex 1:18 have ye done this t, and have saved the H1697
2:14 feared, and said, Surely this t is known. H1697
15 Now when Pharaoh heard this t, he H1697
9: 5 the LORD shall do this t in the land. H1697
6 And the LORD did that t on the H1697
10:15 not any green t in the trees, or in the H3418
12:24 And ye shall observe this t for an H1697
16:14 *lay* a small round t, *as* small as the hoar H2636
16 This *is* the t which the LORD hath H1697
32 And Moses said, This *is* the t which the H1697
18:11 all gods: for in the t wherein they dealt H1697
14 said, What *is* this t that thou doest to H1697
17 him, The t that thou doest *is* not good. H1697
18 *is* with thee: for this t *is* too heavy for H1697
23 If thou shalt do this t, and God H1697
20: 4 or any likeness of *any* t that *is* in heaven
17 his ass, nor any t that *is* thy neighbour's.
22: 9 for any manner of lost t, which *another*
15 if it *be* an hired *t*, it came for his hire.
29: 1 And this *is* the t that thou shalt do unto H1697
33:17 I will do this t also that thou hast H1697
34:10 it *is* a terrible t that I will do with thee.
35: 4 t which the LORD commanded, saying, H1697
Lev 2: 3 and his sons': *it is* a t most holy of the H6944
10 and his sons': *it is* a t most holy of the H6944
4:13 ignorance, and the t be hid from the H1697
5: 2 Or if a soul touch any unclean t, H1697
5 confess that he hath sinned in that *t*:
16 done in the holy t, and shall add the H6944
6: 2 in fellowship, or in a t taken away by

Lev 6: 4 away, or the t which he hath deceitfully H6233
4 him to keep, or the lost t which he found, H9
7 him for any t of all that he hath done H259
7:19 any unclean t shall not be eaten; it
21 touch any unclean t, as the uncleanness
21 unclean t, and eat of the flesh of
8: 5 This is the t which the LORD H1697
9: 6 And Moses said, This is the t which the H1697
11:10 and of any living t which is in the H5315
21 flying creeping t that goeth upon all H8318
35 And every t whereupon any part of their
41 And every creeping t that creepeth H8318
43 with any creeping t that creepeth, H8318
44 t that creepeth upon the earth. H8318
12: 4 touch no hallowed t, nor come into the H6944
13:48 in a skin, or in any t made of skin;
49 in the woof, or in any t of skin; it is a H3627
52 or in linen, or any t of skin, wherein the H3627
53 warp, or in the woof, or in any t of skin; H3627
54 that they wash the t wherein the plague
57 in the woof, or in any t of skin; it is a H3627
58 or whatsoever t of skin it be, which H3627
59 or woof, or any t of skins, to pronounce H3627
15: 4 t, whereon he sitteth, shall be unclean. H3627
6 And he that sitteth on any t whereon he H3627
10 And whosoever toucheth any t that was
20 And every t that she lieth upon in her
20 be unclean: every t also that she sitteth
22 And whosoever toucheth any t that she H3627
23 And if it be on her bed, or on any t H3627
17: 2 them; This is the t which the LORD H1697
19: 8 the hallowed t of the LORD: and that H6944
26 Ye shall not eat any t with the blood:
20:17 it is a wicked t; and they shall be cut
21 it is an unclean t: he hath uncovered his H5079
25 manner of living t that creepeth on the
21:18 hath a flat nose, or any t superfluous,
22: 4 toucheth any t that is unclean by the
5 Or whosoever toucheth any creeping t, H8318
10 There shall no stranger eat of the holy t: H6944
10 hired servant, shall not eat of the holy t. H6944
14 And if a man eat of the holy t H6944
14 give it unto the priest with the holy t. H6944
23 a lamb that hath any t superfluous or
23:37 drink offerings, every t upon his day: H1697
27:23 in that day, as a holy t unto the LORD.
28 Notwithstanding no devoted t, that a
28 devoted t is most holy unto the LORD.
Nu 4:15 not touch any holy t, lest they die. These H6944
16: 9 Seemeth it but a small t unto you, that H4592
13 Is it a small t that thou hast brought us H4592
30 But if the LORD make a new t, and the H1278
17:13 Whosoever cometh any t near unto the
18: 7 office for every t of the altar, and H1697
14 Every t devoted in Israel shall be thine.
15 Every t that openeth the matrix in all
20:19 doing any t else, go through on my feet. H1697
22:38 at all to say any t? the word that God H3972
30: 1 t which the LORD hath commanded. H1697
31:23 Every t that may abide the fire, ye shall H1697
32:20 If ye will do this t, if ye will go armed H1697
35:22 upon him any t without laying of wait, H3627
36: 6 This is the t which the LORD doth H1697
Dt 1:14 And ye answered me, and said, The t H1697
32 Yet in this t ye did not believe the H1697
4:18 The likeness of any t that creepeth on
23 the likeness of any t, which the LORD thy
25 the likeness of any t, and shall do evil in
32 hath been any such t as this great thing
32 great t is, or hath been heard like it? H1697
5: 8 or any likeness of any t that is in heaven
21 his ass, or any t that is thy neighbour's.
7:26 thou be a cursed t like it: but thou shalt H2764
26 shalt utterly abhor it; for it is a cursed t. H2764
8: 9 shalt not lack any t in it; a land whose
12:32 What t soever I command you, observe H1697
13:14 it be truth, and the t certain, that such H1697
17 of the cursed t to thine hand: that the H2764
14: 3 Thou shalt not eat any abominable t. H8441
19 And every creeping t that flieth is H8318
21 Ye shall not eat of any t that dieth of
15:10 that for this t the LORD thy God shall H1697
15 therefore I command thee this t to day. H1697
16: 4 shall there any t of the flesh, which thou
17: 4 it be true, and the t certain, that such H1697
5 that wicked t, unto thy gates, even H1697
18:22 of the LORD, if the t follow not, nor H1697
22 to pass, that is the t which the LORD H1697
22: 3 and with all lost t of thy brother's, which

Dt 22:20 But if this t be true, and the tokens of H1697
23: 9 then keep thee from every wicked t. H1697
14 t in thee, and turn away from thee. H1697
19 usury of any t that is lent upon usury: H1697
24:10 When thou dost lend thy brother any t, H4859
18 therefore I command thee to do this t. H1697
22 therefore I command thee to do this t. H1697
26:11 And thou shalt rejoice in every good t
31:13 not known any t, may hear, and learn
32:47 For it is not a vain t for you; because it H1697
47 life: and through this t ye shall prolong H1697
Jos 4:10 Jordan, until every t was finished that H1697
6:18 from the accursed t, lest ye make H2764
18 of the accursed t, and make the camp H2764
7: 1 in the accursed t: for Achan, the son of H2764
1 of the accursed t: and the anger of the H2764
11 of the accursed t, and have also stolen, H2764
13 is an accursed t in the midst of thee, H2764
13 away the accursed t from among you. H2764
15 with the accursed t shall be burnt with H2764
9:24 because of you, and have done this t. H1697
14: 6 Thou knowest the t that the LORD said H1697
21:45 There failed not ought of any good t H1697
22:20 in the accursed t, and wrath fell on all H2764
24 it for fear of this t, saying, In time to H1697
33 And the t pleased the children of Israel; H1697
23:14 souls, that not one t hath failed of all H1697
14 you, and not one t hath failed thereof. H1697
Jdg 6:29 Who hath done this t? And when they H1697
29 the son of Joash hath done this t. H1697
8:27 after it: which t became a snare unto
11:25 And now art thou any t better than
37 And she said unto her father, Let this t H1697
13: 4 strong drink, and eat not any unclean t:
7 eat any unclean t: for the child shall be
14 She may not eat of any t that cometh of
14 eat any unclean t: all that I commanded
18: 7 to shame in any t; and they were far H1697
10 is no want of any t that is in the earth. H1697
19:19 thy servants: there is no want of any t. H1697
24 but unto this man do not so vile a t. H1697
20: 9 But now this shall be the t which we H1697
21:11 And this is the t that ye shall do, Ye H1697
Ru 3:18 until he have finished the t this day. H1697
1Sa 3:11 Behold, I will do a t in Israel, at which H1697
17 And he said, What is the t that the H1697
17 if thou hide any t from me of all the H1697
4: 7 there hath not been such a t heretofore.
8: 6 But the t displeased Samuel, when they H1697
12:16 and see this great t, which the LORD H1697
14:12 we will shew you a t. And Jonathan said H1697
15: 9 them: but every t that was vile and H4399
18:20 they told Saul, and the t pleased him. H1697
23 it to you a light t to be a king's son in
20: 2 father hide this t from me? it is not so. H1697
26 Nevertheless Saul spake not any t that H3972
39 But the lad knew not any t: only H3972
21: 2 Let no man know any t of the business H3972
22:15 king impute any t unto his servant, nor H1697
24: 6 I should do this t unto my master, the H1697
25:15 missed we any t, as long as we were H3972
26:16 This t is not good that thou hast done. H1697
28:10 punishment happen to thee for this t. H1697
18 LORD done this t unto thee this day. H1697
30:19 spoil, nor any t that they had taken to
2Sa 2: 6 kindness, because ye have done this t. H1697
3:13 with thee: but one t I require of thee, H1697
7:19 And this was yet a small t in thy sight, H6994
11:11 as thy soul liveth, I will not do this t. H1697
25 Joab, Let not this t displease thee, for H1697
27 him a son. But the t that David had H1697
12: 5 that hath done this t shall surely die:
6 did this t, and because he had no pity. H1697
12 t before all Israel, and before the sun. H1697
21 unto him, What t is this that thou hast H1697
13: 2 it hard for him to do any t to her. H3972
12 me; for no such t ought to be done in H3651
20 regard not this t. So Tamar remained H1697
33 the king take the t to his heart, to think H1697
14:13 thought such a t against the people of
13 doth speak this t as one which is faulty, H1697
15 to speak of this t unto my lord the king, H1697
18 I pray thee, the t that I shall ask thee. H1697
20 Joab done this t: and my lord is wise, H1697
21 I have done this t: go therefore, bring H1697
15:11 their simplicity, and they knew not any t.
35 it shall be, that what t soever thou shalt
36 send unto me every t that ye can hear.
17:19 corn thereon; and the t was not known.

2Sa 24: 3 doth my lord the king delight in this t? H1697
1Ki 1:27 Is this t done by my lord the king, and H1697
3:10 Lord, that Solomon had asked this t. H1697
11 hast asked this t, and hast not asked H1697
10: 3 there was not any t hid from the king, H1697
11:10 concerning this t, that he should not go H1697
12:24 to his house; for this t is from me. They H1697
30 And this t became a sin: for the people H1697
13:33 After this t Jeroboam returned not H1697
34 And this t became sin unto the house H1697
14: 5 cometh to ask a t of thee for her son; H1697
13 is found some good t toward the LORD H1697
15: 5 turned not aside from any t that he
16:31 it had been a light t for him to walk in H7043
20: 9 I will do: but this t I may not do. And H1697
24 And do this t, Take the kings away, H1697
33 whether any t would come from him,
2Ki 2:10 And he said, Thou hast asked a hard t: H7185
3:18 And this is but a light t in the sight of H7043
4: 2 not any t in the house, save a pot of oil.
5:13 do some great t, wouldest thou not have H1697
18 In this t the LORD pardon thy servant, H1697
18 the LORD pardon thy servant in this t. H1697
6:11 troubled for this t; and he called his H1697
7: 2 in heaven, might this t be? And he said, H1697
19 might such a t be? And he said, Behold, H1697
8: 9 even of every good t of Damascus, forty H2898
13 do this great t? And Elisha answered, H1697
11: 5 saying, This is the t that ye shall do; A H1697
17:12 said unto them, Ye shall not do this t. H1697
20: 9 LORD will do the t that he hath spoken: H1697
10 And Hezekiah answered, It is a light t H7043
1Ch 2: 7 who transgressed in the t accursed.
11:19 I should do this t: shall I drink the blood H2063
13: 4 t was right in the eyes of all the people. H1697
17:17 And yet this was a small t in thine eyes, H6994
23 Therefore now, LORD, let the t that H1697
21: 3 lord require this t? why will he be a cause
7 And God was displeased with this t; H1697
8 I have done this t: but now, I beseech H1697
26:28 had dedicated any t, it was under the
2Ch 9:20 t accounted of in the days of Solomon. H3972
11: 4 his house: for this t is done of me. And H1697
16:10 him because of this t. And Asa oppressed
23: 4 This is the t that ye shall do; A third H1697
19 was unclean in any t should enter in. H1697
29:36 people: for the t was done suddenly. H1697
30: 4 And the t pleased the king and all the H1697
Ezr 7:27 hath put such a t as this in the king's
9: 3 And when I heard this t, I rent my H1697
10: 2 there is hope in Israel concerning this t.
13 many that have transgressed in this t. H1697
Neh 2:19 said, What is this t that ye do? will ye H1697
13:17 them, What evil t is this that ye do, and H1697
Est 2: 4 the t pleased the king; and he did so. H1697
22 And the t was known to Mordecai, who H1697
5:14 the banquet. And the t pleased Haman; H1697
6:13 all his friends every t that had befallen
8: 5 in his sight, and the t seem right before H1697
Job 3:25 For the t which I greatly feared is come
4:12 Now a t was secretly brought to me, H1697
6: 8 God would grant me the t that I long for!
9:22 This is one t, therefore I said it, He
12:10 living t, and the breath of all mankind. H2416
13:28 And he, as a rotten t, consumeth, as a H7538
14: 4 Who can bring a clean t out of an
15:11 thee? is there any secret t with thee? H1697
22:28 Thou shalt also decree a t, and it shall be
23:14 For he performeth the t that is
26: 3 thou plentifully declared the t as it is?
28:10 and his eye seeth every precious t. H3366
11 the t that is hid bringeth he forth to light.
33:32 If thou hast any t to say, answer me:
39: 8 and he searcheth after every green t. H3387
42: 2 I know that thou canst do every t, and
7 t that is right, as my servant Job hath.
8 the t which is right, like my servant Job.
Ps 2: 1 rage, and the people imagine a vain t? H7385
27: 4 One t have I desired of the LORD, that
33:17 An horse is a vain t for safety: neither H8267
34:10 seek the LORD shall not want any good t.
38:20 because I follow the t that good is.
69:34 seas, and every t that moveth therein.
84:11 and glory: no good t will he withhold
89:34 nor alter the t that is gone out of my lips.
92: 1 It is a good t to give thanks unto the
101: 3 I will set no wicked t before mine eyes: H1697
141: 4 Incline not my heart to any evil t, to H1697
145:16 and satisfiest the desire of every living t. H2416

Ps 150: 6 Let every t that hath breath praise the
Prv 4: 7 Wisdom *is* the principal t; *therefore* get H7225
18:22 *Whoso* findeth a wife findeth a good *t*,
22:18 For *it is* a pleasant t if thou keep them H5273
25: 2 *It is* the glory of God to conceal a t: but H1697
27: 7 to the hungry soul every bitter t is sweet.
Ecc 1: 9 The t that hath been, it *is that* which
9 and *there is* no new t under the sun.
10 Is there *any* t whereof it may be said, H1697
3: 1 To every *t there is* a season, and a time
11 He hath made every *t* beautiful in his
14 be put to it, nor any t taken from it: and H369
19 beasts; even one t befalleth them: as the
5: 2 hasty to utter *any* t before God: for God H1697
6: 5 *any t*: this hath more rest than the other.
7: 8 Better *is* the end of a t than the H1697
8: 1 interpretation of a t? a man's wisdom H1697
3 t; for he doeth whatsoever pleaseth him. H1697
5 shall feel no evil t: and a wise man's H1697
15 man hath no better t under the sun, than
9: 5 know not any t, neither have they any H3972
6 ever in any *t* that is done under the sun.
11: 7 Truly the light *is* sweet, and a pleasant *t*
12:14 with every secret t, whether *it be* good, H5956
Isa 7:13 of David; *Is it* a small t for you to weary H4592
15: 6 the grass faileth, there is no green t. H3418
17:13 like a rolling t before the whirlwind. H1534
19: 7 brooks, and every t sown by the brooks,
29:16 me not? or shall the t framed say of him
21 and turn aside the just for a t of nought.
38: 7 will do this t that he hath spoken; H1697
40:15 he taketh up the isles as a very little t. H1851
41:12 shall be as nothing, and as a t of nought.
43:19 Behold, I will do a new t; now it shall H2319
49: 6 And he said, It is a light t that thou H7043
52:11 touch no unclean *t*; go ye out of the midst
55:11 it shall prosper *in the t* whereto I sent it.
64: 6 But we are all as an unclean *t*, and all our
66: 8 Who hath heard such a t? who hath seen
Jer 2:10 diligently, and see if there be such a t.
19 and see that *it is* an evil *t* and bitter, that
5:30 A wonderful and horrible t is H8186
7:23 But this t commanded I them, saying, H1697
11:13 t, *even* altars to burn incense unto Baal.
14:14 t of nought, and the deceit of their heart.
18:13 of Israel hath done a very horrible t. H8186
22: 4 For if ye do this t indeed, then shall H1697
23:14 an horrible t: they commit adultery, H8186
31:22 created a new t in the earth, A woman H2319
32:27 all flesh: is there any t too hard for me? H1697
33:14 will perform that good t which I have H1697
38: 5 *is* not *he that* can do *any* t against you. H1697
14 will ask thee a t; hide nothing from me. H1697
40: 3 therefore this t is come upon you. H1697
16 t: for thou speakest falsely of Ishmael. H1697
42: 3 may walk, and the t that we may do. H1697
4 pass, *that* whatsoever t the LORD shall H1697
21 your God, nor any *t* for the which he
44: 4 do not this abominable t that I hate. H1697
17 But we will certainly do whatsoever t H1697
Lam 2:13 What t shall I take to witness for thee?
13 for thee? what t shall I liken to thee, H4100
Ezk 8:17 of man? Is it a light t to the house of H7043
14: 9 he hath spoken a t, I the LORD have H1697
16:47 *were* a very little *t*, thou wast corrupted
34:18 *Seemeth it* a small t unto you to have H4592
44:18 with any t that causeth sweat.
29 dedicated t in Israel shall be theirs. H2764
31 The priests shall not eat of any t that is
47: 9 And it shall come to pass, *that* every t H5315
9 t shall live whither the river cometh.
48:12 t most holy by the border of the Levites.
Dan 2: 5 Chaldeans, The t is gone from me: if ye H4406
8 because ye see the t is gone from me. H4406
11 And *it is* a rare t that the king H4406
15 Arioch made the t known to Daniel. H4406
17 and made the t known to Hananiah, H4406
3:29 which speak any t amiss against the God
4:33 The same hour was the t fulfilled upon H4406
5:15 not shew the interpretation of the t: H4406
26 This *is* the interpretation of the t: H4406
6:12 and said, The t *is* true, according to H4406
10: 1 king of Persia a t was revealed unto H1697
1 and the t *was* true, but the time H1697
1 t, and had understanding of the vision. H1697
Hos 6:10 I have seen an horrible t in the house of H8186
8: 3 Israel hath cast off *the t that is* good: the
12 *but* they were counted as a strange t. H2114
Am 6:13 Ye which rejoice in a t of nought, which H1697

Jna 3: 7 t: let them not feed, nor drink water: H3972
Mal 1:14 the Lord a corrupt t: for I *am* a great H7843
Mt 8:33 and told every t, and what was befallen G3956
18:19 as touching any t that they shall ask, it G4229
19:16 t shall I do, that I may have eternal life? G18
20:20 *him*, and desiring a certain t of him. G5100
21:24 will ask you one t, which if ye tell me, I G3056
24:17 down to take any t out of his house: G5100
Mk 1:27 saying, What t is this? what new G5101
4:22 neither was any t kept secret, but that
5:32 about to see her that had done this t. G5124
7:18 that whatsoever t from without G3956
9:22 t, have compassion on us, and help us. G5100
10:21 unto him, One t thou lackest: go thy G1520
11:13 he might find any t thereon: and when G5100
13:15 *therein*, to take any t out of his house: G5100
16: 8 any t to any *man*; for they were afraid. G3762
18 they drink any deadly t, it shall not hurt G5100
Lk 1:35 also that holy t which shall be born G40
2:15 and see this t which is come to pass, G4487
6: 9 I will ask you one t; Is it lawful on the G5101
8:17 neither *any t* hid, that shall not be
9:21 commanded *them* to tell no man that t; G5124
10:42 But one t is needful: and Mary hath G1520
12:11 t ye shall answer, or what ye shall say: G5101
26 If ye then be not able to do that t which
18:22 Yet lackest thou one t: sell all that thou G1520
19: 8 if I have taken any t from any man by G5100
20: 3 will also ask you one t; and answer me: G3056
22:23 of them it was that should do this t. G5124
35 lacked ye any t? And they said, Nothing. G5100
Jn 1: 3 was not any t made that was made. G1520
46 him, Can there any good t come out of G18
5:14 no more, lest a worse t come unto thee. G5100
7: 4 For *there is* no man *that* doeth any t in G5100
9:25 I know not: one t I know, that, whereas G1520
30 is a marvellous t, that ye know not from G2298
14:14 If ye shall ask any t in my name, I will G5100
18:34 Jesus answered him, Sayest thou this t G5124
Act 5: 4 conceived this t in thine heart? thou G4229
10:14 eaten any t that is common or unclean. G3956
28 it is an unlawful t for a man that is a Jew G111
12:12 And when he had considered *the t*, he
17:21 but either to tell, or to hear some new t.) G2537
25 he needed any t, seeing he giveth to all G5100
19:32 Some therefore cried one t, and some G2896
39 But if ye inquire any t concerning other G5100
21:25 observe no such t, save only that they G5108
34 And some cried one t, some another, G994
23:17 for he hath a certain t to tell him. G5100
25: 8 Caesar, have I offended any t at all. G5100
11 committed any t worthy of death, I G5100
26 Of whom I have no certain t to write G5100
26: 8 Why should it be thought a t incredible
10 Which t I also did in Jerusalem: and G3739
26 for this t was not done in a corner. G5124
Ro 7:18 dwelleth no good t: for to will is present G18
8:33 Who shall lay any t to the charge of G1458
9:20 God? Shall the t formed say to him that
13: 6 attending continually upon this very t. G846
8 Owe no man any t, but to love one G3367
14:14 t to be unclean, to him *it is* unclean. G5100
21 wine, nor *any t* whereby thy brother
22 not himself in that t which he alloweth.
1Co 1: 5 That in every t ye are enriched by him, G3956
10 all speak the same t, and *that* there be no G846
2: 2 For I determined not to know any t G5100
3: 7 So then neither is he that planteth any t, G5100
4: 3 But with me it is a very small t that I G1646
8: 2 he knoweth any t, he knoweth nothing G5100
7 this hour eat *it* as a t offered unto an
9:11 t if we shall reap your carnal things? G3173
17 For if I do this t willingly, I have a G5124
10:19 What say I then? that the idol is any t, G5100
19 is offered in sacrifice to idols is any t? G5100
14:30 If *any t* be revealed to another that
35 And if they will learn any t, let them ask G5100
2Co 2:10 To whom ye forgive any t, I *forgive* also: G5100
10 for if I forgave any t, to whom I forgave G1536
3: 5 to think any t as of ourselves; but G5100
5: 5 us for the selfsame t *is* God, who also G846
6: 3 Giving no offence in any t, that the G3367
17 not the unclean *t*; and I will receive you,
7:11 For behold this selfsame t, that ye G846
14 For if I have boasted any t to him of G1536
8: 7 Therefore, as ye abound in every *t*, *in*
9:11 Being enriched in every t to all G3956
10: 5 and every high t that exalteth itself G5313
11:15 Therefore *it is* no great t if his G3173

2Co 12: 8 For this t I besought the Lord thrice, G5127
Gal 4:18 always in *a* good *t*, and not only when I
5: 6 availeth any t, nor uncircumcision; G5100
6:15 availeth any t, nor uncircumcision, G5100
Eph 4:28 with *his* hands the t which is good, that
5:24 *be* to their own husbands in every t. G3956
27 or any such t; but that it should be G5108
6: 8 Knowing that whatsoever good t any G18
Php 1: 6 Being confident of this very t, that he G846
3:13 but *this* one t *I do*, forgetting those G1520
15 and if in any t ye be otherwise minded, G1536
16 by the same rule, let us mind the same t. G846
4: 6 Be careful for nothing; but in every t by G3956
1Th 1: 8 so that we need not to speak any t. G5100
5:18 In every t give thanks: for this is the G3956
2Th 1: 6 Seeing *it is* a righteous t with God to G1342
1Ti 1:10 t that is contrary to sound doctrine; G2087
2Ti 1:14 That good t which was committed unto G2570
Tit 2: 8 ashamed, having no evil t to say of you. G3367
Phlm 6 good t which is in you in Christ Jesus. G18
Heb 10:29 an unholy t, and hath done despite G2839
31 *It is* a fearful t to fall into the hands of G5398
11:40 God having provided some better t for G5100
13: 9 For *it is* a good t that the heart be G2570
Jas 1: 7 that he shall receive any t of the Lord. G5100
1Pt 4:12 some strange t happened unto you: G3581
2Pt 3: 8 of this one t, that one day *is* with G1520
1Jn 2: 8 unto you, which t is true in him and in G3739
5:14 t according to his will, he heareth us: G5100
Rev 2:15 of the Nicolaitans, which t I hate. G3739
9: 4 neither any green t, neither any tree; G5515
21:27 enter into it any t that defileth, neither G3956

THINGS

Gen 7:23 and the creeping t, and the fowl of the H7431
9: 3 as the green herb have I given you all t.
15: 1 After these t the word of the LORD H1697
20: 8 and told all these t in their ears: and H1697
22: 1 And it came to pass after these t, that H1697
20 And it came to pass after these t, that it H1697
24: 1 the LORD had blessed Abraham in all t.
28 told *them of* her mother's house these t. H1697
53 brother and to her mother precious t. H4030
66 And the servant told Isaac all t that he H1697
29:13 his house. And he told Laban all these t. H1697
39: 7 And it came to pass after these t, that H1697
40: 1 And it came to pass after these t, *that* H1697
42:36 *away*: all these t are against me.
45:23 with the good t of Egypt, and ten she H2898
48: 1 And it came to pass after these t, that H1697
Ex 10: 2 thy son's son, what t I have wrought in
12:36 unto them *such t as they required*. And
23:13 And in all *t* that I have said unto you be
25:22 testimony, of all *t* which I will give thee
28:38 of the holy t, which the children of H6944
29:33 And they shall eat those t wherewith the
35 sons, according to all *t* which I have
40: 4 and set in order the t that are to be set in
Lev 2: 8 is made of these t unto the LORD: and
4: 2 LORD *concerning t* which ought not to
13 LORD *concerning t* which should not be
22 his God *concerning t* which should not
27 LORD *concerning t* which ought not to
5: 2 unclean creeping t, and *if* it be hidden H8318
5 in one of these *t*, that he shall confess
15 in the holy t of the LORD; then he H6944
17 any of these t which are forbidden
8:36 So Aaron and his sons did all t which H1697
10:19 LORD; and such t have befallen me: and
11:23 But all *other* flying creeping t, which H8318
29 the creeping t that creep upon the H8318
42 all creeping t that creep upon the H8318
14:11 clean, and those t, before the LORD, *at*
15:10 *any of* those t shall wash his clothes,
27 And whosoever toucheth those t shall be
18:24 Defile not ye yourselves in any of these t:
20:23 these t, and therefore I abhorred them.
22: 2 from the holy t of the children of Israel, H6944
2 holy name *in those t* which they hallow
3 unto the holy t, which the children of H6944
4 not eat of the holy t, until he be clean. H6944
6 t, unless he wash his flesh with water. H6944
7 eat of the holy t; because it *is* his food. H6944
12 may not eat of an offering of the holy t.
15 And they shall not profane the holy t of H6944
16 holy t: for I the LORD do sanctify them. H6944
26:23 these t, but will walk contrary unto me;
Nu 1:50 and over all t that *belong* to it: they
4: 4 the congregation, *about* the most holy t: H6944

Nu 4:15 lest they die. These *t are* the burden of
19 unto the most holy t: Aaron and his H6944
20 the holy t are covered, lest they die. H6944
5: 9 And every offering of all the holy t of H6944
10 And every man's hallowed t shall be H6944
15:13 shall do these t after this manner, in
18: 8 of all the hallowed t of the children of H6944
9 This shall be thine of the most holy t, H6944
19 All the heave offerings of the holy t, H6944
32 t of the children of Israel, lest ye die. H6944
29:39 These *t* ye shall do unto the LORD in
31:20 of goats' *hair,* and all t made of wood.
35:29 So these *t* shall be for a statute of
Dt 1:18 that time all the t which ye should do. H1697
4: 7 God *is* in all *t that* we call upon him *for?*
9 lest thou forget the t which thine eyes H1697
30 and all these t are come upon thee, H1697
6:11 And houses full of all good *t,* which thou
10:21 terrible t, which thine eyes have seen.
12: 8 Ye shall not do after all *the t* that we do
26 Only thy holy t which thou hast, and H6944
18:12 For all that do these t *are* an
25:16 For all that do such t, *and* all that do
26:13 away the hallowed t out of *mine* house, H6944
28:47 of heart, for the abundance of all *t;*
48 and in want of all *t:* and he shall put a
57 for want of all *t* secretly in the siege and
29:29 The secret *t belong* unto the LORD our
29 our God: but those *t which are* revealed
30: 1 when all these t are come upon thee, H1697
32:35 t that shall come upon them make haste.
33:13 for the precious t of heaven, for the H4022
14 the precious t put forth by the moon, H4022
15 And for the chief t of the ancient H7218
15 for the precious t of the lasting hills, H4022
16 And for the precious t of the earth and H4022
Jos 1:17 unto Moses in all t, so will we hearken
2:11 And as soon as we had heard *these t,* our
23 Nun, and told him all *t* that befell them:
11: 1 had heard *those t,* that he sent to Jobab
23:14 of all the good t which the LORD your H1697
15 *that* as all good t are come upon you, H1697
15 bring upon you all evil t, until he have
24:29 And it came to pass after these t, that H1697
Jdg 13:23 shewed us all these *t,* nor would as at this
23 at this time have told us *such t* as these.
18:27 And they took *the t* which Micah had
Ru 4: 7 for to confirm all t; a man plucked off H1697
1Sa 2:23 Why do ye such t? for I hear of your evil H1697
3:12 In that day I will perform against Eli all *t*
17 me of all the t that he said unto thee. H1697
12:21 *ye go* after vain *t,* which cannot profit
24 how great *t* he hath done for you.
15:21 the chief of the t which should have been
19: 7 him all those t. And Jonathan brought H1697
25:37 had told him these t, that his heart died H1697
26:25 shalt both do great *t,* and also shalt still
2Sa 7:21 great t, to make thy servant know *them.* H1420
23 to do for you great t and terrible, for H1420
11:18 Then Joab sent and told David all the t H1697
12: 8 have given unto thee such and such t.
13:21 heard of all these t, he was very wroth. H1697
14:20 God, to know all *t* that *are* in the earth.
23: 5 ordered in all *t,* and sure: for *this is* all
17 it. These t did these three mighty men.
22 These *t* did Benaiah the son of Jehoiada,
24:12 I offer thee three *t;* choose thee one of
23 All these *t* did Araunah, *as* a king, give
1Ki 4:33 of fowl, and of creeping t, and of fishes. H7431
5: 8 considered the t which thou sentest to
7:51 brought in the t which David his father
15:15 And he brought in the t which his H6944
15 dedicated, and the t which himself had
17:17 And it came to pass after these t, *that* H1697
18:36 *that* I have done all these t at thy word. H1697
21: 1 And it came to pass after these t, *that* H1697
26 according to all *t* as did the Amorites,
2Ki 8: 4 all the great t that Elisha hath done. H1419
11: 9 did according to all *t* that Jehoiada the
12: 4 of the dedicated t that is brought into H6944
18 all the hallowed t that Jehoshaphat, H6944
18 his own hallowed t, and all the gold *that* H6944
14: 3 according to all t as Joash his father did.
17: 9 did secretly *those* t that *were* not right H1697
11 wicked t to provoke the LORD to anger: H1697
19:29 shall eat this year such t as grow of
20:13 of his precious t, the silver, and the H5238
15 answered, All *the t* that *are* in mine
23:17 proclaimed these t that thou hast done H1697

2Ki 25:15 the bowls, *and* such t as *were* of gold, *in*
1Ch 4:22 Jashubilehem. And *these are* ancient t. H1697
9:31 over the t that were made in the pans.
11:19 it. These t did these three mightiest.
24 These *t* did Benaiah the son of Jehoiada,
17:19 in making known all *these* great t. H1420
21:10 I offer thee three *t:* choose thee one of
23:13 the most holy t, he and his sons for H6944
28 of all holy t, and the work of the H6944
26:20 over the treasures of the dedicated t. H6944
26 of the dedicated t, which David the H6944
28:12 and of the treasuries of the dedicated t: H6944
14 *He gave* of gold by weight for *t* of gold,
29: 2 my God the gold for *t to be made* of gold,
2 and the silver for *t* of silver, and the
2 and the brass for *t* of brass, the iron for
2 brass, the iron for *t* of iron, and wood for
2 of iron, and wood for *t* of wood; onyx
5 The gold for *t* of gold, and the silver for
5 and the silver for *t* of silver, and for all
14 this sort? for all t *come* of thee, and of
17 offered all these t: and now have I seen
19 and to do all *these t,* and to build the
2Ch 3: 3 Now these *are the t wherein* Solomon
4: 6 wash in them: such t as they offered for
5: 1 brought in *all* the t that David his H6944
12:12 and also in Judah t went well. H1697
15:18 the house of God the t that his father had
19: 3 Nevertheless there are good t found in
21: 3 and of precious t, with fenced cities in H4030
23: 8 did according to all t that Jehoiada the
24: 7 all the dedicated t of the house of the H6944
29:33 And the consecrated t *were* six H6944
31: 5 tithe of all *t* brought they in abundantly.
6 and the tithe of holy t which were H6944
12 tithes and the dedicated *t* faithfully: over
14 of the LORD, and the most holy t. H6944
32: 1 After these t, and the establishment H1697
Ezr 1: 6 t, beside all *that* was willingly offered. H4030
2:63 of the most holy t, till there stood up a H6944
7: 1 Now after these t, in the reign of H1697
9: 1 Now when these t were done, the princes
Neh 6: 8 There are no such t done as thou H1697
16 about us saw *these t,* they were much
7:65 of the most holy t, till there stood *up* a H6944
9: 6 the earth, and all *t* that *are* therein, the
10:33 feasts, and for the holy *t,* and for the sin
12:47 sanctified *holy t* unto the Levites; and
13:26 of Israel sin by these t? yet among many
Est 2: 1 After these t, when the wrath of king H1697
3 let their *t* for purification be given *them:*
9 gave her her t for purification, with
9 with such t as belonged to her, and
12 *other* t for the purifying of the women;)
3: 1 After these t did king Ahasuerus H1697
5:11 and all *the t* wherein the king had
9:20 And Mordecai wrote these t, and sent H1697
Job 5: 9 Which doeth great t and unsearchable;
9 marvellous t without number: H6381
6: 7 The t *that* my soul refused to touch *are*
30 cannot my taste discern perverse t? H1942
8: 2 How long wilt thou speak these *t?* and
9:10 Which doeth great t past finding out;
10:13 And these *t* hast thou hid in thine heart:
12: 3 yea, who knoweth not such t as these? H3644
22 He discovereth deep t out of darkness, H6013
13:20 Only do not two *t* unto me: then will I
26 For thou writest bitter t against me, H4846
14:19 washest away the t which grow *out* of
16: 2 I have heard many such t: miserable
22:18 Yet he filled their houses with good *t:* but
23:14 for me: and many such *t are* with him.
26: 5 Dead *t* are formed from under the
33:29 Lo, all these *t* worketh God oftentimes
37: 5 his voice; great t doeth he, which we
41:30 sharp pointed t upon the mire.
34 He beholdeth all high *t:* he *is* a king over
42: 3 I understood not; t too wonderful for
Ps 8: 6 hands; thou hast put all *t* under his feet:
12: 3 *and* the tongue that speaketh proud t:
15: 5 that doeth these *t* shall never be moved.
17: 2 let thine eyes behold the t that are equal.
31:18 which speak grievous t proudly and H6277
35:11 they laid to my charge *t* that I knew not.
38:12 t, and imagine deceits all the day long. H1942
42: 4 When I remember these *t,* I pour out my
45: 1 I speak of the t which I have made
4 right hand shall teach thee terrible t. H3372
50:21 These *t* hast thou done, and I kept

Ps 57: 2 unto God that performeth *all t* for me.
60: 3 Thou hast shewed thy people hard t: H7186
65: 5 *By* terrible t in righteousness wilt thou
71:19 great t: O God, who *is* like unto thee! H1419
72:18 of Israel, who only doeth wondrous t. H6381
78:12 Marvellous t did he in the sight of their H6382
86:10 doest wondrous t: thou *art* God alone. H6381
87: 3 Glorious t are spoken of thee, O city of H3513
94: 4 *and* speak hard t? *and* all the workers H6277
98: 1 done marvellous t: his right hand, and H6381
103: 5 Who satisfieth thy mouth with good *t; so*
104:25 sea, wherein *are* t creeping innumerable,
106:21 which had done great t in Egypt; H1419
22 of Ham, *and* terrible t by the Red sea. H3372
107:43 Whoso *is* wise, and will observe these *t,*
113: 6 Who humbleth *himself* to behold *the t*
119:18 may behold wondrous t out of thy law. H6381
128 *t to be* right; *and* I hate every false way.
126: 2 The LORD hath done great t for them. H1431
3 The LORD hath done great t for us; H1431
131: 1 in great matters, or in t too high for me.
148:10 Beasts, and all cattle; creeping t, and H7431
Prv 2:12 from the man that speaketh froward t; H8419
3:15 rubies: and all the t thou canst desire are
6:16 These six *t* doth the LORD hate: yea,
8: 6 Hear; for I will speak of excellent t; and H5057
6 the opening of my lips *shall be* right t. H4339
11 rubies; and all the t that may be desired
15:28 mouth of the wicked poureth out evil t. H7451
16: 4 The LORD hath made all *t* for himself:
30 He shutteth his eyes to devise froward t: H8419
22:20 Have not I written to thee excellent t in H7991
23:16 shall rejoice, when thy lips speak right t. H4339
33 and thine heart shall utter perverse t. H8419
24:23 These *t* also *belong* to the wise. *It is* not
26:10 The great *God* that formed all *t* both
28: 5 they that seek the LORD understand all *t.*
10 upright shall have good *t* in possession.
30: 7 Two *t* have I required of thee; deny me
15 There are three *t that* are never satisfied,
15 *yea,* four *t* say not, *It is* enough:
18 There be three *t which* are too wonderful
21 For three *t* the earth is disquieted, and
24 There be four *t which are* little upon the
29 There be three t which go well, yea, four
Ecc 1: 8 All t *are* full of labour; man cannot H1697
11 *There is* no remembrance of former *t;*
11 remembrance of *t* that are to come with
13 concerning all *t* that are done under
6:11 Seeing there be many t that increase H1697
7:15 All *t* have I seen in the days of my
25 and the reason *of t,* and to know the
9: 2 All *t come* alike to all: *there is* one event
3 This *is* an evil among all *t* that are done
10:19 merry: but money answereth all *t.*
11: 9 *t* God will bring thee into judgment.
Isa 12: 5 t: this *is* known in all the earth. H1348
25: 1 done wonderful *t; thy* counsels of old *are*
6 a feast of fat t, a feast of wines on the H8081
6 on the lees, of fat t full of marrow, of H8081
29:16 Surely your turning of t upside down
30:10 not unto us right t, speak unto us smooth
10 unto us smooth t, prophesy deceits:
32: 8 But the liberal deviseth liberal t; and by H5081
8 things; and by liberal t shall he stand. H5081
34: 1 the world, and all t that come forth of it.
38:16 O Lord, by these *t men* live, and in all
16 and in all these *t is* the life of my spirit:
39: 2 of his precious t, the silver, and the H5238
40:26 hath created these *t,* that bringeth out
41:22 shew the former t, what they *be,* that we H7223
22 end of them; or declare us t for to come.
23 Shew the t that are to come hereafter,
42: 9 Behold, the former t are come to pass, H7223
9 to pass, and new t do I declare: before H2319
16 and crooked t straight. These things H4625
16 straight. These t will I do unto them, H1697
20 Seeing many t, but thou observest not; H7227
43: 9 shew us former t? let them bring forth H7223
18 Remember ye not the former t, neither H7223
18 things, neither consider the t of old.
44: 7 people? and the t that are coming, and
9 their delectable t shall not profit; and H2530
24 that maketh all *t;* that stretcheth forth
45: 7 and create evil: I the LORD do all these *t.*
11 Maker, Ask me of t to come concerning
19 righteousness, I declare t that are right.
46: 9 Remember the former t of old: for I *am* H7223
10 ancient times *the t* that are not *yet* done,

T

Isa 47: 7 didst not lay these *t* to thy heart, neither
9 But these two *t* shall come to thee in a
13 from *these t* that shall come upon thee.
48: 3 I have declared the former t from the H7223
6 shewed thee new t from this time, even H2319
6 t, and thou didst not know them. H5341
14 hath declared these *t*? The LORD hath
51:19 These two *t* are come unto thee; who
56: 4 and choose *the t* that please me, and
61:11 garden causeth the t that are sown in it
64: 3 When thou didst terrible t *which* we H3372
11 and all our pleasant t are laid waste. H4261
12 Wilt thou refrain thyself for these *t*, O
65: 4 broth of abominable *t is in* their vessels;
66: 2 For all those *t* hath mine hand made,
2 and all those *t* have been, saith the
8 hath seen such t? Shall the earth be made
Jer 2: 8 and walked after *t that* do not profit.
3: 5 and done evil t as thou couldest. H7451
7 And I said after she had done all these *t*,
4:18 procured these *t* unto thee; this *is* thy
5: 9 Shall I not visit for these *t*? saith the
19 our God all these *t* unto us? then shalt
25 Your iniquities have turned away these *t*,
25 sins have withholden good *t* from you.
29 Shall I not visit for these *t*? saith the
8:13 shall fade; and *the t that* I have given
9: 9 Shall I not visit them for these *t*? saith the
24 for in these *t* I delight, saith the LORD.
10:16 *is* the former of all *t*; and Israel *is* the rod
13:22 come these t upon me? For the greatness
14:22 upon thee: for thou hast made all these *t*.
16:18 of their detestable and abominable t. H8441
19 vanity, and *t* wherein *there is* no profit.
17: 9 The heart *is* deceitful above all *t*, and
18:13 hath heard such t: the virgin of Israel
20: 1 heard that Jeremiah prophesied these t. H1697
5 all the precious t thereof, and all the H3366
21:14 and it shall devour all t round about it.
26:10 Judah heard these t, then they came up H1697
30:15 increased, I have done these t unto thee.
31: 5 plant, and shall eat *them* as common t. H2490
33: 3 and mighty t, which thou knowest not. H1219
42: 5 even according to all t for the which the H1697
44:18 her, we have wanted all *t*, and have been
45: 5 And seekest thou great t for thyself? H1419
51:19 *is* the former of all t: and *Israel is* the rod
Lam 1: 7 all her pleasant t that she had in the H4262
10 all her pleasant t: for she hath seen *that* H4261
11 their pleasant t for meat to relieve the H4262
16 For these *t* I weep; mine eye, mine eye
2:14 vain and foolish t for thee: and they H8602
5:17 For this our heart is faint; for these *t* our
Ezk 5:11 all thy detestable t, and with all thine H8251
7:20 of their detestable t therein: therefore H8251
8:10 form of creeping t, and abominable H7431
11: 5 for I know the t that come into your
18 all the detestable t thereof and all the H8251
21 heart of their detestable t and their H8251
25 all the t that the LORD had shewed me. H1697
16:16 *t* shall not come, neither shall it be *so*.
30 thou doest all these *t*, the work of an
43 me in all these *t*; behold, therefore I also
17:12 ye not what these *t mean*? tell *them*,
15 that doeth such *t*? or shall he break the
18 hath done all these *t*, he shall not escape.
18:10 *that* doeth the like to *any* one of these *t*,
20:40 of your oblations, with all your holy t. H6944
22: 8 Thou hast despised mine holy t, and H6944
25 and precious t; they have made her H3366
26 mine holy t: they have put no difference H6944
23:30 I will do these *t* unto thee, because thou
24:19 these *t are* to us, that thou doest *so*?
27:24 in all sorts *of t*, in blue clothes, and
37:23 their detestable t, nor with any of their H8251
38:10 same time shall t come into thy mind, H1697
20 and all creeping t that creep upon the H7431
42:13 eat the most holy t: there shall they lay H6944
13 they lay the most holy t, and the meat H6944
14 to *those t* which *are* for the people.
44: 8 of mine holy t: but ye have set keepers H6944
13 to any of my holy t, in the most holy H6944
30 And the first of all the firstfruits of all *t*,
Dan 2:10 *that* asked such t at any magician, or H4406
22 He revealeth the deep and secret t: he
40 and subdueth all *t*: and as iron that
7: 8 of man, and a mouth speaking great t. H7260
16 me know the interpretation of the t. H4406
20 that spake very great t, whose look *was* H7260

Dan 10:21 me in these t, but Michael your prince.
11:36 speak marvellous t against the God of H6381
38 and with precious stones, and pleasant t.
43 over all the precious t of Egypt: and the
12: 7 holy people, all these *t* shall be finished.
8 my Lord, what *shall be* the end of these *t*?
Hos 2:18 *with* the creeping t of the ground: and I H7431
8:12 I have written to him the great t of my H7239
9: 3 and they shall eat unclean *t* in Assyria.
14: 9 understand these *t*? prudent, and he shall
Joel 2:20 come up, because he hath done great t. H1431
21 rejoice: for the LORD will do great t. H1431
3: 5 into your temples my goodly pleasant t: H4261
Oba 6 How are *the t* of Esau searched out! *how*
6 out! *how* are his hidden t sought up! H4710
Mic 7:15 Egypt will I shew unto him marvellous *t*.
Hab 1:14 t, *that have* no ruler over them? H7431
Zep 1: 2 I will utterly consume all *t* from off the
Zec 4:10 the day of small t? for they shall rejoice, H6996
8:12 of this people to possess all these *t*.
16 These *are* the t that ye shall do; Speak H1697
17 these *are t* that I hate, saith the LORD.
Mt 1:20 But while he thought on these t, behold,
2: 3 When Herod the king had heard *these t*,
4: 9 And saith unto him, All these t will I G5023
6: 8 t ye have need of, before ye ask him. G3739
32 (For after all these t do the Gentiles G5023
32 knoweth that ye have need of all these t. G5130
33 and all these t shall be added unto you. G5023
34 thought for the t of itself. Sufficient G3588
7:11 heaven give good t to them that ask him? G18
12 Therefore all t whatsoever ye would G3956
9:18 While he spake these t unto them, G5023
11: 4 again those t which ye do hear and see:
25 thou hast hid these t from the wise and G5023
27 All t are delivered unto me of my G3956
12:34 being evil, speak good t? for out of the G18
35 forth good t: and an evil man out G18
35 of the evil treasure bringeth forth evil t. G4190
13: 3 And he spake many t unto them in G4183
17 desired to see *those t* which ye see, and
17 and to hear *those t* which ye hear, and
34 All these t spake Jesus unto the G5023
35 I will utter t which have been kept
41 of his kingdom all t that offend, and G3956
51 these t? They say unto him, Yea, Lord. G3956
52 forth out of his treasure *t* new and old.
56 Whence then hath this *man* all these t? G5023
15:18 But those t which proceed out of the
20 These are *the t* which defile a man: but
16:21 and suffer many t of the elders and G4183
23 savourest not the t that be of God, but G3588
17:11 truly shall first come, and restore all t. G3956
19:20 him, All these t have I kept from my G5023
26 but with God all t are possible. G3956
21:15 saw the wonderful t that he did, and G2297
22 And all t, whatsoever ye shall ask in G3956
23 t? and who gave thee this authority? G5023
24 tell you by what authority I do these t. G5023
27 tell I you by what authority I do these t. G5023
22: 4 t *are* ready: come unto the marriage. G3956
21 unto Caesar the t which are Caesar's; G3588
21 and unto God the t that are God's. G3588
23:20 sweareth by it, and by all t thereon. G3956
36 Verily I say unto you, All these t shall G5023
24: 2 See ye not all these t? verily I say unto G5023
3 when shall these t be? and what *shall* G5023
6 for all *these t* must come to pass, but
33 shall see all these t, know that it is near, G5023
34 shall not pass, till all these t be fulfilled. G5023
25:21 faithful over a few t, I will make thee G3641
21 t: enter thou into the joy of thy lord. G4183
23 faithful over a few t, I will make thee G3641
23 t: enter thou into the joy of thy lord. G4183
27:13 how many t they witness against thee? G4214
19 t this day in a dream because of him. G4183
54 and those t that were done, they
28:11 the chief priests all the t that were done. G537
20 Teaching them to observe all t G3956
Mk 1:44 for thy cleansing those t which Moses
2: 8 Why reason ye these t in your hearts? G5023
3: 8 what great t he did, came unto him. G3745
4: 2 And he taught them many t by G4183
11 all *these* t are done in parables: G3956
19 the lusts of other t entering in, choke G3062
34 he expounded all t to his disciples. G3956
5:19 them how great t the Lord hath done G3745
20 how great t Jesus had done for him: G3745
26 And had suffered many t of many G4183

Mk 6: 2 this *man* these t? and what wisdom *is* G5023
20 he did many t, and heard him gladly. G4183
30 and told him all t, both what they had G3956
34 and he began to teach them many t. G4183
7: 4 And many other t there be, which they G243
8 cups: and many other such like t ye do. G3946
13 delivered: and many such like t do ye. G3946
15 defile him: but the t which come out of
23 All these evil t come from within, and G4190
37 He hath done all t well: he maketh both G3956
8:31 must suffer many t, and be rejected of G4183
33 savourest not the t that be of God, but G3588
33 that be of God, but the t that be of men. G3588
9: 9 tell no man what t they had seen, till G3739
12 and restoreth all t; and how it is written G3956
12 suffer many t, and be set at nought. G4183
23 all t *are* possible to him that believeth. G3956
10:27 God: for with God all t are possible. G3956
32 them what t should happen unto him,
11:11 about upon all t, and now the eventide G3956
23 believe that those t which he saith shall
24 Therefore I say unto you, What t G3956
28 dost thou these t? and who gave thee G5023
28 gave thee this authority to do these t? G5023
29 tell you by what authority I do these t. G5023
33 I tell you by what authority I do these t. G5023
12:17 to Caesar the t that are Caesar's, and G3588
17 and to God the t that are God's. And G3588
13: 4 Tell us, when shall these t be? and what G5023
4 sign when all these t shall be fulfilled? G5023
7 troubled: for *such t* must needs be; but
23 heed: behold, I have foretold you all t. G3956
29 ye shall see these t come to pass, know G5023
30 shall not pass, till all these t be done. G5023
14:36 And he said, Abba, Father, all t *are* G3956
15: 3 of many t: but he answered nothing. G4183
4 how many t they witness against thee. G4214
Lk 1: 1 of those t which are most surely G4229
3 of all t from the very first, to G3956
4 t, wherein thou hast been instructed. G3056
20 the day that these t shall be performed, G5023
45 t which were told her from the Lord.
49 to me great t; and holy *is* his name. G3167
53 He hath filled the hungry with good t; G18
2:18 *it* wondered at those t which were told
19 But Mary kept all these t, and pondered G4487
20 God for all the t that they had heard G3956
33 at those t which were spoken of him.
39 And when they had performed all t G537
3:18 And many other t in his exhortation G4183
4:28 heard these t, were filled with wrath, G5023
5:26 saying, We have seen strange t to day. G3861
27 And after these t he went forth, and G5023
6:46 Lord, Lord, and do not the t which I say?
7: 9 When Jesus heard these t, he marvelled G5023
18 of John shewed him of all these t. G5130
22 and tell John what t ye have seen and G3739
8: 8 he had said these t, he cried, He that G5023
39 shew how great t God hath done unto G3745
39 how great t Jesus had done unto him. G3745
9: 9 I hear such t? And he desired to see him. G5108
22 must suffer many t, and be rejected of G4183
36 any of those t which they had seen. G3762
43 every one at all t which Jesus did, he G3956
10: 1 After these t the Lord appointed other G5023
7 and drinking such t as they give: for the
8 you, eat such t as are set before you: G2068
21 thou hast hid these t from the wise and G5023
22 All t are delivered to me of my Father: G3956
23 *are* the eyes which see the t ye see:
24 desired to see those t which ye see, and
24 and to hear those t which ye hear, and
41 art careful and troubled about many t: G4183
11:27 And it came to pass, as he spake these t, G5023
41 But rather give alms of such t as ye have;
41 and, behold, all t are clean unto you. G3956
53 And as he said these t unto them, the G5023
53 and to provoke him to speak of many t: G4119
12:15 abundance of the t which he possesseth.
20 those t be, which thou hast provided?
30 For all these t do the nations of the G5023
30 knoweth that ye have need of these t. G5130
31 and all these t shall be added unto you. G5023
48 But he that knew not, and did commit t
13: 2 because they suffered such t? G5108
17 And when he had said these t, all his G5023
17 the glorious t that were done by him. G1741
14: 6 could not answer him again to these t. G5023
15 him heard these t, he said unto him, G5023

Lk 14:17 bidden, Come; for all t are now ready. G3956
21 his lord these t. Then the master of G5023
15:26 and asked what these t meant. G5023
16:14 heard all these t: and they derided him. G5023
25 receivedst thy good t, and likewise G18
25 Lazarus evil t: but now he is comforted, G2556
17: 9 t that were commanded him? I trow not.
10 shall have done all those t which are
25 But first must he suffer many t, and be G4183
18:22 Now when Jesus heard these t, he said G5023
27 And he said, The t which are impossible
31 Jerusalem, and all t that are written by G3956
34 And they understood none of these t: G5130
34 knew they the t which were spoken.
19:11 And as they heard these t, he added and G5023
42 in this thy day, the t *which belong* unto G3588
20: 2 doest thou these t? or who is he that G5023
8 tell I you by what authority I do these t. G5023
25 unto Caesar the t which be Caesar's, G3588
25 and unto God the t which be God's. G3588
21: 6 *As for* these t which ye behold, the days G5023
7 when shall these t be? and what sign G5023
7 *be* when these t shall come to pass? G5023
9 terrified: for these t must first come to G5023
22 all t which are written may be fulfilled. G3956
26 looking after those t which are coming
28 And when these t begin to come to G5130
31 So likewise ye, when ye see these t G5023
36 to escape all these t that shall come to G5023
22:37 for the t concerning me have an end. G3588
65 And many other t blasphemously G2087
23: 8 he had heard many t of him; and he G4183
14 touching those t whereof ye accuse him:
31 For if they do these t in a green tree, G5023
48 beholding the t which were done, smote
49 stood afar off, beholding these t. G5023
24: 9 t unto the eleven, and to all the rest. G5023
10 which told these t unto the apostles. G5023
14 And they talked together of all these t G5130
18 hast not known the t which are come to
19 And he said unto them, What t? And G4169
21 is the third day since these t were done. G5023
26 these t, and to enter into his glory? G5023
27 the scriptures the t concerning himself. G3588
35 And they told what t *were done* in the G3588
44 yet with you, that all t must be fulfilled, G3956
48 And ye are witnesses of these t. G5130
Jn 1: 3 All t were made by him; and without G3956
28 These t were done in Bethabara G5023
50 thou? thou shalt see greater t than these.
2:16 doves, Take these t hence; make not G5023
18 unto us, seeing that thou doest these t? G5023
3: 9 and said unto him, How can these t be? G5023
10 of Israel, and knowest not these t? G5023
12 If I have told you earthly t, and ye G1919
12 ye believe, if I tell you *of* heavenly t? G2032
22 After these t came Jesus and his G5023
35 Son, and hath given all t into his hand. G3956
4:25 when he is come, he will tell us all t. G3956
29 Come, see a man, which told me all t G3956
45 him, having seen all the t that he did at G3956
5:16 had done these t on the sabbath day. G5023
19 Father do: for what t soever he doeth,
20 sheweth him all t that himself doeth: G3956
34 these t I say, that ye might be saved. G5023
6: 1 After these t Jesus went over the sea of G5023
59 These t said he in the synagogue, as he G5023
7: 1 After these t Jesus walked in Galilee: G5023
4 do these t, shew thyself to the world. G5023
32 murmured such t concerning him; and G5023
8:26 I have many t to say and to judge of G4183
26 those t which I have heard of him. G5023
28 Father hath taught me, I speak these t. G5023
29 for I do always those t that please him.
10: 6 t they were which he spake unto them. G5101
41 t that John spake of this man were true. G3956
11:11 These t said he: and after that he saith G5023
45 the t which Jesus did, believed on him.
46 and told them what t Jesus had done. G3739
12:16 These t understood not his disciples at G5023
16 they that these t were written of him, G5023
16 *that* they had done these t unto him. G5023
36 of light. These t spake Jesus, and G5023
41 These t said Esaias, when he saw his G5023
13: 3 had given all t into his hands, and G3956
17 If ye know these t, happy are ye if ye do G5023
29 him, Buy *those* t that we have need of
14:25 These t have I spoken unto you, being G5023
26 shall teach you all t, and bring all things G3956

Jn 14:26 and bring all t to your remembrance, G3956
15:11 These t have I spoken unto you, that G5023
15 you friends; for all t that I have heard G3956
17 These t I command you, that ye love G5023
21 But all these t will they do unto you for G5023
16: 1 These t have I spoken unto you, that ye G5023
3 And these t will they do unto you, G5023
4 But these t have I told you, that when G5023
4 them. And these t I said not unto you G5023
6 But because I have said these t unto G5023
12 I have yet many t to say unto you, but G4183
13 speak: and he will shew you t to come.
15 All t that the Father hath are mine: G3956
25 These t have I spoken unto you in G5023
30 thou knowest all t, and needest not that G3956
33 These t I have spoken unto you, that in G5023
17: 7 Now they have known that all t G3956
13 And now come I to thee; and these t I G5023
18: 4 Jesus therefore, knowing all t that G3956
19:24 lots. These t therefore the soldiers did. G5023
28 After this, Jesus knowing that all t were G3956
36 For these t were done, that the G5023
20:18 *that* he had spoken these t unto her. G5023
21: 1 After these t Jesus shewed himself G5023
17 thou knowest all t; thou knowest that I G3956
24 testifieth of these t, and wrote these G5130
24 and wrote these t: and we know that his G5023
25 And there are also many other t which G243
Act 1: 3 the t pertaining to the kingdom of God: G3588
9 And when he had spoken these t, while G5023
2:44 were together, and had all t common; G537
3:18 But those t, which God before had
21 of restitution of all t, which God hath G3956
22 all t whatsoever he shall say unto you. G3956
4:20 For we cannot but speak the t which we
25 rage, and the people imagine vain t? G2756
32 that ought of the t which he possessed G5224
32 was his own; but they had all t common. G537
34 the prices of the t that were sold,
5: 5 came on all them that heard these t. G5023
11 and upon as many as heard these t. G5023
24 heard these t, they doubted of them G3056
32 And we are his witnesses of these t; and G4487
7: 1 Then said the high priest, Are these t G5023
50 Hath not my hand made all these t? G5023
54 When they heard these t, they were cut G5023
8: 6 heed unto those t which Philip spake,
12 Philip preaching the t concerning the G3588
24 t which ye have spoken come upon me. G3367
9:16 For I will shew him how great t he must G3745
10: 8 And when he had declared all *these* t G537
12 and creeping t, and fowls of the air. G2062
33 all t that are commanded thee of God. G3956
39 And we are witnesses of all t which he G3956
11: 6 and creeping t, and fowls of the air. G2062
18 When they heard these t, they held their G5023
22 Then tidings of these t came unto the G846
12:17 Go shew these t unto James, and to G5023
13:39 justified from all t, from which ye could G3956
45 against those t which were spoken by
14:15 And saying, Sirs, why do ye these t? We G5023
15 and the sea, and all t that are therein: G3956
15: 4 all t that God had done with them.
17 saith the Lord, who doeth all these t. G5023
20 and *from* t strangled, and *from* blood.
27 shall also tell *you* the same t by mouth. G846
28 greater burden than these necessary t; G1876
29 blood, and from t strangled, and from
16:14 unto the t which were spoken of Paul.
17: 8 of the city, when they heard these t. G5023
11 daily, whether those t were so. G5023
20 For thou bringest certain strange t to G3579
20 know therefore what these t mean. G5023
22 that in all t ye are too superstitious. G3956
24 God that made the world and all t G3956
25 giveth to all life, and breath, and all t; G2596
18: 1 After these t Paul departed from G5023
17 And Gallio cared for none of those t. G5130
25 diligently the t of the Lord, knowing G3588
19: 8 the t concerning the kingdom of God. G3588
21 After these t were ended, Paul G5023
36 Seeing then that these t cannot be G5130
20:22 knowing the t that shall befall me there:
24 But none of these t move me, neither
30 t, to draw away disciples after them. G1294
35 I have shewed you all t, how that so G3956
21:12 And when we heard these t, both we, G5023
19 particularly what t God had wrought G3739
24 know that those t, whereof they were

Act 21:25 themselves from t offered to idols, and
22:10 all t which are appointed for thee to do. G3956
23:22 that thou hast shewed these t to me. G5023
24: 8 of all these t, whereof we accuse him. G5130
9 assented, saying that these t were so. G5023
13 Neither can they prove the t whereof
14 believing all t which are written in G3956
22 And when Felix heard these t, having G5023
25: 9 there be judged of these t before me? G5130
11 be none of these t whereof these accuse
18 none accusation of such t as I supposed:
26: 2 the t whereof I am accused of the Jews: G3956
9 I ought to do many t contrary to the G4183
16 both of these t which thou hast seen,
16 t in the which I will appear unto thee;
22 saying none other t than those which the
26 For the king knoweth of these t, before G5130
26 that none of these t are hidden from G5130
27:11 than those t which were spoken by Paul.
28:10 laded *us* with such t as were necessary. G3588
24 And some believed the t which were
31 and teaching those t which concern the G3588
Ro 1:20 For the invisible t of him from the G517
20 understood by the t that are made, *even*
23 and fourfooted beasts, and creeping t. G2062
28 to do those t which are not convenient;
30 of evil t, disobedient to parents, G2556
32 commit such t are worthy of death, G5108
2: 1 for thou that judgest doest the same t. G846
2 against them which commit such t. G5108
3 which do such t, and doest the same, G5108
14 do by nature the t contained in the law, G3588
18 will, and approvest the t that are more
3:19 Now we know that what t soever the law
4:17 t which be not as though they were.
6:21 What fruit had ye then in those t
21 for the end of those t *is* death. G1565
8: 5 flesh do mind the t of the flesh; but they G3588
5 are after the Spirit the t of the Spirit. G3588
28 And we know that all t work together G3956
31 What shall we then say to these t? If God G5023
32 he not with him also freely give us all t? G3956
37 Nay, in all these t we are more than G5125
38 nor t present, nor things to come,
38 nor things present, nor t to come,
10: 5 which doeth those t shall live by them. G846
15 of peace, and bring glad tidings of good t! G18
11:36 all t: to whom *be* glory for ever. Amen. G3956
12:16 Mind not high t, but condescend to men G5308
17 Provide t honest in the sight of all men.
14: 2 For one believeth that he may eat all t: G3956
18 For he that in these t serveth Christ *is* G5125
19 Let us therefore follow after the t which
19 t wherewith one may edify another. G3588
20 work of God. All t indeed *are* pure; but G3956
15: 4 For whatsoever t were written G3745
17 Christ in those t which pertain to God.
18 of any of those t which Christ hath not
27 of their spiritual t, their duty is also to G4152
27 also to minister unto them in carnal t. G4559
1Co 1:27 But God hath chosen the foolish t of the G3474
27 hath chosen the weak t of the world to G772
27 to confound the t which are mighty;
28 And base t of the world, and things G36
28 And base things of the world, and t
28 God chosen, *yea*, and t which are not, to
28 are not, to bring to nought t that are:
2: 9 the heart of man, the t which God hath
10 all t, yea, the deep things of God. G3956
10 all things, yea, the deep t of God. G899
11 For what man knoweth the t of a man, G3588
11 him? even so the t of God knoweth no G3588
12 the t that are freely given to us of God. G3588
13 Which t also we speak, not in the G3739
13 comparing spiritual t with spiritual. G4152
14 But the natural man receiveth not the t G3588
15 But he that is spiritual judgeth all t, yet G3956
3:21 man glory in men. For all t are yours; G3956
22 or life, or death, or t present, or things to
22 present, or t to come; all are yours;
4: 5 to light the hidden t of darkness, and G2927
6 And these t, brethren, I have in a figure G5023
13 the offscouring of all t unto this day. G3956
14 I write not these t to shame you, but as G5023
6: 3 much more t that pertain to this life?
4 If then ye have judgments of t pertaining
12 All t are lawful unto me, but all things G3956
12 All things are lawful unto me, but all t G3956
12 not expedient: all t are lawful for me, G3956

1Co 7: 1 Now concerning the t whereof ye wrote
32 careth for the t that belong to the Lord, G3588
33 But he that is married careth for the t G3588
34 careth for the t of the Lord, that she G3588
34 careth for the t of the world, how she G3588
8: 1 Now as touching t offered unto idols, we
4 the eating of those t that are offered in
6 of whom are all t, and we in him; and G3956
6 by whom are all t, and we by him. G3956
10 to eat those t which are offered to idols;
9: 8 Say I these t as a man? or saith not the G5023
11 If we have sown unto you spiritual t, is G4152
11 thing if we shall reap your carnal t? G4559
12 but suffer all t, lest we should hinder G3956
13 about holy t live of the things of G2413
13 things live of the t of the temple? and
15 But I have used none of these t: neither G5130
15 I written these t, that it should be so G5023
22 I am made all t to all men, that I might G3956
25 is temperate in all t. Now they do it to G3956
10: 6 Now these t were our examples, to the G5023
6 not lust after evil t, as they also lusted. G2556
11 Now all these t happened unto them G5023
20 But I say, that the t which the Gentiles
23 All t are lawful for me, but all things G3956
23 All things are lawful for me, but all t G3956
23 not expedient: all t are lawful for me, G3956
23 are lawful for me, but all t edify not. G3956
33 Even as I please all men in all t, not
11: 2 me in all t, and keep the ordinances, G3956
12 also by the woman; but all t of God. G3956
13: 7 Beareth all t, believeth all things, G3956
7 Beareth all things, believeth all t, G3956
7 things, hopeth all t, endureth all things. G3956
7 things, hopeth all things, endureth all t. G3956
11 I became a man, I put away childish t. G3588
14: 7 And even t without life giving sound,
26 Let all t be done unto edifying. G3956
37 that the t that I write unto you
40 Let all t be done decently and in order. G3956
15:27 For he hath put all t under his feet. But G3956
27 when he saith all t are put under him, G3956
27 which did put all t under him. G3956
28 And when all t shall be subdued unto G3956
28 t under him, that God may be all in all. G3956
16:14 Let all your t be done with charity. G3956
2Co 1:13 For we write none other t unto you, than G243
17 lightness? or the t that I purpose, do I
2: 9 of you, whether ye be obedient in all t. G3956
16 life. And who is sufficient for these t? G5023
4: 2 But have renounced the hidden t of G2927
15 For all t are for your sakes, that the G3956
18 While we look not at the t which are
18 are seen, but at the t which are not seen:
18 are not seen: for the t which are seen are
18 but the t which are not seen are eternal.
5:10 one may receive the t done in his body, G3588
17 is a new creature: old t are passed away; G744
17 away; behold, all t are become new. G3956
18 And all t are of God, who hath G3588
6: 4 But in all t approving ourselves as the
10 having nothing, and yet possessing all t. G3956
7:11 what revenge! In all t ye have approved
14 but as we spake all t to you in truth, G3956
16 that I have confidence in you in all t.
8:21 Providing for honest t, not only in the G2570
22 diligent in many t, but now much more G4183
9: 8 in all t, may abound to every good work:
10: 7 Do ye look on t after the outward G3588
13 But we will not boast of t without our
15 Not boasting of t without our measure,
16 line of t made ready to our hand. G3588
11: 6 made manifest among you in all t. G3956
9 supplied: and in all t I have kept myself
28 Beside those t that are without, that
30 the t which concern mine infirmities. G3588
12:19 all t, dearly beloved, for your edifying. G3956
13:10 Therefore I write these t being absent, G5023
Gal 1:20 Now the t which I write unto you,
2:18 For if I build again the t which I G5023
3: 4 Have ye suffered so many t in vain? if it G5118
10 not in all t which are written in G3588
4:24 Which t are an allegory: for these are G3748
5:17 that ye cannot do the t that ye would. G5023
21 t shall not inherit the kingdom of God. G5108
6: 6 unto him that teacheth in all good t. G18
Eph 1:10 together in one all t in Christ, both G3956
11 all t after the counsel of his own will: G3956
22 And hath put all t under his feet, and
Eph 1:22 to be the head over all t to the church,
3: 9 God, who created all t by Jesus Christ: G3956
4:10 all heavens, that he might fill all t.) G3956
15 in all t, which is the head, even Christ: G3956
5: 6 because of these t cometh the wrath of G5023
12 t which are done of them in secret. G2931
13 But all t that are reproved are made G3956
20 Giving thanks always for all t unto God G3956
6: 9 And, ye masters, do the same t unto G846
21 the Lord, shall make known to you all t: G3956
Php 1:10 That ye may approve t that are excellent;
12 brethren, that the t which happened G3588
2: 4 Look not every man on his own t, but G1438
4 but every man also on the t of others. G3588
10 should bow, of t in heaven, and things
10 t in earth, and things under the earth;
10 things in earth, and t under the earth;
14 Do all t without murmurings and G3956
21 For all seek their own, not the t which G3588
3: 1 To write the same t to you, to me indeed G846
7 But what t were gain to me, those I G3748
8 Yea doubtless, and I count all t but loss G3956
8 the loss of all t, and do count them G3956
13 I do, forgetting those t which are behind,
13 forth unto those t which are before,
19 is in their shame, who mind earthly t.) G1919
21 able even to subdue all t unto himself. G3956
4: 8 Finally, brethren, whatsoever t are G3745
8 are true, whatsoever t are honest, G3745
8 whatsoever t are just, whatsoever G3745
8 just, whatsoever t are pure, whatsoever G3745
8 are pure, whatsoever t are lovely, G3745
8 lovely, whatsoever t are of good report; G3745
8 if there be any praise, think on these t. G5023
9 Those t, which ye have both learned, G5023
12 where and in all t I am instructed both G3956
13 I can do all t through Christ which G3956
18 of Epaphroditus the t which were sent G3588
Col 1:16 For by him were all t created, that are G3956
16 all t were created by him, and for him: G3956
17 And he is before all t, and by him all G3956
17 all things, and by him all t consist. G3956
18 in all t he might have the preeminence.
20 to reconcile all t unto himself; by him, G3956
20 they be t in earth, or things in heaven. G3588
20 they be things in earth, or t in heaven. G3588
2:17 Which are a shadow of t to come; but
18 into those t which he hath not seen,
23 Which t have indeed a shew of wisdom G3748
3: 1 Christ, seek those t which are above,
2 Set your affection on t above, not on G3588
2 on things above, not on t on the earth. G3588
14 And above all these t put on charity, G5125
20 Children, obey your parents in all t: for G3956
22 Servants, obey in all t your masters G3956
4: 9 unto you all t which are done here. G3956
1Th 2:14 also have suffered like t of your own G5024
5:21 Prove all t; hold fast that which is good. G3956
2Th 2: 5 I was yet with you, I told you these t? G5023
3: 4 will do the t which we command you.
1Ti 3:11 not slanderers, sober, faithful in all t. G3956
14 These t write I unto thee, hoping to G5023
4: 6 of these t, thou shalt be a good G5023
8 profitable unto all t, having promise of G3956
11 These t command and teach. G5023
15 Meditate upon these t; give thyself G5023
5: 7 And these t give in charge, that they G5023
13 speaking t which they ought not.
21 thou observe these t without preferring G5023
6: 2 the benefit. These t teach and exhort. G5023
11 But thou, O man of God, flee these t; G5023
13 who quickeneth all t, and before Christ G3956
17 God, who giveth us richly all t to enjoy; G3956
2Ti 1:12 For the which cause I also suffer these t: G5023
18 and in how many t he ministered unto G3745
2: 2 And the t that thou hast heard of me
7 Lord give thee understanding in all t. G3956
10 Therefore I endure all t for the elect's G3956
14 Of these t put them in remembrance, G5023
3:14 But continue thou in the t which thou
4: 5 But watch thou in all t, endure G3956
Tit 1: 5 set in order the t that are wanting, and
11 houses, teaching t which they ought not,
15 Unto the pure all t are pure: but unto G3956
2: 1 But speak thou the t which become
3 given to much wine, teachers of good t; G2567
7 In all t shewing thyself a pattern of G3956
9 them well in all t; not answering again;
10 the doctrine of God our Saviour in all t. G3956
Tit 2:15 These t speak, and exhort, and rebuke G5023
3: 8 This is a faithful saying, and these t I G5130
8 t are good and profitable unto men. G5023
Heb 1: 2 all t, by whom also he made the worlds; G3956
3 and upholding all t by the word of his G3956
2: 1 earnest heed to the t which we have
8 Thou hast put all t in subjection under G3956
8 now we see not yet all t put under him. G3956
10 For it became him, for whom are all t, G3956
10 by whom are all t, in bringing many G3956
17 Wherefore in all t it behoved him to be G3956
17 high priest in t pertaining to God, to G4314
3: 4 man; but he that built all t is God. G3956
5 of those t which were to be spoken after;
4:13 in his sight: but all t are naked and G3956
5: 1 for men in t pertaining to God, that G3588
8 he obedience by the t which he suffered;
11 Of whom we have many t to say, and
6: 9 But, beloved, we are persuaded better t G2909
9 things of you, and t that accompany
18 That by two immutable t, in which it G4229
7:13 For he of whom these t are spoken G5023
8: 1 Now of the t which we have spoken this
5 shadow of heavenly t, as Moses was G2032
5 that thou make all t according to the G3956
9: 6 Now when these t were thus ordained, G5130
11 an high priest of good t to come, by a G18
22 And almost all t are by the law purged G3956
23 the patterns of t in the heavens should G3588
23 but the heavenly t themselves with G2032
10: 1 For the law having a shadow of good t to G18
1 the very image of the t, can never with G4229
11: 1 Now faith is the substance of t hoped
1 hoped for, the evidence of t not seen. G4229
3 of God, so that t which are seen were
3 were not made of t which do appear.
7 warned of God of t not seen as yet, G3588
14 For they that say such t declare plainly G5108
20 Jacob and Esau concerning t to come.
12:24 that speaketh better t than that of Abel. G2909
27 removing of those t that are shaken, as
27 are shaken, as of t that are made, that
27 t which cannot be shaken may remain.
13: 5 be content with such t as ye have: for he
18 in all t willing to live honestly. G3956
Jas 2:16 them not those t which are needful to
3: 2 For in many t we offend all. If any man G4183
5 and boasteth great t. Behold, how great G3166
7 of serpents, and of t in the sea, is tamed,
10 My brethren, these t ought not so to be. G5023
5:12 But above all t, my brethren, swear not, G3956
1Pt 1:12 they did minister the t, which are now G846
12 which t the angels desire to look into. G3739
18 with corruptible t, as silver and gold, G5349
4: 7 But the end of all t is at hand: be ye G3956
8 And above all t have fervent charity G3956
11 that God in all t may be glorified G3956
2Pt 1: 3 given unto us all t that pertain unto life G3956
8 For if these t be in you, and abound, G5023
9 But he that lacketh these t is blind, and G5023
10 for if ye do these t, ye shall never fall: G5023
12 of these t, though ye know them, G5130
15 have these t always in remembrance. G5130
2:12 speak evil of the t that they understand
3: 4 fell asleep, all t continue as they were G3956
11 Seeing then that all these t shall be G5130
14 ye look for such t, be diligent that ye G5023
16 in them of these t; in which are some G5130
16 things; in which are some t hard to be G5100
17 ye know these t before, beware lest ye
1Jn 1: 4 And these t write we unto you, that G5023
2: 1 My little children, these t write I unto G5023
15 Love not the world, neither the t that G3588
20 from the Holy One, and ye know all t. G3956
26 These t have I written unto you
27 teacheth you of all t, and is truth, and is G3956
3:20 than our heart, and knoweth all t. G3956
22 do those t that are pleasing in his sight.
5:13 These t have I written unto you that G5023
2Jn 8 that we lose not those t which we have
12 Having many t to write unto you, I G4183
3Jn 2 Beloved, I wish above all t that thou G3956
13 I had many t to write, but I will not G4183
Jude 10 But these speak evil of those t which they
10 in those t they corrupt themselves. G5125
Rev 1: 1 unto his servants t which must shortly
2 of Jesus Christ, and of all t that he saw. G3745
3 and keep those t which are written
19 Write the t which thou hast seen, and

Rev 1:19 hast seen, and the t which are, and the
19 are, and the t which shall be hereafter;
2: 1 write; These t saith he that holdeth G3592
8 write; These t saith the first and the G3592
10 Fear none of those t which thou shalt
12 write; These t saith he which hath G3592
14 But I have a few t against thee, because G3641
14 of Israel, to eat t sacrificed unto idols,
18 write; These t saith the Son of God, G3592
20 Notwithstanding I have a few t against G3641
20 and to eat t sacrificed unto idols.
3: 1 write; These t saith he that hath the G3592
2 Be watchful, and strengthen the t which
7 write; These t saith he that is holy, G3592
14 write; These t saith the Amen, the G3592
4: 1 will shew thee t which must be hereafter.
11 hast created all t, and for thy pleasure G3956
7: 1 And after these t I saw four angels G5023
10: 4 unto me, Seal up those t which the seven
6 heaven, and the t that therein are, and G3588
6 the earth, and the t that therein are, G3588
6 the sea, and the t which are therein, G3588
13: 5 speaking great t and blasphemies; and G3173
18: 1 And after these t I saw another angel G5023
14 from thee, and all t which were dainty G3956
15 The merchants of these t, which were G5130
19: 1 And after these t I heard a great voice G5023
20:12 judged out of those t which were written
21: 4 pain: for the former t are passed away. G4413
5 Behold, I make all t new. And he said G3956
7 He that overcometh shall inherit all t; G3956
22: 6 the t which must shortly be done.
8 And I John saw these t, and heard G5023
8 of the angel which shewed me these t. G5023
16 unto you these t in the churches. I am G5023
18 add unto these t, God shall add unto G5023
19 the t which are written in this book.
20 He which testifieth these t saith, Surely G5023

THINGS'
Col 3: 6 For which t sake the wrath of God

THINK
Gen 40:14 But t on me when it shall be well with H2142
Nu 36: 6 to whom they t best; only to the family H5869
2Sa 13:33 to his heart, to t that all the king's sons H559
2Ch 13: 8 And now ye t to withstand the kingdom H559
Neh 5:19 T upon me, my God, for good, H2142
6: 6 thou and the Jews t to rebel: for which H2803
14 My God, t thou upon Tobiah and H2142
Est 4:13 to answer Esther, T not with thyself H1819
Job 31: 1 eyes; why then should I t upon a maid? H995
41:32 him; *one* would t the deep *to be* hoary. H2803
Ecc 8:17 though a wise *man* t to know *it*, yet shall H559
Isa 10: 7 doth his heart t so; but *it is* in his heart H2803
Jer 23:27 Which t to cause my people to forget H2803
29:11 For I know the thoughts that I t toward H2803
Ezk 38:10 mind, and thou shalt t an evil thought: H2803
Dan 7:25 most High, and t to change times and H5452
Jna 1: 6 God will t upon us, that we perish not. H6245
Zec 11:12 And I said unto them, If ye t good, give H5869
Mt 3: 9 And t not to say within yourselves, We G1380
5:17 T not that I am come to destroy the G3543
6: 7 *do*: for they t that they shall be heard G1380
9: 4 Wherefore t ye evil in your hearts? G1760
10:34 T not that I am come to send peace on G3543
18:12 How t ye? if a man have an hundred G1380
21:28 But what t ye? A *certain* man had two G1380
22:42 Saying, What t ye of Christ? whose son G1380
24:44 as ye t not the Son of man cometh. G1380
26:66 What t ye? They answered and said, He G1380
Mk 14:64 Ye have heard the blasphemy: what t G5316
Lk 12:40 man cometh at an hour when ye t not. G1380
13: 4 fell, and slew them, t ye that they were G1380
Jn 5:39 Search the scriptures; for in them ye t G1380
45 Do not t that I will accuse you to the G1380
11:56 t ye, that he will not come to the feast? G1380
16: 2 you will t that he doeth God service. G1380
Act 13:25 he said, Whom t ye that I am? I am not G5282
17:29 we ought not to t that the Godhead is G3543
26: 2 I t myself happy, king Agrippa, G2233
Ro 12: 3 is among you, not to t *of himself* more G5252
3 than he ought to t; but to think soberly, G5426
3 to think; but to t soberly, according as G5426
1Co 4: 6 learn in us not to t *of men* above that G5426
9 For I t that God hath set forth us the G1380
7:36 But if any man t that he behaveth G3543
40 I t also that I have the Spirit of God. G1380
8: 2 And if any man t that he knoweth any G1380
1Co 12:23 body, which we t to be less honourable, G1380
14:37 If any man t himself to be a prophet, or G1380
2Co 3: 5 of ourselves to t any thing as of G3049
10: 2 wherewith I t to be bold against some, G3049
2 some, which t of us as if we walked G3049
7 let him of himself t this again, that, as G3049
11 Let such an one t this, that, such as we G3049
11:16 I say again, Let no man t me a fool; if G1380
12: 6 lest any man should t of me above that G3049
19 Again, t ye that we excuse ourselves G1380
Gal 6: 3 For if a man t himself to be something, G1380
Eph 3:20 all that we ask or t, according to the G3539
Php 1: 7 Even as it is meet for me to t this of you G5426
4: 8 if *there be* any praise, t on these things. G3049
Jas 1: 7 For let not that man t that he shall G3633
4: 5 Do ye t that the scripture saith in vain, G1380
1Pt 4: 4 Wherein they t it strange that ye run not
12 Beloved, t it not strange concerning the
2Pt 1:13 Yea, I t it meet, as long as I am in this G2233

THINKEST
2Sa 10: 3 Hanun their lord, T thou that David H5869
1Ch 19: 3 said to Hanun, T thou that David doth H5869
Job 35: 2 T thou this to be right, *that* thou saidst, H2803
Mt 17:25 him, saying, What t thou, Simon? of G1380
22:17 Tell us therefore, What t thou? Is it G1380
26:53 T thou that I cannot now pray to my G1380
Lk 10:36 Which now of these three, t thou, was G1380
Act 28:22 of thee what thou t: for as concerning G5426
Ro 2: 3 And t thou this, O man, that judgest G3049

THINKETH
2Sa 18:27 And the watchman said, Me t the H7200
Ps 40:17 But I *am* poor and needy; *yet* the Lord t H2803
Prv 23: 7 For as he t in his heart, so *is* he: Eat H8176
1Co 10:12 Wherefore let him that t he standeth G1380
13: 5 own, is not easily provoked, t no evil; G3049
Php 3: 4 If any other man t that he hath whereof G1380

THINKING
2Sa 4:10 Saul is dead, t to have brought H1931+H1961
5: 6 in hither: t, David cannot come in hither. H559

THIRD
Gen 1:13 and the morning were the t day. H7992
2:14 And the name of the t river *is* Hiddekel: H7992
6:16 and t *stories* shalt thou make it. H7992
22: 4 Then on the t day Abraham lifted up H7992
31:22 And it was told Laban on the t day that H7992
32:19 second, and the t, and all that followed H7992
34:25 And it came to pass on the t day, when H7992
40:20 And it came to pass the t day, *which* H7992
42:18 And Joseph said unto them the t day, H7992
50:23 children of the t *generation*: the H8029
Ex 19: 1 In the t month, when the children of H7992
11 And be ready against the t day: for the H7992
11 third day: for the t day the LORD will H7992
15 the t day: come not at *your* wives. H7969
16 And it came to pass on the t day in the H7992
20: 5 the children unto the t and fourth H8029
28:19 And the t row a ligure, an agate, and H7992
34: 7 unto the t and to the fourth *generation*. H8029
39:12 And the t row, a ligure, an agate, and H7992
Lev 7:17 on the t day shall be burnt with fire. H7992
18 eaten at all on the t day, it shall not be H7992
19: 6 the t day, it shall be burnt in the fire. H7992
7 And if it be eaten at all on the t day, it H7992
Nu 2:24 And they shall go forward in the t rank. H7992
7:24 On the t day Eliab the son of Helon, H7992
14:18 unto the t and fourth *generation*. H8029
15: 6 mingled with the t *part* of an hin of oil. H7992
7 shalt offer the t *part* of an hin of wine, H7992
19:12 He shall purify himself with it on the t H7992
12 not himself the t day, then the seventh H7992
19 the unclean on the t day, and on the H7992
28:14 a bullock, and the t *part* of an hin unto H7992
29:20 And on the t day eleven bullocks, two H7992
31:19 on the t day, and on the seventh day. H7992
Dt 5: 9 the children unto the t and fourth H8029
23: 8 of the LORD in their t generation. H7992
26:12 thine increase the t year, *which is* the H7992
Jos 9:17 unto their cities on the t day. Now their H7992
19:10 And the t lot came up for the children H7992
Jdg 20:30 of Benjamin on the t day, and put H7992
1Sa 3: 8 Samuel again the t time. And he arose H7992
17:13 him Abinadab, and the t Shammah. H7992
19:21 the t time, and they prophesied also. H7992
20: 5 in the field unto the t *day* at even. H7992
12 any time, *or* the t *day*, and, behold, *if* H7992
1Sa 30: 1 come to Ziklag on the t day, that the H7992
2Sa 1: 2 It came even to pass on the t day, that, H7992
3: 3 Carmelite; and the t, Absalom the son H7992
18: 2 And David sent forth a t part of the H7992
2 of Joab, and a t part under the hand H7992
2 brother, and a t part under the hand H7992
1Ki 3:18 And it came to pass the t day after that H7992
6: 6 broad, and the t *was* seven cubits H7992
8 and out of the middle into the t. H7992
12:12 to Rehoboam the t day, as the king had H7992
12 saying, Come to me again the t day. H7992
15:28 Even in the t year of Asa king of Judah H7969
33 In the t year of Asa king of Judah H7969
18: 1 to Elijah in the t year, saying, Go, shew H7992
34 t time. And they did *it* the third time. H8027
34 third time. And they did *it* the t time. H8027
22: 2 And it came to pass in the t year, that H7992
2Ki 1:13 And he sent again a captain of the t H7992
13 his fifty. And the t captain of fifty went H7992
11: 5 that ye shall do; A t part of you that H7992
6 And a t part *shall be* at the gate of Sur; H7992
6 the gate of Sur; and a t part at the gate H7992
18: 1 Now it came to pass in the t year of H7969
19:29 the same; and in the t year sow ye, and H7992
20: 5 heal thee: on the t day thou shalt go up H7992
8 into the house of the LORD the t day? H7992
1Ch 2:13 the second, and Shimma the t, H7992
3: 2 The t, Absalom the son of Maachah the H7992
15 the t Zedekiah, the fourth Shallum. H7992
8: 1 Ashbel the second, and Aharah the t, H7992
39 Jehush the second, and Eliphelet the t. H7992
12: 9 first, Obadiah the second, Eliab the t, H7992
23:19 the t, and Jekameam the fourth. H7992
24: 8 The t to Harim, the fourth to Seorim, H7992
23 Jahaziel the t, Jekameam the fourth. H7992
25:10 The t to Zaccur, *he*, his sons, and his H7992
26: 2 Zebadiah the t, Jathniel the fourth, H7992
4 second, Joah the t, and Sacar the fourth, H7992
11 Hilkiah the second, Tebaliah the t, H7992
27: 5 The t captain of the host for the third H7992
5 The third captain of the host for the t H7992
2Ch 10:12 to Rehoboam on the t day, as the king H7992
12 saying, Come again to me on the t day. H7992
15:10 at Jerusalem in the t month, in the H7992
17: 7 Also in the t year of his reign he sent to H7969
23: 4 This *is* the thing that ye shall do; A t H7992
5 And a t part *shall be* at the king's H7992
5 house; and a t part at the gate of the H7992
27: 5 him, both the second year, and the t. H7992
31: 7 In the t month they began to lay the H7992
Ezr 6:15 And this house was finished on the t H8532
Neh 10:32 yearly with the t part of a shekel for the H7992
Est 1: 3 In the t year of his reign, he made a H7969
5: 1 Now it came to pass on the t day, that H7992
8: 9 at that time in the t month, that *is*, the H7992
Job 42:14 and the name of the t, Keren-happuch. H7992
Isa 19:24 In that day shall Israel be the t with H7992
37:30 the same: and in the t year sow ye, and H7992
Jer 38:14 unto him into the t entry that *is* in the H7992
Ezk 5: 2 Thou shalt burn with fire a t part in the H7992
2 and thou shalt take a t part, *and* smite H7992
2 it with a knife: and a t part thou shalt H7992
12 A t part of thee shall die with the H7992
12 of thee: and a t part shall fall by the H7992
12 and I will scatter a t part into all the H7992
10:14 of a man, and the t the face of a lion, H7992
21:14 be doubled the t time, the sword of the H7992
31: 1 year, in the t *month*, in the first *day* H7992
46:14 of an ephah, and the t part of an hin of H7992
Dan 1: 1 In the t year of the reign of Jehoiakim H7969
2:39 thee, and another t kingdom of brass, H8523
5: 7 and shall be the t ruler in the kingdom. H8523
16 and shalt be the t ruler in the kingdom. H8531
29 he should be the t ruler in the kingdom. H8531
8: 1 In the t year of the reign of king H7969
10: 1 In the t year of Cyrus king of Persia a H7969
Hos 6: 2 After two days will he revive us: in the t H7992
Zec 6: 3 And in the t chariot white horses; and H7992
13: 8 *and* die; but the t shall be left therein. H7992
9 And I will bring the t part through the H7992
Mt 16:21 be killed, and be raised again the t day. G5154
17:23 And they shall kill him, and the t day G5154
20: 3 And he went out about the t hour, and G5154
19 *him*: and the t day he shall rise again. G5154
22:26 Likewise the second also, and the t, G5154
26:44 the t time, saying the same words. G5154
27:64 sure until the t day, lest his disciples G5154
Mk 9:31 that he is killed, he shall rise the t day. G5154
10:34 him: and the t day he shall rise again. G5154

T

Mk 12:21 left he any seed: and the t likewise. G5154
14:41 And he cometh the t time, and saith G5154
15:25 And it was the t hour, and they G5154
Lk 9:22 and be slain, and be raised the t day. G5154
12:38 or come in the t watch, and find *them* G5154
13:32 and the t *day* I shall be perfected. G5154
18:33 death: and the t day he shall rise again. G5154
20:12 And again he sent a t: and they G5154
31 And the t took her; and in like manner G5154
23:22 And he said unto them the t time, Why, G5154
24: 7 be crucified, and the t day rise again. G5154
21 the t day since these things were done. G5154
46 and to rise from the dead the t day: G5154
Jn 2: 1 And the t day there was a marriage in G5154
21:14 This is now the t time that Jesus G5154
17 He saith unto him the t time, Simon, G5154
17 said unto him the t time, Lovest thou G5154
Act 2:15 seeing it is *but* the t hour of the day. G5154
10:40 Him God raised up the t day, and G5154
20: 9 from the t loft, and was taken up dead. G5152
23:23 two hundred, at the t hour of the night; G5154
27:19 And the t *day* we cast out with our own G5154
1Co 15: 4 the t day according to the scriptures: G5154
2Co 12: 2 such an one caught up to the t heaven. G5154
14 Behold, the t time I am ready to come G5154
13: 1 This *is* the t *time* I am coming to you. G5154
Rev 4: 7 like a calf, and the t beast had a face as G5154
6: 5 And when he had opened the t seal, I G5154
5 seal, I heard the t beast say, Come and G5154
8: 7 the earth: and the t part of trees was G5154
8 and the t part of the sea became blood; G5154
9 And the t part of the creatures which G5154
9 the t part of the ships were destroyed. G5154
10 And the t angel sounded, and there fell G5154
10 it fell upon the t part of the rivers, and G5154
11 and the t part of the waters became G5154
12 sounded, and the t part of the sun was G5154
12 smitten, and the t part of the moon, G5154
12 the moon, and the t part of the stars; so G5154
12 the stars; so as the t part of them was G5154
12 for a t part of it, and the night likewise. G5154
9:15 a year, for to slay the t part of men. G5154
18 By these three was the t part of men G5154
11:14 *and*, behold, the t woe cometh quickly. G5154
12: 4 And his tail drew the t part of the stars G5154
14: 9 And the t angel followed them, saying G5154
16: 4 And the t angel poured out his vial G5154
21:19 t, a chalcedony; the fourth, an emerald; G5154

THIRDLY

1Co 12:28 prophets, t teachers, after that G5154

THIRST

Ex 17: 3 and our children and our cattle with t? H6772
Dt 28:48 in hunger, and in t, and in nakedness, H6772
29:19 of mine heart, to add drunkenness to t: H6771
Jdg 15:18 now shall I die for t, and fall into the H6772
2Ch 32:11 by famine and by t, saying, The LORD H6772
Neh 9:15 of the rock for their t, and promisedst H6772
20 and gavest them water for their t. H6772
Job 24:11 tread *their* winepresses, and suffer t. H6770
Ps 69:21 in my t they gave me vinegar to drink. H6772
104:11 the field: the wild asses quench their t. H6772
Isa 5:13 and their multitude dried up with t. H6772
41:17 tongue faileth for t, I the LORD will H6772
49:10 They shall not hunger nor t; neither H6770
50: 2 *there is* no water, and dieth for t. H6772
Jer 2:25 thy throat from t: but thou saidst, There H6773
48:18 *thy* glory, and sit in t; for the spoiler of H6772
Lam 4: 4 of his mouth for t: the young children H6772
Hos 2: 3 her like a dry land, and slay her with t. H6772
Am 8:11 of bread, nor a t for water, but of H6772
13 fair virgins and young men faint for t. H6772
Mt 5: 6 Blessed *are* they which do hunger and t G1372
Jn 4:13 drinketh of this water shall t again: G1372
14 him shall never t; but the water that I G1372
15 I t not, neither come hither to draw. G1372
6:35 he that believeth on me shall never t. G1372
7:37 t, let him come unto me, and drink. G1372
19:28 scripture might be fulfilled, saith, I t. G1372
Ro 12:20 feed him; if he t, give him drink: for in G1372
1Co 4:11 both hunger, and t, and are naked, and G1372
2Co 11:27 in hunger and t, in fastings often, in G1373
Rev 7:16 They shall hunger no more, neither t G1372

THIRSTED

Ex 17: 3 And the people t there for water; and H6770
Isa 48:21 And they t not *when* he led them H6770

THIRSTETH

Ps 42: 2 My soul t for God, for the living God: H6770
63: 1 I seek thee: my soul t for thee, my flesh H6770
143: 6 soul *t* after thee, as a thirsty land. Selah. H6770
Isa 55: 1 Ho, every one that t, come ye to the H6771

THIRSTY

Jdg 4:19 to drink; for I am t. And she opened a H6770
2Sa 17:29 and weary, and t, in the wilderness. H6771
Ps 63: 1 in a dry and t land, where no water is; H5889
107: 5 Hungry and t, their soul fainted in H6771
143: 6 *thirsteth* after thee, as a t land. Selah. H5889
Prv 25:21 and if he be t, give him water to drink: H6771
25 *As* cold waters to a t soul, so *is* good H5889
Isa 21:14 to him that was t, they prevented with H6771
29: 8 or as when a t man dreameth, and, H6771
32: 6 he will cause the drink of the t to fail. H6771
35: 7 a pool, and the t land springs of water: H6774
44: 3 For I will pour water upon him that is t, H6771
65:13 but ye shall be t: behold, my servants H6770
Ezk 19:13 the wilderness, in a dry and t ground. H6772
Mt 25:35 me meat: I was t, and ye gave me drink: G1372
37 and fed *thee*? or t, and gave *thee* drink? G1372
42 meat: I was t, and ye gave me no drink: G1372

THIRTEEN

Gen 17:25 And Ishmael his son *was* t H7969+H6240
Nu 3:43 two hundred and threescore and t. H7969
46 threescore and t of the firstborn of the H7969
29:13 the LORD; t young bullocks, H7969+H6240
14 bullock of the t bullocks, two H7969+H6240
Jos 19: 6 t cities and their villages: H7969+H6240
21: 4 the tribe of Benjamin, t cities. H7969+H6240
6 Manasseh in Bashan, t cities. H7969+H6240
19 t cities with their suburbs. H7969+H6240
33 t cities with their suburbs. H7969+H6240
1Ki 7: 1 his own house t years, and he H7969+H6240
1Ch 6:60 their families *were* t cities. H7969+H6240
62 Manasseh in Bashan, t cities. H7969+H6240
26:11 and brethren of Hosah *were* t. H7969+H6240
Ezk 40:11 the length of the gate, t cubits. H7969+H6240

THIRTEENTH

Gen 14: 4 and in the t year they rebelled. H7969+H6240
1Ch 24:13 The t to Huppah, the H7969+H6240
25:20 The t to Shubael, *he*, his sons, H7969+H6240
Est 3:12 called on the t day of the first H7969+H6240
13 day, *even* upon the t *day* of the H7969+H6240
8:12 upon the t *day* of the twelfth H7969+H6240
9: 1 Adar, on the t day of the same, H7969+H6240
17 On the t day of the month H7969+H6240
18 on the t *day* thereof, and H7969+H6240
Jer 1: 2 in the t year of his reign. H7969+H6240
25: 3 From the t year of Josiah the H7969+H6240

THIRTIETH

2Ki 15:13 in the nine and t year of Uzziah king H7970
17 In the nine and t year of Azariah king H7970
25:27 And it came to pass in the seven and t H7970
2Ch 15:19 the five and t year of the reign of Asa. H7970
16: 1 In the six and t year of the reign of Asa H7970
Neh 5:14 unto the two and t year of Artaxerxes H7970
13: 6 for in the two and t year of Artaxerxes H7970
Jer 52:31 And it came to pass in the seven and t H7970
Ezk 1: 1 Now it came to pass in the t year, in the H7970

THIRTY

Gen 5: 3 And Adam lived an hundred and t H7970
5 nine hundred and t years: and he died. H7970
16 t years, and begat sons and daughters: H7970
6:15 fifty cubits, and the height of it t cubits. H7970
11:12 And Arphaxad lived five and t years, H7970
14 And Salah lived t years, and begat H7970
16 And Eber lived four and t years, and H7970
17 t years, and begat sons and daughters. H7970
18 And Peleg lived t years, and begat Reu: H7970
20 And Reu lived two and t years, and H7970
22 And Serug lived t years, and begat H7970
18:30 there shall t be found there. And H7970
30 he said, I will not do *it*, if I find t there. H7970
25:17 an hundred and t and seven years: and H7970
32:15 T milch camels with their colts, forty H7970
41:46 And Joseph *was* t years old when he H7970
46:15 and his daughters *were* t and three. H7970
47: 9 an hundred and t years: few and evil H7970
Ex 6:16 *were* an hundred t and seven years. H7970
18 *were* an hundred t and three years. H7970
20 an hundred and t and seven years. H7970
12:40 Egypt, *was* four hundred and t years. H7970
Ex 12:41 the four hundred and t years, even the H7970
21:32 unto their master t shekels of silver, H7970
26: 8 The length of one curtain *shall be* t H7970
36:15 The length of one curtain *was* t cubits, H7970
38:24 hundred and t shekels, after the shekel H7970
Lev 12: 4 three and t days; she shall touch H7970
27: 4 then thy estimation shall be t shekels. H7970
Nu 1:35 t and two thousand and two hundred. H7970
37 t and five thousand and four hundred. H7970
2:21 t and two thousand and two hundred. H7970
23 t and five thousand and four hundred. H7970
4: 3 From t years old and upward even H7970
23 From t years old and upward until fifty H7970
30 From t years old and upward even H7970
35 From t years old and upward even H7970
39 From t years old and upward even H7970
40 two thousand and six hundred and t. H7970
43 From t years old and upward even H7970
47 From t years old and upward even H7970
7:13 an hundred and t *shekels*, one silver H7970
19 an hundred and t *shekels*, one silver H7970
25 an hundred and t *shekels*, one silver H7970
31 of an hundred and t *shekels*, one silver H7970
37 an hundred and t *shekels*, one silver H7970
43 of an hundred and t *shekels*, a silver H7970
49 an hundred and t *shekels*, one silver H7970
55 of an hundred and t *shekels*, one silver H7970
61 an hundred and t *shekels*, one silver H7970
67 an hundred and t *shekels*, one silver H7970
73 an hundred and t *shekels*, one silver H7970
79 an hundred and t *shekels*, one silver H7970
85 an hundred and t *shekels*, each bowl H7970
20:29 t days, *even* all the house of Israel. H7970
26: 7 thousand and seven hundred and t. H7970
37 of them, t and two thousand and H7970
51 and a thousand seven hundred and t. H7970
31:35 And t and two thousand persons in all, H7970
36 t thousand and five hundred sheep: H7970
38 And the beeves *were* t and six H7970
39 And the asses *were* t thousand and five H7970
40 LORD'S tribute *was* t and two persons. H7970
43 thousand and t thousand *and* seven H7970
44 And t and six thousand beeves, H7970
45 And t thousand asses and five H7970
Dt 2:14 the brook Zered, *was* t and eight years; H7970
34: 8 the plains of Moab t days: so the days H7970
Jos 7: 5 of them about t and six men: for they H7970
8: 3 Joshua chose out t thousand mighty H7970
12:24 The king of Tirzah, one: all the kings t H7970
Jdg 10: 4 And he had t sons that rode on thirty H7970
4 And he had thirty sons that rode on t H7970
4 and they had t cities, which are called H7970
12: 9 And he had t sons, and thirty H7970
9 And he had thirty sons, and t H7970
9 and took in t daughters from abroad H7970
14 And he had forty sons and t nephews, H7970
14:11 brought t companions to be with him. H7970
12 t sheets and thirty change of garments: H7970
12 thirty sheets and t change of garments: H7970
13 then shall ye give me t sheets and thirty H7970
13 thirty sheets and t change of garments. H7970
19 and slew t men of them, and took H7970
20:31 in the field, about t men of Israel. H7970
39 of Israel about t persons: for they said, H7970
1Sa 4:10 there fell of Israel t thousand footmen. H7970
9:22 bidden, which *were* about t persons. H7970
11: 8 and the men of Judah t thousand. H7970
13: 5 fight with Israel, t thousand chariots, H7970
2Sa 5: 4 David *was* t years old when he began to H7970
5 he reigned t and three years over H7970
6: 1 *the* chosen *men* of Israel, t thousand. H7970
23:13 And three of the t chief went down, and H7970
23 He was more honourable than the t, but H7970
24 *was* one of the t; Elhanan the son of H7970
39 Uriah the Hittite: t and seven in all. H7970
1Ki 2:11 he in Hebron, and t and three years H7970
4:22 for one day was t measures of fine H7970
5:13 and the levy was t thousand men. H7970
6: 2 *cubits*, and the height thereof t cubits. H7970
7: 2 the height thereof t cubits, upon four H7970
6 breadth thereof t cubits: and the porch H7970
23 of t cubits did compass it round about. H7970
16:23 In the t and first year of Asa king of H7970
29 And in the t and eighth year of Asa H7970
20: 1 and *there were* t and two kings with H7970
15 two hundred and t and two: and after them H7970
16 the t and two kings that helped him. H7970
22:31 But the king of Syria commanded his t H7970
42 Jehoshaphat *was* t and five years old H7970

2Ki 8:17 T and two years old was he when he H7970
13:10 In the t and seventh year of Joash king H7970
15: 8 In the t and eighth year of Azariah king H7970
18:14 talents of silver and t talents of gold. H7970
22: 1 and he reigned t and one years in H7970
1Ch 3: 4 Jerusalem he reigned t and three years. H7970
7: 4 for war, six and t thousand *men:* for H7970
7 and two thousand and t and four. H7970
11:15 Now three of the t captains went down H7970
25 among the t, but attained not to the H7970
42 of the Reubenites, and t with him, H7970
12: 4 man among the t, and over the thirty; H7970
4 and over the t; and Jeremiah, and H7970
34 shield and spear t and seven thousand. H7970
15: 7 and his brethren an hundred and t: H7970
19: 7 So they hired t and two thousand H7970
23: 3 from the age of t years and upward: H7970
3 by man, was t and eight thousand. H7970
27: 6 *was* mighty *among* the t, and above the H7970
6 and above the t: and in his course *was* H7970
29:27 he in Hebron, and t and three *years* H7970
2Ch 3:15 two pillars of t and five cubits high, H7970
4: 2 of t cubits did compass it round about. H7970
16:12 And Asa in the t and ninth year of his H7970
20:31 Judah: *he was* t and five years old when H7970
21: 5 Jehoram *was* t and two years old when H7970
20 T and two years old was he when he H7970
24:15 and t years old *was he* when he died. H7970
34: 1 reigned in Jerusalem one and t years. H7970
35: 7 to the number of t thousand, and three H7970
Ezr 1: 9 And this *is* the number of them: t H7970
10 T basons of gold, silver basons of a H7970
2:35 three thousand and six hundred and t. H7970
42 of Shobai, *in* all an hundred t and nine. H7970
65 three hundred t and seven: and *there* H7970
66 Their horses *were* seven hundred t and H7970
67 Their camels, four hundred t and five; H7970
Neh 7:38 three thousand nine hundred and t. H7970
45 of Shobai, an hundred t and eight. H7970
67 three hundred t and seven: and they H7970
68 Their horses, seven hundred t and six: H7970
69 *Their* camels, four hundred t and five: H7970
70 five hundred and t priests' garments. H7970
Est 4:11 to come in unto the king these t days. H7970
Jer 38:10 Take from hence t men with thee, and H7970
52:29 eight hundred t and two persons: H7970
Ezk 40:17 t chambers *were* upon the pavement. H7970
41: 6 over another, and t in order; and they H7970
46:22 *cubits* long and t broad: these four H7970
Dan 6: 7 God or man for t days, save of thee, O H8533
12 or man within t days, save of thee, O H8533
12:12 three hundred and five and t days. H7970
Zec 11:12 weighed for my price t *pieces* of silver. H7970
13 And I took the t *pieces* of silver, and H7970
Mt 13:23 an hundredfold, some sixty, some t. G5144
26:15 with him for t pieces of silver. G5144
27: 3 brought again the t pieces of silver to G5144
9 And they took the t pieces of silver, the G5144
Mk 4: 8 forth, some t, and some sixty, and G5144
Lk 3:23 And Jesus himself began to be about t G5144
Jn 5: 5 had an infirmity t and eight years. G5144
6:19 five and twenty or t furlongs, they see G5144
Gal 3:17 four hundred and t years after, cannot G5144

THIRTYFOLD
Mt 13: 8 an hundredfold, some sixtyfold, some t. G5144
Mk 4:20 t, some sixty, and some an hundred. G5144

THIRTY-THOUSAND See THIRTY and THOUSAND.

THIS See the Appendix.

THISTLE
2Ki 14: 9 of Judah, saying, The t that *was* in H2336
9 *was* in Lebanon, and trode down the t. H2336
2Ch 25:18 of Judah, saying, The t that *was* in H2336
18 *was* in Lebanon, and trode down the t. H2336
Hos 10: 8 the thorn and the t shall come up on H1863

THISTLES
Gen 3:18 Thorns also and t shall it bring forth to H1863
Job 31:40 Let t grow instead of wheat, and cockle H2336
Mt 7:16 men gather grapes of thorns, or figs of t? G5146

THITHER
Gen 19:20 one: Oh, let me escape t, (*is* it not a little H8033
22 Haste thee, escape t; for I cannot do any H8033
22 till thou be come t. Therefore the name H8033
24: 6 that thou bring not my son t again. H8033
Gen 24: 8 my oath: only bring not my son t again. H8033
29: 3 And t were all the flocks gathered: and H8033
39: 1 which had brought him down t. H8033
42: 2 get you down t, and buy for us from H8033
Ex 10:26 must serve the LORD, until we come t. H8033
26:33 mayest bring in t within the vail the H8033
Nu 35: 6 that he may flee t: and to them ye shall H8033
11 t, which killeth any person at unawares. H8033
15 killeth any person unawares may flee t. H8033
Dt 1:37 saying, Thou also shalt not go in t. H8033
38 thee, he shall go in t: encourage him: for H8033
39 they shall go in t, and unto them will H8033
4:42 That the slayer might flee t, which H8033
12: 5 shall ye seek, and t thou shalt come: H8033
6 And t ye shall bring your burnt H8033
11 to dwell there; t shall ye bring all that H8033
19: 3 three parts, that every slayer may flee t. H8033
4 which shall flee t, that he may live: H8033
32:52 thou shalt not go t unto the land which H8033
34: 4 thine eyes, but thou shalt not go over t. H8033
Jos 7: 3 people to labour t; for they *are but* few. H8033
4 So there went up t of the people about H8033
20: 3 may flee t: and they shall be your H8033
9 might flee t, and not die by the hand H8033
Jdg 8:27 and all Israel went t a whoring after it: H8033
9:51 the city, and t fled all the men and H8033
18: 3 and they turned in t, and said unto him, H8033
17 up, *and* came in t, *and* took the graven H8033
19:15 And they turned aside t, to go in *and* to H8033
21:10 And the congregation sent t twelve H8033
1Sa 2:14 unto all the Israelites that came t. H8033
5: 8 the ark of the God of Israel about *t*.
9: 6 to pass: now let us go t; peradventure he
10: 5 thou art come t to the city, that thou H8033
10 And when they came t to the hill, H8033
22 man should yet come t. And the LORD H1988
19:23 And he went t to Naioth in Ramah: and H8033
22: 1 heard *it*, they went down t to him. H8033
30: 7 Abiathar brought t the ephod to David.
2Sa 2: 2 So David went up t, and his two wives H8033
4: 6 And they came t into the midst of the
1Ki 6: 7 before it was brought t: so that there was
19: 9 And he came t unto a cave, and lodged H8033
2Ki 2: 8 divided hither and t, so that they two H2008
14 hither and t: and Elisha went over. H2008
4: 8 passed by, he turned in t to eat bread. H8033
10 he cometh to us, that he shall turn in t. H8033
11 And it fell on a day, that he came t, and H8033
6: 6 and cast *it* in t; and the iron did swim. H8033
9 place; for t the Syrians are come down. H8033
14 Therefore sent he t horses, and H8033
9: 2 And when thou comest t, look out there H8033
17:27 saying, Carry t one of the priests whom H8033
2Ch 1: 6 And Solomon went up t to the brasen H8033
Ezr 10: 6 and *when* he came t, he did eat no H8033
Neh 4:20 ye t unto us: our God shall fight for us. H8033
5:16 *were* gathered t unto the work. H8033
13: 9 the chambers: and t brought I again H8033
Job 1:21 shall I return t: the LORD gave, and H8033
6:20 hoped; they came t, and were ashamed. H5704
Ecc 1: 7 the rivers come, t they return again. H8033
Isa 7:24 shall *men* come t; because all the land H8033
25 shall not come t the fear of briers and H8033
32:20 forth *t* the feet of the ox and the ass.
55:10 and returneth not t, but watereth the H8033
57: 7 t wentest thou up to offer sacrifice. H8033
Jer 22:11 place; He shall not return t any more: H8033
27 desire to return, t shall they not return. H8033
31: 8 a great company shall return t. H2008
40: 4 and convenient for thee to go, t go. H8033
Ezk 1:20 to go, they went, t *was their* spirit to go; H8033
11:18 And they shall come t, and they shall H8033
40: 1 LORD was upon me, and brought me t. H8033
3 And he brought me t, and, behold, *there* H8033
47: 9 waters shall come t: for they shall be H8033
Joel 3:11 round about: t cause thy mighty ones H8033
Mt 2:22 he was afraid to go t: notwithstanding, G1563
Mk 6:33 and ran afoot t out of all cities, and G1563
Lk 17:37 t will the eagles be gathered together. G1563
21: 2 poor widow casting in t two mites. G1563
Jn 7:34 *me*: and where I am, *t* ye cannot come.
36 *me*: and where I am, *t* ye cannot come?
11: 8 to stone thee; and goest thou t again? G1563
18: 2 ofttimes resorted t with his disciples. G1563
3 Pharisees, cometh t with lanterns and G1563
Act 8:30 And Philip ran t to *him*, and heard him G4870
14:19 And there came t *certain* Jews from G1904
16:13 spake unto the women which resorted *t*.
17:10 *t* went into the synagogue of the Jews. G3854
Act 17:13 came t also, and stirred up the people. G1563
25: 4 that he himself would depart shortly *t*.

THITHERWARD
Jdg 18:15 And they turned t, and came to the H8033
Jer 50: 5 with their faces t, *saying*, Come, and let H2008
Ro 15:24 brought on my way t by you, if first I be G1563

THOMAS
Mt 10: 3 Philip, and Bartholomew; T, and G2381
Mk 3:18 and Matthew, and T, and James the *son* G2381
Lk 6:15 Matthew and T, James the *son* of G2381
Jn 11:16 Then said T, which is called Didymus, G2381
14: 5 T saith unto him, Lord, we know not G2381
20:24 But T, one of the twelve, called G2381
26 were within, and T with them: *then* G2381
27 Then saith he to T, Reach hither thy G2381
28 And T answered and said unto him, G2381
29 Jesus saith unto him, T, because thou G2381
21: 2 Simon Peter, and T called Didymus, G2381
Act 1:13 Philip, and T, Bartholomew, and G2381

THONGS
Act 22:25 And as they bound him with t, Paul G2438

THORN
Job 41: 2 nose? or bore his jaw through with a t? H2336
Prv 26: 9 *As* a t goeth up into the hand of a H2336
Isa 55:13 Instead of the t shall come up the fir H5285
Ezk 28:24 nor *any* grieving t of all *that are* round H6975
Hos 10: 8 be destroyed: the t and the thistle shall H6975
Mic 7: 4 *is sharper* than a t hedge: the day of thy H4534
2Co 12: 7 was given to me a t in the flesh, the G4647

THORN-HEDGE See THORN and HEDGE.

THORNS
Gen 3:18 T also and thistles shall it bring forth to H6975
Ex 22: 6 If fire break out, and catch in t, so that H6975
Nu 33:55 in your eyes, and t in your sides, and H6796
Jos 23:13 in your sides, and t in your eyes, until H6796
Jdg 2: 3 but they shall be *as t* in your sides, and
8: 7 the t of the wilderness and with briers. H6975
16 And he took the elders of the city, and t H6975
2Sa 23: 6 *be* all of them as t thrust away, because H6975
2Ch 33:11 among the t, and bound him with H2336
Job 5: 5 it even out of the t, and the robber H6791
Ps 58: 9 Before your pots can feel the t, he shall H329
118:12 as the fire of t: for in the name of the H6975
Prv 15:19 *is* as an hedge of t: but the way of the H2312
22: 5 T *and* snares *are* in the way of the H6791
24:31 And, lo, it was all grown over with t, H7063
Ecc 7: 6 For as the crackling of t under a pot, so H5518
Song 2: 2 As the lily among t, so *is* my love H2336
Isa 5: 6 up briers and t: I will also command H7898
7:19 and upon all t, and upon all bushes. H5285
23 it shall *even* be for briers and t. H7898
24 all the land shall become briers and t. H7898
25 fear of briers and t: but it shall be for H7898
9:18 the briers and t, and shall kindle in the H7898
10:17 devour his t and his briers in one day; H7898
27: 4 set the briers *and* t against me in H7898
32:13 shall come up t *and* briers; yea, upon H6975
33:12 t cut up shall they be burned in the fire. H6975
34:13 And t shall come up in her palaces, H5518
Jer 4: 3 fallow ground, and sow not among t. H6975
12:13 They have sown wheat, but shall reap t: H6975
Ezk 2: 6 though briers and t *be* with thee, and H5544
Hos 2: 6 up thy way with t, and make a wall, H5518
9: 6 them: t *shall be* in their tabernacles. H2336
Nah 1:10 For while *they be* folden together *as* t, H5518
Mt 7:16 men gather grapes of t, or figs of thistles? G173
13: 7 And some fell among t; and the thorns G173
7 And some fell among thorns; and the t G173
22 He also that received seed among the t is G173
27:29 And when they had platted a crown of t, G173
Mk 4: 7 And some fell among t, and the thorns G173
7 And some fell among thorns, and the t G173
18 sown among t; such as hear the word, G173
15:17 a crown of t, and put it about his *head*, G174
Lk 6:44 his own fruit. For of t men do not gather G173
8: 7 And some fell among t; and the thorns G173
7 And some fell among thorns; and the t G173
14 And that which fell among t are they, G173
Jn 19: 2 And the soldiers platted a crown of t, and G173
5 the crown of t, and the purple robe. G174
Heb 6: 8 But that which beareth t and briers *is* G173

T

THOROUGHLY

Ex 21:19 and shall cause *him* to be t healed. H7495
2Ki 11:18 they in pieces t, and slew Mattan the H3190

THOSE

Gen 6: 4 There were giants in the earth in t H1992
15:17 lamp that passed between t pieces. H428
19:25 And he overthrew t cities, and all the H411
24:60 possess the gate of t which hate them.
33: 5 and said, Who *are* t with thee? And he H428
41:35 And let them gather all the food of t H428
42: 5 to buy *corn* among t that came: for the
50: 3 are fulfilled the days of t which are
Ex 2:11 And it came to pass in t days, when H1992
4:21 see that thou do all t wonders before
29:33 And they shall eat t things wherewith the
35:35 work, and of t that devise cunning work.
Lev 11:27 that go on *all* four, t *are* unclean unto H1992
14:11 be made clean, and t things, before the
42 in the place of t stones; and he shall
15:10 that beareth *any of* t things shall wash
27 And whosoever toucheth t things shall
22: 2 not my holy name *in t things* which they
Nu 1:21 T that were numbered of them, *even* of
22 of their fathers, t that were numbered
23 T that were numbered of them, *even* of
25 T that were numbered of them, *even* of
27 T that were numbered of them, *even* of
29 T that were numbered of them, *even* of
31 T that were numbered of them, *even* of
33 T that were numbered of them, *even* of
35 T that were numbered of them, *even* of
37 T that were numbered of them, *even* of
39 T that were numbered of them, *even* of
41 T that were numbered of them, *even* of
43 T that were numbered of them, *even* of
44 These *are* t that were numbered, which
45 So were all t that were numbered of the
2: 4 And his host, and t that were numbered
5 And t that do pitch next unto him *shall*
6 And his host, and t that were numbered
8 And his host, and t that were numbered
11 And his host, and t that were numbered
12 And t which pitch by him *shall be* the
13 And his host, and t that were numbered
15 And his host, and t that were numbered
19 And his host, and t that were numbered
21 And his host, and t that were numbered
23 And his host, and t that were numbered
26 And his host, and t that were numbered
27 And t that encamp by him *shall be* the
28 And his host, and t that were numbered
30 And his host, and t that were numbered
32 These *are* t which were numbered of the
32 of their fathers: all t that were numbered
3:22 T that were numbered of them,
22 and upward, *even* t that were numbered
34 And t that were numbered of them,
38 But t that encamp before the tabernacle
43 month old and upward, of t that were
46 And for t that are to be redeemed of the
4:36 And t that were numbered of them by
38 And t that were numbered of the sons of
40 Even t that were numbered of them,
42 And t that were numbered of the
44 Even t that were numbered of them after
45 These *be* t that were numbered of the
46 All t that were numbered of the Levites,
48 Even t that were numbered of them,
9: 7 And t men said unto him, We *are* H1992
13: 3 of Paran: all t men *were* heads of the
14:22 Because all t men which have seen my H582
37 Even t men that did bring up the evil H582
18:16 And t that are to be redeemed from a
25: 9 And t that died in the plague were
26:18 Gad according to t that were numbered
22 of Judah according to t that were
25 according to t that were numbered
27 according to t that were numbered
34 of Manasseh, and t that were numbered
37 according to t that were numbered
43 according to t that were numbered
47 of Asher according to t that were
54 to t that were numbered of him.
62 And t that were numbered of them were
33:55 come to pass, that t which ye let remain
Dt 7:22 And the LORD thy God will put out t H411
17: 9 that shall be in t days, and inquire; and H1992
18: 9 do after the abominations of t nations. H1992
Dt 19: 5 he shall flee unto one of t cities, and live: H428
17 the judges, which shall be in t days; H1992
20 And t which remain shall hear, and fear,
26: 3 that shall be in t days, and say unto H1992
29: 3 seen, the signs, and t great miracles: H1992
29 LORD our God: but t *things which are*
32:21 to jealousy with *t which are* not a people;
Jos 3:16 Zaretan: and t that came down toward
4:20 And t twelve stones, which they took out H428
10:22 out t five kings unto me out of the cave. H428
23 And they did so, and brought forth t five H428
24 they brought out t kings unto Joshua, H428
11: 1 of Hazor had heard *t things,* that he sent
10 was the head of all t kingdoms. H428
12 And all the cities of t kings, and all the H428
18 Joshua made war a long time with all t H428
17:12 out *the inhabitants of* t cities; but the H428
20: 4 And when he that doth flee unto one of t H428
6 that shall be in t days: then shall the H428
21:16 suburbs; nine cities out of t two tribes. H428
24:17 and which did t great signs in our sight, H428
Jdg 2:16 out of the hand of t that spoiled them.
23 Therefore the LORD left t nations, H428
7: 8 tent, and retained t three hundred men:
11:13 restore t *lands* again peaceably.
12: 5 it was *so,* that when t Ephraimites which
17: 6 In t days *there was* no king in Israel, H1992
18: 1 In t days *there was* no king in Israel: H1992
1 in Israel: and in t days the tribe of the H1992
19: 1 And it came to pass in t days, when H1992
20:27 covenant of God *was* there in t days, H1992
28 stood before it in t days,) saying, Shall H1992
21:25 In t days *there was* no king in Israel: H1992
1Sa 3: 1 in t days; *there was* no open vision. H1992
7:16 Mizpeh, and judged Israel in all t places. H428
10: 9 and all t signs came to pass that day. H428
11: 6 when he heard t tidings, and his anger H428
17:11 When Saul and all Israel heard t words H428
28 whom hast thou left t few sheep in the H2007
18:23 And Saul's servants spake t words in the H428
19: 7 shewed him all t things. And Jonathan H428
25: 9 according to all t words in the name of H428
12 and came and told him all t sayings. H428
27: 8 Amalekites: for t *nations were* of old H2007
28: 1 And it came to pass in t days, that the H1992
3 Saul had put away t that had familiar H1992
9 how he hath cut off t that have familiar
30: 9 where t that were left behind stayed.
20 they drave before t *other* cattle, and H1931
22 *men* of Belial, of t that went with David, H582
2Sa 5:14 And these *be* the names of t that were
16:23 he counselled in t days, *was* as if a man H1992
1Ki 2: 7 and let them be of t that eat at thy table:
3: 2 the name of the LORD, until t days. H1992
4:27 And t officers provided victual for king H428
8: 4 tabernacle, even t did the priests and the
9:21 to destroy, upon t did Solomon levy a
21:27 And it came to pass, when Ahab heard t H428
2Ki 4: 4 pour out into all t vessels, and thou shalt H428
6:22 thou smite t whom thou hast taken
10:32 In t days the LORD began to cut Israel H1992
15:37 In t days the LORD began to send H1992
17: 9 And the children of Israel did secretly *t*
18: 4 made: for unto t days the children of H1992
20: 1 In t days was Hezekiah sick unto H1992
24:15 the mighty of the land, *t* carried he into
1Ch 4:23 These *were* the potters, and t that dwelt
16:42 and cymbals for t that should make a
2Ch 14: 6 he had no war in t years; because the H428
15: 5 And in t times *there was* no peace to H1992
17:19 These waited on the king, beside *t* whom
20:29 on all the kingdoms of *t* countries, when
32:13 of the nations of t lands any ways able
14 Who *was there* among all the gods of t H428
24 In t days Hezekiah was sick to the H1992
Ezr 1: 8 Even t did Cyrus king of Persia bring
2: 1 out of the captivity, of t which had been
62 These sought their register *among* t that
3: 3 of the people of t countries: and they
5: 9 Then asked we t elders, *and* said unto H479
14 of Babylon, t did Cyrus the king take H1994
7:19 house of thy God, *t* deliver thou before
8:35 *Also* the children of t that had been
9: 2 with the people of *t* lands: yea, the hand
4 transgression of t that had been carried
10: 3 of my lord, and of t that tremble at the
8 of t that had been carried away.
Neh 4:17 bare burdens, with t that laded, *every*
5:17 and rulers, beside t that came unto us
Neh 6:17 Moreover in t days the nobles of Judah
7: 6 out of the captivity, of t that had been
64 These sought their register *among* t that
8: 3 and the women, and t that could
10: 1 Now t that sealed *were,* Nehemiah, the
13:15 In t days saw I in Judah *some* treading H1992
23 In t days also saw I Jews *that* had H1992
Est 1: 2 *That* in t days, when the king H1992
2:21 In t days, while Mordecai sat in the H1992
21 and Teresh, of t which kept the door,
3: 9 to the hands of t that have the charge
9: 5 what they would unto t that hated them.
11 On that day the number of t that were
Job 5:11 To set up on high t that be low; that
11 t which mourn may be exalted to safety.
21:22 seeing he judgeth t that are high.
24:13 They are of t that rebel against the light;
19 *so doth* the grave *t which* have sinned.
27:15 T that remain of him shall be buried in
Ps 5:11 But let all t that put their trust in thee
13: 4 against him; *and* t that trouble me
17: 7 *in thee* from t that rise up *against them.*
18:30 he *is* a buckler to all t that trust in him.
39 under me t that rose up against me.
48 liftest me up above t that rise up against
21: 8 right hand shall find out t that hate thee.
37: 9 For evildoers shall be cut off: but t that
40:16 Let all t that seek thee rejoice and be
50: 5 Gather my saints together unto me; t
61: 5 *me* the heritage of t that fear thy name.
63: 9 But t *that* seek my soul, to destroy *it,*
68: 6 he bringeth out t which are bound with
11 *was* the company of t that published *it.*
69: 6 for my sake: let not t that seek thee be
26 the grief of t whom thou hast wounded.
70: 4 Let all t that seek thee rejoice and be
74:23 the tumult of t that rise up against thee
79:11 thou t that are appointed to die;
92:13 T that be planted in the house of the
102:20 to loose t that are appointed to death;
103:18 To such as keep his covenant, and to t
106:46 He made them also to be pitied of all t
109:31 save *him* from t that condemn his soul.
119:79 Let t that fear thee turn unto me, and
79 and t that have known thy testimonies.
132 usest to do unto t that love thy name.
123: 4 the scorning of t that are at ease, *and*
125: 4 Do good, O LORD, unto *t that be* good,
139:21 I grieved with t that rise up against thee?
140: 9 *As for* the head of t that compass me
143: 3 darkness, as t that have been long dead.
145:14 and raiseth up all *t that be* bowed down.
147:11 fear him, in t that hope in his mercy.
Prv 1:12 and whole, as t that go down into the pit:
4:22 For they *are* life unto t that find them,
8:17 I love them that love me; and t that seek
21 That I may cause t that love me to
22:23 and spoil the soul of t that spoiled them.
24:11 death, and *t that are* ready to be slain;
26:28 A lying tongue hateth *t that are* afflicted
31: 6 and wine unto t that be of heavy hearts.
Ecc 1:11 are to come with *t* that shall come after.
5:14 But t riches perish by evil travail: and H1931
7:28 a woman among all t have I not found. H428
8: 8 wickedness deliver t that are given to it.
12: 3 they are few, and t that look out of the
Song 7: 9 the lips of t that are asleep to speak.
8:12 a thousand, and t that keep the fruit
Isa 14:19 *as* the raiment of t that are slain, thrust
27: 7 Hath he smitten him, as he smote t that
35: 8 it; but it *shall be* for t: the wayfaring men,
38: 1 In t days was Hezekiah sick unto H1992
40:11 shall gently lead t that are with young.
56: 8 beside t that are gathered unto him.
60:12 yea, *t* nations shall be utterly wasted.
64: 5 righteousness, *t that* remember thee
5 t is continuance, and we shall be saved. H1992
66: 2 For all t *things* hath mine hand made, H428
2 hand made, and all t *things* have been, H428
19 and I will send t that escape of them H1992
Jer 3:16 in the land, in t days, saith the LORD, H1992
18 In t days the house of Judah shall walk H1992
4:12 *Even* a full wind from t *places* shall H428
5:18 Nevertheless in t days, saith the LORD, H1992
8:16 is in it; the city, and t that dwell therein.
14:15 famine shall t prophets be consumed. H1992
21: 7 into the hand of t that seek their life: and
27:11 and serve him, t will I let remain still
31:29 In t days they shall say no more, The H1992

Jer 31:33 of Israel; After t days, saith the LORD, H1992
36 If t ordinances depart from before me, H428
33:15 In t days, and at that time, will I cause H1992
16 In t days shall Judah be saved, and H1992
38:22 princes, and t *women* shall say, Thy H2007
39: 9 in the city, and t that fell away, that fell
46:26 And I will deliver them into the hand of t
49: 5 of hosts, from all t that be about thee;
36 them toward all t winds; and there shall H428
50: 4 In t days, and in that time, saith the H1992
20 In t days, and in that time, saith the
52:15 in the city, and t that fell away, that fell
Lam 2:22 nor remained: t that I have swaddled
3:62 The lips of t that rose up against me,
Ezk 1:21 When t went, *these* went; and when
21 went; and when t stood, *these* stood; and
21 stood; and when t were lifted up from
18:11 And that doeth not any of t *duties*, but H428
22: 5 *T that be* near, and *those that be* far
5 *Those that be* near, and *t that be* far
28:26 judgments upon all t that despise them
33:24 Son of man, they that inhabit t wastes of H428
34:27 of t that served themselves of them.
38:17 prophesied in t days *many* years that H1992
39:10 and they shall spoil t that spoiled them,
10 t that robbed them, saith the Lord GOD. H428
14 the passengers t that remain upon the
40:25 round about, like t windows: the length H479
42:14 to *t things* which *are* for the people.
Dan 3:22 flame of the fire slew t men that took up H479
4:37 t that walk in pride he is able to abase. H1768
6:24 and they brought t men which had H479
10: 2 In t days I Daniel was mourning three H1992
11: 4 be plucked up, even for others beside t. H428
14 And in t times there shall many stand H1992
Joel 2:16 the children, and t that suck the breasts:
29 in t days will I pour out my spirit. H1992
3: 1 For, behold, in t days, and in that time, H1992
Oba 14 the crossway, to cut off t of his that did
14 thou have delivered up t of his that did
Zep 1: 6 the LORD; and *t* that have not sought
9 In the same day also will I punish all t
Hag 2:16 Since t *days* were, when *one* came to an
22 the chariots, and t that ride in them; and
Zec 3: 4 And he answered and spake unto t that
4:10 of Zerubbabel *with* t seven; they *are* the H428
7: 5 *month*, even t seventy years, did ye H2088
8:23 Thus saith the LORD of hosts; In t days H1992
11:16 shall not visit t that be cut off, neither
13: 6 he shall answer, *T* with which I was
14: 3 and fight against t nations, as when he H1992
Mal 3: 5 and against t that oppress the hireling
Mt 3: 1 In t days came John the Baptist, *G1565*
4:24 and torments, and t which were *G3588*
24 with devils, and t which were lunatick,
24 t that had the palsy; and he healed them.
11: 4 again t things which ye do hear and see:
13:17 have desired to see *t things* which ye see,
17 seen *them*; and to hear *t things* which ye
15:18 But t things which proceed out of the *G3588*
30 him, having with them *t that were* lame,
16:23 that be of God, but t that be of men. *G3588*
21:40 what will he do unto t husbandmen? *G1565*
41 miserably destroy t wicked men, and *G846*
22: 7 t murderers, and burned up their city. *G1565*
10 So t servants went out into the *G1565*
24:19 and to them that give suck in t days! *G1565*
22 And except t days should be shortened, *G1565*
22 elect's sake t days shall be shortened. *G1565*
29 Immediately after the tribulation of t *G1565*
25: 7 Then all t virgins arose, and trimmed *G1565*
19 After a long time the lord of t servants *G1565*
27:54 the earthquake, and t things that were *G3588*
Mk 1: 9 And it came to pass in t days, that *G1565*
44 for thy cleansing t things which Moses
2:20 them, and then shall they fast in t days. *G1565*
6:55 about in beds t that were sick, where *G3588*
7:15 of him, t are they that defile the man. *G1565*
8: 1 In t days the multitude being very *G1565*
10:13 disciples rebuked t that brought *them*. *G3588*
11:23 shall believe that t things which he saith
12: 7 But t husbandmen said among *G1565*
13:17 and to them that give suck in t days! *G1565*
19 For *in* t days shall be affliction, such as *G1565*
20 had shortened t days, no flesh should *G3588*
24 But in t days, after that tribulation, the *G1565*
Lk 1: 1 a declaration of t things which are *G3588*
4 the certainty of t things, wherein thou
24 And after t days his wife Elisabeth *G5025*

Lk 1:39 And Mary arose in t days, and went *G5025*
45 a performance of t things which were *G3588*
2: 1 And it came to pass in t days, that *G1565*
18 And all they that heard *it* wondered at t
33 at t things which were spoken of him. *G3588*
4: 2 of the devil. And in t days he did eat *G1565*
5:35 them, and then shall they fast in t days. *G1565*
6:12 And it came to pass in t days, that he *G5025*
32 for sinners also love t that love them. *G3588*
7:28 For I say unto you, Among t that are
8:12 T by the way side are they that hear; *G3588*
9:36 and told no man in t days any of those *G1565*
36 any of t things which they had seen.
10:24 have desired to see t things which ye see,
24 seen *them*; and to hear t things which ye
12:20 t things be, which thou hast provided?
37 Blessed *are* t servants, whom the lord *G1565*
38 find *them* so, blessed are t servants. *G1565*
13: 4 Or t eighteen, upon whom the tower in *G1565*
14: 7 And he put forth a parable to t which *G3588*
24 For I say unto you, That none of t men *G1565*
17:10 shall have done all t things which are *G3588*
19:27 But t mine enemies, which would not *G1565*
20: 1 And it came to pass, *that* on one of t *G1565*
21:23 that give suck, in t days! for there shall *G1565*
26 and for looking after t things which are
23:14 touching t things whereof ye accuse him:
Jn 2:14 And found in the temple t that sold *G3588*
6:14 Then t men, when they had seen the *G3588*
8:10 where are t thine accusers? hath *G1565*
26 t things which I have heard of him. *G5023*
29 I do always t things that please him. *G3588*
31 Then said Jesus to t Jews which *G3588*
10:32 for which of t works do ye stone me? *G846*
13:29 said unto him, Buy *t things* that we have
17:11 thine own name t whom thou hast given *G846*
12 them in thy name: t that thou gavest me *G846*
Act 1:15 And in t days Peter stood up in the *G5025*
2:18 I will pour out in t days of my Spirit; *G1565*
3:18 But t things, which God before had
24 from Samuel and t that follow after, as *G3588*
6: 1 And in t days, when the number of the *G5025*
7:41 And they made a calf in t days, and *G1565*
8: 6 gave heed unto t things which Philip *G3588*
9:37 And it came to pass in t days, that she *G1565*
13:45 and spake against t things which were *G3588*
16: 3 which were in t quarters: for they knew *G1565*
35 sent the serjeants, saying, Let t men go. *G1565*
17:11 These were more noble than t in *G3588*
11 daily, whether t things were so. *G5023*
18:17 And Gallio cared for none of t things. *G5130*
20: 2 And when he had gone over t parts, *G1565*
21: 5 And when we had accomplished t *G3588*
15 And after t days we took up our *G5025*
24 all may know that t things, whereof they
26:16 hast seen, and of t things in the which I
22 other things than t which the prophets
27:11 t things which were spoken by Paul. *G3588*
28:31 of God, and teaching t things which *G3588*
Ro 1:28 do t things which are not convenient; *G3588*
4:17 dead, and calleth t things which be not *G3588*
6:13 unto God, as t that are alive from the
21 What fruit had ye then in t things
21 for the end of t things *is* death. *G1565*
10: 5 which doeth t things shall live by them. *G846*
15:17 Christ in t things which pertain to God. *G3588*
18 For I will not dare to speak of any of t
1Co 8: 4 As concerning therefore the eating of t *G3588*
10 eat t things which are offered to idols; *G3588*
12:22 Nay, much more t members of the *G3588*
23 And t *members* of the body, which we *G3739*
14:23 and there come in *t that are* unlearned,
2Co 7: 6 Nevertheless God, that comforteth t *G3588*
11:28 Beside t things that are without, that *G3588*
Eph 5:12 For it is a shame even to speak of t *G3588*
Php 3: 7 But what things were gain to me, t I *G5023*
13 thing *I do*, forgetting t things which are *G3588*
13 forth unto t things which are before, *G3588*
4: 3 true yokefellow, help t women which
9 T things, which ye have both learned, *G5023*
Col 2:18 intruding into t things which he hath
3: 1 If ye then be risen with Christ, seek t *G3588*
1Ti 4:10 of all men, specially of t that believe.
5: 8 and specially for t of his own house, he *G3588*
2Ti 2:25 In meekness instructing t that oppose *G3588*
3: 3 fierce, despisers of t that are good,
Heb 3: 5 t things which were to be spoken after; *G3588*
5:14 of full age, *even* t who by reason of use *G3588*
6: 4 For *it is* impossible for t who were once *G3588*

Heb 7:21 (For t priests were made without an *G3588*
27 Who needeth not daily, as t high *G3588*
8:10 of Israel after t days, saith the Lord; *G1565*
10: 1 can never with t sacrifices which they *G846*
3 But in t *sacrifices there is* a *G846*
16 with them after t days, saith the Lord, *G1565*
12:27 the removing of t things that are *G3588*
27 are made, that t things which cannot *G3588*
13:11 For the bodies of t beasts, whose blood *G5130*
Jas 2:16 ye give them not t things which are *G3588*
2Pt 2: 6 unto t that after should live ungodly; *G3588*
18 wantonness, t that were clean escaped *G3588*
1Jn 3:22 t things that are pleasing in his sight. *G3588*
2Jn 8 Look to yourselves, that we lose not t
Jude 10 But these speak evil of t things which *G3745*
10 in t things they corrupt themselves. *G5125*
Rev 1: 3 and keep t things which are written *G3588*
2:10 Fear none of t things which thou shalt *G3588*
13 denied my faith, even in t days wherein *G3588*
4: 9 And when t beasts give glory and *G3588*
9: 4 any tree; but only t men which have *G3588*
6 And in t days shall men seek death, *G1565*
10: 4 unto me, Seal up t things which the
13:14 by *the means of* t miracles which he *G3588*
20:12 were judged out of t things which were *G3588*

THOU See the Appendix.

THOUGH
Gen 31:30 And now, *t* thou wouldest needs be
33:10 seen thy face, as t I had seen the face of
40:10 and it *was* as t it budded, *and* her
Lev 5:17 of the LORD; t he wist *it* not, yet is he
11: 7 And the swine, t he divide the hoof, and
25:35 relieve him: *yea, t he* be a stranger, or a
Nu 18:27 unto you, as t *it were* the corn of the
Dt 29:19 I shall have peace, t I walk in the H3588
Jos 17:18 out the Canaanites, t they have iron H3588
18 iron chariots, *and* t they *be* strong. H3588
Jdg 13:16 said unto Manoah, T thou detain me, I H518
15: 3 the Philistines, t I do them a displeasure.
7 And Samson said unto them, T ye have H518
Ru 2:13 thine handmaid, t I be not like unto one
1Sa 14:39 saveth Israel, t it be in Jonathan H3588+H518
20:20 on the side *thereof*, as t I shot at a mark.
21: 5 common, yea, t it were sanctified this H3588
2Sa 1:21 *as t he had* not *been* anointed with oil.
3:39 And I *am* this day weak, t anointed king;
4: 6 midst of the house, *as t* they would have
18:12 And the man said unto Joab, T I should H3863
1Ki 2:28 after Adonijah, t he turned not after
1Ch 26:10 the chief, (for *t* he was not the firstborn,
2Ch 30:19 God of his fathers, t *he be* not *cleansed*
Neh 1: 9 and do them; t there were of you cast H518
6: 1 left therein; (t at that time I had not H1571
Est 9: 1 power over them, (t it was turned to the
Job 8: 7 T thy beginning was small, yet thy latter
9:15 Whom, t I were righteous, *yet* would I H518
21 *T* I *were* perfect, *yet* would I not know
10:19 I should have been as t I had not been; I
11:12 For vain man would be wise, t man be
13:15 T he slay me, yet will I trust in him: but H2005
14: 8 T the root thereof wax old in the earth, H518
16: 6 T I speak, my grief is not asswaged: and H518
6 and *t* I forbear, what am I eased?
19:17 My breath is strange to my wife, t I
26 And *t* after my skin *worms* destroy this
27 *t* my reins be consumed within me.
20: 6 T his excellency mount up to the
12 T wickedness be sweet in his mouth, H518
12 his mouth, *t* he hide it under his tongue;
13 *T* he spare it, and forsake it not; but
24:23 *T* it be given him *to be* in safety,
27: 8 For what *is* the hope of the hypocrite, t H3588
16 T he heap up silver as the dust, and H518
30:24 to the grave, t they cry in his destruction. H518
39:16 her young ones, as t *they were* not hers:
Ps 23: 4 Yea, t I walk through the valley of the H3588
27: 3 T an host should encamp against me, H518
3 shall not fear: t war should rise against H518
35:14 I behaved myself as t *he had been* my
37:24 T he fall, he shall not be utterly cast
44:19 T thou hast sore broken us in the place
46: 2 Therefore will not we fear, t the earth be
2 be removed, and t the mountains be
3 *T* the waters thereof roar *and* be
3 *and* be troubled, *t* the mountains shake
49:18 T while he lived he blessed his soul: H3588
68:13 T ye have lien among the pots, *yet shall* H518

Ps 78:23 T he had commanded the clouds from
99: 8 that forgavest them, t thou tookest
138: 6 T the LORD *be* high, yet hath he H3588
7 T I walk in the midst of trouble, thou H518
Prv 6:35 rest content, t thou givest many gifts. H3588
11:21 *T* hand *join* in hand, the wicked shall
16: 5 to the LORD: *t* hand *join* in hand, he
27:22 T thou shouldest bray a fool in a mortar H518
28: 6 *that is* perverse *in his* ways, t he *be* rich.
29:19 for t he understand he will not answer.
Ecc 6: 6 Yea, t he live a thousand years twice H432
8:12 T a sinner do evil an hundred times, and
17 the sun: because t a man labour to seek H834
17 find *it*; yea further; t a wise *man* think to H518
Isa 1:18 saith the LORD: t your sins be as scarlet, H518
18 be as white as snow; t they be red like H518
10:22 For t thy people Israel be as the sand of H518
12: 1 I will praise thee: t thou wast angry H3588
30:20 And *t* the Lord give you the bread of
35: 8 men, t fools, shall not err *therein*.
45: 4 thee, t thou hast not known me.
5 I girded thee, t thou hast not known me:
49: 5 again to him, T Israel be not gathered,
63:16 Doubtless thou *art* our father, t H3588
Jer 2:22 For t thou wash thee with nitre, and take H518
4:30 what wilt thou do? T thou clothest H3588
30 with crimson, t thou deckest thee with H3588
30 of gold, t thou rentest thy face H3588
5: 2 And t they say, The LORD liveth; surely H518
22 it cannot pass it: and t the waves thereof
22 t they roar, yet can they not pass over it?
11:11 able to escape; and t they shall cry unto
12: 6 not, t they speak fair words unto thee. H3588
14: 7 O LORD, t our iniquities testify against H518
15: 1 Then said the LORD unto me, T Moses H518
22:24 *As* I live, saith the LORD, t Coniah the H518
30:11 to save thee: t I make a full end of H3588
32: 5 him, saith the LORD: t ye fight with the H3588
33 and not the face: t I taught them, rising
37:10 For t ye had smitten the whole army of H518
46:23 forest, saith the LORD, t it cannot be H3588
49:16 the height of the hill: t thou shouldest H3588
51: 5 of the LORD of hosts; t their land was H3588
53 T Babylon should mount up to heaven, H3588
53 up to heaven, and t she should fortify H518
Lam 3:32 But t he cause grief, yet will he have H3588
Ezk 2: 6 of their words, t briers and thorns *be* H3588
6 their looks, t they *be* a rebellious house.
3: 9 their looks, t they *be* a rebellious house.
8:18 I have pity: and t they cry in mine ears
12: 3 consider, t they *be* a rebellious house. H3588
13 yet shall he not see it, t he shall die there.
14:14 T these three men, Noah, Daniel, and
16 *T* these three men *were* in it, *as* I live,
18 T these three men *were* in it, *as* I live,
20 T Noah, Daniel, and Job, *were* in it, *as* I
26:21 *shalt be* no *more*: t thou be sought for,
28: 2 t thou set thine heart as the heart of God:
32:25 slain by the sword: t their terror was H3588
26 slain by the sword, t they caused their H3588
27 upon their bones, t *they were* the terror H3588
Dan 5:22 thine heart, t thou knewest all this; H6903
9: 9 t we have rebelled against him; H3588
Hos 4:15 T thou, Israel, play the harlot, *yet* let not H518
5: 2 t I *have been* a rebuker of them all.
7:13 against me: t I have redeemed them,
15 T I have bound *and* strengthened their
8:10 Yea, t they have hired among the H3588
9:12 T they bring up their children, H3588+H518
16 bear no fruit: yea, t they bring forth, yet H3588
11: 7 from me: t they called them to the
13:15 T he be fruitful among *his* brethren, an H3588
Am 5:22 T ye offer me burnt offerings H3588+H518
9: 2 T they dig into hell, thence shall mine H518
2 mine hand take them; t they climb up to H518
3 And t they hide themselves in the top of H518
3 out thence; and t they be hid from my H518
4 And t they go into captivity before their H518
Oba 4 T thou exalt *thyself* as the eagle, and H518
4 as the eagle, and t thou set thy nest H518
16 and they shall be as t they had not been.
Mic 5: 2 But thou, Beth-lehem Ephratah, *t* thou
Nah 1:12 Thus saith the LORD; T *they be* quiet, H518
12 he shall pass through. T I have afflicted
Hab 1: 5 ye will not believe, t it be told *you*. H3588
2: 3 speak, and not lie: t it tarry, wait for it; H518
Zec 9: 2 Tyrus, and Zidon, t it be very wise. H3588
10: 6 they shall be as t I had not cast them off: H834
12: 3 be cut in pieces, t all the people of the

Mt 26:33 Peter answered and said unto him, T G1499
35 Peter said unto him, T I should die G2579
60 But found none: yea, t many false G2532
Lk 9:53 face was as t he would go to Jerusalem.
11: 8 I say unto you, T he will not rise and G1499
16:31 persuaded, t one rose from the dead. G1437
18: 4 T I fear not God, nor regard man; G1499
7 unto him, t he bear long with them? G2532
24:28 made as t he would have gone further. G4364
Jn 4: 2 (T Jesus himself baptized not, but his G2544
8: 6 on the ground, *as t he heard them not*.
14 Jesus answered and said unto them, T I G2579
10:38 But if I do, t ye believe not me, believe G2579
11:25 in me, t he were dead, yet shall he live: G2579
12:37 But t he had done so many miracles
Act 3:12 earnestly on us, as t by our own power G5613
13:28 And t they found no cause of death *in*
41 believe, t a man declare it unto you. G1437
17:25 men's hands, as t he needed any thing,
27 t he be not far from every one of us: G2544
23:15 you to morrow, as t ye would inquire G5613
20 the council, as t they would inquire G5613
27:30 under colour as t they would have cast G5613
28: 4 is a murderer, whom, t he hath escaped
17 Men *and* brethren, t I have committed
Ro 4:11 all them that believe, t they be not G1223
17 things which be not as t they were. G5613
7: 3 t she be married to another man.
9: 6 Not as t the word of God hath taken G3754
27 Esaias also crieth concerning Israel, T G1437
1Co 4:15 For t ye have ten thousand instructors G1437
18 Now some are puffed up, as t I would G5613
5: 3 judged already, as t I were present, G5613
7:29 that have wives be as t they had none; G5613
30 And they that weep, as t they wept not; G5613
30 that rejoice, as t they rejoiced not; and G5613
30 they that buy, as t they possessed not; G5613
8: 5 For t there be that are called gods, G2532
9:16 For t I preach the gospel, I have G1437
19 For t I be free from all *men*, yet have I
13: 1 T I speak with the tongues of men and G1437
2 And t I have *the gift of* prophecy, and G1437
2 all knowledge; and t I have all faith, so G1437
3 And t I bestow all my goods to feed *the* G1437
3 feed *the poor*, and t I give my body to G1437
2Co 4:16 For which cause we faint not; but t our G1499
5:16 the flesh: yea, t we have known Christ G1499
20 for Christ, as t God did beseech *you* G5613
7: 8 For t I made you sorry with a letter, I G1499
8 I do not repent, t I did repent: for I G1499
8 you sorry, t *it were* but for a season. G1499
12 Wherefore, t I wrote unto you, *I did it* G1499
8: 9 Jesus Christ, that, t he was rich, yet for
10: 3 For t we walk in the flesh, we do not war
8 For t I should boast somewhat more of G1437
14 *our measure*, as t we reached not unto G5613
11: 6 But t *I be* rude in speech, yet not in G1487
21 I speak as concerning reproach, as t we G3754
12: 6 For t I would desire to glory, I shall not G1437
11 very chiefest apostles, t I be nothing. G1499
15 and be spent for you; t the more G1499
13: 4 For t he was crucified through G2532
7 which is honest, t we be as reprobates. G1161
Gal 1: 8 But t we, or an angel from heaven, G2532
3:15 the manner of men; T *it be* but a man's G3676
4: 1 from a servant, t he be lord of all;
Php 3: 4 T I might also have confidence in the G2539
12 Not as t I had already attained, either G3754
Col 2: 5 For t I be absent in the flesh, yet am I G1487
20 the world, why, as t living in the world, G5613
Phlm 8 Wherefore, t I might be much bold in
Heb 5: 8 T he were a Son, yet learned he G2539
6: 9 accompany salvation, t we thus speak. G1499
7: 5 of their brethren, t they come out of the G2539
12:17 t he sought it carefully with tears. G2539
Jas 2:14 What *doth it* profit, my brethren, t a G1437
3: 4 Behold also the ships, which t *they be* so
1Pt 1: 6 Wherein ye greatly rejoice, t now for a
7 that perisheth, t it be tried with fire, G1161
8 ye love; in whom, t now ye see *him* not,
4:12 is to try you, as t some strange thing
2Pt 1:12 of these things, t ye know *them*, and G2539
2Jn 5 And now I beseech thee, lady, not as t I G5613
Jude 5 in remembrance, t ye once knew this,

THOUGHT

Gen 20:11 And Abraham said, Because I t, Surely H559
38:15 When Judah saw her, he t her *to be* an H2803
48:11 And Israel said unto Joseph, I had not t H6419
Gen 50:20 But as for you, ye t evil against me; *but* H2803
Ex 32:14 evil which he t to do unto his people. H1696
Nu 24:11 Therefore now flee thou to thy place: I t H559
33:56 do unto you, as I t to do unto them. H1819
Dt 15: 9 Beware that there be not a t in thy H1697
19:19 Then shall ye do unto him, as he had t H2161
Jdg 15: 2 And her father said, I verily t that thou H559
20: 5 me by night, *and* t to have slain me: H1819
Ru 4: 4 And I t to advertise thee, saying, Buy *it* H559
1Sa 1:13 therefore Eli t she had been drunken. H2803
9: 5 *caring* for the asses, and take t for us. H1672
18:25 enemies. But Saul t to make David fall H2803
20:26 thing that day: for he t, Something hath H559
2Sa 4:10 him in Ziklag, who *t* that I would have
13: 2 t it hard for him to do any thing to her. H5869
14:13 then hast thou t such a thing against H2803
19:18 and to do what he t good. And Shimei H5869
21:16 with a new *sword*, t to have slain David. H559
2Ki 5:11 and said, Behold, I t, He will surely come H559
2Ch 11:22 his brethren: for *he t* to make him king.
32: 1 cities, and t to win them for himself. H559
Neh 6: 2 of Ono. But they t to do me mischief. H2803
Est 3: 6 And he t scorn to lay hands on H5869
6: 6 Now Haman t in his heart, To whom H559
Job 12: 5 despised in the t of him that is at ease. H6248
42: 2 *that* no t can be withholden from thee. H4209
Ps 48: 9 We have t of thy lovingkindness, O H1819
49:11 Their inward t *is, that* their houses *shall*
64: 6 both the inward t of every one *of them*,
73:16 When I t to know this, it *was* too H2803
119:59 I t on my ways, and turned my feet H2803
139: 2 thou understandest my t afar off. H7454
Prv 24: 9 The t of foolishness *is* sin: and the H2154
30:32 t evil, *lay* thine hand upon thy mouth. H2161
Ecc 10:20 Curse not the king, no not in thy t; and H4093
Isa 14:24 Surely as I have t, so shall it come to H1819
Jer 18: 8 of the evil that I t to do unto them. H2803
Ezk 38:10 thy mind, and thou shalt think an evil t: H4284
Dan 4: 2 I t it good to shew the signs and H6925
6: 3 king t to set him over the whole realm. H6246
Am 4:13 unto man what *is* his t, that maketh the H7808
Zec 1: 6 as the LORD of hosts t to do unto us, H2161
8:14 For thus saith the LORD of hosts; As I t H2161
15 So again have I t in these days to do H2161
Mal 3:16 the LORD, and that t upon his name. H2803
Mt 1:20 But while he t on these things, behold, G1760
6:25 Therefore I say unto you, Take no t for G3309
27 Which of you by taking t can add one G3309
28 And why take ye t for raiment? G3309
31 Therefore take no t, saying, What shall G3309
34 Take therefore no t for the morrow: for G3309
34 morrow shall take t for the things of G3309
10:19 But when they deliver you up, take no t G3309
Mk 13:11 you up, take no t beforehand what ye G4305
14:72 thrice. And when he t thereon, he wept. G1911
Lk 7: 7 Wherefore neither t I myself worthy to G515
9:47 And Jesus, perceiving the t of their G1261
12:11 powers, take ye no t how or what thing G3309
17 And he t within himself, saying, What G1260
22 unto you, Take no t for your life, what G3309
25 And which of you with taking t can add G3309
26 is least, why take ye t for the rest? G3309
19:11 and because they t that the kingdom of G1380
Jn 11:13 of his death: but they t that he had G1380
13:29 For some *of them* t, because Judas had G1380
Act 8:20 because thou hast t that the gift of God G3543
22 t of thine heart may be forgiven thee. G1963
10:19 While Peter t on the vision, the Spirit G1760
12: 9 by the angel; but t he saw a vision. G1380
15:38 But Paul t not good to take him with G515
26: 8 Why should it be t a thing incredible G2919
9 I verily t with myself, that I ought to do G1380
1Co 13:11 as a child, I t as a child: but when G3049
2Co 9: 5 Therefore I t it necessary to exhort the G2233
10: 5 every t to the obedience of Christ; G3540
Php 2: 6 Who, being in the form of God, t it not G2233
1Th 3: 1 we t it good to be left at Athens alone; G2106
Heb 10:29 ye, shall he be t worthy, who hath

THOUGHTEST

Ps 50:21 I kept silence; thou t that I was H1819

THOUGHTS

Gen 6: 5 t of his heart *was* only evil continually. H4284
Jdg 5:15 of Reuben *there were* great t of heart. H2711
1Ch 28: 9 of the t: if thou seek him, he H4284
29:18 imagination of the t of the heart of thy H4284
Job 4:13 In t from the visions of the night, when H5587
17:11 are broken off, *even* the t of my heart. H4180

Job 20: 2 Therefore do my t cause me to H5587
21:27 Behold, I know your t, and the devices H4284
Ps 10: 4 seek *after God*: God *is* not in all his t. H4209
33:11 the t of his heart to all generations. H4284
40: 5 thou hast done, and thy t *which are* to H4284
56: 5 all their t *are* against me for evil. H4284
92: 5 are thy works! *and* thy t are very deep. H4284
94:11 The LORD knoweth the t of man, that H4284
19 In the multitude of my t within me thy H8312
119:113 I hate *vain* t: but thy law do I love. H5588
139:17 How precious also are thy t unto me, O H7454
23 know my heart: try me, and know my t: H8312
146: 4 his earth; in that very day his t perish. H6250
Prv 12: 5 The t of the righteous *are* right: *but* the H4284
15:26 The t of the wicked *are* an abomination H4284
16: 3 LORD, and thy t shall be established. H4284
21: 5 The t of the diligent *tend* only to H4284
Isa 55: 7 man his t: and let him return unto H4284
8 For my t *are* not your thoughts, neither H4284
8 For my thoughts *are* not your t, neither H4284
9 ways, and my t than your thoughts. H4284
9 ways, and my thoughts than your t. H4284
59: 7 blood: their t *are* thoughts of iniquity; H4284
7 their thoughts *are* t of iniquity; wasting H4284
65: 2 *that was* not good, after their own t; H4284
66:18 For I *know* their works and their t: it H4284
Jer 4:14 long shall thy vain t lodge within thee? H4284
6:19 the fruit of their t, because they have H4284
23:20 performed the t of his heart: in the H4209
29:11 For I know the t that I think toward H4284
11 saith the LORD, t of peace, and not of H4284
Dan 2:29 As for thee, O king, thy t came *into thy* H7476
30 thou mightest know the t of thy heart. H7476
4: 5 me afraid, and the t upon my bed and H2031
19 one hour, and his t troubled him. The H7476
5: 6 changed, and his t troubled him, so H7476
10 ever: let not thy t trouble thee, nor let H7476
Mic 4:12 But they know not the t of the LORD, H4284
Mt 9: 4 And Jesus knowing their t said, G1761
12:25 And Jesus knew their t, and said unto G1761
15:19 For out of the heart proceed evil t, G1261
Mk 7:21 evil t, adulteries, fornications, murders, G1261
Lk 2:35 the t of many hearts may be revealed. G1261
5:22 But when Jesus perceived their t, he G1261
6: 8 But he knew their t, and said to the man G1261
11:17 But he, knowing their t, said unto them, G1270
24:38 and why do t arise in your hearts? G1261
Ro 2:15 witness, and *their* t the mean while G3053
1Co 3:20 And again, The Lord knoweth the t of G1261
Heb 4:12 of the t and intents of the heart. G1761
Jas 2: 4 and are become judges of evil t? G1261

THOUSAND

Gen 20:16 given thy brother a t *pieces* of silver: H505
Ex 12:37 t on foot *that were* men, beside children. H505
32:28 of the people that day about three t men. H505
38:25 talents, and a t seven hundred and H505
26 for six hundred t and three thousand H505
26 three t and five hundred and fifty *men*. H505
28 And of the t seven hundred seventy and H505
29 and two t and four hundred shekels. H505
Lev 26: 8 of you shall put ten t to flight: and your H7233
Nu 1:21 *were* forty and six t and five hundred. H505
23 *were* fifty and nine t and three hundred. H505
25 forty and five t six hundred and fifty. H505
27 and fourteen t and six hundred. H505
29 *were* fifty and four t and four hundred. H505
31 *were* fifty and seven t and four hundred. H505
33 Ephraim, *were* forty t and five hundred. H505
35 *were* thirty and two t and two hundred. H505
37 *were* thirty and five t and four hundred. H505
39 threescore and two t and seven hundred. H505
41 *were* forty and one t and five hundred. H505
43 *were* fifty and three t and four hundred. H505
46 were six hundred t and three thousand H505
46 and three t and five hundred and fifty. H505
2: 4 and fourteen t and six hundred. H505
6 *were* fifty and four t and four hundred. H505
8 *were* fifty and seven t and four hundred. H505
9 Judah *were* an hundred t and fourscore H505
9 and fourscore t and six thousand and H505
9 thousand and six t and four hundred, H505
11 *were* forty and six t and five hundred. H505
13 *were* fifty and nine t and three hundred. H505
15 and five t and six hundred and fifty. H505
16 *were* an hundred t and fifty and one H505
16 and fifty and one t and four hundred H505
19 of them, *were* forty t and five hundred. H505
21 *were* thirty and two t and two hundred. H505
Nu 2:23 *were* thirty and five t and four hundred. H505
24 *were* an hundred t and eight thousand H505
24 thousand and eight t and an hundred, H505
26 threescore and two t and seven hundred. H505
28 *were* forty and one t and five hundred. H505
30 *were* fifty and three t and four hundred. H505
31 *were* an hundred t and fifty and seven H505
31 and fifty and seven t and six hundred. H505
32 *were* six hundred t and three thousand H505
32 and three t and five hundred and fifty. H505
3:22 of them *were* seven t and five hundred. H505
28 upward, *were* eight t and six hundred, H505
34 upward, *were* six t and two hundred. H505
39 old and upward, *were* twenty and two t. H505
43 were twenty and two t two hundred and H505
50 he the money; a t three hundred and H505
4:36 were two t seven hundred and fifty. H505
40 were two t and six hundred and thirty. H505
44 families, were three t and two hundred. H505
48 eight t and five hundred and fourscore. H505
7:85 *weighed* two t and four hundred *shekels*, H505
11:21 *am, are* six hundred t footmen; and thou H505
16:49 were fourteen t and seven hundred, H505
25: 9 in the plague were twenty and four t. H505
26: 7 three t and seven hundred and thirty. H505
14 twenty and two t and two hundred. H505
18 of them, forty t and five hundred. H505
22 and sixteen t and five hundred. H505
25 threescore and four t and three hundred. H505
27 of them, threescore t and five hundred. H505
34 them, fifty and two t and seven hundred. H505
37 thirty and two t and five hundred. These H505
41 *were* forty and five t and six hundred. H505
43 threescore and four t and four hundred. H505
47 *were* fifty and three t and four hundred. H505
50 *were* forty and five t and four hundred. H505
51 of Israel, six hundred t and a thousand H505
51 and a t seven hundred and thirty. H505
62 were twenty and three t, all males from a H505
31: 4 Of every tribe a t, throughout all H505+H505
5 of Israel, a t of *every* tribe, twelve H505
5 of *every* tribe, twelve t armed for war. H505
6 And Moses sent them to the war, a t of H505
32 was six hundred t and seventy thousand H505
32 and seventy t and five thousand sheep, H505
32 and seventy thousand and five t sheep, H505
33 And threescore and twelve t beeves, H505
34 And threescore and one t asses, H505
35 And thirty and two t persons in all, of H505
36 three hundred t and seven and thirty H505
36 and thirty t and five hundred sheep: H505
38 And the beeves *were* thirty and six t; of H505
39 And the asses *were* thirty t and five H505
40 And the persons *were* sixteen t; of which H505
43 was three hundred t and thirty thousand H505
43 and thirty t *and* seven thousand H505
43 *and* seven t and five hundred sheep, H505
44 And thirty and six t beeves, H505
45 And thirty t asses and five hundred, H505
46 And sixteen t persons;) H505
52 t seven hundred and fifty shekels. H505
35: 4 city and outward a t cubits round about. H505
5 on the east side two t cubits, and on the H505
5 the south side two t cubits, and on the H505
5 on the west side two t cubits, and on the H505
5 the north side two t cubits; and the city H505
Dt 1:11 your fathers make you a t times so many H505
7: 9 his commandments to a t generations; H505
32:30 How should one chase a t, and two put H505
30 two put ten t to flight, except H7233+H505
Jos 3: 4 and it, about two t cubits by measure: H505
4:13 About forty t prepared for war passed H505
7: 3 two or three t men go up and H505+H505
4 people about three t men: and they fled H505
8: 3 chose out thirty t mighty men of valour, H505
12 And he took about five t men, and set H505
25 *were* twelve t, *even* all the men of Ai. H505
23:10 One man of you shall chase a t: for the H505
Jdg 1: 4 they slew of them in Bezek ten t men. H505
3:29 that time about ten t men, all lusty, and H505
4: 6 take with thee ten t men of the children H505
10 went up with ten t men at his feet: and H505
14 mount Tabor, and ten t men after him. H505
5: 8 or spear seen among forty t in Israel? H505
7: 3 two t; and there remained ten thousand. H505
3 two thousand; and there remained ten t. H505
8:10 them, about fifteen t *men*, all that were H505
10 and twenty t men that drew sword. H505
26 he requested was a t and seven hundred H505
Jdg 9:49 died also, about a t men and women. H505
12: 6 time of the Ephraimites forty and two t. H505
15:11 Then three t men of Judah went to the H505
15 and took it, and slew a t men therewith. H505
16 the jaw of an ass have I slain a t men. H505
16:27 roof about three t men and women, that H505
20: 2 hundred t footmen that drew sword. H505
10 an hundred of a t, and a thousand out H505
10 a thousand, and a t out of ten thousand, H505
10 out of ten t, to fetch victual for the H7233
15 twenty and six t men that drew sword, H505
17 four hundred t men that drew sword: H505
21 that day twenty and two t men. H505
25 eighteen t men; all these drew the sword. H505
34 And there came against Gibeah ten t H505
35 twenty and five t and an hundred men: H505
44 And there fell of Benjamin eighteen t H505
45 in the highways five t men; and pursued H505
45 Gidom, and slew two t men of them. H505
46 were twenty and five t men that drew the H505
21:10 sent thither twelve t men of the H505
1Sa 4: 2 of the army in the field about four t men. H505
10 for there fell of Israel thirty t footmen. H505
6:19 of the people fifty t and threescore and H505
11: 8 t, and the men of Judah thirty thousand. H505
8 thousand, and the men of Judah thirty t. H505
13: 2 Saul chose him three t *men* of Israel; H505
2 of Israel; *whereof* two t were with Saul in H505
2 Beth-el, and a t were with Jonathan H505
5 with Israel, thirty t chariots, and six H505
5 chariots, and six t horsemen, and people H505
15: 4 Telaim, two hundred t footmen, and ten H505
4 footmen, and ten t men of Judah. H505
17: 5 of the coat *was* five t shekels of brass. H505
18 the captain of *their* t, and look how thy H505
18:13 his captain over a t; and he went out and H505
24: 2 Then Saul took three t chosen men out H505
25: 2 great, and he had three t sheep, and a H505
2 sheep, and a t goats: and he was H505
26: 2 of Ziph, having three t chosen men of H505
2Sa 6: 1 all *the* chosen *men* of Israel, thirty t. H505
8: 4 And David took from him a t *chariots*, H505
4 and twenty t footmen: and David H505
5 of the Syrians two and twenty t men. H505
13 the valley of salt, *being* eighteen t *men*. H505
10: 6 of Zoba, twenty t footmen, and of king H505
6 of king Maacah a t men, and of Ish-tob H505
6 men, and of Ish-tob twelve t men. H505
18 the Syrians, and forty t horsemen, and H505
17: 1 choose out twelve t men, and I will arise H505
18: 3 *thou art* worth ten t of us: therefore now H505
7 great slaughter that day of twenty t *men*. H505
12 I should receive a t *shekels* of silver in H505
19:17 And *there were* a t men of Benjamin H505
24: 9 eight hundred t valiant men that drew H505
9 men of Judah *were* five hundred t men. H505
15 Dan even to Beer-sheba seventy t men. H505
1Ki 3: 4 great high place: a t burnt offerings did H505
4:26 And Solomon had forty t stalls of horses H505
26 for his chariots, and twelve t horsemen. H505
32 And he spake three t proverbs: and his H505
32 and his songs were a t and five. H505
5:11 And Solomon gave Hiram twenty t H505
13 all Israel; and the levy was thirty t men. H505
14 And he sent them to Lebanon, ten t a H505
15 And Solomon had threescore and ten t H505
15 fourscore t hewers in the mountains; H505
16 the work, three t and three hundred, H505
7:26 flowers of lilies: it contained two t baths. H505
8:63 two and twenty t oxen, and an hundred H505
63 and twenty t sheep. So the king and H505
10:26 and he had a t and four hundred H505
26 and twelve t horsemen, whom he H505
12:21 and fourscore t chosen men, which were H505
19:18 Yet I have left *me* seven t in Israel, all the H505
20:15 all the children of Israel, *being* seven t. H505
29 an hundred t footmen in one day. H505
30 twenty and seven t of the men *that were* H505
2Ki 3: 4 of Israel an hundred t lambs, and an H505
4 and an hundred t rams, with the wool. H505
5: 5 of silver, and six t *pieces* of gold, and ten H505
13: 7 chariots, and ten t footmen; for the king H505
14: 7 valley of salt ten t, and took Selah by war, H505
15:19 gave Pul a t talents of silver, that H505
18:23 deliver thee two t horses, if thou be able H505
19:35 fourscore and five t: and when they arose H505
24:14 of valour, *even* ten t captives, and all the H505
16 And all the men of might, *even* seven t, H505
16 and smiths a t, all *that were* strong *and* H505

T

1Ch 5:18 *were* four and forty t seven hundred and H505
21 of their camels fifty t, and of sheep two H505
21 two hundred and fifty t, and of asses two H505
21 two t, and of men an hundred thousand. H505
21 two thousand, and of men an hundred t. H505
7: 2 two and twenty t and six hundred. H505
4 war, six and thirty t *men:* for they had H505
5 their genealogies fourscore and seven t. H505
7 twenty and two t and thirty and four. H505
9 valour, *was* twenty t and two hundred. H505
11 *were* seventeen t and two hundred H505
40 *and* to battle *was* twenty and six t men. H505
9:13 of their fathers, a t and seven hundred H505
12:14 an hundred, and the greatest over a t. H505
24 and spear *were* six t and eight hundred, H505
25 for the war, seven t and one hundred. H505
26 Of the children of Levi four t and six H505
27 him *were* three t and seven hundred; H505
29 of Saul, three t: for hitherto the greatest H505
30 And of the children of Ephraim twenty t H505
31 of Manasseh eighteen t, which were H505
33 of war, fifty t, which could keep rank: H505
34 And of Naphtali a t captains, and with H505
34 with shield and spear thirty and seven t. H505
35 war twenty and eight t and six hundred. H505
36 went forth to battle, expert in war, forty t. H505
37 for the battle, an hundred and twenty t. H505
16:15 *which* he commanded to a t generations; H505
18: 4 And David took from him a t chariots, H505
4 chariots, and seven t horsemen, and H505
4 and twenty t footmen: David also H505
5 of the Syrians two and twenty t men. H505
12 Edomites in the valley of salt eighteen t. H505
19: 6 of Ammon sent a t talents of silver to H505
7 So they hired thirty and two t chariots, H505
18 the Syrians seven t *men which fought in* H505
18 chariots, and forty t footmen, and killed H505
21: 5 *they of* Israel were a t thousand and an H505
5 Israel were a thousand t and an hundred H505
5 and an hundred t men that drew sword: H505
5 and ten t men that drew sword. H505
14 and there fell of Israel seventy t men. H505
22:14 LORD an hundred t talents of gold, and H505
14 of gold, and a t thousand talents of H505
14 and a thousand t talents of silver; and H505
23: 3 man by man, was thirty and eight t. H505
4 Of which, twenty and four t *were* to set H505
4 and six t *were* officers and judges: H505
5 Moreover four t *were* porters; and four H505
5 porters; and four t praised the LORD H505
26:30 men of valour, a t and seven hundred, H505
32 of valour, *were* two t and seven hundred H505
27: 1 of every course *were* twenty and four t. H505
2 and in his course *were* twenty and four t. H505
4 course likewise *were* twenty and four t. H505
5 and in his course *were* twenty and four t. H505
7 and in his course *were* twenty and four t. H505
8 and in his course *were* twenty and four t. H505
9 and in his course *were* twenty and four t. H505
10 and in his course *were* twenty and four t. H505
11 and in his course *were* twenty and four t. H505
12 and in his course *were* twenty and four t. H505
13 and in his course *were* twenty and four t. H505
14 and in his course *were* twenty and four t. H505
15 and in his course *were* twenty and four t. H505
29: 4 *Even* three t talents of gold, of the gold of H505
4 of Ophir, and seven t talents of refined H505
7 of God of gold five t talents and ten H505
7 talents and ten t drams, and of silver H7239
7 and of silver ten t talents, and of brass H505
7 and of brass eighteen t talents, and one H505
7 and one hundred t talents of iron. H505
21 that day, *even* a t bullocks, a thousand H505
21 bullocks, a t rams, *and* a thousand H505
21 rams, *and* a t lambs, with their drink H505
2Ch 1: 6 and offered a t burnt offerings upon it. H505
14 and he had a t and four hundred H505
14 and twelve t horsemen, which he H505
2: 2 out threescore and ten t men to bear H505
2 and fourscore t to hew in the H505+H376
2 three t and six hundred to oversee them. H505
10 cut timber, twenty t measures of beaten H505
10 wheat, and twenty t measures of barley, H505
10 barley, and twenty t baths of wine, and H505
10 baths of wine, and twenty t baths of oil. H505
17 t and three thousand and six hundred. H505
17 thousand and three t and six hundred. H505
18 And he set threescore and ten t of them H505
18 and fourscore t *to be* hewers in the H505

2Ch 2:18 and three t and six hundred overseers H505
4: 5 *and* it received and held three t baths. H505
7: 5 of twenty and two t oxen, and an H505
5 and twenty t sheep: so the king and H505
9:25 And Solomon had four t stalls for horses H505
25 and twelve t horsemen; whom he H505
11: 1 and fourscore t chosen *men,* which were H505
12: 3 and threescore t horsemen: and the H505
13: 3 war, *even* four hundred t chosen men: H505
3 with eight hundred t chosen men, *being* H505
17 of Israel five hundred t chosen men. H505
14: 8 three hundred t; and out of Benjamin, H505
8 t: all these *were* mighty men of valour. H505
9 with an host of a t thousand, and three H505
9 host of a thousand t, and three hundred H505
15:11 seven hundred oxen and seven t sheep. H505
17:11 him flocks, seven t and seven hundred H505
11 and seven t and seven hundred he goats. H505
14 mighty men of valour three hundred t. H505
15 with him two hundred and fourscore t. H505
16 two hundred t mighty men of valour. H505
17 men with bow and shield two hundred t. H505
18 fourscore t ready prepared for the war. H505
25: 5 three hundred t choice *men, able* to go H505
6 He hired also an hundred t mighty men H505
11 and smote of the children of Seir ten t. H505
12 And *other* ten t *left* alive did the children H505
13 three t of them, and took much spoil. H505
26:12 of valour *were* two t and six hundred. H505
13 three hundred t and seven thousand H505
13 and seven t and five hundred, that H505
27: 5 of silver, and ten t measures of wheat, H505
5 of wheat, and ten t of barley. So much H505
28: 6 and twenty t in one day, *which were* H505
8 two hundred t, women, sons, and H505
29:33 six hundred oxen and three t sheep. H505
30:24 the congregation a t bullocks and seven H505
24 bullocks and seven t sheep; and the H505
24 to the congregation a t bullocks and ten H505
24 bullocks and ten t sheep: and a great H505
35: 7 number of thirty t, and three thousand H505
7 and three t bullocks: these *were* H505
8 offerings two t and six hundred *small* H505
9 t *small cattle,* and five hundred oxen. H505
Ezr 1: 9 chargers of gold, a t chargers of silver, H505
10 hundred and ten, *and* other vessels a t. H505
11 of silver *were* five t and four hundred. H505
2: 3 The children of Parosh, two t an H505
6 Joab, two t eight hundred and twelve. H505
7 The children of Elam, a t two hundred H505
12 The children of Azgad, a t two hundred H505
14 The children of Bigvai, two t fifty and H505
31 The children of the other Elam, a t two H505
35 The children of Senaah, three t and six H505
37 The children of Immer, a t fifty and two. H505
38 The children of Pashur, a t two hundred H505
39 The children of Harim, a t and H505
64 and two t three hundred *and* threescore, H505
65 *there were* seven t three hundred thirty H505
67 asses, six t seven hundred and twenty. H505
69 threescore and one t drams of gold, and H505
69 of gold, and five t pound of silver, and H505
8:27 Also twenty basons of gold, of a t drams; H505
Neh 3:13 a t cubits on the wall unto the dung gate. H505
7: 8 The children of Parosh, two t an H505
11 two t and eight hundred *and* eighteen. H505
12 The children of Elam, a t two hundred H505
17 The children of Azgad, two t three H505
19 The children of Bigvai, two t threescore H505
34 The children of the other Elam, a t two H505
38 The children of Senaah, three t nine H505
40 The children of Immer, a t fifty and two. H505
41 The children of Pashur, a t two hundred H505
42 The children of Harim, a t and H505
66 and two t three hundred and threescore, H505
67 *there were* seven t three hundred thirty H505
69 six t seven hundred and twenty asses. H505
70 to the treasure a t drams of gold, fifty H505
71 of the work twenty t drams of gold, and H7239
71 two t and two hundred pound of silver. H505
72 gave *was* twenty t drams of gold, and H7239
72 of gold, and two t pound of silver, and H505
Est 3: 9 and I will pay ten t talents of silver to the H505
9:16 seventy and five t, but they laid not their H505
Job 1: 3 His substance also was seven t sheep, H505
3 sheep, and three t camels, and five H505
9: 3 him, he cannot answer him one of a t. H505
33:23 a t, to shew unto man his uprightness: H505
42:12 for he had fourteen t sheep, and six H505

Job 42:12 sheep, and six t camels, and a thousand H505
12 camels, and a t yoke of oxen, and a H505
12 yoke of oxen, and a t she asses. H505
Ps 50:10 *is* mine, *and* the cattle upon a t hills. H505
60:ttl of Edom in the valley of salt twelve t. H505
68:17 The chariots of God *are* twenty t, *even* H7239
84:10 For a day in thy courts *is* better than a t. I H505
90: 4 For a t years in thy sight *are but* as H505
91: 7 A t shall fall at thy side, and ten H505
7 at thy side, and ten t at thy right hand; H7233
105: 8 *which* he commanded to a t generations. H505
Ecc 6: 6 Yea, though he live a t years twice *told,* H505
7:28 one man among a t have I found; but a H505
Song 4: 4 a t bucklers, all shields of mighty men. H505
5:10 and ruddy, the chiefest among ten t. H7233
8:11 thereof was to bring a t *pieces* of silver. H505
12 *must have* a t, and those that keep H505
Isa 7:23 where there were a t vines at a thousand H505
23 vines at a t silverlings, it shall *even* H505
30:17 One t *shall flee* at the rebuke of one; at H505
36: 8 I will give thee two t horses, if thou be H505
37:36 fourscore and five t: and when they arose H505
60:22 A little one shall become a t, and a small H505
Jer 52:28 year three t Jews and three and twenty: H505
30 the persons *were* four t and six hundred. H505
Ezk 45: 1 length of five and twenty t *reeds,* and the H505
1 *shall be* ten t. This *shall be* holy in H505
3 of five and twenty t, and the breadth of H505
3 the breadth of ten t: and in it shall be the H505
5 And the five and twenty t of length, and H505
5 of length, and the ten t of breadth, shall H505
6 of the city five t broad, and five and H505
6 five and twenty t long, over against the H505
47: 3 he measured a t cubits, and he brought H505
4 Again he measured a t, and brought me H505
4 Again he measured a t, and brought me H505
5 Afterward he measured a t; *and it was* a H505
48: 8 of five and twenty t *reeds in* breadth, H505
9 of five and twenty t in length, and of ten H505
9 in length, and of ten t in breadth. H505
10 five and twenty t *in length,* and toward H505
10 the west ten t in breadth, and toward H505
10 toward the east ten t in breadth, and H505
10 five and twenty t in length: and the H505
13 *have* five and twenty t in length, and ten H505
13 in length, and ten t in breadth: all the H505
13 twenty t, and the breadth ten thousand. H505
13 twenty thousand, and the breadth ten t. H505
15 And the five t, that are left in the breadth H505
15 the five and twenty t, shall be a profane H505
16 the north side four t and five hundred, H505
16 the south side four t and five hundred, H505
16 on the east side four t and five hundred, H505
16 the west side four t and five hundred. H505
18 *portion shall be* ten t eastward, and ten H505
18 eastward, and ten t westward: and it H505
20 All the oblation *shall be* five and twenty t H505
20 by five and twenty t: ye shall offer the H505
21 the five and twenty t of the oblation H505
21 the five and twenty t toward the west H505
30 side, four t and five hundred measures. H505
32 And at the east side four t and five H505
33 And at the south side four t and five H505
34 At the west side four t and five hundred, H505
35 *It was* round about eighteen t *measures*: H505
Dan 5: 1 made a great feast to a t of his lords, and H506
1 of his lords, and drank wine before the t. H506
7:10 from before him: t thousands ministered H506
10 unto him, and ten t times ten thousand H7240
10 times ten t stood before him: the H7240
8:14 And he said unto me, Unto two t and H505
12:11 *be* a t two hundred and ninety days. H505
12 t three hundred and five and thirty days. H505
Am 5: 3 city that went out *by* a t shall leave an H505
Jna 4:11 than sixscore t persons that cannot H7239
Mt 14:21 five t men, beside women and children. G4000
15:38 And they that did eat were four t men, G5070
16: 9 t, and how many baskets ye took up? G4000
10 Neither the seven loaves of the four t, G5070
18:24 him, which owed him ten t talents. G3463
Mk 5:13 two t;) and were choked in the sea. G1367
6:44 eat of the loaves were about five t men. G4000
8: 9 about four t: and he sent them away. G5070
19 loaves among five t, how many baskets G4000
20 And when the seven among four t, how G5070
Lk 9:14 For they were about five t men. And he G4000
14:31 he be able with ten t to meet him that G5505
31 that cometh against him with twenty t? G5505
Jn 6:10 men sat down, in number about five t. G4000

Act 2:41 added *unto them* about three t souls. G5153
4: 4 the number of the men was about five t. G5505
19:19 and found *it* fifty t *pieces* of silver. G3461
21:38 four t men that were murderers? G5070
Ro 11: 4 to myself seven t men, who have not G2035
1Co 4:15 For though ye have ten t instructors in G3463
10: 8 and fell in one day three and twenty t. G5505
14:19 ten t words in an *unknown* tongue. G3463
2Pt 3: 8 *is* with the Lord as a t years, and a G5507
8 years, and a t years as one day. G5507
Rev 5:11 of them was ten t times ten thousand, G5505
11 t, and thousands of thousands; G3461+G3461
7: 4 *and* forty *and* four t of all the tribes of G5505
5 Of the tribe of Juda *were* sealed twelve t. G5505
5 *were* sealed twelve t. Of the tribe of Gad G5505
5 Of the tribe of Gad *were* sealed twelve t. G5505
6 Of the tribe of Aser *were* sealed twelve t. G5505
6 *were* sealed twelve t. Of the tribe of G5505
6 tribe of Manasses *were* sealed twelve t. G5505
7 *were* sealed twelve t. Of the tribe of Levi G5505
7 Levi *were* sealed twelve t. Of the tribe of G5505
7 tribe of Issachar *were* sealed twelve t. G5505
8 *were* sealed twelve t. Of the tribe of G5505
8 *were* sealed twelve t. Of the tribe of G5505
8 tribe of Benjamin *were* sealed twelve t. G5505
9:16 *were* two hundred t thousand: and I
16 t: and I heard the number of them. G1417
11: 3 shall prophesy a t two hundred *and* G5507
13 slain of men seven t: and the remnant G5505
12: 6 a t two hundred *and* threescore days. G5507
14: 1 forty *and* four t, having his Father's G5505
3 t, which were redeemed from the earth. G5505
20 space of a t *and* six hundred furlongs. G5507
20: 2 and Satan, and bound him a t years, G5507
3 no more, till the t years should be G5507
4 lived and reigned with Christ a t years. G5507
5 lived not again until the t years were G5507
6 and shall reign with him a t years. G5507
7 And when the t years are expired, G5507
21:16 the reed, twelve t furlongs. The length G5505

THOUSANDS

Gen 24:60 thou *the mother* of t of millions, and let H505
Ex 18:21 *to be* rulers of t, *and* rulers of hundreds, H505
25 the people, rulers of t, rulers of hundreds, H505
20: 6 And shewing mercy unto t of them that H505
34: 7 Keeping mercy for t, forgiving iniquity H505
Nu 1:16 of their fathers, heads of t in Israel. H505
10: 4 *are* heads of the t of Israel, shall gather H505
36 O LORD, unto the many t of Israel. H505
31: 5 So there were delivered out of the t of H505
14 the captains over t, and captains over H505
48 And the officers which *were* over t of the H505
48 host, the captains of t, and captains of H505
52 of the captains of t, and of the captains of H505
54 of the captains of t and of hundreds, and H505
Dt 1:15 you, captains over t, and captains over H505
5:10 And shewing mercy unto t of them that H505
33: 2 he came with ten t of saints: from his H7233
17 they *are* the ten t of Ephraim, and they H7233
17 and they *are* the t of Manasseh. H505
Jos 22:14 of their fathers among the t of Israel. H505
21 and said unto the heads of the t of Israel, H505
30 and heads of the t of Israel which *were* H505
1Sa 8:12 And he will appoint him captains over t, H505
10:19 the LORD by your tribes, and by your t. H505
18: 7 slain his t, and David his ten thousands. H505
7 his thousands, and David his ten t. H7233
8 unto David ten t, and to me they have H7233
8 have ascribed *but* t: and *what* can he H505
21:11 slain his t, and David his ten thousands? H505
11 his thousands, and David his ten t? H7233
22: 7 captains of t, and captains of hundreds; H505
23:23 him out throughout all the t of Judah. H505
29: 2 by hundreds, and by t: but David and his H505
5 slew his t, and David his ten thousands? H505
5 slew his thousands, and David his ten t? H7233
2Sa 18: 1 of t and captains of hundreds over them. H505
4 people came out by hundreds and by t. H505
1Ch 12:20 captains of the t that *were* of Manasseh. H505
13: 1 t and hundreds, *and* with every leader. H505
15:25 the captains over t, went to bring up the H505
26:26 the captains over t and hundreds, and H505
27: 1 and captains of t and hundreds, and H505
28: 1 captains over the t, and captains over the H505
29: 6 and the captains of t and of hundreds, H505
2Ch 1: 2 to the captains of t and of hundreds, and H505
17:14 the captains of t; Adnah the chief, and H505
25: 5 them captains over t, and captains over H505

Ps 3: 6 I will not be afraid of ten t of people, H7233
68:17 thousand, *even* t of angels: the Lord *is* H505
119:72 better unto me than t of gold and silver. H505
144:13 forth t and ten thousands in our streets: H503
13 thousands and ten t in our streets: H7231
Jer 32:18 Thou shewest lovingkindness unto t, and H505
Dan 7:10 him: thousand t ministered unto him, H506
11:12 t: but he shall not be strengthened *by it.* H7239
Mic 5: 2 be little among the t of Judah, *yet* out of H505
6: 7 Will the LORD be pleased with t of rams, H505
7 rams, *or* with ten t of rivers of oil? shall H7233
Act 21:20 how many t of Jews there are which G3461
Jude 14 Lord cometh with ten t of his saints, G3461
Rev 5:11 ten thousand, and t of thousands; G5505
11 times ten thousand, and thousands of t; G5505

THOUSAND-THOUSAND See THOUSAND.

THREAD

Gen 14:23 That I will not *take* from a t even to a H2339
38:28 a scarlet t, saying, This came out first. H8144
30 had the scarlet t upon his hand: and H8144
Jos 2:18 bind this line of scarlet t in the window H2339
Jdg 16: 9 the withs, as a t of tow is broken when H6616
12 brake them from off his arms like a t. H2339
Song 4: 3 Thy lips *are* like a t of scarlet, and thy H2339

THREATEN

Act 4:17 let us straitly t them, that they speak G546

THREATENED

Act 4:21 So when they had further t them, they G4324
1Pt 2:23 he suffered, he t not; but committed G546

THREATENING

Eph 6: 9 them, forbearing t: knowing that your G547

THREATENINGS

Act 4:29 And now, Lord, behold their t: and grant G547
9: 1 And Saul, yet breathing out t and G547

THREE

Gen 5:22 begat Methuselah t hundred years, and H7969
23 And all the days of Enoch were t H7969
6:10 And Noah begat t sons, Shem, Ham, H7969
15 of the ark *shall be* t hundred cubits, the H7969
7:13 wife, and the t wives of his sons with H7969
9:19 These *are* the t sons of Noah: and of H7969
28 And Noah lived after the flood t H7969
11:13 t years, and begat sons and daughters. H7969
15 t years, and begat sons and daughters. H7969
14:14 born in his own house, t hundred and H7969
15: 9 me an heifer of t years old, and a she H8027
9 and a she goat of t years old, and a ram H8027
9 old, and a ram of t years old, and a H8027
18: 2 looked, and, lo, t men stood by him: H7969
6 ready quickly t measures of fine meal, H7969
29: 2 and, lo, there *were* t flocks of sheep H7969
34 I have born him t sons: therefore was H7969
30:36 And he set t days' journey betwixt H7969
38:24 And it came to pass about t months H7969
40:10 And in the vine *were* t branches: and it H7969
12 of it: The t branches *are* three days: H7969
12 of it: The three branches *are* t days: H7969
13 Yet within t days shall Pharaoh lift up H7969
16 *I had* t white baskets on my head: H7969
18 thereof: The t baskets *are* three days: H7969
18 thereof: The three baskets *are* t days: H7969
19 Yet within t days shall Pharaoh lift up H7969
42:17 put them all together into ward t days. H7969
45:22 Benjamin he gave t hundred *pieces* of H7969
46:15 and his daughters *were* thirty and t. H7969
Ex 2: 2 *a* goodly *child,* she hid him t months. H7969
3:18 we beseech thee, t days' journey into H7969
5: 3 us go, we pray thee, t days' journey into H7969
6:18 *were* an hundred thirty and t years. H7969
7: 7 fourscore and t years old, when they H7969
8:27 We will go t days' journey into the H7969
10:22 darkness in all the land of Egypt t days: H7969
23 from his place for t days: but all the H7969
15:22 and they went t days in the wilderness, H7969
21:11 And if he do not these t unto her, then H7969
23:14 T times thou shalt keep a feast unto me H7969
17 T times in the year all thy males shall H7969
25:32 out of the sides of it; t branches of the H7969
32 of the one side, and t branches of the H7969
33 T bowls made like unto almonds, *with* H7969
33 in one branch; and t bowls made like H7969
27: 1 and the height thereof *shall be* t cubits. H7969

Ex 27:14 their pillars t, and their sockets three. H7969
14 their pillars three, and their sockets t. H7969
15 their pillars t, and their sockets three. H7969
15 their pillars three, and their sockets t. H7969
32:28 people that day about t thousand men. H7969
37:18 of the sides thereof; t branches of the H7969
18 one side thereof, and t branches of the H7969
19 T bowls made after the fashion of H7969
19 and a flower; and t bowls made like H7969
38: 1 and t cubits the height thereof. H7969
14 their pillars t, and their sockets three. H7969
14 their pillars three, and their sockets t. H7969
15 their pillars t, and their sockets three. H7969
15 their pillars three, and their sockets t. H7969
26 thousand and t thousand and five H7969
Lev 12: 4 her purifying t and thirty days; H7969+H3117
14:10 blemish, and t tenth deals of fine flour H7969
19:23 as uncircumcised: t years shall it be as H7969
25:21 and it shall bring forth fruit for t years. H7969
27: 6 estimation *shall be* t shekels of silver. H7969
Nu 1:23 fifty and nine thousand and t hundred. H7969
43 fifty and t thousand and four hundred. H7969
46 t thousand and five hundred and fifty. H7969
2:13 fifty and nine thousand and t hundred. H7969
30 fifty and t thousand and four hundred. H7969
32 t thousand and five hundred and fifty. H7969
3:50 a thousand t hundred and threescore H7969
4:44 were t thousand and two hundred. H7969
10:33 of the LORD t days' journey: and the H7969
33 before them in the t days' journey, to H7969
12: 4 Come out ye t unto the tabernacle H7969
4 the congregation. And they t came out. H7969
15: 9 a meat offering of t tenth deals of flour H7969
22:28 thou hast smitten me these t times? H7969
32 thine ass these t times? behold, I went H7969
33 from me these t times: unless she had H7969
24:10 altogether blessed *them* these t times. H7969
26: 7 were forty and t thousand and seven H7969
25 and four thousand and t hundred. H7969
47 fifty and t thousand and four hundred. H7969
62 were twenty and t thousand, all males H7969
28:12 And t tenth deals of flour *for* a meat H7969
20 mingled with oil: t tenth deals shall ye H7969
28 mingled with oil, t tenth deals unto one H7969
29: 3 mingled with oil, t tenth deals for a H7969
9 flour mingled with oil, t tenth deals to a H7969
14 mingled with oil, t tenth deals unto H7969
31:36 was in number t hundred thousand H7969
43 congregation was t hundred thousand H7969
33: 8 and went t days' journey in the H7969
39 t years old when he died in mount Hor. H7969
35:14 Ye shall give t cities on this side H7969
14 side Jordan, and t cities shall ye give in H7969
Dt 4:41 Then Moses severed t cities on this side H7969
14:28 At the end of t years thou shalt bring H7969
16:16 T times in a year shall all thy males H7969
17: 6 At the mouth of two witnesses, or t H7969
19: 2 Thou shalt separate t cities for thee in H7969
3 to inherit, into t parts, that every slayer H8027
7 Thou shalt separate t cities for thee. H7969
9 shalt thou add t cities more for thee, H7969
9 cities more for thee, beside these t: H7969
15 or at the mouth of t witnesses, shall the H7969
Jos 1:11 for within t days ye shall pass over H7969
2:16 hide yourselves there t days, until the H7969
22 and abode there t days, until the H7969
3: 2 And it came to pass after t days, that H7969
7: 3 let about two or t thousand men go up H7969
4 the people about t thousand men: and H7969
9:16 And it came to pass at the end of t days H7969
15:14 And Caleb drove thence the t sons of H7969
17:11 and her towns, *even* t countries. H7969
18: 4 Give out from among you t men for H7969
21:32 and Kartan with her suburbs; t cities. H7969
Jdg 1:20 he expelled thence the t sons of Anak. H7969
7: 6 their mouth, were t hundred men: but H7969
7 Gideon, By the t hundred men that H7969
8 and retained those t hundred men: and H7969
16 And he divided the t hundred men *into* H7969
16 hundred men *into* t companies, and he H7969
20 And the t companies blew the H7969
22 And the t hundred blew the trumpets, H7969
8: 4 over, he, and the t hundred men that H7969
9:22 When Abimelech had reigned t years H7969
43 divided them into t companies, and H7969
10: 2 And he judged Israel twenty and t H7969
11:26 coasts of Arnon, t hundred years? why H7969
14:14 could not in t days expound the riddle. H7969
15: 4 And Samson went and caught t H7969

Jdg 15:11 Then t thousand men of Judah went to H7969
16:15 mocked me these t times, and hast not H7969
27 the roof about t thousand men and H7969
19: 4 he abode with him t days: so they did H7969
1Sa 1:24 up with her, with t bullocks, and one H7969
2:13 with a fleshhook of t teeth in his hand; H7969
21 and bare t sons and two daughters. H7969
9:20 And as for thine asses that were lost t H7969
10: 3 shall meet thee t men going up to God H7969
3 one carrying t kids, and another H7969
3 another carrying t loaves of bread, and H7969
11: 8 of Israel were t hundred thousand, H7969
11 put the people in t companies; and they H7969
13: 2 Saul chose him t thousand *men* of H7969
17 of the Philistines in t companies: one H7969
17:13 And the t eldest sons of Jesse went *and* H7969
13 the names of his t sons that went to the H7969
14 And David *was* the youngest: and the t H7969
20:19 And *when* thou hast stayed t days, *then* H8027
20 And I will shoot t arrows on the side H7969
41 bowed himself t times: and they kissed H7969
21: 5 us about these t days, since I came out, H8032
24: 2 Then Saul took t thousand chosen men H7969
25: 2 great, and he had t thousand sheep, H7969
26: 2 of Ziph, having t thousand chosen men H7969
30:12 *any* water, t days and three nights. H7969
12 *any* water, three days and t nights. H7969
13 left me, because t days agone I fell sick. H7969
31: 6 So Saul died, and his t sons, and his H7969
8 and his t sons fallen in mount Gilboa. H7969
2Sa 2:18 And there were t sons of Zeruiah there, H7969
31 t hundred and threescore men died. H7969
5: 5 and t years over all Israel and Judah. H7969
6:11 the Gittite t months: and the LORD H7969
13:38 went to Geshur, and was there t years. H7969
14:27 And unto Absalom there were born t H7969
18:14 thee. And he took t darts in his hand, H7969
20: 4 t days, and be thou here present. H7969
21: 1 in the days of David t years, year after H7969
16 spear *weighed* t hundred *shekels* of H7969
23: 9 *one* of the t mighty men with David, H7969
13 And t of the thirty chief went down, H7991
16 And the t mighty men brake through H7969
17 it. These things did these t mighty men. H7969
18 chief among t. And he lifted up H7969+H7992
18 his spear against t hundred, *and* slew H7969
18 slew *them,* and had the name among t. H7969
19 Was he not most honourable of t? H7969
19 howbeit he attained not unto the *first* t. H7969
22 had the name among t mighty men. H7969
23 t. And David set him over his guard. H7969
24:12 LORD, I offer thee t *things;* choose thee H7969
13 or wilt thou flee t months before thine H7969
13 or that there be t days' pestilence in thy H7969
1Ki 2:11 and t years reigned he in Jerusalem. H7969
39 And it came to pass at the end of t H7969
4:32 And he spake t thousand proverbs: and H7969
5:16 over the work, t thousand and three H7969
16 thousand and t hundred, which ruled H7969
6:36 And he built the inner court with t rows H7969
7: 4 And *there were* windows *in* t rows, and H7969
4 and light *was* against light *in* t ranks. H7969
5 and light *was* against light *in* t ranks. H7969
12 about *was* with t rows of hewed stones, H7969
25 It stood upon twelve oxen, t looking H7969
25 the north, and t looking toward the H7969
25 the west, and t looking toward the H7969
25 the south, and t looking toward the H7969
27 thereof, and t cubits the height of it. H7969
9:25 And t times in a year did Solomon offer H7969
10:17 And *he made* t hundred shields *of* H7969
17 *of* beaten gold; t pound of gold went H7969
22 of Hiram: once in t years came the H7969
11: 3 princesses, and t hundred concubines: H7969
12: 5 And he said unto them, Depart yet *for* t H7969
15: 2 T years reigned he in Jerusalem. And H7969
17:21 upon the child t times, and cried unto H7969
22: 1 And they continued t years without H7969
2Ki 2:17 they sought t days, but found him not. H7969
3:10 hath called these t kings together, to H7969
13 hath called these t kings together, to H7969
9:32 looked out to him two *or* t eunuchs. H7969
12: 6 But it was *so, that* in the t and H7969+H8141
13: 1 In the t and twentieth year of H7969+H8141
25 his father by war. T times did Joash H7969
17: 5 up to Samaria, and besieged it t years. H7969
18:10 And at the end of t years they took it: H7969
14 king of Judah t hundred talents of H7969
23:31 Jehoahaz *was* twenty and t years old H7969
2Ki 23:31 and he reigned t months in Jerusalem. H7969
24: 1 his servant t years: then he turned H7969
8 reigned in Jerusalem t months. And his H7969
25:17 height of the chapiter t cubits; and the H7969
18 priest, and the t keepers of the door: H7969
1Ch 2: 3 and Shelah: *which* t were born unto H7969
16 Abishai, and Joab, and Asahel, t. H7969
22 And Segub begat Jair, who had t and H7969
3: 4 he reigned thirty and t years. H7969
23 and Hezekiah, and Azrikam, t. H7969
7: 6 Bela, and Becher, and Jediael, t. H7969
10: 6 So Saul died, and his t sons, and all his H7969
11:11 t hundred slain *by him* at one time. H7969
12 Ahohite, who *was one* of the t mighties. H7969
15 Now t of the thirty captains went down H7969
18 And the t brake through the host of the H7969
19 it. These things did these t mightiest. H7969
20 he was chief of the t: for lifting up his H7969
20 up his spear against t hundred, he slew H7969
20 *them,* and had a name among the t. H7969
21 Of the t, he was more honourable than H7969
21 howbeit he attained not to the *first* t. H7969
24 had the name among the t mighties. H7969
25 t: and David set him over his guard. H7969
12:27 *were* t thousand and seven hundred; H7969
29 the kindred of Saul, t thousand: for H7969
39 And there they were with David t days, H7969
13:14 in his house t months. And the LORD H7969
21:10 LORD, I offer thee t *things:* choose thee H7969
12 Either t years' famine; or three months H7969
12 Either three years' famine; or t months H7969
12 *thee;* or else t days the sword of the H7969
23: 8 *was* Jehiel, and Zetham, and Joel, t. H7969
9 and Haran, t. These *were* the chief H7969
23 Mahli, and Eder, and Jeremoth, t. H7969
24:18 The t and twentieth to Delaiah, the H7969
25: 5 Heman fourteen sons and t daughters. H7969
30 The t and twentieth to Mahazioth, *he,* H7969
29: 4 *Even* t thousand talents of gold, of the H7969
27 and t *years* reigned he in Jerusalem. H7969
2Ch 2: 2 the mountain, and t thousand and six H7969
17 and t thousand and six hundred. H7969
18 the mountain, and t thousand and six H7969
4: 4 It stood upon twelve oxen, t looking H7969
4 the north, and t looking toward the H7969
4 the west, and t looking toward the H7969
4 the south, and t looking toward the H7969
5 it received and held t thousand baths. H7969
6:13 cubits broad, and t cubits high, and H7969
7:10 And on the t and twentieth day of the H7969
8:13 the solemn feasts, t times in the year, H7969
9:16 And t hundred shields *made he of* H7969
16 *he of* beaten gold: t hundred *shekels* of H7969
21 of Huram: every t years once came the H7969
10: 5 after t days. And the people departed. H7969
11:17 Solomon strong, t years: for three years H7969
17 three years: for t years they walked in H7969
13: 2 He reigned t years in Jerusalem. His H7969
14: 8 out of Judah t hundred thousand; H7969
9 thousand, and t hundred chariots; and H7969
17:14 men of valour t hundred thousand. H7969
20:25 and they were t days in gathering of H7969
25: 5 and found them t hundred thousand H7969
13 and smote t thousand of them, and H7969
26:13 And under their hand *was* an army, t H7969
29:33 hundred oxen and t thousand sheep. H7969
31:16 Beside their genealogy of males, from t H7969
35: 7 thousand, and t thousand bullocks: H7969
8 *small cattle,* and t hundred oxen. H7969
36: 2 Jehoahaz *was* twenty and t years old H7969
2 and he reigned t months in Jerusalem. H7969
9 and he reigned t months and ten days H7969
Ezr 2: 4 The children of Shephatiah, t hundred H7969
11 of Bebai, six hundred twenty and t. H7969
17 The children of Bezai, t hundred H7969
17 of Bezai, three hundred twenty and t. H7969
19 of Hashum, two hundred twenty and t. H7969
21 Beth-lehem, an hundred twenty and t. H7969
25 seven hundred and forty and t. H7969
28 and Ai, two hundred twenty and t. H7969
32 The children of Harim, t hundred and H7969
34 The children of Jericho, t hundred forty H7969
35 The children of Senaah, t thousand H7969
36 of Jeshua, nine hundred seventy and t. H7969
58 *were* t hundred ninety and two. H7969
64 thousand t hundred *and* threescore, H7969
65 seven thousand t hundred thirty and H7969
6: 4 *With* t rows of great stones, and a row H8532
8: 5 and with him t hundred males. H7969
Ezr 8:15 abode we in tents t days: and I viewed H7969
32 to Jerusalem, and abode there t days. H7969
10: 8 not come within t days, according to H7969
9 Jerusalem within t days. It *was* the H7969
Neh 2:11 So I came to Jerusalem, and was there t H7969
7: 9 The children of Shephatiah, t hundred H7969
17 The children of Azgad, two thousand t H7969
22 The children of Hashum, t hundred H7969
23 The children of Bezai, t hundred H7969
29 and Beeroth, seven hundred forty and t. H7969
32 and Ai, an hundred twenty and t. H7969
35 The children of Harim, t hundred and H7969
36 The children of Jericho, t hundred forty H7969
38 The children of Senaah, t thousand H7969
39 of Jeshua, nine hundred seventy and t. H7969
60 *were* t hundred ninety and two. H7969
66 thousand t hundred and threescore, H7969
67 seven thousand t hundred thirty and H7969
Est 4:16 eat nor drink t days, night or day: I H7969
8: 9 Sivan, on the t and twentieth *day* H7969
9:15 Adar, and slew t hundred men at H7969
Job 1: 2 unto him seven sons and t daughters. H7969
3 sheep, and t thousand camels, and H7969
4 t sisters to eat and to drink with them. H7969
17 made out t bands, and fell upon H7969
2:11 Now when Job's t friends heard of all H7969
32: 1 So these t men ceased to answer Job, H7969
3 Also against his t friends was his wrath H7969
5 t men, then his wrath was kindled. H7969
42:13 He had also seven sons and t H7969
Prv 30:15 give. There are t *things that* are never H7969
18 There be t *things which* are too H7969
21 For t *things* the earth is disquieted, and H7969
29 There be t *things* which go well, yea, H7969
Isa 15: 5 Zoar, an heifer of t years old: for by the H7992
16:14 saying, Within t years, as the years of H7969
17: 6 olive tree, two *or* t berries in the top of H7969
20: 3 and barefoot t years *for* a sign and H7969
Jer 25: 3 day, that *is* the t and twentieth year, H7969
36:23 Jehudi had read t or four leaves, he cut H7969
48:34 *as* an heifer of t years old: for the H7992
52:24 priest, and the t keepers of the door: H7969
28 t thousand Jews and three and twenty: H7969
28 three thousand Jews and t and twenty: H7969
30 In the t and twentieth year of H7969
Ezk 4: 5 of the days, t hundred and ninety H7969
9 lie upon thy side, t hundred and ninety H7969
14:14 Though these t men, Noah, Daniel, and H7969
16 *Though* these t men *were* in it, *as* I live, H7969
18 Though these t men *were* in it, *as* I live, H7969
40:10 eastward *were* t on this side, and three H7969
10 on this side, and t on that side; they H7969
10 three on that side; they t *were* of one H7969
21 And the little chambers thereof *were* t H7969
21 on this side and t on that side; and the H7969
48 of the gate *was* t cubits on this side, H7969
48 on this side, and t cubits on that side. H7969
41: 6 And the side chambers *were* t, one over H7969
16 about on their t stories, over against H7969
22 The altar of wood *was* t cubits high, H7969
42: 3 *was* gallery against gallery in t *stories.* H7992
6 For they *were* in t *stories,* but had not H8027
48:31 the tribes of Israel: t gates northward; H7969
32 five hundred: and t gates; and one gate H7969
33 measures: and t gates; one gate of H7969
34 *with* their t gates; one gate of Gad, H7969
Dan 1: 5 so nourishing them t years, that at the H7969
3:23 And these t men, Shadrach, Meshach, H8532
24 Did not we cast t men bound into the H8532
6: 2 And over these t presidents; of whom H8532
10 upon his knees t times a day, and H8532
13 but maketh his petition t times a day. H8532
7: 5 side, and *it had* t ribs in the mouth of H8532
8 whom there were t of the first horns H8532
20 up, and before whom t fell; even *of* that H8532
24 the first, and he shall subdue t kings. H8532
8:14 two thousand and t hundred days; H7969
10: 2 In those days I Daniel was mourning t H7969
3 at all, till t whole weeks were fulfilled. H7969
11: 2 shall stand up yet t kings in Persia; and H7969
12:12 t hundred and five and thirty days. H7969
Am 1: 3 Thus saith the LORD; For t H7969
6 Thus saith the LORD; For t H7969
9 Thus saith the LORD; For t H7969
11 Thus saith the LORD; For t H7969
13 Thus saith the LORD; For t H7969
2: 1 Thus saith the LORD; For t H7969
4 Thus saith the LORD; For t H7969
6 Thus saith the LORD; For t H7969

Am 4: 4 morning, *and* your tithes after **t** years: H7969
7 *there were* yet **t** months to the harvest: H7969
8 So two *or* **t** cities wandered unto one H7969
Jna 1:17 belly of the fish **t** days and three nights. H7969
17 belly of the fish three days and **t** nights. H7969
3: 3 exceeding great city of **t** days' journey. H7969
Zec 11: 8 **T** shepherds also I cut off in one H7969
Mt 12:40 For as Jonas was **t** days and three *G5140*
40 For as Jonas was three days and **t** *G5140*
40 the Son of man be **t** days and three *G5140*
40 and **t** nights in the heart of the earth. *G5140*
13:33 took, and hid in **t** measures of meal, till *G5140*
15:32 with me now **t** days, and have nothing *G5140*
17: 4 let us make here **t** tabernacles; one for *G5140*
18:16 mouth of two or **t** witnesses every word *G5140*
20 For where two or **t** are gathered *G5140*
26:61 temple of God, and to build it in **t** days. *G5140*
27:40 and buildest *it* in **t** days, save thyself. If *G5140*
63 yet alive, After **t** days I will rise again. *G5140*
Mk 8: 2 me **t** days, and have nothing to eat: *G5140*
31 be killed, and after **t** days rise again. *G5140*
9: 5 and let us make **t** tabernacles; one for *G5140*
14: 5 sold for more than **t** hundred pence, *G5145*
58 hands, and within **t** days I will build *G5140*
15:29 the temple, and buildest *it* in **t** days, *G5140*
Lk 1:56 And Mary abode with her about **t** *G5140*
2:46 And it came to pass, that after **t** days *G5140*
4:25 was shut up **t** years and six months, *G5140*
9:33 and let us make **t** tabernacles; one for *G5140*
10:36 Which now of these **t**, thinkest thou, *G5140*
11: 5 say unto him, Friend, lend me **t** loaves; *G5140*
12:52 **t** against two, and two against three. *G5140*
52 three against two, and two against **t**. *G5140*
13: 7 Behold, these **t** years I come seeking *G5140*
21 took and hid in **t** measures of meal, till *G5140*
Jn 2: 6 containing two or **t** firkins apiece. *G5140*
19 temple, and in **t** days I will raise it up. *G5140*
20 and wilt thou rear it up in **t** days? *G5140*
12: 5 Why was not this ointment sold for **t** *G5145*
21:11 and fifty and **t**: and for all there were *G5140*
Act 2:41 *unto them* about **t** thousand souls. *G5153*
5: 7 And it was about the space of **t** hours *G5140*
7:20 up in his father's house **t** months: *G5140*
9: 9 And he was **t** days without sight, and *G5140*
10:19 said unto him, Behold, **t** men seek thee. *G5140*
11:10 And this was done **t** times: and all were *G511*
11 And, behold, immediately there were **t** *G5140*
17: 2 went in unto them, and **t** sabbath days *G5140*
19: 8 for the space of **t** months, disputing *G5140*
20: 3 And *there* abode **t** months. And when *G5140*
31 by the space of **t** years I ceased not to *G5148*
25: 1 the province, after **t** days he ascended *G5140*
28: 7 us, and lodged us **t** days courteously. *G5140*
11 And after **t** months we departed in a *G5140*
12 at Syracuse, we tarried *there* **t** days. *G5140*
15 forum, and The **t** taverns: whom when *G5140*
17 And it came to pass, that after **t** days *G5140*
1Co 10: 8 fell in one day **t** and twenty thousand. *G5140*
13:13 **t**; but the greatest of these *is* charity. *G5140*
14:27 or at the most *by* **t**, and *that* by course; *G5140*
29 Let the prophets speak two or **t**, and let *G5140*
2Co 13: 1 mouth of two or **t** witnesses shall every *G5140*
Gal 1:18 Then after **t** years I went up to *G5140*
1Ti 5:19 but before two or **t** witnesses. *G5140*
Heb 10:28 mercy under two or **t** witnesses: *G5140*
11:23 he was born, was hid **t** months of his *G5150*
Jas 5:17 by the space of **t** years and six months. *G5140*
1Jn 5: 7 For there are **t** that bear record in *G5140*
7 the Holy Ghost: and these **t** are one. *G5140*
8 And there are **t** that bear witness in *G5140*
8 and the blood: and these **t** agree in one. *G5140*
Rev 6: 6 for a penny, and **t** measures of barley *G5140*
8:13 of the **t** angels, which are yet to sound! *G5140*
9:18 By these **t** was the third part of men *G5140*
11: 9 their dead bodies **t** days and an half, *G5140*
11 And after **t** days and an half the Spirit *G5140*
16:13 And I saw **t** unclean spirits like frogs *G5140*
19 And the great city was divided into **t** *G5140*
21:13 On the east **t** gates; on the north three *G5140*
13 On the east three gates; on the north **t** *G5140*
13 **t** gates; and on the west three gates. *G5140*
13 three gates; and on the west **t** gates. *G5140*

THREEFOLD

Ecc 4:12 him; and a **t** cord is not quickly broken. H8027

THREE-HUNDRED

See THREE and HUNDRED.

THREESCORE

Gen 25: 7 lived, an hundred **t** and fifteen years. H8141
26 *was* **t** years old when she bare them. H8346
46:26 sons' wives, all the souls *were* **t** and six; H8346
27 which came into Egypt, *were* **t** and ten. H7657
50: 3 mourned for him **t** and ten days. H7657
Ex 15:27 wells of water, and **t** and ten palm H7657
38:25 hundred and **t** and fifteen shekels, H7657
Lev 12: 5 of her purifying **t** and six days. H8346+H3117
Nu 1:27 of Judah, *were* **t** and fourteen thousand H7657
39 tribe of Dan, *were* **t** and two thousand H8346
2: 4 of them, *were* **t** and fourteen thousand H7657
26 of them, *were* **t** and two thousand and H8346
3:43 two hundred and **t** and thirteen. H7657
46 two hundred and **t** and thirteen of the H7657
50 three hundred and **t** and five *shekels*, H8346
26:22 of them, **t** and sixteen thousand H7657
25 of them, **t** and four thousand and H8346
27 of them, **t** thousand and five hundred. H8346
43 **t** and four thousand and four hundred. H8346
31:33 And **t** and twelve thousand beeves, H7657
34 And **t** and one thousand asses, H8346
37 was six hundred and **t** and fifteen. H7657
38 the LORD'S tribute *was* **t** and twelve. H7657
39 the LORD'S tribute *was* **t** and one. H8346
33: 9 of water, and **t** and ten palm trees; H7657
Dt 3: 4 not from them, **t** cities, all the region H8346
10:22 into Egypt with **t** and ten persons; and H7657
Jos 13:30 of Jair, which *are* in Bashan, **t** cities: H8346
Jdg 1: 7 And Adoni-bezek said, **T** and ten H7657
8:14 thereof, *even* **t** and seventeen men. H7657
30 And Gideon had **t** and ten sons of his H7657
9: 2 *which are* **t** and ten persons, reign H7657
4 And they gave him **t** and ten *pieces* of H7657
5 of Jerubbaal, *being* **t** and ten persons, H7657
18 slain his sons, **t** and ten persons, upon H7657
24 That the cruelty *done* to the **t** and ten H7657
12:14 that rode on **t** and ten ass colts: and H7657
1Sa 6:19 fifty thousand and **t** and ten men: and H376
2Sa 2:31 *so that* three hundred and **t** men died. H8346
1Ki 4:13 *is* in Bashan, **t** great cities with walls H8346
22 of fine flour, and **t** measures of meal, H8346
5:15 And Solomon had **t** and ten thousand H7657
6: 2 the length thereof *was* **t** cubits, and the H8346
10:14 six hundred **t** and six talents of gold, H8346
2Ki 25:19 of the land, and **t** men of the people of H8346
1Ch 2:21 **t** years old; and she bare him Segub. H8346
23 thereof, *even* **t** cities. All these *belonged* H8346
5:18 hundred and **t**, that went out to the war. H8346
9:13 hundred and **t**; very able men for the H8346
16:38 And Obed-edom with their brethren, **t** H8346
21: 5 *was* four hundred **t** and ten thousand H7657
26: 8 service, *were* **t** and two of Obed-edom. H8346
2Ch 2: 2 And Solomon told out **t** and ten H7657
18 And he set **t** and ten thousand of them H7657
3: 3 **t** cubits, and the breadth twenty cubits. H8346
9:13 hundred and **t** and six talents of gold; H8346
11:21 wives, and **t** concubines; and begat H8346
21 and eight sons, and **t** daughters.) H8346
12: 3 With twelve hundred chariots, and **t** H8346
29:32 brought, was **t** and ten bullocks, an H7657
36:21 kept sabbath, to fulfil **t** and ten years. H7657
Ezr 2: 9 of Zaccai, seven hundred and **t**. H8346
64 and two thousand three hundred *and* **t**, H8346
69 of the work **t** and one thousand drams H7239
6: 3 laid; the height thereof **t** cubits, *and* the H8361
3 cubits, *and* the breadth thereof **t** cubits; H8361
8:10 and with him an hundred and **t** males. H8346
13 and Shemaiah, and with them **t** males. H8346
Neh 7:14 of Zaccai, seven hundred and **t**. H8346
18 of Adonikam, six hundred **t** and seven. H8346
19 The children of Bigvai, two thousand **t** H8346
66 and two thousand three hundred and **t**, H8346
72 and **t** and seven priests' garments. H8346
11: 6 four hundred **t** and eight valiant men. H8346
Ps 90:10 The days of our years *are* **t** years and H7657
Song 3: 7 Behold his bed, which *is* Solomon's; **t** H8346
6: 8 There are **t** queens, and fourscore H8346
Isa 7: 8 Rezin; and within **t** and five years shall H8346
Jer 52:25 of the land; and **t** men of the people of H8346
Ezk 40:14 He made also posts of **t** cubits, even H8346
Dan 3: 1 whose height *was* **t** cubits, *and* the H8361
5:31 *being* about **t** and two years old. H8361
9:25 seven weeks, and **t** and two weeks: the H8346
26 And after **t** and two weeks shall H8346
Zec 1:12 had indignation these **t** and ten years? H7657
Lk 24:13 was from Jerusalem *about* **t** furlongs. *G1835*
Act 7:14 and all his kindred, **t** and fifteen souls. *G1440*
23:23 and horsemen **t** and ten, and spearmen *G1440*
27:37 ship two hundred **t** and sixteen souls. *G1440*
1Ti 5: 9 the number under **t** years old, having *G1835*
Rev 11: 3 *and* **t** days, clothed in sackcloth. *G1835*
12: 6 a thousand two hundred *and* **t** days. *G1835*
13:18 his number *is* Six hundred **t** *and* six. *G1835*

THREESCORE-THOUSAND

See THREESCORE and THOUSAND.

THREE-THOUSAND

See THREE and THOUSAND.

THRESH

Isa 41:15 teeth: thou shalt **t** the mountains, and H1758
Jer 51:33 *it is* time to **t** her: yet a little while, H1869
Mic 4:13 Arise and **t**, O daughter of Zion: for I H1758
Hab 3:12 thou didst **t** the heathen in anger. H1758

THRESHED

Jdg 6:11 and his son Gideon **t** wheat by the H2251
Isa 28:27 For the fitches are not **t** with a H1758
Am 1: 3 because they have **t** Gilead with H1758

THRESHETH

1Co 9:10 **t** in hope should be partaker of his hope. *G248*

THRESHING

Lev 26: 5 And your **t** shall reach unto the H1786
2Sa 24:22 sacrifice, and **t** instruments and *other* H4173
2Ki 13: 7 and had made them like the dust by **t**. H1758
1Ch 21:20 themselves. Now Ornan was **t** wheat. H1758
23 offerings, and the **t** instruments for H4173
Isa 21:10 O my **t**, and the corn of my floor: that H4098
28:27 For the fitches are not threshed with a **t** H2742
28 he will not ever be **t** it, nor break *it with* H1758
41:15 Behold, I will make thee a new sharp **t** H4173
Am 1: 3 Gilead with **t** instruments of iron: H2742

THRESHINGFLOOR

Gen 50:10 And they came to the **t** of Atad, which H1637
Nu 15:20 offering of the **t**, so shall ye heave it. H1637
18:27 **t**, and as the fulness of the winepress. H1637
30 **t**, and as the increase of the winepress. H1637
Ru 3: 2 he winnoweth barley to night in the **t**. H1637
2Sa 6: 6 And when they came to Nachon's **t**, H1637
24:18 LORD in the **t** of Araunah the Jebusite. H1637
21 said, To buy the **t** of thee, to build an H1637
24 **t** and the oxen for fifty shekels of silver. H1637
1Ch 13: 9 And when they came unto the **t** of H1637
21:15 stood by the **t** of Ornan the Jebusite. H1637
18 LORD in the **t** of Ornan the Jebusite. H1637
21 went out of the **t**, and bowed himself H1637
22 the place of *this* **t**, that I may build an H1637
28 him in the **t** of Ornan the Jebusite, H1637
2Ch 3: 1 prepared in the **t** of Ornan the Jebusite. H1637
Jer 51:33 of Babylon *is* like a **t**, *it is* time to thresh H1637

THRESHINGFLOORS

1Sa 23: 1 fight against Keilah, and they rob the **t**. H1637
Dan 2:35 of the summer **t**; and the wind carried H147

THRESHINGPLACE

2Sa 24:16 was by the **t** of Araunah the Jebusite. H1637

THRESHOLD

Jdg 19:27 house, and her hands *were* upon the **t**. H5592
1Sa 5: 4 cut off upon the **t**; only *the stump of* H4670
5 the **t** of Dagon in Ashdod unto this day. H4670
1Ki 14:17 to the **t** of the door, the child died; H5592
Ezk 9: 3 he was, to the **t** of the house. And he H4670
10: 4 *and stood* over the **t** of the house; and H4670
18 from off the **t** of the house, and stood H4670
40: 6 and measured the **t** of the gate, *which* H5592
6 and the other **t** *of the gate, which was* H5592
7 five cubits; and the **t** of the gate by the H5592
43: 8 In their setting of their **t** by my H5592
46: 2 worship at the **t** of the gate: then he H4670
47: 1 from under the **t** of the house eastward: H4670
Zep 1: 9 those that leap on the **t**, which fill their H4670

THRESHOLDS

Neh 12:25 keeping the ward at the **t** of the gates. H624
Ezk 43: 8 threshold by my **t**, and their post by my H5592
Zep 2:14 **t**: for he shall uncover the cedar work. H5592

THREW

2Sa 16:13 and **t** stones at him, and cast dust. H5619
2Ki 9:33 And he said, Throw her down. So they **t** H8058
2Ch 31: 1 the groves, and **t** down the high places H5422
Mk 12:42 **t** in two mites, which make a farthing. *G906*
Lk 9:42 And as he was yet a coming, the devil **t** *G4486*

Act 22:23 off *their* clothes, and t dust into the air, G906

THREWEST
Neh 9:11 persecutors thou t into the deeps, as a H7993

THRICE
Ex 34:23 T in the year shall all your men H6471
24 before the LORD thy God t in the year. H6471
2Ki 13:18 And he smote t, and stayed. H7969+H6471
19 thou shalt smite Syria *but* t. H7969+H6471
Mt 26:34 the cock crow, thou shalt deny me t. G5151
75 t. And he went out, and wept bitterly. G5151
Mk 14:30 cock crow twice, thou shalt deny me t. G5151
72 shalt deny me t. And when he thought G5151
Lk 22:34 shalt t deny that thou knowest me. G5151
61 the cock crow, thou shalt deny me t. G5151
Jn 13:38 not crow, till thou hast denied me t. G5151
Act 10:16 This was done t: and the vessel was G5151
2Co 11:25 T was I beaten with rods, once was I G5151
25 rods, once was I stoned, t I suffered G5151
12: 8 For this thing I besought the Lord t, G5151

THROAT
Ps 5: 9 very wickedness; their t *is* an open H1627
69: 3 I am weary of my crying: my t is dried: H1627
115: 7 not: neither speak they through their t. H1627
Prv 23: 2 And put a knife to thy t, if thou *be* a H3930
Jer 2:25 unshod, and thy t from thirst: but thou H1627
Mt 18:28 the t, saying, Pay me that thou owest. G4155
Ro 3:13 Their t *is* an open sepulchre; with their G2995

THRONE
Gen 41:40 only in the t will I be greater than thou. H3678
Ex 11: 5 that sitteth upon his t, even unto the H3678
12:29 that sat on his t unto the firstborn of H3678
Dt 17:18 he sitteth upon the t of his kingdom, H3678
1Sa 2: 8 make them inherit the t of glory: for the H3678
2Sa 3:10 and to set up the t of David over Israel H3678
7:13 stablish the t of his kingdom for ever. H3678
16 thee: thy t shall be established for ever. H3678
14: 9 and the king and his t *be* guiltless. H3678
1Ki 1:13 my t? why then doth Adonijah reign? H3678
17 after me, and he shall sit upon my t. H3678
20 on the t of my lord the king after him. H3678
24 after me, and he shall sit upon my t? H3678
27 on the t of my lord the king after him? H3678
30 shall sit upon my t in my stead; even so H3678
35 and sit upon my t; for he shall be king H3678
37 and make his t greater than the throne H3678
37 than the t of my lord king David. H3678
46 And also Solomon sitteth on the t of the H3678
47 and make his t greater than thy throne. H3678
47 greater than thy t. And the king bowed H3678
48 my t this day, mine eyes even seeing *it*. H3678
2: 4 thee (said he) a man on the t of Israel. H3678
12 Then sat Solomon upon the t of David H3678
19 sat down on his t, and caused a seat to H3678
24 and set me on the t of David my father, H3678
33 and upon his t, shall there be peace H3678
45 *be* blessed, and the t of David shall be H3678
3: 6 him a son to sit on his t, as *it is* this day. H3678
5: 5 I will set upon thy t in thy room, he H3678
7: 7 Then he made a porch for the t where H3678
8:20 and sit on the t of Israel, as the LORD H3678
25 sight to sit on the t of Israel; so that thy H3678
9: 5 Then I will establish the t of thy H3678
5 not fail thee a man upon the t of Israel. H3678
10: 9 to set thee on the t of Israel: because H3678
18 Moreover the king made a great t of H3678
19 The t had six steps, and the top of the H3678
19 and the top of the t *was* round behind: H3678
16:11 as he sat on his t, *that* he slew all the H3678
22:10 sat each on his t, having put on their H3678
19 LORD sitting on his t, and all the host of H3678
2Ki 10: 3 t, and fight for your master's house. H3678
30 *generation* shall sit on the t of Israel. H3678
11:19 house. And he sat on the t of the kings. H3678
13:13 sat upon his t: and Joash was buried H3678
15:12 sons shall sit on the t of Israel unto the H3678
25:28 to him, and set his t above the throne H3678
28 his throne above the t of the kings that H3678
1Ch 17:12 house, and I will stablish his t for ever. H3678
14 his t shall be established for evermore. H3678
22:10 t of his kingdom over Israel for ever. H3678
28: 5 son to sit upon the t of the kingdom of H3678
29:23 Then Solomon sat on the t of the LORD H3678
2Ch 6:10 and am set on the t of Israel, as the H3678
16 to sit upon the t of Israel; yet so that H3678
7:18 Then will I stablish the t of thy H3678
2Ch 9: 8 to set thee on his t, *to be* king for the H3678
17 Moreover the king made a great t of H3678
18 And *there were* six steps to the t, with a H3678
18 fastened to the t, and stays on each side H3678
18: 9 of them on his t, clothed in *their* robes, H3678
18 sitting upon his t, and all the host of H3678
23:20 set the king upon the t of the kingdom. H3678
Neh 3: 7 t of the governor on this side the river. H3678
Est 1: 2 sat on the t of his kingdom, which H3678
5: 1 sat upon his royal t in the royal house, H3678
Job 26: 9 He holdeth back the face of his t, *and* H3678
36: 7 *are they* on the t; yea, he doth establish H3678
Ps 9: 4 cause; thou satest in the t judging right. H3678
7 he hath prepared his t for judgment. H3678
11: 4 the LORD'S t *is* in heaven: his eyes H3678
45: 6 Thy t, O God, *is* for ever and ever: the H3678
47: 8 God sitteth upon the t of his holiness. H3678
89: 4 build up thy t to all generations. Selah. H3678
14 the habitation of thy t: mercy and truth H3678
29 ever, and his t as the days of heaven. H3678
36 His seed shall endure for ever, and his t H3678
44 and cast his t down to the ground. H3678
93: 2 Thy t *is* established of old: thou *art* H3678
94:20 Shall the t of iniquity have fellowship H3678
97: 2 judgment *are* the habitation of his t. H3678
103:19 The LORD hath prepared his t in the H3678
132:11 fruit of thy body will I set upon thy t. H3678
12 shall also sit upon thy t for evermore. H3678
Prv 16:12 the t is established by righteousness. H3678
20: 8 A king that sitteth in the t of judgment H3678
28 king: and his t is upholden by mercy. H3678
25: 5 t shall be established in righteousness. H3678
29:14 poor, his t shall be established for ever. H3678
Isa 6: 1 sitting upon a t, high and lifted up, and H3678
9: 7 no end, upon the t of David, and upon H3678
14:13 I will exalt my t above the stars of God: H3678
16: 5 And in mercy shall the t be established: H3678
22:23 be for a glorious t to his father's house. H3678
47: 1 ground: *there is* no t, O daughter of the H3678
66: 1 The heaven *is* my t, and the earth *is* my H3678
Jer 1:15 set every one his t at the entering of the H3678
3:17 call Jerusalem the t of the LORD; and H3678
13:13 sit upon David's t, and the priests, and H3678
14:21 do not disgrace the t of thy glory: H3678
17:12 A glorious high t from the beginning *is* H3678
25 sitting upon the t of David, riding in H3678
22: 2 sittest upon the t of David, thou, and H3678
4 sitting upon the t of David, riding in H3678
30 sitting upon the t of David, and ruling H3678
29:16 sitteth upon the t of David, and of all H3678
33:17 to sit upon the t of the house of Israel; H3678
21 to reign upon his t; and with the Levites H3678
36:30 to sit upon the t of David: and his dead H3678
43:10 and will set his t upon these stones that H3678
49:38 And I will set my t in Elam, and will H3678
52:32 him, and set his t above the throne of H3678
32 his throne above the t of the kings that H3678
Lam 5:19 thy t from generation to generation. H3678
Ezk 1:26 the likeness of a t, as the appearance of H3678
26 the likeness of the t *was* the likeness as H3678
10: 1 as the appearance of the likeness of a t. H3678
43: 7 the place of my t, and the place of the H3678
Dan 5:20 t, and they took his glory from him: H3764
7: 9 the pure wool: his t *was like* the fiery H3764
Jna 3: 6 he arose from his t, and he laid his robe H3678
Hag 2:22 And I will overthrow the t of kingdoms, H3678
Zec 6:13 sit and rule upon his t; and he shall be a H3678
13 a priest upon his t: and the counsel of H3678
Mt 5:34 all; neither by heaven; for it is God's t: G2362
19:28 shall sit in the t of his glory, ye also G2362
23:22 sweareth by the t of God, and by him G2362
25:31 then shall he sit upon the t of his glory: G2362
Lk 1:32 give unto him the t of his father David: G2362
Act 2:30 he would raise up Christ to sit on his t; G2362
7:49 Heaven *is* my t, and earth *is* my G2362
12:21 his t, and made an oration unto them. G968
Heb 1: 8 But unto the Son *he saith*, Thy t, O God, G2362
4:16 Let us therefore come boldly unto the t G2362
8: 1 of the t of the Majesty in the heavens; G2362
12: 2 down at the right hand of the t of God. G2362
Rev 1: 4 the seven Spirits which are before his t; G2362
3:21 to sit with me in my t, even as I also G2362
21 am set down with my Father in his t. G2362
4: 2 and, behold, a t was set in heaven, and G2362
2 was set in heaven, and *one* sat on the t. G2362
3 the t, in sight like unto an emerald. G2362
4 And round about the t *were* four and G2362
5 And out of the t proceeded lightnings G2362
5 the t, which are the seven Spirits of God. G2362
Rev 4: 6 And before the t *there was* a sea of G2362
6 in the midst of the t, and round about G2362
6 round about the t, *were* four beasts full G2362
9 on the t, who liveth for ever and ever, G2362
10 that sat on the t, and worship him that G2362
10 cast their crowns before the t, saying, G2362
5: 1 that sat on the t a book written within G2362
6 lo, in the midst of the t and of the four G2362
7 right hand of him that sat upon the t. G2362
11 round about the t and the beasts and G2362
13 t, and unto the Lamb for ever and ever. G2362
6:16 the t, and from the wrath of the Lamb: G2362
7: 9 stood before the t, and before the Lamb, G2362
10 sitteth upon the t, and unto the Lamb. G2362
11 round about the t, and *about* the elders G2362
11 t on their faces, and worshipped God, G2362
15 Therefore are they before the t of God, G2362
15 on the t shall dwell among them. G2362
17 is in the midst of the t shall feed them, G2362
8: 3 the golden altar which was before the t. G2362
12: 5 was caught up unto God, and *to* his t. G2362
14: 3 song before the t, and before the four G2362
5 are without fault before the t of God. G2362
16:17 of heaven, from the t, saying, It is done. G2362
19: 4 sat on the t, saying, Amen; Alleluia. G2362
5 And a voice came out of the t, saying, G2362
20:11 And I saw a great white t, and him that G2362
21: 5 And he that sat upon the t said, G2362
22: 1 out of the t of God and of the Lamb. G2362
3 curse: but the t of God and of the Lamb G2362

THRONES
Ps 122: 5 For there are set t of judgment, the H3678
5 judgment, the t of the house of David. H3678
Isa 14: 9 from their t all the kings of the nations. H3678
Ezk 26:16 down from their t, and lay away their H3678
Dan 7: 9 I beheld till the t were cast down, and H3764
Mt 19:28 t, judging the twelve tribes of Israel. G2362
Lk 22:30 on t judging the twelve tribes of Israel. G2362
Col 1:16 whether *they be* t, or dominions, or G2362
Rev 20: 4 And I saw t, and they sat upon them, G2362

THRONG
Mk 3: 9 of the multitude, lest they should t him. G2346
Lk 8:45 the multitude t thee and press *thee*, G4912

THRONGED
Mk 5:24 much people followed him, and t him. G4918
Lk 8:42 dying. But as he went the people t him. G4846

THRONGING
Mk 5:31 the multitude t thee, and sayest thou, G4918

THROUGH
Gen 6:13 is filled with violence t them; and, H6440
12: 6 And Abram passed t the land unto the H5674
13:17 Arise, walk t the land in the length of it
30:32 I will pass t all thy flock to day, H5674
41:36 that the land perish not t the famine.
Ex 10:15 herbs of the field, t all the land of Egypt.
12:12 For I will pass t the land of Egypt this
23 For the LORD will pass t to smite the H5674
13:17 God led them not *t* the way of the land of
18 But God led the people about, *t* the way
14:16 go on dry *ground* t the midst of the sea.
24 of the Egyptians t the pillar of fire and
19:13 be stoned, or shot t; whether *it be* beast H3384
21 lest they break t unto the LORD to H2040
24 the people break t to come up unto the H2040
21: 6 shall bore his ear t with an aul; and he
36:33 And he made the middle bar to shoot t H8432
Lev 4: 2 If a soul shall sin t ignorance against
13 of Israel sin t ignorance, and the thing
22 done *somewhat* t ignorance *against* any
27 people sin t ignorance, while he doeth
5:15 If a soul commit a trespass, and sin t
18:21 of thy seed pass t *the fire* to Molech, H5674
26: 6 neither shall the sword go t your land.
Nu 13:32 saying, The land, t which we have gone
14: 7 t to search it, *is* an exceeding good land.
15:27 And if any soul sin t ignorance, then he
29 him that sinneth t ignorance, *both for*
20:17 Let us pass, I pray thee, t thy country: we
17 we will not pass t the fields, or through
17 the fields, or t the vineyards, neither
19 *doing* any thing *else*, go t on my feet. H5674
20 And he said, Thou shalt not go t. And H5674
21 to give Israel passage t his border:
21:22 Let me pass t thy land: we will not turn

Nu 21:23 Israel to pass **t** his border: but Sihon
24: 8 and pierce *them* **t** with his arrows.
25: 8 both of them **t**, the man of Israel, and H1856
8 and the woman **t** her belly. So the plague H413
31:16 the children of Israel, **t** the counsel of
23 ye shall make *it* go **t** the fire, and it shall
23 not the fire ye shall make go **t** the water.
33: 8 and passed **t** the midst of the sea H5674
Dt 1:19 from Horeb, we went **t** all that great and
2: 4 Ye *are* to pass **t** the coast of your H5674
7 thy walking **t** this great wilderness:
8 dwelt in Seir, **t** the way of the plain
18 Thou art to pass over **t** Ar, the coast of
27 Let me pass **t** thy land: I will go along by
28 I may drink: only I will pass **t** on my feet;
5:15 thee out thence **t** a mighty hand and by
8:15 Who led thee **t** that great and terrible
9:26 hast redeemed **t** thy greatness, which
15:17 aul, and thrust *it* **t** his ear unto the door,
18:10 daughter to pass **t** the fire, *or* that useth
29:16 came **t** the nations which ye passed by; H7130
31:29 him to anger **t** the work of your hands.
32:47 it *is* your life: and **t** this thing ye shall
33:11 of his hands: smite **t** the loins of them
Jos 1:11 Pass **t** the host, and command the H7130
2:15 Then she let them down by a cord **t** the H1157
3: 2 days, that the officers went **t** the host; H7130
18: 4 they shall rise, and go **t** the land, and
8 Go and walk **t** the land, and describe
9 And the men went and passed **t** the H5674
12 north side, and went up **t** the mountains
24:17 all the people **t** whom we passed: H7130
Jdg 2:22 That **t** them I may prove Israel, whether
3:23 Then Ehud went forth **t** the porch, and
5: 6 and the travellers walked **t** byways.
26 had pierced and stricken **t** his temples. H2498
28 a window, and cried **t** the lattice, Why is
9:54 young man thrust him **t**, and he died. H1856
11:16 Egypt, and walked **t** the wilderness unto
17 I pray thee, pass **t** thy land: but the king
18 Then they went along **t** the wilderness,
19 we pray thee, **t** thy land into my place.
20 But Sihon trusted not Israel to pass **t** his
20:12 And the tribes of Israel sent men **t** all the
1Sa 9: 4 And he passed **t** mount Ephraim, and
4 and passed **t** the land of Shalisha,
4 then they passed **t** the land of Shalim,
4 *were* not: and he passed **t** the land of the
19:12 So Michal let David down **t** a window:
31: 4 and thrust me **t** therewith; lest these H1856
4 and thrust me **t**, and abuse me. But his H1856
2Sa 2:29 all that night **t** the plain, and passed
29 Jordan, and went **t** all Bithron, and they
4: 7 and gat them away **t** the plain all night. H1870
6:16 daughter looked **t** a window, and saw
12:31 made them pass **t** the brickkiln: and
18:14 and thrust them **t** the heart of Absalom,
20:14 And he went **t** all the tribes of Israel unto
22:13 **T** the brightness before him were coals
30 For by thee I have run **t** a troop: by my
23:16 And the three mighty men brake **t** the H1234
24: 2 *was* with him, Go now **t** all the tribes of
8 So when they had gone **t** all the land,
2Ki 1: 2 And Ahaziah fell down **t** a lattice in his
3: 8 The way **t** the wilderness of Edom.
26 swords, to break **t** *even* unto the king of H1234
10:21 And Jehu sent **t** all Israel: and all the
16: 3 his son to pass **t** the fire, according to
17:17 daughters to pass **t** the fire, and used
21: 6 And he made his son pass **t** the fire, and
23:10 his daughter to pass **t** the fire to Molech.
24:20 For **t** the anger of the LORD it came to
1Ch 10: 4 and thrust me **t** therewith; lest these H1856
11:18 And the three brake **t** the host of the H1234
2Ch 19: 4 and he went out again **t** the people from
23:20 and they came **t** the high gate into the H8432
24: 9 And they made a proclamation **t** Judah
30:10 So the posts passed from city to city **t** the
31:18 their daughters, **t** all the congregation:
32: 4 and the brook that ran **t** the midst of the
33: 6 And he caused his children to pass **t** the
Ezr 6:14 and they prospered **t** the prophesying of
Neh 9:11 so that they went **t** the midst of the sea H5674
Est 6: 9 him on horseback **t** the street of the city,
11 him on horseback **t** the street of the city,
Job 7:14 with dreams, and terrifiest me **t** visions:
14: 9 *Yet* **t** the scent of water it will bud, and
20:24 *and* the bow of steel shall strike him **t**. H2498
22:13 know? can he judge **t** the dark cloud?

Job 24:16 In the dark they dig **t** houses, *which* H2864
26:12 understanding he smiteth **t** the proud.
29: 3 *when* by his light I walked *t* darkness;
7 When I went out to the gate **t** the city,
40:24 with his eyes: *his* nose pierceth **t** snares.
41: 2 his nose? or bore his jaw **t** with a thorn?
Ps 8: 8 passeth **t** the paths of the seas.
10: 4 The wicked, **t** the pride of his
18:29 For by thee I have run **t** a troop; and by H7323
19: 4 Their line is gone out **t** all the earth, and
21: 7 For the king trusteth in the LORD, and **t**
23: 4 Yea, though I walk **t** the valley of the
32: 3 waxed old **t** my roaring all the day long.
44: 5 **T** thee will we push down our enemies:
5 down our enemies: **t** thy name will we
60:12 **T** God we shall do valiantly: for he *it is*
66: 3 *thou in* thy works! **t** the greatness of thy
6 dry *land*: they went **t** the flood on foot:
12 our heads; we went **t** fire and through
12 went through fire and **t** water: but thou
68: 7 thou didst march **t** the wilderness; Selah:
73: 9 and their tongue walketh **t** the earth.
78:13 them to pass **t**; and he made the waters
81: 5 when he went out **t** the land of Egypt:
84: 6 *Who* passing **t** the valley of Baca make it
92: 4 For thou, LORD, hast made me glad **t**
106: 9 **t** the depths, as through the wilderness.
9 through the depths, as **t** the wilderness.
107:39 low **t** oppression, affliction, and sorrow.
108:13 **T** God we shall do valiantly: for he *it is*
109:24 My knees are weak **t** fasting; and my
110: 5 The Lord at thy right hand shall strike **t**
115: 7 not: neither speak they **t** their throat.
119:98 Thou **t** thy commandments hast made
104 **T** thy precepts I get understanding:
136:14 And made Israel to pass **t** the midst of it:
16 To him which led his people **t** the
Prv 7: 6 For at the window of my house I looked **t**
8 Passing **t** the street near her corner; and
23 Till a dart strike **t** his liver; as a bird H6398
11: 9 **t** knowledge shall the just be delivered.
18: 1 **T** desire a man, having separated
24: 3 **T** wisdom is an house builded; and by
Ecc 5: 3 For a dream cometh **t** the multitude of
10:18 decayeth; and **t** idleness of the hands
18 of the hands the house droppeth **t**. H1811
Song 2: 9 windows, shewing himself **t** the lattice.
Isa 8: 8 And he shall pass **t** Judah; he shall
21 And they shall pass **t** it, hardly bestead
9:19 **T** the wrath of the LORD of hosts is the
13:15 Every one that is found shall be thrust **t**; H1856
14:19 are slain, thrust **t** with a sword, that go H2944
16: 8 they wandered *t* the wilderness: her
21: 1 in the south pass **t**; *so* it cometh from H2498
23:10 Pass **t** thy land as a river, O daughter of H5674
27: 4 go **t** them, I would burn them together.
28: 7 But they also have erred **t** wine, and
7 through wine, and **t** strong drink are out
7 have erred **t** strong drink, they are H4480
7 are out of the way **t** strong drink; they
15 scourge shall pass **t**, it shall not come H5674
18 **t**, then ye shall be trodden down by it. H5674
30:31 For **t** the voice of the LORD shall the
34:10 none shall pass **t** it for ever and ever.
43: 2 When thou passest **t** the waters, I *will* H5674
2 *be* with thee; and **t** the rivers, they shall
2 when thou walkest **t** the fire, thou shalt H1119
48:21 And they thirsted not *when* he led them **t**
60:15 so that no man went **t** *thee*, I will make H5674
62:10 Go **t**, go through the gates; prepare ye H5674
10 Go through, go **t** the gates; prepare ye H5674
63:13 That led them **t** the deep, as an horse in
Jer 2: 6 of Egypt, that led us **t** the wilderness,
6 the wilderness, **t** a land of deserts and
6 deserts and of pits, **t** a land of drought,
6 shadow of death, **t** a land that no man
6 man passed **t**, and where no man dwelt?
3: 9 And it came to pass **t** the lightness of her
5: 1 Run ye to and fro **t** the streets of
9: 6 the midst of deceit; **t** deceit they refuse to
10 that none can pass **t** *them*; neither can H5674
12 like a wilderness, that none passeth **t**? H5674
12:12 all high places **t** the wilderness: for the
17:24 bring in no burden **t** the gates of this city
32:35 daughters to pass **t** *the fire* unto Molech;
51: 4 and *they that are* thrust **t** in her streets. H1856
52 **t** all her land the wounded shall groan.
52: 3 For **t** the anger of the LORD it came to H5921
Lam 3:44 that *our* prayer should not pass **t**. H5674

Lam 4: 9 **t** for *want of* the fruits of the field. H1856
21 the cup also shall pass **t** unto thee: thou
Ezk 5:17 blood shall pass **t** thee; and I will bring
6: 8 ye shall be scattered **t** the countries.
9: 4 And the LORD said unto him, Go **t** the H5674
4 the midst of the city, **t** the midst of
5 Go ye after him **t** the city, and smite: let
12: 5 Dig thou **t** the wall in their sight, and
7 in the even I digged **t** the wall with mine
12 go forth: they shall dig **t** the wall to carry
14: 5 are all estranged from me **t** their idols.
15 If I cause noisome beasts to pass **t** the
15 man may pass **t** because of the beasts: H5674
17 and say, Sword, go **t** the land; so that I
16:14 for it *was* perfect **t** my comeliness, which
21 cause them to pass **t** *the fire* for them? H5674
36 discovered **t** thy whoredoms with
40 and thrust thee **t** with their swords. H1333
20:23 and disperse them **t** the countries;
26 they caused to pass **t** *the fire* all that H5674
31 your sons to pass **t** the fire, ye pollute H5674
23:37 for them **t** *the fire*, to devour *them*. H5674
29:11 No foot of man shall pass **t** it, nor foot of
11 of beast shall pass **t** it, neither shall it be
12 and will disperse them **t** the countries.
30:23 and will disperse them **t** the countries.
33:28 shall be desolate, that none shall pass **t**. H5674
34: 6 My sheep wandered **t** all the mountains,
36:19 they were dispersed **t** the countries:
39:14 passing **t** the land to bury with
15 And the passengers *that* pass **t** the land,
41:19 *it was* made **t** all the house round about.
46:19 After he brought me **t** the entry, which
47: 3 and he brought me **t** the waters; the
4 and brought me **t** the waters; the waters
4 me **t**; the waters *were* to the loins. H5674
Dan 8:25 And **t** his policy also he shall cause craft
9: 7 and *that are* far off, **t** all the countries
11: 2 and by his strength **t** his riches he shall
10 and overflow, and pass **t**: then shall he H5674
Joel 3:17 shall no strangers pass **t** her any more.
Am 2:10 led you forty years **t** the wilderness, to
5:17 for I will pass **t** thee, saith the LORD. H7130
Jna 3: 7 and published **t** Nineveh by the decree
Mic 2:13 up, and have passed **t** the gate, and are H5674
5: 8 who, if he go **t**, both treadeth down, H5674
Nah 1:12 when he shall pass **t**. Though I have H5674
15 no more pass **t** thee; he is utterly cut off.
3: 4 that selleth nations **t** her whoredoms,
4 and families **t** her witchcrafts.
Hab 1: 6 which shall march **t** the breadth of the
3:12 Thou didst march **t** the land in H6805
14 Thou didst strike **t** with his staves the H5344
15 Thou didst walk **t** the sea with thine
15 thine horses, *t* the heap of great waters.
Zec 1:10 hath sent to walk to and fro **t** the earth.
11 have walked to and fro **t** the earth, and,
17 of hosts; My cities **t** prosperity shall yet
4:10 which run to and fro **t** the whole earth.
12 branches which **t** the two golden pipes H3027
5: 6 This *is* their resemblance **t** all the earth.
6: 7 walk to and fro **t** the earth: and he said,
7 walk to and fro **t** the earth. So they
7 So they walked to and fro **t** the earth.
7:14 no man passed **t** nor returned: for they H5674
9: 8 shall pass **t** them any more: for now
15 make a noise as **t** wine; and they shall
10: 7 shall rejoice as **t** wine: yea, their children
11 And he shall pass **t** the sea with
13: 3 shall thrust him **t** when he prophesieth.
9 And I will bring the third part **t** the fire,
Mt 6:19 and where thieves break **t** and steal: *G1358*
20 where thieves do not break **t** nor steal: *G1358*
9:34 out devils **t** the prince of the devils. *G1722*
12: 1 on the sabbath day **t** the corn; and his *G1223*
43 a man, he walketh **t** dry places, seeking *G1223*
19:24 for a camel to go **t** the eye of a needle, *G1223*
Mk 2:23 And it came to pass, that he went **t** the *G1223*
6:55 And ran **t** that whole region round *G4063*
7:13 Making the word of God of none effect **t**
31 **t** the midst of the coasts of Decapolis. *G303*
9:30 and passed **t** Galilee; and he would *G1223*
10:25 It is easier for a camel to go **t** the eye of *G1223*
11:16 should carry *any* vessel **t** the temple. *G1223*
Lk 1:78 **T** the tender mercy of our God; *G1223*
2:35 (Yea, a sword shall pierce **t** thy own *G1330*
4:14 of him **t** all the region round about. *G2596*
30 But he passing **t** the midst of them *G1223*
5:19 and let him down **t** the tiling with *his* *G1223*

T

Lk 6: 1 first, that he went t the corn fields; and G1223
9: 6 And they departed, and went t the G2596
10:17 devils are subject unto us t thy name. G1722
11:15 t Beelzebub the chief of the devils. G1722
18 say that I cast out devils t Beelzebub. G1722
24 a man, he walketh t dry places, seeking G1223
12:39 have suffered his house to be broken t. G1358
13:22 And he went t the cities and villages, G2596
17: 1 but woe *unto him*, t whom they come! G1223
11 t the midst of Samaria and Galilee. G1223
18:25 For it is easier for a camel to go t a G1223
19: 1 And *Jesus* entered and passed t G1330
Jn 1: 7 Light, that all *men* t him might believe. G1223
3:17 that the world t him might be saved. G1223
4: 4 And he must needs go t Samaria. G1223
8:59 t the midst of them, and so passed by. G1223
15: 3 Now ye are clean t the word which I G1223
17:11 Holy Father, keep t thine own name G1722
17 Sanctify them t thy truth: thy word is G1722
19 also might be sanctified t the truth. G1722
20 which shall believe on me t their word; G1223
20:31 believing ye might have life t his name. G1722
Act 1: 2 up, after that he t the Holy Ghost had G1223
3:16 And his name t faith in his name hath G1909
17 And now, brethren, I wot that t G2596
4: 2 t Jesus the resurrection from the dead. G1722
8:18 And when Simon saw that t laying on G1223
40 and passing t he preached in all the G1330
10:43 witness, that t his name whosoever G1223
12:10 out, and passed on t one street; and G4281
13: 6 And when they had gone t the isle unto G1330
38 men *and* brethren, that t this man is G1223
14:22 and that we must t much tribulation G1223
15: 3 they passed t Phenice and Samaria, G1330
11 But we believe that t the grace of the G1223
41 And he went t Syria and Cilicia, G1330
16: 4 And as they went t the cities, they G1279
17: 1 Now when they had passed t G1353
18:27 them much which had believed t grace: G1223
19: 1 having passed t the upper coasts came G1330
21 when he had passed t Macedonia and G1330
20: 3 he purposed to return t Macedonia. G1223
21: 4 who said to Paul t the Spirit, that he G1223
Ro 1: 8 First, I thank my God t Jesus Christ for G1223
24 up to uncleanness t the lusts of their G1722
2:23 thy boast of the law, t breaking the law G1223
24 the Gentiles t you, as it is written. G1223
3: 7 more abounded t my lie unto his glory; G1722
24 Being justified freely by his grace t the G1223
25 *be* a propitiation t faith in his blood, to G1223
25 that are past, t the forbearance of God; G1722
30 by faith, and uncircumcision t faith. G1223
31 Do we then make void the law t faith? G1223
4:13 or to his seed, t the law, but through G1223
13 the law, but t the righteousness of faith. G1223
20 He staggered not at the promise of God t
5: 1 peace with God t our Lord Jesus Christ: G1223
9 we shall be saved from wrath t him. G1223
11 but we also joy in God t our Lord Jesus G1223
15 *is* the free gift. For if t the offence of one
21 might grace reign t righteousness unto G1223
6:11 alive unto God t Jesus Christ our Lord. G1722
23 *is* eternal life t Jesus Christ our Lord. G1722
7:25 I thank God t Jesus Christ our Lord. So G1223
8: 3 do, in that it was weak t the flesh, God G1223
13 shall die: but if ye t the Spirit do mortify
37 than conquerors t him that loved us. G1223
11:11 forbid: but *rather* t their fall salvation *is*
30 now obtained mercy t their unbelief:
31 not believed, that t your mercy they also
36 For of him, and t him, and to him, *are* G1223
12: 3 For I say, t the grace given unto me, to G1223
15: 4 our learning, that we t patience and G1223
13 in hope, t the power of the Holy Ghost. G1722
17 I have therefore whereof I may glory t G1722
19 T mighty signs and wonders, by the G1722
16:27 To God only wise, *be* glory t Jesus G1223
1Co 1: 1 of Jesus Christ t the will of God, and G1223
4:15 Jesus I have begotten you t the gospel. G1223
8:11 And t thy knowledge shall the weak G1909
10: 1 the cloud, and all passed t the sea; G1223
13:12 For now we see t a glass, darkly; but G1223
15:57 us the victory t our Lord Jesus Christ. G1223
16: 5 when I shall pass t Macedonia: for I do G1330
5 Macedonia: for I do pass t Macedonia. G1330
2Co 3: 4 And such trust have we t Christ to G1223
4:15 grace might t the thanksgiving of G1223
8: 9 poor, that ye t his poverty might be rich.
9:11 causeth t us thanksgiving to God. G1223
2Co 10: 4 carnal, but mighty t God to the pulling
11: 3 beguiled Eve t his subtilty, so your G1722
33 And t a window in a basket was I let G1223
12: 7 above measure t the abundance of the
13: 4 For though he was crucified t G1537
Gal 2:19 For I t the law am dead to the law, that G1223
3: 8 justify the heathen t faith, preached G1537
14 on the Gentiles t Jesus Christ; that we G1722
14 receive the promise of the Spirit t faith. G1223
4: 7 if a son, then an heir of God t Christ. G1223
13 Ye know how t infirmity of the flesh I G1223
5: 5 For we t the Spirit wait for the hope of
10 I have confidence in you t the Lord, G1722
Eph 1: 7 In whom we have redemption t his G1223
2: 7 *his* kindness toward us t Christ Jesus. G1722
8 For by grace are ye saved t faith; and G1223
18 For t him we both have access by one G1223
22 for an habitation of God t the Spirit. G1722
4: 6 *is* above all, and t all, and in you all. G1223
18 the life of God t the ignorance that is G1223
Php 1:19 to my salvation t your prayer, and the G1223
2: 3 *Let* nothing *be done* t strife or G2596
3: 9 but that which is t the faith of Christ, G1223
4: 7 your hearts and minds t Christ Jesus. G1722
13 I can do all things t Christ which G1722
Col 1:14 In whom we have redemption t his G1223
20 And, having made peace t the blood of G1223
22 In the body of his flesh t death, to G1223
2: 8 Beware lest any man spoil you t G1223
12 ye are risen with *him* t the faith of the G1223
2Th 2:13 you to salvation t sanctification of the G1722
16 consolation and good hope t grace, G1722
1Ti 6:10 themselves t with many sorrows. G4044
2Ti 1:10 and immortality to light t the gospel: G1223
3:15 t faith which is in Christ Jesus. G1223
Tit 1: 3 his word t preaching, which is G1722
3: 6 Which he shed on us abundantly t G1223
Phlm 22 for I trust that t your prayers I shall G1223
Heb 2:10 of their salvation perfect t sufferings. G1223
14 part of the same; that t death he might G1223
15 And deliver them who t fear of death
3:13 be hardened t the deceitfulness of sin.
6:12 of them who t faith and patience G1223
9:14 blood of Christ, who t the eternal Spirit G1223
10:10 By the which will we are sanctified t the G1223
20 for us, t the veil, that is to say, his flesh; G1223
11: 3 T faith we understand that the worlds
11 T faith also Sara herself received
28 T faith he kept the passover, and the
29 By faith they passed t the Red sea as by G1224
33 Who t faith subdued kingdoms, G1223
39 report t faith, received not the promise: G1223
12:20 shall be stoned, or thrust t with a dart: G2700
13:20 t the blood of the everlasting covenant, G1722
21 in his sight, t Jesus Christ; to whom G1223
1Pt 1: 2 of God the Father, t sanctification of G1722
5 Who are kept by the power of God t G1223
6 in heaviness t manifold temptations: G1722
22 in obeying the truth t the Spirit unto G1223
4:11 may be glorified t Jesus Christ, to G1223
2Pt 1: 1 faith with us t the righteousness of G1722
2 unto you t the knowledge of God, G1722
3 life and godliness, t the knowledge of G1223
4 corruption that is in the world t lust. G1722
2: 3 And t covetousness shall they with G1722
18 of vanity, they allure t the lusts of the G1722
18 lusts of the flesh, *t much* wantonness,
20 of the world t the knowledge of the G1722
1Jn 4: 9 the world, that we might live t him. G1223
Rev 8:13 an angel flying t the midst of heaven, G1722
18: 3 rich t the abundance of her delicacies. G1537
22:14 and may enter in t the gates into the city.

THROUGHLY

Gen 11: 3 and burn them t. And they had brick H8316
Job 6: 2 Oh that my grief were t weighed, and H8254
Ps 51: 2 Wash me t from mine iniquity, and H7235
Jer 6: 9 hosts, They shall t glean the remnant of H5953
7: 5 For if ye t amend your ways and your H3190
5 your doings; if ye t execute judgment H6213
50:34 his name: he shall t plead their cause, H7378
Ezk 16: 9 Then washed I thee with water; yea, I t
Mt 3:12 Whose fan *is* in his hand, and he will t G1245
Lk 3:17 Whose fan *is* in his hand, and he will t G1245
2Co 11: 6 but we have been t made manifest G1722
2Ti 3:17 That the man of God may be perfect, t G1822

THROUGHOUT

Gen 41:29 of great plenty t all the land of Egypt:
Gen 41:46 and went t all the land of Egypt. H5674
45: 8 house, and a ruler t all the land of Egypt.
Ex 5:12 So the people were scattered abroad t all
7:19 *that* there may be blood t all the land of
21 there was blood t all the land of Egypt.
8:16 may become lice t all the land of Egypt.
17 land became lice t all the land of Egypt.
9: 9 and upon beast, t all the land of Egypt.
16 my name may be declared t all the earth.
22 herb of the field, t the land of Egypt.
25 And the hail smote t all the land of Egypt
11: 6 And there shall be a great cry t all the
12:14 it a feast to the LORD t your generations;
29:42 *This shall be* a continual burnt offering t
30: 8 before the LORD t your generations.
10 atonement upon it t your generations: it
21 him and to his seed t their generations.
31 oil unto me t your generations.
31:13 me and you t your generations; that
16 the sabbath t their generations, *for*
32:27 from gate to gate t the camp, and slay
34: 3 any man be seen t all the mount; neither
35: 3 Ye shall kindle no fire t your habitations
36: 6 it to be proclaimed t the camp, saying,
37:19 and a flower: so t the six branches going
40:15 priesthood t their generations.
38 the house of Israel, t all their journeys.
Lev 3:17 for your generations t all your dwellings,
7:36 *by* a statute for ever t their generations.
10: 9 *be* a statute for ever t your generations:
17: 7 for ever unto them t their generations.
23:14 t your generations in all your dwellings.
21 in all your dwellings t your generations.
31 t your generations in all your dwellings.
25: 9 make the trumpet sound t all your land.
10 proclaim liberty t *all* the land unto all
30 to him that bought it t his generations: it
Nu 1:42 Of the children of Naphtali, t their
52 man by his own standard, t their hosts.
2: 3 camp of Judah pitch t their armies: and
9 t their armies. These shall first set forth.
16 hundred and fifty, t their armies. And
24 and an hundred, t their armies. And
32 of the camps t their hosts *were* six
3:39 of the LORD, t their families, all the
4:22 the sons of Gershon, t the houses of their
38 sons of Gershon, t their families, and by
40 numbered of them, t their families, by
42 of the sons of Merari, t their families, by
10: 8 ordinance for ever t your generations.
25 of all the camps t their hosts: and over
11:10 Then Moses heard the people weep t
15:38 of their garments t their generations,
18:23 *be* a statute for ever t your generations,
26: 2 old and upward, t their fathers' house,
28:14 of every month t the months of the year.
21 offer for every lamb, t the seven lambs:
24 After this manner ye shall offer daily, t
29 A several tenth deal unto one lamb, t the
29: 4 And one tenth deal for one lamb, t the
10 A several tenth deal for one lamb, t the
31: 4 Of every tribe a thousand, t all the tribes
35:29 t your generations in all your dwellings.
Dt 16:18 God giveth thee, t thy tribes: and they
28:40 Thou shalt have olive trees t all thy
52 thou trustedst, t all thy land: and he
52 thee in all thy gates t all thy land, which
Jos 2:22 *them* t all the way, but found *them* not.
6:27 his fame was *noised* t all the country.
16: 1 goeth up from Jericho t mount Beth-el,
22:14 house a prince t all the tribes of Israel;
24: 3 the flood, and led him t all the land of
Jdg 6:35 And he sent messengers t all Manasseh;
7:22 his fellow, even t all the host: and the
24 And Gideon sent messengers t all mount
20: 6 and sent her t all the country of the
10 ten men of an hundred t all the tribes of
1Sa 5:11 a deadly destruction t all the city; the
11: 7 and sent *them* t all the coasts of Israel
13: 3 blew the trumpet t all the land, saying,
19 Now there was no smith found t all the
23:23 him out t all the thousands of Judah.
2Sa 8:14 And he put garrisons in Edom; t all
15:10 But Absalom sent spies t all the tribes of
19: 9 And all the people were at strife t all the
1Ki 1: 3 So they sought for a fair damsel t all the
6:38 the house finished t all the parts thereof,
15:22 Then king Asa made a proclamation t
18: 6 them to pass t it: Ahab went one way

1Ki 22:36 And there went a proclamation t the
2Ki 17: 5 Then the king of Assyria came up t all
1Ch 5:10 their tents t all the east *land* of Gilead. H6440
6:54 Now these *are* their dwelling places t
60 cities t their families *were* thirteen cities.
62 And to the sons of Gershom t their
63 *were given* by lot, t their families, out of
7:40 And the number t the genealogy of them
9:34 Levites *were* chief t their generations;
12:30 famous t the house of their fathers.
21: 4 went t all Israel, and came to Jerusalem.
12 the LORD destroying t all the coasts of
22: 5 of fame and of glory t all countries: I will
26: 6 sons born, that ruled t the house of their
27: 1 month by month t all the months of the
2Ch 8: 6 and t all the land of his dominion.
11:23 of all his children t all the countries of
16: 9 For the eyes of the LORD run to and fro t
17: 9 and went about t all the cities of Judah,
19 king put in the fenced cities t all Judah.
19: 5 And he set judges in the land t all the
20: 3 and proclaimed a fast t all Judah. H5921
25: 5 houses of *their* fathers, t all Judah and
26:14 And Uzziah prepared for them t all the
30: 5 make proclamation t all Israel, from
6 and his princes t all Israel and Judah,
22 and they did eat t the feast seven days,
31:20 And thus did Hezekiah t all Judah, and
34: 7 down all the idols t all the land of Israel,
36:22 a proclamation t all his kingdom, and
Ezr 1: 1 a proclamation t all his kingdom, and
10: 7 And they made proclamation t Judah
Est 1:20 shall be published t all his empire, (for it
3: 6 the Jews that *were* t the whole kingdom
9: 2 in their cities t all the provinces of the
4 his fame went out t all the provinces: for
28 and kept t every generation, every
Ps 72: 5 sun and moon endure, t all generations.
102:24 my days: thy years *are* t all generations.
135:13 memorial, O LORD, t all generations.
145:13 thy dominion *endureth* t all generations.
Jer 17: 3 thy high places for sin, t all thy borders.
Ezk 38:21 And I will call for a sword against him t
Mt 4:24 And his fame went t all Syria: and they *G1519*
Mk 1:28 t all the region round about Galilee. *G1519*
39 And he preached in their synagogues t *G1519*
14: 9 shall be preached t the whole world, *G1519*
Lk 1:65 abroad t all the hill country of Judaea. *G1722*
4:25 when great famine was t all the land; *G1909*
7:17 And this rumour of him went forth t all *G1722*
17 and t all the region round about. *G1722*
8: 1 that he went t every city and village, *G1353*
39 and published t the whole city how *G2596*
23: 5 people, teaching t all Jewry, beginning *G2596*
Jn 19:23 without seam, woven from the top t. *G1223*
Act 8: 1 all scattered abroad t the regions of *G2596*
9:31 Then had the churches rest t all Judaea *G2596*
32 And it came to pass, as Peter passed t *G1223*
42 And it was known t all Joppa; and *G2596*
10:37 was published t all Judaea, and began *G2596*
11:28 be great dearth t all the world: which *G1909*
13:49 the Lord was published t all the region. *G1223*
14:24 And after they had passed t Pisidia, *G1330*
16: 6 Now when they had gone t Phrygia and *G1330*
19:26 but almost t all Asia, this Paul hath
24: 5 among all the Jews t the world, and a *G2596*
26:20 and at Jerusalem, and t all the coasts of *G1519*
Ro 1: 8 faith is spoken of t the whole world. *G1722*
9:17 name might be declared t all the earth. *G1722*
2Co 8:18 *is* in the gospel t all the churches; *G1223*
Eph 3:21 t all ages, world without end. Amen. *G1519*
1Pt 1: 1 strangers scattered t Pontus, Galatia, *G1290*

THROW

Jdg 2: 2 this land; ye shall t down their altars: H5422
6:25 years old, and t down the altar of Baal H2040
2Sa 20:15 Joab battered the wall, to t it down. H5307
2Ki 9:33 And he said, T her down. So they threw H8058
Jer 1:10 and to t down, to build, and to plant. H2040
31:28 down, and to t down, and to destroy, H2040
Ezk 16:39 and they shall t down thine eminent H2040
Mic 5:11 land, and t down all thy strong holds: H2040
Mal 1: 4 build, but I will t down; and they shall H2040

THROWING

Nu 35:17 And if he smite him with t a stone, H3027

THROWN

Ex 15: 1 and his rider hath he t into the sea. H7411
Ex 15:21 and his rider hath he t into the sea. H7411
Jdg 6:32 him, because he hath t down his altar. H5422
2Sa 20:21 his head shall be t to thee over the wall. H7993
1Ki 19:10 thy covenant, t down thine altars, and H2040
14 thy covenant, t down thine altars, and H2040
Jer 31:40 up, nor t down any more for ever. H2040
33: 4 of Judah, which are t down by the H5422
50:15 fallen, her walls are t down: for it *is* the H2040
Lam 2: 2 not pitied: he hath t down in his wrath H2040
17 of old: he hath t down, and hath not H2040
Ezk 29: 5 And I will leave thee *t* into the
38:20 shall be t down, and the steep H2040
Nah 1: 6 fire, and the rocks are t down by him. H5422
Mt 24: 2 upon another, that shall not be t down. *G2647*
Mk 13: 2 upon another, that shall not be t down. *G2647*
Lk 4:35 the devil had t him in the midst, he *G4496*
21: 6 upon another, that shall not be t down. *G2647*
Rev 18:21 city Babylon be t down, and shall be *G906*

THRUST

Ex 11: 1 shall surely t you out hence altogether. H1644
12:39 because they were t out of Egypt, and H1644
Nu 22:25 of the LORD, she t herself unto the H3905
25: 8 Israel into the tent, and t both of them H1856
35:20 But if he t him of hatred, or hurl at him H1920
22 But if he t him suddenly without H1920
Dt 13: 5 of bondage, to t thee out of the way H5080
10 he hath sought to t thee away from the H5080
15:17 Then thou shalt take an aul, and t *it* H5414
33:27 arms: and he shall t out the enemy H1644
Jdg 3:21 his right thigh, and t it into his belly: H8628
6:38 the morrow, and t the fleece together, H2115
9:41 and Zebul t out Gaal and his brethren, H1644
54 young man t him through, and he died. H1856
11: 2 grew up, and they t out Jephthah, and H1644
1Sa 11: 2 you, that I may t out all your right eyes, H5365
31: 4 thy sword, and t me through therewith; H1856
4 come and t me through, and abuse H1856
2Sa 2:16 fellow by the head, and *t* his sword in his
18:14 in his hand, and t them through the H8628
23: 6 of them as thorns t away, because they H5074
1Ki 2:27 So Solomon t out Abiathar from being H1644
2Ki 4:27 came near to t her away. And the man H1920
1Ch 10: 4 thy sword, and t me through therewith; H1856
2Ch 26:20 his forehead, and they t him out from H926
Ps 118:13 Thou hast t sore at me that I might fall: H1760
Isa 13:15 Every one that is found shall be t H1856
14:19 that are slain, t through with a sword, H2944
Jer 51: 4 *they that are* t through in her streets. H1856
Ezk 16:40 and t thee through with their swords. H1333
34:21 Because ye have t with side and with H1920
46:18 by oppression, to t them out of their H3238
Joel 2: 8 Neither shall one t another; they shall H1766
Zec 13: 3 t him through when he prophesieth. H1856
Lk 4:29 And rose up, and t him out of the city, *G1544*
5: 3 him that he would t out a little from the *G1877*
10:15 to heaven, shalt be t down to hell. *G2601*
13:28 of God, and you *yourselves* t out. *G1544*
Jn 20:25 of the nails, and t my hand into his side, *G906*
27 thy hand, and t *it* into my side: and be *G906*
Act 7:27 But he that did his neighbour wrong t *G683*
39 not obey, but t *him* from them, and *G683*
16:24 Who, having received such a charge, t *G906*
37 and now do they t us out privily? nay *G1544*
27:39 if it were possible, to t in the ship. *G1856*
Heb 12:20 be stoned, or t through with a dart: *G2700*
Rev 14:15 sat on the cloud, T in thy sickle, and *G3992*
16 And he that sat on the cloud t in his *G906*
18 sickle, saying, T in thy sharp sickle, *G3992*
19 And the angel t in his sickle into the *G906*

THRUSTETH

Job 32:13 out wisdom: God t him down, not man. H5086

THUMB

Ex 29:20 sons, and upon the t of their right hand, H931
Lev 8:23 ear, and upon the t of his right hand, H931
14:14 and upon the t of his right hand, and H931
17 and upon the t of his right hand, and H931
25 and upon the t of his right hand, and H931
28 and upon the t of his right hand, and H931

THUMBS

Lev 8:24 ear, and upon the t of their right hands, H931
Jdg 1: 6 cut off his t and his great toes. H931+H3027
7 having their t and their great H931+H3027

THUMMIM

Ex 28:30 the Urim and the T; and they shall be H8550
Lev 8: 8 in the breastplate the Urim and the T. H8550
Dt 33: 8 And of Levi he said, *Let* thy T and thy H8550
Ezr 2:63 stood up a priest with Urim and with T. H8550
Neh 7:65 stood *up* a priest with Urim and T. H8550

THUNDER

Ex 9:23 the LORD sent t and hail, and the fire H6963
29 the LORD; *and* the t shall cease, neither H6963
1Sa 2:10 out of heaven shall he t upon them: the H7481
7:10 with a great t on that day upon the H6963
12:17 and he shall send t and rain; that ye H6963
18 the LORD sent t and rain that day: and H6963
Job 26:14 the t of his power who can understand? H7482
28:26 and a way for the lightning of the t: H6963
38:25 of waters, or a way for the lightning of t; H6963
39:19 hast thou clothed his neck with t? H7483
25 the t of the captains, and the shouting. H7482
40: 9 or canst thou t with a voice like him? H7481
Ps 77:18 The voice of thy t *was* in the heaven: H7482
81: 7 the secret place of t: I proved thee at the H7482
104: 7 at the voice of thy t they hasted away. H7482
Isa 29: 6 of hosts with t, and with earthquake, H7482
Mk 3:17 them Boanerges, which is, The sons of t: *G1027*
Rev 6: 1 as it were the noise of t, one of the four *G1027*
14: 2 as the voice of a great t: and I heard the *G1027*

THUNDERBOLTS

Ps 78:48 also to the hail, and their flocks to hot t. H7565

THUNDERED

1Sa 7:10 but the LORD t with a great thunder H7481
2Sa 22:14 The LORD t from heaven, and the most H7481
Ps 18:13 The LORD also t in the heavens, and H7481
Jn 12:29 it t: others said, An angel spake to him. *G1096*

THUNDERETH

Job 37: 4 After it a voice roareth: he t with the H7481
5 God t marvellously with his voice; great H7481
Ps 29: 3 glory t: the LORD *is* upon many waters. H7481

THUNDERINGS

Ex 9:28 no *more* mighty t and hail; and I will H6963
20:18 And all the people saw the t, and the H6963
Rev 4: 5 lightnings and t and voices: and *there* *G1027*
8: 5 t, and lightnings, and an earthquake. *G1027*
11:19 t, and an earthquake, and great hail. *G1027*
19: 6 voice of mighty t, saying, Alleluia: for *G1027*

THUNDERS

Ex 9:33 the LORD: and the t and hail ceased, H6963
34 and the hail and the t were ceased, he H6963
19:16 that there were t and lightnings, and H6963
Rev 10: 3 had cried, seven t uttered their voices. *G1027*
4 And when the seven t had uttered their *G1027*
4 the seven t uttered, and write them not. *G1027*
16:18 And there were voices, and t, and *G1027*

THUS

Gen 2: 1 T the heavens and the earth were
6:22 T did Noah; according to all that God
19:36 T were both the daughters of Lot with
20:16 and with all *other:* t she was reproved.
21:32 T they made a covenant at Beer-sheba:
24:30 his sister, saying, T spake the man H3541
25:22 t? And she went to inquire of the LORD. H2088
34 his way: t Esau despised *his* birthright.
31: 8 If he said t, The speckled shall be thy H3541
8 and if he said t, The ringstraked shall H3541
9 T God hath taken away the cattle of your H430
40 *T* I was; in the day the drought
41 T have I been twenty years in thy H2088
32: 4 And he commanded them, saying, T H3541
4 Jacob saith t, I have sojourned with H3541
36: 8 T dwelt Esau in mount Seir: Esau *is*
37:35 son mourning. T his father wept for him.
42:25 for the way: and t did he unto them. H3651
45: 9 and say unto him, T saith thy son H3541
Ex 3:14 I AM: and he said, T shalt thou say H3541
15 And God said moreover unto Moses, T H3541
4:22 And thou shalt say unto Pharaoh, T H3541
5: 1 in, and told Pharaoh, T saith the LORD H3541
10 people, saying, T saith Pharaoh, I will H3541
15 dealest thou t with thy servants? H3541
7:17 T saith the LORD, In this thou shalt H3541
8: 1 and say unto him, T saith the LORD, H3541
20 and say unto him, T saith the LORD, H3541
9: 1 and tell him, T saith the LORD God H3541
13 and say unto him, T saith the LORD H3541
10: 3 said unto him, T saith the LORD God H3541

T

Ex 11: 4 And Moses said, T saith the LORD, H3541
12:11 And t shall ye eat it; *with* your loins H3602
50 T did all the children of Israel; as the
14:11 t with us, to carry us forth out of Egypt? H2063
30 T the LORD saved Israel that day out of
19: 3 mountain, saying, T shalt thou say to H3541
20:22 And the LORD said unto Moses, T thou H3541
26:17 against another: t shalt thou make for H3651
24 of it unto one ring: t shall it be for them H3651
29:35 And t shalt thou do unto Aaron, and to
32:27 And he said unto them, T saith the H3541
36:22 one from another: t did he make for all H3651
29 to one ring: t he did to both of them H3651
39:32 T was all the work of the tabernacle of
40:16 T did Moses: according to all that the
Lev 15:31 T shall ye separate the children of Israel
16: 3 T shall Aaron come into the holy *place*: H2063
Nu 4:19 But t do unto them, that they may live,
49 to his burden: t were they numbered
8: 7 And t shalt thou do unto them, to H3541
14 T shalt thou separate the Levites from
26 do no service. T shalt thou do unto the H3602
10:28 T *were* the journeyings of the children of H428
11:15 And if thou deal t with me, kill me, I H3602
15:11 T shall it be done for one bullock, or for H3602
18:26 T speak unto the Levites, and say unto
28 T ye also shall offer an heave offering H3651
20:14 the king of Edom, T saith thy brother H3541
21 T Edom refused to give Israel passage
21:31 T Israel dwelt in the land of the H3478
22:16 and said to him, T saith Balak the son H3541
23: 5 unto Balak, and t thou shalt speak. H3541
16 said, Go again unto Balak, and say t. H3541
32: 8 T did your fathers, when I sent them H3541
Dt 7: 5 But t shall ye deal with them; ye shall H3541
9:25 T I fell down before the LORD forty days
20:15 T shalt thou do unto all the cities *which* H3651
29:24 the LORD done t unto this land? what H3662
32: 6 Do ye t requite the LORD, O foolish H2063
Jos 2: 4 hid them, and said t, There came men H3651
6: 3 the city once. T shalt thou do six days. H3541
7:10 wherefore liest thou t upon thy face? H2088
13 to morrow: for t saith the LORD God H3541
20 of Israel, and t and thus have I done: H2063
20 of Israel, and thus and t have I done:
10:25 good courage: for t shall the LORD do H3602
16: 5 to their families was *t*: even the border of
21:13 T they gave to the children of Aaron the
42 about them: t *were* all these cities. H3651
22:16 T saith the whole congregation of the H3541
24: 2 And Joshua said unto all the people, T H3541
Jdg 6: 8 said unto them, T saith the LORD God H3541
8: 1 thou served us t, that thou calledst us H1697
28 T was Midian subdued before the
9:56 T God rendered the wickedness of H430
11:15 And said unto him, T saith Jephthah, H3541
33 very great slaughter. T the children of
13:18 t after my name, seeing it *is* secret? H2088
18: 4 And he said unto them, T and thus H2090
4 And he said unto them, Thus and t H2090
20:43 *T* they inclosed the Benjamites round
1Sa 2:27 said unto him, T saith the LORD, Did H3541
9: 9 to inquire of God, t he spake, Come, H3541
10:18 And said unto the children of Israel, T H3541
11: 9 that came, T shall ye say unto the H3541
14: 9 If they say t unto us, Tarry until we H3541
10 But if they say t, Come up unto us; then H3541
15: 2 T saith the LORD of hosts, I remember H3541
18:25 And Saul said, T shall ye say to David, H3541
20: 7 If he say t, *It is* well; thy servant shall H3541
22 But if I say t unto the young man, H3541
25: 6 And t shall ye say to him that liveth *in* H3541
26:18 And he said, Wherefore doth my lord t H2088
2Sa 6:22 And I will yet be more vile than t, and H2063
7: 5 Go and tell my servant David, T saith H3541
8 my servant David, T saith the LORD of H3541
11:25 Then David said unto the messenger, T H3541
12: 7 Thou *art* the man. T saith the LORD H3541
11 T saith the LORD, Behold, I will raise H3541
31 the brickkiln: and t did he unto all the H3651
15:26 But if he t say, I have no delight in thee; H3541
16: 7 And t said Shimei when he cursed, H3541
17:15 the priests, T and thus did Ahithophel H2063
15 the priests, Thus and t did Ahithophel H2063
15 Israel; and t and thus have I counselled.
15 Israel; and thus and t have I counselled.
21 over the water: for t hath Ahithophel H3602
18:14 Then said Joab, I may not tarry t with H3651
33 and as he went, t he said, O my son H3541

2Sa 24:12 Go and say unto David, T saith the H3541
1Ki 1:48 And also t said the king, Blessed *be* the H3602
2:30 said unto him, T saith the king, Come H3541
30 T said Joab, and thus he answered me. H3541
30 Thus said Joab, and t he answered me.
3:22 *is* my son. T they spake before the king.
5:11 t gave Solomon to Hiram year by year. H3541
9: 8 t unto this land, and to this house? H3602
11:31 thee ten pieces: for t saith the LORD, H3541
12:10 unto him, saying, T shalt thou speak H3541
10 *it* lighter unto us; t shalt thou say unto H3541
24 T saith the LORD, Ye shall not go up, H3541
13: 2 said, O altar, altar, t saith the LORD; H3541
21 from Judah, saying, T saith the LORD, H3541
14: 5 son; for he *is* sick: t and thus shalt thou H2090
5 *is* sick: thus and t shalt thou say unto H2090
7 Go, tell Jeroboam, T saith the LORD H3541
16:12 T did Zimri destroy all the house of
17:14 For t saith the LORD God of Israel, The H3541
20: 2 and said unto him, T saith Ben-hadad, H3541
5 came again, and said, T speaketh H3541
13 of Israel, saying, T saith the LORD, H3541
14 And he said, T saith the LORD, *Even* H3541
28 of Israel, and said, T saith the LORD, H3541
42 And he said unto him, T saith the H3541
21:19 unto him, saying, T saith the LORD, H3541
19 unto him, saying, T saith the LORD, In H3541
22:11 of iron: and he said, T saith the LORD, H3541
27 And say, T saith the king, Put this H3541
2Ki 1: 4 Now therefore t saith the LORD, Thou H3541
6 and say unto him, T saith the LORD, *Is* H3541
11 O man of God, t hath the king said, H3541
16 And he said unto him, T saith the H3541
2:21 in there, and said, T saith the LORD, I H3541
3:16 And he said, T saith the LORD, Make H3541
17 For t saith the LORD, Ye shall not see H3541
4:43 that they may eat: for t saith the LORD, H2063
5: 4 his lord, saying, T and thus said the H3541
4 saying, Thus and t said the maid that H3541
7: 1 of the LORD; T saith the LORD, To H3541
9: 3 his head, and say, T saith the LORD, I H2063
6 said unto him, T saith the LORD God H3541
12 now. And he said, T and thus spake he H3541
12 he said, Thus and t spake he to me, H3541
12 he to me, saying, T saith the LORD, I
18 him, and said, T saith the king, *Is it* H3541
19 to them, and said, T saith the king, *Is it* H3541
10:28 T Jehu destroyed Baal out of Israel. H3541
16:16 T did Urijah the priest, according to all
18:19 ye now to Hezekiah, T saith the great H3541
29 T saith the king, Let not Hezekiah H3541
31 Hearken not to Hezekiah: for t saith H3541
19: 3 And they said unto him, T saith H3541
6 And Isaiah said unto them, T shall ye H3541
6 to your master, T saith the LORD, Be H3541
10 T shall ye speak to Hezekiah king of H3541
20 to Hezekiah, saying, T saith the LORD H3541
32 Therefore t saith the LORD concerning H3541
20: 1 said unto him, T saith the LORD, Set H3541
5 of my people, T saith the LORD, the H3541
21:12 Therefore t saith the LORD God of H3541
22:15 And she said unto them, T saith the H3541
16 T saith the LORD, Behold, I will bring H3541
18 of the LORD, t shall ye say to him, H3541
18 ye say to him, T saith the LORD God H3541
1Ch 15:28 T all Israel brought up the ark of the
17: 4 Go and tell David my servant, T saith H3541
7 Now therefore t shalt thou say unto my H3541
7 my servant David, T saith the LORD of H3541
18: 6 *and* brought gifts. T the LORD preserved
13 David's servants. T the LORD preserved
21:10 Go and tell David, saying, T saith the H3541
11 him, T saith the LORD, Choose thee H3541
24: 4 of Ithamar; and *t* were they divided.
5 T were they divided by lot, one sort with
29:26 T David the son of Jesse reigned over all
2Ch 4:18 T Solomon made all these vessels in
5: 1 T all the work that Solomon made for
7:11 T Solomon finished the house of the
21 t unto this land, and unto this house? H3602
10:10 unto him, saying, T shalt thou answer H3541
10 lighter for us; t shalt thou say unto H3541
11: 4 T saith the LORD, Ye shall not go up, H3541
12: 5 said unto them, T saith the LORD, Ye H3541
13:18 T the children of Israel were brought H3541
18:10 of iron, and said, T saith the LORD, H3541
26 And say, T saith the king, Put this H3541
19: 9 And he charged them, saying, T shall H3541
20:15 king Jehoshaphat, T saith the LORD H3541

2Ch 21:12 prophet, saying, T saith the LORD God H3541
24:11 it to his place again. T they did day by H3541
20 and said unto them, T saith God, Why H3541
22 T Joash the king remembered not the
31:20 And t did Hezekiah throughout all H2063
32:10 T saith Sennacherib king of Assyria, H3541
22 T the LORD saved Hezekiah and the
34:23 And she answered them, T saith the H3541
24 T saith the LORD, Behold, I will bring H3541
26 ye say unto him, T saith the LORD God H3541
36:23 T saith Cyrus king of Persia, All the H3541
Ezr 1: 2 T saith Cyrus king of Persia, The LORD H3541
5: 3 and said t unto them, Who hath H3652
7 t; Unto Darius the king, all peace. H1836
9 said unto them t, Who commanded you H3660
11 And t they returned us answer, saying, H3660
6: 2 roll, and therein *was* a record t written: H3652
Neh 5:13 this promise, even t be he shaken out, H3602
13:18 Did not your fathers t, and did not our H3541
30 T cleansed I them from all strangers,
Est 1:18 deed of the queen. T *shall there arise* too
2:13 Then t came *every* maiden unto the H2088
6: 9 before him, T shall it be done to the H3602
11 before him, T shall it be done unto H3602
9: 5 T the Jews smote all their enemies with
Job 1: 5 in their hearts. T did Job continually. H3602
27:12 *it*; why then are ye t altogether vain? H2088
Ps 38:14 T I was as a man that heareth not, and
63: 4 T will I bless thee while I live: I will lift H3651
73:15 If I say, I will speak t; behold, I should H3644
21 T my heart was grieved, and I was H3588
106:20 T they changed their glory into the
29 T they provoked *him* to anger with their
39 T were they defiled with their own
128: 4 Behold, that t shall the man be blessed H3651
Isa 7: 7 T saith the Lord GOD, It shall not H3541
8:11 For the LORD spake t to me with a H3541
10:24 Therefore t saith the Lord GOD of H3541
21: 6 For t hath the Lord said unto me, Go, H3541
16 For t hath the Lord said unto me, H3541
22:15 T saith the Lord GOD of hosts, Go, get H3541
24:13 When t it shall be in the midst of the H3541
28:16 Therefore t saith the Lord GOD, H3541
29:22 Therefore t saith the LORD, who H3541
30:12 Wherefore t saith the Holy One of H3541
15 For t saith the Lord GOD, the Holy One H3541
31: 4 For t hath the LORD spoken unto me, H3541
36: 4 ye now to Hezekiah, T saith the great H3541
14 T saith the king, Let not Hezekiah H3541
16 Hearken not to Hezekiah: for t saith H3541
37: 3 And they said unto him, T saith H3541
6 And Isaiah said unto them, T shall ye H3541
6 unto your master, T saith the LORD, H3541
10 T shall ye speak to Hezekiah king of H3541
21 Hezekiah, saying, T saith the LORD H3541
33 Therefore t saith the LORD concerning H3541
38: 1 said unto him, T saith the LORD, Set H3541
5 Go, and say to Hezekiah, T saith the H3541
42: 5 T saith God the LORD, he that created H3541
43: 1 But now t saith the LORD that created H3541
14 T saith the LORD, your redeemer, the H3541
16 T saith the LORD, which maketh a way H3541
44: 2 T saith the LORD that made thee, and H3541
6 T saith the LORD the King of Israel, H3541
24 T saith the LORD, thy redeemer, and H3541
45: 1 T saith the LORD to his anointed, to H3541
11 T saith the LORD, the Holy One of H3541
14 T saith the LORD, The labour of Egypt, H3541
18 For t saith the LORD that created the H3541
47:15 T shall they be unto thee with whom H3651
48:17 T saith the LORD, thy Redeemer, the H3541
49: 7 T saith the LORD, the Redeemer of H3541
8 T saith the LORD, In an acceptable H3541
22 T saith the Lord GOD, Behold, I will lift H3541
25 But t saith the LORD, Even the captives H3541
50: 1 T saith the LORD, Where *is* the bill of H3541
51:22 T saith thy Lord the LORD, and thy H3541
52: 3 For t saith the LORD, Ye have sold H3541
4 For t saith the Lord GOD, My people H3541
56: 1 T saith the LORD, Keep ye judgment, H3541
4 For t saith the LORD unto the eunuchs H3541
57:15 For t saith the high and lofty One that H3541
65: 8 T saith the LORD, As the new wine is H3541
13 Therefore t saith the Lord GOD, H3541
66: 1 T saith the LORD, The heaven *is* my H3541
12 For t saith the LORD, Behold, I will H3541
Jer 2: 2 Jerusalem, saying, T saith the LORD; I H3541
5 T saith the LORD, What iniquity have H3541
4: 3 For t saith the LORD to the men of H3541

Jer 4:27 For t hath the LORD said, The whole H3541
5:13 in them: t shall it be done unto them. H3541
14 Wherefore t saith the LORD God of H3541
6: 6 For t hath the LORD of hosts said, Hew H3541
9 T saith the LORD of hosts, They shall H3541
16 T saith the LORD, Stand ye in the H3541
21 Therefore t saith the LORD, Behold, I H3541
22 T saith the LORD, Behold, a people H3541
7: 3 T saith the LORD of hosts, the God of H3541
20 Therefore t saith the Lord GOD; H3541
21 T saith the LORD of hosts, the God of H3541
8: 4 Moreover thou shalt say unto them, T H3541
9: 7 Therefore t saith the LORD of hosts, H3541
15 Therefore t saith the LORD of hosts, H3541
17 T saith the LORD of hosts, Consider ye, H3541
22 Speak, T saith the LORD, Even the H3541
23 T saith the LORD, Let not the wise *man* H3541
10: 2 T saith the LORD, Learn not the way of H3541
11 T shall ye say unto them, The gods that H1836
18 For t saith the LORD, Behold, I will H3541
11: 3 And say thou unto them, T saith the H3541
11 Therefore t saith the LORD, Behold, I H3541
21 Therefore t saith the LORD of the men H3541
22 Therefore t saith the LORD of hosts, H3541
12:14 T saith the LORD against all mine evil H3541
13: 1 T saith the LORD unto me, Go and get H3541
9 T saith the LORD, After this manner H3541
12 them this word; T saith the LORD God H3541
13 Then shalt thou say unto them, T saith H3541
14:10 T saith the LORD unto this people, H3541
10 unto this people, T have they loved to H3651
15 Therefore t saith the LORD concerning H3541
15: 2 shalt tell them, T saith the LORD; Such H3541
19 Therefore t saith the LORD, If thou H3541
16: 3 For t saith the LORD concerning the H3541
5 For t saith the LORD, Enter not into the H3541
9 For t saith the LORD of hosts, the God H3541
17: 5 T saith the LORD; Cursed *be* the man H3541
19 T said the LORD unto me; Go and H3541
21 T saith the LORD; Take heed to H3541
18:11 of Jerusalem, saying, T saith the LORD; H3541
13 Therefore t saith the LORD; Ask ye H3541
23 *t* with them in the time of thine anger.
19: 1 T saith the LORD, Go and get a potter's H3541
3 of Jerusalem; T saith the LORD of H3541
11 And shalt say unto them, T saith the H3541
12 T will I do unto this place, saith the H3651
15 T saith the LORD of hosts, the God of H3541
20: 4 For t saith the LORD, Behold, I will H3541
21: 3 Then said Jeremiah unto them, T shall H3541
4 T saith the LORD God of Israel; Behold, H3541
8 And unto this people thou shalt say, T H3541
12 O house of David, t saith the LORD; H3541
22: 1 T saith the LORD; Go down to the H3541
3 T saith the LORD; Execute ye judgment H3541
6 For t saith the LORD unto the king's H3541
8 the LORD done t unto this great city? H3602
11 For t saith the LORD touching Shallum H3541
18 Therefore t saith the LORD concerning H3541
30 T saith the LORD, Write ye this man H3541
23: 2 Therefore t saith the LORD God of H3541
15 Therefore t saith the LORD of hosts H3541
16 T saith the LORD of hosts, Hearken not H3541
35 T shall ye say every one to his H3541
37 T shalt thou say to the prophet, What H3541
38 the LORD; therefore t saith the LORD; H3541
24: 5 T saith the LORD, the God of Israel; H3541
8 are so evil; surely t saith the LORD, So H3541
25: 8 Therefore t saith the LORD of hosts; H3541
15 For t saith the LORD God of Israel unto H3541
27 Therefore thou shalt say unto them, T H3541
28 say unto them, T saith the LORD of H3541
32 T saith the LORD of hosts, Behold, evil H3541
26: 2 T saith the LORD; Stand in the court of H3541
4 And thou shalt say unto them, T saith H3541
18 of Judah, saying, T saith the LORD of H3541
19 against them? T might we procure great
27: 2 T saith the LORD to me; Make thee H3541
4 unto their masters, T saith the LORD of H3541
4 T shall ye say unto your masters; H3541
16 this people, saying, T saith the LORD; H3541
19 For t saith the LORD of hosts H3541
21 Yea, t saith the LORD of hosts, the God H3541
28: 2 T speaketh the LORD of hosts, the God H3541
11 people, saying, T saith the LORD; Even H3602
13 Go and tell Hananiah, saying, T saith H3541
14 For t saith the LORD of hosts, the God H3541
16 Therefore t saith the LORD; Behold, I H3541
29: 4 T saith the LORD of hosts, the God of H3541

Jer 29: 8 For t saith the LORD of hosts, the God H3541
10 For t saith the LORD, That after H3541
16 *Know* that t saith the LORD of the king H3541
17 T saith the LORD of hosts; Behold, I H3541
21 T saith the LORD of hosts, the God of H3541
24 *T* shalt thou also speak to Shemaiah the
25 T speaketh the LORD of hosts, the God H3541
31 the captivity, saying, T saith the LORD H3541
32 Therefore t saith the LORD; Behold, I H3541
30: 2 T speaketh the LORD God of Israel, H3541
5 For t saith the LORD; We have heard a H3541
12 For t saith the LORD, Thy bruise *is* H3541
18 T saith the LORD; Behold, I will bring H3541
31: 2 T saith the LORD, The people *which* H3541
7 For t saith the LORD; Sing with H3541
15 T saith the LORD; A voice was heard in H3541
16 T saith the LORD; Refrain thy voice H3541
18 Ephraim bemoaning himself *t*; Thou hast
23 T saith the LORD of hosts, the God of H3541
35 T saith the LORD, which giveth the sun H3541
37 T saith the LORD; If heaven above can H3541
32: 3 and say, T saith the LORD, Behold, H3541
14 T saith the LORD of hosts, the God of H3541
15 For t saith the LORD of hosts, the God H3541
28 Therefore t saith the LORD; Behold, I H3541
36 And now therefore t saith the LORD, H3541
42 For t saith the LORD; Like as I have H3541
33: 2 T saith the LORD the maker thereof, H3541
4 For t saith the LORD, the God of Israel, H3541
10 T saith the LORD; Again there shall be H3541
12 T saith the LORD of hosts; Again in H3541
17 For t saith the LORD; David shall never H3541
20 T saith the LORD; If ye can break my H3541
24 even cast them off? t they have despised
25 T saith the LORD; If my covenant *be* H3541
34: 2 T saith the LORD, the God of Israel; Go H3541
2 and tell him, T saith the LORD; Behold, H3541
4 king of Judah; T saith the LORD of H3541
13 T saith the LORD, the God of Israel; I H3541
17 Therefore t saith the LORD; Ye have H3541
35: 8 T have we obeyed the voice of Jonadab
13 T saith the LORD of hosts, the God of H3541
17 Therefore t saith the LORD God of H3541
18 of the Rechabites, T saith the LORD of H3541
19 Therefore t saith the LORD of hosts, H3541
36:29 king of Judah, T saith the LORD; Thou H3541
30 Therefore t saith the LORD of H3541
37: 7 T saith the LORD, the God of Israel; H3541
7 the God of Israel; T shall ye say to the H3541
9 T saith the LORD; Deceive not H3541
21 city were spent. T Jeremiah remained
38: 2 T saith the LORD, He that remaineth in H3541
3 T saith the LORD, This city shall surely H3541
4 be put to death: for t he weakeneth the H3651
17 Then said Jeremiah unto Zedekiah, T H3541
39:16 Ethiopian, saying, T saith the LORD of H3541
42: 9 And said unto them, T saith the LORD, H3541
15 remnant of Judah; T saith the LORD of H3541
18 For t saith the LORD of hosts, the God H3541
43: 7 LORD: t came they *even* to Tahpanhes.
10 And say unto them, T saith the LORD H3541
44: 2 T saith the LORD of hosts, the God of H3541
7 Therefore now t saith the LORD, the H3541
11 Therefore t saith the LORD of hosts, H3541
25 T saith the LORD of hosts, the God of H3541
30 T saith the LORD; Behold, I will give H3541
45: 2 T saith the LORD, the God of Israel, H3541
4 T shalt thou say unto him, The LORD H3541
4 The LORD saith t; Behold, *that* which I H3541
47: 2 T saith the LORD; Behold, waters rise H3541
48: 1 Against Moab t saith the LORD of H3541
40 For t saith the LORD; Behold, he shall H3541
47 LORD. T far *is* the judgment of Moab. H2008
49: 1 Concerning the Ammonites, t saith the H3541
7 Concerning Edom, t saith the LORD of H3541
12 For t saith the LORD; Behold, they H3541
28 shall smite, t saith the LORD; Arise H3541
35 T saith the LORD of hosts; Behold, I H3541
50:18 Therefore t saith the LORD of hosts, H3541
33 T saith the LORD of hosts; The children H3541
51: 1 T saith the LORD; Behold, I will raise H3541
4 T the slain shall fall in the land of the
33 For t saith the LORD of hosts, the God H3541
36 Therefore t saith the LORD; Behold, I H3541
58 T saith the LORD of hosts; The broad H3541
64 And thou shalt say, T shall Babylon H3602
64 weary. T far *are* the words of Jeremiah. H2008
52:27 land of Hamath. T Judah was carried
Ezk 1:11 T *were* their faces: and their wings *were*

Ezk 2: 4 say unto them, T saith the Lord GOD. H3541
3:11 and tell them, T saith the Lord GOD; H3541
27 say unto them, T saith the Lord GOD; H3541
4:13 And the LORD said, Even t shall the H3602
5: 5 T saith the Lord GOD; This *is* H3541
7 Therefore t saith the Lord GOD; H3541
8 Therefore t saith the Lord GOD; H3541
13 T shall mine anger be accomplished,
6: 3 of the Lord GOD; T saith the Lord GOD H3541
11 T saith the Lord GOD; Smite with thine H3541
12 t will I accomplish my fury upon them.
7: 2 Also, thou son of man, t saith the Lord H3541
5 T saith the Lord GOD; An evil, an only H3541
11: 5 said unto me, Speak; T saith the LORD; H3541
5 Thus saith the LORD; T have ye said, O H3651
7 Therefore t saith the Lord GOD; Your H3541
16 Therefore say, T saith the Lord GOD; H3541
17 Therefore say, T saith the Lord GOD; I H3541
12:10 Say thou unto them, T saith the Lord H3541
19 And say unto the people of the land, T H3541
23 Tell them therefore, T saith the Lord H3541
28 Therefore say unto them, T saith the H3541
13: 3 T saith the Lord GOD; Woe unto the H3541
8 Therefore t saith the Lord GOD; H3541
13 Therefore t saith the Lord GOD; I will H3541
15 T will I accomplish my wrath upon the
18 And say, T saith the Lord GOD; Woe to H3541
20 Wherefore t saith the Lord GOD; H3541
14: 4 say unto them, T saith the Lord GOD; H3541
6 house of Israel, T saith the Lord GOD; H3541
21 For t saith the Lord GOD; How much H3541
15: 6 Therefore t saith the Lord GOD; As the H3541
16: 3 And say, T saith the Lord GOD unto H3541
13 T wast thou decked with gold and silver;
19 savour: and *t* it was, saith the Lord GOD.
36 T saith the Lord GOD; Because thy H3541
59 For t saith the Lord GOD; I will even H3541
17: 3 And say, T saith the Lord GOD; A great H3541
9 Say thou, T saith the Lord GOD; Shall it H3541
19 Therefore t saith the Lord GOD; *As* I H3541
22 T saith the Lord GOD; I will also take of H3541
20: 3 say unto them, T saith the Lord GOD; H3541
5 And say unto them, T saith the Lord H3541
27 say unto them, T saith the Lord GOD; H3541
30 house of Israel, T saith the Lord GOD; H3541
39 As for you, O house of Israel, t saith the H3541
47 of the LORD; T saith the Lord GOD; H3541
21: 3 And say to the land of Israel, T saith H3541
9 Son of man, prophesy, and say, T saith H3541
24 Therefore t saith the Lord GOD; H3541
26 T saith the Lord GOD; Remove the H3541
28 prophesy and say, T saith the Lord H3541
22: 3 Then say thou, T saith the Lord GOD, H3541
19 Therefore t saith the Lord GOD; H3541
28 them, saying, T saith the Lord GOD, H3541
23: 4 sons and daughters. T *were* their names;
7 T she committed her whoredoms with
21 T thou calledst to remembrance the
22 Therefore, O Aholibah, t saith the Lord H3541
27 T will I make thy lewdness to cease from
28 For t saith the Lord GOD; Behold, I will H3541
32 T saith the Lord GOD; Thou shalt drink H3541
35 Therefore t saith the Lord GOD; H3541
39 profane it; and, lo, t have they done in H3541
46 For t saith the Lord GOD; I will bring H3541
48 T will I cause lewdness to cease out of
24: 3 say unto them, T saith the Lord GOD; H3541
6 Wherefore t saith the Lord GOD; Woe H3541
9 Therefore t saith the Lord GOD; Woe to H3541
21 Speak unto the house of Israel, T saith H3541
24 T Ezekiel is unto you a sign: according to
25: 3 of the Lord GOD; T saith the Lord GOD; H3541
6 For t saith the Lord GOD; Because thou H3541
8 T saith the Lord GOD; Because that H3541
12 T saith the Lord GOD; Because that H3541
13 Therefore t saith the Lord GOD; I will H3541
15 T saith the Lord GOD; Because the H3541
16 Therefore t saith the Lord GOD; H3541
26: 3 Therefore t saith the Lord GOD; H3541
7 For t saith the Lord GOD; Behold, I will H3541
15 T saith the Lord GOD to Tyrus; Shall H3541
19 For t saith the Lord GOD; When I shall H3541
27: 3 for many isles, T saith the Lord GOD; H3541
28: 2 prince of Tyrus, T saith the Lord GOD; H3541
6 Therefore t saith the Lord GOD; H3541
12 and say unto him, T saith the Lord H3541
22 And say, T saith the Lord GOD; Behold, H3541
25 T saith the Lord GOD; When I shall H3541
29: 3 Speak, and say, T saith the Lord GOD; H3541

Ezk 29: 8 Therefore t saith the Lord GOD; H3541
13 Yet t saith the Lord GOD; At the end of H3541
19 Therefore t saith the Lord GOD; H3541
30: 2 Son of man, prophesy and say, T saith H3541
6 T saith the LORD; They also that H3541
10 T saith the Lord GOD; I will also make H3541
13 T saith the Lord GOD; I will also H3541
19 T will I execute judgments in Egypt: and
22 Therefore t saith the Lord GOD; H3541
31: 7 T was he fair in his greatness, in the
10 Therefore t saith the Lord GOD; H3541
15 T saith the Lord GOD; In the day when
18 To whom art thou t like in glory and in H3602
32: 3 T saith the Lord GOD; I will therefore H3541
11 For t saith the Lord GOD; The sword of H3541
33:10 house of Israel; T ye speak, saying, If H3651
25 Wherefore say unto them, T saith the H3541
27 Say thou t unto them, Thus saith the H3541
27 Say thou thus unto them, T saith the H3541
34: 2 say unto them, T saith the Lord GOD H3541
10 T saith the Lord GOD; Behold, I *am* H3541
11 For t saith the Lord GOD; Behold, I, H3541
17 And *as for* you, O my flock, t saith the H3541
20 Therefore t saith the Lord GOD unto H3541
30 T shall they know that I the LORD their
35: 3 And say unto it, T saith the Lord GOD; H3541
7 T will I make mount Seir most desolate,
13 T with your mouth ye have boasted
14 T saith the Lord GOD; When the whole H3541
36: 2 T saith the Lord GOD; Because the H3541
3 Therefore prophesy and say, T saith H3541
4 of the Lord GOD; T saith the Lord GOD H3541
5 Therefore t saith the Lord GOD; Surely H3541
6 and to the valleys, T saith the Lord H3541
7 Therefore t saith the Lord GOD; I have H3541
13 T saith the Lord GOD; Because they say H3541
22 house of Israel, T saith the Lord GOD; H3541
33 T saith the Lord GOD; In the day that I H3541
37 T saith the Lord GOD; I will yet *for* this H3541
37: 5 T saith the Lord GOD unto these bones; H3541
9 say to the wind, T saith the Lord GOD; H3541
12 say unto them, T saith the Lord GOD; H3541
19 Say unto them, T saith the Lord GOD; H3541
21 And say unto them, T saith the Lord H3541
38: 3 And say, T saith the Lord GOD; Behold, H3541
10 T saith the Lord GOD; It shall also H3541
14 and say unto Gog, T saith the Lord H3541
17 T saith the Lord GOD; *Art* thou he of H3541
23 T will I magnify myself, and sanctify
39: 1 Gog, and say, T saith the Lord GOD; H3541
16 Hamonah. T shall they cleanse the land.
17 And, thou son of man, t saith the Lord H3541
20 T ye shall be filled at my table with
25 Therefore t saith the Lord GOD; Now H3541
43:18 And he said unto me, Son of man, t H3541
20 about: t shalt thou cleanse and purge it.
44: 6 house of Israel, T saith the Lord GOD; H3541
9 T saith the Lord GOD; No stranger, H3541
45: 9 T saith the Lord GOD; Let it suffice H3541
18 T saith the Lord GOD; In the first H3541
46: 1 T saith the Lord GOD; The gate of the H3541
15 T shall they prepare the lamb, and the
16 T saith the Lord GOD; If the prince give H3541
47:13 T saith the Lord GOD; This *shall be* the H3541
Dan 1:16 T Melzar took away the portion of their
2:24 he went and said t unto him; Destroy H3652
25 in haste, and said t unto him, I have H3652
4:10 T *were* the visions of mine head in my
14 He cried aloud, and said t, Hew down H3652
6: 6 t unto him, King Darius, live for ever. H3652
7: 5 said t unto it, Arise, devour much flesh. H3652
23 T he said, The fourth beast shall be the H3652
11:17 ones with him; t shall he do: and he shall
39 T shall he do in the most strong holds
Hos 10: 4 a covenant: t judgment springeth
Am 1: 3 T saith the LORD; For three H3541
6 T saith the LORD; For three H3541
9 T saith the LORD; For three H3541
11 T saith the LORD; For three H3541
13 T saith the LORD; For three H3541
2: 1 T saith the LORD; For three H3541
4 T saith the LORD; For three H3541
6 T saith the LORD; For three H3541
11 *Is it* not even t, O ye children of Israel? H2063
3:11 Therefore t saith the Lord GOD; An H3541
12 T saith the LORD; As the shepherd H3541
4:12 Therefore t will I do unto thee, O Israel: H3541
5: 3 For t saith the Lord GOD; The city that H3541
4 For t saith the LORD unto the house of H3541
Am 5:16 the Lord, saith t; Wailing *shall be* in all H3541
7: 1 T hath the Lord GOD shewed unto me; H3541
4 T hath the Lord GOD shewed unto me: H3541
7 T he shewed me: and, behold, the Lord H3541
11 For t Amos saith, Jeroboam shall die H3541
17 Therefore t saith the LORD; Thy wife H3541
8: 1 T hath the Lord GOD shewed unto me: H3541
Oba 1 The vision of Obadiah. T saith the Lord H3541
Mic 2: 3 Therefore t saith the LORD; Behold, H3541
3: 5 T saith the LORD concerning the H3541
5: 6 entrances thereof: t shall he deliver *us*
Nah 1:12 T saith the LORD; Though *they be* H3541
12 likewise many, yet t shall they be cut H3651
Hag 1: 2 T speaketh the LORD of hosts, saying, H3541
5 Now therefore t saith the LORD of H3541
7 T saith the LORD of hosts; Consider H3541
2: 6 For t saith the LORD of hosts; Yet once, H3541
11 T saith the LORD of hosts; Ask now the H3541
Zec 1: 3 Therefore say thou unto them, T saith H3541
4 have cried, saying, T saith the LORD of H3541
14 Cry thou, saying, T saith the LORD of H3541
16 Therefore t saith the LORD; I am H3541
17 Cry yet, saying, T saith the LORD of H3541
2: 8 For t saith the LORD of hosts; After the H3541
3: 7 T saith the LORD of hosts; If thou wilt H3541
6:12 And speak unto him, saying, T H3541
7: 9 T speaketh the LORD of hosts, saying, H3541
14 they knew not. T the land was desolate
8: 2 T saith the LORD of hosts; I was H3541
3 T saith the LORD; I am returned unto H3541
4 T saith the LORD of hosts; There shall H3541
6 T saith the LORD of hosts; If it be H3541
7 T saith the LORD of hosts; Behold, I H3541
9 T saith the LORD of hosts; Let your H3541
14 For t saith the LORD of hosts; As I H3541
19 T saith the LORD of hosts; The fast of H3541
20 T saith the LORD of hosts; *It shall* yet H3541
23 T saith the LORD of hosts; In those H3541
11: 4 T saith the LORD my God; Feed the H3541
Mal 1: 4 the desolate places; t saith the LORD of
13 the lame, and the sick; t ye brought an
Mt 2: 5 for t it is written by the prophet, *G3779*
3:15 *it to be so* now: for t it becometh us to *G3779*
15: 6 *he shall be free*. T have ye made the *G2532*
26:54 scriptures be fulfilled, that t it must be? *G3779*
Mk 2: 7 Why doth this *man* t speak *G3779*
Lk 1:25 T hath the Lord dealt with me in the *G3779*
2:48 why hast thou t dealt with us? behold, *G3779*
9:34 While he t spake, there came a cloud, *G5023*
11:45 t saying thou reproachest us also. *G5023*
17:30 Even t shall it be in the day when the *G5024*
18:11 The Pharisee stood and prayed t with *G5023*
19:28 And when he had t spoken, he went *G5023*
31 do ye loose *him*? t shall ye say unto *G3779*
22:51 and said, Suffer ye t far. And he *G5127*
23:46 and having said t, he gave up the ghost. *G5023*
24:36 And as they t spake, Jesus himself *G5023*
40 And when he had t spoken, he shewed *G5124*
46 And said unto them, T it is written, *G3779*
46 it is written, and t it beholved Christ to *G3779*
Jn 4: 6 *his* journey, sat t on the well: *and* it was *G3779*
9: 6 When he had t spoken, he spat on the *G5023*
11:43 And when he t had spoken, he cried *G5023*
48 If we let him t alone, all *men* will *G3779*
13:21 When Jesus had t said, he was troubled *G5023*
18:22 And when he had t spoken, one of the *G5023*
20:14 And when she had t said, she turned *G5023*
Act 19:41 And when he had t spoken, he *G5023*
20:36 And when he had t spoken, he kneeled *G5023*
21:11 and feet, and said, T saith the Holy *G3592*
26:24 And as he t spake for himself, Festus *G5023*
30 And when he had t spoken, the king *G5023*
27:35 And when he had t spoken, he took *G5023*
Ro 9:20 formed *it*, Why hast thou made me t? *G3779*
1Co 14:25 And t are the secrets of his heart made *G3779*
2Co 1:17 When I therefore was t minded, did I *G5124*
5:14 us; because we t judge, that if one died *G5124*
Php 3:15 as be perfect, be t minded: and if in any *G5124*
Heb 6: 9 salvation, though we t speak. *G3779*
9: 6 Now when these things were t *G3779*
Rev 9:17 And t I saw the horses in the vision, *G3779*
16: 5 shalt be, because thou hast judged t. *G5023*
18:21 the sea, saying, T with violence shall *G3779*

THY See the Appendix.

THYATIRA
Act 16:14 of the city of T, which worshipped God, *G2363*
Rev 1:11 and unto T, and unto Sardis, and *G2363*
Rev 2:18 And unto the angel of the church in T *G2363*
24 unto the rest in T, as many as have not *G2363*

THYINE
Rev 18:12 scarlet, and all t wood, and all manner *G2367*

THYSELF See the Appendix.

TIBERIAS
Jn 6: 1 the sea of Galilee, which is *the sea* of T. *G5085*
23 other boats from T nigh unto the place *G5085*
21: 1 T; and on this wise shewed he *himself*. *G5085*

TIBERIUS
Lk 3: 1 of the reign of T Caesar, Pontius Pilate *G5086*

TIBHATH
1Ch 18: 8 Likewise from T, and from Chun, cities H2880

TIBNI
1Ki 16:21 people followed T the son of Ginath, to H8402
22 that followed T the son of Ginath: so H8402
22 of Ginath: so T died, and Omri reigned. H8402

TIDAL
Gen 14: 1 king of Elam, and T king of nations; H8413
9 of Elam, and with T king of nations, H8413

TIDE See EVENTIDE and NOONTIDE.

TIDINGS
Gen 29:13 Laban heard the t of Jacob his sister's H8088
Ex 33: 4 And when the people heard these evil t, H1697
1Sa 4:19 she heard the t that the ark of God H8052
11: 4 of Saul, and told the t in the ears of the H1697
5 told him the t of the men of Jabesh. H1697
6 t, and his anger was kindled greatly. H1697
27:11 alive, to bring *t* to Gath, saying, Lest
2Sa 4: 4 years old when the t came of Saul and H8052
10 have brought good t, I took hold of him, H1319
10 have given him a reward for his t: H1309
13:30 were in the way, that t came to David, H8052
18:19 and bear the king t, how that the LORD H1319
20 shalt not bear t this day, but H1309+H376
20 thou shalt bear t another day: but this H1319
20 no t, because the king's son is dead. H1319
22 son, seeing that thou hast no t ready? H1309
25 *be* alone, *there is* t in his mouth. And H1309
26 And the king said, He also bringeth t. H1319
27 *is* a good man, and cometh with good t. H1309
31 and Cushi said, T, my lord the king: for H1319
1Ki 1:42 *art* a valiant man, and bringest good t. H1319
2:28 Then t came to Joab: for Joab had H8052
14: 6 for I *am* sent to thee *with* heavy *t*.
2Ki 7: 9 day *is* a day of good t, and we hold our H1309
1Ch 10: 9 t unto their idols, and to the people. H1319
Ps 112: 7 He shall not be afraid of evil t: his heart H8052
Isa 40: 9 O Zion, that bringest good t, get thee up H1319
9 that bringest good t, lift up thy voice H1319
41:27 to Jerusalem one that bringeth good t. H1319
52: 7 that bringeth good t, that publisheth H1319
7 that bringeth good t of good, that H1319
61: 1 me to preach good t unto the meek; he H1319
Jer 20:15 Cursed *be* the man who brought t to H1319
37: 5 Jerusalem heard t of them, they H8088
49:23 have heard evil t: they are fainthearted; H8052
Ezk 21: 7 answer, For the t; because it cometh: H8052
Dan 11:44 But t out of the east and out of the H8052
Nah 1:15 that bringeth good t, that publisheth H1319
Lk 1:19 unto thee, and to shew thee these glad t. *G2097*
2:10 I bring you good t of great joy, which *G2097*
8: 1 shewing the glad t of the kingdom of *G2097*
Act 11:22 Then t of these things came unto the *G3056*
13:32 And we declare unto you glad t, how *G2097*
21:31 And as they went about to kill him, t *G5334*
Ro 10:15 peace, and bring glad t of good things! *G2097*
1Th 3: 6 and brought us good t of your faith and *G2097*

TIE
1Sa 6: 7 come no yoke, and t the kine to the cart, H631
Prv 6:21 thine heart, *and* t them about thy neck. H6029

TIED
Ex 39:31 And they t unto it a lace of blue, to H5414
1Sa 6:10 milch kine, and t them to the cart, and H631
2Ki 7:10 of man, but horses t, and asses tied, and H631
10 and asses t, and the tents as they *were*. H631
Mt 21: 2 shall find an ass t, and a colt with her: *G1210*
Mk 11: 2 it, ye shall find a colt t, whereon never *G1210*

Mk 11: 4 way, and found the colt t by the door G1210
Lk 19:30 ye shall find a colt t, whereon yet never G1210

TIGLATH-PILESER
2Ki 16: 7 So Ahaz sent messengers to T king of H8407
10 to meet T king of Assyria, and H8407

TIGLATH-PI-LESER
2Ki 15:29 of Israel came T king of Assyria, and H8407

TIKVAH
2Ki 22:14 the son of T, the son of Harhas, keeper H8616
Ezr 10:15 the son of T were employed about H8616

TIKVATH
2Ch 34:22 the son of T, the son of Hasrah, H8616+H8445

TILE
Ezk 4: 1 Thou also, son of man, take thee a t, H3843

TILGATH-PILNESER
1Ch 5: 6 Beerah his son, whom T king of H8407
26 and the spirit of T king of Assyria, and H8407
2Ch 28:20 And T king of Assyria came unto him, H8407

TILING
Lk 5:19 down through the t with *his* couch into G2766

TILL
Gen 2: 5 *there was* not a man to t the ground. H5647
3:19 thou eat bread, t thou return unto the H5704
23 garden of Eden, to t the ground from H5647
19:22 do any thing t thou be come thither. H5704
29: 8 together, and *t* they roll the stone from
38:11 thy father's house, t Shelah my son be H5704
17 thou give *me* a pledge, t thou send *it?* H5704
Ex 15:16 be *as* still as a stone; t thy people pass H5704
16 over, O LORD, t the people pass over, H5704
16:19 Let no man leave of it t the morning. H5704
24 And they laid it up t the morning, as H5704
34:33 And *t* Moses had done speaking with
40:37 not t the day that it was taken up. H5704
Nu 12:15 not t Miriam was brought in *again*. H5704
Dt 17: 5 shalt stone them with stones, t they die.
28:45 and overtake thee, t thou be destroyed; H5704
Jos 5: 6 in the wilderness, t all the people *that* H5704
8 places in the camp, t they were whole. H5704
8: 6 (For they will come out after us) t we H5704
10:20 great slaughter, t they were consumed, H5704
Jdg 3:25 And they tarried t they were ashamed: H5704
6: 4 of the earth, t thou come unto Gaza, H5704
11:33 And he smote them from Aroer, even t H5704
16: 3 And Samson lay t midnight, and arose H5704
19:26 house where her lord *was,* t it was light. H5704
21: 2 and abode there t even before God, and H5704
Ru 1:13 Would ye tarry for them t they were H5704
1Sa 10: 8 shalt thou tarry, t I come to thee, and H5704
16:11 we will not sit down t he come hither. H5704
22: 3 you, t I know what God will do for me. H5704
2Sa 3:35 bread, or ought else, t the sun be down. H6440
9:10 thy servants, shall t the land for him, H5647
1Ki 14:10 man taketh away dung, t it be all gone. H5704
18:28 t the blood gushed out upon them. H5704
2Ki 2:17 And when they urged him t he was H5704
4:20 sat on her knees t noon, and *then* died. H5704
7: 9 peace: if we tarry t the morning light, H5704
10:17 Ahab in Samaria, t he had destroyed H5704
13:17 in Aphek, t thou have consumed *them.* H5704
19 hadst thou smitten Syria t thou hadst H5704
21:16 blood very much, t he had filled H5704
2Ch 26:15 marvellously helped, t he was strong. H3588
29:34 did help them, t the work was ended, H5704
36:16 his people, t *there was* no remedy. H5704
Ezr 2:63 the most holy things, t there stood up a H5704
5: 5 them to cease, t the matter came to H5705
9:14 thou be angry with us t thou hadst H5704
Neh 2: 7 convey me over t I come into Judah; H5704
4:11 not know, neither see, t we come in the H5704
21 of the morning t the stars appeared. H5704
7:65 the most holy things, t there stood *up* a H5704
13:19 not be opened t after the sabbath: and H5704
Job 7:19 me alone t I swallow down my spittle? H5704
8:21 T he fill thy mouth with laughing, and H5704
14: 6 Turn from him, that he may rest, t he H5704
12 So man lieth down, and riseth not: t the H5704
14 time will I wait, t my change come. H5704
27: 5 God forbid that I should justify you: t I H5704
32: 4 Now Elihu had waited t Job had spoken,
Ps 10:15 out his wickedness *t* thou find none.
Ps 18:37 did I turn again t they were consumed. H5704
68:30 of the people, *t every one* submit himself
Prv 7:23 T a dart strike through his liver; as a H5704
29:11 a wise *man* keepeth it in t afterwards.
Ecc 2: 3 lay hold on folly, t I might see what *was* H5704
Song 2: 7 not up, nor awake *my* love, t he please. H5704
3: 5 not up, nor awake *my* love, t he please. H5704
Isa 5: 8 lay field to field, t *there be* no place, H5704
11 until night, *t* wine inflame them!
22:14 t ye die, saith the Lord GOD of hosts. H5704
23:13 people was not, *t* the Assyrian founded
30:17 of five shall ye flee: t ye be left as a
38:13 I reckoned t morning, *that,* as a lion, so H5704
42: 4 He shall not fail nor be discouraged, t H5704
62: 7 And give him no rest, t he establish, H5704
7 he establish, and t he make Jerusalem H5704
Jer 7:32 shall bury in Tophet, t there be no place.
9:16 after them, t I have consumed them. H5704
19:11 in Tophet, t *there be* no place to bury.
23:20 executed, and t he have performed H5704
24:10 among them, t they be consumed from H5704
27:11 and they shall t it, and dwell therein. H5647
49: 9 they will destroy t they have enough. H5704
37 after them, t I have consumed them: H5704
52: 3 and Judah, t he had cast them out H5704
11 him in prison t the day of his death. H5704
Lam 3:50 T the LORD look down, and behold H5704
Ezk 4: 8 t thou hast ended the days of thy siege. H5704
14 my youth up even t now have I not H5704
24:13 any more, t I have caused my fury H5704
28:15 created, t iniquity was found in thee. H5704
34:21 t ye have scattered them abroad; H5704
39:15 he set up a sign by it, t the buriers have H5704
19 And ye shall eat fat t ye be full, and
19 and drink blood t ye be drunken, of my
47:20 sea from the border, t a man come over H5704
Dan 2: 9 to speak before me, t the time be H5705
34 Thou sawest t that a stone was cut out H5705
4:23 the field, t seven times pass over him; H5705
25 pass over thee, t thou know that the H5705
33 with the dew of heaven, t his hairs were H5705
5:21 the dew of heaven; t he knew that the H5705
6:14 and he laboured t the going down of H5705
7: 4 wings: I beheld t the wings thereof were H5705
9 I beheld t the thrones were cast down, H5705
11 I beheld *even* t the beast was slain, H5705
10: 3 all, t three whole weeks were fulfilled. H5704
11:36 and shall prosper t the indignation be H5704
12: 9 up and sealed t the time of the end. H5704
13 But go thou thy way t the end *be*: for
Hos 5:15 I will go *and* return to my place, t they H5704
10:12 to seek the LORD, t he come and rain H5704
Oba 5 not have stolen t they had enough? if the
Jna 4: 5 it in the shadow, t he might see what H5704
Zep 3: 3 they gnaw not the bones t the morrow.
Mt 1:25 And knew her not t she had brought G2193
2: 9 went before them, t it came and stood G2193
5:18 For verily I say unto you, T heaven and G2193
18 wise pass from the law, t all be fulfilled. G2193
26 t thou hast paid the uttermost farthing. G2193
10:11 worthy; and there abide t ye go thence. G2193
23 of Israel, t the Son of man be come. G2193
12:20 t he send forth judgment unto victory. G2193
13:33 of meal, t the whole was leavened. G2193
16:28 not taste of death, t they see the Son of G2193
18:21 me, and I forgive him? t seven times? G2193
30 into prison, t he should pay the debt. G2193
34 to the tormentors, t he should pay all G2193
22:44 t I make thine enemies thy footstool? G2193
23:39 not see me henceforth, t ye shall say, G2193
24:34 not pass, t all these things be fulfilled. G2193
Mk 6:10 there abide t ye depart from that place. G2193
9: 1 not taste of death, t they have seen the G2193
9 they had seen, t the Son of man were G3752
12:36 t I make thine enemies thy footstool. G2193
13:30 not pass, t all these things be done. G3360
Lk 1:80 t the day of his shewing unto Israel. G2193
9:27 death, t they see the kingdom of God. G2193
12:50 am I straitened t it be accomplished! G2193
59 t thou hast paid the very last mite. G2193
13: 8 also, t I shall dig about it, and dung *it*: G2193
21 of meal, t the whole was leavened. G2193
15: 8 house, and seek diligently t she find *it?* G2193
17: 8 and serve me, t I have eaten and G2193
19:13 and said unto them, Occupy t I come. G2193
20:43 T I make thine enemies thy footstool. G2193
21:32 shall not pass away, t all be fulfilled. G2193
Jn 13:38 not crow, t thou hast denied me thrice. G2193
21:22 If I will that he tarry t I come, what *is* G2193
Jn 21:23 he tarry t I come, what *is that* to thee? G2193
Act 7:18 T another king arose, which knew not G891
8:40 in all the cities, t he came to Caesarea. G2193
20:11 even t break of day, so he departed. G891
21: 5 and children, t *we were* out of the city: G2193
23:12 eat nor drink t they had killed Paul. G2193
21 eat nor drink t they have killed him: G2193
25:21 to be kept t I might send him to Caesar. G2193
28:23 the prophets, from morning t evening. G2193
1Co 11:26 ye do shew the Lord's death t he come. G891
15:25 For he must reign, t he hath put all G891
Gal 3:19 of transgressions, t the seed should G891
Eph 4:13 T we all come in the unity of the faith, G3360
Php 1:10 and without offence t the day of Christ; G1519
1Ti 4:13 T I come, give attendance to reading, G2193
Heb 10:13 From henceforth expecting t his G2193
Rev 2:25 which ye have *already* hold fast t I come. G891
7: 3 sea, nor the trees, t we have sealed the G891
15: 8 into the temple, t the seven plagues of G891
20: 3 nations no more, t the thousand years G891

TILLAGE
1Ch 27:26 of the field for t of the ground *was* Ezri H5656
Neh 10:37 have the tithes in all the cities of our t. H5656
Prv 13:23 Much food *is in* the t of the poor: but H5215

TILLED
Ezk 36: 9 unto you, and ye shall be t and sown: H5647
34 And the desolate land shall be t, H5647

TILLER
Gen 4: 2 sheep, but Cain was a t of the ground. H5647

TILLEST
Gen 4:12 When thou t the ground, it shall not H5647

TILLETH
Prv 12:11 He that t his land shall be satisfied with H5647
28:19 He that t his land shall have plenty of H5647

TILON
1Ch 4:20 Ben-hanan, and T. And the sons of Ishi H8436

TIMAEUS
Mk 10:46 of T, sat by the highway side begging. G5090

TIMBER
Ex 31: 5 *them,* and in carving of t, to work in all H6086
Lev 14:45 of it, and the t thereof, and all the H6086
1Ki 5: 6 skill to hew t like unto the Sidonians. H6086
8 thy desire concerning t of cedar, and H6086
8 timber of cedar, and concerning t of fir. H6086
18 t and stones to build the house. H6086
6:10 rested on the house *with* t of cedar. H6086
15:22 of Ramah, and the t thereof, wherewith H6086
2Ki 12:12 stone, and to buy t and hewed stone to H6086
22: 6 t and hewn stone to repair the house. H6086
1Ch 14: 1 to David, and t of cedars, with masons H6086
22:14 for it is in abundance: t also and stone H6086
15 of stone and t, and all manner of H6086
2Ch 2: 8 can skill to cut t in Lebanon; and, H6086
9 Even to prepare me t in abundance: for H6086
10 the hewers that cut t, twenty thousand H6086
14 in stone, and in t, in purple, in blue, H6086
16: 6 of Ramah, and the t thereof, wherewith H6086
34:11 hewn stone, and t for couplings, and to H6086
Ezr 5: 8 great stones, and t is laid in the walls, H636
6: 4 and a row of new t: and let the expenses H636
11 alter this word, let t be pulled down from H636
Neh 2: 8 he may give me t to make beams for H6086
Ezk 26:12 t and thy dust in the midst of the water. H6086
Hab 2:11 the beam out of the t shall answer it. H6086
Zec 5: 4 the t thereof and the stones thereof. H6086

TIMBREL
Ex 15:20 of Aaron, took a t in her hand; and all H8596
Job 21:12 They take the t and harp, and rejoice at H8596
Ps 81: 2 Take a psalm, and bring hither the t, H8596
149: 3 praises unto him with the t and harp. H8596
150: 4 Praise him with the t and dance: praise H8596

TIMBRELS
Ex 15:20 out after her with t and with dances. H8596
Jdg 11:34 to meet him with t and with dances: H8596
2Sa 6: 5 on t, and on cornets, and on cymbals. H8596
1Ch 13: 8 t, and with cymbals, and with trumpets. H8596
Ps 68:25 *them were* the damsels playing with t. H8608

T

TIME
Gen 4: 3 And in process of **t** it came to pass, that H3117
17:21 unto thee at this set **t** in the next year. H4150
18:10 according to the **t** of life; and, lo, Sarah H6256
14 for the LORD? At the **t** appointed I will H4150
14 the **t** of life, and Sarah shall have a son. H6256
21: 2 set **t** of which God had spoken to him. H4150
22 And it came to pass at that **t**, that H6256
22:15 Abraham out of heaven the second **t**, H8145
24:11 of water at the **t** of the evening, *even* H6256
11 the **t** that women go out to draw *water.* H6256
26: 8 been there a long **t**, that Abimelech king H3117
29: 7 day, neither *is it* **t** that the cattle should H6256
34 and said, Now this **t** will my husband H6471
30:33 answer for me in **t** to come, when it H3117
31:10 And it came to pass at the **t** that the H6256
38: 1 And it came to pass at that **t**, that Judah H6256
12 And in process of **t** the daughter of H3117
27 And it came to pass in the **t** of her H6256
39: 5 And it came to pass from the **t** *that* he H227
11 And it came to pass about this **t**, that H3117
41: 5 And he slept and dreamed the second **t**: H8145
43:10 now we had returned this second **t**. H6471
18 sacks at the first **t** are we brought in; H8462
20 indeed down at the first **t** to buy food: H8462
47:29 And the **t** drew nigh that Israel must H3117
Ex 2:23 And it came to pass in process of **t**, that H3117
8:32 his heart at this **t** also, neither would H6471
9: 5 And the LORD appointed a set **t**, H4150
14 For I will at this **t** send all my plagues H6471
18 Behold, to morrow about this **t** I will H6256
27 them, I have sinned this **t**: the LORD *is* H6471
13:14 son asketh thee in **t** to come, saying, H4297
21:19 *for* the loss of his **t**, and shall cause *him* H7674
29 with his horn in **t** past, and it hath been H7674
36 used to push in **t** past, and his H8543+H8032
23:15 thee, in the **t** appointed of the H8543+H8032
34:18 thee, in the **t** of the month Abib: H4150
21 earing **t** and in harvest thou shalt rest. H2758
Lev 13:58 washed the second **t**, and shall be clean. H8145
15:25 days out of the **t** of her separation, or H6256
25 if it run beyond the **t** of her separation; H5921
18:18 nakedness, beside the other in her life *t*.
25:32 may the Levites redeem at any **t**. H5769
50 according to the **t** of an hired servant H3117
26: 5 unto the sowing **t**: and ye shall eat your H2233
Nu 10: 6 When ye blow an alarm the second **t**, H8145
13:20 **t** *was* the time of the firstripe grapes. H3117
20 time *was* the **t** of the firstripe grapes. H3117
14:14 them, by day **t** in a pillar of a cloud, H3119
20:15 in Egypt a long **t**; and the Egyptians H3117
22: 4 *was* king of the Moabites at that **t**. H6256
23:23 according to this **t** it shall be said of H6256
26:10 died, what **t** the fire devoured two
32:10 the same **t**, and he sware, saying, H3117
35:26 But if the slayer shall at any **t** come H3318
Dt 1: 9 And I spake unto you at that **t**, saying, I H6256
16 And I charged your judges at that **t**, H6256
18 And I commanded you at that **t** all the H6256
2:20 therein in old **t**; and the Ammonites H6440
34 And we took all his cities at that **t**, and H6256
3: 4 And we took all his cities at that **t**, there H6256
8 And we took at that **t** out of the hand of H6256
12 possessed at that **t**, from Aroer, which H6256
18 And I commanded you at that **t**, saying, H6256
21 And I commanded Joshua at that **t**, H6256
23 And I besought the LORD at that **t**, H6256
4:14 me at that **t** to teach you statutes H6256
5: 5 and you at that **t**, to shew you the word H6256
6:20 *And* when thy son asketh thee in **t** to H4279
9:19 hearkened unto me at that **t** also. H6471
20 and I prayed for Aaron also the same **t**. H6256
10: 1 At that **t** the LORD said unto me, Hew H6256
8 At that **t** the LORD separated the tribe H6256
10 to the first **t**, forty days and forty H3117
10 unto me at that **t** also, *and* the LORD H6471
16: 9 weeks from *such* **t** *as* thou beginnest *to*
19: 4 whom he hated not in **t** past; H8543+H8032
6 as he hated him not in **t** past. H8543+H8032
14 which they of old **t** have set in thine H7223
20:19 When thou shalt besiege a city a long **t**, H3117
32:35 shall slide in *due* **t**: for the day of their H6256
Jos 2: 5 And it came to pass *about the* **t** of
3:15 all his banks all the **t** of harvest,) H3117
4: 6 *their fathers* in **t** to come, saying, What H4279
21 ask their fathers in **t** to come, saying,
5: 2 At that **t** the LORD said unto Joshua, H6256
2 again the children of Israel the second **t**. H8145
6:16 And it came to pass at the seventh **t**, H6471

Jos 6:26 And Joshua adjured *them* at that **t**, H6256
8:14 all his people, at a **t** appointed, before
10:27 And it came to pass at the **t** of the H6256
42 Joshua take at one **t**, because the LORD H6471
11: 6 morrow about this **t** will I deliver them H6256
10 And Joshua at that **t** turned back, and H6256
18 Joshua made war a long **t** with all those H3117
21 And at that **t** came Joshua, and cut off H6256
22:24 *this* thing, saying, In **t** to come your H4279
27 to our children in **t** to come, Ye have no H4279
28 to our generations in **t** to come, that we H4279
23: 1 And it came to pass a long **t** after that H3117
24: 2 side of the flood in old **t**, *even* Terah, the H5769
Jdg 3:29 And they slew of Moab at that **t** about H6256
4: 4 of Lapidoth, she judged Israel at that **t**. H6256
9: 8 The trees went forth *on a t* to anoint a
10:14 deliver you in the **t** of your tribulation. H6256
11: 4 And it came to pass in process of **t**, that H3117
26 did ye not recover *them* within that **t**? H6256
12: 6 there fell at that **t** of the Ephraimites H6256
13:23 this **t** have told us *such things* as these. H6256
14: 4 for at that **t** the Philistines had H6256
8 And after a **t** he returned to take her, H3117
15: 1 a while after, in the **t** of wheat harvest, H3117
18:31 **t** that the house of God was in Shiloh. H3117
20:15 numbered at that **t** out of the cities H3117
21:14 And Benjamin came again at that **t**; H6256
22 them at this **t**, *that* ye should be guilty. H6256
24 thence at that **t**, every man to his tribe H6256
Ru 4: 7 Now this *was the manner* in former **t** in H6440
1Sa 1: 4 And when the **t** was that Elkanah H3117
20 Wherefore it came to pass, when the **t** H3117
3: 2 And it came to pass at that **t**, when Eli H3117
8 again the third **t**. And he arose and went
4:20 And about the **t** of her death the H6256
7: 2 that the **t** was long; for it was H3117
9:13 up; for about this **t** ye shall find him. H3117
16 To morrow about this **t** I will send thee H6256
24 eat: for unto this **t** hath it been kept for H4150
11: 9 To morrow, by *that t* the sun be hot, ye
13: 8 to the set **t** that Samuel *had appointed:* H4150
14:18 was at that **t** with the children of Israel. H3117
21 before that **t**, which went up with H8032
18:19 But it came to pass at the **t** when H6256
19:21 the third **t**, and they prophesied also.
20:12 to morrow any **t**, *or* the third *day,* and, H6256
35 out into the field at the **t** appointed with
26: 8 and I will not *smite* him the second **t**. H8138
27: 7 And the **t** that David dwelt in H4557+H3117
2Sa 2:11 And the **t** that David was king H4557+H3117
5: 2 Also in **t** past, when Saul was H865+H8543
7: 6 house since the **t** that I brought up the H3117
11 And as since the **t** that I commanded H3117
11: 1 expired, at the **t** when kings go forth H6256
14: 2 that had a long **t** mourned for the dead: H3117
29 again the second **t**, he would not come. H8145
17: 7 hath given *is* not good at this **t**. H6471
20: 5 the set **t** which he had appointed him. H4150
18 to speak in old **t**, saying, They shall H7223
23: 8 eight hundred, whom he slew at one **t**. H6471
13 David in the harvest **t** unto the cave of
20 a lion in the midst of a pit in **t** of snow: H3117
24:15 even to the **t** appointed: and there H6256
1Ki 1: 6 him at any **t** in saying, Why hast H3117
2:26 but I will not at this **t** put thee to death, H3117
8:65 And at that **t** Solomon held a feast, and H6256
9: 2 the second **t**, as he had appeared H8145
11:29 And it came to pass at that **t** when H6256
42 And the **t** that Solomon reigned in H3117
14: 1 At that **t** Abijah the son of Jeroboam H6256
15:23 in the **t** of his old age he was H6256
18:29 until the *t* of the offering of the
34 And he said, Do *it* the second **t**. And H8138
34 did *it* the second **t**. And he said, Do *it* H8138
34 third **t**. And they did *it* the third time. H8027
34 third time. And they did *it* the third **t**. H8027
36 And it came to pass at *the t of* the
44 And it came to pass at the seventh **t**, H7637
19: 2 one of them by to morrow about this **t**. H6256
7 again the second **t**, and touched him, H8145
20: 6 to morrow about this **t**, and they shall H6256
2Ki 3: 6 the same **t**, and numbered all Israel. H3117
4:16 according to the **t** of life, thou shalt H6256
17 said unto her, according to the **t** of life. H6256
5:26 to meet thee? *Is it* a **t** to receive money, H6256
7: 1 morrow about this **t** *shall* a measure of H6256
18 about this **t** in the gate of Samaria: H6256
8:22 Then Libnah revolted at the same **t**. H6256
10: 6 Then he wrote a letter the second **t** to H8145

2Ki 10: 6 by to morrow this **t**. Now the king's H6256
36 And the **t** that Jehu reigned over Israel H3117
16: 6 At that **t** Rezin king of Syria recovered H6256
18:16 At that **t** did Hezekiah cut off *the gold* H6256
20:12 At that **t** Berodach-baladan, the son of H6256
24:10 At that **t** the servants of H6256
1Ch 9:20 in **t** past, *and* the LORD *was* with him. H6440
25 seven days from **t** to time with them. H6256
25 seven days from time to **t** with them. H6256
11: 2 And moreover in **t** past, even when H8543
11 three hundred slain *by him* at one **t**. H6471
12:22 For at *that* **t** day by day there came to H6256
17:10 And since the **t** that I commanded H3117
20: 1 expired, at the **t** that kings go out *to* H6256
4 at which **t** Sibbechai the Hushathite H227
21:28 At that **t** when David saw that the H6256
29:22 king the second **t**, and anointed *him* H8145
27 And the **t** that he reigned over Israel H3117
2Ch 7: 8 Also at the same **t** Solomon kept the H6256
13:18 under at that **t**, and the children of H6256
15:11 the LORD the same **t**, of the spoil *which* H3117
16: 7 And at that **t** Hanani the seer came to H6256
10 *some* of the people the same **t**. H6256
18:34 the **t** of the sun going down he died. H6256
21:10 this day. The same **t** *also* did Libnah H6256
19 in process of **t**, after the end of H3117+H3117
24:11 Now it came to pass, that at what **t** the H6256
25:27 Now after the **t** that Amaziah did turn H6256
28:16 At that **t** did king Ahaz send unto the H6256
22 And in the **t** of his distress did he H6256
30: 3 For they could not keep it at that **t**, H6256
5 a long **t** *in such sort* as it was written. H6256
26 for since the **t** of Solomon the son H3117
35:17 the passover at that **t**, and the feast of H6256
Ezr 4:10 on this side the river, and at such a **t**. H3706
11 on this side the river, and at such a **t**. H3706
15 the same of old **t**: for which cause was H3118
17 beyond the river, Peace, and at such a **t**. H3706
19 found that this city of old **t** hath made H3118
5: 3 At the same **t** came to them Tatnai, H2166
16 and since that **t** even until now hath H116
7:12 heaven, perfect *peace*, and at such a **t**. H3706
8:34 and all the weight was written at that **t**. H6256
10:13 But the people *are* many, and *it is* a **t** of H6256
Neh 2: 6 the king to send me; and I set him a **t**. H2165
4:16 And it came to pass from that **t** forth, H3117
22 Likewise at the same **t** said I unto the H6256
5:14 Moreover from the **t** that I was H3117
6: 1 (though at that **t** I had not set up the H6256
5 fifth **t** with an open letter in his hand; H6471
9:27 them: and in the **t** of their trouble, H6256
32 **t** of the kings of Assyria unto this day. H3117
12:44 And at that **t** were some appointed H3117
13: 6 But in all this *t* was not I at Jerusalem:
21 on you. From that **t** forth came they no H6256
Est 2:19 **t**, then Mordecai sat in the king's gate. H8145
4:14 thy peace at this **t**, *then* shall there H6256
14 to the kingdom for *such* a **t** as this? H6256
8: 9 called at that **t** in the third month, H6256
9:27 to their *appointed* **t** every year; H2165
Job 6:17 What **t** they wax warm, they vanish: H6256
7: 1 *Is there* not an appointed **t** to man H6635
9:19 who shall set me a **t** *to plead*? H3259
14:13 appoint me a set **t**, and remember me! H2706
14 **t** will I wait, till my change come. H6635
15:32 It shall be accomplished before his **t**, H3117
22:16 Which were cut down out of **t**, whose H6256
30: 3 in former **t** desolate and waste. H570
38:23 Which I have reserved against the **t** of H6256
39: 1 Knowest thou the **t** when the wild goats H6256
2 thou the **t** when they bring forth? H6256
18 What **t** she lifteth up herself on high, H6256
Ps 4: 7 more than in the **t** *that* their corn and H6256
21: 9 a fiery oven in the **t** of thine anger: the H6256
27: 5 For in the **t** of trouble he shall hide me H3117
32: 6 unto thee in a **t** when thou mayest be H6256
37:19 They shall not be ashamed in the evil **t**: H6256
39 *he is* their strength in the **t** of trouble. H6256
41: 1 LORD will deliver him in **t** of trouble. H3117
56: 3 What **t** I am afraid, I will trust in thee. H3117
69:13 LORD, *in* an acceptable **t**: O God, in the H6256
71: 9 Cast me not off in the **t** of old age; H6256
78:38 not: yea, many a **t** turned he his anger H7235
81: 3 **t** appointed, on our solemn feast day.
15 their **t** should have endured for ever. H6256
89:47 Remember how short my **t** is: H2465
102:13 upon Zion: for the **t** to favour her, yea, H6256
13 to favour her, yea, the set **t**, is come. H4150
105:19 Until the **t** that his word came: the H6256

Ps 113: 2 from this **t** forth and for evermore.
115:18 But we will bless the LORD from this **t** H6258
119:126 *It is* **t** for *thee*, LORD, to work: *for* they H6256
121: 8 from this **t** forth, and even for evermore.
129: 1 Many a **t** have they afflicted me from H7227
2 Many a **t** have they afflicted me from H7227
Prv 25:13 As the cold of snow in the **t** of harvest, H3117
19 Confidence in an unfaithful man in **t** of H3117
31:25 and she shall rejoice in **t** to come. H3117
Ecc 1:10 already of old **t**, which was before us. H5769
3: 1 a **t** to every purpose under the heaven: H6256
2 A **t** to be born, and a time to die; a time H6256
2 A time to be born, and a **t** to die; a time H6256
2 A time to be born, and a time to die; a **t** H6256
2 a **t** to pluck up *that which is* planted; H6256
3 A **t** to kill, and a time to heal; a time to H6256
3 A time to kill, and a **t** to heal; a time to H6256
3 A time to kill, and a time to heal; a **t** to H6256
3 to break down, and a **t** to build up; H6256
4 A **t** to weep, and a time to laugh; a time H6256
4 A time to weep, and a **t** to laugh; a time H6256
4 A time to weep, and a time to laugh; a **t** H6256
4 a time to mourn, and a **t** to dance; H6256
5 A **t** to cast away stones, and a time to H6256
5 A time to cast away stones, and a **t** to H6256
5 stones together; a **t** to embrace, and a H6256
5 and a **t** to refrain from embracing; H6256
6 A **t** to get, and a time to lose; a time to H6256
6 A time to get, and a **t** to lose; a time to H6256
6 A time to get, and a time to lose; a **t** to H6256
6 a time to keep, and a **t** to cast away; H6256
7 A **t** to rend, and a time to sew; a time to H6256
7 A time to rend, and a **t** to sew; a time to H6256
7 A time to rend, and a time to sew; a **t** to H6256
7 a time to keep silence, and a **t** to speak; H6256
8 A **t** to love, and a time to hate; a time of H6256
8 A time to love, and a **t** to hate; a time of H6256
8 A time to love, and a time to hate; a **t** of H6256
8 to hate; a time of war, and a **t** of peace. H6256
11 beautiful in his **t**: also he hath set the H6256
17 for *there is* a **t** there for every purpose H6256
7:17 why shouldest thou die before thy **t**? H6256
8: 5 heart discerneth both **t** and judgment. H6256
6 Because to every purpose there is **t** and H6256
9 the sun: *there is* a **t** wherein one man H6256
9:11 **t** and chance happeneth to them all. H6256
12 For man also knoweth not his **t**: as the H6256
12 **t**, when it falleth suddenly upon them. H6256
Song 2:12 The flowers appear on the earth; the **t** H6256
Isa 11:11 hand again the second **t** to recover the H8145
13:22 palaces: and her **t** *is* near to come, and H6256
16:13 spoken concerning Moab since that **t**. H227
18: 7 In that **t** shall the present be brought H6256
20: 2 At the same **t** spake the LORD by H6256
26:17 draweth near the **t** of her delivery, is in
28:19 From the **t** that it goeth forth it shall H1767
30: 8 be for the **t** to come for ever and ever: H3117
33: 2 our salvation also in the **t** of trouble. H6256
39: 1 At that **t** Merodach-baladan, the son of H6256
42:14 I have long **t** holden my peace; I have H5769
23 will hearken and hear for the **t** to come? H268
44: 8 I told thee from that **t**, and have declared H227
45:21 this from ancient **t**? *who* hath told it H6924
21 told it from that **t**? *have* not I the LORD? H227
48: 6 things from this **t**, even hidden things, H6258
8 not; yea, from that **t** *that* thine ear was H6256
16 from the **t** that it was, there *am* H6256
49: 8 In an acceptable **t** have I heard thee, H6256
60:22 I the LORD will hasten it in his **t**. H6256
Jer 1:13 me the second **t**, saying, What seest H8145
2:20 For of old **t** I have broken thy yoke, *and*
27 face: but in the **t** of their trouble they H6256
28 can save thee in the **t** of thy trouble: for H6256
3: 4 Wilt thou not from this **t** cry unto me, H6258
17 At that **t** they shall call Jerusalem the H6256
4:11 At that **t** shall it be said to this people H6256
6:15 that fall: at the **t** *that* I visit them they H6256
8: 1 At that **t**, saith the LORD, they shall H6256
7 observe the **t** of their coming; but H6256
12 that fall: in the **t** of their visitation they H6256
15 for a **t** of health, and behold trouble! H6256
10:15 **t** of their visitation they shall perish. H6256
11:12 save them at all in the **t** of their trouble. H6256
14 hear *them* in the **t** that they cry unto H6256
13: 3 came unto me the second **t**, saying, H8145
14: 8 the saviour thereof in **t** of trouble, why H6256
19 for the **t** of healing, and behold trouble! H6256
15:11 the **t** of evil and in the time of affliction. H6256
11 the time of evil and in the **t** of affliction. H6256
Jer 18:23 *thus* with them in the **t** of thine anger. H6256
27: 7 son, until the very **t** of his land come: H6256
30: 7 it: it *is* even the **t** of Jacob's trouble; but H6256
31: 1 At the same **t**, saith the LORD, will I be H6256
33: 1 the second **t**, while he was yet shut
15 In those days, and at that **t**, will I cause H6256
39:10 them vineyards and fields at the same **t**. H3117
46:17 a noise; he hath passed the **t** appointed.
21 upon them, *and* the **t** of their visitation. H6256
49: 8 upon him, the **t** *that* I will visit him. H6256
19 will appoint me the **t**? and who *is* that H3259
50: 4 In those days, and in that **t**, saith the H6256
16 the sickle in the **t** of harvest: for fear of H6256
20 In those days, and in that **t**, saith the H6256
27 day is come, the **t** of their visitation. H6256
31 day is come, the **t** *that* I will visit thee. H6256
44 will appoint me the **t**? and who *is* that H3259
51: 6 iniquity; for this *is* the **t** of the LORD'S H6256
18 **t** of their visitation they shall perish. H6256
33 *it is* **t** to thresh her: yet a little H6256
33 and the **t** of her harvest shall come. H6256
Lam 5:20 us for ever, *and* forsake us so long **t**? H3117
Ezk 4:10 a day: from **t** to time shalt thou eat it. H6256
10 a day: from time to **t** shalt thou eat it. H6256
11 an hin: from **t** to time shalt thou drink. H6256
11 an hin: from time to **t** shalt thou drink. H6256
7: 7 in the land: the **t** is come, the day of H6256
12 The **t** is come, the day draweth near: let H6256
16: 8 thee, behold, thy **t** *was* the time of love; H6256
8 thy time *was* the **t** of love; and I spread H6256
57 as at the **t** of *thy* reproach of the H6256
21:14 be doubled the third **t**, the sword of the
22: 3 of it, that her **t** may come, and maketh H6256
26:20 the people of old **t**, and shall set thee in H5769
27:34 In the **t** *when* thou shalt be broken by H6256
30: 3 day; it shall be the **t** of the heathen. H6256
35: 5 of the sword in the **t** of their calamity, H6256
5 in the **t** *that their* iniquity *had* an end: H6256
38:10 *that* at the same **t** shall things come H3117
17 have spoken in old **t** by my servants the H3117
18 And it shall come to pass at the same **t** H3117
Dan 2: 8 ye would gain the **t**, because ye see the H5732
9 speak before me, till the **t** be changed: H5732
16 he would give him **t**, and that he would H2166
3: 5 *That* at what **t** ye hear the sound of the H5732
7 Therefore at that **t**, when all the people H2166
8 Wherefore at that **t** certain Chaldeans H2166
15 Now if ye be ready that at what **t** ye H5732
4:36 At the same **t** my reason returned unto H2166
7:12 lives were prolonged for a season and **t**. H5732
22 High; and the **t** came that the saints H2166
25 a **t** and times and the dividing of time. H5732
25 a time and times and the dividing of **t**. H5732
8:17 at the **t** of the end *shall be* the vision. H6256
19 for at the **t** appointed the end *shall be*.
23 And in the latter **t** of their kingdom, H319
9:21 me about the **t** of the evening oblation. H6256
10: 1 *was* true, but the **t** appointed *was* long:
11:24 against the strong holds, even for a **t**. H6256
27 yet the end *shall be* at the **t** appointed.
29 At the **t** appointed he shall return, and
35 white, *even* to the **t** of the end: because H6256
35 end: because *it is* yet for a **t** appointed.
40 And at the **t** of the end shall the king of H6256
12: 1 And at that **t** shall Michael stand up, H6256
1 there shall be a **t** of trouble, such as H6256
1 *even* to that same **t**: and at that time thy H6256
1 time: and at that **t** thy people shall be H6256
4 the book, *even* to the **t** of the end: many H6256
7 *it shall be* for a **t**, times, and an half; H4150
9 up and sealed till the **t** of the end. H6256
11 And from the **t** *that* the daily *sacrifice* H6256
Hos 2: 9 my corn in the **t** thereof, and my wine H6256
9:10 fig tree at her first **t**: *but* they went to H7225
10:12 ground: for *it is* **t** to seek the LORD, till H6256
Joel 3: 1 For, behold, in those days, and in that **t**, H6256
Am 5:13 silence in that **t**; for it *is* an evil time. H6256
13 silence in that time; for it *is* an evil **t**. H6256
Jna 3: 1 came unto Jonah the second **t**, saying,
Mic 2: 3 shall ye go haughtily: for this **t** *is* evil. H6256
3: 4 face from them at that **t**, as they have H6256
5: 3 give them up, until the **t** *that* she which H6256
Nah 1: 9 affliction shall not rise up the second **t**. H6471
Hab 2: 3 For the vision *is* yet for an appointed **t**, H4150
Zep 1:12 And it shall come to pass at that **t**, *that* I H6256
3:19 Behold, at that **t** I will undo all that H6256
20 At that **t** will I bring you *again*, even in H6256
20 *again*, even in the **t** that I gather you: H6256
Hag 1: 2 people say, The **t** is not come, the time H6256
Hag 1: 2 time is not come, the **t** that the LORD'S H6256
4 *Is it* **t** for you, O ye, to dwell in your H6256
Zec 10: 1 Ask ye of the LORD rain in the **t** of the H6256
14: 7 pass, *that* at evening **t** it shall be light. H6256
Mal 3:11 **t** in the field, saith the LORD of hosts. H7921
Mt 1:11 **t** they were carried away to Babylon: *G1909*
2: 7 diligently what **t** the star appeared. *G5550*
16 under, according to the **t** which he had *G5550*
4: 6 **t** thou dash thy foot against a stone. *G3379*
17 From that **t** Jesus began to preach, and *G5119*
5:21 said by them of old **t**, Thou shalt not kill; *G744*
25 him; lest at any **t** the adversary deliver *G3379*
27 of old **t**, Thou shalt not commit adultery: *G744*
33 said by them of old **t**, Thou shalt not *G744*
8:29 come hither to torment us before the **t**? *G2540*
11:25 At that **t** Jesus answered and said, I *G2540*
12: 1 At that **t** Jesus went on the sabbath day *G2540*
13:15 closed; lest at any **t** they should see *G3379*
30 harvest: and in the **t** of harvest I will *G2540*
14: 1 At that **t** Herod the tetrarch heard of *G2540*
15 place, and the **t** is now past; send the *G5610*
16:21 From that **t** forth began Jesus to shew *G5119*
18: 1 At the same **t** came the disciples unto *G5610*
21:34 And when the **t** of the fruit drew near, *G2540*
24:21 the world to this **t**, no, nor ever shall be. *G3568*
25:19 After a long **t** the lord of those servants *G5550*
26:16 And from that **t** he sought opportunity *G5119*
18 The Master saith, My **t** is at hand; I will *G2540*
42 He went away again the second **t**, and *G1208*
44 the third **t**, saying the same words. *G5154*
Mk 1:15 And saying, The **t** is fulfilled, and the *G2540*
4:12 lest at any **t** they should be converted, *G3379*
17 so endure but for a **t**: afterward, when *G4340*
6:35 place, and now the **t** *is* far passed: *G5610*
10:30 now in this **t**, houses, and brethren, *G2540*
11:13 but leaves; for the **t** of figs was not *yet*. *G2540*
13:19 God created unto this **t**, neither shall be. *G3568*
33 pray: for ye know not when the **t** is. *G2540*
14:41 And he cometh the third **t**, and saith *G5154*
72 And the second **t** the cock crew. And *G1208*
Lk 1:10 praying without at the **t** of incense. *G5610*
57 Now Elisabeth's full **t** came that she *G5550*
4: 5 of the world in a moment of **t**. *G5550*
11 **t** thou dash thy foot against a stone. *G3379*
27 And many lepers were in Israel in the **t** *G1909*
7:45 woman since the **t** I came in hath not *G3739*
8:13 and in **t** of temptation fall away. *G2540*
27 had devils long **t**, and ware no clothes, *G5550*
9:51 And it came to pass, when the **t** was *G2250*
12: 1 In the mean **t**, when there were *G1722*
56 how is it that ye do not discern this **t**? *G2540*
13:35 see me, until *the* **t** come when ye shall
14:17 And sent his servant at supper **t** to say *G5610*
15:29 I at any **t** thy commandment: *G3763*
16:16 John: since that **t** the kingdom of God *G5119*
18:30 in this present **t**, and in the world to *G2540*
19:44 thou knewest not the **t** of thy visitation. *G2540*
20: 9 and went into a far country for a long **t**. *G5550*
21: 8 I am *Christ*; and the **t** draweth near: go *G2540*
34 lest at any **t** your hearts be overcharged *G3379*
37 And in the day **t** he was teaching in the *G2250*
23: 7 himself also was at Jerusalem at that **t**. *G2250*
22 And he said unto them the third **t**, Why, *G5154*
Jn 1:18 No man hath seen God at any **t**; the *G4455*
3: 4 **t** into his mother's womb, and be born? *G1208*
5: 6 been now a long **t** *in that case*, he saith *G5550*
37 his voice at any **t**, nor seen his shape. *G4455*
6:66 From that ***t*** many of his disciples went
7: 6 Then Jesus said unto them, My **t** is not *G2540*
6 not yet come: but your **t** is alway ready. *G2540*
8 this feast; for my **t** is not yet full come. *G2540*
11:39 him, Lord, by this **t** he stinketh: for he *G2235*
14: 9 I been so long **t** with you, and yet hast *G5550*
16: 2 yea, the **t** cometh, that whosoever *G5610*
4 you, that when the **t** shall come, ye may *G5610*
25 in proverbs: but the **t** cometh, when I *G5610*
21:14 This is now the third **t** that Jesus *G5154*
16 He saith to him again the second **t**, *G1208*
17 He saith unto him the third **t**, Simon, *G5154*
17 unto him the third **t**, Lovest thou me? *G5154*
Act 1: 6 **t** restore again the kingdom to Israel? *G5550*
21 with us all the **t** that the Lord Jesus *G5550*
7:13 And at the second ***t*** Joseph was made
17 But when the **t** of the promise drew *G5550*
20 In which **t** Moses was born, and was *G2540*
8: 1 death. And at that **t** there was a great *G2250*
11 that of long **t** he had bewitched them *G5550*
10:15 him again the second **t**, What God hath *G1208*
11: 8 hath at any **t** entered into my mouth. *G3763*

T

Act 12: 1 Now about that **t** Herod the king *G2540*
13:18 And about the **t** of forty years suffered *G5550*
14: 3 Long **t** therefore abode they speaking *G5550*
28 And there they abode long **t** with the *G5550*
15:21 For Moses of old **t** hath in every city *G1074*
17:21 there spent their **t** in nothing else, but *G2119*
18:20 longer **t** with them, he consented not; *G5550*
23 And after he had spent some **t** *there*, he *G5550*
19:23 And the same **t** there arose no small *G2540*
20:16 not spend the **t** in Asia: for he hasted, *G5551*
24:25 Go thy way for this **t**; when I have a *G3568*
27: 9 Now when much **t** was spent, and *G5550*
Ro 3:26 To declare, *I say*, at this **t** his *G2540*
5: 6 in due **t** Christ died for the ungodly. *G2540*
8:18 of this present **t** *are* not worthy *to be* *G2540*
9: 9 of promise, At this **t** will I come, and *G2540*
11: 5 Even so then at this present **t** also there *G2540*
13:11 And that, knowing the **t**, that now *it is* *G2540*
11 that now *it is* high **t** to awake out of *G5610*
1Co 4: 5 Therefore judge nothing before the **t**, *G2540*
7: 5 *be* with consent for a **t**, that ye may give *G2540*
29 But this I say, brethren, the **t** *is* short: it *G2540*
9: 7 Who goeth a warfare any **t** at his own *G4218*
15: 8 of me also, as of one born out of due **t**. *G1626*
16:12 at all to come at this **t**; but he will come *G3568*
12 come when he shall have convenient **t**. *G2119*
2Co 6: 2 (For he saith, I have heard thee in a **t** *G2540*
2 **t**; behold, now *is* the day of salvation.) *G2540*
8:14 But by an equality, *that* now at this **t** *G2540*
12:14 Behold, the third **t** I am ready to come *G5154*
13: 1 This *is* the third **t** I am coming to you. In
2 present, the second **t**; and being absent
Gal 1:13 my conversation in **t** past in the Jews' *G4218*
4: 2 until the **t** appointed of the father. *G4287*
4 But when the fulness of the **t** was come, *G5550*
5:21 also told *you* in **t** past, that they which
Eph 2: 2 Wherein in **t** past ye walked according *G4218*
11 that ye *being* in **t** past Gentiles in the *G4218*
12 That at that **t** ye were without Christ, *G2540*
5:16 Redeeming the **t**, because the days are *G2540*
Col 3: 7 In the which ye also walked some **t**, *G4218*
4: 5 them that are without, redeeming the **t**. *G2540*
1Th 2: 5 For neither at any **t** used we flattering *G4218*
17 you for a short **t** in presence, not in *G2540*
2Th 2: 6 that he might be revealed in his **t**. *G2540*
1Ti 2: 6 a ransom for all, to be testified in due **t**. *G2540*
6:19 against the **t** to come, that they may *G3195*
2Ti 4: 3 For the **t** will come when they will not *G2540*
6 and the **t** of my departure is at hand. *G2540*
Phlm 11 Which in **t** past was to thee *G4218*
Heb 1: 1 **t** past unto the fathers by the prophets, *G3819*
5 said he at any **t**, Thou art my Son, this *G4218*
13 said he at any **t**, Sit on my right hand, *G4218*
2: 1 lest at any **t** we should let *them* slip. *G3379*
4: 7 after so long a **t**; as it is said, To day *G5550*
16 and find grace to help in **t** of need. *G2121*
5:12 For when for the **t** ye ought to be *G5550*
9: 9 Which *was* a figure for the **t** then *G2540*
10 *on them* until the **t** of reformation. *G2540*
28 the second **t** without sin unto salvation. *G1208*
11:32 And what shall I more say? for the **t** *G5550*
Jas 4:14 for a little **t**, and then vanisheth away. *G3641*
1Pt 1: 5 ready to be revealed in the last **t**. *G2540*
11 Searching what, or what manner of **t** *G2540*
17 the **t** of your sojourning *here* in fear: *G5550*
2:10 Which in **t** past *were* not a people, but *G4218*
3: 5 For after this manner in the old **t** the *G4218*
4: 2 live the rest of *his* **t** in the flesh to the *G5550*
3 For the **t** past of *our* life may suffice us *G5550*
17 For the **t** *is come* that judgment must *G2540*
5: 6 of God, that he may exalt you in due **t**: *G2540*
2Pt 1:21 For the prophecy came not in old **t** by *G4218*
2: 3 now of a long **t** lingereth not, and their *G1597*
13 to riot in the day **t**. Spots *they are* and *G2250*
1Jn 2:18 Little children, it is the last **t**: and as ye *G5610*
18 whereby we know that it is the last **t**. *G5610*
4:12 No man hath seen God at any **t**. If we *G4455*
Jude 18 in the last **t**, who should walk after *G5550*
Rev 1: 3 are written therein: for the **t** *is* at hand. *G2540*
10: 6 that there should be **t** no longer: *G5550*
11:18 is come, and the **t** of the dead, that they *G2540*
12:12 he knoweth that he hath but a short **t**. *G2540*
14 is nourished for a **t**, and times, and half *G2540*
14 half a **t**, from the face of the serpent. *G2540*
14:15 and reap: for the **t** is come for thee to *G5610*
22:10 of this book: for the **t** is at hand. *G2540*

TIMES

Gen 27:36 me these two **t**: he took away my H6471
31: 7 **t**; but God suffered him not to hurt me. H4489
41 and thou hast changed my wages ten **t**. H4489
33: 3 **t**, until he came near to his brother. H6471
43:34 mess was five **t** so much as any of H3027
Ex 23:14 Three **t** thou shalt keep a feast unto me H7272
17 Three **t** in the year all thy males shall H6471
Lev 4: 6 of the blood seven **t** before the LORD, H6471
17 **t** before the LORD, *even* before the vail. H6471
8:11 the altar seven **t**, and anointed the altar H6471
14: 7 from the leprosy seven **t**, and shall H6471
16 his finger seven **t** before the LORD: H6471
27 his left hand seven **t** before the LORD: H6471
51 water, and sprinkle the house seven **t**: H6471
16: 2 he come not at all **t** into the holy *place* H6256
14 of the blood with his finger seven **t**. H6471
19 his finger seven **t**, and cleanse it, and H6471
19:26 ye use enchantment, nor observe **t**. H6049
25: 8 unto thee, seven **t** seven years; and the H6471
26:18 punish you seven **t** more for your sins. H7651
21 I will bring seven **t** more plagues upon H7651
24 punish you yet seven **t** for your sins. H7651
28 will chastise you seven **t** for your sins. H7651
Nu 14:22 **t**, and have not hearkened to my voice; H6471
19: 4 tabernacle of the congregation seven **t**: H6471
22:28 that thou hast smitten me these three **t**? H7272
32 ass these three **t**? behold, I went out to H7272
33 me these three **t**: unless she had turned H7272
24: 1 not, as at other **t**, to seek for H6471+H6471
10 altogether blessed *them* these three **t**. H6471
Dt 1:11 you a thousand **t** so many more as ye H6471
2:10 The Emims dwelt therein in **t** past, a
4:42 and hated him not in **t** past; and that H8543
16:16 Three **t** in a year shall all thy males H6471
18:10 of **t**, or an enchanter, or a witch, H6049
14 unto observers of **t**, and unto diviners: H6049
Jos 6: 4 the city seven **t**, and the priests shall H6471
15 manner seven **t**: only on that day they H6471
15 day they compassed the city seven **t**. H6471
Jdg 13:25 to move him at **t** in the camp of Dan
16:15 me these three **t**, and hast not told me H6471
20 go out as at other **t** before, and H6471+H6471
20:30 against Gibeah, as at other **t**. H6471+H6471
31 as at other **t**, in the highways, H6471+H6471
1Sa 3:10 called as at other **t**, Samuel, Samuel. H6471+H6471
18:10 as at other **t**: and *there was* a H3117+H3117
19: 7 was in his presence, as in **t** past. H865+H8543
20:25 as at other **t**, *even* upon a seat H6471+H6471
41 himself three **t**: and they kissed one H6471
2Sa 3:17 for David in **t** past *to be* king over you: H8543
1Ki 8:59 at all **t**, as the matter shall require: H3117
9:25 And three **t** in a year did Solomon offer H6471
17:21 the child three **t**, and cried unto the H6471
18:43 nothing. And he said, Go again seven **t**. H6471
22:16 him, How many **t** shall I adjure thee H6471
2Ki 4:35 seven **t**, and the child opened his eyes. H6471
5:10 in Jordan seven **t**, and thy flesh shall H6471
14 himself seven **t** in Jordan, according H6471
13:19 smitten five or six **t**; then hadst thou H6471
25 by war. Three **t** did Joash beat him, H6471
19:25 it, *and* of ancient **t** that I have formed H3117
21: 6 the fire, and observed **t**, and used H6049
1Ch 12:32 of the **t**, to know what Israel H6256
21: 3 an hundred **t** so many more as they H6471
29:30 and his might, and the **t** that went over H6256
2Ch 8:13 feasts, three **t** in the year, *even* in H6471
15: 5 And in those **t** *there was* no peace to H6256
18:15 And the king said to him, How many **t** H6471
33: 6 Hinnom: also he observed **t**, and used H6049
Ezr 10:14 come at appointed **t**, and with them the H6256
Neh 4:12 they said unto us ten **t**, From all places H6471
6: 4 Yet they sent unto me four **t** after this H6471
9:28 heaven; and many **t** didst thou deliver H6256
10:34 of our fathers, at **t** appointed year by H6256
13:31 And for the wood offering, at **t** H6256
Est 1:13 which knew the **t**, (for so *was* the king's H6256
9:31 days of Purim in their **t** *appointed*, H2165
Job 19: 3 These ten **t** have ye reproached me: ye H6471
24: 1 Why, seeing **t** are not hidden from the H6256
Ps 9: 9 the oppressed, a refuge in **t** of trouble. H6256
10: 1 *why* hidest thou *thyself* in **t** of trouble? H6256
12: 6 in a furnace of earth, purified seven **t**. H7659
31:15 My **t** *are* in thy hand: deliver me from H6256
34: 1 I will bless the LORD at all **t**: his praise H6256
44: 1 thou didst in their days, in the **t** of old. H3117
62: 8 Trust in him at all **t**; *ye* people, pour out H6256
77: 5 the days of old, the years of ancient **t**. H5769
106: 3 *and* he that doeth righteousness at all **t**. H6256
43 Many **t** did he deliver them; but they H6471
119:20 *that it hath* unto thy judgments at all **t**. H6256
Ps119:164 Seven **t** a day do I praise thee because H7651
Prv 5:19 breasts satisfy thee at all **t**; and be thou H6256
17:17 A friend loveth at all **t**, and a brother is H6256
24:16 For a just *man* falleth seven **t**, and H7651
Ecc 8:12 Though a sinner do evil an hundred **t**,
Isa 14:31 none *shall be* alone in his appointed **t**. H4151
33: 6 be the stability of thy **t**, *and* strength of H6256
37:26 it; *and* of ancient **t**, that I have formed H3117
46:10 and from ancient **t** *the things* that are H6924
Jer 8: 7 her appointed **t**; and the turtle and the H4150
Ezk 12:27 he prophesieth of the **t** *that are* far off. H6256
Dan 1:20 he found them ten **t** better than all the H3027
2:21 And he changeth the **t** and the seasons: H5732
3:19 **t** more than it was wont to be heated. H7655
4:16 him; and let seven **t** pass over him. H5732
23 of the field, till seven **t** pass over him; H5732
25 of heaven, and seven **t** shall pass over H5732
32 as oxen, and seven **t** shall pass over H5732
6:10 his knees three **t** a day, and prayed, H2166
13 but maketh his petition three **t** a day. H2166
7:10 and ten thousand **t** ten thousand stood
25 think to change **t** and laws: and they H2166
25 a time and **t** and the dividing of time. H5732
9:25 again, and the wall, even in troublous **t**. H6256
11: 6 and he that strengthened her in *these* **t**. H6256
14 And in those **t** there shall many stand H6256
12: 7 *it shall be* for a time, **t**, and an half; and H4150
Mt 16: 3 but can ye not *discern* the signs of the **t**? *G2540*
18:21 me, and I forgive him? till seven **t**? *G2034*
22 seven **t**: but, Until seventy times seven. *G2034*
22 seven times: but, Until seventy **t** seven. *G1441*
Lk 17: 4 And if he trespass against thee seven **t** *G2034*
4 a day, and seven **t** in a day turn again *G2034*
21:24 until the **t** of the Gentiles be fulfilled. *G2540*
Act 1: 7 you to know the **t** or the seasons, which *G5550*
3:19 out, when the **t** of refreshing shall come *G2540*
21 receive until the **t** of restitution of all *G5550*
11:10 And this was done three **t**: and all were *G5151*
14:16 Who in **t** past suffered all nations to *G1074*
17:26 determined the **t** before appointed, and *G2540*
30 And the **t** of this ignorance God winked *G5550*
Ro 11:30 For as ye in **t** past have not believed *G4218*
2Co 11:24 Of the Jews five **t** received I forty *stripes* *G3999*
Gal 1:23 persecuted us in **t** past now preacheth *G4218*
4:10 Ye observe days, and months, and **t**, *G2540*
Eph 1:10 of the fulness of **t** he might gather *G2540*
2: 3 conversation in **t** past in the lusts of *G4218*
1Th 5: 1 But of the **t** and the seasons, brethren, *G5550*
1Ti 4: 1 that in the latter **t** some shall depart *G2540*
6:15 Which in his **t** he shall shew, *who is* the *G2540*
2Ti 3: 1 in the last days perilous **t** shall come. *G2540*
Tit 1: 3 But hath in due **t** manifested his word *G2540*
Heb 1: 1 God, who at sundry **t** and in divers *G4181*
1Pt 1:20 but was manifest in these last **t** for you, *G5550*
Rev 5:11 was ten thousand **t** ten thousand, and
12:14 for a time, and **t**, and half a time, from *G2540*

TIMNA

Gen 36:12 And **T** was concubine to Eliphaz Esau's H8555
22 and Hemam; and Lotan's sister *was* **T**. H8555
1Ch 1:36 and Gatam, Kenaz, and **T**, and Amalek. H8555
39 and Homam: and **T** *was* Lotan's sister. H8555

TIMNAH

Gen 36:40 duke **T**, duke Alvah, duke Jetheth, H8555
Jos 15:10 to Beth-shemesh, and passed on to **T**: H8553
57 Cain, Gibeah, and **T**; ten cities with H8553
1Ch 1:51 were; duke **T**, duke Aliah, duke Jetheth, H8555
2Ch 28:18 thereof, and **T** with the villages thereof, H8553

TIMNATH

Gen 38:12 sheepshearers to **T**, he and his friend H8553
13 in law goeth up to **T** to shear his sheep. H8553
14 *is* by the way to **T**; for she saw that H8553
Jdg 14: 1 And Samson went down to **T**, and saw H8553
1 in **T** of the daughters of the Philistines. H8553
2 seen a woman in **T** of the daughters of H8553
5 and his mother, to **T**, and came to the H8553
5 to the vineyards of **T**: and, behold, a H8553

TIMNATH-HERES

Jdg 2: 9 of his inheritance in **T**, in the mount of H8556

TIMNATH-SERAH

Jos 19:50 he asked, *even* **T** in mount Ephraim: H8556
24:30 his inheritance in **T**, which *is* in mount H8556

TIMNITE

Jdg 15: 6 the son in law of the **T**, because he had H8554

TIMON
Act 6: 5 and Nicanor, and T, and Parmenas, G5096

TIMOTHEUS
Act 16: 1 was there, named T, the son of a certain G5095
17:14 sea: but Silas and T abode there still. G5095
15 unto Silas and T for to come to him G5095
18: 5 And when Silas and T were come from G5095
19:22 unto him, T and Erastus; but he G5095
20: 4 of Derbe, and T; and of Asia, Tychicus G5095
Ro 16:21 T my workfellow, and Lucius, and G5095
1Co 4:17 For this cause have I sent unto you T, G5095
16:10 Now if T come, see that he may be with G5095
2Co 1:19 and Silvanus and T, was not yea and G5095
Php 1: 1 Paul and T, the servants of Jesus Christ, G5095
2:19 But I trust in the Lord Jesus to send T G5095
Col 1: 1 by the will of God, and T *our* brother, G5095
1Th 1: 1 Paul, and Silvanus, and T, unto the G5095
3: 2 And sent T, our brother, and minister G5095
6 But now when T came from you unto G5095
2Th 1: 1 Paul, and Silvanus, and T, unto the G5095

TIMOTHY
2Co 1: 1 will of God, and T *our* brother, unto the G5095
1Ti 1: 2 Unto T, *my* own son in the faith: Grace, G5095
18 This charge I commit unto thee, son T, G5095
6:20 O T, keep that which is committed to G5095
2Ti 1: 2 To T, *my* dearly beloved son: Grace, G5095
Phlm 1 Paul, a prisoner of Jesus Christ, and T G5095
Heb 13:23 Know ye that *our* brother T is set at G5095

TIN
Nu 31:22 the brass, the iron, the t, and the lead, H913
Isa 1:25 away thy dross, and take away all thy t: H913
Ezk 22:18 they *are* brass, and t, and iron, and lead, H913
20 iron, and lead, and t, into the midst of H913
27:12 iron, t, and lead, they traded in thy fairs. H913

TINGLE
1Sa 3:11 ears of every one that heareth it shall t. H6750
2Ki 21:12 heareth of it, both his ears shall t. H6750
Jer 19: 3 whosoever heareth, his ears shall t. H6750

TINKLING
Isa 3:16 they go, and making a t with their feet: H5913
18 the bravery of *their* t ornaments *about*
1Co 13: 1 *as* sounding brass, or a t cymbal. G214

TIP
Ex 29:20 and put *it* upon the t of the right ear of H8571
20 and upon the t of the right ear of his H8571
Lev 8:23 put *it* upon the t of Aaron's right ear, H8571
24 the blood upon the t of their right ear, H8571
14:14 put *it* upon the t of the right ear of him H8571
17 put upon the t of the right ear of him H8571
25 put *it* upon the t of the right ear of him H8571
28 his hand upon the t of the right ear of H8571
Lk 16:24 that he may dip the t of his finger in G206

TIPHSAH
1Ki 4:24 the river, from T even to Azzah, over H8607
2Ki 15:16 Then Menahem smote T, and all that H8607

TIRAS
Gen 10: 2 Javan, and Tubal, and Meshech, and T. H8494
1Ch 1: 5 Javan, and Tubal, and Meshech, and T. H8494

TIRATHITES
1Ch 2:55 dwelt at Jabez; the T, the Shimeathites, H8654

TIRE
Ezk 24:17 the dead, bind the t of thine head upon H6287

TIRED
2Ki 9:30 her face, and t her head, and looked H3190

TIRES
Isa 3:18 cauls, and *their* round t like the moon, H7720
Ezk 24:23 And your t *shall be* upon your heads, H6287

TIRHAKAH
2Ki 19: 9 And when he heard say of T king of H8640
Isa 37: 9 And he heard say concerning T king of H8640

TIRHANAH
1Ch 2:48 Caleb's concubine, bare Sheber, and T. H8647

TIRIA
1Ch 4:16 Ziph, and Ziphah, T, and Asareel. H8493

TIRSHATHA
Ezr 2:63 And the T said unto them, that they H8660
Neh 7:65 And the T said unto them, that they H8660
70 the work. The T gave to the treasure H8660
8: 9 And Nehemiah, which *is* the T, and H8660
10: 1 T, the son of Hachaliah, and Zidkijah, H8660

TIRZAH
Nu 26:33 and Noah, Hoglah, Milcah, and T. H8656
27: 1 Noah, and Hoglah, and Milcah, and T. H8656
36:11 For Mahlah, T, and Hoglah, and H8656
Jos 12:24 The king of T, one: all the kings thirty H8656
17: 3 and Noah, Hoglah, Milcah, and T. H8656
1Ki 14:17 and came to T: *and* when she came H8656
15:21 off building of Ramah, and dwelt in T. H8656
33 all Israel in T, twenty and four years. H8656
16: 6 T: and Elah his son reigned in his stead. H8656
8 to reign over Israel in T, two years. H8656
9 him, as he was in T, drinking himself H8656
9 house of Arza steward of *his* house in T. H8656
15 seven days in T. And the people *were* H8656
17 all Israel with him, and they besieged T. H8656
23 twelve years: six years reigned he in T. H8656
2Ki 15:14 went up from T, and came to Samaria, H8656
16 thereof from T: because they opened H8656
Song 6: 4 Thou *art* beautiful, O my love, as T, H8656

TISHBITE
1Ki 17: 1 And Elijah the T, *who was* of the H8664
21:17 the LORD came to Elijah the T, saying, H8664
28 the LORD came to Elijah the T, saying, H8664
2Ki 1: 3 said to Elijah the T, Arise, go up to meet H8664
8 his loins. And he said, It *is* Elijah the T. H8664
9:36 his servant Elijah the T, saying, In the H8664

TITHE
Lev 27:30 And all the t of the land, *whether* of the H4643
32 And concerning the t of the herd, or of H4643
Nu 18:26 for the LORD, *even* a tenth *part* of the t. H4643
Dt 12:17 thy gates the t of thy corn, or of thy H4643
14:22 Thou shalt truly t all the increase of thy H6237
23 his name there, the t of thy corn, of thy H4643
28 bring forth all the t of thine increase H4643
2Ch 31: 5 the field; and the t of all *things* brought H4643
6 brought in the t of oxen and sheep, and H4643
6 sheep, and the t of holy things which H4643
Neh 10:38 shall bring up the t of the tithes unto H4643
13:12 Then brought all Judah the t of the H4643
Mt 23:23 for ye pay t of mint and anise and G586
Lk 11:42 But woe unto you, Pharisees! for ye t G586

TITHES
Gen 14:20 into thy hand. And he gave him t of all. H4643
Lev 27:31 *ought* of his t, he shall add thereto H4643
Nu 18:24 But the t of the children of Israel, which H4643
26 of Israel the t which I have given you H4643
28 LORD of all your t, which ye receive of H4643
Dt 12: 6 and your t, and heave offerings H4643
11 sacrifices, your t, and the heave offering H4643
26:12 of tithing all the t of thine increase the H4643
2Ch 31:12 And brought in the offerings and the t H4643
Neh 10:37 our God; and the t of our ground unto H4643
37 have the t in all the cities of our tillage. H6237
38 the Levites take t: and the Levites shall H6237
38 up the tithe of the t unto the house of H4643
12:44 and for the t, to gather into them H4643
13: 5 vessels, and the t of the corn, the new H4643
Am 4: 4 morning, *and* your t after three years: H4643
Mal 3: 8 we robbed thee? In t and offerings. H4643
10 Bring ye all the t into the storehouse, H4643
Lk 18:12 I fast twice in the week, I give t of all that G586
Heb 7: 5 to take t of the people according G586
6 from them received t of Abraham, and G1183
8 And here men that die receive t; but G1181
9 receiveth t, payed tithes in Abraham. G1181
9 receiveth tithes, payed t in Abraham. G1183

TITHING
Dt 26:12 When thou hast made an end of t all H6237
12 *is* the year of t, and hast given *it* unto H4643

TITLE
2Ki 23:17 Then he said, What t *is* that that I see? H6725
Jn 19:19 And Pilate wrote a t, and put *it* on the G5102
20 This t then read many of the Jews: for G5102

TITLES
Job 32:21 let me give flattering t unto man. H3655
22 For I know not to give flattering t; *in so* H3655

TITTLE
Mt 5:18 one jot or one t shall in no wise pass G2762
Lk 16:17 to pass, than one t of the law to fail. G2762

TITUS
2Co 2:13 I found not T my brother: but taking G5103
7: 6 down, comforted us by the coming of T; G5103
13 we for the joy of T, because his spirit G5103
14 which I *made* before T, is found a truth. G5103
8: 6 Insomuch that we desired T, that as he G5103
16 earnest care into the heart of T for you. G5103
23 Whether *any do inquire of* T, *he is my* G5103
12:18 I desired T, and with *him* I sent a G5103
18 a brother. Did T make a gain of you? G5103
Gal 2: 1 Barnabas, and took T with *me* also. G5103
3 But neither T, who was with me, being G5103
2Ti 4:10 Crescens to Galatia, T unto Dalmatia. G5103
Tit 1: 4 To T, *mine* own son after the common G5103

TIZITE
1Ch 11:45 of Shimri, and Joha his brother, the T, H8491

TO See the Appendix.

TOAH
1Ch 6:34 Jeroham, the son of Eliel, the son of T, H8430

TOB
Jdg 11: 3 dwelt in the land of T: and there were H2897
5 to fetch Jephthah out of the land of T: H2897

TOB-ADONIJAH
2Ch 17: 8 and Tobijah, and T, Levites; and with H2899

TOBIAH
Ezr 2:60 the children of T, the children of H2900
Neh 2:10 When Sanballat the Horonite, and T H2900
19 the Horonite, and T the servant, the H2900
4: 3 Now T the Ammonite *was* by him, and H2900
7 Sanballat, and T, and the Arabians, H2900
6: 1 when Sanballat, and T, and Geshem the H2900
12 me: for T and Sanballat had hired him. H2900
14 My God, think thou upon T and H2900
17 many letters unto T, and *the letters* of H2900
17 and *the letters* of T came unto them. H2900
19 *And* T sent letters to put me in fear. H2900
7:62 the children of T, the children of H2900
13: 4 the house of our God, *was* allied unto T: H2900
7 Eliashib did for T, in preparing him a H2900
8 stuff of T out of the chamber. H2900

TOBIJAH
2Ch 17: 8 Adonijah, and T, and Tob-adonijah, H2900
Zec 6:10 *even* of Heldai, of T, and of Jedaiah, H2900
14 to Helem, and to T, and to Jedaiah, and H2900

TOCHEN
1Ch 4:32 Rimmon, and T, and Ashan, five cities: H8507

TO-DAY See DAY.

TOE
Ex 29:20 and upon the great t of their right foot, H931
Lev 8:23 and upon the great t of his right foot. H931
14:14 and upon the great t of his right foot: H931
17 and upon the great t of his right foot, H931
25 and upon the great t of his right foot: H931
28 and upon the great t of his right foot, H931

TOES
Lev 8:24 and upon the great t of their right feet: H931
Jdg 1: 6 and cut off his thumbs and his great t. H7272
7 and their great t cut off, gathered *their* H7272
2Sa 21:20 on every foot six t, four and twenty in H676
1Ch 20: 6 whose fingers and t *were* four and H676
Dan 2:41 And whereas thou sawest the feet and t, H677
42 And *as* the t of the feet *were* part of iron, H677

TOGARMAH
Gen 10: 3 Gomer; Ashkenaz, and Riphath, and T. H8425
1Ch 1: 6 Aschchenaz, and Riphath, and T. H8425
Ezk 27:14 They of the house of T traded in thy H8425
38: 6 the house of T of the north quarters, H8425

TOGETHER
Gen 1: 9 be gathered t unto one place, and H6960
10 and the gathering t of the waters called H4723
3: 7 leaves t, and made themselves aprons. H8609
13: 6 they might dwell t: for their substance H3162

T

Gen 13: 6 great, so that they could not dwell **t**. H3162
14: 3 All these were joined **t** in the vale of H2266
22: 6 a knife; and they went both of them **t**. H3162
8 offering: so they went both of them **t**. H3162
19 rose up and went **t** to Beer-sheba; and H3162
25:22 And the children struggled **t** within her; H7533
29: 7 should be gathered **t**: water ye the sheep, H622
8 flocks be gathered **t**, and *till* they roll the H622
22 And Laban gathered **t** all the men of the H622
34:30 gather themselves **t** against me, and slay
36: 7 that they might dwell **t**; and the land H3162
42:17 And he put them all **t** into ward three H622
49: 1 Gather yourselves **t**, that I may tell you
2 Gather yourselves **t**, and hear, ye sons H6908
Ex 2:13 the Hebrews strove **t**: and he said to him
3:16 Go, and gather the elders of Israel **t**, and
4:29 **t** all the elders of the children of Israel:
8:14 And they gathered them **t** upon heaps: H6651
15: 8 waters were gathered **t**, the floods stood H6192
19: 8 And all the people answered **t**, and said, H3162
21:18 And if men strive **t**, and one smite
26: 3 The five curtains shall be coupled **t** one H2266
6 couple the curtains **t** with the taches:
11 and couple the tent **t**, that it may be one.
24 And they shall be coupled **t** beneath, and
24 shall be coupled **t** above the head of it H3162
28: 7 edges thereof; and *so* it shall be joined **t**. H2266
30:35 apothecary, tempered **t**, pure *and* holy:
32: 1 themselves **t** unto Aaron, and said H6950
26 of Levi gathered themselves **t** unto him.
35: 1 children of Israel **t**, and said unto them, H6950
36:18 to couple the tent **t**, that it might be one.
29 and coupled **t** at the head thereof, H3162
39: 4 for it, to couple *it* **t**: by the two edges H2266
4 by the two edges was it coupled **t**. H2266
Lev 8: 3 And gather thou all the congregation **t** H6950
4 was gathered **t** unto the door of the H6950
24:10 a man of Israel strove **t** in the camp; H5327
26:25 ye are gathered **t** within your cities, I will
Nu 1:18 all the congregation **t** on the first *day* of H6950
8: 9 assembly of the children of Israel **t**: H6950
10: 7 is to be gathered **t**, ye shall blow, but ye H6950
11:22 be gathered **t** for them, to suffice them?
14:35 that are gathered **t** against me: in this H3259
16: 3 And they gathered themselves **t** against H6950
11 *are* gathered **t** against the LORD: and H3259
20: 2 **t** against Moses and against Aaron. H6950
8 thou the assembly **t**, thou, and Aaron H6950
10 the congregation **t** before the rock, and H6950
21:16 the people **t**, and I will give them water.
23 all his people **t**, and went out against
24:10 and he smote his hands **t**: and Balak said
26:10 swallowed them up **t** with Korah, when
27: 3 themselves **t** against the LORD in H3259
Dt 4:10 me the people **t**, and I will make them H6950
22:10 shalt not plow with an ox and an ass **t**. H3162
11 divers sorts, *as* of woollen and linen **t**. H3162
25: 5 If brethren dwell **t**, and one of them die, H3162
11 When men strive **t** one with another, H3162
31:12 Gather the people **t**, men, and women, H6950
33: 5 *and* the tribes of Israel were gathered **t**. H3162
17 push the people **t** to the ends of the H3162
Jos 8:16 in Ai were called **t** to pursue after them:
9: 2 That they gathered themselves **t**, to H3162
10: 5 themselves **t**, and went up, they and
6 mountains are gathered **t** against us. H6908
11: 5 And when all these kings were met **t**, H3259
5 came and pitched **t** at the waters of H3162
17:10 and they met **t** in Asher on the north, H6293
18: 1 Israel assembled **t** at Shiloh, and set up H6950
22:12 themselves **t** at Shiloh, to go up to H6950
Jdg 4:13 And Sisera gathered **t** all his chariots, H2199
6:33 the east were gathered **t**, and went over, H3162
38 thrust the fleece **t**, and wringed the dew H2115
7:23 themselves **t** out of Naphtali, and H6817
24 themselves **t**, and took the waters H6817
9: 6 And all the men of Shechem gathered **t**,
47 the tower of Shechem were gathered **t**. H6908
10:17 were gathered **t**, and encamped in H6817
17 themselves **t**, and encamped in Mizpeh.
11:20 all his people **t**, and pitched in Jahaz,
12: 1 themselves **t**, and went northward, H6817
4 Then Jephthah gathered **t** all the men H6908
16:23 gathered them **t** for to offer a great
18:22 **t**, and overtook the children of Dan. H2199
19: 6 both of them **t**: for the damsel's father H3162
29 and divided her, *t* with her bones, into
20: 1 was gathered **t** as one man, from Dan H6950
11 against the city, knit **t** as one man. H2270

Jdg 20:14 themselves **t** out of the cities unto
1Sa 5:11 So they sent and gathered **t** all the lords
7: 6 And they gathered **t** to Mizpeh, and H6908
7 were gathered **t** to Mizpeh, the lords H6908
8: 4 **t**, and came to Samuel unto Ramah, H6908
10:17 And Samuel called the people **t** unto the
11:11 so that two of them were not left **t**. H3162
13: 4 people were called **t** after Saul to Gilgal. H6817
5 themselves **t** to fight with Israel, thirty
11 gathered themselves **t** at Michmash;
15: 4 And Saul gathered the people **t**, and H8085
17: 1 Now the Philistines gathered **t** their
1 and were gathered **t** at Shochoh, which
2 Israel were gathered **t**, and pitched by the
10 day; give me a man, that we may fight **t**. H3162
23: 8 And Saul called all the people **t** to war, H8085
25: 1 were gathered **t**, and lamented him, H6908
28: 1 their armies **t** for warfare, to fight H6908
4 themselves **t**, and came and pitched H6908
4 all Israel **t**, and they pitched in Gilboa. H6908
23 eat. But his servants, **t** with the woman,
29: 1 Now the Philistines gathered **t** all their H6908
31: 6 and all his men, that same day **t**. H3162
2Sa 2:13 went out, and met **t** by the pool of H3162
16 so they fell down **t**: wherefore that place H3162
25 themselves **t** after Abner, and became H6908
30 all the people **t**, there lacked of David's H6908
6: 1 Again, David gathered **t** all *the* chosen
10:15 Israel, they gathered themselves **t**. H3162
17 he gathered all Israel **t**, and passed over
12: 3 up: and it grew up **t** with him, and with H3162
28 rest of the people **t**, and encamp against
29 And David gathered all the people **t**, and
14: 6 they two strove **t** in the field, and *there*
16 my son **t** out of the inheritance of God. H3162
20:14 **t**, and went also after him. H6950+H7035
21: 9 and they fell *all* seven **t**, and were put to H3162
23: 9 there gathered **t** to battle, and the men
11 were gathered **t** into a troop, where was
1Ki 3:18 also: and we *were* **t**; *there was* no H3162
5:12 Solomon; and they two made a league **t**.
10:26 And Solomon gathered **t** chariots and
11: 1 strange women, **t** with the daughter of
18:20 the prophets **t** unto mount Carmel. H6908
20: 1 all his host **t**: and *there were* thirty H6908
22: 6 the prophets **t**, about four hundred H6908
2Ki 2: 8 and wrapped *it* **t**, and smote the waters, H1563
3:10 **t**, to deliver them into the hand of Moab!
13 **t**, to deliver them into the hand of Moab.
9:25 I and thou rode **t** after Ahab his father, H6776
10:18 And Jehu gathered all the people **t**, and H6908
1Ch 10: 6 his three sons, and all his house died **t**. H3162
11:13 were gathered **t** to battle, where was
13: 5 So David gathered all Israel **t**, from H6950
15: 3 And David gathered all Israel **t** to H6950
16:35 and gather us **t**, and deliver us from H6908
19: 7 **t** from their cities, and came to battle.
22: 2 And David commanded to gather **t** the H3664
23: 2 And he gathered **t** all the princes of
2Ch 12: 5 Judah, that were gathered **t** to Jerusalem
15:10 So they gathered themselves **t** at H6908
18: 5 Therefore the king of Israel gathered **t** H6908
20: 4 And Judah gathered themselves **t**, to H6908
24: 5 And he gathered **t** the priests and the H6908
25: 5 Moreover Amaziah gathered Judah **t**, H6908
28:24 And Ahaz gathered **t** the vessels of the
29: 4 and gathered them **t** into the east street,
30: 3 gathered themselves **t** to Jerusalem.
32: 4 So there was gathered much people **t**, H6908
6 gathered them **t** to him in the street H6908
34:17 And they have gathered **t** the money H5413
29 Then the king sent and gathered **t** all the
Ezr 2:64 The whole congregation **t** *was* forty and H259
3: 1 themselves **t** as one man to Jerusalem.
9 the sons of Judah, **t**, to set forward the H259
11 And they sang **t** by course in praising
4: 3 but we ourselves **t** will build unto the H3162
6:20 were purified **t**, all of them *were* pure, H259
7:28 and I gathered **t** out of Israel chief men H6908
8:15 And I gathered them **t** to the river that H6908
10: 7 gather themselves **t** unto Jerusalem; H6908
9 themselves **t** unto Jerusalem within H6908
Neh 4: 6 wall was joined **t** unto the half thereof: H7194
8 And conspired all of them **t** to come H3162
6: 2 Come, let us meet **t** in *some one of* the H3162
7 now therefore, and let us take counsel **t**. H3162
10 said, Let us meet **t** in the house of God, H3259
7: 5 heart to gather **t** the nobles, and the H6908
66 The whole congregation **t** *was* forty and H259

Neh 8: 1 And all the people gathered themselves **t**
13 And on the second day were gathered **t**
12:28 themselves **t**, both out of the plain
13:11 them **t**, and set them in their place. H6908
Est 2: 3 they may gather **t** all the fair young H6908
8 were gathered **t** unto Shushan the H6908
19 And when the virgins were gathered **t** H6908
4:16 Go, gather **t** all the Jews that are H3664
8:11 to gather themselves **t**, and to stand for H6950
9: 2 The Jews gathered themselves **t** in their H6950
15 themselves **t** on the fourteenth day H6950
16 themselves **t**, and stood for their lives, H6950
18 assembled **t** on the thirteenth *day* H6950
Job 2:11 an appointment **t** to come to mourn H3162
3:18 *There* the prisoners rest **t**; they hear not H3162
6: 2 and my calamity laid in the balances **t**! H3162
9:32 *and* we should come **t** in judgment. H3162
10: 8 and fashioned me **t** round about; yet H3162
11:10 If he cut off, and shut up, or gather **t**, H6950
16:10 have gathered themselves **t** against me. H3162
17:16 of the pit, when *our* rest **t** *is* in the dust. H3162
19:12 His troops come **t**, and raise up their H3162
24: 4 the poor of the earth hide themselves **t**. H3162
30: 7 under the nettles they were gathered **t**. H5596
34:15 All flesh shall perish **t**, and man shall H3162
38: 7 When the morning stars sang **t**, and all H3162
38 hardness, and the clods cleave fast **t**? H1692
40:13 Hide them in the dust **t**; *and* bind their H3162
17 the sinews of his stones are wrapped **t**. H8276
41:15 *His* scales *are his* pride, shut up **t** *as* H5462
17 stick **t**, that they cannot be sundered. H3920
23 The flakes of his flesh are joined **t**: they H1692
Ps 2: 2 take counsel **t**, against the LORD, and H3162
14: 3 They are all gone aside, they are *all* **t** H3162
31:13 they took counsel **t** against me, they H3162
33: 7 He gathereth the waters of the sea **t** as
34: 3 with me, and let us exalt his name **t**. H3162
35:15 themselves **t**: *yea*, the abjects gathered
15 themselves **t** against me, and I knew
26 to confusion **t** that rejoice at mine H3162
37:38 **t**: the end of the wicked shall be cut off. H3162
40:14 and confounded **t** that seek after my H3162
41: 7 All that hate me whisper **t** against me: H3162
47: 9 The princes of the people are gathered **t**,
48: 4 kings were assembled, they passed by **t**. H3162
49: 2 Both low and high, rich and poor, **t**. H3162
50: 5 Gather my saints **t** unto me; those that
55:14 We took sweet counsel **t**, *and* walked H3162
56: 6 They gather themselves **t**, they hide
71:10 that lay wait for my soul take counsel **t**, H3162
74: 8 us destroy them **t**: they have burned up H3162
83: 5 For they have consulted **t** with one H3162
85:10 Mercy and truth are met **t**; righteousness
88:17 like water; they compassed me about **t**. H3162
94:21 They gather themselves **t** against the H1413
98: 8 clap *their* hands: let the hills be joyful **t** H3162
102:22 When the people are gathered **t**, and the H3162
104:22 **t**, and lay them down in their dens.
122: 3 is builded as a city that is compact **t**: H3162
133: 1 *it is* for brethren to dwell **t** in unity! H3162
140: 2 continually are they gathered **t** *for* war.
147: 2 he gathereth **t** the outcasts of Israel. H3664
Prv 22: 2 The rich and poor meet **t**: the LORD *is*
29:13 The poor and the deceitful man meet **t**:
Ecc 3: 5 to gather stones **t**; a time to embrace, H3664
4: 5 The fool foldeth his hands **t**, and eateth
11 Again, if two lie **t**, then they have heat:
Isa 1:18 Come now, and let us reason **t**, saith the H3198
28 sinners *shall be* **t**, and they that forsake H3162
31 burn **t**, and none shall quench *them*. H3162
8:10 Take counsel **t**, and it shall come to H5779
9:11 against him, and join his enemies **t**; H5526
21 *and* they **t** *shall be* against Judah. H3162
11: 6 **t**; and a little child shall lead them. H3162
7 shall lie down **t**: and the lion shall eat H3162
12 of Israel, and gather **t** the dispersed of H6908
14 them of the east **t**: they shall lay their H3162
13: 4 of nations gathered **t**: the LORD of hosts
18: 6 They shall be left **t** unto the fowls of the H3162
22: 3 All thy rulers are fled **t**, they are bound H3162
3 are bound **t**, *which* have fled from far. H3162
9 gathered **t** the waters of the lower pool. H6908
24:22 And they shall be gathered **t**, *as* prisoners H626
25:11 pride **t** with the spoils of their hands.
26:19 Thy dead *men* shall live, *t with* my dead
27: 4 go through them, I would burn them **t**. H3162
31: 3 shall fall down, and they all shall fail **t**. H3162
34: 4 shall be rolled **t** as a scroll: and all their H1556
40: 5 all flesh shall see *it* **t**: for the mouth of H3162

Isa 41: 1 speak: let us come near **t** to judgment. H3162
19 fir tree, *and* the pine, and the box tree **t**: H3162
20 and understand **t**, that the hand of the H3162
23 we may be dismayed, and behold *it* **t**. H3162
43: 9 Let all the nations be gathered **t**, and let H3162
17 they shall lie down **t**, they shall not rise: H3162
26 Put me in remembrance: let us plead **t**: H3162
44:11 all be gathered **t**, let them stand up; *yet* H6908
11 shall fear, *and* they shall be ashamed **t**. H3162
45: 8 spring up **t**; I the LORD have created it. H3162
16 to confusion **t** *that are* makers of idols. H3162
20 come; draw near **t**, ye *that are* escaped H3162
21 them take counsel **t**: who hath declared H3162
46: 2 They stoop, they bow down **t**; they H3162
48:13 *when* I call unto them, they stand up **t**. H3162
49:18 gather themselves **t**, *and* come to thee. H6908
50: 8 with me? let us stand **t**: who *is* mine H3162
52: 8 with the voice **t** shall they sing: for they H3162
9 Break forth into joy, sing **t**, ye waste H3162
54:15 Behold, they shall surely gather **t**, *but* H1481
15 **t** against thee shall fall for thy sake. H1481
60: 4 gather themselves **t**, they come to thee: H6908
5 Then thou shalt see, and flow **t**, and H5102
7 shall be gathered **t** unto thee, the rams H6908
13 tree, and the box **t**, to beautify the place H3162
62: 9 have brought it **t** shall drink it in the H6908
65: 7 of your fathers **t**, saith the LORD, which H3162
25 The wolf and the lamb shall feed **t**, and H259
66:17 shall be consumed **t**, saith the LORD. H3162
Jer 3:18 they shall come **t** out of the land of the H3162
4: 5 land: cry, gather **t**, and say, Assemble H4390
6:11 of young men **t**: for even the husband H3162
12 fields and wives **t**: for I will stretch out H3162
21 and the sons **t** shall fall upon them; H3162
13:14 and the sons **t**, saith the LORD: I will H3162
31: 8 **t**: a great company shall return thither. H3162
12 and shall flow **t** to the goodness of the H5102
13 men and old **t**: for I will turn their H3162
24 the cities thereof **t**, husbandmen, and H3162
41: 1 there they did eat bread **t** in Mizpah. H3162
46:12 the mighty, *and* they are fallen both **t**. H3162
21 *and* are fled away **t**: they did not stand, H3162
48: 7 *with* his priests and his princes **t**. H3162
49: 3 *and* his priests and his princes **t**. H3162
14 *saying*, Gather ye **t**, and come against H6908
50: 4 children of Judah **t**, going and weeping: H3162
29 Call **t** the archers against Babylon: all H8085
33 *were* oppressed **t**: and all that took H3162
51:27 against her, call **t** against her the H8085
38 They shall roar **t** like lions: they shall H3162
44 shall not flow **t** any more unto him: H5102
Lam 2: 8 the wall to lament; they languished **t**. H3162
Ezk 21:14 smite *thine* hands **t**, and let the sword H3709
17 I will also smite mine hands **t**, and I will H3709
29: 5 not be brought **t**, nor gathered: I have H622
37: 7 and the bones came **t**, bone to his bone. H7126
Dan 2:35 broken to pieces **t**, and became like the H2298
3: 2 king sent to gather **t** the princes, the H3673
3 were gathered **t** unto the dedication H3673
27 being gathered **t**, saw these men, upon H3673
6: 6 princes assembled **t** to the king, and H7284
7 have consulted **t** to establish a royal H3272
11: 6 shall join themselves **t**; for the king's H2266
Hos 1:11 of Israel be gathered **t**, and appoint H3162
11: 8 within me, my repentings are kindled **t**. H3162
Joel 3:11 and gather yourselves **t** round about: H6908
Am 1:15 he and his princes **t**, saith the LORD. H3162
3: 3 Can two walk **t**, except they be agreed? H3162
Mic 2:12 Israel; I will put them **t** as the sheep of H3162
Nah 1:10 For while *they be* folden **t** *as* thorns, H5440
2:10 the knees smite **t**, and much pain *is* in H6375
Zep 2: 1 Gather yourselves **t**, yea, gather H7197
1 yea, gather **t**, O nation not desired; H7197
Zec 10: 4 bow, out of him every oppressor **t**. H3162
12: 3 of the earth be gathered **t** against it.
14:14 shall be gathered **t**, gold, and silver, and
Mt 1:18 before they came **t**, she was found with *G4905*
2: 4 of the people **t**, he demanded of them *G4863*
13: 2 And great multitudes were gathered **t** *G4863*
30 Let both grow **t** until the harvest: and *G4885*
30 reapers, Gather ye **t** first the tares, and *G4816*
18:20 For where two or three are gathered **t** *G4863*
19: 6 hath joined **t**, let not man put asunder. *G4801*
22:10 and gathered **t** all as many as they *G4863*
34 to silence, they were gathered **t**. *G1909*
41 While the Pharisees were gathered **t**, *G4863*
23:37 thy children **t**, even as a hen gathereth *G1996*
24:28 is, there will the eagles be gathered **t**. *G4863*
31 they shall gather **t** his elect from the *G1996*

Mt 26: 3 Then assembled **t** the chief priests, and *G4863*
27:17 Therefore when they were gathered **t**, *G4863*
62 and Pharisees came **t** unto Pilate, *G4863*
Mk 1:33 And all the city was gathered **t** at the *G1996*
2: 2 And straightway many were gathered **t**, *G4863*
15 and sinners sat also **t** with Jesus and his
3:20 And the multitude cometh **t** again, so *G4905*
6:30 And the apostles gathered themselves **t** *G4863*
33 outwent them, and came **t** unto him. *G4905*
7: 1 Then came **t** unto him the Pharisees, *G4863*
9:25 came running **t**, he rebuked the foul *G1998*
10: 9 What therefore God hath joined **t**, let *G4801*
12:28 them reasoning **t**, and perceiving that *G4802*
13:27 and shall gather **t** his elect from the *G1996*
14:56 him, but their witness agreed not **t**. *G2470*
59 But neither so did their witness agree **t**. *G2470*
15:16 and they call **t** the whole band. *G4779*
Lk 5:15 multitudes came **t** to hear, and to be *G4905*
6:38 down, and shaken **t**, and running over, *G4531*
8: 4 were gathered **t**, and were come to him *G4896*
9: 1 Then he called his twelve disciples **t**, *G4779*
11:29 gathered thick **t**, he began to say, This *G1865*
12: 1 there were gathered **t** an innumerable *G1996*
13:11 **t**, and could in no wise lift up *herself*. *G4794*
34 thy children **t**, as a hen *doth gather* *G1996*
15: 6 And when he cometh home, he calleth **t** *G4779*
9 *her* neighbours **t**, saying, Rejoice with
13 son gathered all **t**, and took his journey *G4863*
17:35 Two *women* shall be grinding **t**; the one *G1909*
37 *is*, thither will the eagles be gathered **t**. *G4863*
22:55 down **t**, Peter sat down among them. *G4776*
66 **t**, and led him into their council, saying, *G4863*
23:12 were made friends **t**: for before they *G3326*
13 And Pilate, when he had called **t** the *G4779*
48 And all the people that came **t** to that *G4836*
24:14 And they talked **t** of all these things *G4314*
15 they communed *t* and reasoned, Jesus
33 **t**, and them that were with them, *G4867*
Jn 4:36 and he that reapeth may rejoice **t**. *G3674*
6:13 Therefore they gathered *them* **t**, and *G4863*
11:52 he should gather **t** in one the children *G4863*
53 took counsel **t** for to put him to death. *G4823*
20: 4 So they ran both **t**: and the other *G3674*
7 but wrapped **t** in a place by itself. *G1794*
21: 2 There were **t** Simon Peter, and Thomas *G3674*
Act 1: 4 And, being assembled **t** with *them*,
6 When they therefore were come **t**, they *G4905*
15 **t** were about an hundred and twenty,) *G1909*
2: 6 the multitude came **t**, and were *G4905*
44 And all that believed were **t**, and had all *G1909*
3: 1 Now Peter and John went up **t** into the *G1909*
11 all the people ran **t** unto them in the *G4936*
4: 6 priest, were gathered **t** at Jerusalem. *G4863*
26 were gathered **t** against the Lord, and *G1909*
27 the people of Israel, were gathered **t**, *G4863*
31 were assembled **t**; and they were all *G4863*
5: 9 ye have agreed **t** to tempt the Spirit of *G4856*
21 called the council **t**, and all the senate of *G4779*
10:24 called **t** his kinsmen and near friends. *G4779*
27 in, and found many that were come **t**. *G4905*
12:12 where many were gathered **t** praying. *G4867*
13:44 whole city **t** to hear the word of God. *G4863*
14: 1 they went both **t** into the synagogue *G2596*
27 the church **t**, they rehearsed all that *G4863*
15: 6 And the apostles and elders came **t** for *G4863*
30 multitude **t**, they delivered the epistle: *G4863*
16:22 And the multitude rose up **t** against *G4911*
19:19 their books **t**, and burned them before *G4851*
25 Whom he called **t** with the workmen of *G4867*
32 knew not wherefore they were come **t**. *G4905*
20: 7 the disciples came **t** to break bread, *G4863*
8 chamber, where they were gathered **t**. *G4863*
21:22 **t**: for they will hear that thou art come. *G4905*
30 and the people ran **t**: and they took *G1096*
23:12 of the Jews banded **t**, and bound *G4160*
28:17 chief of the Jews **t**: and when they were *G4779*
17 they were come **t**, he said unto them, *G4905*
Ro 1:12 That is, that I may be comforted **t** with *G4837*
3:12 out of the way, they are **t** become *G260*
6: 5 For if we have been planted **t** in the *G4854*
8:17 *him*, that we may be also glorified **t**. *G4888*
22 and travaileth in pain **t** until now. *G4944*
28 And we know that all things work **t** for *G4903*
15:30 **t** with me in *your* prayers to God for me;
1Co 1:10 be perfectly joined **t** in the same mind *G2675*
3: 9 For we are labourers **t** with God: ye are
5: 4 ye are gathered **t**, and my spirit, with *G4863*
7: 5 prayer; and come **t** again, that Satan *G4905*
11:17 **t** not for the better, but for the worse. *G4905*

1Co 11:18 For first of all, when ye come **t** in the *G4905*
20 When ye come **t** therefore into one *G4905*
33 ye come **t** to eat, tarry one for another. *G4905*
34 that ye come not **t** unto condemnation. *G4905*
12:24 tempered the body **t**, having given more *G4786*
14:23 If therefore the whole church be come **t** *G4905*
26 when ye come **t**, every one of you hath *G4905*
2Co 1:11 Ye also helping **t** by prayer for us, that *G4943*
6: 1 We then, *as* workers **t** *with him*, *G4903*
14 Be ye not unequally yoked **t** with *G2086*
Eph 1:10 he might gather **t** in one all things in
2: 5 us **t** with Christ, (by grace ye are saved;)
6 And hath raised *us* up **t**, and made *us* *G4891*
6 sit **t** in heavenly *places* in Christ Jesus: *G4776*
21 In whom all the building fitly framed **t** *G4883*
22 In whom ye also are builded **t** for an *G4925*
4:16 body fitly joined **t** and compacted by *G4883*
Php 1:27 striving **t** for the faith of the gospel; *G4866*
3:17 Brethren, be followers **t** of me, and *G4831*
Col 2: 2 being knit **t** in love, and unto all *G4822*
13 hath he quickened **t** with him, having *G4806*
19 **t**, increaseth with the increase of God. *G4822*
1Th 4:17 shall be caught up **t** with them in the *G260*
5:10 wake or sleep, we should live **t** with him. *G260*
11 Wherefore comfort yourselves **t**, and *G240*
2Th 2: 1 and *by* our gathering **t** unto him, *G1997*
Heb 10:25 of ourselves **t**, as the manner of some *G1997*
Jas 5: 3 heaped treasure **t** for the last days. *G2343*
1Pt 3: 7 and as being heirs **t** of the grace of life; *G4789*
5:13 The *church that is* at Babylon, elected **t**
Rev 6:14 when it is rolled **t**; and every mountain *G1507*
16:16 And he gathered them **t** into a place *G4863*
19:17 **t** unto the supper of the great God; *G4863*
19 armies, gathered **t** to make war against *G4863*
20: 8 to gather them **t** to battle: the number *G4863*

TOHU
1Sa 1: 1 of **T**, the son of Zuph, an Ephrathite: H8459

TOI
2Sa 8: 9 When **T** king of Hamath heard that H8583
10 Then **T** sent Joram his son unto king H8583
10 had wars with **T**. And *Joram* brought H8583

TOIL
Gen 5:29 our work and **t** of our hands, because H6093
41:51 all my **t**, and all my father's house. H5999
Mt 6:28 grow; they **t** not, neither do they spin: *G2872*
Lk 12:27 they grow: they **t** not, they spin not; *G2872*

TOILED
Lk 5: 5 Master, we have **t** all the night, and *G2872*

TOILING
Mk 6:48 And he saw them **t** in rowing; for the *G928*

TOKEN
Gen 9:12 And God said, This *is* the **t** of the H226
13 and it shall be for a **t** of a covenant H226
17 And God said unto Noah, This *is* the **t** of H226
17:11 a **t** of the covenant betwixt me and you. H226
Ex 3:12 and this *shall be* a **t** unto thee, that I H226
12:13 And the blood shall be to you for a **t** H226
13:16 And it shall be for a **t** upon thine hand, H226
Nu 17:10 to be kept for a **t** against the rebels; and H226
Jos 2:12 my father's house, and give me a true **t**: H226
Ps 86:17 Shew me a **t** for good; that they which H226
Mk 14:44 him had given them a **t**, saying, *G4953*
Php 1:28 is to them an evident **t** of perdition, but *G1732*
2Th 1: 5 *Which is* a manifest **t** of the righteous *G1730*
3:17 is the **t** in every epistle: so I write. *G4592*

TOKENS
Dt 22:15 take and bring forth *the t of* the damsel's
17 and yet these *are the t of* my daughter's
20 But if this thing be true, *and the t of*
Job 21:29 by the way? and do ye not know their **t**, H226
Ps 65: 8 parts are afraid at thy **t**: thou makest the H226
135: 9 *Who* sent **t** and wonders into the midst H226
Isa 44:25 That frustrateth the **t** of the liars, and H226

TOLA
Gen 46:13 And the sons of Issachar; **T**, and H8439
Nu 26:23 their families: *of* **T**, the family of the H8439
Jdg 10: 1 to defend Israel **T** the son of Puah, the H8439
1Ch 7: 1 Now the sons of Issachar *were*, **T**, and H8439
2 And the sons of **T**; Uzzi, and Rephaiah, H8439
2 house, *to wit*, of **T**: *they were* valiant H8439

TOLAD
1Ch 4:29 And at Bilhah, and at Ezem, and at T, H8434

TOLAITES
Nu 26:23 the T: of Pua, the family of the Punites: H8440

TOLD
Gen 3:11 And he said, Who t thee that thou *wast* H5046
9:22 father, and t his two brethren without. H5046
14:13 had escaped, and t Abram the Hebrew; H5046
20: 8 all his servants, and t all these things in H1696
22: 3 unto the place of which God had t him. H559
9 which God had t him of; and Abraham H559
20 things, that it was t Abraham, saying, H5046
24:28 And the damsel ran, and t *them of* her H5046
33 t mine errand. And he said, Speak on. H1696
66 And the servant t Isaac all things that H5608
26:32 came, and t him concerning the H5046
27:42 her elder son were t to Rebekah: and H5046
29:12 And Jacob t Rachel that he *was* her H5046
12 son: and she ran and t her father. H5046
13 house. And he t Laban all these things. H5608
31:20 Syrian, in that he t him not that he fled. H5046
22 And it was t Laban on the third day H5046
37: 5 And Joseph dreamed a dream, and he t H5046
9 dream, and t it his brethren, and H5608
10 And he t *it* to his father, and to his H5608
38:13 And it was t Tamar, saying, Behold thy H5046
24 after, that it was t Judah, saying, H5046
40: 9 And the chief butler t his dream to H5608
41: 8 and Pharaoh t them his dream; but H5608
12 of the guard; and we t him, and he H5608
24 seven good ears: and I t *this* unto the H559
42:29 t him all that befell unto them; saying, H5046
43: 7 brother? and we t him according to the H5046
44:24 father, we t him the words of my lord. H5046
45:26 And t him, saying, Joseph *is* yet alive, H5046
27 And they t him all the words of Joseph, H1696
47: 1 Then Joseph came and t Pharaoh, and H5046
48: 1 things, that *one* t Joseph, Behold, thy H559
2 And *one* t Jacob, and said, Behold, thy H5046
Ex 4:28 And Moses t Aaron all the words of the H5046
5: 1 and Aaron went in, and t Pharaoh, Thus H559
14: 5 And it was t the king of Egypt that the H5046
16:22 of the congregation came and t Moses. H5046
18: 8 And Moses t his father in law all that H5608
19: 9 for ever. And Moses t the words of the H5046
24: 3 And Moses came and t the people all H5608
Lev 21:24 And Moses t *it* unto Aaron, and to his H1696
Nu 11:24 And Moses went out, and t the people H1696
27 And there ran a young man, and t H5046
13:27 And they t him, and said, We came H5608
14:39 And Moses t these sayings unto all the H1696
23:26 said unto Balak, T not I thee, saying, H1696
29:40 And Moses t the children of Israel H559
Dt 17: 4 And it be t thee, and thou hast heard *of* H5046
Jos 2: 2 And it was t the king of Jericho, saying, H559
23 and t him all *things* that befell them: H5608
9:24 it was certainly t thy servants, how that H5046
10:17 And it was t Joshua, saying, The five H5046
Jdg 6:13 which our fathers t us of, saying, Did H5608
7:13 *was* a man that t a dream unto his H5608
9: 7 And when they t *it* to Jotham, he went H5046
25 way by them: and it was t Abimelech. H5046
42 into the field; and they t Abimelech. H5046
47 And it was t Abimelech, that all the H5046
13: 6 Then the woman came and t her H559
6 he *was*, neither t he me his name: H5046
23 this time have t us *such things* as these. H8085
14: 2 And he came up, and t his father and H5046
6 in his hand: but he t not his father or H5046
9 did eat: but he t not them that he had H5046
16 and hast not t *it* me. And he said unto H5046
16 Behold, I have not t *it* my father nor H5046
17 day, that he t her, because she lay H5046
17 upon him: and she t the riddle to the H5046
16: 2 *And it was* t the Gazites, saying, Samson
10 mocked me, and t me lies: now tell me, H1696
13 hast mocked me, and t me lies: tell me H1696
15 t me wherein thy great strength *lieth*. H5046
17 That he t her all his heart, and said H5046
18 And when Delilah saw that he had t her H5046
Ru 3:16 t her all that the man had done to her. H5046
1Sa 3:13 For I have t him that I will judge his H5046
18 And Samuel t him every whit, and hid H5046
4:13 the city, and t *it*, all the city cried out. H5046
14 And the man came in hastily, and t Eli. H5046
8:10 And Samuel t all the words of the LORD H559
9:15 Now the LORD had t Samuel in his ear H1540
1Sa 10:16 And Saul said unto his uncle, He t us H5046
16 whereof Samuel spake, he t him not. H5046
25 Then Samuel t the people the manner H1696
11: 4 of Saul, and t the tidings in the ears H1696
5 t him the tidings of the men of Jabesh. H5608
14: 1 the other side. But he t not his father. H5046
33 Then they t Saul, saying, Behold, the H5046
43 And Jonathan t him, and said, I did H5046
15:12 morning, it was t Samuel, saying, Saul H5046
18:20 they t Saul, and the thing pleased him. H5046
24 And the servants of Saul t him, saying, H5046
26 And when his servants t David these H5046
19: 2 and Jonathan t David, saying, Saul H5046
11 David's wife t him, saying, If thou H5046
18 to Ramah, and t him all that Saul had H5046
19 And it was t Saul, saying, Behold, H5046
21 And when it was t Saul, he sent other H5046
23: 1 Then they t David, saying, Behold, the H5046
7 And it was t Saul that David was come H5046
13 go. And it was t Saul that David was H5046
22 for it is t me *that* he dealeth very subtilly. H559
25 *him*. And they t David: wherefore he H5046
24: 1 that it was t him, saying, Behold, H5046
25:12 and came and t him all those sayings. H5046
14 But one of the young men t Abigail, H5046
19 you. But she t not her husband Nabal. H5046
36 wherefore she t him nothing, less or H5046
37 and his wife had t him these things, H5046
27: 4 And it was t Saul that David was fled to H5046
2Sa 1: 5 young man that t him, How knowest H5046
6 And the young man that t him said, As H5046
13 the young man that t him, Whence *art* H5046
2: 4 of Judah. And they t David, saying, H5046
3:23 were come, they t Joab, saying, Abner H5046
4:10 When one t me, saying, Behold, Saul is H5046
6:12 And it was t king David, saying, The H5046
10: 5 When they t *it* unto David, he sent to H5046
17 And when it was t David, he gathered H5046
11: 5 and t David, and said, I *am* with child. H5046
10 And when they had t David, saying, H5046
18 Then Joab sent and t David all the H5046
14:33 So Joab came to the king, and t him: H5046
15:31 And *one* t David, saying, Ahithophel *is* H5046
17:17 and a wench went and t them; and they H5046
17 them; and they went and t king David. H5046
18 Nevertheless a lad saw them, and t H5046
21 and went and t king David, and said H5046
18:10 And a certain man saw *it*, and t Joab, H5046
11 And Joab said unto the man that t him, H5046
25 And the watchman cried, and t the H5046
19: 1 And it was t Joab, Behold, the king H5046
8 the gate. And they t unto all the people, H5046
21:11 And it was t David what Rizpah the H5046
24:13 So Gad came to David, and t him, and H5046
1Ki 1:23 And they t the king, saying, Behold H5046
51 And it was t Solomon, saying, Behold, H5046
2:29 And it was t king Solomon that Joab H5046
39 of Gath. And they t Shimei, saying, H5046
41 And it was t Solomon that Shimei had H5046
8: 5 not be t nor numbered for multitude. H5608
10: 3 And Solomon t her all her questions: H5046
3 hid from the king, which he t her not. H5046
7 the half was not t me: thy wisdom and H5046
13:11 his sons came and t him all the works H5608
11 king, them they t also to their father. H5608
25 they came and t *it* in the city where the H1696
14: 2 the prophet, which t me that *I should* H1696
18:13 Was it not t my lord what I did when H5046
16 So Obadiah went to meet Ahab, and t H5046
19: 1 And Ahab t Jezebel all that Elijah had H5046
20:17 sent out, and they t him, saying, There H5046
2Ki 1: 7 up to meet you, and t you these words? H1696
4: 7 Then she came and t the man of God. H5046
27 hath hid *it* from me, and hath not t me. H5046
31 t him, saying, The child is not awaked. H5046
5: 4 And *one* went in, and t his lord, saying, H5046
6:10 the man of God t him and warned him H559
13 t him, saying, Behold, *he is* in Dothan. H5046
7:10 of the city: and they t them, saying, We H5046
11 And he called the porters; and they t *it* H5046
15 messengers returned, and t the king. H5046
8: 6 the woman, she t him. So the king H5608
7 sick; and it was t him, saying, The man H5046
14 t me *that* thou shouldest surely recover. H559
9:18 the watchman t, saying, The messenger H5046
20 And the watchman t, saying, He came H5046
36 Wherefore they came again, and t him. H5046
10: 8 And there came a messenger, and t H5046
12:10 up in bags, and t the money that was H4487
2Ki 12:11 And they gave the money, being t, into H8505
18:37 and t him the words of Rab-shakeh. H5046
23:17 And the men of the city t him, *It is* the H559
1Ch 17:25 For thou, O my God, hast t thy servant H1540
19: 5 Then there went *certain*, and t David H5046
17 And it was t David; and he gathered all H5046
2Ch 2: 2 And Solomon t out threescore and ten H5608
5: 6 not be t nor numbered for multitude. H5608
9: 2 And Solomon t her all her questions: H5046
2 hid from Solomon which he t her not. H5046
6 thy wisdom was not t me: *for* thou H5046
20: 2 Then there came some that t H5046
34:18 Then Shaphan the scribe t the king, H5046
Ezr 8:17 and I t them what they H7760+H6310
Neh 2:12 with me; neither t I *any* man what my H5046
16 had I as yet t *it* to the Jews, nor to H5046
18 Then I t them of the hand of my God H5046
Est 2:22 to Mordecai, who t *it* unto Esther the H5046
3: 4 unto them, that they t Haman, to see H5046
4 for he had t them that he *was* a Jew. H5046
4: 4 came and t *it* her. Then was the H5046
7 And Mordecai t him of all that had H5046
9 And Hatach came and t Esther the H5046
12 And they t to Mordecai Esther's words. H5046
5:11 And Haman t them of the glory of his H5608
6: 2 that Mordecai had t of Bigthana and H5046
13 And Haman t Zeresh his wife and all H5608
8: 1 for Esther had t what he *was* unto her. H5046
Job 15:18 Which wise men have t from their H5046
37:20 Shall it be t him that I speak? if a man H5608
Ps 44: 1 our fathers have t us, *what* work thou H5608
52:ttl came and t Saul, and said unto H5046
78: 3 and known, and our fathers have t us. H5608
90: 9 we spend our years as a tale *that is* t.
Ecc 6: 6 years twice *t*, yet hath he seen no good:
Isa 7: 2 And it was t the house of David, H5046
36:22 and t him the words of Rabshakeh. H5046
40:21 heard? hath it not been t you from the H5046
44: 8 afraid: have not I t thee from that time, H8085
45:21 time? *who* hath t it from that time? H5046
52:15 had not been t them shall they see; H5608
Jer 36:20 t all the words in the ears of the king. H5046
38:27 asked him: and he t them according to H5046
Dan 4: 7 soothsayers: and I t the dream before H560
8 and before him I t the dream, *saying*, H560
7: 1 the dream, *and* t the sum of the matters. H560
16 of all this. So he t me, and made me H560
8:26 which was t *is* true: wherefore shut H559
Jna 1:10 of the LORD, because he had t them. H5046
Hab 1: 5 ye will not believe, though it be t *you*. H5608
Zec 10: 2 a lie, and have t false dreams; they H1696
Mt 8:33 into the city, and t every thing, and what *G518*
12:48 said unto him that t him, Who is my *G2036*
14:12 and buried it, and went and t Jesus. *G518*
18:31 and t unto their lord all that was done. *G1285*
24:25 Behold, I have t you before. *G4280*
26:13 hath done, be t for a memorial of her. *G2980*
28: 7 there shall ye see him: lo, I have t you. *G2036*
Mk 5:14 And they that fed the swine fled, and t *it* *G312*
16 And they that saw *it* t them how it *G1334*
33 before him, and t him all the truth. *G2036*
6:30 unto Jesus, and t him all things, both *G518*
9:12 And he answered and t them, Elias *G2036*
16:10 *And* she went and t them that had been *G518*
13 And they went and t *it* unto the residue: *G518*
Lk 1:45 things which were t her from the Lord. *G2980*
2:17 was t them concerning this child. *G2980*
18 which were t them by the shepherds. *G2980*
20 heard and seen, as it was t unto them. *G2980*
8:20 And it was t him *by certain* which said, *G518*
34 and t *it* in the city and in the country. *G518*
36 They also which saw *it* t them by what *G518*
9:10 were returned, t him all that they had *G1334*
36 kept *it* close, and t no man in those days *G518*
13: 1 that season some that t him of the *G518*
18:37 And they t him, that Jesus of Nazareth *G518*
24: 9 And returned from the sepulchre, and t *G518*
10 which t these things unto the apostles. *G3004*
35 And they t what things *were done* in *G1834*
Jn 3:12 If I have t you earthly things, and ye *G2036*
4:29 Come, see a man, which t me all things *G2036*
39 testified, He t me all that ever I did. *G2036*
51 him, and t *him*, saying, Thy son liveth. *G518*
5:15 The man departed, and t the Jews that it *G312*
8:40 a man that hath t you the truth, which *G2980*
9:27 He answered them, I have t you *G2036*
10:25 Jesus answered them, I t you, and ye *G2036*
11:46 and t them what things Jesus had done. *G2036*
14: 2 t you. I go to prepare a place for you. *G2036*

Jn 14:29 And now I have **t** you before it come to G2046
16: 4 But these things have I **t** you, that when G2980
4 remember that I **t** you of them. And G2036
18: 8 Jesus answered, I have **t** you that I am G2036
20:18 Mary Magdalene came and **t** the G518
Act 5:22 not in the prison, they returned, and **t**, G518
25 Then came one and **t** them, saying, G518
9: 6 it shall be **t** thee what thou must do. G2980
12:14 in, and **t** how Peter stood before the gate. G518
16:36 And the keeper of the prison **t** this G518
38 And the serjeants **t** these words unto the G312
22:10 and there it shall be **t** thee of all things G2980
26 *that*, he went and **t** the chief captain, G518
23:16 and entered into the castle, and **t** Paul. G518
30 And when it was **t** me how that the G3377
27:25 God, that it shall be even as it was **t** me. G2980
2Co 7: 7 in you, when he **t** us your earnest desire, G312
13: 2 I **t** you before, and foretell you, as if I G4280
Gal 5:21 as I have also **t** *you* in time past, that G4277
Php 3:18 (For many walk, of whom I have **t** you G3004
1Th 3: 4 For verily, when we were with you, we **t** G4302
2Th 2: 5 I was yet with you, I **t** you these things? G3004
Jude 18 How that they **t** you there should be G3004

TOLERABLE
Mt 10:15 Verily I say unto you, It shall be more **t** G414
11:22 But I say unto you, It shall be more **t** for G414
24 it shall be more **t** for the land of Sodom G414
Mk 6:11 you, It shall be more **t** for Sodom and G414
Lk 10:12 But I say unto you, that it shall be more **t** G414
14 But it shall be more **t** for Tyre and Sidon G414

TOLL
Ezr 4:13 will they not pay **t**, tribute, and custom, H4061
20 the river; and **t**, tribute, and custom, H4061
7:24 **t**, tribute, or custom, upon them. H4061

TOMB
Job 21:32 to the grave, and shall remain in the **t**. H1430
Mt 27:60 And laid it in his own new **t**, which he G3419
Mk 6:29 took up his corpse, and laid it in a **t**. G3419

TOMBS
Mt 8:28 coming out of the **t**, exceeding fierce, so G3419
23:29 ye build the **t** of the prophets, and G5028
Mk 5: 2 of the **t** a man with an unclean spirit, G3419
3 Who had *his* dwelling among the **t**; and G3419
5 and in the **t**, crying, and cutting G3418
Lk 8:27 neither abode in *any* house, but in the **t**. G3418

TO-MORROW See MORROW.

TONGS
Ex 25:38 And the **t** thereof, and the snuffdishes H4457
Nu 4: 9 and his lamps, and his **t**, and his H4457
1Ki 7:49 and the lamps, and the **t** *of* gold, H4457
2Ch 4:21 the lamps, and the **t**, *made he of* gold, H4457
Isa 6: 6 had taken with the **t** from off the altar: H4457
44:12 The smith with the **t** both worketh in H4621

TONGUE
Gen 10: 5 **t**, after their families, in their nations. H3956
Ex 4:10 but I *am* slow of speech, and of a slow **t**. H3956
11: 7 a dog move his **t**, against man or beast: H3956
Dt 28:49 whose **t** thou shalt not understand; H3956
Jos 10:21 **t** against any of the children of Israel. H3956
Jdg 7: 5 of the water with his **t**, as a dog lappeth, H3956
2Sa 23: 2 spake by me, and his word *was* in my **t**. H3956
Ezr 4: 7 **t**, and interpreted in the Syrian tongue. H762
7 tongue, and interpreted in the Syrian **t**. H762
Est 7: 4 I had held my **t**, although the enemy H2790
Job 5:21 the scourge of the **t**: neither shalt thou H3956
6:24 Teach me, and I will hold my **t**: and H2790
30 Is there iniquity in my **t**? cannot my H3956
13:19 if I hold my **t**, I shall give up the ghost. H2790
15: 5 and thou choosest the **t** of the crafty. H3956
20:12 mouth, *though* he hide it under his **t**; H3956
16 of asps: the viper's **t** shall slay him. H3956
27: 4 wickedness, nor my **t** utter deceit. H3956
29:10 The nobles held their peace, and their **t** H3956
33: 2 mouth, my **t** hath spoken in my mouth. H3956
41: 1 **t** with a cord *which* thou lettest down? H3956
Ps 5: 9 open sepulchre; they flatter with their **t**. H3956
10: 7 under his **t** *is* mischief and vanity. H3956
12: 3 *and* the **t** that speaketh proud things: H3956
4 Who have said, With our **t** will we H3956
15: 3 *He that* backbiteth not with his **t**, nor H3956
22:15 a potsherd; and my **t** cleaveth to my H3956
34:13 Keep thy **t** from evil, and thy lips from H3956
35:28 And my **t** shall speak of thy H3956
37:30 wisdom, and his **t** talketh of judgment. H3956
39: 1 that I sin not with my **t**: I will keep my H3956
3 the fire burned: *then* spake I with my **t**, H3956
45: 1 king: my **t** *is* the pen of a ready writer. H3956
50:19 Thou givest thy mouth to evil, and thy **t** H3956
51:14 **t** shall sing aloud of thy righteousness. H3956
52: 2 Thy **t** deviseth mischiefs; like a sharp H3956
4 all devouring words, O *thou* deceitful **t**. H3956
57: 4 and arrows, and their **t** a sharp sword. H3956
64: 3 Who whet their **t** like a sword, *and* H3956
8 So they shall make their own **t** to fall H3956
66:17 mouth, and he was extolled with my **t**. H3956
68:23 *and* the **t** of thy dogs in the same. H3956
71:24 My **t** also shall talk of thy H3956
73: 9 and their **t** walketh through the earth. H3956
109: 2 have spoken against me with a lying **t**. H3956
119:172 My **t** shall speak of thy word: for all thy H3956
120: 2 from lying lips, *and* from a deceitful **t**. H3956
3 shall be done unto thee, thou false **t**? H3956
126: 2 laughter, and our **t** with singing: then H3956
137: 6 If I do not remember thee, let my **t** H3956
139: 4 For *there is* not a word in my **t**, *but*, lo, H3956
Prv 6:17 A proud look, a lying **t**, and hands that H3956
24 the flattery of the **t** of a strange woman. H3956
10:20 The **t** of the just *is as* choice silver: the H3956
31 but the froward **t** shall be cut out. H3956
12:18 a sword: but the **t** of the wise *is* health. H3956
19 ever: but a lying **t** *is* but for a moment. H3956
15: 2 The **t** of the wise useth knowledge H3956
4 A wholesome **t** *is* a tree of life: but H3956
16: 1 the answer of the **t**, *is* from the LORD. H3956
17: 4 lips; *and* a liar giveth ear to a naughty **t**. H3956
20 hath a perverse **t** falleth into mischief. H3956
18:21 Death and life *are* in the power of the **t**: H3956
21: 6 The getting of treasures by a lying **t** *is* a H3956
23 Whoso keepeth his mouth and his **t** H3956
25:15 and a soft **t** breaketh the bone. H3956
23 an angry countenance a backbiting **t**. H3956
26:28 A lying **t** hateth *those that are* afflicted H3956
28:23 favour than he that flattereth with the **t**. H3956
31:26 and in her **t** *is* the law of kindness. H3956
Song 4:11 milk *are* under thy **t**; and the smell of H3956
Isa 3: 8 because their **t** and their doings *are* H3956
11:15 utterly destroy the **t** of the Egyptian H3956
28:11 another **t** will he speak to this people. H3956
30:27 and his **t** as a devouring fire: H3956
32: 4 and the **t** of the stammerers shall H3956
33:19 **t**, *that thou canst* not understand. H3956
35: 6 as an hart, and the **t** of the dumb sing: H3956
41:17 *is* none, *and* their **t** faileth for thirst, I H3956
45:23 knee shall bow, every **t** shall swear. H3956
50: 4 The Lord GOD hath given me the **t** of H3956
54:17 shall prosper; and every **t** *that* shall rise H3956
57: 4 *and* draw out the **t**? *are* ye not children H3956
59: 3 your **t** hath muttered perverseness. H3956
Jer 9: 5 have taught their **t** to speak lies, *and* H3956
8 Their **t** *is as* an arrow shot out; it H3956
18:18 smite him with the **t**, and let us not give H3956
Lam 4: 4 The **t** of the sucking child cleaveth to H3956
Ezk 3:26 And I will make thy **t** cleave to the roof H3956
Dan 1: 4 the learning and the **t** of the Chaldeans. H3956
Hos 7:16 for the rage of their **t**: this *shall be* their H3956
Am 6:10 he say, Hold thy **t**: for we may not make H2013
Mic 6:12 and their **t** *is* deceitful in their mouth. H3956
Hab 1:13 *and* holdest thy **t** when the wicked H2790
Zep 3:13 shall a deceitful **t** be found in their H3956
Zec 14:12 **t** shall consume away in their mouth. H3956
Mk 7:33 his ears, and he spit, and touched his **t**; G1100
35 of his **t** was loosed, and he spake plain. G1100
Lk 1:64 and his **t** *loosed*, and he spake, G1100
16:24 my **t**; for I am tormented in this flame. G1100
Jn 5: 2 **t** Bethesda, having five porches. G1447
Act 1:19 in their proper **t**, Aceldama, that is to G1258
2: 8 in our own **t**, wherein we were born? G1258
26 rejoice, and my **t** was glad; moreover G1100
21:40 unto *them* in the Hebrew **t**, saying, G1258
22: 2 in the Hebrew **t** to them, they kept the G1258
26:14 saying in the Hebrew **t**, Saul, Saul, why G1258
Ro 14:11 to me, and every **t** shall confess to God. G1100
1Co 14: 2 For he that speaketh in an *unknown* **t** G1100
4 He that speaketh in an *unknown* **t** G1100
9 So likewise ye, except ye utter by the **t** G1100
13 *unknown* **t** pray that he may interpret. G1100
14 For if I pray in an *unknown* **t**, my spirit G1100
19 ten thousand words in an *unknown* **t**. G1100
26 a doctrine, hath a **t**, hath a revelation, G1100
27 If any man speak in an *unknown* **t**, *let it* G1100
Php 2:11 And *that* every **t** should confess that G1100
Jas 1:26 bridleth not his **t**, but deceiveth his own G1100
3: 5 Even so the **t** is a little member, and G1100
6 And the **t** *is* a fire, a world of iniquity: G1100
6 of iniquity: so is the **t** among our G1100
8 But the **t** can no man tame; *it is* an G1100
1Pt 3:10 let him refrain his **t** from evil, and his G1100
1Jn 3:18 neither in **t**; but in deed and in truth. G1100
Rev 5: 9 kindred, and **t**, and people, and nation; G1100
9:11 in the Hebrew **t** *is* Abaddon, but in the G1447
11 in the Greek **t** hath *his* name Apollyon. G1673
14: 6 nation, and kindred, and **t**, and people, G1100
16:16 called in the Hebrew **t** Armageddon. G1447

TONGUES
Gen 10:20 after their **t**, in their countries, *and* H3956
31 **t**, in their lands, after their nations. H3956
Ps 31:20 secretly in a pavilion from the strife of **t**. H3956
55: 9 Destroy, O Lord, *and* divide their **t**: for I H3956
78:36 and they lied unto him with their **t**. H3956
140: 3 They have sharpened their **t** like a H3956
Isa 66:18 all nations and **t**; and they shall come, H3956
Jer 9: 3 And they bend their **t** *like* their bow *for* H3956
23:31 that use their **t**, and say, He saith. H3956
Mk 16:17 out devils; they shall speak with new **t**; G1100
Act 2: 3 And there appeared unto them cloven **t** G1100
4 **t**, as the Spirit gave them utterance. G1100
11 in our **t** the wonderful works of God. G1100
10:46 For they heard them speak with **t**, and G1100
19: 6 and they spake with **t**, and prophesied. G1100
Ro 3:13 with their **t** they have used deceit; G1100
1Co 12:10 another *divers* kinds of **t**; to another the G1100
10 to another the interpretation of **t**: G1100
28 helps, governments, diversities of **t**. G1100
30 do all speak with **t**? do all interpret? G1100
13: 1 Though I speak with the **t** of men and G1100
8 fail; whether *there be* **t**, they shall cease; G1100
14: 5 I would that ye all spake with **t**, but G1100
5 he that speaketh with **t**, except he G1100
6 you speaking with **t**, what shall I profit G1100
18 I thank my God, I speak with **t** more G1100
21 With *men of* other **t** and other lips will G2084
22 Wherefore **t** are for a sign, not to them G1100
23 and all speak with **t**, and there come in G1100
39 and forbid not to speak with **t**. G1100
Rev 7: 9 and people, and **t**, stood before the G1100
10:11 peoples, and nations, and **t**, and kings. G1100
11: 9 and kindreds and **t** and nations shall G1100
13: 7 over all kindreds, and **t**, and nations. G1100
16:10 and they gnawed their **t** for pain, G1100
17:15 and multitudes, and nations, and **t**. G1100

TOO
Gen 18:14 Is any thing **t** hard for the LORD? At H6381
Ex 12: 4 And if the household be **t** little for the
18:18 for this thing *is* **t** heavy for thee; thou
36: 7 for all the work to make it, and **t** much.
Nu 11:14 alone, because *it is* **t** heavy for me.
16: 3 unto them, *Ye take* **t** much upon you,
7 *take* **t** much upon you, ye sons of Levi.
22: 6 this people; for they *are* **t** mighty for me:
Dt 1:17 the cause that is **t** hard for you, bring *it*
2:36 there was not one city **t** strong for us: the
12:21 his name there be **t** far from thee, then H7368
14:24 And if the way be **t** long for thee, so that
24 *or* if the place be **t** far from thee, which H7368
17: 8 If there arise a matter **t** hard for thee in
Jos 17:15 if mount Ephraim be **t** narrow for thee. H213
19: 9 of Judah was **t** much for them: therefore
47 of Dan went out *t little* for them:
22:17 *Is* the iniquity of Peor **t** little for us, from
Jdg 7: 2 *are* with thee *are* **t** many for me to give
4 The people *are* yet *t* many; bring them H7227
18:26 saw that they *were* **t** strong for him, he
Ru 1:12 go *your way;* for I am **t** old to have an
2Sa 3:39 the sons of Zeruiah *be* **t** hard for me: the
10:11 And he said, If the Syrians be **t** strong
11 of Ammon be **t** strong for thee, then
12: 8 and if *that had been* **t** little, I would
22:18 hated me: for they were **t** strong for me.
1Ki 1:36 LORD God of my lord the king say so *t*.
8:64 the LORD *was* **t** little to receive the burnt
12:28 unto them, It is **t** much for you to go up
19: 7 because the journey *is* **t** great for thee.
2Ki 3:26 saw that the battle was **t** sore for him, he
6: 1 we dwell with thee is **t** strait for us.
1Ch 19:12 And he said, If the Syrians be **t** strong
12 be **t** strong for thee, then I will help thee.
2Ch 29:34 But the priests were **t** few, so that they
Est 1:18 *there arise* **t** much contempt and wrath.

T

Job 42: 3 **t** wonderful for me, which I knew not.
Ps 18:17 hated me: for they were **t** strong for me.
35:10 from him that is **t** strong for him, yea,
38: 4 an heavy burden they are **t** heavy for me.
73:16 When I thought to know this, it *was* **t**
131: 1 great matters, or in things **t** high for me.
139: 6 *Such* knowledge *is* **t** wonderful for me; it
Prv 24: 7 Wisdom *is* **t** high for a fool: he openeth
30:18 There be three *things which* are **t**
Isa 49:19 shall even now be **t** narrow by reason of
20 ears, The place *is* **t** strait for me: give
Jer 32:17 *and* there is nothing **t** hard for thee:
27 all flesh: is there any thing **t** hard for me?
Act 17:22 that in all things ye are **t** superstitious.

TOOK

Gen 2:15 And the LORD God **t** the man, and put H3947
21 he slept: and he **t** one of his ribs, and H3947
3: 6 *one* wise, she **t** of the fruit thereof, H3947
4:19 And Lamech **t** unto him two wives: the H3947
5:24 God: and he *was* not; for God **t** him. H3947
6: 2 **t** them wives of all which they chose. H3947
8: 9 his hand, and **t** her, and pulled her H3947
20 the LORD; and **t** of every clean beast, H3947
9:23 And Shem and Japheth **t** a garment, H3947
11:29 And Abram and Nahor **t** them wives: H3947
31 And Terah **t** Abram his son, and Lot H3947
12: 5 And Abram **t** Sarai his wife, and Lot H3947
14:11 And they **t** all the goods of Sodom and H3947
12 And they **t** Lot, Abram's brother's son, H3947
15:10 And he **t** unto him all these, and H3947
16: 3 And Sarai Abram's wife **t** Hagar her H3947
17:23 And Abraham **t** Ishmael his son, and H3947
18: 8 And he **t** butter, and milk, and the calf H3947
20: 2 king of Gerar sent, and **t** Sarah. H3947
14 And Abimelech **t** sheep, and oxen, and H3947
21:14 the morning, and **t** bread, and a bottle H3947
21 **t** him a wife out of the land of Egypt. H3947
27 And Abraham **t** sheep and oxen, and H3947
22: 3 his ass, and **t** two of his young men H3947
6 And Abraham **t** the wood of the burnt H3947
6 his son; and he **t** the fire in his hand, H3947
10 hand, and **t** the knife to slay his son. H3947
13 went and **t** the ram, and offered H3947
24: 7 The LORD God of heaven, which **t** me H3947
10 And the servant **t** ten camels of the H3947
22 that the man **t** a golden earring of H3947
61 servant **t** Rebekah, and went his way. H3947
65 she **t** a vail, and covered herself. H3947
67 Sarah's tent, and **t** Rebekah, and she H3947
25: 1 Then again Abraham **t** a wife, and her H3947
20 years old when he **t** Rebekah to wife, H3947
26 out, and his hand **t** hold on Esau's heel;
26:34 And Esau was forty years old when he **t** H3947
27:15 And Rebekah **t** goodly raiment of her H3947
36 two times: he **t** away my birthright; H3947
28: 9 Then went Esau unto Ishmael, and **t** H3947
11 was set; and he **t** of the stones of that H3947
18 in the morning, and **t** the stone that he H3947
29:23 evening, that he **t** Leah his daughter, H3947
30: 9 left bearing, she **t** Zilpah her maid, and H3947
37 And Jacob **t** him rods of green poplar, H3947
31:23 And he **t** his brethren with him, and H3947
45 And Jacob **t** a stone, and set it up *for* a H3947
46 stones; and they **t** stones, and made an H3947
32:13 same night; and **t** of that which came H3947
22 And he rose up that night, and **t** his H3947
23 And he **t** them, and sent them over the H3947
33:11 enough. And he urged him, and he **t** *it*. H3947
34: 2 **t** her, and lay with her, and defiled her. H3947
25 Levi, Dinah's brethren, **t** each man his H3947
26 edge of the sword, and **t** Dinah out of H3947
28 They **t** their sheep, and their oxen, and H3947
29 ones, and their wives **t** they captive, and
36: 2 Esau **t** his wives of the daughters of H3947
6 And Esau **t** his wives, and his sons, and H3947
37:24 And they **t** him, and cast him into a pit: H3947
31 And they **t** Joseph's coat, and killed a H3947
38: 2 and he **t** her, and went in unto her. H3947
6 And Judah **t** a wife for Er his firstborn, H3947
28 and the midwife **t** and bound upon his H3947
39:20 And Joseph's master **t** him, and put H3947
40:11 in my hand: and I **t** the grapes, and H3947
41:42 And Pharaoh **t** off his ring from his H5493
42:24 with them, and **t** from them Simeon, H3947
30 to us, and **t** us for spies of the country. H5414
43:15 And the men **t** that present, and they H3947
15 present, and they **t** double money in H3947
34 And he **t** *and sent* messes unto them H5375
Gen 44:11 Then they speedily **t** down every man H3381
46: 1 And Israel **t** his journey with all that he
6 And they **t** their cattle, and their goods, H3947
47: 2 And he **t** some of his brethren, *even* H3947
48: 1 *is* sick: and he **t** with him his two sons, H3947
13 And Joseph **t** them both, Ephraim in H3947
22 brethren, which I **t** out of the hand of H3947
50:25 And Joseph **t** an oath of the children of
Ex 2: 1 Levi, and **t** *to wife* a daughter of Levi. H3947
3 longer hide him, she **t** for him an ark of H3947
9 the woman **t** the child, and nursed it. H3947
4: 6 and when he **t** it out, behold, his hand H3318
20 And Moses **t** his wife and his sons, and H3947
20 and Moses **t** the rod of God in his hand. H3947
25 Then Zipporah **t** a sharp stone, and cut H3947
6:20 And Amram **t** him Jochebed his H3947
23 And Aaron **t** him Elisheba, daughter of H3947
25 And Eleazar Aaron's son **t** him *one* of H3947
9:10 And they **t** ashes of the furnace, and H3947
10:19 west wind, which **t** away the locusts, H5375
12:34 And the people **t** their dough before it H5375
13:19 And Moses **t** the bones of Joseph with H3947
20 And they **t** their journey from Succoth,
22 He **t** not away the pillar of the cloud by H4185
14: 6 And he made ready his chariot, and **t** H3947
7 And he **t** six hundred chosen chariots, H3947
25 And **t** off their chariot wheels, that they H5493
15:20 sister of Aaron, **t** a timbrel in her hand; H3947
16: 1 And they **t** their journey from Elim, and
17:12 heavy; and they **t** a stone, and put *it* H3947
18: 2 Then Jethro, Moses' father in law, **t** H3947
12 And Jethro, Moses' father in law, **t** a H3947
24: 6 And Moses **t** half of the blood, and put H3947
7 And he **t** the book of the covenant, and H3947
8 And Moses **t** the blood, and sprinkled *it* H3947
32:20 And he **t** the calf which they had made, H3947
33: 7 And Moses **t** the tabernacle, and H3947
34: 4 **t** in his hand the two tables of stone. H3947
34 with him, he **t** the vail off, until he H5493
40:20 And he **t** and put the testimony into the H3947
Lev 6: 4 that which he **t** violently away, or the
8:10 And Moses **t** the anointing oil, and H3947
15 And he slew *it;* and Moses **t** the blood, H3947
16 And he **t** all the fat that *was* upon the H3947
23 And he slew *it;* and Moses **t** of the H3947
25 And he **t** the fat, and the rump, and all H3947
26 the LORD, he **t** one unleavened cake, H3947
28 And Moses **t** them from off their H3947
29 And Moses **t** the breast, and waved it H3947
30 And Moses **t** of the anointing oil, and H3947
9:15 offering, and **t** the goat, which *was* H3947
17 And he brought the meat offering, and **t**
10: 1 the sons of Aaron, **t** either of them his H3947
Nu 1:17 And Moses and Aaron **t** these men H3947
3:49 And Moses **t** the redemption money of H3947
50 the children of Israel **t** he the money; a H3947
7: 6 And Moses **t** the wagons and the oxen, H3947
10:12 And the children of Israel **t** their H5265
13 And they first **t** their journey according
11:25 unto him, and **t** of the spirit that *was* H680
16: 1 son of Peleth, sons of Reuben, **t** *men*: H3947
18 And they **t** every man his censer, and H3947
39 And Eleazar the priest **t** the brasen H3947
47 And Aaron **t** as Moses commanded, H3947
17: 9 they looked, and **t** every man his rod. H3947
20: 9 And Moses **t** the rod from before the H3947
21: 1 Israel, and **t** *some* of them prisoners. H7617
25 And Israel **t** all these cities: and Israel H3947
32 Jaazer, and they **t** the villages thereof, H3920
22:41 that Balak **t** Balaam, and brought H3947
23: 7 And he **t** up his parable, and said, H5375
11 done unto me? I **t** thee to curse mine H3947
18 And he **t** up his parable, and said, Rise H5375
24: 3 And he **t** up his parable, and said, H5375
15 And he **t** up his parable, and said, H5375
20 And when he looked on Amalek, he **t** H5375
21 And he looked on the Kenites, and **t** up H5375
23 And he **t** up his parable, and said, Alas, H5375
25: 7 and **t** a javelin in his hand; H3947
27:22 him: and he **t** Joshua, and set him H3947
31: 9 And the children of Israel **t** *all* the
9 little ones, and **t** the spoil of all their
11 And they **t** all the spoil, and all the H3947
27 between them that **t** the war upon H8610
47 half, Moses **t** one portion of fifty, H3947
51 And Moses and Eleazar the priest **t** the H3947
54 And Moses and Eleazar the priest **t** the H3947
32:39 to Gilead, and **t** it, and dispossessed H3920
41 went and **t** the small towns thereof, H3920
Nu 32:42 And Nobah went and **t** Kenath, and the H3920
33:12 And they **t** their journey out of the
Dt 1:15 So I **t** the chief of your tribes, wise men, H3947
23 And the saying pleased me well: and I **t** H3947
25 And they **t** of the fruit of the land in H3947
2: 1 Then we turned, and **t** our journey into H5265
34 And we **t** all his cities at that time, and H3920
35 Only the cattle we **t** for a prey unto
35 and the spoil of the cities which we **t**. H3920
3: 4 And we **t** all his cities at that time, H3920
4 not a city which we **t** not from them, H3947
7 of the cities, we **t** for a prey to ourselves.
8 And we **t** at that time out of the hand of H3947
14 Jair the son of Manasseh **t** all the H3947
9:17 And I **t** the two tables, and cast them H8610
21 And I **t** your sin, the calf which ye had H3947
10: 6 And the children of Israel **t** their journey
22:14 her, and say, I **t** this woman, and when H3947
24: 3 husband die, which **t** her *to be* his wife; H3947
29: 8 And we **t** their land, and gave it for an H3947
Jos 2: 4 And the woman **t** the two men, and hid H3947
3: 6 the people. And they **t** up the ark of the H5375
4: 8 commanded, and **t** up twelve stones H5375
20 And those twelve stones, which they **t** H3947
6:12 the priests **t** up the ark of the LORD. H5375
20 straight before him, and they **t** the city. H3920
7: 1 of the tribe of Judah, **t** of the accursed H3947
17 of Judah; and he **t** the family of the H3920
21 coveted them, and **t** them; and, behold, H3947
23 And they **t** them out of the midst of the H3947
24 And Joshua, and all Israel with him, **t** H3947
8:12 And he **t** about five thousand men, and H3947
19 **t** it, and hasted and set the city on fire. H3920
23 And the king of Ai they **t** alive, and H8610
27 spoil of that city Israel **t** for a prey unto
9: 4 ambassadors, and **t** old sacks upon H3947
12 This our bread we **t** hot *for* our provision
14 And the men **t** of their victuals, and H3947
10:27 and they **t** them down off the trees, H3381
28 And that day Joshua **t** Makkedah, and H3920
32 of Israel, which **t** it on the second day, H3920
35 And they **t** it on that day, and smote it H3920
37 And they **t** it, and smote it with the H3920
39 And he **t** it, and the king thereof, and H3920
11:10 turned back, and **t** Hazor, and smote H3920
14 the children of Israel **t** for a prey unto
16 So Joshua **t** all that land, the hills, and H3947
17 he **t**, and smote them, and slew them. H3920
19 of Gibeon: all *other* they **t** in battle. H3947
23 So Joshua **t** the whole land, according H3947
15:17 brother of Caleb, **t** it: and he gave him H3920
16: 4 and Ephraim, **t** their inheritance.
19:47 Leshem, and **t** it, and smote it with H3920
24: 3 And I **t** your father Abraham from the H3947
26 law of God, and **t** a great stone, and set H3947
Jdg 1:13 younger brother, **t** it: and he gave him H3920
18 Also Judah **t** Gaza with the coast H3920
3: 6 And they **t** their daughters to be their H3947
21 And Ehud put forth his left hand, and **t** H3947
25 therefore they **t** a key, and opened H3947
28 after him, and **t** the fords of Jordan H3920
4:21 Then Jael Heber's wife **t** a nail of the H3947
21 of the tent, and **t** an hammer in her H7760
5:19 of Megiddo; they **t** no gain of money. H3947
6:27 Then Gideon **t** ten men of his servants, H3947
7: 8 So the people **t** victuals in their hand, H3947
24 together, and **t** the waters unto H3920
25 And they **t** two princes of the H3920
8:12 after them, and **t** the two kings of H3920
16 And he **t** the elders of the city, and H3947
21 Zalmunna, and **t** away the ornaments H3947
9:43 And he **t** the people, and divided them H3947
45 that day; and he **t** the city, and slew the H3920
48 and Abimelech **t** an axe in his hand, H3947
48 the trees, and **t** it, and laid *it* on his H5375
50 encamped against Thebez, and **t** it. H3920
11:13 Because Israel **t** away my land, when H3947
15 Jephthah, Israel **t** not away the land of H3947
12: 5 And the Gileadites **t** the passages of H3920
6 *it* right. Then they **t** him, and slew him at H270
9 he sent abroad, and **t** in thirty daughters H935
13:19 So Manoah **t** a kid with a meat H3947
14: 9 And he **t** thereof in his hands, and went H7287
19 men of them, and **t** their spoil, and H3947
15: 4 foxes, and **t** firebrands, and turned H3947
15 his hand, and **t** it, and slew a thousand H3947
16: 3 at midnight, and **t** the doors of the gate H270
12 Delilah therefore **t** new ropes, and H3947
21 But the Philistines **t** him, and put out his H270

Jdg 16:29 And Samson t hold of the two middle
31 came down, and t him, and brought H5375
17: 2 silver *is* with me; I t it. And his mother H3947
4 and his mother t two hundred *shekels* H3947
18:17 in thither, *and* t the graven image, and H3947
20 was glad, and he t the ephod, and the H3947
27 And they t *the things* which Micah had H3947
19: 1 Ephraim, who t to him a concubine H3947
15 that t them into his house to lodging. H622
25 to him: so the man t his concubine, H2388
28 Then the man t her *up* upon an ass, H3947
29 into his house, he t a knife, and laid H3947
20: 6 And I t my concubine, and cut her in H270
21:23 did so, and t *them* wives, according H5375
Ru 1: 4 And they t them wives of the women of H5375
2:18 And she t *it* up, and went into the city: H5375
4: 2 And he t ten men of the elders of the H3947
13 So Boaz t Ruth, and she was his wife: H3947
16 And Naomi t the child, and laid it in H3947
1Sa 1:24 And when she had weaned him, she t H5927
2:14 up the priest t for himself. So they H3947
5: 1 And the Philistines t the ark of God, H3947
2 When the Philistines t the ark of God, H3947
3 LORD. And they t Dagon, and set him H3947
6:10 And the men did so; and t two milch H3947
12 And the kine t the straight way to the
15 And the Levites t down the ark of the H3381
7: 9 And Samuel t a sucking lamb, and H3947
12 Then Samuel t a stone, and set *it* H3947
8: 3 and t bribes, and perverted judgment. H3947
9:22 And Samuel t Saul and his servant, H3947
24 And the cook t up the shoulder, and H7311
10: 1 Then Samuel t a vial of oil, and poured H3947
11: 7 And he t a yoke of oxen, and hewed H3947
14:32 the spoil, and t sheep, and oxen, and H3947
47 So Saul t the kingdom over Israel, and H3920
52 or any valiant man, he t him unto him. H622
15: 8 And he t Agag the king of the H8610
21 But the people t of the spoil, sheep and H3947
16:13 Then Samuel t the horn of oil, and H3947
20 And Jesse t an ass *laden* with bread, H3947
23 Saul, that David t an harp, and played H3947
17:20 with a keeper, and t, and went, as Jesse H5375
34 a bear, and t a lamb out of the flock: H5375
40 And he t his staff in his hand, and H3947
49 in his bag, and t thence a stone, and H3947
51 the Philistine, and t his sword, and H3947
54 And David t the head of the Philistine, H3947
57 Philistine, Abner t him, and brought H3947
18: 2 And Saul t him that day, and would let H3947
19:13 And Michal t an image, and laid *it* in H3947
24: 2 Then Saul t three thousand chosen H3947
25:18 Then Abigail made haste, and t two H3947
43 David also t Ahinoam of Jezreel; and H3947
26:12 So David t the spear and the cruse of H3947
27: 9 woman alive, and t away the sheep, H3947
28:24 and killed it, and t flour, and kneaded H3947
30:20 And David t all the flocks and the H3947
31: 4 Saul t a sword, and fell upon it. H3947
12 went all night, and t the body of Saul H3947
13 And they t their bones, and buried H3947
2Sa 1:10 was fallen: and I t the crown that *was* H3947
11 Then David t hold on his clothes, and
2: 8 of Saul's host, t Ish-bosheth the son H3947
32 And they t up Asahel, and buried him H5375
3:15 And Ish-bosheth sent, and t her from H3947
27 to Hebron, Joab t him aside in the gate
36 And all the people t notice *of it*, and it H5384
4: 4 and his nurse t him up, and fled: and H5375
7 him, and t his head, and gat them H3947
10 good tidings, I t hold of him, and slew
12 in Hebron. But they t the head of H3947
5: 7 Nevertheless David t the strong hold of H3920
13 And David t *him* more concubines and H3947
6: 6 and t hold of it; for the oxen shook *it*.
7: 8 the LORD of hosts, I t thee from the H3947
15 from him, as I t *it* from Saul, whom H5493
8: 1 them: and David t Metheg-ammah H3947
4 And David t from him a thousand H3920
7 And David t the shields of gold that H3947
8 king David t exceeding much brass. H3947
10: 4 Wherefore Hanun t David's servants, H3947
11: 4 And David sent messengers, and t her; H3947
12: 4 unto him; but t the poor man's lamb, H3947
26 of Ammon, and t the royal city. H3920
29 Rabbah, and fought against it, and t it. H3920
30 And he t their king's crown from off his H3947
13: 8 down. And she t flour, and kneaded H3947
9 And she t a pan, and poured *them* out H3947

2Sa 13:10 hand. And Tamar t the cakes which H3947
11 unto him to eat, he t hold of her, and
15: 5 his hand, and t him, and kissed him. H2388
17:19 And the woman t and spread a H3947
18:14 with thee. And he t three darts in his H3947
17 And they t Absalom, and cast him into H3947
20: 3 and the king t the ten women *his* H3947
9 brother? And Joab t Amasa by the beard H270
10 But Amasa t no heed to the sword that
21: 8 But the king t the two sons of Rizpah H3947
10 And Rizpah the daughter of Aiah t H3947
12 And David went and t the bones of H3947
22:17 He sent from above, he t me; he drew H3947
23:16 by the gate, and t *it*, and brought *it* to H5375
1Ki 1:39 And Zadok the priest t an horn of oil H3947
3: 1 Pharaoh king of Egypt, and t Pharaoh's H3947
20 And she arose at midnight, and t my H3947
4:15 Ahimaaz *was* in Naphtali; he also t H3947
8: 3 came, and the priests t up the ark. H5375
11:18 to Paran: and they t men with them out H3947
12:28 Whereupon the king t counsel, and
13:29 And the prophet t up the carcase of the H5375
14:26 And he t away the treasures of the H3947
26 house; he even t away all: and he took H3947
26 away all: and he t away all the shields H3947
15:12 And he t away the sodomites out of the H5375
18 Then Asa t all the silver and the gold H3947
22 and they t away the stones of Ramah, H5375
16:31 of Nebat, that he t to wife Jezebel the H3947
17:19 me thy son. And he t him out of her H3947
23 And Elijah t the child, and brought him H3947
18: 4 that Obadiah t an hundred prophets, H3947
10 said, *He is* not *there;* he t an oath of the
26 And they t the bullock which was given H3947
31 And Elijah t twelve stones, according H3947
40 escape. And they t them: and Elijah H8610
19:21 And he returned back from him, and t H3947
20:34 which my father t from thy father, I H3947
41 And he hasted, and t the ashes away
22:46 of his father Asa, he t out of the land. H1197
2Ki 2: 8 And Elijah t his mantle, and wrapped H3947
12 him no more: and he t hold of his own
13 He t up also the mantle of Elijah that H7311
14 And he t the mantle of Elijah that fell H3947
3:26 too sore for him, he t with him seven H3947
27 Then he t his eldest son that should H3947
4:37 and t up her son, and went out. H5375
5: 5 he departed, and t with him ten talents H3947
24 And when he came to the tower, he t H3947
6: 7 thee. And he put out his hand, and t it. H3947
8 against Israel, and t counsel with his
7:14 They t therefore two chariot horses; H3947
8: 9 So Hazael went to meet him, and t a H3947
15 the morrow, that he t a thick cloth, and H3947
9:13 Then they hasted, and t every man his H3947
10: 7 to them, that they t the king's sons, and H3947
14 alive. And they t them alive, and slew H8610
15 he t him up to him into the chariot. H5927
31 But Jehu t no heed to walk in the law of
11: 2 sister of Ahaziah, t Joash the son of H3947
4 with them, and t an oath of them in the
9 and they t every man his men H3947
19 And he t the rulers over hundreds, and H3947
12: 9 But Jehoiada the priest t a chest, and H3947
17 against Gath, and t it: and Hazael set H3920
18 And Jehoash king of Judah t all the H3947
13:15 And he t unto him bow and arrows. H3947
18 And he said, Take the arrows. And he t H3947
25 And Jehoash the son of Jehoahaz t H3947
14: 7 ten thousand, and t Selah by war, and H8610
13 And Jehoash king of Israel t Amaziah H8610
14 And he t all the gold and silver, and all H3947
21 And all the people of Judah t Azariah, H3947
15:29 king of Assyria, and t Ijon, and H3947
16: 8 And Ahaz t the silver and gold that was H3947
9 Damascus, and t it, and carried *the* H8610
17 off them; and t down the sea from off H3381
17: 6 the king of Assyria t Samaria, and H3920
18:10 And at the end of three years they t it: H3920
13 the fenced cities of Judah, and t them. H8610
20: 7 of figs. And they t and laid *it* on the H3947
23:11 And he t away the horses that the kings H7673
16 and sent, and t the bones out of the H3947
19 to anger, Josiah t away, and did to H5493
30 people of the land t Jehoahaz the son of H3947
34 to Jehoiakim, and t Jehoahaz away: H3947
24:12 t him in the eighth year of his reign. H3947
25: 6 So they t the king, and brought him up H8610
14 they ministered, t they away. H3947

2Ki 25:15 silver, the captain of the guard t away. H3947
18 And the captain of the guard t Seraiah H3947
19 And out of the city he t an officer that H3947
20 of the guard t these, and brought them H3947
1Ch 2:19 And when Azubah was dead, Caleb t H3947
23 And he t Geshur, and Aram, with the H3947
4:18 daughter of Pharaoh, which Mered t. H3947
5:21 And they t away their cattle; of their
7:15 And Machir t to wife *the sister* of H3947
10: 4 So Saul t a sword, and fell upon it. H3947
9 stripped him, they t his head, and his H5375
12 They arose, all the valiant men, and t H5375
11: 5 David t the castle of Zion, which H3920
18 by the gate, and t *it*, and brought *it* to H5375
14: 3 And David t more wives at Jerusalem: H3947
17: 7 the LORD of hosts, I t thee from the H3947
13 as I t *it* from *him* that was before thee: H5493
18: 1 them, and t Gath and her towns H3947
4 And David t from him a thousand H3920
7 And David t the shields of gold that H3947
19: 4 Wherefore Hanun t David's servants, H3947
20: 2 And David t the crown of their king H3947
23:22 their brethren the sons of Kish t them. H5375
27:23 But David t not the number of them H5375
2Ch 5: 4 came; and the Levites t up the ark. H5375
8:18 to Ophir, and t thence four hundred H3947
10: 6 And king Rehoboam t counsel with the
8 men gave him, and t counsel with the
11:18 And Rehoboam t him Mahalath the H3947
20 And after her he t Maachah the H3947
21 (for he t eighteen wives, and H5375
12: 4 And he t the fenced cities which H3920
9 Jerusalem, and t away the treasures of H3947
9 king's house; he t all: he carried away H3947
13:19 after Jeroboam, and t cities from him, H3920
14: 3 For he t away the altars of the strange H5493
5 Also he t away out of all the cities of H5493
15: 8 the prophet, he t courage, and put away
16: 6 Then Asa the king t all Judah; and they H3947
17: 6 moreover he t away the high places
22:11 of the king, t Joash the son of Ahaziah, H3947
23: 1 himself, and t the captains of H3947
8 commanded, and t every man his men H3947
20 And he t the captains of hundreds, and H3947
24: 3 And Jehoiada t for him two wives; and H5375
11 the chest, and t it, and carried it to his H5375
25:13 thousand of them, and t much spoil. H962
17 Then Amaziah king of Judah t advice,
23 And Joash the king of Israel t Amaziah H8610
24 And *he t* all the gold and the silver, and
26: 1 Then all the people of Judah t Uzziah, H3947
28: 8 daughters, and t also away much spoil
15 name rose up, and t the captives, and H2388
21 For Ahaz t away a portion *out* of the
29:16 And the Levites t *it*, to carry *it* out H6901
30:14 And they arose and t away the altars
14 altars for incense t they away, and cast
23 And the whole assembly t counsel to
32: 3 He t counsel with his princes and his
33:11 of Assyria, which t Manasseh among H3920
15 And he t away the strange gods, and the
34:33 And Josiah t away all the abominations
35:24 His servants therefore t him out of that H5674
36: 1 Then the people of the land t Jehoahaz H3947
4 And Necho t Jehoahaz his brother, H3947
Ezr 2:61 of Barzillai; which t a wife of the H3947
5:14 Nebuchadnezzar t out of the temple H5312
6: 5 Nebuchadnezzar t forth out of the H5312
8:30 So t the priests and the Levites the H6901
Neh 2: 1 before him: and I t up the wine, and H5375
4: 1 he was wroth, and t great indignation,
5:12 the priests, and t an oath of them, that
7:63 children of Barzillai, which t *one* of the H3947
9:25 And they t strong cities, and a fat land, H3920
Est 2: 7 were dead, t for his own daughter. H3947
3:10 And the king t his ring from his hand, H5493
6:11 Then t Haman the apparel and the H3947
8: 2 And the king t off his ring, which he H5493
9:27 The Jews ordained, and t upon them, H6901
Job 1:15 And the Sabeans fell *upon them*, and t H3947
2: 8 And he t him a potsherd to scrape H3947
Ps 18:16 He sent from above, he t me, he drew H3947
22: 9 But thou *art* he that t me out of the H1518
31:13 every side: while they t counsel together
48: 6 Fear t hold upon them there, *and* pain,
55:14 We t sweet counsel together, *and* walked
56:ttl when the Philistines t him in Gath. H270
69: 4 then I restored *that* which I t not away. H1497
71: 6 womb: thou art he that t me out of my H1491

Ps 78:70 He chose David also his servant, and **t** H3947
Prv 12:27 not that which he **t** in hunting: but the
Ecc 2:20 all the labour which I **t** under the sun. H5998
Song 5: 7 of the walls **t** away my veil from me. H5375
Isa 8: 2 And I **t** unto me faithful witnesses to H5749
20: 1 and fought against Ashdod, and **t** it; H3920
36: 1 defenced cities of Judah, and **t** them. H8610
40:14 With whom **t** he counsel, and *who*
Jer 13: 7 and digged, and **t** the girdle from the H3947
25:17 Then **t** I the cup at the LORD'S hand, H3947
26: 8 **t** him, saying, Thou shalt surely die. H8610
27:20 king of Babylon **t** not, when he carried H3947
28: 3 king of Babylon **t** away from this place, H3947
10 Then Hananiah the prophet **t** the yoke H3947
31:32 in the day *that* I **t** them by the hand to H2388
32:10 and sealed *it*, and **t** witnesses, and H5749
11 So I **t** the evidence of the purchase, H3947
35: 3 Then I **t** Jaazaniah the son of Jeremiah, H3947
36:14 the son of Neriah **t** the roll in his hand, H3947
21 the roll: and he **t** it out of Elishama the H3947
32 Then **t** Jeremiah another roll, and gave H3947
37:13 of Hananiah; and he **t** Jeremiah the H8610
14 not to him: so Irijah **t** Jeremiah, and H8610
17 Then Zedekiah the king sent, and **t** him H8610
38: 6 Then **t** they Jeremiah, and cast him H3947
11 So Ebed-melech **t** the men with him, H3947
11 the treasury, and **t** thence old cast H3947
13 with cords, and **t** him up out of the H5927
14 Then Zedekiah the king sent, and **t** H3947
39:14 Even they sent, and **t** Jeremiah out of H3947
40: 2 And the captain of the guard **t** H3947
41:12 Then they **t** all the men, and went to H3947
16 Then **t** Johanan the son of Kareah, and H3947
43: 5 of the forces, **t** all the remnant of H3947
50:33 and all that **t** them captives held them
43 feeble: anguish **t** hold of him, *and* pangs
52: 9 Then they **t** the king, and carried him H8610
18 they ministered, **t** they away. H3947
19 silver, **t** the captain of the guard away. H3947
24 And the captain of the guard **t** Seraiah H3947
25 He **t** also out of the city an eunuch, H3947
26 of the guard **t** them, and brought them H3947
Lam 5:13 They **t** the young men to grind, and the H5375
Ezk 3:12 Then the spirit **t** me up, and I heard H5375
14 So the spirit lifted me up, and **t** me H3947
8: 3 of an hand, and **t** me by a lock of mine H3947
10: 7 the cherubims, and **t** *thereof*, and put *it* H5375
7 with linen: who **t** *it*, and went out. H3947
11:24 Afterwards the spirit **t** me up, and H5375
16:50 therefore I **t** them away as I saw *good*. H5493
17: 3 and **t** the highest branch of the cedar: H3947
5 He **t** also of the seed of the land, and H3947
19: 5 hope was lost, then she **t** another of her H3947
23:10 These discovered her nakedness: they **t** H3947
13 was defiled, *that* they *t* both one way,
29: 7 When they **t** hold of thee by thy hand, H8610
33: 5 of the trumpet, and **t** not warning; his
43: 5 So the spirit **t** me up, and brought me H5375
Dan 1:16 Thus Melzar **t** away the portion of their H5375
3:22 slew those men that **t** up Shadrach, H5267
5:20 throne, and they **t** his glory from him: H5709
31 And Darius the Median **t** the kingdom, H6902
Hos 1: 3 So he went and **t** Gomer the daughter H3947
12: 3 He **t** his brother by the heel in the womb,
13:11 I gave thee a king in mine anger, and **t** H3947
Am 7:15 And the LORD **t** me as I followed the H3947
Jna 1:15 So they **t** up Jonah, and cast him forth H5375
Zec 11: 7 poor of the flock. And I **t** unto me two H3947
10 And I **t** my staff, *even* Beauty, and cut H3947
13 at of them. And I **t** the thirty *pieces* of H3947
Mt 1:24 bidden him, and **t** unto him his wife: G3880
2:14 When he arose, he **t** the young child G3880
21 And he arose, and **t** the young child G3880
8:17 saying, Himself **t** our infirmities, and G2983
9:25 **t** her by the hand, and the maid arose. G2902
13:31 which a man **t**, and sowed in his field: G2983
33 which a woman **t**, and hid in three G2983
14:12 And his disciples came, and **t** up the G142
19 on the grass, and **t** the five loaves, and G2983
20 filled: and they **t** up of the fragments G142
15:36 And he **t** the seven loaves and the G2983
37 filled: and they **t** up of the broken *meat* G142
39 And he sent away the multitude, and **t** G1684
16: 9 and how many baskets ye **t** up? G2983
10 and how many baskets ye **t** up? G2983
22 Then Peter **t** him, and began to rebuke G4355
18:28 hands on him, and **t** *him* by the throat, G2902
20:17 And Jesus going up to Jerusalem **t** the G3880
21:35 And the husbandmen **t** his servants, G2983

Mt 21:46 because they **t** him for a prophet. G2192
22: 6 And the remnant **t** his servants, and G2902
15 Then went the Pharisees, and **t** counsel G2983
24:39 flood came, and **t** them all away; so shall G142
25: 1 ten virgins, which **t** their lamps, and G2983
3 They that *were* foolish **t** their lamps, G2983
3 their lamps, and **t** no oil with them: G2983
4 But the wise **t** oil in their vessels with G2983
15 ability; and straightway **t** his journey. G589
35 drink: I was a stranger, and ye **t** me in: G4863
38 When saw we thee a stranger, and **t** G4863
43 I was a stranger, and ye **t** me not in: G4863
26:26 And as they were eating, Jesus **t** bread, G2983
27 And he **t** the cup, and gave thanks, and G2983
37 And he **t** with him Peter and the two G3880
50 and laid hands on Jesus, and **t** him. G2902
27: 1 of the people **t** counsel against Jesus G2983
6 And the chief priests **t** the silver pieces, G2983
7 And they **t** counsel, and bought with G2983
9 saying, And they **t** the thirty pieces of G2983
24 was made, he **t** water, and washed G2983
27 Then the soldiers of the governor **t** G3880
30 And they spit upon him, and **t** the reed, G2983
31 mocked him, they **t** the robe off from G1562
48 of them ran, and **t** a spunge, and filled G2983
28:15 So they **t** the money, and did as they G2983
Mk 1:31 And he came and **t** her by the hand, G2902
2:12 And immediately he arose, **t** up the bed, G142
3: 6 and straightway **t** counsel with the G4160
4:36 multitude, they **t** him even as he was G3880
5:41 And he **t** the damsel by the hand, and G2902
6:29 **t** up his corpse, and laid it in a tomb. G142
43 And they **t** up twelve baskets full of the G142
7:33 And he **t** him aside from the multitude, G618
8: 6 ground: and he **t** the seven loaves, and G2983
8 filled: and they **t** up of the broken *meat* G142
19 **t** ye up? They say unto him, Twelve. G142
20 fragments **t** ye up? And they said, Seven. G142
23 And he **t** the blind man by the hand, G1949
32 Peter **t** him, and began to rebuke him. G4355
9:27 But Jesus **t** him by the hand, and lifted G2902
36 And he **t** a child, and set him in the G2983
10:16 And he **t** them up in his arms, put *his* G1723
32 afraid. And he **t** again the twelve, and G3880
12: 8 And they **t** him, and killed *him*, and G2983
20 the first **t** a wife, and dying left no seed. G2983
21 And the second **t** her, and died, neither G2983
14:22 And as they did eat, Jesus **t** bread, and G2983
23 And he **t** the cup, and when he had G2983
46 laid their hands on him, and **t** him. G2902
49 teaching, and ye **t** me not: but the G2902
15:20 And when they had mocked him, they **t** G1562
46 And he bought fine linen, and **t** him G2507
Lk 2:28 Then **t** he him up in his arms, and G1209
5:25 before them, and **t** up that whereon he G142
8:54 And he put them all out, and **t** her by G2902
9:10 had done. And he **t** them, and went G3880
16 Then he **t** the five loaves and the two G2983
28 these sayings, he **t** Peter and John and G3880
47 heart, **t** a child, and set him by him, G1949
10:34 him to an inn, and **t** care of him. G1959
35 he departed, he **t** out two pence, and G1544
13:19 seed, which a man **t**, and cast into his G2983
21 It is like leaven, which a woman **t** and G2983
14: 4 And they held their peace. And he **t** G1949
15:13 all together, and **t** his journey into a far G589
18:31 Then he **t** *unto him* the twelve, and G3880
20:29 **t** a wife, and died without children. G2983
30 And the second **t** her to wife, and he G2983
31 And the third **t** her; and in like manner G2983
22:17 And he **t** the cup, and gave thanks, and G1209
19 And he **t** bread, and gave thanks, and G2983
54 Then **t** they him, and led *him*, and G4815
23:53 And he **t** it down, and wrapped it in G2507
24:30 with them, he **t** bread, and blessed *it*, G2983
43 And he **t** *it*, and did eat before them. G2983
Jn 5: 9 was made whole, and **t** up his bed, and G142
6:11 And Jesus **t** the loaves; and when he G2983
24 his disciples, they also **t** shipping, and G1684
8:59 Then **t** they up stones to cast at him: but G142
10:31 Then the Jews **t** up stones again to stone G941
11:41 Then they **t** away the stone *from the* G142
53 Then from that day forth they **t** counsel G4823
12: 3 Then **t** Mary a pound of ointment of G2983
13 **T** branches of palm trees, and went G2983
13: 4 and **t** a towel, and girded himself. G2983
18:12 of the Jews **t** Jesus, and bound him, G4815
19: 1 Then Pilate therefore **t** Jesus, and G2983
16 And they **t** Jesus, and led *him* away. G3880

Jn 19:23 crucified Jesus, **t** his garments, and G2983
27 that disciple **t** her unto his own *home*. G2983
38 came therefore, and **t** the body of Jesus. G142
40 Then **t** they the body of Jesus, and G2983
Act 1:16 which was guide to them that **t** Jesus. G4815
3: 7 And he **t** him by the right hand, and G4084
4:13 and they **t** knowledge of them, G1921
5:33 *to the heart*, and **t** counsel to slay them. G1011
7:21 daughter **t** him up, and nourished G337
43 Yea, ye **t** up the tabernacle of Moloch, G353
9:23 fulfilled, the Jews **t** counsel to kill him: G4823
25 Then the disciples **t** him by night, and G2983
27 But Barnabas **t** him, and brought *him* G1949
10:26 But Peter **t** him up, saying, Stand up; I G1453
12:25 ministry, and **t** with them John, whose G4838
13:29 of him, they **t** *him* down from the G2507
15:39 **t** Mark, and sailed unto Cyprus; G3880
16: 3 with him; and **t** and circumcised him G2983
33 And he **t** them the same hour of the G3880
17: 5 moved with envy, **t** unto them certain G4355
19 And they **t** him, and brought him unto G1949
18:17 Then all the Greeks **t** Sosthenes, the G1949
18 good while, and then **t** his leave of the G657
26 had heard, they **t** him unto *them*, and G4355
19:13 Jews, exorcists, **t** upon them to call G2021
20:14 And when he met with us at Assos, we **t** G353
21: 6 **t** ship; and they returned home again. G1910
11 And when he was come unto us, he **t** G142
15 And after those days we **t** up our
26 Then Paul **t** the men, and the next day G3880
30 ran together: and they **t** Paul, and drew G1949
32 Who immediately **t** soldiers and G3880
33 captain came near, and **t** him, and G1949
23:18 So he **t** him, and brought *him* to the G3880
19 Then the chief captain **t** him by the G1949
31 commanded them, **t** Paul, and brought G353
24: 6 the temple: whom we **t**, and would have G2902
7 violence **t** *him* away out of our hands,
27:35 And when he had thus spoken, he **t** G2983
36 good cheer, and they also **t** *some* meat. G4355
28:15 saw, he thanked God, and **t** courage. G2983
1Co 11:23 night in which he was betrayed **t** bread: G2983
25 After the same manner also *he* **t** the cup,
Gal 2: 1 Barnabas, and **t** Titus with *me* also. G4838
Php 2: 7 reputation, and **t** upon him the form G2983
Col 2:14 **t** it out of the way, nailing it to his cross; G142
Heb 2:14 himself likewise **t** part of the same; that
16 For verily he **t** not on *him the nature of* G1949
16 but he **t** on *him* the seed of Abraham.
8: 9 in the day when I **t** them by the hand to G1949
9:19 to the law, he **t** the blood of calves and G2983
10:34 in my bonds, and **t** joyfully the spoiling G4327
Rev 5: 7 And he came and **t** the book out of the G2983
8: 5 And the angel **t** the censer, and filled it G2983
10:10 And I **t** the little book out of the angel's G2983
18:21 And a mighty angel **t** up a stone like a

TOOKEST

Ps 99: 8 thou **t** vengeance of their inventions.
Ezk 16:18 And **t** thy broidered garments, and H3947

TOOL

Ex 20:25 up thy **t** upon it, thou hast polluted it. H2719
32: 4 it with a graving **t**, after he had made it H2747
Dt 27: 5 shalt not lift up *any* iron *t* upon them.
1Ki 6: 7 nor axe *nor* any **t** of iron heard in the H3627

TOOTH

Ex 21:24 Eye for eye, **t** for tooth, hand for hand, H8127
24 Eye for eye, tooth for **t**, hand for hand, H8127
27 And if he smite out his manservant's **t**, H8127
27 his maidservant's **t**; he shall let him go H8127
Lev 24:20 Breach for breach, eye for eye, **t** for H8127
20 for eye, tooth for **t**: as he hath caused a H8127
Dt 19:21 **t** for tooth, hand for hand, foot for foot. H8127
21 tooth for **t**, hand for hand, foot for foot. H8127
Prv 25:19 *is like* a broken **t**, and a foot out of joint. H8127
Mt 5:38 An eye for an eye, and a **t** for a tooth: G3599
38 An eye for an eye, and a tooth for a **t**: G3599

TOOTH'S

Ex 21:27 he shall let him go free for his **t** sake.

TOP

Gen 11: 4 and a tower, whose **t** *may reach* unto H7218
28:12 on the earth, and the **t** of it reached to
18 a pillar, and poured oil upon the **t** of it.
Ex 17: 9 I will stand on the **t** of the hill with the H7218
10 and Hur went up to the **t** of the hill. H7218

Ex 19:20 Sinai, on the **t** of the mount: and the H7218
20 the **t** of the mount; and Moses went up. H7218
24:17 fire on the **t** of the mount in the H7218
28:32 And there shall be an hole in the **t** of it, H7218
30: 3 it with pure gold, the **t** thereof, and the H1406
34: 2 there to me in the **t** of the mount. H7218
37:26 pure gold, *both* the **t** of it, and the sides H1406
Nu 14:40 gat them up into the **t** of the mountain, H7218
44 to go up unto the hill **t**: nevertheless the H7218
20:28 died there in the **t** of the mount: and H7218
21:20 of Moab, to the **t** of Pisgah, which H7218
23: 9 For from the **t** of the rocks I see him, H7218
14 of Zophim, to the **t** of Pisgah, and built H7218
28 And Balak brought Balaam unto the **t** H7218
Dt 3:27 Get thee up into the **t** of Pisgah, and lift H7218
28:35 sole of thy foot unto the **t** of thy head. H6936
33:16 and upon the **t** of the head of him *that* H6936
34: 1 of Nebo, to the **t** of Pisgah, that *is* over H7218
Jos 15: 8 went up to the **t** of the mountain that H7218
9 And the border was drawn from the **t** H7218
Jdg 6:26 thy God upon the **t** of this rock, in the H7218
9: 7 and stood in the **t** of mount Gerizim, H7218
25 wait for him in the **t** of the mountains, H7218
36 down from the **t** of the mountains. And H7218
51 and gat them up to the **t** of the tower. H1406
15: 8 and dwelt in the **t** of the rock Etam. H5585
11 of Judah went to the **t** of the rock Etam, H5585
16: 3 to the **t** of an hill that *is* before Hebron. H7218
1Sa 9:25 with Saul upon the **t** of the house. H1406
26 called Saul to the **t** of the house, saying, H1406
26:13 and stood on the **t** of an hill afar off; a H7218
2Sa 2:25 one troop, and stood on the **t** of an hill. H7218
15:32 was come to the **t** *of the mount,* where H7218
16: 1 And when David was a little past the **t** H7218
22 a tent upon the **t** of the house; and H1406
1Ki 7:17 *were* upon the **t** of the pillars; seven H7218
18 chapiters that *were* upon the **t**, with H7218
19 And the chapiters that *were* upon the **t** H7218
22 And upon the **t** of the pillars *was* lily H7218
35 And in the **t** of the base *was there* a H7218
35 high: and on the **t** of the base the ledges H7218
41 that *were* on the **t** of the two pillars; H7218
41 which *were* upon the **t** of the pillars; H7218
10:19 The throne had six steps, and the **t** of H7218
18:42 went up to the **t** of Carmel; and he cast H7218
2Ki 1: 9 he sat on the **t** of an hill. And he spake H7218
9:13 *it* under him on the **t** of the stairs, and H1634
23:12 And the altars that *were* on the **t** of the H1406
2Ch 3:15 on the **t** of each of them *was* five cubits. H7218
4:12 *which were* on the **t** of the two pillars, H7218
12 which *were* on the **t** of the pillars; H7218
25:12 them unto the **t** of the rock, and cast H7218
12 down from the **t** of the rock, that they H7218
Est 5: 2 near, and touched the **t** of the sceptre. H7218
Ps 72:16 the earth upon the **t** of the mountains; H7218
102: 7 as a sparrow alone upon the house **t**. H1406
Prv 8: 2 She standeth in the **t** of high places, by H7218
23:34 or as he that lieth upon the **t** of a mast. H7218
Song 4: 8 look from the **t** of Amana, from the H7218
8 of Amana, from the **t** of Shenir and H7218
Isa 2: 2 established in the **t** of the mountains, H7218
17: 6 three berries in the **t** of the uppermost H7218
30:17 as a beacon upon the **t** of a mountain, H7218
42:11 shout from the **t** of the mountains. H7218
Lam 2:19 faint for hunger in the **t** of every street. H7218
4: 1 are poured out in the **t** of every street. H7218
Ezk 17: 4 He cropped off the **t** of his young twigs, H7218
22 crop off from the **t** of his young twigs a H7218
24: 7 her; she set it upon the **t** of a rock; she H6706
8 her blood upon the **t** of a rock, that it H6706
26: 4 her, and make her like the **t** of a rock. H6706
14 And I will make thee like the **t** of a H6706
31: 3 and his **t** was among the thick boughs. H6788
10 he hath shot up his **t** among the thick H6788
14 shoot up their **t** among the thick H6788
43:12 This *is* the law of the house; Upon the **t** H7218
Am 1: 2 and the **t** of Carmel shall wither. H7218
9: 3 themselves in the **t** of Carmel, I will H7218
Mic 4: 1 established in the **t** of the mountains, H7218
Nah 3:10 in pieces at the **t** of all the streets: and H7218
Zec 4: 2 a bowl upon the **t** of it, and his seven H7218
2 lamps, which *are* upon the **t** thereof: H7218
Mt 27:51 in twain from the **t** to the bottom; and *G509*
Mk 15:38 rent in twain from the **t** to the bottom. *G509*
Jn 19:23 seam, woven from the **t** throughout. *G509*
Heb 11:21 *leaning* upon the **t** of his staff. *G206*

TOPAZ
Ex 28:17 *be* a sardius, a **t**, and a carbuncle: *this* H6357
Ex 39:10 *was* a sardius, a **t**, and a carbuncle: this H6357
Job 28:19 The **t** of Ethiopia shall not equal it, H6357
Ezk 28:13 the sardius, **t**, and the diamond, the H6357
Rev 21:20 eighth, beryl; the ninth, a **t**; the tenth, a *G5116*

TOPHEL
Dt 1: 1 between Paran, and **T**, and Laban, and H8603

TOPHET
Isa 30:33 For **T** *is* ordained of old; yea, for the H8613
Jer 7:31 the high places of **T**, which *is* in the H8612
32 no more be called **T**, nor the valley of H8612
32 shall bury in **T**, till there be no place. H8612
19: 6 no more be called **T**, nor The valley of H8612
11 *them* in **T**, till *there be* no place to bury. H8612
12 thereof, and *even* make this city as **T**: H8612
13 as the place of **T**, because of all the H8612
14 Then came Jeremiah from **T**, whither H8612

TOPHETH
2Ki 23:10 And he defiled **T**, which *is* in the valley H8612

TOPS
Gen 8: 5 were the **t** of the mountains seen. H7218
2Sa 5:24 of a going in the **t** of the mulberry trees, H7218
1Ki 7:16 to set upon the **t** of the pillars: the H7218
1Ch 14:15 of going in the **t** of the mulberry trees, H7218
Job 24:24 and cut off as the **t** of the ears of corn. H7218
Isa 2:21 the rocks, and into the **t** of the ragged H5585
15: 3 sackcloth: on the **t** of their houses, and H1406
Ezk 6:13 high hill, in all the **t** of the mountains, H7218
Hos 4:13 They sacrifice upon the **t** of the H7218
Joel 2: 5 Like the noise of chariots on the **t** of H7218

TORCH
Zec 12: 6 wood, and like a **t** of fire in a sheaf; and H3940

TORCHES
Nah 2: 3 *shall be* with flaming **t** in the day of his H6393
4 like **t**, they shall run like the lightnings. H3940
Jn 18: 3 with lanterns and **t** and weapons. *G2985*

TORE See TARE.

TORMENT
Mt 8:29 thou come hither to **t** us before the time? *G928*
Mk 5: 7 I adjure thee by God, that thou **t** me not. *G928*
Lk 8:28 God most high? I beseech thee, **t** me not. *G928*
16:28 lest they also come into this place of **t**. *G931*
1Jn 4:18 because fear hath **t**. He that feareth is *G2851*
Rev 9: 5 months: and their **t** *was* as the torment *G929*
5 **t** of a scorpion, when he striketh a man. *G929*
14:11 And the smoke of their **t** ascendeth up *G929*
18: 7 so much **t** and sorrow give her: *G929*
10 Standing afar off for the fear of her **t**, *G929*
15 for the fear of her **t**, weeping and wailing, *G929*

TORMENTED
Mt 8: 6 at home sick of the palsy, grievously **t**. *G928*
Lk 16:24 cool my tongue; for I am **t** in this flame. *G3600*
25 but now he is comforted, and thou art **t**. *G3600*
Heb 11:37 goatskins; being destitute, afflicted, **t**; *G2558*
Rev 9: 5 that they should be **t** five months: and *G928*
11:10 prophets **t** them that dwelt on the earth. *G928*
14:10 and he shall be **t** with fire and brimstone *G928*
20:10 be **t** day and night for ever and ever. *G928*

TORMENTORS
Mt 18:34 him to the **t**, till he should pay all *G930*

TORMENTS
Mt 4:24 divers diseases and **t**, and those which *G931*
Lk 16:23 And in hell he lift up his eyes, being in **t**, *G931*

TORN
Gen 31:39 That which was **t** *of beasts* I brought H2966
44:28 is **t** in pieces; and I saw him not since: H2963
Ex 22:13 If it be **t** in pieces, *then* let him bring it H2963
13 shall not make good that which was **t**. H2966
31 *any* flesh *that is* **t** of beasts in the field; H2966
Lev 7:24 fat of that which is **t** with beasts, may H2966
17:15 *itself*, or that which was **t** *with beasts,* H2966
22: 8 That which dieth of itself, or is **t** *with* H2966
1Ki 13:26 lion, which hath **t** him, and slain him, H7665
28 not eaten the carcase, nor **t** the ass. H7665
Isa 5:25 their carcases *were* **t** in the midst of the H5478
Jer 5: 6 out thence shall be **t** in pieces: because H2963
Ezk 4:14 dieth of itself, or is **t** in pieces; neither H2966
44:31 itself, or **t**, whether it be fowl or beast. H2966
Hos 6: 1 LORD: for he hath **t**, and he will heal us; H2963
Mal 1:13 *that which was* **t**, and the lame, and the H1497
Mk 1:26 And when the unclean spirit had **t** him, *G4682*

TORTOISE
Lev 11:29 and the mouse, and the **t** after his kind, H6632

TORTURED
Heb 11:35 again: and others were **t**, not accepting *G5178*

TOSS
Isa 22:18 He will surely violently turn and **t** thee H6802
Jer 5:22 the waves thereof **t** themselves, yet can H1607

TOSSED
Ps 109:23 I am **t** up and down as the locust. H5287
Prv 21: 6 **t** to and fro of them that seek death. H5086
Isa 54:11 O thou afflicted, **t** with tempest, *and* not
Mt 14:24 **t** with waves: for the wind was contrary. *G928*
Act 27:18 And we being exceedingly **t** with a *G5492*
Eph 4:14 be no more children, **t** to and fro, and *G2831*
Jas 1: 6 of the sea driven with the wind and **t**. *G4494*

TOSSINGS
Job 7: 4 and I am full of **t** to and fro unto the H5076

TOTTERING
Ps 62: 3 wall *shall ye be, and as* a **t** fence. H1760

TOU
1Ch 18: 9 Now when **T** king of Hamath heard H8583
10 had war with **T**;) and *with him* all H8583

TOUCH
Gen 3: 3 eat of it, neither shall ye **t** it, lest ye die. H5060
20: 6 therefore suffered I thee not to **t** her. H5060
Ex 19:12 up into the mount, or **t** the border of it: H5060
13 There shall not an hand **t** it, but he H5060
Lev 5: 2 Or if a soul **t** any unclean thing, H5060
3 Or if he **t** the uncleanness of man, H5060
6:27 Whatsoever shall **t** the flesh thereof H5060
7:21 Moreover the soul that shall **t** any H5060
11: 8 shall ye not **t**; they *are* unclean to you. H5060
31 whosoever doth **t** them, when they be H5060
12: 4 days; she shall **t** no hallowed thing, nor H5060
Nu 4:15 but they shall not **t** *any* holy thing, lest H5060
16:26 wicked men, and **t** nothing of theirs, H5060
Dt 14: 8 of their flesh, nor **t** their dead carcase. H5060
Jos 9:19 now therefore we may not **t** them. H5060
Ru 2: 9 that they shall not **t** thee? and when H5060
2Sa 14:10 me, and he shall not **t** thee any more. H5060
18:12 that none **t** the young man Absalom. H5060
23: 7 But the man *that* shall **t** them must be H5060
1Ch 16:22 *Saying*, **T** not mine anointed, and do H5060
Job 1:11 But put forth thine hand now, and **t** all H5060
2: 5 But put forth thine hand now, and **t** his H5060
5:19 yea, in seven there shall no evil **t** thee. H5060
6: 7 The things *that* my soul refused to **t** *are* H5060
Ps 105:15 *Saying*, **T** not mine anointed, and do H5060
144: 5 **t** the mountains, and they shall smoke. H5060
Isa 52:11 out from thence, **t** no unclean *thing*; go H5060
Jer 12:14 evil neighbours, that **t** the inheritance H5060
Lam 4:14 so that men could not **t** their garments. H5060
15 depart, depart, **t** not: when they fled H5060
Hag 2:12 with his skirt do **t** bread, or pottage, or H5060
13 by a dead body **t** any of these, shall it H5060
Mt 9:21 For she said within herself, If I may but **t** *G680*
14:36 And besought him that they might only **t** *G680*
Mk 3:10 for to **t** him, as many as had plagues. *G680*
5:28 For she said, If I may **t** but his clothes, I *G680*
6:56 that they might **t** if it were but the border *G680*
8:22 unto him, and besought him to **t** him. *G680*
10:13 to him, that he should **t** them: and *his* *G680*
Lk 6:19 And the whole multitude sought to **t** *G680*
11:46 and ye yourselves **t** not the burdens *G4379*
18:15 that he would **t** them: but when *his* *G680*
Jn 20:17 Jesus saith unto her, **T** me not; for I am *G680*
1Co 7: 1 *It is* good for a man not to **t** a woman. *G680*
2Co 6:17 saith the Lord, and **t** not the unclean *G680*
Col 2:21 (**T** not; taste not; handle not; *G680*
Heb 11:28 destroyed the firstborn should **t** them. *G2345*
12:20 so much as a beast **t** the mountain, it *G2345*

TOUCHED
Gen 26:29 as we have not **t** thee, and as we have H5060
32:25 not against him, he **t** the hollow of his H5060
32 day: because he **t** the hollow of Jacob's H5060
Lev 22: 6 The soul which hath **t** any such shall be H5060
Nu 19:18 and upon him that **t** a bone, or one H5060

T

Nu 31:19 whosoever hath **t** any slain, purify *both* H5060
Jdg 6:21 *was* in his hand, and **t** the flesh and the H5060
1Sa 10:26 a band of men, whose hearts God had **t**. H5060
1Ki 6:27 wing of the one **t** the *one* wall, and the H5060
27 the other cherub **t** the other wall; and H5060
27 **t** one another in the midst of the house. H5060
19: 5 then an angel **t** him, and said unto H5060
7 second time, and **t** him, and said, Arise H5060
2Ki 13:21 was let down, and **t** the bones of Elisha, H5060
Est 5: 2 drew near, and **t** the top of the sceptre. H5060
Job 19:21 friends; for the hand of God hath **t** me. H5060
Isa 6: 7 said, Lo, this hath **t** thy lips; and thine H5060
Jer 1: 9 his hand, and **t** my mouth. And the H5060
Ezk 3:13 creatures that **t** one another, and the H5401
Dan 8: 5 whole earth, and **t** not the ground: and H5060
18 but he **t** me, and set me upright. H5060
9:21 to fly swiftly, **t** me about the time of H5060
10:10 And, behold, an hand **t** me, which set H5060
16 of the sons of men **t** my lips: then I H5060
18 Then there came again and **t** me *one* H5060
Mt 8: 3 And Jesus put forth *his* hand, and **t** him, *G680*
15 And he **t** her hand, and the fever left her: *G680*
9:20 *him*, and **t** the hem of his garment: *G680*
29 Then **t** he their eyes, saying, According *G680*
14:36 as many as **t** were made perfectly whole. *G680*
17: 7 And Jesus came and **t** them, and said, *G680*
20:34 So Jesus had compassion *on them*, and **t** *G680*
Mk 1:41 forth *his* hand, and **t** him, and saith unto *G680*
5:27 in the press behind, and **t** his garment. *G680*
30 in the press, and said, Who **t** my clothes? *G680*
31 thee, and sayest thou, Who **t** me? *G680*
6:56 and as many as **t** him were made whole. *G680*
7:33 his ears, and he spit, and **t** his tongue; *G680*
Lk 5:13 And he put forth *his* hand, and **t** him, *G680*
7:14 And he came and **t** the bier: and they *G680*
8:44 Came behind *him*, and **t** the border of *G680*
45 And Jesus said, Who **t** me? When all *G680*
45 press *thee*, and sayest thou, Who **t** me? *G680*
46 And Jesus said, Somebody hath **t** me: for *G680*
47 what cause she had **t** him, and how she *G680*
22:51 far. And he **t** his ear, and healed him. *G680*
Act 27: 3 And the next *day* we **t** at Sidon. And *G2609*
Heb 4:15 which cannot be **t** with the feeling of *G4834*
12:18 that might be **t**, and that burned with *G5584*

TOUCHETH

Gen 26:11 saying, He that **t** this man or his wife H5060
Ex 19:12 of it: whosoever **t** the mount shall be H5060
29:37 whatsoever **t** the altar shall be holy. H5060
30:29 holy: whatsoever **t** them shall be holy. H5060
Lev 6:18 fire: every one that **t** them shall be holy. H5060
7:19 And the flesh that **t** any unclean *thing* H5060
11:24 whosoever **t** the carcase of them H5060
26 every one that **t** them shall be unclean. H5060
27 unto you: whoso **t** their carcase shall be H5060
36 which **t** their carcase shall be unclean. H5060
39 eat, die; he that **t** the carcase thereof H5060
15: 5 And whosoever **t** his bed shall wash his H5060
7 And he that **t** the flesh of him that hath H5060
10 And whosoever **t** any thing that was H5060
11 And whomsoever he **t** that hath the H5060
12 And the vessel of earth, that he **t** which H5060
19 **t** her shall be unclean until the even. H5060
21 And whosoever **t** her bed shall wash his H5060
22 And whosoever **t** any thing that she sat H5060
23 **t** it, he shall be unclean until the even. H5060
27 And whosoever **t** those things shall be H5060
22: 4 be clean. And whoso **t** any thing *that is* H5060
5 Or whosoever **t** any creeping thing, H5060
Nu 19:11 He that **t** the dead body of any man H5060
13 Whosoever **t** the dead body of any man H5060
16 And whosoever **t** one that is slain with H5060
21 and he that **t** the water of separation H5060
22 And whatsoever the unclean *person* **t** H5060
22 that **t** *it* shall be unclean until even. H5060
Jdg 16: 9 tow is broken when it **t** the fire. So his H7306
Job 4: 5 it **t** thee, and thou art troubled. H5060
Ps 104:32 he **t** the hills, and they smoke. H5060
Prv 6:29 whosoever **t** her shall not be innocent. H5060
Ezk 17:10 the east wind **t** it? it shall wither in H5060
Hos 4: 2 they break out, and blood **t** blood. H5060
Am 9: 5 And the Lord GOD of hosts *is* he that **t** H5060
Zec 2: 8 that **t** you toucheth the apple of his eye. H5060
8 that toucheth you **t** the apple of his eye. H5060
Lk 7:39 *this is* that **t** him: for she is a sinner. *G680*
1Jn 5:18 himself, and that wicked one **t** him not. *G680*

TOUCHING

Gen 27:42 thy brother Esau, as **t** thee, doth comfort
Lev 5:13 for him as **t** his sin that he hath sinned
Nu 8:26 thou do unto the Levites **t** their charge.
1Sa 20:23 And *as* **t** the matter which thou and I
2Ki 22:18 *As* **t** the words which thou hast heard;
Ezr 7:24 Also we certify you, that **t** any of the
Job 37:23 *T* the Almighty, we cannot find him out:
Ps 45: 1 which I have made **t** the king: my tongue
Isa 5: 1 a song of my beloved **t** his vineyard. My
Jer 1:16 against them **t** all their wickedness, H5921
21:11 And **t** the house of the king of Judah,
22:11 For thus saith the LORD **t** Shallum the H413
Ezk 7:13 for the vision *is* **t** the whole multitude
Mt 18:19 agree on earth as **t** any thing that they *G4012*
22:31 But as **t** the resurrection of the dead, *G4012*
Mk 12:26 And as **t** the dead, that they rise: have *G4012*
Lk 23:14 **t** those things whereof ye accuse him:
Act 5:35 what ye intend to do as **t** these men. *G1909*
21:25 As **t** the Gentiles which believe, we have *G4012*
24:21 among them, T the resurrection of *G4012*
26: 2 day before thee **t** all the things whereof *G4012*
Ro 11:28 your sakes: but as **t** the election, *they* *G2596*
1Co 8: 1 Now as **t** things offered unto idols, we *G4012*
16:12 As **t** *our* brother Apollos, I greatly *G4012*
2Co 9: 1 For as **t** the ministering to the saints, it *G4012*
Php 3: 5 the Hebrews; as **t** the law, a Pharisee; *G2596*
6 the church; **t** the righteousness which *G2596*
Col 4:10 son to Barnabas, (**t** whom ye received *G4012*
1Th 4: 9 But as **t** brotherly love ye need not that *G4012*
2Th 3: 4 And we have confidence in the Lord **t** *G1909*

TOW

Jdg 16: 9 withs, as a thread of **t** is broken when it H5296
Isa 1:31 And the strong shall be as **t**, and the H5296
43:17 they are extinct, they are quenched as **t**. H6594

TOWARD

Gen 2:14 *is* it which goeth **t** the east of Assyria.
12: 9 And Abram journeyed, going on still **t**
13:12 the plain, and pitched *his* tent **t** Sodom. H5704
15: 5 said, Look now **t** heaven, and tell the H8064
18: 2 door, and bowed himself **t** the ground,
16 and looked **t** Sodom: and Abraham H6440
22 from thence, and went **t** Sodom: but H5467
19: 1 himself with his face **t** the ground;
28 And he looked **t** Sodom and Gomorrah, H6440
28 and Gomorrah, and **t** all the land of the H6440
20: 1 And Abraham journeyed from thence **t**
25:18 as thou goest **t** Assyria: *and* he died H804
28:10 from Beer-sheba, and went **t** Haran. H2771
30:40 faces of the flocks **t** the ringstraked, and H413
31: 2 and, behold, it *was* not **t** him as before.
5 that it *is* not **t** me as before; but the
21 and set his face *t* the mount Gilead.
48:13 in his right hand **t** Israel's left hand, and
13 in his left hand **t** Israel's right hand, and
Ex 9: 8 it **t** the heaven in the sight of Pharaoh.
10 sprinkled it up **t** heaven; and it became
22 forth thine hand **t** heaven, that there
23 And Moses stretched forth his rod **t**
10:21 out thine hand **t** heaven, that there may
22 And Moses stretched forth his hand **t**
16:10 that they looked **t** the wilderness, and, H413
25:20 one to another; **t** the mercy seat shall
26:35 of the tabernacle **t** the south: and thou
28:27 underneath, **t** the forepart thereof, H4136
34: 8 his head **t** the earth, and worshipped.
36:25 *which is* **t** the north corner, he
39:20 underneath, **t** the forepart of it, over H4136
Lev 9:22 And Aaron lifted up his hand **t** the
13:41 from the part of his head **t** his face, he *is*
Nu 2: 3 And on the east side **t** the rising of the
3:38 the tabernacle **t** the east, *even* before
16:42 that they looked **t** the tabernacle of the
21:11 which *is* before Moab, **t** the sunrising.
20 of Pisgah, which looketh **t** Jeshimon. H6440
23:28 top of Peor, that looketh **t** Jeshimon. H6440
24: 1 but he set his face **t** the wilderness.
32:14 yet the fierce anger of the LORD **t** Israel.
34:15 *near* Jericho eastward, **t** the sunrising.
Dt 4:41 cities on this side Jordan **t** the sunrising;
47 *were* on this side Jordan **t** the sunrising;
28:54 his eye shall be evil **t** his brother, and
54 his brother, and **t** the wife of his bosom,
54 of his bosom, and **t** the remnant of his
56 her eye shall be evil **t** the husband of her
56 and **t** her son, and toward her daughter,
56 and toward her son, and **t** her daughter,
57 And **t** her young one that cometh out
57 her feet, and **t** her children which she
Jos 1: 4 unto the great sea **t** the going down of
15 you on this side Jordan **t** the sunrising.
3:16 that came down **t** the sea of the plain,
8:18 that *is* in thy hand **t** Ai; for I will give it
18 spear that *he had* in his hand **t** the city.
12: 1 other side Jordan **t** the rising of the sun,
13: 5 and all Lebanon, **t** the sunrising, from
15: 4 *From thence* it passed **t** Azmon, and
7 And the border went up **t** Debir from the
7 so northward, looking **t** Gilgal, that *is*
7 and the border passed **t** the waters of
21 the children of Judah **t** the coast of Edom
16: 6 And the border went out **t** the sea to
18:13 And the border went over from thence **t**
17 and went forth **t** Geliloth, which *is* over
18 And passed along **t** the side over against
19:11 And their border went up **t** the sea, and
12 And turned from Sarid eastward **t** the
18 And their border was **t** Jezreel, and
27 And turneth **t** the sunrising to
27 valley of Jiphthah-el **t** the north side of
34 to Judah upon Jordan **t** the sunrising.
Jdg 3:28 the fords of Jordan **t** Moab, and suffered
4: 6 Go and draw **t** mount Tabor, and take
5: 9 My heart *is* **t** the governors of Israel, that
11 the righteous acts *t the inhabitants* of his
8: 3 abated **t** him, when he had said that.
13:20 the flame went up **t** heaven from off the H8064
19: 9 the day draweth **t** evening, I pray you
18 Beth-lehem-judah **t** the side of mount
20:43 ease over against Gibeah **t** the sunrising.
45 And they turned and fled **t** the
1Sa 13:18 to the valley of Zeboim **t** the wilderness.
17:30 And he turned from him **t** another, and H4136
48 ran **t** the army to meet the Philistine.
20:12 *if there be* good **t** David, and I then send
41 arose out of *a place* **t** the south, and fell H681
2Sa 14: 1 that the king's heart *was* **t** Absalom.
15:23 passed over, **t** the way of the wilderness.
24: 5 the midst of the river of Gad, and **t** Jazer:
20 coming on **t** him: and Araunah went
1Ki 7: 9 and *so* on the outside **t** the great court.
25 oxen, three looking **t** the north, and
25 and three looking **t** the west, and three
25 and three looking **t** the south, and three
25 and three looking **t** the east: and the sea
8:22 and spread forth his hands **t** heaven:
29 That thine eyes may be open **t** this house
29 and day, *even* **t** the place of which thou
29 thy servant shall make **t** this place.
30 they shall pray **t** this place: and hear
35 thee; if they pray **t** this place, and
38 and spread forth his hands **t** this house:
42 he shall come and pray **t** this house;
44 unto the LORD **t** the city which thou H1870
44 hast chosen, and *t* the house that I have
48 pray unto thee **t** their land, which thou H1870
14:13 *some* good thing **t** the LORD God of
18:43 Go up now, look **t** the sea. And he went H1870
2Ki 3:14 I would not look **t** thee, nor see thee.
25: 4 and *the king* went the way **t** the plain.
1Ch 9:24 In four quarters were the porters, **t** the
12:15 *both* **t** the east, and toward the west.
15 *both* toward the east, and **t** the west.
26:17 four a day, and **t** Asuppim two *and* two.
2Ch 4: 4 oxen, three looking **t** the north, and
4 and three looking **t** the west, and three
4 and three looking **t** the south, and three
4 and three looking **t** the east: and the sea
6:13 and spread forth his hands **t** heaven,
20 which thy servant prayeth **t** this place.
21 they shall make **t** this place: hear thou
26 *yet* if they pray **t** this place, and confess
34 pray unto thee **t** this city which thou H1870
38 captives, and pray **t** their land, which H1870
38 their fathers, and *t* the city which thou
38 hast chosen, and **t** the house which I
16: 9 heart *is* perfect **t** him. Herein thou hast
20:24 And when Judah came **t** the watch tower
24:16 Israel, both **t** God, and toward his house.
16 Israel, both toward God, and **t** his house.
31:14 Levite, the porter **t** the east, *was* over the
Ezr 3:11 *endureth* for ever **t** Israel. And all the
Neh 3:26 **t** the east, and the tower that lieth out.
12:31 right hand upon the wall **t** the dung gate:
Est 1:13 **t** all that knew law and judgment: H6440
8: 4 out the golden sceptre **t** Esther. So Esther
Job 2:12 dust upon their heads **t** heaven.
11:13 heart, and stretch out thine hands **t** him;

Job 39:26 *and* stretch her wings t the south?
Ps 5: 7 thy fear will I worship t thy holy temple.
25:15 Mine eyes *are* ever t the LORD; for he
28: 2 I lift up my hands t thy holy oracle.
66: 5 *in his* doing t the children of men.
85: 4 and cause thine anger t us to cease.
86:13 For great *is* thy mercy t me: and thou
98: 3 and his truth t the house of Israel: all
103:11 great is his mercy t them that fear him.
116:12 unto the LORD *for* all his benefits t me?
117: 2 For his merciful kindness is great t us:
138: 2 I will worship t thy holy temple, and
Prv 14:35 The king's favour *is* t a wise servant: but
23: 5 they fly away as an eagle t heaven.
Ecc 1: 6 The wind goeth t the south, and turneth
11: 3 and if the tree fall t the south, or toward
3 the south, or t the north, in the place
Song 7: 4 of Lebanon which looketh t Damascus. H6440
10 I *am* my beloved's, and his desire *is* t
Isa 7: 1 of Israel, went up t Jerusalem to war
11:14 of the Philistines t the west; they shall
29:13 t me is taught by the precept of men:
38: 2 Then Hezekiah turned his face t the wall,
49:23 thee with *their* face t the earth, and lick
63: 7 the great goodness t the house of Israel,
15 of thy mercies t me? are they restrained?
66:14 shall be known t his servants, and *his*
14 and *his* indignation t his enemies.
Jer 1:13 pot; and the face thereof *is* t the north. H6440
3:12 Go and proclaim these words t the
4: 6 Set up the standard t Zion: retire, stay
11 in the wilderness t the daughter of my H1870
12: 3 tried mine heart t thee: pull them out
15: 1 my mind *could* not *be* t this people: cast
29:10 my good word t you, in causing you to
11 For I know the thoughts that I think t
31:21 set thine heart t the highway, *even* the
40 of the horse gate t the east, *shall be* holy
46: 6 fall t the north by the river Euphrates.
49:36 will scatter them t all those winds; and
Lam 2:19 lift up thy hands t him for the life of thy
Ezk 1:23 straight, the one t the other: every one
4: 7 Therefore thou shalt set thy face t the
6: 2 Son of man, set thy face t the mountains
14 than the wilderness t Diblath, in all their
8: 3 gate that looketh t the north; where *was*
5 eyes now the way t the north. So I lifted
5 up mine eyes the way t the north, and
14 house which *was* t the north; and,
16 men, with their backs t the temple of the
16 and their faces t the east; and they
16 and they worshipped the sun t the east.
9: 2 gate, which lieth t the north, and every
12:14 And I will scatter t every wind all that
16:42 So will I make my fury t thee to rest, and
63 when I am pacified t thee for all that
17: 6 branches turned t him, and the roots
7 did bend her roots t him, and shot forth
7 forth her branches t him, that he might
21 shall be scattered t all winds: and ye
20:46 Son of man, set thy face t the south, H1870
46 and drop *thy word* t the south, and
21: 2 Son of man, set thy face t Jerusalem, and
2 and drop *thy word* t the holy places, and
24:23 iniquities, and mourn one t another.
33:25 lift up your eyes t your idols, and shed
40: 6 which looketh t the east, and went up H1870
20 court that looked t the north, he H1870
22 gate that looketh t the east; and they H1870
23 against the gate t the north, and toward
23 toward the north, and t the east; and he
24 After that he brought me t the south, H1870
24 and behold a gate t the south: and he H1870
27 in the inner court t the south: and he H1870
27 to gate t the south an hundred cubits. H1870
31 And the arches thereof *were* t the utter
32 into the inner court t the east: and he H1870
34 And the arches thereof *were* t the
37 And the posts thereof *were* t the utter
44 their prospect *was* t the south: one at H1870
44 gate *having* the prospect t the north. H1870
45 whose prospect *is* t the south, *is* for the H1870
46 And the chamber whose prospect *is* t H1870
41:11 chambers *were* t *the place that was* left,
11 *that was* left, one door t the north, and H1870
11 and another door t the south: and the
12 place at the end t the west *was* seventy H1870
14 place t the east, an hundred cubits.
19 So that the face of a man *was* t the palm

Ezk 41:19 face of a young lion t the palm tree on
42: 1 utter court, the way t the north: and he H1870
1 *was* before the building t the north.
4 of one cubit; and their doors t the north.
7 the chambers, t the utter court on the H1870
10 wall of the court t the east, over against H1870
11 which *were* t the north, as long as H1870
12 that *were* t the south *was* a door H1870
12 t the east, as one entereth into them. H1870
15 he brought me forth t the gate whose H1870
15 gate whose prospect *is* t the east, and H1870
43: 1 *even* the gate that looketh t the east: H1870
4 of the gate whose prospect *is* t the east. H1870
17 about; and his stairs shall look t the east.
44: 1 which looketh t the east; and it *was* shut.
46: 1 court that looketh t the east shall be shut
12 gate that looketh t the east, and he shall
19 which looked t the north: and, behold,
47: 1 of the house *stood t* the east, and the
8 waters issue out t the east country, and
15 And this *shall be* the border of the land t
48:10 be *this* holy oblation; t the north five and
10 *in length*, and t the west ten thousand
10 in breadth, and t the east ten thousand
10 in breadth, and t the south five and
17 And the suburbs of the city shall be t the
17 and fifty, and t the south two hundred
17 and fifty, and t the east two hundred
17 and t the west two hundred and fifty.
21 of the oblation t the east border, and
21 twenty thousand t the west border, over
28 Kadesh, *and* to the river t the great sea.
Dan 4: 2 that the high God hath wrought t me. H5974
6:10 in his chamber t Jerusalem, he kneeled H5049
8: 8 notable ones t the four winds of heaven.
9 exceeding great, t the south, and toward
9 t the east, and toward the pleasant *land*.
9 toward the east, and t the pleasant *land*.
18 sleep on my face t the ground: but he
10: 9 on my face, and my face t the ground.
15 face t the ground, and I became dumb.
11: 4 and shall be divided t the four winds of
19 Then he shall turn his face t the fort of
29 return, and come t the south; but it shall
Hos 3: 1 love of the LORD t the children of Israel,
5: 1 for judgment *is* t you, because ye have
Joel 2:20 with his face t the east sea, and his
20 and his hinder part t the utmost sea, and
Jna 2: 4 yet I will look again t thy holy temple.
Zec 6: 6 the grisled go forth t the south country.
8 these that go t the north country have
9: 1 the tribes of Israel, *shall be* t the LORD.
14: 4 the midst thereof t the east and toward
4 the east and t the west, *and there shall*
4 shall remove t the north, and half of
4 the north, and half of it t the south.
8 half of them t the former sea, and half
8 sea, and half of them t the hinder sea: in
Mt 12:49 And he stretched forth his hand t his G1909
14:14 t them, and he healed their sick. G1909
28: 1 as it began to dawn t the first *day* of the G1519
Mk 6:34 with compassion t them, because they G1909
Lk 2:14 and on earth peace, good will t men. G1722
12:21 for himself, and is not rich t God. G1519
13:22 teaching, and journeying t Jerusalem. G1519
24:29 with us: for it is t evening, and the day G4314
Jn 6:17 went over the sea t Capernaum. And it G1519
Act 1:10 And while they looked stedfastly t G1519
8:26 Arise, and go t the south unto the way G2596
20:21 repentance t God, and faith toward G1519
21 God, and faith t our Lord Jesus Christ. G1519
22: 3 was zealous t God, as ye all are this day.
24:15 And have hope t God, which they G1519
16 void of offence t God, and *toward* men. G4314
16 void of offence toward God, and *t* men.
27:12 lieth t the south west and north west. G2596
40 to the wind, and made t shore. G1519
28:14 seven days: and so we went t Rome. G1519
Ro 1:27 in their lust one t another; men with
5: 8 But God commendeth his love t us, in G1519
11:22 fell, severity; but t thee, goodness, if G1909
12:16 *Be* of the same mind one t another. G1519
15: 5 one t another according to Christ Jesus: G1722
1Co 7:36 himself uncomely t his virgin, if she G1909
2Co 1:16 you to be brought on my way t Judaea. G1519
18 But *as* God *is* true, our word t you was G4314
2: 8 that ye would confirm *your* love t him. G1519
7: 4 Great *is* my boldness of speech t you, G4314
7 mind t me; so that I rejoiced the more. G5228

2Co 7:15 is more abundant t you, whilst he G1519
9: 8 all grace abound t you; that ye, always G1519
10: 1 you, but being absent am bold t you: G1519
13: 4 with him by the power of God t you. G1519
Gal 2: 8 same was mighty in me t the Gentiles:) G1519
Eph 1: 8 Wherein he hath abounded t us in all G1519
2: 7 *his* kindness t us through Christ Jesus. G1909
Php 2:30 life, to supply your lack of service t me. G4314
3:14 I press t the mark for the prize of the G2596
Col 4: 5 Walk in wisdom t them that are G4314
1Th 3:12 in love one t another, and toward G1519
12 t all *men*, even as we *do* toward you: G1519
12 toward all *men*, even as we *do* t you: G1519
4:10 And indeed ye do it t all the brethren G1519
12 That ye may walk honestly t them that G4314
5:14 support the weak, be patient t all *men*. G4314
2Th 1: 3 one of you all t each other aboundeth; G1519
Tit 3: 4 of God our Saviour t man appeared, G4314
Phlm 5 t the Lord Jesus, and toward all saints; G4314
5 toward the Lord Jesus, and t all saints; G1519
Heb 6: 1 from dead works, and of faith t God, G1909
10 ye have shewed t his name, in that ye G1519
1Pt 2:19 t God endure grief, suffering wrongfully.
3:21 of a good conscience t God,) by the G1519
1Jn 3:21 us not, *then* have we confidence t God. G4314
4: 9 In this was manifested the love of God t G1722

TOWEL

Jn 13: 4 and took a t, and girded himself. G3012
5 with the t wherewith he was girded. G3012

TOWER

Gen 11: 4 us a city and a t, whose top *may reach* H4026
5 t, which the children of men builded. H4026
35:21 spread his tent beyond the t of Edar. H4026
Jdg 8: 9 again in peace, I will break down this t. H4026
17 And he beat down the t of Penuel, and H4026
9:46 And when all the men of the t of H4026
47 t of Shechem were gathered together. H4026
49 all the men of the t of Shechem died H4026
51 But there was a strong t within the city, H4026
51 and gat them up to the top of the t. H4026
52 And Abimelech came unto the t, and H4026
52 the door of the t to burn it with fire. H4026
2Sa 22: 3 salvation, my high t, and my refuge, my H4869
51 *He is* the t of salvation for his H4024+H1431
2Ki 5:24 And when he came to the t, he took H6076
9:17 And there stood a watchman on the t H4026
17: 9 t of the watchmen to the fenced city. H4026
18: 8 t of the watchmen to the fenced city. H4026
2Ch 20:24 the watch t in the wilderness, H4707+H4708
Neh 3: 1 of it; even unto the t of Meah they H4026
1 sanctified it, unto the t of Hananeel. H4026
11 other piece, and the t of the furnaces. H4026
25 *the wall*, and the t which lieth out from H4026
26 the east, and the t that lieth out. H4026
27 against the great t that lieth out, even H4026
12:38 from beyond the t of the furnaces even H4026
39 fish gate, and the t of Hananeel, and H4026
39 Hananeel, and the t of Meah, even unto H4026
Ps 18: 2 horn of my salvation, *and* my high t. H4869
61: 3 for me, *and* a strong t from the enemy. H4026
144: 2 fortress; my high t, and my deliverer; H4869
Prv 18:10 The name of the LORD *is* a strong t: the H4026
Song 4: 4 Thy neck *is* like the t of David builded H4026
7: 4 Thy neck *is* as a t of ivory; thine eyes H4026
4 thy nose *is* as the t of Lebanon which H4026
Isa 2:15 And upon every high t, and upon every H4026
5: 2 vine, and built a t in the midst of it, H4026
Jer 6:27 I have set thee *for* a t *and* a fortress H969
31:38 LORD from the t of Hananeel unto the H4026
Ezk 29:10 desolate, from the t of Syene even unto H4024
30: 6 down: from the t of Syene shall they fall H4024
Mic 4: 8 And thou, O t of the flock, the strong H4026
Hab 2: 1 set me upon the t, and will watch to see H4692
Zec 14:10 gate, and *from* the t of Hananeel unto H4026
Mt 21:33 in it, and built a t, and let it out to G4444
Mk 12: 1 winefat, and built a t, and let it out to G4444
Lk 13: 4 Or those eighteen, upon whom the t in G4444
14:28 For which of you, intending to build a t, G4444

TOWERS

2Ch 14: 7 *them* walls, and t, gates, and bars, H4026
26: 9 Moreover Uzziah built t in Jerusalem H4026
10 Also he built t in the desert, and digged H4026
15 men, to be on the t and upon the H4026
27: 4 and in the forests he built castles and t. H4026
32: 5 raised *it* up to the t, and another wall H4026
Ps 48:12 go round about her: tell the t thereof. H4026

Song 8:10 I *am* a wall, and my breasts like t: then H4026
Isa 23:13 they set up the t thereof, they raised up H971
30:25 of the great slaughter, when the t fall. H4026
32:14 left; the forts and t shall be for dens for H975
33:18 receiver? where *is* he that counted the t? H4026
Ezk 26: 4 break down her t: I will also scrape her H4026
9 with his axes he shall break down thy t. H4026
27:11 were in thy t: they hanged their shields H4026
Zep 1:16 the fenced cities, and against the high t. H6438
3: 6 I have cut off the nations: their t are H6438

TOWN
Jos 2:15 the t wall, and she dwelt upon the wall. H7023
1Sa 16: 4 And the elders of the t trembled at his H5892
23: 7 into a t that hath gates and bars. H5892
27: 5 a place in some t in the country, that H5892
Hab 2:12 Woe to him that buildeth a t with H5892
Mt 10:11 And into whatsoever city or t ye shall G2968
Mk 8:23 led him out of the t; and when he had G2968
26 into the t, nor tell *it* to any in the town. G2968
26 into the town, nor tell *it* to any in the t. G2968
Lk 5:17 were come out of every t of Galilee, and G2968
Jn 7:42 the t of Bethlehem, where David was? G2968
11: 1 the t of Mary and her sister Martha. G2968
30 Now Jesus was not yet come into the t, G2968

TOWNCLERK
Act 19:35 And when the t had appeased the G1122

TOWNS
Gen 25:16 names, by their t, and by their castles; H2691
Nu 32:41 t thereof, and called them Havoth-jair. H2333
Dt 3: 5 bars; beside unwalled t a great many. H5892
Jos 13:30 and all the t of Jair, which *are* in H2333
15:45 Ekron, with her t and her villages: H1323
47 Ashdod with her t and her villages, H1323
47 Gaza with her t and her villages, unto H1323
17:11 Beth-shean and her t, and Ibleam and H1323
11 Ibleam and her t, and the inhabitants H1323
11 of Dor and her t, and the inhabitants H1323
11 of Endor and her t, and the inhabitants H1323
11 Taanach and her t, and the inhabitants H1323
11 and her t, *even* three countries. H1323
16 and her t, and *they* who *are* of H1323
Jdg 1:27 and her t, nor Taanach and her H1323
27 Taanach and her t, nor the inhabitants H1323
27 of Dor and her t, nor the inhabitants H1323
27 of Ibleam and her t, nor the inhabitants H1323
27 Megiddo and her t: but the Canaanites H1323
11:26 in Heshbon and her t, and in Aroer and H1323
26 in Aroer and her t, and in all the cities H1323
1Ki 4:13 to him *pertained* the t of Jair the son of H2333
1Ch 2:23 Aram, with the t of Jair, from them, H2333
23 with Kenath, and the t thereof, *even* H1323
5:16 and in her t, and in all the suburbs H1323
7:28 Beth-el and the t thereof, and eastward H1323
28 Gezer, with the t thereof; Shechem also H1323
28 also and the t thereof, unto Gaza and H1323
28 thereof, unto Gaza and the t thereof: H1323
29 and her t, Taanach and her towns, H1323
29 Taanach and her t, Megiddo and her H1323
29 Megiddo and her t, Dor and her towns. H1323
29 towns, Dor and her t. In these dwelt the H1323
8:12 built Ono, and Lod, with the t thereof: H1323
18: 1 her t out of the hand of the Philistines. H1323
2Ch 13:19 him, Beth-el with the t thereof, and H1323
19 and Jeshanah with the t thereof, and H1323
19 thereof, and Ephrain with the t thereof. H1323
Est 9:19 in the unwalled t, made the fourteenth H5892
Jer 19:15 city and upon all her t all the evil that I H5892
Zec 2: 4 be inhabited *as* t without walls for the H6519
Mk 1:38 us go into the next t, that I may preach G2969
8:27 his disciples, into the t of Caesarea G2968
Lk 9: 6 and went through the t, preaching the G2968
12 may go into the t and country round G2968

TRACHONITIS
Lk 3: 1 T, and Lysanias the tetrarch of Abilene, G5139

TRADE
Gen 34:10 you; dwell and t ye therein, and get you H5503
21 in the land, and t therein; for the land, H5503
46:32 And the men *are* shepherds, for their t H582
34 That ye shall say, Thy servants' t hath H582
Rev 18:17 and as many as t by sea, stood afar off, G2038

TRADED
Ezk 27:12 iron, tin, and lead, they t in thy fairs. H5414
13 merchants: they t the persons of men H5414
14 They of the house of Togarmah t in thy H5414
17 merchants: they t in thy market wheat H5414
Mt 25:16 talents went and t with the same, and G2038

TRADING
Lk 19:15 how much every man had gained by t. G1281

TRADITION
Mt 15: 2 Why do thy disciples transgress the t of G3862
3 the commandment of God by your t? G3862
6 of God of none effect by your t. G3862
Mk 7: 3 oft, eat not, holding the t of the elders. G3862
5 according to the t of the elders, but eat G3862
8 of God, ye hold the t of men, *as* the G3862
9 of God, that ye may keep your own t. G3862
13 effect through your t, which ye have G3862
Col 2: 8 vain deceit, after the t of men, after the G3862
2Th 3: 6 not after the t which he received of us. G3862
1Pt 1:18 *received* by t from your fathers;

TRADITIONS
Gal 1:14 zealous of the t of my fathers. G3862
2Th 2:15 fast, and hold the t which ye have been G3862

TRAFFICK
Gen 42:34 your brother, and ye shall t in the land. H5503
1Ki 10:15 and of the t of the spice merchants, H4536
Ezk 17: 4 land of t; he set it in a city of merchants. H3667
28: 5 By thy great wisdom *and* by thy t hast H7404
18 by the iniquity of thy t; therefore will I H7404

TRAFFICKERS
Isa 23: 8 t *are* the honourable of the earth? H3667

TRAIN
1Ki 10: 2 with a very great t, with camels that H2428
Prv 22: 6 T up a child in the way he should go: H2596
Isa 6: 1 lifted up, and his t filled the temple. H7757

TRAINED
Gen 14:14 he armed his t *servants*, born in his H2593

TRAITOR
Lk 6:16 Judas Iscariot, which also was the t. G4273

TRAITORS
2Ti 3: 4 T, heady, highminded, lovers of G4273

TRAMPLE
Ps 91:13 and the dragon shalt thou t under feet. H7429
Isa 63: 3 mine anger, and t them in my fury; and H7429
Mt 7: 6 swine, lest they t them under their feet, G2662

TRANCE
Nu 24: 4 falling *into a t*, but having his eyes open:
16 falling *into a t*, but having his eyes open:
Act 10:10 while they made ready, he fell into a t, G1611
11: 5 praying: and in a t I saw a vision, A G1611
22:17 I prayed in the temple, I was in a t; G1611

TRANQUILLITY
Dan 4:27 poor; if it may be a lengthening of thy t. H7963

TRANSFERRED
1Co 4: 6 I have in a figure t to myself and *to* G3345

TRANSFIGURED
Mt 17: 2 And was t before them: and his face G3339
Mk 9: 2 themselves: and he was t before them. G3339

TRANSFORMED
Ro 12: 2 world: but be ye t by the renewing of G3339
2Co 11:14 And no marvel; for Satan himself is t G3345
15 ministers also be t as the ministers of G3345

TRANSFORMING
2Co 11:13 t themselves into the apostles of Christ. G3345

TRANSGRESS
Nu 14:41 now do ye t the commandment H5674
1Sa 2:24 I hear: ye make the LORD'S people to t. H5674
2Ch 24:20 Thus saith God, Why t ye the H5674
Neh 1: 8 saying, *If* ye t, I will scatter you abroad H4603
13:27 this great evil, to t against our God in H4603
Ps 17: 3 am purposed *that* my mouth shall not t. H5674
25: 3 them be ashamed which t without cause. H898
Prv 28:21 for for a piece of bread *that* man will t. H6586
Jer 2:20 saidst, I will not t; when upon every H5674
Ezk 20:38 and them that t against me: I will bring H6586
Am 4: 4 Come to Beth-el, and t; at Gilgal H6586
Mt 15: 2 Why do thy disciples t the tradition of G3845
3 Why do ye also t the commandment G3845
Ro 2:27 letter and circumcision dost t the law? G3848

TRANSGRESSED
Dt 26:13 me: I have not t thy commandments, H5674
Jos 7:11 Israel hath sinned, and they have also t H5674
15 because he hath t the covenant of the H5674
23:16 When ye have t the covenant of the H5674
Jdg 2:20 this people hath t my covenant which H5674
1Sa 14:33 t: roll a great stone unto me this day. H898
15:24 sinned: for I have t the commandment H5674
1Ki 8:50 wherein they have t against thee, and H6586
2Ki 18:12 their God, but t his covenant, *and* all H5674
1Ch 2: 7 of Israel, who t in the thing accursed. H4603
5:25 And they t against the God of their H4603
2Ch 12: 2 because they had t against the LORD, H4603
26:16 destruction: for he t against the LORD H4603
28:19 naked, and t sore against the LORD. H4603
36:14 and the people, t very much after all H4603
Ezr 10:10 them, Ye have t, and have taken strange H4603
13 we are many that have t in this thing. H6586
Isa 24: 5 because they have t the laws, changed H5674
43:27 and thy teachers have t against me. H6586
66:24 of the men that have t against me: for H6586
Jer 2: 8 the pastors also t against me, and the H6586
29 all have t against me, saith the LORD. H6586
3:13 that thou hast t against the LORD thy H6586
33: 8 and whereby they have t against me. H6586
34:18 And I will give the men that have t my H5674
Lam 3:42 We have t and have rebelled: thou hast H6586
Ezk 2: 3 t against me, *even* unto this very day. H6586
18:31 whereby ye have t; and make you a new H6586
Dan 9:11 Yea, all Israel have t thy law, even by H5674
Hos 6: 7 But they like men have t the covenant: H5674
7:13 because they have t against me: though H6586
8: 1 because they have t my covenant, and H5674
Zep 3:11 wherein thou hast t against me: for H6586
Lk 15:29 I serve thee, neither t I at any time thy G3928

TRANSGRESSEST
Est 3: 3 Why t thou the king's commandment? H5674

TRANSGRESSETH
Prv 16:10 the king: his mouth t not in judgment. H4603
Hab 2: 5 Yea also, because he t by wine, *he is* a H898
1Jn 3: 4 Whosoever committeth sin t also the G4160
2Jn 9 Whosoever t, and abideth not in the G3845

TRANSGRESSING
Dt 17: 2 of the LORD thy God, in t his covenant, H5674
Isa 59:13 In t and lying against the LORD, and H6586

TRANSGRESSION
Ex 34: 7 iniquity and t and sin, and that will H6588
Nu 14:18 iniquity and t, and by no means H6588
Jos 22:22 in rebellion, or if in t against the LORD, H4604
1Sa 24:11 *is* neither evil nor t in mine hand, and I H6588
1Ch 9: 1 carried away to Babylon for their t. H4604
10:13 So Saul died for his t which he H4604
2Ch 29:19 did cast away in his t, have we prepared H4604
Ezr 9: 4 because of the t of those that had been H4604
10: 6 t of them that had been carried away. H4604
Job 7:21 And why dost thou not pardon my t, H6588
8: 4 and he have cast them away for their t; H6588
13:23 make me to know my t and my sin. H6588
14:17 My t *is* sealed up in a bag, and thou H6588
33: 9 I am clean without t, I *am* innocent; H6588
34: 6 right? my wound *is* incurable without t. H6588
Ps 19:13 and I shall be innocent from the great t. H6588
32: 1 Blessed *is he whose* t *is* forgiven, *whose* H6588
36: 1 The t of the wicked saith within my H6588
59: 3 not *for* my t, nor *for* my sin, O LORD. H6588
89:32 Then will I visit their t with the rod, H6588
107:17 Fools because of their t, and because of H6588
Prv 12:13 The wicked is snared by the t of *his* H6588
17: 9 He that covereth a t seeketh love; but H6588
19 He loveth t that loveth strife: *and* he H6588
19:11 and *it is* his glory to pass over a t. H6588
28: 2 For the t of a land many *are* the princes H6588
24 and saith, *It is* no t; the same *is* the H6588
29: 6 In the t of an evil man *there is* a snare: H6588
16 When the wicked are multiplied, t H6588
22 and a furious man aboundeth in t. H6588
Isa 24:20 like a cottage; and the t thereof shall be H6588
53: 8 for the t of my people was he stricken. H6588
57: 4 ye not children of t, a seed of falsehood, H6588
58: 1 t, and the house of Jacob their sins. H6588

Isa 59:20 turn from t in Jacob, saith the LORD. H6588
Ezk 33:12 in the day of his t: as for the wickedness H6588
Dan 8:12 by reason of t, and it cast down the H6588
13 *sacrifice*, and the t of desolation, to H6588
9:24 city, to finish the t, and to make an end H6588
Am 4: 4 at Gilgal multiply t; and bring your H6586
Mic 1: 5 For the t of Jacob *is* all this, and for the H6588
5 Israel. What *is* the t of Jacob? *is it* not H6588
3: 8 unto Jacob his t, and to Israel his sin. H6588
6: 7 firstborn *for* my t, the fruit of my body H6588
7:18 and passeth by the t of the remnant of H6588
Act 1:25 t fell, that he might go to his own place. *G3845*
Ro 4:15 wrath: for where no law is, *there is* no t. *G3847*
5:14 of Adam's t, who is the figure of *G3847*
1Ti 2:14 the woman being deceived was in the t. *G3847*
Heb 2: 2 stedfast, and every t and disobedience *G3847*
1Jn 3: 4 also the law: for sin is the t of the law. *G458*

TRANSGRESSIONS
Ex 23:21 pardon your t: for my name *is* in him. H6588
Lev 16:16 because of their t in all their sins: and H6588
21 and all their t in all their sins, putting H6588
Jos 24:19 he will not forgive your t nor your sins. H6588
1Ki 8:50 thee, and all their t wherein they have H6588
Job 31:33 If I covered my t as Adam, by hiding H6588
35: 6 him? or *if* thy t be multiplied, what H6588
36: 9 and their t that they have exceeded. H6588
Ps 5:10 t; for they have rebelled against thee. H6588
25: 7 of my youth, nor my t: according to thy H6588
32: 5 I will confess my t unto the LORD; and H6588
39: 8 Deliver me from all my t: make me not H6588
51: 1 of thy tender mercies blot out my t. H6588
3 For I acknowledge my t: and my sin *is* H6588
65: 3 *for* our t, thou shalt purge them away. H6588
103:12 *so* far hath he removed our t from us. H6588
Isa 43:25 I, *even* I, *am* he that blotteth out thy t H6588
44:22 a thick cloud, thy t, and, as a cloud, thy H6588
50: 1 and for your t is your mother put away. H6588
53: 5 But he *was* wounded for our t, *he was* H6588
59:12 For our t are multiplied before thee, H6588
12 against us: for our t *are* with us; and *as* H6588
Jer 5: 6 because their t are many, *and* their H6588
Lam 1: 5 multitude of her t: her children are gone H6588
14 The yoke of my t is bound by his hand: H6588
22 unto me for all my t: for my sighs *are* H6588
Ezk 14:11 more with all their t; but that they may H6588
18:22 All his t that he hath committed, they H6588
28 turneth away from all his t that he hath H6588
30 t; so iniquity shall not be your ruin. H6588
31 Cast away from you all your t, whereby H6588
21:24 in that your t are discovered, so that H6588
33:10 saying, If our t and our sins *be* upon H6588
37:23 with any of their t: but I will save them H6588
39:24 according to their t have I done unto H6588
Am 1: 3 Thus saith the LORD; For three t of H6588
6 Thus saith the LORD; For three t of H6588
9 Thus saith the LORD; For three t of H6588
11 Thus saith the LORD; For three t of H6588
13 Thus saith the LORD; For three t of the H6588
2: 1 Thus saith the LORD; For three t of H6588
4 Thus saith the LORD; For three t of H6588
6 Thus saith the LORD; For three t of H6588
3:14 That in the day that I shall visit the t of H6588
5:12 For I know your manifold t and your H6588
Mic 1:13 for the t of Israel were found in thee. H6588
Gal 3:19 added because of t, till the seed should *G3847*
Heb 9:15 redemption of the t *that were* under the *G3847*

TRANSGRESSOR
Prv 21:18 the righteous, and the t for the upright. H898
22:12 and he overthroweth the words of the t. H898
Isa 48: 8 and wast called a t from the womb. H6586
Gal 2:18 which I destroyed, I make myself a t. *G3848*
Jas 2:11 kill, thou art become a t of the law. *G3848*

TRANSGRESSORS
Ps 37:38 But the t shall be destroyed together: H6586
51:13 *Then* will I teach t thy ways; and H6586
59: 5 be not merciful to any wicked t. Selah. H898
119:158 I beheld the t, and was grieved; because H898
Prv 2:22 earth, and the t shall be rooted out of it. H898
11: 3 the perverseness of t shall destroy them. H898
6 deliver them: but t shall be taken in *their* H898
13: 2 but the soul of the t *shall eat* violence. H898
15 giveth favour: but the way of t *is* hard. H898
23:28 a prey, and increaseth the t among men. H898
26:10 rewardeth the fool, and rewardeth t. H5674
Isa 1:28 And the destruction of the t and of the H6586
46: 8 men: bring *it* again to mind, O ye t. H6586
53:12 with the t; and he bare the sin H6586
12 many, and made intercession for the t. H6586
Dan 8:23 when the t are come to the full, H6586
Hos 14: 9 in them: but the t shall fall therein. H6586
Mk 15:28 saith, And he was numbered with the t. *G459*
Lk 22:37 among the t: for the things concerning *G459*
Jas 2: 9 sin, and are convinced of the law as t. *G3848*

TRANSLATE
2Sa 3:10 To t the kingdom from the house of H5674

TRANSLATED
Col 1:13 t *us* into the kingdom of his dear Son: *G3179*
Heb 11: 5 By faith Enoch was t that he should not *G3346*
5 because God had t him: for before his *G3346*

TRANSLATION
Heb 11: 5 him: for before his t he had this *G3331*

TRANSPARENT
Rev 21:21 city *was* pure gold, as it were t glass. *G1307*

TRAP
Job 18:10 the ground, and a t for him in the way. H4434
Ps 69:22 *been* for *their* welfare, *let it become* a t. H4170
Jer 5:26 snares; they set a t, they catch men. H4889
Ro 11: 9 a snare, and a t, and a stumblingblock, *G2339*

TRAPS
Jos 23:13 be snares and t unto you, and scourges H4170

TRAVAIL
Gen 38:27 And it came to pass in the time of her t, H3205
Ex 18: 8 sake, *and* all the t that had come upon H8513
Nu 20:14 knowest all the t that hath befallen us: H8513
Ps 48: 6 there, *and* pain, as of a woman in t. H3205
Ecc 1:13 heaven: this sore t hath God given to H6045
2:23 For all his days *are* sorrows, and his t H6045
26 sinner he giveth t, to gather and to heap H6045
3:10 I have seen the t, which God hath given H6045
4: 4 Again, I considered all t, and every H5999
6 hands full *with* t and vexation of spirit. H5999
8 This *is* also vanity, yea, it *is* a sore t. H6045
5:14 But those riches perish by evil t: and he H6045
Isa 23: 4 the sea, saying, I t not, nor bring forth H2342
53:11 He shall see of the t of his soul, *and* H5999
54: 1 thou *that* didst not t with child: for H2342
Jer 4:31 as of a woman in t, *and* the anguish as H2470
6:24 of us, *and* pain, as of a woman in t. H3205
13:21 not sorrows take thee, as a woman in t? H3205
22:23 upon thee, the pain as of a woman in t! H3205
30: 6 a man doth t with child? wherefore H3205
6 t, and all faces are turned into paleness? H3205
49:24 have taken her, as a woman in t. H3205
50:43 of him, *and* pangs as of a woman in t. H3205
Lam 3: 5 me, and compassed *me* with gall and t. H8513
Mic 4: 9 pangs have taken thee as a woman in t. H3205
10 like a woman in t: for now shalt thou go H3205
Jn 16:21 A woman when she is in t hath sorrow, *G5088*
Gal 4:19 My little children, of whom I t in birth *G5605*
1Th 2: 9 our labour and t: for labouring night *G3449*
5: 3 upon them, as t upon a woman with *G5604*
2Th 3: 8 with labour and t night and day, that *G3449*

TRAVAILED
Gen 35:16 and Rachel t, and she had hard labour. H3205
38:28 And it came to pass, when she t, that H3205
1Sa 4:19 and t; for her pains came upon her. H3205
Isa 66: 7 Before she t, she brought forth; before H2342
8 Zion t, she brought forth her children. H2342

TRAVAILEST
Gal 4:27 forth and cry, thou that t not: for the *G5605*

TRAVAILETH
Job 15:20 The wicked man t with pain all *his* H2342
Ps 7:14 Behold, he t with iniquity, and hath H2254
Isa 13: 8 as a woman that t: they shall be amazed H3205
21: 3 of a woman that t: I was bowed down at H3205
Jer 31: 8 child and her that t with child together: H3205
Mic 5: 3 *that* she which t hath brought forth: H3205
Ro 8:22 and t in pain together until now. *G4944*

TRAVAILING
Isa 42:14 will I cry like a t woman; I will destroy H3205
Hos 13:13 The sorrows of a t woman shall come H3205
Rev 12: 2 And she being with child cried, t in *G5605*

TRAVEL
Act 19:29 companions in t, they rushed with one *G4898*
2Co 8:19 of the churches to t with us with this *G4898*

TRAVELLED
Act 11:19 about Stephen t as far as Phenice, and *G1330*

TRAVELLER
2Sa 12: 4 And there came a t unto the rich man, H1982
Job 31:32 the street: *but* I opened my doors to the t. H734

TRAVELLERS
Jdg 5: 6 the t walked through byways. H1980+H5410

TRAVELLETH
Prv 6:11 So shall thy poverty come as one that t, H1980
24:34 So shall thy poverty come *as* one that t; H1980

TRAVELLING
Isa 21:13 ye lodge, O ye t companies of Dedanim. H736
63: 1 in his apparel, t in the greatness of his H6808
Mt 25:14 For *the kingdom of heaven is* as a man t *g589*

TRAVERSING
Jer 2:23 *thou art* a swift dromedary t her ways; H8308

TREACHEROUS
Isa 21: 2 declared unto me; the t dealer dealeth H898
24:16 woe unto me! the t dealers have dealt H898
16 t dealers have dealt very treacherously. H898
Jer 3: 7 not. And her t sister Judah saw *it*. H901
8 of divorce; yet her t sister Judah feared H898
10 And yet for all this her t sister Judah H901
11 hath justified herself more than t Judah. H898
9: 2 *be* all adulterers, an assembly of t men. H898
Zep 3: 4 Her prophets *are* light *and* t persons: her H900

TREACHEROUSLY
Jdg 9:23 men of Shechem dealt t with Abimelech: H898
Isa 21: 2 dealer dealeth t, and the spoiler H898
24:16 dealers have dealt t; yea, the treacherous H898
16 the treacherous dealers have dealt very t. H898
33: 1 spoiled; and dealest t, and they dealt not H898
1 and they dealt not t with thee! when H898
1 t, they shall deal treacherously with thee. H898
1 treacherously, they shall deal t with thee. H898
48: 8 wouldest deal very t, and wast called a H898
Jer 3:20 Surely *as* a wife t departeth from her H898
20 so have ye dealt t with me, O house of H898
5:11 dealt very t against me, saith the LORD. H898
12: 1 are all they happy that deal very t? H898
6 they have dealt t with thee; yea, they H898
Lam 1: 2 t with her, they are become her enemies. H898
Hos 5: 7 They have dealt t against the LORD: for H898
6: 7 there have they dealt t against me. H898
Hab 1:13 them that deal t, *and* holdest thy tongue H898
Mal 2:10 us? why do we deal t every man against H898
11 Judah hath dealt t, and an abomination H898
14 whom thou hast dealt t: yet *is* she thy H898
15 none deal t against the wife of his youth. H898
16 heed to your spirit, that ye deal not t. H898

TREACHERY
2Ki 9:23 said to Ahaziah, *There is* t, O Ahaziah. H4820

TREAD
Dt 11:24 of your feet shall t shall be yours: from H1869
25 shall t upon, as he hath said unto you. H1869
33:29 and thou shalt t upon their high places. H1869
Jos 1: 3 of your foot shall t upon, that have I H1869
1Sa 5: 5 Dagon's house, t on the threshold of H1869
Job 24:11 t *their* winepresses, and suffer thirst. H1869
40:12 and t down the wicked in their place. H1915
Ps 7: 5 *it*; yea, let him t down my life upon the H7429
44: 5 we t them under that rise up against us. H947
60:12 for he *it is that* shall t down our enemies. H947
91:13 Thou shalt t upon the lion and adder: H1869
108:13 for he *it is that* shall t down our enemies. H947
Isa 1:12 this at your hand, to t my courts? H7429
10: 6 prey, and to t them down like H7760+H4823
14:25 my mountains t him under foot: then H947
16:10 the treaders shall t out no wine in *their* H1869
26: 6 The foot shall t it down, *even* the feet of H7429
63: 3 none with me: for I will t them in mine H1869
6 And I will t down the people in mine H947
Jer 25:30 shout, as they that t *the grapes*, against H1869
48:33 none shall t with shouting; *their* H1869
Ezk 26:11 With the hoofs of his horses shall he t H7429
34:18 but ye must t down with your feet H7429

T

Dan 7:23 shall **t** it down, and break it in pieces. H1759
Hos 10:11 *and* loveth to **t** out *the corn*; but I H1758
Mic 1: 3 and **t** upon the high places of the earth. H1869
5: 5 and when he shall **t** in our palaces, H1869
6:15 reap; thou shalt **t** the olives, but thou H1869
Nah 3:14 go into clay, and **t** the morter, make H7429
Zec 10: 5 mighty *men*, which **t** down *their enemies* H947
Mal 4: 3 And ye shall **t** down the wicked; for H6072
Lk 10:19 Behold, I give unto you power to **t** on *G3961*
Rev 11: 2 they **t** under foot forty *and* two months. *G3961*

TREADER
Am 9:13 the reaper, and the **t** of grapes him that H1869

TREADERS
Isa 16:10 be shouting: the **t** shall tread out no H1869

TREADETH
Dt 25: 4 Thou shalt not muzzle the ox when he **t** H7429
Job 9: 8 and **t** upon the waves of the sea. H1869
Isa 41:25 *upon* morter, and as the potter **t** clay. H7429
63: 2 garments like him that **t** in the winefat? H1869
Am 4:13 darkness, and **t** upon the high places H1869
Mic 5: 6 and when he **t** within our borders. H1869
8 go through, both **t** down, and teareth in H7429
1Co 9: 9 of the ox that **t** out the corn. Doth God *G248*
1Ti 5:18 muzzle the ox that **t** out the corn. And, *G248*
Rev 19:15 a rod of iron: and he **t** the winepress of *G3961*

TREADING
Neh 13:15 In those days saw I in Judah *some* **t** H1869
Isa 7:25 of oxen, and for the **t** of lesser cattle. H4823
22: 5 For *it is* a day of trouble, and of **t** down, H4001
Am 5:11 Forasmuch therefore as your **t** *is* upon H1318

TREASON
1Ki 16:20 of Zimri, and his **t** that he wrought, *are* H7195
2Ki 11:14 rent her clothes, and cried, **T**, Treason. H7195
14 rent her clothes, and cried, Treason, **T**. H7195
2Ch 23:13 rent her clothes, and said, **T**, Treason. H7195
13 rent her clothes, and said, Treason, **T**. H7195

TREASURE
Gen 43:23 hath given you **t** in your sacks: I had H4301
Ex 1:11 Pharaoh **t** cities, Pithom and Raamses. H4543
19: 5 shall be a peculiar **t** unto me above all H5459
Dt 28:12 unto thee his good **t**, the heaven to give H214
1Ch 29: 8 gave *them* to the **t** of the house of the H214
Ezr 2:69 They gave after their ability unto the **t** of H214
5:17 made in the king's **t** house, which *is* H1596
7:20 bestow *it* out of the king's **t** house. H1596
Neh 7:70 gave to the **t** a thousand drams of H214
71 fathers gave to the **t** of the work twenty H214
10:38 God, to the chambers, into the **t** house. H214
Ps 17:14 thou fillest with thy hid *t*: they are full of
135: 4 himself, *and* Israel for his peculiar **t**. H5459
Prv 15: 6 In the house of the righteous *is* much **t**: H2633
16 than great **t** and trouble therewith. H214
21:20 *There is* **t** to be desired and oil in the H214
Ecc 2: 8 and the peculiar **t** of kings and of the H5459
Isa 33: 6 of salvation: the fear of the LORD *is* his **t**. H214
Ezk 22:25 have taken the **t** and precious things; H2633
Dan 1: 2 the vessels into the **t** house of his god. H214
Hos 13:15 he shall spoil the **t** of all pleasant vessels. H214
Mt 6:21 For where your **t** is, there will your *G2344*
12:35 A good man out of the good **t** of the *G2344*
35 of the evil **t** bringeth forth evil things. *G2344*
13:44 heaven is like unto **t** hid in a field; the *G2344*
52 forth out of his **t** *things* new and old. *G2344*
19:21 **t** in heaven: and come *and* follow me. *G2344*
Mk 10:21 thou shalt have **t** in heaven: and come, *G2344*
Lk 6:45 A good man out of the good **t** of his *G2344*
45 evil man out of the evil **t** of his heart *G2344*
12:21 So *is* he that layeth up **t** for himself, *G2343*
33 wax not old, a **t** in the heavens that *G2344*
34 For where your **t** is, there will your *G2344*
18:22 have **t** in heaven: and come, follow me. *G2344*
Act 8:27 the charge of all her **t**, and had come to *G1047*
2Co 4: 7 But we have this **t** in earthen vessels, *G2344*
Jas 5: 3 heaped **t** together for the last days. *G2343*

TREASURED
Isa 23:18 it shall not be **t** nor laid up; for her H686

TREASURE-HOUSE See TREASURE and HOUSE.

TREASURER
Ezr 1: 8 of Mithredath the **t**, and numbered H1489
Isa 22:15 get thee unto this **t**, *even* unto Shebna, H5532

TREASURERS
Ezr 7:21 a decree to all the **t** which *are* beyond H1490
Neh 13:13 And I made **t** over the treasuries, H686
Dan 3: 2 the judges, the **t**, the counsellors, the H1411
3 the judges, the **t**, the counsellors, the H1411

TREASURES
Dt 32:34 with me, *and* sealed up among my **t**? H214
33:19 of the seas, and *of* **t** hid in the sand. H8226
1Ki 7:51 among the **t** of the house of the LORD. H214
14:26 And he took away the **t** of the house of H214
26 the LORD, and the **t** of the king's house; H214
15:18 *that were* left in the **t** of the house of the H214
18 the LORD, and the **t** of the king's house, H214
2Ki 12:18 *was* found in the **t** of the house of the H214
14:14 LORD, and in the **t** of the king's house, H214
16: 8 LORD, and in the **t** of the king's house, H214
18:15 LORD, and in the **t** of the king's house. H214
20:13 was found in his **t**: there was nothing in H214
15 my **t** that I have not shewed them. H214
24:13 And he carried out thence all the **t** of the H214
13 the LORD, and the **t** of the king's house, H214
1Ch 26:20 And of the Levites, Ahijah *was* over the **t** H214
20 and over the **t** of the dedicated things. H214
22 *were* over the **t** of the house of the LORD. H214
24 the son of Moses, *was* ruler of the **t**. H214
26 *were* over all the **t** of the dedicated H214
27:25 And over the king's **t** *was* Azmaveth the H214
2Ch 5: 1 put he among the **t** of the house of God. H214
8:15 any matter, or concerning the **t**. H214
12: 9 and took away the **t** of the house of the H214
9 the LORD, and the **t** of the king's house; H214
16: 2 and gold out of the **t** of the house of the H214
25:24 and the **t** of the king's house, the H214
36:18 and small, and the **t** of the house of the H214
18 the LORD, and the **t** of the king, and of H214
Ezr 6: 1 where the **t** were laid up in Babylon. H1596
Neh 12:44 chambers for the **t**, for the offerings, for H214
Job 3:21 not; and dig for it more than for hid **t**; H4301
38:22 Hast thou entered into the **t** of the snow? H214
22 snow? or hast thou seen the **t** of the hail, H214
Prv 2: 4 silver, and searchest for her as *for* hid **t**; H4301
8:21 to inherit substance; and I will fill their **t**. H214
10: 2 **T** of wickedness profit nothing: but H214
21: 6 The getting of **t** by a lying tongue *is* a H214
Isa 2: 7 *any* end of their **t**; their land is also full H214
10:13 and have robbed their **t**, and I have put H6259
30: 6 asses, and their **t** upon the bunches of H214
39: 2 was found in his **t**: there was nothing in H214
4 my **t** that I have not shewed them. H214
45: 3 And I will give thee the **t** of darkness, H214
Jer 10:13 and bringeth forth the wind out of his **t**. H214
15:13 Thy substance and thy **t** will I give to the H214
17: 3 *and* all thy **t** to the spoil, *and* thy H214
20: 5 thereof, and all the **t** of the kings of H214
41: 8 Slay us not: for we have **t** in the field, of H4301
48: 7 thy works and in thy **t**, thou shalt also be H214
49: 4 her **t**, *saying*, Who shall come unto me? H214
50:37 *is* upon her **t**; and they shall be robbed. H214
51:13 abundant in **t**, thine end is come, *and* H214
16 and bringeth forth the wind out of his **t**. H214
Ezk 28: 4 and hast gotten gold and silver into thy **t**: H214
Dan 11:43 But he shall have power over the **t** of H4362
Mic 6:10 Are there yet the **t** of wickedness in the H214
Mt 2:11 had opened their **t**, they presented unto *G2344*
6:19 Lay not up for yourselves **t** upon earth, *G2344*
20 But lay up for yourselves **t** in heaven, *G2344*
Col 2: 3 In whom are hid all the **t** of wisdom *G2344*
Heb 11:26 riches than the **t** in Egypt: for he had *G2344*

TREASUREST
Ro 2: 5 and impenitent heart **t** up unto thyself *G2343*

TREASURIES
1Ch 9:26 the chambers and **t** of the house of God. H214
28:11 thereof, and of the **t** thereof, and of the H1597
12 round about, of the **t** of the house of H214
12 God, and of the **t** of the dedicated things: H214
2Ch 32:27 and he made himself **t** for silver, and for H214
Neh 13:12 and the new wine and the oil unto the **t**. H214
13 And I made treasurers over the **t**, H214
Est 3: 9 the business, to bring *it* into the king's **t**. H1595
4: 7 king's **t** for the Jews, to destroy them. H1595
Ps 135: 7 the rain; he bringeth the wind out of his **t**. H214

TREASURY
Jos 6:19 they shall come into the **t** of the LORD. H214
24 put into the **t** of the house of the LORD. H214
Jer 38:11 the king under the **t**, and took thence old H214
Mt 27: 6 the **t**, because it is the price of blood. *G2878*
Mk 12:41 And Jesus sat over against the **t**, and *G1049*
41 money into the **t**: and many that were *G1049*
43 than all they which have cast into the **t**: *G1049*
Lk 21: 1 rich men casting their gifts into the **t**. *G1049*
Jn 8:20 These words spake Jesus in the **t**, as he *G1049*

TREATISE
Act 1: 1 The former **t** have I made, O *G3056*

TREE
Gen 1:11 seed, *and* the fruit **t** yielding fruit after H6086
12 his kind, and the **t** yielding fruit, whose H6086
29 earth, and every **t**, in the which *is* the H6086
29 *is* the fruit of a **t** yielding seed; to you H6086
2: 9 God to grow every **t** that is pleasant to H6086
9 good for food; the **t** of life also in the H6086
9 the **t** of knowledge of good and evil. H6086
16 **t** of the garden thou mayest freely eat: H6086
17 But of the **t** of the knowledge of good H6086
3: 1 shall not eat of every **t** of the garden? H6086
3 But of the fruit of the **t** which *is* in the H6086
6 And when the woman saw that the **t** H6086
6 to the eyes, and a **t** to be desired to H6086
11 Hast thou eaten of the **t**, whereof I H6086
12 me, she gave me of the **t**, and I did eat. H6086
17 and hast eaten of the **t**, of which I H6086
22 the **t** of life, and eat, and live for ever: H6086
24 way, to keep the way of the **t** of life. H6086
18: 4 feet, and rest yourselves under the **t**: H6086
8 by them under the **t**, and they did eat. H6086
30:37 hazel and chesnut **t**; and pilled white H6196
40:19 hang thee on a **t**; and the birds shall eat H6086
Ex 9:25 the field, and brake every **t** of the field. H6086
10: 5 **t** which groweth for you out of the field: H6086
15:25 shewed him a **t**, *which* when he had H6086
Lev 27:30 of the fruit of the **t**, *is* the LORD'S: *it is* H6086
Nu 6: 4 **t**, from the kernels even to the husk. H1612
Dt 12: 2 upon the hills, and under every green **t**: H6086
19: 5 to cut down the **t**, and the head slippeth H6086
20:19 down (for the **t** of the field *is* man's H6086
21:22 put to death, and thou hang him on a **t**: H6086
23 all night upon the **t**, but thou shalt in H6086
22: 6 in the way in any **t**, or on the ground, H6086
24:20 When thou beatest thine olive **t**, thou H2132
Jos 8:29 And the king of Ai he hanged on a **t** H6086
29 down from the **t**, and cast it at the H6086
Jdg 4: 5 And she dwelt under the palm **t** of H8560
9: 8 unto the olive **t**, Reign thou over us. H2132
9 But the olive **t** said unto them, Should I H2132
10 And the trees said to the fig **t**, Come H8384
11 But the fig **t** said unto them, Should I H8384
1Sa 14: 2 a pomegranate **t** which *is* in Migron: H7416
22: 6 in Gibeah under a **t** in Ramah, having H815
31:13 a **t** at Jabesh, and fasted seven days. H815
1Ki 4:25 and under his fig **t**, from Dan even to H8384
33 And he spake of trees, from the cedar **t** H730
6:23 *of* olive **t**, *each* ten cubits high. H6086
31 doors *of* olive **t**: the lintel *and* side posts H6086
32 The two doors also *were of* olive **t**; and H6086
33 posts *of* olive **t**, a fourth part *of the wall*. H6086
34 And the two doors *were of* fir **t**: the two H6086
14:23 every high hill, and under every green **t**. H6086
19: 4 under a juniper **t**: and he requested for H7574
5 under a juniper **t**, behold, then an angel H7574
2Ki 3:19 fell every good **t**, and stop all wells of H6086
16: 4 on the hills, and under every green **t**. H6086
17:10 every high hill, and under every green **t**: H6086
18:31 every one of his fig **t**, and drink ye every H8384
2Ch 3: 5 he cieled with fir **t**, which he overlaid H6086
28: 4 on the hills, and under every green **t**. H6086
Est 2:23 both hanged on a **t**: and it was written H6086
Job 14: 7 For there is hope of a **t**, if it be cut H6086
19:10 mine hope hath he removed like a **t**. H6086
24:20 and wickedness shall be broken as a **t**. H6086
Ps 1: 3 And he shall be like a **t** planted by the H6086
37:35 and spreading himself like a green bay **t**. H249
52: 8 But I *am* like a green olive **t** in the H2132
92:12 **t**: he shall grow like a cedar in Lebanon. H8558
Prv 3:18 She *is* a **t** of life to them that lay hold H6086
11:30 The fruit of the righteous *is* a **t** of life; H6086
13:12 *when* the desire cometh, *it is* a **t** of life. H6086
15: 4 A wholesome tongue *is* a **t** of life: but H6086
27:18 Whoso keepeth the fig **t** shall eat the H8384
Ecc 11: 3 earth: and if the **t** fall toward the south, H6086
3 where the **t** falleth, there it shall be. H6086
12: 5 and the almond **t** shall flourish, and H8247
Song 2: 3 As the apple **t** among the trees of the H8598
13 The fig **t** putteth forth her green figs, H8384

Song 7: 7 This thy stature is like to a palm t, and H8558
8 I said, I will go up to the palm t, I will H8558
8: 5 up under the apple t: there thy mother H8598
Isa 6:13 be eaten: as a teil t, and as an oak, whose H424
17: 6 of an olive t, two *or* three berries H2132
24:13 of an olive t, and as the gleaning H2132
34: 4 vine, and as a falling *fig* from the fig t. H8384
36:16 every one of his fig t, and drink ye every H8384
40:20 chooseth a t *that* will not rot; he H6086
41:19 cedar, the shittah t, and the myrtle, and H7848
19 the myrtle, and the oil t; I will set in the H6086
19 the desert the fir t, *and* the pine, and the H1265
19 *and* the pine, and the box t together: H8391
44:19 shall I fall down to the stock of a t? H6086
23 O forest, and every t therein: for the H6086
55:13 come up the fir t, and instead of the H1265
13 up the myrtle t: and it shall be to the H1918
56: 3 let the eunuch say, Behold, I *am* a dry t. H6086
57: 5 idols under every green t, slaying the H6086
60:13 unto thee, the fir t, the pine tree, and H1265
13 fir tree, the pine t, and the box together, H8410
65:22 for as the days of a t *are* the days of my H6086
66:17 behind one t in the midst, eating swine's
Jer 1:11 And I said, I see a rod of an almond t. H8247
2:20 t thou wanderest, playing the harlot. H6086
3: 6 t, and there hath played the harlot. H6086
13 under every green t, and ye have not H6086
8:13 nor figs on the fig t, and the leaf shall H8384
10: 3 for *one* cutteth a t out of the forest, the H6086
5 They *are* upright as the palm t, but H8560
11:16 A green olive t, fair, *and* of goodly fruit: H2132
19 Let us destroy the t with the fruit H6086
17: 8 For he shall be as a t planted by the H6086
Ezk 6:13 under every green t, and under every H6086
15: 2 Son of man, What is the vine t more H6086
2 tree more than any t, *or than* a branch H6086
6 GOD; As the vine t among the trees of H6086
17: 5 by great waters, *and* set it *as* a willow t. H6851
24 down the high t, have exalted the low H6086
24 exalted the low t, have dried up the H6086
24 dried up the green t, and have made the H6086
24 have made the dry t to flourish: I the H6086
20:47 every green t in thee, and every dry H6086
47 and every dry t: the flaming flame shall H6086
21:10 the rod of my son, *as* every t. H6086
31: 8 his branches; nor any t in the garden of H6086
34:27 And the t of the field shall yield her H6086
36:30 And I will multiply the fruit of the t, and H6086
41:18 so that a palm t *was* between a cherub H8561
19 toward the palm t on the one side, and H8561
19 toward the palm t on the other side: *it* H8561
Dan 4:10 I saw, and behold a t in the midst of the H363
11 The t grew, and was strong, and the H363
14 Hew down the t, and cut off his branches, H363
20 The t that thou sawest, which grew, and H363
23 saying, Hew the t down, and destroy it; H363
26 the stump of the t roots; thy kingdom H363
Hos 9:10 firstripe in the fig t at her first time: *but* H8384
14: 6 as the olive t, and his smell as Lebanon. H2132
8 a green fir t. From me is thy fruit found. H1265
Joel 1: 7 and barked my fig t: he hath made it H8384
12 The vine is dried up, and the fig t H8384
12 the pomegranate t, the palm tree also, H7416
12 tree, the palm t also, and the apple H8558
12 and the apple t, *even* all the trees of H8598
2:22 do spring, for the t beareth her fruit, H6086
22 t and the vine do yield their strength. H8384
Mic 4: 4 vine and under his fig t; and none shall H8384
Hab 3:17 Although the fig t shall not blossom, H8384
Hag 2:19 the vine, and the fig t, and the H8384
19 and the olive t, hath not brought forth: H6086
Zec 3:10 under the vine and under the fig t. H8384
11: 2 Howl, fir t; for the cedar is fallen; H1265
Mt 3:10 therefore every t which bringeth not G1186
7:17 Even so every good t bringeth forth G1186
17 but a corrupt t bringeth forth evil fruit. G1186
18 A good t cannot bring forth evil fruit, G1186
18 *can* a corrupt t bring forth good fruit. G1186
19 Every t that bringeth not forth good G1186
12:33 Either make the t good, and his fruit G1186
33 or else make the t corrupt, and his fruit G1186
33 corrupt: for the t is known by *his* fruit. G1186
13:32 and becometh a t, so that the birds of G1186
21:19 And when he saw a fig t in the way, he G4808
19 And presently the fig t withered away. G4808
20 How soon is the fig t withered away! G4808
21 *is done* to the fig t, but also if ye shall G4808
24:32 Now learn a parable of the fig t; When G4808
Mk 11:13 And seeing a fig t afar off having G4808
Mk 11:20 saw the fig t dried up from the roots. G4808
21 behold, the fig t which thou cursedst G4808
13:28 Now learn a parable of the fig t; When G4808
Lk 3: 9 of the trees: every t therefore which G1186
6:43 For a good t bringeth not forth corrupt G1186
43 doth a corrupt t bring forth good fruit. G1186
44 For every t is known by his own fruit. G1186
13: 6 *man* had a fig t planted in his vineyard; G4808
7 fruit on this fig t, and find none: cut it G4808
19 and waxed a great t; and the fowls of G1186
17: 6 this sycamine t, Be thou plucked up G4807
19: 4 into a sycomore t to see him: for he was G4809
21:29 Behold the fig t, and all the trees; G4808
23:31 For if they do these things in a green t, G3586
Jn 1:48 thou wast under the fig t, I saw thee. G4808
50 thee under the fig t, believest thou? thou G4808
Act 5:30 Jesus, whom ye slew and hanged on a t. G3586
10:39 whom they slew and hanged on a t: G3586
13:29 from the t, and laid *him* in a sepulchre. G3586
Ro 11:17 thou, being a wild olive t, wert graffed in G65
17 of the root and fatness of the olive t; G1636
24 For if thou wert cut out of the olive t G65
24 into a good olive t: how much more G2565
24 be graffed into their own olive t? G1636
Gal 3:13 Cursed *is* every one that hangeth on a t: G3586
Jas 3:12 Can the fig t, my brethren, bear olive G4808
1Pt 2:24 own body on the t, that we, being dead G3586
Rev 2: 7 I give to eat of the t of life, which is in G3586
6:13 the earth, even as a fig t casteth her G4808
7: 1 the earth, nor on the sea, nor on any t. G1186
9: 4 thing, neither any t; but only those men G1186
22: 2 river, *was there* the t of life, which bare G3586
2 t *were* for the healing of the nations. G3586
14 may have right to the t of life, and may G3586

TREES

Gen 3: 2 eat of the fruit of the t of the garden: H6086
8 LORD God amongst the t of the garden. H6086
23:17 and all the t that *were* in the field, H6086
Ex 10:15 all the fruit of the t which the hail had H6086
15 green thing in the t, or in the herbs of H6086
15:27 and ten palm t: and they encamped H8558
Lev 19:23 all manner of t for food, then ye shall H6086
23:40 boughs of goodly t, branches of palm H6086
40 branches of palm t, and the boughs of H8558
40 the boughs of thick t, and willows of the H6086
26: 4 the t of the field shall yield their fruit. H6086
20 shall the t of the land yield their fruits. H6086
Nu 24: 6 river's side, as the t of lign aloes which
6 *and* as cedar t beside the waters. H730
33: 9 and ten palm t; and they pitched there. H8558
Dt 6:11 and olive t, which thou plantedst H2132
8: 8 and vines, and fig t, and pomegranates; H8384
16:21 thee a grove of any t near unto the altar H6086
20:19 not destroy the t thereof by forcing an H6086
20 Only the t which thou knowest that H6086
20 that they *be* not t for meat, thou shalt H6086
28:40 Thou shalt have olive t throughout all H2132
42 All thy t and fruit of thy land shall the H6086
34: 3 of palm t, unto Zoar. H5892+H8558+H5899
Jos 10:26 them on five t: and they were hanging H6086
26 hanging upon the t until the evening. H6086
27 them down off the t, and cast them into H6086
Jdg 1:16 city of palm t with the H5892+H8558+H5899
3:13 the city of palm t. H5892+H8558+H5899
9: 8 The t went forth *on a time* to anoint a H6086
9 man, and go to be promoted over the t? H6086
10 And the t said to the fig tree, Come H6086
11 fruit, and go to be promoted over the t? H6086
12 Then said the t unto the vine, Come H6086
13 man, and go to be promoted over the t? H6086
14 Then said all the t unto the bramble, H6086
15 And the bramble said unto the t, If in H6086
48 a bough from the t, and took it, and laid H6086
2Sa 5:11 David, and cedar t, and carpenters, and H6086
23 upon them over against the mulberry t. H1057
24 of the mulberry t, that then thou shalt H1057
1Ki 4:33 And he spake of t, from the cedar tree H6086
5: 6 they hew me cedar t out of Lebanon; and H730
10 So Hiram gave Solomon cedar t and fir H6086
10 and fir t *according to* all his desire. H6086
6:29 and palm t and open flowers, within H8561
32 and palm t and open flowers, and H8561
32 the cherubims, and upon the palm t. H8561
35 and palm t and open flowers: and H8561
7:36 lions, and palm t, according to the H8561
9:11 with cedar t and fir trees, and with H6086
11 with cedar trees and fir t, and with gold, H6086
10:11 plenty of almug t, and precious stones. H6086
1Ki 10:12 And the king made of the almug t H6086
12 almug t, nor were seen unto this day. H6086
27 t that *are* in the vale, for abundance. H8256
2Ki 3:25 and felled all the good t: only in H6086
19:23 cut down the tall cedar t thereof, *and* the H730
23 *and* the choice fir t thereof: and I will H1265
1Ch 14:14 upon them over against the mulberry t. H1057
15 of the mulberry t, *that* then thou shalt H1057
16:33 Then shall the t of the wood sing out at H6086
22: 4 Also cedar t in abundance: for the H6086
27:28 And over the olive t and the sycomore H2132
28 and the sycomore t that *were* in the low H8256
2Ch 1:15 as stones, and cedar t made he as the H730
15 t that *are* in the vale for abundance. H8256
2: 8 Send me also cedar t, fir trees, and H6086
8 Send me also cedar trees, fir t, and H1265
8 trees, and algum t, out of Lebanon: for I
3: 5 and set thereon palm t and chains. H8561
9:10 brought algum t and precious stones. H6086
11 And the king made of the algum t H6086
27 as stones, and cedar t made he as the H730
27 he as the sycomore t that *are* in the low H8256
28:15 city of palm t, to their H5892+H8558+H5899
Ezr 3: 7 to bring cedar t from Lebanon to the H6086
Neh 8:15 thick t, to make booths, as *it is* written. H6086
9:25 and fruit t in abundance: so they H6086
10:35 of all fruit of all t, year by year, unto the H6086
37 of all manner of t, of wine and of oil, H6086
Job 40:21 He lieth under the shady t, in the covert H6628
22 The shady t cover him *with* their H6628
Ps 74: 5 he had lifted up axes upon the thick t. H6086
78:47 hail, and their sycomore t with frost. H8256
96:12 then shall all the t of the wood rejoice H6086
104:16 The t of the LORD are full *of sap*; the H6086
17 *as for* the stork, the fir t *are* her house. H1265
105:33 He smote their vines also and their fig t; H8384
33 fig trees; and brake the t of their coasts. H6086
148: 9 Mountains, and all hills; fruitful t, and H6086
Ecc 2: 5 I planted t in them of all *kind of* fruits: H6086
6 the wood that bringeth forth t: H6086
Song 2: 3 As the apple tree among the t of the H6086
4:14 with all t of frankincense; myrrh H6086
Isa 7: 2 t of the wood are moved with the wind. H6086
10:19 And the rest of the t of his forest shall H6086
14: 8 Yea, the fir t rejoice at thee, *and* the H1265
37:24 *and* the choice fir t thereof: and I will H1265
44:14 for himself among the t of the forest: he H6086
55:12 the t of the field shall clap *their* hands. H6086
61: 3 might be called t of righteousness, the H352
Jer 5:17 thy vines and thy fig t: they shall H8384
6: 6 said, Hew ye down t, and cast a mount H6097
7:20 and upon the t of the field, and upon H6086
17: 2 by the green t upon the high hills. H6086
Ezk 15: 2 which is among the t of the forest? H6086
6 tree among the t of the forest, which H6086
17:24 And all the t of the field shall know that H6086
20:28 hill, and all the thick t, and they offered H6086
27: 5 *ship* boards of fir t of Senir: they have H1265
31: 4 little rivers unto all the t of the field. H6086
5 above all the t of the field, and his H6086
8 not hide him: the fir t were not like his H1265
8 and the chesnut t were not like his H6196
9 so that all the t of Eden, that *were* in H6086
14 To the end that none of all the t by the H6086
14 neither their t stand up in their height, H352
15 and all the t of the field fainted for him. H6086
16 the pit: and all the t of Eden, the choice H6086
18 among the t of Eden? yet shalt thou H6086
18 down with the t of Eden unto the H6086
40:16 and upon *each* post *were* palm t. H8561
22 arches, and their palm t, *were* after the H8561
26 and it had palm t, one on this side, and H8561
31 court; and palm t *were* upon the posts H8561
34 court; and palm t *were* upon the posts H8561
37 court; and palm t *were* upon the posts H8561
41:18 and palm t, so that a palm tree *was* H8561
20 t made, and *on* the wall of the temple. H8561
25 and palm t, like as *were* made upon H8561
26 and palm t on the one side and H8561
47: 7 t on the one side and on the other. H6086
12 side, shall grow all t for meat, whose H6086
Hos 2:12 her vines and her fig t, whereof she hath H8384
Joel 1:12 apple tree, *even* all the t of the field, are H6086
19 flame hath burned all the t of the field. H6086
Am 4: 9 and your fig t and your olive trees H8384
9 trees and your olive t increased, the H2132
Nah 2: 3 and the fir t shall be terribly shaken. H1265
3:12 All thy strong holds *shall be like* fig t H8384
Zec 1: 8 among the myrtle t that *were* in the H1918

Zec 1:10 among the myrtle **t** answered and said, H1918
11 among the myrtle **t**, and said, We have H1918
4: 3 And two olive **t** by it, one upon the H2132
11 *are* these two olive **t** upon the right *side* H2132
Mt 3:10 the root of the **t**: therefore every tree *G1186*
21: 8 the **t**, and strawed *them* in the way. *G1186*
Mk 8:24 up, and said, I see men as **t**, walking. *G1186*
11: 8 off the **t**, and strawed *them* in the way. *G1186*
Lk 3: 9 the root of the **t**: every tree therefore *G1186*
21:29 Behold the fig tree, and all the **t**; *G1186*
Jn 12:13 Took branches of palm **t**, and went *G5404*
Jude 12 about of winds; **t** whose fruit withereth, *G1186*
Rev 7: 3 the sea, nor the **t**, till we have sealed the *G1186*
8: 7 the third part of **t** was burnt up, and all *G1186*
11: 4 These are the two olive **t**, and the two *G1636*

TREMBLE

Dt 2:25 **t**, and be in anguish because of thee. H7264
20: 3 not, and do not **t**, neither be ye terrified H2648
Ezr 10: 3 lord, and of those that **t** at the H2730
Job 9: 6 of her place, and the pillars thereof **t**. H6426
26:11 The pillars of heaven **t** and are H7322
Ps 60: 2 Thou hast made the earth to **t**; thou H7493
99: 1 The LORD reigneth; let the people **t**: he H7264
114: 7 **T**, thou earth, at the presence of the H2342
Ecc 12: 3 of the house shall **t**, and the strong men H2111
Isa 5:25 and the hills did **t**, and their carcases H7264
14:16 the earth to **t**, that did shake kingdoms; H7264
32:11 **T**, ye women that are at ease; be H2729
64: 2 *that* the nations may **t** at thy presence! H7264
66: 5 Hear the word of the LORD, ye that **t** at H2730
Jer 5:22 the LORD: will ye not **t** at my presence, H2342
10:10 the earth shall **t**, and the nations shall H7493
33: 9 and they shall fear and **t** for all the H7264
51:29 And the land shall **t** and sorrow: for H7493
Ezk 26:16 ground, and shall **t** at *every* moment, H2729
18 Now shall the isles **t** in the day of thy H2729
32:10 and they shall **t** at *every* moment, every H2729
Dan 6:26 my kingdom men **t** and fear before the H2112
Hos 11:10 then the children shall **t** from the west. H2729
11 They shall **t** as a bird out of Egypt, and H2729
Joel 2: 1 of the land **t**: for the day of the LORD H7264
10 the heavens shall **t**: the sun and the H7493
Am 8: 8 Shall not the land **t** for this, and every H7264
Hab 3: 7 the curtains of the land of Midian did **t**. H7264
Jas 2:19 doest well: the devils also believe, and **t**. *G5425*

TREMBLED

Gen 27:33 And Isaac **t** very exceedingly, and said, H2729
Ex 19:16 all the people that *was* in the camp **t**. H2729
Jdg 5: 4 of Edom, the earth **t**, and the heavens H7493
1Sa 4:13 for his heart **t** for the ark of God. And H2730
14:15 the spoilers, they also **t**, and the earth H2729
16: 4 elders of the town **t** at his coming, and H2729
28: 5 he was afraid, and his heart greatly **t**. H2729
2Sa 22: 8 Then the earth shook and **t**; the H7493
Ezr 9: 4 me every one that **t** at the words of the H2730
Ps 18: 7 Then the earth shook and **t**; the H7493
77:18 the world: the earth **t** and shook. H7264
97: 4 the world: the earth saw, and **t**. H2342
Jer 4:24 I beheld the mountains, and, lo, they **t**, H7493
8:16 the whole land **t** at the sound of the H7493
Dan 5:19 and languages, **t** and feared before H2112
Hab 3:10 The mountains saw thee, *and* they **t**: the H2342
16 When I heard, my belly **t**; my lips H7264
16 into my bones, and I **t** in myself, that I H7264
Mk 16: 8 sepulchre; for they **t** and were amazed: *G2192*
Act 7:32 Then Moses **t**, and durst not behold. *G1096*
24:25 to come, Felix **t**, and answered, Go thy *G1096*

TREMBLETH

Job 37: 1 At this also my heart **t**, and is moved H2729
Ps 104:32 He looketh on the earth, and it **t**: he H7460
119:120 My flesh **t** for fear of thee; and I am H5568
Isa 66: 2 of a contrite spirit, and **t** at my word. H2730

TREMBLING

Ex 15:15 men of Moab, **t** shall take hold upon H7461
Dt 28:65 give thee there a **t** heart, and failing of H7268
1Sa 13: 7 and all the people followed him **t**. H2729
14:15 And there was **t** in the host, in the field, H2731
15 earth quaked: so it was a very great **t**. H2731
Ezr 10: 9 of the house of God, **t** because of *this* H7460
Job 4:14 Fear came upon me, and **t**, which made H7461
21: 6 afraid, and **t** taketh hold on my flesh. H6427
Ps 2:11 the LORD with fear, and rejoice with **t**. H7461
55: 5 Fearfulness and **t** are come upon me, H7461
Isa 51:17 of the cup of **t**, *and* wrung *them* out. H8653
22 hand the cup of **t**, *even* the dregs of the H8653
Jer 30: 5 a voice of **t**, of fear, and not of peace. H2731
Ezk 12:18 thy water with **t** and with carefulness; H7269
26:16 themselves with **t**; they shall sit upon H2731
Dan 10:11 spoken this word unto me, I stood **t**. H7460
Hos 13: 1 When Ephraim spake **t**, he exalted H7578
Zec 12: 2 Jerusalem a cup of **t** unto all the people H7478
Mk 5:33 But the woman fearing and **t**, knowing *G5141*
Lk 8:47 not hid, she came **t**, and falling down *G5141*
Act 9: 6 And he **t** and astonished said, Lord, *G5141*
16:29 **t**, and fell down before Paul and Silas, *G1790*
1Co 2: 3 in weakness, and in fear, and in much **t**. *G5156*
2Co 7:15 how with fear and **t** ye received him. *G5156*
Eph 6: 5 with fear and **t**, in singleness of your *G5156*
Php 2:12 out your own salvation with fear and **t**. *G5156*

TRENCH

1Sa 17:20 he came to the **t**, as the host was going H4570
26: 5 and Saul lay in the **t**, and the people H4570
7 within the **t**, and his spear stuck H4570
2Sa 20:15 and it stood in the **t**: and all the people H2426
1Ki 18:32 and he made a **t** about the altar, as H8585
35 and he filled the **t** also with water. H8585
38 licked up the water that *was* in the **t**. H8585
Lk 19:43 shall cast a **t** about thee, and compass *G5482*

TRESPASS

Gen 31:36 What *is* my **t**? what *is* my sin, that H6588
50:17 I pray thee now, the **t** of thy brethren, H6588
17 thee, forgive the **t** of the servants of the H6588
Ex 22: 9 For all manner of **t**, *whether it be* for ox, H6588
Lev 5: 6 And he shall bring his **t** offering unto the H817
7 he shall bring for his **t**, which he hath H817
15 If a soul commit a **t**, and sin through H4604
15 he shall bring for his **t** unto the LORD a H817
15 shekel of the sanctuary, for a **t** offering: H817
16 **t** offering, and it shall be forgiven him. H817
18 thy estimation, for a **t** offering, unto the H817
19 It *is* a **t** offering: he hath certainly H817
6: 2 If a soul sin, and commit a **t** against H4604
5 appertaineth, in the day of his **t** offering. H819
6 And he shall bring his **t** offering unto the H817
6 for a **t** offering, unto the priest: H817
17 *is* the sin offering, and as the **t** offering. H817
7: 1 Likewise this *is* the law of the **t** offering: H817
2 shall they kill the **t** offering: and the H817
5 by fire unto the LORD: it *is* a **t** offering. H817
7 As the sin offering *is*, so *is* the **t** offering: H817
37 offering, and of the **t** offering, and of the H817
14:12 and offer him for a **t** offering, and the log H817
13 *so is* the **t** offering: it *is* most holy: H817
14 of the blood of the **t** offering, and the H817
17 foot, upon the blood of the **t** offering: H817
21 shall take one lamb *for* a **t** offering to be H817
24 the lamb of the **t** offering, and the log H817
25 And he shall kill the lamb of the **t** H817
25 of the blood of the **t** offering, and put *it* H817
28 the place of the blood of the **t** offering: H817
19:21 And he shall bring his **t** offering unto the H817
21 *even* a ram for a **t** offering. H817
22 with the ram of the **t** offering before the H817
22:16 Or suffer them to bear the iniquity of **t**, H819
26:40 their fathers, with their **t** which they H4604
Nu 5: 6 commit, to do a **t** against the LORD, H4604
7 shall recompense his **t** with the principal H817
8 to recompense the **t** unto, let the H817
8 unto, let the **t** be recompensed unto H817
12 go aside, and commit a **t** against him, H4604
27 and have done **t** against her husband, H4604
6:12 of the first year for a **t** offering: but the H817
18: 9 of theirs, and every **t** offering of theirs, H817
31:16 to commit **t** against the LORD in H4604
Jos 7: 1 But the children of Israel committed a **t** H4604
22:16 of the LORD, What **t** *is* this that ye have H4604
20 of Zerah commit a **t** in the accursed H4604
31 not committed this **t** against the LORD: H4604
1Sa 6: 3 any wise return him a **t** offering: then ye H817
4 Then said they, What *shall be* the **t** H817
8 ye return him *for* a **t** offering, in a coffer H817
17 returned *for* a **t** offering unto the LORD; H817
25:28 I pray thee, forgive the **t** of thine H6588
1Ki 8:31 If any man **t** against his neighbour, H2398
2Ki 12:16 The **t** money and sin money was not H817
1Ch 21: 3 why will he be a cause of **t** to Israel? H819
2Ch 19:10 them that they **t** not against the LORD, H816
10 your brethren: this do, and ye shall not **t**. H816
24:18 Judah and Jerusalem for this their **t**. H819
28:13 our sins and to our **t**: for our trespass is H819
13 trespass: for our **t** is great, and *there is* H819
22 And in the time of his distress did he **t** H4603
2Ch 33:19 and all his sin, and his **t**, and the places H4604
Ezr 9: 2 and rulers hath been chief in this **t**. H4604
6 and our **t** is grown up unto the heavens. H819
7 we *been* in a great **t** unto this day; and H819
13 and for our great **t**, seeing that thou our H819
10:10 strange wives, to increase the **t** of Israel. H819
19 *they offered* a ram of the flock for their **t**. H819
Ezk 15: 8 committed a **t**, saith the Lord GOD. H4604
17:20 **t** that he hath trespassed against me. H4604
18:24 be mentioned: in his **t** that he hath H4604
20:27 they have committed a **t** against me. H4604
40:39 and the sin offering and the **t** offering. H817
42:13 and the **t** offering; for the place *is* holy. H817
44:29 sin offering, and the **t** offering; and every H817
46:20 shall boil the **t** offering and the sin H817
Dan 9: 7 them, because of their **t** that they have H4604
Mt 18:15 Moreover if thy brother shall **t** against *G264*
Lk 17: 3 Take heed to yourselves: If thy brother **t** *G264*
4 And if he **t** against thee seven times in a *G264*

TRESPASSED

Lev 5:19 he hath certainly **t** against the LORD. H816
26:40 which they **t** against me, and that H4603
Nu 5: 7 give *it* unto *him* against whom he hath **t**. H816
Dt 32:51 Because ye **t** against me among the H4603
2Ch 26:18 for thou hast **t**; neither *shall it be* for H4603
29: 6 For our fathers have **t**, and done *that* H4603
30: 7 brethren, which **t** against the LORD H4603
33:23 himself; but Amon **t** more and more. H819
Ezr 10: 2 Ezra, We have **t** against our God, and H4603
Ezk 17:20 his trespass that he hath **t** against me. H4603
18:24 that he hath **t**, and in his sin that he H4603
39:23 because they **t** against me, therefore H4603
26 whereby they have **t** against me, when H4603
Dan 9: 7 trespass that they have **t** against thee. H4603
Hos 8: 1 my covenant, and **t** against my law. H6586

TRESPASSES

Ezr 9:15 before thee in our **t**: for we cannot stand H819
Ps 68:21 of such an one as goeth on still in his **t**. H817
Ezk 39:26 and all their **t** whereby they have H4604
Mt 6:14 For if ye forgive men their **t**, your *G3900*
15 But if ye forgive not men their **t**, neither *G3900*
15 neither will your Father forgive your **t**. *G3900*
18:35 forgive not every one his brother their **t**. *G3900*
Mk 11:25 is in heaven may forgive you your **t**. *G3900*
26 which is in heaven forgive your **t**. *G3900*
2Co 5:19 not imputing their **t** unto them; and *G3900*
Eph 2: 1 who were dead in **t** and sins; *G3900*
Col 2:13 with him, having forgiven you all **t**; *G3900*

TRESPASSING

Lev 6: 7 of all that he hath done in **t** therein. H819
Ezk 14:13 against me by **t** grievously, then will H4603

TRESPASS-OFFERING See TRESPASS and OFFERING.

TRIAL

Job 9:23 he will laugh at the **t** of the innocent. H4531
Ezk 21:13 Because *it is* a **t**, and what if *the sword* H974
2Co 8: 2 How that in a great **t** of affliction the *G1382*
Heb 11:36 And others had **t** of *cruel* mockings *G3984*
1Pt 1: 7 That the **t** of your faith, being much *G1383*
4:12 the fiery **t** which is to try you, *G4451*

TRIBE

Ex 31: 2 of Uri, the son of Hur, of the **t** of Judah: H4294
6 Ahisamach, of the **t** of Dan: and in the H4294
35:30 of Uri, the son of Hur, of the **t** of Judah; H4294
34 the son of Ahisamach, of the **t** of Dan. H4294
38:22 son of Hur, of the **t** of Judah, made all H4294
23 of Ahisamach, of the **t** of Dan, an H4294
Lev 24:11 the daughter of Dibri, of the **t** of Dan:) H4294
Nu 1: 4 be a man of every **t**; every one head of H4294
5 *t of* Reuben; Elizur the son of Shedeur.
21 of them, *even* of the **t** of Reuben, *were* H4294
23 of them, *even* of the **t** of Simeon, *were* H4294
25 of them, *even* of the **t** of Gad, *were* forty H4294
27 of them, *even* of the **t** of Judah, *were* H4294
29 of them, *even* of the **t** of Issachar, *were* H4294
31 of them, *even* of the **t** of Zebulun, *were* H4294
33 of them, *even* of the **t** of Ephraim, *were* H4294
35 them, *even* of the **t** of Manasseh, *were* H4294
37 them, *even* of the **t** of Benjamin, *were* H4294
39 of them, *even* of the **t** of Dan, *were* H4294
41 them, *even* of the **t** of Asher, *were* forty H4294
43 of them, *even* of the **t** of Naphtali, *were* H4294
47 But the Levites after the **t** of their H4294
49 Only thou shalt not number the **t** of H4294

Nu 2: 5 unto him *shall be* the **t** of Issachar: and H4294
7 *Then* the **t** of Zebulun: and Eliab the H4294
12 by him *shall be* the **t** of Simeon: and the H4294
14 Then the **t** of Gad: and the captain of H4294
20 And by him *shall be* the **t** of Manasseh: H4294
22 Then the **t** of Benjamin: and the H4294
27 by him *shall be* the **t** of Asher: and the H4294
29 Then the **t** of Naphtali: and the captain H4294
3: 6 Bring the **t** of Levi near, and present H4294
4:18 Cut ye not off the **t** of the families of the H7626
7:12 son of Amminadab, of the **t** of Judah: H4294
10:15 And over the host of the **t** of the H4294
16 And over the host of the **t** of the H4294
19 And over the host of the **t** of the H4294
20 And over the host of the **t** of the H4294
23 And over the host of the **t** of the H4294
24 And over the host of the **t** of the H4294
26 And over the host of the **t** of the H4294
27 And over the host of the **t** of the H4294
13: 2 of Israel: of every **t** of their fathers shall H4294
4 And these *were* their names: of the **t** of H4294
5 Of the **t** of Simeon, Shaphat the son of H4294
6 Of the **t** of Judah, Caleb the son of H4294
7 Of the **t** of Issachar, Igal the son of H4294
8 Of the **t** of Ephraim, Oshea the son of H4294
9 Of the **t** of Benjamin, Palti the son of H4294
10 Of the **t** of Zebulun, Gaddiel the son of H4294
11 Of the **t** of Joseph, *namely,* of the tribe H4294
11 Of the tribe of Joseph, *namely,* of the **t** H4294
12 Of the **t** of Dan, Ammiel the son of H4294
13 Of the **t** of Asher, Sethur the son of H4294
14 Of the **t** of Naphtali, Nahbi the son of H4294
15 Of the **t** of Gad, Geuel the son of Machi. H4294
18: 2 And thy brethren also of the **t** of Levi, H4294
2 tribe of Levi, the **t** of thy father, bring H7626
31: 4 Of every **t** a thousand, H4294+H4294
5 *every* **t**, twelve thousand armed for war. H4294
6 thousand of *every* **t**, them and Phinehas H4294
32:33 and unto half the **t** of Manasseh the H7626
34:13 unto the nine tribes, and to the half **t**: H4294
14 For the **t** of the children of Reuben H4294
14 fathers, and the **t** of the children of Gad H4294
14 and half the **t** of Manasseh have H4294
15 The two tribes and the half **t** have H4294
18 And ye shall take one prince of every **t**, H4294
19 **t** of Judah, Caleb the son of Jephunneh. H4294
20 And of the **t** of the children of Simeon, H4294
21 Of the **t** of Benjamin, Elidad the son of H4294
22 And the prince of the **t** of the children H4294
23 of Joseph, for the **t** of the children of H4294
24 And the prince of the **t** of the children H4294
25 And the prince of the **t** of the children H4294
26 And the prince of the **t** of the children H4294
27 And the prince of the **t** of the children H4294
28 And the prince of the **t** of the children H4294
36: 3 inheritance of the **t** whereunto they are H4294
4 inheritance of the **t** whereunto they are H4294
4 the inheritance of the **t** of our fathers. H4294
5 **t** of the sons of Joseph hath said well. H4294
6 of the **t** of their father shall they marry. H4294
7 remove from **t** to tribe: for every one H4294
7 from tribe to **t**: for every one of the H4294
7 to the inheritance of the **t** of his fathers. H4294
8 inheritance in any **t** of the children of H4294
8 of the family of the **t** of her father, that H4294
9 remove from *one* **t** to another tribe; but H4294
9 tribe to another **t**; but every one of the H4294
12 in the **t** of the family of their father. H4294
Dt 1:23 twelve men of you, one of a **t**: H376+H7626
3:13 I unto the half **t** of Manasseh; all the H7626
10: 8 At that time the LORD separated the **t** H7626
18: 1 The priests the Levites, *and* all the **t** of H7626
29: 8 Gadites, and to the half **t** of Manasseh. H7626
18 or family, or **t**, whose heart turneth H7626
Jos 1:12 **t** of Manasseh, spake Joshua, saying, H7626
3:12 tribes of Israel, out of every **t** a man. H7626
4: 2 out of the people, out of every **t** a man, H7626
4 children of Israel, out of every **t** a man: H7626
12 of Gad, and half the **t** of Manasseh, H7626
7: 1 of Zerah, of the **t** of Judah, took of the H4294
14 it shall be, *that* the **t** which the LORD H7626
16 tribes; and the **t** of Judah was taken: H7626
18 of Zerah, of the **t** of Judah, was taken. H4294
12: 6 Gadites, and the half **t** of Manasseh. H7626
13: 7 nine tribes, and the half **t** of Manasseh, H7626
14 Only unto the **t** of Levi he gave none H7626
15 And Moses gave unto the **t** of the H4294
24 And Moses gave *inheritance* unto the **t** H4294
29 unto the half **t** of Manasseh: and *this* H7626
Jos 13:29 of the half **t** of the children of H4294
33 But unto the **t** of Levi Moses gave not H7626
14: 2 for the nine tribes, and *for* the half **t**. H4294
3 tribes and an half **t** on the other side H4294
15: 1 *This* then was the lot of the **t** of the H4294
20 This *is* the inheritance of the **t** of the H4294
21 And the uttermost cities of the **t** of the H4294
16: 8 inheritance of the **t** of the children of H4294
17: 1 There was also a lot for the **t** of H4294
18: 4 three men for *each* **t**: and I will send H7626
7 and half the **t** of Manasseh, have H7626
11 And the lot of the **t** of the children of H4294
21 Now the cities of the **t** of the children of H4294
19: 1 *even* for the **t** of the children of Simeon H4294
8 inheritance of the **t** of the children of H4294
23 This *is* the inheritance of the **t** of the H4294
24 And the fifth lot came out for the **t** of H4294
31 This *is* the inheritance of the **t** of the H4294
39 This *is* the inheritance of the **t** of the H4294
40 *And* the seventh lot came out for the **t** H4294
48 This *is* the inheritance of the **t** of the H4294
20: 8 the plain out of the **t** of Reuben, and H4294
8 Gilead out of the **t** of Gad, and Golan in H4294
8 in Bashan out of the **t** of Manasseh. H4294
21: 4 by lot out of the **t** of Judah, and out of H4294
4 and out of the **t** of Simeon, and out H4294
4 out of the **t** of Benjamin, thirteen cities. H4294
5 of the families of the **t** of Ephraim, and H4294
5 and out of the **t** of Dan, and out of the H4294
5 out of the half **t** of Manasseh, ten cities. H4294
6 of the families of the **t** of Issachar, and H4294
6 and out of the **t** of Asher, and out of H4294
6 and out of the **t** of Naphtali, and out H4294
6 and out of the half **t** of Manasseh in H4294
7 *had* out of the **t** of Reuben, and out H4294
7 and out of the **t** of Gad, and out of the H4294
7 out of the **t** of Zebulun, twelve cities. H4294
9 And they gave out of the **t** of the H4294
9 and out of the **t** of the children of H4294
17 And out of the **t** of Benjamin, Gibeon H4294
20 of their lot out of the **t** of Ephraim. H4294
23 And out of the **t** of Dan, Eltekeh with H4294
25 And out of the half **t** of Manasseh, H4294
27 out of the *other* half **t** of Manasseh *they* H4294
28 And out of the **t** of Issachar, Kishon H4294
30 And out of the **t** of Asher, Mishal with H4294
32 And out of the **t** of Naphtali, Kedesh in H4294
34 the Levites, out of the **t** of Zebulun, H4294
36 And out of the **t** of Reuben, Bezer with H4294
38 And out of the **t** of Gad, Ramoth in H4294
22: 1 Gadites, and the half **t** of Manasseh, H4294
7 Now to the *one* half of the **t** of H7626
9 of Gad and the half **t** of Manasseh H7626
10 of Gad and the half **t** of Manasseh built H7626
11 of Gad and the half **t** of Manasseh have H7626
13 and to the half **t** of Manasseh, into the H7626
15 and to the half **t** of Manasseh, unto the H7626
21 of Gad and the half **t** of Manasseh H7626
Jdg 18: 1 and in those days the **t** of the Danites H7626
19 a priest unto a **t** and a family in Israel? H7626
30 were priests to the **t** of Dan until the H7626
20:12 through all the **t** of Benjamin, saying, H7626
21: 3 should be to day one **t** lacking in Israel? H7626
6 is one **t** cut off from Israel this day. H7626
17 that a **t** be not destroyed out of Israel. H7626
24 every man to his **t** and to his family, H7626
1Sa 9:21 all the families of the **t** of Benjamin? H7626
10:20 near, the **t** of Benjamin was taken. H7626
21 When he had caused the **t** of Benjamin H7626
1Ki 7:14 He *was* a widow's son of the **t** of H4294
11:13 *but* will give one **t** to thy son for David H7626
32 (But he shall have one **t** for my servant H7626
36 And unto his son will I give one **t**, that H7626
12:20 house of David, but the **t** of Judah only. H7626
21 of Judah, with the **t** of Benjamin, an H7626
2Ki 17:18 was none left but the **t** of Judah only. H7626
1Ch 5:18 and half the **t** of Manasseh, of valiant H7626
23 And the children of the half **t** of H7626
26 and the half **t** of Manasseh, and H7626
6:60 And out of the **t** of Benjamin; Geba H4294
61 the family of that **t**, *were cities given* out H4294
61 out of the half **t**, *namely, out of* the half H4294
61 half *t* of Manasseh, by lot, ten cities. H4294
62 families out of the **t** of Issachar, and H4294
62 and out of the **t** of Asher, and out of H4294
62 and out of the **t** of Naphtali, and out H4294
62 and out of the **t** of Manasseh in H4294
63 families, out of the **t** of Reuben, and H4294
63 and out of the **t** of Gad, and out of the H4294
1Ch 6:63 out of the **t** of Zebulun, twelve cities. H4294
65 And they gave by lot out of the **t** of the H4294
65 and out of the **t** of the children of H4294
65 and out of the **t** of the children of H4294
66 of their coasts out of the **t** of Ephraim. H4294
70 And out of the half **t** of Manasseh; Aner H4294
71 family of the half **t** of Manasseh, Golan H4294
72 And out of the **t** of Issachar; Kedesh H4294
74 And out of the **t** of Asher; Mashal with H4294
76 And out of the **t** of Naphtali; Kedesh in H4294
77 *given* out of the **t** of Zebulun, Rimmon H4294
78 *them* out of the **t** of Reuben, Bezer in H4294
80 And out of the **t** of Gad; Ramoth in H4294
12:31 And of the half **t** of Manasseh eighteen H4294
37 and of the half **t** of Manasseh, with all H7626
23:14 his sons were named of the **t** of Levi. H7626
26:32 and the half **t** of Manasseh, for every H7626
27:20 **t** of Manasseh, Joel the son of Pedaiah: H7626
21 Of the half *t* of Manasseh in Gilead, Iddo
Ps 78:67 Joseph, and chose not the **t** of Ephraim: H7626
68 But chose the **t** of Judah, the mount H7626
Ezk 47:23 to pass, *that* in what **t** the stranger H7626
Lk 2:36 of Phanuel, of the **t** of Aser: she was of *G5443*
Act 13:21 Cis, a man of the **t** of Benjamin, by the *G5443*
Ro 11: 1 seed of Abraham, *of* the **t** of Benjamin. *G5443*
Php 3: 5 stock of Israel, *of* the **t** of Benjamin, an *G5443*
Heb 7:13 to another **t**, of which no man gave *G5443*
14 out of Juda; of which **t** Moses spake *G5443*
Rev 5: 5 the Lion of the **t** of Juda, the Root of *G5443*
7: 5 Of the **t** of Juda *were* sealed twelve *G5443*
5 thousand. Of the **t** of Reuben *were* *G5443*
5 **t** of Gad *were* sealed twelve thousand. *G5443*
6 Of the **t** of Aser *were* sealed twelve *G5443*
6 thousand. Of the **t** of Nepthalim *were* *G5443*
6 thousand. Of the **t** of Manasses *were* *G5443*
7 Of the **t** of Simeon *were* sealed twelve *G5443*
7 thousand. Of the **t** of Levi *were* sealed *G5443*
7 thousand. Of the **t** of Issachar *were* *G5443*
8 Of the **t** of Zabulon *were* sealed twelve *G5443*
8 thousand. Of the **t** of Joseph *were* *G5443*
8 thousand. Of the **t** of Benjamin *were* *G5443*

TRIBES

Gen 49:16 his people, as one of the **t** of Israel. H7626
28 All these *are* the twelve **t** of Israel: and H7626
Ex 24: 4 according to the twelve **t** of Israel. H7626
28:21 shall they be according to the twelve **t**. H7626
39:14 his name, according to the twelve **t**. H7626
Nu 1:16 princes of the **t** of their fathers, heads H4294
7: 2 the princes of the **t**, and were over them H4294
24: 2 **t**; and the spirit of God came upon him. H7626
26:55 the **t** of their fathers they shall inherit. H4294
30: 1 unto the heads of the **t** concerning the H4294
31: 4 the **t** of Israel, shall ye send to the war. H4294
32:28 fathers of the **t** of the children of Israel: H4294
33:54 to the **t** of your fathers ye shall inherit. H4294
34:13 unto the nine **t**, and to the half tribe: H4294
15 The two **t** and the half tribe have H4294
36: 3 the sons of the *other* **t** of the children of H7626
9 but every one of the **t** of the children of H4294
Dt 1:13 **t**, and I will make them rulers over you. H7626
15 So I took the chief of your **t**, wise men, H7626
15 over tens, and officers among your **t**. H7626
5:23 all the heads of your **t**, and your elders; H7626
12: 5 out of all your **t** to put his name there, H7626
14 in one of thy **t**, there thou shalt offer H7626
16:18 throughout thy **t**: and they shall judge H7626
18: 5 him out of all thy **t**, to stand to minister H7626
29:10 captains of your **t**, your elders, and your H7626
21 evil out of all the **t** of Israel, according H7626
31:28 Gather unto me all the elders of your **t**, H7626
33: 5 the **t** of Israel were gathered together. H7626
Jos 3:12 the **t** of Israel, out of every tribe a man. H7626
4: 5 of the **t** of the children of Israel: H7626
8 to the number of the **t** of the children of H7626
7:14 according to your **t**: and it shall be, *that* H7626
16 **t**; and the tribe of Judah was taken: H7626
11:23 their **t**. And the land rested from war. H7626
12: 7 Joshua gave unto the **t** of Israel *for* a H7626
13: 7 nine **t**, and the half tribe of Manasseh, H7626
14: 1 of the fathers of the **t** of the children of H4294
2 for the nine **t**, and *for* the half tribe. H4294
3 inheritance of two **t** and an half tribe H4294
4 For the children of Joseph were two **t**, H4294
18: 2 of Israel seven **t**, which had not yet H7626
19:51 of the fathers of the **t** of the children of H4294
21: 1 fathers of the **t** of the children of Israel; H4294
16 suburbs; nine cities out of those two **t**. H7626
22:14 throughout all the **t** of Israel; and each H4294

Jos 23: 4 for your **t**, from Jordan, with all H7626
24: 1 And Joshua gathered all the **t** of Israel H7626
Jdg 18: 1 fallen unto them among the **t** of Israel. H7626
20: 2 *even* of all the **t** of Israel, presented H7626
10 throughout all the **t** of Israel, and an H7626
12 And the **t** of Israel sent men through all H7626
21: 5 among all the **t** of Israel that came not H7626
8 one *is there* of the **t** of Israel that came H7626
15 had made a breach in the **t** of Israel. H7626
1Sa 2:28 And did I choose him out of all the **t** of H7626
9:21 the smallest of the **t** of Israel? and my H7626
10:19 by your **t**, and by your thousands. H7626
20 And when Samuel had caused all the **t** H7626
15:17 the head of the **t** of Israel, and the H7626
2Sa 5: 1 Then came all the **t** of Israel to David H7626
7: 7 word with any of the **t** of Israel, whom I H7626
15: 2 Thy servant *is* of one of the **t** of Israel. H7626
10 throughout all the **t** of Israel, saying, H7626
19: 9 throughout all the **t** of Israel, saying, H7626
20:14 And he went through all the **t** of Israel H7626
24: 2 through all the **t** of Israel, from Dan H7626
1Ki 8: 1 all the heads of the **t**, the chief of the H4294
16 city out of all the **t** of Israel to build an H7626
11:31 of Solomon, and will give ten **t** to thee: H7626
32 I have chosen out of all the **t** of Israel:) H7626
35 and will give it unto thee, *even* ten **t**. H7626
14:21 out of all the **t** of Israel, to put his name H7626
18:31 to the number of the **t** of the sons of H7626
2Ki 21: 7 **t** of Israel, will I put my name for ever: H7626
1Ch 27:16 Furthermore over the **t** of Israel: the H7626
22 *were* the princes of the **t** of Israel. H7626
28: 1 the princes of the **t**, and the captains of H7626
29: 6 and princes of the **t** of Israel, and the H7626
2Ch 5: 2 all the heads of the **t**, the chief of the H4294
6: 5 city among all the **t** of Israel to build an H7626
11:16 And after them out of all the **t** of Israel H7626
12:13 out of all the **t** of Israel, to put his name H7626
33: 7 **t** of Israel, will I put my name for ever: H7626
Ezr 6:17 to the number of the **t** of Israel. H7625
Ps 78:55 the **t** of Israel to dwell in their tents. H7626
105:37 not one feeble *person* among their **t**. H7626
122: 4 Whither the **t** go up, the tribes of the H7626
4 Whither the tribes go up, the **t** of the H7626
Isa 19:13 *they that are* the stay of the **t** thereof. H7626
49: 6 to raise up the **t** of Jacob, and to restore H7626
63:17 sake, the **t** of thine inheritance. H7626
Ezk 37:19 Ephraim, and the **t** of Israel his fellows, H7626
45: 8 the house of Israel according to their **t**. H7626
47:13 to the twelve **t** of Israel: Joseph *shall* H7626
21 unto you according to the **t** of Israel. H7626
22 with you among the **t** of Israel. H7626
48: 1 Now these *are* the names of the **t**. From H7626
19 shall serve it out of all the **t** of Israel. H7626
23 As for the rest of the **t**, from the east H7626
29 divide by lot unto the **t** of Israel for H7626
31 the names of the **t** of Israel: three gates H7626
Hos 5: 9 of rebuke: among the **t** of Israel have I H7626
Hab 3: 9 to the oaths of the **t**, *even thy* word. H4294
Zec 9: 1 **t** of Israel, *shall be* toward the LORD. H7626
Mt 19:28 thrones, judging the twelve **t** of Israel. *G5443*
24:30 then shall all the **t** of the earth mourn, *G5443*
Lk 22:30 thrones judging the twelve **t** of Israel. *G5443*
Act 26: 7 Unto which *promise* our twelve **t**, *G1429*
Jas 1: 1 **t** which are scattered abroad, greeting. *G5443*
Rev 7: 4 of all the **t** of the children of Israel. *G5443*
21:12 of the twelve **t** of the children of Israel: *G5443*

TRIBULATION
Dt 4:30 When thou art in **t**, and all these things H6862
Jdg 10:14 them deliver you in the time of your **t**. H6869
1Sa 26:24 and let him deliver me out of all **t**. H6869
Mt 13:21 for a while: for when **t** or persecution *G2347*
24:21 For then shall be great **t**, such as was *G2347*
29 Immediately after the **t** of those days *G2347*
Mk 13:24 But in those days, after that **t**, the sun *G2347*
Jn 16:33 ye shall have **t**: but be of good cheer; *G2347*
Act 14:22 much **t** enter into the kingdom of God. *G2347*
Ro 2: 9 **T** and anguish, upon every soul of man *G2347*
5: 3 also: knowing that **t** worketh patience; *G2347*
8:35 love of Christ? *shall* **t**, or distress, or *G2347*
12:12 Rejoicing in hope; patient in **t**; *G2347*
2Co 1: 4 Who comforteth us in all our **t**, that we *G2347*
7: 4 I am exceeding joyful in all our **t**. *G2347*
1Th 3: 4 **t**; even as it came to pass, and ye know. *G2346*
2Th 1: 6 recompense **t** to them that trouble you; *G2347*
Rev 1: 9 brother, and companion in **t**, and in the *G2347*
2: 9 I know thy works, and **t**, and poverty, *G2347*
10 and ye shall have **t** ten days: be thou *G2347*
22 **t**, except they repent of their deeds. *G2347*
Rev 7:14 came out of great **t**, and have washed *G2347*

TRIBULATIONS
1Sa 10:19 and your **t**; and ye have said unto H6869
Ro 5: 3 And not only *so*, but we glory in **t** also: *G2347*
Eph 3:13 not at my **t** for you, which is your glory. *G2347*
2Th 1: 4 your persecutions and **t** that ye endure: *G2347*

TRIBUTARIES
Dt 20:11 **t** unto thee, and they shall serve thee. H4522
Jdg 1:30 dwelt among them, and became **t**. H4522
33 and of Beth-anath became **t** unto them. H4522
35 Joseph prevailed, so that they became **t**. H4522

TRIBUTARY
Lam 1: 1 the provinces, *how* is she become **t**! H4522

TRIBUTE
Gen 49:15 to bear, and became a servant unto **t**. H4522
Nu 31:28 And levy a **t** unto the LORD of the men H4371
37 And the LORD'S **t** of the sheep was six H4371
38 LORD'S **t** *was* threescore and twelve. H4371
39 the LORD'S **t** *was* threescore and one. H4371
40 LORD'S **t** *was* thirty and two persons. H4371
41 And Moses gave the **t**, *which was* the H4371
Dt 16:10 thy God with a **t** of a freewill offering H4530
Jos 16:10 unto this day, and serve under **t**. H4522
17:13 to **t**; but did not utterly drive them out. H4522
Jdg 1:28 to **t**, and did not utterly drive them out. H4522
2Sa 20:24 And Adoram *was* over the **t**: and H4522
1Ki 4: 6 the son of Abda *was* over the **t**. H4522
9:21 levy a **t** of bondservice unto this day. H4522
12:18 who *was* over the **t**; and all Israel H4522
2Ki 23:33 and put the land to a **t** of an hundred H6066
2Ch 8: 8 Solomon make to pay **t** until this day. H4522
10:18 that *was* over the **t**; and the children of H4522
17:11 presents, and **t** silver; and the Arabians H4853
Ezr 4:13 they not pay toll, **t**, and custom, and *so* H1093
20 toll, **t**, and custom, was paid unto them. H1093
6: 8 goods, *even* of the **t** beyond the river, H4061
7:24 to impose toll, **t**, or custom, upon them. H1093
Neh 5: 4 for the king's **t**, *and that upon* our lands H4060
Est 10: 1 And the king Ahasuerus laid a **t** upon H4522
Prv 12:24 rule: but the slothful shall be under **t**. H4522
Mt 17:24 they that received **t** *money* came to *G1323*
24 and said, Doth not your master pay **t**? *G1323*
25 **t**? of their own children, or of strangers? *G2778*
22:17 it lawful to give **t** unto Caesar, or not? *G2778*
19 Shew me the **t** money. And they *G2778*
Mk 12:14 Is it lawful to give **t** to Caesar, or not? *G2778*
Lk 20:22 Is it lawful for us to give **t** unto Caesar, *G5411*
23: 2 forbidding to give **t** to Caesar, saying *G5411*
Ro 13: 6 For for this cause pay ye **t** also: for they *G5411*
7 Render therefore to all their dues: **t** to *G5411*
7 tribute to whom **t** *is due*; custom to *G5411*

TRICKLETH
Lam 3:49 Mine eye **t** down, and ceaseth not, H5064

TRIED
Dt 21: 5 every controversy and every stroke be **t**:
2Sa 22:31 of the LORD *is* **t**: he *is* a buckler to all H6884
Job 23:10 he hath **t** me, I shall come forth as gold. H974
34:36 My desire *is that* Job may be **t** unto the H974
Ps 12: 6 words: *as* silver **t** in a furnace of earth, H6884
17: 3 night; thou hast **t** me, *and* shalt find H6884
18:30 of the LORD is **t**: he *is* a buckler to all H6884
66:10 us: thou hast **t** us, as silver is tried. H6884
10 us: thou hast tried us, as silver is **t**. H6884
105:19 came: the word of the LORD **t** him. H6884
Isa 28:16 a stone, a **t** stone, a precious corner H976
Jer 12: 3 hast seen me, and **t** mine heart toward H974
Dan 12:10 made white, and **t**; but the wicked shall H6884
Zec 13: 9 try them as gold is **t**: they shall call on my H974
Heb 11:17 By faith Abraham, when he was **t**, *G3985*
Jas 1:12 for when he is **t**, he shall receive the *G1384*
1Pt 1: 7 though it be **t** with fire, might be found *G1381*
Rev 2: 2 evil: and thou hast **t** them which say *G3985*
10 that ye may be **t**; and ye shall have *G3985*
3:18 I counsel thee to buy of me gold **t** in the *G4448*

TRIEST
1Ch 29:17 I know also, my God, that thou **t** the H974
Jer 11:20 righteously, that **t** the reins and the H974
20:12 But, O LORD of hosts, that **t** the H974

TRIETH
Job 34: 3 For the ear **t** words, as the mouth tasteth H974
Ps 7: 9 the righteous God **t** the hearts and reins. H974
Ps 11: 5 The LORD **t** the righteous: but the H974
Prv 17: 3 for gold: but the LORD **t** the hearts. H974
1Th 2: 4 men, but God, which **t** our hearts. *G1381*

TRIMMED
2Sa 19:24 his feet, nor **t** his beard, nor washed H6213
Mt 25: 7 Then all those virgins arose, and **t** their *G2885*

TRIMMEST
Jer 2:33 Why **t** thou thy way to seek love? H3190

TRIUMPH
2Sa 1:20 the daughters of the uncircumcised **t**. H5937
Ps 25: 2 let not mine enemies **t** over me. H5970
41:11 mine enemy doth not **t** over me. H7321
47: 1 shout unto God with the voice of **t**. H7440
60: 8 shoe: Philistia, **t** thou because of me. H7321
92: 4 work: I will **t** in the works of thy hands. H7442
94: 3 the wicked, how long shall the wicked **t**? H5937
106:47 thy holy name, *and* to **t** in thy praise. H7623
108: 9 I cast out my shoe; over Philistia will I **t**. H7321
2Co 2:14 causeth us to **t** in Christ, and maketh *G2358*

TRIUMPHED
Ex 15: 1 the LORD, for he hath **t** gloriously: the H1342
21 the LORD, for he hath **t** gloriously; the H1342

TRIUMPHING
Job 20: 5 That the **t** of the wicked *is* short, and H7445
Col 2:15 shew of them openly, **t** over them in it. *G2358*

TROAS
Act 16: 8 they passing by Mysia came down to **T**. *G5174*
11 Therefore loosing from **T**, we came with *G5174*
20: 5 These going before tarried for us at **T**. *G5174*
6 unto them to **T** in five days; where *G5174*
2Co 2:12 Furthermore, when I came to **T** to *G5174*
2Ti 4:13 The cloak that I left at **T** with Carpus, *G5174*

TROD See TRODDEN and TRODE.

TRODDEN
Dt 1:36 the land that he hath **t** upon, and to his H1869
Jos 14: 9 whereon thy feet have **t** shall be thine H1869
Jdg 5:21 O my soul, thou hast **t** down strength. H1869
Job 22:15 the old way which wicked men have **t**? H1869
28: 8 The lion's whelps have not **t** it, nor the H1869
Ps119:118 Thou hast **t** down all them that err H5541
Isa 5: 5 the wall thereof, and it shall be **t** down: H4823
14:19 of the pit; as a carcase **t** under feet. H947
18: 2 meted out and **t** down, whose land the H4001
7 meted out and **t** under foot, whose land H4001
25:10 and Moab shall be **t** down under him, H1758
10 as straw is **t** down for the dunghill. H1758
28: 3 of Ephraim, shall be **t** under feet: H7429
18 through, then ye shall be **t** down by it. H4823
63: 3 I have **t** the winepress alone; and of the H947
18 adversaries have **t** down thy sanctuary. H947
Jer 12:10 they have **t** my portion under foot, H947
Lam 1:15 The Lord hath **t** under foot all my H5541
15 the Lord hath **t** the virgin, the daughter H1869
Ezk 34:19 that which ye have **t** with your feet; and H4823
Dan 8:13 and the host to be **t** under foot? H4823
Mic 7:10 she be **t** down as the mire of the streets. H4823
Mt 5:13 cast out, and to be **t** under foot of men. *G2662*
Lk 8: 5 side; and it was **t** down, and the fowls *G2662*
21:24 and Jerusalem shall be **t** down of the *G3961*
Heb 10:29 worthy, who hath **t** under foot the Son of *G262*
Rev 14:20 And the winepress was **t** without the *G3961*

TRODE
Jdg 9:27 vineyards, and **t** *the grapes*, and made H1869
20:43 chased them, *and* **t** them down with H1869
2Ki 7:17 and the people **t** upon him in the gate, H7429
20 **t** upon him in the gate, and he died. H7429
9:33 on the horses: and he **t** her under foot. H7429
14: 9 *was* in Lebanon, and **t** down the thistle. H7429
2Ch 25:18 *was* in Lebanon, and **t** down the thistle. H7429
Lk 12: 1 that they **t** one upon another, he *G2662*

TROGYLLIUM
Act 20:15 **T**; and the next *day* we came to Miletus. *G5175*

TROOP
Gen 30:11 And Leah said, A **t** cometh: and she H1409
49:19 Gad, a **t** shall overcome him: but he H1416
1Sa 30: 8 I pursue after this **t**? shall I overtake H1416
2Sa 2:25 one **t**, and stood on the top of an hill. H92
3:22 from *pursuing* a **t**, and brought in a H1416

2Sa 22:30 For by thee I have run through a **t**: by H1416
23:11 together into a **t**, where was a piece of H2416
13 of Adullam: and the **t** of the Philistines H2416
Ps 18:29 For by thee I have run through a **t**; and H1416
Isa 65:11 a table for that **t**, and that furnish the H1409
Jer 18:22 thou shalt bring a **t** suddenly upon H1416
Hos 7: 1 *and* the **t** of robbers spoileth without. H1416
Am 9: 6 hath founded his **t** in the earth; he that H92

TROOPS
Job 6:19 The **t** of Tema looked, the companies of H734
19:12 His **t** come together, and raise up their H1416
Jer 5: 7 themselves by **t** in the harlots' houses.
Hos 6: 9 And as **t** of robbers wait for a man, *so* H1416
Mic 5: 1 Now gather thyself in **t**, O daughter of H1413
1 O daughter of **t**: he hath laid siege H1416
Hab 3:16 the people, he will invade them with his **t**.

TROPHIMUS
Act 20: 4 and of Asia, Tychicus and **T**. *G5161*
21:29 him in the city **T** an Ephesian, whom *G5161*
2Ti 4:20 Erastus abode at Corinth: but **T** have I *G5161*

TROTH See BETROTH.

TROUBLE
Jos 6:18 the camp of Israel a curse, and **t** it. H5916
7:25 us? the LORD shall **t** thee this day. And H5916
Jdg 11:35 art one of them that **t** me: for I have H5916
2Ki 19: 3 day *is* a day of **t**, and of rebuke, and H6869
1Ch 22:14 Now, behold, in my **t** I have prepared H6040
2Ch 15: 4 But when they in their **t** did turn unto H6862
29: 8 them to **t**, to astonishment, H2189+H2113
32:18 to **t** them; that they might take the city. H926
Neh 9:27 in the time of their **t**, when they cried H6869
32 let not all the **t** seem little before thee, H8513
Job 3:26 I rest, neither was I quiet; yet **t** came. H7267
5: 6 neither doth **t** spring out of the ground; H5999
7 Yet man is born unto **t**, as the sparks fly H5999
14: 1 of a woman *is* of few days, and full of **t**. H7267
15:24 **T** and anguish shall make him afraid; H6862
27: 9 Will God hear his cry when **t** cometh H6869
30:25 that was in **t**? was *not* my soul H7186+H3117
34:29 then can make **t**? and when he hideth H7561
38:23 of **t**, against the day of battle and war? H6862
Ps 3: 1 LORD, how are they increased that **t** H6862
9: 9 for the oppressed, a refuge in times of **t**. H6869
13 consider my **t** *which I suffer* of them H6040
10: 1 *why* hidest thou *thyself* in times of **t**? H6869
13: 4 that **t** me rejoice when I am moved. H6862
20: 1 The LORD hear thee in the day of **t**; the H6869
22:11 Be not far from me; for **t** *is* near; for H6869
27: 5 For in the time of **t** he shall hide me in H7451
31: 7 considered my **t**; thou hast known my H6040
9 O LORD, for I am in **t**: mine eye is H6887
32: 7 preserve me from **t**; thou shalt compass H6862
37:39 *he is* their strength in the time of **t**. H6869
41: 1 the LORD will deliver him in time of **t**. H7451
46: 1 and strength, a very present help in **t**. H6869
50:15 And call upon me in the day of **t**: I will H6869
54: 7 For he hath delivered me out of all **t**: H6869
59:16 defence and refuge in the day of my **t**. H6862
60:11 Give us help from **t**: for vain *is* the help H6862
66:14 mouth hath spoken, when I was in **t**. H6862
69:17 servant; for I am in **t**: hear me speedily. H6887
73: 5 They *are* not in **t** *as other* men; neither H5999
77: 2 In the day of my **t** I sought the Lord: H6869
78:33 consume in vanity, and their years in **t**. H928
49 **t**, by sending evil angels *among them*. H6869
81: 7 Thou calledst in **t**, and I delivered thee; H6869
86: 7 In the day of my **t** I will call upon thee: H6869
91:15 in **t**; I will deliver him, and honour him. H6869
102: 2 the day *when* I am in **t**; incline thine ear H6862
107: 6 the LORD in their **t**, *and* he delivered H6862
13 the LORD in their **t**, *and* he saved them H6862
19 Then they cry unto the LORD in their **t**, H6862
26 depths: their soul is melted because of **t**. H7451
28 Then they cry unto the LORD in their **t**, H6862
108:12 Give us help from **t**: for vain *is* the help H6862
116: 3 hold upon me: I found **t** and sorrow. H6869
119:143 **T** and anguish have taken hold on me: H6862
138: 7 Though I walk in the midst of **t**, thou H6869
142: 2 before him; I shewed before him my **t**. H6869
143:11 sake bring my soul out of **t**. H6869
Prv 11: 8 The righteous is delivered out of **t**, and H6869
12:13 *his* lips: but the just shall come out of **t**. H6869
15: 6 but in the revenues of the wicked is **t**. H5916
16 than great treasure and **t** therewith. H4103
25:19 man in time of **t** *is like* a broken tooth, H6869
Isa 1:14 a **t** unto me; I am weary to bear *them*. H2960
8:22 the earth; and behold **t** and darkness, H6869
17:14 And behold at eveningtide **t**; *and* before H1091
22: 5 For *it is* a day of **t**, and of treading H4103
26:16 LORD, in **t** have they visited thee, they H6862
30: 6 into the land of **t** and anguish, from H6869
33: 2 our salvation also in the time of **t**. H6869
37: 3 day *is* a day of **t**, and of rebuke, and H6869
46: 7 he not answer, nor save him out of his **t**. H6869
65:23 nor bring forth for **t**; for they *are* the seed H928
Jer 2:27 their **t** they will say, Arise, and save us. H7451
28 in the time of thy **t**: for *according to* the H7451
8:15 *and* for a time of health, and behold **t**! H1205
11:12 save them at all in the time of their **t**. H7451
14 time that they cry unto me for their **t**. H7451
14: 8 thereof in time of **t**, why shouldest thou H6869
19 for the time of healing, and behold **t**! H1205
30: 7 Jacob's **t**; but he shall be saved out of it. H6869
51: 2 **t** they shall be against her round about. H7451
Lam 1:21 have heard of my **t**; they are glad that H7451
Ezk 7: 7 is come, the day of **t** *is* near, and not H4103
32:13 the foot of man **t** them any more, nor H1804
13 more, nor the hoofs of beasts **t** them. H1804
Dan 4:19 thereof, **t** thee. Belteshazzar answered H927
5:10 let not thy thoughts **t** thee, nor let thy H927
11:44 out of the north shall **t** him: therefore he H926
12: 1 shall be a time of **t**, such as never was H6869
Nah 1: 7 hold in the day of **t**; and he knoweth H6869
Hab 3:16 rest in the day of **t**: when he cometh up H6869
Zep 1:15 That day *is* a day of wrath, a day of **t** H6869
Mt 26:10 them, Why **t** ye the woman? G2873+G3930
Mk 14: 6 And Jesus said, Let her alone; why **t** ye G3930
Lk 7: 6 unto him, Lord, **t** not thyself: for I am G4660
8:49 Thy daughter is dead; **t** not the Master. G4660
11: 7 answer and say, **T** me not: the door is G2873
Act 15:19 Wherefore my sentence is, that we **t** G3926
16:20 being Jews, do exceedingly **t** our city, G1613
20:10 **T** not yourselves; for his life is in him. G2350
1Co 7:28 have **t** in the flesh: but I spare you. G2347
2Co 1: 4 them which are in any **t**, by the comfort G2347
8 ignorant of our **t** which came to us in G2347
Gal 1: 7 there be some that **t** you, and would G5015
5:12 I would they were even cut off which **t** G387
6:17 From henceforth let no man **t** me: for I G3930
2Th 1: 6 tribulation to them that **t** you; G2346
2Ti 2: 9 Wherein I suffer **t**, as an evil doer, *even* G2553
Heb 12:15 up **t** *you*, and thereby many be defiled; G1776

TROUBLED
Gen 34:30 and Levi, Ye have **t** me to make me to H5916
41: 8 that his spirit was **t**; and he sent and H6470
45: 3 him; for they were **t** at his presence. H926
Ex 14:24 cloud, and **t** the host of the Egyptians, H2000
Jos 7:25 And Joshua said, Why hast thou **t** us? H5916
1Sa 14:29 Then said Jonathan, My father hath **t** H5916
16:14 and an evil spirit from the LORD **t** him. H1204
28:21 that he was sore **t**, and said unto him, H926
2Sa 4: 1 were feeble, and all the Israelites were **t**. H926
1Ki 18:18 And he answered, I have not **t** Israel; H5916
2Ki 6:11 of Syria was sore **t** for this thing; and H5590
Ezr 4: 4 Judah, and **t** them in building, H926+H1089
Job 4: 5 faintest; it toucheth thee, and thou art **t**. H926
21: 4 *were so*, why should not my spirit be **t**? H7114
23:15 Therefore am I **t** at his presence: when I H926
34:20 the people shall be **t** at midnight, and H1607
Ps 30: 7 thou didst hide thy face, *and* I was **t**. H926
38: 6 I am **t**; I am bowed down greatly; I go H5753
46: 3 roar *and* be **t**, *though* the mountains H2560
48: 5 marvelled; they were **t**, *and* hasted away. H926
77: 3 I remembered God, and was **t**: I H1993
4 waking: I am so **t** that I cannot speak. H6470
16 they were afraid: the depths also were **t**. H7264
83:17 Let them be confounded and **t** for ever; H926
90: 7 thine anger, and by thy wrath are we **t**. H926
104:29 Thou hidest thy face, they are **t**: thou H926
Prv 25:26 *is as* a **t** fountain, and a corrupt spring. H7515
Isa 32:10 Many days and years shall ye be **t**, ye H7264
11 that are at ease; be **t**, ye careless ones: H7264
57:20 But the wicked *are* like the **t** sea, when H1644
Jer 31:20 my bowels are **t** for him; I will surely H1993
Lam 1:20 my bowels are **t**; mine heart is turned H2560
2:11 my bowels are **t**, my liver is poured H2560
Ezk 7:27 of the land shall be **t**: I will do unto them H926
26:18 *are* in the sea shall be **t** at thy departure. H926
27:35 they shall be **t** in *their* countenance. H7481
Dan 2: 1 was **t**, and his sleep brake from him. H6470
3 and my spirit was **t** to know the dream. H6470
4: 5 my bed and the visions of my head **t** me. H927
19 and his thoughts **t** him. The king spake, H927
Dan 5: 6 and his thoughts **t** him, so that the joints H927
9 Then was king Belshazzar greatly **t**, and H927
7:15 body, and the visions of my head **t** me. H927
28 my cogitations much **t** me, and my H927
Zec 10: 2 were **t**, because *there was* no shepherd. H6031
Mt 2: 3 he was **t**, and all Jerusalem with him. *G5015*
14:26 the sea, they were **t**, saying, It is a spirit; *G5015*
24: 6 see that ye be not **t**: for all *these things* *G2360*
Mk 6:50 For they all saw him, and were **t**. And *G5015*
13: 7 of wars, be ye not **t**: for *such things* *G2360*
Lk 1:12 And when Zacharias saw *him*, he was **t**, *G5015*
29 And when she saw *him*, she was **t** at his *G1298*
10:41 art careful and **t** about many things: *G5182*
24:38 And he said unto them, Why are ye **t**? *G5015*
Jn 5: 4 season into the pool, and **t** the water: *G5015*
7 when the water is **t**, to put me into the *G5015*
11:33 her, he groaned in the spirit, and was **t**, *G5015*
12:27 Now is my soul **t**; and what shall I say? *G5015*
13:21 When Jesus had thus said, he was **t** in *G5015*
14: 1 Let not your heart be **t**: ye believe in *G5015*
27 your heart be **t**, neither let it be afraid. *G5015*
Act 15:24 out from us have **t** you with words, *G5015*
17: 8 And they **t** the people and the rulers of *G5015*
2Co 4: 8 *We are* **t** on every side, yet not *G2346*
7: 5 no rest, but we were **t** on every side; *G2346*
2Th 1: 7 And to you who are **t** rest with us, *G2346*
2: 2 in mind, or be **t**, neither by spirit, nor *G2360*
1Pt 3:14 not afraid of their terror, neither be **t**; *G5015*

TROUBLEDST
Ezk 32: 2 thy rivers, and **t** the waters with thy H1804

TROUBLER
1Ch 2: 7 And the sons of Carmi; Achar, the **t** of H5916

TROUBLES
Dt 31:17 many evils and **t** shall befall them; so H6869
21 many evils and **t** are befallen them, H6869
Job 5:19 He shall deliver thee in six **t**: yea, in H6869
Ps 25:17 The **t** of my heart are enlarged: *O* bring H6869
22 Redeem Israel, O God, out of all his **t**. H6869
34: 6 *him*, and saved him out of all his **t**. H6869
17 and delivereth them out of all their **t**. H6869
71:20 me great and sore **t**, shalt quicken me H6869
88: 3 For my soul is full of **t**: and my life H7451
Prv 21:23 and his tongue keepeth his soul from **t**. H6869
Isa 65:16 the former **t** are forgotten, and because H6869
Mk 13: 8 **t**: these *are* the beginnings of sorrows. *G5016*

TROUBLEST
Mk 5:35 why **t** thou the Master any further? *G4660*

TROUBLETH
1Sa 16:15 now, an evil spirit from God **t** thee. H1204
1Ki 18:17 said unto him, *Art* thou he that **t** Israel? H5916
Job 22:10 about thee, and sudden fear **t** thee; H926
23:16 my heart soft, and the Almighty **t** me: H926
Prv 11:17 soul: but *he that is* cruel **t** his own flesh. H5916
29 He that **t** his own house shall inherit H5916
15:27 He that is greedy of gain **t** his own H5916
Dan 4: 9 in thee, and no secret **t** thee, tell me the H598
Lk 18: 5 Yet because this widow **t** me, I will *G3930*
Gal 5:10 minded: but he that **t** you shall bear his *G5015*

TROUBLING
Job 3:17 There the wicked cease *from* **t**; and H7267
Jn 5: 4 then first after the **t** of the water *G5016*

TROUBLOUS
Dan 9:25 again, and the wall, even in **t** times. H6695

TROUGH
Gen 24:20 pitcher into the **t**, and ran again unto H8268

TROUGHS
Gen 30:38 in the watering **t** when the flocks came H8268
Ex 2:16 filled the **t** to water their father's flock. H7298

TROW
Lk 17: 9 that were commanded him? I **t** not. *G1380*

TRUCEBREAKERS
2Ti 3: 3 Without natural affection, **t**, false *G786*

TRUE
Gen 42:11 We *are* all one man's sons; we *are* **t** H3651
19 If ye *be* **t** *men*, let one of your brethren H3651
31 And we said unto him, We are **t** *men*; H3651
33 I know that ye *are* **t** *men*; leave one of H3651

Gen 42:34 but *that* ye *are* **t** *men: so* will I deliver H3651
Jos 2:12 my father's house, and give me a **t** token: H571
Ru 3:12 And now it is **t** that I *am thy* near H551
2Sa 7:28 God, and thy words be **t**, and thou hast H571
2Ch 9: 5 And she said to the king, *It was* a **t** H571
15: 3 *been* without the **t** God, and without a H571
Ps 19: 9 the LORD *are* **t** *and* righteous altogether. H571
119:160 Thy word *is* **t** *from* the beginning: and H571
Dan 3:14 said unto them, *Is it* **t**, O Shadrach, H6656
24 and said unto the king, **T**, O king. H3330
6:12 said, The thing *is* **t**, according to the law H3330
8:26 which was told *is* **t**: wherefore shut thou H571
10: 1 and the thing *was* **t**, but the time H571
Zec 7: 9 saying, Execute **t** judgment, and shew H571
Mt 22:16 we know that thou art **t**, and teachest the G227
Mk 12:14 know that thou art **t**, and carest for no G227
Lk 16:11 will commit to your trust the **t** *riches*? G228
Jn 1: 9 *That* was the **t** Light, which lighteth G228
3:33 hath set to his seal that God is **t**. G227
4:23 and now is, when the **t** worshippers shall G228
37 And herein is that saying **t**, One soweth, G228
5:31 witness of myself, my witness is not **t**. G227
32 witness which he witnesseth of me is **t**. G227
6:32 giveth you the **t** bread from heaven. G228
7:18 is **t**, and no unrighteousness is in him. G227
28 he that sent me is **t**, whom ye know not. G228
8:13 record of thyself; thy record is not **t**. G227
14 *yet* my record is **t**: for I know whence I G227
16 And yet if I judge, my judgment is **t**: for I G227
17 law, that the testimony of two men is **t**. G227
26 he that sent me is **t**; and I speak to the G227
10:41 that John spake of this man were **t**. G227
15: 1 I am the **t** vine, and my Father is the G228
17: 3 know thee the only **t** God, and Jesus G228
19:35 and his record is **t**: and he knoweth that G228
35 that he saith **t**, that ye might believe. G227
21:24 and we know that his testimony is **t**. G227
Act 12: 9 wist not that it was **t** which was done by G227
Ro 3: 4 God forbid: yea, let God be **t**, but every G227
2Co 1:18 But *as* God *is* **t**, our word toward you G4103
6: 8 and good report: as deceivers, and *yet* **t**; G227
Eph 4:24 created in righteousness and **t** holiness. G225
Php 4: 3 And I entreat thee also, **t** yokefellow, G1103
8 things are **t**, whatsoever things *are* G227
1Th 1: 9 from idols to serve the living and **t** God; G228
1Ti 3: 1 This *is* a **t** saying, If a man desire the G4103
Tit 1:13 This witness is **t**. Wherefore rebuke them G227
Heb 8: 2 A minister of the sanctuary, and of the **t** G228
9:24 the figures of the **t**; but into heaven itself, G228
10:22 Let us draw near with a **t** heart in full G228
1Pt 5:12 is the **t** grace of God wherein ye stand. G227
2Pt 2:22 according to the **t** proverb, The dog *is* G227
1Jn 2: 8 you, which thing is **t** in him and in you: G227
8 is past, and the **t** light now shineth. G228
5:20 know him that is **t**, and we are in him G228
20 are in him that is **t**, *even* in his Son Jesus G228
20 Christ. This is the **t** God, and eternal life. G228
3Jn 12 record; and ye know that our record is **t**. G227
Rev 3: 7 is holy, he that is **t**, he that hath the key G228
14 the faithful and **t** witness, the beginning G228
6:10 O Lord, holy and **t**, dost thou not judge G228
15: 3 and **t** *are* thy ways, thou King of saints. G228
16: 7 **t** and righteous *are* thy judgments. G228
19: 2 For **t** and righteous *are* his judgments: G228
9 unto me, These are the **t** sayings of God. G228
11 *was* called Faithful and **T**, and in G228
21: 5 Write: for these words are **t** and faithful. G228
22: 6 *are* faithful and **t**: and the Lord God of G228

TRULY
Gen 4:24 If Cain shall be avenged sevenfold, **t**
24:49 And now if ye will deal kindly and **t** with H571
47:29 deal kindly and **t** with me; bury me not, H571
48:19 shall be great: but **t** his younger brother H199
Nu 14:21 But *as* **t** *as* I live, all the earth shall be H199
28 Say unto them, *As* **t** *as* I live, saith the
Dt 14:22 Thou shalt **t** tithe all the increase of thy H6237
Jos 2:14 that we will deal kindly and **t** with thee. H571
24 And they said unto Joshua, **T** the LORD H3588
Jdg 9:16 Now therefore, if ye have done **t** and H571
19 If ye then have dealt **t** and sincerely with H571
1Sa 20: 3 he be grieved: but **t** *as* the LORD liveth, H199
Job 36: 4 For **t** my words *shall* not *be* false: he that H551
Ps 62: 1 **T** my soul waiteth upon God: from him H389
73: 1 **T** God *is* good to Israel, *even* to such as H389
116:16 O LORD, **t** I *am* thy servant; I H577+H3588
Prv 12:22 but they that deal **t** *are* his delight. H530
Ecc 11: 7 **T** the light *is* sweet, and a pleasant *thing*
Jer 3:23 **T** in vain *is salvation hoped for* from the H403
3:23 of mountains: **t** in the LORD our God H403
10:19 said, **T** this *is* a grief, and I must bear it. H389
28: 9 known, that the LORD hath **t** sent him. H571
Ezk 18: 9 judgments, to deal **t**; he *is* just, he shall H571
Mic 3: 8 But **t** I am full of power by the spirit of H199
Mt 9:37 The harvest **t** *is* plenteous, but the G3303
17:11 unto them, Elias **t** shall first come, and G3303
27:54 saying, **T** this was the Son of God. G230
Mk 14:38 spirit **t** *is* ready, but the flesh *is* weak. G3303
15:39 he said, **T** this man was the Son of God. G230
Lk 10: 2 them, The harvest **t** *is* great, but the G3303
11:48 **T** ye bear witness that ye allow the deeds G687
20:21 *of any*, but teachest the way of God **t**: G1909
22:22 And **t** the Son of man goeth, as it was G3303
Jn 4:18 is not thy husband: in that saidst thou **t**. G227
20:30 And many other signs **t** did Jesus in the G3303
Act 1: 5 For John **t** baptized with water; but ye G3303
3:22 For Moses **t** said unto the fathers, A G3303
5:23 Saying, The prison **t** found we shut G3303
2Co 12:12 **T** the signs of an apostle were wrought G3303
Heb 7:23 And they **t** were many priests, because G3303
11:15 And **t**, if they had been mindful of that G3303
1Jn 1: 3 with us: and **t** our fellowship *is* with G2532

TRUMP
1Co 15:52 of an eye, at the last **t**: for the trumpet G4536
1Th 4:16 and with the **t** of God: and the dead G4536

TRUMPET
Ex 19:13 not live: when the **t** soundeth long, they H3104
16 the voice of the **t** exceeding loud; so H7782
19 And when the voice of the **t** sounded H7782
20:18 the noise of the **t**, and the mountain H7782
Lev 25: 9 Then shalt thou cause the **t** of the jubile H7782
9 the **t** sound throughout all your land. H7782
Nu 10: 4 And if they blow *but* with one *t*, then the
Jos 6: 5 the sound of the **t**, all the people shall H7782
20 heard the sound of the **t**, and the people H7782
Jdg 3:27 that he blew a **t** in the mountain of H7782
6:34 **t**; and Abi-ezer was gathered after him. H7782
7:16 and he put a **t** in every man's hand, H7782
18 When I blow with a **t**, I and all that *are* H7782
1Sa 13: 3 And Saul blew the **t** throughout all the H7782
2Sa 2:28 So Joab blew a **t**, and all the people H7782
6:15 shouting, and with the sound of the **t**. H7782
15:10 the sound of the **t**, then ye shall say, H7782
18:16 And Joab blew the **t**, and the people H7782
20: 1 and he blew a **t**, and said, We have no H7782
22 And he blew a **t**, and they retired from H7782
1Ki 1:34 the **t**, and say, God save king Solomon. H7782
39 And they blew the **t**; and all the people H7782
41 the sound of the **t**, he said, Wherefore H7782
Neh 4:18 And he that sounded the **t** *was* by me. H7782
20 the sound of the **t**, resort ye thither unto H7782
Job 39:24 believeth he that *it is* the sound of the **t**. H7782
Ps 47: 5 a shout, the LORD with the sound of a **t**. H7782
81: 3 Blow up the **t** in the new moon, in the H7782
150: 3 Praise him with the sound of the **t**: H7782
Isa 18: 3 and when he bloweth a **t**, hear ye. H7782
27:13 day, *that* the great **t** shall be blown, H7782
58: 1 lift up thy voice like a **t**, and shew my H7782
Jer 4: 5 and say, Blow ye the **t** in the land: cry, H7782
19 the sound of the **t**, the alarm of war. H7782
21 standard, *and* hear the sound of the **t**? H7782
6: 1 and blow the **t** in Tekoa, and set up H7782
17 **t**. But they said, We will not hearken. H7782
42:14 the sound of the **t**, nor have hunger of H7782
51:27 the land, blow the **t** among the nations, H7782
Ezk 7:14 They have blown the **t**, even to make all H8619
33: 3 he blow the **t**, and warn the people; H7782
4 the sound of the **t**, and taketh not H7782
5 He heard the sound of the **t**, and took H7782
6 and blow not the **t**, and the people be H7782
Hos 5: 8 Blow ye the cornet in Gibeah, *and* the **t** H2689
8: 1 *Set* the **t** to thy mouth. *He shall come* as H7782
Joel 2: 1 Blow ye the **t** in Zion, and sound an H7782
15 Blow the **t** in Zion, sanctify a fast, call a H7782
Am 2: 2 shouting, *and* with the sound of the **t**: H7782
3: 6 Shall a **t** be blown in the city, and the H7782
Zep 1:16 A day of the **t** and alarm against the H7782
Zec 9:14 GOD shall blow the **t**, and shall go with H7782
Mt 6: 2 do not sound a **t** before thee, as the G4537
24:31 with a great sound of a **t**, and they shall G4536
1Co 14: 8 For if the **t** give an uncertain sound, G4536
15:52 last trump: for the **t** shall sound, and the
Heb 12:19 And the sound of a **t**, and the voice of G4536
Rev 1:10 heard behind me a great voice, as of a **t**, G4536
4: 1 *was* as it were of a **t** talking with me; G4536
8:13 other voices of the **t** of the three angels, G4536
9:14 which had the **t**, Loose the four angels G4536

TRUMPETERS
2Ki 11:14 princes and the **t** by the king, and all H2689
2Ch 5:13 It came even to pass, as the **t** H2690+H2690
29:28 sang, and the **t** sounded: *and* all *this* H2689
Rev 18:22 and of pipers, and **t**, shall be heard no G4538

TRUMPETS
Lev 23:24 of blowing of **t**, an holy convocation.
Nu 10: 2 Make thee two **t** of silver; of a whole H2689
8 shall blow with the **t**; and they shall be H2689
9 an alarm with the **t**; and ye shall be H2689
10 ye shall blow with the **t** over your burnt H2689
29: 1 it is a day of blowing the **t** unto you.
31: 6 and the **t** to blow in his hand. H2689
Jos 6: 4 the ark seven **t** of rams' horns: and H7782
4 and the priests shall blow with the **t**. H7782
6 priests bear seven **t** of rams' horns H7782
8 bearing the seven **t** of rams' horns H7782
8 and blew with the **t**: and the ark of the H7782
9 that blew with the **t**, and the rearward H7782
9 going on, and blowing with the **t**. H7782
13 And seven priests bearing seven **t** of H7782
13 and blew with the **t**: and the armed men H7782
13 going on, and blowing with the **t**. H7782
16 blew with the **t**, Joshua said unto the H7782
20 blew with the **t**: and it came to pass, H7782
Jdg 7: 8 hand, and their **t**: and he sent all *the* H7782
18 then blow ye the **t** also on every side of H7782
19 and they blew the **t**, and brake the H7782
20 And the three companies blew the **t**, H7782
20 their left hands, and the **t** in their right H7782
22 And the three hundred blew the **t**, and H7782
2Ki 9:13 and blew with **t**, saying, Jehu is king. H7782
11:14 and blew with **t**: and Athaliah rent her H2689
12:13 snuffers, basons, **t**, any vessels of gold, H2689
1Ch 13: 8 timbrels, and with cymbals, and with **t**. H2689
15:24 did blow with the **t** before the ark of H2689
28 cornet, and with **t**, and with cymbals, H2689
16: 6 the priests with **t** continually before the H2689
42 and Jeduthun with **t** and cymbals for H2689
2Ch 5:12 and twenty priests sounding with **t**:) H2689
13 *their* voice with the **t** and cymbals and H2689
7: 6 **t** before them, and all Israel stood.
13:12 with sounding **t** to cry alarm against H2689
14 and the priests sounded with the **t**. H2689
15:14 shouting, and with **t**, and with cornets. H2689
20:28 and **t** unto the house of the LORD. H2689
23:13 princes and the **t** by the king: and all H2689
13 and sounded with **t**, also the singers H2689
29:26 of David, and the priests with the **t**. H2689
27 began *also* with the **t**, and with the H2689
Ezr 3:10 their apparel with **t**, and the Levites the H2689
Neh 12:35 And *certain* of the priests' sons with **t**; H2689
41 Zechariah, *and* Hananiah, with **t**; H2689
Job 39:25 He saith among the **t**, Ha, ha; and he H7782
Ps 98: 6 With **t** and sound of cornet make a H2689
Rev 8: 2 God; and to them were given seven **t**. G4536
6 seven **t** prepared themselves to sound. G4536

TRUST
Jdg 9:15 *and* put your **t** in my shadow: and H2620
Ru 2:12 under whose wings thou art come to **t**. H2620
2Sa 22: 3 The God of my rock; in him will I **t**: *he is* H2620
31 he *is* a buckler to all them that **t** in him. H2620
2Ki 18:20 thou **t**, that thou rebellest against me? H982
21 king of Egypt unto all that **t** on him. H982
22 But if ye say unto me, We **t** in the LORD H982
24 and put thy **t** on Egypt for chariots H982
30 Neither let Hezekiah make you **t** in the H982
1Ch 5:20 of them; because they put their **t** in him. H982
2Ch 32:10 **t**, that ye abide in the siege in Jerusalem? H982
Job 4:18 Behold, he put no **t** in his servants; and H539
8:14 off, and whose **t** *shall be* a spider's web. H4009
13:15 Though he slay me, yet will I **t** in him: H3176
15:15 Behold, he putteth no **t** in his saints; yea, H539
31 Let not him that is deceived **t** in vanity: H539
35:14 *is* before him; therefore **t** thou in him. H2342
39:11 Wilt thou **t** him, because his strength *is* H982
Ps 2:12 *are* all they that put their **t** in him. H2620
4: 5 and put your **t** in the LORD. H982
5:11 But let all those that put their **t** in thee H2620
7: 1 O LORD my God, in thee do I put my **t**: H2620
9:10 name will put their **t** in thee: for thou, H982
11: 1 In the LORD put I my **t**: how say ye to H2620
16: 1 me, O God: for in thee do I put my **t**. H2620
17: 7 which put their **t** *in thee* from those H2620
18: 2 in whom I will **t**; my buckler, and the H2620

Ps 18:30 he *is* a buckler to all those that t in him. H2620
20: 7 Some *t* in chariots, and some in horses:
25: 2 O my God, I t in thee: let me not be H982
20 not be ashamed; for I put my t in thee. H2620
31: 1 In thee, O LORD, do I put my t; let me H2620
6 lying vanities: but I t in the LORD. H982
19 that t in thee before the sons of men! H2620
34:22 of them that t in him shall be desolate. H2620
36: 7 their t under the shadow of thy wings. H2620
37: 3 T in the LORD, and do good; *so* shalt H982
5 Commit thy way unto the LORD; t also H982
40 and save them, because they t in him. H2620
40: 3 see *it*, and fear, and shall t in the LORD. H982
4 the LORD his t, and respecteth not the H4009
44: 6 For I will not t in my bow, neither shall H982
49: 6 They that t in their wealth, and boast H982
52: 8 I t in the mercy of God for ever and ever. H982
55:23 out half their days; but I will t in thee. H982
56: 3 What time I am afraid, I will t in thee. H982
4 God I have put my t; I will not fear what H982
11 In God have I put my t: I will not be H982
61: 4 I will t in the covert of thy wings. Selah. H2620
62: 8 T in him at all times; *ye* people, pour out H982
10 T not in oppression, and become not H982
64:10 LORD, and shall t in him; and all the H2620
71: 1 In thee, O LORD, do I put my t: let me H2620
5 GOD: *thou art* my t from my youth. H4009
73:28 I have put my t in the Lord GOD, that H4268
91: 2 and my fortress: my God; in him will I t. H982
4 wings shalt thou t: his truth *shall be thy* H2620
115: 9 O Israel, t thou in the LORD: he *is* their H982
10 O house of Aaron, t in the LORD: he *is* H982
11 Ye that fear the LORD, t in the LORD: he H982
118: 8 *It is* better to t in the LORD than to put H2620
9 *It is* better to t in the LORD than to put H2620
119:42 that reproacheth me: for I t in thy word. H982
125: 1 They that t in the LORD *shall be* as H982
141: 8 thee is my t; leave not my soul destitute. H2620
143: 8 for in thee do I t: cause me to know the H982
144: 2 I t; who subdueth my people under me. H2620
146: 3 Put not your t in princes, *nor* in the son H982
Prv 3: 5 T in the LORD with all thine heart; and H982
22:19 That thy t may be in the LORD, I have H4009
28:25 his t in the LORD shall be made fat. H982
29:25 putteth his t in the LORD shall be safe. H982
30: 5 unto them that put their t in him. H2620
31:11 The heart of her husband doth safely t in H982
Isa 12: 2 Behold, God *is* my salvation; I will t, and H982
14:32 and the poor of his people shall t in it. H2620
26: 4 T ye in the LORD for ever: for in the H982
30: 2 and to t in the shadow of Egypt! H2620
3 your shame, and the t in the shadow of H2622
12 this word, and t in oppression and H982
31: 1 and stay on horses, and t in chariots, H982
36: 5 thou t, that thou rebellest against me? H982
6 king of Egypt to all that t in him. H982
7 But if thou say to me, We t in the LORD H982
9 and put thy t on Egypt for chariots H982
15 Neither let Hezekiah make you t in the H982
42:17 ashamed, that t in graven images, that H982
50:10 no light? let him t in the name of the H982
51: 5 upon me, and on mine arm shall they t. H3176
57:13 he that putteth his t in me shall possess H2620
59: 4 for truth: they t in vanity, and speak H982
Jer 7: 4 T ye not in lying words, saying, The H982
8 Behold, ye t in lying words, that cannot H982
14 name, wherein ye t, and unto the place H982
9: 4 of his neighbour, and t ye not in any H982
28:15 but thou makest this people to t in a lie. H982
29:31 him not, and he caused you to t in a lie: H982
39:18 hast put thy t in me, saith the LORD. H982
46:25 Pharaoh, and *all* them that t in him: H982
49:11 *them* alive; and let thy widows t in me. H982
Ezk 16:15 But thou didst t in thine own beauty, H982
33:13 shall surely live; if he t to his own H982
Hos 10:13 because thou didst t in thy way, in the H982
Am 6: 1 at ease in Zion, and t in the mountain of H982
Mic 7: 5 T ye not in a friend, put ye not H539
Nah 1: 7 and he knoweth them that t in him. H2620
Zep 3:12 they shall t in the name of the LORD. H2620
Mt 12:21 And in his name shall the Gentiles t. G1679
Mk 10:24 is it for them that t in riches to enter G3982
Lk 16:11 will commit to your t the true *riches*? G4100
Jn 5:45 you, *even* Moses, in whom ye t. G1679
Ro 15:12 the Gentiles; in him shall the Gentiles t. G1679
24 come to you: for I t to see you in my G1679
1Co 16: 7 by the way; but I t to tarry a while with G1679
2Co 1: 9 that we should not t in ourselves, but in G3982
10 in whom we t that he will yet deliver *us*; G1679
2Co 1:13 t ye shall acknowledge even to the end; G1679
3: 4 And such t have we through Christ to G4006
5:11 unto God; and I t also are made G1679
10: 7 If any man t to himself that he is G3982
13: 6 But I t that ye shall know that we are G1679
Php 2:19 But I t in the Lord Jesus to send G1679
24 But I t in the Lord that I also myself G3982
3: 4 whereof he might t in the flesh, I more: G3982
1Th 2: 4 of God to be put in t with the gospel, G4100
1Ti 1:11 God, which was committed to my t. G4100
4:10 because we t in the living God, who G1679
6:17 highminded, nor t in uncertain riches, G1679
20 is committed to thy t, avoiding profane G3872
Phlm 22 also a lodging: for I t that through your G1679
Heb 2:13 And again, I will put my t in him. And G2071
13:18 Pray for us: for we t we have a good G3982
2Jn 12 and ink: but I t to come unto you, and G1679
3Jn 14 But I t I shall shortly see thee, and we G1679

TRUSTED

Dt 32:37 their gods, *their* rock in whom they t, H2620
Jdg 11:20 But Sihon t not Israel to pass through his H539
20:36 because they t unto the liers in wait H982
2Ki 18: 5 He t in the LORD God of Israel; so that H982
Ps 13: 5 But I have t in thy mercy; my heart shall H982
22: 4 Our fathers t in thee: they trusted, and H982
4 Our fathers trusted in thee: they t, and H982
5 they t in thee, and were not confounded. H982
8 He t on the LORD *that* he would deliver H1556
26: 1 integrity: I have t also in the LORD; H982
28: 7 my shield; my heart t in him, and I am H982
31:14 But I t in thee, O LORD: I said, Thou *art* H982
33:21 him, because we have t in his holy name. H982
41: 9 friend, in whom I t, which did eat of my H982
52: 7 his strength; but t in the abundance of H982
78:22 Because they believed not in God, and t H982
Isa 47:10 For thou hast t in thy wickedness: thou H982
Jer 13:25 hast forgotten me, and t in falsehood. H982
48: 7 For because thou hast t in thy works and H982
49: 4 daughter? that t in her treasures, *saying*, H982
Dan 3:28 his servants that t in him, and have H7365
Zep 3: 2 not correction; she t not in the LORD; H982
Mt 27:43 He t in God; let him deliver him now, if G3982
Lk 11:22 wherein he t, and divideth his spoils. G3982
18: 9 certain which t in themselves that they G3982
24:21 But we t that it had been he which G1679
Eph 1:12 praise of his glory, who first t in Christ. G4276
13 In whom ye also *t*, after that ye heard the
1Pt 3: 5 women also, who t in God, adorned G1679

TRUSTEDST

Dt 28:52 wherein thou t, throughout all thy land: H982
Jer 5:17 cities, wherein thou t, with the sword. H982
12: 5 *wherein* thou t, *they wearied thee*, then H982

TRUSTEST

2Ki 18:19 What confidence *is* this wherein thou t? H982
21 Now, behold, thou t upon the staff of H982
19:10 thy God in whom thou t deceive thee, H982
Isa 36: 4 What confidence *is* this wherein thou t? H982
6 Lo, thou t in the staff of this broken reed, H982
37:10 thy God, in whom thou t, deceive thee, H982

TRUSTETH

Job 40:23 *and* hasteth not: he t that he can draw H982
Ps 21: 7 For the king t in the LORD, and through H982
32:10 wicked: but he that t in the LORD, mercy H982
34: 8 good: blessed *is* the man *that* t in him. H2620
57: 1 me: for my soul t in thee: yea, in the H2620
84:12 hosts, blessed *is* the man that t in thee. H982
86: 2 my God, save thy servant that t in thee. H982
115: 8 unto them; *so is* every one that t in them. H982
135:18 unto them: *so is* every one that t in them. H982
Prv 11:28 He that t in his riches shall fall: but the H982
16:20 and whoso t in the LORD, happy *is* he. H982
28:26 He that t in his own heart is a fool: but H982
Isa 26: 3 *is* stayed *on thee*: because he t in thee. H982
Jer 17: 5 *be* the man that t in man, and maketh H982
7 Blessed *is* the man that t in the LORD, H982
Hab 2:18 his work t therein, to make dumb idols? H982
1Ti 5: 5 and desolate, t in God, and continueth G1679

TRUSTING

Ps 112: 7 tidings: his heart is fixed, t in the LORD. H982

TRUSTY

Job 12:20 He removeth away the speech of the t, H539

TRUTH

Gen 24:27 of his mercy and his t: I *being* in the way, H571
32:10 and of all the t, which thou hast shewed H571
42:16 *there be any* t in you: or else by the H571
Ex 18:21 such as fear God, men of t, hating H571
34: 6 and abundant in goodness and t, H571
Dt 13:14 and, behold, *if it be* t, *and* the thing H571
32: 4 *are* judgment: a God of t and without H530
Jos 24:14 in sincerity and in t: and put away the H571
Jdg 9:15 unto the trees, If in t ye anoint me king H571
1Sa 12:24 Only fear the LORD, and serve him in t H571
21: 5 said unto him, Of a t women *have been* H518
2Sa 2: 6 And now the LORD shew kindness and t H571
15:20 thy brethren: mercy and t *be* with thee. H571
1Ki 2: 4 to walk before me in t with all their heart H571
3: 6 before thee in t, and in righteousness, H571
17:24 the word of the LORD in thy mouth *is* t. H571
2Ki 19:17 Of a t, LORD, the kings of Assyria have H551
20: 3 before thee in t and with a perfect heart, H571
19 *it not good*, if peace and t be in my days? H571
2Ch 18:15 but the t to me in the name of the LORD? H571
31:20 right and t before the LORD his God. H571
Est 9:30 of Ahasuerus, *with* words of peace and t, H571
Job 9: 2 I know *it is* so of a t: but how should man H551
Ps 15: 2 and speaketh the t in his heart. H571
25: 5 Lead me in thy t, and teach me: for thou H571
10 *are* mercy and t unto such as keep his H571
26: 3 mine eyes: and I have walked in thy t. H571
30: 9 the dust praise thee? shall it declare thy t? H571
31: 5 hast redeemed me, O LORD God of t. H571
33: 4 *is* right; and all his works *are done* in t. H530
40:10 and thy t from the great congregation. H571
11 and thy t continually preserve me. H571
43: 3 O send out thy light and thy t: let them H571
45: 4 because of t and meekness *and* H571
51: 6 Behold, thou desirest t in the inward H571
54: 5 unto mine enemies: cut them off in thy t. H571
57: 3 God shall send forth his mercy and his t. H571
10 the heavens, and thy t unto the clouds. H571
60: 4 be displayed because of the t. Selah. H7189
61: 7 mercy and t, *which* may preserve him. H571
69:13 mercy hear me, in the t of thy salvation. H571
71:22 psaltery, *even* thy t, O my God: unto thee H571
85:10 Mercy and t are met together; H571
11 T shall spring out of the earth; and H571
86:11 in thy t: unite my heart to fear thy name. H571
15 and plenteous in mercy and t. H571
89:14 mercy and t shall go before thy face. H571
49 *which* thou swarest unto David in thy t? H530
91: 4 his t *shall be thy* shield and buckler. H571
96:13 righteousness, and the people with his t. H530
98: 3 He hath remembered his mercy and his t H530
100: 5 and his t *endureth* to all generations. H530
108: 4 and thy t *reacheth* unto the clouds. H571
111: 8 ever, *and are* done in t and uprightness. H571
117: 2 great toward us: and the t of the LORD H571
119:30 I have chosen the way of t: thy judgments H530
43 And take not the word of t utterly out of H571
142 righteousness, and thy law *is* the t. H571
151 LORD; and all thy commandments *are* t. H571
132:11 The LORD hath sworn *in* t unto David; H571
138: 2 and for thy t: for thou hast magnified H571
145:18 upon him, to all that call upon him in t. H571
146: 6 that therein *is*: which keepeth t for ever: H571
Prv 3: 3 Let not mercy and t forsake thee: bind H571
8: 7 For my mouth shall speak t; and H571
12:17 *He that* speaketh t sheweth forth H530
19 The lip of t shall be established for ever: H571
14:22 and t *shall be* to them that devise good. H571
16: 6 By mercy and t iniquity is purged: and H571
20:28 Mercy and t preserve the king: and his H571
22:21 of the words of t; that thou mightest H571
21 words of t to them that send unto thee? H571
23:23 Buy the t, and sell *it* not; *also* wisdom, H571
Ecc 12:10 *was* written *was* upright, *even* words of t. H571
Isa 5: 9 of hosts, Of a t many houses shall be H3808
10:20 the LORD, the Holy One of Israel, in t. H571
16: 5 shall sit upon it in t in the tabernacle of H571
25: 1 *thy* counsels of old *are* faithfulness *and* t. H544
26: 2 nation which keepeth the t may enter in. H529
37:18 Of a t, LORD, the kings of Assyria have H551
38: 3 before thee in t and with a perfect heart, H571
18 down into the pit cannot hope for thy t. H571
19 to the children shall make known thy t. H571
39: 8 there shall be peace and t in my days. H571
42: 3 he shall bring forth judgment unto t. H571
43: 9 justified: or let them hear, and say, *It is* t. H571
48: 1 Israel, *but* not in t, nor in righteousness. H571
59: 4 *any* pleadeth for t: they trust in vanity, H530

Isa 59:14 afar off: for **t** is fallen in the street, H571
15 Yea, **t** faileth; and he *that* departeth H571
61: 8 direct their work in **t**, and I will make an H571
65:16 in the God of **t**; and he that sweareth H543
16 swear by the God of **t**; because the former H543
Jer 4: 2 LORD liveth, in **t**, in judgment, and in H571
5: 1 that seeketh the **t**; and I will pardon it. H530
3 O LORD, *are* not thine eyes upon the **t**? H530
7:28 correction: **t** is perished, and is cut H530
9: 3 not valiant for the **t** upon the earth; for H530
5 and will not speak the **t**: they have taught H571
26:15 thereof: for of a **t** the LORD hath sent H571
33: 6 unto them the abundance of peace and **t**. H571
Dan 2:47 and said, Of a **t** *it is*, that your God *is* H7187
4:37 all whose works *are* **t**, and his ways H7187
7:16 and asked him the **t** of all this. So he H3330
19 Then I would know the **t** of the fourth H3321
8:12 it cast down the **t** to the ground; and it H571
9:13 our iniquities, and understand thy **t**. H571
10:21 in the scripture of **t**: and *there is* none H571
11: 2 And now will I shew thee the **t**. Behold, H571
Hos 4: 1 because *there is* no **t**, nor mercy, nor H571
Mic 7:20 Thou wilt perform the **t** to Jacob, *and* the H571
Zec 8: 3 be called a city of **t**; and the mountain of H571
8 be their God, in **t** and in righteousness. H571
16 ye every man the **t** to his neighbour; H571
16 judgment of **t** and peace in your gates: H571
19 feasts; therefore love the **t** and peace. H571
Mal 2: 6 The law of **t** was in his mouth, and H571
Mt 14:33 saying, Of a **t** thou art the Son of God. *G230*
15:27 And she said, **T**, Lord: yet the dogs eat *G3483*
22:16 the way of God in **t**, neither carest thou *G225*
Mk 5:33 down before him, and told him all the **t**. *G225*
12:14 the way of God in **t**: Is it lawful to give *G225*
32 thou hast said the **t**: for there is one God; *G225*
Lk 4:25 But I tell you of a **t**, many widows were in *G225*
9:27 But I tell you of a **t**, there be some *G230*
12:44 Of a **t** I say unto you, that he will make *G230*
21: 3 And he said, Of a **t** I say unto you, that *G230*
22:59 saying, Of a **t** this *fellow* also was with *G225*
Jn 1:14 of the Father,) full of grace and **t**. *G225*
17 *but* grace and **t** came by Jesus Christ. *G225*
3:21 But he that doeth **t** cometh to the light, *G225*
4:23 in spirit and in **t**: for the Father seeketh *G225*
24 him must worship *him* in spirit and in **t**. *G225*
5:33 John, and he bare witness unto the **t**. *G225*
6:14 did, said, This is of a **t** that prophet that *G230*
7:40 saying, said, Of a **t** this is the Prophet. *G230*
8:32 And ye shall know the **t**, and the truth *G225*
32 And ye shall know the truth, and the **t** *G225*
40 hath told you the **t**, which I have heard of *G225*
44 abode not in the **t**, because there is no *G225*
44 because there is no **t** in him. When he *G225*
45 And because I tell *you* the **t**, ye believe me *G225*
46 if I say the **t**, why do ye not believe me? *G225*
14: 6 Jesus saith unto him, I am the way, the **t**, *G225*
17 *Even* the Spirit of **t**; whom the world *G225*
15:26 *even* the Spirit of **t**, which proceedeth *G225*
16: 7 Nevertheless I tell you the **t**; It is *G225*
13 Howbeit when he, the Spirit of **t**, is come, *G225*
13 guide you into all **t**: for he shall not speak *G225*
17:17 Sanctify them through thy **t**: thy word is *G225*
17 them through thy truth: thy word is **t**. *G225*
19 also might be sanctified through the **t**. *G225*
18:37 witness unto the **t**. Every one that is of *G225*
37 one that is of the **t** heareth my voice. *G225*
38 Pilate saith unto him, What is **t**? And *G225*
Act 4:27 For of a **t** against thy holy child Jesus, *G225*
10:34 and said, Of a **t** I perceive that God is *G225*
26:25 forth the words of **t** and soberness. *G225*
Ro 1:18 men, who hold the **t** in unrighteousness; *G225*
25 Who changed the **t** of God into a lie, and *G225*
2: 2 of God is according to **t** against them *G225*
8 and do not obey the **t**, but obey *G225*
20 of knowledge and of the **t** in the law. *G225*
3: 7 For if the **t** of God hath more abounded *G225*
9: 1 I say the **t** in Christ, I lie not, my *G225*
15: 8 for the **t** of God, to confirm the *G225*
1Co 5: 8 the unleavened *bread* of sincerity and **t**. *G225*
13: 6 not in iniquity, but rejoiceth in the **t**; *G225*
14:25 and report that God is in you of a **t**. *G3689*
2Co 4: 2 of the **t** commending ourselves *G225*
6: 7 By the word of **t**, by the power of God, by *G225*
7:14 spake all things to you in **t**, even so our *G225*
14 which *I made* before Titus, is found a **t**. *G225*
11:10 As the **t** of Christ is in me, no man shall *G225*
12: 6 for I will say the **t**: but *now* I forbear, lest *G225*
13: 8 For we can do nothing against the **t**, but *G225*
8 nothing against the truth, but for the **t**. *G225*
Gal 2: 5 **t** of the gospel might continue with you. *G225*
14 according to the **t** of the gospel, I said *G225*
3: 1 not obey the **t**, before whose eyes Jesus *G225*
4:16 your enemy, because I tell you the **t**? *G226*
5: 7 hinder you that ye should not obey the **t**? *G225*
Eph 1:13 ye heard the word of **t**, the gospel of your *G225*
4:15 But speaking the **t** in love, may grow up *G226*
21 been taught by him, as the **t** is in Jesus: *G225*
25 speak every man **t** with his neighbour: *G225*
5: 9 in all goodness and righteousness and **t**;) *G225*
6:14 loins girt about with **t**, and having on the *G225*
Php 1:18 in pretence, or in **t**, Christ is preached; *G225*
Col 1: 5 before in the word of the **t** of the gospel; *G225*
6 *of it*, and knew the grace of God in **t**: *G225*
1Th 2:13 of men, but as it is in **t**, the word of God, *G230*
2Th 2:10 love of the **t**, that they might be saved. *G225*
12 **t**, but had pleasure in unrighteousness. *G225*
13 of the Spirit and belief of the **t**: *G225*
1Ti 2: 4 and to come unto the knowledge of the **t**. *G225*
7 (I speak the **t** in Christ, *and* lie not;) *G225*
3:15 living God, the pillar and ground of the **t**. *G225*
4: 3 of them which believe and know the **t**. *G225*
6: 5 and destitute of the **t**, supposing that *G225*
2Ti 2:15 ashamed, rightly dividing the word of **t**. *G225*
18 Who concerning the **t** have erred, saying *G225*
25 repentance to the acknowledging of the **t**; *G225*
3: 7 able to come to the knowledge of the **t**. *G225*
8 do these also resist the **t**: men of corrupt *G225*
4: 4 the **t**, and shall be turned unto fables. *G225*
Tit 1: 1 of the **t** which is after godliness; *G225*
14 of men, that turn from the **t**. *G225*
Heb 10:26 knowledge of the **t**, there remaineth no *G225*
Jas 1:18 us with the word of **t**, that we should be a *G225*
3:14 glory not, and lie not against the **t**. *G225*
5:19 Brethren, if any of you do err from the **t**, *G225*
1Pt 1:22 in obeying the **t** through the Spirit unto *G225*
2Pt 1:12 *them*, and be established in the present **t**. *G225*
2: 2 the way of **t** shall be evil spoken of. *G225*
1Jn 1: 6 walk in darkness, we lie, and do not the **t**: *G225*
8 deceive ourselves, and the **t** is not in us. *G225*
2: 4 is a liar, and the **t** is not in him. *G225*
21 ye know not the **t**, but because ye know *G225*
21 ye know it, and that no lie is of the **t**. *G225*
27 of all things, and is **t**, and is no lie, and *G227*
3:18 neither in tongue; but in deed and in **t**. *G225*
19 And hereby we know that we are of the **t**, *G225*
4: 6 we the spirit of **t**, and the spirit of error. *G225*
5: 6 beareth witness, because the Spirit is **t**. *G225*
2Jn 1 whom I love in the **t**; and not I only, but *G225*
1 but also all they that have known the **t**; *G225*
3 the Son of the Father, in **t** and love. *G225*
4 thy children walking in **t**, as we have *G225*
3Jn 1 wellbeloved Gaius, whom I love in the **t**. *G225*
3 and testified of the **t** that is in thee, even *G225*
3 is in thee, even as thou walkest in the **t**. *G225*
4 than to hear that my children walk in **t**. *G225*
8 that we might be fellowhelpers to the **t**. *G225*
12 of all *men*, and of the **t** itself: yea, and we *G225*

TRUTH'S

Ps 115: 1 glory, for thy mercy, *and* for thy **t** sake. H571
2Jn 2 For the **t** sake, which dwelleth in us, and *G225*

TRY

Jdg 7: 4 water, and I will **t** them for thee there: H6884
2Ch 32:31 God left him, to **t** him, that he might H5254
Job 7:18 morning, *and* **t** him every moment? H974
12:11 Doth not the ear **t** words? and the mouth H974
Ps 11: 4 behold, his eyelids **t**, the children of men. H974
26: 2 Examine me, O LORD, and prove me; **t** H6884
139:23 Search me, O God, and know my heart: **t** H974
Jer 6:27 that thou mayest know and **t** their way. H974
9: 7 will melt them, and **t** them; for how shall H974
17:10 I the LORD search the heart, *I* **t** the H974
Lam 3:40 Let us search and **t** our ways, and turn H2713
Dan 11:35 shall fall, to **t** them, and to purge, H6884
Zec 13: 9 is refined, and will **t** them as gold is H974
1Co 3:13 **t** every man's work of what sort it is. *G1381*
1Pt 4:12 trial which is to **t** you, as though some *G3986*
1Jn 4: 1 Beloved, believe not every spirit, but **t** *G1381*
Rev 3:10 to **t** them that dwell upon the earth. *G3985*

TRYING

Jas 1: 3 Knowing *this*, that the **t** of your faith *G1383*

TRYPHENA

Ro 16:12 Salute **T** and Tryphosa, who labour in *G5170*

TRYPHOSA

Ro 16:12 Salute Tryphena and **T**, who labour in *G5173*

TUBAL

Gen 10: 2 Javan, and **T**, and Meshech, and Tiras. H8422
1Ch 1: 5 Javan, and **T**, and Meshech, and Tiras. H8422
Isa 66:19 draw the bow, *to* **T**, and Javan, *to* the H8422
Ezk 27:13 Javan, **T**, and Meshech, they *were* thy H8422
32:26 There *is* Meshech, **T**, and all her H8422
38: 2 and **T**, and prophesy against him, H8422
3 Gog, the chief prince of Meshech and **T**: H8422
39: 1 Gog, the chief prince of Meshech and **T**: H8422

TUBAL-CAIN

Gen 4:22 And Zillah, she also bare **T**, an H8423
22 iron: and the sister of **T** *was* Naamah. H8423

TUMBLED

Jdg 7:13 cake of barley bread **t** into the host of H2015

TUMULT

1Sa 4:14 the noise of this? And the man came H1995
2Sa 18:29 a great **t**, but I knew not what *it was*. H1995
2Ki 19:28 Because thy rage against me and thy **t** H7600
Ps 65: 7 of their waves, and the **t** of the people. H1995
74:23 of thine enemies: the **t** of those that rise H7588
83: 2 For, lo, thine enemies make a **t**: and H1993
Isa 33: 3 At the noise of the **t** the people fled; at H1995
37:29 Because thy rage against me, and thy **t**, H7600
Jer 11:16 noise of a great **t** he hath kindled fire H1999
Hos 10:14 Therefore shall a **t** arise among thy H7588
Am 2: 2 shall die with **t**, with shouting, *and* H7588
Zec 14:13 day, *that* a great **t** from the LORD shall H4103
Mt 27:24 but *that* rather a **t** was made, he took *G2351*
Mk 5:38 and seeth the **t**, and them that wept *G2351*
Act 21:34 certainty for the **t**, he commanded him *G2351*
24:18 neither with multitude, nor with **t**. *G2351*

TUMULTS

Am 3: 9 behold the great **t** in the midst thereof, H4103
2Co 6: 5 In stripes, in imprisonments, in **t**, in *G181*
12:20 backbitings, whisperings, swellings, **t**: *G181*

TUMULTUOUS

Isa 13: 4 of a great people; a **t** noise of the H7588
22: 2 Thou that art full of stirs, a **t** city, a H1993
Jer 48:45 and the crown of the head of the **t** ones. H7588

TURN

Gen 19: 2 And he said, Behold now, my lords, **t** H5493
24:49 I may **t** to the right hand, or to the left. H6437
27:44 days, until thy brother's fury **t** away; H7725
45 Until thy brother's anger **t** away from H7725
Ex 3: 3 And Moses said, I will now **t** aside, and H5493
14: 2 of Israel, that they **t** and encamp before H7725
23:27 all thine enemies **t** their backs unto thee.
32:12 the face of the earth? **T** from thy fierce H7725
Lev 13:16 Or if the raw flesh **t** again, and be H7725
19: 4 **T** ye not unto idols, nor make to H6437
Nu 14:25 To morrow **t** you, and get you into H6437
20:17 way, we will not **t** to the right hand nor H5186
21:22 thy land: we will not **t** into the fields, or H5186
22:23 smote the ass, to **t** her into the way. H5186
26 **t** either to the right hand or to the left. H5186
32:15 For if ye **t** away from after him, he will H7725
34: 4 And your border shall **t** from the south H5437
Dt 1: 7 **T** you, and take your journey, and go to H6437
40 But *as for* you, **t** you, and take your H6437
2: 3 long enough: **t** you northward. H6437
27 **t** unto the right hand nor to the left. H5493
4:30 latter days, if thou **t** to the LORD thy H7725
5:32 **t** aside to the right hand or to the left. H5493
7: 4 For they will **t** away thy son from H5493
11:16 not deceived, and ye **t** aside, and serve H5493
28 your God, but **t** aside out of the way H5493
13: 5 he hath spoken to **t** *you* away from the H5627
17 the LORD may **t** from the fierceness H7725
14:25 Then shalt thou **t** *it* into money, and H5414
16: 7 **t** in the morning, and go unto thy tents. H6437
17:17 that his heart **t** not away: neither shall H5493
20 and that he **t** not aside from the H5493
23:13 and shalt **t** back and cover that H7725
14 thing in thee, and **t** away from thee. H7725
30: 3 That then the LORD thy God will **t** thy H7725
10 law, *and* if thou **t** unto the LORD thy H7725
17 But if thine heart **t** away, so that thou H6437
31:20 fat; then will they **t** unto other gods, H6437
29 *yourselves*, and **t** aside from the way H5493
Jos 1: 7 commanded thee: **t** not from it *to* the H5493

Jos 22:16 God of Israel, to t away this day from H7725
18 But that ye must t away this day from H7725
23 That we have built us an altar to t from H7725
29 against the LORD, and t this day from H7725
23: 6 of Moses, that ye t not aside therefrom H5493
24:20 gods, then he will t and do you hurt, H7725
Jdg 4:18 said unto him, T in, my lord, turn in H5493
18 Turn in, my lord, t in to me; fear not. H5493
11: 8 Therefore we t again to thee now, that H7725
19:11 thee, and let us t in into this city of the H5493
12 him, We will not t aside hither into the H5493
20: 8 will we any *of us* t into his house. H5493
Ru 1:11 And Naomi said, T again, my H7725
12 T again, my daughters, go *your way;* H7725
4: 1 Ho, such a one! t aside, sit down here. H5493
1Sa 12:20 this wickedness: yet t not aside from H5493
21 And t ye not aside: for *then should ye* H5493
14: 7 *is* in thine heart: t thee; behold, I *am* H5186
15:25 my sin, and t again with me, that H5493
30 before Israel, and t again with me, that H5493
22:17 stood about him, T, and slay the priests H5437
18 And the king said to Doeg, T thou, and H5437
2Sa 2:21 And Abner said to him, T thee aside to H5186
21 not t aside from following of him. H5493
22 And Abner said again to Asahel, T thee H5493
23 Howbeit he refused to t aside: H5493
14:19 the king, none can t to the right hand or
24 And the king said, Let him t to his own H5437
15:31 O LORD, I pray thee, t the counsel of
18:30 And the king said *unto him,* T aside, H5437
19:37 Let thy servant, I pray thee, t back H7725
1Ki 8:33 thee, and shall t again to thee, and H7725
35 thy name, and t from their sin, when H7725
9: 6 *But* if ye shall at all t from following H7725
11: 2 *for* surely they will t away your heart H5186
12:27 of this people t again unto their lord, H7725
13: 9 drink water, nor t again by the same H7725
17 water there, nor t again to go by the H7725
17: 3 Get thee hence, and t thee eastward, H6437
22:34 of his chariot, T thine hand, and carry H2015
2Ki 1: 6 said unto us, Go, t again unto the king H7725
4:10 cometh to us, that he shall t in thither. H5493
9:18 to do with peace? t thee behind me. H5437
19 to do with peace? t thee behind me. H5437
17:13 all the seers, saying, T ye from your evil H7725
18:24 How then wilt thou t away the face of H7725
19:28 in thy lips, and I will t thee back by the H7725
20: 5 T again, and tell Hezekiah the captain H7725
1Ch 12:23 to Hebron, to t the kingdom of Saul H5437
14:14 not up after them; t away from them, H5437
2Ch 6:26 thy name, and t from their sin, when H7725
37 captive, and t and pray unto thee H7725
42 O LORD God, t not away the face of H7725
7:14 seek my face, and t from their wicked H7725
19 But if ye t away, and forsake my H7725
15: 4 But when they in their trouble did t H7725
18:33 to his chariot man, T thine hand, that H2015
25:27 Now after the time that Amaziah did t H5493
29:10 his fierce wrath may t away from us. H7725
30: 6 Ye children of Israel, t again unto the H7725
8 of his wrath may t away from you. H7725
9 For if ye t again unto the LORD, your H7725
9 and will not t away *his* face from H2015
35:22 Nevertheless Josiah would not t his H5437
Neh 1: 9 But *if* ye t unto me, and keep my H7725
4: 4 we are despised: and t their reproach H7725
9:26 against them to t them to thee, and H7725
Est 2:12 Now when every maid's t was come to H8447
15 Now when the t of Esther, the daughter H8447
Job 5: 1 and to which of the saints wilt thou t? H6437
14: 6 T from him, that he may rest, till he H8159
23:13 But he *is* in one *mind,* and who can t H7725
24: 4 They t the needy out of the way: the H5186
34:15 and man shall t again unto dust. H7725
Ps 4: 2 O ye sons of men, how long *will ye* t my
7:12 If he t not, he will whet his sword; he H7725
18:37 did I t again till they were consumed. H7725
21:12 Therefore shalt thou make them t their
22:27 remember and t unto the LORD: and H7725
25:16 T thee unto me, and have mercy upon H6437
40: 4 the proud, nor such as t aside to lies. H7750
44:10 Thou makest us to t back from the H7725
56: 9 t back: this I know; for God *is* for me. H7725
60: 1 been displeased; O t thyself to us again. H7725
69:16 *is* good: t unto me according H6437
80: 3 T us again, O God, and cause thy face H7725
7 T us again, O God of hosts, and cause H7725
19 T us again, O LORD God of hosts, H7725
85: 4 T us, O God of our salvation, and cause H7725
Ps 85: 8 saints: but let them not t again to folly. H7725
86:16 O t unto me, and have mercy upon me; H6437
101: 3 that t aside; *it* shall not cleave to me. H7750
104: 9 that they t not again to cover the earth. H7725
106:23 in the breach, to t away his wrath, lest H7725
119:37 T away mine eyes from beholding H5674
39 T away my reproach which I fear: for H5674
79 Let those that fear thee t unto me, and H7725
125: 5 As for such as t aside unto their H5186
126: 4 T again our captivity, O LORD, as the H7725
132:10 For thy servant David's sake t not away H7725
11 David; he will not t from it; Of the fruit H7725
Prv 1:23 T you at my reproof: behold, I will pour H7725
4:15 Avoid it, pass not by it, t from it, and H7847
27 T not to the right hand nor to the left: H5186
9: 4 Whoso *is* simple, let him t in hither: *as* H7725
16 Whoso *is* simple, let him t in hither: H7725
24:18 and he t away his wrath from him. H7725
25:10 to shame, and thine infamy t not away. H7725
29: 8 a snare: but wise *men* t away wrath. H7725
Ecc 3:20 are of the dust, and all t to dust again. H7725
Song 2:17 flee away, t, my beloved, and be H5437
6: 5 T away thine eyes from me, for they H5437
Isa 1:25 And I will t my hand upon thee, and H7725
10: 2 To t aside the needy from judgment, H5186
13:14 shall every man t to his own people, H6437
14:27 stretched out, and who shall t it back? H7725
19: 6 And they shall t the rivers far away; H2186
22:18 He will surely violently t and toss thee H6801
23:17 and she shall t to her hire, and shall H7725
28: 6 to them that t the battle to the gate. H7725
29:21 t aside the just for a thing of nought. H5186
30:11 Get you out of the way, t aside out of H5186
21 ye in it, when ye t to the right hand, and
21 the right hand, and when ye t to the left.
31: 6 T ye unto *him from* whom the children H7725
36: 9 How then wilt thou t away the face of H7725
37:29 in thy lips, and I will t thee back by the H7725
58:13 If thou t away thy foot from the H7725
59:20 unto them that t from transgression H7725
Jer 2:24 occasion who can t her away? all they H7725
35 his anger shall t from me. Behold, I will H7725
3: 7 all these *things,* T thou unto me. But H7725
14 T, O backsliding children, saith the H7725
19 father; and shalt not t away from me. H7725
4:28 not repent, neither will I t back from it. H7725
6: 9 of Israel as a vine: t back thine hand as H7725
8: 4 arise? shall he t away, and not return? H7725
13:16 look for light, he t it into the shadow of H7760
18: 8 I have pronounced, t from their evil, I H7725
20 *and* to t away thy wrath from them. H7725
21: 4 Behold, I will t back the weapons of H5437
25: 5 They said, T ye again now every one H7725
26: 3 If so be they will hearken, and t every H7725
29:14 LORD: and I will t away your captivity, H7725
31:13 old together: for I will t their mourning H2015
18 *to the yoke:* t thou me, and I shall H7725
21 *which* thou wentest: t again, O virgin of H7725
21 of Israel, t again to these thy cities. H7725
32:40 that I will not t away from them, to H7725
44: 5 their ear to t from their wickedness, H7725
49: 8 Flee ye, t back, dwell deep, O H6437
50:16 sword they shall t every one to his H6437
Lam 2:14 thine iniquity, to t away thy captivity; H7725
3:35 To t aside the right of a man before the H5186
40 Let us search and try our ways, and t H7725
5:21 T thou us unto thee, O LORD, and we H7725
Ezk 3:19 Yet if thou warn the wicked, and he t H7725
20 Again, When a righteous *man* doth t H7725
4: 8 and thou shalt not t thee from one side H2015
7:22 My face will I t also from them, and H5437
8: 6 my sanctuary? but t thee yet again, *and* H7725
13 He said also unto me, T thee yet again, H7725
15 O son of man? t thee yet again, *and* H7725
14: 6 GOD; Repent, and t *yourselves* from H7725
6 your idols; and t away your faces from H7725
18:21 But if the wicked will t from all his sins H7725
30 GOD. Repent, and t *yourselves* from all H7725
32 wherefore t *yourselves,* and live ye. H7725
33: 9 of his way to t from it; if he do not H7725
9 it; if he do not t from his way, he shall H7725
11 that the wicked t from his way and live: H7725
11 his way and live: t ye, turn ye from H7725
11 and live: turn ye, t ye from your evil H7725
14 surely die; if he t from his sin, and do H7725
19 But if the wicked t from his H7725
36: 9 For, behold, I *am* for you, and I will t H6437
38: 4 And I will t thee back, and put hooks H7725
12 To take a spoil, and to take a prey; to t H7725
Ezk 39: 2 And I will t thee back, and leave but the H7725
Dan 9:13 that we might t from our iniquities, H7725
11:18 After this shall he t his face unto the H7725
18 he shall cause *it* to t upon him. H7725
19 Then he shall t his face toward the fort H7725
12: 3 and they that t many to righteousness H7725
Hos 5: 4 They will not frame their doings to t H7725
12: 6 Therefore t thou to thy God: keep H7725
14: 2 Take with you words, and t to the H7725
Joel 2:12 Therefore also now, saith the LORD, t H7725
13 garments, and t unto the LORD your H7725
Am 1: 3 and for four, I will not t away *the* H7725
6 and for four, I will not t away *the* H7725
8 and I will t mine hand against Ekron: H7725
9 and for four, I will not t away *the* H7725
11 and for four, I will not t away *the* H7725
13 and for four, I will not t away *the* H7725
2: 1 and for four, I will not t away *the* H7725
4 and for four, I will not t away *the* H7725
6 and for four, I will not t away *the* H7725
7 of the poor, and t aside the way of the H5186
5: 7 Ye who t judgment to wormwood, and H2015
12 a bribe, and they t aside the poor in the H5186
8:10 And I will t your feasts into mourning, H2015
Jna 3: 8 God: yea, let them t every one from his H7725
9 Who can tell *if* God will t and repent, H7725
9 and repent, and t away from his fierce H7725
Mic 7:19 He will t again, he will have H7725
Zep 2: 7 visit them, and t away their captivity. H7725
3: 9 For then will I t to the people a pure H2015
20 the earth, when I t back your captivity H2015
Zec 1: 3 LORD of hosts; T ye unto me, saith the H7725
3 t unto you, saith the LORD of hosts. H7725
4 LORD of hosts; T ye now from your evil H7725
9:12 T you to the strong hold, ye prisoners H7725
10: 9 live with their children, and t again. H7725
13: 7 I will t mine hand upon the little ones. H7725
Mal 2: 6 and did t many away from iniquity. H7725
3: 5 and that t aside the stranger *from* H5186
4: 6 And he shall t the heart of the fathers H7725
Mt 5:39 thy right cheek, t to him the other also. G4762
42 would borrow of thee t not thou away. G654
7: 6 their feet, and t again and rend you. G4762
Mk 13:16 And let him that is in the field not t G1994
Lk 1:16 Israel shall he t to the Lord their God. G1994
17 power of Elias, to t the hearts of the G1994
10: 6 rest upon it: if not, it shall t to you again. G344
17: 4 times in a day t again to thee, saying, G1994
21:13 And it shall t to you for a testimony. G576
Act 13: 8 to t away the deputy from the faith. G1294
46 everlasting life, lo, we t to the Gentiles. G4762
14:15 you that ye should t from these vanities G1994
26:18 To open their eyes, *and* to t *them* from G1994
20 should repent and t to God, and do G1994
Ro 11:26 shall t away ungodliness from Jacob: G654
2Co 3:16 Nevertheless when it shall t to the Lord, G1994
Gal 4: 9 of God, how t ye again to the weak G1994
Php 1:19 For I know that this shall t to my G576
2Ti 3: 5 the power thereof: from such t away. G665
4: 4 And they shall t away *their* ears from the G654
Tit 1:14 of men, that t from the truth. G654
Heb 12:25 we *escape,* if we t away from him that G654
Jas 3: 3 us; and we t about their whole body. G3329
2Pt 2:21 they have known *it,* to t from the holy G1994
Rev 11: 6 over waters to t them to blood, and G4762

TURNED

Gen 3:24 sword which t every way, to keep the H2015
18:22 And the men t their faces from thence, H6437
19: 3 greatly; and they t in unto him, and H5493
38: 1 from his brethren, and t in to a certain H5186
16 And he t unto her by the way, and said, H5186
42:24 And he t himself about from them, and H5437
Ex 3: 4 And when the LORD saw that he t H5493
4: 7 behold, it was t again as his *other* flesh. H7725
7:15 the rod which was t to a serpent shalt H2015
17 the river, and they shall be t to blood. H2015
20 that *were* in the river were t to blood. H2015
23 And Pharaoh t and went into his H6437
10: 6 t himself, and went out from Pharaoh. H6437
19 And the LORD t a mighty strong west H2015
14: 5 his servants was t against the people, H2015
32: 8 They have t aside quickly out of the H5493
15 And Moses t, and went down from the H6437
33:11 unto his friend. And he t again into the H7725
Lev 13: 3 in the plague is t white, and the plague H2015
4 the hair thereof be not t white; then the H2015
10 skin, and it have t the hair white, and H2015
13 the plague: it is all t white: he *is* clean. H2015

T

Lev 13:17 *if* the plague be **t** into white; then the H2015
20 the hair thereof be **t** white; the priest H2015
25 the bright spot be **t** white, and it *be in* H2015
Nu 14:43 because ye are **t** away from the LORD, H7725
20:21 wherefore Israel **t** away from him. H5186
21:33 And they **t** and went up by the way of H6437
22:23 his hand: and the ass **t** aside out of the H5186
33 And the ass saw me, and **t** from me H5186
33 unless she had **t** from me, surely now H5186
25: 4 the LORD may be **t** away from Israel. H7725
11 the priest, hath **t** my wrath away from H7725
33: 7 And they removed from Etham, and **t** H7725
Dt 1:24 And they **t** and went up into the H6437
2: 1 Then we **t**, and took our journey into H6437
8 Ezion-gaber, we **t** and passed by the H6437
3: 1 Then we **t**, and went up the way to H6437
9:12 they are quickly **t** aside out of the way H5493
15 So I **t** and came down from the mount, H6437
16 calf: ye had **t** aside quickly out of H5493
10: 5 And I **t** myself and came down from H6437
23: 5 but the LORD thy God **t** the curse into a H2015
31:18 in that they are **t** unto other gods. H6437
Jos 7:12 their enemies, *but* **t** *their* backs before H6437
26 day. So the LORD **t** from the fierceness H7725
8:20 wilderness **t** back upon the pursuers. H2015
21 they **t** again, and slew the men of Ai. H7725
11:10 And Joshua at that time **t** back, and H7725
19:12 And **t** from Sarid eastward toward the H7725
Jdg 2:17 unto them: they **t** quickly out of the H5493
3:19 But he himself **t** again from the H7725
4:18 And when he had **t** in unto her into the H5493
8:33 children of Israel **t** again, and went a H7925
14: 8 to take her, and he **t** aside to see the H5493
15: 4 firebrands, and **t** tail to tail, and put a H6437
18: 3 Levite: and they **t** in thither, and said H5493
15 And they **t** thitherward, and came to H5493
21 So they **t** and departed, and put the H6437
23 of Dan. And they **t** their faces, and said H5437
26 he **t** and went back unto his house. H6437
19:15 And they **t** aside thither, to go in *and* to H5493
20:41 And when the men of Israel **t** again, the H2015
42 Therefore they **t** *their backs* before the H6437
45 And they **t** and fled toward the H6437
47 But six hundred men **t** and fled to the H6437
48 And the men of Israel **t** again upon the H7725
Ru 3: 8 was afraid, and **t** himself: and, behold, H3943
4: 1 here. And he **t** aside, and sat down. H5493
1Sa 6:12 as they went, and **t** not aside *to* the H5493
8: 3 in his ways, but **t** aside after lucre, and H5186
10: 6 them, and shalt be **t** into another man. H2015
9 And it was *so*, that when he had **t** his H6437
13:17 one company **t** unto the way *that* H6437
18 And another company **t** the way *to* H6437
18 another company **t** *to* the way of the H6437
14:21 even they also *t* to be with the Israelites
47 he **t** himself, he vexed *them*. H6437
15:11 *be* king: for he is **t** back from following H7725
27 And as Samuel **t** about to go away, he H5437
31 So Samuel **t** again after Saul; and Saul H7725
17:30 And he **t** from him toward another, H5437
22:18 Doeg the Edomite **t**, and he fell upon H5437
25:12 So David's young men **t** their way, and H2015
2Sa 1:22 the bow of Jonathan **t** not back, and the H7734
2:19 and in going he **t** not to the right hand H5186
18:30 here. And he **t** aside, and stood still. H5437
19: 2 And the victory that day was **t** into
22:38 **t** not again until I had consumed them. H7725
1Ki 2:15 the kingdom is **t** about, and is become H5437
28 to Joab: for Joab had **t** after Adonijah, H5186
28 though he **t** not after Absalom. And H5186
8:14 And the king **t** his face about, and H5437
10:13 bounty. So she **t** and went to her own H6437
11: 3 and his wives **t** away his heart. H5186
4 was old, *that* his wives **t** away his heart H5186
9 his heart was **t** from the LORD God H5186
15: 5 of the LORD, and **t** not aside from any H5493
18:37 *that* thou hast **t** their heart back again. H5437
20:39 behold, a man **t** aside, and brought H5493
21: 4 upon his bed, and **t** away his face, and H5437
22:32 king of Israel. And they **t** aside to fight H5493
33 that they **t** back from pursuing him. H7725
43 of Asa his father; he **t** not aside from it, H5493
2Ki 1: 5 And when the messengers **t** back unto H7725
5 unto them, Why are ye now **t** back? H7725
2:24 And he **t** back, and looked on them, H6437
4: 8 passed by, he **t** in thither to eat bread. H5493
11 he **t** into the chamber, and lay there. H5493
5:12 clean? So he **t** and went away in a rage. H6437
26 when the man **t** again from his chariot H2015

2Ki 9:23 And Joram **t** his hands, and fled, and H2015
15:20 the king of Assyria **t** back, and stayed H7725
16:18 entry without, **t** he from the house of H5437
20: 2 Then he **t** his face to the wall, and H5437
22: 2 his father, and **t** not aside to the right H5493
23:16 And as Josiah **t** himself, he spied the H6437
25 before him, that **t** to the LORD with all H7725
26 Notwithstanding the LORD **t** not from H7725
34 Josiah his father, and **t** his name to H5437
24: 1 then he **t** and rebelled against him. H7725
1Ch 10:14 he slew him, and **t** the kingdom unto H5437
21:20 And Ornan **t** back, and saw the angel; H7725
2Ch 6: 3 And the king **t** his face, and blessed the H5437
9:12 the king. So she **t**, and went away to her H2015
12:12 wrath of the LORD **t** from him, that he H7725
18:32 they **t** back again from pursuing him. H7725
20:10 **t** from them, and destroyed them not; H5493
29: 6 him, and have **t** away their faces from H5437
6 of the LORD, and **t** *their* backs. H5414
36: 4 and Jerusalem, and **t** his name to H5437
Ezr 6:22 them joyful, and **t** the heart of the king H5437
10:14 of our God for this matter be **t** from us. H7725
Neh 2:15 the wall, and **t** back, and entered by H7725
9:35 neither **t** they from their wicked works. H7725
13: 2 our God **t** the curse into a blessing. H2015
Est 9: 1 (though it was **t** to the contrary, that H2015
22 the month which was **t** unto them from H2015
Job 6:18 The paths of their way are **t** aside; they H3943
16:11 **t** me over into the hands of the wicked. H3399
19:19 they whom I loved are **t** against me. H2015
20:14 *Yet* his meat in his bowels is **t**, *it is* the H2015
28: 5 and under it is **t** up as it were fire. H2015
30:15 Terrors are **t** upon me: they pursue my H2015
31 My harp also is *t* to mourning, and my
31: 7 If my step hath **t** out of the way, and H5186
34:27 Because they **t** back from him, and H5493
37:12 And it is **t** round about by his counsels: H2015
38:14 It is **t** as clay *to* the seal; and they stand H2015
41:22 and sorrow is **t** into joy before him. H1750
28 slingstones are **t** with him into stubble. H2015
42:10 And the LORD **t** the captivity of Job, H7725
Ps 9: 3 When mine enemies are **t** back, they H7725
17 The wicked shall be **t** into hell, *and* all H7725
30:11 Thou hast **t** for me my mourning into H2015
32: 4 is **t** into the drought of summer. Selah. H2015
35: 4 soul: let them be **t** back and brought to H5472
44:18 Our heart is not **t** back, neither have H5472
66: 6 He **t** the sea into dry *land*: they went H2015
20 Blessed *be* God, which hath not **t** away H5493
70: 2 soul: let them be **t** backward, and put H5472
3 Let them be **t** back for a reward of their H7725
78: 9 bows, **t** back in the day of battle. H2015
38 yea, many a time **t** he his anger away, H7725
41 Yea, they **t** back and tempted God, and H7725
44 And had **t** their rivers into blood; and H2015
57 But **t** back, and dealt unfaithfully like H5472
57 they were **t** aside like a deceitful bow. H2015
81:14 **t** my hand against their adversaries. H7725
85: 3 thy wrath: thou hast **t** *thyself* from the H7725
89:43 Thou hast also **t** the edge of his sword, H7725
105:25 He **t** their heart to hate his people, to H2015
29 He **t** their waters into blood, and slew H2015
114: 8 Which **t** the rock *into* a standing water, H2015
119:59 I thought on my ways, and **t** my feet H7725
126: 1 When the LORD **t** again the captivity of H7725
129: 5 Let them all be confounded and **t** back H5472
Ecc 2:12 And I **t** myself to behold wisdom, and H6437
Song 6: 1 is thy beloved **t** aside? that we may H6437
Isa 5:25 his anger is not **t** away, but his hand H7725
9:12 his anger is not **t** away, but his hand H7725
17 his anger is not **t** away, but his hand H7725
21 his anger is not **t** away, but his hand H7725
10: 4 his anger is not **t** away, but his hand H7725
12: 1 is **t** away, and thou comfortedst me. H7725
21: 4 pleasure hath he **t** into fear unto me. H7760
28:27 neither is a cart wheel **t** about upon the H5437
29:17 Lebanon shall be **t** into a fruitful field, H7725
34: 9 And the streams thereof shall be **t** into H2015
38: 2 Then Hezekiah **t** his face toward the H5437
42:17 They shall be **t** back, they shall be H5472
44:20 heart hath **t** him aside, that he cannot H5186
50: 5 not rebellious, neither **t** away back. H5472
53: 6 astray; we have **t** every one to his own H6437
59:14 And judgment is **t** away backward, and H5253
63:10 therefore he was **t** to be their enemy, H2015
Jer 2:21 how then art thou **t** into the degenerate H2015
27 for they have **t** *their* back unto me, H6437
3:10 Judah hath not **t** unto me with her H7725
4: 8 of the LORD is not **t** back from us. H7725

Jer 5:25 Your iniquities have **t** away these H5186
6:12 And their houses shall be **t** unto others, H5437
8: 6 I done? every one **t** to his course, as the H7725
11:10 They are **t** back to the iniquities of their H7725
23:22 they should have **t** them from their evil H7725
30: 6 and all faces are **t** into paleness? H2015
31:18 be **t**; for thou *art* the LORD my God. H7725
19 Surely after that I was **t**, I repented; and H7725
32:33 And they have **t** unto me the back, and H6437
34:11 But afterward they **t**, and caused the H7725
15 And ye were now **t**, and had done right H7725
16 But ye **t** and polluted my name, and H7725
38:22 in the mire, *and* they are **t** away back. H5472
46: 5 dismayed *and* **t** away back? and their H5472
21 for they also are **t** back, *and* are fled H6437
48:39 how hath Moab **t** the back with shame! H6437
50: 6 astray, they have **t** them away *on* the H7725
Lam 1:13 for my feet, he hath **t** me back: he hath H7725
20 mine heart is **t** within me; for I have H2015
3: 3 Surely against me is he **t**; he turneth his H7725
11 He hath **t** aside my ways, and pulled H5493
5: 2 Our inheritance is **t** to strangers, our H2015
15 is ceased; our dance is **t** into mourning. H2015
21 we shall be **t**; renew our days as of old. H7725
Ezk 1: 9 to another; they **t** not when they went; H5437
12 went; *and* they **t** not when they went. H5437
17 sides: *and* they **t** not when they went. H5437
10:11 four sides; they **t** not as they went, but H5437
11 followed it; they **t** not as they went. H5437
16 wheels also **t** not from beside them. H5437
17: 6 whose branches **t** toward him, and the H6437
26: 2 the people: she is **t** unto me: I shall be H5437
42:19 He **t** about to the west side, *and* H5437
Dan 9:16 and thy fury be **t** away from thy city H7725
10: 8 my comeliness was **t** in me into H2015
16 my sorrows are **t** upon me, and I have H2015
Hos 7: 8 the people; Ephraim is a cake not **t**. H2015
11: 8 Zeboim? mine heart is **t** within me, my H2015
14: 4 for mine anger is **t** away from him. H7725
Joel 2:31 The sun shall be **t** into darkness, and H2015
Am 6:12 oxen? for ye have **t** judgment into gall, H2015
Jna 3:10 And God saw their works, that they **t** H7725
Nah 2: 2 For the LORD hath **t** away the H7725
Hab 2:16 right hand shall be **t** unto thee, and H5437
Zep 1: 6 And them that are **t** back from the H5472
Hag 2:17 yet ye *t* not to me, saith the LORD.
Zec 5: 1 Then I **t**, and lifted up mine eyes, and H7725
6: 1 And I **t**, and lifted up mine eyes, and H7725
14:10 All the land shall be **t** as a plain from H5437
Mt 2:22 he **t** aside into the parts of Galilee: *G402*
9:22 But Jesus **t** him about, and when he *G1994*
16:23 But he **t**, and said unto Peter, Get thee *G4762*
Mk 5:30 had gone out of him, **t** him about in the *G1994*
8:33 But when he had **t** about and looked on *G1994*
Lk 2:45 And when they found him not, they **t** *G5290*
7: 9 at him, and **t** him about, and said *G4762*
44 And he **t** to the woman, and said unto *G4762*
9:55 But he **t**, and rebuked them, and said, *G4762*
10:23 And he **t** him unto *his* disciples, and *G4762*
14:25 with him: and he **t**, and said unto them, *G4762*
17:15 he was healed, **t** back, and with a loud *G5290*
22:61 And the Lord **t**, and looked upon Peter. *G4762*
Jn 1:38 Then Jesus **t**, and saw them following, *G4762*
16:20 but your sorrow shall be **t** into joy. *G1096*
20:14 And when she had thus said, she **t** *G4762*
16 Jesus saith unto her, Mary. She **t** *G4762*
Act 2:20 The sun shall be **t** into darkness, and *G3344*
7:39 in their hearts **t** back again into Egypt, *G4762*
42 Then God **t**, and gave them up to *G4762*
9:35 and Saron saw him, and **t** to the Lord. *G1994*
11:21 number believed, and **t** unto the Lord. *G1994*
15:19 from among the Gentiles are **t** to God: *G1994*
16:18 being grieved, **t** and said to the spirit, *G1994*
17: 6 These that have **t** the world upside down *G387*
19:26 persuaded and **t** away much people, *G3172*
1Th 1: 9 you, and how ye **t** to God from idols to *G1994*
1Ti 1: 6 have **t** aside unto vain jangling; *G1824*
5:15 For some are already **t** aside after *G1824*
2Ti 1:15 are in Asia be **t** away from me; of whom *G654*
4: 4 the truth, and shall be **t** unto fables. *G1624*
Heb 11:34 fight, **t** to flight the armies of the aliens. *G2827*
12:13 which is lame be **t** out of the way; but *G1624*
Jas 3: 4 winds, yet are they **t** about with a very *G3329*
4: 9 let your laughter be **t** to mourning, and *G3344*
2Pt 2:22 The dog *is* **t** to his own vomit again; *G1994*
Rev 1:12 And I **t** to see the voice that spake with *G1994*
12 **t**, I saw seven golden candlesticks; *G1994*

TURNEST
1Ki 2: 3 doest, and whithersoever thou **t** thyself: H6437
Job 15:13 That thou **t** thy spirit against God, and H7725
Ps 90: 3 Thou **t** man to destruction; and sayest, H7725

TURNETH
Lev 20: 6 And the soul that **t** after such as have H6437
Dt 29:18 tribe, whose heart **t** away this day from H6437
Jos 7: 8 O Lord, what shall I say, when Israel **t** H2015
19:27 And **t** toward the sunrising to H7725
29 And *then* the coast **t** to Ramah, and to H7725
29 Tyre; and the coast **t** to Hosah; and the H7725
34 And *then* the coast **t** westward to H7725
Job 39:22 neither **t** he back from the sword. H7725
Ps 107:33 He **t** rivers into a wilderness, and the H7760
35 He **t** the wilderness into a standing H7760
146: 9 way of the wicked he **t** upside down. H5791
Prv 15: 1 A soft answer **t** away wrath: but H7725
17: 8 hath it: whithersoever it **t**, it prospereth. H6437
21: 1 of water: he **t** it whithersoever he will. H5186
26:14 *As* the door **t** upon his hinges, so *doth* H5437
28: 9 He that **t** away his ear from hearing the H5493
30:30 among beasts, and **t** not away for any; H7725
Ecc 1: 6 The wind goeth toward the south, and **t** H5437
Song 1: 7 I be as one that **t** aside by the flocks of H5844
Isa 9:13 For the people **t** not unto him that H7725
24: 1 it waste, and **t** it upside down, and H5753
44:25 maketh diviners mad; that **t** wise *men* H7725
Jer 14: 8 man *that* **t** aside to tarry for a night? H5186
49:24 Damascus is waxed feeble, *and* **t** H6437
Lam 1: 8 yea, she sigheth, and **t** backward. H7725
3: 3 Surely against me is he turned; he **t** his H2015
Ezk 18:24 But when the righteous **t** away from his H7725
26 When a righteous *man* **t** away from his H7725
27 Again, when the wicked *man* **t** away H7725
28 Because he considereth, and **t** away H7725
33:12 thereby in the day that he **t** from his H7725
18 When the righteous **t** from his H7725
Am 5: 8 and Orion, and **t** the shadow of death H2015

TURNING
2Ki 21:13 a dish, wiping *it*, and **t** *it* upside down. H2015
2Ch 26: 9 at the **t** *of the wall*, and fortified them. H4740
36:13 from **t** unto the LORD God of Israel. H7725
Neh 3:19 up to the armoury at the **t** *of the wall*. H4740
20 piece, from the **t** *of the wall* unto the H4740
24 the **t** *of the wall*, even unto the corner. H4740
25 Palal the son of Uzai, over against the **t** H4740
Prv 1:32 For the **t** away of the simple shall slay H4878
Isa 29:16 Surely your **t** of things upside down H2017
Ezk 41:24 leaves *apiece*, two **t** leaves; two *leaves* H4142
Mic 2: 4 me! **t** away he hath divided our fields. H7725
Lk 23:28 But Jesus **t** unto them said, Daughters *G4762*
Jn 21:20 Then Peter, **t** about, seeth the disciple *G1994*
Act 3:26 him to bless you, in **t** away every one of *G654*
9:40 and prayed; and **t** *him* to the body said, *G1994*
Jas 1:17 is no variableness, neither shadow of **t**. *G5157*
2Pt 2: 6 And **t** the cities of Sodom and *G5077*
Jude 4 ungodly men, **t** the grace of our God *G3346*

TURTLE
Song 2:12 the voice of the **t** is heard in our land; H8449
Jer 8: 7 times; and the **t** and the crane and the H8449

TURTLEDOVE
Gen 15: 9 years old, and a **t**, and a young pigeon. H8449
Lev 12: 6 a young pigeon, or a **t**, for a sin offering, H8449
Ps 74:19 O deliver not the soul of thy **t** unto the H8449

TURTLEDOVES
Lev 1:14 his offering of **t**, or of young pigeons. H8449
5: 7 hath committed, two **t**, or two young H8449
11 But if he be not able to bring two **t**, or H8449
14:22 And two **t**, or two young pigeons, such H8449
30 And he shall offer the one of the **t**, or of H8449
15:14 shall take to him two **t**, or two young H8449
Lk 2:24 Lord, A pair of **t**, or two young pigeons. *G5167*

TURTLES
Lev 12: 8 shall bring two **t**, or two young pigeons; H8449
15:29 shall take unto her two **t**, or two young H8449
Nu 6:10 day he shall bring two **t**, or two young H8449

TUTORS
Gal 4: 2 But is under **t** and governors until the *G2012*

TWAIN
1Sa 18:21 day be my son in law in *the one of* the **t**. H8147
2Ki 4:33 them **t**, and prayed unto the LORD. H8147
Isa 6: 2 six wings; with **t** he covered his face, H8147
2 his face, and with **t** he covered his feet, H8147
2 covered his feet, and with **t** he did fly. H8147
Jer 34:18 **t**, and passed between the parts thereof, H8147
Ezk 21:19 may come: both **t** shall come forth out H8147
Mt 5:41 compel thee to go a mile, go with him **t**. *G1417*
19: 5 his wife: and they **t** shall be one flesh? *G1417*
6 Wherefore they are no more **t**, but one *G1417*
21:31 Whether of them **t** did the will of *his* *G1417*
27:21 Whether of the **t** will ye that I release *G1417*
51 temple was rent in **t** from the top to the *G1417*
Mk 10: 8 And they **t** shall be one flesh: so then *G1417*
8 then they are no more **t**, but one flesh. *G1417*
15:38 And the veil of the temple was rent in **t** *G1417*
Eph 2:15 of **t** one new man, *so* making peace; *G1417*

TWELFTH
Nu 7:78 On the **t** day Ahira the son of H8147+H6240
1Ki 19:19 he with the **t**: and Elijah passed H8147+H6240
2Ki 8:25 In the **t** year of Joram the son H8147+H6240
17: 1 In the **t** year of Ahaz king of H8147+H6240
25:27 Judah, in the **t** month, on the H8147+H6240
1Ch 24:12 The eleventh to Eliashib, the **t** H8147+H6240
25:19 The **t** to Hashabiah, *he*, his H8147+H6240
27:15 The **t** *captain* for the twelfth H8147+H6240
15 The twelfth *captain* for the **t** H8147+H6240
2Ch 34: 3 and in the **t** year he began to H8147+H6240
Ezr 8:31 Ahava on the **t** *day* of the first H8147+H6240
Est 3: 7 Nisan, in the **t** year of king H8147+H6240
7 month, *to* the **t** *month*, that *is*, H8147+H6240
13 *day* of the **t** month, which is H8147+H6240
8:12 *day* of the **t** month, which *is* H8147+H6240
9: 1 Now in the **t** month, that *is*, H8147+H6240
Jer 52:31 of Judah, in the **t** month, in the H8147+H6240
Ezk 29: 1 tenth *month*, in the **t** *day* of the H8147+H6240
32: 1 And it came to pass in the **t** H8147+H6240
1 year, in the **t** month, in the H8147+H6240
17 It came to pass also in the **t** H8147+H6240
33:21 And it came to pass in the **t** H8147+H6240
Rev 21:20 eleventh, a jacinth; the **t**, an amethyst. *G1428*

TWELVE
Gen 5: 8 and **t** years: and he died. H8147+H6240
14: 4 **T** years they served H8147+H6240
17:20 exceedingly; **t** princes shall he H8147+H6240
25:16 by their castles; **t** princes H8147+H6240
35:22 Now the sons of Jacob were **t**: H8147+H6240
42:13 servants *are* **t** brethren, the H8147+H6240
32 We *be* **t** brethren, sons of our H8147+H6240
49:28 All these *are* the **t** tribes of H8147+H6240
Ex 15:27 where *were* **t** wells of water, H8147+H6240
24: 4 under the hill, and **t** pillars, H8147+H6240
4 to the **t** tribes of Israel. H8147+H6240
28:21 of Israel, **t**, according to their H8147+H6240
21 be according to the **t** tribes. H8147+H6240
39:14 of Israel, **t**, according to their H8147+H6240
14 according to the **t** tribes. H8147+H6240
Lev 24: 5 and bake **t** cakes thereof: two H8147+H6240
Nu 1:44 Israel, *being* **t** men: each one H8147+H6240
7: 3 wagons, and **t** oxen; a wagon H8147+H6240
84 of Israel: **t** chargers of silver, H8147+H6240
84 of silver, **t** silver bowls, twelve H8147+H6240
84 silver bowls, **t** spoons of gold: H8147+H6240
86 The golden spoons *were* **t**, full H8147+H6240
87 offering *were* **t** bullocks, the H8147+H6240
87 the rams **t**, the lambs of the H8147+H6240
87 the first year **t**, with their meat H8147+H6240
87 of the goats for sin offering **t**. H8147+H6240
17: 2 their fathers **t** rods: write thou H8147+H6240
6 houses, *even* **t** rods: and the H8147+H6240
29:17 *ye shall offer* **t** young bullocks, H8147+H6240
31: 5 *every* tribe, **t** thousand armed for war. H8147
33 And threescore and **t** thousand beeves, H8147
38 tribute *was* threescore and **t**. H7657+H8147
33: 9 and in Elim *were* **t** fountains of H8147+H6240
Dt 1:23 **t** men of you, one of a tribe: H8147+H6240
Jos 3:12 Now therefore take you **t** men H8147+H6240
4: 2 Take you **t** men out of the H8147+H6240
3 stood firm, **t** stones, and ye H8147+H6240
4 Then Joshua called the **t** men, H8147+H6240
8 and took up **t** stones out of the H8147+H6240
9 And Joshua set up **t** stones in H8147+H6240
20 And those **t** stones, which they H8147+H6240
8:25 women, *were* **t** thousand, *even* H8147+H6240
18:24 **t** cities with their villages: H8147+H6240
19:15 **t** cities with their villages. H8147+H6240
21: 7 of the tribe of Zebulun, **t** cities. H8147+H6240
40 were *by* their lot **t** cities. H8147+H6240
Jdg 19:29 bones, into **t** pieces, and sent H8147+H6240
Jdg 21:10 sent thither **t** thousand men of H8147+H6240
2Sa 2:15 over by number **t** of Benjamin, H8147+H6240
15 and **t** of the servants of David. H8147+H6240
10: 6 of Ish-tob **t** thousand men. H8147+H6240
17: 1 choose out **t** thousand men, H8147+H6240
1Ki 4: 7 And Solomon had **t** officers H8147+H6240
26 and **t** thousand horsemen. H8147+H6240
7:15 and a line of **t** cubits did H8147+H6240
25 It stood upon **t** oxen, three H8147+H6240
44 And one sea, and **t** oxen under H8147+H6240
10:20 And **t** lions stood there on the H8147+H6240
26 chariots, and **t** thousand H8147+H6240
11:30 on him, and rent it *in* **t** pieces: H8147+H6240
16:23 over Israel, **t** years: six years H8147+H6240
18:31 And Elijah took **t** stones, H8147+H6240
19:19 plowing *with* **t** yoke *of oxen* H8147+H6240
2Ki 3: 1 of Judah, and reigned **t** years. H8147+H6240
21: 1 Manasseh *was* **t** years old H8147+H6240
1Ch 6:63 of the tribe of Zebulun, **t** cities. H8147+H6240
9:22 two hundred and **t**. These were H8147+H6240
15:10 his brethren an hundred and **t**. H8147+H6240
25: 9 his brethren and sons *were* **t**: H8147+H6240
10 sons, and his brethren, *were* **t**: H8147+H6240
11 sons, and his brethren, *were* **t**: H8147+H6240
12 sons, and his brethren, *were* **t**: H8147+H6240
13 sons, and his brethren, *were* **t**: H8147+H6240
14 sons, and his brethren, *were* **t**: H8147+H6240
15 sons, and his brethren, *were* **t**: H8147+H6240
16 sons, and his brethren, *were* **t**: H8147+H6240
17 sons, and his brethren, *were* **t**: H8147+H6240
18 sons, and his brethren, *were* **t**: H8147+H6240
19 sons, and his brethren, *were* **t**: H8147+H6240
20 sons, and his brethren, *were* **t**: H8147+H6240
21 sons, and his brethren, *were* **t**: H8147+H6240
22 sons, and his brethren, *were* **t**: H8147+H6240
23 sons, and his brethren, *were* **t**: H8147+H6240
24 sons, and his brethren, *were* **t**: H8147+H6240
25 sons, and his brethren, *were* **t**: H8147+H6240
26 sons, and his brethren, *were* **t**: H8147+H6240
27 sons, and his brethren, *were* **t**: H8147+H6240
28 sons, and his brethren, *were* **t**: H8147+H6240
29 sons, and his brethren, *were* **t**: H8147+H6240
30 sons, and his brethren, *were* **t**: H8147+H6240
31 sons, and his brethren, *were* **t**. H8147+H6240
2Ch 1:14 chariots, and **t** thousand H8147+H6240
4: 4 It stood upon **t** oxen, three H8147+H6240
15 One sea, and **t** oxen under it. H8147+H6240
9:19 And **t** lions stood there on the H8147+H6240
25 and chariots, and **t** thousand H8147+H6240
12: 3 With **t** hundred chariots, and threescore H505
33: 1 Manasseh *was* **t** years old H8147+H6240
Ezr 2: 6 thousand eight hundred and **t**. H8147+H6240
18 of Jorah, an hundred and **t**. H8147+H6240
6:17 for all Israel, **t** he goats, H8648+H6236
8:24 Then I separated **t** of the chief H8147+H6240
35 God of Israel, **t** bullocks for all H8147+H6240
35 seven lambs, **t** he goats *for* a H8147+H6240
Neh 5:14 king, *that is*, **t** years, I and my H8147+H6240
7:24 of Hariph, an hundred and **t**. H8147+H6240
Est 2:12 that she had been **t** months, H8147+H6240
Ps 60: ttl in the valley of salt **t** thousand. H8147+H6240
Jer 52:20 The two pillars, one sea, and **t** H8147+H6240
21 and a fillet of **t** cubits did H8147+H6240
Ezk 43:16 And the altar *shall be* **t** *cubits* H8147+H6240
16 *cubits* long, **t** broad, square in H8147+H6240
47:13 to the **t** tribes of Israel: H8147+H6240
Dan 4:29 At the end of **t** months he H8648+H6236
Mt 9:20 an issue of blood **t** years, came behind *G1427*
10: 1 And when he had called unto *him* his **t** *G1427*
2 Now the names of the **t** apostles are *G1427*
5 These **t** Jesus sent forth, and *G1427*
11: 1 of commanding his **t** disciples, he *G1427*
14:20 fragments that remained **t** baskets full. *G1427*
19:28 ye also shall sit upon **t** thrones, judging *G1427*
28 thrones, judging the **t** tribes of Israel. *G1427*
20:17 Jerusalem took the **t** disciples apart in *G1427*
26:14 Then one of the **t**, called Judas Iscariot, *G1427*
20 even was come, he sat down with the **t**. *G1427*
47 Judas, one of the **t**, came, and with him *G1427*
53 give me more than **t** legions of angels? *G1427*
Mk 3:14 And he ordained **t**, that they should be *G1427*
4:10 with the **t** asked of him the parable. *G1427*
5:25 which had an issue of blood **t** years, *G1427*
42 was *of the age* of **t** years. And they were *G1427*
6: 7 And he called *unto him* the **t**, and began *G1427*
43 And they took up **t** baskets full of the *G1427*
8:19 took ye up? They say unto him, **T**. *G1427*
9:35 And he sat down, and called the **t**, and *G1427*
10:32 he took again the **t**, and began to tell *G1427*

Mk 11:11 he went out unto Bethany with the **t**. *G1427*
14:10 And Judas Iscariot, one of the **t**, went *G1427*
17 in the evening he cometh with the **t**. *G1427*
20 the **t**, that dippeth with me in the dish. *G1427*
43 Judas, one of the **t**, and with him a great *G1427*
Lk 2:42 And when he was **t** years old, they went *G1427*
6:13 chose **t**, whom also he named apostles; *G1427*
8: 1 of God: and the **t** *were* with him, *G1427*
42 For he had one only daughter, about **t** *G1427*
43 an issue of blood **t** years, which had *G1427*
9: 1 Then he called his **t** disciples together, *G1427*
12 then came the **t**, and said unto him, *G1427*
17 that remained to them **t** baskets. *G1427*
18:31 Then he took *unto him* the **t**, and said *G1427*
22: 3 Iscariot, being of the number of the **t**. *G1427*
14 sat down, and the **t** apostles with him. *G1427*
30 on thrones judging the **t** tribes of Israel. *G1427*
47 Judas, one of the **t**, went before them, *G1427*
Jn 6:13 and filled **t** baskets with the fragments *G1427*
67 Then said Jesus unto the **t**, Will ye also *G1427*
70 I chosen you **t**, and one of you is a devil? *G1427*
71 should betray him, being one of the **t**. *G1427*
11: 9 Jesus answered, Are there not **t** hours *G1427*
20:24 But Thomas, one of the **t**, called *G1427*
Act 6: 2 Then the **t** called the multitude of the *G1427*
7: 8 Jacob; and Jacob *begat* the **t** patriarchs. *G1427*
19: 7 And all the men were about **t**. *G1177*
24:11 there are yet but **t** days since I went up *G1177*
26: 7 Unto which *promise* our **t** tribes, *G1429*
1Co 15: 5 he was seen of Cephas, then of the **t**: *G1427*
Jas 1: 1 Jesus Christ, to the **t** tribes which are *G1427*
Rev 7: 5 Of the tribe of Juda *were* sealed **t** *G1427*
5 *were* sealed **t** thousand. Of the tribe *G1427*
5 tribe of Gad *were* sealed **t** thousand. *G1427*
6 Of the tribe of Aser *were* sealed **t** *G1427*
6 *were* sealed **t** thousand. Of the tribe *G1427*
6 of Manasses *were* sealed **t** thousand. *G1427*
7 Of the tribe of Simeon *were* sealed **t** *G1427*
7 of Levi *were* sealed **t** thousand. Of the *G1427*
7 of Issachar *were* sealed **t** thousand. *G1427*
8 Of the tribe of Zabulon *were* sealed **t** *G1427*
8 *were* sealed **t** thousand. Of the tribe *G1427*
8 of Benjamin *were* sealed **t** thousand. *G1427*
12: 1 and upon her head a crown of **t** stars: *G1427*
21:12 and high, *and* had **t** gates, and at the *G1427*
12 and at the gates **t** angels, and names *G1427*
12 of the **t** tribes of the children of Israel: *G1427*
14 And the wall of the city had **t** *G1427*
14 names of the **t** apostles of the Lamb. *G1427*
16 city with the reed, **t** thousand furlongs. *G1427*
21 And the **t** gates *were* twelve pearls; *G1427*
21 And the twelve gates *were* **t** pearls; *G1427*
22: 2 of life, which bare **t** *manner of* fruits, *G1427*

TWELVE-HUNDRED See TWELVE and HUNDRED.

TWELVE-THOUSAND See TWELVE and THOUSAND.

TWENTIETH

Gen 8:14 **t** day of the month, was the earth dried. H6242
Ex 12:18 the one and **t** day of the month at even. H6242
Nu 10:11 And it came to pass on the **t** *day* of the H6242
1Ki 15: 9 And in the **t** year of Jeroboam king of H6242
2Ki 12: 6 But it was *so, that* in the three and **t** H6242
13: 1 In the three and **t** year of Joash the son H6242
15:30 the **t** year of Jotham the son of Uzziah. H6242
25:27 on the seven and **t** *day* of the month, H6242
1Ch 24:16 The nineteenth to Pethahiah, the **t** to H6242
17 The one and **t** to Jachin, the two and H6242
17 to Jachin, the two and **t** to Gamul, H6242
18 The three and **t** to Delaiah, the four H6242
18 to Delaiah, the four and **t** to Maaziah. H6242
25:27 The **t** to Eliathah, *he,* his sons, and his H6242
28 The one and **t** to Hothir, *he,* his sons, H6242
29 The two and **t** to Giddalti, *he,* his sons, H6242
30 The three and **t** to Mahazioth, *he,* his H6242
31 The four and **t** to Romamti-ezer, *he,* H6242
2Ch 7:10 And on the three and **t** day of the H6242
Ezr 10: 9 month, on the **t** *day* of the month; and H6242
Neh 1: 1 **t** year, as I was in Shushan the palace, H6242
2: 1 Nisan, in the **t** year of Artaxerxes the H6242
5:14 of Judah, from the **t** year even unto the H6242
Est 8: 9 on the three and **t** *day* thereof; and it H6242
Jer 25: 3 *is* the three and **t** year, the word of the H6242
52:30 In the three and **t** year of H6242
31 in the five and **t** *day* of the month, *that* H6242
Ezk 29:17 And it came to pass in the seven and **t** H6242
40: 1 In the five and **t** year of our captivity, H6242
Dan 10: 4 And in the four and **t** day of the first H6242
Hag 1:15 In the four and **t** day of the sixth H6242
2: 1 In the seventh *month,* in the one and **t** H6242
10 In the four and **t** *day* of the ninth H6242
18 from the four and **t** day of the ninth H6242
20 four and **t** *day* of the month, saying, H6242
Zec 1: 7 Upon the four and **t** day of the eleventh H6242

TWENTY

Gen 6: 3 days shall be an hundred and **t** years. H6242
11:24 And Nahor lived nine and **t** years, and H6242
18:31 there shall be **t** found there. And he H6242
23: 1 and seven and **t** years old: *these were* H6242
31:38 This **t** years *have* I *been* with thee; thy H6242
41 Thus have I been **t** years in thy house; I H6242
32:14 Two hundred she goats, and **t** he goats, H6242
14 goats, two hundred ewes, and **t** rams, H6242
15 and ten bulls, **t** she asses, and ten foals. H6242
37:28 to the Ishmeelites for **t** *pieces* of silver: H6242
Ex 26: 2 *shall be* eight and **t** cubits, and the H6242
18 **t** boards on the south side southward. H6242
19 of silver under the **t** boards; two H6242
20 the north side *there shall be* **t** boards: H6242
27:10 And the **t** pillars thereof and their H6242
10 thereof and their **t** sockets *shall be of* H6242
11 long, and his **t** pillars and their twenty H6242
11 pillars and their **t** sockets *of* brass; the H6242
16 *be* an hanging of **t** cubits, *of* blue, and H6242
30:13 (a shekel *is* **t** gerahs:) an half shekel H6242
14 numbered, from **t** years old and above, H6242
36: 9 The length of one curtain *was* **t** and H6242
23 **t** boards for the south side southward: H6242
24 silver he made under the **t** boards; two H6242
25 the north corner, he made **t** boards, H6242
38:10 Their pillars *were* **t**, and their brasen H6242
10 brasen sockets **t**; the hooks of the pillars H6242
11 their pillars *were* **t**, and their sockets of H6242
11 their sockets of brass **t**; the hooks of the H6242
18 fine twined linen: and **t** cubits *was* the H6242
24 of the offering, was **t** and nine talents, H6242
26 be numbered, from **t** years old and H6242
Lev 27: 3 of the male from **t** years old even unto H6242
5 old even unto **t** years old, then thy H6242
5 be of the male **t** shekels, and for the H6242
25 sanctuary: **t** gerahs shall be the shekel. H6242
Nu 1: 3 From **t** years old and upward, all that H6242
18 **t** years old and upward, by their polls. H6242
20 polls, every male from **t** years old and H6242
22 polls, every male from **t** years old and H6242
24 of the names, from **t** years old and H6242
26 of the names, from **t** years old and H6242
28 of the names, from **t** years old and H6242
30 of the names, from **t** years old and H6242
32 of the names, from **t** years old and H6242
34 of the names, from **t** years old and H6242
36 of the names, from **t** years old and H6242
38 of the names, from **t** years old and H6242
40 of the names, from **t** years old and H6242
42 of the names, from **t** years old and H6242
45 of their fathers, from **t** years old and H6242
3:39 and upward, *were* **t** and two thousand. H6242
43 of them, were **t** and two thousand two H6242
47 take *them*: (the shekel *is* **t** gerahs:) H6242
7:86 spoons *was* an hundred and **t** *shekels.* H6242
88 offerings *were* **t** and four bullocks, the H6242
8:24 the Levites: from **t** and five years old H6242
11:19 five days, neither ten days, nor **t** days; H6242
14:29 number, from **t** years old and upward, H6242
18:16 of the sanctuary, which *is* **t** gerahs. H6242
25: 9 in the plague were **t** and four thousand. H6242
26: 2 of Israel, from **t** years old and upward, H6242
4 *Take the sum of the people,* from **t** H6242
14 **t** and two thousand and two hundred. H6242
62 of them were **t** and three thousand, H6242
32:11 up out of Egypt, from **t** years old and H6242
33:39 And Aaron *was* an hundred and **t** and H6242
Dt 31: 2 an hundred and **t** years old this day; I H6242
34: 7 And Moses *was* an hundred and **t** H6242
Jos 15:32 cities *are* **t** and nine, with their villages: H6242
19:30 Ummah also, and Aphek, and Rehob: **t** H6242
Jdg 4: 3 of iron; and **t** years he mightily H6242
7: 3 of the people **t** and two thousand; and H6242
8:10 and **t** thousand men that drew sword. H6242
10: 2 And he judged Israel **t** and three years, H6242
3 and judged Israel **t** and two years. H6242
11:33 to Minnith, *even* **t** cities, and unto the H6242
15:20 in the days of the Philistines **t** years. H6242
16:31 his father. And he judged Israel **t** years. H6242
20:15 out of the cities **t** and six thousand men H6242
21 that day **t** and two thousand men. H6242
Jdg 20:35 that day **t** and five thousand and H6242
46 of Benjamin were **t** and five thousand H6242
1Sa 7: 2 was long; for it was **t** years: and all the H6242
14:14 made, was about **t** men, within as it H6242
2Sa 3:20 to Hebron, and **t** men with him. And H6242
8: 4 horsemen, and **t** thousand footmen: H6242
5 of the Syrians two and **t** thousand men. H6242
9:10 Ziba had fifteen sons and **t** servants. H6242
10: 6 Syrians of Zoba, **t** thousand footmen, H6242
18: 7 slaughter that day of **t** thousand *men.* H6242
19:17 sons and his **t** servants with him; and H6242
21:20 six toes, four and **t** in number; and he H6242
24: 8 at the end of nine months and **t** days. H6242
1Ki 4:23 Ten fat oxen, and **t** oxen out of the H6242
5:11 And Solomon gave Hiram **t** thousand H6242
11 household, and **t** measures of pure oil: H6242
6: 2 breadth thereof **t** *cubits,* and the height H6242
3 of the house, **t** cubits *was* the length H6242
16 And he built **t** cubits on the sides of the H6242
20 And the oracle in the forepart *was* **t** H6242
20 in length, and **t** cubits in breadth, and H6242
20 in breadth, and **t** cubits in the height H6242
8:63 LORD, two and **t** thousand oxen, and H6242
63 an hundred and **t** thousand sheep. So H6242
9:10 And it came to pass at the end of **t** H6242
11 Hiram **t** cities in the land of Galilee. H6242
28 gold, four hundred and **t** talents, and H6242
10:10 an hundred and **t** talents of gold, and H6242
14:20 *were* two and **t** years: and he slept with H6242
15:33 all Israel in Tirzah, **t** and four years. H6242
16: 8 In the **t** and sixth year of Asa king of H6242
10 killed him, in the **t** and seventh year of H6242
15 In the **t** and seventh year of Asa king of H6242
29 over Israel in Samaria **t** and two years. H6242
20:30 a wall fell upon **t** and seven thousand H6242
22:42 and he reigned **t** and five years in H6242
2Ki 4:42 of the firstfruits, **t** loaves of barley, and H6242
8:26 Two and **t** years old *was* Ahaziah when H6242
10:36 in Samaria *was* **t** and eight years. H6242
14: 2 He was **t** and five years old when he H6242
2 reign, and reigned **t** and nine years in H6242
15: 1 In the **t** and seventh year of Jeroboam H6242
27 Israel in Samaria, *and reigned* **t** years. H6242
33 Five and **t** years old was he when he H6242
16: 2 **T** years old *was* Ahaz when he began to H6242
18: 2 **T** and five years old was he when he H6242
2 and he reigned **t** and nine years in H6242
21:19 Amon *was* **t** and two years old when he H6242
23:31 Jehoahaz *was* **t** and three years old H6242
36 Jehoiakim *was* **t** and five years old H6242
24:18 Zedekiah *was* **t** and one years old when H6242
1Ch 2:22 three and **t** cities in the land of Gilead. H6242
7: 2 two and **t** thousand and six hundred. H6242
7 their genealogies **t** and two thousand H6242
9 *was* **t** thousand and two hundred. H6242
40 to battle *was* **t** and six thousand men. H6242
12:28 his father's house **t** and two captains. H6242
30 And of the children of Ephraim **t** H6242
35 And of the Danites expert in war **t** and H6242
37 the battle, an hundred and **t** thousand. H6242
15: 5 and his brethren an hundred and **t**: H6242
6 and his brethren two hundred and **t**: H6242
18: 4 horsemen, and **t** thousand footmen: H6242
5 of the Syrians two and **t** thousand men. H6242
20: 6 toes *were* four and **t**, six *on each hand,* H6242
23: 4 Of which, **t** and four thousand *were* to H6242
24 from the age of **t** years and upward. H6242
27 numbered from **t** years old and above: H6242
27: 1 every course *were* **t** and four thousand. H6242
2 in his course *were* **t** and four thousand. H6242
4 likewise *were* **t** and four thousand. H6242
5 in his course *were* **t** and four thousand. H6242
7 in his course *were* **t** and four thousand. H6242
8 in his course *were* **t** and four thousand. H6242
9 in his course *were* **t** and four thousand. H6242
10 in his course *were* **t** and four thousand. H6242
11 in his course *were* **t** and four thousand. H6242
12 in his course *were* **t** and four thousand. H6242
13 in his course *were* **t** and four thousand. H6242
14 in his course *were* **t** and four thousand. H6242
15 in his course *were* **t** and four thousand. H6242
23 of them from **t** years old and under: H6242
2Ch 2:10 that cut timber, **t** thousand measures H6242
10 of beaten wheat, and **t** thousand H6242
10 of barley, and **t** thousand baths of H6242
10 of wine, and **t** thousand baths of oil. H6242
3: 3 cubits, and the breadth **t** cubits. H6242
4 of the house, **t** cubits, and the height H6242
4 an hundred and **t**: and he overlaid it H6242

2Ch 3: 8 of the house, t cubits, and the breadth H6242
8 the breadth thereof t cubits: and he H6242
11 And the wings of the cherubims *were* t H6242
13 themselves forth t cubits: and they H6242
4: 1 Moreover he made an altar of brass, t H6242
1 length thereof, and t cubits the breadth H6242
5:12 and t priests sounding with trumpets:) H6242
7: 5 a sacrifice of t and two thousand oxen, H6242
5 an hundred and t thousand sheep: so H6242
8: 1 And it came to pass at the end of t H6242
9: 9 an hundred and t talents of gold, and H6242
11:21 and begat t and eight sons, and H6242
13:21 t and two sons, and sixteen daughters. H6242
20:31 and he reigned t and five years in H6242
25: 1 Amaziah *was* t and five years old *when* H6242
1 and he reigned t and nine years in H6242
5 them from t years old and above, H6242
27: 1 Jotham *was* t and five years old when H6242
8 He was five and t years old when he H6242
28: 1 Ahaz *was* t years old when he began to H6242
6 an hundred and t thousand in one day, H6242
29: 1 *he was* five and t years old, and he H6242
1 reigned nine and t years in Jerusalem. H6242
31:17 and the Levites from t years old and H6242
33:21 Amon *was* two and t years old when he H6242
36: 2 Jehoahaz *was* t and three years old H6242
5 Jehoiakim *was* t and five years old H6242
11 Zedekiah *was* one and t years old when H6242
Ezr 1: 9 chargers of silver, nine and t knives, H6242
2:11 The children of Bebai, six hundred t H6242
12 a thousand two hundred t and two. H6242
17 The children of Bezai, three hundred t H6242
19 of Hashum, two hundred t and three. H6242
21 of Beth-lehem, an hundred t and three. H6242
23 The men of Anathoth, an hundred t H6242
26 and Gaba, six hundred t and one. H6242
27 The men of Michmas, an hundred t H6242
28 and Ai, two hundred t and three. H6242
32 children of Harim, three hundred and t. H6242
33 and Ono, seven hundred t and five. H6242
41 of Asaph, an hundred t and eight. H6242
67 six thousand seven hundred and t. H6242
3: 8 the Levites, from t years old and H6242
8:11 Bebai, and with him t and eight males. H6242
19 Merari, his brethren and their sons, t; H6242
20 two hundred and t Nethinims: all of H6242
27 Also t basons of gold, of a thousand H6242
Neh 6:15 So the wall was finished in the t and H6242
7:16 The children of Bebai, six hundred t H6242
17 two thousand three hundred t and two. H6242
22 of Hashum, three hundred t and eight. H6242
23 The children of Bezai, three hundred t H6242
27 The men of Anathoth, an hundred t H6242
30 and Geba, six hundred t and one. H6242
31 Michmas, an hundred and t and two. H6242
32 Beth-el and Ai, an hundred t and three. H6242
35 children of Harim, three hundred and t. H6242
37 and Ono, seven hundred t and one. H6242
69 thousand seven hundred and t asses. H6242
71 of the work t thousand drams of H8147
72 people gave *was* t thousand drams of H8147
9: 1 Now in the t and fourth day of this H6242
11: 8 Sallai, nine hundred t and eight. H6242
12 eight hundred t and two: and Adaiah H6242
14 an hundred t and eight: and their H6242
Est 1: 1 hundred and seven and t provinces:) H6242
8: 9 an hundred t and seven provinces, H6242
9:30 to the hundred t and seven provinces H6242
Ps 68:17 The chariots of God *are* t thousand, H7239
Jer 52: 1 Zedekiah *was* one and t years old when H6242
28 three thousand Jews and three and t: H6242
Ezk 4:10 eat *shall be* by weight, t shekels a day: H6242
8:16 about five and t men, with their backs H6242
11: 1 the gate five and t men; among whom H6242
40:13 five and t cubits, door against door. H6242
21 and the breadth five and t cubits. H6242
25 and the breadth five and t cubits. H6242
29 long, and five and t cubits broad. H6242
30 t cubits long, and five cubits broad. H6242
33 long, and five and t cubits broad. H6242
36 and the breadth five and t cubits. H6242
49 The length of the porch *was* t cubits, H6242
41: 2 forty cubits: and the breadth, t cubits. H6242
4 So he measured the length thereof, t H6242
4 and the breadth, t cubits, before the H6242
10 the wideness of t cubits round about H6242
42: 3 Over against the t *cubits* which *were* H6242
45: 1 the length of five and t thousand *reeds,* H6242
3 length of five and t thousand, and the H6242
Ezk 45: 5 And the five and t thousand of length, H6242
5 for a possession for t chambers. H6242
6 and five and t thousand long, over H6242
12 And the shekel *shall be* t gerahs: twenty H6242
12 And the shekel *shall be* twenty gerahs: t H6242
12 shekels, five and t shekels, fifteen H6242
48: 8 offer of five and t thousand *reeds in* H6242
9 LORD *shall be* of five and t thousand in H6242
10 the north five and t thousand *in length,* H6242
10 the south five and t thousand in length: H6242
13 *shall have* five and t thousand in H6242
13 *shall be* five and t thousand, and the H6242
15 the five and t thousand, shall be a H6242
20 All the oblation *shall be* five and t H6242
20 by five and t thousand: ye shall offer H6242
21 the five and t thousand of the oblation H6242
21 the five and t thousand toward the H6242
Dan 6: 1 an hundred and t princes, which H6243
10:13 me one and t days: but, lo, Michael, H6242
Hag 2:16 to an heap of t *measures,* there were H6242
16 out of the press, there were *but* t. H6242
Zec 5: 2 the length thereof *is* t cubits, and the H6242
Lk 14:31 cometh against him with t thousand? *G1501*
Jn 6:19 about five and t or thirty furlongs, they *G1501*
Act 1:15 together were about an hundred and t,) *G1501*
27:28 And sounded, and found *it* t fathoms: *G1501*
1Co 10: 8 fell in one day three and t thousand. *G1501*
Rev 4: 4 *were* four and t seats: and upon the *G1501*
4 I saw four and t elders sitting, clothed *G1501*
10 The four and t elders fall down before *G1501*
5: 8 and four *and* t elders fell down before *G1501*
14 And the four *and* t elders fell down and *G1501*
11:16 And the four and t elders, which sat *G1501*
19: 4 And the four and t elders and the four *G1501*

TWENTY'S

Gen 18:31 he said, I will not destroy *it* for t sake. H6242

TWENTY-THOUSAND See TWENTY and THOUSAND.

TWICE

Gen 41:32 unto Pharaoh t; *it is* because the thing H6471
Ex 16: 5 shall be t as much as they gather daily. H4932
22 day they gathered t as much bread, two H4932
Nu 20:11 he smote the rock t: and the water came H6471
1Sa 18:11 David avoided out of his presence t. H6471
1Ki 11: 9 Israel, which had appeared unto him t, H6471
2Ki 6:10 and saved himself there, not once nor t. H8147
Neh 13:20 lodged without Jerusalem once or t. H8147
Job 33:14 For God speaketh once, yea t, *yet man* H8147
40: 5 yea, t; but I will proceed no further. H8147
42:10 gave Job t as much as he had before. H4932
Ps 62:11 God hath spoken once; t have I heard H8147
Ecc 6: 6 Yea, though he live a thousand years t H6471
Mk 14:30 cock crow t, thou shalt deny me thrice. *G1364*
72 the cock crow t, thou shalt deny me *G1364*
Lk 18:12 I fast t in the week, I give tithes of all *G1364*
Jude 12 fruit, t dead, plucked up by the roots; *G1364*

TWIGS

Ezk 17: 4 He cropped off the top of his young t, H3242
22 the top of his young t a tender one, and H3127

TWILIGHT

1Sa 30:17 And David smote them from the t even H5399
2Ki 7: 5 And they rose up in the t, to go unto the H5399
7 Wherefore they arose and fled in the t, H5399
Job 3: 9 Let the stars of the t thereof be dark; let H5399
24:15 waiteth for the t, saying, No eye shall H5399
Prv 7: 9 In the t, in the evening, in the black and H5399
Ezk 12: 6 *it* forth in the t: thou shalt cover thy H5939
7 *it* forth in the t, *and* I bare *it* upon *my* H5939
12 *his* shoulder in the t, and shall go forth: H5939

TWINED

Ex 26: 1 curtains *of* fine t linen, and blue, and H7806
31 and scarlet, and fine t linen of cunning H7806
36 fine t linen, wrought with needlework. H7806
27: 9 the court *of* fine t linen of an hundred H7806
16 scarlet, and fine t linen, wrought with H7806
18 fine t linen, and their sockets *of* brass. H7806
28: 6 and fine t linen, with cunning work. H7806
8 purple, and scarlet, and fine t linen. H7806
15 and *of* fine t linen, shalt thou make it. H7806
36: 8 curtains *of* fine t linen, and blue, and H7806
35 and scarlet, and fine t linen: *with* H7806
37 scarlet, and fine t linen, of needlework; H7806
38: 9 *were of* fine t linen, an hundred cubits: H7806
16 court round about *were* of fine t linen. H7806
Ex 38:18 scarlet, and fine t linen: and twenty H7806
39: 2 purple, and scarlet, and fine t linen. H7806
5 scarlet, and fine t linen; as the LORD H7806
8 purple, and scarlet, and fine t linen. H7806
24 and purple, and scarlet, *and* t *linen.* H7806
28 linen, and linen breeches *of* fine t linen, H7806
29 And a girdle *of* fine t linen, and blue, H7806

TWINKLING

1Co 15:52 In a moment, in the t of an eye, at the *G4493*

TWINS

Gen 25:24 behold, *there were* t in her womb. H8380
38:27 that, behold, t *were* in her womb. H8380
Song 4: 2 bear t, and none *is* barren among them. H8382
5 that are t, which feed among the lilies. H8380
6: 6 every one beareth t, and *there is* not one H8382
7: 3 *are* like two young roes *that are* t. H8380

TWO

Gen 1:16 And God made t great lights; the H8147
4:19 And Lamech took unto him t wives: the H8147
5:18 And Jared lived an hundred sixty and t H8147
20 hundred sixty and t years: and he died. H8147
26 t years, and begat sons and daughters: H8147
28 eighty and t years, and begat a son: H8147
6:19 And of every living thing of all flesh, t H8147
20 after his kind, t of every *sort* shall come H8147
7: 2 not clean by t, the male and his female. H8147
9 There went in t and two unto Noah H8147
9 There went in two and t unto Noah H8147
15 unto Noah into the ark, t and two of all H8147
15 the ark, two and t of all flesh, wherein H8147
9:22 father, and told his t brethren without. H8147
10:25 And unto Eber were born t sons: the H8147
11:10 begat Arphaxad t years after the flood: H8147
19 And Peleg lived after he begat Reu t H8147
20 And Reu lived t and thirty years, and H8147
21 And Reu lived after he begat Serug t H8147
23 And Serug lived after he begat Nahor t H8147
32 And the days of Terah were t hundred H8147
19: 1 And there came t angels to Sodom at H8147
8 Behold now, I have t daughters which H8147
15 thy wife, and thy t daughters, which H8147
16 the hand of his t daughters; the LORD H8147
30 the mountain, and his t daughters with H8147
30 dwelt in a cave, he and his t daughters. H8147
22: 3 his ass, and took t of his young men H8147
24:22 a shekel weight, and t bracelets for her H8147
25:23 And the LORD said unto her, T nations H8147
23 in thy womb, and t manner of people H8147
27: 9 fetch me from thence t good kids of the H8147
36 me these t times: he took away H6471
29:16 And Laban had t daughters: the name H8147
31:33 tent, and into the t maidservants' tents; H8147
41 years for thy t daughters, and six years H8147
32: 7 herds, and the camels, into t bands; H8147
10 Jordan; and now I am become t bands. H8147
14 T hundred she goats, and twenty he
14 goats, t hundred ewes, and twenty rams,
22 night, and took his t wives, and his two H8147
22 two wives, and his t womenservants, H8147
33: 1 Rachel, and unto the t handmaids. H8147
34:25 were sore, that t of the sons of Jacob, H8147
40: 2 And Pharaoh was wroth against t *of* H8147
41: 1 And it came to pass at the end of t full
50 And unto Joseph were born t sons H8147
42:37 saying, Slay my t sons, if I bring him H8147
44:27 Ye know that my wife bare me t *sons:* H8147
45: 6 For these t years *hath* the famine *been* in
46:27 him in Egypt, *were* t souls: all the souls H8147
48: 1 his t sons, Manasseh and Ephraim. H8147
5 And now thy t sons, Ephraim and H8147
49:14 ass couching down between t burdens:
Ex 2:13 day, behold, t men of the Hebrews H8147
4: 9 not believe also these t signs, neither H8147
12: 7 strike *it* on the t side posts and on the H8147
22 the lintel and the t side posts with the H8147
23 the lintel, and on the t side posts, the H8147
16:22 as much bread, t omers for one *man:* H8147
29 day the bread of t days; abide ye every
18: 3 And her t sons; of which the name of H8147
6 and thy wife, and her t sons with her. H8147
21:21 he continue a day or t, he shall not be
25:10 *of* shittim wood: t cubits and a half *shall*
12 thereof; and t rings *shall be* in the H8147
12 of it, and t rings in the other side of it. H8147
17 seat *of* pure gold: t cubits and a half
18 And thou shalt make t cherubims *of* H8147

Ex 25:18 them, in the t ends of the mercy seat. H8147
19 the cherubims on the t ends thereof. H8147
22 from between the t cherubims which H8147
23 *of* shittim wood: t cubits *shall be* the
35 And *there shall be* a knop under t H8147
35 and a knop under t branches of the H8147
35 and a knop under t branches of the H8147
26:17 T tenons *shall there be* in one board, H8147
19 the twenty boards; t sockets under one H8147
19 one board for his t tenons, and two H8147
19 his two tenons, and t sockets under H8147
19 under another board for his t tenons. H8147
21 And their forty sockets *of* silver; t H8147
21 and t sockets under another board. H8147
23 And t boards shalt thou make for the H8147
23 corners of the tabernacle in the t sides.
24 both; they shall be for the t corners. H8147
25 sixteen sockets; t sockets under one H8147
25 and t sockets under another board. H8147
27 the tabernacle, for the t sides westward.
27: 7 upon the t sides of the altar, to bear it. H8147
28: 7 It shall have the t shoulderpieces H8147
7 joined at the t edges thereof; and *so* H8147
9 And thou shalt take t onyx stones, and H8147
11 shalt thou engrave the t stones with the H8147
12 And thou shalt put the t stones upon H8147
12 upon his t shoulders for a memorial. H8147
14 And t chains *of* pure gold at the ends; H8147
23 the breastplate t rings of gold, and H8147
23 and shalt put the t rings on the two H8147
23 rings on the t ends of the breastplate. H8147
24 And thou shalt put the t wreathen H8147
24 of gold in the t rings *which are* on the H8147
25 And *the other* t ends of the two H8147
25 And *the other* two ends of the t H8147
25 shalt fasten in the t ouches, and put H8147
26 And thou shalt make t rings of gold, H8147
26 shalt put them upon the t ends of the H8147
27 And t *other* rings of gold thou shalt H8147
27 put them on the t sides of the ephod H8147
29: 1 bullock, and t rams without blemish, H8147
3 with the bullock and the t rams. H8147
13 the liver, and the t kidneys, and the fat H8147
22 the liver, and the t kidneys, and the fat H8147
38 upon the altar; t lambs of the first year H8147
30: 2 shall it be: and t cubits *shall be* the
4 And t golden rings shalt thou make to H8147
4 the crown of it, by the t corners thereof, H8147
4 thereof, upon the t sides of it shalt thou H8147
23 half so much, *even* t hundred and fifty
23 calamus t hundred and fifty *shekels*,
31:18 him upon mount Sinai, t tables of H8147
32:15 the mount, and the t tables of the H8147
34: 1 Moses, Hew thee t tables of stone like H8147
4 And he hewed t tables of stone like H8147
4 took in his hand the t tables of stone. H8147
29 Sinai with the t tables of testimony H8147
36:22 One board had t tenons, equally H8147
24 the twenty boards; t sockets under one H8147
24 one board for his t tenons, and two H8147
24 his two tenons, and t sockets under H8147
24 under another board for his t tenons. H8147
26 And their forty sockets of silver; t H8147
26 and t sockets under another board. H8147
28 And t boards made he for the corners H8147
28 corners of the tabernacle in the t sides.
30 of silver, under every board t sockets. H8147
37: 1 *of* shittim wood: t cubits and a half *was*
3 corners of it; even t rings upon the one H8147
3 it, and t rings upon the other side of it. H8147
6 seat *of* pure gold: t cubits and a half *was*
7 And he made t cherubims *of* gold, H8147
7 them, on the t ends of the mercy seat; H8147
8 he the cherubims on the t ends thereof. H8147
10 And he made the table *of* shittim wood: t
21 And a knop under t branches of the H8147
21 and a knop under t branches of the H8147
21 and a knop under t branches of the H8147
25 foursquare; and t cubits *was* the height
27 And he made t rings of gold for it H8147
27 thereof, by the t corners of it, upon the H8147
27 of it, upon the t sides thereof, to be H8147
38:29 t thousand and four hundred shekels.
39: 4 by the t edges was it coupled together. H8147
16 And they made t ouches *of* gold, and H8147
16 *of* gold, and t gold rings; and put H8147
16 rings; and put the t rings in the two H8147
16 rings in the t ends of the breastplate. H8147
17 And they put the t wreathen chains of H8147

Ex 39:17 t rings on the ends of the breastplate. H8147
18 And the t ends of the two wreathen H8147
18 And the two ends of the t wreathen H8147
18 fastened in the t ouches, and put them H8147
19 And they made t rings of gold, and put H8147
19 and put *them* on the t ends of the H8147
20 And they made t *other* golden rings, H8147
20 put them on the t sides of the ephod H8147
Lev 3: 4 And the t kidneys, and the fat that *is* on H8147
10 And the t kidneys, and the fat that *is* H8147
15 And the t kidneys, and the fat that *is* H8147
4: 9 And the t kidneys, and the fat that *is* H8147
5: 7 hath committed, t turtledoves, or two H8147
7 two turtledoves, or t young pigeons, H8147
11 But if he be not able to bring t H8147
11 two turtledoves, or t young pigeons, H8147
7: 4 And the t kidneys, and the fat that *is* on H8147
8: 2 sin offering, and t rams, and a basket H8147
16 the liver, and the t kidneys, and their H8147
25 the liver, and the t kidneys, and their H8147
12: 5 she shall be unclean t weeks, as in her
8 she shall bring t turtles, or two young H8147
8 two turtles, or t young pigeons; the H8147
14: 4 that is to be cleansed t birds alive *and* H8147
10 And on the eighth day he shall take t he H8147
22 And t turtledoves, or two young H8147
22 And two turtledoves, or t young H8147
49 And he shall take to cleanse the house t H8147
15:14 shall take to him t turtledoves, or two H8147
14 two turtledoves, or t young pigeons, H8147
29 she shall take unto her t turtles, or two H8147
29 her two turtles, or t young pigeons, and H8147
16: 1 the death of the t sons of Aaron, when H8147
5 children of Israel t kids of the goats for H8147
7 And he shall take the t goats, and H8147
8 And Aaron shall cast lots upon the t H8147
23:13 And the meat offering thereof *shall be* t H8147
17 Ye shall bring out of your habitations t H8147
17 two wave loaves of t tenth deals: they H8147
18 bullock, and t rams: they shall be *for* H8147
19 a sin offering, and t lambs of the first H8147
20 LORD, with the t lambs: they shall be H8147
24: 5 t tenth deals shall be in one cake. H8147
6 And thou shalt set them in t rows, six H8147
Nu 1:35 and t thousand and two hundred. H8147
35 thirty and two thousand and t hundred.
39 and t thousand and seven hundred. H8147
2:21 and t thousand and two hundred. H8147
21 thirty and two thousand and t hundred.
26 and t thousand and seven hundred. H8147
3:34 *were* six thousand and t hundred.
39 upward, *were* twenty and t thousand. H8147
43 them, were twenty and t thousand two H8147
43 t hundred and threescore and thirteen.
46 to be redeemed of the t hundred and
4:36 t thousand seven hundred and fifty.
40 t thousand and six hundred and thirty.
44 were three thousand and t hundred.
6:10 And on the eighth day he shall bring t H8147
10 two turtles, or t young pigeons, to the H8147
7: 3 oxen; a wagon for t of the princes, and H8147
7 T wagons and four oxen he gave unto H8147
17 And for a sacrifice of peace offerings, t H8147
23 And for a sacrifice of peace offerings, t H8147
29 And for a sacrifice of peace offerings, t H8147
35 And for a sacrifice of peace offerings, t H8147
41 And for a sacrifice of peace offerings, t H8147
47 And for a sacrifice of peace offerings, t H8147
53 And for a sacrifice of peace offerings, t H8147
59 And for a sacrifice of peace offerings, t H8147
65 And for a sacrifice of peace offerings, t H8147
71 And for a sacrifice of peace offerings, t H8147
77 And for a sacrifice of peace offerings, t H8147
83 And for a sacrifice of peace offerings, t H8147
85 vessels *weighed* t thousand and four
89 t cherubims: and he spake unto him. H8147
9:22 Or *whether it were* t days, or a month, or
10: 2 Make thee t trumpets of silver; of a H8147
11:19 Ye shall not eat one day, nor t days, nor
26 But there remained t *of the* men in the H8147
31 t cubits *high* upon the face of the earth.
13:23 bare it between t upon a staff; and *they* H8147
15: 6 *for* a meat offering t tenth deals of flour H8147
16: 2 the children of Israel, t hundred and fifty
17 man his censer, t hundred and fifty
35 and consumed the t hundred and fifty
22:22 ass, and his t servants *were* with him. H8147
26:10 the fire devoured t hundred and fifty
14 and t thousand and two hundred. H8147

Nu 26:14 and two thousand and t hundred.
34 and t thousand and seven hundred. H8147
37 of them, thirty and t thousand and five H8147
28: 3 unto the LORD; t lambs of the first year H8147
9 And on the sabbath day t lambs of the H8147
9 without spot, and t tenth deals of flour H8147
11 unto the LORD; t young bullocks, and H8147
12 one bullock; and t tenth deals of flour H8147
19 unto the LORD; t young bullocks, and H8147
20 a bullock, and t tenth deals for a ram; H8147
27 unto the LORD; t young bullocks, one H8147
28 bullock, t tenth deals unto one ram, H8147
29: 3 a bullock, *and* t tenth deals for a ram, H8147
9 a bullock, *and* t tenth deals to one ram, H8147
13 young bullocks, t rams, *and* fourteen H8147
14 thirteen bullocks, t tenth deals to each H8147
14 tenth deals to each ram of the t rams, H8147
17 young bullocks, t rams, fourteen lambs H8147
20 And on the third day eleven bullocks, t H8147
23 And on the fourth day ten bullocks, t H8147
26 And on the fifth day nine bullocks, t H8147
29 And on the sixth day eight bullocks, t H8147
32 seven bullocks, t rams, *and* fourteen H8147
31:27 And divide the prey into t parts; between
35 And thirty and t thousand persons in H8147
40 tribute *was* thirty and t persons. H8147
34:15 The t tribes and the half tribe have H8147
35: 5 on the east side t thousand cubits, and
5 on the south side t thousand cubits, and
5 on the west side t thousand cubits, and
5 on the north side t thousand cubits; and
6 to them ye shall add forty and t cities. H8147
Dt 3: 8 out of the hand of the t kings of the H8147
21 done unto these t kings: so shall the H8147
4:13 he wrote them upon t tables of stone. H8147
47 Og king of Bashan, t kings of the H8147
5:22 he wrote them in t tables of stone, and H8147
9:10 And the LORD delivered unto me t H8147
11 the LORD gave me the t tables of stone, H8147
15 burned with fire: and the t tables of the H8147
15 of the covenant *were* in my t hands. H8147
17 And I took the t tables, and cast them H8147
17 cast them out of my t hands, and brake H8147
10: 1 unto me, Hew thee t tables of stone like H8147
3 wood, and hewed t tables of stone like H8147
3 having the t tables in mine hand. H8147
14: 6 the cleft into t claws, *and* cheweth H8147
17: 6 At the mouth of t witnesses, or three H8147
18: 3 and the t cheeks, and the maw.
19:15 at the mouth of t witnesses, or at the H8147
21:15 If a man have t wives, one beloved, and H8147
32:30 a thousand, and t put ten thousand to H8147
Jos 2: 1 Nun sent out of Shittim t men to spy H8147
4 And the woman took the t men, and H8147
10 ye did unto the t kings of the Amorites, H8147
23 So the t men returned, and descended H8147
3: 4 you and it, about t thousand cubits by
6:22 But Joshua had said unto the t men H8147
7: 3 go up; but let about t or three thousand
21 garment, and t hundred shekels of
9:10 And all that he did to the t kings of the H8147
14: 3 the inheritance of t tribes and an half H8147
4 For the children of Joseph were t tribes, H8147
15:60 and Rabbah; t cities with their villages: H8147
19:30 twenty and t cities with their villages. H8147
21:16 nine cities out of those t tribes. H8147
25 with her suburbs; t cities. H8147
27 Beesh-terah with her suburbs; t cities. H8147
24:12 you, *even* the t kings of the Amorites; H8147
Jdg 3:16 a dagger which had t edges, of a cubit H8147
5:30 man a damsel *or* t; to Sisera a prey of
7: 3 the people twenty and t thousand; and H8147
25 And they took t princes of the H8147
8:12 and took the t kings of Midian, Zebah H8147
9:44 of the city: and the t *other* companies H8147
10: 3 and judged Israel twenty and t years. H8147
11:37 me: let me alone t months, that I may H8147
38 he sent her away *for* t months: and she H8147
39 And it came to pass at the end of t H8147
12: 6 the Ephraimites forty and t thousand. H8147
15: 4 a firebrand in the midst between t tails. H8147
13 they bound him with t new cords, and H8147
16: 3 of the city, and the t posts, and went H8147
28 avenged of the Philistines for my t eyes. H8147
29 And Samson took hold of the t middle H8147
17: 4 his mother took t hundred *shekels* of
19:10 *were* with him t asses saddled, his H6771
20:21 that day twenty and t thousand men. H8147
45 and slew t thousand men of them.

Ru 1: 1 Moab, he, and his wife, and his **t** sons. H8147
2 and the name of his **t** sons Mahlon and H8147
3 died; and she was left, and her **t** sons. H8147
5 was left of her **t** sons and her husband. H8147
7 she was, and her **t** daughters in law H8147
8 And Naomi said unto her **t** daughters H8147
19 So they **t** went until they came to H8147
4:11 like Leah, which **t** did build the house H8147
1Sa 1: 2 And he had **t** wives; the name of the H8147
3 in Shiloh. And the **t** sons of Eli, Hophni H8147
2:21 three sons and **t** daughters. And the H8147
34 come upon thy **t** sons, on Hophni and H8147
4: 4 and the **t** sons of Eli, Hophni H8147
11 taken; and the **t** sons of Eli, Hophni H8147
17 the people, and thy **t** sons also, Hophni H8147
6: 7 a new cart, and take **t** milch kine, on H8147
10 And the men did so; and took **t** milch H8147
10: 2 then thou shalt find **t** men by Rachel's H8147
4 thee, and give thee **t** *loaves* of bread; H8147
11:11 so that **t** of them were not left together. H8147
13: 1 he had reigned **t** years over Israel, H8147
2 of Israel; *whereof* **t** thousand were with
14:49 and the names of his **t** daughters *were* H8147
15: 4 them in Telaim, **t** hundred thousand
18:27 of the Philistines **t** hundred men; and
23:18 And they **t** made a covenant before the H8147
25:13 men; and **t** hundred abode by the stuff.
18 Then Abigail made haste, and took **t**
18 loaves, and **t** bottles of wine, and H8147
18 of raisins, and **t** hundred cakes of figs,
27: 3 David with his **t** wives, Ahinoam the H8147
28: 8 and he went, and **t** men with him, and H8147
30: 5 And David's **t** wives were taken H8147
10 four hundred men: for **t** hundred abode
12 a cake of figs, and **t** clusters of raisins: H8147
18 away: and David rescued his **t** wives. H8147
21 And David came to the **t** hundred men,
2Sa 1: 1 and David had abode **t** days in Ziklag; H8147
2: 2 So David went up thither, and his **t** H8147
10 and reigned **t** years. But the house H8147
4: 2 And Saul's son had **t** men *that were* H8147
8: 2 ground; even with **t** lines measured he H8147
5 Syrians **t** and twenty thousand men. H8147
12: 1 him, There were **t** men in one city; the H8147
13:23 And it came to pass after **t** full years,
14: 6 And thy handmaid had **t** sons, and H8147
6 two sons, and they **t** strove together in H8147
26 the hair of his head at **t** hundred shekels
28 So Absalom dwelt **t** full years in
15:11 And with Absalom went **t** hundred men
27 city in peace, and your **t** sons with you, H8147
36 there with them their **t** sons, Ahimaaz H8147
16: 1 and upon them **t** hundred *loaves* of
18:24 And David sat between the **t** gates: and H8147
21: 8 But the king took the **t** sons of Rizpah H8147
23:20 many acts, he slew **t** lionlike men of H8147
1Ki 2: 5 *and* what he did to the **t** captains of the H8147
32 who fell upon **t** men more righteous H8147
39 of three years, that **t** of the servants of H8147
3:16 Then came there **t** women, *that were* H8147
18 us in the house, save we **t** in the house. H8147
25 the living child in **t**, and give half to the H8147
5:12 and they **t** made a league together. H8147
14 in Lebanon, *and* **t** months at home: H8147
6:23 And within the oracle he made **t** H8147
32 The **t** doors also *were of* olive tree; and H8147
34 And the **t** doors *were of* fir tree: the two H8147
34 And the two doors *were of* fir tree: the **t** H8147
34 **t** leaves of the other door *were* folding. H8147
7:15 For he cast **t** pillars of brass, of H8147
16 And he made **t** chapiters *of* molten H8147
18 And he made the pillars, and **t** rows H8147
20 And the chapiters upon the **t** pillars H8147
20 *were* **t** hundred in rows round
24 *were* cast in **t** rows, when it was cast. H8147
26 of lilies: it contained **t** thousand baths.
41 The **t** pillars, and the *two* bowls of the H8147
41 The two pillars, and the *t* bowls of the
41 on the top of the **t** pillars; and the two H8147
41 pillars; and the **t** networks, to cover the H8147
41 to cover the **t** bowls of the chapiters H8147
42 for the **t** networks, *even* two H8147
42 networks, *even* **t** rows of pomegranates H8147
42 to cover the **t** bowls of the chapiters H8147
8: 7 For the cherubims spread forth *their* **t**
9 *There was* nothing in the ark save the **t** H8147
63 unto the LORD, **t** and twenty thousand H8147
9:10 had built the **t** houses, the house of H8147
10:16 And king Solomon made **t** hundred

1Ki 10:19 seat, and **t** lions stood beside the stays. H8147
11:29 and they **t** *were* alone in the field: H8147
12:28 and made **t** calves *of* gold, and said H8147
14:20 reigned *were* **t** and twenty years: and H8147
15:25 Judah, and reigned over Israel **t** years. H8147
16: 8 to reign over Israel in Tirzah, **t** years.
21 of Israel divided into **t** parts: half of the H2677
24 of Shemer for **t** talents of silver, and
29 Israel in Samaria twenty and **t** years. H8147
17:12 I *am* gathering **t** sticks, that I may go H8147
18:21 halt ye between **t** opinions? if the LORD H8147
23 Let them therefore give us **t** bullocks; H8147
32 as would contain **t** measures of seed.
20: 1 *were* thirty and **t** kings with him, and H8147
15 and they were **t** hundred and thirty two:
15 hundred and thirty **t**: and after them he H8147
16 the thirty and **t** kings that helped him. H8147
27 before them like **t** little flocks of kids; H8147
21:10 And set **t** men, sons of Belial, before H8147
13 And there came in **t** men, children of H8147
22:31 his thirty and **t** captains that had rule H8147
51 of Judah, and reigned **t** years over Israel.
2Ki 1:14 and burnt up the **t** captains of the H8147
2: 6 will not leave thee. And they **t** went on. H8147
7 afar off: and they **t** stood by Jordan. H8147
8 so that they **t** went over on dry ground. H8147
12 own clothes, and rent them in **t** pieces. H8147
24 there came forth **t** she bears out of the H8147
24 and tare forty and **t** children of them. H8147
4: 1 unto him my **t** sons to be bondmen. H8147
5:17 to thy servant **t** mules' burden of earth?
22 mount Ephraim **t** young men of the H8147
22 of silver, and **t** changes of garments. H8147
23 And Naaman said, Be content, take **t**
23 him, and bound **t** talents of silver in H8147
23 two talents of silver in **t** bags, with two H8147
23 silver in two bags, with **t** changes of H8147
23 laid *them* upon **t** of his servants; and H8147
7: 1 for a shekel, and **t** measures of barley for
14 They took therefore **t** chariot horses; H8147
16 for a shekel, and **t** measures of barley for
18 to the king, saying, **T** measures of barley
8:17 Thirty and **t** years old was he when he H8147
26 **T** and twenty years old *was* Ahaziah H8147
9:32 looked out to him **t** *or* three eunuchs. H8147
10: 4 and said, Behold, **t** kings stood not H8147
8 Lay ye them in **t** heaps at the entering H8147
14 house, *even* **t** and forty men; neither H8147
11: 7 And **t** parts of all you that go forth on H8147
15: 2 and he reigned **t** and fifty years in H8147
23 Israel in Samaria, *and reigned* **t** years.
27 In the **t** and fiftieth year of Azariah H8147
17:16 images, *even* **t** calves, and made a H8147
18:23 I will deliver thee **t** thousand horses, if
21: 5 the **t** courts of the house of the LORD. H8147
19 Amon *was* twenty and **t** years old when H8147
19 and he reigned **t** years in Jerusalem. H8147
23:12 had made in the **t** courts of the house H8147
25: 4 of the gate between **t** walls, which *is* by
16 The **t** pillars, one sea, and the bases H8147
1Ch 1:19 And unto Eber were born **t** sons: the H8147
4: 5 And Ashur the father of Tekoa had **t** H8147
5:21 and of sheep **t** hundred and fifty
21 and of asses **t** thousand, and of men
7: 2 in the days of David **t** and twenty H8147
7 and **t** thousand and thirty and four. H8147
9 *was* twenty thousand and **t** hundred.
11 thousand and **t** hundred *soldiers*, fit
9:22 in the gates *were* **t** hundred and twelve.
11:21 than the **t**; for he was their captain: H8147
22 many acts; he slew **t** lionlike men of H8147
12:28 father's house twenty and **t** captains. H8147
32 heads of them *were* **t** hundred; and all
15: 6 and his brethren **t** hundred and twenty:
8 the chief, and his brethren **t** hundred:
18: 5 Syrians **t** and twenty thousand men. H8147
19: 7 So they hired thirty and **t** thousand H8147
24:17 The one and twentieth to Jachin, the **t** H8147
25: 7 was **t** hundred fourscore and eight.
29 The **t** and twentieth to Giddalti, *he*, his H8147
26: 8 *were* threescore and **t** of Obed-edom. H8147
17 a day, and toward Asuppim **t** *and* two. H8147
17 a day, and toward Asuppim two *and* **t**. H8147
18 four at the causeway, *and* **t** at Parbar. H8147
32 And his brethren, men of valour, *were* **t**
2Ch 3:10 And in the most holy house he made **t** H8147
15 Also he made before the house **t** pillars H8147
4: 3 sea round about. **T** rows of oxen *were* H8147
12 *To wit*, the **t** pillars, and the pommels, H8147

2Ch 4:12 on the top of the **t** pillars, and the two H8147
12 pillars, and the **t** wreaths to cover the H8147
12 to cover the **t** pommels of the chapiters
13 on the **t** wreaths; two rows of H8147
13 on the two wreaths; **t** rows of H8147
13 to cover the **t** pommels of the chapiters H8147
5:10 *There was* nothing in the ark save the **t** H8147
7: 5 of twenty and **t** thousand oxen, and H8147
8:10 officers, *even* **t** hundred and fifty, that
9:15 And king Solomon made **t** hundred
18 place, and **t** lions standing by the stays: H8147
13:21 and **t** sons, and sixteen daughters. H8147
14: 8 and drew bows, **t** hundred and fourscore
17:15 him **t** hundred and fourscore thousand.
16 and with him **t** hundred thousand
17 bow and shield **t** hundred thousand.
21: 5 Jehoram *was* thirty and **t** years old H8147
19 after the end of **t** years, his bowels fell H8147
20 Thirty and **t** years old was he when he H8147
22: 2 Forty and **t** years old *was* Ahaziah H8147
24: 3 And Jehoiada took for him **t** wives; and H8147
26: 3 reigned fifty and **t** years in Jerusalem. H8147
12 valour *were* **t** thousand and six hundred.
28: 8 of their brethren **t** hundred thousand,
29:32 hundred rams, *and* **t** hundred lambs: all
33: 5 the **t** courts of the house of the LORD. H8147
21 Amon *was* **t** and twenty years old when H8147
21 reign, and reigned **t** years in Jerusalem. H8147
35: 8 passover offerings **t** thousand and six
Ezr 2: 3 The children of Parosh, **t** thousand an
3 thousand an hundred seventy and **t**. H8147
4 three hundred seventy and **t**. H8147
6 **t** thousand eight hundred and twelve.
7 The children of Elam, a thousand **t**
10 of Bani, six hundred forty and **t**. H8147
12 The children of Azgad, a thousand **t**
12 a thousand two hundred twenty and **t**. H8147
14 The children of Bigvai, **t** thousand fifty
19 The children of Hashum, **t** hundred
24 The children of Azmaveth, forty and **t**. H8147
27 of Michmas, an hundred twenty and **t**. H8147
28 The men of Beth-el and Ai, **t** hundred
29 The children of Nebo, fifty and **t**. H8147
31 a thousand **t** hundred fifty and four.
37 of Immer, a thousand fifty and **t**. H8147
38 The children of Pashur, a thousand **t**
58 *were* three hundred ninety and **t**. H8147
60 of Nekoda, six hundred fifty and **t**. H8147
64 *was* forty and **t** thousand three hundred
65 *were* among them **t** hundred singing
66 their mules, **t** hundred forty and five;
6:17 hundred bullocks, **t** hundred rams, four
8: 4 and with him **t** hundred males.
9 with him **t** hundred and eighteen males.
20 of the Levites, **t** hundred and twenty
27 drams; and **t** vessels of fine copper, H8147
10:13 a work of one day or **t**: for we are many H8147
Neh 5:14 year even unto the **t** and thirtieth year H8147
6:15 of *the month* Elul, in fifty and **t** days. H8147
7: 8 The children of Parosh, **t** thousand an H8147
8 thousand an hundred seventy and **t**. H8147
9 three hundred seventy and **t**. H8147
10 of Arah, six hundred fifty and **t**. H8147
11 of Jeshua and Joab, **t** thousand and eight
12 The children of Elam, a thousand **t**
17 The children of Azgad, **t** thousand H8147
17 thousand three hundred twenty and **t**. H8147
19 The children of Bigvai, **t** thousand
28 The men of Beth-azmaveth, forty and **t**. H8147
31 an hundred and twenty and **t**. H8147
33 The men of the other Nebo, fifty and **t**. H8147
34 a thousand **t** hundred fifty and four.
40 of Immer, a thousand fifty and **t**. H8147
41 The children of Pashur, a thousand **t**
60 *were* three hundred ninety and **t**. H8147
62 of Nekoda, six hundred forty and **t**. H8147
66 *was* forty and **t** thousand three hundred
67 and they had **t** hundred forty and five
68 their mules, **t** hundred forty and five:
71 drams of gold, and **t** thousand and two
71 thousand and **t** hundred pound of silver.
72 drams of gold, and **t** thousand pound of
11:12 twenty and **t**: and Adaiah the son H8147
13 And his brethren, chief of the fathers, **t**
13 hundred forty and **t**: and Amashai the H8147
18 All the Levites in the holy city *were* **t**
19 gates, *were* an hundred seventy and **t**. H8147
12:31 and appointed **t** great *companies of* H8147
40 So stood the **t** *companies of them that* H8147

Neh 13: 6 for in the t and thirtieth year of H8147
Est 2:21 sat in the king's gate, t of the king's H8147
6: 2 Bigthana and Teresh, t of the king's H8147
9:27 would keep these t days according to H8147
Job 13:20 Only do not t *things* unto me: then will H8147
42: 7 and against thy t friends: for ye have H8147
Prv 30: 7 T *things* have I required of thee; deny H8147
15 The horseleach hath t daughters, H8147
Ecc 4: 9 T *are* better than one; because they H8147
11 Again, if t lie together, then they have H8147
12 And if one prevail against him, t shall H8147
Song 4: 5 Thy t breasts *are* like two young roes H8147
5 Thy two breasts *are* like t young roes H8147
6:13 As it were the company of t armies.
7: 3 Thy t breasts *are* like two young roes H8147
3 Thy two breasts *are* like t young roes H8147
8:12 that keep the fruit thereof t hundred.
Isa 7: 4 for the t tails of these smoking H8147
21 shall nourish a young cow, and t sheep; H8147
17: 6 of an olive tree, t *or* three berries in the H8147
22:11 Ye made also a ditch between the t walls
36: 8 and I will give thee t thousand horses, if
45: 1 before him the t leaved gates; and the
47: 9 But these t *things* shall come to thee in H8147
51:19 These t *things* are come unto thee; who H8147
Jer 2:13 For my people have committed t evils; H8147
3:14 one of a city, and t of a family, and I H8147
24: 1 The LORD shewed me, and, behold, t H8147
28: 3 Within t full years will I bring again into
11 within the space of t full years. And the
33:24 saying, The t families which the LORD H8147
39: 4 gate betwixt the t walls: and he went H8147
52: 7 gate between the t walls, which *was* by H8147
20 The t pillars, one sea, and twelve H8147
29 eight hundred thirty and t persons: H8147
Ezk 1:11 stretched upward; t *wings* of every one H8147
11 to another, and t covered their bodies. H8147
23 every one had t, which covered on this H8147
23 and every one had t, which covered on H8147
21:19 Also, thou son of man, appoint thee t H8147
21 way, at the head of the t ways, to use H8147
23: 2 Son of man, there were t women, the H8147
35:10 Because thou hast said, These t nations H8147
10 nations and these t countries shall be H8147
37:22 they shall be no more t nations, neither H8147
22 into t kingdoms any more at all: H8147
40: 9 and the posts thereof, t cubits; and the H8147
39 And in the porch of the gate *were* t H8147
39 on this side, and t tables on that side, to
40 north gate, *were* t tables; and on the H8147
40 at the porch of the gate, *were* t tables. H8147
41: 3 post of the door, t cubits; and the door, H8147
18 a cherub; and *every* cherub had t faces; H8147
22 and the length thereof t cubits; and the H8147
23 temple and the sanctuary had t doors. H8147
24 And the doors had t leaves *apiece*, two H8147
24 And the doors had two leaves *apiece*, t H8147
24 two turning leaves; t *leaves* for the one H8147
24 door, and t leaves for the other *door*. H8147
43:14 settle *shall be* t cubits, and the breadth H8147
45:15 And one lamb out of the flock, out of t
46:19 *was* a place on the t sides westward.
47:13 of Israel: Joseph *shall have* t portions.
48:17 be toward the north t hundred and fifty,
17 toward the south t hundred and fifty,
17 toward the east t hundred and fifty, and
17 and toward the west t hundred and fifty.
Dan 5:31 *being* about threescore and t years old. H8648
8: 3 a ram which had *t* horns: and the *two*
3 *two* horns: and the *t* horns *were* high;
6 And he came to the ram that had *t*
7 and brake his t horns: and there was H8147
14 And he said unto me, Unto t thousand
20 The ram which thou sawest having *t*
9:25 threescore and t weeks: the street shall H8147
26 And after threescore and t weeks shall H8147
12: 5 there stood other t, the one on this side H8147
11 a thousand t hundred and ninety days.
Hos 6: 2 After t days will he revive us: in the third
10:10 bind themselves in their t furrows. H8147
Am 1: 1 of Israel, t years before the earthquake.
3: 3 Can t walk together, except they be H8147
12 mouth of the lion t legs, or a piece of an H8147
4: 8 So t *or* three cities wandered unto one H8147
Zec 4: 3 And t olive trees by it, one upon the H8147
11 What *are* these t olive trees upon the H8147
12 What *be these* t olive branches which H8147
12 which through the t golden pipes H8147
14 Then said he, These *are* the t anointed H8147
Zec 5: 9 there came out t women, and the wind H8147
6: 1 out from between t mountains; and the H8147
11: 7 I took unto me t staves; the one I called H8147
13: 8 saith the LORD, t parts therein shall be H8147
Mt 2:16 thereof, from t years old and under, *G1332*
4:18 sea of Galilee, saw t brethren, Simon *G1417*
21 he saw other t brethren, James *the* *G1417*
6:24 No man can serve t masters: for either *G1417*
8:28 there met him t possessed with devils, *G1417*
9:27 And when Jesus departed thence, t *G1417*
10:10 Nor scrip for *your* journey, neither t *G1417*
29 Are not t sparrows sold for a farthing? *G1417*
11: 2 of Christ, he sent t of his disciples, *G1417*
14:17 have here but five loaves, and t fishes. *G1417*
19 loaves, and the t fishes, and looking *G1417*
18: 8 than having t hands or two feet to *G1417*
8 or t feet to be cast into everlasting fire. *G1417*
9 having t eyes to be cast into hell fire. *G1417*
16 with thee one or t more, that in the *G1417*
16 in the mouth of t or three witnesses *G1417*
19 Again I say unto you, That if t of you *G1417*
20 For where t or three are gathered *G1417*
20:21 that these my t sons may sit, the one *G1417*
24 indignation against the t brethren. *G1417*
30 And, behold, t blind men sitting by the *G1417*
21: 1 of Olives, then sent Jesus t disciples, *G1417*
28 But what think ye? A *certain* man had t *G1417*
22:40 On these t commandments hang all the *G1417*
24:40 Then shall t be in the field; the one *G1417*
41 T *women shall be* grinding at the mill; *G1417*
25:15 five talents, to another t, and to another *G1417*
17 And likewise he that *had received* t, he *G1417*
17 *received* two, he also gained other t. *G1417*
22 He also that had received t talents *G1417*
22 unto me t talents: behold, I have *G1417*
22 gained t other talents beside them. *G1417*
26: 2 Ye know that after t days is *the feast of* *G1417*
37 And he took with him Peter and the t *G1417*
60 none. At the last came t false witnesses, *G1417*
27:38 Then were there t thieves crucified with *G1417*
Mk 5:13 sea, (they were about t thousand;) and *G1367*
6: 7 send them forth by t and two; and gave *G1417*
7 them forth by two and t; and gave them *G1417*
9 with sandals; and not put on t coats. *G1417*
37 we go and buy t hundred pennyworth *G1250*
38 they knew, they say, Five, and t fishes. *G1417*
41 five loaves and the t fishes, he looked *G1417*
41 the t fishes divided he among them all. *G1417*
9:43 than having t hands to go into hell, *G1417*
45 life, than having t feet to be cast into *G1417*
47 having t eyes to be cast into hell fire: *G1417*
11: 1 he sendeth forth t of his disciples, *G1417*
4 where t ways met; and they loose him. *G296*
12:42 in t mites, which make a farthing. *G1417*
14: 1 After t days was *the feast of* the *G1417*
13 And he sendeth forth t of his disciples, *G1417*
15:27 And with him they crucify t thieves; the *G1417*
16:12 in another form unto t of them, as they *G1417*
Lk 2:24 pair of turtledoves, or t young pigeons. *G1417*
3:11 He that hath t coats, let him impart *G1417*
5: 2 And saw t ships standing by the lake: *G1417*
7:19 And John calling *unto him* t of his *G1417*
41 which had t debtors: the one owed *G1417*
9: 3 money; neither have t coats apiece. *G1417*
13 but five loaves and t fishes; except we *G1417*
16 Then he took the five loaves and the t *G1417*
30 And, behold, there talked with him t *G1417*
32 and the t men that stood with him. *G1417*
10: 1 and sent them t and two before his face
1 sent them two and t before his face into *G1417*
35 he took out t pence, and gave *them* *G1417*
12: 6 Are not five sparrows sold for t *G1417*
52 three against t, and two against three. *G1417*
52 three against two, and t against three. *G1417*
15:11 And he said, A certain man had t sons: *G1417*
16:13 No servant can serve t masters: for *G1417*
17:34 I tell you, in that night there shall be t *G1417*
35 T *women* shall be grinding together; *G1417*
36 T *men* shall be in the field; the one *G1417*
18:10 T men went up into the temple to pray; *G1417*
19:29 of Olives, he sent t of his disciples, *G1417*
21: 2 poor widow casting in thither t mites. *G1417*
22:38 And they said, Lord, behold, here *are* t *G1417*
23:32 And there were also t other, *G1417*
24: 4 behold, t men stood by them *G1417*
13 And, behold, t of them went that same *G1417*
Jn 1:35 after John stood, and t of his disciples; *G1417*
37 And the t disciples heard him speak, *G1417*
40 One of the t which heard John *speak*, *G1417*
Jn 2: 6 containing t or three firkins apiece. *G1417*
4:40 with them: and he abode there t days. *G1417*
43 Now after t days he departed thence, *G1417*
6: 7 Philip answered him, T hundred *G1250*
9 barley loaves, and t small fishes: but *G1417*
8:17 law, that the testimony of t men is true. *G1417*
11: 6 he was sick, he abode t days still in the *G1417*
19:18 Where they crucified him, and t other *G1417*
20:12 And seeth t angels in white sitting, the *G1417*
21: 2 of Zebedee, and t other of his disciples. *G1417*
8 land, but as it were t hundred cubits,) *G1250*
Act 1:10 t men stood by them in white apparel; *G1417*
23 And they appointed t, Joseph called *G1417*
24 whether of these t thou hast chosen, *G1417*
7:29 land of Madian, where he begat t sons. *G1417*
9:38 they sent unto him t men, desiring *him* *G1417*
10: 7 he called t of his household servants, *G1417*
12: 6 sleeping between t soldiers, bound with *G1417*
6 bound with t chains: and the keepers *G1417*
19:10 And this continued by the space of t *G1417*
22 So he sent into Macedonia t of them *G1417*
34 about the space of t hours cried out, *G1417*
21:33 *him* to be bound with t chains; and *G1417*
23:23 And he called unto *him* t centurions, *G1417*
23 Make ready t hundred soldiers to *G1250*
23 ten, and spearmen t hundred, at the *G1250*
24:27 But after t years Porcius Festus came *G1333*
27:37 And we were in all in the ship t *G1250*
41 And falling into a place where t seas *G1337*
28:30 And Paul dwelt t whole years in his *G1333*
1Co 6:16 body? for t, saith he, shall be one flesh. *G1417*
14:27 tongue, *let it be* by t, or at the most *by* *G1417*
29 Let the prophets speak t or three, and *G1417*
2Co 13: 1 In the mouth of t or three witnesses *G1417*
Gal 4:22 For it is written, that Abraham had t *G1417*
24 for these are the t covenants; the one *G1417*
Eph 5:31 his wife, and they t shall be one flesh. *G1417*
Php 1:23 For I am in a strait betwixt t, having a *G1417*
1Ti 5:19 but before t or three witnesses. *G1417*
Heb 6:18 That by t immutable things, in which *it* *G1417*
10:28 mercy under t or three witnesses: *G1417*
Rev 2:12 hath the sharp sword with t edges; *G1366*
9:12 there come t woes more hereafter. *G1417*
16 horsemen *were* t hundred thousand *G1417*
11: 2 tread under foot forty *and* t months. *G1417*
3 And I will give *power* unto my t *G1417*
3 a thousand t hundred *and* threescore *G1250*
4 These are the t olive trees, and the two *G1417*
4 These are the two olive trees, and the t *G1417*
10 because these t prophets tormented *G1417*
12: 6 t hundred *and* threescore days. *G1417*
14 And to the woman were given t wings *G1417*
13: 5 him to continue forty *and* t months. *G1417*
11 earth; and he had t horns like a lamb, *G1417*

TWOEDGED

Ps 149: 6 mouth, and a t sword in their hand; H6374
Prv 5: 4 as wormwood, sharp as a t sword. H6310
Heb 4:12 and sharper than any t sword, piercing *G1366*
Rev 1:16 mouth went a sharp t sword: and his *G1366*

TWOFOLD

Mt 23:15 t more the child of hell than yourselves. *G1366*

TWO-HUNDRED See TWO and HUNDRED.

TWO-THOUSAND See TWO and THOUSAND.

TYCHICUS

Act 20: 4 and of Asia, T and Trophimus. *G5190*
Eph 6:21 *and* how I do, T, a beloved brother and *G5190*
Col 4: 7 All my state shall T declare unto you, *G5190*
2Ti 4:12 And T have I sent to Ephesus. *G5190*
Tit 3:12 unto thee, or T, be diligent to come *G5190*

TYRANNUS

Act 19: 9 disputing daily in the school of one T. *G5181*

TYRE

Jos 19:29 and to the strong city T; and the coast H6865
2Sa 5:11 And Hiram king of T sent messengers H6865
24: 7 And came to the strong hold of T, and H6865
1Ki 5: 1 And Hiram king of T sent his servants H6865
7:13 sent and fetched Hiram out of T. H6865
14 *was* a man of T, a worker in brass: and H6876
9:11 (*Now* Hiram the king of T had H6865
12 And Hiram came out from T to see the H6865
1Ch 14: 1 Now Hiram king of T sent messengers H6865
22: 4 T brought much cedar wood to David. H6876

2Ch 2: 3 to Huram the king of T, saying, As thou H6865
11 Then Huram the king of T answered in H6865
14 *was* a man of T, skilful to work in gold, H6876
Ezr 3: 7 and to them of T, to bring cedar trees H6876
Neh 13:16 There dwelt men of T also therein, H6876
Ps 45:12 And the daughter of T *shall be there* H6865
83: 7 Philistines with the inhabitants of T; H6865
87: 4 Philistia, and T, with Ethiopia; this H6865
Isa 23: 1 The burden of T. Howl, ye ships of H6865
5 they be sorely pained at the report of T. H6865
8 Who hath taken this counsel against T, H6865
15 in that day, that T shall be forgotten H6865
15 seventy years shall T sing as an harlot. H6865
17 LORD will visit T, and she shall turn to H6865
Joel 3: 4 to do with me, O T, and Zidon, and all H6865
Mt 11:21 had been done in T and Sidon, they *G5184*
22 more tolerable for T and Sidon at the *G5184*
15:21 into the coasts of T and Sidon. *G5184*
Mk 3: 8 and they about T and Sidon, a great *G5184*
7:24 into the borders of T and Sidon, and *G5184*
31 from the coasts of T and Sidon, he *G5184*
Lk 6:17 the sea coast of T and Sidon, which *G5184*
10:13 had been done in T and Sidon, which *G5184*
14 But it shall be more tolerable for T and *G5184*
Act 12:20 with them of T and Sidon: but they *G5183*
21: 3 and landed at T: for there the ship was *G5184*
7 finished *our* course from T, we came to *G5184*

TYRUS
Jer 25:22 And all the kings of T, and all the kings H6865
27: 3 and to the king of T, and to the king of H6865
47: 4 *and* to cut off from T and Zidon every H6865
Ezk 26: 2 Son of man, because that T hath said H6865
3 against thee, O T, and will cause many H6865
4 And they shall destroy the walls of T, H6865
7 I will bring upon T Nebuchadrezzar H6865
Ezk 26:15 Thus saith the Lord GOD to T; Shall not H6865
27: 2 of man, take up a lamentation for T; H6865
3 And say unto T, O thou that art situate H6865
3 the Lord GOD; O T, thou hast said, I *am* H6865
8 O T, *that* were in thee, were thy pilots. H6865
32 What *city is* like T, like the destroyed in H6865
28: 2 Son of man, say unto the prince of T, H6865
12 upon the king of T, and say unto him, H6865
29:18 service against T: every head *was* made H6865
18 nor his army, for T, for the service that H6865
Hos 9:13 Ephraim, as I saw T, *is* planted in a H6865
Am 1: 9 transgressions of T, and for four, I will H6865
10 But I will send a fire on the wall of T, H6865
Zec 9: 2 T, and Zidon, though it be very wise. H6865
3 And T did build herself a strong hold, H6865

U

UCAL
Prv 30: 1 spake unto Ithiel, even unto Ithiel and U, H401

UEL
Ezr 10:34 sons of Bani; Maadai, Amram, and U, H177

ULAI
Dan 8: 2 in a vision, and I was by the river of U. H195
16 *the banks of* U, which called, and said, H195

ULAM
1Ch 7:16 and his sons *were* U and Rakem. H198
17 And the sons of U; Bedan. These *were* the H198
8:39 his brother *were*, U his firstborn, Jehush H198
40 And the sons of U were mighty men of H198

ULLA
1Ch 7:39 And the sons of U; Arah, and Haniel, H5925

UMMAH
Jos 19:30 U also, and Aphek, and Rehob: twenty H5981

UNACCUSTOMED
Jer 31:18 as a bullock **u** *to the yoke*: turn H3808+H3925

UNADVISEDLY
Ps 106:33 spirit, so that he spake **u** with his lips. H981

UNAWARES
Gen 31:20 And Jacob stole away **u** to H3820+H3824
26 hast stolen away **u** to me, and carried H3824
Nu 35:11 thither, which killeth any person at **u**. H7684
15 killeth any person **u** may flee thither. H7684
Dt 4:42 his neighbour **u**, and hated him H1097+H1847
Jos 20: 3 killeth *any* person **u** *and* unwittingly H7684
9 *any* person at **u** might flee thither, and H7684
Ps 35: 8 Let destruction come upon him at **u**; H3045
Lk 21:34 life, and *so* that day come upon you **u**. *G160*
Gal 2: 4 And that because of false brethren **u** *G3920*
Heb 13: 2 some have entertained angels **u**. *G2990*
Jude 4 For there are certain men crept in **u**, *G3921*

UNBELIEF
Mt 13:58 mighty works there because of their **u**. *G570*
17:20 Because of your **u**: for verily I say unto *G570*
Mk 6: 6 And he marvelled because of their **u**. And *G570*
9:24 tears, Lord, I believe; help thou mine **u**. *G570*
16:14 them with their **u** and hardness of heart, *G570*
Ro 3: 3 **u** make the faith of God without effect? *G570*
4:20 of God through **u**; but was strong in faith, *G570*
11:20 Well; because of **u** they were broken off, *G570*
23 And they also, if they abide not still in **u**, *G570*
30 now obtained mercy through their **u**: *G543*
32 For God hath concluded them all in **u**, *G543*
1Ti 1:13 mercy, because I did *it* ignorantly in **u**. *G570*
Heb 3:12 of **u**, in departing from the living God. *G570*
19 that they could not enter in because of **u**. *G570*
4: 6 preached entered not in because of **u**: *G543*
11 any man fall after the same example of **u**. *G543*

UNBELIEVERS
Lk 12:46 will appoint him his portion with the **u**. *G571*
1Co 6: 6 law with brother, and that before the **u**. *G571*
14:23 or **u**, will they not say that ye are mad? *G571*
2Co 6:14 together with **u**: for what fellowship hath *G571*

UNBELIEVING
Act 14: 2 But the **u** Jews stirred up the Gentiles, *G544*
1Co 7:14 For the **u** husband is sanctified by the *G571*
14 the wife, and the **u** wife is sanctified by *G571*
15 But if the **u** depart, let him depart. A *G571*
Tit 1:15 are defiled and **u** *is* nothing pure; but *G571*
Rev 21: 8 But the fearful, and **u**, and the *G571*

UNBLAMEABLE
Col 1:22 and **u** and unreproveable in his sight: *G299*
1Th 3:13 To the end he may stablish your hearts **u** *G273*

UNBLAMEABLY
1Th 2:10 and justly and **u** we behaved ourselves *G274*

UNCERTAIN
1Co 14: 8 For if the trumpet give an **u** sound, who *G82*
1Ti 6:17 nor trust in **u** riches, but in the living *G83*

UNCERTAINLY
1Co 9:26 I therefore so run, not as **u**; so fight I, not *G84*

UNCHANGEABLE
Heb 7:24 continueth ever, hath an **u** priesthood. *G531*

UNCIRCUMCISED
Gen 17:14 And the **u** man child whose flesh of his H6189
34:14 is **u**; for that *were* a reproach unto us: H6190
Ex 6:12 Pharaoh hear me, who *am* of **u** lips? H6189
30 Behold, I *am* of **u** lips, and how shall H6189
12:48 land: for no **u** person shall eat thereof. H6189
Lev 19:23 the fruit thereof as **u**: three years shall it H6188
23 as **u** unto you: it shall not be eaten of. H6189
26:41 if then their **u** hearts be humbled, H6189
Jos 5: 7 for they were **u**, because they had not H6189
Jdg 14: 3 to take a wife of the **u** Philistines? And H6189
15:18 thirst, and fall into the hand of the **u**? H6189
1Sa 14: 6 garrison of these **u**: it may be that the H6189
17:26 for who *is* this **u** Philistine, that he H6189
36 the bear: and this **u** Philistine shall be H6189
31: 4 lest these **u** come and thrust me H6189
2Sa 1:20 lest the daughters of the **u** triumph. H6189
1Ch 10: 4 lest these **u** come and abuse me. H6189
Isa 52: 1 come into thee the **u** and the unclean. H6189
Jer 6:10 their ear *is* **u**, and they cannot hearken: H6189
9:25 *them which are* circumcised with the **u**; H6190
26 *these* nations *are* **u**, and all the house of H6189
26 the house of Israel *are* **u** in the heart. H6189
Ezk 28:10 Thou shalt die the deaths of the **u** by H6189
31:18 in the midst of the **u** with *them that be* H6189
32:19 go down, and be thou laid with the **u**. H6189
21 down, they lie **u**, slain by the sword. H6189
24 are gone down **u** into the nether parts H6189
25 him: all of them **u**, slain by the sword: H6189
26 him: all of them **u**, slain by the sword, H6189
27 *are* fallen of the **u**, which are gone down H6189
28 in the midst of the **u**, and shalt lie with H6189
29 shall lie with the **u**, and with them that H6189
30 and they lie **u** with *them that be* slain H6189
32 in the midst of the **u** with *them that are* H6189
44: 7 *sanctuary* strangers, **u** in heart, and H6189
Ezk 44: 7 in heart, and **u** in flesh, to be in my H6189
9 Lord GOD; No stranger, **u** in heart, nor H6189
9 in heart, nor **u** in flesh, shall enter H6189
Act 7:51 Ye stiffnecked and **u** in heart and ears, *G564*
11: 3 Saying, Thou wentest in to men **u**, and *G203*
Ro 4:11 *he had yet* being **u**: that he might be the *G203*
12 Abraham, which *he had* being *yet* **u**. *G203*
1Co 7:18 let him not become **u**. Is any called in *G1986*

UNCIRCUMCISION
Ro 2:25 of the law, thy circumcision is made **u**. *G203*
26 Therefore if the **u** keep the righteousness *G203*
26 not his **u** be counted for circumcision? *G203*
27 And shall not **u** which is by nature, if it *G203*
3:30 by faith, and **u** through faith. *G203*
4: 9 *only*, or upon the **u** also? for we say that *G203*
10 in circumcision, or in **u**? Not in *G203*
10 Not in circumcision, but in **u**. *G203*
1Co 7:18 called in **u**? let him not be circumcised. *G203*
19 Circumcision is nothing, and **u** is *G203*
Gal 2: 7 the gospel of the **u** was committed unto *G203*
5: 6 nor **u**; but faith which worketh by love. *G203*
6:15 any thing, nor **u**, but a new creature. *G203*
Eph 2:11 who are called U by that which is called *G203*
Col 2:13 your sins and the **u** of your flesh, hath he *G203*
3:11 circumcision nor **u**, Barbarian, Scythian, *G203*

UNCLE
Lev 10: 4 sons of Uzziel the **u** of Aaron, and said H1730
25:49 Either his **u**, or his uncle's son, may H1730
1Sa 10:14 And Saul's **u** said unto him and to his H1730
15 And Saul's **u** said, Tell me, I pray thee, H1730
16 And Saul said unto his **u**, He told us H1730
14:50 host *was* Abner, the son of Ner, Saul's **u**. H1730
1Ch 27:32 Also Jonathan David's **u** was a H1730
Est 2:15 of Abihail the **u** of Mordecai, who had H1730
Jer 32: 7 son of Shallum thine **u** shall come unto H1730
Am 6:10 And a man's **u** shall take him up, and H1730

UNCLEAN
Lev 5: 2 Or if a soul touch any **u** thing, whether H2931
2 *be* a carcase of an **u** beast, or a carcase H2931
2 or a carcase of **u** cattle, or the carcase H2931
2 or the carcase of **u** creeping things, and H2931
2 from him; he also shall be **u**, and guilty. H2931
7:19 And the flesh that toucheth any **u** *thing* H2931
21 that shall touch any **u** *thing, as* the H2931
21 of man, or *any* **u** beast, or any H2931
21 any abominable **u** *thing*, and eat of the H2931
10:10 and unholy, and between **u** and clean; H2931
11: 4 divideth not the hoof; he *is* **u** unto you. H2931
5 divideth not the hoof; he *is* **u** unto you. H2931
6 divideth not the hoof; he *is* **u** unto you. H2931
7 he cheweth not the cud; he *is* **u** to you. H2931
8 shall ye not touch; they *are* **u** to you. H2931
24 And for these ye shall be **u**: whosoever H2930
24 of them shall be **u** until the even. H2930
25 his clothes, and be **u** until the even. H2930
26 the cud, *are* **u** unto you: every one H2931
26 every one that toucheth them shall be **u**. H2930
27 *all* four, those *are* **u** unto you: whoso H2931
27 their carcase shall be **u** until the even. H2930
28 his clothes, and be **u** until the even: H2930
28 until the even: they *are* **u** unto you. H2931

U

Lev 11:29 These also *shall be* **u** unto you among H2931
31 These *are* **u** to you among all that H2931
31 they be dead, shall be **u** until the even. H2930
32 doth fall, it shall be **u**; whether *it be* any H2930
32 **u** until the even; so it shall be cleansed. H2930
33 *is* in it shall be **u**; and ye shall break it. H2930
34 cometh shall be **u**: and all drink that H2930
34 be drunk in every *such* vessel shall be **u**. H2930
35 falleth shall be **u**; *whether it be* oven, H2930
35 *are* **u**, and shall be unclean unto you. H2931
35 *are* unclean, and shall be **u** unto you. H2931
36 which toucheth their carcase shall be **u**. H2930
38 fall thereon, it *shall be* **u** unto you. H2931
39 thereof shall be **u** until the even. H2930
40 his clothes, and be **u** until the even: he H2930
40 his clothes, and be **u** until the even. H2930
43 make yourselves **u** with them, that ye H2930
47 To make a difference between the **u** H2931
12: 2 child: then she shall be **u** seven days; H2930
2 for her infirmity shall she be **u**. H2930
5 then she shall be **u** two weeks, as in her H2930
13: 3 look on him, and pronounce him **u**. H2930
8 shall pronounce him **u**: it *is* a leprosy. H2930
11 pronounce him **u**, and shall not shut H2930
11 and shall not shut him up: for he *is* **u**. H2931
14 flesh appeareth in him, he shall be **u**. H2930
15 him to be **u**: *for* the raw flesh *is* unclean: H2930
15 *for* the raw flesh *is* **u**: it *is* a leprosy. H2931
20 shall pronounce him **u**: it *is* a plague of H2930
22 shall pronounce him **u**: it *is* a plague. H2930
25 him **u**: it *is* the plague of leprosy. H2930
27 him **u**: it *is* the plague of leprosy. H2930
30 pronounce him **u**: it *is* a dry scall, *even* H2930
36 shall not seek for yellow hair; he *is* **u**. H2931
44 He is a leprous man, he *is* **u**: the priest H2931
44 him utterly **u**; his plague *is* in his head. H2930
45 his upper lip, and shall cry, **U**, unclean. H2931
45 his upper lip, and shall cry, Unclean, **u**. H2931
46 be defiled; he *is* **u**: he shall dwell alone; H2931
51 the plague *is* a fretting leprosy; it *is* **u**. H2931
55 be not spread; it *is* **u**; thou shalt burn it H2931
59 it clean, or to pronounce it **u**. H2930
14:36 be not made **u**: and afterward the priest H2930
40 them into an **u** place without the city: H2931
41 off without the city into an **u** place: H2931
44 *is* a fretting leprosy in the house: it *is* **u**. H2931
45 forth out of the city into an **u** place. H2931
46 it is shut up shall be **u** until the even. H2930
57 To teach when *it is* **u**, and when *it is* H2931
15: 2 of his flesh, *because of* his issue he *is* **u**. H2931
4 hath the issue, is **u**: and every thing, H2930
4 thing, whereon he sitteth, shall be **u**. H2930
5 in water, and be **u** until the even. H2930
6 in water, and be **u** until the even. H2930
7 in water, and be **u** until the even. H2930
8 in water, and be **u** until the even. H2930
9 upon that hath the issue shall be **u**. H2930
10 him shall be **u** until the even: and H2930
10 in water, and be **u** until the even. H2930
11 in water, and be **u** until the even. H2930
16 flesh in water, and be **u** until the even. H2930
17 with water, and be **u** until the even. H2930
18 in water, and be **u** until the even. H2930
19 toucheth her shall be **u** until the even. H2930
20 shall be **u**: every thing also that H2930
20 also that she sitteth upon shall be **u**. H2930
21 in water, and be **u** until the even. H2930
22 in water, and be **u** until the even. H2930
23 toucheth it, he shall be **u** until the even. H2930
24 him, he shall be **u** seven days; and all H2930
24 all the bed whereon he lieth shall be **u**. H2930
25 days of her separation: she *shall be* **u**. H2931
26 **u**, as the uncleanness of her separation. H2931
27 things shall be **u**, and shall wash his H2930
27 in water, and be **u** until the even. H2930
33 and of him that lieth with her that is **u**. H2931
17:15 **u** until the even: then shall he be clean. H2930
20:21 wife, it *is* an **u** thing: he hath uncovered H5079
25 clean beasts and **u**, and between H2931
25 and between **u** fowls and clean: and H2931
25 which I have separated from you as **u**. H2930
22: 4 any thing *that is* **u** *by* the dead, or a H2931
5 he may be made **u**, or a man of whom H2930
6 any such shall be **u** until even, and H2930
27:11 And if *it be* any **u** beast, of which they H2931
27 And if *it be* of an **u** beast, then he shall H2931
Nu 6: 7 He shall not make himself **u** for his H2930
9:10 posterity shall be **u** by reason of a dead H2931
18:15 firstling of **u** beasts shalt thou redeem. H2931
Nu 19: 7 and the priest shall be **u** until the even. H2930
8 in water, and shall be **u** until the even. H2930
10 his clothes, and be **u** until the even: H2930
11 body of any man shall be **u** seven days. H2930
13 be **u**; his uncleanness *is* yet upon him. H2931
14 *is* in the tent, shall be **u** seven days. H2930
15 hath no covering bound upon it, *is* **u**. H2931
16 man, or a grave, shall be **u** seven days. H2930
17 And for an **u** *person* they shall take of H2931
19 sprinkle upon the **u** on the third day, H2931
20 But the man that shall be **u**, and shall H2930
20 not been sprinkled upon him; he *is* **u**. H2931
21 of separation shall be **u** until even. H2930
22 And whatsoever the **u** *person* toucheth H2931
22 toucheth shall be **u**; and the soul that H2930
22 that toucheth *it* shall be **u** until even. H2930
Dt 12:15 given thee: the **u** and the clean may eat H2931
22 **u** and the clean shall eat *of* them alike. H2931
14: 7 the hoof; *therefore* they *are* **u** unto you. H2931
8 not the cud, it *is* **u** unto you: ye shall H2931
10 scales ye may not eat; it *is* **u** unto you. H2931
19 And every creeping thing that flieth *is* **u** H2931
15:22 Thou shalt eat it within thy gates: the **u** H2931
23:14 that he see no **u** thing in thee, and turn H6172
26:14 thereof for *any* **u** *use*, nor given *ought* H2931
Jos 22:19 possession *be* **u**, *then* pass ye over unto H2931
Jdg 13: 4 strong drink, and eat not any **u** *thing*: H2931
7 neither eat any **u** *thing*: for the child H2932
14 drink, nor eat any **u** *thing*: all that I H2932
2Ch 23:19 *was* **u** in any thing should enter in. H2931
Ezr 9:11 go to possess it, is an **u** land with the H5079
Job 14: 4 bring a clean *thing* out of an **u**? not one. H2931
36:14 in youth, and their life *is* among the **u**. H6945
Ecc 9: 2 the clean, and to the **u**; to him that H2931
Isa 6: 5 I *am* a man of **u** lips, and I dwell in the H2931
5 of a people of **u** lips: for mine eyes have H2931
35: 8 of holiness; the **u** shall not pass over H2931
52: 1 into thee the uncircumcised and the **u**. H2931
11 thence, touch no **u** *thing*; go ye out of H2931
64: 6 But we are all as an **u** *thing*, and all our H2931
Lam 4:15 They cried unto them, Depart ye; *it is* **u**; H2931
Ezk 22:26 between the **u** and the clean, and have H2931
44:23 to discern between the **u** and the clean. H2931
Hos 9: 3 and they shall eat **u** *things* in Assyria. H2931
Hag 2:13 Then said Haggai, If *one that is* **u** by a H2931
13 of these, shall it be **u**? And the priests H2930
13 priests answered and said, It shall be **u**. H2930
14 and that which they offer there *is* **u**. H2931
Zec 13: 2 and the **u** spirit to pass out of the land. H2932
Mt 10: 1 power *against* **u** spirits, to cast them G169
12:43 When the **u** spirit is gone out of a man, G169
Mk 1:23 a man with an **u** spirit; and he cried out, G169
26 And when the **u** spirit had torn him, and G169
27 even the **u** spirits, and they do obey him. G169
3:11 And **u** spirits, when they saw him, fell G169
30 Because they said, He hath an **u** spirit. G169
5: 2 out of the tombs a man with an **u** spirit, G169
8 him, Come out of the man, *thou* **u** spirit. G169
13 leave. And the **u** spirits went out, and G169
6: 7 two; and gave them power over **u** spirits; G169
7:25 daughter had an **u** spirit, heard of him, G169
Lk 4:33 **u** devil, and cried out with a loud voice, G169
36 the **u** spirits, and they come out. G169
6:18 And they that were vexed with **u** spirits: G169
8:29 (For he had commanded the **u** spirit to G169
9:42 Jesus rebuked the **u** spirit, and healed G169
11:24 When the **u** spirit is gone out of a man, G169
Act 5:16 were vexed with **u** spirits: and they were G169
8: 7 For **u** spirits, crying with loud voice, G169
10:14 eaten any thing that is common or **u**. G169
28 I should not call any man common or **u**. G169
11: 8 common or **u** hath at any time entered G169
Ro 14:14 *there is* nothing **u** of itself: but to him G2839
14 any thing to be **u**, to him *it is* unclean. G2839
14 any thing to be unclean, to him *it is* **u**. G2839
1Co 7:14 your children **u**; but now are they holy. G169
2Co 6:17 not the **u** *thing*; and I will receive you, G169
Eph 5: 5 no whoremonger, nor **u** person, nor G169
Heb 9:13 sprinkling the **u**, sanctifieth to the G2840
Rev 16:13 And I saw three **u** spirits like frogs *come* G169
18: 2 and a cage of every **u** and hateful bird. G169

UNCLEANNESS

Lev 5: 3 Or if he touch the **u** of man, whatsoever H2932
3 of man, whatsoever **u** *it be* that a man H2932
7:20 the LORD, having his **u** upon him, even H2932
21 *thing, as* the **u** of man, or *any* unclean H2932
14:19 cleansed from his **u**; and afterward he H2932
15: 3 And this shall be his **u** in his issue: H2932
Lev 15: 3 be stopped from his issue, it *is* his **u**. H2932
25 of the issue of her **u** shall be as the days H2932
26 be unclean, as the **u** of her separation. H2932
30 before the LORD for the issue of her **u**. H2932
31 Israel from their **u**; that they die not in H2932
31 die not in their **u**, when they defile my H2932
16:16 because of the **u** of the children of H2932
16 among them in the midst of their **u**. H2932
19 it from the **u** of the children of Israel. H2932
18:19 as long as she is put apart for her **u**. H2932
22: 3 the LORD, having his **u** upon him, that H2932
5 **u**, whatsoever uncleanness he hath; H2930
5 uncleanness, whatsoever **u** he hath; H2932
Nu 5:19 hast not gone aside to **u** *with another* H2932
19:13 shall be unclean; his **u** *is* yet upon him. H2932
Dt 23:10 clean by reason of **u** that chanceth him H7137
24: 1 hath found some **u** in her: then let him H6172
2Sa 11: 4 her **u**: and she returned unto her house. H2932
2Ch 29:16 out all the **u** that they found in the H2932
Ezr 9:11 it from one end to another with their **u**. H2932
Ezk 36:17 me as the **u** of a removed woman. H2932
39:24 According to their **u** and according to H2932
Zec 13: 1 of Jerusalem for sin and for **u**. H5079
Mt 23:27 full of dead *men's* bones, and of all **u**. G167
Ro 1:24 Wherefore God also gave them up to **u** G167
6:19 servants to **u** and to iniquity unto G167
2Co 12:21 not repented of the **u** and fornication G167
Gal 5:19 Adultery, fornication, **u**, lasciviousness, G167
Eph 4:19 to work all **u** with greediness. G167
5: 3 But fornication, and all **u**, or G167
Col 3: 5 the earth; fornication, **u**, inordinate G167
1Th 2: 3 *was* not of deceit, nor of **u**, nor in guile: G167
4: 7 For God hath not called us unto **u**, but G167
2Pt 2:10 the flesh in the lust of **u**, and despise G3394

UNCLEANNESSES

Ezk 36:29 I will also save you from all your **u**: and H2932

UNCLE'S

Lev 20:20 And if a man shall lie with his **u** wife, H1733
20 uncovered his **u** nakedness: they shall H1730
25:49 Either his uncle, or his **u** son, may H1730
Est 2: 7 that *is*, Esther, his **u** daughter: for she H1730
Jer 32: 8 So Hanameel mine **u** son came to me H1730
9 of Hanameel my **u** son, that *was* in H1730
12 of Hanameel mine **u** *son*, and in the H1730

UNCLOTHED

2Co 5: 4 that we would be **u**, but clothed upon, G1562

UNCOMELY

1Co 7:36 behaveth himself **u** toward his virgin, if G807
12:23 **u** *parts* have more abundant comeliness. G809

UNCONDEMNED

Act 16:37 beaten us openly **u**, being Romans, and G178
22:25 to scourge a man that is a Roman, and **u**? G178

UNCORRUPTIBLE

Ro 1:23 And changed the glory of the **u** God into G862

UNCORRUPTNESS

Tit 2: 7 in doctrine *shewing* **u**, gravity, sincerity, G90

UNCOVER

Lev 10: 6 Ithamar, his sons, **U** not your heads, H6544
18: 6 to **u** *their* nakedness: I *am* the LORD. H1540
7 shalt thou not **u**: she *is* thy mother; thou H1540
7 thou shalt not **u** her nakedness. H1540
8 thou not **u**: it *is* thy father's nakedness. H1540
9 *even* their nakedness thou shalt not **u**. H1540
10 not **u**: for theirs *is* thine own nakedness. H1540
11 sister, thou shalt not **u** her nakedness. H1540
12 Thou shalt not **u** the nakedness of thy H1540
13 Thou shalt not **u** the nakedness of thy H1540
14 Thou shalt not **u** the nakedness of thy H1540
15 Thou shalt not **u** the nakedness of thy H1540
15 wife; thou shalt not **u** her nakedness. H1540
16 Thou shalt not **u** the nakedness of thy H1540
17 Thou shalt not **u** the nakedness of a H1540
17 daughter, to **u** her nakedness; *for* they H1540
18 to vex *her*, to **u** her nakedness, beside H1540
19 unto a woman to **u** her nakedness, as H1540
20:18 and shall **u** her nakedness; he hath H1540
19 And thou shalt not **u** the nakedness of H1540
21:10 not **u** his head, nor rend his clothes; H6544
Nu 5:18 the LORD, and **u** the woman's head, H6544
Ru 3: 4 shalt go in, and **u** his feet, and lay thee H1540
Isa 47: 2 Take the millstones, and grind meal: **u** H1540

Isa 47: 2 leg, **u** the thigh, pass over the rivers. H1540
Zep 2:14 for he shall **u** the cedar work. H6168

UNCOVERED
Gen 9:21 drunken; and he was **u** within his tent. H1540
Lev 20:11 his father's wife hath **u** his father's H1540
17 their people: he hath **u** his sister's H1540
18 and she hath **u** the fountain of her H1540
20 wife, he hath **u** his uncle's nakedness: H1540
21 unclean thing: he hath **u** his brother's H1540
Ru 3: 7 and **u** his feet, and laid her down. H1540
2Sa 6:20 of Israel to day, who **u** himself to day in H1540
Isa 20: 4 *their* buttocks **u**, to the shame of Egypt. H2834
22: 6 *and* horsemen, and Kir **u** the shield. H6168
47: 3 Thy nakedness shall be **u**, yea, thy H1540
Jer 49:10 But I have made Esau bare, I have **u** H1540
Ezk 4: 7 **u**, and thou shalt prophesy against it. H2834
Hab 2:16 and let thy foreskin be **u**: the cup of the H6188
Mk 2: 4 for the press, they **u** the roof where he *G648*
1Co 11: 5 with *her* head **u** dishonoureth her head: *G177*
13 it comely that a woman pray unto God **u**? *G177*

UNCOVERETH
Lev 20:19 sister: for he **u** his near kin: they shall H6168
Dt 27:20 wife; because he **u** his father's skirt. H1540
2Sa 6:20 the vain fellows shamelessly **u** himself! H1540

UNCTION
1Jn 2:20 But ye have an **u** from the Holy One, *G5545*

UNDEFILED
Ps 119: 1 Blessed *are* the **u** in the way, who walk H8549
Song 5: 2 my love, my dove, my **u**: for my head is H8535
6: 9 My dove, my **u** is *but* one; she *is* the H8535
Heb 7:26 *who is* holy, harmless, **u**, separate from *G283*
13: 4 in all, and the bed **u**: but whoremongers *G283*
Jas 1:27 Pure religion and **u** before God and the *G283*
1Pt 1: 4 To an inheritance incorruptible, and **u**, *G283*

UNDER See the Appendix.

UNDERGIRDING
Act 27:17 up, they used helps, **u** the ship; and, *G5269*

UNDERNEATH
Ex 28:27 two sides of the ephod **u**, toward the H4295
39:20 two sides of the ephod **u**, toward the H4295
Dt 33:27 The eternal God *is thy* refuge, and **u** *are* H8478

UNDERSETTERS
1Ki 7:30 thereof had **u**: under the laver *were* H3802
30 **u** molten, at the side of every addition. H3802
34 And *there were* four **u** to the four H3802
34 *and* the **u** *were* of the very base itself. H3802

UNDERSTAND
Gen 11: 7 they may not **u** one another's speech. H8085
41:15 thou canst **u** a dream to interpret it. H8085
Nu 16:30 pit; then ye shall **u** that these men have H3045
Dt 9: 3 **U** therefore this day, that the LORD thy H3045
6 **U** therefore, that the LORD thy God H3045
28:49 a nation whose tongue thou shalt not **u**; H8085
2Ki 18:26 language; for we **u** *it*: and talk not with H8085
1Ch 28:19 the LORD made me **u** in writing by *his* H7919
Neh 8: 3 those that could **u**; and the ears of all the H995
7 the people to **u** the law: and the people H995
8 sense, and caused *them* to **u** the reading. H995
13 scribe, even to **u** the words of the law. H7919
Job 6:24 and cause me to **u** wherein I have erred. H995
23: 5 me, and **u** what he would say unto me. H995
26:14 but the thunder of his power who can **u**? H995
32: 9 wise: neither do the aged **u** judgment. H995
36:29 Also can *any* **u** the spreadings of the H995
Ps 14: 2 were any that did **u**, *and* seek God. H7919
19:12 Who can **u** *his* errors? cleanse thou me H995
53: 2 were *any* that did **u**, that did seek God. H7919
82: 5 They know not, neither will they **u**; they H995
92: 6 knoweth not; neither doth a fool **u** this. H995
94: 8 **U**, ye brutish among the people: and *ye* H995
107:43 shall **u** the lovingkindness of the LORD. H995
119:27 Make me to **u** the way of thy precepts: so H995
100 I **u** more than the ancients, because I H995
Prv 1: 6 To **u** a proverb, and the interpretation; H995
2: 5 Then shalt thou **u** the fear of the LORD, H995
9 Then shalt thou **u** righteousness, and H995
8: 5 O ye simple, **u** wisdom: and, ye fools, be H995
14: 8 The wisdom of the prudent *is* to **u** his H995
19:25 understanding, *and* he will **u** knowledge. H995
20:24 how can a man then **u** his own way? H995
Prv 28: 5 Evil men **u** not judgment: but they that H995
5 but they that seek the LORD **u** all *things*. H995
29:19 for though he **u** he will not answer. H995
Isa 6: 9 ye indeed, but **u** not; and see ye indeed, H995
10 their ears, and **u** with their heart, and H995
28: 9 shall he make to **u** doctrine? *them that* H995
19 shall be a vexation only *to* **u** the report. H995
32: 4 The heart also of the rash shall **u** H995
33:19 tongue, *that thou canst* not **u**. H998
36:11 language; for we **u** *it*: and speak not to H8085
41:20 and consider, and **u** together, that the H7919
43:10 believe me, and **u** that I *am* he: before H995
44:18 *and* their hearts, that they cannot **u**. H7919
56:11 *that* cannot **u**: they all look to their H995
Jer 9:12 Who *is* the wise man, that may **u** this? H995
Ezk 3: 6 thou canst not **u**. Surely, had I sent thee H8085
Dan 8:16 Gabriel, make this *man* to **u** the vision. H995
17 he said unto me, **U**, O son of man: for at H995
9:13 from our iniquities, and **u** thy truth. H7919
23 **u** the matter, and consider the vision. H995
25 Know therefore and **u**, *that* from the H7919
10:11 greatly beloved, **u** the words that I speak H995
12 didst set thine heart to **u**, and to chasten H995
14 Now I am come to make thee **u** what H995
11:33 And they that **u** among the people shall H7919
12:10 shall **u**; but the wise shall understand. H995
10 shall understand; but the wise shall **u**. H995
Hos 4:14 the people *that* doth not **u** shall fall. H995
14: 9 Who *is* wise, and he shall **u** these *things*? H995
Mic 4:12 the LORD, neither **u** they his counsel: for H995
Mt 13:13 they hear not, neither do they **u**. *G4920*
14 and shall not **u**; and seeing ye shall *G4920*
15 ears, and should **u** with *their* heart, *G4920*
15:10 and said unto them, Hear, and **u**: *G4920*
17 Do not ye yet **u**, that whatsoever *G3539*
16: 9 Do ye not yet **u**, neither remember the *G3539*
11 How is it that ye do not **u** that I spake *it* *G3539*
24:15 holy place, (whoso readeth, let him **u**:) *G3539*
Mk 4:12 may hear, and not **u**; lest at any time *G4920*
7:14 unto me every one *of you*, and **u**: *G4920*
8:17 **u**? have ye your heart yet hardened? *G4920*
21 unto them, How is it that ye do not **u**? *G4920*
13:14 him that readeth **u**,) then let them that *G3539*
14:68 know not, neither **u** I what thou sayest. *G1987*
Lk 8:10 not see, and hearing they might not **u**. *G4920*
24:45 that they might **u** the scriptures, *G4920*
Jn 8:43 Why do ye not **u** my speech? *even* *G1097*
12:40 *their* eyes, nor **u** with *their* heart, and *G3539*
Act 24:11 Because that thou mayest **u**, that there *G1097*
28:26 and shall not **u**; and seeing ye shall *G4920*
27 *their* ears, and **u** with *their* heart, and *G4920*
Ro 15:21 and they that have not heard shall **u**. *G4920*
1Co 12: 3 Wherefore I give you to **u**, that no man *G1107*
13: 2 *of* prophecy, and **u** all mysteries, and *G1492*
Eph 3: 4 Whereby, when ye read, ye may **u** my *G3539*
Php 1:12 But I would ye should **u**, brethren, that *G1097*
Heb 11: 3 Through faith we **u** that the worlds *G3539*
2Pt 2:12 things that they **u** not; and shall utterly *G50*

UNDERSTANDEST
Job 15: 9 not? *what* **u** thou, which *is* not in us? H995
Ps 139: 2 uprising, thou **u** my thought afar off. H995
Jer 5:15 knowest not, neither **u** what they say. H8085
Act 8:30 and said, **U** thou what thou readest? *G1097*

UNDERSTANDETH
1Ch 28: 9 all hearts, and **u** all the imaginations H995
Job 28:23 God **u** the way thereof, and he knoweth H995
Ps 49:20 Man *that is* in honour, and **u** not, is like H995
Prv 8: 9 They *are* all plain to him that **u**, and right H995
14: 6 but knowledge *is* easy unto him that **u**. H995
Jer 9:24 in this, that he **u** and knoweth me, that H7919
Mt 13:19 the kingdom, and **u** *it* not, then cometh *G4920*
23 the word, and **u** *it*; which also beareth *G4920*
Ro 3:11 There is none that **u**, there is none that *G4920*
1Co 14: 2 God: for no man **u** *him*; howbeit in the *G191*
16 seeing he **u** not what thou sayest? *G1492*

UNDERSTANDING
Ex 31: 3 in wisdom, and in **u**, and in knowledge, H8394
35:31 in wisdom, in **u**, and in knowledge, and H8394
36: 1 put wisdom and **u** to know how to H8394
Dt 1:13 Take you wise men, and **u**, and known H995
4: 6 wisdom and your **u** in the sight of the H998
6 this great nation *is* a wise and **u** people. H995
32:28 counsel, neither *is there any* **u** in them. H8394
1Sa 25: 3 a woman of good **u**, and of a beautiful H7922
1Ki 3: 9 Give therefore thy servant an **u** heart to H8085
11 asked for thyself **u** to discern judgment; H995
1Ki 3:12 thee a wise and an **u** heart; so that there H995
4:29 And God gave Solomon wisdom and **u** H8394
7:14 with wisdom, and **u**, and cunning to H8394
1Ch 12:32 *were men* that had **u** of the times, to H998
22:12 Only the LORD give thee wisdom and **u**, H998
2Ch 2:12 with prudence and **u**, that might build an H998
13 endued with **u**, of Huram my father's, H998
26: 5 who had **u** in the visions of God: H995
Ezr 8:16 for Joiarib, and for Elnathan, men of **u**. H995
18 us a man of **u**, of the sons of Mahli, H7922
Neh 8: 2 could hear with **u**, upon the first day of H995
10:28 one having knowledge, and having **u**; H995
Job 12: 3 But I have **u** as well as you; I *am* not H3824
12 *is* wisdom; and in length of days **u**. H8394
13 and strength, he hath counsel and **u**. H8394
20 and taketh away the **u** of the aged. H2940
17: 4 For thou hast hid their heart from **u**: H7922
20: 3 the spirit of my **u** causeth me to answer. H998
26:12 by his **u** he smiteth through the proud. H8394
28:12 be found? and where *is* the place of **u**? H998
20 wisdom? and where *is* the place of **u**? H998
28 *is* wisdom; and to depart from evil *is* **u**. H998
32: 8 of the Almighty giveth them **u**. H995
34:10 me, ye men of **u**: far be it from God, *that* H3824
16 If now *thou hast* **u**, hear this: hearken to H998
34 Let men of **u** tell me, and let a wise H3824
38: 4 of the earth? declare, if thou hast **u**. H998
36 parts? or who hath given **u** to the heart? H998
39:17 neither hath he imparted to her **u**. H998
Ps 32: 9 *which* have no **u**: whose mouth must be H995
47: 7 of all the earth: sing ye praises with **u**. H7919
49: 3 the meditation of my heart *shall be* of **u**. H8394
111:10 of wisdom: a good **u** have all they that H7922
119:34 Give me **u**, and I shall keep thy law; yea, I H995
73 **u**, that I may learn thy commandments. H995
99 I have more **u** than all my teachers: for H7919
104 Through thy precepts I get **u**: therefore I H995
125 I *am* thy servant; give me **u**, that I may H995
130 giveth light; it giveth **u** unto the simple. H995
144 *is* everlasting: give me **u**, and I shall live. H995
169 LORD: give me **u** according to thy word. H995
147: 5 and of great power: his **u** *is* infinite. H8394
Prv 1: 2 instruction; to perceive the words of **u**; H998
5 man of **u** shall attain unto wise counsels: H995
2: 2 wisdom, *and* apply thine heart to **u**; H8394
3 *and* liftest up thy voice for **u**; H8394
6 of his mouth *cometh* knowledge and **u**. H8394
11 Discretion shall preserve thee, **u** shall H8394
3: 4 So shalt thou find favour and good **u** in H7922
5 heart; and lean not unto thine own **u**. H998
13 wisdom, and the man *that* getteth **u**. H8394
19 by **u** hath he established the heavens. H8394
4: 1 of a father, and attend to know **u**. H998
5 Get wisdom, get **u**: forget *it* not; neither H998
7 wisdom: and with all thy getting get **u**. H998
5: 1 my wisdom, *and* bow thine ear to my **u**: H8394
6:32 a woman lacketh **u**: he *that* doeth it H3820
7: 4 *art* my sister; and call **u** *thy* kinswoman: H998
7 the youths, a young man void of **u**, H3820
8: 1 Doth not wisdom cry? and **u** put forth H8394
5 and, ye fools, be ye of an **u** heart. H995
14 sound wisdom: I *am* **u**; I have strength. H998
9: 4 him that wanteth **u**, she saith to him, H3820
6 foolish, and live; and go in the way of **u**. H998
10 and the knowledge of the holy *is* **u**. H998
16 him that wanteth **u**, she saith to him, H3820
10:13 In the lips of him that hath **u** wisdom is H995
13 *is* for the back of him that is void of **u**. H3820
23 mischief: but a man of **u** hath wisdom. H8394
11:12 but a man of **u** holdeth his peace. H8394
12:11 that followeth vain *persons is* void of **u**. H3820
13:15 Good **u** giveth favour: but the way of H7922
14:29 *He that is* slow to wrath *is* of great **u**: H8394
33 of him that hath **u**: but *that which is* in H995
15:14 The heart of him that hath **u** seeketh H995
21 but a man of **u** walketh uprightly. H8394
32 but he that heareth reproof getteth **u**. H3820
16:16 to get **u** rather to be chosen than silver! H998
22 **U** *is* a wellspring of life unto him that H7922
17:18 A man void of **u** striketh hands, *and* H3820
24 Wisdom *is* before him that hath **u**; but H995
27 *and* a man of **u** is of an excellent spirit. H8394
28 shutteth his lips *is esteemed* a man of **u**. H995
18: 2 A fool hath no delight in **u**, but that his H8394
19: 8 soul: he that keepeth **u** shall find good. H8394
25 **u**, *and* he will understand knowledge. H995
20: 5 water; but a man of **u** will draw it out. H8394
21:16 out of the way of **u** shall remain in the H7919
30 *There is* no wisdom nor **u** nor counsel H8394

Prv 23:23 not; *also* wisdom, and instruction, and **u**. H998
24: 3 builded; and by **u** it is established: H8394
30 by the vineyard of the man void of **u**; H3820
28: 2 but by a man of **u** *and* knowledge the H995
11 the poor that hath **u** searcheth him out. H995
16 The prince that wanteth **u** *is* also a H8394
30: 2 *any* man, and have not the **u** of a man. H998
Ecc 9:11 riches to men of **u**, nor yet favour to men H995
Isa 11: 2 of wisdom and **u**, the spirit of counsel H998
3 And shall make him of quick **u** in the H7306
27:11 for it *is* a people of no **u**: therefore he that H998
29:14 the **u** of their prudent *men* shall be hid. H998
16 say of him that framed it, He had no **u**? H995
24 in spirit shall come to **u**, and they that H998
40:14 and shewed to him the way of **u**? H8394
28 is weary? *there is* no searching of his **u**. H8394
44:19 knowledge nor **u** to say, I have burned H8394
Jer 3:15 shall feed you with knowledge and **u**. H7919
4:22 they have none **u**: they *are* wise to do evil, H995
5:21 and without **u**; which have eyes, and H3820
51:15 hath stretched out the heaven by his **u**. H8394
Ezk 28: 4 With thy wisdom and with thine **u** thou H8394
Dan 1: 4 in knowledge, and **u** science, and such H995
17 Daniel had **u** in all visions and dreams. H995
20 And in all matters of wisdom *and* **u**, that H998
2:21 and knowledge to them that know **u**: H999
4:34 heaven, and mine **u** returned unto me, H4486
5:11 father light and **u** and wisdom, like the H7924
12 and knowledge, and **u**, interpreting of H7924
14 thee, and *that* light and **u** and excellent H7924
8:23 and **u** dark sentences, shall stand up. H995
9:22 now come forth to give thee skill and **u**. H998
10: 1 the thing, and had **u** of the vision. H998
11:35 And *some* of them of **u** shall fall, to try H7919
Hos 13: 2 to their own **u**, all of it the work of H8394
Oba 7 under thee: *there is* none **u** in him. H8394
8 Edom, and **u** out of the mount of Esau? H8394
Mt 15:16 And Jesus said, Are ye also yet without **u**? G801
Mk 7:18 Are ye so without **u** also? Do ye not G801
12:33 and with all the **u**, and with all the soul, G4907
Lk 1: 3 had perfect **u** of all things from the G3877
2:47 were astonished at his **u** and answers. G4907
24:45 Then opened he their **u**, that they might G3563
Ro 1:31 Without **u**, covenantbreakers, without G801
1Co 1:19 bring to nothing the **u** of the prudent. G4907
14:14 spirit prayeth, but my **u** is unfruitful. G3563
15 I will pray with the **u** also: I will sing G3563
15 spirit, and I will sing with the **u** also. G3563
19 five words with my **u**, that *by my voice* I G3563
20 Brethren, be not children in **u**: howbeit G5424
20 malice be ye children, but in **u** be men. G5424
Eph 1:18 The eyes of your **u** being enlightened; G1271
4:18 Having the **u** darkened, being G1271
5:17 Wherefore be ye not unwise, but **u** G4920
Php 4: 7 which passeth all **u**, shall keep your G3563
Col 1: 9 of his will in all wisdom and spiritual **u**; G4907
2: 2 the full assurance of **u**, to the G4907
1Ti 1: 7 Desiring to be teachers of the law; **u** G3539
2Ti 2: 7 and the Lord give thee **u** in all things. G4907
1Jn 5:20 hath given us an **u**, that we may know G1271
Rev 13:18 Here is wisdom. Let him that hath **u** G3563

UNDERSTOOD

Gen 42:23 And they knew not that Joseph **u** *them;* H8085
Dt 32:29 O that they were wise, *that* they **u** this, H7919
1Sa 4: 6 And they **u** that the ark of the LORD H3045
26: 4 David therefore sent out spies, and **u** H3045
2Sa 3:37 For all the people and all Israel **u** that H3045
Neh 8:12 because they had **u** the words that were H995
13: 7 And I came to Jerusalem, and **u** of the H995
Job 13: 1 all *this*, mine ear hath heard and **u** it. H995
42: 3 have I uttered that I **u** not; things too H995
Ps 73:17 the sanctuary of God; *then* **u** I their end. H995
81: 5 *where* I heard a language *that* I **u** not. H3045
106: 7 Our fathers **u** not thy wonders in Egypt; H7919
Isa 40:21 not **u** from the foundations of the earth? H995
44:18 They have not known nor **u**: for he hath H995
Dan 8:27 astonished at the vision, but none **u** *it.* H995
9: 2 In the first year of his reign I Daniel **u** by H995
10: 1 *was* long: and he **u** the thing, and had H995
12: 8 And I heard, but I **u** not: then said I, O H995
Mt 13:51 Jesus saith unto them, Have ye **u** all G4920
16:12 Then **u** they how that he bade *them* not G4920
17:13 Then the disciples **u** that he spake unto G4920
26:10 When Jesus **u** *it*, he said unto them, G1097
Mk 9:32 But they **u** not that saying, and were G50
Lk 2:50 And they **u** not the saying which he G4920
9:45 But they **u** not this saying, and it was hid G50
18:34 And they **u** none of these things: and G4920
Jn 8:27 They **u** not that he spake to them of the G1097
10: 6 them: but they **u** not what things they G1097
12:16 These things **u** not his disciples at the G1097
Act 7:25 would have **u** how that God by his G4920
25 would deliver them: but they **u** not. G4920
23:27 him, having **u** that he was a Roman. G3129
34 And when he **u** that *he was* of Cilicia; G4441
Ro 1:20 clearly seen, being **u** by the things that G3539
1Co 13:11 I spake as a child, I **u** as a child, I G5426
14: 9 words easy to be **u**, how shall it be G2154
2Pt 3:16 things hard to be **u**, which they that are G1425

UNDERTAKE

Isa 38:14 O LORD, I am oppressed; **u** for me. H6148

UNDERTOOK

Est 9:23 And the Jews **u** to do as they had H6901

UNDO

Isa 58: 6 of wickedness, to **u** the heavy burdens, H5425
Zep 3:19 Behold, at that time I will **u** all that H6213

UNDONE

Nu 21:29 Woe to thee, Moab! thou art **u**, O people H6
Jos 11:15 he left nothing **u** of all that the LORD H5493
Isa 6: 5 Then said I, Woe *is* me! for I am **u**; H1820
Mt 23:23 have done, and not to leave the other **u**. G863
Lk 11:42 have done, and not to leave the other **u**. G863

UNDRESSED

Lev 25: 5 **u**: *for* it is a year of rest unto the land. H5139
11 nor gather *the grapes* in it of thy vine **u**. H5139

UNEQUAL

Ezk 18:25 not my way equal? are not your ways **u**? H8505
29 my ways equal? are not your ways **u**? H8505

UNEQUALLY

2Co 6:14 Be ye not **u** yoked together with G2086

UNFAITHFUL

Prv 25:19 Confidence in an **u** man in time of H898

UNFAITHFULLY

Ps 78:57 But turned back, and dealt **u** like their H898

UNFEIGNED

2Co 6: 6 kindness, by the Holy Ghost, by love **u**, G505
1Ti 1: 5 and *of* a good conscience, and *of* faith **u**: G505
2Ti 1: 5 When I call to remembrance the **u** faith G505
1Pt 1:22 the Spirit unto **u** love of the brethren, G505

UNFRUITFUL

Mt 13:22 choke the word, and he becometh **u**. G175
Mk 4:19 in, choke the word, and it becometh **u**. G175
1Co 14:14 prayeth, but my understanding is **u**. G175
Eph 5:11 And have no fellowship with the **u** works G175
Tit 3:14 for necessary uses, that they be not **u**. G175
2Pt 1: 8 *be* barren nor **u** in the knowledge of G175

UNGIRDED

Gen 24:32 the house: and he **u** his camels, and H6605

UNGODLINESS

Ro 1:18 from heaven against all **u** and G763
11:26 and shall turn away **u** from Jacob: G763
2Ti 2:16 for they will increase unto more **u**. G763
Tit 2:12 Teaching us that, denying **u** and worldly G763

UNGODLY

2Sa 22: 5 the floods of **u** men made me afraid; H1100
2Ch 19: 2 thou help the **u**, and love them that H7563
Job 16:11 God hath delivered me to the **u**, and H5760
34:18 *art* wicked? *and* to princes, *Ye are* **u**? H7563
Ps 1: 1 the counsel of the **u**, nor standeth in the H7563
4 The **u** *are* not so: but *are* like the chaff H7563
5 Therefore the **u** shall not stand in the H7563
6 but the way of the **u** shall perish. H7563
3: 7 thou hast broken the teeth of the **u**. H7563
18: 4 the floods of **u** men made me afraid. H1100
43: 1 against an **u** nation: O deliver H3808+H2623
73:12 Behold, these *are* the **u**, who prosper in H7563
Prv 16:27 An **u** man diggeth up evil: and in his H1100
19:28 An **u** witness scorneth judgment: and H1100
Ro 4: 5 **u**, his faith is counted for righteousness. G765
5: 6 in due time Christ died for the **u**. G765
1Ti 1: 9 for the **u** and for sinners, for G765
1Pt 4:18 where shall the **u** and the sinner appear? G765
2Pt 2: 5 in the flood upon the world of the **u**; G765
2: 6 unto those that after should live **u**; G764
3: 7 day of judgment and perdition of **u** men. G765
Jude 4 condemnation, **u** men, turning the grace G765
15 all that are **u** among them of all their G765
15 them of all their **u** deeds which they have G763
15 which they have **u** committed, and of all G764
15 **u** sinners have spoken against him. G765
18 who should walk after their own **u** lusts. G763

UNHOLY

Lev 10:10 and **u**, and between unclean and clean; H2455
1Ti 1: 9 and for sinners, for **u** and profane, for G462
2Ti 3: 2 disobedient to parents, unthankful, **u**, G462
Heb 10:29 he was sanctified, an **u** thing, and hath G2839

UNICORN

Nu 23:22 he hath as it were the strength of an **u**. H7214
24: 8 the strength of an **u**: he shall eat up the H7214
Job 39: 9 Will the **u** be willing to serve thee, or H7214
10 Canst thou bind the **u** with his band in H7214
Ps 29: 6 calf; Lebanon and Sirion like a young **u**. H7214
92:10 an **u**: I shall be anointed with fresh oil. H7214

UNICORNS

Dt 33:17 *like* the horns of **u**: with them he shall H7214
Ps 22:21 hast heard me from the horns of the **u**. H7214
Isa 34: 7 And the **u** shall come down with them, H7214

UNITE

Ps 86:11 thy truth: **u** my heart to fear thy name. H3161

UNITED

Gen 49: 6 be not thou **u**: for in their anger they H3161

UNITY

Ps 133: 1 *it is* for brethren to dwell together in **u**! H3162
Eph 4: 3 Endeavouring to keep the **u** of the G1775
13 Till we all come in the **u** of the faith, G1775

UNJUST

Ps 43: 1 me from the deceitful and **u** man. H5766
Prv 11: 7 perish: and the hope of **u** *men* perisheth. H205
28: 8 He that by usury and **u** gain increaseth H8636
29:27 An **u** man *is* an abomination to the H5766
Zep 3: 5 not; but the **u** knoweth no shame. H5767
Mt 5:45 sendeth rain on the just and on the **u**. G94
Lk 16: 8 And the lord commended the **u** steward, G93
10 is **u** in the least is unjust also in much. G94
10 is unjust in the least is **u** also in much. G94
18: 6 And the Lord said, Hear what the **u** G93
11 **u**, adulterers, or even as this publican. G94
Act 24:15 of the dead, both of the just and **u**. G94
1Co 6: 1 before the **u**, and not before the saints? G94
1Pt 3:18 the just for the **u**, that he might bring G94
2Pt 2: 9 and to reserve the **u** unto the day of G94
Rev 22:11 He that is **u**, let him be unjust still: and G91
11 He that is unjust, let him be **u** still: and G91

UNJUSTLY

Ps 82: 2 How long will ye judge **u**, and accept H5766
Isa 26:10 will he deal **u**, and will not behold H5765

UNKNOWN

Act 17:23 TO THE U GOD. Whom therefore G57
1Co 14: 2 For he that speaketh in an *u* tongue
4 He that speaketh in an *u* tongue edifieth
13 Wherefore let him that speaketh in an *u*
14 For if I pray in an *u* tongue, my spirit
19 than ten thousand words in an *u* tongue.
27 If any man speak in an *u* tongue, *let it be*
2Co 6: 9 As **u**, and *yet* well known; as dying, and, G50
Gal 1:22 And was **u** by face unto the churches of G50

UNLADE

Act 21: 3 for there the ship was to **u** her burden. G670

UNLAWFUL

Act 10:28 how that it is an **u** thing for a man that G111
2Pt 2: 8 soul from day to day with *their* **u** deeds;) G459

UNLEARNED

Act 4:13 that they were **u** and ignorant men, they G62
1Co 14:16 the room of the **u** say Amen at thy G2399
23 in *those that are* **u**, or unbelievers, will G2399
24 not, or *one* **u**, he is convinced of all, G2399
2Ti 2:23 But foolish and **u** questions avoid, G521
2Pt 3:16 which they that are **u** and unstable G261

UNLEAVENED
Gen 19: 3 and did bake **u** bread, and they did eat. H4682
Ex 12: 8 with fire, and **u** bread; *and* with bitter H4682
15 Seven days shall ye eat **u** bread; even H4682
17 And ye shall observe *the feast of* **u** H4682
18 even, ye shall eat **u** bread, until the one H4682
20 your habitations shall ye eat **u** bread. H4682
39 And they baked **u** cakes of the dough H4682
13: 6 Seven days thou shalt eat **u** bread, and H4682
7 **U** bread shall be eaten seven days; and H4682
23:15 Thou shalt keep the feast of **u** bread: H4682
15 (thou shalt eat **u** bread seven days, as H4682
29: 2 And **u** bread, and cakes unleavened H4682
2 And unleavened bread, and cakes **u** H4682
2 oil, and wafers **u** anointed with oil: *of* H4682
23 of the **u** bread that *is* before the LORD: H4682
34:18 The feast of **u** bread shalt thou keep. H4682
18 days thou shalt eat **u** bread, as I H4682
Lev 2: 4 the oven, *it shall be* **u** cakes of fine flour H4682
4 with oil, or **u** wafers anointed with oil. H4682
5 shall be *of* fine flour **u**, mingled with oil. H4682
6:16 his sons eat: with **u** bread shall it be H4682
7:12 of thanksgiving **u** cakes mingled with H4682
12 with oil, and **u** wafers anointed with H4682
8: 2 and two rams, and a basket of **u** bread; H4682
26 And out of the basket of **u** bread, that H4682
26 he took one **u** cake, and a cake of H4682
23: 6 *is* the feast of **u** bread unto the LORD: H4682
6 LORD: seven days ye must eat **u** bread. H4682
Nu 6:15 And a basket of **u** bread, cakes of fine H4682
15 oil, and wafers of **u** bread anointed H4682
17 with the basket of **u** bread: the priest H4682
19 of the ram, and one **u** cake out of the H4682
19 basket, and one **u** wafer, and shall put H4682
9:11 eat it with **u** bread and bitter *herbs*. H4682
28:17 seven days shall **u** bread be eaten. H4682
Dt 16: 3 shalt thou eat **u** bread therewith, *even* H4682
8 Six days thou shalt eat **u** bread: and on H4682
16 in the feast of **u** bread, and in the feast H4682
Jos 5:11 after the passover, **u** cakes, and H4682
Jdg 6:19 ready a kid, and **u** cakes of an ephah of H4682
20 the flesh and the **u** cakes, and lay *them* H4682
21 the flesh and the **u** cakes; and there H4682
21 the flesh and the **u** cakes. Then the H4682
1Sa 28:24 *it*, and did bake **u** bread thereof: H4682
2Ki 23: 9 of the **u** bread among their brethren. H4682
1Ch 23:29 and for the **u** cakes, and for *that* H4682
2Ch 8:13 in the feast of **u** bread, and in the feast H4682
30:13 keep the feast of **u** bread in the second H4682
21 kept the feast of **u** bread seven days H4682
35:17 and the feast of **u** bread seven days. H4682
Ezr 6:22 And kept the feast of **u** bread seven H4682
Ezk 45:21 of seven days; **u** bread shall be eaten. H4682
Mt 26:17 Now the first *day* of the *feast of* **u** bread G106
Mk 14: 1 passover, and of **u** bread: and the chief G106
12 And the first day of **u** bread, when they G106
Lk 22: 1 Now the feast of **u** bread drew nigh, G106
7 Then came the day of **u** bread, when the G106
Act 12: 3 also. (Then were the days of **u** bread.) G106
20: 6 after the days of **u** bread, and came unto G106
1Co 5: 7 lump, as ye are **u**. For even Christ our G106
8 with the **u** *bread* of sincerity and truth. G106

UNLESS
Lev 22: 6 **u** he wash his flesh with water. H3588+H518
Nu 22:33 these three times: **u** she had turned from H194
2Sa 2:27 *As* God liveth, **u** thou hadst H3588+H3884
Ps 27:13 *I had fainted*, **u** I had believed to see H3884
94:17 **U** the LORD *had been* my help, my soul H3884
119:92 **U** thy law *had been* my delights, I H3884
Prv 4:16 away, **u** they cause *some* to fall. H518+H3808
1Co 15: 2 **u** ye have believed in vain. G1622+G1508

UNLOOSE
Mk 1: 7 I am not worthy to stoop down and **u**. G3089
Lk 3:16 I am not worthy to **u**: he shall baptize G3089
Jn 1:27 shoe's latchet I am not worthy to **u**. G3089

UNMARRIED
1Co 7: 8 I say therefore to the **u** and widows, It is G22
11 But and if she depart, let her remain **u**, or G22
32 He that is **u** careth for the things G22
34 and a virgin. The **u** woman careth for G22

UNMERCIFUL
Ro 1:31 without natural affection, implacable, **u**: G415

UNMINDFUL
Dt 32:18 Of the Rock *that* begat thee thou art **u**, H7876

UNMOVEABLE
Act 27:41 fast, and remained **u**, but the hinder part G761
1Co 15:58 be ye stedfast, **u**, always abounding in G277

UNNI
1Ch 15:18 and Jehiel, and U, Eliab, and Benaiah, H6042
20 and Jehiel, and U, and Eliab, and H6042
Neh 12: 9 Also Bakbukiah and U, their brethren, H6042

UNOCCUPIED
Jdg 5: 6 the highways were **u**, and the travellers H2308

UNPERFECT
Ps 139:16 yet being **u**; and in thy book all H1564

UNPREPARED
2Co 9: 4 me, and find you **u**, we (that we say not, G532

UNPROFITABLE
Job 15: 3 Should he reason with **u** talk? or with H5532
Mt 25:30 And cast ye the **u** servant into outer G888
Lk 17:10 you, say, We are **u** servants: we have G888
Ro 3:12 are together become **u**; there is none that G889
Tit 3: 9 about the law; for they are **u** and vain. G512
Phlm 11 Which in time past was to thee **u**, but G890
Heb 13:17 and not with grief: for that *is* **u** for you. G255

UNPROFITABLENESS
Heb 7:18 before for the weakness and **u** thereof. G512

UNPUNISHED
Prv 11:21 shall not be **u**: but the seed of the H5352
16: 5 hand *join* in hand, he shall not be **u**. H5352
17: 5 that is glad at calamities shall not be **u**. H5352
19: 5 A false witness shall not be **u**, and *he* H5352
9 A false witness shall not be **u**, and *he* H5352
Jer 25:29 should ye be utterly **u**? Ye shall not be H5352
29 Ye shall not be **u**: for I will call for a H5352
30:11 and will not leave thee altogether **u**. H5352
46:28 yet will I not leave thee wholly **u**. H5352
49:12 shall altogether go **u**? thou shalt not go H5352
12 go **u**, but thou shalt surely drink *of it*. H5352

UNQUENCHABLE
Mt 3:12 but he will burn up the chaff with **u** fire. G762
Lk 3:17 but the chaff he will burn with fire **u**. G762

UNREASONABLE
Act 25:27 For it seemeth to me **u** to send a G249
2Th 3: 2 And that we may be delivered from **u** G824

UNREBUKEABLE
1Ti 6:14 without spot, **u**, until the appearing of G423

UNREPROVEABLE
Col 1:22 holy and unblameable and **u** in his sight: G410

UNRIGHTEOUS
Ex 23: 1 with the wicked to be an **u** witness. H2555
Job 27: 7 he that riseth up against me as the **u**. H5767
Ps 71: 4 out of the hand of the **u** and cruel man. H5765
Isa 10: 1 Woe unto them that decree **u** decrees, H205
55: 7 his way, and the **u** man his thoughts: H205
Lk 16:11 been faithful in the **u** mammon, who will G94
Ro 3: 5 we say? *Is* God **u** who taketh vengeance? G94
1Co 6: 9 Know ye not that the **u** shall not inherit G94
Heb 6:10 For God *is* not **u** to forget your work and G94

UNRIGHTEOUSLY
Dt 25:16 *and* all that do **u**, *are* an abomination H5766

UNRIGHTEOUSNESS
Lev 19:15 Ye shall do no **u** in judgment: thou H5766
35 Ye shall do no **u** in judgment, in H5766
Ps 92:15 *he is* my rock, and *there is* no **u** in him. H5766
Jer 22:13 his house by **u**, and his H3808+H6664
Lk 16: 9 of the mammon of **u**; that, when ye fail, G93
Jn 7:18 the same is true, and no **u** is in him. G93
Ro 1:18 ungodliness and **u** of men, who hold the G93
18 of men, who hold the truth in **u**; G93
29 Being filled with all **u**, fornication, G93
2: 8 truth, but obey **u**, indignation and wrath, G93
3: 5 But if our **u** commend the righteousness G93
6:13 *as* instruments of **u** unto sin: but yield G93
9:14 What shall we say then? *Is there* **u** with G93
2Co 6:14 hath righteousness with **u**? and what G458
2Th 2:10 And with all deceivableness of **u** in them G93
12 not the truth, but had pleasure in **u**. G93
Heb 8:12 For I will be merciful to their **u**, and their G93
2Pt 2:13 And shall receive the reward of **u**, *as* they G93
15 *son* of Bosor, who loved the wages of **u**; G93
1Jn 1: 9 us *our* sins, and to cleanse us from all **u**. G93
5:17 All **u** is sin: and there is a sin not unto G93

UNRIPE
Job 15:33 He shall shake off his **u** grape as the H1154

UNRULY
1Th 5:14 warn them that are **u**, comfort the G813
Tit 1: 6 faithful children not accused of riot or **u**. G506
10 For there are many **u** and vain talkers G506
Jas 3: 8 *it is* an **u** evil, full of deadly poison. G183

UNSATIABLE
Ezk 16:28 thou wast **u**; yea, thou hast H1115+H7654

UNSAVOURY
2Sa 22:27 the froward thou wilt shew thyself **u**. H6617
Job 6: 6 Can that which is **u** be eaten without H8602

UNSEARCHABLE
Job 5: 9 Which doeth great things and **u**; H369+H2714
Ps 145: 3 praised; and his greatness *is* **u**. H369+H2714
Prv 25: 3 and the heart of kings *is* **u**. H369+H2714
Ro 11:33 of God! how **u** *are* his judgments, and G419
Eph 3: 8 the Gentiles the **u** riches of Christ; G421

UNSEEMLY
Ro 1:27 working that which is **u**, and receiving in G808
1Co 13: 5 Doth not behave itself **u**, seeketh not her G807

UNSHOD
Jer 2:25 Withhold thy foot from being **u**, and thy H3182

UNSKILFUL
Heb 5:13 For every one that useth milk *is* **u** in the G552

UNSPEAKABLE
2Co 9:15 Thanks *be* unto God for his **u** gift. G411
12: 4 and heard **u** words, which it is not G731
1Pt 1: 8 ye rejoice with joy **u** and full of glory: G412

UNSPOTTED
Jas 1:27 *and* to keep himself **u** from the world. G784

UNSTABLE
Gen 49: 4 **U** as water, thou shalt not excel; H6349
Jas 1: 8 A double minded man *is* **u** in all his G182
2Pt 2:14 from sin; beguiling **u** souls: an heart G793
3:16 are unlearned and **u** wrest, as *they do* G793

UNSTOPPED
Isa 35: 5 and the ears of the deaf shall be **u**. H6605

UNTAKEN
2Co 3:14 the same veil **u** away in the G3361+G343

UNTEMPERED
Ezk 13:10 and, lo, others daubed it with **u** *morter*: H8602
11 Say unto them which daub *it* with **u** H8602
14 have daubed with **u** *morter*, and bring H8602
15 daubed it with **u** *morter*, and will say H8602
22:28 daubed them with **u** *morter*, seeing H8602

UNTHANKFUL
Lk 6:35 for he is kind unto the **u** and *to* the evil. G884
2Ti 3: 2 disobedient to parents, **u**, unholy, G884

UNTIL See the Appendix.

UNTIMELY
Job 3:16 Or as an hidden **u** birth I had not been; H5309
Ps 58: 8 away: *like* the **u** birth of a woman, *that* H5309
Ecc 6: 3 I say, *that* an **u** birth *is* better than he. H5309
Rev 6:13 a fig tree casteth her **u** figs, when she is G3653

UNTO See the Appendix.

UNTOWARD
Act 2:40 Save yourselves from this **u** generation. G4646

UNWALLED
Dt 3: 5 and bars; beside **u** towns a great many. H6521
Est 9:19 that dwelt in the **u** towns, made the H6519
Ezk 38:11 go up to the land of **u** villages; I will go to

UNWASHEN
Mt 15:20 to eat with **u** hands defileth not a man. G449

Mk 7: 2 is to say, with **u**, hands, they found fault. *G449*
5 the elders, but eat bread with **u** hands? *G449*

UNWEIGHED
1Ki 7:47 And Solomon left all the vessels ***u***,

UNWISE
Dt 32: 6 people and **u**? *is* not he thy H3808+H2450
Hos 13:13 him: he *is* an **u** son; for he H3808+H2450
Ro 1:14 both to the wise, and to the **u**. *G453*
Eph 5:17 Wherefore be ye not **u**, but *G878*

UNWITTINGLY
Lev 22:14 And if a man eat *of* the holy thing **u**, H7684
Jos 20: 3 unawares *and* **u** may flee H1097+H1847
5 his neighbour **u**, and hated him H1097+H1847

UNWORTHILY
1Co 11:27 cup of the Lord, **u**, shall be guilty of the *G371*
29 For he that eateth and drinketh **u**, eateth *G371*

UNWORTHY
Act 13:46 yourselves **u** of everlasting life, *G3756+G514*
1Co 6: 2 are ye **u** to judge the smallest matters? *G370*

UP See the Appendix.

UPBRAID
Jdg 8:15 with whom ye did **u** me, saying, *Are* the H2778
Mt 11:20 Then began he to **u** the cities wherein *G3679*

UPBRAIDED
Mk 16:14 they sat at meat, and **u** them with their *G3679*

UPBRAIDETH
Jas 1: 5 and **u** not; and it shall be given him. *G3679*

UPHARSIN
Dan 5:25 was written, MENE, MENE, TEKEL, **U**. H6537

UPHAZ
Jer 10: 9 and gold from **U**, the work of the H210
Dan 10: 5 loins *were* girded with fine gold of **U**: H210

UPHELD
Isa 63: 5 unto me; and my fury, it **u** me. H5564

UPHOLD
Ps 51:12 salvation; and **u** me *with thy* free spirit. H5564
54: 4 the Lord *is* with them that **u** my soul. H5564
119:116 **U** me according unto thy word, that I H5564
Prv 29:23 but honour shall **u** the humble in spirit. H8551
Isa 41:10 thee; yea, I will **u** thee with the right H8551
42: 1 Behold my servant, whom I **u**; mine H8551
63: 5 that *there was* none to **u**: therefore mine H5564
Ezk 30: 6 Thus saith the LORD; They also that **u** H5564

UPHOLDEN
Job 4: 4 Thy words have **u** him that was falling, H6965
Prv 20:28 the king: and his throne is **u** by mercy. H5582

UPHOLDEST
Ps 41:12 And as for me, thou **u** me in mine H8551

UPHOLDETH
Ps 37:17 broken: but the LORD **u** the righteous. H5564
24 for the LORD **u** *him with* his hand. H5564
63: 8 hard after thee: thy right hand **u** me. H8551
145:14 The LORD **u** all that fall, and raiseth up H5564

UPHOLDING
Heb 1: 3 of his person, and **u** all things by the *G5342*

UPON See the Appendix.

UPPER
Ex 12: 7 side posts and on the **u** door post of the H4947
Lev 13:45 **u** lip, and shall cry, Unclean, unclean. H8222
Dt 24: 6 No man shall take the nether or the **u** H7393
Jos 15:19 the **u** springs, and the nether springs. H5942
16: 5 Ataroth-addar, unto Beth-horon the **u**; H5945
Jdg 1:15 the **u** springs and the nether springs. H5942
2Ki 1: 2 a lattice in his **u** chamber that *was* in H5944
18:17 by the conduit of the **u** pool, which *is* in H5945
23:12 on the top of the **u** chamber of Ahaz, H5944
1Ch 7:24 nether, and the **u**, and Uzzen-sherah.) H5945
28:11 thereof, and of the **u** chambers thereof, H5944
2Ch 3: 9 he overlaid the **u** chambers with gold. H5944
8: 5 Also he built Beth-horon the **u**, and H5945
2Ch 32:30 This same Hezekiah also stopped the **u** H5945
Isa 7: 3 of the conduit of the **u** pool in the H5945
36: 2 by the conduit of the **u** pool in the H5945
Ezk 42: 5 Now the **u** chambers *were* shorter: for H5945
Zep 2:14 shall lodge in the **u** lintels of it; *their* H3730
Mk 14:15 And he will shew you a large **u** room *G508*
Lk 22:12 And he shall shew you a large **u** room *G508*
Act 1:13 went up into an **u** room, where abode *G5253*
9:37 washed, they laid *her* in an **u** chamber. *G5253*
39 him into the **u** chamber: and all the *G5253*
19: 1 passed through the **u** coasts came to *G510*
20: 8 And there were many lights in the **u** *G5250*

UPPERMOST
Gen 40:17 And in the **u** basket *there was* of all H5945
Isa 17: 6 in the top of the **u** bough, four *or* five in
9 bough, and an **u** branch, which they left
Mt 23: 6 And love the **u** rooms at feasts, and the *G4411*
Mk 12:39 synagogues, and the **u** rooms at feasts: *G4411*
Lk 11:43 Pharisees! for ye love the **u** seats in the *G4410*

UPRIGHT
Gen 37: 7 and also stood **u**; and, behold, your H5324
Ex 15: 8 the floods stood **u** as an heap, *and* the H5324
Lev 26:13 bands of your yoke, and made you go **u**. H6968
1Sa 29: 6 thou hast been **u**, and thy going out and H3477
2Sa 22:24 I was also **u** before him, and have kept H8549
26 **u** man thou wilt shew thyself upright. H8549
26 upright man thou wilt shew thyself **u**. H8552
2Ch 29:34 Levites *were* more **u** in heart to sanctify H3477
Job 1: 1 was perfect and **u**, and one that feared H3477
8 earth, a perfect and an **u** man, one that H3477
2: 3 earth, a perfect and an **u** man, one that H3477
8: 6 If thou *wert* pure and **u**; surely now he H3477
12: 4 the just **u** *man is* laughed to scorn. H8549
17: 8 **U** *men* shall be astonied at this, and H3477
Ps 7:10 *is* of God, which saveth the **u** in heart. H3477
11: 2 they may privily shoot at the **u** in heart. H3477
7 his countenance doth behold the **u**. H3477
18:23 I was also **u** before him, and I kept H8549
25 **u** man thou wilt shew thyself upright; H8549
25 upright man thou wilt shew thyself **u**; H8552
19:13 over me: then shall I be **u**, and I shall be H8552
20: 8 and fallen: but we are risen, and stand **u**.
25: 8 Good and **u** *is* the LORD: therefore will H3477
32:11 shout for joy, all *ye that are* **u** in heart. H3477
33: 1 righteous: *for* praise is comely for the **u**. H3477
36:10 and thy righteousness to the **u** in heart. H3477
37:14 to slay such as be of **u** conversation. H3477
18 The LORD knoweth the days of the **u**: H8549
37 the **u**: for the end of *that* man *is* peace. H3477
49:14 feed on them; and the **u** shall have H3477
64:10 him; and all the **u** in heart shall glory. H3477
92:15 To shew that the LORD *is* **u**: *he is* my H3477
94:15 and all the **u** in heart shall follow it. H3477
97:11 and gladness for the **u** in heart. H3477
111: 1 of the **u**, and *in* the congregation. H3477
112: 2 the generation of the **u** shall be blessed. H3477
4 Unto the **u** there ariseth light in the H3477
119:137 Righteous *art* thou, O LORD, and **u** *are* H3477
125: 4 and *to them that are* **u** in their hearts. H3477
140:13 name: the **u** shall dwell in thy presence. H3477
Prv 2:21 For the **u** shall dwell in the land, and H3477
10:29 *is* strength to the **u**: but destruction H8537
11: 3 The integrity of the **u** shall guide them: H3477
6 The righteousness of the **u** shall deliver H3477
11 By the blessing of the **u** the city is H3477
20 *as are* **u** in *their* way *are* his delight. H8549
12: 6 the mouth of the **u** shall deliver them. H3477
13: 6 Righteousness keepeth *him that is* **u** in H8537
14:11 the tabernacle of the **u** shall flourish. H3477
15: 8 but the prayer of the **u** *is* his delight. H3477
16:17 The highway of the **u** *is* to depart from H3477
21:18 and the transgressor for the **u**. H3477
29 but *as for* the **u**, he directeth his way. H3477
28:10 **u** shall have good *things* in possession. H8549
29:10 The bloodthirsty hate the **u**: but the just H8535
27 the just: and *he that is* **u** in the way *is* H3477
Ecc 7:29 hath made man **u**; but they have sought H3477
12:10 *was* written *was* **u**, *even* words of truth. H3476
Song 1: 4 love more than wine: the **u** love thee. H4339
Isa 26: 7 most **u**, dost weigh the path of the just. H3477
Jer 10: 5 They *are* **u** as the palm tree, but speak H4749
Dan 8:18 but he touched me, and set me **u**. H5977
10:11 thee, and stand **u**: for unto thee am I H5977
11:17 kingdom, and **u** ones with him; thus H3477
Mic 7: 2 and *there is* none **u** among men: they H3477
4 as a brier: the most **u** *is sharper* than a H3477
Hab 2: 4 is lifted up is not **u** in him: but the just H3474
Act 14:10 Said with a loud voice, Stand **u** on thy *G3717*

UPRIGHTLY
Ps 15: 2 He that walketh **u**, and worketh H8549
58: 1 do ye judge **u**, O ye sons of men? H4339
75: 2 receive the congregation I will judge **u**. H4339
84:11 will he withhold from them that walk **u**. H8549
Prv 2: 7 *he is* a buckler to them that walk **u**. H8537
10: 9 He that walketh **u** walketh surely: but H8537
15:21 but a man of understanding walketh **u**. H3474
28:18 Whoso walketh **u** shall be saved: but *he* H8549
Isa 33:15 and speaketh **u**; he that despiseth the H4339
Am 5:10 and they abhor him that speaketh **u**. H8549
Mic 2: 7 words do good to him that walketh **u**? H3477
Gal 2:14 But when I saw that they walked not **u** *G3716*

UPRIGHTNESS
Dt 9: 5 Not for thy righteousness, or for the **u** H3476
1Ki 3: 6 and in **u** of heart with thee; and H3483
9: 4 of heart, and in **u**, to do according to all H3476
1Ch 29:17 and hast pleasure in **u**. As for me, in the H4339
17 As for me, in the **u** of mine heart I have H3476
Job 4: 6 thy hope, and the **u** of thy ways? H8537
33: 3 My words *shall be of* the **u** of my heart: H3476
23 a thousand, to shew unto man his **u**: H3476
Ps 9: 8 minister judgment to the people in **u**. H4339
25:21 Let integrity and **u** preserve me; for I H3476
111: 8 and ever, *and are* done in truth and **u**. H3477
119: 7 I will praise thee with **u** of heart, when H3476
143:10 *is* good; lead me into the land of **u**. H4334
Prv 2:13 Who leave the paths of **u**, to walk in the H3476
14: 2 He that walketh in his **u** feareth the H3476
28: 6 Better *is* the poor that walketh in his **u**, H8537
Isa 26: 7 The way of the just *is* **u**: thou, most H4339
10 in the land of **u** will he deal unjustly, H5229
57: 2 in their beds, *each one* walking *in* his **u**. H5228

UPRISING
Ps 139: 2 and mine **u**, thou understandest H6965

UPROAR
1Ki 1:41 *is this* noise of the city being in an **u**? H1993
Mt 26: 5 lest there be an **u** among the people. *G2351*
Mk 14: 2 *day*, lest there be an **u** of the people. *G2351*
Act 17: 5 all the city on an **u**, and assaulted the *G2350*
19:40 for this day's **u**, there being no cause *G4714*
20: 1 And after the **u** was ceased, Paul called *G2351*
21:31 band, that all Jerusalem was in an **u**. *G4797*
38 days madest an **u**, and leddest out into *G387*

UPSIDE
2Ki 21:13 *it*, and turning *it* **u** down. H5921+H6440
Ps 146: 9 way of the wicked he turneth **u** down.
Isa 24: 1 and turneth it **u** down, and H5921+H6440
29:16 Surely your turning of things **u** down
Act 17: 6 the world **u** down are come hither also; *G389*

UPWARD
Gen 7:20 Fifteen cubits **u** did the waters prevail; H4605
Ex 38:26 twenty years old and **u**, for six hundred H4605
Nu 1: 3 From twenty years old and **u**, all that H4605
18 twenty years old and **u**, by their polls. H4605
20 **u**, all that were able to go forth to war; H4605
22 **u**, all that were able to go forth to war; H4605
24 **u**, all that were able to go forth to war; H4605
26 **u**, all that were able to go forth to war; H4605
28 **u**, all that were able to go forth to war; H4605
30 **u**, all that were able to go forth to war; H4605
32 **u**, all that were able to go forth to war; H4605
34 **u**, all that were able to go forth to war; H4605
36 **u**, all that were able to go forth to war; H4605
38 **u**, all that were able to go forth to war; H4605
40 **u**, all that were able to go forth to war; H4605
42 **u**, all that were able to go forth to war; H4605
45 years old and **u**, all that were able to H4605
3:15 old and **u** shalt thou number them. H4605
22 a month old and **u**, *even* those that were H4605
28 a month old and **u**, *were* eight thousand H4605
34 **u**, *were* six thousand and two hundred. H4605
39 and **u**, *were* twenty and two thousand. H4605
40 **u**, and take the number of their names. H4605
43 a month old and **u**, of those that were H4605
4: 3 From thirty years old and **u** even until H4605
23 From thirty years old and **u** until fifty H4605
30 From thirty years old and **u** even unto H4605
35 From thirty years old and **u** even unto H4605
39 From thirty years old and **u** even unto H4605
43 From thirty years old and **u** even unto H4605
47 From thirty years old and **u** even unto H4605

Nu 8:24 five years old and u they shall go in to H4605
14:29 u, which have murmured against me, H4605
26: 2 years old and u, throughout their H4605
4 twenty years old and u; as the LORD H4605
62 a month old and u: for they were not H4605
32:11 years old and u, shall see the land H4605
Jdg 1:36 up to Akrabbim, from the rock, and u. H4605
1Sa 9: 2 u *he was* higher than any of the people. H4605
10:23 of the people from his shoulders and u. H4605
2Ki 3:21 armour, and u, and stood in the border. H4605
19:30 take root downward, and bear fruit u. H4605
1Ch 23: 3 of thirty years and u: and their number H4605
24 from the age of twenty years and u. H4605
2Ch 31:16 years old and u, *even* unto every one H4605
17 and u, in their charges by their courses; H4605
Ezr 3: 8 years old and u, to set forward the work H4605
Job 5: 7 is born unto trouble, as the sparks fly u. H1361
Ecc 3:21 of man that goeth u, and the spirit of H4605
Isa 8:21 their king and their God, and look u. H4605
37:31 take root downward, and bear fruit u: H4605
38:14 eyes fail *with looking* u: O LORD, I am H4791
Ezk 1:11 *were* stretched u; two *wings* of every H4605
27 of his loins even u, and from the H4605
8: 2 his loins even u, as the appearance of H4605
41: 7 about still u to the side chambers: H4605
7 the house went still u round about the H4605
7 the house *was still* u, and so increased H4605
43:15 the altar and u *shall be* four horns. H4605
Hag 2:15 from this day and u, from before a H4605
18 Consider now from this day and u, H4605

UR
Gen 11:28 land of his nativity, in U of the Chaldees. H218
31 with them from U of the Chaldees, to go H218
15: 7 thee out of U of the Chaldees, to give H218
1Ch 11:35 Sacar the Hararite, Eliphal the son of U, H218
Neh 9: 7 him forth out of U of the Chaldees, and H218

URBANE
Ro 16: 9 Salute U, our helper in Christ, and G3773

URGE
Lk 11:53 began to u *him* vehemently, and G1758

URGED
Gen 33:11 enough. And he u him, and he took *it*. H6484
Jdg 16:16 her words, and u him, *so* that his soul H509
19: 7 u him: therefore he lodged there again. H6484
2Ki 2:17 And when they u him till he was H6484
5:16 And he u him to take *it*; but he refused. H6484
23 talents. And he u him, and bound two H6555

URGENT
Ex 12:33 And the Egyptians were u upon the H2388
Dan 3:22 was u, and the furnace exceeding H2685

URI
Ex 31: 2 of U, the son of Hur, of the tribe of Judah: H221
35:30 of U, the son of Hur, of the tribe of Judah; H221
38:22 And Bezaleel the son of U, the son of H221
1Ki 4:19 Geber the son of U *was* in the country of H221
1Ch 2:20 And Hur begat U, and Uri begat Bezaleel. H221
20 And Hur begat Uri, and U begat H221
2Ch 1: 5 Bezaleel the son of U, the son of Hur, had H221
Ezr 10:24 the porters; Shallum, and Telem, and U. H221

URIAH
2Sa 11: 3 of Eliam, the wife of U the Hittite? H223
6 *saying*, Send me U the Hittite. And Joab H223
6 the Hittite. And Joab sent U to David. H223
7 And when U was come unto him, David H223
8 And David said to U, Go down to thy H223
8 wash thy feet. And U departed out of the H223
9 But U slept at the door of the king's H223
10 told David, saying, U went not down H223
10 David said unto U, Camest thou not from H223
11 And U said unto David, The ark, and H223
12 And David said to U, Tarry here to day H223
12 let thee depart. So U abode in Jerusalem H223
14 to Joab, and sent *it* by the hand of U. H223
15 saying, Set ye U in the forefront of the H223
16 that he assigned U unto a place where he H223
17 of David; and U the Hittite died also. H223
21 Thy servant U the Hittite is dead also. H223
24 thy servant U the Hittite is dead also. H223
26 And when the wife of U heard that Uriah H223
26 And when the wife of Uriah heard that U H223
12: 9 thou hast killed U the Hittite with the H223
10 the wife of U the Hittite to be thy wife. H223

2Sa 23:39 U the Hittite: thirty and seven in all. H223
1Ki 15: 5 save only in the matter of U the Hittite. H223
1Ch 11:41 U the Hittite, Zabad the son of Ahlai, H223
Ezr 8:33 the son of U the priest; and with H223
Isa 8: 2 to record, U the priest, and Zechariah H223

URIAH'S
2Sa 12:15 the child that U wife bare unto David, H223

URIAS
Mt 1: 6 of her *that had been the wife* of U; G3774

URIEL
1Ch 6:24 Tahath his son, U his son, Uzziah his H222
15: 5 Of the sons of Kohath; U the chief, and H222
11 for the Levites, for U, Asaiah, and Joel, H222
2Ch 13: 2 the daughter of U of Gibeah. And there H222

URIJAH
2Ki 16:10 and king Ahaz sent to U the priest the H223
11 And U the priest built an altar according H223
11 from Damascus: so U the priest made *it* H223
15 And king Ahaz commanded U the H223
16 Thus did U the priest, according to all H223
Neh 3: 4 the son of U, the son of Koz. And H223
21 the son of U the son of Koz another H223
8: 4 and Anaiah, and U, and Hilkiah, and H223
Jer 26:20 of the LORD, U the son of Shemaiah H223
21 to death: but when U heard it, he was H223
23 And they fetched forth U out of Egypt, H223

URIM
Ex 28:30 of judgment the U and the Thummim; H224
Lev 8: 8 breastplate the U and the Thummim. H224
Nu 27:21 the judgment of U before the LORD: at H224
Dt 33: 8 and thy U *be* with thy holy one, H224
1Sa 28: 6 by dreams, nor by U, nor by prophets. H224
Ezr 2:63 up a priest with U and with Thummim. H224
Neh 7:65 stood *up* a priest with U and Thummim. H224

US See the Appendix.

USE
Lev 7:24 other u: but ye shall in no wise eat of it. H4399
19:26 ye u enchantment, nor observe times. H5172
Nu 10: 2 that thou mayest u them for the calling H1961
15:39 eyes, after which ye u to go a whoring:
Dt 26:14 for *any* unclean *u*, nor given *ought*
2Sa 1:18 of Judah *the u of* the bow: behold, *it*
1Ch 12: 2 bows, and could u both the right hand H3231
28:15 according to the u of every candlestick. H5656
Jer 23:31 that u their tongues, and say, He saith. H3947
31:23 As yet they shall u this speech in the H559
46:11 in vain shalt thou u many medicines; *for*
Ezk 12:23 they shall no more u it as a proverb in H4912
16:44 proverbs shall u *this* proverb against H4911
18: 2 What mean ye, that ye u this proverb H4911
3 any more to u this proverb in Israel. H4911
21:21 the two ways, to u divination: he made H7080
Mt 5:44 despitefully u you, and persecute you; G1908
6: 7 But when ye pray, u not vain repetitions, G945
Lk 6:28 pray for them which despitefully u you. G1908
Act 14: 5 u *them* despitefully, and to stone them, G5195
Ro 1:26 u into that which is against nature: G5540
27 the natural u of the woman, burned G5540
1Co 7:21 thou mayest be made free, u *it* rather. G5530
31 And they that u this world, as not G5530
2Co 1:17 thus minded, did I u lightness? or the G5530
3:12 hope, we u great plainness of speech: G5530
13:10 being present I should u sharpness, G5530
Gal 5:13 unto liberty; only *u* not liberty for an
Eph 4:29 is good to the u of edifying, that it may G5532
1Ti 1: 8 the law *is* good, if a man u it lawfully; G5530
3:10 then let them u the office of a deacon,
5:23 Drink no longer water, but u a little G5530
2Ti 2:21 u, *and* prepared unto every good work. G2173
Heb 5:14 who by reason of u have their senses G1838
1Pt 4: 9 U hospitality one to another without G5382

USED
Ex 21:36 Or if it be known that the ox hath u to
Lev 7:24 beasts, may be u in any other use: but H6213
Jdg 14:10 a feast; for so u the young men to do.
20 whom he had u as his friend.
2Ki 17:17 through the fire, and u divination and H7080
21: 6 times, and u enchantments, and
2Ch 33: 6 times, and u enchantments, and
6 and u witchcraft, and dealt
Jer 2:24 A wild ass u to the wilderness, *that* H3928

Ezk 22:29 The people of the land have u H6231
35:11 which thou hast u out of thy hatred H6213
Hos 12:10 visions, and u similitudes, by the
Mk 2:18 and of the Pharisees u to fast: and they G2258
Act 8: 9 in the same city u sorcery, and G3096
19:19 Many of them also which u curious G4238
27:17 Which when they had taken up, they u G5530
Ro 3:13 tongues they have u deceit; the poison G1387
1Co 9:12 we have not u this power; but suffer G5530
15 But I have u none of these things: G5530
1Th 2: 5 For neither at any time u we G1096+G1722
1Ti 3:13 For they that have u the office of a G1247
Heb 10:33 companions of them that were so u. G390

USES
Tit 3:14 necessary u, that they be not unfruitful. G5532

USEST
Ps119:132 u to do unto those that love thy name. H4941

USETH
Dt 18:10 the fire, *or* that u divination, *or* an H7080
Est 6: 8 which the king *u* to wear, and the horse
Prv 15: 2 The tongue of the wise u knowledge
18:23 The poor u entreaties; but the rich H1696
Jer 22:13 by wrong; *that* u his neighbour's service
Ezk 16:44 Behold, every one that u proverbs shall
Heb 5:13 For every one that u milk *is* unskilful in G3348

USING
Col 2:22 Which all are to perish with the u;) after G671
1Pt 2:16 As free, and not u *your* liberty for a G2192

USURER
Ex 22:25 be to him as an u, neither shalt thou lay H5383

USURP
1Ti 2:12 to teach, nor to u authority over the G831

USURY
Ex 22:25 neither shalt thou lay upon him u. H5392
Lev 25:36 Take thou no u of him, or increase: but H5392
37 thy money upon u, nor lend him thy H5392
Dt 23:19 Thou shalt not lend upon u to thy H5391
19 to thy brother; u of money, usury of H5392
19 usury of money, u of victuals, usury of H5392
19 u of any thing that is lent upon usury: H5392
19 usury of any thing that is lent upon u: H5391
20 thou mayest lend upon u; but unto thy H5391
20 not lend upon u: that the LORD thy God H5391
Neh 5: 7 unto them, Ye exact u, every one of his H4855
10 corn: I pray you, let us leave off this u. H4855
Ps 15: 5 *He that* putteth not out his money to u, H5392
Prv 28: 8 He that by u and unjust gain H5392
Isa 24: 2 of u, so with the giver of usury to him. H5383
2 of usury, so with the giver of u to him. H5378
Jer 15:10 neither lent on u, nor men have lent to H5383
10 u; *yet* every one of them doth curse me. H5383
Ezk 18: 8 He *that* hath not given forth upon u, H5392
13 Hath given forth upon u, and hath H5392
17 hath not received u nor increase, hath H5392
22:12 thou hast taken u and increase, and H5392
Mt 25:27 should have received mine own with u. G5110
Lk 19:23 I might have required mine own with u? G5110

US-WARD
Ps 40: 5 *which are* to u: they cannot be reckoned H413
Eph 1:19 of his power to u who believe, G2248
2Pt 3: 9 is longsuffering to u, not willing that G2248

UTHAI
1Ch 9: 4 U the son of Ammihud, the son of H5793
Ezr 8:14 Of the sons also of Bigvai; U, and H5793

UTMOST
Gen 49:26 unto the u bound of the everlasting H8379
Nu 22:36 of Arnon, which *is* in the u coast. H7097
41 he might see the u *part* of the people. H7097
23:13 shalt see but the u part of them, and H7097
Dt 34: 2 and all the land of Judah, unto the u sea, H314
Jer 9:26 all *that are* in the u corners, that dwell H7112
25:23 Buz, and all *that are* in the u corners, H7112
49:32 *that are* in the u corners; and I will H7112
50:26 Come against her from the u border, H7093
Joel 2:20 part toward the u sea, and his stink shall H314
Lk 11:31 she came from the u parts of the earth G4009

UTTER
Lev 5: 1 not u *it*, then he shall bear his iniquity. H5046

Jos 2:14 Our life for yours, if ye **u** not this our H5046
20 And if thou **u** this our business, then H5046
Jdg 5:12 awake, awake, **u** a song: arise, Barak, H1696
1Ki 20:42 I appointed to **u** destruction, therefore
Job 8:10 thee, and **u** words out of their heart? H3318
15: 2 Should a wise man **u** vain knowledge, H6030
27: 4 wickedness, nor my tongue **u** deceit. H1897
33: 3 and my lips shall **u** knowledge clearly. H4448
Ps 78: 2 a parable: I will **u** dark sayings of old: H5042
94: 4 *How long* shall they **u** *and* speak hard H5042
106: 2 Who can **u** the mighty acts of the H4448
119:171 My lips shall **u** praise, when thou hast H5042
145: 7 They shall abundantly **u** the memory of H5042
Prv 14: 5 not lie: but a false witness will **u** lies. H6315
23:33 and thine heart shall **u** perverse things. H1696
Ecc 1: 8 man cannot **u** *it*: the eye is not satisfied H1696
5: 2 heart be hasty to **u** *any* thing before H3318
Isa 32: 6 hypocrisy, and to **u** error against the H1696
48:20 ye, tell this, **u** it *even* to the end of H3318
Jer 1:16 And I will **u** my judgments against H1696
25:30 from on high, and **u** his voice from his H5414
Ezk 24: 3 And **u** a parable unto the rebellious H4911
40:31 *were* toward the **u** court; and palm H2435
37 *were* toward the **u** court; and palm H2435
42: 1 Then he brought me forth into the **u** H2435
3 which *was* for the **u** court, *was* gallery H2435
7 toward the **u** court on the forepart H2435
8 that *were* in the **u** court *was* fifty H2435
9 one goeth into them from the **u** court. H2435
14 holy *place* into the **u** court, but there H2435
44:19 And when they go forth into the **u** H2435
19 *even* into the **u** court to the people, H2435
46:20 into the **u** court, to sanctify the people. H2435
21 Then he brought me forth into the **u** H2435
47: 2 without unto the **u** gate by the way that H2351
Joel 2:11 And the LORD shall **u** his voice before H5414
3:16 roar out of Zion, and **u** his voice from H5414
Am 1: 2 roar from Zion, and **u** his voice from H5414
Nah 1: 8 he will make an **u** end of the place H3617
9 he will make an **u** end: affliction shall H3617
Zec 14:11 there shall be no more **u** destruction; but
Mt 13:35 in parables; I will **u** things which have G2044
1Co 14: 9 So likewise ye, except ye **u** by the G1325
2Co 12: 4 which it is not lawful for a man to **u**. G2980

UTTERANCE
Act 2: 4 other tongues, as the Spirit gave them **u**. G669
1Co 1: 5 by him, in all **u**, and *in* all knowledge; G3056
2Co 8: 7 *in* faith, and **u**, and knowledge, and G3056
Eph 6:19 And for me, that **u** may be given unto G3056
Col 4: 3 open unto us a door of **u**, to speak the G3056

UTTERED
Nu 30: 6 she vowed, or **u** ought out of her lips, H4008
8 and that which she **u** with her lips, H4008
Jdg 11:11 and Jephthah **u** all his words before H1696
2Sa 22:14 heaven, and the most High **u** his voice. H5414
Neh 6:19 before me, and **u** my words to him. H3318
Job 26: 4 To whom hast thou **u** words? and H5046
42: 3 therefore have I **u** that I understood H5046
Ps 46: 6 he **u** his voice, the earth melted. H5414
66:14 Which my lips have **u**, and my mouth H6475
Jer 48:34 Jahaz, have they **u** their voice, from H5414
51:55 great waters, a noise of their voice is **u**: H5414
Hab 3:10 by: the deep **u** his voice, *and* lifted H5414
Ro 8:26 for us with groanings which cannot be **u**. G215
Heb 5:11 to be **u**, seeing ye are dull of hearing. G3004
Rev 10: 3 cried, seven thunders **u** their voices. G2980
4 And when the seven thunders had **u** G2980
4 seven thunders **u**, and write them not. G2980

UTTERETH
Job 15: 5 For thy mouth **u** thine iniquity, and thou H502
Ps 19: 2 Day unto day **u** speech, and night unto H5042
Prv 1:20 Wisdom crieth without; she **u** her voice H5414
21 gates: in the city she **u** her words, *saying*, H559
10:18 lips, and he that **u** a slander, *is* a fool. H3318
29:11 A fool **u** all his mind: but a wise *man* H3318
Jer 10:13 When he **u** his voice, *there is* a H5414
51:16 When he **u** *his* voice, *there is* a H5414
Mic 7: 3 the great *man*, he **u** his mischievous H1696

UTTERING
Isa 59:13 **u** from the heart words of falsehood. H1897

UTTERLY
Ex 17:14 of Joshua: for I will **u** put out the H4229
22:17 If her father **u** refuse to give her unto H3985
20 the LORD only, he shall be **u** destroyed.
Ex 23:24 but thou shalt **u** overthrow them, and H2040
Lev 13:44 **u** unclean; his plague *is* in his head. H2930
26:44 to destroy them **u**, and to break my H3615
Nu 15:31 that soul shall **u** be cut off; his iniquity H3772
21: 2 hand, then I will **u** destroy their cities. H2763
3 and they **u** destroyed them and H2763
30:12 But if her husband hath **u** made them H6565
Dt 2:34 at that time, and **u** destroyed the men, H2763
3: 6 And we **u** destroyed them, as we did H2763
6 king of Heshbon, **u** destroying the men,
4:26 that ye shall soon **u** perish from off the H6
26 days upon it, but shall **u** be destroyed. H8045
7: 2 smite them, *and* **u** destroy them; thou H2763
26 it: *but* thou shalt **u** detest it, and thou H8262
26 shalt **u** abhor it; for it *is* a cursed thing. H8581
12: 2 Ye shall **u** destroy all the places, wherein H6
13:15 destroying it **u**, and all that *is* therein, H2763
20:17 But thou shalt **u** destroy them; *namely*, H2763
31:29 For I know that after my death ye will **u** H7843
Jos 2:10 Sihon and Og, whom ye **u** destroyed. H2763
6:21 And they **u** destroyed all that *was* in H2763
8:26 **u** destroyed all the inhabitants of Ai. H2763
10: 1 taken Ai, and had **u** destroyed it; as he H2763
28 king thereof he **u** destroyed, them, and H2763
35 *were* therein he **u** destroyed that day, H2763
37 it **u**, and all the souls that *were* therein. H2763
39 of the sword, and **u** destroyed all the H2763
40 remaining, but **u** destroyed all that H2763
11:11 edge of the sword, **u** destroying *them*: H2763
12 the sword, *and* he **u** destroyed them, as H2763
20 destroy them **u**, *and* that they might H2763
21 destroyed them **u** with their cities. H2763
17:13 to tribute; but did not **u** drive them out. H3423
Jdg 1:17 Zephath, and **u** destroyed it. And the H2763
28 tribute, and did not **u** drive them out. H3423
15: 2 that thou hadst **u** hated her; therefore H8130
21:11 shall do, Ye shall **u** destroy every male, H2763
1Sa 15: 3 Now go and smite Amalek, and **u**
8 alive, and **u** destroyed all the people
9 and would not **u** destroy them: but every
9 vile and refuse, that they destroyed **u**. H2763
15 God; and the rest we have **u** destroyed.
18 and said, Go and **u** destroy the sinners
20 and have **u** destroyed the Amalekites.
21 which should have been **u** destroyed, to
27:12 made his people Israel **u** to abhor him; H887
2Sa 17:10 of a lion, shall **u** melt: for all Israel H4549
23: 7 be **u** burned with fire in the *same* place. H8313
1Ki 9:21 also were not able **u** to destroy, upon
2Ki 19:11 them **u**: and shalt thou be delivered? H2763
1Ch 4:41 and destroyed them **u** unto this day, and
2Ch 20:23 of mount Seir, **u** to slay and destroy
31: 1 until they had **u** destroyed them all.
32:14 that my fathers **u** destroyed, that could
Neh 9:31 sake thou didst not **u** consume them,
Ps 37:24 Though he fall, he shall not be **u** cast
73:19 they are **u** consumed with terrors. H5486
89:33 will I not **u** take from him, nor suffer
119: 8 keep thy statutes: O forsake me not **u**. H3966
43 And take not the word of truth **u** out of H3966
Song 8: 7 house for love, it would **u** be contemned. H936
Isa 2:18 And the idols he shall **u** abolish. H3632
6:11 man, and the land be **u** desolate, H8077
11:15 And the LORD shall **u** destroy the tongue
24: 3 The land shall be **u** emptied, and H1238
3 The land shall be utterly emptied, and **u** H962
19 The earth is **u** broken down, the earth is
34: 2 armies: he hath **u** destroyed them, he
37:11 them **u**; and shalt thou be delivered? H2763
40:30 weary, and the young men shall **u** fall: H3782
56: 3 The LORD hath **u** separated me from his H914
60:12 yea, *those* nations shall be **u** wasted. H2717
Jer 9: 4 for every brother will **u** supplant, and H6117
12:17 But if they will not obey, I will **u** pluck H5428
14:19 Hast thou **u** rejected Judah? hath thy H3988
23:39 Therefore, behold, I, even I, will **u** H5377
25: 9 about, and will **u** destroy them, and
29 and should ye be **u** unpunished? Ye H5352
50:21 Pekod: waste and **u** destroy after them,
26 destroy her **u**: let nothing of her be left. H2763
51: 3 young men; destroy ye **u** all her host. H2763
58 of Babylon shall be **u** broken, and her H6209
Lam 5:22 But thou hast **u** rejected us; thou art H3988
Ezk 9: 6 Slay **u** old *and* young, both maids, and H4889
17:10 shall it not **u** wither, when the east H3001
27:31 And they shall make themselves **u** bald H7144
29:10 the land of Egypt **u** waste *and* desolate, H2721
Dan 11:44 to destroy, and **u** to make away many.
Hos 1: 6 of Israel; but I will **u** take them away. H5375
Hos 10:15 shall the king of Israel **u** be cut off. H1820
Am 9: 8 that I will not **u** destroy the house of H8045
Mic 2: 4 *and* say, We be **u** spoiled: he hath H7703
Nah 1:15 more pass through thee; he is **u** cut off. H3605
Zep 1: 2 I will **u** consume all *things* from off the H622
Zec 11:17 and his right eye shall be **u** darkened. H3543
1Co 6: 7 Now therefore there is **u** a fault among G3654
2Pt 2:12 shall **u** perish in their own corruption; G2704
Rev 18: 8 and she shall be **u** burned with fire: for G2618

UTTERMOST
Ex 26: 4 thou make in the **u** edge of *another* H7020
36:11 he made in the **u** side of *another* H7020
17 And he made fifty loops upon the **u** H7020
Nu 11: 1 *that were* in the **u** parts of the camp. H7097
20:16 in Kadesh, a city in the **u** of thy border: H7097
Dt 11:24 even unto the **u** sea shall your coast be. H314
Jos 15: 1 *was* the **u** part of the south coast. H7097
5 bay of the sea at the **u** part of Jordan: H7097
21 And the **u** cities of the tribe of the H7097
1Sa 14: 2 And Saul tarried in the **u** part of H7097
1Ki 6:24 cherub: from the **u** part of the one wing H7098
24 the **u** part of the other *were* ten cubits. H7098
2Ki 7: 5 were come to the **u** part of the camp of H7097
8 And when these lepers came to the **u** H7097
Neh 1: 9 cast out unto the **u** part of the heaven, H7097
Ps 2: 8 **u** parts of the earth *for* thy possession. H657
65: 8 They also that dwell in the **u** parts are H7098
139: 9 *and* dwell in the **u** parts of the sea; H319
Isa 7:18 fly that *is* in the **u** part of the rivers of H7097
24:16 From the **u** part of the earth have we H3671
Mt 5:26 till thou hast paid the **u** farthing. G2078
12:42 she came from the **u** parts of the earth G4009
Mk 13:27 winds, from the **u** part of the earth to the G206
27 part of the earth to the **u** part of heaven. G206
Act 1: 8 and unto the **u** part of the earth. G2075
24:22 down, I will know the **u** of your matter. G1231
1Th 2:16 the wrath is come upon them to the **u**. G5056
Heb 7:25 save them to the **u** that come unto God G3838

UZ
Gen 10:23 And the children of Aram; U, and Hul, H5780
36:28 The children of Dishan *are* these; U, H5780
1Ch 1:17 U, and Hul, and Gether, and Meshech. H5780
42 The sons of Dishan; U, and Aran. H5780
Job 1: 1 There was a man in the land of U, H5780
Jer 25:20 of the land of U, and all the kings of H5780
Lam 4:21 in the land of U; the cup also shall pass H5780

UZAI
Neh 3:25 Palal the son of U, over against the H186

UZAL
Gen 10:27 And Hadoram, and U, and Diklah, H187
1Ch 1:21 Hadoram also, and U, and Diklah, H187

UZZA
2Ki 21:18 in the garden of U: and Amon his son H5798
26 in the garden of U: and Josiah his son H5798
1Ch 6:29 his son, Shimei his son, U his son, H5798
8: 7 them, and begat U, and Ahihud. H5798
13: 7 and U and Ahio drave the cart. H5798
9 of Chidon, U put forth his hand to H5798
10 kindled against U, and he smote him, H5798
11 a breach upon U: wherefore that place H5798
Ezr 2:49 The children of U, the children of H5798
Neh 7:51 children of U, the children of Phaseah, H5798

UZZAH
2Sa 6: 3 in Gibeah: and U and Ahio, the sons H5798
6 threshingfloor, U put forth *his hand* to H5798
7 kindled against U; and God smote him H5798
8 a breach upon U: and he called the H5798

UZZEN-SHERAH
1Ch 7:24 the nether, and the upper, and U.) H242

UZZI
1Ch 6: 5 begat Bukki, and Bukki begat U, H5813
6 And U begat Zerahiah, and Zerahiah H5813
51 Bukki his son, U his son, Zerahiah his H5813
7: 2 And the sons of Tola; U, and Rephaiah, H5813
3 And the sons of U; Izrahiah: and the H5813
7 And the sons of Bela; Ezbon, and U, H5813
9: 8 Elah the son of U, the son of Michri, H5813
Ezr 7: 4 The son of Zerahiah, the son of U, the H5813
Neh 11:22 at Jerusalem *was* U the son of Bani, the H5813
12:19 And of Joiarib, Mattenai; of Jedaiah, U; H5813
42 and Eleazar, and U, and Jehohanan, H5813

UZZIA

1Ch 11:44 **U** the Ashterathite, Shama and Jehiel H5814

UZZIAH

2Ki 15:13 thirtieth year of **U** king of Judah; and H5818
30 twentieth year of Jotham the son of **U**. H5818
32 the son of **U** king of Judah to reign. H5818
34 to all that his father **U** had done. H5818
1Ch 6:24 Tahath his son, Uriel his son, **U** his H5818
27:25 castles, *was* Jehonathan the son of **U**: H5818
2Ch 26: 1 Then all the people of Judah took **U**, H5818
3 Sixteen years old *was* **U** when he began H5818
8 And the Ammonites gave gifts to **U**: and H5818
9 Moreover **U** built towers in Jerusalem H5818
11 Moreover **U** had an host of fighting H5818
14 And **U** prepared for them throughout H5818
18 And they withstood **U** the king, and H5818
2Ch 26:18 not unto thee, **U**, to burn incense unto H5818
19 Then **U** was wroth, and *had* a censer in H5818
21 And **U** the king was a leper unto the H5818
22 Now the rest of the acts of **U**, first and H5818
23 So **U** slept with his fathers, and they H5818
27: 2 to all that his father **U** did: howbeit he H5818
Ezr 10:21 and Shemaiah, and Jehiel, and **U**. H5818
Neh 11: 4 the son of **U**, the son of Zechariah, H5818
Isa 1: 1 in the days of **U**, Jotham, Ahaz, *and* H5818
6: 1 In the year that king **U** died I saw also H5818
7: 1 of Jotham, the son of **U**, king of Judah, H5818
Hos 1: 1 in the days of **U**, Jotham, Ahaz, *and* H5818
Am 1: 1 in the days of **U** king of Judah, and H5818
Zec 14: 5 in the days of **U** king of Judah: and H5818

UZZIEL

Ex 6:18 and Hebron, and **U**: and the years of H5816
22 And the sons of **U**; Mishael, and H5816
Lev 10: 4 the sons of **U** the uncle of Aaron, H5816
Nu 3:19 Amram, and Izehar, Hebron, and **U**. H5816
30 *shall be* Elizaphan the son of **U**. H5816
1Ch 4:42 and Rephaiah, and **U**, the sons of Ishi. H5816
6: 2 Amram, Izhar, and Hebron, and **U**. H5816
18 Amram, and Izhar, and Hebron, and **U**. H5816
7: 7 and Uzzi, and **U**, and Jerimoth, and Iri, H5816
15:10 Of the sons of **U**; Amminadab the chief, H5816
23:12 Amram, Izhar, Hebron, and **U**, four. H5816
20 Of the sons of **U**; Michah the first, and H5816
24:24 *Of* the sons of **U**; Michah: of the sons of H5816
25: 4 Mattaniah, **U**, Shebuel, and Jerimoth, H5816
2Ch 29:14 the sons of Jeduthun; Shemaiah, and **U**. H5816
Neh 3: 8 Next unto him repaired **U** the son of H5816

UZZIELITES

Nu 3:27 and the family of the **U**: these *are* the H5817
1Ch 26:23 the Izharites, the Hebronites, *and* the **U**: H5817

V

VAGABOND

Gen 4:12 and a **v** shalt thou be in the earth. H5110
14 be a fugitive and a **v** in the earth; and it H5110
Act 19:13 Then certain of the **v** Jews, exorcists, *G4022*

VAGABONDS

Ps 109:10 Let his children be continually **v**, and H5128

VAIL

Gen 24:65 she took a **v**, and covered herself. H6809
38:14 and covered her with a **v**, and wrapped H6809
19 and laid by her **v** from her, and put on H6809
Ex 26:31 And thou shalt make a **v** *of* blue, and H6532
33 And thou shalt hang up the **v** under the H6532
33 in thither within the **v** the ark of the H6532
33 and the **v** shall divide unto you H6532
35 table without the **v**, and the candlestick H6532
27:21 without the **v**, which *is* before the H6532
30: 6 And thou shalt put it before the **v** that H6532
34:33 with them, he put a **v** on his face. H4533
34 him, he took the **v** off, until he came H4533
35 and Moses put the **v** upon his face H4533
35:12 mercy seat, and the **v** of the covering, H6532
36:35 And he made a **v** *of* blue, and purple, H6532
38:27 the sockets of the **v**; an hundred sockets H6532
39:34 skins, and the **v** of the covering, H6532
40: 3 testimony, and cover the ark with the **v**. H6532
21 and set up the **v** of the covering, and H6532
22 tabernacle northward, without the **v**. H6532
26 tent of the congregation before the **v**: H6532
Lev 4: 6 LORD, before the **v** of the sanctuary. H6532
17 before the LORD, *even* before the **v**. H6532
16: 2 *place* within the **v** before the mercy H6532
12 beaten small, and bring *it* within the **v**: H6532
15 his blood within the **v**, and do with that H6532
21:23 Only he shall not go in unto the **v**, nor H6532
24: 3 Without the **v** of the testimony, in the H6532
Nu 4: 5 down the covering **v**, and cover the ark H6532
18: 7 and within the **v**; and ye shall serve: I H6532
Ru 3:15 Also he said, Bring the **v** that *thou hast* H4304
2Ch 3:14 And he made the **v** *of* blue, and purple, H6532
Isa 25: 7 the **v** that is spread over all nations. H4541

VAILS

Isa 3:23 the fine linen, and the hoods, and the **v**. H7289

VAIN

Ex 5: 9 and let them not regard **v** words. H8267
20: 7 LORD thy God in **v**; for the LORD will H7723
7 him guiltless that taketh his name in **v**. H7723
Lev 26:16 seed in **v**, for your enemies shall eat it. H7385
20 And your strength shall be spent in **v**: H7385
Dt 5:11 LORD thy God in **v**: for the LORD will H7723
11 *him* guiltless that taketh his name in **v**. H7723
32:47 For it *is* not a **v** thing for you; because H7386
Jdg 9: 4 Abimelech hired **v** and light persons, H7386
11: 3 were gathered **v** men to Jephthah, and H7386
1Sa 12:21 *then should ye go* after **v** *things*, which H8414
21 cannot profit nor deliver; for they *are* **v**. H8414
25:21 Now David had said, Surely in **v** have I H8267
2Sa 6:20 as one of the **v** fellows shamelessly H7386
2Ki 17:15 and became **v**, and went after the H1891
18:20 Thou sayest, (but *they are but* **v** H8193
2Ch 13: 7 And there are gathered unto him **v** H7386
Job 9:29 *If* I be wicked, why then labour I in **v**? H1892
11:11 For he knoweth **v** men: he seeth H7723
12 For **v** man would be wise, though man H5014
15: 2 Should a wise man utter **v** knowledge, H7307
16: 3 Shall **v** words have an end? or what H7307
21:34 How then comfort ye me in **v**, seeing in H1892
27:12 *it*; why then are ye thus altogether **v**? H1891
35:16 Therefore doth Job open his mouth in **v**; H1892
39:16 hers: her labour is in **v** without fear; H7385
41: 9 Behold, the hope of him is in **v**: shall not H3576
Ps 2: 1 rage, and the people imagine a **v** thing? H7385
26: 4 I have not sat with **v** persons, neither H7723
33:17 An horse *is* a **v** thing for safety: neither H8267
39: 6 Surely every man walketh in a **v** shew:
6 they are disquieted in **v**: he heapeth up H1892
60:11 Give us help from trouble: for **v** *is* the H7723
62:10 and become not **v** in robbery: if riches H1891
73:13 Verily I have cleansed my heart *in* **v**, H7385
89:47 wherefore hast thou made all men in **v**? H7723
108:12 Give us help from trouble: for **v** *is* the H7723
119:113 I hate ***v*** thoughts: but thy law do I love.
127: 1 they labour in **v** that build it: except H7723
1 the city, the watchman waketh *but* in **v**. H7723
2 *It is* **v** for you to rise up early, to sit up H7723
139:20 *and* thine enemies take *thy name* in **v**. H7723
Prv 1:17 Surely in **v** the net is spread in the sight H2600
12:11 **v** *persons is* void of understanding. H7386
28:19 **v** *persons* shall have poverty enough. H7386
30: 9 steal, and take the name of my God *in* **v**.
31:30 Favour *is* deceitful, and beauty *is* **v**: *but* H1892
Ecc 6:12 life, all the days of his **v** life which he H1892
Isa 1:13 Bring no more **v** oblations; incense is H7723
30: 7 For the Egyptians shall help in **v**, and to H1892
36: 5 I say, *sayest thou*, (but *they are but* **v** H8193
45:18 he created it not in **v**, he formed it to be H8414
19 Seek ye me in **v**: I the LORD speak H8414
49: 4 Then I said, I have laboured in **v**, I have H7385
4 for nought, and in **v**: *yet* surely my H1892
65:23 They shall not labour in **v**, nor bring H7385
Jer 2: 5 walked after vanity, and are become **v**? H1891
30 In **v** have I smitten your children; they H7723
3:23 Truly in **v** *is salvation hoped for* from H8267
4:14 shall thy **v** thoughts lodge within thee? H205
30 with painting, in **v** shalt thou make H7723
6:29 **v**: for the wicked are not plucked away. H7723
8: 8 Lo, certainly in **v** made he *it*; the pen H8267
8 made he *it*; the pen of the scribes *is* in **v**. H8267
10: 3 For the customs of the people *are* **v**: for H1892
23:16 they make you **v**: they speak a vision H1891
46:11 of Egypt: in **v** shalt thou use many H7723
50: 9 expert man; none shall return in **v**. H7387
51:58 shall labour in **v**, and the folk in the fire, H7385
Lam 2:14 Thy prophets have seen **v** and foolish H7723
4:17 as yet failed for our **v** help: in our H1892
Ezk 6:10 in **v** that I would do this evil unto them. H2600
12:24 For there shall be no more any **v** vision H7723
13: 7 Have ye not seen a **v** vision, and have H7723
Zec 10: 2 they comfort in **v**: therefore they went H1892
Mal 3:14 Ye have said, It *is* **v** to serve God: and H7723
Mt 6: 7 But when ye pray, use not **v** repetitions,
15: 9 But in **v** they do worship me, teaching *G3155*
Mk 7: 7 Howbeit in **v** do they worship me, *G3155*
Act 4:25 rage, and the people imagine **v** things? *G2756*
Ro 1:21 but became **v** in their imaginations, *G3154*
13: 4 not the sword in **v**: for he is the minister *G1500*
1Co 3:20 the thoughts of the wise, that they are **v**. *G3152*
15: 2 unto you, unless ye have believed in **v**. *G1500*
10 me was not in **v**; but I laboured more *G2756*
14 preaching **v**, and your faith *is* also vain. *G2756*
14 preaching vain, and your faith *is* also **v**. *G2756*
17 your faith *is* **v**; ye are yet in your sins. *G3152*
58 that your labour is not in **v** in the Lord. *G2756*
2Co 6: 1 that ye receive not the grace of God in **v**. *G2756*
9: 3 you should be in **v** in this behalf; that, *G2758*
Gal 2: 2 means I should run, or had run, in **v**. *G2756*
21 by the law, then Christ is dead in **v**. *G1432*
3: 4 Have ye suffered so many things in **v**? if *G1500*
4 so many things in vain? if *it be* yet in **v**. *G1500*
4:11 I have bestowed upon you labour in **v**. *G1500*
5:26 Let us not be desirous of **v** glory, *G2755*
Eph 5: 6 Let no man deceive you with **v** words: *G2756*
Php 2:16 not run in **v**, neither laboured in vain. *G2756*
16 not run in vain, neither laboured in **v**. *G2756*
Col 2: 8 philosophy and **v** deceit, after the *G2756*
1Th 2: 1 in unto you, that it was not in **v**: *G2756*
3: 5 tempted you, and our labour be in **v**. *G2756*
1Ti 1: 6 have turned aside unto **v** jangling; *G3150*
6:20 avoiding profane *and* **v** babblings, and *G2757*
2Ti 2:16 But shun profane *and* **v** babblings: for *G2757*
Tit 1:10 For there are many unruly and **v** *G3151*
3: 9 the law; for they are unprofitable and **v**. *G3152*
Jas 1:26 his own heart, this man's religion *is* **v**. *G3152*
2:20 But wilt thou know, O **v** man, that faith *G2756*
4: 5 Do ye think that the scripture saith in **v**, *G2761*
1Pt 1:18 and gold, from your **v** conversation *G3152*

VAINGLORY

Php 2: 3 *Let* nothing *be done* through strife or **v**; *G2754*

VAINLY

Col 2:18 seen, **v** puffed up by his fleshly mind, *G1500*

VAJEZATHA

Est 9: 9 and Arisai, and Aridai, and **V**, H2055

VALE

Gen 14: 3 All these were joined together in the **v** H6010
8 battle with them in the **v** of Siddim; H6010
10 And the **v** of Siddim *was full of* H6010
37:14 **v** of Hebron, and he came to Shechem. H6010
Dt 1: 7 hills, and in the **v**, and in the south, and H8219
Jos 10:40 south, and of the **v**, and of the springs, H8219
1Ki 10:27 trees that *are* in the **v**, for abundance. H8219
2Ch 1:15 trees that *are* in the **v** for abundance. H8219
Jer 33:13 in the cities of the **v**, and in the cities of H8219

VALIANT

1Sa 14:52 or any **v** man, he took him unto him. H2428
16:18 and a mighty **v** man, and a man of H2428
18:17 only be thou **v** for me, and H1121+H2428
26:15 *Art* not thou a **v** man? and who *is* like
31:12 All the **v** men arose, and went all night, H2428
2Sa 2: 7 and be ye **v**: for your master H1121+H2428
11:16 place where he knew that **v** men *were*. H2428
13:28 you? be courageous, and be **v**. H1121+H2428
17:10 And he also *that is* **v**, whose H1121+H2428
10 and *they* which *be* with him *are* **v** men. H2428

V

2Sa 23:20 the son of a v man, of Kabzeel, who H2428
24: 9 thousand v men that drew the sword; H2428
1Ki 1:42 *art* a v man, and bringest good tidings. H2428
1Ch 5:18 of Manasseh, of v men, men able to H2428
7: 2 of Tola: *they were* v men of might in H1368
5 of Issachar *were* v men of might, H1368
10:12 They arose, all the v men, and took H2428
11:22 the son of a v man of Kabzeel, who H2428
26 Also the v men of the armies *were,* H1368
28: 1 and with all the v men, unto Jerusalem. H2428
2Ch 13: 3 with an army of v men of war, *even* H1368
26:17 priests of the LORD, *that were* v men: H2428
28: 6 *which were* all v men; because they had H2428
Neh 11: 6 hundred threescore and eight v men. H2428
Song 3: 7 threescore v men *are* about it, of H1368
7 men *are* about it, of the v of Israel. H1368
Isa 10:13 put down the inhabitants like a v *man:* H3524
33: 7 Behold, their v ones shall cry without: H691
Jer 9: 3 but they are not v for the truth upon H1396
46:15 Why are thy v *men* swept away? they H47
Nah 2: 3 is made red, the v men *are* in scarlet: H2428
Heb 11:34 strong, waxed v in fight, turned to *G2478*

VALIANTEST
Jdg 21:10 men of the v, and commanded H1121+H2428

VALIANTLY
Nu 24:18 for his enemies; and Israel shall do v. H2428
1Ch 19:13 behave ourselves v for our people, and H2388
Ps 60:12 Through God we shall do v: for he *it is* H2428
108:13 Through God we shall do v: for he *it is* H2428
118:15 the right hand of the LORD doeth v. H2428
16 the right hand of the LORD doeth v. H2428

VALLEY
Gen 14:17 v of Shaveh, which *is* the king's dale. H6010
26:17 tent in the v of Gerar, and dwelt there. H5158
19 And Isaac's servants digged in the v, H5158
Nu 14:25 dwelt in the v.) To morrow turn you, H6010
21:12 removed, and pitched in the v of Zared. H5158
20 And from Bamoth *in* the v, that *is* in the H1516
32: 9 For when they went up unto the v of H5158
Dt 1:24 the v of Eshcol, and searched it out. H5158
3:16 Arnon half the v, and the border even H5158
29 So we abode in the v over against H1516
4:46 On this side Jordan, in the v over H1516
21: 4 unto a rough v, which is neither eared H5158
4 strike off the heifer's neck there in the v: H5158
6 over the heifer that is beheaded in the v: H5158
34: 3 And the south, and the plain of the v of H1237
6 And he buried him in a v in the land of H1516
Jos 7:24 they brought them unto the v of Achor. H6010
26 called, The v of Achor, unto this day. H6010
8:11 *there was* a v between them and Ai. H1516
13 went that night into the midst of the v. H6010
10:12 and thou, Moon, in the v of Ajalon. H6010
11: 2 v, and in the borders of Dor on the west, H8219
8 and unto the v of Mizpeh eastward; H1237
16 of Goshen, and the v, and the plain, and H8219
16 of Israel, and the v of the same; H8219
17 Baal-gad in the v of Lebanon under H1237
12: 7 Baal-gad in the v of Lebanon even unto H1237
13:19 Zareth-shahar in the mount of the v, H6010
27 And in the v, Beth-aram, and H6010
15: 7 Debir from the v of Achor, and so H6010
8 And the border went up by the v of the H1516
8 *lieth* before the v of Hinnom westward, H1516
8 end of the v of the giants northward: H6010
33 *And* in the v, Eshtaol, and Zoreah, and H8219
17:16 in the land of the v have chariots of H6010
16 and *they* who *are* of the v of Jezreel. H6010
18:16 *lieth* before the v of the son of Hinnom, H1516
16 which *is* in the v of the giants on the H6010
16 descended to the v of Hinnom, to the H1516
21 and Beth-hoglah, and the v of Keziz, H6010
19:14 thereof are in the v of Jiphthah-el: H1516
27 and to the v of Jiphthah-el toward H1516
Jdg 1: 9 and in the south, and in the v. H8219
19 the v, because they had chariots of iron. H6010
34 not suffer them to come down to the v: H6010
5:15 on foot into the v. For the divisions of H6010
6:33 over, and pitched in the v of Jezreel. H6010
7: 1 of them, by the hill of Moreh, in the v. H6010
8 of Midian was beneath him in the v. H6010
12 lay along in the v like grasshoppers for H6010
16: 4 v of Sorek, whose name *was* Delilah. H5158
18:28 man; and it was in the v that *lieth* by H6010
1Sa 6:13 harvest in the v: and they lifted up their H6010
13:18 the v of Zeboim toward the wilderness. H1516
1Sa 15: 5 a city of Amalek, and laid wait in the v. H5158
17: 2 and pitched by the v of Elah, and set H6010
3 side: and *there was* a v between them. H1516
19 v of Elah, fighting with the Philistines. H6010
52 thou come to the v, and to the gates of H1516
21: 9 thou slewest in the v of Elah, behold, it H6010
31: 7 other side of the v, and *they* that *were* H6010
2Sa 5:18 spread themselves in the v of Rephaim. H6010
22 spread themselves in the v of Rephaim. H6010
8:13 v of salt, *being* eighteen thousand *men.* H1516
23:13 Philistines pitched in the v of Rephaim. H6010
2Ki 2:16 some v. And he said, Ye shall not send. H1516
3:16 the LORD, Make this v full of ditches. H5158
17 see rain; yet that v shall be filled with H5158
14: 7 He slew of Edom in the v of salt ten H1516
23:10 which *is* in the v of the children of H1516
1Ch 4:14 the father of the v of Charashim; for H1516
39 of the v, to seek pasture for their flocks. H1516
10: 7 that *were* in the v saw that they fled, H6010
11:15 encamped in the v of Rephaim. H6010
14: 9 spread themselves in the v of Rephaim. H6010
13 spread themselves abroad in the v. H6010
18:12 in the v of salt eighteen thousand. H1516
2Ch 14:10 in the v of Zephathah at Mareshah. H1516
20:26 themselves in the v of Berachah; for H6010
26 The v of Berachah, unto this day. H6010
25:11 and went to the v of salt, and smote of H1516
26: 9 gate, and at the v gate, and at the H1516
28: 3 Moreover he burnt incense in the v of H1516
33: 6 the fire in the v of the son of Hinnom: H1516
14 of Gihon, in the v, even to the entering H5158
35:22 and came to fight in the v of Megiddo. H1237
Neh 2:13 by the gate of the v, even before the H1516
15 by the gate of the v, and *so* returned. H1516
3:13 The v gate repaired Hanun, and the H1516
11:30 from Beer-sheba unto the v of Hinnom. H1516
35 Lod, and Ono, the v of craftsmen. H1516
Job 21:33 The clods of the v shall be sweet unto H5158
39:21 He paweth in the v, and rejoiceth in *his* H6010
Ps 23: 4 Yea, though I walk through the v of the H1516
60: 6 and mete out the v of Succoth. H6010
ttl Edom in the v of salt twelve thousand. H1516
84: 6 *Who* passing through the v of Baca H6010
108: 7 and mete out the v of Succoth. H6010
Prv 30:17 the ravens of the v shall pick it out, and H5158
Song 6:11 the fruits of the v, *and* to see whether H5158
Isa 17: 5 gathereth ears in the v of Rephaim. H6010
22: 1 The burden of the v of vision. What H1516
5 of hosts in the v of vision, breaking H1516
28: 4 the head of the fat v, shall be a fading H1516
21 be wroth as *in* the v of Gibeon, that he H6010
40: 4 Every v shall be exalted, and every H1516
63:14 As a beast goeth down into the v, the H1237
65:10 of flocks, and the v of Achor a place for H6010
Jer 2:23 see thy way in the v, know what thou H1516
7:31 which *is* in the v of the son of Hinnom, H1516
32 called Tophet, nor the v of the son of H1516
32 of Hinnom, but the v of slaughter: for H1516
19: 2 And go forth unto the v of the son of H1516
6 called Tophet, nor The v of the son of H1516
6 son of Hinnom, but The v of slaughter. H1516
21:13 O inhabitant of the v, *and* rock of the H6010
31:40 And the whole v of the dead bodies, H6010
32:35 Baal, which *are* in the v of the son of H1516
44 in the cities of the v, and in the cities of H8219
47: 5 their v: how long wilt thou cut thyself? H6010
48: 8 shall escape: the v also shall perish, H6010
49: 4 thy flowing v, O backsliding daughter? H6010
Ezk 37: 1 midst of the v which *was* full of bones, H1237
2 the open v; and, lo, *they were* very dry. H1237
39:11 in Israel, the v of the passengers on H1516
11 they shall call *it* The v of Hamon-gog. H1516
15 have buried it in the v of Hamon-gog. H1516
Hos 1: 5 the bow of Israel in the v of Jezreel. H6010
2:15 thence, and the v of Achor for a door H6010
Joel 3: 2 down into the v of Jehoshaphat, and H6010
12 come up to the v of Jehoshaphat: for H6010
14 Multitudes, multitudes in the v of H6010
14 the LORD *is* near in the v of decision. H6010
18 LORD, and shall water the v of Shittim. H5158
Mic 1: 6 thereof into the v, and I will discover H1516
Zec 12:11 of Hadadrimmon in the v of Megiddon. H1237
14: 4 *shall be* a very great v; and half of the H1516
5 And ye shall flee *to* the v of the H1516
5 for the v of the mountains shall H1516
Lk 3: 5 Every v shall be filled, and every *G5327*

VALLEYS
Nu 24: 6 As the v are they spread forth, as H5158
Dt 8: 7 depths that spring out of v and hills; H1237
11:11 *is* a land of hills and v, *and* drinketh H1237
Jos 9: 1 hills, and in the v, and in all the coasts H8219
12: 8 In the mountains, and in the v, and in H8219
1Ki 20:28 he *is* not God of the v, therefore will I H6010
1Ch 12:15 all *them* of the v, *both* toward the east, H6010
27:29 in the v *was* Shaphat the son of Adlai: H6010
Job 30: 6 To dwell in the clifts of the v, *in* caves of H5158
39:10 or will he harrow the v after thee? H6010
Ps 65:13 with flocks; the v also are covered over H6010
104: 8 go down by the v unto the place which H1237
10 He sendeth the springs into the v, *which* H5158
Song 2: 1 the rose of Sharon, *and* the lily of the v. H6010
Isa 7:19 in the desolate v, and in the holes of the H5158
22: 7 pass, *that* thy choicest v shall be full of H6010
28: 1 v of them that are overcome with wine! H1516
41:18 in the midst of the v: I will make the H1237
57: 5 in the v under the clifts of the rocks? H5158
Jer 49: 4 Wherefore gloriest thou in the v, thy H6010
Ezk 6: 3 rivers, and to the v; Behold, I, *even* I, H1516
7:16 like doves of the v, all of them H1516
31:12 and in all the v his branches are fallen, H1516
32: 5 and fill the v with thy height. H1516
35: 8 hills, and in thy v, and in all thy rivers, H1516
36: 4 the rivers, and to the v, to the desolate H1516
6 rivers, and to the v, Thus saith the Lord H1516
Mic 1: 4 him, and the v shall be cleft, as wax H6010

VALOUR
Jos 1:14 all the mighty men of v, and help them; H2428
6: 2 king thereof, *and* the mighty men of v. H2428
8: 3 men of v, and sent them away by night. H2428
10: 7 with him, and all the mighty men of v. H2428
Jdg 3:29 men of v; and there escaped not a man. H2428
6:12 *is* with thee, thou mighty man of v. H2428
11: 1 a mighty man of v, and he *was* the son H2428
18: 2 coasts, men of v, from Zorah, and from H2428
20:44 thousand men; all these *were* men of v. H2428
46 drew the sword; all these *were* men of v. H2428
1Ki 11:28 a mighty man of v: and Solomon seeing H2428
2Ki 5: 1 a mighty man in v, *but he was* a leper. H2428
24:14 the mighty men of v, *even* ten thousand H2428
1Ch 5:24 mighty men of v, famous men, *and* H2428
7: 7 mighty men of v; and were reckoned H2428
9 mighty men of v, *was* twenty thousand H2428
11 mighty men of v, *were* seventeen H2428
40 mighty men of v, chief of the princes. H2428
8:40 were mighty men of v, archers, and had H2428
12:21 men of v, and were captains in the host. H2428
25 mighty men of v for the war, seven H2428
28 And Zadok, a young man mighty of v, H2428
30 mighty men of v, famous throughout H2428
26: 6 father: for they *were* mighty men of v. H2428
30 his brethren, men of v, a thousand and H2428
31 mighty men of v at Jazer of Gilead. H2428
32 And his brethren, men of v, *were* two H2428
2Ch 13: 3 chosen men, *being* mighty men of v. H2428
14: 8 all these *were* mighty men of v. H2428
17:13 mighty men of v, *were* in Jerusalem. H2428
14 men of v three hundred thousand. H2428
16 hundred thousand mighty men of v. H2428
17 a mighty man of v, and with him armed H2428
25: 6 mighty men of v out of Israel for an H2428
26:12 v *were* two thousand and six hundred. H2428
32:21 all the mighty men of v, and the leaders H2428
Neh 11:14 And their brethren, mighty men of v, an H2428

VALUE
Lev 27: 8 the priest shall v him; according to his H6186
8 that vowed shall the priest v him. H6186
12 And the priest shall v it, whether it be H6186
Job 13: 4 of lies, ye *are* all physicians of no v. H457
Mt 10:31 Fear ye not therefore, ye are of more v *G1308*
27: 9 they of the children of Israel did v; *G5091*
Lk 12: 7 ye are of more v than many sparrows. *G1308*

VALUED
Lev 27:16 seed *shall be* v at fifty shekels of silver.
Job 28:16 It cannot be v with the gold of Ophir, H5541
19 it, neither shall it be v with pure gold. H5541
Mt 27: 9 of him that was v, whom they of the *G5091*

VALUEST
Lev 27:12 v it, *who art* the priest, so shall it be. H6187

VANIAH
Ezr 10:36 V, Meremoth, Eliashib, H2057

VANISH

Job 6:17 What time they wax warm, they v: H6789
Isa 51: 6 the heavens shall v away like smoke, H4414
1Co 13: 8 *there be* knowledge, it shall v away. *G2673*
Heb 8:13 and waxeth old *is* ready to v away. *G854*

VANISHED

Jer 49: 7 from the prudent? is their wisdom v? H5628
Lk 24:31 knew him; and he v out of their sight. *G1096*

VANISHETH

Job 7: 9 *As* the cloud is consumed and v away: H3212
Jas 4:14 for a little time, and then v away. *G853*

VANITIES

Dt 32:21 to anger with their v: and I will move H1892
1Ki 16:13 God of Israel to anger with their v. H1892
26 God of Israel to anger with their v. H1892
Ps 31: 6 I have hated them that regard lying v: H1892
Ecc 1: 2 Vanity of v, saith the Preacher, vanity H1892
2 the Preacher, vanity of v; all *is* vanity. H1892
5: 7 *are* also *divers* v: but fear thou God. H1892
12: 8 Vanity of v, saith the preacher; all *is* H1892
Jer 8:19 graven images, *and* with strange v? H1892
10: 8 and foolish: the stock *is* a doctrine of v. H1892
14:22 Are there *any* among the v of the H1892
Jna 2: 8 They that observe lying v forsake their H1892
Act 14:15 turn from these v unto the living God, *G3152*

VANITY

2Ki 17:15 and they followed v, and became vain, H1892
Job 7: 3 So am I made to possess months of v, H7723
16 alway: let me alone; for my days *are* v. H1892
15:31 Let not him that is deceived trust in v: H7723
31 vanity: for v shall be his recompence. H7723
35 forth v, and their belly prepareth deceit. H205
31: 5 If I have walked with v, or if my foot H7723
35:13 Surely God will not hear v, neither will H7723
Ps 4: 2 ye love v, *and* seek after leasing? Selah. H7385
10: 7 under his tongue *is* mischief and v. H205
12: 2 They speak v every one with his H7723
24: 4 his soul unto v, nor sworn deceitfully. H7723
39: 5 at his best state *is* altogether v. Selah. H1892
11 a moth: surely every man *is* v. Selah. H1892
41: 6 *me*, he speaketh v: his heart gathereth H7723
62: 9 Surely men of low degree *are* v, *and* H1892
9 they *are* altogether *lighter* than v. H1892
78:33 in v, and their years in trouble. H1892
94:11 the thoughts of man, that they *are* v. H1892
119:37 Turn away mine eyes from beholding v; H7723
144: 4 Man is like to v: his days *are* as a H1892
8 Whose mouth speaketh v, and their H7723
11 mouth speaketh v, and their right hand H7723
Prv 13:11 Wealth *gotten* by v shall be H1892
21: 6 a lying tongue *is* a v tossed to and fro H1892
22: 8 He that soweth iniquity shall reap v: and H205
30: 8 Remove far from me v and lies: give H7723
Ecc 1: 2 V of vanities, saith the Preacher, vanity H1892
2 Vanity of vanities, saith the Preacher, v H1892
2 the Preacher, vanity of vanities; all *is* v. H1892
14 behold, all *is* v and vexation of spirit. H1892
2: 1 pleasure: and, behold, this also *is* v. H1892
11 behold, all *was* v and vexation of spirit, H1892
15 I said in my heart, that this also *is* v. H1892
17 me: for all *is* v and vexation of spirit. H1892
19 wise under the sun. This *is* also v. H1892
21 portion. This also *is* v and a great evil. H1892
23 not rest in the night. This is also v. H1892
26 This also *is* v and vexation of spirit. H1892
3:19 preeminence above a beast: for all *is* v. H1892
4: 4 This *is* also v and vexation of spirit. H1892
7 Then I returned, and I saw v under the H1892
8 This *is* also v, yea, it *is* a sore travail. H1892
16 this also *is* v and vexation of spirit. H1892
5:10 abundance with increase: this *is* also v. H1892
6: 2 it: this *is* v, and it *is* an evil disease. H1892
4 For he cometh in with v, and departeth H1892
9 this *is* also v and vexation of spirit. H1892
11 that increase v, what *is* man the better? H1892
7: 6 *is* the laughter of the fool: this also *is* v. H1892
15 in the days of my v: there is a just *man* H1892
8:10 where they had so done: this *is* also v. H1892
14 There is a v which is done upon the H1892
14 the righteous: I said that this also *is* v. H1892
9: 9 of the life of thy v, which he hath given H1892
9 sun, all the days of thy v: for that *is* thy H1892
11: 8 they shall be many. All that cometh *is* v. H1892
10 thy flesh: for childhood and youth *are* v. H1892
12: 8 V of vanities, saith the preacher; all *is* H1892
Ecc 12: 8 of vanities, saith the preacher; all *is* v. H1892
Isa 5:18 of v, and sin as it were with a cart rope: H7723
30:28 with the sieve of v: and *there shall be* a H7723
40:17 to him less than nothing, and v. H8414
23 he maketh the judges of the earth as v. H8414
41:29 Behold, they *are* all v; their works *are* H205
44: 9 *are* all of them v; and their delectable H8414
57:13 them all away; v shall take *them*: but H1892
58: 9 forth of the finger, and speaking v; H205
59: 4 for truth: they trust in v, and speak lies; H8414
Jer 2: 5 walked after v, and are become vain? H1892
10:15 They *are* v, *and* the work of errors: in H1892
16:19 v, and *things* wherein *there is* no profit. H1892
18:15 have burned incense to v, and they have H7723
51:18 They *are* v, the work of errors: in the H1892
Ezk 13: 6 They have seen v and lying divination, H7723
8 ye have spoken v, and seen lies, H7723
9 prophets that see v, and that divine lies: H7723
23 Therefore ye shall see no more v, nor H7723
21:29 Whiles they see v unto thee, whiles they H7723
22:28 *morter*, seeing v, and divining lies unto H7723
Hos 12:11 surely they are v: they sacrifice bullocks H7723
Hab 2:13 shall weary themselves for very v? H7385
Zec 10: 2 For the idols have spoken v, and the H205
Ro 8:20 For the creature was made subject to v, *G3153*
Eph 4:17 Gentiles walk, in the v of their mind, *G3153*
2Pt 2:18 swelling *words* of v, they allure through *G3153*

VANTAGE See ADVANTAGE.

VAPOUR

Job 36:27 down rain according to the v thereof: H108
33 it, the cattle also concerning the v. H5927
Ps 148: 8 Fire, and hail; snow, and v; stormy H7008
Act 2:19 blood, and fire, and v of smoke: *G822*
Jas 4:14 life? It is even a v, that appeareth for a *G822*

VAPOURS

Ps 135: 7 He causeth the v to ascend from the H5387
Jer 10:13 he causeth the v to ascend from the H5387
51:16 he causeth the v to ascend from the H5387

VARIABLENESS

Jas 1:17 is no v, neither shadow of turning. *G3883*

VARIANCE

Mt 10:35 For I am come to set a man at v *G1369*
Gal 5:20 Idolatry, witchcraft, hatred, v, *G2054*

VASHNI

1Ch 6:28 And the sons of Samuel; the firstborn V, H2059

VASHTI

Est 1: 9 Also V the queen made a feast for the H2060
11 To bring V the queen before the king H2060
12 But the queen V refused to come at the H2060
15 What shall we do unto the queen V H2060
16 and the princes, V the queen hath not H2060
17 commanded V the queen to be brought H2060
19 be not altered, That V come no more H2060
2: 1 he remembered V, and what she had H2060
4 be queen instead of V. And the thing H2060
17 head, and made her queen instead of V. H2060

VAUNT

Jdg 7: 2 hands, lest Israel v themselves against H6286

VAUNTETH

1Co 13: 4 charity v not itself, is not puffed up, *G4068*

VEHEMENT

Song 8: 6 of fire, *which hath a* most v flame. H3050
Jna 4: 8 God prepared a v east wind; and the H2759
2Co 7:11 fear, yea, *what* v desire, yea, *what* zeal, *G1972*

VEHEMENTLY

Mk 14:31 But he spake the more v, If I should die *G1537*
Lk 6:48 the stream beat v upon that house, and *G4366*
49 stream did beat v, and immediately it *G4366*
11:53 began to urge *him* v, and to provoke *G1171*
23:10 and scribes stood and v accused him. *G2159*

VEIL

Song 5: 7 of the walls took away my v from me. H7289
Mt 27:51 And, behold, the v of the temple was *G2665*
Mk 15:38 And the v of the temple was rent in *G2665*
Lk 23:45 And the sun was darkened, and the v *G2665*
2Co 3:13 And not as Moses, *which* put a v over *G2571*
14 the same v untaken away in the *G2571*
2Co 3:14 which *v* is done away in Christ.
15 Moses is read, the v is upon their heart. *G2571*
16 to the Lord, the v shall be taken away. *G2571*
Heb 6:19 which entereth into that within the v; *G2665*
9: 3 And after the second v, the tabernacle *G2665*
10:20 through the v, that is to say, his flesh; *G2665*

VEIN

Job 28: 1 Surely there is a v for the silver, and a H4161

VENGEANCE

Gen 4:15 slayeth Cain, v shall be taken on him H5358
Dt 32:35 To me *belongeth* v, and recompence; H5359
41 I will render v to mine enemies, and H5359
43 and will render v to his adversaries, H5359
Jdg 11:36 the LORD hath taken v for thee of thine H5360
Ps 58:10 when he seeth the v: he shall wash his H5359
94: 1 O LORD God, to whom v belongeth; O H5360
1 to whom v belongeth, shew thyself. H5360
99: 8 thou tookest v of their inventions. H5358
149: 7 To execute v upon the heathen, *and* H5360
Prv 6:34 he will not spare in the day of v. H5359
Isa 34: 8 For *it is* the day of the LORD'S v, *and* H5359
35: 4 God will come *with* v, *even* God *with* a H5359
47: 3 v, and I will not meet *thee as* a man. H5359
59:17 the garments of v *for* clothing, and was H5359
61: 2 and the day of v of our God; to comfort H5359
63: 4 For the day of v *is* in mine heart, and H5359
Jer 11:20 let me see thy v on them: for unto thee H5360
20:12 let me see thy v on them: for unto thee H5360
46:10 of hosts, a day of v, that he may avenge H5360
50:15 down: for it *is* the v of the LORD: take H5360
15 of the LORD: take v upon her; as she H5358
28 in Zion the v of the LORD our God, H5360
28 the LORD our God, the v of his temple. H5360
51: 6 of the LORD'S v; he will render unto H5360
11 it; because it *is* the v of the LORD, the H5360
11 of the LORD, the v of his temple. H5360
36 cause, and take v for thee; and I will H5358
Lam 3:60 Thou hast seen all their v *and* all their H5360
Ezk 24: 8 fury to come up to take v; I have set her H5359
25:12 of Judah by taking v, and hath greatly H5359
14 And I will lay my v upon Edom by the H5360
14 shall know my v, saith the Lord GOD. H5360
15 and have taken v with a despiteful H5359
17 And I will execute great v upon them H5360
17 when I shall lay my v upon them. H5360
Mic 5:15 And I will execute v in anger and fury H5359
Nah 1: 2 LORD will take v on his adversaries, H5358
Lk 21:22 For these be the days of v, that all *G1557*
Act 28: 4 the sea, yet v suffereth not to live. *G1349*
Ro 3: 5 who taketh v? (I speak as a man) *G3709*
12:19 V *is* mine; I will repay, saith the Lord. *G1557*
2Th 1: 8 In flaming fire taking v on them that *G1557*
Heb 10:30 For we know him that hath said, V *G1557*
Jude 7 example, suffering the v of eternal fire. *G1349*

VENISON

Gen 25:28 eat of *his* v: but Rebekah loved Jacob. H6718
27: 3 go out to the field, and take me *some* v; H6720
5 to the field to hunt *for* v, *and* to bring *it*. H6718
7 Bring me v, and make me savoury H6718
19 eat of my v, that thy soul may bless me. H6718
25 will eat of my son's v, that my soul may H6718
31 his son's v, that thy soul may bless me. H6718
33 he that hath taken v, and brought *it* me, H6718

VENOM

Dt 32:33 of dragons, and the cruel v of asps. H7219

VENOMOUS

Act 28: 4 And when the barbarians saw the *v*

VENT

Job 32:19 v; it is ready to burst like new bottles. H6605

VENTURE

1Ki 22:34 And a *certain* man drew a bow at a v, H8537
2Ch 18:33 And a *certain* man drew a bow at a v, H8537

VERIFIED

Gen 42:20 v, and ye shall not die. And they did so. H539
1Ki 8:26 I pray thee, be v, which thou spakest H539
2Ch 6:17 let thy word be v, which thou hast spoken H539

VERILY

Gen 42:21 And they said one to another, We *are* v H61
Ex 31:13 of Israel, saying, V my sabbaths ye shall H389
Jdg 15: 2 And her father said, I v thought that H559

1Ki 1:43 said to Adonijah, V our lord king David H61
2Ki 4:14 Gehazi answered, V she hath no child, H61
1Ch 21:24 Nay; but I will v buy it for the full price: H7069
Job 19:13 acquaintance are v estranged from me. H389
Ps 37: 3 in the land, and v thou shalt be fed. H530
39: 5 before thee: v every man at his best H389
58:11 So that a man shall say, V *there is* a H389
11 v he is a God that judgeth in the earth. H389
66:19 *But* v God hath heard *me;* he hath H403
73:13 V I have cleansed my heart *in* vain, and H389
Isa 45:15 V thou *art* a God that hidest thyself, O H403
Jer 15:11 The LORD said, V it shall be H518+H3808
11 well with thy remnant; v I will cause the H518
Mt 5:18 For v I say unto you, Till heaven and G281
26 V I say unto thee, Thou shalt by no G281
6: 2 have glory of men. V I say unto you, G281
5 be seen of men. V I say unto you, They G281
16 unto men to fast. V I say unto you, They G281
8:10 that followed, V I say unto you, I have G281
10:15 V I say unto you, It shall be more G281
23 ye into another: for v I say unto you, Ye G281
42 name of a disciple, v I say unto you, he G281
11:11 V I say unto you, Among them that are G281
13:17 For v I say unto you, That many G281
16:28 V I say unto you, There be some G281
17:20 your unbelief: for v I say unto you, If ye G281
18: 3 And said, V I say unto you, Except ye be G281
13 And if so be that he find it, v I say unto G281
18 V I say unto you, Whatsoever ye shall G281
19:23 Then said Jesus unto his disciples, V I G281
28 And Jesus said unto them, V I say unto G281
21:21 Jesus answered and said unto them, V I G281
31 saith unto them, V I say unto you, That G281
23:36 V I say unto you, All these things shall G281
24: 2 all these things? v I say unto you, There G281
34 V I say unto you, This generation shall G281
47 V I say unto you, That he shall make G281
25:12 But he answered and said, V I say unto G281
40 and say unto them, V I say unto you, G281
45 Then shall he answer them, saying, V I G281
26:13 V I say unto you, Wheresoever this G281
21 And as they did eat, he said, V I say unto G281
34 Jesus said unto him, V I say unto thee, G281
Mk 3:28 V I say unto you, All sins shall be G281
6:11 against them. V I say unto you, It shall G281
8:12 seek after a sign? v I say unto you, There G281
9: 1 And he said unto them, V I say unto G281
12 told them, Elias v cometh first, and G3303
41 ye belong to Christ, v I say unto you, he G281
10:15 V I say unto you, Whosoever shall not G281
29 And Jesus answered and said, V I say G281
11:23 For v I say unto you, That whosoever G281
12:43 saith unto them, V I say unto you, That G281
13:30 V I say unto you, that this generation G281
14: 9 V I say unto you, Wheresoever this G281
18 did eat, Jesus said, V I say unto you, One G281
25 V I say unto you, I will drink no more of G281
30 And Jesus saith unto him, V I say unto G281
Lk 4:24 And he said, V I say unto you, No G281
11:51 and the temple: v I say unto you, It G3483
12:37 find watching: v I say unto you, that G281
13:35 you desolate: and v I say unto you, Ye G281
18:17 V I say unto you, Whosoever shall not G281
29 And he said unto them, V I say unto G281
21:32 V I say unto you, This generation shall G281
23:43 And Jesus said unto him, V I say unto G281
Jn 1:51 And he saith unto him, V, verily, I say G281
51 And he saith unto him, Verily, v, I say G281
3: 3 Jesus answered and said unto him, V, G281
3 said unto him, Verily, v, I say unto thee, G281
5 Jesus answered, V, verily, I say unto thee, G281
5 Jesus answered, Verily, v, I say unto thee, G281
11 V, verily, I say unto thee, We speak that G281
11 Verily, v, I say unto thee, We speak that G281
5:19 said unto them, V, verily, I say unto you, G281
19 unto them, Verily, v, I say unto you, The G281
24 V, verily, I say unto you, He that heareth G281
24 Verily, v, I say unto you, He that heareth G281
25 V, verily, I say unto you, The hour is G281
25 Verily, v, I say unto you, The hour is G281
6:26 Jesus answered them and said, V, verily, G281
26 Jesus answered them and said, Verily, v, G281
32 Then Jesus said unto them, V, verily, I G281
32 Then Jesus said unto them, Verily, v, I G281
47 V, verily, I say unto you, He that G281
47 Verily, v, I say unto you, He that G281
53 Then Jesus said unto them, V, verily, I G281
53 Then Jesus said unto them, Verily, v, I G281
8:34 Jesus answered them, V, verily, I say G281
Jn 8:34 Jesus answered them, Verily, v, I say G281
51 V, verily, I say unto you, If a man keep G281
51 Verily, v, I say unto you, If a man keep G281
58 Jesus said unto them, V, verily, I say unto G281
58 Jesus said unto them, Verily, v, I say unto G281
10: 1 V, verily, I say unto you, He that entereth G281
1 Verily, v, I say unto you, He that entereth G281
7 Then said Jesus unto them again, V, G281
7 them again, Verily, v, I say unto you, I G281
12:24 V, verily, I say unto you, Except a corn of G281
24 Verily, v, I say unto you, Except a corn of G281
13:16 V, verily, I say unto you, The servant is G281
16 Verily, v, I say unto you, The servant is G281
20 V, verily, I say unto you, He that G281
20 Verily, v, I say unto you, He that G281
21 testified, and said, V, verily, I say unto G281
21 and said, Verily, v, I say unto you, that G281
38 thy life for my sake? V, verily, I say unto G281
38 my sake? Verily, v, I say unto thee, The G281
14:12 V, verily, I say unto you, He that G281
12 Verily, v, I say unto you, He that G281
16:20 V, verily, I say unto you, That ye shall G281
20 Verily, v, I say unto you, That ye shall G281
23 ask me nothing. V, verily, I say unto you, G281
23 me nothing. Verily, v, I say unto you, G281
21:18 V, verily, I say unto thee, When thou G281
18 Verily, v, I say unto thee, When thou G281
Act 16:37 us out privily? nay v; but let them come G1063
19: 4 Then said Paul, John v baptized with G3303
22: 3 I am v a man *which am* a Jew, born in G3303
26: 9 I v thought with myself, that I ought to G3303
Ro 2:25 For circumcision v profiteth, if thou G3303
10:18 But I say, Have they not heard? Yes v, G3304
15:27 It hath pleased them v; and their G1063
1Co 5: 3 For I v, as absent in body, but present G3303
9:18 What is my reward then? *V* that, when I
14:17 For thou v givest thanks well, but the G3303
Gal 3:21 have given life, v righteousness should G3689
1Th 3: 4 For v, when we were with you, we told G2532
Heb 2:16 For v he took not on *him the nature of* G1222
3: 5 And Moses v *was* faithful in all his G3303
6:16 For men v swear by the greater: and an G3303
7: 5 And v they that are of the sons of Levi, G3303
18 For there is v a disannulling of the G3303
9: 1 Then v the first *covenant* had also G3303
12:10 For they v for a few days chastened *us* G3303
1Pt 1:20 Who v was foreordained before the G3303
1Jn 2: 5 But whoso keepeth his word, in him v is G230

VERITY

Ps 111: 7 The works of his hands *are* v and H571
1Ti 2: 7 a teacher of the Gentiles in faith and v. G225

VERMILION

Jer 22:14 *is* cieled with cedar, and painted with v. H8350
Ezk 23:14 of the Chaldeans pourtrayed with v, H8350

VERY

Gen 1:31 behold, *it was* v good. And the evening H3966
4: 5 was v wroth, and his countenance fell. H3966
12:14 beheld the woman that she *was* v fair. H3966
13: 2 And Abram *was* v rich in cattle, in H3966
18:20 and because their sin is v grievous; H3966
21:11 And the thing was v grievous in H3966
24:16 And the damsel *was* v fair to look H3966
26:13 and grew until he became v great: H3966
27:21 whether thou *be* my v son Esau or not. H2088
24 And he said, *Art* thou my v son Esau? H2088
33 And Isaac trembled v exceedingly, and H1419
34: 7 and they were v wroth, because he had H3966
41:19 after them, poor and v ill favoured and H3966
31 following; for it *shall be* v grievous. H3966
49 sand of the sea, v much, until he left H3966
47:13 the famine *was* v sore, so that the land H3966
50: 9 and it was a v great company. H3966
10 with a great and v sore lamentation: H3966
Ex 1:20 multiplied, and waxed v mighty. H3966
8:28 shall not go v far away: entreat for me. H7368
9: 3 *there shall be* a v grievous murrain. H3966
16 And in v deed for this *cause* have I H199
18 cause it to rain a v grievous hail, such H3966
24 with the hail, v grievous, such as there H3966
10:14 coasts of Egypt: v grievous *were they;* H3966
11: 3 man Moses *was* v great in the land of H3966
12:38 flocks, and herds, *even* v much cattle. H3966
30:36 And thou shalt beat *some* of it v small, H1854
Nu 6: 9 And if any man die v suddenly by him, H6621
11:33 smote the people with a v great plague. H3966
12: 3 (Now the man Moses *was* v meek, H3966
Nu 13:28 *are* walled, *and* v great: and moreover H3966
16:15 And Moses was v wroth, and said unto H3966
22:17 For I will promote thee unto v great H3966
32: 1 of Gad had a v great multitude of H3966
Dt 9:20 And the LORD was v angry with Aaron H3966
21 it, *and* ground *it* v small, *even* until it H3190
20:15 the cities *which are* v far off from thee, H3966
27: 8 all the words of this law v plainly. H3190
28:43 get up above thee v high; and thou H4605
43 high; and thou shalt come down v low. H4295
54 among you, and v delicate, his eye H3966
30:14 But the word *is* v nigh unto thee, in thy H3966
32:20 *be:* for they *are* a v froward generation,
Jos 1: 7 Only be thou strong and v courageous, H3966
3:16 up upon an heap v far from the city H3966
8: 4 v far from the city, but be ye all ready: H3966
9: 9 And they said unto him, From a v far H3966
13 old by reason of the v long journey. H3966
22 us, saying, We *are* v far from you; H3966
10:20 them with a v great slaughter, till H3966
27 mouth, *which remain* until this v day. H6106
11: 4 with horses and chariots v many. H3966
13: 1 yet v much land to be possessed. H3966
22: 8 tents, and with v much cattle, with H3966
8 iron, and with v much raiment: divide H3966
23: 6 Be ye therefore v courageous to keep H3966
Jdg 3:17 of Moab: and Eglon *was* a v fat man. H3966
11:33 the vineyards, with a v great slaughter. H3966
35 hast brought me v low, and thou art H3766
13: 6 an angel of God, v terrible: but I asked H3966
18: 9 and, behold, it *is* v good: and *are* ye H3966
Ru 1:20 Almighty hath dealt v bitterly with me. H3966
1Sa 2:17 the young men was v great before the H3966
22 Now Eli was v old, and heard all that H3966
4:10 and there was a v great slaughter; for H3966
5: 9 the city with a v great destruction: and H3966
11 the hand of God was v heavy there. H3966
14:15 quaked: so it was a v great trembling. H430
20 *and there was* a v great discomfiture. H3966
31 to Aijalon: and the people were v faint. H3966
18: 8 And Saul was v wroth, and the saying H3966
15 himself v wisely, he was afraid of him. H3966
19: 4 works *have been* to thee-ward v good: H3966
20: 7 peace: but if he be v wroth, *then* be H2734
23:22 it is told me *that* he dealeth v subtilly. H6191
25: 2 and the man *was* v great, and he had H3966
15 But the men *were* v good unto us, and H3966
34 For in v deed, *as* the LORD God of Israel H199
36 him, for he *was* v drunken: wherefore H3966
26: 4 that Saul was come in v deed. H3559
2Sa 1:26 brother Jonathan: v pleasant hast thou H3966
2:17 And there was a v sore battle that day; H3966
3: 8 Then was Abner v wroth for the words H3966
11: 2 woman *was* v beautiful to look upon. H3966
12:15 wife bare unto David, and it was v sick.
13: 3 and Jonadab *was* a v subtil man. H3966
21 of all these things, he was v wroth. H3966
36 also and all his servants wept v sore. H3966
18:17 wood, and laid a v great heap of stones H3966
19:32 Now Barzillai was a v aged man, *even* H3966
32 Mahanaim; for he *was* a v great man. H3966
24:10 thy servant; for I have done v foolishly. H3966
1Ki 1: 4 And the damsel *was* v fair, and H3966
6 and he also *was a* v goodly *man;* and H3966
15 and the king was v old; and Abishag H3966
7:34 the undersetters *were* of the v base itself.
10: 2 And she came to Jerusalem with a v H3966
2 that bare spices, and v much gold, and H3966
10 of gold, and of spices v great store, and H3966
19:10 And he said, I have been v jealous for H7065
14 And he said, I have been v jealous for H7065
21:26 And he did v abominably in following H3966
2Ki 14:26 Israel, *that it was* v bitter: for *there was* H3966
17:18 Therefore the LORD was v angry with H3966
21:16 shed innocent blood v much, till he had H3966
1Ch 9:13 and threescore; v able men for the work
18: 8 brought David v much brass, H3966
21: 8 thy servant; for I have done v foolishly. H3966
13 hand of the LORD; for v great *are* his H3966
23:17 but the sons of Rehabiah were v many. H4605
2Ch 6:18 But will God in v deed dwell with men on H552
7: 8 Israel with him, a v great congregation, H3966
9: 1 at Jerusalem, with a v great company, H3966
14:13 and they carried away v much spoil. H3966
16: 8 a huge host, with v many chariots and H3966
14 they made a v great burning for him. H3966
20:35 king of Israel, who did v wickedly:
24:24 the LORD delivered a v great host into H3966
30:13 second month, a v great congregation. H3966

2Ch 32:29 God had given him substance v much. H3966
33:14 and raised it up a v great height, and H3966
36:14 transgressed v much after all the H4604
Ezr 10: 1 unto him out of Israel a v great H3966
1 children: for the people wept v sore. H7235
Neh 1: 7 We have dealt v corruptly against thee, H2254
2: 2 of heart. Then I was v sore afraid, H3966
4: 7 to be stopped, then they were v wroth, H3966
5: 6 And I was v angry when I heard their H3966
8:17 so. And there was v great gladness. H3966
Est 1:12 v wroth, and his anger burned in him. H3966
Job 1: 3 she asses, and a v great household; so H3966
2:13 for they saw that *his* grief was v great. H3966
15:10 With us *are* both the grayheaded and v H3453
32: 6 young, and ye *are* v old; wherefore I H3453
Ps 5: 9 their inward part *is* v wickedness; their H1942
35: 8 into that v destruction let him fall.
46: 1 God *is* our refuge and strength, a v H3966
50: 3 be v tempestuous round about him. H3966
71:19 Thy righteousness also, O God, *is* v H5704
79: 8 prevent us: for we are brought v low. H3966
89: 2 shalt thou establish in the v heavens.
92: 5 thy works! *and* thy thoughts are v deep. H3966
93: 5 Thy testimonies are v sure: holiness H3966
104: 1 my God, thou art v great; thou art H3966
105:12 number; yea, v few, and strangers in it.
119:107 I am afflicted v much: quicken H5704+H3966
138 *are* righteous and v faithful. H3966
140 Thy word *is* v pure: therefore thy H3966
142: 6 Attend unto my cry; for I am brought v H3966
146: 4 earth; in that v day his thoughts perish.
147:15 *upon* earth: his word runneth v swiftly. H5704
Prv 17: 9 repeateth a matter separateth v friends.
27:15 A continual dropping in a v rainy day H5464
Isa 1: 9 had left unto us a v small remnant, we H4592
5: 1 hath a vineyard in a v fruitful hill:
10:25 For yet a v little while, and the H4213
16: 6 of Moab; *he is* v proud: *even* of his H3966
14 remnant *shall be* v small *and* feeble. H4592
24:16 dealers have dealt v treacherously. H899
29:17 *Is* it not yet a v little while, and H4213
30:19 more: he will be v gracious unto thee at H2603
31: 1 because they are v strong; but they look H3966
33:17 shall behold the land that is v far off. H4801
40:15 he taketh up the isles as a v little thing. H1851
47: 6 hast thou v heavily laid thy yoke. H3966
48: 8 thou wouldest deal v treacherously, and H898
52:13 be exalted and extolled, and be v high. H3966
64: 9 Be not wroth v sore, O LORD, neither H3966
12 hold thy peace, and afflict us v sore? H3966
Jer 2:12 be ye v desolate, saith the LORD. H3966
4:19 I am pained at my v heart; my heart H7023
5:11 Judah have dealt v treacherously against H898
12: 1 all they happy that deal v treacherously? H899
14:17 a great breach, with a v grievous blow. H3966
18:13 of Israel hath done a v horrible thing. H3966
20:15 is born unto thee; making him v glad. H8055
24: 2 One basket *had* v good figs, *even* like H3966
2 other basket *had* v naughty figs, which H3966
3 Figs; the good figs, v good; and the evil, H3966
3 good; and the evil, v evil, that cannot H3966
27: 7 his son's son, until the v time of his land
40:12 wine and summer fruits v much. H3966
46:20 Egypt *is like* a v fair heifer, *but* H3304
Lam 5:22 thou art v wroth against us. H5704+H3966
Ezk 2: 3 against me, *even* unto this v day. H6106
16:47 as *if that were* a v little *thing*, thou wast H6985
27:25 v glorious in the midst of the seas. H3966
33:32 And, lo, thou *art* unto them as a v H5690
37: 2 behold, *there were* v many in the open H3966
2 open valley; and, lo, *they were* v dry. H3966
40: 2 and set me upon a v high mountain, by H3966
47: 7 of the river *were* v many trees on the H3966
9 there shall be a v great multitude of H3966
Dan 2:12 For this cause the king was angry and v H7690
6:19 Then the king arose v early in the
7:20 mouth that spake v great things, whose H7260
8: 8 Therefore the he goat waxed v great: H3966
11:25 up to battle with a v great and mighty H3966
Joel 2:11 for his camp *is* v great: for *he is* strong H3966
11 and v terrible; and who can abide it? H3966
Am 5:20 even v dark, and no brightness in it? H651
Jna 4: 1 Jonah exceedingly, and he was v angry. H2734
Hab 2:13 shall labour in the v fire, and the H1767
13 shall weary themselves for v vanity? H1767
Zec 1:15 And I am v sore displeased with the H1419
8: 4 with his staff in his hand for v age. H7230
9: 2 Tyrus, and Zidon, though it be v wise. H3966
5 *shall see it*, and be v sorrowful, and H3966
Zec 14: 4 *there shall be* a v great valley; and half H3966
Mt 10:30 But the v hairs of your head are all G2532
15:28 was made whole from that v hour. G1565
17:18 the child was cured from that v hour. G1565
18:31 done, they were v sorry, and came and G4970
21: 8 And a v great multitude spread their G4118
24:24 possible, they shall deceive the v elect. G2532
26: 7 an alabaster box of v precious ointment, G927
37 and began to be sorrowful and v heavy. G85
Mk 8: 1 In those days the multitude being v G3827
14: 3 of spikenard v precious; and she brake G4185
33 to be sore amazed, and to be v heavy; G85
16: 2 And v early in the morning the first G3029
4 was rolled away: for it was v great. G4970
Lk 1: 3 all things from the v first, to write unto
9: 5 city, shake off the v dust from your feet G2532
10:11 Even the v dust of your city, which
12: 7 But even the v hairs of your head are G2532
59 till thou hast paid the v last mite. G2532
18:23 And when he heard this, he was v G4970
23 was very sorrowful: for he was v rich. G4970
24 And when Jesus saw that he was v G4036
19:17 been faithful in a v little, have thou G1646
48 the people were v attentive to hear him. G1582
24: 1 Now upon the first *day* of the week, v
Jn 7:26 know indeed that this is the v Christ? G230
8: 4 was taken in adultery, in the v act. G1888
12: 3 of spikenard, v costly, and anointed G4186
14:11 or else believe me for the v works' sake.
Act 9:22 Damascus, proving that this is v Christ. G846
10:10 And he became v hungry, and would
24: 2 and that v worthy deeds are done G2735
25:10 done no wrong, as thou v well knowest. G2566
Ro 10:20 But Esaias is v bold, and saith, I was G662
13: 6 attending continually upon this v thing. G846
1Co 4: 3 But with me it is a v small thing that I G1646
2Co 9: 2 and your zeal hath provoked v many. G4119
11: 5 a whit behind the v chiefest apostles. G5228
12:11 am I behind the v chiefest apostles, G3029
15 And I will v gladly spend and be spent G2236
Php 1: 6 Being confident of this v thing, that he G846
1Th 5:13 And to esteem them v highly in love for G5228
23 And the v God of peace sanctify you G846
2Ti 1:17 me out v diligently, and found *me*. G4708
18 me at Ephesus, thou knowest v well. G957
Heb 10: 1 come, *and* not the v image of the things, G846
Jas 3: 4 turned about with a v small helm, G1646
5:11 Lord is v pitiful, and of tender mercy. G4184

VESSEL

Lev 6:28 But the earthen v wherein it is sodden H3627
11:32 whether *it be* any v of wood, or H3627
32 sack, whatsoever v *it be*, wherein *any* H3627
33 And every earthen v, whereinto *any* of H3627
34 drunk in every *such* v shall be unclean. H3627
14: 5 in an earthen v over running water: H3627
50 in an earthen v over running water: H3627
15:12 And the v of earth, that he toucheth H3627
12 v of wood shall be rinsed in water. H3627
Nu 5:17 in an earthen v; and of the dust that H3627
19:15 And every open v, which hath no H3627
17 water shall be put thereto in a v: H3627
Dt 23:24 but thou shalt not put *any* in thy v. H3627
1Sa 21: 5 it were sanctified this day in the v. H3627
1Ki 17:10 a little water in a v, that I may drink. H3627
2Ki 4: 6 Bring me yet a v. And he said unto her, H3627
6 *is* not a v more. And the oil stayed. H3627
Ps 2: 9 dash them in pieces like a potter's v. H3627
31:12 man out of mind: I am like a broken v. H3627
Prv 25: 4 there shall come forth a v for the finer. H3627
Isa 30:14 of the potters' v that is broken in H5035
66:20 a clean v into the house of the LORD. H3627
Jer 18: 4 And the v that he made of clay was H3627
4 it again another v, as seemed good to H3627
19:11 a potter's v, that cannot be made H3627
22:28 idol? *is he* a v wherein *is* no pleasure? H3627
25:34 and ye shall fall like a pleasant v. H3627
32:14 v, that they may continue many days. H3627
48:11 emptied from v to vessel, neither hath H3627
11 from vessel to v, neither hath he gone H3627
38 Moab like a v wherein *is* no pleasure, H3627
51:34 me an empty v, he hath swallowed me H3627
Ezk 4: 9 put them in one v, and make thee bread H3627
15: 3 take a pin of it to hang any v thereon? H3627
Hos 8: 8 Gentiles as a v wherein *is* no pleasure. H3627
Mk 11:16 should carry *any* v through the temple. G4632
Lk 8:16 covereth it with a v, or putteth *it* under G4632
Jn 19:29 Now there was set a v full of vinegar: G4632
Act 9:15 for he is a chosen v unto me, to bear G4632
Act 10:11 and a certain v descending unto him, G4632
16 This was done thrice: and the v was G4632
11: 5 a vision, A certain v descend, as it had G4632
Ro 9:21 lump to make one v unto honour, and G4632
1Th 4: 4 his v in sanctification and honour; G4632
2Ti 2:21 he shall be a v unto honour, sanctified, G4632
1Pt 3: 7 as unto the weaker v, and as being heirs G4632

VESSELS

Gen 43:11 in the land in your v, and carry down H3627
Ex 7:19 in *v of* wood, and in *vessels of* stone.
19 in *vessels of* wood, and in *v of* stone.
25:39 gold shall he make it, with all these v. H3627
27: 3 the v thereof thou shalt make *of* brass. H3627
19 All the v of the tabernacle in all the H3627
30:27 And the table and all his v, and the H3627
27 and his v, and the altar of incense, H3627
28 with all his v, and the laver and his foot. H3627
35:13 The table, and his staves, and all his v, H3627
16 and all his v, the laver and his foot, H3627
37:16 And he made the v which *were* upon H3627
24 gold made he it, and all the v thereof. H3627
38: 3 And he made all the v of the altar, the H3627
3 all the v thereof made he *of* brass. H3627
30 grate for it, and all the v of the altar, H3627
39:36 The table, *and* all the v thereof, and the H3627
37 all the v thereof, and the oil for light, H3627
39 and all his v, the laver and his foot, H3627
40 pins, and all the v of the service of the H3627
40: 9 all the v thereof: and it shall be holy. H3627
10 and all his v, and sanctify the altar: H3627
Lev 8:11 altar and all his v, both the laver and H3627
Nu 1:50 and over all the v thereof, and over all H3627
50 and all the v thereof; and they shall H3627
3:31 the altars, and the v of the sanctuary H3627
36 v thereof, and all that serveth thereto, H3627
4: 9 and all the oil v thereof, wherewith H3627
10 And they shall put it and all the v H3627
14 And they shall put upon it all the v H3627
14 the basons, all the v of the altar; and H3627
15 and all the v of the sanctuary, as H3627
16 in the sanctuary, and in the v thereof. H3627
7: 1 the altar and all the v thereof, and had H3627
85 all the silver v *weighed* two thousand H3627
18: 3 not come nigh the v of the sanctuary H3627
19:18 tent, and upon all the v, and upon the H3627
Jos 6:19 But all the silver, and gold, and v of H3627
24 the gold, and the v of brass and of iron, H3627
Ru 2: 9 go unto the v, and drink of *that* which H3627
1Sa 9: 7 is spent in our v, and *there is* not a H3627
21: 5 I came out, and the v of the young men H3627
2Sa 8:10 brought with him v of silver, and H3627
10 and v of gold, and vessels of brass: H3627
10 and vessels of gold, and v of brass: H3627
17:28 and earthen v, and wheat, and barley, H3627
1Ki 7:45 and all these v, which Hiram made H3627
47 And Solomon left all the v *unweighed*, H3627
48 And Solomon made all the v that H3627
51 the gold, and the v, did he put among H3627
8: 4 and all the holy v that *were* in the H3627
10:21 And all king Solomon's drinking v *were* H3627
21 *of* gold, and all the v of the house of the H3627
25 man his present, v of silver, and vessels H3627
25 of silver, and v of gold, and garments, H3627
15:15 of the LORD, silver, and gold, and v. H3627
2Ki 4: 3 Then he said, Go, borrow thee v abroad H3627
3 *even* empty v; borrow not a few. H3627
4 out into all those v, and thou shalt set H3627
5 *the* v to her; and she poured out.
6 And it came to pass, when the v were H3627
7:15 of garments and v, which the Syrians H3627
12:13 trumpets, any v of gold, or vessels of H3627
13 any vessels of gold, or v of silver, of the H3627
14:14 silver, and all the v that were found in H3627
23: 4 the LORD all the v that were made for H3627
24:13 cut in pieces all the v of gold which H3627
25:14 and all the v of brass wherewith H3627
16 brass of all these v was without weight. H3627
1Ch 9:28 of the ministering v, that they should H3627
29 to oversee the v, and all the instruments H3627
18: 8 sea, and the pillars, and the v of brass. H3627
10 of v of gold and silver and brass. H3627
22:19 and the holy v of God, into the house H3627
23:26 nor any v of it for the service thereof. H3627
28:13 v of service in the house of the LORD. H3627
2Ch 4:18 Thus Solomon made all these v in great H3627
19 And Solomon made all the v that *were* H3627
5: 5 and all the holy v that *were* in the H3627
9:20 And all the drinking v of king Solomon H3627

2Ch 9:20 *of* gold, and all the v of the house of the H3627
24 man his present, v of silver, and vessels H3627
24 of silver, and v of gold, and raiment, H3627
15:18 had dedicated, silver, and gold, and v. H3627
24:14 were made v for the house of the H3627
14 of the LORD, *even* v to minister, and to H3627
14 and spoons, and v of gold and silver. H3627
25:24 silver, and all the v that were found in H3627
28:24 And Ahaz gathered together the v of H3627
24 cut in pieces the v of the house of God, H3627
29:18 offering, with all the v thereof, and the H3627
18 shewbread table, with all the v thereof. H3627
19 Moreover all the v, which king Ahaz in H3627
36: 7 Nebuchadnezzar also carried of the v H3627
10 with the goodly v of the house of the H3627
18 And all the v of the house of God, great H3627
19 and destroyed all the goodly v thereof. H3627
Ezr 1: 6 their hands with v of silver, with gold, H3627
7 Also Cyrus the king brought forth the v H3627
10 and ten, *and* other v a thousand. H3627
11 All the v of gold and of silver *were* five H3627
5:14 And the v also of gold and silver of the H3984
15 And said unto him, Take these v, go, H3984
6: 5 And also let the golden and silver v of H3984
7:19 The v also that are given thee for the H3984
8:25 the gold, and the v, *even* the offering of H3627
26 silver, and silver v an hundred talents, H3627
27 two v of fine copper, precious as gold. H3627
28 the LORD; the v *are* holy also; and the H3627
30 the gold, and the v, to bring *them* to H3627
33 the gold and the v weighed in the house H3627
Neh 10:39 where *are* the v of the sanctuary, and H3627
13: 5 and the v, and the tithes of the H3627
9 I again the v of the house of God, H3627
Est 1: 7 And they gave *them* drink in v of gold, H3627
7 of gold, (the v being diverse one from H3627
Isa 18: 2 by the sea, even in v of bulrushes upon H3627
22:24 and the issue, all v of small quantity, H3627
24 quantity, from the v of cups, even to all H3627
24 of cups, even to all the v of flagons. H3627
52:11 ye clean, that bear the v of the LORD. H3627
65: 4 broth of abominable *things is in* their v; H3627
Jer 14: 3 with their v empty; they were ashamed H3627
27:16 Behold, the v of the LORD'S house H3627
18 of hosts, that the v which are left in the H3627
19 residue of the v that remain in this city, H3627
21 concerning the v that remain *in* the H3627
28: 3 into this place all the v of the LORD'S H3627
6 to bring again the v of the LORD'S H3627
40:10 put *them* in your v, and dwell in your H3627
48:12 empty his v, and break their bottles. H3627
49:29 and all their v, and their camels; and H3627
52:18 and all the v of brass wherewith H3627
20 brass of all these v was without weight. H3627
Ezk 27:13 of men and v of brass in thy market. H3627
Dan 1: 2 with part of the v of the house of God: H3627
2 the v into the treasure house of his god. H3627
5: 2 the golden and silver v which his father H3984
3 Then they brought the golden v that H3984
23 have brought the v of his house before H3984
11: 8 their precious v of silver and of gold; H3627
Hos 13:15 shall spoil the treasure of all pleasant v. H3627
Hag 2:16 *v* out of the press, there were *but* twenty.
Mt 13:48 the good into v, but cast the bad away. *G30*
25: 4 But the wise took oil in their v with their *G30*
Mk 7: 4 cups, and pots, brasen v, and of tables. *G5473*
Ro 9:22 the v of wrath fitted to destruction: *G4632*
23 of his glory on the v of mercy, which he *G4632*
2Co 4: 7 But we have this treasure in earthen v, *G4632*
2Ti 2:20 there are not only v of gold and of *G4632*
Heb 9:21 and all the v of the ministry. *G4632*
Rev 2:27 a rod of iron; as the v of a potter shall *G4632*
18:12 and all manner v of ivory, and all *G4632*
12 and all manner v of most precious *G4632*

VESTMENTS
2Ki 10:22 the vestry, Bring forth v for all the H3830
22 of Baal. And he brought them forth v. H4403

VESTRY
2Ki 10:22 him that *was* over the v, Bring forth H4458

VESTURE
Dt 22:12 thy v, wherewith thou coverest *thyself.* H3682
Ps 22:18 among them, and cast lots upon my v. H3830
102:26 a garment; as a v shalt thou change H3830
Mt 27:35 them, and upon my v did they cast lots. *G2441*
Jn 19:24 them, and for my v they did cast lots. *G2441*
Heb 1:12 And as a v shalt thou fold them up, and *G4018*
Rev 19:13 And he *was* clothed with a v dipped in *G2440*
16 And he hath on *his* v and on his thigh a *G2440*

VESTURES
Gen 41:42 arrayed him in v of fine linen, and put H899

VEX
Ex 22:21 Thou shalt neither v a stranger, nor H3238
Lev 18:18 to her sister, to v *her,* to uncover her H6887
19:33 thee in your land, ye shall not v him. H3238
Nu 25:17 V the Midianites, and smite them: H6887
18 For they v you with their wiles, H6887
33:55 v you in the land wherein ye dwell. H6887
2Sa 12:18 will he then v himself, if we tell H6213+H7451
2Ch 15: 6 for God did v them with all adversity. H2000
Job 19: 2 How long will ye v my soul, and break H3013
Ps 2: 5 and v them in his sore displeasure. H926
Isa 7: 6 Let us go up against Judah, and v it, H6973
11:13 Judah, and Judah shall not v Ephraim. H6887
Ezk 32: 9 I will also v the hearts of many people, H3707
Hab 2: 7 awake that shall v thee, and thou shalt H2111
Act 12: 1 *his* hands to v certain of the church. *G2559*

VEXATION
Dt 28:20 upon thee cursing, v, and rebuke, in all H4103
Ecc 1:14 behold, all *is* vanity and v of spirit. H7469
17 I perceived that this also is v of spirit. H7475
2:11 all *was* vanity and v of spirit, and *there* H7469
17 me: for all *is* vanity and v of spirit. H7469
22 his labour, and of the v of his heart, H7475
26 God. This also *is* vanity and v of spirit. H7469
4: 4 This *is* also vanity and v of spirit. H7469
6 hands full *with* travail and v of spirit. H7469
16 Surely this also *is* vanity and v of spirit. H7475
6: 9 this *is* also vanity and v of spirit. H7469
Isa 9: 1 such as *was* in her v, when at the first H4164
28:19 be a v only *to* understand the report. H2113
65:14 of heart, and shall howl for v of spirit. H7667

VEXATIONS
2Ch 15: 5 came in, but great v *were* upon all the H4103

VEXED
Nu 20:15 the Egyptians v us, and our fathers: H7489
Jdg 2:18 them that oppressed them and v them. H1766
10: 8 And that year they v and oppressed the H7492
16:16 him, *so* that his soul was v unto death; H7114
1Sa 14:47 he turned himself, he v *them.* H7561
2Sa 13: 2 And Amnon was so v, that he fell sick H3334
2Ki 4:27 for her soul *is* v within her: and the H4843
Neh 9:27 enemies, who v them: and in the time H6887
Job 27: 2 and the Almighty, *who* hath v my soul; H4843
Ps 6: 2 O LORD, heal me; for my bones are v. H926
3 My soul is also sore v: but thou, O LORD, H926
10 ashamed and sore v: let them return *and* H926
Isa 63:10 But they rebelled, and v his holy Spirit: H6087
Ezk 22: 5 thee, *which art* infamous *and* much v. H4103
7 they v the fatherless and the widow. H3238
29 robbery, and have v the poor and H3238
Mt 15:22 daughter is grievously v with a devil. *G1139*
17:15 is lunatick, and sore v: for ofttimes he *G3958*
Lk 6:18 And they that were v with unclean *G3791*
Act 5:16 and them which were v with unclean *G3791*
2Pt 2: 7 And delivered just Lot, v with the filthy *G2669*
8 and hearing, v *his* righteous soul from *G928*

VIAL
1Sa 10: 1 Then Samuel took a v of oil, and H6378
Rev 16: 2 poured out his v upon the earth; and *G5357*
3 And the second angel poured out his v *G5357*
4 And the third angel poured out his v *G5357*
8 And the fourth angel poured out his v *G5357*
10 And the fifth angel poured out his v *G5357*
12 And the sixth angel poured out his v *G5357*
17 And the seventh angel poured out his v *G5357*

VIALS
Rev 5: 8 harps, and golden v full of odours, *G5357*
15: 7 seven golden v full of the wrath of God, *G5357*
16: 1 v of the wrath of God upon the earth. *G5357*
17: 1 had the seven v, and talked with me, *G5357*
21: 9 had the seven v full of the seven last *G5357*

VICTORY
2Sa 19: 2 And the v that day was *turned* into H8668
23:10 wrought a great v that day; and the H8668
12 and the LORD wrought a great v. H8668
1Ch 29:11 the glory, and the v, and the majesty: H5331
Ps 98: 1 his holy arm, hath gotten him the v. H3467
Isa 25: 8 He will swallow up death in v; and the H5331
Mt 12:20 till he send forth judgment unto v. *G3534*
1Co 15:54 is written, Death is swallowed up in v. *G3534*
55 *is* thy sting? O grave, where *is* thy v? *G3534*
57 us the v through our Lord Jesus Christ. *G3534*
1Jn 5: 4 and this is the v that overcometh the *G3529*
Rev 15: 2 had gotten the v over the beast, and *G3528*

VICTUAL
Ex 12:39 had they prepared for themselves any v. H6720
Jdg 20:10 thousand, to fetch v for the people, that H6720
1Ki 4:27 And those officers provided v for king H3557
2Ch 11:11 and store of v, and of oil and wine. H3978
23 and he gave them v in abundance. And H4202

VICTUALS
Gen 14:11 and all their v, and went their way. H400
Lev 25:37 usury, nor lend him thy v for increase. H400
Dt 23:19 of money, usury of v, usury of any thing H400
Jos 1:11 Prepare you v; for within three days H6720
9:11 to us, saying, Take v with you for the H6720
14 And the men took of their v, and asked H6718
Jdg 7: 8 So the people took v in their hand, and H6720
17:10 and thy v. So the Levite went in. H4241
1Sa 22:10 him, and gave him v, and gave him the H6720
1Ki 4: 7 which provided v for the king and his H3557
11:18 appointed him v, and gave him land. H3899
Neh 10:31 bring ware or any v on the sabbath day H7668
13:15 *them* in the day wherein they sold v. H6715
Jer 40: 5 him v and a reward, and let him go. H737
44:17 of v, and were well, and saw no evil. H3899
Mt 14:15 into the villages, and buy themselves v. *G1033*
Lk 9:12 get v: for we are here in a desert place. *G1979*

VIEW
Jos 2: 1 saying, Go v the land, even Jericho. H7200
7: 2 saying, Go up and v the country. And H7270
2Ki 2: 7 went, and stood to v afar off: and they H5048
15 which *were* to v at Jericho saw him, H5048

VIEWED
Jos 7: 2 And the men went up and v Ai. H7270
Ezr 8:15 three days: and I v the people, and the H995
Neh 2:13 the dung port, and v the walls of H7663
15 night by the brook, and v the wall, and H7663

VIGILANT
1Ti 3: 2 of one wife, v, sober, of good behaviour, *G3524*
1Pt 5: 8 Be sober, be v; because your adversary *G1127*

VILE
Dt 25: 3 thy brother should seem v unto thee. H7034
Jdg 19:24 but unto this man do not so v a thing. H5039
1Sa 3:13 v, and he restrained them not. H7043
15: 9 thing *that was* v and refuse, that they H5240
2Sa 6:22 And I will yet be more v than thus, and H7043
Job 18: 3 as beasts, *and* reputed v in your sight? H2933
40: 4 Behold, I am v; what shall I answer H7043
Ps 15: 4 In whose eyes a v person is contemned; H959
Isa 32: 5 The v person shall be no more called H5036
6 For the v person will speak villany, and H5036
Jer 15:19 precious from the v, thou shalt be as my H2151
29:17 make them like v figs, that cannot be H8182
Lam 1:11 and consider; for I am become v. H2151
Dan 11:21 And in his estate shall stand up a v H959
Nah 1:14 I will make thy grave; for thou art v. H7043
3: 6 v, and will set thee as a gazing-stock. H5034
Ro 1:26 For this cause God gave them up unto v *G819*
Php 3:21 Who shall change our v body, that it *G5014*
Jas 2: 2 come in also a poor man in v raiment; *G4508*

VILELY
2Sa 1:21 of the mighty is v cast away, the shield H1602

VILER
Job 30: 8 base men: they were v than the earth. H5217

VILEST
Ps 12: 8 every side, when the v men are exalted. H2149

VILLAGE
Mt 21: 2 Saying unto them, Go into the v over *G2968*
Mk 11: 2 your way into the v over against you: *G2968*
Lk 8: 1 every city and v, preaching and *G2968*
9:52 and entered into a v of the Samaritans, *G2968*
56 save *them.* And they went to another v. *G2968*
10:38 into a certain v: and a certain woman *G2968*
17:12 And as he entered into a certain v, there *G2968*
19:30 Saying, Go ye into the v over against *G2968*

Lk 24:13 that same day to a **v** called Emmaus, G2968
28 And they drew nigh unto the **v**, whither G2968

VILLAGES

Ex 8:13 out of the **v**, and out of the fields. H2691
Lev 25:31 But the houses of the **v** which have no H3691
Nu 21:25 in Heshbon, and in all the **v** thereof. H1323
32 and they took the **v** thereof, and drove H1323
32:42 Kenath, and the **v** thereof, and called it H1323
Jos 13:23 families, the cities and the **v** thereof. H2691
28 their families, the cities, and their **v**. H2691
15:32 cities *are* twenty and nine, with their **v**: H2691
36 fourteen cities with their **v**: H2691
41 Makkedah; sixteen cities with their **v**: H2691
44 and Mareshah; nine cities with their **v**: H2691
45 Ekron, with her towns and her **v**: H2691
46 all that *lay* near Ashdod, with their **v**: H2691
47 Ashdod with her towns and her **v**, Gaza H2691
47 her towns and her **v**, unto the river of H2691
51 and Giloh; eleven cities with their **v**: H2691
54 and Zior; nine cities with their **v**: H2691
57 and Timnah; ten cities with their **v**: H2691
59 and Eltekon; six cities with their **v**: H2691
60 and Rabbah; two cities with their **v**: H2691
62 Salt, and En-gedi; six cities with their **v**. H2691
16: 9 of Manasseh, all the cities with their **v**. H2691
18:24 and Gaba; twelve cities with their **v**: H2691
28 fourteen cities with their **v**. This *is* the H2691
19: 6 Sharuhen; thirteen cities and their **v**: H2691
7 and Ashan; four cities and their **v**: H2691
8 And all the **v** that *were* round about H2691
15 Beth-lehem: twelve cities with their **v**. H2691
16 their families, these cities with their **v**. H2691
22 at Jordan: sixteen cities with their **v**. H2691
23 to their families, the cities and their **v**. H2691
30 twenty and two cities with their **v**. H2691
31 their families, these cities with their **v**. H2691
38 nineteen cities with their **v**. H2691
39 to their families, the cities and their **v**. H2691
48 their families, these cities with their **v**. H2691
21:12 But the fields of the city, and the **v** H2691
Jdg 5: 7 *The inhabitants of* the **v** ceased, they H6520
11 *inhabitants* of his **v** in Israel: then shall H6520
1Sa 6:18 and of country **v**, even unto the great H3724
1Ch 4:32 And their **v** *were*, Etam, and Ain, H2691
33 And all their **v** that *were* round about H2691
6:56 But the fields of the city, and the **v** H2691
9:16 dwelt in the **v** of the Netophathites. H2691
22 genealogy in their **v**, whom David and H2691
25 *were* in their **v**, *were* to come after H2691
27:25 cities, and in the **v**, and in the castles, H3723
2Ch 28:18 Shocho with the **v** thereof, and Timnah H1323
18 Timnah with the **v** thereof, Gimzo also H1323
18 and the **v** thereof: and they dwelt there. H1323
Neh 6: 2 in *some one of* the **v** in the plain of H3715
11:25 And for the **v**, with their fields, *some* of H2691
25 and *in* the **v** thereof, and at Dibon, H2691
25 at Dibon, and *in* the **v** thereof, and at H1323
25 and at Jekabzeel, and *in* the **v** thereof, H1323
27 at Beer-sheba, and *in* the **v** thereof, H1323
28 and at Mekonah, and in the **v** thereof, H1323
30 Zanoah, Adullam, and *in* their **v**, at H2691
30 and *in* the **v** thereof. And they dwelt H1323
31 and Aija, and Beth-el, and *in* their **v**, H1323
12:28 and from the **v** of Netophathi; H2691
29 builded them **v** round about Jerusalem. H2691
Est 9:19 Therefore the Jews of the **v**, that dwelt H6521
Ps 10: 8 He sitteth in the lurking places of the **v**: H2691
Song 7:11 forth into the field; let us lodge in the **v**. H3723
Isa 42:11 lift up *their voice*, the **v** *that* Kedar doth H2691
Ezk 38:11 the land of unwalled **v**; I will go to them H6519
Hab 3:14 the head of his **v**: they came out as a H6518
Mt 9:35 all the cities and **v**, teaching in their G2968
14:15 into the **v**, and buy themselves victuals. G2968
Mk 6: 6 he went round about the **v**, teaching. G2968
36 and into the **v**, and buy themselves G2968
56 And whithersoever he entered, into **v**, G2968
Lk 13:22 And he went through the cities and **v**, G2968
Act 8:25 gospel in many **v** of the Samaritans. G2968

VILLANY

Isa 32: 6 For the vile person will speak **v**, and his H5039
Jer 29:23 Because they have committed **v** in H5039

VINE

Gen 40: 9 my dream, behold, a **v** *was* before me; H1612
10 And in the **v** *were* three branches: and H1612
49:11 Binding his foal unto the **v**, and his H1612
11 colt unto the choice **v**; he washed his H8321
Lev 25: 5 the grapes of thy **v** undressed: *for* it is a H5139
11 *the grapes* in it of thy **v** undressed. H5139
Nu 6: 4 is made of the **v** tree, from the kernels H3196
Dt 32:32 For their **v** *is* of the vine of Sodom, and H1612
32 For their vine *is* of the **v** of Sodom, and H1612
Jdg 9:12 Then said the trees unto the **v**, Come H1612
13 And the **v** said unto them, Should I H1612
13:14 that cometh of the **v**, neither let her H1612
1Ki 4:25 man under his **v** and under his fig tree, H1612
2Ki 4:39 herbs, and found a wild **v**, and gathered H1612
18:31 man of his own **v**, and every one of his H1612
2Ch 26:10 *also,* and **v** dressers in the mountains, H3755
Job 15:33 grape as the **v**, and shall cast off his H1612
Ps 80: 8 Thou hast brought a **v** out of Egypt: H1612
14 heaven, and behold, and visit this **v**; H1612
128: 3 Thy wife *shall be* as a fruitful **v** by the H1612
Song 6:11 to see whether the **v** flourished, *and* the H1612
7: 8 **v**, and the smell of thy nose like apples; H1612
12 let us see if the **v** flourish, *whether* the H1612
Isa 5: 2 with the choicest **v**, and built a tower in H8321
16: 8 languish, *and* the **v** of Sibmah: the H1612
9 of Jazer the **v** of Sibmah: I will water H1612
24: 7 The new wine mourneth, the **v** H1612
32:12 for the pleasant fields, for the fruitful **v**. H1612
34: 4 **v**, and as a falling *fig* from the fig tree. H1612
36:16 ye every one of his **v**, and every one of H1612
Jer 2:21 Yet I had planted thee a noble **v**, wholly H8321
21 plant of a strange **v** unto me? H1612
6: 9 of Israel as a **v**: turn back thine hand H1612
8:13 *be* no grapes on the **v**, nor figs on the fig H1612
48:32 O **v** of Sibmah, I will weep for thee with H1612
Ezk 15: 2 Son of man, What is the **v** tree more H1612
6 the Lord GOD; As the **v** tree among the H1612
17: 6 And it grew, and became a spreading **v** H1612
6 so it became a **v**, and brought forth H1612
7 and, behold, this **v** did bend her roots H1612
8 bear fruit, that it might be a goodly **v**. H1612
19:10 Thy mother *is* like a **v** in thy blood, H1612
Hos 10: 1 Israel *is* an empty **v**, he bringeth forth H1612
14: 7 and grow as the **v**: the scent thereof H1612
Joel 1: 7 He hath laid my **v** waste, and barked H1612
12 The **v** is dried up, and the fig tree H1612
2:22 tree and the **v** do yield their strength. H1612
Mic 4: 4 But they shall sit every man under his **v** H1612
Nah 2: 2 out, and marred their **v** branches. H1612
Hag 2:19 yea, as yet the **v**, and the fig tree, and H1612
Zec 3:10 under the **v** and under the fig tree. H1612
8:12 For the seed *shall be* prosperous; the **v** H1612
Mal 3:11 neither shall your **v** cast her fruit H1612
Mt 26:29 of this fruit of the **v**, until that day when G288
Mk 14:25 of the fruit of the **v**, until that day that I G288
Lk 22:18 **v**, until the kingdom of God shall come. G288
Jn 15: 1 I am the true **v**, and my Father is the G288
4 **v**; no more can ye, except ye abide in me. G288
5 I am the **v**, ye *are* the branches: He that G288
Jas 3:12 olive berries? either a **v**, figs? so *can* no G288
Rev 14:18 the clusters of the **v** of the earth; for her G288
19 and gathered the **v** of the earth, and cast G288

VINEDRESSERS

2Ki 25:12 of the land *to be* **v** and husbandmen. H3755
Isa 61: 5 alien *shall be* your plowmen and your **v**. H3755
Jer 52:16 of the land for **v** and for husbandmen. H3755
Joel 1:11 howl, O ye **v**, for the wheat and for H3755

VINEGAR

Nu 6: 3 and shall drink no **v** of wine, or vinegar H2558
3 of wine, or **v** of strong drink, neither H2558
Ru 2:14 thy morsel in the **v**. And she sat beside H2558
Ps 69:21 in my thirst they gave me **v** to drink. H2558
Prv 10:26 As **v** to the teeth, and as smoke to the H2558
25:20 weather, *and as* **v** upon nitre, so *is* he H2558
Mt 27:34 They gave him **v** to drink mingled with G3690
48 and filled *it* with **v**, and put *it* on a reed, G3690
Mk 15:36 a spunge full of **v**, and put *it* on a reed, G3690
Lk 23:36 coming to him, and offering him **v**, G3690
Jn 19:29 Now there was set a vessel full of **v**: and G3690
29 filled a spunge with **v**, and put *it* upon G3690
30 had received the **v**, he said, It is G3690

VINES

Nu 20: 5 or of figs, or of **v**, or of pomegranates; H1612
Dt 8: 8 A land of wheat, and barley, and **v**, and H1612
Ps 78:47 He destroyed their **v** with hail, and H1612
105:33 He smote their **v** also and their fig H1612
Song 2:13 green figs, and the **v** *with* the tender H1612
15 the **v**: for our vines *have* tender grapes. H3754
15 the vines: for our **v** *have* tender grapes. H3754
Isa 7:23 there were a thousand **v** at a thousand H1612
Jer 5:17 shall eat up thy **v** and thy fig trees: they H1612
31: 5 Thou shalt yet plant **v** upon the H3754
Hos 2:12 And I will destroy her **v** and her fig H1612
Hab 3:17 fruit *be* in the **v**; the labour of the olive H1612

VINEYARD

Gen 9:20 *be* an husbandman, and he planted a **v**: H3754
Ex 22: 5 If a man shall cause a field or **v** to be H3754
5 of his own **v**, shall he make restitution. H3754
23:11 deal with thy **v**, *and* with thy oliveyard. H3754
Lev 19:10 And thou shalt not glean thy **v**, neither H3754
10 *every* grape of thy **v**; thou shalt leave H3754
25: 3 thy **v**, and gather in the fruit thereof; H3754
4 neither sow thy field, nor prune thy **v**. H3754
Dt 20: 6 hath planted a **v**, and hath not *yet* eaten H3754
22: 9 Thou shalt not sow thy **v** with divers H3754
9 sown, and the fruit of thy **v**, be defiled. H3754
23:24 thy neighbour's **v**, then thou mayest eat H3754
24:21 the grapes of thy **v**, thou shalt not glean H3754
28:30 thou shalt plant a **v**, and shalt not H3754
1Ki 21: 1 Jezreelite had a **v**, which *was* in Jezreel, H3754
2 Give me thy **v**, that I may have it for H3754
2 give thee for it a better **v** than it; *or,* if it H3754
6 him, Give me thy **v** for money; or else, H3754
6 will give thee *another* **v** for it: and he H3754
6 he answered, I will not give thee my **v**. H3754
7 thee the **v** of Naboth the Jezreelite. H3754
15 take possession of the **v** of Naboth the H3754
16 up to go down to the **v** of Naboth the H3754
18 *he is* in the **v** of Naboth, whither H3754
Ps 80:15 And the **v** which thy right hand hath H3657
Prv 24:30 **v** of the man void of understanding; H3754
31:16 the fruit of her hands she planteth a **v**. H3754
Song 1: 6 *but* mine own **v** have I not kept. H3754
8:11 Solomon had a **v** at Baal-hamon; he let H3754
11 he let out the **v** unto keepers; every H3754
12 My **v**, which *is* mine, *is* before me: thou, H3754
Isa 1: 8 left as a cottage in a **v**, as a lodge in a H3754
3:14 ye have eaten up the **v**; the spoil of the H3754
5: 1 touching his **v**. My wellbeloved hath H3754
1 hath a **v** in a very fruitful hill: H3754
3 judge, I pray you, betwixt me and my **v**. H3754
4 done more to my **v**, that I have not done H3754
5 I will do to my **v**: I will take away the H3754
7 For the **v** of the LORD of hosts *is* the H3754
10 Yea, ten acres of **v** shall yield one bath, H3754
27: 2 In that day sing ye unto her, A **v** of red H3754
Jer 12:10 Many pastors have destroyed my **v**, H3754
35: 7 seed, nor plant **v**, nor have *any*: but all H3754
9 neither have we **v**, nor field, nor seed: H3754
Mic 1: 6 *and* as plantings of a **v**: and I will pour H3754
Mt 20: 1 the morning to hire labourers into his **v**. G290
2 a penny a day, he sent them into his **v**. G290
4 Go ye also into the **v**, and whatsoever is G290
7 Go ye also into the **v**; and whatsoever is G290
8 So when even was come, the lord of the **v** G290
21:28 and said, Son, go work to day in my **v**. G290
33 which planted a **v**, and hedged it round G290
39 and cast *him* out of the **v**, and slew *him*. G290
40 When the lord therefore of the **v** cometh, G290
41 men, and will let out *his* **v** unto other G290
Mk 12: 1 man planted a **v**, and set an hedge about G290
2 the husbandmen of the fruit of the **v**. G290
8 and killed *him*, and cast *him* out of the **v**. G290
9 What shall therefore the lord of the **v** do? G290
9 and will give the **v** unto others. G290
Lk 13: 6 fig tree planted in his **v**; and he came and G290
7 Then said he unto the dresser of his **v**, G289
20: 9 man planted a **v**, and let it forth to G290
10 of the fruit of the **v**: but the husbandmen G290
13 Then said the lord of the **v**, What shall I G290
15 So they cast him out of the **v**, and killed G290
15 shall the lord of the **v** do unto them? G290
16 and shall give the **v** to others. And when G290
1Co 9: 7 who planteth a **v**, and eateth not of the G290

VINEYARDS

Nu 16:14 of fields and **v**: wilt thou put out the H3754
20:17 or through the **v**, neither will we drink H3754
21:22 fields, or into the **v**; we will not drink *of* H3754
22:24 in a path of the **v**, a wall *being* on this H3754
Dt 6:11 thou diggedst not, **v** and olive trees, H3754
28:39 Thou shalt plant **v**, and dress *them*, but H3754
Jos 24:13 in them; of the **v** and oliveyards which H3754
Jdg 9:27 and gathered their **v**, and trode *the* H3754
11:33 unto the plain of the **v**, with a very great H3754
14: 5 and came to the **v** of Timnath: and, H3754
15: 5 standing corn, with the **v** *and* olives. H3754
21:20 saying, Go and lie in wait in the **v**; H3754

Jdg 21:21 come ye out of the v, and catch you H3754
1Sa 8:14 And he will take your fields, and your v, H3754
15 your seed, and of your v, and give to his H3754
22: 7 of you fields and v, *and* make you all H3754
2Ki 5:26 oliveyards, and v, and sheep, and oxen, H3754
18:32 a land of bread and v, a land of oil olive H3754
19:29 and plant v, and eat the fruits thereof. H3754
1Ch 27:27 And over the v *was* Shimei the H3754
27 the increase of the v for the wine cellars H3754
Neh 5: 3 our lands, v, and houses, that we H3754
4 tribute, *and that upon* our lands and v. H3754
5 for other men have our lands and v. H3754
11 their lands, their v, their oliveyards, H3754
9:25 wells digged, v, and oliveyards, and H3754
Job 24:18 earth: he beholdeth not the way of the v. H3754
Ps 107:37 And sow the fields, and plant v, which H3754
Ecc 2: 4 I builded me houses; I planted me v: H3754
Song 1: 6 me the keeper of the v; *but* mine own H3754
14 cluster of camphire in the v of En-gedi. H3754
7:12 Let us get up early to the v; let us see if H3754
Isa 16:10 field; and in the v there shall be no H3754
36:17 of corn and wine, a land of bread and v. H3754
37:30 and plant v, and eat the fruit thereof. H3754
65:21 shall plant v, and eat the fruit of them. H3754
Jer 32:15 v shall be possessed again in this land. H3754
39:10 them v and fields at the same time. H3754
Ezk 28:26 houses, and plant v; yea, they shall H3754
Hos 2:15 And I will give her her v from thence, H3754
Am 4: 9 gardens and your v and your fig trees H3754
5:11 v, but ye shall not drink wine of them. H3754
17 And in all v *shall be* wailing: for I will H3754
9:14 they shall plant v, and drink the wine H3754
Zep 1:13 plant v, but not drink the wine thereof. H3754

VINTAGE
Lev 26: 5 reach unto the v, and the vintage shall H1210
5 vintage, and the v shall reach unto the H1210
Jdg 8: 2 Ephraim better than the v of Abi-ezer? H1210
Job 24: 6 and they gather the v of the wicked. H3754
Isa 16:10 I have made *their* v shouting to cease.
24:13 the gleaning grapes when the v is done. H1210
32:10 careless women: for the v shall fail, the H1210
Jer 48:32 upon thy summer fruits and upon thy v. H1210
Mic 7: 1 of the v: *there is* no cluster to H1210
Zec 11: 2 for the forest of the v is come down. H1208

VIOL
Isa 5:12 And the harp, and the v, the tabret, and H5035
Am 6: 5 That chant to the sound of the v, *and* H5035

VIOLATED
Ezk 22:26 Her priests have v my law, and have H2554

VIOLENCE
Gen 6:11 God, and the earth was filled with v. H2555
13 the earth is filled with v through them; H2555
Lev 6: 2 by v, or hath deceived his neighbour; H1498
2Sa 22: 3 my saviour; thou savest me from v. H2555
Ps 11: 5 and him that loveth v his soul hateth. H2555
55: 9 for I have seen v and strife in the city. H2555
58: 2 weigh the v of your hands in the earth. H2555
72:14 from deceit and v: and precious shall H2555
73: 6 a chain; v covereth them *as* a garment. H2555
Prv 4:17 of wickedness, and drink the wine of v. H2555
10: 6 but v covereth the mouth of the wicked. H2555
11 but v covereth the mouth of the wicked. H2555
13: 2 the soul of the transgressors *shall eat* v. H2555
28:17 A man that doeth v to the blood of *any* H6231
Isa 53: 9 v, neither *was any* deceit in his mouth. H2555
59: 6 and the act of v *is* in their hands. H2555
60:18 V shall no more be heard in thy land, H2555
Jer 6: 7 her wickedness: v and spoil is heard in H2555
20: 8 For since I spake, I cried out, I cried v H2555
22: 3 no wrong, do no v to the stranger, the H2554
17 and for oppression, and for v, to do *it*. H4835
51:35 The v done to me and to my flesh *be* H2555
46 and v in the land, ruler against ruler. H2555
Ezk 7:11 V is risen up into a rod of wickedness: H2555
23 bloody crimes, and the city is full of v. H2555
8:17 the land with v, and have returned to H2555
12:19 of the v of all them that dwell therein. H2555
18: 7 spoiled none by v, hath given his bread H1500
12 hath spoiled by v, hath not restored the H1500
16 hath spoiled by v, *but* hath given his H1500
18 his brother by v, and did *that* which H1499
28:16 the midst of thee with v, and thou hast H2555
45: 9 of Israel: remove v and spoil, and H2555
Joel 3:19 wilderness, for the v *against* the H2555
Am 3:10 store up v and robbery in their palaces. H2555
Am 6: 3 and cause the seat of v to come near; H2555
Oba 10 For *thy* v against thy brother Jacob H2555
Jna 3: 8 and from the v that *is* in their hands. H2555
Mic 2: 2 and take *them* by v; and houses, and H1497
6:12 For the rich men thereof are full of v, H2555
Hab 1: 2 unto thee *of* v, and thou wilt not save! H2555
3 for spoiling and v *are* before me: and H2555
9 They shall come all for v: their faces H2555
2: 8 blood, and *for* the v of the land, of the H2555
17 For the v of Lebanon shall cover thee, H2555
17 blood, and for the v of the land, of the H2555
Zep 1: 9 their masters' houses with v and deceit. H2555
3: 4 sanctuary, they have done v to the law. H2554
Mal 2:16 for *one* covereth v with his garment, H2555
Mt 11:12 v, and the violent take it by force. G971
Lk 3:14 unto them, Do v to no man, neither G1286
Act 5:26 them without v: for they feared the G970
21:35 of the soldiers for the v of the people. G970
24: 7 great v took *him* away out of our hands, G970
27:41 part was broken with the v of the waves. G970
Heb 11:34 Quenched the v of fire, escaped the G1411
Rev 18:21 saying, Thus with v shall that great city G3731

VIOLENT
2Sa 22:49 hast delivered me from the v man. H2555
Ps 7:16 own head, and his v dealing shall come H2555
18:48 hast delivered me from the v man. H2555
86:14 the assemblies of v *men* have sought H6184
140: 1 evil man: preserve me from the v man; H2555
4 preserve me from the v man; who have H2555
11 shall hunt the v man to overthrow *him*. H2555
Prv 16:29 A v man enticeth his neighbour, and H2555
Ecc 5: 8 of the poor, and v perverting of H1499
Mt 11:12 violence, and the v take it by force. G973

VIOLENTLY
Gen 21:25 servants had v taken away. H1497
Lev 6: 4 that which he took v away, or the thing H1500
Dt 28:31 thine ass *shall be* v taken away from H1497
Job 20:19 *because* he hath v taken away an house H1497
24: 2 *Some* remove the landmarks; they v H1497
Isa 22:18 He will surely v turn and toss thee *like* a
Lam 2: 6 And he hath v taken away his H2554
Mt 8:32 herd of swine ran v down a steep place G3729
Mk 5:13 and the herd ran v down a steep place G3729
Lk 8:33 and the herd ran v down a steep place G3729

VIOLS
Isa 14:11 the noise of thy v: the worm is spread H5035
Am 5:23 for I will not hear the melody of thy v. H5035

VIPER
Isa 30: 6 young and old lion, the v and fiery flying H660
59: 5 which is crushed breaketh out into a v. H660
Act 28: 3 fire, there came a v out of the heat, and G2191

VIPERS
Mt 3: 7 O generation of v, who hath warned you G2191
12:34 O generation of v, how can ye, being G2191
23:33 *Ye* serpents, *ye* generation of v, how can G2191
Lk 3: 7 O generation of v, who hath warned you G2191

VIPER'S
Job 20:16 He shall suck the poison of asps: the v H660

VIRGIN
Gen 24:16 to look upon, a v, neither had any man H1330
43 that when the v cometh forth to draw H5959
Lev 21: 3 And for his sister a v, that is nigh unto H1330
14 shall take a v of his own people to wife. H1330
Dt 22:19 evil name upon a v of Israel: and she H1330
23 If a damsel *that is* a v be betrothed H1330
28 If a man find a damsel *that is* a v, which H1330
32:25 man and the v, the suckling *also* with H1330
2Sa 13: 2 for she *was* a v; and Amnon thought H1330
1Ki 1: 2 the king a young v: and let her stand H1330
2Ki 19:21 him; The v the daughter of Zion H1330
Isa 7:14 a sign; Behold, a v shall conceive, and H5959
23:12 O thou oppressed v, daughter of Zidon: H1330
37:22 him; The v, the daughter of Zion, H1330
47: 1 Come down, and sit in the dust, O v H1330
62: 5 For *as* a young man marrieth a v, *so* H1330
Jer 14:17 not cease: for the v daughter of my H1330
18:13 such things: the v of Israel hath done H1330
31: 4 shalt be built, O v of Israel: thou shalt H1330
13 Then shall the v rejoice in the dance, H1330
21 turn again, O v of Israel, turn again H1330
46:11 Go up into Gilead, and take balm, O v, H1330
Lam 1:15 hath trodden the v, the daughter of H1330
Lam 2:13 comfort thee, O v daughter of Zion? for H1330
Joel 1: 8 Lament like a v girded with sackcloth H1330
Am 5: 2 The v of Israel is fallen; she shall no H1330
Mt 1:23 Behold, a v shall be with child, and G3933
Lk 1:27 To a v espoused to a man whose name G3933
1Co 7:28 sinned; and if a v marry, she hath not G3933
34 a wife and a v. The unmarried woman G3933
36 toward his v, if she pass the flower G3933
37 heart that he will keep his v, doeth well. G3933
2Co 11: 2 present *you as* a chaste v to Christ. G3933

VIRGINITY
Lev 21:13 And he shall take a wife in her v. H1331
Dt 22:15 v unto the elders of the city in the gate: H1331
17 *of* my daughter's v. And they shall H1331
20 *of* v be not found for the damsel: H1331
Jdg 11:37 and bewail my v, I and my fellows. H1331
38 bewailed her v upon the mountains. H1331
Ezk 23: 3 there they bruised the teats of their v. H1331
8 the breasts of her v, and poured their H1331
Lk 2:36 an husband seven years from her v; G3932

VIRGINS
Ex 22:17 pay money according to the dowry of v. H1330
Jdg 21:12 hundred young v, that had known no H1330
2Sa 13:18 *that were* v apparelled. Then his H1330
Est 2: 2 be fair young v sought for the king: H1330
3 all the fair young v unto Shushan the H1330
17 more than all the v; so that he set the H1330
19 And when the v were gathered together H1330
Ps 45:14 of needlework: the v her companions H1330
Song 1: 3 forth, therefore do the v love thee. H5959
6: 8 concubines, and v without number. H5959
Isa 23: 4 nourish up young men, *nor* bring up v. H1330
Lam 1: 4 v are afflicted, and she *is* in bitterness. H1330
18 my sorrow: my v and my young men H1330
2:10 with sackcloth: the v of Jerusalem hang H1330
21 in the streets: my v and my young men H1330
Am 8:13 In that day shall the fair v and young H1330
Mt 25: 1 be likened unto ten v, which took their G3933
7 Then all those v arose, and trimmed G3933
11 Afterward came also the other v, G3933
Act 21: 9 four daughters, v, which did prophesy. G3933
1Co 7:25 Now concerning v I have no G3933
Rev 14: 4 for they are v. These are they which G3933

VIRGIN'S
Lk 1:27 of David; and the v name *was* Mary. G3933

VIRTUE
Mk 5:30 in himself that v had gone out of him, G1411
Lk 6:19 went v out of him, and healed *them* all. G1411
8:46 for I perceive that v is gone out of me. G1411
Php 4: 8 if *there be* any v, and if *there be* any G703
2Pt 1: 3 of him that hath called us to glory and v: G703
5 to your faith v; and to virtue knowledge; G703
5 to your faith virtue; and to v knowledge; G703

VIRTUOUS
Ru 3:11 doth know that thou *art* a v woman. H2428
Prv 12: 4 A v woman *is* a crown to her husband: H2428
31:10 Who can find a v woman? for her price H2428

VIRTUOUSLY
Prv 31:29 Many daughters have done v, but thou H2428

VISAGE
Isa 52:14 As many were astonied at thee; his v H4758
Lam 4: 8 Their v is blacker than a coal; they are H8389
Dan 3:19 fury, and the form of his v was changed H600

VISIBLE
Col 1:16 and that are in earth, v and invisible, G3707

VISION
Gen 15: 1 unto Abram in a v, saying, Fear not, H4236
Nu 12: 6 v, *and* will speak unto him in a dream. H4759
24: 4 which saw the v of the Almighty, falling H4236
16 *which* saw the v of the Almighty, falling H4236
1Sa 3: 1 in those days; *there was* no open v. H2377
15 And Samuel feared to shew Eli the v. H4759
2Sa 7:17 this v, so did Nathan speak unto David. H2384
1Ch 17:15 this v, so did Nathan speak unto David. H2377
2Ch 32:32 they *are* written in the v of Isaiah the H2377
Job 20: 8 be chased away as a v of the night. H2384
33:15 In a dream, in a v of the night, when H2384
Ps 89:19 Then thou spakest in v to thy holy one, H2377
Prv 29:18 Where *there is* no v, the people perish: H2377
Isa 1: 1 The v of Isaiah the son of Amoz, which H2377

Isa 21: 2 A grievous v is declared unto me; the H2380
22: 1 The burden of the valley of v. What H2384
5 in the valley of v, breaking down the H2384
28: 7 they err in v, they stumble *in* judgment. H7203
29: 7 her, shall be as a dream of a night v. H2377
11 And the v of all is become unto you as H2380
Jer 14:14 unto you a false v and divination, and H2377
23:16 vain: they speak a v of their own heart, H2377
Lam 2: 9 prophets also find no v from the LORD. H2377
Ezk 7:13 yet alive: for the v *is* touching the whole H2377
26 shall they seek a v of the prophet; but H2377
8: 4 to the v that I saw in the plain. H4758
11:24 brought me in a v by the Spirit of God H4758
24 the v that I had seen went up from me. H4758
12:22 are prolonged, and every v faileth? H2377
23 are at hand, and the effect of every v. H2377
24 For there shall be no more any vain v H2377
27 of Israel say, The v that he seeth *is* for H2377
13: 7 Have ye not seen a vain v, and have ye H4236
43: 3 appearance of the v which I saw, *even* H4758
3 according to the v that I saw when I H4758
3 *were* like the v that I saw by the river H4758
Dan 2:19 Daniel in a night v. Then Daniel blessed H2376
7: 2 Daniel spake and said, I saw in my v H2376
8: 1 king Belshazzar a v appeared unto me, H2377
2 And I saw in a v; and it came to pass, H2377
2 in a v, and I was by the river of Ulai. H2377
13 long *shall be* the v *concerning* the daily H2377
15 had seen the v, and sought for the H2377
16 make this *man* to understand the v. H4758
17 for at the time of the end *shall be* the v. H2377
26 And the v of the evening and the H4758
26 up the v; for it *shall be* for many days. H2377
27 at the v, but none understood *it*. H4758
9:21 I had seen in the v at the beginning, H2377
23 the matter, and consider the v. H4758
24 and to seal up the v and prophecy, and H2377
10: 1 thing, and had understanding of the v. H4758
7 And I Daniel alone saw the v: for the H4759
7 me saw not the v; but a great quaking H4759
8 alone, and saw this great v, and there H4759
14 days: for yet the v *is* for *many* days. H2377
16 me, O my lord, by the v my sorrows are H4759
11:14 to establish the v; but they shall fall. H2377
Oba 1 The v of Obadiah. Thus saith the Lord H2377
Mic 3: 6 that ye shall not have a v; and it shall be H2377
Nah 1: 1 book of the v of Nahum the Elkoshite. H2377
Hab 2: 2 and said, Write the v, and make *it* plain H2377
3 For the v *is* yet for an appointed time, H2377
Zec 13: 4 every one of his v, when he hath H2384
Mt 17: 9 saying, Tell the v to no man, until the G3705
Lk 1:22 that he had seen a v in the temple: for G3701
24:23 had also seen a v of angels, which said G3701
Act 9:10 said the Lord in a v, Ananias. And he G3705
12 And hath seen in a v a man named G3705
10: 3 He saw in a v evidently about the ninth G3705
17 himself what this v which he had seen G3705
19 While Peter thought on the v, the Spirit G3705
11: 5 in a trance I saw a v, A certain vessel G3705
12: 9 by the angel; but thought he saw a v. G3705
16: 9 And a v appeared to Paul in the night; G3705
10 And after he had seen the v, G3705
18: 9 in the night by a v, Be not afraid, but G3705
26:19 not disobedient unto the heavenly v: G3701
Rev 9:17 And thus I saw the horses in the v, and G3706

VISIONS
Gen 46: 2 And God spake unto Israel in the v of H4759
2Ch 9:29 and in the v of Iddo the seer against H2378
26: 5 in the v of God: and as long H7200
Job 4:13 In thoughts from the v of the night, H2384
7:14 dreams, and terrifiest me through v: H2384
Ezk 1: 1 were opened, and I saw v of God. H4759
8: 3 and brought me in the v of God to H4759
13:16 and which see v of peace for her, and H2377
40: 2 In the v of God brought he me into the H4759
43: 3 the city: and the v *were* like the vision H4759
Dan 1:17 understanding in all v and dreams. H2377
2:28 v of thy head upon thy bed, are these; H2376
4: 5 bed and the v of my head troubled me. H2376
9 thee, tell me the v of my dream that I H2376
10 Thus *were* the v of mine head in my H2376
13 I saw in the v of my head upon my bed, H2376
7: 1 had a dream and v of his head upon H2376
7 After this I saw in the night v, and H2376
13 I saw in the night v, and, behold, *one* H2376
15 and the v of my head troubled me. H2376
Hos 12:10 and I have multiplied v, and used H2377
Joel 2:28 dreams, your young men shall see v: H2384
Act 2:17 men shall see v, and your old men shall G3706
2Co 12: 1 come to v and revelations of the Lord. G3701

VISIT
Gen 50:24 God will surely v you, and bring you H6485
25 God will surely v you, and ye shall H6485
Ex 13:19 God will surely v you; and ye shall H6485
32:34 I v I will visit their sin upon them. H6485
34 I visit I will v their sin upon them. H6485
Lev 18:25 And the land is defiled: therefore I do v H6485
Job 5:24 v thy habitation, and shalt not sin. H6485
7:18 And *that* thou shouldest v him every H6485
Ps 59: 5 of Israel, awake to v all the heathen: be H6485
80:14 heaven, and behold, and v this vine; H6485
89:32 Then will I v their transgression with H6485
106: 4 thy people: O v me with thy salvation; H6485
Isa 23:17 that the LORD will v Tyre, and she H6485
Jer 3:16 neither shall they v *it*; neither shall *that* H6485
5: 9 Shall I not v for these *things*? saith the H6485
29 Shall I not v for these *things*? saith the H6485
6:15 at the time *that* I v them they shall be H6485
9: 9 Shall I not v them for these *things*? H6485
14:10 their iniquity, and v their sins. H6485
15:15 me, and v me, and revenge me H6485
23: 2 behold, I will v upon you the evil of H6485
27:22 be until the day that I v them, saith the H6485
29:10 at Babylon I will v you, and perform H6485
32: 5 there shall he be until I v him, saith the H6485
49: 8 upon him, the time *that* I will v him. H6485
50:31 day is come, the time *that* I will v thee. H6485
Lam 4:22 captivity: he will v thine iniquity, O H6485
Hos 2:13 And I will v upon her the days of H6485
8:13 v their sins: they shall return to Egypt. H6485
9: 9 their iniquity, he will v their sins. H6485
Am 3:14 That in the day that I shall v the H6485
14 him I will also v the altars of Beth-el: H6485
Zep 2: 7 v them, and turn away their captivity. H6485
Zec 11:16 *which* shall not v those that be cut off, H6485
Act 7:23 to v his brethren the children of Israel. G1980
15:14 at the first did v the Gentiles, to take G1980
36 us go again and v our brethren in every G1980
Jas 1:27 Father is this, To v the fatherless and G1980

VISITATION
Nu 16:29 be visited after the v of all men; *then* H6486
Job 10:12 and thy v hath preserved my spirit. H6486
Isa 10: 3 And what will ye do in the day of v, and H6486
Jer 8:12 in the time of their v they shall be cast H6486
10:15 in the time of their v they shall perish. H6486
11:23 of Anathoth, *even* the year of their v. H6486
23:12 *even* the year of their v, saith the LORD. H6486
46:21 upon them, *and* the time of their v. H6486
48:44 the year of their v, saith the LORD. H6486
50:27 for their day is come, the time of their v. H6486
51:18 in the time of their v they shall perish. H6486
Hos 9: 7 The days of v are come, the days of H6486
Mic 7: 4 v cometh; now shall be their perplexity. H6486
Lk 19:44 thou knewest not the time of thy v. G1984
1Pt 2:12 shall behold, glorify God in the day of v. G1984

VISITED
Gen 21: 1 And the LORD v Sarah as he had said, H6485
Ex 3:16 I have surely v you, and *seen* that H6485
4:31 the LORD had v the children of Israel, H6485
Nu 16:29 men, or if they be v after the visitation H6485
Jdg 15: 1 that Samson v his wife with a kid; H6485
Ru 1: 6 had v his people in giving them bread. H6485
1Sa 2:21 And the LORD v Hannah, so that she H6485
Job 35:15 But now, because *it is* not *so*, he hath v H6485
Ps 17: 3 heart; thou hast v *me* in the night; thou H6485
Prv 19:23 satisfied; he shall not be v with evil. H6485
Isa 24:22 and after many days shall they be v. H6485
26:14 hast thou v and destroyed them, H6485
16 LORD, in trouble have they v thee, they H6485
29: 6 Thou shalt be v of the LORD of hosts H6485
Jer 6: 6 this *is* the city to be v; she *is* wholly H6485
23: 2 and have not v them: behold, I will H6485
Ezk 38: 8 After many days thou shalt be v: in the H6485
Zec 10: 3 of hosts hath v his flock the house of H6485
Mt 25:36 me: I was sick, and ye v me: I was in G1980
43 sick, and in prison, and ye v me not. G1980
Lk 1:68 for he hath v and redeemed his people, G1980
78 the dayspring from on high hath v us, G1980
7:16 us; and, That God hath v his people. G1980

VISITEST
Ps 8: 4 and the son of man, that thou v him? H6485
65: 9 Thou v the earth, and waterest it: thou H6485
Heb 2: 6 or the son of man, that thou v him? G1980

VISITETH
Job 31:14 when he v, what shall I answer him? H6485

VISITING
Ex 20: 5 *am* a jealous God, v the iniquity of the H6485
34: 7 clear *the guilty;* v the iniquity of the H6485
Nu 14:18 clearing *the guilty*, v the iniquity of the H6485
Dt 5: 9 *am* a jealous God, v the iniquity of the H6485

VOCATION
Eph 4: 1 of the v wherewith ye are called, G2821

VOICE
Gen 3: 8 And they heard the v of the LORD God H6963
10 And he said, I heard thy v in the H6963
17 unto the v of thy wife, and hast H6963
4:10 thou done? the v of thy brother's blood H6963
23 Zillah, Hear my v; ye wives of Lamech, H6963
16: 2 Abram hearkened to the v of Sarai. H6963
21:12 v; for in Isaac shall thy seed be called. H6963
16 against *him*, and lift up her v, and wept. H6963
17 And God heard the v of the lad; and the H6963
17 hath heard the v of the lad where he *is*. H6963
22:18 because thou hast obeyed my v. H6963
26: 5 Because that Abraham obeyed my v, H6963
27: 8 Now therefore, my son, obey my v H6963
13 only obey my v, and go fetch me *them*. H6963
22 and said, The v *is* Jacob's voice, but H6963
22 v, but the hands *are* the hands of Esau. H6963
38 And Esau lifted up his v, and wept. H6963
43 Now therefore, my son, obey my v; and H6963
29:11 Rachel, and lifted up his v, and wept. H6963
30: 6 also heard my v, and hath given me H6963
39:14 to lie with me, and I cried with a loud v: H6963
15 that I lifted up my v and cried, that he H6963
18 And it came to pass, as I lifted up my v H6963
Ex 3:18 And they shall hearken to thy v: and H6963
4: 1 hearken unto my v: for they will say, H6963
8 hearken to the v of the first sign, that H6963
8 they will believe the v of the latter sign. H6963
9 hearken unto thy v, that thou shalt take H6963
5: 2 I should obey his v to let Israel go? I H6963
15:26 hearken to the v of the LORD thy God, H6963
18:19 Hearken now unto my v, I will give thee H6963
24 So Moses hearkened to the v of his H6963
19: 5 Now therefore, if ye will obey my v H6963
16 the mount, and the v of the trumpet H6963
19 And when the v of the trumpet H6963
19 spake, and God answered him by a v. H6963
23:21 Beware of him, and obey his v, provoke H6963
22 But if thou shalt indeed obey his v, and H6963
24: 3 with one v, and said, All the words H6963
32:18 And he said, *It is* not the v of *them that* H6963
18 neither *is it* the v of *them that* cry for H6963
Lev 5: 1 And if a soul sin, and hear the v of H6963
Nu 7:89 then he heard the v of one speaking H6963
14: 1 lifted up their v, and cried; and the H6963
22 times, and have not hearkened to my v; H6963
20:16 he heard our v, and sent an angel, and H6963
21: 3 And the LORD hearkened to the v of H6963
Dt 1:34 And the LORD heard the v of your H6963
45 to your v, nor give ear unto you. H6963
4:12 fire: ye heard the v of the words, but H6963
12 saw no similitude; only *ye heard* a v. H6963
30 God, and shalt be obedient unto his v; H6963
33 Did *ever* people hear the v of God H6963
36 thee to hear his v, that he might instruct H6963
5:22 with a great v: and he added no more. H6963
23 when ye heard the v out of the midst of H6963
24 we have heard his v out of the midst of H6963
25 us: if we hear the v of the LORD our H6963
26 that hath heard the v of the living God H6963
28 And the LORD heard the v of your H6963
28 I have heard the v of the words of this H6963
8:20 unto the v of the LORD your God. H6963
9:23 him not, nor hearkened to his v. H6963
13: 4 and obey his v, and ye shall serve him, H6963
18 When thou shalt hearken to the v of the H6963
15: 5 hearken unto the v of the LORD thy H6963
18:16 not hear again the v of the LORD my H6963
21:18 will not obey the v of his father, or the H6963
18 his father, or the v of his mother, and H6963
20 our v; *he is* a glutton, and a drunkard. H6963
26: 7 LORD heard our v, and looked on our H6963
14 hearkened to the v of the LORD my H6963
17 judgments, and to hearken unto his v: H6963
27:10 Thou shalt therefore obey the v of the H6963
14 unto all the men of Israel with a loud v, H6963
28: 1 diligently unto the v of the LORD thy H6963

V

Dt 28: 2 unto the v of the LORD thy God. H6963
15 not hearken unto the v of the LORD thy H6963
45 not unto the v of the LORD thy God, H6963
62 not obey the v of the LORD thy God. H6963
30: 2 and shalt obey his v according to all H6963
8 And thou shalt return and obey the v of H6963
10 If thou shalt hearken unto the v of the H6963
20 thou mayest obey his v, and that thou H6963
33: 7 Hear, LORD, the v of Judah, and bring H6963
Jos 5: 6 obeyed not the v of the LORD: unto H6963
6:10 any noise with your v, neither shall *any* H6963
10:14 unto the v of a man: for the LORD H6963
22: 2 my v in all that I commanded you: H6963
24:24 will we serve, and his v will we obey. H6963
Jdg 2: 2 obeyed my v: why have ye done this? H6963
4 the people lifted up their v, and wept. H6963
20 and have not hearkened unto my v; H6963
6:10 ye dwell: but ye have not obeyed my v. H6963
9: 7 and lifted up his v, and cried, and said H6963
13: 9 And God hearkened to the v of H6963
18: 3 they knew the v of the young man the H6963
25 him, Let not thy v be heard among us, H6963
20:13 not hearken to the v of their brethren H6963
Ru 1: 9 and they lifted up their v, and wept. H6963
14 And they lifted up their v, and wept H6963
1Sa 1:13 lips moved, but her v was not heard: H6963
2:25 not unto the v of their father, because H6963
8: 7 Hearken unto the v of the people in all H6963
9 Now therefore hearken unto their v: H6963
19 to obey the v of Samuel; and they H6963
22 unto their v, and make them a king. H6963
12: 1 unto your v in all that ye said unto H6963
14 serve him, and obey his v, and not rebel H6963
15 But if ye will not obey the v of the H6963
15: 1 unto the v of the words of the LORD. H6963
19 thou not obey the v of the LORD, but H6963
20 I have obeyed the v of the LORD, and H6963
22 as in obeying the v of the LORD? H6963
24 I feared the people, and obeyed their v. H6963
19: 6 And Saul hearkened unto the v of H6963
24:16 said, *Is* this thy v, my son David? And H6963
16 And Saul lifted up his v, and wept. H6963
25:35 to thy v, and have accepted thy person. H6963
26:17 And Saul knew David's v, and said, *Is* H6963
17 said, *Is* this thy v, my son David? And H6963
17 David said, *It is* my v, my lord, O king. H6963
28:12 she cried with a loud v: and the woman H6963
18 Because thou obeyedst not the v of the H6963
21 hath obeyed thy v, and I have put my H6963
22 hearken thou also unto the v of thine H6963
23 unto their v. So he arose from the H6963
30: 4 him lifted up their v and wept, until H6963
2Sa 3:32 the king lifted up his v, and wept at the H6963
12:18 hearken unto our v: how will he then H6963
13:14 hearken unto her v: but, being stronger H6963
36 and lifted up their v and wept: and the H6963
15:23 And all the country wept with a loud v, H6963
19: 4 cried with a loud v, O my son Absalom, H6963
35 I hear any more the v of singing men H6963
22: 7 he did hear my v out of his temple, and H6963
14 and the most High uttered his v. H6963
1Ki 8:55 of Israel with a loud v, saying, H6963
17:22 And the LORD heard the v of Elijah; H6963
18:26 us. But *there was* no v, nor any that H6963
29 *there was* neither v, nor any to answer, H6963
19:12 the fire: and after the fire a still small v. H6963
13 *there came* a v unto him, and said, H6963
20:25 he hearkened unto their v, and did so. H6963
36 not obeyed the v of the LORD, behold, H6963
2Ki 4:31 but *there was* neither v, nor hearing. H6963
7:10 no man there, neither v of man, but H6963
10: 6 hearken unto my v, take ye the heads of H6963
18:12 Because they obeyed not the v of the H6963
28 and cried with a loud v in the Jews' H6963
19:22 thou exalted *thy* v, and lifted up thine H6963
1Ch 15:16 sounding, by lifting up the v with joy. H6963
2Ch 5:13 they lifted up *their* v with the trumpets H6963
15:14 LORD with a loud v, and with shouting, H6963
20:19 God of Israel with a loud v on high. H6963
30:27 the people: and their v was heard, and H6963
32:18 Then they cried with a loud v in the H6963
Ezr 3:12 loud v; and many shouted aloud for joy: H6963
10:12 v, As thou hast said, so must we do. H6963
Neh 9: 4 with a loud v unto the LORD their God. H6963
Job 2:12 they lifted up their v, and wept; and H6963
3: 7 be solitary, let no joyful v come therein. H7445
18 they hear not the v of the oppressor. H6963
4:10 The roaring of the lion, and the v of the H6963
16 *was* silence, and I heard a v, *saying*, H6963

Job 9:16 that he had hearkened unto my v. H6963
30:31 my organ into the v of them that weep. H6963
33: 8 I have heard the v of *thy* words, *saying*, H6963
34:16 this: hearken to the v of my words. H6963
37: 2 Hear attentively the noise of his v, and H6963
4 After it a v roareth: he thundereth with H6963
4 with the v of his excellency; and H6963
4 will not stay them when his v is heard. H6963
5 with his v; great things doeth he, H6963
38:34 Canst thou lift up thy v to the clouds, H6963
40: 9 canst thou thunder with a v like him? H6963
Ps 3: 4 I cried unto the LORD with my v, and H6963
5: 2 Hearken unto the v of my cry, my King, H6963
3 My v shalt thou hear in the morning, O H6963
6: 8 LORD hath heard the v of my weeping. H6963
18: 6 God: he heard my v out of his temple, H6963
13 gave his v; hail *stones* and coals of fire. H6963
19: 3 language, *where* their v is not heard. H6963
26: 7 That I may publish with the v of H6963
27: 7 Hear, O LORD, *when* I cry with my v: H6963
28: 2 Hear the v of my supplications, when I H6963
6 hath heard the v of my supplications. H6963
29: 3 The v of the LORD *is* upon the waters: H6963
4 The v of the LORD *is* powerful; the H6963
4 the v of the LORD *is* full of majesty. H6963
5 The v of the LORD breaketh the cedars; H6963
7 The v of the LORD divideth the flames H6963
8 The v of the LORD shaketh the H6963
9 The v of the LORD maketh the hinds to H6963
31:22 nevertheless thou heardest the v of my H6963
42: 4 of God, with the v of joy and praise, H6963
44:16 For the v of him that reproacheth and H6963
46: 6 he uttered his v, the earth melted. H6963
47: 1 shout unto God with the v of triumph. H6963
55: 3 Because of the v of the enemy, because H6963
17 and cry aloud: and he shall hear my v. H6963
58: 5 Which will not hearken to the v of H6963
64: 1 Hear my v, O God, in my prayer: H6963
66: 8 make the v of his praise to be heard: H6963
19 he hath attended to the v of my prayer. H6963
68:33 send out his v, *and that* a mighty voice. H6963
33 send out his voice, *and that* a mighty v. H6963
74:23 Forget not the v of thine enemies: the H6963
77: 1 I cried unto God with my v, *even* unto H6963
1 with my v; and he gave ear unto me. H6963
18 The v of thy thunder *was* in the heaven: H6963
81:11 to my v; and Israel would none of me. H6963
86: 6 attend to the v of my supplications. H6963
93: 3 up their v; the floods lift up their waves. H6963
95: 7 of his hand. To day if ye will hear his v, H6963
98: 5 with the harp, and the v of a psalm. H6963
102: 5 By reason of the v of my groaning my H6963
103:20 hearkening unto the v of his word. H6963
104: 7 At thy rebuke they fled; at the v of thy H6963
106:25 hearkened not unto the v of the LORD. H6963
116: 1 hath heard my v *and* my supplications. H6963
118:15 The v of rejoicing and salvation *is* in H6963
119:149 Hear my v according unto thy H6963
130: 2 Lord, hear my v: let thine ears be H6963
2 attentive to the v of my supplications. H6963
140: 6 the v of my supplications, O LORD. H6963
141: 1 ear unto my v, when I cry unto thee. H6963
142: 1 I cried unto the LORD with my v; with H6963
1 my voice; with my v unto the LORD did H6963
Prv 1:20 she uttereth her v in the streets: H6963
2: 3 *and* liftest up thy v for understanding; H6963
5:13 And have not obeyed the v of my H6963
8: 1 cry? and understanding put forth her v? H6963
4 Unto you, O men, I call; and my v *is* to H6963
27:14 friend with a loud v, rising early in the H6963
Ecc 5: 3 v *is known* by multitude of words. H6963
6 v, and destroy the work of thine hands? H6963
10:20 the air shall carry the v, and that which H6963
12: 4 shall rise up at the v of the bird, and all H6963
Song 2: 8 The v of my beloved! behold, he H6963
12 the v of the turtle is heard in our land; H6963
14 let me hear thy v; for sweet *is* thy voice, H6963
14 *is* thy v, and thy countenance *is* comely. H6963
5: 2 I sleep, but my heart waketh: *it is* the v H6963
8:13 hearken to thy v: cause me to hear *it*. H6963
Isa 6: 4 door moved at the v of him that cried, H6963
8 Also I heard the v of the Lord, saying, H6963
10:30 Lift up thy v, O daughter of Gallim: H6963
13: 2 exalt the v unto them, shake the H6963
15: 4 and Elealeh: their v shall be heard *even* H6963
24:14 They shall lift up their v, they shall sing H6963
28:23 Give ye ear, and hear my v; hearken, H6963
29: 4 of the dust, and thy v shall be, as of one H6963
30:19 unto thee at the v of thy cry; when he H6963

Isa 30:30 cause his glorious v to be heard, and H6963
31 For through the v of the LORD shall the H6963
31: 4 be afraid of their v, nor abase himself H6963
32: 9 are at ease; hear my v, ye careless H6963
36:13 and cried with a loud v in the Jews' H6963
37:23 thou exalted *thy* v, and lifted up thine H6963
40: 3 The v of him that crieth in the H6963
6 The v said, Cry. And he said, What H6963
9 tidings, lift up thy v with strength; lift *it* H6963
42: 2 cause his v to be heard in the street. H6963
11 thereof lift up *their* v, the villages *that*
48:20 Chaldeans, with a v of singing declare H6963
50:10 that obeyeth the v of his servant, that H6963
51: 3 thanksgiving, and the v of melody. H6963
52: 8 Thy watchmen shall lift up the v; with H6963
8 the voice; with the v together shall they H6963
58: 1 Cry aloud, spare not, lift up thy v like a H6963
4 to make your v to be heard on high. H6963
65:19 people: and the v of weeping shall be H6963
19 more heard in her, nor the v of crying. H6963
66: 6 A v of noise from the city, a voice from H6963
6 A voice of noise from the city, a v from H6963
6 from the temple, a v of the LORD that H6963
Jer 3:13 have not obeyed my v, saith the LORD. H6963
21 A v was heard upon the high places, H6963
25 not obeyed the v of the LORD our God. H6963
4:15 For a v declareth from Dan, and H6963
16 out their v against the cities of Judah. H6963
31 For I have heard a v as of a woman in H6963
31 her first child, the v of the daughter of H6963
6:23 no mercy; their v roareth like the sea; H6963
7:23 saying, Obey my v, and I will be your H6963
28 obeyeth not the v of the LORD their H6963
34 of Jerusalem, the v of mirth, and the H6963
34 of mirth, and the v of gladness, the H6963
34 of gladness, the v of the bridegroom, H6963
34 and the v of the bride: for the H6963
8:19 Behold the v of the cry of the daughter H6963
9:10 can *men* hear the v of the cattle; both H6963
13 obeyed my v, neither walked therein; H6963
19 For a v of wailing is heard out of Zion, H6963
10:13 When he uttereth his v, *there is* a H6963
11: 4 saying, Obey my v, and do them, H6963
7 and protesting, saying, Obey my v. H6963
16: 9 in your days, the v of mirth, and the H6963
9 of mirth, and the v of gladness, the H6963
9 of gladness, the v of the bridegroom, H6963
9 the bridegroom, and the v of the bride. H6963
18:10 it obey not my v, then I will repent of H6963
19 to the v of them that contend with me. H6963
22:20 cry; and lift up thy v in Bashan, and cry H6963
21 thy youth, that thou obeyedst not my v. H6963
25:10 Moreover I will take from them the v of H6963
10 of mirth, and the v of gladness, the H6963
10 of gladness, the v of the bridegroom, H6963
10 and the v of the bride, the sound H6963
30 on high, and utter his v from his holy H6963
36 A v of the cry of the shepherds, and an H6963
26:13 and obey the v of the LORD your God; H6963
30: 5 We have heard a v of trembling, of H6963
19 and the v of them that make merry: H6963
31:15 Thus saith the LORD; A v was heard in H6963
16 Thus saith the LORD; Refrain thy v H6963
32:23 obeyed not thy v, neither walked in thy H6963
33:11 The v of joy, and the voice of gladness, H6963
11 The voice of joy, and the v of gladness, H6963
11 of gladness, the v of the bridegroom, H6963
11 and the v of the bride, the voice H6963
11 of the bride, the v of them that shall H6963
35: 8 Thus have we obeyed the v of Jonadab H6963
38:20 I beseech thee, the v of the LORD, H6963
40: 3 not obeyed his v, therefore this thing H6963
42: 6 evil, we will obey the v of the LORD our H6963
6 we obey the v of the LORD our God. H6963
13 obey the v of the LORD your God, H6963
21 not obeyed the v of the LORD your H6963
43: 4 obeyed not the v of the LORD, to dwell H6963
7 obeyed not the v of the LORD: thus H6963
44:23 have not obeyed the v of the LORD, nor H6963
46:22 The v thereof shall go like a serpent; for H6963
48: 3 A v of crying *shall be* from Horonaim, H6963
34 they uttered their v, from Zoar *even* H6963
50:28 The v of them that flee and escape out H6963
42 shew mercy: their v shall roar like the H6963
51:16 When he uttereth *his* v, *there is* a H6963
55 of her the great v; when her waves do H6963
55 waters, a noise of their v is uttered: H6963
Lam 3:56 Thou hast heard my v: hide not thine H6963
Ezk 1:24 waters, as the v of the Almighty, the H6963

Ezk 1:24 of the Almighty, the **v** of speech, as the H6963
25 And there was a **v** from the firmament H6963
28 face, and I heard a **v** of one that spake. H6963
3:12 heard behind me a **v** of a great rushing, H6963
8:18 with a loud **v**, *yet* will I not hear them. H6963
9: 1 He cried also in mine ears with a loud **v**, H6963
10: 5 outer court, as the **v** of the Almighty H6963
11:13 cried with a loud **v**, and said, Ah Lord H6963
19: 9 holds, that his **v** should no more be H6963
21:22 to lift up the **v** with shouting, to H6963
23:42 And a **v** of a multitude being at ease H6963
27:30 And shall cause their **v** to be heard H6963
33:32 hath a pleasant **v**, and can play well on H6963
43: 2 of the east: and his **v** *was* like a noise of H6963
Dan 4:31 mouth, there fell a **v** from heaven, H7032
6:20 with a lamentable **v** unto Daniel: *and* H7032
7:11 I beheld then because of the **v** of the H7032
8:16 And I heard a man's **v** between *the* H6963
9:10 Neither have we obeyed the **v** of the H6963
11 not obey thy **v**; therefore the curse H6963
14 which he doeth: for we obeyed not his **v**. H6963
10: 6 brass, and the **v** of his words like the H6963
6 of his words like the **v** of a multitude. H6963
9 Yet heard I the **v** of his words: and H6963
9 when I heard the **v** of his words, then H6963
Joel 2:11 And the LORD shall utter his **v** before H6963
3:16 of Zion, and utter his **v** from Jerusalem; H6963
Am 1: 2 Zion, and utter his **v** from Jerusalem; H6963
Jna 2: 2 of hell cried I, *and* thou heardest my **v**. H6963
9 But I will sacrifice unto thee with the **v** H6963
Mic 6: 1 mountains, and let the hills hear thy **v**. H6963
9 The LORD'S **v** crieth unto the city, and H6963
Nah 2: 7 **v** of doves, tabering upon their breasts. H6963
13 the earth, and the **v** of thy messengers H6963
Hab 3:10 his **v**, *and* lifted up his hands on high. H6963
16 quivered at the **v**: rottenness entered H6963
Zep 1:14 greatly, *even* the **v** of the day of the H6963
2:14 lintels of it; *their* **v** shall sing in the H6963
3: 2 She obeyed not the **v**; she received not H6963
Hag 1:12 people, obeyed the **v** of the LORD their H6963
Zec 6:15 obey the **v** of the LORD your God. H6963
11: 3 *There is* a **v** of the howling of the H6963
3 glory is spoiled: a **v** of the roaring of H6963
Mt 2:18 In Rama was there a **v** heard, G5456
3: 3 saying, The **v** of one crying in the G5456
17 And lo a **v** from heaven, saying, This is G5456
12:19 shall any man hear his **v** in the streets. G5456
17: 5 and behold a **v** out of the cloud, which G5456
27:46 cried with a loud **v**, saying, Eli, Eli, G5456
50 with a loud **v**, yielded up the ghost. G5456
Mk 1: 3 The **v** of one crying in the wilderness, G5456
11 And there came a **v** from heaven, G5456
26 cried with a loud **v**, he came out of him. G5456
5: 7 And cried with a loud **v**, and said, What G5456
9: 7 them: and a **v** came out of the cloud, G5456
15:34 cried with a loud **v**, saying, Eloi, Eloi, G5456
37 And Jesus cried with a loud **v**, and gave G5456
Lk 1:42 And she spake out with a loud **v**, and G5456
44 For, lo, as soon as the **v** of thy G5456
3: 4 saying, The **v** of one crying in the G5456
22 upon him, and a **v** came from heaven, G5456
4:33 devil, and cried out with a loud **v**, G5456
8:28 and with a loud **v** said, What have I to G5456
9:35 And there came a **v** out of the cloud, G5456
36 And when the **v** was past, Jesus was G5456
11:27 lifted up her **v**, and said unto him, G5456
17:15 back, and with a loud **v** glorified God, G5456
19:37 God with a loud **v** for all the mighty G5456
23:46 And when Jesus had cried with a loud **v**, G5456
Jn 1:23 He said, I *am* the **v** of one crying in the G5456
3:29 **v**: this my joy therefore is fulfilled. G5456
5:25 shall hear the **v** of the Son of God: and G5456
28 that are in the graves shall hear his **v**, G5456
37 his **v** at any time, nor seen his shape. G5456
10: 3 the sheep hear his **v**: and he calleth his G5456
4 sheep follow him: for they know his **v**. G5456
5 for they know not the **v** of strangers. G5456
16 they shall hear my **v**; and there shall be G5456
27 My sheep hear my **v**, and I know them, G5456
11:43 with a loud **v**, Lazarus, come forth. G5456
12:28 Then came there a **v** from heaven, G5456
30 Jesus answered and said, This **v** came G5456
18:37 one that is of the truth heareth my **v**. G5456
Act 2:14 lifted up his **v**, and said unto them, G5456
4:24 they lifted up their **v** to God with one G5456
7:31 *it*, the **v** of the Lord came unto him, G5456
57 Then they cried out with a loud **v**, and G5456
60 cried with a loud **v**, Lord, lay not this G5456
8: 7 For unclean spirits, crying with loud **v**, G5456
Act 9: 4 And he fell to the earth, and heard a **v** G5456
7 hearing a **v**, but seeing no man. G5456
10:13 And there came a **v** to him, Rise, Peter; G5456
15 And the **v** *spake* unto him again the G5456
11: 7 And I heard a **v** saying unto me, Arise, G5456
9 But the **v** answered me again from G5456
12:14 And when she knew Peter's **v**, she G5456
22 *It is* the **v** of a god, and not of a man. G5456
14:10 Said with a loud **v**, Stand upright on thy G5456
16:28 But Paul cried with a loud **v**, saying, Do G5456
19:34 a Jew, all with one **v** about the space of G5456
22: 7 and heard a **v** saying unto me, Saul, G5456
9 not the **v** of him that spake to me. G5456
14 and shouldest hear the **v** of his mouth. G5456
24:21 Except it be for this one **v**, that I cried G5456
26:10 put to death, I gave my **v** against *them*. G5586
14 earth, I heard a **v** speaking unto me, G5456
24 said with a loud **v**, Paul, thou art beside G5456
1Co 14:11 meaning of the **v**, I shall be unto him G5456
19 that *by my* **v** I might teach others
Gal 4:20 my **v**; for I stand in doubt of you. G5456
1Th 4:16 a shout, with the **v** of the archangel, G5456
Heb 3: 7 Ghost saith, To day if ye will hear his **v**, G5456
15 if ye will hear his **v**, harden not your G5456
4: 7 will hear his **v**, harden not your hearts. G5456
12:19 And the sound of a trumpet, and the **v** G5456
19 voice of words; which **v** they that heard
26 Whose **v** then shook the earth: but now G5456
2Pt 1:17 there came such a **v** to him from the G5456
18 And this **v** which came from heaven we G5456
2:16 **v** forbad the madness of the prophet. G5456
Rev 1:10 behind me a great **v**, as of a trumpet, G5456
12 And I turned to see the **v** that spake G5456
15 and his **v** as the sound of many waters. G5456
3:20 any man hear my **v**, and open the door, G5456
4: 1 and the first **v** which I heard *was* as G5456
5: 2 with a loud **v**, Who is worthy to open G5456
11 And I beheld, and I heard the **v** of G5456
12 Saying with a loud **v**, Worthy is the G5456
6: 6 And I heard a **v** in the midst of the four G5456
7 seal, I heard the **v** of the fourth beast G5456
10 And they cried with a loud **v**, saying, G5456
7: 2 cried with a loud **v** to the four angels, G5456
10 And cried with a loud **v**, saying, G5456
8:13 saying with a loud **v**, Woe, woe, woe, to G5456
9:13 and I heard a **v** from the four horns G5456
10: 3 And cried with a loud **v**, as *when* a lion G5456
4 and I heard a **v** from heaven saying G5456
7 But in the days of the **v** of the seventh G5456
8 And the **v** which I heard from heaven G5456
11:12 And they heard a great **v** from heaven G5456
12:10 And I heard a loud **v** saying in heaven, G5456
14: 2 And I heard a **v** from heaven, as the G5456
2 heaven, as the **v** of many waters, and G5456
2 waters, and as the **v** of a great thunder: G5456
2 **v** of harpers harping with their harps: G5456
7 Saying with a loud **v**, Fear God, and G5456
9 them, saying with a loud **v**, If any man G5456
13 And I heard a **v** from heaven saying G5456
15 crying with a loud **v** to him that sat on G5456
16: 1 And I heard a great **v** out of the temple G5456
17 there came a great **v** out of the temple G5456
18: 2 And he cried mightily with a strong **v**, G5456
4 And I heard another **v** from heaven, G5456
22 And the **v** of harpers, and musicians, G5456
23 all in thee; and the **v** of the bridegroom G5456
19: 1 And after these things I heard a great **v** G5456
5 And a **v** came out of the throne, saying, G5456
6 And I heard as it were the **v** of a great G5456
6 and as the **v** of many waters, and G5456
6 many waters, and as the **v** of mighty G5456
17 he cried with a loud **v**, saying to all the G5456
21: 3 And I heard a great **v** out of heaven G5456

VOICES

Jdg 21: 2 and lifted up their **v**, and wept sore; H6963
1Sa 11: 4 the people lifted up their **v**, and wept. H6963
Lk 17:13 And they lifted up *their* **v**, and said, G5456
23:23 And they were instant with loud **v**, G5456
23 crucified. And the **v** of them and of the G5456
Act 13:27 not, nor yet the **v** of the prophets which G5456
14:11 they lifted up their **v**, saying in the G5456
22:22 lifted up their **v**, and said, Away with G5456
1Co 14:10 so many kinds of **v** in the world, and G5456
Rev 4: 5 and thunderings and **v**: and *there were* G5456
8: 5 and there were **v**, and thunderings, and G5456
13 of the other **v** of the trumpet of the G5456
10: 3 cried, seven thunders uttered their **v**. G5456
4 had uttered their **v**, I was about to G5456
Rev 11:15 there were great **v** in heaven, saying, G5456
19 lightnings, and **v**, and thunderings, and G5456
16:18 And there were **v**, and thunders, and G5456

VOID

Gen 1: 2 And the earth was without form, and **v**; H922
Nu 30:12 hath utterly made them **v** on the day he H6565
12 them **v**; and the LORD shall forgive her. H6565
13 it, or her husband may make it **v**. H6565
15 But if he shall any ways make them **v** H6565
Dt 32:28 For they *are* a nation **v** of counsel, H6
1Ki 22:10 their robes, in a **v** place in the entrance H1637
2Ch 18: 9 and they sat in a **v** place at the entering H1637
Ps 89:39 Thou hast made **v** the covenant of thy H5010
119:126 to work: *for* they have made **v** thy law. H6565
Prv 7: 7 a young man **v** of understanding, H2638
10:13 back of him that is **v** of understanding. H2638
11:12 He that is **v** of wisdom despiseth his H2638
12:11 vain *persons is* **v** of understanding. H2638
17:18 A man **v** of understanding striketh H2638
24:30 of the man **v** of understanding; H2638
Isa 55:11 not return unto me **v**, but it shall H7387
Jer 4:23 without form, and **v**; and the heavens, H922
19: 7 And I will make **v** the counsel of Judah H1238
Nah 2:10 She is empty, and **v**, and waste: and the H4003
Act 24:16 a conscience **v** of offence toward God, G677
Ro 3:31 Do we then make **v** the law through G2673
4:14 **v**, and the promise made of none effect: G2758
1Co 9:15 any man should make my glorying **v**. G2758

VOLUME

Ps 40: 7 Then said I, Lo, I come: in the **v** of the H4039
Heb 10: 7 Then said I, Lo, I come (in the **v** of the G2777

VOLUNTARILY

Ezk 46:12 or peace offerings **v** unto the LORD, H5071

VOLUNTARY

Lev 1: 3 offer it of his own **v** will at the door of H7522
7:16 *be* a vow, or a **v** offering, it shall be H5071
Ezk 46:12 Now when the prince shall prepare a **v** H5071
Col 2:18 of your reward in a **v** humility and G2309

VOMIT

Job 20:15 and he shall **v** them up again: God H6958
Prv 23: 8 thou **v** up, and lose thy sweet words. H6958
25:16 lest thou be filled therewith, and **v** it. H6958
26:11 As a dog returneth to his **v**, *so* a fool H6892
Isa 19:14 as a drunken *man* staggereth in his **v**. H6892
28: 8 For all tables are full of **v** *and* H6892
Jer 48:26 in his **v**, and he also shall be in derision. H6892
2Pt 2:22 turned to his own **v** again; and the sow G1829

VOMITED

Jna 2:10 and it **v** out Jonah upon the dry *land*. H6958

VOMITETH

Lev 18:25 the land itself **v** out her inhabitants. H6958

VOPHSI

Nu 13:14 tribe of Naphtali, Nahbi the son of **V**. H2058

VOW

Gen 28:20 And Jacob vowed a **v**, saying, If God will H5088
31:13 thou vowedst a **v** unto me: now arise, H5088
Lev 7:16 But if the sacrifice of his offering *be* a **v**, H5088
22:21 LORD to accomplish *his* **v**, or a freewill H5088
23 but for a **v** it shall not be accepted. H5088
27: 2 make a singular **v**, the persons *shall be* H5088
Nu 6: 2 *themselves* to **v** a vow of a Nazarite, H5087
2 to vow a **v** of a Nazarite, to separate H5088
5 All the days of the **v** of his separation H5088
21 according to the **v** which he vowed, so H5088
15: 3 in performing a **v**, or in a freewill H5088
8 a **v**, or peace offerings unto the LORD: H5088
21: 2 And Israel vowed a **v** unto the LORD, H5088
30: 2 If a man **v** a vow unto the LORD, or H5087
2 If a man vow a **v** unto the LORD, or H5088
3 If a woman also **v** a vow unto the H5087
3 If a woman also vow a **v** unto the H5088
4 And her father hear her **v**, and her bond H5088
8 he shall make her **v** which she vowed, H5088
9 But every **v** of a widow, and of her that H5088
13 Every **v**, and every binding oath to H5088
Dt 12:11 choice vows which ye **v** unto the LORD: H5087
23:18 thy God for any **v**: for even both these H5088
21 When thou shalt **v** a vow unto the H5087
21 When thou shalt vow a **v** unto the H5088
22 But if thou shalt forbear to **v**, it shall be H5087

V

Jdg 11:30 And Jephthah vowed a v unto the H5088
39 *according* to his v which he had vowed: H5088
1Sa 1:11 And she vowed a v, and said, O LORD H5088
21 the LORD the yearly sacrifice, and his v. H5088
2Sa 15: 7 let me go and pay my v, which I have H5088
8 For thy servant vowed a v while I H5088
Ps 65: 1 and unto thee shall the v be performed. H5088
76:11 V, and pay unto the LORD your God: let H5087
Ecc 5: 4 When thou vowest a v unto God, defer H5088
5 Better *is it* that thou shouldest not v, H5087
5 than that thou shouldest v and not pay. H5087
Isa 19:21 yea, they shall v a vow unto the LORD, H5087
21 a v unto the LORD, and perform *it*. H5088
Act 18:18 *his* head in Cenchrea: for he had a v. G2171
21:23 have four men which have a v on them; G2171

VOWED
Gen 28:20 And Jacob v a vow, saying, If God will H5087
Lev 27: 8 ability that v shall the priest value him. H5087
Nu 6:21 Nazarite who hath v, *and of* his offering H5087
21 the vow which he v, so he must do after H5087
21: 2 And Israel v a vow unto the LORD, and H5087
30: 6 when she v, or uttered ought out H5088
8 her vow which she v, and that which H5921
10 And if she v in her husband's house, or H5087
Dt 23:23 as thou hast v unto the LORD thy H5087
Jdg 11:30 And Jephthah v a vow unto the LORD, H5087
39 vow which he had v: and she knew no H5087
1Sa 1:11 And she v a vow, and said, O LORD of H5087
2Sa 15: 7 I have v unto the LORD, in Hebron. H5087
2Sa 15: 8 For thy servant v a vow while I abode H5087
Ps 132: 2 How he sware unto the LORD, *and* v H5087
Ecc 5: 4 in fools: pay that which thou hast v. H5087
Jer 44:25 vows that we have v, to burn incense to H5087
Jna 2: 9 that I have v. Salvation *is* of the LORD. H5087

VOWEDST
Gen 31:13 *and* where thou v a vow unto me: now H5087

VOWEST
Dt 12:17 thy vows which thou v, nor thy freewill H5087
Ecc 5: 4 When thou v a vow unto God, defer not H5087

VOWETH
Mal 1:14 his flock a male, and v, and sacrificeth H5087

VOWS
Lev 22:18 his oblation for all his v, and for all his H5088
23:38 beside all your v, and beside all your H5088
Nu 29:39 feasts, beside your v, and your freewill H5088
30: 4 at her: then all her v shall stand, and H5088
5 not any of her v, or of her bonds H5088
7 heard *it*: then her v shall stand, and her H5088
11 her not: then all her v shall stand, and H5088
12 lips concerning her v, or concerning the H5088
14 all her v, or all her bonds, which H5088
Dt 12: 6 hand, and your v, and your freewill H5088
11 choice v which ye vow unto the LORD: H5088
17 nor any of thy v which thou vowest, H5088
26 thou hast, and thy v, thou shalt take, H5088
Job 22:27 hear thee, and thou shalt pay thy v. H5088
Ps 22:25 pay my v before them that fear him. H5088
50:14 and pay thy v unto the most High: H5088
56:12 Thy v *are* upon me, O God: I will render H5088
61: 5 For thou, O God, hast heard my v: thou H5088
8 for ever, that I may daily perform my v. H5088
66:13 burnt offerings: I will pay thee my v, H5088
116:14 I will pay my v unto the LORD now in H5088
18 I will pay my v unto the LORD now in H5088
Prv 7:14 with me; this day have I payed my v. H5088
20:25 *is* holy, and after v to make inquiry. H5088
31: 2 my womb? and what, the son of my v? H5088
Jer 44:25 perform our v that we have vowed, H5088
25 your v, and surely perform your vows. H5088
25 your vows, and surely perform your v. H5088
Jna 1:16 a sacrifice unto the LORD, and made v. H5088
Nah 1:15 perform thy v: for the wicked shall H5088

VOYAGE
Act 27:10 I perceive that this v will be with hurt G4144

VULTURE
Lev 11:14 And the v, and the kite after his kind; H1676
Dt 14:13 And the glede, and the kite, and the v H1772

VULTURES
Isa 34:15 there shall the v also be gathered, every H1772

VULTURE'S
Job 28: 7 and which the v eye hath not seen: H344

W

WAFER
Ex 29:23 bread, and one w out of the basket of H7550
Lev 8:26 bread, and one w, and put *them* on the H7550
Nu 6:19 one unleavened w, and shall put *them* H7550

WAFERS
Ex 16:31 taste of it *was* like w *made* with honey. H6838
29: 2 with oil, and w unleavened anointed H7550
Lev 2: 4 oil, or unleavened w anointed with oil. H7550
7:12 and unleavened w anointed with oil, H7550
Nu 6:15 with oil, and w of unleavened bread H7550

WAG
Jer 18:16 shall be astonished, and w his head. H5110
Lam 2:15 thee; they hiss and w their head at the H5128
Zep 2:15 by her shall hiss, *and* w his hand. H5128

WAGES
Gen 29:15 nought? tell me, what *shall* thy w *be*? H4909
30:28 And he said, Appoint me thy w, and I H7939
31: 7 and changed my w ten times; but God H4909
8 shall be thy w; then all the cattle bare H7939
41 and thou hast changed my w ten times. H4909
Ex 2: 9 I will give *thee* thy w. And the woman H7939
Lev 19:13 rob *him*: the w of him that is hired H6468
Jer 22:13 w, and giveth him not for his work; H2600
Ezk 29:18 yet had he no w, nor his army, for H7939
19 prey; and it shall be the w for his army. H7939
Hag 1: 6 he that earneth w earneth wages *to* H7936
6 w *to put it* into a bag with holes. H7936
Mal 3: 5 the hireling in *his* w, the widow, and the H7939
Lk 3:14 *any* falsely; and be content with your w. G3800
Jn 4:36 And he that reapeth receiveth w, and G3408
Ro 6:23 For the w of sin *is* death; but the gift of G3800
2Co 11: 8 I robbed other churches, taking w *of* G3800
2Pt 2:15 who loved the w of unrighteousness; G3408

WAGGING
Mt 27:39 And they that passed by reviled him, w G2795
Mk 15:29 by railed on him, w their heads, and G2795

WAGON
Nu 7: 3 twelve oxen; a w for two of the princes, H5699

WAGONS
Gen 45:19 this do ye; take you w out of the land of H5699
21 Joseph gave them w, according to the H5699
27 when he saw the w which Joseph had H5699
46: 5 their wives, in the w which Pharaoh H5699
Nu 7: 3 six covered w, and twelve oxen; a H5699
6 And Moses took the w and the oxen, H5699
Nu 7: 7 Two w and four oxen he gave unto the H5699
8 And four w and eight oxen he gave H5699
Ezk 23:24 with chariots, w, and wheels, and with H7393

WAIL
Ezk 32:18 Son of man, w for the multitude of H5091
Mic 1: 8 Therefore I will w and howl, I will go H5594
Rev 1: 7 shall w because of him. Even so, Amen. G2875

WAILED
Mk 5:38 and them that wept and w greatly. G214

WAILING
Est 4: 3 and weeping, and w; and many lay in H4553
Jer 9:10 take up a weeping and w, and for the H5092
18 and take up a w for us, that our eyes H5092
19 For a voice of w is heard out of Zion, H5092
20 your daughters w, and every one her H5092
Ezk 7:11 neither *shall there be* w for them. H5089
27:31 with bitterness of heart *and* bitter w. H4553
32 And in their w they shall take up a H5204
Am 5:16 the Lord, saith thus; W *shall be* in all H4553
16 such as are skilful of lamentation to w. H4553
17 And in all vineyards *shall be* w: for I H4553
Mic 1: 8 I will make a w like the dragons, and H4553
Mt 13:42 there shall be w and gnashing of teeth. G2805
50 there shall be w and gnashing of teeth. G2805
Rev 18:15 the fear of her torment, weeping and w, G3996
19 weeping and w, saying, Alas, alas, that G3996

WAIT
Ex 21:13 And if a man lie not in w, but God H6658
Nu 3:10 and they shall w on their priest's office: H8104
8:24 they shall go in to w upon the service of H6633
35:20 hurl at him by laying of w, that he die; H6660
22 him any thing without laying of w, H6660
Dt 19:11 and lie in w for him, and rise up H693
Jos 8: 4 ye shall lie in w against the city, *even* H693
13 and their liers in w on the west of the H6119
Jdg 9:25 And the men of Shechem set liers in w H693
32 that *is* with thee, and lie in w in the field: H693
34 w against Shechem in four companies. H693
35 that *were* with him, from lying in w. H3993
43 and laid w in the field, and looked, H693
16: 2 *him* in, and laid w for him all night in H693
9 Now *there were* men lying in w, abiding H693
12 And *there were* liers in w abiding in the H693
20:29 And Israel set liers in w round about H693
33 and the liers in w of Israel came forth H693
36 in w which they had set beside Gibeah. H693
37 And the liers in w hasted, and rushed H693
37 and the liers in w drew *themselves* H693
Jdg 20:38 and the liers in w, that they should make H693
21:20 saying, Go and lie in w in the vineyards; H693
1Sa 15: 2 Israel, how he laid *w* for him in the way,
5 city of Amalek, and laid w in the valley. H693
22: 8 against me, to lie in w, as at this day? H693
13 rise against me, to lie in w, as at this day? H693
2Ki 6:33 should I w for the LORD any longer? H3176
1Ch 23:28 Because their office *was* to w on the H3027
2Ch 5:11 *and* did not *then* w by course: H8104
13:10 and the Levites *w* upon *their* business: H8104
Ezr 8:31 and of such as lay in w by the way. H693
Job 14:14 time will I w, till my change come. H3176
17:13 If I w, the grave *is* mine house: I have H6960
31: 9 *if* I have laid w at my neighbour's door; H693
38:40 dens, *and* abide in the covert to lie in w? H695
Ps 10: 9 He lieth in w secretly as a lion in his den: H693
9 his den: he lieth in w to catch the poor: H693
25: 3 Yea, let none that w on thee be H6960
5 salvation; on thee do I w all the day. H6960
21 preserve me; for I w on thee. H6960
27:14 W on the LORD: be of good courage, H6960
14 thine heart: w, I say, on the LORD. H6960
37: 7 Rest in the LORD, and w patiently for H2342
9 off: but those that w upon the LORD, H6960
34 W on the LORD, and keep his way, and H6960
39: 7 And now, Lord, what w I for? my hope H6960
52: 9 done *it*: and I will w on thy name; for *it* H6960
56: 6 my steps, when they w for my soul. H6960
59: 3 For, lo, they lie in w for my soul: the H693
9 *Because of* his strength will I w upon H8104
62: 5 My soul, w thou only upon God; for my H1826
69: 3 mine eyes fail while I w for my God. H3176
6 Let not them that w on thee, O Lord H6960
71:10 w for my soul take counsel together, H8104
104:27 These w all upon thee; that thou H7663
123: 2 so our eyes *w* upon the LORD our
130: 5 I w for the LORD, my soul doth wait, H6960
5 I wait for the LORD, my soul doth w, H6960
145:15 The eyes of all w upon thee; and thou H7663
Prv 1:11 If they say, Come with us, let us lay w for H693
18 And they lay w for their *own* blood; they H693
7:12 streets, and lieth in w at every corner.) H693
12: 6 The words of the wicked *are* to lie in w H693
20:22 w on the LORD, and he shall save thee. H6960
23:28 She also lieth in w as *for* a prey, and H693
24:15 Lay not w, O wicked *man*, against the H693
Isa 8:17 And I will w upon the LORD, that H2442
30:18 And therefore will the LORD w, that he H2442
18 blessed *are* all they that w for him. H2442
40:31 But they that w upon the LORD shall H6960
42: 4 earth: and the isles shall w for his law. H3176
49:23 shall not be ashamed that w for me. H6960

Isa 51: 5 the isles shall w upon me, and on mine H6960
59: 9 overtake us: we w for light, but behold H6960
60: 9 Surely the isles shall w for me, and the H6960
Jer 5:26 *men*: they lay w, as he that setteth H7789
9: 8 his mouth, but in heart he layeth his w. H696
14:22 therefore we will w upon thee: for thou H6960
Lam 3:10 He *was* unto me *as* a bear lying in w, *and* H693
25 The LORD *is* good unto them that w for H6960
26 w for the salvation of the LORD. H1748
4:19 they laid w for us in the wilderness. H693
Hos 6: 9 And as troops of robbers w for a man, H2442
7: 6 whiles they lie in w: their baker sleepeth H693
12: 6 and w on thy God continually. H6960
Mic 7: 2 men: they all lie in w for blood; they H693
7 the LORD; I will w for the God of my H3176
Hab 2: 3 though it tarry, w for it; because it will H2442
Zep 3: 8 Therefore w ye upon me, saith the H2442
Mk 3: 9 small ship should w on him because of G4342
Lk 11:54 Laying w for him, and seeking to catch G1748
12:36 And ye yourselves like unto men that w G4327
Act 1: 4 Jerusalem, but w for the promise of the G4037
20: 3 the Jews laid w for him, as he was G1096
19 befell me by the lying in w of the Jews: G1917
23:16 of their lying in w, he went and entered G1749
21 for there lie in w for him of them more G1748
30 that the Jews laid w for the man, I sent G1917
25: 3 laying w in the way to kill him. G1747
Ro 8:25 not, *then* do we with patience w for *it*. G553
12: 7 Or ministry, *let us* w on *our* ministering:
1Co 9:13 and they which w at the altar are G4332
Gal 5: 5 For we through the Spirit w for the hope G553
Eph 4:14 whereby they lie in w to deceive; G3180
1Th 1:10 And to w for his Son from heaven, G362

WAITED

Gen 49:18 I have w for thy salvation, O LORD. H6960
1Ki 20:38 So the prophet departed, and w for the H5975
2Ki 5: 2 maid; and she w on Naaman's wife. H6440
1Ch 6:32 and *then* they w on their office H5975
33 And these *are* they that w with their H5975
9:18 Who hitherto *w* in the king's gate
2Ch 7: 6 And the priests w on their offices: the H5975
17:19 These w on the king, beside *those* H8334
35:15 and the porters *w* at every gate; they
Neh 12:44 the priests and for the Levites that w. H5975
Job 6:19 the companies of Sheba w for them. H6960
15:22 darkness, and he is w for of the sword. H6822
29:21 Unto me *men* gave ear, and w, and kept H3176
23 And they w for me as for the rain; and H3176
30:26 I w for light, there came darkness. H3176
32: 4 Now Elihu had w till Job had spoken, H2442
11 Behold, I w for your words; I gave ear H3176
16 When I had w, (for they spake not, but H3176
Ps 40: 1 I w patiently for the LORD; and he H6960
106:13 They soon forgat his works; they w not H2442
119:95 The wicked have w for me to destroy H6960
Isa 25: 9 *is* our God; we have w for him, and he H6960
9 LORD; we have w for him, we will be H6960
26: 8 O LORD, have we w for thee; the desire H6960
33: 2 unto us; we have w for thee: be thou H6960
Ezk 19: 5 Now when she saw that she had w, *and* H3176
Mic 1:12 For the inhabitant of Maroth w H2342
Zec 11:11 of the flock that w upon me knew that H8104
Mk 15:43 which also w for the kingdom of G4327
Lk 1:21 And the people w for Zacharias, and G4328
23:51 also himself w for the kingdom of God. G4327
Act 10: 7 of them that w on him continually; G4342
24 And Cornelius w for them, and had G4328
17:16 Now while Paul w for them at Athens, G1551
1Pt 3:20 of God w in the days of Noah, G1551

WAITETH

Job 24:15 The eye also of the adulterer w for the H8104
Ps 33:20 Our soul w for the LORD: he *is* our help H2442
62: 1 Truly my soul w upon God: from him H1747
65: 1 Praise w for thee, O God, in Sion: and H1747
130: 6 My soul w for the Lord more than they
Prv 27:18 w on his master shall be honoured. H8104
Isa 64: 4 hath prepared for him that w for him. H2442
Dan 12:12 Blessed *is* he that w, and cometh to the H2442
Mic 5: 7 not for man, nor w for the sons of men. H3176
Ro 8:19 of the creature w for the manifestation G553
Jas 5: 7 the husbandman w for the precious G1551

WAITING

Nu 8:25 they shall cease w upon the service H6635
Prv 8:34 at my gates, w at the posts of my doors. H8104
Lk 2:25 just and devout, w for the consolation G4327
8:40 him: for they were all w for him. G4328
Jn 5: 3 w for the moving of the water. G1551
Ro 8:23 within ourselves, w for the adoption, *to* G553
1Co 1: 7 So that ye come behind in no gift; w for G553
2Th 3: 5 God, and into the patient w for Christ. G5281

WAKE

Jer 51:39 sleep, and not w, saith the LORD. H6974
57 sleep, and not w, saith the King, whose H6974
Joel 3: 9 Prepare war, w up the mighty men, H5782
1Th 5:10 Who died for us, that, whether we w or G1127

WAKED

Zec 4: 1 came again, and w me, as a man that H5782

WAKENED

Joel 3:12 Let the heathen be w, and come up to H5782
Zec 4: 1 me, as a man that is w out of his sleep, H5782

WAKENETH

Isa 50: 4 *him that is* weary: he w morning by H5782
4 he w mine ear to hear as the learned. H5782

WAKETH

Ps 127: 1 the city, the watchman w *but* in vain. H8245
Song 5: 2 I sleep, but my heart w: *it is* the voice of H5782

WAKING

Ps 77: 4 Thou holdest mine eyes w: I am so H8109

WALK

Gen 13:17 Arise, w through the land in the length H1980
17: 1 God; w before me, and be thou perfect. H1980
24:40 before whom I w, will send his angel H1980
48:15 and Isaac did w, the God which fed me H1980
Ex 16: 4 whether they will w in my law, or no. H3212
18:20 w, and the work that they must do. H3212
21:19 If he rise again, and w abroad upon his H1980
Lev 18: 3 neither shall ye w in their ordinances. H3212
4 to w therein: I *am* the LORD your God. H3212
20:23 And ye shall not w in the manners of H3212
26: 3 If ye w in my statutes, and keep my H3212
12 And I will w among you, and will be H1980
21 And if ye w contrary unto me, and will H3212
23 things, but will w contrary unto me; H1980
24 Then will I also w contrary unto you, H1980
27 unto me, but w contrary unto me; H1980
28 Then I will w contrary unto you also in H1980
Dt 5:33 Ye shall w in all the ways which the H3212
8: 6 God, to w in his ways, and to fear him. H3212
19 thy God, and w after other gods, and H1980
10:12 the LORD thy God, to w in all his ways, H3212
11:22 your God, to w in all his ways, and H3212
13: 4 Ye shall w after the LORD your God, H3212
5 thee to w in. So shalt thou put H3212
19: 9 thy God, and to w ever in his ways; H3212
26:17 be thy God, and to w in his ways, and H3212
28: 9 the LORD thy God, and w in his ways. H1980
29:19 peace, though I w in the imagination H3212
30:16 LORD thy God, to w in his ways, and to H3212
Jos 18: 8 saying, Go and w through the land, H1980
22: 5 your God, and to w in all his ways, and H3212
Jdg 2:22 way of the LORD to w therein, as their H3212
5:10 that sit in judgment, and w by the way. H1980
1Sa 2:30 thy father, should w before me for ever: H1980
35 shall w before mine anointed for ever. H1980
8: 5 art old, and thy sons w not in thy ways: H1980
1Ki 2: 3 the LORD thy God, to w in his ways, to H3212
4 to their way, to w before me in truth H3212
3:14 And if thou wilt w in my ways, to keep H3212
14 did w, then I will lengthen thy days. H1980
6:12 if thou wilt w in my statutes, and H3212
12 to w in them; then will I H3212
8:23 that w before thee with all their heart: H1980
25 way, that they w before me as thou H3212
36 they should w, and give rain upon H3212
58 unto him, to w in all his ways, and H3212
61 the LORD our God, to w in his statutes, H3212
9: 4 And if thou wilt w before me, as David H3212
11:38 thee, and wilt w in my ways, and do H1980
16:31 light thing for him to w in the sins of H3212
2Ki 10:31 But Jehu took no heed to w in the law H3212
23: 3 the LORD, to w after the LORD, and H3212
2Ch 6:14 that w before thee with all their hearts: H1980
16 to their way to w in my law, as thou H3212
27 they should w; and send rain upon H3212
31 That they may fear thee, to w in thy H3212
7:17 And as for thee, if thou wilt w before H3212
34:31 the LORD, to w after the LORD, and H3212
Neh 5: 9 ought ye not to w in the fear of our God H3212
Neh 10:29 into an oath, to w in God's law, which H3212
Ps 12: 8 The wicked w on every side, when the H1980
23: 4 Yea, though I w through the valley of H3212
26:11 But as for me, I will w in mine H3212
48:12 W about Zion, and go round about her: H5437
56:13 w before God in the light of the living? H1980
78:10 of God, and refused to w in his law; H3212
82: 5 understand; they w on in darkness: all H1980
84:11 withhold from them that w uprightly. H1980
86:11 Teach me thy way, O LORD; I will w in H1980
89:15 sound: they shall w, O LORD, in the H1980
30 If his children forsake my law, and w H3212
101: 2 unto me? I will w within my house with H1980
115: 7 they, but they w not: neither speak they H1980
116: 9 I will w before the LORD in the land of H1980
119: 1 the way, who w in the law of the LORD. H1980
3 They also do no iniquity: they w in his H1980
45 And I will w at liberty: for I seek thy H1980
138: 7 Though I w in the midst of trouble, H3212
143: 8 should w; for I lift up my soul unto thee. H3212
Prv 1:15 My son, w not thou in the way with H3212
2: 7 *is* a buckler to them that w uprightly. H1980
13 to w in the ways of darkness; H3212
20 That thou mayest w in the way of good H3212
3:23 Then shalt thou w in thy way safely, H3212
Ecc 4:15 I considered all the living which w H1980
6: 8 that knoweth to w before the living? H1980
11: 9 of thy youth, and w in the ways of thine H1980
Isa 2: 3 ways, and we will w in his paths: for H3212
5 O house of Jacob, come ye, and let us w H3212
3:16 Zion are haughty, and w with stretched H3212
8:11 not w in the way of this people, saying, H3212
30: 2 That w to go down into Egypt, and H1980
21 This *is* the way, w ye in it, when ye turn H3212
35: 9 *there*: but the redeemed shall w *there*: H1980
40:31 weary; *and* they shall w, and not faint. H3212
42: 5 it, and spirit to them that w therein: H1980
24 for they would not w in his ways, H1980
50:11 with sparks: w in the light of your H3212
59: 9 for brightness, *but* we w in darkness. H1980
Jer 3:17 neither shall they w any more after the H3212
18 of Judah shall w with the house of H3212
6:16 *is* the good way, and w therein, and ye H3212
16 But they said, We will not w *therein*. H3212
25 Go not forth into the field, nor w by the H3212
7: 6 neither w after other gods to your hurt: H3212
9 w after other gods whom ye know not; H1980
23 be my people: and w ye in all the ways H1980
9: 4 every neighbour will w with slanders. H1980
13:10 my words, which w in the imagination H1980
10 of their heart, and w after other gods, H3212
16:12 for, behold, ye w every one after the H1980
18:12 no hope: but we will w after our own H3212
15 to w in paths, *in* a way not cast up; H3212
23:14 adultery, and w in lies: they strengthen H1980
26: 4 hearken to me, to w in my law, which I H3212
31: 9 I will cause them to w by the rivers of H3212
42: 3 may w, and the thing that we may do. H3212
Lam 5:18 which is desolate, the foxes w upon it. H1980
Ezk 11:20 That they may w in my statutes, and H3212
20:18 in the wilderness, W ye not in the H3212
19 I *am* the LORD your God; w in my H3212
33:15 he had robbed, w in the statutes of life, H1980
36:12 Yea, I will cause men to w upon you, H3212
27 and cause you to w in my statutes, and H3212
37:24 they shall also w in my judgments, and H3212
42: 4 And before the chambers *was* a w of H4109
Dan 4:37 that w in pride he is able to abase. H1981
9:10 LORD our God, to w in his laws, which H3212
Hos 11:10 They shall w after the LORD: he shall H3212
14: 9 and the just shall w in them: but the H3212
Joel 2: 8 they shall w every one in his path: H3212
Am 3: 3 Can two w together, except they be H3212
Mic 4: 2 ways, and we will w in his paths: for H3212
5 For all people will w every one in the H3212
5 god, and we will w in the name of the H3212
6: 8 mercy, and to w humbly with thy God? H3212
16 of Ahab, and ye w in their counsels; H3212
Nah 2: 5 stumble in their w; they shall make H1979
Hab 3:15 Thou didst w through the sea with H1869
19 he will make me to w upon mine high H1869
Zep 1:17 men, that they shall w like blind men, H1980
Zec 1:10 sent to w to and fro through the earth. H1980
3: 7 hosts; If thou wilt w in my ways, and if H3212
7 places to w among these that stand by. H1980
6: 7 to go that they might w to and fro H1980
7 Get you hence, w to and fro through H1980
10:12 and they shall w up and down in his H1980
Mt 9: 5 be forgiven thee; or to say, Arise, and w? G4043

W

Mt 11: 5 and the lame w, the lepers are cleansed, G4043
15:31 whole, the lame to w, and the blind to G4043
Mk 2: 9 say, Arise, and take up thy bed, and w? G4043
7: 5 asked him, Why w not thy disciples G4043
Lk 5:23 forgiven thee; or to say, Rise up and w? G4043
7:22 see, the lame w, the lepers are cleansed, G4043
11:44 w over *them* are not aware *of them.* G4043
13:33 Nevertheless I must w to day, and to G4198
20:46 which desire to w in long robes, and G4043
24:17 one to another, as ye w, and are sad? G4043
Jn 5: 8 unto him, Rise, take up thy bed, and w. G4043
11 said unto me, Take up thy bed, and w. G4043
12 said unto thee, Take up thy bed, and w? G4043
7: 1 for he would not w in Jewry, because G4043
8:12 me shall not w in darkness, but shall G4043
11: 9 the day? If any man w in the day, he G4043
10 But if a man w in the night, he G4043
12:35 the light with you. W while ye have the G4043
Act 3: 6 Jesus Christ of Nazareth rise up and w. G4043
12 or holiness we had made this man to w? G4043
14:16 all nations to w in their own ways. G4198
21:21 neither to w after the customs. G4043
Ro 4:12 only, but who also w in the steps of that G4748
6: 4 so we also should w in newness of life. G4043
8: 1 Christ Jesus, who w not after the flesh, G4043
4 in us, who w not after the flesh, but G4043
13:13 Let us w honestly, as in the day; not in G4043
1Co 3: 3 are ye not carnal, and w as men? G4043
7:17 him w. And so ordain I in all churches. G4043
2Co 5: 7 (For we w by faith, not by sight:) G4043
6:16 in them, and w in *them*; and I will be G1704
10: 3 For though we w in the flesh, we do not G4043
Gal 5:16 *This* I say then, W in the Spirit, and ye G4043
25 If we live in the Spirit, let us also w in G4748
6:16 And as many as w according to this G4748
Eph 2:10 ordained that we should w in them. G4043
4: 1 you that ye w worthy of the vocation G4043
17 Lord, that ye henceforth w not as other G4043
17 Gentiles w, in the vanity of their mind, G4043
5: 2 And w in love, as Christ also hath loved G4043
8 light in the Lord: w as children of light: G4043
15 See then that ye w circumspectly, not G4043
Php 3:16 attained, let us w by the same rule, let G4748
17 w so as ye have us for an ensample. G4043
18 (For many w, of whom I have told you G4043
Col 1:10 That ye might w worthy of the Lord G4043
2: 6 Christ Jesus the Lord, *so* w ye in him: G4043
4: 5 W in wisdom toward them that are G4043
1Th 2:12 That ye would w worthy of God, who G4043
4: 1 how ye ought to w and to please God, G4043
12 That ye may w honestly toward them G4043
2Th 3:11 there are some which w among you G4043
2Pt 2:10 But chiefly them that w after the flesh G4198
1Jn 1: 6 with him, and w in darkness, we lie, G4043
7 But if we w in the light, as he is in the G4043
2: 6 himself also so to w, even as he walked. G4043
2Jn 6 And this is love, that we w after his G4043
6 from the beginning, ye should w in it. G4043
3Jn 4 to hear that my children w in truth. G4043
Jude 18 should w after their own ungodly lusts. G4198
Rev 3: 4 and they shall w with me in white: for G4043
9:20 which neither can see, nor hear, nor w: G4043
16:15 he w naked, and they see his shame. G4043
21:24 are saved shall w in the light of it: and G4043

WALKED

Gen 5:22 And Enoch w with God after he begat H1980
24 And Enoch w with God: and he *was* H1980
6: 9 his generations, *and* Noah w with God. H1980
Ex 2: 5 and her maidens w along by the river's H1980
14:29 But the children of Israel w upon dry H1980
Lev 26:40 also they have w contrary unto me; H1980
41 And *that* I also have w contrary unto H3212
Jos 5: 6 For the children of Israel w forty years H1980
Jdg 2:17 which their fathers w in, obeying the H1980
5: 6 and the travellers w through byways. H3212
11:16 up from Egypt, and w through the H3212
1Sa 8: 3 And his sons w not in his ways, but H1980
12: 2 you: and I have w before you from my H1980
2Sa 2:29 And Abner and his men w all that H1980
7: 6 have w in a tent and in a tabernacle. H1980
7 In all *the places* wherein I have w with H1980
11: 2 off his bed, and w upon the roof of the H1980
1Ki 3: 6 according as he w before thee in truth, H1980
8:25 before me as thou hast w before me. H1980
9: 4 David thy father w, in integrity of heart, H1980
11:33 and have not w in my ways, to do *that* H1980
15: 3 And he w in all the sins of his father, H3212
26 of the LORD, and w in the way of his H3212

1Ki 15:34 sight of the LORD, and w in the way of H3212
16: 2 Israel; and thou hast w in the way of H3212
26 For he w in all the way of Jeroboam the H3212
22:43 And he w in all the ways of Asa his H3212
52 of the LORD, and w in the way of his H3212
2Ki 4:35 Then he returned, and w in the house H3212
8:18 And he w in the way of the kings of H3212
27 And he w in the way of the house of H3212
13: 6 Israel sin, *but* w therein: and there H1980
11 who made Israel sin: *but* he w therein. H1980
16: 3 But he w in the way of the kings of H3212
17: 8 And w in the statutes of the heathen, H3212
19 their God, but w in the statutes of H3212
22 For the children of Israel w in all the H3212
20: 3 now how I have w before thee in truth H1980
21:21 And he w in all the way that his father H3212
21 way that his father w in, and served the H1980
22 and w not in the way of the LORD. H1980
22: 2 of the LORD, and w in all the way of H3212
1Ch 17: 6 Wheresoever I have w with all Israel, H1980
8 thou hast w, and have cut off all H1980
2Ch 6:16 in my law, as thou hast w before me. H1980
7:17 David thy father w, and do according to H1980
11:17 w in the way of David and Solomon. H1980
17: 3 because he w in the first ways of H1980
4 God of his father, and w in his H1980
20:32 And he w in the way of Asa his father, H3212
21: 6 And he w in the way of the kings of H3212
12 Because thou hast not w in the ways of H1980
13 But hast w in the way of the kings of H3212
22: 3 He also w in the ways of the house of H1980
5 He w also after their counsel, and went H1980
28: 2 For he w in the ways of the kings of H3212
34: 2 sight of the LORD, and w in the ways of H3212
Est 2:11 And Mordecai w every day before the H1980
Job 29: 3 *when* by his light I w *through* darkness; H3212
31: 5 If I have w with vanity, or if my foot H1980
7 and mine heart w after mine eyes, and H1980
38:16 hast thou w in the search of the depth? H1980
Ps 26: 1 Judge me, O LORD; for I have w in H1980
3 mine eyes: and I have w in thy truth. H1980
55:14 We took sweet counsel together, *and* w H1980
81:12 lust: *and* they w in their own counsels. H3212
13 unto me, *and* Israel had w in my ways! H1980
142: 3 w have they privily laid a snare for me. H1980
Isa 9: 2 The people that w in darkness have H1980
20: 3 Isaiah hath w naked and barefoot H1980
38: 3 thee, how I have w before thee in truth H1980
Jer 2: 5 w after vanity, and are become vain? H3212
8 and w after *things that* do not profit. H1980
7:24 their ear, but w in the counsels *and* H3212
8: 2 whom they have w, and whom they H1980
9:13 not obeyed my voice, neither w therein; H1980
14 But have w after the imagination of H3212
11: 8 their ear, but w every one in the H3212
16:11 the LORD, and have w after other gods, H3212
32:23 not thy voice, neither w in thy law; they H1980
44:10 they feared, nor w in my law, nor in my H1980
23 of the LORD, nor w in his law, nor in H1980
Ezk 5: 6 my statutes, they have not w in them. H1980
7 you, *and* have not w in my statutes, H1980
11:12 for ye have not w in my statutes, H1980
16:47 Yet hast thou not w after their ways, H1980
18: 9 Hath w in my statutes, and hath kept H1980
17 judgments, hath w in my statutes; he H1980
20:13 wilderness: they w not in my statutes, H1980
16 judgments, and w not in my statutes, H1980
21 against me: they w not in my statutes, H1980
23:31 Thou hast w in the way of thy sister; H1980
28:14 of God; thou hast w up and down in the H1980
Dan 4:29 At the end of twelve months he w in the H1981
Hos 5:11 he willingly w after the commandment. H1980
Am 2: 4 err, after the which their fathers have w: H1980
Nah 2:11 lion, *even* the old lion, w, *and* the lion's H1980
Zec 1:11 said, We have w to and fro through H1980
6: 7 So they w to and fro through the earth. H1980
Mal 2: 6 in his lips: he w with me in peace and H1980
3:14 and that we have w mournfully before H1980
Mt 14:29 ship, he w on the water, to go to Jesus. G4043
Mk 1:16 Now as he w by the sea of Galilee, he G4043
5:42 damsel arose, and w; for she was *of the* G4043
16:12 as they w, and went into the country. G4043
Jn 1:36 And looking upon Jesus as he w, he G4043
5: 9 up his bed, and w: and on the same day G4043
6:66 went back, and w no more with him. G4043
7: 1 After these things Jesus w in Galilee: G4043
10:23 And Jesus w in the temple in Solomon's G4043
11:54 Jesus therefore w no more openly G4043
Act 3: 8 And he leaping up stood, and w, and G4043

Act 14: 8 his mother's womb, who never had w: G4043
10 on thy feet. And he leaped and w. G4043
2Co 10: 2 of us as if we w according to the flesh. G4043
12:18 a gain of you? w we not in the same G4043
18 spirit? *w we* not in the same steps? G4043
Gal 2:14 But when I saw that they w not G3716
Eph 2: 2 Wherein in time past ye w according to G4043
Col 3: 7 In the which ye also w some time, G4043
1Pt 4: 3 Gentiles, when we w in lasciviousness, G4198
1Jn 2: 6 himself also so to walk, even as he w. G4043

WALKEDST

Jn 21:18 thyself, and w whither thou wouldest: G4043

WALKEST

Dt 6: 7 and when thou w by the way, and H3212
11:19 and when thou w by the way, when H3212
1Ki 2:42 goest out, and w abroad any whither, H1980
Isa 43: 2 thee: when thou w through the fire, H3212
Act 21:24 also w orderly, and keepest the law. G4748
Ro 14:15 *thy* meat, now w thou not charitably. G4043
3Jn 3 is in thee, even as thou w in the truth. G4043

WALKETH

Gen 24:65 man *is* this that w in the field to meet H1980
Dt 23:14 For the LORD thy God w in the midst of H1980
1Sa 12: 2 And now, behold, the king w before H1980
Job 18: 8 by his own feet, and he w upon a snare. H1980
22:14 not; and he w in the circuit of heaven. H1980
34: 8 of iniquity, and w with wicked men. H3212
Ps 1: 1 Blessed *is* the man that w not in the H1980
15: 2 He that w uprightly, and worketh H1980
39: 6 Surely every man w in a vain shew: H1980
73: 9 and their tongue w through the earth. H1980
91: 6 *Nor* for the pestilence *that* w in H1980
101: 6 w in a perfect way, he shall serve me. H1980
104: 3 who w upon the wings of the wind: H1980
128: 1 feareth the LORD; that w in his ways. H1980
Prv 6:12 A naughty person, a wicked man, w H1980
10: 9 He that w uprightly walketh surely: but H1980
9 He that walketh uprightly w surely: but H3212
13:20 He that w with wise *men* shall be wise: H1980
14: 2 He that w in his uprightness feareth the H1980
15:21 a man of understanding w uprightly. H1980
19: 1 Better *is* the poor that w in his H1980
20: 7 The just *man* w in his integrity: his H1980
28: 6 Better *is* the poor that w in his H1980
18 Whoso w uprightly shall be saved: but H1980
26 whoso w wisely, he shall be delivered. H1980
Ecc 2:14 head; but the fool w in darkness: and I H1980
10: 3 Yea also, when he that is a fool w by H1980
Isa 33:15 He that w righteously, and speaketh H1980
50:10 of his servant, that w *in* darkness, and H1980
65: 2 people, which w in a way *that was* not H1980
Jer 10:23 *is* not in man that w to direct his steps. H1980
23:17 every one that w after the imagination H1980
Ezk 11:21 But *as for them* whose heart w after the H1980
Mic 2: 7 words do good to him that w uprightly? H1980
Mt 12:43 out of a man, he w through dry places, G1330
Lk 11:24 out of a man, he w through dry places, G1330
Jn 12:35 you: for he that w in darkness knoweth G4043
2Th 3: 6 every brother that w disorderly, and G4043
1Pt 5: 8 as a roaring lion, w about, seeking G4043
1Jn 2:11 is in darkness, and w in darkness, and G4043
Rev 2: 1 right hand, who w in the midst of the G4043

WALKING

Gen 3: 8 of the LORD God w in the garden in the H1980
Dt 2: 7 he knoweth thy w through this great H3212
1Ki 3: 3 And Solomon loved the LORD, w in the H3212
16:19 sight of the LORD, in w in the way of H3212
Job 1: 7 earth, and from w up and down in it. H1980
2: 2 earth, and from w up and down in it. H1980
31:26 it shined, or the moon w *in* brightness; H1980
Ecc 10: 7 princes w as servants upon the earth. H1980
Isa 3:16 and wanton eyes, w and mincing *as* H1980
20: 2 And he did so, w naked and barefoot. H1980
57: 2 beds, *each one* w in his uprightness. H1980
Jer 6:28 They *are* all grievous revolters, w with H1980
Dan 3:25 four men loose, w in the midst of the H1981
Mic 2:11 If a man w in the spirit and falsehood H1980
Mt 4:18 And Jesus, w by the sea of Galilee, saw G4043
14:25 Jesus went unto them, w on the sea. G4043
26 And when the disciples saw him w on G4043
Mk 6:48 unto them, w upon the sea, and would G4043
49 But when they saw him w upon the sea, G4043
8:24 up, and said, I see men as trees, w. G4043
11:27 and as he was w in the temple, there G4043
Lk 1: 6 righteous before God, w in all the G4198

Jn 6:19 they see Jesus w on the sea, and *G4043*
Act 3: 8 w, and leaping, and praising God. *G4043*
9 And all the people saw him w and *G4043*
9:31 were edified; and w in the fear of the *G4198*
2Co 4: 2 of dishonesty, not w in craftiness, nor *G4043*
2Pt 3: 3 days scoffers, w after their own lusts, *G4198*
2Jn 4 of thy children w in truth, as we have *G4043*
Jude 16 These are murmurers, complainers, w *G4198*

WALL

Gen 49: 6 in their selfwill they digged down a w. H7794
22 a well; *whose* branches run over the w: H7791
Ex 14:22 the waters *were* a w unto them on their H2346
29 the waters *were* a w unto them on their H2346
Lev 14:37 which in sight *are* lower than the w; H7023
25:31 which have no w round about them H2346
Nu 22:24 of the vineyards, a w *being* on this side, H1447
24 *being* on this side, and a w on that side. H1447
25 thrust herself unto the w, and crushed H7023
25 against the w: and he smote her again. H7023
35: 4 *shall reach* from the w of the city and H7023
Jos 2:15 town w, and she dwelt upon the wall. H2346
15 town wall, and she dwelt upon the w. H2346
6: 5 shout; and the w of the city shall fall H2346
20 shout, that the w fell down flat, so that H2346
1Sa 18:11 David even to the w *with it*. And David H7023
19:10 David even to the w with the javelin; H7023
10 javelin into the w: and David fled, and H7023
20:25 upon a seat by the w: and Jonathan H7023
25:16 They were a w unto us both by night H2346
22 light any that pisseth against the w. H7023
34 light any that pisseth against the w. H7023
31:10 his body to the w of Beth-shan. H2346
12 his sons from the w of Beth-shan, and H2346
2Sa 11:20 not that they would shoot from the w? H2346
21 him from the w, that he died in Thebez? H2346
21 went ye nigh the w? then say thou, Thy H2346
24 And the shooters shot from off the w H2346
18:24 the gate unto the w, and lifted up his H2346
20:15 Joab battered the w, to throw it down. H2346
21 head shall be thrown to thee over the w. H2346
22:30 by my God have I leaped over a w. H7791
1Ki 3: 1 and the w of Jerusalem round about. H2346
4:33 out of the w: he spake also of beasts, H7023
6: 5 And against the w of the house he built H7023
6 for without *in the* w of the house he
27 touched the *one* w, and the wing of the H7023
27 touched the other w; and their wings H7023
31 *and* side posts *were* a fifth part *of the w*.
33 posts *of* olive tree, a fourth part *of the w*.
9:15 and Millo, and the w of Jerusalem, and H2346
14:10 against the w, *and* him that is shut H7023
16:11 that pisseth against a w, neither of his H7023
20:30 city; and *there* a w fell upon twenty and H2346
21:21 against the w, and him that is shut H7023
23 shall eat Jezebel by the w of Jezreel. H2426
2Ki 3:27 offering upon the w. And there was H2346
4:10 I pray thee, on the w; and let us set for H7023
6:26 by upon the w, there cried a woman H2346
30 by upon the w, and the people looked, H2346
9: 8 against the w, and him that is shut H7023
33 sprinkled on the w, and on the horses: H7023
14:13 brake down the w of Jerusalem from H2346
18:26 the ears of the people that *are* on the w. H2346
27 which sit on the w, that they may eat H2346
20: 2 Then he turned his face to the w, and H7023
2Ch 3:11 reaching to the w of the house: and the H7023
12 reaching to the w of the house: and the H7023
25:23 brake down the w of Jerusalem from H2346
26: 6 brake down the w of Gath, and the wall H2346
6 of Gath, and the w of Jabneh, and the H2346
6 of Jabneh, and the w of Ashdod, and H2346
9 the turning *of the w*, and fortified them.
27: 3 and on the w of Ophel he built much. H2346
32: 5 built up all the w that was broken, and H2346
5 and another w without, and repaired H2346
18 that *were* on the w, to affright them, H2346
33:14 Now after this he built a w without the H2346
36:19 brake down the w of Jerusalem, and H2346
Ezr 5: 3 build this house, and to make up this w? H846
9: 9 give us a w in Judah and in Jerusalem. H1447
Neh 1: 3 and reproach: the w of Jerusalem also H2346
2: 8 house, and for the w of the city, and for H2346
15 and viewed the w, and turned back, and H2346
17 let us build up the w of Jerusalem, that H2346
3: 8 fortified Jerusalem unto the broad w. H2346
13 cubits on the w unto the dung gate. H2346
15 thereof, and the w of the pool of Siloah H2346
19 to the armoury at the turning *of the w*.
Neh 3:20 the turning *of the w* unto the door of the
24 turning *of the w*, even unto the corner.
25 the turning *of the w*, and the tower which
27 that lieth out, even unto the w of Ophel. H2346
4: 1 we builded the w, he was wroth, and H2346
3 he shall even break down their stone w. H2346
6 So built we the w; and all the wall was H2346
6 So built we the wall; and all the w was H2346
10 so that we are not able to build the w. H2346
13 places behind the w, *and* on the higher H2346
15 of us to the w, every one unto his work. H2346
17 They which builded on the w, and they H2346
19 upon the w, one far from another. H2346
5:16 in the work of this w, neither bought we H2346
6: 1 I had builded the w, and *that* there was H2346
6 thou buildest the w, that thou mayest H2346
15 So the w was finished in the twenty and H2346
7: 1 Now it came to pass, when the w was H2346
12:27 And at the dedication of the w of H2346
30 the people, and the gates, and the w. H2346
31 of Judah upon the w, and appointed H2346
31 hand upon the w toward the dung gate: H2346
37 going up of the w, above the house of H2346
38 the people upon the w, from beyond the H2346
38 of the furnaces even unto the broad w; H2346
13:21 lodge ye about the w? if ye do *so* again, I H2346
Ps 18:29 and by my God have I leaped over a w. H7791
62: 3 w *shall ye be, and as* a tottering fence. H7023
Prv 18:11 and as an high w in his own conceit. H2346
24:31 the stone w thereof was broken down. H1444
Song 2: 9 behind our w, he looketh forth at H3796
8: 9 If she *be* a w, we will build upon her a H2346
10 I *am* a w, and my breasts like towers: H2346
Isa 2:15 high tower, and upon every fenced w, H2346
5: 5 break down the w thereof, and it shall H1447
22:10 have ye broken down to fortify the w. H2346
25: 4 ones *is* as a storm *against* the w. H7023
30:13 out in a high w, whose breaking cometh H2346
36:11 the ears of the people that *are* on the w. H2346
12 that sit upon the w, that they may eat H2346
38: 2 the w, and prayed unto the LORD, H7023
59:10 We grope for the w like the blind, and H7023
Jer 15:20 a fenced brasen w: and they shall fight H2346
49:27 And I will kindle a fire in the w of H2346
51:44 him: yea, the w of Babylon shall fall. H2346
Lam 2: 8 to destroy the w of the daughter of H2346
8 w to lament; they languished together. H2346
18 Their heart cried unto the Lord, O w of H2346
Ezk 4: 3 and set it *for* a w of iron between thee H7023
8: 7 when I looked, behold a hole in the w. H7023
8 man, dig now in the w: and when I had H7023
8 I had digged in the w, behold a door. H7023
10 pourtrayed upon the w round about. H7023
12: 5 Dig thou through the w in their sight, H7023
7 through the w with mine hand; I H7023
12 dig through the w to carry out thereby: H7023
13:10 and one built up a w, and, lo, others H2434
12 Lo, when the w is fallen, shall it not be H7023
14 So will I break down the w that ye have H7023
15 wrath upon the w, and upon them that H7023
15 say unto you, The w *is* no *more*, neither H7023
23:14 upon the w, the images of the H7023
38:20 and every w shall fall to the ground. H2346
40: 5 And behold a w on the outside of the H2346
41: 5 After he measured the w of the house, H7023
6 entered into the w which *was* of the H7023
6 they had not hold in the w of the house. H7023
9 The thickness of the w, which *was* for H7023
12 broad; and the w of the building *was* H7023
17 and by all the w round about within H7023
20 trees made, and *on* the w of the temple. H7023
42: 7 And the w that *was* without over H1447
10 thickness of the w of the court toward H1444
12 directly before the w toward the east, H1448
20 four sides: it had a w round about, five H2346
43: 8 my posts, and the w between me and H7023
Dan 5: 5 upon the plaister of the w of the king's H3797
9:25 and the w, even in troublous times. H2742
Hos 2: 6 a w, that she shall not find her paths. H1447
Joel 2: 7 shall climb the w like men of war; and H2346
9 shall run upon the w, they shall climb H2346
Am 1: 7 But I will send a fire on the w of Gaza, H2346
10 But I will send a fire on the w of Tyrus, H2346
14 But I will kindle a fire in the w of H2346
5:19 hand on the w, and a serpent bit him. H7023
7: 7 stood upon a w *made* by a plumbline, H2346
Nah 2: 5 make haste to the w thereof, and the H2346
3: 8 the sea, *and* her w *was* from the sea? H2346
Hab 2:11 For the stone shall cry out of the w, and H7023
Zec 2: 5 will be unto her a w of fire round H2346
Act 9:25 and let *him* down by the w in a basket. *G5038*
23: 3 thee, *thou* whited w: for sittest thou to *G5109*
2Co 11:33 down by the w, and escaped his hands. *G5038*
Eph 2:14 the middle w of partition *between us*; *G3320*
Rev 21:12 And had a w great and high, *and* had *G5038*
14 And the w of the city had twelve *G5038*
15 the gates thereof, and the w thereof. *G5038*
17 And he measured the w thereof, an *G5038*
18 And the building of the w of it was *of* *G5038*
19 And the foundations of the w of the city *G5038*

WALLED

Lev 25:29 house in a w city, then he may redeem H2346
30 that *is* in the w city shall be established H2346
Nu 13:28 and the cities *are* w, *and* very great: and H1219
Dt 1:28 *are* great and w up to heaven; and H1219

WALLOW

Jer 6:26 sackcloth, and w thyself in ashes: make H6428
25:34 Howl, ye shepherds, and cry; and w H6428
48:26 Moab also shall w in his vomit, and he H5606
Ezk 27:30 they shall w themselves in the ashes: H6428

WALLOWED

2Sa 20:12 And Amasa w in blood in the midst of H1556
Mk 9:20 he fell on the ground, and w foaming. *G2947*

WALLOWING

2Pt 2:22 that was washed to her w in the mire. *G2946*

WALLS

Lev 14:37 the plague *be* in the w of the house with H7023
39 plague be spread in the w of the house; H7023
Dt 3: 5 All these cities *were* fenced with high w, H2346
28:52 thy high and fenced w come down, H2346
1Ki 4:13 great cities with w and brasen bars: H2346
6: 5 about, *against* the w of the house H7023
6 not be fastened in the w of the house. H7023
15 And he built the w of the house within H7023
15 the house, and the w of the cieling: *and* H7023
16 both the floor and the w with boards of H7023
29 And he carved all the w of the house H7023
2Ki 25: 4 the gate between two w, which *is* by the H2346
10 down the w of Jerusalem round about. H2346
1Ch 29: 4 to overlay the w of the houses *withal*: H7023
2Ch 3: 7 the posts, and the w thereof, and the H7023
7 gold; and graved cherubims on the w. H7023
8: 5 fenced cities, with w, gates, and bars; H2346
14: 7 make about *them* w, and towers, gates, H2346
Ezr 4:12 w *thereof*, and joined the foundations. H7792
13 builded, and the w set up *again, then* H7792
16 *again*, and the w thereof set up, by this H7792
5: 8 is laid in the w, and this work goeth H3797
9 build this house, and to make up these w? H846
Neh 2:13 and viewed the w of Jerusalem, which H2346
4: 7 heard that the w of Jerusalem were H2346
Job 24:11 *Which* make oil within their w, *and* H7791
Ps 51:18 Zion: build thou the w of Jerusalem. H2346
55:10 about it upon the w thereof: mischief H2346
122: 7 Peace be within thy w, *and* prosperity H2426
Prv 25:28 *that is* broken down, *and* without w. H2346
Song 5: 7 of the w took away my veil from me. H2346
Isa 22: 5 the w, and of crying to the mountains. H7023
11 between the two w for the water of the H2346
25:12 high fort of thy w shall he bring down, H2346
26: 1 will *God* appoint *for* w and bulwarks. H2346
49:16 thy w *are* continually before me. H2346
56: 5 and within my w a place and a name H2346
60:10 shall build up thy w, and their kings H2346
18 thy w Salvation, and thy gates Praise. H2346
62: 6 I have set watchmen upon thy w, O H2346
Jer 1:15 against all the w thereof round about, H2346
18 pillar, and brasen w against the whole H2346
5:10 Go ye up upon her w, and destroy; but H8284
21: 4 you without the w, and I will assemble H2346
39: 4 w: and he went out the way of the plain. H2346
8 and brake down the w of Jerusalem. H2346
50:15 are fallen, her w are thrown down: for H2346
51:12 Set up the standard upon the w of H2346
58 hosts; The broad w of Babylon shall be H2346
52: 7 between the two w, which *was* by the H2346
14 all the w of Jerusalem round about. H2346
Lam 2: 7 of the enemy the w of her palaces; they H2346
Ezk 26: 4 And they shall destroy the w of Tyrus, H2346
9 of war against thy w, and with his axes H2346
10 cover thee: thy w shall shake at the H2346
12 shall break down thy w, and destroy thy H2346
27:11 *were* upon thy w round about, and the H2346

Ezk 27:11 shields upon thy w round about; they H2346
33:30 thee by the w and in the doors of H7023
38:11 w, and having neither bars nor gates, H2346
41:13 the w thereof, an hundred cubits long; H7023
22 thereof, and the w thereof, *were* of H7023
25 made upon the w; and *there were* thick H7023
Mic 7:11 *In* the day that thy w are to be built, *in* H1447
Zec 2: 4 *as* towns without w for the multitude of H6519
Heb 11:30 By faith the w of Jericho fell down, after *G5038*

WANDER
Gen 20:13 God caused me to w from my father's H8582
Nu 14:33 And your children shall w in the H7462
32:13 he made them w in the wilderness forty H5128
Dt 27:18 the blind to w out of the way. And H7686
Job 12:24 and causeth them to w in a wilderness H8582
38:41 cry unto God, they w for lack of meat. H8582
Ps 55: 7 Lo, *then* would I w far off, *and* remain H5074
59:15 Let them w up and down for meat, and H5128
107:40 causeth them to w in the wilderness, H8582
119:10 let me not w from thy commandments. H7686
Isa 47:15 thy youth: they shall w every one to his H8582
Jer 14:10 have they loved to w, they have not H5128
48:12 shall cause him to w, and shall empty H6808
Am 8:12 And they shall w from sea to sea, and H5128

WANDERED
Gen 21:14 and w in the wilderness of Beer-sheba. H8582
Jos 14:10 *children of* Israel w in the wilderness: H1980
Ps 107: 4 They w in the wilderness in a solitary H8582
Isa 16: 8 *even* unto Jazer, they w *through* the H8582
Lam 4:14 They have w *as* blind *men* in the H5128
15 fled away and w, they said among the H5128
Ezk 34: 6 My sheep w through all the mountains, H7686
Am 4: 8 So two *or* three cities w unto one city, H5128
Heb 11:37 the sword: they w about in sheepskins *G4022*
38 not worthy:) they w in deserts, and *in* *G4105*

WANDERERS
Jer 48:12 send unto him w, that shall cause him H6808
Hos 9:17 and they shall be w among the nations. H5074

WANDEREST
Jer 2:20 green tree thou w, playing the harlot. H6808

WANDERETH
Job 15:23 He w abroad for bread, *saying*, Where H5074
Prv 21:16 The man that w out of the way of H8582
27: 8 As a bird that w from her nest, so *is* a H5074
8 nest, so *is* a man that w from his place. H5074
Isa 16: 3 the outcasts; bewray not him that w. H5074
Jer 49: 5 and none shall gather up him that w. H5074

WANDERING
Gen 37:15 behold, *he was* w in the field: and the H8582
Prv 26: 2 As the bird by w, as the swallow by H5110
Ecc 6: 9 Better *is* the sight of the eyes than the w H1980
Isa 16: 2 For it shall be, *that*, as a w bird cast out H5074
1Ti 5:13 And withal they learn *to be* idle, w *G4022*
Jude 13 their own shame; w stars, to whom is *G4107*

WANDERINGS
Ps 56: 8 Thou tellest my w: put thou my tears H5112

WANT
Dt 28:48 nakedness, and in w of all *things:* and H2640
57 she shall eat them for w of all *things* H2640
Jdg 18:10 *is* no w of any thing that *is* in the earth. H4270
19:19 thy servants: *there is* no w of any thing. H4270
Job 24: 8 embrace the rock for w of a shelter. H1097
30: 3 For w and famine *they were* solitary; H2639
31:19 If I have seen any perish for w of H1097
Ps 23: 1 LORD *is* my shepherd; I shall not w. H2637
34: 9 for *there is* no w to them that fear him. H4270
10 the LORD shall not w any good *thing*. H2637
Prv 6:11 travelleth, and thy w as an armed man. H4270
10:21 many: but fools die for w of wisdom. H2638
13:23 is *that is* destroyed for w of judgment. H3808
25 soul: but the belly of the wicked shall w. H2637
14:28 honour: but in the w of people *is* the H657
21: 5 but of every one *that is* hasty only to w. H4270
22:16 to the rich, *shall* surely *come* to w. H4270
24:34 travelleth; and thy w as an armed man. H4270
Isa 34:16 fail, none shall w her mate: for my H6485
Jer 33:17 David shall never w a man to sit upon H3772
18 Neither shall the priests the Levites w a H3772
35:19 w a man to stand before me for ever. H3772
Lam 4: 9 through for *w of* the fruits of the field.
Ezk 4:17 That they may w bread and water, and H2637
Am 4: 6 your cities, and w of bread in all your H2640
Mk 12:44 but she of her w did cast in all that she *G5304*
Lk 15:14 in that land; and he began to be in w. *G5302*
2Co 8:14 *be a supply* for their w, that their *G5303*
14 for your w: that there may be equality: *G5303*
9:12 only supplieth the w of the saints, but *G5303*
Php 4:11 Not that I speak in respect of w: for I *G5304*

WANTED
Jer 44:18 unto her, we have w all *things*, and H2637
Jn 2: 3 And when they w wine, the mother of *G5302*
2Co 11: 9 with you, and w, I was chargeable to *G5302*

WANTETH
Dt 15: 8 for his need, *in that* which he w. H2637
Prv 9: 4 that w understanding, she saith to him, H2638
16 that w understanding, she saith to him, H2638
10:19 In the multitude of words there w not H2308
28:16 The prince that w understanding *is* H2638
Ecc 6: 2 honour, so that he w nothing for his H2638
Song 7: 2 goblet, *which* w not liquor: thy belly H2637

WANTING
2Ki 10:19 priests; let none be w: for I have a great H6485
19 shall be w, he shall not live. But H6485
Prv 19: 7 *with* words, *yet* they *are* w *to him*. H3808
Ecc 1:15 that which is w cannot be numbered. H2642
Dan 5:27 in the balances, and art found w. H2627
Tit 1: 5 the things that are w, and ordain elders *G3007*
3:13 that nothing be w unto them. *G3007*
Jas 1: 4 may be perfect and entire, w nothing. *G3007*

WANTON
Isa 3:16 forth necks and w eyes, walking and H8265
1Ti 5:11 wax w against Christ, they will marry; *G2691*
Jas 5: 5 earth, and been w; ye have nourished *G4684*

WANTONNESS
Ro 13:13 and w, not in strife and envying. *G766*
2Pt 2:18 *through much* w, those that were clean *G766*

WANTS
Jdg 19:20 *let* all thy w *lie* upon me; only lodge H4270
Php 2:25 and he that ministered to my w. *G5532*

WAR
Gen 14: 2 *That these* made w with Bera king of H4421
Ex 1:10 falleth out any w, they join also unto H4421
13:17 they see w, and they return to Egypt: H4421
15: 3 The LORD *is* a man of w: the LORD *is* H4421
17:16 LORD *will have* w with Amalek from H4421
32:17 *There is* a noise of w in the camp. H4421
Nu 1: 3 able to go forth to w in Israel: thou and H6635
20 all that were able to go forth to w; H6635
22 all that were able to go forth to w; H6635
24 all that were able to go forth to w; H6635
26 all that were able to go forth to w; H6635
28 all that were able to go forth to w; H6635
30 all that were able to go forth to w; H6635
32 all that were able to go forth to w; H6635
34 all that were able to go forth to w; H6635
36 all that were able to go forth to w; H6635
38 all that were able to go forth to w; H6635
40 all that were able to go forth to w; H6635
42 all that were able to go forth to w; H6635
45 that were able to go forth to w in Israel; H6635
10: 9 And if ye go to w in your land against H4421
26: 2 all that are able to go to w in Israel. H6635
31: 3 unto the w, and let them go against H6635
4 tribes of Israel, shall ye send to the w. H6635
5 tribe, twelve thousand armed for w. H6635
6 And Moses sent them to the w, a H6635
6 the priest, to the w, with the holy H6635
21 unto the men of w which went to the H6635
27 that took the w upon them, who went H4421
28 of the men of w which went out to H4421
32 which the men of w had caught, was H6635
36 that went out to w, was in number three H6635
49 sum of the men of w which *are* under H4421
53 (*For* the men of w had taken spoil, H6635
32: 6 brethren go to w, and shall ye sit here? H4421
20 ye will go armed before the LORD to w, H4421
27 man armed for w, before the LORD to H6635
Dt 1:41 w, ye were ready to go up into the hill. H4421
2:14 of the men of w were wasted out from H4421
16 all the men of w were consumed and H4421
3:18 of Israel, all *that are* meet for the w. H2428
4:34 by wonders, and by w, and by a mighty H4421
20:12 but will make w against thee, then thou H4421
Dt 20:19 time, in making w against it to take it, H3898
20 w with thee, until it be subdued. H4421
21:10 When thou goest forth to w against H4421
24: 5 shall not go out to w, neither shall he be H6635
Jos 4:13 About forty thousand prepared for w H6635
5: 4 all the men of w, died in the wilderness H4421
6 *that were* men of w, which came out of H4421
6: 3 the city, all *ye* men of w, *and* go round H4421
8: 1 all the people of w with thee, and arise, H4421
3 all the people of w, to go up against Ai: H4421
11 And all the people, *even the people* of w H4421
10: 5 before Gibeon, and made w against it. H3898
7 all the people of w with him, and all the H4421
24 of the men of w which went with him, H4421
11: 7 So Joshua came, and all the people of w H4421
18 Joshua made w a long time with all H4421
23 tribes. And the land rested from w. H4421
14:11 for w, both to go out, and to come in. H4421
15 And the land had rest from w. H4421
17: 1 w, therefore he had Gilead and Bashan. H4421
22:12 at Shiloh, to go up to w against them. H6635
Jdg 3: 2 to teach them w, at the least such as H4421
10 and went out to w: and the LORD H4421
5: 8 They chose new gods; then *was* w in H3901
11: 4 of Ammon made w against Israel. H3898
5 of Ammon made w against Israel, the H3898
27 me wrong to w against me: the LORD H3898
18:11 men appointed with weapons of w. H4421
16 their weapons of w, which *were* of the H4421
17 *that were* appointed with weapons of w. H4421
20:17 drew sword: all these *were* men of w. H4421
21:22 his wife in the w: for ye did not give H4421
1Sa 8:12 of w, and instruments of his chariots. H4421
14:52 And there was sore w against the H4421
16:18 man, and a man of w, and prudent in H4421
17:33 and he a man of w from his youth. H4421
18: 5 over the men of w, and he was accepted H4421
19: 8 And there was w again: and David H4421
23: 8 the people together to w, to go down to H4421
28:15 the Philistines make w against me, and H3898
2Sa 1:27 fallen, and the weapons of w perished! H4421
3: 1 Now there was long w between the H4421
6 And it came to pass, while there was w H4421
11: 7 people did, and how the w prospered. H4421
18 David all the things concerning the w; H4421
19 the matters of the w unto the king, H4421
17: 8 of w, and will not lodge with the people. H4421
21:15 Moreover the Philistines had yet w H4421
22:35 He teacheth my hands to w; so that a H4421
1Ki 2: 5 shed the blood of w in peace, and put H4421
5 put the blood of w upon his girdle that H4421
9:22 they *were* men of w, and his servants, H4421
14:30 And there was w between Rehoboam H4421
15: 6 And there was w between Rehoboam H4421
7 was w between Abijam and Jeroboam. H4421
16 And there was w between Asa and H4421
32 And there was w between Asa and H4421
20:18 they be come out for w, take them alive. H4421
22: 1 without w between Syria and Israel. H4421
2Ki 8:28 son of Ahab to the w against Hazael H4421
13:25 his father by w. Three times did Joash H4421
14: 7 and took Selah by w, and called the H4421
16: 5 up to Jerusalem to w: and they besieged H4421
18:20 strength for the w. Now on whom dost H4421
24:16 strong *and* apt for w, even them the H4421
25: 4 and all the men of w *fled* by night by H4421
19 set over the men of w, and five men of H4421
1Ch 5:10 And in the days of Saul they made w H4421
18 and skilful in w, *were* four and forty H4421
18 and threescore, that went out to the w. H6635
19 And they made w with the Hagarites, H4421
22 slain, because the w *was* of God. And H4421
7: 4 bands of soldiers for w, six and thirty H4421
11 *soldiers*, fit to go out for w *and* battle. H6635
40 that were apt to the w *and* to battle *was* H6635
12: 1 the mighty men, helpers of the w. H4421
8 *and* men of w *fit* for the battle, that H6635
23 armed to the w, *and* came to David H6635
24 eight hundred, ready armed to the w. H6635
25 w, seven thousand and one hundred. H6635
33 forth to battle, expert in w, with all H4421
33 all instruments of w, fifty thousand, H4421
35 And of the Danites expert in w twenty H4421
36 to battle, expert in w, forty thousand. H4421
37 of instruments of w for the battle, an H6635
38 All these men of w, that could keep H4421
18:10 Hadarezer had w with Tou;) and *with* H4421
20: 4 that there arose w at Gezer with the H4421
5 And there was w again with the H4421

1Ch 20: 6 And yet again there was w at Gath, H4421
28: 3 *been* a man of w, and hast shed blood. H4421
2Ch 6:34 If thy people go out to w against their H4421
8: 9 but they *were* men of w, and chief of his H4421
13: 2 was w between Abijah and Jeroboam. H4421
3 of valiant men of w, *even* four hundred H4421
14: 6 rest, and he had no w in those years; H4421
15:19 And there was no *more* w unto the five H4421
17:10 they made no w against Jehoshaphat. H3898
13 and the men of w, mighty men of H4421
18 thousand ready prepared for the w. H6635
18: 3 and *we will be* with thee in the w. H4421
22: 5 king of Israel to w against Hazael king H4421
25: 5 w, that could handle spear and shield. H6635
26:11 that went out to w by bands, according H6635
13 that made w with mighty power, H4421
28:12 up against them that came from the w, H6635
32: 6 And he set captains of w over the H4421
33:14 of w in all the fenced cities of Judah. H2428
35:21 house wherewith I have w: for God H4421
Job 5:20 and in w from the power of the sword. H4421
10:17 me; changes and w *are* against me. H6635
38:23 trouble, against the day of battle and w? H4421
Ps 18:34 He teacheth my hands to w, so that a H4421
27: 3 not fear: though w should rise against H4421
55:21 than butter, but w *was* in his heart: his H7128
68:30 thou the people *that* delight in w. H7128
120: 7 peace: but when I speak, they *are* for w. H4421
140: 2 are they gathered together *for* w. H4421
144: 1 my hands to w, *and* my fingers to fight: H7128
Prv 20:18 counsel: and with good advice make w. H4421
24: 6 shalt make thy w: and in multitude of H4421
Ecc 3: 8 hate; a time of w, and a time of peace. H4421
8: 8 no discharge in *that* w; neither shall H4421
9:18 Wisdom *is* better than weapons of w: H7128
Song 3: 8 They all hold swords, *being* expert in w: H4421
Isa 2: 4 neither shall they learn w any more. H4421
3: 2 The mighty man, and the man of w, the H4421
25 by the sword, and thy mighty in the w. H4421
7: 1 Jerusalem to w against it, but could H4421
21:15 bow, and from the grievousness of w. H4421
36: 5 and strength for w: now on whom dost H4421
37: 9 forth to make w with thee. And when H3898
41:12 thee: they that w against thee shall be H4421
42:13 like a man of w: he shall cry, yea, roar; H4421
Jer 4:19 sound of the trumpet, the alarm of w. H4421
6: 4 Prepare ye w against her; arise, and let H4421
23 for w against thee, O daughter of Zion. H4421
21: 2 Babylon maketh w against us; if so be H3898
4 back the weapons of w that *are* in your H4421
28: 8 of w, and of evil, and of pestilence. H4421
38: 4 of the men of w that remain in this H4421
39: 4 and all the men of w, then they fled, and H4421
41: 3 were found there, *and* the men of w. H4421
16 mighty men of w, and the women, and H4421
42:14 we shall see no w, nor hear the sound H4421
48:14 *are* mighty and strong men for the w? H4421
49: 2 will cause an alarm of w to be heard in H4421
26 and all the men of w shall be cut off in H4421
50:30 and all her men of w shall be cut off in H4421
51:20 *and* weapons of w: for with thee will I H4421
32 fire, and the men of w are affrighted. H4421
52: 7 up, and all the men of w fled, and went H4421
25 of the men of w; and seven men of them H4421
Ezk 17:17 for him in the w, by casting up mounts, H4421
26: 9 And he shall set engines of w against H6904
27:10 army, thy men of w: they hanged the H4421
27 and all thy men of w, that *are* in thee, H4421
32:27 their weapons of w: and they have laid H4421
39:20 with all men of w, saith the Lord GOD. H4421
Dan 7:21 I beheld, and the same horn made w H7129
9:26 of the w desolations are determined. H4421
Joel 2: 7 the wall like men of w; and they shall H4421
3: 9 the Gentiles; Prepare w, wake up the H4421
9 men of w draw near; let them come up: H4421
Mic 2: 8 pass by securely as men averse from w. H4421
3: 5 they even prepare w against him. H4421
4: 3 neither shall they learn w any more. H4421
Lk 14:31 Or what king, going to make w against G4171
23:11 And Herod with his men of w set him G4753
2Co 10: 3 in the flesh, we do not w after the flesh: G4754
1Ti 1:18 by them mightest w a good warfare; G4754
Jas 4: 1 of your lusts that w in your members? G4754
2 w, yet ye have not, because ye ask not. G4170
1Pt 2:11 fleshly lusts, which w against the soul; G4754
Rev 11: 7 pit shall make w against them, and G4171
12: 7 And there was w in heaven: Michael G4171
17 and went to make w with the remnant G4171
13: 4 beast? who is able to make w with him? G4170
Rev 13: 7 And it was given unto him to make w G4171
17:14 These shall make w with the Lamb, G4170
19:11 he doth judge and make w. G4170
19 together to make w against him that G4171

WARD
Gen 40: 3 And he put them in w in the house of H4929
4 and they continued a season in w. H4929
7 with him in the w of his lord's house, H4929
41:10 and put me in w in the captain of the H4929
42:17 And he put them all together into w H4929
Lev 24:12 And they put him in w, that the mind of H4929
Nu 15:34 And they put him in w, because it was H4929
2Sa 20: 3 and put them in w, and fed them, but H4931
1Ch 12:29 had kept the w of the house of Saul. H4931
25: 8 And they cast lots, w against *ward*, as H4931
8 And they cast lots, ward against *w*, as
26:16 of the going up, w against ward. H4929
16 of the going up, ward against w. H4929
Neh 12:24 the man of God, w over against ward. H4929
24 the man of God, ward over against w. H4929
25 the w at the thresholds of the gates. H4929
45 porters kept the w of their God, and the H4931
45 of their God, and the w of the H4931
Isa 21: 8 and I am set in my w whole nights: H4931
Jer 37:13 a captain of the w *was* there, whose H6488
Ezk 19: 9 And they put him in w in chains, and H5474
Act 12:10 and the second w, they came unto the G5438

WARDROBE
2Ki 22:14 keeper of the w; (now she dwelt in H899
2Ch 34:22 keeper of the w; (now she dwelt in H899

WARDS
1Ch 9:23 the house of the tabernacle, by w. H4931
26:12 the chief men, *having* w one against H4931
Neh 13:30 appointed the w of the priests and the H4931

WARE
Neh 10:31 And *if* the people of the land bring w or H4728
13:16 and all manner of w, and sold on the H4377
20 sellers of all kind of w lodged without H4465
Lk 8:27 long time, and w no clothes, neither G1737
Act 14: 6 They were w of *it*, and fled unto Lystra G4894
2Ti 4:15 Of whom be thou w also; for he hath G5442

WARES
Jer 10:17 Gather up thy w out of the land, O H3666
Ezk 27:16 multitude of the w of thy making: they H4639
18 multitude of the w of thy making, for H4639
33 When thy w went forth out of the seas, H5801
Jna 1: 5 and cast forth the w that *were* in the H3627

WARFARE
1Sa 28: 1 together for w, to fight with Israel. H6635
Isa 40: 2 unto her, that her w is accomplished, H6635
1Co 9: 7 Who goeth a w any time at his own G4754
2Co 10: 4 (For the weapons of our w *are* not G4752
1Ti 1:18 thou by them mightest war a good w; G4752

WARM
2Ki 4:34 and the flesh of the child waxed w. H2552
Job 6:17 What time they wax w, they vanish: H2215
37:17 How thy garments *are* w, when he H2525
Ecc 4:11 have heat: but how can one be w *alone*? H3179
Isa 44:15 take thereof, and w himself; yea, he H2552
16 saith, Aha, I am w, I have seen the fire: H2552
47:14 a coal to w at, *nor* fire to sit before it. H2552
Hag 1: 6 you, but there is none w; and he that H2527

WARMED
Job 31:20 were *not* w with the fleece of my sheep; H2552
Mk 14:54 the servants, and w himself at the fire. G2328
Jn 18:18 cold: and they w themselves: and Peter G2328
18 Peter stood with them, and w himself. G2328
25 And Simon Peter stood and w himself. G2328
Jas 2:16 Depart in peace, be *ye* w and filled; G2328

WARMETH
Job 39:14 eggs in the earth, and w them in dust, H2552
Isa 44:16 satisfied: yea, he w *himself*, and saith, H2552

WARMING
Mk 14:67 And when she saw Peter w himself, she G2328

WARN
2Ch 19:10 ye shall even w them that they trespass H2094
Ezk 3:18 nor speakest to w the wicked from his H2094
19 Yet if thou w the wicked, and he turn H2094
Ezk 3:21 Nevertheless if thou w the righteous H2094
33: 3 he blow the trumpet, and w the people; H2094
7 at my mouth, and w them from me. H2094
8 dost not speak to w the wicked from H2094
9 Nevertheless, if thou w the wicked of H2094
Act 20:31 w every one night and day with tears. G3560
1Co 4:14 you, but as my beloved sons I w *you*. G3560
1Th 5:14 Now we exhort you, brethren, w them G3560

WARNED
2Ki 6:10 God told him and w him of, and saved H2094
Ps 19:11 Moreover by them is thy servant w: *and* H2094
Ezk 3:21 is w; also thou hast delivered thy soul. H2094
33: 6 the people be not w; if the sword come, H2094
Mt 2:12 And being w of God in a dream that G5537
22 being w of God in a dream, G5537
3: 7 w you to flee from the wrath to come? G5263
Lk 3: 7 w you to flee from the wrath to come? G5263
Act 10:22 of the Jews, was w from God by an holy G5537
Heb 11: 7 By faith Noah, being w of God of things G5537

WARNING
Jer 6:10 To whom shall I speak, and give w, that H5749
Ezk 3:17 my mouth, and give them w from me. H2094
18 givest him not w, nor speakest to warn H2094
20 not given him w, he shall die in his sin, H2094
33: 4 and taketh not w; if the sword come, H2094
5 and took not w; his blood shall be upon H2094
5 he that taketh w shall deliver his soul. H2094
Col 1:28 Whom we preach, w every man, and G3560

WARP
Lev 13:48 Whether *it be* in the w, or woof; of H8359
49 skin, either in the w, or in the woof, or H8359
51 either in the w, or in the woof, or in H8359
52 that garment, whether w or woof, in H8359
53 either in the w, or in the woof, or in H8359
56 skin, or out of the w, or out of the woof: H8359
57 either in the w, or in the woof, or in H8359
58 And the garment, either w, or woof, or H8359
59 or linen, either in the w, or woof, or any H8359

WARRED
Nu 31: 7 And they w against the Midianites, as H6633
42 Moses divided from the men that w, H6633
Jos 24: 9 Moab, arose and w against Israel, and H3898
1Ki 14:19 of Jeroboam, how he w, and how he H3898
20: 1 besieged Samaria, and w against it. H3898
22:45 and how he w, *are* they not written H3898
2Ki 6: 8 Then the king of Syria w against Israel, H3898
14:28 and his might, how he w, and how he H3898
2Ch 26: 6 And he went forth and w against the H3898

WARRETH
2Ti 2: 4 No man that w entangleth himself with G4754

WARRING
2Ki 19: 8 king of Assyria w against Libnah: for H3898
Isa 37: 8 king of Assyria w against Libnah: for H3898
Ro 7:23 But I see another law in my members, w G497

WARRIOR
Isa 9: 5 For every battle of the w *is* with H5431

WARRIORS
1Ki 12:21 men, which were w, to fight against the H4421
2Ch 11: 1 *men*, which were w, to fight against H4421

WARS
Nu 21:14 in the book of the w of the LORD, What H4421
Jdg 3: 1 as had not known all the w of Canaan; H4421
2Sa 8:10 Hadadezer had w with Toi. And *Joram* H4421
1Ki 5: 3 his God for the w which were about H4421
1Ch 22: 8 hast made great w: thou shalt not build H4421
2Ch 12:15 And *there were* w between Rehoboam H4421
16: 9 from henceforth thou shalt have w. H4421
27: 7 and all his w, and his ways, lo, they H4421
Ps 46: 9 He maketh w to cease unto the end of H4421
Mt 24: 6 And ye shall hear of w and rumours of G4171
6 and rumours of w: see that ye be not G4171
Mk 13: 7 And when ye shall hear of w and G4171
7 and rumours of w, be ye not troubled: G4171
Lk 21: 9 But when ye shall hear of w and G4171
Jas 4: 1 From whence *come* w and fightings G4171

WAS See the Appendix.

WASH
Gen 18: 4 be fetched, and w your feet, and rest H7364

W

Gen 19: 2 all night, and w your feet, and ye shall H7364
24:32 and water to w his feet, and the men's H7364
Ex 2: 5 came down to w *herself* at the river; H7364
19:10 morrow, and let them w their clothes, H3526
29: 4 and shalt w them with water. H7364
17 in pieces, and w the inwards of him, H7364
30:18 foot *also of* brass, to w *withal*: and thou H7364
19 For Aaron and his sons shall w their H7364
20 they shall w with water, that they H7364
21 So they shall w their hands and their H7364
40:12 congregation, and w them with water. H7364
30 altar, and put water there, to w *withal*. H7364
Lev 1: 9 But his inwards and his legs shall he w H7364
13 But he shall w the inwards and the legs H7364
6:27 thou shalt w that whereon it was H3526
9:14 And he did w the inwards and the legs, H7364
11:25 of them shall w his clothes, and be H3526
28 of them shall w his clothes, and be H3526
40 carcase of it shall w his clothes, and be H3526
40 carcase of it shall w his clothes, and be H3526
13: 6 he shall w his clothes, and be clean. H3526
34 he shall w his clothes, and be clean. H3526
54 that they w *the thing* wherein the H3526
58 *be*, which thou shalt w, if the plague be H3526
14: 8 And he that is to be cleansed shall w H3526
8 off all his hair, and w himself in water, H7364
9 off: and he shall w his clothes, also he H3526
9 also he shall w his flesh in water, and H7364
47 And he that lieth in the house shall w H3526
47 eateth in the house shall w his clothes. H3526
15: 5 his bed shall w his clothes, and bathe H3526
6 the issue shall w his clothes, and bathe H3526
7 the issue shall w his clothes, and bathe H3526
8 then he shall w his clothes, and bathe H3526
10 *of* those things shall w his clothes, and H3526
11 in water, he shall w his clothes, and H3526
13 his cleansing, and w his clothes, and H3526
16 him, then he shall w all his flesh in H7364
21 her bed shall w his clothes, and bathe H3526
22 she sat upon shall w his clothes, and H3526
27 unclean, and shall w his clothes, and H3526
16: 4 therefore shall he w his flesh in water, H7364
24 And he shall w his flesh with water in H7364
26 the scapegoat shall w his clothes, and H3526
28 And he that burneth them shall w his H3526
17:15 he shall both w his clothes, and bathe H3526
16 But if he w *them* not, nor bathe his H3526
22: 6 things, unless he w his flesh with water. H7364
Nu 8: 7 and let them w their clothes, and *so* H3526
19: 7 Then the priest shall w his clothes, and H3526
8 And he that burneth her shall w his H3526
10 of the heifer shall w his clothes, and be H3526
19 himself, and w his clothes, and bathe H3526
21 separation shall w his clothes; and he H3526
31:24 And ye shall w your clothes on the H3526
Dt 21: 6 slain *man*, shall w their hands over the H7364
23:11 on, he shall w *himself* with water: H7364
Ru 3: 3 W thyself therefore, and anoint thee, H7364
1Sa 25:41 to w the feet of the servants of my lord. H7364
2Sa 11: 8 to thy house, and w thy feet. And Uriah H7364
2Ki 5:10 him, saying, Go and w in Jordan seven H7364
12 of Israel? may I not w in them, and be H7364
13 when he saith to thee, W, and be clean? H7364
2Ch 4: 6 and five on the left, to w in them: such H7364
6 but the sea *was* for the priests to w in. H7364
Job 9:30 If I w myself with snow water, and H7364
Ps 26: 6 I will w mine hands in innocency: so H7364
51: 2 W me throughly from mine iniquity, H3526
7 w me, and I shall be whiter than snow. H3526
58:10 w his feet in the blood of the wicked. H7364
Isa 1:16 W you, make you clean; put away the H7364
Jer 2:22 For though thou w thee with nitre, and H3526
4:14 O Jerusalem, w thine heart from H3526
Ezk 23:40 whom thou didst w thyself, paintedst H7364
Mt 6:17 anoint thine head, and w thy face; *G3538*
15: 2 w not their hands when they eat bread. *G3538*
Mk 7: 3 Jews, except they w *their* hands oft, eat *G3538*
4 except they w, they eat not. And many *G907*
Lk 7:38 and began to w his feet with tears, and *G1026*
Jn 9: 7 And said unto him, Go, w in the pool of *G3538*
11 pool of Siloam, and w: and I went and *G3538*
13: 5 and began to w the disciples' feet, and *G3538*
6 unto him, Lord, dost thou w my feet? *G3538*
8 him, Thou shalt never w my feet. Jesus *G3538*
8 I w thee not, thou hast no part with me. *G3538*
10 not save to w *his* feet, but is clean *G3538*
14 ye also ought to w one another's feet. *G3538*
Act 22:16 be baptized, and w away thy sins, calling *G628*

WASHED

Gen 43:24 water, and they w their feet; and he H7364
31 And he w his face, and went out, and H7364
49:11 choice vine; he w his garments in wine, H3526
Ex 19:14 the people; and they w their clothes. H3526
40:31 And Moses and Aaron and his sons w H7364
32 w; as the LORD commanded Moses. H7364
Lev 8: 6 and his sons, and w them with water. H7364
21 And he w the inwards and the legs in H7364
13:55 after that it is w: and, behold, *if* the H3526
58 w the second time, and shall be clean. H3526
15:17 shall be w with water, and be H3526
Nu 8:21 purified, and they w their clothes; and H3526
Jdg 19:21 w their feet, and did eat and drink. H7364
2Sa 12:20 the earth, and w, and anointed *himself*, H7364
19:24 his beard, nor w his clothes, from the H3526
1Ki 22:38 And *one* w the chariot in the pool of H7857
38 his blood; and they w his armour; H7364
2Ch 4: 6 offering they w in them; but the sea H1740
Job 29: 6 When I w my steps with butter, and the H7364
Ps 73:13 *in* vain, and w my hands in innocency. H7364
Prv 30:12 and *yet* is not w from their filthiness. H7364
Song 5: 3 w my feet; how shall I defile them? H7364
12 of waters, w with milk, *and* fitly set. H7364
Isa 4: 4 When the Lord shall have w away the H7364
Ezk 16: 4 neither wast thou w in water to supple H7364
9 Then w I thee with water; yea, I H7364
9 yea, I throughly w away thy blood from H7857
40:38 gates, where they w the burnt offering. H1740
Mt 27:24 he took water, and w *his* hands before *G633*
Lk 7:44 feet: but she hath w my feet with tears, *G1026*
11:38 that he had not first w before dinner. *G907*
Jn 9: 7 way therefore, and w, and came seeing. *G3538*
11 and I went and w, and I received sight. *G3538*
15 upon mine eyes, and I w, and do see. *G3538*
13:10 Jesus saith to him, He that is w needeth *G3068*
12 So after he had w their feet, and had *G3538*
14 If I then, *your* Lord and Master, have w *G3538*
Act 9:37 w, they laid *her* in an upper chamber. *G3068*
16:33 of the night, and w *their* stripes; and *G3068*
1Co 6:11 And such were some of you: but ye are w, *G628*
1Ti 5:10 if she have w the saints' feet, if she *G3538*
Heb 10:22 and our bodies w with pure water. *G3068*
2Pt 2:22 was w to her wallowing in the mire. *G3068*
Rev 1: 5 w us from our sins in his own blood, *G3068*
7:14 and have w their robes, and made *G4150*

WASHEST

Job 14:19 The waters wear the stones: thou w H7857

WASHING

Lev 13:56 dark after the w of it; then he shall rend H3526
2Sa 11: 2 he saw a woman w herself; and the H7364
Neh 4:23 *that* every one put them off for w. H4325
Song 4: 2 came up from the w; whereof every one H7367
6: 6 go up from the w, whereof every one H7367
Mk 7: 4 to hold, *as* the w of cups, and pots, *G909*
8 of men, *as* the w of pots and cups: and *G909*
Lk 5: 2 gone out of them, and were w *their* nets. *G637*
Eph 5:26 it with the w of water by the word, *G3067*
Tit 3: 5 saved us, by the w of regeneration, and *G3067*

WASHINGS

Heb 9:10 and drinks, and divers w, and carnal *G909*

WASHPOT

Ps 60: 8 Moab *is* my w; over Edom will I H5518+H7366
108: 9 Moab *is* my w; over Edom will I H5518+H7366

WAST

Gen 3:11 And he said, Who told thee that thou *w*
19 for out of it w thou taken: for dust
33:10 of God, and thou w pleased with me.
40:13 former manner when thou w his butler. H1961
Dt 5:15 And remember that thou w a servant H1961
15:15 And thou shalt remember that thou w H1961
16:12 And thou shalt remember that thou w H1961
23: 7 because thou w a stranger in his land. H1961
24:18 But thou shalt remember that thou w a H1961
22 And thou shalt remember that thou w H1961
25:18 thee, when thou *w* faint and weary; and
28:60 Egypt, which thou w afraid of; and they
Ru 3: 2 maidens thou w? Behold, he winnoweth
1Sa 15:17 And Samuel said, When thou *w* little in
17 in thine own sight, *w* thou not *made* the
2Sa 1:14 And David said unto him, How w thou
25 *thou w* slain in thine high places.
5: 2 king over us, thou w he that leddest out H1961
1Ch 11: 2 was king, thou *w* he that leddest out and
Job 15: 7 born? or w thou made before the hills?
38: 4 Where w thou when I laid the H1961
21 Knowest thou *it*, because thou w then
Ps 99: 8 our God: thou w a God that forgavest H1961
114: 5 thou Jordan, *that* thou w driven back?
Isa 12: 1 thee: though thou w angry with me,
14: 3 bondage wherein thou w made to serve,
33: 1 Woe to thee that spoilest, and thou *w*
43: 4 Since thou w precious in my sight, thou
48: 8 w called a transgressor from the womb.
54: 6 when thou w refused, saith thy God.
57:10 hand; therefore thou w not grieved.
Jer 2:36 of Egypt, as thou w ashamed of Assyria.
50:24 Babylon, and thou w not aware: thou art
Ezk 16: 4 in the day thou w born thy navel was not
4 not cut, neither w thou washed in water
4 w not salted at all, nor swaddled at all.
5 thee; but thou w cast out in the open
5 thy person, in the day that thou w born.
6 thee *when thou w* in thy blood, Live; yea,
6 thee *when thou w* in thy blood, Live.
7 grown, whereas thou *w* naked and bare.
13 Thus w thou decked with gold and
13 and oil: and thou w exceeding beautiful,
22 youth, when thou w naked and bare, H1961
22 and bare, *and* w polluted in thy blood. H1961
28 because thou w unsatiable; yea, thou
29 and yet thou w not satisfied herewith.
47 little *thing*, thou w corrupted more than
21:30 w created, in the land of thy nativity.
24:13 thee, and thou w not purged, thou shalt
26:17 destroyed, *that* w inhabited of seafaring
17 city, which w strong in the sea, she
27:25 thy market: and thou w replenished, and
28:13 in thee in the day that thou w created.
14 have set thee *so*: thou w upon the holy H1961
15 Thou *w* perfect in thy ways from the day
15 w created, till iniquity was found in thee.
Oba 11 Jerusalem, even thou w as one of them.
Mt 26:69 Thou also w with Jesus of Galilee. *G2258*
Mk 14:67 thou also w with Jesus of Nazareth. *G2258*
Jn 1:48 thou w under the fig tree, I saw thee. *G5607*
9:34 unto him, Thou w altogether born in *G1080*
21:18 unto thee, When thou w young, thou *G2258*
Rev 5: 9 seals thereof: for thou w slain, and hast
11:17 which art, and w, and art to come; *G2258*
16: 5 which art, and w, and shalt be, because *G2258*

WASTE

Lev 26:31 And I will make your cities w, and bring H2723
33 shall be desolate, and your cities w. H2723
Nu 21:30 and we have laid them w even unto H8074
Dt 32:10 land, and in the w howling wilderness; H8414
1Ki 17:14 of meal shall not w, neither shall the H3615
2Ki 19:25 lay w fenced cities *into* ruinous heaps. H7582
1Ch 17: 9 w them any more, as at the beginning, H1086
Neh 2: 3 sepulchres, *lieth* w, and the gates H2720
17 Jerusalem *lieth* w, and the gates thereof H2720
Job 30: 3 in former time desolate and w. H4875
38:27 To satisfy the desolate and w *ground*; H4875
Ps 79: 7 Jacob, and laid w his dwelling place. H8074
80:13 The boar out of the wood doth w it, H3765
Isa 5: 6 And I will lay it w: it shall not be H1326
17 manner, and the w places of the fat H2723
15: 1 Ar of Moab is laid w, *and* brought to H7703
1 Moab is laid w, *and* brought to silence; H7703
23: 1 for it is laid w, so that there is no house, H7703
14 of Tarshish: for your strength is laid w. H7703
24: 1 and maketh it w, and turneth it upside H1110
33: 8 The highways lie w, the wayfaring man H8074
34:10 it shall lie w; none shall pass through H2717
37:18 w all the nations, and their countries, H2717
26 w defenced cities *into* ruinous heaps. H7582
42:15 I will make w mountains and hills, and H2717
49:17 that made thee w shall go forth of thee. H2717
19 For thy w and thy desolate places, and H2723
51: 3 comfort all her w places; and he will H2723
52: 9 Break forth into joy, sing together, ye w H2723
58:12 shall build the old w places: thou shalt H2723
61: 4 shall repair the w cities, the desolations H2721
64:11 and all our pleasant things are laid w. H2723
Jer 2:15 made his land w: his cities are burned H8047
4: 7 shall be laid w, without an inhabitant. H5327
27:17 wherefore should this city be laid w? H2723
46:19 w and desolate without an inhabitant. H8047
49:13 a reproach, a w, and a curse; and all H2721
50:21 of Pekod: w and utterly destroy H2717
Ezk 5:14 Moreover I will make thee w, and a H2723
6: 6 the cities shall be laid w, and the high H2717

Ezk 6: 6 your altars may be laid w and made H2717
12:20 shall be laid w, and the land shall be H2717
19: 7 and he laid w their cities; and the H2717
26: 2 I shall be replenished, *now* she is laid w: H2717
29: 9 be desolate and w; and they shall know H2723
10 of Egypt utterly w *and* desolate, from H2723
12 cities *that are* laid w shall be desolate H2717
30:12 make the land w, and all that is therein, H8074
35: 4 I will lay thy cities w, and thou shalt be H2723
36:35 of Eden; and the w and desolate and H2720
38 feasts; so shall the w cities be filled H2720
38: 8 have been always w: but it is brought H2723
Joel 1: 7 He hath laid my vine w, and barked my H8047
Am 7: 9 of Israel shall be laid w; and I will rise H2717
9:14 shall build the w cities, and inhabit H8074
Mic 5: 6 And they shall w the land of Assyria H7462
Nah 2:10 She is empty, and void, and w: and the H1110
3: 7 say, Nineveh is laid w: who will bemoan H7703
Zep 3: 6 made their streets w, that none passeth H2717
Hag 1: 4 your cieled houses, and this house *lie* w? H2720
9 house that *is* w, and ye run every man H2720
Mal 1: 3 w for the dragons of the wilderness. H8077
Mt 26: 8 saying, To what purpose *is* this w? *G684*
Mk 14: 4 Why was this w of the ointment made? *G684*

WASTED

Nu 14:33 your carcases be w in the wilderness. H8552
24:22 Nevertheless the Kenite shall be w, until H1197
Dt 2:14 men of war were w out from among the H8552
1Ki 17:16 *And* the barrel of meal w not, neither H3615
1Ch 20: 1 of the army, and w the country of the H7843
Ps 137: 3 song; and they that w us *required of us* H8437
Isa 6:11 answered, Until the cities be w without H7582
19: 5 and the river shall be w and dried up. H2717
60:12 yea, *those* nations shall be utterly w. H2717
Jer 44: 6 they are w *and* desolate, as at this day. H2723
Ezk 30: 7 be in the midst of the cities *that are* w. H2717
Joel 1:10 The field is w, the land mourneth; for H7703
10 for the corn is w: the new wine is dried H7703
Lk 15:13 w his substance with riotous living. *G1287*
16: 1 unto him that he had w his goods. *G1287*
Gal 1:13 persecuted the church of God, and w it: *G4199*

WASTENESS

Zep 1:15 distress, a day of w and desolation, a H7722

WASTER

Prv 18: 9 work is brother to him that is a great w. H7843
Isa 54:16 and I have created the w to destroy. H7843

WASTES

Isa 61: 4 And they shall build the old w, they H2723
Jer 49:13 the cities thereof shall be perpetual w. H2723
Ezk 33:24 Son of man, they that inhabit those w H2723
27 that *are* in the w shall fall by the sword, H2723
36: 4 to the desolate w, and to the cities that H2723
10 inhabited, and the w shall be builded: H2723
33 in the cities, and the w shall be builded. H2723

WASTETH

Job 14:10 But man dieth, and w away: yea, man H2522
Ps 91: 6 for the destruction *that* w at noonday. H7736
Prv 19:26 He that w *his* father, *and* chaseth away H7703

WASTING

Isa 59: 7 w and destruction *are* in their paths. H7701
60:18 be heard in thy land, w nor destruction H7701

WATCH

Gen 31:49 And Mizpah; for he said, The LORD w H6822
Ex 14:24 in the morning w the LORD looked unto H821
Jdg 7:19 of the middle w; and they had but newly H821
19 but newly set the w: and they blew the H8104
1Sa 11:11 host in the morning w, and slew the H821
19:11 David's house, to w him, and to slay H8104
2Sa 13:34 man that kept the w lifted up his eyes, H6822
2Ki 11: 5 be keepers of the w of the king's house; H4931
6 shall ye keep the w of the house, that it H4931
7 shall keep the w of the house of the H4931
2Ch 20:24 And when Judah came toward the w H4707
23: 6 people shall keep the w of the LORD. H4931
Ezr 8:29 W ye, and keep *them*, until ye weigh H8245
Neh 4: 9 our God, and set a w against them day H4929
7: 3 every one in his w, and every one *to be* H4929
Job 7:12 a whale, that thou settest a w over me? H4929
14:16 my steps: dost thou not w over my sin? H8104
Ps 90: 4 when it is past, and *as* a w in the night. H821
102: 7 I w, and am as a sparrow alone upon H8245
130: 6 than they that w for the morning: *I say,* H8104
Ps 130: 6 *more than* they that w for the morning. H8104
141: 3 Set a w, O LORD, before my mouth; H8108
Isa 21: 5 Prepare the table, w in the watchtower, H6822
29:20 and all that w for iniquity are cut off: H8245
Jer 5: 6 a leopard shall w over their cities: H8245
31:28 and to afflict; so will I w over them, to H8245
44:27 Behold, I will w over them for evil, and H8245
51:12 Babylon, make the w strong, set up the H4929
Nah 2: 1 the munition, w the way, make *thy* H6822
Hab 2: 1 I will stand upon my w, and set me H4931
1 tower, and will w to see what he will H6822
Mt 14:25 And in the fourth w of the night Jesus *G5438*
24:42 W therefore: for ye know not what *G1127*
43 known in what w the thief would come, *G5438*
25:13 W therefore, for ye know neither the *G1127*
26:38 death: tarry ye here, and w with me. *G1127*
40 could ye not w with me one hour? *G1127*
41 W and pray, that ye enter not into *G1127*
27:65 Pilate said unto them, Ye have a w: go *G2892*
66 sure, sealing the stone, and setting a w. *G2892*
28:11 some of the w came into the city, *G2892*
Mk 6:48 and about the fourth w of the night he *G5438*
13:33 Take ye heed, w and pray: for ye know *G69*
34 work, and commanded the porter to w. *G1127*
35 W ye therefore: for ye know not when *G1127*
37 what I say unto you I say unto all, W. *G1127*
14:34 unto death: tarry ye here, and w. *G1127*
37 thou? couldest not thou w one hour? *G1127*
38 W ye and pray, lest ye enter into *G1127*
Lk 2: 8 keeping w over their flock by night. *G5438*
12:38 And if he shall come in the second w, or *G5438*
38 come in the third w, and find *them* so, *G5438*
21:36 W ye therefore, and pray always, that ye *G69*
Act 20:31 Therefore w, and remember, that by the *G1127*
1Co 16:13 W ye, stand fast in the faith, quit you *G1127*
Col 4: 2 Continue in prayer, and w in the same *G1127*
1Th 5: 6 as *do* others; but let us w and be sober. *G1127*
2Ti 4: 5 But w thou in all things, endure *G3525*
Heb 13:17 for they w for your souls, as they *G69*
1Pt 4: 7 ye therefore sober, and w unto prayer. *G3525*
Rev 3: 3 thou shalt not w, I will come on thee *G1127*

WATCHED

Ps 59:ttl sent, and they w the house to kill him. H8104
Jer 20:10 it. All my familiars w for my halting, H8104
31:28 pass, *that* like as I have w over them, to H8245
Lam 4:17 w for a nation *that* could not save *us*. H6822
Dan 9:14 Therefore hath the LORD w upon the H8245
Mt 24:43 he would have w, and would not have *G1127*
27:36 And sitting down they w him there; *G5083*
Mk 3: 2 And they w him, whether he would *G3906*
Lk 6: 7 And the scribes and Pharisees w him, *G3906*
12:39 he would have w, and not have suffered *G1127*
14: 1 on the sabbath day, that they w him. *G2258*
20:20 And they w *him*, and sent forth spies, *G3906*
Act 9:24 w the gates day and night to kill him. *G3906*

WATCHER

Dan 4:13 and, behold, a w and an holy one came H5894
23 And whereas the king saw a w and an H5894

WATCHERS

Jer 4:16 Jerusalem, *that* w come from a far H5341
Dan 4:17 This matter *is* by the decree of the w, H5894

WATCHES

Neh 7: 3 and appoint w of the inhabitants of H4931
12: 9 *were* over against them in the w. H4931
Ps 63: 6 bed, *and* meditate on thee in the *night* w. H821
119:148 Mine eyes prevent the *night* w, that I H821
Lam 2:19 beginning of the w pour out thine heart H821

WATCHETH

Ps 37:32 The wicked w the righteous, and H6822
Ezk 7: 6 An end is come, the end is come: it w H6974
Rev 16:15 Blessed *is* he that w, and keepeth his *G1127*

WATCHFUL

Rev 3: 2 Be w, and strengthen the things which *G1127*

WATCHING

1Sa 4:13 by the wayside w: for his heart trembled H6822
Prv 8:34 Blessed *is* the man that heareth me, w H8245
Lam 4:17 vain help: in our w we have watched H6836
Mt 27:54 that were with him, w Jesus, saw the *G5083*
Lk 12:37 he cometh shall find w: verily I say unto *G1127*
Eph 6:18 in the Spirit, and w thereunto with all *G69*

WATCHINGS

2Co 6: 5 in tumults, in labours, in w, in fastings; *G70*
11:27 In weariness and painfulness, in w *G70*

WATCHMAN

2Sa 18:24 the two gates: and the w went up to the H6822
25 And the w cried, and told the king. And H6822
26 And the w saw another man running: H6822
26 running: and the w called unto the H6822
27 And the w said, Me thinketh the H6822
2Ki 9:17 And there stood a w on the tower in H6822
18 behind me. And the w told, saying, The H6822
20 And the w told, saying, He came even H6822
Ps 127: 1 keep the city, the w waketh *but* in vain. H8104
Isa 21: 6 set a w, let him declare what he seeth. H6822
11 to me out of Seir, W, what of the night? H8104
11 what of the night? W, what of the night? H8104
12 The w said, The morning cometh, and H8104
Ezk 3:17 Son of man, I have made thee a w unto H6822
33: 2 of their coasts, and set him for their w: H6822
6 But if the w see the sword come, and H6822
7 I have set thee a w unto the house of H6822
Hos 9: 8 The w of Ephraim *was* with my God: H6822

WATCHMAN'S

Ezk 33: 6 his blood will I require at the w hand. H6822

WATCHMEN

1Sa 14:16 And the w of Saul in Gibeah of H6822
2Ki 17: 9 the tower of the w to the fenced city. H5341
18: 8 the tower of the w to the fenced city. H5341
Song 3: 3 The w that go about the city found me: H8104
5: 7 The w that went about the city found H8104
Isa 52: 8 Thy w shall lift up the voice; with the H6822
56:10 His w *are* blind: they are all ignorant, H6822
62: 6 I have set w upon thy walls, O H8104
Jer 6:17 Also I set w over you, *saying*, Hearken H6822
31: 6 For there shall be a day, *that* the w H5341
51:12 watch strong, set up the w, prepare the H8104
Mic 7: 4 the day of thy w *and* thy visitation H6822

WATCHTOWER

Isa 21: 5 Prepare the table, watch in the w, eat, H6844
8 upon the w in the daytime, and H4707

WATER

Gen 2:10 And a river went out of Eden to w the H8248
16: 7 by a fountain of w in the wilderness, by H4325
18: 4 Let a little w, I pray you, be fetched, and H4325
21:14 and a bottle of w, and gave *it* unto H4325
15 And the w was spent in the bottle, and H4325
19 she saw a well of w; and she went, and H4325
19 bottle with w, and gave the lad drink. H4325
25 of a well of w, which Abimelech's H4325
24:11 the city by a well of w at the time of the H4325
11 the time that women go out to draw *w*. H7579
13 Behold, I stand *here* by the well of w; H4325
13 the men of the city come out to draw w: H4325
17 thee, drink a little w of thy pitcher. H4325
19 said, I will draw w for thy camels also, H7579
20 to draw *w*, and drew for all his camels. H7579
32 the camels, and w to wash his feet, and H4325
43 Behold, I stand by the well of w; and it H4325
43 forth to draw *w*, and I say to her, Give H7579
43 thee, a little w of thy pitcher to drink; H4325
45 the well, and drew *w*: and I said unto H7579
26:18 And Isaac digged again the wells of w, H4325
19 and found there a well of springing w. H4325
20 saying, The w *is* ours: and he called H4325
32 and said unto him, We have found w. H4325
29: 7 w ye the sheep, and go *and* feed *them*. H8248
8 the well's mouth; then we w the sheep. H8248
37:24 the pit *was* empty, *there was* no w in it. H4325
43:24 and gave *them* w, and they washed H4325
49: 4 Unstable as w, thou shalt not excel; H4325
Ex 2:10 said, Because I drew him out of the w. H4325
16 came and drew *w*, and filled the troughs
16 the troughs to w their father's flock. H8248
19 *w* enough for us, and watered the flock.
4: 9 shalt take of the w of the river, and H4325
9 dry *land*: and the w which thou takest H4325
7:15 he goeth out unto the w; and thou shalt H4325
18 shall lothe to drink of the w of the river. H4325
19 upon all their pools of w, that they may H4325
21 not drink of the w of the river; and H4325
24 about the river for w to drink; for they H4325
24 could not drink of the w of the river. H4325
8:20 forth to the w; and say unto him, Thus H4325
12: 9 sodden at all with w, but roast *with* fire; H4325

Ex 15:22 days in the wilderness, and found no w. H4325
27 twelve wells of w, and threescore and H4325
17: 1 *there was* no w for the people to drink. H4325
2 and said, Give us w that we may drink. H4325
3 And the people thirsted there for w; and H4325
6 there shall come w out of it, that the H4325
20: 4 or that *is* in the w under the earth: H4325
23:25 thy bread, and thy w; and I will take H4325
29: 4 and shalt wash them with w. H4325
30:18 the altar, and thou shalt put w therein. H4325
20 shall wash with w, that they die not; or H4325
32:20 *it* upon the w, and made the children H4325
34:28 bread, nor drink w. And he wrote upon H4325
40: 7 and the altar, and shalt put w therein. H4325
12 congregation, and wash them with w. H4325
30 altar, and put w there, to wash *withal*. H4325
Lev 1: 9 shall he wash in w: and the priest shall H4325
13 and the legs with w: and the priest shall H4325
6:28 shall be both scoured, and rinsed in w. H4325
8: 6 and his sons, and washed them with w. H4325
21 and the legs in w; and Moses burnt the H4325
11:32 it must be put into w, and it shall be H4325
34 *that* on which *such* w cometh shall be H4325
36 *there is* plenty of w, shall be clean: but H4325
38 But if *any* w be put upon the seed, and H4325
14: 5 in an earthen vessel over running w: H4325
6 bird *that was* killed over the running w: H4325
8 and wash himself in w, that he may be H4325
9 his flesh in w, and he shall be clean. H4325
50 in an earthen vessel over running w: H4325
51 w, and sprinkle the house seven times: H4325
52 with the running w, and with the living H4325
15: 5 in w, and be unclean until the even. H4325
6 in w, and be unclean until the even. H4325
7 in w, and be unclean until the even. H4325
8 in w, and be unclean until the even. H4325
10 in w, and be unclean until the even. H4325
11 rinsed his hands in w, he shall wash his H4325
11 in w, and be unclean until the even. H4325
12 vessel of wood shall be rinsed in w. H4325
13 flesh in running w, and shall be clean. H4325
16 in w, and be unclean until the even. H4325
17 with w, and be unclean until the even. H4325
18 in w, and be unclean until the even. H4325
21 in w, and be unclean until the even. H4325
22 in w, and be unclean until the even. H4325
27 in w, and be unclean until the even. H4325
16: 4 wash his flesh in w, and *so* put them on. H4325
24 And he shall wash his flesh with w in H4325
26 w, and afterward come into the camp. H4325
28 bathe his flesh in w, and afterward he H4325
17:15 and bathe *himself* in w, and be unclean H4325
22: 6 things, unless he wash his flesh with w. H4325
Nu 5:17 And the priest shall take holy w in an H4325
17 priest shall take, and put *it* into the w: H4325
18 the bitter w that causeth the curse: H4325
19 this bitter w that causeth the curse: H4325
22 And this w that causeth the curse shall H4325
23 he shall blot *them* out with the bitter w: H4325
24 to drink the bitter w that causeth the H4325
24 the curse: and the w that causeth the H4325
26 shall cause the woman to drink the w. H4325
27 her to drink the w, then it shall come to H4325
27 husband, that the w that causeth the H4325
8: 7 them: Sprinkle w of purifying upon H4325
19: 7 bathe his flesh in w, and afterward he H4325
8 his clothes in w, and bathe his flesh H4325
8 w, and shall be unclean until the even. H4325
9 of Israel for a w of separation: it *is* a H4325
13 because the w of separation was not H4325
17 w shall be put thereto in a vessel: H4325
18 and dip *it* in the w, and sprinkle *it* upon H4325
19 himself in w, and shall be clean at even. H4325
20 of the LORD: the w of separation hath H4325
21 sprinkleth the w of separation shall H4325
21 that toucheth the w of separation shall H4325
20: 2 And there was no w for the H4325
5 neither *is* there any w to drink. H4325
8 give forth his w, and thou shalt bring H4325
8 forth to them w out of the rock: so thou H4325
10 must we fetch you w out of this rock? H4325
11 twice: and the w came out abundantly, H4325
13 This *is* the w of Meribah; because the H4325
17 we drink *of* the w of the wells: we will H4325
19 cattle drink of thy w, then I will pay for H4325
24 against my word at the w of Meribah. H4325
21: 5 *is there any* w; and our soul loatheth H4325
16 people together, and I will give them w. H4325
24: 7 He shall pour the w out of his buckets, H4325

Nu 27:14 sanctify me at the w before their eyes: H4325
14 their eyes: that *is* the w of Meribah in H4325
31:23 purified with the w of separation: and H4325
23 the fire ye shall make go through the w. H4325
33: 9 fountains of w, and threescore and H4325
14 where was no w for the people to drink. H4325
Dt 2: 6 ye shall also buy w of them for money, H4325
28 eat; and give me w for money, that I H4325
8: 7 a land of brooks of w, of fountains and H4325
15 *there was* no w; who brought thee forth H4325
15 thee forth w out of the rock of flint; H4325
9: 9 I neither did eat bread nor drink w: H4325
18 bread, nor drink w, because of all your H4325
11: 4 how he made the w of the Red sea to H4325
11 *and* drinketh w of the rain of heaven: H4325
12:16 ye shall pour it upon the earth as w. H4325
24 thou shalt pour it upon the earth as w. H4325
15:23 shalt pour it upon the ground as w. H4325
23: 4 bread and with w in the way, when ye H4325
11 wash *himself* with w: and when the sun H4325
29:11 of thy wood unto the drawer of thy w: H4325
Jos 2:10 dried up the w of the Red sea for you, H4325
3: 8 to the brink of the w of Jordan, ye shall H4325
15 dipped in the brim of the w, (for Jordan H4325
7: 5 of the people melted, and became as w. H4325
9:21 wood and drawers of w unto all the H4325
23 drawers of w for the house of my God. H4325
27 and drawers of w for the congregation, H4325
15: 9 the fountain of the w of Nephtoah, and H4325
19 me also springs of w. And he gave her H4325
16: 1 by Jericho, unto the w of Jericho on the H4325
Jdg 1:15 me also springs of w. And Caleb gave H4325
4:19 I pray thee, a little w to drink; for I am H4325
5: 4 dropped, the clouds also dropped w. H4325
11 the places of drawing w, there shall they H4857
25 He asked w, *and* she gave *him* milk; she H4325
6:38 dew out of the fleece, a bowl full of w. H4325
7: 4 down unto the w, and I will try them H4325
5 people unto the w: and the LORD said H4325
5 lappeth of the w with his tongue, as H4325
6 down upon their knees to drink w. H4325
15:19 and there came w thereout; and when H4325
1Sa 7: 6 Mizpeh, and drew w, and poured *it* out H4325
9:11 w, and said unto them, Is the seer here? H4325
25:11 Shall I then take my bread, and my w, H4325
26:11 and the cruse of w, and let us go. H4325
12 and the cruse of w from Saul's bolster; H4325
16 the cruse of w that *was* at his bolster. H4325
30:11 he did eat; and they made him drink w; H4325
12 *any* w, three days and three nights. H4325
2Sa 14:14 For we must needs die, and *are* as w H4325
17:20 over the brook of w. And when they had H4325
21 pass quickly over the w: for thus hath H4325
21:10 of harvest until w dropped upon them H4325
23:15 give me drink of the w of the well of H4325
16 and drew w out of the well of H4325
1Ki 13: 8 I eat bread nor drink w in this place: H4325
9 bread, nor drink w, nor turn again by H4325
16 nor drink w with thee in this place: H4325
17 no bread nor drink w there, nor turn H4325
18 and drink w. *But* he lied unto him. H4325
19 eat bread in his house, and drank w. H4325
22 bread and drunk w in the place, of the H4325
22 and drink no w; thy carcase shall not H4325
14:15 is shaken in the w, and he shall root up H4325
17:10 a little w in a vessel, that I may drink. H4325
18: 4 a cave, and fed them with bread and w.) H4325
5 all fountains of w, and unto all brooks: H4325
13 a cave, and fed them with bread and w? H4325
33 four barrels with w, and pour *it* on the H4325
35 And the w ran round about the altar; H4325
35 and he filled the trench also with w. H4325
38 licked up the w that *was* in the trench. H4325
19: 6 and a cruse of w at his head. And he H4325
22:27 w of affliction, until I come in peace. H4325
2Ki 2:19 w *is* naught, and the ground barren. H4325
3: 9 and there was no w for the host, and H4325
11 which poured w on the hands of Elijah. H4325
17 shall be filled with w, that ye may drink, H4325
19 stop all wells of w, and mar every good H4325
20 there came w by the way of Edom, H4325
20 and the country was filled with w. H4325
22 shone upon the w, and the Moabites H4325
22 the w on the other side *as* red as blood: H4325
25 all the wells of w, and felled all the good H4325
6: 5 head fell into the w: and he cried, and H4325
22 set bread and w before them, that they H4325
8:15 and dipped *it* in w, and spread *it* on his H4325
20:20 and brought w into the city, *are* they H4325

1Ch 11:17 give me drink of the w of the well of H4325
18 and drew w out of the well of H4325
2Ch 18:26 w of affliction, until I return in peace. H4325
32: 4 of Assyria come, and find much w? H4325
Ezr 10: 6 no bread, nor drink w: for he mourned H4325
Neh 3:26 over against the w gate toward the H4325
8: 1 *was* before the w gate; and they spake H4325
3 that *was* before the w gate from the H4325
16 in the street of the w gate, and in the H4325
9:15 broughtest forth w for them out of the H4325
20 and gavest them w for their thirst. H4325
12:37 David, even unto the w gate eastward. H4325
13: 2 bread and with w, but hired Balaam H4325
Job 8:11 mire? can the flag grow without w? H4325
9:30 If I wash myself with snow w, and make H1119
14: 9 *Yet* through the scent of w it will bud, H4325
15:16 *is* man, which drinketh iniquity like w? H4325
22: 7 Thou hast not given w to the weary to H4325
34: 7 Job, *who* drinketh up scorning like w? H4325
36:27 For he maketh small the drops of w: H4325
Ps 1: 3 by the rivers of w, that bringeth forth H4325
6: 6 to swim; I w my couch with my tears. H4529
22:14 I am poured out like w, and all my H4325
42: 1 As the hart panteth after the w brooks, H4325
63: 1 a dry and thirsty land, where no w is; H4325
65: 9 *which* is full of w: thou preparest them H4325
66:12 fire and through w: but thou broughtest H4325
72: 6 grass: as showers *that* w the earth. H2222
77:17 The clouds poured out w: the skies sent H4325
79: 3 Their blood have they shed like w H4325
88:17 w; they compassed me about together. H4325
107:35 w, and dry ground into watersprings. H4325
109:18 like w, and like oil into his bones. H4325
114: 8 w, the flint into a fountain of waters. H4325
Prv 8:24 *were* no fountains abounding with w. H4325
17:14 one letteth out w: therefore leave off H4325
20: 5 of man *is like* deep w; but a man of H4325
21: 1 w: he turneth it whithersoever he will. H4325
25:21 if he be thirsty, give him w to drink: H4325
27:19 As in w face *answereth* to face, so the H4325
30:16 is not filled with w; and the fire *that* H4325
Ecc 2: 6 I made me pools of w, to water H4325
6 I made me pools of water, to w H8248
Isa 1:22 become dross, thy wine mixed with w: H4325
30 fadeth, and as a garden that hath no w. H4325
3: 1 stay of bread, and the whole stay of w, H4325
12: 3 Therefore with joy shall ye draw w out H4325
14:23 and pools of w: and I will sweep it with H4325
16: 9 of Sibmah: I will w thee with my tears, H7301
21:14 of Tema brought w to him that was H4325
22:11 two walls for the w of the old pool: but H4325
27: 3 I the LORD do keep it; I will w it every H8248
30:14 or to take w *withal* out of the pit. H4325
20 of adversity, and the w of affliction, yet H4325
32: 2 as rivers of w in a dry place, as the H4325
35: 7 land springs of w: in the habitation of H4325
37:25 I have digged, and drunk w; and with H4325
41:17 *When* the poor and needy seek w, and H4325
18 of w, and the dry land springs of water. H4325
18 of water, and the dry land springs of w. H4325
44: 3 For I will pour w upon him that is H4325
4 the grass, as willows by the w courses. H4325
12 faileth: he drinketh no w, and is faint. H4325
49:10 by the springs of w shall he guide them. H4325
50: 2 *there is* no w, and dieth for thirst. H4325
58:11 like a spring of w, whose waters fail not. H4325
63:12 arm, dividing the w before them, to H4325
Jer 2:13 broken cisterns, that can hold no w. H4325
8:14 and given us w of gall to drink, because H4325
9:15 and give them w of gall to drink. H4325
13: 1 it upon thy loins, and put it not in w. H4325
14: 3 *and* found no w; they returned with H4325
23:15 them drink the w of gall: for from the H4325
38: 6 *there was* no w, but mire: so Jeremiah H4325
Lam 1:16 down with w, because the comforter H4325
2:19 thine heart like w before the face of the H4325
3:48 with rivers of w for the destruction H4325
5: 4 We have drunken our w for money; our H4325
Ezk 4:11 Thou shalt drink also w by measure, H4325
16 w by measure, and with astonishment: H4325
17 That they may want bread and w, and H4325
7:17 feeble, and all knees shall be weak *as* w. H4325
12:18 w with trembling and with carefulness; H4325
19 and drink their w with astonishment, H4325
16: 4 thou washed in w to supple *thee*; thou H4325
9 Then washed I thee with w; yea, I H4325
17: 7 w it by the furrows of her plantation. H8248
21: 7 shall be weak *as* w: behold, it cometh, H4325
24: 3 a pot, set *it* on, and also pour w into it: H4325

Ezk 26:12 and thy dust in the midst of the w. H4325
31:14 height, all that drink w: for they are all H4325
16 all that drink w, shall be comforted H4325
32: 6 I will also w with thy blood the land H8248
36:25 Then will I sprinkle clean w upon you, H4325
Dan 1:12 give us pulse to eat, and w to drink. H4325
Hos 2: 5 my bread and my w, my wool and my H4325
5:10 pour out my wrath upon them like w. H4325
10: 7 king is cut off as the foam upon the w. H4325
Joel 3:18 and shall w the valley of Shittim. H8248
Am 4: 8 one city, to drink w; but they were not H4325
8:11 nor a thirst for w, but of hearing the H4325
Jna 3: 7 thing: let them not feed, nor drink w: H4325
Nah 2: 8 But Nineveh *is* of old like a pool of w: H4325
Hab 3:10 the overflowing of the w passed by: the H4325
Zec 9:11 prisoners out of the pit wherein *is* no w. H4325
Mt 3:11 I indeed baptize you with w unto G5204
16 out of the w: and, lo, the heavens G5204
10:42 ones a cup of cold w only in the name of
14:28 thou, bid me come unto thee on the w. G5204
29 ship, he walked on the w, to go to Jesus. G5204
17:15 falleth into the fire, and oft into the w. G5204
27:24 made, he took w, and washed *his* hands G5204
Mk 1: 8 I indeed have baptized you with w: but G5204
10 up out of the w, he saw the heavens G5204
9:41 shall give you a cup of w to drink in my G5204
14:13 man bearing a pitcher of w: follow him. G5204
Lk 3:16 baptize you with w; but one mightier G5204
7:44 thou gavest me no w for my feet: but G5204
8:23 were filled *with* w, and were in jeopardy.
24 the raging of the w: and they ceased, G5204
25 the winds and w, and they obey him. G5204
16:24 the tip of his finger in w, and cool my G5204
22:10 a pitcher of w; follow him into the G5204
Jn 1:26 I baptize with w: but there standeth G5204
31 therefore am I come baptizing with w. G5204
33 to baptize with w, the same said unto G5204
2: 7 w. And they filled them up to the brim. G5204
9 had tasted the w that was made wine, G5204
9 which drew the w knew;) the governor G5204
3: 5 a man be born of w and *of* the Spirit, G5204
23 there was much w there: and they G5204
4: 7 of Samaria to draw w: Jesus saith unto G5204
10 and he would have given thee living w. G5204
11 whence then hast thou that living w? G5204
13 drinketh of this w shall thirst again: G5204
14 But whosoever drinketh of the w that I G5204
14 thirst; but the w that I shall give him G5204
14 of w springing up into everlasting life. G5204
15 Sir, give me this w, that I thirst not, G5204
46 he made the w wine. And there was G5204
5: 3 waiting for the moving of the w. G5204
4 and troubled the w: whosoever then G5204
4 troubling of the w stepped in was made G5204
7 no man, when the w is troubled, to put G5204
7:38 of his belly shall flow rivers of living w. G5204
13: 5 After that he poureth w into a bason, G5204
19:34 forthwith came there out blood and w. G5204
Act 1: 5 For John truly baptized with w; but ye G5204
8:36 unto a certain w: and the eunuch said, G5204
36 w; what doth hinder me to be baptized? G5204
38 both into the w, both Philip and the G5204
39 up out of the w, the Spirit of the Lord G5204
10:47 Can any man forbid w, that these G5204
11:16 indeed baptized with w; but ye shall be G5204
Eph 5:26 it with the washing of w by the word, G5204
1Ti 5:23 Drink no longer w, but use a little wine G5202
Heb 9:19 and of goats, with w, and scarlet wool, G5204
10:22 and our bodies washed with pure w. G5204
Jas 3:11 at the same place sweet *w* and bitter?
12 no fountain both yield salt w and fresh. G5204
1Pt 3:20 that is, eight souls were saved by w. G5204
2Pt 2:17 These are wells without w, clouds that G504
3: 5 standing out of the w and in the water: G5204
5 standing out of the water and in the w: G5204
6 was, being overflowed with w, perished: G5204
1Jn 5: 6 This is he that came by w and blood, G5204
6 Christ; not by w only, but by water and G5204
6 water only, but by w and blood. And it G5204
8 the Spirit, and the w, and the blood: G5204
Jude 12 *they are* without w, carried about of G504
Rev 12:15 out of his mouth w as a flood after the G5204
16:12 and the w thereof was dried up, G5204
21: 6 of the fountain of the w of life freely. G5204
22: 1 And he shewed me a pure river of w of G5204
17 will, let him take the w of life freely. G5204

WATER-BROOKS See WATER and BROOKS.

WATERCOURSE
2Ch 32:30 the upper w of Gihon, and H4161+H4325
Job 38:25 Who hath divided a w for the H8585

WATERED
Gen 2: 6 and w the whole face of the ground. H8248
13:10 that it *was* well w every where, before H4945
29: 2 out of that well they w the flocks: and a H8248
3 well's mouth, and w the sheep, and put H8248
10 well's mouth, and w the flock of Laban H8248
Ex 2:17 up and helped them, and w their flock. H8248
19 *water* enough for us, and w the flock. H8248
Prv 11:25 that watereth shall be w also himself. H3384
Isa 58:11 shalt be like a w garden, and like a H7302
Jer 31:12 soul shall be as a w garden; and they H7302
1Co 3: 6 I have planted, Apollos w; but God gave G4222

WATEREDST
Dt 11:10 w *it* with thy foot, as a garden of herbs: H8248

WATEREST
Ps 65: 9 Thou visitest the earth, and w it: thou H7783
10 Thou w the ridges thereof abundantly: H7301

WATERETH
Ps 104:13 He w the hills from his chambers: the H8248
Prv 11:25 he that w shall be watered also himself. H7301
Isa 55:10 not thither, but w the earth, and H7301
1Co 3: 7 that w; but God that giveth the increase. G4222
8 Now he that planteth and he that w are G4222

WATERFLOOD
Ps 69:15 Let not the w overflow me, H7641+H4325

WATERING
Gen 30:38 the gutters in the w troughs when the H4325
Job 37:11 Also by w he wearieth the thick cloud: H7377
Lk 13:15 from the stall, and lead *him* away to w? G4222

WATERPOT
Jn 4:28 The woman then left her w, and went G5201

WATERPOTS
Jn 2: 6 And there were set there six w of stone, G5201
7 Jesus saith unto them, Fill the w with G5201

WATERS
Gen 1: 2 of God moved upon the face of the w. H4325
6 in the midst of the w, and let it divide H4325
6 and let it divide the w from the waters. H4325
6 and let it divide the waters from the w. H4325
7 and divided the w which *were* under H4325
7 from the w which *were* above the H4325
9 And God said, Let the w under the H4325
10 together of the w called he Seas: and H4325
20 And God said, Let the w bring forth H4325
21 which the w brought forth abundantly, H4325
22 and fill the w in the seas, and let H4325
6:17 do bring a flood of w upon the earth, to H4325
7: 6 the flood of w was upon the earth. H4325
7 the ark, because of the w of the flood. H4325
10 the w of the flood were upon the earth. H4325
17 the earth; and the w increased, and H4325
18 And the w prevailed, and were H4325
18 and the ark went upon the face of the w. H4325
19 And the w prevailed exceedingly upon H4325
20 Fifteen cubits upward did the w H4325
24 And the w prevailed upon the earth an H4325
8: 1 over the earth, and the w asswaged; H4325
3 And the w returned from off the earth H4325
3 and fifty days the w were abated. H4325
5 And the w decreased continually until H4325
7 the w were dried up from off the earth. H4325
8 him, to see if the w were abated from H4325
9 the ark, for the w *were* on the face of H4325
11 the w were abated from off the earth. H4325
13 of the month, the w were dried up from H4325
9:11 any more by the w of a flood; neither H4325
15 of all flesh; and the w shall no more H4325
Ex 7:17 hand upon the w which *are* in the river, H4325
19 hand upon the w of Egypt, upon their H4325
20 and smote the w that *were* in the river, H4325
20 and all the w that *were* in the river H4325
8: 6 his hand over the w of Egypt; and the H4325
14:21 sea dry *land*, and the w were divided. H4325
22 dry *ground*: and the w *were* a wall unto H4325
26 the sea, that the w may come again H4325
28 And the w returned, and covered the H4325
29 of the sea; and the w *were* a wall unto H4325
Ex 15: 8 And with the blast of thy nostrils the w H4325
10 they sank as lead in the mighty w. H4325
19 brought again the w of the sea upon H4325
23 not drink of the w of Marah, for they H4325
25 he had cast into the w, the waters were H4325
25 the waters, the w were made sweet: H4325
27 and they encamped there by the w. H4325
Lev 11: 9 of all that *are* in the w: whatsoever hath H4325
9 and scales in the w, in the seas, and in H4325
10 all that move in the w, and of any living H4325
10 thing which *is* in the w, they *shall be* an H4325
12 fins nor scales in the w, that *shall be* an H4325
46 moveth in the w, and of every creature H4325
Nu 21:22 not drink *of* the w of the well: *but* we H4325
24: 6 *and* as cedar trees beside the w. H4325
7 *shall be* in many w, and his king shall H4325
Dt 4:18 fish that *is* in the w beneath the earth: H4325
5: 8 or that *is* in the w beneath the earth: H4325
10: 7 to Jotbath, a land of rivers of w. H4325
14: 9 of all that *are* in the w: all that have fins H4325
32:51 of Israel at the w of Meribah-Kadesh, H4325
33: 8 thou didst strive at the w of Meribah; H4325
Jos 3:13 shall rest in the w of Jordan, *that* the H4325
13 of Jordan, *that* the w of Jordan shall be H4325
13 be cut off *from* the w that come down H4325
16 That the w which came down from H4325
4: 7 Then ye shall answer them, That the w H4325
7 over Jordan, the w of Jordan were cut H4325
18 dry land, that the w of Jordan returned H4325
23 For the LORD your God dried up the w H4325
5: 1 had dried up the w of Jordan from H4325
11: 5 the w of Merom, to fight against Israel. H4325
7 them by the w of Merom suddenly; H4325
15: 7 passed toward the w of En-shemesh, H4325
18:15 went out to the well of w of Nephtoah: H4325
Jdg 5:19 in Taanach by the w of Megiddo; they H4325
7:24 before them the w unto Beth-barah H4325
24 the w unto Beth-barah and Jordan. H4325
2Sa 5:20 as the breach of w. Therefore he called H4325
12:27 Rabbah, and have taken the city of w. H4325
22:12 dark w, *and* thick clouds of the skies. H4325
17 he took me; he drew me out of many w; H4325
2Ki 2: 8 and smote the w, and they were divided H4325
14 and smote the w, and said, Where *is* H4325
14 had smitten the w, they parted hither H4325
21 the spring of the w, and cast the salt in H4325
21 I have healed these w; there shall not be H4325
22 So the w were healed unto this day, H4325
5:12 better than all the w of Israel? may I H4325
18:31 drink ye every one the w of his cistern: H4325
19:24 I have digged and drunk strange w, and H4325
1Ch 14:11 the breaking forth of w: therefore they H4325
2Ch 32: 3 men to stop the w of the fountains H4325
Neh 9:11 the deeps, as a stone into the mighty w. H4325
Job 3:24 my roarings are poured out like the w. H4325
5:10 earth, and sendeth w upon the fields: H4325
11:16 *and* remember *it* as w *that* pass away: H4325
12:15 Behold, he withholdeth the w, and they H4325
14:11 *As* the w fail from the sea, and the H4325
19 The w wear the stones: thou washest H4325
22:11 see; and abundance of w cover thee. H4325
24:18 He *is* swift as the w; their portion is H4325
19 Drought and heat consume the snow w: H4325
26: 5 the w, and the inhabitants thereof. H4325
8 He bindeth up the w in his thick H4325
10 He hath compassed the w with bounds, H4325
27:20 Terrors take hold on him as w, a H4325
28: 4 *even the* w forgotten of the foot:
25 and he weigheth the w by measure. H4325
29:19 My root *was* spread out by the w, and H4325
30:14 breaking in *of* w: in the desolation they
37:10 and the breadth of the w is straitened. H4325
38:25 w, or a way for the lightning of thunder; H7858
30 The w are hid as *with* a stone, and the H4325
34 that abundance of w may cover thee? H4325
Ps 18:11 dark w *and* thick clouds of the skies. H4325
15 Then the channels of w were seen, and H4325
16 he took me, he drew me out of many w. H4325
23: 2 he leadeth me beside the still w. H4325
29: 3 The voice of the LORD *is* upon the w: H4325
3 thundereth: the LORD *is* upon many w. H4325
32: 6 w they shall not come nigh unto him. H4325
33: 7 He gathereth the w of the sea together H4325
46: 3 *Though* the w thereof roar *and* be H4325
58: 7 Let them melt away as w *which* run H4325
69: 1 Save me, O God; for the w are come in H4325
2 deep w, where the floods overflow me. H4325
14 that hate me, and out of the deep w. H4325
73:10 w of a full *cup* are wrung out to them. H4325

W

Ps 74:13 the heads of the dragons in the w. H4325
77:16 The w saw thee, O God, the waters saw H4325
16 The waters saw thee, O God, the w saw H4325
19 w, and thy footsteps are not known. H4325
78:13 he made the w to stand as an heap. H4325
16 and caused w to run down like rivers. H4325
20 Behold, he smote the rock, that the w H4325
81: 7 proved thee at the w of Meribah. Selah. H4325
93: 4 than the noise of many w, *yea, than* the H4325
104: 3 his chambers in the w: who maketh the H4325
6 the w stood above the mountains. H4325
105:29 He turned their w into blood, and slew H4325
41 He opened the rock, and the w gushed H4325
106:11 And the w covered their enemies: there H4325
32 They angered *him* also at the w of H4325
107:23 in ships, that do business in great w; H4325
114: 8 water, the flint into a fountain of w. H4325
119:136 Rivers of w run down mine eyes, H4325
124: 4 Then the w had overwhelmed us, the H4325
5 Then the proud w had gone over our H4325
136: 6 the w: for his mercy *endureth* for ever. H4325
144: 7 w, from the hand of strange children; H4325
147:18 his wind to blow, *and* the w flow. H4325
148: 4 and ye w that *be* above the heavens. H4325
Prv 5:15 Drink w out of thine own cistern, and H4325
15 and running w out of thine own well. H5140
16 abroad, *and* rivers of w in the streets. H4325
8:29 decree, that the w should not pass his H4325
9:17 Stolen w are sweet, and bread *eaten* in H4325
18: 4 *are as* deep w, *and* the wellspring H4325
25:25 *As* cold w to a thirsty soul, so *is* good H4325
30: 4 hath bound the w in a garment? who H4325
Ecc 11: 1 Cast thy bread upon the w: for thou H4325
Song 4:15 of living w, and streams from Lebanon. H4325
5:12 of w, washed with milk, *and* fitly set. H4325
8: 7 Many w cannot quench love, neither H4325
Isa 8: 6 refuseth the w of Shiloah that go softly, H4325
7 up upon them the w of the river, strong H4325
11: 9 of the LORD, as the w cover the sea. H4325
15: 6 For the w of Nimrim shall be desolate: H4325
9 For the w of Dimon shall be full of H4325
17:12 a rushing like the rushing of mighty w! H4325
13 the rushing of many w: but *God* shall H4325
18: 2 upon the w, *saying*, Go, ye swift H4325
19: 5 And the w shall fail from the sea, and H4325
8 spread nets upon the w shall languish. H4325
22: 9 together the w of the lower pool. H4325
23: 3 And by great w the seed of Sihor, the H4325
28: 2 a flood of mighty w overflowing, shall H4325
17 the w shall overflow the hiding place. H4325
30:25 *and* streams of w in the day of the H4325
32:20 Blessed *are* ye that sow beside all w, H4325
33:16 shall be given him; his w *shall be* sure. H4325
35: 6 w break out, and streams in the desert. H4325
36:16 ye every one the w of his own cistern; H4325
40:12 Who hath measured the w in the H4325
43: 2 When thou passest through the w, I *will* H4325
16 in the sea, and a path in the mighty w; H4325
20 because I give w in the wilderness, *and* H4325
48: 1 come forth out of the w of Judah, which H4325
21 he caused the w to flow out of the rock H4325
21 the rock also, and the w gushed out. H4325
51:10 dried the sea, the w of the great deep; H4325
54: 9 For this *is as* the w of Noah unto me: H4325
9 sworn that the w of Noah should no H4325
55: 1 come ye to the w, and he that hath no H4325
57:20 rest, whose w cast up mire and dirt. H4325
58:11 like a spring of water, whose w fail not. H4325
64: 2 fire causeth the w to boil, to make thy H4325
Jer 2:13 fountain of living w, *and* hewed them H4325
18 to drink the w of Sihor? or what hast H4325
18 of Assyria, to drink the w of the river? H4325
6: 7 As a fountain casteth out her w, so she H4325
9: 1 Oh that my head were w, and mine eyes H4325
18 tears, and our eyelids gush out with w. H4325
10:13 *is* a multitude of w in the heavens, and H4325
14: 3 little ones to the w: they came to the H4325
15:18 unto me as a liar, *and as* w *that* fail? H4325
17: 8 planted by the w, and *that* spreadeth H4325
13 the LORD, the fountain of living w. H4325
18:14 shall the cold flowing w that come from H4325
31: 9 by the rivers of w in a straight way, H4325
41:12 him by the great w that *are* in Gibeon. H4325
46: 7 whose w are moved as the rivers? H4325
8 Egypt riseth up like a flood, and *his* w H4325
47: 2 Thus saith the LORD; Behold, w rise up H4325
48:34 the w also of Nimrim shall be desolate. H4325
50:38 A drought *is* upon her w; and they shall H4325
51:13 O thou that dwellest upon many w, H4325
Jer 51:16 *is* a multitude of w in the heavens; and H4325
55 great w, a noise of their voice is uttered: H4325
Lam 3:54 W flowed over mine head; *then* I said, I H4325
Ezk 1:24 the noise of great w, as the voice of the H4325
17: 5 *it* by great w, *and* set it *as* a willow tree. H4325
8 It was planted in a good soil by great w, H4325
19:10 planted by the w: she was fruitful and H4325
10 full of branches by reason of many w. H4325
26:19 thee, and great w shall cover thee; H4325
27:26 thee into great w: the east wind hath H4325
34 in the depths of the w thy merchandise H4325
31: 4 The w made him great, the deep set H4325
5 the multitude of w, when he shot forth. H4325
7 branches: for his root was by great w. H4325
14 all the trees by the w exalt themselves H4325
15 and the great w were stayed: and I H4325
32: 2 and troubledst the w with thy feet, and H4325
13 beside the great w; neither shall the foot H4325
14 Then will I make their w deep, and H4325
34:18 drunk of the deep w, but ye must foul H4325
43: 2 w: and the earth shined with his glory. H4325
47: 1 and, behold, w issued out from under H4325
1 the east, and the w came down from H4325
2 there ran out w on the right side. H4325
3 the w; the waters *were* to the ankles. H4325
3 the waters; the w *were* to the ankles. H4325
4 me through the w; the waters *were* to H4325
4 the waters; the w *were* to the knees. H4325
4 me through; the w *were* to the loins. H4325
5 pass over: for the w were risen, waters H4325
5 waters were risen, w to swim in, a river H4325
8 Then said he unto me, These w issue H4325
8 into the sea, the w shall be healed. H4325
9 because these w shall come thither: H4325
12 because their w they issued out of the H4325
19 from Tamar *even* to the w of strife *in* H4325
48:28 Tamar *unto* the w of strife *in* Kadesh, H4325
Dan 12: 6 *was* upon the w of the river, How long H4325
7 *was* upon the w of the river, when he H4325
Joel 1:20 for the rivers of w are dried up, and the H4325
3:18 shall flow with w, and a fountain shall H4325
Am 5: 8 that calleth for the w of the sea, and H4325
24 But let judgment run down as w, and H4325
9: 6 that calleth for the w of the sea, and H4325
Jna 2: 5 The w compassed me about, *even* to H4325
Mic 1: 4 w *that are* poured down a steep place. H4325
Nah 3: 8 *that had* the w round about it, whose H4325
14 Draw thee w for the siege, fortify thy H4325
Hab 2:14 of the LORD, as the w cover the sea. H4325
3:15 horses, *through* the heap of great w. H4325
Zec 14: 8 And it shall be in that day, *that* living w H4325
Mt 8:32 into the sea, and perished in the w. G5204
Mk 9:22 fire, and into the w, to destroy him: but G5204
2Co 11:26 *In* journeyings often, *in* perils of w, *in* G4215
Rev 1:15 and his voice as the sound of many w. G5204
7:17 living fountains of w: and God shall G5204
8:10 the rivers, and upon the fountains of w; G5204
11 third part of the w became wormwood; G5204
11 of the w, because they were made bitter. G5204
11: 6 and have power over w to turn them to G5204
14: 2 the voice of many w, and as the voice of G5204
7 and the sea, and the fountains of w. G5204
16: 4 fountains of w; and they became blood. G5204
5 And I heard the angel of the w say, G5204
17: 1 great whore that sitteth upon many w: G5204
15 And he saith unto me, The w which G5204
19: 6 the voice of many w, and as the voice of G5204

WATERSPOUTS
Ps 42: 7 at the noise of thy w: all thy waves and H6794

WATERSPRINGS
Ps 107:33 and the w into dry ground; H4161+H4325
35 water, and dry ground into w. H4161+H4325

WAVE
Ex 29:24 his sons; and shalt w them *for* a wave H5130
24 them *for* a w offering before the LORD. H8573
26 consecration, and w it *for* a wave H5130
26 and wave it *for* a w offering before the H8573
27 the breast of the w offering, and the H8573
Lev 7:30 *for* a w offering before the LORD. H8573
34 For the w breast and the heave H8573
8:27 them *for* a w offering before the LORD. H8573
29 and waved it *for* a w offering before the H8573
9:21 waved *for* a w offering before the H8573
10:14 And the w breast and heave shoulder H8573
15 The heave shoulder and the w breast H8573
15 by fire of the fat, to w *it for* a wave H5130
Lev 10:15 to wave *it for* a w offering before the H8573
14:12 the log of oil, and w them *for* a wave H5130
12 them *for* a w offering before the LORD: H8573
24 and the priest shall w them *for* a wave H5130
24 them *for* a w offering before the LORD: H8573
23:11 And he shall w the sheaf before the H5130
11 after the sabbath the priest shall w it. H5130
12 And ye shall offer that day when ye w H5130
15 the sheaf of the w offering; seven H8573
17 habitations two w loaves of two tenth H8573
20 And the priest shall w them with the H5130
20 firstfruits *for* a w offering before the H8573
Nu 5:25 hand, and shall w the offering before H5130
6:20 And the priest shall w them *for* a wave H5130
20 And the priest shall wave them *for* a w H8573
20 the priest, with the w breast and heave H8573
18:11 their gift, with all the w offerings of the H8573
18 be thine, as the w breast and as the H8573
Jas 1: 6 wavereth is like a w of the sea driven G2830

WAVED
Ex 29:27 heave offering, which is w, and which is H5130
Lev 7:30 w *for* a wave offering before the LORD. H5130
8:27 his sons' hands, and w them *for* a wave H5130
29 And Moses took the breast, and w it *for* H5130
9:21 shoulder Aaron w *for* a wave offering H5130
14:21 offering to be w, to make an atonement H8573

WAVE-LOAF See WAVE and LOAF.

WAVE-OFFERING See WAVE and OFFERING.

WAVERETH
Jas 1: 6 For he that w is like a wave of the G1252

WAVERING
Heb 10:23 w; (for he *is* faithful that promised;) G186
Jas 1: 6 But let him ask in faith, nothing w. For G1252

WAVES
2Sa 22: 5 When the w of death compassed me, H4867
Job 9: 8 and treadeth upon the w of the sea. H1116
38:11 and here shall thy proud w be stayed? H1530
Ps 42: 7 w and thy billows are gone over me. H4867
65: 7 of their w, and the tumult of the people. H1530
88: 7 hast afflicted *me* with all thy w. Selah. H4867
89: 9 the w thereof arise, thou stillest them. H1530
93: 3 up their voice; the floods lift up their w. H1796
4 *yea, than* the mighty w of the sea. H4867
107:25 wind, which lifteth up the w thereof. H1530
29 a calm, so that the w thereof are still. H1530
Isa 48:18 thy righteousness as the w of the sea: H1530
51:15 the sea, whose w roared: The LORD H1530
Jer 5:22 pass it: and though the w thereof toss H1530
31:35 the sea when the w thereof roar; The H1530
51:42 with the multitude of the w thereof. H1530
55 voice; when her w do roar like great H1530
Ezk 26: 3 as the sea causeth his w to come up. H1530
Jna 2: 3 thy billows and thy w passed over me. H1530
Zec 10:11 shall smite the w in the sea, and all the H1530
Mt 8:24 covered with the w: but he was asleep. G2949
14:24 with w: for the wind was contrary. G2949
Mk 4:37 of wind, and the w beat into the ship, G2949
Lk 21:25 perplexity; the sea and the w roaring; G4535
Act 27:41 was broken with the violence of the w. G2949
Jude 13 Raging w of the sea, foaming out their G2949

WAX
Ex 22:24 And my wrath shall w hot, and I will kill
32:10 my wrath may w hot against them, and
11 doth thy wrath w hot against thy people,
22 anger of my lord w hot: thou knowest
Lev 25:47 And if a sojourner or stranger w rich by
47 *dwelleth* by him w poor, and sell himself
1Sa 3: 2 began to w dim, *that* he could not see;
Job 6:17 What time they w warm, they vanish:
14: 8 Though the root thereof w old in the
Ps 22:14 my heart is like w; it is melted in the H1749
68: 2 *them* away: as w melteth before the H1749
97: 5 The hills melted like w at the presence H1749
102:26 all of them shall w old like a garment; as
Isa 17: 4 and the fatness of his flesh shall w lean.
29:22 neither shall his face now w pale.
50: 9 lo, they all shall w old as a garment; the
51: 6 and the earth shall w old like a garment,
Jer 6:24 thereof: our hands w feeble: anguish
Mic 1: 4 shall be cleft, as w before the fire, *and* H1749
Mt 24:12 abound, the love of many shall w cold. G5594
Lk 12:33 bags which w not old, a treasure in G3822

1Ti 5:11 they have begun to w wanton against G2691
2Ti 3:13 But evil men and seducers shall w G4298
Heb 1:11 they all shall w old as doth a garment; G3822

WAXED
Gen 18:12 saying, After I am w old shall I have
26:13 And the man w great, and went forward,
41:56 the famine w sore in the land of Egypt.
Ex 1: 7 multiplied, and w exceeding mighty;
20 people multiplied, and w very mighty.
16:21 and when the sun w hot, it melted.
19:19 long, and w louder and louder, H2390
32:19 and Moses' anger w hot, and he cast the
Nu 11:23 the LORD'S hand w short? thou shalt see
Dt 8: 4 Thy raiment w not old upon thee,
32:15 But Jeshurun w fat, and kicked: thou art
Jos 23: 1 that Joshua w old and stricken in age.
1Sa 2: 5 she that hath many children is w feeble.
2Sa 3: 1 of David: but David w stronger and H1980
1 house of Saul w weaker and weaker. H1980
21:15 the Philistines: and David w faint.
2Ki 4:34 child; and the flesh of the child w warm.
1Ch 11: 9 So David w greater and greater: for the H1980
2Ch 13:21 But Abijah w mighty, and married
17:12 And Jehoshaphat w great exceedingly; H1980
24:15 But Jehoiada w old, and was full of days
Neh 9:21 w not old, and their feet swelled not.
Est 9: 4 man Mordecai w greater and greater. H1980
Ps 32: 3 When I kept silence, my bones w old
Jer 49:24 Damascus is w feeble, and turneth
50:43 and his hands w feeble: anguish took
Dan 8: 8 Therefore the he goat w very great: and
9 a little horn, which w exceeding great,
10 And it w great, even to the host of
Mt 13:15 For this people's heart is w gross, and G3975
Lk 1:80 And the child grew, and w strong in G2901
2:40 And the child grew, and w strong in G2901
13:19 and it grew, and w a great tree; and the G1096
Act 13:46 Then Paul and Barnabas w bold, and G3955
28:27 For the heart of this people is w gross, G3975
Heb 11:34 made strong, w valiant in fight, turned G1096
Rev 18: 3 of the earth are w rich through the G4147

WAXEN
Gen 19:13 the cry of them is w great before the face
Lev 25:25 If thy brother be w poor, and hath sold
35 And if thy brother be w poor, and fallen
39 by thee be w poor, and be sold unto
Dt 29: 5 clothes are not w old upon you, and thy
5 and thy shoe is not w old upon thy foot.
31:20 themselves, and w fat; then will they
32:15 kicked: thou art w fat, thou art grown
Jos 17:13 of Israel were w strong, that they put
Jer 5:27 they are become great, and w rich.
28 They are w fat, they shine: yea, they
Ezk 16: 7 hast increased and w great, and thou art

WAXETH
Ps 6: 7 it w old because of all mine enemies.
Heb 8:13 and w old is ready to vanish away. G1095

WAXING
Php 1:14 in the Lord, w confident by my bonds, G3982

WAY
Gen 3:24 w, to keep the way of the tree of life. H2015
24 way, to keep the w of the tree of life. H1870
6:12 had corrupted his w upon the earth. H1870
12:19 behold thy wife, take her, and go thy w.
14:11 and all their victuals, and went their w. H3212
16: 7 by the fountain in the w to Shur. H1870
18:16 went with them to bring them on the w. H7971
19 shall keep the w of the LORD, to do H1870
33 And the LORD went his w, as soon as H3212
21:16 him a good w off, as it were a bowshot: H7368
24:27 I being in the w, the LORD led me to H1870
40 and prosper thy w; and thou shalt take H1870
42 now thou do prosper my w which I go: H1870
48 had led me in the right w to take my H1870
56 prospered my w; send me away that H1870
61 servant took Rebekah, and went his w. H3212
62 And Isaac came from the w of the well H935
25:34 his w: thus Esau despised his birthright. H3212
28:20 keep me in this w that I go, and will H1870
32: 1 And Jacob went on his w, and the H1870
33:16 So Esau returned that day on his w H1870
35: 3 and was with me in the w which I went. H1870
16 was but a little w to come to Ephrath: H776
19 the w to Ephrath, which is Beth-lehem. H1870
Gen 38:14 which is by the w to Timnath; for she H1870
16 And he turned unto her by the w, and H1870
21 was openly by the w side? And they H1870
42:25 for the w: and thus did he unto them. H1870
38 befall him by the w in the which ye go, H1870
45:21 and gave them provision for the w. H1870
23 bread and meat for his father by the w. H1870
24 them, See that ye fall not out by the w. H1870
48: 7 of Canaan in the w, when yet there was H1870
7 was but a little w to come unto Ephrath: H776
7 w of Ephrath; the same is Beth-lehem. H1870
49:17 Dan shall be a serpent by the w, an H1870
Ex 2:12 And he looked this w and that way, H3541
12 And he looked this way and that w, and H3541
4:24 And it came to pass by the w in the inn, H1870
5:20 w, as they came forth from Pharaoh: H7125
13:17 not through the w of the land of the H1870
18 through the w of the wilderness of H1870
21 to lead them the w; and by night in a H1870
18: 8 w, and how the LORD delivered them. H1870
20 shew them the w wherein they must H1870
27 and he went his w into his own land.
23:20 to keep thee in the w, and to bring thee H1870
32: 8 aside quickly out of the w which I H1870
33: 3 people: lest I consume thee in the w. H1870
13 shew me now thy w, that I may know H1870
Nu 13:17 Get you up this w southward, and go up
14:25 the wilderness by the w of the Red sea. H1870
20:17 by the king's high w, we will not turn to H1870
19 will go by the high w: and if I and my H4546
21: 1 Israel came by the w of the spies; then H1870
4 mount Hor by the w of the Red sea, to H1870
4 much discouraged because of the w. H1870
22 high w, until we be past thy borders. H1870
33 And they turned and went up by the w H1870
22:22 stood in the w for an adversary against H1870
23 standing in the w, and his sword drawn H1870
23 aside out of the w, and went into the H1870
23 smote the ass, to turn her into the w. H1870
26 where was no w to turn either to the H1870
31 standing in the w, and his sword drawn H1870
32 because thy w is perverse before me: H1870
34 thou stoodest in the w against me: now H1870
24:25 to his place: and Balak also went his w. H1870
Dt 1: 2 w of mount Seir unto Kadesh-barnea.) H1870
19 ye saw by the w of the mountain of H1870
22 again by what w we must go up, and H1870
31 his son, in all the w that ye went, until H1870
33 Who went in the w before you, to H1870
33 w ye should go, and in a cloud by day. H1870
40 the wilderness by the w of the Red sea. H1870
2: 1 wilderness by the w of the Red sea, as H1870
8 in Seir, through the w of the plain from H1870
8 by the w of the wilderness of Moab. H1870
27 along by the high w, I will neither turn H1870
3: 1 Then we turned, and went up the w to H1870
6: 7 walkest by the w, and when thou liest H1870
8: 2 And thou shalt remember all the w H1870
9:12 aside out of the w which I commanded H1870
16 quickly out of the w which the LORD H1870
11:19 walkest by the w, when thou liest down, H1870
28 aside out of the w which I command H1870
30 Jordan, by the w where the sun goeth H1870
13: 5 thee out of the w which the LORD thy H1870
14:24 And if the w be too long for thee, so H1870
17:16 shall henceforth return no more that w. H1870
19: 3 Thou shalt prepare thee a w, and divide H1870
6 him, because the w is long, and slay H1870
22: 4 ox fall down by the w, and hide thyself H1870
6 before thee in the w in any tree, or on H1870
23: 4 with water in the w, when ye came forth H1870
24: 9 Miriam by the w, after that ye were H1870
25:17 unto thee by the w, when ye were come H1870
18 How he met thee by the w, and smote H1870
27:18 w. And all the people shall say, Amen. H1870
28: 7 one w, and flee before thee seven ways. H1870
25 shalt go out one w against them, and H1870
68 with ships, by the w whereof I spake H1870
31:29 turn aside from the w which I have H1870
Jos 1: 8 shalt make thy w prosperous, and then H1870
2: 7 And the men pursued after them the w H1870
16 and afterward may ye go your w. H1870
22 all the w, but found them not. H1870
3: 4 ye may know the w by which ye must H1870
4 ye have not passed this w heretofore. H1870
5: 4 by the w, after they came out of Egypt. H1870
5 wilderness by the w as they came forth H1870
7 had not circumcised them by the w. H1870
8:15 and fled by the w of the wilderness. H1870
Jos 8:20 no power to flee this w or that way: and H2008
20 this way or that w: and the people that H2008
10:10 them along the w that goeth up to H1870
12: 3 on the east, the w to Beth-jeshimoth; H1870
23:14 And, behold, this day I am going the w H1870
24:17 us in all the w wherein we went, and H1870
Jdg 2:17 quickly out of the w which their fathers H1870
19 own doings, nor from their stubborn w. H1870
22 they will keep the w of the LORD to H1870
5:10 that sit in judgment, and walk by the w. H1870
8:11 And Gideon went up by the w of them H1870
9:25 w by them: and it was told Abimelech. H1870
18: 5 our w which we go shall be prosperous. H1870
6 the LORD is your w wherein ye go. H1870
22 And when they were a good w from the H7368
26 And the children of Dan went their w: H1870
19: 5 of bread, and afterward go your w. H3212
9 on your w, that thou mayest go home. H1870
14 And they passed on and went their w; H3212
27 went out to go his w: and, behold, the H1870
20:42 of Israel unto the w of the wilderness; H1870
Ru 1: 7 the w to return unto the land of Judah. H1870
12 Turn again, my daughters, go your w; H1870
1Sa 1:18 woman went her w, and did eat, and H1870
6: 9 And see, if it goeth up by the w of his H1870
12 And the kine took the straight w to the H1870
12 way to the w of Beth-shemesh, and H1870
9: 6 can shew us our w that we should go. H1870
8 give to the man of God, to tell us our w. H1870
12:23 will teach you the good and the right w: H1870
13:17 turned unto the w that leadeth to H1870
18 And another company turned the w to H1870
18 turned to the w of the border that H1870
15: 2 in the w, when he came up from Egypt. H1870
20 and have gone the w which the LORD H1870
17:52 fell down by the w to Shaaraim, even H1870
20:22 w: for the LORD hath sent thee away. H3212
24: 3 sheepcotes by the w, where was a cave; H1870
7 up out of the cave, and went on his w. H1870
25:12 So David's young men turned their w, H1870
26: 3 Jeshimon, by the w. But David abode in H1870
25 on his w, and Saul returned to his place. H1870
28:22 strength, when thou goest on thy w. H1870
30: 2 them away, and went on their w. H1870
2Sa 2:24 by the w of the wilderness of Gibeon. H1870
13:30 they were in the w, that tidings came to H1870
34 by the w of the hill side behind him. H1870
15: 2 stood beside the w of the gate: and it H1870
23 over, toward the w of the wilderness. H1870
16:13 men went by the w, Shimei went along H1870
18:23 the w of the plain, and overran Cushi. H1870
19:36 Thy servant will go a little w over Jordan
22:31 As for God, his w is perfect; the word of H1870
33 power: and he maketh my w perfect. H1870
1Ki 1:49 and rose up, and went every man his w. H1870
2: 2 I go the w of all the earth: be thou H1870
4 take heed to their w, to walk before me H1870
8:25 take heed to their w, that they walk H1870
32 to bring his w upon his head; and H1870
36 them the good w wherein they should H1870
11:29 found him in the w; and he had clad H1870
13: 9 again by the same w that thou camest. H1870
10 So he went another w, and returned not H1870
10 not by the w that he came to Beth-el. H1870
12 unto them, What w went he? For his H1870
12 had seen what w the man of God went, H1870
17 again to go by the w that thou camest. H1870
24 met him by the w, and slew him: and H1870
24 was cast in the w, and the ass stood by H1870
25 the carcase cast in the w, and the lion H1870
26 back from the w heard thereof, he said, H1870
28 carcase cast in the w, and the ass and H1870
33 not from his evil w, but made again of H1870
15:26 and walked in the w of his father, and H1870
34 and walked in the w of Jeroboam, and H1870
16: 2 hast walked in the w of Jeroboam, and H1870
19 in walking in the w of Jeroboam, and H1870
26 For he walked in all the w of Jeroboam H1870
18: 6 it: Ahab went one w by himself, and H1870
6 Obadiah went another w by himself. H1870
7 And as Obadiah was in the w, behold, H1870
19:15 Go, return on thy w to the wilderness of H1870
20:38 for the king by the w, and disguised H1870
22:24 and said, Which w went the spirit of the H335
52 and walked in the w of his father, and H1870
52 father, and in the w of his mother, and H1870
52 and in the w of Jeroboam the son H1870
2Ki 2:23 was going up by the w, there came forth H1870
3: 8 And he said, Which w shall we go up? H1870

2Ki 3: 8 The **w** through the wilderness of Edom. H1870
20 came water by the **w** of Edom, and the H1870
4:29 hand, and go thy **w**: if thou meet any H1870
5:19 peace. So he departed from him a little **w**. H776
6:19 This *is* not the **w**, neither *is* this the city: H1870
7:15 and, lo, all the **w** *was* full of garments H1870
8:18 And he walked in the **w** of the kings of H1870
27 And he walked in the **w** of the house of H1870
9:27 saw *this*, he fled by the **w** of the garden H1870
10:12 he *was* at the shearing house in the **w**, H1870
11:16 and she went by the **w** by the which the H1870
19 and came by the **w** of the gate of the H1870
16: 3 But he walked in the **w** of the kings of H1870
19:28 back by the **w** by which thou camest. H1870
33 By the **w** that he came, by the same H1870
21:21 And he walked in all the **w** that his H1870
22 and walked not in the **w** of the LORD. H1870
22: 2 walked in all the **w** of David his father, H1870
25: 4 by night by the **w** of the gate between H1870
4 *the king* went the **w** toward the plain. H1870
2Ch 6:16 take heed to their **w** to walk in my law, H1870
23 by recompensing his **w** upon his own H1870
27 them the good **w**, wherein they should H1870
34 enemies by the **w** that thou shalt send H1870
11:17 walked in the **w** of David and Solomon. H1870
18:23 and said, Which **w** went the spirit of H1870
20:32 And he walked in the **w** of Asa his H1870
21: 6 And he walked in the **w** of the kings of H1870
13 But hast walked in the **w** of the kings of H1870
Ezr 8:21 of him a right **w** for us, and for our H1870
22 the enemy in the **w**: because we had H1870
31 and of such as lay in wait by the **w**. H1870
Neh 8:10 Then he said unto them, Go your **w**, eat H1870
12 And all the people went their **w** to eat, H1870
9:12 light in the **w** wherein they should go. H1870
19 lead them in the **w**; neither the pillar of H1870
19 and the **w** wherein they should go. H1870
Est 4:17 So Mordecai went his **w**, and did H5674
Job 3:23 *Why is light given* to a man whose **w** is H1870
6:18 The paths of their **w** are turned aside; H1870
8:19 Behold, this *is* the joy of his **w**, and out H1870
12:24 in a wilderness *where there is* no **w**. H1870
16:22 shall go the **w** *whence* I shall not return. H734
17: 9 The righteous also shall hold on his **w**, H1870
18:10 the ground, and a trap for him in the **w**. H5410
19: 8 He hath fenced up my **w** that I cannot H734
12 and raise up their **w** against me, and H1870
21:29 the **w**? and do ye not know their tokens, H1870
31 Who shall declare his **w** to his face? H1870
22:15 Hast thou marked the old **w** which H734
23:10 But he knoweth the **w** that I take: *when* H1870
11 My foot hath held his steps, his **w** have H1870
24: 4 They turn the needy out of the **w**: the H1870
18 beholdeth not the **w** of the vineyards. H1870
24 taken out of the **w** as all *other*, and cut H7092
28:23 God understandeth the **w** thereof, and H1870
26 a **w** for the lightning of the thunder: H1870
29:25 I chose out their **w**, and sat chief, and H1870
31: 7 If my step hath turned out of the **w**, and H1870
36:23 Who hath enjoined him his **w**? or who H1870
38:19 Where *is* the **w** *where* light dwelleth? H1870
24 By what **w** is the light parted, *which* H1870
25 or a **w** for the lightning of thunder; H1870
Ps 1: 1 standeth in the **w** of sinners, nor sitteth H1870
6 For the LORD knoweth the **w** of the H1870
6 but the **w** of the ungodly shall perish. H1870
2:12 ye perish *from* the **w**, when his wrath is H1870
5: 8 make thy **w** straight before my face. H1870
18:30 *As for* God, his **w** *is* perfect: the word of H1870
32 strength, and maketh my **w** perfect. H1870
25: 8 therefore will he teach sinners in the **w**. H1870
9 and the meek will he teach his **w**. H1870
12 he teach in the **w** *that* he shall choose. H1870
27:11 Teach me thy **w**, O LORD, and lead me H1870
32: 8 teach thee in the **w** which thou shalt go: H1870
35: 3 Draw out also the spear, and stop *the w*
6 Let their **w** be dark and slippery: and H1870
36: 4 himself in a **w** *that is* not good; he H1870
37: 5 Commit thy **w** unto the LORD; trust H1870
7 prospereth in his **w**, because of the man H1870
23 the LORD: and he delighteth in his **w**. H1870
34 Wait on the LORD, and keep his **w**, and H1870
44:18 have our steps declined from thy **w**; H734
49:13 This their **w** *is* their folly: yet their H1870
67: 2 That thy **w** may be known upon earth, H1870
77:13 Thy **w**, O God, *is* in the sanctuary: who H1870
19 Thy **w** *is* in the sea, and thy path in the H1870
78:50 He made a **w** to his anger; he spared H5410
80:12 they which pass by the **w** do pluck her? H1870
Ps 85:13 and shall set *us* in the **w** of his steps. H1870
86:11 Teach me thy **w**, O LORD; I will walk in H1870
89:41 All that pass by the **w** spoil him: he is a H1870
101: 2 wisely in a perfect **w**. O when wilt thou H1870
6 in a perfect **w**, he shall serve me. H1870
102:23 He weakened my strength in the **w**; he H1870
107: 4 **w**; they found no city to dwell in. H1870
7 And he led them forth by the right **w**, H1870
40 in the wilderness, *where there is* no **w**. H1870
110: 7 He shall drink of the brook in the **w**: H1870
119: 1 Blessed *are* the undefiled in the **w**, who H1870
9 young man cleanse his **w**? by taking heed H734
14 I have rejoiced in the **w** of thy H1870
27 Make me to understand the **w** of thy H1870
29 Remove from me the **w** of lying: and H1870
30 I have chosen the **w** of truth: thy H1870
32 I will run the **w** of thy commandments, H1870
33 Teach me, O LORD, the **w** of thy H1870
37 vanity; *and* quicken thou me in thy **w**. H1870
101 every evil **w**, that I might keep thy word. H734
104 therefore I hate every false **w**. H734
128 *to be* right; *and* I hate every false **w**. H734
139:24 And see if *there be any* wicked **w** in me, H1870
24 me, and lead me in the **w** everlasting. H1870
142: 3 my path. In the **w** wherein I walked have H734
143: 8 me to know the **w** wherein I should H1870
146: 9 and widow: but the **w** of the wicked he H1870
Prv 1:15 My son, walk not thou in the **w** with H1870
31 **w**, and be filled with their own devices. H1870
2: 8 and preserveth the **w** of his saints. H1870
12 To deliver thee from the **w** of the evil H1870
20 That thou mayest walk in the **w** of good H1870
3:23 Then shalt thou walk in thy **w** safely, H1870
4:11 I have taught thee in the **w** of wisdom; I H1870
14 and go not in the **w** of evil *men*. H1870
19 The **w** of the wicked *is* as darkness: H1870
5: 8 Remove thy **w** far from her, and come H1870
6:23 reproofs of instruction *are* the **w** of life: H1870
7: 8 corner; and he went the **w** to her house, H1870
27 Her house *is* the **w** to hell, going down H1870
8: 2 by the **w** in the places of the paths. H1870
13 **w**, and the froward mouth, do I hate. H1870
20 I lead in the **w** of righteousness, in the H734
22 of his **w**, before his works of old. H1870
9: 6 live; and go in the **w** of understanding. H1870
10:17 He *is in* the **w** of life that keepeth H734
29 The **w** of the LORD *is* strength to the H1870
11: 5 shall direct his **w**: but the wicked shall H1870
20 *as are* upright in *their* **w** *are* his delight. H1870
12:15 The **w** of a fool *is* right in his own eyes: H1870
26 but the **w** of the wicked seduceth them. H1870
28 In the **w** of righteousness *is* life; and *in* H734
13: 6 *that is* upright in the **w**: but wickedness H1870
15 but the **w** of transgressors *is* hard. H1870
14: 8 his **w**: but the folly of fools *is* deceit. H1870
12 There is a **w** which seemeth right unto H1870
15: 9 The **w** of the wicked *is* an abomination H1870
10 **w**: *and* he that hateth reproof shall die. H734
19 The **w** of the slothful *man is* as an H1870
19 but the **w** of the righteous *is* made plain. H734
24 The **w** of life *is* above to the wise, that he H734
16: 9 A man's heart deviseth his **w**: but the H1870
17 that keepeth his **w** preserveth his soul. H1870
25 There is a **w** that seemeth right unto a H1870
29 leadeth him into the **w** *that is* not good. H1870
31 *if* it be found in the **w** of righteousness. H1870
19: 3 perverteth his **w**: and his heart fretteth H1870
20:14 when he is gone his **w**, then he boasteth.
24 can a man then understand his own **w**? H1870
21: 2 Every **w** of a man *is* right in his own H1870
8 The **w** of man *is* froward and strange: H1870
16 The man that wandereth out of the **w** H1870
29 *as for* the upright, he directeth his **w**. H1870
22: 5 Thorns *and* snares *are* in the **w** of the H1870
6 Train up a child in the **w** he should go: H1870
23:19 be wise, and guide thine heart in the **w**. H1870
26:13 *is* a lion in the **w**; a lion *is* in the streets. H1870
28:10 astray in an evil **w**, he shall fall himself H1870
29:27 in the **w** *is* abomination to the wicked. H1870
30:19 The **w** of an eagle in the air; the way of H1870
19 The way of an eagle in the air; the **w** of H1870
19 upon a rock; the **w** of a ship in the H1870
19 sea; and the **w** of a man with a maid. H1870
20 Such *is* the **w** of an adulterous woman; H1870
Ecc 9: 7 Go thy **w**, eat thy bread with joy, and H3212
10: 3 walketh by the **w**, his wisdom faileth H1870
11: 5 As thou knowest not what *is* the **w** of H1870
12: 5 *shall be* in the **w**, and the almond tree H1870
Song 1: 8 women, go thy **w** forth by the footsteps H1870
Isa 3:12 to err, and destroy the **w** of thy paths. H1870
8:11 not walk in the **w** of this people, saying, H1870
9: 1 afflict *her by* the **w** of the sea, beyond H1870
15: 5 go it up; for in the **w** of Horonaim they H1870
26: 7 The **w** of the just *is* uprightness: thou, H734
8 Yea, in the **w** of thy judgments, O LORD, H734
28: 7 are out of the **w**; the priest and the H8582
7 they are out of the **w** through strong H8582
30:11 Get you out of the **w**, turn aside out of H1870
21 saying, This *is* the **w**, walk ye in it, when H1870
35: 8 And an highway shall be there, and a **w**, H1870
8 shall be called The **w** of holiness; the H1870
37:29 back by the **w** by which thou camest. H1870
34 By the **w** that he came, by the same H1870
40: 3 Prepare ye the **w** of the LORD, make H1870
14 shewed to him the **w** of understanding? H1870
27 O Israel, My **w** is hid from the LORD, H1870
41: 3 the **w** *that* he had not gone with his feet. H734
42:16 And I will bring the blind by a **w** *that* H1870
43:16 which maketh a **w** in the sea, and a H1870
19 I will even make a **w** in the wilderness, H1870
48:15 and he shall make his **w** prosperous. H1870
17 thee by the **w** *that* thou should-est go. H1870
49:11 And I will make all my mountains a **w**, H1870
51:10 sea a **w** for the ransomed to pass over? H1870
53: 6 one to his own **w**; and the LORD hath H1870
55: 7 Let the wicked forsake his **w**, and the H1870
56:11 all look to their own **w**, every one for his H1870
57:10 greatness of thy **w**; *yet* saidst thou not, H1870
14 cast ye up, prepare the **w**, take up the H1870
14 out of the **w** of my people. H1870
17 went on frowardly in the **w** of his heart. H1870
59: 8 The **w** of peace they know not; and H1870
62:10 prepare ye the **w** of the people; cast up, H1870
65: 2 walketh in a **w** *that was* not good, H1870
Jer 2:17 thy God, when he led thee by the **w**? H1870
18 And now what hast thou to do in the **w** H1870
18 thou to do in the **w** of Assyria, to drink H1870
23 Baalim? see thy **w** in the valley, know H1870
33 Why trimmest thou thy **w** to seek love? H1870
36 to change thy **w**? thou also shalt be H1870
3:21 have perverted their **w**, *and* they have H1870
4: 7 the Gentiles is on his **w**; he is gone forth H5265
18 Thy **w** and thy doings have procured H1870
5: 4 they know not the **w** of the LORD, *nor* H1870
5 have known the **w** of the LORD, *and* H1870
6:16 where *is* the good **w**, and walk therein, H1870
25 nor walk by the **w**; for the sword of the H1870
27 that thou mayest know and try their **w**. H1870
10: 2 Thus saith the LORD, Learn not the **w** H1870
23 O LORD, I know that the **w** of man *is* H1870
12: 1 doth the **w** of the wicked prosper? H1870
18:11 one from his evil **w**, and make your H1870
15 to walk in paths, *in* a **w** not cast up; H1870
21: 8 you the **w** of life, and the way of death. H1870
8 you the way of life, and the **w** of death. H1870
23:12 Wherefore their **w** shall be unto them H1870
22 evil **w**, and from the evil of their doings. H1870
25: 5 one from his evil **w**, and from the evil of H1870
35 And the shepherds shall have no **w** to H6
26: 3 man from his evil **w**, that I may repent H1870
28:11 And the prophet Jeremiah went his **w**. H1870
31: 9 in a straight **w**, wherein they shall not H1870
21 the highway, *even* the **w** *which* thou H1870
32:39 heart, and one **w**, that they may fear me H1870
35:15 man from his evil **w**, and amend your H1870
36: 3 man from his evil **w**; that I may forgive H1870
7 one from his evil **w**: for great *is* the H1870
39: 4 by night, by the **w** of the king's garden, H1870
4 and he went out the **w** of the plain. H1870
42: 3 may shew us the **w** wherein we may H1870
48:19 O inhabitant of Aroer, stand by the **w**, H1870
50: 5 They shall ask the **w** to Zion with their H1870
52: 7 by night by the **w** of the gate between H1870
7 and they went by the **w** of the plain. H1870
Ezk 3:18 from his wicked **w**, to save his life; the H1870
19 from his wicked **w**, he shall die in his H1870
7:27 them after their **w**, and according to H1870
8: 5 eyes now the **w** toward the north. So H1870
5 up mine eyes the **w** toward the north, H1870
9: 2 And, behold, six men came from the **w** H1870
10 recompense their **w** upon their head. H1870
11:21 recompense their **w** upon their own H1870
13:22 his wicked **w**, by promising him life: H1870
14:22 ye shall see their **w** and their doings: H1870
16:25 every head of the **w**, and hast made thy H1870
27 which are ashamed of thy lewd **w**. H1870
31 the head of every **w**, and makest thine H1870
43 recompense thy **w** upon *thine* head, H1870

Ezk 18:25 Yet ye say, The w of the Lord is not H1870
25 w equal? are not your ways unequal? H1870
29 Yet saith the house of Israel, The w of H1870
21:16 Go thee one w or other, *either* on the
19 *it* at the head of the w to the city. H1870
20 Appoint a w, that the sword may come H1870
21 the parting of the w, at the head of the H1870
22:31 my wrath: their own w have I H1870
23:13 was defiled, *that* they *took* both one w, H1870
31 Thou hast walked in the w of thy sister; H1870
33: 8 the wicked from his w, that wicked *man* H1870
9 the wicked of his w to turn from it; if he H1870
9 not turn from his w, he shall die in his H1870
11 turn from his w and live: turn ye, turn H1870
17 thy people say, The w of the Lord is not H1870
17 but as for them, their w is not equal. H1870
20 Yet ye say, The w of the Lord is not H1870
36:17 it by their own w and by their doings: H1870
17 their doings: their w was before me as H1870
19 according to their w and according to H1870
42: 1 the utter court, the w toward the north: H1870
4 breadth inward, a w of one cubit; and H1870
11 And the w before them *was* like the H1870
12 door in the head of the w, *even* the way H1870
12 the way, *even* the w directly before the H1870
43: 2 came from the w of the east: and his H1870
4 the house by the w of the gate whose H1870
44: 1 Then he brought me back the w of the H1870
3 shall enter by the w of the porch of *that* H1870
3 and shall go out by the w of the same. H1870
4 Then brought he me the w of the north H1870
46: 2 And the prince shall enter by the w of H1870
8 shall go in by the w of the porch of *that* H1870
8 and he shall go forth by the w thereof. H1870
9 entereth in by the w of the north gate to H1870
9 shall go out by the w of the south gate; H1870
9 that entereth by the w of the south gate H1870
9 go forth by the w of the north gate: he H1870
9 not return by the w of the gate whereby H1870
47: 2 Then brought he me out of the w of the H1870
2 led me about the w without unto the H1870
2 the utter gate by the w that looketh H1870
15 the w of Hethlon, as men go to Zedad; H1870
48: 1 to the coast of the w of Hethlon, as one H1870
Dan 12: 9 And he said, Go thy w, Daniel: for the H3212
13 But go thou thy w till the end *be*: for H3212
Hos 2: 6 I will hedge up thy w with thorns, and H1870
6: 9 murder in the w by consent: for they H1870
10:13 w, in the multitude of thy mighty men. H1870
13: 7 a leopard by the w will I observe *them*: H1870
Am 2: 7 and turn aside the w of the meek: and a H1870
Jna 3: 8 every one from his evil w, and from the H1870
10 from their evil w; and God repented of H1870
Nah 1: 3 LORD hath his w in the whirlwind and H1870
2: 1 watch the w, make *thy* loins strong, H1870
Zec 10: 2 they went their w as a flock, they were
Mal 2: 8 But ye are departed out of the w; ye H1870
3: 1 shall prepare the w before me: and the H1870
Mt 2:12 into their own country another w. G3598
3: 3 w of the Lord, make his paths straight. G3598
4:15 *by* the w of the sea, beyond Jordan, G3598
5:24 altar, and go thy w; first be reconciled G5217
25 thou art in the w with him; lest at any G3598
7:13 gate, and broad *is* the w, that leadeth to G3598
14 and narrow *is* the w, which leadeth G3598
8: 4 man; but go thy w, shew thyself to the G5217
13 centurion, Go thy w; and as thou hast G5217
28 so that no man might pass by that w. G3598
30 And there was a good w off from them G3112
10: 5 Go not into the w of the Gentiles, and G3598
11:10 which shall prepare thy w before thee. G3598
13: 4 *seeds* fell by the w side, and the fowls G3598
19 is he which received seed by the w side. G3598
25 tares among the wheat, and went his w. G565
15:32 away fasting, lest they faint in the w. G3598
20: 4 I will give you. And they went their w. G565
14 Take *that* thine *is*, and go thy w: I will G5217
17 apart in the w, and said unto them, G3598
30 men sitting by the w side, when they G3598
21: 8 garments in the w; others cut down G3598
8 the trees, and strawed *them* in the w. G3598
19 And when he saw a fig tree in the w, he G3598
32 For John came unto you in the w of G3598
22:16 and teachest the w of God in truth, G3598
22 and left him, and went their w. G565
27:65 go your w, make *it* as sure as ye can. G5217
Mk 1: 2 which shall prepare thy w before thee. G3598
3 w of the Lord, make his paths straight. G3598
44 man: but go thy w, shew thyself to the G5217
Mk 2:11 thy bed, and go thy w into thine house. G5217
4: 4 some fell by the w side, and the fowls G3598
15 And these are they by the w side, where G3598
7:29 w; the devil is gone out of thy daughter. G5217
8: 3 the w: for divers of them came from far. G3598
27 and by the w he asked his disciples, G3598
9:33 ye disputed among yourselves by the w? G3598
34 But they held their peace: for by the w G3598
10:17 And when he was gone forth into the w, G3598
21 lackest: go thy w, sell whatsoever thou G5217
32 And they were in the w going up to G3598
52 And Jesus said unto him, Go thy w; thy G5217
52 his sight, and followed Jesus in the w. G3598
11: 2 And saith unto them, Go your w into G5217
4 And they went their w, and found the colt G565
8 garments in the w: and others cut down G3598
8 the trees, and strawed *them* in the w. G3598
12:12 and they left him, and went their w. G565
14 but teachest the w of God in truth: Is it G3598
16: 7 But go your w, tell his disciples and G5217
Lk 1:79 to guide our feet into the w of peace. G3598
3: 4 w of the Lord, make his paths straight. G3598
4:30 through the midst of them went his w, G4198
5:19 And when they could not find by what *w*
7:22 them, Go your w, and tell John what G4198
27 which shall prepare thy w before thee. G3598
8: 5 some fell by the w side; and it was G3598
12 Those by the w side are they that hear; G3598
39 thee. And he went his w, and published G565
9:57 they went in the w, a certain *man* said G3598
10: 4 nor shoes: and salute no man by the w. G3598
31 certain priest that w: and when he saw G3598
12:58 *as thou art* in the w, give diligence that G3598
14:32 Or else, while the other is yet a great w G4206
15:20 he was yet a great w off, his father saw G3112
17:19 And he said unto him, Arise, go thy w: G4198
18:35 blind man sat by the w side begging: G3598
19: 4 tree to see him: for he was to pass that *w*.
32 And they that were sent went their w, G565
36 went, they spread their clothes in the w. G3598
20:21 *of any*, but teachest the w of God truly: G3598
22: 4 And he went his w, and communed with G565
24:32 with us by the w, and while he opened G3598
35 *were done* in the w, and how he was G3598
Jn 1:23 Make straight the w of the Lord, as G3598
4:28 her w into the city, and saith to the men, G565
50 Jesus saith unto him, Go thy w; thy son G4198
50 spoken unto him, and he went his w. G4198
8:21 them, I go my w, and ye shall seek me, G5217
9: 7 Sent.) He went his w therefore, and G565
10: 1 other w, the same is a thief and a robber. G237
11:28 said, she went her w, and called Mary her G565
14: 4 And whither I go ye know, and the w ye G3598
5 goest; and how can we know the w? G3598
6 Jesus saith unto him, I am the w, the G3598
16: 5 But now I go my w to him that sent me; G5217
18: 8 ye seek me, let these go their w: G5217
Act 8:26 the south unto the w that goeth down G3598
36 And as they went on *their* w, they came G3598
39 more: and he went on his w rejoicing. G3598
9: 2 found any of this w, whether they were G3598
15 But the Lord said unto him, Go thy w: G4198
17 And Ananias went his w, and entered G565
17 unto thee in the w as thou camest, hath G3598
27 seen the Lord in the w, and that he had G3598
15: 3 And being brought on their w by the G4311
16:17 which shew unto us the w of salvation. G3598
18:25 This man was instructed in the w of the G3598
26 unto him the w of God more perfectly. G3598
19: 9 but spake evil of that w before the G3598
23 there arose no small stir about that w. G3598
21: 5 and went our w; and they all brought G4198
5 all brought us on our w, with wives and G4311
22: 4 And I persecuted this w unto the death, G3598
24:14 that after the w which they call heresy, G3598
22 knowledge of *that* w, he deferred them, G3598
25 answered, Go thy w for this time; when G4198
25: 3 laying wait in the w to kill him. G3598
26:13 At midday, O king, I saw in the w a G3598
Ro 3: 2 Much every w: chiefly, because that G5158
12 They are all gone out of the w, they are G1578
17 And the w of peace have they not G3598
14:13 or an occasion to fall in *his* brother's w.
15:24 to be brought on my w thitherward by G4311
1Co 10:13 also make a w to escape, that ye may G1545
12:31 yet shew I unto you a more excellent w. G3598
16: 7 For I will not see you now by the w; but G3938
2Co 1:16 to be brought on my w toward Judaea. G4311
Php 1:18 What then? notwithstanding, every w, G5158
Col 2:14 it out of the w, nailing it to his cross; G3319
1Th 3:11 Jesus Christ, direct our w unto you. G3598
2Th 2: 7 *will let*, until he be taken out of the w. G3319
Heb 5: 2 that are out of the w; for that he himself G4105
9: 8 that the w into the holiest of all G3598
10:20 By a new and living w, which he hath G3598
12:13 out of the w; but let it rather be healed. G1624
Jas 1:24 and goeth his w, and straightway G565
2:25 and had sent *them* out another w? G3598
5:20 the error of his w shall save a soul from G3598
2Pt 2: 2 the w of truth shall be evil spoken of. G3598
15 Which have forsaken the right w, and G3598
15 following the w of Balaam *the son* of G3598
21 to have known the w of righteousness, G3598
3: 1 pure minds by w of remembrance: G1722
Jude 11 have gone in the w of Cain, and ran G3598
Rev 16:12 dried up, that the w of the kings of the G3598

WAYFARING

Jdg 19:17 his eyes, he saw a w man in the street of H732
2Sa 12: 4 to dress for the w man that was come H732
Isa 33: 8 The highways lie waste, the w H5674+H734
35: 8 for those: the w men, though H1982+H1870
Jer 9: 2 a lodging place of w men; that I might H732
14: 8 in the land, and as a w man *that* turneth H732

WAYMARKS

Jer 31:21 Set thee up w, make thee high heaps: set H6725

WAYS

Gen 19: 2 and go on your w. And they said, Nay; H1870
Lev 20: 4 And if the people of the land do any w H5956
26:22 and your *high* w shall be desolate. H1870
Nu 30:15 But if he shall any w make them void H6565
Dt 5:33 Ye shall walk in all the w which the H1870
8: 6 God, to walk in his w, and to fear him. H1870
10:12 to walk in all his w, and to love him, H1870
11:22 in all his w, and to cleave unto him; H1870
19: 9 to walk ever in his w; then shalt thou H1870
26:17 and to walk in his w, and to keep his H1870
28: 7 one way, and flee before thee seven w. H1870
9 of the LORD thy God, and walk in his w. H1870
25 and flee seven w before them: and shalt H1870
29 not prosper in thy w: and thou shalt be H1870
30:16 God, to walk in his w, and to keep his H1870
32: 4 *is* perfect: for all his w *are* judgment: a H1870
Jos 22: 5 and to walk in all his w, and to keep his H1870
1Sa 8: 3 And his sons walked not in his w, but H1870
5 walk not in thy w: now make us a king H1870
18:14 all his w; and the LORD *was* with him. H1870
2Sa 22:22 For I have kept the w of the LORD, and H1870
1Ki 2: 3 to walk in his w, to keep his statutes, H1870
3:14 And if thou wilt walk in my w, to keep H1870
8:39 according to his w, whose heart thou H1870
58 him, to walk in all his w, and to keep his H1870
11:33 not walked in my w, to do *that which is* H1870
38 wilt walk in my w, and do *that is* right H1870
22:43 And he walked in all the w of Asa his H1870
2Ki 17:13 Turn ye from your evil w, and keep my H1870
2Ch 6:30 unto all his w, whose heart thou H1870
31 to walk in thy w, so long as they live H1870
7:14 from their wicked w; then will I hear H1870
13:22 of Abijah, and his w, and his sayings, H1870
17: 3 he walked in the first w of his father H1870
6 And his heart was lifted up in the w of H1870
21:12 not walked in the w of Jehoshaphat thy H1870
12 nor in the w of Asa king of Judah, H1870
22: 3 He also walked in the w of the house of H1870
27: 6 his w before the LORD his God. H1870
7 his wars, and his w, lo, they *are* written H1870
28: 2 For he walked in the w of the kings of H1870
26 Now the rest of his acts and of all his w, H1870
32:13 of those lands any w able to deliver H3201
34: 2 and walked in the w of David his H1870
Job 4: 6 thy hope, and the uprightness of thy w? H1870
13:15 will maintain mine own w before him. H1870
21:14 we desire not the knowledge of thy w. H1870
22: 3 *to him*, that thou makest thy w perfect? H1870
28 and the light shall shine upon thy w. H1870
24:13 they know not the w thereof, nor abide H1870
23 he resteth; yet his eyes *are* upon their w. H1870
26:14 Lo, these *are* parts of his w: but how H1870
30:12 up against me the w of their destruction. H734
31: 4 Doth not he see my w, and count all my H1870
34:11 every man to find according to *his* w. H734
21 For his eyes *are* upon the w of man, H1870
27 and would not consider any of his w: H1870
40:19 He *is* the chief of the w of God: he that H1870
Ps 10: 5 His w are always grievous; thy H1870

Ps 18:21 For I have kept the w of the LORD, and H1870
25: 4 Shew me thy w, O LORD; teach me thy H1870
39: 1 I said, I will take heed to my w, that I H1870
51:13 *Then* will I teach transgressors thy w; H1870
81:13 me, *and* Israel had walked in my w! H1870
84: 5 thee; in whose heart *are* the w *of them*. H4546
91:11 over thee, to keep thee in all thy w. H1870
95:10 heart, and they have not known my w: H1870
103: 7 He made known his w unto Moses, his H1870
119: 3 also do no iniquity: they walk in his w. H1870
5 O that my w were directed to keep thy H1870
15 precepts, and have respect unto thy w. H734
26 I have declared my w, and thou H1870
59 I thought on my w, and turned my feet H1870
168 for all my w *are* before thee. H1870
125: 5 their crooked w, the LORD shall lead H6128
128: 1 feareth the LORD; that walketh in his w. H1870
138: 5 Yea, they shall sing in the w of the H1870
139: 3 and art acquainted *with* all my w. H1870
145:17 The LORD *is* righteous in all his w, and H1870
Prv 1:19 So *are* the w of every one that is greedy H734
2:13 to walk in the w of darkness; H1870
15 Whose w *are* crooked, and *they* froward H734
3: 6 In all thy w acknowledge him, and he H1870
17 Her w *are* ways of pleasantness, and all H1870
17 Her ways *are* w of pleasantness, and all H1870
31 oppressor, and choose none of his w. H1870
4:26 feet, and let all thy w be established. H1870
5: 6 path of life, her w are moveable, *that* H4570
21 For the w of man *are* before the eyes of H1870
6: 6 sluggard; consider her w, and be wise: H1870
7:25 Let not thine heart decline to her w, go H1870
8:32 for blessed *are they that* keep my w. H1870
9:15 call passengers who go right on their w: H734
10: 9 that perverteth his w shall be known. H1870
14: 2 *that is* perverse in his w despiseth him. H1870
12 but the end thereof *are* the w of death. H1870
14 filled with his own w: and a good man H1870
16: 2 All the w of a man *are* clean in his own H1870
7 When a man's w please the LORD, he H1870
25 but the end thereof *are* the w of death. H1870
17:23 the bosom to pervert the w of judgment. H734
19:16 *but* he that despiseth his w shall die. H1870
22:25 Lest thou learn his w, and get a snare to H734
23:26 heart, and let thine eyes observe my w. H1870
28: 6 *is* perverse *in his* w, though he *be* rich. H1870
18 *is* perverse *in his* w shall fall at once. H1870
31: 3 thy w to that which destroyeth kings. H1870
27 She looketh well to the w of her H1979
Ecc 11: 9 and walk in the w of thine heart, and H1870
Song 3: 2 and in the broad w I will seek him H7339
Isa 2: 3 teach us of his w, and we will walk in H1870
42:24 not walk in his w, neither were they H1870
45:13 I will direct all his w: he shall build my H1870
49: 9 shall feed in the w, and their pastures H1870
55: 8 *are* your w my ways, saith the LORD. H1870
8 *are* your ways my w, saith the LORD. H1870
9 the earth, so are my w higher than your H1870
9 higher than your w, and my thoughts H1870
57:18 I have seen his w, and will heal him: I H1870
58: 2 to know my w, as a nation that did H1870
13 doing thine own w, nor finding thine H1870
63:17 us to err from thy w, *and* hardened our H1870
64: 5 thee in thy w: behold, thou art wroth; H1870
66: 3 have chosen their own w, and their soul H1870
Jer 2:23 *art* a swift dromedary traversing her w; H1870
33 thou also taught the wicked ones thy w. H1870
3: 2 lien with. In the w hast thou sat for H1870
13 hast scattered thy w to the strangers H1870
6:16 Thus saith the LORD, Stand ye in the w, H1870
7: 3 Amend your w and your doings, and H1870
5 For if ye throughly amend your w and H1870
23 and walk ye in all the w that I have H1870
12:16 learn the w of my people, to swear H1870
15: 7 *since* they return not from their w. H1870
16:17 For mine eyes *are* upon all their w: they H1870
17:10 according to his w, *and* according to the H1870
18:11 make your w and your doings good. H1870
15 to stumble in their w *from* the ancient H1870
23:12 them as slippery *w* in the darkness: they
26:13 Therefore now amend your w and your H1870
32:19 open upon all the w of the sons of men: H1870
19 according to his w, and according to the H1870
Lam 1: 4 The w of Zion do mourn, because none H1870
3: 9 He hath inclosed my w with hewn H1870
11 He hath turned aside my w, and pulled H1870
40 Let us search and try our w, and turn H1870
Ezk 7: 3 thee according to thy w, and will H1870
4 recompense thy w upon thee, and thine H1870

Ezk 7: 8 thee according to thy w, and will H1870
9 thee according to thy w and thine H1870
14:23 when ye see their w and their doings: H1870
16:47 Yet hast thou not walked after their w, H1870
47 corrupted more than they in all thy w. H1870
61 Then thou shalt remember thy w, and H1870
18:23 he should return from his w, and live? H1870
25 my way equal? are not your w unequal? H1870
29 w equal? are not your ways unequal? H1870
29 ways equal? are not your w unequal? H1870
30 according to his w, saith the Lord GOD. H1870
20:43 And there shall ye remember your w, H1870
44 to your wicked w, nor according to your H1870
21:19 appoint thee two w, that the sword of H1870
21 head of the two w, to use divination: he H1870
24:14 according to thy w, and according to H1870
28:15 Thou *wast* perfect in thy w from the H1870
33:11 w; for why will ye die, O house of Israel? H1870
20 I will judge you every one after his w. H1870
36:31 your own evil w, and your doings that H1870
32 for your own w, O house of Israel. H1870
Dan 4:37 *are* truth, and his w judgment: and those H735
5:23 *are* all thy w, hast thou not glorified: H735
Hos 4: 9 their w, and reward them their doings. H1870
9: 8 w, *and* hatred in the house of his God. H1870
12: 2 according to his w; according to his H1870
14: 9 them? for the w of the LORD *are* right, H1870
Joel 2: 7 w, and they shall not break their ranks: H1870
Mic 4: 2 teach us of his w, and we will walk in H1870
Nah 2: 4 in the broad w: they shall seem like H7339
Hab 3: 6 hills did bow: his w *are* everlasting. H1979
Hag 1: 5 the LORD of hosts; Consider your w. H1870
7 the LORD of hosts; Consider your w. H1870
Zec 1: 4 from your evil w, and *from* your evil H1870
6 according to our w, and according to H1870
3: 7 wilt walk in my w, and if thou wilt keep H1870
Mal 2: 9 my w, but have been partial in the law. H1870
Mt 8:33 and went their w into the city, and told *G565*
22: 5 of *it*, and went their w, one to his farm, *G565*
Mk 11: 4 where two w met; and they loose him. *G296*
Lk 1:76 the face of the Lord to prepare his w; *G3598*
3: 5 and the rough w *shall be* made smooth; *G3598*
10: 3 Go your w: behold, I send you forth as *G5217*
10 you not, go your w out into the streets of
Jn 11:46 But some of them went their w to the *G565*
Act 2:28 Thou hast made known to me the w of *G3598*
13:10 cease to pervert the right w of the Lord? *G3598*
14:16 all nations to walk in their own w. *G3598*
Ro 3:16 Destruction and misery *are* in their w: *G3598*
11:33 judgments, and his w past finding out! *G3598*
1Co 4:17 of my w which be in Christ, *G3598*
Heb 3:10 heart; and they have not known my w. *G3598*
Jas 1: 8 minded man *is* unstable in all his w. *G3598*
11 shall the rich man fade away in his w. *G4197*
2Pt 2: 2 their pernicious w; by reason of whom *G684*
Rev 15: 3 and true *are* thy w, thou King of saints. *G3598*
16: 1 angels, Go your w, and pour out the *G5217*

WAYSIDE

1Sa 4:13 upon a seat by the w watching: for his H1870
Ps 140: 5 a net by the w; they have set H3027+H4570

WE See the Appendix.

WEAK

Nu 13:18 they *be* strong or w, few or many; H7504
Jdg 16: 7 shall I be w, and be as another man. H2470
11 shall I be w, and be as another man. H2470
17 become w, and be like any *other* man. H2470
2Sa 3:39 And I *am* this day w, though anointed H7390
17: 2 he *is* weary and w handed, and will H7504
2Ch 15: 7 be w: for your work shall be rewarded. H7503
Job 4: 3 thou hast strengthened the w hands. H7504
Ps 6: 2 O LORD; for I *am* w: O LORD, heal me; H536
109:24 My knees are w through fasting; and H3782
Isa 14:10 w as we? art thou become like unto us? H2470
35: 3 Strengthen ye the w hands, and H7504
Ezk 7:17 and all knees shall be w *as* water. H3212
16:30 How w is thine heart, saith the Lord H535
21: 7 all knees shall be w *as* water: behold, it H3212
Joel 3:10 into spears: let the w say, I *am* strong. H2523
Mt 26:41 spirit indeed *is* willing, but the flesh *is* w. *G772*
Mk 14:38 spirit truly *is* ready, but the flesh *is* w. *G772*
Act 20:35 to support the w, and to remember the *G770*
Ro 4:19 And being not w in faith, he considered *G770*
8: 3 do, in that it was w through the flesh, *G770*
14: 1 Him that is w in the faith receive ye, *but* *G770*
2 things: another, who is w, eateth herbs. *G770*
21 stumbleth, or is offended, or is made w. *G770*

Ro 15: 1 of the w, and not to please ourselves. *G102*
1Co 1:27 hath chosen the w things of the world to *G772*
4:10 in Christ; we *are* w, but ye *are* strong; ye *G772*
8: 7 and their conscience being w is defiled. *G772*
9 a stumblingblock to them that are w. *G770*
10 of him which is w be emboldened to eat *G772*
11 And through thy knowledge shall the w *G770*
12 their w conscience, ye sin against Christ. *G770*
9:22 To the w became I as weak, that I might *G772*
22 To the weak became I as w, that I might *G772*
22 I might gain the w: I am made all things *G772*
11:30 For this cause many *are* w and sickly *G772*
2Co 10:10 *is* w, and *his* speech contemptible. *G772*
11:21 we had been w. Howbeit whereinsoever *G770*
29 Who is w, and I am not weak? who is *G770*
29 Who is weak, and I am not w? who is *G770*
12:10 sake: for when I am w, then am I strong. *G770*
13: 3 you-ward is not w, but is mighty in you. *G770*
4 For we also are w in him, but we shall *G770*
9 For we are glad, when we are w, and ye *G770*
Gal 4: 9 ye again to the w and beggarly elements, *G772*
1Th 5:14 support the w, be patient toward all *men*. *G772*

WEAKEN

Isa 14:12 the ground, which didst w the nations! H2522

WEAKENED

Ezr 4: 4 Then the people of the land w the H7503
Neh 6: 9 hands shall be w from the work, that H7503
Ps 102:23 He w my strength in the way; he H6031

WEAKENETH

Job 12:21 and w the strength of the mighty. H7503
Jer 38: 4 to death: for thus he w the hands of the H7503

WEAKER

2Sa 3: 1 the house of Saul waxed w and weaker. H1980
1 the house of Saul waxed weaker and w. H1800
1Pt 3: 7 wife, as unto the w vessel, and as being *G772*

WEAKNESS

1Co 1:25 and the w of God is stronger than men. *G772*
2: 3 And I was with you in w, and in fear, and *G769*
15:43 it is sown in w; it is raised in power: *G769*
2Co 12: 9 is made perfect in w. Most gladly *G769*
13: 4 For though he was crucified through w, *G769*
Heb 7:18 for the w and unprofitableness thereof. *G772*
11:34 of the sword, out of w were made strong, *G769*

WEALTH

Gen 34:29 And all their w, and all their little ones, H2428
Dt 8:17 of *mine* hand hath gotten me this w. H2428
18 giveth thee power to get w, that he may H2428
Ru 2: 1 a mighty man of w, of the family of H2428
1Sa 2:32 in all *the w* which *God* shall give
2Ki 15:20 the mighty men of w, of each man fifty H2428
2Ch 1:11 not asked riches, w, or honour, nor the H5233
12 thee riches, and w, and honour, such as H5233
Ezr 9:12 peace or their w for ever: that ye may H2896
Est 10: 3 seeking the w of his people, and H2896
Job 21:13 They spend their days in w, and in a H2896
31:25 If I rejoiced because my w *was* great, H2428
Ps 44:12 dost not increase *thy w* by their price.
49: 6 They that trust in their w, and boast H2428
10 perish, and leave their w to others. H2428
112: 3 W and riches *shall be* in his house: and H1952
Prv 5:10 Lest strangers be filled with thy w; and H3581
10:15 The rich man's w *is* his strong city: the H1952
13:11 W *gotten* by vanity shall be H1952
22 w of the sinner *is* laid up for the just. H2428
18:11 The rich man's w *is* his strong city, and H1952
19: 4 W maketh many friends; but the poor H1952
Ecc 5:19 given riches and w, and hath given him H5233
6: 2 hath given riches, w, and honour, so H5233
Zec 14:14 and the w of all the heathen round H2428
Act 19:25 know that by this craft we have our w. *G2142*
1Co 10:24 his own, but every man another's *w*. *G2142*

WEALTHY

Ps 66:12 thou broughtest us out into a w *place*. H7310
Jer 49:31 Arise, get you up unto the w nation, H7961

WEANED

Gen 21: 8 And the child grew, and was w: and H1580
8 feast the *same* day that Isaac was w. H1580
1Sa 1:22 *up* until the child be w, and *then* I will H1580
23 until thou have w him; only the LORD H1580
23 and gave her son suck until she w him. H1580
24 And when she had w him, she took him H1580

1Ki 11:20 whom Tahpenes w in Pharaoh's house: H1580
Ps 131: 2 as a child that is w of his mother: my H1580
2 mother: my soul is even as a w child. H1580
Isa 11: 8 of the asp, and the w child shall put his H1580
28: 9 them that are w from the milk, and H1580
Hos 1: 8 Now when she had w Lo-ruhamah, she H1580

WEAPON
Nu 35:18 Or if he smite him with an hand w of H3627
Dt 23:13 have a paddle upon thy w; and it shall be, H240
2Ch 23:10 man having his w in his hand, from the H7973
Neh 4:17 work, and with the other hand held a w. H7973
Job 20:24 He shall flee from the iron w, and the H5402
Isa 54:17 No w that is formed against thee shall H3627
Ezk 9: 1 man with his destroying w in his hand. H3627
2 man a slaughter w in his hand; and H3627

WEAPONS
Gen 27: 3 Now therefore take, I pray thee, thy w, H3627
Dt 1:41 on every man his w of war, ye were H3627
Jdg 18:11 hundred men appointed with w of war. H3627
16 with their w of war, which were H3627
17 that were appointed with w of war. H3627
1Sa 21: 8 my sword nor my w with me, because H3627
2Sa 1:27 How are the mighty fallen, and the w of H3627
2Ki 11: 8 man with his w in his hand: and he H3627
11 man with his w in his hand, round H3627
2Ch 23: 7 every man with his w in his hand; and H3627
Ecc 9:18 Wisdom is better than w of war: but H3627
Isa 13: 5 LORD, and the w of his indignation, H3627
Jer 21: 4 I will turn back the w of war that are in H3627
22: 7 every one with his w: and they shall cut H3627
50:25 brought forth the w of his indignation: H3627
51:20 Thou art my battle axe and w of war: H3627
Ezk 32:27 to hell with their w of war: and they H3627
39: 9 on fire and burn the w, both the shields H5402
10 shall burn the w with fire: and they H5402
Jn 18: 3 with lanterns and torches and w. G3696
2Co 10: 4 (For the w of our warfare are not G3696

WEAR
Ex 18:18 Thou wilt surely w away, both thou, H5034
Dt 22: 5 The woman shall not w that which H1961
11 Thou shalt not w a garment of divers H3847
1Sa 2:28 to burn incense, to w an ephod before H5375
22:18 five persons that did w a linen ephod. H5375
Est 6: 8 the king useth to w, and the horse that H3847
Job 14:19 The waters w the stones: thou washest H7833
Isa 4: 1 own bread, and w our own apparel: H3847
Dan 7:25 High, and shall w out the saints of the H1080
Zec 13: 4 they w a rough garment to deceive: H3847
Mt 11: 8 w soft clothing are in kings' houses. G5409
Lk 9:12 And when the day began to w away, G2827

WEARETH
Jas 2: 3 And ye have respect to him that w the G5409

WEARIED
Gen 19:11 that they w themselves to find the door. H3811
Isa 43:23 an offering, nor w thee with incense. H3021
24 thou hast w me with thine iniquities. H3021
47:13 Thou art w in the multitude of thy H3811
57:10 Thou art w in the greatness of thy way; H3021
Jer 4:31 for my soul is w because of murderers. H5888
12: 5 and they have w thee, then how canst H3811
5 trustedst, they w thee, then how wilt
Ezk 24:12 She hath w herself with lies, and her H3811
Mic 6: 3 have I w thee? testify against me. H3811
Mal 2:17 Ye have w the LORD with your words. H3021
17 Wherein have we w him? When ye say, H3021
Jn 4: 6 therefore, being w with his journey, sat G2872
Heb 12: 3 lest ye be w and faint in your minds. G2577

WEARIETH
Job 37:11 Also by watering he w the thick cloud: H2959
Ecc 10:15 The labour of the foolish w every one of H3021

WEARINESS
Ecc 12:12 end; and much study is a w of the flesh. H3024
Mal 1:13 Ye said also, Behold, what a w is it! and H4972
2Co 11:27 In w and painfulness, in watchings G2873

WEARING
1Sa 14: 3 priest in Shiloh, w an ephod. And the H5375
Jn 19: 5 Then came Jesus forth, w the crown of G5409
1Pt 3: 3 w of gold, or of putting on of apparel; G4025

WEARISOME
Job 7: 3 and w nights are appointed to me. H5999

WEARY
Gen 27:46 And Rebekah said to Isaac, I am w of H6973
Dt 25:18 faint and w; and he feared not God. H3023
Jdg 4:21 for he was fast asleep and w. So he died. H5774
8:15 give bread unto thy men that are w? H3287
2Sa 16:14 w, and refreshed themselves there. H5889
17: 2 And I will come upon him while he is w H3023
29 and w, and thirsty, in the wilderness. H5889
23:10 his hand was w, and his hand clave H3021
Job 3:17 troubling; and there the w be at rest. H3019
10: 1 My soul is w of my life; I will leave my H5354
16: 7 But now he hath made me w: thou hast H3811
22: 7 Thou hast not given water to the w to H5889
Ps 6: 6 I am w with my groaning; all the night H3021
68: 9 thine inheritance, when it was w. H3811
69: 3 I am w of my crying: my throat is H3021
Prv 3:11 LORD; neither be w of his correction: H6973
25:17 lest he be w of thee, and so hate thee. H7646
Isa 1:14 trouble unto me; I am w to bear them. H3811
5:27 None shall be w nor stumble among H5889
7:13 w men, but will ye weary my God also? H3811
13 weary men, but will ye w my God also? H3811
16:12 seen that Moab is w on the high place, H3811
28:12 ye may cause the w to rest; and this is H5889
32: 2 the shadow of a great rock in a w land. H5889
40:28 not, neither is w? there is no searching H3021
30 Even the youths shall faint and be w, H3021
31 be w; and they shall walk, and not faint. H3021
43:22 but thou hast been w of me, O Israel. H3021
46: 1 they are a burden to the w beast. H5889
50: 4 to him that is w: he wakeneth morning H3287
Jer 2:24 seek her will not w themselves; in her H3286
6:11 of the LORD; I am w with holding in: I H3811
9: 5 and w themselves to commit iniquity. H3811
15: 6 destroy thee; I am w with repenting. H3811
20: 9 w with forbearing, and I could not stay. H3811
31:25 For I have satiated the w soul, and I H5889
51:58 the folk in the fire, and they shall be w. H3286
64 w. Thus far are the words of Jeremiah. H3286
Hab 2:13 shall w themselves for very vanity? H3286
Lk 18: 5 lest by her continual coming she w me. G5299
Gal 6: 9 And let us not be w in well doing: for in G1573
2Th 3:13 But ye, brethren, be not w in well G1573

WEASEL
Lev 11:29 the earth; the w, and the mouse, and H2467

WEATHER
Job 37:22 Fair w cometh out of the north: with H2091
Prv 25:20 a garment in cold w, and as vinegar H3117
Mt 16: 2 say, It will be fair w: for the sky is red. G2105
3 And in the morning, It will be foul w to G5494

WEAVE
Isa 19: 9 that w networks, shall be confounded. H707
59: 5 They hatch cockatrice' eggs, and w the H707

WEAVER
Ex 35:35 linen, and of the w, even of them that do H707
Isa 38:12 I have cut off like a w my life: he will cut H707

WEAVER'S
1Sa 17: 7 And the staff of his spear was like a w H707
2Sa 21:19 staff of whose spear was like a w beam. H707
1Ch 11:23 was a spear like a w beam; and he went H707
20: 5 whose spear staff was like a w beam. H707
Job 7: 6 My days are swifter than a w shuttle,

WEAVEST
Jdg 16:13 unto her, If thou w the seven locks of my H707

WEB
Jdg 16:13 the seven locks of my head with the w. H4545
14 the pin of the beam, and with the w. H4545
Job 8:14 and whose trust shall be a spider's w. H1004
Isa 59: 5 weave the spider's w: he that eateth of H6980

WEBS
Isa 59: 6 Their w shall not become garments, H6980

WEDDING
Mt 22: 3 to the w: and they would not come. G1062
8 Then saith he to his servants, The w is G1062
10 and the w was furnished with guests. G1062
11 a man which had not on a w garment: G1062
12 a w garment? And he was speechless. G1062
Lk 12:36 return from the w; that when he cometh G1062
14: 8 of any man to a w, sit not down in the G1062

WEDGE
Jos 7:21 of silver, and a w of gold of fifty shekels H3956
24 the garment, and the w of gold, and his H3956
Isa 13:12 even a man than the golden w of Ophir. H3800

WEDLOCK
Ezk 16:38 as women that break w and shed blood H5003

WEEDS
Jna 2: 5 the w were wrapped about my head. H5488

WEEK
Gen 29:27 Fulfil her w, and we will give thee this H7620
28 And Jacob did so, and fulfilled her w: H7620
Dan 9:27 many for one w: and in the midst of H7620
27 in the midst of the w he shall cause the H7620
Mt 28: 1 the first day of the w, came Mary G4521
Mk 16: 2 the first day of the w, they came unto G4521
9 the first day of the w, he appeared first G4521
Lk 18:12 I fast twice in the w, I give tithes of all G4521
24: 1 Now upon the first day of the w, very G4521
Jn 20: 1 The first day of the w cometh Mary G4521
19 the first day of the w, when the doors G4521
Act 20: 7 And upon the first day of the w, when G4521
1Co 16: 2 Upon the first day of the w let every G4521

WEEKS
Ex 34:22 And thou shalt observe the feast of w, of H7620
Lev 12: 5 be unclean two w, as in her separation: H7620
Nu 28:26 the LORD, after your w be out, ye shall H7620
Dt 16: 9 Seven w shalt thou number unto thee: H7620
9 number the seven w from such time as H7620
10 And thou shalt keep the feast of w unto H7620
16 and in the feast of w, and in the feast of H7620
2Ch 8:13 of w, and in the feast of tabernacles. H7620
Jer 5:24 unto us the appointed w of the harvest. H7620
Dan 9:24 Seventy w are determined upon thy H7620
25 shall be seven w, and threescore and H7620
25 and two w: the street shall be built H7620
26 And after threescore and two w shall H7620
10: 2 I Daniel was mourning three full w. H7620
3 at all, till three whole w were fulfilled. H7620

WEEP
Gen 23: 2 to mourn for Sarah, and to w for her. H1058
43:30 sought where to w; and he entered into H1058
Nu 11:10 Then Moses heard the people w H1058
13 this people? for they w unto me, saying, H1058
1Sa 11: 5 people that they w? And they told him H1058
30: 4 until they had no more power to w. H1058
2Sa 1:24 Ye daughters of Israel, w over Saul, H1058
12:21 didst fast and w for the child, while H1058
2Ch 34:27 thy clothes, and w before me; I have H1058
Neh 8: 9 mourn not, nor w. For all the people H1058
Job 27:15 in death: and his widows shall not w. H1058
30:25 Did not I w for him that was in trouble? H1058
31 my organ into the voice of them that w. H1058
Ecc 3: 4 A time to w, and a time to laugh; a time H1058
Isa 15: 2 the high places, to w: Moab shall howl H1065
22: 4 from me; I will w bitterly, labour not H1065
30:19 thou shalt w no more: he will be H1058
33: 7 ambassadors of peace shall w bitterly. H1058
Jer 9: 1 tears, that I might w day and night for H1058
13:17 it, my soul shall w in secret places for H1058
17 mine eye shall w sore, and run down H1830
22:10 W ye not for the dead, neither bemoan H1058
10 bemoan him: but w sore for him that H1058
48:32 O vine of Sibmah, I will w for thee with H1058
Lam 1:16 For these things I w; mine eye, mine eye H1058
Ezk 24:16 nor w, neither shall thy tears run down. H1058
23 shall not mourn nor w; but ye shall pine H1058
27:31 and they shall w for thee with H1058
Joel 1: 5 Awake, ye drunkards, and w; and howl, H1058
2:17 of the LORD, w between the porch H1058
Mic 1:10 Declare ye it not at Gath, w ye not at H1058
Zec 7: 3 saying, Should I w in the fifth month, H1058
Mk 5:39 w? the damsel is not dead, but sleepeth. G2799
Lk 6:21 are ye that w now: for ye shall laugh. G2799
25 laugh now! for ye shall mourn and w. G2799
7:13 on her, and said unto her, W not. G2799
8:52 W not; she is not dead, but sleepeth. G2799
23:28 of Jerusalem, w not for me, but weep G2799
28 w for yourselves, and for your children. G2799
Jn 11:31 She goeth unto the grave to w there. G2799
16:20 you, That ye shall w and lament, but G2799
Act 21:13 What mean ye to w and to break mine G2799
Ro 12:15 do rejoice, and w with them that weep. G2799
15 do rejoice, and weep with them that w. G2799
1Co 7:30 And they that w, as though they wept G2799

W

Jas 4: 9 Be afflicted, and mourn, and w: let your G2799
5: 1 Go to now, *ye* rich men, w and howl for G2799
Rev 5: 5 And one of the elders saith unto me, W G2799
18:11 And the merchants of the earth shall w G2799

WEEPEST
1Sa 1: 8 to her, Hannah, why w thou? and why H1058
Jn 20:13 And they say unto her, Woman, why w G2799
15 Jesus saith unto her, Woman, why w G2799

WEEPETH
2Sa 19: 1 the king w and mourneth for Absalom. H1058
2Ki 8:12 And Hazael said, Why w my lord? And H1058
Ps 126: 6 He that goeth forth and w, bearing H1058
Lam 1: 2 She w sore in the night, and her tears H1058

WEEPING
Nu 25: 6 of Israel, who *were* w *before* the door of H1058
Dt 34: 8 so the days of w *and* mourning for H1065
2Sa 3:16 went with her along w behind her to H1058
15:30 and they went up, w as they went up. H1058
Ezr 3:13 the noise of the w of the people: for the H1065
10: 1 when he had confessed, w and casting H1058
Est 4: 3 and fasting, and w, and wailing; and H1065
Job 16:16 My face is foul with w, and on my H1065
Ps 6: 8 the LORD hath heard the voice of my w. H1065
30: 5 in his favour *is* life: w may endure for a H1065
102: 9 bread, and mingled my drink with w, H1065
Isa 15: 3 every one shall howl, w abundantly. H1065
5 up of Luhith with w shall they go it up; H1065
16: 9 Therefore I will bewail with the w of H1065
22:12 of hosts call to w, and to mourning, and H1065
65:19 and the voice of w shall be no more H1065
Jer 3:21 the high places, w *and* supplications of H1065
9:10 For the mountains will I take up a w H1065
31: 9 They shall come with w, and with H1065
15 *and* bitter w; Rahel weeping for her H1065
15 weeping; Rahel w for her children H1058
16 thy voice from w, and thine eyes from H1065
41: 6 to meet them, w all along as he went: H1058
48: 5 Luhith continual w shall go up; for in H1065
32 for thee with the w of Jazer: thy plants H1065
50: 4 going and w: they shall go, and seek H1058
Ezk 8:14 there sat women w for Tammuz. H1058
Joel 2:12 and with w, and with mourning: H1065
Mal 2:13 with tears, with w, and with crying out, H1065
Mt 2:18 heard, lamentation, and w, and great G2805
18 mourning, Rachel w *for* her children, G2799
8:12 there shall be w and gnashing of teeth. G2805
22:13 there shall be w and gnashing of teeth. G2805
24:51 there shall be w and gnashing of teeth. G2805
25:30 there shall be w and gnashing of teeth. G2805
Lk 7:38 And stood at his feet behind *him* w, and G2799
13:28 There shall be w and gnashing of teeth, G2805
Jn 11:33 When Jesus therefore saw her w, and G2799
33 and the Jews also w which came with G2799
20:11 at the sepulchre w: and as she wept, she G2799
Act 9:39 stood by him w, and shewing the coats G2799
Php 3:18 now tell you even w, *that they are* the G2799
Rev 18:15 the fear of her torment, w and wailing, G2799
19 their heads, and cried, w and wailing, G2799

WEIGH
1Ch 20: 2 and found it to w a talent of gold, and H4948
Ezr 8:29 Watch ye, and keep *them*, until ye w H8254
Ps 58: 2 Yea, in heart ye work wickedness; ye w H6424
Isa 26: 7 upright, dost w the path of the just. H6424
46: 6 They lavish gold out of the bag, and w H8254
Ezk 5: 1 thee balances to w, and divide the *hair*. H4948

WEIGHED
Gen 23:16 and Abraham w to Ephron the silver, H8254
Nu 7:85 all the silver vessels *w* two thousand and
1Sa 2: 3 knowledge, and by him actions are w. H8505
17: 7 his spear's head *w* six hundred shekels
2Sa 14:26 he polled it:) he w the hair of his head H8254
21:16 of whose spear *w* three hundred *shekels*
Ezr 8:25 And w unto them the silver, and the H8254
26 I even w unto their hand six hundred H8254
33 and the vessels w in the house of our H8254
Job 6: 2 Oh that my grief were throughly w, and H8254
28:15 shall silver be w *for* the price thereof. H8254
31: 6 Let me be w in an even balance, that H8254
Isa 40:12 in a measure, and w the mountains in H8254
Jer 32: 9 in Anathoth, and w him the money, H8254
10 and w *him* the money in the balances. H8254
Dan 5:27 TEKEL; Thou art w in the balances, H8625
Zec 11:12 w for my price thirty *pieces* of silver. H8254

WEIGHETH
Job 28:25 and he w the waters by measure. H8505
Prv 16: 2 own eyes; but the LORD w the spirits. H8505

WEIGHING
Nu 7:85 Each charger of silver *w* an hundred and
86 full of incense, *w* ten *shekels* apiece,

WEIGHT
Gen 24:22 of half a shekel w, and two bracelets for H4948
22 for her hands of ten *shekels* w of gold; H4948
43:21 sack, our money in full w: and we have H4948
Ex 30:34 of each shall there be a like *w:* H4948
Lev 19:35 in meteyard, in w, or in measure. H4948
26:26 w: and ye shall eat, and not be satisfied. H4948
Nu 7:13 silver charger, the w thereof *was* an H4948
19 silver charger, the w whereof *was* an H4948
25 silver charger, the w whereof *was* an H4948
31 charger of the w of an hundred and H4948
37 silver charger, the w whereof *was* an H4948
43 charger of the w of an hundred and H4948
49 silver charger, the w whereof *was* an H4948
55 charger of the w of an hundred and H4948
61 silver charger, the w whereof *was* an H4948
67 silver charger, the w whereof *was* an H4948
73 silver charger, the w whereof *was* an H4948
79 silver charger, the w whereof *was* an H4948
Dt 25:15 *But* thou shalt have a perfect and just w, H68
Jos 7:21 of fifty shekels w, then I coveted them, H4948
Jdg 8:26 And the w of the golden earrings that H4948
1Sa 17: 5 of mail; and the w of the coat *was* five H4948
2Sa 12:30 off his head, the w whereof *was* a talent H4948
14:26 at two hundred shekels after the king's w. H68
21:16 sons of the giant, the w of whose spear H4948
16 *shekels* of brass in w, he being girded H4948
1Ki 7:47 was the w of the brass found out. H4948
10:14 Now the w of gold that came to H4948
2Ki 25:16 brass of all these vessels was without w. H4948
1Ch 21:25 place six hundred shekels of gold by w. H4948
22: 3 and brass in abundance without w; H4948
14 brass and iron without w; for it is in H4948
28:14 *He gave* of gold by w for *things* of gold, H4948
14 of silver by w, for all instruments H4948
15 Even the w for the candlesticks of gold, H4948
15 their lamps of gold, by w for every H4948
15 of silver by w, *both* for the candlestick, H4948
16 And by w *he gave* gold for the tables of H4948
17 *he gave gold* by w for every bason; and H4948
17 *silver* by w for every bason of silver: H4948
18 refined gold by w; and gold for the H4948
2Ch 3: 9 And the w of the nails *was* fifty shekels H4948
4:18 w of the brass could not be found out. H4948
9:13 Now the w of gold that came to H4948
Ezr 8:30 the Levites the w of the silver, and the H4948
34 By number *and* by w of every one: and H4948
34 and all the w was written at that time. H4948
Job 28:25 To make the w for the winds; and he H4948
Prv 11: 1 to the LORD: but a just w *is* his delight. H68
16:11 A just w and balance *are* the LORD'S: H6425
Jer 52:20 brass of all these vessels was without w. H4948
Ezk 4:10 eat *shall be* by w, twenty shekels a day: H4946
16 shall eat bread by w, and with care; and H4948
Zec 5: 8 the w of lead upon the mouth thereof. H68
Jn 19:39 and aloes, about an hundred pound *w*.
2Co 4:17 more exceeding *and* eternal w of glory; G922
Heb 12: 1 us lay aside every w, and the sin which G3591
Rev 16:21 *stone* about the w of a talent: and men G5006

WEIGHTIER
Mt 23:23 have omitted the w *matters* of the law, G926

WEIGHTS
Lev 19:36 Just balances, just w, a just ephah, and a H68
Dt 25:13 Thou shalt not have in thy bag divers w, H68
Prv 16:11 all the w of the bag *are* his work. H68
20:10 Divers w, *and* divers measures, both of H68
23 Divers w *are* an abomination unto the H68
Mic 6:11 balances, and with the bag of deceitful w? H68

WEIGHTY
Prv 27: 3 A stone *is* heavy, and the sand w; but a H5192
2Co 10:10 For *his* letters, say they, *are* w and G926

WELFARE
Gen 43:27 And he asked them of *their* w, and said, H7965
Ex 18: 7 of *their* w; and they came into the tent. H7965
1Ch 18:10 to inquire of his w, and to congratulate H7965
Neh 2:10 to seek the w of the children of Israel. H2896
Job 30:15 and my w passeth away as a cloud. H3444
Ps 69:22 *been* for *their* w, *let it become* a trap. H7965
Jer 38: 4 not the w of this people, but the hurt. H7965

WELL
Gen 4: 7 If thou doest w, shalt thou not be H3190
7 if thou doest not w, sin lieth at the door. H3190
12:13 that it may be w with me for thy sake; H3190
16 And he entreated Abram w for her H3190
13:10 that it *was* w watered every where, H4945
16:14 Wherefore the w was called H875
18:11 *were* old *and* w stricken in age; *and*
21:19 and she saw a w of water; and she went, H875
25 because of a w of water, which H875
30 unto me, that I have digged this w. H875
24: 1 And Abraham was old, *and* w stricken
11 the city by a w of water at the time H875
13 Behold, I stand *here* by the w of water; H5869
16 w, and filled her pitcher, and came up. H5869
20 ran again unto the w to draw *water,* and H875
29 ran out unto the man, unto the w. H5869
30 behold, he stood by the camels at the w. H5869
42 And I came this day unto the w, and H5869
43 Behold, I stand by the w of water; and H5869
45 down unto the w, and drew *water:* and H5869
62 And Isaac came from the way of the w
25:11 and Isaac dwelt by the w Lahai-roi. H883
26:19 and found there a w of springing water. H875
20 w Esek; because they strove with him. H875
21 And they digged another w, and strove H875
22 and digged another w; and for that they H875
25 and there Isaac's servants digged a w. H875
32 concerning the w which they had digged, H875
29: 2 And he looked, and behold a w in the H875
2 by it; for out of that w they watered the H875
6 And he said unto them, *Is* he w? And H7965
6 they said, *He is* w: and, behold, Rachel H7965
17 Rachel was beautiful and w favoured. H3303
32: 9 kindred, and I will deal w with thee: H3190
37:14 see whether it be w with thy brethren, H7965
14 thy brethren, and w with the flocks; H7965
39: 6 was *a* goodly *person,* and w favoured. H3303
40:14 But think on me when it shall be w with H3190
41: 2 of the river seven w favoured kine and H3303
4 did eat up the seven w favoured and fat H3303
18 w favoured; and they fed in a meadow: H3303
43:27 *Is* your father w, the old man of whom H7965
45:16 it pleased Pharaoh w, and his servants.
49:22 a w; *whose* branches run over the wall: H5869
Ex 1:20 Therefore God dealt w with the H3190
2:15 land of Midian: and he sat down by a w. H875
4:14 that he can speak w. And also, behold, H1696
10:29 And Moses said, Thou hast spoken w, I H3651
Lev 24:16 stone him: as w the stranger, as he that
22 Ye shall have one manner of law, as w
Nu 11:18 to eat? for *it was* w with us in Egypt: H2895
13:30 it; for we are w able to overcome it.
21:16 to Beer: that *is* the w whereof the LORD H875
17 this song, Spring up, O w; sing ye unto it: H875
18 The princes digged the w, the nobles of H875
22 *of* the waters of the w: *but* we will go H875
36: 5 tribe of the sons of Joseph hath said w. H3651
Dt 1:17 hear the small as w as the great; ye shall
23 And the saying pleased me w: and I H5869
3:20 your brethren, as w as unto you, and
4:40 that it may go w with thee, and with H3190
5:14 thy maidservant may rest as w as thou.
16 and that it may go w with thee, in the H3190
28 have w said all that they have spoken. H3190
29 that it might be w with them, and with H3190
33 and *that it may be* w with you, and *that* H2895
6: 3 *it*; that it may be w with thee, and that H3190
18 that it may be w with thee, and that H3190
7:18 of them: *but* shalt w remember what H2142
12:25 Thou shalt not eat it; that it may go w H3190
28 that it may go w with thee, and with H3190
15:16 thine house, because he is w with thee; H2895
18:17 w *spoken that* which they have spoken. H3190
19:13 from Israel, that it may go w with thee. H2895
20: 8 brethren's heart faint as w as his heart.
22: 7 that it may be w with thee, and *that* H3190
Jos 8:33 of the LORD, as w the stranger, as he
18:15 out to the w of waters of Nephtoah: H4599
Jdg 7: 1 pitched beside the w of Harod: so that H5878
9:16 if ye have dealt w with Jerubbaal and H2896
14: 3 Get her for me; for she pleaseth me w.
7 the woman; and she pleased Samson w.
20:48 of the sword, as w the men of *every* city,
Ru 3: 1 for thee, that it may be w with thee? H3190
13 part of a kinsman, w; let him do the H2896

1Sa 9:10 Then said Saul to his servant, **W** said; H2896
16:16 play with his hand, and thou shalt be **w**. H2895
17 that can play **w**, and bring *him* to me. H3190
23 and was **w**, and the evil spirit departed H2895
18:26 it pleased David **w** to be the king's son H3474
19:22 came to a great **w** that *is* in Sechu: and H953
20: 7 If he say thus, *It is* **w**; thy servant shall H2896
24:18 thou hast dealt **w** with me: forasmuch H2896
19 will he let him go **w** away? wherefore H2896
20 And now, behold, I know **w** that thou
25:31 shall have dealt **w** with my lord, then H3190
2Sa 3:13 And he said, **W**; I will make a league H2896
26 the **w** of Sirah: but David knew *it* not. H953
6:19 of Israel, as **w** to the women as men,
11:25 devoureth one as **w** as another: make H2090
17: 4 And the saying pleased Absalom **w**, and H3474
18 **w** in his court; whither they went down. H875
21 came up out of the **w**, and went and told H875
18:28 the king, All is **w**. And he fell down to H7965
19: 6 died this day, then it had pleased thee **w**.
23:15 **w** of Beth-lehem, which *is* by the gate! H953
16 water out of the **w** of Beth-lehem, that H953
1Ki 2:18 And Bath-sheba said, **W**; I will speak H2896
8:18 thou didst **w** that it was in thine heart. H2895
18:24 answered and said, It is **w** spoken. H2896
2Ki 4:23 nor sabbath. And she said, *It shall be* **w**. H7965
26 say unto her, *Is it* **w** with thee? *is it* well H7965
26 with thee? *is it* **w** with thy husband? H7965
26 thy husband? *is it* **w** with the child? H7965
26 the child? And she answered, *It is* **w**. H7965
5:21 chariot to meet him, and said, *Is* all **w**? H7965
22 And he said, All *is* **w**. My master hath H7965
7: 9 We do not **w**: this day *is* a day of H3651
9:11 unto him, *Is* all **w**? wherefore came this H7965
10:30 thou hast done **w** in executing *that* H2895
25:24 of Babylon; and it shall be **w** with you. H3190
1Ch 11:17 the **w** of Beth-lehem, that *is* at the gate! H953
18 water out of the **w** of Beth-lehem, that H953
25: 8 ward against *ward*, as **w** the small as the
26:13 And they cast lots, as **w** the small as the
2Ch 6: 8 didst **w** in that it was in thine heart: H2895
12:12 and also in Judah things went **w**. H2896
31:15 courses, as **w** to the great as to the small:
Neh 2:13 before the dragon **w**, and to the dung H5869
Job 12: 3 But I have understanding as **w** as you; I H71
33:31 Mark **w**, O Job, hearken unto me: hold H7181
Ps 48:13 Mark ye **w** her bulwarks, consider her H3820
49:18 thee, when thou doest **w** to thyself. H3190
73: 2 gone; my steps had **w** nigh slipped. H369
78:29 So they did eat, and were **w** filled: for H3966
84: 6 it a **w**; the rain also filleth the pools. H4599
87: 7 As **w** the singers as the players on
119:65 Thou hast dealt **w** with thy servant, O H2896
128: 2 thou *be*, and *it shall be* **w** with thee. H2896
139:14 and *that* my soul knoweth right **w**. H3966
Prv 5:15 and running waters out of thine own **w**. H875
10:11 The mouth of a righteous *man is* a **w** of H4726
11:10 When it goeth **w** with the righteous, the H2898
13:10 but with the **w** advised *is* wisdom.
14:15 the prudent *man* looketh **w** to his going. H995
24:32 Then I saw, *and* considered *it* **w**: I looked
27:23 of thy flocks, *and* look **w** to thy herds. H3820
30:29 There be three *things* which go **w**, yea, H2895
31:27 She looketh **w** to the ways of her H6822
Ecc 8:12 that it shall be **w** with them that fear H2896
13 But it shall not be **w** with the wicked, H2896
Song 4:15 A fountain of gardens, a **w** of living H875
Isa 1:17 Learn to do **w**; seek judgment, relieve H3190
3:10 that *it shall be* **w** *with him*: for they H2896
24 and instead of **w** set hair baldness; and H4639
25: 6 marrow, of wines on the lees **w** refined.
33:23 they could not **w** strengthen their mast, H3653
42:21 The LORD is **w** pleased for his H2654
Jer 1:12 me, Thou hast **w** seen: for I will hasten H3190
7:23 you, that it may be **w** unto you. H3190
15:11 The LORD said, Verily it shall be **w** H2896
11 to entreat thee **w** in the time of evil and H2896
22:15 justice, *and* then *it was* **w** with him? H2896
16 needy; then *it was* **w** *with him*: *was* not H2896
38:20 be **w** unto thee, and thy soul shall live. H3190
39:12 Take him, and look **w** to him, H5869+H7760
40: 4 I will look **w** unto thee: but if H7760+H5869
9 of Babylon, and it shall be **w** with you. H3190
42: 6 that it may be **w** with us, when we obey H3190
44:17 victuals, and were **w**, and saw no evil. H2896
Ezk 24: 5 *and* make it boil **w**, and let them seethe H7571
10 spice it **w**, and let the bones be burned. H4841
33:32 and can play **w** on an instrument: for H2895
44: 5 Son of man, mark **w**, and behold with H3820

Ezk 44: 5 thereof; and mark **w** the entering in of H3820
47:14 And ye shall inherit it, one as **w** as
Dan 1: 4 no blemish, but **w** favoured, and skilful H2896
3:15 I have made; **w**: but if ye worship not,
Jna 4: 4 Then said the LORD, Doest thou **w** to H3190
9 And God said to Jonah, Doest thou **w** to H3190
9 I do **w** to be angry, *even* unto death. H3190
Zec 8:15 these days to do **w** unto Jerusalem and H3190
Mt 3:17 beloved Son, in whom I am **w** pleased. G2106
12:12 is lawful to do **w** on the sabbath days. G2573
18 whom my soul is **w** pleased: I will put G2106
15: 7 Ye hypocrites, **w** did Esaias prophesy G2573
17: 5 in whom I am **w** pleased; hear ye him. G2106
25:21 His lord said unto him, **W** done, *thou* G2095
23 His lord said unto him, **W** done, good G2095
Mk 1:11 beloved Son, in whom I am **w** pleased. G2106
7: 6 He answered and said unto them, **W** G2573
9 And he said unto them, Full **w** ye reject G2573
37 done all things **w**: he maketh both the G2573
12:28 answered them **w**, asked him, Which is G2573
32 And the scribe said unto him, **W**, G2573
Lk 1: 7 they both were *now* **w** stricken in years. G4260
18 man, and my wife **w** stricken in years. G4260
3:22 beloved Son; in thee I am **w** pleased. G2106
6:26 all men shall speak **w** of you! for so did G2573
13: 9 And if it bear fruit, *w*: and if not, *then*
19:17 And he said unto him, **W**, thou good G2095
20:39 said, Master, thou hast **w** said. G2573
Jn 2:10 and when men have **w** drunk, then that G3184
4: 6 Now Jacob's **w** was there. Jesus G4077
6 the **w**: *and* it was about the sixth hour. G4077
11 with, and the **w** is deep: from whence G5421
12 which gave us the **w**, and drank thereof G5421
14 shall be in him a **w** of water springing G4077
17 Thou hast **w** said, I have no husband: G2573
8:48 unto him, Say we not **w** that thou art a G2573
11:12 Lord, if he sleep, he shall do **w**. G4982
13:13 and Lord: and ye say **w**; for *so* I am. G2573
18:23 the evil: but if **w**, why smitest thou me? G2573
Act 10:33 and thou hast **w** done that thou art G2573
47 received the Holy Ghost as **w** as we? G2532
15:29 yourselves, ye shall do **w**. Fare ye well. G2095
29 yourselves, ye shall do well. Fare ye **w**. G4517
16: 2 Which was **w** reported of by the G3140
25:10 no wrong, as thou very **w** knowest. G2573
28:25 spoken one word, **W** spake the Holy G2573
Ro 2: 7 continuance in **w** doing seek for glory G18
11:20 **W**; because of unbelief they were G2573
16: 5 house. Salute my **w** beloved Epaenetus,
1Co 7:37 that he will keep his virgin, doeth **w**. G2573
38 in marriage doeth **w**; but he that giveth G2573
9: 5 a sister, a wife, as **w** as other apostles, G2532
10: 5 But with many of them God was not **w** G2106
14:17 For thou verily givest thanks **w**, but the G2573
2Co 6: 9 As unknown, and *yet* **w** known; as G1921
11: 4 accepted, ye might **w** bear with *him*. G2573
Gal 4:17 They zealously affect you, *but* not **w**; G2573
5: 7 Ye did run **w**; who did hinder you that G2573
6: 9 And let us not be weary in **w** doing: for G2570
Eph 6: 3 That it may be **w** with thee, and thou G2095
Php 4:14 Notwithstanding ye have **w** done, that G2573
Col 3:20 for this is **w** pleasing unto the Lord. G2101
2Th 3:13 But ye, brethren, be not weary in **w** G2569
1Ti 3: 4 One that ruleth **w** his own house, G2573
12 their children and their own houses **w**. G2573
13 the office of a deacon **w** purchase to G2573
5:10 **W** reported of for good works; if she G3140
17 Let the elders that rule **w** be counted G2573
2Ti 1:18 me at Ephesus, thou knowest very **w**. G957
Tit 2: 9 **w** in all *things*; not answering again; G2101
Heb 4: 2 preached, as **w** as unto them: but the G2509
13:16 with such sacrifices God is **w** pleased. G2100
Jas 2: 8 love thy neighbour as thyself, ye do **w**: G2573
19 **w**: the devils also believe, and tremble. G2573
1Pt 2:14 and for the praise of them that do **w**. G17
15 For so is the will of God, that with **w** G15
20 but if, when ye do **w**, and suffer *for it*, ye G15
3: 6 as long as ye do **w**, and are not afraid G15
17 ye suffer for **w** doing, than for evil doing. G15
4:19 in **w** doing, as unto a faithful Creator. G16
2Pt 1:17 beloved Son, in whom I am **w** pleased. G2106
19 whereunto ye do **w** that ye take heed, G2573
3Jn 6 after a godly sort, thou shalt do **w**: G2573

WELLBELOVED

Song 1:13 A bundle of myrrh *is* my **w** unto me; he H1730
Isa 5: 1 Now will I sing to my **w** a song of my H3039
1 **w** hath a vineyard in a very fruitful hill: H3039
Mk 12: 6 Having yet therefore one son, his **w**, he G27

3Jn 1 The elder unto the **w** Gaius, whom I love G27

WELLFAVOURED

Nah 3: 4 of the **w** harlot, the mistress H2896+H2580

WELL-NIGH See WELL and NIGH.

WELLPLEASING

Php 4:18 smell, a sacrifice acceptable, **w** to God. G2101
Heb 13:21 in you that which is **w** in his sight, G2101

WELLS

Gen 26:15 For all the **w** which his father's servants H875
18 And Isaac digged again the **w** of water, H875
Ex 15:27 where *were* twelve **w** of water, and H5869
Nu 20:17 *of* the water of the **w**: we will go by the H875
Dt 6:11 filledst not, and **w** digged, which thou H953
2Ki 3:19 tree, and stop all **w** of water, and mar H4599
25 stopped all the **w** of water, and felled H4599
2Ch 26:10 and digged many **w**: for he had much H953
Neh 9:25 full of all goods, **w** digged, vineyards, H953
Isa 12: 3 ye draw water out of the **w** of salvation. H4599
2Pt 2:17 These are **w** without water, clouds that G4077

WELL'S

Gen 29: 2 a great stone *was* upon the **w** mouth. H875
3 rolled the stone from the **w** mouth, and H875
3 again upon the **w** mouth in his place. H875
8 the **w** mouth; then we water the sheep. H875
10 rolled the stone from the **w** mouth, and H875
2Sa 17:19 a covering over the **w** mouth, and spread H875

WELLSPRING

Prv 16:22 Understanding *is* a **w** of life unto him H4726
18: 4 the **w** of wisdom *as* a flowing brook. H4726

WEN

Lev 22:22 or having a **w**, or scurvy, or scabbed, H2990

WENCH

2Sa 17:17 the city: and a **w** went and told them; H8198

WENT

Gen 2: 6 But there **w** up a mist from the earth, H5927
10 And a river **w** out of Eden to water the H3318
4:16 And Cain **w** out from the presence of H3318
7: 7 And Noah **w** in, and his sons, and his H935
9 There **w** in two and two unto Noah into H935
15 And they **w** in unto Noah into the ark, H935
16 And they that **w** in, went in male and H935
16 And they that went in, **w** in male and H935
18 the ark **w** upon the face of the waters. H3212
8: 7 And he sent forth a raven, which **w** H3318
18 And Noah **w** forth, and his sons, and H3318
19 after their kinds, **w** forth out of the ark. H3318
9:18 And the sons of Noah, that **w** forth of H3318
23 their shoulders, and **w** backward, and H3212
10:11 Out of that land **w** forth Asshur, and H3318
11:31 wife; and they **w** forth with them from H3318
12: 4 unto him; and Lot **w** with him: and H3212
5 Haran; and they **w** forth to go into the H3318
10 land: and Abram **w** down into Egypt to H3381
13: 1 And Abram **w** up out of Egypt, he, and H5927
3 And he **w** on his journeys from the H3212
5 And Lot also, which **w** with Abram, H1980
14: 8 And there **w** out the king of Sodom, H3318
11 and all their victuals, and **w** their way. H3212
17 And the king of Sodom **w** out to meet H3318
24 of the men which **w** with me, Aner, H1980
15:17 that, when the sun **w** down, and it was H935
16: 4 And he **w** in unto Hagar, and she H935
17:22 him, and God **w** up from Abraham. H5927
18:16 **w** with them to bring them on the way. H1980
22 from thence, and **w** toward Sodom: but H3212
33 And the LORD **w** his way, as soon as he H3212
19: 6 And Lot **w** out at the door unto them, H3318
14 And Lot **w** out, and spake unto his sons H3318
28 **w** up as the smoke of a furnace. H5927
30 And Lot **w** up out of Zoar, and dwelt in H5927
33 and the firstborn **w** in, and lay with her H935
21:16 And she **w**, and sat her down over H3212
19 of water; and she **w**, and filled the bottle H3212
22: 3 and rose up, and **w** unto the place of H3212
6 and they **w** both of them together. H3212
8 so they **w** both of them together. H3212
13 and Abraham **w** and took the ram, and H3212
19 and they rose up and **w** together to H3212
23:10 that **w** in at the gate of his city, saying, H935
18 before all that **w** in at the gate of his city. H935

Gen 24:10 and he arose, and w to Mesopotamia, H3212
16 her: and she w down to the well, and H3381
45 her shoulder; and she w down unto the H3381
61 servant took Rebekah, and w his way. H3212
63 And Isaac w out to meditate in the field H3318
25:22 And she w to inquire of the LORD. H3212
34 and rose up, and w his way: thus Esau H3212
26: 1 And Isaac w unto Abimelech king H3212
13 And the man waxed great, and w H3212
23 And he w up from thence to H5927
26 Then Abimelech w to him from Gerar, H1980
27: 5 his son. And Esau w to the field to hunt H3212
14 And he w, and fetched, and brought H3212
22 And Jacob w near unto Isaac his H5066
28: 5 And Isaac sent away Jacob: and he w H3212
9 Then w Esau unto Ishmael, and took H3212
10 And Jacob w out from Beer-sheba, and H3318
10 from Beer-sheba, and w toward Haran. H3212
29: 1 Then Jacob w on his journey, and came H5375
10 that Jacob w near, and rolled the H5066
23 her to him; and he w in unto her. H935
30 And he w in also unto Rachel, and he H935
30: 4 to wife: and Jacob w in unto her. H935
14 And Reuben w in the days of wheat H3212
16 and Leah w out to meet him, and H3318
31:19 And Laban w to shear his sheep: and H1980
33 And Laban w into Jacob's tent, and into H935
33 *them* not. Then w he out of Leah's tent, H3318
32: 1 And Jacob w on his way, and the H1980
21 So w the present over before him: and H5674
34: 1 w out to see the daughters of the land. H3318
6 And Hamor the father of Shechem w H3318
24 hearkened all that w out of the gate of H3318
24 all that w out of the gate of his city. H3318
26 out of Shechem's house, and w out. H3318
35: 3 and was with me in the way which I w. H1980
13 And God w up from him in the place H5927
22 that land, that Reuben w and lay with H3212
36: 6 land of Canaan; and w into the country H3212
37:12 And his brethren w to feed their H3212
17 And Joseph w after his brethren, and H3212
38: 1 that time, that Judah w down from his H3381
2 and he took her, and w in unto her. H935
9 to pass, when he w in unto his brother's H935
11 w and dwelt in her father's house. H3212
12 was comforted, and w up unto his H5927
19 And she arose, and w away, and laid H3212
39:11 time, that *Joseph* w into the house to do H935
41:45 Joseph w out over *all* the land of Egypt. H3318
46 And Joseph w out from the presence H3318
46 and w throughout all the land of Egypt. H5674
42: 3 And Joseph's ten brethren w down to H3381
43:15 and rose up, and w down to Egypt, and H3381
31 And he washed his face, and w out, H3318
44:28 And the one w out from me, and I said, H3318
45:25 And they w up out of Egypt, and came H5927
46:29 his chariot, and w up to meet Israel his H5927
47:10 And Jacob blessed Pharaoh, and w out H3318
49: 4 defiledst thou *it*: he w up to my couch. H5927
50: 7 And Joseph w up to bury his father: H5927
7 and with him w up all the servants of H5927
9 And there w up with him both chariots H5927
14 and all that w up with him to bury H5927
18 And his brethren also w and fell down H3212
Ex 2: 1 And there w a man of the house of H3212
8 maid w and called the child's mother. H3212
11 grown, that he w out unto his brethren, H3318
13 And when he w out the second day, H3318
4:18 And Moses w and returned to Jethro H3212
27 Moses. And he w, and met him in the H3212
29 And Moses and Aaron w and gathered H3212
5: 1 And afterward Moses and Aaron w in, H935
10 And the taskmasters of the people w H3318
7:10 And Moses and Aaron w in unto H935
23 And Pharaoh turned and w into his H935
8:12 And Moses and Aaron w out from H3318
30 And Moses w out from Pharaoh, and H3318
9:33 And Moses w out of the city from H3318
10: 6 himself, and w out from Pharaoh. H3318
14 And the locusts w up over all the land H5927
18 And he w out from Pharaoh, and H3318
11: 8 w out from Pharaoh in a great anger. H3318
12:28 And the children of Israel w away, and H3212
38 And a mixed multitude w up also with H5927
41 LORD w out from the land of Egypt. H3318
13:18 children of Israel w up harnessed out H5927
21 And the LORD w before them by day in H1980
14: 8 of Israel w out with an high hand. H3318
19 And the angel of God, which w before H1980
Ex 14:19 removed and w behind them; and the H3212
19 pillar of the cloud w from before their H5265
22 And the children of Israel w into the H935
23 And the Egyptians pursued, and w in H935
15:19 For the horse of Pharaoh w in with his H935
19 w on dry *land* in the midst of the sea. H1980
20 and all the women w out after her with H3318
22 the Red sea, and they w out into the H3318
22 of Shur; and they w three days in the H3212
16:27 And it came to pass, *that* there w out H3318
17:10 and Hur w up to the top of the hill. H5927
18: 7 And Moses w out to meet his father in H3318
27 and he w his way into his own land. H3212
19: 3 And Moses w up unto God, and the H5927
14 And Moses w down from the mount H3381
20 the top of the mount; and Moses w up. H5927
25 So Moses w down unto the people, and H3381
24: 9 Then w up Moses, and Aaron, Nadab, H5927
13 and Moses w up into the mount of God. H5927
15 And Moses w up into the mount, and a H5927
18 And Moses w into the midst of the cloud, H935
32:15 And Moses turned, and w down from H3381
33: 7 which sought the LORD w out unto the H3318
8 And it came to pass, when Moses w out H3318
34: 4 in the morning, and w up unto mount H5927
34 But when Moses w in before the LORD H935
35 again, until he w in to speak with him. H935
38:26 for every one that w to be numbered, H5674
40:32 When they w into the tent of the H935
36 of Israel w onward in all their journeys: H5265
Lev 9: 8 Aaron therefore w unto the altar, and H7126
23 And Moses and Aaron w into the H935
10: 2 And there w out fire from the LORD, H3318
5 So they w near, and carried them in H7126
16:23 he put on when he w into the holy *place*, H935
24:10 *was* an Egyptian, w out among the H3318
Nu 8:22 And after that w the Levites in to do H935
10:14 In the first *place* w the standard of the H5265
33 of the LORD w before them in the three H5265
34 by day, when they w out of the camp. H5265
11: 8 *And* the people w about, and gathered H7751
24 And Moses w out, and told the people H3318
26 were written, but w not out unto the H3318
31 And there w forth a wind from the H5265
13:21 So they w up, and searched the land H5927
26 And they w and came to Moses, and to H3212
31 But the men that w up with him said, H5927
14:24 he w; and his seed shall possess it. H935
38 that w to search the land, lived *still*. H1980
16:25 And Moses rose up and w unto Dathan H3212
33 to them, w down alive into the H3381
17: 8 the morrow Moses w into the tabernacle H935
20: 6 And Moses and Aaron w from the H935
15 How our fathers w down into Egypt, H3381
27 and they w up into mount Hor H5927
21:16 And from thence *they* w to Beer: that *is*
18 from the wilderness *they* w to Mattanah:
23 together, and w out against Israel into H3318
33 And they turned and w up by the way H5927
33 king of Bashan w out against them, he, H3318
22:14 rose up, and they w unto Balak, and H935
21 ass, and w with the princes of Moab. H3212
22 because he w: and the angel of the H1980
23 of the way, and w into the field: and H3212
26 And the angel of the LORD w further, H5674
32 times? behold, I w out to withstand H3318
35 So Balaam w with the princes of Balak. H3212
36 was come, he w out to meet him unto H3318
39 And Balaam w with Balak, and they H3212
23: 3 tell thee. And he w to an high place. H3212
24: 1 to bless Israel, he w not, as at other H1980
25 And Balaam rose up, and w and H3212
25 to his place: and Balak also w his way. H1980
25: 8 And he w after the man of Israel into the H935
26: 4 which w forth out of the land of Egypt. H3318
31:13 the congregation, w forth to meet them H3318
21 men of war which w to the battle, This *is* H935
27 upon them, who w out to battle, and H3318
28 men of war which w out to battle: one H3318
36 of them that w out to war, was in H3318
32: 9 For when they w up unto the valley of H5927
39 son of Manasseh w to Gilead, and took H3212
41 And Jair the son of Manasseh w and H1980
42 And Nobah w and took Kenath, and H1980
33: 1 of Israel, which w forth out of the land H3318
3 children of Israel w out with an high H3318
8 wilderness, and w three days' journey H3212
23 And they w from Kehelathah, and H5265
29 And they w from Mithcah, and pitched H5265
Nu 33:33 And they w from Hor-hagidgad, and H5265
38 And Aaron the priest w up into mount H5927
Dt 1:19 from Horeb, we w through all that H3212
24 And they turned and w up into the H5927
31 that ye w, until ye came into this place. H1980
33 Who w in the way before you, to search H1980
43 and w presumptuously up into the hill. H5927
2:13 Zered. And we w over the brook Zered. H5674
3: 1 Then we turned, and w up the way to H5927
5: 5 and w not up into the mount;) saying, H5927
10: 3 like unto the first, and w up into the H5927
22 Thy fathers w down into Egypt with H3381
26: 5 my father, and he w down into Egypt, H3381
29:26 For they w and served other gods, and H3212
31: 1 And Moses w and spake these words H3212
14 Moses and Joshua w, and presented H3212
33: 2 his right hand *w* a fiery law for them.
34: 1 And Moses w up from the plains of H5927
Jos 2: 1 Jericho. And they w, and came into an H3212
5 that the men w out: whither the men H3318
5 whither the men w I wot not: pursue H1980
22 And they w, and came unto the H3212
3: 2 that the officers w through the host; H5674
6 the covenant, and w before the people. H3212
5:13 his hand: and Joshua w unto him, and H3212
6: 1 Israel: none w out, and none came in. H3318
9 And the armed men w before the H1980
13 ark of the LORD w on continually, and H1980
13 the armed men w before them; but the H1980
20 so that the people w up into the city, H5927
23 And the young men that were spies w in, H935
7: 2 And the men w up and viewed Ai. H5927
4 So there w up thither of the people H5927
8: 9 forth: and they w to lie in ambush, and H3212
10 the people, and w up, he and the elders H5927
11 *were* with him, w up, and drew nigh, H5927
13 of the city, Joshua w that night into the H3212
14 men of the city w out against Israel to H3318
17 in Ai or Beth-el, that w not out after H3318
9: 4 They did work wilily, and w and made H3212
6 And they w to Joshua unto the camp at H3212
10: 5 together, and w up, they and all their H5927
9 *and* w up from Gilgal all night. H5927
24 men of war which w with him, Come H1980
36 And Joshua w up from Eglon, and all H5927
11: 4 And they w out, they and all their hosts H3318
14: 8 Nevertheless my brethren that w up H5927
15: 3 And it w out to the south side to H3318
3 to Hezron, and w up to Adar, and H5927
4 Azmon, and w out unto the river of H3318
6 And the border w up to Beth-hogla, H5927
6 and the border w up to the stone of H5927
7 And the border w up toward Debir H5927
8 And the border w up by the valley of H5927
8 and the border w up to the top of the H5927
9 of Nephtoah, and w out to the cities of H3318
10 the north side, and w down to H3381
11 And the border w out unto the side of H3318
11 Baalah, and w out unto Jabneel; and H3318
15 And he w up thence to the inhabitants H5927
16: 6 And the border w out toward the sea to H3318
6 and the border w about eastward unto H5437
7 And it w down from Janohah to H3381
7 came to Jericho, and w out at Jordan. H3318
8 The border w out from Tappuah H3212
17: 7 and the border w along on the right H1980
18: 8 And the men arose, and w away: and H3212
8 them that w to describe the land, H1980
9 And the men w and passed through the H3212
12 and the border w up to the side of H5927
12 the north side, and w up through the H5927
13 And the border w over from thence H5674
15 and the border w out on the west, and H3318
15 on the west, and w out to the well of H3318
17 And was drawn from the north, and w H3318
17 to En-shemesh, and w forth toward H3318
18 northward, and w down unto Arabah: H3381
19:11 And their border w up toward the sea, H5927
47 And the coast of the children of Dan w H3318
47 children of Dan w up to fight against H5927
22: 6 away: and they w unto their tents. H3212
24: 4 and his children w down into Egypt. H3381
11 And ye w over Jordan, and came unto H5674
17 way wherein we w, and among all the H1980
Jdg 1: 3 into thy lot. So Simeon w with him. H3212
4 And Judah w up; and the LORD H5927
9 And afterward the children of Judah w H3381
10 And Judah w against the Canaanites H3212
11 And from thence he w against the H3212

Jdg 1:16 father in law, w up out of the city of H5927
16 they w and dwelt among the people. H3212
17 And Judah w with Simeon his brother, H3212
22 And the house of Joseph, they also w H5927
26 And the man w into the land of the H3212
2: 6 children of Israel w every man unto his H3212
15 Whithersoever they w out, the hand of H3318
17 judges, but they w a whoring after other
3:10 he judged Israel, and w out to war: and H3318
13 and Amalek, and w and smote Israel, H3212
19 all that stood by him w out from him. H3318
22 And the haft also w in after the blade; H935
23 Then Ehud w forth through the porch, H3318
27 the children of Israel w down with him H3381
28 hand. And they w down after him, and H3381
4: 9 arose, and w with Barak to Kedesh. H3212
10 to Kedesh; and he w up with ten H5927
10 his feet: and Deborah w up with him. H5927
14 thee? So Barak w down from mount H3381
18 And Jael w out to meet Sisera, and said H3318
21 in her hand, and w softly unto him, and H935
6:19 And Gideon w in, and made ready a kid, H935
33 together, and w over, and pitched in H5674
7:11 the host. Then w he down with Phurah H3381
8: 8 And he w up thence to Penuel, and H5927
11 And Gideon w up by the way of them H5927
27 and all Israel w thither a whoring after
29 And Jerubbaal the son of Joash w and H3212
33 turned again, and w a whoring after
9: 1 And Abimelech the son of Jerubbaal w H3212
5 And he w unto his father's house at H935
6 of Millo, and w, and made Abimelech H3212
7 And when they told *it* to Jotham, he w H3212
8 The trees w forth *on a time* to anoint a H1980
21 And Jotham ran away, and fled, and w H3212
26 his brethren, and w over to Shechem: H5674
27 And they w out into the fields, and H3318
27 made merry, and w into the house of H935
35 And Gaal the son of Ebed w out, and H3318
39 And Gaal w out before the men of H3318
42 that the people w out into the field; and H3318
50 Then w Abimelech to Thebez, and H3212
52 against it, and w hard unto the door H5066
11: 3 men to Jephthah, and w out with him. H3318
5 elders of Gilead w to fetch Jephthah out H3212
11 Then Jephthah w with the elders of H3212
18 Then they w along through the H3212
38 two months: and she w with her H3212
40 *That* the daughters of Israel w yearly to H3212
12: 1 together, and w northward, and said H5674
13:11 And Manoah arose, and w after his H3212
20 For it came to pass, when the flame w H5927
14: 1 And Samson w down to Timnath, and H3381
5 Then w Samson down, and his father H3381
7 And he w down, and talked with the H3381
9 in his hands, and w on eating, and H1980
10 So his father w down unto the woman: H3381
18 day before the sun w down, What *is* H935
19 upon him, and he w down to Ashkelon, H3381
19 and he w up to his father's house. H5927
15: 4 And Samson w and caught three H3212
8 slaughter: and he w down and dwelt in H3381
9 Then the Philistines w up, and pitched H5927
11 Then three thousand men of Judah w H3381
16: 1 Then w Samson to Gaza, and saw there H3212
1 saw there an harlot, and w in unto her. H935
3 the two posts, and w away with them, H5265
14 of his sleep, and w away with the pin of H5265
19 him, and his strength w from him. H5493
17:10 and thy victuals. So the Levite w in. H3212
18:11 And there w from thence of the family H5265
12 And they w up, and pitched in H5927
14 Then answered the five men that w to H1980
17 And the five men that w to spy out the H1980
17 to spy out the land w up, *and* came in H5927
18 And these w into Micah's house, and H935
20 image, and w in the midst of the people. H935
26 And the children of Dan w their way: H3212
26 he turned and w back unto his house. H7725
19: 2 against him, and w away from him H3212
3 And her husband arose, and w after H3212
14 And they passed on and w their way; H3212
14 way; and the sun w down upon them H935
15 and when he w in, he sat him down H935
18 from thence *am* I: and I w to H3212
23 of the house, w out unto them, and H3318
27 of the house, and w out to go his way: H3318
20: 1 Then all the children of Israel w out, H3318
18 And the children of Israel arose, and w H5927

Jdg 20:20 And the men of Israel w out to battle H3318
23 (And the children of Israel w up and H5927
25 And Benjamin w forth against them H3318
26 all the people, w up, and came unto H5927
30 And the children of Israel w up against H5927
31 And the children of Benjamin w out H3318
21:23 caught: and they w and returned unto H3212
24 his family, and they w out from thence H3318
Ru 1: 1 Beth-lehem-judah w to sojourn in the H3212
7 Wherefore she w forth out of the place H3318
7 law with her; and they w on the way to H3212
19 So they two w until they came to H3212
21 I w out full, and the LORD hath H1980
2: 3 And she w, and came, and gleaned in H3212
18 And she took *it* up, and w into the city: H935
3: 6 And she w down unto the floor, and H3381
7 was merry, he w to lie down at the end H935
15 laid *it* on her: and she w into the city. H935
4: 1 Then w Boaz up to the gate, and sat H5927
13 his wife: and when he w in unto her, the H935
1Sa 1: 3 And this man w up out of his city H5927
7 by year, when she w up to the house of H5927
18 So the woman w her way, and did eat, H3212
21 and all his house, w up to offer unto H5927
22 But Hannah w not up; for she said unto H5927
2:11 And Elkanah w to Ramah to his house. H3212
20 And they w unto their own home. H1980
3: 3 And ere the lamp of God w out in the H3518
5 down again. And he w and lay down. H3212
6 Samuel arose and w to Eli, and said, H3212
8 And he arose and w to Eli, and said, H3212
9 So Samuel w and lay down in his place. H3212
4: 1 all Israel. Now Israel w out against the H3318
5:12 and the cry of the city w up to heaven. H5927
6:12 *and* w along the highway, H1980
12 lowing as they w, and turned not aside H1980
12 of the Philistines w after them unto the H1980
7: 7 of the Philistines w up against Israel. H5927
11 And the men of Israel w out of Mizpeh, H3318
16 And he w from year to year in circuit to H1980
9: 9 (Beforetime in Israel, when a man w to H3212
10 let us go. So they w unto the city where H3212
11 *And* as they w up the hill to the city, H5927
14 And they w up into the city: *and* when H5927
26 arose, and they w out both of them, he H3318
10:14 servant, Whither w ye? And he said, To H1980
26 And Saul also w home to Gibeah; and H1980
26 Gibeah; and there w with him a band H3212
11:15 And all the people w to Gilgal; and H3212
13: 7 And *some of* the Hebrews w over H5674
10 came; and Saul w out to meet him, that H3318
20 But all the Israelites w down to the H3381
23 And the garrison of the Philistines w H3318
14:16 they w on beating down *one another.* H3212
19 of the Philistines w on and increased: H3212
21 that time, which w up with them into H5927
46 Then Saul w up from following the H5927
46 the Philistines w to their own place. H1980
15:34 Then Samuel w to Ramah; and Saul H3212
34 w up to his house to Gibeah of Saul. H5927
16:13 So Samuel rose up, and w to Ramah. H3212
17: 4 And there w out a champion out of the H3318
7 and one bearing a shield w before him. H1980
12 sons: and the man w among men *for* an H935
13 And the three eldest sons of Jesse w H3212
13 his three sons that w to the battle *were* H1980
15 But David w and returned from Saul to H1980
20 keeper, and took, and w, as Jesse had H3212
35 And I w out after him, and smote him, H3318
41 man that bare the shield *w* before him.
18: 5 And David w out whithersoever Saul H3318
13 w out and came in before the people. H3318
16 he w out and came in before them. H3318
27 Wherefore David arose and w, he and H3212
30 Then the princes of the Philistines w H3318
30 to pass, after they w forth, *that* David H3318
19: 8 And there was war again: and David w H3318
12 and he w, and fled, and escaped. H3212
18 he and Samuel w and dwelt in Naioth. H3212
22 Then w he also to Ramah, and came to H3212
23 And he w thither to Naioth in Ramah: H3212
23 him also, and he w on, and prophesied, H3212
20:11 they w out both of them into the field. H3318
35 that Jonathan w out into the field at H3318
42 departed: and Jonathan w into the city. H935
21:10 Saul, and w to Achish the king of Gath. H935
22: 1 heard *it*, they w down thither to him. H3381
3 And David w thence to Mizpeh of H3212
23: 5 So David and his men w to Keilah, and H3212

1Sa 23:13 out of Keilah, and w whithersoever H1980
16 And Jonathan Saul's son arose, and w H3212
18 the wood, and Jonathan w to his house. H1980
24 And they arose, and w to Ziph before H3212
25 Saul also and his men w to seek *him.* H3212
26 And Saul w on this side of the H3212
28 after David, and w against the H3212
29 And David w up from thence, and H5927
24: 2 of all Israel, and w to seek David and H3212
3 a cave; and Saul w in to cover his feet: H935
7 up out of the cave, and w on *his* way. H3212
8 David also arose afterward, and w out H3318
22 Saul. And Saul w home; but David and H3212
25: 1 and w down to the wilderness of Paran. H3381
12 their way, and w again, and came and H7725
13 his sword: and there w up after David H9527
42 of hers that w after her; and she went H1980
42 went after her; and she w after the H3212
26: 2 Then Saul arose, and w down to the H3381
13 Then David w over to the other side, H5674
25 prevail. So David w on his way, and H3212
27: 8 And David and his men w up, and H5927
28: 8 raiment, and he w, and two men with H3212
25 they rose up, and w away that night. H3212
29:11 And the Philistines w up to Jezreel. H5927
30: 2 *them* away, and w on their way. H3212
9 So David w, he and the six hundred H3212
21 Besor: and they w forth to meet David, H3318
22 of those that w with David, and said, H1980
22 Because they w not with us, we will H1980
31: 3 And the battle w sore against Saul, and
12 All the valiant men arose, and w all H3212
2Sa 1: 4 And David said unto him, How w the H1961
2: 2 So David w up thither, and his two H5927
12 Saul, w out from Mahanaim to Gibeon. H3318
13 the servants of David, w out, and met H3318
15 Then there arose and w over by H5674
24 and the sun w down when they were H935
29 passed over Jordan, and w through all H3212
32 Joab and his men w all night, and they H3212
3:16 And her husband w with her along H3212
19 and Abner w also to speak in the H3212
21 sent Abner away; and he w in peace. H3212
4: 5 and Baanah, w, and came about the H3212
5: 6 And the king and his men w to H3212
10 And David w on, and grew great, and H3212
17 heard *of it*, and w down to the hold. H3381
6: 2 And David arose, and w with all the H3212
4 ark of God: and Ahio w before the ark. H1980
12 of God. So David w and brought up the H3212
7:18 Then w king David in, and sat before the H935
23 Israel, whom God w to redeem for a H1980
8: 3 of Zobah, as he w to recover his border H3212
6 preserved David whithersoever he w. H1980
14 preserved David whithersoever he w. H1980
10:16 of the host of Hadarezer *w* before them.
11: 9 his lord, and w not down to his house. H3381
10 saying, Uriah w not down unto his H3381
13 and at even he w out to lie on his bed H3318
13 his lord, but w not down to his house. H3381
17 And the men of the city w out, and H3318
21 died in Thebez? why w ye nigh the wall? H5066
22 So the messenger w, and came and H3212
12:16 w in, and lay all night upon the earth. H935
17 And the elders of his house arose, *and w*
24 his wife, and w in unto her, and lay H935
29 together, and w to Rabbah, and fought H3212
13: 8 So Tamar w to her brother Amnon's H3212
9 And they w out every man from him. H3318
19 her hand on her head, and w on crying. H3212
37 But Absalom fled, and w to Talmai, the H3212
38 So Absalom fled, and w to Geshur, and H3212
14:23 So Joab arose and w to Geshur, and H3212
15: 9 in peace. So he arose, and w to Hebron. H3212
11 And with Absalom w two hundred men H1980
11 called; and they w in their simplicity, H1980
16 And the king w forth, and all his H3318
17 And the king w forth, and all the H3318
24 and Abiathar w up, until all the people H5927
30 And David w up by the ascent of H5927
30 and wept as he w up, and had his head H5927
30 covered, and he w barefoot: and all the H1980
30 they w up, weeping as they went up. H5927
30 they went up, weeping as they w up. H5927
16:13 And as David and his men w by the H3212
13 by the way, Shimei w along on the hill's H1980
13 and cursed as he w, and threw stones at H1980
22 and Absalom w in unto his father's H935
17:17 city: and a wench w and told them; and H1980

2Sa 17:17 them; and they **w** and told king David. H3212
18 told Absalom: but they **w** both of them H3212
18 well in his court; whither they **w** down. H3381
21 of the well, and **w** and told king David, H3212
25 an Israelite, that **w** in to Abigail the H935
18: 6 So the people **w** out into the field H3318
9 and the mule **w** under the thick boughs H935
9 the mule that *was* under him **w** away. H5674
24 the watchman **w** up to the roof over H3212
33 And the king was much moved, and **w** H5927
33 wept: and as he **w**, thus he said, O my H3212
19:17 and they **w** over Jordan before the king. H6743
18 And there **w** over a ferry boat to carry H5674
19 my lord the king **w** out of Jerusalem, H3318
31 Rogelim, and **w** over Jordan with the H5674
39 And all the people **w** over Jordan. And H5674
40 Then the king **w** on to Gilgal, and H5674
40 and Chimham **w** on with him: and all H5674
20: 2 So every man of Israel **w** up from after H5927
3 and fed them, but **w** not in unto them. H935
5 So Amasa **w** to assemble *the men of* H3212
7 And there **w** out after him Joab's men, H3318
7 men: and they **w** out of Jerusalem, to H3318
8 *is* in Gibeon, Amasa **w** before them. And H935
8 thereof; and as he **w** forth it fell out. H3318
13 all the people **w** on after Joab, to H5674
14 And he **w** through all the tribes of H5674
14 gathered together, and **w** also after him. H935
22 Then the woman **w** unto all the people in H935
21:12 And David **w** and took the bones of H3212
15 with Israel; and David **w** down, and his H3381
22: 9 There **w** up a smoke out of his nostrils, H5927
23:13 And three of the thirty chief **w** down, H3381
17 of the men that **w** in jeopardy of their H1980
20 men of Moab: he **w** down also and slew H3381
21 his hand; but he **w** down to him with a H3381
24: 4 of the host **w** out from the presence H3318
7 and they **w** out to the south of Judah, H3318
19 Gad, **w** up as the LORD commanded. H5927
20 him: and Araunah **w** out, and bowed H3318
1Ki 1:15 And Bath-sheba **w** in unto the king into H935
38 and the Pelethites, **w** down, and caused H3381
49 and rose up, and **w** every man his way. H3212
50 and arose, and **w**, and caught hold on H3212
2: 8 in the day when I **w** to Mahanaim: but H3212
19 Bath-sheba therefore **w** unto king H935
34 So Benaiah the son of Jehoiada **w** up, H5927
40 his ass, and **w** to Gath to Achish to H3212
40 **w**, and brought his servants from Gath. H3212
46 of Jehoiada; which **w** out, and fell upon H3318
3: 4 And the king **w** to Gibeon to sacrifice H3212
6: 8 the house: and they **w** up with winding H5927
8:66 the king, and **w** unto their tents joyful H3212
10: 5 by which he **w** up unto the house of H5927
13 So she turned and **w** to her own H3212
16 *shekels* of gold **w** to one target. H5927
17 pound of gold **w** to one shield: and the H5927
29 And a chariot came up and **w** out of H3318
11: 5 For Solomon **w** after Ashtoreth the H3212
6 of the LORD, and **w** not fully after the
24 *Zobah:* and they **w** to Damascus, and H3212
29 when Jeroboam **w** out of Jerusalem, H3318
12: 1 And Rehoboam **w** to Shechem: for all H3212
25 **w** out from thence, and built Penuel. H3318
30 sin: for the people **w** *to worship* before H3212
13:10 So he **w** another way, and returned not H3212
12 them, What way **w** he? For his sons had H1980
12 man of God **w**, which came from Judah. H1980
14 And **w** after the man of God, and found H3212
19 So he **w** back with him, and did eat H7725
28 And he **w** and found his carcase cast in H3212
14: 4 did so, and arose, and **w** to Shiloh, and H3212
28 And it was *so*, when the king **w** into the H935
15:17 And Baasha king of Israel **w** up against H5927
16:10 And Zimri **w** in and smote him, and H935
17 And Omri **w** up from Gibbethon, and H5927
18 was taken, that he **w** into the palace of H935
31 Zidonians, and **w** and served Baal, and H3212
17: 5 So he **w** and did according unto the H3212
5 of the LORD: for he **w** and dwelt by the H3212
10 So he arose and **w** to Zarephath. And H3212
15 And she **w** and did according to the H3212
18: 2 And Elijah **w** to shew himself unto H3212
6 it: Ahab **w** one way by himself, H1980
6 Obadiah **w** another way by himself. H1980
16 So Obadiah **w** to meet Ahab, and told H3212
16 told him: and Ahab **w** to meet Elijah. H3212
42 So Ahab **w** up to eat and to drink. And H5927
42 to drink. And Elijah **w** up to the top of H5927
1Ki 18:43 the sea. And he **w** up, and looked, and H5927
45 rain. And Ahab rode, and **w** to Jezreel. H3212
19: 3 And when he saw *that*, he arose, and **w** H3212
4 But he himself **w** a day's journey into H1980
8 and drink, and **w** in the strength of that H3212
13 in his mantle, and **w** out, and stood in H3318
21 Then he arose, and **w** after Elijah, and H3212
20: 1 chariots: and he **w** up and besieged H5927
16 And they **w** out at noon. But H3318
17 of the provinces **w** out first; and H3318
21 And the king of Israel **w** out, and smote H3318
26 **w** up to Aphek, to fight against Israel. H5927
27 all present, and **w** against them: and H3212
39 said, Thy servant **w** out into the midst H3318
43 And the king of Israel **w** to his house H3212
21:27 and lay in sackcloth, and **w** softly. H1980
22:24 But Zedekiah the son of Chenaanah **w** H5674
24 and said, Which way **w** the spirit of the H5674
29 king of Judah **w** up to Ramoth-gilead. H5927
30 disguised himself, and **w** into the battle. H935
36 And there **w** a proclamation H5674
48 for gold: but they **w** not; for the ships H1980
2Ki 1: 9 with his fifty. And he **w** up to him: and, H5927
13 captain of fifty **w** up, and came and fell H5927
15 and **w** down with him unto the king. H3381
2: 1 that Elijah **w** with Elisha from Gilgal. H3212
2 leave thee. So they **w** down to Beth-el. H3381
6 will not leave thee. And they two **w** on. H3212
7 of the prophets **w**, and stood to view H1980
8 so that they two **w** over on dry ground. H5674
11 And it came to pass, as they still **w** on, H1980
11 **w** up by a whirlwind into heaven. H5927
13 fell from him, and **w** back, and stood H7725
14 hither and thither: and Elisha **w** over. H5674
21 And he **w** forth unto the spring of the H3318
23 And he **w** up from thence unto Beth-el: H5927
25 And he **w** from thence to mount H3212
3: 6 And king Jehoram **w** out of Samaria H3318
7 And he **w** and sent to Jehoshaphat the H3212
9 So the king of Israel **w**, and the king of H3212
12 and the king of Edom **w** down to him. H3381
24 them: but they **w** forward smiting the H5221
25 the slingers **w** about *it*, and smote it. H5437
4: 5 So she **w** from him, and shut the door H3212
18 he **w** out to his father to the reapers. H3318
21 And she **w** up, and laid him on the bed H5927
21 shut *the door* upon him, and **w** out. H3318
25 So she **w** and came unto the man of H3212
31 Wherefore he **w** again to meet him, H7725
33 He **w** in therefore, and shut the door H935
34 And he **w** up, and lay upon the child, H5927
35 to and fro; and **w** up, and stretched H5927
37 Then she **w** in, and fell at his feet, and H935
37 and took up her son, and **w** out. H3318
39 And one **w** out into the field to gather H3318
5: 4 And *one* **w** in, and told his lord, saying, H935
11 But Naaman was wroth, and **w** away, H3212
12 So he turned and **w** away in a rage. H3212
14 Then **w** he down, and dipped himself H3381
25 But he **w** in, and stood before his H935
25 And he said, Thy servant **w** no whither. H1980
26 And he said unto him, **W** not mine H1980
27 seed for ever. And he **w** out from his H3318
6: 4 So he **w** with them. And when they H3212
23 away, and they **w** to their master. So H3212
24 host, and **w** up, and besieged Samaria. H5927
7: 8 of the camp, they **w** into one tent, and H935
8 and raiment, and **w** and hid *it*; and H3212
8 carried thence *also*, and **w** and hid *it*. H3212
15 And they **w** after them unto Jordan: H3212
16 And the people **w** out, and spoiled the H3318
8: 2 of God: and she **w** with her household, H3212
3 and she **w** forth to cry unto the H3318
9 So Hazael **w** to meet him, and took a H3212
21 So Joram **w** over to Zair, and all the H5674
28 And he **w** with Joram the son of Ahab H3212
29 And king Joram **w** back to be healed in H7725
29 king of Judah **w** down to see Joram H3381
9: 4 man the prophet, **w** to Ramoth-gilead. H3212
6 And he arose, and **w** into the house; and H935
16 So Jehu rode in a chariot, and **w** to H3212
18 So there **w** one on horseback to meet H3212
21 king of Judah **w** out, each in his H3318
21 chariot, and they **w** out against Jehu, H3318
24 and the arrow **w** out at his heart, and H3318
35 And they **w** to bury her: but they found H3212
10: 9 morning, that he **w** out, and stood, and H3318
23 And Jehu **w**, and Jehonadab the son of H935
24 And when they **w** in to offer sacrifices H935
2Ki 10:25 and **w** to the city of the house of Baal. H3212
11:16 And they laid hands on her; and she **w** H935
18 And all the people of the land **w** into the H935
12:17 Then Hazael king of Syria **w** up, and H5927
18 Syria: and he **w** away from Jerusalem. H5927
13: 5 so that they **w** out from under the H3318
14:11 Jehoash king of Israel **w** up; and he and H5927
15:14 For Menahem the son of Gadi **w** up H5927
16: 9 the king of Assyria **w** up against H5927
10 And king Ahaz **w** to Damascus to meet H3212
17: 5 all the land, and **w** up to Samaria, and H5927
15 became vain, and **w** after the heathen H3212
18: 7 whithersoever he **w** forth: and he H3318
17 And they **w** up and came to Jerusalem. H5927
19: 1 and **w** into the house of the LORD. H935
14 it: and Hezekiah **w** up into the house of H5927
35 angel of the LORD **w** out, and smote in H3318
36 **w** and returned, and dwelt at Nineveh. H3212
22:14 and Asahiah, **w** unto Huldah the H3212
23: 2 And the king **w** up into the house of the H5927
29 king of Egypt **w** up against the king H5927
29 and king Josiah **w** against him; and he H3212
24:12 And Jehoiachin the king of Judah **w** out H3318
25: 4 *the king* **w** the way toward the plain. H3212
1Ch 2:21 And afterward Hezron **w** in to the H935
4:39 And they **w** to the entrance of Gedor, H3212
42 hundred men, **w** to mount Seir, having H1980
5:18 and threescore, that **w** out to the war. H3318
25 their fathers, and **w** a whoring after the
6:15 And Jehozadak **w** *into captivity*, when H1980
7:23 And when he **w** in to his wife, she H935
23 because it **w** evil with his house. H1961
10: 3 And the battle **w** sore against Saul, and
11: 4 And David and all Israel **w** to H3212
6 of Zeruiah **w** first up, and was chief. H5927
15 Now three of the thirty captains **w** H3381
22 of Moab: also he **w** down and slew a H3381
23 beam; and he **w** down to him with a H3381
12:15 These *are* they that **w** over Jordan in H5674
17 And David **w** out to meet them, and H3318
20 As he **w** to Ziklag, there fell to him of H3212
33 Of Zebulun, such as **w** forth to battle, H3318
36 And of Asher, such as **w** forth to battle, H3318
13: 6 And David **w** up, and all Israel, to H5927
14: 8 all the Philistines **w** up to seek David. H5927
8 heard *of it*, and **w** out against them. H3318
17 And the fame of David **w** out into all H3318
15:25 over thousands, **w** to bring up the ark H1980
16:20 And *when* they **w** from nation to H1980
17:21 Israel, whom God **w** to redeem *to be* H1980
18: 3 unto Hamath, as he **w** to stablish his H3212
6 preserved David whithersoever he **w**. H1980
13 preserved David whithersoever he **w**. H1980
19: 5 Then there **w** *certain*, and told David H3212
16 of the host of Hadarezer **w** before them.
21: 4 departed, and **w** throughout all Israel, H1980
19 And David **w** up at the saying of Gad, H5927
21 and saw David, and **w** out of the H3318
27: 1 came in and **w** out month by month H3318
29:30 and the times that **w** over him, and H5674
2Ch 1: 3 with him, **w** to the high place that H3212
6 And Solomon **w** up thither to the H5927
8: 3 And Solomon **w** to Hamath-zobah, and H3212
17 Then **w** Solomon to Ezion-geber, and H1980
18 the sea; and they **w** with the servants of H935
9: 4 by which he **w** up into the house of H5927
12 So she turned, and **w** away to her own H3212
15 *shekels* of beaten gold **w** to one target. H5927
16 *shekels* of gold **w** to one shield. And the H5927
21 For the king's ships **w** to Tarshish with H1980
10: 1 And Rehoboam **w** to Shechem: for to H3212
16 house. So all Israel **w** to their tents. H3212
12:12 and also in Judah things **w** well. H1961
14:10 Then Asa **w** out against him, and they H3318
15: 2 And he **w** out to meet Asa, and said H3318
5 no peace to him that **w** out, nor to him H3318
17: 9 with them, and **w** about throughout all H5437
18: 2 And after *certain* years he **w** down to H3381
12 And the messenger that **w** to call H1980
23 and said, Which way **w** the spirit of the H5674
28 king of Judah **w** up to Ramoth-gilead. H5927
29 himself; and they **w** to the battle. H935
19: 2 And Jehu the son of Hanani the seer **w** H3318
4 Jerusalem: and he **w** out again through H3318
20:20 in the morning, and **w** forth into the H3318
20 and as they **w** forth, Jehoshaphat H3318
21 of holiness, as they **w** out before the H3318
21: 9 Then Jehoram **w** forth with his princes, H5674
22: 5 their counsel, and **w** with Jehoram the H3212

2Ch 22: 6 king of Judah **w** down to see Jehoram H3381
7 he was come, he **w** out with Jehoram H3318
23: 2 And they **w** about in Judah, and H5437
17 Then all the people **w** to the house of H935
25:11 his people, and **w** to the valley of salt, H3212
21 So Joash the king of Israel **w** up; and H5927
26: 6 And he **w** forth and warred against the H3318
11 of fighting men, that **w** out to war by H3318
16 his God, and **w** into the temple of the H935
17 And Azariah the priest **w** in after him, H935
28: 9 *was* Oded: and he **w** out before the host H3318
29:16 And the priests **w** into the inner part of H935
18 Then they **w** in to Hezekiah the king, H935
20 and **w** up to the house of the LORD. H5927
30: 6 So the posts **w** with the letters from the H3212
31: 1 that were present **w** out to the cities of H3318
34:22 king *had appointed*, **w** to Huldah the H3212
30 And the king **w** up into the house of the H5927
35:20 and Josiah **w** out against him. H3318
Ezr 2: 1 of the province that **w** up out of the H5927
59 And these *were* they which **w** up from H5927
4:23 their companions, they **w** up in haste to H236
5: 8 Be it known unto the king, that we **w** H236
7: 6 This Ezra **w** up from Babylon; and he H5927
7 And there **w** up *some* of the children of H5927
8: 1 of them that **w** up with me from H5927
10: 6 house of God, and **w** into the chamber H3212
Neh 2:13 And I **w** out by night by the gate of the H3318
14 Then I **w** on to the gate of the fountain, H5674
15 Then **w** I up in the night by the brook, H5927
16 And the rulers knew not whither I **w**, or H1980
7: 6 of the province, that **w** up out of the H5927
61 And these *were* they which **w** up *also* H5927
8:12 And all the people **w** their way to eat, H3212
16 So the people **w** forth, and brought H3318
9:11 them, so that they **w** through the midst H5674
24 So the children **w** in and possessed the H935
12: 1 the Levites that **w** up with Zerubbabel H5927
31 *whereof one* **w** on the right hand upon H8418
32 And after them **w** Hoshaiah, and half H3212
37 them, they **w** up by the stairs of the H5927
38 *that gave* thanks **w** over against *them*, H1980
Est 2:14 In the evening she **w**, and on the morrow H935
3:15 The posts **w** out, being hastened by the H3318
4: 1 with ashes, and **w** out into the midst of H3318
6 So Hatach **w** forth to Mordecai unto H3318
17 So Mordecai **w** his way, and did H5674
5: 9 Then **w** Haman forth that day joyful H3318
7: 7 of wine in his wrath *w* into the palace
8 As the word **w** out of the king's mouth, H3318
8:14 upon mules *and* camels **w** out, being H3318
15 And Mordecai **w** out from the presence H3318
9: 4 and his fame **w** out throughout all the H1980
Job 1: 4 And his sons **w** and feasted *in their* H1980
12 **w** forth from the presence of the LORD. H3318
2: 7 So **w** Satan forth from the presence of H3318
18:20 as they that **w** before were affrighted. H6923
29: 7 When I **w** out to the gate through the H3318
30:28 I **w** mourning without the sun: I stood H1980
31:34 kept silence, *and* **w** not out of the door? H3318
42: 9 the Naamathite **w**, and did according H3212
Ps 18: 8 There **w** up a smoke out of his nostrils, H5927
42: 4 the multitude, I **w** with them to the H1718
66: 6 He turned the sea into dry *land*: they **w** H5674
12 over our heads; we **w** through fire and H935
68:25 The singers **w** before, the players on H6923
73:17 Until I **w** into the sanctuary of God; *then* H935
77:17 a sound: thine arrows also **w** abroad. H1980
81: 5 when he **w** out through the land H3318
105:13 When they **w** from one nation to H1980
106:32 so that it **w** ill with Moses for their sakes:
39 **w** a whoring with their own inventions.
114: 1 When Israel **w** out of Egypt, the house H3318
119:67 Before I was afflicted I **w** astray: but H7683
133: 2 **w** down to the skirts of his garments; H3381
Prv 7: 8 corner; and he **w** the way to her house, H6805
24:30 I **w** by the field of the slothful, and by H5674
Ecc 2:20 Therefore I **w** about to cause my heart H5437
Song 5: 7 The watchmen that **w** about the city H5437
6:11 I **w** down into the garden of nuts to see H3381
Isa 7: 1 king of Israel, **w** up toward Jerusalem H5927
8: 3 And I **w** unto the prophetess; and she H7126
37: 1 and **w** into the house of the LORD. H935
14 it: and Hezekiah **w** up unto the house H5927
36 Then the angel of the LORD **w** forth, H3318
37 **w** and returned, and dwelt at Nineveh. H3212
48: 3 and they **w** forth out of my mouth, H3318
51:23 and as the street, to them that **w** over. H5674
52: 4 GOD, My people **w** down aforetime H3381
Isa 57:17 **w** on frowardly in the way of his heart. H3212
60:15 so that no man **w** through *thee*, I will H5674
Jer 3: 8 not, but **w** and played the harlot also. H3212
7:24 and **w** backward, and not forward. H1961
11:10 words; and they **w** after other gods to H1980
13: 5 So I **w**, and hid it by Euphrates, as the H3212
7 Then I **w** to Euphrates, and digged, H3212
18: 3 Then I **w** down to the potter's house, H3381
22:11 his father, which **w** forth out of this H3318
26:21 was afraid, and fled, and **w** into Egypt; H935
28: 4 of Judah, that **w** into Babylon, saith the H935
11 And the prophet Jeremiah **w** his way. H3212
31: 2 Israel, when I **w** to cause him to rest. H1980
36:12 Then he **w** down into the king's house, H3381
20 And they **w** in to the king into the court, H935
37: 4 Now Jeremiah came in and **w** out H3318
12 Then Jeremiah **w** forth out of H3318
38: 8 Ebed-melech **w** forth out of the king's H3318
11 men with him, and **w** into the house of H935
39: 4 they fled, and **w** forth out of the city H3318
4 and he **w** out the way of the plain. H3318
40: 6 Then **w** Jeremiah unto Gedaliah the son H935
41: 6 And Ishmael the son of Nethaniah **w** H3318
6 all along as he **w**: and it came to pass, H1980
12 Then they took all the men, and **w** to H3212
14 and **w** unto Johanan the son of Kareah. H3212
15 eight men, and **w** to the Ammonites. H3212
44: 3 anger, in that they **w** to burn incense, H3212
51:59 when he **w** with Zedekiah the king H3212
52: 7 of war fled, and **w** forth out of the city H3318
7 and they **w** by the way of the plain. H3212
Ezk 1: 9 not when they **w**; they went every one H3212
9 they **w** every one straight forward. H3212
12 And they **w** every one straight forward: H3212
12 **w**; *and* they turned not when they went. H3212
12 went; *and* they turned not when they **w**. H3212
13 of lamps: it **w** up and down among H1980
13 and out of the fire **w** forth lightning. H3318
17 When they **w**, they went upon their four H3212
17 When they went, they **w** upon their H3212
17 sides: *and* they turned not when they **w**. H3212
19 And when the living creatures **w**, the H3212
19 went, the wheels **w** by them: and when H3212
20 was to go, they **w**, thither *was their* H3212
21 When those **w**, *these* went; and when H3212
21 When those went, *these* **w**; and when H3212
24 And when they **w**, I heard the noise of H3212
3:14 me away, and I **w** in bitterness, in the H3212
23 Then I arose, and **w** forth into the H3318
8:10 So I **w** in and saw; and behold every H935
11 and a thick cloud of incense **w** up. H5927
9: 2 **w** in, and stood beside the brasen altar. H935
7 And they **w** forth, and slew in the city. H3318
10: 2 over the city. And he **w** in in my sight. H935
3 **w** in; and the cloud filled the inner court. H935
4 Then the glory of the LORD **w** up from H7311
6 he **w** in, and stood beside the wheels. H935
7 with linen: who took *it*, and **w** out. H3318
11 When they **w**, they went upon their four H3212
11 When they went, they **w** upon their H3212
11 turned not as they **w**, but to the place H3212
11 followed it; they turned not as they **w**. H3212
16 And when the cherubims **w**, the wheels H3212
16 went, the wheels **w** by them: and when H3212
19 sight: when they **w** out, the wheels also H3318
22 they **w** every one straight forward. H3212
11:23 And the glory of the LORD **w** up from H5927
24 vision that I had seen **w** up from me. H5927
16:14 And thy renown **w** forth among the H3318
19: 6 And he **w** up and down among the H1980
20:16 for their heart **w** after their idols. H1980
23:44 Yet they **w** in unto her, as they go in unto H935
44 the harlot: so **w** they in unto Aholah H935
24:12 her great scum **w** not forth out of her: H3318
25: 3 of Judah, when they **w** into captivity; H1980
27:33 When thy wares **w** forth out of the seas, H3318
31:15 the day when he **w** down to the grave I H3381
17 They also **w** down into hell with him H3381
36:20 whither they **w**, they profaned my holy H935
21 among the heathen, whither they **w**. H935
22 among the heathen, whither ye **w**. H935
39:23 the house of Israel **w** into captivity for
40: 6 the east, and **w** up the stairs thereof, H5927
22 the east; and they **w** up unto it by seven H5927
49 whereby they **w** up to it: and *there were* H5927
41: 3 Then **w** he inward, and measured the H935
7 about of the house **w** still upward round
44:10 me, when Israel **w** astray, which went H8582
10 astray, which **w** astray away from me H8582
Ezk 44:15 children of Israel **w** astray from me, H8582
47: 3 line in his hand **w** forth eastward, he H3318
48:11 my charge, which **w** not astray when H8552
11 **w** astray, as the Levites went astray. H8552
11 went astray, as the Levites **w** astray. H8552
Dan 2:13 And the decree **w** forth that the wise H5312
16 Then Daniel **w** in, and desired of the H5954
17 Then Daniel **w** to his house, and made H236
24 Therefore Daniel **w** in unto Arioch, H5954
24 *men* of Babylon: he **w** and said thus unto H236
6:10 was signed, he **w** into his house; and H5954
18 Then the king **w** to his palace, and H236
18 before him: and his sleep **w** from him. H5075
19 and **w** in haste unto the den of lions. H236
Hos 1: 3 So he **w** and took Gomer the daughter H3212
2:13 jewels, and she **w** after her lovers, and H3212
5:13 *saw* his wound, then **w** Ephraim to the H3212
9:10 first time: *but* they **w** to Baal-peor, and H935
11: 2 *As* they called them, so they **w** from H1980
Am 5: 3 The city that **w** out *by* a thousand shall H3318
3 and that which **w** forth *by* an hundred H3318
19 a bear met him; or **w** into the house, and H935
Jna 1: 3 of the LORD, and **w** down to Joppa; H3381
3 fare thereof, and **w** down into it, to go H3381
2: 6 I **w** down to the bottoms of the H3381
3: 3 So Jonah arose, and **w** unto Nineveh, H3212
4: 5 So Jonah **w** out of the city, and sat on H3318
Nah 3:10 Yet *was* she carried away, she **w** into H1980
Hab 3: 5 Before him **w** the pestilence, and H3212
5 and burning coals **w** forth at his feet. H3318
11 thine arrows they **w**, *and* at the shining H1980
Zec 2: 3 talked with me **w** forth, and another H3318
3 and another angel **w** out to meet him, H3318
5: 5 Then the angel that talked with me **w** H3318
6: 7 And the bay **w** forth, and sought to go H3318
8:10 *any* peace to him that **w** out or came in H3318
10: 2 therefore they **w** their way as a flock, H5265
Mt 2: 9 saw in the east, **w** before them, till it G4254
3: 5 Then **w** out to him Jerusalem, and all G1607
16 And Jesus, when he was baptized, **w** up G305
4:23 And Jesus **w** about all Galilee, teaching G4013
24 And his fame **w** throughout all Syria: G565
5: 1 And seeing the multitudes, he **w** up into G305
8:32 come out, they **w** into the herd of swine: G565
33 And they that kept them fled, and **w** G565
9:25 were put forth, he **w** in, and took her by G1525
26 And the fame hereof **w** abroad into all G1831
32 As they **w** out, behold, they brought to G1831
35 And Jesus **w** about all the cities and G4018
11: 7 John, What **w** ye out into the G1831
8 But what **w** ye out for to see? A man G1831
9 But what **w** ye out for to see? A G1831
12: 1 At that time Jesus **w** on the sabbath G4198
9 thence, he **w** into their synagogue: G2064
14 Then the Pharisees **w** out, and held a G1831
13: 1 The same day **w** Jesus out of the house, G1831
2 him, so that he **w** into a ship, and sat; G1684
3 saying, Behold, a sower **w** forth to sow; G1831
25 tares among the wheat, and **w** his way. G565
36 away, and **w** into the house: and G2064
46 of great price, **w** and sold all that he G565
14:12 and buried it, and **w** and told Jesus. G2064
14 And Jesus **w** forth, and saw a great G1831
23 away, he **w** up into a mountain G305
25 Jesus **w** unto them, walking on the sea. G565
15:21 Then Jesus **w** thence, and departed into G1831
29 the sea of Galilee; and **w** up into a G305
18:13 ninety and nine which **w** not astray. G4105
28 But the same servant **w** out, and found G1831
30 And he would not: but **w** and cast him G565
19:22 that saying, he **w** away sorrowful: for G565
20: 1 which **w** out early in the morning G1821
3 And he **w** out about the third hour, and G1821
4 I will give you. And they **w** their way. G565
5 Again he **w** out about the sixth and G1831
6 And about the eleventh hour he **w** out, G1831
21: 6 And the disciples **w**, and did as Jesus G4198
9 And the multitudes that **w** before, and G4254
12 And Jesus **w** into the temple of God, G1525
17 And he left them, and **w** out of the city G1831
29 not: but afterward he repented, and **w**. G565
30 answered and said, I *go*, sir: and **w** not. G565
33 husbandmen, and **w** into a far country: G589
22: 5 But they made light of *it*, and **w** their G565
10 So those servants **w** out into the G1831
15 Then **w** the Pharisees, and took G4198
22 and left him, and **w** their way. G565
24: 1 And Jesus **w** out, and departed from G1831
25: 1 and **w** forth to meet the bridegroom. G1831

W

Mt 25:10 And while they w to buy, the bridegroom G565
10 that were ready w in with him to the G1525
16 the five talents w and traded with the G4198
18 But he that had received one w and G565
25 And I was afraid, and w and hid thy G565
26:14 Judas Iscariot, w unto the chief priests, G4198
30 they w out into the mount of Olives. G1831
39 And he w a little farther, and fell on his G4281
42 He w away again the second time, and G565
44 And he left them, and w away again, G565
58 palace, and w in, and sat with the G1525
75 thrice. And he w out, and wept bitterly. G1831
27: 5 departed, and w and hanged himself. G565
53 resurrection, and w into the holy city, G1525
58 He w to Pilate, and begged the body of G4334
66 So they w, and made the sepulchre sure, G4198
28: 9 And as they w to tell his disciples, G4198
16 Then the eleven disciples w away into G4198
Mk 1: 5 And there w out unto him all the land G1607
20 with the hired servants, and w after him. G565
21 And they w into Capernaum; and G1531
35 before day, he w out, and departed into G1831
45 But he w out, and began to publish *it* G1831
2:12 up the bed, and w forth before them G1831
13 And he w forth again by the sea side; G1831
23 And it came to pass, that he w through G3899
23 w, to pluck the ears of corn. G3598+G4160
26 How he w into the house of God in the G1525
3: 6 And the Pharisees w forth, and G1831
19 him: and they w into an house. G2064
21 heard *of it*, they w out to lay hold on G1831
4: 3 Hearken; Behold, there w out a sower G1831
5:13 unclean spirits w out, and entered into G1831
14 w out to see what it was that was done. G1831
24 And *Jesus* w with him; and much people G565
6: 1 And he w out from thence, and came G1831
6 w round about the villages, teaching. G4013
12 And they w out, and preached that G1831
24 And she w forth, and said unto her G1831
27 he w and beheaded him in the prison, G565
51 And he w up unto them into the ship; G305
7:24 And from thence he arose, and w into G565
8:27 And Jesus w out, and his disciples, into G1831
10:22 And he was sad at that saying, and w G565
32 and Jesus w before them: and they G4254
46 And they came to Jericho: and as he w G1607
11: 4 And they w their way, and found the colt G565
9 And they that w before, and they that G4254
11 he w out unto Bethany with the twelve. G1831
15 and Jesus w into the temple, and G1525
19 And when even was come, he w out of G1607
12: 1 husbandmen, and w into a far country. G589
12 and they left him, and w their way. G565
13: 1 And as he w out of the temple, one of G1607
14:10 And Judas Iscariot, one of the twelve, w G565
16 And his disciples w forth, and came G1831
26 they w out into the mount of Olives. G1831
35 And he w forward a little, and fell on G4281
39 And again he w away, and prayed, and G565
68 sayest. And he w out into the porch; G1831
15:43 of God, came, and w in boldly unto G1525
16: 8 And they w out quickly, and fled from G1831
10 *And* she w and told them that had been G4198
12 as they walked, and w into the country. G4198
13 And they w and told *it* unto the residue: G565
20 And they w forth, and preached every G1831
Lk 1: 9 when he w into the temple of the Lord. G1525
39 And Mary arose in those days, and w G4198
2: 1 days, that there w out a decree from G1831
3 And all w to be taxed, every one into G4198
4 And Joseph also w up from Galilee, out G305
41 Now his parents w to Jerusalem every G4198
42 years old, they w up to Jerusalem after G305
44 in the company, w a day's journey; and G2064
51 And he w down with them, and came G2597
4:14 Galilee: and there w out a fame of him G1831
16 custom was, he w into the synagogue G1525
30 through the midst of them w his way, G4198
37 And the fame of him w out into every G1607
42 he departed and w into a desert place: G4198
5:15 But so much the more w there a fame G1330
19 of the multitude, they w upon the G305
27 And after these things he w forth, and G1831
6: 1 the first, that he w through the corn G1279
4 How he w into the house of God, and G1525
12 days, that he w out into a mountain G1831
19 him: for there w virtue out of him, and G1831
7: 6 Then Jesus w with them. And when he G4198
11 day after, that he w into a city called G4198
Lk 7:11 w with him, and much people. G4848
17 And this rumour of him w forth G1831
24 John, What w ye out into the G1831
25 But what w ye out for to see? A man G1831
26 But what w ye out for to see? A G1831
36 with him. And he w into the Pharisee's G1525
8: 1 afterward, that he w throughout every G1353
2 out of whom w seven devils, G1831
5 A sower w out to sow his seed: and as G1831
22 day, that he w into a ship with his G1684
27 And when he w forth to land, there met G1831
33 Then w the devils out of the man, and G1831
34 they fled, and w and told *it* in the city G565
35 Then they w out to see what was done; G1831
37 great fear: and he w up into the ship, G1684
39 done unto thee. And he w his way, and G565
42 But as he w the people thronged him. G5217
9: 6 And they departed, and w through the G1330
10 he took them, and w aside privately G5298
28 and w up into a mountain to pray. G305
52 his face: and they w, and entered into a G4198
56 *them*. And they w to another village. G4198
57 And it came to pass, that, as they w in G4198
10:30 A certain *man* w down from Jerusalem G2597
34 And w to *him*, and bound up his G4334
38 Now it came to pass, as they w, that he G4198
11:37 and he w in, and sat down to meat. G1525
13:22 And he w through the cities and G1279
14: 1 And it came to pass, as he w into the G2064
25 And there w great multitudes with him: G4848
15:15 And he w and joined himself to a G4198
16:30 but if one w unto them from the G4198
17:11 And it came to pass, as he w to G4198
14 that, as they w, they were cleansed. G5217
29 But the same day that Lot w out of G1831
18:10 Two men w up into the temple to pray; G305
14 I tell you, this man w down to his G2597
39 And they which w before rebuked him, G4254
19:12 certain nobleman w into a far country G4198
28 And when he had thus spoken, he w G4198
32 And they that were sent w their way, and G565
36 And as he w, they spread their clothes G4198
45 And he w into the temple, and began to G1525
20: 9 and w into a far country for a long time. G589
21:37 and at night he w out, and abode in the G1831
22: 4 And he w his way, and communed with G565
13 And they w, and found as he had said G565
39 And he came out, and w, as he was G4198
47 one of the twelve, w before them, and G4281
62 And Peter w out, and wept bitterly. G1831
23:52 This *man* w unto Pilate, and begged G4334
24:13 And, behold, two of them w that same G2258
15 himself drew near, and w with them. G4848
24 were with us w to the sepulchre, and G565
28 whither they w: and he made as though G4198
29 spent. And he w in to tarry with them. G1525
Jn 2:12 After this he w down to Capernaum, G2597
13 at hand, and Jesus w up to Jerusalem, G305
4:28 left her waterpot, and w her way into the G565
30 Then they w out of the city, and came G1831
43 he departed thence, and w into Galilee. G565
45 the feast: for they also w unto the feast. G2064
47 Judaea into Galilee, he w unto him, and G565
50 spoken unto him, and he w his way. G4198
5: 1 of the Jews; and Jesus w up to Jerusalem. G305
4 For an angel w down at a certain G2597
6: 1 After these things Jesus w over the sea of G565
3 And Jesus w up into a mountain, and G424
16 his disciples w down unto the sea, G2597
17 And entered into a ship, and w over the G2064
21 the ship was at the land whither they w. G5217
22 and that Jesus w not with his disciples G4897
66 From that *time* many of his disciples w G565
7:10 were gone up, then w he also up unto the G305
14 Now about the midst of the feast Jesus w G305
53 And every man w unto his own house. G4198
8: 1 Jesus w unto the mount of Olives. G4198
9 *own* conscience, w out one by one, G1831
59 hid himself, and w out of the temple, G1831
9: 7 Sent.) He w his way therefore, and G565
11 I w and washed, and I received sight. G565
10:40 And w away again beyond Jordan into G565
11:20 Jesus was coming, w and met him: but G5221
28 And when she had so said, she w her G565
31 rose up hastily and w out, followed her, G1831
46 But some of them w their ways to the G565
54 the Jews; but w thence unto a country G565
55 hand: and many w out of the country up G305
12:11 Jews w away, and believed on Jesus. G5217
Jn 12:13 Took branches of palm trees, and w G1831
13: 3 he was come from God, and w to God; G5217
30 He then having received the sop w G1831
18: 1 spoken these words, he w forth with his G1831
4 come upon him, w forth, and said unto G1831
6 they w backward, and fell to the ground. G565
15 high priest, and w in with Jesus into G4897
16 door without. Then w out that other G1831
28 and they themselves w not into the G1525
29 Pilate then w out unto them, and said, G1831
38 had said this, he w out again unto the G1831
19: 4 Pilate therefore w forth again, and G1831
9 And w again into the judgment hall, G1525
17 And he bearing his cross w forth into a G1831
20: 3 Peter therefore w forth, and that other G1831
5 the linen clothes lying; yet w he not in. G1525
6 him, and w into the sepulchre, G1525
8 Then w in also that other disciple, G1525
10 Then the disciples w away again unto G565
21: 3 go with thee. They w forth, and entered G1831
11 Simon Peter w up, and drew the net to G305
23 Then w this saying abroad among the G1831
Act 1:10 heaven as he w up, behold, two men G4198
13 And when they were come in, they w up G305
21 Jesus w in and out among us, G1525+G1831
3: 1 Now Peter and John w up together into G305
4:23 And being let go, they w to their own G2064
5:26 Then w the captain with the officers, G565
7:15 So Jacob w down into Egypt, and died, G2597
8: 4 w every where preaching the word. G1330
5 Then Philip w down to the city of G2718
27 And he arose and w: and, behold, a G4198
36 And as they w on *their* way, they came G4198
38 still: and they w down both into the G2597
39 more: and he w on his way rejoicing. G4198
9: 1 of the Lord, w unto the high priest, G4334
17 And Ananias w his way, and entered G565
29 Grecians: but they w about to slay him. G2021
39 Then Peter arose and w with them. G4905
10: 9 On the morrow, as they w on their G3596
9 nigh unto the city, Peter w up upon the G305
21 Then Peter w down to the men which G2597
23 the morrow Peter w away with them, G1831
27 And as he talked with him, he w in, G1525
38 with power: who w about doing good, G1330
12: 9 And he w out, and followed him; and G1831
10 accord: and they w out, and passed on G1831
17 he departed, and w into another place. G4198
19 to death. And he w down from Judaea G2718
13:11 a darkness; and he w about seeking G4013
14 in Pisidia, and w into the synagogue G1525
14: 1 that they w both together into the G1525
25 in Perga, they w down into Attalia: G2597
15:24 that certain which w out from us have G1831
38 and w not with them to the work. G4905
41 And he w through Syria and Cilicia, G1330
16: 4 And as they w through the cities, they G1279
13 And on the sabbath we w out of the city G1831
16 And it came to pass, as we w to prayer, G4198
40 And they w out of the prison, and G1831
17: 2 And Paul, as his manner was, w in G1525
10 *thither* w into the synagogue of the Jews. G549
18:22 the church, he w down to Antioch. G2597
23 he departed, and w over *all* the country G1330
19: 8 And he w into the synagogue, and G1525
12 and the evil spirits w out of them. G1831
20:10 And Paul w down, and fell on him, and G2597
13 And we w before to ship, and sailed G4281
21: 2 Phenicia, we w aboard, and set forth. G1910
5 we departed and w our way; and they G4198
15 up our carriages, and w up to Jerusalem. G305
16 There w with us also *certain* of the G4905
18 And the *day* following Paul w in with G1524
31 And as they w about to kill him, tidings G2212
22: 5 the brethren, and w to Damascus, to G4198
26 When the centurion heard *that*, he w G4334
23:16 lying in wait, he w and entered into the G3854
19 him by the hand, and w *with him* aside G402
24:11 since I w up to Jerusalem for to worship. G305
25: 6 more than ten days, he w down unto G2597
26:12 Whereupon as I w to Damascus with G4198
21 in the temple, and w about to kill *me*. G3987
28:14 seven days: and so we w toward Rome. G2064
Ro 10:18 verily, their sound w into all the earth, G1831
2Co 2:13 them, I w from thence into Macedonia. G1831
8:17 of his own accord he w unto you. G1831
Gal 1:17 Neither w I up to Jerusalem to them G424
17 before me; but I w into Arabia, and G565
18 Then after three years I w up to G424

Gal 2: 1 Then fourteen years after I **w** up again to G305
2 And I **w** up by revelation, and G305
1Ti 1: 3 at Ephesus, when I **w** into Macedonia, G4198
18 the prophecies which **w** before on thee, G4254
Heb 9: 6 the priests **w** always into the first G1524
7 But into the second *w* the high priest
11: 8 he **w** out, not knowing whither he went. G1831
8 he went out, not knowing whither he **w**. G2064
1Pt 3:19 By which also he **w** and preached unto G4198
1Jn 2:19 They **w** out from us, but they were not G1831
19 with us: but *they w out*, that they might
3Jn 7 **w** forth, taking nothing of the Gentiles. G1831
Rev 1:16 out of his mouth **w** a sharp twoedged G1607
6: 2 he **w** forth conquering, and to conquer. G1831
4 And there **w** out another horse *that* G1831
10: 9 And I **w** unto the angel, and said unto G565
12:17 the woman, and **w** to make war with the G565
16: 2 And the first **w**, and poured out his vial G565
20: 9 And they **w** up on the breadth of the G305

WENTEST
Gen 49: 4 because thou **w** up to thy father's bed; H5927
Jdg 5: 4 LORD, when thou **w** out of Seir, when H3318
8: 1 us not, when thou **w** to fight with the H1980
1Sa 10: 2 asses which thou **w** to seek are found: H1980
2Sa 7: 9 thou **w**, and have cut off all H1980
16:17 friend? why **w** thou not with thy friend? H1980
19:25 **w** not thou with me, Mephibosheth? H1980
Ps 68: 7 O God, when thou **w** forth before thy H3318
Isa 57: 7 thither **w** thou up to offer sacrifice. H5927
9 And thou **w** to the king with ointment, H7788
Jer 2: 2 espousals, when thou **w** after me in the H3212
31:21 way *which* thou **w**: turn again, O virgin H1980
Hab 3:13 Thou **w** forth for the salvation of thy H3318
Act 11: 3 Saying, Thou **w** in to men G1525

WEPT
Gen 21:16 *him*, and lift up her voice, and **w**. H1058
27:38 And Esau lifted up his voice, and **w**. H1058
29:11 Rachel, and lifted up his voice, and **w**. H1058
33: 4 his neck, and kissed him: and they **w**. H1058
37:35 mourning. Thus his father **w** for him. H1058
42:24 from them, and **w**; and returned to H1058
43:30 entered into *his* chamber, and **w** there. H1058
45: 2 And he **w** aloud: and the Egyptians and H1065
14 **w**; and Benjamin wept upon his neck. H1058
14 wept; and Benjamin **w** upon his neck. H1058
15 all his brethren, and **w** upon them: and H1058
46:29 neck, and **w** on his neck a good while. H1058
50: 1 face, and **w** upon him, and kissed him. H1058
17 Joseph **w** when they spake unto him. H1058
Ex 2: 6 and, behold, the babe **w**. And she had H1058
Nu 11: 4 of Israel also **w** again, and said, Who H1058
18 flesh: for ye have **w** in the ears of the H1058
20 you, and have **w** before him, saying, H1058
14: 1 and cried; and the people **w** that night. H1058
Dt 1:45 And ye returned and **w** before the H1058
34: 8 And the children of Israel **w** for Moses H1058
Jdg 2: 4 the people lifted up their voice, and **w**. H1058
14:16 And Samson's wife **w** before him, and H1058
17 And she **w** before him the seven days, H1058
20:23 went up and **w** before the LORD until H1058
26 the house of God, and **w**, and sat there H1058
21: 2 and lifted up their voices, and **w** sore; H1058
Ru 1: 9 and they lifted up their voice, and **w**. H1058
14 And they lifted up their voice, and **w** H1058
1Sa 1: 7 her; therefore she **w**, and did not eat. H1058
10 prayed unto the LORD, and **w** sore. H1058
11: 4 the people lifted up their voices, and **w**. H1058
20:41 one another, and **w** one with another, H1058
24:16 And Saul lifted up his voice, and **w**. H1058
30: 4 up their voice and **w**, until they had no H1058
2Sa 1:12 And they mourned, and **w**, and fasted H1058
3:32 up his voice, and **w** at the grave of H1058
32 grave of Abner; and all the people **w**. H1058
34 And all the people **w** again over him. H1058
12:22 yet alive, I fasted and **w**: for I said, Who H1058
13:36 up their voice and **w**: and the king also H1058
36 also and all his servants **w** very sore. H1058
15:23 And all the country **w** with a loud H1058
30 of *mount* Olivet, and **w** as he went up, H1058
18:33 over the gate, and **w**: and as he went, H1058
2Ki 8:11 was ashamed: and the man of God **w**. H1058
13:14 unto him, and **w** over his face, and H1058
20: 3 in thy sight. And Hezekiah **w** sore. H1058
22:19 thy clothes, and **w** before me; I also H1058
Ezr 3:12 before their eyes, **w** with a loud voice; H1058
10: 1 children: for the people **w** very sore. H1058
Neh 1: 4 I sat down and **w**, and mourned *certain* H1058
8: 9 For all the people **w**, when they heard H1058
Job 2:12 their voice, and **w**; and they rent every H1058
Ps 69:10 When I **w**, *and chastened* my soul with H1058
137: 1 yea, we **w**, when we remembered Zion. H1058
Isa 38: 3 in thy sight. And Hezekiah **w** sore. H1058
Hos 12: 4 angel, and prevailed: he **w**, and made H1058
Mt 26:75 thrice. And he went out, and **w** bitterly. G2799
Mk 5:38 and them that **w** and wailed greatly. G2799
14:72 And when he thought thereon, he **w**. G2799
16:10 been with him, as they mourned and **w**. G2799
Lk 7:32 mourned to you, and ye have not **w**. G2799
8:52 And all **w**, and bewailed her: but he G2799
19:41 near, he beheld the city, and **w** over it, G2799
22:62 And Peter went out, and **w** bitterly. G2799
Jn 11:35 Jesus **w**. G1145
20:11 and as she **w**, she stooped down, G2799
Act 20:37 And they all **w** sore, and fell on Paul's G1096
1Co 7:30 And they that weep, as though they **w** G2799
Rev 5: 4 And I **w** much, because no man was G2799

WERE See the Appendix.

WERT
Job 8: 6 If thou **w** pure and upright; surely now
Song 8: 1 O that thou *w* as my brother, that sucked
Ro 11:17 a wild olive tree, **w** graffed in among
24 For if thou **w** cut out of the olive tree
24 by nature, and **w** graffed contrary to
Rev 3:15 nor hot: I would thou **w** cold or hot. G1498

WEST
Gen 12: 8 Beth-el on the **w**, and Hai on the east: H3220
28:14 abroad to the **w**, and to the east, and H3220
Ex 10:19 a mighty strong **w** wind, which took H3220
27:12 of the court on the **w** side *shall be* H3220
38:12 And for the **w** side *were* hangings of H3220
Nu 2:18 On the **w** side *shall be* the standard of H3220
34: 6 a border: this shall be your **w** border. H3220
35: 5 cubits, and on the **w** side two thousand H3220
Dt 33:23 possess thou the **w** and the south. H3220
Jos 8: 9 and Ai, on the **w** side of Ai: but Joshua H3220
12 and Ai, on the **w** side of the city. H3220
13 liers in wait on the **w** of the city, Joshua H3220
11: 2 and in the borders of Dor on the **w**, H3220
3 east and on the **w**, and *to* the Amorite, H3220
12: 7 side Jordan on the **w**, from Baal-gad in H3220
15:12 And the **w** border *was* to the great sea, H3220
18:14 of Judah: this *was* the **w** quarter. H3220
15 went out on the **w**, and went out to the H3220
19:34 to Asher on the **w** side, and to Judah H3220
1Ki 7:25 toward the **w**, and three looking toward H3220
1Ch 9:24 toward the east, **w**, north, and south. H3220
12:15 *both* toward the east, and toward the **w**. H4628
2Ch 4: 4 toward the **w**, and three looking toward H3220
32:30 down to the **w** side of the city of David. H4628
33:14 of David, on the **w** side of Gihon, in the H4628
Ps 75: 6 nor from the **w**, nor from the south. H4628
103:12 As far as the east is from the **w**, *so* far H4628
107: 3 **w**, from the north, and from the south. H4628
Isa 11:14 toward the **w**; they shall spoil them H3220
43: 5 the east, and gather thee from the **w**; H4628
45: 6 sun, and from the **w**, that *there is* none H4628
49:12 the **w**; and these from the land of Sinim. H3220
59:19 LORD from the **w**, and his glory from H4628
Ezk 41:12 end toward the **w** *was* seventy cubits H3220
42:19 He turned about to the **w** side, *and* H3220
45: 7 the city, from the **w** side westward, and H3220
7 the **w** border unto the east border. H3220
47:20 The **w** side also *shall be* the great sea H3220
20 against Hamath. This *is* the **w** side. H3220
48: 1 his sides east *and* **w**; a *portion for* Dan. H3220
2 unto the **w** side, a *portion for* Asher. H3220
3 unto the **w** side, a *portion for* Naphtali. H3220
4 the **w** side, a *portion for* Manasseh. H3220
5 unto the **w** side, a *portion for* Ephraim. H3220
6 unto the **w** side, a *portion for* Reuben. H3220
7 unto the **w** side, a *portion for* Judah. H3220
8 east side unto the **w** side, shall be the H3220
8 the east side unto the **w** side: and the H3220
10 and toward the **w** ten thousand in H3220
16 **w** side four thousand and five hundred. H3220
17 toward the **w** two hundred and fifty. H3220
21 toward the **w** border, over against H3220
23 **w** side, Benjamin *shall have* a *portion*. H3220
24 **w** side, Simeon *shall have* a *portion*. H3220
25 unto the **w** side, Issachar a *portion*. H3220
26 unto the **w** side, Zebulun a *portion*. H3220
27 side unto the **w** side, Gad a *portion*. H3220
34 At the **w** side four thousand and five H3220
Dan 8: 5 goat came from the **w** on the face of the H4628
Hos 11:10 the children shall tremble from the **w**. H3220
Zec 8: 7 and from the **w** country; H3996+H8121
14: 4 and toward the **w**, *and there shall be* a H3220
Mt 8:11 from the east and **w**, and shall sit down G1424
24:27 even unto the **w**; so shall also the G1424
Lk 12:54 rise out of the **w**, straightway ye say, G1424
13:29 the east, and *from* the **w**, and from the G1424
Act 27:12 toward the south **w** and north west. G3047
12 toward the south west and north **w**. G5566
Rev 21:13 three gates; and on the **w** three gates. G1424

WESTERN
Nu 34: 6 And *as for* the **w** border, ye shall even H3220

WESTWARD
Gen 13:14 and southward, and eastward, and **w**: H3220
Ex 26:22 And for the sides of the tabernacle **w** H3220
27 of the tabernacle, for the two sides **w**. H3220
36:27 And for the sides of the tabernacle **w** he H3220
32 boards of the tabernacle for the sides **w**. H3220
Nu 3:23 shall pitch behind the tabernacle **w**. H3220
Dt 3:27 lift up thine eyes **w**, and northward, and H3220
Jos 5: 1 the side of Jordan **w**, and all the kings of H3220
15: 8 valley of Hinnom **w**, which *is* at the end H3220
10 from Baalah **w** unto mount Seir, and H3220
16: 3 And goeth down **w** to the coast of H3220
8 The border went out from Tappuah **w** H3220
18:12 the mountains **w**; and the goings out H3220
19:26 to Carmel **w**, and to Shihor-libnath; H3220
34 And *then* the coast turneth **w** to H3220
22: 7 on this side Jordan **w**. And when Joshua H3220
23: 4 off, even unto the great sea **w**. H3996+H8121
1Ch 7:28 Naaran, and **w** Gezer, with the towns H4628
26:16 *the lot came forth* **w**, with the gate H4628
18 At Parbar **w**, four at the causeway, *and* H4628
30 this side Jordan **w** in all the business of H4628
Ezk 45: 7 from the west side **w**, and from the east H3220
46:19 there *was* a place on the two sides **w**. H3220
48:18 and ten thousand **w**: and it shall be over H3220
21 east border, and **w** over against the five H3220
Dan 8: 4 I saw the ram pushing **w**, and H3220

WEST-WIND See WEST and WIND.

WET
Job 24: 8 They are **w** with the showers of the H7372
Dan 4:15 the field; and let it be **w** with the dew of H6647
23 the field; and let it be **w** with the dew of H6647
25 and they shall **w** thee with the dew of H6647
33 and his body was **w** with the dew of H6647
5:21 and his body was **w** with the dew of H6647

WHALE
Job 7:12 *Am* I a sea, or a **w**, that thou settest a H8577
Ezk 32: 2 and thou *art* as a **w** in the seas: and H8577

WHALES
Gen 1:21 And God created great **w**, and every H8577

WHALE'S
Mt 12:40 three nights in the **w** belly; so shall the G2785

WHAT
Gen 2:19 *them* unto Adam to see **w** he would call H4100
3:13 unto the woman, **W** *is* this *that* thou H4100
4:10 And he said, **W** hast thou done? the H4100
9:24 and knew **w** his younger son H853+H834
12:18 Abram, and said, **W** *is* this *that* thou H4100
15: 2 And Abram said, Lord GOD, **w** wilt H4100
20: 9 said unto him, **W** hast thou done unto H4100
9 done unto us? and **w** have I offended H4100
10 And Abimelech said unto Abraham, **W** H4100
21:17 said unto her, **W** aileth thee, Hagar? H4100
29 And Abimelech said unto Abraham, **W** H4100
23:15 shekels of silver; **w** *is* that betwixt me H4100
24:65 For she *had* said unto the servant, **W** H4310
25:32 **w** profit shall this birthright do to me? H4100
26:10 And Abimelech said, **W** *is* this thou H4100
27:37 **w** shall I do now unto thee, my son? H4100
46 of the land, **w** good shall my life do me? H4100
29:15 nought? tell me, **w** *shall* thy wages *be?* H4100
25 he said to Laban, **W** *is* this thou hast H4100
30:31 And he said, **W** shall I give thee? And H4100
31:26 And Laban said to Jacob, **W** hast thou H4100
32 discern thou **w** *is* thine with me, and H4100
36 said to Laban, **W** *is* my trespass? what H4100
36 *is* my trespass? **w** *is* my sin, that thou H4100
37 all my stuff, **w** hast thou found of H4100

Gen 31:43 seest *is* mine: and w can I do this day H4100
32:27 And he said unto him, W *is* thy name? H4100
33: 8 And he said, W *meanest* thou by all H4310
15 me. And he said, W needeth it? let me H4100
34:11 and w ye shall say unto me I will give. H834
37:10 said unto him, W *is* this dream that H4100
15 asked him, saying, W seekest thou? H4100
20 shall see w will become of his dreams. H4100
26 And Judah said unto his brethren, W H4100
38:16 And she said, W wilt thou give me, that H4100
18 And he said, W pledge shall I give thee? H834
39: 8 wotteth not w *is* with me in the house, H4100
41:25 Pharaoh w he *is* about to do. H853+H834
28 unto Pharaoh: W God *is* about to do he H834
55 Go unto Joseph; w he saith to you, do. H834
42:28 W *is* this *that* God hath done unto us? H4100
44:15 And Joseph said unto them, W deed *is* H4100
16 And Judah said, W shall we say unto H4100
16 say unto my lord? w shall we speak? or H4100
46:33 and shall say, W *is* your occupation? H4100
47: 3 said unto his brethren, W *is* your H4100
Ex 2: 4 And his sister stood afar off, to wit w H4100
3:13 shall say to me, W *is* his name? what H4100
13 *is* his name? w shall I say unto them? H4100
4: 2 And the LORD said unto him, W *is* that H4100
12 mouth, and teach thee w thou shalt say. H834
15 and will teach you w ye shall do. H853+H834
6: 1 Now shalt thou see w I will do to H853+H834
10: 2 of thy son's son, w things I have H853+H834
26 we know not with w we must serve the H4100
12:26 unto you, W mean ye by this service? H4100
13:14 to come, saying, W *is* this? that thou H4100
15:24 Moses, saying, W shall we drink? H4100
16: 7 w *are* we, that ye murmur against us? H4100
8 against him: and w *are* we? your H4100
15 for they wist not w it *was*. And Moses H4100
17: 4 LORD, saying, W shall I do unto this H4100
18:14 the people, he said, W *is* this thing that H4100
19: 4 Ye have seen w I did unto the Egyptians, H834
23:11 may eat: and w they leave the beasts
32: 1 Egypt, we wot not w is become of him. H4100
21 And Moses said unto Aaron, W did H4100
23 Egypt, we wot not w is become of him. H4100
33: 5 that I may know w to do unto thee. H4100
Lev 15: 9 And w saddle soever he rideth upon that H834
17: 3 W man soever *there be* of the house of H376
22: 4 W man soever of the seed of Aaron *is* a H376
25:20 And if ye shall say, W shall we eat the H4100
Nu 9: 8 still, and I will hear w the LORD will H4100
10:32 it shall be, that w goodness the LORD H834
13:18 And see the land, w it *is*; and the H4100
19 And w the land *is* that they dwell in, H4100
19 good or bad; and w cities *they be* that H4100
20 And w the land *is*, whether it *be* fat or H4100
15:34 not declared w should be done to him. H4100
16:11 the LORD: and w *is* Aaron, that ye H4100
21:14 of the LORD, W he did in the Red sea, H4100
22: 9 and said, W men *are* these with thee? H4100
19 w the LORD will say unto me more. H4100
28 unto Balaam, W have I done unto thee, H4100
23:11 And Balak said unto Balaam, W hast H4100
17 unto him, W hath the LORD spoken? H4100
23 and of Israel, W hath God wrought! H4100
24:13 *but* w the LORD saith, that will I speak? H834
14 will advertise thee w this people shall do H834
26:10 company died, w time the fire devoured
31:50 for the LORD, w every man hath gotten, H834
Dt 1:22 us word again by w way we must go up, H834
22 go up, and into w cities we shall come. H853
33 to shew you by w way ye should go, and H834
3:24 thy mighty hand: for w God *is there* in H4310
4: 3 Your eyes have seen w the LORD H853+H834
7 For w nation *is there so* great, who H4310
8 And w nation *is there so* great, that H4310
6:20 time to come, saying, W *mean* the H4100
7:18 well remember w the LORD thy H853+H834
8: 2 thee, to know w *was* in thine H853+H834
10:12 And now, Israel, w doth the LORD thy H4100
11: 4 And w he did unto the army of Egypt, H834
5 And w he did unto you in the wilderness, H834
6 And w he did unto Dathan and Abiram, H834
12:32 W thing soever I command you, observe H853
20: 5 the people, saying, W man *is there* that H4310
6 And w man *is he* that hath planted a H4310
7 And w man *is there* that hath H4310
8 they shall say, W man *is there that is* H4310
24: 9 Remember w the LORD thy God H853+H834
25:17 Remember w Amalek did unto H853+H834
29:24 w *meaneth* the heat of this great anger? H4100

Dt 32:20 them, I will see w their end *shall be*: for H4100
Jos 2:10 out of Egypt; and w ye did unto the two H834
4: 6 saying, W *mean* ye by these stones? H4100
21 to come, saying, W *mean* these stones? H4100
5:14 him, W saith my lord unto his servant? H4100
7: 8 O Lord, w shall I say, when Israel H4100
9 w wilt thou do unto thy great name? H4100
19 w thou hast done; hide *it* not from me. H4100
9: 3 Gibeon heard w Joshua had done H853+H834
15:18 Caleb said unto her, W wouldest thou? H4100
22:16 of the LORD, W trespass *is* this that H4100
24 children, saying, W have ye to do with H4100
24: 7 eyes have seen w I have done in H853+H834
Jdg 1:14 and Caleb said unto her, W wilt thou? H4100
7:11 And thou shalt hear w they say; and H4100
8: 2 And he said unto them, W have I done H4100
3 and Zeeb: and w was I able to do in H4100
18 and Zalmunna, W manner of men *were* H375
9:48 *were* with him, W ye have seen me do, H4100
10:18 one to another, W man *is he* that will H4310
11:12 of Ammon, saying, W hast thou to do H4100
13: 8 us, and teach us w we shall do unto the H4100
17 of the LORD, W *is* thy name, that when H4310
14: 6 or his mother w he had done. H853+H834
18 the sun went down, W *is* sweeter than H4100
18 than honey? and w *is* stronger than a H4100
15:11 *are* rulers over us? w *is* this *that* thou H4100
16: 5 *lieth*, and by w *means* we may prevail H4100
18: 3 thee hither? and w makest thou in this H4100
3 in this *place*? and w hast thou here? H4100
8 brethren said unto them, W *say* ye? H4100
14 therefore consider w ye have to do. H4100
18 said the priest unto them, W do ye? H4100
23 said unto Micah, W aileth thee, that H4100
24 are gone away: and w have I more? and H4100
24 have I more? and w *is* this *that* ye say H4100
24 this *that* ye say unto me, W aileth thee? H4100
19:24 and do with them w seemeth good unto
20:12 saying, W wickedness *is* this that H4100
21: 8 And they said, W one *is there* of the H4310
Ru 2:18 in law saw w she had gleaned: H853+H834
3: 4 he will tell thee w thou shalt do. H853+H834
4: 5 Then said Boaz, W day thou buyest the
1Sa 1:23 said unto her, Do w seemeth thee good;
3:17 And he said, W *is* the thing that *the* H4100
18 LORD: let him do w seemeth him good.
4: 6 shout, they said, W *meaneth* the noise H4100
14 crying, he said, W *meaneth* the noise H4100
16 And he said, W is there done, my son? H4100
5: 8 them, and said, W shall we do with the H4100
6: 2 diviners, saying, W shall we do to the H4100
4 Then said they, W *shall be* the trespass H4100
9: 7 behold, *if* we go, w shall we bring the H4100
7 to bring to the man of God: w have we? H4100
10: 2 you, saying, W shall I do for my son? H4100
8 and shew thee w thou shalt do. H853+H834
11 one to another, W *is* this *that* is come H4100
15 I pray thee, w Samuel said unto you. H4100
11: 5 and Saul said, W *aileth* the people that H4100
13:11 And Samuel said, W hast thou done? H4100
14:40 unto Saul, Do w seemeth good unto thee.
43 Then Saul said to Jonathan, Tell me w H4100
15:14 And Samuel said, W *meaneth* then this H4100
16 I will tell thee w the LORD hath H853+H834
16: 3 I will shew thee w thou shalt do: H853+H834
17:26 by him, saying, W shall be done to the H4100
29 And David said, W have I now done? *Is* H4100
18: 8 w *can* he have more but the kingdom?
18 Who *am* I? and w *is* my life, *or* my H4310
19: 3 of thee; and w I see, that I will tell thee. H4100
20: 1 before Jonathan, W have I done? what H4100
1 have I done? w *is* mine iniquity? and H4100
1 iniquity? and w *is* my sin before thy H4100
10 or w *if* thy father answer thee roughly? H4100
32 shall he be slain? w hath he done? H4100
21: 2 I send thee, and w I have commanded H834
3 Now therefore w is under thine hand? H4100
3 in mine hand, or w there is present.
22: 3 you, till I know w God will do for me. H4100
25:17 Now therefore know and consider w H4100
26:18 his servant? for w have I done? or what H4100
18 have I done? or w evil *is* in mine hand? H4100
28: 2 shalt know w thy servant can do. H853+H834
9 thou knowest w Saul hath done, H853+H834
13 Be not afraid: for w sawest thou? And H4100
14 And he said unto her, W form *is* he of? H4100
15 make known unto me w I shall do. H4100
29: 3 of the Philistines, W *do* these Hebrews H4100
8 And David said unto Achish, But w H4100

1Sa 29: 8 have I done? and w hast thou found in H4100
2Sa 3:24 the king, and said, W hast thou done? H4100
7:18 I, O Lord GOD? and w *is* my house, that H4310
20 And w can David say more unto thee? H4100
23 And w one nation in the earth *is* like H4310
9: 8 And he bowed himself, and said, W *is* H4100
12:21 Then said his servants unto him, W H4100
14: 5 And the king said unto her, W aileth H4100
15: 2 him, and said, Of w city *art* thou? And H4310
21 liveth, surely in w place my lord the king H834
35 it shall be, *that* w thing soever thou H3605
16: 2 And the king said unto Ziba, W H4100
10 And the king said, W have I to do with H4100
20 Give counsel among you w we shall do. H4100
17: 5 and let us hear likewise w he saith. H4100
18: 4 And the king said unto them, W seemeth H834
21 Go tell the king w thou hast seen. And H834
29 a great tumult, but I knew not w *it was*. H4100
19:18 and to do w he thought good. And
22 And David said, W have I to do with H4100
27 do therefore w *is* good in thine eyes.
28 thine own table. W right therefore have H4100
35 thy servant taste w I eat or what I H853+H834
35 what I eat or w I drink? can I hear H853+H834
37 him w shall seem good unto thee. H853+H834
21: 3 the Gibeonites, W shall I do for you? H4100
4 W ye shall say, *that* will I do for you. H4100
11 And it was told David w Rizpah H853+H834
24:13 advise, and see w answer I shall return H4100
17 but these sheep, w have they done? let H4100
22 take and offer up w *seemeth* good unto
1Ki 1:16 And the king said, W wouldest thou? H4100
2: 5 Moreover thou knowest also w H853+H834
5 did to me, *and* w he did to the two H834
9 man, and knowest w thou oughtest to do H834
3: 5 and God said, Ask w I shall give thee. H4100
8:38 W prayer and supplication soever be H3605
9:13 And he said, W cities *are* these which H4100
11:22 Then Pharaoh said unto him, But w H4100
12: 9 And he said unto them, W counsel give H4100
16 the king, saying, W portion have we in H4100
13:12 unto them, W way went he? For H335+H2088
12 his sons had seen w way the man of God H834
14: 3 tell thee w shall become of the child. H4100
14 of Jeroboam that day: but w? even now. H4100
16: 5 of Baasha, and w he did, and his might, H834
17:18 And she said unto Elijah, W have I to H4100
18: 9 And he said, W have I sinned, that H4100
13 Was it not told my lord w I did H853+H834
19: 9 unto him, W doest thou here, Elijah? H4100
13 and said, W doest thou here, Elijah? H4100
20 back again: for w have I done to thee? H4100
20:22 mark, and see w thou doest: for H853+H834
22:14 LORD liveth, w the LORD saith H853+H834
2Ki 1: 7 And he said unto them, W manner of H4100
2: 9 unto Elisha, Ask w I shall do for thee, H4100
3:13 the king of Israel, W have I to do with H4100
4: 2 And Elisha said unto her, W shall I do H4100
2 do for thee? tell me, w hast thou in the H4100
13 us with all this care; w *is* to be done for H4100
14 And he said, W then *is* to be done for H4100
43 And his servitor said, W, should I set H4100
6:28 And the king said unto her, W aileth H4100
33 *is* of the LORD; w should I wait for the H4100
7:12 now shew you w the Syrians have H853+H834
8:13 And Hazael said, But w, *is* thy servant a H4100
14 who said to him, W said Elisha to thee? H4100
9:18 And Jehu said, W hast thou to do with H4100
19 Jehu answered, W hast thou to do with H4100
22 And he answered, W peace, so long as H4100
18:19 king of Assyria, W confidence *is* this H4100
19:11 Behold, thou hast heard w the H853+H834
20: 8 And Hezekiah said unto Isaiah, W H4100
14 said unto him, W said these men? and H4100
15 And he said, W have they seen in thine H4100
22:19 thou heardest w I spake against this H834
23:17 Then he said, W title *is* that that I see? H4100
1Ch 12:32 times, to know w Israel ought to do; the H4100
17:16 I, O LORD God, and w *is* mine house, H4310
18 W can David *speak* more to thee for H4100
21 And w one nation in the earth *is* like H4310
21:12 advise thyself w word I shall bring H4100
17 *as for* these sheep, w have they done? let
29:14 But who *am* I, and w *is* my people, that H4310
2Ch 1: 7 said unto him, Ask w I shall give thee. H4100
6:29 *Then* w prayer *or* what supplication H834
29 *Then* what prayer *or* w supplication
10: 6 yet lived, saying, W counsel give ye *me* H349
9 And he said unto them, W advice give H4100

2Ch 10:16 the king, saying, W portion have we in H4100
18:13 w my God saith, that will I speak. H853+H834
19: 6 And said to the judges, Take heed w ye H4100
10 And w cause soever shall come to you H3602
20:12 we w to do: but our eyes *are* upon thee. H4100
24:11 Now it came to pass, that at w time the
25: 9 man of God, But w shall we do for the H4100
32:13 Know ye not w I and my fathers have H4100
35:21 to him, saying, W have I to do with H4100
Ezr 5: 4 this manner, W are the names of the H4479
6: 8 Moreover I make a decree w ye H3964+H1768
8:17 and I told them w they should say unto H1697
9:10 And now, O our God, w shall we say H4100
Neh 2: 4 Then the king said unto me, For w dost H4100
12 told I *any* man w my God had put in H4100
16 whither I went, or w I did; neither had I H4100
19 us, and said, W *is* this thing that ye H4100
4: 2 and said, W do these feeble Jews? H4100
20 In w place *therefore* ye hear the sound H4100
13:17 said unto them, W evil thing *is* this that H834
Est 1:15 W shall we do unto the queen Vashti H4100
2: 1 Vashti, and w she had done, and H853+H834
1 and w was decreed against her. H853+H834
11 did, and w should become of her. H4100
15 nothing but w Hegai the king's H853+H834
4: 5 to know w it *was*, and why it *was*. H4100
5: 3 Then said the king unto her, W wilt H4100
3 queen Esther? and w *is* thy request? it H4100
6 banquet of wine, W *is* thy petition? and H4100
6 be granted thee: and w *is* thy request? H4100
6: 3 And the king said, W honour and H4100
6 said unto him, W shall be done unto H4100
7: 2 the banquet of wine, W *is* thy petition, H4100
2 granted thee: and w *is* thy request? and H4100
8: 1 for Esther had told w he *was* unto her. H4100
9: 5 and did w they would unto those H4100
12 sons of Haman; w have they done in H4100
12 provinces? now w *is* thy petition? and H4100
12 be granted thee: or w *is* thy request H4100
Job 2:10 women speaketh. W? shall we receive H1571
6:11 W *is* my strength, that I should hope? H4100
11 should hope? and w *is* mine end, that I H4100
17 W time they wax warm, they vanish:
25 How forcible are right words! but w H4100
7:17 W *is* man, that thou shouldest magnify H4100
20 I have sinned; w shall I do unto thee, O H4100
9:12 who will say unto him, W dost thou? H4100
11: 8 *It is* as high as heaven; w canst thou H4100
8 deeper than hell; w canst thou know? H4100
13: 2 W ye know, *the same* do I know also: I
13 may speak, and let come on me w *will*. H4100
15: 9 W knowest thou, that we know not? H4100
9 that we know not? *w* understandest
12 thee away? and w do thy eyes wink at, H4100
14 W *is* man, that he should be clean? and H4100
16: 3 Shall vain words have an end? or w H4100
6 and *though* I forbear, w am I eased? H4100
21:15 W *is* the Almighty, that we should H4100
15 serve him? and w profit should we H4100
21 For w pleasure *hath* he in his house H4100
31 who shall repay him *w* he hath done?
22:17 and w can the Almighty do for them? H4100
23: 5 understand w he would say unto me. H4100
13 *w* his soul desireth, even *that* he doeth.
27: 8 For w *is* the hope of the hypocrite, H4100
31: 2 For w portion of God *is there* from H4100
2 from above? and *w* inheritance of the
14 W then shall I do when God riseth up? H4100
14 when he visiteth, w shall I answer him? H4100
32:11 reasons, whilst ye searched out w to say.
34: 4 let us know among ourselves w *is* good. H4100
7 W man *is* like Job, *who* drinketh up H4310
33 not I: therefore speak w thou knowest. H4100
35: 3 For thou saidst, W advantage will it be H4100
3 unto thee? *and*, W profit shall I have, H4100
6 If thou sinnest, w doest thou against H4100
6 be multiplied, w doest thou unto him? H4100
7 If thou be righteous, w givest thou him? H4100
7 him? or w receiveth he of thine hand? H4100
37:19 Teach us w we shall say unto him; *for* H4100
38:24 By w way is the light parted, H335+H2088
39:18 W time she lifteth up herself on high, she
40: 4 Behold, I am vile; w shall I answer H4100
Ps 8: 4 W is man, that thou art mindful of H4100
11: 3 If the foundations be destroyed, w can H4100
25:12 W man *is* he that feareth the LORD? H4310
30: 9 W profit *is there* in my blood, when I H4100
34:12 W man *is he that* desireth life, *and* H4310
39: 4 w it *is; that* I may know how frail I *am*. H4310

Ps 39: 7 And now, Lord, w wait I for? my hope H4100
44: 1 have told us, *w* work thou didst in their
46: 8 Come, behold the works of the LORD, w H834
50:16 But unto the wicked God saith, W hast H4100
56: 3 W time I am afraid, I will trust in thee.
4 I will not fear w flesh can do unto me. H4100
11 not be afraid w man can do unto me. H4100
66:16 will declare w he hath done for my soul. H834
85: 8 I will hear w God the LORD will speak: H4100
89:48 W man *is he that* liveth, and shall not H4310
114: 5 W *ailed* thee, O thou sea, that thou H4100
116:12 W shall I render unto the LORD *for* all H4100
118: 6 I will not fear: w can man do unto me? H4100
120: 3 W shall be given unto thee? or what H4100
3 What shall be given unto thee? or w H4100
144: 3 LORD, w *is* man, that thou takest H4100
Prv 4:19 they know not at w they stumble. H4100
10:32 The lips of the righteous know w is H4100
23: 1 diligently w *is* before thee: H853+H834
25: 8 lest *thou know not* w to do in the end H4100
27: 1 knowest not w a day may bring forth. H4100
30: 4 ends of the earth? w *is* his name, and H4100
4 w *is* his son's name, if thou canst tell? H4100
31: 2 W, my son? and what, the son of my H4100
2 What, my son? and w, the son of my H4100
2 my womb? and w, the son of my vows? H4100
Ecc 1: 3 W profit hath a man of all his labour H4100
2: 2 *It is* mad: and of mirth, W doeth it? H4100
3 till I might see w *was* that good for the H335
12 and folly: for w *can* the man *do* that H4100
22 For w hath man of all his labour, and H4100
3: 9 W profit hath he that worketh in that H4100
22 bring him to see w shall be after him? H4100
5:11 eat them: and w good *is there* to the H4100
16 shall he go: and w profit hath he that H4100
6: 8 For w hath the wise more than the fool? H4100
8 than the fool? w hath the poor, that H4100
11 increase vanity, w *is* man the better? H4100
12 For who knoweth w is good for man in H4100
12 w shall be after him under the sun? H4100
7:10 Say not thou, W is *the cause* that the H4100
8: 4 who may say unto him, W doest thou? H4100
10:14 a man cannot tell w shall be; and what H4100
14 w shall be after him, who can tell him? H4100
11: 2 not w evil shall be upon the earth. H4100
5 As thou knowest not w *is* the way of the H4100
Song 5: 9 W *is* thy beloved more than *another* H4100
9 among women? w *is* thy beloved more H4100
6:13 look upon thee. W will ye see in the H4100
8: 8 hath no breasts: w shall we do for our H4100
Isa 1:11 To w purpose *is* the multitude of your H4100
3:15 W mean ye *that* ye beat my people to H4100
5: 4 W could have been done more to my H4100
5 And now go to; I will tell you w I H853+H834
10: 3 And w will ye do in the day of H4100
14:32 W shall *one* then answer the H4100
19:12 let them know w the LORD of hosts H4100
21: 6 a watchman, let him declare w he seeth. H834
11 of Seir, Watchman, w of the night? H4100
11 the night? Watchman, w of the night? H4100
22: 1 The burden of the valley of vision. W H4100
16 W hast thou here? and whom hast thou H4100
33:13 Hear, ye *that are* far off, w I have done; H834
36: 4 the king of Assyria, W confidence *is* this H834
37:11 Behold, thou hast heard w the kings of H4100
38:15 W shall I say? he hath both spoken H4100
22 Hezekiah also had said, W *is* the sign H4100
39: 3 said unto him, W said these men? and H4100
4 Then said he, W have they seen in H4100
40: 6 The voice said, Cry. And he said, W H4100
18 To whom then will ye liken God? or w H4100
41:22 and shew us w we shall happen: let H853+H834
22 the former things, w they *be*, that we H4100
45: 9 that fashioneth it, W makest thou? or H4100
10 unto *his* father, W begettest thou? or to H4100
10 woman, W hast thou brought forth? H4100
52: 5 Now therefore, w have I here, saith the H4100
64: 4 God, beside thee, *w* he hath prepared for
Jer 1:11 saying, Jeremiah, w seest thou? And I H4100
13 time, saying, W seest thou? And I said, H4100
2: 5 Thus saith the LORD, W iniquity have H4100
18 And now w hast thou to do in the way H4100
18 of Sihor? or w hast thou to do in the H4100
23 in the valley, know w thou hast done: H4100
4:30 And *when* thou *art* spoiled, w wilt thou H4100
5:15 not, neither understandest w they say. H4100
31 so: and w will ye do in the end thereof? H4100
6:18 congregation, w *is* among them. H853+H834
20 To w purpose cometh there to me H4100

Jer 7:12 first, and see w I did to it for the H853+H834
17 Seest thou not w they do in the cities of H4100
8: 6 saying, W have I done? every H4100
9 of the LORD; and w wisdom *is* in them? H4100
9:12 may declare it, for w the land perisheth H4100
11:15 W hath my beloved to do in mine H4100
13:21 W wilt thou say when he shall punish H4100
16:10 evil against us? or w *is* our iniquity? or H4100
10 *is* our iniquity? or w *is* our sin that we H4100
18: 7 *At w* instant I shall speak concerning a
9 And *at w* instant I shall speak
23:25 I have heard w the prophets said, H853+H834
28 word faithfully. W *is* the chaff to the H4100
33 ask thee, saying, W *is* the burden of the H4100
33 say unto them, W burden? I will even H4100
35 one to his brother, W hath the LORD H4100
35 and, W hath the LORD spoken? H4100
37 Thus shalt thou say to the prophet, W H4100
37 thee? and, W hath the LORD spoken? H4100
24: 3 Then said the LORD unto me, W seest H4100
32:24 the pestilence: and w thou hast spoken is H834
33:24 Considerest thou not w this people H4100
37:18 unto king Zedekiah, W have I offended H4100
38:25 unto us now w thou hast said unto H4100
25 death; also w the king said unto thee: H4100
48:19 her that escapeth, *and* say, W is done? H4100
Lam 2:13 W thing shall I take to witness for thee? H4100
13 witness for thee? w thing shall I liken to H4100
13 of Jerusalem? w shall I equal to thee, H4100
5: 1 Remember, O LORD, w is come upon H4100
Ezk 2: 8 But thou, son of man, hear w I H853+H834
8: 6 of man, seest thou w they do? *even* the H4100
12 hast thou seen w the ancients of the H834
12: 9 house, said unto thee, W doest thou? H4100
22 Son of man, w *is* that proverb *that* ye H4100
15: 2 Son of man, W is the vine tree more H4100
17:12 Know ye not w these *things mean*? H4100
18: 2 W mean ye, that ye use this proverb H4100
19: 2 And say, W *is* thy mother? A lioness: H4100
20:29 Then I said unto them, W *is* the high H4100
21:13 Because *it is* a trial, and w if *the sword* H4100
24:19 thou not tell us w these *things are* to us, H4100
27:32 over thee, *saying*, W *city is* like Tyrus, H4100
33:30 pray you, and hear w is the word that H4100
37:18 not shew us w thou *meanest* by these? H4100
47:23 And it shall come to pass, *that* in w tribe H834
Dan 2:22 he knoweth w *is* in the darkness, and H4101
23 unto me now w we desired of thee: H1768
28 king Nebuchadnezzar w shall be in the H4101
29 upon thy bed, w should come to pass H4101
29 known to thee w shall come to pass. H4101
45 known to the king w shall come to pass H4101
3: 5 *That* at w time ye hear the sound of the H1768
15 Now if ye be ready that at w time ye H1768
4:35 hand, or say unto him, W doest thou? H4101
8:19 thee know w shall be in the last H853+H834
10:14 thee understand w shall befall thy H853+H834
12: 8 w *shall be* the end of these *things*? H4100
Hos 6: 4 O Ephraim, w shall I do unto thee? O H4100
4 thee? O Judah, w shall I do unto thee? H4100
9: 5 W will ye do in the solemn day, and in H4100
14 Give them, O LORD: w wilt thou give? H4100
10: 3 LORD; w then should a king do to us? H4100
14: 8 Ephraim *shall say*, W have I to do any H4100
Joel 3: 4 Yea, and w have ye to do with me, O H4100
Am 4:13 unto man w *is* his thought, that H4100
5:18 of the LORD! to w end *is* it for you? the H4100
7: 8 And the LORD said unto me, Amos, w H4100
8: 2 And he said, Amos, w seest thou? And I H4100
Jna 1: 6 and said unto him, W meanest thou, O H4100
8 evil *is* upon us; W *is* thine occupation? H4100
8 comest thou? w *is* thy country? and H4100
8 and of w people *art* thou? H335+H2088
11 Then said they unto him, W shall we H4100
4: 5 might see w would become of the city. H4100
Mic 1: 5 house of Israel. W *is* the transgression H4310
5 not Samaria? and w *are* the high places H4310
6: 1 Hear ye now w the LORD saith; Arise, H834
3 O my people, w have I done unto thee? H4100
5 O my people, remember now w Balak H4100
5 consulted, and w Balaam the son of H4100
8 He hath shewed thee, O man, w *is* H4100
8 what *is* good; and w doth the LORD H4100
Nah 1: 9 W do ye imagine against the LORD? he H4100
Hab 2: 1 will watch to see w he will say unto me, H4100
1 w I shall answer when I am reproved. H4100
18 W profiteth the graven image that the H4100
Zec 1: 9 Then said I, O my lord, w *are* these? H4100
9 unto me, I will shew thee w these *be*. H4100

Zec 1:19 talked with me, W *be* these? And he H4100
21 Then said I, W come these to do? And H4100
2: 2 Jerusalem, to see w *is* the breadth H4100
2 thereof, and w *is* the length thereof. H4100
4: 2 And said unto me, W seest thou? And I H4100
4 with me, saying, W *are* these, my lord? H4100
5 w these be? And I said, No, my lord. H4100
11 said unto him, W *are* these two olive H4100
12 said unto him, W *be these* two olive H4100
13 w these *be*? And I said, No, my lord. H4100
5: 2 And he said unto me, W seest thou? H4100
5 eyes, and see w *is* this that goeth forth. H4100
6 And I said, W *is it*? And he said, This *is* H4100
6: 4 talked with me, W *are* these, my lord? H4100
13: 6 And *one* shall say unto him, W *are* H4100
Mal 1:13 Ye said also, Behold, w a weariness *is it*!
3:13 LORD. Yet ye say, W have we spoken H4100
14 to serve God: and w profit *is it* that we H4100
Mt 2: 7 diligently w time the star appeared. G3588
5:46 For if ye love them which love you, w G5101
47 And if ye salute your brethren only, w G5101
6: 3 left hand know w thy right hand doeth: G5101
8 Father knoweth w things ye have need G3739
25 for your life, w ye shall eat, or what G5101
25 ye shall eat, or w ye shall drink; nor yet G5101
25 yet for your body, w ye shall put on. Is G5101
31 Therefore take no thought, saying, W G5101
31 shall we eat? or, W shall we drink? or, G5101
7: 2 For with w judgment ye judge, ye shall G3739
2 judged: and with w measure ye mete, it G3739
9 Or w man is there of you, whom if his G5101
8:27 But the men marvelled, saying, W G4217
29 And, behold, they cried out, saying, W G5101
33 every thing, and w was befallen to the G3588
9:13 But go ye and learn w *that* meaneth, I G5101
10:19 thought how or w ye shall speak: for it G5101
19 you in that same hour w ye shall speak. G5101
27 W I tell you in darkness, *that* speak ye G3739
27 ye in light: and w ye hear in the ear, G3739
11: 7 concerning John, W went ye out into G5101
8 But w went ye out for to see? A man G5101
9 But w went ye out for to see? A G5101
12: 3 Have ye not read w David did, when he G5101
7 But if ye had known w *this* meaneth, I G5101
11 And he said unto them, W man shall G5101
16:26 For w is a man profited, if he shall gain G5101
26 his own soul? or w shall a man give in G5101
17:25 him, saying, W thinkest thou, Simon? G5101
18:31 So when his fellowservants saw w was G3588
19: 6 but one flesh. W therefore God hath G3739
16 Good Master, w good thing shall I do, G5101
20 I kept from my youth up: w lack I yet? G5101
27 thee; w shall we have therefore? G5101
20:15 Is it not lawful for me to do w I will G3739
21 And he said unto her, W wilt thou? She G5101
22 said, Ye know not w ye ask. Are ye able G5101
32 said, W will ye that I shall do unto you? G5101
21:16 And said unto him, Hearest thou w G5101
23 and said, By w authority doest thou G4169
24 you by w authority I do these things. G4169
27 I you by w authority I do these things. G4169
28 But w think ye? A *certain* man had two G5101
40 w will he do unto those husbandmen? G5101
22:17 Tell us therefore, W thinkest thou? Is it G5101
42 Saying, W think ye of Christ? whose G5101
24: 3 things be? and w *shall be* the sign of G5101
42 Watch therefore: for ye know not w G4169
43 had known in w watch the thief would G4169
26: 8 saying, To w purpose *is* this waste? G5101
15 And said *unto them*, W will ye give me, G5101
40 saith unto Peter, W, could ye not watch G3779
62 thou nothing? w *is it which* these G5101
65 blasphemy; w further need have we G5101
66 W think ye? They answered and said, G5101
70 all, saying, I know not w thou sayest. G5101
27: 4 said, W *is that* to us? see thou *to that*. G5101
22 Pilate saith unto them, W shall I do G5101
23 And the governor said, Why, w evil G5101
Mk 1:24 Saying, Let *us* alone; w have we to do G5101
27 saying, W thing is this? what G5101
27 thing is this? w new doctrine *is* this? G5101
2:25 ye never read w David did, when he G5101
3: 8 w great things he did, came unto him. G3745
4:24 And he said unto them, Take heed w ye G5101
24 ye hear: with w measure ye mete, it G3739
30 w comparison shall we compare it? G4169
41 to another, W manner of man G5101+G686
5: 7 voice, and said, W have I to do with G5101
9 And he asked him, W *is* thy name? And G5101

Mk 5:14 went out to see w it was that was done. G5101
33 knowing w was done in her, came G3739
6: 2 these things? and w wisdom *is* this G5101
10 And he said unto them, In w place G3699
24 unto her mother, W shall I ask? And G5101
30 all things, both w they had done, and G3745
30 they had done, and w they had taught. G3745
8:36 For w shall it profit a man, if he shall G5101
37 Or w shall a man give in exchange for G5101
9: 6 For he wist not w to say; for they were G5101
9 tell no man w things they had seen, G3739
10 one with another w the rising from the G5101
16 And he asked the scribes, W question G5101
33 house he asked them, W was it that ye G5101
10: 3 them, W did Moses command you? G5101
9 W therefore God hath joined together, G3739
17 Good Master, w shall I do that I may G5101
32 w things should happen unto him, G3588
36 And he said unto them, W would ye G5101
38 Ye know not w ye ask: can ye drink G5101
51 and said unto him, W wilt thou that I G5101
11: 5 unto them, W do ye, loosing the colt? G5101
24 Therefore I say unto you, W things G3745
28 And say unto him, By w authority G4169
29 you by w authority I do these things. G4169
33 you by w authority I do these things. G4169
12: 9 W shall therefore the lord of the G5101
13: 1 him, Master, see w manner of stones G4217
1 of stones and w buildings *are here*! G4217
4 things be? and w *shall be* the sign when G5101
11 beforehand w ye shall speak, neither G5101
37 And w I say unto you I say unto all, G3739
14: 8 She hath done w she could: she is come G3739
36 not w I will, but what thou wilt. G5101
36 not what I will, but w thou wilt. G5101
40 neither wist they w to answer him. G5101
60 thou nothing? w *is it which* these G5101
63 W need we any further witnesses? G5101
64 Ye have heard the blasphemy: w think G5101
68 understand I w thou sayest. And he G5101
15:12 again unto them, W will ye then that I G5101
14 Then Pilate said unto them, Why, w G5101
24 upon them, w every man should take. G5101
Lk 1:29 w manner of salutation this should be. G4217
66 saying, W manner of child G5101+G686
3:10 And the people asked him, saying, W G5101
12 said unto him, Master, w shall we do? G5101
14 of him, saying, And w shall we do? And G5101
4:34 Saying, Let *us* alone; w have we to do G5101
36 saying, W a word *is* this! for with G5101
5:19 And when they could not find by w *way* G4169
22 unto them, W reason ye in your hearts? G5101
6: 3 so much as this, w David did, when G3739
11 with another w they might do to Jesus. G5101
32 For if ye love them which love you, w G4169
33 do good to you, w thank have ye? for G4169
34 ye hope to receive, w thank have ye? for G4169
7:22 way, and tell John w things ye have G3739
24 concerning John, W went ye out into G5101
25 But w went ye out for to see? A man G5101
26 But w went ye out for to see? A G5101
31 this generation? and to w are they like? G5101
39 known who and w manner of woman G4217
8: 9 And his disciples asked him, saying, W G5101
25 to another, W manner of man G5101+G686
28 a loud voice said, W have I to do with G5101
30 And Jesus asked him, saying, W is thy G5101
34 When they that fed *them* saw w was G3588
35 Then they went out to see w was done; G3588
36 They also which saw *it* told them by w G4459
47 all the people for w cause she had G3739
56 they should tell no man w was done. G3588
9:25 For w is a man advantaged, if he gain G5101
33 one for Elias: not knowing w he said. G3739
55 know not w manner of spirit ye are of. G3634
10:25 w shall I do to inherit eternal life? G5101
26 He said unto him, W is written in the G5101
12:11 no thought how or w thing ye shall G5101
11 thing ye shall answer, or w ye shall say: G5101
12 you in the same hour w ye ought to say. G3739
17 himself, saying, W shall I do, because G5101
22 for your life, w ye shall eat; neither G5101
22 neither for the body, w ye shall put on. G5101
29 And seek not ye w ye shall eat, or what G5101
29 And seek not ye what ye shall eat, or w G5101
39 the house had known w hour the thief G4169
49 and w will I, if it be already kindled? G5101
57 of yourselves judge ye not w is right? G3588
13:18 Then said he, Unto w is the kingdom of G5101

Lk 14:31 Or w king, going to make war against G5101
15: 4 W man of you, having an hundred G5101
8 Either w woman having ten pieces of G5101
26 and asked w these things meant. G5101
16: 3 within himself, W shall I do? for my G5101
4 I am resolved w to do, that, when I am G5101
18: 6 And the Lord said, Hear w the unjust G5101
18 w shall I do to inherit eternal life? G5101
36 pass by, he asked w it meant. G5101
41 Saying, W wilt thou that I shall do unto G5101
19:48 And could not find w they might do: G5101
20: 2 saying, Tell us, by w authority doest G4169
8 I you by w authority I do these things. G4169
13 Then said the lord of the vineyard, W G5101
15 and killed *him*. W therefore shall the G5101
17 And he beheld them, and said, W is G5101
21: 7 things be? and w sign *will there be* G5101
14 to meditate before w ye shall answer:
22:49 about him saw w would follow, they G3588
60 And Peter said, Man, I know not w G3739
71 And they said, W need we any further G5101
23:22 third time, Why, w evil hath he done? I G5101
31 a green tree, w shall be done in the dry? G5101
34 for they know not w they do. And they G5101
47 Now when the centurion saw w was G3588
24:17 And he said unto them, W manner of G5101
19 And he said unto them, W things? And G4169
35 And they told w things *were done* in G3588
Jn 1:21 And they asked him, W then? Art thou G5101
22 that sent us. W sayest thou of thyself? G5101
38 saith unto them, W seek ye? They said G5101
2: 4 Jesus saith unto her, Woman, w have I G5101
18 said unto him, W sign shewest thou G5101
25 of man: for he knew w was in man. G5101
3:32 And w he hath seen and heard, that he G3739
4:22 Ye worship ye know not w: we know G3739
22 not what: we know w we worship: for G3739
27 yet no man said, W seekest thou? or, G5101
5:12 Then asked they him, W man is that G5101
19 of himself, but w he seeth the Father G5100
19 the Father do: for w things soever he G5100
6: 6 for he himself knew w he would do. G5101
9 fishes: but w are they among so many? G5101
28 Then said they unto him, W shall we G5101
30 They said therefore unto him, W sign G5101
30 and believe thee? w dost thou work? G5101
62 *W* and if ye shall see the Son of man
7:36 W *manner of* saying is this that he G5101
51 it hear him, and know w he doeth? G5101
8: 5 should be stoned: but w sayest thou? G5101
9:17 They say unto the blind man again, W G5101
21 But by w means he now seeth, we know G4459
26 Then said they to him again, W did he G5101
10: 6 they understood not w things they were G5101
11:46 and told them w things Jesus had done. G3739
47 a council, and said, W do we? for this G5101
56 in the temple, W think ye, that he will G5101
12: 6 the bag, and bare w was put therein. G3588
27 Now is my soul troubled; and w shall I G5101
33 This he said, signifying w death he G4169
49 a commandment, w I should say, and G5101
49 I should say, and w I should speak. G5101
13: 7 Jesus answered and said unto him, W I G3739
12 them, Know ye w I have done to you? G5101
28 Now no man at the table knew for w G5101
15: 7 w ye will, and it shall be done unto you. G3739
15 knoweth not w his lord doeth: but G5101
16:17 themselves, W is this that he saith G5101
18 They said therefore, W is this that he G5101
18 A little while? we cannot tell w he saith. G5101
18:21 which heard me, w I have said unto G5101
21 unto them: behold, they know w I said. G3739
29 them, and said, W accusation bring ye G5101
32 signifying w death he should die. G4169
35 thee unto me: w hast thou done? G5101
38 Pilate saith unto him, W is truth? And G5101
19:22 Pilate answered, W I have written I G3739
21:19 This spake he, signifying by w death he G4169
21 Jesus, Lord, and w *shall* this man *do*? G5101
22 come, w *is that* to thee? follow thou me. G5101
23 he tarry till I come, w *is that* to thee? G5101
Act 2:12 one to another, W meaneth this? G5101
37 Men *and* brethren, w shall we do? G5101
4: 7 they asked, By w power, or by what G4169
7 or by w name, have ye done this? G4169
9 man, by w means he is made whole; G5101
16 Saying, W shall we do to these men? for G5101
5: 7 not knowing w was done, came in. G3588
35 heed to yourselves w ye intend to do as G5101

Act 7:40 Egypt, we wot not w is become of him. *G5101*
49 *is* my footstool: w house will ye build *G4169*
49 the Lord: or w *is* the place of my rest? *G5101*
8:30 Understandest thou w thou readest? *G3739*
36 w doth hinder me to be baptized? *G5101*
9: 6 said, Lord, w wilt thou have me to *G5101*
6 it shall be told thee w thou must do. *G5101*
10: 4 afraid, and said, W is it, Lord? And he *G5101*
6 he shall tell thee w thou oughtest to do. *G5101*
15 the second time, W God hath cleansed, *G3739*
17 Now while Peter doubted in himself w *G5101*
21 w *is* the cause wherefore ye are come? *G5101*
29 for w intent ye have sent for me? *G5101*
11: 9 from heaven, W God hath cleansed, *G3739*
17 w was I, that I could withstand God? *G5101*
12:18 soldiers, w was become of Peter. *G5101+G687*
13:12 Then the deputy, when he saw w was *G3588*
14:11 And when the people saw w Paul had *G3739*
15:12 and Paul, declaring w miracles and *G3745*
16:30 and said, Sirs, w must I do to be saved? *G5101*
17:18 And some said, W will this babbler *G5101*
19 May we know w this new doctrine, *G5101*
20 know therefore w these things mean. *G5101*
19: 3 And he said unto them, Unto w then *G5101*
35 *Ye* men of Ephesus, w man is there that *G5101*
20:18 into Asia, after w manner I have been *G4459*
21:13 Then Paul answered, W mean ye to *G5101*
19 particularly w things God had wrought *G3739*
22 W is it therefore? the multitude must *G5101*
33 who he was, and w he had done. *G5101*
22:10 And I said, W shall I do, Lord? And the *G5101*
15 all men of w thou hast seen and heard. *G3739*
26 w thou doest: for this man is a Roman. *G5101*
23:19 *him,* W is that thou hast to tell me? *G5101*
30 thee w *they had* against him. Farewell. *G3588*
34 *letter,* he asked of w province he was. *G4169*
28:22 But we desire to hear of thee w thou *G3739*
Ro 3: 1 W advantage then hath the Jew? or *G5101*
1 or w profit *is there* of circumcision? *G5101*
3 For w if some did not believe? shall *G5101*
5 of God, w shall we say? *Is* God *G5101*
9 W then? are we better *than they*? No, in *G5101*
19 Now we know that w things soever the *G3745*
27 It is excluded. By w law? of works? Nay: *G4169*
4: 1 W shall we say then that Abraham our *G5101*
3 For w saith the scripture? Abraham *G5101*
21 And being fully persuaded that, w he *G3739*
6: 1 W shall we say then? Shall we continue *G5101*
15 W then? shall we sin, because we are *G5101*
21 W fruit had ye then in those things *G5101*
7: 7 W shall we say then? *Is* the law sin? *G5101*
15 For that which I do I allow not: for w I *G3739*
15 that do I not; but w I hate, that do I. *G3739*
8: 3 For w the law could not do, in that it *G3588*
24 is not hope: for w a man seeth, why *G3739*
26 for we know not w we should pray for *G5101*
27 the hearts knoweth w *is* the mind of the *G5101*
31 W shall we then say to these things? If *G5101*
9:14 W shall we say then? *Is there* *G5101*
22 W if God, willing to shew *his* wrath, and
30 W shall we say then? That the Gentiles, *G5101*
10: 8 But w saith it? The word is nigh thee, *G5101*
11: 2 Wot ye not w the scripture saith of *G5101*
4 But w saith the answer of God unto *G5101*
7 W then? Israel hath not obtained that *G5101*
15 of the world, w *shall* the receiving *of* *G5101*
12: 2 that ye may prove w *is* that good, and *G5101*
1Co 2:11 For w man knoweth the things of a *G5101*
3:13 try every man's work of w sort it is. *G3697*
4: 7 *another*? and w hast thou that thou *G5101*
21 W will ye? shall I come unto you with a *G5101*
5:12 For w have I to do to judge them also *G5101*
6:16 W? know ye not that he which is joined *G2228*
19 W? know ye not that your body is the *G2228*
7:16 For w knowest thou, O wife, whether *G5101*
36 let him do w he will, he sinneth not: *G3739*
9:18 W is my reward then? *Verily* that, *G5101*
10:15 I speak as to wise men; judge ye w I *G3739*
19 W say I then? that the idol is any thing, *G5101*
11:22 W? have ye not houses to eat and to *G1063*
22 that have not? W shall I say to you? *G5101*
14: 6 with tongues, w shall I profit you, *G5101*
7 shall it be known w is piped or harped? *G3588*
9 shall it be known w is spoken? for ye *G3588*
15 W is it then? I will pray with the spirit, *G5101*
16 he understandeth not w thou sayest? *G5101*
36 W? came the word of God out from you? *G2228*
15: 2 ye keep in memory w I preached unto *G5101*
10 But by the grace of God I am w I am: *G3739*

1Co 15:29 Else w shall they do which are baptized *G5101*
32 at Ephesus, w advantageth it me, *G5101*
35 up? and with w body do they come? *G4169*
2Co 1:13 things unto you, than w ye read or *G3739*
6:14 with unbelievers: for w fellowship hath *G5101*
14 and w communion hath light *G5101*
15 And w concord hath Christ with Belial? *G5101*
15 with Belial? or w part hath he that *G5101*
16 And w agreement hath the temple of *G5101*
7:11 after a godly sort, w carefulness it *G4214*
11 in you, yea, *w* clearing of yourselves,
11 of yourselves, yea, *w* indignation, yea,
11 *what* indignation, yea, *w* fear, yea, *what*
11 *what* fear, yea, *w* vehement desire, yea,
11 desire, yea, *w* zeal, yea, *what* revenge!
11 *what* zeal, yea, *w* revenge! In all *things*
11:12 But w I do, that I will do, that I may cut *G3739*
12:13 For w is it wherein ye were inferior to *G5101*
Gal 4:30 Nevertheless w saith the scripture? *G5101*
Eph 1:18 that ye may know w is the hope of his *G5101*
18 of his calling, and w the riches of the *G5101*
19 And w *is* the exceeding greatness of his *G5101*
3: 9 And to make all *men* see w *is* the *G5101*
18 with all saints w *is* the breadth, and *G5101*
4: 9 (Now that he ascended, w is it but that *G5101*
5:10 Proving w is acceptable unto the Lord. *G5101*
17 understanding w the will of the Lord *is.* *G5101*
Php 1:18 W then? notwithstanding, every way, *G5101*
22 labour: yet w I shall choose I wot not. *G5101*
3: 7 But w things were gain to me, those I *G3748*
Col 1:27 To whom God would make known w *is* *G5101*
2: 1 For I would that ye knew w great *G2245*
1Th 1: 5 as ye know w manner of men we *G3634*
9 For they themselves shew of us w *G3697*
2:19 For w *is* our hope, or joy, or crown of *G5101*
3: 9 For w thanks can we render to God *G5101*
4: 2 For ye know w commandments we *G5101*
2Th 2: 6 And now ye know w withholdeth that *G3588*
1Ti 1: 7 w they say, nor whereof they affirm. *G3739*
2Ti 2: 7 Consider w I say; and the Lord give *G3739*
3:11 at Lystra; w persecutions I endured: *G3634*
Heb 2: 6 testified, saying, W is man, that thou *G5101*
7:11 received the law,) w further need *was* *G5101*
11:32 And w shall I more say? for the time *G5101*
12: 7 as with sons; for w son is he whom the *G5101*
13: 6 I will not fear w man shall do unto me. *G5101*
Jas 1:24 forgetteth w manner of man he was. *G3697*
2:14 W *doth it* profit, my brethren, though a *G5101*
16 needful to the body; w *doth it* profit? *G5101*
4:14 Whereas ye know not w *shall be* on the *G3588*
14 on the morrow. For w *is* your life? It is *G4169*
1Pt 1:11 Searching w, or what manner of time *G5101*
11 Searching what, or w manner *G1519+G5101*
2:20 For w glory *is it*, if, when ye be buffeted *G4169*
4:17 *it* first *begin* at us, w shall the end *be* of *G5101*
2Pt 3:11 things shall be dissolved, w manner *of* *G4217*
1Jn 3: 1 Behold, w manner of love the Father *G4217*
2 not yet appear w we shall be: but we *G5101*
Jude 10 know not: but w they know naturally, *G3745*
Rev 1:11 and the last: and, W thou seest, write *G3739*
2: 7 He that hath an ear, let him hear w the *G5101*
11 He that hath an ear, let him hear w the *G5101*
17 He that hath an ear, let him hear w the *G5101*
29 He that hath an ear, let him hear w the *G5101*
3: 3 know w hour I will come upon thee. *G4169*
6 He that hath an ear, let him hear w the *G5101*
13 He that hath an ear, let him hear w the *G5101*
22 He that hath an ear, let him hear w the *G5101*
7:13 saying unto me, W are these which are *G5101*
18:18 W *city is* like unto this great city! *G5101*

WHATSOEVER

Gen 2:19 call them: and w Adam called H3605+H834
8:19 every fowl, *and* w creepeth upon the H3605
19:12 and w thou hast in the H3605+H834
31:16 w God hath said unto thee, do. H3605+H834
39:22 prison; and w they did there, he H3605+H834
Ex 13: 2 Sanctify unto me all the firstborn, w H3605
21:30 of his life w is laid upon him. H3605+H834
29:37 holy: w toucheth the altar shall be holy. H3605
30:29 holy: w toucheth them shall be holy. H3605
Lev 5: 3 of man, w uncleanness *it be* that H3605
4 or to do good, w *it be* that a man H3605+H834
6:27 W shall touch the flesh thereof shall be H3605
7:27 W soul *it be* that eateth any manner of H3605
11: 3 W parteth the hoof, and is H3605
9 that *are* in the waters: w hath fins and H3605
12 W hath no fins nor scales in the waters, H3605
27 And w goeth upon his paws, among all H3605

Lev 11:32 And upon w *any* of them, when they H3605
32 or skin, or sack, w vessel *it be,* wherein H3605
33 *any* of them falleth, w *is* in it shall be H3605
42 W goeth upon the belly, and H3605
42 the belly, and w goeth upon *all* four, H3605
42 upon *all* four, or w hath more feet H3605
13:58 warp, or woof, or w thing of skin *it be,* H3605
15:26 and w she sitteth upon H3605+H3627
17: 8 And thou shalt say unto them, W H376+H834
10 And w man *there be* of the house H376+H834
13 And w man *there be* of the H376+H834
21:18 For w man *he be* that hath a blemish, H3605
22: 5 uncleanness, w uncleanness he hath; H3605
18 say unto them, W *he be* of the H376+H834
20 *But* w hath a blemish, *that* shall ye not H3605
23:29 For w soul *it be* that shall not be H3605
30 And w soul *it be* that doeth any work in H3605
27:32 the flock, *even* of w passeth under the H3605
Nu 5:10 things shall be his: w any man giveth the H834
18:13 *And* w is first ripe in the land, which H834
19:22 And w the unclean *person* toucheth H3605
22:17 and I will do w thou sayest unto H3605+H834
23: 3 to meet me: and w he sheweth H1697+H4100
30:12 heard *them; then* w proceeded out of H3605
Dt 2:37 unto w the LORD our God forbad us. H3605
12: 8 every man w *is* right in his own eyes. H3605
15 in all thy gates, w thy soul lusteth after, H3605
20 eat flesh, w thy soul lusteth after. H3605
21 eat in thy gates w thy soul lusteth after. H3605
14:10 And w hath not fins and scales H3605+H834
26 money for w thy soul lusteth H3605+H834
26 drink, or for w thy soul desireth: H3605+H834
Jdg 10:15 do thou unto us w seemeth good unto H3605
11:31 Then it shall be, that w cometh forth of H834
1Sa 14:36 And they said, Do w seemeth good H3605
20: 4 Then said Jonathan unto David, W thy H4100
25: 8 I pray thee, w cometh to thine H853+H834
2Sa 3:36 them: as w the king did pleased H3605+H834
15:15 *ready to do* w my lord the king H3605+H834
19:38 unto thee: and w thou shalt H3605+H834
1Ki 8:37 of their cities; w plague, whatsoever H3605
37 whatsoever plague, w sickness *there be;* H834
10:13 all her desire, w she asked, beside *that* H3605
20: 6 it shall be, *that* w is pleasant in thine H3605
2Ch 6:28 w sore or whatsoever sickness *there be:* H3605
28 whatsoever sore or w sickness *there be:* H3605
9:12 all her desire, w she asked, beside *that* H3605
Ezr 7:18 And w shall seem good to thee, H4101+H1768
20 And w more shall be needful for the
21 the river, that w Ezra the H3605+H3627
23 W is commanded by the God H3605+H3627
Est 2:13 the king; w she desired H853+H3605+H834
Job 37:12 they may do w he commandeth H3605+H834
41:11 *w is* under the whole heaven is mine.
Ps 1: 3 and w he doeth shall prosper. H3605+H834
8: 8 *w* passeth through the paths of the seas.
115: 3 he hath done w he hath pleased. H3605+H834
135: 6 W the LORD pleased, *that* did H3605+H834
Ecc 2:10 And w mine eyes desired I kept H3605+H834
3:14 I know that, w God doeth, it H3605+H834
8: 3 for he doeth w pleaseth him. H3605+H834
9:10 W thy hand findeth to do, do *it* H3605+H834
Jer 1: 7 send thee, and w I command H3605+H834
42: 4 come to pass, *that* w thing the LORD H3605
44:17 But we will certainly do w thing H853+H3605
Mt 5:37 for w is more than these cometh of evil. *G3588*
7:12 Therefore all things w ye would *G3745+G302*
10:11 And into w city or town ye shall *G3739+G302*
14: 7 to give her w she would ask. *G3739+G1437*
15: 5 *It is* a gift, by w thou mightest *G3739+G1437*
17 Do not ye yet understand, that w *G3956*
16:19 heaven: and w thou shalt bind *G3739+G1437*
19 in heaven: and w thou shalt loose on *G1437*
17:12 done unto him w they listed. Likewise *G3745*
18:18 Verily I say unto you, W ye *G3745+G1437*
18 in heaven: and w ye shall loose *G3745+G1437*
20: 4 vineyard, and w is right I will *G3739+G1437*
7 w is right, *that* shall ye receive. *G3739+G1437*
21:22 And all things, w ye shall ask in *G3745+G302*
23: 3 All therefore w they bid you *G3745+G302*
28:20 Teaching them to observe all things w I *G3745*
Mk 6:22 Ask of me w thou wilt, and I *G3739+G1437*
23 And he sware unto her, W *G3739+G1437*
7:11 is to say, a gift, by w thou mightest be *G1437*
18 not perceive, that w thing from without *G3956*
9:13 w they listed, as it is written of him. *G3745*
10:21 go thy way, sell w thou hast, and give *G3745*
35 do for us w we shall desire. *G3739+G1437*
11:23 to pass; he shall have w he saith. *G3739+G302*

Mk 13:11 but w shall be given you G3739+G1437
Lk 4:23 heal thyself: w we have heard done G3745
9: 4 And w house ye enter into, there G3739+G302
10: 5 And into w house ye enter, first G3739+G302
8 And into w city ye enter, and G3739+G302
10 But into w city ye enter, and G3739+G302
35 of him; and w thou spendest G3748+G302
12: 3 Therefore w ye have spoken in G3745
Jn 2: 5 W he saith unto you, do *it*. G3748+G302
5: 4 was made whole of w disease he had. G1221
11:22 But I know, that even now, w G3748+G302
12:50 is life everlasting: w I speak therefore, G3739
14:13 And w ye shall ask in my name, G3748+G302
26 remembrance, w I have said unto you. G3739
15:14 Ye are my friends, if ye do w I G3745
16 remain: that w ye shall ask of G3748+G302
16:13 of himself; but w he shall hear, G3745+G302
23 say unto you, W ye shall ask the G3748+G302
17: 7 Now they have known that all things w G3745
Act 3:22 things w he shall say unto you. G3748+G302
4:28 For to do w thy hand and thy counsel G3745
Ro 14:23 not of faith: for w *is* not of faith is sin. G3956
15: 4 For w things were written aforetime G3745
16: 2 ye assist her in w business she G3739+G302
1Co 10:25 W is sold in the shambles, *that* eat, G3956
27 be disposed to go; w is set before you, G3956
31 or w ye do, do all to the glory of God. G5100
Gal 2: 6 be somewhat, (w they were, it G3697+G4218
6: 7 mocked: for w a man soweth, G3739+G1437
Eph 5:13 light: for w doth make manifest is light. G3956
6: 8 Knowing that w good G3739+G1437+G5100
Php 4: 8 Finally, brethren, w things are true, G3745
8 things are true, w things *are* honest, G3745
8 things *are* honest, w things *are* just, G3745
8 things *are* just, w things *are* pure, G3745
8 things *are* pure, w things *are* lovely, G3745
8 things *are* lovely, w things *are* of good G3745
11 have learned, in w state I am, G3588+G3739
Col 3:17 And w ye do in word G3956+G3754+G5100
23 And w ye do, do it G3956+G3754+G1437
1Jn 3:22 And w we ask, we receive of G3739+G1437
5: 4 For w is born of God overcometh the G3956
15 he hear us, w we ask, we know G3739+G302
3Jn 5 faithfully w thou doest to the G3739+G1437
Rev 18:22 no craftsman, of w craft *he be*, shall be G3956
21:27 that defileth, neither *w* worketh

WHEAT

Gen 30:14 And Reuben went in the days of w H2406
Ex 9:32 But the w and the rie were not smitten: H2406
34:22 of the firstfruits of w harvest, and the H2406
Nu 18:12 the wine, and of the w, the firstfruits of H1715
Dt 8: 8 A land of w, and barley, and vines, and H2406
32:14 the fat of kidneys of w; and thou didst H2406
Jdg 6:11 Gideon threshed w by the winepress, to H2406
15: 1 in the time of w harvest, that Samson H2406
Ru 2:23 harvest and of w harvest; and dwelt H2406
1Sa 6:13 *were* reaping their w harvest in the H2406
12:17 *Is it* not w harvest to day? I will call H2406
2Sa 4: 6 have fetched w; and they smote him H2406
17:28 vessels, and w, and barley, and flour, H2406
1Ki 5:11 thousand measures of w *for* food to his H2406
1Ch 21:20 Now Ornan was threshing w. H2406
23 the w for the meat offering; I give it all. H2406
2Ch 2:10 of beaten w, and twenty thousand H2406
15 Now therefore the w, and the barley, the H2406
27: 5 measures of w, and ten thousand of H2406
Ezr 6: 9 God of heaven, w, salt, wine, and oil, H2591
7:22 measures of w, and to an hundred H2591
Job 31:40 Let thistles grow instead of w, and H2406
Ps 81:16 the finest of the w: and with honey out H2406
147:14 *and* filleth thee with the finest of the w. H2406
Prv 27:22 in a mortar among w with a pestle, *yet* H7383
Song 7: 2 *like* an heap of w set about with lilies. H2406
Isa 28:25 in the principal w and the appointed H2406
Jer 12:13 They have sown w, but shall reap H2406
23:28 *is* the chaff to the w? saith the LORD. H1250
31:12 of the LORD, for w, and for wine, and H1715
41: 8 in the field, of w, and of barley, and of H2406
Ezk 4: 9 Take thou also unto thee w, and barley, H2406
27:17 traded in thy market w of Minnith, and H2406
45:13 of an homer of w, and ye shall give the H2406
Joel 1:11 for the w and for the barley; H2406
2:24 And the floors shall be full of w, and the H1250
Am 5:11 him burdens of w: ye have built houses H1250
8: 5 we may set forth w, making the ephah H1250
6 shoes; *yea*, and sell the refuse of the w? H1250
Mt 3:12 and gather his w into the garner; but G4621
13:25 tares among the w, and went his way. G4621
13:29 tares, ye root up also the w with them. G4621
30 them: but gather the w into my barn. G4621
Lk 3:17 will gather the w into his garner; but G4621
16: 7 measures of w. And he said unto him, G4621
22:31 *to have* you, that he may sift *you* as w: G4621
Jn 12:24 Except a corn of w fall into the ground G4621
Act 27:38 ship, and cast out the w into the sea. G4621
1Co 15:37 chance of w, or of some other *grain*: G4621
Rev 6: 6 say, A measure of w for a penny, and G4621
18:13 and fine flour, and w, and beasts, and G4621

WHEATEN

Ex 29: 2 oil: *of* w flour shalt thou make them. H2406

WHEEL

1Ki 7:32 of a w *was* a cubit and half a cubit. H212
33 work of a chariot w: their axletrees, and H212
Ps 83:13 O my God, make them like a w; as the H1534
Prv 20:26 wicked, and bringeth the w over them. H212
Ecc 12: 6 or the w broken at the cistern. H1534
Isa 28:27 neither is a cart w turned about upon H212
28 nor break *it with* the w of his cart, nor H1536
Ezk 1:15 behold one w upon the earth by the H212
16 as it were a w in the middle of a wheel. H212
16 as it were a wheel in the middle of a w. H212
10: 9 cherubims, one w by one cherub, and H212
9 and another w by another cherub: and H212
10 if a w had been in the midst of a wheel. H212
10 if a wheel had been in the midst of a w. H212
13 cried unto them in my hearing, O w. H1534

WHEELS

Ex 14:25 And took off their chariot w, that they H212
Jdg 5:28 why tarry the w of his chariots? H6471
1Ki 7:30 And every base had four brasen w, and H212
32 And under the borders *were* four w; and H212
32 the axletrees of the w *were joined* to the H212
33 And the work of the w *was* like the work H212
Isa 5:28 like flint, and their w like a whirlwind: H1534
Jer 18: 3 and, behold, he wrought a work on the w. H70
47: 3 rumbling of his w, the fathers shall not H1534
Ezk 1:16 The appearance of the w and their work H212
19 went, the w went by them: and when H212
19 up from the earth, the w were lifted up. H212
20 spirit to go; and the w were lifted up over H212
20 spirit of the living creature *was* in the w. H212
21 from the earth, the w were lifted up over H212
21 spirit of the living creature *was* in the w. H212
3:13 the noise of the w over against them, H212
10: 2 Go in between the w, *even* under the H1534
6 from between the w, from between the H1534
6 then he went in, and stood beside the w. H212
9 And when I looked, behold the four w by H212
9 the w *was* as the colour of a beryl stone. H212
12 wings, and the w, *were* full of eyes round H212
12 about, *even* the w that they four had. H212
13 As for the w, it was cried unto them in H212
16 And when the cherubims went, the w H212
16 w also turned not from beside them. H212
19 they went out, the w also *were* beside H212
11:22 wings, and the w beside them; and the H212
23:24 wagons, and w, and with an assembly H1534
26:10 and of the w, and of the chariots, H1534
Dan 7: 9 fiery flame, *and* his w *as* burning fire. H1535
Nah 3: 2 the rattling of the w, and of the pransing H212

WHELM See OVERWHELM.

WHELP

Gen 49: 9 Judah *is* a lion's w: from the prey, my H1482
Dt 33:22 And of Dan he said, Dan *is* a lion's w: H1482
Nah 2:11 lion's w, and none made *them* afraid? H1482

WHELPS

2Sa 17: 8 bear robbed of her w in the field: and thy
Job 4:11 the stout lion's w are scattered abroad. H1121
28: 8 The lion's w have not trodden it, nor H1121
Prv 17:12 Let a bear robbed of her w meet a man,
Jer 51:38 like lions: they shall yell as lions' w. H1484
Ezk 19: 2 nourished her w among young lions. H1482
3 And she brought up one of her w: it H1482
5 of her w, *and* made him a young lion. H1482
Hos 13: 8 *is* bereaved of *her* w, and will rend the
Nah 2:12 enough for his w, and strangled for his H1484

WHEN See the Appendix.

WHENCE

Gen 3:23 to till the ground from w he was taken.
16: 8 And he said, Hagar, Sarai's maid, w H335
24: 5 unto the land from w thou camest?
29: 4 w *be* ye? And they said, Of Haran *are* we. H370
42: 7 he said unto them, W come ye? And they H370
Nu 11:13 W should I have flesh to give unto all H370
23:13 place, from w thou mayest see H834+H8033
Dt 9:28 Lest the land w thou broughtest H834+H8033
11:10 of Egypt, from w ye came out, H834+H8033
Jos 2: 4 men unto me, but I wist not w they *were*: H370
9: 8 them, Who *are* ye? and from w come ye? H370
20: 6 own house, unto the city from w he fled. H834
Jdg 13: 6 asked him not w he *was*, neither H335+H2088
17: 9 And Micah said unto him, W comest H370
19:17 Whither goest thou? and w comest thou? H370
1Sa 25:11 whom I know not w they *be*? H834+H2088
30:13 thou? and w *art* thou? And he H335+H2088
2Sa 1: 3 him, From w comest thou? And H335+H2088
13 that told him, W *art* thou? And H335+H2088
2Ki 5:25 said unto him, W *comest thou*, Gehazi? H370
6:27 do not help thee, w shall I help thee? out H370
20:14 men? and from w came they unto thee? H370
Neh 4:12 From all places w ye shall return unto H370
Job 1: 7 And the LORD said unto Satan, W H370
2: 2 And the LORD said unto Satan, From w H335
10:21 Before I go w I shall not return, *even* to
16:22 I shall go the way *w* I shall not return.
28:20 W then cometh wisdom? and where *is* H370
Ps 121: 1 unto the hills, from w cometh my help. H370
Ecc 1: 7 the place from w the rivers come, thither
Isa 30: 6 anguish, from w *come* the young and H1992
39: 3 men? and from w came they unto thee? H370
47:11 not know from w it riseth: and mischief
51: 1 look unto the rock *w* ye are hewn, and to
1 to the hole of the pit *w* ye are digged.
Jer 29:14 into the place w I caused you to H834+H8033
Jna 1: 8 occupation? and w comest thou? what *is* H370
Nah 3: 7 her? w shall I seek comforters for thee? H370
Mt 12:44 into my house from w I came out; and G3606
13:27 in thy field? from w hath it tares? G4159
54 and said, W hath this *man* this G4159
56 W then hath this *man* all these things? G4159
15:33 And his disciples say unto him, W G4159
21:25 The baptism of John, w was it? from G4159
Mk 6: 2 saying, From w hath this *man* these G4159
8: 4 him, From w can a man satisfy these G4159
12:37 him Lord; and w is he *then* his son? G4159
Lk 1:43 And w *is* this to me, that the mother of G4159
11:24 return unto my house w I came out. G3606
13:25 say unto you, I know you not w ye are: G4159
27 I know you not w ye are; depart from G4159
20: 7 that they could not tell w *it was*. G4159
Jn 1:48 Nathanael saith unto him, W knowest G4159
2: 9 wine, and knew not w it was: (but the G4159
3: 8 but canst not tell w it cometh, and G4159
4:11 w then hast thou that living water? G4159
6: 5 he saith unto Philip, W shall we buy G4159
7:27 Howbeit we know this man w he is: but G4159
27 cometh, no man knoweth w he is. G4159
28 me, and ye know w I am: and I am not G4159
8:14 record is true: for I know w I came, and G4159
14 cannot tell w I come, and whither I go. G4159
9:29 this *fellow*, we know not from w he is. G4159
30 ye know not from w he is, and *yet* he G4159
19: 9 saith unto Jesus, W art thou? But Jesus G4159
Act 14:26 And thence sailed to Antioch, from w G3606
Php 3:20 is in heaven; from w also we look for G3739
Heb 11:15 of that *country* from w they came out, G3739
19 w also he received him in a figure. G3606
Jas 4: 1 From w *come* wars and fightings G4159
Rev 2: 5 Remember therefore from w thou art G4159
7:13 in white robes? and w came they? G4159

WHENSOEVER

Gen 30:41 And it came to pass, w the stronger H3605
Mk 14: 7 you always, and w ye will ye may do G3752
Ro 15:24 W I take my journey into G5613+G1437

WHERE

Gen 2:11 land of Havilah, w *there is* gold; H834+H8033
3: 9 Adam, and said unto him, W *art* thou? H335
4: 9 And the LORD said unto Cain, W *is* Abel H335
13: 3 unto the place w his tent had been at H834
10 well watered every w, before the LORD
14 from the place w thou art northward,
18: 9 And they said unto him, W *is* Sarah thy H346
19: 5 and said unto him, W *are* the men which H346
27 to the place w he stood before the LORD: H834
20:15 *is* before thee: dwell w it pleaseth thee.
21:17 hath heard the voice of the lad w he *is*. H834

Gen 22: 7 but w *is* the lamb for a burnt offering?
27:33 and said, Who? w *is* he that hath taken H645
31:13 I *am* the God of Beth-el, w thou H834
13 the pillar, *and* w thou vowedst a vow H834
33:19 And he bought a parcel of a field, w he H834
35:13 him in the place w he talked with him. H834
14 And Jacob set up a pillar in the place w H834
15 the place w God spake with him, Beth-el. H834
27 w Abraham and Isaac sojourned. H834
37:16 me, I pray thee, w they feed *their flocks.* H375
38:21 that place, saying, W *is* the harlot, that H346
39:20 the prison, a place w the king's prisoners H834
40: 3 prison, the place w Joseph *was* bound. H834
43:30 and he sought *w* to weep; and he entered
Ex 2:20 And he said unto his daughters, And w H346
5:11 Go ye, get you straw w ye can find it: yet H834
9:26 Only in the land of Goshen, w the
12:13 upon the houses w ye *are:* and when I H834
30 not a house w *there was* not one dead. H834
15:27 And they came to Elim, w *were* twelve H8033
18: 5 w he encamped at the mount of God: H8033
20:21 unto the thick darkness w God *was.* H8033
24 oxen: in all places w I record my name I H834
27:18 breadth fifty every w, and the height five
29:42 the LORD: w I will meet you, H834+H8033
30: 6 w I will meet with thee. H834+H8033
36 congregation, w I will meet with H834+H8033
Lev 4:12 camp unto a clean place, w the ashes are H413
12 wood with fire: w the ashes are poured H5921
24 kill it in the place w they kill the burnt H834
33 the place w they kill the burnt offering. H834
6:25 In the place w the burnt offering is H834
7: 2 In the place w they kill the burnt offering H834
14:13 And he shall slay the lamb in the place w H834
Nu 9:17 and in the place w the cloud abode, H834
13:22 unto Hebron; w Ahiman, Sheshai, and H8033
17: 4 w I will meet with you. H834+H8033
22:26 in a narrow place, w *was* no way to turn H834
33:14 w was no water for the people to drink. H8033
54 shall be in the place w his lot falleth; H8033
Dt 1:31 And in the wilderness, w thou hast seen H834
8:15 and drought, w *there was* no water; H834
11:10 ye came out, w thou sowedst thy seed, H834
30 side Jordan, by the way w the sun goeth
18: 6 out of all Israel, w he sojourned, H834+H8033
23:16 in one of thy gates, w it liketh him best:
32:37 And he shall say, W *are* their gods, *their* H335
Jos 4: 3 out of the place w the priests' feet stood
3 lodging place, w ye shall lodge this night. H834
8 unto the place w they lodged, and laid H413
9 in the place w the feet of the priests
Jdg 5:27 w he bowed, there he fell down dead. H834
6:13 befallen us? and w *be* all his miracles H346
9:38 Then said Zebul unto him, W *is* now thy H346
17: 8 to sojourn w he could find *a place:* H834
9 and I go to sojourn w I may find *a place.* H834
18:10 hands; a place w *there is* no want of any H834
19:26 w her lord *was,* till it was light. H834+H8033
20:22 array in the place w they put H834+H8033
Ru 1: 7 of the place w she was, and her H834+H8033
16 I will go; and w thou lodgest, I will lodge: H834
17 W thou diest, will I die, and there will I H834
2:19 And her mother in law said unto her, W H645
19 to day? and w wroughtest thou? blessed H375
3: 4 the place w he shall lie, and H834+H8033
1Sa 3: 3 of the LORD, w the ark of God H834+H8033
6:14 and stood there, w *there was* a great H8033
9:10 the city w the man of God *was.* H834+H8033
18 pray thee, w the seer's house *is.* H335+H2088
10: 5 the hill of God, w *is* the garrison H834+H8033
14 that *they were* no w, we came to Samuel. H369
14:11 w they had hid themselves. H834+H8033
19: 3 father in the field w thou *art,* and I will H834
22 he asked and said, W *are* Samuel and H375
20:19 to the place w thou didst hide H834+H8033
23:22 and see his place w his haunt *is, and* H834
23 the lurking places w he hideth H834+H8033
24: 3 by the way, w *was* a cave; and Saul H8033
26: 5 to the place w Saul had pitched: H834+H8033
5 the place w Saul lay, and Abner H834+H8033
16 And now see w the king's spear *is,* and H335
30: 9 w those that were left behind stayed.
31 to all the places w David himself H834+H8033
2Sa 2:23 to the place w Asahel fell down H834+H8033
9: 4 And the king said unto him, W *is* he? H375
11:16 place w he knew that valiant men *were.* H834
15:32 *of the mount,* w he worshipped H834+H8033
16: 3 And the king said, And w *is* thy master's H346
17:12 him in some place w he shall be H834+H8033
2Sa 17:20 the house, they said, W *is* Ahimaaz and H346
18: 7 W the people of Israel were slain before H8033
21:12 of Beth-shan, w the Philistines had H8033
19 the Philistines, w Elhanan the son of
20 And there was yet a battle in Gath, w
23:11 into a troop, w was a piece of ground H8033
1Ki 4:28 unto the place w *the officers* H834+H8033
7: 7 for the throne w he might judge, H834+H8033
8 And his house w he dwelt *had* H834+H8033
13:25 *it* in the city w the old prophet dwelt. H834
17:19 up into a loft, w he abode, and H834+H8033
21:19 the LORD, In the place w dogs licked the H834
2Ki 2:14 waters, and said, W *is* the LORD God of H346
4: 8 to Shunem, w *was* a great woman; H8033
6: 1 now, the place w we dwell with H834+H8033
2 us a place there, w we may dwell. And H8033
6 And the man of God said, W fell it? And H575
13 And he said, Go and spy w he *is,* that I H351
18:34 W *are* the gods of Hamath, and of H346
34 and of Arpad? w *are* the gods of H346
19:13 W *is* the king of Hamath, and the king of H346
23: 7 of the LORD, w the women wove H834+H8033
8 high places w the priests had H834+H8033
1Ch 11: 4 which *is* Jebus; w the Jebusites *were,* H8033
13 together to battle, w was a parcel of
13: 2 our brethren every w, *that are* left in all
20: 6 And yet again there was war at Gath, w
2Ch 3: 1 in mount Moriah, w *the LORD* appeared H834
25: 4 in the book of Moses, w the LORD H834
36:20 away to Babylon; w they were servants
Ezr 1: 4 in any place w he sojourneth, let H834+H8033
6: 1 house of the rolls, w the treasures were H8536
3 be builded, the place w they offered H1768
Neh 10:39 the chambers, w *are* the vessels of the H8033
13: 5 a great chamber, w aforetime they laid H8033
Est 1: 6 *W were* white, green, and blue,
7: 5 queen, Who is he, and w is he, that durst H335
Job 4: 7 or w were the righteous cut off? H375
9:24 judges thereof; if not, w, *and* who *is* he? H645
10:22 order, and w the light *is* as darkness.
12:24 in a wilderness *w there is* no way.
14:10 man giveth up the ghost, and w *is* he?
15:23 for bread, *saying,* W *is* it? he knoweth H346
17:15 And w *is* now my hope? as for my H346+H645
20: 7 which have seen him shall say, W *is* he? H335
21:28 For ye say, W *is* the house of the prince? H346
28 w *are* the dwelling places of the wicked? H346
23: 3 Oh that I knew w I might find him! *that* I
9 On the left hand, w he doth work, but I
28: 1 silver, and a place for gold w they fine *it.*
12 But w shall wisdom be found? and where H370
12 w *is* the place of understanding? H335+H2088
20 Whence then cometh wisdom? and w *is* H335
34:22 nor shadow of death, w the workers of H8033
35:10 But none saith, W *is* God my maker, H335
36:16 strait *into* a broad place, w *there is* no
38: 4 W wast thou when I laid the foundations H375
19 W *is* the way *where* light dwelleth? and H335
19 Where *is* the way w light dwelleth? and H335
19 *as for* darkness, w *is* the place thereof, H335
26 To cause it to rain on the earth, *w* no
39:30 blood: and w the slain *are,* there *is* she. H834
40:20 food, w all the beasts of the field play. H8033
Ps 19: 3 *There is* no speech nor language, *w* their
26: 8 and the place w thine honour dwelleth.
42: 3 continually say unto me, W *is* thy God? H346
10 they say daily unto me, W *is* thy God? H346
53: 5 There were they in great fear, *w* no fear
63: 1 in a dry and thirsty land, w no water is;
69: 2 I sink in deep mire, w *there is* no
2 deep waters, w the floods overflow me.
79:10 Wherefore should the heathen say, W *is* H346
81: 5 the land of Egypt: *w* I heard a language
84: 3 a nest for herself, w she may lay her H834
89:49 Lord, w *are* thy former H346
104:17 W the birds make their nests: *as* H834+H8033
107:40 in the wilderness, *w there is* no way.
115: 2 Wherefore should the heathen say, W *is* H346
Prv 11:14 W no counsel *is,* the people fall: but in
14: 4 W no oxen *are,* the crib *is* clean: but
15:17 Better *is* a dinner of herbs w love is, H8033
26:20 W no wood is, *there* the fire goeth out: so H657
20 the fire goeth out: so w *there is* no
29:18 W *there is* no vision, the people perish:
Ecc 1: 5 and hasteth to his place w he arose. H8033
8: 4 W the word of a king *is, there is* power: H834
10 w they had so done: this *is* also vanity. H834
11: 3 place w the tree falleth, there it shall be.
Song 1: 7 Tell me, O thou whom my soul loveth, w H349
Song 1: 7 thou feedest, w thou makest *thy flock* H349
Isa 7:23 place shall be, w there were a thousand H834
10: 3 for help? and w will ye leave your glory? H575
19:12 W *are* they? where *are* thy wise *men?* H335
12 Where *are* they? w *are* thy wise *men?* H645
29: 1 Woe to Ariel, to Ariel, the city *w* David
30:32 And *in* every place w the grounded staff
33:18 Thine heart shall meditate terror. W *is* H346
18 *is* the scribe? w *is* the receiver? where H346
18 w *is* he that counted the towers?
35: 7 of dragons, w each lay, *shall be* grass
36:19 W *are* the gods of Hamath and Arphad? H346
19 Hamath and Arphad? w *are* the gods of H346
37:13 W *is* the king of Hamath, and the king of H346
49:21 I was left alone; these, w *had* they *been?* H375
50: 1 Thus saith the LORD, W *is* the bill of H335
51:13 and w *is* the fury of the oppressor? H346
57: 8 thou lovedst their bed w thou sawest *it.* H3027
63:11 his people, *saying,* W *is* he that brought H346
11 of his flock? w *is* he that put his holy H346
15 and of thy glory: w *is* thy zeal and thy H346
64:11 Our holy and our beautiful house, w our H834
66: 1 *is* my footstool: w *is* the house that ye H335
1 unto me? and w *is* the place of my rest? H335
Jer 2: 6 Neither said they, W *is* the LORD that H346
6 passed through, and w no man dwelt? H8033
8 The priests said not, W *is* the LORD? H346
28 But w *are* thy gods that thou hast made H346
3: 2 places, and see w thou hast not been lien H375
6:16 for the old paths, w *is* the good way, and H335
7:12 *was* in Shiloh, w I set my name H834+H8033
13: 7 from the place w I had hid it: H834+H8033
20 from the north: w *is* the flock *that* was H346
16:13 and night; w I will not shew you favour. H834
17:15 Behold, they say unto me, W *is* the word H346
22:26 country, w ye were not born; H834+H8033
35: 7 in the land w ye *be* strangers. H834+H8033
36:19 Jeremiah; and let no man know w ye be. H375
37:19 W *are* now your prophets which H346
38: 9 in the place w he is: for *there is* no H8478
39: 5 Hamath, w he gave judgment upon him.
42:14 the land of Egypt, w we shall see no war, H834
52: 9 Hamath; w he gave judgment upon him.
Lam 2:12 They say to their mothers, W *is* corn and H346
Ezk 3:15 of Chebar, and I sat w they sat, and H8033
6:13 oak, the place w they did offer H834+H8033
8: 3 the north; w *was* the seat of the H834+H8033
11:16 the countries w they shall come. H834+H8033
17 out of the countries w ye have been H834
13:12 not be said unto you, W *is* the daubing H346
17:10 it shall wither in the furrows w it grew. H5921
16 surely in the place w the king *dwelleth*
20:38 out of the country w they sojourn, and
21:30 thee in the place w thou wast created, in H834
34:12 of all places w they have been H834+H8033
40:38 w they washed the burnt offering. H8033
42:13 chambers, w the priests that H834+H8033
43: 7 of my feet, w I will dwell in the H834+H8033
46:20 *is* the place w the priests shall H834+H8033
20 the sin offering, w they shall bake the H834
24 them that boil, w the ministers H834+H8033
Dan 8:17 So he came near w I stood: and when he
Hos 1:10 pass, *that* in the place w it was said unto H834
13:10 I will be thy king: w *is any other* that H645
Joel 2:17 say among the people, W *is* their God? H346
Am 3: 5 upon the earth, w no gin *is* for him? shall
Mic 7:10 said unto me, W is the LORD thy God? H346
Nah 2:11 W *is* the dwelling of the lions, and the H346
11 young lions, w the lion, *even* the H834+H8033
3:17 and their place is not known w they *are.* H335
Zep 3:19 land w they have been put to shame.
Zec 1: 5 Your fathers, w *are* they? and the H346
Mal 1: 6 if then I *be* a father, w *is* mine honour? H346
6 if I *be* a master, w *is* my fear? saith the H346
2:17 in them; or, W *is* the God of judgment? H346
Mt 2: 2 Saying, W is he that is born King of the *G4226*
4 of them w Christ should be born. *G4226*
9 and stood over w the young child was. *G3757*
6:19 upon earth, w moth and rust doth *G3699*
19 and w thieves break through and steal: *G3699*
20 in heaven, w neither moth nor rust *G3699*
20 rust doth corrupt, and w thieves do not *G3699*
21 For w your treasure is, there will your *G3699*
8:20 Son of man hath not w to lay *his* head. *G4226*
13: 5 Some fell upon stony places, w they *G3699*
18:20 For w two or three are gathered *G3757*
25:24 man, reaping w thou hast not sown, *G3699*
24 and gathering w thou hast not strawed: *G3606*
26 that I reap w I sowed not, and gather *G3699*

Mt 25:26 not, and gather w I have not strawed: *G3606*
26:17 saying unto him, W wilt thou that we *G4226*
57 the high priest, w the scribes and the *G3699*
28: 6 Come, see the place w the Lord lay. *G3699*
16 w Jesus had appointed them. *G3757*
Mk 2: 4 the roof w he was: and when they *G3699*
4: 5 And some fell on stony ground, w it *G3699*
15 And these are they by the way side, w *G3699*
5:40 entereth in w the damsel was lying. *G3699*
6:55 that were sick, w they heard he was. *G3699*
9:44 W their worm dieth not, and the fire is *G3699*
46 W their worm dieth not, and the fire is *G3699*
48 W their worm dieth not, and the fire is *G3699*
11: 4 w two ways met; and they loose him. *G296*
13:14 prophet, standing w it ought not, (let *G3699*
14:12 said unto him, W wilt thou that we go *G4226*
14 house, The Master saith, W is the *G4226*
14 the guestchamber, w I shall eat the *G3699*
15:47 *mother* of Joses beheld w he was laid. *G4226*
16: 6 here: behold the place w they laid him. *G3699*
20 preached every w, the Lord working *G3837*
Lk 4:16 And he came to Nazareth, w he had *G3757*
17 he found the place w it was written, *G3757*
8:25 And he said unto them, W is your *G4226*
9: 6 the gospel, and healing every w. *G3837*
58 Son of man hath not w to lay *his* head. *G4226*
10:33 journeyed, came w he was: and when *G2596*
12:17 I have no room w to bestow my fruits? *G4226*
33 heavens that faileth not, w no thief *G3699*
34 For w your treasure is, there will your *G3699*
17:17 not ten cleansed? but w *are* the nine? *G4226*
37 said unto him, W, Lord? And he said *G4226*
22: 9 And they said unto him, W wilt thou *G4226*
10 him into the house w he entereth in. *G3757*
11 Master saith unto thee, W is the *G4226*
11 the guestchamber, w I shall eat the *G3699*
Jn 1:28 beyond Jordan, w John was baptizing. *G3699*
38 interpreted, Master,) w dwellest thou? *G4226*
39 came and saw w he dwelt, and abode *G4226*
3: 8 The wind bloweth w it listeth, and thou *G3699*
4:20 is the place w men ought to worship. *G3699*
46 Cana of Galilee, w he made the water *G3699*
6:23 unto the place w they did eat bread, *G3699*
62 Son of man ascend up w he was before? *G3699*
7:11 him at the feast, and said, W is he? *G4226*
34 and w I am, *thither* ye cannot come. *G3699*
36 and w I am, *thither* ye cannot come? *G3699*
42 the town of Bethlehem, w David was? *G3699*
8:10 unto her, Woman, w are those thine *G4226*
19 Then said they unto him, W is thy *G4226*
9:12 Then said they unto him, W is he? He *G4226*
10:40 into the place w John at first baptized; *G3699*
11: 6 days still in the same place w he was. *G3699*
30 was in that place w Martha met him. *G3699*
32 Then when Mary was come w Jesus *G3699*
34 And said, W have ye laid him? They *G4226*
41 *from the place* w the dead was laid. *G3757*
57 if any man knew w he were, he should *G4226*
12: 1 came to Bethany, w Lazarus was which *G3699*
26 follow me; and w I am, there shall also *G3699*
14: 3 that w I am, *there* ye may be also. *G3699*
17:24 me, be with me w I am; that they may *G3699*
18: 1 the brook Cedron, w was a garden, into *G3699*
19:18 W they crucified him, and two other *G3699*
20 the Jews: for the place w Jesus was *G3699*
41 Now in the place w he was crucified *G3699*
20: 2 and we know not w they have laid him. *G4226*
12 the feet, w the body of Jesus had lain. *G3699*
13 and I know not w they have laid him. *G4226*
15 him hence, tell me w thou hast laid *G4226*
19 doors were shut w the disciples were *G3699*
Act 1:13 an upper room, w abode both Peter, *G3757*
2: 2 filled all the house w they were sitting. *G3757*
4:31 place was shaken w they were *G1722+G3739*
7:29 land of Madian, w he begat two sons. *G3757*
33 for the place w thou standest is *G1722+G3739*
8: 4 went every w preaching the word. *G1330*
11:11 the house w I was, sent from *G1722+G3739*
12:12 was Mark; w many were gathered *G3757*
15:36 in every city w we have *G1722+G3739*
16:13 by a river side, w prayer was wont to *G3757*
17: 1 w was a synagogue of the Jews: *G3699*
30 all men every w to repent: *G3837*
20: 6 in five days; w we abode seven days. *G3757*
8 w they were gathered together. *G3757*
21:28 all *men* every w against the people, *G3837*
25:10 judgment seat, w I ought to be judged: *G3757*
27:41 And falling into a place w two seas met, *G337*
28:14 W we found brethren, and were *G3757*
Act 28:22 know that every w it is spoken against. *G3837*
Ro 3:27 W *is* boasting then? It is excluded. By *G4226*
4:15 Because the law worketh wrath: for w *G3757*
5:20 abound. But w sin abounded, grace *G3757*
9:26 *that* in the place w it was said unto *G3757*
15:20 the gospel, not w Christ was named, *G3699*
1Co 1:20 W *is* the wise? where *is* the scribe? *G4226*
20 Where *is* the wise? w *is* the scribe? *G4226*
20 *is* the scribe? w *is* the disputer of this *G4226*
4:17 as I teach every w in every church. *G3837*
12:17 If the whole body *were* an eye, w *were* *G4226*
17 *were* hearing, w *were* the smelling? *G4226*
19 And if they were all one member, w *G4226*
15:55 O death, w *is* thy sting? O grave, where *G4226*
55 O death, where *is* thy sting? O grave, w *G4226*
2Co 3:17 Now the Lord is that Spirit: and w the *G3757*
Gal 4:15 W is then the blessedness ye spake of? *G5101*
Php 4:12 to abound: every w and in all things I *G3956*
Col 3: 1 which are above, w Christ sitteth on the *G3757*
11 W there is neither Greek nor Jew, *G3699*
1Ti 2: 8 I will therefore that men pray every w, *G5117*
Heb 9:16 For w a testament *is*, there must also of *G3699*
10:18 Now w remission of these *is, there is* no *G3699*
Jas 3:16 For w envying and strife *is*, there *is* *G3699*
1Pt 4:18 scarcely be saved, w shall the ungodly *G4226*
2Pt 3: 4 And saying, W is the promise of his *G4226*
Rev 2:13 I know thy works, and w thou dwellest, *G4226*
13 dwellest, *even* w Satan's seat *is*: and *G3699*
13 slain among you, w Satan dwelleth. *G3699*
11: 8 Egypt, w also our Lord was crucified. *G3699*
12: 6 into the wilderness, w she hath a place *G3699*
14 into her place, w she is nourished for *G3699*
17:15 thou sawest, w the whore sitteth, are *G3757*
20:10 fire and brimstone, w the beast and the *G3699*

WHEREABOUT

1Sa 21: 2 of the business w I send thee, and what H834

WHEREAS

Gen 31:37 W thou hast searched all my stuff, H3588
Dt 19: 6 and slay him; w he *was* not worthy of
28:62 And ye shall be left few in number, w ye H834
1Sa 24:17 me good, w I have rewarded thee evil.
2Sa 7: 6 W I have not dwelt in *any* house since H3588
15:20 W thou camest *but* yesterday, should I
1Ki 8:18 my father, W it was in thine H3282+H834
12:11 And now w my father did lade you with
2Ki 13:19 consumed *it*: w now thou shalt smite H6258
2Ch 10:11 For w my father put a heavy yoke upon H6258
28:13 hither: for w we have offended against H3588
Job 22:20 W our substance is not cut down, but H518
Ecc 4:14 For out of prison he cometh to reign; w H3588
Isa 37:21 God of Israel, W thou hast prayed to H834
60:15 W thou hast been forsaken and hated, H8478
Jer 4:10 w the sword reacheth unto the soul.
Ezk 13: 7 a lying divination, w ye say, The LORD
16: 7 is grown, w thou *wast* naked and bare.
34 in thy whoredoms, w none followeth
35:10 will possess it; w the LORD was there:
36:34 shall be tilled, w it lay desolate H8478+H834
Dan 2:41 And w thou sawest the feet and toes, H1768
43 And w thou sawest iron mixed with H1768
4:23 And w the king saw a watcher and an H1768
26 And w they commanded to leave the H1768
8:22 Now that being broken, w four stood up
Mal 1: 4 W Edom saith, We are impoverished, H3588
Jn 9:25 I know, that, w I was blind, now I see.
1Co 3: 3 For ye are yet carnal: for w *there is* *G3699*
Jas 4:14 W ye know not what *shall be* on the *G3748*
1Pt 2:12 the Gentiles: that, w they speak *G1722+G3739*
3:16 that, w they speak evil *G1722+G3739*
2Pt 2:11 W angels, which are greater in power *G3699*

WHEREBY

Gen 15: 8 And he said, Lord GOD, w shall I know H4100
44: 5 lord drinketh, and w indeed he divineth?
Lev 22: 5 any creeping thing, w he may be made H834
Nu 5: 8 w an atonement shall be made for him. H834
17: 5 of Israel, w they murmur against you. H834
Dt 7:19 stretched out arm, w the LORD thy God H834
28:20 of thy doings, w thou hast forsaken me. H834
1Sa 20:33 him to smite him: w Jonathan knew that
Ps 45: 5 enemies; *w* the people fall under thee.
8 palaces, w they have made thee glad. H4482
68: 9 a plentiful rain, w thou didst confirm
Jer 3: 8 And I saw, when for all the causes w H834
17:19 of the people, w the kings of Judah come H834
23: 6 and this *is* his name w he shall be called, H834
33: 8 all their iniquity, w they have sinned H834
Jer 33: 8 all their iniquities, w they have sinned, H834
8 w they have transgressed against me. H834
Ezk 18:31 transgressions, w ye have transgressed; H834
20:25 and judgments w they should not live;
39:26 and all their trespasses w they have H834
40:49 *me* by the steps w they went up to it: and H834
46: 9 by the way of the gate w he came in, but H834
47:13 *be* the border, w ye shall inherit the land H834
Zep 2: 8 of Ammon, w they have reproached H834
Lk 1:18 And Zacharias said unto the angel, W *G2596*
78 mercy of our God; w the dayspring *G1722*
Act 4:12 among men, w we must be saved. *G1722*
11:14 Who shall tell thee words, w thou and *G1722*
19:40 there being no cause w we may give an *G4012*
Ro 8:15 of adoption, w we cry, Abba, Father. *G1722*
14:21 nor *any thing* w thy brother stumbleth, *G1722*
Eph 3: 4 W, when ye read, ye may understand *G4314*
4:14 craftiness, w they lie in wait to deceive; *G4314*
30 And grieve not the holy Spirit of God, w *G1722*
Php 3:21 to the working w he is able even to *G3588*
Heb 12:28 let us have grace, w we may serve God *G1223*
2Pt 1: 4 W are given unto us exceeding great *G1223*
3: 6 W the world that then was, being *G1223*
1Jn 2:18 w we know that it is the last time. *G3606*

WHEREFORE

Gen 10: 9 the LORD: w it is said, Even H5921+H3651
16:14 W the well was called H5921+H3651
18:13 And the LORD said unto Abraham, W H4100
21:10 W she said unto Abraham, Cast out this
31 W he called that place Beer-sheba;
24:31 of the LORD; w standest thou without?
26:27 And Isaac said unto them, W come ye H4069
29:25 w then hast thou beguiled me? H4100+H2063
31:27 W didst thou flee away secretly, and H4100
30 house, *yet* w hast thou stolen my gods? H4100
32:29 And he said, W *is* it *that* thou dost H4100
38:10 the LORD: w he slew him also.
40: 7 saying, W look ye *so* sadly to day? H4069
43: 6 And Israel said, W dealt ye *so* ill with H4100
44: 4 W have ye rewarded evil for good? H4100
7 And they said unto him, W saith my H4100
47:19 W shall we die before thine eyes, both H4100
22 w they sold not their lands. H5921+H3651
50:11 the Egyptians: w the name of it H5921+H3651
Ex 2:13 the wrong, W smitest thou thy fellow? H4100
5: 4 said unto them, W do ye, Moses and H4100
14 *and* demanded, W have ye not fulfilled H4069
15 W dealest thou thus with thy servants? H4100
22 and said, Lord, w hast thou *so* evil H4100
6: 6 W say unto the children of Israel, I *am* H3651
14:11 wilderness? w hast thou dealt H4100+H2063
15 And the LORD said unto Moses, W H4100
17: 2 W the people did chide with Moses, and
2 ye with me? w do ye tempt the LORD? H4100
3 Moses, and said, W *is* this *that* thou H4100
20:11 the seventh day: w the LORD H5921+H3651
31:16 W the children of Israel shall keep the
32:12 W should the Egyptians speak, and H4100
Lev 10:17 W have ye not eaten the sin offering in H4069
13:25 out of the burning: w the priest shall
25:18 W ye shall do my statutes, and keep my
Nu 9: 7 body of a man: w are we kept back, H4100
11:11 And Moses said unto the LORD, W H4100
11 thy servant? and w have I not found
12: 8 shall he behold: w then were ye not H4069
14: 3 And w hath the LORD brought us unto H4100
41 And Moses said, W now do ye H4100
16: 3 LORD *is* among them: w then lift ye up H4069
20: 5 And w have ye made us to come up out H4100
21 border: w Israel turned away from him.
21: 5 against Moses, W have ye brought us H4100
14 W it is said in the book of the H5921+H3651
27 W they that speak in proverbs H5921+H3651
22:32 said unto him, W hast thou smitten H4100
37 thee to call thee? w camest thou not H4100
25:12 W say, Behold, I give unto him my H3651
32: 5 W, said they, if we have found grace in
7 And w discourage ye the heart of the
Dt 7:12 W it shall come to pass, if ye hearken to
10: 9 W Levi hath no part nor H5921+H3651
19: 7 W I command thee, saying, H5921+H3651
29:24 Even all nations shall say, W H5921+H4100
Jos 5: 9 from off you. W the name of the place
7: 5 in the going down: w the hearts of the
7 And Joshua said, Alas, O Lord GOD, w H4100
10 up; w liest thou thus upon thy face? H4100
26 of his anger. W the name of H5921+H3651
9:11 W our elders and all the inhabitants of

Jos 9:22 them, saying, W have ye beguiled us, H4100
10: 3 W Adoni-zedek king of Jerusalem sent
Jdg 2: 3 W I also said, I will not drive them out
10:13 gods: w I will deliver you no more. H3651
11:27 W I have not sinned against thee, but
12: 1 unto Jephthah, W passedst thou over H4069
3 into my hand: w then are ye come up H4100
15:19 and he revived: w he called the H5921+H3651
18:12 in Judah: w they called that place
Ru 1: 7 W she went forth out of the place where
1Sa 1:20 W it came to pass, when the time was
2:17 W the sin of the young men was very
29 W kick ye at my sacrifice and at mine H4100
30 W the LORD God of Israel saith, I said H3651
4: 3 elders of Israel said, W hath the LORD H4100
6: 5 W ye shall make images of your
6 W then do ye harden your hearts, as H4100
9:21 w then speakest thou so to me? H4100
14:27 with the oath: w he put forth the end
15:19 W then didst thou not obey the voice of H4100
16:19 W Saul sent messengers unto Jesse, and
18:15 W when Saul saw that he behaved
21 be against him. W Saul said to David,
27 W David arose and went, he and his
19: 5 and didst rejoice: w then wilt thou sin H4100
24 all that night. W they say, *Is* H5921+H3651
20:27 Jonathan his son, W cometh not the H4069
31 nor thy kingdom. W now send and fetch
32 and said unto him, W shall he be slain? H4100
21:14 w *then* have ye brought him to me? H4100
23:25 they told David: w he came down into a
28 W Saul returned from pursuing after
24: 9 And David said to Saul, W hearest H4100
19 him go well away? w the LORD reward
25: 8 will shew thee. W let the young men find
36 he *was* very drunken: w she told him
26:15 to thee in Israel? w then hast thou not H4100
18 And he said, W doth my lord thus H4100
27: 6 Ziklag that day: w Ziklag pertaineth H3651
28: 9 out of the land: w then layest thou a H4100
16 Then said Samuel, W then dost thou H4100
29: 7 W now return, and go in peace, that
10 W now rise up early in the morning with
2Sa 2:16 they fell down together: w that place was
22 following me: w should I smite thee H4100
23 Howbeit he refused to turn aside: w
3: 7 said to Abner, W hast thou gone in H4069
5: 8 *be chief and captain.* W they said, The
7:22 W thou art great, O LORD H5921+H3651
10: 4 W Hanun took David's servants, and
11:20 he say unto thee, W approached ye so H4069
12: 9 W hast thou despised the H4069
23 But now he is dead, w should I fast? H4100
14:13 And the woman said, W then hast thou H4100
31 said unto him, W have thy servants set H4100
32 to the king, to say, W am I come from H4100
15:19 to Ittai the Gittite, W goest thou also H4100
16:10 shall then say, W hast thou done so? H4069
18:22 Joab said, W wilt thou run, my H4100+H2088
19:12 and my flesh: w then are ye the last H4100
25 said unto him, W wentest not thou H4100
35 and singing women? w then should thy H4100
42 *is* near of kin to us: w then be ye angry H4100
21: 3 W David said unto the Gibeonites, What
24:21 And Araunah said, W is my lord the H4069
1Ki 1: 2 W his servants said unto him, Let there
11 W Nathan spake unto Bath-sheba the
41 trumpet, he said, W *is this* noise of the H4069
11:11 W the LORD said unto Solomon,
12:15 W the king hearkened not unto the
16:16 also slain the king: w all Israel made
20: 9 W he said unto the messengers of
22:34 of the harness: w he said unto the driver
2Ki 4:23 And he said, W wilt thou go to him to H4069
31 voice, nor hearing. W he went again to
5: 7 of his leprosy? w consider, I H3588+H389
8 the king, saying, W hast thou rent thy H4100
7: 7 W they arose and fled in the twilight,
9:11 him, *Is* all well? w came this mad *fellow* H4069
36 W they came again, and told him. And
17:26 W they spake to the king of Assyria,
19: 4 God hath heard: w lift up *thy* prayer for
1Ch 13:11 breach upon Uzza: w that place is called
19: 4 W Hanun took David's servants, and
21: 4 against Joab. W Joab departed, and
29:10 W David blessed the LORD before all the
2Ch 5: 3 W all the men of Israel assembled
19: 7 W now let the fear of the LORD be upon
22: 4 W he did evil in the sight of the LORD

2Ch 25:10 to go home again: w their anger was
15 W the anger of the LORD was kindled
28: 5 W the LORD his God delivered him into
29: 8 W the wrath of the LORD was upon
34 the burnt offerings: w their brethren the
33:11 W the LORD brought upon them the
Neh 2: 2 W the king said unto me, Why *is* thy
Est 3: 6 people of Mordecai: w Haman sought to
9:26 W they called these days H5921+H3651
Job 3:20 W is light given to him that is in H4100
10: 2 w thou contendest with me. H5921+H4100
18 W then hast thou brought me forth out H4100
13:14 W do I take my flesh in my H5921+H4100
24 W hidest thou thy face, and holdest me H4100
18: 3 W are we counted as beasts, *and* H4069
21: 7 W do the wicked live, become old, yea, H4069
32: 6 ye *are* very old; w I was afraid, H5921+H3651
33: 1 W, Job, I pray thee, hear my speeches, H199
42: 6 W I abhor *myself*, and repent H5921+H3651
Ps 10:13 W doth the wicked contemn H5921+H4100
44:24 W hidest thou thy face, *and* forgettest H4100
49: 5 W should I fear in the days of evil, H4100
79:10 W should the heathen say, Where *is* H4100
89:47 my time is: w hast thou made H5921+H4100
115: 2 W should the heathen say, Where *is* H4100
Prv 17:16 W *is there* a price in the hand H4100+H2088
Ecc 3:22 W I perceive that *there is* nothing better,
4: 2 W I praised the dead which are already
5: 6 it *was* an error: w should God be angry H4100
Isa 5: 4 not done in it? w, when I looked that H4069
10:12 W it shall come to pass, *that* when the
16:11 W my bowels shall sound like H5921+H3651
24:15 W glorify ye the LORD in the H5921+H3651
28:14 W hear the word of the LORD, ye H3651
29:13 W the Lord said, Forasmuch as this
30:12 W thus saith the Holy One of Israel, H3651
37: 4 God hath heard: w lift up *thy* prayer for
50: 2 W, when I came, *was there* no man? H4069
55: 2 W do ye spend money for *that which is* H4100
58: 3 W have we fasted, *say they*, and thou H4100
3 thou seest not? *w* have we afflicted our
63: 2 W *art thou* red in thine apparel, and H4069
Jer 2: 9 W I will yet plead with you, saith the H3651
29 W will ye plead with me? ye all have H4100
31 land of darkness? w say my people, We H4069
5: 6 W a lion out of the forest shall H5921+H3651
14 W thus saith the LORD God of hosts, H3651
19 when ye shall say, W doeth the H8478+H4100
12: 1 of *thy* judgments: W doth the way of H4069
1 the wicked prosper? *w* are all they happy
13:22 And if thou say in thine heart, W come H4069
16:10 unto thee, W hath the LORD H5921+H4100
20:18 W came I forth out of the womb to see
22: 8 neighbour, W hath the LORD H5921+H4100
28 *is* no pleasure? w are they cast out, he H4069
23:12 W their way shall be unto them as H3651
27:17 live: w should this city be laid waste? H4100
30: 6 travail with child? w do I see every man H4069
32: 3 him up, saying, W dost thou prophesy, H4069
37:15 W the princes were wroth with
40:15 shall know *it*: w should he slay thee, H4100
44: 6 W my fury and mine anger was poured
7 the God of Israel; W commit ye *this* H4100
46: 5 W have I seen them dismayed *and* H4069
49: 4 W gloriest thou in the valleys, thy H4100
51:52 W, behold, the days come, saith the H3651
Lam 3:39 W doth a living man complain, a man H4100
5:20 W dost thou forget us for ever, *and* H4100
Ezk 5:11 W, *as* I live, saith the Lord GOD; Surely, H3651
7:24 W I will bring the worst of the heathen,
13:20 W thus saith the Lord GOD; Behold, I H3651
16:35 W, O harlot, hear the word of the H3651
18:32 GOD: w turn *yourselves*, and live ye.
20:10 W I caused them to go forth out of the
25 W I gave them also statutes *that were*
30 W say unto the house of Israel, Thus H3651
21: 7 unto thee, W sighest thou? that H5981+H4100
23: 9 W I have delivered her into the hand of H3651
24: 6 W thus saith the Lord GOD; Woe to the H3651
33:25 W say unto them, Thus saith the Lord H3651
36:18 W I poured my fury upon them for the
43: 8 w I have consumed them in mine anger.
Dan 3: 8 W at that time certain H6903+H3606+H1836
4:27 W, O king, let my counsel be acceptable H3861
6: 9 W king Darius signed H3606+H1836+H6903
8:26 was told *is* true: w shut thou up the
10:20 Then said he, Knowest thou w I come H4100
Joel 2:17 rule over them: w should they say H4100
Jna 1:14 W they cried unto the LORD, and said,

Hab 1:13 look on iniquity: w lookest thou upon H4100
Mal 2:14 Yet ye say, W? Because the LORD hath H4100
15 of the spirit. And w one? That he might H4100
Mt 6:30 W, if God so clothe the grass of the field, G1161
7:20 W by their fruits ye shall know G686+G1065
9: 4 W think ye evil in your hearts? G2443+G5101
12:12 than a sheep? W it is lawful to do well G5620
31 W I say unto you, All manner G1223+G5124
14:31 little faith, w didst thou doubt? G1519+G5101
18: 8 W if thy hand or thy foot offend thee, G1161
19: 6 W they are no more twain, but one G5620
23:31 W ye be witnesses unto yourselves, G5620
34 W, behold, I send unto you G1223+G5124
24:26 W if they shall say unto you, Behold, he G3767
26:50 him, Friend, w art thou come? G1909+G3739
27: 8 W that field was called, The field of G1352
Lk 7: 7 W neither thought I myself worthy to G1352
47 W I say unto thee, Her sins, G3739+G5484
19:23 W then gavest not thou my money into G1302
Jn 9:27 and ye did not hear: w would ye hear *it* G5101
Act 1:21 W of these men which have companied G3767
6: 3 W, brethren, look ye out among you G3767
10:21 *is* the cause w ye are come? G1223+G3739
13:35 W he saith also in another *psalm*, G1352
15:19 W my sentence is, that we trouble not G1352
19:32 w they were come together. G5101+G1752
38 W if Demetrius, and the craftsmen G3767
20:26 W I take you to record this day, that I G1352
22:24 know w they cried so G1223+G3739+G156
30 the certainty w he was accused of the G5101
23:28 the cause w they accused him, G1223+G3739
24:26 might loose him: w he sent for him the G1352
25:26 unto my lord. W I have brought him G1352
26: 3 w I beseech thee to hear me patiently. G1352
27:25 W, sirs, be of good cheer: for I believe G1352
34 W I pray you to take *some* meat: for G1352
Ro 1:24 W God also gave them up to G1352
5:12 W, as by one man sin entered G1223+G5124
7: 4 W, my brethren, ye also are become G5620
12 W the law *is* holy, and the G5620
9:32 W? Because *they sought it* not by faith, G1302
13: 5 W *ye* must needs be subject, not only G1352
15: 7 W receive ye one another, as Christ G1352
1Co 4:16 W I beseech you, be ye followers of me. G3767
8:13 W, if meat make my brother to offend, I G1355
10:12 W let him that thinketh he standeth G5620
14 W, my dearly beloved, flee from G1355
11:27 W whosoever shall eat this bread, and G5620
33 W, my brethren, when ye come together G5620
12: 3 W I give you to understand, that no G1352
14:13 W let him that speaketh in an G1355
22 W tongues are for a sign, not to them G5620
39 W, brethren, covet to prophesy, and G5620
2Co 2: 8 W I beseech you that ye would confirm G1352
5: 9 W we labour, that, whether present or G1352
16 W henceforth know we no man after G5620
6:17 W come out from among them, and be G1352
7:12 W, though I wrote unto you, *I did it* not G686
8:24 W shew ye to them, and before the G3767
11:11 W? because I love you not? God G1302
Gal 3:19 W then *serveth* the law? It was added G5101
24 W the law was our schoolmaster *to* G5620
4: 7 W thou art no more a servant, but a G5620
Eph 1:15 W I also, after I heard of your G1223+G5124
2:11 W remember, that ye *being* in time G1352
3:13 W I desire that ye faint not at my G1352
4: 8 W he saith, When he ascended up on G1352
25 W putting away lying, speak every G1352
5:14 W he saith, Awake thou that sleepest, G1352
17 W be ye not unwise, but G1223+G5124
6:13 W take unto you the whole G1223+G5124
Php 2: 9 W God also hath highly exalted him, G1352
12 W, my beloved, as ye have always G5620
Col 2:20 W if ye be dead with Christ from the G3767
1Th 2:18 W we would have come unto you, even G1352
3: 1 W when we could no longer forbear, G1352
4:18 W comfort one another with these G5620
5:11 W comfort yourselves together, and G1352
2Th 1:11 W also we pray always for you, G1519+G3739
2Ti 1: 6 W I put thee in remembrance G1223+G3739
Tit 1:13 This witness is true. W rebuke G1223+G3739
Phlm 8 W, though I might be much bold in G1352
Heb 2:17 W in all things it behoved him to be G3606
3: 1 W, holy brethren, partakers of the G3606
7 W (as the Holy Ghost saith, To day if G1352
10 W I was grieved with that generation, G1352
7:25 W he is able also to save them to the G3606
8: 3 and sacrifices: w *it is* of necessity that G3606
10: 5 W when he cometh into the world, he G1352

Heb 11:16 is, an heavenly: w God is not ashamed G1352
12: 1 W seeing we also are compassed about G5105
12 W lift up the hands which hang down, G1352
28 W we receiving a kingdom which G1352
13:12 W Jesus also, that he might sanctify the G1352
Jas 1:19 W, my beloved brethren, let every man G5620
21 W lay apart all filthiness and G1352
4: 6 But he giveth more grace. W he saith, G1352
1Pt 1:13 W gird up the loins of your mind, be G1352
2: 1 W laying aside all malice, and all guile, G3767
6 W also it is contained in the scripture, G1352
4:19 W let them that suffer according to the G5620
2Pt 1:10 W the rather, brethren, give diligence G1352
12 W I will not be negligent to put you G1352
3:14 W, beloved, seeing that ye look for such G1352
1Jn 3:12 brother. And w slew he him? G5484+G5101
3Jn 10 W, if I come, I will remember G1223+G5124
Rev 17: 7 And the angel said unto me, W didst G1302

WHEREIN
Gen 1:30 upon the earth, w *there is* life, *I have* H834
6:17 to destroy all flesh, w *is* the breath of life, H834
7:15 two of all flesh, w *is* the breath of life. H834
17: 8 seed after thee, the land w thou art a
21:23 and to the land w thou hast sojourned. H834
28: 4 inherit the land w thou art a stranger,
36: 7 and the land w they were strangers
37: 1 And Jacob dwelt in the land w his father
Ex 1:14 field: all their service, w they made them H834
6: 4 their pilgrimage, w they were strangers. H834
12: 7 post of the houses, w they shall eat it. H834
18:11 w they dealt proudly *he was* above them. H834
20 them the way w they must walk, and
22:27 for his skin: w shall he sleep? and H4100
33:16 For w shall it be known here that I and H4100
Lev 4:23 Or if his sin, w he hath sinned, come to H834
5:18 his ignorance w he erred and wist *it* H834
6:28 But the earthen vessel w it is sodden H834
11:32 vessel *it be*, w *any* work is done, it H834
36 Nevertheless a fountain or pit, w *there is*
13:46 All the days w the plague *shall be* in him H834
52 any thing of skin, w the plague is: for it H834
54 wash *the thing* w the plague *is*, and he H834
57 shalt burn that w the plague *is* with fire. H834
18: 3 After the doings of the land of Egypt, w H834
Nu 12:11 not the sin upon us, w we have done H834
11 done foolishly, and w we have sinned. H834
19: 2 without spot, w *is* no blemish, *and* upon H834
31:10 And they burnt all their cities w they
33:55 and shall vex you in the land w ye dwell. H834
35:33 So ye shall not pollute the land w ye *are*: H834
34 ye shall inhabit, w I dwell: for I the H8432
Dt 8: 9 A land w thou shalt eat bread without H834
15 wilderness, *w were* fiery serpents,
12: 2 Ye shall utterly destroy all the places, w H834
7 w the LORD thy God hath blessed thee. H834
17: 1 bullock, or sheep, w is blemish, *or* any H834
28:52 walls come down, w thou trustedst, H2004
Jos 8:24 in the wilderness w they chased them, H834
10:27 into the cave w they had been H834+H8033
22:19 of the LORD, w the LORD'S H834+H8033
33 w the children of Reuben and Gad dwelt. H834
24:17 us in all the way w we went, and among H834
Jdg 16: 5 him, and see w his great strength *lieth*, H4100
6 me, I pray thee, w thy great strength H4100
15 not told me w thy great strength *lieth*. H4100
18: 6 before the LORD *is* your way w ye go. H834
1Sa 6:15 that *was* with it, w the jewels of gold H834
14:38 and see w this sin hath been this day. H4100
2Sa 7: 7 In all *the places* w I have walked with all H834
1Ki 2:26 afflicted in all w my father was afflicted.
8:21 for the ark, w *is* the covenant H834+H8033
36 them the good way w they should walk, H834
50 transgressions w they have transgressed H834
13:31 me in the sepulchre w the man of God *is* H834
2Ki 12: 2 w Jehoiada the priest instructed him. H834
14: 6 of the law of Moses, w the LORD H834
17:29 in their cities w they dwelt. H834+H8033
18:19 What confidence *is* this w thou trustest? H834
23:23 year of king Josiah, *w* this passover was
2Ch 3: 3 Now these *are the things* w Solomon was
6:11 And in it have I put the ark, w *is* H834+H8033
27 the good way, w they should walk; and H834
8: 1 of twenty years, w Solomon had built the H834
33:19 and the places w he built high places, H834
Ezr 5: 7 They sent a letter unto him, w was H1459
Neh 6: 6 W *was* written, It is reported among the
9:12 them light in the way w they should go.
19 light, and the way w they should go. H834
Neh 13:15 *them* in the day w they sold victuals. H834
Est 5:11 and all *the things* w the king had H834
8:11 W the king granted the Jews which *were* H834
9:22 As the days w the Jews rested from their H834
Job 3: 3 Let the day perish w I was born, and the
6:16 reason of the ice, *and* w the snow is hid:
24 cause me to understand w I have erred. H4100
38:26 *is; on* the wilderness, w *there is* no man;
Ps 74: 2 this mount Zion, w thou hast dwelt.
90:15 Make us glad according to the days *w*
15 us, *and* the years w we have seen evil.
104:20 Thou makest darkness, and it is night: w
25 *So is* this great and wide sea, w *are* H8033
142: 3 path. In the way w I walked have they H2098
143: 8 to know the way w I should walk; for I H2098
Ecc 2:19 over all my labour w I have laboured,
19 laboured, and w I have shewed myself
22 w he hath laboured under the sun?
3: 9 he that worketh in that w he laboureth? H834
8: 9 the sun: *there is* a time w one man ruleth H834
Isa 2:22 nostrils: for w is he to be accounted of? H4100
14: 3 bondage w thou wast made to serve, H834
33:21 *and* streams; w shall go no galley with
36: 4 What confidence *is* this w thou trustest? H834
47:12 of thy sorceries, w thou hast laboured H834
65:12 and did choose *that* w I delighted not. H834
Jer 5:17 fenced cities, w thou trustedst, H834+H2004
7:14 by my name, w ye trust, and unto the H834
12: 5 the land of peace, *w* thou trustedst, *they*
16:19 vanity, and *things w there is* no profit.
20:14 Cursed *be* the day w I was born: let not H834
14 day w my mother bare me be blessed. H834
22:28 idol? *is he* a vessel w *is* no pleasure?
31: 9 waters in a straight way, w they shall not
36:14 thine hand the roll w thou hast read in H834
41: 9 Now the pit w Ishmael had cast all the H834
42: 3 shew us the way w we may walk, and the H834
48:38 vessel w *is* no pleasure, saith the LORD.
51:43 a wilderness, a land w no man dwelleth, H834
Ezk 20:34 of the countries w ye are scattered, with H834
41 out of the countries w ye have been
43 all your doings, w ye have been defiled; H834
23:19 days of her youth, w she had played the H834
26:10 enter into a city w is made a breach.
32: 6 thy blood the land w thou swimmest,
37:23 dwellingplaces, w they have sinned, and H834
25 Jacob my servant, w your fathers have H834
42:14 lay their garments w they minister; for H834
44:19 off their garments w they ministered, H834
Hos 2:13 days of Baalim, w she burned incense H834
8: 8 the Gentiles as a vessel w *is* no pleasure.
Jna 4:11 that great city, w are more than sixscore
Mic 6: 3 unto thee? and w have I wearied thee? H4100
Zep 3:11 ashamed for all thy doings, w thou hast H834
Zec 9:11 prisoners out of the pit w *is* no water.
Mal 1: 2 LORD. Yet ye say, W hast thou loved H4100
6 ye say, W have we despised thy name? H4100
7 altar; and ye say, W have we polluted H4100
2:17 words. Yet ye say, W have we wearied H4100
3: 7 hosts. But ye said, W shall we return? H4100
8 me. But ye say, W have we robbed H4100
Mt 11:20 the cities w most of his mighty G1722+G3739
25:13 w the Son of man cometh. G1722+G3739
Mk 2: 4 bed w the sick of the palsy lay. G1909+G3739
Lk 1: 4 w thou hast been instructed. G4012+G3739
25 me in the days w he looked on *me*, to G3739
11:22 his armour w he trusted, and G1909+G3739
23:53 in stone, w never man before was laid. G3757
Jn 19:41 w was never man yet laid. G1722+G3739
Act 2: 8 own tongue, w we were born? G1722+G3739
7: 4 into this land, w ye now dwell. G1519+G3739
10:12 W were all manner of G1722+G3739
Ro 2: 1 judgest: for w thou judgest G1722+G3739
5: 2 into this grace w we stand, and G1722+G3739
7: 6 being dead w we were held; G1722+G3739
1Co 7:20 in the same calling w he was called. G3739
24 Brethren, let every man, w he G1722+G3739
15: 1 have received, and w ye stand; G1722+G3739
2Co 11:12 occasion; that w they glory, G1722+G3739
12:13 For what is it w ye were inferior to G3739
Eph 1: 6 of his grace, w he hath made G1722+G3739
8 W he hath abounded toward us in all G3739
2: 2 W in time past ye walked G1722+G3739
5:18 And be not drunk with wine, w G1722+G3739
Php 4:10 again; w ye were also careful, G1909+G3739
Col 2:12 Buried with him in baptism, w G1722+G3739
2Ti 2: 9 W I suffer trouble, as an evil G1722+G3739
Heb 6:17 W God, willing more G1722+G3739
9: 2 made; the first, w *was* the G1722+G3739
Heb 9: 4 with gold, w *was* the golden G1722+G3739
1Pt 1: 6 W ye greatly rejoice, though G1722+G3739
3:20 was a preparing, w few, that is, G1519+G3739
4: 4 W they think it strange that ye G1722+G3739
5:12 true grace of God w ye stand. G1519+G3739
2Pt 3:12 the day of God, w the heavens G1223+G3739
13 w dwelleth righteousness. G1722+G3739
Rev 2:13 in those days w Antipas *was* G1722+G3739
18:19 great city, w were made rich G1722+G3739

WHEREINSOEVER
2Co 11:21 Howbeit w any is bold, G1722+G3739+G302

WHEREINTO
Lev 11:33 vessel, w *any* of them H834+H413+H8432
Nu 14:24 into the land w he went; and his H824+H8432
Jn 6:22 save that one w his disciples were G1519

WHEREOF
Gen 3:11 eaten of the tree, w I commanded thee H834
Lev 6:30 And no sin offering, w *any* of the blood H834
13:24 Or if there be *any* flesh, in the skin w
27: 9 And if *it be* a beast, w men bring an H834
Nu 5: 3 not their camps, in the midst w I dwell. H834
7:19 the weight w *was* an hundred and
25 the weight w *was* an hundred and
37 the weight w *was* an hundred and
49 the weight w *was* an hundred and
61 the weight w *was* an hundred and
67 the weight w *was* an hundred and
73 the weight w *was* an hundred and
79 the weight w *was* an hundred and
21:16 that *is* the well w the LORD spake unto H834
Dt 13: 2 come to pass, w he spake unto thee, H834
28:27 the itch, w thou canst not be healed. H834
68 ships, by the way w I spake unto thee, H834
Jos 14:12 Now therefore give me this mountain, w H834
20: 2 cities of refuge, w I spake unto you by H834
22: 9 their possession, w they were possessed, H834
1Sa 10:16 w Samuel spake, he told him not. H834
13: 2 *men* of Israel; *w* two thousand were
2Sa 12:30 head, the weight w *was* a talent of gold
2Ki 13:14 sick of his sickness w he died. And Joash H834
17:12 For they served idols, w the LORD had H834
2Ch 3: 8 house, the length w *was* according to the
6:20 upon the place w thou hast said that H834
24:14 king and Jehoiada, w were made vessels
33: 4 of the LORD, w the LORD had said, H834
Neh 12:31 *that gave* thanks, w *one* went on the
Job 6: 4 me, the poison w drinketh up my spirit: H834
Ps 46: 4 *There is* a river, the streams w shall
57: 6 w they are fallen *themselves*. Selah.
126: 3 done great things for us; *w* we are glad.
Ecc 1:10 Is there *any* thing w it may be said, See,
Song 4: 2 up from the washing; w every one bear
6: 6 from the washing, w every one beareth
Jer 32:36 this city, w ye say, It shall be delivered H834
43 And fields shall be bought in this land, w H834
42:16 and the famine, w ye were afraid, shall H834
Ezk 32:15 be destitute of that w it was full, when I
39: 8 GOD; this *is* the day w I have spoken. H834
Dan 9: 2 of the years, w the word of the LORD H834
Hos 2:12 and her fig trees, w she hath said, These H834
Lk 23:14 touching those things w ye accuse him: G3739
Act 2:32 This Jesus hath God raised up, w we all G3739
3:15 from the dead; w we are witnesses. G3739
17:19 this new doctrine, w thou speakest, *is*? G5259
31 whom he hath ordained; *w* he hath given
21:24 know that those things, w they were G3739
24: 8 of all these things, w we accuse him. G3739
13 Neither can they prove the things w G4012
25:11 of these things w these accuse me, no G3739
26: 2 the things w I am accused of the Jews: G3739
Ro 4: 2 he hath *w* to glory; but not before God.
6:21 in those things w ye are now ashamed? G3739
15:17 I have therefore w I may glory through
1Co 7: 1 Now concerning the things w ye wrote G3739
2Co 9: 5 your bounty, w ye had notice before,
Eph 3: 7 W I was made a minister, according to G3739
Php 3: 4 w he might trust in the flesh, I more:
Col 1: 5 for you in heaven, w ye heard before in G3739
23 heaven; w I Paul am made a minister; G3739
25 W I am made a minister, according to G3739
1Ti 1: 7 what they say, nor w they affirm. G4012
6: 4 strifes of words, w cometh envy, strife, G1537
Heb 2: 5 the world to come, w we speak. G4012
10:15 *W* the Holy Ghost also is a witness to us:
12: 8 But if ye be without chastisement, w all G3739
13:10 We have an altar, w they have no right G1537

1Jn 4: 3 of antichrist, w ye have heard that G3739

WHEREON

Gen 28:13 of Isaac: the land w thou liest, to H834+H5921
Ex 3: 5 the place w thou standest *is* holy ground. H834
8:21 and also the ground w they *are*. H834+H5921
Lev 6:27 wash that w it was sprinkled H834+H5921
15: 4 Every bed, w he lieth that hath H834+H5921
4 w he sitteth, shall be unclean. H834+H5921
6 on *any* thing w he sat that hath H834+H5921
17 and every skin, w is the seed of H834+H5921
23 on any thing w she sitteth, when H834+H5921
24 bed w he lieth shall be unclean. H834+H5921
26 Every bed w she lieth all the H834+H5921
Dt 11:24 Every place w the soles of your feet shall H834
Jos 5:15 for the place w thou standest *is* H834+H5921
14: 9 Surely the land w thy feet have trodden H834
1Sa 6:18 *stone of* Abel, w they set down H834+H5921
2Ch 4:19 tables w the shewbread *was set;* H834+H5921
32:10 of Assyria, W do ye trust, that H5921+H4100
Est 7: 8 upon the bed w Esther *was*. Then said
Job 24:23 *Though* it be given him *to be* in safety, w
Song 4: 4 an armoury, w there hang a H5921+H4100
Isa 36: 6 on Egypt; w if a man lean, it H834+H5921
Ezk 37:20 And the sticks w thou writest H834+H5921
Mk 11: 2 a colt tied, w never man sat; G1909+G3739
Lk 4:29 of the hill w their city was G1909+G3739
5:25 and took up that w he lay, and G1909+G3739
19:30 a colt tied, w yet never man G1909+G3739
Jn 4:38 I sent you to reap that w ye bestowed G3739

WHERESOEVER

Lev 13:12 even to his foot, w the priest looketh; H3605
2Ki 8: 1 and sojourn w thou canst sojourn: H834
12: 5 w any breach shall be found. H834+H8033
1Ch 17: 6 W I have walked with all Israel, H3605+H834
Jer 40: 5 the people: or go w it seemeth H413+H3605
Dan 2:38 And w the children of men dwell, the H3606
Mt 24:28 For w the carcase is, there will G3699+G1437
26:13 Verily I say unto you, W this G3699+G1437
Mk 9:18 And w he taketh him, he teareth G3699+G302
14: 9 Verily I say unto you, W this G3699+G302
14 And w he shall go in, say ye to G3699+G1437
Lk 17:37 said unto them, W the body *is*, thither G3699

WHERETO

Job 30: 2 Yea, w *might* the strength of their H4100
Isa 55:11 it shall prosper *in the thing* w I sent it. H834
Php 3:16 Nevertheless, w we have G1519+G3739

WHEREUNTO

Nu 36: 3 of the tribe w they are received: so H834
4 of the tribe w they are received: so H834
Dt 4:26 from off the land w ye go over Jordan to H834
2Ch 8:11 holy, w the ark of the LORD hath come. H834
Est 10: 2 of Mordecai, w the king advanced him,
Ps 71: 3 Be thou my strong habitation, w I may
Jer 22:27 But to the land w they desire to return, H834
Ezk 5: 9 not done, and w I will not do any more H834
20:29 the high place w ye go? And the H834+H8033
Mt 11:16 But w shall I liken this generation? It is G5101
Mk 4:30 And he said, W shall we liken the G5101
Lk 7:31 And the Lord said, W then shall I liken G5101
13:18 of God like? and w shall I resemble it? G5101
20 And again he said, W shall I liken the G5101
Act 5:24 doubted of them w this would grow. G5101
13: 2 Saul for the work w I have called them. G3739
27: 8 havens; nigh w was the city *of* Lasea. G3739
Gal 4: 9 w ye desire again to be in bondage? G3739
Col 1:29 W I also labour, striving G1519+G3739
2Th 2:14 W he called you by our gospel, G1519+G3739
1Ti 2: 7 W I am ordained a preacher, G1519+G3739
4: 6 of good doctrine, w thou hast attained. G3739
6:12 on eternal life, w thou art also G1519+G3739
2Ti 1:11 W I am appointed a preacher, G1519+G3739
1Pt 2: 8 w also they were appointed. G1519+G3739
3:21 The like figure w *even* baptism doth G3739
2Pt 1:19 word of prophecy; w ye do well that ye G3739

WHEREUPON

Lev 11:35 And every *thing* w *any part* of H834+H5921
Jdg 16:26 may feel the pillars w the house H834+H5921
1Ki 7:48 of gold, w the shewbread *was*, H834+H5921
12:28 W the king took counsel, and made two
2Ch 12: 6 W the princes of Israel and the king
Job 38: 6 W are the foundations thereof H5921+H4100
Ezk 9: 3 the cherub, w he was, to the H834+H5921
23:41 before it, w thou hast set mine H5921
24:25 eyes, and that w they set their minds,

Ezk 40:41 eight tables, w they slew *their sacrifices*. H413
42 and one cubit high: w also they laid the H413
Am 4: 7 piece w it rained not withered. H834+H5921
Mt 14: 7 W he promised with an oath to give her G3606
Act 24:18 W certain Jews from Asia G1722+G3739
26:12 W as I went to Damascus with G1722+G3739
19 W, O king Agrippa, I was not G3606
Heb 9:18 W neither the first *testament* was G3606

WHEREWITH

Gen 27:41 of the blessing w his father blessed him: H834
Ex 3: 9 w the Egyptians oppress them.
4:17 rod in thine hand, w thou shalt do signs. H834
16:32 may see the bread w I have fed you in H834
17: 5 and thy rod, w thou smotest the river, H834
29:33 And they shall eat those things w the H834
Nu 3:31 of the sanctuary w they minister, and
48 And thou shalt give the money, w the
4: 9 vessels thereof, w they minister unto it: H834
12 of ministry, w they minister in the H834
14 all the vessels thereof, w they minister H834
16:39 brasen censers, w they that were burnt H834
25:18 For they vex you with their wiles, w they H834
30: 4 vow, and her bond w she hath bound her H834
4 w she hath bound her soul shall stand. H834
5 or of her bonds w she hath bound her H834
6 out of her lips, w she bound her soul; H834
7 bonds w she bound her soul shall stand. H834
8 with her lips, w she bound her soul, H834
9 that is divorced, w they have bound their H834
11 bond w she bound her soul shall stand. H834
35:17 throwing a stone, w he may die, and he H834
18 weapon of wood, w he may die, and he H834
23 Or with any stone, w a man may die, H834
Dt 9:19 hot displeasure, w the LORD was wroth H834
15:14 winepress: *of that* w the LORD thy God H834
22:12 of thy vesture, w thou coverest *thyself*. H834
28:53 w thine enemies shall distress thee: H834
55 in the straitness, w thine enemies shall H834
57 siege and straitness, w thine enemy shall H834
67 fear of thine heart w thou shalt fear, and H834
33: 1 And this *is* the blessing, w Moses the H834
Jos 8:26 For Joshua drew not his hand back, w he H834
Jdg 6:15 And he said unto him, Oh my Lord, w H4100
9: 4 of Baal-berith, w Abimelech hired vain
9 I leave my fatness, w by me they honour H834
38 *is* now thy mouth, w thou saidst, Who *is* H834
16: 6 *lieth*, and w thou mightest be bound H4100
10 I pray thee, w thou mightest be bound. H4100
13 told me lies: tell me w thou mightest be H4100
1Sa 6: 2 tell us w we shall send it to his place. H4100
8: 8 even unto this day, w they have forsaken
29: 4 to us: for w should he reconcile H4100
2Sa 13:15 so that the hatred w he hated her *was* H834
15 than the love w he had loved her. And H834
21: 3 I do for you? and w shall I make the H4100
1Ki 8:59 And let these my words, w I have made H834
15:22 and the timber thereof, w Baasha had H834
26 and in his sin w he made Israel to sin. H834
30 by his provocation w he provoked the H834
34 and in his sin w he made Israel to sin. H834
16:26 and in his sin w he made Israel to sin, H834
21:22 the provocation w thou hast provoked H834
22:22 And the LORD said unto him, W? And H4100
2Ki 13:12 did, and his might w he fought against H834
21:16 beside his sin w he made Judah to sin, H834
23:26 of his great wrath, w his anger was H834
25:14 brass w they ministered, took they away. H834
1Ch 18: 8 very much brass, w Solomon made the
2Ch 2:17 the numbering w David his father had H834
16: 6 and the timber thereof, w Baasha was H834
18:20 him. And the LORD said unto him, W? H4100
35:21 against the house w I have war: for God
Neh 9:34 w thou didst testify against them. H834
Job 15: 3 or with speeches w he can do no good?
Ps 79:12 w they have reproached thee, O Lord. H834
89:51 W thine enemies have reproached, O H834
51 O LORD; w they have reproached H834
93: 1 with strength, *w* he hath girded himself:
109:19 for a girdle w he is girded continually.
119:42 So shall I have w to answer him that H1697
129: 7 W the mower filleth not his hand; nor he
Song 3:11 with the crown w his mother crowned
Isa 28:12 To whom he said, This *is* the rest *w* ye
37: 6 thou hast heard, w the servants of the H834
Jer 18:10 the good, w I said I would benefit them. H834
19: 9 and straitness, w their enemies, and H834
21: 4 *are* in your hands, w ye fight against the H834
33:16 this *is the name* w she shall be called, H834

Jer 52:18 brass w they ministered, took they away. H834
Lam 1:12 is done unto me, w the LORD hath H834
Ezk 13:12 *is* the daubing w ye have daubed *it*? H834
20 your pillows, w ye there hunt the souls H834
16:19 oil, and honey, w I fed thee, thou hast
29:20 *for* his labour w he served against it, H834
32:16 This *is* the lamentation w they shall
36:18 and for their idols *w* they had polluted it:
40:42 the instruments w they slew the burnt
Dan 2: 1 dreamed dreams, w his spirit was
Mic 6: 6 W shall I come before the LORD, *and* H4100
Zec 14:12 And this shall be the plague w the LORD H834
18 be the plague, w the LORD will smite H834
Mal 2: 5 to him *for* the fear w he feared me, and H834
Mt 5:13 his savour, w shall it be salted? G1722+G5101
Mk 3:28 w soever they shall blaspheme: G1722+G5101
9:50 his saltness, w will ye season G1722+G5101
Lk 14:34 savour, w shall it be seasoned? G1722+G5101
17: 8 him, Make ready w I may sup, and gird G5101
Jn 13: 5 *them* with the towel w he was girded. G3739
17:26 *it*: that the love w thou hast loved me G3739
Ro 14:19 and things w one may edify another. G1519
2Co 1: 4 w we ourselves are comforted of God. G3739
7: 7 the consolation w he was comforted in G3739
10: 2 that confidence, w I think to be bold G3739
Gal 5: 1 Stand fast therefore in the liberty w G3739
Eph 2: 4 mercy, for his great love w he loved us, G3739
4: 1 worthy of the vocation w ye are called, G3739
6:16 of faith, w ye shall be able G1722+G3739
1Th 3: 9 w we joy for your sakes before our God; G3739
Heb 10:29 of the covenant, w he was G1722+G3739

WHEREWITHAL

Ps 119: 9 W shall a young man cleanse his way?
Mt 6:31 we drink? or, W shall we be clothed? G5101

WHET

Dt 32:41 If I w my glittering sword, and mine H8150
Ps 7:12 If he turn not, he will w his sword; he H3913
64: 3 Who w their tongue like a sword, *and* H8150
Ecc 10:10 If the iron be blunt, and he do not w H7043

WHETHER

Gen 18:21 I will go down now, and see w they have
24:21 his peace, to wit w the LORD had made
27:21 son, w thou *be* my very son Esau or not.
31:39 it, *w* stolen by day, or stolen by night. H1589
37:14 Go, I pray thee, see w it be well with thy
32 know now w it *be* thy son's coat or no.
42:16 may be proved, w *there be any* truth in
43: 6 to tell the man w ye had yet a brother? H5750
Ex 4:18 in Egypt, and see w they be yet alive. H5750
12:19 w he be a stranger, or born in the land.
16: 4 them, w they will walk in my law, or no.
19:13 or shot through; w *it be* beast or man, it H518
21:31 W he have gored a son, or have gored a H176
22: 4 in his hand alive, w it be ox, or ass, or H5704
8 the judges, *to see* w he have put his H3808
9 For all manner of trespass, *w it be* for
34:19 thy cattle, *w* ox or sheep, *that is male*.
Lev 3: 1 he offer *it* of the herd; *w it be* a male or H518
5: 1 and *is* a witness, w he hath seen or H176
2 Or if a soul touch any unclean thing, w *it* H176
7:26 no manner of blood, *w it be* of fowl or of
11:32 it shall be unclean; *w it be* any vessel of
35 shall be unclean; *w it be* oven, or ranges
13:47 plague of leprosy is in, *w it be* a woollen
48 W *it be* in the warp, or woof; of linen, or
48 w in a skin, or in any thing made of skin; H176
52 He shall therefore burn that garment, w H176
55 inward, w it *be* bare within or without. H176
15: 3 in his issue: w his flesh run with his
16:29 and do no work at all, *w it be* one of your
17:15 torn *with beasts*, *w it be* one of your own
18: 9 of thy mother, *w she be* born at home,
22:28 And *w it be* cow or ewe, ye shall not kill
27:12 And the priest shall value it, w it be good H996
14 shall estimate it, w it be good or bad: as H996
26 it; *w it be* ox, or sheep: it *is* the LORD'S. H518
30 And all the tithe of the land, *w* of the
33 He shall not search w it be good or bad, H996
Nu 9:21 they journeyed: *w it was* by day or by H176
22 Or *w it were* two days, or a month, or a H176
11:23 thou shalt see now w my word shall
13:18 w they *be* strong or weak, few or many;
19 *is* that they dwell in, w it *be* good or bad;
19 dwell in, w in tents, or in strong holds;
20 And what the land *is*, w it *be* fat or lean,
20 it *be* fat or lean, w there be wood therein,

W

Nu 15:30 presumptuously, *w he be* born in the H4480
18:15 unto the LORD, *w it be* of men or beasts,
Dt 4:32 unto the other, w there hath been *any*
8: 2 *was* in thine heart, w thou wouldest keep
13: 3 you, to know w ye love the LORD your H518
18: 3 offer a sacrifice, *w it be* ox or sheep; and
22: 6 or on the ground, *w they be* young ones,
24:14 *that is* poor and needy, *w he be* of thy
Jos 24:15 ye will serve; w the gods which your H518
Jdg 2:22 That through them I may prove Israel, w
3: 4 Israel by them, to know w they would H4100
9: 2 the men of Shechem, W *is* better for you,
18: 5 that we may know w our way which we H518
Ru 3:10 not young men, w poor or rich.
2Sa 12:22 I said, Who can tell w GOD will be H518
15:21 the king shall be, w in death or life, even H518
1Ki 20:18 And he said, W they be come out for H518
18 take them alive; or w they be come out H518
33 Now the men did diligently observe w H518
2Ki 1: 2 of Ekron w I shall recover of this disease.
2Ch 14:11 with thee to help, w with many, or with H996
15:13 be put to death, w small or great, H4480
13 small or great, w man or woman.
Ezr 2:59 and their seed, w they *were* of Israel: H518
5:17 *is* there at Babylon, w it be *so*, that a H2006
7:26 upon him, *w it be* unto death, or H2006
Neh 7:61 nor their seed, w they *were* of Israel. H518
Est 3: 4 they told Haman, to see w Mordecai's
4:11 that whosoever, w man or woman, shall
14 and who knoweth w thou art come to the H518
Job 34:29 can behold him? *w it be done* against a
33 will recompense it, w thou refuse, or H3588
33 thou refuse, or w thou choose; and not H3588
37:13 He causeth it to come, w for correction, H518
Prv 20:11 Even a child is known by his doings, w H518
11 his work *be* pure, and *w it be* right. H518
29: 9 man, w he rage or laugh, *there is* no rest.
Ecc 2:19 And who knoweth w he shall be a wise H518
5:12 The sleep of a labouring man *is* sweet, w H518
11: 6 thou knowest not w shall prosper, either H335
6 that, or w they both *shall be* alike good. H518
12:14 thing, *w it be* good, or whether *it be* evil. H518
14 thing, whether *it be* good, or *w it be* evil.
Song 6:11 valley, *and* to see w the vine flourished,
7:12 if the vine flourish, *w* the tender grape
Jer 30: 6 Ask ye now, and see w a man doth H518
42: 6 W *it be* good, or whether *it be* evil, we H518
6 Whether *it be* good, or *w it be* evil, we H518
Ezk 2: 5 And they, w they will hear, or whether H518
5 And they, whether they will hear, or w H518
7 words unto them, w they will hear, or H518
7 they will hear, or w they will forbear: for H518
3:11 saith the Lord GOD; w they will hear, or H518
11 they will hear, or w they will forbear. H518
44:31 of itself, or torn, w it be fowl or beast. H4480
Mt 9: 5 For w is easier, to say, *Thy* sins be *G5101*
21:31 W of them twain did the will of *his* *G5101*
23:17 *Ye* fools and blind: for w *is* greater, the *G5101*
19 *Ye* fools and blind: for w *is* greater, the *G5101*
26:63 us w thou be the Christ, the Son of God. *G1487*
27:21 said unto them, W of the twain will ye *G5101*
49 The rest said, Let be, let us see w Elias *G1487*
Mk 2: 9 W is it easier to say to the sick of the *G5101*
3: 2 And they watched him, w he would *G1487*
15:36 w Elias will come to take him down. *G1487*
44 him w he had been any while dead. *G1487*
Lk 3:15 of John, w he were the Christ, or not; *G3379*
5:23 W is easier, to say, Thy sins be forgiven *G5101*
6: 7 watched him, w he would heal on the *G1487*
14:28 cost, w he have *sufficient* to finish *it*? *G1487*
31 and consulteth w he be able with ten *G1487*
22:27 For w *is* greater, he that sitteth at meat, *G5101*
23: 6 he asked w the man were a Galilaean. *G1487*
Jn 7:17 know of the doctrine, w it be of God, or *G4220*
17 it be of God, or *w* I speak of myself. *G1487*
9:25 He answered and said, W he be a *G1487*
Act 1:24 shew w of these two thou hast chosen, *G3739*
4:19 and said unto them, W it be right in the *G1487*
5: 8 unto her, Tell me w ye sold the land for *G1487*
9: 2 any of this way, w they were men or *G1487*
10:18 And called, and asked w Simon, which *G1487*
17:11 daily, w those things were so. *G1487*
19: 2 as heard w there be any Holy Ghost. *G1487*
25:20 I asked *him* w he would go to *G1487*
Ro 6:16 to whom ye obey; w of sin unto death, *G2273*
12: 6 that is given to us, w prophecy, *let us* *G1535*
14: 8 For w we live, we live unto the Lord; *G1437*
8 the Lord; and w we die, we die unto *G1437*
8 die unto the Lord: w we live therefore, *G1437*
1Co 1:16 I know not w I baptized any other. *G1536*
3:22 W Paul, or Apollos, or Cephas, or the *G1535*
7:16 For what knowest thou, O wife, w thou *G1487*
16 O man, w thou shalt save *thy* wife? *G1487*
8: 5 that are called gods, w in heaven or in *G1535*
10:31 W therefore ye eat, or drink, or *G1535*
12:13 into one body, *w we be* Jews or *G1535*
13 Jews or Gentiles, *w we be* bond or free; *G1535*
26 And w one member suffer, all the *G1535*
13: 8 Charity never faileth: but w *there be* *G1535*
8 they shall fail; w *there be* tongues, they *G1535*
8 they shall cease; w *there be* knowledge, *G1535*
14: 7 life giving sound, w pipe or harp, *G1535*
15:11 Therefore *w it were* I or they, so we *G1535*
2Co 1: 6 And w we be afflicted, *it is* for your *G1535*
6 we also suffer: or w we be comforted, *it* *G1535*
2: 9 of you, w ye be obedient in all things. *G1487*
5: 9 Wherefore we labour, that, w present *G1535*
10 that he hath done, *w it be* good or bad. *G1535*
13 For w we be beside ourselves, *it is* to *G1535*
13 or w we be sober, *it is* for your cause. *G1535*
8:23 W *any do inquire of Titus, he is my* *G1535*
12: 2 years ago, (w in the body, I cannot *G1535*
2 I cannot tell; or w out of the body, I *G1535*
3 And I knew such a man, (w in the body, *G1535*
13: 5 Examine yourselves, w ye be in the *G1487*
Eph 6: 8 of the Lord, *w he be* bond or free. *G1535*
Php 1:18 every way, w in pretence, or in truth, *G1535*
20 in my body, *w it be* by life, or by death. *G1535*
27 of Christ: that w I come and see you, *G1535*
Col 1:16 and invisible, *w they be* thrones, or *G1535*
20 by him, *I say*, *w they be* things in earth, *G1535*
1Th 5:10 Who died for us, that, w we wake or *G1535*
2Th 2:15 been taught, w by word, or our epistle. *G1535*
1Pt 2:13 sake: w it be to the king, as supreme; *G1487*
1Jn 4: 1 but try the spirits w they are of God: *G1487*

WHICH See the Appendix.

WHILE
Gen 8:22 W the earth remaineth, seedtime and H5750
19:16 And w he lingered, the men laid hold
25: 6 away from Isaac his son, w he yet lived,
29: 9 And w he yet spake with them, Rachel
45: 1 stood no man with him, w Joseph made
46:29 neck, and wept on his neck a good w. H5750
Ex 33:22 And it shall come to pass, w my glory H5704
22 cover thee with my hand w I pass by: H5704
34:29 of his face shone w he talked with him.
Lev 4:27 ignorance, w he doeth *somewhat*
14:46 the house all the w that it is shut up H3117
26:43 enjoy her sabbaths, w she lieth desolate
Nu 11:33 And w the flesh *was* yet between their
15:32 And w the children of Israel were in the
23:15 offering, w I meet *the LORD* yonder.
25:11 children of Israel, w he was zealous for
Dt 19: 6 pursue the slayer, w his heart is hot, H3588
31:27 stiff neck: behold, w I am yet alive with
Jos 14:10 this word unto Moses, w *the children of* H834
Jdg 3:26 And Ehud escaped w they tarried, and H5704
11:26 W Israel dwelt in Heshbon and her H3478
14:17 the seven days, w their feast lasted: and
15: 1 But it came to pass within a w after, in H3117
16:27 that beheld w Samson made sport. H8123
1Sa 2:13 priest's servant came, w the flesh was in
7: 2 And it came to pass, w the ark abode in H3117
9:27 but stand thou still a w, that I may shew H3117
14:19 And it came to pass, w Saul talked unto H5704
20:14 And thou shalt not only w yet I live shew H518
22: 4 all the w that David was in the hold. H3117
25: 7 them, all the w they were in Carmel. H3117
16 and day, all the w we were with them H3117
27:11 his manner all the w he dwelleth in the H3117
2Sa 3: 6 And it came to pass, w there was war
35 David to eat meat w it was yet day,
7:19 house for a great w to come. And *is* this H7350
12:18 for they said, Behold, w the child was yet
21 weep for the child, *w it was* alive; but
22 And he said, W the child was yet alive, I
13:30 And it came to pass, w they were in the
15: 8 For thy servant vowed a vow w I abode
12 *even* from Giloh, w he offered sacrifices.
17: 2 And I will come upon him w he *is* weary
18:14 heart of Absalom, w he *was* yet alive in H5750
19:32 the king of sustenance w he lay at
24:13 thine enemies, w they pursue thee? or
1Ki 1:14 Behold, w thou yet talkest there with the
22 And, lo, w she yet talked with the king,
42 And w he yet spake, behold, Jonathan
1Ki 3:20 son from beside me, w thine handmaid
6: 7 heard in the house, w it was in building.
12: 6 Solomon his father w he yet lived, and
17: 7 And it came to pass after a w, that the H3117
18:45 And it came to pass in the mean w, that H3541
2Ki 6:33 And w he yet talked with them, behold,
1Ch 12: 1 to David to Ziklag, w he yet kept himself
17:17 house for a great w to come, and hast
21:12 before thy foes, w that the sword of thine
2Ch 10: 6 before Solomon his father w he yet lived,
14: 7 gates, and bars, *w* the land *is* yet before
15: 2 LORD *is* with you, w ye be with him; and
26:19 burn incense: and w he was wroth with
34: 3 For in the eighth year of his reign, w he
Neh 7: 3 the sun be hot; and w they stand by, let H5704
Est 2:21 In those days, w Mordecai sat in the
6:14 And w they *were* yet talking with him,
Job 1:16 W he *was* yet speaking, there came also
17 W he *was* yet speaking, there came also
18 W he *was* yet speaking, there came also
20:23 shall rain *it* upon him w he is eating.
24:24 They are exalted for a little w, but are H4592
27: 3 All the w my breath *is* in me, and the H5750
Ps 7: 2 *it* in pieces, w *there is* none to deliver.
31:13 *was* on every side: w they took counsel
37:10 For yet a little w, and the wicked *shall* H4592
39: 1 a bridle, w the wicked is before me. H5750
3 My heart was hot within me, w I was
42: 3 day and night, w they continually say
10 reproach me; w they say daily unto me,
49:18 Though w he lived he blessed his soul:
63: 4 Thus will I bless thee w I live: I will lift
69: 3 mine eyes fail w I wait for my God.
78:30 w their meat *was* yet in their mouths,
88:15 up: w I suffer thy terrors I am distracted.
104:33 praise to my God w I have my being. H5750
146: 2 W I live will I praise the LORD: I will
2 unto my God w I have any being. H5750
Prv 8:26 W as yet he had not made the earth, nor
19:18 Chasten thy son w there is hope, and H3588
31:15 She riseth also w it is yet night, and
Ecc 9: 3 *is* in their heart w they live, and after
12: 1 days of thy youth, w the evil days come H5750
2 W the sun, or the light, or the moon, or H5750
Song 1:12 W the king *sitteth* at his table, my H5750
Isa 10:25 For yet a very little w, and the H4592
28: 4 w it is yet in his hand he eateth it up.
29:17 *Is* it not yet a very little w, and Lebanon H4592
55: 6 Seek ye the LORD w he may be found,
6 be found, call ye upon him w he is near:
63:18 *it* but a little w: our adversaries have H4705
65:24 and w they are yet speaking, I will hear.
Jer 13:16 mountains, and, w ye look for light, he
15: 9 sun is gone down w *it was* yet day: she
33: 1 the second time, w he was yet shut up in
39:15 unto Jeremiah, w he was shut up in the
40: 5 Now w he was not yet gone back, *he*
51:33 her: yet a little w, and the time of her
Lam 1:19 ghost in the city, w they sought their H3588
Ezk 9: 8 And it came to pass, w they were slaying
Dan 4:31 W the word *was* in the king's mouth, H5751
Hos 1: 4 for yet a little *w*, and I will avenge the
Nah 1:10 For w *they be* folden together *as* H5704
10 *as* thorns, and w they are drunken *as*
Hag 2: 6 once, it *is* a little w, and I will shake the H4592
Zec 14:12 consume away w they stand upon their
Mt 1:20 But w he thought on these things,
9:18 W he spake these things unto them,
12:46 W he yet talked to the people, behold, *G2089*
13:21 but dureth for a w: for when tribulation *G4340*
25 But w men slept, his enemy came and *G1722*
29 But he said, Nay; lest w ye gather up the
14:22 side, w he sent the multitudes away. *G2193*
17: 5 W he yet spake, behold, a bright cloud
22 And w they abode in Galilee, Jesus said
22:41 W the Pharisees were gathered *G1161*
25: 5 W the bridegroom tarried, they all *G1161*
10 And w they went to buy, the bridegroom
26:36 Sit ye here, w I go and pray yonder. *G2193*
47 And w he yet spake, lo, Judas, one of *G2089*
73 And after a w came unto *him* they that *G3397*
27:63 that deceiver said, w he was yet alive,
28:13 by night, and stole him *away* w we slept.
Mk 1:35 rising up a great w before day, he went *G3029*
2:19 fast, w the bridegroom *G1722+G3739*
5:35 W he yet spake, there came from the *G2089*
6:31 place, and rest a w: for there were many *G3641*
45 Bethsaida, w he sent away the people. *G2193*
12:35 And Jesus answered and said, w he

Mk 14:32 his disciples, Sit ye here, w I shall pray. G2193
43 And immediately, w he yet spake,
15:44 him whether he had been any w dead. G3819
Lk 1: 8 And it came to pass, that w he G1722
2: 6 And so it was, that, w they were there, G1722
5:34 fast, w the bridegroom G1722+G3739
8:13 root, which for a w believe, and in time G2540
49 W he yet spake, there cometh one from
9:34 W he thus spake, there came a cloud, G1161
43 power of God. But w they wondered
10:13 they had a great w ago repented, sitting
14:32 Or else, w the other is yet a great way off,
18: 4 And he would not for a w: but G5550
22:47 And w he yet spake, behold a multitude,
58 And after a little w another saw him, G1024
60 w he yet spake, the cock crew.
24:15 And it came to pass, that, w they G1722
32 burn within us, w he talked with us by G5613
32 and w he opened to us the scriptures? G5613
41 And w they yet believed not for joy, G2089
44 I spake unto you, w I was yet with you,
51 And it came to pass, w he blessed G1722
Jn 4:31 In the mean w his disciples prayed G3342
5: 7 the pool: but w I am coming, G1722+G3739
7:33 them, Yet a little w am I with you, and G5550
9: 4 him that sent me, w it is day: the night G2193
12:35 them, Yet a little w is the light with you. G5550
35 with you. Walk w ye have the light, lest G2193
36 W ye have light, believe in the light, G2193
13:33 Little children, yet a little w I am with G3397
14:19 Yet a little w, and the world seeth me no G3397
16:16 A little w, and ye shall not see me: and G3397
16 and again, a little w, and ye shall see G3397
17 unto us, A little w, and ye shall not see G3397
17 and again, a little w, and ye shall see G3397
18 A little w? we cannot tell what he saith. G3397
19 of that I said, A little w, and ye shall not G3397
19 again, a little w, and ye shall see me? G3397
17:12 W I was with them in the world, I kept G3753
Act 1: 9 And when he had spoken these things, w
10 And w they looked stedfastly toward G5613
9:39 Dorcas made, w she was with them.
10:10 w they made ready, he fell into a trance,
17 Now w Peter doubted in himself what G5613
19 W Peter thought on the vision, the G1161
44 W Peter yet spake these words, the Holy
15: 7 know how that a good w ago God made G2250
17:16 Now w Paul waited for them at Athens,
18:18 *there* yet a good w, and then took his G2425
19: 1 And it came to pass, that, w G1722+G3588
20:11 and talked a long w, even till break of G1909
22:17 to Jerusalem, even w I prayed in the
24:20 in me, w I stood before the council,
25: 8 W he answered for himself, Neither
27:33 And w the day was coming on, G891+G3739
28: 6 had looked a great w, and saw no harm G1909
Ro 2:15 thoughts the mean w accusing or else
5: 8 w we were yet sinners, Christ died for us.
7: 3 So then if, w *her* husband liveth, she be
1Co 3: 4 For w one saith, I am of Paul; and G3752
8:13 I will eat no flesh w the world standeth,
16: 7 w with you, if the Lord permit. G5550+G5099
2Co 4:18 W we look not at the things which are G4648
Gal 2:17 But if, w we seek to be justified by Christ,
1Ti 5: 6 But she that liveth in pleasure is dead w
6:10 of all evil: which w some coveted after,
Heb 3:13 But exhort one another daily, w it is G891
15 W it is said, To day if ye will hear his G1722
9: 8 made manifest, w as the first tabernacle
17 no strength at all w the testator liveth. G3753
10:37 For yet a little w, and he that shall come G3397
1Pt 3: 2 W they behold your chaste conversation
20 in the days of Noah, w the ark was a
5:10 ye have suffered a w, make you perfect, G3641
2Pt 2:13 own deceivings w they feast with you;
19 W they promise them liberty, they

WHILES
Ezk 21:29 W they see vanity unto thee, whiles they
29 Whiles they see vanity unto thee, w they
44:17 come upon them, w they minister in the
Dan 5: 2 Belshazzar, w he tasted the wine,
9:20 And w I *was* speaking, and praying, H5750
21 Yea, w I *was* speaking in prayer, even H5750
Hos 7: 6 heart like an oven, w they lie in wait:
Mt 5:25 quickly, w thou art in the G2193+G3755
Act 5: 4 W it remained, was it not thine own?
2Co 9:13 W by the experiment of this

WHILST
Jdg 6:31 be put to death w *it is yet* morning: if H5704
Neh 6: 3 w I leave it, and come down to you? H834
Job 8:12 W *it is* yet in his greenness, *and* not cut H5704
32:11 reasons, w ye searched out what to say. H5704
Ps 141:10 Let the wicked fall into their own nets, w
Jer 17: 2 W their children remember their altars
2Co 5: 6 knowing that, w we are at home in the
7:15 toward you, w he remembereth the
Heb 10:33 Partly, w ye were made a gazingstock
33 and partly, w ye became companions

WHIP
Prv 26: 3 A w for the horse, a bridle for the ass, H7752
Nah 3: 2 The noise of a w, and the noise of the H7752

WHIPS
1Ki 12:11 you with w, but I will chastise you H7752
14 you with w, but I will chastise you H7752
2Ch 10:11 you with w, but I *will chastise you* H7752
14 you with w, but I *will chastise you* H7752

WHIRLETH
Ecc 1: 6 unto the north; it w about continually, H1980

WHIRLWIND
2Ki 2: 1 into heaven by a w, that Elijah went H5591
11 and Elijah went up by a w into heaven. H5591
Job 37: 9 Out of the south cometh the w: and cold H5492
38: 1 answered Job out of the w, and said, H5591
40: 6 LORD unto Job out of the w, and said, H5591
Ps 58: 9 with a w, both living, and in *his* wrath. H8175
Prv 1:27 cometh as a w; when distress and H5492
10:25 As the w passeth, so *is* the wicked no H5492
Isa 5:28 like flint, and their wheels like a w: H5492
17:13 and like a rolling thing before the w. H5492
40:24 the w shall take them away as stubble. H5591
41:16 away, and the w shall scatter them: H5591
66:15 his chariots like a w, to render his anger H5492
Jer 4:13 *shall be* as a w: his horses are swifter H5492
23:19 Behold, a w of the LORD is gone forth H5591
19 fury, even a grievous w: it shall fall H5591
25:32 and a great w shall be raised up from H5591
30:23 Behold, the w of the LORD goeth forth H5591
23 fury, a continuing w: it shall fall with H5591
Ezk 1: 4 And I looked, and, behold, a w H7307+H5591
Dan 11:40 against him like a w, with chariots, and H8175
Hos 8: 7 they shall reap the w: it hath no stalk: H5492
13: 3 is driven with the w out of the floor, H5590
Am 1:14 with a tempest in the day of the w: H5492
Nah 1: 3 his way in the w and in the storm, and H5492
Hab 3:14 came out as a w to scatter me: their H5590
Zec 7:14 But I scattered them with a w among H5590

WHIRLWINDS
Isa 21: 1 of the sea. As w in the south pass H5492
Zec 9:14 and shall go with w of the south. H5591

WHISPER
Ps 41: 7 All that hate me w together against me: H3907
Isa 29: 4 and thy speech shall w out of the dust. H6850

WHISPERED
2Sa 12:19 that his servants w, David perceived H3907

WHISPERER
Prv 16:28 A froward man soweth strife: and a w H5372

WHISPERERS
Ro 1:29 murder, debate, deceit, malignity; w, G5588

WHISPERINGS
2Co 12:20 backbitings, w, swellings, tumults: G5587

WHIT
Dt 13:16 thereof every w, for the LORD thy God: H3632
1Sa 3:18 And Samuel told him every w, and hid H1697
Jn 7:23 every w whole on the sabbath day? G3650
13:10 every w: and ye are clean, but not all. G3650
2Co 11: 5 For I suppose I was not a w behind the G3367

WHITE
Gen 30:35 one that had *some* w in it, and all the H3836
37 tree; and pilled w strakes in them, and H3836
37 the w appear which *was* in the rods. H3836
40:16 *I had* three w baskets on my head: H2751
49:12 with wine, and his teeth w with milk. H3836
Ex 16:31 coriander seed, w; and the taste of it H3836
Lev 13: 3 plague is turned w, and the plague in H3836
Lev 13: 4 If the bright spot *be* w in the skin of his H3836
4 be not turned w; then the priest shall H3836
10 *if* the rising *be* w in the skin, and it H3836
10 turned the hair w, and *there be* quick H3836
13 the plague: it is all turned w: he *is* clean. H3836
16 unto w, he shall come unto the priest; H3836
17 be turned into w; then the priest shall H3836
19 And in the place of the boil there be a w H3836
19 or a bright spot, w, and somewhat H3836
20 hair thereof be turned w; the priest shall H3836
21 *there be* no w hairs therein, and *if* H3836
24 that burneth have a w bright spot, H3836
24 bright spot, somewhat reddish, or w; H3836
25 spot be turned w, and it *be in* sight H3836
26 *there be* no w hair in the bright spot, H3836
38 flesh bright spots, *even* w bright spots; H3836
39 flesh *be* darkish w; it *is* a freckled spot H3836
42 or bald forehead, a w reddish sore; it *is* a H125
43 of the sore *be* w reddish in his bald head, H125
Nu 12:10 *became* leprous, w as snow: and Aaron
Jdg 5:10 Speak, ye that ride on w asses, ye that H6715
2Ki 5:27 from his presence a leper *as* w as snow.
2Ch 5:12 *being* arrayed in w linen, having
Est 1: 6 *Where were* w, green, and blue, H2353
6 and blue, and w, and black, marble. H1858
8:15 of blue and w, and with a great crown H2353
Job 6: 6 or is there *any* taste in the w of an egg? H7388
Ps 68:14 kings in it, it was *w* as snow in Salmon.
Ecc 9: 8 Let thy garments be always w; and let H3836
Song 5:10 My beloved *is* w and ruddy, the chiefest H6703
Isa 1:18 they shall be as w as snow; though they H3835
Ezk 27:18 in the wine of Helbon, and w wool. H6713
Dan 7: 9 garment *was* w as snow, and the hair H2358
11:35 and to make *them* w, *even* to the time of H3835
12:10 Many shall be purified, and made w, H3835
Joel 1: 7 away; the branches thereof are made w. H3835
Zec 1: 8 *were there* red horses, speckled, and w. H3836
6: 3 And in the third chariot w horses; and H3836
6 country; and the w go forth after them; H3836
Mt 5:36 canst not make one hair w or black. G3022
17: 2 and his raiment was w as the light. G3022
28: 3 lightning, and his raiment w as snow: G3022
Mk 9: 3 exceeding w as snow; so as no fuller G3022
3 so as no fuller on earth can w them. G3021
16: 5 w garment; and they were affrighted. G3022
Lk 9:29 and his raiment *was* w *and* glistering. G3022
Jn 4:35 for they are w already to harvest. G3022
20:12 And seeth two angels in w sitting, the G3022
Act 1:10 two men stood by them in w apparel; G3022
Rev 1:14 His head and *his* hairs *were* w like G3022
14 white like wool, as w as snow; and his G3022
2:17 and will give him a w stone, and in the G3022
3: 4 walk with me in w: for they are worthy. G3022
5 shall be clothed in w raiment; and I G3022
18 be rich; and w raiment, that thou G3022
4: 4 sitting, clothed in w raiment; and they G3022
6: 2 And I saw, and behold a w horse: and G3022
11 And w robes were given unto every one G3022
7: 9 w robes, and palms in their hands; G3022
13 in w robes? and whence came they? G3022
14 made them w in the blood of the Lamb. G3021
14:14 And I looked, and behold a w cloud, G3022
15: 6 in pure and w linen, and having their G2986
19: 8 linen, clean and w: for the fine linen is G2986
11 and behold a w horse; and he that sat G3022
14 him upon w horses, clothed in fine G3022
14 clothed in fine linen, w and clean. G3022
20:11 And I saw a great w throne, and him G3022

WHITED
Mt 23:27 for ye are like unto w sepulchres, which G2867
Act 23: 3 smite thee, *thou* w wall: for sittest thou G2867

WHITER
Ps 51: 7 wash me, and I shall be w than snow. H3835
Lam 4: 7 snow, they were w than milk, they were H6705

WHITHER
Gen 16: 8 camest thou? and w wilt thou go? And H575
20:13 me; at every place w we shall come, say H4725
28:15 thee in all *places* w thou goest, and will H834
32:17 *art* thou? and w goest thou? and whose H575
37:30 said, The child *is* not; and I, w shall I go? H575
Ex 21:13 thee a place w he shall flee. H834+H8033
34:12 of the land w thou goest, lest H834+H5921
Lev 18: 3 of Canaan, w I bring you, shall H834+H8033
20:22 that the land, w I bring you to H834+H8033
Nu 13:27 unto the land w thou sentest us, H834+H8033
15:18 ye come into the land w I bring you,

W

Nu 35:25 of his refuge, **w** he was fled: and H834+H8033
26 city of his refuge, **w** he was fled; H834+H8033
Dt 1:28 **W** shall we go up? our brethren H834+H8033
3:21 the kingdoms **w** thou passest. H834+H8033
4: 5 in the land **w** ye go to possess it. H834+H8033
14 land **w** ye go over to possess it. H834+H8033
27 **w** the LORD shall lead you. H834+H8033
6: 1 in the land **w** ye go to possess it: H834+H8033
7: 1 into the land **w** thou goest to H834+H8033
11: 8 possess the land, **w** ye go to possess it; H834
10 For the land, **w** thou goest in to H834+H8033
11 But the land, **w** ye go to possess H834+H8033
29 in unto the land **w** thou goest to H834+H8033
12:29 before thee, **w** thou goest to H834+H8033
21:14 shalt let her go **w** she will; but thou shalt
23:12 camp, **w** thou shalt go forth abroad: H8033
20 land **w** thou goest to possess it. H834+H8033
28:21 land, **w** thou goest to possess it. H834+H8033
37 **w** the LORD shall lead thee. H834+H8033
63 land **w** thou goest to possess it. H834+H8033
30: 1 all the nations, **w** the LORD thy H834+H8033
3 all the nations, **w** the LORD thy H834+H8033
16 land **w** thou goest to possess it. H834+H8033
18 upon the land, **w** thou passest H834+H8033
31:13 ye live in the land **w** ye go over H834+H8033
16 of the land, **w** they go *to be* H834+H8033
32:47 in the land, **w** ye go over Jordan H834+H8033
50 And die in the mount **w** thou H834+H8033
Jos 2: 5 the men went out: **w** the men went I wot H575
Jdg 19:17 **W** goest thou? and whence comest thou? H575
Ru 1:16 after thee: for **w** thou goest, I will H413+H834
1Sa 10:14 and to his servant, **W** went ye? And he H575
27:10 And Achish said, **W** have ye made a H413
2Sa 2: 1 And David said, **W** shall I go up? And he H575
13:13 And I, **w** shall I cause my shame to go? H575
15:20 us? seeing I go **w** I may, return H5921+H834
17:18 a well in his court; **w** they went down. H8033
1Ki 2:36 there, and go not forth thence any **w**. H575
42 abroad any **w**, that thou shalt surely H575
8:47 in the land **w** they were carried H834+H8033
18:10 or kingdom, **w** my lord hath not sent H834
12 carry thee **w** I know not; and H5921+H834
21:18 **w** he is gone down to possess it. H834+H8033
2Ki 5:25 And he said, Thy servant went no **w**. H575
2Ch 6:37 in the land **w** they are carried H834+H8033
38 of their captivity, **w** they have carried H834
10: 2 who *was* in Egypt, **w** he had fled from H834
Neh 2:16 And the rulers knew not **w** I went, or H575
Ps 122: 4 **W** the tribes go up, the tribes of the H8033
139: 7 **W** shall I go from thy spirit? or whither H575
7 Whither shall I go from thy spirit? or **w** H575
Ecc 9:10 in the grave, **w** thou goest. H834+H8033
Song 6: 1 **W** is thy beloved gone, O thou fairest H575
1 among women? **w** is thy beloved turned H575
Isa 20: 6 expectation, **w** we flee for help H834+H8033
Jer 8: 3 in all the places **w** I have driven H834+H8033
15: 2 they say unto thee, **W** shall we go forth? H575
16:15 all the lands **w** he had driven H834+H8033
19:14 Then came Jeremiah from Tophet, **w** the H834
22:12 But he shall die in the place **w** H834+H8033
23: 3 of all countries **w** I have driven H834+H8033
8 all countries **w** I had driven H834+H8033
24: 9 all places **w** I shall drive them. H834+H8033
29: 7 And seek the peace of the city **w** H834+H8033
14 all the places **w** I have driven H834+H8033
18 nations **w** I have driven them: H834+H8033
30:11 of all nations **w** I have scattered H834+H8033
32:37 of all countries, **w** I have driven H834+H8033
40: 4 land *is* before thee: **w** it seemeth good H413
12 of all places **w** they were driven, H834+H8033
42:22 **w** ye desire to go *and* to sojourn. H834+H8033
43: 5 all nations, **w** they had been H834+H8033
44: 8 land of Egypt, **w** ye be gone to H834+H8033
45: 5 a prey in all places **w** thou goest. H834+H8033
46:28 all the nations **w** I have driven H834+H8033
49:36 be no nation **w** the outcasts of H834+H8033
Ezk 1:12 forward: **w** the spirit was to H834+H8033
4:13 the Gentiles, **w** I will drive them. H834+H8033
6: 9 the nations **w** they shall be H834+H8033
10:11 but to the place **w** the head looked they H834
12:16 the heathen **w** they come; and H834+H8033
29:13 people **w** they were scattered: H834+H8033
36:20 the heathen, **w** they went, they H834+H8033
21 the heathen, **w** they went. H834+H8033
22 among the heathen, **w** ye went. H834+H8033
37:21 the heathen, **w** they be gone, H834+H8033
47: 9 shall live **w** the river cometh. H834+H8033
Dan 9: 7 the countries **w** thou hast driven H834+H8033
Joel 3: 7 out of the place **w** ye have sold H834+H8033
Zec 2: 2 Then said I, **W** goest thou? And he said H575
5:10 with me, **W** do these bear the ephah? H575
Lk 10: 1 and place, **w** he himself would come. *G3757*
24:28 And they drew nigh unto the village, **w** *G3757*
Jn 3: 8 it cometh, and **w** it goeth: so is every *G4226*
6:21 the ship was at the land **w** they went. *G1519*
7:35 themselves, **W** will he go, that we shall *G4226*
8:14 I came, and **w** I go; but ye cannot *G4226*
14 cannot tell whence I come, and **w** I go. *G4226*
21 in your sins: **w** I go, ye cannot come. *G3699*
22 he saith, **W** I go, ye cannot come. *G3699*
12:35 in darkness knoweth not **w** he goeth. *G4226*
13:33 unto the Jews, **W** I go, ye cannot come; *G3699*
36 Simon Peter said unto him, Lord, **w** *G4226*
36 answered him, **W** I go, thou canst not *G3699*
14: 4 And **w** I go ye know, and the way ye *G3699*
5 we know not **w** thou goest; and how *G4226*
16: 5 none of you asketh me, **W** goest thou? *G4226*
18:20 and in the temple, **w** the Jews always *G3699*
21:18 and walkedst **w** thou wouldest: but *G3699*
18 and carry *thee* **w** thou wouldest not. *G3699*
Heb 6:20 **W** the forerunner is for us entered, *G3699*
11: 8 he went out, not knowing **w** he went. *G4226*
1Jn 2:11 and knoweth not **w** he goeth, because *G4226*

WHITHERSOEVER

Jos 1: 7 mayest prosper **w** thou goest. H3605+H834
9 God *is* with thee **w** thou goest. H3605+H834
16 do, and **w** thou sendest us, we will go. H834
Jdg 2:15 **W** they went out, the hand of H3605+H834
1Sa 14:47 and **w** he turned himself, H3605+H834
18: 5 And David went out **w** Saul sent H3605+H834
23:13 Keilah, and went **w** they could go. And it H834
2Sa 7: 9 And I was with thee **w** thou H3605+H834
8: 6 preserved David **w** he went. H3605+H834
14 preserved David **w** he went. H3605+H834
1Ki 2: 3 **w** thou turnest thyself: H3605+H834+H8033
8:44 their enemy, **w** thou shalt send them, H1870
2Ki 18: 7 he prospered **w** he went forth: H3605+H834
1Ch 17: 8 And I have been with thee **w** H3605+H834
18: 6 preserved David **w** he went. H3605+H834
13 preserved David **w** he went. H3605+H834
Est 4: 3 And in every province, **w** the king's H4725
8:17 province, and in every city, **w** the king's H4725
Prv 17: 8 hath it: **w** it turneth, it H413+H3605+H834
21: 1 he turneth it **w** he will. H5921+H3605+H834
Ezk 1:20 **W** the spirit was to go, H5921+H834+H8033
21:16 hand, *or* on the left, **w** thy face *is* set. H575
47: 9 **w** the rivers H413+H3605+H834+H8033
Mt 8:19 Master, I will follow thee **w** thou goest. *G3699*
Mk 6:56 And **w** he entered, into villages, or *G3699*
Lk 9:57 Lord, I will follow thee **w** thou goest. *G3699*
1Co 16: 6 ye may bring me on my journey **w** I go. *G3757*
Jas 3: 4 very small helm, **w** the governor listeth. *G3699*
Rev 14: 4 follow the Lamb **w** he goeth. These *G3699*

WHO See the Appendix.

WHOLE

Gen 2: 6 the **w** face of the ground. H854+H3605
11 the **w** land of Havilah, H854+H3605
13 the **w** land of Ethiopia. H854+H3605
7:19 under the **w** heaven, were covered. H3605
8: 9 on the face of the **w** earth: then he put H3605
9:19 of them was the **w** earth overspread. H3605
11: 1 And the **w** earth was of one language, H3605
4 abroad upon the face of the **w** earth. H3605
13: 9 *Is* not the **w** land before thee? separate H3605
47:28 years: so the **w** age of Jacob was an
Ex 10:15 For they covered the face of the **w** earth,
12: 6 month: and the **w** assembly of the H3605
16: 2 And the **w** congregation of the children H3605
3 this **w** assembly with hunger. H854+H3605
10 spake unto the **w** congregation of the H3605
19:18 and the **w** mount quaked greatly. H3605
29:18 And thou shalt burn the **w** ram H854+H3605
Lev 3: 9 fat thereof, *and* the **w** rump, it shall he H8549
4:12 Even the **w** bullock shall he H854+H3605
13 And if the **w** congregation of Israel sin H3605
7:14 And of it he shall offer one out of the **w** H3605
8:21 burnt the **w** ram upon the altar: H854+H3605
10: 6 let your brethren, the **w** house of Israel, H3605
25:29 redeem it within a **w** year after it is H8552
Nu 3: 7 the charge of the **w** congregation before H3605
8: 9 gather the **w** assembly of the H854+H3605
10: 2 of silver; of a **w** piece shalt thou make H4749
11:20 *But* even a **w** month, until it come out H3117
21 flesh, that they may eat a **w** month. H3117
14: 2 Aaron: and the **w** congregation said H3605
Nu 14:29 you, according to your **w** number, from H3605
20: 1 of Israel, *even* the **w** congregation, into H3605
22 And the children of Israel, *even* the **w** H3605
Dt 2:25 *that are* under the **w** heaven, who shall H3605
4:19 unto all nations under the **w** heaven. H3605
27: 6 LORD thy God of **w** stones: and thou H8003
29:23 *And that* the **w** land thereof *is* H3605
33:10 and **w** burnt sacrifice upon thine altar. H3632
Jos 5: 8 places in the camp, till they were **w**. H2421
8:31 Moses, an altar of **w** stones, over which H8003
10:13 hasted not to go down about a **w** day. H8549
11:23 So Joshua took the **w** land, H854+H3605
18: 1 And the **w** congregation of the children H3605
22:12 heard *of it*, the **w** congregation of the H3605
16 Thus saith the **w** congregation of the H3605
18 with the **w** congregation of Israel. H3605
Jdg 19: 2 and was there four **w** months. H3117
21:13 And the **w** congregation sent *some* to H3605
2Sa 1: 9 me, because my life *is* yet **w** in me. H3605
3:19 good to the **w** house of Benjamin. H3605
6:19 *even* among the **w** multitude of Israel, H3605
14: 7 And, behold, the **w** family is risen H3605
1Ki 6:22 And the **w** house he overlaid with gold, H3605
22 house: also the **w** altar that *was* by the H3605
11:34 Howbeit I will not take the **w** kingdom H3605
2Ki 9: 8 For the **w** house of Ahab shall perish: H3605
2Ch 6: 3 face, and blessed the **w** congregation of H3605
15:15 him with their **w** desire; and he was H3605
16: 9 fro throughout the **w** earth, to shew H3605
26:12 The **w** number of the chief of the H3605
30:23 And the **w** assembly took counsel to H3605
33: 8 according to the **w** law and the statutes H3605
Ezr 2:64 The **w** congregation together *was* forty H3605
Neh 7:66 The **w** congregation together *was* forty H3605
Est 3: 6 *were* throughout the **w** kingdom of H3605
Job 5:18 he woundeth, and his hands make **w**. H7495
28:24 earth, *and* seeth under the **w** heaven; H3605
34:13 or who hath disposed the **w** world? H3605
37: 3 He directeth it under the **w** heaven, H3605
41:11 *is* under the **w** heaven is mine. H3605
Ps 9: 1 I will praise *thee*, O LORD, with my **w** H3605
48: 2 Beautiful for situation, the joy of the **w** H3605
51:19 offering and **w** burnt offering: then H3632
72:19 ever: and let the **w** earth be filled *with* H3605
97: 5 the presence of the Lord of the **w** earth. H3605
105:16 the land: he brake the **w** staff of bread. H3605
111: 1 the LORD with *my* **w** heart, in the H3605
119: 2 *and that* seek him with the **w** heart. H3605
10 With my **w** heart have I sought thee: O H3605
34 yea, I shall observe it with *my* **w** heart. H3605
58 I entreated thy favour with *my* **w** heart: H3605
69 will keep thy precepts with *my* **w** heart. H3605
145 I cried with *my* **w** heart; hear me, O
138: 1 I will praise thee with my **w** heart: before
Prv 1:12 **w**, as those that go down into the pit: H8549
16:33 The lot is cast into the lap; but the **w** H3605
26:26 be shewed before the *w* congregation.
Ecc 12:13 Let us hear the conclusion of the **w** H3605
13 for this *is* the **w** *duty* of man. H3605
Isa 1: 5 and more: the **w** head is sick, and the H3605
5 head is sick, and the **w** heart faint. H3605
3: 1 and the staff, the **w** stay of bread, and H3605
1 stay of bread, and the **w** stay of water, H3605
6: 3 of hosts: the **w** earth *is* full of his glory. H3605
10:12 performed his **w** work upon mount H3605
13: 5 his indignation, to destroy the **w** land. H3605
14: 7 The **w** earth is at rest, *and* is quiet: they H3605
26 upon the **w** earth: and this *is* the H3605
29 Rejoice not thou, **w** Palestina, because H3605
31 Howl, O gate; cry, O city; thou, **w** H3605
21: 8 and I am set in my ward **w** nights: H3605
28:22 even determined upon the **w** earth. H3605
54: 5 God of the **w** earth shall he be called. H3605
Jer 1:18 walls against the **w** land, against the H3605
3:10 **w** heart, but feignedly, saith the LORD. H3605
4:20 is cried; for the **w** land is spoiled: H3605
27 For thus hath the LORD said, The **w** H3605
29 The **w** city shall flee for the noise of the H3605
7:15 brethren, *even* the **w** seed of Ephraim. H3605
8:16 from Dan: the **w** land trembled at the H3605
12:11 unto me; the **w** land is made desolate, H3605
13:11 unto me the **w** house of Israel and H3605
11 of Israel and the **w** house of Judah, H3605
15:10 of contention to the **w** earth! I have H3605
19:11 that cannot be made **w** again: and they H7495
24: 7 shall return unto me with their **w** heart. H3605
25:11 And this **w** land shall be a desolation, H3605
31:40 And the **w** valley of the dead bodies, H3605
32:41 my **w** heart and with my whole soul. H3605

Jer 32:41 my whole heart and with my w soul. H3605
35: 3 and the w house of the Rechabites; H3605
37:10 For though ye had smitten the w army H3605
45: 4 I will pluck up, even this w land. H3605
50:23 How is the hammer of the w earth cut H3605
51:41 is the praise of the w earth surprised! H3605
47 of Babylon: and her w land shall be H3605
Lam 2:15 of beauty, The joy of the w earth? H3605
Ezk 5:10 in thee, and the w remnant of thee will H3605
7:13 *is* touching the w multitude thereof, H3605
10:12 And their w body, and their backs, and H3605
15: 5 Behold, when it was w, it was meet for H8549
32: 4 fill the beasts of the w earth with thee. H3605
35:14 Thus saith the Lord GOD; When the w H3605
37:11 bones are the w house of Israel: behold, H3605
39:25 mercy upon the w house of Israel, and H3605
43:11 they may keep the w form thereof, and H3605
12 the mountain the w limit thereof round H3605
45: 6 it shall be for the w house of Israel. H3605
Dan 2:35 great mountain, and filled the w earth. H3606
48 made him ruler over the w province of H3606
6: 1 which should be over the w kingdom; H3606
3 thought to set him over the w realm. H3606
7:23 and shall devour the w earth, and shall H3606
27 under the w heaven, shall be given H3606
8: 5 on the face of the w earth, and touched H3605
9:12 evil: for under the w heaven hath not H3605
10: 3 at all, till three w weeks were fulfilled. H3117
11:17 the strength of his w kingdom, and H3605
Am 1: 6 away captive the w captivity, to deliver H8003
9 delivered up the w captivity to Edom, H8003
3: 1 of Israel, against the w family which I H3605
Mic 4:13 substance unto the Lord of the w earth. H3605
Zep 1:18 LORD'S wrath; but the w land shall be H3605
Zec 4:10 run to and fro through the w earth. H3605
14 that stand by the Lord of the w earth. H3605
5: 3 the face of the w earth: for every one H3605
Mal 3: 9 ye have robbed me, *even* this w nation. H3605
Mt 5:29 thy w body should be cast into hell. G3650
30 thy w body should be cast into hell. G3650
6:22 single, thy w body shall be full of light. G3650
23 But if thine eye be evil, thy w body shall G3650
8:32 and, behold, the w herd of swine ran G3956
34 And, behold, the w city came out to G3956
9:12 They that be w need not a physician, G2480
21 but touch his garment, I shall be w. G4982
22 hath made thee w. And the woman was G4982
22 woman was made w from that hour. G4982
12:13 and it was restored w, like as the other. G5199
13: 2 the w multitude stood on the shore. G3956
33 of meal, till the w was leavened. G3650
14:36 as touched were made perfectly w. G1295
15:28 was made w from that very hour. G2390
31 the maimed to be w, the lame to walk, G5199
16:26 if he shall gain the w world, and lose G3650
26:13 be preached in the w world, *there* shall G3650
27:27 unto him the w band *of soldiers*. G3650
Mk 2:17 They that are w have no need of the G2480
3: 5 his hand was restored w as the other. G5199
4: 1 in the sea; and the w multitude was by G3956
5:28 I may touch but his clothes, I shall be w. G4982
34 hath made thee w; go in peace, and be G4982
34 go in peace, and be w of thy plague. G5199
6:55 And ran through that w region round G3650
56 as many as touched him were made w. G4982
8:36 the w world, and lose his own soul? G3650
10:52 hath made thee w. And immediately he G4982
12:33 all w burnt offerings and sacrifices. G3646
14: 9 throughout the w world, *this* also that G3650
15: 1 scribes and the w council, and bound G3650
16 and they call together the w band. G3650
33 over the w land until the ninth hour. G3650
Lk 1:10 And the w multitude of the people were G3956
5:31 They that are w need not a physician; G5198
6:10 his hand was restored w as the other. G5199
19 And the w multitude sought to touch G3956
7:10 found the servant w that had been sick. G5198
8:37 Then the w multitude of the country of G537
39 throughout the w city how great things G3650
48 thy faith hath made thee w; go in peace. G4982
50 believe only, and she shall be made w. G4982
9:25 if he gain the w world, and lose G3650
11:34 eye is single, thy w body also is full of G3650
36 If thy w body therefore *be* full of light, G3650
36 no part dark, the w shall be full of light, G3650
13:21 of meal, till the w was leavened. G3650
17:19 go thy way: thy faith hath made thee w. G4982
19:37 mount of Olives, the w multitude of the G537
21:35 that dwell on the face of the w earth. G3956

Lk 23: 1 And the w multitude of them arose, and G537
Jn 4:53 and himself believed, and his w house. G3650
5: 4 made w of whatsoever disease he had. G5199
6 saith unto him, Wilt thou be made w? G5199
9 And immediately the man was made w, G5199
11 He answered them, He that made me w, G5199
14 thou art made w: sin no more, lest a G5199
15 it was Jesus, which had made him w. G5199
7:23 man every whit w on the sabbath day? G5199
11:50 and that the w nation perish not. G3650
Act 4: 9 man, by what means he is made w; G4982
10 doth this man stand here before you w. G5199
6: 5 And the saying pleased the w G3956
9:34 maketh thee w: arise, and make thy G2390
11:26 to pass, that a w year they assembled G3650
13:44 w city together to hear the word of God. G3956
15:22 and elders, with the w church, to send G3650
19:29 And the w city was filled with G3650
28:30 And Paul dwelt two w years in his own G3650
Ro 1: 8 is spoken of throughout the w world. G3650
8:22 For we know that the w creation G3956
16:23 Gaius mine host, and of the w church, G3650
1Co 5: 6 a little leaven leaveneth the w lump? G3650
12:17 If the w body *were* an eye, where *were* G3650
17 the hearing? If the w *were* hearing, G3650
14:23 If therefore the w church be come G3650
Gal 5: 3 that he is a debtor to do the w law. G3650
9 A little leaven leaveneth the w lump. G3650
Eph 3:15 Of whom the w family in heaven and G3956
4:16 From whom the w body fitly joined G3956
6:11 Put on the w armour of God, that ye may
13 Wherefore take unto you the w armour
1Th 5:23 *I pray God* your w spirit and soul and G3648
Tit 1:11 who subvert w houses, teaching things G3650
Jas 2:10 For whosoever shall keep the w law, G3650
3: 2 *and* able also to bridle the w body. G3650
3 us; and we turn about their w body. G3650
6 that it defileth the w body, and setteth G3650
1Jn 2: 2 but also for *the sins of* the w world. G3650
5:19 and the w world lieth in wickedness. G3650
Rev 12: 9 deceiveth the w world: he was cast out G3650
16:14 the earth and of the w world, to gather G3650

WHOLESOME

Prv 15: 4 A w tongue *is* a tree of life: but H4832
1Ti 6: 3 consent not to w words, *even* the words G5198

WHOLLY

Lev 6:22 unto the LORD; it shall be w burnt. H3632
23 shall be w burnt: it shall not be eaten. H3632
19: 9 thou shalt not w reap the corners of H3615
Nu 3: 9 his sons: they *are* w given unto him out H5414
4: 6 over *it* a cloth w of blue, and shall put H3632
8:16 For they *are* w given unto me from H5414
32:11 because they have not w followed me: H4390
12 for they have w followed the LORD. H4390
Dt 1:36 because he hath w followed the LORD. H4390
Jos 14: 8 but I w followed the LORD my God. H4390
9 hast w followed the LORD my God. H4390
14 he w followed the LORD God of Israel. H4390
Jdg 17: 3 said, I had w dedicated the silver H6942
1Sa 7: 9 a burnt offering w unto the LORD: and H3632
1Ch 28:21 people *will be* w at thy commandment. H3605
Job 21:23 One dieth in his full strength, being w H3605
Isa 22: 1 thou art w gone up to the housetops? H3605
Jer 2:21 Yet I had planted thee a noble vine, w a H3605
6: 6 she *is* w oppression in the midst of her. H3605
13:19 of it, it shall be w carried away captive. H7965
42:15 God of Israel; If ye w set your faces to H7760
46:28 yet will I not leave thee w unpunished. H5352
50:13 but it shall be w desolate: every one H3605
Ezk 11:15 all the house of Israel w, *are* they unto H3605
Am 8: 8 it shall rise up w as a flood; and it shall H3605
9: 5 it shall rise up w like a flood; and shall H3605
Act 17:16 when he saw the city w given to idolatry.
1Th 5:23 sanctify you w; and *I pray God* your G3651
1Ti 4:15 things; give thyself w to them; that thy G2468

WHOM See the Appendix.

WHOMSOEVER

Gen 31:32 With w thou findest thy gods, let him not H834
44: 9 With w of thy servants it be found, both H834
Lev 15:11 And w he toucheth that hath the H3605+H834
Jdg 7: 4 with thee; and of w I say unto thee, This H834
11:24 to possess? So w the LORD our H3605+H834
Dan 4:17 and giveth it to w he will, and setteth H4479
25 of men, and giveth it to w he will. H4479
32 of men, and giveth it to w he will. H4479

Dan 5:21 *that* he appointeth over it w he will. H4479
Mt 11:27 *he* to w the Son will reveal *him*. G3739+G1437
21:44 broken: but on w it shall fall, it G3739+G302
26:48 a sign, saying, W I shall kiss, G3739+G302
Mk 14:44 a token, saying, W I shall kiss, G3739+G302
15: 6 them one prisoner, w they desired. G3746
Lk 4: 6 me; and to w I will I give it. G3739+G1437
12:48 For unto w much is given, G3956+G3739
20:18 broken; but on w it shall fall, it G3739+G302
Jn 13:20 He that receiveth w I send G1437+G5100
Act 8:19 power, that on w I lay hands, he G3739+G302
1Co 16: 3 And when I come, w ye shall G3739+G1437

WHORE

Lev 19:29 cause her to be a w; lest the land fall to H2181
21: 7 They shall not take a wife *that is* a w, or H2181
9 by playing the w, she profaneth her H2181
Dt 22:21 in Israel, to play the w in her father's H2181
23:17 There shall be no w of the daughters of H6948
18 Thou shalt not bring the hire of a w, or H2181
Jdg 19: 2 And his concubine played the w H2181
Prv 23:27 For a w *is* a deep ditch; and a strange H2181
Isa 57: 3 the seed of the adulterer and the w. H2181
Ezk 16:28 Thou hast played the w also with the H2181
Rev 17: 1 great w that sitteth upon many waters: G4204
15 thou sawest, where the w sitteth, are G4204
16 shall hate the w, and shall make her G4204
19: 2 judged the great w, which did corrupt G4204

WHOREDOM

Gen 38:24 she *is* with child by w. And Judah said, H2183
Lev 19:29 the land fall to w, and the land become H2181
20: 5 him, to commit w with Molech, from H2181
Nu 25: 1 commit w with the daughters of Moab. H2181
Jer 3: 9 lightness of her w, that she defiled the H2184
13:27 the lewdness of thy w, *and* thine H2184
Ezk 16:17 men, and didst commit w with them, H2181
33 come unto thee on every side for thy w. H8457
20:30 commit ye w after their abominations? H2181
23: 8 virginity, and poured their w upon her. H8457
17 her with their w, and she was polluted H8457
27 thee, and thy w *brought* from the land H2184
43: 7 kings, by their w, nor by the carcases H2184
9 Now let them put away their w, and the H2184
Hos 1: 2 great w, *departing* from the LORD. H2181
4:10 they shall commit w, and shall not H2181
11 W and wine and new wine take away H2184
13 shall commit w, and your spouses shall H2181
14 they commit w, nor your spouses when H2181
18 have committed w continually: her H2181
5: 3 committest w, *and* Israel is defiled. H2181
6:10 *is* the w of Ephraim, Israel is defiled. H2184

WHOREDOMS

Nu 14:33 and bear your w, until your carcases H2184
2Ki 9:22 so long as the w of thy mother Jezebel H2183
2Ch 21:13 like to the w of the house of Ahab, H2181
Jer 3: 2 with thy w and with thy wickedness. H2184
Ezk 16:20 *Is this* of thy w a small matter, H8457
22 and thy w thou hast not remembered H8457
25 that passed by, and multiplied thy w. H8457
26 thy w, to provoke me to anger. H8457
34 *other* women in thy w, whereas none H8457
34 thee to commit w: and in that thou H2181
36 through thy w with thy lovers, and H8457
23: 3 And they committed w in Egypt; they H2181
3 they committed w in their youth: there H2181
7 Thus she committed her w with them, H8457
8 Neither left she her w *brought* from H8457
11 she, and in her w more than her sister H8457
11 more than her sister in *her* w. H2183
14 And *that* she increased her w: for when H8457
18 So she discovered her w, and H8457
19 Yet she multiplied her w, in calling to H8457
29 nakedness of thy w shall be discovered, H2183
29 both thy lewdness and thy w. H8457
35 bear thou also thy lewdness and thy w. H8457
43 commit w with her, and she *with them*? H8457
Hos 1: 2 unto thee a wife of w and children of H2183
2 and children of w: for the land hath H2183
2: 2 put away her w out of her sight, and H2183
4 children; for they *be* the children of w. H2183
4:12 for the spirit of w hath caused *them* to H2183
5: 4 for the spirit of w *is* in the midst of H2183
Nah 3: 4 Because of the multitude of the w of the H2183
4 w, and families through her witchcrafts. H2183

WHOREMONGER

Eph 5: 5 For this ye know, that no w, nor G4205

WHOREMONGERS
1Ti 1:10 For w, for them that defile themselves G4205
Heb 13: 4 but w and adulterers God will judge. G4205
Rev 21: 8 murderers, and w, and sorcerers, and G4205
22:15 sorcerers, and w, and murderers, and G4205

WHORES
Ezk 16:33 They give gifts to all w: but thou givest H2181
Hos 4:14 are separated with w, and they sacrifice H2181

WHORE'S
Jer 3: 3 and thou hadst a w forehead, thou H2181

WHORING
Ex 34:15 and they go a w after their gods, and H2181
16 daughters go a w after their gods, and H2181
16 make thy sons go a w after their gods. H2181
Lev 17: 7 they have gone a w. This shall be a H2181
20: 5 off, and all that go a w after him, to H2181
6 wizards, to go a w after them, I will H2181
Nu 15:39 own eyes, after which ye use to go a w: H2181
Dt 31:16 rise up, and go a w after the gods of the H2181
Jdg 2:17 but they went a w after other gods, and H2181
8:27 went thither a w after it: which thing H2181
33 again, and went a w after Baalim, and H2181
1Ch 5:25 and went a w after the gods of the H2181
2Ch 21:13 of Jerusalem to go a w, like to the H2181
Ps 73:27 all them that go a w from thee. H2181
106:39 went a w with their own inventions. H2181
Ezk 6: 9 eyes, which go a w after their idols: and H2181
23:30 thou hast gone a w after the heathen, H2181
Hos 4:12 have gone a w from under their God. H2181
9: 1 thou hast gone a w from thy God, thou H2181

WHORISH
Prv 6:26 For by means of a w woman *a man is* H2181
Ezk 6: 9 broken with their w heart, which hath H2181
16:30 the work of an imperious w woman; H2181

WHOSE See the Appendix.

WHOSO
Gen 9: 6 W sheddeth man's blood, by man shall
Lev 11:27 *are* unclean unto you: w toucheth their H3605
22: 4 he be clean. And w toucheth any thing
Nu 35:30 W killeth any person, the murderer H3605
Dt 19: 4 that he may live: W killeth his neighbour H834
2Ch 23:14 of the ranges: and w followeth her, let
Ps 50:23 W offereth praise glorifieth me: and to
101: 5 W privily slandereth his neighbour, him
107:43 W *is* wise, and will observe these H4310
Prv 1:33 But w hearkeneth unto me shall dwell
6:32 *But* w committeth adultery with a
8:35 For w findeth me findeth life, and shall
9: 4 W *is* simple, let him turn in hither: *as* H4310
16 W *is* simple, let him turn in hither: and H4310
12: 1 W loveth instruction loveth knowledge:
13:13 W despiseth the word shall be
16:20 and w trusteth in the LORD, happy *is* he.
17: 5 W mocketh the poor reproacheth his
13 W rewardeth evil for good, evil shall not
18:22 *W* findeth a wife findeth a good *thing*,
20: 2 the roaring of a lion: *w* provoketh him to
20 W curseth his father or his mother, his
21:13 W stoppeth his ears at the cry of the
23 W keepeth his mouth and his tongue
25:14 W boasteth himself of a false gift *is like* H376
26:27 W diggeth a pit shall fall therein: and he
27:18 W keepeth the fig tree shall eat the fruit
28: 7 W keepeth the law *is* a wise son: but he
10 W causeth the righteous to go astray in
13 shall not prosper: but w confesseth and
18 W walketh uprightly shall be saved: but
24 W robbeth his father or his mother, and
26 w walketh wisely, he shall be delivered.
29: 3 W loveth wisdom rejoiceth his father: H376
24 W is partner with a thief hateth his own
25 The fear of man bringeth a snare: but w
Ecc 7:26 hands *as* bands: w pleaseth God shall
8: 5 W keepeth the commandment shall feel
10: 8 fall into it; and w breaketh an hedge,
9 W removeth stones shall be hurt
Dan 3: 6 And w falleth not down and H4479
11 And w falleth not down and H4479
Zec 14:17 And it shall be, *that* w will not come up H834
Mt 18: 5 And w shall receive one such G3739+G302
6 But w shall offend one of these G3739+G302
19: 9 adultery: and w marrieth her which G3588
23:20 W therefore shall swear by the altar, G3588
Mt 23:21 And w shall swear by the temple, G3588
24:15 place, (w readeth, let him understand:) G3588
Mk 7:10 thy mother; and, W curseth father or G3588
Jn 6:54 W eateth my flesh, and drinketh my G3588
Jas 1:25 But w looketh into the perfect law of G3588
1Jn 2: 5 But w keepeth his word, in him G3739+G302
3:17 But w hath this world's good, G3739+G302

WHOSOEVER
Gen 4:15 unto him, Therefore w slayeth Cain, H3605
Ex 12:15 of your houses: for w eateth leavened H3605
19 your houses: for w eateth that which is H3605
19:12 the border of it: w toucheth the mount H3605
22:19 W lieth with a beast shall surely be put H3605
30:33 W compoundeth *any* like it, or H834+H376
33 *any* like it, or w putteth *any* of it upon H834
38 W shall make like unto that, to H834+H376
31:14 be put to death: for w doeth *any* work H3605
15 holy to the LORD: w doeth *any* work in H3605
32:24 And I said unto them, W hath any H4310
33 And the LORD said unto Moses, W hath H834
35: 2 rest to the LORD: w doeth work therein H3605
5 unto the LORD: w *is* of a willing heart, H3605
Lev 7:25 For w eateth the fat of the beast, of H3605
11:24 And for these ye shall be unclean: w H3605
25 And w beareth *ought* of the carcase of H3605
31 all that creep: w doth touch them, H3605
15: 5 And w toucheth his bed shall wash his H376
10 And w toucheth any thing that was H3605
19 seven days: and w toucheth her shall H3605
21 And w toucheth her bed shall wash his H3605
22 And w toucheth any thing that she sat H3605
27 And w toucheth those things shall be H3605
17:14 thereof: w eateth it shall be cut off. H3605
18:29 For w shall commit any of these H3605+H834
19:20 And w lieth carnally with a woman, that H376
20: 2 the children of Israel, W *he be* of the H376
21:17 Speak unto Aaron, saying, W *he be* of H376
22: 3 Say unto them, W *he be* of all your seed H376
5 Or w toucheth any creeping thing, H376
21 And w offereth a sacrifice of peace H376
24:15 W curseth his God shall bear his sin. H376
Nu 5: 2 an issue, and w is defiled by the dead: H3605
15:14 And if a stranger sojourn with you, or w H834
17:13 W cometh any thing near unto the H3605
19:13 W toucheth the dead body of any man H3605
16 And w toucheth one that is slain H3605+H834
31:19 the camp seven days: w hath killed any H3605
19 any person, and w hath touched any H3605
Dt 18:19 And it shall come to pass, *that* w will not H376
Jos 1:18 W *he be* that doth rebel against thy H376
2:19 And it shall be, *that* w shall go out of the H834
19 *be* guiltless: and w shall be with H3605+H834
20: 9 them, that w killeth *any* person H3605+H834
Jdg 7: 3 people, saying, W *is* fearful and afraid, H3605
1Sa 11: 7 saying, W cometh not forth after H4310
2Sa 5: 8 And David said on that day, W getteth H834
14:10 And the king said, W saith *ought* unto
17: 9 at the first, that w heareth it will say, H8085
1Ki 13:33 priests of the high places: w would, he
2Ki 10:19 *to do* to Baal; w shall be H3605+H834
21:12 and Judah, that w heareth of it, both H3605
1Ch 11: 6 And David said, W smiteth the H3605
26:28 dedicated; *and* w had dedicated *any* H3605
2Ch 13: 9 lands? so that w cometh to consecrate H3605
15:13 That w would not seek the LORD God of H3605
23: 7 in his hand; and w *else* cometh into the H3605
Ezr 1: 4 And w remaineth in any place where H3605
6:11 Also I have made a decree, that w shall H3605
7:26 And w will not do the law of thy God, H3605
10: 8 And that w would not come within three H834
Est 4:11 do know, that w, whether man or H3605
Prv 6:29 w toucheth her shall not be innocent. H3605
20: 1 and w is deceived thereby is not wise.
27:16 W hideth her hideth the wind, and the
Isa 54:15 *but* not by me: w shall gather together H4310
59: 8 w goeth therein shall not know peace. H3605
Jer 19: 3 which w heareth, his ears shall tingle. H3605
Ezk 33: 4 Then w heareth the sound of the H8085
Dan 5: 7 wise *men* of Babylon, W shall read this H3605
6: 7 firm decree, that w shall ask a petition H3605
Joel 2:32 And it shall come to pass, *that* w shall H834
Mt 5:19 W therefore shall break one of G3739+G1437
19 of heaven: but w shall do and G3739+G302
21 not kill; and w shall kill shall be G3739+G302
22 But I say unto you, That w is angry G3956
22 judgment: and w shall say to his G3739+G302
22 council: but w shall say, Thou G3739+G302
28 But I say unto you, That w looketh on a G3956
Mt 5:31 It hath been said, W shall put G3739+G302
32 But I say unto you, That w shall G3739+G302
32 adultery: and w shall marry G3739+G1437
39 resist not evil: but w shall smite thee on G3748
41 And w shall compel thee to go a mile, G3748
7:24 Therefore w heareth these G3956+G3748
10:14 And w shall not receive you, G3739+G1437
32 W therefore shall confess me G3956+G3748
33 But w shall deny me before men, him G3748
42 And w shall give to drink unto G3739+G1437
11: 6 And blessed is *he*, w shall not G3739+G1437
12:32 And w speaketh a word against G3739+G302
32 him: but w speaketh against G3739+G302
50 For w shall do the will of my G3748+G302
13:12 For w hath, to him shall be given, and G3748
12 abundance: but w hath not, from him G3748
15: 5 But ye say, W shall say to *his* G3739+G302
16:25 For w will save his life shall lose G3739+G302
25 lose it: and w will lose his life G3739+G302
18: 4 W therefore shall humble himself as G3748
19: 9 And I say unto you, W shall put G3739+G302
20:26 you: but w will be great among G3739+G1437
27 And w will be chief among G3739+G1437
21:44 And w shall fall on this stone shall be G3588
23:12 And w shall exalt himself shall be G3748
16 which say, W shall swear by the G3739+G302
16 is nothing; but w shall swear by G3739+G302
18 And, W shall swear by the G3739+G1437
18 it is nothing; but w sweareth by G3739+G302
Mk 3:35 For w shall do the will of God, G3739+G302
6:11 And w shall not receive you, nor G3745+G302
8:34 said unto them, W will come after me, G3748
35 For w will save his life shall lose G3739+G302
35 lose it; but w shall lose his life G3739+G302
38 W therefore shall be ashamed of G3739+G302
9:37 W shall receive one of such G3739+G1437
37 me: and w shall receive me, G3739+G1437
41 For w shall give you a cup of G3739+G302
42 And w shall offend one of *these* G3739+G302
10:11 And he saith unto them, W G3739+G1437
15 Verily I say unto you, W shall G3739+G1437
43 you: but w will be great among G3739+G1437
44 And w of you will be the G3739+G302
11:23 For verily I say unto you, That w G3739+G302
Lk 6:47 W cometh to me, and heareth my G3956
7:23 And blessed is *he*, w shall not G3739+G1437
8:18 ye hear: for w hath, to him shall G3739+G302
18 be given; and w hath not, from G3739+G302
9: 5 And w will not receive you, G3745+G302
24 For w will save his life shall lose G3739+G302
24 lose it: but w will lose his life G3739+G302
26 For w shall be ashamed of me G3739+G302
48 And said unto them, W shall G3739+G1437
48 me: and w shall receive me G3739+G1437
12: 8 Also I say unto you, W G3956+G3739+G302
10 And w shall speak a word G3956+G3739
14:11 For w exalteth himself shall be abased; G3956
27 And w doth not bear his cross, and G3748
33 So likewise, w he be of you that G3956
16:18 W putteth away his wife, and marrieth G3956
18 adultery: and w marrieth her that is G3956
17:33 W shall seek to save his life G3739+G1437
33 lose it; and w shall lose his life G3739+G1437
18:17 Verily I say unto you, W shall G3739+G1437
20:18 W shall fall upon that stone shall be G3956
Jn 3:15 That w believeth in him should not G3956
16 begotten Son, that w believeth in him G3956
4:13 Jesus answered and said unto her, W G3956
14 But w drinketh of the water that G3739+G302
5: 4 the water: w then first after the G3588
8:34 W committeth sin is the servant of sin. G3956
11:26 And w liveth and believeth in me shall G3956
12:46 I am come a light into the world, that w G3956
16: 2 the time cometh, that w killeth you will G3956
19:12 Caesar's friend: w maketh himself a G3956
Act 2:21 to pass, *that* w shall call G3956+G3739+G302
10:43 through his name w believeth in him G3956
13:26 of Abraham, and w among you feareth G3588
Ro 2: 1 O man, w thou art that judgest: G3956
9:33 rock of offence: and w believeth on him G3956
10:11 For the scripture saith, W believeth on G3956
13 For w shall call upon G3956+G3739+G302
13: 2 W therefore resisteth the power, G3588
1Co 11:27 Wherefore w shall eat this G3739+G302
Gal 5: 4 effect unto you, w of you are justified G3748
10 bear his judgment, w he be. G3748+G302
Jas 2:10 For w shall keep the whole law, and yet G3748
4: 4 with God? w therefore will be G3739+G302
1Jn 2:23 W denieth the Son, the same hath not G3956

1Jn 3: 4 W committeth sin transgresseth also G3956
6 W abideth in him sinneth not: G3956
6 in him sinneth not: w sinneth hath not G3956
9 W is born of God doth not commit sin; G3956
10 of the devil: w doeth not righteousness G3956
15 W hateth his brother is a murderer: G3956
4:15 W shall confess that Jesus is the G3739+G302
5: 1 W believeth that Jesus is the Christ is G3956
18 We know that w is born of God sinneth G3956
2Jn 9 W transgresseth, and abideth not in G3956
Rev 14:11 and w receiveth the mark of his name. G1536
20:15 And w was not found written in the G1536
22:15 and w loveth and maketh a lie. G3956
17 athirst come. And w will, let him take G3588

WHY

Gen 4: 6 And the LORD said unto Cain, W art H4100
6 and w is thy countenance fallen? H4100
12:18 done unto me? w didst thou not tell me H4100
19 W saidst thou, She *is* my sister? so I H4100
25:22 said, If *it be* so, w *am* I thus? And she H4100
27:45 fetch thee from thence: w should I be H4100
42: 1 sons, W do ye look one upon another? H4100
47:15 Give us bread: for w should we die in H4100
Ex 1:18 said unto them, W have ye done this H4069
2:20 And where *is* he? w *is* it *that* ye have H4100
3: 3 great sight, w the bush is not burnt. H4069
5:22 people? w *is* it *that* thou hast sent me? H4100
14: 5 and they said, W have we done this, H4100
17: 2 said unto them, W chide ye with me? H4100
18:14 to the people? w sittest thou thyself H4069
32:11 and said, LORD, w doth thy wrath wax H4100
Nu 11:20 saying, W came we forth out of Egypt? H4100
20: 4 And w have ye brought up the H4100
27: 4 W should the name of our father be H4100
Dt 5:25 Now therefore w should we die? for this H4100
Jos 5: 4 And this *is* the cause w Joshua did H4100
7:25 And Joshua said, W hast thou troubled H4100
17:14 Joshua, saying, W hast thou given me H4069
Jdg 2: 2 obeyed my voice: w have ye done this? H4100
5:16 W abodest thou among the sheepfolds, H4100
17 Gilead abode beyond Jordan: and w H4100
28 the lattice, W is his chariot *so* long H4069
28 w tarry the wheels of his chariots? H4069
6:13 the LORD be with us, w then is all this H4100
8: 1 said unto him, W hast thou served us H4100
9:28 Shechem: for w should we serve him? H4100
11: 7 house? and w are ye come unto me H4069
26 hundred years? w therefore did ye not H4069
13:18 said unto him, W askest thou thus H4100
15:10 And the men of Judah said, W are ye H4100
21: 3 And said, O LORD God of Israel, w is H4100
Ru 1:11 my daughters: w will ye go with me? H4100
21 again empty: w *then* call ye me Naomi, H4100
2:10 said unto him, W have I found grace H4069
1Sa 1: 8 to her, Hannah, w weepest thou? and H4100
8 thou? and w eatest thou not? and H4100
8 thou not? and w is thy heart grieved? H4100
2:23 And he said unto them, W do ye such H4100
6: 3 w his hand is not removed from you. H4100
17: 8 said unto them, W are ye come out to H4100
28 and he said, W camest thou down H4100
19:17 And Saul said unto Michal, W hast H4100
17 me, Let me go; w should I kill thee? H4100
20: 2 shew it me: and w should my father H4060
8 me thyself; for w shouldest thou bring H4100
21: 1 said unto him, W *art* thou alone, and H4069
22:13 And Saul said unto him, W have ye H4100
27: 5 dwell there: for w should thy servant H4100
28:12 to Saul, saying, W hast thou deceived H4100
15 And Samuel said to Saul, W hast thou H4100
2Sa 3:24 came unto thee; w *is* it *that* thou hast H4100
7: 7 W build ye not me an house of cedar? H4100
11:10 from *thy* journey? w *then* didst thou H4069
21 he died in Thebez? w went ye nigh the H4100
13: 4 And he said unto him, W *art* thou, H4069
26 unto him, W should he go with thee? H4100
16: 9 unto the king, W should this dead dog H4100
17 w wentest thou not with thy friend? H4100
18:11 sawest *him*, and w didst thou not smite H4069
19:10 Now therefore w speak ye not a word H4100
11 of Judah, saying, W are ye the last to H4100
29 And the king said unto him, W H4100
36 with the king: and w should the king H4100
41 unto the king, W have our brethren the H4069
43 in David than ye: w then did ye despise H4069
20:19 a mother in Israel: w wilt thou swallow H4100
24: 3 may see *it*: but w doth my lord the king H4100
1Ki 1: 6 time in saying, W hast thou done so? H4069

1Ki 1:13 throne? w then doth Adonijah reign? H4069
2:22 unto his mother, And w dost thou ask H4100
43 W then hast thou not kept the oath of H4100
9: 8 they shall say, W hath the LORD done H4100
14: 6 thou wife of Jeroboam; w feignest thou H4100
21: 5 said unto him, W is thy spirit so sad, H4100
2Ki 1: 5 unto them, W are ye now turned back? H4100
7: 3 to another, W sit we here until we die? H4100
8:12 And Hazael said, W weepeth my lord? H4069
12: 7 said unto them, W repair ye not the H4069
14:10 tarry at home: for w shouldest thou H4100
1Ch 17: 6 people, saying, W have ye not built me H4100
21: 3 lord's servants? w then doth my lord H4100
3 w will he be a cause of trespass to Israel? H4100
2Ch 7:21 so that he shall say, W hath the LORD H4100
24: 6 and said unto him, W hast thou not H4069
20 Thus saith God, W transgress ye the H4100
25:15 said unto him, W hast thou sought H4100
16 counsel? forbear; w shouldest thou be H4100
19 now at home; w shouldest thou meddle H4100
32: 4 the land, saying, W should the kings of H4100
Ezr 4:22 ye fail not to do this: w should damage H4101
7:23 of heaven: for w should there be wrath H4101
Neh 2: 2 Wherefore the king said unto me, W *is* H4069
3 the king live for ever: w should not my H4069
6: 3 come down: w should the work cease, H4100
13:11 rulers, and said, W is the house of God H4069
21 said unto them, W lodge ye about the H4069
Est 3: 3 unto Mordecai, W transgressest thou H4069
4: 5 to know what it *was*, and w it *was*. H4100
Job 3:11 W died I not from the womb? *why* did I H4100
11 Why died I not from the womb? *w* did I
12 W did the knees prevent me? or why H4069
12 Why did the knees prevent me? or w H4069
23 W *is light given* to a man whose way is H4100
7:20 preserver of men? w hast thou set me H4100
21 And w dost thou not pardon my H4100
9:29 *If* I be wicked, w then labour I in vain? H4100
15:12 W doth thine heart carry thee away? H4100
19:22 W do ye persecute me as God, and are H4100
28 But ye should say, W persecute we H4100
21: 4 *so*, w should not my spirit be troubled? H4069
24: 1 W, seeing times are not hidden from H4069
27:12 *it*; w then are ye thus altogether vain? H4100
31: 1 I made a covenant with mine eyes; w H4100
33:13 W dost thou strive against him? for he H4069
Ps 2: 1 W do the heathen rage, and the people H4100
10: 1 W standest thou afar off, O LORD? *why* H4100
1 Why standest thou afar off, O LORD? *w*
22: 1 My God, my God, w hast thou forsaken H4100
1 hast thou forsaken me? *w art thou so* far
42: 5 W art thou cast down, O my soul? and
5 O my soul? and *w* art thou disquieted
9 I will say unto God my rock, W hast H4100
9 forgotten me? w go I mourning because H4100
11 W art thou cast down, O my soul? and H4100
11 O my soul? and w art thou disquieted H4100
43: 2 For thou *art* the God of my strength: w H4100
2 dost thou cast me off? w go I mourning H4100
5 W art thou cast down, O my soul? and H4100
5 O my soul? and w art thou disquieted H4100
44:23 Awake, w sleepest thou, O Lord? arise, H4100
52: 1 W boastest thou thyself in mischief, O H4100
68:16 W leap ye, ye high hills? *this is* the hill H4100
74: 1 O God, w hast thou cast *us* off for ever? H4100
1 cast *us* off for ever? *w* doth thine anger
11 W withdrawest thou thy hand, even thy H4100
80:12 W hast thou *then* broken down her H4100
88:14 LORD, w castest thou off my soul? *why* H4100
14 LORD, why castest thou off my soul? *w*
Prv 5:20 And w wilt thou, my son, be ravished
22:27 If thou hast nothing to pay, w should H4100
Ecc 2:15 even to me; and w was I then more H4100
7:16 wise: w shouldest thou destroy thyself? H4100
17 w shouldest thou die before thy time? H4100
Song 1: 7 to rest at noon: for w should I be as one H4100
Isa 1: 5 W should ye be stricken any more? ye H4100
40:27 W sayest thou, O Jacob, and speakest, H4100
63:17 O LORD, w hast thou made us to err H4100
Jer 2:14 he a homeborn *slave*? w is he spoiled? H4069
33 W trimmest thou thy way to seek love? H4100
36 W gaddest thou about so much to H4100
8: 5 W *then* is this people of Jerusalem H4069
14 W do we sit still? assemble yourselves, H4100
19 her king in her? W have they provoked H4069
22 no physician there? w then is not the H4069
14: 8 in time of trouble, w shouldest thou be H4100
9 W shouldest thou be as a man H4100
19 soul lothed Zion? w hast thou smitten H4069

Jer 15:18 W is my pain perpetual, and my H4100
26: 9 W hast thou prophesied in the name of H4069
27:13 W will ye die, thou and thy people, by H4100
29:27 Now therefore w hast thou not H4100
30:15 W criest thou for thine affliction? thy H4100
36:29 this roll, saying, W hast thou written H4069
46:15 W are thy valiant *men* swept away? H4069
49: 1 hath he no heir? w *then* doth their king H4069
Ezk 18:19 Yet say ye, W? doth not the son bear the H4069
31 for w will ye die, O house of Israel? H4100
33:11 for w will ye die, O house of Israel? H4100
Dan 1:10 your drink: for w should he see your H4100
2:15 king's captain, W *is* the decree *so* hasty H4100
Jna 1:10 said unto him, W hast thou done this? H4100
Mic 4: 9 Now w dost thou cry out aloud? *is there* H4100
Hab 1: 3 W dost thou shew me iniquity, and H4100
Hag 1: 9 did blow upon it. W? saith the H3282+H4100
Mal 2:10 one God created us? w do we deal H4069
Mt 6:28 And w take ye thought for raiment? G5101
7: 3 And w beholdest thou the mote that is G5101
8:26 And he saith unto them, W are ye G5101
9:11 said unto his disciples, W eateth your G1302
14 of John, saying, W do we and the G1302
13:10 said unto him, W speakest thou unto G1302
15: 2 W do thy disciples transgress the G1302
3 and said unto them, W do ye also G1302
16: 8 O ye of little faith, w reason ye among G5101
17:10 And his disciples asked him, saying, W G5101
19 and said, W could not we cast him out? G1302
19: 7 They say unto him, W did Moses then G5101
17 And he said unto him, W callest thou G5101
20: 6 them, W stand ye here all the day idle? G5101
21:25 unto us, W did ye not then believe him? G1302
22:18 said, W tempt ye me, *ye* hypocrites? G5101
26:10 he said unto them, W trouble ye the G5101
27:23 And the governor said, W, what evil G1063
46 my God, w hast thou forsaken me? G2444
Mk 2: 7 W doth this *man* thus speak G5101
8 he said unto them, W reason ye these G5101
18 and say unto him, W do the disciples of G1302
24 unto him, Behold, w do they on the G5101
4:40 And he said unto them, W are ye so G5101
5:35 daughter is dead: w troublest thou the G5101
39 saith unto them, W make ye this ado, G5101
7: 5 asked him, W walk not thy disciples G1302
8:12 his spirit, and saith, W doth this G5101
17 saith unto them, W reason ye, because G5101
9:11 And they asked him, saying, W say the G3754
28 privately, W could not we cast him out? G3754
10:18 And Jesus said unto him, W callest G5101
11: 3 And if any man say unto you, W do ye G5101
31 will say, W then did ye not believe him? G1302
12:15 said unto them, W tempt ye me? bring G5101
14: 4 and said, W was this waste of the G5101
6 And Jesus said, Let her alone; w G5101
15:14 Then Pilate said unto them, W, what G1063
34 my God, w hast thou forsaken me? G5101
Lk 2:48 unto him, Son, w hast thou thus dealt G5101
5:30 his disciples, saying, W do ye eat and G1302
33 And they said unto him, W do the G1302
6: 2 said unto them, W do ye that which is G5101
41 And w beholdest thou the mote that is G5101
46 And w call ye me, Lord, Lord, and do G5101
12:26 is least, w take ye thought for the rest? G5101
57 Yea, and w even of yourselves judge ye G5101
13: 7 it down; w cumbereth it the ground? G2444
18:19 And Jesus said unto him, W callest G5101
19:31 And if any man ask you, W do ye loose G1302
33 said unto them, W loose ye the colt? G5101
20: 5 will say, W then believed ye him not? G1302
23 and said unto them, W tempt ye me? G5101
22:46 And said unto them, W sleep ye? rise G5101
23:22 the third time, W, what evil hath he G1063
24: 5 W seek ye the living among the dead? G5101
38 And he said unto them, W are ye G5101
38 and w do thoughts arise in your hearts? G1302
Jn 1:25 said unto him, W baptizest thou then, G5101
4:27 thou? or, W talkest thou with her? G5101
7:19 the law? W go ye about to kill me? G5101
45 them, W have ye not brought him? G1302
8:43 W do ye not understand my speech? G1302
46 I say the truth, w do ye not believe me? G1302
9:30 and said unto them, W herein is a G1063
10:20 a devil, and is mad; w hear ye him? G5101
12: 5 W was not this ointment sold for three G1302
13:37 Peter said unto him, Lord, w cannot I G1302
18:21 W askest thou me? ask them which G5101
23 the evil: but if well, w smitest thou me? G5101
20:13 And they say unto her, Woman, w G5101

Jn 20:15 Jesus saith unto her, Woman, w G5101
Act 1:11 Which also said, Ye men of Galilee, w G5101
3:12 Ye men of Israel, w marvel ye at this? G5101
12 ye at this? or w look ye so earnestly G5101
4:25 David hast said, W did the heathen G2444
5: 3 But Peter said, Ananias, w hath Satan G1302
4 in thine own power? w hast thou G5101
7:26 w do ye wrong one to another? G2444
9: 4 him, Saul, Saul, w persecutest thou me? G5101
14:15 And saying, Sirs, w do ye these things? G5101
15:10 Now therefore w tempt ye God, to put a G5101
22: 7 me, Saul, Saul, w persecutest thou me? G5101
16 And now w tarriest thou? arise, and be G5101
26: 8 W should it be thought a thing G5101
14 Saul, Saul, w persecutest thou me? G5101
Ro 3: 7 w yet am I also judged as a sinner? G5101
8:24 a man seeth, w doth he yet hope for? G5101
9:19 Thou wilt say then unto me, W doth he G5101
20 formed *it*, W hast thou made me thus? G5101
14:10 But w dost thou judge thy brother? or G5101
10 judge thy brother? or w dost thou set at G5101
1Co 4: 7 didst receive *it*, w dost thou glory, as G5101
6: 7 one with another. W do ye not rather G1302
7 take wrong? w do ye not rather *suffer* G1302
10:29 of the other: for w is my liberty judged G2444
30 For if I by grace be a partaker, w am I G5101
15:29 w are they then baptized for the dead? G5101
30 And w stand we in jeopardy every G5101
Gal 2:14 as do the Jews, w compellest thou the G5101
5:11 preach circumcision, w do I yet suffer G5101
Col 2:20 of the world, w, as though living in G5101

WICKED

Gen 13:13 But the men of Sodom *were* w and H7451
18:23 also destroy the righteous with the w? H7563
25 the righteous with the w: and that the H7563
25 should be as the w, that be far from H7563
38: 7 And Er, Judah's firstborn, was w in the H7451
Ex 9:27 *is* righteous, and I and my people *are* w. H7563
23: 1 the w to be an unrighteous witness. H7563
7 slay thou not: for I will not justify the w. H7563
Lev 20:17 his nakedness; it *is* a w thing; and they H2617
Nu 16:26 the tents of these w men, and touch H7563
Dt 15: 9 a thought in thy w heart, saying, The H1100
17: 5 have committed that w thing, unto thy H7451
23: 9 then keep thee from every w thing. H7451
25: 1 the righteous, and condemn the w. H7563
2 And it shall be, if the w man *be* worthy H7563
1Sa 2: 9 his saints, and the w shall be silent in H7563
24:13 from the w: but mine hand shall H7563
30:22 Then answered all the w men and *men* H7451
2Sa 3:34 falleth before w men, *so* fellest thou. H5766
4:11 How much more, when w men have H7563
1Ki 8:32 condemning the w, to bring his way H7563
2Ki 17:11 and wrought w things to provoke the H7451
2Ch 6:23 by requiting the w, by recompensing his H7563
7:14 turn from their w ways; then will I hear H7451
24: 7 For the sons of Athaliah, that w H4849
Neh 9:35 turned they from their w works. H7451
Est 7: 6 and enemy *is* this w Haman. Then H7451
9:25 by letters that his w device, which he H7451
Job 3:17 There the w cease *from* troubling; and H7563
8:22 place of the w shall come to nought. H7563
9:22 *it*, He destroyeth the perfect and the w. H7563
24 the hand of the w: he covereth the faces H7563
29 *If* I be w, why then labour I in vain? H7561
10: 3 and shine upon the counsel of the w? H7563
7 Thou knowest that I am not w; and H7561
15 If I be w, woe unto me; and *if* I be H7561
11:20 But the eyes of the w shall fail, and they H7563
15:20 The w man travaileth with pain all *his* H7563
16:11 turned me over into the hands of the w. H7563
18: 5 Yea, the light of the w shall be put out, H7563
21 Surely such *are* the dwellings of the w, H5767
20: 5 That the triumphing of the w *is* short, H7563
22 hand of the w shall come upon him. H6011
29 This *is* the portion of a w man from H7563
21: 7 Wherefore do the w live, become old, H7563
16 the counsel of the w is far from me. H7563
17 How oft is the candle of the w put out! H7563
28 where *are* the dwelling places of the w? H7563
30 That the w is reserved to the day of H7451
22:15 Hast thou marked the old way which w H205
18 but the counsel of the w is far from me. H7563
24: 6 and they gather the vintage of the w. H7563
27: 7 Let mine enemy be as the w, and he H7563
13 This *is* the portion of a w man with H7563
29:17 And I brake the jaws of the w, and H5767
31: 3 *Is* not destruction to the w? and a H5767

Job 34: 8 of iniquity, and walketh with w men. H7562
18 *Is it fit* to say to a king, *Thou art* w? *and* H1100
26 He striketh them as w men in the open H7563
36 end because of *his* answers for w men. H205
36: 6 He preserveth not the life of the w: but H7563
17 the judgment of the w: judgment and H7563
38:13 that the w might be shaken out of it? H7563
15 And from the w their light is H7563
40:12 and tread down the w in their place. H7563
Ps 7: 9 Oh let the wickedness of the w come to H7563
11 and God is angry *with the* w every day.
9: 5 destroyed the w, thou hast put out their H7563
16 he executeth: the w is snared in the H7563
17 The w shall be turned into hell, *and* all H7563
10: 2 The w in *his* pride doth persecute the H7563
3 For the w boasteth of his heart's desire, H7563
4 The w, through the pride of his H7563
13 Wherefore doth the w contemn God? H7563
15 Break thou the arm of the w and the H7563
11: 2 For, lo, the w bend *their* bow, they H7563
5 the righteous: but the w and him that H7563
6 Upon the w he shall rain snares, fire H7563
12: 8 The w walk on every side, when the H7563
17: 9 From the w that oppress me, *from* my H7563
13 my soul from the w, *which is* thy sword: H7563
22:16 assembly of the w have inclosed me: H7489
26: 5 of evil doers; and will not sit with the w. H7563
27: 2 When the w, *even* mine enemies and H7489
28: 3 Draw me not away with the w, and with H7563
31:17 upon thee: let the w be ashamed, *and* H7563
32:10 Many sorrows *shall be* to the w: but he H7563
34:21 Evil shall slay the w: and they that hate H7563
36: 1 The transgression of the w saith within H7563
11 let not the hand of the w remove me. H7563
37: 7 man who bringeth w devices to pass. H4209
10 For yet a little while, and the w *shall* H7563
12 The w plotteth against the just, and H7563
14 The w have drawn out the sword, and H7563
16 *is* better than the riches of many w. H7563
17 For the arms of the w shall be broken: H7563
20 But the w shall perish, and the enemies H7563
21 The w borroweth, and payeth not H7563
28 but the seed of the w shall be cut off. H7563
32 The w watcheth the righteous, and H7563
34 when the w are cut off, thou shalt see *it*. H7563
35 I have seen the w in great power, and H7563
38 the end of the w shall be cut off. H7563
40 them from the w, and save them, H7563
39: 1 with a bridle, while the w is before me. H7563
50:16 But unto the w God saith, What hast H7563
55: 3 the oppression of the w: for they cast H7563
58: 3 The w are estranged from the womb: H7563
10 shall wash his feet in the blood of the w. H7563
59: 5 merciful to any w transgressors. Selah. H205
64: 2 counsel of the w; from the insurrection H7489
68: 2 let the w perish at the presence of God. H7563
71: 4 of the hand of the w, out of the hand of H7563
73: 3 *when* I saw the prosperity of the w. H7563
74:19 the multitude *of the* w: forget not the
75: 4 and to the w, Lift not up the horn: H7563
8 thereof, all the w of the earth shall H7563
10 All the horns of the w also will I cut off; H7563
82: 2 and accept the persons of the w? Selah. H7563
4 rid *them* out of the hand of the w. H7563
91: 8 behold and see the reward of the w. H7563
92: 7 When the w spring as the grass, and H7563
11 *desire* of the w that rise up against me. H7489
94: 3 LORD, how long shall the w, how long H7563
3 wicked, how long shall the w triumph? H7563
13 until the pit be digged for the w. H7563
97:10 them out of the hand of the w. H7563
101: 3 I will set no w thing before mine eyes: I H1100
4 from me: I will not know a w *person*. H7451
8 I will early destroy all the w of the land; H7563
8 off all w doers from the city of the LORD. H205
104:35 earth, and let the w be no more. Bless H7563
106:18 company; the flame burned up the w. H7563
109: 2 For the mouth of the w and the mouth H7563
6 Set thou a w man over him: and let H7563
112:10 The w shall see *it*, and be grieved; he H7563
10 away: the desire of the w shall perish. H7563
119:53 because of the w that forsake thy law. H7563
61 The bands of the w have robbed me: H7563
95 The w have waited for me to destroy H7563
110 The w have laid a snare for me: yet I H7563
119 Thou puttest away all the w of the H7563
155 Salvation *is* far from the w: for they H7563
125: 3 For the rod of the w shall not rest upon H7562
129: 4 he hath cut asunder the cords of the w. H7563

Ps 139:19 Surely thou wilt slay the w, O God: H7563
24 And see if *there be any* w way in me, H6090
140: 4 the hands of the w; preserve me from H7563
8 Grant not, O LORD, the desires of the w: H7563
8 further not his w device; *lest* they exalt H7563
141: 4 thing, to practise w works with men H7562
10 Let the w fall into their own nets, whilst H7563
145:20 love him: but all the w will he destroy. H7563
146: 9 way of the w he turneth upside down. H7563
147: 6 he casteth the w down to the ground. H7563
Prv 2:14 *and* delight in the frowardness of the w; H7451
22 But the w shall be cut off from the H7563
3:25 the desolation of the w, when it cometh. H7563
33 *is* in the house of the w: but he blesseth H7563
4:14 Enter not into the path of the w, and go H7563
19 The way of the w *is* as darkness: they H7563
5:22 His own iniquities shall take the w H7563
6:12 A naughty person, a w man, walketh H205
18 An heart that deviseth w imaginations, H205
9: 7 a w *man getteth* himself a blot. H7563
10: 3 he casteth away the substance of the w. H7563
6 violence covereth the mouth of the w. H7563
7 but the name of the w shall rot. H7563
11 violence covereth the mouth of the w. H7563
16 *tendeth* to life: the fruit of the w to sin. H7563
20 silver: the heart of the w *is* little worth. H7563
24 The fear of the w, it shall come upon H7563
25 As the whirlwind passeth, so *is* the w H7563
27 the years of the w shall be shortened. H7563
28 the expectation of the w shall perish. H7563
30 but the w shall not inhabit the earth. H7563
32 mouth of the w *speaketh* frowardness. H7563
11: 5 the w shall fall by his own wickedness. H7563
7 When a w man dieth, *his* expectation H7563
8 trouble, and the w cometh in his stead. H7563
10 when the w perish, *there is* shouting. H7563
11 it is overthrown by the mouth of the w. H7563
18 The w worketh a deceitful work: but to H7563
21 *Though* hand *join* in hand, the w shall H7451
23 *but* the expectation of the w *is* wrath. H7563
31 much more the w and the sinner. H7563
12: 2 a man of w devices will he condemn. H4209
5 *but* the counsels of the w *are* deceit. H7563
6 The words of the w *are* to lie in wait for H7563
7 The w are overthrown, and *are* not: but H7563
10 the tender mercies of the w *are* cruel. H7563
12 The w desireth the net of evil *men*: but H7563
13 The w is snared by the transgression of H7451
21 but the w shall be filled with mischief. H7563
26 but the way of the w seduceth them. H7563
13: 5 A righteous *man* hateth lying: but a w H7563
9 but the lamp of the w shall be put out. H7563
17 A w messenger falleth into mischief: H7563
25 soul: but the belly of the w shall want. H7563
14:11 The house of the w shall be H7563
17 and a man of w devices is hated. H4209
19 and the w at the gates of the righteous. H7563
32 The w is driven away in his H7563
15: 6 but in the revenues of the w is trouble. H7563
8 The sacrifice of the w *is* an H7563
9 The way of the w *is* an abomination H7563
26 The thoughts of the w *are* an H7451
28 mouth of the w poureth out evil things. H7563
29 The LORD *is* far from the w: but he H7563
16: 4 yea, even the w for the day of evil. H7563
17: 4 A w doer giveth heed to false lips; *and* H7489
15 He that justifieth the w, and he that H7563
23 A w *man* taketh a gift out of the bosom H7563
18: 3 When the w cometh, *then* cometh also H7563
5 the person of the w, to overthrow the H7563
19:28 the mouth of the w devoureth iniquity. H7563
20:26 A wise king scattereth the w, and H7563
21: 4 heart, *and* the plowing of the w, *is* sin. H7563
7 The robbery of the w shall destroy H7563
10 The soul of the w desireth evil: his H7563
12 considereth the house of the w: *but God* H7563
12 the w for *their* wickedness. H7563
18 The w *shall be* a ransom for the H7563
27 The sacrifice of the w *is* abomination: H7563
27 *when* he bringeth it with a w mind? H2154
29 A w man hardeneth his face: but *as for* H7563
24:15 Lay not wait, O w *man*, against the H7563
16 again: but the w shall fall into mischief. H7563
19 *men*, neither be thou envious at the w; H7563
20 the candle of the w shall be put out. H7563
24 He that saith unto the w, Thou *art* H7563
25: 5 Take away the w *from* before the king, H7563
26 down before the w *is as* a troubled H7563
26:23 Burning lips and a w heart *are like* a H7451

Prv 28: 1 The **w** flee when no man pursueth: but H7563
4 They that forsake the law praise the **w**: H7563
12 but when the **w** rise, a man is hidden. H7563
15 *so is* a **w** ruler over the poor people. H7563
28 When the **w** rise, men hide themselves: H7563
29: 2 the **w** beareth rule, the people mourn. H7563
7 *but* the **w** regardeth not to know *it*. H7563
12 hearken to lies, all his servants *are* **w**. H7563
16 When the **w** are multiplied, H7563
27 in the way *is* abomination to the **w**. H7563
Ecc 3:17 righteous and the **w**: for *there is* a time H7563
7:15 and there is a **w** *man* that prolongeth H7563
17 Be not over much **w**, neither be thou H7561
8:10 And so I saw the **w** buried, who had H7563
13 But it shall not be well with the **w**, H7563
14 to the work of the **w**; again, there be H7563
14 again, there be **w** *men*, to whom it H7563
9: 2 and to the **w**; to the good and to the H7563
Isa 3:11 Woe unto the **w**! *it shall be* ill *with him*: H7563
5:23 Which justify the **w** for reward, and H7563
11: 4 the breath of his lips shall he slay the **w**. H7563
13:11 *their* evil, and the **w** for their iniquity; H7563
14: 5 of the **w**, *and* the sceptre of the rulers. H7563
26:10 Let favour be shewed to the **w**, *yet* will H7563
32: 7 evil: he deviseth **w** devices to destroy H2154
48:22 *is* no peace, saith the LORD, unto the **w**. H7563
53: 9 And he made his grave with the **w**, and H7563
55: 7 Let the **w** forsake his way, and the H7563
57:20 But the **w** *are* like the troubled sea, H7563
21 *is* no peace, saith my God, to the **w**. H7563
Jer 2:33 thou also taught the **w** ones thy ways. H7451
5:26 For among my people are found **w** H7563
28 the deeds of the **w**: they judge not the H7451
6:29 in vain: for the **w** are not plucked away. H7451
12: 1 the way of the **w** prosper? *wherefore* H7563
15:21 of the hand of the **w**, and I will redeem H7451
17: 9 and desperately **w**: who can know it? H605
23:19 fall grievously upon the head of the **w**. H7563
25:31 *are* **w** to the sword, saith the LORD. H7563
30:23 fall with pain upon the head of the **w**. H7563
Ezk 3:18 When I say unto the **w**, Thou shalt H7563
18 to warn the **w** from his wicked way, H7563
18 wicked from his **w** way, to save his life; H7563
18 his life; the same **w** *man* shall die in his H7563
19 Yet if thou warn the **w**, and he turn not H7563
19 nor from his **w** way, he shall die in H7563
7:21 a prey, and to the **w** of the earth for a H7563
8: 9 the **w** abominations that they do here. H7451
11: 2 and give **w** counsel in this city: H7451
13:22 the hands of the **w**, that he should not H7451
22 from his **w** way, by promising him life: H7563
18:20 wickedness of the **w** shall be upon him. H7563
21 But if the **w** will turn from all his sins H7563
23 Have I any pleasure at all that the **w** H7563
24 that the **w** *man* doeth, shall he H7563
27 Again, when the **w** *man* turneth away H7563
20:44 not according to your **w** ways, nor H7451
21: 3 off from thee the righteous and the **w**. H7563
4 righteous and the **w**, therefore shall my H7563
25 And thou, profane **w** prince of Israel, H7563
29 *are* slain, of the **w**, whose day is come, H7563
30:12 the hand of the **w**: and I will make the H7451
33: 8 When I say unto the **w**, O wicked *man*, H7563
8 When I say unto the wicked, O **w** *man*, H7563
8 speak to warn the **w** from his way, that H7563
8 from his way, that **w** *man* shall die in H7563
9 Nevertheless, if thou warn the **w** of his H7563
11 in the death of the **w**; but that the H7563
11 but that the **w** turn from his way and H7563
12 the wickedness of the **w**, he shall not fall H7563
14 Again, when I say unto the **w**, Thou H7563
15 *If* the **w** restore the pledge, give again H7563
19 But if the **w** turn from his wickedness, H7563
Dan 12:10 and tried; but the **w** shall do wickedly: H7563
10 and none of the **w** shall understand; H7563
Mic 6:10 in the house of the **w**, and the scant H7563
11 Shall I count *them* pure with the **w** H7562
Nah 1: 3 not at all acquit *the* **w**: the LORD hath his
11 evil against the LORD, a **w** counsellor. H1100
15 thy vows: for the **w** shall no more pass H1100
Hab 1: 4 go forth: for the **w** doth compass about H7563
13 tongue when the **w** devoureth *the man* H7563
3:13 of the house of the **w**, by discovering the H7563
Zep 1: 3 with the **w**; and I will cut off man H7563
Mal 3:18 righteous and the **w**, between him that H7563
4: 3 And ye shall tread down the **w**; for they H7563
Mt 12:45 other spirits more **w** than himself, and G4191
45 shall it be also unto this **w** generation. G4190
13:19 then cometh the **w** *one*, and catcheth G4190
13:38 the tares are the children of the **w** *one*; G4190
49 and sever the **w** from among the just, G4190
16: 4 A **w** and adulterous generation seeketh G4190
18:32 unto him, O thou **w** servant, I forgave G4190
21:41 destroy those **w** men, and will let out G2556
25:26 unto him, *Thou* **w** and slothful servant, G4190
Lk 11:26 other spirits more **w** than himself; and G4191
19:22 will I judge thee, *thou* **w** servant. Thou G4190
Act 2:23 by **w** hands have crucified and slain: G459
18:14 of wrong or **w** lewdness, O *ye* Jews, G4190
1Co 5:13 from among yourselves that **w** person. G4190
Eph 6:16 to quench all the fiery darts of the **w**. G4190
Col 1:21 by **w** works, yet now hath he reconciled G4190
2Th 2: 8 And then shall that **W** be revealed, G459
3: 2 and **w** men: for all *men* have not faith. G4190
2Pt 2: 7 with the filthy conversation of the **w**: G113
3:17 of the **w**, fall from your own stedfastness. G113
1Jn 2:13 overcome the **w** one. I write unto you, G4190
14 you, and ye have overcome the **w** one. G4190
3:12 Not as Cain, *who* was of that **w** one, G4190
5:18 and that **w** one toucheth him not. G4190

WICKEDLY

Gen 19: 7 said, I pray you, brethren, do not so **w**. H7489
Dt 9:18 ye sinned, in doing **w** in the sight of the H7451
Jdg 19:23 you, do not *so* **w**; seeing that this man H7489
1Sa 12:25 But if ye shall still do **w**, ye shall be H7489
2Sa 22:22 and have not **w** departed from my God. H7561
24:17 and I have done **w**: but these sheep, H5753
2Ki 21:11 *and* hath done **w** above all that the H7489
2Ch 6:37 we have done amiss, and have dealt **w**; H7561
20:35 Ahaziah king of Israel, who did very **w**: H7561
22: 3 his mother was his counsellor to do **w**. H7561
Neh 9:33 hast done right, but we have done **w**: H7561
Job 13: 7 Will ye speak **w** for God? and talk H5766
34:12 Yea, surely God will not do **w**, neither H7561
Ps 18:21 and have not **w** departed from my God. H7561
73: 8 They are corrupt, and speak **w** H7451
74: 3 enemy hath done **w** in the sanctuary. H7489
106: 6 committed iniquity, we have done **w**. H7561
139:20 For they speak against thee **w**, *and* H4209
Dan 9: 5 and have done **w**, and have rebelled, H7561
15 day; we have sinned, we have done **w**. H7561
11:32 And such as do **w** against the covenant H7561
12:10 the wicked shall do **w**: and none of the H7561
Mal 4: 1 and all that do **w**, shall be stubble: and H7564

WICKEDNESS

Gen 6: 5 And GOD saw that the **w** of man *was* H7451
39: 9 I do this great **w**, and sin against God? H7451
Lev 18:17 they *are* her near kinswomen: it *is* **w**. H2154
19:29 and the land become full of **w**. H2154
20:14 her mother, it *is* **w**: they shall be burnt H2154
14 they; that there be no **w** among you. H2154
Dt 9: 4 land: but for the **w** of these nations the H7564
5 land: but for the **w** of these nations the H7564
27 people, nor to their **w**, nor to their sin: H7562
13:11 more any such **w** as this is among you. H7451
17: 2 that hath wrought **w** in the sight of the H7451
28:20 quickly; because of the **w** of thy doings, H7455
Jdg 9:56 Thus God rendered the **w** of H7451
20: 3 of Israel, Tell *us*, how was this **w**? H7451
12 What **w** *is* this that is done among you? H7451
1Sa 12:17 and see that your **w** *is* great, which ye H7451
20 have done all this **w**: yet turn not aside H7451
24:13 As saith the proverb of the ancients, **W** H7562
25:39 hath returned the **w** of Nabal upon his H7451
2Sa 3:39 the doer of evil according to his **w**. H7451
7:10 **w** afflict them any more, as beforetime, H5766
1Ki 1:52 if **w** shall be found in him, he shall die. H7451
2:44 knowest all the **w** which thine heart is H7451
44 return thy **w** upon thine own head; H7451
8:47 done perversely, we have committed **w**; H7561
21:25 himself to work **w** in the sight of the H7451
2Ki 21: 6 he wrought much **w** in the sight of the H7451
1Ch 17: 9 the children of **w** waste them any more, H5766
Job 4: 8 iniquity, and sow **w**, reap the same. H5999
11:11 For he knoweth vain men: he seeth **w** H205
14 and let not **w** dwell in thy tabernacles. H5766
20:12 Though **w** be sweet in his mouth, H7451
22: 5 *Is* not thy **w** great? and thine iniquities H7451
24:20 and **w** shall be broken as a tree. H5766
27: 4 My lips shall not speak **w**, nor my H5766
34:10 God, *that he should do* **w**; and *from* the H7562
35: 8 Thy **w** *may hurt* a man as thou *art*; and H7562
Ps 5: 4 in **w**: neither shall evil dwell with thee. H7562
9 part *is* very **w**; their throat *is* an open H1942
7: 9 Oh let the **w** of the wicked come to an H7451
10:15 *man*: seek out his **w** *till* thou find none. H7562
Ps 28: 4 according to the **w** of their endeavours: H7455
45: 7 and hatest **w**: therefore God, thy God, H7562
52: 7 *and* strengthened himself in his **w**. H1942
55:11 **W** *is* in the midst thereof: deceit and H1942
15 down quick into hell: for **w** *is* in their H7451
58: 2 Yea, in heart ye work **w**; ye weigh the H5766
84:10 my God, than to dwell in the tents of **w**. H7562
89:22 upon him; nor the son of **w** afflict him. H5766
94:23 off in their own **w**; *yea*, the LORD our H7451
107:34 for the **w** of them that dwell therein. H7451
Prv 4:17 For they eat the bread of **w**, and drink H7562
8: 7 For my mouth shall speak truth; and **w** H7562
10: 2 Treasures of **w** profit nothing: but H7562
11: 5 but the wicked shall fall by his own **w**. H7564
12: 3 A man shall not be established by **w**: H7562
13: 6 way: but **w** overthroweth the sinner. H7564
14:32 The wicked is driven away in his **w**: but H7451
16:12 to kings to commit **w**: for the throne is H7562
21:12 overthroweth the wicked for *their* **w**. H7451
26:26 by deceit, his **w** shall be shewed before H7451
30:20 her mouth, and saith, I have done no **w**. H205
Ecc 3:16 of judgment, *that* **w** *was* there; and the H7562
7:15 *man* that prolongeth *his life* in his **w**. H7451
25 and to know the **w** of folly, even of H7562
8: 8 **w** deliver those that are given to it. H7562
Isa 9:18 For **w** burneth as the fire: it shall H7564
47:10 For thou hast trusted in thy **w**: thou H7451
58: 4 with the fist of **w**: ye shall not fast as H7562
6 loose the bands of **w**, to undo the heavy H7562
Jer 1:16 touching all their **w**, who have forsaken H7451
2:19 Thine own **w** shall correct thee, and thy H7451
3: 2 with thy whoredoms and with thy **w**. H7451
4:14 O Jerusalem, wash thine heart from **w**, H7451
18 thee; this *is* thy **w**, because it is bitter, H7451
6: 7 casteth out her **w**: violence and spoil is H7451
7:12 I did to it for the **w** of my people Israel. H7451
8: 6 him of his **w**, saying, What have H7451
12: 4 wither, for the **w** of them that dwell H7451
14:16 for I will pour their **w** upon them. H7451
20 We acknowledge, O LORD, our **w**, *and* H7562
22:22 ashamed and confounded for all thy **w**. H7451
23:11 have I found their **w**, saith the LORD. H7451
14 return from his **w**: they are all of them H7451
33: 5 **w** I have hid my face from this city. H7451
44: 3 Because of their **w** which they have H7451
5 **w**, to burn no incense unto other gods. H7451
9 Have ye forgotten the **w** of your H7451
9 your fathers, and the **w** of the kings of H7451
9 of Judah, and the **w** of their wives, and H7451
9 and your own **w**, and the wickedness H7451
9 and the **w** of your wives, which H7451
Lam 1:22 Let all their **w** come before thee; and do H7451
Ezk 3:19 he turn not from his **w**, nor from his H7562
5: 6 my judgments into **w** more than the H7564
7:11 Violence is risen up into a rod of **w**: H7562
16:23 And it came to pass after all thy **w**, H7451
57 Before thy **w** was discovered, as at the H7451
18:20 the **w** of the wicked shall be upon him. H7564
27 turneth away from his **w** that he hath H7564
31:11 him: I have driven him out for his **w**. H7562
33:12 as for the **w** of the wicked, he shall H7564
12 he turneth from his **w**; neither shall the H7562
19 But if the wicked turn from his **w**, and H7564
Hos 7: 1 and the **w** of Samaria: for they H7451
2 all their **w**: now their own doings H7451
3 They make the king glad with their **w**, H7451
9:15 All their **w** *is* in Gilgal: for there I hated H7451
15 them: for the **w** of their doings I will H7455
10:13 Ye have plowed **w**, ye have reaped H7562
15 of your great **w**: in a morning shall H7451
Joel 3:13 the fats overflow; for their **w** *is* great. H7451
Jna 1: 2 it; for their **w** is come up before me. H7451
Mic 6:10 Are there yet the treasures of **w** in the H7562
Nah 3:19 hath not thy **w** passed continually? H7451
Zec 5: 8 And he said, This *is* **w**. And he cast it H7564
Mal 1: 4 them, The border of **w**, and, The people H7564
3:15 they that work **w** are set up; yea, *they* H7564
Mt 22:18 But Jesus perceived their **w**, and said, G4189
Mk 7:22 Thefts, covetousness, **w**, deceit, G4189
Lk 11:39 inward part is full of ravening and **w**. G4189
Act 8:22 Repent therefore of this thy **w**, and pray G2549
25: 5 this man, if there be any **w** in him. G824
Ro 1:29 fornication, **w**, covetousness, G4189
1Co 5: 8 leaven of malice and **w**; but with the G4189
Eph 6:12 against spiritual **w** in high *places*. G4189
1Jn 5:19 of God, and the whole world lieth in **w**. G4190

WIDE

Dt 15: 8 But thou shalt open thine hand **w** unto H6605

Dt 15:11 open thine hand w unto thy brother, to H6605
1Ch 4:40 the land *was* w, and quiet, and H7342+H3027
Job 29:23 their mouth w *as* for the latter rain.
30:14 They came *upon me* as a w breaking in H7342
Ps 35:21 Yea, they opened their mouth w H7337
81:10 open thy mouth w, and I will fill it. H7337
104:25 *So is* this great and w sea, H7342+H3027
Prv 13: 3 w his lips shall have destruction. H6589
21: 9 with a brawling woman in a w house. H2267
25:24 a brawling woman and in a w house. H2267
Isa 57: 4 whom make ye a w mouth, *and* draw H7337
Jer 22:14 That saith, I will build me a w house H4060
Nah 3:13 thy land shall be set w open unto thine H6605
Mt 7:13 Enter ye in at the strait gate: for w *is* G4116

WIDENESS

Ezk 41:10 And between the chambers *was* the w H7341

WIDOW

Gen 38:11 in law, Remain a w at thy father's house, H490
Ex 22:22 Ye shall not afflict any w, or fatherless H490
Lev 21:14 A w, or a divorced woman, or profane, *or* H490
22:13 But if the priest's daughter be a w, or H490
Nu 30: 9 But every vow of a w, and of her that is H490
Dt 10:18 of the fatherless and w, and loveth the H490
14:29 fatherless, and the w, which *are* within H490
16:11 the fatherless, and the w, that *are* among H490
14 and the w, that *are* within thy gates. H490
24:19 and for the w: that the LORD thy God H490
20 stranger, for the fatherless, and for the w. H490
21 stranger, for the fatherless, and for the w. H490
26:12 fatherless, and the w, that they may eat H490
13 and to the w, according to all thy H490
27:19 w. And all the people shall say, Amen. H490
2Sa 14: 5 a w woman, and mine husband is dead. H490
1Ki 11:26 *was* Zeruah, a w woman, even he lifted H490
17: 9 a w woman there to sustain thee. H490
10 the city, behold, the w woman *was* there H490
20 evil upon the w with whom I sojourn, H490
Job 24:21 beareth not: and doeth not good to the w. H490
31:16 or have caused the eyes of the w to fail; H490
Ps 94: 6 They slay the w and the stranger, and H490
109: 9 children be fatherless, and his wife a w. H490
146: 9 the fatherless and w: but the way of the H490
Prv 15:25 but he will establish the border of the w. H490
Isa 1:17 judge the fatherless, plead for the w. H490
23 doth the cause of the w come unto them. H490
47: 8 I shall not sit *as* a w, neither shall I know H490
Jer 7: 6 the fatherless, and the w, and shed not H490
22: 3 the fatherless, nor the w, neither shed H490
Lam 1: 1 is she become as a w! she *that was* great H490
Ezk 22: 7 have they vexed the fatherless and the w. H490
44:22 for their wives a w, nor her that is put H490
22 of Israel, or a w that had a priest before. H490
Zec 7:10 And oppress not the w, nor the H490
Mal 3: 5 in *his* wages, the w, and the fatherless, H490
Mk 12:42 And there came a certain poor w, and G5503
43 That this poor w hath cast more in, G5503
Lk 2:37 And she *was* a w of about fourscore G5503
4:26 of Sidon, unto a woman *that was* a w. G5503
7:12 and she was a w: and much people of G5503
18: 3 And there was a w in that city; and she G5503
5 Yet because this w troubleth me, I will G5503
21: 2 And he saw also a certain poor w G5503
3 poor w hath cast in more than they all: G5503
1Ti 5: 4 But if any w have children or nephews, G5503
5 Now she that is a w indeed, and G5503
9 Let not a w be taken into the number G5503
Rev 18: 7 and am no w, and shall see no sorrow. G5503

WIDOWHOOD

Gen 38:19 her, and put on the garments of her w. H491
2Sa 20: 3 unto the day of their death, living in w. H491
Isa 47: 9 of children, and w: they shall come upon H489
54: 4 the reproach of thy w any more. H491

WIDOWS

Ex 22:24 shall be w, and your children fatherless. H490
Job 22: 9 Thou hast sent w away empty, and the H490
27:15 in death: and his w shall not weep. H490
Ps 68: 5 of the w, *is* God in his holy habitation. H490
78:64 and their w made no lamentation. H490
Isa 9:17 their fatherless and w: for every one *is* an H490
10: 2 of my people, that w may be their prey, H490
Jer 15: 8 Their w are increased to me above the H490
18:21 children, and *be* w; and let their men be H490
49:11 *them* alive; and let thy w trust in me. H490
Lam 5: 3 and fatherless, our mothers *are* as w. H490
Ezk 22:25 made her many w in the midst thereof. H490

Lk 4:25 But I tell you of a truth, many w were G5503
Act 6: 1 because their w were neglected in the G5503
9:39 and all the w stood by him weeping, G5503
41 the saints and w, presented her alive. G5503
1Co 7: 8 I say therefore to the unmarried and w, G5503
1Ti 5: 3 Honour w that are widows indeed. G5503
3 Honour widows that are w indeed. G5503
11 But the younger w refuse: for when G5503
16 believeth have w, let them relieve them, G5503
16 it may relieve them that are w indeed. G5503
Jas 1:27 the fatherless and w in their affliction, G5503

WIDOW'S

Gen 38:14 And she put her w garments off from H491
Dt 24:17 nor take a w raiment to pledge: H490
1Ki 7:14 He *was* a w son of the tribe of Naphtali, H490
Job 24: 3 they take the w ox for a pledge. H490
29:13 and I caused the w heart to sing for joy. H490

WIDOWS'

Mt 23:14 for ye devour w houses, and for a G5503
Mk 12:40 Which devour w houses, and for a G5503
Lk 20:47 Which devour w houses, and for a G5503

WIDTH See WIDENESS.

WIFE

Gen 2:24 unto his w: and they shall be one flesh. H802
25 man and his w, and were not ashamed. H802
3: 8 and Adam and his w hid themselves H802
17 the voice of thy w, and hast eaten of the H802
21 Unto Adam also and to his w did the H802
4: 1 And Adam knew Eve his w; and she H802
17 And Cain knew his w; and she conceived, H802
25 And Adam knew his w again; and she H802
6:18 and thy w, and thy sons' wives with thee. H802
7: 7 his sons, and his w, and his sons' wives H802
13 Noah, and Noah's w, and the three wives H802
8:16 Go forth of the ark, thou, and thy w, and H802
18 and his w, and his sons' wives with him: H802
11:29 name of Abram's w *was* Sarai; and the H802
29 name of Nahor's w, Milcah, the daughter H802
31 his son Abram's w; and they went forth H802
12: 5 And Abram took Sarai his w, and Lot his H802
11 he said unto Sarai his w, Behold now, I H802
12 say, This *is* his w: and they will kill me, H802
17 plagues because of Sarai Abram's w. H802
18 didst thou not tell me that she *was* thy w? H802
19 have taken her to me to w: now therefore H802
19 behold thy w, take *her*, and go thy way. H802
20 him away, and his w, and all that he had. H802
13: 1 Egypt, he, and his w, and all that he had, H802
16: 1 Now Sarai Abram's w bare him no H802
3 And Sarai Abram's w took Hagar her H802
3 her to her husband Abram to be his w. H802
17:15 As for Sarai thy w, thou shalt not call her H802
19 And God said, Sarah thy w shall bear H802
18: 9 thy w? And he said, Behold, in the tent. H802
10 and, lo, Sarah thy w shall have a son. H802
19:15 Arise, take thy w, and thy two daughters, H802
16 the hand of his w, and upon the hand H802
26 But his w looked back from behind him, H802
20: 2 And Abraham said of Sarah his w, She *is* H802
3 thou hast taken; for she *is* a man's w. H1166
7 Now therefore restore the man *his* w; for H802
12 of my mother; and she became my w. H802
14 Abraham, and restored him Sarah his w. H802
17 and his w, and his maidservants; H802
18 because of Sarah Abraham's w. H802
21:21 took him a w out of the land of Egypt. H802
23:19 buried Sarah his w in the cave of the H802
24: 3 shalt not take a w unto my son of the H802
4 and take a w unto my son Isaac. H802
7 shalt take a w unto my son from thence. H802
15 Bethuel, son of Milcah, the w of Nahor, H802
36 And Sarah my master's w bare a son to H802
37 Thou shalt not take a w to my son of the H802
38 my kindred, and take a w unto my son. H802
40 and thou shalt take a w for my son of my H802
51 son's w, as the LORD hath spoken. H802
67 she became his w; and he loved her: and H802
25: 1 Then again Abraham took a w, and her H802
10 was Abraham buried, and Sarah his w. H802
20 he took Rebekah to w, the daughter of H802
21 And Isaac entreated the LORD for his w, H802
21 of him, and Rebekah his w conceived. H802
26: 7 asked *him* of his w; and he said, She *is* H802
7 to say, *She is* my w; lest, *said he*, the men H802
8 Isaac *was* sporting with Rebekah his w. H802

Gen 26: 9 of a surety she *is* thy w: and how saidst H802
10 have lien with thy w, and thou shouldest H802
11 or his w shall surely be put to death. H802
34 when he took to w Judith the daughter H802
27:46 if Jacob take a w of the daughters of H802
28: 1 not take a w of the daughters of Canaan. H802
2 and take thee a w from thence of the H802
6 to take him a w from thence; and that H802
6 not take a w of the daughters of Canaan; H802
9 son, the sister of Nebajoth, to be his w. H802
29:21 Give *me* my w, for my days are fulfilled, H802
28 gave him Rachel his daughter to w also. H802
30: 4 to w: and Jacob went in unto her. H802
9 her maid, and gave her Jacob to w. H802
34: 4 Hamor, saying, Get me this damsel to w. H802
8 daughter: I pray you give her him to w. H802
12 unto me: but give me the damsel to w. H802
36:10 son of Adah the w of Esau, Reuel the son H802
10 the son of Bashemath the w of Esau. H802
12 these *were* the sons of Adah Esau's w. H802
13 were the sons of Bashemath Esau's w. H802
14 of Zibeon, Esau's w: and she bare to Esau H802
17 *are* the sons of Bashemath Esau's w. H802
18 Esau's w; duke Jeush, duke Jaalam, H802
18 the daughter of Anah, Esau's w. H802
38: 6 And Judah took a w for Er his firstborn, H802
8 unto thy brother's w, and marry her, and H802
9 unto his brother's w, that he spilled *it* on H802
12 of Shuah Judah's w died; and Judah was H802
14 and she was not given unto him to w. H802
39: 7 that his master's w cast her eyes upon H802
8 unto his master's w, Behold, my master H802
9 thou *art* his w: how then can I do this H802
19 the words of his w, which she spake unto H802
41:45 and he gave him to w Asenath the H802
44:27 Ye know that my w bare me two *sons*: H802
46:19 The sons of Rachel Jacob's w; Joseph, H802
49:31 and Sarah his w; there they buried Isaac H802
31 Rebekah his w; and there I buried Leah. H802
Ex 2: 1 of Levi, and took *to w* a daughter of Levi.
4:20 And Moses took his w and his sons, and H802
6:20 his father's sister to w; and she bare him H802
23 sister of Naashon, to w; and she bare him H802
25 of Putiel to w; and she bare him H802
18: 2 Moses' w, after he had sent her back, H802
5 his sons and his w unto Moses into the H802
6 and thy w, and her two sons with her. H802
20:17 thy neighbour's w, nor his manservant, H802
21: 3 then his w shall go out with him. H802
4 If his master have given him a w, and she H802
4 or daughters; the w and her children H802
5 w, and my children; I will not go out free: H802
10 If he take him another *w*; her food, her
22:16 he shall surely endow her to be his w. H802
Lev 18: 8 The nakedness of thy father's w shalt H802
14 not approach to his w: she *is* thine aunt. H802
15 w; thou shalt not uncover her nakedness. H802
16 brother's w: it *is* thy brother's nakedness. H802
18 Neither shalt thou take a w to her sister, H802
20 neighbour's w, to defile thyself with her. H802
20:10 with *another* man's w, *even he* that H802
10 his neighbour's w, the adulterer and the H802
11 with his father's w hath uncovered his H802
14 And if a man take a w and her mother, it H802
20 And if a man shall lie with his uncle's w, H1733
21 And if a man shall take his brother's w, it H802
21: 7 They shall not take a w *that is* a whore, H802
13 And he shall take a w in her virginity. H802
14 shall take a virgin of his own people to w. H802
Nu 5:12 unto them, If any man's w go aside, and H802
14 he be jealous of his w, and she be defiled: H802
14 jealous of his w, and she be not defiled: H802
15 Then shall the man bring his w unto the H802
29 This *is* the law of jealousies, when a w H802
30 he be jealous over his w, and shall set the H802
26:59 And the name of Amram's w *was* H802
30:16 a man and his w, between the father and H802
36: 8 of Israel, shall be w unto one of the H802
Dt 5:21 thy neighbour's w, neither shalt thou H802
13: 6 daughter, or the w of thy bosom, or thy H802
20: 7 hath betrothed a w, and hath not taken H802
21:11 that thou wouldest have her to thy w; H802
13 be her husband, and she shall be thy w. H802
22:13 If any man take a w, and go in unto her, H802
16 unto this man to w, and he hateth her; H802
19 w; he may not put her away all his days. H802
24 his neighbour's w: so thou shalt put away H802
29 and she shall be his w; because he hath H802
30 A man shall not take his father's w, nor H802

Dt 24: 1 When a man hath taken a w, and H802
2 she may go and be another man's w.
3 husband die, which took her *to be* his w; H802
4 her again to be his w, after that she is H802
5 When a man hath taken a new w, he H802
5 cheer up his w which he hath taken. H802
25: 5 have no child, the w of the dead shall not H802
5 take her to him to w, and perform the H802
7 to take his brother's w, then let his H2994
7 let his brother's w go up to the gate H2994
9 Then shall his brother's w come unto H2994
11 another, and the w of the one draweth H802
27:20 lieth with his father's w; because he H802
28:30 Thou shalt betroth a w, and another man H802
54 and toward the w of his bosom, and H802
Jos 15:16 him will I give Achsah my daughter to w. H802
17 he gave him Achsah his daughter to w. H802
Jdg 1:12 him will I give Achsah my daughter to w. H802
13 he gave him Achsah his daughter to w. H802
4: 4 And Deborah, a prophetess, the w of H802
17 the tent of Jael the w of Heber the Kenite: H802
21 Then Jael Heber's w took a nail of the H802
5:24 Blessed above women shall Jael the w of H802
11: 2 And Gilead's w bare him sons; and his H802
13: 2 and his w *was* barren, and bare not. H802
11 And Manoah arose, and went after his w, H802
19 and Manoah and his w looked on. H802
20 Manoah and his w looked on *it*, and fell H802
21 and to his w. Then Manoah knew H802
22 And Manoah said unto his w, We shall H802
23 But his w said unto him, If the LORD H802
14: 2 now therefore get her for me to w. H802
3 goest to take a w of the uncircumcised H802
15 unto Samson's w, Entice thy husband, H802
16 And Samson's w wept before him, and H802
20 But Samson's w was *given* to his H802
15: 1 Samson visited his w with a kid; and he H802
1 I will go in to my w into the chamber. H802
6 he had taken his w, and given her to his H802
21: 1 us give his daughter unto Benjamin to w. H802
18 *be* he that giveth a w to Benjamin. H802
21 you every man his w of the daughters of H802
22 to each man his w in the war: for ye did H802
Ru 1: 1 of Moab, he, and his w, and his two sons. H802
2 the name of his w Naomi, and the name H802
4: 5 the Moabitess, the w of the dead, to raise H802
10 Moreover Ruth the Moabitess, the w of H802
10 to be my w, to raise up the name H802
13 So Boaz took Ruth, and she was his w: H802
1Sa 1: 4 to Peninnah his w, and to all her sons H802
19 his w; and the LORD remembered her. H802
2:20 And Eli blessed Elkanah and his w, and H802
4:19 And his daughter in law, Phinehas' w, H802
14:50 And the name of Saul's w *was* Ahinoam, H802
18:17 will I give thee to w: only be thou valiant H802
19 given unto Adriel the Meholathite to w. H802
27 Saul gave him Michal his daughter to w. H802
19:11 Michal David's w told him, saying, If H802
25: 3 the name of his w Abigail: and *she was* H802
14 Abigail, Nabal's w, saying, Behold, David H802
37 of Nabal, and his w had told him these H802
39 with Abigail, to take her to him to w. H802
40 us unto thee, to take thee to him to w. H802
42 messengers of David, and became his w. H802
44 daughter, David's w, to Phalti the son of H802
27: 3 and Abigail the Carmelitess, Nabal's w. H802
30: 5 Abigail the w of Nabal the Carmelite. H802
22 to every man his w and his children, that H802
2Sa 2: 2 and Abigail Nabal's w the Carmelite. H802
3: 3 of Abigail the w of Nabal the Carmelite; H802
5 w. These were born to David in Hebron. H802
14 saying, Deliver *me* my w Michal, which I H802
11: 3 of Eliam, the w of Uriah the Hittite? H802
11 and to lie with my w? *as* thou livest, and H802
26 And when the w of Uriah heard that H802
27 she became his w, and bare him a son. H802
12: 9 and hast taken his w *to be* thy wife, and H802
9 his wife *to be* thy w, and hast slain him H802
10 the w of Uriah the Hittite to be thy wife. H802
10 the wife of Uriah the Hittite to be thy w. H802
15 w bare unto David, and it was very sick. H802
24 And David comforted Bath-sheba his w, H802
1Ki 2:17 give me Abishag the Shunammite to w. H802
21 be given to Adonijah thy brother to w. H802
4:11 Taphath the daughter of Solomon to w: H802
15 Basmath the daughter of Solomon to w: H802
7: 8 he had taken *to w*, like unto this porch.
9:16 present unto his daughter, Solomon's w. H802
11:19 he gave him to w the sister of his own H802

1Ki 11:19 own w, the sister of Tahpenes the queen. H802
14: 2 And Jeroboam said to his w, Arise, I pray H802
2 known to be the w of Jeroboam; and get H802
4 And Jeroboam's w did so, and arose, H802
5 Behold, the w of Jeroboam cometh H802
6 said, Come in, thou w of Jeroboam; why H802
17 And Jeroboam's w arose, and departed, H802
16:31 that he took to w Jezebel the daughter H802
21: 5 But Jezebel his w came to him, and said H802
7 And Jezebel his w said unto him, Dost H802
25 LORD, whom Jezebel his w stirred up. H802
2Ki 5: 2 maid; and she waited on Naaman's w. H802
8:18 of Ahab was his w: and he did evil in the H802
14: 9 to my son to w: and there passed by H802
22:14 the prophetess, the w of Shallum the son H802
1Ch 2:18 of Azubah *his* w, and of Jerioth: her sons H802
24 w bare him Ashur the father of Tekoa. H802
26 Jerahmeel had also another w, whose H802
29 And the name of the w of Abishur *was* H802
35 his servant to w; and she bare him Attai. H802
3: 3 Abital: the sixth, Ithream by Eglah his w. H802
4:18 And his w Jehudijah bare Jered the H802
19 And the sons of *his* w Hodiah the sister H802
7:15 And Machir took to w *the sister* of H802
16 And Maachah the w of Machir bare a H802
23 And when he went in to his w, she H802
8: 9 And he begat of Hodesh his w, Jobab, H802
2Ch 8:11 for he said, My w shall not dwell in the H802
11:18 the son of David to w, *and* Abihail the H802
21: 6 of Ahab to w: and he wrought *that* H802
22:11 of king Jehoram, the w of Jehoiada the H802
25:18 to my son to w: and there passed by H802
34:22 the prophetess, the w of Shallum the son H802
Ezr 2:61 which took a w of the daughters of H802
Neh 7:63 to w, and was called after their name. H802
Est 5:10 called for his friends, and Zeresh his w. H802
14 Then said Zeresh his w and all his H802
6:13 And Haman told Zeresh his w and all his H802
13 and Zeresh his w unto him, If Mordecai H802
Job 2: 9 Then said his w unto him, Dost thou still H802
19:17 My breath is strange to my w, though I H802
31:10 *Then* let my w grind unto another, and H802
Ps 109: 9 Let his children be fatherless, and his w H802
128: 3 Thy w *shall be* as a fruitful vine by the H802
Prv 5:18 and rejoice with the w of thy youth. H802
6:29 So he that goeth in to his neighbour's w; H802
18:22 *Whoso* findeth a w findeth a good *thing*, H802
19:13 of a w *are* a continual dropping. H802
14 and a prudent w *is* from the LORD. H802
Ecc 9: 9 Live joyfully with the w whom thou H802
Isa 54: 1 of the married w, saith the LORD. H1166
6 in spirit, and a w of youth, when thou H802
Jer 3: 1 They say, If a man put away his w, and H802
20 Surely *as* a w treacherously departeth H802
5: 8 one neighed after his neighbour's w. H802
6:11 husband with the w shall be taken, the H802
16: 2 Thou shalt not take thee a w, neither H802
Ezk 16:32 *But as* a w that committeth adultery, H802
18: 6 his neighbour's w, neither hath come H802
11 and defiled his neighbour's w, H802
15 Israel, hath not defiled his neighbour's w, H802
22:11 with his neighbour's w; and another hath H802
24:18 and at even my w died; and I did in the H802
33:26 w: and shall ye possess the land? H802
Hos 1: 2 take unto thee a w of whoredoms and H802
2: 2 for she *is* not my w, neither *am* I her H802
12:12 for a w, and for a wife he kept *sheep*. H802
12 for a wife, and for a w he kept *sheep*. H802
Am 7:17 Therefore thus saith the LORD; Thy w H802
Mal 2:14 thee and the w of thy youth, against H802
14 companion, and the w of thy covenant. H802
15 treacherously against the w of his youth. H802
Mt 1: 6 of her *that had been the* w of Urias;
20 unto thee Mary thy w: for that which is G1135
24 bidden him, and took unto him his w: G1135
5:31 shall put away his w, let him give her a G1135
32 shall put away his w, saving for the G1135
14: 3 Herodias' sake, his brother Philip's w. G1135
18:25 to be sold, and his w, and children, and G1135
19: 3 man to put away his w for every cause? G1135
5 his w: and they twain shall be one flesh? G1135
9 shall put away his w, except *it be* for G1135
10 be so with *his* w, it is not good to marry. G1135
29 or mother, or w, or children, or lands, G1135
22:24 w, and raise up seed unto his brother. G1135
25 he had married a w, deceased, and, G1060
25 no issue, left his w unto his brother: G1135
28 Therefore in the resurrection whose w G1135
27:19 seat, his w sent unto him, saying, G1135

Mk 6:17 Philip's w: for he had married her. G1135
18 lawful for thee to have thy brother's w. G1135
10: 2 a man to put away *his* w? tempting him. G1135
7 father and mother, and cleave to his w; G1135
11 shall put away his w, and marry G1135
29 or mother, or w, or children, or lands, G1135
12:19 die, and leave *his* w *behind him*, and G1135
19 w, and raise up seed unto his brother. G1135
20 first took a w, and dying left no seed. G1135
23 they shall rise, whose w shall she be of G1135
23 be of them? for the seven had her to w. G1135
Lk 1: 5 of Abia: and his w *was* of the daughters G1135
13 is heard; and thy w Elisabeth shall bear G1135
18 man, and my w well stricken in years. G1135
24 And after those days his w Elisabeth G1135
2: 5 To be taxed with Mary his espoused w, G1135
3:19 brother Philip's w, and for all the evils G1135
8: 3 And Joanna the w of Chuza Herod's G1135
14:20 And another said, I have married a w, G1135
26 and mother, and w, and children, and G1135
16:18 Whosoever putteth away his w, and G1135
17:32 Remember Lot's w. G1135
18:29 or brethren, or w, or children, for the G1135
20:28 die, having a w, and he die without G1135
28 w, and raise up seed unto his brother. G1135
29 took a w, and died without children. G1135
30 And the second took her to w, and he G1135
33 Therefore in the resurrection whose w G1135
33 of them is she? for seven had her to w. G1135
Jn 19:25 *w* of Cleophas, and Mary Magdalene.
Act 5: 1 with Sapphira his w, sold a possession, G1135
2 And kept back *part* of the price, his w G1135
7 after, when his w, not knowing what G1135
18: 2 Italy, with his w Priscilla; (because that G1135
24:24 came with his w Drusilla, which was G1135
1Co 5: 1 that one should have his father's w. G1135
7: 2 man have his own w, and let every G1135
3 Let the husband render unto the w due G1135
3 likewise also the w unto the husband. G1135
4 The w hath not power of her own body, G1135
4 not power of his own body, but the w. G1135
10 Let not the w depart from *her* husband: G1135
11 and let not the husband put away *his* w. G1135
12 brother hath a w that believeth not, G1135
14 sanctified by the w, and the unbelieving G1135
14 the unbelieving w is sanctified by the G1135
16 For what knowest thou, O w, whether G1135
16 O man, whether thou shalt save *thy* w? G1135
27 Art thou bound unto a w? seek not to be G1135
27 thou loosed from a w? seek not a wife. G1135
27 thou loosed from a wife? seek not a w. G1135
33 of the world, how he may please *his* w. G1135
34 There is difference *also* between a w G1135
39 The w is bound by the law as long as G1135
9: 5 lead about a sister, a w, as well as other G1135
Eph 5:23 For the husband is the head of the w, G1135
28 He that loveth his w loveth himself. G1135
31 his w, and they two shall be one flesh. G1135
33 so love his w even as himself; and G1135
33 w *see* that she reverence *her* husband. G1135
1Ti 3: 2 the husband of one w, vigilant, sober, of G1135
12 husbands of one w, ruling their children G1135
5: 9 old, having been the w of one man, G1135
Tit 1: 6 the husband of one w, having faithful G1135
1Pt 3: 7 honour unto the w, as unto the weaker G1134
Rev 19: 7 and his w hath made herself ready. G1135
21: 9 I will shew thee the bride, the Lamb's w. G1135

WIFE'S

Gen 3:20 And Adam called his w name Eve; H802
20:11 and they will slay me for my w sake. H802
36:39 city *was* Pau; and his w name *was* H802
Lev 18:11 The nakedness of thy father's w H802
Jdg 11: 2 him sons; and his w sons grew up, and H802
1Ch 1:50 *was* Pai; and his w name *was* Mehetabel, H802
8:29 of Gibeon; whose w name *was* Maachah: H802
9:35 Jehiel, whose w name *was* Maachah: H802
Mt 8:14 his w mother laid, and sick of a fever. G3994
Mk 1:30 But Simon's w mother lay sick of a G3994
Lk 4:38 And Simon's w mother was taken with G3994

WILD

Gen 16:12 And he will be a w man; his hand *will* H6501
Lev 26:22 I will also send w beasts among you, H7704
Dt 14: 5 deer, and the w goat, and the pygarg, H689
5 pygarg, and the w ox, and the chamois. H8377
1Sa 17:46 of the air, and to the w beasts of the H2416
24: 2 his men upon the rocks of the w goats. H3277
2Sa 2:18 Asahel *was as* light of foot as a w roe. H7704

2Ki 4:39 and found a w vine, and gathered H7704
39 gathered thereof w gourds his lap full, H7704
14: 9 there passed by a w beast that *was* in H7704
2Ch 25:18 there passed by a w beast that *was* in H7704
Job 6: 5 Doth the w ass bray when he hath H6501
11:12 though man be born *like* a w ass's colt. H6501
24: 5 Behold, *as* w asses in the desert, go H6501
39: 1 Knowest thou the time when the w H3277
5 Who hath sent out the w ass free? or H6501
5 hath loosed the bands of the w ass? H6171
15 or that the w beast may break them. H7704
Ps 50:11 and the w beasts of the field *are* mine. H2123
80:13 the w beast of the field doth devour it. H2123
104:11 field: the w asses quench their thirst. H6501
18 The high hills *are* a refuge for the w H3277
Isa 5: 2 grapes, and it brought forth w grapes. H891
4 forth grapes, brought it forth w grapes? H891
13:21 But w beasts of the desert shall lie H6728
22 And the w beasts of the islands shall cry H338
32:14 a joy of w asses, a pasture of flocks; H6501
34:14 The w beasts of the desert shall also H6728
14 also meet with the w beasts of the island, H338
51:20 the streets, as a w bull in a net: they are H8377
Jer 2:24 A w ass used to the wilderness, *that* H6501
14: 6 And the w asses did stand in the high H6501
50:39 Therefore the w beasts of the desert H6728
39 of the desert with the w beasts of the H338
Dan 5:21 *was* with the w asses: they fed him H6167
Hos 8: 9 For they are gone up to Assyria, a w H6501
13: 8 like a lion: the w beast shall tear them. H7704
Mt 3: 4 and his meat was locusts and w honey. *G66*
Mk 1: 6 and he did eat locusts and w honey; *G66*
13 and was with the w beasts; and the *G2342*
Act 10:12 beasts of the earth, and w beasts, and *G2342*
11: 6 beasts of the earth, and w beasts, and *G2342*
Ro 11:17 off, and thou, being a w olive tree, wert *G65*
24 olive tree which is w by nature, and wert *G65*

WILD-ASS See WILD and ASS.

WILDERNESS
Gen 14: 6 Seir, unto El-paran, which *is* by the w. H4057
16: 7 w, by the fountain in the way to Shur. H4057
21:14 and wandered in the w of Beer-sheba. H4057
20 dwelt in the w, and became an archer. H4057
21 And he dwelt in the w of Paran: and his H4057
36:24 the mules in the w, as he fed the asses of H4057
37:22 this pit that *is* in the w, and lay no hand H4057
Ex 3:18 days' journey into the w, that we may H4057
4:27 Go into the w to meet Moses. And H4057
5: 1 they may hold a feast unto me in the w. H4057
7:16 serve me in the w: and, behold, hitherto H4057
8:27 journey into the w, and sacrifice to the H4057
28 your God in the w; only ye shall not go H4057
13:18 the way of the w of the Red sea: and H4057
20 in Etham, in the edge of the w. H4057
14: 3 in the land, the w hath shut them in. H4057
11 us away to die in the w? wherefore hast H4057
12 than that we should die in the w. H4057
15:22 went out into the w of Shur; and they H4057
22 days in the w, and found no water. H4057
16: 1 Israel came unto the w of Sin, which *is* H4057
2 against Moses and Aaron in the w: H4057
3 us forth into this w, to kill this whole H4057
10 looked toward the w, and, behold, the H4057
14 upon the face of the w *there lay* a small H4057
32 fed you in the w, when I brought you H4057
17: 1 from the w of Sin, after their journeys, H4057
18: 5 Moses into the w, where he encamped H4057
19: 1 day came they *into* the w of Sinai. H4057
2 had pitched in the w; and there Israel H4057
Lev 7:38 unto the LORD, in the w of Sinai. H4057
16:10 to let him go for a scapegoat into the w. H4057
21 by the hand of a fit man into the w: H4057
22 and he shall let go the goat in the w. H4057
Nu 1: 1 unto Moses in the w of Sinai, in the H4057
19 so he numbered them in the w of Sinai. H4057
3: 4 the LORD, in the w of Sinai, and they H4057
14 unto Moses in the w of Sinai, saying, H4057
9: 1 unto Moses in the w of Sinai, in the H4057
5 at even in the w of Sinai: according H4057
10:12 out of the w of Sinai; and the cloud H4057
12 and the cloud rested in the w of Paran. H4057
31 to encamp in the w, and thou mayest be H4057
12:16 and pitched in the w of Paran. H4057
13: 3 them from the w of Paran: all those H4057
21 the land from the w of Zin unto Rehob, H4057
26 of Israel, unto the w of Paran, to H4057
14: 2 or would God we had died in this w! H4057
Nu 14:16 therefore he hath slain them in the w. H4057
22 Egypt and in the w, and have tempted H4057
25 into the w by the way of the Red sea. H4057
29 Your carcases shall fall in this w; and H4057
32 your carcases, they shall fall in this w. H4057
33 wander in the w forty years, and bear H4057
33 until your carcases be wasted in the w. H4057
35 me: in this w they shall be consumed, H4057
15:32 Israel were in the w, they found a man H4057
16:13 to kill us in the w, except thou make H4057
20: 4 the LORD into this w, that we and our H4057
21: 5 of Egypt to die in the w? for *there is* no H4057
11 at Ijeabarim, in the w which *is* before H4057
13 which *is* in the w that cometh out of H4057
18 from the w *they went* to Mattanah: H4057
23 Israel into the w: and he came to Jahaz, H4057
24: 1 but he set his face toward the w. H4057
26:64 the children of Israel in the w of Sinai. H4057
65 surely die in the w. And there was not H4057
27: 3 Our father died in the w, and he was not H4057
14 of Meribah in Kadesh in the w of Zin. H4057
32:13 wander in the w forty years, until all H4057
15 w; and ye shall destroy all this people. H4057
33: 6 in Etham, which *is* in the edge of the w. H4057
8 of the sea into the w, and went three H4057
8 the w of Etham, and pitched in Marah. H4057
11 Red sea, and encamped in the w of Sin. H4057
12 w of Sin, and encamped in Dophkah. H4057
15 and pitched in the w of Sinai. H4057
36 in the w of Zin, which *is* Kadesh. H4057
34: 3 shall be from the w of Zin along by the H4057
Dt 1: 1 side Jordan in the w, in the plain over H4057
19 great and terrible w, which ye saw by H4057
31 And in the w, where thou hast seen how H4057
40 into the w by the way of the Red sea. H4057
2: 1 journey into the w by the way of the H4057
7 through this great w: these forty years H4057
8 passed by the way of the w of Moab. H4057
26 And I sent messengers out of the w of H4057
4:43 *Namely,* Bezer in the w, in the plain H4057
8: 2 forty years in the w, to humble thee, H4057
15 great and terrible w, *wherein were* fiery H4057
16 Who fed thee in the w with manna, H4057
9: 7 to wrath in the w: from the day that H4057
28 brought them out to slay them in the w. H4057
11: 5 And what he did unto you in the w, H4057
24 be yours: from the w and Lebanon, H4057
29: 5 And I have led you forty years in the w: H4057
32:10 the waste howling w; he led him about, H3452
51 in the w of Zin; because ye sanctified H4057
Jos 1: 4 From the w and this Lebanon even H4057
5: 4 of war, died in the w by the way, after H4057
5 *were* born in the w by the way as they H4057
6 forty years in the w, till all the people H4057
8:15 them, and fled by the way of the w. H4057
20 the w turned back upon the pursuers. H4057
24 Ai in the field, in the w wherein they H4057
12: 8 and in the w, and in the south country; H4057
14:10 wandered in the w: and now, lo, I *am* H4057
15: 1 of Edom the w of Zin southward *was* H4057
61 In the w, Beth-arabah, Middin, and H4057
16: 1 on the east, to the w that goeth up from H4057
18:12 out thereof were at the w of Beth-aven. H4057
20: 8 Bezer in the w upon the plain out H4057
24: 7 and ye dwelt in the w a long season. H4057
Jdg 1:16 of Judah into the w of Judah, which H4057
8: 7 the thorns of the w and with briers. H4057
16 and thorns of the w and briers, and H4057
11:16 through the w unto the Red sea, and H4057
18 Then they went along through the w, H4057
22 and from the w even unto Jordan. H4057
20:42 the way of the w; but the battle overtook H4057
45 And they turned and fled toward the w H4057
47 turned and fled to the w unto the rock H4057
1Sa 4: 8 Egyptians with all the plagues in the w. H4057
13:18 to the valley of Zeboim toward the w. H4057
17:28 few sheep in the w? I know thy pride, H4057
23:14 And David abode in the w in strong H4057
14 a mountain in the w of Ziph. And Saul H4057
15 David *was* in the w of Ziph in a wood. H4057
24 his men *were* in the w of Maon, in the H4057
25 and abode in the w of Maon. And when H4057
25 pursued after David in the w of Maon. H4057
24: 1 Behold, David *is* in the w of En-gedi. H4057
25: 1 and went down to the w of Paran. H4057
4 And David heard in the w that Nabal H4057
14 out of the w to salute our master; H4057
21 *fellow* hath in the w, so that nothing H4057
26: 2 went down to the w of Ziph, having H4057
1Sa 26: 2 him, to seek David in the w of Ziph. H4057
3 abode in the w, and he saw that Saul H4057
3 that Saul came after him into the w. H4057
2Sa 2:24 Giah by the way of the w of Gibeon. H4057
15:23 passed over, toward the way of the w. H4057
28 See, I will tarry in the plain of the w, H4057
16: 2 such as be faint in the w may drink. H4057
17:16 in the plains of the w, but speedily pass H4057
29 and weary, and thirsty, in the w. H4057
1Ki 2:34 was buried in his own house in the w. H4057
9:18 And Baalath, and Tadmor in the w, in H4057
19: 4 journey into the w, and came and sat H4057
15 on thy way to the w of Damascus: and H4057
2Ki 3: 8 The way through the w of Edom. H4057
1Ch 5: 9 the entering in of the w from the river H4057
6:78 Bezer in the w with her suburbs, and H4057
12: 8 the hold to the w men of might, *and* H4057
21:29 made in the w, and the altar of the H4057
2Ch 1: 3 servant of the LORD had made in the w. H4057
8: 4 And he built Tadmor in the w, and all H4057
20:16 end of the brook, before the w of Jeruel. H4057
20 forth into the w of Tekoa: and as they H4057
24 tower in the w, they looked unto the H4057
24: 9 servant of God *laid* upon Israel in the w. H4057
Neh 9:19 them not in the w: the pillar of the cloud H4057
21 them in the w, *so that* they lacked H4057
Job 1:19 wind from the w, and smote the four H4057
12:24 to wander in a w *where there is* no way. H8414
24: 5 for a prey: the w *yieldeth* food for them H6160
30: 3 w in former time desolate and waste. H6723
38:26 *is; on* the w, wherein *there is* no man; H4057
39: 6 Whose house I have made the w, and H6160
Ps 29: 8 The voice of the LORD shaketh the w; H4057
8 the LORD shaketh the w of Kadesh. H4057
55: 7 far off, *and* remain in the w. Selah. H4057
63: ttl David, when he was in the w of Judah. H4057
65:12 They drop *upon* the pastures of the w: H4057
68: 7 thou didst march through the w; Selah: H3452
72: 9 They that dwell in the w shall bow H6728
74:14 *be* meat to the people inhabiting the w. H6728
78:15 He clave the rocks in the w, and gave H4057
17 by provoking the most High in the w. H6723
19 said, Can God furnish a table in the w? H4057
40 How oft did they provoke him in the w, H4057
52 and guided them in the w like a flock. H4057
95: 8 as *in* the day of temptation in the w: H4057
102: 6 I am like a pelican of the w: I am like an H4057
106: 9 through the depths, as through the w. H4057
14 But lusted exceedingly in the w, and H4057
26 them, to overthrow them in the w: H4057
107: 4 They wandered in the w in a solitary H4057
33 He turneth rivers into a w, and the H4057
35 He turneth the w into a standing water, H4057
40 wander in the w, *where there is* no way. H8414
136:16 the w: for his mercy *endureth* for ever. H4057
Prv 21:19 *It is* better to dwell in the w, than with a H4057
Song 3: 6 Who *is* this that cometh out of the w H4057
8: 5 Who *is* this that cometh up from the w, H4057
Isa 14:17 *That* made the world as a w, and H4057
16: 1 from Sela to the w, unto the mount of H4057
8 *through* the w: her branches are H4057
23:13 them that dwell in the w: they set up the H6728
27:10 and left like a w: there shall the calf H4057
32:15 on high, and the w be a fruitful field, H4057
16 Then judgment shall dwell in the w, and H4057
33: 9 Sharon is like a w; and Bashan and H6160
35: 1 The w and the solitary place shall be H4057
6 sing: for in the w shall waters break H4057
40: 3 The voice of him that crieth in the w, H4057
41:18 I will make the w a pool of water, and H4057
19 I will plant in the w the cedar, the H4057
42:11 Let the w and the cities thereof lift up H4057
43:19 a way in the w, *and* rivers in the desert. H4057
20 I give waters in the w, *and* rivers in the H4057
50: 2 make the rivers a w: their fish stinketh, H4057
51: 3 he will make her w like Eden, and her H4057
63:13 in the w, *that* they should not stumble? H4057
64:10 Thy holy cities are a w, Zion is a H4057
10 Zion is a w, Jerusalem a desolation. H4057
Jer 2: 2 in the w, in a land *that was* not sown. H4057
6 led us through the w, through a land of H4057
24 A wild ass used to the w, *that* snuffeth H4057
31 Have I been a w unto Israel? a land H4057
3: 2 as the Arabian in the w; and thou hast H4057
4:11 the high places in the w toward the H4057
26 place *was* a w, and all the cities thereof H4057
9: 2 Oh that I had in the w a lodging place H4057
10 the habitations of the w a lamentation, H4057
12 up like a w, that none passeth through? H4057

Jer 9:26 that dwell in the w: for all *these* nations H4057
12:10 made my pleasant portion a desolate w. H4057
12 through the w: for the sword of the H4057
13:24 that passeth away by the wind of the w. H4057
17: 6 the w, *in* a salt land and not inhabited. H4057
22: 6 a w, *and* cities *which* are not inhabited. H4057
23:10 places of the w are dried up, and their H4057
31: 2 found grace in the w; *even* Israel, when H4057
48: 6 lives, and be like the heath in the w. H4057
50:12 *shall be* a w, a dry land, and a desert. H4057
51:43 a dry land, and a w, a land wherein no H6160
Lam 4: 3 cruel, like the ostriches in the w. H4057
19 they laid wait for us in the w. H4057
5: 9 our lives because of the sword of the w. H4057
Ezk 6:14 desolate than the w toward Diblath, in H4057
19:13 And now she *is* planted in the w, in a H4057
20:10 of Egypt, and brought them into the w. H4057
13 against me in the w: they walked not in H4057
13 upon them in the w, to consume them. H4057
15 unto them in the w, that I would not H4057
17 did I make an end of them in the w. H4057
18 But I said unto their children in the w, H4057
21 my anger against them in the w. H4057
23 them also in the w, that I would scatter H4057
35 And I will bring you into the w of the H4057
36 fathers in the w of the land of Egypt, H4057
23:42 brought Sabeans from the w, which put H4057
29: 5 And I will leave thee *thrown* into the w, H4057
34:25 safely in the w, and sleep in the woods. H4057
Hos 2: 3 make her as a w, and set her like a dry H4057
14 the w, and speak comfortably unto her. H4057
9:10 I found Israel like grapes in the w; I saw H4057
13: 5 I did know thee in the w, in the land of H4057
15 come up from the w, and his spring H4057
Joel 1:19 pastures of the w, and the flame hath H4057
20 hath devoured the pastures of the w. H4057
2: 3 w; yea, and nothing shall escape them. H4057
22 pastures of the w do spring, for the tree H4057
3:19 shall be a desolate w, for the violence H4057
Am 2:10 w, to possess the land of the Amorite. H4057
5:25 in the w forty years, O house of Israel? H4057
6:14 in of Hemath unto the river of the w. H6160
Zep 2:13 Nineveh a desolation, *and* dry like a w. H4057
Mal 1: 3 heritage waste for the dragons of the w. H4057
Mt 3: 1 Baptist, preaching in the w of Judaea, *G2048*
3 one crying in the w, Prepare ye the way *G2048*
4: 1 into the w to be tempted of the devil. *G2048*
11: 7 w to see? A reed shaken with the wind? *G2048*
15:33 in the w, as to fill so great a multitude? *G2047*
Mk 1: 3 The voice of one crying in the w, *G2048*
4 John did baptize in the w, and preach *G2048*
12 the Spirit driveth him into the w. *G2048*
13 And he was there in the w forty days, *G2048*
8: 4 these *men* with bread here in the w? *G2047*
Lk 3: 2 unto John the son of Zacharias in the w. *G2048*
4 one crying in the w, Prepare ye the way *G2048*
4: 1 and was led by the Spirit into the w, *G2048*
5:16 And he withdrew himself into the w, *G2048*
7:24 went ye out into the w for to see? A reed *G2048*
8:29 and was driven of the devil into the w.) *G2048*
15: 4 and nine in the w, and go after that *G2048*
Jn 1:23 one crying in the w, Make straight the *G2048*
3:14 the serpent in the w, even so must the *G2048*
6:49 Your fathers did eat manna in the w, *G2048*
11:54 country near to the w, into a city called *G2048*
Act 7:30 to him in the w of mount Sina an angel *G2048*
36 in the Red sea, and in the w forty years. *G2048*
38 in the church in the w with the angel *G2048*
42 *by the space of* forty years in the w? *G2048*
44 of witness in the w, as he had *G2048*
13:18 suffered he their manners in the w. *G2048*
21:38 out into the w four thousand men *G2048*
1Co 10: 5 for they were overthrown in the w. *G2048*
2Co 11:26 *in* perils in the w, *in* perils in the sea, *G2047*
Heb 3: 8 in the day of temptation in the w: *G2048*
17 sinned, whose carcases fell in the w? *G2048*
Rev 12: 6 And the woman fled into the w, where *G2048*
14 she might fly into the w, into her place, *G2048*
17: 3 in the spirit into the w: and I saw a *G2048*

WILD-GOAT See WILD and GOAT.

WILD-OX See WILD and OX.

WILES
Nu 25:18 For they vex you with their w, H5231
Eph 6:11 able to stand against the w of the devil. *G3180*

WILFULLY
Heb 10:26 For if we sin w after that we have *G1596*

WILILY
Jos 9: 4 They did work w, and went and made H6195

WILL
Gen 2:18 I w make him an help meet for him. H6213
3:15 And I w put enmity between thee and H7896
16 Unto the woman he said, I w greatly H7235
6: 7 And the LORD said, I w destroy man H4229
13 behold, I w destroy them with the earth.
18 But with thee w I establish my covenant;
7: 4 For yet seven days, and I w cause it to
4 w I destroy from off the face of the earth.
8:21 said in his heart, I w not again curse the
21 his youth; neither w I again smite any
9: 5 And surely your blood of your lives w I
5 of every beast w I require it, and at the
5 brother w I require the life of man.
11 And I w establish my covenant with you;
15 And I w remember my covenant, which H2142
16 in the cloud; and I w look upon it, that H7200
11: 6 and now nothing w be restrained from
12: 1 house, unto a land that I w shew thee: H7200
2 And I w make of thee a great nation, H6213
2 nation, and I w bless thee, and make H1288
3 And I w bless them that bless thee, and H1288
7 Unto thy seed w I give this land: and
12 w kill me, but they will save thee alive. H2026
12 will kill me, but they w save thee alive.
13: 9 left hand, then I w go to the right; or if
9 to the right hand, then I w go to the left.
15 thee w I give it, and to thy seed for ever.
16 And I w make thy seed as the dust of H7760
17 breadth of it; for I w give it unto thee. H5414
14:23 That I w not *take* from a thread even to
23 and that I w not take any thing that
15:14 whom they shall serve, w I judge: and
16:10 said unto her, I w multiply thy seed H7235
12 And he w be a wild man; his hand *will*
12 And he will be a wild man; his hand *w*
17: 2 And I w make my covenant between H5414
2 thee, and w multiply thee exceedingly. H7235
6 And I w make thee exceeding fruitful,
6 fruitful, and I w make nations of thee, H5414
7 And I w establish my covenant H6965
8 And I w give unto thee, and to thy seed H5414
8 possession; and I w be their God.
16 And I w bless her, and give thee a son H1288
16 also of her: yea, I w bless her, and she H1288
19 his name Isaac: and I w establish my H6965
20 blessed him, and w make him fruitful,
20 make him fruitful, and w multiply him H7235
20 and I w make him a great nation. H5414
21 But my covenant w I establish with
18: 5 And I w fetch a morsel of bread, and H3947
10 And he said, I w certainly return unto H7725
14 time appointed I w return unto thee, H7725
19 For I know him, that he w command his
21 I w go down now, and see whether they H3381
21 is come unto me; and if not, I w know. H3045
26 I w spare all the place for their sakes. H5375
28 there forty and five, I w not destroy *it.*
29 he said, I w not do *it* for forty's sake.
30 be angry, and I w speak: Peradventure
30 said, I w not do *it,* if I find thirty there.
31 said, I w not destroy *it* for twenty's sake.
32 Lord be angry, and I w speak yet but this
32 he said, I w not destroy *it* for ten's sake.
19: 2 but we w abide in the street all night.
9 in to sojourn, and he w needs be a judge:
9 be a judge: now w we deal worse with
13 For we w destroy this place, because the
14 for the LORD w destroy this city. But H7843
21 thing also, that I w not overthrow this
32 wine, and we w lie with him, that we
20:11 and they w slay me for my wife's sake.
21: 6 *so that* all that hear w laugh with me. H6711
13 And also of the son of the bondwoman w
18 hand; for I w make him a great nation. H7760
24 And Abraham said, I w swear.
22: 2 of the mountains which I w tell thee of. H559
5 ass; and I and the lad w go yonder and
8 And Abraham said, My son, God w H7200
17 That in blessing I w bless thee, and in
17 in multiplying I w multiply thy seed as
23:13 thee, hear me: I w give thee money for H5414
13 *it* of me, and I w bury my dead there.

Gen 24: 3 And I w make thee swear by the LORD,
5 the woman w not be willing to follow
7 Unto thy seed w I give this land; he shall
8 And if the woman w not be willing to
14 shall say, Drink, and I w give thy camels
19 drink, she said, I w draw *water* for thy H7579
33 eat: but he said, I w not eat, until I have
39 the woman w not follow me.
40 whom I walk, w send his angel with H7971
44 drink thou, and I w also draw for thy
46 and said, Drink, and I w give thy camels
49 And now if ye w deal kindly and truly H3426
57 And they said, We w call the damsel, H7121
58 go with this man? And she said, I w go.
26: 3 Sojourn in this land, and I w be with
3 be with thee, and w bless thee; for unto H1288
3 and unto thy seed, I w give all these H5414
3 countries, and I w perform the oath H6965
4 And I w make thy seed to multiply as the
4 of heaven, and w give unto thy seed all H5414
24 I *am* with thee, and w bless thee, and H1288
27: 9 of the goats; and I w make them savoury
12 My father peradventure w feel me, and H4959
25 And he said, Bring *it* near to me, and I w H398
41 at hand; then w I slay my brother Jacob.
45 to him: then I w send, and fetch thee H7971
28:13 liest, to thee w I give it, and to thy seed;
15 And, behold, I *am* with thee, and w H8104
15 thou goest, and w bring thee again into
15 into this land; for I w not leave thee,
20 saying, If God w be with me, and will
20 be with me, and w keep me in this way H8104
20 way that I go, and w give me bread to H5414
22 me I w surely give the tenth unto thee. H6237
29:18 And Jacob loved Rachel; and said, I w H5647
27 Fulfil her week, and we w give thee this H5414
32 now therefore my husband w love me. H157
34 Now this time w my husband be joined
35 and she said, Now w I praise the LORD:
30:13 for the daughters w call me blessed: and
20 a good dowry; now w my husband dwell
28 Appoint me thy wages, and I w give *it.* H5414
31 me, I w again feed *and* keep thy flock: H7725
32 I w pass through all thy flock to day,
31: 3 and to thy kindred; and I w be with thee.
52 *be* witness, that I w not pass over this
32: 9 thy kindred, and I w deal well with thee:
11 I fear him, lest he w come and smite me, H935
12 And thou saidst, I w surely do thee H3190
20 us. For he said, I w appease him with H3722
20 me, and afterward I w see his face; H7200
20 face; peradventure he w accept of me.
26 I w not let thee go, except thou bless me.
33:12 and let us go, and I w go before thee.
13 them one day, all the flock w die. H4191
14 his servant: and I w lead on softly,
34:11 and what ye shall say unto me I w give. H5414
12 and gift, and I w give according as ye H5414
15 But in this w we consent unto you: If ye
15 unto you: If ye w be as we *be,* that every
16 Then w we give our daughters unto you,
16 unto you, and we w take your H3947
16 to us, and we w dwell with you, and H3427
16 with you, and we w become one people.
17 But if ye w not hearken unto us, to be
17 be circumcised; then w we take our
17 we take our daughter, and we w be gone.
22 Only herein w the men consent unto us
23 unto them, and they w dwell with us. H3427
35: 3 to Beth-el; and I w make there an altar H6213
12 and Isaac, to thee I w give it, and to thy H5414
12 to thy seed after thee w I give the land.
37:13 come, and I w send thee unto them. H7971
20 some pit, and we w say, Some evil beast H559
20 shall see what w become of his dreams.
35 and he said, For I w go down into the
38:17 And he said, I w send *thee* a kid from H7971
41:32 and God w shortly bring it to pass. H4116
40 in the throne w I be greater than thou.
42:34 ye *are* true *men:* so w I deliver you your
36 *is* not, and ye w take Benjamin *away:*
37 hand, and I w bring him to thee again.
43: 4 us, we w go down and buy thee food:
5 But if thou wilt not send *him,* we w not
8 with me, and we w arise and go; that H6965
9 I w be surety for him; of my hand shalt
44: 9 and we also w be my lord's bondmen.
26 be with us, then w we go down: for we
31 *with us,* that he w die: and thy servants H4191

Gen 45:11 And there w I nourish thee; for yet *there*
18 unto me: and I w give you the good of H5414
28 yet alive: I w go and see him before I die.
46: 3 for I w there make of thee a great nation:
4 I w go down with thee into Egypt; and I
4 into Egypt; and I w also surely bring thee
31 his father's house, I w go up, and shew
47:16 your cattle; and I w give you for your H5414
18 said unto him, We w not hide *it* from my
19 and we and our land w be servants unto
25 lord, and we w be Pharaoh's servants.
30 But I w lie with my fathers, and thou
30 And he said, I w do as thou hast said. H6213
48: 4 And said unto me, Behold, I w make
4 thee, and I w make of thee a multitude H5414
4 of people; and w give this land to thy H5414
9 I pray thee, unto me, and I w bless them.
49: 7 for it was cruel: I w divide them in H2505
50: 5 and bury my father, and I w come again.
15 they said, Joseph w peradventure hate
15 hate us, and w certainly requite us
21 Now therefore fear ye not: I w nourish H3557
24 I die: and God w surely visit you, and H6485
25 saying, God w surely visit you, and H6485
Ex 2: 9 it for me, and I w give *thee* thy wages.
3: 3 And Moses said, I w now turn aside, and
10 Come now therefore, and I w send thee
12 And he said, Certainly I w be with thee;
17 And I have said, I w bring you up out of
19 And I am sure that the king of Egypt w
20 And I w stretch out my hand, and smite
20 my wonders which I w do in the midst
20 thereof: and after that he w let you go.
21 And I w give this people favour in the
4: 1 But, behold, they w not believe me, nor
1 my voice: for they w say, The LORD hath
8 And it shall come to pass, if they w not
8 they w believe the voice of the latter sign.
9 And it shall come to pass, if they w not
12 Now therefore go, and I w be with thy
14 he seeth thee, he w be glad in his heart.
15 in his mouth: and I w be with thy mouth,
15 and w teach you what ye shall do.
21 in thine hand: but I w harden his heart,
23 I w slay thy son, *even* thy firstborn.
5: 2 not the LORD, neither w I let Israel go.
10 saith Pharaoh, I w not give you straw.
6: 1 thou see what I w do to Pharaoh: for
6 the LORD, and I w bring you out from
6 Egyptians, and I w rid you out of their
6 bondage, and I w redeem you with a
7 And I w take you to me for a people, and
7 me for a people, and I w be to you a God:
8 And I w bring you in unto the land,
8 and to Jacob; and I w give it you for an
7: 3 And I w harden Pharaoh's heart, and
17 the LORD: behold, I w smite with the rod
8: 2 I w smite all thy borders with frogs:
8 my people; and I w let the people go,
21 go, behold, I w send swarms *of flies*
22 And I w sever in that day the land of
23 And I w put a division between my
26 their eyes, and w they not stone us?
27 We w go three days' journey into the
28 And Pharaoh said, I w let you go, that ye
29 from thee, and I w entreat the LORD that
9:14 For I w at this time send all my plagues
15 For now I w stretch out my hand, that I
18 Behold, to morrow about this time I w
28 w let you go, and ye shall stay no longer.
29 out of the city, I w spread abroad my
30 that ye w not yet fear the LORD God.
10: 4 w I bring the locusts into thy coast:
9 And Moses said, We w go with our
9 and with our herds w we go; for we *must*
10 be so with you, as I w let you go, and
29 well, I w see thy face again no more.
11: 1 And the LORD said unto Moses, Yet w I
1 afterwards he w let you go hence: when
4 w I go out into the midst of Egypt:
8 and after that I w go out. And he went
12:12 For I w pass through the land of Egypt
12 this night, and w smite all the firstborn
12 I w execute judgment: I *am* the LORD.
13 I see the blood, I w pass over you, and
23 For the LORD w pass through to smite
23 posts, the LORD w pass over the door,
23 pass over the door, and w not suffer the
25 which the LORD w give you, according

Ex 12:48 with thee, and w keep the passover to
13:19 of Israel, saying, God w surely visit you;
14: 3 For Pharaoh w say of the children of
4 And I w harden Pharaoh's heart, that he
4 after them; and I w be honoured upon
13 LORD, which he w shew to you to day:
17 And I, behold, I w harden the hearts of
17 follow them: and I w get me honour
15: 1 spake, saying, I w sing unto the LORD,
2 he *is* my God, and I w prepare him an
2 my father's God, and I w exalt him.
9 The enemy said, I w pursue, I will
9 The enemy said, I will pursue, I w
9 I will overtake, I w divide the spoil; my
9 upon them; I w draw my sword, my
26 all his statutes, I w put none of these
16: 4 unto Moses, Behold, I w rain bread from
4 whether they w walk in my law, or no.
23 bake *that* which ye w bake *to day*, and
23 and seethe that ye w seethe; and that
17: 6 Behold, I w stand before thee there upon
9 to morrow I w stand on the top of the
14 ears of Joshua: for I w utterly put out the
16 *that* the LORD w *have* war with Amalek
18:19 Hearken now unto my voice, I w give
19: 5 Now therefore, if ye w obey my voice
8 LORD hath spoken we w do. And Moses
11 day the LORD w come down in the sight
20: 7 in vain; for the LORD w not hold him
19 with us, and we w hear: but let not God
24 I w come unto thee, and I will bless thee.
24 I will come unto thee, and I w bless thee.
21: 5 and my children; I w not go out free:
13 his hand; then I w appoint thee a place
22 woman's husband w lay upon him; and
22:23 at all unto me, I w surely hear their cry;
24 And my wrath shall wax hot, and I w kill
27 me, that I w hear; for I *am* gracious.
23: 7 thou not: for I w not justify the wicked.
21 him not; for he w not pardon your
22 that I speak; then I w be an enemy unto
23 and the Jebusites: and I w cut them off.
25 thy water; and I w take sickness away
26 land: the number of thy days I w fulfil.
27 I w send my fear before thee, and will
27 I will send my fear before thee, and w
27 thou shalt come, and I w make all thine
28 And I w send hornets before thee, which
29 I w not drive them out from before thee
30 By little and little I w drive them out
31 And I w set thy bounds from the Red sea
31 desert unto the river: for I w deliver the
33 gods, it w surely be a snare unto thee.
24: 3 which the LORD hath said w we do.
7 hath said w we do, and be obedient.
12 and be there: and I w give thee tables of
25:22 And there I w meet with thee, and I will
22 And there I will meet with thee, and I w
22 of all *things* which I w give thee in
29:42 I w meet you, to speak there unto thee.
43 And there I w meet with the children of
44 And I w sanctify the tabernacle of the
44 and the altar: I w sanctify also both
45 And I w dwell among the children of
45 children of Israel, and w be their God.
30: 6 the testimony, where I w meet with thee.
36 where I w meet with thee: it shall
32:10 and I w make of thee a great nation.
13 saidst unto them, I w multiply your seed
13 I have spoken of w I give unto your seed,
30 sin: and now I w go up unto the LORD;
33 against me, him w I blot out of my book.
34 I visit I w visit their sin upon them.
33: 1 Jacob, saying, Unto thy seed w I give it:
2 And I w send an angel before thee; and I
2 angel before thee; and I w drive out the
3 and honey: for I w not go up in the midst
5 people: I w come up into the midst
14 shall go *with thee*, and I w give thee rest.
17 And the LORD said unto Moses, I w do
19 And he said, I w make all my goodness
19 before thee, and I w proclaim the name
19 before thee; and w be gracious to whom
19 to whom I w be gracious, and will
19 will be gracious, and w shew mercy on
19 shew mercy on whom I w shew mercy.
22 passeth by, that I w put thee in a clift of
22 of the rock, and w cover thee with my
23 And I w take away mine hand, and thou

Ex 34: 1 the first: and I w write upon *these* tables
7 and sin, and that w by no means clear
10 all thy people I w do marvels, such as
10 it *is* a terrible thing that I w do with thee.
24 For I w cast out the nations before thee,
Lev 1: 3 his own voluntary w at the door of the H7522
2: 1 And when any w offer a meat offering
9: 4 to day the LORD w appear unto you. H7200
10: 3 spake, saying, I w be sanctified in them
3 all the people I w be glorified. And
16: 2 he die not: for I w appear in the cloud H7200
17:10 manner of blood; I w even set my face
10 w cut him off from among his people.
19: 5 LORD, ye shall offer it at your own w. H7522
20: 3 And I w set my face against that man, H5414
3 that man, and w cut him off from
5 Then I w set my face against that man, H7760
5 his family, and w cut him off, and all
6 after them, I w even set my face against
6 w cut him off from among his people.
24 their land, and I w give it unto you to H5414
22:18 in Israel, that w offer his oblation for
18 which they w offer unto the LORD
19 *Ye shall offer* at your own w a male H7522
29 And when ye w offer a sacrifice of
29 unto the LORD, offer *it* at your own w. H7522
32 holy name; but I w be hallowed among
23:30 soul w I destroy from among his people.
25:21 Then I w command my blessing upon H6680
26: 4 Then I w give you rain in due season,
6 And I w give peace in the land, and ye
6 *you* afraid: and I w rid evil beasts out of
9 For I w have respect unto you, and make
11 And I w set my tabernacle among you: H5414
12 And I w walk among you, and will be H1980
12 And I will walk among you, and w be
14 But if ye w not hearken unto me, and
14 and w not do all these commandments;
15 judgments, so that ye w not do all my
16 I also w do this unto you; I will even H6213
16 I also will do this unto you; I w even
17 And I w set my face against you, and H5414
18 And if ye w not yet for all this hearken
18 unto me, then I w punish you seven H3256
19 And I w break the pride of your power; H7665
19 your power; and I w make your heaven H5414
21 And if ye walk contrary unto me, and w H14
21 hearken unto me; I w bring seven times
22 I w also send wild beasts among you,
23 And if ye w not be reformed by me by
23 things, but w walk contrary unto me;
24 Then w I also walk contrary unto you,
24 unto you, and w punish you yet seven H5221
25 And I w bring a sword upon you, that H935
25 your cities, I w send the pestilence H7971
27 And if ye w not for all this hearken unto
28 Then I w walk contrary unto you also H1980
28 in fury; and I, even I, w chastise you H3256
30 And I w destroy your high places, and H8045
31 And I w make your cities waste, and H5414
31 desolation, and I w not smell the savour
32 And I w bring the land into desolation:
33 And I w scatter you among the H2219
33 the heathen, and w draw out a sword
36 left *alive* of you I w send a faintness into H935
42 Then w I remember my covenant with
42 with Abraham w I remember; and I will
42 remember; and I w remember the land. H2142
44 land of their enemies, I w not cast them
44 away, neither w I abhor them, to destroy
45 But I w for their sakes remember the
27:13 But if he w at all redeem it, then he shall
15 And if he that sanctified it w redeem his
19 And if he that sanctified the field w in
20 And if he w not redeem the field, or if he
31 And if a man w at all redeem *ought* of
Nu 6:27 children of Israel; and I w bless them. H1288
9: 8 them, Stand still, and I w hear what the H8085
8 the LORD w command concerning you. H6680
14 among you, and w keep the passover
10:29 the LORD said, I w give it you: come H5414
29 with us, and we w do thee good: for the
30 And he said unto him, I w not go; but I
30 I will not go; but I w depart to mine own
32 do unto us, the same w we do unto thee.
11:17 And I w come down and talk with thee
17 with thee there: and I w take of the spirit H680
17 *is* upon thee, and w put *it* upon them; H7760
18 w give you flesh, and ye shall eat. H5414

Nu 11:21 thou hast said, I **w** give them flesh, that H5414
12: 6 you, *I* the LORD **w** make myself known
6 *and* **w** speak unto him in a dream.
8 With him **w** I speak mouth to mouth,
14: 8 If the LORD delight in us, then he **w** H935
11 Moses, How long **w** this people provoke
11 me? and how long **w** it be ere they
12 I **w** smite them with the pestilence, and H5221
12 them, and **w** make of thee a greater H6213
14 And they **w** tell *it* to the inhabitants of H559
15 heard the fame of thee **w** speak, saying, H559
24 me fully, him **w** I bring into the land
28 spoken in mine ears, so **w** I do to you:
31 be a prey, them **w** I bring in, and they
35 I the LORD have said, I **w** surely do it
40 we *be here,* and **w** go up unto the place
43 therefore the LORD **w** not be with you.
15: 3 And **w** make an offering by fire unto the
14 generations, and **w** offer an offering
16: 5 the LORD **w** shew who *are* his, and H3045
5 *who is* holy; and **w** cause *him* to come
5 **w** he cause to come near unto him.
12 of Eliab: which said, We **w** not come up:
14 eyes of these men? we **w** not come up.
17: 4 the testimony, where I **w** meet with you.
5 blossom: and I **w** make to cease from
20:17 thy country: we **w** not pass through the
17 the vineyards, neither **w** we drink *of* the
17 of the wells: we **w** go by the king's *high*
17 *high* way, we **w** not turn to the right
19 unto him, We **w** go by the high way: H5927
19 of thy water, then I **w** pay for it: I will
19 I will pay for it: I **w** only, without *doing*
21: 2 then I **w** utterly destroy their cities.
16 together, and I **w** give them water.
22 Let me pass through thy land: we **w** not
22 into the vineyards; we **w** not drink *of* the
22 of the well: *but* we **w** go along by the
22: 8 this night, and I **w** bring you word again,
17 For I **w** promote thee unto very great
17 honour, and I **w** do whatsoever thou H6213
19 what the LORD **w** say unto me more. H1696
34 it displease thee, I **w** get me back again.
23: 3 offering, and I **w** go: peradventure the
3 the LORD **w** come to meet me: and H7136
3 he sheweth me I **w** tell thee. And he H5046
27 I pray thee, I **w** bring thee unto another H3947
27 peradventure it **w** please God that thou
24:13 *but* what the LORD saith, that **w** I speak?
14 *therefore, and* I **w** advertise thee what H3289
32:15 For if ye turn away from after him, he **w**
16 him, and said, We **w** build sheepfolds H1129
17 But we ourselves **w** go ready armed
18 We **w** not return unto our houses, until
19 For we **w** not inherit with them on
20 And Moses said unto them, If ye **w** do H6213
20 ye **w** go armed before the LORD to war,
21 And **w** go all of you armed over Jordan
23 But if ye **w** not do so, behold, ye have
23 and be sure your sin **w** find you out.
25 servants **w** do as my lord commandeth. H6213
27 But thy servants **w** pass over, every man
29 children of Reuben **w** pass with you over
30 But if they **w** not pass over with you
31 hath said unto thy servants, so **w** we do.
32 We **w** pass over armed before the LORD
33:55 But if ye **w** not drive out the inhabitants
Dt 1:13 and I **w** make them rulers over you. H7760
17 you, bring *it* unto me, and I **w** hear it. H8085
22 you, and said, We **w** send men before us,
36 see it, and to him **w** I give the land that
39 **w** I give it, and they shall possess it.
41 against the LORD, we **w** go up and fight,
2: 5 Meddle not with them; for I **w** not give
9 in battle: for I **w** not give thee of their
19 with them: for I **w** not give thee of the
25 This day **w** I begin to put the dread of
27 Let me pass through thy land: I **w** go
27 by the high way, I **w** neither turn unto
28 drink: only I **w** pass through on my feet;
3: 2 Fear him not: for I **w** deliver him, and all
4:10 together, and I **w** make them hear my
31 a merciful God;) he **w** not forsake thee,
5:11 in vain: for the LORD **w** not hold *him*
25 for this great fire **w** consume us: if we H398
27 unto thee; and we **w** hear *it,* and do *it.* H8085
31 here by me, and I **w** speak unto thee all
7: 4 For they **w** turn away thy son from
4 other gods: so **w** the anger of the LORD

Dt 7:10 destroy them: he **w** not be slack to him
10 hateth him, he **w** repay him to his face.
13 And he **w** love thee, and bless thee, and H157
13 multiply thee: he **w** also bless the fruit of
15 And the LORD **w** take away from thee all
15 all sickness, and **w** put none of the evil H7760
15 upon thee; but **w** lay them upon all H5414
16 gods; for that *w be* a snare unto thee.
20 Moreover the LORD thy God **w** send H7971
22 And the LORD thy God **w** put out those
9:14 heaven: and I **w** make of thee a nation H6213
10: 2 And I **w** write on the tables the words H3789
11:14 That I **w** give *you* the rain of your land H5414
15 And I **w** send grass in thy fields for thy H5414
23 Then **w** the LORD drive out all these
28 And a curse, if ye **w** not obey the
12:20 thou shalt say, I **w** eat flesh, because thy H398
30 serve their gods? even so **w** I do likewise.
15:16 And it shall be, if he say unto thee, I **w**
17:12 And the man that **w** do presumptuously,
12 and **w** not hearken unto the
14 and shalt say, I **w** set a king over me, H7760
18:15 The LORD thy God **w** raise up unto thee
18 I **w** raise them up a Prophet from among
18 unto thee, and **w** put my words in his H5414
19 *that* whosoever **w** not hearken unto my
19 in my name, I **w** require *it* of him. H1875
20:12 And if it **w** make no peace with thee, but
12 with thee, but **w** make war against thee,
21:14 go whither she **w**; but thou shalt not sell H5315
18 son, which **w** not obey the voice of
18 him, **w** not hearken unto them:
20 and rebellious, he **w** not obey our voice;
23:21 the LORD thy God **w** surely require it of H1875
25: 7 a name in Israel, he **w** not perform the H14
9 that **w** not build up his brother's house.
28: 1 the LORD thy God **w** set thee on high H5414
27 The LORD **w** smite thee with the botch H5221
55 So that he **w** not give to any of them of
59 Then the LORD **w** make thy plagues
60 Moreover he **w** bring upon thee all the H7725
61 book of this law, them **w** the LORD bring
63 you; so the LORD **w** rejoice over you to H7797
29:20 The LORD **w** not spare him, but then the H14
30: 3 That then the LORD thy God **w** turn thy H7725
3 upon thee, and **w** return and gather thee
4 from thence **w** the LORD thy God gather
4 thee, and from thence **w** he fetch thee:
5 And the LORD thy God **w** bring thee into H935
5 possess it; and he **w** do thee good, and
6 And the LORD thy God **w** circumcise H4135
7 And the LORD thy God **w** put all these H5414
9 And the LORD thy God **w** make thee
9 for the LORD **w** again rejoice over thee H7725
31: 3 The LORD thy God, he **w** go over before
3 thee, *and* he **w** destroy these nations H8045
6 thee; he **w** not fail thee, nor forsake thee.
8 go before thee; he **w** be with thee, he will
8 be with thee, he **w** not fail thee, neither
16 and this people **w** rise up, and go a
16 among them, and **w** forsake me, and H5800
17 in that day, and I **w** forsake them, and H5800
17 them, and I **w** hide my face from them,
17 them; so that they **w** say in that day, Are H559
18 And I **w** surely hide my face in that day H5641
20 waxen fat; then **w** they turn unto other
23 I sware unto them: and I **w** be with thee.
29 For I know that after my death ye **w** H7843
29 you; and evil **w** befall you in the latter H7122
29 days; because ye **w** do evil in the sight H6213
32: 1 Give ear, O ye heavens, and I **w** speak;
3 Because I **w** publish the name of the
7 ask thy father, and he **w** shew thee; thy H5046
7 thee; thy elders, and they **w** tell thee. H559
20 And he said, I **w** hide my face from H5641
20 face from them, I **w** see what their end H7200
21 vanities: and I **w** move them to jealousy
21 *are* not a people; I **w** provoke them to
23 I **w** heap mischiefs upon them; I will H5595
23 I will heap mischiefs upon them; I **w** H3615
24 destruction: I **w** also send the teeth of
41 on judgment; I **w** render vengeance to H7725
41 and **w** reward them that hate me.
42 I **w** make mine arrows drunk with
43 his people: for he **w** avenge the blood of H5358
43 his servants, and **w** render vengeance H7725
43 adversaries, and **w** be merciful unto his
33:16 and *for* the good **w** of him that dwelt in H7522
34: 4 Jacob, saying, I **w** give it unto thy seed: H5414

Jos 1: 5 with Moses, *so* I **w** be with thee: I will
5 thee: I **w** not fail thee, nor forsake thee.
16 us we **w** do, and whithersoever H6213
16 whithersoever thou sendest us, we **w** go.
17 in all things, so **w** we hearken unto thee:
18 and **w** not hearken unto thy
2:12 kindness, that ye **w** also shew kindness
13 And *that* ye **w** save alive my father, and
14 we **w** deal kindly and truly with thee. H6213
17 And the men said unto her, We *w be*
19 his head, and we *w be* guiltless: and
20 business, then we **w** be quit of thine oath
3: 5 the LORD **w** do wonders among you. H6213
7 Joshua, This day **w** I begin to magnify
7 as I was with Moses, *so* I **w** be with thee.
10 you, and *that* he **w** without fail drive out
7:12 accursed: neither **w** I be with you any
8: 5 that *are* with me, **w** approach unto the H7126
5 at the first, that we **w** flee before them, H5127
6 (For they **w** come out after us) till we
6 the city; for they **w** say, They flee before H559
6 first: therefore we **w** flee before them. H5127
7 your God **w** deliver it into your hand. H5414
18 toward Ai; for I **w** give it into thine H5414
9:20 This we **w** do to them; we will even let H6213
20 This we will do to them; we **w** even let
11: 6 about this time **w** I deliver them up all
13: 6 the Sidonians, them **w** I drive out from
14:12 if so be the LORD *w be* with me, then I
15:16 **w** I give Achsah my daughter to wife.
18: 4 *each* tribe: and I **w** send them, and they
22:18 the LORD? and it **w** be, *seeing* ye rebel to
18 that to morrow he **w** be wroth with the
23:13 the LORD your God **w** no more drive out
24:15 this day whom ye **w** serve; whether the H5647
15 and my house, we **w** serve the LORD. H5647
18 in the land: *therefore* **w** we also serve the
19 *is* a jealous God; he **w** not forgive your
20 gods, then he **w** turn and do you hurt, H7725
21 Joshua, Nay; but we **w** serve the LORD. H5647
24 **w** we serve, and his voice will we obey.
24 will we serve, and his voice **w** we obey.
Jdg 1: 3 and I likewise **w** go with thee into thy H1980
12 **w** I give Achsah my daughter to wife.
24 the city, and we **w** shew thee mercy. H6213
2: 1 I **w** never break my covenant with you.
3 Wherefore I also said, I **w** not drive them
21 I also **w** not henceforth drive out any
22 whether they **w** keep the way of the H8104
4: 7 And I **w** draw unto thee to the river H4900
7 and I **w** deliver him into thine hand. H5414
8 go with me, then I **w** go: but if thou wilt H1980
8 wilt not go with me, *then* I **w** not go.
9 And she said, I **w** surely go with thee: H1980
22 him, Come, and I **w** shew thee the man H7200
5: 3 ye princes; I, *even* I, **w** sing unto the H7891
3 unto the LORD; I **w** sing *praise* to the H2167
6:16 And the LORD said unto him, Surely I **w**
18 said, I **w** tarry until thou come again. H3427
31 stood against him, **W** ye plead for Baal?
31 ye plead for Baal? **w** ye save him? he that
31 save him? he that **w** plead for him, let H7378
37 Behold, I **w** put a fleece of wool in the H3322
39 against me, and I **w** speak but this once:
7: 4 the water, and I **w** try them for thee H6884
7 men that lapped **w** I save you, and
8: 7 mine hand, then I **w** tear your flesh H1758
9 in peace, I **w** break down this tower.
23 And Gideon said unto them, I **w** not rule
25 And they answered, We **w** willingly H5414
10:13 gods: wherefore I **w** deliver you no more.
18 man *is he* that **w** begin to fight against H2490
11:24 out from before us, them **w** we possess.
31 and I **w** offer it up for a burnt offering.
12: 1 **w** burn thine house upon thee with fire. H8313
13:16 thou detain me, I **w** not eat of thy bread:
14:12 And Samson said unto them, I **w** now
12 and find *it* out, then I **w** give you thirty H5414
15: 1 a kid; and he said, I **w** go in to my wife
7 ye have done this, yet **w** I be avenged of
7 of you, and after that I **w** cease. H2308
12 that ye **w** not fall upon me yourselves.
13 saying, No; but we **w** bind thee fast, and H631
13 but surely we **w** not kill thee. And they
16: 5 afflict him: and we **w** give thee every one
17 then my strength **w** go from me, and I H5493
20 his sleep, and said, I **w** go out as at other
17: 3 now therefore I **w** restore it unto thee. H7725
10 and a priest, and I **w** give thee ten H5414

Jdg 17:13 I that the LORD **w** do me good, seeing
19:12 And his master said unto him, We **w** not
12 of Israel; we **w** pass over to Gibeah.
24 concubine; them I **w** bring out now, and
20: 8 man, saying, We **w** not any *of us* go to
8 **w** we any *of us* turn into his house.
9 thing which we **w** do to Gibeah; *we will* H6213
9 to Gibeah; *we w go up* by lot against it;
10 And we **w** take ten men of an hundred H3947
28 I **w** deliver them into thine hand. H5414
21: 7 the LORD that we **w** not give them of our
22 complain, that we **w** say unto them, Be
Ru 1:10 And they said unto her, Surely we **w**
11 my daughters: why **w** ye go with me? *are*
16 thou goest, I **w** go; and where thou
16 thou lodgest, I **w** lodge: thy people *shall* H3885
17 Where thou diest, **w** I die, and there will
17 Where thou diest, will I die, and there **w**
3: 4 and he **w** tell thee what thou shalt do. H5046
5 All that thou sayest unto me I **w** do. H6213
11 And now, my daughter, fear not; I **w** do H6213
13 morning, *that* if he **w** perform unto thee
13 part: but if he **w** not do the part of a H2654
13 to thee, then **w** I do the part of a
18 how the matter **w** fall: for the man will
18 fall: for the man **w** not be in rest, until he
4: 4 after thee. And he said, I **w** redeem *it*.
1Sa 1:11 a man child, then I **w** give him unto the
22 her husband, *I w not go up* until the
22 and *then* I **w** bring him, that he may
2: 9 He **w** keep the feet of his saints, and the
15 **w** not have sodden flesh of thee, but raw.
16 *me* now: and if not, I **w** take *it* by force.
30 that honour me I **w** honour, and they
31 Behold, the days come, that I **w** cut off
35 And I **w** raise me up a faithful priest,
35 in my mind: and I **w** build him a sure
3:11 Samuel, Behold, I **w** do a thing in Israel,
12 In that day I **w** perform against Eli all
12 when I begin, I **w** also make an end.
13 For I have told him that I **w** judge his
6: 5 peradventure he **w** lighten his hand
7: 3 him only: and he **w** deliver you out of the
5 and I **w** pray for you unto the LORD.
8 God for us, that he **w** save us out of the
8:11 And he said, This **w** be the manner of
11 reign over you: He **w** take your sons, and
12 And he **w** appoint him captains over
12 over fifties; and *w set them* to ear his
13 And he **w** take your daughters *to be*
14 And he **w** take your fields, and your
15 And he **w** take the tenth of your seed,
16 And he **w** take your menservants, and
17 He **w** take the tenth of your sheep: and
18 the LORD **w** not hear you in that day.
19 said, Nay; but we **w** have a king over us;
9: 8 of silver: *that* **w** I give to the man of
13 to eat: for the people **w** not eat until he
16 To morrow about this time I **w** send thee
19 and to morrow I **w** let thee go, and will
19 and **w** tell thee all that *is* in thine heart.
10: 2 at Zelzah; and they **w** say unto thee, The
4 And they **w** salute thee, and give thee H7592
6 And the spirit of the LORD **w** come upon
8 and, behold, I **w** come down unto thee,
11: 1 a covenant with us, and we **w** serve thee.
2 On this *condition* **w** I make *a covenant*
3 man to save us, we **w** come out to thee.
10 To morrow we **w** come out unto you,
12: 3 eyes therewith? and I **w** restore it you.
10 of our enemies, and we **w** serve thee.
14 If ye **w** fear the LORD, and serve him,
15 But if ye **w** not obey the voice of the
16 which the LORD **w** do before your eyes.
17 *Is it* not wheat harvest to day? I **w** call
22 For the LORD **w** not forsake his people
23 **w** teach you the good and the right way:
13:12 Therefore said I, The Philistines **w** come
14: 6 may be that the LORD **w** work for us: for
8 Then said Jonathan, Behold, we **w** pass
8 and we **w** discover ourselves unto them.
9 to you; then we **w** stand still in our place,
9 in our place, and **w** not go up unto them.
10 unto us; then we **w** go up: for the LORD
12 up to us, and we **w** shew you a thing.
40 Jonathan my son **w** be on the other side.
15:16 Saul, Stay, and I **w** tell thee what the
26 And Samuel said unto Saul, I **w** not
29 And also the Strength of Israel **w** not lie
1Sa 16: 1 with oil, and go, I **w** send thee to Jesse
2 go? if Saul hear *it*, he **w** kill me. And the
3 And call Jesse to the sacrifice, and I **w**
11 for we **w** not sit down till he come hither.
17: 9 to kill me, then **w** we be your servants:
25 him, the king **w** enrich him with great
25 with great riches, and **w** give him his
32 **w** go and fight with this Philistine.
37 paw of the bear, he **w** deliver me out of
44 Come to me, and I **w** give thy flesh unto
46 This day **w** the LORD deliver thee into
46 mine hand; and I **w** smite thee, and take
46 from thee; and I **w** give the carcases of
47 and he **w** give you into our hands.
18:11 And Saul cast the javelin; for he said, I **w**
17 Merab, her **w** I give thee to wife: only
21 And Saul said, I **w** give him her, that she
19: 3 And I **w** go out and stand beside my
3 thou *art*, and I **w** commune with my
3 of thee; and what I see, that I **w** tell thee.
20: 2 behold, my father **w** do nothing either
2 small, but that he **w** shew it me: and why
4 thy soul desireth, I **w** even do *it* for thee.
13 *to do* thee evil, then I **w** shew it thee, and
18 be missed, because thy seat **w** be empty.
20 And I **w** shoot three arrows on the side
21 And, behold, I **w** send a lad, *saying*, Go,
22: 3 you, till I know what God **w** do for me.
7 ye Benjamites; **w** the son of Jesse give
23: 4 **w** deliver the Philistines into thine hand.
11 **W** the men of Keilah deliver me up into
11 up into his hand? **w** Saul come down, as
11 And the LORD said, He **w** come down.
12 Then said David, **W** the men of Keilah
12 the LORD said, They **w** deliver *thee* up.
23 the certainty, and I **w** go with you: and it
23 be in the land, that I **w** search him out
24: 4 thee, Behold, I **w** deliver thine enemy
10 thee; and I said, I **w** not put forth mine
19 For if a man find his enemy, **w** he let
25: 8 Ask thy young men, and they **w** shew
28 for the LORD **w** certainly make my lord
26: 6 Joab, saying, Who **w** go down with me to
6 Abishai said, I **w** go down with thee.
8 and I **w** not *smite* him the second time.
21 my son David: for I **w** no more do thee
27:11 So did David, and so *w be* his manner all
28: 2 David, Therefore **w** I make thee keeper
19 Moreover the LORD **w** also deliver Israel
23 But he refused, and said, I **w** not eat. But
30:15 I **w** bring thee down to this company.
22 not with us, we **w** not give them *ought*
24 For who **w** hearken unto you in this
2Sa 2: 6 unto you: and I also **w** requite you this
26 thou not that it **w** be bitterness in the
3:13 And he said, Well; I **w** make a league
18 servant David I **w** save my people Israel
21 And Abner said unto David, I **w** arise
21 will arise and go, and **w** gather all Israel
5:19 David, Go up: for I **w** doubtless deliver
6:21 therefore **w** I play before the LORD.
22 And I **w** yet be more vile than thus, and
22 vile than thus, and **w** be base in mine
7:10 Moreover I **w** appoint a place for my
10 my people Israel, and **w** plant them, that
11 thee that he **w** make thee an house.
12 with thy fathers, I **w** set up thy seed after
12 bowels, and I **w** establish his kingdom.
13 my name, and I **w** stablish the throne of
14 I **w** be his father, and he shall be my son.
14 commit iniquity, I **w** chasten him with
27 servant, saying, I **w** build thee an house:
9: 7 him, Fear not: for I **w** surely shew thee
7 father's sake, and **w** restore thee all the
10: 2 Then said David, I **w** shew kindness
11 for thee, then I **w** come and help thee.
11:11 *as* thy soul liveth, I **w** not do this thing.
12 and to morrow I **w** let thee depart. So
12:11 Thus saith the LORD, Behold, I **w** raise
11 thine own house, and I **w** take thy wives
12 For thou didst *it* secretly: but I **w** do this
18 our voice: how **w** he then vex himself,
22 tell *whether* GOD **w** be gracious to me,
13:13 for he **w** not withhold me from thee.
14: 7 he slew; and we **w** destroy the heir also:
8 and I **w** give charge concerning thee.
15 handmaid said, I **w** now speak unto the
15 **w** perform the request of his handmaid.
16 For the king **w** hear, to deliver his
2Sa 14:17 the LORD thy God **w** be with thee.
15: 8 to Jerusalem, then I **w** serve the LORD.
21 or life, even there also **w** thy servant be.
25 of the LORD, he **w** bring me again, and
28 See, I **w** tarry in the plain of the
34 say unto Absalom, I **w** be thy servant, O
34 hitherto, so *w* I now also *be* thy servant:
16:12 It may be that the LORD **w** look on mine
12 and that the LORD **w** requite me good
18 his **w** I be, and with him will I abide.
18 his will I be, and with him **w** I abide.
19 presence, so **w** I be in thy presence.
17: 1 men, and I **w** arise and pursue after
2 And I **w** come upon him while he *is*
2 weak handed, and **w** make him afraid:
2 shall flee; and I **w** smite the king only:
3 And I **w** bring back all the people unto
8 of war, and **w** not lodge with the people.
9 *other* place: and it **w** come to pass, when
9 heareth it **w** say, There is a slaughter
12 be found, and we **w** light upon him as
13 that city, and we **w** draw it into the river,
18: 2 I **w** surely go forth with you myself also.
3 if we flee away, they **w** not care for us;
3 if half of us die, **w** they care for us: but
4 seemeth you best I **w** do. And the king
19: 7 go not forth, there **w** not tarry one with
7 this night: and that **w** be worse unto thee
26 thy servant said, I **w** saddle me an ass,
33 and I **w** feed thee with me in Jerusalem.
36 Thy servant **w** go a little way over Jordan
38 with me, and I **w** do to him that which
38 shalt require of me, *that* **w** I do for thee.
20:21 him only, and I **w** depart from the city.
21: 4 And the Gibeonites said unto him, We **w**
4 What ye shall say, *that* **w** I do for you.
6 unto us, and we **w** hang them up unto
6 choose. And the king said, I **w** give *them*.
22: 3 The God of my rock; in him **w** I trust: *he*
4 I **w** call on the LORD, *who is* worthy to
29 and the LORD **w** lighten my darkness.
50 Therefore I **w** give thanks unto thee, O
50 and I **w** sing praises unto thy name.
24:24 Nay; but I **w** surely buy *it* of thee
24 thee at a price: neither **w** I offer burnt
1Ki 1: 5 himself, saying, I **w** be king: and he
14 the king, I also **w** come in after thee, and
30 stead; even so **w** I certainly do this day.
51 he **w** not slay his servant with the sword.
52 And Solomon said, If he **w** shew himself
2: 8 I **w** not put thee to death with the sword.
17 the king, (for he **w** not say thee nay,)
18 And Bath-sheba said, Well; I **w** speak for
20 on, my mother: for I **w** not say thee nay.
26 of death: but I **w** not at this time put
30 And he said, Nay; but I **w** die here. And
38 king hath said, so **w** thy servant do. And
3:14 did walk, then I **w** lengthen thy days.
5: 5 Thy son, whom I **w** set upon thy throne
6 and unto thee **w** I give hire for thy
8 to me for: *and* I **w** do all thy desire
9 unto the sea: and I **w** convey them by sea
9 appoint me, and **w** cause them to be
6:12 walk in them; then **w** I perform my word
13 And I **w** dwell among the children of
13 and **w** not forsake my people Israel.
8:27 But **w** God indeed dwell on the earth?
9: 5 Then I **w** establish the throne of thy
6 or your children, and **w** not keep my
7 Then **w** I cut off Israel out of the land
7 for my name, **w** I cast out of my sight;
11: 2 *for* surely they **w** turn away your heart
11 thee, I **w** surely rend the kingdom
11 from thee, and **w** give it to thy servant.
12 Notwithstanding in thy days I **w** not do
12 *but* I **w** rend it out of the hand of thy son.
13 Howbeit I **w** not rend away all the
13 the kingdom; *but* **w** give one tribe to thy
31 of Israel, Behold, I **w** rend the kingdom
31 Solomon, and **w** give ten tribes to thee:
34 Howbeit I **w** not take the whole kingdom
34 of his hand: but I **w** make him prince all
35 But I **w** take the kingdom out of his son's
35 and **w** give it unto thee, *even* ten tribes.
36 And unto his son **w** I give one tribe, that
37 And I **w** take thee, and thou shalt reign
38 servant did; that I **w** be with thee, and
38 for David, and **w** give Israel unto thee.
39 And I **w** for this afflict the seed of David,

1Ki 12: 4 upon us, lighter, and we **w** serve thee.
7 then they **w** be thy servants for ever.
11 a heavy yoke, I **w** add to your yoke: my
11 but I **w** chastise you with scorpions.
14 yoke heavy, and I **w** add to your yoke:
14 but I **w** chastise you with scorpions.
13: 7 thyself, and I **w** give thee a reward.
8 half thine house, I **w** not go in with thee,
8 in with thee, neither **w** I eat bread nor
16 in with thee: neither **w** I eat bread nor
14:10 Therefore, behold, I **w** bring evil upon
10 house of Jeroboam, and **w** cut off from
10 and left in Israel, and **w** take away the
16: 3 Behold, I **w** take away the posterity of
3 of his house; and **w** make thy house like
18: 1 Ahab; and I **w** send rain upon the earth.
15 I **w** surely shew myself unto him to day.
23 no fire *under:* and I **w** dress the other
24 of your gods, and I **w** call on the name of
19:20 mother, and *then* I **w** follow thee. And he
20: 6 Yet I **w** send my servants unto thee to
9 at the first I **w** do: but this thing I may
13 behold, I **w** deliver it into thine
22 king of Syria **w** come up against thee.
25 for chariot: and we **w** fight against them
28 the valleys, therefore **w** I deliver all this
31 Israel: peradventure he **w** save thy life.
34 from thy father, I **w** restore; and thou
34 Then *said Ahab,* I **w** send thee away
21: 2 unto my house: and I **w** give thee for it a
2 I **w** give thee the worth of it in money.
4 for he had said, I **w** not give thee the
6 if it please thee, I **w** give thee *another*
6 answered, I **w** not give thee my vineyard.
7 thine heart be merry: I **w** give thee the
21 Behold, I **w** bring evil upon thee, and
21 evil upon thee, and **w** take away thy
21 thy posterity, and **w** cut off from Ahab
22 And **w** make thine house like the house
29 before me, I **w** not bring the evil in
29 days **w** I bring the evil upon his house.
22:14 the LORD saith unto me, that **w** I speak.
21 the LORD, and said, I **w** persuade him.
22 And he said, I **w** go forth, and I will be
22 I will go forth, and I **w** be a lying spirit in
30 Jehoshaphat, I **w** disguise myself, and
2Ki 2: 2 *as* thy soul liveth, I **w** not leave thee. So
3 that the LORD **w** take away thy master
4 *as* thy soul liveth, I **w** not leave thee. So
5 that the LORD **w** take away thy master
6 **w** not leave thee. And they two went on.
3: 7 And he said, I **w** go up: I *am* as thou
18 of the LORD: he **w** deliver the Moabites
4:30 *as* thy soul liveth, I **w** not leave thee. And
5: 5 Go to, go, and I **w** send a letter unto the
11 I thought, He **w** surely come out to me,
16 whom I stand, I **w** receive none. And he
17 earth? for thy servant **w** henceforth offer
20 the LORD liveth, I **w** run after him, and
6: 3 thy servants. And he answered, I **w** go.
11 and said unto them, **W** ye not shew me
19 follow me, and I **w** bring you to the man
28 to day, and we **w** eat my son to morrow.
7: 4 If we say, We **w** enter into the city, then
9 some mischief **w** come upon us: now
12 his servants, I **w** now shew you what
9: 8 shall perish: and I **w** cut off from Ahab
9 And I **w** make the house of Ahab like the
26 the LORD; and I **w** requite thee in this
10: 5 thy servants, and **w** do all that thou shalt
5 shalt bid us; we **w** not make any king:
6 ye *be* mine, and *if* ye **w** hearken unto my
18:14 thou puttest on me **w** I bear. And the
21 if a man lean, it **w** go into his hand, and
23 king of Assyria, and I **w** deliver thee two
30 saying, The LORD **w** surely deliver us,
32 you, saying, The LORD **w** deliver us.
19: 4 It may be the LORD thy God **w** hear all
4 the living God; and **w** reprove the words
7 Behold, I **w** send a blast upon him, and
7 own land; and I **w** cause him to fall by
23 of Lebanon, and **w** cut down the tall
23 fir trees thereof: and I **w** enter into the
28 ears, therefore I **w** put my hook in thy
28 in thy lips, and I **w** turn thee back by the
34 For I **w** defend this city, to save it, for
20: 5 thy tears: behold, I **w** heal thee: on the
6 And I **w** add unto thy days fifteen years;
6 fifteen years; and I **w** deliver thee and

2Ki 20: 6 of Assyria; and I **w** defend this city for
8 sign that the LORD **w** heal me, and that I
9 that the LORD **w** do the thing that he
21: 4 said, In Jerusalem **w** I put my name.
7 of Israel, **w** I put my name for ever:
8 Neither **w** I make the feet of Israel move
8 only if they **w** observe to do according
13 And I **w** stretch over Jerusalem the line
13 of Ahab: and I **w** wipe Jerusalem as *a*
14 And I **w** forsake the remnant of mine
22:16 Thus saith the LORD, Behold, I **w** bring
20 Behold therefore, I **w** gather thee unto
20 see all the evil which I **w** bring upon this
23:27 And the LORD said, I **w** remove Judah
27 Israel, and **w** cast off this city Jerusalem
1Ch 12:19 away, saying, He **w** fall to his master
14:10 up; for I **w** deliver them into thine hand.
16:18 Saying, Unto thee **w** I give the land of
17: 9 Also I **w** ordain a place for my people
9 my people Israel, and **w** plant them, and
10 Israel. Moreover I **w** subdue all thine
10 that the LORD **w** build thee an house.
11 thy fathers, that I **w** raise up thy seed
11 thy sons; and I **w** establish his kingdom.
12 He shall build me an house, and I **w**
13 I **w** be his father, and he shall be my son:
13 be my son: and I **w** not take my mercy
14 But I **w** settle him in mine house and in
19: 2 And David said, I **w** shew kindness unto
12 be too strong for thee, then I **w** help thee.
21: 3 **w** he be a cause of trespass to Israel?
24 Ornan, Nay; but I **w** verily buy it for the
24 the full price: for I **w** not take *that* which
22: 5 all countries: I **w** *therefore* now make
9 a man of rest; and I **w** give him rest from
9 be Solomon, and I **w** give peace and
10 be my son, and I ***w be*** his father; and I
10 *will be* his father; and I **w** establish the
28: 6 him *to be* my son, and I **w** be his father.
7 Moreover I **w** establish his kingdom for
9 if thou seek him, he **w** be found of thee;
9 forsake him, he **w** cast thee off for ever.
20 God, *even* my God, ***w be*** with thee; he
20 *will be* with thee; he **w** not fail thee, nor
21 ***w be*** wholly at thy commandment.
2Ch 1:12 unto thee; and I **w** give thee riches, and
2:10 And, behold, I **w** give to thy servants, the
16 And we **w** cut wood out of Lebanon, as
16 shalt need: and we **w** bring it to thee in
6:18 But **w** God in very deed dwell with men
7:14 wicked ways; then **w** I hear from heaven,
14 from heaven, and **w** forgive their sin,
14 forgive their sin, and **w** heal their land.
18 Then **w** I stablish the throne of thy
20 Then **w** I pluck them up by the roots out
20 for my name, **w** I cast out of my sight,
20 out of my sight, and **w** make it *to be a*
10: 4 he put upon us, and we **w** serve thee.
7 to them, they **w** be thy servants for ever.
11 yoke upon you, I **w** put more to your
11 but I ***w*** *chastise you* with scorpions.
14 your yoke heavy, but I **w** add thereto: my
14 but I ***w*** *chastise you* with scorpions.
12: 7 *therefore* I **w** not destroy them, but
7 destroy them, but I **w** grant them some
15: 2 if ye seek him, he **w** be found of you; but
2 but if ye forsake him, he **w** forsake you.
18: 3 and *we* ***w be*** with thee in the war.
5 for God **w** deliver *it* into the king's hand.
13 even what my God saith, that **w** I speak.
20 LORD, and said, I **w** entice him. And the
21 And he said, I **w** go out, and be a lying
29 Jehoshaphat, I **w** disguise myself, and
29 myself, and **w** go to the battle; but
20:17 them: for the LORD ***w be*** with you.
21:14 Behold, with a great plague **w** the LORD
28:23 them, *therefore* **w** I sacrifice to them,
30: 6 Isaac, and Israel, and he **w** return to the
9 and merciful, and **w** not turn away *his*
33: 7 of Israel, **w** I put my name for ever:
8 Neither **w** I any more remove the foot of
8 so that they **w** take heed to do all that
34:24 Thus saith the LORD, Behold, I **w** bring
28 Behold, I **w** gather thee to thy fathers,
28 all the evil that I **w** bring upon this place,
Ezr 4: 3 we ourselves together **w** build unto the
13 set up *again, then* **w** they not pay toll,
7:18 the gold, that do after the **w** of your God.
26 And whosoever **w** not do the law of thy

Ezr 10: 4 unto thee: we also ***w be*** with thee: be of
Neh 1: 8 *If* ye transgress, I **w** scatter you abroad
9 of the heaven, *yet* **w** I gather them from
9 from thence, and **w** bring them unto the
2:19 that ye do? **w** ye rebel against the king?
20 The God of heaven, he **w** prosper us;
20 we his servants **w** arise and build: but
4: 2 do these feeble Jews? **w** they fortify
2 fortify themselves? **w** they sacrifice? will
2 will they sacrifice? **w** they make an end
2 an end in a day? **w** they revive the stones
12 shall return unto us *they* ***w be upon you.***
5: 8 the heathen; and **w** ye even sell your
12 Then said they, We **w** restore *them,* and
12 restore *them,* and **w** require nothing of
12 of them; so **w** we do as thou sayest.
6:10 the temple: for they **w** come to slay thee;
10 in the night **w** they come to slay thee.
11 the temple to save his life? I **w** not go in.
10:39 we **w** not forsake the house of our God.
13:21 if ye do *so* again, I **w** lay hands on you.
Est 3: 9 be destroyed: and I **w** pay ten thousand
4:16 and my maidens **w** fast likewise; and so
16 likewise; and so **w** I go in unto the king,
5: 8 I **w** do to morrow as the king hath said.
7: 8 said the king, **W** he force the queen also
Job 1:11 hath, and he **w** curse thee to thy face. H3808
2: 4 all that a man hath **w** he give for his life.
5 his flesh, and he **w** curse thee to thy face.
5: 1 Call now, if there be any that **w** answer
6:24 Teach me, and I **w** hold my tongue: and
7:11 Therefore I **w** not refrain my mouth; I
11 my mouth; I **w** speak in the anguish
11 **w** complain in the bitterness of my soul.
8:20 Behold, God **w** not cast away a perfect
20 *man,* neither **w** he help the evil doers:
9: 3 If he **w** contend with him, he cannot H2654
12 who **w** say unto him, What doest thou?
13 *If* God **w** not withdraw his anger, the
18 He **w** not suffer me to take my breath,
23 If the scourge slay suddenly, he **w** laugh
27 If I say, I **w** forget my complaint, I will
27 If I say, I will forget my complaint, I **w**
10: 1 My soul is weary of my life; I **w** leave my
1 I **w** speak in the bitterness of my soul.
2 I **w** say unto God, Do not condemn me;
15 *if* I be righteous, *yet* **w** I not lift up my
11:11 also; **w** he not then consider *it?*
13: 7 **W** ye speak wickedly for God? and talk
8 **W** ye accept his person? will ye contend
8 Will ye accept his person? **w** ye contend
10 He **w** surely reprove you, if ye do secretly
13 I may speak, and let come on me what ***w.***
15 Though he slay me, yet **w** I trust in him:
15 **w** maintain mine own ways before him.
19 Who *is* he *that* **w** plead with me? for
20 Only do not two *things* unto me: then **w** I
22 Then call thou, and I **w** answer: or let me
14: 7 be cut down, that it **w** sprout again, and
7 the tender branch thereof **w** not cease.
9 *Yet* through the scent of water it **w** bud,
14 time **w** I wait, till my change come.
15 Thou shalt call, and I **w** answer thee:
15:17 I **w** shew thee, hear me; and that *which* I
17 and that *which* I have seen I **w** declare;
17: 3 who *is* he *that* **w** strike hands with me?
18: 2 How long ***w it be ere*** ye make an end of
2 mark, and afterwards we **w** speak.
19: 2 How long **w** ye vex my soul, and break
5 If indeed ye **w** magnify *yourselves*
22: 4 **W** he reprove thee for fear of thee? will
4 Will he reprove thee for fear of thee? **w**
23: 6 **W** he plead against me with *his* great
24:25 And if *it be* not *so* now, who **w** make me
27: 5 I **w** not remove mine integrity from me.
6 My righteousness I hold fast, and **w** not
9 **W** God hear his cry when trouble
10 **W** he delight himself in the Almighty?
10 Almighty? **w** he always call upon God?
11 I **w** teach you by the hand of God: *that*
11 *is* with the Almighty **w** I not conceal.
30:24 Howbeit he **w** not stretch out *his* hand to
32:10 Therefore I said, Hearken to me; I also **w**
14 **w** I answer him with your speeches.
17 *I said,* I **w** answer also my part, I also
17 my part, I also **w** shew mine opinion.
20 I **w** speak, that I may be refreshed: I will
20 I will speak, that I may be refreshed: I **w**
33:12 Behold, *in* this thou art not just: I **w**

Job 33:26 He shall pray unto God, and he w be
26 he w render unto man his righteousness.
28 He w deliver his soul from going into the
31 unto me: hold thy peace, and I w speak.
34:12 Yea, surely God w not do wickedly,
12 w the Almighty pervert judgment.
23 For he w not lay upon man more than
31 chastisement, I w not offend any more:
32 if I have done iniquity, I w do no more.
33 Should it be according to thy mind? he w
35: 3 For thou saidst, What advantage w it be
4 I w answer thee, and thy companions
13 Surely God w not hear vanity, neither
13 vanity, neither w the Almighty regard it.
36: 2 Suffer me a little, and I w shew thee that
3 I w fetch my knowledge from afar, and
3 w ascribe righteousness to my Maker.
19 W he esteem thy riches? no, not gold,
37: 4 w not stay them when his voice is heard.
23 and in plenty of justice: he w not afflict.
38: 3 Gird up now thy loins like a man; for I w
39: 9 W the unicorn be willing to serve thee,
10 or w he harrow the valleys after thee?
12 Wilt thou believe him, that he w bring
40: 4 I w lay mine hand upon my mouth.
5 Once have I spoken; but I w not answer:
5 yea, twice; but I w proceed no further.
7 Gird up thy loins now like a man: I w
14 Then w I also confess unto thee that
41: 3 W he make many supplications unto
3 thee? w he speak soft words unto thee?
4 W he make a covenant with thee? wilt
12 I w not conceal his parts, nor his power,
42: 4 Hear, I beseech thee, and I w speak: I
4 and I will speak: I w demand of thee,
8 for you: for him w I accept: lest I deal
Ps 2: 7 I w declare the decree: the LORD hath
3: 6 I w not be afraid of ten thousands of
4: 2 O ye sons of men, how long w ye turn my
2 shame? how long w ye love vanity, and
3 the LORD w hear when I call unto him.
6 There be many that say, Who w shew us
8 I w both lay me down in peace, and
5: 2 and my God: for unto thee w I pray.
3 in the morning w I direct my prayer
3 my prayer unto thee, and w look up.
6 w abhor the bloody and deceitful man.
7 But as for me, I w come into thy house in
7 fear w I worship toward thy holy temple.
6: 9 the LORD w receive my prayer.
7:12 If he turn not, he w whet his sword; he
17 I w praise the LORD according to his
17 righteousness: and w sing praise to the
9: 1 I w praise thee, O LORD, with my whole
1 I w shew forth all thy marvellous works.
2 I w be glad and rejoice in thee: I will sing
2 I will be glad and rejoice in thee: I w sing
9 The LORD also w be a refuge for the
10 And they that know thy name w put
14 of Zion: I w rejoice in thy salvation.
10: 4 his countenance, w not seek after God:
11 he hideth his face; he w never see it.
12: 4 Who have said, With our tongue w we
5 of the needy, now w I arise, saith the
5 saith the LORD; I w set him in safety
13: 6 I w sing unto the LORD, because he hath
16: 4 offerings of blood w I not offer, nor take
7 I w bless the LORD, who hath given me
17:15 As for me, I w behold thy face in
18: 1 I w love thee, O LORD, my strength.
2 in whom I w trust; my buckler, and
3 I w call upon the LORD, who is worthy
28 LORD my God w enlighten my darkness.
49 Therefore w I give thanks unto thee, O
20: 5 We w rejoice in thy salvation, and in the
5 of our God we w set up our banners:
6 his anointed; he w hear him from his
7 in horses: but we w remember the name
21:13 so w we sing and praise thy power.
22:22 I w declare thy name unto my brethren:
22 of the congregation w I praise thee.
25 congregation: I w pay my vows before
23: 4 the shadow of death, I w fear no evil: for
6 of my life: and I w dwell in the house of
25: 8 therefore w he teach sinners in the way.
9 The meek w he guide in judgment: and
9 and the meek w he teach his way.
14 him; and he w shew them his covenant.
26: 4 neither w I go in with dissemblers.
Ps 26: 5 evil doers; and w not sit with the wicked.
6 I w wash mine hands in innocency: so
6 so w I compass thine altar, O LORD:
11 But as for me, I w walk in mine integrity:
12 in the congregations w I bless the LORD.
27: 3 rise against me, in this w I be confident.
4 of the LORD, that w I seek after; that I
6 me: therefore w I offer in his tabernacle
6 sacrifices of joy; I w sing, yea, I will sing
6 yea, I w sing praises unto the LORD.
8 said unto thee, Thy face, LORD, w I seek.
10 me, then the LORD w take me up.
12 Deliver me not over unto the w of mine H5315
28: 1 Unto thee w I cry, O LORD my rock; be
7 and with my song w I praise him.
29:11 The LORD w give strength unto his
11 the LORD w bless his people with peace.
30: 1 I w extol thee, O LORD; for thou hast
12 God, I w give thanks unto thee for ever.
31: 7 I w be glad and rejoice in thy mercy: for
32: 5 have I not hid. I said, I w confess my
8 I w instruct thee and teach thee in the
8 shalt go: I w guide thee with mine eye.
34: 1 I w bless the LORD at all times: his
11 Come, ye children, hearken unto me: I w
35:18 I w give thee thanks in the great
18 I w praise thee among much people.
37:33 The LORD w not leave him in his hand,
38:18 For I w declare mine iniquity; I will be
18 For I will declare mine iniquity; I w be
39: 1 I said, I w take heed to my ways, that I
1 not with my tongue: I w keep my mouth
40: 8 I delight to do thy w, O my God: yea, thy H7522
41: 1 LORD w deliver him in time of trouble.
2 The LORD w preserve him, and keep
2 deliver him unto the w of his enemies. H5315
3 The LORD w strengthen him upon the
42: 6 me: therefore w I remember thee from
8 Yet the LORD w command his
9 I w say unto God my rock, Why hast
43: 4 Then w I go unto the altar of God, unto
4 the harp w I praise thee, O God my God.
44: 5 Through thee w we push down our
5 through thy name w we tread them
6 For I w not trust in my bow, neither shall
45:17 I w make thy name to be remembered in
46: 2 Therefore w not we fear, though the
10 Be still, and know that I am God: I w be
10 the heathen, I w be exalted in the earth.
48: 8 God: God w establish it for ever. Selah.
14 ever: he w be our guide even unto death.
49: 4 I w incline mine ear to a parable: I will
4 I will incline mine ear to a parable: I w
15 But God w redeem my soul from the
18 his soul: and men w praise thee, when
50: 7 Hear, O my people, and I w speak; O
7 O Israel, and I w testify against thee:
8 I w not reprove thee for thy sacrifices or
9 I w take no bullock out of thy house, nor
13 W I eat the flesh of bulls, or drink the
15 w deliver thee, and thou shalt glorify me.
21 as thyself: but I w reprove thee, and set
23 aright w I shew the salvation of God.
51:13 Then w I teach transgressors thy ways;
52: 9 I w praise thee for ever, because thou
9 hast done it: and I w wait on thy name;
54: 6 I w freely sacrifice unto thee: I will
6 I will freely sacrifice unto thee: I w
55:16 As for me, I w call upon God; and the
17 Evening, and morning, and at noon, w I
23 out half their days; but I w trust in thee.
56: 3 What time I am afraid, I w trust in thee.
4 In God I w praise his word, in God I have
4 I w not fear what flesh can do unto me.
10 In God w I praise his word: in the LORD
10 word: in the LORD w I praise his word.
11 In God have I put my trust: I w not be
12 Thy vows are upon me, O God: I w
57: 1 of thy wings w I make my refuge, until
2 I w cry unto God most high; unto God
7 heart is fixed: I w sing and give praise.
8 and harp: I myself w awake early.
9 I w praise thee, O Lord, among the
9 I w sing unto thee among the nations.
58: 5 Which w not hearken to the voice of
59: 9 Because of his strength w I wait upon
16 But I w sing of thy power; yea, I will sing
16 But I will sing of thy power; yea, I w sing
17 Unto thee, O my strength, w I sing: for
Ps 60: 6 God hath spoken in his holiness; I w
6 I will rejoice, I w divide Shechem, and
8 Moab is my washpot; over Edom w I
9 Who w bring me into the strong city?
9 strong city? who w lead me into Edom?
61: 2 From the end of the earth w I cry unto
4 I w abide in thy tabernacle for ever: I
4 w trust in the covert of thy wings. Selah.
8 So w I sing praise unto thy name for
62: 3 How long w ye imagine mischief against
63: 1 O God, thou art my God; early w I seek
4 Thus w I bless thee while I live: I will lift
4 Thus will I bless thee while I live: I w lift
7 in the shadow of thy wings w I rejoice.
66:13 I w go into thy house with burnt
13 burnt offerings: I w pay thee my vows,
15 I w offer unto thee burnt sacrifices of
15 I w offer bullocks with goats. Selah.
16 fear God, and I w declare what he hath
18 in my heart, the Lord w not hear me:
68:16 in; yea, the LORD w dwell in it for ever.
22 The Lord said, I w bring again from
22 from Bashan, I w bring my people again
69:30 I w praise the name of God with a song,
30 and w magnify him with thanksgiving.
35 For God w save Zion, and will build the
35 For God will save Zion, and w build the
71:14 But I w hope continually, and will yet
14 But I will hope continually, and w yet
16 I w go in the strength of the Lord GOD: I
16 of the Lord GOD: I w make mention of
22 I w also praise thee with the psaltery,
22 O my God: unto thee w I sing with the
73:15 If I say, I w speak thus; behold, I should
75: 2 the congregation I w judge uprightly.
9 But I w declare for ever; I will sing
9 But I will declare for ever; I w sing
10 All the horns of the wicked also w I cut
77: 7 W the Lord cast off for ever? and will he
7 Will the Lord cast off for ever? and w he
10 And I said, This is my infirmity: but I w
11 I w remember the works of the LORD:
11 surely I w remember thy wonders of old.
12 I w meditate also of all thy work, and
78: 2 I w open my mouth in a parable: I will
2 I will open my mouth in a parable: I w
4 We w not hide them from their children,
79:13 of thy pasture w give thee thanks for
13 thee thanks for ever: we w shew forth thy
80:18 So w not we go back from thee: quicken
18 us, and we w call upon thy name.
81: 8 Hear, O my people, and I w testify unto
10 open thy mouth wide, and I w fill it.
82: 2 How long w ye judge unjustly, and
5 They know not, neither w they
84: 4 they w be still praising thee. Selah.
11 shield: the LORD w give grace and glory:
11 no good thing w he withhold from them
85: 8 I w hear what God the LORD will speak:
8 I will hear what God the LORD w speak:
8 will speak: for he w speak peace unto his
86: 7 In the day of my trouble I w call upon
11 Teach me thy way, O LORD; I w walk in
12 I w praise thee, O Lord my God, with all
12 and I w glorify thy name for evermore.
87: 4 I w make mention of Rahab and
89: 1 I w sing of the mercies of the LORD for
1 with my mouth w I make known thy
4 Thy seed w I establish for ever, and
23 And I w beat down his foes before his
25 I w set his hand also in the sea, and his
27 Also I w make him my firstborn, higher
28 My mercy w I keep for him for
29 His seed also w I make to endure for
32 Then w I visit their transgression with
33 Nevertheless my lovingkindness w I not
34 My covenant w I not break, nor alter the
35 my holiness that I w not lie unto David.
91: 2 I w say of the LORD, He is my refuge
2 my fortress: my God; in him w I trust.
14 me, therefore w I deliver him: I will set
14 will I deliver him: I w set him on high,
15 He shall call upon me, and I w answer
15 I will answer him: I w be with him in
15 I w deliver him, and honour him.
16 With long life w I satisfy him, and shew
92: 4 I w triumph in the works of thy hands.
94: 8 people: and ye fools, when w ye be wise?
14 For the LORD w not cast off his people,

Ps 94:14 neither **w** he forsake his inheritance.
16 Who **w** rise up for me against the
16 the evildoers? *or* who **w** stand up for me
95: 7 his hand. To day if ye **w** hear his voice,
101: 1 I **w** sing of mercy and judgment: unto
1 judgment: unto thee, O LORD, **w** I sing.
2 I **w** behave myself wisely in a perfect
2 thou come unto me? I **w** walk within my
3 I **w** set no wicked thing before mine eyes:
4 from me: I **w** not know a wicked *person*.
5 his neighbour, him **w** I cut off: him that
5 look and a proud heart **w** not I suffer.
8 I **w** early destroy all the wicked of the
102:17 He **w** regard the prayer of the destitute,
103: 9 He **w** not always chide: neither will he
9 He will not always chide: neither **w** he
104:33 I **w** sing unto the LORD as long as I live:
33 as long as I live: I **w** sing praise to my
34 My meditation of him shall be sweet: I **w**
105:11 Saying, Unto thee **w** I give the land of
107:43 Whoso *is* wise, and **w** observe these
108: 1 O God, my heart is fixed; I **w** sing and
2 Awake, psaltery and harp: I *myself* **w**
3 I **w** praise thee, O LORD, among the
3 the people: and I **w** sing praises unto
7 God hath spoken in his holiness; I **w**
7 I will rejoice, I **w** divide Shechem, and
9 Moab *is* my washpot; over Edom **w** I
9 out my shoe; over Philistia **w** I triumph.
10 Who **w** bring me into the strong city?
10 strong city? who **w** lead me into Edom?
109:30 I **w** greatly praise the LORD with my
30 I **w** praise him among the multitude.
110: 4 The LORD hath sworn, and **w** not
111: 1 Praise ye the LORD. I **w** praise the LORD
5 he **w** ever be mindful of his covenant.
112: 5 he **w** guide his affairs with discretion.
115:12 The LORD hath been mindful of us: he **w**
12 he will bless *us*; he **w** bless the house of
12 of Israel; he **w** bless the house of Aaron.
13 He **w** bless them that fear the LORD,
18 But we **w** bless the LORD from this time
116: 2 **w** I call upon *him* as long as I live.
9 I **w** walk before the LORD in the land of
13 I **w** take the cup of salvation, and call
14 I **w** pay my vows unto the LORD now in
17 I **w** offer to thee the sacrifice of
17 and **w** call upon the name of the LORD.
18 I **w** pay my vows unto the LORD now in
118: 6 The LORD *is* on my side; I **w** not fear:
10 the name of the LORD **w** I destroy them.
11 the name of the LORD I **w** destroy them.
12 the name of the LORD I **w** destroy them.
19 of righteousness: I **w** go into them, *and* I
19 go into them, *and* I **w** praise the LORD:
21 I **w** praise thee: for thou hast heard me,
24 made; we **w** rejoice and be glad in it.
28 Thou *art* my God, and I **w** praise thee:
28 thee: *thou art* my God, I **w** exalt thee.
119: 7 I **w** praise thee with uprightness of
8 I **w** keep thy statutes: O forsake me not
15 I **w** meditate in thy precepts, and have
16 I **w** delight myself in thy statutes: I will
16 I will delight myself in thy statutes: I **w**
32 I **w** run the way of thy commandments,
45 And I **w** walk at liberty: for I seek thy
46 I **w** speak of thy testimonies also before
46 before kings, and **w** not be ashamed.
47 And I **w** delight myself in thy
48 My hands also **w** I lift up unto thy
48 loved; and I **w** meditate in thy statutes.
62 At midnight I **w** rise to give thanks unto
69 lie against me: *but* I **w** keep thy precepts
74 They that fear thee **w** be glad when they
78 cause: *but* I **w** meditate in thy precepts.
93 I **w** never forget thy precepts: for with
95 me: *but* I **w** consider thy testimonies.
106 I have sworn, and I **w** perform *it*, that I
106 that I **w** keep thy righteous judgments.
115 Depart from me, ye evildoers: for I **w**
117 I shall be safe: and I **w** have respect unto
134 of man: so **w** I keep thy precepts.
145 hear me, O LORD: I **w** keep thy statutes.
121: 1 I **w** lift up mine eyes unto the hills, from
3 He **w** not suffer thy foot to be moved: he
3 he that keepeth thee **w** not slumber.
122: 8 sakes, I **w** now say, Peace *be* within thee.
9 of the LORD our God I **w** seek thy good.
132: 3 Surely I **w** not come into the tabernacle

Ps 132: 4 I **w** not give sleep to mine eyes, *or*
7 We **w** go into his tabernacles: we will
7 We will go into his tabernacles: we **w**
11 unto David; he **w** not turn from it; Of
11 fruit of thy body **w** I set upon thy throne.
12 If thy children **w** keep my covenant and
14 This *is* my rest for ever: here **w** I dwell;
15 I **w** abundantly bless her provision: I will
15 I will abundantly bless her provision: I **w**
16 I **w** also clothe her priests with salvation:
17 There **w** I make the horn of David to
18 His enemies **w** I clothe with shame: but
135:14 For the LORD **w** judge his people, and he
14 his people, and he **w** repent himself
138: 1 I **w** praise thee with my whole heart:
1 before the gods **w** I sing praise unto thee.
2 I **w** worship toward thy holy temple, and
8 The LORD **w** perfect *that which*
139:14 I **w** praise thee; for I am fearfully *and*
140:12 I know that the LORD **w** maintain the
143:10 Teach me to do thy **w**; for thou *art* my
144: 9 I **w** sing a new song unto thee, O God:
9 of ten strings **w** I sing praises unto thee.
145: 1 I **w** extol thee, my God, O king; and I will
1 I will extol thee, my God, O king; and I **w**
2 Every day **w** I bless thee; and I will
2 Every day will I bless thee; and I **w**
5 I **w** speak of the glorious honour of thy
6 acts: and I **w** declare thy greatness.
19 He **w** fulfil the desire of them that fear
19 also **w** hear their cry, and will save them.
19 also will hear their cry, and **w** save them.
20 him: but all the wicked **w** he destroy.
146: 2 While I live **w** I praise the LORD: I will
2 While I live will I praise the LORD: I **w**
149: 4 he **w** beautify the meek with salvation.
Prv 1: 5 A wise *man* **w** hear, and will increase
5 A wise *man* will hear, and **w** increase
22 How long, ye simple ones, **w** ye love
23 Turn you at my reproof: behold, I **w**
23 I **w** make known my words unto you.
26 I also **w** laugh at your calamity; I will
26 I also will laugh at your calamity; I **w**
28 Then shall they call upon me, but I **w** not
3:28 I **w** give; when thou hast it by thee.
6:26 adulteress **w** hunt for the precious life.
34 he **w** not spare in the day of vengeance.
35 He **w** not regard any ransom; neither
35 any ransom; neither **w** he rest content,
7:20 *and* **w** come home at the day appointed.
8: 6 Hear; for I **w** speak of excellent things;
21 substance; and I **w** fill their treasures.
9: 8 rebuke a wise man, and he **w** love thee.
9 Give *instruction* to a wise *man*, and he **w**
9 just *man*, and he **w** increase in learning.
10: 3 The LORD **w** not suffer the soul of the
8 The wise in heart **w** receive
12: 2 a man of wicked devices **w** he condemn.
14: 5 A faithful witness **w** not lie: but a false
5 not lie: but a false witness **w** utter lies.
15:12 him: neither **w** he go unto the wise.
25 The LORD **w** destroy the house of the
25 he **w** establish the border of the widow.
16:14 of death: but a wise man **w** pacify it.
18:14 The spirit of a man **w** sustain his
19: 6 Many **w** entreat the favour of the prince:
17 which he hath given **w** he pay him again.
24 in *his* bosom, and **w** not so much as
25 Smite a scorner, and the simple **w**
25 *and* he **w** understand knowledge.
20: 3 strife: but every fool **w** be meddling.
4 The sluggard **w** not plow by reason of
5 a man of understanding **w** draw it out.
6 Most men **w** proclaim every one his own
22 Say not thou, I **w** recompense evil; *but*
21: 1 water: he turneth it whithersoever he **w**. H2654
22: 6 when he is old, he **w** not depart from it.
23 For the LORD **w** plead their cause, and
23: 9 Speak not in the ears of a fool: for he **w**
35 when shall I awake? I **w** seek it yet again.
24:29 Say not, I **w** do so to him as he hath
29 hath done to me: I **w** render to the man
26:27 rolleth a stone, it **w** return upon him.
27:22 **w** not his foolishness depart from him.
28: 8 gather it for him that **w** pity the poor.
21 a piece of bread *that* man **w** transgress.
29:19 A servant **w** not be corrected by words:
19 though he understand he **w** not answer.
31:12 She **w** do him good and not evil all the

Ecc 2: 1 I said in mine heart, Go to now, I **w**
4:10 For if they fall, the one **w** lift up his
13 king, who **w** no more be admonished. H3045
5:12 of the rich **w** not suffer him to sleep.
7: 2 men; and the living **w** lay *it* to his heart.
23 said, I **w** be wise; but it *was* far from me.
10:11 Surely the serpent **w** bite without
12 the lips of a fool **w** swallow up himself.
11: 9 *things* God **w** bring thee into judgment.
Song 1: 4 Draw me, we **w** run after thee: the king
4 his chambers: we **w** be glad and rejoice
4 rejoice in thee, we **w** remember thy love
11 We **w** make thee borders of gold with
3: 2 I **w** rise now, and go about the city in the
2 the broad ways I **w** seek him whom my
4: 6 flee away, I **w** get me to the mountain
6:13 look upon thee. What **w** ye see in the
7: 8 I said, I **w** go up to the palm tree, I will
8 I said, I will go up to the palm tree, I **w**
12 bud forth: there **w** I give thee my loves.
8: 9 If she *be* a wall, we **w** build upon her a
9 we **w** inclose her with boards of cedar.
Isa 1: 5 any more? ye **w** revolt more and more:
15 forth your hands, I **w** hide mine eyes
15 **w** not hear: your hands are full of blood.
24 One of Israel, Ah, I **w** ease me of mine
25 And I **w** turn my hand upon thee, and
26 And I **w** restore thy judges as at the first,
2: 3 of Jacob; and he **w** teach us of his ways,
3 his ways, and we **w** walk in his paths: for
3: 4 And I **w** give children *to be* their princes,
7 In that day shall he swear, saying, I **w**
14 The LORD **w** enter into judgment with
17 Therefore the Lord **w** smite with a scab
17 the LORD **w** discover their secret parts.
18 In that day the Lord **w** take away the
4: 1 man, saying, We **w** eat our own bread,
5 And the LORD **w** create upon every
5: 1 Now **w** I sing to my wellbeloved a song
5 And now go to; I **w** tell you what I will do
5 And now go to; I will tell you what I **w** do
5 to my vineyard: I **w** take away the hedge
6 And I **w** lay it waste: it shall not be
6 briers and thorns: I **w** also command the
26 And he **w** lift up an ensign to the nations
26 from far, and **w** hiss unto them from
6: 8 I send, and who **w** go for us? Then said
7: 9 son. If ye **w** not believe, surely ye
12 But Ahaz said, I **w** not ask, neither will I
12 But Ahaz said, I will not ask, neither **w** I
13 men, but **w** ye weary my God also?
8:17 And I **w** wait upon the LORD, that
17 the house of Jacob, and I **w** look for him.
9: 7 of the LORD of hosts **w** perform this.
10 The bricks are fallen down, but we **w**
10 but we **w** change *them into* cedars.
14 Therefore the LORD **w** cut off from
10: 3 And what **w** ye do in the day of
3 from far? to whom **w** ye flee for help?
3 help? and where **w** ye leave your glory?
6 I **w** send him against an hypocritical
6 of my wrath **w** I give him a charge,
12 on Jerusalem, I **w** punish the fruit of the
12: 1 say, O LORD, I **w** praise thee: though
2 Behold, God *is* my salvation; I **w** trust,
13:11 And I **w** punish the world for *their* evil,
11 iniquity; and I **w** cause the arrogancy
11 **w** lay low the haughtiness of the terrible.
12 I **w** make a man more precious than fine
13 Therefore I **w** shake the heavens, and
17 Behold, I **w** stir up the Medes against
14: 1 For the LORD **w** have mercy on Jacob,
1 on Jacob, and **w** yet choose Israel, and
13 For thou hast said in thine heart, I **w**
13 into heaven, I **w** exalt my throne above
13 the stars of God: I **w** sit also upon the
14 I **w** ascend above the heights of the
14 of the clouds; I **w** be like the most High.
22 For I **w** rise up against them, saith the
23 I **w** also make it a possession for the
23 pools of water: and I **w** sweep it with the
25 That I **w** break the Assyrian in my land,
30 down in safety: and I **w** kill thy root with
15: 9 be full of blood: for I **w** bring more upon
16: 9 Therefore I **w** bewail with the weeping of
9 vine of Sibmah: I **w** water thee with my
18: 4 For so the LORD said unto me, I **w** take
4 will take my rest, and I **w** consider in my
19: 2 And I **w** set the Egyptians against the

Isa 19: 3 thereof; and I **w** destroy the counsel
4 And the Egyptians **w** I give over into the
21:12 if ye **w** inquire, inquire ye: return, come.
22: 4 away from me; I **w** weep bitterly, labour
17 Behold, the LORD **w** carry thee away
17 captivity, and **w** surely cover thee.
18 He **w** surely violently turn and toss thee
19 And I **w** drive thee from thy station, and
20 pass in that day, that I **w** call my servant
21 And I **w** clothe him with thy robe, and
21 with thy girdle, and I **w** commit thy
22 And the key of the house of David **w** I lay
23 And I **w** fasten him *as* a nail in a sure
23:17 that the LORD **w** visit Tyre, and she shall
25: 1 O LORD, thou *art* my God; I **w** exalt thee,
1 I will exalt thee, I **w** praise thy name; for
7 And he **w** destroy in this mountain the
8 He **w** swallow up death in victory; and
8 and the Lord GOD **w** wipe away tears
9 for him, and he **w** save us: this *is* the
9 we **w** be glad and rejoice in his salvation.
26: 1 **w** *God* appoint *for* walls and bulwarks.
9 spirit within me **w** I seek thee early: for
9 of the world **w** learn righteousness.
10 shewed to the wicked, *yet* **w** he not learn
10 of uprightness **w** he deal unjustly, and
10 **w** not behold the majesty of the LORD.
11 is lifted up, they **w** not see: *but* they shall
13 only **w** we make mention of thy name.
27: 3 I the LORD do keep it; I **w** water it every
3 *any* hurt it, I **w** keep it night and day.
11 he that made them **w** not have mercy on
11 formed them **w** shew them no favour.
28:11 tongue **w** he speak to this people.
17 Judgment also **w** I lay to the line, and
28 Bread *corn* is bruised; because he **w** not
29: 2 Yet I **w** distress Ariel, and there shall be
3 And I **w** camp against thee round about,
3 round about, and **w** lay siege against
3 mount, and I **w** raise forts against thee.
14 Therefore, behold, I **w** proceed to do a
30: 6 serpent, they **w** carry their riches upon
9 *that* **w** not hear the law of the LORD: H14
16 But ye said, No; for we **w** flee upon
16 ye flee: and, We **w** ride upon the swift;
18 And therefore **w** the LORD wait, that he
18 you, and therefore **w** he be exalted, that
19 weep no more: he **w** be very gracious
19 when he shall hear it, he **w** answer thee.
32 in battles of shaking **w** he fight with it.
31: 2 Yet he also *is* wise, and **w** bring evil, and
2 will bring evil, and **w** not call back his
2 his words: but **w** arise against the house
4 against him, *he* **w** not be afraid of their
5 As birds flying, so **w** the LORD of hosts
5 defending also he **w** deliver *it; and*
5 *it; and* passing over he **w** preserve it.
32: 6 For the vile person **w** speak villany, and
6 villany, and his heart **w** work iniquity, to
6 he **w** cause the drink of the thirsty to fail.
33:10 Now **w** I rise, saith the LORD; now will I
10 Now will I rise, saith the LORD; now **w** I
10 will I be exalted; now **w** I lift up myself.
21 But there the glorious LORD *w be* unto
22 the LORD *is* our king; he **w** save us.
35: 4 not: behold, your God **w** come *with*
4 a recompence; he **w** come and save you.
36: 6 if a man lean, it **w** go into his hand, and
8 king of Assyria, and I **w** give thee two
15 saying, The LORD **w** surely deliver us:
18 saying, The LORD **w** deliver us. Hath
37: 4 It may be the LORD thy God **w** hear the
4 the living God, and **w** reprove the words
7 Behold, I **w** send a blast upon him, and
7 own land; and I **w** cause him to fall by
24 of Lebanon; and I **w** cut down the tall
24 fir trees thereof: and I **w** enter into the
29 ears, therefore **w** I put my hook in thy
29 in thy lips, and I **w** turn thee back by the
35 For I **w** defend this city to save it for
38: 5 I **w** add unto thy days fifteen years.
6 And I **w** deliver thee and this city out of
6 king of Assyria: and I **w** defend this city.
7 **w** do this thing that he hath spoken;
8 Behold, I **w** bring again the shadow of
12 a weaver my life: he **w** cut me off with
13 *that*, as a lion, so **w** he break all my
20 me: therefore we **w** sing my songs to the
40:10 Behold, the Lord GOD **w** come with

Isa 40:18 To whom then **w** ye liken God? or what
18 what likeness **w** ye compare unto him?
20 a tree *that* **w** not rot; he seeketh unto
25 To whom then **w** ye liken me, or shall I
41:10 for I *am* thy God: I **w** strengthen thee;
10 thee; yea, I **w** help thee; yea, I will
10 help thee; yea, I **w** uphold thee with the
13 For I the LORD thy God **w** hold thy right
13 saying unto thee, Fear not; I **w** help thee.
14 ye men of Israel; I **w** help thee, saith the
15 Behold, I **w** make thee a new sharp
17 for thirst, I the LORD **w** hear them, I the
17 I the God of Israel **w** not forsake them.
18 I **w** open rivers in high places, and
18 of the valleys: I **w** make the wilderness
19 I **w** plant in the wilderness the cedar, the
19 and the oil tree; I **w** set in the desert the
27 behold them: and I **w** give to Jerusalem
42: 6 in righteousness, and **w** hold thine hand,
6 thine hand, and **w** keep thee, and give
8 and my glory **w** I not give to another,
14 myself: *now* **w** I cry like a travailing
14 woman; I **w** destroy and devour at once.
15 I **w** make waste mountains and hills,
15 all their herbs; and I **w** make the rivers
15 rivers islands, and I **w** dry up the pools.
16 And I **w** bring the blind by a way *that*
16 they knew not; I **w** lead them in paths
16 they have not known: I **w** make darkness
16 **w** I do unto them, and not forsake them.
21 sake; he **w** magnify the law, and
23 Who among you **w** give ear to this? *who*
23 ear to this? *who* **w** hearken and hear for
43: 2 the waters, I *w be* with thee; and through
4 thee: therefore **w** I give men for thee,
5 Fear not: for I *am* with thee: I **w** bring
6 I **w** say to the north, Give up; and to the
13 my hand: I **w** work, and who shall let it?
19 Behold, I **w** do a new thing; now it shall
19 ye not know it? I **w** even make a way in
25 own sake, and **w** not remember thy sins.
44: 2 the womb, *which* **w** help thee; Fear not,
3 For I **w** pour water upon him that is
3 the dry ground: I **w** pour my spirit upon
15 to burn: for he **w** take thereof, and warm
26 I **w** raise up the decayed places thereof:
27 That saith to the deep, Be dry, and I **w**
45: 1 before him; and I **w** loose the loins of
2 I **w** go before thee, and make the
2 places straight: I **w** break in pieces the
3 And I **w** give thee the treasures of
13 and I **w** direct all his ways: he
46: 4 *even* to hoar hairs **w** I carry *you*: I have
4 I have made, and I **w** bear; even I will
4 even I **w** carry, and will deliver *you*.
4 even I will carry, and **w** deliver *you*.
5 To whom **w** ye liken me, and make *me*
10 shall stand, and I **w** do all my pleasure:
11 I have spoken *it*, I **w** also bring it to pass;
11 to pass; I have purposed *it*, I **w** also do it.
13 not tarry: and I **w** place salvation in Zion
47: 3 shall be seen: I **w** take vengeance, and
3 and I **w** not meet *thee as* a man.
48: 6 Thou hast heard, see all this; and **w** not
9 For my name's sake **w** I defer mine
9 and for my praise **w** I refrain for thee,
11 for mine own sake, **w** I do *it*: for how
11 and I **w** not give my glory unto another.
14 hath loved him: he **w** do his pleasure on
49: 3 O Israel, in whom I **w** be glorified.
6 of Israel: I **w** also give thee for a light
8 I helped thee: and I **w** preserve thee, and
11 And I **w** make all my mountains a way,
13 and **w** have mercy upon his afflicted.
15 they may forget, yet **w** I not forget thee.
22 Thus saith the Lord GOD, Behold, I **w** lift
25 be delivered: for I **w** contend with him
25 with thee, and I **w** save thy children.
26 And I **w** feed them that oppress thee
50: 7 For the Lord GOD **w** help me; therefore
8 *He is* near that justifieth me; who **w**
9 Behold, the Lord GOD **w** help me; who *is*
51: 3 For the LORD shall comfort Zion: he **w**
3 places; and he **w** make her wilderness
4 from me, and I **w** make my judgment
23 But I **w** put it into the hand of them that
52:12 for the LORD **w** go before you; and the
12 the God of Israel *w be* your rearward.
53:12 Therefore **w** I divide him *a portion* with

Isa 54: 7 but with great mercies **w** I gather thee.
8 kindness **w** I have mercy on thee,
11 behold, I **w** lay thy stones with fair
12 And I **w** make thy windows of agates,
55: 3 shall live; and I **w** make an everlasting
7 the LORD, and he **w** have mercy upon
7 to our God, for he **w** abundantly pardon.
56: 5 Even unto them **w** I give in mine house
5 sons and of daughters: I **w** give them an
7 Even them **w** I bring to my holy
8 of Israel saith, Yet **w** I gather *others* to
12 Come ye, *say they*, I **w** fetch wine, and
12 fetch wine, and we **w** fill ourselves with
57:12 I **w** declare thy righteousness, and thy
16 For I **w** not contend for ever, neither will
16 For I will not contend for ever, neither **w**
18 I have seen his ways, and **w** heal him: I
18 and will heal him: I **w** lead him also, and
19 near, saith the LORD; and I **w** heal him.
58:14 in the LORD; and I **w** cause thee to ride
59: 2 *his* face from you, that he **w** not hear.
18 accordingly he **w** repay, fury to his
18 to the islands he **w** repay recompence.
60: 7 and I **w** glorify the house of my glory.
12 For the nation and kingdom that **w** not
13 I **w** make the place of my feet glorious.
15 through *thee*, I **w** make thee an eternal
17 For brass I **w** bring gold, and for iron I
17 gold, and for iron I **w** bring silver, and
17 and for stones iron: I **w** also make thy
22 I the LORD **w** hasten it in his time.
61: 8 offering; and I **w** direct their work in
8 in truth, and I **w** make an everlasting
10 I **w** greatly rejoice in the LORD, my soul
11 so the Lord GOD **w** cause righteousness
62: 1 For Zion's sake **w** I not hold my peace,
1 Jerusalem's sake I **w** not rest, until the
8 his strength, Surely I **w** no more give thy
63: 3 *was* none with me: for I **w** tread them in
3 garments, and I **w** stain all my raiment.
6 And I **w** tread down the people in mine
6 **w** bring down their strength to the earth.
7 I **w** mention the lovingkindnesses of the
8 *that* **w** not lie: so he was their Saviour.
65: 6 Behold, *it is* written before me: I **w** not
6 keep silence, but **w** recompense, even
7 the hills: therefore **w** I measure their
8 a blessing *is* in it: so **w** I do for my
9 And I **w** bring forth a seed out of Jacob,
12 Therefore **w** I number you to the sword,
19 And I **w** rejoice in Jerusalem, and joy in
24 before they call, I **w** answer; and while
24 while they are yet speaking, I **w** hear.
66: 2 but to this *man* **w** I look, *even* to *him*
4 I also **w** choose their delusions, and will
4 I also will choose their delusions, and **w**
12 For thus saith the LORD, Behold, I **w**
13 comforteth, so **w** I comfort you; and ye
15 For, behold, the LORD **w** come with fire,
16 For by fire and by his sword **w** the LORD
18 it shall come, that I **w** gather all nations
19 And I **w** set a sign among them, and I
19 them, and I **w** send those that escape
21 And I **w** also take of them for priests *and*
22 new earth, which I **w** make, shall remain
Jer 1:12 for I **w** hasten my word to perform it.
15 For, lo, I **w** call all the families of the
16 And I **w** utter my judgments against
2: 9 Wherefore I **w** yet plead with you, saith
9 with your children's children **w** I plead.
20 and thou saidst, I **w** not transgress;
24 all they that seek her **w** not weary
25 loved strangers, and after them **w** I go.
27 trouble they **w** say, Arise, and save us.
29 Wherefore **w** ye plead with me? ye all
31 are lords; we **w** come no more unto thee?
35 from me. Behold, I **w** plead with thee,
3: 5 **W** he reserve *his anger* for ever? will he
5 Will he reserve *his anger* for ever? **w** he
12 the LORD; *and* I **w** not cause mine anger
12 LORD, *and* I **w** not keep *anger* for ever.
14 unto you: and I **w** take you one of a city,
14 of a family, and I **w** bring you to Zion:
15 And I **w** give you pastors according to
22 Return, ye backsliding children, *and* I **w**
4: 6 stay not: for I **w** bring evil from the
12 now also **w** I give sentence against them.
27 be desolate; yet **w** I not make a full end.
28 purposed *it*, and **w** not repent, neither

Jer 4:28 not repent, neither w I turn back from it.
30 w despise thee, they will seek thy life.
30 will despise thee, they w seek thy life.
5: 1 that seeketh the truth; and I w pardon it.
5 I w get me unto the great men, and will
5 I will get me unto the great men, and w
14 word, behold, I w make my words in thy
15 Lo, I w bring a nation upon you from
18 LORD, I w not make a full end with you.
22 Fear ye not me? saith the LORD: w ye
31 so: and what w ye do in the end thereof?
6:11 with holding in: I w pour it out upon the
12 together: for I w stretch out my hand
16 But they said, We w not walk *therein*.
17 But they said, We w not hearken.
19 Hear, O earth: behold, I w bring evil
21 LORD, Behold, I w lay stumblingblocks
7: 3 and I w cause you to dwell in this place.
7 Then w I cause you to dwell in this place,
9 W ye steal, murder, and commit
14 Therefore w I do unto *this* house, which
15 And I w cast you out of my sight, as I
16 intercession to me: for I w not hear thee.
23 my voice, and I w be your God, and ye
27 them; but they w not hearken to thee:
27 unto them; but they w not answer thee.
34 Then w I cause to cease from the cities of
8:10 Therefore w I give their wives unto
13 I w surely consume them, saith the
17 For, behold, I w send serpents,
17 among you, which *w* not *be* charmed,
9: 4 for every brother w utterly supplant, and
4 every neighbour w walk with slanders.
5 And they w deceive every one his
5 one his neighbour, and w not speak the
7 of hosts, Behold, I w melt them, and try
10 For the mountains w I take up a weeping
11 And I w make Jerusalem heaps, *and* a
11 of dragons; and I w make the cities of
15 of Israel; Behold, I w feed them, *even*
16 I w scatter them also among the
16 have known: and I w send a sword after
25 saith the LORD, that I w punish all *them*
10:18 For thus saith the LORD, Behold, I w
18 w distress them, that they may find *it so*.
11: 4 ye be my people, and I w be your God:
8 heart: therefore I w bring upon them all
11 LORD, Behold, I w bring evil upon them,
11 cry unto me, I w not hearken unto them.
14 for them: for I w not hear *them* in the
22 of hosts, Behold, I w punish them: the
23 of them: for I w bring evil upon the men
12:14 to inherit; Behold, I w pluck them out of
15 plucked them out I w return, and have
15 on them, and w bring them again, every
16 And it shall come to pass, if they w
17 But if they w not obey, I will utterly
17 But if they will not obey, I w utterly
13: 9 After this manner w I mar the pride of
13 LORD, Behold, I w fill all the inhabitants
14 And I w dash them one against another,
14 saith the LORD: I w not pity, nor spare,
17 But if ye w not hear it, my soul shall
24 Therefore w I scatter them as the stubble
26 Therefore w I discover thy skirts upon
14:10 accept them; he w now remember their
12 When they fast, I w not hear their cry;
12 and an oblation, I w not accept them:
12 accept them: but I w consume them by
13 I w give you assured peace in this place.
16 I w pour their wickedness upon them.
22 God? therefore we w wait upon thee: for
15: 3 And I w appoint over them four kinds,
4 And I w cause them to be removed into
6 therefore w I stretch out my hand
7 And I w fan them with a fan in the gates
7 gates of the land; I w bereave *them* of
7 *them* of children, I w destroy my people,
9 residue of them w I deliver to the sword
11 remnant; verily I w cause the enemy to
13 Thy substance and thy treasures w I give
14 And I w make *thee* to pass with thine
19 If thou return, then w I bring thee again,
20 And I w make thee unto this people a
21 And I w deliver thee out of the hand of
21 the wicked, and I w redeem thee out of
16: 9 of Israel; Behold, I w cause to cease out
13 Therefore w I cast you out of this land
13 night; where I w not shew you favour.

Jer 16:15 driven them: and I w bring them again
16 Behold, I w send for many fishers, saith
16 fish them; and after w I send for many
18 And first I w recompense their iniquity
21 Therefore, behold, I w this once cause
21 them to know, I w cause them to know
17: 3 O my mountain in the field, I w give thy
4 I gave thee; and I w cause thee to serve
27 But if ye w not hearken unto me to
27 sabbath day; then w I kindle a fire in the
18: 2 there I w cause thee to hear my words.
8 from their evil, I w repent of the evil that
10 my voice, then I w repent of the good,
12 is no hope: but we w walk after our own
12 own devices, and we w every one do the
14 W *a man* leave the snow of Lebanon
17 I w scatter them as with an east wind
17 the enemy; I w shew them the back,
19: 3 of Israel; Behold, I w bring evil upon this
7 And I w make void the counsel of Judah
7 in this place; and I w cause them to fall
7 and their carcases w I give to be meat
8 And I w make this city desolate, and an
9 And I w cause them to eat the flesh of
11 of hosts; Even so w I break this people
12 Thus w I do unto this place, saith the
15 of Israel; Behold, I w bring upon this city
20: 4 For thus saith the LORD, Behold, I w
4 behold *it*: and I w give all Judah into the
5 Moreover I w deliver all the strength of
5 the kings of Judah w I give into the hand
9 Then I said, I w not make mention of
10 *say they*, and we w report it. All my
10 Peradventure he w be enticed, and we
21: 2 so be that the LORD w deal with us
4 God of Israel; Behold, I w turn back the
4 the walls, and I w assemble them into
5 And I myself w fight against you with an
6 And I w smite the inhabitants of this
7 And afterward, saith the LORD, I w
14 But I w punish you according to the fruit
14 the LORD: and I w kindle a fire in the
22: 5 But if ye w not hear these words, I swear
6 *yet* surely I w make thee a wilderness,
7 And I w prepare destroyers against thee,
14 That saith, I w build me a wide house
21 *but* thou saidst, I w not hear. This *hath*
25 And I w give thee into the hand of them
26 And I w cast thee out, and thy mother
23: 2 them: behold, I w visit upon you the evil
3 And I w gather the remnant of my flock
3 driven them, and w bring them again to
4 And I w set up shepherds over them
5 the LORD, that I w raise unto David a
12 fall therein: for I w bring evil upon them,
15 Behold, I w feed them with wormwood,
33 I w even forsake you, saith the LORD.
34 I w even punish that man and his house.
39 Therefore, behold, I, even I, w utterly
39 forget you, and I w forsake you, and the
40 And I w bring an everlasting reproach
24: 5 Like these good figs, so w I acknowledge
6 For I w set mine eyes upon them for
6 for good, and I w bring them again to
6 to this land: and I w build them, and not
6 I w plant them, and not pluck *them* up.
7 And I w give them an heart to know me,
7 my people, and I w be their God: for they
8 saith the LORD, So w I give Zedekiah the
9 And I w deliver them to be removed into
10 And I w send the sword, the famine, and
25: 6 of your hands; and I w do you no hurt.
9 Behold, I w send and take all the
9 my servant, and w bring them against
9 round about, and w utterly destroy
10 Moreover I w take from them the voice
12 *that* I w punish the king of Babylon,
12 and w make it perpetual desolations.
13 And I w bring upon that land all my
14 of them also: and I w recompense them
16 of the sword that I w send among them.
27 of the sword which I w send among you.
29 be unpunished: for I w call for a sword
31 the nations, he w plead with all flesh;
31 with all flesh; he w give them *that are*
26: 3 If so be they w hearken, and turn every
4 the LORD; If ye w not hearken to me, to
6 Then w I make this house like Shiloh,
6 like Shiloh, and w make this city a curse

Jer 26:13 and the LORD w repent him of the evil
27: 8 kingdom which w not serve the same
8 Babylon, and that w not put their neck
8 that nation w I punish, saith the LORD,
11 serve him, those w I let remain still in
13 Why w ye die, thou and thy people, by
13 that w not serve the king of Babylon?
22 the LORD; then w I bring them up, and
28: 3 Within two full years w I bring again
4 And I w bring again to this place
4 w break the yoke of the king of Babylon.
11 the LORD; Even so w I break the yoke of
16 LORD; Behold, I w cast thee from off the
29:10 at Babylon I w visit you, and perform
12 unto me, and I w hearken unto you.
14 And I w be found of you, saith the
14 saith the LORD: and I w turn away your
14 captivity, and I w gather you from all
14 the LORD; and I w bring you again into
17 of hosts; Behold, I w send upon them the
17 the pestilence, and w make them like
18 And I w persecute them with the sword,
18 the pestilence, and w deliver them to be
21 name; Behold, I w deliver them into the
32 LORD; Behold, I w punish Shemaiah the
32 the good that I w do for my people, saith
30: 3 saith the LORD, that I w bring again the
3 the LORD: and I w cause them to return
8 of hosts, *that* I w break his yoke from
8 off thy neck, and w burst thy bonds, and
9 their king, whom I w raise up unto them.
10 O Israel: for, lo, I w save thee from afar,
11 scattered thee, yet w I not make a full
11 full end of thee: but I w correct thee in
11 w not leave thee altogether unpunished.
16 that prey upon thee w I give for a prey.
17 For I w restore health unto thee, and I
17 health unto thee, and I w heal thee of thy
18 Thus saith the LORD; Behold, I w bring
19 make merry: and I w multiply them, and
19 shall not be few; I w also glorify them,
20 and I w punish all that oppress them.
21 of them; and I w cause him to draw
22 And ye shall be my people, and I w be
31: 1 At the same time, saith the LORD, w I be
4 Again I w build thee, and thou shalt be
8 Behold, I w bring them from the north
9 with supplications w I lead them: I will
9 will I lead them: I w cause them to walk
10 scattered Israel w gather him, and keep
13 old together: for I w turn their mourning
13 into joy, and w comfort them, and make
14 And I w satiate the soul of the priests
20 troubled for him; I w surely have mercy
27 the LORD, that I w sow the house of
28 and to afflict; so w I watch over them, to
31 saith the LORD, that I w make a new
33 But this *shall be* the covenant that I w
33 saith the LORD, I w put my law in their
33 in their hearts; and w be their God, and
34 the LORD: for I w forgive their iniquity,
34 and I w remember their sin no more.
37 out beneath, I w also cast off all the seed
32: 3 LORD, Behold, I w give this city into the
28 LORD; Behold, I w give this city into the
37 Behold, I w gather them out of all
37 in great wrath; and I w bring them again
37 and I w cause them to dwell safely:
38 And they shall be my people, and I w be
39 And I w give them one heart, and one
40 And I w make an everlasting covenant
40 with them, that I w not turn away from
40 them good; but I w put my fear in their
41 Yea, I w rejoice over them to do them
41 do them good, and I w plant them in this
42 this people, so w I bring upon them all
44 of the south: for I w cause their captivity
33: 3 Call unto me, and I w answer thee, and
6 Behold, I w bring it health and cure, and
6 and cure, and I w cure them, and will
6 cure them, and w reveal unto them the
7 And I w cause the captivity of Judah and
7 return, and w build them, as at the first.
8 And I w cleanse them from all their
8 against me; and I w pardon all their
11 of the LORD. For I w cause to return the
14 the LORD, that I w perform that good
15 In those days, and at that time, w I
22 sea measured: so w I multiply the seed

Jer 33:26 Then **w** I cast away the seed of Jacob,
26 servant, *so* that I **w** not take *any* of his
26 and Jacob: for I **w** cause their captivity
34: 2 LORD; Behold, I **w** give this city into the
5 for thee; and they **w** lament thee, *saying*,
17 to the famine; and I **w** make you to be
18 And I **w** give the men that have
20 I **w** even give them into the hand of their
21 and his princes **w** I give into the hand
22 Behold, I **w** command, saith the LORD,
22 it with fire: and I **w** make the cities of
35: 6 But they said, We **w** drink no wine: for
13 of Jerusalem, **W** ye not receive
17 of Israel; Behold, I **w** bring upon Judah
36: 3 It may be that the house of Judah **w** hear
7 It may be they **w** present their
7 the LORD, and **w** return every one from
16 **w** surely tell the king of all these words.
31 And I **w** punish him and his seed and his
31 iniquity; and I **w** bring upon them, and
38:14 unto Jeremiah, I **w** ask thee a thing; hide
16 us this soul, I **w** not put thee to death,
16 to death, neither **w** I give thee into the
25 from us, and we **w** not put thee to death;
39:16 of Israel; Behold, I **w** bring my words
17 But I **w** deliver thee in that day, saith the
18 For I **w** surely deliver thee, and thou
40: 4 come; and I **w** look well unto thee:
10 As for me, behold, I **w** dwell at Mizpah
10 Chaldeans, which **w** come unto us: but
15 I pray thee, and I **w** slay Ishmael the son
42: 4 *you*; behold, I **w** pray unto the LORD
4 shall answer you, I **w** declare *it* unto you;
4 you; I **w** keep nothing back from you.
6 *it be* evil, we **w** obey the voice of the
10 If ye **w** still abide in this land, then will I
10 If ye will still abide in this land, then **w** I
10 *you* down, and I **w** plant you, and not
12 And I **w** shew mercies unto you, that he
13 But if ye say, We **w** not dwell in this
14 Saying, No; but we **w** go into the land of
14 hunger of bread; and there **w** we dwell:
17 from the evil that I **w** bring upon them.
20 say, so declare unto us, and we **w** do *it*.
43:10 God of Israel; Behold, I **w** send and take
10 my servant, and **w** set his throne upon
12 And I **w** kindle a fire in the houses of the
44:11 of Israel; Behold, I **w** set my face against
12 And I **w** take the remnant of Judah, that
13 For I **w** punish them that dwell in the
16 the LORD, we **w** not hearken unto thee.
17 But we **w** certainly do whatsoever thing
25 hand, saying, We **w** surely perform our
25 unto her: ye **w** surely accomplish your
27 Behold, I **w** watch over them for evil,
29 the LORD, that I **w** punish you in this
30 Thus saith the LORD; Behold, I **w** give
45: 4 which I have built **w** I break down, and
4 I **w** pluck up, even this whole land.
5 not: for, behold, I **w** bring evil upon all
5 LORD: but thy life **w** I give unto thee for
46: 8 and he saith, I **w** go up, *and* will cover
8 I will go up, *and* **w** cover the earth; I will
8 cover the earth; I **w** destroy the city and
25 saith; Behold, I **w** punish the multitude
26 And I **w** deliver them into the hand of
27 for, behold, I **w** save thee from afar
28 I *am* with thee; for I **w** make a full end of
28 driven thee: but I **w** not make a full end
28 **w** I not leave thee wholly unpunished.
47: 4 for the LORD **w** spoil the Philistines,
6 O thou sword of the LORD, how long ***w** it*
48:12 saith the LORD, that I **w** send unto him
31 Therefore **w** I howl for Moab, and I will
31 Therefore will I howl for Moab, and I **w**
32 O vine of Sibmah, I **w** weep for thee with
35 Moreover I **w** cause to cease in Moab,
44 in the snare: for I **w** bring upon it, *even*
47 Yet **w** I bring again the captivity of
49: 2 the LORD, that I **w** cause an alarm of
5 Behold, I **w** bring a fear upon thee, saith
6 And afterward I **w** bring again the
8 of Dedan; for I **w** bring the calamity of
8 upon him, the time *that* I **w** visit him.
9 they **w** destroy till they have enough.
11 Leave thy fatherless children, I **w**
15 For, lo, I **w** make thee small among the
16 as high as the eagle, I **w** bring thee down
19 of the strong: but I **w** suddenly make

Jer 49:19 *is* like me? and who **w** appoint me the
19 *is* that shepherd that **w** stand before me?
27 And I **w** kindle a fire in the wall of
32 cattle a spoil: and I **w** scatter into all
32 corners; and I **w** bring their calamity
35 of hosts; Behold, I **w** break the bow of
36 And upon Elam **w** I bring the four winds
36 of heaven, and **w** scatter them toward
37 For I **w** cause Elam to be dismayed
37 their life: and I **w** bring evil upon them,
37 the LORD; and I **w** send the sword after
38 And I **w** set my throne in Elam, and will
38 And I will set my throne in Elam, and **w**
39 the latter days, *that* I **w** bring again the
50: 9 For, lo, I **w** raise and cause to come up
18 of Israel; Behold, I **w** punish the king of
19 And I **w** bring Israel again to his
20 for I **w** pardon them whom I reserve.
31 day is come, the time *that* I **w** visit thee.
32 raise him up: and I **w** kindle a fire in his
42 they *are* cruel, and **w** not shew mercy:
44 of the strong: but I **w** make them
44 *is* like me? and who **w** appoint me the
44 *is* that shepherd that **w** stand before me?
51: 1 Thus saith the LORD; Behold, I **w** raise
2 And **w** send unto Babylon fanners, that
6 he **w** render unto her a recompence.
14 *saying*, Surely I **w** fill thee with men, as
20 war: for with thee **w** I break in pieces the
20 and with thee **w** I destroy kingdoms;
21 And with thee **w** I break in pieces the
21 and with thee **w** I break in pieces the
22 With thee also **w** I break in pieces man
22 and with thee **w** I break in pieces old
22 and with thee **w** I break in pieces the
23 I **w** also break in pieces with thee the
23 and with thee **w** I break in pieces the
23 **w** I break in pieces captains and rulers.
24 And I **w** render unto Babylon and to all
25 all the earth: and I **w** stretch out mine
25 and **w** make thee a burnt mountain.
36 LORD; Behold, I **w** plead thy cause, and
36 for thee; and I **w** dry up her sea, and
39 In their heat I **w** make their feasts, and I
39 make their feasts, and I **w** make them
40 I **w** bring them down like lambs to the
44 And I **w** punish Bel in Babylon, and I
44 in Babylon, and I **w** bring forth out of his
47 days come, that I **w** do judgment upon
52 the LORD, that I **w** do judgment upon
57 And I **w** make drunk her princes, and
64 from the evil that I **w** bring upon her:
Lam 3:24 saith my soul; therefore **w** I hope in him.
31 For the Lord **w** not cast off for ever:
32 But though he cause grief, yet **w** he have
4:16 hath divided them; he **w** no more regard
22 of Zion; he **w** no more carry thee away
22 into captivity: he **w** visit thine iniquity, O
22 of Edom; he **w** discover thy sins.
Ezk 2: 1 upon thy feet, and I **w** speak unto thee.
5 And they, whether they **w** hear, or
5 or whether they **w** forbear, (for they *are*
7 whether they **w** hear, or whether they
7 **w** forbear: for they *are* most rebellious.
3: 7 But the house of Israel **w** not hearken H14
7 unto thee; for they **w** not hearken unto H14
11 **w** hear, or whether they will forbear.
11 will hear, or whether they **w** forbear.
18 but his blood **w** I require at thine hand.
20 but his blood **w** I require at thine hand.
22 the plain, and I **w** there talk with thee.
26 And I **w** make thy tongue cleave to the
27 But when I speak with thee, I **w** open thy
4: 8 And, behold, I **w** lay bands upon thee,
13 the Gentiles, whither I **w** drive them.
16 of man, behold, I **w** break the staff of
5: 2 and I **w** draw out a sword after them.
8 against thee, and **w** execute judgments
9 And I **w** do in thee that which I have not
9 and whereunto I **w** not do any more the
10 their fathers; and I **w** execute judgments
10 of thee **w** I scatter into all the winds.
11 therefore **w** I also diminish *thee*;
11 eye spare, neither **w** I have any pity.
12 about thee; and I **w** scatter a third part
12 and I **w** draw out a sword after them.
13 and I **w** cause my fury to rest
13 upon them, and I **w** be comforted: and
14 Moreover I **w** make thee waste, and a

Ezk 5:16 *and* which I **w** send to destroy you:
16 destroy you: and I **w** increase the famine
16 you, and **w** break your staff of bread:
17 So **w** I send upon you famine and evil
17 thee; and I **w** bring the sword upon
6: 3 Behold, I, *even* I, **w** bring a sword upon
3 you, and I **w** destroy your high places.
4 be broken: and I **w** cast down your slain
5 And I **w** lay the dead carcases of the
5 their idols; and I **w** scatter your bones
8 Yet **w** I leave a remnant, that ye may
12 thus **w** I accomplish my fury upon them.
14 So **w** I stretch out my hand upon them,
7: 3 Now *is* the end *come* upon thee, and I **w**
3 upon thee, and **w** judge thee according
3 to thy ways, and **w** recompense upon
4 spare thee, neither **w** I have pity: but I
4 I have pity: but I **w** recompense thy ways
8 Now **w** I shortly pour out my fury upon
8 upon thee: and I **w** judge thee according
8 to thy ways, and **w** recompense thee for
9 And mine eye shall not spare, neither **w**
9 will I have pity: I **w** recompense thee
21 And I **w** give it into the hands of the
22 My face **w** I turn also from them, and
24 Wherefore I **w** bring the worst of the
24 their houses: I **w** also make the pomp
27 shall be troubled: I **w** do unto them after
27 to their deserts **w** I judge them; and they
8:18 Therefore **w** I also deal in fury: mine eye
18 not spare, neither **w** I have pity: and
18 with a loud voice, *yet* **w** I not hear them.
9:10 not spare, neither **w** I have pity, *but* I
10 will I have pity, *but* I **w** recompense their
11: 7 I **w** bring you forth out of the midst of it.
8 Ye have feared the sword; and I **w** bring
9 And I **w** bring you out of the midst
9 and **w** execute judgments among you.
10 Ye shall fall by the sword; I **w** judge you
11 *but* I **w** judge you in the border of Israel:
16 the countries, yet **w** I be to them as a
17 the Lord GOD; I **w** even gather you from
17 and I **w** give you the land of Israel.
19 And I **w** give them one heart, and I will
19 And I will give them one heart, and I **w**
19 within you; and I **w** take the stony heart
19 flesh, and **w** give them an heart of flesh:
20 shall be my people, and I **w** be their God.
21 abominations, I **w** recompense their way
12: 3 it may be they **w** consider, though they
13 My net also **w** I spread upon him, and he
13 taken in my snare: and I **w** bring him to
14 And I **w** scatter toward every wind all
14 and I **w** draw out the sword after them.
16 But I **w** leave a few men of them from
23 the Lord GOD; I **w** make this proverb to
25 For I *am* the LORD: I **w** speak, and the
25 O rebellious house, **w** I say the word,
25 and **w** perform it, saith the Lord GOD.
13:13 Therefore thus saith the Lord GOD; I **w**
14 So **w** I break down the wall that ye have
15 Thus **w** I accomplish my wrath upon the
15 *morter*, and **w** say unto you, The wall
18 to hunt souls! **W** ye hunt the souls of
18 of my people, and **w** ye save the souls
19 And **w** ye pollute me among my people
20 *them* fly, and I **w** tear them from your
20 your arms, and **w** let the souls go, *even*
21 Your kerchiefs also **w** I tear, and deliver
23 divinations: for I **w** deliver my people
14: 4 I the LORD **w** answer him that cometh
7 me; I the LORD **w** answer him by myself:
8 And I **w** set my face against that man,
8 that man, and **w** make him a sign and
8 a proverb, and I **w** cut him off from the
9 that prophet, and I **w** stretch out my
9 upon him, and **w** destroy him from the
13 grievously, then **w** I stretch out mine
13 hand upon it, and **w** break the staff of
13 bread thereof, and **w** send famine upon
13 it, and **w** cut off man and beast from it:
15: 3 to do any work? or **w** *men* take a pin of it
6 so **w** I give the inhabitants of Jerusalem.
7 And I **w** set my face against them; they
8 And I **w** make the land desolate, because
16:27 thee unto the **w** of them that hate thee, H5315
37 Behold, therefore I **w** gather all thy
37 thou hast hated; I **w** even gather them
37 about against thee, and **w** discover thy

Ezk 16:38 And I w judge thee, as women that break
38 I w give thee blood in fury and jealousy.
39 And I w also give thee into their hand,
41 women: and I w cause thee to cease
42 So w I make my fury toward thee to rest,
42 I w be quiet, and will be no more angry.
42 I will be quiet, and w be no more angry.
43 therefore I also w recompense thy way
53 her daughters, then *w I bring again* the
59 For thus saith the Lord GOD; I w even
60 Nevertheless I w remember my covenant
60 of thy youth, and I w establish unto thee
61 thy younger: and I w give them unto thee
62 And I w establish my covenant with
17:19 it w I recompense upon his own head.
20 And I w spread my net upon him, and
20 taken in my snare, and I w bring him to
20 to Babylon, and w plead with him there
22 Thus saith the Lord GOD; I w also take
22 high cedar, and w set *it*; I will crop off
22 and will set *it*; I w crop off from the top
22 a tender one, and w plant *it* upon an
23 In the mountain of the height of Israel w
18:21 But if the wicked w turn from all his sins
30 Therefore I w judge you, O house of
31 for why w ye die, O house of Israel?
20: 3 Lord GOD, I w not be inquired of by you.
8 then I said, I w pour out my fury upon
31 Lord GOD, I w not be inquired of by you.
32 all, that ye say, We w be as the heathen,
33 with fury poured out, w I rule over you:
34 And I w bring you out from the people,
34 the people, and w gather you out of the
35 And I w bring you into the wilderness of
35 and there w I plead with you face to face.
36 w I plead with you, saith the Lord GOD.
37 And I w cause you to pass under the rod,
37 the rod, and I w bring you into the bond
38 And I w purge out from among you the
38 against me: I w bring them forth out
39 hereafter *also*, if ye w not hearken unto
40 serve me: there w I accept them, and
40 accept them, and there w I require your
41 I w accept you with your sweet savour,
41 scattered; and I w be sanctified in you
47 GOD; Behold, I w kindle a fire in thee,
21: 3 *am* against thee, and w draw forth my
3 of his sheath, and w cut off from thee the
4 Seeing then that I w cut off from thee the
17 I w also smite mine hands together, and
17 together, and I w cause my fury to rest:
23 oaths: but he w call to remembrance
27 I w overturn, overturn, overturn, it: and
27 whose right it is; and I w give it *him*.
30 into his sheath? I w judge thee in the
31 And I w pour out mine indignation upon
31 upon thee, I w blow against thee in
22:14 I the LORD have spoken *it*, and w do *it*.
15 And I w scatter thee among the heathen,
15 w consume thy filthiness out of thee.
19 behold, therefore I w gather you into the
20 it, to melt *it*; so w I gather *you* in mine
20 and I w leave *you there*, and melt you.
21 Yea, I w gather you, and blow upon you
23:22 GOD; Behold, I w raise up thy lovers
22 w bring them against thee on every side;
24 round about: and I w set judgment
25 And I w set my jealousy against thee,
27 Thus w I make thy lewdness to cease
28 For thus saith the Lord GOD; Behold, I w
30 I w do these *things* unto thee, because
31 w I give her cup into thine hand.
43 old in adulteries, W they now commit
46 For thus saith the Lord GOD; I w bring
46 w give them to be removed and spoiled.
48 Thus w I cause lewdness to cease out of
24: 9 city! I w even make the pile for fire great.
14 to pass, and I w do *it*; I will not go back,
14 and I will do *it*; I w not go back, neither
14 go back, neither w I spare, neither will
14 I spare, neither w I repent; according to
21 GOD; Behold, I w profane my sanctuary,
25: 4 Behold, therefore I w deliver thee to the
5 And I w make Rabbah a stable for
7 Behold, therefore I w stretch out mine
7 upon thee, and w deliver thee for a spoil
7 to the heathen; and I w cut thee off from
7 the people, and I w cause thee to perish
7 of the countries: I w destroy thee; and

Ezk 25: 9 Therefore, behold, I w open the side of
10 the Ammonites, and w give them in
11 And I w execute judgments upon Moab;
13 Therefore thus saith the Lord GOD; I w
13 upon Edom, and w cut off man and
13 from it; and I w make it desolate from
14 And I w lay my vengeance upon Edom
16 GOD; Behold, I w stretch out mine hand
16 the Philistines, and I w cut off the
17 And I w execute great vengeance upon
26: 3 thee, O Tyrus, and w cause many
4 down her towers: I w also scrape her
7 For thus saith the Lord GOD; Behold, I w
13 And I w cause the noise of thy songs to
14 And I w make thee like the top of a rock:
21 I w make thee a terror, and thou *shalt be*
28: 7 Behold, therefore I w bring strangers
16 hast sinned: therefore I w cast thee as
16 of God: and I w destroy thee, O covering
17 of thy brightness: I w cast thee to the
17 to the ground, I w lay thee before kings,
18 traffick; therefore w I bring forth a fire
18 devour thee, and I w bring thee to ashes
22 thee, O Zidon; and I w be glorified in the
23 For I w send into her pestilence, and
29: 4 But I w put hooks in thy jaws, and I will
4 But I will put hooks in thy jaws, and I w
4 thy scales, and I w bring thee up out of
5 And I w leave thee *thrown* into the
8 GOD; Behold, I w bring a sword upon
10 thy rivers, and I w make the land of
12 And I w make the land of Egypt desolate
12 desolate forty years: and I w scatter the
12 w disperse them through the countries.
13 the end of forty years w I gather the
14 And I w bring again the captivity of
14 of Egypt, and w cause them to return
15 the nations: for I w diminish them, that
19 GOD; Behold, I w give the land of Egypt
21 In that day w I cause the horn of the
21 Israel to bud forth, and I w give thee the
30:10 Thus saith the Lord GOD; I w also make
12 And I w make the rivers dry, and sell the
12 of the wicked: and I w make the land
13 Thus saith the Lord GOD; I w also
13 the idols, and I w cause *their* images to
13 and I w put a fear in the land of Egypt.
14 And I w make Pathros desolate, and will
14 And I will make Pathros desolate, and w
14 Zoan, and w execute judgments in No.
15 And I w pour my fury upon Sin, the
15 and I w cut off the multitude of No.
16 And I w set fire in Egypt: Sin shall have
19 Thus w I execute judgments in Egypt:
22 king of Egypt, and w break his arms, the
22 w cause the sword to fall out of his hand.
23 And I w scatter the Egyptians among the
23 w disperse them through the countries.
24 And I w strengthen the arms of the king
24 in his hand: but I w break Pharaoh's
25 But I w strengthen the arms of the king
26 And I w scatter the Egyptians among the
32: 3 Thus saith the Lord GOD; I w therefore
4 Then w I leave thee upon the land, I will
4 Then will I leave thee upon the land, I w
4 the open field, and w cause all the fowls
4 upon thee, and I w fill the beasts of the
5 And I w lay thy flesh upon the
6 I w also water with thy blood the land
7 And when I shall put thee out, I w cover
7 thereof dark; I w cover the sun with a
8 All the bright lights of heaven w I make
9 I w also vex the hearts of many people,
10 Yea, I w make many people amazed at
12 By the swords of the mighty w I cause
13 I w destroy also all the beasts thereof
14 Then w I make their waters deep, and
33: 6 w I require at the watchman's hand.
8 but his blood w I require at thine hand.
11 for why w ye die, O house of Israel?
20 I w judge you every one after his ways.
27 *is* in the open field w I give to the beasts
28 For I w lay the land most desolate, and
31 words, but they w not do them: for with
33 And when this cometh to pass, (lo, it w
34:10 shepherds; and I w require my flock at
10 any more; for I w deliver my flock from
11 Behold, I, *even* I, w both search my
12 *are* scattered; so w I seek out my sheep,

Ezk 34:12 out my sheep, and w deliver them out of
13 And I w bring them out from the people,
13 the countries, and w bring them to their
14 I w feed them in a good pasture, and
15 I w feed my flock, and I will cause them
15 I will feed my flock, and I w cause them
16 I w seek that which was lost, and bring
16 driven away, and w bind up *that which*
16 *was* broken, and w strengthen that
16 was sick: but I w destroy the fat and the
16 the strong; I w feed them with judgment.
20 Behold, I, *even* I, w judge between the fat
22 Therefore w I save my flock, and they
22 and I w judge between cattle and cattle.
23 And I w set up one shepherd over them,
24 And I the LORD w be their God, and my
25 And I w make with them a covenant of
25 of peace, and w cause the evil beasts
26 And I w make them and the places
26 a blessing; and I w cause the shower to
29 And I w raise up for them a plant of
35: 3 against thee, and I w stretch out mine
3 thee, and I w make thee most desolate.
4 I w lay thy cities waste, and thou shalt
6 the Lord GOD, I w prepare thee unto
7 Thus w I make mount Seir most
8 And I w fill his mountains with his slain
9 I w make thee perpetual desolations,
10 be mine, and we w possess it; whereas
11 the Lord GOD, I w even do according to
11 them; and I w make myself known
14 earth rejoiceth, I w make thee desolate.
15 it was desolate, so w I do unto thee: thou
36: 9 For, behold, I *am* for you, and I w turn
10 And I w multiply men upon you, all the
11 And I w multiply upon you man and
11 bring fruit: and I w settle you after your
11 old estates, and w do better *unto you*
12 Yea, I w cause men to walk upon you,
15 Neither w I cause *men* to hear in thee
23 And I w sanctify my great name, which
24 For I w take you from among the
24 and w bring you into your own land.
25 Then w I sprinkle clean water upon you,
25 and from all your idols, w I cleanse you.
26 A new heart also w I give you, and a new
26 and a new spirit w I put within you: and
26 within you: and I w take away the stony
26 flesh, and I w give you an heart of flesh.
27 And I w put my spirit within you, and
28 shall be my people, and I w be your God.
29 I w also save you from all your
29 and I w call for the corn, and
29 for the corn, and w increase it, and lay
30 And I w multiply the fruit of the tree,
33 all your iniquities I w also cause *you* to
36 I the LORD have spoken *it*, and I w do *it*.
37 Thus saith the Lord GOD; I w yet *for* this
37 I w increase them with men like a flock.
37: 5 bones; Behold, I w cause breath to enter
6 And I w lay sinews upon you, and will
6 And I will lay sinews upon you, and w
12 O my people, I w open your graves, and
19 Lord GOD; Behold, I w take the stick of
19 his fellows, and w put them with him,
21 GOD; Behold, I w take the children of
21 they be gone, and w gather them on
22 And I w make them one nation in the
23 but I w save them out of all
23 have sinned, and w cleanse them: so
23 they be my people, and I w be their God.
26 Moreover I w make a covenant of peace
26 with them: and I w place them, and
26 them, and w set my sanctuary in
27 be with them: yea, I w be their God, and
38: 4 And I w turn thee back, and put hooks
4 thy jaws, and I w bring thee forth, and
11 And thou shalt say, I w go up to the land
11 villages; I w go to them that are at
16 latter days, and I w bring thee against
21 And I w call for a sword against him
22 And I w plead against him with
22 with blood; and I w rain upon him, and
23 Thus w I magnify myself, and sanctify
23 myself; and I w be known in the eyes
39: 2 And I w turn thee back, and leave but
2 part of thee, and w cause thee to come
2 north parts, and w bring thee upon the
3 And I w smite thy bow out of thy left

Ezk 39: 3 thy left hand, and w cause thine arrows
4 that *is* with thee: I w give thee unto the
6 And I w send a fire on Magog, and
7 So w I make my holy name known in the
7 Israel; and I w not *let them* pollute
11 pass in that day, *that* I w give unto Gog a
21 And I w set my glory among the
25 the Lord GOD; Now w I bring again the
25 and w be jealous for my holy name;
29 Neither w I hide my face any more from
43: 7 of my feet, where I w dwell in the midst
9 I w dwell in the midst of them for ever.
27 and I w accept you, saith the Lord GOD.
44:14 But I w make them keepers of the charge
Dan 2: 4 and we w shew the interpretation.
5 from me: if ye w not make known unto
7 and we w shew the interpretation of it.
9 But if ye w not make known unto me the
24 w shew unto the king the interpretation.
25 of Judah, that w make known unto the
36 This *is* the dream; and we w tell the
3:17 w deliver *us* out of thine hand, O king.
18 O king, that we w not serve thy gods, nor H383
4:17 it to whomsoever he w, and setteth up H6634
25 men, and giveth it to whomsoever he w. H6634
32 men, and giveth it to whomsoever he w. H6634
35 doeth according to his w in the army of H6634
5:12 called, and he w shew the interpretation.
17 to another; yet I w read the writing unto
21 he appointeth over it whomsoever he w. H6634
6:16 servest continually, he w deliver thee.
8: 4 according to his w, and became great. H7522
19 And he said, Behold, I w make thee
10:20 thee? and now w I return to fight with
21 But I w shew thee that which is noted in
11: 2 And now w I shew thee the truth.
3 dominion, and do according to his w. H7522
16 to his own w, and none shall stand H7522
36 do according to his w; and he shall exalt H7522
Hos 1: 4 a little *while*, and I w avenge the blood of
4 house of Jehu, and w cause to cease the
5 at that day, that I w break the bow of
6 Lo-ruhamah: for I w no more have
6 of Israel; but I w utterly take them away.
7 But I w have mercy upon the house of
7 of Judah, and w save them by the LORD
7 their God, and w not save them by bow,
9 not my people, and I w not be your *God*.
2: 4 And I w not have mercy upon her
5 for she said, I w go after my lovers, that
6 Therefore, behold, I w hedge up thy way
7 shall she say, I w go and return to my
9 Therefore w I return, and take away my
9 thereof, and w recover my wool and
10 And now w I discover her lewdness in
11 I w also cause all her mirth to cease, her
12 And I w destroy her vines and her fig
12 given me: and I w make them a forest,
13 And I w visit upon her the days of
14 Therefore, behold, I w allure her, and
15 And I w give her her vineyards from
17 For I w take away the names of Baalim
18 And in that day w I make a covenant for
18 the ground: and I w break the bow and
18 and w make them to lie down safely.
19 And I w betroth thee unto me for ever;
19 me for ever; yea, I w betroth thee unto
20 I w even betroth thee unto me in
21 And it shall come to pass in that day, I w
21 saith the LORD, I w hear the heavens,
23 And I w sow her unto me in the earth;
23 in the earth; and I w have mercy upon
23 mercy; and I w say to *them which were*
3: 3 for *another* man: so w I also *be* for thee.
4: 5 in the night, and I w destroy thy mother.
6 knowledge, I w also reject thee, that
6 of thy God, I w also forget thy children.
7 w I change their glory into shame.
9 like priest: and I w punish them for their
14 I w not punish your daughters when
16 w feed them as a lamb in a large place.
5: 4 They w not frame their doings to turn
10 bound: *therefore* I w pour out my wrath
12 Therefore *w* I *be* unto Ephraim as a
14 For I *w be* unto Ephraim as a lion, and
14 of Judah: I, *even* I, w tear and go away; I
14 w take away, and none shall rescue *him*.
15 I w go *and* return to my place, till they
15 in their affliction they w seek me early.
Hos 6: 1 he hath torn, and he w heal us; he hath
1 he hath smitten, and he w bind us up.
2 After two days w he revive us: in the
2 in the third day he w raise us up, and we
7:12 When they shall go, I w spread my net
12 net upon them; I w bring them down as
12 of the heaven; I w chastise them, as their
8: 5 long *w it be* ere they attain to innocency?
10 the nations, now w I gather them, and
13 them not; now w he remember their
14 fenced cities: but I w send a fire upon his
9: 5 What w ye do in the solemn day, and in
9 *therefore* he w remember their iniquity,
9 their iniquity, he w visit their sins.
12 their children, yet w I bereave them, *that*
15 of their doings I w drive them out of
15 of mine house, I w love them no more:
16 bring forth, yet w I slay *even* the beloved
17 My God w cast them away, because they
10:11 her fair neck: I w make Ephraim to ride;
11: 9 I w not execute the fierceness of mine
9 of mine anger, I w not return to destroy
9 of thee: and I w not enter into the city.
11 of Assyria: and I w place them in their
12: 2 with Judah, and w punish Jacob
2 to his doings w he recompense him.
9 the land of Egypt w yet make thee to
13: 7 Therefore I w be unto them as a lion: as
7 a leopard by the way w I observe *them*:
8 I w meet them as a bear *that is* bereaved
8 *of her whelps*, and w rend the caul of
8 heart, and there w I devour them like a
10 I w be thy king: where *is any other* that
14 I w ransom them from the power of the
14 of the grave; I w redeem them from
14 death: O death, I w be thy plagues; O
14 plagues; O grave, I w be thy destruction:
14: 2 so w we render the calves of our lips.
3 Asshur shall not save us; we w not ride
3 horses: neither w we say any more to
4 I w heal their backsliding, I will love
4 I will heal their backsliding, I w love
5 I w be as the dew unto Israel: he shall
Joel 1:19 O LORD, to thee w I cry: for the fire hath
2:14 Who knoweth *if* he w return and repent,
18 Then w the LORD be jealous for his
19 Yea, the LORD w answer and say unto
19 people, Behold, I w send you corn, and
19 therewith: and I w no more make you a
20 But I w remove far off from you the
20 *army*, and w drive him into a land
21 rejoice: for the LORD w do great things.
23 and he w cause to come down
25 And I w restore to you the years that the
28 afterward, *that* I w pour out my spirit
29 in those days w I pour out my spirit.
30 And I w shew wonders in the heavens
3: 2 I w also gather all nations, and will
2 I will also gather all nations, and w
2 of Jehoshaphat, and w plead with them
4 coasts of Palestine? w ye render me a
4 swiftly *and* speedily w I return your
7 Behold, I w raise them out of the place
7 have sold them, and w return your
8 And I w sell your sons and your
12 for there w I sit to judge all the heathen
16 but the LORD *w be* the hope of his
21 For I w cleanse their blood *that* I have
Am 1: 2 And he said, The LORD w roar from
3 and for four, I w not turn away *the*
4 But I w send a fire into the house of
5 I w break also the bar of Damascus, and
6 Gaza, and for four, I w not turn away *the*
7 But I w send a fire on the wall of Gaza,
8 And I w cut off the inhabitant from
8 from Ashkelon, and I w turn mine hand
9 and for four, I w not turn away *the*
10 But I w send a fire on the wall of Tyrus,
11 and for four, I w not turn away *the*
12 But I w send a fire upon Teman, which
13 and for four, I w not turn away *the*
14 But I w kindle a fire in the wall of
2: 1 and for four, I w not turn away *the*
2 But I w send a fire upon Moab, and it
3 And I w cut off the judge from the midst
3 midst thereof, and w slay all the princes
4 and for four, I w not turn away *the*
5 But I w send a fire upon Judah, and it
6 and for four, I w not turn away *the*
Am 2: 7 and his father w go in unto the *same*
3: 2 I w punish you for all your iniquities.
4 W a lion roar in the forest, when he hath
4 he hath no prey? w a young lion cry out
7 Surely the Lord GOD w do nothing, but
8 The lion hath roared, who w not fear?
14 Israel upon him I w also visit the altars
15 And I w smite the winter house with the
4: 2 upon you, that he w take you away with
12 Therefore thus w I do unto thee, O
12 Israel: *and* because I w do this unto thee,
5:15 God of hosts w be gracious unto the
17 I w pass through thee, saith the LORD.
21 I hate, I despise your feast days, and I w
22 meat offerings, I w not accept *them*:
22 *them*: neither w I regard the peace
23 for I w not hear the melody of thy viols.
27 Therefore w I cause you to go into
6: 8 palaces: therefore w I deliver up the city
11 and he w smite the great house
12 Shall horses run upon the rock? w *one*
14 But, behold, I w raise up against you a
7: 8 the Lord, Behold, I w set a plumbline in
8 I w not again pass by them any more:
9 be laid waste; and I w rise against the
8: 2 I w not again pass by them any more.
5 Saying, When w the new moon be gone,
7 I w never forget any of their works.
9 Lord GOD, that I w cause the sun to go
9 I w darken the earth in the clear day:
10 And I w turn your feasts into mourning,
10 lamentation; and I w bring up sackcloth
10 upon every head; and I w make it as the
11 Lord GOD, that I w send a famine in the
9: 1 all of them; and I w slay the last of them
2 to heaven, thence w I bring them down:
3 top of Carmel, I w search and take them
3 of the sea, thence w I command the
4 their enemies, thence w I command the
4 slay them: and I w set mine eyes upon
8 kingdom, and I w destroy it from off the
8 earth; saving that I w not utterly destroy
9 For, lo, I w command, and I will sift the
9 For, lo, I will command, and I w sift the
11 In that day w I raise up the tabernacle of
11 thereof; and I w raise up his ruins, and
11 and I w build it as in the days of old:
14 And I w bring again the captivity of my
15 And I w plant them upon their land, and
Oba 4 w I bring thee down, saith the LORD.
Jna 1: 6 God w think upon us, that we perish not.
2: 4 I w look again toward thy holy temple.
9 But I w sacrifice unto thee with the voice
9 of thanksgiving; I w pay *that* that I have
3: 9 Who can tell *if* God w turn and repent,
Mic 1: 3 out of his place, and w come down, and
6 Therefore I w make Samaria as an heap
6 of a vineyard: and I w pour down the
6 I w discover the foundations thereof.
7 the idols thereof w I lay desolate: for she
8 Therefore I w wail and howl, I will go
8 Therefore I will wail and howl, I w go
8 and naked: I w make a wailing like
15 Yet w I bring an heir unto thee, O
2:11 do lie, *saying*, I w prophesy unto thee
12 I w surely assemble, O Jacob, all of thee;
12 O Jacob, all of thee; I w surely gather the
12 of Israel; I w put them together as
3: 4 the LORD, but he w not hear them: he
4 not hear them: he w even hide his face
11 for money: yet w they lean upon the
4: 2 of Jacob; and he w teach us of his ways,
2 his ways, and we w walk in his paths: for
5 For all people w walk every one in the
5 of his god, and we w walk in the name of
6 In that day, saith the LORD, w I
6 that halteth, and I w gather her that is
7 And I w make her that halted a
13 of Zion: for I w make thine horn iron,
13 horn iron, and I w make thy hoofs brass:
13 people: and I w consecrate their gain
5: 3 Therefore w he give them up, until the
10 the LORD, that I w cut off thy horses out
10 of thee, and I w destroy thy chariots:
11 And I w cut off the cities of thy land, and
12 And I w cut off witchcrafts out of thine
13 Thy graven images also w I cut off, and
14 And I w pluck up thy groves out of the
14 midst of thee: so w I destroy thy cities.

Mic 5:15 And I w execute vengeance in anger and
6: 2 his people, and he w plead with Israel.
7 W the LORD be pleased with thousands
13 Therefore also w I make *thee* sick in
14 thou deliverest w I give up to the sword.
7: 7 Therefore I w look unto the LORD; I will
7 Therefore I will look unto the LORD; I w
7 God of my salvation: my God w hear me.
9 I w bear the indignation of the LORD,
9 for me: he w bring me forth to the
15 w I shew unto him marvellous *things*.
19 He w turn again, he will have
19 He will turn again, he w have
19 upon us; he w subdue our iniquities;
Nah 1: 2 furious; the LORD w take vengeance on
3 in power, and w not at all acquit *the*
8 But with an overrunning flood he w
9 the LORD? he w make an utter end:
12 afflicted thee, I w afflict thee no more.
13 For now w I break his yoke from off
13 thee, and w burst thy bonds in sunder.
14 house of thy gods w I cut off the graven
14 I w make thy grave; for thou art vile.
2:13 of hosts, and I w burn her chariots in
13 thy young lions: and I w cut off thy prey
3: 5 of hosts; and I w discover thy skirts
5 thy face, and I w shew the nations thy
6 And I w cast abominable filth upon thee,
6 vile, and w set thee as a gazing-stock.
7 is laid waste: who w bemoan her?
Hab 1: 5 marvellously: for *I* w work a work in
5 ye w not believe, though it be told *you*.
2: 1 I w stand upon my watch, and set me
1 the tower, and w watch to see what he
1 to see what he w say unto me, and what
3 it w surely come, it will not tarry.
3 it will surely come, it w not tarry.
3:16 he w invade them with his troops.
18 Yet I w rejoice in the LORD, I will joy in
18 Yet I will rejoice in the LORD, I w joy in
19 The LORD God *is* my strength, and he w
19 hinds' *feet*, and he w make me to walk
Zep 1: 2 I w utterly consume all *things* from off
3 I w consume man and beast; I will
3 I will consume man and beast; I w
3 the wicked; and I w cut off man from off
4 I w also stretch out mine hand upon
4 of Jerusalem; and I w cut off the
8 sacrifice, that I w punish the princes,
9 In the same day also w I punish all those
12 at that time, *that* I w search Jerusalem
12 w not do good, neither will he do evil.
12 will not do good, neither w he do evil.
17 And I w bring distress upon men, that
2: 5 of the Philistines, I w even destroy thee.
11 The LORD *w be* terrible unto them: for
11 unto them: for he w famish all the gods
13 And he w stretch out his hand against
13 destroy Assyria; and w make Nineveh a
3: 5 the midst thereof; he w not do iniquity:
9 For then w I turn to the people a pure
11 me: for then I w take away out of the
12 I w also leave in the midst of thee an
17 thee *is* mighty; he w save, he will rejoice
17 he will save, he w rejoice over thee with
17 thee with joy; he w rest in his love, he
17 his love, he w joy over thee with singing.
18 I w gather *them that are* sorrowful for
19 Behold, at that time I w undo all that
19 afflict thee: and I w save her that halteth,
19 driven out; and I w get them praise and
20 At that time I w bring you *again*, even in
20 I gather you: for I w make you a name
Hag 1: 8 the house; and I w take pleasure in it,
8 it, and I w be glorified, saith the LORD.
2: 6 a little while, and I w shake the heavens,
7 And I w shake all nations, and the desire
7 shall come: and I w fill this house with
9 w I give peace, saith the LORD of hosts.
19 forth: from this day w I bless *you*.
21 I w shake the heavens and the earth;
22 And I w overthrow the throne of
22 throne of kingdoms, and I w destroy the
22 of the heathen; and I w overthrow the
23 In that day, saith the LORD of hosts, w I
23 the LORD, and w make thee as a signet:
Zec 1: 3 of hosts, and I w turn unto you, saith
9 unto me, I w shew thee what these *be*.
2: 5 For I, saith the LORD, w be unto her a

Zec 2: 5 and w be the glory in the midst of her.
9 For, behold, I w shake mine hand upon
10 lo, I come, and I w dwell in the midst of
11 my people: and I w dwell in the midst of
3: 4 I w clothe thee with change of raiment.
7 my courts, and I w give thee places to
8 I w bring forth my servant the BRANCH.
9 eyes: behold, I w engrave the graving
9 of hosts, and I w remove the iniquity
5: 4 I w bring it forth, saith the LORD of
6:15 come to pass, if ye w diligently obey the
8: 3 unto Zion, and w dwell in the midst of
7 of hosts; Behold, I w save my people
8 And I w bring them, and they shall dwell
8 my people, and I w be their God, in truth
11 But now I *w* not *be* unto the residue of
12 their dew; and I w cause the remnant of
13 house of Israel; so w I save you, and ye
21 to seek the LORD of hosts: I w go also.
23 a Jew, saying, We w go with you: for we
9: 4 Behold, the Lord w cast her out, and he
4 her out, and he w smite her power in the
6 I w cut off the pride of the Philistines.
7 And I w take away his blood out of his
8 And I w encamp about mine house
10 And I w cut off the chariot from
12 declare *that* I w render double unto thee;
10: 6 And I w strengthen the house of Judah,
6 of Judah, and I w save the house of
6 of Joseph, and I w bring them again to
6 the LORD their God, and w hear them.
8 I w hiss for them, and gather them; for I
9 And I w sow them among the people:
10 I w bring them again also out of the land
10 of Assyria; and I w bring them into the
12 And I w strengthen them in the LORD;
11: 6 For I w no more pity the inhabitants of
6 LORD: but, lo, I w deliver the men every
6 out of their hand I w not deliver *them*.
7 And I w feed the flock of slaughter, *even*
9 Then said I, I w not feed you: that that
16 For, lo, I w raise up a shepherd in the
12: 2 Behold, I w make Jerusalem a cup of
3 And in that day w I make Jerusalem a
4 In that day, saith the LORD, I w smite
4 madness: and I w open mine eyes upon
4 of Judah, and w smite every horse of
6 In that day w I make the governors of
9 in that day, *that* I w seek to destroy all
10 And I w pour upon the house of David,
13: 2 of hosts, *that* I w cut off the names of
2 and also I w cause the prophets and
7 I w turn mine hand upon the little ones.
9 And I w bring the third part through the
9 the fire, and w refine them as silver
9 is refined, and w try them as gold is
9 on my name, and I w hear them: I will
9 I will hear them: I w say, It *is* my people:
14: 2 For I w gather all nations against
12 the LORD w smite all the people
17 And it shall be, *that* whoso w not come
18 the LORD w smite the heathen that
Mal 1: 4 but we w return and build the
4 shall build, but I w throw down; and
5 say, The LORD w be magnified from the
8 unto thy governor; w he be pleased with
9 God that he w be gracious unto us:
9 been by your means: w he regard your
10 w I accept an offering at your hand.
2: 2 If ye w not hear, and if ye will not lay *it*
2 If ye will not hear, and if ye w not lay *it*
2 the LORD of hosts, I w even send a curse
2 upon you, and I w curse your blessings:
3 Behold, I w corrupt your seed, and
12 The LORD w cut off the man that doeth
13 receiveth *it* with good w at your hand. H7522
3: 1 Behold, I w send my messenger, and he
5 And I w come near to you to judgment;
5 to judgment; and I w be a swift witness
7 unto me, and I w return unto you, saith
8 W a man rob God? Yet ye have robbed
10 LORD of hosts, if I w not open you the
11 And I w rebuke the devourer for your
17 my jewels; and I w spare them, as a man
4: 5 Behold, I w send you Elijah the prophet
Mt 2:13 w seek the young child to destroy him. G3195
3:12 Whose fan *is* in his hand, and he w
12 the garner; but he w burn up the chaff
4: 9 And saith unto him, All these things w I

Mt 4:19 me, and I w make you fishers of men.
5:40 And if any man w sue thee at the law, G2309
6:10 Thy kingdom come. Thy w be done in G2307
14 your heavenly Father w also forgive you:
15 w your Father forgive your trespasses.
21 For where your treasure is, there w G2071
24 for either he w hate the one, and love
24 other; or else he w hold to the one, and
7: 9 son ask bread, w he give him a stone?
10 Or if he ask a fish, w he give him a
21 the w of my Father which is in heaven. G2307
22 Many w say to me in that day, Lord,
23 And then w I profess unto them, I never
24 and doeth them, I w liken him unto a
8: 3 him, saying, I w; be thou clean. And G2309
7 And Jesus saith unto him, I w come and
19 I w follow thee whithersoever thou goest.
9:13 *that* meaneth, I w have mercy, and not G2309
15 them? but the days w come, when the
38 w send forth labourers into his harvest.
10:17 But beware of men: for they w deliver
17 they w scourge you in their synagogues;
32 before men, him w I confess also before
33 before men, him w I also deny before my
11:14 And if ye w receive *it*, this is Elias, G2309
27 to whomsoever the Son w reveal *him*. G1014
28 are heavy laden, and I w give you rest.
12: 7 *this* meaneth, I w have mercy, and not
11 w he not lay hold on it, and lift *it* out?
18 is well pleased: I w put my spirit upon
29 man? and then he w spoil his house.
44 Then he saith, I w return into my house
50 For whosoever shall do the w of my G2307
13:30 time of harvest I w say to the reapers,
35 prophet, saying, I w open my mouth in
35 in parables; I w utter things which have
15:32 to eat: and I w not send them away G2309
16: 2 *It w be* fair weather: for the sky is red.
3 And in the morning, *It w be* foul weather
18 upon this rock I w build my church; and
19 And I w give unto thee the keys of the
24 If any *man* w come after me, let him G2309
25 For whosoever w save his life shall lose G2309
25 w lose his life for my sake shall find it.
18:14 Even so it is not the w of your Father G2307
16 But if he w not hear *thee, then* take with G191
26 patience with me, and I w pay thee all.
29 patience with me, and I w pay thee all.
20: 4 I w give you. And they went their way.
14 Take *that* thine *is*, and go thy way: I w G2309
15 Is it not lawful for me to do what I w G2309
26 but whosoever w be great among you, G2309
27 And whosoever w be chief among you, G2309
32 said, What w ye that I shall do unto you?
21: 3 them; and straightway he w send them.
24 unto them, I also w ask you one thing,
24 tell me, I in like wise w tell you by what
25 From heaven; he w say unto us, Why did
29 He answered and said, I w not: but G2309
31 Whether of them twain did the w of *his* G2307
37 son, saying, They w reverence my son.
40 what w he do unto those husbandmen?
41 They say unto him, He w miserably
41 wicked men, and w let out *his* vineyard
44 it shall fall, it w grind him to powder.
23: 4 they *themselves* w not move them with G2309
24:28 For wheresoever the carcase is, there w G4863
25:21 over a few things, I w make thee ruler
23 over a few things, I w make thee ruler
26:15 And said *unto them*, What w ye give me,
15 will ye give me, and I w deliver him unto
18 time is at hand; I w keep the passover at
29 But I say unto you, I w not drink G4095
31 for it is written, I w smite the shepherd,
32 But after I am risen again, I w go before
33 of thee, *yet* w I never be offended.
35 die with thee, yet w I not deny thee.
39 nevertheless not as I w, but as thou *wilt*. G2309
42 me, except I drink it, thy w be done. G2307
27:17 unto them, Whom w ye that I release
21 of the twain w ye that I release unto
42 from the cross, and we w believe him.
43 him now, if he w have him: for he said,
49 see whether Elias w come to save him.
63 yet alive, After three days I w rise again.
28:14 we w persuade him, and secure you.
Mk 1:17 I w make you to become fishers of men.
41 and saith unto him, I w; be thou clean. G2309
2:20 But the days w come, when the

Mk 2:22 and the bottles w be marred: but new
3:27 goods, except he w first bind the strong G1210
27 man; and then he w spoil his house.
35 For whosoever shall do the w of God, G2307
4:13 and how then w ye know all parables?
6:22 thou wilt, and I w give *it* thee.
23 shalt ask of me, I w give *it* thee, unto the
25 asked, saying, I w that thou give me by G2309
8: 3 own houses, they w faint by the way: for
34 them, Whosoever w come after me, let G2309
35 For whosoever w save his life shall lose G2309
9:50 wherewith w ye season it? Have salt
10:43 but whosoever w be great among you, G2309
44 And whosoever of you w be the G2309
11: 3 and straightway he w send him hither.
26 But if ye do not forgive, neither w your G863
29 said unto them, I w also ask of you one G1905
29 and answer me, and I w tell you by what
31 w say, Why then did ye not believe him?
12: 6 them, saying, They w reverence my son.
9 vineyard do? he w come and destroy the
9 and w give the vineyard unto others.
14: 7 whensoever ye w ye may do them good: G2309
15 And he w shew you a large upper room
25 Verily I say unto you, I w drink no more
27 for it is written, I w smite the shepherd,
28 But after that I am risen, I w go before
29 all shall be offended, yet *w* not I.
31 die with thee, I w not deny thee in any G533
36 not what I w, but what thou wilt. G2309
58 We heard him say, I w destroy this
58 I w build another made without hands.
15: 9 But Pilate answered them, saying, W ye
12 unto them, What w ye then that I shall
36 whether Elias w come to take him down.
Lk 2:14 on earth peace, good w toward men. G2107
3:17 Whose fan *is* in his hand, and he w
17 his floor, and w gather the wheat into
17 chaff he w burn with fire unquenchable.
4: 6 him, All this power w I give thee, and the
6 me; and to whomsoever I w I give it. G2309
23 And he said unto them, Ye w surely say G2046
5: 5 at thy word I w let down the net.
13 him, saying, I w: be thou clean. And G2309
35 But the days w come, when the
37 else the new wine w burst the bottles,
6: 9 Then said Jesus unto them, I w ask you
47 them, I w shew you to whom he is like:
7:42 which of them w love him most?
9: 5 And whosoever w not receive you, G1209
23 And he said to *them* all, If any *man* w G2309
24 For whosoever w save his life shall lose G2309
24 it: but whosoever w lose his life for my
57 I w follow thee whithersoever thou goest.
61 And another also said, Lord, I w follow
10:22 and *he* to whom the Son w reveal *him*. G1014
35 when I come again, I w repay thee.
11: 2 w be done, as in heaven, so in earth. G2307
8 I say unto you, Though he w not rise and
8 his importunity he w rise and give him
11 that is a father, w he give him a stone?
11 a fish, w he for a fish give him a serpent?
12 Or if he shall ask an egg, w he offer him
24 none, he saith, I w return unto my house
49 wisdom of God, I w send them prophets
12: 5 But I w forewarn you whom ye shall
18 And he said, This w I do: I will pull down
18 And he said, This will I do: I w pull down
18 w I bestow all my fruits and my goods.
19 And I w say to my soul, Soul, thou hast
28 more *w he clothe* you, O ye of little faith?
34 For where your treasure is, there w G2071
36 for their lord, when he w return from the
37 meat, and w come forth and serve them.
44 Of a truth I say unto you, that he w make
46 The lord of that servant w come in a day
46 is not aware, and w cut him in sunder,
46 him in sunder, and w appoint him his
47 knew his lord's w, and prepared not G2307
47 w, shall be beaten with many *stripes*. G2307
48 much, of him they w ask the more.
49 and what w I, if it be already kindled?
55 There w be heat; and it cometh to pass.
13:24 w seek to enter in, and shall not be able.
31 depart hence: for Herod w kill thee. G2309
14: 5 into a pit, and w not straightway pull G385
15:18 I w arise and go to my father, and will
18 I will arise and go to my father, and w
16:11 w commit to your trust the true *riches*?

Lk 16:13 for either he w hate the one, and love
13 other; or else he w hold to the one, and
30 unto them from the dead, they w repent.
31 prophets, neither w they be persuaded,
17: 1 but that offences w come: but woe *unto*
7 or feeding cattle, w say unto him by and
8 And w not rather say unto him, Make
22 the disciples, The days w come, when ye
37 w the eagles be gathered together. G4863
18: 5 troubleth me, I w avenge her, lest by her
8 I tell you that he w avenge them G4160
19:14 w not have this *man* to reign over us. G2309
22 of thine own mouth w I judge thee, *thou*
20: 3 said unto them, I w also ask you one G2065
5 he w say, Why then believed ye him not?
6 men; all the people w stone us: for they
13 What shall I do? I w send my beloved
13 w reverence *him* when they see him.
18 it shall fall, it w grind him to powder.
21: 6 ye behold, the days w come, in the which
7 be? and what sign *w there be* when these
15 For I w give you a mouth and wisdom,
22:16 For I say unto you, I w not any more G5315
18 For I say unto you, I w not drink of the G4095
42 not my w, but thine, be done. G2307
67 them, If I tell you, ye w not believe: G4100
68 And if I also ask *you*, ye w not answer G611
23:16 I w therefore chastise him, and release G630
22 w therefore chastise him, and let *him* go. G630
25 but he delivered Jesus to their w. G2307
Jn 1:13 blood, nor of the w of the flesh, nor of G2307
13 flesh, nor of the w of man, but of God. G2307
2:19 temple, and in three days I w raise it up.
4:25 when he is come, he w tell us all things.
34 meat is to do the w of him that sent me, G2307
48 signs and wonders, ye w not believe. G4100
5:20 doeth: and he w shew him greater works
21 even so the Son quickeneth whom he w. G2309
30 seek not mine own w, but the will of the G2307
30 the w of the Father which hath sent me. G2307
40 And ye w not come to me, that ye G2309
43 come in his own name, him ye w receive.
45 Do not think that I w accuse you to the
6:37 cometh to me I w in no wise cast out. G1544
38 own w, but the will of him that sent me. G2307
38 own will, but the w of him that sent me. G2307
39 And this is the Father's w which hath G2307
40 And this is the w of him that sent me, G2307
40 life: and I w raise him up at the last day.
44 and I w raise him up at the last day.
51 the bread that I w give is my flesh, which
51 which I w give for the life of the world.
54 life; and I w raise him up at the last day.
67 Then said Jesus unto the twelve, W ye G2309
7:17 If any man w do his will, he shall know G2309
17 If any man will do his w, he shall know G2307
31 Christ cometh, w he do more miracles
35 Whither w he go, that we shall G3195
35 shall not find him? w he go unto the G3195
8:22 Then said the Jews, W he kill himself?
44 lusts of your father ye w do. He was a G2309
9:27 *it* again? w ye also be his disciples? G2309
31 God, and doeth his w, him he heareth. G2307
10: 5 And a stranger w they not follow, but
5 not follow, but w flee from him: for they
11:22 thou wilt ask of God, God w give *it* thee.
48 If we let him thus alone, all *men* w
56 ye, that he w not come to the feast? G2064
12:26 serve me, him w *my* Father honour. G5091
28 both glorified *it*, and w glorify *it* again.
32 And I, if I be lifted up from the earth, w
13:37 now? I w lay down my life for thy sake.
14: 3 a place for you, I w come again, and
13 in my name, that w I do, that the Father
14 If ye shall ask any thing in my name, I w
16 And I w pray the Father, and he shall
18 I w not leave you comfortless: I will G863
18 I will not leave you comfortless: I w
21 of my Father, and I w love him, and will
21 love him, and w manifest myself to him.
23 If a man love me, he w keep my words:
23 and my Father w love him, and we will
23 love him, and we w come unto him, and
26 whom the Father w send in my name, he
30 Hereafter I w not talk much with you: G2980
15: 7 ye w, and it shall be done unto you. G2309
20 me, they w also persecute you; G1377
20 kept my saying, they w keep yours also.
21 But all these things w they do unto you

Jn 15:26 is come, whom I w send unto you from
16: 2 you w think that he doeth God service.
3 And these things w they do unto you,
7 the Comforter w not come unto you; G2064
7 but if I depart, I w send him unto you.
8 And when he is come, he w reprove the
13 of truth, is come, he w guide you into all
13 and he w shew you things to come.
22 have sorrow: but I w see you again, and
23 the Father in my name, he w give *it* you.
26 you, that I w pray the Father for you:
17:24 Father, I w that they also, whom thou G2309
26 thy name, and w declare *it*: that the love
18:39 one at the passover: w ye therefore that I
20:15 hast laid him, and I w take him away.
25 my hand into his side, I w not believe. G4100
21:22 Jesus saith unto him, If I w that he G2309
23 not die; but, If I w that he tarry till I G2309
Act 2:17 last days, saith God, I w pour out of my
18 my handmaidens I w pour out in those
19 And I w shew wonders in heaven above,
3:23 *that* every soul, which w not hear that G191
5:38 work be of men, it w come to nought:
6: 4 But we w give ourselves continually to
7: 7 be in bondage w I judge, said God: and G2919
34 And now come, I w send thee into Egypt.
43 and I w carry you away beyond Babylon.
49 what house w ye build me? saith the
9:16 For I w shew him how great things he
13:22 own heart, which shall fulfil all my w. G2307
34 I w give you the sure mercies of David.
36 own generation by the w of God, fell on G1012
15:16 After this I w return, and will build
16 After this I will return, and w build
16 is fallen down; and I w build again the
16 again the ruins thereof, and I w set it up:
17:18 some said, What w this babbler say? G2309
31 in the which he w judge the world in G3195
32 We w hear thee again of this *matter*.
18: 6 henceforth I w go unto the Gentiles.
15 *it*; for I w be no judge of such *matters*. G1014
21 in Jerusalem: but I w return again unto
21 if God w. And he sailed from Ephesus. G2309
21:14 saying, The w of the Lord be done. G2307
22 for they w hear that thou art come.
22:14 know his w, and see that Just One, G2307
18 for they w not receive thy testimony G3858
21 And he said unto me, Depart: for I w
23:14 w eat nothing until we have slain Paul.
21 with an oath, that they w neither eat nor
35 I w hear thee, said he, when thine
24:22 I w know the uttermost of your matter.
25 a convenient season, I w call for thee.
26:16 things in the which I w appear unto thee;
27:10 that this voyage w be with hurt and G3195
28:28 the Gentiles, and *that* they w hear it.
Ro 1:10 by the w of God to come unto you. G2307
2: 6 Who w render to every man according
18 And knowest *his* w, and approvest the G2307
4: 8 Blessed *is* the man to whom the Lord w G3049
5: 7 For scarcely for a righteous man w one G599
7:18 good thing: for to w is present with me; G2309
8:27 for the saints according to *the w of* God.
9: 9 w I come, and Sarah shall have a son.
15 For he saith to Moses, I w have mercy on
15 mercy on whom I w have mercy, and I
15 have mercy, and I w have compassion
15 on whom I w have compassion.
18 on whom he w *have mercy*, and whom G2309
18 *mercy*, and whom he w he hardeneth. G2309
19 find fault? For who hath resisted his w? G1013
25 As he saith also in Osee, I w call them
28 For he w finish the work, and cut *it* short
28 work w the Lord make upon the earth. G4160
10:19 First Moses saith, I w provoke you to
19 *and* by a foolish nation I w anger you.
12: 2 and acceptable, and perfect, w of God. G2307
19 *is* mine; I w repay, saith the Lord.
15: 9 For this cause I w confess to thee among
18 For I w not dare to speak of any of G5111
24 into Spain, I w come to you: for I trust
28 this fruit, I w come by you into Spain.
32 with joy by the w of God, and may with G2307
1Co 1: 1 w of God, and Sosthenes *our* brother, G2307
19 For it is written, I w destroy the wisdom
19 of the wise, and w bring to nothing the
4: 5 Lord come, who both w bring to light the
5 of darkness, and w make manifest the
19 But I w come to you shortly, if the Lord

1Co 4:19 if the Lord w, and will know, not G2309
19 if the Lord will, and w know, not the
21 What w ye? shall I come unto you with a
6:12 for me, but I w not be brought under G1850
14 w also raise up us by his own power. G1825
7:36 he w, he sinneth not: let them marry. G2309
37 over his own w, and hath so decreed G2307
37 that he w keep his virgin, doeth well.
39 to whom she w; only in the Lord. G2309
8:13 brother to offend, I w eat no flesh while
9:17 but if against my w, a dispensation *of the* G210
10:13 *is* faithful, who w not suffer you to be G1439
13 ye are able; but w with the temptation G4160
11:34 the rest w I set in order when I come.
12:11 dividing to every man severally as he w. G1014
14:15 What is it then? I w pray with the spirit,
15 with the spirit, and I w pray with the
15 also: I w sing with the spirit,
15 I w sing with the understanding also.
21 and other lips w I speak unto this
21 that w they not hear me, saith the Lord.
23 w they not say that ye are mad?
25 down on *his* face he w worship God, and
35 And if they w learn any thing, let them G2309
15:35 But some *man* w say, How are the dead
16: 3 *your* letters, them w I send to bring your
5 Now I w come unto you, when I shall
6 And it may be that I w abide, yea, and
7 For I w not see you now by the way; but G2309
8 But I w tarry at Ephesus until Pentecost.
12 the brethren: but his w was not at all to G2307
12 at this time; but he w come when he
2Co 1: 1 Christ by the w of God, and Timothy G2307
10 whom we trust that he w yet deliver *us*; G4506
6:16 as God hath said, I w dwell in them, and
16 in *them*; and I w be their God, and they
17 the unclean *thing*; and I w receive you,
18 And w be a Father unto you, and ye shall
8: 5 the Lord, and unto us by the w of God. G2307
11 *was* a readiness to w, so *there may be* a G2309
10:11 we are absent, such *w we be* also in deed
13 But we w not boast of things without G2744
11: 9 unto you, and *so* w I keep *myself*.
12 But what I do, that I w do, that I may cut
18 many glory after the flesh, I w glory also.
30 If I must needs glory, I w glory of the
12: 1 to glory. I w come to visions and
5 Of such an one w I glory: yet of myself I
5 I w not glory, but in mine infirmities. G2744
6 not be a fool; for I w say the truth: but
9 gladly therefore w I rather glory in my
14 to you; and I w not be burdensome G2655
15 And I w very gladly spend and be spent
21 *And* lest, when I come again, my God w
13: 2 that, if I come again, I w not spare: G5339
Gal 1: 4 to the w of God and our Father: G2307
5:10 the Lord, that ye w be none otherwise
Eph 1: 1 Christ by the w of God, to the saints G2307
5 according to the good pleasure of his w, G2307
9 us the mystery of his w, according to his G2307
11 all things after the counsel of his own w: G2307
5:17 what the w of the Lord *is*. G2307
6: 6 doing the w of God from the heart; G2307
7 With good w doing service, as to the G2133
Php 1: 6 good work in you w perform *it* until the
15 and strife; and some also of good w: G2107
18 I therein do rejoice, yea, and w rejoice.
2:13 to w and to do of *his* good pleasure. G2309
20 For I have no man likeminded, who w
23 soon as I shall see how it w go with me.
Col 1: 1 w of God, and Timotheus *our* brother, G2307
9 knowledge of his w in all wisdom and G2307
2:23 a shew of wisdom in w worship, and
4:12 and complete in all the w of God. G2307
1Th 4: 3 For this is the w of God, *even* your G2307
14 sleep in Jesus w God bring with him. G71
5:18 for this is the w of God in Christ Jesus G2307
24 *is* he that calleth you, who also w do *it*.
2Th 2: 7 *w let*, until he be taken out of the way.
3: 4 w do the things which we command you.
1Ti 2: 4 Who w have all men to be saved, and to
8 I w therefore that men pray every G1014
5:11 wanton against Christ, they w marry; G2309
14 I w therefore that the younger women G1014
6: 9 But they that w be rich fall into G1014
2Ti 1: 1 Christ by the w of God, according to G2307
2:12 *him*: if we deny *him*, he also w deny us:
16 they w increase unto more ungodliness.
17 And their word w eat as doth a canker:
2Ti 2:25 if God peradventure w give them
26 who are taken captive by him at his w. G2307
3:12 Yea, and all that w live godly in Christ G2309
4: 3 For the time w come when they will not
3 For the time will come when they w not G430
18 evil work, and w preserve *me* unto his
Tit 3: 8 and these things I w that thou affirm G1014
Phlm 19 mine own hand, I w repay *it*: albeit I do
Heb 1: 5 thee? And again, I w be to him a Father,
2: 4 the Holy Ghost, according to his own w? G2308
12 Saying, I w declare thy name unto my
12 of the church w I sing praise unto thee.
13 And again, I w put my trust in him. And
3: 7 saith, To day if ye w hear his voice,
15 While it is said, To day if ye w hear his
4: 7 w hear his voice, harden not your hearts.
6: 3 And this w we do, if God permit.
14 Saying, Surely blessing I w bless thee,
14 thee, and multiplying I w multiply thee.
7:21 Lord sware and w not repent, Thou *art* G3338
8: 8 saith the Lord, when I w make a new
10 For this *is* the covenant that I w make
10 saith the Lord; I w put my laws into their
10 their hearts: and I w be to them a God,
12 For I w be merciful to their
12 their iniquities w I remember no more.
10: 7 it is written of me,) to do thy w, O God. G2307
9 Then said he, Lo, I come to do thy w, O G2307
10 By the which w we are sanctified G2307
16 This *is* the covenant that I w make with
16 saith the Lord, I w put my laws into their
16 and in their minds w I write them;
17 And their sins and iniquities w I
30 unto me, I w recompense, saith the
36 w of God, ye might receive the promise. G2307
37 shall come w come, and will not tarry.
37 shall come will come, and w not tarry. G5549
13: 4 and adulterers God w judge.
5 I w never leave thee, nor forsake thee.
6 w not fear what man shall do unto me. G5399
21 work to do his w, working in you that G2307
23 whom, if he come shortly, I w see you.
Jas 1:18 Of his own w begat he us with the word G1014
2:18 and I w shew thee my faith by my works.
4: 4 therefore w be a friend of the world G1014
7 Resist the devil, and he w flee from you.
8 Draw nigh to God, and he w draw nigh
13 or to morrow we w go into such a city,
15 For that ye *ought* to say, If the Lord w, G2309
1Pt 2:15 For so is the w of God, that with well G2307
3:10 For he that w love life, and see good G2309
13 And who *is* he that w harm you, if ye be
17 For *it is* better, if the w of God be so, G2307
4: 2 to the lusts of men, but to the w of God. G2307
3 to have wrought the w of the Gentiles, G2307
19 according to the w of God commit the G2307
2Pt 1:12 Wherefore I w not be negligent to put G272
15 Moreover I w endeavour that ye may be
21 in old time by the w of man: but holy G2307
3:10 But the day of the Lord w come as a thief
1Jn 2:17 doeth the w of God abideth for ever. G2307
5:14 thing according to his w, he heareth us: G2307
3Jn 10 Wherefore, if I come, I w remember his
13 I had many things to write, but I w not G2309
Jude 5 I w therefore put you in remembrance, G1014
Rev 2: 5 first works; or else I w come unto thee
5 unto thee quickly, and w remove thy
7 that overcometh w I give to eat of the
10 death, and I w give thee a crown of life.
16 Repent; or else I w come unto thee
16 thee quickly, and w fight against them
17 that overcometh w I give to eat of the
17 manna, and w give him a white stone,
22 Behold, I w cast her into a bed, and
23 And I w kill her children with death; and
23 and hearts: and I w give unto every one
24 I w put upon you none other burden.
26 to him w I give power over the nations:
28 And I w give him the morning star.
3: 3 shalt not watch, I w come on thee as a
3 know what hour I w come upon thee.
5 raiment; and I w not blot out his name G1813
5 the book of life, but I w confess his name
9 Behold, I w make them of the synagogue
9 do lie; behold, I w make them to come
10 my patience, I also w keep thee from the
12 Him that overcometh w I make a pillar
12 no more out: and I w write upon him the
12 and *I w write upon him* my new name.
Rev 3:16 nor hot, I w spue thee out of my mouth. G3195
20 open the door, I w come in to him, and
20 and w sup with him, and he with me.
21 To him that overcometh w I grant to sit
4: 1 up hither, and I w shew thee things
11: 3 And I w give *power* unto my two
5 And if any man w hurt them, fire G2309
5 and if any man w hurt them, he must G2309
6 with all plagues, as often as they w. G2309
17: 1 me, Come hither; I w shew unto thee the
7 thou marvel? I w tell thee the mystery
17 hearts to fulfil his w, and to agree, and G1106
21: 3 *is* with men, and he w dwell with them,
6 and the end. I w give unto him that is
7 I w be his God, and he shall be my son.
9 I w shew thee the bride, the Lamb's wife.
22:17 w, let him take the water of life freely. G2309

WILLETH

Ro 9:16 So then *it is* not of him that w, nor of G2309

WILLING

Gen 24: 5 woman will not be w to follow me unto H14
8 And if the woman will not be w to follow H14
Ex 35: 5 whosoever *is* of a w heart, let him bring H5081
21 his spirit made w, *and* they brought the H5068
22 as many as were w hearted, *and* H5081
29 The children of Israel brought a w H5071
29 heart made them w to bring for all H5068
1Ch 28: 9 heart and with a w mind: for the LORD H2655
21 every w skilful man, for any H5081
29: 5 And who *then* is w to consecrate his H5068
Job 39: 9 Will the unicorn be w to serve thee, or H14
Ps 110: 3 Thy people *shall be* w in the day of thy H5071
Isa 1:19 If ye be w and obedient, ye shall eat the H14
Mt 1:19 a just *man*, and not w to make her a G2309
26:41 spirit indeed *is* w, but the flesh *is* weak. G4289
Mk 15:15 And *so* Pilate, w to content the people, G1014
Lk 10:29 But he, w to justify himself, said unto G2309
22:42 Saying, Father, if thou be w, remove G1014
23:20 Pilate therefore, w to release Jesus, G2309
Jn 5:35 w for a season to rejoice in his light. G2309
Act 24:27 room: and Felix, w to shew the Jews a G2309
25: 9 But Festus, w to do the Jews a pleasure, G2309
27:43 But the centurion, w to save Paul, kept G1014
Ro 9:22 *What* if God, w to shew *his* wrath, and G2309
2Co 5: 8 We are confident, *I say*, and w rather G2106
8: 3 *their* power *they were* w of themselves; G830
12 For if there be first a w mind, *it is* G4288
1Th 2: 8 of you, we were w to have imparted G2106
1Ti 6:18 ready to distribute, w to communicate; G2843
Heb 6:17 Wherein God, w more abundantly to G1014
13:18 in all things w to live honestly. G2309
2Pt 3: 9 to us-ward, not w that any should G1014

WILLINGLY

Ex 25: 2 man that giveth it w with his heart ye H5068
Jdg 5: 2 when the people w offered themselves. H5068
9 themselves w among the people. H5068
8:25 And they answered, We will w give H5414
1Ch 29: 6 the rulers of the king's work, offered w, H5068
9 for that they offered w, because with H5068
9 heart they offered w to the LORD: and H5068
14 be able to offer so w after this sort? for H5068
17 of mine heart I have w offered all these H5068
17 are present here, to offer w unto thee. H5068
2Ch 17:16 son of Zichri, who w offered himself H5068
35: 8 And his princes gave w unto the H5071
Ezr 1: 6 things, beside all *that* was w offered. H5068
3: 5 of every one that w offered a freewill H5068
7:16 priests, offering w for the house of their H5069
Neh 11: 2 all the men, that w offered themselves to
Prv 31:13 flax, and worketh w with her hands. H2656
Lam 3:33 For he doth not afflict w nor grieve the H3820
Hos 5:11 he w walked after the commandment. H2974
Jn 6:21 Then they w received him into the ship: G2309
Ro 8:20 to vanity, not w, but by reason of him G1635
1Co 9:17 For if I do this thing w, I have a reward: G1635
Phlm 14 not be as it were of necessity, but w. G2596
1Pt 5: 2 by constraint, but w; not for filthy lucre, G1596
2Pt 3: 5 For this they w are ignorant of, that by G2309

WILLOW

Ezk 17: 5 *it* by great waters, *and* set it *as* a w tree. H6851

WILLOWS

Lev 23:40 of thick trees, and w of the brook; and H6155
Job 40:22 the w of the brook compass him about. H6155
Ps 137: 2 We hanged our harps upon the w in H6155

Isa 15: 7 they carry away to the brook of the **w**. H6155
44: 4 the grass, as **w** by the water courses. H6155

WILT

Gen 13: 9 from me: if *thou* **w** *take* the left hand,
15: 2 And Abram said, Lord GOD, what **w**
16: 8 thou? and whither **w** thou go? And she
18:23 And Abraham drew near, and said, **W**
24 within the city: **w** thou also destroy and
28 the fifty righteous: **w** thou destroy all the
20: 4 **w** thou slay also a righteous nation?
21:23 by God that thou **w** not deal falsely with
23:13 saying, But if thou **w** *give it,* I pray thee,
24:58 and said unto her, **W** thou go with this
26:29 That thou **w** do us no hurt, as we have
30:31 any thing: if thou **w** do this thing for me,
38:16 she said, What **w** thou give me, that thou
17 And she said, **W** thou give *me* a pledge,
43: 4 If thou **w** send our brother with us, we H3426
5 But if thou **w** not send *him,* we will not
Ex 4:13 by the hand *of him whom* thou **w** send.
8:21 Else, if thou **w** not let my people go,
9: 2 For if thou refuse to let *them* go, and **w**
17 my people, that thou **w** not let them go?
10: 3 How long **w** thou refuse to humble
13:13 a lamb; and if thou **w** not redeem it, then
15:26 And said, If thou **w** diligently hearken to
26 thy God, and **w** do that which is right
26 right in his sight, and **w** give ear to his
18:18 Thou **w** surely wear away, both thou,
20:25 And if thou **w** make me an altar of stone,
32:32 Yet now, if thou **w** forgive their sin—;
33:12 know whom thou **w** send with me. Yet
Nu 16:14 and vineyards: **w** thou put out the eyes
22 one man sin, and **w** thou be wroth with
21: 2 and said, If thou **w** indeed deliver this
Dt 23:13 be, when thou **w** ease thyself abroad,
28:15 But it shall come to pass, if thou **w** not
58 If thou **w** not observe to do all the words
30:17 away, so that thou **w** not hear, but shalt
Jos 7: 9 what **w** thou do unto thy great name?
Jdg 1:14 and Caleb said unto her, What **w** thou?
4: 8 And Barak said unto her, If thou **w** go
8 thou **w** not go with me, *then* I will not go.
6:36 And Gideon said unto God, If thou **w** H3426
37 I know that thou **w** save Israel by mine
11:24 **W** not thou possess that which Chemosh
13:16 thy bread: and if thou **w** offer a burnt
Ru 4: 4 my people. If thou **w** redeem *it,* redeem
4 *it:* but if thou **w** not redeem *it, then* tell
1Sa 1:11 of hosts, if thou **w** indeed look on the
11 thine handmaid, but **w** give unto thine
14 And Eli said unto her, How long **w** thou
14:37 the Philistines? **w** thou deliver them into
16: 1 Samuel, How long **w** thou mourn for
19: 5 wherefore then **w** thou sin against
21: 9 the ephod: if thou **w** take that, take *it:* for
24:21 LORD, that thou **w** not cut off my seed
21 me, and that thou **w** not destroy my
25:17 what thou **w** do; for evil is determined
30:15 by God, that thou **w** neither kill me, nor
2Sa 5:19 to the Philistines? **w** thou deliver them
13: 4 from day to day? **w** thou not tell me?
18:22 said, Wherefore **w** thou run, my son,
20:19 in Israel: why **w** thou swallow up the
22:26 With the merciful thou **w** shew thyself
26 man thou **w** shew thyself upright.
27 With the pure thou **w** shew thyself pure;
27 froward thou **w** shew thyself unsavoury.
28 And the afflicted people thou **w** save: but
24:13 in thy land? or **w** thou flee three months
1Ki 3:14 And if thou **w** walk in my ways, to keep
6:12 art in building, if thou **w** walk in my
9: 4 And if thou **w** walk before me, as David
4 **w** keep my statutes and my judgments:
11:38 And it shall be, if thou **w** hearken unto
38 thee, and **w** walk in my ways, and
12: 7 saying, If thou **w** be a servant unto this
7 this day, and **w** serve them, and answer
13: 8 the king, If thou **w** give me half thine
22: 4 And he said unto Jehoshaphat, **W** thou
2Ki 3: 7 against me: **w** thou go with me against
4:23 And he said, Wherefore **w** thou go to
8:12 the evil that thou **w** do unto the children
12 their strong holds **w** thou set on fire, and
12 their young men **w** thou slay with the
12 the sword, and **w** dash their children,
18:24 How then **w** thou turn away the face of
1Ch 14:10 Philistines? and **w** thou deliver them into
17:25 servant that thou **w** build him an house:
2Ch 7:17 And as for thee, if thou **w** walk before
18: 3 king of Judah, **W** thou go with me to
20: 9 affliction, then thou **w** hear and help.
12 O our God, **w** thou not judge them? for
25: 8 But if thou **w** go, do *it,* be strong for the
Neh 2: 6 be? and when **w** thou return? So it
Est 5: 3 Then said the king unto her, What **w**
Job 4: 2 *If* we assay to commune with thee, **w**
5: 1 and to which of the saints **w** thou turn?
7:19 How long **w** thou not depart from me,
8: 2 How long **w** thou speak these *things*?
9:28 know that thou **w** not hold me innocent.
10: 9 and **w** thou bring me into dust again?
14 **w** not acquit me from mine iniquity.
13:25 **W** thou break a leaf driven to and fro?
25 fro? and **w** thou pursue the dry stubble?
14:15 answer thee: thou **w** have a desire to the
30:23 For I know *that* thou **w** bring me *to*
34:17 **w** thou condemn him that is most just?
38:39 **W** thou hunt the prey for the lion? or fill
39:11 **W** thou trust him, because his strength
11 great? or **w** thou leave thy labour to him?
12 **W** thou believe him, that he will bring
40: 8 **W** thou also disannul my judgment? wilt
8 Wilt thou also disannul my judgment? **w**
41: 4 Will he make a covenant with thee? **w**
5 **W** thou play with him as *with* a bird? or
5 or **w** thou bind him for thy maidens?
Ps 5:12 For thou, LORD, **w** bless the righteous;
12 **w** thou compass him as *with* a shield.
10:13 said in his heart, Thou **w** not require *it.*
17 the humble: thou **w** prepare their heart,
17 heart, thou **w** cause thine ear to hear:
13: 1 How long **w** thou forget me, O LORD? for
1 how long **w** thou hide thy face from me?
16:10 For thou **w** not leave my soul in hell;
10 in hell; neither **w** thou suffer thine Holy
11 Thou **w** shew me the path of life: in thy
17: 6 I have called upon thee, for thou **w** hear
18:25 With the merciful thou **w** shew thyself
25 man thou **w** shew thyself upright;
26 With the pure thou **w** shew thyself pure;
26 froward thou **w** shew thyself froward.
27 For thou **w** save the afflicted people; but
27 people; but **w** bring down high looks.
28 For thou **w** light my candle: the LORD
35:17 Lord, how long **w** thou look on? rescue
38:15 For in thee, O LORD, do I hope: thou **w**
41: 2 earth: and thou **w** not deliver him unto
3 thou **w** make all his bed in his sickness.
51:17 heart, O God, thou **w** not despise.
56:13 soul from death: *w* not *thou deliver* my
60:10 *W* not thou, O God, *which* hadst cast us
61: 6 Thou **w** prolong the king's life: *and* his
65: 5 *By* terrible things in righteousness **w**
79: 5 How long, LORD? **w** thou be angry for
80: 4 O LORD God of hosts, how long **w** thou
81: 8 O Israel, if thou **w** hearken unto me;
85: 5 **W** thou be angry with us for ever? wilt
5 Wilt thou be angry with us for ever? **w**
6 **W** thou not revive us again: that thy
86: 7 call upon thee: for thou **w** answer me.
88:10 **W** thou shew wonders to the dead? shall
89:46 How long, LORD? **w** thou hide thyself for
101: 2 way. O when **w** thou come unto me?
108:11 **W** not *thou,* O God, *who* hast cast us off?
11 cast us off? and **w** not thou, O God, go
119:82 word, saying, When **w** thou comfort me?
84 of thy servant? when **w** thou execute
138: 7 of trouble, thou **w** revive me: thou shalt
139:19 Surely thou **w** slay the wicked, O God:
Prv 2: 1 My son, if thou **w** receive my words, and
5:20 And why **w** thou, my son, be ravished
6: 9 How long **w** thou sleep, O sluggard?
9 when **w** thou arise out of thy sleep?
23: 5 **W** thou set thine eyes upon that which is
Isa 26: 3 Thou **w** keep *him* in perfect peace,
12 LORD, thou **w** ordain peace for us: for
27: 8 forth, thou **w** debate with it: he stayeth
36: 9 How then **w** thou turn away the face of
38:12 *even* to night **w** thou make an end of me.
13 *even* to night **w** thou make an end of me.
16 **w** thou recover me, and make me to live.
58: 5 ashes *under him*? **w** thou call this a fast,
64:12 **W** thou refrain thyself for these *things,* O
12 *things,* O LORD? **w** thou hold thy peace,
Jer 3: 4 **W** thou not from this time cry unto me,
4: 1 If thou **w** return, O Israel, saith the
1 unto me: and if thou **w** put away thine
30 And *when* thou *art* spoiled, what **w** thou
12: 5 how **w** thou do in the swelling of Jordan?
13:21 What **w** thou say when he shall punish
27 thee, O Jerusalem! **w** thou not be made
15:18 to be healed? **w** thou be altogether unto
31:22 How long **w** thou go about, O thou
38:15 *it* unto thee, **w** thou not surely put me
15 counsel, **w** thou not hearken unto me?
17 of Israel; If thou **w** assuredly go forth
18 But if thou **w** not go forth to the king of
47: 5 their valley: how long **w** thou cut thyself?
Lam 1:21 hast done *it:* thou **w** bring the day *that*
Ezk 9: 8 Ah Lord GOD! **w** thou destroy all the
11:13 Ah Lord GOD! **w** thou make a full end
20: 4 **W** thou judge them, son of man, wilt
4 Wilt thou judge them, son of man, **w**
22: 2 Now, thou son of man, **w** thou judge,
2 wilt thou judge, **w** thou judge the bloody
23:36 me; Son of man, **w** thou judge Aholah
24:19 And the people said unto me, **W** thou
28: 9 **W** thou yet say before him that slayeth
37:18 unto thee, saying, **W** thou not shew us
Hos 9:14 Give them, O LORD: what **w** thou give?
Mic 7:19 and thou **w** cast all their sins into
20 Thou **w** perform the truth to Jacob, *and*
Hab 1: 2 I cry, and thou **w** not hear! *even* cry out
2 thee *of* violence, and thou **w** not save!
Zep 3: 7 I said, Surely thou **w** fear me, thou wilt
7 I said, Surely thou wilt fear me, thou **w**
Zec 1:12 of hosts, how long **w** thou not have
3: 7 Thus saith the LORD of hosts; If thou **w**
7 my ways, and if thou **w** keep my charge,
Mt 4: 9 if thou **w** fall down and worship me.
7: 4 Or how **w** thou say to thy brother, Let G2309
8: 2 if thou **w**, thou canst make me clean. G2309
13:28 said unto him, **W** thou then that we go G2309
15:28 thee even as thou **w**. And her daughter G2309
17: 4 us to be here: if thou **w**, let us make here G2309
19:17 God: but if thou **w** enter into life, keep G2309
21 Jesus said unto him, If thou **w** be G2309
20:21 And he said unto her, What **w** thou? G2309
26:17 saying unto him, Where **w** thou that we G2309
39 nevertheless not as I will, but as thou **w**.
Mk 1:40 If thou **w**, thou canst make me clean. G2309
6:22 thou **w**, and I will give *it* thee. G2309
10:51 unto him, What **w** thou that I should G2309
14:12 unto him, Where **w** thou that we go G2309
36 not what I will, but what thou **w**. G2309
Lk 4: 7 If thou therefore **w** worship me, all shall
5:12 if thou **w**, thou canst make me clean. G2309
9:54 *this,* they said, Lord, **w** thou that we G2309
18:41 Saying, What **w** thou that I shall do G2309
22: 9 And they said unto him, Where **w** thou
Jn 2:20 and **w** thou rear it up in three days? G1453
5: 6 unto him, **W** thou be made whole? G2309
11:22 thou **w** ask of God, God will give *it* thee.
13:38 Jesus answered him, **W** thou lay down
14:22 how is it that thou **w** manifest thyself G3195
Act 1: 6 of him, saying, Lord, **w** thou at this time
2:27 Because thou **w** not leave my soul in G1459
27 in hell, neither **w** thou suffer thine Holy
7:28 **W** thou kill me, as thou diddest the G2309
9: 6 said, Lord, what **w** thou have me to do? G2309
13:10 of all righteousness, **w** thou not cease to
25: 9 Paul, and said, **W** thou go up to
Ro 9:19 Thou **w** say then unto me, Why doth he
11:19 Thou **w** say then, The branches were
13: 3 but to the evil. **W** thou then not be G2309
Phlm 21 that thou **w** also do more than I say. G4160
Jas 2:20 But **w** thou know, O vain man, that G2309

WIMPLES

Isa 3:22 and the **w**, and the crisping pins, H4304

WIN

2Ch 32: 1 and thought to **w** them for himself. H1234
Php 3: 8 them *but* dung, that I may **w** Christ, G2770

WIND

Gen 8: 1 ark: and God made a **w** to pass over the H7307
41: 6 with the east **w** sprung up after them. H6921
23 with the east **w**, sprung up after them: H6921
27 east **w** shall be seven years of famine. H6921
Ex 10:13 brought an east **w** upon the land all H7307
13 the east **w** brought the locusts. H7307
19 strong west **w**, which took away the H7307
14:21 by a strong east **w** all that night, and H7307
15:10 Thou didst blow with thy **w**, the sea H7307

Nu 11:31 And there went forth a w from the H7307
2Sa 22:11 he was seen upon the wings of the w. H7307
1Ki 18:45 with clouds and w, and there was a H7307
19:11 and a great and strong w rent the H7307
11 *was* not in the w: and after the wind H7307
11 and after the w an earthquake; *but* H7307
2Ki 3:17 Ye shall not see w, neither shall ye see H7307
Job 1:19 And, behold, there came a great w H7307
6:26 of one that is desperate, *which are* as w? H7307
7: 7 O remember that my life *is* w: mine eye H7307
8: 2 words of thy mouth *be like* a strong w? H7307
15: 2 and fill his belly with the east w? H6921
21:18 They are as stubble before the w, and as H7307
27:21 The east w carrieth him away, and he H6921
30:15 my soul as the w: and my welfare H7307
22 Thou liftest me up to the w; thou H7307
37:17 he quieteth the earth by the south *w*?
21 but the w passeth, and cleanseth them. H7307
38:24 scattereth the east w upon the earth? H6921
Ps 1: 4 the chaff which the w driveth away. H7307
18:10 yea, he did fly upon the wings of the w. H7307
42 dust before the w: I did cast them out H7307
35: 5 Let them be as chaff before the w: and H7307
48: 7 the ships of Tarshish with an east w. H7307
78:26 He caused an east w to blow in the H6921
26 by his power he brought in the south w. H8486
39 *were but* flesh; a w that passeth away, H7307
83:13 like a wheel; as the stubble before the w. H7307
103:16 For the w passeth over it, and it is H7307
104: 3 who walketh upon the wings of the w: H7307
107:25 w, which lifteth up the waves thereof. H7307
135: 7 he bringeth the w out of his treasuries. H7307
147:18 his w to blow, *and* the waters flow. H7307
148: 8 vapour; stormy w fulfilling his word: H7307
Prv 11:29 shall inherit the w: and the fool *shall be* H7307
25:14 gift *is like* clouds and w without rain. H7307
23 The north w driveth away rain: so *doth* H7307
27:16 Whosoever hideth her hideth the w, and H7307
30: 4 hath gathered the w in his fists? who H7307
Ecc 1: 6 The w goeth toward the south, and H7307
6 and the w returneth again according H7307
5:16 hath he that hath laboured for the w? H7307
11: 4 He that observeth the w shall not sow; H7307
Song 4:16 Awake, O north w; and come, thou south;
Isa 7: 2 trees of the wood are moved with the w. H7307
11:15 with his mighty w shall he shake his H7307
17:13 before the w, and like a rolling thing H7307
26:18 brought forth w; we have not wrought H7307
27: 8 his rough w in the day of the east wind. H7307
8 his rough wind in the day of the east w. H6921
32: 2 place from the w, and a covert from the H7307
41:16 Thou shalt fan them, and the w shall H7307
29 molten images *are* w and confusion. H7307
57:13 thee; but the w shall carry them all H7307
64: 6 like the w, have taken us away. H7307
Jer 2:24 snuffeth up the w at her pleasure; in H7307
4:11 Jerusalem, A dry w of the high places H7307
12 *Even* a full w from those *places* shall H7307
5:13 And the prophets shall become w, and H7307
10:13 forth the w out of his treasures. H7307
13:24 away by the w of the wilderness. H7307
14: 6 snuffed up the w like dragons; their H7307
18:17 I will scatter them as with an east w H7307
22:22 The w shall eat up all thy pastors, and H7307
51: 1 that rise up against me, a destroying w; H7307
16 forth the w out of his treasures. H7307
Ezk 5: 2 scatter in the w; and I will draw out H7307
12:14 And I will scatter toward every w all H7307
13:11 shall fall; and a stormy w shall rend *it*. H7307
13 rend *it* with a stormy w in my fury; and H7307
17:10 when the east w toucheth it? it shall H7307
19:12 and the east w dried up her fruit: her H7307
27:26 waters: the east w hath broken thee in H7307
37: 9 Prophesy unto the w, prophesy, son of H7307
9 and say to the w, Thus saith the Lord H7307
Dan 2:35 and the w carried them away, H7308
Hos 4:19 The w hath bound her up in her wings, H7307
8: 7 For they have sown the w, and they H7307
12: 1 Ephraim feedeth on w, and followeth H7307
1 after the east w: he daily increaseth H6921
13:15 *his* brethren, an east w shall come, the H6921
15 shall come, the w of the LORD shall H7307
Am 4:13 and createth the w, and declareth unto H7307
Jna 1: 4 But the LORD sent out a great w into H7307
4: 8 a vehement east w; and the sun beat H7307
Hab 1: 9 sup up *as* the east w, and they shall H6921
Zec 5: 9 women, and the w *was* in their wings; H7307
Mt 11: 7 to see? A reed shaken with the w? G417
14:24 with waves: for the w was contrary. G417
14:30 But when he saw the w boisterous, he G417
32 were come into the ship, the w ceased. G417
Mk 4:37 And there arose a great storm of w, and G417
39 And he arose, and rebuked the w, and G417
39 w ceased, and there was a great calm. G417
41 that even the w and the sea obey him? G417
6:48 in rowing; for the w was contrary unto G417
51 into the ship; and the w ceased: and they G417
Lk 7:24 for to see? A reed shaken with the w? G417
8:23 down a storm of w on the lake; and they G417
24 and rebuked the w and the raging of the G417
12:55 And when *ye see* the south w blow, ye G3558
Jn 3: 8 The w bloweth where it listeth, and G4151
6:18 And the sea arose by reason of a great w G417
Act 2: 2 a rushing mighty w, and it filled all the G4157
27: 7 Cnidus, the w not suffering us, we G417
13 And when the south w blew softly, G3558
14 it a tempestuous w, called Euroclydon. G417
15 not bear up into the w, we let *her* drive. G417
40 to the w, and made toward shore. G4154
28:13 one day the south w blew, and we came G3558
Eph 4:14 about with every w of doctrine, by the G417
Jas 1: 6 of the sea driven with the w and tossed. G416
Rev 6:13 figs, when she is shaken of a mighty w. G417
7: 1 the earth, that the w should not blow on G417

WINDING

1Ki 6: 8 and they went up with w stairs into the H3583
Ezk 41: 7 And *there was* an enlarging, and a w H5437
7 chambers: for the w about of the house H4141

WINDOW

Gen 6:16 A w shalt thou make to the ark, and in H6672
8: 6 the w of the ark which he had made: H2474
26: 8 looked out at a w, and saw, and, H2474
Jos 2:15 a cord through the w: for her house *was* H2474
18 thread in the w which thou didst let H2474
21 and she bound the scarlet line in the w. H2474
Jdg 5:28 The mother of Sisera looked out at a w, H2474
1Sa 19:12 So Michal let David down through a w: H2474
2Sa 6:16 looked through a w, and saw king H2474
2Ki 9:30 tired her head, and looked out at a w. H2474
32 And he lifted up his face to the w, and H2474
13:17 And he said, Open the w eastward. And H2474
1Ch 15:29 Saul looking out at a w saw king David H2474
Prv 7: 6 For at the w of my house I looked H2474
Act 20: 9 And there sat in a w a certain young G2376
2Co 11:33 And through a w in a basket was I let G2376

WINDOWS

Gen 7:11 up, and the w of heaven were opened. H699
8: 2 The fountains also of the deep and the w H699
1Ki 6: 4 And for the house he made w of H2474
7: 4 And *there were* w *in* three rows, and H8261
5 *were* square, with the w: and light *was* H8260
2Ki 7: 2 LORD would make w in heaven, might H699
19 should make w in heaven, might such H699
Ecc 12: 3 those that look out of the w be darkened, H699
Song 2: 9 w, shewing himself through the lattice. H2474
Isa 24:18 in the snare: for the w from on high are H699
54:12 And I will make thy w of agates, and H8121
60: 8 as a cloud, and as the doves to their w? H699
Jer 9:21 For death is come up into our w, *and* is H2474
22:14 cutteth him out w; and *it is* cieled with H2474
Ezk 40:16 And *there were* narrow w to the little H2474
16 to the arches: and w *were* round about H2474
22 And their w, and their arches, and their H2474
25 And *there were* w in it and in the H2474
25 about, like those w: the length *was* fifty H2474
29 and *there were* w in it and in the arches H2474
33 and *there were* w therein and in the H2474
36 thereof, and the w to it round about: H2474
41:16 The door posts, and the narrow w, and H2474
16 the w, and the windows were covered; H2474
16 the windows, and the w *were* covered; H2474
26 And *there were* narrow w and palm H2474
Dan 6:10 his house; and his w being open in his H3551
Joel 2: 9 they shall enter in at the w like a thief. H2474
Zep 2:14 shall sing in the w; desolation *shall be* H2474
Mal 3:10 not open you the w of heaven, and pour H699

WINDS

Job 28:25 To make the weight for the w; and he H7307
Jer 49:32 scatter into all w them *that are* in the H7307
36 And upon Elam will I bring the four w H7307
36 toward all those w; and there shall be H7307
Ezk 5:10 of thee will I scatter into all the w. H7307
12 part into all the w, and I will draw out H7307
17:21 toward all w: and ye shall know that H7307
37: 9 from the four w, O breath, and breathe H7307
Dan 7: 2 behold, the four w of the heaven strove H7308
8: 8 ones toward the four w of heaven. H7307
11: 4 toward the four w of heaven; and not H7307
Zec 2: 6 four w of the heaven, saith the LORD. H7307
Mt 7:25 came, and the w blew, and beat upon G417
27 came, and the w blew, and beat upon G417
8:26 and rebuked the w and the sea; and G417
27 that even the w and the sea obey him! G417
24:31 w, from one end of heaven to the other. G417
Mk 13:27 elect from the four w, from the uttermost G417
Lk 8:25 the w and water, and they obey him. G417
Act 27: 4 Cyprus, because the w were contrary. G417
Jas 3: 4 *are* driven of fierce w, yet are they turned G417
Jude 12 carried about of w; trees whose fruit G417
Rev 7: 1 holding the four w of the earth, that the G417

WINDY

Ps 55: 8 I would hasten my escape from the w H7307

WINE

Gen 9:21 And he drank of the w, and was H3196
24 And Noah awoke from his w, and knew H3196
14:18 forth bread and w: and he *was* the H3196
19:32 Come, let us make our father drink w, H3196
33 And they made their father drink w H3196
34 make him drink w this night also; and H3196
35 And they made their father drink w H3196
27:25 and he brought him w, and he drank. H3196
28 of the earth, and plenty of corn and w: H8492
37 with corn and w have I sustained him: H8492
49:11 his garments in w, and his clothes in H3196
12 His eyes *shall be* red with w, and his H3196
Ex 29:40 part of an hin of w *for* a drink offering. H3196
Lev 10: 9 Do not drink w nor strong drink, thou, H3196
23:13 *shall be* of w, the fourth *part* of an hin. H3196
Nu 6: 3 He shall separate *himself* from w and H3196
3 no vinegar of w, or vinegar of strong H3196
20 after that the Nazarite may drink w. H3196
15: 5 And the fourth *part* of an hin of w for a H3196
7 of w, *for* a sweet savour unto the LORD. H3196
10 half an hin of w, *for* an offering made H3196
18:12 all the best of the w, and of the wheat, H8492
28: 7 cause the strong w to be poured unto H7941
14 be half an hin of w unto a bullock, and H3196
Dt 7:13 thy corn, and thy w, and thine oil, the H8492
11:14 in thy corn, and thy w, and thine oil. H8492
12:17 thy corn, or of thy w, or of thy oil, or the H8492
14:23 of thy corn, of thy w, and of thine oil, H8492
26 for sheep, or for w, or for strong drink, H3196
16:13 hast gathered in thy corn and thy w: H3342
18: 4 The firstfruit *also* of thy corn, of thy w, H8492
28:39 drink *of the* w, nor gather *the grapes*; H3196
51 leave thee *either* corn, w, or oil, *or* the H8492
29: 6 have ye drunk w or strong drink: that H3196
32:33 Their w *is* the poison of dragons, and H3196
38 *and* drank the w of their drink H3196
33:28 a land of corn and w; also his heavens H8492
Jos 9: 4 w bottles, old, and rent, and bound up; H3196
13 And these bottles of w, which we filled, H3196
Jdg 9:13 Should I leave my w, which cheereth H8492
13: 4 and drink not w nor strong drink, and H3196
7 and now drink no w nor strong drink, H3196
14 let her drink w or strong drink, nor H3196
19:19 there is bread and w also for me, and H3196
1Sa 1:14 be drunken? put away thy w from thee. H3196
15 drunk neither w nor strong drink, but H3196
24 and a bottle of w, and brought him unto H3196
10: 3 and another carrying a bottle of w: H3196
16:20 and a bottle of w, and a kid, and sent H3196
25:18 and two bottles of w, and five sheep H3196
37 when the w was gone out of Nabal, H3196
2Sa 6:19 *flesh*, and a flagon *of w*. So all the people
13:28 is merry with w, and when I say unto H3196
16: 1 of summer fruits, and a bottle of w. H3196
2 to eat; and the w, that such as be faint H3196
2Ki 18:32 a land of corn and w, a land of bread H8492
1Ch 9:29 fine flour, and the w, and the oil, and H3196
12:40 of raisins, and w, and oil, and oxen, H3196
16: 3 a good piece of flesh, and a flagon *of w*.
27:27 the w cellars *was* Zabdi the Shiphmite: H3196
2Ch 2:10 of w, and twenty thousand baths of oil. H3196
15 the oil, and the w, which my lord hath H3196
11:11 and store of victual, and of oil and w. H3196
31: 5 the firstfruits of corn, w, and oil, and H8492
32:28 of corn, and w, and oil; and stalls for H8492
Ezr 6: 9 wheat, salt, w, and oil, according to H2562
7:22 hundred baths of w, and to an hundred H2562
Neh 2: 1 the king, *that* w *was* before him: and H3196

Neh 2: 1 and I took up the w, and gave *it* unto H3196
5:11 the w, and the oil, that ye exact of them. H8492
15 them bread and w, beside forty shekels H3196
18 of all sorts of w: yet for all this required H3196
10:37 of trees, of w and of oil, unto the H8492
39 corn, of the new w, and the oil, unto the H8492
13: 5 the corn, the new w, and the oil, which H8492
12 new w and the oil unto the treasuries. H8492
15 Judah *some* treading w presses on the H8492
15 asses; as also w, grapes, and figs, and H3196
Est 1: 7 and royal w in abundance, according H3196
10 king was merry with w, he commanded H3196
5: 6 Esther at the banquet of w, What *is* thy H3196
7: 2 day at the banquet of w, What *is* thy H3196
7 the banquet of w in his wrath *went* into H3196
8 of the banquet of w; and Haman was H3196
Job 1:13 w in their eldest brother's house: H3196
18 w in their eldest brother's house: H3196
32:19 Behold, my belly *is* as w *which* hath no H3196
Ps 4: 7 *that* their corn and their w increased. H8492
60: 3 us to drink the w of astonishment. H3196
75: 8 *is* a cup, and the w is red; it is full of H3196
78:65 man that shouteth by reason of w. H3196
104:15 And w *that* maketh glad the heart of H3196
Prv 3:10 thy presses shall burst out with new w. H8492
4:17 and drink the w of violence. H3196
9: 2 her w; she hath also furnished her table. H3196
5 drink of the w *which* I have mingled. H3196
20: 1 W *is* a mocker, strong drink *is* raging: H3196
21:17 that loveth w and oil shall not be rich. H3196
23:30 They that tarry long at the w; they that H3196
30 the wine; they that go to seek mixed w. H4469
31 Look not thou upon the w when it is H3196
31: 4 to drink w; nor for princes strong drink: H3196
6 w unto those that be of heavy hearts. H3196
Ecc 2: 3 to give myself unto w, yet acquainting H3196
9: 7 with joy, and drink thy w with a merry H3196
10:19 A feast is made for laughter, and w H3196
Song 1: 2 his mouth: for thy love *is* better than w. H3196
4 love more than w: the upright love thee. H3196
4:10 is thy love than w! and the smell of H3196
5: 1 I have drunk my w with my milk: eat, H3196
7: 9 like the best w for my beloved, that H3196
8: 2 w of the juice of my pomegranate. H3196
Isa 1:22 Thy silver is become dross, thy w H5435
5:11 until night, *till* w inflame them! H3196
12 and pipe, and w, are in their feasts: but H3196
22 mighty to drink w, and men of strength H3196
16:10 shall tread out no w in *their* presses; I H3196
22:13 and drinking w: let us eat and drink; H3196
24: 7 The new w mourneth, the vine H8492
9 They shall not drink w with a song; H3196
11 *There is* a crying for w in the streets; all H3196
27: 2 sing ye unto her, A vineyard of red w. H2561
28: 1 of them that are overcome with w! H3196
7 But they also have erred through w, and H3196
7 swallowed up of w, they are out of the H3196
29: 9 but not with w; they stagger, but not H3196
36:17 and w, a land of bread and vineyards. H8492
49:26 as with sweet w: and all flesh shall H6071
51:21 afflicted, and drunken, but not with w: H3196
55: 1 eat; yea, come, buy w and milk without H3196
56:12 Come ye, *say they,* I will fetch w, and we H3196
62: 8 thy w, for the which thou hast laboured: H8492
65: 8 Thus saith the LORD, As the new w is H8492
Jer 13:12 shall be filled with w: and they shall say H3196
12 that every bottle shall be filled with w? H3196
23: 9 like a man whom w hath overcome, H3196
25:15 unto me; Take the w cup of this fury at H3196
31:12 for wheat, and for w, and for oil, and H8492
35: 2 chambers, and give them w to drink. H3196
5 pots full of w, and cups, and I said H3196
5 cups, and I said unto them, Drink ye w. H3196
6 But they said, We will drink no w: for H3196
6 no w, *neither ye,* nor your sons for ever: H3196
8 us, to drink no w all our days, we, our H3196
14 sons not to drink w, are performed; for H3196
40:10 but ye, gather ye w, and summer fruits, H3196
12 w and summer fruits very much. H3196
48:33 and I have caused w to fail from the H3196
51: 7 of her w; therefore the nations are mad. H3196
Lam 2:12 *is* corn and w? when they swooned H3196
Ezk 27:18 in the w of Helbon, and white wool. H3196
44:21 Neither shall any priest drink w, when H3196
Dan 1: 5 meat, and of the w which he drank: so H3196
8 meat, nor with the w which he drank: H3196
16 their meat, and the w that they should H3196
5: 1 and drank w before the thousand. H2562
2 Belshazzar, whiles he tasted the w, H2562
Dan 5: 4 They drank w, and praised the gods of H2562
23 have drunk w in them; and thou hast H2562
10: 3 came flesh nor w in my mouth, neither H3196
Hos 2: 8 her corn, and w, and oil, and multiplied H8492
9 time thereof, and my w in the season H8492
22 the corn, and the w, and the oil; and H8492
3: 1 to other gods, and love flagons of w. H6025
4:11 Whoredom and w and new wine take H3196
11 Whoredom and wine and new w take H8492
7: 5 with bottles of w; he stretched out his H3196
14 corn and w, *and* they rebel against me. H8492
9: 2 them, and the new w shall fail in her. H8492
4 They shall not offer w *offerings* to the H3196
14: 7 thereof *shall be* as the w of Lebanon. H3196
Joel 1: 5 all ye drinkers of w, because of the new H3196
5 new w; for it is cut off from your mouth. H6071
10 new w is dried up, the oil languisheth. H8492
2:19 you corn, and w, and oil, and ye shall H8492
24 the fats shall overflow with w and oil. H8492
3: 3 sold a girl for w, that they might drink. H3196
18 drop down new w, and the hills shall H6071
Am 2: 8 they drink the w of the condemned *in* H3196
12 But ye gave the Nazarites w to drink; H3196
5:11 but ye shall not drink w of them. H3196
6: 6 That drink w in bowls, and anoint H3196
9:13 sweet w, and all the hills shall melt. H6071
14 and drink the w thereof; they shall also H3196
Mic 2:11 unto thee of w and of strong drink; H3196
6:15 and sweet w, but shalt not drink wine. H8492
15 and sweet wine, but shalt not drink w. H3196
Hab 2: 5 transgresseth by w, *he is* a proud man, H3196
Zep 1:13 vineyards, but not drink the w thereof. H3196
Hag 1:11 and upon the new w, and upon the oil, H8492
2:12 or pottage, or w, or oil, or any meat, H3196
Zec 9:15 a noise as through w; and they shall be H3196
17 men cheerful, and new w the maids. H8492
10: 7 rejoice as through w: yea, their children H3196
Mt 9:17 Neither do men put new w into old *G3631*
17 break, and the w runneth out, and the *G3631*
17 but they put new w into new bottles, *G3631*
Mk 2:22 And no man putteth new w into old *G3631*
22 else the new w doth burst the bottles, *G3631*
22 the bottles, and the w is spilled, and the *G3631*
22 new w must be put into new bottles. *G3631*
15:23 And they gave him to drink w mingled *G3631*
Lk 1:15 drink neither w nor strong drink; and *G3631*
5:37 And no man putteth new w into old *G3631*
37 else the new w will burst the bottles, *G3631*
38 But new w must be put into new *G3631*
39 No man also having drunk old w
7:33 drinking w; and ye say, He hath a devil. *G3631*
10:34 pouring in oil and w, and set him on his *G3631*
Jn 2: 3 And when they wanted w, the mother of *G3631*
3 Jesus saith unto him, They have no w. *G3631*
9 that was made w, and knew not whence *G3631*
10 set forth good w; and when men have *G3631*
10 thou hast kept the good w until now. *G3631*
4:46 he made the water w. And there was a *G3631*
Act 2:13 said, These men are full of new w. *G1098*
Ro 14:21 eat flesh, nor to drink w, nor *any thing* *G3631*
Eph 5:18 And be not drunk with w, wherein is *G3631*
1Ti 3: 3 Not given to w, no striker, not greedy of *G3943*
8 to much w, not greedy of filthy lucre; *G3631*
5:23 but use a little w for thy stomach's sake *G3631*
Tit 1: 7 to w, no striker, not given to filthy lucre; *G3943*
2: 3 to much w, teachers of good things; *G3631*
1Pt 4: 3 lusts, excess of w, revellings, *G3632*
Rev 6: 6 and *see* thou hurt not the oil and the w. *G3631*
14: 8 of the w of the wrath of her fornication. *G3631*
10 The same shall drink of the w of the *G3631*
16:19 of the w of the fierceness of his wrath. *G3631*
17: 2 drunk with the w of her fornication. *G3631*
18: 3 For all nations have drunk of the w of *G3631*
13 frankincense, and w, and oil, and fine *G3631*

WINEBIBBER
Mt 11:19 man gluttonous, and a w, a friend of *G3630*
Lk 7:34 a w, a friend of publicans and sinners! *G3630*

WINEBIBBERS
Prv 23:20 Be not among w; among H3196+H5433

WINE-CELLARS See WINE and CELLARS.

WINE-CUP See WINE and CUP.

WINEFAT
Isa 63: 2 like him that treadeth in the w? H1660
Mk 12: 1 *a place for* the w, and built a tower, and *G5276*

WINEPRESS
Nu 18:27 and as the fulness of the w. H3342
30 and as the increase of the w. H3342
Dt 15:14 and out of thy w: *of that* wherewith the H3342
Jdg 6:11 by the w, to hide *it* from the Midianites. H1660
7:25 they slew at the w of Zeeb, and pursued H3342
2Ki 6:27 out of the barnfloor, or out of the w? H3342
Isa 5: 2 it, and also made a w therein: and he H3342
63: 3 I have trodden the w alone; and of the H6333
Lam 1:15 virgin, the daughter of Judah, *as* in a w. H1660
Hos 9: 2 The floor and the w shall not feed H3342
Mt 21:33 and digged a w in it, and built a tower, *G3025*
Rev 14:19 *it* into the great w of the wrath of God. *G3025*
20 And the w was trodden without the *G3025*
20 came out of the w, even unto the horse *G3025*
19:15 he treadeth the w of the fierceness and *G3025*

WINEPRESSES
Job 24:11 *and* tread *their* w, and suffer thirst. H3342
Jer 48:33 to fail from the w: none shall tread with H3342
Zec 14:10 tower of Hananeel unto the king's w. H3342

WINES
Isa 25: 6 fat things, a feast of w on the lees, of fat H8105
6 marrow, of w on the lees well refined. H8105

WING
1Ki 6:24 And five cubits *was* the one w of the H3671
24 cubits the other w of the cherub: from H3671
24 part of the one w unto the uttermost H3671
27 so that the w of the one touched H3671
27 *one* wall, and the w of the other cherub H3671
2Ch 3:11 cubits long: one w *of the one cherub* H3671
11 and the other w *was likewise* five H3671
11 reaching to the w of the other cherub. H3671
12 And *one* w of the other cherub *was* five H3671
12 and the other w *was* five cubits *also,* H3671
12 joining to the w of the other cherub. H3671
Isa 10:14 the w, or opened the mouth, or peeped. H3671
Ezk 17:23 all fowl of every w; in the shadow of the H3671

WINGED
Gen 1:21 kind, and every w fowl after his kind: H3671
Dt 4:17 of any w fowl that flieth in the air, H3671

WINGS
Ex 19: 4 eagles' w, and brought you unto myself. H3671
25:20 stretch forth *their* w on high, covering H3671
20 seat with their w, and their faces *shall* H3671
37: 9 And the cherubims spread out *their* w H3671
9 covered with their w over the mercy H3671
Lev 1:17 And he shall cleave it with the w H3671
Dt 32:11 abroad her w, taketh them, beareth H3671
11 taketh them, beareth them on her w: H84
Ru 2:12 under whose w thou art come to trust. H3671
2Sa 22:11 he was seen upon the w of the wind. H3671
1Ki 6:27 forth the w of the cherubims, so H3671
27 wall; and their w touched one another H3671
8: 6 *even* under the w of the cherubims. H3671
7 forth *their* two w over the place of the H3671
1Ch 28:18 spread out *their* w, and covered the ark
2Ch 3:11 And the w of the cherubims *were* H3671
13 The w of these cherubims spread H3671
5: 7 *even* under the w of the cherubims: H3671
8 For the cherubims spread forth *their* w H3671
Job 39:13 *Gavest thou* the goodly w unto the H3671
13 or w and feathers unto the ostrich? H84
26 *and* stretch her w toward the south? H3671
Ps 17: 8 eye, hide me under the shadow of thy w, H3671
18:10 yea, he did fly upon the w of the wind. H3671
36: 7 their trust under the shadow of thy w. H3671
55: 6 And I said, Oh that I had w like a dove! H83
57: 1 in the shadow of thy w will I make my H3671
61: 4 I will trust in the covert of thy w. Selah. H3671
63: 7 in the shadow of thy w will I rejoice. H3671
68:13 *shall ye be* as the w of a dove covered H3671
91: 4 and under his w shalt thou trust: his H3671
104: 3 who walketh upon the w of the wind: H3671
139: 9 *If* I take the w of the morning, *and* H3671
Prv 23: 5 make themselves w; they fly away as an H3671
Ecc 10:20 that which hath w shall tell the matter. H3671
Isa 6: 2 each one had six w; with twain he H3671
8: 8 out of his w shall fill the breadth H3671
18: 1 Woe to the land shadowing with w, H3671
40:31 mount up with w as eagles; they shall H83
Jer 48: 9 Give w unto Moab, that it may flee and H6731
40 and shall spread his w over Moab. H3671
49:22 and spread his w over Bozrah: and at H3671
Ezk 1: 6 four faces, and every one had four w. H3671

Ezk 1: 8 of a man under their w on their four H3671
8 they four had their faces and their w. H3671
9 Their w were joined one to another; H3671
11 Thus were their faces: and their w were H3671
11 upward; two w of every one were joined
23 And under the firmament were their w H3671
24 the noise of their w, like the noise of H3671
24 when they stood, they let down their w. H3671
25 they stood, and had let down their w. H3671
3:13 I heard also the noise of the w of the H3671
10: 5 And the sound of the cherubims' w was H3671
8 the form of a man's hand under their w. H3671
12 hands, and their w, and the wheels, H3671
16 lifted up their w to mount up from the H3671
19 And the cherubims lifted up their w, H3671
21 every one four w; and the likeness of H3671
21 the hands of a man was under their w. H3671
11:22 Then did the cherubims lift up their w, H3671
17: 3 eagle with great w, longwinged, full of H3671
7 eagle with great w and many feathers: H3671
Dan 7: 4 lion, and had eagle's w: I beheld till the H1611
4 I beheld till the w thereof were plucked, H1611
6 the back of it four w of a fowl; the beast H1611
Hos 4:19 The wind hath bound her up in her w, H3671
Zec 5: 9 wind was in their w; for they had wings H3671
9 for they had w like the wings of a stork: H3671
9 had wings like the w of a stork: and H3671
Mal 4: 2 healing in his w; and ye shall go forth, H3671
Mt 23:37 under her w, and ye would not! G4420
Lk 13:34 brood under her w, and ye would not! G4420
Rev 4: 8 each of them six w about him; and they G4420
9: 9 the sound of their w was as the sound G4420
12:14 And to the woman were given two w of G4420

WINK
Job 15:12 thee away? and what do thy eyes w at, H7335
Ps 35:19 me: neither let them w with the eye that H7169

WINKED
Act 17:30 And the times of this ignorance God w G5237

WINKETH
Prv 6:13 He w with his eyes, he speaketh with H7169
10:10 He that w with the eye causeth sorrow: H7169

WINNETH
Prv 11:30 tree of life; and he that w souls is wise. H3947

WINNOWED
Isa 30:24 w with the shovel and with the fan. H2219

WINNOWETH
Ru 3: 2 w barley to night in the threshingfloor. H2219

WINTER
Gen 8:22 w, and day and night shall not cease. H2779
Ps 74:17 earth: thou hast made summer and w. H2779
Song 2:11 For, lo, the w is past, the rain is over H5638
Isa 18: 6 beasts of the earth shall w upon them. H2778
Am 3:15 And I will smite the w house with the H2779
Zec 14: 8 sea: in summer and in w shall it be. H2779
Mt 24:20 in the w, neither on the sabbath day: G5494
Mk 13:18 pray ye that your flight be not in the w. G5494
Jn 10:22 feast of the dedication, and it was w. G5494
Act 27:12 not commodious to w in, the more part G3915
12 and there to w; which is an haven of G3914
1Co 16: 6 will abide, yea, and w with you, that ye G3914
2Ti 4:21 Do thy diligence to come before w. G5494
Tit 3:12 for I have determined there to w. G3914

WINTERED
Act 28:11 which had w in the isle, whose sign G3914

WINTERHOUSE
Jer 36:22 Now the king sat in the w in the ninth H2779

WIPE
2Ki 21:13 Ahab: and I will w Jerusalem as a man H4229
Neh 13:14 this, and w not out my good deeds H4229
Isa 25: 8 the Lord GOD will w away tears from H4229
Lk 7:38 tears, and did w them with the hairs G1591
10:11 cleaveth on us, we do w off against you: G631
Jn 13: 5 feet, and to w them with the towel G1591
Rev 7:17 shall w away all tears from their eyes. G1813
21: 4 And God shall w away all tears from G1813

WIPED
Prv 6:33 and his reproach shall not be w away. H4229
Lk 7:44 and w them with the hairs of her head. G1591
Jn 11: 2 ointment, and w his feet with her hair, G1591
12: 3 the feet of Jesus, and w his feet with her G1591

WIPETH
2Ki 21:13 as a man w a dish, wiping it, and H4229
Prv 30:20 she eateth, and w her mouth, and H4229

WIPING
2Ki 21:13 dish, w it, and turning it upside down. H4229

WINGS (cont.) – WISDOM

WIRES
Ex 39: 3 and cut it into w, to work it in the blue, H6616

WISDOM
Ex 28: 3 with the spirit of w, that they may make H2451
31: 3 the spirit of God, in w, and in H2451
6 hearted I have put w, that they may H2451
35:26 stirred them up in w spun goats' hair. H2451
31 spirit of God, in w, in understanding, H2451
35 Them hath he filled with w of heart, to H2451
36: 1 the LORD put w and understanding H2451
2 the LORD had put w, even every one H2451
Dt 4: 6 them; for this is your w and your H2451
34: 9 full of the spirit of w; for Moses had laid H2451
2Sa 14:20 according to the w of an angel of God, H2451
20:22 the people in her w. And they cut off the H2451
1Ki 2: 6 Do therefore according to thy w, and let H2451
3:28 w of God was in him, to do judgment. H2451
4:29 And God gave Solomon w and H2451
30 And Solomon's w excelled the wisdom H2451
30 And Solomon's wisdom excelled the w H2451
30 the east country, and all the w of Egypt. H2451
34 people to hear the w of Solomon, from H2451
34 of the earth, which had heard of his w. H2451
5:12 And the LORD gave Solomon w, as he H2451
7:14 and he was filled with w, and H2451
10: 4 w, and the house that he had built, H2451
6 mine own land of thy acts and of thy w. H2451
7 was not told me: thy w and prosperity H2451
8 before thee, and that hear thy w. H2451
23 kings of the earth for riches and for w. H2451
24 his w, which God had put in his heart. H2451
11:41 he did, and his w, are they not written H2451
1Ch 22:12 Only the LORD give thee w and H7922
2Ch 1:10 Give me now w and knowledge, that I H2451
11 but hast asked w and knowledge for H2451
12 W and knowledge is granted unto thee; H2451
9: 3 had seen the w of Solomon, and the H2451
5 own land of thine acts, and of thy w: H2451
6 greatness of thy w was not told me: for H2451
7 continually before thee, and hear thy w. H2451
22 the kings of the earth in riches and w. H2451
23 his w, that God had put in his heart. H2451
Ezr 7:25 And thou, Ezra, after the w of thy God, H2452
Job 4:21 go away? they die, even without w. H2451
6:13 Is not my help in me? and is w driven H8454
11: 6 shew thee the secrets of w, that they are H2451
12: 2 No doubt but ye are the people, and w H2451
12 With the ancient is w; and in length of H2451
13 With him is w and strength, he hath H2451
16 With him is strength and w: the H8454
13: 5 your peace! and it should be your w. H2451
15: 8 and dost thou restrain w to thyself? H2451
26: 3 him that hath no w? and how hast thou H2451
28:12 But where shall w be found? and where H2451
18 for the price of w is above rubies. H2451
20 Whence then cometh w? and where is H2451
28 the Lord, that is w; and to depart from H2451
32: 7 and multitude of years should teach w. H2451
13 w: God thrusteth him down, not man. H2451
33:33 hold thy peace, and I shall teach thee w. H2451
34:35 and his words were without w. H7919
36: 5 not any: he is mighty in strength and w. H3820
38:36 Who hath put w in the inward parts? or H2451
37 Who can number the clouds in w? or H2451
39:17 Because God hath deprived her of w, H2451
26 Doth the hawk fly by thy w, and stretch H998
Ps 37:30 The mouth of the righteous speaketh w, H2451
49: 3 My mouth shall speak of w; and the H2454
51: 6 part thou shalt make me to know w. H2451
90:12 that we may apply our hearts unto w. H2451
104:24 are thy works! in w hast thou made H2451
105:22 his pleasure; and teach his senators w. H2449
111:10 is the beginning of w: a good H2451
136: 5 To him that by w made the heavens: H8394
Prv 1: 2 To know w and instruction; to perceive H2451
3 To receive the instruction of w, justice, H7919
7 but fools despise w and instruction. H2451
20 W crieth without; she uttereth her H2454
2: 2 So that thou incline thine ear unto w, H2451
6 For the LORD giveth w: out of his H2451
7 He layeth up sound w for the righteous: H8454
10 When w entereth into thine heart, and H2451
3:13 Happy is the man that findeth w, and H2451
19 The LORD by w hath founded the H2451
21 eyes: keep sound w and discretion: H8454
4: 5 Get w, get understanding: forget it not; H2451
7 W is the principal thing; therefore get H2451
7 therefore get w: and with all thy getting H2451
11 I have taught thee in the way of w; I H2451
5: 1 My son, attend unto my w, and bow H2451
7: 4 Say unto w, Thou art my sister; and call H2451
8: 1 Doth not w cry? and understanding put H2451
5 O ye simple, understand w: and, ye H6195
11 For w is better than rubies; and all the H2451
12 I w dwell with prudence, and find out H2451
14 Counsel is mine, and sound w: I am H8454
9: 1 W hath builded her house, she hath H2454
10 the beginning of w: and the knowledge H2451
10:13 understanding w is found: but a rod H2451
21 feed many: but fools die for want of w. H3820
23 but a man of understanding hath w. H2451
31 The mouth of the just bringeth forth w: H2451
11: 2 cometh shame: but with the lowly is w. H2451
12 He that is void of w despiseth his H3820
12: 8 according to his w: but he that is of a H7922
13:10 but with the well advised is w. H2451
14: 6 A scorner seeketh w, and findeth it not: H2451
8 The w of the prudent is to understand H2451
33 W resteth in the heart of him that hath H2451
15:21 Folly is joy to him that is destitute of w: H3820
33 of w; and before honour is humility. H2451
16:16 How much better is it to get w than H2451
17:16 to get w, seeing he hath no heart to it? H2451
24 W is before him that hath H2451
18: 1 seeketh and intermeddleth with all w. H8454
4 the wellspring of w as a flowing brook. H2451
19: 8 He that getteth w loveth his own soul: H3820
21:30 There is no w nor understanding nor H2451
23: 4 not to be rich: cease from thine own w. H998
9 for he will despise the w of thy words. H7922
23 Buy the truth, and sell it not; also w, H2451
24: 3 Through w is an house builded; and by H2451
7 W is too high for a fool: he openeth not H2454
14 So shall the knowledge of w be unto thy H2451
29: 3 Whoso loveth w rejoiceth his father: H2451
15 The rod and reproof give w: but a child H2451
30: 3 I neither learned w, nor have the H2451
31:26 She openeth her mouth with w; and in H2451
Ecc 1:13 and search out by w concerning all H2451
16 have gotten more w than all they that H2451
16 great experience of w and knowledge. H2451
17 And I gave my heart to know w, and to H2451
18 For in much w is much grief: and he H2451
2: 3 mine heart with w; and to lay hold on H2451
9 also my w remained with me. H2451
12 And I turned myself to behold w, and H2451
13 Then I saw that w excelleth folly, as far H2451
21 For there is a man whose labour is in w, H2451
26 good in his sight w, and knowledge, and H2451
7:11 W is good with an inheritance: and by H2451
12 For w is a defence, and money is a H2451
12 that w giveth life to them that have it. H2451
19 W strengtheneth the wise more than H2451
23 All this have I proved by w: I said, I will H2451
25 and to seek out w, and the reason of H2451
8: 1 a thing? a man's w maketh his face to H2451
16 When I applied mine heart to know w, H2451
9:10 nor w, in the grave, whither thou goest. H2451
13 This w have I seen also under the sun, H2451
15 and he by his w delivered the city; yet H2451
16 Then said I, W is better than strength: H2451
16 the poor man's w is despised, and his H2451
18 W is better than weapons of war: but H2451
10: 1 that is in reputation for w and honour. H2451
3 by the way, his w faileth him, and he H3820
10 strength: but w is profitable to direct. H2451
Isa 10:13 it, and by my w; for I am prudent: and H2451
11: 2 him, the spirit of w and understanding, H2451
29:14 a wonder: for the w of their wise men H2451
33: 6 And w and knowledge shall be the H2451
47:10 seeth me. Thy w and thy knowledge, H2451
Jer 8: 9 of the LORD; and what w is in them? H2451
9:23 wise man glory in his w, neither let the H2451
10:12 the world by his w, and hath stretched H2451
49: 7 the LORD of hosts; Is w no more in H2451
7 from the prudent? is their w vanished? H2451
51:15 the world by his w, and hath stretched H2451

Ezk 28: 4 With thy w and with thine H2451
5 By thy great w *and* by thy traffick hast H2451
7 w, and they shall defile thy brightness. H2451
12 sum, full of w, and perfect in beauty. H2451
17 hast corrupted thy w by reason of thy H2451
Dan 1: 4 and skilful in all w, and cunning in H2451
17 in all learning and w: and Daniel had H2451
20 And in all matters of w *and* H2451
2:14 with counsel and w to Arioch the H2942
20 ever and ever: for w and might are his: H2452
21 kings: he giveth w unto the wise, and H2452
23 hast given me w and might, and hast H2452
30 to me for *any* w that I have more than H2452
5:11 and w, like the wisdom of the H2452
11 wisdom, like the w of the gods, was H2452
14 and excellent w is found in thee. H2452
Mic 6: 9 and *the man of* w shall see thy name: H8454
Mt 11:19 But w is justified of her children. G4678
12:42 earth to hear the w of Solomon; and, G4678
13:54 *man* this w, and *these* mighty works? G4678
Mk 6: 2 things? and what w *is* this which is G4678
Lk 1:17 the disobedient to the w of the just; to G5428
2:40 w: and the grace of God was upon him. G4678
52 And Jesus increased in w and stature, G4678
7:35 But w is justified of all her children. G4678
11:31 earth to hear the w of Solomon; and, G4678
49 Therefore also said the w of God, I will G4678
21:15 For I will give you a mouth and w, G4678
Act 6: 3 the Holy Ghost and w, whom we may G4678
10 And they were not able to resist the w G4678
7:10 gave him favour and w in the sight of G4678
22 And Moses was learned in all the w of G4678
Ro 11:33 O the depth of the riches both of the w G4678
1Co 1:17 the gospel: not with w of words, lest the G4678
19 For it is written, I will destroy the w of G4678
20 God made foolish the w of this world? G4678
21 For after that in the w of God the world G4678
21 of God the world by w knew not God, it G4678
22 a sign, and the Greeks seek after w: G4678
24 the power of God, and the w of God. G4678
30 is made unto us w, and righteousness, G4678
2: 1 of speech or of w, declaring unto you G4678
4 enticing words of man's w, but in G4678
5 the w of men, but in the power of God. G4678
6 Howbeit we speak w among them that G4678
6 yet not the w of this world, nor of G4678
7 But we speak the w of God in a G4678
7 *even* the hidden *w*, which God ordained
13 which man's w teacheth, but which G4678
3:19 For the w of this world is foolishness G4678
12: 8 the Spirit the word of w; to another the G4678
2Co 1:12 not with fleshly w, but by the grace of G4678
Eph 1: 8 toward us in all w and prudence; G4678
17 you the spirit of w and revelation in the G4678
3:10 by the church the manifold w of God, G4678
Col 1: 9 in all w and spiritual understanding; G4678
28 every man in all w; that we may present G4678
2: 3 In whom are hid all the treasures of w G4678
23 Which things have indeed a shew of w G4678
3:16 in you richly in all w; teaching and G4678
4: 5 Walk in w toward them that are G4678
Jas 1: 5 If any of you lack w, let him ask of God, G4678
3:13 his works with meekness of w. G4678
15 This w descendeth not from above, but G4678
17 But the w that is from above is first G4678
2Pt 3:15 according to the w given unto him hath G4678
Rev 5:12 and riches, and w, and strength, and G4678
7:12 and glory, and w, and thanksgiving, G4678
13:18 Here is w. Let him that hath G4678
17: 9 And here *is* the mind which hath w. The G4678

WISE

Gen 3: 6 to make *one* w, she took of the fruit H7919
41: 8 Egypt, and all the w men thereof: and H2450
33 w, and set him over the land of Egypt. H2450
39 *is* none so discreet and w as thou *art*: H2450
Ex 7:11 Then Pharaoh also called the w men H2450
22:23 If thou afflict them in any w, and they H6031
23: 8 gift blindeth the w, and perverteth the H6493
28: 3 unto all *that are* w hearted, whom I H2450
31: 6 of all that are w hearted I have put H2450
35:10 And every w hearted among you shall H2450
25 And all the women that were w hearted H2450
36: 1 and every w hearted man, in whom H2450
2 and every w hearted man, in whose H2450
4 And all the w men, that wrought all the H2450
8 And every w hearted man among them H2450
Lev 7:24 other use: but ye shall in no w eat of it. H398
19:17 heart: thou shalt in any w rebuke thy H3198
Lev 27:19 field will in any w redeem it, then he H1350
Nu 6:23 saying, On this w ye shall bless the H3541
Dt 1:13 Take you w men, and understanding, H2450
15 So I took the chief of your tribes, w H2450
4: 6 *is* a w and understanding people. H2450
16:19 the eyes of the w, and pervert the words H2450
17:15 Thou shalt in any w set *him* king over H7760
21:23 thou shalt in any w bury him that day; H6912
22: 7 *But* thou shalt in any w let the dam go, H7971
32:29 O that they were w, *that* they H2449
Jos 6:18 And ye, in any w keep *yourselves* from H7535
23:12 Else if ye do in any w go back, and H7725
Jdg 5:29 Her w ladies answered her, yea, she H2450
1Sa 6: 3 not empty; but in any w return him a H7725
2Sa 14: 2 fetched thence a w woman, and said H2450
20 and my lord *is* w, according to the H2450
20:16 Then cried a w woman out of the city, H2450
1Ki 2: 9 for thou *art* a w man, and knowest H2450
3:12 I have given thee a w and an H2450
26 child, and in no w slay it. But the other H4191
27 no w slay it: she *is* the mother thereof. H4191
5: 7 David a w son over this great people. H2450
11:22 Nothing: howbeit let me go in any w. H7971
1Ch 26:14 his son, a w counsellor, they cast H7922
27:32 was a counsellor, a w man, and a scribe: H995
2Ch 2:12 to David the king a w son, endued with H2450
Est 1:13 Then the king said to the w men, which H2450
6:13 Then said his w men and Zeresh his H2450
Job 5:13 He taketh the w in their own craftiness: H2450
9: 4 *He is* w in heart, and mighty in H2450
11:12 For vain man would be w, though man H3823
15: 2 Should a w man utter vain knowledge, H2450
18 Which w men have told from their H2450
17:10 I cannot find *one* w *man* among you. H2450
22: 2 is w may be profitable unto himself? H7919
32: 9 Great men are not *always* w: neither do H2449
34: 2 Hear my words, O ye w *men*; and give H2450
34 me, and let a w man hearken unto me. H2450
37:24 respecteth not any *that are* w of heart. H2450
Ps 2:10 Be w now therefore, O ye kings: be H7919
19: 7 the LORD *is* sure, making w the simple. H2449
36: 3 he hath left off to be w, *and* to do good. H7919
37: 8 fret not thyself in any w to do evil. H389
49:10 For he seeth *that* w men die, likewise H2450
94: 8 people: and *ye* fools, when will ye be w? H7919
107:43 Whoso *is* w, and will observe these H2450
Prv 1: 5 A w *man* will hear, and will increase H2450
5 shall attain unto w counsels:
6 words of the w, and their dark sayings. H2450
3: 7 Be not w in thine own eyes: fear the H2450
35 The w shall inherit glory: but shame H2450
6: 6 sluggard; consider her ways, and be w: H2449
8:33 Hear instruction, and be w, and refuse H2449
9: 8 rebuke a w man, and he will love thee. H2450
9 Give *instruction* to a w *man*, and he H2450
12 If thou be w, thou shalt be wise for H2449
12 If thou be wise, thou shalt be w for H2449
10: 1 The proverbs of Solomon. A w son H2450
5 He that gathereth in summer *is* a w H7919
8 The w in heart will receive H2450
14 W *men* lay up knowledge: but the H2450
19 sin: but he that refraineth his lips *is* w. H7919
11:29 fool *shall be* servant to the w of heart. H2450
30 of life; and he that winneth souls *is* w. H2450
12:15 he that hearkeneth unto counsel *is* w. H2450
18 but the tongue of the w *is* health. H2450
13: 1 A w son *heareth* his father's H2450
14 The law of the w *is* a fountain of life, to H2450
20 He that walketh with w *men* shall be H2450
20 wise *men* shall be w: but a companion H2449
14: 1 Every w woman buildeth her house: H2454
3 the lips of the w shall preserve them. H2450
16 A w *man* feareth, and departeth from H2450
24 The crown of the w *is* their riches: *but* H2450
35 The king's favour *is* toward a w H7919
15: 2 The tongue of the w useth knowledge H2450
7 The lips of the w disperse knowledge: H2450
12 him: neither will he go unto the w. H2450
20 A w son maketh a glad father: but a H2450
24 The way of life *is* above to the w, that he H7919
31 the reproof of life abideth among the w. H2450
16:14 of death: but a w man will pacify it. H2450
21 The w in heart shall be called prudent: H2450
23 The heart of the w teacheth his mouth, H2450
17: 2 A w servant shall have rule over a son H7919
10 A reproof entereth more into a w man H995
28 his peace, is counted w: *and* he that H2450
18:15 the ear of the w seeketh knowledge. H2450
19:20 that thou mayest be w in thy latter end. H2449
Prv 20: 1 whosoever is deceived thereby is not w. H2449
26 A w king scattereth the wicked, and H2450
21:11 simple is made w: and when the wise H2449
11 wise: and when the w is instructed, he H2450
20 the w; but a foolish man spendeth it up. H2450
22 A w *man* scaleth the city of the mighty, H2450
22:17 the words of the w, and apply thine H2450
23:15 My son, if thine heart be w, my heart H2449
19 Hear thou, my son, and be w, and guide H2449
24 a w *child* shall have joy of him. H2450
24: 5 A w man *is* strong; yea, a man of H2450
6 For by w counsel thou shalt make thy
23 These *things* also *belong* to the w. *It is* H2450
25:12 *is* a w reprover upon an obedient ear. H2450
26: 5 folly, lest he be w in his own conceit. H2450
12 Seest thou a man w in his own conceit? H2450
27:11 My son, be w, and make my heart glad, H2449
28: 7 Whoso keepeth the law *is* a w son: but H995
11 The rich man *is* w in his own conceit; H2450
29: 8 a snare: but w *men* turn away wrath. H2450
9 *If* a w man contendeth with a foolish H2450
11 A fool uttereth all his mind: but a w H2450
30:24 the earth, but they *are* exceeding w: H2450
Ecc 2:14 The w man's eyes *are* in his head; but H2450
15 was I then more w? Then I said in my H2449
16 For *there is* no remembrance of the w H2450
16 And how dieth the w *man*? as the fool. H2450
19 he shall be a w *man* or a fool? yet shall H2450
19 w under the sun. This *is* also vanity. H2449
4:13 Better *is* a poor and a w child than an H2450
6: 8 For what hath the w more than the H2450
7: 4 The heart of the w *is* in the house of H2450
5 *It is* better to hear the rebuke of the w, H2450
7 Surely oppression maketh a w man H2450
16 w: why shouldest thou destroy thyself? H2449
19 Wisdom strengtheneth the w more H2450
23 said, I will be w; but it *was* far from me. H2449
8: 1 Who *is* as the w *man*? and who H2450
5 no evil thing: and a w man's heart H2450
17 further; though a w *man* think to know H2450
9: 1 righteous, and the w, and their works, H2450
11 yet bread to the w, nor yet riches to men H2450
15 Now there was found in it a poor w H2450
17 The words of w *men are* heard in quiet H2450
10: 2 A w man's heart *is* at his right hand; H2450
12 The words of a w man's mouth *are* H2450
12: 9 the preacher was w, he still taught the H2450
11 The words of the w *are* as goads, and H2450
Isa 5:21 Woe unto *them that are* w in their own H2450
19:11 the counsel of the w counsellors of H2450
11 son of the w, the son of ancient kings? H2450
12 Where *are* they? where *are* thy w *men*? H2450
29:14 the wisdom of their w *men* shall perish, H2450
31: 2 Yet he also *is* w, and will bring evil, and H2450
44:25 mad; that turneth w *men* backward, H2450
Jer 4:22 they *are* w to do evil, but to do H2450
8: 8 How do ye say, We *are* w, and the law H2450
9 The w *men* are ashamed, they are H2450
9:12 Who *is* the w man, that may H2450
23 Thus saith the LORD, Let not the w H2450
10: 7 as among all the w *men* of the nations, H2450
18:18 counsel from the w, nor the word from H2450
50:35 upon her princes, and upon her w *men*. H2450
51:57 princes, and her w *men*, her captains, H2450
Ezk 27: 8 thy mariners: thy w *men*, O Tyrus, *that* H2450
9 The ancients of Gebal and the w *men* H2450
Dan 2:12 to destroy all the w *men* of Babylon. H2445
13 And the decree went forth that the w H2445
14 forth to slay the w *men* of Babylon: H2445
18 with the rest of the w *men* of Babylon. H2445
21 wisdom unto the w, and knowledge to H2445
24 to destroy the w *men* of Babylon: he H2445
24 Destroy not the w *men* of Babylon: H2445
27 cannot the w *men*, the astrologers, H2445
48 over all the w *men* of Babylon. H2445
4: 6 to bring in all the w *men* of Babylon H2445
18 as all the w *men* of my kingdom H2445
5: 7 and said to the w *men* of Babylon, H2445
8 Then came in all the king's w *men*: but H2445
15 And now the w *men*, the astrologers, H2445
12: 3 And they that be w shall shine as the H7919
10 but the w shall understand. H7919
Hos 14: 9 Who *is* w, and he shall understand H2450
Oba 8 even destroy the w *men* out of Edom, H2450
Zec 9: 2 Tyrus, and Zidon, though it be very w. H2449
Mt 1:18 Jesus Christ was on this w: When as his G3779
2: 1 w men from the east to Jerusalem, G3097
7 privily called the w men, inquired of G3097
16 mocked of the w men, was exceeding G3097

Mt 2:16 had diligently inquired of the **w** men. *G3097*
5:18 **w** pass from the law, till all be fulfilled. *G3364*
7:24 liken him unto a **w** man, which built *G5429*
10:16 **w** as serpents, and harmless as doves. *G5429*
42 you, he shall in no **w** lose his reward. *G3364*
11:25 things from the **w** and prudent, and *G4680*
21:24 if ye tell me, I in like **w** will tell you by *G2504*
23:34 you prophets, and **w** men, and scribes: *G4680*
24:45 Who then is a faithful and **w** servant, *G5429*
25: 2 And five of them were **w**, and five *were* *G5429*
4 But the **w** took oil in their vessels with *G5429*
8 And the foolish said unto the **w**, Give us *G5429*
9 But the **w** answered, saying, *Not so*; *G5429*
Mk 14:31 in any **w**. Likewise also said they all. *G3364*
Lk 10:21 things from the **w** and prudent, and *G4680*
12:42 that faithful and **w** steward, whom *his* *G5429*
13:11 and could in no **w** lift up *herself*. *G1519*
18:17 a little child shall in no **w** enter therein. *G3364*
Jn 6:37 cometh to me I will in no **w** cast out. *G3364*
21: 1 and on this **w** shewed he *himself*. *G3779*
Act 7: 6 And God spake on this **w**, That his seed *G3779*
13:34 he said on this **w**, I will give you the *G3779*
41 ye shall in no **w** believe, though a man *G3364*
Ro 1:14 both to the **w**, and to the unwise. *G4680*
22 Professing themselves to be **w**, they *G4680*
3: 9 *they*? No, in no **w**: for we have before *G3843*
10: 6 speaketh on this **w**, Say not in thine *G3779*
11:25 lest ye should be **w** in your own *G5429*
12:16 estate. Be not **w** in your own conceits. *G5429*
16:19 I would have you **w** unto that which is *G4680*
27 To God only **w**, *be* glory through Jesus *G4680*
1Co 1:19 the wisdom of the **w**, and will bring to *G4680*
20 Where *is* the **w**? where *is* the scribe? *G4680*
26 that not many **w** men after the flesh, *G4680*
27 world to confound the **w**; and God hath *G4680*
3:10 unto me, as a **w** masterbuilder, I have *G4680*
18 you seemeth to be **w** in this world, let *G4680*
18 him become a fool, that he may be **w**. *G4680*
19 He taketh the **w** in their own craftiness. *G4680*
20 thoughts of the **w**, that they are vain. *G4680*
4:10 sake, but ye *are* **w** in Christ; we *are* *G5429*
6: 5 that there is not a **w** man among you? *G4680*
10:15 I speak as to **w** men; judge ye what I *G4680*
2Co 10:12 among themselves, are not **w**. *G4920*
11:19 fools gladly, seeing ye *yourselves* are **w**. *G5429*
Eph 5:15 circumspectly, not as fools, but as **w**, *G4680*
1Ti 1:17 invisible, the only **w** God, *be* honour *G4680*
2Ti 3:15 are able to make thee **w** unto salvation *G4679*
Heb 4: 4 *day* on this **w**, And God did rest the *G3779*
Jas 3:13 Who *is* a **w** man and endued with *G4680*
Jude 25 To the only **w** God our Saviour, *be* *G4680*
Rev 21:27 And there shall in no **w** enter into it *G3364*

WISE-HEARTED See WISE and HEARTED.

WISELY
Ex 1:10 Come on, let us deal **w** with them; lest H2449
1Sa 18: 5 behaved himself **w**: and Saul set him H7919
14 And David behaved himself **w** in all his H7919
15 himself very **w**, he was afraid of him. H7919
30 himself more **w** than all the servants H7919
2Ch 11:23 And he dealt **w**, and dispersed of all his H995
Ps 58: 5 of charmers, charming never so **w**. H2449
64: 9 for they shall **w** consider of his doing. H7919
101: 2 I will behave myself **w** in a perfect way. H7919
Prv 16:20 He that handleth a matter **w** shall find H7919
21:12 The righteous *man* **w** considereth the H7919
28:26 whoso walketh **w**, he shall be delivered. H2451
Ecc 7:10 dost not inquire **w** concerning this. H2451
Lk 16: 8 he had done **w**: for the children of this *G5430*

WISE-MEN See WISE and MEN.

WISER
1Ki 4:31 For he was **w** than all men; than Ethan H2449
Job 35:11 maketh us **w** than the fowls of heaven? H2449
Ps 119:98 hast made me **w** than mine enemies: H2449
Prv 9: 9 and he will be yet **w**: teach a just *man*, H2449
26:16 The sluggard *is* **w** in his own conceit H2450
Ezk 28: 3 Behold, thou *art* **w** than Daniel; there is H2450
Lk 16: 8 generation **w** than the children of light. *G5429*
1Co 1:25 Because the foolishness of God is **w** *G4680*

WISH
Job 33: 6 Behold, I *am* according to thy **w** in H6310
Ps 40:14 and put to shame that **w** me evil. H2655
73: 7 they have more than heart could **w**. H4906
Ro 9: 3 For I could **w** that myself were *G2172*
2Co 13: 9 this also we **w**, *even* your perfection. *G2172*
3Jn 2 Beloved, I **w** above all things that thou *G2172*

WISHED
Jna 4: 8 he fainted, and **w** in himself to die, and H7592
Act 27:29 out of the stern, and **w** for the day. *G2172*

WISHING
Job 31:30 mouth to sin by **w** a curse to his soul. H7592

WIST
Ex 16:15 It *is* manna: for they **w** not what it *was*. H3045
34:29 that Moses **w** not that the skin of H3045
Lev 5:17 the LORD; though he **w** *it* not, yet is he H3045
18 **w** *it* not, and it shall be forgiven him. H3045
Jos 2: 4 unto me, but I **w** not whence they *were*: H3045
8:14 the plain; but he **w** not that *there were* H3045
Jdg 16:20 myself. And he **w** not that the LORD H3045
Mk 9: 6 For he **w** not what to say; for they were *G1492*
14:40 neither **w** they what to answer him. *G1492*
Lk 2:49 ye sought me? **w** ye not that I must be *G1492*
Jn 5:13 And he that was healed **w** not who it *G1492*
Act 12: 9 followed him; and **w** not that it was *G1492*
23: 5 Then said Paul, I **w** not, brethren, that *G1492*

WIT
Gen 24:21 held his peace, to **w** whether the LORD H3045
Ex 2: 4 And his sister stood afar off, to **w** what H3045
Jos 17: 1 of Joseph; *to* **w**, for Machir the firstborn
1Ki 2:32 *thereof, to* **w**, Abner the son of Ner,
7:50 doors of the house, *to* **w**, of the temple.
13:23 for him the ass, *to* **w**, for the prophet
2Ki 10:29 after them, *to* **w**, the golden calves that
1Ch 7: 2 father's house, *to* **w**, of Tola: *they were*
27: 1 their number, *to* **w**, the chief fathers and
2Ch 4:12 *To* **w**, the two pillars, and the pommels,
25: 7 *to* **w**, *with* all the children of Ephraim.
10 Then Amaziah separated them, *to* **w**, the
31: 3 the burnt offerings, *to* **w**, for the morning
Neh 11: 3 in their cities, *to* **w**, Israel, the priests,
Est 2:12 accomplished, *to* **w**, six months with oil
Jer 25:18 *To* **w**, Jerusalem, and the cities of Judah,
34: 9 of them, *to* **w**, of a Jew his brother.
Ezk 13:16 *To* **w**, the prophets of Israel which
Ro 8:23 *to* **w**, the redemption of our body.
2Co 5:19 To **w**, that God was in Christ, *G5613*
8: 1 Moreover, brethren, we do you to **w** of *G1107*

WITCH
Ex 22:18 Thou shalt not suffer a **w** to live. H3784
Dt 18:10 of times, or an enchanter, or a **w**, H3784

WITCHCRAFT
1Sa 15:23 For rebellion *is as* the sin of **w**, and H7081
2Ch 33: 6 and used **w**, and dealt with a familiar H3784
Gal 5:20 Idolatry, **w**, hatred, variance, *G5331*

WITCHCRAFTS
2Ki 9:22 mother Jezebel and her **w** *are so* many? H3785
Mic 5:12 And I will cut off **w** out of thine hand; H3785
Nah 3: 4 the mistress of **w**, that selleth nations H3785
4 and families through her **w**. H3785

WITH See the Appendix.

WITHAL
Ex 25:29 **w**: *of* pure gold shalt thou make them. H2004
30: 4 be for places for the staves to bear it **w**. H1992
18 *of* brass, to wash *w*: and thou shalt put it
36: 3 to make it *w*. And they brought yet
37:16 and his covers to cover **w**, *of* pure gold. H2004
27 to be places for the staves to bear it **w**.
38: 7 **w**; he made the altar hollow with boards.
40:30 the altar, and put water there, to wash *w*.
Lev 5: 3 shall be defiled **w**, and it be hid from
6:30 to reconcile **w** in the holy *place*, shall
11:21 their feet, to leap **w** upon the earth; H2004
19:24 shall be holy to praise the LORD *w*.
Nu 4: 7 covers to cover **w**: and the continual H5262
Jdg 7:20 hands to blow *w*: and they cried, The
1Sa 16:12 he *was* ruddy, *and* **w** of a beautiful H5973
1Ki 19: 1 had done, and **w** how he had slain all
2Ki 23:26 that Manasseh had provoked him **w**.
1Ch 29: 4 to overlay the walls of the houses *w*:
2Ch 24:14 and to offer *w*, and spoons, and vessels
26:15 and great stones **w**. And his name spread
Est 6: 9 may array the man *w* whom the king
Job 2: 8 **w**; and he sat down among the ashes.
Ps 141:10 their own nets, whilst that I **w** escape. H3162
Prv 22:18 thee; they shall **w** be fitted in thy lips. H3162
Isa 30:14 hearth, or to take water *w* out of the pit.
23 shalt sow the ground **w**; and bread of the
Mk 10:39 I am baptized **w** shall ye be baptized: *G907*
Lk 6:38 **w** it shall be measured to you again.
Act 25:27 **w** to signify the crimes *laid* against him.
1Co 12: 7 Spirit is given to every man to profit **w**. *G4851*
Col 4: 3 **W** praying also for us, that God would *G260*
1Ti 5:13 And **w** they learn *to be* idle, wandering *G260*
Phlm 22 But **w** prepare me also a lodging: for I *G260*

WITHDRAW
1Sa 14:19 Saul said unto the priest, **W** thine hand. H622
Job 9:13 *If* God will not **w** his anger, the proud H7725
13:21 **W** thine hand far from me: and let not H7368
33:17 That he may **w** man *from his* purpose, H5493
Prv 25:17 **W** thy foot from thy neighbour's house; H3365
Ecc 7:18 also from this **w** not thine hand: for H3240
Isa 60:20 shall thy moon **w** itself: for the LORD H622
Joel 2:10 dark, and the stars shall **w** their shining: H622
3:15 and the stars shall **w** their shining. H622
2Th 3: 6 Christ, that ye **w** yourselves from every *G4724*
1Ti 6: 5 gain is godliness: from such **w** thyself. *G868*

WITHDRAWEST
Ps 74:11 Why **w** thou thy hand, even thy right H7725

WITHDRAWETH
Job 36: 7 He **w** not his eyes from the righteous: H1639

WITHDRAWN
Dt 13:13 you, and have **w** the inhabitants of H5080
Song 5: 6 but my beloved had **w** himself, *and* was H2559
Lam 2: 8 out a line, he hath not **w** his hand from H7725
Ezk 18: 8 *that* hath **w** his hand from iniquity, H7725
Hos 5: 6 find *him*; he hath **w** himself from them. H2502
Lk 22:41 And he was **w** from them about a stone's *G645*

WITHDREW
Neh 9:29 in them;) and **w** the shoulder, H5414+H5637
Ezk 20:22 Nevertheless I **w** mine hand, and H7725
Mt 12:15 But when Jesus knew *it*, he **w** himself *G402*
Mk 3: 7 But Jesus **w** himself with his disciples to *G402*
Lk 5:16 And he **w** himself into the wilderness, *G2258*
Gal 2:12 they were come, he **w** and separated *G5288*

WITHER
Ps 1: 3 leaf also shall not **w**; and whatsoever he H5034
37: 2 like the grass, and **w** as the green herb. H5034
Isa 19: 6 dried up: the reeds and flags shall **w**. H7060
7 **w**, be driven away, and be no *more*. H3001
40:24 and they shall **w**, and the whirlwind H3001
Jer 12: 4 of every field **w**, for the wickedness H3001
Ezk 17: 9 thereof, that it **w**? it shall wither in all H3001
9 it wither? it shall **w** in all the leaves of H3001
10 shall it not utterly **w**, when the east H3001
10 it shall **w** in the furrows where it grew. H3001
Am 1: 2 mourn, and the top of Carmel shall **w**. H3001

WITHERED
Gen 41:23 And, behold, seven ears, **w**, thin, *and* H6798
Ps 102: 4 My heart is smitten, and **w** like grass; H3001
11 that declineth; and I am **w** like grass. H3001
Isa 15: 6 for the hay is **w** away, the grass faileth, H3001
27:11 When the boughs thereof are **w**, they H3001
Lam 4: 8 bones; it is **w**, it is become like a stick. H3001
Ezk 19:12 broken and **w**; the fire consumed them. H3001
Joel 1:12 trees of the field, are **w**: because joy is H3001
12 joy is **w** away from the sons of men. H3001
17 are broken down; for the corn is **w**. H3001
Am 4: 7 the piece whereupon it rained not **w**. H3001
Jna 4: 7 day, and it smote the gourd that it **w**. H3001
Mt 12:10 had *his* hand **w**. And they asked him, *G3584*
13: 6 because they had no root, they **w** away. *G3583*
21:19 ever. And presently the fig tree **w** away. *G3583*
20 How soon is the fig tree **w** away! *G3583*
Mk 3: 1 was a man there which had a **w** hand. *G3583*
3 which had the **w** hand, Stand forth. *G3583*
4: 6 and because it had no root, it **w** away. *G3583*
11:21 fig tree which thou cursedst is **w** away. *G3583*
Lk 6: 6 was a man whose right hand was **w**. *G3584*
8 which had the **w** hand, Rise up, and *G3584*
8: 6 it **w** away, because it lacked moisture. *G3583*
Jn 5: 3 **w**, waiting for the moving of the water. *G3584*
15: 6 as a branch, and is **w**; and men gather *G3583*

WITHERETH
Job 8:12 cut down, it **w** before any *other* herb. H3001
Ps 90: 6 up; in the evening it is cut down, and **w**. H3001
129: 6 which **w** afore it groweth up: H3001

Isa 40: 7 The grass w, the flower fadeth: because H3001
8 The grass w, the flower fadeth: but the H3001
Jas 1:11 heat, but it w the grass, and the flower *G3583*
1Pt 1:24 w, and the flower thereof falleth away: *G3583*
Jude 12 trees whose fruit w, without fruit, twice *G5352*

WITHHELD
Gen 20: 6 heart; for I also w thee from sinning H2820
22:12 not w thy son, thine only *son* from me. H2820
16 and hast not w thy son, thine only *son:* H2820
30: 2 w from thee the fruit of the womb? H4513
Job 31:16 If I have w the poor from *their* desire, H4513
Ecc 2:10 not from them, I w not my heart from H4513

WITHHELDEST
Neh 9:20 them, and w not thy manna from H4513

WITHHOLD
Gen 23: 6 dead; none of us shall w from thee his H3607
2Sa 13:13 king; for he will not w me from thee. H4513
Job 4: 2 but who can w himself from speaking? H6113
Ps 40:11 W not thou thy tender mercies from H3607
84:11 he w from them that walk uprightly. H4513
Prv 3:27 W not good from them to whom it is H4513
23:13 W not correction from the child: for *if* H4513
Ecc 11: 6 in the evening w not thine hand: for H3240
Jer 2:25 W thy foot from being unshod, and thy H4513

WITHHOLDEN
1Sa 25:26 the LORD hath w thee from coming to H4513
Job 22: 7 thou hast w bread from the hungry. H4513
38:15 And from the wicked their light is w, H4513
42: 2 *that* no thought can be w from thee. H1219
Ps 21: 2 hast not w the request of his lips. Selah. H4513
Jer 3: 3 Therefore the showers have been w, H4513
5:25 your sins have w good *things* from you. H4513
Ezk 18:16 any, hath not w the pledge, neither H2254
Joel 1:13 is w from the house of your God. H4513
Am 4: 7 And also I have w the rain from you, H4513

WITHHOLDETH
Job 12:15 Behold, he w the waters, and they dry H6113
Prv 11:24 and *there is* that w more than is meet, H2820
26 He that w corn, the people shall curse H4513
2Th 2: 6 And now ye know what w that he *G2722*

WITHIN
Gen 6:14 shalt pitch it w and without with pitch. H1004
9:21 and he was uncovered w his tent. H8432
18:12 Therefore Sarah laughed w herself, H7130
24 Peradventure there be fifty righteous w H8432
26 fifty righteous w the city, then I will H8432
25:22 And the children struggled together w H7130
39:11 none of the men of the house there w. H1004
40:13 Yet w three days shall Pharaoh lift up H7969
19 Yet w three days shall Pharaoh lift up H7969
Ex 20:10 nor thy stranger that *is* w thy gates:
25:11 it with pure gold, w and without shalt H1004
26:33 bring in thither w the vail the ark of the H1004
37: 2 And he overlaid it with pure gold w H1004
Lev 10:18 was not brought in w the holy *place*: ye H6441
13:55 *whether* it *be* bare w or without. H7146
14:41 to be scraped w round about, and they H1004
16: 2 into the holy *place* w the vail before the H1004
12 beaten small, and bring *it* w the vail: H1004
15 bring his blood w the vail, and do with H1004
25:29 he may redeem it w a whole year after H5701
29 is sold; *w* a full year may he redeem it. H8537
30 And if it be not redeemed w the space H5701
26:25 are gathered together w your cities, I will H413
Nu 4:10 all the vessels thereof w a covering of H413
18: 7 of the altar, and w the vail; and ye shall H1004
Dt 5:14 thy stranger that *is* w thy gates; that thy
12:12 and the Levite that *is* w your gates;
17 Thou mayest not eat w thy gates the
18 the Levite that *is* w thy gates: and thou
14:27 And the Levite that *is* w thy gates; thou
28 year, and shalt lay *it* up w thy gates:
29 the widow, which *are* w thy gates, shall
15: 7 of thy brethren w any of thy gates in thy
22 Thou shalt eat it w thy gates: the
16: 5 the passover w any of thy gates, which
11 the Levite that *is* w thy gates, and the
14 and the widow, that *are* w thy gates.
17: 2 If there be found among you, w any of
8 of controversy w thy gates: then shalt
23:10 camp, he shall not come w the camp: H8432
24:14 that *are* in thy land w thy gates:
26:12 they may eat w thy gates, and be filled;
Dt 28:43 The stranger that *is* w thee shall get up H7130
31:12 thy stranger that *is* w thy gates, that they
32:25 The sword without, and terror w, shall H2315
Jos 1:11 you victuals; for w three days ye shall
19: 1 inheritance was w the inheritance of H8432
9 inheritance w the inheritance of them. H8432
21:41 All the cities of the Levites w the H8432
Jdg 7:16 pitchers, and lamps w the pitchers. H8432
9:51 But there was a strong tower w the city, H8432
11:18 but came not w the border of Moab:
26 did ye not recover *them* w that time?
14:12 declare it me w the seven days of the
15: 1 But it came to pass w a while after, in
1Sa 13:11 thou camest not w the days appointed,
14:14 about twenty men, w as it were an half
25:36 heart *was* merry w him, for he *was* very H5921
37 died w him, and he became *as* a stone. H7130
26: 7 Saul lay sleeping w the trench, and his
2Sa 7: 2 but the ark of God dwelleth w curtains. H8432
20: 4 w three days, and be thou here present.
1Ki 6:15 And he built the walls of the house w H1004
16 built *them* for it w, *even* for the oracle, H1004
18 And the cedar of the house w *was* H6441
19 in the house w, to set there the ark H6441
21 So Solomon overlaid the house w with H6441
23 And w the oracle he made two
27 And he set the cherubims w the inner H8432
29 trees and open flowers, w and without. H6441
30 he overlaid with gold, w and without. H6441
7: 8 *had* another court w the porch, *which* H1004
9 sawed with saws, w and without, even H1004
31 And the mouth of it w the chapiter and H1004
2Ki 4:27 her soul *is* vexed w her: and the LORD
6:30 *he had* sackcloth w upon his flesh. H1004
7:11 and they told *it* to the king's house w. H6441
11: 8 he that cometh w the ranges, let him be
2Ch 3: 4 and he overlaid it w with pure gold. H6441
Ezr 4:15 moved sedition w the same of old time: H4481
10: 8 And that whosoever would not come w
9 unto Jerusalem w three days. It *was* the
Neh 4:22 his servant lodge w Jerusalem, that in H8432
6:10 the house of God, w the temple, and let H8432
Job 6: 4 For the arrows of the Almighty *are* w H5978
14:22 pain, and his soul w him shall mourn. H5921
19:27 *though* my reins be consumed w me. H2436
20:13 it not; but keep it still w his mouth: H8432
14 is turned, *it is* the gall of asps w him. H7130
24:11 *Which* make oil w their walls, *and* tread H996
32:18 For I am full of matter, the spirit w me H990
Ps 36: 1 the wicked saith w my heart, *that there* H7130
39: 3 My heart was hot w me, while I was H7130
40: 8 O my God: yea, thy law *is* w my heart. H8432
10 I have not hid thy righteousness w my H8432
42: 6 O my God, my soul is cast down w me: H5921
11 art thou disquieted w me? hope thou in H5921
43: 5 thou disquieted w me? hope in God: for H5921
45:13 The king's daughter *is* all glorious w: H6441
51:10 O God; and renew a right spirit w me. H7130
55: 4 My heart is sore pained w me: and the H7130
94:19 In the multitude of my thoughts w me H7130
101: 2 walk w my house with a perfect heart. H7130
7 shall not dwell w my house: he that H7130
103: 1 all that is w me, *bless* his holy name. H7130
109:22 needy, and my heart is wounded w me. H7130
122: 2 Our feet shall stand w thy gates, O
7 Peace be w thy walls, *and* prosperity
7 thy walls, *and* prosperity w thy palaces.
8 sakes, I will now say, Peace *be* w thee.
142: 3 When my spirit was overwhelmed w H5921
143: 4 Therefore is my spirit overwhelmed w H5921
4 within me; my heart w me is desolate. H8432
147:13 he hath blessed thy children w thee. H7130
Prv 22:18 if thou keep them w thee; they shall H990
26:24 his lips, and layeth up deceit w him; H7130
Ecc 9:14 *There was* a little city, and few men w it;
Song 4: 1 *hast* doves' eyes w thy locks: thy hair *is* H1157
3 a piece of a pomegranate w thy locks. H1157
6: 7 *are* thy temples w thy locks. H1157
Isa 7: 8 *is* Rezin; and w threescore and five years
16:14 spoken, saying, W three years, as the
21:16 said unto me, W a year, according to H5750
26: 9 with my spirit w me will I seek thee H7130
56: 5 in mine house and w my walls a place
60:18 nor destruction w thy borders; but thou
63:11 *is* he that put his holy Spirit w him? H7130
Jer 4:14 shall thy vain thoughts lodge w thee? H7130
23: 9 Mine heart w me is broken because of H7130
28: 3 W two full years will I bring again into H5750
11 neck of all nations w the space of two H5750
Lam 1:20 mine heart is turned w me; for I have H7130
Ezk 1:27 of fire round about w it, from the H1004
2:10 and it *was* written w and without: and H6440
3:24 me, Go, shut thyself w thine house. H8432
7:15 and the famine w: he that *is* in the field H1004
11:19 put a new spirit w you; and I will take H7130
12:24 divination w the house of Israel. H8432
36:26 spirit will I put w you: and I will take H7130
27 And I will put my spirit w you, and H7130
40: 7 the porch of the gate w *was* one reed. H1004
8 also the porch of the gate w, one reed. H1004
16 and to their posts w the gate round H6441
43 And w *were* hooks, an hand broad, H1004
41: 9 place of the side chambers that *were* w. H1004
17 about w and without, by measure. H6442
44:17 in the gates of the inner court, and w. H1004
Dan 6:12 any God or man w thirty days, save of H5705
11:20 the kingdom: but w few days he shall be
Hos 11: 8 heart is turned w me, my repentings are
Jna 2: 7 When my soul fainted w me I H5921
Mic 3: 3 for the pot, and as flesh w the caldron. H8432
5: 6 and when he treadeth w our borders.
Zep 3: 3 Her princes w her *are* roaring lions; her H7130
Zec 12: 1 and formeth the spirit of man w him. H7130
Mt 3: 9 And think not to say w yourselves, We *G1722*
9: 3 w themselves, This *man* blasphemeth. *G1722*
21 For she said w herself, If I may but *G1722*
23:25 w they are full of extortion and excess. *G2081*
26 first that *which is* w the cup and *G1787*
27 outward, but are w full of dead *men's* *G2081*
28 w ye are full of hypocrisy and iniquity. *G2081*
Mk 2: 8 they so reasoned w themselves, he said *G1722*
7:21 For from w, out of the heart of men, *G2081*
23 All these evil things come from w, and *G2081*
14: 4 had indignation w themselves, and *G4314*
58 with hands, and w three days I will *G1223*
Lk 3: 8 begin not to say w yourselves, We have *G1722*
7:39 saw *it*, he spake w himself, saying, This *G1722*
49 him began to say w themselves, Who is *G1722*
11: 7 And he from w shall answer and say, *G2081*
40 is without make that which is w also? *G2081*
12:17 And he thought w himself, saying, *G1722*
16: 3 Then the steward said w himself, What *G1722*
17:21 behold, the kingdom of God is w you. *G1787*
18: 4 afterward he said w himself, Though I *G1722*
19:44 and thy children w thee; and they shall *G1722*
24:32 our heart burn w us, while he talked *G1722*
Jn 20:26 his disciples were w, and Thomas with *G2080*
Act 5:23 we had opened, we found no man w. *G2080*
Ro 8:23 ourselves groan w ourselves, waiting *G1722*
1Co 5:12 do not ye judge them that are w? *G2080*
2Co 7: 5 without *were* fightings, w *were* fears. *G2081*
Heb 6:19 and which entereth into that w the veil; *G2082*
Rev 4: 8 *were* full of eyes w: and they rest not *G2081*
5: 1 a book written w and on the backside, *G2081*

WITHOUT
See the Appendix.

WITHS
Jdg 16: 7 me with seven green w that were never H3499
8 up to her seven green w which had not H3499
9 And he brake the w, as a thread of tow H3499

WITHSTAND
Nu 22:32 I went out to w thee, because *thy* way H7854
2Ch 13: 7 tenderhearted, and could not w them. H2388
8 And now ye think to w the kingdom of H2388
20: 6 might, so that none is able to w thee? H3320
Est 9: 2 no man could w them; for the H5975+H6440
Ecc 4:12 him, two shall w him; and a threefold H5975
Dan 11:15 the south shall not w, neither his chosen H5975
15 neither *shall there be any* strength to w. H5975
Act 11:17 Christ; what was I, that I could w God? *G2967*
Eph 6:13 ye may be able to w in the evil day, and *G436*

WITHSTOOD
2Ch 26:18 And they w Uzziah the king, and said H5975
Dan 10:13 the kingdom of Persia w me one and H5975
Act 13: 8 by interpretation) w them, seeking to *G436*
Gal 2:11 But when Peter was come to Antioch, I w *G436*
2Ti 3: 8 Now as Jannes and Jambres w Moses, so *G436*
4:15 also; for he hath greatly w our words. *G436*

WITNESS
Gen 21:30 w unto me, that I have digged this well. H5713
31:44 let it be for a w between me and thee. H5707
48 And Laban said, This heap *is* a w H5707
50 us; see, God *is* w betwixt me and thee. H5707
52 This heap *be* w, and *this* pillar *be* H5707

Gen 31:52 and *this* pillar *be* w, that I will not pass H5713
Ex 20:16 Thou shalt not bear false w against thy H5707
22:13 let him bring it *for* w, *and* he shall not H5707
23: 1 with the wicked to be an unrighteous w. H5707
Lev 5: 1 swearing, and *is* a w, whether he hath H5707
Nu 5:13 and *there be* no w against her, neither H5707
17: 7 before the LORD in the tabernacle of w. H5715
8 the tabernacle of w; and, behold, the H5715
18: 2 *minister* before the tabernacle of w. H5715
35:30 of witnesses: but one w shall not testify H5707
Dt 4:26 I call heaven and earth to w against H5749
5:20 Neither shalt thou bear false w against H5707
17: 6 of one w he shall not be put to death. H5707
19:15 One w shall not rise up against a man H5707
16 If a false w rise up against any man to H5707
18 and, behold, *if* the w *be* a false witness, H5707
18 witness *be* a false w, *and* hath testified H5707
31:19 w for me against the children of Israel. H5707
21 against them as a w; for it shall not be H5707
26 it may be there for a w against thee. H5707
Jos 22:27 But *that* it *may be* a w between us, and H5707
28 but it *is* a w between us and you. H5707
34 a w between us that the LORD *is* God. H5707
24:27 stone shall be a w unto us; for it hath H5713
27 a w unto you, lest ye deny your God. H5713
Jdg 11:10 The LORD be w between us, if we do H8085
1Sa 12: 3 Behold, here I *am*: w against me before H6030
5 And he said unto them, The LORD *is* w H5707
5 his anointed *is* w this day, that ye have H5707
5 my hand. And they answered, *He is* w. H5707
1Ki 21:10 him, to bear w against him, saying, H5749
2Ch 24: 6 of Israel, for the tabernacle of w? H5715
Job 16: 8 *which* is a w *against me*: and my H5707
8 rising up in me beareth w to my face. H6030
19 Also now, behold, my w *is* in heaven, H5707
29:11 when the eye saw *me*, it gave w to me: H5749
Ps 89:37 and *as* a faithful w in heaven. Selah. H5707
Prv 6:19 A false w *that* speaketh lies, and he H5707
12:17 righteousness: but a false w deceit. H5707
14: 5 A faithful w will not lie: but a false H5707
5 will not lie: but a false w will utter lies. H5707
25 A true w delivereth souls: but a H5707
25 souls: but a deceitful *w* speaketh lies.
19: 5 A false w shall not be unpunished, and H5707
9 A false w shall not be unpunished, and H5707
28 An ungodly w scorneth judgment: and H5707
21:28 A false w shall perish: but the man that H5707
24:28 Be not a w against thy neighbour H5707
25:18 A man that beareth false w against his H5707
Isa 3: 9 The shew of their countenance doth w H6030
19:20 And it shall be for a sign and for a w H5707
55: 4 Behold, I have given him *for* a w to the H5707
Jer 29:23 I know, and *am* a w, saith the LORD. H5707
42: 5 a true and faithful w between us, if we H5707
Lam 2:13 What thing shall I take to w for thee? H5749
Mic 1: 2 let the Lord GOD be w against you, the H5707
Mal 2:14 LORD hath been w between thee and H5749
3: 5 I will be a swift w against the sorcerers, H5707
Mt 15:19 thefts, false w, blasphemies: G5577
19:18 not steal, Thou shalt not bear false w, G5576
24:14 in all the world for a w unto all nations; G3142
26:59 w against Jesus, to put him to death; G5577
62 what *is it which* these w against thee? G2649
27:13 how many things they w against thee? G2649
Mk 10:19 steal, Do not bear false w, Defraud not, G5576
14:55 council sought for w against Jesus to G3141
56 For many bare false w against him, but G5576
56 him, but their w agreed not together. G3141
57 and bare false w against him, saying, G5576
59 But neither so did their w agree G3141
60 what *is it which* these w against thee? G2649
15: 4 how many things they w against thee. G2649
Lk 4:22 And all bare him w, and wondered at G3140
11:48 Truly ye bear w that ye allow the deeds G3140
18:20 w, Honour thy father and thy mother. G5576
22:71 we any further w? for we ourselves have G3141
Jn 1: 7 The same came for a w, to bear witness G3141
7 The same came for a witness, to bear w G3140
8 but *was sent* to bear w of that Light. G3140
15 John bare w of him, and cried, saying, G3140
3:11 we have seen; and ye receive not our w. G3141
26 whom thou barest w, behold, the same G3140
28 Ye yourselves bear me w, that I said, I G3140
5:31 If I bear w of myself, my witness is not G3140
31 If I bear witness of myself, my w is not G3141
32 There is another that beareth w of me; G3140
32 w which he witnesseth of me is true. G3141
33 Ye sent unto John, and he bare w unto G3140
36 But I have greater w than *that* of John: G3141
Jn 5:36 w of me, that the Father hath sent me. G3140
37 sent me, hath borne w of me. Ye have G3140
8:18 I am one that bear w of myself, and the G3140
18 Father that sent me beareth w of me. G3140
10:25 my Father's name, they bear w of me. G3140
15:27 And ye also shall bear w, because ye G3140
18:23 spoken evil, bear w of the evil: but if G3140
37 that I should bear w unto the truth. G3140
Act 1:22 to be a w with us of his resurrection. G3144
4:33 gave the apostles w of the resurrection G3142
7:44 Our fathers had the tabernacle of w in G3142
10:43 To him give all the prophets w, that G3140
14:17 himself without w, in that he did good, G267
15: 8 hearts, bare them w, giving them the G3140
22: 5 As also the high priest doth bear me w, G3140
15 For thou shalt be his w unto all men of G3144
23:11 so must thou bear w also at Rome. G3140
26:16 a minister and a w both of these things G3144
Ro 1: 9 For God is my w, whom I serve with my G3144
2:15 also bearing w, and *their* thoughts G4828
8:16 The Spirit itself beareth w with our G4828
9: 1 also bearing me w in the Holy Ghost, G4828
13: 9 not bear false w, Thou shalt not covet; G5576
1Th 2: 5 nor a cloak of covetousness; God *is* w: G3144
Tit 1:13 This w is true. Wherefore rebuke them G3141
Heb 2: 4 God also bearing *them* w, both with G4901
10:15 *Whereof* the Holy Ghost also is a w to G3140
11: 4 he obtained w that he was righteous, G3140
Jas 5: 3 of them shall be a w against you, and G3142
1Pt 5: 1 an elder, and a w of the sufferings of G3144
1Jn 1: 2 seen *it*, and bear w, and shew unto you G3140
5: 6 beareth w, because the Spirit is truth. G3140
8 And there are three that bear w in G3140
9 If we receive the w of men, the witness G3141
9 If we receive the witness of men, the w G3141
9 for this is the w of God which he hath G3141
10 of God hath the w in himself: he that G3141
3Jn 6 Which have borne w of thy charity G3140
Rev 1: 5 *who is* the faithful w, *and* the first G3144
3:14 w, the beginning of the creation of God; G3144
20: 4 beheaded for the w of Jesus, and for the G3141

WITNESSED

1Ki 21:13 the men of Belial w against him, *even* H5749
Ro 3:21 being w by the law and the prophets; G3140
1Ti 6:13 Pontius Pilate w a good confession; G3140
Heb 7: 8 *them*, of whom it is w that he liveth. G3140

WITNESSES

Nu 35:30 by the mouth of w: but one witness H5707
Dt 17: 6 At the mouth of two w, or three H5707
6 or three w, shall he that is worthy H5707
7 The hands of the w shall be first upon H5707
19:15 the mouth of two w, or at the mouth of H5707
15 three w, shall the matter be established. H5707
Jos 24:22 the people, Ye *are* w against yourselves H5707
22 to serve him. And they said, *We are* w. H5707
Ru 4: 9 all the people, Ye *are* w this day, that I H5707
10 the gate of his place: ye *are* w this day. H5707
11 said, *We are* w. The LORD make the H5707
Job 10:17 Thou renewest thy w against me, and H5707
Ps 27:12 mine enemies: for false w are risen up H5707
35:11 False w did rise up; they laid to my H5707
Isa 8: 2 And I took unto me faithful w to H5707
43: 9 bring forth their w, that they may be H5707
10 Ye *are* my w, saith the LORD, and my H5707
12 my w, saith the LORD, that I *am* God. H5707
44: 8 *it*? ye *are* even my w. Is there a God H5707
9 they *are* their own w; they see not, nor H5707
Jer 32:10 sealed *it*, and took w, and weighed *him* H5707
12 presence of the w that subscribed the H5707
25 money, and take w; for the city is given H5707
44 seal *them*, and take w in the land of H5707
Mt 18:16 three w every word may be established. G3144
23:31 Wherefore ye be w unto yourselves, G3140
26:60 many false w came, *yet* found they G5575
60 they none. At the last came two false w, G5575
65 need have we of w? behold, now ye have G3144
Mk 14:63 and saith, What need we any further w? G3144
Lk 24:48 And ye are w of these things. G3144
Act 1: 8 you: and ye shall be w unto me both in G3144
2:32 God raised up, whereof we all are w. G3144
3:15 raised from the dead; whereof we are w. G3144
5:32 And we are his w of these things; and G3144
6:13 And set up false w, which said, This G3144
7:58 *him*: and the w laid down their clothes G3144
10:39 And we are w of all things which he did G3144
41 Not to all the people, but unto w G3144
13:31 who are his w unto the people. G3144
1Co 15:15 Yea, and we are found false w of God; G5575
2Co 13: 1 w shall every word be established. G3144
1Th 2:10 Ye *are* w, and God *also*, how holily and G3144
1Ti 5:19 accusation, but before two or three w. G3144
6:12 a good profession before many w. G3144
2Ti 2: 2 me among many w, the same commit G3144
Heb 10:28 without mercy under two or three w: G3144
12: 1 so great a cloud of w, let us lay aside G3144
Rev 11: 3 And I will give *power* unto my two w, G3144

WITNESSETH

Jn 5:32 the witness which he w of me is true. G3140
Act 20:23 Save that the Holy Ghost w in every G1263

WITNESSING

Act 26:22 unto this day, w both to small and G3140

WITS'

Ps 107:27 a drunken man, and are at their w end. H2451

WITTINGLY

Gen 48:14 w; for Manasseh *was* the firstborn. H7919

WITTY

Prv 8:12 and find out knowledge of w inventions.

WIVES

Gen 4:19 And Lamech took unto him two w: the H802
23 And Lamech said unto his w, Adah and H802
23 Hear my voice; ye w of Lamech, hearken H802
6: 2 took them w of all which they chose. H802
18 and thy wife, and thy sons' w with thee. H802
7: 7 wife, and his sons' w with him, into the H802
13 w of his sons with them, into the ark; H802
8:16 and thy sons, and thy sons' w with thee. H802
18 and his wife, and his sons' w with him: H802
11:29 And Abram and Nahor took them w: the H802
28: 9 and took unto the w which he had H802
30:26 Give *me* my w and my children, for H802
31:17 and set his sons and his w upon camels; H802
50 shalt take *other* w beside my daughters, H802
32:22 night, and took his two w, and his two H802
34:21 w, and let us give them our daughters. H802
29 ones, and their w took they captive, and H802
36: 2 Esau took his w of the daughters of H802
6 And Esau took his w, and his sons, and H802
37: 2 of Zilpah, his father's w: and Joseph H802
45:19 your w, and bring your father, and come. H802
46: 5 ones, and their w, in the wagons which H802
26 w, all the souls *were* threescore and six; H802
Ex 19:15 the third day: come not at *your* w. H802
22:24 sword; and your w shall be widows, and H802
32: 2 in the ears of your w, of your sons, and of H802
Nu 14: 3 the sword, that our w and our children H802
16:27 tents, and their w, and their sons, and H802
32:26 Our little ones, our w, our flocks, and all H802
Dt 3:19 But your w, and your little ones, and H802
17:17 Neither shall he multiply w to himself, H802
21:15 If a man have two w, one beloved, and H802
29:11 Your little ones, your w, and thy stranger H802
Jos 1:14 Your w, your little ones, and your cattle, H802
Jdg 3: 6 to be their w, and gave their daughters H802
8:30 of his body begotten: for he had many w. H802
21: 7 How shall we do for w for them that H802
7 will not give them of our daughters to w? H802
14 they gave them w which they had saved H802
16 shall we do for w for them that remain, H802
18 Howbeit we may not give them w of our H802
23 so, and took *them* w, according to their H802
Ru 1: 4 And they took them w of the women of H802
1Sa 1: 2 And he had two w; the name of the one H802
25:43 and they were also both of them his w. H802
27: 3 *even* David with his two w, Ahinoam the H802
30: 3 with fire; and their w, and their sons, and H802
5 And David's two w were taken captives, H802
18 away: and David rescued his two w. H802
2Sa 2: 2 So David went up thither, and his two w H802
5:13 concubines and w out of Jerusalem, H802
12: 8 and thy master's w into thy bosom, and H802
11 and I will take thy w before thine eyes, H802
11 lie with thy w in the sight of this sun. H802
19: 5 of thy w, and the lives of thy concubines; H802
1Ki 11: 3 And he had seven hundred w, princesses, H802
3 and his w turned away his heart. H802
4 was old, *that* his w turned away his H802
8 And likewise did he for all his strange w, H802
20: 3 Thy silver and thy gold *is* mine; thy w H802
5 thy gold, and thy w, and thy children; H802
7 unto me for my w, and for my children, H802

2Ki 4: 1 woman of the **w** of the sons of the H802
24:15 and the king's **w**, and his officers, and H802
1Ch 4: 5 of Tekoa had two **w**, Helah and Naarah. H802
7: 4 *men*: for they had many **w** and sons. H802
8: 8 away; Hushim and Baara *were* his **w**. H802
14: 3 And David took more **w** at Jerusalem: H802
2Ch 11:21 above all his **w** and his concubines: H802
21 (for he took eighteen **w**, and threescore H802
23 in abundance. And he desired many **w**. H802
13:21 married fourteen **w**, and begat twenty H802
20:13 little ones, their **w**, and their children. H802
21:14 children, and thy **w**, and all thy goods: H802
17 sons also, and his **w**; so that there was H802
24: 3 And Jehoiada took for him two **w**; and he H802
29: 9 and our **w** *are* in captivity for this. H802
31:18 little ones, their **w**, and their sons, and H802
Ezr 10: 2 have taken strange **w** of the people of the H802
3 to put away all the **w**, and such as are H802
10 **w**, to increase the trespass of Israel. H802
11 of the land, and from the strange **w**. H802
14 have taken strange **w** in our cities come H802
17 **w** by the first day of the first month. H802
18 had taken strange **w**: *namely*, of the sons H802
19 put away their **w**; and *being* guilty, *they* H802
44 All these had taken strange **w**: and *some* H802
44 them had **w** by whom they had children. H802
Neh 4:14 daughters, your **w**, and your houses. H802
5: 1 their **w** against their brethren the Jews. H802
10:28 law of God, their **w**, their sons, and their H802
12:43 rejoice with great joy: the **w** also and the H802
13:23 **w** of Ashdod, of Ammon, *and* of Moab: H802
27 against our God in marrying strange **w**? H802
Est 1:20 it is great,) all the **w** shall give to their H802
Isa 13:16 shall be spoiled, and their **w** ravished. H802
Jer 6:12 *with their* fields and **w** together: for I will H802
8:10 Therefore will I give their **w** unto others, H802
14:16 them, them, their **w**, nor their sons, nor H802
18:21 and let their **w** be bereaved of their H802
29: 6 Take ye **w**, and beget sons and H802
6 and take **w** for your sons, and give H802
23 their neighbours' **w**, and have spoken H802
35: 8 we, our **w**, our sons, nor our daughters; H802
38:23 So they shall bring out all thy **w** and thy H802
44: 9 of their **w**, and your own wickedness, H802
9 of your **w**, which they have committed H802
15 knew that their **w** had burned incense H802
25 Ye and your **w** have both spoken with H802
Ezk 44:22 Neither shall they take for their **w** a H802
Dan 5: 2 his princes, his **w**, and his concubines, H7695
3 **w**, and his concubines, drank in them. H7695
23 thou, and thy lords, thy **w**, and thy H7695
6:24 and their **w**; and the lions had the H5389
Zec 12:12 apart, and their **w** apart; the family of H802
12 of Nathan apart, and their **w** apart; H802
13 apart, and their **w** apart; the family of H802
13 of Shimei apart, and their **w** apart; H802
14 every family apart, and their **w** apart. H802
Mt 19: 8 **w**: but from the beginning it was not so. G1135
Lk 17:27 they married **w**, they were given in G1060
Act 21: 5 on our way, with **w** and children, till *we* G1135
1Co 7:29 have **w** be as though they had none; G1135
Eph 5:22 **W**, submit yourselves unto your own G1135
24 unto Christ, so *let* the **w** *be* to their own G1135
25 Husbands, love your **w**, even as Christ G1135
28 So ought men to love their **w** as their G1135
Col 3:18 **W**, submit yourselves unto your own G1135
19 Husbands, love *your* **w**, and be not G1135
1Ti 3:11 Even so *must their* **w** *be* grave, not G1135
1Pt 3: 1 Likewise, ye **w**, *be* in subjection to your G1135
1 be won by the conversation of the **w**; G1135

WIVES'

1Ti 4: 7 But refuse profane and old **w** fables, G1126

WIZARD

Lev 20:27 spirit, or that is a **w**, shall surely be put H3049
Dt 18:11 spirits, or a **w**, or a necromancer. H3049

WIZARDS

Lev 19:31 neither seek after **w**, to be defiled by H3049
20: 6 spirits, and after **w**, to go a whoring H3049
1Sa 28: 3 spirits, and the **w**, out of the land. H3049
9 spirits, and the **w**, out of the land: H3049
2Ki 21: 6 spirits and **w**: he wrought much H3049
23:24 spirits, and the **w**, and the images, and H3049
2Ch 33: 6 spirit, and with **w**: he wrought much H3049
Isa 8:19 spirits, and unto **w** that peep, and that H3049
19: 3 that have familiar spirits, and to the **w**. H3049

WOE

Nu 21:29 **W** to thee, Moab! thou art undone, O H188
1Sa 4: 7 And they said, **W** unto us! for there hath H188
8 **W** unto us! who shall deliver us out of H188
Job 10:15 If I be wicked, **w** unto me; and *if* I be H480
Ps 120: 5 **W** is me, that I sojourn in Mesech, *that* I H190
Prv 23:29 Who hath **w**? who hath sorrow? who hath H188
Ecc 4:10 up his fellow: but **w** to him *that is* alone H337
10:16 **W** to thee, O land, when thy king *is* a H337
Isa 3: 9 they hide *it* not. **W** unto their soul! for H188
11 **W** unto the wicked! *it shall be* ill *with* H188
5: 8 **W** unto them that join house to house, H1945
11 **W** unto them that rise up early in the H1945
18 **W** unto them that draw iniquity with H1945
20 **W** unto them that call evil good, and H1945
21 **W** unto *them that are* wise in their own H1945
22 **W** unto *them that are* mighty to drink H1945
6: 5 Then said I, **W** *is* me! for I am undone; H188
10: 1 **W** unto them that decree unrighteous H1945
17:12 **W** to the multitude of many people, H1945
18: 1 **W** to the land shadowing with wings, H1945
24:16 my leanness, **w** unto me! the treacherous H188
28: 1 **W** to the crown of pride, to the H1945
29: 1 **W** to Ariel, to Ariel, the city *where* H1945
15 **W** unto them that seek deep to hide H1945
30: 1 **W** to the rebellious children, saith the H1945
31: 1 **W** to them that go down to Egypt for H1945
33: 1 **W** to thee that spoilest, and thou *wast* H1945
45: 9 **W** unto him that striveth with his H1945
10 **W** unto him that saith unto *his* father, H1945
Jer 4:13 eagles. **W** unto us! for we are spoiled. H188
31 her hands, *saying*, **W** *is* me now! for my H188
6: 4 us go up at noon. **W** unto us! for the day H188
10:19 **W** is me for my hurt! my wound is H188
13:27 the hills in the fields. **W** unto thee, O H188
15:10 **W** is me, my mother, that thou hast H188
22:13 **W** unto him that buildeth his house by H1945
23: 1 **W** be unto the pastors that destroy and H1945
45: 3 Thou didst say, **W** is me now! for the H188
48: 1 the God of Israel; **W** unto Nebo! for it is H1945
46 **W** be unto thee, O Moab! the people of H188
50:27 to the slaughter: **w** unto them! for their H1945
Lam 5:16 The crown is fallen *from* our head: **w** H188
Ezk 2:10 lamentations, and mourning, and **w**. H1958
13: 3 Thus saith the Lord GOD; **W** unto the H1945
18 And say, Thus saith the Lord GOD; **W** H1945
16:23 (**w**, woe unto thee! saith the Lord GOD;) H188
23 (woe, **w** unto thee! saith the Lord GOD;) H188
24: 6 Wherefore thus saith the Lord GOD; **W** H188
9 Therefore thus saith the Lord GOD; **W** to H188
30: 2 Lord GOD; Howl ye, **W** worth the day! H1929
34: 2 the shepherds; **W** *be* to the shepherds H1945
Hos 7:13 **W** unto them! for they have fled from H188
9:12 *be* a man *left*: yea, **w** also to them when I H188
Am 5:18 **W** unto you that desire the day of the H1945
6: 1 **W** to them *that are* at ease in Zion, and H1945
Mic 2: 1 **W** to them that devise iniquity, and H1945
7: 1 **W** is me! for I am as when they have H480
Nah 3: 1 **W** to the bloody city! it *is* all full of lies H1945
Hab 2: 6 him, and say, **W** to him that increaseth H1945
9 **W** to him that coveteth an evil H1945
12 **W** to him that buildeth a town with H1945
15 **W** unto him that giveth his neighbour H1945
19 **W** unto him that saith to the wood, H1945
Zep 2: 5 **W** unto the inhabitants of the sea H1945
3: 1 **W** to her that is filthy and polluted, to H1945
Zec 11:17 **W** to the idol shepherd that leaveth the H1945
Mt 11:21 **W** unto thee, Chorazin! woe unto thee, G3759
21 Woe unto thee, Chorazin! **w** unto thee, G3759
18: 7 **W** unto the world because of offences! G3759
7 come; but **w** to that man by whom G3759
23:13 But **w** unto you, scribes and Pharisees, G3759
14 **W** unto you, scribes and Pharisees, G3759
15 **W** unto you, scribes and Pharisees, G3759
16 **W** unto you, *ye* blind guides, which G3759
23 **W** unto you, scribes and Pharisees, G3759
25 **W** unto you, scribes and Pharisees, G3759
27 **W** unto you, scribes and Pharisees, G3759
29 **W** unto you, scribes and Pharisees, G3759
24:19 And **w** unto them that are with child, G3759
26:24 of him: but **w** unto that man by whom G3759
Mk 13:17 But **w** to them that are with child, and G3759
14:21 of him: but **w** to that man by whom G3759
Lk 6:24 But **w** unto you that are rich! for ye G3759
25 **W** unto you that are full! for ye shall G3759
25 ye shall hunger. **W** unto you that laugh G3759
26 **W** unto you, when all men shall speak G3759
10:13 **W** unto thee, Chorazin! woe unto thee, G3759
13 Woe unto thee, Chorazin! **w** unto thee, G3759
Lk 11:42 But **w** unto you, Pharisees! for ye tithe G3759
43 **W** unto you, Pharisees! for ye love the G3759
44 **W** unto you, scribes and Pharisees, G3759
46 And he said, **W** unto you also, *ye* G3759
47 **W** unto you! for ye build the sepulchres G3759
52 **W** unto you, lawyers! for ye have taken G3759
17: 1 **w** *unto him*, through whom they come! G3759
21:23 But **w** unto them that are with child, G3759
22:22 determined: but **w** unto that man by G3759
1Co 9:16 **w** is unto me, if I preach not the gospel! G3759
Jude 11 **W** unto them! for they have gone in the G3759
Rev 8:13 with a loud voice, **W**, woe, woe, to the G3759
13 with a loud voice, Woe, **w**, woe, to the G3759
13 voice, Woe, woe, **w**, to the inhabiters of G3759
9:12 One **w** is past; *and*, behold, there come G3759
11:14 The second **w** is past; *and*, behold, the G3759
14 behold, the third **w** cometh quickly. G3759
12:12 dwell in them. **W** to the inhabiters of G3759

WOEFUL

Jer 17:16 have I desired the **w** day; thou knowest: H605

WOES

Rev 9:12 there come two **w** more hereafter. G3759

WOLF

Gen 49:27 Benjamin shall ravin *as* a **w**: in the H2061
Isa 11: 6 The **w** also shall dwell with the lamb, H2061
65:25 The **w** and the lamb shall feed together, H2061
Jer 5: 6 slay them, *and* a **w** of the evenings H2061
Jn 10:12 sheep are not, seeth the **w** coming, and G3074
12 fleeth: and the **w** catcheth them, and G3074

WOLVES

Ezk 22:27 thereof *are* like **w** ravening the prey, to H2061
Hab 1: 8 than the evening **w**: and their horsemen H2061
Zep 3: 3 *are* evening **w**; they gnaw not the bones H2061
Mt 7:15 but inwardly they are ravening **w**. G3074
10:16 in the midst of **w**: be ye therefore wise G3074
Lk 10: 3 I send you forth as lambs among **w**. G3074
Act 20:29 shall grievous **w** enter in among you, G3074

WOMAN

Gen 2:22 he a **w**, and brought her unto the man. H802
23 **W**, because she was taken out of Man. H802
3: 1 he said unto the **w**, Yea, hath God said, H802
2 And the **w** said unto the serpent, We H802
4 And the serpent said unto the **w**, Ye shall H802
6 And when the **w** saw that the tree *was* H802
12 And the man said, The **w** whom thou H802
13 And the LORD God said unto the **w**, H802
13 hast done? And the **w** said, The serpent H802
15 thee and the **w**, and between thy seed H802
16 Unto the **w** he said, I will greatly H802
12:11 know that thou *art* a fair **w** to look upon: H802
14 beheld the **w** that she *was* very fair. H802
15 the **w** was taken into Pharaoh's house. H802
20: 3 a dead man, for the **w** which thou hast H802
24: 5 Peradventure the **w** will not be willing to H802
8 And if the **w** will not be willing to follow H802
39 Peradventure the **w** will not follow me. H802
44 *let* the same *be* the **w** whom the LORD H802
46:10 and Shaul the son of a Canaanitish **w**.
Ex 2: 2 And the **w** conceived, and bare a son: H802
9 And the **w** took the child, and nursed it. H802
3:22 But every **w** shall borrow of her H802
6:15 **w**: these *are* the families of Simeon. H3669
11: 2 and every **w** of her neighbour, jewels H802
21:22 If men strive, and hurt a **w** with child, so H802
28 If an ox gore a man or a **w**, that they die: H802
29 hath killed a man or a **w**; the ox shall be H802
35:29 every man and **w**, whose heart made H802
36: 6 neither man nor **w** make any more work H802
Lev 12: 2 of Israel, saying, If a **w** have conceived H802
13:29 If a man or **w** have a plague upon the H802
38 If a man also or a **w** have in the skin of H802
15:18 The **w** also with whom man shall lie *with* H802
19 And if a **w** have an issue, *and* her issue H802
25 And if a **w** have an issue of her blood H802
33 man, and of the **w**, and of him that lieth H5347
18:17 the nakedness of a **w** and her daughter, H802
19 Also thou shalt not approach unto a **w** to H802
23 neither shall any **w** stand before a beast H802
19:20 And whosoever lieth carnally with a **w**, H802
20:13 as he lieth with a **w**, both of them have H802
16 And if a **w** approach unto any beast, and H802
16 thou shalt kill the **w**, and the beast: they H802
18 And if a man shall lie with a **w** having H802
27 A man also or **w** that hath a familiar H802

Lev 21: 7 shall they take a w put away from her H802
14 A widow, or a divorced w, or profane, H1644
24:10 And the son of an Israelitish w, whose H802
10 of the Israelitish w and a man of Israel
Nu 5: 6 When a man or w shall commit any sin H802
18 And the priest shall set the w before the H802
19 and say unto the w, If no man have lain H802
21 Then the priest shall charge the w with H802
21 shall say unto the w, The LORD make H802
22 to rot: And the w shall say, Amen, amen. H802
24 And he shall cause the w to drink the H802
26 shall cause the w to drink the water. H802
27 the w shall be a curse among her people. H802
28 And if the w be not defiled, but be clean; H802
30 and shall set the w before the LORD, and H802
31 and this w shall bear her iniquity. H802
6: 2 When either man or w shall separate H802
12: 1 of the Ethiopian w whom he had H802
1 for he had married an Ethiopian w. H802
25: 6 a Midianitish w in the sight of Moses, H4084
8 of Israel, and the w through her belly. So H802
14 the Midianitish w, *was* Zimri, the son H4084
15 And the name of the Midianitish w that H802
30: 3 If a w also vow a vow unto the LORD, H802
31:17 and kill every w that hath known man H802
Dt 15:12 or an Hebrew w, be sold unto thee, and H5680
17: 2 giveth thee, man or w, that hath wrought H802
5 forth that man or that w, which have H802
5 that man or that w, and shalt stone them H802
21:11 a beautiful w, and hast a desire unto H802
22: 5 The w shall not wear that which H802
14 and say, I took this w, and when I came H802
22 If a man be found lying with a w H802
22 that lay with the w, and the woman: so H802
22 the woman, and the w: so shalt thou put H802
28:56 The tender and delicate w among you,
29:18 you man, or w, or family, or tribe, whose H802
Jos 2: 4 And the w took the two men, and hid H802
6:21 the city, both man and w, young and old, H802
22 out thence the w, and all that she hath, H802
Jdg 4: 9 into the hand of a w. And Deborah arose, H802
9:53 And a certain w cast a piece of a H802
54 say not of me, A w slew him. And his H802
11: 2 for thou *art* the son of a strange w. H802
13: 3 appeared unto the w, and said unto her, H802
6 Then the w came and told her husband, H802
9 again unto the w as she sat in the field: H802
10 And the w made haste, and ran, and H802
11 spakest unto the w? And he said, I *am*. H802
13 all that I said unto the w let her beware. H802
24 And the w bare a son, and called his H802
14: 1 Timnath, and saw a w in Timnath of the H802
2 said, I have seen a w in Timnath of the H802
3 *Is there* never a w among the daughters H802
7 with the w; and she pleased Samson well. H802
10 So his father went down unto the w: and H802
16: 4 that he loved a w in the valley of Sorek, H802
19:26 Then came the w in the dawning of the H802
27 and, behold, the w his concubine was H802
20: 4 And the Levite, the husband of the w H802
21:11 and every w that hath lain by man. H802
Ru 1: 5 of them; and the w was left of her two H802
3: 8 himself: and, behold, a w lay at his feet. H802
11 doth know that thou *art* a virtuous w. H802
14 be known that a w came into the floor. H802
4:11 The LORD make the w that is come into H802
12 LORD shall give thee of this young w. H5291
1Sa 1:15 my lord, I *am* a w of a sorrowful spirit: H802
18 in thy sight. So the w went her way, and H802
23 his word. So the w abode, and gave her H802
26 my lord, I *am* the w that stood by thee H802
2:20 thee seed of this w for the loan which is H802
15: 3 but slay both man and w, infant and H802
20:30 perverse rebellious *w*, do not I know that
25: 3 and *she was* a w of good understanding, H802
27: 9 neither man nor w alive, and took away H802
11 And David saved neither man nor w H802
28: 7 Seek me a w that hath a familiar H802
7 a w that hath a familiar spirit at En-dor. H802
8 they came to the w by night: and he said, H802
9 And the w said unto him, Behold, thou H802
11 Then said the w, Whom shall I bring up H802
12 And when the w saw Samuel, she cried H802
12 a loud voice: and the w spake to Saul, H802
13 thou? And the w said unto Saul, I saw H802
21 And the w came unto Saul, and saw that H802
23 together with the w, compelled him; and H802
24 And the w had a fat calf in the house; H802
2Sa 3: 8 me to day with a fault concerning this w? H802

2Sa 11: 2 the roof he saw a w washing herself; and H802
2 the w *was* very beautiful to look upon. H802
3 And David sent and inquired after the w. H802
5 And the w conceived, and sent and told H802
21 did not a w cast a piece of a millstone H802
13:17 said, Put now this w out from me, and
14: 2 thence a wise w, and said unto her, I H802
2 oil, but be as a w that had a long time H802
4 And when the w of Tekoah spake to the H802
5 a widow w, and mine husband is dead. H802
8 And the king said unto the w, Go to thine H802
9 And the w of Tekoah said unto the king, H802
12 Then the w said, Let thine handmaid, I H802
13 And the w said, Wherefore then hast H802
18 and said unto the w, Hide not from me, I H802
18 w said, Let my lord the king now speak. H802
19 in all this? And the w answered and said, H802
27 she was a w of a fair countenance. H802
17:19 And the w took and spread a covering H802
20 came to the w to the house, they said, H802
20 Jonathan? And the w said unto them, H802
20:16 Then cried a wise w out of the city, Hear, H802
17 near unto her, the w said, *Art* thou Joab? H802
21 from the city. And the w said unto Joab, H802
22 Then the w went unto all the people in H802
1Ki 3:17 And the one w said, O my lord, I and this H802
17 my lord, I and this w dwell in one house; H802
18 delivered, that this w was delivered also: H802
22 And the other w said, Nay; but the living H802
26 Then spake the w whose the living child H802
11:26 Zeruah, a widow w, even he lifted up *his* H802
14: 5 she shall feign herself *to be* another *w*.
17: 9 a widow w there to sustain thee. H802
10 behold, the widow w *was* there gathering H802
17 *that* the son of the w, the mistress of the H802
24 And the w said to Elijah, Now by this I H802
2Ki 4: 1 Now there cried a certain w of the wives H802
8 Shunem, where *was* a great w; and she H802
17 And the w conceived, and bare a son at H802
6:26 wall, there cried a w unto him, saying, H802
28 answered, This w said unto me, Give thy H802
30 heard the words of the w, that he rent his H802
8: 1 Then spake Elisha unto the w, whose son H802
2 And the w arose, and did after the H802
3 years' end, that the w returned out of the H802
5 that, behold, the w, whose son he had H802
5 O king, this *is* the w, and this *is* her son, H802
6 And when the king asked the w, she told H802
9:34 now this cursed *w*, and bury her: for she
1Ch 16: 3 both man and w, to every one a loaf of H802
2Ch 2:14 The son of a w of the daughters of Dan, H802
15:13 small or great, whether man or w. H802
24: 7 For the sons of Athaliah, that wicked w,
Est 4:11 whether man or w, shall come unto the H802
Job 14: 1 Man *that is* born of a w *is* of few days, H802
15:14 born of a w, that he should be righteous? H802
25: 4 how can he be clean *that is* born of a w? H802
31: 9 If mine heart have been deceived by a w, H802
Ps 48: 6 there, *and* pain, as of a w in travail.
58: 8 of a w, *that* they may not see the sun. H802
113: 9 He maketh the barren w to keep house, H6135
Prv 2:16 To deliver thee from the strange w, *even* H802
5: 3 For the lips of a strange w drop *as* an H2114
20 with a strange w, and embrace the H2114
6:24 To keep thee from the evil w, from the H802
24 the flattery of the tongue of a strange w.
26 For by means of a whorish w *a man is* H802
32 *But* whoso committeth adultery with a w H802
7: 5 from the strange w, from the stranger H802
10 And, behold, there met him a w *with* the H802
9:13 A foolish w *is* clamorous: *she is* simple, H802
11:16 A gracious w retaineth honour: and H802
22 *so is* a fair w which is without discretion. H802
12: 4 A virtuous w *is* a crown to her husband: H802
14: 1 Every wise w buildeth her house: but the H802
20:16 and take a pledge of him for a strange w.
21: 9 than with a brawling w in a wide house. H802
19 than with a contentious and an angry w. H802
23:27 ditch; and a strange w *is* a narrow pit.
25:24 with a brawling w and in a wide house. H802
27:13 and take a pledge of him for a strange w.
15 rainy day and a contentious w are alike. H802
30:20 Such *is* the way of an adulterous w; she H802
23 For an odious w when she is married;
31:10 Who can find a virtuous w? for her price H802
30 *is* vain: *but* a w *that* feareth the LORD, H802
Ecc 7:26 And I find more bitter than death the w, H802
28 a w among all those have I not found. H802
Isa 13: 8 be in pain as a w that travaileth: they

Isa 21: 3 as the pangs of a w that travaileth: I was
26:17 Like as a w with child, *that* draweth near
42:14 w; I will destroy and devour at once. H3205
45:10 to the w, What hast thou brought forth? H802
49:15 Can a w forget her sucking child, that H802
54: 6 For the LORD hath called thee as a w H802
Jer 4:31 For I have heard a voice as of a w in
6: 2 of Zion to a comely and delicate *w*.
24 hold of us, *and* pain, as of a w in travail.
13:21 not sorrows take thee, as a w in travail? H802
22:23 upon thee, the pain as of a w in travail!
30: 6 on his loins, as a w in travail, and all
31: 8 and the lame, the w with child and her
22 in the earth, A w shall compass a man. H5347
44: 7 from you man and w, child and suckling, H802
48:41 shall be as the heart of a w in her pangs. H802
49:22 be as the heart of a w in her pangs. H802
24 have taken her, as a w in travail.
50:43 of him, *and* pangs as of a w in travail.
51:22 in pieces man and w; and with thee will I H802
Lam 1:17 is as a menstruous w among them. H5079
Ezk 16:30 the work of an imperious whorish w; H802
18: 6 hath come near to a menstruous w, H802
23:44 as they go in unto a w that playeth the H802
36:17 me as the uncleanness of a removed w. H5079
Hos 3: 1 unto me, Go yet, love a w beloved of *her* H802
13:13 The sorrows of a travailing w shall H3205
Mic 4: 9 pangs have taken thee as a w in travail.
10 of Zion, like a w in travail: for now shalt
Zec 5: 7 w that sitteth in the midst of the ephah. H802
Mt 5:28 looketh on a w to lust after her hath *G1135*
9:20 And, behold, a w, which was diseased *G1135*
22 the w was made whole from that hour. *G1135*
13:33 unto leaven, which a w took, and hid in *G1135*
15:22 And, behold, a w of Canaan came out *G1135*
28 said unto her, O w, great *is* thy faith: be *G1135*
22:27 And last of all the w died also. *G1135*
26: 7 There came unto him a w having an *G1135*
10 trouble ye the w? for she hath wrought *G1135*
13 also this, that this w hath done, be told *G3778*
Mk 5:25 And a certain w, which had an issue of *G1135*
33 But the w fearing and trembling, *G1135*
7:25 For a *certain* w, whose young daughter *G1135*
26 The w was a Greek, a Syrophenician by *G1135*
10:12 And if a w shall put away her husband, *G1135*
12:22 left no seed: last of all the w died also. *G1135*
14: 3 there came a w having an alabaster *G1135*
Lk 4:26 of Sidon, unto a w *that was* a widow. *G1135*
7:37 And, behold, a w in the city, which was *G1135*
39 what manner of w *this is* that toucheth *G1135*
44 And he turned to the w, and said unto *G1135*
44 Seest thou this w? I entered into thine *G1135*
45 Thou gavest me no kiss: but this w *G3778*
46 anoint: but this w hath anointed my *G3778*
50 And he said to the w, Thy faith hath *G1135*
8:43 And a w having an issue of blood *G1135*
47 And when the w saw that she was not *G1135*
10:38 village: and a certain w named Martha *G1135*
11:27 things, a certain w of the company *G1135*
13:11 And, behold, there was a w which had *G1135*
12 W, thou art loosed from thine infirmity. *G1135*
16 And ought not this w, being a daughter *G3778*
21 It is like leaven, which a w took and hid *G1135*
15: 8 Either what w having ten pieces of *G1135*
20:32 Last of all the w died also. *G1135*
22:57 And he denied him, saying, W, I know *G1135*
Jn 2: 4 Jesus saith unto her, W, what have I to *G1135*
4: 7 There cometh a w of Samaria to draw *G1135*
9 Then saith the w of Samaria unto him, *G1135*
9 of me, which am a w of Samaria? for *G1135*
11 The w saith unto him, Sir, thou hast *G1135*
15 The w saith unto him, Sir, give me this *G1135*
17 The w answered and said, I have no *G1135*
19 The w saith unto him, Sir, I perceive *G1135*
21 Jesus saith unto her, W, believe me, the *G1135*
25 The w saith unto him, I know that *G1135*
27 he talked with the w: yet no man said, *G1135*
28 The w then left her waterpot, and went *G1135*
39 the saying of the w, which testified, He *G1135*
42 And said unto the w, Now we believe, *G1135*
8: 3 unto him a w taken in adultery; and *G1135*
4 They say unto him, Master, this w was *G1135*
9 alone, and the w standing in the midst. *G1135*
10 saw none but the w, he said unto her, *G1135*
10 he said unto her, W, where are those *G1135*
16:21 A w when she is in travail hath sorrow, *G1135*
19:26 unto his mother, W, behold thy son! *G1135*
20:13 And they say unto her, W, why weepest *G1135*
15 Jesus saith unto her, W, why weepest *G1135*

Act 9:36 Dorcas: this w was full of good works G3778
16: 1 son of a certain w, which was a Jewess, G1135
14 And a certain w named Lydia, a seller G1135
17:34 Areopagite, and a w named Damaris, G1135
Ro 1:27 the natural use of the w, burned in their G2338
7: 2 For the w which hath an husband is G1135
1Co 7: 1 *It is* good for a man not to touch a w. G1135
2 and let every w have her own husband. G1538
13 And the w which hath an husband that G1135
34 The unmarried w careth for the things G22
11: 3 the head of the w *is* the man; and the G1135
5 But every w that prayeth or G1135
6 For if the w be not covered, let her also G1135
6 it be a shame for a w to be shorn or G1135
7 God: but the w is the glory of the man. G1135
8 For the man is not of the w; but the G1135
8 of the woman; but the w of the man. G1135
9 Neither was the man created for the w; G1135
9 for the woman; but the w for the man. G1135
10 For this cause ought the w to have G1135
11 man without the w, neither the woman G1135
11 the w without the man, in the Lord. G1135
12 For as the w *is* of the man, even so *is* G1135
12 also by the w; but all things of God. G1135
13 that a w pray unto God uncovered? G1135
15 But if a w have long hair, it is a glory to G1135
Gal 4: 4 Son, made of a w, made under the law, G1135
1Th 5: 3 w with child; and they shall not escape. G3588
1Ti 2:11 Let the w learn in silence with all G1135
12 But I suffer not a w to teach, nor to G1135
14 And Adam was not deceived, but the w G1135
5:16 If any man or w that believeth have
Rev 2:20 sufferest that w Jezebel, which calleth G1135
12: 1 in heaven; a w clothed with the sun, G1135
4 stood before the w which was ready to G1135
6 And the w fled into the wilderness, G1135
13 w which brought forth the man *child*. G1135
14 And to the w were given two wings of a G1135
15 a flood after the w, that he might cause G1135
16 And the earth helped the w, and the G1135
17 And the dragon was wroth with the w, G1135
17: 3 and I saw a w sit upon a scarlet G1135
4 And the w was arrayed in purple and G1135
6 And I saw the w drunken with the G1135
7 the mystery of the w, and of the beast G1135
9 mountains, on which the w sitteth. G1135
18 And the w which thou sawest is that G1135

WOMANKIND

Lev 18:22 mankind, as with w: it *is* abomination. H802

WOMAN'S

Gen 38:20 from the w hand: but he found her not. H802
Ex 21:22 according as the w husband will lay H802
Lev 24:11 And the Israelitish w son blasphemed H802
Nu 5:18 and uncover the w head, and put the H802
25 offering out of the w hand, and shall H802
Dt 22: 5 a man put on a w garment: for all that H802
1Ki 3:19 And this w child died in the night; H802

WOMB

Gen 25:23 nations *are* in thy w, and two manner of H990
24 behold, *there were* twins in her w. H990
29:31 opened her w: but Rachel *was* barren. H7358
30: 2 withheld from thee the fruit of the w? H990
22 hearkened to her, and opened her w. H7358
38:27 travail, that, behold, twins *were* in her w. H990
49:25 blessings of the breasts, and of the w: H7356
Ex 13: 2 openeth the w among the children H7358
Nu 8:16 as open every w, *even instead of* the H7358
12:12 when he cometh out of his mother's w. H7358
Dt 7:13 the fruit of thy w, and the fruit of thy H990
Jdg 13: 5 unto God from the w: and he shall begin H990
7 God from the w to the day of his death. H990
16:17 from my mother's w: if I be shaven, then H990
Ru 1:11 my w, that they may be your husbands? H4578
1Sa 1: 5 but the LORD had shut up her w. H7358
6 because the LORD had shut up her w. H7358
Job 1:21 I out of my mother's w, and naked shall I H990
3:10 w, nor hid sorrow from mine eyes. H990
11 Why died I not from the w? *why* did I H7358
10:18 forth out of the w? Oh that I had given H7358
19 been carried from the w to the grave. H990
24:20 The w shall forget him; the worm shall H7358
31:15 Did not he that made me in the w make H990
15 and did not one fashion us in the w? H7358
18 I have guided her from my mother's w;) H990
38: 8 forth, *as if* it had issued out of the w? H7358
29 Out of whose w came the ice? and the H990
Ps 22: 9 But thou *art* he that took me out of the w: H990
10 I was cast upon thee from the w: thou H7358
58: 3 The wicked are estranged from the w: H7358
71: 6 up from the w: thou art he that took H990
110: 3 of holiness from the w of the morning: H7358
127: 3 *and* the fruit of the w *is his* reward. H990
139:13 thou hast covered me in my mother's w. H990
Prv 30:16 The grave; and the barren w; the earth H7356
31: 2 of my w? and what, the son of my vows? H990
Ecc 5:15 As he came forth of his mother's w, H990
11: 5 *do grow* in the w of her that is with child: H990
Isa 13:18 the w; their eye shall not spare children. H990
44: 2 thee from the w, *which* will help thee; H990
24 thee from the w, I *am* the LORD that H990
46: 3 the belly, which are carried from the w: H7356
48: 8 wast called a transgressor from the w. H990
49: 1 called me from the w; from the bowels of H990
5 me from the w *to be* his servant, to H990
15 on the son of her w? yea, they may forget, H990
66: 9 forth, and shut *the* w? saith thy God.
Jer 1: 5 forth out of the w I sanctified thee, *and* H7358
20:17 Because he slew me not from the w; or H7358
17 and her w *to be* always great *with me*. H7358
18 Wherefore came I forth out of the w to H7358
Ezk 20:26 that openeth the w, that I might make H7356
Hos 9:11 from the w, and from the conception. H990
14 them a miscarrying w and dry breasts. H7358
16 I slay *even* the beloved *fruit* of their w. H990
12: 3 He took his brother by the heel in the w, H990
Mt 19:12 *their* mother's w: and there are some G2836
Lk 1:15 Holy Ghost, even from his mother's w. G2836
31 conceive in thy w, and bring forth a G1064
41 babe leaped in her w; and Elisabeth was G2836
42 and blessed *is* the fruit of thy w. G2836
44 ears, the babe leaped in my w for joy. G2836
2:21 angel before he was conceived in the w. G2836
23 the w shall be called holy to the Lord;) G3388
11:27 Blessed *is* the w that bare thee, and G2836
Jn 3: 4 time into his mother's w, and be born? G2836
Act 3: 2 lame from his mother's w was carried, G2836
14: 8 his mother's w, who never had walked: G2836
Ro 4:19 neither yet the deadness of Sarah's w: G3388
Gal 1:15 mother's w, and called *me* by his grace, G2836

WOMBS

Gen 20:18 fast closed up all the w of the house of H7358
Lk 23:29 barren, and the w that never bare, and G2836

WOMEN

Gen 14:16 goods, and the w also, and the people. H802
18:11 to be with Sarah after the manner of w. H802
24:11 the time that w go out to draw *water*.
31:35 for the custom of w *is* upon me. And he H802
33: 5 And he lifted up his eyes, and saw the w H802
Ex 1:16 to the Hebrew w, and see *them* upon H5680
19 the Hebrew w *are* not as the Egyptian H5680
19 as the Egyptian w; for they *are* lively, and H802
2: 7 of the Hebrew w, that she may nurse H5680
15:20 hand; and all the w went out after her H802
35:22 And they came, both men and w, as H802
25 And all the w that were wise hearted did H802
26 And all the w whose heart stirred them H802
38: 8 of *the* w assembling, which assembled
Lev 26:26 staff of your bread, ten w shall bake your H802
Nu 31: 9 And the children of Israel took *all* the w H802
15 them, Have ye saved all the w alive? H5347
18 But all the w children, that have not H802
35 persons in all, of w that had not known H802
Dt 2:34 the men, and the w, and the little ones, of H802
3: 6 the men, w, and children, of every city. H802
20:14 But the w, and the little ones, and the H802
31:12 Gather the people together, men, and w, H802
Jos 8:25 day, both of men and w, *were* twelve H802
35 of Israel, with the w, and the little ones, H802
Jdg 5:24 Blessed above w shall Jael the wife of H802
24 blessed shall she be above w in the tent. H802
9:49 died also, about a thousand men and w. H802
51 fled all the men and w, and all they of the H802
16:27 Now the house was full of men and w; H802
27 w, that beheld while Samson made sport. H802
21:10 the sword, with the w and the children. H802
14 saved alive of the w of Jabesh-gilead: H802
16 the w are destroyed out of Benjamin? H802
Ru 1: 4 And they took them wives of the w of H802
4:14 And the w said unto Naomi, Blessed *be* H802
17 And the w her neighbours gave it a
1Sa 2:22 they lay with the w that assembled *at* the H802
4:20 And about the time of her death the w
15:33 sword hath made w childless, so shall H802
1Sa 15:33 childless among w. And Samuel hewed H802
18: 6 the Philistine, that the w came out of all H802
7 And the w answered *one another* as they H802
21: 4 have kept themselves at least from w. H802
5 him, Of a truth w *have been* kept from H802
22:19 both men and w, children and sucklings, H802
30: 2 And had taken the w captives, that *were* H802
2Sa 1:26 me was wonderful, passing the love of w. H802
6:19 as well to the w as men, to every one H802
15:16 And the king left ten w, *which were* H802
19:35 men and singing w? wherefore then
20: 3 the king took the ten w *his* concubines, H802
1Ki 3:16 Then came there two w, *that were* H802
11: 1 But king Solomon loved many strange w, H802
1 daughter of Pharaoh, w of the Moabites,
2Ki 8:12 children, and rip up their w with child.
15:16 *it; and* all the w therein that were with
23: 7 the w wove hangings for the grove. H802
2Ch 28: 8 thousand, w, sons, and daughters, H802
35:25 and the singing w spake of Josiah in
Ezr 2:65 two hundred singing men and singing w.
10: 1 of men and w and children: for the H802
Neh 7:67 forty and five singing men and singing w.
8: 2 both of men and w, and all that could H802
3 the men and the w, and those that could H802
13:26 even him did outlandish w cause to sin. H802
Est 1: 9 a feast for the w *in* the royal house which H802
17 abroad unto all w, so that they shall H802
2: 3 to the house of the w, unto the custody of H802
3 keeper of the w; and let their things for H802
8 to the custody of Hegai, keeper of the w. H802
9 unto the best *place* of the house of the w. H802
12 to the manner of the w, (for so were the H802
12 *other* things for the purifying of the w;) H802
13 the house of the w unto the king's house. H802
14 second house of the w, to the custody of H802
15 the keeper of the w, appointed. And H802
17 above all the w, and she obtained grace H802
3:13 little children and w, in one day, *even* H802
8:11 little ones and w, and *to take* the spoil H802
Job 2:10 as one of the foolish w speaketh. What? H5036
42:15 And in all the land were no w found *so* H802
Ps 45: 9 thy honourable w: upon thy right hand H3368
Prv 22:14 The mouth of strange w *is* a deep pit: H2114
23:33 Thine eyes shall behold strange w, and H2114
31: 3 Give not thy strength unto w, nor thy H802
Ecc 2: 8 me men singers and w singers, and the
Song 1: 8 fairest among w, go thy way forth by H802
5: 9 fairest among w? what *is* thy beloved H802
6: 1 fairest among w? whither is thy beloved H802
Isa 3:12 oppressors, and w rule over them. O my H802
4: 1 And in that day seven w shall take hold H802
19:16 In that day shall Egypt be like unto w: H802
27:11 be broken off: the w come, *and* set them H802
32: 9 Rise up, ye w that are at ease; hear my H802
10 ye careless w: for the vintage shall H982
11 Tremble, ye w that are at ease; be
Jer 7:18 the fire, and the w knead *their* dough, to H802
9:17 for the mourning w, that they may come;
17 send for cunning *w*, that they may come:
20 Yet hear the word of the LORD, O ye w, H802
38:22 And, behold, all the w that are left in the H802
22 princes, and those *w* shall say, Thy
40: 7 him men, and w, and children, and of H802
41:16 of war, and the w, and the children, and H802
43: 6 *Even* men, and w, and children, and the H802
44:15 gods, and all the w that stood by, a great H802
20 men, and to the w, and to all the people H802
24 and to all the w, Hear the word of the H802
50:37 shall become as w: a sword *is* upon her H802
51:30 they became as w: they have burned her H802
Lam 2:20 done this. Shall the w eat their fruit, *and* H802
4:10 The hands of the pitiful w have sodden H802
5:11 They ravished the w in Zion, *and* the H802
Ezk 8:14 there sat w weeping for Tammuz. H802
9: 6 little children, and w: but come not near H802
13:18 GOD; Woe to the *w* that sew pillows to
16:34 And the contrary is in thee from *other* w H802
38 And I will judge thee, as w that break
41 the sight of many w: and I will cause thee H802
23: 2 Son of man, there were two w, the H802
10 famous among w; for they had executed H802
44 Aholah and unto Aholibah, the lewd w.
45 after the manner of w that shed blood;
48 of the land, that all w may be taught not H802
Dan 11:17 the daughter of w, corrupting her: but H802
37 nor the desire of w, nor regard any god: H802
Hos 13:16 their w with child shall be ripped up.
Am 1:13 they have ripped up the w with child of

Mic 2: 9 The w of my people have ye cast out H802
Nah 3:13 midst of thee *are* w: the gates of thy land H802
Zec 5: 9 came out two w, and the wind *was* in H802
8: 4 old men and old w dwell in the streets H2205
14: 2 rifled, and the w ravished; and half of H802
Mt 11:11 that are born of w there hath not risen G1135
14:21 thousand men, beside w and children. G1135
15:38 thousand men, beside w and children. G1135
24:41 Two w *shall be* grinding at the mill; the
27:55 And many w were there beholding afar G1135
28: 5 and said unto the w, Fear not ye: for I G1135
Mk 15:40 There were also w looking on afar off: G1135
41 and many other w which came up with G243
Lk 1:28 *is* with thee: blessed *art* thou among w. G1135
42 w, and blessed *is* the fruit of thy womb. G1135
7:28 that are born of w there is not a greater G1135
8: 2 And certain w, which had been healed G1135
17:35 Two w shall be grinding together; the
23:27 of people, and of w, which also G1135
49 And all his acquaintance, and the w G1135
55 And the w also, which came with him G1135
24:10 James, and other w *that were* with them,
22 Yea, and certain w also of our G1135
24 the w had said: but him they saw not. G1135
Act 1:14 with the w, and Mary the mother G1135
5:14 Lord, multitudes both of men and w.) G1135
8: 3 men and w committed *them* to prison. G1135
12 they were baptized, both men and w. G1135
9: 2 they were men or w, he might bring G1135
13:50 and honourable w, and the chief men of G1135
16:13 unto the w which resorted *thither*. G1135
17: 4 multitude, and of the chief w not a few. G1135
12 of honourable w which were Greeks, G1135
22: 4 delivering into prisons both men and w. G1135
Ro 1:26 for even their w did change the natural G2338
1Co 14:34 Let your w keep silence in the G1135
35 a shame for w to speak in the church. G1135
Php 4: 3 help those w which laboured with G846
1Ti 2: 9 In like manner also, that w adorn G1135
10 But (which becometh w professing G1135
5: 2 The elder w as mothers; the younger as G4245
14 I will therefore that the younger w G3501
2Ti 3: 6 lead captive silly w laden with sins, led G1133
Tit 2: 3 The aged w likewise, that *they be* in G4247
4 That they may teach the young w to be G3501
Heb 11:35 W received their dead raised to life G1135
1Pt 3: 5 old time the holy w also, who trusted in G1135
Rev 9: 8 And they had hair as the hair of w, and G1135
14: 4 not defiled with w; for they are virgins. G1135

WOMEN'S
Est 2:11 the court of the w house, to know how H802

WOMENSERVANTS
Gen 20:14 menservants, and w, and gave *them* H8198
32: 5 menservants, and w: and I have sent to H8198
22 and his two w, and his eleven sons, H8198

WON
1Ch 26:27 Out of the spoils w in battles did they
Prv 18:19 A brother offended *is harder to be w*
1Pt 3: 1 be w by the conversation of the wives; G2770

WONDER
Dt 13: 1 dreams, and giveth thee a sign or a w, H4159
2 And the sign or the w come to pass, H4159
28:46 and for a w, and upon thy seed for ever. H4159
2Ch 32:31 to inquire of the w that was *done* in the H4159
Ps 71: 7 I am as a w unto many; but thou *art* H4159
Isa 20: 3 and w upon Egypt and upon Ethiopia; H4159
29: 9 Stay yourselves, and w; cry ye out, and H8539
14 work and a w: for the wisdom of their H6382
Jer 4: 9 astonished, and the prophets shall w. H8539
Hab 1: 5 and regard, and w marvellously: for *I* H8539
Act 3:10 were filled with w and amazement at G2285
13:41 Behold, ye despisers, and w, and perish: G2296
Rev 12: 1 And there appeared a great w in G4592
3 And there appeared another w in G4592
17: 8 on the earth shall w, whose names were G2296

WONDERED
Isa 59:16 *was* no man, and w that *there was* no H8074
63: 5 to help; and I w that *there was* none H8074
Zec 3: 8 for they *are* men w at: for, behold, I will H4159
Mt 15:31 Insomuch that the multitude w, when G2296
Mk 6:51 in themselves beyond measure, and w. G2296
Lk 2:18 And all they that heard *it* w at those G2296
4:22 And all bare him witness, and w at the G2296
8:25 And they being afraid w, saying one to G2296
9:43 But while they w every one at all things G2296
11:14 out, the dumb spake; and the people w. G2296
24:41 not for joy, and w, he said unto them, G2296
Act 7:31 When Moses saw *it*, he w at the sight: G2296
8:13 with Philip, and w, beholding the G1839
Rev 13: 3 and all the world w after the beast. G2296
17: 6 I saw her, I w with great admiration. G2296

WONDERFUL
Dt 28:59 make thy plagues w, and the plagues of H6381
2Sa 1:26 me was w, passing the love of women. H6381
2Ch 2: 9 I am about to build *shall be* w great. H6381
Job 42: 3 things too w for me, which I knew not. H6381
Ps 40: 5 Many, O LORD my God, *are* thy w H6381
78: 4 and his w works that he hath done. H6381
107: 8 *for* his w works to the children of men! H6381
15 *for* his w works to the children of men! H6381
21 *for* his w works to the children of men! H6381
31 *for* his w works to the children of men! H6381
111: 4 He hath made his w works to be H6381
119:129 Thy testimonies *are* w: therefore doth H6382
139: 6 *Such* knowledge *is* too w for H6383+H6383
Prv 30:18 There be three *things which* are too w H6381
Isa 9: 6 name shall be called W, Counsellor, The H6382
25: 1 thou hast done w *things; thy* counsels H6382
28:29 w in counsel, *and* excellent in working. H6381
Jer 5:30 A w and horrible thing is committed in H8047
Mt 7:22 and in thy name done many w works? G1411
21:15 scribes saw the w things that he did, G2297
Act 2:11 in our tongues the w works of God. G3167

WONDERFULLY
1Sa 6: 6 he had wrought w among them, did H5953
Ps 139:14 I am fearfully *and* w made: marvellous H6395
Lam 1: 9 therefore she came down w: she had no H6382
Dan 8:24 he shall destroy w, and shall prosper, H6381

WONDERING
Gen 24:21 And the man w at her held his peace, to H7583
Lk 24:12 and departed, w in himself at that G2296
Act 3:11 that is called Solomon's, greatly w. G1569

WONDERS
Ex 3:20 Egypt with all my w which I will do in H6381
4:21 thou do all those w before Pharaoh, H4159
7: 3 signs and my w in the land of Egypt. H4159
11: 9 unto you; that my w may be multiplied H4159
10 And Moses and Aaron did all these w H4159
15:11 in holiness, fearful *in* praises, doing w? H6382
Dt 4:34 by signs, and by w, and by war, and by H4159
6:22 And the LORD shewed signs and w, H4159
7:19 the signs, and the w, and the mighty H4159
26: 8 and with signs, and with w: H4159
34:11 In all the signs and the w, which the H4159
Jos 3: 5 the LORD will do w among you. H6381
1Ch 16:12 his w, and the judgments of his mouth; H4159
Neh 9:10 And shewedst signs and w upon H4159
17 mindful of thy w that thou didst among H6381
Job 9:10 out; yea, and w without number. H6381
Ps 77:11 surely I will remember thy w of old. H6382
14 Thou *art* the God that doest w: thou H6382
78:11 And forgat his works, and his w that he H6381
43 in Egypt, and his w in the field of Zoan: H4159
88:10 Wilt thou shew w to the dead? shall the H6382
12 Shall thy w be known in the dark? and H6382
89: 5 And the heavens shall praise thy w, O H6382
96: 3 the heathen, his w among all people. H6381
105: 5 his w, and the judgments of his mouth; H4159
27 them, and w in the land of Ham. H4159
106: 7 Our fathers understood not thy w in H6381
107:24 of the LORD, and his w in the deep. H6381
135: 9 *Who* sent tokens and w into the midst H4159
136: 4 To him who alone doeth great w: for his H6381
Isa 8:18 for signs and for w in Israel from the H4159
Jer 32:20 Which hast set signs and w in the land H4159
21 signs, and with w, and with a strong H4159
Dan 4: 2 the signs and w that the high God hath H8540
3 mighty *are* his w! his kingdom *is* an H8540
6:27 signs and w in heaven and in earth, H8540
12: 6 long *shall it be to* the end of these w? H6382
Joel 2:30 And I will shew w in the heavens and H4159
Mt 24:24 great signs and w; insomuch that, if *it* G5059
Mk 13:22 shew signs and w, to seduce, if *it were* G5059
Jn 4:48 ye see signs and w, ye will not believe. G5059
Act 2:19 And I will shew w in heaven above, and G5059
22 by miracles and w and signs, which G5059
43 w and signs were done by the apostles. G5059
4:30 that signs and w may be done by the G5059
5:12 many signs and w wrought among the G5059
6: 8 w and miracles among the people. G5059
7:36 he had shewed w and signs in the land G5059
14: 3 signs and w to be done by their hands. G5059
15:12 what miracles and w God had wrought G5059
Ro 15:19 Through mighty signs and w, by the G5059
2Co 12:12 in signs, and w, and mighty deeds. G5059
2Th 2: 9 with all power and signs and lying w, G5059
Heb 2: 4 both with signs and w, and with divers G5059
Rev 13:13 And he doeth great w, so that he G4592

WONDROUS
1Ch 16: 9 unto him, talk ye of all his w works. H6381
Job 37:14 still, and consider the w works of God. H6381
16 of the clouds, the w works of him H4652
Ps 26: 7 and tell of all thy w works. H6381
71:17 hitherto have I declared thy w works. H6381
72:18 God of Israel, who only doeth w things. H6381
75: 1 thy name is near thy w works declare. H6381
78:32 still, and believed not for his w works. H6381
86:10 For thou *art* great, and doest w things: H6381
105: 2 unto him: talk ye of all his w works. H6381
106:22 W works in the land of Ham, *and* H6381
119:18 I may behold w things out of thy law. H6381
27 precepts: so shall I talk of thy w works. H6381
145: 5 of thy majesty, and of thy w works. H6381
Jer 21: 2 w works, that he may go up from us. H6381

WONDROUSLY
Jdg 13:19 w; and Manoah and his wife looked on. H6381
Joel 2:26 that hath dealt w with you: and my H6381

WONT
Ex 21:29 But if the ox were w to push with his H5056
Nu 22:30 w to do so unto thee? And he said, Nay. H5532
1Sa 30:31 himself and his men were w to haunt. H1980
2Sa 20:18 Then she spake, saying, They were w to H1696
Dan 3:19 times more than it was w to be heated. H2370
Mt 27:15 Now at *that* feast the governor was w G1486
Mk 10: 1 and, as he was w, he taught them again. G1486
Lk 22:39 and went, as he was w, to the mount of G2596
Act 16:13 where prayer was w to be made; and G3543

WOOD
Gen 6:14 Make thee an ark of gopher w; rooms H6086
22: 3 his son, and clave the w for the burnt H6086
6 And Abraham took the w of the burnt H6086
7 the fire and the w: but where *is* the H6086
9 altar there, and laid the w in order, and H6086
9 and laid him on the altar upon the w. H6086
Ex 7:19 in *vessels of* w, and in *vessels of* stone. H6086
25: 5 red, and badgers' skins, and shittim w, H6086
10 an ark *of* shittim w: two cubits and a H6086
13 shittim w, and overlay them with gold. H6086
23 a table *of* shittim w: two cubits *shall be* H6086
28 staves *of* shittim w, and overlay them H6086
26:15 tabernacle *of* shittim w standing up. H6086
26 And thou shalt make bars *of* shittim w; H6086
32 pillars of shittim w overlaid with gold:
37 pillars *of* shittim w, and overlay them
27: 1 an altar *of* shittim w, five cubits long, H6086
6 shittim w, and overlay them with brass. H6086
30: 1 upon: *of* shittim w shalt thou make it. H6086
5 shittim w, and overlay them with gold. H6086
35: 7 red, and badgers' skins, and shittim w, H6086
24 was found shittim w for any work of H6086
33 *them*, and in carving of w, to make any H6086
36:20 tabernacle *of* shittim w, standing up. H6086
31 And he made bars of shittim w; five for H6086
36 pillars *of* shittim w, and overlaid them
37: 1 And Bezaleel made the ark *of* shittim w: H6086
4 And he made staves *of* shittim w, and H6086
10 And he made the table *of* shittim w: two H6086
15 And he made the staves *of* shittim w, H6086
25 altar *of* shittim w: the length of it *was* H6086
28 And he made the staves *of* shittim w, H6086
38: 1 offering *of* shittim w: five cubits *was* the H6086
6 And he made the staves *of* shittim w, H6086
Lev 1: 7 and lay the w in order upon the fire: H6086
8 in order upon the w that *is* on the fire H6086
12 in order on the w that *is* on the fire H6086
17 altar, upon the w that *is* upon the fire: H6086
3: 5 which *is* upon the w that *is* on the fire: H6086
4:12 burn him on the w with fire: where the H6086
6:12 the priest shall burn w on it every H6086
11:32 *it be* any vessel of w, or raiment, or H6086
14: 4 and cedar w, and scarlet, and hyssop: H6086
6 it, and the cedar w, and the scarlet, and H6086
49 and cedar w, and scarlet, and hyssop: H6086
51 And he shall take the cedar w, and the H6086

W

Lev 14:52 with the cedar **w**, and with the hyssop, H6086
15:12 vessel of **w** shall be rinsed in water. H6086
Nu 13:20 whether there be **w** therein, or not. And H6086
19: 6 And the priest shall take cedar **w**, and H6086
31:20 of goats' *hair*, and all things made of **w**. H6086
35:18 hand weapon of **w**, wherewith he may H6086
Dt 4:28 of men's hands, **w** and stone, which H6086
10: 1 the mount, and make thee an ark of **w**. H6086
3 And I made an ark *of* shittim **w**, and H6086
19: 5 As when a man goeth into the **w** with H3293
5 his neighbour to hew **w**, and his hand H6086
28:36 thou serve other gods, **w** and stone. H6086
64 fathers have known, *even* **w** and stone. H6086
29:11 of thy **w** unto the drawer of thy water: H6086
17 and their idols, **w** and stone, silver and H6086
Jos 9:21 let them be hewers of **w** and drawers of H6086
23 and hewers of **w** and drawers of water H6086
27 day hewers of **w** and drawers of water H6086
17:15 get thee up to the **w** *country*, and cut H3293
18 be thine; for it *is* a **w**, and thou shalt cut H3293
Jdg 6:26 sacrifice with the **w** of the grove which H6086
1Sa 6:14 and they clave the **w** of the cart, and H6086
14:25 And all *they of* the land came to a **w**; H3293
26 come into the **w**, behold, the honey H3293
23:15 *was* in the wilderness of Ziph in a **w**. H2793
16 **w**, and strengthened his hand in God. H2793
18 the **w**, and Jonathan went to his house. H2793
19 holds in the **w**, in the hill of Hachilah, H2793
2Sa 6: 5 *made of* fir **w**, even on harps, and H6086
18: 6 and the battle was in the **w** of Ephraim; H3293
8 the country: and the **w** devoured more H3293
17 into a great pit in the **w**, and laid a very H3293
24:22 *other* instruments of the oxen for **w**. H6086
1Ki 6:15 on the inside with **w**, and covered the H6086
18:23 and lay *it* on **w**, and put no fire *under*: H6086
23 and lay *it* on **w**, and put no fire *under*: H6086
33 And he put the **w** in order, and cut the H6086
33 laid *him* on the **w**, and said, Fill four H6086
33 *it* on the burnt sacrifice, and on the **w**. H6086
38 sacrifice, and the **w**, and the stones, and H6086
2Ki 2:24 bears out of the **w**, and tare forty and H3293
6: 4 they came to Jordan, they cut down **w**. H6086
19:18 of men's hands, **w** and stone: therefore H6086
1Ch 16:33 Then shall the trees of the **w** sing out at H3293
21:23 instruments for **w**, and the wheat for H6086
22: 4 Tyre brought much cedar **w** to David. H6086
29: 2 of iron, and **w** for *things* of wood; H6086
2 wood for *things* of **w**; onyx stones, and H6086
2Ch 2:16 And we will cut **w** out of Lebanon, as H6086
Neh 8: 4 upon a pulpit of **w**, which they had H6086
10:34 the people, for the **w** offering, to bring H6086
13:31 And for the **w** offering, at times H6086
Job 41:27 iron as straw, *and* brass as rotten **w**. H6086
Ps 80:13 The boar out of the **w** doth waste it, H3293
83:14 As the fire burneth a **w**, and as the H3293
96:12 then shall all the trees of the **w** rejoice H3293
132: 6 we found it in the fields of the **w**. H3293
141: 7 cutteth and cleaveth *w* upon the earth.
Prv 26:20 Where no **w** is, *there* the fire goeth out: H6086
21 *As* coals *are* to burning coals, and **w** to H6086
Ecc 2: 6 the **w** that bringeth forth trees: H3293
10: 9 **w** shall be endangered thereby. H6086
Song 2: 3 the trees of the **w**, so *is* my beloved H3293
3: 9 himself a chariot of the **w** of Lebanon. H6086
Isa 7: 2 trees of the **w** are moved with the wind. H3293
10:15 should lift up *itself*, *as if it were* no **w**. H6086
30:33 *is* fire and much **w**; the breath of the H6086
37:19 of men's hands, **w** and stone: therefore H6086
45:20 that set up the **w** of their graven image, H6086
60:17 silver, and for **w** brass, and for stones H6086
Jer 5:14 this people **w**, and it shall devour them. H6086
7:18 The children gather **w**, and the fathers H6086
28:13 the yokes of **w**; but thou shalt make H6086
46:22 against her with axes, as hewers of **w**. H6086
Lam 5: 4 water for money; our **w** is sold unto us. H6086
13 grind, and the children fell under the **w**. H6086
Ezk 15: 3 Shall **w** be taken thereof to do any H6086
20:32 of the countries, to serve **w** and stone. H6086
24:10 Heap on **w**, kindle the fire, consume the H6086
39:10 So that they shall take no **w** out of the H6086
41:16 door, cieled with **w** round about, and H6086
22 The altar of **w** *was* three cubits high, H6086
22 thereof, *were* of **w**: and he said unto me, H6086
Dan 5: 4 of brass, of iron, of **w**, and of stone. H636
23 of brass, iron, **w**, and stone, which see H636
Mic 7:14 dwell solitarily *in* the **w**, in the midst of H3293
Hab 2:19 Woe unto him that saith to the **w**, H6086
Hag 1: 8 Go up to the mountain, and bring **w**, H6086
Zec 12: 6 of fire among the **w**, and like a torch of H6086
1Co 3:12 silver, precious stones, **w**, hay, stubble; *G3586*
2Ti 2:20 silver, but also of **w** and of earth; and *G3585*
Rev 9:20 and stone, and of **w**: which neither can *G3585*
18:12 and all thyine **w**, and all manner vessels *G3586*
12 **w**, and of brass, and iron, and marble, *G3586*

WOOD-OFFERING See WOOD and OFFERING.

WOODS
Ezk 34:25 in the wilderness, and sleep in the **w**. H3264

WOOF
Lev 13:48 Whether *it be* in the warp, or **w**; of H6154
49 the warp, or in the **w**, or in any thing of H6154
51 warp, or in the **w**, or in a skin, *or* in any H6154
52 whether warp or **w**, in woollen or in H6154
53 or in the **w**, or in any thing of skin; H6154
56 skin, or out of the warp, or out of the **w**: H6154
57 the warp, or in the **w**, or in any thing of H6154
58 And the garment, either warp, or **w**, or H6154
59 in the warp, or **w**, or any thing of skins, H6154

WOOL
Jdg 6:37 Behold, I will put a fleece of **w** in the H6785
2Ki 3: 4 an hundred thousand rams, with the **w**. H6785
Ps 147:16 He giveth snow like **w**: he scattereth the H6785
Prv 31:13 She seeketh **w**, and flax, and worketh H6785
Isa 1:18 be red like crimson, they shall be as **w**. H6785
51: 8 worm shall eat them like **w**: but my H6785
Ezk 27:18 in the wine of Helbon, and white **w**. H6785
34: 3 you with the **w**, ye kill them that are H6785
44:17 garments; and no **w** shall come upon H6785
Dan 7: 9 head like the pure **w**: his throne *was like* H6015
Hos 2: 5 **w** and my flax, mine oil and my drink. H6785
9 will recover my **w** and my flax *given* to H6785
Heb 9:19 water, and scarlet **w**, and hyssop, and *G2053*
Rev 1:14 *were* white like **w**, as white as snow; *G2053*

WOOLLEN
Lev 13:47 *it be* a **w** garment, or a linen garment; H6785
48 of linen, or of **w**; whether in a skin, or H6785
52 warp or woof, in **w** or in linen, or any H6785
59 in a garment of **w** or linen, either in the H6785
19:19 of linen and **w** come upon thee. H8162
Dt 22:11 divers sorts, *as of* **w** and linen together. H6785

WORD
Gen 15: 1 After these things the **w** of the LORD H1697
4 And, behold, the **w** of the LORD *came* H1697
30:34 I would it might be according to thy **w**. H1697
37:14 and bring me **w** again. So he sent him H1697
41:40 unto thy **w** shall all my people H6310
44: 2 to the **w** that Joseph had spoken. H1697
18 I pray thee, speak a **w** in my lord's ears, H1697
Ex 8:10 *it* according to thy **w**: that thou mayest H1697
13 And the LORD did according to the **w** H1697
31 And the LORD did according to the **w** H1697
9:20 He that feared the **w** of the LORD H1697
21 And he that regarded not the **w** of the H1697
12:35 according to the **w** of Moses; and they H1697
14:12 *Is* not this the **w** that we did tell thee in H1697
32:28 according to the **w** of Moses: and there H1697
Lev 10: 7 they did according to the **w** of Moses. H1697
Nu 3:16 **w** of the LORD, as he was commanded. H6310
51 according to the **w** of the LORD, as the H6310
4:45 **w** of the LORD by the hand of Moses. H6310
11:23 **w** shall come to pass unto thee or not. H1697
13:26 and brought back **w** unto them, and H1697
14:20 I have pardoned according to thy **w**: H1697
15:31 Because he hath despised the **w** of the H1697
20:24 against my **w** at the water of Meribah. H6310
22: 8 I will bring you **w** again, as the LORD H1697
18 go beyond the **w** of the LORD my God, H6310
20 them; but yet the **w** which I shall say H1697
35 men: but only the **w** that I shall speak H1697
38 say any thing? the **w** that God putteth H1697
23: 5 And the LORD put a **w** in Balaam's H1697
16 and put a **w** in his mouth, and said, H1697
27:21 the LORD: at his **w** shall they go out, H6310
21 go out, and at his **w** they shall come in, H6310
30: 2 not break his **w**, he shall do according H1697
36: 5 Israel according to the **w** of the LORD, H6310
Dt 1:22 the land, and bring us **w** again by what H1697
25 and brought us **w** again, and said, *It is* H1697
4: 2 Ye shall not add unto the **w** which I H1697
5: 5 to shew you the **w** of the LORD: for ye H1697
8: 3 only, but by every *w* that proceedeth out
9: 5 he may perform the **w** which the LORD H1697
18:20 to speak a **w** in my name, which H1697
Dt 18:21 **w** which the LORD hath not spoken? H1697
21: 5 and by their **w** shall every controversy H6310
30:14 But the **w** *is* very nigh unto thee, in thy H1697
33: 9 observed thy **w**, and kept thy covenant. H565
34: 5 Moab, according to the **w** of the LORD. H6310
Jos 1:13 Remember the **w** which Moses the H1697
6:10 neither shall *any* **w** proceed out of your H1697
8:27 unto the **w** of the LORD which H1697
35 There was not a **w** of all that Moses H1697
14: 7 him **w** again as *it was* in mine heart. H1697
10 LORD spake this **w** unto Moses, while H1697
19:50 According to the **w** of the LORD they H6310
22: 9 **w** of the LORD by the hand of Moses. H6310
32 of Israel, and brought them **w** again. H1697
1Sa 1:23 establish his **w**. So the woman abode, H1697
3: 1 before Eli. And the **w** of the LORD was H1697
7 **w** of the LORD yet revealed unto him. H1697
21 Samuel in Shiloh by the **w** of the LORD. H1697
4: 1 And the **w** of Samuel came to all Israel. H1697
9:27 that I may shew thee the **w** of God. H1697
15:10 Then came the **w** of the LORD unto H1697
23 hast rejected the **w** of the LORD, he H1697
26 hast rejected the **w** of the LORD, and H1697
2Sa 3:11 And he could not answer Abner a **w** H1697
7: 4 night, that the **w** of the LORD came H1697
7 of Israel spake I a **w** with any of the H1697
25 And now, O LORD God, the **w** that thou H1697
14:12 thee, speak *one* **w** unto my lord the H1697
17 Then thine handmaid said, The **w** of H1697
15:28 there come **w** from you to certify me. H1697
19:10 ye not a **w** of bringing the king back? H2790
14 so that they sent *this* **w** unto the king,
22:31 *As for* God, his way *is* perfect; the **w** of H565
23: 2 by me, and his **w** *was* in my tongue. H4405
24: 4 Notwithstanding the king's **w** prevailed H1697
11 the morning, the **w** of the LORD came H1697
1Ki 2: 4 That the LORD may continue his **w** H1697
23 not spoken this **w** against his own life. H1697
27 that he might fulfil the **w** of the LORD, H1697
30 brought the king **w** again, saying, Thus H1697
42 me, The **w** *that* I have heard *is* good. H1697
6:11 And the **w** of the LORD came to H1697
12 will I perform my **w** with thee, which I H1697
8:20 And the LORD hath performed his **w** H1697
26 And now, O God of Israel, let thy **w**, I H1697
56 hath not failed one **w** of all his good H1697
12:22 But the **w** of God came unto Shemaiah H1697
24 therefore to the **w** of the LORD, and H1697
24 according to the **w** of the LORD. H1697
13: 1 out of Judah by the **w** of the LORD unto H1697
2 And he cried against the altar in the **w** H1697
5 of God had given by the **w** of the LORD. H1697
9 For so was it charged me by the **w** of H1697
17 For it was said to me by the **w** of the H1697
18 unto me by the **w** of the LORD, saying, H1697
20 the table, that the **w** of the LORD came H1697
26 unto the **w** of the LORD: therefore H6310
26 according to the **w** of the LORD, which H1697
32 For the saying which he cried by the **w** H1697
14:18 according to the **w** of the LORD, which H1697
16: 1 Then the **w** of the LORD came to Jehu H1697
7 of Hanani came the **w** of the LORD H1697
12 according to the **w** of the LORD, which H1697
34 according to the **w** of the LORD, which H1697
17: 1 rain these years, but according to my **w**. H1697
2 And the **w** of the LORD came unto him, H1697
5 unto the **w** of the LORD: for he H1697
8 And the **w** of the LORD came unto him, H1697
16 according to the **w** of the LORD, which H1697
24 **w** of the LORD in thy mouth *is* truth. H1697
18: 1 days, that the **w** of the LORD came to H1697
21 And the people answered him not a **w**. H1697
31 unto whom the **w** of the LORD came, H1697
36 I have done all these things at thy **w**. H1697
19: 9 and, behold, the **w** of the LORD *came* H1697
20: 9 departed, and brought him **w** again. H1697
35 neighbour in the **w** of the LORD, Smite H1697
21: 4 because of the **w** which Naboth the H1697
17 And the **w** of the LORD came to Elijah H1697
28 And the **w** of the LORD came to Elijah H1697
22: 5 pray thee, at the **w** of the LORD to day. H1697
13 one mouth: let thy **w**, I pray thee, be like H1697
13 thee, be like the **w** of one of them, and H1697
19 And he said, Hear thou therefore the **w** H1697
38 the **w** of the LORD which he spake. H1697
2Ki 1:16 to inquire of his **w**? therefore thou shalt H1697
17 So he died according to the **w** of the H1697
3:12 And Jehoshaphat said, The **w** of the H1697
4:44 according to the **w** of the LORD. H1697

2Ki 6:18 blindness according to the **w** of Elisha. H1697
7: 1 Then Elisha said, Hear ye the **w** of the H1697
16 shekel, according to the **w** of the LORD. H1697
9:26 according to the **w** of the LORD. H1697
36 said, This *is* the **w** of the LORD, which H1697
10:10 nothing of the **w** of the LORD, which H1697
14:25 according to the **w** of the LORD God of H1697
15:12 This *was* the **w** of the LORD which he H1697
18:28 **w** of the great king, the king of Assyria: H1697
36 answered him not a **w**: for the king's H1697
19:21 This *is* the **w** that the LORD hath H1697
20: 4 **w** of the LORD came to him, saying, H1697
16 Hezekiah, Hear the **w** of the LORD. H1697
19 Good *is* the **w** of the LORD which H1697
22: 9 brought the king **w** again, and said, H1697
20 And they brought the king **w** again. H1697
23:16 according to the **w** of the LORD which H1697
24: 2 according to the **w** of the LORD, which H1697
1Ch 10:13 *even* against the **w** of the LORD, which H1697
11: 3 to the **w** of the LORD by Samuel. H1697
10 to the **w** of the LORD concerning Israel. H1697
12:23 him, according to the **w** of the LORD. H6310
15:15 according to the **w** of the LORD. H1697
16:15 of his covenant; the **w** *which* he H1697
17: 3 the **w** of God came to Nathan, saying, H1697
6 Israel, spake I a **w** to any of the judges H1697
21: 4 Nevertheless the king's **w** prevailed H1697
6 the king's **w** was abominable to Joab. H1697
12 thyself what **w** I shall bring again to H1697
22: 8 But the **w** of the LORD came to me, H1697
2Ch 6:10 performed his **w** that he hath spoken: H1697
17 of Israel, let thy **w** be verified, which H1697
10:15 might perform his **w**, which he spake by H1697
11: 2 But the **w** of the LORD came to H1697
12: 7 themselves, the **w** of the LORD came to H1697
18: 4 pray thee, at the **w** of the LORD to day. H1697
12 one assent; let thy **w** therefore, I pray H1697
18 Again he said, Therefore hear the **w** of H1697
30:12 of the princes, by the **w** of the LORD. H1697
34:16 brought the king **w** back again, saying, H1697
21 have not kept the **w** of the LORD, to do H1697
28 So they brought the king **w** again. H1697
35: 6 **w** of the LORD by the hand of Moses. H1697
36:21 To fulfil the **w** of the LORD by the H1697
22 king of Persia, that the **w** of the LORD H1697
Ezr 1: 1 of Persia, that the **w** of the LORD by the H1697
6:11 shall alter this **w**, let timber be pulled H6600
10: 5 do according to this **w**. And they sware. H1697
Neh 1: 8 Remember, I beseech thee, the **w** that H1697
Est 1:21 did according to the **w** of Memucan: H1697
7: 8 in the house? As the **w** went out of the H1697
Job 2:13 and none spake a **w** unto him: for they H1697
Ps 17: 4 Concerning the works of men, by the **w** H1697
18:30 *As for* God, his way *is* perfect: the **w** of H565
33: 4 For the **w** of the LORD *is* right; and all H1697
6 By the **w** of the LORD were the heavens H1697
56: 4 In God I will praise his **w**, in God I have H1697
10 In God will I praise *his* **w**: in the LORD H1697
10 word: in the LORD will I praise *his* **w**. H1697
68:11 The Lord gave the **w**: great *was* the H565
103:20 hearkening unto the voice of his **w**. H1697
105: 8 for ever, the **w** *which* he commanded H1697
19 Until the time that his **w** came: the H1697
19 Until the time that his word came: the **w** H565
28 and they rebelled not against his **w**. H1697
106:24 pleasant land, they believed not his **w**: H1697
107:20 He sent his **w**, and healed them, and H1697
119: 9 taking heed *thereto* according to thy **w**. H1697
11 Thy **w** have I hid in mine heart, that I H565
16 in thy statutes: I will not forget thy **w**. H1697
17 servant, *that* I may live, and keep thy **w**. H1697
25 quicken thou me according to thy **w**. H1697
28 thou me according unto thy **w**. H1697
38 Stablish thy **w** unto thy servant, who *is* H565
41 *even* thy salvation, according to thy **w**. H565
42 reproacheth me: for I trust in thy **w**. H1697
43 And take not the **w** of truth utterly out H1697
49 Remember the **w** unto thy servant, H1697
50 affliction: for thy **w** hath quickened me. H565
58 be merciful unto me according to thy **w**. H565
65 servant, O LORD, according unto thy **w**. H1697
67 I went astray: but now have I kept thy **w**. H565
74 see me; because I have hoped in thy **w**. H1697
76 according to thy **w** unto thy servant. H565
81 for thy salvation: *but* I hope in thy **w**. H1697
82 Mine eyes fail for thy **w**, saying, When H565
89 For ever, O LORD, thy **w** is settled in H1697
101 every evil way, that I might keep thy **w**. H1697
105 Thy **w** *is* a lamp unto my feet, and a H1697
Ps119:107 me, O LORD, according unto thy **w**. H1697
114 place and my shield: I hope in thy **w**. H1697
116 Uphold me according unto thy **w**, that I H565
123 and for the **w** of thy righteousness. H565
133 Order my steps in thy **w**: and let not any H565
140 Thy **w** *is* very pure: therefore thy servant H565
147 morning, and cried: I hoped in thy **w**. H1697
148 watches, that I might meditate in thy **w**. H565
154 me: quicken me according to thy **w**. H565
158 was grieved; because they kept not thy **w**. H565
160 Thy **w** *is* true *from* the beginning: and H1697
161 but my heart standeth in awe of thy **w**. H1697
162 I rejoice at thy **w**, as one that findeth H565
169 me understanding according to thy **w**. H1697
170 thee: deliver me according to thy **w**. H565
172 My tongue shall speak of thy **w**: for all H565
130: 5 soul doth wait, and in his **w** do I hope. H1697
138: 2 magnified thy **w** above all thy name. H565
139: 4 For *there is* not a **w** in my tongue, *but*, H4405
147:15 *upon* earth: his **w** runneth very swiftly. H1697
18 He sendeth out his **w**, and melteth H1697
19 He sheweth his **w** unto Jacob, H1697+H1697
148: 8 vapour; stormy wind fulfilling his **w**: H1697
Prv 12:25 it stoop: but a good **w** maketh it glad. H1697
13:13 Whoso despiseth the **w** shall be H1697
14:15 The simple believeth every **w**: but the H1697
15:23 **w** *spoken* in due season, how good *is it*! H1697
25:11 A **w** fitly spoken *is like* apples of gold in H1697
30: 5 Every **w** of God *is* pure: he *is* a shield H565
Ecc 8: 4 Where the **w** of a king *is*, *there is* H1697
Isa 1:10 Hear the **w** of the LORD, ye rulers of H1697
2: 1 The **w** that Isaiah the son of Amoz saw H1697
3 and the **w** of the LORD from Jerusalem. H1697
5:24 despised the **w** of the Holy One of Israel. H565
8:10 to nought; speak the **w**, and it shall not H1697
20 **w**, *it is* because *there is* no light in them. H1697
9: 8 The Lord sent a **w** into Jacob, and it H1697
16:13 This *is* the **w** that the LORD hath H1697
24: 3 for the LORD hath spoken this **w**. H1697
28:13 But the **w** of the LORD was unto them H1697
14 Wherefore hear the **w** of the LORD, ye H1697
29:21 That make a man an offender for a **w**, H1697
30:12 Because ye despise this **w**, and trust in H1697
21 And thine ears shall hear a **w** behind H1697
36:21 answered him not a **w**: for the king's H1697
37:22 This *is* the **w** which the LORD hath H1697
38: 4 Then came the **w** of the LORD to H1697
39: 5 Hear the **w** of the LORD of hosts: H1697
8 Good *is* the **w** of the LORD which H1697
40: 8 the **w** of our God shall stand for ever. H1697
41:28 I asked of them, could answer a **w**. H1697
44:26 That confirmeth the **w** of his servant, H1697
45:23 I have sworn by myself, the **w** is gone H1697
50: 4 how to speak a **w** in season to *him that* H1697
55:11 So shall my **w** be that goeth forth out of H1697
66: 2 a contrite spirit, and trembleth at my **w**. H1697
5 Hear the **w** of the LORD, ye that H1697
5 tremble at his **w**; Your brethren that H1697
Jer 1: 2 To whom the **w** of the LORD came in H1697
4 Then the **w** of the LORD came unto me, H1697
11 Moreover the **w** of the LORD came H1697
12 for I will hasten my **w** to perform it. H1697
13 And the **w** of the LORD came unto me H1697
2: 1 Moreover the **w** of the LORD came to H1697
4 Hear ye the **w** of the LORD, O house of H1697
31 O generation, see ye the **w** of the LORD. H1697
5:13 wind, and the **w** *is* not in them: thus H1696
14 ye speak this **w**, behold, I will make H1697
6:10 behold, the **w** of the LORD is unto H1697
7: 1 The **w** that came to Jeremiah from the H1697
2 there this **w**, and say, Hear the word H1697
2 and say, Hear the **w** of the LORD, all *ye* H1697
8: 9 have rejected the **w** of the LORD; and H1697
9:20 Yet hear the **w** of the LORD, O ye H1697
20 ear receive the **w** of his mouth, and H1697
10: 1 Hear ye the **w** which the LORD H1697
11: 1 The **w** that came to Jeremiah from the H1697
13: 2 So I got a girdle according to the **w** of H1697
3 And the **w** of the LORD came unto me H1697
8 Then the **w** of the LORD came unto me, H1697
12 unto them this **w**; Thus saith the LORD H1697
14: 1 The **w** of the LORD that came to H1697
17 Therefore thou shalt say this **w** unto H1697
15:16 eat them; and thy **w** was unto me the H1697
16: 1 The **w** of the LORD came also unto me, H1697
17:15 *is* the **w** of the LORD? let it come now. H1697
20 And say unto them, Hear ye the **w** of H1697
18: 1 The **w** which came to Jeremiah from H1697
5 Then the **w** of the LORD came to me, H1697
Jer 18:18 the wise, nor the **w** from the prophet. H1697
19: 3 And say, Hear ye the **w** of the LORD, O H1697
20: 8 spoil; because the **w** of the LORD was H1697
9 his name. But *his* **w** was in mine heart as
21: 1 The **w** which came unto Jeremiah from H1697
11 Judah, *say*, Hear ye the **w** of the LORD; H1697
22: 1 king of Judah, and speak there this **w**, H1697
2 And say, Hear the **w** of the LORD, O H1697
29 O earth, earth, earth, hear the **w** of the H1697
23:18 and heard his **w**? who hath marked his H1697
18 who hath marked his **w**, and heard *it*? H1697
28 he that hath my **w**, let him speak my H1697
28 let him speak my **w** faithfully. What *is* H1697
29 *Is* not my **w** like as a fire? saith the H1697
36 for every man's **w** shall be his burden; H1697
38 ye say this **w**, The burden of the LORD, H1697
24: 4 Again the **w** of the LORD came unto H1697
25: 1 The **w** that came to Jeremiah H1697
3 year, the **w** of the LORD hath come H1697
26: 1 came this **w** from the LORD, saying, H1697
2 to speak unto them; diminish not a **w**: H1697
27: 1 Judah came this **w** unto Jeremiah from H1697
18 But if they *be* prophets, and if the **w** of H1697
28: 7 Nevertheless hear thou now this **w** that H1697
9 peace, when the **w** of the prophet shall H1697
12 Then the **w** of the LORD came unto H1697
29:10 and perform my good **w** toward you, in H1697
20 Hear ye therefore the **w** of the LORD, H1697
30 Then came the **w** of the LORD unto H1697
30: 1 The **w** that came to Jeremiah from the H1697
31:10 Hear the **w** of the LORD, O ye nations, H1697
32: 1 The **w** that came to Jeremiah from the H1697
6 And Jeremiah said, The **w** of the LORD H1697
8 according to the **w** of the LORD, and H1697
8 I knew that this *was* the **w** of the LORD. H1697
26 Then came the **w** of the LORD unto H1697
33: 1 Moreover the **w** of the LORD came H1697
19 And the **w** of the LORD came unto H1697
23 Moreover the **w** of the LORD came to H1697
34: 1 The **w** which came unto Jeremiah from H1697
4 Yet hear the **w** of the LORD, O H1697
5 pronounced the **w**, saith the LORD. H1697
8 *This is* the **w** that came unto Jeremiah H1697
12 Therefore the **w** of the LORD came to H1697
35: 1 The **w** which came unto Jeremiah from H1697
12 Then came the **w** of the LORD unto H1697
36: 1 king of Judah, *that* this **w** came unto H1697
27 Then the **w** of the LORD came to H1697
37: 6 Then came the **w** of the LORD unto the H1697
17 said, Is there *any* **w** from the LORD? H1697
38:21 the **w** that the LORD hath shewed me: H1697
39:15 Now the **w** of the LORD came unto H1697
40: 1 The **w** that came to Jeremiah from the H1697
42: 7 **w** of the LORD came unto Jeremiah. H1697
15 And now therefore hear the **w** of the H1697
43: 8 Then came the **w** of the LORD unto H1697
44: 1 The **w** that came to Jeremiah H1697
16 *As for* the **w** that thou hast spoken unto H1697
24 women, Hear the **w** of the LORD, all H1697
26 Therefore hear ye the **w** of the LORD, H1697
45: 1 The **w** that Jeremiah the prophet spake H1697
46: 1 The **w** of the LORD which came to H1697
13 The **w** that the LORD spake to H1697
47: 1 The **w** of the LORD that came to H1697
49:34 The **w** of the LORD that came to H1697
50: 1 The **w** that the LORD spake against H1697
51:59 The **w** which Jeremiah the prophet H1697
Lam 2:17 he hath fulfilled his **w** that he had H565
Ezk 1: 3 The **w** of the LORD came expressly H1697
3:16 **w** of the LORD came unto me, saying, H1697
17 therefore hear the **w** at my mouth, and H1697
6: 1 And the **w** of the LORD came unto me, H1697
3 of Israel, hear the **w** of the Lord GOD; H1697
7: 1 Moreover the **w** of the LORD came H1697
11:14 Again the **w** of the LORD came unto H1697
12: 1 The **w** of the LORD also came unto me, H1697
8 And in the morning came the **w** of the H1697
17 Moreover the **w** of the LORD came to H1697
21 And the **w** of the LORD came unto me, H1697
25 will speak, and the **w** that I shall speak H1697
25 will I say the **w**, and will perform it, H1697
26 Again the **w** of the LORD came to me, H1697
28 any more, but the **w** which I have H1697
13: 1 And the **w** of the LORD came unto me, H1697
2 own hearts, Hear ye the **w** of the LORD; H1697
6 to hope that they would confirm the **w**. H1697
14: 2 And the **w** of the LORD came unto me, H1697
12 The **w** of the LORD came again to me, H1697
15: 1 And the **w** of the LORD came unto me, H1697

Book	Ref	Context	Strong's
Ezk	16: 1	Again the w of the LORD came unto	H1697
	35	Wherefore, O harlot, hear the w of the	H1697
	17: 1	And the w of the LORD came unto me,	H1697
	11	Moreover the w of the LORD came	H1697
	18: 1	The w of the LORD came unto me	H1697
	20: 2	Then came the w of the LORD unto me,	H1697
	45	Moreover the w of the LORD came	H1697
	46	and drop *thy w* toward the south, and	
	47	south, Hear the w of the LORD; Thus	H1697
	21: 1	And the w of the LORD came unto me,	H1697
	2	and drop *thy w* toward the holy places,	
	8	Again the w of the LORD came unto	H1697
	18	The w of the LORD came unto me	H1697
	22: 1	Moreover the w of the LORD came	H1697
	17	And the w of the LORD came unto me,	H1697
	23	And the w of the LORD came unto me,	H1697
	23: 1	The w of the LORD came again unto	H1697
	24: 1	w of the LORD came unto me, saying,	H1697
	15	Also the w of the LORD came unto me,	H1697
	20	Then I answered them, The w of the	H1697
	25: 1	The w of the LORD came again unto	H1697
	3	Hear the w of the Lord GOD; Thus	H1697
	26: 1	w of the LORD came unto me, saying,	H1697
	27: 1	The w of the LORD came again unto	H1697
	28: 1	The w of the LORD came again unto	H1697
	11	Moreover the w of the LORD came	H1697
	20	Again the w of the LORD came unto	H1697
	29: 1	w of the LORD came unto me, saying,	H1697
	17	w of the LORD came unto me, saying,	H1697
	30: 1	The w of the LORD came again unto	H1697
	20	w of the LORD came unto me, saying,	H1697
	31: 1	w of the LORD came unto me, saying,	H1697
	32: 1	w of the LORD came unto me, saying,	H1697
	17	w of the LORD came unto me, saying,	H1697
	33: 1	Again the w of the LORD came unto	H1697
	7	shalt hear the w at my mouth, and	H1697
	23	Then the w of the LORD came unto me,	H1697
	30	w that cometh forth from the LORD.	H1697
	34: 1	And the w of the LORD came unto me,	H1697
	7	Therefore, ye shepherds, hear the w of	H1697
	9	Therefore, O ye shepherds, hear the w	H1697
	35: 1	Moreover the w of the LORD came	H1697
	36: 1	of Israel, hear the w of the LORD:	H1697
	4	of Israel, hear the w of the Lord GOD;	H1697
	16	Moreover the w of the LORD came	H1697
	37: 4	ye dry bones, hear the w of the LORD.	H1697
	15	The w of the LORD came again unto	H1697
	38: 1	And the w of the LORD came unto me,	H1697
Dan	3:28	the king's w, and yielded their bodies,	H4406
	4:17	demand by the w of the holy ones: to	H3983
	31	While the w *was* in the king's mouth,	H4406
	9: 2	years, whereof the w of the LORD came	H1697
	10:11	this w unto me, I stood trembling.	H1697
Hos	1: 1	The w of the LORD that came unto	H1697
	2	The beginning of the w of the LORD by	H1696
	4: 1	Hear the w of the LORD, ye children of	H1697
Joel	1: 1	The w of the LORD that came to Joel	H1697
	2:11	that executeth his w: for the day of the	H1697
Am	3: 1	Hear this w that the LORD hath spoken	H1697
	4: 1	Hear this w, ye kine of Bashan, that *are*	H1697
	5: 1	Hear ye this w which I take up against	H1697
	7:16	Now therefore hear thou the w of the	H1697
	16	not *thy w* against the house of Isaac.	
	8:12	w of the LORD, and shall not find *it*.	H1697
Jna	1: 1	Now the w of the LORD came unto	H1697
	3: 1	And the w of the LORD came unto	H1697
	3	according to the w of the LORD. Now	H1697
	6	For w came unto the king of Nineveh,	H1697
Mic	1: 1	The w of the LORD that came to Micah	H1697
	4: 2	and the w of the LORD from Jerusalem.	H1697
Hab	3: 9	the tribes, *even thy* w. Selah. Thou didst	H562
Zep	1: 1	The w of the LORD which came unto	H1697
	2: 5	the Cherethites! the w of the LORD *is*	H1697
Hag	1: 1	the month, came the w of the LORD by	H1697
	3	Then came the w of the LORD by	H1697
	2: 1	month, came the w of the LORD by the	H1697
	5	*According to* the w that I covenanted	H1697
	10	of Darius, came the w of the LORD by	H1697
	20	And again the w of the LORD came	H1697
Zec	1: 1	Darius, came the w of the LORD unto	H1697
	7	Darius, came the w of the LORD unto	H1697
	4: 6	saying, This *is* the w of the LORD unto	H1697
	8	Moreover the w of the LORD came	H1697
	6: 9	And the w of the LORD came unto me,	H1697
	7: 1	Darius, *that* the w of the LORD came	H1697
	4	Then came the w of the LORD of hosts	H1697
	8	And the w of the LORD came unto	H1697
	8: 1	Again the w of the LORD of hosts came	H1697
	18	And the w of the LORD of hosts came	H1697
Zec	9: 1	The burden of the w of the LORD in the	H1697
	11:11	me knew that it *was* the w of the LORD.	H1697
	12: 1	The burden of the w of the LORD for	H1697
Mal	1: 1	The burden of the w of the LORD to	H1697
Mt	2: 8	*him*, bring me w again, that I may come	G518
	13	until I bring thee w: for Herod will seek	G2036
	4: 4	but by every w that proceedeth out	G4487
	8: 8	w only, and my servant shall be healed.	G3056
	16	*his* w, and healed all that were sick:	G3056
	12:32	And whosoever speaketh a w against	G3056
	36	But I say unto you, That every idle w	G4487
	13:19	When any one heareth the w of the	G3056
	20	the w, and anon with joy receiveth it;	G3056
	21	of the w, by and by he is offended.	G3056
	22	that heareth the w; and the care of this	G3056
	22	the w, and he becometh unfruitful.	G3056
	23	that heareth the w, and understandeth	G3056
	15:23	But he answered her not a w. And his	G3056
	18:16	witnesses every w may be established.	G4487
	22:46	to answer him a w, neither durst any	G3056
	26:75	And Peter remembered the w of Jesus,	G4487
	27:14	And he answered him to never a w;	G4487
	28: 8	joy; and did run to bring his disciples w.	G518
Mk	2: 2	and he preached the w unto them.	G3056
	4:14	The sower soweth the w.	G3056
	15	side, where the w is sown; but when	G3056
	15	the w that was sown in their hearts.	G3056
	16	w, immediately receive it with gladness;	G3056
	18	sown among thorns; such as hear the w,	G3056
	19	the w, and it becometh unfruitful.	G3056
	20	such as hear the w, and receive *it*, and	G3056
	33	spake he the w unto them, as they	G3056
	5:36	As soon as Jesus heard the w that was	G3056
	7:13	Making the w of God of none effect	G3056
	14:72	called to mind the w that Jesus said	G4487
	16:20	the w with signs following. Amen.	G3056
Lk	1: 2	eyewitnesses, and ministers of the w;	G3056
	38	thy w. And the angel departed from her.	G4487
	2:29	depart in peace, according to thy w:	G4487
	3: 2	high priests, the w of God came unto	G4487
	4: 4	by bread alone, but by every w of God.	G4487
	32	his doctrine: for his w was with power.	G3056
	36	saying, What a w *is* this! for with	G3056
	5: 1	him to hear the w of God, he stood by	G3056
	5	at thy w I will let down the net.	G4487
	7: 7	in a w, and my servant shall be healed.	G3056
	8:11	is this: The seed is the w of God.	G3056
	12	taketh away the w out of their hearts,	G3056
	13	hear, receive the w with joy; and these	G3056
	15	having heard the w, keep *it*, and bring	G3056
	21	which hear the w of God, and do it.	G3056
	10:39	also sat at Jesus' feet, and heard his w.	G3056
	11:28	that hear the w of God, and keep it.	G3056
	12:10	And whosoever shall speak a w against	G3056
	22:61	remembered the w of the Lord, how he	G3056
	24:19	and w before God and all the people:	G3056
Jn	1: 1	In the beginning was the W, and the	G3056
	1	Word, and the W was with God, and	G3056
	1	was with God, and the W was God.	G3056
	14	And the W was made flesh, and dwelt	G3056
	2:22	and the w which Jesus had said.	G3056
	4:41	more believed because of his own w;	G3056
	50	the man believed the w that Jesus had	G3056
	5:24	He that heareth my w, and believeth on	G3056
	38	And ye have not his w abiding in you:	G3056
	8:31	my w, *then* are ye my disciples indeed;	G3056
	37	because my w hath no place in you.	G3056
	43	*even* because ye cannot hear my w.	G3056
	10:35	unto whom the w of God came, and the	G3056
	12:48	judgeth him: the w that I have spoken,	G3056
	14:24	sayings: and the w which ye hear is not	G3056
	15: 3	Now ye are clean through the w which I	G3056
	20	Remember the w that I said unto you,	G3056
	25	But *this cometh to pass*, that the w	G3056
	17: 6	them me; and they have kept thy w.	G3056
	14	I have given them thy w; and the world	G3056
	17	Sanctify them through thy truth: thy w	G3056
	20	shall believe on me through their w;	G3056
Act	2:41	Then they that gladly received his w	G3056
	4: 4	which heard the w believed; and the	G3056
	29	with all boldness they may speak thy w,	G3056
	31	they spake the w of God with boldness.	G3056
	6: 2	leave the w of God, and serve tables.	G3056
	4	to prayer, and to the ministry of the w.	G3056
	7	And the w of God increased; and the	G3056
	8: 4	went every where preaching the w.	G3056
	14	had received the w of God, they sent	G3056
	25	and preached the w of the Lord,	G3056
	10:36	The w which *God* sent unto the	G3056
Act	10:37	That w, *I say*, ye know, which was	G4487
	44	fell on all them which heard the w.	G3056
	11: 1	had also received the w of God.	G3056
	16	Then remembered I the w of the Lord,	G4487
	19	the w to none but unto the Jews only.	G3056
	12:24	But the w of God grew and multiplied.	G3056
	13: 5	they preached the w of God in the	G3056
	7	Saul, and desired to hear the w of God.	G3056
	15	w of exhortation for the people, say on.	G3056
	26	to you is the w of this salvation sent.	G3056
	44	city together to hear the w of God.	G3056
	46	necessary that the w of God should first	G3056
	48	and glorified the w of the Lord: and as	G3056
	49	And the w of the Lord was published	G3056
	14: 3	unto the w of his grace, and granted	G3056
	25	And when they had preached the w in	G3056
	15: 7	hear the w of the gospel, and believe.	G3056
	35	w of the Lord, with many others also.	G3056
	36	the w of the Lord, *and see* how they do.	G3056
	16: 6	the Holy Ghost to preach the w in Asia,	G3056
	32	And they spake unto him the w of the	G3056
	17:11	they received the w with all readiness	G3056
	13	that the w of God was preached	G3056
	18:11	teaching the w of God among them.	G3056
	19:10	in Asia heard the w of the Lord Jesus,	G3056
	20	So mightily grew the w of God and	G3056
	20:32	to God, and to the w of his grace, which	G3056
	22:22	unto this w, and *then* lifted up their	G3056
	28:25	had spoken one w, Well spake the Holy	G4487
Ro	9: 6	Not as though the w of God hath taken	G3056
	9	For this *is* the w of promise, At this	G3056
	10: 8	But what saith it? The w is nigh thee,	G4487
	8	that is, the w of faith, which we preach;	G4487
	17	hearing, and hearing by the w of God.	G4487
	15:18	the Gentiles obedient, by w and deed,	G3056
1Co	4:20	For the kingdom of God *is* not in w, but	G3056
	12: 8	For to one is given by the Spirit the w of	G3056
	8	the w of knowledge by the same Spirit;	G3056
	14:36	What? came the w of God out from	G3056
2Co	1:18	But *as* God *is* true, our w toward you	G3056
	2:17	which corrupt the w of God: but as of	G3056
	4: 2	nor handling the w of God deceitfully;	G3056
	5:19	unto us the w of reconciliation.	G3056
	6: 7	By the w of truth, by the power of God,	G3056
	10:11	such as we are in w by letters when we	G3056
	13: 1	witnesses shall every w be established.	G4487
Gal	5:14	For all the law is fulfilled in one w, *even*	G3056
	6: 6	Let him that is taught in the w	G3056
Eph	1:13	that ye heard the w of truth, the gospel	G3056
	5:26	it with the washing of water by the w,	G4487
	6:17	of the Spirit, which is the w of God:	G4487
Php	1:14	more bold to speak the w without fear.	G3056
	2:16	Holding forth the w of life; that I may	G3056
Col	1: 5	in the w of the truth of the gospel;	G3056
	25	to me for you, to fulfil the w of God;	G3056
	3:16	Let the w of Christ dwell in you richly	G3056
	17	And whatsoever ye do in w or deed, *do*	G3056
1Th	1: 5	For our gospel came not unto you in w	G3056
	6	received the w in much affliction,	G3056
	8	For from you sounded out the w of the	G3056
	2:13	when ye received the w of God which ye	G3056
	13	*it* not *as* the w of men, but as it is	G3056
	13	as it is in truth, the w of God, which	G3056
	4:15	For this we say unto you by the w of the	G3056
2Th	2: 2	by spirit, nor by w, nor by letter as from	G3056
	15	taught, whether by w, or our epistle.	G3056
	17	stablish you in every good w and work.	G3056
	3: 1	for us, that the w of the Lord may have	G3056
	14	And if any man obey not our w by this	G3056
1Ti	4: 5	For it is sanctified by the w of God and	G3056
	12	of the believers, in w, in conversation,	G3056
	5:17	they who labour in the w and doctrine.	G3056
2Ti	2: 9	bonds; but the w of God is not bound.	G3056
	15	rightly dividing the w of truth.	G3056
	17	And their w will eat as doth a canker:	G3056
	4: 2	Preach the w; be instant in season, out	G3056
Tit	1: 3	But hath in due times manifested his w	G3056
	9	Holding fast the faithful w as he hath	G3056
	2: 5	that the w of God be not blasphemed.	G3056
Heb	1: 3	all things by the w of his power, when	G4487
	2: 2	For if the w spoken by angels was	G3056
	4: 2	them: but the w preached did not profit	G3056
	12	For the w of God *is* quick, and	G3056
	5:13	the w of righteousness: for he is a babe.	G3056
	6: 5	And have tasted the good w of God,	G4487
	7:28	infirmity; but the w of the oath, which	G3056
	11: 3	framed by the w of God, so that things	G4487
	12:19	entreated that the w should not be	G3056
	27	And this *w*, Yet once more, signifieth the	

Heb 13: 7 unto you the **w** of God: whose faith *G3056*
22 suffer the **w** of exhortation: for I *G3056*
Jas 1:18 Of his own will begat he us with the **w** *G3056*
21 **w**, which is able to save your souls. *G3056*
22 But be ye doers of the **w**, and not *G3056*
23 For if any be a hearer of the **w**, and not *G3056*
3: 2 any man offend not in **w**, the same *is* a *G3056*
1Pt 1:23 by the **w** of God, which liveth *G3056*
25 But the **w** of the Lord endureth for ever. *G4487*
25 And this is the **w** which by the gospel *G4487*
2: 2 of the **w**, that ye may grow thereby: *G3050*
8 stumble at the **w**, being disobedient: *G3056*
3: 1 if any obey not the **w**, they also may *G3056*
1 also may without the **w** be won by the *G3056*
2Pt 1:19 We have also a more sure **w** of *G3056*
3: 5 of, that by the **w** of God the heavens *G3056*
7 now, by the same **w** are kept in store, *G3056*
1Jn 1: 1 hands have handled, of the **W** of life; *G3056*
10 make him a liar, and his **w** is not in us. *G3056*
2: 5 But whoso keepeth his **w**, in him verily *G3056*
7 is the **w** which ye have heard *G3056*
14 are strong, and the **w** of God abideth in *G3056*
3:18 My little children, let us not love in **w**, *G3056*
5: 7 the Father, the **W**, and the Holy Ghost: *G3056*
Rev 1: 2 Who bare record of the **w** of God, and *G3056*
9 Patmos, for the **w** of God, and for the *G3056*
3: 8 my **w**, and hast not denied my name. *G3056*
10 Because thou hast kept the **w** of my *G3056*
6: 9 were slain for the **w** of God, and for the *G3056*
12:11 Lamb, and by the **w** of their testimony; *G3056*
19:13 and his name is called The **W** of God. *G3056*
20: 4 Jesus, and for the **w** of God, and which *G3056*

WORDS

Gen 24:30 he heard the **w** of Rebekah his sister, H1697
52 heard their **w**, he worshipped the H1697
27:34 And when Esau heard the **w** of his H1697
42 And these **w** of Esau her elder son were H1697
31: 1 And he heard the **w** of Laban's sons, H1697
34:18 And their **w** pleased Hamor, and H1697
37: 8 the more for his dreams, and for his **w**. H1697
39:17 him according to these **w**, saying, The H1697
19 master heard the **w** of his wife, which H1697
42:16 in prison, that your **w** may be proved, H1697
20 me; so shall your **w** be verified, and ye H1697
43: 7 the tenor of these **w**: could we certainly H1697
44: 6 and he spake unto them these same **w**. H1697
7 my lord these **w**? God forbid that thy H1697
10 unto your **w**: he with whom H1697+H3651
24 father, we told him the **w** of my lord. H1697
45:27 And they told him all the **w** of Joseph, H1697
49:21 *is* a hind let loose: he giveth goodly **w**. H561
Ex 4:15 unto him, and put **w** in his mouth: and H1697
28 And Moses told Aaron all the **w** of the H1697
30 And Aaron spake all the **w** which the H1697
5: 9 therein; and let them not regard vain **w**. H1697
19: 6 These *are* the **w** which thou shalt speak H1697
7 **w** which the LORD commanded him. H1697
8 the **w** of the people unto the LORD. H1697
9 told the **w** of the people unto the LORD. H1697
20: 1 And God spake all these **w**, saying, H1697
23: 8 and perverteth the **w** of the righteous. H1697
24: 3 the people all the **w** of the LORD, and H1697
3 and said, All the **w** which the LORD H1697
4 And Moses wrote all the **w** of the H1697
8 made with you concerning all these **w**. H1697
34: 1 *these* tables the **w** that were in the first H1697
27 Write thou these **w**: for after the tenor H1697
27 after the tenor of these **w** I have made a H1697
28 the tables the **w** of the covenant, the H1697
35: 1 These *are* the **w** which the LORD hath H1697
Nu 11:24 told the people the **w** of the LORD, and H1697
12: 6 And he said, Hear now my **w**: If there be H1697
16:31 of speaking all these **w**, that the ground H1697
22: 7 and spake unto him the **w** of Balak. H1697
24: 4 He hath said, which heard the **w** of God, H561
16 He hath said, which heard the **w** of God, H561
Dt 1: 1 These *be* the **w** which Moses spake H1697
34 **w**, and was wroth, and sware, saying, H1697
2:26 of Heshbon with **w** of peace, saying, H1697
4:10 them hear my **w**, that they may learn H1697
12 heard the voice of the **w**, but saw no H1697
36 his **w** out of the midst of the fire. H1697
5:22 These **w** the LORD spake unto all your H1697
28 the voice of your **w**, when ye spake unto H1697
28 the voice of the **w** of this people, which H1697
6: 6 And these **w**, which I command thee H1697
9:10 to all the **w**, which the LORD spake H1697
10: 2 And I will write on the tables the **w** that H1697
Dt 11:18 Therefore shall ye lay up these my **w** in H1697
12:28 Observe and hear all these **w** which I H1697
13: 3 Thou shalt not hearken unto the **w** of H1697
16:19 and pervert the **w** of the righteous. H1697
17:19 to keep all the **w** of this law and these H1697
18:18 and will put my **w** in his mouth; and he H1697
19 not hearken unto my **w** which he shall H1697
27: 3 upon them all the **w** of this law, when H1697
8 stones all the **w** of this law very plainly. H1697
26 not *all* the **w** of this law to do them. H1697
28:14 from any of the **w** which I command H1697
58 If thou wilt not observe to do all the **w** H1697
29: 1 These *are* the **w** of the covenant, which H1697
9 Keep therefore the **w** of this covenant, H1697
19 he heareth the **w** of this curse, that he H1697
29 that *we* may do all the **w** of this law. H1697
31: 1 And Moses went and spake these **w** H1697
12 and observe to do all the **w** of this law: H1697
24 an end of writing the **w** of this law in a H1697
28 I may speak these **w** in their ears, and H1697
30 **w** of this song, until they were ended. H1697
32: 1 and hear, O earth, the **w** of my mouth. H561
44 And Moses came and spake all the **w** of H1697
45 end of speaking all these **w** to all Israel: H1697
46 hearts unto all the **w** which I testify H1697
46 to observe to do, all the **w** of this law. H1697
33: 3 thy feet; *every one* shall receive of thy **w**. H1703
Jos 1:18 not hearken unto thy **w** in all that thou H1697
2:21 And she said, According unto your **w**, H1697
3: 9 and hear the **w** of the LORD your God. H1697
8:34 And afterward he read all the **w** of the H1697
22:30 him, heard the **w** that the children of H1697
24:26 And Joshua wrote these **w** in the book H1697
27 hath heard all the **w** of the LORD which H561
Jdg 2: 4 the LORD spake these **w** unto all the H1697
9: 3 of Shechem all these **w**: and their hearts H1697
30 the city heard the **w** of Gaal the son of H1697
11:10 us, if we do not so according to thy **w**. H1697
11 all his **w** before the LORD in Mizpeh. H1697
28 the **w** of Jephthah which he sent him. H1697
13:12 And Manoah said, Now let thy **w** come H1697
16:16 daily with her **w**, and urged him, *so* that H1697
1Sa 3:19 did let none of his **w** fall to the ground. H1697
8:10 And Samuel told all the **w** of the LORD H1697
21 And Samuel heard all the **w** of the H1697
15: 1 unto the voice of the **w** of the LORD. H1697
24 LORD, and thy **w**: because I feared the H1697
17:11 When Saul and all Israel heard those **w** H1697
23 to the same **w**: and David heard *them*. H1697
31 And when the **w** were heard which H1697
18:23 And Saul's servants spake those **w** in H1697
26 told David these **w**, it pleased David H1697
21:12 And David laid up these **w** in his heart, H1697
24: 7 with these **w**, and suffered them not H1697
9 thou men's **w**, saying, Behold, David H1697
16 end of speaking these **w** unto Saul, that H1697
25: 9 **w** in the name of David, and ceased. H1697
24 and hear the **w** of thine handmaid. H1697
26:19 the king hear the **w** of his servant. If H1697
28:20 because of the **w** of Samuel: and there H1697
21 thy **w** which thou spakest unto me. H1697
2Sa 3: 8 Then was Abner very wroth for the **w** H1697
7:17 According to all these **w**, and according H1697
28 that God, and thy **w** be true, and thou H1697
14: 3 him. So Joab put the **w** in her mouth. H1697
19 **w** in the mouth of thine handmaid: H1697
19:43 back our king? And the **w** of the men of H1697
43 fiercer than the **w** of the men of Israel. H1697
20:17 him, Hear the **w** of thine handmaid. H1697
22: 1 And David spake unto the LORD the **w** H1697
23: 1 Now these *be* the last **w** of David. H1697
1Ki 1:14 come in after thee, and confirm thy **w**. H1697
3:12 Behold, I have done according to thy **w**: H1697
5: 7 Hiram heard the **w** of Solomon, that he H1697
8:59 And let these my **w**, wherewith I have H1697
10: 7 Howbeit I believed not the **w**, until I H1697
12: 7 and speak good **w** to them, then they H1697
13:11 that day in Beth-el: the **w** which he had H1697
21:27 Ahab heard those **w**, that he rent his H1697
22:13 Behold now, the **w** of the prophets H1697
2Ki 1: 7 up to meet you, and told you these **w**? H1697
6:12 king of Israel the **w** that thou speakest H1697
30 the king heard the **w** of the woman, H1697
18:20 Thou sayest, (but *they are but* vain **w**,) *I* H1697
27 to speak these **w**? *hath he* not *sent me* H1697
37 and told him the **w** of Rab-shakeh. H1697
19: 4 God will hear all the **w** of Rab-shakeh, H1697
4 will reprove the **w** which the LORD thy H1697
6 Be not afraid of the **w** which thou hast H1697
2Ki 19:16 see: and hear the **w** of Sennacherib, H1697
22:11 had heard the **w** of the book of the law, H1697
13 concerning the **w** of this book that is H1697
13 unto the **w** of this book, to do H1697
16 *even* all the **w** of the book which the H1697
18 *touching* the **w** which thou hast heard; H1697
23: 2 in their ears all the **w** of the book of the H1697
3 to perform the **w** of this covenant that H1697
16 proclaimed, who proclaimed these **w**. H1697
24 perform the **w** of the law which were H1697
1Ch 17:15 According to all these **w**, and according H1697
23:27 For by the last **w** of David the Levites H1697
25: 5 king's seer in the **w** of God, to lift up the H1697
2Ch 9: 6 Howbeit I believed not their **w**, until I H1697
10: 7 and speak good **w** to them, they will be H1697
11: 4 they obeyed the **w** of the LORD, and H1697
15: 8 And when Asa heard these **w**, and the H1697
18:12 Behold, the **w** of the prophets *declare* H1697
29:15 of the king, by the **w** of the LORD, to H1697
30 the LORD with the **w** of David, and of H1697
32: 8 upon the **w** of Hezekiah king of Judah. H1697
33:18 his God, and the **w** of the seers that H1697
34:19 **w** of the law, that he rent his clothes. H1697
21 concerning the **w** of the book that is H1697
26 the **w** which thou hast heard; H1697
27 thou heardest his **w** against this place, H1697
30 in their ears all the **w** of the book of the H1697
31 to perform the **w** of the covenant which H1697
35:22 not unto the **w** of Necho from the H1697
36:16 and despised his **w**, and misused his H1697
Ezr 7:11 a scribe of the **w** of the commandments H1697
9: 4 trembled at the **w** of the God of Israel, H1697
Neh 1: 1 The **w** of Nehemiah the son of H1697
4 I heard these **w**, that I sat down and H1697
2:18 as also the king's **w** that he had spoken H1697
5: 6 when I heard their cry and these **w**. H1697
6: 6 be their king, according to these **w**. H1697
7 king according to these **w**. Come now H1697
19 and uttered my **w** to him. *And* Tobiah H1697
8: 9 wept, when they heard the **w** of the law. H1697
12 the **w** that were declared unto them. H1697
13 even to understand the **w** of the law. H1697
9: 8 performed thy **w**; for thou *art* righteous: H1697
Est 4: 9 and told Esther the **w** of Mordecai. H1697
12 And they told to Mordecai Esther's **w**. H1697
9:26 for all the **w** of this letter, and *of* H1697
30 Ahasuerus, *with* **w** of peace and truth, H1697
Job 4: 4 Thy **w** have upholden him that was H4405
6: 3 sea: therefore my **w** are swallowed up. H1697
10 not concealed the **w** of the Holy One. H561
25 How forcible are right **w**! but what doth H561
26 Do ye imagine to reprove **w**, and the H4405
8: 2 **w** of thy mouth *be like* a strong wind? H561
10 tell thee, and utter **w** out of their heart? H4405
9:14 choose out my **w** *to reason* with him? H1697
11: 2 Should not the multitude of **w** be H1697
12:11 Doth not the ear try **w**? and the mouth H4405
15:13 and lettest *such* **w** go out of thy mouth? H4405
16: 3 Shall vain **w** have an end? or what H1697
4 I could heap up **w** against you, and H4405
18: 2 **w**? mark, and afterwards we will speak. H4405
19: 2 my soul, and break me in pieces with **w**? H4405
23 Oh that my **w** were now written! oh H4405
22:22 mouth, and lay up his **w** in thine heart. H561
23: 5 I would know the **w** *which* he would H4405
12 have esteemed the **w** of his mouth more H561
26: 4 To whom hast thou uttered **w**? and H4405
29:22 After my **w** they spake not again; and H1697
31:40 of barley. The **w** of Job are ended. H1697
32:11 Behold, I waited for your **w**; I gave ear H1697
12 convinced Job, *or* that answered his **w**: H561
14 Now he hath not directed *his* **w** against H4405
33: 1 my speeches, and hearken to all my **w**. H1697
3 My **w** *shall be of* the uprightness of my H561
5 If thou canst answer me, set *thy* **w** in
8 I have heard the voice of *thy* **w**, *saying*, H4405
34: 2 Hear my **w**, O ye wise *men*; and give ear H4405
3 For the ear trieth **w**, as the mouth H4405
16 hear this: hearken to the voice of my **w**. H4405
35 and his **w** *were* without wisdom. H1697
37 us, and multiplieth his **w** against God. H561
35:16 he multiplieth **w** without knowledge. H4405
36: 4 For truly my **w** *shall* not *be* false: he H4405
38: 2 counsel by **w** without knowledge? H4405
41: 3 thee? will he speak soft *w* unto thee?
42: 7 had spoken these **w** unto Job, the H1697
Ps 5: 1 Give ear to my **w**, O LORD, consider my H561
7:ttl the **w** of Cush the Benjamite. H1697
12: 6 The **w** of the LORD *are* pure words: *as* H565

Ps 12: 6 The words of the LORD *are* pure w: *as* H565
18:ttl the LORD the w of this song in the day H1697
19: 4 the earth, and their w to the end of the H4405
14 Let the w of my mouth, and the H561
22: 1 me, *and from* the w of my roaring? H1697
36: 3 The w of his mouth *are* iniquity and H1697
50:17 and castest my w behind thee. H1697
52: 4 Thou lovest all devouring w, O *thou* H1697
54: 2 Hear my prayer, O God; give ear to the w H561
55:21 *The* w of his mouth were smoother than
21 in his heart: his w were softer than oil, H1697
56: 5 Every day they wrest my w: all their H1697
59:12 *For* the sin of their mouth *and* the w of H1697
64: 3 *to shoot* their arrows, *even* bitter w: H1697
78: 1 incline your ears to the w of my mouth. H561
106:12 Then believed they his w; they sang his H1697
107:11 Because they rebelled against the w of H561
109: 3 They compassed me about also with w H1697
119:57 I have said that I would keep thy w. H1697
103 How sweet are thy w unto my taste! *yea,* H565
130 The entrance of thy w giveth light; it H1697
139 mine enemies have forgotten thy w. H1697
138: 4 when they hear the w of thy mouth. H561
141: 6 they shall hear my w; for they are sweet. H561
Prv 1: 2 to perceive the w of understanding; H561
6 w of the wise, and their dark sayings. H1697
21 in the city she uttereth her w, *saying,* H561
23 you, I will make known my w unto you. H1697
2: 1 My son, if thou wilt receive my w, and H561
16 the stranger *which* flattereth with her w; H561
4: 4 w: keep my commandments, and live. H1697
5 neither decline from the w of my mouth. H561
20 My son, attend to my w; incline thine H1697
5: 7 and depart not from the w of my mouth. H561
6: 2 Thou art snared with the w of thy H561
2 thou art taken with the w of thy mouth. H561
7: 1 My son, keep my w, and lay up my H561
5 the stranger *which* flattereth with her w. H561
24 and attend to the w of my mouth. H561
8: 8 All the w of my mouth *are* in H561
10:19 In the multitude of w there wanteth not H1697
12: 6 The w of the wicked *are* to lie in wait H1697
15: 1 wrath: but grievous w stir up anger. H1697
26 *the* w of the pure *are* pleasant words. H1697
26 but *the words* of the pure *are* pleasant w. H561
16:24 Pleasant w *are as* an honeycomb, sweet H561
17:27 He that hath knowledge spareth his w: H561
18: 4 The w of a man's mouth *are as* deep H1697
8 The w of a talebearer *are* as wounds, H1697
19: 7 *with* w, *yet* they *are* wanting *to him.* H561
27 *causeth* to err from the w of knowledge. H561
22:12 overthroweth the w of the transgressor. H1697
17 Bow down thine ear, and hear the w of H1697
21 the certainty of the w of truth; that thou H561
21 w of truth to them that send unto thee? H561
23: 8 thou vomit up, and lose thy sweet w. H1697
9 for he will despise the wisdom of thy w. H4405
12 and thine ears to the w of knowledge. H561
26:22 The w of a talebearer *are* as wounds, H1697
29:19 A servant will not be corrected by w: for H1697
20 Seest thou a man *that is* hasty in his w? H1697
30: 1 The w of Agur the son of Jakeh, *even* H1697
6 Add thou not unto his w, lest he reprove H1697
31: 1 The w of king Lemuel, the prophecy H1697
Ecc 1: 1 The w of the Preacher, the son of H1697
5: 2 upon earth: therefore let thy w be few. H1697
3 fool's voice *is known* by multitude of w. H1697
7 of dreams and many w *there are* also H1697
7:21 Also take no heed unto all w that are H1697
9:16 *is* despised, and his w are not heard. H1697
17 The w of wise *men are* heard in quiet H1697
10:12 The w of a wise man's mouth *are* H1697
13 The beginning of the w of his mouth *is* H1697
14 A fool also is full of w: a man cannot tell H1697
12:10 out acceptable w: and *that which was* H1697
10 written *was* upright, *even* w of truth. H1697
11 The w of the wise *are* as goads, and as H1697
Isa 29:11 unto you as the w of a book that is H1697
18 the deaf hear the w of the book, and the H1697
31: 2 will not call back his w: but will arise H1697
32: 7 w, even when the needy speaketh right. H561
36: 5 *they are but* vain w) *I have* counsel and H1697
12 to speak these w? *hath he* not *sent me* H1697
13 w of the great king, the king of Assyria. H1697
22 rent, and told him the w of Rabshakeh. H1697
37: 4 thy God will hear the w of Rabshakeh, H1697
4 will reprove the w which the LORD thy H1697
6 Be not afraid of the w that thou hast H1697
17 see: and hear all the w of Sennacherib, H1697
Isa 41:26 yea, *there is* none that heareth your w. H561
51:16 And I have put my w in thy mouth, and H1697
58:13 pleasure, nor speaking *thine own* w: H1697
59:13 uttering from the heart w of falsehood. H1697
21 thee, and my w which I have put in H1697
Jer 1: 1 The w of Jeremiah the son of Hilkiah, H1697
9 Behold, I have put my w in thy mouth. H1697
3:12 Go and proclaim these w toward the H1697
5:14 I will make my w in thy mouth fire, H1697
6:19 my w, nor to my law, but rejected it. H1697
7: 4 Trust ye not in lying w, saying, The H1697
8 Behold, ye trust in lying w, that cannot H1697
27 Therefore thou shalt speak all these w H1697
11: 2 Hear ye the w of this covenant, and H1697
3 that obeyeth not the w of this covenant, H1697
6 me, Proclaim all these w in the cities of H1697
6 ye the w of this covenant, and do them. H1697
8 upon them all the w of this covenant, H1697
10 to hear my w; and they went after H1697
12: 6 though they speak fair w unto thee. H2896
13:10 refuse to hear my w, which walk in the H1697
15:16 Thy w were found, and I did eat them; H1697
16:10 people all these w, and they shall say H1697
18: 2 there I will cause thee to hear my w. H1697
18 and let us not give heed to any of his w. H1697
19: 2 there the w that I shall tell thee, H1697
15 necks, that they might not hear my w. H1697
22: 5 But if ye will not hear these w, I swear H1697
23: 9 and because of the w of his holiness. H1697
16 not unto the w of the prophets that H1697
22 people to hear my w, then they should H1697
30 my w every one from his neighbour. H1697
36 perverted the w of the living God, of H1697
25: 8 hosts; Because ye have not heard my w, H1697
13 upon that land all my w which I have H1697
30 them all these w, and say unto them, H1697
26: 2 house, all the w that I command thee H1697
5 To hearken to the w of my servants the H1697
7 these w in the house of the LORD. H1697
12 this city all the w that ye have heard. H1697
15 you to speak all these w in your ears. H1697
20 land according to all the w of Jeremiah: H1697
21 princes, heard his w, the king sought to H1697
27:12 to all these w, saying, Bring your H1697
14 Therefore hearken not unto the w of H1697
16 not to the w of your prophets that H1697
28: 6 LORD perform thy w which thou hast H1697
29: 1 Now these *are* the w of the letter that H1697
19 not hearkened to my w, saith the LORD, H1697
23 and have spoken lying w in my name, H1697
30: 2 Write thee all the w that I have spoken H1697
4 And these *are* the w that the LORD H1697
34: 6 spake all these w unto Zedekiah king H1697
18 not performed the w of the covenant H1697
35:13 to hearken to my w? saith the LORD. H1697
14 The w of Jonadab the son of Rechab, H1697
36: 2 therein all the w that I have spoken H1697
4 of Jeremiah all the w of the LORD, H1697
6 my mouth, the w of the LORD in the H1697
8 w of the LORD in the LORD'S house. H1697
10 Then read Baruch in the book the w of H1697
11 out of the book all the w of the LORD, H1697
13 unto them all the w that he had heard, H1697
16 had heard all the w, they were afraid H1697
16 will surely tell the king of all these w. H1697
17 thou write all these w at his mouth? H1697
18 all these w unto me with his mouth, H1697
20 told all the w in the ears of the king. H1697
24 of his servants that heard all these w. H1697
27 the roll, and the w which Baruch wrote H1697
28 in it all the former w that were in the H1697
32 of Jeremiah all the w of the book which H1697
32 added besides unto them many like w. H1697
37: 2 hearken unto the w of the LORD, which H1697
38: 1 heard the w that Jeremiah had spoken H1697
4 in speaking such w unto them: for this H1697
24 know of these w, and thou shalt not die. H1697
27 to all these w that the king had H1697
39:16 I will bring my w upon this city for evil, H1697
42: 4 according to your w; and it shall come H1697
43: 1 the people all the w of the LORD their H1697
1 had sent him to them, *even* all these w, H1697
44:28 whose w shall stand, mine, or theirs. H1697
29 may know that my w shall surely stand H1697
45: 1 he had written these w in a book at the H1697
51:60 w that are written against Babylon. H1697
61 shalt see, and shalt read all these w; H1697
64 weary. Thus far *are* the w of Jeremiah. H1697
Ezk 2: 6 be afraid of their w, though briers and H1697
Ezk 2: 6 not afraid of their w, nor be dismayed H1697
7 And thou shalt speak my w unto them, H1697
3: 4 and speak with my w unto them. H1697
6 hard language, whose w thou canst not H1697
10 Son of man, all my w that I shall speak H1697
12:28 shall none of my w be prolonged any H1697
33:31 and they hear thy w, but they will not H1697
32 they hear thy w, but they do them not. H1697
35:13 your w against me: I have heard *them.* H1697
Dan 2: 9 lying and corrupt w to speak before H4406
5:10 *Now* the queen, by reason of the w of H4406
6:14 Then the king, when he heard *these* w, H4406
7:11 the voice of the great w which the horn H4406
25 And he shall speak *great* w against the H4406
9:12 And he hath confirmed his w, which he H1697
10: 6 of his w like the voice of a multitude. H1697
9 Yet heard I the voice of his w: and when H1697
9 the voice of his w, then was I in a deep H1697
11 understand the w that I speak unto H1697
12 thy God, thy w were heard, and I am H1697
12 were heard, and I am come for thy w. H1697
15 And when he had spoken such w unto H1697
12: 4 But thou, O Daniel, shut up the w, and H1697
9 Daniel: for the w *are* closed up and H1697
Hos 6: 5 slain them by the w of my mouth: and H561
10: 4 They have spoken w, swearing falsely in H1697
14: 2 Take with you w, and turn to the LORD: H1697
Am 1: 1 The w of Amos, who was among the H1697
7:10 the land is not able to bear all his w. H1697
8:11 but of hearing the w of the LORD: H1697
Mic 2: 7 doings? do not my w do good to him H1697
Hag 1:12 their God, and the w of Haggai the H1697
Zec 1: 6 But my w and my statutes, which I H1697
13 *with* good w *and* comfortable words. H1697
13 *with* good words *and* comfortable w. H1697
7: 7 *Should ye* not *hear* the w which the H1697
12 the law, and the w which the LORD of H1697
8: 9 these days these w by the mouth of the H1697
Mal 2:17 Ye have wearied the LORD with your w. H1697
3:13 Your w have been stout against me, H1697
Mt 10:14 nor hear your w, when ye depart out G3056
12:37 For by thy w thou shalt be justified, G3056
37 and by thy w thou shalt be condemned. G3056
22:22 When they had heard *these* w, they
24:35 away, but my w shall not pass away. G3056
26:44 the third time, saying the same w. G3056
Mk 8:38 of me and of my w in this adulterous G3056
10:24 were astonished at his w. But Jesus G3056
12:13 of the Herodians, to catch him in *his* w. G3056
13:31 away: but my w shall not pass away. G3056
14:39 and prayed, and spake the same w. G3056
Lk 1:20 thou believest not my w, which shall be G3056
3: 4 As it is written in the book of the w of G3056
4:22 at the gracious w which proceeded out G3056
9:26 of me and of my w, of him shall the Son G3056
20:20 take hold of his w, that so they might G3056
26 And they could not take hold of his w G4487
21:33 away: but my w shall not pass away. G3056
23: 9 many w; but he answered him nothing. G3056
24: 8 And they remembered his w, G4487
11 And their w seemed to them as idle G4487
44 These *are* the w which I spake unto G3056
Jn 3:34 sent speaketh the w of God: for God G4487
5:47 his writings, how shall ye believe my w? G4487
6:63 nothing: the w that I speak unto you, G4487
68 we go? thou hast the w of eternal life. G4487
7: 9 When he had said these w unto them, G5023
8:20 These w spake Jesus in the treasury, as G4487
30 As he spake these w, many believed on G5023
47 He that is of God heareth God's w: ye G4487
9:22 These *w* spake his parents, because they
40 him heard these w, and said unto him, G5023
10:21 Others said, These are not the w of him G4487
12:47 And if any man hear my w, and believe G4487
48 and receiveth not my w, hath one that G4487
14:10 Father in me? the w that I speak unto G4487
23 he will keep my w: and my Father will G3056
15: 7 If ye abide in me, and my w abide in G4487
17: 1 These w spake Jesus, and lifted up his G5023
8 For I have given unto them the w which G4487
18: 1 When Jesus had spoken these w, he G5023
Act 2:14 known unto you, and hearken to my w: G4487
22 Ye men of Israel, hear these w; Jesus of G3056
40 And with many other w did he testify G3056
5: 5 And Ananias hearing these w fell G3056
20 to the people all the w of this life. G4487
6:11 w against Moses, and *against* God. G4487
13 w against this holy place, and the law: G4487
7:22 and was mighty in w and in deeds. G3056

Act 10:22 into his house, and to hear **w** of thee. *G4487*
44 While Peter yet spake these **w**, the Holy *G4487*
11:14 Who shall tell thee **w**, whereby thou and *G4487*
13:42 that these **w** might be preached *G4487*
15:15 And to this agree the **w** of the prophets; *G3056*
24 troubled you with **w**, subverting your *G3056*
32 with many **w**, and confirmed *them*. *G3056*
16:38 And the serjeants told these **w** unto the *G4487*
18:15 But if it be a question of **w** and names, *G3056*
20:35 to remember the **w** of the Lord Jesus, *G3056*
38 Sorrowing most of all for the **w** which *G3056*
24: 4 hear us of thy clemency a few **w**. *G4935*
26:25 forth the **w** of truth and soberness. *G4487*
28:29 And when he had said these **w**, the Jews *G5023*
Ro 10:18 and their **w** unto the ends of the world. *G4487*
16:18 belly; and by good **w** and fair speeches *G5542*
1Co 1:17 not with wisdom of **w**, lest the cross of *G3056*
2: 4 not with enticing **w** of man's wisdom, *G3056*
13 we speak, not in the **w** which man's *G3056*
14: 9 by the tongue **w** easy to be understood, *G3056*
19 had rather speak five **w** with my *G3056*
19 ten thousand **w** in an *unknown* tongue. *G3056*
2Co 12: 4 unspeakable **w**, which it is not lawful *G4487*
Eph 3: 3 the mystery; (as I wrote afore in few **w**, *G3641*
5: 6 Let no man deceive you with vain **w**: for *G3056*
Col 2: 4 should beguile you with enticing **w**. *G4086*
1Th 2: 5 used we flattering **w**, as ye know, nor a *G3056*
4:18 comfort one another with these **w**. *G3056*
1Ti 4: 6 up in the **w** of faith and of good *G3056*
6: 3 not to wholesome **w**, *even* the words of *G3056*
3 words, *even* the **w** of our Lord Jesus *G3588*
4 and strifes of **w**, whereof cometh envy, *G3055*
2Ti 1:13 Hold fast the form of sound **w**, which *G3056*
2:14 strive not about **w** to no profit, *but* to *G3054*
4:15 for he hath greatly withstood our **w**. *G3056*
Heb 12:19 and the voice of **w**; which *voice* they *G4487*
13:22 have written a letter unto you in few **w**. *G1024*
2Pt 2: 3 they with feigned **w** make merchandise *G3056*
18 For when they speak great swelling **w** of
3: 2 That ye may be mindful of the **w** which *G4487*
3Jn 10 us with malicious **w**: and not content *G3056*
Jude 16 great swelling **w**, having men's persons
17 But, beloved, remember ye the **w** which *G4487*
Rev 1: 3 they that hear the **w** of this prophecy, *G3056*
17:17 until the **w** of God shall be fulfilled. *G4487*
21: 5 Write: for these **w** are true and faithful. *G3056*
22:18 that heareth the **w** of the prophecy of *G3056*
19 away from the **w** of the book of this *G3056*

WORD'S
2Sa 7:21 For thy **w** sake, and according to thine H1697
Mk 4:17 **w** sake, immediately they are offended.

WORE See WARE.

WORK
Gen 2: 2 God ended his **w** which he had made; H4399
2 day from all his **w** which he had made. H4399
3 all his **w** which God created and made. H4399
5:29 us concerning our **w** and toil of our H4639
Ex 5: 9 Let there more **w** be laid upon the men, H5656
11 ought of your **w** shall be diminished. H5656
18 Go therefore now, *and* **w**; for there shall H5647
12:16 no manner of **w** shall be done in them, H4399
14:31 And Israel saw that great **w** which the H3027
18:20 walk, and the **w** that they must do. H4639
20: 9 shalt thou labour, and do all thy **w**: H4399
10 shalt not do any **w**, thou, nor thy son, H4399
23:12 Six days thou shalt do thy **w**, and on the H4639
24:10 feet as it were a paved **w** of a sapphire H4639
25:18 *of* gold, *of* beaten **w** shalt thou make H4749
31 gold: *of* beaten **w** shall the candlestick H4749
36 it *shall be* one beaten **w** *of* pure gold. H4749
26: 1 of cunning **w** shalt thou make them. H4639
31 **w**: with cherubims shall it be made: H4639
28: 6 and fine twined linen, with cunning **w**. H4639
8 according to the **w** thereof; *even of* H4639
11 With the **w** of an engraver in stone, *like* H4639
14 *of* wreathen **w** shalt thou make them, H4639
15 with cunning **w**; after the work of the H4639
15 work; after the **w** of the ephod thou H4639
22 at the ends *of* wreathen **w** *of* pure gold. H4639
32 a binding of woven **w** round about the H4639
31: 4 To devise cunning works, to **w** in gold, H6213
5 to **w** in all manner of workmanship. H6213
14 doeth *any* **w** therein, that soul shall H4399
15 Six days may **w** be done; but in the H4399
15 doeth *any* **w** in the sabbath day, H4399
32:16 And the tables *were* the **w** of God, and H4639
Ex 34:10 *art* shall see the **w** of the LORD: for it *is* H4639
21 Six days thou shalt **w**, but on the H5647
35: 2 Six days shall **w** be done, but on the H4399
2 doeth **w** therein shall be put to death. H4399
21 offering to the **w** of the tabernacle of H4399
24 for any **w** of the service, brought *it*. H4399
29 for all manner of **w**, which the LORD H4399
32 And to devise curious works, to **w** in H6213
33 to make any manner of cunning **w**. H4399
35 of heart, to **w** all manner of work, H6213
35 all manner of **w**, of the engraver, and H4399
35 of them that do any **w**, and of those that H4399
35 and of those that devise cunning **w**. H4284
36: 1 to know how to **w** all manner of work H6213
1 all manner of **w** for the service of the H4399
2 him up to come unto the **w** to do it: H4399
3 brought for the **w** of the service of the H4399
4 that wrought all the **w** of the sanctuary, H4399
4 man from his **w** which they made; H4399
5 for the service of the **w**, which the LORD H4399
6 make any more **w** for the offering of H4399
7 for all the **w** to make it, and too much. H4399
8 that wrought the **w** of the tabernacle H4399
8 of cunning **w** made he them. H4639
35 cherubims made he it of cunning **w**. H4639
37:17 pure gold: *of* beaten **w** made he the H4749
22 all of it *was* one beaten **w** *of* pure gold. H4749
29 according to the **w** of the apothecary. H4639
38:24 All the gold that was occupied for the **w** H4399
24 the work in all the **w** of the holy *place*, H4399
39: 3 *it into* wires, to **w** *it* in the blue, and in H6213
3 and in the fine linen, *with* cunning **w**. H4639
5 according to the **w** thereof; *of* gold, H4639
8 *of* cunning **w**, like the work of the H4639
8 work, like the **w** of the ephod; *of* gold, H4639
15 at the ends, *of* wreathen **w** *of* pure gold. H4639
22 of the ephod *of* woven **w**, all *of* blue. H4639
27 *of* woven **w** for Aaron, and for his sons, H4639
32 Thus was all the **w** of the tabernacle of H5656
42 so the children of Israel made all the **w**. H5656
43 And Moses did look upon all the **w**, H4399
40:33 the court gate. So Moses finished the **w**. H4399
Lev 11:32 *it be*, wherein *any* **w** is done, it must be H4399
13:51 a skin, *or* in any **w** that is made of skin; H4399
16:29 souls, and do no **w** at all, *whether it be* H4399
23: 3 Six days shall **w** be done: but the H4399
3 ye shall do no **w** *therein*: it *is* the H4399
7 ye shall do no servile **w** therein. H4399
8 ye shall do no servile **w** *therein*. H4399
21 shall do no servile **w** *therein: it shall be* H4399
25 Ye shall do no servile **w** *therein*: but ye H4399
28 And ye shall do no **w** in that same day: H4399
30 *be* that doeth any **w** in that same day, H4399
31 Ye shall do no manner of **w**: *it shall be* a H4399
35 ye shall do no servile **w** *therein*. H4399
36 *and* ye shall do no servile **w** *therein*. H4399
Nu 4: 3 the host, to do the **w** in the tabernacle H4399
23 service, to do the **w** in the tabernacle of H5656
30 service, to do the **w** of the tabernacle of H5656
35 the service, for the **w** in the tabernacle H5656
39 the service, for the **w** in the tabernacle H5656
43 the service, for the **w** in the tabernacle H5656
8: 4 And this **w** of the candlestick *was of* H4639
4 *was* beaten **w**: according unto the H4749
28:18 do no manner of servile **w** *therein*: H4399
25 convocation; ye shall do no servile **w**. H4399
26 convocation; ye shall do no servile **w**: H4399
29: 1 ye shall do no servile **w**: it is a day of H4399
7 souls: ye shall not do any **w** *therein*: H4399
12 shall do no servile **w**, and ye shall keep H4399
35 ye shall do no servile **w** *therein*: H4399
31:20 of skins, and all **w** of goats' *hair*, and H4639
Dt 4:28 And there ye shall serve gods, the **w** of H4639
5:13 thou shalt labour, and do all thy **w**: H4399
14 shalt not do any **w**, thou, nor thy son, H4399
14:29 the **w** of thine hand which thou doest. H4639
15:19 thou shalt do no **w** with the firstling of H5647
16: 8 thy God: thou shalt do no **w** *therein*. H4399
24:19 bless thee in all the **w** of thine hands. H4639
27:15 the LORD, the **w** of the hands of the H4639
28:12 to bless all the **w** of thine hand: and H4639
30: 9 plenteous in every **w** of thine hand, in H4639
31:29 to anger through the **w** of your hands. H4639
32: 4 *He is* the Rock, his **w** *is* perfect: for all H6467
33:11 and accept the **w** of his hands: smite H6467
Jos 9: 4 They did **w** wilily, and went and made H6213
Jdg 19:16 old man from his **w** out of the field at H4639
Ru 2:12 The LORD recompense thy **w**, and a full H6467
1Sa 8:16 and your asses, and put *them* to his **w**. H4399
1Sa 14: 6 the LORD will **w** for us: for *there is* no H6213
1Ki 5:16 *were* over the **w**, three thousand and H4399
16 over the people that wrought in the **w**. H4399
6:35 with gold fitted upon the carved **w**. H2707
7: 8 was of the like **w**. Solomon made also H4639
14 and cunning to **w** all works in brass. H6213
14 to king Solomon, and wrought all his **w**. H4399
17 *And* nets of checker **w**, and wreaths of H4639
17 wreaths of chain **w**, for the chapiters H4639
19 *were* of lily **w** in the porch, four cubits. H4639
22 the pillars *was* lily **w**: so was the work of H4639
22 so was the **w** of the pillars finished. H4399
28 And the **w** of the bases *was* on this H4639
29 *were* certain additions made of thin **w**. H4639
31 round *after* the **w** of the base, a cubit H4639
33 And the **w** of the wheels *was* like the H4639
33 *was* like the **w** of a chariot wheel: H4639
40 of doing all the **w** that he made king H4399
51 So was ended all the **w** that king H4399
9:23 over Solomon's **w**, five hundred and H4399
23 over the people that wrought in the **w**. H4399
16: 7 to anger with the **w** of his hands, in H4639
21:20 to **w** evil in the sight of the LORD, H6213
25 did sell himself to **w** wickedness in the H6213
2Ki 12:11 of them that did the **w**, that had the H4399
19:18 no gods, but the **w** of men's hands, H4639
22: 5 hand of the doers of the **w**, that have the H4399
5 it to the doers of the **w** which *is* in the H4399
9 of them that do the **w**, that have the H4399
25:17 and the wreathen **w**, and pomegranates H7639
17 had the second pillar with wreathen **w**. H7639
1Ch 4:23 there they dwelt with the king for his **w**. H4399
6:49 for all the **w** of the *place* most holy, H4399
9:13 the **w** of the service of the house of God. H4399
19 *were* over the **w** of the service, keepers H4399
33 employed in *that* **w** day and night. H4399
16:37 continually, as every day's **w** required: H1697
22:15 of cunning men for every manner of **w**. H4399
23: 4 to set forward the **w** of the house of the H4399
24 polls, that did the **w** for the service of H4399
28 the **w** of the service of the house of God; H4639
27:26 And over them that did the **w** of the H4399
28:13 and for all the **w** of the service of the H4399
20 finished all the **w** for the service of the H4399
29: 1 and tender, and the **w** *is* great: for the H4399
5 for all manner of **w** *to be made* by the H4399
6 rulers of the king's **w**, offered willingly, H4399
2Ch 2: 7 a man cunning to **w** in gold, and in H6213
14 man of Tyre, skilful to **w** in gold, and in H6213
18 hundred overseers to set the people a **w**. H5647
3:10 image **w**, and overlaid them with gold. H4639
4: 5 the brim of it like the **w** of the brim of a H4639
11 finished the **w** that he was to make H4399
5: 1 Thus all the **w** that Solomon made for H4399
8: 9 servants for his **w**; but they *were* men H4399
16 Now all the **w** of Solomon was H4399
15: 7 be weak: for your **w** shall be rewarded. H6468
16: 5 building of Ramah, and let his **w** cease. H4399
24:12 it to such as did the **w** of the service of H4399
13 So the workmen wrought, and the **w** H4399
29:34 help them, till the **w** was ended, and H4399
31:21 And in every **w** that he began in the H4639
32:19 *which were* the **w** of the hands of man. H4639
34:12 And the men did the **w** faithfully: and H4399
13 that wrought the **w** in any manner of H4399
Ezr 2:69 the treasure of the **w** threescore and H4399
3: 8 the **w** of the house of the LORD. H4399
4:24 Then ceased the **w** of the house of God H5673
5: 8 the walls, and this **w** goeth fast on, and H5673
6: 7 Let the **w** of this house of God alone; let H5673
22 their hands in the **w** of the house of H4399
10:13 neither *is this* a **w** of one day or two: H4399
Neh 2:16 the rulers, nor to the rest that did the **w**. H4399
18 strengthened their hands for *this* good **w**.
3: 5 not their necks to the **w** of their Lord. H5656
4: 6 thereof: for the people had a mind to **w**. H6213
11 slay them, and cause the **w** to cease. H4399
15 of us to the wall, every one unto his **w**. H4399
16 wrought in the **w**, and the other half of H4399
17 wrought in the **w**, and with the other H4399
19 of the people, The **w** *is* great and large, H4399
21 So we laboured in the **w**: and half of H4399
5:16 Yea, also I continued in the **w** of this H4399
16 *were* gathered thither unto the **w**. H4399
6: 3 I *am* doing a great **w**, so that I cannot H4399
3 why should the **w** cease, whilst I leave H4399
9 from the **w**, that it be not done. H4399
16 that this **w** was wrought of our God. H4399
7:70 gave unto the **w**. The Tirshatha gave H4399

Neh 7:71 the treasure of the w twenty thousand H4399
10:33 *for* all the w of the house of our God. H4399
11:12 And their brethren that did the w of the H4399
13:10 the w, were fled every one to his field. H4399
Job 1:10 hast blessed the w of his hands, and his H4639
7: 2 hireling looketh for *the reward of* his w: H6467
10: 3 despise the w of thine hands, and H3018
14:15 have a desire to the w of thine hands. H4639
23: 9 On the left hand, where he doth w, but I H6213
24: 5 they forth to their w; rising betimes for H6467
34:11 For the w of a man shall he render unto H6467
19 for they all *are* the w of his hands. H4639
36: 9 Then he sheweth them their w, and H6467
24 Remember that thou magnify his w, H6467
37: 7 man; that all men may know his w. H4639
Ps 8: 3 When I consider thy heavens, the w of H4639
9:16 w of his own hands. Higgaion. Selah. H6467
28: 4 them after the w of their hands; render H4639
44: 1 have told us, *what* w thou didst in their H6467
58: 2 Yea, in heart ye w wickedness; ye H6466
62:12 to every man according to his w. H4639
64: 9 and shall declare the w of God; for they H6467
74: 6 But now they break down the carved w H6603
77:12 I will meditate also of all thy w, and talk H6467
90:16 Let thy w appear unto thy servants, H6467
17 establish thou the w of our hands upon H4639
17 the w of our hands establish thou it. H4639
92: 4 me glad through thy w: I will triumph in H6467
95: 9 tempted me, proved me, and saw my w. H6467
101: 3 eyes: I hate the w of them that turn H6213
102:25 the heavens *are* the w of thy hands. H4639
104:23 Man goeth forth unto his w and to his H6467
111: 3 His w *is* honourable and glorious: and H6467
115: 4 Their idols *are* silver and gold, the w of H4639
119:126 *It is* time for *thee*, LORD, to w: *for* they H6213
135:15 silver and gold, the w of men's hands. H4639
141: 4 with men that w iniquity: and let me H6466
143: 5 works; I muse on the w of thy hands. H4639
Prv 11:18 The wicked worketh a deceitful w: but H6468
16:11 all the weights of the bag *are* his w. H4639
18: 9 He also that is slothful in his w is H4399
20:11 his w *be* pure, and whether *it be* right. H6467
21: 8 but *as for* the pure, his w *is* right. H6467
24:27 Prepare thy w without, and make it fit H4399
29 render to the man according to his w. H6467
Ecc 2:17 Therefore I hated life; because the w H4639
3:11 can find out the w that God maketh H4639
17 there for every purpose and for every w. H4639
4: 3 the evil w that is done under the sun. H4639
4 and every right w, that for this a man H4639
5: 6 and destroy the w of thine hands? H4639
7:13 Consider the w of God: for who can H4639
8: 9 heart unto every w that is done under H4639
11 Because sentence against an evil w is H4639
14 according to the w of the wicked; H4639
14 according to the w of the righteous: I H4639
17 Then I beheld all the w of God, that a H4639
17 find out the w that is done under the H4639
9:10 might; for *there is* no w, nor device, nor H4639
12:14 For God shall bring every w into H4639
Song 7: 1 w of the hands of a cunning workman. H4639
Isa 2: 8 they worship the w of their own hands, H4639
5:12 regard not the w of the LORD, neither H6467
19 *and* hasten his w, that we may see *it*: H4639
10:12 his whole w upon mount Zion and H4639
17: 8 look to the altars, the w of his hands, H4639
19: 9 Moreover they that w in fine flax, and H5647
14 to err in every w thereof, as a drunken H4639
15 Neither shall there be *any* w for Egypt, H4639
25 and Assyria the w of my hands, and H4639
28:21 he may do his w, his strange work; and H4639
21 work, his strange w; and bring to pass H4639
29:14 do a marvellous w among this people, H6381
14 *even* a marvellous w and a wonder: for H6381
16 clay: for shall the w say of him that H4639
23 But when he seeth his children, the w H4639
31: 2 the help of them that w iniquity. H6466
32: 6 villany, and his heart will w iniquity, to H6213
17 And the w of righteousness shall be H4639
37:19 no gods, but the w of men's hands, H4639
40:10 *is* with him, and his w before him. H6468
41:24 Behold, ye *are* of nothing, and your w H6467
43:13 my hand: I will w, and who shall let it? H6466
45: 9 thou? or thy w, He hath no hands? H6467
11 the w of my hands command ye me. H6467
49: 4 the LORD, and my w with my God. H6468
54:16 an instrument for his w; and I have H4639
60:21 w of my hands, that I may be glorified. H4639
61: 8 I will direct their w in truth, and I will H6468
Isa 62:11 *is* with him, and his w before him. H6468
64: 8 and we all *are* the w of thy hand. H4639
65: 7 their former w into their bosom. H6468
22 shall long enjoy the w of their hands. H4639
Jer 10: 3 of the forest, the w of the hands of the H4639
9 from Uphaz, the w of the workman, H4639
9 they *are* all the w of cunning *men*. H4639
15 They *are* vanity, *and* the w of errors: in H4639
17:22 neither do ye any w, but hallow ye the H4399
24 the sabbath day, to do no w therein; H4399
18: 3 behold, he wrought a w on the wheels. H4399
22:13 wages, and giveth him not for his w; H6467
31:16 from tears: for thy w shall be rewarded, H6468
32:19 Great in counsel, and mighty in w: for H5950
30 the w of their hands, saith the LORD. H4639
48:10 Cursed *be* he that doeth the w of the H4399
50:25 for this *is* the w of the Lord GOD of H4399
29 according to her w; according to all that H6467
51:10 in Zion the w of the LORD our God. H4639
18 They *are* vanity, the w of errors: in the H4639
Lam 3:64 according to the w of their hands. H4639
4: 2 the w of the hands of the potter! H4639
Ezk 1:16 wheels and their w *was* like unto the H4639
16 and their w *was* as it were a wheel H4639
15: 3 thereof to do any w? or will *men* take a H4399
4 of it is burned. Is it meet for *any* w? H4399
5 it was meet for no w: how much less H4399
5 meet yet for *any* w, when the fire hath H4399
16:10 I clothed thee also with broidered w, H7553
13 and broidered w; thou didst eat fine H7553
30 the w of an imperious whorish woman; H4639
27: 7 Fine linen with broidered w from Egypt H7553
16 w, and fine linen, and coral, and agate. H7553
24 and broidered w, and in chests of rich H7553
33:26 Ye stand upon your sword, ye w H6213
Dan 11:23 with him he shall w deceitfully: for he H6213
Hos 6: 8 Gilead *is* a city of them that w iniquity, H6466
13: 2 all of it the w of the craftsmen: they H4639
14: 3 any more to the w of our hands, *Ye are* H4639
Mic 2: 1 iniquity, and w evil upon their beds! H6466
5:13 no more worship the w of thine hands. H4639
Hab 1: 5 for *I* will w a work in your days, H6466
5 for *I* will work a w in your days, *which* H6467
2:18 the maker of his w trusteth therein, to H3336
3: 2 LORD, revive thy w in the midst of the H6467
Zep 2:14 for he shall uncover the cedar w. H731
Hag 1:14 came and did w in the house of the H4399
2: 4 the LORD, and w: for I *am* with you, H6213
14 and so *is* every w of their hands; and H4639
Mal 3:15 yea, they that w wickedness are set H6213
Mt 7:23 depart from me, ye that w iniquity. *G2038*
21:28 said, Son, go w to day in my vineyard. *G2038*
26:10 she hath wrought a good w upon me. *G2041*
Mk 6: 5 And he could there do no mighty w, *G1411*
13:34 to every man his w, and commanded *G2041*
14: 6 her? she hath wrought a good w on me. *G2041*
Lk 13:14 men ought to w: in them therefore come *G2038*
Jn 4:34 of him that sent me, and to finish his w. *G2041*
5:17 My Father worketh hitherto, and I w. *G2038*
6:28 do, that we might w the works of God? *G2038*
29 unto them, This is the w of God, that ye *G2041*
30 see, and believe thee? what dost thou w? *G2038*
7:21 I have done one w, and ye all marvel. *G2041*
9: 4 I must w the works of him that sent *G2038*
4 the night cometh, when no man can w. *G2038*
10:33 For a good w we stone thee not; but *G2041*
17: 4 the w which thou gavest me to do. *G2041*
Act 5:38 w be of men, it will come to nought: *G2041*
13: 2 the w whereunto I have called them. *G2041*
41 and perish: for I w a work in your days, *G2038*
41 for I work a w in your days, a work *G2041*
41 in your days, a w which ye shall in no *G2041*
14:26 of God for the w which they fulfilled. *G2041*
15:38 and went not with them to the w. *G2041*
27:16 we had much w to come by the boat: *G2480*
Ro 2:15 Which shew the w of the law written in *G2041*
7: 5 by the law, did w in our members to *G1754*
8:28 And we know that all things w together *G4903*
9:28 For he will finish the w, and cut *it* short *G3056*
28 w will the Lord make upon the earth. *G3056*
11: 6 grace: otherwise w is no more work. *G2041*
6 grace: otherwise work is no more w. *G2041*
14:20 For meat destroy not the w of God. All *G2041*
1Co 3:13 Every man's w shall be made manifest: *G2041*
13 try every man's w of what sort it is. *G2041*
14 If any man's w abide which he hath *G2041*
15 If any man's w shall be burned, he *G2041*
9: 1 our Lord? are not ye my w in the Lord? *G2041*
15:58 always abounding in the w of the Lord, *G2041*
1Co 16:10 worketh the w of the Lord, as I also *do*. *G2041*
2Co 9: 8 all *things*, may abound to every good w: *G2041*
Gal 6: 4 But let every man prove his own w, and *G2041*
Eph 4:12 the saints, for the w of the ministry, for *G2041*
19 to w all uncleanness with greediness. *G2039*
Php 1: 6 begun a good w in you will perform *G2041*
2:12 more in my absence, w out your own *G2716*
30 Because for the w of Christ he was nigh *G2041*
Col 1:10 in every good w, and increasing in the *G2041*
1Th 1: 3 Remembering without ceasing your w *G2041*
4:11 own business, and to w with your own *G2038*
2Th 1:11 and the w of faith with power: *G2041*
2: 7 doth already w: only he who now letteth *G1754*
17 stablish you in every good word and w. *G2041*
3:10 any would not w, neither should he eat. *G2038*
12 they w, and eat their own bread. *G2038*
1Ti 3: 1 office of a bishop, he desireth a good w. *G2041*
5:10 have diligently followed every good w. *G2041*
2Ti 2:21 use, *and* prepared unto every good w. *G2041*
4: 5 afflictions, do the w of an evangelist, *G2041*
18 from every evil w, and will preserve *me* *G2041*
Tit 1:16 and unto every good w reprobate. *G2041*
3: 1 to be ready to every good w, *G2041*
Heb 6:10 to forget your w and labour of love, *G2041*
13:21 Make you perfect in every good w to do *G2041*
Jas 1: 4 But let patience have *her* perfect w, that *G2041*
25 w, this man shall be blessed in his deed. *G2041*
3:16 *is*, there *is* confusion and every evil w. *G4229*
1Pt 1:17 to every man's w, pass the time of your *G2041*
Rev 22:12 every man according as his w shall be. *G2041*

WORKED See WROUGHT.

WORKER

1Ki 7:14 a man of Tyre, a w in brass: and he H2790

WORKERS

2Ki 23:24 Moreover the *w with* familiar spirits,
1Ch 22:15 hewers and w of stone and timber, H2796
Job 31: 3 *punishment* to the w of iniquity? H6466
34: 8 Which goeth in company with the w of H6466
22 the w of iniquity may hide themselves. H6466
Ps 5: 5 thy sight: thou hatest all w of iniquity. H6466
6: 8 Depart from me, all ye w of iniquity; H6466
14: 4 Have all the w of iniquity no H6466
28: 3 and with the w of iniquity, which speak H6466
36:12 There are the w of iniquity fallen: they H6466
37: 1 thou envious against the w of iniquity. H6213
53: 4 Have the w of iniquity no knowledge? H6466
59: 2 Deliver me from the w of iniquity, and H6466
64: 2 the insurrection of the w of iniquity: H6466
92: 7 grass, and when all the w of iniquity do H6466
9 all the w of iniquity shall be scattered. H6466
94: 4 all the w of iniquity boast themselves? H6466
16 up for me against the w of iniquity? H6466
125: 5 forth with the w of iniquity: *but* peace H6466
141: 9 me, and the gins of the w of iniquity. H6466
Prv 10:29 *shall be* to the w of iniquity. H6466
21:15 *shall be* to the w of iniquity. H6466
Lk 13:27 depart from me, all *ye* w of iniquity. *G2040*
1Co 12:29 *are* all teachers? *are* all w of miracles? *G1411*
2Co 6: 1 We then, *as* w together *with him*, *G4903*
11:13 For such *are* false apostles, deceitful w, *G2040*
Php 3: 2 Beware of dogs, beware of evil w, *G2040*

WORKETH

Job 33:29 Lo, all these *things* w God oftentimes H6466
Ps 15: 2 He that walketh uprightly, and w H6466
101: 7 He that w deceit shall not dwell within H6213
Prv 11:18 The wicked w a deceitful work: but to H6213
26:28 by it; and a flattering mouth w ruin. H6213
31:13 She seeketh wool, and flax, and w H6213
Ecc 3: 9 What profit hath he that w in that H6213
Isa 44:12 The smith with the tongs both w in the H6466
12 hammers, and w it with the strength H6466
64: 5 Thou meetest him that rejoiceth and w H6213
Dan 6:27 He delivereth and rescueth, and he w H5648
Jn 5:17 But Jesus answered them, My Father w *G2038*
Act 10:35 w righteousness, is accepted with him. *G2038*
Ro 2:10 to every man that w good, to the Jew *G2038*
4: 4 Now to him that w is the reward not *G2038*
5 But to him that w not, but believeth on *G2038*
15 Because the law w wrath: for where no *G2716*
5: 3 knowing that tribulation w patience; *G2716*
13:10 Love w no ill to his neighbour: *G2038*
1Co 12: 6 it is the same God which w all in all. *G1754*
11 But all these w that one and the *G1754*
16:10 he w the work of the Lord, as I also *do*. *G2038*
2Co 4:12 So then death w in us, but life in you. *G1754*

2Co 4:17 but for a moment, w for us a far more G2716
7:10 For godly sorrow w repentance to G2716
10 of: but the sorrow of the world w death. G2716
Gal 3: 5 the Spirit, and w miracles among you, G1754
5: 6 but faith which w by love. G1754
Eph 1:11 of him who w all things after the G1754
2: 2 now w in the children of disobedience: G1754
3:20 according to the power that w in us, G1754
Php 2:13 For it is God which w in you both to G1754
Col 1:29 to his working, which w in me mightily. G1754
1Th 2:13 effectually w also in you that believe. G1754
Jas 1: 3 that the trying of your faith w patience. G2716
20 For the wrath of man w not the G2716
Rev 21:27 *whatsoever* w abomination, or *maketh* G4160

WORKFELLOW
Ro 16:21 Timotheus my w, and Lucius, and G4904

WORKING
Ps 52: 2 like a sharp razor, w deceitfully. H6213
74:12 For God *is* my King of old, w salvation H6466
Isa 28:29 in counsel, *and* excellent in w. H8454
Ezk 46: 1 shall be shut the six w days; but on the H4639
Mk 16:20 where, the Lord w with *them*, and G4903
Ro 1:27 another; men with men w that which is G2716
7:13 it might appear sin, w death in me by G2716
1Co 4:12 And labour, w with our own hands: G2038
9: 6 have not we power to forbear w? G2038
12:10 To another the w of miracles; to G1755
Eph 1:19 according to the w of his mighty power, G1753
3: 7 me by the effectual w of his power. G1753
4:16 to the effectual w in the measure of G1753
28 let him labour, w with *his* hands the G2038
Php 3:21 according to the w whereby he is able G1753
Col 1:29 to his w, which worketh in me mightily. G1753
2Th 2: 9 *Even him*, whose coming is after the w G1753
3:11 w not at all, but are busybodies. G2038
Heb 13:21 to do his will, w in you that which is G4160
Rev 16:14 For they are the spirits of devils, w G4160

WORKMAN
Ex 35:35 and of the cunning w, and of the H2803
38:23 and a cunning w, and an embroiderer H2803
Song 7: 1 the work of the hands of a cunning w. H542
Isa 40:19 The w melteth a graven image, and the H2796
20 him a cunning w to prepare a graven H2796
Jer 10: 3 of the hands of the w, with the axe. H2796
9 the work of the w, and of the hands of H2796
Hos 8: 6 For from Israel *was* it also: the w made H2796
Mt 10:10 staves: for the w is worthy of his meat. G2040
2Ti 2:15 unto God, a w that needeth not to G2040

WORKMANSHIP
Ex 31: 3 in knowledge, and in all manner of w, H4399
5 of timber, to work in all manner of w. H4399
35:31 in knowledge, and in all manner of w; H4399
2Ki 16:10 of it, according to all the w thereof. H4639
1Ch 28:21 for all manner of w every willing skilful H4399
Ezk 28:13 and gold: the w of thy tabrets and of H4399
Eph 2:10 For we are his w, created in Christ Jesus G4161

WORKMEN
2Ki 12:14 But they gave that to the w, and H4399+H6213
15 on w: for they dealt faithfully. H6213+H4399
1Ch 22:15 Moreover *there are* w with H6213+H4399
25: 1 number of the w according to H582+H4399
2Ch 24:13 So the w wrought, and the H4399+H6213
34:10 the hand of the w that had the H6213+H4399
10 gave it to the w that wrought H6213+H4399
17 and to the hand of the w. H6213+H4399
Ezr 3: 9 forward the w in the house of H6213+H4399
Isa 44:11 ashamed: and the w, they *are* of men: H2796
Act 19:25 Whom he called together with the w of G2040

WORKMEN'S
Jdg 5:26 right hand to the w hammer; and with H6001

WORKS
Ex 5: 4 their w? get you unto your burdens. H4639
13 saying, Fulfil your w, *your* daily tasks, H4639
23:24 nor do after their w: but thou shalt H4639
31: 4 To devise cunning w, to work in gold, H4284
35:32 And to devise curious w, to work in H4284
Nu 16:28 me to do all these w; for *I have* not *done* H4639
Dt 2: 7 blessed thee in all the w of thy hand: he H4639
3:24 to thy w, and according to thy might? H4639
15:10 thee in all thy w, and in all that thou H4639
16:15 and in all the w of thine hands, H4639
Jos 24:31 had known all the w of the LORD, that H4639
Jdg 2: 7 w of the LORD, that he did for Israel. H4639
10 yet the w which he had done for Israel. H4639
1Sa 8: 8 According to all the w which they have H4639
19: 4 w *have been* to thee-ward very good: H4639
1Ki 7:14 to work all w in brass. And he came H4399
13:11 told him all the w that the man of God H4639
2Ki 22:17 to anger with all the w of their hands; H4639
1Ch 16: 9 unto him, talk ye of all his wondrous w. H6381
12 Remember his marvellous w that he H6381
24 his marvellous w among all nations. H6381
28:19 upon me, *even* all the w of this pattern. H4399
2Ch 20:37 hath broken thy w. And the ships were H4639
32:30 And Hezekiah prospered in all his w. H4639
34:25 to anger with all the w of their hands; H4639
Neh 6:14 to these their w, and on the prophetess H4639
9:35 turned they from their wicked w. H4611
Job 34:25 Therefore he knoweth their w, and he H4566
37:14 and consider the wondrous w of God. H6381
16 the wondrous w of him which is perfect H4652
Ps 8: 6 over the w of thy hands; thou hast H4639
9: 1 I will shew forth all thy marvellous w. H6381
14: 1 w, *there is* none that doeth good. H5949
17: 4 Concerning the w of men, by the word H6468
26: 7 and tell of all thy wondrous w. H6381
28: 5 Because they regard not the w of the H6468
33: 4 *is* right; and all his w *are done* in truth. H4639
15 hearts alike; he considereth all their w. H4639
40: 5 *are* thy wonderful w *which* thou hast H6381
46: 8 Come, behold the w of the LORD, what H4659
66: 3 *art thou in* thy w! through the greatness H4639
5 Come and see the w of God: *he is* H4659
71:17 have I declared thy wondrous w. H6381
73:28 Lord GOD, that I may declare all thy w. H4399
75: 1 name is near thy wondrous w declare. H6381
77:11 I will remember the w of the LORD: H4611
78: 4 and his wonderful w that he hath done. H6381
7 and not forget the w of God, but keep H4611
11 And forgat his w, and his wonders that H5949
32 and believed not for his wondrous w. H6381
86: 8 *are there any* w like unto thy works.
8 *are there any works* like unto thy w. H4639
92: 4 I will triumph in the w of thy hands. H4639
5 O LORD, how great are thy w! *and* thy H4639
103:22 Bless the LORD, all his w in all places H4639
104:13 earth is satisfied with the fruit of thy w. H4639
24 O LORD, how manifold are thy w! in H4639
31 for ever: the LORD shall rejoice in his w. H4639
105: 2 unto him: talk ye of all his wondrous w. H6381
5 Remember his marvellous w that he H6381
106:13 They soon forgat his w; they waited not H4639
22 Wondrous w in the land of Ham, *and* H6381
35 the heathen, and learned their w. H4639
39 with their own w, and went a whoring H4639
107: 8 his wonderful w to the children of men! H6381
15 his wonderful w to the children of men! H6381
21 his wonderful w to the children of men! H6381
22 and declare his w with rejoicing. H4639
24 These see the w of the LORD, and his H4639
31 his wonderful w to the children of men! H6381
111: 2 The w of the LORD *are* great, sought H4639
4 He hath made his wonderful w to be H6381
6 the power of his w, that he may give H4639
7 The w of his hands *are* verity and H4639
118:17 live, and declare the w of the LORD. H4639
119:27 so shall I talk of thy wondrous w. H6381
138: 8 forsake not the w of thine own hands. H4639
139:14 w; and *that* my soul knoweth right well. H4639
141: 4 to practise wicked w with men that H5949
143: 5 thy w; I muse on the work of thy hands. H6467
145: 4 One generation shall praise thy w to H4639
5 of thy majesty, and of thy wondrous w. H1697
9 his tender mercies *are* over all his w. H4639
10 All thy w shall praise thee, O LORD; H4639
17 in all his ways, and holy in all his w. H4639
Prv 7:16 with carved *w*, with fine linen of Egypt.
8:22 of his way, before his w of old. H4659
16: 3 Commit thy w unto the LORD, and thy H4639
24:12 render to *every* man according to his w? H6467
31:31 let her own w praise her in the gates. H4639
Ecc 1:14 I have seen all the w that are done H4639
2: 4 I made me great w; I builded me H4639
11 Then I looked on all the w that my H4639
3:22 rejoice in his own w; for that *is* his H4639
9: 1 the wise, and their w, *are* in the hand of H5652
7 heart; for God now accepteth thy w. H4639
11: 5 not the w of God who maketh all. H4639
Isa 26:12 thou also hast wrought all our w in us. H4639
29:15 LORD, and their w are in the dark, and H4639
41:29 Behold, they *are* all vanity; their w *are* H4639
Isa 57:12 and thy w; for they shall not profit thee. H4639
59: 6 with their w: their works *are* works H4639
6 with their works: their w *are* works of H4639
6 their works *are* w of iniquity, and the H4639
66:18 For I *know* their w and their thoughts: H4639
Jer 1:16 worshipped the w of their own hands. H4639
7:13 done all these w, saith the LORD, and H4639
21: 2 w, that he may go up from us. H6381
25: 6 to anger with the w of your hands; and H4639
7 the w of your hands to your own hurt. H4639
14 according to the w of their own hands. H4639
44: 8 unto wrath with the w of your hands, H4639
48: 7 For because thou hast trusted in thy w H4639
Ezk 6: 6 down, and your w may be abolished. H4639
Dan 4:37 heaven, all whose w *are* truth, and his H4567
9:14 in all his w which he doeth: for H4639
Am 8: 7 Surely I will never forget any of their w. H4639
Jna 3:10 And God saw their w, that they turned H4639
Mic 6:16 are kept, and all the w of the house of H4639
Mt 5:16 may see your good w, and glorify your G2041
7:22 in thy name done many wonderful w? G1411
11: 2 w of Christ, he sent two of his disciples, G2041
20 of his mighty w were done, because G1411
21 for if the mighty w, which were done in G1411
23 for if the mighty w, which have been G1411
13:54 *man* this wisdom, and *these* mighty w? G1411
58 And he did not many mighty w there G1411
14: 2 w do shew forth themselves in him. G1411
16:27 reward every man according to his w. G4234
23: 3 after their w: for they say, and do not. G2041
5 But all their w they do for to be seen of G2041
Mk 6: 2 mighty w are wrought by his hands? G1411
14 w do shew forth themselves in him. G1411
Lk 10:13 for if the mighty w had been done in G1411
19:37 for all the mighty w that they had seen; G1411
Jn 5:20 w than these, that ye may marvel. G2041
36 *that* of John: for the w which the Father G2041
36 to finish, the same w that I do, bear G2041
6:28 do, that we might work the w of God? G2041
7: 3 also may see the w that thou doest. G2041
7 I testify of it, that the w thereof are evil. G2041
8:39 ye would do the w of Abraham. G2041
9: 3 but that the w of God should be made G2041
4 I must work the w of him that sent me, G2041
10:25 ye believed not: the w that I do in my G2041
32 Jesus answered them, Many good w G2041
32 for which of those w do ye stone me? G2041
37 If I do not the w of my Father, believe G2041
38 me, believe the w: that ye may know, G2041
14:10 that dwelleth in me, he doeth the w. G2041
12 on me, the w that I do shall he do G2041
12 also; and greater *w* than these shall he G2041
15:24 If I had not done among them the w G2041
Act 2:11 in our tongues the wonderful w of God. G3167
7:41 rejoiced in the w of their own hands. G2041
9:36 good w and almsdeeds which she did. G2041
15:18 Known unto God are all his w from the G2041
26:20 to God, and do w meet for repentance. G2041
Ro 3:27 law? of w? Nay: but by the law of faith. G2041
4: 2 For if Abraham were justified by w, he G2041
6 God imputeth righteousness without w, G2041
9:11 stand, not of w, but of him that calleth;) G2041
32 as it were by the w of the law. For they G2041
11: 6 And if by grace, then *is it* no more of w: G2041
6 But if *it be* of w, then is it no more G2041
13: 3 For rulers are not a terror to good w, G2041
12 cast off the w of darkness, and let G2041
2Co 11:15 whose end shall be according to their w. G2041
Gal 2:16 justified by the w of the law, but by the G2041
16 and not by the w of the law: for by the G2041
16 w of the law shall no flesh be justified. G2041
3: 2 w of the law, or by the hearing of faith? G2041
5 w of the law, or by the hearing of faith? G2041
10 For as many as are of the w of the law G2041
5:19 Now the w of the flesh are manifest, G2041
Eph 2: 9 Not of w, lest any man should boast. G2041
10 Jesus unto good w, which God hath G2041
5:11 the unfruitful w of darkness, but rather G2041
Col 1:21 wicked w, yet now hath he reconciled G2041
1Ti 2:10 professing godliness) with good w. G2041
5:10 Well reported of for good w; if she have G2041
25 Likewise also the good w *of some* are G2041
6:18 be rich in good w, ready to distribute, G2041
2Ti 1: 9 according to our w, but according to his G2041
3:17 throughly furnished unto all good w. G2041
4:14 Lord reward him according to his w: G2041
Tit 1:16 know God; but in w they deny *him*, G2041
2: 7 thyself a pattern of good w: in doctrine G2041
14 a peculiar people, zealous of good w. G2041

Tit 3: 5 Not by w of righteousness which we *G2041*
8 to maintain good w. These things are *G2041*
14 to maintain good w for necessary uses, *G2041*
Heb 1:10 the heavens are the w of thine hands: *G2041*
2: 7 didst set him over the w of thy hands: *G2041*
3: 9 proved me, and saw my w forty years. *G2041*
4: 3 rest: although the w were finished from *G2041*
4 did rest the seventh day from all his w. *G2041*
10 from his own w, as God *did* from his. *G2041*
6: 1 from dead w, and of faith toward God, *G2041*
9:14 from dead w to serve the living God? *G2041*
10:24 to provoke unto love and to good w: *G2041*
Jas 2:14 and have not w? can faith save him? *G2041*
17 Even so faith, if it hath not w, is dead, *G2041*
18 faith, and I have w: shew me thy faith *G2041*
18 faith without thy w, and I will shew thee *G2041*
18 and I will shew thee my faith by my w. *G2041*
20 vain man, that faith without w is dead? *G2041*
21 our father justified by w, when he had *G2041*
22 wrought with his w, and by works was *G2041*
22 and by w was faith made perfect? *G2041*
24 Ye see then how that by w a man is *G2041*
25 the harlot justified by w, when she had *G2041*
26 is dead, so faith without w is dead also. *G2041*
3:13 his w with meekness of wisdom. *G2041*
1Pt 2:12 may by *your* good w, which they shall *G2041*
2Pt 3:10 w that are therein shall be burned up. *G2041*
1Jn 3: 8 he might destroy the w of the devil. *G2041*
12 Because his own w were evil, and his *G2041*
Rev 2: 2 I know thy w, and thy labour, and thy *G2041*
5 and do the first w; or else I will come *G2041*
9 I know thy w, and tribulation, and *G2041*
13 I know thy w, and where thou dwellest, *G2041*
19 I know thy w, and charity, and service, *G2041*
19 w; and the last *to be* more than the first. *G2041*
23 every one of you according to your w. *G2041*
26 and keepeth my w unto the end, to him *G2041*
3: 1 stars; I know thy w, that thou hast a *G2041*
2 not found thy w perfect before God. *G2041*
8 I know thy w: behold, I have set before *G2041*
15 I know thy w, that thou art neither cold *G2041*
9:20 not of the w of their hands, that *G2041*
14:13 labours; and their w do follow them. *G2041*
15: 3 *are* thy w, Lord God Almighty; *G2041*
18: 6 according to her w: in the cup which *G2041*
20:12 in the books, according to their w. *G2041*
13 judged every man according to their w. *G2041*

WORK'S
1Th 5:13 in love for their w sake. *And* be at *G2041*

WORKS'
Jn 14:11 or else believe me for the very w sake. *G2041*

WORLD
1Sa 2: 8 and he hath set the w upon them. H8398
2Sa 22:16 of the w were discovered, at H8398
1Ch 16:30 Fear before him, all the earth: the w H8398
Job 18:18 into darkness, and chased out of the w. H8398
34:13 or who hath disposed the whole w? H8398
37:12 upon the face of the w in the earth. H8398
Ps 9: 8 And he shall judge the w in H8398
17:14 from men of the w, *which have* their H2465
18:15 of the w were discovered at H8398
19: 4 to the end of the w. In them hath he set H8398
22:27 All the ends of the w shall remember H776
24: 1 the w, and they that dwell therein. H8398
33: 8 of the w stand in awe of him. H8398
49: 1 give ear, all *ye* inhabitants of the w: H2465
50:12 the w *is* mine, and the fulness thereof. H8398
73:12 in the w; they increase *in* riches. H5769
77:18 the w: the earth trembled and shook. H8398
89:11 *is* thine: *as for* the w and the fulness H8398
90: 2 formed the earth and the w, even from H8398
93: 1 himself: the w also is stablished, that H8398
96:10 LORD reigneth: the w also shall be H8398
13 earth: he shall judge the w with H8398
97: 4 His lightnings enlightened the w: the H8398
98: 7 the w, and they that dwell therein. H8398
9 judge the w, and the people with equity. H8398
Prv 8:26 nor the highest part of the dust of the w. H8398
Ecc 3:11 he hath set the w in their heart, so that H5769
Isa 13:11 And I will punish the w for *their* evil, H8398
14:17 *That* made the w as a wilderness, and H8398
21 nor fill the face of the w with cities. H8398
18: 3 All ye inhabitants of the w, and dwellers H8398
23:17 of the w upon the face of the earth. H776
24: 4 fadeth away, the w languisheth *and* H8398
26: 9 of the w will learn righteousness. H8398
Isa 26:18 have the inhabitants of the w fallen. H8398
27: 6 bud, and fill the face of the w with fruit. H8398
34: 1 w, and all things that come forth of it. H8398
38:11 no more with the inhabitants of the w. H2309
45:17 nor confounded w without end. H5769
62:11 unto the end of the w, Say ye to the H776
64: 4 For since the beginning of the w *men* H5769
Jer 10:12 established the w by his wisdom, and H8398
25:26 kingdoms of the w, which *are* upon the H776
51:15 established the w by his wisdom, and H8398
Lam 4:12 inhabitants of the w, would not have H8398
Nah 1: 5 yea, the w, and all that dwell therein. H8398
Mt 4: 8 of the w, and the glory of them; *G2889*
5:14 Ye are the light of the w. A city that is *G2889*
12:32 in this w, neither in the *world* to come. *G165*
32 in this world, neither in the *w* to come.
13:22 the care of this w, and the deceitfulness *G165*
35 secret from the foundation of the w. *G2889*
38 The field is the w; the good seed are the *G2889*
39 of the w; and the reapers are the angels. *G165*
40 the fire; so shall it be in the end of this w. *G165*
49 So shall it be at the end of the w: the *G165*
16:26 shall gain the whole w, and lose his own *G2889*
18: 7 Woe unto the w because of offences! *G2889*
24: 3 of thy coming, and of the end of the w? *G165*
14 in all the w for a witness unto all *G3625*
21 the w to this time, no, nor ever shall be. *G2889*
25:34 for you from the foundation of the w: *G2889*
26:13 in the whole w, *there* shall also this, *G2889*
28:20 alway, *even* unto the end of the w. Amen. *G165*
Mk 4:19 And the cares of this w, and the *G165*
8:36 the whole w, and lose his own soul? *G2889*
10:30 and in the w to come eternal life. *G165*
14: 9 the whole w, *this* also that she hath *G2889*
16:15 Go ye into all the w, and preach the *G2889*
Lk 1:70 which have been since the w began: *G165*
2: 1 that all the w should be taxed. *G3625*
4: 5 of the w in a moment of time. *G3625*
9:25 w, and lose himself, or be cast away? *G2889*
11:50 w, may be required of this generation; *G2889*
12:30 do the nations of the w seek after: and *G2889*
16: 8 for the children of this w are in their *G165*
18:30 and in the w to come life everlasting. *G165*
20:34 this w marry, and are given in marriage: *G165*
35 to obtain that w, and the resurrection *G165*
Jn 1: 9 every man that cometh into the w. *G2889*
10 He was in the w, and the world was *G2889*
10 He was in the world, and the w was *G2889*
10 made by him, and the w knew him not. *G2889*
29 which taketh away the sin of the w. *G2889*
3:16 For God so loved the w, that he gave his *G2889*
17 For God sent not his Son into the w to *G2889*
17 to condemn the w; but that the world *G2889*
17 that the w through him might be saved. *G2889*
19 light is come into the w, and men loved *G2889*
4:42 indeed the Christ, the Saviour of the w. *G2889*
6:14 prophet that should come into the w. *G2889*
33 from heaven, and giveth life unto the w. *G2889*
51 which I will give for the life of the w. *G2889*
7: 4 do these things, shew thyself to the w. *G2889*
7 The w cannot hate you; but me it *G2889*
8:12 I am the light of the w: he that followeth *G2889*
23 ye are of this w; I am not of this world. *G2889*
23 ye are of this world; I am not of this w. *G2889*
26 and I speak to the w those things which *G2889*
9: 5 As long as I am in the w, I am the light *G2889*
5 am in the world, I am the light of the w. *G2889*
32 Since the w began was it not heard that *G165*
39 I am come into this w, that they which *G2889*
10:36 and sent into the w, Thou blasphemest; *G2889*
11: 9 not, because he seeth the light of this w. *G2889*
27 of God, which should come into the w. *G2889*
12:19 behold, the w is gone after him. *G2889*
25 in this w shall keep it unto life eternal. *G2889*
31 Now is the judgment of this w: now *G2889*
31 shall the prince of this w be cast out. *G2889*
46 I am come a light into the w, that *G2889*
47 to judge the w, but to save the world. *G2889*
47 to judge the world, but to save the w. *G2889*
13: 1 depart out of this w unto the Father, *G2889*
1 in the w, he loved them unto the end. *G2889*
14:17 *Even* the Spirit of truth; whom the w *G2889*
19 Yet a little while, and the w seeth me no *G2889*
22 thyself unto us, and not unto the w? *G2889*
27 you: not as the w giveth, give I unto *G2889*
30 this w cometh, and hath nothing in me. *G2889*
31 But that the w may know that I love the *G2889*
15:18 If the w hate you, ye know that it hated *G2889*
19 If ye were of the w, the world would love *G2889*
Jn 15:19 If ye were of the world, the w would *G2889*
19 ye are not of the w, but I have chosen *G2889*
19 of the w, therefore the world hateth you. *G2889*
19 the world, therefore the w hateth you. *G2889*
16: 8 he will reprove the w of sin, and of *G2889*
11 because the prince of this w is judged. *G2889*
20 lament, but the w shall rejoice: and ye *G2889*
21 for joy that a man is born into the w. *G2889*
28 am come into the w: again, I leave the *G2889*
28 I leave the w, and go to the Father. *G2889*
33 have peace. In the w ye shall have *G2889*
33 of good cheer; I have overcome the w. *G2889*
17: 5 which I had with thee before the w was. *G2889*
6 me out of the w: thine they were, and *G2889*
9 I pray for them: I pray not for the w, but *G2889*
11 And now I am no more in the w, but *G2889*
11 these are in the w, and I come to thee. *G2889*
12 While I was with them in the w, I kept *G2889*
13 I speak in the w, that they might have *G2889*
14 I have given them thy word; and the w *G2889*
14 of the w, even as I am not of the world. *G2889*
14 of the world, even as I am not of the w. *G2889*
15 take them out of the w, but that thou *G2889*
16 They are not of the w, even as I am not *G2889*
16 of the world, even as I am not of the w. *G2889*
18 As thou hast sent me into the w, even so *G2889*
18 so have I also sent them into the w. *G2889*
21 w may believe that thou hast sent me. *G2889*
23 in one; and that the w may know that *G2889*
24 me before the foundation of the w. *G2889*
25 O righteous Father, the w hath not *G2889*
18:20 openly to the w; I ever taught in the *G2889*
36 is not of this w: if my kingdom were *G2889*
36 were of this w, then would my servants *G2889*
37 came I into the w, that I should bear *G2889*
21:25 that even the w itself could not contain *G2889*
Act 3:21 all his holy prophets since the w began. *G165*
11:28 throughout all the w: which came to *G3625*
15:18 all his works from the beginning of the w. *G165*
17: 6 w upside down are come hither also; *G3625*
24 God that made the w and all things *G2889*
31 he will judge the w in righteousness by *G3625*
19:27 whom all Asia and the w worshippeth. *G3625*
24: 5 throughout the w, and a ringleader of *G3625*
Ro 1: 8 is spoken of throughout the whole w. *G2889*
20 the creation of the w are clearly seen, *G2889*
3: 6 for then how shall God judge the w? *G2889*
19 the w may become guilty before God. *G2889*
4:13 should be the heir of the w, *was* not to *G2889*
5:12 sin entered into the w, and death by sin; *G2889*
13 (For until the law sin was in the w: but *G2889*
10:18 and their words unto the ends of the w. *G3625*
11:12 the riches of the w, and the diminishing *G2889*
15 the reconciling of the w, what *shall* the *G2889*
12: 2 And be not conformed to this w: but be *G165*
16:25 which was kept secret since the w began, *G166*
1Co 1:20 *is* the disputer of this w? hath not God *G165*
20 God made foolish the wisdom of this w? *G2889*
21 of God the w by wisdom knew not *G2889*
27 things of the w to confound the wise; *G2889*
27 weak things of the w to confound the *G2889*
28 And base things of the w, and things *G2889*
2: 6 the wisdom of this w, nor of the princes *G165*
6 princes of this w, that come to nought: *G165*
7 ordained before the w unto our glory: *G165*
8 Which none of the princes of this w *G165*
12 the spirit of the w, but the spirit which *G2889*
3:18 to be wise in this w, let him become a *G165*
19 For the wisdom of this w is foolishness *G2889*
22 or Cephas, or the w, or life, or death, or *G2889*
4: 9 unto the w, and to angels, and to men. *G2889*
13 made as the filth of the w, *and are* the *G2889*
5:10 the fornicators of this w, or with the *G2889*
10 for then must ye needs go out of the w. *G2889*
6: 2 shall judge the w? and if the world shall *G2889*
2 world? and if the w shall be judged by *G2889*
7:31 And they that use this w, as not abusing *G2889*
31 for the fashion of this w passeth away. *G2889*
33 of the w, how he may please *his* wife. *G2889*
34 w, how she may please *her* husband. *G2889*
8: 4 *is* nothing in the w, and that *there is* *G2889*
13 eat no flesh while the w standeth, lest I *G165*
10:11 upon whom the ends of the w are come. *G165*
11:32 should not be condemned with the w. *G2889*
14:10 of voices in the w, and none of them *is* *G2889*
2Co 1:12 w, and more abundantly to you-ward. *G2889*
4: 4 In whom the god of this w hath blinded *G165*
5:19 reconciling the w unto himself, not *G2889*
7:10 but the sorrow of the w worketh death. *G2889*

Gal 1: 4 this present evil w, according to the will G165
4: 3 in bondage under the elements of the w: G2889
6:14 by whom the w is crucified unto me, G2889
14 is crucified unto me, and I unto the w. G2889
Eph 1: 4 foundation of the w, that we should be G2889
21 this w, but also in that which is to come: G165
2: 2 to the course of this w, according to the G2889
12 no hope, and without God in the w: G2889
3: 9 beginning of the w hath been hid in God, G165
21 all ages, w without end. Amen. G165
6:12 the darkness of this w, against spiritual G165
Php 2:15 whom ye shine as lights in the w; G2889
Col 1: 6 as *it is* in all the w; and bringeth forth G2889
2: 8 of the w, and not after Christ. G2889
20 the rudiments of the w, why, as though G2889
20 in the w, are ye subject to ordinances, G2889
1Ti 1:15 w to save sinners; of whom I am chief. G2889
3:16 on in the w, received up into glory. G2889
6: 7 For we brought nothing into *this* w, *and* G2889
17 Charge them that are rich in this w, that G165
2Ti 1: 9 us in Christ Jesus before the w began, G166
4:10 loved this present w, and is departed G165
Tit 1: 2 cannot lie, promised before the w began; G166
2:12 righteously, and godly, in this present w; G165
Heb 1: 6 into the w, he saith, And let all G3625
2: 5 the w to come, whereof we speak. G3625
4: 3 finished from the foundation of the w. G2889
6: 5 of God, and the powers of the w to come, G165
9:26 foundation of the w: but now once in G2889
26 in the end of the w hath he appeared to G165
10: 5 Wherefore when he cometh into the w, G2889
11: 7 condemned the w, and became heir of G2889
38 (Of whom the w was not worthy:) they G2889
Jas 1:27 to keep himself unspotted from the w. G2889
2: 5 the poor of this w rich in faith, and G2889
3: 6 And the tongue *is* a fire, a w of iniquity: G2889
4: 4 friendship of the w is enmity with God? G2889
4 a friend of the w is the enemy of God. G2889
1Pt 1:20 foundation of the w, but was manifest G2889
5: 9 in your brethren that are in the w. G2889
2Pt 1: 4 corruption that is in the w through lust. G2889
2: 5 And spared not the old w, but saved G2889
5 in the flood upon the w of the ungodly; G2889
20 the pollutions of the w through the G2889
3: 6 Whereby the w that then was, being G2889
1Jn 2: 2 but also for *the sins of* the whole w. G2889
15 Love not the w, neither the things *that* G2889
15 *that are* in the w. If any man love the G2889
15 w, the love of the Father is not in him. G2889
16 For all that *is* in the w, the lust of the G2889
16 life, is not of the Father, but is of the w. G2889
17 And the w passeth away, and the lust G2889
3: 1 of God: therefore the w knoweth us not, G2889
13 Marvel not, my brethren, if the w hate G2889
4: 1 false prophets are gone out into the w. G2889
3 and even now already is it in the w. G2889
4 that is in you, than he that is in the w. G2889
5 They are of the w: therefore speak they G2889
5 of the w, and the world heareth them. G2889
5 of the world, and the w heareth them. G2889
9 the w, that we might live through him. G2889
14 sent the Son *to be* the Saviour of the w. G2889
17 because as he is, so are we in this w. G2889
5: 4 God overcometh the w: and this is the G2889
4 that overcometh the w, *even* our faith. G2889
5 Who is he that overcometh the w, but G2889
19 and the whole w lieth in wickedness. G2889
2Jn 7 entered into the w, who confess not that G2889
Rev 3:10 come upon all the w, to try them that G3625
11:15 The kingdoms of this w are become *the* G2889
12: 9 the whole w: he was cast out into G3625
13: 3 and all the w wondered after the beast. G1093
8 slain from the foundation of the w. G2889
16:14 and of the whole w, to gather them to G3625
17: 8 foundation of the w, when they behold G2889

WORLDLY
Tit 2:12 ungodliness and w lusts, we should live G2886
Heb 9: 1 of divine service, and a w sanctuary. G2886

WORLDS
Heb 1: 2 all things, by whom also he made the w; G165
11: 3 Through faith we understand that the w G165

WORLD'S
1Jn 3:17 But whoso hath this w good, and seeth G2889

WORM
Ex 16:24 stink, neither was there any w therein. H7415
Job 17:14 w, *Thou art* my mother, and my sister. H7415
24:20 The womb shall forget him; the w shall H7415
25: 6 How much less man, *that is* a w? and H7415
6 and the son of man, *which is* a w? H8438
Ps 22: 6 But I *am* a w, and no man; a reproach H8438
Isa 14:11 of thy viols: the w is spread under thee, H7415
41:14 Fear not, thou w Jacob, *and* ye men of H8438
51: 8 garment, and the w shall eat them like H5580
66:24 me: for their w shall not die, neither H8438
Jna 4: 7 But God prepared a w when the H8438
Mk 9:44 Where their w dieth not, and the fire is G4663
46 Where their w dieth not, and the fire is G4663
48 Where their w dieth not, and the fire is G4663

WORMS
Ex 16:20 and it bred w, and stank: and Moses H8438
Dt 28:39 *the grapes;* for the w shall eat them. H8438
Job 7: 5 My flesh is clothed with w and clods of H7415
19:26 And *though* after my skin *w* destroy this
21:26 in the dust, and the w shall cover them. H7415
Isa 14:11 under thee, and the w cover thee. H8438
Mic 7:17 of their holes like w of the earth: they H2119
Act 12:23 was eaten of w, and gave up the ghost. G4662

WORMWOOD
Dt 29:18 you a root that beareth gall and w; H3939
Prv 5: 4 But her end is bitter as w, sharp as a H3939
Jer 9:15 w, and give them water of gall to drink. H3939
23:15 feed them with w, and make them drink H3939
Lam 3:15 he hath made me drunken with w. H3939
19 and my misery, the w and the gall. H3939
Am 5: 7 Ye who turn judgment to w, and leave H3939
Rev 8:11 And the name of the star is called W: and G894
11 of the waters became w; and many men G894

WORSE
Gen 19: 9 now will we deal w with thee, than with H7489
2Sa 19: 7 and that will be w unto thee than all H7489
1Ki 16:25 did w than all that *were* before him. H7489
2Ki 14:12 And Judah was put to the w before H5062
1Ch 19:16 were put to the w before Israel, they H5062
19 were put to the w before Israel, they H5062
2Ch 6:24 And if thy people Israel be put to the w H5062
25:22 And Judah was put to the w before H5062
33: 9 to err, *and* to do w than the heathen, H7451
Jer 7:26 neck: they did w than their fathers. H7489
16:12 And ye have done w than your fathers; H7489
Dan 1:10 he see your faces w liking than the H2196
Mt 9:16 the garment, and the rent is made w. G5501
12:45 of that man is w than the first. Even G5501
27:64 the last error shall be w than the first. G5501
Mk 2:21 from the old, and the rent is made w. G5501
5:26 nothing bettered, but rather grew w, G5501
Lk 11:26 *state* of that man is w than the first. G5501
Jn 2:10 then that which is w: *but* thou hast kept G1640
5:14 no more, lest a w thing come unto thee. G5501
1Co 8: 8 neither, if we eat not, are we the w. G5302
11:17 not for the better, but for the w. G2276
1Ti 5: 8 the faith, and is w than an infidel. G5501
2Ti 3:13 But evil men and seducers shall wax w G5501
13 and w, deceiving, and being deceived. G1909
2Pt 2:20 end is w with them than the beginning. G5501

WORSHIP
Gen 22: 5 yonder and w, and come again to you. H7812
Ex 24: 1 of the elders of Israel; and w ye afar off. H7812
34:14 For thou shalt w no other god: for the H7812
Dt 4:19 be driven to w them, and serve them, H7812
8:19 and serve them, and w them, I testify H7812
11:16 and serve other gods, and w them; H7812
26:10 God, and w before the LORD thy God: H7812
30:17 and w other gods, and serve them; H7812
Jos 5:14 to the earth, and did w, and said unto H7812
1Sa 1: 3 of his city yearly to w and to sacrifice H7812
15:25 again with me, that I may w the LORD. H7812
30 me, that I may w the LORD thy God. H7812
1Ki 9: 6 go and serve other gods, and w them: H7812
12:30 went *to w* before the one, *even* unto Dan.
2Ki 5:18 of Rimmon to w there, and he leaneth H7812
17:36 ye w, and to him shall ye do sacrifice. H7812
18:22 shall w before this altar in Jerusalem? H7812
1Ch 16:29 w the LORD in the beauty of holiness. H7812
2Ch 7:19 go and serve other gods, and w them; H7812
32:12 saying, Ye shall w before one altar, and H7812
Ps 5: 7 fear will I w toward thy holy temple. H7812
22:27 of the nations shall w before thee. H7812
29 shall eat and w: all they that go down H7812
29: 2 w the LORD in the beauty of holiness. H7812
45:11 for he *is* thy Lord; and w thou him. H7812
66: 4 All the earth shall w thee, and shall H7812
81: 9 neither shalt thou w any strange god. H7812
86: 9 shall come and w before thee, O Lord; H7812
95: 6 O come, let us w and bow down: let us H7812
96: 9 O w the LORD in the beauty of H7812
97: 7 themselves of idols: w him, all *ye* gods. H7812
99: 5 Exalt ye the LORD our God, and w at H7812
9 Exalt the LORD our God, and w at his H7812
132: 7 tabernacles: we will w at his footstool. H7812
138: 2 I will w toward thy holy temple, and H7812
Isa 2: 8 Their land also is full of idols; they w H7812
20 to w, to the moles and to the bats; H7812
27:13 of Egypt, and shall w the LORD in the H7812
36: 7 Jerusalem, Ye shall w before this altar? H7812
46: 6 it a god: they fall down, yea, they w. H7812
49: 7 princes also shall w, because of the H7812
66:23 come to w before me, saith the LORD. H7812
Jer 7: 2 enter in at these gates to w the LORD. H7812
13:10 them, and to w them, shall even be H7812
25: 6 them, and to w them, and provoke H7812
26: 2 which come to w in the LORD'S house, H7812
44:19 make her cakes to w her, and pour out H6087
Ezk 46: 2 and he shall w at the threshold of the H7812
3 Likewise the people of the land shall w H7812
9 the north gate to w shall go out by the H7812
Dan 3: 5 ye fall down and w the golden image H5457
10 fall down and w the golden image: H5457
12 not thy gods, nor w the golden image H5457
14 serve my gods, nor w the golden image H5457
15 ye fall down and w the image which I H5457
15 *well:* but if ye w not, ye shall be cast H5457
18 serve thy gods, nor w the golden image H5457
28 nor w any god, except their own God. H5457
Mic 5:13 no more w the work of thine hands. H7812
Zep 1: 5 And them that w the host of heaven H7812
5 and them that w *and* that swear by the H7812
2:11 and *men* shall w him, every one from H7812
Zec 14:16 year to year to w the King, the LORD H7812
17 earth unto Jerusalem to w the King, the H7812
Mt 2: 2 star in the east, and are come to w him. G4352
8 that I may come and w him also. G4352
4: 9 thee, if thou wilt fall down and w me. G4352
10 Thou shalt w the Lord thy God, and G4352
15: 9 But in vain they do w me, teaching *for* G4576
Mk 7: 7 Howbeit in vain do they w me, G4576
Lk 4: 7 If thou therefore wilt w me, all shall be G4352
8 Thou shalt w the Lord thy God, and G4352
14:10 shalt thou have w in the presence of G1391
Jn 4:20 is the place where men ought to w. G4352
21 nor yet at Jerusalem, w the Father. G4352
22 Ye w ye know not what: we know what G4352
22 what we w: for salvation is of the Jews. G4352
23 worshippers shall w the Father in spirit G4352
23 for the Father seeketh such to w him. G4352
24 God *is* a Spirit: and they that w him G4352
24 him must w *him* in spirit and in truth. G4352
12:20 them that came up to w at the feast: G4352
Act 7:42 gave them up to w the host of heaven; G3000
43 which ye made to w them: and I will G4352
8:27 and had come to Jerusalem for to w, G4352
17:23 ye ignorantly w, him declare I unto you. G2151
18:13 men to w God contrary to the law. G4576
24:11 since I went up to Jerusalem for to w. G4352
14 they call heresy, so w I the God of my G3000
1Co 14:25 on *his* face he will w God, and report G4352
Php 3: 3 For we are the circumcision, which w G3000
Col 2:23 of wisdom in will w, and humility, and G1479
Heb 1: 6 And let all the angels of God w him. G4352
Rev 3: 9 them to come and w before thy feet, G4352
4:10 on the throne, and w him that liveth for G4352
9:20 they should not w devils, and idols of G4352
11: 1 and the altar, and them that w therein. G4352
13: 8 the earth shall w him, whose names G4352
12 dwell therein to w the first beast, whose G4352
15 as would not w the image of the beast G4352
14: 7 is come: and w him that made heaven, G4352
9 voice, If any man w the beast and his G4352
11 day nor night, who w the beast and his G4352
15: 4 shall come and w before thee; for thy G4352
19:10 And I fell at his feet to w him. And he G4352
10 of Jesus: w God: for the testimony G4352
22: 8 I fell down to w before the feet of the G4352
9 keep the sayings of this book: w God. G4352

WORSHIPPED
Gen 24:26 down his head, and w the LORD. H7812
48 And I bowed down my head, and w the H7812
52 their words, he w the LORD, *bowing* H7812
Ex 4:31 then they bowed their heads and w. H7812

Ex 12:27 And the people bowed the head and w. H7812
32: 8 calf, and have w it, and have sacrificed H7812
33:10 up and w, every man *in* his tent door. H7812
34: 8 his head toward the earth, and w. H7812
Dt 17: 3 other gods, and w them, either the sun, H7812
29:26 other gods, and w them, gods whom H7812
Jdg 7:15 thereof, that he w, and returned into the H7812
1Sa 1:19 early, and w before the LORD, and H7812
28 the LORD. And he w the LORD there. H7812
15:31 again after Saul; and Saul w the LORD. H7812
2Sa 12:20 of the LORD, and w: then he came to H7812
15:32 *the mount,* where he w God, behold, H7812
1Ki 9: 9 gods, and have w them, and served H7812
11:33 me, and have w Ashtoreth the goddess H7812
16:31 and went and served Baal, and w him. H7812
22:53 For he served Baal, and w him, and H7812
2Ki 17:16 a grove, and w all the host of heaven, H7812
21: 3 king of Israel; and w all the host of H7812
21 that his father served, and w them: H7812
1Ch 29:20 heads, and w the LORD, and the king. H7812
2Ch 7: 3 the pavement, and w, and praised the H7812
22 on other gods, and w them, and served H7812
29:28 And all the congregation w, and the H7812
29 with him bowed themselves, and w. H7812
30 and they bowed their heads and w. H7812
33: 3 and made groves, and w all the host of H7812
Neh 8: 6 their heads, and w the LORD with *their* H7812
9: 3 confessed, and w the LORD their God. H7812
Job 1:20 and fell down upon the ground, and w, H7812
Ps 106:19 They made a calf in Horeb, and w the H7812
Jer 1:16 and w the works of their own hands. H7812
8: 2 whom they have w: they shall not be H7812
16:11 them, and have w them, and have H7812
22: 9 and w other gods, and served them. H7812
Ezk 8:16 and they w the sun toward the east. H7812
Dan 2:46 upon his face, and w Daniel, and H5457
3: 7 fell down *and* w the golden image that H5457
Mt 2:11 fell down, and w him: and when they G4352
8: 2 And, behold, there came a leper and w G4352
9:18 a certain ruler, and w him, saying, My G4352
14:33 the ship came and w him, saying, Of a G4352
15:25 Then came she and w him, saying, G4352
18:26 The servant therefore fell down, and w G4352
28: 9 and held him by the feet, and w him. G4352
17 And when they saw him, they w him: G4352
Mk 5: 6 saw Jesus afar off, he ran and w him, G4352
15:19 him, and bowing *their* knees w him. G4352
Lk 24:52 And they w him, and returned to G4352
Jn 4:20 Our fathers w in this mountain; and ye G4352
9:38 And he said, Lord, I believe. And he w G4352
Act 10:25 and fell down at his feet, and w *him.* G4352
16:14 of Thyatira, which w God, heard *us*: G4576
17:25 Neither is w with men's hands, as G2323
18: 7 Justus, *one* that w God, whose house G4576
Ro 1:25 God into a lie, and w and served the G4573
2Th 2: 4 God, or that is w; so that he as God G4574
Heb 11:21 and w, *leaning* upon the top of his staff. G4352
Rev 5:14 and w him that liveth for ever and ever. G4352
7:11 the throne on their faces, and w God, G4352
11:16 seats, fell upon their faces, and w God, G4352
13: 4 And they w the dragon which gave G4352
4 the beast: and they w the beast, saying, G4352
16: 2 and *upon* them which w his image. G4352
19: 4 fell down and w God that sat on the G4352
20 and them that w his image. These both G4352
20: 4 which had not w the beast, neither his G4352

WORSHIPPER
Jn 9:31 if any man be a w of God, and doeth G2318
Act 19:35 of the Ephesians is a w of the great G3511

WORSHIPPERS
2Ki 10:19 that he might destroy the w of Baal. H5647
21 Israel: and all the w of Baal came, so H5647
22 for all the w of Baal. And he brought H5647
23 and said unto the w of Baal, Search, H5647
23 of the LORD, but the w of Baal only. H5647
Jn 4:23 is, when the true w shall worship the G4353
Heb 10: 2 because that the w once purged should G3000

WORSHIPPETH
Neh 9: 6 all; and the host of heaven w thee. H7812
Isa 44:15 a god, and w *it*; he maketh it a graven H7812
17 down unto it, and w *it*, and prayeth H7812
Dan 3: 6 And whoso falleth not down and w H5457
11 And whoso falleth not down and w, *that* H5457
Act 19:27 whom all Asia and the world w. G4576

WORSHIPPING
2Ki 19:37 And it came to pass, as he was w in the H7812
2Ch 20:18 fell before the LORD, w the LORD. H7812
Isa 37:38 And it came to pass, as he was w in the H7812
Mt 20:20 with her sons, w *him*, and desiring a G4352
Col 2:18 humility and w of angels, intruding G2356

WORST
Ezk 7:24 Wherefore I will bring the w of the H7451

WORTH
Gen 23: 9 money as it is w he shall give it me for H4392
15 My lord, hearken unto me: the land *is* w H702
Lev 27:23 unto him the w of thy estimation, *even* H4373
Dt 15:18 thee; for he hath been w a double hired H7939
2Sa 18: 3 but now *thou art* w ten thousand of us: H3644
1Ki 21: 2 I will give thee the w of it in money. H4242
Job 24:25 a liar, and make my speech nothing w? H408
Prv 10:20 silver: the heart of the wicked *is* little w.
Ezk 30: 2 Lord GOD; Howl ye, Woe w the day! H1929

WORTHIES
Nah 2: 5 He shall recount his w: they shall stumble H117

WORTHILY
Ru 4:11 and do thou w in Ephratah, and be H2428

WORTHY
Gen 32:10 I am not w of the least of all the H6994
Dt 17: 6 shall he that is w of death be put to
19: 6 he *was* not w of death, inasmuch H4941
21:22 And if a man have committed a sin w H4941
22:26 in the damsel no sin *w* of death: for as
25: 2 And it shall be, if the wicked man *be* w H1121
1Sa 1: 5 But unto Hannah he gave a w portion; H639
26:16 liveth, ye *are* w to die, because ye have H1121
2Sa 22: 4 I will call on the LORD, *who is* w to be
1Ki 1:52 shew himself a w man, there shall not H2428
2:26 fields; for thou *art* w of death: but I will H376
Ps 18: 3 I will call upon the LORD, *who is* w to be
Jer 26:11 This man *is* w to die; for he hath H4941
16 This man *is* not w to die: for he hath H4941
Mt 3:11 shoes I am not w to bear: he shall G2425
8: 8 Lord, I am not w that thou shouldest G2425
10:10 staves: for the workman is w of his meat. G514
11 it is w; and there abide till ye go thence. G514
13 And if the house be w, let your peace G514
13 it be not w, let your peace return to you. G514
37 than me is not w of me: and he that G514
37 daughter more than me is not w of me. G514
38 and followeth after me, is not w of me. G514
22: 8 but they which were bidden were not w. G514
Mk 1: 7 I am not w to stoop down and unloose. G2425
Lk 3: 8 Bring forth therefore fruits w of G514
16 shoes I am not w to unloose: he shall G2425
7: 4 he was w for whom he should do this: G514
6 for I am not w that thou shouldest G2425
7 Wherefore neither thought I myself w to G515
10: 7 for the labourer is w of his hire. Go not G514
12:48 did commit things w of stripes, shall be G514
15:19 And am no more w to be called thy son: G514
21 and am no more w to be called thy son. G514
20:35 But they which shall be accounted w to G2661
21:36 may be accounted w to escape all these G2661
23:15 lo, nothing w of death is done unto him. G514
Jn 1:27 shoe's latchet I am not w to unloose. G514
Act 5:41 w to suffer shame for his name. G2661
13:25 shoes of *his* feet I am not w to loose. G514
23:29 laid to his charge w of death or of bonds. G514
24: 2 and that very w deeds are done unto G2735
25:11 any thing w of death, I refuse not G514
25 nothing w of death, and that he G514
26:31 doeth nothing w of death or of bonds. G514
Ro 1:32 such things are w of death, not only do G514
8:18 time *are* not w *to be compared* with G514
Eph 4: 1 you that ye walk w of the vocation G516
Col 1:10 That ye might walk w of the Lord unto G516
1Th 2:12 That ye would walk w of God, who hath G516
2Th 1: 5 ye may be counted w of the kingdom of G2661
11 would count you w of *this* calling, and G515
1Ti 1:15 This *is* a faithful saying, and w of all G514
4: 9 This *is* a faithful saying and w of all G514
5:17 Let the elders that rule well be counted w G515
18 And, The labourer *is* w of his reward. G514
6: 1 their own masters w of all honour, that G514
Heb 3: 3 For this *man* was counted w of more G515
10:29 shall he be thought w, who hath trodden G515
11:38 (Of whom the world was not w:) they G514
Jas 2: 7 Do not they blaspheme that w name by G2570
Rev 3: 4 walk with me in white: for they are w. G514
4:11 Thou art w, O Lord, to receive glory and G514
5: 2 a loud voice, Who is w to open the book, G514
4 no man was found w to open and to G514
9 saying, Thou art w to take the book, and G514
12 Saying with a loud voice, W is the Lamb G514
16: 6 given them blood to drink; for they are w. G514

WOT
Gen 21:26 And Abimelech said, I w not who hath H3045
44:15 ye have done? w ye not that such a man H3045
Ex 32: 1 Egypt, we w not what is become of him. H3045
23 Egypt, we w not what is become of him. H3045
Nu 22: 6 of the land: for I w that he whom thou H3045
Jos 2: 5 the men went I w not: pursue after H3045
Act 3:17 And now, brethren, I w that through G1492
7:40 Egypt, we w not what is become of him. G1492
Ro 11: 2 which he foreknew. W ye not what the G1492
Php 1:22 labour: yet what I shall choose I w not. G1107

WOTTETH
Gen 39: 8 my master w not what *is* with me H3045

WOULD See the Appendix.

WOULDEST See the Appendix.

WOUND
Ex 21:25 Burning for burning, w for wound, H6482
25 Burning for burning, wound for w, H6482
Dt 32:39 I make alive; I w, and I heal: neither *is* H4272
1Ki 22:35 of the w into the midst of the chariot. H4347
Job 34: 6 Should I lie against my right? my w *is* H2671
Ps 68:21 But God shall w the head of his H4272
110: 6 shall w the heads over many countries. H4272
Prv 6:33 A w and dishonour shall he get; and his H5061
20:30 The blueness of a w cleanseth away H6482
Isa 30:26 and healeth the stroke of their w. H4347
Jer 10:19 Woe is me for my hurt! my w is H4347
15:18 Why is my pain perpetual, and my w H4347
30:12 *is* incurable, *and* thy w *is* grievous. H4347
14 thee with the w of an enemy, with the H4347
Hos 5:13 Judah *saw* his w, then went Ephraim H4205
13 he not heal you, nor cure you of your w. H4205
Oba 7 bread have laid a w under thee: *there is* H4204
Mic 1: 9 For her w *is* incurable; for it is come H4347
Nah 3:19 *There is* no healing of thy bruise; thy w H4347
Jn 19:40 body of Jesus, and w it in linen clothes G1210
Act 5: 6 And the young men arose, w him up, G4958
1Co 8:12 against the brethren, and w their weak G5180
Rev 13: 3 and his deadly w was healed: and all G4127
12 first beast, whose deadly w was healed. G4127
14 had the w by a sword, and did live. G4127

WOUNDED
Dt 23: 1 He that is w in the stones, or hath his H1795
Jdg 9:40 w, *even* unto the entering of the gate. H2491
1Sa 17:52 of Ekron. And the w of the Philistines H2491
31: 3 him; and he was sore w of the archers. H2342
2Sa 22:39 And I have consumed them, and w H4272
1Ki 20:37 him, so that in smiting he w *him*. H6481
22:34 carry me out of the host; for I am w. H2470
2Ki 8:28 and the Syrians w Joram. H5221
1Ch 10: 3 hit him, and he was w of the archers. H2342
2Ch 18:33 carry me out of the host; for I am w. H2470
35:23 Have me away; for I am sore w. H2470
Job 24:12 the soul of the w crieth out: yet God H2491
Ps 18:38 I have w them that they were not able H4272
64: 7 an arrow; suddenly shall they be w. H4347
69:26 to the grief of those whom thou hast w. H2491
109:22 needy, and my heart is w within me. H2490
Prv 7:26 For she hath cast down many w: yea, H2491
18:14 infirmity; but a w spirit who can bear? H5218
Song 5: 7 smote me, they w me; the keepers of H6481
Isa 51: 9 hath cut Rahab, *and* w the dragon? H2490
53: 5 But he *was* w for our transgressions, *he* H2490
Jer 30:14 not; for I have w thee with the wound H5221
37:10 remained *but* w men among them, *yet* H1856
51:52 through all her land the w shall groan. H2491
Lam 2:12 swooned as the w in the streets of the H2491
Ezk 26:15 of thy fall, when the w cry, when the H2491
28:23 streets; and the w shall be judged in the H2491
30:24 with the groanings of a deadly w *man*. H2491
Joel 2: 8 fall upon the sword, they shall not be w. H1214
Zec 13: 6 I was w *in* the house of my friends. H5221
Mk 12: 4 cast stones, and w *him* in the head, and
Lk 10:30 his raiment, and w *him*, and departed, G4127
20:12 And again he sent a third: and they w G5135
Act 19:16 they fled out of that house naked and w. G5135

Rev 13: 3 And I saw one of his heads as it were **w** G4969

WOUNDEDST
Hab 3:13 anointed; thou **w** the head out of the H4272

WOUNDETH
Job 5:18 up: he **w**, and his hands make whole. H4272

WOUNDING
Gen 4:23 to my **w**, and a young man to my hurt. H6482

WOUNDS
2Ki 8:29 in Jezreel of the **w** which the Syrians H4347
9:15 in Jezreel of the **w** which the Syrians H4347
2Ch 22: 6 because of the **w** which were given him H4347
Job 9:17 and multiplieth my **w** without cause. H6482
Ps 38: 5 My **w** stink *and* are corrupt because of H2250
147: 3 in heart, and bindeth up their **w**. H6094
Prv 18: 8 The words of a talebearer *are* as **w**, and H3859
23:29 who hath **w** without cause? who H6482
26:22 The words of a talebearer *are* as **w**, and H3859
27: 6 Faithful *are* the **w** of a friend; but the H6482
Isa 1: 6 in it; *but* **w**, and bruises, and putrifying H6482
Jer 6: 7 before me continually *is* grief and **w**. H4347
30:17 will heal thee of thy **w**, saith the LORD; H4347
Zec 13: 6 What *are* these **w** in thine hands? Then H4347
Lk 10:34 And went to *him*, and bound up his **w**, G5134

WOVE
2Ki 23: 7 the women **w** hangings for the grove. H707

WOVEN
Ex 28:32 have a binding of **w** work round about H707
39:22 And he made the robe of the ephod *of* **w** H707
27 And they made coats *of* fine linen *of* **w** H707
Jn 19:23 seam, **w** from the top throughout. G5307

WRAP
Isa 28:20 than that he can **w** himself *in it*. H3664
Mic 7: 3 his mischievous desire: so they **w** it up. H5686

WRAPPED
Gen 38:14 with a vail, and **w** herself, and sat in an H5968
1Sa 21: 9 behold, it *is here* **w** in a cloth behind H3874
1Ki 19:13 Elijah heard *it*, that he **w** his face in his H3874
2Ki 2: 8 And Elijah took his mantle, and **w** *it* H1563
Job 8:17 His roots are **w** about the heap, *and* H5440
40:17 the sinews of his stones are **w** together. H8276
Ezk 21:15 bright, *it is* **w** up for the slaughter. H4593
Jna 2: 5 the weeds were **w** about my head. H2280
Mt 27:59 the body, he **w** it in a clean linen cloth, G1794
Mk 15:46 him down, and **w** him in the linen, and G1750
Lk 2: 7 firstborn son, and **w** him in swaddling G4683
12 find the babe **w** in swaddling clothes, G4683
23:53 And he took it down, and **w** it in linen, G1794
Jn 20: 7 but **w** together in a place by itself. G1794

WRATH
Gen 39:19 servant to me; that his **w** was kindled. H639
49: 7 fierce; and their **w**, for it was cruel: I H5678
Ex 15: 7 **w**, *which* consumed them as stubble. H2740
22:24 And my **w** shall wax hot, and I will kill H639
32:10 Now therefore let me alone, that my **w** H639
11 why doth thy **w** wax hot against thy H639
12 from thy fierce **w**, and repent of this evil H639
Lev 10: 6 lest ye die, and lest **w** come upon all the H7107
Nu 1:53 testimony, that there be no **w** upon the H7110
11:33 it was chewed, the **w** of the LORD was H639
16:46 them: for there is **w** gone out from the H7110
18: 5 **w** any more upon the children of Israel. H7110
25:11 hath turned my **w** away from the H2534
Dt 9: 7 LORD thy God to **w** in the wilderness: H7107
8 the LORD to **w**, so that the LORD was H7107
22 ye provoked the LORD to **w**. H7107
11:17 And *then* the LORD'S **w** be kindled H639
29:23 overthrew in his anger, and in his **w**: H2534
28 land in anger, and in **w**, and in great H2534
32:27 Were it not that I feared the **w** of the H3708
Jos 9:20 even let them live, lest **w** be upon us, H7110
22:20 accursed thing, and **w** fell on all the H7110
1Sa 28:18 his fierce **w** upon Amalek, therefore H639
2Sa 11:20 And if so be that the king's **w** arise, and H2534
2Ki 22:13 for great *is* the **w** of the LORD that is H2534
17 therefore my **w** shall be kindled against H2534
23:26 of his great **w**, wherewith his anger H639
1Ch 27:24 not, because there fell **w** for it against H7110
2Ch 12: 7 and my **w** shall not be poured H2534
12 And when he humbled himself, the **w** of H639
19: 2 *is* **w** upon thee from before the LORD. H7110
19:10 the LORD, and *so* **w** come upon you, H7110
24:18 and idols: and **w** came upon Judah and H7110
28:11 for the fierce **w** of the LORD *is* upon you. H639
13 and *there is* fierce **w** against Israel. H639
29: 8 Wherefore the **w** of the LORD was H7110
10 that his fierce **w** may turn away from us. H639
30: 8 of his **w** may turn away from you. H639
32:25 there was **w** upon him, and upon H7110
26 so that the **w** of the LORD came not H7110
34:21 for great *is* the **w** of the LORD that is H2534
25 therefore my **w** shall be poured out H2534
36:16 until the **w** of the LORD arose against H2534
Ezr 5:12 of heaven unto **w**, he gave them into the H7265
7:23 should there be **w** against the realm of H7109
8:22 **w** *is* against all them that forsake him. H639
10:14 until the fierce **w** of our God for this H639
Neh 13:18 yet ye bring more **w** upon Israel by H2740
Est 1:18 *there arise* too much contempt and **w**. H7110
2: 1 After these things, when the **w** of king H2534
3: 5 reverence, then was Haman full of **w**. H2534
7: 7 of wine in his **w** *went* into the palace H2534
10 Then was the king's **w** pacified. H2534
Job 5: 2 For **w** killeth the foolish man, and envy H3708
14:13 me secret, until thy **w** be past, that thou H639
16: 9 He teareth *me* in his **w**, who hateth me: H639
19:11 He hath also kindled his **w** against me, H639
29 Be ye afraid of the sword: for **w** H2534
20:23 cast the fury of his **w** upon him, and H639
28 *goods* shall flow away in the day of his **w**. H639
21:20 he shall drink of the **w** of the Almighty. H2534
30 shall be brought forth to the day of **w**. H5678
32: 2 Then was kindled the **w** of Elihu the son H639
2 Job was his **w** kindled, because he H639
3 Also against his three friends was his **w** H639
5 *these* three men, then his **w** was kindled. H639
36:13 But the hypocrites in heart heap up **w**: H639
18 Because *there is* **w**, *beware* lest he take H2534
40:11 Cast abroad the rage of thy **w**: and H639
42: 7 the Temanite, My **w** is kindled against H639
Ps 2: 5 Then shall he speak unto them in his **w**, H639
12 the way, when his **w** is kindled but a H639
21: 9 in his **w**, and the fire shall devour them. H639
37: 8 Cease from anger, and forsake **w**: fret H2534
38: 1 O LORD, rebuke me not in thy **w**: H7110
55: 3 upon me, and in **w** they hate me. H639
58: 9 a whirlwind, both living, and in *his* **w**. H2740
59:13 Consume *them* in **w**, consume *them*, H2534
76:10 Surely the **w** of man shall praise thee: H2534
10 the remainder of **w** shalt thou restrain. H2534
78:31 The **w** of God came upon them, and slew H639
38 away, and did not stir up all his **w**. H2534
49 of his anger, **w**, and indignation, and H5678
79: 6 Pour out thy **w** upon the heathen that H2534
85: 3 Thou hast taken away all thy **w**: thou H5678
88: 7 Thy **w** lieth hard upon me, and thou H2534
16 Thy fierce **w** goeth over me; thy terrors H2740
89:46 for ever? shall thy **w** burn like fire? H2534
90: 7 anger, and by thy **w** are we troubled. H2534
9 away in thy **w**: we spend our years H5678
11 even according to thy fear, *so is* thy **w**. H5678
95:11 Unto whom I sware in my **w** that they H639
102:10 Because of thine indignation and thy **w**: H7110
106:23 his **w**, lest he should destroy *them*. H2534
40 Therefore was the **w** of the LORD H639
110: 5 strike through kings in the day of his **w**. H639
124: 3 when their **w** was kindled against us: H639
138: 7 hand against the **w** of mine enemies, H639
Prv 11: 4 Riches profit not in the day of **w**: but H5678
23 *but* the expectation of the wicked *is* **w**. H5678
12:16 A fool's **w** is presently known: but a H3708
14:29 *He that is* slow to **w** *is* of great H639
35 **w** is *against* him that causeth shame. H5678
15: 1 A soft answer turneth away **w**: but H2534
16:14 The **w** of a king *is as* messengers of H2534
19:12 The king's **w** *is* as the roaring of a lion; H2197
19 A man of great **w** shall suffer H2534
21:14 and a reward in the bosom strong **w**. H2534
24 *is* his name, who dealeth in proud **w**. H5678
24:18 him, and he turn away his **w** from him. H639
27: 3 a fool's **w** *is* heavier than them both. H3708
4 **W** is cruel, and anger *is* outrageous; H2534
29: 8 into a snare: but wise *men* turn away **w**. H639
30:33 so the forcing of **w** bringeth forth strife. H639
Ecc 5:17 much sorrow and **w** with his sickness. H7110
Isa 9:19 Through the **w** of the LORD of hosts is H5678
10: 6 the people of my **w** will I give him a H5678
13: 9 cruel both with **w** and fierce anger, to H5678
13 of her place, in the **w** of the LORD of H5678
14: 6 He who smote the people in **w** with a H5678
Isa 16: 6 and his **w**: *but* his lies *shall* not *be* so. H5678
54: 8 In a little **w** I hid my face from thee for H7110
60:10 thee: for in my **w** I smote thee, but in H7110
Jer 7:29 and forsaken the generation of his **w**. H5678
10:10 king: at his **w** the earth shall tremble, H7110
18:20 *and* to turn away thy **w** from them. H2534
21: 5 in anger, and in fury, and in great **w**. H7110
32:37 my fury, and in great **w**; and I will bring H7110
44: 8 In that ye provoke me unto **w** with the H3707
48:30 I know his **w**, saith the LORD; but *it* H5678
50:13 Because of the **w** of the LORD it shall H7110
Lam 2: 2 down in his **w** the strong holds of H5678
3: 1 hath seen affliction by the rod of his **w**. H5678
Ezk 7:12 for **w** *is* upon all the multitude thereof. H2740
14 my **w** *is* upon all the multitude thereof. H2740
19 in the day of the **w** of the LORD: they H5678
13:15 Thus will I accomplish my **w** upon the H2534
21:31 in the fire of my **w**, and deliver thee into H5678
22:21 you in the fire of my **w**, and ye shall be H5678
31 with the fire of my **w**: their own way H5678
38:19 *and* in the fire of my **w** have I spoken, H5678
Hos 5:10 pour out my **w** upon them like water. H5678
13:11 anger, and took *him* away in my **w**. H5678
Am 1:11 perpetually, and he kept his **w** for ever: H5678
Nah 1: 2 and he reserveth *w* for his enemies.
Hab 3: 2 make known; in **w** remember mercy. H7267
8 rivers? *was* thy **w** against the sea, that H5678
Zep 1:15 That day *is* a day of **w**, a day of trouble H5678
18 the day of the LORD'S **w**; but the whole H5678
Zec 7:12 a great **w** from the LORD of hosts. H7110
8:14 provoked me to **w**, saith the LORD of H7107
Mt 3: 7 warned you to flee from the **w** to come? G3709
Lk 3: 7 warned you to flee from the **w** to come? G3709
4:28 heard these things, were filled with **w**, G2372
21:23 in the land, and **w** upon this people. G3709
Jn 3:36 life; but the **w** of God abideth on him. G3709
Act 19:28 they were full of **w**, and cried out, G2372
Ro 1:18 For the **w** of God is revealed from G3709
2: 5 up unto thyself **w** against the day of G3709
5 against the day of **w** and revelation of G3709
8 unrighteousness, indignation and **w**, G3709
4:15 Because the law worketh **w**: for where G3709
5: 9 we shall be saved from **w** through him. G3709
9:22 *What* if God, willing to shew *his* **w**, and G3709
22 the vessels of **w** fitted to destruction: G3709
12:19 give place unto **w**: for it is written, G3709
13: 4 to *execute* **w** upon him that doeth evil. G3709
5 only for **w**, but also for conscience sake. G3709
Gal 5:20 **w**, strife, seditions, heresies, G2372
Eph 2: 3 nature the children of **w**, even as others. G3709
4:26 let not the sun go down upon your **w**: G3950
31 Let all bitterness, and **w**, and anger, G2372
5: 6 things cometh the **w** of God upon the G3709
6: 4 your children to **w**: but bring them up G3949
Col 3: 6 For which things' sake the **w** of God G3709
8 all these; anger, **w**, malice, blasphemy, G2372
1Th 1:10 which delivered us from the **w** to come. G3709
2:16 **w** is come upon them to the uttermost. G3709
5: 9 For God hath not appointed us to **w**, but G3709
1Ti 2: 8 holy hands, without **w** and doubting. G3709
Heb 3:11 So I sware in my **w**, They shall not enter G3709
4: 3 I have sworn in my **w**, if they shall enter G3709
11:27 not fearing the **w** of the king: for he G2372
Jas 1:19 swift to hear, slow to speak, slow to **w**: G3709
20 For the **w** of man worketh not the G3709
Rev 6:16 throne, and from the **w** of the Lamb: G3709
17 For the great day of his **w** is come; and G3709
11:18 And the nations were angry, and thy **w** G3709
12:12 unto you, having great **w**, because he G2372
14: 8 of the wine of the **w** of her fornication. G2372
10 of the wine of the **w** of God, which is G2372
19 the great winepress of the **w** of God. G2372
15: 1 for in them is filled up the **w** of God. G2372
7 **w** of God, who liveth for ever and ever. G2372
16: 1 vials of the **w** of God upon the earth. G2372
19 of the wine of the fierceness of his **w**. G3709
18: 3 of the wine of the **w** of her fornication, G2372
19:15 the fierceness and **w** of Almighty God. G3709

WRATHFUL
Ps 69:24 and let thy **w** anger take hold of them. H2740
Prv 15:18 A **w** man stirreth up strife: but *he that* H2534

WRATHS
2Co 12:20 envyings, **w**, strifes, backbitings, G2372

WREATH
2Ch 4:13 on each **w**, to cover the two pommels H7639

WREATHED
Lam 1:14 his hand: they are w, *and* come up upon H8276

WREATHEN
Ex 28:14 at the ends; *of* w work shalt thou make H5688
14 and fasten the w chains to the ouches. H5688
22 at the ends *of* w work *of* pure gold. H5688
24 And thou shalt put the two w *chains* of H5688
25 And *the other* two ends of the two w H5688
39:15 at the ends, *of* w work *of* pure gold. H5688
17 And they put the two w chains of gold H5688
18 And the two ends of the two w chains H5688
2Ki 25:17 three cubits; and the w work, and H7639
17 had the second pillar with w work. H7639

WREATHS
1Ki 7:17 *And* nets of checker work, and w of H1434
2Ch 4:12 pillars, and the two w to cover the two H7639
13 on the two w; two rows of H7639

WRECK See SHIPWRECK.

WREST
Ex 23: 2 to decline after many to w *judgment*: H5186
6 Thou shalt not w the judgment of thy H5186
Dt 16:19 Thou shalt not w judgment; thou shalt H5186
Ps 56: 5 Every day they w my words: all their H6087
2Pt 3:16 and unstable w, as *they do* also the *G4761*

WRESTLE
Eph 6:12 For we w not against flesh and blood, *G2076*

WRESTLED
Gen 30: 8 wrestlings have I w with my sister, and H6617
32:24 And Jacob was left alone; and there w a H79
25 thigh was out of joint, as he w with him. H79

WRESTLINGS
Gen 30: 8 And Rachel said, With great w have I H5319

WRETCHED
Ro 7:24 O w man that I am! who shall deliver *G5005*
Rev 3:17 not that thou art w, and miserable, and *G5005*

WRETCHEDNESS
Nu 11:15 in thy sight; and let me not see my w. H7451

WRING
Lev 1:15 the altar, and w off his head, and burn H4454
5: 8 offering first, and w off his head from H4454
Ps 75: 8 shall w *them* out, *and* drink *them*. H4680

WRINGED
Jdg 6:38 together, and w the dew out of the H4680

WRINGING
Prv 30:33 butter, and the w of the nose bringeth H4330

WRINKLE
Eph 5:27 having spot, or w, or any such thing; *G4512*

WRINKLES
Job 16: 8 And thou hast filled me with w, *which* is H7059

WRITE
Ex 17:14 And the LORD said unto Moses, W this H3789
34: 1 the first: and I will w upon *these* tables H3789
27 And the LORD said unto Moses, W H3789
Nu 5:23 And the priest shall w these curses in a H3789
17: 2 twelve rods: w thou every man's name H3789
3 And thou shalt w Aaron's name upon H3789
Dt 6: 9 And thou shalt w them upon the posts H3789
10: 2 And I will w on the tables the words H3789
11:20 And thou shalt w them upon the door H3789
17:18 that he shall w him a copy of this law H3789
24: 1 in her: then let him w her a bill of H3789
3 husband hate her, and w her a bill of H3789
27: 3 And thou shalt w upon them all the H3789
8 And thou shalt w upon the stones all H3789
31:19 Now therefore w ye this song for you, H3789
2Ch 26:22 Isaiah the prophet, the son of Amoz, w. H3789
Ezr 5:10 that we might w the names of the men H3790
Neh 9:38 *covenant*, and w *it*; and our princes, H3789
Est 8: 8 W ye also for the Jews, as it liketh you, H3789
Prv 3: 3 w them upon the table of thine heart: H3789
7: 3 Bind them upon thy fingers, w them H3789
Isa 8: 1 a great roll, and w in it with a man's H3789
10: 1 decrees, and that w grievousness *which* H3789
19 shall be few, that a child may w them. H3789
Isa 30: 8 Now go, w it before them in a table, H3789
Jer 22:30 Thus saith the LORD, W ye this man H3789
30: 2 of Israel, saying, W thee all the words H3789
31:33 inward parts, and w it in their hearts; H3789
36: 2 Take thee a roll of a book, and w H3789
17 thou w all these words at his mouth? H3789
28 Take thee again another roll, and w in H3789
Ezk 24: 2 Son of man, w thee the name of the H3789
37:16 one stick, and w upon it, For Judah, H3789
16 take another stick, and w upon it, For H3789
43:11 the laws thereof: and w *it* in their sight, H3789
Hab 2: 2 me, and said, W the vision, and make H3789
Mk 10: 4 And they said, Moses suffered to w a *G1125*
Lk 1: 3 the very first, to w unto thee in order, *G1125*
16: 6 bill, and sit down quickly, and w fifty. *G1125*
7 him, Take thy bill, and w fourscore. *G1125*
Jn 1:45 w, Jesus of Nazareth, the son of Joseph. *G1125*
19:21 the Jews to Pilate, W not, The King of *G1125*
Act 15:20 But that we w unto them, that they *G1989*
25:26 Of whom I have no certain thing to w *G1125*
26 had, I might have somewhat to w. *G1125*
1Co 4:14 I w not these things to shame you, but *G1125*
14:37 the things that I w unto you are the *G1125*
2Co 1:13 For we w none other things unto you, *G1125*
2: 9 For to this end also did I w, that I might *G1125*
9: 1 it is superfluous for me to w to you: *G1125*
13: 2 being absent now I w to them which *G1125*
10 Therefore I w these things being *G1125*
Gal 1:20 Now the things which I w unto you, *G1125*
Php 3: 1 in the Lord. To w the same things to *G1125*
1Th 4: 9 ye need not that I w unto you: for ye *G1125*
5: 1 ye have no need that I w unto you. *G1125*
2Th 3:17 is the token in every epistle: so I w. *G1125*
1Ti 3:14 These things w I unto thee, hoping to *G1125*
Heb 8:10 their mind, and w them in their hearts: *G1924*
10:16 and in their minds will I w them; *G1924*
2Pt 3: 1 This second epistle, beloved, I now w *G1125*
1Jn 1: 4 And these things w we unto you, that *G1125*
2: 1 My little children, these things w I unto *G1125*
7 Brethren, I w no new commandment *G1125*
8 Again, a new commandment I w unto *G1125*
12 I w unto you, little children, because *G1125*
13 I w unto you, fathers, because ye have *G1125*
13 the beginning. I w unto you, young *G1125*
13 the wicked one. I w unto you, little *G1125*
2Jn 12 Having many things to w unto you, I *G1125*
12 you, I would not w with paper and ink:
3Jn 13 I had many things to w, but I will not *G1125*
13 I will not with ink and pen w unto thee: *G1125*
Jude 3 Beloved, when I gave all diligence to w *G1125*
3 was needful for me to w unto you, and *G1125*
Rev 1:11 What thou seest, w in a book, and send *G1125*
19 W the things which thou hast seen, and *G1125*
2: 1 of Ephesus w; These things saith he *G1125*
8 church in Smyrna w; These things saith *G1125*
12 in Pergamos w; These things saith he *G1125*
18 in Thyatira w; These things saith the *G1125*
3: 1 church in Sardis w; These things saith *G1125*
7 in Philadelphia w; These things saith he *G1125*
12 out: and I will w upon him the name *G1125*
12 and *I will w upon him* my new name.
14 of the Laodiceans w; These things saith *G1125*
10: 4 I was about to w: and I heard a voice *G1125*
4 thunders uttered, and w them not. *G1125*
14:13 saying unto me, W, Blessed *are* the *G1125*
19: 9 And he saith unto me, W, Blessed *are* *G1125*
21: 5 he said unto me, W: for these words are *G1125*

WRITER
Jdg 5:14 they that handle the pen of the w. H5608
Ps 45: 1 king: my tongue *is* the pen of a ready w. H5608

WRITER'S
Ezk 9: 2 with linen, with a w inkhorn by his H5608
3 which *had* the w inkhorn by his side; H5608

WRITEST
Job 13:26 For thou w bitter things against me, H3789
Ezk 37:20 And the sticks whereon thou w shall be H3789

WRITETH
Ps 87: 6 The LORD shall count, when he w up H3789

WRITING
Ex 32:16 of God, and the w *was* the writing of H4385
16 the w of God, graven upon the tables. H4385
39:30 wrote upon it a w, *like to* the engravings H4385
Dt 10: 4 to the first w, the ten commandments, H4385
31:24 made an end of w the words of this law H3789
1Ch 28:19 me understand in w by *his* hand upon H3791
2Ch 2:11 of Tyre answered in w, which he sent to H3791
21:12 And there came a w to him from Elijah H4385
35: 4 according to the w of David king of H3791
4 according to the w of Solomon his son. H4385
36:22 kingdom, and *put it* also in w, saying, H4385
Ezr 1: 1 kingdom, and *put it* also in w, saying, H4385
4: 7 of Persia; and the w of the letter *was* H3791
Est 1:22 according to the w thereof, and to H3791
3:12 according to the w thereof, and *to* H3791
14 The copy of the w for a commandment H3791
4: 8 Also he gave him the copy of the w of H3791
8: 8 king's ring: for the w which is written H3791
9 according to the w thereof, and unto H3791
9 w, and according to their language. H3791
13 The copy of the w for a commandment H3791
9:27 according to their w, and according to H3791
Isa 38: 9 The w of Hezekiah king of Judah, when H4385
Ezk 13: 9 they be written in the w of the house of H3791
Dan 5: 7 shall read this w, and shew me the H3792
8 could not read the w, nor make known H3792
15 should read this w, and make known H3792
16 canst read the w, and make known to H3792
17 yet I will read the w unto the king, and H3792
24 sent from him; and this w was written. H3792
25 And this *is* the w that was written, H3792
6: 8 and sign the w, that it be not changed, H3792
9 Wherefore king Darius signed the w H3792
10 Now when Daniel knew that the w was H3792
Mt 5:31 let him give her a w of divorcement:
19: 7 w of divorcement, and to put her away? *G975*
Lk 1:63 And he asked for a w table, and wrote, *G4098*
Jn 19:19 on the cross. And the w was, JESUS OF *G1125*

WRITINGS
Jn 5:47 But if ye believe not his w, how shall ye *G1121*

WRITING-TABLE See WRITING and TABLE.

WRITTEN
Ex 24:12 I have w; that thou mayest teach them. H3789
31:18 of stone, w with the finger of God. H3789
32:15 the tables *were* w on both their sides; H3789
15 one side and on the other *were* they w. H3789
32 thee, out of thy book which thou hast w. H3789
Nu 11:26 of them that were w, but went not out H3789
Dt 9:10 two tables of stone w with the finger of H3789
10 and on them *was* w according to all the
28:58 of this law that are w in this book, that H3789
61 which *is* not w in the book of this law, H3789
29:20 curses that are w in this book shall lie H3789
21 that are w in this book of the law: H3789
27 it all the curses that are w in this book: H3789
30:10 statutes which are w in this book of the H3789
Jos 1: 8 to all that is w therein: for then thou H3789
8:31 of Israel, as it is w in the book of the H3789
34 to all that is w in the book of the law. H3789
10:13 *Is* not this w in the book of Jasher? H3789
23: 6 to do all that is w in the book of the law H3789
2Sa 1:18 behold, *it is* w in the book of Jasher.) H3789
1Ki 2: 3 as it is w in the law of Moses, H3789
11:41 w in the book of the acts of Solomon? H3789
14:19 behold, they *are* w in the book of the H3789
29 he did, *are* they not w in the book of the H3789
15: 7 he did, *are* they not w in the book of the H3789
23 built, *are* they not w in the book of the H3789
31 he did, *are* they not w in the book of the H3789
16: 5 might, *are* they not w in the book of the H3789
14 he did, *are* they not w in the book of the H3789
20 *are* they not w in the book of the H3789
27 *are* they not w in the book of the H3789
21:11 *and* as it *was* w in the letters which H3789
22:39 built, *are* they not w in the book of the H3789
45 *are* they not w in the book of the H3789
2Ki 1:18 he did, *are* they not w in the book of the H3789
8:23 he did, *are* they not w in the book of the H3789
10:34 might, *are* they not w in the book of the H3789
12:19 he did, *are* they not w in the book of the H3789
13: 8 might, *are* they not w in the book of the H3789
12 Judah, *are* they not w in the book of the H3789
14: 6 unto that which is w in the book of the H3789
15 Judah, *are* they not w in the book of the H3789
18 *are* they not w in the book of the H3789
28 Israel, are they not w in the book of the H3789
15: 6 he did, *are* they not w in the book of the H3789
11 behold, they *are* w in the book of the H3789
15 behold, they *are* w in the book of the H3789
21 he did, *are* they not w in the book of the H3789
26 behold, they *are* w in the book of the H3789

2Ki 15:31 behold, they *are* **w** in the book of the H3789
36 he did, *are* they not **w** in the book of the H3789
16:19 he did, *are* they not **w** in the book of the H3789
20:20 city, *are* they not **w** in the book of the H3789
21:17 *are* they not **w** in the book of the H3789
25 he did, *are* they not **w** in the book of the H3789
22:13 unto all that which is **w** concerning us. H3789
23: 3 that were **w** in this book. And all H3789
21 as *it is* **w** in the book of this covenant. H3789
24 the law which were **w** in the book that H3789
28 he did, *are* they not **w** in the book of the H3789
24: 5 he did, *are* they not **w** in the book of the H3789
1Ch 4:41 And these **w** by name came in the days H3789
9: 1 behold, they *were* **w** in the book of the H3789
16:40 to all that is **w** in the law of the LORD, H3789
29:29 last, behold, they *are* **w** in the book of H3789
2Ch 9:29 and last, *are* they not **w** in the book of H3789
12:15 and last, *are* they not **w** in the book of H3789
13:22 *are* **w** in the story of the prophet Iddo. H3789
16:11 last, lo, they *are* **w** in the book of the H3789
20:34 behold, they *are* **w** in the book of Jehu H3789
23:18 of the LORD, as *it is* **w** in the law of H3789
24:27 behold, they *are* **w** in the story of the H3789
25: 4 but *did* as *it is* **w** in the law in the book H3789
26 *are* they not **w** in the book of the kings H3789
27: 7 ways, lo, they *are* **w** in the book of the H3789
28:26 behold, they *are* **w** in the book of the H3789
30: 5 *it* of a long *time in such sort* as it was **w**. H3789
18 than it was **w**. But Hezekiah prayed H3789
31: 3 feasts, as *it is* **w** in the law of the LORD. H3789
32:32 behold, they *are* **w** in the vision of H3789
33:18 *are* **w** in the book of the kings of Israel.
19 *are* **w** among the sayings of the seers. H3789
34:21 to do after all that is **w** in this book. H3789
24 the curses that are **w** in the book which H3789
31 the covenant which are **w** in this book. H3789
35:12 unto the LORD, as *it is* **w** in the book of H3789
25 behold, they *are* **w** in the lamentations. H3789
26 *which was* **w** in the law of the LORD, H3789
27 behold, they *are* **w** in the book of the H3789
36: 8 behold, they *are* **w** in the book of the H3789
Ezr 3: 2 **w** in the law of Moses the man of God. H3789
4 as *it is* **w**, and *offered* the daily H3789
4: 7 of the letter *was* **w** in the Syrian tongue, H3789
5: 7 **w** thus; Unto Darius the king, all peace. H3790
6: 2 a roll, and therein *was* a record thus **w**: H3790
18 as it is **w** in the book of Moses. H3792
8:34 and all the weight was **w** at that time. H3789
Neh 6: 6 Wherein *was* **w**, It is reported among H3789
7: 5 up at the first, and found **w** therein, H3789
8:14 And they found **w** in the law which the H3789
15 of thick trees, to make booths, as *it is* **w**. H3789
10:34 the LORD our God, as *it is* **w** in the law: H3789
36 our cattle, as *it is* **w** in the law, and the H3789
12:23 of the fathers, *were* **w** in the book of the H3789
13: 1 and therein was found **w**, that the H3789
Est 1:19 him, and let it be **w** among the laws of H3789
2:23 a tree: and it was **w** in the book of the H3789
3: 9 If it please the king, let it be **w** that they H3789
12 and there was **w** according to all that H3789
12 it **w**, and sealed with the king's ring. H3789
6: 2 And it was found **w**, that Mordecai had H3789
8: 5 his eyes, let it be **w** to reverse the letters H3789
8 writing which is **w** in the king's name, H3789
9 and it was **w** according to all that H3789
9:23 and as Mordecai had **w** unto them; H3789
32 of Purim; and it was **w** in the book. H3789
10: 2 him, *are* they not **w** in the book of the H3789
Job 19:23 Oh that my words were now **w**! oh that H3789
31:35 and *that* mine adversary had **w** a book. H3789
Ps 40: 7 in the volume of the book *it is* **w** of me, H3789
69:28 living, and not be **w** with the righteous. H3789
102:18 This shall be **w** for the generation to H3789
139:16 *members* were **w**, *which* in continuance H3789
149: 9 To execute upon them the judgment **w**: H3789
Prv 22:20 Have not I **w** to thee excellent things in H3789
Ecc 12:10 **w** *was* upright, *even* words of truth. H3789
Isa 4: 3 is **w** among the living in Jerusalem: H3789
65: 6 Behold, *it is* **w** before me: I will not H3789
Jer 17: 1 The sin of Judah *is* **w** with a pen of H3789
13 depart from me shall be **w** in the earth, H3789
25:13 it, *even* all that is **w** in this book, which H3789
36: 6 which thou hast **w** from my mouth, the H3789
29 Why hast thou **w** therein, saying, The H3789
45: 1 when he had **w** these words in a book H3789
51:60 words that are **w** against Babylon. H3789
Ezk 2:10 me; and it *was* **w** within and without: H3789
10 and *there was* **w** therein lamentations, H3789
13: 9 shall they be **w** in the writing of the H3789

Dan 5:24 sent from him; and this writing was **w**. H7560
25 And this *is* the writing that was **w**, H7560
9:11 the oath that *is* **w** in the law of Moses H3789
13 As *it is* **w** in the law of Moses, all this H3789
12: 1 one that shall be found **w** in the book. H3789
Hos 8:12 I have **w** to him the great things of my H3789
Mal 3:16 was **w** before him for them H3789
Mt 2: 5 Judaea: for thus it is **w** by the prophet, *G1125*
4: 4 But he answered and said, It is **w**, Man *G1125*
6 down: for it is **w**, He shall give his *G1125*
7 Jesus said unto him, It is **w** again, *G1125*
10 Satan: for it is **w**, Thou shalt worship *G1125*
11:10 For this is *he*, of whom it is **w**, Behold, I *G1125*
21:13 And said unto them, It is **w**, My house *G1125*
26:24 The Son of man goeth as it is **w** of him: *G1125*
31 me this night: for it is **w**, I will smite the *G1125*
27:37 his accusation **w**, THIS IS JESUS THE *G1125*
Mk 1: 2 As it is **w** in the prophets, Behold, I *G1125*
7: 6 you hypocrites, as it is **w**, This people *G1125*
9:12 and how it is **w** of the Son of man, that *G1125*
13 they listed, as it is **w** of him. *G1125*
11:17 them, Is it not **w**, My house shall be *G1125*
14:21 The Son of man indeed goeth, as it is **w** *G1125*
27 me this night: for it is **w**, I will smite the *G1125*
15:26 was **w** over, THE KING OF THE JEWS. *G1924*
Lk 2:23 (As it is **w** in the law of the Lord, Every *G1125*
3: 4 As it is **w** in the book of the words of *G1125*
4: 4 him, saying, It is **w**, That man shall not *G1125*
8 behind me, Satan: for it is **w**, Thou shalt *G1125*
10 For it is **w**, He shall give his angels *G1125*
17 he found the place where it was **w**, *G1125*
7:27 This is *he*, of whom it is **w**, Behold, I *G1125*
10:20 because your names are **w** in heaven. *G1125*
26 He said unto him, What is **w** in the *G1125*
18:31 all things that are **w** by the prophets *G1125*
19:46 Saying unto them, It is **w**, My house is *G1125*
20:17 is this then that is **w**, The stone which *G1125*
21:22 all things which are **w** may be fulfilled. *G1125*
22:37 For I say unto you, that this that is **w** *G1125*
23:38 And a superscription also was **w** over *G1125*
24:44 which were **w** in the law of Moses, *G1125*
46 And said unto them, Thus it is **w**, and *G1125*
Jn 2:17 that it was **w**, The zeal of thine house *G1125*
6:31 in the desert; as it is **w**, He gave them *G1125*
45 It is **w** in the prophets, And they shall *G1125*
8:17 It is also **w** in your law, that the *G1125*
10:34 Jesus answered them, Is it not **w** in *G1125*
12:14 a young ass, sat thereon; as it is **w**, *G1125*
16 these things were **w** of him, and *that* *G1125*
15:25 be fulfilled that is **w** in their law, They *G1125*
19:20 **w** in Hebrew, *and* Greek, *and* Latin. *G1125*
22 Pilate answered, What I have **w** I have *G1125*
22 What I have written I have **w**. *G1125*
20:30 disciples, which are not **w** in this book: *G1125*
31 But these are **w**, that ye might believe *G1125*
21:25 which, if they should be **w** every one, I *G1125*
25 the books that should be **w**. Amen. *G1125*
Act 1:20 For it is **w** in the book of Psalms, Let *G1125*
7:42 of heaven; as it is **w** in the book of the *G1125*
13:29 all that was **w** of him, they took *him* *G1125*
33 again; as it is also **w** in the second *G1125*
15:15 the words of the prophets; as it is **w**, *G1125*
21:25 believe, we have **w** *and* concluded that *G1989*
23: 5 priest: for it is **w**, Thou shalt not speak *G1125*
24:14 are **w** in the law and in the prophets: *G1125*
Ro 1:17 as it is **w**, The just shall live by faith. *G1125*
2:15 Which shew the work of the law **w** in *G1123*
24 the Gentiles through you, as it is **w**. *G1125*
3: 4 every man a liar; as it is **w**, That thou *G1125*
10 As it is **w**, There is none righteous, no, *G1125*
4:17 (As it is **w**, I have made thee a father of *G1125*
23 Now it was not **w** for his sake alone, *G1125*
8:36 As it is **w**, For thy sake we are killed all *G1125*
9:13 As it is **w**, Jacob have I loved, but Esau *G1125*
33 As it is **w**, Behold, I lay in Sion a *G1125*
10:15 be sent? as it is **w**, How beautiful are the *G1125*
11: 8 (According as it is **w**, God hath given *G1125*
26 be saved: as it is **w**, There shall come *G1125*
12:19 wrath: for it is **w**, Vengeance *is* mine; *G1125*
14:11 For it is **w**, *As* I live, saith the Lord, *G1125*
15: 3 but, as it is **w**, The reproaches of them *G1125*
4 For whatsoever things were **w** *G4270*
4 aforetime were **w** for our learning, that *G4270*
9 *his* mercy; as it is **w**, For this cause I will *G1125*
15 Nevertheless, brethren, I have **w** the *G1125*
21 But as it is **w**, To whom he was not *G1125*
1Co 1:19 For it is **w**, I will destroy the wisdom of *G1125*
31 That, according as it is **w**, He that *G1125*
2: 9 But as it is **w**, Eye hath not seen, nor ear *G1125*

1Co 3:19 with God. For it is **w**, He taketh the wise *G1125*
4: 6 that which is **w**, that no one of you be *G1125*
5:11 But now I have **w** unto you not to keep *G1125*
9: 9 For it is **w** in the law of Moses, Thou *G1125*
10 no doubt, *this* is **w**: that he that ploweth *G1125*
15 neither have I **w** these things, that it *G1125*
10: 7 of them; as it is **w**, The people sat down *G1125*
11 and they are **w** for our admonition, *G1125*
14:21 In the law it is **w**, With *men of* other *G1125*
15:45 And so it is **w**, The first man Adam was *G1125*
54 is **w**, Death is swallowed up in victory. *G1125*
2Co 3: 2 Ye are our epistle **w** in our hearts, *G1449*
3 ministered by us, **w** not with ink, but *G1449*
7 But if the ministration of death, **w** *and* *G1722*
4:13 according as it is **w**, I believed, and *G1125*
8:15 As it is **w**, He that *had gathered* much *G1125*
9: 9 (As it is **w**, He hath dispersed abroad; *G1125*
Gal 3:10 the curse: for it is **w**, Cursed *is* every one *G1125*
10 are **w** in the book of the law to do them. *G1125*
13 for us: for it is **w**, Cursed *is* every one *G1125*
4:22 For it is **w**, that Abraham had two sons, *G1125*
27 For it is **w**, Rejoice, *thou* barren that *G1125*
6:11 Ye see how large a letter I have **w** unto *G1125*
Phlm 19 I Paul have **w** *it* with mine own hand, I *G1125*
Heb 10: 7 it is **w** of me,) to do thy will, O God. *G1125*
12:23 which are **w** in heaven, and to God *G583*
13:22 I have **w** a letter unto you in few words. *G1989*
1Pt 1:16 Because it is **w**, Be ye holy; for I am *G1125*
5:12 I suppose, I have **w** briefly, exhorting, *G1125*
2Pt 3:15 given unto him hath **w** unto you; *G1125*
1Jn 2:14 I have **w** unto you, fathers, because ye *G1125*
14 beginning. I have **w** unto you, young *G1125*
21 I have not **w** unto you because ye know *G1125*
26 These *things* have I **w** unto you *G1125*
5:13 These things have I **w** unto you that *G1125*
Rev 1: 3 are **w** therein: for the time *is* at hand. *G1125*
2:17 the stone a new name **w**, which no man *G1125*
5: 1 the throne a book **w** within and on the *G1125*
13: 8 names are not **w** in the book of life of *G1125*
14: 1 his Father's name **w** in their foreheads. *G1125*
17: 5 And upon her forehead *was* a name **w**, *G1125*
8 names were not **w** in the book of life *G1125*
19:12 **w**, that no man knew, but he himself. *G1125*
16 his thigh a name **w**, KING OF KINGS, *G1125*
20:12 things which were **w** in the books, *G1125*
15 And whosoever was not found **w** in the *G1125*
21:12 and names **w** thereon, which are *G1924*
27 which are **w** in the Lamb's book of life. *G1125*
22:18 the plagues that are **w** in this book: *G1125*
19 the things which are **w** in this book. *G1125*

WRONG

Gen 16: 5 And Sarai said unto Abram, My **w** *be* H2555
Ex 2:13 **w**, Wherefore smitest thou thy fellow? H7563
Dt 19:16 to testify against him *that which is* **w**; H5627
Jdg 11:27 but thou doest me **w** to war against me: H7451
1Ch 12:17 seeing *there is* no **w** in mine hands, the H2555
16:21 He suffered no man to do them **w**: yea, H6231
Est 1:16 hath not done **w** to the king only, but H5753
Job 19: 7 Behold, I cry out of **w**, but I am not H2555
Ps 105:14 He suffered no man to do them **w**: yea, H6231
Jer 22: 3 and do no **w**, do no violence to the H3238
13 and his chambers by **w**; *that* useth his H4941
Lam 3:59 O LORD, thou hast seen my **w**: judge H5792
Hab 1: 4 therefore **w** judgment proceedeth. H6127
Mt 20:13 I do thee no **w**: didst not thou agree *G91*
Act 7:24 And seeing one *of them* suffer **w**, he *G91*
26 brethren; why do ye **w** one to another? *G91*
27 But he that did his neighbour **w** thrust *G91*
18:14 If it were a matter of **w** or wicked *G92*
25:10 I done no **w**, as thou very well knowest. *G91*
1Co 6: 7 do ye not rather take **w**? why do ye not *G91*
8 Nay, ye do **w**, and defraud, and that *your* *G91*
2Co 7:12 that had done the **w**, nor for his cause *G91*
12 cause that suffered **w**, but that our care *G91*
12:13 burdensome to you? forgive me this **w**. *G93*
Col 3:25 But he that doeth **w** shall receive for the *G91*
25 receive for the **w** which he hath done: *G91*

WRONGED

2Co 7: 2 Receive us; we have **w** no man, we have *G91*
Phlm 18 If he hath **w** thee, or oweth *thee* ought, *G91*

WRONGETH

Prv 8:36 But he that sinneth against me **w** his H2554

WRONGFULLY

Job 21:27 *which* ye **w** imagine against me. H2554
Ps 35:19 Let not them that are mine enemies **w** H8267

Ps 38:19 and they that hate me **w** are multiplied. H8267
69: 4 mine enemies **w**, are mighty: then I H8267
119:86 they persecute me **w**; help thou me. H8267
Ezk 22:29 they have oppressed the stranger **w**. H4941
1Pt 2:19 toward God endure grief, suffering **w**. *G95*

WROTE

Ex 24: 4 And Moses **w** all the words of the H3789
34:28 water. And he **w** upon the tables the H3789
39:30 *of* pure gold, and **w** upon it a writing, H3789
Nu 33: 2 And Moses **w** their goings out H3789
Dt 4:13 he **w** them upon two tables of stone. H3789
5:22 no more. And he **w** them in two tables H3789
10: 4 And he **w** on the tables, according to H3789
31: 9 And Moses **w** this law, and delivered it H3789
22 Moses therefore **w** this song the same H3789
Jos 8:32 And he **w** there upon the stones a copy H3789
32 of Moses, which he **w** in the presence of H3789
24:26 And Joshua **w** these words in the book H3789
1Sa 10:25 of the kingdom, and **w** *it* in a book, and H3789
2Sa 11:14 that David **w** a letter to Joab, and H3789
15 And he **w** in the letter, saying, Set ye H3789
1Ki 21: 8 So she **w** letters in Ahab's name, and H3789
9 And she **w** in the letters, saying, H3789
2Ki 10: 1 And Jehu **w** letters, and sent to H3789
6 Then he **w** a letter the second time to H3789
17:37 which he **w** for you, ye shall observe H3789
1Ch 24: 6 *one* of the Levites, **w** them before the H3789
2Ch 30: 1 Israel and Judah, and **w** letters also to H3789
32:17 He **w** also letters to rail on the LORD H3789
Ezr 4: 6 of his reign, **w** they *unto him* an H3789
7 And in the days of Artaxerxes **w** H3789
8 the scribe **w** a letter against Jerusalem H3790
9 Then *w* Rehum the chancellor, and
Est 8: 5 Agagite, which he **w** to destroy the Jews H3789
10 And he **w** in the king Ahasuerus' name, H3789
9:20 And Mordecai **w** these things, and sent H3789
29 Mordecai the Jew, **w** with all authority, H3789
Jer 36: 4 and Baruch **w** from the mouth of H3789
18 and I **w** *them* with ink in the book. H3789
27 **w** at the mouth of Jeremiah, saying, H3789
32 son of Neriah; who **w** therein from the H3789
51:60 So Jeremiah **w** in a book all the evil H3789
Dan 5: 5 a man's hand, and **w** over against the H3790
5 king saw the part of the hand that **w**. H3790
6:25 Then king Darius **w** unto all people, H3790
7: 1 his bed: then he **w** the dream, *and* told H3790
Mk 10: 5 of your heart he **w** you this precept. *G1125*
12:19 Master, Moses **w** unto us, If a man's *G1125*
Lk 1:63 And he asked for a writing table, and **w**, *G1125*
20:28 Saying, Master, Moses **w** unto us, If *G1125*
Jn 5:46 have believed me: for he **w** of me. *G1125*
8: 6 and with *his* finger **w** on the ground, *as* *G1125*
8 And again he stooped down, and **w** on *G1125*
19:19 And Pilate **w** a title, and put *it* on the *G1125*
21:24 of these things, and **w** these things: and *G1125*
Act 15:23 And they **w** *letters* by them after this *G1125*
18:27 the brethren **w**, exhorting the disciples *G1125*
23:25 And he **w** a letter after this manner: *G1125*
Ro 16:22 I Tertius, who **w** *this* epistle, salute you *G1125*
1Co 5: 9 I **w** unto you in an epistle not to *G1125*
7: 1 things whereof ye **w** unto me: *It is* good *G1125*
2Co 2: 3 And I **w** this same unto you, lest, when *G1125*
4 and anguish of heart I **w** unto you with *G1125*
7:12 Wherefore, though I **w** unto you, *I did* *G1125*
Eph 3: 3 the mystery; (as I **w** afore in few words, *G4270*
Phlm 21 Having confidence in thy obedience I **w** *G1125*
2Jn 5 lady, not as though I **w** a new *G1125*
3Jn 9 I **w** unto the church: but Diotrephes, *G1125*

WROTH

Gen 4: 5 was very **w**, and his countenance fell. H2734
6 **w**? and why is thy countenance fallen? H2734
31:36 And Jacob was **w**, and chode with H2734
34: 7 and they were very **w**, because he had H2734
40: 2 And Pharaoh was **w** against two *of* his H7107
41:10 Pharaoh was **w** with his servants, and H7107
Ex 16:20 stank: and Moses was **w** with them. H7107
Nu 16:15 And Moses was very **w**, and said unto H2734
22 thou be **w** with all the congregation? H7107
31:14 And Moses was **w** with the officers of H7107
Dt 1:34 words, and was **w**, and sware, saying, H7107
3:26 But the LORD was **w** with me for your H5674
9:19 the LORD was **w** against you to destroy H7107
Jos 22:18 to morrow he will be **w** with the whole H7107
1Sa 18: 8 And Saul was very **w**, and the saying H2734
20: 7 but if he be very **w**, *then* be sure that H2734
29: 4 Philistines were **w** with him; and the H7107
2Sa 3: 8 Then was Abner very **w** for the words H2734
13:21 heard of all these things, he was very **w**. H2734
22: 8 moved and shook, because he was **w**. H2734
2Ki 5:11 But Naaman was **w**, and went away, H7107
13:19 And the man of God was **w** with him, H7107
2Ch 16:10 Then Asa was **w** with the seer, and put H3707
26:19 Then Uzziah was **w**, and *had* a censer H2196
19 and while he was **w** with the priests, H2196
28: 9 your fathers was **w** with Judah, he hath H2534
Neh 4: 1 the wall, he was **w**, and took great H2734
7 to be stopped, then they were very **w**, H2734
Est 1:12 very **w**, and his anger burned in him. H7107
2:21 kept the door, were **w**, and sought to lay H7107
Ps 18: 7 and were shaken, because he was **w**. H2734
78:21 *this*, and was **w**: so a fire was kindled H5674
59 When God heard *this*, he was **w**, and H5674
62 sword; and was **w** with his inheritance. H5674
89:38 thou hast been **w** with thine anointed. H5674
Isa 28:21 he shall be **w** as *in* the valley of Gibeon, H7264
47: 6 I was **w** with my people, I have polluted H7107
54: 9 not be **w** with thee, nor rebuke thee. H7107
57:16 will I be always **w**: for the spirit should H7107
17 was I **w**, and smote him: I hid H7107
17 I hid me, and was **w**, and he went on H7107
64: 5 behold, thou art **w**; for we have sinned: H7107
9 Be not **w** very sore, O LORD, neither H7107
Jer 37:15 Wherefore the princes were **w** with H7107
Lam 5:22 rejected us; thou art very **w** against us. H7107
Mt 2:16 was exceeding **w**, and sent forth, and *G2373*
18:34 And his lord was **w**, and delivered him *G3710*
22: 7 *thereof*, he was **w**: and he sent forth his *G3710*
Rev 12:17 And the dragon was **w** with the *G3710*

WROUGHT

Gen 34: 7 because he had **w** folly in Israel in lying H6213
Ex 10: 2 things I have **w** in Egypt, and my signs H5953
26:36 fine twined linen, **w** with needlework.
27:16 fine twined linen, **w** with needlework: H4639
36: 1 Then **w** Bezaleel and Aholiab, and H6213
4 And all the wise men, that **w** all the H6213
8 among them that **w** the work of the H6213
39: 6 And they **w** onyx stones inclosed in H6213
Lev 20:12 to death: they have **w** confusion; their H6213
Nu 23:23 Jacob and of Israel, What hath God **w**! H6466
31:51 the gold of them, *even* all **w** jewels. H4639
Dt 13:14 such abomination is **w** among you; H6213
17: 2 woman, that hath **w** wickedness in the H6213
4 *that* such abomination is **w** in Israel: H6213
21: 3 hath not been **w** with, *and* which hath H5647
22:21 because she hath **w** folly in Israel, to H6213
31:18 which they shall have **w**, in that they are H6213
Jos 7:15 and because he hath **w** folly in Israel. H6213
Jdg 20:10 all the folly that they have **w** in Israel. H6213
Ru 2:19 whom she had **w**, and said, The man's H6213
19 name with whom I **w** to day *is* Boaz. H6213
1Sa 6: 6 when he had **w** wonderfully among H5953
11:13 the LORD hath **w** salvation in Israel. H6213
14:45 die, who hath **w** this great salvation H6213
45 for he hath **w** with God this day. So H6213
19: 5 and the LORD **w** a great salvation for H6213
2Sa 18:13 Otherwise I should have **w** falsehood H6213
23:10 and the LORD **w** a great victory that H6213
12 and the LORD **w** a great victory. H6213
1Ki 5:16 over the people that **w** in the work. H6213
7:14 to king Solomon, and **w** all his work. H6213
26 brim thereof was **w** like the brim of a H4639
1Ki 9:23 rule over the people that **w** in the work. H6213
16:20 treason that he **w**, *are* they not written H7194
25 But Omri **w** evil in the eyes of the H6213
2Ki 3: 2 And he **w** evil in the sight of the LORD; H6213
12:11 that **w** upon the house of the LORD, H6213
17:11 before them; and **w** wicked things to H6213
21: 6 and wizards: he **w** much wickedness in H6213
1Ch 4:21 **w** fine linen, of the house of Ashbea, H5656
22: 2 hew **w** stones to build the house of God. H1496
2Ch 3:14 fine linen, and **w** cherubims thereon. H5927
21: 6 to wife: and he **w** *that which was* evil H6213
24:12 and also such as **w** iron and brass to H2796
13 So the workmen **w**, and the work was H6213
31:20 all Judah, and **w** *that which was* good H6213
33: 6 with wizards: he **w** much evil in the H6213
34:10 the workmen that **w** in the house of the H6213
13 of all that **w** the work in any manner H6213
Neh 4:16 of my servants **w** in the work, and the H6213
17 one of his hands **w** in the work, and H6213
6:16 that this work was **w** of our God. H6213
9:18 Egypt, and had **w** great provocations; H6213
26 to thee, and they **w** great provocations. H6213
Job 12: 9 that the hand of the LORD hath **w** this? H6213
36:23 or who can say, Thou hast **w** iniquity? H6466
Ps 31:19 *which* thou hast **w** for them that trust H6466
45:13 within: her clothing *is* of **w** gold. H4865
68:28 O God, that which thou hast **w** for us. H6466
78:43 How he had **w** his signs in Egypt, and H7760
139:15 **w** in the lowest parts of the earth. H7551
Ecc 2:11 my hands had **w**, and on the labour H6213
17 the work that is **w** under the sun *is* H6213
Isa 26:12 for thou also hast **w** all our works in us. H6466
18 wind; we have not **w** any deliverance in H6213
41: 4 Who hath **w** and done *it*, calling the H6466
Jer 11:15 *seeing* she hath **w** lewdness with many, H6213
18: 3 behold, he **w** a work on the wheels. H6213
Ezk 20: 9 But I **w** for my name's sake, that it H6213
14 But I **w** for my name's sake, that it H6213
22 mine hand, and **w** for my name's sake, H6213
44 when I have **w** with you for my name's H6213
29:20 they **w** for me, saith the Lord GOD. H6213
Dan 4: 2 that the high God hath **w** toward me. H5648
Jna 1:11 us? for the sea **w**, and was tempestuous. H1980
13 **w**, and was tempestuous against them. H1980
Zep 2: 3 earth, which have **w** his judgment; seek H6466
Mt 20:12 Saying, These last have **w** *but* one *G4160*
26:10 for she hath **w** a good work upon me. *G2038*
Mk 6: 2 such mighty works are **w** by his hands? *G1096*
14: 6 ye her? she hath **w** a good work on me. *G2038*
Jn 3:21 made manifest, that they are **w** in God. *G2038*
Act 5:12 and wonders **w** among the people; *G1096*
15:12 had **w** among the Gentiles by them. *G4160*
18: 3 abode with them, and **w**: for by their *G2038*
19:11 And God **w** special miracles by the *G4160*
21:19 **w** among the Gentiles by his ministry. *G4160*
Ro 7: 8 commandment, **w** in me all manner of *G2716*
15:18 Christ hath not **w** by me, to make the *G2716*
2Co 5: 5 Now he that hath **w** us for the selfsame *G2716*
7:11 what carefulness it **w** in you, yea, *what* *G2716*
12:12 Truly the signs of an apostle were **w** *G2716*
Gal 2: 8 (For he that **w** effectually in Peter to *G1754*
Eph 1:20 Which he **w** in Christ, when he raised *G1754*
2Th 3: 8 for nought; but **w** with labour and *G2038*
Heb 11:33 kingdoms, **w** righteousness, obtained *G2038*
Jas 2:22 Seest thou how faith **w** with his works, *G4903*
1Pt 4: 3 may suffice us to have **w** the will of the *G2716*
2Jn 8 **w**, but that we receive a full reward. *G2038*
Rev 19:20 false prophet that **w** miracles before *G4160*

WROUGHTEST

Ru 2:19 to day? and where **w** thou? blessed be H6213

WRUNG

Lev 1:15 shall be **w** out at the side of the altar: H4680
5: 9 the blood shall be **w** out at the bottom H4680
Ps 73:10 waters of a full *cup* are **w** out to them. H4680
Isa 51:17 the cup of trembling, *and* **w** *them* out. H4680

Y

YARN

1Ki 10:28 Egypt, and linen **y**: the king's merchants H4723
28 received the linen **y** at a price. H4723
2Ch 1:16 Egypt, and linen **y**: the king's merchants H4723
2Ch 1:16 received the linen **y** at a price. H4723

YE See the Appendix.

YEA See the Appendix.

YEAR

Gen 7:11 In the six hundredth **y** of Noah's life, in H8141
8:13 and first **y**, in the first *month*, the H8141
14: 4 and in the thirteenth **y** they rebelled. H8141
5 And in the fourteenth **y** came H8141

Gen 17:21 unto thee at this set time in the next **y**. H8141
26:12 in the same **y** an hundredfold: and H8141
47:17 with bread for all their cattle for that **y**. H8141
18 When that **y** was ended, they came H8141
18 him the second **y**, and said unto him, H8141
Ex 12: 2 *shall be* the first month of the **y** to you. H8141
5 a male of the first **y**: ye shall take *it* out H8141
13:10 ordinance in his season from **y** to year. H3117
10 ordinance in his season from year to **y**. H3117
23:11 But the seventh **y** thou shalt let it rest
14 thou shalt keep a feast unto me in the **y**. H8141
16 *is* in the end of the **y**, when thou hast H8141
17 Three times in the **y** all thy males shall H8141
29 from before thee in one **y**; lest the land H8141
29:38 of the first **y** day by day continually. H8141
30:10 of it once in a **y** with the blood of the H8141
10 once in the **y** shall he make atonement H8141
34:23 Thrice in the **y** shall all your men H8141
24 before the LORD thy God thrice in the **y**. H8141
40:17 in the second **y**, on the first *day* of the H8141
Lev 9: 3 **y**, without blemish, for a burnt offering; H8141
12: 6 bring a lamb of the first **y** for a burnt H8141
14:10 lamb of the first **y** without blemish, H8141
16:34 all their sins once a **y**. And he did as the H8141
19:24 But in the fourth **y** all the fruit thereof H8141
25 And in the fifth **y** shall ye eat of the H8141
23:12 **y** for a burnt offering unto the LORD. H8141
18 of the first **y**, and one young bullock, H8141
19 first **y** for a sacrifice of peace offerings. H8141
41 seven days in the **y**. *It shall be* a statute H8141
25: 4 But in the seventh **y** shall be a sabbath H8141
5 *for* it is a **y** of rest unto the land. H8141
10 And ye shall hallow the fiftieth **y**, and H8141
11 A jubile shall that fiftieth **y** be unto H8141
13 In the **y** of this jubile ye shall return H8141
20 we eat the seventh **y**? behold, we shall H8141
21 you in the sixth **y**, and it shall bring H8141
22 And ye shall sow the eighth **y**, and eat H8141
22 until the ninth **y**; until her fruits come H8141
28 bought it until the **y** of jubile: and in H8141
29 it within a whole **y** after it is sold; H8141
29 sold; *within* a full **y** may he redeem it. H3117
30 the space of a full **y**, then the house that H8141
33 shall go out in *the* **y** *of* jubile: for the
40 shall serve thee unto the **y** of jubile: H8141
50 him from the **y** that he was sold to H8141
50 sold to him unto the **y** of jubile: and the H8141
52 few years unto the **y** of jubile, then he H8141
54 shall go out in the **y** of jubile, *both* he, H8141
27:17 If he sanctify his field from the **y** of H8141
18 even unto the **y** of the jubile, and it H8141
23 *even* unto the **y** of the jubile: and he H8141
24 In the **y** of the jubile the field shall H8141
Nu 1: 1 in the second **y** after they were come H8141
6:12 bring a lamb of the first **y** for a trespass H8141
14 lamb of the first **y** without blemish for H8141
14 lamb of the first **y** without blemish for H8141
7:15 lamb of the first **y**, for a burnt offering: H8141
17 lambs of the first **y**: this *was* the offering H8141
21 lamb of the first **y**, for a burnt offering: H8141
23 lambs of the first **y**: this *was* the offering H8141
27 lamb of the first **y**, for a burnt offering: H8141
29 lambs of the first **y**: this *was* the offering H8141
33 lamb of the first **y**, for a burnt offering: H8141
35 lambs of the first **y**: this *was* the offering H8141
39 lamb of the first **y**, for a burnt offering: H8141
41 lambs of the first **y**: this *was* the offering H8141
45 lamb of the first **y**, for a burnt offering: H8141
47 lambs of the first **y**: this *was* the offering H8141
51 lamb of the first **y**, for a burnt offering: H8141
53 lambs of the first **y**: this *was* the offering H8141
57 lamb of the first **y**, for a burnt offering: H8141
59 lambs of the first **y**: this *was* the offering H8141
63 lamb of the first **y**, for a burnt offering: H8141
65 lambs of the first **y**: this *was* the offering H8141
69 lamb of the first **y**, for a burnt offering: H8141
71 lambs of the first **y**: this *was* the offering H8141
75 lamb of the first **y**, for a burnt offering: H8141
77 lambs of the first **y**: this *was* the offering H8141
81 lamb of the first **y**, for a burnt offering: H8141
83 lambs of the first **y**: this *was* the offering H8141
87 lambs of the first **y** twelve, with their H8141
88 lambs of the first **y** sixty. This *was* the H8141
9: 1 of the second **y** after they were come H8141
22 days, or a month, or a **y**, that the cloud H3117
10:11 in the second **y**, that the cloud was H8141
14:34 each day for a **y**, shall ye bear your H8141
15:27 she goat of the first **y** for a sin offering. H8141
28: 3 lambs of the first **y** without spot day by H8141
Nu 28: 9 lambs of the first **y** without spot, and H8141
11 seven lambs of the first **y** without spot; H8141
14 month throughout the months of the **y**. H8141
19 lambs of the first **y**: they shall be unto H8141
27 one ram, seven lambs of the first **y**; H8141
29: 2 lambs of the first **y** without blemish: H8141
8 lambs of the first **y**; they shall be unto H8141
13 first **y**; they shall be without blemish: H8141
17 lambs of the first **y** without spot: H8141
20 lambs of the first **y** without blemish; H8141
23 lambs of the first **y** without blemish: H8141
26 lambs of the first **y** without spot: H8141
29 lambs of the first **y** without blemish: H8141
32 lambs of the first **y** without blemish: H8141
36 lambs of the first **y** without blemish: H8141
33:38 in the fortieth **y** after the children of H8141
Dt 1: 3 And it came to pass in the fortieth **y**, in H8141
11:12 of the **y** even unto the end of the year. H8141
12 of the year even unto the end of the **y**. H8141
14:22 that the field bringeth forth **y** by year. H8141
22 that the field bringeth forth year by **y**. H8141
28 **y**, and shalt lay *it* up within thy gates: H8141
15: 9 The seventh **y**, the year of release, H8141
9 The seventh year, the **y** of release, is at H8141
12 **y** thou shalt let him go free from thee. H8141
20 the LORD thy God **y** by year in the H8141
20 thy God year by **y** in the place which H8141
16:16 Three times in a **y** shall all thy males H8141
24: 5 free at home one **y**, and shall cheer up H8141
26:12 increase the third **y**, *which is* the year of H8141
12 year, *which is* the **y** of tithing, and hast H8141
31:10 **y** of release, in the feast of tabernacles, H8141
Jos 5:12 of the fruit of the land of Canaan that **y**. H8141
Jdg 10: 8 And that **y** they vexed and oppressed H8141
11:40 Jephthah the Gileadite four days in a **y**. H8141
17:10 of silver by the **y**, and a suit of apparel, H3117
1Sa 1: 7 And *as* he did so **y** by year, when she H8141
7 And *as* he did so year by **y**, when she H8141
2:19 *it* to him from **y** to year, when she H3117
19 him from year to **y**, when she came up H3117
7:16 And he went from **y** to year in circuit to H8141
16 And he went from year to **y** in circuit to H8141
13: 1 Saul reigned one **y**; and when he had H8141
27: 7 was a full **y** and four months. H3117
2Sa 11: 1 And it came to pass, after the **y** was H8141
21: 1 of David three years, **y** after year; and H8141
1 years, year after **y**; and David inquired H8141
1Ki 4: 7 man his month in a **y** made provision. H8141
5:11 thus gave Solomon to Hiram **y** by year. H8141
11 thus gave Solomon to Hiram year by **y**. H8141
6: 1 and eightieth **y** after the children of H8141
1 in the fourth **y** of Solomon's reign over H8141
37 In the fourth **y** was the foundation of H8141
38 And in the eleventh **y**, in the month Bul, H8141
9:25 And three times in a **y** did Solomon H8141
10:14 to Solomon in one **y** was six hundred H8141
25 horses, and mules, a rate **y** by year. H8141
25 horses, and mules, a rate year by **y**. H8141
14:25 And it came to pass in the fifth **y** of H8141
15: 1 Now in the eighteenth **y** of king H8141
9 And in the twentieth **y** of Jeroboam H8141
25 in the second **y** of Asa king of Judah, H8141
28 Even in the third **y** of Asa king of Judah H8141
33 In the third **y** of Asa king of Judah H8141
16: 8 In the twenty and sixth **y** of Asa king of H8141
10 and seventh **y** of Asa king of Judah, H8141
15 In the twenty and seventh **y** of Asa king H8141
23 In the thirty and first **y** of Asa king of H8141
29 And in the thirty and eighth **y** of Asa H8141
18: 1 to Elijah in the third **y**, saying, Go, shew H8141
20:22 the return of the **y** the king of Syria will H8141
26 at the return of the **y**, that Ben-hadad H8141
22: 2 And it came to pass in the third **y**, that H8141
41 in the fourth **y** of Ahab king of Israel. H8141
51 the seventeenth **y** of Jehoshaphat king H8141
2Ki 1:17 in the second **y** of Jehoram the son H8141
3: 1 the eighteenth **y** of Jehoshaphat king H8141
8:16 And in the fifth **y** of Joram the son of H8141
25 In the twelfth **y** of Joram the son of H8141
26 he reigned one **y** in Jerusalem. And his H8141
9:29 And in the eleventh **y** of Joram the son H8141
11: 4 And the seventh **y** Jehoiada sent and H8141
12: 1 In the seventh **y** of Jehu Jehoash began H8141
6 and twentieth **y** of king Jehoash the H8141
13: 1 In the three and twentieth **y** of Joash H8141
10 In the thirty and seventh **y** of Joash H8141
20 the land at the coming in of the **y**. H8141
14: 1 In the second **y** of Joash son of H8141
23 In the fifteenth **y** of Amaziah the son of H8141
2Ki 15: 1 In the twenty and seventh **y** of H8141
8 In the thirty and eighth **y** of Azariah H8141
13 nine and thirtieth **y** of Uzziah king of H8141
17 In the nine and thirtieth **y** of Azariah H8141
23 In the fiftieth **y** of Azariah king of H8141
27 In the two and fiftieth **y** of Azariah king H8141
30 **y** of Jotham the son of Uzziah. H8141
32 In the second **y** of Pekah the son of H8141
16: 1 In the seventeenth **y** of Pekah the son H8141
17: 1 In the twelfth **y** of Ahaz king of Judah H8141
4 as *he had done* **y** by year: therefore the H8141
4 *had done* year by **y**: therefore the king H8141
6 In the ninth **y** of Hoshea the king of H8141
18: 1 Now it came to pass in the third **y** of H8141
9 And it came to pass in the fourth **y** of H8141
9 *was* the seventh **y** of Hoshea son of H8141
10 *even* in the sixth **y** of Hezekiah, that *is* H8141
10 that *is* the ninth **y** of Hoshea king of H8141
13 Now in the fourteenth **y** of king H8141
19:29 Ye shall eat this **y** such things as grow H8141
29 and in the second **y** that which H8141
29 and in the third **y** sow ye, and reap, H8141
22: 3 And it came to pass in the eighteenth **y** H8141
23:23 But in the eighteenth **y** of king Josiah, H8141
24:12 took him in the eighth **y** of his reign. H8141
25: 1 And it came to pass in the ninth **y** of H8141
2 unto the eleventh **y** of king Zedekiah. H8141
8 which *is* the nineteenth **y** of king H8141
27 seven and thirtieth **y** of the captivity of H8141
27 of Babylon in the **y** that he began to H8141
1Ch 20: 1 And it came to pass, that after the **y** H8141
26:31 In the fortieth **y** of the reign of David H8141
27: 1 all the months of the **y**, of every course H8141
2Ch 3: 2 month, in the fourth **y** of his reign. H8141
8:13 three times in the **y**, *even* in the feast of H8141
9:13 to Solomon in one **y** was six hundred H8141
24 horses, and mules, a rate **y** by year. H8141
24 horses, and mules, a rate year by **y**. H8141
12: 2 And it came to pass, *that* in the fifth **y** H8141
13: 1 Now in the eighteenth **y** of king H8141
15:10 in the fifteenth **y** of the reign of Asa. H8141
19 five and thirtieth **y** of the reign of Asa. H8141
16: 1 In the six and thirtieth **y** of the reign of H8141
12 And Asa in the thirty and ninth **y** of his H8141
13 in the one and fortieth **y** of his reign. H8141
17: 7 Also in the third **y** of his reign he sent H8141
22: 2 and he reigned one **y** in Jerusalem. His H8141
23: 1 And in the seventh **y** Jehoiada H8141
24: 5 of your God from **y** to year, and see H8141
5 your God from year to **y**, and see that ye H8141
23 And it came to pass at the end of the **y**, H8141
27: 5 him the same **y** an hundred talents H8141
5 him, both the second **y**, and the third. H8141
29: 3 He in the first **y** of his reign, in the first H8141
34: 3 For in the eighth **y** of his reign, while he H8141
3 and in the twelfth **y** he began to purge H8141
8 Now in the eighteenth **y** of his reign, H8141
35:19 In the eighteenth **y** of the reign of H8141
36:10 And when the **y** was expired, king H8141
22 Now in the first **y** of Cyrus king of H8141
Ezr 1: 1 Now in the first **y** of Cyrus king of H8141
3: 8 Now in the second **y** of their coming H8141
4:24 **y** of the reign of Darius king of Persia. H8140
5:13 But in the first **y** of Cyrus the king of H8140
6: 3 In the first **y** of Cyrus the king *the same* H8140
15 sixth **y** of the reign of Darius the king. H8140
7: 7 in the seventh **y** of Artaxerxes the king. H8141
8 which *was* in the seventh **y** of the king. H8141
Neh 1: 1 **y**, as I was in Shushan the palace, H8141
2: 1 in the twentieth **y** of Artaxerxes the H8141
5:14 from the twentieth **y** even unto the two H8141
14 two and thirtieth **y** of Artaxerxes the H8141
10:31 **y**, and the exaction of every debt. H8141
34 at times appointed **y** by year, to burn H8141
34 appointed year by **y**, to burn upon the H8141
35 **y** by year, unto the house of the LORD: H8141
35 year by **y**, unto the house of the LORD: H8141
13: 6 two and thirtieth **y** of Artaxerxes king H8141
Est 1: 3 In the third **y** of his reign, he made a H8141
2:16 Tebeth, in the seventh **y** of his reign. H8141
3: 7 in the twelfth **y** of king Ahasuerus, H8141
9:27 to their *appointed* time every **y**; H8141
Job 3: 6 the days of the **y**, let it not come into H8141
Ps 65:11 Thou crownest the **y** with thy H8141
Isa 6: 1 In the **y** that king Uzziah died I saw H8141
14:28 In the **y** that king Ahaz died was this H8141
20: 1 In the **y** that Tartan came unto H8141
21:16 unto me, Within a **y**, according to the H8141
29: 1 add ye **y** to year; let them kill sacrifices. H8141

Isa 29: 1 add ye year to y; let them kill sacrifices. H8141
34: 8 *and* the y of recompences for H8141
36: 1 Now it came to pass in the fourteenth y H8141
37:30 Ye shall eat *this* y such as groweth of H8141
30 and the second y that which springeth H8141
30 and in the third y sow ye, and reap, H8141
61: 2 To proclaim the acceptable y of the H8141
63: 4 and the y of my redeemed is come. H8141
Jer 1: 2 Judah, in the thirteenth y of his reign. H8141
3 of the eleventh y of Zedekiah the son H8141
11:23 Anathoth, *even* the y of their visitation. H8141
17: 8 be careful in the y of drought, neither H8141
23:12 y of their visitation, saith the LORD. H8141
25: 1 in the fourth y of Jehoiakim the son H8141
1 y of Nebuchadrezzar king of Babylon; H8141
3 From the thirteenth y of Josiah the son H8141
3 and twentieth y, the word of the LORD H8141
28: 1 And it came to pass the same y, in the H8141
1 in the fourth y, *and* in the fifth month, H8141
16 face of the earth: this y thou shalt die, H8141
17 died the same y in the seventh month. H8141
32: 1 LORD in the tenth y of Zedekiah king H8141
1 the eighteenth y of Nebuchadrezzar. H8141
36: 1 And it came to pass in the fourth y of H8141
9 And it came to pass in the fifth y of H8141
39: 1 In the ninth y of Zedekiah king of H8141
2 *And* in the eleventh y of Zedekiah, in H8141
45: 1 in the fourth y of Jehoiakim the son H8141
46: 2 in the fourth y of Jehoiakim the son H8141
48:44 y of their visitation, saith the LORD. H8141
51:46 shall both come *one* y, and after that in H8141
46 that in *another* y *shall come* a rumour, H8141
59 in the fourth y of his reign. And *this* H8141
52: 4 And it came to pass in the ninth y of H8141
5 unto the eleventh y of king Zedekiah. H8141
12 the nineteenth y of Nebuchadrezzar H8141
28 in the seventh y three thousand Jews H8141
29 In the eighteenth y of Nebuchadrezzar H8141
30 In the three and twentieth y of H8141
31 seven and thirtieth y of the captivity of H8141
31 in the *first* y of his reign lifted up H8141
Ezk 1: 1 Now it came to pass in the thirtieth y, in H8141
2 fifth y of king Jehoiachin's captivity, H8141
4: 6 I have appointed thee each day for a y. H8141
8: 1 And it came to pass in the sixth y, in the H8141
20: 1 And it came to pass in the seventh y, in H8141
24: 1 Again in the ninth y, in the tenth H8141
26: 1 And it came to pass in the eleventh y, in H8141
29: 1 In the tenth y, in the tenth *month*, in the H8141
17 and twentieth y, in the first *month*, in H8141
30:20 And it came to pass in the eleventh y, in H8141
31: 1 And it came to pass in the eleventh y, in H8141
32: 1 And it came to pass in the twelfth y, in H8141
17 It came to pass also in the twelfth y, in H8141
33:21 And it came to pass in the twelfth y of H8141
40: 1 In the five and twentieth y of our H8141
1 beginning of the y, in the tenth *day* of H8141
1 in the fourteenth y after that the city H8141
46:13 *of* a lamb of the first y without blemish: H8141
17 it shall be his to the y of liberty; after it H8141
Dan 1: 1 In the third y of the reign of Jehoiakim H8141
21 *even* unto the first y of king Cyrus. H8141
2: 1 And in the second y of the reign of H8141
7: 1 In the first y of Belshazzar king of H8140
8: 1 In the third y of the reign of king H8141
9: 1 In the first y of Darius the son of H8141
2 In the first y of his reign I Daniel H8141
10: 1 In the third y of Cyrus king of Persia a H8141
11: 1 Also I in the first y of Darius the Mede, H8141
Mic 6: 6 burnt offerings, with calves of a y old? H8141
Hag 1: 1 In the second y of Darius the king, in H8141
15 in the second y of Darius the king. H8141
2:10 in the second y of Darius, came the H8141
Zec 1: 1 In the eighth month, in the second y of H8141
7 in the second y of Darius, came the H8141
7: 1 And it came to pass in the fourth y of H8141
14:16 even go up from y to year to worship H8141
16 go up from year to y to worship the H8141
Lk 2:41 every y at the feast of the passover. *G2596*
3: 1 Now in the fifteenth y of the reign of *G2094*
4:19 To preach the acceptable y of the Lord. *G1763*
13: 8 let it alone this y also, till I shall dig *G2094*
Jn 11:49 priest that same y, said unto them, Ye *G1763*
51 high priest that y, he prophesied that *G1763*
18:13 which was the high priest that same y. *G1763*
Act 11:26 to pass, that a whole y they assembled *G1763*
18:11 And he continued *there* a y and six *G1763*
2Co 8:10 to do, but also to be forward a y ago. *G4070*
9: 2 was ready a y ago; and your zeal hath *G4070*
Heb 9: 7 alone once every y, not without blood, *G1763*
25 holy place every y with blood of others; *G2596*
10: 1 sacrifices which they offered y by year *G1763*
1 offered year by y continually make the *G2596*
3 again *made* of sins every y. *G2596*
Jas 4:13 a y, and buy and sell, and get gain: *G1763*
Rev 9:15 a y, for to slay the third part of men. *G1763*

YEARLY

Lev 25:53 *And* as a y hired servant shall he be H8141
Jdg 11:40 *That* the daughters of Israel went y to H3117
21:19 LORD in Shiloh y *in a place* which *is* on H3117
1Sa 1: 3 And this man went up out of his city y H3117
21 the LORD the y sacrifice, and his vow. H3117
2:19 her husband to offer the y sacrifice. H3117
20: 6 *is* a y sacrifice there for all the family. H3117
Neh 10:32 charge ourselves y with the third part H8141
Est 9:21 and the fifteenth day of the same, y, H8141

YEARN

Gen 43:30 for his bowels did y upon his brother: H3648

YEARNED

1Ki 3:26 for her bowels y upon her son, and she H3648

YEARS

Gen 1:14 and for seasons, and for days, and y: H8141
5: 3 and thirty y, and begat *a son* in his H8141
4 y: and he begat sons and daughters: H8141
5 nine hundred and thirty y: and he died. H8141
6 And Seth lived an hundred and five y, H8141
7 seven y, and begat sons and daughters: H8141
8 hundred and twelve y: and he died. H8141
9 And Enos lived ninety y, and begat H8141
10 fifteen y, and begat sons and daughters: H8141
11 nine hundred and five y: and he died. H8141
12 And Cainan lived seventy y, and begat H8141
13 forty y, and begat sons and daughters: H8141
14 nine hundred and ten y: and he died. H8141
15 And Mahalaleel lived sixty and five y, H8141
16 thirty y, and begat sons and daughters: H8141
17 hundred ninety and five y: and he died. H8141
18 sixty and two y, and he begat Enoch: H8141
19 y, and begat sons and daughters: H8141
20 hundred sixty and two y: and he died. H8141
21 And Enoch lived sixty and five y, and H8141
22 y, and begat sons and daughters: H8141
23 were three hundred sixty and five y: H8141
25 eighty and seven y, and begat Lamech: H8141
26 two y, and begat sons and daughters: H8141
27 hundred sixty and nine y: and he died. H8141
28 eighty and two y, and begat a son: H8141
30 five y, and begat sons and daughters: H8141
31 seventy and seven y: and he died. H8141
32 And Noah was five hundred y old: and H8141
6: 3 days shall be an hundred and twenty y. H8141
7: 6 And Noah *was* six hundred y old when H8141
9:28 the flood three hundred and fifty y. H8141
29 nine hundred and fifty y: and he died. H8141
11:10 Shem *was* an hundred y old, and begat H8141
10 begat Arphaxad two y after the flood: H8141
11 y, and begat sons and daughters. H8141
12 And Arphaxad lived five and thirty y, H8141
13 three y, and begat sons and daughters. H8141
14 And Salah lived thirty y, and begat H8141
15 three y, and begat sons and daughters. H8141
16 And Eber lived four and thirty y, and H8141
17 thirty y, and begat sons and daughters. H8141
18 And Peleg lived thirty y, and begat Reu: H8141
19 nine y, and begat sons and daughters. H8141
20 And Reu lived two and thirty y, and H8141
21 seven y, and begat sons and daughters. H8141
22 And Serug lived thirty y, and begat H8141
23 y, and begat sons and daughters. H8141
24 And Nahor lived nine and twenty y, and H8141
25 y, and begat sons and daughters. H8141
26 And Terah lived seventy y, and begat H8141
32 and five y: and Terah died in Haran. H8141
12: 4 y old when he departed out of Haran. H8141
14: 4 Twelve y they served Chedorlaomer, H8141
15: 9 an heifer of three y old, and a she goat H8027
9 a she goat of three y old, and a ram of H8027
9 old, and a ram of three y old, and a H8027
13 they shall afflict them four hundred y; H8141
16: 3 had dwelt ten y in the land of Canaan, H8141
16 And Abram *was* fourscore and six y H8141
17: 1 And when Abram was ninety y old and H8141
17 him that is an hundred y old? and shall H8141
17 shall Sarah, that is ninety y old, bear? H8141
Gen 17:24 And Abraham *was* ninety y old and H8141
25 And Ishmael his son *was* thirteen y old, H8141
21: 5 And Abraham was an hundred y old, H8141
23: 1 seven and twenty y old: *these were* the H8141
1 *these were* the y of the life of Sarah. H8141
25: 7 And these *are* the days of the y of H8141
7 an hundred threescore and fifteen y. H8141
8 full *of y;* and was gathered to his people.
17 And these *are* the y of the life of H8141
17 thirty and seven y: and he gave up the H8141
20 And Isaac was forty y old when he took H8141
26 threescore y old when she bare them. H8141
26:34 And Esau was forty y old when he took H8141
29:18 y for Rachel thy younger daughter. H8141
20 And Jacob served seven y for Rachel; H8141
27 shalt serve with me yet seven other y. H8141
30 and served with him yet seven other y. H8141
31:38 This twenty y *have* I *been* with thee; H8141
41 Thus have I been twenty y in thy house; H8141
41 thee fourteen y for thy two daughters, H8141
41 daughters, and six y for thy cattle: and H8141
35:28 Isaac were an hundred and fourscore y. H8141
37: 2 *being* seventeen y old, was feeding the H8141
41: 1 at the end of two full y, that Pharaoh H8141
26 The seven good kine *are* seven y; and H8141
26 good ears *are* seven y: the dream *is* one. H8141
27 them *are* seven y; and the seven empty H8141
27 east wind shall be seven y of famine. H8141
29 Behold, there come seven y of great H8141
30 after them seven y of famine; and all H8141
34 land of Egypt in the seven plenteous y. H8141
35 food of those good y that come, and lay H8141
36 against the seven y of famine, which H8141
46 And Joseph *was* thirty y old when he H8141
47 And in the seven plenteous y the earth H8141
48 food of the seven y, which were in the H8141
50 two sons before the y of famine came, H8141
53 And the seven y of plenteousness, that H8141
54 And the seven y of dearth began to H8141
45: 6 For these two y *hath* the famine *been* in H8141
6 yet *there are* five y, in the which *there* H8141
11 yet *there are* five y of famine; lest thou, H8141
47: 9 The days of the y of my pilgrimage *are* H8141
9 and thirty y: few and evil have the H8141
9 the days of the y of my life been, and H8141
9 unto the days of the y of the life of my H8141
28 Egypt seventeen y: so the whole age of H8141
28 was an hundred forty and seven y. H8141
50:22 and Joseph lived an hundred and ten y. H8141
26 an hundred and ten y old: and they H8141
Ex 6:16 and Merari: and the y of the life of Levi H8141
16 *were* an hundred thirty and seven y. H8141
18 Uzziel: and the y of the life of Kohath H8141
18 *were* an hundred thirty and three y. H8141
20 Moses: and the y of the life of Amram H8141
20 an hundred and thirty and seven y. H8141
7: 7 And Moses *was* fourscore y old, and H8141
7 y old, when they spake unto Pharaoh. H8141
12:40 Egypt, *was* four hundred and thirty y. H8141
41 and thirty y, even the selfsame day H8141
16:35 eat manna forty y, until they came to a H8141
21: 2 If thou buy an Hebrew servant, six y he H8141
23:10 And six y thou shalt sow thy land, and H8141
30:14 from twenty y old and above, shall H8141
38:26 from twenty y old and upward, for H8141
Lev 19:23 three y shall it be as uncircumcised H8141
25: 3 Six y thou shalt sow thy field, and six H8141
3 thy field, and six y thou shalt prune thy H8141
8 seven sabbaths of y unto thee, seven H8141
8 seven times seven y; and the space of H8141
8 seven sabbaths of y shall be unto thee H8141
8 shall be unto thee forty and nine y. H8141
15 According to the number of y after the H8141
15 of y of the fruits he shall sell unto thee: H8141
16 According to the multitude of y thou H8141
16 to the fewness of y thou shalt diminish H8141
16 *the* y of the fruits doth he sell unto thee. H8141
21 and it shall bring forth fruit for three y. H8141
27 Then let him count the y of the sale H8141
50 the number of y, according to the time H8141
51 If *there be* yet many y *behind,* H8141
52 And if there remain but few y unto the H8141
52 unto his y shall he give him again H8141
54 And if he be not redeemed in these y, H8141
27: 3 male from twenty y old even unto sixty H8141
3 old even unto sixty y old, even thy H8141
5 And if *it be* from five y old even unto H8141
5 old even unto twenty y old, then thy H8141
6 old even unto five y old, then thy H8141

Lev 27: 7 And if *it be* from sixty y old and above; H8141
18 according to the y that remain, even H8141
Nu 1: 3 From twenty y old and upward, all that H8141
18 y old and upward, by their polls. H8141
20 male from twenty y old and upward, H8141
22 male from twenty y old and upward, H8141
24 from twenty y old and upward, all H8141
26 from twenty y old and upward, all H8141
28 from twenty y old and upward, all H8141
30 from twenty y old and upward, all H8141
32 from twenty y old and upward, all H8141
34 from twenty y old and upward, all H8141
36 from twenty y old and upward, all H8141
38 from twenty y old and upward, all H8141
40 from twenty y old and upward, all H8141
42 from twenty y old and upward, all H8141
45 from twenty y old and upward, all H8141
4: 3 From thirty y old and upward even H8141
3 even until fifty y old, all that enter into H8141
23 From thirty y old and upward until H8141
23 and upward until fifty y old shalt thou H8141
30 From thirty y old and upward even H8141
30 even unto fifty y old shalt thou number H8141
35 From thirty y old and upward even H8141
35 even unto fifty y old, every one that H8141
39 From thirty y old and upward even H8141
39 even unto fifty y old, every one that H8141
43 From thirty y old and upward even H8141
43 even unto fifty y old, every one that H8141
47 From thirty y old and upward even H8141
47 even unto fifty y old, every one that H8141
8:24 twenty and five y old and upward they H8141
25 And from the age of fifty y they shall H8141
13:22 built seven y before Zoan in Egypt.) H8141
14:29 from twenty y old and upward, which H8141
33 the wilderness forty y, and bear your H8141
34 *even* forty y, and ye shall know my H8141
26: 2 Israel, from twenty y old and upward, H8141
4 from twenty y old and upward; as H8141
32:11 from twenty y old and upward, shall H8141
13 the wilderness forty y, until all the H8141
33:39 three y old when he died in mount Hor. H8141
Dt 2: 7 these forty y the LORD thy God *hath* H8141
14 *was* thirty and eight y; until all the H8141
8: 2 thee these forty y in the wilderness, to H8141
4 neither did thy foot swell, these forty y. H8141
14:28 At the end of three y thou shalt bring H8141
15: 1 At the end of *every* seven y thou shalt H8141
12 and serve thee six y; then in the seventh H8141
18 in serving thee six y: and the LORD thy H8141
29: 5 And I have led you forty y in the H8141
31: 2 and twenty y old this day; I can no H8141
10 end of *every* seven y, in the solemnity of H8141
32: 7 of old, consider the y of many H8141
34: 7 and twenty y old when he died: his H8141
Jos 5: 6 For the children of Israel walked forty y H8141
13: 1 Now Joshua was old *and* stricken in y; H3117
1 *and* stricken in y, and there remaineth H3117
14: 7 Forty y old *was* I when Moses the H8141
10 forty and five y, even since the LORD H8141
10 I *am* this day fourscore and five y old. H8141
24:29 died, *being* an hundred and ten y old. H8141
Jdg 2: 8 died, *being* an hundred and ten y old. H8141
3: 8 served Chushan-rishathaim eight y. H8141
11 And the land had rest forty y. And H8141
14 Eglon the king of Moab eighteen y. H8141
30 And the land had rest fourscore y. H8141
4: 3 of iron; and twenty y he mightily H8141
5:31 his might. And the land had rest forty y. H8141
6: 1 them into the hand of Midian seven y. H8141
25 bullock of seven y old, and throw down H8141
8:28 quietness forty y in the days of Gideon. H8141
9:22 When Abimelech had reigned three y H8141
10: 2 y, and died, and was buried in Shamir. H8141
3 and judged Israel twenty and two y. H8141
8 of Israel: eighteen y, all the children of H8141
11:26 three hundred y? why therefore did ye H8141
12: 7 And Jephthah judged Israel six y. Then H8141
9 his sons. And he judged Israel seven y. H8141
11 Israel; and he judged Israel ten y. H8141
14 ass colts: and he judged Israel eight y. H8141
13: 1 into the hand of the Philistines forty y. H8141
15:20 in the days of the Philistines twenty y. H8141
16:31 father. And he judged Israel twenty y. H8141
Ru 1: 4 and they dwelled there about ten y. H8141
1Sa 4:15 Now Eli was ninety and eight y old; H8141
18 heavy. And he had judged Israel forty y. H8141
7: 2 for it was twenty y: and all the house of H8141
13: 1 when he had reigned two y over Israel, H8141
1Sa 29: 3 days, or these y, and I have found no H8141
2Sa 2:10 Ish-bosheth Saul's son *was* forty y old H8141
10 and reigned two y. But the house of H8141
11 of Judah was seven y and six months. H8141
4: 4 feet. He was five y old when the tidings H8141
5: 4 David *was* thirty y old when he began H8141
4 began to reign, *and* he reigned forty y. H8141
5 over Judah seven y and six months: H8141
5 and three y over all Israel and Judah. H8141
13:23 And it came to pass after two full y, that H8141
38 went to Geshur, and was there three y. H8141
14:28 So Absalom dwelt two full y in H8141
15: 7 And it came to pass after forty y, that H8141
19:32 man, *even* fourscore y old: and he had H8141
35 I *am* this day fourscore y old: *and* can I H8141
21: 1 of David three y, year after year; and H8141
24:13 him, Shall seven y of famine come unto H8141
1Ki 1: 1 *and* stricken in y; and they covered him H3117
2:11 Israel *were* forty y: seven years reigned H8141
11 *were* forty years: seven y reigned he in H8141
11 and three y reigned he in Jerusalem. H8141
39 at the end of three y, that two of the H8141
6:38 of it. So was he seven y in building it. H8141
7: 1 thirteen y, and he finished all his house. H8141
9:10 the end of twenty y, when Solomon had H8141
10:22 once in three y came the navy of H8141
11:42 in Jerusalem over all Israel *was* forty y. H8141
14:20 two and twenty y: and he slept with his H8141
21 *was* forty and one y old when he began H8141
21 reigned seventeen y in Jerusalem, the H8141
15: 2 Three y reigned he in Jerusalem. And H8141
10 And forty and one y reigned he in H8141
25 of Judah, and reigned over Israel two y. H8141
33 all Israel in Tirzah, twenty and four y. H8141
16: 8 to reign over Israel in Tirzah, two y. H8141
23 twelve y: six years reigned he in Tirzah. H8141
23 twelve years: six y reigned he in Tirzah. H8141
29 Israel in Samaria twenty and two y. H8141
17: 1 rain these y, but according to my word. H8141
22: 1 And they continued three y without H8141
42 Jehoshaphat *was* thirty and five y old H8141
42 twenty and five y in Jerusalem. And his H8141
51 of Judah, and reigned two y over Israel. H8141
2Ki 3: 1 king of Judah, and reigned twelve y. H8141
8: 1 shall also come upon the land seven y. H8141
2 in the land of the Philistines seven y. H8141
17 Thirty and two y old was he when he H8141
17 and he reigned eight y in Jerusalem. H8141
26 Two and twenty y old *was* Ahaziah H8141
10:36 in Samaria *was* twenty and eight y. H8141
11: 3 y. And Athaliah did reign over the land. H8141
21 Seven y old *was* Jehoash when he H8141
12: 1 to reign; and forty y reigned he in H8141
13: 1 in Samaria, *and reigned* seventeen y. H8141
10 in Samaria, *and reigned* sixteen y. H8141
14: 2 He was twenty and five y old when he H8141
2 twenty and nine y in Jerusalem. And H8141
17 son of Jehoahaz king of Israel fifteen y. H8141
21 which *was* sixteen y old, and made him H8141
23 Samaria, *and reigned* forty and one y. H8141
15: 2 Sixteen y old was he when he began to H8141
2 two and fifty y in Jerusalem. And his H8141
17 Israel, *and reigned* ten y in Samaria. H8141
23 Israel in Samaria, *and reigned* two y. H8141
27 Israel in Samaria, *and reigned* twenty y. H8141
33 Five and twenty y old was he when he H8141
33 he reigned sixteen y in Jerusalem. And H8141
16: 2 Twenty y old *was* Ahaz when he began H8141
2 reigned sixteen y in Jerusalem, and did H8141
17: 1 to reign in Samaria over Israel nine y. H8141
5 up to Samaria, and besieged it three y. H8141
18: 2 Twenty and five y old was he when he H8141
2 twenty and nine y in Jerusalem. His H8141
10 And at the end of three y they took it: H8141
20: 6 And I will add unto thy days fifteen y; H8141
21: 1 Manasseh *was* twelve y old when he H8141
1 fifty and five y in Jerusalem. And his H8141
19 Amon *was* twenty and two y old when H8141
19 he reigned two y in Jerusalem. And his H8141
22: 1 Josiah *was* eight y old when he began H8141
1 thirty and one y in Jerusalem. And his H8141
23:31 Jehoahaz *was* twenty and three y old H8141
36 Jehoiakim *was* twenty and five y old H8141
36 he reigned eleven y in Jerusalem. And H8141
24: 1 his servant three y: then he turned and H8141
8 Jehoiachin *was* eighteen y old when he H8141
18 Zedekiah *was* twenty and one y old H8141
18 he reigned eleven y in Jerusalem. And H8141
1Ch 2:21 y old; and she bare him Segub. H8141
1Ch 3: 4 he reigned seven y and six months: and H8141
4 Jerusalem he reigned thirty and three y. H8141
23: 3 the age of thirty y and upward: and H8141
24 from the age of twenty y and upward. H8141
27 from twenty y old and above: H8141
27:23 of them from twenty y old and under: H8141
29:27 Israel *was* forty y; seven years reigned H8141
27 *was* forty years; seven y reigned he in H8141
27 and three y reigned he in Jerusalem. H8141
2Ch 8: 1 the end of twenty y, wherein Solomon H8141
9:21 every three y once came the ships H8141
30 in Jerusalem over all Israel forty y. H8141
11:17 strong, three y: for three years they H8141
17 years: for three y they walked in the H8141
12:13 *was* one and forty y old when he began H8141
13 reigned seventeen y in Jerusalem, the H8141
13: 2 He reigned three y in Jerusalem. His H8141
14: 1 In his days the land was quiet ten y. H8141
6 no war in those y; because the LORD H8141
18: 2 And after *certain* y he went down to H8141
20:31 *he was* thirty and five y old when he H8141
31 twenty and five y in Jerusalem. And his H8141
21: 5 Jehoram *was* thirty and two y old when H8141
5 and he reigned eight y in Jerusalem. H8141
19 the end of two y, his bowels fell out by H3117
20 Thirty and two y old was he when he
20 in Jerusalem eight y, and departed H8141
22: 2 Forty and two y old *was* Ahaziah when H8141
12 y: and Athaliah reigned over the land. H8141
24: 1 Joash *was* seven y old when he began H8141
1 he reigned forty y in Jerusalem. His H8141
15 and thirty y old *was he* when he died. H8141
25: 1 Amaziah *was* twenty and five y old H8141
1 twenty and nine y in Jerusalem. And H8141
5 them from twenty y old and above, and H8141
25 son of Jehoahaz king of Israel fifteen y. H8141
26: 1 who *was* sixteen y old, and made him H8141
3 Sixteen y old *was* Uzziah when he H8141
3 fifty and two y in Jerusalem. His H8141
27: 1 Jotham *was* twenty and five y old when H8141
1 he reigned sixteen y in Jerusalem. His H8141
8 He was five and twenty y old when he H8141
8 and reigned sixteen y in Jerusalem. H8141
28: 1 Ahaz *was* twenty y old when he began H8141
1 he reigned sixteen y in Jerusalem: but H8141
29: 1 five and twenty y old, and he reigned H8141
1 nine and twenty y in Jerusalem. And H8141
31:16 of males, from three y old and upward, H8141
17 from twenty y old and upward, in H8141
33: 1 Manasseh *was* twelve y old when he H8141
1 he reigned fifty and five y in Jerusalem: H8141
21 Amon *was* two and twenty y old when H8141
21 reign, and reigned two y in Jerusalem. H8141
34: 1 Josiah *was* eight y old when he began H8141
1 reigned in Jerusalem one and thirty y. H8141
36: 2 Jehoahaz *was* twenty and three y old H8141
5 Jehoiakim *was* twenty and five y old H8141
5 he reigned eleven y in Jerusalem: and H8141
9 Jehoiachin *was* eight y old when he H8141
11 Zedekiah *was* one and twenty y old H8141
11 and reigned eleven y in Jerusalem. H8141
21 sabbath, to fulfil threescore and ten y. H8141
Ezr 3: 8 from twenty y old and upward, to H8141
5:11 these many y ago, which a great king H8140
Neh 5:14 *that is*, twelve y, I and my brethren H8141
9:21 Yea, forty y didst thou sustain them in H8141
30 Yet many y didst thou forbear them, H8141
Job 10: 5 days of man? *are* thy y as man's days, H8141
15:20 number of y is hidden to the oppressor. H8141
16:22 When a few y are come, then I shall go H8141
32: 7 multitude of y should teach wisdom. H8141
36:11 in prosperity, and their y in pleasures. H8141
26 the number of his y be searched out. H8141
42:16 hundred and forty y, and saw his sons, H8141
Ps 31:10 with grief, and my y with sighing: my H8141
61: 6 life: *and* his y as many generations. H8141
77: 5 I have considered the days of old, the y H8141
10 y of the right hand of the most High. H8141
78:33 in vanity, and their y in trouble. H8141
90: 4 For a thousand y in thy sight *are but* as H8141
9 we spend our y as a tale *that is told*. H8141
10 The days of our y *are* threescore years H8141
10 The days of our years *are* threescore y H8141
10 *they be* fourscore y, yet *is* their strength H8141
15 *and* the y *wherein* we have seen evil. H8141
95:10 Forty y long was I grieved with *this* H8141
102:24 thy y *are* throughout all generations. H8141
27 But thou *art* the same, and thy y shall H8141
Prv 4:10 and the y of thy life shall be many. H8141

Prv 5: 9 unto others, and thy y unto the cruel: H8141
9:11 and the y of thy life shall be increased. H8141
10:27 the y of the wicked shall be shortened. H8141
Ecc 6: 3 and live many y, so that the days of his H8141
3 the days of his y be many, and his soul H8141
6 Yea, though he live a thousand y twice H8141
11: 8 But if a man live many y, *and* rejoice in H8141
12: 1 come not, nor the y draw nigh, when H8141
Isa 7: 8 and five y shall Ephraim be broken, H8141
15: 5 Zoar, an heifer of three y old: for by the
16:14 Within three y, as the years of an H8141
14 three years, as the y of an hireling, and H8141
20: 3 and barefoot three y *for* a sign and H8141
21:16 according to the y of an hireling, and H8141
23:15 be forgotten seventy y, according to the H8141
15 seventy y shall Tyre sing as an harlot. H8141
17 the end of seventy y, that the LORD will H8141
32:10 Many days and y shall ye be troubled, H8141
38: 5 I will add unto thy days fifteen y. H8141
10 I am deprived of the residue of my y. H8141
15 all my y in the bitterness of my soul. H8141
65:20 die an hundred y old; but the sinner H8141
20 an hundred y old shall be accursed. H8141
Jer 25:11 serve the king of Babylon seventy y. H8141
12 when seventy y are accomplished, *that* H8141
28: 3 Within two full y will I bring again into H8141
11 the space of two full y. And the prophet H8141
29:10 That after seventy y be accomplished H8141
34:14 At the end of seven y let ye go every H8141
14 served thee six y, thou shalt let him go H8141
48:34 *as* an heifer of three y old: for the waters
52: 1 Zedekiah *was* one and twenty y old H8141
1 he reigned eleven y in Jerusalem. And H8141
Ezk 4: 5 For I have laid upon thee the y of their H8141
22: 4 *even* unto thy y: therefore have I made H8141
29:11 it, neither shall it be inhabited forty y. H8141
12 be desolate forty y: and I will scatter the H8141
13 At the end of forty y will I gather the H8141
38: 8 in the latter y thou shalt come into H8141
17 y that I would bring thee against them? H8141
39: 9 they shall burn them with fire seven y: H8141
Dan 1: 5 them three y, that at the end thereof H8141
5:31 *being* about threescore and two y old. H8140
9: 2 the number of the y, whereof the word H8141
2 y in the desolations of Jerusalem. H8141
11: 6 And in the end of y they shall join H8141
8 *more* y than the king of the north. H8141
13 come after certain y with a great army H8141
Joel 2: 2 it, *even* to the y of many generations. H8141
25 And I will restore to you the y that the H8141
Am 1: 1 of Israel, two y before the earthquake. H8141
2:10 Egypt, and led you forty y through the H8141
4: 4 morning, *and* your tithes after three y: H3117
5:25 wilderness forty y, O house of Israel? H8141
Hab 3: 2 in the midst of the y, in the midst of the H8141
2 in the midst of the y make known; in H8141
Zec 1:12 indignation these threescore and ten y? H8141
7: 3 myself, as I have done these so many y? H8141
5 y, did ye at all fast unto me, *even* to me? H8141
Mal 3: 4 as in the days of old, and as in former y. H8141
Mt 2:16 thereof, from two y old and under, *G1332*
9:20 of blood twelve y, came behind *him*, *G2094*
Mk 5:25 which had an issue of blood twelve y, *G2094*
42 *of the age* of twelve y. And they were *G2094*
Lk 1: 7 they both were *now* well stricken in y. *G2250*
18 old man, and my wife well stricken in y. *G2250*
2:36 an husband seven y from her virginity; *G2094*
37 and four y, which departed not *G2094*
42 And when he was twelve y old, they *G2094*
3:23 to be about thirty y of age, being (as *G2094*
4:25 was shut up three y and six months, *G2094*
8:42 about twelve y of age, and she lay a *G2094*
43 of blood twelve y, which had spent all *G2094*
12:19 laid up for many y; take thine ease, eat, *G2094*
13: 7 these three y I come seeking fruit *G2094*
11 of infirmity eighteen y, and was bowed *G2094*
16 lo, these eighteen y, be loosed from this *G2094*
15:29 Lo, these many y do I serve thee, *G2094*
Jn 2:20 Then said the Jews, Forty and six y was *G2094*
5: 5 had an infirmity thirty and eight y. *G2094*
8:57 y old, and hast thou seen Abraham? *G2094*
Act 4:22 For the man was above forty y old, on *G2094*
7: 6 and entreat *them* evil four hundred y. *G2094*
23 And when he was full forty y old, it *G5063*
30 And when forty y were expired, there *G2094*
36 Red sea, and in the wilderness forty y. *G2094*
42 *the space of* forty y in the wilderness? *G2094*
9:33 bed eight y, and was sick of the palsy. *G2094*
13:18 And about the time of forty y suffered *G5063*
Act 13:20 and fifty y, until Samuel the prophet. *G2094*
21 of Benjamin, by the space of forty y. *G2094*
19:10 by the space of two y; so that all they *G2094*
20:31 by the space of three y I ceased not to *G5148*
24:10 hast been of many y a judge unto this *G2094*
17 Now after many y I came to bring alms *G2094*
27 But after two y Porcius Festus came *G1333*
28:30 And Paul dwelt two whole y in his own *G1333*
Ro 4:19 about an hundred y old, neither yet the *G1541*
15:23 desire these many y to come unto you; *G2094*
2Co 12: 2 above fourteen y ago, (whether in the *G2094*
Gal 1:18 Then after three y I went up to *G2094*
2: 1 Then fourteen y after I went up again *G2094*
3:17 and thirty y after, cannot disannul, *G2094*
4:10 days, and months, and times, and y. *G1763*
1Ti 5: 9 y old, having been the wife of one man, *G2094*
Heb 1:12 art the same, and thy y shall not fail. *G2094*
3: 9 proved me, and saw my works forty y. *G2094*
17 But with whom was he grieved forty y? *G2094*
11:24 By faith Moses, when he was come to y, *G3173*
Jas 5:17 by the space of three y and six months. *G1763*
2Pt 3: 8 y, and a thousand years as one day. *G2094*
8 years, and a thousand y as one day. *G2094*
Rev 20: 2 Satan, and bound him a thousand y, *G2094*
3 till the thousand y should be fulfilled: *G2094*
4 and reigned with Christ a thousand y. *G2094*
5 until the thousand y were finished. *G2094*
6 and shall reign with him a thousand y. *G2094*
7 And when the thousand y are expired, *G2094*

YEAR'S
Ex 34:22 the feast of ingathering at the y end. H8141
2Sa 14:26 it was at every y end that he polled *it:* H8141

YEARS'
2Ki 8: 3 And it came to pass at the seven y end, H8141
1Ch 21:12 Either three y famine; or three months H8141

YELL
Jer 51:38 like lions: they shall y as lions' whelps. H5286

YELLED
Jer 2:15 him, *and* y, and they made H5414+H6963

YELLOW
Lev 13:30 *and there be* in it a y thin hair; then the H6669
32 there be in it no y hair, and the scall *be* H6669
36 shall not seek for y hair; he *is* unclean. H6669
Ps 68:13 silver, and her feathers with y gold. H3422

YES
Mt 17:25 He saith, Y. And when he was come *G3483*
Mk 7:28 and said unto him, Y, Lord: yet the dogs *G3483*
Ro 3:29 of the Gentiles? Y, of the Gentiles also: *G3483*
10:18 But I say, Have they not heard? Y *G3304*

YESTERDAY
Ex 5:14 brick both y and to day, as heretofore? H8543
1Sa 20:27 of Jesse to meat, neither y, nor to day? H8543
2Sa 15:20 Whereas thou camest *but* y, should I H8543
2Ki 9:26 Surely I have seen y the blood of Naboth, H570
Job 8: 9 (For we *are but of* y, and know nothing, H8543
Ps 90: 4 thy sight *are but* as y when it is past, and H865
Jn 4:52 Y at the seventh hour the fever left him. *G5504*
Act 7:28 kill me, as thou diddest the Egyptian y? *G5504*
Heb 13: 8 Jesus Christ the same y, and to day, and *G5504*

YESTERNIGHT
Gen 19:34 Behold, I lay y with my father: let us H570
31:29 spake unto me y, saying, Take thou heed H570
42 labour of my hands, and rebuked *thee* y. H570

YET See the Appendix.

YIELD
Gen 4:12 shall not henceforth y unto thee her H5414
49:20 *be* fat, and he shall y royal dainties. H5414
Lev 19:25 that it may y unto you the increase H3254
25:19 And the land shall y her fruit, and ye H5414
26: 4 and the land shall y her increase, and H5414
4 the trees of the field shall y their fruit. H5414
20 land shall not y her increase, neither H5414
20 shall the trees of the land y their fruits. H5414
Dt 11:17 and that the land y not her fruit; and H5414
2Ch 30: 8 fathers *were, but* y yourselves unto the H5414
Ps 67: 6 *Then* shall the earth y her increase; *and* H5414
85:12 good; and our land shall y her increase. H5414
107:37 which may y fruits of increase. H6213
Prv 7:21 she caused him to y, with the flattering H5186
Isa 5:10 Yea, ten acres of vineyard shall y one H6213
10 the seed of an homer shall y an ephah. H6213
Ezk 34:27 And the tree of the field shall y her H5414
27 the earth shall y her increase, and they H5414
36: 8 branches, and y your fruit to my people H5375
Hos 8: 7 the bud shall y no meal: if so be it yield, H6213
7 be it y, the strangers shall swallow it up. H6213
Joel 2:22 fig tree and the vine do y their strength. H5414
Hab 3:17 and the fields shall y no meat; the flock H6213
Mk 4: 8 ground, and did y fruit that sprang up *G1325*
Act 23:21 But do not thou y unto them: for there *G3982*
Ro 6:13 Neither y ye your members *as* *G3936*
13 unto sin: but y yourselves unto God, *G3936*
16 Know ye not, that to whom ye y *G3936*
19 even so now y your members servants *G3936*
Jas 3:12 fountain both y salt water and fresh. *G4160*

YIELDED
Gen 49:33 into the bed, and y up the ghost, and H1478
Nu 17: 8 bloomed blossoms, and y almonds. H1580
Dan 3:28 king's word, and y their bodies, that H3052
Mt 27:50 again with a loud voice, y up the ghost. *G863*
Mk 4: 7 up, and choked it, and it y no fruit. *G1325*
Act 5:10 at his feet, and y up the ghost: and the *G1634*
Ro 6:19 flesh: for as ye have y your members *G3936*
Rev 22: 2 *of* fruits, *and* y her fruit every month: *G591*

YIELDETH
Neh 9:37 And it y much increase unto the kings H7325
Job 24: 5 y food for them *and* for *their* children.
Prv 12:12 but the root of the righteous y *fruit.* H5414
Heb 12:11 afterward it y the peaceable fruit of *G591*

YIELDING
Gen 1:11 grass, the herb y seed, *and* the fruit tree H2232
11 *and* the fruit tree y fruit after his kind, H6213
12 grass, *and* herb y seed after his kind, H2232
12 kind, and the tree y fruit, whose seed H6213
29 a tree y seed; to you it shall be for meat. H2232
Ecc 10: 4 thy place; for y pacifieth great offences. H4832
Jer 17: 8 neither shall cease from y fruit. H6213

YOKE
Gen 27:40 shalt break his y from off thy neck. H5923
Lev 26:13 of your y, and made you go upright. H5923
Nu 19: 2 blemish, *and* upon which never came y: H5923
Dt 21: 3 *and* which hath not drawn in the y; H5923
28:48 and he shall put a y of iron upon thy H5923
1Sa 6: 7 hath come no y, and tie the kine to the H5923
11: 7 And he took a y of oxen, and hewed H6776
14:14 of land, *which a* y *of oxen might plow.* H6776
1Ki 12: 4 Thy father made our y grievous: now H5923
4 and his heavy y which he put upon us, H5923
9 saying, Make the y which thy father did H5923
10 Thy father made our y heavy, but make H5923
11 you with a heavy y, I will add to your H5923
11 I will add to your y: my father hath H5923
14 father made your y heavy, and I will H5923
14 and I will add to your y: my father *also* H5923
19:19 *with* twelve y *of oxen* before him, H6776
21 him, and took a y of oxen, and slew H6776
2Ch 10: 4 Thy father made our y grievous: now H5923
4 and his heavy y that he put upon us, H5923
9 the y that thy father did put upon us? H5923
10 Thy father made our y heavy, but make H5923
11 For whereas my father put a heavy y H5923
11 put more to your y: my father chastised H5923
14 My father made your y heavy, but I will H5923
Job 1: 3 and five hundred y of oxen, and five H6776
42:12 y of oxen, and a thousand she asses. H6776
Isa 9: 4 For thou hast broken the y of his H5923
10:27 shoulder, and his y from off thy neck, H5923
27 thy neck, and the y shall be destroyed H5923
14:25 foot: then shall his y depart from off H5923
47: 6 hast thou very heavily laid thy y. H5923
58: 6 go free, and that ye break every y? H4133
9 midst of thee the y, the putting forth of H4133
Jer 2:20 For of old time I have broken thy y, *and* H5923
5: 5 broken the y, *and* burst the bonds. H5923
27: 8 their neck under the y of the king of H5923
11 their neck under the y of the king of H5923
12 your necks under the y of the king of Babylon. H5923
28: 2 broken the y of the king of Babylon. H5923
4 will break the y of the king of Babylon. H5923
10 Then Hananiah the prophet took the y H4133
11 so will I break the y of Nebuchadnezzar H5923
12 had broken the y from off the neck of H4133
14 I have put a y of iron upon the neck H5923
30: 8 I will break his y from off thy neck, and H5923

Jer 31:18 *to the y*: turn thou me, and I
51:23 and his y of oxen; and with thee H6776
Lam 1:14 The y of my transgressions is bound by H5923
3:27 *It is* good for a man that he bear the y H5923
Ezk 34:27 the bands of their y, and delivered them H5923
Hos 11: 4 that take off the y on their jaws, and I H5923
Nah 1:13 For now will I break his y from off thee, H4132
Mt 11:29 Take my y upon you, and learn of me; *G2218*
30 For my y *is* easy, and my burden is *G2218*
Lk 14:19 And another said, I have bought five y *G2201*
Act 15:10 ye God, to put a y upon the neck of the *G2218*
Gal 5: 1 entangled again with the y of bondage. *G2218*
1Ti 6: 1 as are under the y count their own *G2218*

YOKED
2Co 6:14 Be ye not unequally y together with *G2086*

YOKEFELLOW
Php 4: 3 And I entreat thee also, true y, help *G4805*

YOKES
Jer 27: 2 and y, and put them upon thy neck, H4133
28:13 hast broken the y of wood; but thou H4133
13 but thou shalt make for them y of iron. H4133
Ezk 30:18 break there the y of Egypt: and the H4133

YONDER
Gen 22: 5 y and worship, and come again to you. H3541
Nu 16:37 thou the fire y; for they are hallowed. H1973
23:15 burnt offering, while I meet *the LORD* y. H3541
32:19 For we will not inherit with them on y H5676
2Ki 4:25 servant, Behold, *y is* that Shunammite:
Mt 17:20 Remove hence to y place; and it shall *G1563*
26:36 Sit ye here, while I go and pray y. *G1563*

YOU See the Appendix.

YOUNG
Gen 4:23 my wounding, and a y man to my hurt. H3206
14:24 Save only that which the y men have H5288
15: 9 old, and a turtledove, and a y pigeon. H1469
18: 7 unto a y man; and he hasted to dress it. H5288
19: 4 y, all the people from every quarter: H5288
22: 3 took two of his y men with him, and H5288
5 And Abraham said unto his y men, H5288
19 So Abraham returned unto his y men, H5288
31:38 have not cast their y, and the rams of H7921
33:13 and herds with y *are* with me: and if H5763
34:19 And the y man deferred not to do the H5288
41:12 And *there was* there with us a y man, H5288
Ex 10: 9 And Moses said, We will go with our y H5288
23:26 There shall nothing cast their y, nor be H7921
24: 5 And he sent y men of the children of H5288
29: 1 Take one y bullock, and two H1121+H1241
33:11 the son of Nun, a y man, departed not H5288
Lev 1:14 offering of turtledoves, or of y pigeons. H1121
4: 3 he hath sinned, a y bullock H1121+H1241
14 shall offer a y bullock for the H1121+H1241
5: 7 or two y pigeons, unto the LORD; H1121
11 or two y pigeons, then he that H1121
9: 2 Take thee a y calf for a sin H1121+H1241
12: 6 burnt offering, and a y pigeon, or a H1121
8 two turtles, or two y pigeons; the one H1121
14:22 And two turtledoves, or two y pigeons, H1121
30 or of the y pigeons, such as he can get; H1121
15:14 or two y pigeons, and come H1121
29 two turtles, or two y pigeons, and bring H1121
16: 3 *place*: with a y bullock for a sin H1121+H1241
22:28 not kill it and her y both in one day. H1121
23:18 year, and one y bullock, and H1121+H1241
Nu 6:10 two turtles, or two y pigeons, to the H1121
7:15 One y bullock, one ram, one H1121+H1241
21 One y bullock, one ram, one H1121+H1241
27 One y bullock, one ram, one H1121+H1241
33 One y bullock, one ram, one H1121+H1241
39 One y bullock, one ram, one H1121+H1241
45 One y bullock, one ram, one H1121+H1241
51 One y bullock, one ram, one H1121+H1241
57 One y bullock, one ram, one H1121+H1241
63 One y bullock, one ram, one H1121+H1241
69 One y bullock, one ram, one H1121+H1241
75 One y bullock, one ram, one H1121+H1241
81 One y bullock, one ram, one H1121+H1241
8: 8 Then let them take a y bullock H1121+H1241
8 oil, and another y bullock shalt H1121+H1241
11:27 And there ran a y man, and told H5288
28 Moses, *one* of his y men, answered and H979
15:24 shall offer one y bullock for a H1121+H1241
23:24 lift up himself as a y lion: he shall not lie
Nu 28:11 LORD; two y bullocks, and one H1121+H1241
19 LORD; two y bullocks, and one H1121+H1241
27 the LORD; two y bullocks, one H1121+H1241
29: 2 LORD; one y bullock, one ram, H1121+H1241
8 savour; one y bullock, one H1121+H1241
13 thirteen y bullocks, two rams, H1121+H1241
17 *offer* twelve y bullocks, two H1121+H1241
Dt 22: 6 *whether they be* y ones, or eggs, and the H667
6 sitting upon the y, or upon the eggs, thou H667
6 thou shalt not take the dam with the y: H1121
7 go, and take the y to thee; that it may H1121
28:50 of the old, nor shew favour to the y: H5288
57 And toward her y one that cometh out H7988
32:11 fluttereth over her y, spreadeth abroad H1469
25 destroy both the y man and the virgin, H970
Jos 6:21 man and woman, y and old, and ox, H5288
23 And the y men that were spies went in, H5288
Jdg 6:25 Take thy father's y bullock, even the H6499
8:14 And caught a y man of the men of H5288
9:54 Then he called hastily unto the y man H5288
54 slew him. And his y man thrust him H5288
14: 5 behold, a y lion roared against him. H3715
10 there a feast; for so used the y men to do. H970
17: 7 And there was a y man out of H5288
11 y man was unto him as one of his sons. H5288
12 the Levite; and the y man became his H5288
18: 3 the voice of the y man the Levite: and H5288
15 to the house of the y man the Levite, H5288
19:19 and for the y man *which is* with thy H5288
21:12 four hundred y virgins, that had H5291
Ru 2: 9 I not charged the y men that they shall H5288
9 of *that* which the y men have drawn. H5288
15 commanded his y men, saying, Let her H5288
21 keep fast by my y men, until they have H5288
3:10 not y men, whether poor or rich. H970
4:12 LORD shall give thee of this y woman. H5291
1Sa 1:24 LORD in Shiloh: and the child *was* y. H5288
2:17 Wherefore the sin of the y men was H5288
8:16 and your goodliest y men, and your H970
9: 2 *was* Saul, a choice y man, and a goodly: H970
11 city, they found y maidens going out H5291
14: 1 Saul said unto the y man that bare his H5288
6 And Jonathan said to the y man that H5288
17:58 son *art* thou, *thou* y man? And David H5288
20:22 But if I say thus unto the y man, H5291
21: 4 hallowed bread; if the y men have kept H5288
5 the vessels of the y men are holy, and H5288
25: 5 And David sent out ten y men, and H5288
5 said unto the y men, Get you up to H5288
8 Ask thy y men, and they will shew thee. H5288
8 Wherefore let the y men find favour in H5288
9 And when David's y men came, they H5288
12 So David's y men turned their way, and H5288
14 But one of the y men told Abigail, H5288
25 saw not the y men of my lord, whom H5288
27 unto the y men that follow my lord. H5288
26:22 of the y men come over and fetch it. H5288
30:13 he said, I *am* a y man of Egypt, servant H5288
17 save four hundred y men, which rode H5288
2Sa 1: 5 And David said unto the y man that H5288
6 And the y man that told him said, As I H5288
13 And David said unto the y man that H5288
15 And David called one of the y men, and H5288
2:14 And Abner said to Joab, Let the y men H5288
21 hold on one of the y men, and take thee H5288
4:12 And David commanded his y men, and H5288
9:12 And Mephibosheth had a y son, whose H6996
13:32 have slain all the y men the king's sons; H5288
34 But Absalom fled. And the y man that H5288
14:21 bring the y man Absalom again. H5288
16: 2 fruit for the y men to eat; and the H5288
18: 5 for my sake with the y man, *even* with H5288
12 that none *touch* the y man Absalom. H5288
15 And ten y men that bare Joab's armour H5288
29 And the king said, Is the y man H5288
32 And the king said unto Cushi, Is the y H5288
32 to do *thee* hurt, be as *that* y man *is*. H5288
1Ki 1: 2 my lord the king a y virgin: and let her H5291
11:28 Solomon seeing the y man that he was H5288
12: 8 and consulted with the y men that were H3206
10 And the y men that were grown up H3206
14 the counsel of the y men, saying, My H3206
20:14 *Even* by the y men of the princes of H5288
15 Then he numbered the y men of the H5288
17 And the y men of the princes of the H5288
19 So these y men of the princes of the H5288
2Ki 4:22 thee, one of the y men, and one of the H5288
5:22 Ephraim two y men of the sons of the H5288
6:17 the eyes of the y man; and he saw: and, H5288
2Ki 8:12 set on fire, and their y men wilt thou slay H970
9: 4 So the y man, *even* the young man the H5288
4 So the young man, *even* the y man the H5288
1Ch 12:28 And Zadok, a y man mighty of valour, H5288
22: 5 And David said, Solomon my son *is* y H5288
29: 1 hath chosen, *is yet* y and tender, and H5288
2Ch 10: 8 took counsel with the y men that were H3206
10 And the y men that were brought up H3206
14 the advice of the y men, saying, My H3206
13: 7 Rehoboam was y and tenderhearted, H5288
9 himself with a y bullock and H1121+H1241
34: 3 while he was yet y, he began to seek H5288
36:17 who slew their y men with the sword H970
17 compassion upon y man or maiden, old H970
Ezr 6: 9 they have need of, both y bullocks, and H1123
Est 2: 2 be fair y virgins sought for the king: H5291
3 all the fair y virgins unto Shushan H5291
3:13 all Jews, both y and old, little children H5288
8:10 on mules, camels, *and* y dromedaries: H1121
Job 1:19 and it fell upon the y men, and they are H5288
4:10 and the teeth of the y lions, are broken. H3715
19:18 Yea, y children despised me; I arose, and
29: 8 The y men saw me, and hid H5288
32: 6 and said, I *am* y, and ye *are* H6810+H3117
38:39 lion? or fill the appetite of the y lions, H3715
41 his food? when his y ones cry unto God, H3206
39: 3 y ones, they cast out their sorrows. H3206
4 Their y ones are in good liking, they H1121
16 She is hardened against her y ones, as H1121
30 Her y ones also suck up blood: and H667
Ps 17:12 it were a y lion lurking in secret places. H3715
29: 6 Lebanon and Sirion like a y unicorn. H1121
34:10 The y lions do lack, and suffer hunger: H3715
37:25 I have been y, and *now* am old; yet have H5288
58: 6 the great teeth of the y lions, O LORD. H3715
78:63 The fire consumed their y men; and H970
71 From following the ewes great with y H5763
84: 3 she may lay her y, *even* thine altars, O H667
91:13 and adder: the y lion and the dragon H3715
104:21 The y lions roar after their prey, and H3715
119: 9 Wherewithal shall a y man cleanse his H5288
147: 9 his food, *and* to the y ravens which cry. H1121
148:12 Both y men, and maidens; old men, and H970
Prv 1: 4 To give subtilty to the simple, to the y H5288
7: 7 youths, a y man void of understanding, H5288
20:29 The glory of y men *is* their strength: and H970
30:17 pick it out, and the y eagles shall eat it. H1121
Ecc 11: 9 Rejoice, O y man, in thy youth; and let H970
Song 2: 9 My beloved is like a roe or a y hart: H6082
17 a y hart upon the mountains of Bether. H6082
4: 5 Thy two breasts *are* like two y roes that H6082
7: 3 Thy two breasts *are* like two y roes *that* H6082
8:14 a y hart upon the mountains of spices. H6082
Isa 5:29 they shall roar like y lions: yea, they H3715
7:21 shall nourish a y cow, and two sheep; H1241
9:17 have no joy in their y men, neither shall H970
11: 6 the calf and the y lion and the fatling H3715
7 shall feed; their y ones shall lie down H3206
13:18 *Their* bows also shall dash the y men to H5288
20: 4 captives, y and old, naked and H5288
23: 4 I nourish up y men, *nor* bring up virgins. H970
30: 6 whence *come* the y and old lion, the H3833
6 upon the shoulders of y asses, and their
24 The oxen likewise and the y asses that
31: 4 as the lion and the y lion roaring on his H3715
8 and his y men shall be discomfited. H970
40:11 shall gently lead those that are with y. H5763
30 and the y men shall utterly fall: H5288+H970
62: 5 For *as* a y man marrieth a virgin, *so* H970
Jer 2:15 The y lions roared upon him, *and* H3715
6:11 the assembly of y men together: for even H970
9:21 without, *and* the y men from the streets. H970
11:22 punish them: the y men shall die by the H970
15: 8 the mother of the y men a spoiler at H970
18:21 y men *be* slain by the sword in battle. H970
31:12 for oil, and for the y of the flock and of H1121
13 rejoice in the dance, both y men and old H970
48:15 and his chosen y men are gone down H970
49:26 Therefore her y men shall fall in her H970
50:30 Therefore shall her y men fall in the H970
51: 3 her y men; destroy ye utterly all her host. H970
22 in pieces old and y; and with thee will I H5288
22 break in pieces the y man and the maid; H970
Lam 1:15 me to crush my y men: the Lord hath H970
18 and my y men are gone into captivity. H970
2:19 for the life of thy y children, that faint
21 The y and the old lie on the ground in H5288
21 my virgins and my y men are fallen by H970
4: 3 give suck to their y ones: the daughter H1482

Lam 4: 4 for thirst: the y children ask bread, *and*
5:13 They took the y men to grind, and the H970
14 the gate, the y men from their musick. H970
Ezk 9: 6 Slay utterly old *and* y, both maids, and H970
17: 4 He cropped off the top of his y twigs, H3242
22 off from the top of his y twigs a tender H3127
19: 2 nourished her whelps among y lions. H3715
3 it became a y lion, and it learned H3715
5 of her whelps, *and* made him a y lion. H3715
6 lions, he became a y lion, and learned H3715
23: 6 y men, horsemen riding upon horses. H970
12 horses, all of them desirable y men. H970
23 of them desirable y men, captains and H970
30:17 The y men of Aven and of Pi-beseth H970
31: 6 bring forth their y, and under his shadow
32: 2 Thou art like a y lion of the nations, H3715
38:13 with all the y lions thereof, shall say H3715
41:19 side, and the face of a y lion toward the H3715
43:19 a y bullock for a sin offering. H1121+H1241
23 shalt offer a y bullock without H1121+H1241
25 also prepare a y bullock, and a H1121+H1241
45:18 shalt take a y bullock without H1121+H1241
46: 6 *it shall be* a y bullock without H1121+H1241
Hos 5:14 as a lion, and as a y lion to the house of H3715
Joel 2:28 dreams, your y men shall see visions: H970
Am 2:11 and of your y men for Nazarites. *Is* H970
3: 4 no prey? will a y lion cry out of his den, H3715
4:10 of Egypt: your y men have I slain with H970
8:13 In that day shall the fair virgins and y H970
Mic 5: 8 of the forest, as a y lion among the H3715
Nah 2:11 of the y lions, where the lion, H3715
13 shall devour thy y lions: and I will cut H3715
3:10 into captivity: her y children also were
Zec 2: 4 him, Run, speak to this y man, saying, H5288
9:17 y men cheerful, and new wine the maids. H970
11: 3 of the roaring of y lions; for the pride of H3715
16 shall seek the y one, nor heal that that H5288
Mt 2: 8 diligently for the y child; and when ye *G3813*
9 and stood over where the y child was. *G3813*
11 they saw the y child with Mary his *G3813*
13 and take the y child and his mother, *G3813*
13 will seek the y child to destroy him. *G3813*
14 When he arose, he took the y child and *G3813*
20 Saying, Arise, and take the y child and *G3813*
20 are dead which sought the y child's life. *G3813*
21 And he arose, and took the y child and *G3813*
19:20 The y man saith unto him, All these *G3495*
22 But when the y man heard that saying, *G3495*
Mk 7:25 For a *certain* woman, whose y *G2365*
10:13 And they brought y children to him, *G3813*
14:51 And there followed him a certain y *G3495*
51 *body*; and the y men laid hold on him: *G3495*
16: 5 they saw a y man sitting on the right *G3495*
Lk 2:24 A pair of turtledoves, or two y pigeons. *G3502*
7:14 he said, Y man, I say unto thee, Arise. *G3495*
Jn 12:14 And Jesus, when he had found a y ass, *G3678*
21:18 thee, When thou wast y, thou girdedst *G3501*
Act 2:17 and your y men shall see visions, *G3495*
5: 6 And the y men arose, wound him up, *G3501*
10 the ghost: and the y men came in, and *G3495*
7:19 they cast out their y children, to the *G1025*
58 a y man's feet, whose name was Saul. *G3495*
20: 9 And there sat in a window a certain y *G3495*
12 And they brought the y man alive, and *G3816*
23:17 said, Bring this y man unto the chief *G3495*
18 me to bring this y man unto thee, who *G3495*
22 So the chief captain *then* let the y man *G3495*
Tit 2: 4 That they may teach the y women to be *G3501*
6 Y men likewise exhort to be sober *G3501*
1Jn 2:13 I write unto you, y men, because ye *G3495*
14 written unto you, y men, because ye *G3495*

YOUNGER
Gen 9:24 what his y son had done unto him. H6996
19:31 And the firstborn said unto the y, Our H6810
34 firstborn said unto the y, Behold, I lay H6810
35 that night also: and the y arose, and lay H6810
38 And the y, she also bare a son, and H6810
25:23 people; and the elder shall serve the y. H6810
27:15 and put them upon Jacob her y son: H6996
42 called Jacob her y son, and said unto H6996
29:16 and the name of the y *was* Rachel. H6996
18 seven years for Rachel thy y daughter. H6996
26 to give the y before the firstborn. H6810
43:29 said, *Is* this your y brother, of whom ye H6996
48:14 head, who *was* the y, and his left hand H6810
19 be great: but truly his y brother shall be H6996
Jdg 1:13 And Othniel the son of Kenaz, Caleb's y H6996
3: 9 the son of Kenaz, Caleb's y brother. H6996
15: 2 *is* not her y sister fairer than she? H6996
1Sa 14:49 Merab, and the name of the y Michal: H6996
1Ch 24:31 fathers over against their y brethren. H6996
Job 30: 1 But now *they that are* y than I H6810+H3117
Ezk 16:46 thy left hand: and thy y sister, that H6996
61 elder and thy y: and I will give them H6996
Lk 15:12 And the y of them said to *his* father, *G3501*
13 And not many days after the y son *G3501*
22:26 let him be as the y; and he that is chief, *G3501*
Ro 9:12 unto her, The elder shall serve the y. *G1640*
1Ti 5: 1 as a father; *and* the y men as brethren; *G3501*
2 The elder women as mothers; the y as *G3501*
11 But the y widows refuse: for when they *G3501*
14 I will therefore that the y women *G3501*
1Pt 5: 5 Likewise, ye y, submit yourselves unto *G3501*

YOUNGEST
Gen 42:13 and, behold, the y *is* this day with our H6996
15 except your y brother come hither. H6996
20 But bring your y brother unto me; so H6996
32 one *is* not, and the y *is* this day with H6996
34 And bring your y brother unto me: H6996
43:33 birthright, and the y according to his H6810
44: 2 mouth of the y, and his corn money. H6996
12 and left at the y: and the cup was found H6996
23 Except your y brother come down H6996
26 go down: if our y brother be with us, H6996
26 face, except our y brother *be* with us. H6996
Jos 6:26 his y *son* shall he set up the gates of it. H6810
Jdg 9: 5 yet Jotham the y son of Jerubbaal was H6996
1Sa 16:11 remaineth yet the y, and, behold, he H6996
17:14 And David *was* the y: and the three H6996
1Ki 16:34 thereof in his y *son* Segub, according H6810
2Ch 21:17 him, save Jehoahaz, the y of his sons. H6996
22: 1 made Ahaziah his y son king in his H6996

YOUR See the Appendix.

YOURS See the Appendix.

YOURSELVES See the Appendix.

YOUTH
Gen 8:21 *is* evil from his y; neither will I again H5271
43:33 according to his y: and the men H6812
46:34 cattle from our y even until now, both H5271
Lev 22:13 house, as in her y, she shall eat of her H5271
Nu 30: 3 *being* in her father's house in her y; H5271
16 *being yet* in her y in her father's house. H5271
Jdg 8:20 *and* slay them. But the y drew not his H5288
20 for he feared, because he *was* yet a y. H5288
1Sa 17:33 y, and he a man of war from his youth. H5271
33 youth, and he a man of war from his y. H5271
42 for he was *but* a y, and ruddy, and of a H5288
55 whose son *is* this y? And Abner said, *As* H5288
2Sa 19: 7 that befell thee from thy y until now. H5271
1Ki 18:12 I thy servant fear the LORD from my y. H5271
Job 13:26 me to possess the iniquities of my y. H5271
20:11 His bones are full *of the sin* of his y, H5934
29: 4 As I was in the days of my y, when the H2779
30:12 Upon *my* right *hand* rise the y; they H6526
31:18 (For from my y he was brought up with H5271
33:25 he shall return to the days of his y: H5934
36:14 They die in y, and their life *is* among H5290
Ps 25: 7 Remember not the sins of my y, nor my H5271
71: 5 Lord GOD: *thou art* my trust from my y. H5271
17 O God, thou hast taught me from my y: H5271
88:15 to die from *my* y up: *while* I suffer thy H5290
89:45 The days of his y hast thou shortened: H5934
103: 5 *so that* thy y is renewed like the eagle's. H5271
110: 3 the morning: thou hast the dew of thy y. H3208
127: 4 a mighty man; so *are* children of the y. H5271
129: 1 me from my y, may Israel now say: H5271
2 me from my y: yet they have not H5271
144:12 grown up in their y; *that* our daughters H5271
Prv 2:17 Which forsaketh the guide of her y, and H5271
5:18 and rejoice with the wife of thy y. H5271
Ecc 11: 9 Rejoice, O young man, in thy y; and let H3208
9 in the days of thy y, and walk in the ways H979
10 flesh: for childhood and y *are* vanity. H7839
12: 1 in the days of thy y, while the evil days H979
Isa 47:12 laboured from thy y; if so be thou shalt H5271
15 from thy y: they shall wander every H5271
54: 4 forget the shame of thy y, and shalt not H5934
6 and a wife of y, when thou wast refused, H5271
Jer 2: 2 the kindness of thy y, the love of thine H5271
3: 4 My father, thou *art* the guide of my y? H5271
24 our fathers from our y; their flocks and H5271
25 fathers, from our y even unto this day, H5271
22:21 thy y, that thou obeyedst not my voice. H5271
31:19 because I did bear the reproach of my y. H5271
32:30 me from their y: for the children of H5271
48:11 Moab hath been at ease from his y, and H5271
Lam 3:27 for a man that he bear the yoke in his y. H5271
Ezk 4:14 for from my y up even till now have H5271
16:22 the days of thy y, when thou wast naked H5271
43 the days of thy y, but hast fretted me H5271
60 in the days of thy y, and I will establish H5271
23: 3 in their y: there were their breasts H5271
8 Egypt: for in her y they lay with her, H5271
19 the days of her y, wherein she had H5271
21 lewdness of thy y, in bruising thy teats H5271
21 by the Egyptians for the paps of thy y. H5271
Hos 2:15 as in the days of her y, and as in the day H5271
Joel 1: 8 with sackcloth for the husband of her y. H5271
Zec 13: 5 taught me to keep cattle from my y. H5271
Mal 2:14 and the wife of thy y, against whom H5271
15 treacherously against the wife of his y. H5271
Mt 19:20 I kept from my y up: what lack I yet? *G3503*
Mk 10:20 all these have I observed from my y. *G3503*
Lk 18:21 All these have I kept from my y up. *G3503*
Act 26: 4 My manner of life from my y, which *G3503*
1Ti 4:12 Let no man despise thy y; but be thou *G3503*

YOUTHFUL
2Ti 2:22 Flee also y lusts: but follow *G3512*

YOUTHS
Prv 7: 7 y, a young man void of understanding, H1121
Isa 40:30 Even the y shall faint and be weary, H5288

YOU-WARD
2Co 1:12 in the world, and more abundantly to y. *G5209*
13: 3 to y is not weak, but is mighty in you. *G5209*
Eph 3: 2 the grace of God which is given me to y: *G5209*

Z

ZAANAIM
Jdg 4:11 unto the plain of Z, which *is* by Kedesh. H6815

ZAANAN
Mic 1:11 the inhabitant of Z came not forth in H6630

ZAANANNIM
Jos 19:33 from Allon to Z, and Adami, Nekeb, H6815

ZAAVAN
Gen 36:27 *are* these; Bilhan, and Z, and Akan. H2190

ZABAD
1Ch 2:36 begat Nathan, and Nathan begat Z, H2066
37 And Z begat Ephlal, and Ephlal begat H2066
7:21 And Z his son, and Shuthelah his son, H2066
11:41 Uriah the Hittite, Z the son of Ahlai, H2066
2Ch 24:26 against him; Z the son of Shimeath H2066
Ezr 10:27 and Jeremoth, and Z, and Aziza. H2066
10:33 Mattathah, Z, Eliphelet, Jeremai, H2066
43 Of the sons of Nebo; Jeiel, Mattithiah, Z, H2066

ZABBAI
Ezr 10:28 Jehohanan, Hananiah, Z, *and* Athlai. H2079
Neh 3:20 After him Baruch the son of Z earnestly H2079

ZABBUD
Ezr 8:14 Of the sons also of Bigvai; Uthai, and Z, H2072

ZABDI
Jos 7: 1 Carmi, the son of Z, the son of Zerah, of H2067
17 man by man; and Z was taken: H2067
18 Carmi, the son of Z, the son of Zerah, of H2067
1Ch 8:19 And Jakim, and Zichri, and Z, H2067
27:27 the wine cellars *was* Z the Shiphmite: H2067
Neh 11:17 Micha, the son of Z, the son of Asaph, H2067

ZABDIEL
1Ch 27: 2 the son of Z: and in his course *were* H2068
Neh 11:14 *was* Z, the son of *one of* the great men. H2068

ZABUD
1Ki 4: 5 the officers: and Z the son of Nathan H2071

ZABULON
Mt 4:13 in the borders of Z and Nephthalim: *G2194*
15 The land of Z, and the land of *G2194*
Rev 7: 8 Of the tribe of Z *were* sealed twelve *G2194*

ZACCAI
Ezr 2: 9 The children of Z, seven hundred and H2140
Neh 7:14 The children of Z, seven hundred and H2140

ZACCHAEUS
Lk 19: 2 And, behold, *there was* a man named Z, *G2195*
5 and said unto him, Z, make haste, and *G2195*
8 And Z stood, and said unto the Lord; *G2195*

ZACCHUR
1Ch 4:26 his son, Z his son, Shimei his son. H2139

ZACCUR
Nu 13: 4 tribe of Reuben, Shammua the son of Z. H2139
1Ch 24:27 Beno, and Shoham, and Z, and Ibri. H2139
25: 2 Of the sons of Asaph; Z, and Joseph, H2139
10 The third to Z, *he,* his sons, and his H2139
Neh 3: 2 next to them builded Z the son of Imri. H2139
10:12 Z, Sherebiah, Shebaniah, H2139
12:35 the son of Z, the son of Asaph: H2139
13:13 *was* Hanan the son of Z, the son of H2139

ZACHARIAH
2Ki 14:29 and Z his son reigned in his stead. H2148
15: 8 Azariah king of Judah did Z the son of H2148
11 And the rest of the acts of Z, behold, H2148
18: 2 name also *was* Abi, the daughter of Z. H2148

ZACHARIAS
Mt 23:35 unto the blood of Z son of Barachias, *G2197*
Lk 1: 5 priest named Z, of the course of Abia: *G2197*
12 And when Z saw *him,* he was troubled, *G2197*
13 unto him, Fear not, Z: for thy prayer is *G2197*
18 And Z said unto the angel, Whereby *G2197*
21 And the people waited for Z, and *G2197*
40 And entered into the house of Z, and *G2197*
59 him Z, after the name of his father. *G2197*
67 And his father Z was filled with the *G2197*
3: 2 John the son of Z in the wilderness. *G2197*
11:51 unto the blood of Z, which perished *G2197*

ZACHER
1Ch 8:31 And Gedor, and Ahio, and Z. H2144

ZADOK
2Sa 8:17 And Z the son of Ahitub, and H6659
15:24 And lo Z also, and all the Levites *were* H6659
25 And the king said unto Z, Carry back H6659
27 The king said also unto Z the priest, H6659
29 Z therefore and Abiathar carried the H6659
35 And *hast thou* not there with thee Z H6659
35 tell *it* to Z and Abiathar the priests. H6659
17:15 Then said Hushai unto Z and to H6659
18:19 Then said Ahimaaz the son of Z, Let me H6659
22 Then said Ahimaaz the son of Z yet H6659
27 the son of Z. And the king said, He H6659
19:11 And king David sent to Z and to H6659
20:25 And Sheva *was* scribe: and Z and H6659
1Ki 1: 8 But Z the priest, and Benaiah the son H6659
26 But me, *even* me thy servant, and Z the H6659
32 And king David said, Call me Z the H6659
34 And let Z the priest and Nathan the H6659
38 So Z the priest, and Nathan the H6659
39 And Z the priest took an horn of oil out H6659
44 And the king hath sent with him Z the H6659
45 And Z the priest and Nathan the H6659
2:35 over the host: and Z the priest did the H6659
4: 2 he had; Azariah the son of Z the priest, H6659
1Ki 4: 4 and Z and Abiathar *were* the priests: H6659
2Ki 15:33 name *was* Jerusha, the daughter of Z. H6659
1Ch 6: 8 And Ahitub begat Z, and Zadok begat H6659
8 And Ahitub begat Zadok, and Z begat H6659
12 And Ahitub begat Z, and Zadok begat H6659
12 And Ahitub begat Zadok, and Z begat H6659
53 Z his son, Ahimaaz his son. H6659
9:11 the son of Z, the son of Meraioth, H6659
12:28 And Z, a young man mighty of valour, H6659
15:11 And David called for Z and Abiathar H6659
16:39 And Z the priest, and his brethren the H6659
18:16 And Z the son of Ahitub, and H6659
24: 3 And David distributed them, both Z of H6659
6 and the princes, and Z the priest, and H6659
31 the king, and Z, and Ahimelech, and H6659
27:17 the son of Kemuel: of the Aaronites, Z: H6659
29:22 the chief governor, and Z *to be* priest. H6659
2Ch 27: 1 also *was* Jerushah, the daughter of Z. H6659
31:10 of the house of Z answered him, and H6659
Ezr 7: 2 The son of Shallum, the son of Z, the H6659
Neh 3: 4 unto them repaired Z the son of Baana. H6659
29 After them repaired Z the son of H6659
10:21 Meshezabeel, Z, Jaddua, H6659
11:11 the son of Z, the son of Meraioth, H6659
13:13 the priest, and Z the scribe, and of the H6659
Ezk 40:46 *are* the sons of Z among the sons of H6659
43:19 that be of the seed of Z, which approach H6659
44:15 the sons of Z, that kept the charge H6659
48:11 of the sons of Z; which have kept my H6659

ZADOK'S
2Sa 15:36 sons, Ahimaaz Z *son,* and Jonathan H6659

ZAHAM
2Ch 11:19 children; Jeush, and Shamariah, and Z. H2093

ZAIR
2Ki 8:21 So Joram went over to Z, and all the H6811

ZALAPH
Neh 3:30 the sixth son of Z, another piece. After H6764

ZALMON
Jdg 9:48 And Abimelech gat him up to mount Z, H6756
2Sa 23:28 Z the Ahohite, Maharai the H6756

ZALMONAH
Nu 33:41 from mount Hor, and pitched in Z. H6758
42 And they departed from Z, and pitched H6758

ZALMUNNA
Jdg 8: 5 after Zebah and Z, kings of Midian. H6759
6 of Zebah and Z now in thine hand, H6759
7 Zebah and Z into mine hand, then H6759
10 Now Zebah and Z *were* in Karkor, and H6759
12 And when Zebah and Z fled, he H6759
12 and Z, and discomfited all the host. H6759
15 Behold Zebah and Z, with whom ye did H6759
15 of Zebah and Z now in thine hand, H6759
18 Then said he unto Zebah and Z, What H6759
21 Then Zebah and Z said, Rise thou, and H6759
21 slew Zebah and Z, and took away the H6759
Ps 83:11 all their princes as Zebah, and as Z: H6759

ZAMZUMMIMS
Dt 2:20 time; and the Ammonites call them Z; H2157

ZANOAH
Jos 15:34 And Z, and En-gannim, Tappuah, and H2182
56 And Jezreel, and Jokdeam, and Z, H2182
1Ch 4:18 the father of Z. And these *are* the sons H2182
Neh 3:13 the inhabitants of Z; they built it, and H2182
11:30 Z, Adullam, and *in* their villages, at H2182

ZAPHNATHPAANEAH
Gen 41:45 And Pharaoh called Joseph's name Z; H6847

ZAPHON
Jos 13:27 and Succoth, and Z, the rest of the H6829

ZARA
Mt 1: 3 And Judas begat Phares and Z of *G2196*

ZARAH
Gen 38:30 his hand: and his name was called Z. H2226

ZAREAH
Neh 11:29 And at En-rimmon, and at Z, and at H6881

ZAREATHITES
1Ch 2:53 them came the Z, and the Eshtaulites. H6882

ZARED
Nu 21:12 removed, and pitched in the valley of Z. H2218

ZAREPHATH
1Ki 17: 9 Arise, get thee to Z, which *belongeth* to H6886
10 So he arose and went to Z. And when he H6886
Oba 20 *even* unto Z; and the captivity of H6886

ZARETAN
Jos 3:16 that *is* beside Z: and those that came H6891

ZARETH-SHAHAR
Jos 13:19 And Kirjathaim, and Sibmah, and Z in H6890

ZARHITES
Nu 26:13 Of Zerah, the family of the Z: of Shaul, H2227
20 Pharzites: of Zerah, the family of the Z. H2227
Jos 7:17 the family of the Z: and he brought the H2227
17 Z man by man; and Zabdi was taken: H2227
1Ch 27:11 Hushathite, of the Z: and in his course H2227
13 of the Z: and in his course *were* H2227

ZARTANAH
1Ki 4:12 which *is* by Z beneath Jezreel, from H6891

ZARTHAN
1Ki 7:46 the clay ground between Succoth and Z. H6891

ZATTHU
Neh 10:14 Parosh, Pahath-moab, Elam, Z, Bani, H2240

ZATTU
Ezr 2: 8 The children of Z, nine hundred forty H2240
10:27 And of the sons of Z; Elioenai, Eliashib, H2240
Neh 7:13 The children of Z, eight hundred forty H2240

ZAVAN
1Ch 1:42 The sons of Ezer; Bilhan, and Z, *and* H2190

ZAZA
1Ch 2:33 Z. These were the sons of Jerahmeel. H2117

ZEAL
2Sa 21: 2 z to the children of Israel and Judah.) H7065
2Ki 10:16 me, and see my z for the LORD. So they H7068
19:31 the z of the LORD *of hosts* shall do this. H7068
Ps 69: 9 For the z of thine house hath eaten me H7068
119:139 My z hath consumed me, because mine H7068
Isa 9: 7 even for ever. The z of the LORD of H7068
37:32 the z of the LORD of hosts shall do this. H7068
59:17 and was clad with z as a cloak. H7068
63:15 glory: where *is* thy z and thy strength, H7068
Ezk 5:13 have spoken *it* in my z, when I have H7068
Jn 2:17 The z of thine house hath eaten me up. *G2205*
Ro 10: 2 that they have a z of God, but not *G2205*
2Co 7:11 desire, yea, *what* z, yea, *what* revenge! *G2205*
9: 2 and your z hath provoked very many. *G2205*
Php 3: 6 Concerning z, persecuting the church; *G2205*
Col 4:13 he hath a great z for you, and them *G2205*

ZEALOUS
Nu 25:11 while he was z for my sake among H7065
13 because he was z for his God, and H7065
Act 21:20 believe; and they are all z of the law: *G2207*
22: 3 z toward God, as ye all are this day. *G2207*
1Co 14:12 Even so ye, forasmuch as ye are z of *G2207*
Gal 1:14 z of the traditions of my fathers. *G2207*
Tit 2:14 a peculiar people, z of good works. *G2207*
Rev 3:19 chasten: be z therefore, and repent. *G2206*

ZEALOUSLY
Gal 4:17 They z affect you, *but* not well; yea, *G2206*
18 But *it is* good to be z affected always in *G2206*

ZEBADIAH
1Ch 8:15 And Z, and Arad, and Ader, H2069
17 And Z, and Meshullam, and Hezeki, H2069
12: 7 And Joelah, and Z, the sons of Jeroham H2069
26: 2 second, Z the third, Jathniel the fourth, H2069
27: 7 of Joab, and Z his son after him: and H2069
2Ch 17: 8 and Nethaniah, and Z, and Asahel, and H2069
19:11 of the LORD; and Z the son of Ishmael, H2069
Ezr 8: 8 And of the sons of Shephatiah; Z the H2069
10:20 of the sons of Immer; Hanani, and Z. H2069

ZEBAH
Jdg 8: 5 Z and Zalmunna, kings of Midian. H2078
6 *Are* the hands of Z and Zalmunna now H2078
7 hath delivered Z and Zalmunna into H2078
10 Now Z and Zalmunna *were* in Karkor, H2078
12 And when Z and Zalmunna fled, he H2078
12 kings of Midian, Z and Zalmunna, and H2078
15 and said, Behold Z and Zalmunna, H2078
15 *Are* the hands of Z and Zalmunna now H2078
18 Then said he unto Z and Zalmunna, H2078
21 Then Z and Zalmunna said, Rise thou, H2078
21 arose, and slew Z and Zalmunna, and H2078
Ps 83:11 all their princes as Z, and as Zalmunna: H2078

ZEBAIM
Ezr 2:57 of Pochereth of Z, the children of Ami. H6380
Neh 7:59 of Pochereth of Z, the children of Amon. H6380

ZEBEDEE
Mt 4:21 James *the son* of Z, and John his G2199
21 in a ship with Z their father, mending G2199
10: 2 *the son* of Z, and John his brother; G2199
26:37 and the two sons of Z, and began to be G2199
Mk 1:19 saw James the *son* of Z, and John his G2199
20 left their father Z in the ship with the G2199
3:17 And James the *son* of Z, and John the G2199
10:35 And James and John, the sons of Z, G2199
Lk 5:10 John, the sons of Z, which were partners G2199
Jn 21: 2 *sons* of Z, and two other of his disciples. G2199

ZEBEDEE'S
Mt 20:20 Then came to him the mother of Z G2199
27:56 Joses, and the mother of Z children. G2199

ZEBINA
Ezr 10:43 Zabad, Z, Jadau, and Joel, Benaiah. H2081

ZEBOIIM
Gen 14: 2 Z, and the king of Bela, which is Zoar. H6636
8 and the king of Z, and the king of Bela H6636

ZEBOIM
Gen 10:19 and Admah, and Z, even unto Lasha. H6636
Dt 29:23 Admah, and Z, which the LORD H6636
1Sa 13:18 the valley of Z toward the wilderness. H6650
Neh 11:34 Hadid, Z, Neballat, H6650
Hos 11: 8 *how* shall I set thee as Z? mine heart is H6636

ZEBUB See BAAL-ZEBUB.

ZEBUDAH
2Ki 23:36 Z, the daughter of Pedaiah of Rumah. H2080

ZEBUL
Jdg 9:28 of Jerubbaal? and Z his officer? serve H2083
30 And when Z the ruler of the city heard H2083
36 people, he said to Z, Behold, there come H2083
36 mountains. And Z said unto him, Thou H2083
38 Then said Z unto him, Where *is* now H2083
41 at Arumah: and Z thrust out Gaal and H2083

ZEBULONITE
Jdg 12:11 And after him Elon, a Z, judged Israel; H2075
12 And Elon the Z died, and was buried in H2075

ZEBULUN
Gen 30:20 six sons: and she called his name Z. H2074
35:23 Levi, and Judah, and Issachar, and Z: H2074
46:14 And the sons of Z; Sered, and Elon, and H2074
49:13 Z shall dwell at the haven of the sea; H2074
Ex 1: 3 Issachar, Z, and Benjamin, H2074
Nu 1: 9 Of Z; Eliab the son of Helon. H2074
30 Of the children of Z, by their H2074
31 of the tribe of Z, *were* fifty and seven H2074
2: 7 *Then* the tribe of Z: and Eliab the son of H2074
7 *shall be* captain of the children of Z. H2074
7:24 prince of the children of Z, *did offer*: H2074
10:16 of Z *was* Eliab the son of Helon. H2074
13:10 Of the tribe of Z, Gaddiel the son of H2074
26:26 *Of* the sons of Z after their families: of H2074
34:25 of Z, Elizaphan the son of Parnach. H2074
Dt 27:13 and Asher, and Z, Dan, and Naphtali. H2074
33:18 And of Z he said, Rejoice, Zebulun, in H2074
18 And of Zebulun he said, Rejoice, Z, in H2074
Jos 19:10 for the children of Z according to their H2074
16 of the children of Z according to their H2074
27 and reacheth to Z, and to the valley of H2074
34 and reacheth to Z on the south side, H2074
21: 7 and out of the tribe of Z, twelve cities. H2074
Jos 21:34 out of the tribe of Z, Jokneam with her H2074
Jdg 1:30 Neither did Z drive out the inhabitants H2074
4: 6 of Naphtali and of the children of Z? H2074
10 And Barak called Z and Naphtali to H2074
5:14 and out of Z they that handle the H2074
18 Z and Naphtali *were* a people *that* H2074
6:35 Asher, and unto Z, and unto Naphtali; H2074
12:12 buried in Aijalon in the country of Z. H2074
1Ch 2: 1 Levi, and Judah, Issachar, and Z, H2074
6:63 and out of the tribe of Z, twelve cities. H2074
77 out of the tribe of Z, Rimmon with her H2074
12:33 Of Z, such as went forth to battle, expert H2074
40 unto Issachar and Z and Naphtali, H2074
27:19 Of Z, Ishmaiah the son of Obadiah: of H2074
2Ch 30:10 even unto Z: but they laughed them H2074
11 and Manasseh and of Z humbled H2074
18 Issachar, and Z, had not cleansed H2074
Ps 68:27 of Z, *and* the princes of Naphtali. H2074
Isa 9: 1 the land of Z and the land of Naphtali, H2074
Ezk 48:26 side unto the west side, Z a *portion*. H2074
27 And by the border of Z, from the east H2074
33 one gate of Issachar, one gate of Z. H2074

ZEBULUNITES
Nu 26:27 These *are* the families of the Z H2075

ZECHARIAH
1Ch 5: 7 reckoned, *were* the chief, Jeiel, and Z, H2148
9:21 *And* Z the son of Meshelemiah *was* H2148
37 And Gedor, and Ahio, and Z, and H2148
15:18 the second *degree*, Z, Ben, and Jaaziel, H2148
20 And Z, and Aziel, and Shemiramoth, H2148
24 and Amasai, and Z, and Benaiah, and H2148
16: 5 Asaph the chief, and next to him Z, H2148
24:25 *was* Isshiah: of the sons of Isshiah; Z. H2148
26: 2 And the sons of Meshelemiah *were*, Z H2148
11 the third, Z the fourth: all the sons H2148
14 Then for Z his son, a wise counsellor, H2148
27:21 Iddo the son of Z: of Benjamin, Jaasiel H2148
2Ch 17: 7 to Obadiah, and to Z, and to Nethaneel, H2148
20:14 Then upon Jahaziel the son of Z, the son H2148
21: 2 and Jehiel, and Z, and Azariah, and H2148
24:20 And the spirit of God came upon Z the H2148
26: 5 And he sought God in the days of Z, H2148
29: 1 name *was* Abijah, the daughter of Z. H2148
13 of the sons of Asaph; Z, and Mattaniah: H2148
34:12 of Merari; and Z and Meshullam, of H2148
35: 8 Hilkiah and Z and Jehiel, rulers of H2148
Ezr 5: 1 the prophet, and Z the son of Iddo, H2148
6:14 the prophet and Z the son of Iddo. And H2148
8: 3 sons of Pharosh; Z: and with him were H2148
11 And of the sons of Bebai; Z the son of H2148
16 Nathan, and for Z, and for Meshullam, H2148
10:26 And of the sons of Elam; Mattaniah, Z, H2148
Neh 8: 4 and Hashbadana, Z, *and* Meshullam. H2148
11: 4 of Uzziah, the son of Z, the son of H2148
5 Joiarib, the son of Z, the son of Shiloni. H2148
12 of Amzi, the son of Z, the son of Pashur, H2148
12:16 Of Iddo, Z; of Ginnethon, Meshullam; H2148
35 with trumpets; *namely*, Z the son of H2148
41 Z, *and* Hananiah, with trumpets; H2148
Isa 8: 2 priest, and Z the son of Jeberechiah. H2148
Zec 1: 1 word of the LORD unto Z, the son of H2148
7 word of the LORD unto Z, the son of H2148
7: 1 LORD came unto Z in the fourth *day* of H2148
8 word of the LORD came unto Z, saying, H2148

ZEDAD
Nu 34: 8 goings forth of the border shall be to Z: H6657
Ezk 47:15 sea, the way of Hethlon, as men go to Z; H6657

ZEDEKIAH
1Ki 22:11 And Z the son of Chenaanah made him H6667
24 But Z the son of Chenaanah went near, H6667
2Ki 24:17 his stead, and changed his name to Z. H6667
18 Z *was* twenty and one years old when H6667
20 Z rebelled against the king of Babylon. H6667
25: 2 unto the eleventh year of king Z. H6667
7 And they slew the sons of Z before his H6667
7 put out the eyes of Z, and bound him H6667
1Ch 3:15 the third Z, the fourth Shallum. H6667
16 Jehoiakim: Jeconiah his son, Z his son. H6667
2Ch 18:10 And Z the son of Chenaanah had made H6667
23 Then Z the son of Chenaanah came H6667
36:10 LORD, and made Z his brother king H6667
11 Z *was* one and twenty years old when H6667
Jer 1: 3 the eleventh year of Z the son of Josiah H6667
21: 1 the LORD, when king Z sent unto him H6667
3 unto them, Thus shall ye say to Z: H6667
Jer 21: 7 I will deliver Z king of Judah, and his H6667
24: 8 So will I give Z the king of Judah, and H6667
27: 3 to Jerusalem unto Z king of Judah; H6667
12 I spake also to Z king of Judah H6667
28: 1 of the reign of Z king of Judah, in the H6667
29: 3 of Hilkiah, (whom Z king of Judah sent H6667
21 son of Kolaiah, and of Z the son of H6667
22 make thee like Z and like Ahab, whom H6667
32: 1 the tenth year of Z king of Judah, which H6667
3 For Z king of Judah had shut him up, H6667
4 And Z king of Judah shall not escape H6667
5 And he shall lead Z to Babylon, and H6667
34: 2 Go and speak to Z king of Judah, and H6667
4 Yet hear the word of the LORD, O Z H6667
6 unto Z king of Judah in Jerusalem, H6667
8 after that the king Z had made a H6667
21 And Z king of Judah and his princes H6667
36:12 son of Shaphan, and Z the son of H6667
37: 1 And king Z the son of Josiah reigned H6667
3 And Z the king sent Jehucal the son of H6667
17 Then Z the king sent, and took him H6667
18 Moreover Jeremiah said unto king Z, H6667
21 Then Z the king commanded that they H6667
38: 5 Then Z the king said, Behold, he *is* in H6667
14 Then Z the king sent, and took H6667
15 Then Jeremiah said unto Z, If I declare H6667
16 So Z the king sware secretly unto H6667
17 Then said Jeremiah unto Z, Thus saith H6667
19 And Z the king said unto Jeremiah, I H6667
24 Then said Z unto Jeremiah, Let no man H6667
39: 1 In the ninth year of Z king of Judah, in H6667
2 *And* in the eleventh year of Z, in the H6667
4 And it came to pass, *that* when Z the H6667
5 and overtook Z in the plains of Jericho: H6667
6 slew the sons of Z in Riblah before his H6667
44:30 his life; as I gave Z king of Judah into H6667
49:34 of the reign of Z king of Judah, saying, H6667
51:59 he went with Z the king of Judah into H6667
52: 1 Z *was* one and twenty years old when H6667
3 Z rebelled against the king of Babylon. H6667
5 unto the eleventh year of king Z. H6667
8 and overtook Z in the plains of Jericho; H6667
10 slew the sons of Z before his eyes: he H6667
11 Then he put out the eyes of Z; and the H6667

ZEDEKIAH'S
Jer 39: 7 Moreover he put out Z eyes, and bound H6667

ZEEB
Jdg 7:25 Oreb and Z; and they slew Oreb H2062
25 the rock Oreb, and Z they slew at the H2062
25 at the winepress of Z, and pursued H2062
25 Z to Gideon on the other side Jordan. H2062
8: 3 of Midian, Oreb and Z: and what was I H2062
Ps 83:11 Make their nobles like Oreb, and like Z: H2062

ZELAH
Jos 18:28 And Z, Eleph, and Jebusi, which *is* H6762
2Sa 21:14 of Benjamin in Z, in the sepulchre of H6762

ZELEK
2Sa 23:37 Z the Ammonite, Naharai the H6768
1Ch 11:39 Z the Ammonite, Naharai the H6768

ZELOPHEHAD
Nu 26:33 And Z the son of Hepher had no sons, H6765
33 of the daughters of Z *were* Mahlah, and H6765
27: 1 Then came the daughters of Z, the son H6765
7 The daughters of Z speak right: thou H6765
36: 2 of Z our brother unto his daughters. H6765
6 the daughters of Z, saying, Let them H6765
10 Moses, so did the daughters of Z: H6765
11 the daughters of Z, were married unto H6765
Jos 17: 3 But Z, the son of Hepher, the son of H6765
1Ch 7:15 *was* Z: and Zelophehad had daughters. H6765
15 *was* Zelophehad: and Z had daughters. H6765

ZELOTES
Lk 6:15 *son* of Alphaeus, and Simon called Z, G2208
Act 1:13 Z, and Judas *the brother* of James. G2208

ZELZAH
1Sa 10: 2 of Benjamin at Z; and they will say unto H6766

ZEMARAIM
Jos 18:22 And Beth-arabah, and Z, and Beth-el, H6787
2Ch 13: 4 And Abijah stood up upon mount Z, H6787

ZEMARITE
Gen 10:18 And the Arvadite, and the **Z**, and the H6786
1Ch 1:16 And the Arvadite, and the **Z**, and the H6786

ZEMIRA
1Ch 7: 8 And the sons of Becher; **Z**, and Joash, H2160

ZENAN
Jos 15:37 **Z**, and Hadashah, and Migdal-gad, H6799

ZENAS
Tit 3:13 Bring **Z** the lawyer and Apollos on their *G2211*

ZEPHANIAH
2Ki 25:18 chief priest, and **Z** the second priest, H6846
1Ch 6:36 of Joel, the son of Azariah, the son of **Z**, H6846
Jer 21: 1 son of Melchiah, and **Z** the son of H6846
29:25 at Jerusalem, and to **Z** the son of H6846
29 And **Z** the priest read this letter in the H6846
37: 3 son of Shelemiah and **Z** the son of H6846
52:24 chief priest, and **Z** the second priest, H6846
Zep 1: 1 which came unto **Z** the son of Cushi, H6846
Zec 6:10 go into the house of Josiah the son of **Z**; H6846
14 to Hen the son of **Z**, for a memorial in H6846

ZEPHATH
Jdg 1:17 that inhabited **Z**, and utterly destroyed H6857

ZEPHATHAH
2Ch 14:10 in array in the valley of **Z** at Mareshah. H6859

ZEPHI
1Ch 1:36 and Omar, **Z**, and Gatam, Kenaz, H6825

ZEPHO
Gen 36:11 Omar, **Z**, and Gatam, and Kenaz. H6825
15 duke Omar, duke **Z**, duke Kenaz, H6825

ZEPHON
Nu 26:15 their families: of **Z**, the family of the H6827

ZEPHONITES
Nu 26:15 the family of the **Z**: of Haggi, the family H6831

ZER
Jos 19:35 And the fenced cities *are* Ziddim, **Z**, and H6863

ZERAH
Gen 36:13 Nahath, and **Z**, Shammah, and Mizzah: H2226
17 Nahath, duke **Z**, duke Shammah, duke H2226
33 And Bela died, and Jobab the son of **Z** H2226
46:12 and Pharez, and **Z**: but Er and Onan H2226
Nu 26:13 Of **Z**, the family of the Zarhites: of H2226
20 of **Z**, the family of the Zarhites. H2226
Jos 7: 1 of Zabdi, the son of **Z**, of the tribe of H2226
18 of **Z**, of the tribe of Judah, was taken. H2226
24 Achan the son of **Z**, and the silver, and H2226
22:20 Did not Achan the son of **Z** commit a H2226
1Ch 1:37 The sons of Reuel; Nahath, **Z**, H2226
44 son of **Z** of Bozrah reigned in his stead. H2226
2: 4 and **Z**. All the sons of Judah *were* five. H2226
6 And the sons of **Z**; Zimri, and Ethan, H2226
4:24 Nemuel, and Jamin, Jarib, **Z**, *and* Shaul: H2226
6:21 Joah his son, Iddo his son, **Z** his son, H2226
41 The son of Ethni, the son of **Z**, the son H2226
9: 6 And of the sons of **Z**; Jeuel, and their H2226
2Ch 14: 9 And there came out against them **Z** the H2226
Neh 11:24 of the children of **Z** the son of Judah, H2226

ZERAHIAH
1Ch 6: 6 And Uzzi begat **Z**, and Zerahiah begat H2228
6 And Uzzi begat Zerahiah, and **Z** begat H2228
51 Bukki his son, Uzzi his son, **Z** his son, H2228
Ezr 7: 4 The son of **Z**, the son of Uzzi, the son of H2228
8: 4 of **Z**, and with him two hundred males. H2228

ZERED
Dt 2:13 **Z**. And we went over the brook Zered. H2218
13 Zered. And we went over the brook **Z**. H2218
14 over the brook **Z**, *was* thirty and eight H2218

ZEREDA
1Ki 11:26 an Ephrathite of **Z**, Solomon's servant, H6868

ZEREDATHAH
2Ch 4:17 the clay ground between Succoth and **Z**. H6868

ZERERATH
Jdg 7:22 to Beth-shittah in **Z**, *and* to the border H6888

ZERESH
Est 5:10 called for his friends, and **Z** his wife. H2238
14 Then said **Z** his wife and all his friends H2238
6:13 And Haman told **Z** his wife and all his H2238
13 his wise men and **Z** his wife unto him, H2238

ZERETH
1Ch 4: 7 And the sons of Helah *were*, **Z**, and H6889

ZERI
1Ch 25: 3 Gedaliah, and **Z**, and Jeshaiah, H6874

ZEROR
1Sa 9: 1 of Abiel, the son of **Z**, the son of H6872

ZERUAH
1Ki 11:26 name *was* **Z**, a widow woman, even H6871

ZERUBBABEL
1Ch 3:19 And the sons of Pedaiah *were*, **Z**, and H2216
19 and the sons of **Z**; Meshullam, and H2216
Ezr 2: 2 Which came with **Z**: Jeshua, Nehemiah, H2216
3: 2 the priests, and **Z** the son of Shealtiel, H2216
8 month, began **Z** the son of Shealtiel, H2216
4: 2 Then they came to **Z**, and to the chief of H2216
3 But **Z**, and Jeshua, and the rest of the H2216
5: 2 Then rose up **Z** the son of Shealtiel, and H2217
Neh 7: 7 Who came with **Z**, Jeshua, Nehemiah, H2216
12: 1 Levites that went up with **Z** the son of H2216
47 And all Israel in the days of **Z**, and in H2216
Hag 1: 1 the prophet unto **Z** the son of Shealtiel, H2216
12 Then **Z** the son of Shealtiel, and Joshua H2216
14 And the LORD stirred up the spirit of **Z** H2216
2: 2 Speak now to **Z** the son of Shealtiel, H2216
4 Yet now be strong, O **Z**, saith the LORD; H2216
21 Speak to **Z**, governor of Judah, saying, I H2216
23 will I take thee, O **Z**, my servant, the son H2216
Zec 4: 6 of the LORD unto **Z**, saying, Not by H2216
7 mountain? before **Z** *thou shalt become* H2216
9 The hands of **Z** have laid the H2216
10 in the hand of **Z** *with* those seven; they H2216

ZERUIAH
1Sa 26: 6 to Abishai the son of **Z**, brother to Joab, H6870
2Sa 2:13 And Joab the son of **Z**, and the servants H6870
18 And there were three sons of **Z** there, H6870
3:39 men the sons of **Z** *be* too hard for me: H6870
8:16 And Joab the son of **Z** *was* over the H6870
14: 1 Now Joab the son of **Z** perceived that H6870
16: 9 Then said Abishai the son of **Z** unto the H6870
10 with you, ye sons of **Z**? so let him curse, H6870
17:25 of Nahash, sister to **Z** Joab's mother. H6870
18: 2 of Abishai the son of **Z**, Joab's brother, H6870
19:21 But Abishai the son of **Z** answered and H6870
22 you, ye sons of **Z**, that ye should this H6870
21:17 But Abishai the son of **Z** succoured H6870
23:18 of Joab, the son of **Z**, was chief among H6870
37 armourbearer to Joab the son of **Z**, H6870
1Ki 1: 7 Joab the son of **Z**, and with Abiathar the H6870
2: 5 Joab the son of **Z** did to me, *and* what H6870
22 the priest, and for Joab the son of **Z**. H6870
1Ch 2:16 Whose sisters *were* **Z**, and Abigail. And H6870
16 **Z**; Abishai, and Joab, and Asahel, three. H6870
11: 6 son of **Z** went first up, and was chief. H6870
39 the armourbearer of Joab the son of **Z**, H6870
18:12 Moreover Abishai the son of **Z** slew of H6870
15 And Joab the son of **Z** *was* over the H6870
26:28 Joab the son of **Z**, had dedicated; *and* H6870
27:24 Joab the son of **Z** began to number, but H6870

ZETHAM
1Ch 23: 8 chief *was* Jehiel, and **Z**, and Joel, three. H2241
26:22 The sons of Jehieli; **Z**, and Joel his H2241

ZETHAN
1Ch 7:10 and **Z**, and Tharshish, and Ahishahar. H2133

ZETHAR
Est 1:10 and Abagtha, **Z**, and Carcas, the seven H2242

ZIA
1Ch 5:13 and Jachan, and **Z**, and Heber, seven. H2127

ZIBA
2Sa 9: 2 whose name *was* **Z**. And when they had H6717
2 thou **Z**? And he said, Thy servant *is he*. H6717
3 unto him? And **Z** said unto the king, H6717
4 Where *is* he? And **Z** said unto the king, H6717
9 Then the king called to **Z**, Saul's H6717
9:10 **Z** had fifteen sons and twenty servants. H6717
11 Then said **Z** unto the king, According H6717
12 of **Z** *were* servants unto Mephibosheth. H6717
16: 1 top *of the hill*, behold, **Z** the servant of H6717
2 And the king said unto **Z**, What H6717
2 by these? And **Z** said, The asses *be* for H6717
3 master's son? And **Z** said unto the king, H6717
4 Then said the king to **Z**, Behold, thine H6717
4 And **Z** said, I humbly beseech H6717
19:17 with him, and **Z** the servant of the H6717
29 have said, Thou and **Z** divide the land. H6717

ZIBEON
Gen 36: 2 of Anah the daughter of **Z** the Hivite; H6649
14 the daughter of **Z**, Esau's wife: and she H6649
20 Lotan, and Shobal, and **Z**, and Anah, H6649
24 And these *are* the children of **Z**; both H6649
24 as he fed the asses of **Z** his father. H6649
29 duke Shobal, duke **Z**, duke Anah, H6649
1Ch 1:38 and Shobal, and **Z**, and Anah, and H6649
40 And the sons of **Z**; Aiah, and Anah. H6649

ZIBIA
1Ch 8: 9 and **Z**, and Mesha, and Malcham, H6644

ZIBIAH
2Ki 12: 1 mother's name *was* **Z** of Beer-sheba. H6645
2Ch 24: 1 name also *was* **Z** of Beer-sheba. H6645

ZICHRI
Ex 6:21 of Izhar; Korah, and Nepheg, and **Z**. H2147
1Ch 8:19 And Jakim, and **Z**, and Zabdi, H2147
23 And Abdon, and **Z**, and Hanan, H2147
27 And Jaresiah, and Eliah, and **Z**, the H2147
9:15 Micah, the son of **Z**, the son of Asaph; H2147
26:25 and **Z** his son, and Shelomith his son. H2147
27:16 Eliezer the son of **Z**: of the Simeonites, H2147
2Ch 17:16 the son of **Z**, who willingly offered H2147
23: 1 the son of **Z**, into covenant with him. H2147
28: 7 And **Z**, a mighty man of Ephraim, slew H2147
Neh 11: 9 And Joel the son of **Z** *was* their H2147
12:17 Of Abijah, **Z**; of Miniamin, of Moadiah, H2147

ZIDDIM
Jos 19:35 And the fenced cities *are* **Z**, Zer, and H6661

ZIDKIJAH
Neh 10: 1 Tirshatha, the son of Hachaliah, and **Z**, H6667

ZIDON
Gen 49:13 of ships; and his border *shall be* unto **Z**. H6721
Jos 11: 8 chased them unto great **Z**, and unto H6721
19:28 and Kanah, *even* unto great **Z**; H6721
Jdg 1:31 the inhabitants of **Z**, nor of Ahlab, nor H6721
10: 6 Syria, and the gods of **Z**, and the gods of H6721
18:28 it *was* far from **Z**, and they had no H6721
2Sa 24: 6 they came to Dan-jaan, and about to **Z**, H6721
1Ki 17: 9 *belongeth* to **Z**, and dwell there: behold, H6721
1Ch 1:13 And Canaan begat **Z** his firstborn, and H6721
Ezr 3: 7 oil, unto them of **Z**, and to them of Tyre, H6722
Isa 23: 2 the merchants of **Z**, that pass over the H6721
4 Be thou ashamed, O **Z**: for the sea hath H6721
12 virgin, daughter of **Z**: arise, pass over to H6721
Jer 25:22 all the kings of **Z**, and the kings of the H6721
27: 3 and to the king of **Z**, by the hand of the H6721
47: 4 off from Tyrus and **Z** every helper that H6721
Ezk 27: 8 The inhabitants of **Z** and Arvad were H6721
28:21 Son of man, set thy face against **Z**, and H6721
22 against thee, O **Z**; and I will be glorified H6721
Joel 3: 4 me, O Tyre, and **Z**, and all the coasts of H6721
Zec 9: 2 Tyrus, and **Z**, though it be very wise. H6721

ZIDONIANS
Jdg 10:12 The **Z** also, and the Amalekites, and H6722
18: 7 the manner of the **Z**, quiet and secure; H6722
7 **Z**, and had no business with *any* man. H6722
1Ki 11: 1 Ammonites, Edomites, **Z**, *and* Hittites; H6722
5 the goddess of the **Z**, and after Milcom H6722
33 the goddess of the **Z**, Chemosh the god H6722
16:31 king of the **Z**, and went and served H6722
2Ki 23:13 of the **Z**, and for Chemosh the H6722
1Ch 22: 4 for the **Z** and they of Tyre brought H6722
Ezk 32:30 of them, and all the **Z**, which are gone H6722

ZIF
1Ki 6: 1 in the month **Z**, which *is* the second H2099
37 house of the LORD laid, in the month **Z**: H2099

ZIHA
Ezr 2:43 The Nethinims: the children of Z, the H6727
Neh 7:46 The Nethinims: the children of Z, the H6727
11:21 Z and Gispa *were* over the Nethinims. H6727

ZIKLAG
Jos 15:31 And Z, and Madmannah, and H6860
19: 5 And Z, and Beth-marcaboth, and H6860
1Sa 27: 6 Then Achish gave him Z that day: H6860
6 day: wherefore Z pertaineth unto the H6860
30: 1 men were come to Z on the third day, H6860
1 the south, and Z, and smitten Ziklag, H6860
1 and smitten Z, and burned it with fire; H6860
14 of Caleb; and we burned Z with fire. H6860
26 And when David came to Z, he sent of H6860
2Sa 1: 1 and David had abode two days in Z; H6860
4:10 and slew him in Z, who *thought* that I H6860
1Ch 4:30 at Bethuel, and at Hormah, and at Z, H6860
12: 1 came to David to Z, while he yet kept H6860
20 As he went to Z, there fell to him of H6860
Neh 11:28 And at Z, and at Mekonah, and in the H6860

ZILLAH
Gen 4:19 *was* Adah, and the name of the other Z. H6741
22 And Z, she also bare Tubal-cain, an H6741
23 wives, Adah and Z, Hear my voice; ye H6741

ZILPAH
Gen 29:24 Leah Z his maid *for* an handmaid. H2153
30: 9 Z her maid, and gave her Jacob to wife. H2153
10 And Z Leah's maid bare Jacob a son. H2153
12 And Z Leah's maid bare Jacob a second H2153
35:26 And the sons of Z, Leah's handmaid; H2153
37: 2 with the sons of Z, his father's wives: H2153
46:18 These *are* the sons of Z, whom Laban H2153

ZILTHAI
1Ch 8:20 And Elienai, and Z, and Eliel, H6769
12:20 and Elihu, and Z, captains of the H6769

ZIMMAH
1Ch 6:20 Libni his son, Jahath his son, Z his son, H2155
42 The son of Ethan, the son of Z, the son H2155
2Ch 29:12 the son of Z, and Eden the son of Joah: H2155

ZIMRAN
Gen 25: 2 And she bare him Z, and Jokshan, and H2175
1Ch 1:32 she bare Z, and Jokshan, and Medan, H2175

ZIMRI
Nu 25:14 woman, *was* Z, the son of Salu, a prince H2174
1Ki 16: 9 And his servant Z, captain of half *his* H2174
10 And Z went in and smote him, and H2174
12 Thus did Z destroy all the house of H2174
15 king of Judah did Z reign seven days in H2174
16 heard say, Z hath conspired, and H2174
18 And it came to pass, when Z saw that H2174
20 Now the rest of the acts of Z, and his H2174
2Ki 9:31 *Had* Z peace, who slew his master? H2174
1Ch 2: 6 And the sons of Zerah; Z, and Ethan, H2174
8:36 and Z; and Zimri begat Moza, H2174
36 and Zimri; and Z begat Moza, H2174
9:42 and Z; and Zimri begat Moza; H2174
42 and Zimri; and Z begat Moza; H2174
Jer 25:25 And all the kings of Z, and all the kings H2174

ZIN
Nu 13:21 the wilderness of Z unto Rehob, as men H6790
20: 1 into the desert of Z in the first month: H6790
27:14 in the desert of Z, in the strife of the H6790
14 in Kadesh in the wilderness of Z. H6790
33:36 in the wilderness of Z, which *is* Kadesh. H6790
34: 3 the wilderness of Z along by the coast H6790
4 and pass on to Z: and the going forth H6790
Dt 32:51 in the wilderness of Z; because ye H6790
Jos 15: 1 the wilderness of Z southward *was* the H6790
3 passed along to Z, and ascended up on H6790

ZINA
1Ch 23:10 And the sons of Shimei *were*, Jahath, Z, H2126

ZION
2Sa 5: 7 hold of Z: the same *is* the city of David. H6726
1Ki 8: 1 out of the city of David, which *is* Z. H6726
2Ki 19:21 the daughter of Z hath despised thee, H6726
31 out of mount Z: the zeal of the LORD H6726
1Ch 11: 5 castle of Z, which *is* the city of David. H6726
2Ch 5: 2 out of the city of David, which *is* Z. H6726
Ps 2: 6 I set my king upon my holy hill of Z. H6726
Ps 9:11 Z: declare among the people his doings. H6726
14 of Z: I will rejoice in thy salvation. H6726
14: 7 *were come* out of Z! when the LORD H6726
20: 2 sanctuary, and strengthen thee out of Z; H6726
48: 2 earth, *is* mount Z, *on* the sides of the H6726
11 Let mount Z rejoice, let the daughters H6726
12 Walk about Z, and go round about her: H6726
50: 2 Out of Z, the perfection of beauty, God H6726
51:18 Do good in thy good pleasure unto Z: H6726
53: 6 *were come* out of Z! When God bringeth H6726
69:35 For God will save Z, and will build the H6726
74: 2 this mount Z, wherein thou hast dwelt. H6726
76: 2 tabernacle, and his dwelling place in Z. H6726
78:68 of Judah, the mount Z which he loved. H6726
84: 7 *one of them* in Z appeareth before God. H6726
87: 2 The LORD loveth the gates of Z more H6726
5 And of Z it shall be said, This and that H6726
97: 8 Z heard, and was glad; and the H6726
99: 2 The LORD *is* great in Z; and he *is* high H6726
102:13 *and* have mercy upon Z: for the time to H6726
16 When the LORD shall build up Z, he H6726
21 To declare the name of the LORD in Z, H6726
110: 2 of thy strength out of Z: rule thou in the H6726
125: 1 *shall be* as mount Z, *which* cannot be H6726
126: 1 of Z, we were like them that dream. H6726
128: 5 The LORD shall bless thee out of Z: and H6726
129: 5 and turned back that hate Z. H6726
132:13 For the LORD hath chosen Z; he hath H6726
133: 3 the mountains of Z: for there the LORD H6726
134: 3 heaven and earth bless thee out of Z. H6726
135:21 Blessed be the LORD out of Z, which H6726
137: 1 yea, we wept, when we remembered Z. H6726
3 *saying*, Sing us *one* of the songs of Z. H6726
146:10 *even* thy God, O Z, unto all generations. H6726
147:12 O Jerusalem; praise thy God, O Z. H6726
149: 2 the children of Z be joyful in their King. H6726
Song 3:11 Go forth, O ye daughters of Z, and H6726
Isa 1: 8 And the daughter of Z is left as a H6726
27 Z shall be redeemed with judgment, H6726
2: 3 his paths: for out of Z shall go forth the H6726
3:16 the daughters of Z are haughty, and H6726
17 the daughters of Z, and the LORD will H6726
4: 3 *that he that is* left in Z, and *he that* H6726
4 of the daughters of Z, and shall have H6726
5 place of mount Z, and upon her H6726
8:18 of hosts, which dwelleth in mount Z. H6726
10:12 work upon mount Z and on Jerusalem, H6726
24 that dwellest in Z, be not afraid of the H6726
32 the daughter of Z, the hill of Jerusalem. H6726
12: 6 Cry out and shout, thou inhabitant of Z: H6726
14:32 hath founded Z, and the poor of his H6726
16: 1 unto the mount of the daughter of Z. H6726
18: 7 of the LORD of hosts, the mount Z. H6726
24:23 reign in mount Z, and in Jerusalem, H6726
28:16 Behold, I lay in Z for a foundation a H6726
29: 8 nations be, that fight against mount Z. H6726
30:19 For the people shall dwell in Z at H6726
31: 4 for mount Z, and for the hill thereof. H6726
9 *is* in Z, and his furnace in Jerusalem. H6726
33: 5 Z with judgment and righteousness. H6726
14 The sinners in Z are afraid; fearfulness H6726
20 Look upon Z, the city of our H6726
34: 8 recompences for the controversy of Z. H6726
35:10 return, and come to Z with songs and H6726
37:22 the daughter of Z, hath despised thee, H6726
32 out of mount Z: the zeal of the LORD H6726
40: 9 O Z, that bringest good tidings, get thee H6726
41:27 The first *shall say* to Z, Behold, behold H6726
46:13 place salvation in Z for Israel my glory. H6726
49:14 But Z said, The LORD hath forsaken H6726
51: 3 For the LORD shall comfort Z: he will H6726
11 with singing unto Z; and everlasting joy H6726
16 and say unto Z, Thou *art* my people. H6726
52: 1 Awake, awake; put on thy strength, O Z; H6726
2 of thy neck, O captive daughter of Z. H6726
7 that saith unto Z, Thy God reigneth! H6726
8 when the LORD shall bring again Z. H6726
59:20 And the Redeemer shall come to Z, and H6726
60:14 LORD, The Z of the Holy One of Israel. H6726
61: 3 To appoint unto them that mourn in Z, H6726
62:11 ye to the daughter of Z, Behold, thy H6726
64:10 Thy holy cities are a wilderness, Z is a H6726
66: 8 for as soon as Z travailed, she brought H6726
Jer 3:14 of a family, and I will bring you to Z: H6726
4: 6 Set up the standard toward Z: retire, H6726
31 of the daughter of Z, *that* bewaileth H6726
6: 2 I have likened the daughter of Z to a H6726
23 for war against thee, O daughter of Z. H6726
8:19 *Is* not the LORD in Z? *is* not her king in H6726
Jer 9:19 For a voice of wailing is heard out of Z, H6726
14:19 hath thy soul lothed Z? why hast thou H6726
26:18 LORD of hosts; Z shall be plowed *like* H6726
30:17 This *is* Z, whom no man seeketh after. H6726
31: 6 us go up to Z unto the LORD our God. H6726
12 sing in the height of Z, and shall flow H6726
50: 5 They shall ask the way to Z with their H6726
28 to declare in Z the vengeance of the H6726
51:10 in Z the work of the LORD our God. H6726
24 in Z in your sight, saith the LORD. H6726
35 the inhabitant of Z say; and my blood H6726
Lam 1: 4 The ways of Z do mourn, because none H6726
6 And from the daughter of Z all her H6726
17 Z spreadeth forth her hands, *and there* H6726
2: 1 the daughter of Z with a cloud in his H6726
4 of Z: he poured out his fury like fire. H6726
6 to be forgotten in Z, and hath despised H6726
8 of the daughter of Z: he hath stretched H6726
10 The elders of the daughter of Z sit upon H6726
13 O virgin daughter of Z? for thy breach *is* H6726
18 of the daughter of Z, let tears run down H6726
4: 2 The precious sons of Z, comparable to H6726
11 kindled a fire in Z, and it hath devoured H6726
22 O daughter of Z; he will no more carry H6726
5:11 They ravished the women in Z, *and* the H6726
18 Because of the mountain of Z, which is H6726
Joel 2: 1 Blow ye the trumpet in Z, and sound an H6726
15 Blow the trumpet in Z, sanctify a fast, H6726
23 Be glad then, ye children of Z, and H6726
32 for in mount Z and in Jerusalem shall H6726
3:16 The LORD also shall roar out of Z, and H6726
17 God dwelling in Z, my holy mountain: H6726
21 cleansed: for the LORD dwelleth in Z. H6726
Am 1: 2 will roar from Z, and utter his voice H6726
6: 1 Woe to them *that are* at ease in Z, and H6726
Oba 17 But upon mount Z shall be deliverance, H6726
21 up on mount Z to judge the mount H6726
Mic 1:13 sin to the daughter of Z: for the H6726
3:10 They build up Z with blood, and H6726
12 Therefore shall Z for your sake be H6726
4: 2 shall go forth of Z, and the word of the H6726
7 Z from henceforth, even for ever. H6726
8 of the daughter of Z, unto thee shall it H6726
10 forth, O daughter of Z, like a woman in H6726
11 be defiled, and let our eye look upon Z. H6726
13 Arise and thresh, O daughter of Z: for I H6726
Zep 3:14 Sing, O daughter of Z; shout, O Israel; H6726
16 *and to* Z, Let not thine hands be slack. H6726
Zec 1:14 and for Z with a great jealousy. H6726
17 Z, and shall yet choose Jerusalem. H6726
2: 7 Deliver thyself, O Z, that dwellest *with* H6726
10 Sing and rejoice, O daughter of Z: for, H6726
8: 2 I was jealous for Z with great jealousy, H6726
3 I am returned unto Z, and will dwell in H6726
9: 9 Rejoice greatly, O daughter of Z; shout, H6726
13 up thy sons, O Z, against thy sons, O H6726

ZION'S
Isa 62: 1 For Z sake will I not hold my peace, H6726

ZIOR
Jos 15:54 and Z; nine cities with their villages: H6730

ZIPH
Jos 15:24 Z, and Telem, and Bealoth, H2128
55 Maon, Carmel, and Z, and Juttah, H2128
1Sa 23:14 in the wilderness of Z. And Saul sought H2128
15 *was* in the wilderness of Z in a wood. H2128
24 And they arose, and went to Z before H2128
26: 2 to the wilderness of Z, having three H2128
2 to seek David in the wilderness of Z. H2128
1Ch 2:42 was the father of Z; and the sons of H2128
4:16 And the sons of Jehaleleel; Z, and H2128
2Ch 11: 8 And Gath, and Mareshah, and Z, H2128

ZIPHAH
1Ch 4:16 And the sons of Jehaleleel; Ziph, and Z, H2129

ZIPHIMS
Ps 54: ttl of David, when the Z came and said to H2130

ZIPHION
Gen 46:16 And the sons of Gad; Z, and Haggi, H6837

ZIPHITES
1Sa 23:19 Then came up the Z to Saul to Gibeah, H2130
26: 1 And the Z came unto Saul to Gibeah, H2130

ZIPHRON
Nu 34: 9 And the border shall go on to **Z**, and the H2202

ZIPPOR
Nu 22: 2 And Balak the son of **Z** saw all that H6834
4 And Balak the son of **Z** *was* king of the H6834
10 Balak the son of **Z**, king of Moab, hath H6834
16 Balak the son of **Z**, Let nothing, I pray H6834
23:18 hear; hearken unto me, thou son of **Z**: H6834
Jos 24: 9 Then Balak the son of **Z**, king of Moab, H6834
Jdg 11:25 Balak the son of **Z**, king of Moab? did he H6834

ZIPPORAH
Ex 2:21 and he gave Moses **Z** his daughter. H6855
4:25 Then **Z** took a sharp stone, and cut off H6855
18: 2 father in law, took **Z**, Moses' wife, after H6855

ZITHRI
Ex 6:22 Uzziel; Mishael, and Elzaphan, and **Z**. H5644

ZIZ
2Ch 20:16 up by the cliff of **Z**; and ye shall find H6732

ZIZA
1Ch 4:37 And **Z** the son of Shiphi, the son of H2124
2Ch 11:20 and Attai, and **Z**, and Shelomith. H2124

ZIZAH
1Ch 23:11 And Jahath was the chief, and **Z** the H2125

ZOAN
Nu 13:22 built seven years before **Z** in Egypt.) H6814
Ps 78:12 in the land of Egypt, *in* the field of **Z**. H6814
43 Egypt, and his wonders in the field of **Z**: H6814
Isa 19:11 Surely the princes of **Z** *are* fools, the H6814
13 The princes of **Z** are become fools, the H6814
30: 4 For his princes were at **Z**, and his H6814
Ezk 30:14 in **Z**, and will execute judgments in No. H6814

ZOAR
Gen 13:10 land of Egypt, as thou comest unto **Z**. H6820
14: 2 and the king of Bela, which is **Z**. H6820
8 of Bela (the same *is* **Z**;) and they joined H6820
19:22 the name of the city was called **Z**. H6820
23 upon the earth when Lot entered into **Z**. H6820
30 And Lot went up out of **Z**, and dwelt in H6820
30 feared to dwell in **Z**: and he dwelt in a H6820
Dt 34: 3 of Jericho, the city of palm trees, unto **Z**. H6820
Isa 15: 5 *shall flee* unto **Z**, an heifer of three years H6820
Jer 48:34 uttered their voice, from **Z** *even* unto H6820

ZOBA
2Sa 10: 6 and the Syrians of **Z**, twenty thousand H6678
8 and the Syrians of **Z**, and of Rehob, and H6678

ZOBAH
1Sa 14:47 against the kings of **Z**, and against the H6678
2Sa 8: 3 son of Rehob, king of **Z**, as he went to H6678
5 Hadadezer king of **Z**, David slew of the H6678
12 of Hadadezer, son of Rehob, king of **Z**. H6678
23:36 Igal the son of Nathan of **Z**, Bani the H6678
1Ki 11:23 fled from his lord Hadadezer king of **Z**: H6678
24 David slew them *of* **Z**: and they went to
1Ch 18: 3 And David smote Hadarezer king of **Z** H6678
5 Hadarezer king of **Z**, David slew of the H6678
9 all the host of Hadarezer king of **Z**; H6678
19: 6 out of Syria-maachah, and out of **Z**. H6678

ZOBEBAH
1Ch 4: 8 And Coz begat Anub, and **Z**, and the H6637

ZOHAR
Gen 23: 8 entreat for me to Ephron the son of **Z**, H6714
25: 9 of **Z** the Hittite, which *is* before Mamre; H6714
46:10 and Jachin, and **Z**, and Shaul the son of H6714
Ex 6:15 and Jachin, and **Z**, and Shaul the son of H6714

ZOHELETH
1Ki 1: 9 by the stone of **Z**, which *is* by En-rogel, H2120

ZOHETH
1Ch 4:20 sons of Ishi *were*, **Z**, and Ben-zoheth. H2105

ZOPHAH
1Ch 7:35 And the sons of his brother Helem; **Z**, H6690
36 The sons of **Z**; Suah, and Harnepher, H6690

ZOPHAI
1Ch 6:26 *As for* Elkanah: the sons of Elkanah; **Z** H6689

ZOPHAR
Job 2:11 the Shuhite, and **Z** the Naamathite: for H6691
11: 1 Then answered **Z** the Naamathite, and H6691
20: 1 Then answered **Z** the Naamathite, and H6691
42: 9 the Shuhite *and* **Z** the Naamathite H6691

ZOPHIM
Nu 23:14 And he brought him into the field of **Z**, H6839

ZORAH
Jos 19:41 was **Z**, and Eshtaol, and Ir-shemesh, H6881
Jdg 13: 2 And there was a certain man of **Z**, of the H6881
25 camp of Dan between **Z** and Eshtaol. H6881
16:31 him between **Z** and Eshtaol in the H6881
18: 2 of valour, from **Z**, and from Eshtaol, to H6881
8 And they came unto their brethren to **Z** H6881
11 of the Danites, out of **Z** and out of H6881
2Ch 11:10 And **Z**, and Aijalon, and Hebron, which H6881

ZORATHITES
1Ch 4: 2 Lahad. These *are* the families of the **Z**. H6882

ZOREAH
Jos 15:33 *And* in the valley, Eshtaol, and **Z**, and H6881

ZORITES
1Ch 2:54 and half of the Manahethites, the **Z**. H6882

ZOROBABEL
Mt 1:12 begat Salathiel; and Salathiel begat **Z**; *G2216*
13 And **Z** begat Abiud; and Abiud begat *G2216*
Lk 3:27 was *the son* of **Z**, which was *the son* of *G2216*

ZUAR
Nu 1: 8 Of Issachar; Nethaneel the son of **Z**. H6686
2: 5 the son of **Z** *shall be* captain of the H6686
7:18 son of **Z**, prince of Issachar, did offer: H6686
23 the offering of Nethaneel the son of **Z**. H6686
10:15 of Issachar *was* Nethaneel the son of **Z**. H6686

ZUPH
1Sa 1: 1 of Tohu, the son of **Z**, an Ephrathite: H6689
9: 5 to the land of **Z**, Saul said to his servant H6689
1Ch 6:35 The son of **Z**, the son of Elkanah, the H6689

ZUR
Nu 25:15 the daughter of **Z**; he *was* head over a H6698
31: 8 and Rekem, and **Z**, and Hur, and Reba, H6698
Jos 13:21 and Rekem, and **Z**, and Hur, and Reba, H6698
1Ch 8:30 And his firstborn son Abdon, and **Z**, H6698
9:36 And his firstborn son Abdon, then **Z**, H6698

ZURIEL
Nu 3:35 of Merari *was* **Z** the son of Abihail: H6700

ZURISHADDAI
Nu 1: 6 Of Simeon; Shelumiel the son of **Z**. H6701
2:12 Simeon *shall be* Shelumiel the son of **Z**. H6701
7:36 On the fifth day Shelumiel the son of **Z**, H6701
41 the offering of Shelumiel the son of **Z**. H6701
10:19 of Simeon *was* Shelumiel the son of **Z**. H6701

ZUZIMS
Gen 14: 5 Karnaim, and the **Z** in Ham, and the H2104

Appendix

of

Pronouns, Prepositions, Common Words, etc.

APNDX

A

2Th 1:5, 6; **2:**3, 11; **3:**15

1Ti 1:5[2], 8, 9, 13[2], 15, 16, 18, 19; **2:**2, 6, 7[2], 12; **3:**1[4], 2, 3, 5, 6, 7, 9, 10, 13[2]; **4:**2, 6, 9; **5:**1, 5, 9, 23; **6:**9, 12, 13, 19

2Ti 1:7, 11[2]; **2:**3, 4, 5, 11, 15, 17, 20, 21[2], 22; **3:**5, 15; **4:**7, 8

Tit 1:1, 7, 8[2], 12; **2:**7, 14; **3:**8, 10

Phlm 1, 9, 15, 16[3], 17, 22

Heb 1:4, 5[2], 7, 8, 11, 12; **2:**2, 6, 7, 9, 17; **3:**5[2], 6; **4:**1, 4, 7[2], 9, 12, 14; **5:**6, 8, 13; **6:**18; **7:**2, 3, 5, 12, 16, 17, 18, 19, 21, 22[2]; **8:**2, 4, 6[2], 8, 10[2], 13; **9:**1, 2, 9, 11, 16, 17; **10:**1, 3, 5, 15, 20, 22, 27, 31, 32, 33, 34, 37; **11:**2, 4, 6, 8, 9, 10, 11, 14, 16[2], 19, 21, 23, 25, 35, 39; **12:**1, 10, 19, 20[2], 28, 29; **13:**9, 18, 22

Jas 1:1, 6, 8, 11, 18, 23[4], 25[2]; **2:**2[3], 3, 11, 14, 15, 18, 24; **3:**2, 4, 5[3], 6[2], 11, 12, 13[2]; **4:**4, 11[2], 13[2], 14[2]; **5:**3, 5, 16, 17, 20[2]

1Pt 1:3, 6, 19, 22; **2:**4, 5, 6, 8[2], 9[3], 10, 16, 19; **3:**4, 9, 15, 16, 20, 21; **4:**15[3], 16, 19; **5:**1[2], 2, 4, 8, 10, 12, 14

2Pt 1:1, 17, 19[3]; **2:**3, 5, 17, 19; **3:**8[2], 10[2], 13

1Jn 1:10; **2:**4, 8, 22; **3:**15; **4:**20[2]; **5:**10, 16[2], 17

2Jn 4, 5, 7, 8

3Jn 6

Jude 9, 22

Rev 1:10[2], 11, 13[2], 14, 15, 16; **2:**10, 14[2], 17[2], 18, 20[2], 22, 27[2]; **3:**1, 3, 4, 8, 12; **4:**1[2], 2, 3[3], 6, 7[5]; **5:**1, 2[2], 6, 9, 12; **6:**2[3], 4, 5[2], 6[4], 8, 10, 11, 12, 13[2], 14; **7:**2, 9, 10; **8:**3, 8, 10[2], 12, 13; **9:**1, 2[2], 5[2], 11, 13, 15[3]; **10:**1[2], 2, 3[2], 4; **11:**1[2], 3, 12[2], 13; **12:**1[3], 3, 5[2], 6[2], 10, 12, 14[3], 15; **13:**1, 2[3], 5, 11[2], 14, 16, 18; **14:**1, 2[2], 3, 7, 9, 13, 14[3], 15, 17, 18, 20; **15:**2; **16:**1, 2, 3, 15, 16, 17, 18, 21[2]; **17:**3[2], 4, 5, 10; **18:**2[2], 7, 21[3], 22, 23; **19:**1, 5, 6, 11, 12[2], 13, 15[2], 16, 17, 20; **20:**1, 2, 3[2], 4, 6, 11; **21:**1[2], 2, 3, 10, 11[2], 12, 15, 17, 19, 20[3], 27; **22:**1, 15

ABOUT

Gen 23:17; **35:**5; **37:**7; **38:**24; **39:**11; **41:**25, 28, 42, 48; **42:**24; **46:**34

Ex 7:24; **9:**18; **11:**4; **12:**37; **13:**18; **16:**13; **19:**12, 23; **25:**11, 24, 25[2]; **27:**17; **28:**32, 33[2], 34; **29:**16, 20; **30:**3[2]; **32:**28; **37:**2, 11, 12[2], 26[2]; **38:**16, 20, 31[2]; **39:**23, 25, 26; **40:**8, 33

Lev 1:5, 11; **3:**2, 8, 13; **6:**5; **7:**2; **8:**15, 19, 24; **9:**12, 18; **14:**41; **16:**18; **25:**31, 44

Nu 1:50, 53; **2:**2; **3:**26, 37; **4:**4, 14, 26, 32; **11:**8, 24, 31, 32; **16:**24, 34, 49; **22:**4; **32:**33; **34:**12; **35:**2, 4

Dt 6:14; **12:**10; **13:**7; **17:**14; **21:**2; **25:**19; **31:**21; **32:**10

Jos 2:5; **3:**4; **4:**13; **6:**3, 11, 15; **7:**3, 4, 5; **8:**12; **10:**13; **11:**6; **15:**12; **16:**6; **18:**20; **19:**8; **21:**11, 42, 44; **23:**1

Jdg 2:12, 14; **3:**29; **7:**21; **8:**10, 26; **9:**49; **16:**27; **17:**2; **19:**22; **20:**5, 29, 31, 39, 43

Ru 1:4, 19; **2:**17

1Sa 1:20; **4:**2, 20; **5:**8[2], 9, 10; **9:**13, 16, 22, 26; **13:**15; **14:**2, 14, 21; **15:**12, 27; **17:**42; **20:**12; **21:**5; **22:**2, 6, 7, 17; **23:**13, 26; **25:**13, 38; **26:**5, 7; **31:**9

2Sa 3:12; **4:**5; **5:**9; **7:**1; **14:**20; **18:**15; **20:**26; **22:**6, 12; **24:**6

1Ki 2:5, 15; **3:**1; **4:**24, 31; **5:**3; **6:**5[3], 6, 29; **7:**12, 15, 18, 20, 23[2], 24[2], 36; **8:**14; **18:**32, 35; **19:**2; **20:**6; **22:**6, 36

2Ki 1:8; **3:**25; **4:**16; **6:**14, 17; **7:**1, 18; **8:**21; **11:**7, 8, 11; **17:**15; **23:**5; **25:**1, 4, 10, 17

1Ch 4:33; **6:**55; **9:**27; **10:**9; **11:**8[2]; **15:**22; **18:**17; **22:**9; **28:**12

2Ch 2:9; **4:**2, 3[2]; **13:**13; **14:**7, 14; **15:**15; **17:**9, 10; **18:**31, 34; **20:**30; **23:**2, 7, 10; **26:**6; **33:**14; **34:**6

Ezr 1:6; **10:**15

Neh 5:17; **6:**16; **12:**28, 29; **13:**21

Job 1:5, 10[3]; **8:**17; **10:**8; **11:**18; **16:**13; **19:**12; **20:**23; **22:**10; **29:**5; **30:**18; **37:**12; **40:**22; **41:**14

Ps 3:6; **7:**7; **17:**9; **18:**5, 11; **27:**6; **32:**7, 10; **34:**7; **40:**12; **44:**13; **48:**12[2]; **49:**5; **50:**3; **55:**10; **59:**6, 14; **73:**6; **76:**11; **78:**28; **79:**3, 4; **88:**17[2]; **89:**7, 8; **97:**2, 3; **109:**3; **118:**10, 11[2], 12; **125:**2[2]; **128:**3; **139:**11; **140:**9; **142:**7

Prv 1:9; **3:**3; **6:**21; **20:**19

Ecc 1:6[2]; **2:**20; **12:**5

Song 3:2, 3, 7; **5:**7; **7:**2

Isa 3:18; **15:**8; **23:**16; **26:**20; **28:**27; **29:**3; **42:**25; **49:**18; **50:**11; **60:**4

Jer 1:15; **2:**36; **4:**17; **6:**3; **12:**9; **14:**18; **17:**26; **21:**14; **25:**9; **31:**22, 39; **32:**44; **33:**13; **41:**14; **46:**5, 14; **48:**17, 39; **49:**5; **50:**14, 15, 29, 32; **51:**2; **52:**4, 7, 14, 22, 23

Lam 1:17; **2:**3, 22; **3:**7

Ezk 1:4, 18, 27[2], 28; **4:**2; **5:**2, 5, 6, 7[2], 12, 14, 15; **6:**5, 13; **8:**10, 16; **10:**12; **11:**12; **12:**14; **16:**10, 37, 57[2]; **23:**24; **27:**11[2]; **28:**24, 26; **31:**4; **32:**22, 23, 24, 25, 26; **34:**26; **36:**4, 7, 36; **37:**2; **40:**5, 14, 16[2], 17, 25, 29, 30, 33, 36, 43; **41:**5, 6, 7[3], 8, 10, 11, 12, 16[2], 17, 19; **42:**15, 16, 17, 19, 20; **43:**12, 13, 17[2], 20; **45:**1, 2[2]; **46:**23[3]; **47:**2; **48:**35

Dan 5:7, 16, 29, 31; **9:**16, 21

Hos 7:2; **11:**12

Joel 3:11, 12

Am 3:11

Jna 2:3, 5[3], 6

Nah 3:8

Hab 1:4

Zec 2:5; **7:**7; **9:**8; **12:**2, 6; **14:**14

Mt 1:11; **3:**4, 5; **4:**23; **8:**18; **9:**22, 35; **14:**21, 35; **18:**6; **20:**3, 5, 6, 9; **21:**33; **27:**46

Mk 1:6, 28; **2:**2; **3:**5, 8, 32, 34[2]; **4:**10; **5:**13, 30, 32; **6:**6, 36, 44, 48, 55[2]; **8:**9, 33; **9:**8, 14, 42; **10:**23; **11:**11; **12:**1; **14:**51; **15:**17

Lk 1:56, 65; **2:**9, 37, 49; **3:**3, 23; **4:**14, 37; **6:**10; **7:**9, 17; **8:**37, 42; **9:**12, 14, 28; **10:**40, 41; **12:**35; **13:**8; **17:**2; **19:**43; **22:**41, 49, 59; **23:**44; **24:**13

Jn 1:39; **3:**25; **4:**6; **6:**10, 19; **7:**14, 19, 20; **10:**24; **11:**18, 44; **19:**14, 39; **20:**7; **21:**20

Act 1:15; **2:**10, 41; **3:**3; **4:**4; **5:**7, 16, 36; **9:**3, 29; **10:**3, 9, 38; **11:**19; **12:**1, 8; **13:**11, 18, 20; **14:**6, 20; **15:**2; **18:**14; **19:**7, 23, 34; **20:**3; **21:**31; **22:**6[2]; **24:**6; **25:**7, 15, 24; **26:**13, 21; **27:**27, 30

Ro 4:19; **10:**3; **15:**19

1Co 9:5, 13

2Co 4:10

Eph 4:14; **6:**14

1Ti 5:13; **6:**4

2Ti 2:14

Tit 3:9

Heb 8:5; **9:**4; **11:**30, 37; **12:**1; **13:**9

Jas 3:3, 4

1Pt 5:8

Jude 7, 9, 12

Rev 1:13; **4:**3, 4, 6, 8; **5:**11; **7:**11[2]; **8:**1; **10:**4; **16:**21; **20:**9

ABOVE

Gen 1:7, 20; **3:**14[2]; **6:**16; **7:**17; **27:**39; **28:**13; **48:**22; **49:**25, 26

Ex 18:11; **19:**5; **20:**4; **25:**21, 22; **26:**14, 24; **28:**27, 28; **29:**13, 22; **30:**14; **36:**19; **39:**20, 21; **40:**19, 20

Lev 3:4, 10, 15; **4:**9; **7:**4; **8:**16, 25; **9:**10, 19; **11:**21; **27:**7

Nu 3:49; **4:**25; **12:**3; **16:**3

Dt 4:39; **5:**8; **7:**6, 14; **10:**15; **14:**2; **17:**20; **25:**3; **26:**19; **28:**1, 13, 43; **30:**5

Jos 2:11; **3:**13, 16

Jdg 5:24[2]

1Sa 2:29

2Sa 22:17, 49

1Ki 7:3, 11, 20, 25, 29, 31; **8:**7, 23; **14:**9, 22; **16:**30

2Ki 21:11; **25:**28

1Ch 5:2; **16:**25; **23:**27; **27:**6; **29:**3, 11

2Ch 2:5; **4:**4; **5:**8; **11:**21; **24:**20; **25:**5; **34:**4

Neh 3:28; **7:**2; **8:**5; **9:**5; **12:**37, 39[3]

Est 2:17; **3:**1; **5:**11

Job 3:4; **18:**16; **28:**18; **31:**2, 28

Ps 8:1; **10:**5; **18:**16, 48; **27:**6; **45:**7; **50:**4; **57:**5[2], 11[2]; **78:**23; **95:**3; **96:**4; **97:**9[2]; **99:**2; **103:**11; **104:**6; **108:**4, 5[2]; **113:**4[2]; **119:**127[2]; **135:**5; **136:**6; **137:**6; **138:**2; **144:**7; **148:**4, 13

Prv 8:28; **15:**24; **31:**10

Ecc 2:7; **3:**19

Isa 2:2; **6:**2; **7:**11; **14:**13, 14; **45:**8

Jer 4:28; **15:**8; **17:**9; **31:**37; **35:**4; **52:**32

Lam 1:13

Ezk 1:22, 26[2]; **10:**1, 19; **11:**22; **16:**43; **29:**15; **31:**5; **37:**8; **41:**17, 20

Dan 6:3; **11:**5, 36, 37

Am 2:9

Mic 4:1

Nah 3:16

Mt 10:24[2]

Lk 3:20; **6:**40; **13:**2, 4

Jn 3:31[3]; **6:**13; **8:**23; **19:**11

Act 2:19; **4:**22; **26:**13

Ro 10:6; **14:**5

1Co 4:6; **10:**13; **15:**6

2Co 1:8; **11:**23; **12:**2, 6, 7[2]

Gal 1:14; **4:**26

Eph 1:21; **3:**20; **4:**6, 10; **6:**16

Php 2:9

Col 3:1, 2, 14

2Th 2:4

Phlm 16

Heb 1:9; **10:**8

Jas 1:17; **3:**15, 17; **5:**12

1Pt 4:8

3Jn 2

ACCORDING

Gen 6:22; **7:**5; **18:**10, 14, 21; **21:**23; **25:**13, 16; **27:**8, 19; **30:**34; **33:**14; **34:**12; **36:**40, 43; **39:**17; **40:**5; **41:**11, 12, 40, 54; **43:**7, 33[2]; **44:**2, 7, 10; **45:**21; **47:**12; **49:**28; **50:**6, 12

Ex 6:16, 17, 19, 25, 26; **8:**10, 13, 31; **12:**3, 4[2], 21, 25, 35; **16:**16[2], 18, 21; **17:**1; **21:**22, 31; **22:**17; **24:**4; **25:**9, 35; **26:**30; **28:**8, 10, 21[2]; **29:**35, 41[2]; **30:**37; **31:**11; **32:**28; **36:**1; **37:**21, 29; **38:**21; **39:**5, 14[3], 32, 42; **40:**16

Lev 4:3, 35; **5:**10, 12; **9:**16; **10:**7; **12:**2; **25:**15[2], 16[3], 50[2], 51, 52; **26:**21; **27:**8, 16, 17, 18, 25, 27[2]

Nu 1:18, 20, 22, 24, 26, 28, 30, 32, 34, 36, 38, 40, 42, 54; **2:**10, 18, 34[2]; **3:**16, 20, 22, 34, 51; **4:**31, 33, 37, 41, 45, 49[3]; **6:**21; **7:**5, 7, 8; **8:**4, 20; **9:**3[2], 5, 12, 14[2], 20[2]; **10:**13, 14, 18, 22, 28; **14:**17, 19, 20, 29; **15:**12[2], 24; **17:**2[2], 6; **18:**16; **23:**23; **24:**2; **26:**18, 22, 25, 27, 37, 43, 47, 50, 53, 54, 55, 56; **29:**6, 18, 21, 24, 27, 30, 33, 37, 40; **30:**2; **33:**2[2], 54; **34:**14[2]; **35:**8, 24; **36:**5

Dt 1:3, 30, 41, 46; **3:**24[2]; **4:**34; **9:**10; **10:**4, 9, 10; **12:**15; **16:**10, 17; **17:**10[2], 11[2]; **18:**16; **23:**23; **24:**8; **25:**2; **26:**13, 14; **29:**21; **30:**2; **31:**5; **32:**8; **34:**5

Jos 1:7, 8, 17; **2:**21; **4:**5, 8, 10; **7:**14[2]; **8:**8, 27, 34; **10:**32, 35, 37; **11:**23[2]; **12:**7; **13:**15, 24; **15:**12, 13, 20; **16:**5; **17:**4; **18:**4, 10, 11, 20, 21, 28; **19:**1, 8, 10, 16, 17, 23, 24, 31, 32, 39, 40, 48, 50; **21:**33, 44; **22:**9; **24:**5

Jdg 8:35; **9:**16; **11:**10, 36, 39; **20:**10; **21:**23

Ru 3:6

1Sa 2:35; **6:**4, 18; **8:**8; **13:**8; **14:**7; **17:**23; **23:**20; **25:**9, 30

2Sa 3:39; **7:**17[2], 21, 22; **9:**11; **14:**20; **22:**21[2], 25[2]; **24:**19

1Ki 2:6; **3:**6, 12; **4:**28; **5:**6, 10; **6:**3, 38; **7:**9, 36; **8:**32, 39, 43, 56; **9:**4, 11; **11:**37; **12:**24; **13:**5, 26; **14:**18, 24; **15:**29; **16:**12, 34; **17:**1, 5, 15, 16; **18:**31; **20:**4; **21:**26; **22:**38, 53

2Ki 1:17; **2:**22; **4:**16, 17, 44; **5:**14; **6:**18; **7:**16; **9:**26; **10:**17, 30; **11:**9; **14:**3, 6, 25; **15:**3, 34; **16:**3, 10, 11, 16; **17:**13; **18:**3; **21:**8[2]; **22:**13; **23:**16, 19, 25, 32, 35[2], 37; **24:**2, 3, 9, 19

1Ch 6:19, 32, 49; **9:**9; **11:**3, 10; **12:**23; **15:**15; **16:**40; **17:**15[2], 17, 19, 20; **23:**11, 31; **24:**3, 4, 19; **25:**1, 2, 6; **26:**13, 31; **28:**15

2Ch 3:4, 8; **4:**7; **6:**23, 30, 33; **7:**17, 18; **8:**13, 14; **17:**14; **23:**8; **24:**6; **25:**5; **26:**4, 11; **27:**2; **29:**2, 15, 25; **30:**6, 16, 19; **31:**2, 16; **32:**25; **33:**8; **34:**32; **35:**4[2], 5, 6, 10, 12, 13, 15, 16, 26

Ezr 3:4, 7; **6:**9, 13, 14[2], 17; **7:**6, 9, 14; **9:**1; **10:**3[2], 5, 8

Neh 2:8; **5:**12, 13, 19; **6:**6, 7, 14; **8:**18; **9:**27, 28; **12:**24, 45; **13:**22, 24

APNDX

Est 1:7, 8^{2}, 15, 21, 22^{2}; **2:**12, 18; **3:**12^{2}; **4:**16, 17; **8:**9^{4}; **9:**13, 27^{2}, 31

Job 1:5; **20:**18; **33:**6; **34:**11, 33; **36:**27; **42:**9

Ps 7:8^{2}, 17; **18:**20^{2}, 24^{2}; **20:**4; **25:**7; **28:**4^{2}; **33:**22; **35:**24; **48:**10; **51:**1^{2}; **62:**12; **69:**16; **74:**5; **78:**72; **79:**11; **90:**11, 15; **103:**10; **106:**45; **109:**26; **119:**9, 25, 28, 41, 58, 65, 76, 91, 107, 116, 124, 149^{2}, 154, 156, 159, 169, 170; **150:**2

Prv 12:8; **24:**12, 29; **26:**4, 5

Ecc 1:6; **8:**14^{2}

Isa 8:20; **9:**3; **10:**26; **21:**16; **23:**15; **27:**7; **44:**13; **59:**18; **63:**7^{3}

Jer 2:28; **3:**15; **11:**4, 13^{2}; **13:**2; **17:**10^{2}; **21:**2, 14; **25:**14^{2}; **26:**20; **27:**12; **31:**32; **32:**8, 11, 19^{2}; **35:**10, 18; **36:**8; **38:**27; **40:**3; **42:**4, 5, 20; **50:**21, 29^{2}; **52:**2

Lam 3:32, 64

Ezk 4:4, 5, 9; **5:**7; **7:**3, 8, 9, 27; **8:**4; **14:**4; **18:**24, 30; **20:**44^{2}; **23:**24; **24:**14^{2}, 24; **25:**14^{2}; **35:**11^{2}; **36:**19^{2}; **39:**24^{2}; **40:**24, 28, 29, 32, 33, 35; **42:**11^{2}, 12; **43:**3^{2}; **44:**24; **45:**8, 25^{4}; **46:**7; **47:**10, 12, 13, 21

Dan 4:8, 35; **6:**8, 12; **8:**4; **9:**16; **11:**3, 4, 16, 36

Hos 3:1; **9:**10; **10:**1^{2}; **12:**2^{2}; **13:**2, 6

Jna 3:3

Mic 7:15

Hab 3:9

Hag 2:5

Zec 1:6^{2}; **5:**3^{2}

Mal 2:9

Mt 2:16; **9:**29; **16:**27; **25:**15

Mk 7:5

Lk 1:9, 38; **2:**22, 24, 29, 39; **5:**14; **12:**47; **23:**56

Jn 7:24; **18:**31

Act 2:30; **4:**35; **7:**44; **11:**29; **13:**23; **22:**3, 12; **24:**6

Ro 1:3, 4; **2:**2, 6, 16; **4:**18; **8:**27, 28; **9:**3, 11; **10:**2; **11:**5, 8; **12:**3, 6^{2}; **15:**5; **16:**25^{2}, 26

1Co 1:31; **3:**8, 10; **15:**3, 4

2Co 1:17; **4:**13; **5:**10; **8:**12^{2}; **9:**7; **10:**2, 13, 15; **11:**15; **13:**10

Gal 1:4; **2:**14; **3:**29; **6:**16

Eph 1:4, 5, 7, 9, 11, 19; **2:**2^{2}; **3:**7, 11, 16, 20; **4:**7, 16, 22; **6:**5

Php 1:20; **3:**21; **4:**19

Col 1:11, 25, 29; **3:**22

2Th 1:12

1Ti 1:11, 18; **6:**3

2Ti 1:1, 8, 9^{2}; **2:**8; **4:**14

Tit 1:1, 3; **3:**5, 7

Heb 2:4; **7:**5; **8:**4, 5, 9; **9:**19

Jas 2:8

1Pt 1:2, 3, 14, 17; **3:**7; **4:**6^{2}, 19

2Pt 1:3; **2:**22; **3:**13, 15

1Jn 5:14

Rev 2:23; **18:**6; **20:**12, 13; **21:**17; **22:**12

ACCORDINGLY

Isa 59:18

AFTER

Gen 1:11, 12^{2}, 21^{2}, 24^{2}, 25^{3}, 26; **4:**17; **5:**3, 4, 7, 10, 13, 16, 19, 22, 26, 30; **6:**4, 20^{3}; **7:**10, 14^{4}; **8:**3, 19; **9:**9, 28; **10:**1, 5^{2}, 20^{2}, 31^{3}, 32^{2}; **11:**10, 11, 13, 15, 17, 19, 21, 23, 25; **13:**14; **14:**17; **15:**1; **16:**3, 13; **17:**7^{2}, 8, 9, 10, 19; **18:**5, 11, 12, 19, 25; **19:**6, 31; **22:**1, 20; **23:**19; **24:**55, 67; **25:**11, 26; **26:**18^{2}; **31:**23, 30, 36; **32:**29; **33:**2, 7; **35:**5, 12; **36:**40; **37:**17; **38:**24; **39:**7, 19; **40:**1, 13; **41:**3, 6, 19, 23, 27, 30; **44:**4; **45:**15, 23; **48:**1, 4, 6^{2}; **50:**14

Ex 3:20; **5:**19; **7:**25; **10:**14; **11:**8; **14:**4, 8, 9, 10, 23, 28; **15:**20; **16:**1; **17:**1; **18:**2; **21:**9; **23:**2, 24; **25:**9, 40; **28:**15, 43; **29:**29; **30:**12, 13, 24, 25, 32, 35; **32:**4; **33:**8; **34:**15, 16^{2}, 27; **37:**19; **38:**24, 25, 26

Lev 5:15; **11:**14, 15, 16, 19, 22^{4}, 29; **13:**7, 35, 55, 56; **14:**8, 43^{3}, 48; **15:**28; **16:**1; **17:**7; **18:**3^{2}; **19:**31; **20:**5, 6^{3}; **23:**11, 15, 16; **25:**15, 29, 46, 48; **26:**33; **27:**3, 18

Nu 1:1, 2, 18, 20, 22, 24, 26, 28, 30, 32, 34, 36, 38, 40, 42, 47; **2:**34; **3:**15, 47, 50; **4:**2, 15, 29, 34^{2}, 44, 46^{2}; **6:**19, 20, 21; **7:**13, 19, 25, 31, 37, 43, 49, 55, 61, 67, 73, 79, 85, 86, 88; **8:**15, 22; **9:**1, 17; **12:**14; **13:**25; **14:**34; **15:**13, 39^{2}; **16:**29; **18:**16; **25:**8, 13; **26:**1, 12, 15, 20, 23, 26, 28, 35, 37, 38, 41, 42^{2}, 44, 48, 57; **27:**21; **28:**24, 26; **29:**18, 21, 24, 27, 30, 33, 37; **30:**15; **32:**15, 42; **33:**3, 38; **35:**28

Dt 1:4, 8; **3:**11, 14; **4:**37, 40, 45, 46; **6:**14; **8:**19; **9:**4; **10:**15; **11:**4, 28; **12:**8, 15, 20, 21, 25, 28, 30^{2}; **13:**2, 4; **14:**13, 14, 15, 18, 26; **16:**13; **18:**9; **20:**18; **21:**13; **22:**2; **24:**4, 9; **28:**14; **29:**22; **31:**16, 27, 29

Jos 1:1; **2:**5, 7^{2}; **3:**2, 3; **5:**4, 11, 12; **6:**9, 13, 15; **7:**25; **8:**6, 16^{2}, 17^{2}; **9:**16; **10:**14, 19; **13:**23, 28; **19:**47; **20:**5; **22:**27; **23:**1; **24:**6, 20, 29

Jdg 1:1, 6; **2:**10, 17; **3:**22, 28^{2}, 31; **4:**14, 16^{2}; **5:**14; **6:**34, 35; **7:**23; **8:**5, 12, 27, 33; **10:**1, 3; **12:**8, 11, 13; **13:**11, 18; **14:**8; **15:**1, 7; **16:**22; **18:**7, 29; **19:**3; **20:**45

Ru 1:15, 16; **2:**2, 3, 7, 9, 18; **4:**4

1Sa 1:9^{2}, 20; **5:**9; **6:**12; **7:**2; **8:**3; **10:**5; **11:**5, 7^{2}; **12:**21; **13:**4, 14; **14:**12, 13^{2}, 22, 36, 37; **15:**31; **17:**27, 30^{2}, 35, 53; **18:**30; **20:**37, 38; **22:**20; **23:**25, 28; **24:**8, 14^{4}, 21; **25:**13, 19, 38, 42^{2}; **26:**3, 18; **30:**8

2Sa 1:1, 6, 10; **2:**1, 19, 24, 25, 28; **3:**26; **5:**13; **7:**12; **8:**1; **10:**1; **11:**1, 3; **12:**28; **13:**1, 17, 18, 23; **14:**26; **15:**1, 7, 13, 16, 17, 18; **17:**1, 6^{2}, 21; **18:**16, 18, 22; **20:**2, 6, 7^{2}, 10, 11, 13^{2}, 14; **21:**1, 14, 18; **23:**4, 9, 10, 11; **24:**10

1Ki 1:6, 13, 14, 17, 20, 24, 27, 30, 35, 40; **2:**28^{2}; **3:**12, 18; **6:**1; **7:**11, 31, 37; **9:**21; **11:**2, 4, 5^{2}, 6, 10, 15; **12:**14; **13:**14, 23^{2}, 31, 33; **15:**4; **16:**24; **17:**7, 13, 17; **18:**1, 28; **19:**11, 12^{2}, 20, 21; **20:**15; **21:**1

2Ki 1:1; **5:**20, 21^{2}; **6:**24; **7:**14, 15; **8:**2; **9:**25, 27; **10:**29; **14:**17, 19, 22; **17:**15, 33, 34^{4}, 40; **18:**5; **21:**2; **23:**3, 25; **25:**5

1Ch 2:24; **5:**1, 25; **6:**31; **7:**4, 9; **8:**8; **9:**25; **10:**2^{2}; **11:**12; **14:**14; **15:**13; **17:**11; **18:**1; **19:**1; **20:**1, 4; **23:**24; **24:**30; **27:**1, 7, 34; **28:**8; **29:**14, 21

2Ch 1:12; **2:**17; **3:**3; **4:**20; **8:**8, 13; **10:**5, 14; **11:**16, 20; **13:**9, 19; **17:**4; **18:**2, 19^{2}; **20:**1, 35; **21:**18, 19; **22:**4, 5; **23:**21; **24:**4, 17; **25:**14, 15, 20, 25, 27^{2}; **26:**2, 17; **28:**3; **30:**16; **31:**2; **32:**1, 9; **33:**14; **34:**3, 21, 31; **35:**4, 5, 20; **36:**14

Ezr 2:61, 69; **3:**10; **5:**4, 12; **7:**1, 18, 25; **9:**10, 13; **10:**16

Neh 3:16, 17, 18, 20, 21, 22, 23^{2}, 24, 25, 27, 29^{2}, 30^{2}, 31; **4:**13; **5:**8; **6:**4^{2}; **7:**63; **9:**28; **10:**34; **11:**8; **12:**32, 38; **13:**6, 19

Est 1:22; **2:**1, 12; **3:**1, 12; **8:**9; **9:**26

Job 3:1; **10:**6^{2}; **18:**20; **19:**26; **21:**3, 21, 33; **29:**22; **30:**5^{2}; **31:**7; **37:**4; **39:**8, 10; **41:**32; **42:**7, 8, 16

Ps 4:2; **10:**4; **16:**4; **27:**4; **28:**4; **35:**4; **38:**12; **40:**14; **42:**1^{2}; **49:**11, 17; **51:**ttl; **54:**3; **63:**8; **68:**25; **70:**2; **78:**34; **86:**14; **103:**10; **104:**21; **110:**4; **119:**40, 85, 88, 150; **143:**6; **144:**12

Prv 2:3; **6:**25; **7:**22; **15:**9; **20:**7, 25; **21:**21; **28:**19

Ecc 1:11; **2:**12, 18; **3:**22; **4:**16; **6:**12; **7:**14; **9:**3; **10:**14; **11:**1; **12:**2

Song 1:4

Isa 1:23; **5:**17; **10:**24, 26; **11:**3^{2}; **23:**15, 17; **24:**22; **43:**10; **44:**13; **45:**14; **49:**20; **51:**1; **65:**2

Jer 2:2, 5, 8, 23, 25; **3:**7, 17; **5:**8; **7:**6, 9; **8:**2; **9:**14^{2}, 16, 22; **11:**10; **12:**6, 15; **13:**6, 9, 10; **16:**11, 12, 16; **18:**12; **23:**17; **24:**1; **25:**6, 26; **28:**12; **29:**2, 10; **30:**17, 18; **31:**19^{2}, 33; **32:**18, 39; **34:**8; **35:**15; **36:**27; **39:**5; **40:**1; **41:**4, 16; **42:**7, 16; **49:**37; **50:**21; **51:**46; **52:**8

Ezk 5:2, 12; **6:**9; **7:**27; **9:**5; **11:**12, 21; **12:**14; **16:**23, 47^{2}; **20:**16, 24, 30^{2}; **23:**15, 30, 45^{2}, 48; **29:**16; **33:**20, 31; **34:**6; **36:**11; **38:**8; **39:**14, 26; **40:**1, 21, 22, 24; **41:**5; **43:**13; **44:**10, 26; **45:**11; **46:**12, 17, 19; **48:**31

Dan 2:39; **3:**29; **4:**26; **7:**6, 7, 24; **8:**1; **9:**26; **11:**13, 18, 23

Hos 2:5, 7, 13; **5:**8, 11; **6:**2; **7:**4; **11:**10; **12:**1

Joel 2:2

Am 2:4, 7; **4:**4, 10; **7:**1

Zec 2:8; **6:**6; **7:**14

Mt 1:12; **3:**11; **5:**6, 28; **6:**9, 32; **10:**38; **12:**39; **15:**12, 23; **16:**4, 24; **17:**1; **18:**32; **23:**3; **24:**29; **25:**19; **26:**2, 32, 73; **27:**31, 53, 63

Mk 1:7, 14, 17, 20, 36; **2:**1; **4:**28; **8:**12, 25, 31, 34; **9:**2, 31; **12:**34; **13:**24; **14:**1, 28, 70; **16:**12, 14, 19

Lk 1:24, 59; **2:**27, 42, 46; **5:**27; **6:**1; **7:**11; **9:**23, 28; **10:**1; **12:**4, 5, 30; **13:**9; **14:**27, 29; **15:**4, 13; **17:**23; **19:**14; **20:**40; **21:**8, 26; **22:**20, 58, 59; **23:**26, 55

Jn 1:15, 27, 30, 35; **2:**6, 12; **3:**22; **4:**43; **5:**1, 4; **6:**1, 23; **7:**1; **8:**15; **11:**7, 11; **12:**19; **13:**5, 12, 27; **19:**28, 38; **20:**26; **21:**1, 14

Act 1:2, 3, 8; **3:**24; **5:**4, 7, 37^{2}; **7:**5, 7, 36, 45; **9:**23; **10:**24, 37, 41; **12:**4; **13:**15, 20, 22, 25, 36; **14:**24; **15:**1, 13, 16, 17, 23, 33, 36; **16:**7, 10; **17:**27; **18:**1, 18, 23; **19:**4, 21^{2}; **20:**1, 6, 18, 29, 30; **21:**1, 15, 21, 36; **22:**29; **23:**3, 25; **24:**1, 10, 14, 17, 24, 27; **25:**1, 13, 26; **26:**5; **27:**14, 21; **28:**6, 11, 13, 17, 25

Ro 2:5; **3:**11; **5:**14; **6:**19; **7:**22; **8:**1^{2}, 4^{2}, 5^{2}, 12, 13; **9:**30, 31; **10:**20; **14:**19

1Co 1:21, 22, 26; **7:**7^{2}, 40; **10:**6, 18; **11:**25; **12:**28; **14:**1; **15:**6, 7, 32

2Co 5:16^{2}; **7:**9, 11; **9:**14; **10:**3, 7; **11:**17, 18

Gal 1:11, 18; **2:**1, 14; **3:**15, 17, 25; **4:**9, 23, 29^{2}

Eph 1:11, 13^{2}, 15; **4:**24

Php 1:8; **2:**26; **3:**12

Col 2:8^{3}, 22; **3:**10

1Th 2:2

2Th 2:9; **3:**6

1Ti 5:15, 24; **6:**10, 11

2Ti 4:3

Tit 1:1, 4; **3:**4, 10

Heb 3:5; **4:**7, 11; **5:**6, 10; **6:**15, 20; **7:**2, 11^{2}, 15, 16^{2}, 17, 21; **8:**10; **9:**3, 17, 27; **10:**12, 15, 16, 26, 32, 36; **11:**8, 30; **12:**10

Jas 3:9

1Pt 3:5; **5:**10

2Pt 1:15; **2:**6, 10, 20, 21; **3:**3

2Jn 6

3Jn 6

Jude 7, 11, 16, 18

Rev 4:1; **7:**1, 9; **11:**11; **12:**15; **13:**3; **15:**5; **18:**1, 14; **19:**1; **20:**3

AGAINST

Gen 4:8; **14:**15; **15:**10; **16:**12^{2}; **20:**6; **21:**16^{2}; **30:**2; **32:**25; **34:**30; **37:**18; **39:**9; **40:**2^{3}; **41:**36; **42:**22, 36; **43:**18, 25; **44:**18; **50:**20

Ex 1:10; **4:**14; **7:**15; **8:**12; **9:**17; **10:**16^{2}; **11:**7^{2}; **12:**12; **14:**2, 5, 25, 27; **15:**7, 24; **16:**2, 7^{2}, 8^{3}; **17:**3; **19:**11, 15; **20:**16; **23:**29, 33; **25:**27, 37; **26:**17, 35; **28:**27; **32:**10, 11, 12, 33; **37:**14; **39:**20; **40:**24

Lev 4:2^{2}, 13, 14, 22, 27; **5:**19; **6:**2; **17:**10; **19:**16, 18; **20:**3, 5^{2}, 6; **26:**17, 40

Nu 5:6, 7, 12, 13, 27; **8:**2, 3; **10:**9, 21; **11:**18, 33; **12:**1, 8, 9; **13:**31; **14:**2^{2}, 9, 27^{2}, 29, 35, 36; **16:**3^{2}, 11^{2}, 19, 38, 41^{2}, 42^{2}; **17:**5, 10; **20:**2^{2}, 18, 20, 24; **21:**1, 5^{2}, 7^{2}, 23^{2}, 26, 33; **22:**5, 22, 25, 34; **23:**23^{2}; **24:**10; **25:**3, 4; **26:**9^{3}; **27:**3, 14; **30:**9; **31:**3, 7, 16; **32:**13, 23; **35:**30

Dt 1:1, 26, 41, 43, 44; **2:**15, 19, 32; **3:**1, 29; **4:**26, 46; **5:**20; **6:**15; **7:**4; **8:**19; **9:**7, 16, 19, 23, 24; **11:**17, 30; **15:**9^{2}; **19:**11, 15, 16^{2}, 18; **20:**1, 3, 4, 10, 12, 18, 19^{2}, 20; **21:**10; **22:**14, 17, 26; **23:**4, 9; **24:**15; **28:**7^{2}, 25, 48, 49; **29:**7, 20, 27; **30:**19; **31:**17, 19, 21, 26, 27, 28; **32:**49, 51; **33:**11; **34:**1, 6

Jos 1:18; **3:**16; **5:**13; **7:**1, 13, 20; **8:**3, 4, 5, 14^{2}, 22, 33^{2}; **9:**1, 18; **10:**5, 6, 21, 25, 29, 31^{2}, 34^{2}, 36, 38; **11:**5, 7, 20; **18:**17, 18; **19:**47; **22:**11, 12, 16^{2}, 18, 19^{2}, 22, 29, 31, 33; **23:**16; **24:**9, 11, 22

Jdg 1:1^{2}, 3, 5, 8, 9, 10, 11, 22; **2:**14, 15, 20; **3:**8, 10, 12; **4:**24; **5:**14, 20, 23; **6:**2, 3, 4, 31, 32, 39; **7:**2, 22, 24; **9:**18, 31, 33, 34, 43, 45, 50, 52; **10:**7, 9^{3}, 10, 18; **11:**4, 5, 8, 9, 12, 20, 25^{2}, 27^{2}, 32; **12:**1, 3^{2}; **14:**4, 5; **15:**10, 14; **16:**5; **18:**9; **19:**2, 10; **20:**5, 9, 11, 14, 18, 19, 20^{2}, 23^{2}, 24, 25, 28, 30^{2}, 31, 34, 43

Ru 1:13, 21

1Sa 2:25^{2}; **3:**12; **4:**1, 2; **5:**9; **7:**6, 7, 10, 13; **9:**14; **11:**1; **12:**3, 5, 9, 12, 14, 15^{3}, 23; **14:**5^{2}, 20, 33, 34, 47^{6}, 52; **15:**7, 18; **17:**2, 9, 21, 28, 33, 35, 55; **18:**21; **19:**4^{3}, 5; **20:**30; **22:**8^{2}, 13^{2}; **23:**1, 3, 9, 28; **24:**6, 7, 10, 11; **25:**17^{2}, 20, 22, 34; **26:**9, 11, 19, 23; **27:**10^{3}; **28:**15; **29:**8; **30:**23; **31:**1, 3

ALL

36; 12:4, 17, 18; 13:7; 14:2, 10, 20; 15:11[2], 13, 14, 33; 16:4, 15, 19, 24, 26

1Co 1:2, 5[2], 10; 2:10, 15; 3:21, 22; 4:13; 6:12[3]; 7:7, 17; 8:1, 6[2]; 9:12, 19[2], 22[3], 24, 25; 10:1[2], 2, 3, 4, 11, 17, 23[4], 31, 33[2]; 11:2, 5, 12, 18; 12:6[2], 11, 12, 13[2], 19, 26[2], 29[4], 30[3]; 13:2[3], 3, 7[4]; 14:5, 18, 21, 23, 24[3], 26, 31[3], 33, 40; 15:3, 7, 8, 10, 19, 22[2], 24[2], 25, 27[3], 28[4], 29, 39, 51[2]; 16:12, 14, 20, 24

2Co 1:1[2], 3, 4, 20; 2:3[2], 5, 9; 3:2, 18; 4:15; 5:10, 14[2], 15, 17, 18; 6:4, 10; 7:1, 4, 11, 13, 14, 15, 16; 8:7, 18; 9:8[3], 11, 13; 10:6; 11:6, 9, 28; 12:12, 19; 13:2, 13, 14

Gal 1:2; 2:14; 3:8, 10, 22, 26, 28; 4:1, 12, 26; 5:14; 6:6, 10

Eph 1:3, 8, 10, 11, 15, 21, 22[2], 23[2]; 2:3, 21; 3:8, 9[2], 18, 19, 20, 21; 4:2, 6[4], 10[2], 13, 15, 19, 31[2]; 5:3, 9, 13, 20; 6:13, 16[2], 18[3], 21, 24

Php 1:1, 4, 7[2], 8, 9, 13[2], 20, 25; 2:14, 17, 21, 26, 29; 3:8[2], 21; 4:5, 7, 12, 13, 18, 19, 22, 23

Col 1:4, 6, 9, 10, 11[2], 16[2], 17[2], 18, 19, 20, 28; 2:2, 3, 9, 10, 13, 19, 22; 3:8, 11[2], 14, 16, 17, 20, 22; 4:7, 9, 12

1Th 1:2, 7; 2:15; 3:7, 9, 12, 13; 4:6, 10[2]; 5:5, 14, 15, 21, 22, 26, 27

2Th 1:3, 4, 10, 11; 2:4, 9, 10, 12; 3:2, 11, 16[2], 18

1Ti 1:15, 16; 2:1[2], 2[2], 4, 6, 11; 3:4, 11; 4:8, 9, 10, 15; 5:2, 20; 6:1, 10, 13, 17

2Ti 1:15; 2:7, 10, 24; 3:9, 11, 12, 16, 17; 4:2, 5, 8, 16, 17, 21

Tit 1:15; 2:7, 9, 10[2], 11, 14, 15; 3:2[2], 15[2]

Phlm 5

Heb 1:2, 3, 6, 11, 14; 2:8[3], 10[2], 11, 15, 17; 3:2, 4, 5, 16; 4:4, 13, 15; 5:9; 6:16; 7:2, 7; 8:5, 11; 9:3, 8, 17, 19[2], 21, 22; 10:10; 11:13, 39; 12:8, 14, 23; 13:4, 18, 24[2], 25

Jas 1:2, 5, 8, 21; 2:10; 3:2; 4:16; 5:12

1Pt 1:15, 24[2]; 2:1[3], 17, 18; 3:8; 4:7, 8, 11; 5:5, 7, 10, 14

2Pt 1:3, 5; 3:4, 9, 11[2], 16

1Jn 1:5, 7, 9; 2:16, 19, 20, 27; 3:20; 5:17

2Jn 1

3Jn 2, 12

Jude 3, 15[4]

Rev 1:2, 7; 2:23; 3:10; 4:11; 5:6, 13; 7:4, 9, 11, 17; 8:3, 7; 11:6; 12:5; 13:3, 7, 8, 12, 16; 14:8; 15:4; 18:3, 12[3], 14[2], 17, 19, 21, 22[2], 23[3], 24; 19:5, 17, 18, 21; 21:4, 5, 7, 8, 19, 25; 22:21

ALONG

Ex 2:5; 9:23

Nu 21:22; 34:3

Dt 2:27

Jos 10:10; 15:3[2], 6, 10, 11; 16:2; 17:7; 18:18, 19; 19:13

Jdg 7:12, 13; 9:25, 37; 11:18, 26; 20:37

1Sa 6:12; 28:20

2Sa 3:16; 16:13

2Ki 11:11

2Ch 23:10

Jer 41:6

ALSO

Gen 1:16; 2:9; 3:6, 18, 21, 22; 4:4, 22, 26; 6:3, 4, 11; 7:3; 8:2, 8; 10:21; 12:15; 13:5, 16; 14:7, 16[2]; 15:14; 16:13; 17:16; 18:12, 23, 24; 19:21, 34, 35, 38; 20:4, 6; 21:13; 22:20, 24; 24:14, 19, 44, 46[2], 53; 26:21; 27:31, 34, 38, 45; 29:27, 28, 30[2], 33; 30:3, 6, 15, 30; 31:15; 32:6, 18; 33:7; 35:17; 37:7; 38:10, 11, 22, 24; 40:15, 16; 42:22; 43:8, 13; 44:9, 10, 16, 29; 45:20; 46:4, 34; 47:3, 18; 48:11, 19[2]; 50:18, 23

Ex 1:10; 2:19; 3:9; 4:9, 14; 6:4, 5; 7:11[2], 23; 8:21, 32; 10:24, 25, 26; 12:32[2], 38; 15:4; 18:23; 19:22; 21:6, 29, 35; 23:9; 24:11; 25:23; 29:15, 22, 44; 30:18[2], 23; 31:13; 33:12, 17; 35:14; 37:12, 26

Lev 5:2; 7:16; 8:8, 9; 9:4, 18; 11:29, 40; 13:18, 38, 47; 14:9; 15:18, 20; 18:19, 28; 20:13, 27; 22:12; 23:27, 39; 26:16, 22, 24, 28, 39, 40, 41, 42[2], 43

Nu 3:1; 4:22; 6:17; 9:2; 10:10; 11:4, 10; 12:2; 15:15; 16:10, 17, 34; 18:2, 3, 8, 28; 20:11; 22:19, 33; 24:12, 18, 24, 25; 27:13; 28:26; 30:3; 31:8; 33:4; 35:2

Dt 1:37[2]; 2:6, 11, 12, 20; 3:3, 17, 20; 7:13; 8:5; 9:8, 19, 20; 10:10, 14; 15:17; 18:4; 20:6; 23:12; 26:13; 28:51, 61; 29:15; 31:2; 32:24, 25; 33:28

Jos 1:15; 2:12; 7:11[3]; 10:30, 39; 13:3, 22; 15:19; 17:1, 2, 9; 19:30; 20:1; 22:7; 24:5, 18

Jdg 1:15, 18, 22; 2:3, 10, 21; 3:22, 31; 5:4, 15; 6:35; 7:18; 8:9, 22, 31; 9:2, 19, 49; 10:9, 10, 12; 15:5; 17:2; 19:10, 16, 19; 20:48

Ru 1:5, 12[2], 17; 2:16, 21; 3:15; 4:5

1Sa 1:6, 28; 2:15, 26; 3:12, 17; 4:17[2]; 8:8, 20; 10:11, 12, 26; 12:14; 13:4; 14:15, 21, 22, 44; 15:1, 23, 29; 17:38; 18:5; 19:11, 20, 21, 22, 23, 24[2]; 20:15; 22:17; 23:17, 25; 24:8; 25:13, 22, 43[2]; 26:25; 28:19[2], 22; 30:21

2Sa 1:4[2], 18; 2:2, 6, 7, 24; 3:9, 12, 19[2], 35; 4:2; 5:2, 15, 18; 7:11, 19; 8:3, 11; 10:14; 11:12, 17, 21, 24; 12:13, 14; 13:36; 14:7; 15:19[2], 21, 23, 24, 27, 34; 17:5, 10; 18:2, 22, 26; 19:13, 40, 43; 20:14, 26; 21:20; 22:10, 20, 24, 36, 41, 44, 49; 23:20

1Ki 1:6, 14, 22, 33, 46, 48; 2:5, 22, 23; 3:13, 18; 4:13, 15, 28, 33; 6:22, 32, 33; 7:2, 8, 20, 31; 8:24; 9:21; 10:11, 12; 12:14; 13:5, 11, 18, 24; 14:23, 24; 15:13; 16:7, 16; 17:20; 18:35; 19:2; 20:3, 10; 21:19, 23; 22:22

2Ki 1:11; 2:13, 14; 3:18; 5:1; 6:31; 7:4, 8; 8:1; 9:27; 10:2, 5; 11:17; 13:6; 16:14; 17:19; 18:2; 21:11; 22:19; 23:5, 19, 27; 24:4

1Ch 1:14, 21, 51; 2:9, 26, 49; 3:6, 18; 6:3, 48, 67, 79; 7:10, 12, 25, 28; 8:13, 18, 32; 9:29, 38; 10:13; 11:10, 22, 26; 12:38; 13:2; 15:27; 16:6, 25, 30, 38; 17:9, 17; 18:4, 11; 20:2, 6; 21:23; 22:4, 14, 17; 23:26; 24:30; 26:6, 10; 27:4, 30, 32; 28:13, 14, 15, 17, 21; 29:9, 17

2Ch 2:8, 14; 3:7, 12, 15; 4:2, 6, 8, 14, 16, 19; 5:6, 12; 7:6, 8; 8:5, 14; 9:4, 10; 12:5, 9, 12; 13:2, 3, 11; 14:5, 15; 15:16; 17:7, 11; 18:21; 19:11; 20:1; 21:4, 10, 13, 17; 22:2, 3, 5; 23:13, 18; 24:1, 7, 12, 20; 25:6, 24; 26:3, 10[2], 20; 27:1, 5; 28:2, 4, 5, 8, 18[2]; 29:7, 22, 27, 35; 30:1, 12; 31:1, 3, 6, 19; 32:5, 17, 28, 30; 33:4, 6, 19; 34:13, 27; 35:9; 36:7, 13, 22

Ezr 1:1, 7; 3:4, 7; 4:20; 5:10, 14; 6:5, 11; 7:19, 24; 8:6, 14, 16, 20, 27, 28, 35; 10:4, 23, 24, 28

Neh 1:3; 2:6, 18; 3:3, 8, 29; 5:3, 4, 9, 11, 13, 16, 18; 6:7, 19; 7:61; 8:7, 18; 9:13, 20, 23, 37; 10:32, 36; 11:1, 15, 22, 31; 12:9, 10, 22, 29, 43[2]; 13:15, 16, 22, 23

Est 1:9, 16; 2:8; 3:11; 4:8, 16; 5:12; 7:8, 9; 8:8; 9:13, 15

Job 1:3, 6, 16, 17, 18; 2:1; 5:25; 7:1; 9:11, 20; 11:11, 19; 12:15; 13:2, 16, 27; 14:2; 16:4, 12, 17, 19; 17:6, 7, 9; 19:11; 20:9; 22:28; 24:15, 22; 30:11, 31; 31:28; 32:3, 10, 17[2]; 33:6, 19; 36:1, 10, 29, 33; 37:1, 11; 39:30; 40:8, 14; 42:9, 10, 11, 13

Ps 1:3; 5:11; 6:3; 7:13; 9:9; 16:7, 9; 18:7, 9, 13, 19, 23, 35, 40; 19:10, 13; 26:1; 27:7; 28:9; 29:6; 35:3; 37:4, 5; 38:10, 12, 20; 40:2; 45:10; 52:6; 55:10; 60:7; 62:12; 65:8, 13[2]; 68:1, 8, 18; 69:11, 21, 31, 36; 71:18, 19, 22, 24; 72:8, 12, 15; 74:16; 75:10; 76:2; 77:12, 16, 17; 78:14, 16, 20, 21, 27, 46, 48, 55, 62, 70; 81:16; 83:8; 84:6; 89:5, 11, 21, 25, 27, 29, 43; 92:11; 93:1; 95:4; 96:10; 99:4; 105:23, 33, 36, 37; 106:9, 16, 27, 28, 32, 42, 46; 107:32, 38; 108:8; 109:3, 10, 25; 119:3, 23, 24, 41, 46, 48; 132:12, 16; 139:17; 141:5; 145:19; 148:6, 14

Prv 1:26; 4:4; 9:2; 11:25; 17:26; 18:3, 9; 19:2; 21:13; 23:23, 28; 24:23; 25:1; 26:4; 28:16; 30:31; 31:15, 28

Ecc 1:5, 17; 2:1, 7, 8, 9, 14, 15, 19, 21, 23, 24, 26; 3:11, 13; 4:4, 8, 14, 16[2]; 5:7, 10, 16, 17, 19; 6:3, 9; 7:6, 14, 18, 21, 22; 8:10, 14, 16; 9:3, 6, 12, 13; 10:3, 14; 11:2; 12:5

Song 1:16; 7:8

Isa 2:7[2], 8; 5:2, 6; 6:1, 8; 7:13, 20; 8:5; 11:6, 13; 12:2; 13:3, 16, 18; 14:10, 13, 23; 17:3; 19:8, 13; 21:12; 22:9, 11; 23:12; 24:5; 26:12, 21; 28:7, 17, 29; 29:19, 24; 30:5, 22; 31:2, 5; 32:4, 7; 33:2; 34:3, 11, 14[2], 15; 38:22; 40:24; 44:19; 45:16; 46:11[2]; 48:12, 13, 19, 21; 49:6, 7; 56:6; 57:8, 15, 18; 60:14, 16, 17, 21; 62:3; 66:4, 21

Jer 1:3; 2:8, 16, 33, 34, 36; 3:6, 8; 4:12; 6:14, 17; 7:27; 9:16; 10:5; 13:23; 14:5; 16:1, 8; 19:5; 20:1; 23:14[2]; 25:14; 26:20; 27:6, 12, 16; 28:14; 29:24; 30:19, 20; 31:36, 37; 33:21; 35:15; 36:6; 38:25; 39:6; 40:5; 41:3; 43:13; 46:21[2]; 48:2, 7, 8, 26[2], 34; 49:17; 50:24[2]; 51:22, 23; 52:10, 17, 18, 22, 25

Lam 2:9; 3:8, 16; 4:21

Ezk 1:5, 10; 3:13, 21; 4:1, 2, 4, 9, 11; 5:3, 11; 7:2, 18, 22, 24; 8:13, 18; 9:1, 10; 10:16, 17, 19; 12:1, 13; 13:21; 16:10, 11, 17, 19, 24, 26, 28, 39[2], 40, 41, 43, 52[2]; 17:5, 7, 13, 22; 18:4; 19:4; 20:12, 15, 23, 25, 28, 39; 21:9, 17, 19; 23:26, 35, 37; 24:3, 5, 15, 25; 25:13; 26:4; 27:19; 30:6, 10, 13, 18; 31:17; 32:6, 9, 13, 17; 33:30; 36:1, 26, 29, 33; 37:24, 27; 38:10; 39:16; 40:8, 12, 14, 42; 41:8, 14; 43:21, 25; 44:30; 45:5; 47:20

Dan 6:22; 7:6; 8:25[2]; 10:6; 11:1, 8, 14, 17, 22, 41, 42

Hos 2:11; 3:3; 4:3, 5, 6[2]; 5:5; 6:11; 7:11; 8:6; 9:12; 10:6, 8; 11:3; 12:2, 10

Joel 1:12, 20; 2:12, 29; 3:2, 6, 16

Am 1:5; 2:10; 3:14; 4:6, 7; 7:6, 12; 9:14

Jna 4:11

Mic 3:3; 4:11; 5:13; 6:13; 7:12

Nah 3:10, 11[2]

Hab 1:8; 2:5, 15, 16

Zep 1:4, 9, 13; 2:12; 3:12

Zec 3:7[2]; 4:9; 8:6, 21; 9:2, 5, 11; 10:10; 11:8[2]; 12:7; 13:2; 14:14

Mal 1:13; 2:9

Mt 2:8; 3:10; 5:39, 40; 6:14, 21; 10:4, 32, 33; 12:45; 13:22, 23, 26, 29; 15:3, 16; 16:1, 18; 17:12; 18:33, 35; 19:3, 28; 20:4, 7; 21:21, 24; 22:26, 27; 23:26, 28; 24:27, 37, 39, 44; 25:11, 17, 22, 41, 44; 26:13, 35, 69, 71, 73; 27:41, 44, 57

Mk 1:19, 38; 2:15, 21, 26, 28; 3:19; 4:36; 5:16; 7:18; 8:7, 34, 38; 11:25, 29; 12:6, 22; 14:9, 31, 67; 15:31, 40, 41, 43

Lk 1:3, 35, 36; 2:4, 35; 3:9, 12, 21; 4:23, 41, 43; 5:10, 36, 39; 6:4, 5, 6, 13, 14, 16, 29[2], 31, 32, 33, 34, 36; 7:8, 49; 8:36; 9:61; 10:1, 39; 11:1, 4, 18, 30, 34[2], 40, 45, 46, 49; 12:8[2], 34, 40, 54; 13:6, 8; 14:12[2], 26; 16:1, 10[2], 14, 22, 28; 17:24, 26, 28; 18:15; 19:9, 19; 20:3, 11, 12, 31, 32; 21:2; 22:20, 24, 39, 56, 58, 59, 68; 23:7, 27, 32, 35, 36, 38, 51, 55; 24:22, 23

Jn 3:23; 4:45; 5:18, 19, 27; 6:24, 36, 67; 7:3, 10, 47, 52; 8:17, 19; 9:15, 27, 40; 10:16; 11:16, 33, 52; 12:9, 10, 18, 26, 42; 13:9, 14, 32, 34; 14:1, 3, 7, 12, 19; 15:20[2], 23, 27; 17:1, 18, 19, 20, 21, 24; 18:2, 5, 17, 25; 19:23, 39; 20:8; 21:3, 20, 25

Act 1:3, 11; 2:22, 26; 3:17; 5:2, 16, 32, 37; 7:45; 8:13, 19; 9:32; 10:26, 45; 11:1, 18, 30; 12:3; 13:5, 9, 22, 33, 35; 14:1, 5, 15; 15:27, 32, 35[2]; 17:6, 12, 13, 28[2]; 19:17, 19, 21, 27; 20:21, 30; 21:13, 16, 24, 28; 22:5[2], 20, 29; 23:11, 30, 33, 35; 24:6, 9, 15, 26; 25:22, 24; 26:10, 26, 29; 27:10, 12, 36; 28:9, 10

Ro 1:6, 13, 15, 16, 24, 27; 2:9, 10, 12, 15; 3:7, 29[2]; 4:6, 9, 11, 12, 16, 21, 24; 5:2, 3, 11, 15; 6:4, 5, 8, 11; 7:4; 8:11, 17, 21, 23, 26, 29, 30[3], 32, 34; 9:1, 10, 24, 25, 27; 11:1, 5, 16, 21, 22, 23, 31[2]; 13:5, 6; 15:7, 14[3], 22, 27; 16:2, 4, 7

1Co 1:8, 16; 2:13; 4:8; 5:12; 6:14; 7:3, 4, 22, 34, 40; 9:8; 10:6, 9, 10, 13; 11:1, 6, 12, 19, 23, 25; 12:12; 13:12; 14:15[2], 19, 34; 15:1, 2, 3, 8, 14, 18, 21, 28, 40, 42, 48[2], 49; 16:4, 10

2Co 1:5, 6, 7, 11, 14[2], 22; 2:9, 10; 3:6; 4:10, 11, 13, 14; 5:5, 11; 6:1, 13; 8:6[2], 7, 10, 11, 14, 19, 21; 9:6[2], 12; 10:11, 14; 11:15, 18, 21; 13:4, 9

Gal 2:1, 10, 13, 17; 5:21, 25; 6:1, 7

Eph 1:11, 13[2], 15, 21; 2:3, 22; 4:9, 10; 5:2, 25; 6:9, 21

Php 1:15, 20, 29; 2:4, 5, 9, 18, 19, 24, 27; 3:4, 12, 20; 4:3[2], 10, 15

Col 1:6, 7, 8, 9, 29; 2:11, 12; 3:4, 7, 8, 13, 15; 4:1, 3[2], 16

1Th 1:5, 8; 2:8, 10, 13[2], 14; 3:6; 4:6, 8, 14; 5:11, 24

2Th 1:5, 11

1Ti 2:9; 3:10; 5:13, 20, 25; 6:12

2Ti 1:5, 12; 2:2, 5, 10, 11, 12[2], 20, 22; 3:1, 8, 9; 4:8, 15

Tit 3:3, 14

Phlm 9, 21, 22

Heb 1:2; 2:4, 14; 3:2; 4:10; 5:2, 3, 5, 6; 7:2^{2}, 9, 12, 25; 8:3, 6; 9:1, 16; 10:15; 11:11, 19, 32; 12:1, 26; 13:3, 12

Jas 1:11; 2:2, 11, 19, 25, 26; 3:2, 4; 5:8

1Pt 2:5, 6, 8, 18, 21; 3:1, 5, 18, 19, 21; 4:6, 13; 5:1^{2}

2Pt 1:19; 2:1; 3:10, 15, 16^{2}, 17

1Jn 1:3; 2:2, 6, 23, 24; 3:4; 4:11, 21; 5:1

2Jn 1

3Jn 12

Jude 8, 14

Rev 1:7, 9; 2:6, 15; 3:10, 21; 6:11; 11:8; 14:17

AM

Gen 4:9; 15:1, 7; 17:1; 18:12, 13, 27; 22:1, 7, 11; 23:4; 24:24, 34; 25:22, 30, 32; 26:24^{2}; 27:1, 2, 11, 18, 19, 24, 32, 46; 28:13, 15; 30:2, 13; 31:11, 13; 32:10^{2}; 35:11; 37:13; 38:25; 41:44; 43:14; 45:3, 4; 46:2, 3; 49:29; 50:19

Ex 3:4, 6, 8, 11, 14^{3}, 19; 4:10^{2}; 6:2, 6, 7, 8, 12, 29, 30; 7:5, 17; 8:22; 9:29; 10:2; 12:12; 14:4, 18; 15:26; 16:12; 18:6; 20:2, 5; 22:27; 29:46^{2}; 31:13

Lev 8:35; 10:13; 11:44^{2}, 45^{2}; 18:2, 4, 5, 6, 21, 30; 19:2, 3, 4, 10, 12, 14, 16, 18, 25, 28, 30, 31, 32, 34, 36, 37; 20:7, 8, 24, 26; 21:8, 12; 22:2, 3, 8, 30, 31, 32, 33; 23:22, 43; 24:22; 25:17, 38, 55; 26:1, 2, 13, 44, 45

Nu 3:13, 41, 45; 10:10; 11:14, 21; 15:41^{2}; 18:20; 22:30, 37, 38

Dt 1:9, 42; 5:6, 9; 26:3; 29:6; 31:2, 27; 32:39

Jos 5:14; 14:10, 11; 17:14; 23:2, 14

Jdg 4:19; 6:10, 15; 8:5; 9:2; 13:11; 17:9; 18:4; 19:18^{2}

Ru 1:12; 2:10; 3:9, 12; 4:4

1Sa 1:8, 15, 26; 3:4, 5, 6, 8, 16; 4:16; 9:19, 21; 12:2, 3; 14:7; 16:2, 5; 17:8, 43, 58; 18:18, 23; 22:12; 28:15; 30:13

2Sa 1:3, 7, 8, 13, 26; 2:20; 3:8, 39; 7:18; 9:8; 11:5; 14:5, 15, 32; 15:26; 19:20, 22, 35; 20:17, 19; 24:14

1Ki 3:7; 8:20; 13:14, 18, 31; 14:6; 17:12; 18:8, 12, 36; 19:4, 10, 14; 20:4, 13, 28; 22:4, 34

2Ki 2:10; 3:7; 5:7; 16:7; 18:25; 19:23; 21:12

1Ch 17:16; 21:13; 29:14

2Ch 2:6, 9; 6:10^{2}; 18:3, 33; 35:23

Ezr 9:6

Neh 6:3, 11

Est 5:12

Job 1:15, 16, 17, 19; 7:3, 4, 8, 12, 20; 9:20, 28, 32; 10:7, 15; 11:4; 12:3, 4; 13:2, 16:6; 19:7, 10, 15, 20; 21:6; 23:15^{2}; 30:9^{2}, 19, 29; 32:6, 18; 33:6^{2}, 9^{2}; 34:5; 40:4

Ps 6:2, 6; 13:4; 17:3; 22:2, 6, 14; 25:16; 28:7; 31:9, 12^{2}, 22; 35:3; 37:25; 38:6^{2}, 8, 17; 39:4, 10, 12; 40:12, 17; 46:10; 50:7; 52:8; 56:3; 69:2, 3, 8, 17, 20, 29; 70:5; 71:7, 18; 73:23; 77:4; 81:10; 86:1, 2; 88:4^{2}, 8, 15^{2}; 102:2, 6^{2}, 7, 11; 109:22, 23^{2}; 116:16^{2}; 119:19, 63, 83, 94, 107, 120, 125, 141; 120:7; 139:14, 18, 21; 142:6; 143:12

Prv 8:14; 20:9; 26:19; 30:2

Ecc 1:16

Song 1:5, 6; 2:1, 5, 16; 5:1, 8; 6:3; 7:10; 8:10

Isa 1:11, 14; 6:5^{2}, 8; 10:13; 19:11; 21:8; 29:12; 33:24; 36:10; 37:24; 38:10, 14; 41:4, 10^{2}; 42:8; 43:3, 5, 10, 11, 12, 13, 15, 25; 44:5, 6^{2}, 16, 24; 45:3, 5, 6, 18, 22; 46:4, 9^{2}; 47:8, 10; 48:12^{3}, 16, 17; 49:21, 23, 26; 51:12, 15; 52:6; 56:3; 58:9; 60:16; 65:1^{2}, 5

Jer 1:6, 7, 8, 19; 2:23, 35; 3:12, 14; 4:19; 6:11^{2}; 8:21^{2}; 9:24; 15:6, 16, 20; 20:7; 21:13; 23:9, 23, 30, 31, 32; 24:7; 26:14; 29:23; 30:11; 31:9; 32:27; 36:5; 38:19; 42:11; 46:28; 50:31; 51:25

Lam 1:11, 14, 20; 3:1, 54, 63

Ezk 5:8; 6:7, 9, 10, 13, 14; 7:4, 9, 27; 11:10, 12; 12:11, 15, 16, 20, 25; 13:8, 9, 14, 20, 21, 23; 14:8; 15:7; 16:62, 63; 20:5, 7, 12, 19, 20, 26, 38, 42, 44; 21:3; 22:16, 26; 23:49; 24:24, 27; 25:5, 7, 11, 17; 26:3, 6; 27:3; 28:2, 9, 22^{2}, 23, 24, 26; 29:3, 6, 9, 10, 16, 21; 30:8, 19, 22, 25, 26; 32:15; 33:29; 34:10, 27, 30, 31; 35:3, 4, 9, 12, 15; 36:9, 11, 23, 38; 37:6, 13; 38:3, 23; 39:1, 6, 7, 22, 27, 28; 44:28^{2}

Dan 9:22, 23; 10:11, 12, 14, 20

Hos 2:2; 11:9; 12:8, 9; 13:4; 14:8

Joel 2:27^{2}; 3:10, 17

Am 2:13

Jna 1:9; 2:4

Mic 3:8; 7:1

Nah 2:13; 3:5

Hab 2:1

Zep 2:15

Hag 1:13; 2:4

Zec 1:14, 15, 16; 8:3; 10:6; 11:5; 13:5^{2}

Mal 1:14; 3:6

Mt 3:11, 17; 5:17^{2}; 8:8, 9; 9:13, 28; 10:34, 35; 11:29; 15:24; 16:13, 15; 17:5; 18:20; 20:15, 22, 23; 22:32; 24:5; 26:32, 61; 27:24, 43; 28:20

Mk 1:7, 11; 8:27, 29; 10:38, 39; 12:26; 13:6; 14:28, 62

Lk 1:18, 19^{2}; 3:16, 22; 4:43; 5:8; 7:6, 8; 9:18, 20; 12:49, 50, 51; 15:19, 21; 16:3, 4^{2}, 24; 18:11; 21:8; 22:27, 33, 58, 70

Jn 1:20, 21, 23, 27, 31; 3:28^{2}; 4:9, 26; 5:7, 43; 6:35, 41, 48, 51; 7:28^{2}, 29, 33, 34, 36; 8:12, 16, 18, 23^{2}, 24, 28, 58; 9:5^{2}, 9, 39; 10:7, 9, 10, 11, 14^{2}, 36; 11:15, 25; 12:26, 46; 13:13, 19, 33; 14:3, 6, 10, 11, 20; 15:1, 5; 16:28, 32; 17:10, 11, 14, 16, 24; 18:5, 6, 8, 17, 25, 35, 37; 19:21; 20:17

Act 7:32, 34; 9:5, 10; 10:21, 26; 13:25^{3}; 18:6, 10; 20:26; 21:13, 39^{2}; 22:3^{2}, 8; 23:6^{2}; 24:21; 26:2, 6, 7, 15, 25, 26, 29; 27:23; 28:20

Ro 1:14, 15, 16; 3:7; 7:14, 24; 8:38; 11:1, 3, 13; 14:14; 15:14, 29; 16:19

1Co 1:12; 3:4^{2}; 4:4; 9:1^{2}, 2, 22; 10:30; 11:1; 12:15^{2}, 16^{2}; 13:1, 2, 12; 15:9^{2}, 10^{2}; 16:17

2Co 7:4^{2}, 14; 10:1^{2}, 2; 11:2, 21, 22^{3}, 23, 29; 12:10^{2}, 11^{2}, 14; 13:1

Gal 2:19, 20; 4:11, 12^{2}, 16, 18

Eph 3:8; 6:20

Php 1:17, 23; 3:12; 4:11, 12, 18

Col 1:23, 25; 2:5; 4:3

1Ti 1:15; 2:7

2Ti 1:5, 11, 12^{2}; 4:6

Jas 1:13

1Pt 1:16; 5:1

2Pt 1:13, 17

Rev 1:8, 9, 11, 17, 18^{2}; 2:23; 3:17, 21; 18:7; 19:10; 21:6; 22:9, 13, 16

AMONG

Gen 17:10, 12, 23; 23:6, 10; 24:3; 30:32^{2}, 33^{2}, 35, 41; 34:22, 30^{2}; 35:2; 36:30; 40:20; 42:5; 47:6

Ex 2:5; 7:5; 9:20; 10:2; 12:31, 49; 13:2, 13; 15:11; 17:7; 25:8; 28:1; 29:45, 46; 30:12, 13, 14; 31:14; 32:25; 34:9, 10, 19; 35:5, 10; 36:8

Lev 6:18, 29; 7:6, 33, 34; 11:2, 3, 13, 27, 29, 31, 42; 15:31; 16:16, 29; 17:4, 8, 9, 10^{2}, 12, 13; 18:26, 29; 19:8, 16, 34; 20:3, 5, 6, 14, 18; 21:1, 4, 10, 15; 22:3, 32; 23:29, 30; 24:10; 25:33, 45; 26:11, 12, 22, 25, 33, 38

Nu 1:47, 49; 2:33; 3:12^{2}, 41^{2}, 42, 45; 4:2, 18; 5:21, 27; 8:6, 14, 16, 19^{2}; 9:7, 13, 14; 11:1, 3, 4, 20, 21; 12:6; 13:2; 14:11, 13, 14, 42; 15:14, 23, 26, 29^{2}, 30; 16:3, 21, 33, 45, 47; 17:6; 18:6, 20^{2}, 23, 24; 19:10, 20; 21:6; 23:9, 21; 25:7, 11, 14; 26:62^{2}, 64; 27:4^{2}, 7; 31:16, 17; 32:30; 33:4, 54; 35:6, 15, 34

Dt 1:13, 15, 42; 2:14, 15, 16; 4:3, 27^{2}; 6:15; 7:14^{2}, 20, 21; 13:1, 11, 13, 14; 14:6; 15:4, 7; 16:11; 17:2, 7, 15; 18:2, 10, 18; 19:19, 20; 21:9, 11, 21; 22:21, 24; 23:10, 16; 24:7; 26:11; 28:37, 54, 56, 64, 65; 29:17, 18^{2}; 30:1; 31:16, 17; 32:26, 34, 46, 51

Jos 3:5, 10; 4:6; 7:11, 12, 13, 21; 8:9, 33, 35; 9:7, 16, 22; 10:1; 13:13, 22; 14:3, 15; 15:13; 16:9, 10; 17:4^{2}, 6, 9; 18:2, 4, 7; 19:49; 20:4, 9; 22:7, 14, 19, 31; 23:7^{2}, 12; 24:5, 17, 23

Jdg 1:16, 29, 30, 32, 33; 3:5; 5:8, 9, 13, 14, 16; 10:16; 12:4^{2}; 14:3^{2}; 18:1, 25; 20:12, 16; 21:5, 12

Ru 2:7, 15; 4:10

1Sa 2:8; 4:3, 17; 6:6; 7:3; 9:2, 22; 10:10, 11^{2}, 12, 22, 23, 24; 14:15, 30, 34, 39; 15:6^{2}, 33; 16:1; 17:12; 19:24; 22:14; 31:9

2Sa 6:19^{2}; 15:31; 16:20; 17:9; 19:28; 22:50; 23:8, 18^{2}, 22

1Ki 3:13; 5:6; 6:13; 7:51; 8:53; 9:7; 11:20; 14:7; 21:9, 12

2Ki 4:13; 9:2; 11:2; 17:25, 26; 18:5, 35; 20:15; 23:9

1Ch 4:23; 7:5; 11:20, 24, 25; 12:1, 4; 16:8, 24^{2}, 31; 18:14; 21:6; 23:6; 24:4^{2}; 26:12^{2}, 19^{2}, 30, 31^{3}; 27:6; 28:4

2Ch 5:1; 6:5; 7:13, 20; 11:22; 20:25; 22:11; 24:16, 23; 26:6; 28:15; 31:19^{2}; 32:14; 33:11, 19; 35:13; 36:23

Ezr 1:3; 2:62, 65; 10:18

Neh 1:8; 4:11; 5:17; 6:6; 7:64; 9:17; 10:34; 11:17; 13:26

Est 1:19; 3:8; 4:3; 9:21, 28; 10:3

Job 1:6; 2:1, 8; 15:19; 17:10; 18:19; 28:10; 30:5, 7; 33:23; 34:4, 37; 36:14; 39:25; 41:6; 42:15

Ps 9:11; 12:1; 18:49; 21:10; 22:18, 28; 31:11^{2}; 35:18; 44:11, 14^{2}; 45:9, 12; 46:10; 55:15; 57:4^{2}, 9^{2}; 67:2; 68:13, 17, 18, 25; 74:9; 77:14; 78:45, 49, 60; 79:10; 80:6; 82:1; 86:8; 88:5; 89:6; 94:8; 96:3^{2}, 10; 99:6^{2}; 104:10, 12; 105:1, 27, 37; 106:27, 35, 47; 108:3^{2}; 109:30; 110:6; 126:2; 136:11

Prv 1:14; 6:19; 7:7^{2}; 14:9; 15:31; 17:2; 23:20^{2}, 28; 27:22; 30:14, 30; 31:23

Ecc 6:1; 7:28^{2}; 9:3, 17

Song 1:8; 2:2^{2}, 3^{2}, 16; 4:2, 5; 5:9, 10; 6:1, 3, 6

Isa 2:4; 4:3; 5:27; 8:15, 16; 10:16; 12:4; 24:13; 29:14, 19; 33:14^{2}; 36:20; 39:4; 41:28; 42:23; 43:9, 12; 44:4, 14; 48:14; 50:10; 51:18; 57:6; 61:9^{2}; 65:4; 66:19^{2}

Jer 3:19; 4:3; 5:26; 6:15, 18, 27; 8:12, 17; 9:16; 10:7; 11:9^{2}; 12:14; 14:22; 18:13; 24:10; 25:16, 27; 29:18, 32; 31:7; 32:20; 37:4, 10; 39:14; 40:1, 5, 6, 11; 41:8^{2}; 44:8; 46:18; 48:27; 49:15^{2}; 50:2, 23, 46; 51:27, 41

Lam 1:1^{2}, 2, 3, 17; 2:9; 4:15, 20

Ezk 1:1, 13; 2:5, 6; 3:15, 25; 4:13; 5:14; 6:8, 9, 13; 9:2; 11:1, 9, 16^{2}; 12:10, 12, 15, 16; 13:19; 15:2, 6; 16:14; 18:18; 19:2^{2}, 6, 11; 20:9, 23, 38; 22:15, 26, 30; 23:10; 25:10; 27:24, 36; 28:19, 25; 29:12^{2}; 30:23, 26^{2}; 31:3, 10, 14, 18; 32:9, 21; 33:6, 33; 34:12, 24; 35:11; 36:19, 21, 22, 23, 24, 30; 37:21; 39:6, 21, 28; 40:46; 44:9; 47:22^{4}

Dan 1:6, 19; 4:35; 7:8; 11:24, 33

Hos 5:9; 7:7, 8; 8:8, 10; 9:17; 10:14; 13:15

Joel 2:17, 19, 25; 3:2, 9

Am 1:1; 2:16; 4:10; 9:9

Oba 1, 2, 4

Mic 3:11; 4:3; 5:2, 8^{3}; 7:2

Nah 3:8

Hab 1:5

Zep 3:20

Hag 2:3, 5

Zec 1:8, 10, 11; 3:7; 7:14; 8:13; 10:9; 12:6, 8; 14:13

Mal 1:10, 11^{2}, 14

Mt 2:6; 4:23; 9:35; 11:11; 12:11; 13:7, 22, 25, 32, 49; 16:7, 8; 20:26^{2}, 27; 21:38; 23:11; 26:5; 27:35, 56; 28:15

Mk 1:27; 4:7, 18; 5:3; 6:4, 41; 8:16, 19, 20; 9:33, 34; 10:26, 43^{2}; 12:7; 13:10; 15:31, 40; 16:3

Lk 1:1, 25, 28, 42; 2:44; 4:36; 7:16, 28; 8:7, 14; 9:46, 48; 10:3, 30, 36; 16:15; 19:2, 39; 20:14; 22:17, 23, 24, 26, 27, 37, 55; 24:5, 47

Jn 1:14, 26; 6:9, 43, 52; 7:12, 35^{2}, 43; 8:7; 9:16; 10:19; 11:54, 56; 12:19, 20, 42; 15:24; 16:17, 19; 19:24^{2}; 21:23

Act 1:21; 2:22; 3:23; 4:12, 15, 17, 34; 5:12, 34; 6:3, 8; 10:22; 12:18; 13:26; 14:14; 15:7, 12, 19, 22; 17:33, 34; 18:11; 20:25, 29, 32; 21:19, 21, 34; 23:10; 24:5, 21; 25:5, 6; 26:3, 4, 18; 27:22; 28:4, 25, 29

Ro 1:5, 6, 13^{2}; 2:24; 8:29; 11:17; 12:3; 15:9; 16:7

1Co 1:10, 11; 2:2, 6; 3:3, 18; 5:1^{2}, 2, 13; 6:5, 7; 11:18, 19^{2}, 30; 15:12

2Co 1:19; 6:17; 10:1, 12; 11:6, 26; 12:12, 21

Gal 1:16; 2:2; 3:1, 5

Eph 2:3; 3:8; 5:3

AMONGST

AN

AND

15:1, 2, 3, 5, 7, 8, 10, 14[2], 15, 16[2], 17, 18, 22[2], 23, 24[2], 25[4], 26[2], 27, 28[2], 29, 30, 31, 32, 33[3], 34, 35, 36[3], 37, 38[2], 39[5], 40[2]; **16:**1[3], 2[2], 3[4], 4, 5[4], 6, 7[3], 8, 9, 10[3], 11[2], 12[2], 13, 14[2], 15[2], 16[4], 17[5], 18[5], 19[2], 20[2], 22[3], 23, 24, 25[4], 26[2], 27[7], 28, 30[3], 31, 32[5], 33[3], 34, 35[3], 36, 37, 38, 39[2], 40, 41, 42[4], 43[2], 44, 45, 46[5], 47[5], 48[3], 49, 50[2]; **17:**1, 2, 3, 4, 5[2], 6[3], 7, 8[5], 9[3], 10[2], 11, 12; **18:**1[5], 2[3], 3[3], 4[3], 5[2], 6, 7[4], 8[2], 9[3], 11[3], 12[2], 13, 15, 16, 17, 18[2], 19[3], 20[2], 21, 22, 23, 25, 26, 27[2], 28, 30, 31[2], 32; **19:**1[2], 2, 3[2], 4[2], 5[3], 6[4], 7[3], 8[3], 9[3], 10[4], 12, 13[2], 14, 15, 16, 17[2], 18[6], 19[6], 20, 21[2], 22[2]; **20:**1[3], 2[3], 3[2], 4[2], 5, 6[4], 7, 8[6], 9, 10[3], 11[5], 12[2], 13, 14, 15[3], 16[4], 18, 19[3], 20[3], 22[2], 23[2], 25[2], 26[4], 27[2], 28[5], 29; **21:**1[2], 2[2], 3[5], 4[2], 5[3], 6[3], 7[3], 8[3], 9[3], 10[2], 11[2], 12, 13[2], 14, 15[2], 16[2], 18, 19[2], 20, 21, 23[4], 24[2], 25[3], 26, 27, 28, 29, 30, 32[3], 33[4], 34[4], 35[3]; **22:**1[2], 2, 3[2], 4[2], 5, 6[2], 7[4], 8[3], 9[2], 10, 11, 12, 13[2], 14[3], 15[2], 16[2], 17, 18[3], 20[3], 21[3], 22[3], 23[5], 24, 25[3], 26[2], 27[3], 28[2], 29, 30[2], 31[4], 32, 33[3], 34, 35, 36, 37, 38, 39[2], 40[4], 41[2]; **23:**1[3], 2[4], 3[4], 4[4], 5[3], 6[3], 7[3], 9[2], 10[2], 11[2], 12[2], 13[3], 14[4], 15, 16[4], 17[3], 18[3], 19[2], 20[2], 21, 23, 24[2], 25, 26, 27, 28, 29[3], 30[3]; **24:**1, 2[3], 3[3], 5, 6, 7[3], 8[2], 9[2], 10[4], 12, 13, 14[2], 15[3], 16, 17[3], 18[2], 19, 20[2], 21[4], 23[2], 24[4], 25[4]; **25:**1[2], 2[3], 3[2], 4[2], 5, 6[3], 7[2], 8[3], 9[2], 10, 13[3], 15[2], 16, 17, 18; **26:**1[2], 2, 3[2], 4[2], 7[4], 8, 9[5], 10[4], 14[2], 18, 19[3], 20, 21, 22[2], 25[2], 27, 28, 29, 31[2], 32[2], 33[4], 34[3], 36, 37[2], 40[3], 41[3], 43[2], 46, 47[2], 50[3], 51[2], 52, 54, 56, 57, 58, 59[4], 60[3], 61[2], 62[3], 63, 64, 65[2]; **27:**1[4], 2[4], 3[2], 5, 6, 7, 8[2], 9, 10, 11[3], 12[2], 13, 15, 17[3], 18[2], 19[3], 20, 21[3], 22[4], 23[2]; **28:**1, 2[2], 3, 4, 5, 7, 8[2], 9[3], 10, 11[2], 12[2], 13, 14[3], 15[2], 16, 17, 19[2], 20[2], 22, 24, 25, 28, 30, 31[2]; **29:**1, 2[2], 3[2], 4, 5, 6[4], 7[2], 8, 9[2], 11[3], 12[2], 13[2], 14, 15, 16[2], 17, 18[3], 19[3], 20, 21[3], 22[3], 23[2], 24[2], 25[2], 26[2], 27[3], 28[3], 29[2], 30[3], 31[2], 32[2], 33[3], 34[2], 37[2], 38[3], 39[4], 40; **30:**1, 3, 4[4], 5, 6, 7[3], 8[2], 9, 10, 11[4], 12, 13, 16[2]; **31:**1, 3[3], 6[3], 7[2], 8[5], 9[5], 10[2], 11[3], 12[5], 13[3], 14[2], 15, 16, 17, 19[4], 20[4], 21, 22[2], 23[2], 24[3], 25, 26[3], 27[2], 28[4], 29, 30[3], 31[2], 32[3], 33[2], 34[2], 35[2], 36[4], 37[3], 38[3], 39[3], 40[2], 41, 42, 43[3], 44[2], 45[2], 46, 47[2], 48[2], 49[2], 50[2], 51[2], 52[3], 54[4]; **32:**1[3], 2[4], 3[8], 4, 5, 6[3], 7, 9, 10[2], 11[2], 12, 13[2], 14, 15, 16[3], 17, 20, 21, 22[4], 23, 24[2], 25[2], 26, 28[2], 29[3], 31[2], 33[4], 34[3], 35[3], 36[3], 37[3], 38[4], 39[3], 40[2], 41[3], 42[4]; **33:**1, 2[2], 3, 5[2], 6[2], 7[3], 8[4], 9[6], 10[2], 11[2], 12[2], 13[2], 14[2], 15[2], 16[2], 17[2], 18[2], 19[2], 20[2], 21[2], 22[2], 23[2], 24[2], 25[2], 26[2], 27[2], 28[2], 29[2], 30[2], 31[2], 32[2], 33[2], 34[2], 35[2], 36[2], 37[2], 38[2], 39[3], 40, 41[2], 42[2], 43[2], 44[2], 45[2], 46[2], 47[2], 48[2], 49, 50, 51, 52[3], 53[2], 54[3], 55[2]; **34:**1, 2, 3, 4[5], 5[2], 6, 7, 8, 9[2], 10, 11[3], 12[2], 13[2], 14[2], 15, 16, 17, 18, 19, 20, 22, 24, 25, 26, 27, 28; **35:**1, 2, 3[4], 4[2], 5[5], 6[3], 7, 8, 9, 10, 12, 13, 14, 15[2], 16, 17[2], 18, 23[2], 24, 25[3], 27[2], 32, 33; **36:**1[3], 2[2], 3[2], 4, 5, 8, 11[3], 12[2], 13

Dt 1:1[4], 3, 4, 7[7], 8[3], 9, 10, 11, 12[2], 13[3], 14[2], 15[6], 16[4], 17[2], 18, 19[3], 20, 21, 22[5], 23[2], 24[4], 25[4], 27[2], 28[3], 31, 33, 34[3], 36[2], 39[4], 40, 41[3], 42, 43[2], 44[3], 45[2]; **2:**1[2], 2, 4[2], 6, 8[3], 9, 10[2], 12, 13[2], 14[2], 16, 19, 20, 21[4], 22[2], 23[2], 24[3], 25[3], 26, 28, 29, 30, 31[2], 32, 33[4], 34[4], 35, 36; **3:**1[3], 2[4], 3[2], 4, 5, 6[2], 7, 8, 9, 10[3], 11, 12[4], 13[2], 14[2], 15, 16[3], 17[2], 18, 19[2], 20[2], 21, 23, 24[2], 25[2], 26[2], 27[5], 28[3]; **4:**1[3], 5, 6[4], 8[2], 9[3], 10[2], 11[4], 12, 13[2], 14[2], 16, 19[5], 20, 21[2], 22, 23, 25[5], 26, 27[2], 28[2], 29, 30[2], 32, 33, 34[6], 36[2], 37[2], 38, 39[2], 40[3], 42[2], 43[2], 44, 45[2], 46, 47[2], 49; **5:**1[5], 5[2], 9, 10[2], 13, 14, 15[3], 16[2], 22[4], 23[2], 24[4], 26, 27[4], 28[2], 29[2], 31[3], 33[2]; **6:**1, 2[4], 3[3], 5[3], 6, 7[5], 8[2], 9[2], 10[3], 11[4], 13[2], 15, 17[2], 18[4], 20[3], 21, 22[4], 23, 24, 25; **7:**1[8], 2[2], 4, 5[3], 8[2], 9[2], 10, 11[2], 12[3], 13[7], 15[2], 16, 18, 19[4], 20, 21, 22[2], 23, 24[2], 26; **8:**1[3], 2[2], 3[3], 6, 7[2], 8[5], 9, 10, 11[2], 12[3], 13[5], 14, 15[3], 16, 17[2], 19[4]; **9:**1[2], 2[2], 3[2], 5[2], 7, 9, 10[2], 11[2], 12, 13, 14[3], 15[3], 16[3], 17[3], 18[2], 19, 20[2], 21[5], 22[3], 23[2], 25, 26[2], 27, 28, 29[2]; **10:**1[2], 2[2], 3[3], 4[2], 5[4], 6[3], 7, 8, 10[4], 11[2], 12[4], 13, 14, 15, 16, 17[2], 18[3], 20[2], 21[2], 22[2]; **11:**1[4], 2[3], 3[3], 4[3], 5, 6[6], 8[2], 9[3], 10, 11[2], 13[3], 14[3], 15[2], 16[3], 17[4], 18[2], 19[3], 20[2], 21, 22, 23[2], 24, 25, 26, 28, 29[2], 31[2], 32[2]; **12:**1, 2[2], 3[5], 5, 6[8], 7[3], 9, 10[2], 11[3], 12[6], 14, 15[3], 18[6], 20, 21[2], 22[2], 23, 25, 26[2], 27[4], 28[3], 29[2], 30, 31; **13:**1, 2[2], 3, 4[5], 5[2], 6, 9, 10, 11[3], 13[2], 14[4], 15[2], 16[4], 17[4]; **14:**2, 4, 5[6], 6[3], 7[2], 8, 9, 10[2], 12[2], 13[3], 14, 15[4], 16[2], 17[3], 18[4], 19, 23[4], 24, 25[2], 26[4], 27, 28, 29[6]; **15:**2, 6[2], 8, 9[4], 10[2], 11, 12[2], 13, 14[2], 15[2], 16[2], 17[3], 18, 19, 20, 21, 22[2]; **16:**1, 2, 4, 7[4], 8, 10, 11[9], 12[3], 13, 14[8], 15, 16[3], 18[2], 19, 20; **17:**3[3], 4[5], 5, 7, 8[5], 9[4], 10[2], 11, 12[3], 13[3], 14[3], 17, 18, 19[3], 20[2]; **18:**1[2], 3[4], 4[2], 5, 6[2], 12, 14, 17, 18[2], 19, 21; **19:**1[3], 3, 4, 5[4], 6[2], 8[2], 9, 10, 11[4], 12[2], 17, 18[3], 20[3], 21; **20:**1[3], 2[2], 3[2], 5[4], 6[4], 7[4], 8[4], 9, 11[3], 12, 13, 14[4], 17[3], 19, 20[2]; **21:**1, 2[2], 3[2], 4[2], 5[4], 6, 7[2], 8[2], 10[2], 11[2], 12[2], 13[7], 14, 15[4], 18[2], 19[3], 20[3], 21[3], 22[3]; **22:**1, 2[3], 3[3], 4, 6, 7[2], 9, 10, 11, 13[2], 14[4], 15[2], 16[2], 17[3], 18[2], 19[3], 20, 21, 22, 23[2], 24[2], 25[2], 26, 27[2], 28[3], 29; **23:**4[2], 11, 13[4], 14[2], 21, 23; **24:**1[4], 2[2], 3[4], 4, 5, 7[2], 8, 11, 12, 13[2], 14, 15[2], 18, 19[2], 20, 21, 22; **25:**1[2], 2[2], 3[2], 5[4], 6, 7[2], 8[3], 9[4], 10, 11[3], 13, 14, 15[2], 16, 18[3]; **26:**1[3], 2[2], 3[2], 4[2], 5[6], 6[3], 7[4], 8[5], 9[3], 10[3], 11[4], 12[3], 13[3], 14, 15[3], 16[3], 17[5], 18[2], 19[4]; **27:**1, 2[2], 3[2], 4, 5, 6, 7[3], 8, 9[3], 10[2], 11, 12[5], 13[4], 14[2], 15[3], 16, 17, 18, 19[2], 20, 21, 22, 23, 24, 25, 26; **28:**1[2], 2[2], 3, 4[3], 5, 6, 7, 8[2], 9, 10[2], 11[3], 12[3], 13[5], 14, 15[2], 16, 17, 18[2], 19, 20[2], 22[7], 23[2], 24, 25[2], 26[3], 27[3], 28[2], 29[5], 30[3], 31[3], 32[4], 33[3], 35, 36[3], 37[2], 38, 39, 41, 42, 43, 44[2], 45[3], 46[3], 47, 48[4], 51[2], 52[3], 53[3], 54[3], 55, 56[4], 57[3], 58, 59[4], 60, 61, 62, 63[4], 64[3], 65[3], 66[4], 67[2], 68[4]; **29:**2[4], 3, 4[2], 5[2], 7[3], 8[4], 9, 10, 11, 12, 13[3], 14, 15, 16, 17[4], 18[2], 19, 20[3], 21, 22[2], 23[6], 26[3], 27, 28[4], 29; **30:**1[3], 2[4], 3[3], 4, 5[4], 6[3], 7[2], 8[3], 9[3], 10[3], 12[2], 13[2], 14, 15[3], 16[5], 17[2], 18, 19[4], 20[4]; **31:**1[2], 2[3], 3[3], 4[3], 5, 6, 7[4], 8, 9[3], 10, 12[6], 13[2], 14[5], 15[2], 16[5], 17[5], 18, 19, 20[7], 21[2], 22, 23[4], 24, 26, 27[2], 28[3], 29[2], 30; **32:**1[2], 2, 4[2], 5, 6[2], 7[2], 10, 12, 13[2], 14[4], 15[2], 18, 19[2], 20, 21, 22[3], 24[2], 25[2], 27[2], 30[2], 32, 33, 34, 35[2], 36[2], 37, 38[3], 39[3], 40, 41[2], 42[3], 43[3], 44[3], 45, 46, 47, 48, 49, 50[3]; **33:**1, 2[3], 3, 5[2], 6[2], 7[4], 8[3], 9[2], 10[2], 11[2], 12[3], 13[2], 14[2], 15[2], 16[4], 17[3], 18[2], 19, 20[2], 21[3], 22, 23[3], 24[2], 25[2], 26, 27[3], 28, 29[3]; **34:**1[2], 2[4], 3[2], 4[2], 6, 7[2], 8[2], 9[3], 10, 11[3], 12[2]

Jos 1:2, 4[2], 6, 7, 8[2], 9, 11, 12[3], 13, 14[2], 15[2], 16[2], 18[2]; **2:**1[4], 2, 3, 4[3], 5, 6, 7[2], 8, 9[3], 10[2], 11[2], 12, 13[6], 14[3], 15, 16[3], 17, 18[4], 19[3], 20, 21[4], 22[4], 23[4], 24; **3:**1[5], 2, 3[3], 4, 5, 6[4], 7, 8, 9[2], 10[8], 13[2], 14[2], 15[2], 16[4], 17[2]; **4:**1, 3[3], 5[2], 7, 8[4], 9[2], 10[2], 11[2], 12[3], 14, 15, 18[3], 19[2], 20, 21; **5:**1[2], 2, 3[2], 4, 6, 7, 8, 9, 10[2], 11[2], 12, 13[5], 14[4], 15[2]; **6:**1, 2[3], 3[2], 4[3], 5[4], 6[3], 7[3], 8[3], 9[3], 10, 11[2], 12[2], 13[4], 14[2], 15[2], 16, 17[3], 18[3], 19[3], 20[3], 21[6], 22[2], 23[8], 24[5], 25[4], 26[3], 27; **7:**1, 2[5], 3[4], 4, 5[4], 6[4], 7[2], 9[4], 10, 11[4], 13, 14[3], 15[3], 16[2], 17[4], 18[2], 19[3], 20[4], 21[5], 22[3], 23[4], 24[13], 25[3], 26; **8:**1[5], 2[4], 3[3], 4, 5[3], 7, 8, 9[3], 10[4], 11[5], 12[3], 13[2], 14[4], 15[3], 16[3], 17[3], 18[2], 19[6], 20[4], 21[4], 22[3], 23[2], 24[3], 25[2], 27, 28[2], 29[4], 31[2], 32, 33[6], 34[2], 35[2]; **9:**1[5], 2, 3[2], 4[6], 5[5], 6[3], 7[2], 8[3], 9[2], 10[2], 11[3], 12, 13[4], 14[2], 15[3], 16[2], 17[5], 18[2], 21[2], 22[2], 23[3], 24[4], 25[2], 26[2], 27[3]; **10:**1[5], 2[2], 3[3], 4[2], 5[4], 6[3], 7[2], 8, 9, 10[5], 11[3], 12[2], 13[3], 14, 15[2], 16, 17, 18[2], 19[2], 20[2], 21, 22, 23[3], 24[4], 25[2], 26[4], 27[4], 28[5], 29[2], 30[4], 31[4], 32[3], 33[2], 34[4], 35[3], 36[3], 37[6], 38[3], 39[7], 40[4], 41[2], 42[2], 43[2]; **11:**1[3], 2[4], 3[7], 4[3], 5[2], 6[2], 7[2], 8[5], 9[2], 10[3], 11[2], 12[4], 14[2], 15, 16[6], 17[3], 20, 21[4], 22, 23[2]; **12:**1[2], 2[3], 3[3], 4[2], 5[5], 6[4], 7[2], 8[7], 24; **13:**1[4], 2, 3[2], 4, 5[2], 6, 7, 8, 9[2], 10, 11[5], 12[2], 13, 15, 16[3], 17[3], 18[3], 19[3], 20[3], 21[6], 23[3], 24, 25[3], 26[3], 27[5], 28, 29[2], 30[2], 31[3]; **14:**1[3], 2, 3, 4[2], 5, 6[2], 7, 9[2], 10[4], 11, 12[2], 13[2], 15[2]; **15:**2, 3[6], 4[2], 5[2], 6[3], 7[4], 8[2], 9[3], 10[4], 11[5], 12[2], 13, 14[3], 15[2], 16[2], 17[2], 18[3], 19[2], 21[3], 22[3], 23[3], 24[2], 25[3], 26[2], 27[3], 28[3], 29[2], 30[3], 31[3], 32[5], 33[3], 34[3], 35[2], 36[4], 37[2], 38[3], 39[2], 40[3], 41[3], 42[2], 43[3], 44[3], 45, 47[4], 48[3], 49[2], 50[3], 51[3], 52[2], 53[3], 54[3], 55[2], 56[3], 57, 58, 59[3], 60, 61, 62[3]; **16:**1, 2[2], 3[3], 4, 5, 6[3], 7[4], 8, 9, 10[2]; **17:**1, 2[5], 3[3], 4[3], 5[2], 6, 7[2], 9[2], 10[4], 11[13], 14[2], 15[3], 16[4], 17[3], 18[3]; **18:**1[3], 2, 3, 4[5], 5[2], 6, 7[3], 8[6], 9[4], 10[2], 11[3], 12[4], 13[2], 14[3], 15[3], 16[4], 17[4], 18[2], 19[2], 20, 21[2], 22[3], 23[3], 24[3], 25[2], 26[3], 27[3], 28[3]; **19:**1[2], 2[2], 3[3], 4[3], 5[3], 6[3], 7[3], 8, 10[2], 11[4], 12[3], 13[2], 14[2], 15[5], 17, 18[3], 19[3], 20[3], 21[4], 22[4], 23, 24, 25[4], 26[5], 27[5], 28[4], 29[4], 30[3], 33[4], 34[5], 35[3], 36[3], 37[3], 38[4], 39, 40, 41[3], 42[3], 43[3], 44[3], 45[3], 46[2], 47[6], 50[2], 51[2]; **20:**3[2], 4[3], 5[2], 6[4], 7[3], 8[3], 9[2]; **21:**1[2], 2, 3[2], 4[4], 5[3], 6[4], 7[2], 8, 9[2], 11, 12, 13, 14[2], 15[2], 16[3], 17, 18, 20, 21, 22[2], 23, 25[2], 27[2], 28, 30, 31, 32[3], 34[2], 36[2], 37, 38[2], 41, 43[3], 44[2]; **22:**1[2], 2[2], 4[3], 5[6], 6[2], 7, 8[6], 9[4], 10[3], 11[3], 12, 13[3], 14[2], 15[4], 18, 19, 20[2], 21[3], 22, 24, 25[2], 27[4], 28, 29, 30[5], 31[3], 32[4], 33[4], 34[2]; **23:**1[2], 2[7], 3, 5[3], 6, 9, 12[4], 13[3], 14[4], 16[4]; **24:**1[6], 2[3], 3[4], 4[4], 5[3], 6[4], 7[6], 8[4], 9[3], 11[9], 12, 13[4], 14[5], 15[2], 16[2], 17[4], 18, 19, 20[3], 21, 22[2], 23, 24[2], 25[2], 26[3], 27, 29[2], 30, 31[3], 32[2], 33[2]

Jdg 1:2, 3[2], 4[4], 5[4], 6[4], 7[5], 8[3], 9[3], 10[4], 11[2], 12[2], 13[2], 14[3], 15[3], 16[3], 17[4], 18[2], 19[2], 20[2], 21, 22[2], 23, 24[3], 25[2], 26[3], 27[5], 28[2], 30, 33, 34, 35, 36[2]; **2:**1[4], 2, 3, 4[2], 5[2], 6, 7[2], 8[2], 9, 10[2], 11[2], 12[4], 13[3], 14[3], 15[2], 17[2], 18[3], 19[3], 20[3]; **3:**3[3], 4, 5[5], 6[3], 7[4], 8[2], 9, 10[5], 11[2], 12[2], 13[5], 15, 16, 17[2], 18, 19[2], 20[4], 21[3], 22[3], 23[2], 24, 25[4], 26[3], 27[3], 28[4], 29[3], 30, 31[2]; **4:**1, 2, 3[2], 4, 5[3], 6[6], 7[3], 8, 9[3], 10[4], 11, 12, 13[2], 14[2], 15[4], 16[3], 17, 18[3], 19[4], 20[3], 21[5], 22[5], 24[2]; **5:**1, 4, 6, 10, 12, 14, 15[2], 17[2], 18, 19, 25, 26[3], 28, 31; **6:**1[2], 2[4], 3[3], 4[3], 5[4], 6[2], 7, 8, 9[4], 10, 11[3], 12[2], 13[3], 14[3], 15[2], 16[2], 17, 18[3], 19[6], 20[5], 21[5], 22, 23, 24, 25[3], 26[3], 27[3], 28[3], 29[3], 30, 31, 33[4], 34[2], 35[5], 36, 37[2], 38[3], 39[3], 40[2]; **7:**1[2], 2, 3[5], 4[4], 5, 6, 7[3], 8[4], 9, 11[2], 12[4], 13[6], 14[3], 15[4], 16[3], 17[3], 18[3], 19[4], 20[6], 21[4], 22[4], 23[4], 24[5], 25[7]; **8:**1[2], 2, 3[2], 4[3], 5[3], 6[2], 7[3], 8[3], 9, 10[3], 11[3], 12[5], 13, 14[5], 15[4], 16[4], 17[2], 18[2], 19, 20[2], 21[6], 22[2], 23, 24, 25[3], 26[5], 27[4], 28, 29[2], 30[2], 31, 32[2], 33[3], 34; **9:**1[3], 2[2], 3[2], 4[3], 5[3], 6[4], 7[5], 8, 9[2], 10[2], 11[2], 12, 13[3], 14, 15[4], 16[4], 17[2], 18[4], 19[3], 20[5], 21[4], 23[2], 24[3], 25[3], 26[3], 27[8], 28[3], 29[3], 30, 31[3], 32[2], 33[4], 34[3], 35[4], 36[2], 37[3], 38, 39[2], 40[4], 41[3], 42[2], 43[7], 44[5], 45[5], 46, 47, 48[8], 49[5], 50[2], 51[5], 52[3], 53[2], 54[4], 55, 57[2]; **10:**1[2], 2[4], 3[3], 4[2], 5[2], 6[10], 7[3], 8[2], 9[2], 10[2], 11[3], 12[4], 13, 14, 15, 16[3], 17[3], 18[2]; **11:**1[2], 2[4], 3[3], 4, 5, 6[2], 7[3], 8[3], 9[2], 10, 11[3], 12, 13[2], 14, 15, 16[2], 17[2], 18[4], 19[2], 20[2], 21[3], 22[2], 23, 25, 26[4], 27, 29[4], 30[2], 31, 32, 33[2], 34[4], 35[4], 36, 37[4], 38[4], 39[3]; **12:**1[4], 2[3], 3[3], 4[3], 5[2], 6[4], 7[2], 8, 9[4], 10, 11[2], 12[2], 13, 14[4], 15[2]; **13:**1[2], 2[3], 3[4], 4[2], 5[3], 6[2], 7[2], 8[2], 9[2], 10[4], 11[5], 12[2], 13, 15, 16[2], 17, 18, 19[4], 20[3], 21, 22, 23, 24[4], 25[2]; **14:**1[2], 2[4], 3[2], 4, 5[4], 6[3], 7[3], 8[4], 9[6], 10, 11, 12[3], 13[2], 14[3], 15[2], 16[6], 17[3], 18[3], 19[7]; **15:**1, 2, 3, 4[5], 5[4], 6[5], 7[2], 8[4], 9[2], 10[2], 11[2], 12[2], 13[4], 14[4], 15[4], 16, 17[2], 18[5], 19[3], 20; **16:**1[2], 2[4], 3[8], 4, 5[5], 6[2], 7[2], 8, 9[2], 10[2], 11[2], 12[4], 13[3], 14[5], 15[2], 16[2], 17[3], 18[3], 19[5], 20[5], 21[4], 23, 24[2], 25[4], 26, 27[4], 28[3], 29[3], 30[4], 31[6]; **17:**1, 2[3], 3[2], 4[4], 5[4], 7[2], 8[2], 9[3], 10[6], 11[2], 12[3]; **18:**1, 2[4], 3[4], 4[4], 5, 6, 7[6], 8[3], 9[4], 10, 11[2], 12[2], 13[2], 14[4], 15[3], 16, 17[7], 18[4], 19[5], 20[5], 21[4], 22[2], 23[3], 24[5], 25[2], 26[3], 27[6], 28[5], 29, 30[3], 31; **19:**1, 2[3], 3[6], 4[4], 5[3], 6[5], 7, 8[4], 9[4], 10[3], 11[4], 12, 13[2], 14[3], 15[3], 16[2], 17[3], 18[3], 19[5], 20, 21[4], 22[2], 23[2], 24[3], 25[4], 26, 27[5], 28[4], 29[4], 30[2]; **20:**1, 2, 4[3], 5[4], 6[4], 7, 8, 10[3], 12, 13, 15[2], 16, 17, 18[5], 19[2], 20[2], 21[3], 22[2], 23[4], 24, 25[2], 26[7], 27, 28[2], 29, 30[2], 31[5], 32[2], 33[3], 34[2], 35[4], 37[4], 38, 39[2], 40, 41, 42, 43[2], 44, 45[5], 46, 47[2], 48[3]; **21:**2[4], 3, 4[4], 5, 6[2], 8[2], 9, 10[4], 11[2], 12[2], 13[2], 14[3], 15, 17, 19, 20, 21[4], 22, 23[6], 24[3]

Ru 1:1[3], 2[6], 3[3], 4[3], 5[4], 7[2], 8[2], 9[2], 10, 11, 12, 14[3], 15[2], 16[3], 17[3], 19[2], 20, 21[2], 22[2]; **2:**1[2], 2[3], 3[4], 4[3], 6[2], 7[3], 9[3], 10[2], 11[6], 12, 13, 14[8], 15[2], 16[3], 17[2], 18[5], 19[4], 20[3], 21, 22, 23[2]; **3:**2, 3[4], 4[5], 5, 6[2], 7[6], 8[3], 9[2], 10, 11, 12, 13, 14[3], 15[4], 16[2], 17; **4:**1[4], 2[3], 3, 4[4], 6, 7[3], 9[4], 10, 11[5], 12, 13[3], 14, 15[2], 16[3], 17[2], 19[2], 20[2], 21[2], 22[2]

1Sa 1:1, 2[3], 3[4], 4[3], 6, 7[2], 8[2], 9, 10[3], 11[5], 12, 14, 15[2], 16, 17[2], 18[3], 19[6], 20, 21[3], 22[2], 23[2], 24[5], 25[2], 26, 27, 28; **2:**1[2], 3, 4, 5[2], 6[2], 7[2], 8[3], 9, 10[2], 11[2], 13, 14, 15, 16[3], 19, 20[4], 21[4], 22[2], 23, 26[3], 27[2], 28[2], 29[2], 30[2], 31, 32[2], 33[3], 34[2], 35[4], 36[4]; **3:**1[2], 2[2], 3[2], 4, 5[5], 6[5], 8[5], 9[2], 10[3], 11, 13, 14, 15[3], 16[2], 17[2], 18[3], 19[3], 20, 21; **4:**1[3], 2[3], 3, 4[2], 5, 6[2], 7[2], 9[2], 10[4], 11[3], 12[3], 13[3], 14[3], 15[2], 16[3], 17[6], 18[5], 19[5], 20, 21[3], 22; **5:**1[2], 2, 3[3], 4[3], 6[3], 7[2], 8[4], 9[4], 10[2], 11[4], 12[2]; **6:**1, 2[2], 3[2], 4[2], 5[4], 6[2], 7[3], 8[4], 9, 10[4], 11[3], 12[4], 13[4], 14[4], 15[5], 16, 17, 18[2], 19[4], 20[2], 21[2]; **7:**1[4], 2[2], 3[5], 4[2], 5[2], 6[6], 7[2], 8, 9[4], 10[3], 11[3], 12[3], 13[2], 14[4], 15, 16[4], 17[3]; **8:**1, 2, 3[3], 4, 5[2], 6, 7, 8, 9, 10, 11[4], 12[6], 13[3], 14[4], 15[4], 16[5], 17, 18[2], 19, 20[3], 21[2], 22[3]; **9:**2[4], 3[3], 4[4], 5[3], 6[2], 7, 8[2], 9, 11[2], 12[2], 13, 14[2], 16, 17, 18, 19[4], 20[3], 21[3], 22[4], 23, 24[5], 25, 26[5], 27[2]; **10:**1[3], 2[3], 3[4], 4[2], 5[5], 6[3], 7, 8[4], 9[2], 10[3], 11, 12[2], 13, 14[4], 15, 16, 17, 18[4], 19[4], 20, 21[2], 22, 23[4], 24[3], 25[3], 26[2], 27[2]; **11:**1[3], 2[2], 3[2], 4[3], 5[3], 6[2], 7[6], 8[2], 9[4], 10, 11[4], 12, 13, 14[2], 15[5]; **12:**1[2], 2[5], 3[2], 4, 5[3], 6[3], 7, 8[3], 9[4], 10[5], 11[6], 12, 13[2], 14[4], 16, 17[3], 18[4], 19, 20, 21, 23, 24, 25; **13:**1, 2[3], 3[3], 4[3], 5[5], 6[4], 7[3], 8[2], 9[3], 10[2], 11[4], 12[2], 13, 14, 15[3], 16[3], 17, 18[2], 20[3], 21[4], 22[2], 23; **14:**1, 2[2], 3[2], 4[4], 5, 6[2], 7, 8, 9, 10, 11[2], 12[5], 13[5], 14[2], 15[4], 16[3], 17[3], 18, 19[3], 20[5], 21, 23, 24, 25[2], 26, 27[3], 28[2], 31[2], 32[6], 33, 34[8], 35, 36[4], 37, 38[3], 40[3], 41[2], 42[3], 43[3], 44[2], 45, 46, 47[6], 48[3], 49[4], 50[2], 51[2], 52[2]; **15:**3[7], 4[3], 5[2], 6, 7, 8[2], 9[8], 11[3], 12[5], 13[2], 14[2], 15[3], 16[2], 17[2], 18[4], 19, 20[4], 21, 22[3], 23[2], 24[3], 25, 26[2], 27[2], 28[2], 29, 30[2], 31, 32[2], 33[2], 34, 35[2]; **16:**1[2], 2[3], 3[3], 4[4], 5[5], 6[2], 8[2], 9, 10, 11[5], 12[5], 13[3], 14, 15, 16[2], 17[2], 18[6], 19, 20[4], 21[4], 22, 23[4]; **17:**1[3], 2[4], 3[3], 4[2], 5[3], 6[2], 7[3], 8[5], 9[3], 10, 11[2], 12[2], 13[5], 14[2], 15, 16[3], 17[3], 18[3], 19[2], 20[6], 21, 22[4], 23[3], 24[2], 25[4], 26[2], 27, 28[5], 29, 30[3], 31[2], 32[2], 33[2], 34[4], 35[6], 36[2], 37[3], 38[2], 39[4], 40[5], 41[3], 42[4], 43[2], 44[3], 45[2], 46[4], 47[3], 48[4], 49[5], 50[3], 51[6], 52[7], 53[2], 54[2], 55[2], 56, 57[2], 58[2]; **18:**1[2], 2[2], 3, 4[5], 5[5], 6[3], 7[3], 8[5], 9[2], 10[4], 11[2], 12[2], 13[3], 14[2], 16[2], 17[2], 18[2], 20[3], 21[2], 22[3], 23[3], 24, 25, 26[2], 27[6], 28[3], 29[2], 30; **19:**1[2], 2[3], 3[4], 4[3], 5[3], 6[2], 7[4], 8[5], 9[2], 10[4], 11[2], 12[3], 13[4], 14, 15, 16, 17[3], 18[6], 19, 20[4], 21[4], 22[5], 23[4], 24[4]; **20:**1[4], 2[2], 3[5], 5[2], 9, 11[3], 12[4], 13[3], 14, 17, 18, 19[3], 20, 21[2], 23[3], 24, 25[4], 27[2], 28, 29[4], 30[2], 31, 32[2], 33, 34, 35[2], 36[2], 37[2], 38[3], 39, 40[2], 41[5], 42[7]; **21:**1[3], 2[5], 4[2], 5[4], 7, 8[2], 9[2], 10[3], 11[2], 12[2], 13[4]; **22:**1[3], 2[5], 3[4], 4[2], 5[3], 6[2], 7[3], 8[2], 9, 10[3], 11[2], 12[2], 13[4], 14[4], 16[2], 17[4], 18[6],

APNDX

19^6, 20^2, 21, 22; **23:**1, 2^4, 3, 4^2, 5^4, 6, 7^3, 8^2, 9^2, 11, 12^2, 13^5, 14^3, 15^2, 16^3, 17^4, 18^3, 20, 21, 22^3, 23^4, 24^3, 25^4, 26^6, 27, 28, 29^2; **24:**1, 2^2, 3^4, 4^2, 5, 6, 7^2, 8^4, 9, 10^2, 11^3, 12^2, 15^5, 16^3, 17, 18, 20^2, 21, 22^3; **25:**1^6, 2^5, 3^5, 4, 5^4, 6^3, 7, 8^2, 9^2, 10^3, 11^3, 12^3, 13^5, 14, 15, 16, 17^2, 18^7, 19, 20^4, 21, 22, 23^4, 24^4, 25, 26^3, 27, 28, 29^2, 30^2, 32, 33^3, 34, 35^2, 36^3, 37^2, 38, 39^4, 40, 41^3, 42^5, 43; **26:**1, 2, 3^2, 4, 5^6, 6^3, 7^4, 8, 9^2, 10, 11^2, 12^3, 13, 14^3, 15^2, 16^2, 17^3, 18, 21, 22^4, 23, 24^2, 25^2; **27:**1^2, 2^2, 3^3, 4^2, 5, 7^2, 8^5, 9^9, 10^4, 11^2, 12; **28:**1^3, 2^2, 3^4, 4^5, 5^2, 6, 7^2, 8^7, 9^2, 10, 11, 12^2, 13^2, 14^6, 15^4, 16, 17^2, 19^2, 20^2, 21^5, 22^2, 23^3, 24^6, 25^4; **29:**1, 2^3, 3^2, 4^3, 5, 6^3, 7, 8^2, 9^2, 10^2, 11^2; **30:**1^5, 2^2, 3^5, 4^2, 5^2, 6^2, 7^2, 8^3, 9^2, 10, 11^5, 12^4, 13^4, 14^3, 15^3, 16^4, 17^3, 18^2, 19, 20^3, 21^4, 22^4, 23, 25^2, 26, 27^2, 28^3, 29^3, 30^3, 31^3; **31:**1^2, 2^5, 3^3, 4^4, 5^2, 6^3, 7^7, 8^2, 9^4, 10^2, 11, 12^5, 13^3

2Sa 1:1, 2^3, 3^2, 4^6, 5^2, 6^3, 7^3, 8^2, 9, 10^4, 11^2, 12^6, 13^2, 14, 15^4, 16, 17^2, 22, 23^3, 27; **2:**1^4, 2^2, 3^2, 4^3, 5^3, 6^3, 7^2, 8, 9^6, 10, 11^2, 12^2, 13^5, 14^3, 15^2, 16^2, 17^3, 18^4, 19^2, 20^2, 21^3, 22, 23^4, 24^2, 25^3, 26, 27, 28^2, 29^5, 30^3, 31^2, 32^5; **3:**1^4, 2^2, 3^2, 4^2, 5, 6^2, 7^2, 8^3, 9, 10^2, 11, 12^2, 13, 14, 15^2, 16^2, 17, 18, 19^3, 20^3, 21^6, 22^4, 23^3, 24^2, 25^3, 26, 27^2, 28^2, 29^2, 30, 31^5, 32^4, 33^2, 34, 35^2, 36^2, 37, 38^2, 39^2; **4:**1^2, 2^2, 3^2, 4^7, 5^3, 6^4, 7^5, 8^4, 9^3, 10, 11, 12^6; **5:**1^2, 2^3, 3^2, 4, 5^4, 6^3, 8^6, 9^3, 10^3, 11^5, 12^2, 13^4, 14^4, 15^3, 16^3, 17^2, 18, 19^2, 20^3, 21^3, 22^2, 23^2, 24, 25^2; **6:**2^2, 3^4, 4^2, 5^6, 6^2, 7^3, 8^2, 9^2, 11^3, 12^3, 13^2, 14^2, 15^2, 16^4, 17^4, 18^2, 19^3, 20^2, 21^2, 22^3; **7:**1^2, 3, 4, 5, 6, 9^3, 10^2, 11^2, 12^3, 13, 14^2, 16^2, 17, 18^3, 19^2, 20, 21, 23^5, 24, 25^3, 26^2, 28^3, 29; **8:**1^3, 2^5, 4^4, 5^2, 6^3, 7^2, 8^2, 10^5, 11, 12^5, 13, 14^3, 15^3, 16^2, 17^3, 18^3; **9:**1, 2^3, 3^2, 4^2, 5, 6^3, 7^3, 8^2, 9^2, 10^4, 12^2, 13; **10:**1^2, 2^2, 3^3, 4^3, 5^2, 6^5, 7^2, 8^6, 9^2, 10, 11^2, 12^3, 13^3, 14^3, 15, 16^4, 17^5, 18^4, 19^2; **11:**1^5, 2^4, 3^3, 4^5, 5^4, 6^2, 7^3, 8^4, 9, 10, 11^8, 12^3, 13^4, 14^2, 15^3, 16, 17^4, 18, 19, 20^2, 22^2, 23^3, 24^3, 25^2, 26, 27^4; **12:**1^4, 2, 3^6, 4^4, 5^2, 6^2, 7^2, 8^6, 9^2, 10, 11^3, 12, 13^2, 15^3, 16^3, 17^2, 18^3, 19, 20^7, 21^2, 22^2, 24^6, 25^2, 26^2, 27^3, 28^3, 29^4, 30^3, 31^7; **13:**1^2, 2^2, 3, 4^2, 5^6, 6^3, 7, 8^5, 9^4, 10^3, 11^2, 12, 13^2, 14, 15, 16, 17^2, 18^2, 19^4, 20, 22, 23^2, 24^3, 25^2, 26, 27, 28^2, 29^3, 30^2, 31^3, 32^2, 34^3, 35, 36^5, 37^2, 38^2, 39; **14:**2^5, 3^2, 4^3, 5^3, 6^4, 7^5, 8^2, 9^4, 10^2, 11, 12, 13, 14, 15, 16, 17, 18^2, 19^4, 20, 21, 22^4, 23^2, 24^3, 26, 27^2, 28, 29, 30^3, 31^2, 32^2, 33^4; **15:**1^3, 2^5, 3^2, 4, 5^3, 6, 7^2, 9^2, 11^3, 12^2, 13, 14^4, 15, 16^3, 17^3, 18^4, 19^2, 20^3, 21^3, 22^5, 23^3, 24^4, 25^3, 27^2, 29^2, 30^6, 31^2, 32^2, 34, 35^3, 36^2, 37; **16:**1^5, 2^5, 3^3, 4, 5^2, 6^5, 7^2, 8^2, 9, 10, 11^3, 12, 13^5, 14^3, 15^3, 16, 17, 18^4, 19, 21^2, 22, 23^2; **17:**1^2, 2^5, 3, 4^2, 5, 6, 7, 8^4, 9, 10^2, 11, 12^3, 13, 14^2, 15^5, 16^2, 17^5, 18^2, 19^4, 20^5, 21^5, 22^2, 23^7, 24^2, 25, 26, 27^3, 28^9, 29^7; **18:**1^3, 2^4, 4^4, 5^4, 6, 7, 8, 9^7, 10^3, 11^5, 12^3, 13, 14^2, 15^3, 16^2, 17^4, 18^3, 19, 20, 21^2, 22, 23^2, 24^5, 25^5, 26^4, 27^3, 28^4, 29^3, 30^4, 31^2, 32^3, 33^4; **19:**1^2, 2, 3, 4, 5^6, 6^2, 7^2, 8^3, 9^3, 10, 11^2, 12, 13^3, 14^2, 15^2, 16^2, 17^5, 18^3, 19, 21, 22, 23, 24^2, 25, 26^2, 27, 29^2, 30, 31^2, 32, 33^2, 34, 35^3, 36, 37^3, 38^3, 39^4, 40^3, 41^5, 42, 43^4; **20:**1^3, 2, 3^4, 4, 6^3, 7^5, 8^3, 9^2, 10^4, 11^3, 12^3, 14^5, 15^5, 17^3, 18, 19^2, 20^2, 21^2, 22^5, 23^2, 24^2, 25^3, 26; **21:**1^3, 2^5, 3, 4^2, 5^2, 6^2, 7, 8^2, 9^4, 10^3, 11, 12^3, 13^3, 14^4, 15^4, 16, 17^2, 18, 19, 20^4, 21, 22^2; **22:**1^2, 2^3, 3^2, 7^3, 8^2, 9, 10^2, 11^3, 12^2, 14, 15^3, 16, 18, 22, 23, 24, 26, 27, 28, 29, 32, 33^2, 34, 36, 38^2, 39^2, 43, 46, 47^2, 48, 49, 50, 51^2; **23:**1^2, 2, 4, 5^2, 7^2, 9^2, 10^4, 11^3, 12^3, 13^3, 14^2, 15^2, 16^4, 17, 18^4, 20^2, 21^4, 22, 23, 39; **24:**1^3, 2, 3^2, 4^3, 5^3, 6^3, 7^4, 8, 9^3, 10^3, 12, 13^3, 14^2, 15, 16^3, 17^4, 18^2, 19, 20^5, 21^2, 22^4, 23, 24^2, 25^4

1Ki 1:1^2, 2^3, 3^2, 4^3, 5^3, 6^3, 7^3, 8^5, 9^5, 10^3, 11, 12, 13^3, 14, 15^3, 16^3, 17^2, 18^2, 19^6, 20, 21, 22, 23^2, 24^2, 25^9, 26^3, 27, 28^3, 29^2, 30, 31^2, 32^4, 33^2, 34^4, 35^3, 36^2, 37, 38^6, 39^4, 40^3, 41^3, 42^3, 43^2, 44^6, 45^3, 46, 47^3, 48, 49^3, 50^4, 51, 52, 53^4; **2:**1, 2, 3^5, 4, 5^5, 6, 7, 8^2, 9, 10, 11^3, 12, 13^3, 14, 15^3, 16^2, 17, 18, 19^5, 20, 21, 22^5, 23, 24^2, 25^2, 26^2, 28^2, 29^2, 30^5, 31^4, 32^4, 33^4, 34^3, 35^2, 36^5, 37, 38^2, 39^2, 40^5, 41^2, 42^6, 43, 45^2, 46^2; **3:**1^5, 3^2, 4, 5, 6^4, 7^2, 8, 9, 10, 11^2, 12, 13^2, 14^2, 15^7, 16, 17^3, 18^2, 19, 20^4, 21, 22^4, 23^3, 24^2, 25^3, 26^2, 27^2, 28^2; **4:**2, 3, 4^3, 5^3, 6^2, 7^2, 8, 9^3, 10, 12^2, 13, 16, 19^2, 20^3, 21^3, 22^2, 23^5, 24, 25^3, 26^2, 27^2, 28^2, 29^3, 30^2, 31^4, 32^3, 33^4, 34; **5:**1, 2, 5, 6^2, 7^2, 8^3, 9^4, 10, 11^2, 12^4, 13^2, 14^3, 15^3, 16, 17^3, 18^4; **6:**1^2, 2^3, 3^2, 4, 5^3, 6^2, 7, 8^2, 9^3, 10^2, 11, 12^2, 13^2, 14, 15^4, 16^2, 17, 18^2, 19, 20^5, 21^2, 22, 23, 24^2, 25^2, 26, 27^4, 28, 29^4, 30^2, 31^2, 32^6, 34^2, 35^4, 36^2, 38^2; **7:**1, 2^2, 3, 4^2, 5^3, 6^5, 7, 8, 9^2, 10^2, 11^2, 12^3, 13^2, 14^6, 15, 16^2, 17^3, 18^3, 19, 20^2, 21^5, 22, 23^3, 24, 25^5, 26^2, 27^3, 28^2, 29^5, 30^3, 31^4, 32^4, 33^4, 34^2, 35^3, 36^3, 37, 38^2, 39^3, 40^3, 41^2, 42, 43^2, 44^2, 45^4, 46, 47, 48^2, 49^4, 50^7, 51^3; **8:**1, 2, 3^2, 4^4, 5^3, 6, 7^2, 8^3, 10, 14^3, 15^2, 17, 18, 20^4, 21, 22^2, 23^2, 24, 26, 27, 28^2, 29, 30^4, 31^2, 32^3, 33^4, 34^2, 35^3, 36^3, 38^2, 39^3, 42^3, 43^2, 44^2, 45^2, 46^2, 47^3, 48^4, 49^2, 50^3, 51, 52, 54^2, 55^2, 58^3, 59^3, 60, 61, 62^2, 63^5, 64^4, 65^3, 66^4; **9:**1^3, 3^4, 4^4, 6^4, 7^3, 8^4, 9^4, 10^2, 11^2, 12^2, 13^2, 14, 15^7, 16^4, 17^2, 18^2, 19^6, 20^2, 22^5, 23, 25^3, 26, 27, 28^4; **10:**1, 2^4, 3, 4^2, 5^6, 6^2, 7^3, 8, 9, 10^4, 11^2, 12^3, 13^3, 14, 15^3, 16, 17^2, 18, 19^3, 20^2, 21^2, 22^3, 23, 24, 25^6, 26^6, 27^2, 28^2, 29^6; **11:**1, 3^3, 4, 5, 6^2, 7, 8^2, 9, 10, 11^3, 13, 14, 15, 17, 18^6, 19, 20^2, 21^2, 22, 23, 24^5, 25^3, 26, 27^2, 28^2, 29^3, 30^2, 31^2, 32, 33^5, 34, 35, 36, 37^3, 38^6, 39, 40^3, 41^3, 42, 43^3; **12:**1, 2^2, 3^4, 4^2, 5^2, 6^2, 7^4, 8^2, 9, 10, 11, 12, 13^2, 14^2, 18, 20^3, 21^2, 23^3, 24, 25^3, 26, 27^2, 28^2, 29^2, 30, 31^2, 32^3, 33^3; **13:**1^2, 2^4, 3^2, 4^2, 5, 6^6, 7^3, 8, 10, 11^2, 12, 13^2, 14^4, 15, 16, 18^2, 19^2, 20, 21^2, 22^3, 23^2, 24^4, 25^5, 26^2, 27^2, 28^4, 29^5, 30^2, 31, 32, 33, 34^2; **14:**2^3, 3^4, 4^4, 5^2, 6, 7, 8^4, 9^3, 10^4, 11, 12, 13^2, 15^2, 16^2, 17^4, 18^2, 19^2, 20^4, 21^4, 22^2, 23^3, 24^2, 25, 26^3, 27^2, 28^2, 29, 30^2, 31^4; **15:**2, 3^2, 4, 5, 6^2, 7^3, 8^3, 9, 10^3, 11, 12^2, 13^3, 15^4, 16^2, 17^2, 18^4, 19^5, 20^5, 21^2, 22^4, 23^3, 24^3, 25^2, 26^3, 27^3, 28, 29, 30, 31, 32^2, 33, 34^3; **16:**2^3, 3^2, 4, 5^2, 6^2, 7^3, 8, 9, 10^5, 11, 13^2, 14, 15^2, 16^2, 17^3, 18^3, 19, 20, 21, 22, 23, 24^3, 25, 26, 27, 28^2, 29^4, 30, 31^4, 32, 33^2, 34; **17:**1, 2, 3^2, 4^2, 5^2, 6^5, 7, 8, 9, 10^4, 11^2, 12^6, 13^5, 15^5, 16, 17^2, 18^2, 19^4, 20^2, 21^3, 22^3, 23^4, 24^2; **18:**1^2, 2^2, 3, 4^3, 5^3, 6, 7^4, 8, 9, 10^2, 11, 12^4, 13^2, 14^2, 15, 16^2, 17, 18^3, 19^4, 20, 21^3, 22, 23^7, 24^5, 25^3, 26^4, 27^3, 28^3, 29^2, 30^3, 31, 32^2, 33^6, 34^4, 35^2, 36^5, 37, 38^5, 39^2, 40^4, 41^2, 42^4, 43^5, 44^3, 45^5, 46^3; **19:**1^2, 2, 3^4, 4^4, 5^4, 6^6, 7^4, 8^5, 9^4, 10^4, 11^7, 12^2, 13^5, 14^4, 15^2, 16^2, 17^2, 18, 19^4, 20^6, 21^8; **20:**1^8, 2^2, 3^2, 4^3, 5^5, 6^4, 7^6, 8^2, 9^2, 10^3, 11^2, 12^3, 13^2, 14^3, 15^3, 16^3, 17^3, 18, 19, 20^4, 21^4, 22^4, 23^2, 24^2, 25^6, 26^2, 27^4, 28^4, 29^3, 30^4, 31^3, 32^4, 33^3, 34^3, 35^2, 36^2, 37^2, 38^2, 39^5, 40^3, 41^3, 42^2, 43^3; **21:**1, 2^2, 3, 4^5, 5, 6^3, 7^3, 8^3, 9^2, 10^4, 11^3, 12, 13^5, 14, 15^2, 16, 17, 19^3, 20^2, 21^4, 22^3, 23, 24, 26, 27^5, 28; **22:**1^2, 2, 3^3, 4^2, 5, 6^2, 7, 8^2, 9, 10^3, 11^2, 12^2, 13^2, 14, 15^3, 16, 17^2, 18, 19^3, 20^4, 21^3, 22^6, 23, 24^2, 25, 26^3, 27^3, 28^2, 29, 30^4, 31, 32^3, 33, 34^3, 35^4, 36^2, 37^2, 38^3, 39^3, 40, 41, 42^4, 43^2, 44, 45^2, 46, 50^3, 51, 52^4, 53^2

2Ki 1:2^4, 3, 4, 5, 6^3, 7^2, 8^3, 9^3, 10^7, 11^2, 12^7, 13^7, 14, 15^3, 16, 17; **2:**1, 2^3, 3^3, 4^3, 5^3, 6^4, 7^3, 8^5, 9^2, 10, 11^5, 12^6, 13^2, 14^6, 15^3, 16^4, 17^2, 18, 19^2, 20^3, 21^3, 23^4, 24^6, 25^2; **3:**1, 2^2, 4^3, 6^2, 7^4, 8^2, 9^5, 10, 11^2, 12^3, 13^3, 14, 15, 16, 17^2, 18, 19^5, 20^2, 21^3, 22^3, 23^2, 24^2, 25^6, 26, 27^4; **4:**1^2, 2^2, 4^4, 5^3, 6^3, 7^5, 8^3, 9, 10^5, 11^3, 12^2, 13^2, 14^3, 15^2, 16^2, 17^2, 18, 19^2, 20^3, 21^4, 22^4, 23^2, 24^2, 25^2, 26^2, 27^4, 29^4, 30^4, 31^3, 32^2, 33^2, 34^7, 35^6, 36^3, 37^4, 38^5, 39^5, 40^3, 41^3, 42^4, 43^2, 44^2; **5:**1, 2^3, 3, 4^3, 5^6, 6, 7^4, 8^2, 9^2, 10^4, 11^6, 12^3, 13^4, 14^3, 15^5, 16, 17, 18^2, 19, 20, 21^2, 22^2, 23^5, 24^4, 25^3, 26^8, 27^2; **6:**1, 2^3, 3^3, 4, 5^2, 6^5, 7^2, 8^2, 9, 10^3, 11^2, 12, 13^4, 14^4, 15^4, 16, 17^6, 18^3, 19^2, 20^4, 21, 22^5, 23^4, 24^3, 25^3, 26, 27, 28^3, 29^3, 30^4, 31, 32^3, 33^2; **7:**1, 2^2, 3^2, 4^4, 5^2, 6^3, 7^5, 8^{13}, 9^2, 10^5, 11^2, 12^3, 13^4, 14^2, 15^5, 16^3, 17^3, 18^2, 19^3, 20^2; **8:**1^4, 2^4, 3^3, 4, 5^4, 6^2, 7^3, 8^3, 9^4, 10, 11^2, 12^5, 13^2, 14^2, 15^4, 16, 17^2, 18^2, 19, 20, 21^5, 23^2, 24^3, 26^3, 27^2, 28^2, 29^2; **9:**1^4, 2^4, 3^4, 5^4, 6^4, 7^2, 8^3, 9^2, 10^4, 11^3, 12^3, 13^3, 14, 15, 16^2, 17^6, 18^3, 19^2, 20^3, 21^6, 22^3, 23^3, 24^4, 25^2, 26^3, 27^5, 28^2, 29, 30^4, 31, 32^3, 33^4, 34^4, 35^3, 36^2, 37; **10:**1^4, 2^3, 3^3, 4, 5^4, 6^2, 7^4, 8^3, 9^4, 11^3, 12^4, 13^4, 14^4, 15^6, 16^2, 17, 18^2, 19, 20^2, 21^4, 22^2, 23^4, 24^3, 25^7, 26^2, 27^3, 29, 30^2, 32, 33^3, 34^2, 35^3, 36^2; **11:**1^2, 2^3, 3^2, 4^7, 5, 6^2, 7, 8^4, 9^3, 10^2, 11^2, 12^7, 13^2, 14^7, 15^2, 16^3, 17^4, 18^5, 19^7, 20^3; **12:**1^2, 2, 3, 4^2, 5, 6, 7^2, 8, 9^3, 10^4, 11^3, 12^5, 14, 16, 17^3, 18^8, 19^2, 20^3, 21^4; **13:**1^2, 2^2, 3^3, 4^2, 5^2, 6, 7^3, 8^2, 9^3, 10^2, 11, 12^3, 13^3, 14^4, 15^4, 16^3, 17^5, 18^5, 19^2, 20^3, 21^5, 23^5, 24, 25^2; **14:**2^4, 3, 4, 5, 7^2, 9^3, 10^3, 11^2, 12^2, 13^3, 14^6, 15^2, 16^3, 17, 18, 19^2, 20^2, 21^2, 22, 23^2, 24, 27, 28^4, 29^2; **15:**1, 2^3, 3, 4, 5^3, 6^2, 7^2, 8, 9, 10^4, 11, 12, 13^2, 14^4, 15^2, 16^3, 17^2, 18, 19^2, 20^2, 21^2, 22^2, 23, 24, 25^5, 26^2, 27^2, 28, 29^8, 30^4, 31^2, 33^3, 34, 35, 36, 37, 38^3; **16:**2^2, 3, 4^4, 5^2, 6^3, 7^3, 8^4, 9^4, 10^4, 11, 12^3, 13^4, 14^3, 15^9, 17^4, 18^2, 20^3; **17:**2, 3^2, 4^3, 5^2, 6^4, 7, 8^2, 9^2, 10^3, 11^2, 13^5, 15^6, 16^5, 17^5, 18, 20^3, 21^3, 24^8, 25, 26^2, 27^3, 28^2, 29, 30^3, 31^4, 32, 33, 34, 35, 36^3, 37^5, 38, 39, 41^2; **18:**2^3, 3, 4^4, 6, 7^4, 8, 9^2, 10, 11^4, 12^2, 13, 14^3, 15^2, 16^2, 17^7, 18^3, 19, 20, 21, 22^3, 23, 24^2, 25, 26^3, 27^2, 28^2, 30, 31^4, 32^6, 34^2, 36, 37^3; **19:**1^3, 2^3, 3^4, 4, 6, 7^3, 8, 9, 11, 12^3, 13^3, 14^4, 15^3, 16^3, 17, 18^2, 21, 22^3, 23^5, 24^2, 25, 26^3, 27^3, 28^3, 29^6, 30^2, 31, 33, 34, 35^4, 36^3, 37^4; **20:**1^3, 2, 3^3, 4, 5, 6^5, 7^4, 8^2, 9, 10, 11^2, 12, 13^7, 14^3, 15^2, 16, 17, 18^2, 19^2, 20^5, 21^2; **21:**1^3, 2, 3^4, 4, 5, 6^5, 7^3, 8, 9, 10, 11^2, 12, 13^4, 14^4, 15, 17^2, 18^3, 19^3, 20, 21^3, 22^2, 23^2, 24^2, 26^2; **22:**1^3, 2^3, 3, 5^2, 6^4, 8^3, 9^4, 10^2, 11, 12^5, 13^2, 14^5, 15, 16, 17^2, 19^5, 20^3; **23:**1^3, 2^8, 3^7, 4^7, 5^5, 6^4, 7, 8^3, 10, 11^2, 12^4, 13^3, 14^3, 15^5, 16^5, 17^2, 18, 19^2, 20^3, 21, 24^5, 25^3, 27^3, 28, 29^2, 30^6, 31^3, 32, 33^3, 34^5, 35^3, 36^3, 37; **24:**1^2, 2^5, 4, 5, 6, 7, 8^2, 9, 10, 11^2, 12^6, 13^3, 14^5, 15^5, 16^4, 17^2, 18^3, 19, 20; **25:**1^4, 2, 3^2, 4^3, 5^3, 6^2, 7^4, 8, 9^4, 10, 11, 12, 13^4, 14^5, 15^4, 16, 17^5, 18^3, 19^4, 20^2, 21^2, 22, 23^6, 24^5, 25^4, 26^4, 27^3, 28^2, 29^2, 30

1Ch 1:4, 5^6, 6^3, 7^3, 8^2, 9^7, 10, 11^4, 12^3, 13^2, 14^2, 15^3, 16^3, 17^8, 18^2, 19^2, 20^4, 21^2, 22^3, 23^3, 28, 29^2, 30^2, 31, 32^7, 33^5, 34^2, 35^3, 36^4, 37, 38^7, 39^3, 40^5, 41^4, 42^3, 43, 44, 45, 46^2, 47, 48, 49, 50^3, 51; **2:**1^2, 2^2, 3^4, 4^2, 5, 6^5, 7, 8, 9^2, 10^2, 11^2, 12^2, 13^3, 16^4, 17^2, 18^4, 19, 20^2, 21^2, 22^2, 23^3, 24, 25^5, 27^3, 28^4, 29^3, 30^2, 31^3, 32^3, 33^2, 34, 35^2, 36^2, 37^2, 38^2, 39^2, 40^2, 41^2, 42, 43^4, 44^2, 45^2, 46^4, 47^6, 48, 49^2, 52^2, 53^5, 54^2, 55^2; **3:**4^4, 5^4, 6^2, 7^3, 8^3, 9, 10, 15, 16, 17, 18^3, 19^5, 20^4, 21^2, 22^6, 23^3, 24^7; **4:**1^3, 2^3, 3^4, 4^2, 5^2, 6^4, 7^3, 8^3, 9^2, 10^5, 11, 12^3, 13^3, 14^2, 15^3, 16^3, 17^7, 18^4, 19^2, 20^5, 21^2, 22^6, 23^2, 24^2, 26, 27^2, 28^3, 29^3, 30^3, 31^4, 32^4, 33^2, 34^3, 35^2, 36^7, 37, 38, 39, 40^5, 41^5, 42^4, 43^2; **5:**1, 2, 3^2, 7^2, 8^2, 9, 10^2, 11, 12^3, 13^7, 16^3, 17, 18^7, 19^3, 20^4, 21^5, 22, 23^3, 24^8, 25^2, 26^9; **6:**1, 2^3, 3^5, 5^2, 6^2, 7, 8^2, 9^2, 10, 11^2, 12^2, 13^2, 14^2, 15^2, 16, 17^2, 18^4, 19^2, 23^2, 24, 25^2, 26, 28^2, 31, 32^2, 33, 39, 44, 49^4, 50, 55^2, 56, 57^4, 58, 59^2, 60^3, 61, 62^4, 63^2, 64, 65^3, 66, 67, 68^2, 69^2, 70^2, 71, 72, 73^2, 74^2, 75^2, 76^3, 78^2, 79, 80^2, 81^2; **7:**1^2, 2^8, 3^4, 4^3, 5^2, 6^2, 7^9, 8^9, 9^2, 10^7, 11^2, 12^2, 13^3, 15^4, 16^5, 17, 18^3, 19^4, 20^5, 21^4, 22^2, 23^3, 24^3, 25^3, 28^7, 29^5, 30^4, 31^2, 32^4, 33^3, 34^3, 35^4, 36^4, 37^5, 38^3, 39^3, 40^4; **8:**1, 2, 3^3, 4^3, 5^3, 6^2, 7^5, 8^2, 9^4, 10^3, 11^2, 12^3, 13, 14^2, 15^3, 16^3, 17^4, 18^2, 19^3, 20^3, 21^3, 22^3, 23^3, 24^3, 25^2, 26^3, 27^3, 29, 30^5, 31^3, 32^2, 33^6, 34^2, 35^4, 36^5, 37, 38^5, 39^2, 40^4; **9:**1^2, 2, 3^4, 5^2, 6^3, 7, 8^3, 9^3, 10^3, 11, 12^2, 13^3, 14, 15^3, 16^2, 17^5, 19^3, 20^2, 21, 22^2, 23, 24, 25, 26^2, 27^2, 28^2, 29^6, 30, 31, 32, 33^2, 35, 36^5, 37^4, 38^2, 39^6, 40^2, 41^4, 42^5, 43^2, 44^5; **10:**1^2, 2^5, 3^3, 4^3, 5^2, 6^2, 7^6, 8^2, 9^4, 10^2, 11, 12^5, 13, 14^2; **11:**1, 2^4, 3^2, 4^2, 5, 6^3, 7, 8^2, 9, 10, 11, 12, 13^2, 14^4, 15, 16^2, 17^2, 18^4, 19, 20^2, 22, 23^5, 24, 25, 42, 43, 44, 45, 46^3, 47^2; **12:**1, 2^3, 3^4, 4^6, 5^4, 6^4, 7^2, 8^4, 14, 15^2, 16^2, 17^4, 18^4, 19, 20^6, 21^2, 23^2, 24^2, 25, 26, 27^3, 28^3, 29, 30^2, 31^2, 32^2, 34^4, 35^3, 36, 37^4, 38, 39^2, 40^{11}; **13:**1^3, 2^5, 3, 4, 6^2, 7^3, 8^8, 9, 10^3, 11, 12, 14^3; **14:**1^2, 2, 3^3, 4^2, 5^3, 6^3, 7^3, 8^3, 9^2, 10^3, 11, 12^2, 13, 14^2, 15, 16, 17^2; **15:**1^3, 2, 3, 4^2, 5^2, 6^2, 7^2, 8, 9, 10^2, 11^6, 12^2, 14, 15, 16^3, 17^2, 18^{12}, 19, 20^8, 21^6, 22, 23^2, 24^9, 25^2, 26^2, 27^4, 28^4, 29^3; **16:**1^3, 2^2, 3^4, 4^4, 5^9, 6, 7, 11, 12, 16, 17^2, 19, 20^2, 22, 25, 27^2, 28, 29, 31^2, 32^2, 35^4, 36^3, 37, 38^3, 39^2, 40^2, 41^3, 42^5, 43^2; **17:**3, 4, 5, 8^3, 9^3, 10, 11^2, 12, 13^2, 14^2, 15, 16^4, 17^2, 19, 21^2, 22, 23^2, 24, 26^2, 27; **18:**1^3, 2^3, 3, 4^3, 5^2, 6^2, 7^2, 8^3, 10^5, 11^5, 13^2, 14^2, 15^2, 16^3, 17^3; **19:**1, 2^2, 3^2, 4^3, 5^4, 6^5, 7^6, 8^2, 9^3, 10^2, 11^2, 12, 13^3, 14^2, 15^2, 16^3, 17^5, 18^3, 19^2; **20:**1^6, 2^5, 3^6, 4^2, 5^2, 6^5, 8^2; **21:**1^2, 2^3, 3, 4^2, 5^5, 6, 7, 8, 9, 10, 11, 12, 13, 14, 15^5, 16^4, 17^3, 18, 19, 20^3, 21^4, 23^4, 24, 26^5, 27^2, 29; **22:**1, 2^2, 3^3, 4, 5^4, 6, 7, 8, 9^3, 10^3, 11^2, 12^2, 13^2, 14^5, 15^3, 16^4, 18^3, 19^3; **23:**1, 2^2, 3^3, 4^3, 5, 6^2, 7, 8^2, 9^2, 10^3, 11^3, 12, 13^4, 15, 17^2, 19, 20, 21^2, 22^3, 23^2, 24, 26, 27, 28^3, 29^6, 30^3, 31^2, 32^3; **24:**1^2, 2^3, 3^2, 4^3, 5^2, 6^7, 17^2, 18^2, 20, 23, 26, 27^3, 30^2, 31^4; **25:**1^5, 2^3, 3^4, 4^3, 5^2, 6^2, 7, 8, 9, 10, 11, 12, 13, 14, 15, 16, 17, 18, 19, 20, 21, 22, 23, 24, 25, 26, 27, 28^2, 29^2, 30^2, 31^2; **26:**2, 4^2, 7^3, 8^3, 9^2, 11, 13, 14^2, 15, 16, 17^2, 18, 19, 20^2, 22, 23^2, 24, 25^5, 26^4, 28^6, 29^2, 30^4, 31, 32^4; **27:**1^5, 2^2, 4^3, 5^2, 6^2, 7^3, 8^2, 9^2, 10^2, 11^2, 12^2, 13^2, 14^2, 15^2, 23, 25^4, 26, 27, 28^3, 29^2, 30, 31, 32^2, 33^2, 34^3; **28:**1^9, 2^4, 3, 4^2, 5, 6^3, 7, 8^3, 9^4, 10, 11^5, 12^3, 13^3, 15^4, 16^2, 17^4, 18^3, 20^3, 21^4; **29:**1^2, 2^7, 3^2, 4, 5^3, 6^3, 7^5, 8, 9, 10^2, 11^6, 12^6, 13, 14^2, 15^2, 16, 17^2, 18^2, 19^4, 20^5, 21^4, 22^5, 23^2, 24^3, 25^2, 27^3, 28^3, 29^3, 30^4

2Ch 1:1^3, 2^3, 3, 5^2, 6^2, 7, 8^2, 10^2, 11^3, 12^4, 13, 14^6, 15^3, 16^2, 17^6; **2:**1^2, 2^5, 3^2, 4^6, 5, 6, 7^8, 8^2, 10^4, 12^3, 13, 14^7, 15^2, 16^3, 17^5, 18^5; **3:**2, 3, 4^4, 5^3, 6^2, 7^3, 8^3, 9^2, 10^2, 11^2, 12^2, 13^2, 14^5, 15^2, 16^4, 17^4; **4:**1^2, 2^2, 3, 4^5, 5^4, 6^2, 7^3, 8^3, 9^3, 10, 11^4, 12^3, 13, 14, 15, 16^3, 17, 19^2, 21^4, 22^6; **5:**1^4, 2, 4^2, 5^4, 6^2, 7, 8^2, 9^2, 11^2, 12^5, 13^6; **6:**2, 3^3, 4, 6, 10^2, 11, 12^2, 13^6, 14^2, 15^2, 18, 19^2, 20, 21^2, 22^2, 23^3,

20; **148:**3, 4, 5, 6, 7, 8^2, 9^2, 10^2, 11^2, 12^2, 13; **149:**1, 3, 6, 7, 8; **150:**3, 4^2

Prv 1:2, 3^2, 4, 5^2, 6^2, 7, 8, 9, 12, 16, 18, 22^2, 24^2, 25, 27^2, 29, 31, 32, 33; **2:**1, 2, 3, 4, 5, 6, 8, 9^2, 10, 14, 15, 17, 18, 20, 21, 22; **3:**2^2, 3, 4^2, 5, 6, 7, 8, 9, 10, 13, 14, 15, 16^2, 17, 18, 20, 21, 22, 23, 24, 26, 28^2, 31; **4:**1, 3, 4^2, 6^2, 7, 8, 10^2, 12, 14, 15, 16, 17, 18, 22, 24, 25, 26; **5:**1, 2, 3, 7, 8, 9, 10, 11^2, 12^2, 13, 14, 15, 16, 17, 18, 19^2, 20^2, 21, 22, 23; **6:**3^2, 5, 6, 8, 11, 17, 19, 20, 21, 22, 23^2, 26, 27, 28, 33^2; **7:**1, 2^2, 4, 7, 8, 9, 10^2, 11, 12, 13^2, 15, 17, 20, 23, 24; **8:**1, 4, 5, 6, 7, 9, 10^2, 11, 12, 13^3, 14, 15, 16, 17, 18^2, 19, 21, 30, 31, 33^2, 35; **9:**5, 6^2, 7, 8, 9^2, 10, 11, 13, 16, 17, 18; **10:**18, 22, 26; **11:**7, 8, 10, 15, 16, 24^2, 25, 29, 30, 31; **12:**7, 9^2, 14, 28; **13:**4, 5, 18, 22; **14:**6, 10, 13, 14, 16^2, 17, 19, 22, 26; **15:**3, 10, 11, 16, 17, 23, 30, 33; **16:**1, 3, 6^2, 11, 13, 15, 16, 18, 20, 21, 23, 24, 27, 28, 29, 32; **17:**1, 2, 3, 4, 5, 6, 15, 17, 18, 19, 20, 21, 25, 27, 28; **18:**1, 3, 4, 6, 7, 8, 10, 11, 12, 13, 15, 16, 17, 18, 19, 20, 21^2, 22, 24; **19:**1, 2, 3, 5, 6, 9, 11, 13, 14^2, 15, 17, 18, 20, 22, 23, 24, 25^3, 26^2, 28, 29; **20:**1, 4, 10, 11, 12, 13, 15, 16, 18, 22, 23, 25, 26, 28^2, 29; **21:**3, 4^2, 6, 8, 11, 14, 17, 18, 19, 20, 21^2, 22, 23, 24, 26; **22:**1^2, 2, 3^2, 4^3, 5, 6, 7, 8, 10^2, 12, 16, 17^2, 20, 23, 24, 25; **23:**2, 7, 8, 10, 12, 14, 18, 19^2, 21^2, 22, 23^3, 24, 25^2, 26, 27, 28, 32, 33, 35^2; **24:**2, 3, 4^2, 6, 9, 11, 12^2, 13, 14, 16, 17, 18^2, 21^2, 22, 25, 27^2, 28, 30, 31^3, 32^2, 34; **25:**3^2, 4, 5, 6, 9, 10, 12, 14, 15, 16, 17, 18^2, 19, 20, 21, 22, 24, 26, 28; **26:**1, 3, 6, 10, 17, 18, 19, 21, 22, 23, 24, 27, 28; **27:**2^2, 3, 4, 9, 10, 11, 12^2, 13, 15, 16, 20, 21, 23, 24, 25^2, 26, 27^2; **28:**2, 8, 13, 15, 22, 24; **29:**1, 6, 13, 15, 17, 22, 24, 27; **30:**1, 2, 4, 6, 8, 9^4, 10, 11, 12, 13, 14^2, 16^2, 17^2, 19, 20^2, 21, 22, 23, 28, 30, 31, 33; **31:**2^2, 5^2, 6, 7^2, 9^2, 12, 13^2, 15^2, 16, 17, 19, 22, 24^2, 25^2, 26, 27, 28^2, 30, 31

Ecc 1:4, 5^2, 6^2, 9^2, 13^2, 14^2, 15, 16^2, 17^3, 18; **2:**1, 2, 3, 5^2, 7^3, 8^6, 9, 10^2, 11^4, 12^3, 14, 15, 16, 17, 19^2, 21^3, 22, 23, 24^2, 26^4; **3:**1, 2^2, 3^2, 4^2, 5^2, 6^2, 7^2, 8^2, 12, 13^3, 14, 15^2, 16^2, 17^2, 18, 20, 21; **4:**1^4, 4^2, 5, 6, 7, 8^2, 12^2, 13^2, 16; **5:**1, 2^2, 3, 5, 6, 7, 8^3, 11, 14^2, 15, 16^2, 17^2, 18^3, 19^4; **6:**1, 2^2, 3^3, 4^2, 7, 9, 10; **7:**1, 2, 7, 8, 11, 12, 15, 20, 24, 25^5, 26^3; **8:**1^2, 2, 4, 5^2, 6, 8, 9, 10^3, 12, 15^2, 16; **9:**1^2, 2^5, 3^2, 6^2, 7, 8, 9, 11^2, 12, 13, 14^4, 15, 16; **10:**1, 3, 6, 7, 8, 9, 10, 11, 13, 14, 16, 17^2, 18, 19, 20^2; **11:**2, 3, 4, 6, 7, 8, 9^3, 10^2; **12:**3^3, 4^3, 5^5, 7, 9^3, 10, 11, 12^2, 13

Song 1:4, 8, 17; **2:**1, 3, 4, 6, 7, 10^2, 11, 12, 13^2, 14, 16, 17^2; **3:**2^2, 4^2, 5, 6, 11^2; **4:**2, 3, 6^2, 8, 10, 11^2, 14^3, 15, 16^2; **5:**2, 4, 5^2, 6, 10, 11, 12, 16; **6:**2, 3, 6, 8^2, 9^3, 10, 11^2; **7:**5, 6, 7, 8, 9, 10, 12, 13^2; **8:**2, 3, 8, 9, 10, 12, 14

Isa 1:1^2, 2^3, 3, 5^2, 6^2, 7, 8, 9, 11^2, 13, 14, 15, 18, 19, 20, 23^2, 24, 25^3, 26^2, 27, 28^3, 29, 30, 31^4; **2:**1, 2^3, 3^6, 4^4, 5, 6^2, 7, 9^2, 10^2, 11^2, 12^3, 13^3, 14^2, 15^2, 16^2, 17^3, 18, 19^3, 20^2, 21^2; **3:**1^3, 2^4, 3^4, 4^2, 5^3, 6, 8^2, 9, 12^2, 13, 14, 15, 16^4, 17, 18^2, 19^2, 20^4, 21, 22^3, 23^3, 24^5, 25, 26^3; **4:**1^2, 2^3, 3^2, 4^2, 5^4, 6^4; **5:**2^7, 3^3, 5^4, 6^2, 7^2, 9, 10, 12^4, 13^2, 14^5, 15^3, 16, 17, 18, 19^3, 20^3, 21, 22, 23, 24^3, 25^4, 26^3, 28^2, 29^3, 30^4; **6:**1^2, 2^2, 3^2, 4^2, 5, 7^4, 8, 9^3, 10^6, 11^3, 12^2, 13^3; **7:**1^2, 2^3, 3, 4^3, 5, 6^3, 8^3, 9^2, 13, 14^2, 15^2, 16, 17^2, 18^2, 19^5, 20^2, 21^2, 22^2, 23^2, 24^2, 25^3; **8:**1, 2^3, 3^3, 4^2, 6^2, 7^4, 8^3, 9^4, 10^2, 11, 13^2, 14^3, 15^5, 17^2, 18^2, 19^3, 20, 21^6, 22^4; **9:**1^2, 3^2, 4, 5^2, 6^2, 7^4, 8, 9^3, 11, 12^2, 14^2, 15^2, 16, 17^3, 18^3, 19, 20^4, 21^2; **10:**1, 2^2, 3^3, 4, 5, 6^3, 7, 10^2, 11^2, 12^2, 13^4, 14^3, 16, 17^5, 18^4, 19, 20^2, 24, 25^2, 26^2, 27^3, 33^2, 34^2; **11:**1^2, 2^4, 3^2, 4^3, 5^2, 6^5, 7^3, 8^2, 10^2, 11^8, 12^3, 13^2, 14^2, 15^4, 16; **12:**1^2, 2^2, 4, 6; **13:**5, 7, 8^2, 9^2, 10^2, 11^4, 13^2, 14^3, 15, 16, 17, 18, 19^2, 21^3, 22^4; **14:**1^4, 2^6, 3^3, 4, 5, 6, 7, 8, 10, 11^2, 16, 17, 19, 20, 22^4, 23^2, 24, 25^2, 26, 27^3, 29, 30^4, 31, 32; **15:**1^2, 2^3, 3, 4^2, 7, 8, 9; **16:**5^4, 6^2, 8, 9^2, 10^3, 11, 12, 14^3; **17:**1, 2, 3^2, 4^2, 5^3, 7, 8, 9^2, 10^2, 11^2, 12, 13^3, 14^3; **18:**2^3, 3^2, 4^2, 5^3, 6^3, 7^3; **19:**1^3, 2^4, 3^6, 4^2, 5^3, 6^4, 7^2, 8^2, 9, 10^2, 12^2, 14, 16^2, 17, 18, 19, 20^5, 21^5, 22^5, 23^3, 24, 25^2; **20:**1^2, 2^4, 3^4, 4^3, 5^3, 6^2; **21:**2, 5, 7^3, 8^2, 9^4, 10, 12, 15^2, 16, 17; **22:**5^3, 6^3, 7^2, 8^2, 9, 10^2, 12^4, 13^5, 14, 15, 16^2, 17, 18^2, 19^2, 20, 21^5, 22^4, 23^2, 24^2, 25^3; **23:**3^2, 9, 12, 13, 15, 17^3, 18^3; **24:**1^3, 2, 3, 4^2, 6^2, 12, 13, 17^2, 18^3, 20^5, 21^2, 22^3, 23^3; **25:**1, 6, 7^2, 8^2, 9^3, 10, 11^2, 12^2; **26:**1, 6, 8, 10, 11, 14^2, 17, 19^2, 20, 21; **27:**1^3, 3, 4, 5, 6^2, 9^2, 10^4, 11^2, 12^2, 13^4; **28:**2^2, 4^2, 5, 6^2, 7^2, 8, 9^2, 10, 11, 12, 13^5, 15^2, 17^3, 18^2, 19^2, 20, 21, 23^2, 24, 25^4, 26, 27, 29; **29:**2^3, 3^3, 4^5, 5, 6^4, 7^3, 8^5, 9^2, 10^2, 11^2, 12^2, 13^2, 14^2, 15^3, 17^2, 18^3, 19, 20^2, 21^2, 23^2, 24; **30:**1, 2^2, 3, 4, 5, 6^4, 7, 8^2, 10, 12^3, 14, 15^3, 16, 17, 18^2, 20^2, 21^2, 22, 23^3, 24^2, 25^3, 26^2, 27^2, 28^2, 29, 30^5, 32^3, 33^2; **31:**1^3, 2^3, 3^5, 4^2, 5, 7, 8^2, 9^3; **32:**1, 2^2, 3^2, 4, 6^3, 8, 10, 11^2, 13, 14, 15^2, 16, 17^3, 18^3, 19, 20; **33:**1^4, 4^2, 5, 6^3, 9^4, 12, 13, 15^2, 21, 24; **34:**1^3, 2, 3^2, 4^4, 5, 6^3, 7^4, 8, 9^3, 10, 11^4, 12, 13^4, 14^2, 15^3, 16^2, 17^2; **35:**1^3, 2^4, 3, 4, 5, 6^2, 7^3, 8^3, 10^6; **36:**1, 2^2, 3^2, 4, 5, 6, 7^3, 8, 9^2, 10^2, 11^3, 12^2, 13^2, 16^4, 17^3, 19^2, 21, 22^3; **37:**1^3, 2^3, 3^4, 4, 6, 7^3, 8, 9^2, 11, 12^3, 13^3, 14^4, 15, 16, 17^3, 18, 19^2, 22, 23^3, 24^5, 25^2, 26, 27^3, 28^3, 29^3, 30^6, 31^2, 32, 34, 35, 36^4, 37^3, 38^4; **38:**1^3, 2, 3^4, 5, 6^3, 7, 9, 12, 15, 16^2, 21^2; **39:**1^2, 2^7, 3^3, 4, 6, 7^2, 8; **40:**2, 4^4, 5^2, 6^2, 10^2, 11^2, 12^4, 14^4, 15, 16, 17^2, 19^2, 22^2, 24^3, 26, 27^2, 29, 30^2, 31^3; **41:**1, 2^2, 3, 4^2, 5^2, 6, 7^2, 9^3, 11^2, 12^2, 14^2, 15^2, 16^4, 17^3, 18^2, 19^4, 20^4, 22^2, 23, 24, 25^3, 26, 27, 28^2, 29; **42:**3, 4, 5^3, 6^3, 7, 8, 9, 10^3, 11, 12, 14^2, 15^4, 16^3, 18, 19, 21, 22^4, 23, 24, 25^3; **43:**1, 2, 3, 4^2, 5, 6^2, 8, 9^3, 10^3, 11, 12^2, 13^2, 14^2, 16, 17^2, 19, 20^2, 25, 27, 28^2; **44:**1, 2^2, 3^2, 4, 5^3, 6^3, 7^5, 8, 9^2, 11^2, 12^4, 13^2, 14^3, 15^4, 16^2, 17^4, 18, 19^3, 21, 22, 23^2, 24, 25^2, 26^3, 27, 28^2; **45:**1^2, 2^2, 3^2, 4, 5, 6^2, 7^2, 8^3, 11^2, 12^2, 13^2, 14^5, 16, 18^2, 20^2, 21^3, 22^2, 23, 24^2, 25; **46:**1, 3, 4^4, 5^2, 6^3, 7^2, 8, 9^2, 10^2, 13^2; **47:**1^2, 2, 3, 5, 6, 7, 8, 9^2, 10^3, 11^2, 12, 13; **48:**1^2, 2, 3^3, 4^2, 5^2, 6^2, 7, 8, 9, 11, 12, 13, 14^2, 15, 16^2, 18, 19, 21^2; **49:**1, 2^2, 3, 4^2, 5^2, 6^2, 7^4, 8^3, 9, 11^2, 12^3, 13^3, 14, 17, 18^3, 19^3, 21^4, 22^3, 23^4, 25^2, 26^4; **50:**1, 2, 3, 5, 6^2, 7, 10^2, 11; **51:**1, 2^3, 3^4, 4^2, 5^2, 6^4, 8^2, 9, 11^5, 12, 13^4, 14, 16^4, 17, 19^3, 21, 22, 23^2; **52:**1, 2, 3, 4, 5, 10, 12, 13^2, 14, 15; **53:**1, 2^2, 3^4, 4^2, 5, 6, 7^2, 8^2, 9^2, 10, 11, 12^4; **54:**1, 2^2, 3^3, 4, 5, 6^2, 10, 11^2, 12^3, 13^2, 14, 16^2, 17^2; **55:**1^4, 2^3, 3^3, 4, 5^2, 7^4, 9, 10^5, 11, 12^3, 13^2; **56:**1^2, 2^2, 4^2, 5^3, 6^2, 7^2, 11, 12^3; **57:**1^2, 3, 4, 7, 8^3, 9^4, 11^3, 12, 13, 14, 15^4, 16, 17^3, 18^3, 19^2, 20; **58:**1^2, 2^2, 3^3, 4^2, 5^3, 6^2, 7^2, 8^2, 9^3, 10^3, 11^5, 12^3, 13^2, 14^2; **59:**2^2, 3, 4^2, 5^2, 6, 7^2, 8, 10, 11, 12^2, 13^4, 14^3, 15^3, 16^3, 17^3, 19, 20^2, 21^2; **60:**1, 2^2, 3^2, 4^2, 5^3, 6^3, 7, 8, 9^3, 10^2, 11, 12, 13^2, 14^2, 15, 16^3, 17^4, 18, 19, 20, 22; **61:**1, 2, 4^2, 5^4, 6, 7, 8^2, 9^2, 10, 11^2; **62:**1^2, 2^3, 3, 4^2, 5, 7^2, 8^2, 9^2, 11, 12^2; **63:**2, 3^4, 4, 5^4, 6^3, 7^3, 9^4, 10^2, 11, 15^4, 16, 17; **64:**5^2, 6^3, 7^2, 8^2, 11^2, 12; **65:**3, 4^3, 7^2, 8, 9^4, 10^2, 11, 12^2, 14, 15^2, 16^2, 17^2, 18^2, 19^3, 21^4, 22^3, 23, 24^2, 25^3; **66:**1^2, 2^3, 3, 4^2, 5, 9^2, 10, 11^2, 12^2, 13, 14^4, 15^2, 16^2, 17^3, 18^4, 19^5, 20^5, 21^2, 22^2, 23^2, 24^3

Jer 1:5^2, 7, 9^2, 10^5, 11, 13^3, 15^4, 16^3, 17^2, 18^3, 19; **2:**2, 3, 4, 5^2, 6^3, 7^3, 8^3, 9, 10^4, 12, 13, 15^2, 16, 18, 19^4, 20^3, 22, 25^2, 26^2, 27^3, 37^2; **3:**1^2, 2^3, 3^2, 5, 6^2, 7^2, 8^3, 9^3, 10, 11, 12^4, 13^2, 14^3, 15^2, 16^2, 17, 18, 19^3, 21^2, 22, 23, 24^2, 25^3; **4:**1, 2^4, 3^2, 4^3, 5^4, 6, 7^2, 8, 9^4, 10, 11, 13, 15, 16, 18, 20, 21, 22, 23^4, 24^2, 25^2, 26^3, 28^2, 29^3, 30, 31; **5:**1^5, 2, 5^3, 6^2, 7^2, 9, 10, 11, 12, 13^2, 14^2, 17^5, 19^2, 20, 21^3, 22, 23^2, 24, 25, 27, 28, 30, 31^3; **6:**1^3, 2, 4, 5^2, 6, 7^2, 10^2, 11, 12^2, 13, 16^4, 18, 20, 21^3, 22, 23^3, 24, 25, 26, 27^2, 28; **7:**2^2, 3^2, 5^2, 6^2, 7, 9^4, 10^3, 12, 13^4, 14^2, 15, 17, 18^3, 20^6, 21, 23^3, 24^3, 25, 28, 29^3, 31^2, 33^3, 34^3; **8:**1^4, 2^7, 3, 4^2, 6, 7^3, 8, 9^2, 10, 13^2, 14^3, 15^2, 16^3, 17, 19, 20; **9:**1^2, 2, 3^2, 4^2, 5^3, 7, 10^3, 11^3, 12^2, 13^2, 14, 15, 16, 17^2, 18^3, 20^3, 21^2, 22^2, 24^2, 26^6; **10:**2, 4^2, 6, 7, 8, 9^3, 10^2, 11^2, 12, 13^2, 14, 15, 16, 18, 19, 20^3, 21^2, 22^2, 25^4; **11:**2^2, 3, 4^2, 5^2, 6^2, 7, 9^2, 10^2, 11, 12^2, 13, 15, 16^2, 17, 18^2, 19^2, 20, 22, 23; **12:**2, 3^2, 4^2, 5^2, 6, 11, 13, 14, 15^4, 16, 17; **13:**1^3, 2, 3, 4^2, 5, 6^2, 7^3, 9, 10^2, 11^4, 12, 13^3, 14^2, 15, 16^3, 17^2, 18, 19, 20, 21, 22^2, 25, 27^2; **14:**2^2, 3^4, 5, 6, 8, 9, 10, 12^4, 14^3, 15^3, 16^3, 17^2, 18^2, 19^4, 20; **15:**1^2, 2^4, 3^5, 4, 6, 7, 8, 9^2, 10, 11, 12, 13^2, 14, 15^2, 16^3, 18^2, 19^2, 20^3, 21^2; **16:**3^3, 4^4, 5, 6, 8, 9^3, 10^2, 11^5, 12, 13^2, 15^2, 16^5, 18^3, 19^4, 20, 21^2; **17:**1^2, 2, 3^2, 4^2, 5^2, 6^2, 7, 8^3, 9, 10, 11^3, 13, 14^2, 18, 19^3, 20^3, 21, 24, 25^5, 26^{10}, 27^3; **18:**2^2, 3, 4, 7^3, 9^3, 11^4, 12^2, 15, 16^2, 17, 18^3, 19, 20, 21^4, 22; **19:**1^3, 2^2, 3^2, 4^3, 7^6, 8^3, 9^5, 11^3, 12^2, 13^3, 14^2, 15; **20:**2, 3, 4^6, 5^5, 6^6, 7^2, 8^2, 9^2, 10^3, 11, 12^2, 16^4, 17, 18; **21:**1, 4^2, 5^4, 6^2, 7^8, 8^2, 9^4, 10^2, 11, 12^2, 13, 14^2; **22:**1, 2^3, 3^3, 4^3, 6^2, 7^3, 8^2, 9^2, 12, 13^2, 14^4, 15^4, 16, 17^4, 19, 20^3, 22^2, 25^3, 26^3, 28^2, 30; **23:**1, 2^3, 3^4, 4^2, 5^4, 6^2, 8^3, 9^2, 10^2, 11, 12, 13^2, 14^2, 15, 16, 17, 18^3, 20, 22^2, 23, 24, 28, 29, 31, 32^3, 33, 34^4, 35^2, 36, 37, 38, 39^4, 40^2; **24:**1^4, 2, 3^2, 6^5, 7^3, 8^4, 9^3, 10^3; **25:**2, 3^3, 4^2, 5^4, 6^4, 9^8, 10^3, 11^3, 12^4, 13, 14^3, 15, 16^3, 17, 18^4, 19^3, 20^7, 21^2, 22^3, 23^3, 24^2, 25^3, 26^4, 27^4, 28, 29, 30^2, 32, 33, 34^4, 35, 36, 37, 38; **26:**2, 3, 4, 5, 6, 7^2, 8^2, 9^2, 10, 11^2, 12^2, 13^3, 14, 15^2, 16^2, 17, 18^3, 19^3, 20^2, 21^4, 22^2, 23^3; **27:**2^2, 3^5, 4, 5^3, 6^2, 7^5, 8^5, 10^2, 11^3, 12^3, 13^2, 15^2, 16, 17, 18^3, 19^3, 20^2, 21^2, 22^2; **28:**1^3, 3, 4, 5, 6, 7, 8^4, 10, 11^2, 13, 14^2; **29:**1^3, 2^5, 3, 5^3, 6^6, 7^2, 8, 10, 11, 12^3, 13^2, 14^5, 16^2, 17^2, 18^6, 19, 21^2, 22^2, 23^3, 25^2, 26^2, 28^3, 29, 31^2, 32; **30:**3^3, 4^2, 5, 6^2, 8^2, 9, 10^5, 11, 12, 16^3, 17, 18^3, 19^5, 20^2, 21^4, 22^2, 24; **31:**1, 4^2, 5, 6, 7^2, 8^4, 9^2, 10^3, 11, 12^8, 13^3, 14^2, 15, 16^2, 17, 18^2, 19, 23^2, 24^3, 25, 26^2, 27^2, 28^6, 29, 31, 33^3, 34^3, 35^2, 37, 39^2, 40^3; **32:**2, 3^2, 4^3, 5^2, 6, 8^2, 9^2, 10^4, 11^2, 12^2, 13, 14^2, 15^2, 17^3, 18, 19^2, 20^4, 21^5, 22^2, 23^2, 24^5, 25^2, 28^2, 29^4, 30, 31, 32^4, 33^3, 35^2, 36^3, 37^4, 38^2, 39^3, 40, 41^2, 43, 44^8; **33:**3^3, 4^2, 5^2, 6^4, 7^3, 8^3, 9^5, 10^4, 11^3, 12^2, 13^4, 14, 15^3, 16^2, 18^2, 19, 20^3, 21, 22, 25^3, 26^3; **34:**1^4, 2^3, 3^5, 5^2, 7^2, 9, 10^3, 11^4, 14, 15^3, 16^5, 17^3, 18^2, 19^3, 20^3, 21^4, 22^5; **35:**2^3, 3^3, 4, 5^3, 10^2, 11^2, 13^2, 14, 15^5, 17^2, 18^3; **36:**1, 2^3, 3, 4, 5, 6^2, 7^2, 8, 9^2, 12^6, 14^2, 15^2, 16^2, 17, 18, 19^2, 20^2, 21^3, 22, 23^2, 25^2, 26^3, 27, 28, 29^4, 30^2, 31^6, 32^2; **37:**1, 3^2, 4, 5, 8^4, 10^2, 11, 13^2, 14, 15^2, 16^2, 17^4, 21; **38:**1^3, 2^2, 4, 6^3, 8, 9, 10, 11^4, 12^3, 13^2, 14^2, 15, 17^3, 18^2, 19^2, 20, 22^4, 23^3, 24, 25^3, 27^2, 28; **39:**1^2, 2, 3^2, 4^4, 5^2, 7, 8^3, 9, 10^2, 12^2, 13^3, 14^2, 16^3, 17, 18; **40:**1, 2^2, 3^2, 4^3, 5^3, 6, 7^5, 8^6, 9^4, 10^4, 11^4, 12^3, 13, 14, 15^3; **41:**1^2, 2^3, 3^2, 4^2, 5^4, 6^2, 7^3, 8^4, 9, 10^3, 11, 12^2, 13, 14^2, 15, 16^4, 17^2; **42:**1^3, 2^2, 3, 4, 5, 7, 8^2, 9, 10^3, 11, 12^2, 14, 15^2, 16^2, 17^2, 18^6, 20^2, 21, 22^2; **43:**1, 2^2, 3, 4^2, 5, 6^6, 9, 10^4, 11^4, 12^5, 13; **44:**1^3, 2^3, 3, 4, 6^5, 7^2, 8^2, 9^5, 10, 11, 12^9, 13, 15, 17^6, 18^3, 19^3, 20^2, 21^5, 22^3, 23^2, 24, 25^4, 27^3, 28, 29, 30^2; **45:**3, 4, 5; **46:**3^2, 4^3, 5^4, 6, 8^4, 9^5, 10^3, 11, 12^2, 13, 14^4, 16^3, 18, 19, 21^2, 22, 23, 25^4, 26^4, 27^6; **47:**2^5, 3, 4^2, 6, 7; **48:**1^2, 2, 3, 6, 7^3, 8^3, 9, 10, 11^3, 12^2, 13, 14, 15^2, 16, 17^2, 18^2, 19^3, 20, 21^3, 22^3, 23^3, 24^3, 25, 26, 28^2, 29^3, 31, 32, 33^4, 34, 35, 36, 37^2, 38, 39, 40, 41^2, 42, 43^2, 44, 45^3, 46; **49:**1, 2^2, 3^4, 5^2, 6, 10^4, 11, 12, 13^2, 14^3, 15, 16, 17, 18^2, 19^3, 20, 22^3, 23, 24^3, 26, 27^2, 28^2, 29^4, 30, 32^4, 33^2, 36^3, 37^3, 38^3; **50:**1, 2^3, 3^2, 4^4, 5, 7, 8^2, 9^2, 10, 11, 12, 13, 16^2, 17, 18, 19^5, 20^4, 21^3, 22, 23, 24^3, 25, 26, 28, 30, 32^5, 33^2, 34, 35^3, 36^2, 37^4, 38^2, 39^2, 40^2, 41^2, 42^3, 43^2, 44^3, 45, 46; **51:**1, 2^2, 3^2, 4, 6, 8, 9^2, 10, 12, 13, 14, 15, 16^2, 17, 19, 20^2, 21^4, 22^5, 23^5, 24^2, 25^3, 26, 27, 28^2, 29^2, 31, 32^3, 33, 35^2, 36^3, 37^2, 39^3, 41, 43, 44^3, 45, 46^4, 47^2, 48^2, 50, 52, 53, 54, 55, 56, 57^6, 58^4, 59, 61^3, 63^2, 64^3; **52:**1^3, 2, 3, 4^4, 6, 7^3, 8^2, 9, 10, 11^3, 13^4, 14, 15^3, 16, 17^3, 18^5, 19^8, 20, 21^3, 22^4, 23^3, 24^3, 25^3, 26, 27^2, 28^2, 29, 30^3, 31^4, 32^2, 33^2, 34

Lam 1:1, 2, 3, 4, 6^2, 7^3, 8, 11, 12, 13^2, 14, 17, 18^2, 19, 21, 22^2; **2:**1^2, 2^2, 3, 4, 5^2, 6^4, 8, 9^2, 10, 11, 12, 14^3, 15, 16, 17^2, 18, 20^3, 21^3, 22; **3:**2, 4, 5^2, 8, 10, 11, 12, 14, 17, 18^2, 19^2, 20, 26, 28, 37, 38, 40^2, 42, 43, 45, 47^2, 49, 50, 53, 60, 61, 62, 63, 66; **4:**4, 6, 11^2, 12^2, 13, 15, 21^2; **5:**1, 3, 5, 6, 7^2, 11, 13, 20, 21

Ezk 1:1, 3, 4^5, 5, 6^2, 7^3, 8^3, 10^2, 11^2, 12^2, 13^4, 14^2, 16^4, 17, 18, 19^2, 20, 21^2, 22, 23^2, 24, 25^2, 26^2, 27^3, 28^2; **2:**1^2, 2^2, 3^2, 4^2, 5, 6^3, 7, 8, 9^2, 10^6; **3:**1, 2, 3^3, 4^2, 5, 6, 7, 8, 10, 11^3, 12, 13^2, 14^2, 15^2, 16, 17, 18, 19, 20^3, 21, 22^3, 23^3, 24^3, 25^2, 26^2, 27^2; **4:**1^2, 2^4, 3^5, 4, 5, 6^2, 7^2, 8^2, 9^8, 10, 12^2, 13, 15, 16^4, 17^3; **5:**1^4, 2^4, 3, 4^2, 5, 6^3, 7, 8, 9^2, 10^3, 11, 12^4, 13^3, 14, 15^4, 16^3, 17^5; **6:**1, 2, 3^4, 4^3, 5^2, 6^6, 7^2, 9^3, 10^2, 11^3, 12^3, 13^2, 14^2; **7:**3^3, 4^3, 7, 8^3, 9^3, 15^4, 16, 17, 18^3, 19^2, 20, 21^3, 22^2, 23, 24^2, 25^2, 26^2, 27^4; **8:**1^2, 2^2, 3^5, 4, 5, 6, 7^2, 8, 9^2, 10^4, 11^3, 13, 14, 15, 16^6, 17^2, 18; **9:**2^5, 3^2, 4^3, 5^2, 6^4, 7^4, 8^4, 9^4, 10, 11; **10:**1, 2^5, 3, 4^3, 5, 6^2, 7^4, 8, 9^3, 10, 12^5, 14^4, 15, 16^2, 17, 18, 19^4, 20, 21^2, 22^2; **11:**1^4, 2, 3, 5^2, 6, 7, 8, 9^3, 10, 12, 13^3, 15, 16, 17^2, 18^3, 19^4, 20^4, 21, 22^2, 23^2, 24; **12:**2^2, 3^2, 4, 5, 6, 7^3, 8, 10, 11, 12^2, 13^2, 14^3, 15^2, 16^2, 18^2, 19^3, 20^3, 21, 22, 23^2, 25^2, 27; **13:**1, 2, 3, 6^3, 7, 8, 9^3, 10^3, 11^2, 13^2, 14^4, 15^2, 16^2, 17, 18^3, 19^3, 20^2, 21^3, 22, 23; **14:**1, 2, 3, 4^3, 6^2, 7^3, 8^5, 9^3, 10, 11, 13^4, 14, 15, 17^2, 19^2, 20, 21^4, 22^4, 23^3; **15:**1, 4, 5, 7^3, 8; **16:**3^3, 4, 6^2, 7^5, 8^5, 9, 10^3, 11^2, 12^3, 13^8, 14, 15^2, 16^3, 17^3, 18^4, 19^3, 20^2, 21, 22^4, 23, 24, 25^3, 26, 27^2, 28, 29, 31^2, 33, 34^3, 36^3, 37^2, 38^4, 39^6, 40^2, 41^4, 42^3, 43, 45^4, 46^4, 48, 49^3, 50^2, 51, 52, 53^3, 54, 55^4, 57, 58, 60, 61^3, 62^2, 63^2; **17:**1, 2, 3^2, 4, 5^2, 6^5, 7^3, 8, 9, 12^3, 13^3, 15^2, 16, 17^2, 18, 19, 20^4, 21^3, 22^3, 23^4, 24^3; **18:**2, 5^2, 6, 7^2, 8, 9, 10, 11^2, 12^2, 13, 14^2, 16, 18, 19^3, 20, 21^3, 23^2, 24^3, 26^2, 27^2, 28, 30, 31^2, 32; **19:**2, 3^2, 4, 5^2, 6^4, 7^4, 8, 9^2, 10, 11^3, 12^3, 13^2, 14^2; **20:**1^2, 3, 5^3, 6, 7, 8, 10, 11^2, 12, 13^2, 15, 16, 19^2, 20^3, 22, 23, 24^2, 25, 26, 27, 28^4, 29, 30, 31, 32^2, 33^2, 34^4, 35^2, 37^2, 38^4, 39^2, 40^2, 41^2, 42, 43^3, 44, 46^2, 47^4, 48; **21:**1, 2^2, 3^4, 4, 6, 7^6, 9^2, 11^2, 12, 13, 14^2, 15, 17, 19, 20, 22, 23, 25, 26^2, 27^2, 28^3,

31^3; **22:**3, 4^4, 5^2, 7^2, 8, 9, 11^3, 12^3, 13, 14, 15^3, 16^2, 17, 18^3, 20^7, 21^2, 22, 23, 25, 26^5, 27, 28^2, 29^3, 30^2; **23:**3^2, 4^6, 5^2, 6, 7, 8^2, 10^3, 11^2, 12, 14, 16^2, 17^4, 18, 20, 22, 23^6, 24^7, 25^6, 26, 27, 29^6, 30, 32^2, 33^2, 34^3, 35^2, 36, 37^3, 38, 39, 40^3, 41^3, 42^3, 43, 44, 45^3, 46^2, 47^4, 49^3; **24:**3^3, 4, 5^3, 6, 10^2, 11^2, 12, 13, 14^2, 17^3, 18^2, 19, 21^3, 22, 23^3, 24, 25^2, 27^4; **25:**2, 3^3, 4^3, 5^3, 6^2, 7^4, 8, 9, 10, 11^2, 12^2, 13^4, 14^4, 15, 16^2, 17^2; **26:**1, 3, 4^3, 5, 6^2, 7^4, 8^3, 9^2, 10^2, 11, 12^7, 13^2, 14, 16^4, 17^3, 19, 20^2, 21; **27:**3, 7, 8, 9, 10^3, 11, 12, 13^2, 14^2, 15, 16^4, 17^5, 18, 19^3, 21^3, 22^3, 23^3, 24^3, 25^2, 27^5, 29^2, 30^3, 31^4, 32^2, 33, 34, 35, 36; **28:**2^2, 4^3, 5^2, 7^2, 8, 9, 12^2, 13^5, 14^2, 16^2, 18, 19, 21, 22^4, 23^3, 24^2, 25, 26^4; **29:**2^2, 3^2, 4^3, 5^3, 6, 7^3, 8^2, 9^4, 10^3, 12^4, 14^3, 16, 17^2, 18, 19^4, 21^2; **30:**2, 4^4, 5^5, 6, 7^2, 8^2, 9, 11^3, 12^4, 13^3, 14^3, 15^2, 16^3, 17^2, 18^2, 19, 20, 21, 22^3, 23^2, 24^3, 25^3, 26^3; **31:**1, 2, 3^3, 4, 5^2, 6^2, 8, 10^2, 12^6, 13, 15^4, 16^2, 17, 18^2; **32:**1, 2^5, 3, 4^2, 5^2, 6, 7^3, 8, 10^2, 12^2, 14, 15, 16, 18^2, 19, 20, 22, 23, 24, 26, 27^2, 28, 29^2, 30^3, 31^2, 32^2; **33:**2^2, 3, 4^2, 5, 6^3, 7, 10^2, 11, 13, 14^2, 16, 18, 19^2, 21, 22^3, 24, 25^3, 26^2, 27^3, 28^2, 30^3, 31^3, 32^2, 33; **34:**1, 2, 3, 4, 5^2, 6^2, 8^2, 10^2, 11, 12^2, 13^5, 14^2, 15, 16^4, 17^3, 18, 19^2, 20, 21^2, 22^3, 23^3, 24^2, 25^4, 26^3, 27^5, 28^2, 29^2, 30, 31^2; **35:**2, 3^3, 4^2, 5, 6, 7^2, 8^3, 9^2, 10^2, 11^2, 12^2, 13, 15^2; **36:**1, 3^4, 4^4, 5, 6^4, 8, 9^3, 10^3, 11^7, 12^3, 13, 17, 18, 19^3, 20^2, 23^2, 24^2, 25^2, 26^3, 27^4, 28^3, 29^3, 30^2, 31^3, 32, 33, 34, 35^5, 36^2, 38; **37:**1^2, 2^3, 3^2, 4, 5, 6^6, 7^3, 8^3, 9^2, 10^3, 11, 12^3, 13^2, 14^4, 16^4, 17^2, 18, 19^4, 20, 21^3, 22^3, 23^2, 24^4, 25^5, 26^3, 27, 28; **38:**1, 2^2, 3^2, 4^6, 5^2, 6^3, 7^3, 8^2, 9^3, 10, 11^2, 12^3, 13^4, 14, 15^3, 16^2, 18, 19, 20^7, 21, 22^7, 23^3; **39:**1^2, 2^4, 3^2, 4^3, 6^3, 7^2, 8, 9^8, 10^2, 11^5, 12, 13, 14, 15, 16, 17^4, 18^2, 19^2, 20^2, 21^3, 22, 23^2, 24^2, 25^2, 26^2, 27^2, 28; **40:**1^2, 2, 3^4, 4^3, 5^4, 6^3, 7^4, 9^2, 10^4, 11^2, 12^3, 13, 15, 16^5, 17^2, 18, 19, 20^2, 21^6, 22^5, 23^3, 24^3, 25^4, 26^4, 27^2, 28^2, 29^7, 30^3, 31^3, 32^2, 33^7, 34^4, 35^2, 36^4, 37^4, 38^2, 39^4, 40^2, 41, 42^6, 43^2, 44^2, 45, 46, 47^2, 48^5, 49^4; **41:**1^2, 2^5, 3^3, 4^2, 5, 6^3, 7^3, 9, 10, 11^3, 12^2, 13^2, 14, 15^4, 16^4, 17^3, 18^4, 19, 20^2, 21, 22^5, 23^2, 24^2, 25^3, 26^5; **42:**1^2, 2, 3, 4^2, 5, 6, 7, 8, 9, 10, 11^4, 12, 13^4, 14^2, 15, 19, 20^2; **43:**2^3, 3^3, 4, 5^2, 6^2, 7^3, 8^3, 9^2, 10, 11^{11}, 13^5, 14^4, 15^2, 16, 17^5, 18^2, 19, 20^5, 21, 22^2, 23, 24^3, 25, 26^2, 27^4; **44:**1, 2, 3, 4^3, 5^5, 6, 7^3, 8, 10, 11^3, 12^2, 13^2, 14, 15^2, 16^2, 17^3, 18, 19^4, 23^4, 24^5, 25, 26, 27, 28^2, 29^3, 30^2; **45:**1^2, 2, 3^5, 4^2, 5^3, 6^3, 7^6, 8^2, 9^3, 10^2, 11^2, 12^2, 13, 15^3, 17^8, 18, 19^4, 20^2, 22^2, 23^3, 24^3, 25^2; **46:**1, 2^5, 3, 4^2, 5^3, 6^3, 7^4, 8^2, 9, 10^2, 11^5, 12^3, 14^2, 15^2, 19, 20, 21^2, 22, 23^2; **47:**1^2, 2^2, 3^2, 4^2, 5, 6^2, 7, 8^2, 9^3, 10, 11, 12^4, 14^2, 15, 16, 17^4, 18^5, 19^2, 22^3, 23; **48:**1, 2, 3, 4, 5, 6, 7, 8^4, 9^2, 10^7, 12, 13^5, 14, 15^4, 16^8, 17^8, 18^4, 19, 20^2, 21^8, 22^2, 24, 25, 26, 27, 28^2, 29, 30^2, 31, 32^4, 33^3, 34, 35

Dan 1:1, 2^2, 3^3, 4^6, 5^2, 6, 7^3, 9, 10^2, 11, 12^2, 13^2, 14, 15^2, 16^2, 17^4, 19^3, 20^3, 21; **2:**1^2, 2^4, 3^2, 4, 5^2, 6^4, 7^2, 8, 9^2, 10, 11^2, 12^2, 13^3, 14, 15, 16^2, 17^2, 18, 20^3, 21^4, 22^2, 23^3, 24^2, 25, 26^2, 27, 28^2, 29, 30, 31^2, 32^2, 33, 34^2, 35^5, 36, 37^2, 38^3, 39^2, 40^4, 41^3, 42^3, 43, 44^4, 45^4, 46^3, 47^3, 48^3, 49^2; **3:**1, 2^2, 3^3, 4, 5^2, 6^2, 7^3, 8, 9, 10^3, 11^2, 12, 13^2, 14^2, 15^4, 16^2, 17, 19^3, 20^3, 21^3, 22^2, 23^2, 24^4, 25^3, 26^5, 27^3, 28^5, 29^3, 30; **4:**1, 2, 3^2, 4, 5^2, 7^2, 8^2, 9^2, 10^2, 11^3, 12^4, 13^2, 14^4, 15^3, 16^2, 17^3, 19^4, 20^2, 21^3, 22^3, 23^7, 24, 25^5, 26, 27^2, 30^2, 32^4, 33^4, 34^6, 35^4, 36^6, 37^4; **5:**1, 2^3, 3^3, 4^3, 5^2, 6^2, 7^6, 9^2, 10^3, 11^4, 12^5, 13^2, 14^3, 15^2, 16^5, 17^3, 18^3, 19^6, 20^2, 21^5, 22, 23^9, 24, 25, 26, 27, 28^2, 29^3, 31^2; **6:**1, 2^2, 3^2, 4, 6^2, 7^3, 8^2, 9, 10^3, 11^2, 12^3, 13, 14^2, 15^2, 16^3, 17^4, 18^2, 19, 20^3, 22^2, 23^2, 24^6, 25, 26^4, 27^4, 28; **7:**1^2, 2^2, 3, 4^4, 5^4, 6^2, 7^8, 8^3, 9^3, 10^3, 11^2, 12, 13^3, 14^5, 15, 16^2, 18^2, 19^2, 20^4, 21^2, 22^2, 23^3, 24^4, 25^7, 26^2, 27^5, 28; **8:**2^4, 3^4, 4^3, 5^3, 6^2, 7^7, 8^2, 9^3, 10^4, 11^2, 12^4, 13^3, 14^2, 15^2, 16^2, 17^2, 18, 19, 20, 21^2, 23^2, 24^6, 25^3, 26^2, 27^4; **9:**3^4, 4^6, 5^4, 6^2, 7^3, 8, 9, 11, 12^2, 13, 14, 15^2, 16^3, 17^2, 18^3, 19^2, 20^5, 22^4, 23^2, 24^7, 25^5, 26^6, 27^5; **10:**1^3, 4^2, 5^2, 6^5, 7, 8^3, 9^2, 10^2, 11^3, 12^2, 13^2, 15^2, 16^4, 18^2, 19^3, 20^2, 21; **11:**1, 2^3, 3^2, 4^3, 5^4, 6^4, 7^3, 8^4, 9, 10^5, 11^4, 12^2, 13^3, 14, 15^3, 16^2, 17^2, 18, 19^2, 21^2, 22^2, 23^2, 24^4, 25^4, 26^2, 27^2, 28^3, 29, 30^3, 31^4, 32^2, 33^3, 35^3, 36^5, 38^4, 39^3, 40^7, 41^3, 42, 43^4, 44^2, 45^2; **12:**1^3, 2^3, 3^3, 4^3, 5^2, 6, 7^5, 8, 9^2, 10^3, 11^3, 12^3, 13

Hos 1:1^2, 2^2, 3^2, 4^3, 5, 6^3, 7^2, 8, 9, 10, 11^3; **2:**1, 2, 3^4, 4, 5^3, 6, 7^3, 8^4, 9^4, 10^2, 11^2, 12^4, 13^5, 14^2, 15^4, 16^2, 17, 18^7, 19^4, 20, 21^2, 22^4, 23^4; **3:**1, 2^2, 3^2, 4^5, 5^4; **4:**2^5, 3^2, 5^2, 8, 9^3, 10^2, 11^2, 12^2, 13^4, 14, 15, 19; **5:**1^3, 2, 3^2, 4, 5^2, 6, 8, 11, 12, 13^2, 14^3, 15^2; **6:**1^3, 2, 3^2, 4, 5, 6^2, 8, 9; **7:**1^3, 2, 3, 7, 9^2, 10^2, 14^3, 15; **8:**1, 4^2, 7, 10, 13^2, 14^3; **9:**2^2, 3, 5, 7, 8, 10^2, 11^2, 14, 17; **10:**5, 6, 8^3, 10, 11^3, 12, 14; **11:**1, 2, 4^2, 6^3, 7, 9^2, 11^2, 12^2; **12:**1^4, 2, 3, 4^3, 6^2, 8, 9, 10^2, 12^3, 13^2, 14; **13:**2^4, 3^2, 4, 6, 8^2, 10^2, 11, 15^2, 16; **14:**2^2, 5, 6^2, 7, 8, 9^3

Joel 1:2, 3^2, 4^2, 5^2, 6^2, 7^2, 9, 11, 12^2, 13^2, 14^2, 15, 16, 19, 20; **2:**1, 2^3, 3^3, 4, 7^2, 8, 9, 10^2, 11^3, 12^3, 13^6, 14^3, 16^2, 17^3, 18, 19^5, 20^5, 21, 22, 23^3, 24^3, 25^3, 26^4, 27^4, 28^3, 29^2, 30^4, 31^2, 32^3; **3:**1^2, 2^4, 3^3, 4^5, 5^2, 6, 7, 8^3, 10, 11^2, 12, 15^2, 16^4, 17, 18^5, 19, 20

Am 1:1, 2^4, 3, 5^3, 6, 8^4, 9^2, 11^4, 13, 14, 15^2; **2:**1, 2^3, 3^2, 4^3, 5, 6^2, 7^3, 8^2, 9^2, 10, 11^2, 12, 14, 15, 16; **3:**5, 6^2, 9^4, 10, 11^2, 12, 13, 14^2, 15^3; **4:**1, 2, 3^2, 4^3, 5^3, 6^2, 7^4, 9^4, 10^2, 11^2, 12, 13^3; **5:**3, 4, 5^2, 6^3, 7, 8^4, 10, 11, 12^2, 14^2, 15^2, 16^3, 17, 18, 19^3, 20^2, 21, 22, 24, 25, 26; **6:**1, 2^2, 3, 4^3, 5, 6, 7, 8, 9, 10^4, 11^2, 12, 14; **7:**1^2, 2, 4^3, 7, 8^2, 9^3, 11, 12^2, 13, 14^2, 15^2, 16, 17^5; **8:**1, 2^2, 3, 5^3, 6^2, 8^4, 9^2, 10^6, 12^4, 13, 14^3; **9:**1^4, 3^4, 4^4, 5^5, 6^2, 7^2, 8, 9, 11^3, 12, 13^3, 14^6, 15^2

Oba 1^2, 4, 7, 8, 9, 10, 11^2, 16^2, 17^2, 18^6, 19^5, 20^2, 21^2

Jna 1:2, 3^3, 4, 5^4, 6, 7^3, 8^2, 9^3, 10, 11, 12^2, 13, 14^2, 15^2, 16^2, 17^2; **2:**2^3, 3^2, 7, 10^2; **3:**1, 2, 3, 4^4, 5^2, 6^4, 7^3, 8^3, 9^2, 10^3; **4:**1, 2^5, 5^3, 6^2, 7, 8^4, 9^2, 10, 11^3

Mic 1:1^2, 2^2, 3^2, 4^3, 5^2, 6^3, 7^4, 8^3, 16; **2:**1, 2^6, 4^2, 10, 11^2, 13^4; **3:**1^2, 2^2, 3^4, 5^2, 6^3, 7, 8^3, 9^2, 10, 11^3, 12^2; **4:**1^2, 2^7, 3^4, 4^2, 5^2, 6^2, 7^3, 8, 10^3, 11, 13^5; **5:**4^3, 5^3, 6^3, 7, 8^3, 9, 10^2, 11^2, 12^2, 13^2, 14, 15^2; **6:**1, 2^2, 3, 4^3, 5, 6, 8^3, 9^2, 10, 11, 12^2, 14^3, 15, 16^3; **7:**2, 3^2, 4, 9^2, 10, 12^4, 14, 16, 17, 18, 19, 20

Nah 1:2^3, 3^4, 4^4, 5^3, 6^2, 7, 8, 10, 12, 13, 14^2; **2:**2, 3, 5, 6, 7^2, 9, 10^6, 11^3, 12^3, 13^4; **3:**1, 2^3, 3^4, 4, 5^3, 6^3, 7^2, 8, 9^3, 10^2, 14, 16, 17^2, 18

Hab 1:2^2, 3^4, 4, 5^2, 6, 7^2, 8^3, 9, 10^3, 11^2, 12, 13^2, 14, 15^2, 16^2, 17; **2:**1^3, 2^3, 3, 5^3, 6^3, 7^2, 8^2, 10, 11, 12, 13, 15, 16^2, 17^3, 18, 19^2; **3:**2, 3^2, 4^2, 5, 6^3, 7, 8, 10^2, 11^2, 16, 17^2, 19^2

Zep 1:3^4, 4^3, 5^4, 6^2, 8^3, 9, 10^3, 12^2, 13^2, 14, 15^4, 16^2, 17^3; **2:**4^2, 6^3, 7^2, 8^2, 9^4, 10, 11, 13^4, 14^2, 15^2; **3:**1, 4, 7, 11, 12^2, 13^2, 14, 16, 19^4, 20

Hag 1:1, 4, 6^2, 8^4, 9^3, 10, 11^9, 12^3, 14^5, 15; **2:**1, 2^2, 3, 4^3, 6^4, 7^3, 8, 9, 10, 12^3, 13^2, 14^4, 15^2, 17^2, 18^2, 19^3, 20^2, 21, 22^6, 23

Zec 1:3, 4, 5, 6^4, 7, 8^4, 9, 10^3, 11^5, 12^3, 13^2, 14, 15^2, 16, 17^2, 18^2, 19^3, 20, 21; **2:**1^2, 2^2, 3^2, 4^2, 5, 6, 9^2, 10^2, 11^4, 12^2; **3:**1^2, 2, 3, 4^4, 5^3, 6, 7^3, 8, 9, 10; **4:**1^2, 2^5, 3^2, 4, 5^2, 6, 7, 9, 10^2, 11^2, 12^2, 13^3; **5:**1^3, 2^3, 3, 4^5, 5^2, 6^2, 7^2, 8^3, 9^5, 11^3; **6:**1^5, 2, 3^3, 4, 5^2, 6^2, 7^6, 8, 9, 10^3, 11^3, 12^3, 13^5, 14^4, 15^4; **7:**1, 2^2, 3^2, 5^3, 6^3, 7^3, 8, 9^2, 10^2, 11^2, 12, 13^2; **8:**2, 3^3, 4^2, 5^2, 7, 8^5, 12^3, 13^3, 14, 15, 16, 17^2, 18, 19^6, 20, 21^2, 22^2; **9:**1, 2^2, 3^3, 4^2, 5^5, 6^2, 7^4, 8^3, 9^3, 10^6, 13^2, 14^4, 15^6, 16, 17^2; **10:**1, 2^2, 3^2, 5^3, 6^5, 7^3, 8^2, 9^4, 10^4, 11^5, 12^3; **11:**5^3, 6^3, 7^4, 8^2, 9^2, 10^2, 11^2, 12^2, 13^3, 14, 15, 16, 17^2; **12:**1^2, 2, 3, 4^3, 5, 6^4, 7, 8^2, 9, 10^6, 12^3, 13^2, 14; **13:**1^2, 2^4, 3^4, 4, 6, 7^3, 8^2, 9^5; **14:**1, 2^5, 3, 4^6, 5^3, 6, 8^3, 9^2, 10^3, 11^2, 12^3, 13^3, 14^4, 15^3, 16^2, 17, 18^2, 19, 20, 21^5

Mal 1:3^3, 4^3, 5^2, 6^3, 7, 8^3, 9, 11^2, 12, 13^4, 14^3; **2:**1, 2^2, 3^2, 4, 5^3, 6^3, 7, 9, 11^3, 12^2, 13^2, 14^2, 15^3, 17; **3:**1^2, 2^2, 3^5, 4^2, 5^8, 7^2, 8, 10^2, 11^2, 12, 14^2, 15, 16^4, 17^2, 18^3; **4:**1^3, 2^2, 3, 4, 5, 6^3

Mt 1:2^3, 3^4, 4^3, 5^3, 6^2, 7^3, 8^3, 9^3, 10^3, 11^2, 12^2, 13^3, 14^3, 15^3, 16, 17^2, 19, 21^2, 23^2, 24, 25^2; **2:**2, 3, 4^2, 5, 6, 8^5, 9^2, 11^6, 12, 13^5, 14^2, 15, 16^4, 18^3, 20^3, 21^4, 23^2; **3:**2, 4^4, 5^2, 6, 7, 9, 10^2, 11, 12^2, 14, 15, 16^4, 17; **4:**2^2, 3, 4, 5, 6^2, 8^2, 9^2, 10, 11^2, 13^3, 15, 16^2, 17, 18^2, 19^2, 20^2, 21^3, 22^3, 23^4, 24^7, 25^5; **5:**1^2, 2^2, 6, 11^2, 12, 13, 15^2, 16, 18, 19^2, 20, 21, 22, 23, 24^3, 25^2, 29^3, 30^3, 32, 38, 40^2, 41, 42, 43, 44^2, 45^3, 47; **6:**2, 4, 5^2, 6^2, 12, 13^3, 17, 18, 19^3, 20, 24^3, 25, 28, 29, 30, 33^2; **7:**2, 3, 4, 5, 6^2, 7^3, 8^2, 12, 13^2, 14^2, 19, 22^2, 23, 24, 25^5, 26^2, 27^6, 28, 29; **8:**2^2, 3^3, 4^2, 5, 6, 7^2, 8^2, 9^6, 10, 11^5, 12, 13^3, 14^2, 15^4, 16^2, 17, 19^2, 20^2, 21^2, 22, 23, 24, 25^2, 26^4, 27, 28, 29, 30, 32^4, 33^4, 34^2; **9:**1^3, 2^2, 3, 4, 5, 6, 7^2, 8, 9^4, 10^4, 11^2, 13^2, 14, 15^2, 16, 17^3, 18^3, 19^3, 20^2, 22^2, 23^3, 24, 25^2, 26, 27^2, 28^2, 30^2, 33^2, 35^5, 36; **10:**1^3, 2^2, 3^3, 4, 5^2, 7, 11^2, 12, 13, 14, 15, 16, 17, 18^3, 21^4, 22, 25, 26, 27, 28^2, 29, 35^2, 36, 37, 38^2, 39, 40, 41, 42; **11:**1^2, 3, 4^3, 5^3, 6, 7, 9, 12^2, 13, 14, 16, 17^3, 18, 19^4, 21^2, 22, 23, 25^4, 27^2, 28^2, 29^3, 30; **12:**1^3, 3, 4, 5, 7, 9, 10^2, 11^3, 13^2, 14, 15^2, 16, 18, 20, 21, 22^4, 23^2, 25^3, 26, 27, 29^2, 30, 31, 32, 33^2, 35, 37, 38, 39^3, 40^2, 41^2, 42^2, 43, 44^2, 45^4, 46, 47, 48^2, 49^3, 50^2; **13:**1, 2^3, 3, 4^3, 5, 6^2, 7^3, 8, 10^2, 11, 12, 13, 14^4, 15^6, 16, 17^4, 19^2, 20, 21, 22^3, 23^2, 25^2, 26, 27, 28, 30^2, 31, 32^2, 33, 34, 36^2, 37, 39, 40, 41^2, 42^2, 44^3, 46^2, 47, 48^2, 49, 50^2, 52, 53, 54^3, 55^4, 56, 57^2, 58; **14:**2^2, 3^2, 5, 6, 8, 9^2, 10^2, 11^3, 12^5, 13, 14^4, 15^3, 17^2, 19^7, 20^3, 21^2, 22^2, 23^2, 25, 26^2, 28^2, 29^2, 30, 31^3, 32, 33, 34, 35^2, 36^2; **15:**1, 3, 4^2, 6, 8, 10^3, 12, 13, 14, 15, 16, 17, 18, 21^2, 22^2, 23^2, 24, 25, 26^2, 27, 28^2, 29^4, 30^4, 31^2, 32^3, 33, 34^3, 35, 36^6, 37^3, 38^2, 39^3; **16:**1, 2, 3^2, 4^4, 5, 6^2, 7, 9, 10, 11, 12, 14^2, 16^2, 17^3, 18^3, 19^3, 21^5, 22, 23, 24^2, 25, 26, 27; **17:**1^3, 2^3, 3^2, 4^3, 5, 6^2, 7^4, 8, 9, 10, 11^3, 12, 14^2, 15^2, 16^2, 17^2, 18^3, 19, 20^3, 21, 22, 23^3, 24^2, 25, 27^5; **18:**2^2, 3^2, 5, 6, 8, 9^2, 12^4, 13^2, 15^2, 17^2, 18, 21^2, 24, 25^4, 26^2, 27^2, 28^3, 29^3, 30^2, 31^2, 34^2; **19:**1^2, 2^2, 3, 4^3, 5^4, 7, 9^3, 12^2, 13^2, 14, 15^2, 16^2, 17, 19^2, 21^5, 24, 26, 27^2, 28, 29^2, 30; **20:**2, 3^2, 4^3, 5^2, 6^3, 7, 8, 9, 10, 11, 12^2, 13, 14, 16, 17^2, 18^3, 19^4, 20, 21^2, 22^2, 23^3, 24, 25^2, 27, 28, 29, 30, 31, 32^3, 34^3; **21:**1^2, 2^3, 3^2, 5^2, 6^2, 7^4, 8^2, 9^2, 10, 11, 12^5, 13, 14^3, 15^4, 16^3, 17^3, 19^4, 20, 21^3, 22, 23^4, 24^2, 25, 27^3, 28^2, 29^2, 30^5, 31, 32^3, 33^5, 34, 35^4, 36, 38, 39^3, 41, 42, 43, 44, 45^2; **22:**1^3, 3^2, 4^2, 5, 6^3, 7^3, 9, 10^3, 11, 12^2, 13^4, 15, 16^2, 18, 19, 20^2, 21, 22^2, 23, 24, 25^2, 26, 27, 29, 32^2, 33, 35, 37^2, 38, 39, 40, 46; **23:**1, 2, 3^2, 4^2, 5, 6^2, 7^2, 8, 9, 12^2, 13, 14^2, 15^3, 17, 18, 19, 20, 21^2, 22^2, 23^6, 24, 25^3, 26, 27^2, 28, 29^2, 30, 34^6, 35, 37^2; **24:**1^3, 2, 3^3, 4^2, 5, 6^2, 7^4, 9^2, 10^3, 11^2, 12, 14^2, 19^2, 22, 24^3, 27, 29^3, 30^4, 31^2, 32, 35, 36, 38^2, 39^2, 40, 41, 43, 45, 48, 49^3, 50, 51^3; **25:**1, 2^2, 3, 5, 6, 7, 8, 9^2, 10^3, 12, 14, 15^3, 16^2, 17, 18^2, 19, 20^2, 21, 22, 23, 24^2, 25^3, 26^3, 27, 28, 29, 30^2, 31, 32^2, 33, 35^3, 36^3, 37^2, 38^2, 39, 40^2, 41, 42^2, 43^4, 44, 46; **26:**1, 2, 3^2, 4^2, 7, 9, 15^3, 16, 18^2, 19^2, 21, 22^2, 23^2, 25, 26^5, 27^3, 30, 31, 33, 36^2, 37^4, 38, 39^3, 40^3, 41, 42, 43^2, 44^3, 45^3, 47^4, 49^3, 50^3, 51^4, 53, 55^2, 56, 57^2, 58^2, 59^2, 61^2, 62^2, 63^2, 64, 66, 67^2, 69, 71^2, 72, 73^2, 74^2, 75^3; **27:**1, 2^2, 3^2, 4, 5^4, 6^2, 7^2, 9, 10, 11^3, 12^2, 14, 16, 20^2, 21, 23, 24, 25^2, 26, 27, 28^2, 29^4, 30^3, 31^3, 32, 33, 34, 35^3, 36, 37, 38, 39, 40^2, 41, 42, 46, 48^5, 51^3, 52^2, 53^3, 54^2, 55, 56^3, 58, 59, 60^3, 61^2, 62, 64^2, 66^2; **28:**1, 2^4, 3, 4^2, 5^2, 7^3, 8^3, 9^4, 10, 11, 12^2, 13, 14^2, 15^2, 17, 18^3, 19^3, 20

Mk 1:4, 5^3, 6^4, 7^2, 9^2, 10^2, 11, 12, 13^3, 15^3, 16, 17^2, 18^2, 19^2, 20^3, 21^3, 22^2, 23^2, 25^2, 26^2, 27^2, 28, 29^3, 30, 31^5, 32^2, 33, 34^3, 35^3, 36^2, 37, 38, 39^2, 40^3, 41^3, 42^2, 43^2, 44^2, 45^3; **2:**1^2, 2^2, 3, 4^2, 6, 8, 9^2, 11^2, 12^3, 13^3, 14^4, 15^4, 16^5, 18^5, 19, 20, 21, 22^3, 23^2, 24, 25^3, 26^2, 27^2; **3:**1^2, 2, 3, 4, 5^3, 6^2, 7^2, 8^5, 9, 11^2, 12, 13^3, 14^2, 15^2, 16, 17^3, 18^8, 19^2, 20, 21, 22^2, 23^2, 24, 25, 26^2, 27^2, 28, 31^2, 32^3, 33, 34^3, 35^2; **4:**1^4, 2^2, 4^3, 5^2, 6, 7^4, 8^6, 9, 10, 11, 12^4, 13^2, 15^2, 16, 17^2, 18, 19^4, 20^4, 21^2, 24^2, 25, 26, 27^5, 30, 32^2, 33, 34, 35, 36^2, 37^2, 38^3, 39^5, 40, 41^3; **5:**1, 2, 3, 4^3, 5^4, 6, 7^2, 9^2, 10, 12, 13^5, 14^4, 15^6, 16^2, 17, 18, 19^2, 20^3, 21^2, 22^2, 23^3, 24^3, 25, 26^3, 27, 29^2, 30^2, 31^2, 32, 33^3, 34^2, 37^3, 38^4, 39^2, 40^4, 41^2, 42^3, 43^2; **6:**1^3, 2^3, 3^5, 4^2, 5^2, 6^2, 7^4, 8, 9, 10, 11^2, 12^2, 13^3, 14^3, 15, 17^2, 19, 20^4, 21^2, 22^5, 23, 24^3, 25^3, 26^2, 27^4, 28^3, 29^3, 30^3, 31^4, 32, 33^5, 34^3, 35^3, 36^2, 37^4, 38^3, 39, 40^2, 41^6, 42^2, 43^2, 44, 45^2, 46, 47^2, 48^3, 49, 50^3, 51^4, 53^2, 54, 55^2, 56^3; **7:**1, 2, 3, 4^4, 5, 6, 8^2, 9, 10^2, 12, 13, 14^2, 17, 18, 19, 20, 23, 24^5, 25^2, 26, 27, 28^2, 29, 30^2, 31^2, 32^3, 33^4, 34^2, 35^3, 36, 37^2; **8:**1^2, 2, 3, 4, 5^2, 6^6, 7^3, 8^2, 9^2, 10^2, 11^2, 12^2, 13^2, 15^2, 16, 17, 18^2, 20^2, 21, 22^3, 23^4, 24^2, 25^3, 26, 27^3, 28^2, 29^3, 30, 31^6, 32^3, 33, 34^3, 35, 36, 38^2; **9:**1, 2^5, 3, 4^2, 5^5, 7^2, 8, 9, 10, 11, 12^5, 13, 14^2, 15^2, 16, 17^2, 18^6, 19, 20^4, 21^2, 22^3, 24^2, 25^2, 26^4, 27^2, 28, 29^2, 30^3, 31^3, 32, 33^2, 35^4, 36^3, 37, 38^3, 42^2, 43, 44, 45, 46, 47, 48, 49, 50; **10:**1^4, 2^2, 3^2, 4^2, 5^2, 6, 7^2, 8, 10, 11^2, 12^2, 13^2, 14^2, 16^2, 17^3, 18, 19, 20^2, 21^5, 22^2, 23^2, 24^2, 26, 27, 28, 29^3, 30^6, 31, 32^6, 33^4, 34^5, 35^2, 36, 37, 38, 39^3, 40, 41^2, 42^2, 44, 45, 46^3, 47^2, 48, 49^3, 50^2, 51^2, 52^3; **11:**1^2, 2^3, 3^2, 4^3, 5, 6^2, 7^3, 8^3, 9^2, 11^4, 12, 13^2, 14^3, 15^6, 16, 17, 18^3, 19, 20, 21, 22, 23^2, 24, 25, 27^4, 28^2, 29^4, 31, 33^3; **12:**1^6, 2, 3^3, 4^4, 5^4, 7, 8^3, 9^2, 10, 11, 12^3, 13^2, 14^2, 16^4, 17^3, 18, 19^3, 20^2, 21^3, 22^2, 24, 26^3, 28^3, 29, 30^4, 31, 32^2, 33^6, 34^2, 35^2, 37^2, 38^2, 39^2, 40, 41^3, 42^2, 43^2; **13:**1^2, 2, 3^4, 4, 5, 6, 7^2, 8^4, 9^3, 10, 11, 12^3, 13, 15, 16, 17, 18, 20, 21, 22^3, 24, 25^2, 26^2, 27^2, 28, 31, 32, 33, 34^3, 37; **14:**1^4, 3^3, 4^2, 5^2, 6, 7, 10, 11^3, 12^2, 13^3, 14, 15^2, 16^4, 17, 18^2, 19^3, 20^2, 22^5, 23^3, 24, 26, 27^2, 30, 32^2, 33^5, 34^2, 35^3, 36, 37^3, 38, 39^3, 40, 41^3, 43^5, 44^2, 45^3, 46^2, 47^3, 48^3, 49, 50^2, 51^2, 52^2, 53^4, 54^3, 55^3, 57^2, 58, 60^2, 61^2, 62^3,

63, 64, 65[5], 66, 67[3], 68[2], 69[2], 70[3], 71, 72[3]; **15:**1[6], 2[2], 3, 4, 7, 8, 12[2], 13, 14, 15[2], 16[2], 17[3], 18, 19[3], 20[3], 21[2], 22, 23, 24, 25[2], 26, 27[2], 28[2], 29[3], 30, 32[3], 33, 34, 35, 36[4], 37[2], 38, 39[2], 40[3], 41[2], 42, 43[2], 44[2], 45, 46[5], 47[2]; **16:**1[4], 2, 3, 4, 5[2], 6, 7, 8[3], 10[3], 11[2], 12, 13[2], 14[2], 15[2], 16, 17, 18[2], 19, 20[3]

Lk 1:2, 5[2], 6[2], 7[2], 8, 10, 11, 12[2], 13[2], 14[3], 15[2], 16, 17[3], 18[2], 19[3], 20[2], 21[2], 22[3], 23, 24[2], 26, 27, 28[2], 29[2], 30, 31[3], 32[2], 33[2], 35[3], 36[2], 38[2], 39[2], 40[2], 41[2], 42[3], 43, 45, 46, 47, 49, 50, 52, 53, 55, 56[2], 57, 58[3], 59[2], 60[2], 61, 62, 63[3], 64[4], 65[2], 66[2], 67[2], 68, 69, 71, 72, 75, 76, 79, 80[3]; **2:**1, 2, 3, 4[2], 6, 7[3], 8, 9[3], 10, 12, 13[2], 14, 15[2], 16[4], 17, 18, 19, 20[3], 21, 22, 24, 25[4], 26, 27[2], 28[2], 32, 33[2], 34[4], 36[2], 37[4], 38[2], 39, 40[3], 42, 43[3], 44[2], 45, 46[2], 47[2], 48[3], 49, 50, 51[3], 52[4]; **3:**1[4], 2, 3, 5[4], 6, 8, 9[2], 10, 11[2], 12, 13, 14[4], 15[2], 16, 17[2], 18, 19, 21, 22[2], 23; **4:**1[2], 2[2], 3, 4, 5, 6[3], 8[3], 9[3], 11, 12, 13, 14[2], 15, 16[3], 17[2], 18, 20[4], 21, 22[3], 23, 24, 25, 27[2], 28, 29[3], 31[2], 32, 33[2], 35[4], 36[4], 37, 38[4], 39[5], 40[2], 41[3], 42[5], 43, 44; **5:**1, 2[2], 3[4], 4, 5[2], 6[2], 7[4], 9, 10[3], 11[2], 12[2], 13[3], 14[3], 15[2], 16[2], 17[5], 18[3], 19[2], 20, 21[2], 23, 24[2], 25[3], 26[3], 27[3], 28[2], 29[3], 30[3], 31, 33[4], 34, 35, 36[2], 37[3], 38; **6:**1[3], 2, 3[2], 4[3], 5, 6[3], 7[2], 8[4], 10[3], 11[2], 12[2], 13[2], 14[3], 15[2], 16[2], 17[8], 18[2], 19[2], 20[2], 22[3], 23, 25, 28, 29[2], 30, 31, 33, 34, 35[5], 37[3], 38[3], 39, 41, 42, 45, 46[2], 47[2], 48[4], 49[3]; **7:**2[2], 3[2], 4, 5, 6, 7, 8[6], 9[2], 10, 11[3], 12[3], 13[2], 14[4], 15[3], 16[3], 17[2], 18, 19, 21[4], 22[2], 23, 24, 25, 26, 29[2], 30, 31[2], 32[4], 33, 34[4], 36[3], 37, 38[5], 39, 40[2], 41, 42, 43[2], 44[3], 48, 49, 50; **8:**1[4], 2[2], 3[3], 4[2], 5[3], 6[2], 7[3], 8[4], 9, 10[2], 12[2], 13[2], 14[5], 15[2], 17, 18, 19[2], 20[2], 21[4], 22[2], 23[3], 24[6], 25[4], 26, 27[2], 28[2], 29[4], 30[2], 31, 32[3], 33[3], 34[3], 35[4], 37[2], 39[3], 40, 41[4], 42, 43, 44[2], 45[4], 46, 47[3], 48, 50, 51[5], 52[2], 53, 54[3], 55[3], 56; **9:**1[3], 2[2], 3, 4[2], 5, 6[3], 7, 8[2], 9[2], 10[3], 11[4], 12[5], 13[3], 14, 15[2], 16[4], 17[3], 18[2], 19, 21[2], 22[5], 23[3], 25, 26[3], 28[4], 29[3], 30[2], 31, 32[3], 33[4], 34[2], 35, 36[3], 37, 38, 39[4], 40[2], 41[3], 42[5], 43, 45[2], 47[2], 48[2], 49[3], 50, 51, 52[3], 53, 54[3], 55[2], 56, 57, 58[2], 59[2], 60, 61, 62[2]; **10:**1[3], 4, 5, 6, 7[2], 8[2], 9[2], 10[2], 13[2], 14, 15, 16[2], 17, 18, 19[3], 21[4], 22[3], 23[2], 24[4], 25[2], 27[5], 28[2], 29, 30[4], 31[2], 32[3], 33, 34[6], 35[4], 37[2], 38, 39[2], 40[2], 41[3], 42; **11:**1, 2, 4[2], 5[3], 6, 7[4], 8[2], 9[4], 10[2], 14[4], 16, 17, 19, 22[2], 23, 24, 25[2], 26[4], 27[3], 28, 29[2], 31[2], 32[2], 37[3], 38, 39[3], 41, 42[5], 43, 44[2], 45, 46[2], 47, 48, 49[3], 51, 52, 53[3], 54; **12:**3, 4[2], 6, 10, 11[3], 13, 14, 15[2], 16, 17, 18[4], 19[2], 21, 22, 23, 24, 25, 27, 28, 29, 30, 31, 33, 35, 36[2], 37[3], 38[2], 39[2], 42[2], 45[6], 46[3], 47[2], 48[2], 49, 50, 52, 53[3], 54[2], 55[2], 56, 57, 58[2]; **13:**2, 4, 6[3], 7, 8[2], 9[2], 10, 11[3], 12[3], 13[3], 14[4], 15[2], 16, 17[2], 18, 19[4], 20, 21, 22[3], 23, 24, 25[5], 26[2], 28[5], 29[5], 30[2], 31, 32[5], 33[2], 34[2], 35; **14:**1, 2, 3[2], 4[4], 5[2], 6, 7, 9[4], 10, 11, 12, 14, 15, 16, 17, 18[3], 19[2], 20[2], 21[6], 22[2], 23[3], 25[3], 26[7], 27[2], 28, 29, 30, 31, 32; **15:**1, 2[3], 3, 4[2], 5, 6[2], 7, 8[2], 9[2], 11, 12[2], 13[3], 14[2], 15[3], 16[2], 17[3], 18[3], 19, 20[6], 21[3], 22[3], 23[4], 24[3], 25[3], 26[2], 27[3], 28[3], 29[2], 31[2], 32[4]; **16:**1[2], 2[2], 5, 6[4], 7[4], 8, 9, 10, 12, 13[3], 14[2], 15, 16[2], 17[2], 18[2], 19[2], 20, 21[2], 22[3], 23[3], 24[4], 25[2], 26[2], 29, 30, 31[2]; **17:**2, 3, 4[2], 5, 6[3], 7[2], 8[6], 11[2], 12, 13[2], 14[2], 15[2], 16[2], 17, 19, 20[2], 22[2], 23, 25, 26, 27[2], 29[2], 31[2], 33, 34, 35, 36, 37[3]; **18:**1[2], 3[2], 4, 6, 7[2], 9[2], 10, 11, 13, 14, 15, 16[2], 18, 19, 20, 21, 22[3], 23, 24, 26, 27, 28, 29, 30, 31[2], 32[3], 33[3], 34[2], 35, 36, 37, 38, 39, 40[3], 41, 42, 43[3]; **19:**1[2], 2[2], 3[2], 4[2], 5[4], 6[3], 7, 8[3], 9, 10, 11[3], 12, 13[3], 14, 15, 17, 18, 19, 20, 21, 22[2], 24[2], 25, 26, 27, 28, 29[2], 30, 31, 32[2], 33, 34, 35[3], 36, 37[2], 38, 39, 40[2], 41[2], 43[2], 44[3], 45[3], 47[3], 48; **20:**1[3], 2, 3[3], 5, 6, 7, 8, 9[2], 10[2], 11[4], 12[3], 15, 16[3], 17[2], 19[3], 20[3], 21[3], 23, 24[2], 25[2], 26[3], 27, 28[2], 29[2], 30[2], 31[4], 34[2], 35, 36, 37[2], 40, 41, 42, 46[3], 47; **21:**1[2], 2, 3, 5[2], 7[2], 8[2], 9[2], 10, 11[5], 12[3], 13, 15, 16[5], 17, 20, 21[2], 23[2], 24[3], 25[5], 26, 27[2], 28[2], 29[2], 30, 33, 34[4], 36[2], 37[3], 38; **22:**2[2], 4[3], 5[2], 6[2], 8[3], 9, 10, 11, 12, 13[3], 14[2], 15, 17[4], 19[4], 22, 23, 24, 25[2], 26, 29, 30[2], 31, 32, 33[2], 34, 35[4], 36[3], 37, 38[2], 39[3], 40, 41[3], 43, 44[2], 45[2], 46[2], 47[3], 50[2], 51[4], 52[3], 53, 54[3], 55[2], 56[2], 57, 58[3], 59, 60[2], 61[3], 62[2], 63[2], 64[2], 65, 66[4], 67, 68, 70, 71; **23:**1[2], 2[2], 3[3], 4, 5, 7, 8[2], 10[3], 11[4], 12[2], 13[3], 14, 15, 16, 18[2], 19, 22[2], 23[3], 24, 25[2], 26[2], 27[3], 28, 29[2], 30, 32, 33[3], 34[2], 35[2], 36[2], 37, 38[3], 39[2], 41, 42, 43, 44[2], 45[2], 46[2], 48[2], 49[2], 50[3], 51, 52, 53[3], 54[2], 55[3], 56[4]; **24:**1, 2, 3[2], 4, 5[2], 7[2], 8, 9[3], 10[3], 11[2], 12[3], 13, 14, 15[3], 17[2], 18[2], 19[4], 20[3], 21, 22, 23, 24[2], 25, 26, 27[2], 28[2], 29[2], 30[4], 31[3], 32[2], 33[4], 34, 35[2], 36[2], 37[2], 38[2], 39[3], 40[2], 41[2], 42[2], 43[2], 44[3], 46[3], 47[2], 48, 49, 50[3], 51[2], 52[2], 53[2]

Jn 1:1[2], 3, 4, 5[2], 10[2], 11, 14[4], 15, 16[2], 17, 19[2], 20[2], 21[3], 24, 25[2], 29, 31, 32[2], 33[2], 34[2], 35, 36, 37[2], 38[2], 39[3], 40, 41, 42[2], 43[2], 44, 45[2], 46[2], 47, 48, 49, 50, 51[3]; **2:**1[2], 2[2], 3, 6, 7, 8[3], 9, 10[2], 11[2], 12[4], 13[2], 14[4], 15[5], 16, 17, 18, 19[2], 20[2], 22[2], 25; **3:**2, 3, 4, 5, 6, 8[2], 9, 10[2], 11[2], 12, 13, 14, 19[2], 22[3], 23[3], 25, 26[3], 27, 29, 31, 32[3], 35, 36; **4:**1, 3, 4, 6, 10[3], 11, 12[3], 13, 16, 17, 18, 20, 23[2], 24[2], 27[2], 28[2], 30, 34, 35[2], 36[3], 37[2], 38, 39, 40, 41, 42[2], 43, 46, 47[2], 48, 50[2], 51[2], 52, 53[2]; **5:**1, 4, 5[2], 6, 8, 9[4], 11, 12, 13, 14, 15, 16[2], 17, 19, 20[2], 21, 24[2], 25[2], 27, 29[2], 30, 32, 33, 35[2], 37, 38, 39, 40, 43, 44; **6:**2, 3[2], 4, 5, 6, 9, 10, 11[4], 13[2], 15, 16, 17[4], 18, 19[3], 21, 22, 24, 25, 26[2], 29, 30, 33, 35[2], 36, 37, 39, 40[3], 42[2], 43, 44, 45[2], 49, 50, 51, 53, 54[2], 55, 56[2], 57, 58, 62, 63, 64, 65, 66, 69[2], 70; **7:**3, 4, 11, 12, 14, 15, 16, 18, 19, 20, 21[2], 22, 26, 28[2], 29, 31[2], 32[2], 33, 34[2], 35, 36[2], 37[2], 42, 44, 45[2], 51, 52[2], 53; **8:**2[4], 3[3], 6, 7, 8[2], 9[3], 10, 11[2], 14[3], 16[2], 18, 20, 21[2], 23, 25, 26[2], 28, 29, 32[3], 33, 35, 38, 39, 42, 44[3], 45, 46, 48[2], 49, 50[2], 52[2], 53, 55[2], 56[2], 57, 59[2]; **9:**1, 2, 6[2], 7[3], 8[2], 11[7], 14[2], 15[2], 16, 18, 19, 20[2], 24, 25, 27, 28, 30[2], 31, 34[3], 35, 36, 37[2], 38[2], 39[2], 40[2]; **10:**1, 3[3], 4[2], 5, 8, 9[3], 10[3], 12[5], 13, 14[2], 15, 16[4], 18, 20[2], 22[2], 23, 24, 25, 27[2], 28[2], 29, 30, 33, 35, 36, 38[2], 40[2], 41[2], 42; **11:**1, 2, 5[2], 8, 11, 15, 19[2], 20, 25, 26[2], 28[3], 29, 31[2], 32, 33[2], 34[2], 37, 38, 41[2], 42, 43, 44[4], 45, 46, 47[2], 48[3], 49, 50, 51, 52, 54, 55[2], 56, 57; **12:**2, 3[3], 5, 6[2], 9, 11, 13[2], 14, 16, 17, 20, 21, 22[3], 23, 24, 25, 26, 27, 28, 29, 30, 32, 34, 36[2], 38, 40[3], 41, 44, 45, 47[2], 48, 49, 50; **13:**2, 3[2], 4[3], 5[2], 6, 7, 9, 10, 12[2], 13[2], 14, 20, 21[2], 26, 27, 30, 31, 32, 33; **14:**3[3], 4[2], 5, 6, 7[2], 8, 9[2], 10, 11, 12, 13, 16[2], 17, 19, 20[2], 21[4], 22, 23[4], 24, 26, 28, 29, 30, 31; **15:**1, 2, 4, 5, 6[4], 7[2], 10, 11, 16[3], 22, 24[2], 27; **16:**3, 4, 5, 8[3], 10, 13, 14, 15, 16[3], 17[4], 19[4], 20[2], 22[3], 23, 24, 26, 27, 28[2], 29, 30, 32[2]; **17:**1[2], 3[2], 5, 6[2], 8[3], 10[3], 11[2], 12, 13[2], 14, 19, 21, 22, 23[3], 25, 26[3]; **18:**1, 2, 3[4], 4, 5, 6, 7, 10[2], 12[3], 13, 15[3], 16[2], 18[5], 19, 20[2], 22, 25[3], 27, 28[2], 29, 30, 31, 33[2], 35, 37, 38[2]; **19:**1, 2[3], 3[2], 4, 5[2], 6[2], 7, 9[2], 10, 12, 13, 14[3], 16[2], 17, 18[2], 19[3], 20[3], 23[2], 24, 25[2], 26, 27, 29[3], 30[2], 31, 32[3], 33, 34[2], 35[3], 37, 38[3], 39[3], 40, 41; **20:**1, 2[4], 3[2], 4[2], 5[2], 6[2], 7, 8[2], 11[2], 12[2], 13[2], 14[3], 15, 16, 17[4], 18[2], 19[2], 20[2], 22[2], 23, 25[2], 26[4], 27[4], 28[3], 29, 30, 31; **21:**1, 2[4], 3[2], 6[3], 7, 8, 9[2], 11[4], 12[2], 13[3], 17, 18[3], 19, 20, 21, 24[2], 25

Act 1:1, 3, 4, 7, 8[4], 9[2], 10, 13[8], 14[3], 15[3], 16, 17, 18[2], 19, 20[2], 21, 23[2], 24[2], 25, 26[3]; **2:**1, 2[2], 3[2], 4[2], 5, 6, 7[2], 8, 9[6], 10[4], 11, 12[2], 14[3], 17[5], 18[3], 19[4], 20[2], 21, 22[2], 23[3], 26, 29[3], 30, 33[2], 36, 37[3], 38[2], 39[2], 40[2], 41, 42[4], 43[3], 44[2], 45[3], 46[3], 47[2]; **3:**1, 2, 3, 4, 5, 6[2], 7[4], 8[5], 9[2], 10[3], 11[2], 12, 13[3], 14[2], 15, 16[2], 17, 19, 20, 23, 24[2], 25[2]; **4:**1[3], 2, 3[2], 4, 5[3], 6[5], 7, 8, 10, 13[4], 14, 16, 18[2], 19[2], 20, 23[3], 24[5], 25, 26[2], 27[2], 28, 29[2], 30[2], 31[3], 32[2], 33[2], 34, 35[2], 36[2], 37[2]; **5:**2[3], 3, 4, 5[3], 6[3], 7, 8[2], 9, 10[4], 11[2], 12[3], 13, 14[2], 15[2], 16[2], 17[2], 18[2], 19[2], 20, 21[6], 22[2], 23, 24[2], 25[2], 26, 27[2], 28[2], 29[2], 30, 31[2], 32[2], 33, 34, 35, 36[2], 37[2], 38[2], 40[4], 41, 42[3]; **6:**1, 2[2], 3, 4, 5[8], 6, 7[3], 8[3], 9[4], 10[2], 11, 12[6], 13[2], 14, 15; **7:**2[2], 3[3], 4[2], 5[2], 6[3], 7[3], 8[5], 9, 10[5], 11[3], 13[2], 14[3], 15[2], 16[2], 17, 19, 20[2], 21[2], 22[3], 23, 24[3], 26[2], 27, 29, 30, 31, 32[3], 34[3], 35[2], 36[3], 38, 39, 41[3], 42[2], 43[2], 46, 49, 51[2], 52[2], 53, 54, 55[2], 56[2], 57[2], 58[3], 59[2], 60[3]; **8:**1[4], 2[2], 3[2], 5, 6[2], 7[2], 8, 9, 11, 12[2], 13[3], 14, 17, 18, 22, 23, 24, 25[3], 26[2], 27[4], 28, 29, 30[3], 31[3], 32, 33, 34[2], 35[2], 36[2], 37[3], 38[4], 39[2], 40; **9:**1[2], 2, 3[2], 4[2], 5[2], 6[5], 7, 8[3], 9[2], 10[3], 11[3], 12[2], 14, 15[2], 17[4], 18[4], 19, 20, 21[2], 22, 23, 24[2], 25, 26[2], 27[4], 28[2], 29[2], 30, 31[5], 32, 33[2], 34[3], 35[3], 36, 37[2], 38[2], 39[4], 40[5], 41[4], 42[2], 43; **10:**2[2], 3, 4[4], 5[2], 7[2], 8, 9, 10[2], 11[3], 12[3], 13[2], 15, 16, 17, 18[2], 20[2], 21, 22[4], 23[3], 24[4], 25[3], 27[2], 28, 30[3], 31[2], 32, 33, 34, 35, 37, 38[2], 39[3], 40, 41, 42[3], 45, 46, 48; **11:**1[2], 2, 3, 4, 5[2], 6[4], 7[2], 10[2], 11, 12[2], 13[3], 14, 15, 18, 19[2], 20[2], 21[3], 22, 23[2], 24[3], 26[4], 27, 28[2], 30[2]; **12:**2, 3, 4[2], 6[2], 7[5], 8[5], 9[3], 10[4], 11[3], 12, 13, 14[2], 15, 16[2], 17[4], 19[5], 20[3], 21[2], 22[2], 23[3], 24, 25[3]; **13:**1[5], 2[2], 3[3], 4, 5[2], 6, 7[2], 10[2], 11[5], 13[2], 14[2], 15[3], 16[2], 17[2], 18, 19, 20[2], 21[2], 22[2], 25, 26[2], 27, 28, 29[2], 31, 32, 34, 36[2], 38, 39, 41[2], 42, 43[2], 44, 45[2], 46[3], 48[3], 49, 50[5], 51, 52[2]; **14:**1[3], 2, 3[2], 4[2], 5[3], 6[3], 7, 8, 9, 10[2], 11, 12[2], 13[2], 14[2], 15[5], 17[3], 18, 19[3], 20[2], 21[4], 22[2], 23[2], 24, 25, 26, 27[3], 28; **15:**1[2], 2[5], 3[3], 4[4], 5, 6[2], 7[4], 8, 9[2], 12[3], 13[2], 15, 16[3], 17, 20[3], 22[3], 23[5], 24, 25, 27, 28, 29[3], 30, 32[3], 33, 35[2], 36[3], 37, 38, 39[3], 40[2], 41[2]; **16:**1[3], 2, 3[2], 4[2], 5[2], 6[2], 8, 9[3], 10, 11, 12[3], 13[3], 14, 15[4], 16, 17[2], 18[3], 19[3], 20, 21, 22[3], 23, 24, 25[4], 26[3], 27[3], 29[4], 30[2], 31[3], 32[3], 33[4], 34[2], 35, 36[2], 37[3], 38[2], 39[4], 40[4]; **17:**1, 2[3], 3[3], 4[5], 5[4], 6[2], 7, 8[2], 9[2], 10[2], 11, 12, 13, 14[2], 15[3], 17[2], 18[3], 19[2], 21, 22, 23, 24[2], 25[2], 26[3], 27, 28[2], 29, 30, 32[2], 34[3]; **18:**1, 2[2], 3[2], 4[3], 5[3], 6[3], 7[2], 8[3], 9, 10, 11[2], 12[2], 14, 15[2], 16, 17[2], 18[5], 19[3], 21, 22[3], 23[3], 24[2], 25[2], 26[3], 27, 28; **19:**1[2], 2, 3[2], 6[3], 7, 8[3], 9[2], 10[2], 11, 12[2], 14[2], 15[3], 16[4], 17[4], 18[3], 19[3], 20, 21, 22, 23, 25, 26[2], 27[2], 28[2], 29[3], 30, 31, 32[2], 33[3], 35[2], 36, 38[2], 41; **20:**1[3], 2[2], 3[2], 4[7], 6[2], 7[2], 8, 9[4], 10[3], 11[3], 12[2], 13[2], 14[2], 15[5], 17[2], 18, 19[2], 20[3], 21[2], 22, 23, 24, 25, 28, 31[2], 32[3], 34, 35, 36[2], 37[3], 38; **21:**1[4], 2[2], 3[2], 4, 5[6], 6[2], 7[3], 8[4], 9, 10, 11[5], 12[2], 13, 14, 15[2], 16, 17, 18[2], 19, 20[3], 21, 24[4], 25[4], 26, 27[2], 28[4], 30[5], 31, 32[4], 33[4], 34[2], 35, 37, 38, 39, 40[3]; **22:**1, 2[2], 3[2], 4[3], 5[2], 6[2], 7[2], 8[2], 9[2], 10[4], 11, 12, 13[3], 14[3], 15, 16[3], 17, 18[2], 19[2], 20[3], 21, 22[3], 23[3], 24, 25[2], 26, 27, 28[2], 29[2], 30[4]; **23:**1[2], 2, 3, 4, 6[3], 7[3], 9[3], 10[3], 11[2], 12[2], 13, 14[3], 15, 16[3], 17, 18[3], 19[2], 20, 21, 22, 23[4], 24[2], 25, 27[2], 28, 30[2], 31, 32, 33, 34[2], 35; **24:**1[2], 2[2], 3, 5[2], 6, 7, 9, 12, 14, 15[2], 16[2], 17, 19, 22[2], 23[3], 24[2], 25[3], 26, 27; **25:**2[2], 3, 4, 5, 6[2], 7[3], 9[2], 13[2], 14, 15, 16, 17, 19, 20[2], 23[4], 24[3], 25, 26, 27; **26:**1, 3, 6[2], 7, 10[2], 11[3], 12, 13, 14[2], 15[2], 16[3], 17, 18[3], 20[5], 21, 22[2], 23[3], 24, 25, 29[2], 30[4], 31; **27:**1[2], 2, 3[3], 4, 5[2], 6[2], 7[2], 8, 9, 10[3], 11, 12[4], 13, 15[2], 16, 17[2], 18, 19, 20[2], 21[4], 22, 23, 24, 27, 28[4], 29, 30, 31, 32, 33[2], 35[3], 36, 37[2], 38[2], 39, 40[4], 41[3], 42[2], 43[2], 44[3]; **28:**1, 2[3], 3[3], 4, 5[2], 6[2], 7, 8[5], 9, 10, 11[2], 12, 13[4], 14[2], 15[3], 16, 17[3], 20, 21, 23[3], 24[2], 25, 26[4], 27[6], 28, 29[2], 30[2], 31

Ro 1:4, 5, 7[2], 12, 14[2], 16, 18, 20, 21, 23[4], 25[2], 27[2], 28; **2:**3[2], 4[2], 5[2], 7[2], 8[2], 9[2], 10[2], 12, 15, 17[2], 18[2], 19, 20, 27[2], 29[2]; **3:**4, 8[2], 9, 14, 16, 17, 19, 21, 22, 23, 26, 30; **4:**3, 7, 11, 12, 14, 17, 19, 21, 22, 25; **5:**2, 3, 4[2], 5, 11, 12[2], 15, 16, 17; **6:**13, 19, 22[2]; **7:**6, 9, 10, 11, 12[3], 23; **8:**2, 3, 6, 10, 17[2], 22, 23, 27, 28, 30[2]; **9:**2, 4[5], 5, 9, 10, 15, 17, 18, 21, 22, 23, 25, 26, 28, 29[2], 33[2]; **10:**1, 3, 8, 9, 10, 12, 14[2], 15[2], 17, 18, 19, 20, 21; **11:**3[3], 6, 7, 8, 9[4], 10, 12, 14, 16, 17[4], 20, 22, 23, 24, 26[2], 29, 33[2], 35, 36[2]; **12:**2[3], 4, 5, 14, 15; **13:**2, 3, 9, 11, 12, 13[3], 14; **14:**3, 6[3], 7, 8, 9[3], 11, 14, 17[3], 18, 19, 23; **15:**1, 4, 5, 6, 9[2], 10, 11[2], 12[2], 13, 14, 18, 19[2], 21, 23, 24, 26, 27, 28, 29, 30, 31, 32; **16:**2[2], 3, 7[2], 9, 12, 13[2], 14, 15[4], 17[2], 18[2], 19, 20, 21[3], 23[2], 25, 26

1Co 1:1, 2, 3[2], 5, 10[2], 12[3], 14, 16, 19, 22, 23, 24[2], 25, 27, 28[3], 30[3]; **2:**1, 2, 3[3], 4[3]; **3:**1, 2, 3[3], 4, 5, 8[2], 10, 13, 16, 20, 23[2]; **4:**1, 5[2], 6[2], 7, 8, 9[2], 11[4], 12, 13, 17, 19, 21; **5:**1, 2[2], 4, 8[2]; **6:**1, 2, 6, 8[2], 11[2], 13[3], 14[2], 15, 19, 20; **7:**2, 3, 4, 5[2], 6, 7, 8, 10, 11[2], 12, 13[2], 14, 17, 19, 28[2], 30[3], 31, 34[2], 35[2], 36, 37, 40; **8:**2, 4, 5, 6[3], 7, 11, 12; **9:**4, 5[2], 6, 7[2], 10, 13, 20, 23, 25, 27; **10:**1, 2[2], 3, 4[2], 7[2], 8[2], 9, 10, 11, 17, 20[2], 21[2], 26, 27, 28[2]; **11:**2, 3[2], 7, 18, 21[2], 22[2], 24[2], 26, 27[2], 28[2], 29[2], 30[2], 34[2]; **12:**3, 5, 6, 11, 12[2], 13, 16, 19, 21, 23[2], 26, 27, 28, 31; **13:**1[2], 2[5], 3[3], 4, 9, 13; **14:**1, 3[2], 7, 10, 11, 15[2], 21[2], 23[2], 24, 25[3], 27[2], 28[2], 29, 31, 32, 35, 39, 40; **15:**1, 4[2], 5, 8, 10, 11, 14[2], 15, 17, 20, 24[2], 28, 30, 32, 34, 35, 37, 38, 39, 40[2], 41[2], 44, 45, 46, 48, 49, 50, 52[2], 53, 54, 56; **16:**3, 4, 6[2], 9[2], 15, 16[2], 17[2], 18, 19

2Co 1:1, 2[2], 3, 6[3], 7, 10, 12[2], 13, 15, 16[3], 17, 18, 19[3], 20, 21, 22; **2:**3, 4, 7, 12, 14, 15, 16[2]; **3:**2, 4, 7, 13, 17; **4:**5, 7, 13[2], 14, 17; **5:**8[2], 11, 12, 15[2], 18[2], 19; **6:**2, 7, 8[3], 9[3], 10, 14, 15, 16[4], 17[3], 18[3]; **7:**1, 3, 7, 13, 15[2]; **8:**2, 3, 4, 5[2], 7[4], 8, 10, 12, 13, 15, 18, 19[2], 22, 23[2], 24[2]; **9:**2, 4, 5[2], 6, 8, 10[2], 13[2], 14; **10:**1, 5[2], 6, 8, 10[2], 12, 16; **11:**1, 9[4], 14, 25, 27[3], 29[2], 31, 33[2]; **12:**1, 3, 4, 7, 9, 12[2], 14, 15[2], 18, 20, 21[5]; **13:**2[3], 9[2], 10, 11[2], 14[2]

Gal 1:1, 2, 3[2], 4, 5, 7, 13, 14, 15, 16, 17, 18, 21, 22, 24; **2:**1, 2[2], 4, 9[4], 12, 13, 14, 15, 16, 20[2]; **3:**5, 6, 8, 12, 16[3], 17[2], 19, 29[2]; **4:**2, 6, 7, 9, 10[3], 14, 15, 18, 20, 25[2], 27, 30; **5:**1, 11, 15, 16, 17[2], 21, 24[2]; **6:**2, 4[2], 9, 14, 16[3]

Eph 1:1, 2[2], 3, 4, 8, 10, 15, 17, 18, 19, 20, 21[4], 22[2]; **2:**1[2], 3[2], 6[2], 8, 12[2], 14, 16, 17[3], 19[2], 20[2]; **3:**5, 6[2], 9, 10, 12, 15, 17, 18[3], 19; **4:**2, 4, 6[3], 8, 11[5], 13, 14[3], 16, 17, 21, 23, 24[2], 26, 30, 31[4], 32; **5:**2[3], 3, 5, 9[2], 11, 14[2], 18, 19[3], 20, 23, 25, 26, 27, 29, 30, 31[3], 32, 33; **6:**2, 3, 4[2], 5, 7, 9, 10, 12, 13, 14, 15, 17[2], 18[3], 19, 21[2], 22, 23[2]

Php 1:1[2], 2[2], 7[2], 9[3], 10, 11, 13, 14, 15[2], 18[2], 19, 20, 21, 23, 25[3], 27, 28[2], 30; **2:**1, 7[2], 8[2], 9, 10[2], 11, 12, 13, 14, 15[2], 17[3], 18, 25[3], 26, 27, 28, 29; **3:**3[2], 8[2], 9, 10[2], 13, 15, 17, 18, 19; **4:**1[2], 2, 3[2], 4, 6, 7[2], 8, 9[4], 12[4], 15, 16, 18, 20[2]

Col 1:1, 2[3], 3, 4, 6[2], 9[2], 10, 11, 13, 16[3], 17[2], 18, 20, 21[2], 22[2], 23[3], 24, 26, 28; **2:**1[2], 2[3], 3, 4, 5[2], 7[2], 8[2], 10[2], 13[2], 14, 15[2], 18, 19[3], 22, 23[2]; **3:**3, 5, 10, 11, 12, 13, 14, 15[2],

16^{3}, 17^{2}, 19, 23^{2}, 25; **4**:1, 2, 7^{2}, 8, 9, 10, 11, 12, 13^{2}, 14, 15^{2}, 16^{2}, 17

1Th 1:1^{5}, 3^{3}, 5^{2}, 6^{2}, 7, 8, 9^{2}, 10; **2**:2, 9^{2}, 10^{3}, 11^{2}, 12, 15^{4}, 18, 20; **3**:2^{4}, 4, 5, 6^{3}, 7, 10^{2}, 11^{2}, 12^{3}; **4**:1^{3}, 4, 6^{2}, 10^{2}, 11^{3}, 12, 14, 15, 16^{2}, 17^{2}; **5**:1, 3^{2}, 5, 6, 7, 8^{2}, 11, 12^{3}, 13^{2}, 15, 23^{4}

2Th 1:1^{3}, 2^{2}, 3, 4^{2}, 7, 8, 9, 10, 11^{2}, 12^{2}; **2**:1, 3, 4, 6, 8^{2}, 9^{2}, 10, 11, 13, 15, 16^{3}, 17^{2}; **3**:1, 2^{2}, 3, 4^{2}, 5^{2}, 6, 8^{2}, 12^{2}, 14^{2}

1Ti 1:1, 2^{2}, 4, 5^{2}, 9^{4}, 10, 12, 13^{2}, 14^{2}, 15, 17^{2}, 19, 20; **2**:1, 2^{3}, 3, 4, 5^{2}, 7^{3}, 8, 9, 14, 15^{2}; **3**:7, 10, 12, 13, 15, 16; **4**:1, 3^{2}, 4, 5, 6, 7^{2}, 8, 9, 10, 11, 16^{2}; **5**:1, 4^{2}, 5^{4}, 7, 8^{2}, 13^{3}, 16, 17, 18, 21^{2}, 23, 24, 25; **6**:1, 2^{3}, 3^{2}, 4, 5, 7, 8^{2}, 9^{4}, 10, 11, 12, 13, 15^{2}, 16, 20^{2}

2Ti 1:2^{2}, 3, 5^{2}, 7^{2}, 9^{2}, 10^{2}, 11^{2}, 12, 13, 15, 16, 17, 18; **2**:2, 5, 7, 16, 17^{2}, 18, 19, 20^{4}, 21^{2}, 23, 24, 26; **3**:6, 7, 8, 12, 13^{3}, 14, 15, 16; **4**:1^{3}, 2, 4^{2}, 6, 8, 10, 11, 12, 13, 17^{3}, 18^{3}, 19^{2}, 21^{4}

Tit 1:1^{2}, 4^{2}, 5, 9, 10^{2}, 14, 15^{2}, 16^{2}; **2**:9, 12^{2}, 13^{2}, 14, 15^{2}; **3**:1, 3^{3}, 4, 5, 8^{2}, 9^{4}, 10, 11, 13, 14

Phlm 1^{2}, 2^{3}, 3^{2}, 5^{2}, 7, 9, 11, 16

Heb 1:1, 3^{2}, 5^{2}, 6^{2}, 7^{2}, 8, 9, 10^{2}, 11, 12^{3}; **2**:2^{2}, 3, 4^{3}, 7^{2}, 9, 10, 11, 13^{3}, 14, 15, 17; **3**:1, 5, 6, 9, 10^{2}, 18; **4**:4, 5, 6, 12^{7}, 13, 16; **5**:1, 2, 3, 4, 7^{3}, 9, 11, 12^{2}, 14; **6**:1, 2^{3}, 3, 4^{2}, 5^{2}, 6, 7, 8^{2}, 9, 10^{2}, 11, 12, 14, 15, 16, 19^{2}; **7**:1, 2, 5, 6, 7, 8, 9, 11, 15, 18, 20, 21, 23, 26, 27; **8**:2^{2}, 3, 5, 8, 9, 10^{3}, 11^{2}, 12^{2}, 13; **9**:1, 2^{2}, 3, 4^{3}, 5, 7, 9, 10^{3}, 11, 12, 13^{2}, 15, 19^{5}, 21, 22^{2}, 27, 28; **10**:1, 4, 5, 6, 8^{3}, 11^{2}, 16, 17^{2}, 20, 21, 22, 24^{2}, 25, 27, 29^{2}, 30, 33^{2}, 34^{2}, 37^{2}; **11**:4, 5, 6, 7, 8, 9, 10, 11, 12^{2}, 13^{4}, 15, 17, 20, 21, 22, 23, 28, 32^{6}, 35, 36^{3}, 37, 38^{3}, 39; **12**:1^{2}, 2^{2}, 3, 5, 6, 8, 9^{2}, 12, 13, 14, 15, 18^{3}, 19^{2}, 20, 21^{2}, 22^{2}, 23^{3}, 24^{2}, 27, 28; **13**:3, 4^{2}, 5, 6, 8^{2}, 9, 16, 17^{2}, 21, 22, 24

Jas 1:1, 4, 5^{2}, 6, 11^{2}, 14, 15, 17^{2}, 21^{2}, 22, 23, 24^{2}, 25, 26, 27^{4}; **2**:2, 3^{3}, 4, 5, 6, 9, 10, 12, 13, 14, 15, 16^{2}, 18^{2}, 19, 22, 23^{3}, 24, 25; **3**:2, 3, 4, 5, 6^{3}, 7^{4}, 9, 10, 11, 12, 13, 14^{2}, 16^{2}, 17^{3}, 18; **4**:1, 2^{4}, 3, 4, 7, 8^{2}, 9^{3}, 10, 11^{2}, 12, 13^{4}, 14, 15, 17; **5**:1, 2, 3^{3}, 4, 5, 6^{2}, 7^{2}, 10, 11^{2}, 12, 14, 15^{3}, 16, 17^{3}, 18^{3}, 19, 20

1Pt 1:1, 2^{2}, 3, 4^{2}, 7^{2}, 8, 10, 11, 13, 17, 18, 19, 21^{2}, 23, 24^{2}, 25; **2**:1^{4}, 4, 6, 8^{2}, 11, 14, 16, 18, 20, 25; **3**:3, 4, 6, 7, 10^{2}, 11^{2}, 12, 13, 14^{2}, 15^{2}, 19, 22^{3}; **4**:3, 5, 7, 8, 11^{2}, 14, 17, 18^{2}; **5**:1^{2}, 4, 5^{2}, 11^{2}, 12, 13

2Pt 1:1^{2}, 2^{2}, 3^{2}, 4, 5^{2}, 6^{3}, 7^{2}, 8, 9^{2}, 10, 11, 12, 16, 17, 18, 19; **2**:1, 2, 3^{2}, 4, 5, 6^{2}, 7, 8, 9, 10, 11, 12^{2}, 13^{2}, 14, 15, 20^{2}, 22; **3**:2^{2}, 4, 5^{2}, 7^{2}, 8, 10^{2}, 11, 12^{2}, 13, 14, 15, 16, 18^{3}

1Jn 1:1, 2^{4}, 3^{3}, 4, 5^{2}, 6^{2}, 7, 8, 9^{2}, 10; **2**:1, 2^{2}, 3, 4^{2}, 8^{2}, 9, 10, 11^{2}, 14^{2}, 16^{2}, 17^{2}, 18, 20, 21, 22, 24, 25, 27^{4}, 28^{2}; **3**:2, 3, 5^{2}, 9, 10, 12^{3}, 15, 16, 17^{2}, 18, 19^{2}, 20, 22^{2}, 23^{2}, 24^{3}; **4**:3^{3}, 4, 5, 6, 7^{2}, 10, 12, 13, 14^{2}, 15, 16^{4}, 20, 21; **5**:1, 2, 3, 4, 6^{3}, 7^{2}, 8^{4}, 11^{2}, 12, 13, 14, 15, 16, 17, 18, 19^{2}, 20^{4}

2Jn 1^{2}, 2, 3^{3}, 5, 6, 7, 9^{2}, 10, 12^{2}

3Jn 2, 3, 5, 10^{3}, 12^{3}, 13, 14

Jude 1^{3}, 2^{2}, 3, 4^{2}, 6, 7^{3}, 8, 11^{2}, 14, 15^{2}, 16, 22, 23, 24, 25^{3}

Rev 1:1^{2}, 2^{2}, 3^{2}, 4^{4}, 5^{4}, 6^{5}, 7^{3}, 8^{4}, 9^{4}, 10, 11^{10}, 12^{2}, 13^{2}, 14^{2}, 15^{2}, 16^{3}, 17^{3}, 18^{4}, 19^{2}, 20^{2}; **2**:2^{6}, 3^{4}, 5^{3}, 8^{3}, 9^{4}, 10^{2}, 12, 13^{3}, 14, 16, 17^{2}, 18^{2}, 19^{6}, 20^{2}, 21^{2}, 22, 23^{4}, 24^{2}, 26^{2}, 27, 28; **3**:1^{3}, 2, 3^{4}, 4, 5^{2}, 7^{4}, 8^{3}, 9^{3}, 12^{4}, 14^{2}, 16, 17^{7}, 18^{3}, 19^{2}, 20^{4}, 21; **4**:1^{3}, 2^{3}, 3^{3}, 4^{5}, 5^{4}, 6^{4}, 7^{4}, 8^{6}, 9^{4}, 10^{4}, 11^{4}; **5**:1^{2}, 2^{2}, 3, 4^{2}, 5^{2}, 6^{5}, 7^{2}, 8^{4}, 9^{6}, 10^{3}, 11^{6}, 12^{6}, 13^{10}, 14^{5}; **6**:1^{3}, 2^{6}, 3^{2}, 4^{4}, 5^{5}, 6^{4}, 7^{2}, 8^{8}, 9^{2}, 10^{3}, 11^{3}, 12^{4}, 13, 14^{3}, 15^{8}, 16^{4}, 17; **7**:1, 2^{3}, 4^{4}, 9^{6}, 10^{2}, 11^{5}, 12^{7}, 13^{2}, 14^{4}, 15^{3}, 17^{2}; **8**:1, 2^{2}, 3^{3}, 4, 5^{7}, 6, 7^{5}, 8^{3}, 9^{3}, 10^{4}, 11^{3}, 12^{6}, 13^{2}; **9**:1^{3}, 2^{4}, 3^{2}, 4, 5^{2}, 6^{4}, 7^{3}, 8^{2}, 9^{2}, 10^{3}, 11, 12, 13^{2}, 15^{4}, 16^{2}, 17^{8}, 18^{2}, 19^{3}, 20^{6}; **10**:1^{4}, 2^{3}, 3^{2}, 4^{3}, 5^{2}, 6^{7}, 8^{4}, 9^{5}, 10^{4}, 11^{4}; **11**:1^{5}, 2^{3}, 3^{3}, 4, 5^{3}, 6^{2}, 7^{3}, 8^{2}, 9^{6}, 10^{3}, 11^{4}, 12^{3}, 13^{5}, 14, 15^{5}, 16^{3}, 17^{3}, 18^{8}, 19^{7}; **12**:1^{3}, 2^{2}, 3^{4}, 4^{3}, 5^{3}, 6^{2}, 7^{4}, 8, 9^{3}, 10^{5}, 11^{3}, 12^{2}, 13, 14^{3}, 15, 16^{3}, 17^{3}; **13**:1^{5}, 2^{6}, 3^{3}, 4^{2}, 5^{4}, 6^{3}, 7^{5}, 8, 10, 11^{3}, 12^{3}, 13, 14^{2}, 15^{2}, 16^{4}, 17, 18^{2}; **14**:1^{4}, 2^{3}, 3^{6}, 4, 5, 6^{5}, 7^{5}, 8, 9^{3}, 10^{3}, 11^{5}, 12, 13^{2}, 14^{4}, 15^{2}, 16^{2}, 17, 18^{3}, 19^{3}, 20^{3}; **15**:1^{2}, 2^{5}, 3^{4}, 4^{2}, 5^{2}, 6^{3}, 7^{2}, 8^{3}; **16**:1^{2}, 2^{5}, 3^{3}, 4^{3}, 5^{3}, 6^{2}, 7^{2}, 8^{2}, 9^{3}, 10^{3}, 11^{3}, 12^{2}, 13^{3}, 14, 15^{2}, 16, 17^{2}, 18^{5}, 19^{3}, 20^{2}, 21^{2}; **17**:1^{2}, 2, 3^{2}, 4^{6}, 5^{2}, 6^{3}, 7^{3}, 8^{6}, 9, 10^{4}, 11^{4}, 12, 13^{2}, 14^{5}, 15^{4}, 16^{5}, 17^{2}, 18; **18**:1^{2}, 2^{5}, 3^{2}, 4^{2}, 5, 6, 7^{4}, 8^{3}, 9^{3}, 11^{2}, 12^{13}, 13^{14}, 14^{4}, 15, 16^{6}, 17^{4}, 18, 19^{3}, 20^{2}, 21^{3}, 22^{6}, 23^{3}, 24^{3}; **19**:1^{4}, 2^{2}, 3^{3}, 4^{4}, 5^{3}, 6^{3}, 7^{3}, 8^{2}, 9^{2}, 10^{3}, 11^{6}, 12^{2}, 13^{2}, 14^{2}, 15^{4}, 16^{3}, 17^{3}, 18^{7}, 19^{4}, 20^{3}, 21^{2}; **20**:1^{2}, 2^{3}, 3^{4}, 4^{8}, 6^{3}, 7, 8^{2}, 9^{5}, 10^{6}, 11^{4}, 12^{5}, 13^{4}, 14^{2}, 15; **21**:1^{4}, 2, 3^{5}, 4^{2}, 5^{3}, 6^{3}, 7^{2}, 8^{8}, 9^{2}, 10^{3}, 11, 12^{5}, 13, 14^{2}, 15^{3}, 16^{5}, 17^{3}, 18^{2}, 19, 21^{2}, 22^{2}, 23^{2}, 24^{3}, 25, 26^{2}, 27; **22**:1^{2}, 2^{3}, 3^{3}, 4^{2}, 5^{4}, 6^{3}, 8^{4}, 9^{2}, 10, 11^{3}, 12^{2}, 13^{3}, 14, 15^{6}, 16^{3}, 17^{5}, 19^{3}

ANY

Gen 3:1; **4**:15; **8**:12, 21^{2}; **9**:11^{2}; **14**:23; **17**:5, 12; **18**:14; **19**:12, 22; **22**:12; **24**:16; **30**:31; **31**:14; **35**:10; **36**:31; **39**:9, 23; **42**:16; **43**:34; **47**:6

Ex 1:10; **8**:29; **9**:29; **10**:15, 23; **11**:6, 7; **12**:39; **16**:24; **20**:4^{3}, 10, 17; **21**:23; **22**:9, 10, 20, 22, 23, 25, 31; **24**:14^{2}; **30**:32, 33^{2}; **31**:14, 15; **32**:24; **34**:3, 10, 24; **35**:24, 33, 35; **36**:6

Lev 1:2; **2**:1, 11^{2}; **4**:2^{2}, 13, 22, 27^{2}; **5**:2, 11, 17; **6**:3, 7, 27, 30; **7**:8, 15, 18, 19, 21^{3}, 24, 26, 27; **11**:10, 32^{3}, 33, 35, 37^{2}, 38^{2}, 39, 43, 44; **13**:24, 48, 49, 51, 52, 53, 57, 59; **15**:2, 6, 10^{2}, 16, 22, 23, 24; **17**:10, 12, 13; **18**:6, 21, 23^{2}, 24, 26^{3}, 29, 30; **19**:17, 18, 26, 28^{2}; **20**:2, 4, 16, 25; **21**:5, 9, 11, 17, 18; **22**:4, 5, 6, 11, 23, 24, 25; **23**:22, 30; **24**:17; **25**:25, 32, 49; **26**:1; **27**:9, 11, 19, 20

Nu 4:15; **5**:6, 10, 12; **6**:3, 9; **9**:10, 12; **14**:23; **15**:27; **17**:13; **18**:5, 20; **19**:11, 13; **20**:5, 19; **21**:5, 9; **22**:38^{2}; **23**:23; **29**:7; **30**:5, 15; **31**:19^{2}; **35**:11, 15, 22, 23, 26, 30^{2}; **36**:3, 8

Dt 2:19, 37; **4**:16, 17^{2}, 18^{2}, 23, 25, 32; **5**:8^{3}, 14^{2}, 21, 25; **7**:7; **8**:9; **12**:17; **13**:11; **14**:1, 3, 21; **15**:7, 21^{2}; **16**:4, 5, 21, 22; **17**:1^{2}, 2, 3, 15; **18**:6, 10, 16; **19**:11, 15^{3}, 16, 20; **21**:23; **22**:1, 6, 7, 8, 13; **23**:10, 18, 19, 24; **24**:5, 7, 10, 13; **26**:14; **27**:5, 15, 21; **28**:14, 55; **29**:23; **30**:4; **31**:13; **32**:28, 39

Jos 1:5; **2**:11^{2}, 19; **5**:1, 12; **6**:10^{2}, 18; **7**:12; **8**:31; **10**:21; **11**:11, 14; **13**:33; **20**:3, 9; **21**:45; **23**:12, 13

Jdg 2:14, 21; **4**:20^{2}; **11**:25; **13**:4, 7, 14^{2}; **16**:17; **18**:7^{2}, 10, 28; **19**:19; **20**:8^{2}; **21**:1, 12

Ru 1:11; **2**:22

1Sa 2:2, 13, 16; **3**:17; **5**:5; **6**:3; **9**:2; **10**:23; **12**:3, 4; **13**:22; **14**:24^{2}, 28, 52^{2}; **18**:25; **20**:12, 26, 39; **21**:2; **22**:15; **25**:15, 22, 34; **27**:1^{2}; **30**:2, 12, 19

2Sa 2:1, 28; **7**:6, 7, 10, 22; **9**:1, 3; **10**:19; **13**:2; **14**:10, 11, 14, 32; **15**:2, 4, 5, 11; **19**:22, 28, 29, 35, 42; **21**:4, 5

1Ki 1:6; **2**:36, 42; **3**:12, 13; **5**:6; **6**:7; **8**:31, 38; **10**:3, 20; **11**:22; **15**:5, 17, 29; **18**:26, 29^{2}; **20**:33, 39

2Ki 2:21; **4**:2, 29^{2}; **6**:33; **10**:5, 14, 24; **12**:4, 5, 13; **14**:26^{3}; **18**:5, 33; **21**:8; **23**:25; **24**:7

1Ch 1:43; **17**:6, 9, 20; **19**:19; **23**:26; **26**:28; **27**:1; **28**:21; **29**:25

2Ch 1:12; **2**:14; **6**:5, 29; **8**:15; **9**:9, 19, 20; **23**:19; **32**:13, 15; **33**:8; **34**:13

Ezr 1:4; **7**:24

Neh 2:12^{2}; **5**:16; **10**:31

Job 4:20; **5**:1, 4; **6**:6; **7**:10; **8**:12; **9**:33; **10**:22; **15**:11; **16**:17; **18**:19; **20**:9; **21**:22; **22**:3; **25**:3; **31**:7, 19^{2}; **32**:21; **33**:13, 27, 32; **34**:27, 31; **36**:5, 29; **37**:24

Ps 4:6; **14**:2; **33**:17; **34**:10; **37**:8; **38**:3; **49**:7; **53**:2; **59**:5; **74**:9^{2}; **81**:9; **86**:8; **91**:10; **109**:12; **115**:17; **119**:133; **135**:17; **139**:24; **141**:4; **146**:2; **147**:20

Prv 1:17; **6**:35; **14**:34; **28**:17; **30**:2, 30; **31**:5

Ecc 1:10, 11; **2**:10; **3**:14; **5**:2; **6**:5; **9**:5^{2}, 6^{2}

Isa 1:5; **2**:4, 7^{2}; **19**:15; **26**:18; **27**:3; **30**:20; **33**:20; **35**:9; **36**:18; **44**:8; **51**:18; **52**:14; **53**:9; **54**:4; **56**:2; **59**:4; **62**:4

Jer 3:16, 17; **5**:1; **9**:4; **10**:20; **14**:22; **17**:22; **18**:18; **20**:9; **22**:11, 30; **23**:24; **31**:12, 40; **32**:27; **33**:26; **34**:10; **35**:7; **36**:24; **37**:17; **38**:5; **42**:21; **44**:26; **48**:9; **49**:33; **50**:40; **51**:43, 44

Lam 1:12; **3**:49

Ezk 5:9, 11; **7**:11, 13; **9**:6; **12**:24, 28; **14**:11; **15**:2, 3^{2}, 4, 5; **16**:5, 41, 63; **18**:3, 7, 8, 10, 11, 16, 23; **21**:5; **23**:27; **24**:13; **27**:36; **28**:19, 24; **29**:15; **31**:8; **32**:13; **33**:6; **34**:10, 29; **36**:14, 15^{3}; **37**:22, 23^{2}; **39**:7, 10, 15, 28, 29; **44**:9, 13, 18, 21, 31; **46**:16

Dan 2:10, 30^{2}; **3**:28, 29; **6**:4, 5, 7, 12; **8**:4; **11**:15, 37

Hos 13:10; **14**:3, 8

Joel 2:2; **3**:17

Am 6:10; **7**:8, 13; **8**:2, 7

Oba 18

Jna 3:7

Mic 4:3

Zep 3:15

Hag 2:12, 13

Zec 8:10^{2}; **9**:8; **13**:3

Mal 2:13

Mt 4:6; **5**:25, 40; **10**:5; **11**:27; **12**:19; **13**:15, 19; **16**:24; **18**:19; **21**:3; **22**:16, 46^{2}; **24**:17, 23

Mk 1:44; **4**:12, 22, 23; **5**:4, 35; **7**:16; **8**:26; **9**:8, 22, 30, 35; **11**:3, 13, 16^{2}, 25; **12**:21, 34; **13**:5, 15, 21; **14**:31, 63; **15**:44; **16**:8^{2}, 18

Lk 3:14; **4**:11, 40; **8**:17, 27, 43; **9**:23, 36; **10**:19; **11**:11; **14**:8, 26; **15**:29; **19**:8^{2}, 31; **20**:21, 27, 28, 36, 40; **21**:34; **22**:16, 35, 71; **24**:41

Jn 1:3, 18, 46; **2**:25; **4**:33; **5**:37; **6**:46, 51; **7**:4, 17, 37, 48, 51; **8**:33; **9**:22, 31, 32; **10**:9, 28; **11**:9, 57; **12**:26^{2}, 47; **14**:14; **16**:30; **18**:31; **21**:5

Act 4:12, 32, 34; **9**:2; **10**:14, 28, 47; **11**:8; **13**:15; **17**:25; **19**:2, 38, 39; **24**:12, 20; **25**:5, 8, 11, 16, 17, 24; **27**:12, 22, 34, 42; **28**:21^{2}

Ro 1:10; **6**:2; **8**:9, 33, 39; **9**:11; **11**:14; **13**:8, 9; **14**:13, 14, 21; **15**:18

1Co 1:15, 16; **2**:2; **3**:7, 12, 14, 15, 17, 18; **5**:11; **6**:1, 12; **7**:12, 18^{2}, 36; **8**:2^{2}, 3, 9, 10; **9**:7, 15, 27; **10**:19^{2}, 27, 28; **11**:16, 34; **14**:27, 30, 35, 37, 38; **16**:22

2Co 1:4; **2**:5, 10^{2}; **3**:5; **5**:17; **6**:3; **7**:14; **8**:23; **10**:7; **11**:3, 21; **12**:6, 17

Gal 1:8, 9^{2}; **2**:2; **5**:6; **6**:15

Eph 2:9; **5**:5, 27; **6**:8

Php 2:1^{4}; **3**:4, 11, 15; **4**:8^{2}

Col 2:4, 8, 23; **3**:13^{2}

1Th 1:8; **2**:5, 9; **4**:6; **5**:15

2Th 2:3; **3**:8^{2}, 10, 14

1Ti 1:10; **5**:4, 8, 16; **6**:3

Tit 1:6

Heb 1:5, 13; **2**:1; **3**:12, 13; **4**:1, 11, 12, 13; **10**:38; **12**:15^{2}, 16, 19

Jas 1:5, 7, 13, 23, 26; **3**:2; **5**:12, 13^{2}, 14, 19

1Pt 3:1, 6; **4**:11^{2}, 16

2Pt 1:20; **3**:9

1Jn 2:1, 15, 27; **4**:12; **5**:14, 16

2Jn 10

Rev 3:20; **7**:1, 16^{2}; **9**:4^{2}; **11**:5^{2}; **12**:8; **13**:9; **14**:9; **18**:11, 22; **21**:4, 27; **22**:18, 19

ARE

Gen 2:4; **6**:9; **7**:2, 8; **9**:2, 19; **10**:1, 20, 31, 32; **11**:10, 27; **18**:5, 24; **19**:5, 15; **20**:7, 16; **25**:7, 12, 13, 16^{2}, 17, 19, 23; **27**:22, 41, 46; **29**:4, 21; **31**:12, 15, 43^{3}, 49; **32**:17; **33**:5, 8, 13^{2}, 15; **34**:21, 22; **35**:2, 26; **36**:1, 5, 9, 10, 13, 16, 17^{3}, 18, 19^{2}, 20, 21, 24, 26, 27, 28, 29, 30, 31, 40; **37**:2, 17; **38**:25^{2}; **40**:12, 18; **41**:26^{2}, 27; **42**:9^{2}, 10, 11^{3}, 12, 13, 14, 16, 21, 31^{2}, 33, 34^{2}, 36; **43**:18; **44**:16; **45**:6, 11, 16; **46**:8, 18, 22, 25, 31, 32; **47**:1^{2}, 3, 4, 5, 9; **48**:5, 8, 9; **49**:5^{2}, 28; **50**:3^{2}

Ex 1:1, 9, 19^{3}; **2**:18; **3**:7; **4**:18, 19; **5**:5, 16, 17^{2}; **6**:15, 16, 19, 24, 25, 26, 27^{2}; **7**:17; **8**:21; **9**:27; **10**:8, 11; **12**:13; **14**:3; **15**:4; **16**:7, 8^{2}, 16; **19**:6; **21**:1; **24**:14; **25**:22, 26; **28**:3, 4, 24; **29**:33; **30**:13, 14; **31**:6; **32**:2, 22; **33**:5, 16; **35**:1; **39**:6; **40**:4

Lev 4:12^{2}, 13; **5**:17; **10**:14; **11**:2^{2}, 8, 9, 13^{2}, 26, 27, 28, 31, 32, 35, 42; **12**:6; **14**:37; **16**:4; **18**:17, 24; **23**:2, 4, 17, 37, 42; **25**:7, 23, 33, 42, 44, 45, 55^{2}; **26**:25, 36, 39, 46; **27**:34

Nu 1:3, 5, 17, 44; **2**:32; **3**:1, 2, 3, 9, 13, 18, 20, 21, 27, 33, 46^{2}; **4**:15, 20, 41; **6**:13; **8**:16, 17; **9**:7^{2}; **10**:4, 29, 31; **11**:21; **13**:16, 28, 30, 31, 32; **14**:9, 35, 43^{2}; **15**:13, 15; **16**:3, 5, 11, 37, 38; **18**:6, 16, 17, 18; **20**:16; **22**:4, 6, 9, 12; **24**:3, 5, 6, 15; **26**:2, 7, 14, 18, 22, 25, 27, 30, 34, 35, 36, 37^{2}, 41, 42^{2}, 47, 50, 57, 58, 63; **27**:1; **30**:14, 16; **31**:12, 49; **32**:14; **33**:1, 2, 51; **34**:17, 19, 29; **35**:33; **36**:3, 4, 13

Dt 1:2, 10, 11, 20, 28; **2**:4, 25; **3**:18; **4**:4, 20, 30, 32, 45; **5**:3; **6**:1, 14; **7**:6, 17, 20; **8**:9; **9**:12, 29; **11**:12, 30; **12**:1, 9; **13**:7, 13; **14**:1, 2, 4, 7, 9, 12, 29; **16**:11, 14; **17**:14; **18**:12; **20**:2, 15^{2}; **21**:2, 6; **22**:5, 17; **23**:8, 18; **24**:14; **25**:16; **27**:12; **28**:58; **29**:1, 5,

APNDX

20, 21, 27, 29; 30:1, 10; 31:17, 18, 21; 32:4, 5, 20, 21, 28, 32^{2}, 37; 33:3, 17^{3}, 27

Jos 2:3^{2}; 3:8; 4:9; 6:17^{2}, 19; 7:3, 21; 8:5; 9:8^{2}, 9, 11, 13, 22, 23, 25; 10:6, 17; 12:1, 7; 13:14, 17, 30, 32; 14:1; 15:32; 16:3; 17:3, 9, 16^{2}; 18:3; 19:14, 29, 35, 51; 21:9; 22:10, 17; 23:14, 15; 24:22^{2}, 23

Jdg 3:1; 5:11; 6:2; 7:2^{2}, 4, 18; 8:6, 15^{2}; 9:2, 18; 10:4^{2}; 11:7^{2}; 12:3, 4; 15:10^{2}, 11, 12; 18:9, 24; 19:18; 20:7, 13, 32, 39; 21:16

Ru 1:11; 4:9, 10, 11, 18

1Sa 2:3, 4^{2}, 8; 4:8, 17; 6:17; 9:20; 10:2, 7; 12:2, 21; 16:11, 16; 17:8; 19:22; 20:21, 22; 21:5; 26:16; 29:10

2Sa 1:4^{3}, 19, 25, 27; 3:28; 5:1, 8; 7:9; 11:11; 13:33; 14:14, 20; 15:3, 13, 15; 16:4, 21; 17:2, 10, 12, 16; 19:11, 12^{3}; 20:19; 22:28, 39; 24:14

1Ki 1:20, 45; 4:8, 13; 8:8; 9:13; 10:8^{2}, 27; 11:41; 13:3, 32; 14:19, 29; 15:7, 23, 31; 16:5, 14, 20, 27; 18:22, 25; 20:3, 17, 23, 31; 22:39, 45

2Ki 1:5, 18; 3:23; 5:12; 6:9, 16; 7:12, 13^{5}; 8:23; 9:22; 10:2^{2}, 5, 13^{2}, 34; 12:19; 13:8, 12; 14:15, 18, 28; 15:6, 11, 15, 21, 26, 31, 36; 16:19; 18:20, 26, 34^{2}, 35; 19:3, 4; 20:14, 15, 20; 21:17, 25; 23:28; 24:5

1Ch 1:29, 31, 33, 43, 54; 2:1, 18, 55; 4:2, 4, 12, 18, 22; 5:14; 6:19, 31, 33, 50, 54, 65; 7:8, 33; 8:6^{2}, 38, 40; 9:33, 44; 11:1, 10; 12:1, 15, 18, 23; 13:2^{2}; 14:4; 15:12; 16:14, 26, 27^{2}; 17:8; 19:3; 21:3, 13; 22:15; 24:1; 26:19; 29:15^{2}, 17, 29

2Ch 1:15; 2:7; 3:3; 6:37; 7:14; 8:11; 9:7^{2}, 27, 29; 11:10; 12:15; 13:7, 8, 9, 10, 22; 16:11; 17:14; 19:3; 20:12, 34; 23:6; 24:26, 27; 25:26; 26:18; 27:7; 28:10, 26; 29:9, 19; 30:6; 32:32; 33:18, 19; 34:21, 24, 31; 35:25, 27; 36:8

Ezr 2:1; 4:10, 12; 5:4, 11; 6:6, 9; 7:13, 19, 21, 25; 8:1, 13, 28^{3}; 9:6, 15; 10:3, 13^{3}

Neh 1:3^{3}, 10; 2:3, 17^{2}; 4:2, 4, 10, 19; 5:2, 5, 17; 6:8; 7:6; 9:6, 36^{2}, 37; 10:39; 11:3, 7; 12:1

Est 1:16; 3:8; 4:16; 7:4; 8:5, 9; 9:13; 10:2

Job 1:19; 3:8, 19, 22, 24; 4:9, 10, 11, 19, 20; 5:4^{2}; 6:3, 4, 7, 16, 17, 18, 21^{2}, 25, 26; 7:1, 3, 6^{2}, 8, 16; 8:9^{2}, 13, 17; 9:25, 26; 10:5^{2}, 17, 20; 11:6; 12:2, 6, 16; 13:4^{2}, 12, 23; 14:5^{2}, 21; 15:10, 11, 15, 28; 16:2, 22; 17:1^{2}, 2, 7, 11^{2}; 18:3, 21; 19:3, 13, 19, 22; 20:11, 25; 21:7, 9, 18, 22, 24^{2}, 28, 33; 22:10, 12, 14, 19, 29; 23:14; 24:1, 8, 13, 17, 23, 24^{3}; 25:2, 5; 26:5, 11, 14; 27:12; 28:4^{2}, 6; 30:1, 15, 17, 30; 31:40; 32:6, 9; 34:18, 19, 21, 25; 35:5; 36:7^{2}, 20; 37:17, 24; 38:6, 30, 35; 39:4, 30; 40:17, 18^{2}; 41:14, 15, 17, 18, 23^{2}, 25, 28, 29, 30

Ps 1:4^{2}; 2:12; 3:1^{2}; 6:2; 9:3, 6, 15; 10:5^{2}, 8, 16; 12:4, 6, 8; 14:1, 3^{2}; 16:3, 6, 11; 17:2, 10, 14^{2}; 18:38; 19:8, 9, 10; 20:8^{2}; 21:11; 22:14; 25:10, 15, 17, 19; 27:12; 31:10, 15; 32:11; 33:4; 34:15^{2}, 18, 19; 35:19, 20; 36:3, 6, 12^{2}; 37:23, 28, 34; 38:4^{2}, 5, 7, 14, 19^{3}, 20; 39:6; 40:5^{3}, 12; 42:7; 44:13, 22^{2}; 45:5; 47:9; 49:14; 50:11; 51:17; 53:1, 3; 54:3; 55:4, 5, 10; 56:5, 8, 12; 57:4^{2}, 6; 58:3, 4; 59:3, 7; 62:9^{3}; 65:5, 8, 13^{2}; 68:6, 17; 69:1, 4^{2}, 5, 9, 19; 71:13, 24^{2}; 72:20; 73:1, 4, 5^{2}, 8, 10, 12, 19^{2}, 27; 74:20; 75:3; 76:5, 6; 77:19; 79:1, 4^{2}, 8, 11; 82:5, 6^{2}; 83:5; 84:1, 4, 5; 85:10; 86:8, 14; 87:3, 7; 88:5; 89:7, 11, 14, 49; 90:4, 5^{2}, 7^{2}, 9, 10; 92:5^{2}; 93:5; 94:11; 95:4, 7; 96:5, 6^{2}; 97:2^{2}; 100:3; 102:3^{2}, 8^{2}, 11, 20, 22, 24, 25; 103:6, 14, 15; 104:16, 17, 18, 24, 25, 28, 29, 30; 105:7; 106:3; 107:17, 27, 29, 30, 38, 39; 109:2, 4, 24; 111:2, 7^{2}, 8; 113:6; 115:4, 8, 15, 16; 116:11; 118:12; 119:1, 2, 21, 24, 39, 75, 84, 85, 86, 91, 98, 99, 103, 111, 129, 137, 138, 143, 150, 151, 156, 157, 168, 172; 120:7; 122:5; 123:3, 4; 124:7; 125:2, 4; 126:3; 127:3, 4^{2}; 135:15, 18; 139:12, 14, 17, 18; 140:2; 141:6^{2}, 7, 8; 142:6; 144:4; 145:9; 146:8

Prv 1:19; 2:15; 3:15, 17^{2}, 20; 4:22, 23; 5:6, 11, 21; 6:16, 23; 8:8, 9, 11, 18, 32; 9:17, 18^{2}; 10:6; 11:20^{4}; 12:5^{2}, 6, 7^{2}, 10, 22^{2}; 13:8; 14:4, 12, 18; 15:3, 11, 15, 22^{2}, 26^{2}; 16:2, 11^{2}, 13, 24, 25; 17:6^{2}, 15, 24; 18:4, 7, 8, 19, 21; 19:7, 13, 14, 21, 29; 20:7, 10, 15, 23, 24; 22:3, 4, 5, 26; 23:3; 24:11^{2}, 21; 25:1; 26:7, 21, 22, 23, 25, 28; 27:6^{2}, 12, 15, 20^{2}, 24, 25, 26^{2}; 28:1, 2; 29:2, 12, 16; 30:12, 13^{2}, 14, 15^{2}, 18, 24^{2}, 25, 26, 29; 31:8, 21, 25

Ecc 1:8, 11, 13, 14; 2:14, 23; 3:18, 20; 4:1, 2^{2}, 9; 5:7, 11; 7:19, 21; 8:8, 13; 9:1, 3, 12^{3}, 16, 17; 10:12; 11:10; 12:3, 11^{2}

Song 1:10, 17; 3:7; 4:2^{2}, 3^{2}, 5^{2}, 11, 13; 5:11, 12, 13, 14, 15; 6:6, 7, 8; 7:1^{2}, 3^{2}, 9, 13; 8:6

Isa 1:4^{2}, 7, 14, 15, 23; 2:6, 13, 14; 3:8, 12, 16; 4:2; 5:12, 13^{2}, 21, 22, 28; 7:2; 8:18; 9:10^{2}, 16^{2}; 10:8, 14, 20, 29; 14:19; 16:4, 7, 8^{3}; 17:2; 19:11, 12^{2}, 13^{3}; 21:3; 22:2, 3^{4}, 9; 23:8^{2}; 24:6^{2}, 17, 18, 21, 22; 25:1; 26:9, 14^{2}; 27:7, 9, 11; 28:1^{2}, 7^{3}, 8, 9, 15, 27^{2}; 29:9, 15, 20; 30:18, 27; 31:1^{2}, 3; 32:7, 9, 11, 20; 33:13^{2}, 14, 23; 35:4; 36:5, 11, 19^{2}, 20; 37:3; 39:3; 40:11, 15^{2}, 17^{2}, 22; 41:23^{2}, 24, 29^{3}; 42:9, 17, 22^{3}; 43:10, 12, 17^{2}; 44:7, 8, 9^{2}, 11; 45:16, 19, 20, 24; 46:1, 2, 3^{2}, 10, 12; 48:1^{2}, 7; 49:9, 16; 51:1^{2}, 19, 20; 52:7; 53:5; 54:1; 55:8^{2}, 9^{2}; 56:8, 10^{3}, 11^{2}; 57:1, 4, 6, 20; 58:7; 59:3, 6, 7^{2}, 10, 12^{2}; 60:8; 61:1, 9, 11; 63:8, 15, 19; 64:6^{2}, 8^{2}, 9, 10, 11; 65:5, 11, 16^{2}, 22, 23, 24

Jer 2:5^{2}, 11, 15, 28^{2}, 31; 4:13^{2}, 17, 20, 22^{2}; 5:3, 4^{2}, 6^{2}, 7, 10, 16, 23, 26, 27^{2}, 28; 6:4, 20, 23, 28^{3}, 29^{2}; 7:4, 10; 8:8, 9^{2}, 16, 20; 9:3, 10^{3}, 19^{2}, 25, 26^{3}; 10:2, 3, 5, 8, 9, 15, 20^{3}, 21; 11:10, 16; 12:1, 4, 9, 12; 13:22, 23; 14:2, 7, 9, 18, 22; 15:2^{4}, 8; 16:3, 17^{2}, 20; 18:6; 21:4, 7; 22:6, 17, 20, 28^{2}; 23:10, 11, 14, 26; 24:2, 3, 5, 8; 25:12, 22, 23, 26, 31, 34, 37; 27:5, 18; 29:1, 4, 16, 17, 22, 25; 30:4, 6; 31:20, 29; 32:19, 24, 35; 33:4, 10; 34:21; 35:14; 37:19; 38:19, 22^{3}; 40:15; 41:12; 42:2, 11; 43:11^{3}; 44:2, 6, 10, 14, 24, 27, 28; 46:5^{2}, 7, 8, 12, 15, 21^{3}, 23^{2}; 48:14, 15, 17, 32, 36, 41, 46; 49:23, 32; 50:2^{2}, 11, 15^{2}, 37, 38, 42; 51:4, 7, 18, 30, 32^{2}, 43, 51^{2}, 56, 60, 64

Lam 1:2^{2}, 4^{2}, 5^{2}, 6^{2}, 14, 16, 18, 20, 21, 22; 2:9^{2}, 11, 21; 3:22, 23; 4:1, 2, 5, 8, 9, 18, 19; 5:3^{2}, 5, 7, 12, 17

Ezk 2:4, 5, 7; 3:7, 26, 27; 5:2, 5, 6, 7^{2}, 14, 15; 7:9; 11:2, 7, 12, 15; 12:2, 10, 14, 20, 22, 23, 27; 13:4; 14:5; 16:7, 27, 38, 52, 57; 18:2, 4, 25, 29^{2}; 20:3, 30, 34; 21:14, 24^{2}, 29; 22:9, 18^{2}, 19, 27; 23:45; 24:19; 25:9; 26:6, 18, 19; 27:4, 27; 28:8, 24, 25; 29:12^{2}; 30:7^{2}; 31:12^{3}, 14; 32:20, 21, 22, 23, 24, 25, 26, 27^{2}, 28, 29, 30^{2}, 32; 33:24, 27, 30; 34:3, 12, 30, 31; 35:8, 12^{2}; 36:2, 3^{2}, 4^{2}, 7, 8, 20^{2}, 35^{2}, 36; 37:11^{3}; 38:7, 11, 12^{2}, 20, 22; 40:46; 42:13, 14^{2}; 43:13, 18, 27; 44:10; 45:14; 46:24; 48:1^{2}, 11, 15, 29, 30

Dan 1:10; 2:20, 28; 3:12, 16; 4:3^{2}, 18, 35, 37; 5:23; 7:17^{2}, 24; 8:20, 23; 9:7^{2}, 16^{2}, 19, 24, 26; 10:16; 12:9

Hos 1:9, 10^{2}; 2:12; 4:4, 6, 14; 5:2; 6:5; 7:2, 4, 7^{2}, 9, 16; 8:9; 9:6, 7^{2}, 15; 11:7, 8; 12:7, 11^{2}; 14:3, 9

Joel 1:6, 7, 12, 17^{2}, 18^{2}, 20

Am 4:1; 5:16; 6:1^{2}, 6; 9:7, 8, 12

Oba 6^{2}

Jna 4:11

Mic 1:4, 5^{2}, 16; 2:7, 13; 4:11; 6:10, 12, 16; 7:6, 11

Nah 1:3, 6, 10; 2:3; 3:13, 17^{2}

Hab 1:3^{2}, 6, 7, 8^{2}, 15; 3:6

Zep 1:6, 8, 11^{2}, 12; 3:3^{2}, 4, 6^{2}, 18^{2}

Hag 1:6

Zec 1:5, 9, 10, 15, 19, 21^{2}; 3:8; 4:2, 4, 10, 11, 14; 6:4, 5, 6, 10, 15; 8:16, 17; 11:2; 13:6

Mal 1:4; 2:8; 3:6, 7, 9, 15^{2}

Mt 1:17^{3}; 2:2, 18, 20; 5:3, 4, 5, 6, 7, 8, 9, 10^{2}, 11, 13, 14, 15; 6:5, 26; 7:15; 8:26; 9:12, 17, 37; 10:2, 28, 29, 30, 31; 11:5^{2}, 8, 11, 27, 28; 12:5, 48; 13:15, 16, 38^{2}, 39, 40, 56; 15:16, 20; 17:26; 18:20; 19:6, 12^{2}, 26, 30; 20:22^{2}, 25; 22:4^{3}, 14^{2}, 21^{2}, 30^{2}; 23:8, 13, 25, 27^{2}, 28, 31, 37; 24:8, 19; 25:8; 26:55

Mk 2:17^{2}; 4:11^{2}, 15, 16^{2}, 17, 18^{2}, 20^{2}, 40; 5:9; 6:2, 3; 7:15, 18; 9:23; 10:8, 27, 31, 42; 12:17^{2}, 25^{3}; 13:1, 8, 17, 25, 32; 14:36, 48

Lk 1:1; 4:18; 5:20, 31^{2}, 38; 6:21^{2}, 22, 24, 25; 7:22^{2}, 25^{2}, 28, 31, 32, 47^{2}, 48; 8:12, 13, 14^{2}, 15, 21; 9:12, 55, 61; 10:2, 8, 9, 17, 20^{2}, 22, 23; 11:7, 21, 28, 41, 44^{2}; 12:6, 7^{2}, 24, 37, 38; 13:14, 23, 25, 27, 30^{2}, 34; 14:17; 16:8, 15; 17:10^{2}, 17, 18; 18:11, 27^{2}, 31; 19:42; 20:34, 35, 36^{2}, 37; 21:21^{3}, 22, 23, 26; 22:10, 25, 28, 38; 23:29^{2}; 24:17^{2}, 18, 38, 44, 48

Jn 3:21; 4:35^{2}, 38; 5:28, 39; 6:9, 49, 58, 63^{2}, 64, 69; 7:7, 23, 47, 49; 8:10, 23^{2}, 31, 37, 44, 47, 53; 9:28, 40; 10:8, 12, 16, 21, 26, 30, 34; 11:9; 13:10, 11, 17, 35; 14:2; 15:3, 5, 6, 14, 19; 16:15, 30; 17:7, 9, 10^{2}, 11^{2}, 14, 16, 22; 20:23^{2}, 29, 30, 31; 21:25

Act 2:7, 13, 15, 32, 39; 3:15, 25; 5:9, 25, 32; 7:1, 26; 10:4, 21, 31, 33^{2}, 39; 13:27, 31, 39; 14:11, 15^{2}; 15:18, 19, 23; 16:17, 21, 28; 17:6, 22, 28, 29; 19:15, 26, 37, 38^{2}, 40; 20:32; 21:20^{2}, 21^{2}, 24; 22:3, 10; 23:15, 21, 35; 24:2, 11, 14; 25:5, 24; 26:3, 18, 26; 28:27

Ro 1:6, 15, 20^{3}, 28, 32; 2:2, 8, 13, 14, 18, 19; 3:9^{2}, 12^{2}, 15, 16, 19, 25; 4:7^{3}, 12, 14; 6:2, 4, 13, 14, 15, 16, 21; 7:4, 6; 8:1, 5^{2}, 8, 9, 12, 14^{2}, 16, 18, 24, 28, 36^{2}, 37; 9:4, 5, 6^{2}, 7^{2}, 8^{3}, 26; 10:15, 19; 11:14, 16, 28^{2}, 29, 33, 36; 12:5; 13:1, 3, 6; 14:8, 20; 15:1, 14, 26, 27; 16:7, 10, 11, 14, 15, 18

1Co 1:2, 5, 11^{2}, 18, 24, 26, 27, 28^{3}, 30; 2:6, 12, 14^{2}; 3:2, 3^{2}, 4, 8, 9^{3}, 16, 17, 20, 21, 22, 23; 4:8^{2}, 9, 10^{6}, 11^{2}, 13^{2}, 18, 19; 5:2, 4, 7, 12^{2}, 13; 6:2, 4, 11^{3}, 12^{3}, 15, 19, 20^{2}; 7:14, 23, 33; 8:4, 5, 6^{2}, 8^{2}, 9, 10; 9:1, 2, 12, 13, 20^{2}, 21^{2}; 10:11^{2}, 13, 17^{2}, 18, 22, 23^{3}; 11:19, 30, 32^{2}; 12:4, 5, 6, 12, 13, 20, 22, 27, 29^{4}; 14:10, 12, 22, 23^{2}, 25, 32, 34, 37; 15:2, 6, 15, 17, 18^{2}, 19, 23, 27, 29^{2}, 35, 40, 48^{4}; 16:9, 18

2Co 1:1, 4^{2}, 7, 14^{2}, 20, 24; 2:11, 15^{2}, 16, 17; 3:2, 3, 5, 18; 4:3, 8^{2}, 11, 15, 18^{6}; 5:4, 6^{3}, 8, 11^{2}, 17^{2}, 18, 20; 6:12^{2}, 16; 7:3, 6; 8:23; 10:4, 7, 10, 11^{3}, 12, 14; 11:13, 19, 22^{3}, 23, 28; 13:4, 6, 9^{3}

Gal 1:2, 6; 2:15, 17; 3:3^{2}, 7^{2}, 9, 10^{3}, 25, 26, 28, 29; 4:6, 8, 9, 12, 24^{2}, 28, 31; 5:4^{2}, 17, 18, 19^{2}, 24; 6:1, 10, 13

Eph 1:1, 10^{2}; 2:5, 8, 10, 11, 13, 19, 20, 22; 4:1, 4, 25, 30; 5:4, 8, 12, 13^{2}, 16, 30; 6:5

Php 1:1, 7, 10, 11, 13, 14; 2:21; 3:3, 13^{2}, 18; 4:3, 8^{6}, 21, 22

Col 1:2, 16^{2}; 2:3, 10, 11, 12, 17, 20, 22; 3:1, 3, 5, 15; 4:5, 9, 11^{2}, 13, 15

1Th 2:10, 14, 15, 19, 20; 3:3; 4:9, 10, 12, 13, 15^{2}, 17; 5:4, 5^{2}, 7, 8, 12, 14

2Th 1:3, 7; 2:13; 3:11^{2}, 12

1Ti 2:2; 3:7; 5:3, 15, 16, 24, 25^{2}; 6:1, 2^{2}, 17

2Ti 1:15^{2}; 2:19, 20, 26; 3:3, 6, 15

Tit 1:5, 10, 12, 15^{2}; 3:8, 9, 15

Phlm 7

Heb 1:10, 14; 2:10^{2}, 11^{2}, 14, 18; 3:6, 14; 4:13, 15; 5:2, 11, 12, 14; 6:9; 7:5, 13; 8:4; 9:15, 17, 22, 24; 10:8, 10, 14, 39; 11:3; 12:1, 8^{2}, 11, 18, 22, 23, 27^{2}; 13:3, 11

Jas 1:1; 2:4^{2}, 7, 9, 16; 3:4^{2}, 9; 5:2^{2}, 4, 17

1Pt 1:5, 6, 12; 2:5, 9, 10, 14, 25; 3:6^{2}, 9, 12^{2}, 14; 4:6, 13, 14; 5:1, 9^{2}, 14

2Pt 1:4; 2:10^{2}, 11, 13, 15, 17^{2}, 19, 20; 3:5, 7^{2}, 10, 16^{2}

1Jn 2:5, 12, 14, 15, 18; 3:2, 10, 19, 22; 4:1^{2}, 4, 5, 6, 17; 5:3, 7^{2}, 8, 19, 20

2Jn 7

Jude 1, 4, 7, 12^{2}, 15, 16

Rev 1:3, 4^{2}, 11, 19, 20^{2}; 2:2^{3}, 9^{3}, 18; 3:2, 4, 9^{2}; 4:5, 11; 5:6, 8, 13^{2}; 7:13^{2}, 14, 15; 8:13; 9:14; 10:6^{3}; 11:4, 15; 13:8; 14:4^{3}, 5, 12, 13, 18; 15:3^{2}, 4; 16:6, 7, 14; 17:9, 10^{2}, 12, 14^{2}, 15; 18:3, 14^{2}; 19:2, 9^{3}; 20:7, 8, 10; 21:4, 5, 12, 16, 22, 24, 27; 22:6, 14, 15, 18, 19

ART

Gen 3:9, 14, 19; 4:6, 11; 12:11, 13; 13:14; 16:11; 17:8; 20:3; 23:6; 24:23, 47, 60; 26:16, 29; 27:18, 24, 32; 28:4; 29:14, 15; 32:17; 39:9; 41:39; 44:18; 45:19; 46:30; 47:8; 49:3, 8, 9

Ex 4:25, 26; 18:18; 30:25, 35; 33:3; 34:10

Lev 27:12

Nu 14:14^{2}; 21:29

Dt 2:18; 4:30, 38; 7:6, 19; 8:10, 12; 9:1, 6; 14:2, 21, 24; 17:14; 18:9; 26:1; 27:3, 9; 28:10; 32:15^{3}, 18; 33:29

Jos 5:13; 13:1; 17:17

Jdg 8:18; 11:2, 12, 25, 35; 12:5; 13:3, 11

Ru 2:9, 11, 12; 3:9^{2}, 11, 16

1Sa 8:5; 10:2, 5; 17:28, 33^{2}, 58; 19:3; 21:1; 24:17; 26:14, 15; 28:12; 29:9; 30:13

2Sa 1:8, 13; 2:20; 7:22, 24, 28; 9:2; 12:7; 13:4; 15:2, 19, 27; 16:8^{2}, 21; 18:3; 19:13; 20:9, 17; 22:29

1Ki 1:42; 2:9, 26; 6:12; 13:14, 18; 17:18, 24; 18:7, 17, 36, 37; 20:36; 22:4

2Ki 1:4, 6, 16; 3:7; 4:4; 19:15, 19

1Ch 17:26; 29:11

2Ch 14:11; 16:14; 18:3; 20:6, 7; 25:16

Ezr 7:14; 9:15

Neh 2:2; 9:6, 7, 8, 17, 31, 33

Est 4:14

Job 4:5; 15:7; 17:14^2; 22:3; 30:21; 31:24; 33:12; 34:18; 35:8

Ps 2:7; 3:3; 5:4; 8:4; 10:14; 16:2; 22:1, 3, 9, 10; 23:4; 25:5; 31:3, 4, 14; 32:7; 40:17; 42:5^2, 11^2; 43:2, 5^2; 44:4; 45:2; 63:1; 65:5; 66:3; 68:35; 70:5; 71:3, 5^2, 6, 7; 76:4, 7^2; 77:14; 83:18; 86:5, 10^2, 15; 89:17, 26; 90:2; 92:8; 93:2; 97:9^2; 102:27; 104:1^2; 110:4; 118:21, 28^2; 119:12, 57, 68, 114, 137, 151; 137:8; 139:3, 8^2; 140:6; 142:5; 143:10

Prv 6:2^2, 3; 7:4; 24:24

Ecc 10:17

Song 1:15^2, 16; 2:14; 4:1^2, 7; 6:4; 7:6

Isa 14:8, 10^2, 12^2, 19, 31; 22:1, 2; 25:1; 26:15; 37:16, 20; 41:8, 9; 43:1; 44:17, 21^2; 45:15; 47:8, 13; 48:4; 49:3; 51:9, 10, 12, 16; 57:8, 10; 63:2, 16^2; 64:5, 8

Jer 2:21, 23, 27; 3:4, 22; 4:30; 10:6; 12:1, 2; 14:9, 22; 15:6; 17:14, 17; 20:7; 22:6; 31:18; 39:17; 49:12; 50:24^2; 51:20

Lam 5:22

Ezk 3:5; 16:7, 34, 45^2, 54; 22:4^2, 5, 24; 23:30; 26:17; 27:3^2; 28:2, 3, 14; 31:2, 18; 32:2^2; 33:32; 38:13, 17; 40:4

Dan 2:26, 37, 38; 4:18, 22; 5:13^2, 27^2; 9:23

Hos 2:23^2

Oba 2, 5

Jna 1:8; 4:2

Mic 2:7

Nah 1:14; 3:8

Hab 1:12, 13; 2:16

Zec 4:7

Mt 2:6; 5:25; 6:9; 8:29; 11:3, 23; 14:33; 16:14, 16, 17, 18, 23; 22:16; 25:24; 26:50, 73; 27:11

Mk 1:11, 24^2; 3:11; 8:29; 12:14, 34; 14:61, 70^2; 15:2

Lk 1:28^2, 42; 3:22; 4:34^2, 41; 7:19, 20; 10:15, 41; 11:2; 12:58; 13:12; 14:8, 10; 15:31; 16:25; 19:21; 22:32, 58, 67, 70; 23:3, 40; 24:18

Jn 1:19, 21^2, 22, 42, 49^2; 3:2, 10; 4:12, 19; 5:14; 6:69; 7:52; 8:25, 48, 53, 57; 9:28; 11:27; 17:21; 18:17, 25, 33, 37; 19:9, 12; 21:12

Act 4:24; 8:23; 9:5; 10:33; 12:15; 13:33; 17:29; 21:22, 38; 22:8, 27; 26:1, 15, 24

Ro 2:1^2, 17, 19^2; 3:4; 9:20; 14:4

1Co 7:21, 27^2

Gal 4:7

1Ti 6:12

Heb 1:5, 12; 2:6; 5:5, 6; 7:17, 21; 12:5

Jas 2:11; 4:11, 12

Rev 2:5, 9; 3:1, 15, 16, 17; 4:11; 5:9; 11:17^2; 15:4; 16:5^2

AS

Gen 3:5, 22; 4:20^2, 21; 7:9, 16; 8:21; 9:3; 10:9, 19^2, 30; 11:2; 12:4; 13:10^2, 16; 16:6; 17:4, 15, 20, 23; 18:5, 25, 33^2; 19:8, 14, 28; 21:1^2, 4, 16; 22:14, 17^2; 23:9^2; 24:22, 51; 25:18; 26:4, 29^2; 27:4, 9, 12, 14, 19, 23, 27, 30^2, 42, 46; 28:6, 14; 31:2, 5, 26; 32:12, 25, 28, 31; 33:10, 14; 34:12, 15, 22, 31; 35:18; 36:24; 38:11, 29; 39:10, 18; 40:10, 22; 41:13, 19, 21, 38, 39^2, 49, 54; 42:27, 35; 43:6, 17, 34; 44:1^2, 3^2, 15, 17, 18; 47:11, 21, 30; 48:5, 7, 20^2; 49:4, 9^2, 16, 27; 50:6, 12, 20^2

Ex 1:17, 19; 2:14; 4:6, 7; 5:7, 13, 14, 20; 7:6, 10, 13, 20, 22; 8:15, 19, 27; 9:12, 17, 18, 24, 29^2, 30, 35; 10:10, 14; 11:6; 12:25, 28, 31, 32, 36, 48, 50; 13:11; 14:28; 15:5, 7, 8, 10, 16^2; 16:5^2, 10, 14^2, 22, 24, 34; 17:10; 18:21; 19:18; 21:7, 22^2; 22:25; 23:15; 24:10^2; 27:8; 28:32; 30:37; 32:1, 13, 17, 19^2, 23; 33:9, 11; 34:4, 10, 18; 35:22^2; 38:21; 39:1, 5, 6, 7, 21, 23, 26, 29, 31, 43; 40:15, 19, 21, 23, 25, 27, 29, 32

Lev 2:12; 4:10, 20, 21, 26^2, 31, 35; 5:13^2; 6:17^2; 7:7, 10^2, 19, 21; 8:4, 9, 13, 17, 21, 29, 31, 34; 9:7, 10, 15, 21; 10:5, 15, 18; 11:4; 12:5; 13:43; 14:6, 13, 22, 30, 31, 35; 15:25, 26^2; 16:15, 34; 18:19^2, 22, 28; 19:16, 18, 23^2, 34^2; 20:6, 13, 25; 22:13; 24:16^2, 19, 20, 22^2, 23; 25:31, 39, 40^2, 42, 46, 53; 26:19^2, 34^2, 35^2, 36, 37; 27:12, 14, 21, 23

Nu 1:19; 2:17, 33; 3:16, 42, 51; 4:15, 29, 49; 5:4; 8:3, 16, 19, 21, 22; 9:15, 18^2; 10:31; 11:7^2, 8, 12, 31^3; 12:10, 12; 13:21, 33; 14:15, 17, 19, 21^2, 28^3, 32; 15:14, 15, 20, 36; 16:31, 40^3, 45, 47; 17:11; 18:6, 7, 18^2, 24, 27^2, 30^2; 20:9, 27; 21:34; 22:4, 8; 23:2, 22, 24^2, 30; 24:1, 6^4, 8, 9^2; 26:4; 27:11, 13, 17, 22, 23; 28:8^2; 31:7, 31, 41, 47; 32:25, 27, 31; 33:56; 34:6; 36:10

Dt 1:10, 11^2, 17^2, 19, 21, 31, 40, 44; 2:1, 5, 10, 11, 12, 14, 21, 22, 29, 30; 3:2, 6, 20^2; 4:5, 7, 8, 20, 32, 33, 38; 5:12, 14^2, 16, 26, 31, 32; 6:3, 8, 16, 19, 24, 25; 8:5, 18, 20; 9:3^2, 18, 21^2, 25; 10:5, 9, 15, 22; 11:4, 10^2, 18, 21, 25; 12:9, 12, 15^2, 16, 19^2, 20, 21, 22, 24; 13:6, 11, 17; 14:7; 15:6, 21, 22^2, 23; 16:9, 10, 17; 17:14, 16; 18:2, 7, 14; 19:5, 6, 8, 19; 20:8^2, 17; 22:11, 26; 23:23; 24:8; 26:15, 18, 19; 27:3; 28:9, 29, 49^2, 62, 63; 29:13^2, 28; 30:9; 31:3, 4, 13^2, 21; 32:2^4, 10, 11, 31, 50; 33:20, 25; 34:9

Jos 1:3, 5, 15, 17^2; 2:7^2, 11^2; 3:7, 13^2, 15; 4:8^2, 12, 14, 18, 23; 5:5, 14; 6:22; 7:5; 8:2, 5, 6, 15, 19^2, 29^2, 31^2, 33^3; 9:4, 21, 25; 10:1, 2, 11, 28, 30, 39^2, 40; 11:4, 9, 12, 13, 15, 20; 13:6, 8, 14, 33; 14:2, 5, 7, 10, 11^4, 12; 15:18, 63; 17:14; 21:8; 22:4; 23:5, 8, 9, 10, 15; 24:15

Jdg 1:7, 20; 2:3, 15^2, 22; 3:1^2, 2; 4:22; 5:31; 6:5, 16, 27, 36, 37; 7:5, 12, 17; 8:8, 18, 19, 21, 33^2; 9:33^3, 36, 48; 11:36; 13:9, 23^2; 14:6, 20; 15:10, 11, 14; 16:7, 9, 11, 20; 17:8, 11; 19:22; 20:1, 8, 11, 30, 31, 32, 39, 48^2

Ru 1:8; 3:10, 13

1Sa 1:7, 12, 26, 28^2; 2:2, 16^2; 3:10; 4:9; 5:10; 6:6, 12; 7:10; 9:11, 13^2, 20, 27; 10:7; 12:15, 23; 13:5, 7, 10^2; 14:14, 39, 45; 15:22^2, 23^2, 27, 33; 16:7; 17:20^2, 23, 36, 55, 57; 18:1, 3, 6, 7, 10; 19:6, 7, 9, 20; 20:3^2, 13, 17, 20, 21, 23, 25, 31^2, 36, 41^2, 42; 22:8, 13, 14; 23:11; 24:4, 13, 18; 25:15^2, 20, 25, 26^3, 29, 34, 37; 26:10, 16, 20, 24; 27:8; 28:10, 17; 29:6, 8, 9, 10^2; 30:24

2Sa 1:6, 21; 2:18^2, 23^2, 27; 3:9, 33, 34, 36; 4:4, 6, 9; 5:20, 25; 6:16, 18^2, 19^2, 20; 7:10, 11, 15, 25; 8:3; 9:8, 11^2; 10:2; 11:11^2, 25^2; 12:3, 5; 13:13^2, 29, 35, 36^2; 14:2, 11, 13, 14, 17, 19, 25; 15:10^2, 21^2, 26, 30^2, 34; 16:2, 5, 13^2, 19, 23; 17:3, 8, 10, 11, 12^2; 18:32, 33; 19:3, 14, 18, 27, 30; 20:8; 22:23, 31, 43^3, 45^2; 23:4^2, 6; 24:19, 23

1Ki 1:29, 30, 37, 41; 2:3, 24^2, 31, 38; 3:6^2, 14; 4:20, 29; 5:5, 12; 8:20, 24, 25, 43, 53, 57, 59, 61; 9:2, 4, 5; 10:10, 27^2; 11:4, 6, 11, 33, 38^2; 12:12, 17; 13:6, 18, 20, 21; 14:6, 7, 8, 10, 15; 15:3, 11; 16:2, 9, 11^2, 31; 17:1, 11, 12, 13; 18:7, 10, 12^2, 15, 32^2; 19:2, 5; 20:11, 12, 34, 36^4, 39, 40; 21:11^2, 26; 22:4^3, 14, 17

2Ki 1:16; 2:2^2, 4^2, 6^2, 11, 19, 23; 3:7^3, 14, 22^2; 4:8^2, 30^2, 40; 5:16, 20, 27^2; 6:5, 26; 7:7, 10, 13^2, 17, 18; 8:5, 18, 19, 27; 9:17, 22, 31, 37; 10:2^2, 12, 15, 25^2; 11:8^2, 14; 12:9; 13:5, 21, 23; 14:3, 4, 5^2; 15:9; 17:2, 4, 11, 23, 41; 19:12, 26^4, 29, 37; 21:3, 13, 20; 22:18; 23:16, 21, 27; 24:13; 25:15, 22

1Ch 5:1; 6:26; 12:8^2, 20, 33, 36; 14:16; 15:15, 29; 16:37; 17:1, 9, 13, 23; 18:3; 21:3, 15, 17, 21; 22:7, 11; 23:24; 24:19; 25:8^3; 26:13^2, 21; 28:2, 7; 29:11, 15^2, 17, 23, 25

2Ch 1:12, 15^3; 2:3, 16^2; 3:16; 4:6; 5:13^2; 6:8, 10, 15, 16, 31, 33; 7:17^2, 18; 8:7, 14; 9:9, 27^2; 10:12, 17; 11:16; 13:10, 15; 16:3; 18:3^2, 13, 16; 20:9, 20, 21, 33; 21:6, 7; 23:3, 13, 18^2; 24:12^2; 25:4, 16; 26:5^2; 29:8, 31^2; 30:5, 7, 8; 31:3, 5^2, 15^2; 32:17, 19; 33:22, 23; 34:26; 35:12, 18; 36:21^2

Ezr 2:62; 3:1, 2, 4^2; 4:2, 3; 6:18, 21; 7:14, 25, 27, 28; 8:27, 31; 9:7, 13, 15; 10:3, 12

Neh 1:1; 2:16, 18; 5:5^2, 12; 6:8, 11^2; 7:64; 8:1, 15; 9:10, 11, 23, 24; 10:34, 36; 13:15

Est 2:9, 20^2; 3:11; 4:14; 5:5, 8, 13; 6:10; 7:8; 8:8; 9:2, 22, 23^2, 27^2, 31^2

Job 2:10; 3:6, 16^2; 4:8; 5:7, 14, 25, 26; 6:7, 15^2, 26; 7:2^2, 9, 20; 9:26^2, 32; 10:4, 5^2, 9, 10, 16, 19, 22^2; 11:8^2, 16, 17, 20; 12:3^3, 4, 5; 13:9, 28^2; 14:2, 6, 11; 15:24, 33^2; 16:4, 21; 17:6, 7, 10, 15; 18:3, 20; 19:11, 22; 20:8^2; 21:4, 18^2, 33; 22:2, 8, 24^2; 23:10; 24:5, 14, 17, 18, 20, 24^2; 26:3; 27:2, 6, 7^2, 16^2, 18^2, 20, 21; 28:5^2; 29:2^2, 4, 14, 18, 23^2, 25^2; 30:5, 14, 15^2, 18; 31:18, 33, 36, 37; 32:19; 34:3, 26; 35:8; 37:18; 38:8, 14^2, 19, 30; 39:16, 20; 40:15, 18; 41:5, 15, 20, 24^4, 27^2, 29; 42:7, 9, 10^2, 15

Ps 5:7, 12; 10:5, 9; 11:1; 12:6; 14:4; 17:8, 12^2, 15; 18:30, 42^2, 44^2; 19:5^2; 21:9; 22:13; 25:10; 26:11; 27:12; 31:12; 32:9^2; 33:7, 22; 34:18; 35:5, 13, 14^2; 37:2, 6^2, 14, 20, 22; 38:4, 10, 13^2, 14; 39:5^2, 12; 40:4, 16; 41:12; 42:1, 10; 44:22; 48:6, 8; 50:21; 53:4; 55:16, 20; 58:3^2, 7^2, 8, 9; 61:6; 62:3^2; 63:2, 5; 65:3; 66:10; 68:2^2, 13, 14, 15^2, 17, 21; 69:13; 70:4; 71:7; 72:5^2, 6, 7, 17^2; 73:1, 2, 5, 6^2, 19, 20, 22; 74:5; 77:13; 78:8, 13, 15, 27^2, 65; 83:9^3, 10, 11^2, 13, 14^2; 87:7^2; 88:4; 89:10, 11, 29, 36, 37^2; 90:4^2, 5^2, 9; 92:7; 95:8^2; 102:3, 7, 26; 103:11, 12^2, 13, 15^3, 18; 104:2, 6, 17, 33^2; 106:9; 107:10; 109:17^2, 18^2, 19, 23, 29; 116:2^2; 118:12; 119:14^2, 70^2, 111, 132, 162; 122:3; 123:2^2; 124:6, 7; 125:1, 2, 5^2; 126:4; 127:4; 128:3; 129:6; 131:2^2; 133:3^2; 137:8; 139:12, 16; 140:9; 141:2^2, 7; 143:3, 6; 144:4, 12^2; 147:20

Prv 1:12^2, 27^2; 2:4^2; 3:12; 4:18, 19; 5:3, 4^2, 19; 6:5^2, 11^2; 7:2, 22^2, 23; 8:26, 30; 9:4, 16; 10:20, 23, 25, 26^2; 11:19, 20, 22, 28; 12:4; 15:19; 16:14, 15, 24, 27; 17:8, 14; 18:4^2, 8, 11; 19:12^2, 24; 20:2, 19; 21:1, 8, 29; 23:5, 7, 28, 34^2; 24:29, 34^2; 25:12, 13, 16, 20^2, 25, 26; 26:1^2, 2^2, 8, 9, 11, 14, 18, 21, 22; 27:8, 19, 21; 28:1, 4, 15; 30:14^2; 31:8

Ecc 2:8, 13^2, 15, 16; 3:19; 4:1; 5:15^2, 16; 6:12; 7:6, 26; 8:1, 13; 9:2^2, 12^2; 10:5, 7; 11:5; 12:7, 11^2

Song 1:3, 5^2, 7, 14; 2:2, 3; 4:1, 11; 5:11^2, 12, 13^2, 14^2, 15^3; 6:4^3, 5, 6, 7, 10^4, 13; 7:4^2, 8; 8:1, 6^4, 10

Isa 1:7, 8^3, 9, 18^4, 26^2, 30^2, 31^2; 3:9, 12, 16; 5:18, 24^3; 6:13^2; 7:2; 8:6; 9:1, 3, 4, 18, 19; 10:9^3, 10, 11, 14^2, 15^3, 18, 20, 22, 26, 32; 11:9, 16; 13:4, 6, 8^2, 14^2, 17, 19; 14:10, 17, 19^2, 24^2; 16:2, 3, 14; 17:3, 5^2, 6, 9, 13; 19:14; 20:3; 21:1, 3; 22:16, 23; 23:5, 10, 15; 24:2^6, 13^2, 22; 25:4, 5, 10, 11; 26:17, 18, 19, 20; 27:7, 9; 28:2^2, 4, 21^2; 29:2, 4, 5, 7, 8^2, 11, 13, 16, 17; 30:13, 14, 17^2, 22, 26^2, 27, 28, 29^2; 31:4, 5; 32:2^3; 33:4, 11, 12^2; 34:4^3; 35:1, 6; 37:12, 27^4, 30, 38; 38:12, 13, 14, 19; 40:6, 15^3, 17, 22^3, 23, 24, 31; 41:2^2, 11, 12^2, 15, 25^2; 42:13, 19^3; 43:17; 44:4^2, 7, 22^2; 47:3, 4, 8, 14; 48:18^2, 19; 49:18^3, 26; 50:4, 9; 51:9, 12, 13, 20, 23^2; 52:14; 53:2^2, 3, 7^2; 54:6, 9^2; 55:9, 10; 56:12; 58:2, 4, 5, 8, 10; 59:10^3, 12, 17^2, 21; 60:8^2; 61:10^2, 11^2; 62:1^2, 5^2; 63:13, 14; 64:2, 6^3; 65:8, 22; 66:3^4, 8^2, 13, 20, 22

Jer 2:26, 36; 3:2, 5, 20; 4:13^2, 17, 31^2; 5:8, 9, 16, 19, 26, 27, 29; 6:7, 9^2, 23, 24, 26; 7:14, 15; 8:6; 9:8, 9, 22^2; 10:5, 6, 7; 11:5; 12:8, 9, 16; 13:5, 10, 11, 21^2, 24; 14:8^2, 9^2; 15:2^4, 18^2, 19; 16:4; 17:8, 11, 16, 22; 18:4, 6^2, 17; 19:11, 12, 13; 20:9, 11, 16; 21:7; 22:23, 24; 23:12, 14^2, 27, 29, 34; 24:8; 25:18, 30, 38; 26:11, 14^2, 18; 27:13; 30:6, 20; 31:5, 10, 12, 18, 23, 28; 32:20, 31, 42; 33:7, 11, 22; 38:16; 39:12; 40:3, 10; 41:6^2; 42:2, 18; 43:11^3, 12; 44:6, 13, 14, 16, 17, 22, 23, 30; 46:7^2, 18^3, 22, 26; 48:8, 13, 34, 40, 41; 49:16^2, 18, 22^2, 24; 50:8, 9, 11^2, 15, 18, 26, 37, 40, 43; 51:14, 27, 30, 38, 49

Lam 1:1, 15, 17, 20, 22; 2:4, 5, 6, 7, 12, 22; 3:6, 10^2, 12, 45; 4:2, 6, 14, 17^2; 5:3, 21

Ezk 1:1, 4, 10, 13, 14, 15, 16, 18, 22, 24^2, 26^2, 27^3, 28; 3:3, 9, 23; 4:12; 5:11; 7:17, 20; 8:1, 2^3; 9:10, 11; 10:1^2, 5, 9, 10^2, 11^2, 13; 11:16, 21; 12:4^2, 7^2, 11, 23; 14:10, 16, 18, 20; 15:6; 16:4, 7, 31, 32, 38, 44, 47, 48^2, 50, 57, 59; 17:5, 16, 19; 18:3, 4, 18; 20:3, 31, 32^2, 33, 36, 39; 21:7, 10, 23; 22:20, 22; 23:16^2, 18, 20, 44; 24:18, 22; 26:3, 10; 28:2, 6, 16; 30:9, 18; 32:2; 33:11, 12, 17, 27, 31^2, 32; 34:8, 12, 17, 19; 35:6, 11, 15; 36:17, 38^2; 37:7^2, 10; 38:16; 40:2, 40; 41:21, 25; 42:6, 9, 11^4, 12; 43:22; 46:5, 7, 11, 12; 47:10, 14^2, 15, 22; 48:1, 8, 11, 23

Dan 1:4, 13, 17; 2:29, 30, 40^3, 41, 42, 43, 45; 4:18, 25, 32, 33, 35; 5:12; 6:4, 10, 22; 7:4, 9^2, 12, 28; 8:5, 15, 18; 9:7, 12, 13, 15; 10:4, 6^2, 17; 11:29^2, 32; 12:1, 3^2

Hos 1:10; 2:3^2, 15^2; 4:4, 7, 16^2; 5:12^2, 14^2; 6:3^3, 4^2, 5, 9; 7:4, 6, 7, 12^2; 8:1, 8, 12; 9:1, 4, 9, 10^2, 11, 13; 10:4, 7^2, 11, 14; 11:2, 4, 8^2, 11^2; 12:9, 11; 13:3^4, 7^2, 8; 14:5^3, 6^2, 7^3

Joel 1:15; 2:2, 3, 4^2, 5, 32

Am 2:9, 13; 3:12; 4:11^2; 5:11, 14, 16, 19, 24^2; 7:15; 8:8^2, 10^2; 9:5, 7, 9, 11

Oba 4, 11, 15, 16^2

Jna 1:14

Mic 1:4^2, 6^2, 8, 16; 2:8^2, 12^2; 3:3^2, 4, 12^2; 4:9, 12; 5:7^2, 8^2, 15; 7:1^2, 4, 10, 14

Nah 1:10^3; 2:2, 7; 3:6, 15^2, 17^2

Hab 1:8, 9^2, 14^2; 2:5^2, 14; 3:4, 14^2

Zep 1:8, 17^2; 2:2, 9^3

Hag 1:12; 2:3, 19, 23

Zec 1:4, 6; 2:4, 6; 4:1; 5:3^2; 7:3, 12, 13; 8:11, 13, 14; 9:1, 3^2, 7^2, 11, 13, 14, 15^2, 16^3; 10:2, 3, 5, 6, 7, 8; 12:8^3, 10^2, 11; 13:9^2; 14:3, 5, 10, 15

Mal 2:9; 3:3^2, 4^2, 17; 4:1, 2

Mt 1:18, 24; 5:48; 6:2, 5, 7, 10, 12, 16; 7:29^2; 8:13; 9:9, 10, 15^2, 32, 36; 10:7, 16^3, 25^2; 11:7; 12:13, 40; 13:40, 43; 14:5, 36^2; 15:28, 33; 17:2^2, 9, 20; 18:3, 4, 17, 19, 25, 33; 19:19; 20:14, 28, 29; 21:6, 18, 23, 26; 22:9^2, 10^2, 30, 31, 39; 23:37; 24:3, 21, 27, 37, 38, 44; 25:14, 32, 40, 45; 26:7, 19, 21, 24, 26, 39^2, 55; 27:10, 32, 65^2; 28:1, 3, 4, 6, 9, 15

Mk 1:2, 16, 22^2, 42^2; 2:2, 14, 15, 19^2, 23; 3:5, 10^2, 20; 4:4, 18, 20, 26, 33, 36; 5:36^2; 6:15, 31, 34, 56^2; 7:4, 6, 8; 8:24; 9:3^2, 9, 13, 26; 10:1, 15, 32, 46; 11:2^2, 6, 20, 27; 12:25, 26, 31, 33; 13:1, 3, 19, 34; 14:3, 16, 18, 21, 22, 45^2, 48, 66; 15:8; 16:7, 10, 12, 14

Lk 1:1, 2, 23^2, 44^2, 55, 70; 2:15, 20, 23, 43; 3:4, 15, 23; 4:16; 5:1, 14, 17; 6:3, 10, 22, 31, 34, 36, 40; 8:5, 6^2, 23, 42; 9:18, 29, 33, 34, 42, 53, 54, 57; 10:3, 7, 8, 18, 27, 33, 38; 11:1^2, 2, 8^2, 27, 30, 36, 37, 41, 44, 53; 12:58; 13:34; 14:1, 22; 15:19, 25, 30^2; 17:6, 11, 12, 14, 24, 26, 28; 18:11^2, 13, 17, 35; 19:9, 11, 32, 33, 36; 20:1; 21:5, 6, 35; 22:13, 22, 26^2, 27, 29, 31, 39, 44, 52, 56, 66^2; 23:7^2, 14, 24, 26; 24:4, 5, 11, 17, 24, 28, 30, 36, 39, 50^2

Jn 1:12^2, 14, 23, 36; 3:14; 4:51; 5:21, 23, 26, 30; 6:11^2, 31, 57, 58, 59; 7:10, 28, 38; 8:6, 20, 28, 30; 9:1, 5^2, 29; 10:15, 26; 11:20^2, 29^2, 56; 12:14, 50; 13:15, 33, 34; 14:27, 31; 15:4, 6, 9, 10, 12; 16:21^2; 17:2^3, 11, 14, 16, 18, 21, 22, 23; 18:6^2; 19:40; 20:9, 11, 21; 21:8, 9^2

Act 1:10, 11, 19; 2:2, 3, 4, 15, 22, 39^2, 45, 47; 3:6, 11, 12, 17, 24^2; 4:1, 6^2, 34^2, 35; 5:11^2, 35, 36^2, 37^2; 6:15; 7:5^2, 26, 28, 31, 40, 42, 44, 48, 51; 8:3, 16, 32, 36; 9:3, 17, 18, 32, 38; 10:9, 11, 25, 27, 29^2, 45^2, 47^2; 11:5, 15^2, 17^2, 19^2, 22^2; 12:13, 18^2; 13:1, 2, 17, 25, 33, 34, 48^2; 14:20; 15:8, 11, 15, 24; 16:4, 16; 17:2, 14, 23, 25, 28, 29; 19:2; 20:3, 9; 21:10, 25, 31, 37; 22:3, 5, 6, 23, 25; 23:11, 15, 20, 31; 24:10, 25; 25:10, 18; 26:12, 24, 29; 27:25, 27, 30^2; 28:10, 15^2, 22

Ro 1:13, 15^2, 17, 21, 28; 2:12^4, 24; 3:4, 5, 7, 8^2, 10; 4:1, 6, 17^2; 5:12, 15, 16, 18, 19, 21; 6:3, 4, 13^3, 19; 7:1^2, 2; 8:14^2, 26, 36^2; 9:5, 6, 13, 25, 27, 29^2, 32, 33; 10:15; 11:8, 13, 26, 28^2, 30; 12:3, 4, 18^2; 13:9, 13; 14:11; 15:3, 7, 9, 15, 21; 16:2

1Co 1:6, 31; 2:9; 3:1^3, 3, 5, 10, 15; 4:1, 7, 8, 9, 13, 14, 17, 18; 5:1^2, 3^2, 7; 7:7, 8, 17^2, 25, 29, 30^3, 31, 39^2; 8:1, 2, 4, 5, 7; 9:5^3, 8, 20^2, 21, 22, 26^2; 10:6, 7^2, 8, 9, 10, 13, 15, 33; 11:1, 2, 5, 7, 12, 25^2, 26^2; 12:2, 11, 12, 18; 13:1, 11^3, 12; 14:12, 33, 34; 15:8, 22, 38, 48^2, 49, 58; 16:1, 2, 10, 12

2Co 1:5, 7, 14^2, 18, 23; 2:17^3; 3:1, 3, 5, 13, 18^2; 4:1, 13; 5:20; 6:1, 4, 8, 9^3, 10^3, 13, 16; 7:14; 8:5, 6, 7, 11, 15; 9:1, 3, 5^2, 7, 9; 10:2, 7, 9, 11, 14^3; 11:2, 3, 10, 12, 15, 16, 17, 21^2, 23; 12:20^2; 13:2, 7

Gal 1:9; 2:7, 14^2; 3:6, 10^2, 16^2, 27^2; 4:1^2, 12^2, 14^2, 28, 29; 5:14, 21; 6:10, 12^2, 16^2

Eph 1:4; 2:3; 3:3, 5; 4:4, 17, 21, 32; 5:1, 2, 3, 8, 15^2, 22, 23, 24, 25, 28, 29, 33; 6:5, 6^2, 7, 20

Php 1:7^2, 20, 27; 2:8, 12^2, 15, 22, 23; 3:5, 12, 15^2, 17; 4:15

Col 1:6^2, 7; 2:1^2, 6, 7, 20; 3:12, 13, 18, 22, 23; 4:4

1Th 1:5; 2:2, 4^2, 5, 6, 7, 11^2, 13^2, 14; 3:4, 6, 12; 4:1, 5, 6, 9, 11, 13; 5:2, 3, 4, 6, 11

2Th 1:3; 2:2^2, 4; 3:1, 15^2

1Ti 1:3; 5:1^2, 2^2; 6:1^2

2Ti 2:3, 9, 17; 3:8, 9

Tit 1:5, 7, 9; 2:3

Phlm 9, 14, 16, 17

Heb 1:4, 11, 12; 2:14; 3:2, 3, 5, 6, 7, 8, 15; 4:2^2, 3^2, 7, 10, 15; 5:3, 4, 6, 12; 6:19; 7:9, 20, 27; 8:5; 9:8, 9, 25, 27; 10:25^2; 11:7, 9, 12^4, 27, 29; 12:5, 7, 16, 20, 27; 13:3^2, 5, 17

Jas 1:10; 2:8, 9, 12, 26; 5:3, 5, 17

1Pt 1:14, 15, 18^2, 19, 24^2; 2:2, 4, 5, 11, 12, 13, 14, 16^2, 25; 3:6^3, 7^2, 8, 16; 4:1, 10^2, 11^2, 12, 13, 15^4, 16, 19; 5:3, 8, 12

2Pt 1:3, 13^2, 14, 19, 21; 2:1, 12, 13; 3:4, 8^2, 9, 10, 15, 16^2

1Jn 1:7; 2:6, 18, 27^2; 3:2, 3, 7, 12, 23; 4:17

2Jn 4, 5, 6

3Jn 2, 3

Jude 7, 10

Rev 1:10, 14^3, 15^2, 16, 17; 2:24^3, 27^2; 3:3, 19^2, 21; 4:1, 7; 5:6, 13; 6:1, 11, 12^2, 13, 14; 8:8, 10, 12; 9:2, 3, 5, 7^2, 8^2, 9^2, 17; 10:1^2, 3, 7, 9, 10^3; 11:6^2; 12:4^2, 15; 13:2^2, 3, 11, 15^2; 14:2^2, 3; 15:2; 16:3, 15, 18; 17:12^2; 18:6, 17^2; 19:6^3, 12; 20:8; 21:2, 11, 16^2, 21; 22:1, 12

AT

Gen 3:24; 4:7; 6:6; 8:6; 9:5^3; 13:3, 4; 14:17; 17:21; 18:14; 19:1, 6, 11; 20:13; 21:2, 22, 32; 22:19; 23:10, 18; 24:11, 21, 30, 55, 57, 63; 25:32; 26:8; 27:41; 28:19; 31:10; 33:10, 19; 38:1, 5, 11; 41:1, 21; 43:16, 18, 19, 20, 25, 33; 44:12^2; 45:3; 48:3; 49:13, 19, 23, 27

Ex 2:5; 4:25; 5:23; 8:32; 9:14; 12:9, 18^2, 22, 29, 41; 16:6, 12, 13; 18:5, 22, 26; 19:15, 17; 22:23, 26; 28:7, 14, 22; 29:39, 41, 42; 30:8; 32:4; 33:8, 9, 10; 34:22; 35:15; 36:29; 38:8; 39:15; 40:8, 28

Lev 1:3, 15; 3:2; 4:7^2, 18^2, 25, 30, 34; 5:9; 6:20; 7:18; 8:15, 31, 33, 35; 9:9; 13:5, 37; 14:11; 15:24; 16:2, 7, 29; 17:6; 18:9; 19:5, 7, 20; 22:19, 29; 23:5, 32; 25:32; 26:32; 27:10, 13, 16, 31, 33

Nu 3:39; 4:27; 6:6, 18; 9:2, 3, 5, 11, 15, 18^2, 23^3; 10:3; 11:6, 20, 35; 13:30; 16:34; 19:19; 20:24; 21:11, 15, 30, 33, 34; 22:4, 20, 38; 23:25^2; 24:1; 27:14, 21^2; 28:4, 8; 30:4, 6, 7, 11, 14^2; 31:12; 33:14, 16, 17, 19, 21, 26, 27, 30, 32, 34, 35, 38; 34:5, 9, 12; 35:11, 20, 26

Dt 1:4, 9, 16, 18; 2:32, 34; 3:1, 2, 4, 8, 12, 18, 21, 23; 4:14, 46; 5:5; 6:24; 7:21, 22; 8:16, 19; 9:11, 18, 19, 22^3, 25; 10:1, 8, 10; 14:28; 15:1, 9; 16:4, 6^4; 17:6^2; 19:15^2; 21:14; 23:24; 24:5, 15; 28:29, 67; 31:10; 32:35, 51; 33:3, 8^2

Jos 5:2, 3, 10; 6:16, 26; 7:7; 8:5, 6, 14, 29; 9:6, 10, 14, 16; 10:10, 16, 17, 21, 27, 42; 11:5, 10, 21; 12:4^2; 15:4, 5, 7, 8, 11, 63; 16:3, 7, 8; 17:9; 18:1, 9, 12, 14, 19^2; 19:22, 29, 33, 51; 20:4, 9; 21:2, 3; 22:11, 12

Jdg 3:2, 29; 4:4, 10; 5:27^2, 28; 7:25; 8:18; 9:5, 41; 11:39; 12:2, 6^2, 10; 13:23^2, 25; 14:4; 16:3, 20, 28, 30; 18:27, 29; 19:16, 22, 26, 27; 20:15, 16, 20, 30, 31, 32, 33; 21:14, 22, 24

Ru 2:14; 3:7, 8^2, 10, 14

1Sa 2:22, 29^2; 3:2, 10, 11; 6:10; 9:8; 10:2; 13:11; 14:18; 16:4; 17:1, 15; 18:10, 19; 19:19, 22; 20:5^2, 6, 16, 20, 25, 33, 35; 21:1, 4; 22:8, 13, 14; 23:29; 25:1, 24; 26:7, 8, 11, 16; 27:3; 28:7; 30:8, 21; 31:13

2Sa 2:32; 3:30, 32; 4:5; 6:4; 8:3; 9:7, 10, 11, 13; 10:5, 8; 11:1^2, 9, 13; 13:5, 6; 14:26^2; 15:8, 14; 16:3, 6^2, 13, 23; 17:7, 9; 19:9, 28, 32, 42; 20:3, 8, 18; 21:18; 22:16^2; 23:8; 24:8, 24

1Ki 1:6; 2:7, 8, 26, 39; 3:20; 5:14; 7:30; 8:2, 9, 59, 61, 65; 9:2, 6, 8, 10; 10:22, 26, 28; 11:29; 12:27; 13:20; 14:1, 6; 15:18, 27; 18:19, 27, 36^2, 44; 19:6; 20:9, 16, 22, 26; 22:5, 20, 28, 34, 35, 48

2Ki 2:3, 5, 15, 18; 4:17, 37; 5:9, 20; 6:32; 7:3; 8:3, 22, 29; 9:7, 24, 27, 30, 31; 10:8, 12, 14; 11:6^2; 12:4; 13:20; 14:10, 11, 13, 20; 16:6, 10; 17:25; 18:10, 16, 33; 19:21, 36; 20:12; 23:6, 8, 11, 15, 29, 33; 24:3, 10; 25:21, 25

1Ch 2:55; 4:28, 29^3, 30^3, 31^3; 8:29; 9:34, 38; 11:11, 13, 16, 17; 12:22, 32; 13:3; 14:3; 15:13, 29; 16:33, 39; 17:9; 19:5; 20:1^2, 4^2, 6; 21:19, 28, 29^2; 23:30; 26:18^3, 31; 28:7, 21

2Ch 1:3, 4, 6, 13, 14, 15, 16; 3:1; 5:10, 12; 7:8; 8:1, 14, 17; 9:1, 25; 13:18; 14:10; 15:10, 15, 16; 16:2, 7; 18:4, 9, 19, 33; 19:4; 20:16; 22:5, 6^2; 23:5^2, 13^2, 19; 24:8^2, 11, 21, 23; 25:19, 21, 23; 26:9^3; 28:16; 30:1, 3, 5, 13, 21; 31:13; 32:9, 33; 33:14; 35:15, 17, 23; 36:3, 7

Ezr 1:2; 2:68; 3:8; 4:10, 11, 17, 24; 5:2, 3, 17^2; 6:2, 3, 5^2, 9, 12, 17, 18; 7:12; 8:17^2, 21, 29, 34; 9:4, 5; 10:3, 14

Neh 2:12; 3:19; 4:22; 5:17; 6:1, 7; 7:5; 9:37; 10:34; 11:1, 2, 4, 6, 22, 24, 25^3, 26^3, 27^2, 28^2, 29^3, 30^2, 31, 32; 12:25, 27, 37^2, 44; 13:6, 19, 31

Est 1:12; 4:8, 14; 5:6, 13; 6:10; 7:2, 3^2; 8:3, 9, 14; 9:14, 15, 18

Job 2:10; 3:13, 17; 5:22, 23; 9:23; 12:5; 15:12, 23; 16:4, 12; 17:8; 18:12, 20; 19:25; 21:12, 23; 22:21; 23:15; 26:11; 27:23; 29:21; 31:9, 29; 34:20; 37:1; 39:22, 27; 41:9, 26, 29

Ps 7:4; 9:3; 10:5; 11:2; 12:5; 16:8, 11; 18:12, 15^2; 25:13; 30:4, ttl; 34:1; 35:8, 26; 37:13; 39:5, 12; 42:7; 52:6; 55:6, 17, 20; 59:6, 8, 14; 62:8; 64:4^2, 7; 65:8; 68:2, 8^2, 12, 29; 73:3; 74:6; 76:6; 80:16; 81:7; 83:9, 10; 91:6, 7^2; 97:5^2, 12; 99:5, 9; 104:7^2; 105:22; 106:3, 7^2, 32; 107:27; 109:6, 31; 110:1, 5; 114:7^2; 118:13; 119:20, 45, 62, 162; 123:4; 132:6, 7; 135:21; 141:7

Prv 1:23, 25, 26; 4:19; 5:11, 19; 7:6, 12, 19, 20; 8:3^4, 34^2; 9:14; 14:9, 19; 16:7; 17:5, 17; 20:21; 21:13; 23:30, 32; 24:19; 28:18; 29:21; 30:17

Ecc 5:6, 8; 10:2^2; 12:4, 6^2

Song 1:7, 12; 2:9; 7:13; 8:11

Isa 1:12, 26^2; 6:4; 7:3, 23; 9:1; 10:26, 28, 29, 32; 13:6, 8; 14:7, 8, 9; 16:2, 4; 17:7, 14; 19:1, 19; 20:2; 21:3^2; 22:7; 23:5^2; 26:11; 27:13; 28:15; 29:5; 30:2, 4, 13, 17^2, 19^2; 32:9, 11; 33:3^2; 37:22, 37; 39:1; 42:14; 47:14; 50:2^2; 51:17, 20; 52:14, 15; 59:10; 60:4, 14; 64:1, 2, 3; 66:2, 5, 8

Jer 1:15, 17; 2:12, 24; 3:17; 4:9, 11, 19, 26; 5:22; 6:4, 15^2; 7:2, 12; 8:1, 12, 16; 10:2^2, 10, 18; 11:12; 15:8; 17:11, 27; 18:7, 9; 20:16; 23:23, 32; 25:15, 17, 28, 33; 26:19; 27:18; 29:10, 25; 31:1, 12; 32:20; 33:7, 11, 15; 34:8, 14, 16^2; 35:11; 36:10, 17, 27; 39:10; 40:10; 41:3; 43:9; 44:1^3, 6, 22, 23; 45:1; 46:27; 47:3^3; 48:11, 41; 49:17, 21^2, 22; 50:11, 13, 14, 46; 51:31, 49

Lam 1:7, 20; 2:15^2; 3:56^2

Ezk 2:6; 3:9, 15, 16, 17, 18, 20; 8:5, 16; 9:6^2; 10:19; 11:1; 12:4, 23; 14:3; 16:4^2, 25, 46^2, 57; 18:23; 20:32; 21:19, 21^2, 22; 22:13^2; 23:42; 24:18; 26:10, 15, 16^2, 18; 27:3, 28, 35, 36; 28:19; 29:7, 13; 30:18; 31:16; 32:10^2; 33:6, 7, 8; 34:10; 35:15; 36:8, 11; 37:22; 38:10, 11, 18, 20; 39:20; 40:40^2, 44^2; 41:12; 44:11, 17, 25; 46:2, 3, 19; 47:1, 7; 48:28, 32, 33, 34

Dan 1:5, 15, 18; 2:10; 3:5, 7, 8, 15; 4:4, 8, 29, 34, 36; 5:3; 6:24; 8:1, 2, 17, 19, 27; 9:7, 15, 21, 23; 10:3; 11:27^2, 29, 40^2, 43; 12:1^2, 13

Hos 1:5; 2:16; 4:12; 5:8; 9:10; 11:7

Joel 1:15; 2:1, 9

Am 3:5, 9; 4:3^2, 4; 6:1; 7:13; 8:9

Oba 7

Mic 1:10^2; 3:4; 7:16

Nah 1:3, 5^2; 3:10

Hab 1:10; 2:3, 5, 19; 3:5, 11^2, 16

Zep 1:7^2, 12; 2:4; 3:19, 20

Zec 1:11, 15; 3:1, 8; 7:5; 11:13; 12:8; 14:7, 14

Mal 1:10, 13; 2:7, 8, 13

Mt 3:2; 4:6, 17; 5:25, 34, 40; 7:13, 28; 8:6; 9:9, 10; 10:7, 35; 11:22, 25; 12:1, 41; 13:15, 49; 14:1, 9; 15:17, 30; 18:1, 29; 19:4; 22:33; 23:6, 24; 24:33, 41; 25:6, 27; 26:7, 18^2, 45, 46, 60; 27:15

Mk 1:15, 22, 32, 33; 2:14, 15; 4:12; 5:22, 23; 6:3; 7:25; 9:12; 10:22, 24; 11:1, 18; 12:2, 4, 17, 39; 13:29, 35^3; 14:3, 42, 54; 15:6, 34; 16:2, 14

Lk 1:10, 14, 29; 2:18, 33, 41, 47; 4:11, 18, 22, 32; 5:5, 8, 9, 27; 7:9, 37, 38, 49; 8:19, 26, 35, 41; 9:31, 43^2, 61^2; 10:14, 32, 39; 11:5, 32; 12:40, 46; 13:1, 24, 25; 14:10, 14, 15, 17; 15:29; 16:20; 17:16; 19:5, 23, 29, 30, 37, 42; 20:10, 26, 37, 40, 46; 21:30, 31, 34, 37; 22:27^2, 30, 40; 23:7^2, 11, 12, 17, 18; 24:12, 22, 27, 30, 47

Jn 1:18; 2:10, 13, 23; 4:21, 45^2, 46, 47, 52, 53; 5:2, 4, 28, 37; 6:21, 39, 40, 41, 44, 54, 61; 7:2, 11, 23; 8:7, 9, 59; 10:22, 40; 11:24, 32, 49, 55; 12:2, 16, 20; 13:28; 14:20; 16:4, 26; 18:16, 38, 39; 19:11, 39, 42; 20:11, 12^2, 19; 21:1, 20

Act 1:6, 19; 2:5, 14; 3:1, 2, 10^2, 12; 4:6, 11, 18, 35, 37; 5:2, 9, 10, 15; 7:13, 26, 29, 31, 58; 8:1^2, 14, 35, 40; 9:10, 13, 19, 22, 27, 28, 32, 35, 36; 10:11, 25, 30; 11:8, 15; 12:13; 13:1, 5, 12, 27; 14:8; 15:14; 16:2, 4, 25; 17:13, 16, 30; 18:22, 24; 19:1, 17, 26, 27; 20:5, 14, 15^2, 16, 18; 21:3, 11, 13, 24; 22:3; 23:11, 23; 25:4, 8, 10, 15, 23, 24; 26:4^2, 13, 20, 32; 27:3; 28:12

Ro 1:10, 15; 3:26; 4:20; 8:34; 9:9, 32; 11:5; 13:12; 14:10; 15:26; 16:1

1Co 1:2; 7:39; 8:10; 9:7, 13; 11:34; 14:16, 27, 35; 15:6, 23, 29, 32, 52; 16:8, 12^2

2Co 1:1; 4:18^2; 5:6; 8:14

Gal 4:12, 13

Eph 1:1, 20; 2:12; 3:13

Php 1:1; 2:10; 4:5, 10

Col 1:2; 2:1

1Th 2:2, 5, 19; 3:1, 13; 5:13

2Th 2:2; 3:11

1Ti 1:3; 5:4

2Ti 1:18; 2:26; 3:11^3; 4:1, 6, 8, 13, 16, 20^2

Tit 2:5

Heb 1:1, 5, 13; 2:1, 3; 7:13; 9:17; 12:2; 13:23

Jas 3:11

1Pt 1:7, 13; 2:8; 4:7, 17^2; 5:13

1Jn 1:5; 2:28; 4:12

Rev 1:3, 17; 3:20; 8:3; 18:14, 21, 22^2, 23^2; 19:2, 10; 21:12, 25; 22:10

BE

Gen 1:3, 6, 9, 14^2, 15, 22, 28, 29; 2:18, 23, 24; 3:5^2, 6, 12, 16; 4:7^2, 12, 14^2, 15, 24; 6:3, 15, 19, 21; 8:17; 9:1, 2, 3, 6, 7, 11^2, 13, 14, 16, 20, 25^2, 26^2, 27; 10:8; 11:4, 6; 12:2, 3, 13; 13:8^2, 16; 14:19, 20; 15:4^2, 5^2, 13, 15; 16:2, 3, 5, 10, 12^2; 17:1, 4, 5^2, 7, 8, 10, 11, 12, 13^2, 14, 15, 16^2, 17; 18:4, 11, 18, 24, 25^3, 29, 30^2, 31, 32^2; 19:9, 15, 17, 22; 20:9; 21:10, 12^2, 30; 22:14, 18; 23:8; 24:5, 8^2, 14, 27, 41^2, 44, 51, 60; 25:22, 23^2, 24; 26:3, 4, 11, 22, 28; 27:13, 21, 29^3, 33, 39, 45; 28:3, 9, 14^2, 20, 21, 22; 29:4, 7, 8, 15, 26, 29, 34; 30:32, 33, 34; 31:3, 8^2, 30, 44, 52^2; 32:12, 18, 28; 33:14; 34:7, 10, 15^3, 17^2, 22^2, 23, 30; 35:2, 10^2, 11^2; 36:43; 37:14, 27, 32, 35; 38:9, 11, 15, 23, 24, 29; 39:10; 40:14; 41:21, 27, 30, 31^2, 36^2, 40^3, 52; 42:15, 16^3, 19^2, 20, 32, 33; 43:3, 5, 9, 11, 14, 23, 29; 44:9^2, 10^3, 17, 26^2, 30, 34; 45:5, 6, 10; 46:15; 47:19^2, 24, 25; 48:5, 6^2, 16, 19^2, 21; 49:6, 7, 8, 10, 12, 13^2, 17, 20, 26, 29; 50:18

Ex 1:16^2; 2:4; 3:12^2; 4:12, 14, 15, 16^4, 18; 5:8, 9, 11, 18, 21; 6:7, 14^2; 7:1, 17, 19; 8:10, 21, 22, 23; 9:3, 9, 15, 16, 19^2, 22, 28, 29; 10:5, 7, 10, 14, 21^2, 24, 26; 11:6^2, 9; 12:2^2, 4, 5, 13^2, 14, 15, 16^4, 19^3, 25, 32, 33, 42^2, 46, 48^2, 49; 13:3, 5, 6, 7^3, 9^2, 11, 12, 14, 16; 14:4; 15:9, 14, 15, 16; 16:5, 8, 12, 23, 26, 32, 33, 34; 17:4; 18:10, 19^2, 21, 22^2, 23; 19:5, 6, 11, 12, 13^2, 15; 20:12, 20, 26; 21:4, 7, 8, 12, 15, 16^2, 17, 19^2, 20, 21, 22, 28^3, 29^2, 30, 31, 32, 34, 36^2; 22:2^3, 3^3, 4^2, 5, 6, 7^2, 8^2, 9^2, 10, 11, 12, 13, 14, 15^2, 16, 19, 20, 24, 25, 30, 31; 23:1, 12, 13^2, 22, 26, 30, 33; 24:7, 12; 25:7, 10, 12, 14, 15^2, 17, 20, 23, 27, 28, 31^2, 34, 35, 36^2, 38; 26:2, 3^2, 6, 7, 8^2, 11, 16^2, 17, 20, 24^4, 25, 31, 32, 37; 27:1^2, 2, 5, 7^2, 9, 10^2, 11, 12, 13, 14, 15, 16^2, 17^2, 18, 19, 21; 28:7, 8, 11, 16^3, 17^2, 18, 20, 21^2, 28^2, 30, 32^2, 35^2, 37^2, 38^3, 43^2; 29:9, 10, 21, 26, 28^2, 29^3, 34, 37^2, 42, 43, 45; 30:2^4, 4, 12, 13, 16, 21, 25, 29^2, 31, 32^2, 33, 34, 36, 37, 38; 31:14^2, 15^2; 32:4, 8; 33:16^2, 19^2, 23; 34:2, 3, 12, 25; 35:2^3, 9, 27, 29; 36:6, 18, 34; 37:3, 27; 38:5, 26; 39:7, 21^2, 37; 40:4, 9, 10, 15

Lev 1:3, 4, 9, 10, 14, 15; 2:1, 2, 3, 4, 5^2, 7^2, 10, 11, 12, 13; 3:1^2, 6, 12, 17; 4:2, 12, 13^2, 15, 20, 22, 26, 27^2, 31, 35; 5:2^3, 3^4, 4^3, 5^2, 7, 9, 10, 11, 13^2, 16, 17, 18; 6:4, 7, 9, 12^2, 13, 16, 17, 18^2, 21, 22, 23^2, 25, 26, 27, 28^3, 30^2; 7:6, 9, 14, 15, 16^3, 17, 18^4, 19^3, 20, 21, 24, 25, 26, 27^2, 30, 31, 36; 8:5, 33; 10:3^2, 9, 14, 15; 11:7, 10, 11, 12, 13, 20, 23, 24^2, 25, 26, 27, 28, 29, 31^2, 32^6, 33, 34^4, 35^4, 36^2, 37^2, 38^2, 39, 40^2, 41^2, 43, 44, 45^2, 47^2; 12:2^2, 3, 4, 5, 7, 8^2; 13:2^2, 3, 4^3, 5, 6^2, 7, 9, 10^2, 14, 15, 16, 17, 19^2, 20^2, 21^3, 24, 25^2, 26^3, 27, 28, 30^2, 31, 32^2, 33, 34^3, 36, 37, 39, 42, 43, 45, 46^3, 47, 48, 49^2, 51, 52, 53, 55^2, 56, 58^4; 14:2^2, 3, 4, 5, 7, 8^2, 9^2, 11, 14, 17, 18, 19, 20, 21^2, 22, 25, 28, 29, 31, 34, 36, 37, 39, 41, 44, 46, 53; 15:3^2, 4, 5, 6, 7, 8, 9, 10^2, 11, 12^2, 13, 16, 17^2, 18, 19^3, 20^2, 21, 22, 23^2, 24^3, 25^2, 26^2, 27^2, 28^2; 16:4^2, 10^2, 17, 29^2, 30, 31, 34; 17:3, 4^2, 7, 8, 9, 10, 13^2, 14, 15^3; 18:9, 29; 19:2, 6^2, 7^2, 8, 20^2, 22, 23^2, 24, 29, 31, 34; 20:2^2, 7, 9^2, 10, 11^2, 12^2, 13^2, 14^2, 15, 16^2, 17, 18, 21, 26^2, 27^2; 21:1, 3, 6^2, 8, 9, 17, 18, 20; 22:3^2, 4, 5, 6, 7, 12, 13, 18, 20, 21^3, 23, 25^2, 27^2, 28, 30, 32, 33; 23:2, 3, 10, 11, 13^2, 14, 15, 17^2, 18, 20, 21^2, 27^2, 29^3, 30, 31, 32, 34, 35, 36, 37, 39^2, 41; 24:3, 5, 7, 9, 12, 16^2, 17, 19, 20, 21; 25:4, 6, 7, 8, 10, 11, 12, 23, 25, 26, 28, 30^2, 31^2, 34, 35^2, 38, 39^2, 40, 42, 44, 45, 46, 48, 49, 50^2, 51, 53, 54; 26:12^2, 13, 17, 20, 22, 23, 25, 26, 32, 33, 34, 41, 43, 44, 45; 27:2, 3^2, 4^2, 5^2, 6^3, 7^3, 8, 9^2, 10, 11, 12^2, 14^2, 15, 16^2, 18, 19, 20, 21^2, 25^2, 26^2, 27^3, 28, 29^3, 32, 33^3

Nu 1:4, 51^2, 53; 2:3, 5^2, 7, 10^2, 12^2, 14, 18^2, 20^2, 22, 25^2, 27^2, 29; 3:10, 12, 13, 24, 25, 30, 31, 32, 36, 38^2, 45, 46, 48; 4:4, 7, 27, 28, 45; 5:6, 8^2, 9, 10^2, 13^5, 14^4, 19, 20, 27^2, 28^3, 30, 31; 6:5^2, 12, 13, 25; 7:5; 8:14, 19; 9:10^2, 13; 10:7, 8, 9^2, 10, 31, 32^2, 35; 11:16, 20, 22^2; 12:6, 12, 14^3; 13:18, 19^2, 20^3, 28, 31; 14:3, 11, 17, 21, 31, 33, 35, 40, 42, 43; 15:2, 11, 14, 15^2, 16, 19, 24^2, 25, 26, 28, 30^2, 31^2, 34, 35, 39, 40, 41; 16:7^2, 16, 22, 26, 29, 38, 40^2; 17:3, 10, 13; 18:2, 4, 5, 7, 9^2, 10, 13, 14, 15^2, 16, 18, 23, 27, 30; 19:7, 8, 9, 10^2, 11, 12^2, 13^2, 14, 16, 17, 19, 20^2, 21^2, 22^2; 20:24, 26; 21:22, 27; 22:11; 23:9, 10, 23; 24:7^3, 18^2, 20, 22; 25:4; 26:53, 54, 55, 56; 27:4, 11, 13, 17, 20; 28:7^2, 14, 15, 17, 18, 19, 20, 24, 26, 31; 29:3, 8, 9, 13, 14, 18, 21, 24, 27, 30, 33, 37; 31:2, 23^2, 24; 32:5, 22^3, 23, 26, 29, 32; 33:54, 55; 34:3^2, 4, 5, 6, 7, 8, 9^2, 12^2; 35:3, 5^2, 6, 7, 8, 10, 11, 12, 14, 15, 16, 17, 18, 21, 27, 29, 30, 31, 33; 36:3^4, 4^3, 8

Dt 1:1, 17, 21, 29, 39, 42; 2:4, 25; 4:19, 20, 26, 27, 30; 5:16, 29, 33; 6:2, 3, 6, 8, 10, 11, 15, 18, 25; 7:4, 6, 10, 14^2, 16, 18, 20, 21, 23, 24, 25, 26; 8:14, 19, 20; 10:5, 16; 11:8, 15, 16, 17^2, 18, 21, 24^2, 25; 12:11, 21, 23, 27, 30^2; 13:5, 9, 14, 16^2; 14:2, 19, 24^2, 29; 15:4, 7, 9^3, 10, 12, 16, 17, 21^2; 16:4, 8; 17:2, 4^2, 6^2, 7, 9, 18, 19, 20; 18:3^2, 10, 13, 22; 19:10^2, 15, 17, 18; 20:1, 2, 3, 9, 11^3, 20^2; 21:1^2, 3, 5, 8^2, 13^2, 14, 15, 16, 22^2, 23; 22:2^2, 6^2, 7, 9, 19, 20^2, 22, 23, 28, 29; 23:10, 11, 13, 14, 17, 21, 22; 24:2, 3, 4, 5^2, 7, 12, 13, 14, 15, 16^3, 19, 20, 21; 25:1, 2^4, 6^2, 9, 10, 15, 19; 26:1, 3, 12, 17, 18, 19; 27:2, 4^2, 15, 16, 17, 18, 19, 20, 21, 22, 23, 24, 25, 26; 28:3^2, 4, 5, 6^2, 7, 10, 13^2, 16^2, 17, 18, 19^2, 20, 23^2, 24, 25^2, 26, 27, 29, 31^4, 32^2, 33, 34, 35, 44^2, 45, 46, 51, 54, 56, 61, 62, 63, 68; 29:13, 18^2; 30:4, 17; 31:6^2, 7, 8^2, 16, 17^2, 19, 21, 23^2, 26; 32:20, 24, 38, 43, 50; 33:6, 7^2, 8, 13, 20, 24^2, 25^2, 28, 29

Jos 1:4, 5^2, 6, 7, 9^3, 17, 18^3; 2:3, 14, 16, 17, 19^6, 20, 21; 3:4, 7, 13; 4:6, 7; 6:17, 26; 7:12, 14^2, 15^2; 8:1, 4, 8; 9:6, 13, 20, 21, 23; 10:25^2; 11:6; 13:1; 14:9, 12^3; 15:4; 17:15^2, 18^3; 20:3, 6; 21:13, 21, 27, 32, 38; 22:18^2, 19, 22, 27, 28, 34; 23:4, 6, 13, 16; 24:27^2

Jdg 2:3^2; 3:6; 4:9, 20; 5:24^2, 31; 6:13^2, 16, 23, 31^2, 37^2, 39^3; 7:4, 11, 17; 8:5; 9:9, 11, 13, 24, 31, 33; 10:18; 11:6, 8, 9, 10, 26, 27, 31^2, 37; 13:5, 7, 8; 14:11; 15:3, 7; 16:6, 7^2, 9, 10, 11^2, 12, 13, 14, 17^2, 20, 28; 17:2, 10; 18:5, 9, 19^3, 25; 19:6^2, 9, 20, 28; 20:9; 21:3, 5, 17^3, 18, 22^3

Ru 1:11, 16, 17; 2:4, 9, 12, 13, 19, 20; 3:1, 4, 10, 13, 14, 18; 4:10^2, 11, 12, 14^2, 15

1Sa 1:14, 22, 28; 2:9, 10, 28, 30^2, 31, 32, 33, 34; 3:9, 14, 20; 4:9^2, 19; 5:8; 6:3^2, 4; 8:11^2, 13^3, 17, 20; 9:13^2, 16; 10:1, 6, 7, 21; 11:3, 7, 9, 13; 12:15, 25; 13:14; 14:6, 10, 21, 24^2, 28, 39, 40^2; 15:1, 11, 13, 18, 33; 16:16; 17:9^3, 25, 26, 27, 36, 37; 18:17^3, 18, 21^3, 22, 23, 25, 26, 27; 19:6, 11, 22; 20:3, 7^2, 8, 9, 12, 13, 18^2, 23, 29, 31, 32, 42; 22:3, 15, 23; 23:3, 17^2, 20, 21, 23; 24:12, 13, 15, 20^2; 25:6^3, 10, 11, 24, 26, 27, 29, 31, 32, 33^2, 39, 41; 26:9, 19^2, 24, 25; 27:11, 12; 28:13, 19; 29:4^2, 10; 30:24

2Sa 1:5, 16, 21^2; 2:5, 7^2, 26^2; 3:12, 17, 35, 39; 5:2, 8, 14, 24; 6:22^3; 7:8, 11, 12, 14^2, 16^2, 24, 26^2, 28, 29; 10:5, 11^2, 12; 11:15, 20, 24; 12:9, 10, 22, 28; 13:12, 13, 15, 25, 28^2; 14:2^2, 9^2, 14^2, 15, 17^2, 25, 32; 15:20, 21^2, 33, 34^2, 35; 16:2^2, 12, 18, 19, 21; 17:3, 8^2, 9, 10, 11, 12^2, 13^2, 16, 17, 20; 18:25, 28, 32; 19:7, 13, 21, 22^2, 35, 37, 42, 43; 20:1, 4, 20^2, 21; 21:5, 6; 22:4^2, 44, 45, 46, 47^2; 23:1, 3, 4, 5, 6^2, 7^2, 8, 17; 24:3, 13, 17, 21, 22

1Ki 1:2, 5, 21, 35^2, 37, 48, 52; 2:2, 7, 19, 21, 24, 33, 37^2, 39, 45^2; 3:8, 13, 26; 5:6, 7, 9; 6:6; 8:5, 15, 16^2, 26, 29^2, 31, 33, 37^4, 38, 46, 51, 52, 53, 56, 57, 59, 61; 9:3, 7, 8; 10:9, 27^2; 11:37, 38^2; 12:7^2, 10; 13:2^2, 3^2, 6; 14:2^3, 5^2, 6, 10; 17:1, 4; 18:21, 24, 27, 31, 36; 19:15, 16^2; 20:6, 18^2, 23, 25, 39^2, 40; 21:7; 22:3, 13, 22

2Ki 1:10, 12, 13, 14, 15; 2:9^2, 10^2, 16, 21; 3:17; 4:1, 10, 13^2, 14, 23; 5:10, 12, 13, 17, 22, 23; 6:3, 8, 16^2; 7:1, 2, 12, 18, 19; 8:13, 29; 9:10, 15^2, 37; 10:6, 9, 15, 19^2, 23, 24; 11:5, 6^2, 8^2, 15, 17; 12:5, 15; 14:6^3; 15:19; 16:15; 18:23, 29, 30; 19:4, 6, 10, 11, 25, 26, 29; 20:8, 17^2, 18, 19; 22:17^2, 20; 23:27; 25:12, 24^2

1Ch 1:10; 4:10; 5:1; 6:17; 9:22; 11:2, 6; 12:17^3, 18^2; 13:2; 14:15; 15:16; 16:15, 25^2, 30^2, 31, 36, 38; 17:7, 9, 10, 11^3, 13^2, 14, 21, 23, 24^3, 27^2; 19:5, 12^2, 13; 21:3^2, 12, 17^3, 22; 22:5^2, 9^3, 10^2, 11, 13^2, 16^2, 19; 28:4^2, 6^2, 7, 9, 10, 20^3, 21^3; 29:2^2, 5, 10, 14, 22^2

2Ch 1:9; 2:8, 9, 12, 14, 18^2; 4:18; 5:6, 13; 6:4, 5^2, 6^2, 17, 20, 22, 24, 28^4, 29, 36, 40^2, 41; 7:13, 15, 16^2, 18, 20, 21, 22; 9:8^2; 10:7^2, 10; 11:22; 12:7, 8; 13:8, 9; 15:2^2, 7^3, 13; 18:3, 10, 12, 14, 21; 19:7, 11^2; 20:2, 15, 17^2, 20; 22:6; 23:4, 5^2, 7^2, 14, 16; 25:8, 14, 16; 26:15, 18; 29:11, 24; 30:7, 8, 19; 31:4; 32:7^3, 14; 33:4; 34:25^2, 28; 35:3; 36:22, 23

Ezr 1:1, 3; 4:12, 13^2, 15, 16, 21^2; 5:8, 15, 17^2; 6:3^2, 4, 5, 6, 8^2, 9, 11^3, 12; 7:20, 21, 23^2, 24, 26^2, 27; 9:12, 14^2; 10:3, 4^2, 8, 14

Neh 1:6, 11; 2:3, 6, 7, 17; 4:5, 7, 12, 14, 22; 5:5, 8, 13, 14; 6:6, 7, 9^2, 13; 7:3^3, 5; 8:10, 11; 9:5; 10:38; 11:23; 13:5, 19^4

Est 1:17^2, 19^2, 20, 22; 2:2, 3, 4, 9; 3:9^2, 14^2; 4:14; 5:3, 6^2, 14^3; 6:6, 8, 9^2, 11, 13; 7:2^2, 3, 4^2; 8:5^2, 13^2; 9:1, 12^2, 13^2, 14, 25, 28

Job 1:5, 21; 3:4, 6, 7, 9, 17; 4:2, 17^2; 5:1, 11^2, 21^2, 22, 23^2, 24, 25; 6:3, 6, 14, 28, 29; 7:4, 21; 8:2, 14^2, 22; 9:2, 29; 10:15^2; 11:2^2, 12^2, 14, 15, 17^2, 18, 20; 12:14^2; 13:5, 16, 18; 14:7, 12^2, 13; 15:14^2, 29, 31, 32^2, 34; 17:8, 9; 18:2, 4^2, 5, 6^2, 7, 12^2, 14, 15, 16^2, 18, 20; 19:4, 27, 29; 20:8^2, 12, 18, 21, 22, 26; 21:2, 4, 5, 30, 32, 33; 22:2^2, 21, 23, 25, 28; 23:7; 24:20^2, 23^2, 25; 25:4^2; 27:7, 14^2, 15, 19; 28:12, 15^2, 16, 17, 18, 19; 31:6, 8, 11, 22, 28, 31; 32:20; 33:3, 7, 21, 23, 25, 26, 30; 34:10, 20^2, 29, 30, 31, 33, 36; 35:2, 3^2, 6, 7; 36:4, 8^2, 16^2, 26; 37:6, 20^2; 38:11, 13, 15; 39:9; 40:8; 41:9, 17, 23, 32; 42:2

Ps 1:3; 2:10^2, 12; 3:2, 6; 4:4, 6; 5:11; 6:10^2; 7:3; 9:2, 9, 17, 18, 19, 20; 10:2, 6^2; 11:3, 6; 13:2; 14:7; 15:5; 16:4, 8; 17:15; 18:3^2, 45, 46^2; 19:10, 13^2, 14; 21:7, 13; 22:11, 19, 25, 26, 29, 30, 31; 24:7; 25:2, 3^2, 20; 26:11; 27:1, 3, 6, 14; 28:1^2, 6; 30:6, 10, 12; 31:1, 2, 7, 17^3, 18, 21, 24; 32:6, 9^2, 10, 11; 33:22; 34:1, 2, 18, 21, 22; 35:4^2, 5, 6, 9, 22, 26^2, 27^2; 36:2^2, 3, 8, 12; 37:1, 2, 3, 9, 10^2, 14, 15, 17, 18, 19^2, 20, 22^3, 24, 28, 36, 38^2; 38:18, 21; 39:13; 40:5^2, 13, 14^2, 15, 16^2; 41:2, 4, 10, 13; 42:8; 45:12, 14^2, 15, 16, 17; 46:2^2, 3, 5, 10^3; 48:1, 11, 14; 49:3, 16; 50:3, 22; 51:4^2, 7^2, 13, 19; 53:6; 55:6, 20, 22; 56:1, 2, 11; 57:1^3, 5^2, 11^2; 58:3, 7; 59:5, 12, 13, 15; 60:4, 5; 62:2, 3^2, 6, 9; 63:5, 10, 11; 64:7, 10; 65:1, 4; 66:8, 9, 20; 67:1, 2, 4; 68:1, 3, 13, 19, 23, 35; 69:6^2, 14, 23, 25, 28^2, 32; 70:2^2, 3, 4^2; 71:1, 3, 6, 8, 12, 13^2; 72:14, 15^3, 16, 17^2, 18, 19^2; 74:14; 75:10; 76:7, 8, 11^2; 77:2, 7, 9; 78:6, 8; 79:2, 5, 10; 80:3, 4, 7, 17, 19; 81:9; 83:1, 4, 17^2; 84:4, 10; 85:5; 86:3, 17; 87:5, 7; 88:11, 12; 89:2, 6^2, 7^2, 16, 17, 21, 24^2, 37, 52; 90:10, 14, 17; 91:4, 5, 15; 92:7, 9, 10, 13, 14; 93:1; 94:8, 13; 96:4^2, 10^2, 11, 12; 97:1, 7; 98:8; 99:1; 100:4; 101:6; 102:18^2, 26, 28; 104:5, 34^2, 35^2; 106:8, 46, 48; 107:30; 108:5, 6; 109:7^2, 8, 9, 10, 12^2, 13^2, 14^2, 15, 17, 19, 20, 28, 29; 110:3; 111:4, 5; 112:2^2, 3, 6^2, 7, 8, 9, 10; 113:2, 3, 9; 118:24, 26; 119:6, 46, 58, 74, 76, 78, 80^2, 116, 117, 122, 128, 132; 120:3^2; 121:3; 122:7, 8; 124:6; 125:1^2, 4, 5; 127:5; 128:2^2, 3, 4; 129:5, 6, 8; 130:2, 4; 132:9; 135:21; 137:8^2, 9; 138:6; 139:11, 24; 140:10, 11; 141:2, 5^3; 143:2, 7; 144:1, 12^2, 13, 14^3; 145:3, 14; 148:4; 149:2, 5, 6

Prv 1:9, 31, 33; 2:22^2; 3:7, 8, 10, 11, 15, 22, 24^2, 25, 26, 35; 4:10, 12, 26; 5:10^2, 16,

APNDX

17, 18, 19^2, 20, 22; **6:**1, 6, 15, 18, 27, 28, 29, 31, 33; **8:**5, 6, 11^2, 33; **9:**9, 11^2, 12^2; **10:**9, 24, 27, 28, 29, 30, 31; **11:**6, 9, 18, 21^2, 25^2, 26, 29, 31; **12:**3^2, 8^2, 11, 14^2, 19, 21, 24; **13:**4, 9, 11, 13^2, 18^2, 20^2, 21; **14:**11, 14^2, 22; **16:**3, 5, 7, 16, 19, 21, 31; **17:**5, 11, 14; **18:**19, 20^2; **19:**2, 5, 9, 20, 23; **20:**3, 11^2, 13, 17, 20, 21^2; **21:**13, 15, 17^2, 18, 20; **22:**1, 5, 9, 11, 13, 18, 19, 26; **23:**2, 3, 4, 15, 17, 18, 19, 20, 25, 34; **24:**1^2, 4, 8, 11, 14^3, 17, 19, 20^2, 25, 28; **25:**5, 7^2, 16, 17, 21^2; **26:**4, 5, 26; **27:**11, 14, 18, 23; **28:**2, 6, 9, 18, 20^2, 22, 25, 26; **29:**1, 14, 19, 25; **30:**6, 9^2, 10, 18, 24, 29; **31:**6, 30

Ecc 1:9^2, 10, 11, 13, 15^2; **2:**16, 18, 19; **3:**2, 10, 14^2, 15, 22; **4:**11, 13; **5:**1, 2^3, 6, 8, 10; **6:**3^2, 4, 11, 12; **7:**9^2, 14, 16, 17^2, 23, 26; **8:**1, 3, 7^2, 12^2, 13, 14^2, 15, 17; **9:**8; **10:**9^2, 10, 14^2; **11:**2, 3^2, 6, 8; **12:**2, 3, 4^2, 5^3, 6^3, 12, 14^2

Song 1:4, 7; **2:**17; **7:**8; **8:**1, 3, 7, 8, 9^2, 14

Isa 1:5, 18^4, 19, 20, 26, 27, 28^2, 29^2, 30, 31; **2:**2^2, 6, 11^3, 12^2, 17^3, 22; **3:**4, 5, 6^2, 7, 10, 11^2, 24; **4:**1, 2^2, 3, 5, 6; **5:**5^2, 6, 8^2, 9, 15^3, 16^2, 24, 27^3, 28, 29; **6:**10, 11^2, 12, 13^3; **7:**4^2, 8^2, 9, 16, 23^2, 25^2; **8:**4, 9^3, 12, 13^2, 14, 15^3, 21, 22; **9:**1, 5, 6^2, 7, 19, 20^2, 21; **10:**2, 17, 18, 19, 22, 24, 27^2, 30, 33^2; **11:**5, 9, 10^2, 11, 13, 16^2; **12:**2; **13:**7, 8^4, 10, 14, 15, 16^2, 19, 20^2, 21, 22; **14:**1, 14, 15, 20^2, 29, 31; **15:**2, 4^2, 6, 9; **16:**2^2, 4, 5, 6, 10^2, 14^2; **17:**1, 2, 3, 4, 5^2, 6, 9^2, 11, 13; **18:**6, 7; **19:**1, 5, 6, 7^2, 9, 10, 15, 16^2, 17^2, 18, 19, 20, 21, 22, 23, 24, 25; **20:**5, 6; **21:**17; **22:**7, 14, 18, 21, 23, 25^3; **23:**2, 4, 5, 15, 16, 18^3; **24:**2, 3, 9, 13^2, 18, 20^2, 22^3, 23; **25:**2^2, 5, 9^2, 10; **26:**1, 10, 11, 20; **27:**9, 10, 11, 12, 13; **28:**3, 4, 5, 10, 13, 18^2, 19, 21, 22^2, 28; **29:**2^2, 4^3, 5^3, 6, 7, 8^2, 14, 16, 17^2, 22; **30:**3, 5, 8, 13, 14, 15^2, 16, 17, 18^2, 19, 20, 23, 25, 26^2, 28, 30, 31, 32; **31:**4, 8, 9; **32:**2, 3, 4, 5^2, 10, 11, 14^3, 15^3, 17, 19; **33:**1, 2^2, 4, 6, 10, 12^2, 16^3, 20^3, 21, 24; **34:**3^2, 4^2, 5, 7, 9, 10, 12^2, 13, 15; **35:**1, 2, 4, 5^2, 7, 8^3, 9^2; **36:**8, 14, 15; **37:**4, 6, 10, 11, 26, 27, 30; **38:**7; **39:**6^2, 7, 8; **40:**4^3, 5, 9, 20, 24^2, 25, 30, 31; **41:**6, 7, 10, 11^2, 12, 22, 23; **42:**2, 4, 17^2; **43:**2^2, 9^3, 10, 26; **44:**8, 9, 11^3, 15, 21, 26^2, 27, 28^2; **45:**1, 14, 16, 17^2, 18, 22, 24, 25; **46:**5, 13; **47:**1, 3^2, 5, 7, 11, 12^3, 14^2, 15; **48:**11, 14; **49:**3, 5^4, 6^2, 9, 11, 13, 19^2, 22, 23^2, 24, 25^2, 26; **50:**7^2; **51:**3, 6^2, 7, 8, 11, 12^2, 14, 19; **52:**3, 11, 12, 13^2; **53:**11; **54:**3, 4^3, 5, 9, 10^2, 13^2, 14^2; **55:**6, 11, 12, 13^2; **56:**1, 5, 6, 7^2, 12; **57:**16; **58:**4, 8, 10, 11, 12^2; **60:**2, 4, 5^2, 7, 11^3, 12, 18, 19^2, 20^2, 21^2; **61:**3^2, 5, 6, 7, 9, 10; **62:**2, 3, 4^4, 8, 12; **63:**3, 10, 16; **64:**5, 9; **65:**10, 13^3, 17, 18, 19, 20^2, 25; **66:**5^2, 8^2, 10, 11^2, 12^2, 13, 14, 16, 17, 24^2

Jer 1:8, 17; **2:**10, 12^3, 36; **3:**1, 3, 16^2, 17; **4:**7, 9, 11, 13, 14, 27, 28, 29; **5:**1, 6, 9, 13, 29; **6:**6, 8, 11, 12, 15, 22; **7:**20^2, 23^3, 32^2, 33, 34; **8:**2^3, 3, 12, 13, 14, 17; **9:**2, 9; **10:**2, 5^2, 10, 21; **11:**3, 4^2, 5, 11, 19, 23; **12:**13, 16; **13:**10, 11, 12^2, 15, 19^3, 21, 27^2; **14:**8, 9, 15^2, 16; **15:**1, 4, 11, 18^2, 19; **16:**4^5, 6, 14; **17:**5, 6, 8^3, 11, 13^2, 14^2, 17, 18^4, 27; **18:**14, 16, 20, 21^4, 22, 23; **19:**6, 7, 8, 11^2, 13; **20:**6, 10, 11^2, 14^2, 15, 16, 17, 18; **21:**2, 9, 10; **22:**19, 22, 23; **23:**1, 3, 4^2, 6^2, 12^2, 26, 36, 40; **24:**2, 3, 7^2, 8, 9^2, 10; **25:**11, 16^2, 27, 28, 29^2, 32, 33^3, 36; **26:**3, 9^2, 18; **27:**16, 17, 18^2, 22^2; **28:**9; **29:**4, 6, 7, 8^2, 10, 14^2, 17, 18^2, 22, 26; **30:**7, 10^3, 13, 16^2, 18, 19^2, 20^2, 21, 22^2; **31:**1^2, 4^2, 6, 12, 14, 15, 16, 18, 30, 33^3, 37, 38, 40^2; **32:**4, 5, 15, 36, 38^2, 43; **33:**9, 10^2, 12, 16^2, 20, 21, 22, 24, 25, 26; **34:**3, 16, 17, 20; **35:**7; **36:**3, 7, 19, 30; **37:**17, 20; **38:**3, 4, 17, 18, 20, 22, 23^2; **39:**16, 17, 18; **40:**9, 15; **42:**2, 5, 6^3, 11^2, 17, 18^2; **44:**8^2, 12^3, 26, 27^2, 29; **46:**10, 11, 19, 23, 24^2, 26, 27^2; **47:**2, 6^3, 7; **48:**2^2, 3, 4, 6, 7, 8, 9, 10^2, 13, 26, 28, 30, 33, 34, 37^2, 38, 39, 41, 42, 43, 44, 46; **49:**2^4, 5^2, 10, 13, 17^2, 22, 23, 26, 32, 33, 36, 37; **50:**5, 8, 9^2, 10^2, 12^3, 13^3, 19, 20^3, 26, 30, 36, 37, 38, 39^2, 41; **51:**2, 6, 8^2, 26, 29, 35, 46, 47, 58^3, 62, 63, 64

Lam 1:12, 17, 21; **2:**6, 20; **3:**6, 29^2; **4:**9^2, 21^2; **5:**6, 21

Ezk 2:6^6, 8; **3:**9^2, 12, 20, 26^2; **4:**3^2, 7, 10, 17; **5:**12, 13^2, 15, 16; **6:**4^2, 6^6, 8, 9, 13; **7:**4, 11, 16, 17^2, 18, 19^2, 24, 25, 26, 27^2; **9:**4; **11:**3, 11^2, 16, 20^2; **12:**3^2, 11, 13, 19, 20^2, 24, 25, 28^2; **13:**9^3, 11, 12, 13, 14^2, 21^2; **14:**3, 9, 10, 11^3, 15, 16^2, 18, 22^3; **15:**3, 5; **16:**16, 20, 25, 28, 42^2, 52, 54, 61, 63; **17:**8, 14, 15, 20, 21, 23; **18:**5, 13, 20^2, 22, 24, 30; **19:**9, 14^2; **20:**3, 9, 12, 14, 20, 22, 31^2, 32^2, 41, 47^2, 48; **21:**7^4, 11^2, 12^3, 13, 14, 15, 23^2, 24^2, 26, 27, 32^3; **22:**5^2, 14, 21, 22; **23:**25, 29, 32, 33, 46, 48; **24:**8, 10, 11^3, 12, 13, 23, 25, 27^3; **25:**10; **26:**2, 5, 6, 13, 14^2, 16, 17, 18, 20, 21^3; **27:**7, 30, 34, 35^3, 36^2; **28:**9, 19^3, 22^2, 23, 24, 25; **29:**5, 7, 9, 11, 12, 14, 15, 16, 19; **30:**3, 4^2, 7^2, 8, 11, 13, 16, 18, 21^2; **31:**13, 16, 17, 18^2; **32:**6, 10, 12, 15, 19, 25, 27, 28, 30^2, 31, 32; **33:**4, 5, 6, 10, 12, 13, 16, 27^2, 28; **34:**2, 10, 14, 22, 23, 24, 26, 27, 28, 29; **35:**4, 10, 15; **36:**3, 9, 10^2, 12, 23, 25, 28^2, 32^2, 33, 34, 37, 38; **37:**19, 20, 21, 22^3, 23^2, 24, 25, 26, 27^3, 28; **38:**7^2, 8, 9, 16^2, 19, 20, 21, 23; **39:**4, 12, 13^2, 16, 19^2, 20, 25, 28; **42:**13; **43:**10, 11, 12, 13^3, 14^2, 15^2, 16, 17^3, 19, 27; **44:**2^3, 7, 11, 14, 17, 28, 29, 30, 31; **45:**1^3, 2, 3, 4^2, 6, 7^2, 8, 11^2, 12^2, 17, 21; **46:**1^3, 2, 4, 5^2, 6^2, 11, 16^2, 17^2, 18; **47:**5, 8, 9^2, 10^2, 11^2, 12^2, 13, 15, 17, 20, 22; **48:**8^2, 9, 10^2, 11, 12, 13, 15^2, 16, 17, 18^3, 20, 21^3, 22, 28, 31, 35

Dan 1:13; **2:**5^2, 9, 13^2, 20, 28, 40, 41^2, 42, 44^2; **3:**6, 11, 15^2, 17, 18, 19, 28, 29^2; **4:**1, 15^2, 16^2, 19, 23^2, 25, 26, 27^2, 32; **5:**7^2, 10, 12, 16^2, 17, 29; **6:**1, 7, 8, 12, 15, 17, 25, 26^2; **7:**14, 23^2, 24, 25, 27; **8:**13^2, 14, 17, 19^2, 24, 25, 26; **9:**16, 25^2, 26^2, 27; **10:**19^3; **11:**2, 4^3, 5^3, 6, 10^2, 11^2, 12^2, 15, 16, 17, 19, 20, 22^2, 25, 27^2, 28, 29, 30, 32, 34, 36^2, 41, 43; **12:**1^3, 3, 4, 6, 7^2, 8, 10, 11^2, 13

Hos 1:9, 10^3, 11^2; **2:**4, 16, 17; **3:**3^2; **4:**3, 6, 9, 19; **5:**9^2, 12, 14; **7:**4, 16; **8:**4, 5, 6, 7, 8, 11; **9:**4^3, 6, 12, 17; **10:**2, 6^2, 8, 10, 14, 15; **11:**5; **13:**3, 7, 10, 14^3, 15^2, 16^2; **14:**5, 6, 7

Joel 1:11; **2:**2, 6, 8, 10, 18, 19, 21, 22, 23, 24, 26^2, 27, 31, 32^2; **3:**12, 15, 16, 17, 19^2

Am 3:3, 6^3, 11^2, 12, 14; **5:**6, 14, 15^2, 16, 17, 20; **6:**2, 7; **7:**3, 6, 9^2, 11, 17^2; **8:**3^2, 5, 8; **9:**1, 3, 5, 15

Oba 9^2, 10, 15, 16, 17^2, 18^2, 21

Jna 1:4, 6, 11, 12; **3:**4, 7, 8; **4:**4, 6, 9^2

Mic 1:2, 4^2, 7^2, 14; **2:**4, 11; **3:**6^3, 7, 12; **4:**1^2, 10^2, 11; **5:**2^2, 4, 5, 7, 8, 9^2; **6:**7, 14^2; **7:**4, 8, 10, 11^2, 13, 16^2, 17

Nah 1:10^2, 12^2, 14; **2:**3^2, 5, 6^2, 7^2, 13; **3:**11^2, 12^2, 13

Hab 1:5, 10; **2:**5, 7, 9, 14, 16^3; **3:**17^3

Zep 1:10, 17, 18^2; **2:**3^2, 4^2, 5, 6, 7, 9, 11, 12, 14; **3:**7, 8, 11^2, 13, 14, 16^2

Hag 1:2, 8; **2:**4^3, 9, 12, 13^2

Zec 1:4, 9, 16^2, 17, 19; **2:**4, 5^2, 9, 11^2, 13; **3:**9; **4:**5, 12, 13; **5:**3^2, 11; **6:**13^2, 14; **8:**3, 5, 6^2, 8^2, 9^2, 11, 12, 13^2, 19; **9:**1^2, 2, 4, 5^3, 7^2, 10^2, 14, 15, 16; **10:**5^2, 6, 7^2, 10, 11; **11:**5, 9^2, 16, 17^3; **12:**2, 3^2, 5, 6, 8^2, 10, 11; **13:**1, 2, 4, 7, 8^2; **14:**1, 2^2, 4, 6, 7^3, 8^2, 9^2, 10^2, 11^2, 12, 13, 14, 15^2, 17^2, 18, 19, 20^2, 21^2

Mal 1:5, 6^2, 8, 9, 11^3, 14; **2:**4; **3:**4, 5, 10^2, 12, 17; **4:**1, 3

Mt 1:22, 23; **2:**4, 13, 15, 18, 23^2; **3:**13, 14, 15; **4:**1, 3^2, 6, 14; **5:**4, 6, 9, 12, 13^3, 14, 18, 19^2, 21, 22^3, 24, 25, 29, 30, 37, 45, 48; **6:**1, 4, 5^2, 7, 8, 9, 10, 16, 21, 22^2, 23^3, 31, 33; **7:**1, 2^2, 7^2, 8, 13, 14, 26; **8:**3, 8, 12^2, 13, 17; **9:**2^2, 5, 12, 15, 21, 22, 29; **10:**13^2, 15, 16, 18, 19, 21, 22^2, 23, 25, 26^2, 36; **11:**6, 22, 23, 24; **12:**11, 17, 27, 31^2, 32^2, 37^2, 39, 40, 45; **13:**12^2, 15, 35, 40, 42, 49, 50; **14:**9, 27^2, 28; **15:**5, 6, 13, 14, 28, 31; **16:**2, 3, 4, 19^2, 21^2, 22^2, 23^2, 28; **17:**4, 7, 9, 17, 20, 22, 23; **18:**3, 7, 8, 9, 12, 13, 16, 17, 18^2, 19, 25^2; **19:**5, 9, 10, 12, 21, 25, 30^2; **20:**16^2, 18, 22, 23^2, 26^3, 27^2, 28, 33; **21:**4, 13, 21^3, 43, 44; **22:**13, 28; **23:**4, 5, 7, 8, 10, 11, 12^2, 26, 31; **24:**2^2, 3^2, 6, 7, 9^2, 10, 13, 14, 16, 20, 21^2, 22^3, 27, 28, 29^2, 34, 37, 39, 40^2, 41^2, 43, 44, 51; **25:**1, 9, 29^2, 30, 32; **26:**2, 5, 13^2, 31^2, 33^2, 37, 39, 42, 46, 54^2, 56, 63; **27:**22, 23, 25, 26, 35, 40, 42, 49, 58, 64^2; **28:**10

Mk 1:41; **2:**5, 9, 20, 22^2; **3:**14, 24, 25, 26, 28; **4:**12^2, 21^2, 22, 24^2, 25^2, 31, 39; **5:**18, 23, 28, 34, 36, 43; **6:**9, 11, 27, 50^2; **7:**4, 11^2, 24, 27, 34; **8:**12, 31^2, 33^2, 38^2; **9:**1, 5, 12, 19, 34, 35^2, 43, 45^2, 47, 49^2; **10:**8, 12, 26, 31, 33, 38, 39, 40, 41, 43^3, 44^2, 45, 49^2; **11:**2, 10, 17, 23^2; **12:**7, 23; **13:**2^2, 4^3, 7^3, 8^2, 9^2, 10, 11, 12, 13^2, 14, 18, 19^2, 20, 24, 25, 30; **14:**2, 9^2, 19, 27^2, 29, 33^2, 49, 64; **15:**15; **16:**6, 16^2

Lk 1:15^2, 20^3, 29, 32^2, 33, 34, 35^2, 37, 38, 45, 57, 60, 66, 68, 71, 76; **2:**1, 3, 5, 6, 10, 12, 23, 34, 35, 49; **3:**5^4, 7, 12, 14, 23; **4:**3^2, 7, 9; **5:**13, 15, 23, 35, 37, 38; **6:**17, 20, 21, 35^2, 36, 37^3, 38^2, 40; **7:**7, 23; **8:**9, 12, 17^2, 18^2, 38, 43, 48, 50; **9:**22^3, 25, 26^2, 27, 33, 41, 44, 46, 48, 51; **10:**5, 6, 11, 12, 14, 15, 42; **11:**2^2, 9^2, 10, 18, 19, 29, 30, 35, 36^2, 46, 50, 51; **12:**2^2, 3^2, 4, 9, 10^2, 19, 20^2, 26, 29, 31, 34, 35, 39, 40, 45, 47, 48^2, 49, 50^2, 52, 53, 55, 58; **13:**14, 16, 23, 24, 28, 30^2, 32, 33; **14:**8, 11^2, 12, 14^2, 23, 26, 27, 31, 33^2, 34; **15:**7, 14, 19, 21, 23, 24, 32; **16:**2, 21, 31; **17:**6^2, 24, 25, 26, 30, 31, 34^3, 35^2, 36^2, 37; **18:**13, 14^2, 26, 31, 32^2, 40; **19:**7, 15, 19, 26^2, 38; **20:**6, 13, 14, 18, 25^2, 35; **21:**6^2, 7^2, 8, 9, 11^2, 15, 16^2, 17, 22^2, 23, 24^3, 25, 26, 32, 34, 36; **22:**7, 16, 24, 26^2, 37, 42^2, 52; **23:**23, 24, 31, 32, 35, 37, 39, 43; **24:**7^2, 20, 36, 44, 47, 49

Jn 1:25, 31, 42; **3:**2, 3, 4^2, 5, 7, 9, 14, 17, 20, 21, 27; **4:**14; **5:**6, 34; **6:**12, 20, 45; **7:**4, 17, 23; **8:**5, 33^2, 36, 41, 55; **9:**3, 22, 25, 27, 31, 39; **10:**9, 16, 24, 35; **11:**4; **12:**23, 26, 31, 32, 34, 36, 38, 40, 42; **13:**18, 24, 32; **14:**1, 3, 13, 17, 21, 27^2; **15:**7, 8, 11, 25; **16:**1, 20^2, 24, 32, 33; **17:**11, 12, 19, 21^2, 22, 23, 24, 26; **18:**9, 28, 32, 36; **19:**16, 24^2, 28, 31^2, 36^2; **20:**15, 19, 21, 26, 27; **21:**18, 25^2

Act 1:5, 8, 20, 22^2; **2:**14, 20, 21, 24, 25, 38, 47; **3:**14, 19^2, 23, 25; **4:**9, 10, 12, 19, 28, 30; **5:**31, 36, 38, 39^2; **7:**7, 35; **8:**20, 22, 36; **9:**6, 17; **10:**42, 47, 48; **11:**14, 16, 28; **12:**19; **13:**11, 22, 28, 38, 39, 42, 47^2; **14:**3, 9; **15:**1^2, 11, 24; **16:**13, 15, 30, 31; **17:**18, 27; **18:**6, 9, 15^2; **19:**2, 26, 27^3, 36^2, 39, 40; **20:**16; **21:**13, 14^2, 24, 26, 33, 34, 37; **22:**5, 10, 15, 16, 24^2; **23:**3, 11, 29, 35; **24:**4, 15, 21; **25:**4, 5, 6, 9, 10, 11^2, 17, 19, 20, 21^2; **26:**3, 8, 23, 28; **27:**10, 20, 22^2, 24, 25^2, 26, 31; **28:**27, 28

Ro 1:1, 4, 7^2, 11, 12, 19, 22; **2:**12, 13, 25, 26; **3:**4^2, 8, 19, 20, 25, 26; **4:**11^3, 13, 14, 16^2, 17, 18, 24; **5:**9, 10, 15, 19; **6:**5, 6, 8, 11, 17; **7:**2, 3^4, 4, 10; **8:**4, 6^2, 7, 9, 10, 17^2, 18^2, 21, 26, 29^2, 31^2, 39; **9:**7, 17, 26, 27^2, 33; **10:**1, 9, 11, 13, 15; **11:**6, 9, 10, 12, 15^2, 16^2, 17, 19, 20, 22, 23, 24^2, 25^3, 26, 35, 36; **12:**2^2, 9, 10, 16^2, 18, 21; **13:**1^2, 3, 4, 5, 9; **14:**4, 5, 9, 14, 15, 16; **15:**5, 12, 16^2, 24^2, 31^2, 32, 33; **16:**11, 20, 24, 27

1Co 1:1, 2, 3, 8, 10^2, 17; **3:**13^2, 15^2, 18^2; **4:**2, 3, 6, 16, 17; **5:**2, 5, 7, 11; **6:**2, 5, 7, 9, 12, 16; **7:**5, 11, 12, 13, 18, 21, 23, 25, 26, 27, 29, 34, 39^2; **8:**5^2, 10; **9:**2, 10, 12, 15, 19, 23, 27; **10:**1, 7, 13^2, 21, 27, 30, 33; **11:**1, 6^5, 16, 18, 19^2, 27, 31, 32; **12:**13^2, 22, 23, 25, 26; **13:**3, 8^3, 10; **14:**7, 9^2, 10, 11^2, 20^3, 23, 26, 27, 28, 30, 31, 34, 37, 38^2, 40; **15:**9, 12, 13, 14, 15, 17, 22, 26, 28^3, 33, 37, 51, 52^2, 54, 57, 58; **16:**2, 4, 6, 10, 13, 14, 22, 23, 24

2Co 1:2, 3, 4, 6^2, 7, 11, 16, 17; **2:**4, 7, 9, 14; **3:**3, 7, 8, 9, 16; **4:**3, 7, 10, 11; **5:**2, 3^2, 4^2, 8^2, 9, 10, 13^2, 17, 20, 21^2; **6:**3, 13, 14, 16^2, 17, 18^2; **7:**10, 11; **8:**9, 10, 11, 12, 13, 14^3, 16, 23; **9:**3^2, 4, 5, 15; **10:**2^2, 8, 11, 15; **11:**3, 6, 7, 12, 15^2; **12:**6^2, 7^2, 11, 13, 14, 15^2, 16, 20^2; **13:**1, 5^2, 7, 11^4, 14

Gal 1:3, 5, 7, 8, 9, 10; **2:**3, 6^2, 9, 11, 16^2, 17; **3:**4, 8, 9, 15^2, 18, 22, 23, 24, 29; **4:**1, 9, 12, 18, 19, 20, 21, 30; **5:**1, 2, 10^2, 15, 18, 26; **6:**1^2, 3, 7, 9, 12, 16, 18

Eph 1:2, 3, 4, 12, 22; **3:**6, 10, 16, 18, 19, 21; **4:**14, 21, 23, 26, 31, 32; **5:**1, 3, 7, 17, 18^2, 24, 27, 31^2; **6:**3, 5, 8, 10, 11, 13, 16, 19, 23, 24

Php 1:2, 10, 20^3, 23, 26, 27^2, 30; **2:**1, 2, 3, 5, 6, 15, 17, 19, 28; **3:**9, 15^3, 17, 21; **4:**2, 5, 6^2, 8^2, 9, 11, 12^3, 20, 23

Col 1:2, 9, 12, 16, 20, 23; **2:**2, 5, 20; **3:**1, 15, 19, 21; **4:**6, 16, 18

1Th 1:1; **2:**4, 9, 16; **3:**1, 3, 5; **4:**11, 13, 17^2; **5:**6, 7, 8, 13, 14, 23, 27, 28

2Th 1:5, 7, 9, 10^2, 12; **2:**2^2, 3, 6, 7, 8, 10, 12; **3:**1, 2, 8, 13, 14, 16, 18

1Ti 1:7, 10, 17; **2:**1, 4, 6, 12, 15; **3:**2, 8, 10, 11, 12; **4:**3, 4^2, 6, 12; **5:**7, 9, 13, 16, 17, 22, 25; **6:**1, 8, 9, 16, 17, 18, 21

2Ti 1:4, 8^2, 15; **2:**1, 2, 4, 6, 11, 15, 21, 24; **3:**2, 9, 17; **4:**2, 4, 6, 15, 16, 17, 18, 22^2

Tit 1:6, 7, 9, 11, 13; **2:**2, 3, 4, 5^2, 6, 8^2, 9; **3:**1^2, 2, 7, 8, 12, 13, 14, 15

Phlm 8, 14, 22, 25

Heb 1:5^2, 12, 14; **2:**3, 17^2; **3:**5, 12, 13; **4:**15; **5:**5, 11, 12^2; **6:**8, 12; **7:**11; **8:**4, 10^2, 12; **9:**16, 23; **10:**2, 13, 29; **11:**16, 18, 24, 40; **12:**3, 8, 9, 10, 11, 13^2, 15, 16, 18, 19, 20, 27, 28; **13:**2, 5^2, 9^2, 19, 21, 25

Jas 1:4, 5, 13, 18, 19, 22, 23, 25, 26; **2:**12, 15, 16; **3:**1, 4, 10, 17; **4:**4, 9^2, 14; **5:**3, 7, 8, 9, 12, 15, 16

1Pt 1:2, 3, 5, 6, 7^2, 13^2, 15, 16, 21; **2:**3, 6, 7, 13, 18, 20; **3:**1^2, 3, 4, 7, 8^3, 13, 14^2, 15, 16, 17; **4:**6, 7, 11^2, 13^2, 14, 16, 17, 18; **5:**1, 5^2, 8^2, 11, 14

2Pt 1:2, 4, 8[2], 11, 12[2], 15; 2:1, 2, 4, 9, 12; 3:2, 8, 10, 11[2], 12, 14[2], 16, 18

1Jn 1:4; 2:19, 28; 3:1, 2[2]; 4:10, 14

2Jn 2, 3, 12

3Jn 2, 8, 14

Jude 2, 18, 19, 25

Rev 1:4, 6, 19; 2:10[2], 11, 19, 27; 3:2, 5, 18[2], 19; 4:1; 5:13; 6:11[2], 17; 7:12; 9:5; 10:6, 7, 9; 11:5, 9, 18; 12:2, 4, 15; 13:10, 15; 14:10; 16:5, 12; 17:17; 18:4, 8, 21[2], 22[4], 23; 19:7, 8; 20:3[2], 6, 7, 10; 21:3[3], 4[2], 7[2], 25[2]; 22:3[2], 4, 5, 6, 11[4], 12, 21

BECAME

Gen 2:7, 10; 6:4; 19:26; 20:12; 21:20; 24:67; 26:13; 44:32; 47:20, 26; 49:15

Ex 2:10; 4:3, 4; 7:10, 12; 8:17[2]; 9:10, 24; 36:13

Nu 12:10; 26:10

Dt 26:5

Jos 7:5; 14:14; 24:32

Jdg 1:30, 33, 35; 8:27; 15:14; 17:5, 12

Ru 4:16

1Sa 10:12; 16:21; 18:29; 22:2; 25:37, 42

2Sa 2:25; 4:4; 8:2, 6, 14; 11:27

1Ki 11:24; 12:30; 13:6, 33, 34

2Ki 17:3, 15; 24:1

1Ch 18:2, 6, 13; 19:19

2Ch 27:6

Neh 9:25

Est 8:17

Ps 69:11; 83:10; 109:25

Jer 51:30

Ezk 17:6[2]; 19:3, 6; 23:10; 31:5; 34:5, 8[2]; 36:4

Dan 2:35[2]; 8:4; 10:15

Oba 12

Mt 28:4

Mk 9:3

Act 10:10

Ro 1:21, 22; 6:18

1Co 9:20, 22; 13:11

2Co 8:9

Php 2:8

1Th 1:6; 2:14

Heb 2:10; 5:9; 7:26; 10:33; 11:7

Rev 6:12[2]; 8:8, 11; 16:3, 4

BECAMEST

1Ch 17:22

Ezk 16:8

BECAUSE

Gen 2:3, 23; 3:10, 14, 17, 20; 5:29; 7:7; 11:9; 12:13, 17; 16:11; 18:20[2]; 19:13; 20:11, 18; 21:11, 12[2], 13, 25, 31; 22:16, 18; 25:21, 28; 26:5, 7, 9, 20; 27:20, 23, 41, 46; 28:11; 29:15, 33, 34; 30:18, 20; 31:30, 31; 32:32; 33:11[2]; 34:7, 13, 19, 27; 35:7; 36:7; 37:3; 38:15, 26; 39:9, 23; 41:32, 57; 43:18[2], 32; 46:30; 47:20; 49:4

Ex 1:12, 19, 21; 2:10; 4:26; 5:21; 8:12; 9:11; 12:39; 13:8; 14:11; 17:7[2], 16; 18:15; 19:18; 29:33, 34; 32:35; 40:35

Lev 6:4, 9; 10:13; 11:4, 5, 6; 14:48; 15:2; 16:16[2]; 19:8, 20; 20:3; 21:23; 22:7, 25; 26:10, 35, 43[3]

Nu 3:13; 6:7, 12; 7:9; 9:13; 11:3, 14, 20, 34; 12:1; 13:24; 14:16, 22, 24, 43; 15:31, 34; 19:13, 20; 20:12, 13, 24; 21:4; 22:3[2], 22, 29, 32; 25:13; 26:62; 27:4; 30:5, 14; 32:11, 17, 19; 35:28

Dt 1:27, 36; 2:5, 9, 19, 25; 4:3, 37; 7:7, 8[2]; 8:20; 9:18, 25, 28[2]; 12:20; 13:5, 10; 14:8, 29; 15:2, 10, 16[2]; 16:15; 18:12; 19:6; 20:3; 21:14; 22:19, 21, 24[2], 29; 23:4[2], 5, 7; 24:1; 27:20; 28:20, 45, 47, 55, 62; 29:25; 31:17, 29; 32:3, 19, 47, 51[2]; 33:21

Jos 2:9, 11, 24; 5:1, 6, 7; 6:1, 17, 25; 7:12, 15[2]; 9:9, 18, 20, 24[2]; 10:2[2], 42; 11:6; 14:9, 14; 17:1, 6; 20:5; 22:31; 23:3

Jdg 1:19; 2:18, 20; 3:12; 5:23; 6:2, 6, 7, 22, 27, 30[2], 31, 32; 8:20, 24; 9:18; 10:10; 11:13; 12:4; 13:22; 14:17; 15:6; 18:28; 20:36; 21:15, 22

1Sa 1:6, 20; 2:1, 25; 3:13; 4:21[2]; 6:19[2]; 8:18; 9:13, 16; 10:1; 12:10, 22; 13:11, 14; 14:29; 15:23, 24; 16:7; 17:32; 18:3, 12, 16; 19:4[2]; 20:17, 18, 34; 21:8; 22:17[2]; 24:5; 25:28; 26:12, 16, 21; 28:18, 20; 30:6, 13, 16, 22

2Sa 1:9, 10, 12; 2:6; 3:11, 30; 6:8, 12; 8:10; 10:5; 12:6[2], 10, 14, 25; 13:22; 14:15, 26; 16:8, 10; 18:20; 19:21, 26, 42; 21:1, 7; 22:8, 20; 23:6

1Ki 1:50; 2:7, 26[2]; 3:2, 11, 19; 7:47; 8:11, 33, 35, 64; 9:9; 10:9; 11:9, 33, 34; 14:13, 15, 16; 15:5, 13, 30; 16:7; 17:7; 19:7, 14; 20:28, 36, 42; 21:2, 4, 6, 20, 29

2Ki 1:3, 6, 16, 17; 5:1; 8:12, 29; 9:14; 10:30; 13:4, 23; 15:16; 17:26; 18:12; 19:28; 21:11, 15; 22:7, 13, 17, 19; 23:26

1Ch 1:19; 4:9, 41; 5:9, 20, 22; 7:21, 23; 9:27; 12:1; 13:10, 11; 14:2; 15:13, 22; 16:33, 41; 18:10; 19:2; 21:8, 30; 22:8; 23:28; 27:23, 24; 28:3; 29:3, 9

2Ch 1:11; 2:11; 6:24, 26; 7:2, 6, 7, 22; 8:11; 9:8; 12:2, 5, 14; 13:18; 14:6, 7; 15:16; 16:7, 8, 10; 17:3; 20:37; 21:3, 7, 10, 12; 22:6[2], 9; 24:16, 20, 24; 25:16, 20; 26:20; 27:6; 28:6, 9, 19, 23; 30:3; 34:21, 25, 27; 35:14; 36:15

Ezr 3:3, 11[2]; 4:14; 8:22; 9:4, 15; 10:6, 9

Neh 4:9; 5:3, 9, 15, 18; 6:18; 8:12; 9:37, 38; 13:2, 29

Est 1:15; 8:7; 9:3, 24

Job 3:10; 6:20; 8:9; 11:16, 18; 15:27; 17:12; 18:15; 20:19[2]; 23:17; 29:12; 30:11; 31:25[2]; 32:1, 2, 3, 4; 34:27, 36; 35:12, 15; 36:18; 38:21[2]; 39:11, 17

Ps 5:8, 11; 6:7[2]; 7:6; 8:2; 13:6; 14:6; 16:8; 18:7, 19; 27:11; 28:5, 6; 31:10; 33:21; 37:1, 7[2], 40; 38:3[2], 5, 20; 39:9; 41:11; 42:9; 43:2; 44:3; 45:4; 48:11; 52:9; 53:5; 55:3[2], 19; 59:9; 60:4, 8; 63:3, 7; 68:29; 69:7, 18; 78:22; 86:17; 91:9, 14[2]; 97:8; 102:10; 106:33; 107:11, 17[2], 26, 30; 109:16, 21; 116:1, 2; 118:1; 119:53, 56, 62, 74, 100, 136, 139, 158, 164; 122:9

Prv 1:24; 21:7; 22:22; 24:13, 19

Ecc 2:17, 18; 4:9; 5:20; 8:6, 11, 13, 15, 17; 10:15; 12:3, 5, 9

Song 1:3, 6[2]; 3:8

Isa 2:6; 3:8, 16; 5:13, 24; 6:5; 7:5, 24; 8:20; 10:27; 14:20, 29; 15:1[2]; 17:9, 10; 19:16, 17, 20; 22:4; 24:5; 26:3; 28:15, 28; 30:12; 31:1[2]; 32:14; 37:29; 40:7; 43:20; 48:4; 49:7; 50:2; 51:13; 53:9, 12; 55:5; 60:5, 9; 61:1; 64:7; 65:12, 16[2]; 66:4

Jer 2:35[2]; 4:4, 17, 18[2], 19, 28, 31; 5:6, 14; 6:19, 30; 7:13; 8:14, 19; 9:10, 13, 19[2]; 10:5; 12:4, 11, 13; 13:17, 25; 14:4, 5, 6, 16; 15:4, 17; 16:11, 18; 17:13; 18:15; 19:4, 8, 13, 15; 20:8, 17; 21:12; 22:9, 15; 23:9[3], 10, 38; 25:8, 16, 27, 37, 38[2]; 26:3; 28:16; 29:15, 19, 23, 25, 31, 32; 30:14, 15, 17; 31:15, 19; 32:24, 32; 35:16, 17, 18; 39:18; 40:3; 41:9, 18[2]; 44:3, 22[2], 23[2]; 46:15, 21, 23; 47:4; 48:7, 36, 42, 45; 50:7, 11[3], 13, 24; 51:11, 51, 55, 56

Lam 1:3[2], 4, 8, 16[2]; 2:11; 3:22, 28, 51; 5:9, 10, 18

Ezk 3:20, 21; 5:7, 9, 11; 6:9; 7:19; 12:19; 13:8, 10[2], 22; 14:5, 15; 15:8; 16:15, 28, 36, 43, 63; 18:18, 28; 20:16, 24; 21:7, 13, 24[2], 28; 22:19; 23:30[2], 35, 45; 24:13; 25:3, 6, 8, 12, 15; 26:2; 28:2, 5, 6, 17; 29:6, 9, 20; 31:5, 10; 33:29; 34:5, 8[2], 21; 35:5, 10, 15; 36:2, 3, 6, 13; 39:23; 44:2, 7, 12; 47:9, 12

Dan 2:8; 3:22, 29; 4:9; 6:3, 23; 7:11; 9:7, 8, 11, 16; 11:35

Hos 4:1, 6, 10, 13, 19; 5:1, 11; 7:13; 8:1, 11; 9:6, 17; 10:3, 5[2], 13, 15; 11:5, 6

Joel 1:5, 11, 12, 18; 2:20; 3:5, 19

Am 1:3, 6, 9, 11, 13; 2:1, 4, 6; 4:12

Jna 1:10

Mic 2:1, 10; 6:13; 7:9, 13, 17, 18

Nah 3:4, 11

Hab 1:16; 2:3, 5, 8[2], 17

Zep 1:17; 2:10; 3:11

Hag 1:9

Zec 8:10; 9:8[2]; 10:2, 5; 11:2

Mal 2:2, 14

Mt 2:18; 5:36; 7:14; 9:36; 11:20, 25; 12:41; 13:5, 6, 11, 13, 21, 58; 14:5; 15:32; 16:7, 8; 17:20; 18:7, 32; 19:8; 20:7, 15, 31; 21:46; 23:29; 24:12; 26:31, 33; 27:6, 19

Mk 1:34; 3:9, 30; 4:5, 6, 29; 5:4; 6:6, 34; 7:19; 8:2, 16, 17; 9:38, 41; 11:18; 12:24; 14:27; 15:42; 16:14

Lk 1:7, 20; 2:4, 7; 4:18; 5:19; 8:6, 30; 9:7, 49, 53; 10:20; 11:8[2], 18; 12:17; 13:2, 14; 15:27; 16:8; 17:9; 18:5; 19:3, 11[2], 17, 21, 31, 44; 23:8

Jn 1:50; 2:24; 3:18, 19, 23, 29; 4:41, 42; 5:16, 18, 27, 30; 6:2, 26[2], 41; 7:1, 7, 22, 23, 30, 39, 43; 8:22, 37, 43, 44, 45, 47; 9:16, 22; 10:13, 17, 26, 33, 36; 11:9, 10, 42; 12:6, 11, 30, 39, 42; 13:29; 14:12, 17, 19, 28; 15:19, 21, 27; 16:3, 4, 6, 9, 10, 11, 16, 17, 21, 27, 32; 17:14; 19:7, 31, 42; 20:13, 29; 21:17

Act 2:6, 24, 27; 4:21; 6:1; 8:11, 20; 10:45; 12:3, 20, 23; 13:27; 14:12; 16:3; 17:18, 31; 18:2, 3; 20:16; 22:29, 30; 24:11; 25:20; 26:2, 3; 27:4, 9, 12; 28:2[2], 18, 20

Ro 1:19, 21; 3:2; 4:15; 5:5; 6:15, 19; 8:7, 10[2], 21, 27; 9:7, 28, 32; 11:20; 14:23; 15:15

1Co 1:25; 2:14; 3:13; 6:7; 11:10; 12:15, 16; 15:9, 15

2Co 2:13; 5:14; 7:13; 11:7, 11

Gal 2:4, 11; 3:19; 4:6, 16

Eph 4:18; 5:6, 16

Php 1:7; 2:26, 30; 4:17

1Th 2:8, 9, 13; 4:6

2Th 1:3, 10; 2:10, 13; 3:9

1Ti 1:13; 4:10; 5:12; 6:2[2]

Phlm 7

Heb 3:19; 4:6; 6:13; 7:23, 24; 8:9; 10:2; 11:5, 11, 23

Jas 1:10; 4:2, 3

1Pt 1:16; 2:21; 5:8

1Jn 2:8, 11, 12, 13[3], 14[2], 21[2]; 3:1, 9, 12, 14, 16, 22; 4:1, 4, 9, 13, 17, 18, 19; 5:6, 10

3Jn 7

Jude 16

Rev 1:7; 2:4, 14, 20; 3:10, 16, 17; 5:4; 8:11; 11:10, 17; 12:12; 14:8; 16:5, 11, 21

BECOME

Gen 3:22; 9:15; 18:18; 24:35; 32:10; 34:16; 37:20; 48:19[2]

Ex 4:9; 7:9, 19; 8:16; 9:9; 15:2, 6; 23:29; 32:1, 23

Lev 19:29

Nu 5:24, 27

Dt 27:9; 28:37

Jos 9:13

Jdg 16:17

1Sa 28:16

2Sa 7:24

1Ki 2:15; 14:3

2Ki 21:14; 22:19

Est 2:11

Job 7:5; 15:28; 21:7; 30:19, 21

Ps 14:3; 28:1; 53:3; 62:10; 69:8, 22[2]; 79:4; 109:7; 118:14, 21, 22; 119:83

Prv 29:21

Isa 1:21, 22; 7:24; 12:2; 14:10[2]; 19:11, 13; 29:11; 34:9; 35:7; 59:6; 60:22

Jer 2:5; 3:1; 5:13, 27; 7:11; 10:21; 22:5; 26:18; 49:13; 50:23, 37; 51:37, 41

Lam 1:1[2], 2, 6, 11; 4:1, 3, 8

Ezk 22:4, 18, 19; 26:5; 36:35[2]; 37:17

Dan 4:22; 9:16; 11:23

Hos 12:8; 13:15, 16

Jna 4:5

Mic 3:12

Zep 1:13; 2:15

Zec 4:7

Mt 18:3; 21:42

Mk 1:17; 12:10

Lk 20:17

Jn 1:12

Act 4:11; 7:40; 12:18

Ro 3:12, 19; 4:18; 6:22; 7:4, 13

1Co 3:18; 7:18; 8:9; 13:1; 15:20

2Co 5:17; 12:11

Gal 4:16; 5:4

Tit 2:1

Phlm 6

Heb 5:12

Jas 2:4, 11

Rev 11:15; 18:2

BECOMETH

Ps 93:5

Prv 10:4; 17:7, 18

Ecc 4:14

Mt 3:15; 13:22, 32

Mk 4:19, 32

Ro 16:2

Eph 5:3

Php 1:27

1Ti 2:10

Tit 2:3

BEEN

Gen 13:3; 26:8; 31:5, 38, 41, 42; 38:26; 45:6; 46:32, 34; 47:9

Ex 2:22; 9:18; 14:12; 18:3; 21:29; 34:10

Lev 10:19; 13:7

Nu 19:20

Dt 2:7; 4:32^2; 9:7, 24; 15:18; 21:3; 31:27

Jos 7:7; 9:4; 10:27; 23:9

Jdg 16:8, 17

Ru 2:11

1Sa 1:13; 4:7, 9, 17; 9:24; 14:29, 30, 38; 15:21; 18:19; 19:4; 20:13; 21:5; 25:28, 34; 29:3, 6, 8

2Sa 1:21, 26; 12:8; 13:20, 32; 14:32^2; 15:34

1Ki 1:37; 2:26; 14:8; 16:31; 17:7; 19:10, 14

2Ki 4:13; 20:12

1Ch 17:8; 28:3; 29:25

2Ch 1:12; 15:3; 23:9

Ezr 2:1; 4:18, 19^2, 20; 5:16; 8:35; 9:2, 4, 7^2, 8; 10:6, 8

Neh 2:1; 5:15; 7:6; 13:10

Est 2:6^2, 12; 4:11; 6:3; 7:4

Job 3:13^2, 16; 10:19^3; 22:9; 31:9, 27; 38:17; 42:11

Ps 25:6; 27:9; 35:14; 37:25; 42:3; 50:8, 18; 59:16; 60:1; 61:3; 63:7; 69:22; 71:6; 73:14; 85:1; 89:38; 90:1; 94:17; 115:12; 119:54, 71, 92; 124:1, 2; 143:3

Prv 7:26

Ecc 1:9, 10, 16; 2:12; 3:15^2; 4:3, 16; 6:10

Isa 1:6, 9^2; 5:4; 17:10; 23:16; 25:4; 26:17, 18^2; 30:24; 38:9; 39:1; 40:21; 42:14; 43:4, 22; 48:18, 19^2; 49:21; 52:15; 57:11; 60:15; 66:2

Jer 2:31; 3:2, 3^2; 4:17; 15:9; 20:17; 22:21; 28:8; 32:31; 34:14; 42:18; 43:5; 44:18; 48:11^2; 50:6, 29; 51:5, 7

Ezk 2:5; 4:14; 10:10; 11:17; 16:31; 20:41, 43; 22:13; 28:13; 29:6; 33:33; 34:12; 38:8

Dan 5:15; 9:12^2

Hos 5:1, 2

Joel 1:2; 2:2

Oba 16

Mic 5:2

Zep 3:19

Zec 1:2

Mal 1:9; 2:9, 14; 3:13

Mt 1:6; 5:31, 33, 38, 43; 11:21, 23^2; 13:35; 23:30^2; 25:21, 23; 26:9, 24^2

Mk 5:4^2, 18; 6:49; 8:2; 14:5^2, 21; 15:44; 16:10, 11

Lk 1:4, 70; 2:44; 4:16; 7:10; 8:2; 10:13^2; 16:11, 12; 19:17; 24:21

Jn 5:6; 9:18; 11:21, 32, 39; 12:1, 38; 14:9; 15:27

Act 1:16; 4:13, 16; 5:26; 6:15; 7:52; 9:18; 10:11; 11:5; 13:1, 46; 14:19, 26; 15:7; 16:27; 19:21; 20:18; 23:10, 27; 24:10, 19, 26; 25:14; 26:32

Ro 6:5; 9:29^2; 11:34; 15:22, 27; 16:2

1Co 1:11; 12:13

2Co 11:6, 21, 25; 12:11

Gal 3:1, 21^2, 27; 4:15; 5:13

Eph 3:9; 4:21

Php 2:26

Col 1:26; 2:7; 4:11

1Th 2:6

2Th 2:15

1Ti 5:9

2Ti 3:14

Tit 1:9

Heb 8:7^2; 11:15; 13:9

Jas 3:7; 5:5

2Pt 2:21

1Jn 2:19

Rev 5:6; 17:2

BEFORE

Gen 2:5^2; 6:11, 13; 7:1; 10:9^2; 11:28; 12:15; 13:9, 10, 13; 17:1, 18; 18:8, 22; 19:4, 13, 27; 20:15; 23:3, 12, 17, 18, 19; 24:7, 15, 33, 40, 45, 51; 25:9, 18; 27:4, 7^2, 10, 33; 29:26; 30:30, 33, 38, 39, 41; 31:2, 5, 32, 35, 37; 32:3, 16, 17, 20, 21; 33:3, 12, 14^2, 18; 34:10; 36:31; 37:18; 40:9; 41:43, 46, 50; 42:6, 24; 43:9, 14, 15, 33, 34; 44:14; 45:1, 5, 7, 28; 46:28; 47:6, 7, 10, 19; 48:5, 15, 20; 49:8, 30; 50:13, 16, 18

Ex 4:3, 21; 6:12, 30; 7:9, 10^2; 8:20, 26; 9:10, 11, 13; 10:1, 3, 10, 14; 11:10; 12:34; 13:21, 22; 14:2^2, 9, 19^2; 16:9, 33, 34; 17:5, 6; 18:12; 19:2, 7; 20:3, 20; 21:1; 22:9; 23:15, 17, 20, 23, 27, 28^2, 29, 30, 31; 25:30; 27:21^2; 28:12, 25, 29, 30^2, 35, 38; 29:10, 11, 23, 24, 25, 26, 42; 30:6^2, 8, 16, 36; 32:1, 5, 23, 34; 33:2, 19^2; 34:3, 6, 10, 11, 20, 23, 24^2, 34; 39:18; 40:5, 6, 23, 25, 26

Lev 1:3, 5, 11; 3:1, 7, 8, 12, 13; 4:4^2, 6^2, 7, 14, 15^2, 17^2, 18, 24; 6:7, 14^2, 25; 7:30; 8:26, 27, 29; 9:2, 4, 5^2, 21, 24; 10:1, 2, 3, 4, 15, 17, 19; 12:7; 14:11, 12, 16, 18, 23, 24, 27, 29, 31, 36; 15:14, 15, 30; 16:1, 2, 7, 10, 12, 13, 14, 15, 18, 30; 17:4; 18:23, 24, 27, 28, 30; 19:14, 22, 32; 20:23; 23:11, 20, 28, 40; 24:3, 4, 6, 8; 26:7, 8, 17, 37^2; 27:8, 11

Nu 3:4^2, 6, 7, 38^2; 5:16, 18, 25, 30; 6:12, 16, 20; 7:3^2, 10; 8:9, 10, 11, 13^2, 21, 22^2; 9:6^2; 10:9, 10, 33, 35; 11:6, 20; 13:22, 30; 14:5, 10, 14, 37, 42, 43; 15:15, 25, 28; 16:2, 7, 9, 16, 17, 38, 40, 43; 17:4, 7, 9, 10; 18:2, 19; 19:3, 4; 20:3, 8, 9, 10; 21:11; 22:32; 25:4, 6; 26:61; 27:2^3, 5, 14, 17^2, 19^2, 21^2, 22^2; 31:50, 54; 32:4, 17, 20, 21^2, 22^4, 27, 29^2, 32; 33:7^2, 8, 47, 52, 55; 35:12; 36:1^2

Dt 1:8, 21, 22, 30^2, 33, 38, 42, 45; 2:12, 21, 22, 31, 33; 3:18, 28; 4:8, 10, 32, 34, 38, 44; 5:7; 6:19, 22, 25; 7:1, 2, 22, 24; 8:20; 9:2, 3^2, 4^2, 5, 17, 18, 25; 10:8, 11; 11:23, 25, 26, 32; 12:7, 12, 18^2, 29, 30; 14:23, 26; 15:20; 16:11, 16^2; 17:12, 18; 18:7, 12; 19:17^2; 21:16; 22:6, 17; 23:14; 24:4, 13; 25:2; 26:4, 5, 10^2, 13; 27:7; 28:7^2, 25^2, 31^2, 66; 29:2, 10, 15; 30:1, 15, 19; 31:3^3, 5, 8, 11^2, 21; 32:52; 33:1, 10, 27

Jos 1:5, 14; 2:8; 3:1, 6^2, 10, 11, 14; 4:5, 7, 12, 13, 18, 23^2; 5:1; 6:4, 5, 6, 7, 8, 9, 13^2, 20, 26; 7:4, 5, 6, 8, 12^2, 13, 23; 8:5, 6^2, 10, 11, 14, 15, 33^2, 35; 9:24; 10:5, 8, 10, 11, 12, 14; 11:6; 13:3, 6, 25; 14:15; 15:7, 8, 15; 17:4^3, 7; 18:1, 6, 8, 10, 14, 16; 19:11, 46, 51; 20:6, 9; 21:44; 22:27, 29; 23:5, 9^2, 13; 24:1, 8, 12^2, 18

Jdg 1:10, 11, 23; 2:3, 14, 21; 3:2, 27; 4:14, 15, 23; 5:5^2; 6:9, 18; 7:24; 8:13, 28; 9:39, 40; 11:9, 11, 23, 24, 33; 12:5; 14:16, 17, 18; 16:3, 20; 18:6, 21; 20:23, 26^2, 28, 32, 35, 39, 42; 21:2

Ru 3:14; 4:4^2

1Sa 1:12, 15, 19, 22; 2:11, 15, 17, 18, 21, 28, 30, 35; 3:1; 4:2, 3, 17; 5:3, 4; 6:20; 7:6, 10; 8:11, 20; 9:12, 13, 15, 19, 24^2, 27; 10:5, 8, 19, 25; 11:15^2; 12:2^2, 3^2, 7, 16; 14:13, 21; 15:30^2, 33; 16:6, 8, 10, 16, 21, 22; 17:7, 31, 41, 57; 18:13, 16; 19:24; 20:1^2; 21:6, 7, 13; 22:4; 23:18, 24; 25:19, 23; 26:1, 3, 19, 20; 28:22, 25^2; 30:20; 31:1

2Sa 2:14, 17, 24; 3:28, 31, 34; 5:3, 20, 24; 6:4, 5, 14, 16, 17, 21^4; 7:15, 16, 18, 23, 26, 29; 10:6, 9, 13, 14, 15, 16, 18, 19; 11:13; 12:11, 12^2, 20; 13:9; 14:33; 15:1, 18; 18:7, 28; 19:8, 13, 17, 18, 28; 20:8; 21:9; 22:13, 23, 24; 24:13, 20

1Ki 1:2, 5, 23^2, 25, 28, 32; 2:4, 26, 45; 3:6, 12, 15, 16, 22, 24; 6:3^2, 7, 17, 21; 7:6^2, 49; 8:5, 8, 22, 23, 25^2, 28, 31, 33, 50, 54, 59, 62, 64^2, 65; 9:3, 4, 6, 25; 10:8; 11:7, 36; 12:6, 8, 30; 13:6; 14:9, 24; 15:3; 16:25, 30, 33; 17:1, 3, 5; 18:15, 46; 19:11^2, 19; 20:27; 21:10, 13, 26, 29^2; 22:10, 21

2Ki 1:13; 2:9, 15; 3:14, 24; 4:12, 31, 38, 43, 44; 5:15, 16, 23, 25; 6:22, 32; 8:9; 10:4; 11:18; 14:12; 15:10; 16:3, 14; 17:2, 8, 11; 18:5, 22; 19:14, 15, 26, 32; 20:3; 21:2, 9, 11; 22:10, 19^2; 23:3, 13, 25; 25:7, 29

1Ch 1:43; 5:25; 6:32; 10:1; 11:3, 13; 13:8, 10; 14:15; 15:24; 16:1, 4, 6, 29, 30, 37^2, 39; 17:8, 13, 16, 21, 24, 25, 27; 19:7, 9, 10, 14^2, 15, 16^2, 18, 19; 21:12, 30; 22:5, 18^2; 23:13, 31; 24:2, 6^2; 28:4; 29:10, 15, 22, 25

2Ch 1:5, 6, 10, 12, 13; 2:4, 6; 3:15, 17; 4:20; 5:6, 9; 6:12, 13, 14, 16, 19, 22, 24^2, 36; 7:4, 6, 7, 17, 19; 8:12, 14; 9:7, 11; 10:6, 8; 13:13, 14, 15, 16; 14:5, 7, 12^2, 13^2; 15:8; 18:9, 20; 19:2, 11; 20:5, 7, 9, 13, 16, 18, 21; 23:17; 24:14; 25:8, 14, 22; 26:19; 27:6; 28:3, 9, 14; 29:11, 19, 23; 30:9; 31:20; 32:12; 33:2, 7, 9, 12, 19, 23; 34:18, 24, 27^3, 31; 36:12

Ezr 3:12; 4:18, 23; 7:19, 28^2; 8:21, 29; 9:15^2; 10:1, 6

Neh 1:4, 6; 2:1, 13; 4:2, 5^2; 5:15; 6:19; 8:1, 2, 3^3; 9:8, 11, 24, 28, 32, 35; 12:36; 13:4, 19

Est 1:3, 11, 16, 17, 19; 2:11, 23; 3:7; 4:2, 6, 8; 6:1, 9, 11, 13^2; 7:6, 8, 9; 8:1, 3, 4, 5; 9:11, 25

Job 1:6; 2:1^2; 3:24; 4:15, 16, 19; 8:12, 16; 10:21; 13:15, 16; 15:4, 7, 32; 18:20; 21:8, 18, 33; 23:4, 17; 26:6; 30:11; 33:5; 35:14; 41:10, 22; 42:10, 11

Ps 5:8; 16:8; 18:6, 12, 22, 23, 42; 22:25, 27, 29; 23:5; 26:3; 31:19, 22; 34:ttl; 35:5; 36:1; 38:9, 17; 39:1, 5, 13; 41:12; 42:2; 44:15; 50:3, 8, 21; 51:3; 52:9; 54:3; 56:13; 57:6; 58:9; 61:7; 62:8; 68:1, 2, 3, 4, 7, 25; 69:19, 22; 72:9, 11; 73:22; 78:55; 79:11; 80:2, 9; 83:13; 84:7; 85:13; 86:9, 14; 88:1, 2; 89:14, 23, 36; 90:2, 8; 95:2, 6; 96:6, 9, 13; 97:3; 98:6, 9; 100:2; 101:3; 102:28, ttl; 105:17; 106:23; 109:15; 116:9; 119:30, 46, 67, 168, 169, 170; 138:1; 139:5; 141:2, 3; 142:2^2; 147:17

Prv 4:25; 5:21; 8:22, 25^2, 30; 14:19; 15:11, 33; 16:18^2; 17:14, 24; 18:12^2, 13, 16; 22:29^2; 23:1; 25:5, 26; 26:26; 27:4; 30:7

Ecc 1:10, 16; 2:7, 9, 26; 3:14; 4:16; 5:2, 6; 6:8; 7:17; 8:12, 13; 9:1

Song 8:12

Isa 1:12, 16; 7:16; 8:4^2; 9:3, 12; 13:16; 17:13^2, 14; 23:18; 24:23; 28:4; 30:8, 11; 36:7; 37:14, 27, 33; 38:3; 40:10, 17; 41:1, 2; 42:9, 16; 43:10, 13; 45:1^2, 2; 47:14; 48:5, 7, 19; 49:16; 52:12; 53:2, 7; 55:12; 57:16; 58:8; 59:12; 61:11; 62:11; 63:12; 65:6, 12, 24; 66:4, 7^2, 22, 23

Jer 1:5^2, 17; 2:22; 6:7, 21; 7:10; 8:2; 9:13; 13:16^2; 15:1, 9, 19; 17:16; 18:17, 20, 23; 19:7; 21:8; 24:1; 26:4; 28:8^2; 29:21; 30:20; 31:36^2; 32:12, 13, 30, 31; 33:9, 18, 24; 34:5, 15, 18; 35:5, 19; 36:7, 9, 22; 37:20; 38:10, 26; 39:6, 16; 40:4; 42:2, 9; 44:10^2; 47:1; 49:19, 37^2; 50:8, 44; 52:10, 33

Lam 1:5, 6, 22; 2:3, 19; 3:35

Ezk 2:10; 3:20; 4:1; 6:4, 5; 8:1, 11; 9:6; 14:1, 3, 4, 7; 16:18, 19, 50, 57; 20:1, 9, 14, 41; 21:6; 22:30; 23:24, 41; 28:9, 17; 30:24; 32:10; 33:31; 36:17, 23; 37:20; 38:16; 40:12, 22, 26, 47; 41:4, 12, 22; 42:1, 2, 4, 8, 11, 12, 13; 43:24; 44:3, 4, 11, 12, 15, 22; 45:7^2; 46:3, 9

Dan 1:5, 13, 18, 19; 2:2, 9, 10, 11, 24, 25, 31, 36; 3:3, 13; 4:6, 7, 8^2; 5:1, 13, 15, 17, 19, 23; 6:10, 11, 12, 13, 18, 22^2, 26; 7:7, 8, 10^2, 13, 20; 8:3, 4, 6, 7, 15; 9:10, 13, 18, 20; 10:12, 16; 11:16, 22

Hos 7:2

Joel 1:16; 2:3^2, 6, 10, 11, 31

Am 1:1; 2:9; 4:3; 9:4

Jna 1:2; 4:2

Mic 1:4; 2:13^2; 6:1, 4, 6^3

Nah 1:6; 2:1

Hab 1:3; 2:20; 3:5

Zep 2:2^4; 3:20

Hag 1:12; 2:14, 15

Zec 2:13; 3:1, 3, 4, 8, 9; 4:7; 6:5; 7:2; 8:10, 21, 22; 12:8; 14:4, 5, 20

Mal 2:5, 9; 3:1, 11, 14, 16; 4:5

Mt 1:18; 2:9; 5:12, 16, 24; 6:1, 2, 8; 7:6; 8:29; 10:18, 32^2, 33^2; 11:10^2; 14:6, 8, 22; 17:2; 21:9, 31; 24:25, 38; 25:32; 26:32, 34, 70, 75; 27:11, 24, 29; 28:7

Mk 1:2^2, 35; 2:12; 3:11; 5:33; 6:41, 45; 8:6^2, 7; 9:2; 10:32; 11:9; 13:9; 14:28, 30, 72; 15:42; 16:7

Lk 1:6, 8, 17, 75, 76; 2:21, 26, 31; 5:18, 19, 25; 7:27^2; 8:28, 47^2; 9:16, 52; 10:1, 8; 11:6, 38; 12:6, 8^2, 9^2; 14:2; 15:18; 16:15; 18:39; 19:4, 27, 28; 20:26; 21:12^2, 14, 36; 22:15, 34, 47, 61; 23:12, 14, 53; 24:19, 43

Jn 1:15^2, 27, 30^2, 48; 3:28; 5:7; 6:62; 7:51; 8:58; 9:8; 10:4, 8; 11:55; 12:1, 37; 13:1, 19; 14:29; 15:18; 17:5, 24

Act 1:16; 2:20, 25, 31; 3:18, 20; 4:10, 28; 5:23, 27, 36; 6:6; 7:2, 40, 45, 46, 52; 8:32; 9:15; 10:4, 17, 30, 33, 41; 12:6, 14; 13:24; 14:13; 16:29, 34; 17:26; 18:17; 19:9, 19; 20:5, 13; 21:29, 38; 22:30; 23:1, 30, 33; 24:19, 20; 25:9, 16, 26^2; 26:2, 26; 27:24

Ro 2:13; 3:9, 18, 19; 4:2, 17; 9:29; 14:10, 22; 16:7

1Co 2:7; 4:5; 6:1^2, 6; 10:27; 11:21

2Co 1:15; 5:10; 7:3, 14; 8:10, 24; 9:5^2; 12:19; 13:2

Gal 1:9, 17, 20; 2:12, 14; 3:1, 8, 17, 23; 5:21

Eph 1:4^2; 2:10

Php 3:13

Col 1:5, 17

1Th 2:2; 3:4, 9, 13

1Ti 1:13, 18; 5:4, 19, 20, 21^2, 24; 6:12, 13^2

2Ti 1:9; 2:14; 4:1, 21

Tit 1:2

Heb 6:18; 7:18; 10:15; 11:5; 12:1, 2

Jas 1:27; 2:6; 5:9

1Pt 1:20

2Pt 2:11; 3:2, 17

1Jn 2:28; 3:19

3Jn 6

Jude 4, 17, 24

Rev 1:4; 2:14; 3:2, 5^2, 8, 9; 4:5, 6^2, 10^2; 5:8; 7:9^2, 11, 15; 8:2, 3, 4; 9:13; 10:11; 11:4, 16; 12:4, 10; 13:12; 14:3^2, 5; 15:4; 16:19; 19:20; 20:12; 22:8

BEING

Gen 18:12; 19:16; 21:4; 24:27; 34:30; 35:29; 37:2; 50:26

Ex 12:34; 13:15; 22:14; 28:16; 32:18; 39:9

Lev 21:4; 24:8

Nu 1:44; 22:24; 30:3, 16; 31:32; 32:38

Dt 3:13; 17:8; 22:24; 32:31

Jos 9:23; 21:10; 24:29

Jdg 2:8; 9:5

1Sa 2:18; 15:23, 26; 26:13

2Sa 8:13; 13:4, 14; 19:3; 21:16

1Ki 1:41; 2:27; 11:17; 15:13; 16:7; 20:15

2Ki 8:16; 10:6; 12:11

1Ch 9:19; 24:6

2Ch 5:12; 13:3; 15:16; 21:20; 26:21

Ezr 6:11; 10:19

Neh 6:11

Est 1:3, 7; 3:15; 8:14

Job 4:7; 21:23; 42:17

Ps 49:12; 65:6; 69:4; 78:9, 38; 83:4; 104:33; 107:10; 139:16; 146:2

Prv 3:26; 29:1

Song 3:8, 10

Isa 3:26; 17:1; 40:13; 65:20

Jer 2:25; 12:11; 17:16; 31:36; 34:9; 40:1; 48:2, 42

Ezk 17:10; 23:42; 47:8; 48:22

Dan 3:27; 5:31; 6:10; 8:22; 9:21

Mt 1:19, 23, 24; 2:12, 22; 7:11; 12:34; 14:8

Mk 3:5; 5:41; 8:1; 9:33; 14:3; 15:22, 34

Lk 1:74; 2:5; 3:1^2, 2, 19, 21, 23; 4:1, 2, 15; 7:29, 30; 8:25; 11:13; 13:16; 14:21; 16:23; 20:36; 21:12; 22:3, 44

Jn 1:38, 41; 4:6, 9; 5:13; 6:71; 7:50; 8:9; 10:33; 11:49, 51; 13:2; 14:25; 18:26; 19:38; 20:19, 26

Act 1:3, 4; 2:23, 30, 33; 3:1; 4:2, 23, 36; 5:2; 7:55; 13:4, 12; 14:8; 15:3, 21, 25, 32, 40; 16:18, 20, 21, 37; 17:28; 18:25; 19:40; 20:9; 22:11; 26:11; 27:2, 18

Ro 1:20, 29; 2:18; 3:21, 24; 4:11, 12, 19, 21; 5:1, 9, 10; 6:9, 18, 22; 7:6; 9:11; 10:3; 11:17; 12:5; 15:16

1Co 4:12^2, 13; 7:18, 21, 22^2; 8:7; 9:21; 10:17; 12:12

2Co 5:3, 4; 8:17; 9:11; 10:1; 11:9; 12:16; 13:2, 10^2

Gal 1:14; 2:3, 14; 3:13

Eph 1:11, 18; 2:11, 12, 20; 3:17; 4:18, 19

Php 1:6, 11; 2:2, 6, 8; 3:10

Col 1:10; 2:2, 13

1Th 2:8, 17

1Ti 2:14; 3:6, 10

2Ti 1:4; 3:13

Tit 1:16; 3:7, 11

Phlm 9

Heb 1:3, 4; 2:18; 4:1, 2; 5:9; 7:2, 12; 9:11; 11:4, 7, 37; 13:3

Jas 1:25; 2:17

1Pt 1:7, 23; 2:8, 24; 3:5, 7, 18, 22; 5:3^2

2Pt 3:6, 12, 17

Rev 1:12; 12:2; 14:4

BETWEEN

Gen 3:15^2; 9:12, 13, 15, 16, 17; 10:12; 13:3, 7, 8^2; 15:17; 16:5, 14; 17:2, 7, 10; 20:1; 31:44, 48, 49; 48:12; 49:10, 14

Ex 8:23; 9:4; 11:7; 13:9, 16; 14:2, 20; 16:1; 18:16; 22:11; 25:22; 26:33; 28:33; 30:18; 31:13, 17; 39:25^2; 40:7, 30

Lev 10:10^2; 11:47^2; 20:25^2; 26:46

Nu 7:89; 11:33; 13:23; 16:48; 21:13; 26:56; 30:16^2; 31:27^2; 35:24

Dt 1:1, 16^2, 39; 5:5; 6:8; 11:18; 14:1; 17:8^3; 19:17; 25:1; 28:57; 33:12

Jos 3:4; 8:9, 11, 12; 18:11; 22:25, 27, 28, 34; 24:7

Jdg 4:5, 17; 9:23; 11:10, 27; 13:25; 15:4; 16:25, 31; 20:38

1Sa 4:4; 7:12, 14; 14:4, 42; 17:1, 3, 6; 20:3, 23, 42^2; 24:12, 15; 26:13

2Sa 3:1, 6; 6:2; 18:9, 24; 19:35; 21:7^2

1Ki 3:9; 5:12; 7:28, 29, 46; 14:30; 15:6, 7, 16, 19^2, 32; 18:6, 21, 42; 22:1, 34

2Ki 9:24; 11:17^2; 16:14; 19:15; 25:4

1Ch 13:6; 21:16

2Ch 4:17; 12:15; 13:2; 16:3^2; 18:33; 19:10^2; 23:16^3

Neh 3:32

Job 41:16

Ps 80:1; 99:1

Prv 18:18

Isa 22:11; 37:16; 59:2

Jer 7:5; 34:18, 19; 42:5; 52:7

Lam 1:3

Ezk 4:3; 8:3, 16; 10:2^2, 6^2, 7^2; 18:8; 20:12, 20; 22:26^2; 34:17^2, 20^2, 22; 40:7; 41:10, 18; 42:20; 43:8; 44:23^2; 47:16; 48:22

Dan 7:5; 8:5, 16, 21; 11:45

Hos 2:2

Joel 2:17

Jna 4:11

Zec 5:9; 6:1, 13; 9:7; 11:14

Mal 2:14; 3:18^2

Mt 18:15; 23:35

Lk 11:51; 16:26; 23:12

Jn 3:25

Act 12:6; 15:9, 39; 23:7; 26:31

Ro 1:24; 10:12

1Co 6:5; 7:34

Eph 2:14

1Ti 2:5

BUT

Gen 2:6, 17, 20; 3:3; 4:2, 5; 6:8, 18; 8:9; 9:4; 11:30; 12:12; 13:13; 15:4, 10, 16; 16:6; 17:5, 15, 21; 18:15, 22, 27, 32; 19:2, 4, 10, 14, 26; 20:3^2, 4, 12; 21:23, 26; 22:7; 23:6, 13; 24:4, 33, 38; 25:6, 28; 26:29; 27:22, 38; 28:17, 19; 29:17, 20, 31; 30:42; 31:5, 7, 29, 33, 34, 35, 47; 32:28; 34:12, 15, 17; 35:8, 10, 16, 18; 37:11, 22, 35; 38:20; 39:8, 9, 21; 40:14, 22, 23; 41:8, 21, 24, 54; 42:4, 7, 8, 10, 12, 20, 34; 43:5, 34; 44:17; 45:8, 22; 46:12; 47:18, 30; 48:7, 19, 21; 49:19, 24; 50:20^2

Ex 1:12, 16, 17^2; 2:15, 17; 3:22; 4:1, 10, 21; 5:16, 17; 6:3, 9; 7:4, 12; 8:15, 18, 29; 9:6, 30, 32; 10:8, 20, 23, 27; 11:7; 12:9, 44; 13:15, 18; 14:9, 16, 20, 29; 15:19; 16:8, 20, 26; 17:12; 18:22, 26; 19:13, 24; 20:10, 19; 21:13, 14, 18, 28, 29^2; 22:15; 23:11, 22, 24; 24:2; 29:14, 33; 31:15; 32:18; 33:11, 23; 34:13, 20, 21, 34; 35:2; 36:38; 40:37

Lev 1:9, 13, 17; 2:12; 5:8, 11; 6:28; 7:16, 17, 20, 24, 31; 8:17; 9:10; 10:6; 11:4, 5, 6, 11, 23, 36, 38; 12:5; 13:6, 7, 14, 21^2, 23, 26^2, 28, 33, 35, 37; 14:9, 53; 15:28; 16:10; 17:16; 19:14, 15, 18, 24, 34; 20:24; 21:2, 4, 14; 22:11, 13^2, 20, 23, 32; 23:3, 8, 25; 25:4, 17, 28, 31, 34, 36, 40, 43, 46, 52; 26:14, 15, 23, 27, 45; 27:8, 13, 18, 21, 29

Nu 1:47, 50, 53; 2:33; 3:38; 4:15, 19, 20; 5:8, 20, 28; 6:12; 7:9; 8:26; 9:13, 22; 10:4, 7^2, 30; 11:6, 20, 26^2; 12:14; 13:31; 14:10, 21, 24, 31, 32, 38, 41, 44; 15:30; 16:9, 30, 41; 18:2, 17, 23, 24; 19:12, 20; 21:22, 23; 22:20, 24, 35; 23:13, 26; 24:1, 4, 11, 13, 16, 17^2, 20; 26:33, 64; 27:3; 28:19, 27; 29:8, 36; 30:5, 8, 9, 12, 14, 15; 31:18; 32:17, 23, 27, 30; 33:55; 35:8, 20, 22, 26, 28, 30, 31, 33; 36:9

Dt 1:17, 26, 38, 40, 43, 45; 2:11, 12, 21, 30; 3:7, 19, 26, 28; 4:4, 9, 12, 20, 22^2, 26, 29; 5:3, 14, 31; 7:5, 8, 15, 18, 23, 26; 8:3, 18; 9:4, 5, 19; 10:12; 11:7, 11, 28; 12:5, 10, 14, 18; 13:9; 14:7, 12, 20; 15:3, 6^2, 8; 16:6; 17:6, 16; 18:14, 20, 22; 19:11, 13, 21; 20:12, 14, 16, 17; 21:14, 17, 23; 22:7, 20, 25, 26; 23:5, 11, 20, 22, 24, 25; 24:5, 18; 25:15; 26:14; 28:15, 38, 39, 40, 41, 65; 29:15, 20, 29; 30:14, 17^2; 32:15, 52; 34:4, 6

Jos 1:8, 14; 2:4, 6, 22; 5:5, 12, 14; 6:13, 19, 22; 7:1, 3^2, 12; 8:4, 9, 14; 9:12, 19, 21; 10:16, 19, 30, 37, 40; 11:13, 14, 20; 13:13, 33; 14:3, 8; 15:63; 16:10; 17:3^2, 8, 12, 13, 14, 18; 18:7; 21:12; 22:3, 5, 7, 18, 19, 27, 28; 23:8, 9, 13; 24:4, 10, 12, 15, 21

Jdg 1:6, 19, 21, 25, 27, 29, 30, 32, 33, 35; 2:2, 3, 17^2; 3:15, 16, 19; 4:8, 16; 5:31; 6:10, 13, 34, 39^2; 7:6, 10, 19; 8:20; 9:9, 11, 20, 51; 11:16, 17^2, 18, 20^2, 27; 13:3, 6, 7, 9, 21, 23; 14:4, 6, 9, 13, 16, 20; 15:1^2, 13^2, 19; 16:21; 17:6; 19:10^2, 16, 18, 24, 25, 28; 20:9, 13, 14, 32, 34, 40, 42, 47

Ru 1:14, 17; 2:8; 3:3, 13; 4:4

1Sa 1:2, 5^2, 11, 13, 15, 22; 2:15, 16, 18, 25, 30; 4:20; 5:6; 6:3, 9; 7:10; 8:3, 6, 7, 19; 9:4^2, 7, 27; 10:12, 16, 19, 27^2; 12:10, 12, 15^2, 20, 23, 25; 13:8, 14, 16, 20, 22; 14:1, 10, 26, 27, 37, 39, 41, 43; 15:3, 9^2, 19, 21; 16:7^2, 14; 17:9, 15, 33, 42, 45, 50, 54; 18:8^2, 16, 17, 19, 25^2; 19:2, 10; 20:2, 3^2, 5, 7, 13, 15, 22, 39; 21:4, 6; 22:17, 23; 23:14, 24, 27; 24:7, 10, 12, 13, 22; 25:3, 14, 15, 19, 25, 29, 31, 37, 44; 26:3, 7, 11, 19, 23; 28:23^2; 29:2, 8; 30:2, 6, 10, 24; 31:4

2Sa 2:8, 10, 21, 31; 3:1, 13, 22, 26; 4:12; 5:17, 23; 6:10; 7:2, 6, 15, 19; 8:4; 9:10; 10:11; 11:1, 9, 13, 27; 12:3, 4, 12, 17, 19, 21, 23^2; 13:3, 9, 14, 16, 20, 21, 25, 27, 34, 37; 14:2, 6, 25, 29; 15:3, 10, 20, 26, 34; 16:18; 17:16, 18; 18:3^2, 20^2, 22, 23, 29; 19:4, 21, 27, 28, 37; 20:2, 3, 5, 10, 21; 21:2, 7, 8, 17; 22:19, 28, 42^2; 23:6, 7, 12, 16, 21, 23; 24:3, 17, 24

1Ki 1:1, 4, 8, 10, 19, 26, 52; 2:7, 8, 9, 26, 30, 33; 3:7, 11, 21, 22^2, 23, 26^2; 5:4; 7:1, 31; 8:16, 19, 27, 41; 9:6^2, 22^2, 24; 11:1, 10, 12, 13, 22, 32, 34, 35, 39; 12:8, 10, 11, 14, 17, 20, 22; 13:18, 22, 33; 14:4, 9, 14; 15:14; 16:22, 25; 17:1, 12, 13; 18:12, 18, 21, 22, 25, 26; 19:4, 11^2, 12; 20:9, 16, 23, 27, 28, 30; 21:5, 15, 25, 29; 22:8^2, 16, 18, 24, 30, 31, 48, 49

2Ki 1:3, 4, 6, 16; 2:10, 17, 19; 3:2, 5, 11, 15, 18, 24, 26; 4:27, 31, 41; 5:1, 11, 15, 16^2, 17, 20^2, 25; 6:5, 12, 19, 32^2; 7:2, 4, 10, 19; 8:13; 9:15, 18, 27, 35; 10:4, 9, 18, 19, 23, 31; 11:2, 15; 12:3, 6, 7, 9, 14; 13:6, 7, 11, 19, 22; 14:6^2, 11, 19, 27; 15:25; 16:3, 5; 17:2, 14, 18, 19, 36, 39, 40; 18:6, 12, 20^2, 22, 27, 36; 19:18, 27; 20:10; 21:9; 22:18; 23:9, 23, 35; 25:12, 25

1Ch 2:30, 34; 4:27; 5:1, 2; 6:49, 56; 7:14; 10:4; 11:18^2, 25; 12:17, 19; 13:13; 15:2; 16:5, 19, 26; 17:1, 5, 14; 18:4; 19:3, 12, 18; 20:1, 7; 21:3, 6, 8, 13, 17^2, 24, 30; 22:8; 23:11, 17, 22; 24:2; 27:23, 24; 28:3, 9; 29:1, 14

2Ch 1:4, 11; 2:6; 4:6; 5:9; 6:2, 6, 8, 9, 18, 32; 7:19; 8:8, 9^2; 10:8, 10, 11, 14^2, 17, 18; 11:2; 12:7; 13:10, 11, 13, 21; 15:2, 4, 5, 17; 16:12; 17:4; 18:6, 7^2, 15, 17, 29, 31; 19:6; 20:10, 12, 15; 21:3, 13, 20; 22:10, 11; 23:6^2, 7; 24:15, 19, 22, 25; 25:2, 4^3, 7, 8, 9, 13, 20, 27; 26:16, 18; 28:1, 9, 10, 20, 21, 23, 27; 29:34; 30:8, 10, 18; 32:8, 9, 25; 33:2, 10, 22, 23, 25; 35:13, 21^2, 22; 36:13, 16

Ezr 2:59, 62; 3:6, 12; 4:3^2; 5:5, 12, 13; 8:22; 9:9; 10:13

Neh 1:9; 2:2, 14, 19, 20; 3:3, 5, 14, 15; 4:1, 7; 5:15^2; 6:2, 8, 12; 7:4, 61, 64; 9:16, 17^2, 28, 29, 33; 11:3, 21; 13:2, 6, 24

Est 1:12, 16, 17; 2:15; 3:2, 15; 4:4, 11, 14; 5:9, 12; 6:12, 13; 7:4; 9:10, 15, 16^2, 18, 25

Job 1:11; 2:5, 6, 10; 3:9, 21; 4:2, 5, 16; 5:3, 15; 6:1, 14, 25; 7:21; 8:9, 15^2; 9:2, 11, 15, 18, 35; 11:5, 20; 12:2, 3, 7; 13:4, 15; 14:10, 21, 22; 16:5, 7, 12, 20; 17:10; 19:7^2, 28; 20:5, 13; 21:1; 22:8, 18, 20; 23:6, 8^2, 9, 10, 13; 24:24; 26:1, 14^2; 27:17, 19; 28:12; 30:1; 31:32; 32:8, 16; 35:10, 12, 15; 36:6, 7, 12, 13, 17; 37:21; 38:11; 40:5^2; 42:5

Ps 1:2, 4, 6; 2:12; 3:3; 4:3; 5:7, 11; 6:3; 7:9; 9:7, 20; 11:5; 13:5; 15:4; 16:3; 18:18, 27, 41^2; 20:7, 8; 22:2, 3, 6, 9, 19, 24; 26:11; 28:3; 30:5^2; 31:6, 11, 14; 32:10; 34:10, 19; 35:13, 15, 20; 37:9, 11, 17, 20, 21, 28, 36, 38, 39; 38:13, 19; 40:17; 41:10; 44:3, 7, 9; 49:15; 50:16, 21; 52:7, 8; 55:13, 21, 23^2; 59:8, 16; 62:4; 63:9, 11^2; 64:7; 66:12, 19; 68:3, 6, 21; 69:13, 20^2, 29; 70:5; 71:7, 14; 73:2, 4, 25, 26, 28; 74:6; 75:7, 8, 9, 10; 77:10; 78:7, 30, 38, 39, 50, 52, 53, 57, 68; 81:11, 15; 82:7; 85:8; 86:15; 88:13; 89:24, 38; 90:4; 91:7; 92:8, 10; 94:15, 22; 96:5; 102:12, 26, 27; 103:17; 105:12; 106:7, 14, 15, 25, 35, 43; 109:4, 16, 21, 28^2; 115:1, 3, 5^2, 6^2, 7^2, 16, 18; 118:10, 11, 13, 17, 18; 119:23, 61, 67, 69, 70, 78, 81, 87, 95, 96, 113, 161, 163; 120:7; 125:1, 5; 127:1, 5; 130:4; 132:18; 135:16^2, 17; 136:15; 138:6; 139:4, 12; 141:8; 142:4; 145:20; 146:9

Prv 1:7, 25, 28^2, 33; 2:22; 3:1, 32, 33, 34, 35; 4:18; 5:4; 6:31, 32; 8:36; 9:12, 18; 10:1, 2, 3, 4, 5, 6, 7, 8, 9, 10, 11, 12, 13, 14, 17, 19, 21, 23, 24, 25, 27, 28, 29, 30, 31, 32; 11:1, 2, 3, 4, 5, 6, 9, 11, 12, 13, 14, 17, 18, 20, 21, 23, 24, 26, 27, 28; 12:1, 2, 3, 4, 5, 6, 7, 8, 10, 11, 12, 13, 15, 16, 17, 18, 19^2, 20, 21, 22, 23, 24, 25, 26, 27; 13:1, 2, 3, 4, 5, 6, 8, 9, 10, 11, 12, 13, 15, 16, 17, 18, 19, 20, 21, 23, 24, 25; 14:1, 2, 3, 4, 5, 6, 8, 9, 11, 12, 15, 16, 18, 20, 21, 22, 23, 24, 25, 28, 29, 30, 31, 32, 33, 34, 35; 15:1, 2, 4, 5, 6, 7, 8, 9, 13, 14, 15, 18, 19, 20, 21, 22, 25, 26, 27, 28, 29, 32; 16:2, 9, 14, 22, 25, 33; 17:3, 9, 22, 24; 18:2, 14, 17, 23; 19:4, 12, 16; 20:3, 5, 6, 14, 15, 17, 21, 22; 21:2, 5, 8, 12, 13, 15, 20, 26, 28, 29, 31; 22:3, 15; 23:7, 17; 24:16, 25; 25:2; 27:3, 4, 6, 7, 12; 28:1, 2, 4, 5, 7, 10, 11, 12, 13, 14, 16, 18, 19, 20, 25, 26, 27, 28; 29:2, 3, 4, 6, 7, 8, 10, 11, 15, 16, 18, 23, 25, 26; 30:24, 26; 31:29, 30

Ecc 1:4; 2:14, 26; 3:12; 4:1, 10, 11; 5:7, 12, 14; 6:2; 7:4, 12, 14, 23, 26, 28^2, 29; 8:13; 9:5, 11, 18; 10:2, 10, 12, 19; 11:8, 9

Song 1:5, 6; 3:1, 2, 4^2; 5:2, 6^3; 6:9

Isa 1:3, 6, 20, 21; 5:6, 7^2, 12, 16, 25; 6:9^2, 13; 7:1, 12, 13, 25; 8:14; 9:5, 10^2, 12, 17, 21; 10:4, 7, 20; 11:4, 14; 13:21; 14:19; 16:6, 12, 14; 17:11, 13; 22:11; 24:16; 26:11, 13; 28:7, 13, 27; 29:8^2, 9^2, 13, 23; 30:1^2, 5, 16, 20; 31:1, 2, 8; 32:8; 33:21; 34:11, 12; 35:8, 9; 36:5^2, 7, 12, 21; 37:19, 28; 38:17; 40:8, 31; 41:8; 42:19, 20^2, 22; 43:1, 22^2, 24; 45:17; 46:2; 47:9; 48:1, 10; 49:14, 25; 51:6, 8, 15, 21, 23; 53:5; 54:7, 8, 10, 15; 55:10, 11; 57:3, 13^2, 20; 59:2, 9^2, 11^2; 60:2, 10, 18, 19; 61:6; 62:4, 9; 63:10, 18; 64:6, 8; 65:6, 11, 12, 13^3, 14, 18, 20; 66:2, 4, 5

Jer 1:7, 19; 2:7, 11, 25, 27, 28, 34; 3:1, 7, 8, 10, 19; 4:22; 5:3^2, 5, 10, 23; 6:16, 17, 19; 7:12, 13^2, 23, 24^2, 26, 27^2, 28, 32; 8:6, 7, 15; 9:3, 8, 14, 24; 10:5, 8, 10, 19, 24; 11:8^2, 12, 19, 20; 12:3, 13^2, 17; 13:11, 14, 17; 14:12, 13; 15:19, 20; 16:4, 15; 17:6, 8, 18^2, 22, 23^2, 24, 27; 18:12, 23; 19:6; 20:3, 9, 11, 12; 21:9, 14; 22:5, 10, 12, 17^2, 21, 27; 23:8, 22, 38; 25:3, 4; 26:5, 15, 21; 27:11, 18; 28:13, 15; 29:19; 30:7, 9, 11; 31:30, 33; 32:4, 23, 34, 40; 33:5; 34:3, 5, 11, 14, 16; 35:6, 7, 10, 11, 14^2, 15, 16, 17^2; 36:20, 25, 26^2, 31; 37:2, 10, 14; 38:2, 4, 6, 18, 20, 21, 23, 25; 39:5, 10, 12, 17, 18; 40:4, 10, 14, 16; 41:8, 11, 15; 42:2, 13, 14, 21; 43:3, 5; 44:5, 14, 17, 18; 45:5; 46:17, 20, 27, 28^2; 48:30, 45; 49:10, 12, 19, 39; 50:13, 44; 51:9, 26, 62; 52:8, 16

Lam 1:19; 2:14; 3:2, 32; 5:22

Ezk 2:8; 3:5, 7, 14, 18, 19, 20, 25, 27; 7:4, 14, 16, 20, 26; 8:6; 9:6, 10; 10:11; 11:7, 11, 12, 21; 12:16, 23, 28; 14:11, 14, 16, 18, 20; 16:5, 15, 32, 33, 43, 47, 51, 61; 17:14, 15; 18:5, 7, 11, 16, 21, 24; 19:12; 20:8, 9, 13, 14, 16, 18, 24, 39; 21:23; 22:30; 24:23; 28:9; 29:4, 16; 30:24, 25; 32:27; 33:5, 6^2, 8, 9, 11, 13, 17, 19, 24, 31^2, 32; 34:3, 4, 8, 16, 18^2, 28; 36:8, 21, 22; 37:8, 23; 38:8; 39:2, 28; 41:6; 42:6, 14; 44:8, 13, 14, 15, 22, 25; 46:1, 2, 9^2, 17^2, 18; 47:11

Dan 1:4, 8; 2:6, 9^2, 28, 30^2, 41, 43, 44, 49; 3:15, 18; 4:7, 8, 18; 5:8, 15, 20, 23; 6:4, 13; 7:18, 26, 28; 8:3, 4, 7, 17, 18, 22, 24, 25, 27; 9:7, 18, 26; 10:1, 7, 13^2, 21^2; 11:6^2, 7, 10, 11, 12, 14, 16, 17, 18, 19, 20, 21, 25, 27, 29, 32, 34, 38, 41, 43, 44; 12:4, 8, 10^2, 13

Hos 1:6, 7; 2:7^2; 5:6; 6:7; 7:16; 8:4, 6, 12, 13, 14; 9:3, 8, 10, 13; 10:11; 11:3, 5, 12; 13:1, 4, 9; 14:9

Joel 2:20; 3:16, 20

Am 1:4, 7, 10, 12, 14; 2:2, 5, 12; 3:7, 8; 4:8; 5:5, 11^2, 24, 26; 6:6, 14; 7:13, 14; 8:11

Oba 12, 17

Jna 1:3, 4, 5, 13; 2:9; 3:8; 4:1, 7

Mic 1:12; 3:4, 8; 4:1, 4, 12; 5:2; 6:8, 14^2, 15^3

Nah 1:8; 2:8^2; 3:17

Hab 2:3, 4, 5, 20

Zep 1:13^2, 18; 3:5, 7

Hag 1:6^3; 2:16^2

Zec 1:4, 6, 15, 21; 4:6; 7:11, 14; 8:11, 13; 9:7; 11:6, 16; 13:5, 8; 14:7^2, 11

Mal 1:4^2, 12, 14; 2:8, 9; 3:2, 7, 8; 4:2

Mt 1:20; 2:19, 22; 3:7, 11, 12, 14; 4:4^2; 5:13^2, 15, 17, 19, 22^2, 28, 32, 33, 34, 37, 39^2, 44; 6:3, 6, 7, 13, 15, 17, 18, 20, 23, 33; 7:3, 15, 17, 21; 8:4, 8, 12, 20, 22, 24, 27; 9:6, 8, 12^2, 13^2, 14, 15, 17, 18, 21, 22, 24, 25, 31, 34, 36, 37; 10:6, 13, 17, 19, 20, 22, 23, 28^2, 30, 33, 34; 11:8, 9, 16, 19, 22, 24, 27; 12:2, 3, 4, 6, 7, 15, 24^2, 28, 31, 32, 36, 39^2, 48; 13:8, 11, 12, 16, 20, 21, 23, 25, 26, 29, 30, 32, 38, 48, 57; 14:6, 16, 17, 24, 27, 30; 15:3, 5, 8, 9, 11, 13, 18, 20, 23, 24^2, 26; 16:3, 4, 12, 15, 17, 23^2; 17:12^2, 21; 18:6, 7, 16, 17, 22, 25, 28, 30; 19:6, 8, 11, 14, 17^2, 22, 26^2, 30; 20:10, 12, 13, 16, 22, 23^2, 25, 26^2, 28, 31; 21:13, 19, 21, 26, 28, 29, 32, 37, 38, 44, 46; 22:5, 7, 8, 14, 18, 30, 31, 32, 34; 23:3, 4, 5, 8, 11, 13, 16, 18, 25, 27, 28; 24:6, 13, 20, 22, 35, 36^2, 37, 43, 48; 25:4, 9^2, 12, 18, 29, 33, 46; 26:5, 8, 11, 24, 29, 32, 39, 41, 54, 56, 58, 60, 63, 70; 27:20, 23, 24; 28:17

Mk 1:8, 30, 44, 45^2; 2:6, 7, 10, 17^2, 18, 20, 22, 26; 3:4, 7, 26, 29^2; 4:6, 11, 15, 17, 22, 29, 32, 34; 5:6, 19, 26, 28, 33, 39, 40; 6:4^2, 9, 16, 19, 49, 56; 7:5, 6, 11, 15, 19, 24, 27, 36; 8:28, 29, 33^2, 35; 9:13, 22, 27, 29, 32, 34, 37, 39, 50; 10:6, 8, 14, 18, 24, 27, 30, 31, 38, 40^2, 42, 43^2, 45, 48; 11:13, 17, 23, 26, 32; 12:7, 12, 14, 15, 25, 27, 32, 44; 13:7, 9, 11^3, 13, 14, 17, 20, 23, 24, 31, 32^2; 14:2, 7, 21, 28, 29, 31, 36, 38, 49, 56, 59, 61, 68, 71; 15:3, 5, 9, 11, 23; 16:7, 16

Lk 1:13, 60; 2:19, 37, 44, 51; 3:16, 17, 19; 4:4, 25, 26, 30; 5:2, 14, 15, 21, 22, 24, 30, 31, 32, 33, 35, 38; 6:4, 8, 24, 27, 35, 40, 41, 49; 7:7, 25, 26, 28, 30, 35, 44, 45, 46, 47; 8:10, 15, 16, 23, 27, 38, 42, 50, 52^2, 56; 9:9, 13^2, 19, 20, 24, 27, 32, 43, 45, 55, 56, 58, 59, 60, 61; 10:2, 10, 12, 14, 20, 22^2, 29, 33, 40, 42; 11:4, 15, 17, 20, 22, 28, 29, 33, 34, 39, 41, 42; 12:5, 7, 9, 10, 20, 31, 45, 48, 50, 51, 56; 13:3, 5, 27; 14:10, 13, 34, 35; 15:20, 22, 30; 16:15, 25^2, 30; 17:1^2, 7, 17, 25, 29; 18:4, 13, 15, 16, 39; 19:14, 27, 42, 46, 47; 20:6, 10, 14, 18, 21, 23, 35, 38; 21:4, 7, 9^2, 12, 18, 23, 33; 22:21, 22, 26^2, 27, 32, 36, 42, 48, 53, 56; 23:9, 21, 25, 28^2, 40, 41; 24:6, 16, 21, 24, 29, 37, 49

Jn 1:8, 12, 13, 17, 20, 26, 31, 33; 2:9, 10, 21, 24; 3:8, 13, 15, 16, 17, 18, 21, 28, 29, 30, 36; 4:2, 14^2, 23, 32; 5:7, 17, 18, 19, 22, 24, 30, 34^2, 36, 42, 47; 6:9, 20, 22, 26, 27, 32, 36, 38, 39, 64; 7:6, 7, 10^2, 12, 16, 18, 22, 24, 26, 27, 28, 29, 30, 39, 41, 44, 49; 8:5, 6, 10, 12, 14, 16, 26, 28, 35, 37, 40, 42, 49, 55^2, 59; 9:3, 9, 18, 21, 28, 31, 41; 10:1, 2, 5, 6, 8, 10, 12, 18, 26, 33, 38, 39, 41; 11:4, 10, 11, 13, 20, 22, 30, 42, 46, 51, 52, 54; 12:2, 6, 8, 9, 10, 16, 24, 27, 30, 37, 42, 44, 47, 49; 13:7, 9, 10^2, 18, 36; 14:6, 10, 17, 19, 24, 26, 31; 15:15, 16, 19^2, 21, 22, 24, 25, 26; 16:4, 5, 6, 7, 12, 13, 20^2, 21, 22, 25^2, 33; 17:9, 11, 12, 15, 20, 25; 18:16, 23, 28, 36, 39, 40; 19:9, 12, 13, 15^2, 21, 24, 33, 34, 38; 20:7, 11, 17, 24, 25, 27, 31; 21:4^2, 8, 18, 23

Act 1:4, 5, 8; 2:14, 15, 16, 34; 3:6, 14, 18; 4:15, 17, 19, 20, 32; 5:1, 3, 4, 13, 19, 21, 22, 23, 39; 6:4; 7:9, 12, 17, 25, 27, 39, 47, 55; 8:9, 12, 20, 40; 9:7, 8, 15, 21, 22, 24, 26, 27, 29, 40; 10:10, 14, 26, 28, 35, 41; 11:4, 8, 9, 16, 19; 12:5, 9, 14, 15, 16, 17, 20, 24; 13:8, 14, 25, 30, 37, 45, 46, 50, 51; 14:2, 4; 15:5, 11, 20, 38; 16:1, 7, 18, 28, 37^2; 17:5, 13, 14, 21, 30; 18:9, 15, 19, 21^2; 19:9^2, 15, 22, 26, 27, 34, 39; 20:20, 24; 21:13, 24, 39; 22:9, 28; 23:6, 8, 9, 21, 29; 24:7, 11, 14, 27; 25:4, 9, 11, 19, 21, 25; 26:16, 20, 25^2, 29; 27:10, 14, 21, 22, 27, 39, 41, 43; 28:6, 16, 19, 22

Ro 1:13, 21, 32; 2:2, 5, 8^2, 10, 13, 25, 29^2; 3:4, 5, 21, 27; 4:2, 4, 5^2, 10, 12, 13, 16, 20, 24; 5:3, 8, 11, 13, 15, 16, 20; 6:10, 11, 13, 14, 15, 17^2, 22, 23; 7:2, 3, 6, 7, 8, 9, 13, 14, 15, 17, 18, 19, 20, 23, 25; 8:1, 4, 5, 6, 9^2, 10, 11, 13, 15, 20, 23, 24, 25, 26, 32; 9:7, 8, 10, 11, 13, 16, 20, 24, 31, 32; 10:2, 6, 8, 16, 18, 19, 20, 21; 11:4, 6, 7, 11, 15, 18^2, 20, 22, 28; 12:2, 3, 16, 19, 21; 13:1, 3, 4, 5, 8, 14; 14:1, 10, 13, 14, 15, 17, 20; 15:3, 21, 23, 25; 16:4, 18, 19, 26

1Co 1:10, 14, 17, 18, 23, 24, 27, 30; 2:4, 5, 7, 9, 10, 11, 12, 13, 14, 15, 16; 3:1, 5, 6, 7, 10, 15; 4:3, 4, 10^3, 14, 19^2, 20; 5:3, 8, 11, 13; 6:6, 11^3, 12^2, 13^2, 17, 18; 7:4^2, 6, 7, 9, 10, 11, 12, 14, 15^2, 17, 19, 21, 28^2, 29, 32, 33, 34, 35, 36, 37, 38, 39, 40; 8:1, 3, 4, 6^2, 8, 9, 12; 9:12, 15, 17, 21, 24, 25, 27; 10:5, 13^3, 20, 23^2, 24, 28, 29, 33; 11:3, 5, 6, 7, 8, 9, 12, 15, 16, 17, 28, 32; 12:3, 4, 5, 6, 7, 11, 14, 18, 20^2, 24, 25, 31; 13:6, 8, 10, 11, 12^2, 13; 14:1, 2, 3, 4, 5, 14, 17, 20, 22^3, 24, 28, 33, 34, 38; 15:6, 10^3, 13, 20, 23, 27, 35, 37, 38, 39, 40, 46, 51, 57; 16:7, 8, 11, 12^2

2Co 1:9^2, 12, 18, 19, 24; 2:1, 2, 4, 5^2, 13, 17^2; 3:3^2, 5, 6^2, 7, 14, 15, 18; 4:2^2, 3, 5, 7, 8, 9^2, 12, 16, 17, 18^2; 5:4, 11, 12, 15; 6:4, 12; 7:5, 7, 8, 9, 10, 12, 14; 8:5, 8, 10, 14, 16, 17, 19, 21, 22; 9:6, 12; 10:1, 2, 4, 10, 12, 13^2, 15, 17, 18; 11:3, 6^2, 12, 17; 12:5, 6, 14^2, 16, 19; 13:3, 4, 6, 7, 8

Gal 1:1, 7, 8, 11, 12, 15, 17, 19, 23; 2:2, 3, 6, 7, 11, 12, 14, 16, 17, 20; 3:11, 12, 15, 16, 18, 20, 22, 23, 25; 4:2, 4, 7, 9, 14, 17, 18, 23^2, 26, 29, 31; 5:6, 10, 13, 15, 18, 22; 6:4, 8, 13, 14, 15

Eph 1:21; 2:4, 13, 19; 4:7, 9, 15, 20, 28, 29; 5:3, 4, 8, 11, 13, 15, 17, 18, 27, 29, 32; 6:4, 6, 12, 21

Php 1:12, 17, 20, 22, 28, 29; 2:3, 4, 7, 12, 19, 22, 24, 25, 27^2; 3:1, 7, 8^2, 9, 12, 13; 4:6, 10^2, 15, 17, 18, 19

Col 1:26; 2:17; 3:8, 11, 22, 25

1Th 1:5, 8; 2:2, 4^2, 7, 8, 13, 17, 18; 3:6; 4:7, 8, 9, 10, 13; 5:1, 4, 6, 8, 9, 15

2Th 2:12, 13; 3:3, 8, 9, 11, 13, 15

1Ti 1:8, 9, 13; 2:10, 12^2, 14; 3:3, 15; 4:7, 8, 12; 5:1, 4, 6, 8, 11, 13, 19, 23; 6:2, 4, 6, 9, 11, 17

2Ti 1:7, 8, 9, 10, 17; 2:9, 14, 16, 20^2, 22, 23, 24; 3:5, 9, 10, 11, 13, 14; 4:3, 5, 8, 13, 16, 20

Tit 1:3, 8, 15^2, 16; 2:1, 10; 3:2, 4, 5, 9

Phlm 11, 14^2, 16^2, 22

Heb 1:8, 11, 12, 13; 2:6, 8, 9, 16; 3:4, 6, 13, 17, 18; 4:2, 13, 15; 5:4, 5, 14; 6:8, 9, 12; 7:3, 6, 8, 16, 19, 21, 24, 28; 8:6; 9:7, 11, 12, 23, 24, 26, 27; 10:3, 5, 12, 25, 27, 32, 38, 39^2; 11:6, 13, 16; 12:8, 10, 11, 13, 22, 26^2; 13:4, 14, 16, 19

Jas 1:4, 6, 10, 11, 14, 22, 25^2, 26; 2:6, 9, 20; 3:8, 14, 15, 17; 4:6^2, 11^2, 16; 5:12^2

1Pt 1:12, 15, 19, 20, 23, 25; 2:4, 7, 9, 10^2, 16, 18, 20, 23, 25; 3:4, 9, 12, 14, 15, 18, 21; 4:2, 6, 7, 13, 14, 15, 16; 5:2^2, 3, 10

2Pt 1:9, 16, 21; 2:1, 4, 5, 10, 12, 16, 22; 3:7, 8, 9^2, 10, 18

1Jn 1:7; 2:2, 5, 7, 11, 16, 17, 19^{2}, 20, 21, 22, 23, 27^{2}; 3:2, 17, 18; 4:1, 10, 18; 5:5, 6, 18

2Jn 1, 5, 8, 12

3Jn 9, 11^{2}, 13, 14

Jude 6, 9, 10^{2}, 17, 20

Rev 2:6, 9^{2}, 14, 24, 25; 3:5, 9; 9:4, 5, 11; 10:7, 9; 11:2; 12:12; 14:3; 17:12; 19:12; 20:5, 6; 21:8, 27; 22:3

BY

Gen 7:2^{2}, 3; 9:6, 11; 10:5, 32; 14:6, 15; 16:2, 7^{2}; 18:2, 8; 19:36; 20:3; 21:23, 28, 29; 22:13, 16; 23:20; 24:3, 11, 13, 30, 43; 25:11, 13, 16^{2}; 26:18; 27:40; 29:2; 30:3, 27, 40; 31:24, 31, 39^{2}, 40, 53; 32:16; 33:8; 35:4; 36:37, 40; 37:28; 38:14, 16, 18, 19, 20, 21, 24, 25; 39:10^{2}, 12, 16; 41:1, 3, 31, 32, 47; 42:15, 16, 23, 38; 43:32^{3}; 45:1, 7, 23, 24; 47:13; 48:7; 49:17, 22, 24, 25^{2}

Ex 2:3, 5, 15, 23^{2}; 3:7, 19; 4:4, 13, 24; 6:3^{2}; 7:4, 15; 8:24; 9:35; 12:14, 17, 26, 31, 51; 13:3, 14, 16, 21^{3}, 22^{2}; 14:2, 9, 20, 21; 15:16, 27; 16:3^{2}; 18:8, 13, 14; 19:19; 20:26; 21:3^{2}, 4; 22:25, 26; 23:30; 25:14; 26:9^{2}; 28:28; 29:11, 18, 25, 28, 32, 38, 41, 43; 30:4, 6, 20; 31:2; 32:13, 27; 33:6, 12, 17, 21, 22^{2}; 34:6, 7; 35:29, 30; 36:16^{2}; 37:3, 5, 27; 38:21; 39:4, 21; 40:29, 38^{2}

Lev 1:5, 9, 13, 16, 17; 2:2, 3, 9, 10, 11, 14, 16; 3:3, 4, 5, 9^{2}, 10, 11, 14, 15, 16; 4:9, 35; 5:12, 15, 17; 6:2, 17, 18; 7:4, 5, 25, 30, 34, 35, 36; 8:21, 28, 36; 10:11, 12, 13, 15^{2}; 16:21, 31; 19:12, 31; 20:25^{3}; 21:6, 9, 21; 22:4, 22, 27; 23:8, 13, 18, 25, 27, 36^{2}, 37; 24:7, 8, 9^{2}; 25:39, 47^{3}; 26:7, 8, 23^{2}, 26, 46; 27:2

Nu 1:2^{2}, 3, 17, 18^{2}, 20^{3}, 22^{3}, 24^{2}, 26^{2}, 28^{2}, 30^{2}, 32^{2}, 34^{2}, 36^{2}, 38^{2}, 40^{2}, 42, 45, 52^{2}; 2:2, 12, 17, 20, 25, 27, 32, 34; 3:15, 17, 18, 19, 20, 26^{2}, 43, 47, 49; 4:2, 22, 26^{2}, 29, 32, 36, 37, 38, 40, 42, 45, 49; 5:2, 19; 6:9, 11; 7:84; 9:6, 7, 10, 16^{2}, 21^{2}, 23; 10:13, 34; 11:31; 12:2^{2}; 13:3, 22, 29^{2}; 14:3, 14^{2}, 18, 25, 36, 37, 43; 15:3, 10, 13, 14, 23, 24, 25, 28; 16:40; 18:8^{2}, 11, 17, 19, 32; 20:17, 18, 19, 23; 21:1, 4, 18, 22, 33; 22:1, 5; 23:3, 6, 15, 17; 24:6; 26:3, 55, 63^{2}; 27:2, 23; 28:2, 3^{2}, 6, 8, 13, 19, 24; 29:6, 13, 36; 30:3, 10; 31:12, 17, 18, 35; 33:2, 10, 48, 49, 50, 54; 34:3, 13, 18; 35:1, 20, 30, 33; 36:2^{2}, 13^{2}

Dt 1:2, 7, 19, 22, 33^{3}, 40; 2:1, 8^{2}, 27, 30, 36^{2}; 3:12; 4:34^{7}, 48; 5:5, 15, 31; 6:7, 13; 7:22; 8:3^{2}; 9:29^{2}; 10:20; 11:19, 30; 12:30; 14:22; 15:20; 16:1; 18:1; 20:19; 21:5, 17; 22:4; 23:10^{2}; 24:9; 25:2, 11, 17, 18; 27:16; 28:10, 68; 29:16; 33:12, 14^{2}, 29

Jos 2:12, 15, 18; 3:4^{2}; 4:6; 5:1, 4, 5, 7, 13; 7:14^{2}, 16, 17, 18; 8:3, 15; 9:13, 18, 19; 10:18; 11:7, 23; 13:6, 14, 16, 22, 29, 31, 32; 14:2^{2}; 15:1, 6, 8; 16:1, 6, 8; 17:2^{2}; 18:9, 20; 19:49, 51; 20:2, 8, 9; 21:2, 4, 5, 6, 7, 8^{2}, 9, 40^{2}; 22:9, 10; 23:4, 7; 24:26

Jdg 2:18; 3:1, 4^{2}, 15, 19^{2}; 4:11; 5:10, 19, 22; 6:11, 25, 27^{2}, 28, 30, 36, 37; 7:1, 5, 7, 12; 8:11; 9:6, 9, 25, 32, 34, 37^{2}; 11:18, 26; 16:5, 26; 17:10; 18:3, 16, 28; 19:11, 14; 20:5, 9; 21:7, 11, 12

Ru 2:8, 21, 23; 4:1

1Sa 1:7, 9, 26; 2:3, 9, 16, 23, 28; 3:21; 4:13, 18, 20; 5:2; 6:8, 9; 9:23; 10:2, 19^{2}, 21; 11:7, 9; 14:4, 6^{2}, 36; 16:9, 20; 17:2, 23, 26, 35, 43, 52; 18:25, 30; 20:7, 9, 19, 25^{2}; 23:7; 24:3, 21; 25:13, 16, 20, 22, 34; 26:3, 7, 24^{2}; 27:1; 28:6^{3}, 8^{2}, 10, 15^{2}, 17; 29:1, 2^{2}; 30:15, 24

2Sa 1:6, 12; 2:13, 15, 16, 24; 3:5, 18; 6:2, 7; 10:2, 8; 11:14; 12:14, 25; 13:31, 32, 34; 15:30, 36; 16:2, 13; 17:11, 17, 22; 18:4^{3}, 23; 19:3, 7, 37; 20:9, 11, 12, 21; 21:10^{2}, 22^{2}; 22:9, 30^{2}, 35; 23:2, 4, 15, 16; 24:16

1Ki 1:9^{2}, 17, 27, 30; 2:8, 23, 25, 29, 42; 3:5; 4:12, 20; 5:9, 11, 14; 6:21, 22; 7:20; 8:38^{2}, 43, 53, 56; 9:8; 10:5, 25, 29; 12:15; 13:1^{2}, 2, 5, 9^{2}, 10, 17^{2}, 18, 24^{3}, 25^{2}, 28, 32; 14:4, 18; 15:13, 29, 30; 16:7, 12, 13^{2}, 34; 17:3, 5, 16, 20, 24; 18:4, 6^{2}, 13, 24; 19:2, 11, 19; 20:14^{2}, 38, 39^{2}; 21:1, 23; 22:8, 19, 28

2Ki 2:1, 7, 11, 13, 23; 3:11, 20; 4:8, 9, 27; 5:1, 2; 6:14, 26, 30; 8:8, 21; 9:27^{2}, 36; 10:6, 10, 33; 11:11, 14^{2}, 16^{2}, 19; 13:7, 25; 14:7, 9, 25, 27; 16:15; 17:4, 6, 13^{3}, 23; 18:11, 17, 31; 19:7, 11, 23, 28^{2}, 33^{2}; 20:11; 21:10; 23:3, 7, 11; 24:2; 25:4^{3}

1Ch 1:48; 3:3; 4:38, 41; 5:7, 10, 17; 6:15, 61, 63, 65^{2}, 78; 7:4, 5, 7, 9, 11, 29; 8:28; 9:1, 22, 23, 28; 11:3, 11, 14, 18; 12:22, 31; 14:11; 15:16; 16:41; 17:21; 18:3; 19:4, 9; 20:8^{2}; 21:15, 25, 26; 23:3^{2}, 24^{2}, 27, 31; 24:5, 27; 26:16, 25; 27:1; 28:1, 12, 14^{2}, 15^{2}, 16, 17^{2}, 18, 19; 29:5, 8

2Ch 1:17; 2:16; 3:3; 5:11, 14; 6:23^{4}, 33, 34; 7:6, 12, 14, 20, 21; 8:14, 18; 9:4, 18, 24; 10:15; 12:7; 13:5; 16:14; 18:7, 27; 19:5; 20:15, 16; 21:9, 15^{3}, 19; 22:7; 23:10^{2}, 13, 15, 18^{2}; 24:11^{2}, 13; 25:18; 26:11^{2}, 15; 28:15; 29:9, 15, 25, 27; 30:12, 21; 31:6, 15, 17^{2}, 19^{2}; 32:11^{2}; 33:8; 34:14; 35:4, 6, 20; 36:13, 15, 21, 22

Ezr 1:1, 8; 2:62; 3:4, 11; 4:16, 23; 5:5; 6:9; 7:23; 8:3, 18, 20, 31, 33, 34^{2}; 9:11; 10:16, 17, 44

Neh 1:10^{2}; 2:6, 13^{2}, 15^{2}; 3:15, 23, 25; 4:3, 12, 18^{2}; 7:3, 5, 64; 8:14, 18; 9:9, 12^{2}, 14, 19^{2}, 30; 10:29, 34, 35; 12:37; 13:18, 25, 26

Est 1:12, 15; 2:14; 3:13, 15; 7:7; 8:5, 10, 14; 9:25

Job 4:9^{2}; 6:16; 9:11; 11:7; 15:30; 16:12; 17:7; 18:8, 9; 20:29; 21:29; 22:30; 26:12, 13; 27:11; 28:8, 9, 25; 29:3, 19; 30:4, 18; 31:9, 11, 23, 28, 30, 33; 33:18; 35:9^{2}; 36:12, 22, 31, 32; 37:10, 11, 12, 17, 19; 38:2, 24; 39:9, 26; 41:18, 25; 42:5

Ps 1:3; 5:10; 9:16; 10:10; 17:4, 7; 18:8, 29^{2}, 34; 19:11; 30:7; 33:6^{2}, 16^{2}, 17; 37:23; 38:8; 39:10; 41:11; 44:3, 12, 16; 48:4; 49:7; 50:5; 54:1^{2}; 56:7; 59:11; 63:10, 11; 65:5, 6; 66:7; 68:4; 71:6; 72:3; 73:23; 74:7, 13; 77:20; 78:17, 18, 26, 49, 55, 64, 65, 72; 79:10; 80:12; 88:9; 89:35, 39, 41; 90:7^{2}, 10; 91:5^{2}; 94:20; 102:5; 104:8^{2}, 12; 106:22; 107:7; 119:9; 121:6^{2}; 128:3; 129:8; 134:1; 136:5, 8, 9; 137:1; 140:5; 147:4

Prv 3:19^{2}, 20, 28, 29; 4:15; 6:26; 7:26; 8:2, 15, 16, 30; 9:11; 11:5, 11^{2}; 12:3, 13, 14; 13:2, 10, 11^{2}; 14:4; 15:13, 23; 16:6^{2}, 12; 20:4, 11, 18, 28; 21:6; 22:4; 24:3, 4, 6, 30^{2}; 25:15; 26:2^{2}, 6, 17^{2}, 26, 28; 27:9; 28:2, 8; 29:4, 19; 30:27; 31:18

Ecc 1:13; 5:3, 9, 14; 7:3, 11, 23, 26, 27; 9:1, 15; 10:3, 18; 12:11, 12

Song 1:7, 8; 2:7^{2}; 3:1, 5^{2}; 5:4, 12; 7:4

Isa 1:7; 3:5^{2}, 25; 4:1, 4^{2}, 5^{2}; 7:20^{2}; 9:1; 10:13^{2}, 34; 13:15; 15:5; 18:2; 19:7^{3}; 20:2; 22:3, 5, 14; 23:3; 26:13; 27:7, 9, 12; 28:18, 19^{3}; 29:13; 32:8; 34:17; 36:2, 16; 37:7, 11, 24^{2}, 29^{2}, 34^{2}; 38:8, 16; 40:26^{3}; 41:3; 42:16; 43:1, 7; 44:4, 5^{2}, 24; 45:3, 4, 23; 46:3; 48:1^{2}, 17; 49:10, 19; 50:4; 51:18, 19; 52:12; 53:11; 54:15; 60:19; 62:2, 8^{2}; 63:12, 19; 64:4; 65:1, 5, 15, 16; 66:16^{2}

Jer 2:8, 17, 34; 4:26; 5:7^{2}, 22, 31; 6:5, 25; 7:10, 11, 14, 30; 8:3, 5; 10:12^{3}, 14; 11:21, 22^{2}; 12:16^{2}; 13:5, 24; 14:9, 12^{3}, 15; 15:16; 16:4^{2}; 17:2, 8^{2}, 11, 19, 20, 21; 18:21^{2}; 19:2, 7^{2}; 20:2, 4; 21:9^{3}; 22:2, 4, 5, 8, 13^{2}; 23:27, 32^{2}; 25:29; 27:3, 5^{2}, 8, 13^{3}; 29:3, 19, 22; 31:9, 32, 35^{2}; 32:17, 34, 36^{3}; 33:4^{2}; 34:4, 15; 35:4; 37:2; 38:2^{3}, 11, 23; 39:4^{3}, 18; 41:12, 17; 42:17^{3}, 22^{3}; 44:12^{4}, 13^{3}, 15, 18^{2}, 26, 27^{2}; 46:2, 6, 10, 18; 48:19; 49:3, 9, 13, 17; 50:1, 13; 51:14, 15^{3}, 17^{2}; 52:7^{5}

Lam 1:12, 14; 2:15, 21; 3:1; 5:12

Ezk 1:1, 3, 15, 19; 3:15, 23; 4:10, 11, 16^{2}; 5:12, 14; 6:11^{3}, 12^{2}; 8:3; 9:2, 3, 11; 10:9^{3}, 15, 16, 20, 22; 11:10, 24; 12:3, 4, 7; 13:19, 22; 14:3, 7, 13, 14, 20; 16:6, 8, 15, 25, 36, 56, 61; 17:5, 7, 8, 9, 14, 17, 18, 21; 18:7, 12, 16, 18; 19:7, 10^{2}; 20:3, 31^{2}; 21:12; 22:7^{2}, 12; 23:21, 25^{2}; 24:6, 21; 25:12, 13, 14, 15; 26:6, 10, 11; 27:12, 16, 34; 28:5^{2}, 10, 16, 17, 18^{2}, 23; 29:7; 30:5, 6, 10, 12, 17; 31:7, 9, 12, 14, 18; 32:12, 20, 21, 22, 23, 24, 25, 26, 29^{2}, 30, 31; 33:27, 30; 34:13; 35:5; 36:17^{2}, 34, 37; 37:2, 18; 38:17; 39:15, 23; 40:2, 5, 7, 18, 22, 28, 38, 41, 49^{2}; 41:7, 17^{2}; 42:20; 43:3, 4, 6, 7^{2}, 8^{3}, 13; 44:2^{2}, 3^{2}; 45:1; 46:2^{2}, 8^{2}, 9^{5}, 14, 16, 18, 21; 47:2, 12, 16, 18, 22; 48:2, 3, 4, 5, 6, 7, 8, 12, 20, 24, 25, 26, 27, 28, 29

Dan 4:17^{2}, 27^{2}, 30; 5:10; 7:2, 8, 16; 8:2, 11, 12, 24, 25; 9:2, 3, 5, 10, 11, 12, 18, 19; 10:4, 16; 11:2, 12, 16, 18, 21, 32, 33^{4}; 12:7

Hos 1:2, 7^{6}; 2:17; 4:2; 6:5^{2}, 9; 7:4, 16; 8:4, 9; 11:3; 12:3^{2}, 10^{2}, 13^{2}; 13:7, 16; 14:1

Am 2:8; 4:2; 5:3^{2}; 6:8, 10, 13; 7:2, 4, 5, 7, 8, 11, 17^{2}; 8:2, 5, 7, 8, 14; 9:5, 10, 12

Oba 5, 9

Jna 2:2; 3:7

Mic 2:2, 5, 8, 12, 13; 3:8; 7:18

Nah 1:6

Hab 1:16; 2:4, 5, 10, 12; 3:10, 13

Zep 1:5^{2}, 18; 2:12, 15; 3:6

Hag 1:1, 3; 2:1, 10, 13, 22

Zec 1:8; 3:5, 7; 4:3, 6^{3}, 14; 5:4; 7:7, 12; 8:9; 9:8, 11

Mal 1:1, 9; 2:10

Mt 1:22; 2:5, 14, 15, 17, 23; 3:3; 4:4^{2}, 14, 15, 18; 5:21, 26, 27, 33, 34, 35^{2}, 36; 6:27; 7:16, 20; 8:17, 28; 9:25; 11:12; 12:17, 24, 27^{2}, 28, 33, 37^{2}; 13:1, 4, 14, 19, 21^{2}, 35; 14:13; 15:3, 5^{2}, 6; 17:21; 18:7, 28; 20:30^{2}; 21:4, 23, 24, 27; 22:1, 31; 23:16^{2}, 18^{2}, 20^{3}, 21^{3}, 22^{3}; 24:15; 26:4, 24, 63, 73; 27:9, 32, 35, 39, 64; 28:9, 13

Mk 1:16, 31; 2:13, 14; 3:22; 4:1^{2}, 2, 4, 15; 5:4, 7, 21, 22, 41; 6:2, 7, 25^{2}, 32, 39, 40^{2}, 48; 7:11^{2}, 26; 8:3, 23, 27; 9:2, 27, 29^{2}, 33, 34; 10:1, 46; 11:4, 20, 28, 29, 33; 12:1, 36; 13:14; 14:1, 19, 21, 47, 69, 70; 15:21, 29, 35

Lk 1:61, 70, 77; 2:8, 18, 26, 27; 3:19; 4:1, 4^{2}; 5:1, 2, 15, 17, 19; 6:44; 8:4, 5, 12, 20, 36, 54; 9:7, 14, 47; 10:4, 19, 31^{2}, 32; 11:3, 19^{2}; 13:17; 16:22; 17:6, 7^{2}; 18:5, 31, 35, 36, 37; 19:8, 15, 24; 20:2, 8; 21:9^{2}, 16, 24; 22:22, 56; 23:8; 24:4, 12, 32

Jn 1:3, 10, 17^{2}, 42; 3:2, 34; 5:2; 6:15, 18, 57^{2}; 7:50; 8:9^{2}, 59; 9:1, 7, 21; 10:1, 2, 3, 9; 11:39, 42; 12:11, 29; 13:35; 14:6; 16:30; 18:22; 19:7, 25, 26, 39; 20:7; 21:19

Act 1:3, 10, 16, 25; 2:16, 22^{2}, 23^{2}, 33, 43; 3:7, 12, 16, 18, 21; 4:7^{2}, 9, 10^{2}, 16, 25, 30^{2}, 36; 5:10, 12, 15, 19; 6:10; 7:25, 35, 42, 53; 9:8, 13, 25^{2}, 36, 39; 10:6, 22, 32, 36; 11:4, 5, 28, 30; 12:9, 20; 13:4, 8, 11, 19, 21, 36, 39^{2}, 45; 14:3; 15:3, 7, 9, 12, 23, 27, 40; 16:2, 8, 13, 16; 17:10, 23, 29, 31; 18:3, 9, 21, 28; 19:10, 11, 13, 25; 20:16, 19, 31; 21:19; 22:11, 20, 24, 25; 23:2, 4, 10, 11, 19, 31; 24:2^{2}, 8, 21; 25:14; 26:18; 27:2, 11, 12, 13, 16, 23; 28:16, 25

Ro 1:2, 4, 5, 10^{2}, 12, 17, 20; 2:7, 12, 14, 16, 27^{2}; 3:20^{2}, 21, 22, 24, 27^{2}, 28, 30; 4:2, 16; 5:1, 2^{2}, 5, 9, 10^{2}, 11, 12^{2}, 15^{2}, 16^{2}, 17^{3}, 18^{2}, 19^{2}, 21; 6:4^{2}; 7:2, 4, 5, 7, 8, 11^{2}, 13^{2}; 8:11, 14, 20, 24; 9:10^{2}, 32^{2}; 10:5, 17^{2}, 19^{2}; 11:6, 14, 20, 24; 12:1, 2; 14:14; 15:16, 18^{2}, 19, 24, 28, 32; 16:18, 26

1Co 1:4, 5, 9, 10, 11, 21^{2}; 2:10; 3:5, 13, 15; 4:4; 6:2, 11, 14; 7:6, 14^{2}, 39; 8:6^{2}, 9; 9:22, 27; 10:30; 11:12; 12:3^{2}, 8^{2}, 9^{2}, 13; 14:6^{4}, 9, 19, 27^{3}, 30, 31; 15:2, 10, 21^{2}, 31; 16:2, 3, 7

2Co 1:1, 4, 5, 11^{3}, 12, 16, 19^{2}, 20, 24; 2:2, 14; 3:3, 10, 18; 4:2, 14, 16; 5:7^{2}, 18, 20; 6:6^{6}, 7^{3}, 8^{2}; 7:6, 7^{2}, 9, 13; 8:5, 8^{2}, 14, 19, 20; 9:12, 13, 14; 10:1, 9, 11, 12, 15; 11:3, 26^{2}, 33; 12:17; 13:4^{2}

Gal 1:1^{2}, 12, 15, 22; 2:2^{2}, 5, 15, 16^{5}, 17, 20, 21; 3:2^{2}, 3, 5^{2}, 11^{2}, 18, 19, 21, 22, 24, 26; 4:8, 22^{2}, 23; 5:4, 5, 6, 13; 6:14

Eph 1:1, 5; 2:3, 5, 8, 11^{2}, 13, 16, 18; 3:3, 5, 6, 7, 9, 10, 12, 16, 17, 21; 4:14, 16, 21; 5:13, 26

Php 1:11, 14, 20^{2}, 26, 28; 3:9, 11, 16; 4:6, 19

Col 1:1, 16^{2}, 17, 20^{2}, 21; 2:11, 18, 19; 3:17; 4:18

1Th 3:3, 5, 7; 4:1, 2, 15; 5:9, 27

2Th 2:1^{2}, 2^{3}, 3, 14, 15; 3:12, 14, 16

1Ti 1:1, 18; 4:5, 14; 5:21

2Ti 1:1, 6, 10, 14; 2:26; 3:16; 4:17

Tit 1:9; 3:5^{2}, 7

Phlm 6, 7

Heb 1:1, 2^{2}, 3^{2}, 4; 2:2, 3^{2}, 9, 10; 3:4, 16; 5:3, 8, 14; 6:7, 13^{2}, 16, 17, 18; 7:2, 11, 19, 21, 22, 23, 25; 8:6, 9; 9:11, 12^{2}, 15, 22, 26; 10:1, 8, 10, 14, 19, 20, 33, 38; 11:2, 3, 4^{3}, 5, 7^{3}, 8, 9, 12, 17, 20, 21, 22, 23, 24, 27, 29^{2}, 30, 31; 13:11, 15

Jas 2:7, 12, 18, 21, 22, 24^{2}, 25; 5:4, 12^{3}, 17

1Pt 1:3, 5, 12, 18, 21, 23, 25; 2:5, 12, 14, 24; 3:1, 18, 19, 20, 21; 5:2, 10, 12

2Pt 1:4, 13, 21^{2}; 2:2; 3:1, 2, 5, 7

1Jn 3:24; 5:2, 6^{3}

3Jn 14

Jude 1, 12, 23

Rev 1:1; 5:9; 8:13; 9:2, 18[4], 20; 10:6; 12:11[2]; 13:14[2]; 14:20; 18:15, 17, 19, 23; 21:25

DID

Gen 3:6[2], 12, 13, 21; 6:22[2]; 7:5, 20; 11:9[2]; 18:8, 13; 19:3[2]; 21:1; 22:1, 23; 24:54; 25:28, 34; 26:20, 30; 27:25; 29:25, 28; 30:40, 41; 31:46, 54; 35:5; 38:10, 11; 39:3, 6, 19, 22, 23; 40:17, 23; 41:4, 12, 20; 42:20, 25; 43:3, 17, 30, 32; 44:2; 45:5, 21; 47:22; 48:15; 50:12, 15, 16, 17

Ex 1:11, 17; 2:13; 4:30; 5:8, 19; 6:8; 7:6[2], 10, 11, 20, 22[2], 23; 8:7, 13, 17, 18, 24, 31; 9:6, 7; 10:11, 15; 11:10; 12:28[2], 35, 50[2], 51; 13:8; 14:4, 12, 31; 16:3, 17, 18, 24, 35[2]; 17:2, 6, 10; 18:7, 14, 24; 19:4; 24:11; 32:12, 21, 28; 33:4; 34:28; 35:24, 25; 36:22, 29; 39:3, 21, 32[2], 43; 40:16[2]

Lev 4:20; 8:4, 9, 36; 9:14; 10:7; 16:15, 34; 24:23; 26:35; 27:24

Nu 1:54[2]; 2:34; 4:37, 41; 5:4[2]; 7:18, 24, 30, 36; 8:3, 20[2], 22; 9:5; 10:21; 11:5, 25; 14:22, 37; 17:11[2]; 20:27; 21:14; 22:37; 23:2, 30; 25:2; 27:22; 31:31; 32:8; 36:10

Dt 1:30, 32; 2:12, 22, 29; 3:6; 4:3, 4, 33, 34; 5:23; 7:7, 18; 8:3, 4; 9:9, 18; 11:3, 4, 5, 6, 7; 12:30; 24:9; 25:17; 29:2; 31:4; 32:12, 38; 33:9; 34:9

Jos 2:10, 11[2]; 4:8, 18, 20, 23; 5:4, 11, 12, 14, 15; 6:14; 9:4, 9, 10, 26; 10:23, 28[2], 30[2], 39, 42; 11:9, 12, 13, 15[2]; 12:6; 13:12, 22, 32; 14:5; 17:13; 22:20, 33; 24:5, 13, 17

Jdg 1:21, 27, 28, 29, 30, 31, 32, 33; 2:7, 11, 17, 22; 3:7, 12, 16; 4:1; 5:17; 6:1, 13, 20, 27[2], 40; 8:1, 15, 25; 9:27, 56, 57; 10:6, 11, 12; 11:7, 25[2], 26, 39; 13:1, 19, 21; 14:9; 15:11; 16:21; 17:6; 19:4, 6, 8, 21; 21:22, 23, 25

Ru 2:14, 19; 3:6; 4:11

1Sa 1:7[2], 18; 2:11, 14, 22, 27, 28[2]; 3:7, 19; 4:20; 6:6, 10; 7:4, 14; 9:24; 12:7; 13:6; 14:32, 43; 15:2; 16:4; 19:5; 20:34; 21:11; 22:15, 17, 18; 25:4; 27:11; 28:24, 25; 30:11

2Sa 1:2; 2:3; 3:36; 5:25; 7:17; 8:11; 9:6, 13; 11:7[2], 13, 20, 21; 12:3, 6, 17, 20, 31; 13:8, 29; 14:4; 15:6; 17:15; 19:19, 28, 43; 20:6; 21:6; 22:7[2], 11, 23, 37, 43[3]; 23:17, 22; 24:23

1Ki 1:16, 31; 2:5[2], 35, 42; 3:4, 14, 21; 5:18; 7:15, 18, 23, 46, 51; 8:4, 64; 9:21, 22, 24, 25; 10:29; 11:6[2], 7, 8, 16, 25, 33, 38, 41; 12:9, 11, 32; 13:19, 22; 14:4, 16, 21, 22, 24, 29; 15:4, 5, 7, 11[2], 23, 26, 28, 31, 34; 16:5, 7, 12, 14, 15, 19, 25, 27, 30, 33, 34; 17:5, 15[2], 16; 18:13, 34[2]; 19:6, 8, 21; 20:25, 33[2]; 21:11, 13, 25, 26[2]; 22:18, 39, 52

2Ki 1:18; 2:18; 4:1, 28[2], 44; 6:6, 29; 7:8; 8:2, 18[2], 23, 25, 27[2]; 9:27, 34; 10:19, 34; 11:3, 9, 10; 12:2, 11, 19; 13:2, 7, 8, 11, 12, 25; 14:3[3], 4, 15, 24, 28; 15:3, 6, 8, 9, 18, 21, 24, 26, 28, 31, 34[2], 36; 16:2, 16, 19; 17:2, 9, 11, 14, 22, 40[2], 41; 18:3[2], 4, 11, 13, 16; 21:2, 3, 9, 11, 17, 20[2], 25; 22:2; 23:9, 12, 13, 19, 24, 28, 32, 37; 24:3, 5, 9, 11, 19; 25:11, 13, 27, 29

1Ch 4:27; 9:22; 11:19, 24; 14:16; 15:13, 24; 17:15; 23:24; 26:27; 27:26; 29:22

2Ch 1:7; 2:7; 4:2, 3, 16, 17; 5:5, 11; 8:8, 9; 10:9; 12:14; 13:20; 14:2; 15:4, 6; 18:16, 17; 19:8; 20:35[2]; 21:6, 10; 22:4; 23:8; 24:2, 7, 11, 12; 25:2, 4, 12, 27; 26:4[2], 22; 27:2[3], 5; 28:1, 16, 22; 29:2, 19, 34; 30:18, 22, 24; 31:20, 21; 32:3, 9, 33; 33:2, 17, 22[2]; 34:2, 6, 12, 32; 35:3, 12, 18; 36:5, 8, 9, 12

Ezr 1:8, 11; 5:14; 6:13, 21; 10:6, 16

Neh 2:16[2]; 3:3; 5:13, 15; 9:25, 28; 11:12; 13:7, 10, 18[2], 26[2]

Est 1:8, 21; 2:4, 11, 20; 3:1, 2, 5; 4:17; 5:12; 8:1; 9:5

Job 1:5; 2:10; 3:11, 12; 6:22; 28:27; 30:25; 31:13, 15[2], 32, 34[2]; 42:9, 11

Ps 14:2; 18:10[2], 22, 36, 37, 42[2]; 31:11; 35:11, 15; 41:9; 44:3; 45:9; 51:5; 53:2[2]; 55:12; 66:6; 68:12; 78:12, 25, 29, 33, 36, 38, 40; 102:19; 105:35; 106:34, 43; 119:23[2]; 135:6; 139:16; 142:1

Prv 1:29

Isa 5:25; 6:2; 9:1; 10:10; 13:1; 14:16; 20:2; 22:12; 38:14[2]; 42:24; 48:3; 53:4; 58:2; 65:12[4]; 66:4[3]

Jer 7:12, 26; 11:8; 14:6[2]; 15:4, 16; 22:15; 26:19[2]; 31:19; 36:8; 37:2; 38:12; 41:1; 44:19, 21; 46:15, 17, 21; 52:2, 21, 33

Lam 1:7[2]; 4:5

Ezk 3:3; 6:13; 11:22; 12:7; 16:49; 17:7; 18:18; 20:8[2], 17; 24:18; 27:25; 31:6; 34:6, 8; 43:22; 46:12

Dan 1:15; 3:24; 4:7, 33; 6:10; 7:9; 8:4, 27; 10:3

Hos 2:8; 9:17; 10:9; 13:5

Am 1:11[3]; 5:19; 7:4

Oba 14[2]

Jna 3:10; 4:8

Nah 2:12

Hab 1:1; 3:6, 7

Hag 1:9, 12, 14

Zec 1:4, 6, 21; 7:5, 6[3]; 9:3

Mal 2:6, 15

Mt 1:24; 2:22; 9:19; 12:3, 4; 13:58; 14:20; 15:7, 37, 38; 17:2; 19:7; 20:5; 21:6, 15, 25, 31, 36, 42; 25:44, 45[2]; 26:12, 19, 21, 67; 27:9, 35, 51; 28:4, 8, 15

Mk 1:4, 6, 32; 2:25, 26; 3:8; 4:8; 5:20; 6:20, 42, 44; 8:6, 8; 10:3; 11:31; 12:44[2]; 14:18, 22, 59, 65; 15:19

Lk 4:2; 6:1, 3, 4, 10, 23, 26, 49; 7:38; 9:15, 17, 43, 53, 54; 11:40; 12:47, 48; 15:16; 17:9, 27, 28; 19:22; 24:32, 43

Jn 1:45; 2:11, 23, 24; 4:29, 39, 45, 54; 5:16; 6:2, 14, 23, 26, 31, 49, 58; 7:5, 19; 8:40; 9:2, 18, 22, 26, 27; 10:8, 41; 11:45; 12:36, 42; 15:24; 18:15, 26, 34; 19:24[2]; 20:4, 30; 21:7, 25

Act 2:22, 26, 31, 40, 46; 3:17[2]; 4:25; 5:28; 6:8; 7:27, 35, 51; 8:6; 9:9, 36; 10:39, 41; 11:17, 30; 12:8; 14:17; 15:8, 14; 16:18; 19:14; 21:9; 26:10[2], 22

Ro 1:26, 28; 3:3; 5:20; 7:5; 8:29[2], 30; 10:19

1Co 4:8; 10:3, 4; 15:27

2Co 1:17; 2:9; 5:20; 7:8, 12; 8:5; 12:16, 17, 18

Gal 2:12; 4:8; 5:7[2]

Php 4:14

2Th 3:8

1Ti 1:13

2Ti 4:14

Heb 3:16; 4:2, 4, 10; 7:19, 27; 9:9

1Pt 1:11, 12; 2:22

Rev 12:4; 13:14; 19:2; 21:23

DIDST

Gen 12:18; 18:15; 20:6; 21:26; 31:27[2], 39

Ex 15:10; 40:15

Nu 21:34

Dt 3:2; 9:7; 32:14; 33:8[2]

Jos 2:18; 8:2

Jdg 12:1; 13:8

1Sa 3:6, 8; 15:19[3]; 19:5; 20:19; 25:25

2Sa 11:10; 12:12, 21[2]; 13:16; 18:11; 19:28

1Ki 1:13; 2:44; 8:18, 53; 20:9; 21:10

1Ch 17:22

2Ch 2:3[2]; 6:8; 16:8; 20:7; 34:27[2]

Neh 9:7, 9, 10, 11, 17, 21, 22, 28, 30, 31, 34

Ps 22:4, 9; 30:7; 39:9; 40:6; 44:1, 2[2]; 60:10; 68:7, 9[2]; 73:18; 74:13, 15; 76:8; 80:9

Isa 14:12; 22:8; 47:6, 7[2]; 48:6; 54:1[2]; 57:9[3]; 63:14; 64:3

Jer 32:22; 36:17; 45:3

Lam 1:10

Ezk 16:13[2], 15, 16, 17, 36; 23:40; 27:33; 29:7; 35:15

Dan 10:12

Hos 10:13

Hab 3:8, 9, 12[2], 14, 15

Mt 13:27; 14:31; 20:13

Lk 7:46; 19:21

Jn 17:8

Act 11:3

1Co 4:7[2]

Heb 2:7

Rev 17:7

DO

Gen 6:17; 9:13; 11:6[2]; 16:6; 18:5, 17, 19, 25[2], 29, 30; 19:7, 8[2], 22; 21:23; 22:12; 24:42; 25:32; 26:29; 27:37, 46; 30:31; 31:16, 29, 43; 32:12; 34:14, 19; 37:13; 39:9, 11; 40:8; 41:9, 25, 28, 34, 55; 42:1, 18, 22; 43:11; 44:7, 17; 45:17, 19; 47:30

Ex 1:16; 3:20; 4:15, 17, 21; 5:4, 17; 6:1; 8:8, 26; 9:5; 15:26; 17:2, 4; 18:16, 20, 23; 19:8; 20:9, 10; 21:7, 11; 22:30; 23:2, 12, 22, 24; 24:3, 7, 14; 29:1, 35, 41; 31:11; 32:14, 18; 33:5, 17; 34:10[2], 15; 35:1, 19, 35; 36:2; 39:1, 41

Lev 4:2, 3, 20[2]; 5:1, 4[2]; 8:34; 9:6; 10:9; 16:15, 16, 29; 18:3[2], 4, 5, 25; 19:15, 29, 35, 37; 20:4, 8, 22; 21:6, 15, 23; 22:9, 16, 31; 23:3, 7, 8, 21, 25, 28, 31, 35, 36; 25:18[2], 45; 26:3, 14, 15, 16; 27:11

Nu 2:5; 3:7, 8; 4:3, 19, 23, 30, 37, 41, 47; 5:6; 6:21; 7:5; 8:7, 15, 19, 22, 26[2]; 9:14; 10:29, 32[2]; 11:27; 14:28, 35, 41; 15:12, 13, 14[2], 20, 39, 40; 16:6, 9, 28; 18:6, 23; 21:34; 22:17, 18, 20, 30; 23:19, 26; 24:13, 14, 18; 28:18, 25, 26; 29:1, 7, 12, 35, 39; 30:2; 31:19; 32:20, 23, 24, 25, 31; 33:56[2]

Dt 1:14, 18, 44; 3:2, 21, 24; 4:1, 5, 6, 14, 25; 5:1, 13, 14, 27, 31, 32; 6:1, 3, 18, 24, 25; 7:11, 12, 19; 8:1, 16, 19; 11:22, 32; 12:1, 4, 8[2], 14, 25, 30, 31, 32; 13:11, 18; 15:5, 17, 19; 16:8, 12; 17:10[2], 11, 12, 13, 19; 18:7, 9, 12, 14; 19:9, 19; 20:3, 15, 18; 21:9; 22:3[3], 5, 26; 24:8[2], 18, 22; 25:16[2]; 26:16[2]; 27:10, 26; 28:1, 13, 15, 20, 58, 63; 29:9[2], 14, 29; 30:5, 8, 12, 13, 14; 31:4, 5, 12, 29; 32:6, 46; 34:11

Jos 1:2, 7, 8, 16; 2:24; 3:5; 6:3; 7:9; 8:2, 8; 9:20, 25[2]; 10:25; 22:5, 24, 27; 23:6, 12; 24:13, 20

Jdg 6:27; 7:17[3]; 8:3; 9:33, 48[2]; 10:15; 11:10, 12, 36; 13:8, 12, 17; 14:10; 15:3, 10; 17:13; 18:14[2], 18; 19:23[2], 24[2]; 20:9, 10; 21:7, 11, 16

Ru 1:17; 2:9; 3:4, 5, 11, 13[3]; 4:11

1Sa 1:23; 2:23, 35; 3:11, 17, 18; 5:8; 6:2, 6; 7:3; 8:8; 10:2, 7, 8; 11:10; 12:16, 25; 14:7, 36, 40, 44; 16:3; 20:2, 4, 13[2], 30; 22:3; 24:4, 6; 25:17, 22; 26:21, 25; 28:2, 15; 29:3; 30:23

2Sa 3:8, 9[2], 18, 35; 7:3, 23, 25; 9:11; 10:12; 11:11; 12:9, 12; 13:2, 12[2]; 15:4, 5, 15, 26; 16:10, 11, 20; 17:6; 18:4, 32; 19:13, 18, 19, 22[2], 27, 37, 38[2]; 20:6, 17; 21:3, 4; 23:17; 24:12

1Ki 1:30; 2:6, 9, 23, 31, 38; 3:28; 5:8; 8:32, 39, 43[2]; 9:1, 4; 10:9; 11:12, 33, 38; 12:6, 27; 14:8; 17:13, 18; 18:34[2]; 19:2; 20:9[2], 10, 24; 22:22

2Ki 2:9; 3:13; 4:2, 16, 28; 5:13; 6:15, 27, 31; 7:9; 8:12, 13; 9:18, 19; 10:5[2], 19; 11:5; 17:12, 15, 17, 34[2], 36, 37, 41; 18:12; 19:31; 20:9; 21:8, 9; 22:9, 13

1Ch 11:19; 12:32; 13:4; 16:21, 22, 40; 17:2, 23; 19:13; 21:8, 10, 23; 28:7, 10, 20; 29:19

2Ch 6:23, 33; 7:17; 9:8; 14:4; 18:21; 19:6, 7, 9, 10; 20:12; 22:3; 23:4; 25:8, 9; 30:12; 32:10; 33:8, 9; 34:16, 21; 35:6, 21

Ezr 4:2[2], 3, 22; 6:8; 7:10, 18[2], 21, 26; 10:4, 5, 11, 12

Neh 1:9; 2:12, 19; 4:2; 5:9, 12[2]; 6:2, 13; 9:24, 29; 10:29; 13:17, 21, 27

Est 1:8, 15; 3:11; 4:11; 5:5, 8; 6:6, 10; 7:5; 9:13, 23

Job 6:4, 26; 7:20; 9:13; 10:2; 11:8; 13:2, 9, 10, 14, 20; 15:3, 12; 16:4; 17:10; 19:22; 20:2; 21:7, 29; 22:17; 24:1; 31:14; 32:9; 34:10, 12, 32; 36:28; 37:12, 24; 39:1; 41:8; 42:2

Ps 2:1; 7:1; 11:3; 12:2; 16:1; 25:1, 5; 31:1; 34:10, 14, 16; 36:3; 37:3, 8, 27; 38:15; 40:8; 41:7; 50:16; 51:18; 56:4, 11; 58:1[2]; 60:12; 64:4; 71:1; 75:1[2]; 80:12; 82:3; 83:9; 86:4; 89:50; 92:7; 95:10; 103:18, 20, 21; 104:20; 105:14, 15; 107:23; 108:13; 109:21; 111:10; 118:6; 119:3, 21, 35, 83, 109, 113, 132, 141, 153, 157, 163, 164, 176; 125:4; 129:8; 130:5; 131:1; 137:6; 139:21; 143:8, 10

Prv 2:14; 3:27; 6:3, 30; 8:13; 10:23; 14:22; 17:7; 19:7[2], 19; 20:30; 21:3, 7, 15; 24:8, 29; 25:8; 28:12; 31:12

Ecc 2:3, 11, 12; 3:12; 4:8; 5:1; 6:6; 8:11, 12; 9:10[2]; 10:10; 11:5

Song 1:3; 8:8

Isa 1:16, 17; 5:5; 9:13; 10:3, 11; 14:21; 19:15, 21; 23:4; 24:4, 7, 18; 27:3; 28:21; 29:13, 14; 37:32; 38:7, 19; 41:23[2]; 42:9,

16; 43:19; 45:7; 46:10, 11; 48:11, 14; 55:2; 56:1; 57:4; 58:4; 64:6; 65:8

Jer 2:8, 18^2; 4:22^2, 30; 5:28, 31; 7:10, 14, 17, 19^2; 8:8, 14; 9:7; 10:5^2; 11:4, 6, 8, 15; 12:5; 13:12, 23^2; 14:7, 21^2; 17:22, 24; 18:6, 8, 10, 12; 19:12; 22:3^2, 4, 15, 17; 23:24, 32; 25:6; 26:3, 14; 28:6; 29:32; 30:6; 31:20; 32:23, 35, 40, 41; 33:9, 18; 36:3; 38:5; 39:12^2; 40:16; 42:2, 3, 5, 20; 44:4, 17; 50:15, 21, 29; 51:47, 52, 55

Lam 1:4, 22; 2:11

Ezk 2:4; 5:9^2; 6:10; 7:27; 8:6, 9, 12, 13; 11:20; 15:3; 16:5; 18:5, 21; 20:11, 13, 19, 21^2; 21:24; 22:14; 23:30, 48; 24:14, 22, 24; 25:8, 14; 33:9, 14, 19, 31, 32; 34:2; 35:11, 15; 36:11, 22, 27, 32, 36, 37; 37:24, 28; 39:17; 43:11; 44:13; 45:20, 25

Dan 3:14; 4:26; 9:18, 19; 11:3, 16, 17, 24, 27, 28, 30, 32^3, 36, 39; 12:10

Hos 4:18; 6:4^2; 7:10, 15; 9:5; 10:3, 15; 12:1; 14:8

Joel 1:18; 2:21, 22^2; 3:4

Am 3:7, 10; 4:12^2

Jna 1:11; 3:10; 4:9

Mic 2:3, 7^2, 11; 6:8; 7:3

Nah 1:9

Zep 1:12^2; 3:5, 13

Hag 2:3, 12

Zec 1:5, 6, 21; 5:10; 8:15, 16; 9:12; 12:7

Mal 1:10; 2:2, 10; 4:1, 3

Mt 5:6, 15, 19, 44, 46, 47^2; 6:1, 2^2, 7, 20, 26, 28, 32; 7:12^2, 16; 8:9, 29; 9:14, 17, 28; 11:3, 4; 12:2^2, 12, 27, 50; 13:13, 41; 14:2; 15:2, 3, 9, 17; 16:9, 11, 13; 17:25; 18:10, 35; 19:16, 18; 20:13, 15, 32; 21:21, 24, 27, 40; 22:29; 23:3^3, 5; 26:72; 27:19, 22

Mk 1:24, 27; 2:18, 24; 3:4^2, 35; 5:7; 6:5, 14; 7:7, 8, 12, 13, 18; 8:18, 21, 27; 9:22, 39; 10:17, 19^4, 35, 36, 51; 11:3, 5, 26, 28, 29, 33^2; 12:9, 24, 27; 13:11; 14:7; 15:8, 12

Lk 2:27; 3:10, 11, 12, 14^2; 4:23, 34; 5:30, 33; 6:2^2, 9^2, 11, 27, 31^2, 33^3, 35, 44, 46; 7:4, 8; 8:21, 28; 10:11, 25, 28, 37; 11:19, 39; 12:4, 17, 18, 26, 30, 56; 13:32; 15:29; 16:3, 4; 17:10; 18:18, 20^4, 41; 19:31, 48; 20:8, 13, 15; 22:19, 23; 23:31, 34; 24:38

Jn 2:4, 5; 3:2, 11; 4:34; 5:19^2, 30, 36, 45; 6:6, 28, 38; 7:4, 17, 26, 31; 8:11, 28, 29, 38, 39, 41, 43, 44, 46, 49; 9:15, 16, 33; 10:25, 32, 37, 38; 11:12, 47; 13:7, 15, 17, 27; 14:12^3, 13, 14, 31; 15:5, 14, 21; 16:3, 19, 31; 17:4; 21:21

Act 1:1; 2:11, 37; 4:16, 28; 5:35; 7:26, 51^2; 9:6^2; 10:6; 14:15; 15:29, 36; 16:20, 28, 30, 37; 17:7; 19:36; 21:23; 22:10^2; 23:21; 24:10, 16; 25:9; 26:9, 20

Ro 1:28, 32^2; 2:3, 8, 14; 3:8, 31; 7:15^3, 16, 17, 19^2, 20^2, 21; 8:3, 5, 13, 25; 12:8, 15; 13:3, 4; 15:31

1Co 5:12^2; 6:2, 7^2, 8; 7:36; 9:3, 13, 17, 23, 25; 10:22, 31^2; 11:24, 25, 26; 12:30^2; 15:29, 35; 16:1, 5, 10

2Co 1:17; 3:1; 5:4; 7:8; 8:1, 10, 23; 10:3, 7; 11:8, 12^2; 12:19; 13:7^2, 8

Gal 1:10^2; 2:10, 14^2, 21; 3:10; 4:21; 5:3, 11, 17, 21; 6:10

Eph 3:20; 6:9, 21

Php 1:18; 2:13, 14, 18; 3:8, 13; 4:9, 13

Col 1:9; 3:13, 17^2, 23^2

1Th 3:12; 4:10, 11; 5:6, 11, 24

2Th 3:4^2

1Ti 1:4; 6:2, 18

2Ti 2:23; 3:8; 4:5, 9, 21

Phlm 14, 19, 21

Heb 3:10; 4:3, 13; 6:3, 10, 11; 10:7, 9; 11:3, 29; 13:6, 16, 17, 19, 21

Jas 1:16; 2:6, 7, 8, 11^2, 12; 4:5, 15, 17; 5:19

1Pt 1:21; 2:14, 20; 3:6, 11, 12; 4:11

2Pt 1:10, 19; 3:16

1Jn 1:6; 2:3; 3:22; 4:14; 5:16

3Jn 6

Rev 2:5; 3:9, 18; 9:19; 13:14; 14:13; 19:10; 21:24; 22:9, 14

DOEST

Gen 4:7^2; 21:22

Ex 18:14, 17

Dt 12:28; 14:29; 15:18

Jdg 11:27

2Sa 3:25

1Ki 2:3; 19:9, 13; 20:22

Job 9:12; 35:6^2

Ps 49:18; 77:14; 86:10; 119:68

Ecc 8:4

Jer 11:15; 15:5

Ezk 12:9; 16:30; 24:19

Dan 4:35

Jna 4:4, 9

Mt 6:2, 3; 21:23

Mk 11:28

Lk 20:2

Jn 2:18; 3:2; 7:3; 13:27

Act 22:26

Ro 2:1, 3

Jas 2:19

3Jn 5^2

DOETH

Gen 31:12

Ex 31:14, 15; 35:2

Lev 4:27; 6:3; 23:30

Nu 15:30; 24:23

Job 5:9; 9:10; 23:13; 24:21; 37:5

Ps 1:3; 14:1, 3; 15:3, 5; 53:1, 3; 72:18; 106:3; 118:15, 16; 136:4

Prv 6:32; 11:17; 15:7; 17:21, 22; 28:17

Ecc 2:2; 3:14^2; 7:20; 8:3

Isa 49:18; 56:2

Jer 5:19; 48:10

Ezk 17:15; 18:10, 11, 14, 24^2, 27

Dan 4:35; 9:14

Am 9:12

Mal 2:12, 17

Mt 6:3; 7:21, 24, 26; 8:9

Lk 6:47, 49; 7:8

Jn 3:20, 21; 5:19^2, 20; 7:4, 51; 9:31; 11:47; 14:10; 15:15; 16:2

Act 15:17; 26:31

Ro 2:9; 3:12; 10:5; 13:4

1Co 6:18; 7:37, 38^2

Gal 3:5, 12

Eph 6:8

Col 3:25

Jas 4:17

1Jn 2:17, 29; 3:7, 10

3Jn 10, 11^2

Rev 13:13

DOING

Gen 31:28; 44:5

Ex 15:11

Nu 20:19

Dt 9:18

1Ki 7:40; 16:19; 22:43

2Ki 21:16

1Ch 22:16

2Ch 20:32

Ezr 9:1

Neh 6:3

Job 32:22

Ps 64:9; 66:5; 118:23

Isa 56:2; 58:13^2

Mt 21:42; 24:46

Mk 12:11

Lk 12:43

Act 10:38; 24:20

Ro 2:7; 12:20

2Co 8:11

Gal 6:9

Eph 6:6, 7

2Th 3:13

1Ti 4:16; 5:21

1Pt 2:15; 3:17^2; 4:19

DOINGS

Lev 18:3^2

Dt 28:20

Jdg 2:19

1Sa 25:3

2Ch 17:4

Ps 9:11; 77:12

Prv 20:11

Isa 1:16; 3:8, 10; 12:4

Jer 4:4, 18; 7:3, 5; 11:18; 17:10; 18:11; 21:12, 14; 23:2, 22; 25:5; 26:3, 13; 32:19; 35:15; 44:22

Ezk 14:22, 23; 20:43, 44; 21:24; 24:14; 36:17, 19, 31

Hos 4:9; 5:4; 7:2; 9:15; 12:2

Mic 2:7; 3:4; 7:13

Zep 3:7, 11

Zec 1:4, 6

DOST

Gen 32:29; 44:4

Dt 9:5; 24:10, 11

Jdg 14:16

1Sa 24:14; 28:16

1Ki 2:22; 21:7

2Ki 18:20

2Ch 6:26

Neh 2:4

Job 2:9; 7:21; 10:8; 14:3, 16; 15:8; 30:20; 33:13; 37:15, 16

Ps 39:11; 43:2; 44:12; 99:4

Prv 4:8

Ecc 7:10

Song 5:9

Isa 26:7; 36:5

Jer 32:3; 40:14; 48:18

Lam 5:20

Ezk 2:6; 32:19; 33:8

Mic 4:9

Hab 1:3

Lk 10:40; 23:40

Jn 6:30; 9:34, 35; 10:24; 13:6

Ro 2:21, 22^2, 27; 14:10^2

1Co 4:7

Rev 6:10

DOTH

Gen 3:5; 27:42; 45:3

Ex 11:7; 31:13; 32:11

Lev 11:31, 32; 25:16

Nu 5:21; 16:7; 36:6

Dt 1:20, 25, 31; 5:24; 8:3^2; 9:4, 5; 10:12, 18; 16:19; 18:12; 20:16; 31:6, 8

Jos 1:18; 20:4

Jdg 4:20

Ru 3:11

1Sa 9:13; 23:19; 26:1, 18, 20

2Sa 10:3; 14:13^2, 14^2; 19:8, 20; 24:3, 24

1Ki 1:11, 13; 22:8

2Ki 2:15; 5:7

1Ch 19:3; 21:3

2Ch 6:33; 32:11

Job 1:9; 4:21; 5:6; 6:5, 25; 8:3^2; 12:11; 15:12; 16:13; 17:2; 22:13; 23:9; 24:19; 25:3; 31:4; 35:16; 36:7; 39:26, 27; 41:18

Ps 1:2; 10:2, 8, 9, 13; 11:7; 29:9; 41:11; 54:ttl; 59:7; 68:33; 73:11; 74:1; 77:8; 80:13^2; 92:6; 119:129; 130:5; 147:2

Prv 6:16; 8:1; 14:10; 22:5; 24:12^2; 25:23; 26:14; 27:9, 24; 29:6; 30:11; 31:11

Ecc 10:1

Song 2:6

Isa 1:3^2, 23; 3:1, 9; 10:7; 28:24^2, 25, 26^2; 30:33; 42:11; 44:14; 52:6; 59:9

Jer 2:11; 10:7; 12:1; 14:10; 15:10; 23:14; 30:6; 31:10; 49:1; 51:43

Lam 1:1; 3:33, 39; 5:8

Ezk 3:20, 21; 18:19; 20:49

Hos 4:14; **5**:5

Mic 6:8

Hab 1:4^{2}

Zep 3:5

Mt 6:19, 20; **12**:24; **17**:24; **18**:12; **19**:9; **22**:43; **24**:42; **26**:46

Mk 2:7, 22; **8**:12

Lk 1:46; **6**:43; **11**:36; **13**:15, 34; **14**:27; **15**:4, 8; **17**:9; **22**:26

Jn 2:10; **6**:61; **7**:51; **9**:19; **10**:17

Act 4:10; **8**:36; **22**:5; **26**:24

Ro 8:24; **9**:19; **14**:6

1Co 9:9; **11**:14; **13**:5; **15**:50

2Co 1:10; **3**:9

Eph 5:13

Col 1:6

1Th 2:11

2Th 2:7

2Ti 2:17

Heb 1:11; **12**:1

Jas 2:14, 16; **3**:11; **5**:6

1Pt 3:21; **5**:13

1Jn 3:2, 9

3Jn 10

Rev 19:11

EVEN

Gen 6:17; **9**:3; **10**:9, 19, 21; **13**:3, 10; **14**:23; **19**:1, 4, 9; **20**:5; **21**:10; **23**:7, 10; **24**:11; **26**:28; **27**:34, 38; **34**:29; **35**:14; **37**:18; **42**:28; **44**:18; **46**:18, 34; **47**:2, 21; **49**:22, 25

Ex 3:1; **4**:16, 22, 23; **9**:18; **10**:12, 21; **11**:5; **12**:15, 18^{2}, 19, 38, 41; **14**:23; **16**:6, 12, 13; **18**:14; **23**:31; **25**:9, 19; **27**:5; **28**:1, 8, 17, 42; **29**:27, 28, 39, 41; **30**:8, 21, 23, 33, 38; **32**:29; **35**:35; **36**:2; **37**:3, 9; **38**:21, 24; **39**:37, 43

Lev 1:2; **2**:14; **3**:14; **4**:12, 17; **5**:12; **6**:5, 15; **7**:8, 20, 21, 25, 27; **8**:9; **11**:11, 22, 24, 25, 27, 28, 31, 32, 39, 40^{2}; **13**:12, 18, 30, 38; **14**:9, 31, 46; **15**:5, 6, 7, 8, 10^{2}, 11, 16, 17, 18, 19, 21, 22, 23, 27; **16**:32; **17**:5, 9, 10, 13, 15; **18**:9, 10, 29; **19**:21; **20**:6, 10; **22**:6; **23**:2, 4, 5, 16, 18, 32^{3}; **24**:7; **26**:16, 28, 34, 43; **27**:3^{2}, 5, 6, 18, 23, 24, 32

Nu 1:21, 23, 25, 27, 29, 31, 33, 35, 37, 39, 41, 43, 46; **3**:22, 38, 47; **4**:3, 14, 30, 35, 39, 40, 43, 44, 47, 48; **5**:8, 26; **6**:4; **7**:10; **8**:8, 16; **9**:3, 5, 11, 13, 15, 21; **11**:20; **12**:8; **14**:19, 34^{2}, 37, 45; **15**:23; **16**:5^{2}; **17**:6; **18**:21, 26, 29; **19**:7, 8, 10, 19, 21, 22; **20**:1, 22, 29; **21**:24, 26, 30^{2}; **25**:13, 14; **27**:21; **28**:4, 8; **31**:47, 51; **32**:4, 33^{2}; **33**:49; **34**:2, 6; **36**:10

Dt 1:44; **2**:22, 23, 36; **3**:16^{2}, 17^{2}; **4**:5, 13, 19, 20, 24, 30, 48, 49; **5**:3, 23; **9**:9, 11, 21; **10**:15; **11**:12, 24; **12**:5, 22, 30, 31; **13**:7; **16**:3, 4, 6; **17**:5, 12; **18**:20; **20**:14; **21**:3; **22**:26; **23**:2, 3, 16, 18, 23; **25**:18; **26**:9; **28**:59, 64^{2}, 67^{2}; **29**:24; **31**:21; **32**:31, 39; **33**:4

Jos 1:2, 4; **2**:1, 24; **3**:16; **5**:4, 10; **6**:17, 25; **7**:5, 11^{2}; **8**:4, 11, 13, 25, 28; **9**:20, 27; **10**:41^{2}; **11**:4, 17^{2}; **12**:2, 3, 7; **13**:3, 8, 24, 27, 31; **14**:10, 11; **15**:1, 5, 13, 46; **16**:5; **17**:11, 17; **19**:1, 28, 32, 50; **21**:20; **23**:4, 12; **24**:2, 12, 18

Jdg 3:1, 9; **4**:13; **5**:3, 5, 11, 15; **6**:3, 25; **7**:22; **8**:14, 19, 27; **9**:40; **11**:13, 22^{2}, 33^{2}, 36; **18**:15; **19**:16; **20**:1, 2, 23, 26, 33; **21**:2

Ru 2:7, 15, 17

1Sa 3:20; **5**:6; **6**:18, 19; **7**:14; **8**:8, 14; **14**:21, 22; **17**:40, 52; **18**:4, 11; **19**:10; **20**:4, 5, 16, 25; **25**:25, 27; **26**:8; **27**:3, 8; **28**:3, 17; **30**:17, 26

2Sa 1:2, 12; **2**:5; **3**:9, 10, 15; **6**:5, 19; **7**:6, 23; **8**:2; **10**:4; **11**:13, 23; **14**:25; **15**:12, 21; **17**:11; **18**:5; **19**:11, 14, 32; **20**:2, 21; **22**:42; **23**:4; **24**:2, 7, 15^{2}

1Ki 1:26, 30^{2}, 37, 48; **2**:22; **4**:12, 24, 25, 29, 33; **6**:16^{3}; **7**:7, 9, 10, 42, 51; **8**:4, 6, 29, 39, 65; **11**:26, 35; **12**:27, 30, 33; **13**:34; **14**:14, 26; **15**:13, 28; **16**:7; **18**:22, 26; **19**:10, 14; **20**:3, 14, 15; **21**:11, 13, 19; **22**:35

2Ki 3:24, 26; **4**:3; **5**:22; **7**:6, 7, 13; **8**:6, 9; **9**:4, 6, 20; **10**:3, 14, 33; **11**:2, 5, 7; **12**:4; **14**:10, 29; **15**:20; **17**:16; **18**:8, 10, 21; **19**:15, 19, 22; **20**:14; **21**:15; **22**:16; **24**:14, 16^{2}; **25**:22, 23

1Ch 2:23; **4**:15, 39, 42; **5**:8, 24, 26; **6**:39; **10**:13; **11**:2, 8; **12**:2, 40; **13**:5; **14**:16; **16**:16, 19; **17**:7, 24^{2}; **20**:3; **21**:2, 12, 17; **23**:24, 30; **24**:31; **25**:7; **26**:12, 21, 31; **28**:15, 19, 20, 21; **29**:4, 21

2Ch 2:3, 9; **5**:7, 13^{2}; **6**:21, 33, 39; **8**:10, 13^{2}; **9**:26; **11**:6; **13**:3, 5; **17**:7, 8; **18**:13, 21, 34; **19**:10; **20**:4; **24**:14; **25**:13, 19; **26**:8, 19; **28**:10, 27; **30**:5, 10, 18, 27; **31**:16; **33**:14; **34**:6, 11, 24, 27, 33

Ezr 1:8; **3**:3; **4**:5, 11; **5**:1, 16; **6**:8; **7**:11, 21; **8**:25, 26; **9**:1

Neh 2:13; **3**:1, 10, 21, 24, 27; **4**:3^{2}, 13; **5**:8, 11, 13, 14, 15; **8**:13; **9**:6; **12**:23, 37, 38, 39, 43; **13**:26

Est 1:1, 4; **2**:18; **3**:6, 13; **4**:2; **5**:3, 6; **6**:10; **7**:2

Job 4:8, 21; **5**:5; **6**:9; **10**:21; **15**:26; **17**:5, 11; **18**:13; **21**:6; **23**:2, 3, 13; **24**:17; **25**:5; **28**:4; **31**:6; **34**:17; **36**:16; **41**:9; **42**:16

Ps 18:6, 41; **21**:4; **24**:9; **26**:12; **27**:2; **35**:23; **39**:2, ttl; **40**:3; **45**:12; **47**:9; **48**:14; **50**:1, 7; **55**:19; **57**:4^{2}; **59**:12; **64**:3; **65**:4; **67**:6; **68**:8, 17, 19, 24, 26; **71**:16, 22; **73**:1; **74**:3, 11; **76**:7; **77**:1; **78**:6, 54; **84**:2, 3; **90**:2, 11; **91**:9; **105**:17, 20; **106**:7, 38; **107**:43; **108**:1; **109**:16; **113**:8; **115**:16; **118**:27; **119**:41, 112; **121**:8; **125**:2; **131**:2; **133**:2, 3; **136**:22; **137**:7; **139**:10, 11; **146**:10; **148**:14

Prv 2:16; **3**:12; **8**:16; **14**:13, 20; **16**:4, 7; **17**:15, 28; **20**:11, 12; **22**:19; **23**:15; **28**:9; **30**:1^{2}

Ecc 2:12, 15; **3**:19; **4**:16; **7**:25; **9**:1; **11**:5; **12**:10

Song 4:2

Isa 1:6, 13; **4**:3; **5**:9; **7**:6, 17, 23; **8**:7, 8; **9**:7, 9; **10**:21, 23; **13**:3, 5, 12; **14**:9, 18; **15**:4; **16**:6, 8; **18**:2; **19**:13, 22, 24; **20**:4; **22**:15, 24; **23**:4; **24**:15, 16; **25**:5, 10, 12; **26**:5^{2}, 6; **27**:1; **28**:22; **29**:7, 8, 14; **32**:7; **35**:2, 4; **37**:16, 20, 23; **38**:11, 12, 13; **39**:3; **40**:30; **41**:3, 12, 28; **43**:7, 11, 19, 25; **44**:8, 17, 28; **45**:4, 12, 24; **46**:4^{3}; **47**:15; **48**:5, 6, 7, 11, 15, 20; **49**:10, 19, 25; **51**:12, 22; **55**:3; **56**:5, 7; **57**:6, 7, 9, 11; **65**:6; **66**:2

Jer 3:25; **4**:12; **6**:11, 13^{2}, 19; **7**:11, 15, 25; **8**:10^{2}; **9**:15, 22; **10**:11; **11**:7, 13, 23; **12**:6^{2}, 12; **13**:10, 13, 14, 18; **15**:13; **16**:5; **17**:4, 10, 27; **19**:11, 12; **21**:5; **22**:25; **23**:12, 19, 33, 34, 39; **24**:2; **25**:3, 13, 31, 33; **28**:6, 11; **29**:23; **30**:7; **31**:2, 19, 21; **32**:9, 20, 31; **33**:10, 24; **34**:20; **36**:2, 12; **39**:3, 12, 14; **40**:7, 8, 12; **41**:1, 3, 5, 10, 16; **42**:1, 2, 5, 8; **43**:1, 6, 7; **44**:10, 12^{2}, 15; **45**:4; **46**:25; **48**:32, 34^{3}, 44; **49**:37; **50**:7, 21; **51**:9, 56, 60

Lam 4:3

Ezk 1:27^{2}; **2**:3; **4**:1, 13, 14; **5**:8; **6**:3; **7**:14; **8**:2^{2}, 6; **9**:1; **10**:2, 5, 12; **11**:15, 17; **12**:4, 7; **13**:10, 13, 20; **14**:10, 22; **16**:19, 37, 59; **17**:9, 16, 19; **18**:11, 18; **20**:11, 13, 21, 31; **21**:13, 28; **22**:4, 18; **23**:34; **24**:2, 4, 9, 18; **29**:10; **30**:3; **32**:6, 16, 18, 31, 32; **33**:18; **34**:11, 20, 23, 30; **35**:6, 11, 15; **36**:2, 10, 12; **37**:19, 25; **38**:4; **39**:17; **40**:14; **41**:17; **42**:12; **43**:1, 3, 8, 13, 14^{2}; **44**:6, 7, 10, 19; **47**:10, 19; **48**:3, 6, 10, 28

Dan 1:21; **2**:43; **4**:15, 23; **5**:14; **6**:26; **7**:11, 18, 20; **8**:1, 10, 11, 15; **9**:5, 11, 21, 25, 27; **11**:1, 4, 10, 11, 24^{2}, 30, 35, 41; **12**:1, 4

Hos 2:20; **5**:14; **9**:16; **12**:5

Joel 1:2, 12; **2**:2, 12, 14

Am 2:11; **3**:11; **5**:1, 20; **8**:4, 12, 14

Oba 7, 8, 11, 20

Jna 2:5; **3**:5; **4**:9

Mic 1:9; **2**:2, 8, 10, 11; **3**:4, 5; **4**:7, 8, 10; **7**:12^{2}

Nah 2:11; **3**:12

Hab 1:2; **3**:9, 13

Zep 1:14, 18; **2**:5, 9, 11; **3**:8, 10, 15, 20

Hag 2:18

Zec 3:2; **6**:10, 13; **7**:1, 5^{2}; **8**:23; **9**:7, 10^{2}, 12; **11**:7, 10, 14; **12**:6; **14**:16, 17

Mal 1:10, 11, 12; **2**:2, 3; **3**:1, 7, 9, 15

Mt 5:46, 47, 48; **6**:29; **7**:12, 17; **8**:16, 27; **9**:18; **11**:26; **12**:8, 45; **13**:12; **15**:28; **18**:14, 33; **20**:8, 14, 28; **23**:8, 10, 28, 37; **24**:27, 33; **25**:29; **26**:20, 38; **27**:57; **28**:20

Mk 1:27, 32; **4**:25, 35, 36, 41; **6**:2, 47; **10**:45; **11**:6, 19; **12**:44; **13**:22, 29, 35; **14**:30, 54; **15**:42

Lk 1:2, 15; **2**:15; **6**:33; **8**:18, 25; **9**:54; **10**:11, 17, 21; **12**:7, 41, 57; **17**:30; **18**:11; **19**:26, 32, 37, 42, 44; **20**:37; **24**:24

Jn 1:12; **3**:13, 14; **5**:21, 23, 45; **6**:16, 57; **8**:9, 25, 41, 43; **10**:15; **11**:22, 37; **12**:50; **14**:17, 31; **15**:10, 26; **17**:14, 16, 18, 22; **20**:21; **21**:25

Act 2:39; **4**:10; **5**:37, 39; **9**:17; **10**:41; **11**:5; **12**:15; **15**:8, 11; **20**:11; **22**:17; **26**:11; **27**:25

Ro 1:13, 20, 26, 28; **3**:22; **4**:6, 17; **5**:7, 14, 18, 21; **6**:4, 19; **7**:4; **8**:23, 34; **9**:10, 17, 24, 30; **10**:8; **11**:5, 31; **15**:3, 6

1Co 1:6; **2**:7, 11; **3**:1, 5; **4**:11; **5**:7; **7**:7, 8; **9**:14; **10**:33; **11**:1, 5, 12, 14; **12**:2; **13**:12; **14**:7, 12; **15**:22, 24; **16**:1

2Co 1:3, 8, 13, 14, 19; **3**:10, 15, 18; **7**:14; **10**:7, 13; **11**:12; **13**:9

Gal 2:16; **3**:6; **4**:3, 14, 29; **5**:12, 14

Eph 1:10; **2**:3, 5, 15; **4**:4, 15, 32; **5**:12, 23, 25, 29, 33

Php 1:7, 15; **2**:8; **3**:15, 18, 21; **4**:16

Col 1:14, 26; **3**:13

1Th 1:10; **2**:2, 4, 7, 14, 18, 19; **3**:4, 12, 13; **4**:3, 5, 13, 14; **5**:11

2Th 2:9, 16; **3**:1, 10

1Ti 3:11; **6**:3

2Ti 2:9

Tit 1:12, 15

Phlm 19

Heb 1:9; **4**:12; **5**:14; **6**:20; **7**:4; **11**:12, 19

Jas 2:17; **3**:5, 9; **4**:1, 14

1Pt 1:9; **2**:8, 21; **3**:4, 6, 21; **4**:10

2Pt 1:14; **2**:1^{2}; **3**:15

1Jn 2:6, 9, 18, 25, 27; **3**:3, 7; **4**:3; **5**:4, 6, 20

3Jn 2, 3

Jude 7, 23

Rev 1:7; **2**:13^{2}, 27; **3**:4, 21; **6**:13; **14**:20; **16**:7; **17**:11; **18**:6; **21**:11; **22**:20

EVERY

Gen 1:21^{2}, 25, 26, 28, 29^{2}, 30^{4}, 31; **2**:5^{2}, 9, 16, 19^{3}, 20; **3**:1, 14, 24; **4**:14, 22; **6**:5, 17, 19^{2}, 20^{2}; **7**:2, 4, 8, 14^{5}, 21^{2}, 23; **8**:1, 17^{2}, 19^{3}, 20^{2}, 21; **9**:2^{2}, 3, 5^{2}, 10^{3}, 12, 15, 16; **10**:5; **13**:10; **16**:12^{2}; **17**:10, 12, 23; **19**:4; **20**:13; **27**:29; **30**:33, 35; **32**:16; **34**:15, 22, 23, 24; **41**:48; **42**:25, 35; **43**:21; **44**:1, 11^{2}, 13; **45**:1; **46**:34; **47**:20; **49**:28

Ex 1:1, 22^{2}; **3**:22; **7**:12; **9**:19, 22, 25^{2}; **10**:5, 12, 15; **11**:2^{2}; **12**:3, 4, 16, 44; **13**:12, 13; **14**:7; **16**:4, 16^{3}, 18, 21^{2}, 29; **18**:22^{2}, 26; **25**:2; **26**:2; **27**:18; **28**:21; **29**:36; **30**:7, 12, 13, 14; **31**:14; **32**:27^{4}, 29; **33**:7, 8, 10; **34**:19; **35**:10, 21^{2}, 22, 23, 24^{2}, 29; **36**:1, 2^{2}, 3, 4, 8, 30; **38**:26^{2}; **39**:14

Lev 2:13; **6**:12, 18, 23; **7**:6, 10; **11**:15, 21, 26^{2}, 33, 34, 35, 41, 46^{2}; **15**:4^{2}, 12, 17^{2}, 20^{2}, 26; **17**:15; **19**:3, 8, 10; **20**:9; **23**:37; **24**:8; **25**:10^{2}, 13; **27**:28

Nu 1:2, 4^{2}, 20, 22, 52^{2}; **2**:2, 17, 34; **3**:15; **4**:19, 30, 35, 39, 43, 47, 49; **5**:2^{2}, 9, 10; **7**:5; **8**:16, 17; **11**:10; **13**:2^{2}; **15**:12; **16**:3, 17^{2}, 18, 27; **17**:2^{2}, 6, 9; **18**:7, 9^{4}, 10, 11, 13, 14, 15, 29, 31; **19**:15; **21**:8; **23**:2, 4, 14, 30; **25**:5; **26**:54; **28**:10, 14, 21; **29**:14; **30**:4, 9, 11, 13^{2}; **31**:4, 5, 6, 17^{2}, 23, 50, 53; **32**:18, 27, 29; **33**:54; **34**:18; **35**:8, 15; **36**:7, 8^{2}, 9

Dt 1:16, 22, 41; **2**:34; **3**:6, 20; **4**:4; **8**:3; **11**:24; **12**:2, 8, 13, 31; **13**:16; **14**:6, 14, 19; **15**:1, 2; **16**:17; **19**:3; **20**:13; **21**:5^{2}; **23**:9; **24**:16; **26**:11; **28**:61^{2}; **30**:9; **31**:10; **33**:3

Jos 1:3; **3**:12; **4**:2, 4, 5, 10; **6**:5, 20; **11**:14; **21**:42; **24**:28

Jdg 2:6; **5**:30; **7**:5^{2}, 7, 8, 16, 18, 21, 22; **8**:24, 25, 34; **9**:49, 55; **16**:5; **17**:6; **20**:16, 48; **21**:11^{2}, 21, 24^{2}, 25

1Sa 2:36; **3**:11, 18; **4**:10; **8**:22; **10**:25; **12**:11; **13**:2, 20; **14**:20, 34^{3}, 47; **15**:9; **20**:15; **22**:2^{3}, 7; **23**:14; **25**:10, 13^{2}; **26**:23; **27**:3; **30**:6, 22

2Sa 2:3, 16, 27; **6**:19^{2}; **13**:9, 29, 37; **14**:26; **15**:4, 30, 36; **18**:17; **19**:8; **20**:1, 2, 12, 22; **21**:20^{2}

1Ki 1:49; **4**:25, 27, 28; **5**:3, 4; **7**:30^{2}, 36, 38^{2}; **8**:38, 39; **9**:8; **10**:25; **11**:15, 16; **12**:24; **14**:23^{2}; **19**:18; **20**:20, 24; **22**:17, 28, 36^{2}

2Ki 3:19^{4}, 25^{2}; **6**:2; **8**:9; **9**:13; **11**:8, 9, 11; **12**:4^{2}, 5; **14**:6, 12; **16**:4; **17**:10^{2}, 29^{2}; **18**:31^{3}; **23**:35; **25**:9, 30

1Ch 9:27, 32; **13:**1, 2; **16:**3^2, 37, 43; **22:**15, 18; **23:**30; **26:**13, 32; **27:**1; **28:**14, 15^2, 16, 17^2, 21

2Ch 1:2; **2:**14; **6:**29, 30; **7:**21; **8:**13, 14^2; **9:**21, 24; **10:**16; **11:**4, 12, 23; **13:**11^3; **14:**7; **18:**16; **20:**23, 27; **23:**7, 8, 10; **25:**4, 22; **28:**4, 24, 25; **29:**35; **30:**17, 18; **31:**1, 2, 16, 19, 21; **32:**22; **35:**15

Ezr 2:1; **3:**4, 5; **6:**5; **8:**34; **9:**4; **10:**14

Neh 3:28; **4:**15, 17, 18, 22, 23; **5:**7, 13; **7:**3^2, 6; **8:**16; **10:**28, 31; **11:**3, 20, 23; **12:**47; **13:**10, 30

Est 1:8, 22^4; **2:**11, 12, 13; **3:**12^4, 14; **4:**3; **6:**13; **8:**9^2, 11, 13, 17^2; **9:**27, 28^4

Job 1:4, 10; **2:**11, 12; **7:**18^2; **12:**10; **18:**11; **19:**10; **20:**22; **21:**33; **24:**6; **28:**10; **34:**11; **36:**25; **37:**7; **39:**8; **40:**11, 12; **42:**2, 11^2

Ps 7:11; **12:**2, 8; **29:**9; **31:**13; **32:**6; **39:**5, 6, 11; **50:**10; **53:**3; **56:**5; **58:**8; **62:**12; **63:**11; **64:**6; **65:**12; **68:**30; **69:**34; **71:**18, 21; **73:**14; **84:**7; **92:**2; **104:**11; **115:**8; **119:**101, 104, 128, 160; **128:**1; **135:**18; **145:**2, 16; **150:**6

Prv 1:19; **2:**9; **3:**18; **7:**12; **13:**16; **14:**1, 15; **15:**3; **16:**5; **19:**6; **20:**3, 6, 18; **21:**2, 5; **24:**12, 26; **27:**7, 24; **29:**26; **30:**5

Ecc 3:1^2, 11, 13, 17^2; **4:**4; **5:**19; **8:**6, 9; **10:**3, 15; **12:**14^2

Song 3:8; **4:**2; **6:**6; **8:**11

Isa 1:23; **2:**12^2, 15^2; **3:**5^2; **4:**3, 5; **7:**22, 23; **9:**5, 17^2, 20; **13:**7, 14^2, 15^2; **14:**18; **15:**2, 3; **16:**7; **19:**2^2, 7, 14, 17; **24:**10; **27:**3; **30:**25^2, 32; **31:**7; **33:**2; **34:**15; **36:**16^3; **40:**4^2; **41:**6^2; **43:**7; **44:**23; **45:**23^2; **47:**15; **51:**13; **52:**5; **53:**6; **54:**17; **55:**1; **56:**6, 11; **57:**5; **58:**6

Jer 1:15; **2:**20^2; **3:**6^2, 13; **4:**29; **5:**6, 8; **6:**3, 13^2, 25; **8:**6, 10^2; **9:**4^3, 5, 20; **10:**14^2; **11:**8; **12:**4, 15^2; **13:**12^2; **15:**10; **16:**12, 16^2; **17:**10; **18:**11, 12, 16; **19:**8, 9; **20:**7, 10; **22:**7, 8; **23:**17, 27, 30, 35^2, 36; **25:**5; **26:**3; **29:**26; **30:**6, 16; **31:**25, 30^2, 34^2; **32:**19; **34:**9^2, 10^2, 14, 15, 16^2, 17^2; **35:**15; **36:**3, 7; **37:**10; **43:**6; **47:**4; **48:**8, 37^2; **49:**5, 17, 29; **50:**13, 16^2, 42; **51:**6, 9, 17^2, 29, 45, 56; **52:**34

Lam 2:19; **3:**23; **4:**1

Ezk 1:6^2, 9, 11, 12, 23^2; **6:**13^3; **7:**16; **8:**10, 11, 12; **9:**1, 2; **10:**14, 19, 21^2, 22; **11:**5; **12:**14, 22, 23; **13:**18; **14:**4, 7; **16:**15, 24, 25^2, 31^2, 33, 44; **17:**23; **18:**30; **19:**8; **20:**7, 8, 28, 39, 47^2; **21:**7^2, 10; **22:**6; **23:**22; **24:**4; **26:**16; **28:**13, 23; **29:**18^2; **32:**10^2; **33:**20, 26, 30; **34:**6, 8; **36:**3; **37:**21; **38:**20, 21; **39:**4, 17^3; **40:**7; **41:**5^2, 10, 18; **43:**25; **44:**5, 29, 30^2; **45:**20; **46:**13, 14, 15, 18, 21; **47:**9^2

Dan 3:10, 29; **6:**12, 26; **11:**36; **12:**1

Hos 4:3; **9:**1

Joel 2:7, 8

Am 2:8; **4:**3, 4; **8:**3, 8, 10

Oba 9

Jna 1:5, 7; **3:**8

Mic 4:4, 5; **7:**2

Hab 1:10

Zep 2:11, 15; **3:**5, 19

Hag 1:9; **2:**14, 22

Zec 3:10; **5:**3^2; **7:**9; **8:**4, 10, 16; **10:**1, 4; **11:**6, 9; **12:**4^2, 12, 14; **13:**4; **14:**13, 16, 21

Mal 1:11; **2:**10, 17

Mt 3:10; **4:**4; **7:**8, 17, 19, 21, 26; **8:**33; **9:**35^2; **12:**25^2, 36; **13:**47, 52; **15:**13; **16:**27; **18:**16, 35; **19:**3, 29; **20:**9, 10; **25:**15, 29; **26:**22

Mk 1:45; **7:**14; **8:**25; **9:**49^2; **13:**34; **15:**24; **16:**15, 20

Lk 2:3, 23, 41; **3:**5^2, 9; **4:**4, 37, 40; **5:**17; **6:**30, 40, 44; **8:**1, 4; **9:**6, 43; **10:**1; **11:**4, 10, 17; **16:**5, 16, 19; **18:**14; **19:**15, 26, 43

Jn 1:9; **2:**10; **3:**8, 20; **6:**7, 40, 45; **7:**23, 53; **13:**10; **15:**2^2; **16:**32; **18:**37; **19:**23; **21:**25

Act 2:5, 6, 8, 38, 43, 45; **3:**23, 26; **4:**35; **5:**16, 42; **8:**3, 4; **10:**35; **11:**29; **13:**27; **14:**23; **15:**21^2, 36; **16:**26; **17:**27, 30; **18:**4; **20:**23, 31; **21:**26, 28; **22:**19; **26:**11; **28:**2, 22

Ro 1:16; **2:**6, 9, 10; **3:**2, 4, 19; **10:**4; **12:**3^2, 5; **13:**1; **14:**5^2, 11^2, 12; **15:**2

1Co 1:2, 5, 12; **3:**5, 8, 10, 13^2; **4:**5, 17^2; **6:**18; **7:**2^2, 7, 17^2, 20, 24; **8:**7; **9:**25; **10:**24; **11:**3, 4, 5, 21; **12:**7, 11, 18; **14:**26; **15:**23, 30, 38; **16:**2, 16

2Co 2:14; **4:**2, 8; **5:**10; **7:**5; **8:**7; **9:**7, 8, 11; **10:**5^2; **13:**1

Gal 3:10, 13; **5:**3; **6:**4, 5

Eph 1:21; **4:**7, 14, 16^2, 25; **5:**24, 33

Php 1:3, 4, 18; **2:**4^2, 9, 10, 11; **4:**6, 12, 21

Col 1:10, 15, 23, 28^3; **4:**6

1Th 1:8; **2:**11; **4:**4; **5:**18

2Th 1:3; **2:**17; **3:**6, 17

1Ti 2:8; **4:**4; **5:**10

2Ti 2:19, 21; **4:**18

Tit 1:5, 16; **3:**1

Phlm 6

Heb 2:2, 9; **3:**4; **5:**1, 13; **6:**11; **8:**3, 11^2; **9:**7, 19, 25; **10:**3, 11; **12:**1, 6; **13:**21

Jas 1:14, 17^2, 19; **3:**7, 16

1Pt 1:17; **2:**13; **3:**15; **4:**10

1Jn 2:29; **3:**3; **4:**1, 2, 3, 7; **5:**1

Rev 1:7; **2:**23; **5:**8, 9, 13; **6:**11, 14, 15^2; **14:**6; **16:**3, 20, 21; **18:**2^2, 17; **20:**13; **21:**21; **22:**2, 12, 18

FOR

Gen 1:14^3, 15, 29, 30; **2:**5, 9, 17, 18, 20^2; **3:**5, 6, 17, 19^2, 22; **4:**23, 25; **5:**24; **6:**3, 7, 12, 13, 21^3; **7:**1, 4; **8:**9^2, 21^2; **9:**3, 6, 12, 13; **10:**25; **11:**3^2; **12:**10, 13, 16; **13:**6, 8, 15^2, 17; **14:**13; **15:**6, 16; **16:**10, 13; **17:**4, 5, 7, 8, 13, 15, 19, 20; **18:**5, 14, 15, 19, 24, 26, 28, 29, 31, 32; **19:**8, 13, 14, 17, 21, 22, 30; **20:**3^2, 6, 7^2, 11, 18; **21:**2, 7, 10, 12, 16, 17, 18, 30; **22:**2, 3, 7, 8, 12, 13, 16; **23:**2^2, 8, 9^2, 13, 18, 20; **24:**10, 14, 19, 20, 22, 23, 31^2, 32, 40, 44^2, 62, 65; **25:**21, 30; **26:**3, 7^2, 9, 14, 15, 16, 18, 21, 22^3, 24^2; **27:**5, 9, 36^2, 37, 41; **28:**11, 15, 18^2, 22; **29:**2, 9, 15, 18, 20^2, 21, 24, 25, 27, 32; **30:**13, 15, 16, 26^2, 27^2, 30^2, 31, 33^2; **31:**12, 14, 15, 16, 18, 31, 32, 35, 41^2, 44, 45, 49, 52; **32:**10, 11, 12, 13, 20, 26, 28, 30; **33:**10, 17, 19; **34:**8, 14, 21^3, 22; **35:**18; **36:**7; **37:**7, 8^2, 17, 27, 28, 34, 35^2; **38:**6, 11, 14, 16; **39:**5; **40:**15, 17; **41:**8, 19, 31, 32, 36, 49, 51, 52, 55, 57; **42:**2, 4, 5, 18, 19, 23, 25, 27, 30, 33, 38; **43:**5, 9^2, 10, 16, 18, 25, 30, 32^4; **44:**4, 14, 17, 18, 22, 26, 32^3, 34; **45:**3, 5, 6, 11, 19^2, 20, 21, 23, 26; **46:**3, 32, 34; **47:**4^4, 13, 14, 15^2, 16, 17^6, 19, 20^2, 21, 22, 23^2, 24^5; **48:**4, 7, 10, 14, 18; **49:**6, 7^2, 13, 18, 30; **50:**3^3, 5, 10, 13^2, 17, 19, 20

Ex 1:5, 11, 18, 19; **2:**3, 7, 9, 19, 22; **3:**5, 6, 7, 15; **4:**1, 19; **5:**7, 8, 18, 23; **6:**1, 7, 8, 9^2; **7:**9, 12, 24^2; **8:**8, 9^3, 17, 25^2, 26, 28; **9:**2, 11, 14, 15, 16^2, 19, 27, 28, 30, 31, 32; **10:**1, 5, 9, 10, 11, 12, 15, 16, 23, 26, 28; **12:**3, 4^2, 12, 13, 14^2, 15, 17^2, 19, 21, 23, 24^2, 30, 31, 33, 39^2, 42, 44, 48; **13:**3, 9^3, 16^3, 17, 19; **14:**3, 12^2, 13^2, 14, 25^2; **15:**1, 17, 18, 19, 21, 23, 25, 26; **16:**3, 4, 7, 8, 9, 15, 16^2, 22, 23, 25, 27, 29, 32, 33; **17:**1, 3, 14^2, 16; **18:**1^2, 3, 4, 8, 9, 11, 12, 18^2, 19, 22; **19:**2, 5, 7, 9, 11, 23; **20:**5, 7, 11, 20, 25; **21:**2, 6, 19, 21, 23, 24^4, 25^3, 26, 27, 30, 36; **22:**1^2, 2, 3^3, 9^6, 13, 15, 21, 27^3; **23:**7, 8, 9, 15, 21^2, 23, 31, 33; **24:**14; **25:**6^3, 12, 26, 27; **26:**14, 15, 17, 18, 19^2, 20, 22, 23, 24^2, 26, 27^3, 29^2, 36, 37^2; **27:**4, 6, 9^3, 11, 12, 16, 20, 21; **28:**2^3, 4, 12^2, 29, 40^5, 43; **29:**9, 22, 24, 25^2, 26, 27^2, 28^2, 36^3, 37, 40, 41; **30:**4^2, 12, 15, 16^2, 19, 21, 37^2; **31:**10, 11, 13, 14^2, 16, 17^2; **32:**1^2, 7, 12, 13, 18^2, 23^3, 25, 29, 30; **33:**3^2, 5, 16, 17, 20; **34:**7, 9^2, 10, 12, 14^2, 18, 24, 27; **35:**8^3, 9^2, 14^2, 15, 17, 19, 21^2, 24, 27^2, 28^3, 29; **36:**1, 3, 5, 6, 7^2, 14, 19, 20, 22, 23^2, 24^2, 25, 27, 28, 31, 32^3, 34, 36, 37; **37:**3, 12, 13, 14, 27^2; **38:**4, 5^2, 11, 12, 13, 15, 17, 18, 21, 24, 26^3, 27, 28, 30; **39:**1, 4, 7, 27^2, 37, 38, 40^2, 41; **40:**5, 15, 38

Lev 1:4^2, 10, 14; **2:**11, 12^2, 14; **3:**6, 7, 16, 17; **4:**3^2, 8, 14, 20^2, 21, 26, 28, 31^2, 32, 33, 35; **5:**6^3, 7^3, 8, 10^3, 11^3, 13, 15^2, 16^2, 18^2; **6:**6, 7^2, 15, 17, 18, 20, 21, 22, 23^2, 26; **7:**5, 7, 12, 13, 14, 15, 19, 25, 30, 32, 33, 34^2, 36; **8:**2, 14^2, 18, 21, 27, 28, 29^2, 33, 34, 35; **9:**2^2, 3^2, 4^2, 7^3, 8, 15^2, 18^2, 21; **10:**7, 9, 12, 13, 14, 15^2, 17; **11:**24, 35^2, 42, 44^2, 45^2; **12:**2, 6^4, 7^2, 8^3; **13:**7, 11, 15, 28, 36, 52; **14:**4, 6, 10, 12^2, 13, 18, 19, 20, 21^3, 23, 24, 29, 31^3, 34, 53, 54, 55, 56^3; **15:**13, 15^4, 30^4; **16:**2, 3^2, 5^2, 6^3, 8^2, 9, 10, 11^4, 15, 16^2, 17^3, 18, 24^2, 26, 27^2, 29, 30^2, 31, 33^5, 34^2; **17:**5, 6, 7, 11^4, 14^3; **18:**10, 13, 17, 19, 24, 27, 29; **19:**2, 10, 21, 22^2, 23, 28, 34; **20:**7, 9, 19, 23, 26; **21:**1, 2^6, 3^2, 6, 7, 8^2, 11^2, 12, 15, 18, 23; **22:**9, 16, 18^3, 20^2, 23^2, 25, 27; **23:**11, 12, 13, 14, 18, 19^2, 20^2, 21, 28^2, 29, 31, 34, 41; **24:**2, 3, 7, 9, 18, 20^3, 22^3; **25:**4, 5, 6^6, 7^2, 12, 16, 17, 21, 23^3, 24, 30, 33, 34, 37, 42, 46^3, 51, 55; **26:**1, 9, 16, 18^2, 20, 24, 27, 28, 44^2, 45; **27:**2, 5, 6, 7, 10^3, 34

Nu 1:44, 48; **3:**13, 25, 26^2, 38, 41, 46; **4:**16, 24, 25, 26^2, 29, 35, 39, 43; **5:**8, 15^2; **6:**7^4, 11^4, 12, 14^3, 17, 20^2, 21; **7:**3^2, 10, 11, 13, 15, 16, 17, 19^2, 21, 22, 23, 25, 27, 28, 29, 31, 33, 34, 35, 37, 39, 40, 41, 43, 45, 46, 47, 49, 51, 52, 53, 55, 57, 58, 59, 61, 63, 64, 65, 67, 69, 70, 71, 73, 75, 76, 77, 79, 81, 82, 83, 87^2, 88; **8:**8, 11, 12^3, 13, 15, 16, 17^2, 18, 19, 21; **9:**14^2; **10:**2^2, 6, 8^2, 10, 29, 33; **11:**13, 14, 18^2, 22^2, 29, 32; **12:**1; **13:**30, 31; **14:**3, 9^2, 11, 13, 14, 32, 34, 40, 42, 43; **15:**5^2, 6^2, 7^2, 8^2, 10^2, 11^3, 15^3, 16^2, 20, 24^3, 25^3, 27, 28^2, 29^3, 39; **16:**11, 28, 34, 37, 38^2, 39, 46^2, 47; **17:**3^2, 6, 8, 10; **18:**4, 6, 7, 8, 9^2, 11, 16, 17^2, 19^2, 21^2, 23, 26^2, 31^2; **19:**9^3, 10^2, 17^2; **20:**2, 19, 24, 29; **21:**5, 7^2, 13, 24, 26, 28, 34; **22:**6^3, 12, 13, 17, 22, 29, 34; **23:**9; **24:**1, 18, 20, 24; **25:**11, 13^2, 18^2; **26:**53, 62, 65; **27:**14, 21; **28:**2^2, 3, 5, 6, 7^2, 9, 12^4, 13^2, 15, 19, 20^2, 21, 22^2, 23, 27, 30; **29:**2, 3^2, 4, 5^2, 6, 8, 10, 11, 16, 18^3, 19, 21^3, 22, 24^3, 25, 27^3, 28, 30^3, 31, 33^3, 34, 37^3, 38, 39^4; **31:**5, 18, 29, 50^2, 53^2, 54^2; **32:**1, 4, 5, 9, 12, 15, 16^2, 19, 24^2, 27, 29, 36; **33:**4, 14, 53, 54; **34:**2, 6^2, 7, 14, 23; **35:**2, 3^3, 6^2, 11, 12, 13, 15^3, 21, 29, 31, 32, 33, 34; **36:**2, 7, 11

Dt 1:10, 14, 17^2, 30^2, 37, 38, 40, 42; **2:**5^2, 6^2, 7, 9^3, 15, 19^2, 28^2, 30, 35, 36; **3:**2, 7, 11, 18, 19, 22^2, 24, 26, 27, 28; **4:**1, 3, 6, 7^2, 15, 21^2, 24, 31, 32, 34, 38, 40; **5:**5, 9, 11, 23, 25, 26, 29, 31; **6:**8, 15, 24; **7:**4, 6, 7, 16, 21, 25, 26; **8:**7, 10, 18; **9:**4^2, 5^3, 6^2, 12, 19, 20; **10:**13, 17, 19, 21, 22; **11:**2, 10, 12, 15, 18, 22, 25, 31; **12:**9, 23, 28, 31^2; **13:**3, 16^2; **14:**1, 2, 7, 21, 24, 26^6, 27; **15:**4^2, 6, 8, 10, 11, 17, 18; **16:**1, 3, 19; **17:**1, 8; **18:**5^2, 12, 14^2; **19:**2, 7, 9, 10, 11, 15^2, 21^5; **20:**1, 4^2, 16, 19^2, 20; **21:**5, 14, 17^2, 23^2; **22:**5, 8, 20, 26, 27; **23:**3, 6, 7, 14, 18^2, 21; **24:**4^2, 6, 15, 16^3, 19^3, 20^3, 21^3; **25:**11, 16, 19; **26:**1, 3, 14^2; **28:**20, 32, 34, 38, 39, 40, 41, 46^3, 47, 56, 57^2, 62, 67^2, 68; **29:**8, 13, 16, 26, 29; **30:**9^3, 11, 12, 13, 20; **31:**6, 7, 18, 19^2, 20, 21^2, 23, 26, 27, 29; **32:**4, 9, 20, 22, 28, 31, 32, 35, 36^2, 40^2, 43, 47^2, 49; **33:**2, 7, 9, 13^3, 14^2, 15^2, 16^2, 19, 21; **34:**8^2, 9

Jos 1:6^2, 8, 9, 11; **2:**3, 5, 10^2, 11, 14, 15, 24; **3:**4, 5, 15; **4:**7^2, 10, 13, 23, 24; **5:**6, 7, 13^2, 15; **6:**16; **7:**1, 3, 5, 9, 11, 13; **8:**2^2, 6^2, 7, 18, 26, 27, 28; **9:**9, 11, 12, 22, 23, 27^2; **10:**4, 6, 8, 14^2, 18, 19, 24, 25, 42; **11:**6, 10, 13, 14, 20, 23; **12:**6, 7; **13:**6, 7, 12, 32; **14:**1, 2^2, 3, 4^3, 9, 11, 12, 13; **15:**19, 63; **16:**9; **17:**1^3, 2^7, 15^2, 16, 18^2; **18:**4, 6, 7, 8, 10; **19:**1, 9^2, 10, 17, 24, 32, 40, 47, 49, 51; **20:**2, 6, 9^2; **21:**2, 4, 10, 12, 13, 21^2, 26, 27, 32, 38, 40; **22:**17, 24, 25, 26^2, 28^2, 29^3, 34; **23:**2^5, 3^2, 4, 9^2, 10^2, 13; **24:**1^4, 13, 15, 17, 18, 19, 27, 31, 32

Jdg 1:1, 15, 32, 34; **2:**7, 10, 15, 18; **3:**20, 28; **4:**3, 5, 9^2, 14, 17, 19, 21; **5:**2, 15, 16, 30; **6:**4, 5^3, 22, 31^3, 38, 40; **7:**2, 4, 9, 12^2, 14, 15; **8:**5, 10, 11, 20, 21, 22, 24, 30; **9:**2, 3, 5, 17^2, 21, 25, 28; **10:**16; **11:**2, 18, 31, 35, 36, 37, 38; **12:**6, 9; **13:**5^2, 7, 15, 16, 20; **14:**2, 3^2, 4, 10; **15:**18; **16:**2, 17, 18^2, 19, 23^2, 24, 25^2, 28; **17:**3; **18:**1, 9, 10, 19, 26; **19:**6, 15, 19^4; **20:**6, 10, 27, 28, 36, 39, 41; **21:**5, 6, 7^2, 9, 15, 16^2, 17, 18, 22^2

Ru 1:6, 12, 13^4, 16, 20; **2:**13^2, 16; **3:**1, 9, 10, 11, 17, 18; **4:**4, 6^2, 7, 8, 15

1Sa 1:5, 6, 16^2, 22^2, 27; **2:**2, 3, 5, 8, 9, 14, 15^2, 17, 20, 23, 24, 25, 30^2, 32, 35, 36; **3:**5, 6, 8, 9, 10, 13^3, 14, 21; **4:**7^2, 10, 13^2, 18, 19, 20, 22; **5:**7, 11; **6:**2, 4, 8, 17^6; **7:**2, 5, 8, 9^2, 17; **8:**7, 11^2; **9:**5^2, 7, 9, 12^2, 13^2, 14, 16, 19, 20^2, 24^2; **10:**2^2, 7; **11:**2, 13; **12:**19^2, 21^2, 22^2, 23^2, 24^2; **13:**6, 7, 13^2, 19, 21^4; **14:**6^2, 10, 12, 18, 24, 26, 30, 39, 44, 45; **15:**2, 6, 11, 15, 23, 24, 26, 29, 35; **16:**1^2, 7^2, 11, 12, 22; **17:**8, 12, 17, 20, 21, 26, 28, 31, 33, 39^2, 42, 47; **18:**11, 17^2; **19:**5^2, 13, 16; **20:**4, 6^2, 8^2, 9, 15, 17, 21, 22, 23, 26, 29, 31^2, 34^2, 42; **21:**6, 8, 9, 10; **22:**3, 8, 10, 13, 15^2, 23; **23:**4, 7, 10, 17, 21, 22, 26^2, 27; **24:**10, 11, 17, 19^2; **25:**8, 11, 17^2, 21, 25, 28, 34, 36, 39; **26:**9, 12, 15, 18, 19, 20, 21, 23; **27:**1, 4, 5, 8, 12; **28:**1, 2, 9, 10, 12, 13, 15, 17, 20; **29:**4, 6; **30:**6^3, 8, 10, 12, 24, 25, 26; **31:**4

2Sa 1:9, 12^4, 16, 21, 26; **2:**7, 26; **3:**6, 8, 14, 17, 18, 22, 27, 28, 37, 39; **4:**2, 7, 10; **5:**12, 19, 24; **6:**6, 7, 17; **7:**3, 5, 10, 13^2, 16^2, 19, 20, 21, 22, 23^3, 24^2, 25, 26, 27, 29^3; **8:**4, 10; **9:**1, 7^2, 10, 11, 13; **10:**2, 11^2, 12^2; **11:**4, 22, 25, 26; **12:**4^2, 12, 16, 18, 21, 22; **13:**2^3, 12, 13^2, 18, 22, 32^2, 33, 37, 39; **14:**2, 7, 13, 14, 16, 17, 19, 25, 26, 29, 32,

APNDX

33; **15**:2, 6, 8, 12[2], 14, 19, 34; **16**:2[2], 3, 11, 12; **17**:8, 10, 11, 14, 17, 21, 29[3]; **18**:3[3], 5, 8, 12, 13, 16, 18[2], 31, 33; **19**:1, 2[2], 6[2], 7, 8, 9, 20, 21, 22, 26, 28, 32, 38, 42; **20**:11; **21**:1[2], 3, 4[2], 8, 10, 14; **22**:18[2], 22, 23[2], 29, 30, 31, 32, 40, 51[2]; **23**:5; **24**:2, 10, 11, 14, 22[2], 24, 25

1Ki 1:2, 3, 25, 31, 35, 42, 51; **2**:7, 9, 15, 17, 18, 19[2], 20, 22[6], 26, 28, 33[2], 36, 37[2], 42[2], 45; **3**:4, 6, 8, 9, 11[3], 26, 28; **4**:7, 22, 24, 26, 27[2], 28, 31; **5**:1[2], 3, 6[2], 8, 9, 11; **6**:2, 4, 6, 8, 16[3], 31, 33; **7**:7, 8, 12[2], 15, 17[3], 18, 36, 40, 42[2], 45, 50[2], 51; **8**:5, 7, 11, 13[2], 17, 20, 21, 36, 39, 41, 42, 43, 44, 46, 48, 51, 52, 53, 64, 66[2]; **9**:3, 5, 7, 15, 16[2], 19[2], 24; **10**:9, 12[3], 22, 23[2], 26, 27, 29[4]; **11**:2, 4, 5, 7[2], 8, 12, 13[2], 15, 16, 31, 32[2], 34, 38, 39[2]; **12**:1, 2, 5, 7, 15, 17, 24, 28, 30; **13**:6, 9, 12, 17, 23[2], 32; **14**:4, 5[3], 6, 9, 11, 13[2], 15, 18, 23; **15**:4, 27; **16**:7, 13, 19, 24, 26, 31, 32; **17**:5, 12, 13[2], 14; **18**:4, 23, 25[2], 27, 41; **19**:3, 4[2], 7, 10[2], 14, 20; **20**:7[5], 9, 10[2], 18[2], 22, 25[2], 34, 38, 39, 42[2]; **21**:2[2], 4, 6[2], 15[2], 22; **22**:6, 8, 12, 15, 34, 43, 48[2], 53

2Ki 2:2, 4, 6, 9, 18; **3**:2, 9[2], 13, 17, 26, 27; **4**:2, 10, 13[3], 14, 24, 27, 38, 39, 40, 41, 43; **5**:3, 17, 27; **6**:1, 5, 9, 11[2], 16, 23, 25[2], 33; **7**:1[2], 6, 7, 16[2], 18[2], 20; **8**:1[2], 3[2], 5[2], 18, 19, 27; **9**:8, 16, 20, 25, 34; **10**:3, 10, 16, 19, 20, 22, 24, 31; **11**:15; **12**:7[2], 12[2], 13, 15, 21; **13**:4, 7, 17; **14**:6[3], 10, 26[3], 28; **15**:14; **16**:8, 9, 15, 18[2]; **17**:4, 7, 12, 21, 22, 32, 37[2]; **18**:4, 6, 20, 24[2], 26, 29, 31, 36; **19**:3, 4, 8, 18, 31, 34[3]; **20**:1, 6[2], 10, 12; **21**:3[2], 5, 7; **22**:13[4]; **23**:4[3], 7, 13[3]; **24**:3, 4[2], 7, 16, 20; **25**:3, 16, 22, 26, 30

1Ch 4:14, 23, 39, 40, 41, 42; **5**:1, 2, 20, 22; **6**:26, 49[2], 54, 70; **7**:4[2], 11; **9**:1, 13, 26, 33; **10**:4, 13[2]; **11**:9, 19, 20, 21; **12**:8, 18, 19, 21, 22, 25, 29, 37, 39[2], 40; **13**:3, 4, 9; **14**:2, 10, 15; **15**:1[2], 2[2], 3, 11[3], 12, 13[2], 22, 23, 24; **16**:1, 17[2], 21, 25, 26, 34[3], 36, 41, 42; **17**:2, 5, 9, 12, 14[2], 17[2], 18[2], 19, 22[2], 23, 24, 25, 27[3]; **18**:10; **19**:3, 5, 12[2], 13[2]; **21**:6, 8, 13, 17, 22, 23[3], 24[3], 25, 29, 30; **22**:1, 3[3], 4, 5[2], 6[2], 7, 9, 10[2], 14[2], 15, 18; **23**:13[2], 24, 25[2], 26, 27, 28, 29[7]; **24**:5, 6[2]; **25**:6[2], 9; **26**:5, 6, 8[2], 10, 13, 14, 29[2], 31, 32; **27**:2, 3, 5, 7, 8, 9, 10, 11, 12, 13, 14, 15, 24, 26, 27; **28**:2[4], 3, 4[2], 5, 6, 7, 8[4], 9[2], 10[2], 13[3], 14[4], 15[7], 16[3], 17[4], 18[2], 20[2], 21[3]; **29**:1[3], 2[6], 3, 5[3], 7, 9, 10, 11, 14, 15, 16, 17, 18, 19, 21

2Ch 1:3, 4[3], 9, 10, 11, 15, 17[4]; **2**:1[2], 4[3], 5, 8, 9, 12[2]; **3**:3, 6; **4**:6[2], 9, 11[2], 16, 18, 19, 22; **5**:1, 6, 8, 11, 13[3], 14; **6**:2[3], 7, 8, 9, 10[2], 13, 27, 30, 32, 33, 34, 36, 38; **7**:3[3], 6, 7, 9, 10, 12, 16[2], 17, 20; **8**:7, 9, 11[2], 14; **9**:6, 8[2], 11, 21, 25; **10**:1, 7, 10, 11, 15, 17; **11**:4, 5, 14[2], 15[3], 17, 21, 22; **12**:13; **13**:5, 8, 10, 11, 12[2]; **14**:3, 6, 11, 13, 14[2]; **15**:3, 6, 7, 9, 15; **16**:9, 10, 14[2]; **17**:18; **18**:2[2], 5, 7, 8, 11, 32, 33; **19**:6[3], 7, 8[2], 11; **20**:7, 8, 9, 12, 15, 17, 21[2], 23, 25, 26, 27, 30, 33; **21**:6, 7, 19; **22**:1, 3, 4, 7, 9, 11; **23**:6, 8, 14; **24**:3, 6[2], 7, 14, 18, 24, 25[2]; **25**:4[3], 6, 7, 8[2], 9, 20; **26**:8, 10[2], 14, 15, 16, 18[2], 21, 23; **28**:2[2], 6, 10, 11, 13[2], 17, 19[2], 21, 23; **29**:6, 9[2], 11, 21[4], 23, 24[3], 25, 32, 34, 35, 36; **30**:2, 3, 5, 8, 9[2], 14, 17[2], 18[2], 24, 26; **31**:2[2], 3[5], 10, 16, 18; **32**:1, 7[3], 15, 20, 25, 26, 27[6], 28[3], 29; **33**:3[2], 4, 5, 7, 8, 22; **34**:3, 11, 21[3], 26; **35**:7[2], 8, 9, 14[4], 15[2], 21, 23, 24, 25; **36**:17, 21

Ezr 1:4; **2**:68; **3**:3, 11[2], 12, 13; **4**:2, 14, 15; **6**:8, 9, 10, 11, 17[2], 18, 20[4], 22; **7**:9, 10, 16, 19, 20, 23[2]; **8**:16[11], 17, 20, 21[3], 22[2], 23, 35[2]; **9**:2[3], 6, 7, 8, 9, 10, 12[3], 13[2], 15[2]; **10**:1, 4, 6, 9, 13, 14, 19

Neh 1:5, 6, 11; **2**:3, 4, 6, 8[3], 14, 18; **4**:4[2], 5, 6, 14, 18, 20, 23; **5**:2[2], 4, 5, 18[3], 19[2]; **6**:6, 9, 10, 12, 13, 16, 18; **7**:2; **8**:4, 5, 9, 10[3], 11, 17; **9**:5, 8, 10, 15[3], 20, 31[2], 33, 35, 36; **10**:30, 32[2], 33[8], 34, 39; **11**:23[3], 25; **12**:29, 43, 44[8], 46; **13**:1, 5, 6, 7, 10, 13, 14[2], 25, 31[3]

Est 1:8, 9, 11, 13, 17, 20, 22; **2**:2, 3, 7[2], 9, 10, 12[2], 15, 20; **3**:2, 4, 6, 8, 13, 14; **4**:2, 5, 7, 8, 14[2], 16; **5**:4, 8, 9, 10; **6**:3[2], 4, 7; **7**:4[2], 7[2], 9[2], 10; **8**:1, 6, 8[2], 11[2], 13, 17; **9**:2, 4[2], 15, 16, 26, 31[2]; **10**:3

Job 1:4, 5, 9; **2**:4[2], 11, 13; **3**:6, 9, 13, 14, 21[3], 24, 25; **4**:11, 20; **5**:2, 18, 23, 27; **6**:3, 4, 8, 10, 19, 21, 22, 27, 28; **7**:2, 16, 21; **8**:4, 6, 8, 9; **9**:17, 32; **10**:16; **11**:4, 11, 12, 15; **13**:7[2], 8, 16, 19, 24, 26; **14**:7, 16, 20; **15**:5, 22, 23, 25, 31, 34; **16**:12, 17, 21[2]; **17**:1, 4, 10[2], 15; **18**:4, 8, 10[2]; **19**:15, 17, 21, 24, 25, 27, 29; **20**:2, 5, 7, 18, 21; **21**:4, 14, 19, 21, 28; **22**:4, 6[2], 8, 17, 26; **23**:7, 14[2], 16; **24**:3, 5[3], 8, 15, 16, 17, 24; **27**:8, 14, 22; **28**:1[2], 5, 15[2], 17, 18, 24, 25, 26[2]; **29**:13, 23[3]; **30**:3, 4, 23[2], 25[2], 26[2]; **31**:2, 11, 12, 18, 19, 23, 28; **32**:11, 16, 18, 22; **33**:10, 13, 14, 26, 32; **34**:3, 5, 9, 11, 19, 21, 23, 36, 37; **35**:3; **36**:4, 7, 21, 27, 31; **37**:6, 13[3], 19; **38**:3, 7, 9, 10, 19, 25[2], 39, 41[2]; **41**:4[2], 5; **42**:3, 7, 8[3], 10, 12

Ps 1:6; **2**:8[2]; **3**:2, 3, 5, 7; **4**:3, 8; **5**:2, 4, 7, 9, 10, 11, 12; **6**:2[2], 4, 5, 8; **7**:6, 7, 9, 13; **8**:5; **9**:4, 5, 7[2], 9, 10, 12, 18[2]; **10**:3, 5, 6, 14, 16; **11**:2, 7; **12**:1[2], 5[2], 7; **13**:1; **14**:5; **16**:1, 10, 11; **17**:6, 15; **18**:17[2], 21, 22, 27, 28, 29, 30, 31, 39, 50; **19**:4, 9; **21**:3, 4, 6[2], 7, 11; **22**:11[2], 16, 21, 24, 26, 28, 30; **23**:3, 4, 6; **24**:2; **25**:5, 6, 7, 11[2], 15, 16, 19, 20, 21; **26**:1, 3, 11; **27**:5, 12; **28**:9; **29**:10; **30**:1, 5[2], 11, 12; **31**:2, 3[2], 4[2], 7, 9, 10, 13, 16, 17, 19[2], 21, 22, 23; **32**:4, 6, 11; **33**:1[2], 4, 9, 11, 12, 17, 20, 21; **34**:9; **35**:2, 7[3], 10, 12, 13, 14, 20, 27; **36**:2, 9; **37**:2, 7, 9, 10, 13, 17, 18, 22, 24, 27, 28[2], 29, 37; **38**:2, 4[2], 7, 10, 12, 15, 16, 17, 18[2], 20; **39**:7, 11, 12; **40**:1, 12, 15; **41**:4, 12[2]; **42**:2[2], 4, 5[2], 11, ttl; **43**:2, 5; **44**:3, 4, 6, 8, 10, 11, 12, 16, 21, 22[2], 23, 25, 26[2], ttl; **45**:2, 6, 11, 17, ttl; **46**:ttl; **47**:2, 4, 7, 9, ttl; **48**:2, 3, 4, 8, 14[2], ttl; **49**:7, 8[2], 9, 10, 11, 15, 17, ttl; **50**:6, 8, 10, 12; **51**:3, 16; **52**:5, 8, 9[2]; **53**:5; **54**:3, 6, 7; **55**:3, 6, 9, 12, 15, 16, 18; **56**:1, 2, 5, 6, 9[2], 13; **57**:1, 2, 6, 10; **58**:11; **59**:3[4], 7, 9, 12[2], 15, 16, 17; **60**:2, 11, 12; **61**:3[2], 4, 5, 7, 8; **62**:5, 8, 12; **63**:1[2], 10; **64**:9; **65**:1, 3, 9, 13; **66**:7, 10, 16; **67**:4[2]; **68**:10, 16, 18[2], 28; **69**:1, 3, 6[2], 7, 9, 13, 16, 17, 20[2], 21, 22, 26, 33, 35; **70**:3; **71**:3, 5, 10[2], 11, 12, 15, 24[2]; **72**:12, 15, 17, 19, ttl; **73**:2, 3, 4, 14, 16, 26, 27, 28; **74**:1, 4, 10, 12, 19, 20; **75**:1, 6, 8, 9; **77**:7, 8[2]; **78**:5, 18, 20, 29, 32[2], 37, 39, 58, 69; **79**:5, 7, 8, 9[2], 13; **80**:15, 17; **81**:4[2], 5, 15; **82**:8; **83**:2, 5, 10, 17; **84**:2[2], 3, 10, 11, ttl; **85**:5, 8, ttl; **86**:1, 2, 3, 4, 5, 7, 10, 12, 13, 17; **87**:ttl; **88**:3, ttl; **89**:1, 2[2], 4, 6, 11, 17, 18, 28[2], 29, 36, 37, 46, 52; **90**:4, 7, 9, 10; **91**:5[2], 6[2], 11; **92**:4, 7, 8, 9[2], ttl; **93**:5; **94**:13, 14, 16[2]; **95**:3, 7; **96**:4, 5, 13[2]; **97**:9, 11[2]; **98**:1, 9; **99**:3, 5, 9; **100**:5; **102**:3, 9, 10, 12, 13, 14, 18, 19; **103**:6, 9, 11, 14, 15, 16; **104**:5, 8, 14[2], 17, 18[2], 19, 31; **105**:8, 10[2], 14, 16, 17, 32, 38, 39, 42; **106**:1[3], 8, 13, 31[2], 32, 43, 45; **107**:1[3], 8[2], 9, 15[2], 16, 21[2], 25, 31[2], 34, 36; **108**:4, 12, 13; **109**:2, 4, 5[2], 19, 21[2], 22, 31; **110**:4; **111**:3, 8, 9, 10; **112**:3, 6, 9; **113**:2; **115**:1[2], 18; **116**:7, 8, 12; **117**:2[2]; **118**:1[2], 2, 3, 4, 12, 21, 29[3]; **119**:20, 22, 28, 35, 39, 42, 43, 44, 45, 50, 66, 71, 76, 77, 78, 81, 82, 83, 85, 89, 91, 93, 94, 95, 98, 99, 102, 110, 111[2], 115, 118, 120, 122[2], 123[2], 126[2], 131[2], 152, 153, 155, 160, 166, 168, 172, 173, 174, 176; **120**:7[2]; **121**:8; **122**:5, 6, 8; **123**:3; **125**:1, 2, 3, 5; **126**:2, 3; **127**:2[2], ttl; **128**:2; **130**:5, 6[3], 7; **131**:1, 3; **132**:5[2], 9, 10, 12, 13[2], 14[2], 16, 17; **133**:1, 3[2]; **135**:3[2], 4[2], 5, 7, 12, 13, 14; **136**:1[3], 2[2], 3[2], 4[2], 5[2], 6[2], 7[2], 8[2], 9[2], 10[2], 11[2], 12[2], 13[2], 14[2], 15[2], 16[2], 17[2], 18[2], 19[2], 20[2], 21[3], 22[2], 23[2], 24[2], 25[2], 26[2]; **137**:3; **138**:2[3], 5, 8; **139**:4, 6, 13, 14, 20; **140**:2, 5[2], 9; **141**:5, 6, 9; **142**:3, 4, 6[2], 7; **143**:2, 3, 8[2], 10, 11[2], 12; **145**:1, 2, 21; **146**:5, 6, 7, 10; **147**:1[2], 8, 13, 20; **148**:5, 6, 13; **149**:4; **150**:2

Prv 1:9, 11[2], 16, 18[2], 29, 32; **2**:3, 4[2], 6, 7, 18, 21; **3**:2, 12, 14, 26, 32; **4**:2, 3, 13, 16, 17, 22, 23; **5**:3, 21; **6**:1, 23, 26[2], 34; **7**:6, 19, 23, 26; **8**:6, 7, 11, 32, 35; **9**:4, 11, 12, 14, 16; **10**:13, 21; **11**:15[2]; **12**:6, 19[2]; **13**:22, 23; **16**:4[2], 12, 26[2]; **17**:3[2], 13, 17, 26; **18**:6, 16; **19**:10[2], 18, 19, 29[2]; **20**:3, 16[2]; **21**:8, 12, 18[2], 25, 29; **22**:9, 11, 18, 23, 26; **23**:3, 5, 7, 9, 11, 13, 18, 21, 27, 28; **24**:2, 6, 7, 16, 20, 22, 27; **25**:3[2], 4, 7, 13, 16, 22, 27; **26**:1, 3[3], 25; **27**:1, 10, 13[2], 21[2], 24[2], 26, 27[4]; **28**:2, 8, 21[2]; **29**:5, 14, 19; **30**:8, 18, 21[2], 22, 23, 30; **31**:4[3], 8, 10, 21[2]

Ecc 1:4, 18; **2**:3, 10, 12, 16[2], 17, 21[2], 22, 23, 24, 25, 26; **3**:12, 14, 17[3], 19[2], 22[2]; **4**:4, 8, 9, 10[2], 14; **5**:1, 2, 3, 4, 7, 8, 9, 13, 16, 18[2], 20; **6**:2, 4, 7, 8, 12[3]; **7**:2, 3, 5, 6, 9, 10, 12, 13, 18, 20, 22; **8**:3, 7[2], 15, 16; **9**:1, 4[2], 5[2], 6, 7, 9, 10, 12; **10**:1, 4, 17[2], 19, 20; **11**:1, 2, 6, 7, 8, 9, 10; **12**:13, 14

Song 1:2, 7; **2**:5, 11, 14, 15; **3**:10; **4**:4; **5**:2, 4; **6**:5; **7**:6, 9, 13; **8**:6, 7, 8[2], 11

Isa 1:2, 17, 20, 29[2], 30; **2**:3, 10[2], 12, 19[2], 20, 21[2], 22; **3**:1, 7, 8, 9, 10, 11, 12, 14; **4**:2, 5, 6[3]; **5**:7[3], 20[4], 23, 25; **6**:5[2], 8; **7**:4[2], 6, 8, 13, 16, 18[2], 22[2], 23, 25[2]; **8**:4, 10, 11, 14[5], 17, 18[2], 19; **9**:4, 5, 6, 7, 12, 13, 16, 17[2], 18, 21; **10**:3, 4, 8, 13[2], 17[2], 22, 23, 25, 26; **11**:4, 9, 10, 12, 16; **12**:2, 5, 6; **13**:3, 6, 10, 11[2], 17; **14**:1, 2, 9[2], 13, 21[2], 22, 23, 27, 29, 31; **15**:5[3], 6[2], 8, 9[2]; **16**:2, 4, 7[2], 8, 9[3], 11[2]; **17**:2; **18**:4, 5; **19**:10, 15, 20[3]; **20**:3, 6; **21**:6, 15, 16, 17; **22**:5, 11, 13, 16, 23, 25; **23**:1, 4, 13, 14, 18[3]; **24**:3, 11, 14, 18; **25**:1, 2, 4, 8, 9[2], 10[2]; **26**:1, 4[2], 5, 8, 9, 11, 12[2], 19, 20, 21[2]; **27**:11; **28**:5[2], 6[2], 8, 10, 11, 15, 16, 19, 20, 21, 22, 26, 27; **29**:10, 11, 14, 16, 20[2], 21[3]; **30**:4, 7, 8[2], 15, 16, 18[2], 19, 31, 33[2]; **31**:1, 4[4], 7[2], 9; **32**:6, 10, 12[3], 14[2], 15, 17; **33**:2, 5, 22; **34**:2, 5, 6, 8[2], 10[2], 13, 14, 16, 17[2]; **35**:1, 6, 8; **36**:5, 9[2], 11, 14, 16, 21; **37**:3, 4, 8, 19, 32, 35[3]; **38**:1, 14, 17[2], 18[2], 21[2]; **39**:1, 8; **40**:2[2], 3, 5, 8, 10, 16, 26; **41**:7, 10[2], 13, 17, 22, 28; **42**:4, 6[2], 21, 22[2], 23, 24[2]; **43**:1, 3[3], 4[2], 5, 7[2], 14, 21, 25; **44**:3, 7, 10, 14, 15[2], 17, 18, 21, 22, 23[2]; **45**:4, 13, 18, 22; **46**:9, 13; **47**:1, 4, 5, 7, 9[2], 10; **48**:2, 8, 9[3], 11[3], 21; **49**:4, 6, 8, 10, 13, 19, 20, 23[2], 25; **50**:1[2], 2, 7; **51**:2, 3, 4[2], 6[2], 8[2], 10, 19; **52**:1, 3[2], 4, 5, 8, 9, 12[2], 15; **53**:2, 5[2], 8[2], 10, 11, 12; **54**:1, 3, 4[3], 5, 6, 7, 8, 9[2], 10, 14[2], 15, 16; **55**:2[2], 4, 5[2], 7, 8, 9, 10, 12, 13[2]; **56**:1, 4, 7[2], 11; **57**:8, 12, 15, 16[3], 17; **58**:4, 5, 14; **59**:3, 4[2], 9[2], 10, 11[2], 12[3], 14, 17[2], 21[2]; **60**:1, 2, 9, 10, 12, 17[4], 19, 20, 21; **61**:3[3], 7[2], 8[2], 10, 11; **62**:1[2], 4, 5, 8[2], 10; **63**:3, 4, 8, 17; **64**:3, 4[3], 5, 7, 9, 12; **65**:1, 5, 8[2], 10[2], 11, 14[3], 15[2], 17, 18[2], 20, 22, 23[2]; **66**:2, 5, 8, 10[2], 12, 15, 16, 18, 20, 21[2], 22, 24

Jer 1:6, 7, 8, 12, 15, 18, 19; **2**:10, 11, 13, 20, 22, 25, 27, 28, 37; **3**:2, 5, 8, 10, 12[2], 14, 18, 21, 22, 23, 24, 25; **4**:3, 6, 8[2], 13, 15, 20, 22, 27, 28, 29, 31[2]; **5**:4, 5, 7, 9, 10, 11, 22, 26, 29; **6**:1, 4[2], 6, 11, 12, 13, 16[2], 23, 25, 26[2], 27, 29; **7**:5, 7, 12, 16[3], 22, 29, 30, 32, 33[2], 34; **8**:2, 10, 11, 14, 15[2], 16, 17, 21; **9**:1, 2, 3[3], 4, 7[2], 9, 10[2], 12, 17[2], 18, 19, 21, 24, 26; **10**:2, 3[2], 5, 7, 14, 16, 18, 19, 21, 25; **11**:7, 13, 14[4], 17[2], 20, 23; **12**:3[2], 4, 6, 12; **13**:7, 10, 11[5], 15, 16, 17, 18, 21, 22; **14**:4, 7[2], 8, 11[2], 16, 17, 19[3], 20, 21, 22; **15**:2[4], 4, 5, 13, 14, 15, 16, 17, 20; **16**:3, 4[2], 5[2], 6[2], 7[4], 9, 12, 16[2], 17; **17**:3, 4[2], 6, 8, 14, 16, 25; **18**:18, 20[4], 22[2]; **19**:5, 7[2]; **20**:4, 8, 10[2], 11, 12, 13; **21**:2[2], 9, 10[3]; **22**:4, 6, 10[3], 11, 13, 17[4], 18[2], 20, 22, 30; **23**:10[2], 11, 12, 15, 18, 27, 34, 36[2]; **24**:5, 6[2], 7, 9; **25**:5, 12, 14, 15, 29[3], 31, 34, 36, 38; **26**:11, 14, 15[2], 16; **27**:10, 14, 15, 16, 19; **28**:4, 13, 14; **29**:6, 7[2], 8, 9, 10, 11, 13, 26, 28, 32; **30**:3, 5, 7, 8, 10, 11, 12, 14[2], 15[2], 16, 17, 21; **31**:6, 7[2], 9, 11, 12[4], 13, 15[2], 16, 18, 20[2], 22, 25, 30, 34[2], 35[2], 36, 37, 40; **32**:3, 7, 8[2], 15, 17, 19, 25[2], 27, 30[2], 31, 39[2], 42, 44[2]; **33**:4, 5, 9[2], 11[4], 17, 26; **34**:5[2], 7, 11[2], 16[2], 17, 20; **35**:6[2], 9, 11[2], 14, 19; **36**:7, 31; **37**:3, 4, 9, 10, 11, 15, 17; **38**:2[2], 4[2], 5, 9[2], 27; **39**:16[2], 18[2]; **40**:4, 10, 16; **41**:8, 9, 18; **42**:2[3], 5, 10, 11, 18, 20[2], 21; **43**:1, 3, 7, 11[3]; **44**:11, 13, 14, 16, 17, 27[2], 29; **45**:3, 5[3]; **46**:5, 10[2], 11, 12, 14, 19, 21, 22, 27, 28[2]; **47**:3, 4; **48**:1, 5[2], 7, 9, 14, 18, 20, 26, 27[3], 31[3], 32, 34, 36[2], 37, 38, 40, 44, 46; **49**:3[2], 8, 12, 13, 15, 19, 23, 30, 33[2], 37; **50**:3, 9, 14, 15, 16, 20[2], 24, 25, 27, 29, 31, 38, 39, 44; **51**:2, 5, 6, 8[2], 9, 11, 12, 17, 19, 20, 26[3], 29, 33, 36, 37, 46, 48[2], 51, 56, 62; **52**:3, 6, 16[2], 34

Lam 1:5[2], 9, 10, 11[2], 13, 16, 18, 19, 20[2], 22[2]; **2**:11, 13[2], 14[2], 16, 19[2]; **3**:12, 25, 26, 27, 31[2], 33, 39, 48; **4**:4, 6, 9[2], 13, 17[3], 18, 19; **5**:4, 17[2], 19, 20

Ezk 1:10, 13, 18, 20, 21; **2**:4, 5, 7; **3**:3, 5, 7[2], 26, 27; **4**:3, 5, 6, 14, 15, 17; **5**:4, 6, 16; **6**:9, 11[2]; **7**:6, 8, 11, 12, 13[2], 14, 16, 20, 21[2], 22, 23; **8**:12, 14, 17; **9**:4, 9, 10; **10**:10, 13, 17; **11**:5, 12, 21; **12**:2, 3, 4, 6[2], 7, 24, 25[2], 27; **13**:5, 16, 19[2], 23; **14**:7, 21; **15**:4[2], 5[2], 6; **16**:4, 14[2], 19, 21, 33, 52, 56, 59, 61, 63; **17**:17, 20; **18**:17, 18, 26, 31, 32; **19**:1, 11, 14; **20**:6, 9, 14, 16, 22, 28[2], 31, 39, 40, 42, 43, 44; **21**:7, 12, 15, 21, 22, 28, 32[2]; **22**:10, 30[2]; **23**:8, 10, 14, 20, 21, 28, 34, 37, 39, 40[2], 46; **24**:7, 9, 17, 23; **25**:4, 5[2], 6, 7, 15; **26**:5[2], 7, 14, 17, 19, 21; **27**:2, 3, 5, 15, 18, 20, 31[2], 32; **28**:10, 23; **29**:3, 5, 15, 18[2], 19, 20[2]; **30**:3, 9, 18; **31**:7, 11, 14[2], 15[3]; **32**:2, 10[2], 11, 16[3], 18, 32; **33**:2, 11, 12[2], 13[2], 17, 24, 28, 31, 32; **34**:8, 10[2], 11, 17, 19, 29; **36**:5, 8, 9[2], 18[2], 21, 22[2], 24, 29, 31[2], 32[2], 37[2]; **37**:11, 16[4], 25[2], 26, 28; **38**:7, 19, 21; **39**:5, 10, 17, 19, 23, 25, 29; **40**:4, 17, 42, 45, 46; **41**:6, 7, 9, 24[2]; **42**:3[2], 5, 6, 8, 13, 14[2]; **43**:7, 9, 19, 22, 24, 25; **44**:3, 8, 11, 14[2], 22, 25[6], 28; **45**:1, 2[2], 4[3], 5[3], 6, 7, 14, 15[4], 16, 17, 20[2], 22[3], 23, 24[3]; **46**:5[2], 7[3], 14, 15, 17; **47**:1, 5, 9, 12[3], 14, 22; **48**:1[2], 2, 3, 4, 5, 6, 7, 10[2], 11, 14, 15[3], 18, 21[2], 22, 23, 29

Dan 1:7, 10, 17; **2**:2, 4, 9[2], 12, 20[2], 23, 29, 30[3], 35, 37, 44; **3**:9; **4**:12, 18, 19, 21, 22, 30[2], 34, 36; **5**:10, 19; **6**:6, 7, 21, 23, 26[2]; **7**:12, 18[2], 28; **8**:8, 15, 17, 19, 22, 26[2]; **9**:12, 14[2], 16[2], 17, 18[3], 19[2], 20, 23, 24, 26, 27[2]; **10**:7, 8, 11, 12[2], 14[2], 17[3], 19; **11**:4[2], 6, 13, 17, 18, 23, 24, 25, 27, 30, 35, 36, 37, 39; **12**:1, 3, 7[2], 9, 13

FROM

19, 26; **8:**4, 6, 7, 16, 29; **9:**6, 8, 9, 22, 23, 24; **10:**6, 7, 9, 11^{2}, 29, 31, 34, 36, 41; **11:**17, 21^{6}, 23; **12:**1, 2^{3}, 3^{2}, 7; **13:**3, 4, 5, 6^{2}, 9, 16, 26^{2}, 30; **14:**7, 15; **15:**2^{2}, 4, 5, 7, 9, 10, 46; **16:**1^{2}, 2, 7, 8; **17:**7; **18:**4, 12, 13, 14, 15, 17; **19:**12, 13, 29, 33^{2}, 34; **20:**3, 6; **22:**9, 16, 17, 18, 23, 25, 29, 32^{2}; **23:**1, 4, 5^{2}, 9, 13^{2}, 15, 16; **24:**3, 8, 12, 17, 18

Jdg 1:11, 14, 36^{2}; **2:**1, 3, 19^{2}, 21; **3:**3, 19^{2}, 20, 21, 27; **4:**11, 13, 14; **5:**5^{2}, 11, 20; **6:**8, 9, 11, 13, 14; **7:**3; **8:**13, 22; **9:**20^{3}, 35, 36, 48; **10:**11^{4}, 16; **11:**3, 13, 16, 22^{2}, 23, 24, 29, 31, 33; **12:**9; **13:**5, 7, 20; **15:**13, 14; **16:**12, 17^{2}, 19, 20; **17:**2, 3, 8; **18:**2^{3}, 7, 11, 22, 28; **19:**2, 16, 18^{2}, 30; **20:**1, 13, 31, 32; **21:**6, 8, 19, 24

Ru 1:6, 13, 16; **2:**4, 7, 8; **4:**10^{2}

1Sa 1:14; **2:**8, 19, 30, 33; **3:**17^{2}, 18, 20; **4:**4, 18, 21, 22; **5:**1; **6:**3, 5^{3}, 7, 20; **7:**3, 14^{2}, 16; **9:**2, 25; **10:**2, 3, 5, 9, 23; **12:**2, 20; **13:**5, 8, 11, 15; **14:**17, 21, 31, 46; **15:**2, 6^{2}, 7, 11, 15, 23, 26, 28; **16:**1, 13, 14^{2}, 15, 16, 23^{2}; **17:**15, 24, 26, 30, 33, 46, 53, 57; **18:**6, 9, 10, 12, 13; **19:**8, 9; **20:**1, 2, 9, 15^{2}, 34; **21:**4, 5, 6; **22:**15; **23:**13, 28, 29; **24:**1, 13; **25:**10, 26^{2}, 33^{2}, 34, 39^{2}; **26:**12^{2}, 19; **28:**15, 16, 23; **30:**17, 25; **31:**1, 12

2Sa 1:1, 2, 3, 4, 22^{2}; **2:**12, 19, 21, 22, 26, 27, 30; **3:**10^{2}, 15^{2}, 22, 26^{2}, 28, 29; **4:**11; **5:**9, 13, 25; **6:**2^{2}, 12; **7:**1, 8^{2}, 11, 15^{2}, 23^{2}; **8:**4, 8^{2}, 13; **9:**5; **10:**14; **11:**2^{2}, 4, 8, 10, 15, 20, 21, 24; **12:**10, 17, 20, 30; **13:**4, 9^{2}, 13, 17, 32; **14:**14, 18, 19, 25, 32; **15:**12^{2}, 14, 18, 28; **17:**11; **18:**13, 16; **19:**7, 24, 31; **20:**2^{2}, 20, 21, 22; **21:**5, 10, 12^{2}, 13; **22:**3, 4, 14, 17, 18^{2}, 22, 23, 24, 44, 49^{2}; **23:**11, 17; **24:**2, 4, 15^{2}, 21, 25

1Ki 1:45, 53; **2:**15, 27, 31^{2}, 33, 40, 41; **3:**20; **4:**12, 21, 24, 25, 33, 34; **5:**9; **6:**24; **7:**7, 9, 23; **8:**35, 51, 53, 54^{2}, 65; **9:**6, 12, 28; **10:**3, 11^{2}; **11:**9, 11, 23; **12:**2, 15, 24, 25; **13:**4, 5, 12, 14, 21, 26, 33, 34; **14:**7, 8, 10; **15:**5, 13, 19; **16:**17; **18:**12^{2}, 26; **19:**17, 21; **20:**33, 34, 36^{2}, 41; **21:**21; **22:**24, 33, 43

2Ki 1:4, 6, 10^{2}, 12^{2}, 14; **2:**1, 3, 5, 9, 10, 13, 14, 21, 23, 25^{2}; **3:**27; **4:**5, 27, 42; **5:**19, 21, 22, 24, 26, 27; **6:**32; **8:**14, 20, 22; **9:**2, 8; **10:**21, 29^{2}, 31, 33^{2}; **11:**2^{2}, 11, 19; **12:**18; **13:**5, 6, 11, 17, 23; **14:**13, 24, 25, 27; **15:**9, 14, 16, 18, 24, 28; **16:**3, 6, 11^{2}, 12, 14^{2}, 17^{2}, 18; **17:**7, 8, 9, 13, 21^{2}, 22, 24^{5}, 27, 28, 33; **18:**6, 8, 14, 16^{2}, 17; **19:**8; **20:**14^{3}, 18; **21:**16; **23:**6, 8, 12, 17, 22, 26, 30; **24:**7, 15, 20; **25:**5

1Ch 2:23; **4:**10; **5:**9, 23; **9:**25; **10:**1; **11:**8, 13; **13:**5^{2}; **14:**14, 16; **16:**20^{2}, 23, 35; **17:**5^{2}, 7^{2}, 8, 13^{2}, 21; **18:**4, 8^{2}, 11^{6}; **19:**7; **20:**2; **21:**2, 22, 26; **22:**9; **23:**3, 24, 27; **27:**23

2Ch 1:4, 13^{2}; **4:**2; **5:**9; **6:**21^{2}, 23, 25, 26, 27, 30, 32, 33^{2}, 35, 39^{2}; **7:**1, 8, 14^{2}; **8:**15; **9:**2, 10, 26; **10:**2; **11:**4, 14; **12:**12; **13:**19; **15:**8, 16; **16:**3, 9; **18:**23, 31, 32; **19:**2, 4; **20:**2, 10, 32; **21:**8, 10^{2}, 12; **22:**11^{2}; **23:**10, 20; **24:**5, 23, 25; **25:**5, 12, 13, 14, 23, 27; **26:**18, 19, 20, 21; **28:**8, 12; **29:**6, 10; **30:**5, 6, 8, 9, 10; **31:**16, 17; **32:**22^{2}, 23; **33:**8; **34:**3, 33; **35:**11, 15, 18, 21, 22^{2}; **36:**12, 13, 20

Ezr 1:11; **2:**59, 62; **3:**6, 7, 8, 13; **4:**12, 14, 21; **6:**6, 11, 21; **7:**6, 9; **8:**1, 31^{2}; **9:**1, 5, 8, 11; **10:**6, 8, 11^{2}, 14

Neh 1:9; **3:**15, 20, 21, 24, 25, 28; **4:**5, 12, 16, 19, 21; **5:**13^{2}, 14^{2}, 17; **6:**9; **7:**61, 64; **8:**3, 18; **9:**2, 13, 15, 19, 20, 27, 28, 35; **10:**28; **11:**30, 31; **12:**28, 29, 38, 39; **13:**3, 21, 28, 30

Est 1:1, 7, 19; **2:**6; **3:**7^{2}, 8, 10; **4:**4, 14; **7:**7; **8:**2, 9, 15; **9:**16, 22^{3}, 28^{2}

Job 1:7^{2}, 12, 16, 19; **2:**2^{3}, 7^{2}, 11; **3:**4, 10, 11, 17, 19; **4:**2, 13, 20; **5:**4, 15^{3}, 20^{2}, 21; **6:**13, 14, 23^{2}; **7:**19; **8:**18; **9:**34; **10:**14, 19; **13:**20, 21; **14:**6, 11; **15:**18; **17:**4; **18:**17, 18; **19:**9, 13^{2}; **20:**24, 29; **21:**9, 14, 16; **22:**6, 7, 17, 18, 22, 23; **23:**7, 12, 17; **24:**1, 9, 10, 12; **26:**4, 5; **27:**5; **28:**4^{2}, 11, 21^{2}, 28; **30:**5, 10; **31:**2^{2}, 16, 18^{2}, 22^{2}, 23; **33:**17^{2}, 18^{2}, 24, 28, 30; **34:**10^{2}, 27; **35:**3; **36:**3, 7, 10; **38:**15; **39:**22, 29; **42:**2

Ps 2:3, 12; **3:**ttl; **6:**8; **7:**1; **9:**13; **12:**1, 5, 7; **13:**1; **14:**2; **17:**2, 4, 7, 9^{2}, 13, 14^{2}; **18:**3, 16, 17^{2}, 21, 22, 23, 43, 48^{2}, ttl^{2}; **19:**6^{2}, 12, 13^{2}; **20:**2, 6; **21:**10^{2}; **22:**1^{2}, 10^{2}, 11, 19, 20^{2}, 21^{2}, 24; **24:**5^{2}; **27:**9; **30:**3; **31:**11, 15^{2}, 20^{2}, 22; **32:**7; **33:**13, 14, 19; **34:**4, 13^{2}, 14, 16; **35:**10^{2}, 17^{2}, 22; **37:**8, 27, 40; **38:**9, 10, 11, 21; **39:**2, 8, 10; **40:**10, 11; **41:**13; **42:**6^{2}; **43:**1; **44:**7, 10, 18; **49:**14, 15; **50:**1, 4; **51:**2^{2}, 9, 11^{2}, 14; **53:**2; **55:**1, 8, 11, 12, 18; **56:**13^{2}; **57:**3^{2}, ttl; **58:**3; **59:**1^{2}, 2^{2}; **60:**11; **61:**2, 3; **62:**1, 4, 5; **64:**1, 2^{2}; **66:**20; **68:**20, 22^{2}, 26; **69:**5, 14, 17; **71:**5, 6, 12, 17, 20; **72:**8^{2}, 14; **73:**27^{2}; **75:**6^{3}; **76:**8; **78:**4, 23, 30, 42, 50, 70, 71; **80:**14, 18; **81:**6^{2}; **83:**4; **84:**7, 11; **85:**3, 11; **86:**13; **88:**5, 8, 14, 15, 18; **89:**33, 48; **90:**2; **91:**3^{2}; **93:**2; **94:**13; **96:**2; **101:**4, 8; **102:**2, 19^{2}; **103:**4, 12^{2}, 17; **104:**13, 21; **105:**13^{2}; **106:**10^{2}, 47, 48; **107:**2, 3^{4}, 20, 41; **108:**12; **109:**15, 17, 20, 31; **110:**3; **113:**2, 3; **114:**1; **115:**18; **116:**8^{3}; **119:**10, 19, 21, 22, 29, 37, 51, 101, 102, 110, 115, 118, 134, 150, 155, 157, 160; **120:**2^{2}; **121:**1, 2, 7, 8; **125:**2; **129:**1, 2; **130:**8; **131:**3; **132:**11; **135:**7; **136:**11, 24; **139:**7^{2}, 12, 15, 19; **140:**1^{2}, 4^{2}; **141:**9; **142:**6; **143:**7, 9; **144:**7^{2}, 10, 11; **148:**1, 7

Prv 1:15, 33; **2:**12^{2}, 16^{2}, 22; **3:**7, 21, 26, 27; **4:**5, 15, 21, 24^{2}, 27; **5:**7, 8; **6:**5^{2}, 24^{2}; **7:**5^{2}; **8:**23^{2}; **10:**2; **11:**4; **13:**14, 19; **14:**7, 14, 16, 27; **15:**24, 29; **16:**1, 6, 17; **17:**13; **19:**4, 7, 14, 27; **20:**3, 9; **21:**23; **22:**5, 6, 15, 27; **23:**4, 13, 14; **24:**18; **25:**4, 5, 17, 25; **27:**8^{2}, 22; **28:**9; **29:**21, 26; **30:**8, 12, 14^{2}; **31:**14

Ecc 1:7; **2:**10^{2}, 24; **3:**5, 11, 14; **7:**18, 23, 26; **8:**10; **10:**5; **11:**10^{2}; **12:**11

Song 3:4; **4:**1, 2, 8^{6}, 15; **5:**7; **6:**5^{2}, 6; **8:**5

Isa 1:6, 15, 16; **2:**3, 6, 22; **3:**1^{2}; **4:**4, 6^{3}; **5:**23, 26^{2}; **6:**6; **7:**17^{2}; **8:**17, 18; **9:**7, 14; **10:**2^{2}, 3, 27^{2}; **11:**11^{8}, 12, 16; **13:**5^{2}, 6, 20; **14:**3^{3}, 9^{2}, 12, 22, 25^{2}, 31; **16:**1, 4; **17:**1, 3^{2}; **18:**2, 7^{2}; **19:**5; **20:**2^{2}, 6; **21:**1^{2}, 15^{4}; **22:**3, 4, 14, 19^{2}, 24; **23:**1; **24:**14, 16, 18^{2}; **25:**4^{2}, 8^{2}; **27:**12; **28:**9^{2}, 19, 22, 29; **29:**13, 15; **30:**6, 11, 14, 27; **31:**6, 8; **32:**2^{2}, 15; **33:**15^{3}; **34:**4^{2}, 10, 17; **36:**2; **37:**8, 14, 20; **38:**7, 12^{2}, 13, 17; **39:**3^{3}, 7; **40:**21^{2}, 27^{2}; **41:**2, 4, 9^{2}, 25^{2}, 26; **42:**7, 10, 11; **43:**5^{2}, 6^{2}; **44:**2, 8, 24; **45:**6^{2}, 8, 21^{2}; **46:**3^{2}, 7, 10^{2}, 11^{2}, 12; **47:**11, 12, 13, 14, 15; **48:**3, 5, 6, 7, 8^{2}, 16^{2}, 19, 20; **49:**1^{3}, 5, 12^{4}, 24; **50:**6; **51:**4, 8; **52:**2^{2}, 11; **53:**3, 8^{2}; **54:**8, 10, 14^{2}; **55:**10; **56:**2^{2}, 3, 6, 11; **57:**1; **58:**7, 9, 13^{2}; **59:**2, 9, 11, 13^{2}, 15, 19^{2}, 20, 21; **60:**4, 6, 9; **63:**1^{2}, 15^{2}, 16, 17^{2}; **64:**7; **65:**16; **66:**6^{2}, 23^{2}

Jer 2:5, 25^{2}, 35, 37; **3:**1, 4, 19, 20, 23^{2}, 24, 25; **4:**6, 7^{2}, 8, 12, 14, 15^{2}, 16, 28; **5:**15, 25; **6:**8, 13^{2}, 20^{2}, 22^{2}; **7:**1, 28, 34^{2}; **8:**10^{2}, 13, 16; **9:**2, 3, 21^{2}; **10:**9^{2}, 11^{2}, 13; **11:**1, 4, 15, 19; **12:**2, 12, 14; **13:**6, 7, 20, 25; **15:**7, 19; **16:**5, 15^{2}, 16^{2}, 17^{2}, 19; **17:**4, 5, 8, 12, 13, 16, 26^{6}; **18:**1, 8, 11, 14^{2}, 15, 18^{3}, 20, 22, 23; **19:**14; **20:**13, 17; **21:**1, 2, 7^{3}; **22:**20, 21; **23:**8, 14, 15, 22^{2}, 30; **24:**1, 10; **25:**3, 5^{2}, 10, 30^{2}, 32^{2}, 33; **26:**1, 3, 10; **27:**1, 10, 16, 20; **28:**3, 6, 10, 11, 12, 16; **29:**1^{2}, 2, 4, 14^{2}, 20; **30:**1, 8, 10^{2}, 21; **31:**8^{2}, 11, 13, 16^{3}, 34, 36^{2}, 38; **32:**1, 30, 31^{2}, 40^{2}; **33:**5, 8; **34:**1, 8, 12, 14, 21; **35:**1, 15; **36:**1, 2^{2}, 3, 4, 6, 7, 9, 29, 32; **37:**5, 9, 11, 17; **38:**10, 14, 25; **40:**1^{2}, 4; **41:**5^{3}, 6, 14, 15, 16^{3}; **42:**1, 4, 8, 11, 17; **43:**5, 12; **44:**5, 7, 12; **46:**16, 27^{2}; **47:**4; **48:**2, 3, 10, 11^{2}, 18, 33^{3}, 34^{2}, 42, 44, 45; **49:**5, 7, 14, 16, 19^{2}, 32, 36, 38; **50:**6, 9^{2}, 16, 26, 39, 41^{2}, 44^{2}; **51:**16, 25, 45, 48, 53, 54^{2}, 64; **52:**3, 8, 29

Lam 1:6, 13, 14, 16; **2:**1, 3, 8, 9; **3:**17, 18, 50, 66; **5:**14^{2}, 16, 19

Ezk 1:19, 21, 25, 27^{2}; **3:**12, 17, 18, 19^{2}, 20; **4:**8, 10, 11, 14; **6:**9; **7:**20, 22, 26^{2}; **8:**2^{2}, 6; **9:**2, 3; **10:**2, 4, 6^{2}, 7, 16^{2}, 18, 19; **11:**15, 17, 18, 23, 24; **12:**3, 16^{3}, 19; **13:**20, 22; **14:**5, 6^{2}, 7, 8, 9, 11, 13, 17, 19, 21; **15:**7; **16:**9, 34, 41, 42; **17:**22; **18:**8, 17, 21, 23, 24, 26, 27, 28, 30, 31; **19:**8; **20:**17, 34, 38, 41, 47; **21:**3, 4^{2}; **22:**5, 26; **23:**8, 17, 18^{2}, 22, 27^{2}, 28, 40, 42; **24:**13, 16, 25; **25:**7, 9^{2}, 13^{2}; **26:**4, 7, 16; **27:**5, 7^{2}, 29; **28:**3, 15, 16, 18, 25; **29:**10, 13; **30:**6, 9; **31:**12; **32:**13; **33:**6, 7, 8, 9^{2}, 11^{2}, 12, 14, 18, 19, 30; **34:**10^{2}, 13^{2}; **35:**7; **36:**24, 25^{2}, 29, 33; **37:**9, 21; **38:**8, 15; **39:**2, 22, 23, 24, 27, 29; **40:**13, 15, 19, 23, 27; **41:**7, 16, 20; **42:**6, 9^{2}; **43:**2, 9, 14^{2}, 15; **44:**10^{2}, 15; **45:**7^{3}, 9; **46:**18; **47:**1^{3}, 10, 15, 17, 18^{5}, 19, 20; **48:**1, 2, 3, 4, 5, 6, 7, 8^{2}, 22^{2}, 23, 24, 25, 26, 27, 28, 35

Dan 2:1, 5, 8, 15; **3:**17; **4:**3, 13, 14^{2}, 16, 23, 25, 31^{2}, 32, 33, 34; **5:**20^{2}, 21, 24; **6:**18, 20, 27; **7:**3^{2}, 4, 7, 10, 19, 23, 24; **8:**5; **9:**5^{2}, 13, 16, 25; **10:**12; **11:**22; **12:**11

Hos 1:2; **2:**2, 15; **4:**12; **5:**3, 6; **7:**4, 13; **8:**6; **9:**1, 11^{3}, 12; **10:**5, 9; **11:**2, 7, 10; **12:**9; **13:**4, 14^{3}, 15; **14:**4, 8

Joel 1:5, 9, 12, 13, 15, 16; **2:**20; **3:**6, 16, 20

Am 1:2^{2}, 5^{2}, 8^{2}; **2:**3, 9^{2}, 10, 14; **3:**1, 5, 11; **4:**7; **5:**11, 12, 19, 23; **6:**2, 14; **8:**12^{2}; **9:**3, 7^{2}, 8

Oba 1

Jna 1:3^{2}, 10, 15; **2:**6; **3:**5, 6^{2}, 8^{2}, 9, 10; **4:**3, 6

Mic 1:2, 12, 16; **2:**3, 4, 8^{2}, 9^{2}; **3:**2^{2}, 3, 4; **4:**2, 7, 10; **5:**2^{2}, 6, 7; **6:**5; **7:**5, 12^{5}, 20

Nah 1:13; **2:**13; **3:**7, 8

Hab 1:8, 12; **2:**9; **3:**3^{2}, 17

Zep 1:2, 3, 4, 6, 10^{3}; **2:**11; **3:**10

Hag 1:10^{2}; **2:**15^{2}, 18^{3}, 19

Zec 1:4^{2}; **2:**6; **3:**4^{2}; **6:**1, 5, 10; **7:**12; **8:**7^{2}; **9:**5, 7, 10^{4}; **13:**5; **14:**2, 5, 8, 10^{3}, 13, 16

Mal 1:5, 11; **2:**6; **3:**5, 7^{2}

Mt 1:17^{3}, 21, 24; **2:**1, 16; **3:**7, 13, 17; **4:**17, 21, 25^{5}; **5:**18, 29, 30, 42; **6:**13; **7:**23; **8:**1, 11, 30; **9:**9, 15, 16, 22; **11:**12, 25; **12:**15, 38, 42, 44; **13:**12, 27, 35, 49; **14:**2; **15:**8, 18, 27, 28, 29; **16:**1, 21, 22; **17:**9^{2}, 18; **18:**8, 9, 35; **19:**1, 8, 12, 20; **20:**8, 29; **21:**8, 25^{2}, 43; **22:**46; **23:**34, 35; **24:**1, 29, 31^{2}; **25:**28, 29, 32^{2}, 34, 41; **26:**16, 39, 42, 47; **27:**31, 40, 42, 45, 51, 55, 64; **28:**2^{2}, 7, 8

Mk 1:9, 11, 42, 45; **2:**20, 21; **3:**7^{2}, 8^{3}, 22; **4:**25; **5:**35; **6:**1, 2, 10, 14, 16; **7:**1, 4, 6, 15, 17, 18, 21, 23, 24, 31, 33; **8:**3, 4, 11; **9:**9^{2}, 10; **10:**1, 6, 20; **11:**12, 20, 30, 31; **12:**2, 25, 34; **13:**19, 27^{2}; **14:**35, 36, 43, 52; **15:**20, 30, 32, 38; **16:**3, 8

Lk 1:2, 3, 15, 26, 38, 45, 48, 50, 52, 71^{2}, 78; **2:**1, 4, 15, 36, 37; **3:**7, 22; **4:**1, 9, 13, 42; **5:**3, 8, 10, 13, 35; **6:**17, 22; **7:**6; **8:**18, 37, 49; **9:**5, 7, 33, 37, 39, 45, 54; **10:**7, 18, 21, 30, 42; **11:**4, 7, 16, 22, 31, 50, 51; **12:**36, 52, 58; **13:**12, 15, 16, 27, 29^{4}; **16:**3, 18, 21, 26^{2}, 30, 31; **17:**7, 29; **18:**21, 34; **19:**8, 24, 26^{2}, 39, 42; **20:**4, 5, 35; **21:**11; **22:**41, 42, 43, 45; **23:**5, 49, 55; **24:**2, 9, 13, 46, 49, 51

Jn 1:6, 19, 32; **2:**22; **3:**2, 13, 27, 31^{2}; **4:**11; **5:**24, 34, 41, 44; **6:**23, 31, 32^{2}, 33, 38, 41, 42, 50, 51, 58, 64, 66; **7:**29; **8:**23^{2}, 25, 42, 44; **9:**1, 29, 30; **10:**5, 18, 32; **11:**41, 53; **12:**1, 9, 17, 27, 28, 32, 36; **13:**3, 4; **14:**7; **15:**26^{2}, 27; **16:**22, 27, 28, 30; **17:**8, 15; **18:**3, 28, 36; **19:**11, 12, 23, 27; **20:**1, 9; **21:**8, 14

Act 1:4, 11, 12^{2}, 22^{2}, 25; **2:**2, 40, 46; **3:**2, 15, 19, 23, 24, 26; **4:**2, 10; **5:**38, 41; **7:**3, 4, 33, 39; **8:**10, 26, 33; **9:**3, 8, 14, 18; **10:**17, 21, 22, 23, 37, 41; **11:**4, 5, 9, 11, 27; **12:**7, 10, 11, 19, 25; **13:**4, 8, 13^{2}, 14, 29, 30, 31, 34, 39^{2}, 46; **14:**8, 15, 17, 19, 26; **15:**1, 18, 19, 20^{4}, 24, 29^{5}, 33, 38^{2}, 39; **16:**11, 12; **17:**3, 27, 31, 33; **18:**1, 2^{2}, 5, 6, 16, 21; **19:**9, 12^{2}, 35; **20:**6, 9, 17, 18, 20, 26; **21:**1^{2}, 7, 10, 25^{4}; **22:**5, 6, 22, 29, 30; **23:**10, 21; **24:**18; **25:**1, 7; **26:**4, 5, 10, 12, 13, 17^{2}, 18^{2}, 23, 26; **27:**4, 21, 34, 43; **28:**13, 15, 17, 23

Ro 1:4, 7, 17, 18, 20; **4:**24; **5:**9, 14; **6:**4, 7, 9, 13, 17, 18, 20, 22; **7:**2, 3, 4, 6, 24; **8:**2, 11^{2}, 21, 35, 39; **9:**3; **10:**6, 7, 9; **11:**15, 26; **15:**19, 22, 31

1Co 1:3^{2}; **4:**7; **5:**2, 13; **7:**10, 27; **9:**19; **10:**14; **14:**36; **15:**12, 20, 41, 47

2Co 1:2^{2}, 10; **2:**3, 13; **3:**1, 18; **5:**2, 6, 8; **6:**17; **7:**1; **11:**3, 9^{2}, 12; **12:**8

Gal 1:1, 3^{2}, 4, 6, 8, 15; **2:**12; **3:**13; **4:**1, 24; **5:**4; **6:**17

Eph 1:2^{2}, 20; **2:**12^{2}; **3:**9; **4:**16, 18, 31; **5:**14; **6:**6, 23

Php 1:2^{2}, 5; **3:**20; **4:**15, 18

Col 1:2, 13, 18, 23, 26^{2}; **2:**12, 19, 20; **4:**16

1Th 1:1, 8, 9, 10^{3}; **2:**17; **3:**6; **4:**3, 16; **5:**22

2Th 1:2, 7, 9^{2}; **2:**2, 13; **3:**2, 3, 6

1Ti 1:2, 6; **4:**1, 3; **5:**13; **6:**5, 10

2Ti 1:2, 3, 15; **2:**8, 19, 21; **3:**5, 15; **4:**4, 18

Tit 1:4, 14; **2:**14

Phlm 3

Heb 3:12; **4:**3, 4, 10^{2}; **5:**1, 7; **6:**1, 7; **7:**1, 6, 26; **8:**11; **9:**14; **10:**13, 22; **11:**15, 19^{2}; **12:**25^{2}; **13:**20

Jas 1:17^{2}, 27; **3:**15, 17; **4:**1, 7; **5:**19, 20^{2}

1Pt 1:3, 12, 18^{2}, 21; **2:**11; **3:**10; **4:**1

2Pt 1:9, 17^{2}, 18; **2:**8, 14, 18, 21; **3:**4, 17

1Jn 1:1, 7, 9; **2:**7^{2}, 13, 14, 19, 20, 24^{2}; **3:**8, 11, 14, 17; **4:**21; **5:**21

2Jn 3^{2}, 4, 5, 6

Jude 14, 24

Rev 1:4^{2}, 5^{2}; **2:**5; **3:**10, 12; **6:**4, 16^{2}; **7:**2, 17; **8:**10; **9:**1, 6, 13; **10:**1, 4, 8; **11:**11, 12; **12:**14; **13:**8, 13; **14:**2, 3, 4, 13^{3}, 18; **15:**8^{2}; **16:**17; **17:**8; **18:**1, 4, 14^{2}; **20:**1, 9, 11; **21:**2, 4, 10; **22:**19^{2}

HAD

Gen 1:31; 2:2^2, 3, 5, 8, 22; 3:1; 4:4, 5; 5:4; 6:6, 12; 7:9, 16; 8:6; 9:24; 11:3^2, 30; 12:1, 4, 5^2, 16, 20; 13:1, 3, 4, 5; 14:13; 16:1, 3, 4, 5; 17:23; 18:8, 33; 19:17; 20:4, 18; 21:1^2, 2, 4, 9, 25; 22:3, 9; 23:16; 24:1, 2, 15, 16, 19, 21, 22, 29, 45, 48, 65^2, 66; 25:5, 6; 26:8, 14, 15^2, 18^3, 32; 27:17, 30, 31; 28:6, 9, 18; 29:16, 20; 30:9, 25, 35, 38, 43; 31:18^2, 19, 21, 25, 32, 34, 42; 32:23; 33:10, 19; 34:5, 7, 13, 19, 27; 35:16; 36:6; 38:15, 30; 39:1, 4, 5^3, 6^2, 13; 40:1, 16, 22; 41:21^2, 43, 54; 43:2^2, 6, 10^2, 23; 44:2; 45:27^2; 46:1, 5, 6; 47:11, 22, 27; 48:11; 49:33; 50:14

Ex 2:6^2, 16, 25; 4:28^2, 30, 31^2; 5:14; 7:10, 13, 22, 25; 8:12, 15, 19; 9:12, 35; 10:15, 23; 12:28, 39; 13:17, 19; 14:12; 15:25; 16:3, 18^2; 17:10; 18:1^2, 2, 8^2, 9^2, 24; 19:2; 31:18; 32:4, 20, 25, 29; 33:5; 34:4, 32, 33; 35:25, 29; 36:1, 2, 3, 7, 22; 39:43^3; 40:23

Lev 10:5, 19; 21:3; 24:23

Nu 1:48; 3:4; 7:1^3; 8:4, 22; 12:1^2, 14; 13:32; 14:2^2, 24; 16:31, 39; 20:3; 21:9, 26; 22:2, 33^2; 23:2, 30; 26:33, 65; 27:3; 30:6; 31:32, 35, 53; 32:1, 9, 13; 33:4

Dt 1:3, 4, 39, 41; 2:12; 7:8; 9:16^4, 21, 25; 10:5, 15; 19:19; 29:26; 31:24; 32:30^2; 34:9

Jos 2:6^2, 11; 4:4; 5:1, 5, 7, 8, 12^2; 6:8, 10, 22^2, 23, 25; 7:7, 24, 25; 8:13, 18, 19, 20, 21, 24, 26, 33; 9:3, 4, 16, 18, 21; 10:1^6, 13, 20, 27, 32, 33, 35, 37, 39^2; 11:1, 14; 14:3, 15; 17:1, 3, 6^2, 8, 11; 18:2; 19:2, 9, 49; 21:4, 5, 6, 7, 10, 20, 45; 22:7; 23:1; 24:31^2

Jdg 1:8^2, 19; 2:6, 7, 10, 15^2; 3:1, 11, 12, 16, 18, 20, 30; 4:3, 11, 18, 24; 5:26, 31; 6:3, 27; 7:19; 8:3, 8, 19, 24, 30^2, 34, 35; 9:22; 10:4^2; 11:34, 39; 12:9, 14; 14:4, 6^2, 9, 18^2, 20; 15:5, 6, 17, 19; 16:8, 18; 17:3^2, 5; 18:1, 7, 27^2, 28; 19:6, 17; 20:36; 21:1, 5, 12, 14, 15

Ru 1:6^2; 2:1, 17, 18^2, 19; 3:7, 16

1Sa 1:2^3, 5, 6, 9^2, 13, 20, 24; 3:8; 4:18; 5:9^2; 6:6, 16, 19^2; 7:14; 9:2, 15; 10:9, 13, 20, 21, 26; 13:1, 4^2, 8, 10, 21; 14:11, 17, 22, 24, 30^2; 15:35; 17:5, 6, 12, 20, 21, 39, 40; 18:1; 19:18; 20:34, 37; 22:21; 24:5, 10, 16, 18; 25:2, 21, 34, 35, 37, 44; 26:5; 28:3^3, 20, 24; 30:1, 2, 4, 12^2, 16^2, 18, 19, 21; 31:11

2Sa 1:1, 21; 2:27, 30, 31; 3:7, 17, 22, 30; 4:2, 4; 5:12^2, 17, 25; 6:8, 13, 17, 18, 22, 23; 7:1; 8:9, 10^2, 11; 9:2, 10, 12; 11:10, 13, 22, 27; 12:2, 3^2, 6, 8; 13:1, 3, 10, 11, 15, 18, 22, 23, 28, 29, 36; 14:2, 6, 32, 33; 15:2, 24, 30; 16:23; 17:14, 18, 20; 18:18, 33; 19:6^3, 8, 24, 32, 43; 20:3, 5, 8; 21:2, 11, 12^3, 15, 20; 22:1, 38; 23:8, 18, 20, 21, 22; 24:8, 10

1Ki 1:6, 41; 2:28, 41; 3:1, 10, 21, 28; 4:2, 7, 11, 14, 24^2, 26, 34; 5:1^2, 15; 6:22; 7:8^2, 20, 28, 30^2, 37, 51; 8:11, 54, 66; 9:1, 2, 10, 11, 12, 16, 19, 24, 27; 10:4^2, 7, 15, 19, 22, 24, 26, 28; 11:3, 9, 10, 15, 16, 29; 12:8, 12, 32^2, 33^2; 13:4, 5, 11^2, 12, 23^3, 28, 31; 14:22^2, 26; 15:3, 12, 13, 15^2, 20, 22, 29; 16:31, 32; 17:7; 19:1^2; 21:1, 4^2, 11^2; 22:31, 53

2Ki 1:17^2; 2:14; 3:2; 4:12, 15, 17, 20; 5:1, 2^2, 7, 8^2, 13; 6:23, 30; 7:6, 15, 17, 18; 8:1, 5^2, 29; 9:14, 15, 31; 10:1, 17, 25; 11:15; 12:6, 11, 18; 13:7^2, 23^2, 25; 14:5; 15:3, 9, 34; 16:11, 18; 17:4^2, 7^3, 8, 12, 15, 20, 23, 28, 29, 35; 18:4, 16, 18; 19:8; 20:11, 12^2; 21:3, 7, 16, 24; 22:11; 23:5, 8, 11, 12^2, 13, 15, 19^2, 26, 29, 32, 37; 24:7, 9, 13^2, 19, 20; 25:16, 17, 22, 23

1Ch 2:22, 26, 34^2, 52; 4:5, 22, 27^2, 40; 6:31, 32, 49, 66; 7:4, 15; 8:8, 38, 40; 9:23, 28, 31, 44; 10:9, 11, 13; 11:10, 11, 20, 22, 24; 12:15, 29, 32, 39; 13:11, 14; 14:2, 4, 12; 15:3, 27; 16:1, 2; 18:9, 10^2; 19:6, 17; 21:28; 23:11, 17, 22; 24:2, 19, 28; 26:9, 10, 26, 28^2; 27:23; 28:2^2, 12; 29:25

2Ch 1:3, 4^3, 5, 12, 14, 16; 2:17; 3:1; 5:1, 14; 6:13^2; 7:1, 2, 6, 7, 10; 8:1, 2, 6, 11, 12, 14, 18; 9:3^2, 6, 12, 23, 25; 10:2, 6; 11:14, 15; 12:1^2, 2, 9, 13; 14:6^3, 8; 15:8, 11, 15, 16, 18^2; 16:14; 17:2, 5, 9, 13; 18:1, 2, 10, 30; 20:21, 23, 27, 29, 33; 21:2, 6, 7, 10; 22:1, 7, 9^2; 23:8, 9, 18, 21; 24:7, 10, 14, 16, 22, 24; 25:3; 26:5, 10, 11, 19, 20; 28:3, 6, 17, 18^2; 29:2, 22, 29, 34, 36; 30:2, 3^2, 5, 17, 18; 31:1, 10; 32:27, 29; 33:2, 3, 4, 7^2, 9, 15, 22, 23, 25; 34:4, 7^2, 8, 9, 10, 11, 19, 22; 35:20, 24; 36:13, 14, 15, 17, 20, 21

Ezr 1:5, 7^2; 2:1^2; 3:7, 12; 5:12, 14; 6:13, 21, 22; 7:6, 10; 8:20, 22, 25, 35; 9:4; 10:1^2, 6, 8, 17, 18, 44^3

Neh 1:2; 2:1, 9, 12, 16, 18; 4:6, 15, 18; 5:15^2; 6:1^2, 12^2, 18; 7:1, 6^2, 67; 8:1, 4, 12, 14, 17; 9:18^2, 28^2; 10:28; 11:16; 12:29, 43; 13:3, 5, 10, 23

Est 1:8; 2:1, 6^3, 7, 10^2, 12, 15, 20^2; 3:2, 4, 6, 12; 4:5, 7^2, 17; 5:5, 11^2, 12; 6:2, 4, 13, 14; 7:4^2, 9^2, 10; 8:1, 2, 3, 16, 17; 9:1, 16, 23^2, 24^2, 26^2, 31^2

Job 2:11; 3:13, 15, 16, 26; 6:20; 9:16^3; 10:18^2, 19; 22:8; 24:16; 29:12; 31:25, 31, 35; 32:3^2, 4^2, 16; 38:8; 42:7, 10, 11^2, 12, 13

Ps 27:13^2; 35:14; 42:4; 51:ttl; 55:6; 73:2; 74:5; 78:11, 23, 24^2, 43, 44, 54; 81:13^2; 84:10; 89:7; 94:17^2; 105:26; 106:21, 23; 119:51, 56, 87, 92; 124:1, 2, 3, 4^2, 5

Prv 8:26; 24:31

Ecc 1:16; 2:7^2, 11^2, 18; 4:1^2; 8:10^2

Song 3:4; 5:6; 8:11

Isa 1:9; 6:2, 6; 22:11; 26:13; 29:16; 37:8; 38:9, 17, 21, 22; 39:1^2; 41:3; 48:18, 19; 49:21; 52:15^2; 53:9; 59:10; 60:10

Jer 2:21; 3:7, 8; 4:23; 5:7; 6:15; 8:12; 9:2; 11:19; 13:7; 16:15; 19:14; 23:8, 22^2; 24:1^2, 2^2; 25:17; 26:8^2, 19; 28:12; 29:1; 32:3, 16; 34:8, 10, 11, 15^2, 16, 18; 36:4, 11, 13, 16, 23, 25, 27, 32; 37:4, 10, 15, 16; 38:1, 7, 27; 39:5, 10; 40:1^2, 7^2, 11^2; 41:2, 4, 9^3, 10, 11, 14, 16^3, 18; 43:1^2, 5, 6; 44:15, 17, 20; 45:1; 52:2, 3, 20, 25

Lam 1:7, 9; 2:17^2

Ezk 1:5, 6^2, 8^2, 10^3, 16, 23^2, 25, 27; 3:6; 8:8; 9:3, 11; 10:6, 10^2, 12, 14, 21; 11:24, 25; 16:14, 17; 17:3, 18; 19:5, 11; 20:6, 15, 24^3, 28; 23:10, 19, 32, 39; 29:18^2; 33:15, 21, 22; 35:5^2; 36:18^2, 21^2; 40:10, 26, 31, 34, 37; 41:6, 18, 23, 24; 42:6, 15, 20; 44:22, 25; 47:3, 7

Dan 1:4, 9, 11, 17, 18; 2:24; 3:2, 3^2, 7, 27^2; 4:12, 21; 5:2; 6:24^2; 7:1, 4, 5, 6^2, 7^2, 12, 20; 8:3, 5, 6^2, 15; 9:21; 10:1, 11, 15, 19

Hos 1:8; 2:23; 12:3, 4

Am 7:2

Oba 5, 16

Jna 1:10, 17; 3:10; 4:10

Nah 3:8

Hab 3:4

Hag 1:12

Zec 1:12; 5:9; 7:2; 10:6; 11:10

Mal 2:15

Mt 1:6, 24, 25; 2:3, 4, 7, 9, 11, 16; 3:4; 4:2, 12, 24; 7:28; 9:8; 10:1; 11:1, 2, 21, 23; 12:7, 10; 13:5^2, 6, 46^2, 53; 14:3, 13, 21, 23, 35; 16:5; 17:8; 18:24, 25^2, 32, 33^2; 19:1, 22; 20:2, 11, 34; 21:28, 32, 45; 22:11, 22, 25, 28, 34^2; 23:30; 24:43; 25:16, 17, 18, 20, 22, 24; 26:1, 8, 19, 24^2, 30, 57; 27:2, 3, 16, 18, 26, 29, 31, 34, 50, 59, 60; 28:12, 16

Mk 1:19, 22, 26, 37, 42; 2:4, 25; 3:1, 3, 5, 8, 10^2; 4:5^2, 6, 36; 5:3, 4^2, 15, 18, 19, 20, 25, 26^3, 27, 30, 32, 40; 6:17^2, 18, 19, 30^2, 31, 41, 46, 49, 53; 7:14, 25, 32; 8:7, 9, 14^2, 23, 33, 34; 9:8, 9, 34, 36; 10:22; 11:6, 11; 12:12, 22, 23, 28, 44; 13:20; 14:4, 16, 21, 23, 26, 44; 15:7^2, 8, 10, 15, 20, 24, 44; 16:1, 9, 10, 11^2, 14, 19

Lk 1:3, 7, 22, 58; 2:17, 20, 26, 36, 39, 43; 3:19; 4:13, 16, 17, 33, 35, 40; 5:4, 6, 9, 11; 6:8; 7:1, 10, 13, 39, 41, 42; 8:2, 8, 27, 29^2, 39, 42, 43, 47; 9:8, 10, 11, 36; 10:13^2, 33, 39; 11:38; 12:39; 13:1, 6, 11, 14, 17; 14:2; 15:9, 11, 14, 20; 16:1^2, 8; 17:6; 19:15^2, 28, 32, 37; 20:19, 33; 21:4; 22:13, 55, 61, 64; 23:8, 13, 25, 46, 51; 24:1, 14, 21, 23, 24, 37, 40

Jn 2:9, 15, 22^2; 4:1, 18, 50; 5:4, 5, 6, 13, 15, 16, 18, 46; 6:11, 13, 14, 19, 23, 25, 60; 7:9; 8:3, 10, 19; 9:6, 8, 15, 18^2, 22, 35^2; 11:6, 13, 17, 21, 28, 32, 43, 45, 46, 57; 12:1, 6, 9, 14, 16, 18, 37; 13:3, 12^2, 21, 26, 29^2; 14:7; 15:22^3, 24^3; 17:5; 18:1, 6, 18, 22, 24, 38; 19:23, 30; 20:12, 14, 18^2, 20, 22; 21:15, 19

Act 1:2^2, 9, 17; 2:30, 44, 45; 3:10, 12, 18; 4:7, 13, 15, 21, 23, 31, 32, 35; 5:23, 27, 34, 40; 6:6, 15; 7:5, 17, 36, 44^3, 60; 8:11^2, 14, 25, 27^2; 9:18, 19, 27^3, 31, 33, 37, 38, 41; 10:8, 11, 17^2, 24, 31; 11:1, 5, 6, 13, 23, 26; 12:4, 12, 16, 17, 19, 25; 13:1, 3, 5, 6, 19, 22, 24, 29, 36; 14:8, 9, 11, 18, 19, 21^2, 23^2, 24, 25, 26, 27^3; 15:2, 4, 7, 12, 13, 30, 31, 33; 16:6, 10^2, 23, 27, 34, 40; 17:1, 9, 13; 18:2, 18, 22, 23, 26, 27; 19:6, 13, 21, 35, 41; 20:2^2, 11, 13, 16, 36; 21:1, 3, 5, 6, 7, 9, 19^2, 29^2, 33, 40; 22:29; 23:7, 12, 13, 30, 34; 24:10, 19; 25:6, 12, 14, 19, 21, 25, 26; 26:30, 32; 27:4, 5, 7, 13, 16, 17, 28, 30, 35^2, 38, 40; 28:3, 6, 9, 11, 18, 19, 23, 25, 29^2

Ro 1:2; 4:11, 12, 21; 5:14; 6:21; 7:7^3; 9:10, 23, 29^2

1Co 1:15; 2:8; 7:29; 11:24, 25; 14:19

2Co 1:9, 12; 2:13; 3:10; 7:5, 12; 8:6, 15^4; 9:5; 11:21

Gal 1:23; 2:2; 3:21; 4:15, 22

Eph 2:3

Php 2:26^2, 27; 3:12

1Th 1:9; 2:2

2Th 2:12

Tit 1:5

Heb 1:3; 2:14; 3:16, 17; 4:8; 5:7; 6:15; 7:6; 8:7; 9:1, 4^2, 19; 10:2, 6, 12, 15, 34; 11:5^2, 11, 15^2, 17, 26, 31, 36; 12:9

Jas 2:21, 25^2

1Pt 2:10

2Pt 2:21

1Jn 2:7, 19

2Jn 5

3Jn 13

Rev 1:16; 4:4, 7, 8; 5:6, 8; 6:2, 3, 5^2, 7, 9, 12; 8:1, 6, 9; 9:8, 9, 10, 11, 14, 19; 10:2, 3, 4, 10; 13:11, 14^2, 15, 17; 14:18^2; 15:2; 16:2; 17:1; 18:19; 19:12, 20; 20:4^2; 21:9, 12^2, 14, 15, 23; 22:8

HAST

Gen 3:11, 13, 14, 17^2; 4:10, 14; 12:18; 15:3; 18:5; 19:12^2, 19^2, 21; 20:3, 9^3, 10; 21:23, 29; 22:12, 16^2, 18; 24:14^2; 26:10; 27:20, 36, 38, 45; 29:25^2; 30:15; 31:26^2, 28^2, 30, 36, 37^2, 41; 32:10, 28^2; 33:9; 37:10; 38:23, 29; 39:17; 45:10, 11; 47:25, 30

Ex 3:12; 4:10; 5:22^2, 23; 9:19; 10:29; 12:44; 13:12; 14:11^2; 15:7, 13^3, 16, 17; 17:3; 20:25; 23:16^2; 29:36; 32:11, 21, 32; 33:1, 12^3, 17^2

Nu 5:19, 20; 11:11, 21; 14:17, 19; 16:13, 14; 22:28, 29, 30, 32; 23:11^2; 24:10; 27:13

Dt 1:14, 31; 2:7; 3:24; 4:33; 8:10, 12^2, 13; 9:2, 12, 26^2; 12:26; 13:2, 6; 16:13; 17:4; 21:8, 10, 11, 14; 22:3, 9; 23:23^2; 24:19; 26:10, 12^2, 13, 14, 15, 17; 28:20; 32:18

Jos 2:17, 20; 7:7, 19, 25; 14:9; 15:19; 17:14, 17

Jdg 1:15; 5:21; 6:36, 37; 8:1, 22; 9:38; 11:12, 35, 36; 14:16^2; 15:11, 18; 16:10, 13, 15^2; 18:3

Ru 2:11^2, 13^2, 19; 3:10, 15

1Sa 1:17; 4:20; 12:4^2; 13:11, 13^2, 14; 14:43; 15:23, 26; 17:28, 45; 19:17; 20:8, 19, 30; 22:13^2; 24:17, 18^2, 19; 25:6, 7, 31, 33; 26:15, 16; 28:12, 15; 29:4, 6, 8

2Sa 1:26; 3:7, 24^2; 6:22; 7:18, 19, 21, 24, 25^2, 27, 28, 29; 11:19; 12:9^4, 10^2, 14, 21; 14:13; 15:35; 16:8, 10; 18:21, 22; 19:5, 6; 22:36, 37, 40^2, 41, 44^2, 49^2

1Ki 1:6, 11, 24, 27; 2:8, 26, 43; 3:6^3, 7, 8, 11^5, 13; 8:24^2, 25, 29, 36, 44, 48; 9:3^2, 13; 11:11, 22; 13:21^2, 22; 14:8, 9^3; 16:2^2; 17:13, 20; 18:18, 37; 20:13, 25, 36, 40, 42; 21:19, 20^2, 22

2Ki 1:16; 2:10; 4:2, 13; 5:8; 6:22; 9:18, 19; 10:30^2; 14:10; 17:26; 19:6, 11, 15, 20, 22^2, 23^2, 25; 20:19; 22:18, 19^2; 23:17

1Ch 17:8, 16, 17^2, 19, 21, 23^2, 25, 26; 22:8^3; 28:3^2, 20; 29:17

2Ch 1:8^2, 9, 11^3; 6:15^3, 16^2, 17, 20, 27^2, 34, 38; 16:7, 9; 19:3^2; 20:11, 37; 21:12, 13^3; 24:6; 25:15, 16^2, 19; 26:18; 34:26

Ezr 9:11, 13^2; 10:12

Neh 1:10; 6:7; 9:6, 8, 33, 37

Est 6:10^2, 13

Job 1:8, 10^2; 2:3; 4:3^2, 4; 7:20; 10:4, 9, 10, 11^2, 12, 13, 18; 11:4; 14:5; 15:8; 16:7, 8; 17:4; 22:6, 7^2, 9, 15; 26:2, 3^2, 4; 33:8, 32; 34:16; 36:17, 21, 23; 37:18; 38:4, 12, 16^2, 17, 18, 22^2; 39:19^2; 40:9

Ps 3:7^2; 4:1, 7; 7:6; 8:1, 2, 3, 5^2, 6; 9:4, 5^3, 6, 10; 10:14, 17; 16:2; 17:3^3; 18:35, 36, 39^2, 40, 43^2, 48; 21:2^2, 5, 6^2; 22:1, 15, 21; 27:9; 30:1^2, 2, 3^2, 7, 11^2; 31:5, 7^2, 8^2, 19^2; 35:22; 39:5; 40:5, 6^2; 42:9; 44:7^2, 9, 11^2, 19; 50:16, 18, 21; 51:8; 52:9; 53:5; 56:13; 59:16; 60:1^3, 2^2, 3^2, 4; 61:3, 5^2;

63:7; 65:9; 66:10^2, 12; 68:10, 18^3, 28; 69:19, 26^2; 71:3, 17, 19, 20, 23; 73:23, 27; 74:1, 2^3, 16, 17^2; 77:14, 15; 80:8^2, 12; 85:1^2, 2^2, 3^2; 86:9, 13, 17; 88:6, 7, 8^2, 18; 89:10^2, 11, 12, 13, 38^2, 39^2, 40^2, 42^2, 43^2, 44, 45^2, 47; 90:1, 8, 15; 91:9; 92:4; 102:10, 25; 104:8, 9, 24, 26; 108:11; 109:27; 110:3; 116:8, 16; 118:13, 21; 119:4, 21, 49, 65, 75, 90, 93, 98, 102, 118, 138, 152, 171; 137:8; 138:2; 139:1, 5, 13^2; 140:7

Prv 3:28; 6:1; 22:27; 23:8; 24:14; 25:16; 30:32^2

Ecc 5:4; 7:22

Song 1:15; 4:1, 9^2

Isa 2:6; 3:6; 9:3, 4; 14:13, 20; 17:10^2; 22:16^3; 23:16; 25:1, 2, 4; 26:12, 14, 15^2; 37:6, 11, 16, 21, 23^2, 24^2, 26; 38:17^2; 39:8; 40:28^2; 43:4, 22^2, 23^2, 24^4; 45:4, 5, 10; 47:6, 10^3, 12, 15; 48:6; 49:20; 51:13, 17^2, 23; 57:6^2, 7, 8^3, 10, 11^3; 60:15; 62:8; 63:17; 64:7^2

Jer 1:12; 2:17^2, 18^2, 19, 23, 27, 28, 33; 3:1, 2^3, 5, 6, 13^2; 4:10, 19; 5:3^2; 12:2, 3, 5; 13:4, 21, 25; 14:19^2, 22; 15:6, 10, 17; 20:6, 7^2; 26:9; 28:6, 13, 16; 29:25, 27; 30:13; 31:18; 32:17, 20^2, 21, 22, 23, 24, 25; 36:6, 14, 29^2; 38:25; 39:18; 44:16; 48:7; 50:24; 51:62, 63

Lam 1:21^2, 22; 2:20, 21^2, 22; 3:17, 42, 43^3, 44, 45, 56, 58^2, 59, 60, 61; 5:22

Ezk 3:19, 20, 21; 4:6, 8; 5:11; 8:12, 15, 17; 9:11; 16:7, 17, 18, 19, 20^3, 21, 22, 24^2, 25^3, 26^2, 28^2, 29, 31, 37^3, 43^2, 47, 48, 51^3, 52^3, 54, 58, 59^2, 63; 22:4^4, 8^2, 12^3, 13; 23:30, 31, 35, 41; 25:6; 27:3; 28:2, 4^2, 5, 6, 13, 14, 16, 17, 18; 31:10; 32:9; 33:9; 35:5^2, 6, 10, 11, 12; 36:13; 38:13; 43:23; 47:6

Dan 2:23^3; 3:10, 12^2, 18; 5:22, 23^3; 6:12, 13; 9:7, 15^2; 10:19

Hos 4:6^2; 9:1^2; 10:9; 13:9; 14:1

Oba 15

Jna 1:10, 14; 2:6; 4:10^2

Mic 7:20

Nah 3:16

Hab 1:12^2; 2:8, 10^2

Zep 3:11

Zec 1:12

Mal 1:2; 2:14

Mt 5:26; 6:6; 8:13; 11:25^2; 17:27; 18:15; 19:21; 20:12; 21:16; 25:21, 23, 24^2, 25; 26:25, 64; 27:46

Mk 10:21; 12:32; 15:34

Lk 1:4, 30; 2:31, 48; 7:43; 10:21^2, 28; 11:27; 12:19, 20, 59; 13:26; 14:22; 15:30; 18:22; 19:17; 20:39; 24:18

Jn 2:10; 4:11^2, 17, 18^2; 6:68; 7:20; 8:48, 52, 57; 9:37; 11:41, 42; 13:8, 38; 14:9; 17:2^2, 3, 7, 9, 11, 18, 21, 23^3, 24^2, 25, 26; 18:35; 20:15, 29^2

Act 1:24; 2:28; 4:24, 25, 27; 5:4^2; 8:20, 21; 10:33; 22:15; 23:11, 19, 22; 24:10; 25:12; 26:16

Ro 2:20; 9:20; 14:22

1Co 4:7; 7:28; 8:10

Col 4:17

1Ti 4:6; 6:12

2Ti 1:13; 2:2; 3:10, 14^3, 15

Phlm 5

Heb 1:9, 10; 2:8; 10:5, 6

Jas 2:18

Rev 1:19; 2:2^2, 3^4, 4, 6, 13, 14, 15; 3:1, 3, 4, 8^3, 10, 11; 4:11; 5:9, 10; 11:17^2; 16:5, 6

HATH

Gen 1:20; 3:1, 3; 4:11, 25; 5:29; 14:20; 16:2, 11; 17:14; 18:19; 19:13, 19; 21:6, 12, 17, 26; 22:20; 23:9; 24:27, 35^2, 36^2, 44, 51, 56; 26:22; 27:27, 33, 35, 36^2; 29:32, 33^2; 30:2, 6^3, 18, 20, 23, 27, 30; 31:1^2, 5, 7, 9, 15^2, 16^2, 42; 33:5, 11; 37:20, 33; 38:24, 26; 39:8^2, 9, 14; 41:25, 39, 51, 52; 42:28; 43:23; 44:16; 45:6, 8, 9; 46:32, 34; 47:18; 48:9, 11

Ex 3:13, 14, 15, 18; 4:1, 5, 11; 5:3, 23; 7:16; 9:18; 10:12; 12:25; 13:9; 14:3; 15:1^2, 4, 6, 21^2; 16:6, 9, 15, 16, 23, 29; 17:16; 18:10^2; 19:8; 21:8^2, 29^3, 36^2; 22:11; 24:3, 7, 8; 32:24, 33; 35:1, 10, 30, 31, 34, 35

Lev 4:3, 22, 23, 28^2, 35; 5:1, 5, 6, 7, 10, 13, 16, 19; 6:2, 4^2, 5, 7, 10; 7:8; 8:34^2; 10:6, 11, 15, 17; 11:9, 12, 42; 12:7; 13:4, 7, 12, 13, 17, 31, 33, 41, 50; 14:43^2, 48; 15:2, 4, 6, 7, 8, 9, 11^2, 12, 13, 32, 33; 16:20; 17:2, 4; 19:8, 22^2; 20:3, 9, 11, 17, 18^2, 20, 21, 27; 21:3, 17, 18^2, 20^2, 21^2, 23; 22:4, 5, 6, 20, 23; 24:14, 19, 20; 25:25, 28; 27:22, 28

Nu 5:2, 7, 27; 6:9, 21; 10:29; 12:2^2; 14:3, 16, 24, 40; 15:22, 23, 31^2; 16:5, 9, 10, 28, 29; 19:2, 15, 20^2; 20:14, 16; 21:28, 29; 22:10; 23:7, 8^2, 12, 17, 19^2, 20, 21^2, 22, 23; 24:3^2, 4, 6, 8, 11, 15^2, 16; 25:11; 27:4; 30:1, 4^2, 5, 12^2, 15; 31:17, 19^2, 50; 32:7, 21, 24, 31; 36:5

Dt 1:10, 11, 21^2, 27, 36^2; 2:7^2; 3:18, 20, 21; 4:3, 7, 8, 19, 20, 23, 32^2, 34; 5:12, 16, 24, 26, 32, 33; 6:3, 17, 19, 20, 25; 7:1, 6, 8; 8:10, 17; 9:3, 4^2, 28; 10:9, 21, 22; 11:4, 25, 29; 12:7, 12, 15, 20, 21^2; 13:5, 10, 12, 17; 14:2, 10, 24, 27, 29; 15:14, 18; 16:10, 11, 17; 17:2, 3, 16; 18:2, 5, 14, 21, 22^2; 19:1, 8, 18; 20:5^2, 6^2, 7^2, 13, 14, 17; 21:1, 3^2, 5, 10, 16, 17; 22:3, 17, 19, 21, 24, 29; 23:1; 24:1^2, 5^2; 25:10, 19; 26:9^2, 11, 16, 18^2, 19^2; 27:3; 28:9, 52, 53, 55; 29:4, 13^2, 22, 24; 30:1, 3; 31:2, 3, 7; 32:6^2, 27

Jos 1:13^2, 15; 2:9, 14, 24; 6:16, 22; 7:11, 15^3; 8:31; 10:4, 19; 14:10; 17:14; 18:3; 22:4, 25; 23:3^2, 5, 9^2, 10, 13, 14^2, 15, 16; 24:20, 27

Jdg 1:7; 2:20; 3:28; 4:6, 14; 6:13, 25, 29^2, 30^2, 31, 32; 7:2, 14, 15; 8:3, 7; 11:23, 36^2; 13:10; 15:6, 10; 16:17, 18, 23, 24; 18:4, 10; 21:11

Ru 1:20, 21^3; 2:7, 11, 20; 4:14, 15

1Sa 1:27; 2:5^2, 8; 3:17; 4:3, 7, 17; 6:7, 9; 7:12; 9:24; 10:1, 2, 22, 24; 11:13; 12:13, 22, 24; 13:14^2; 14:10, 12, 29, 38, 45^2; 15:11, 16, 22, 23, 26, 28^2, 33; 16:8, 9, 10, 22; 17:36; 18:7, 22; 19:4; 20:13, 15, 22, 26, 29^2, 32; 21:2^2, 11; 22:8^2; 23:7^2, 10, 11, 22; 25:21^2, 26, 27, 28, 30, 31, 34, 39^3; 26:8; 27:12; 28:7^2, 9^2, 17^2, 18, 21; 29:3; 30:23^2

2Sa 1:16; 3:9, 18, 23, 29; 4:8, 9; 5:20; 6:12; 7:27; 9:3, 11; 10:3^2; 12:5, 13; 13:20, 24, 30, 32; 14:19, 20, 22, 30; 15:4; 16:8^2, 10, 11, 21; 17:6, 7, 21; 18:19, 28, 31; 19:27, 42; 20:21; 22:21, 25, 36; 23:5

1Ki 1:19^3, 25^2, 26, 29, 37, 43, 44, 48, 51; 2:24^2, 31, 38; 5:4, 7; 8:15, 20, 56^2; 9:8, 9; 12:11; 13:3, 26^2; 14:11; 16:16^2; 18:10; 19:18; 22:23^2, 28

2Ki 1:9, 11; 2:2, 4, 6, 16; 3:7, 10, 13; 4:2, 14, 27^2; 5:20, 22; 6:29, 32; 7:6; 8:1, 4, 9, 10, 13; 10:10; 14:10; 17:26; 18:22^2, 27^2, 33; 19:4^2, 16, 21^3; 20:9; 21:11^3; 22:10, 16

1Ch 14:11; 15:2; 16:12, 17; 17:25; 19:3; 22:11, 18^2; 23:25; 28:4, 5^2, 10; 29:1

2Ch 2:11^2, 12, 15; 6:1, 4, 10^2; 7:21, 22; 8:11; 13:6; 14:7; 15:3; 18:22^2, 27; 20:37; 23:3; 24:20; 25:8, 16; 28:9; 29:8, 11; 30:8; 31:10; 32:12; 34:18; 36:23^2

Ezr 1:2^2; 4:3, 18, 19^2; 5:3, 16; 6:12; 7:27, 28; 9:2, 8, 9^2

Neh 9:32

Est 1:15, 16; 5:5, 8; 6:3

Job 1:10, 11, 12, 16, 21; 2:4; 3:23; 5:16; 6:5; 7:8; 9:4^2; 10:12; 12:9, 13; 13:1^2; 16:7, 11, 12^2; 17:6, 9; 19:6^2, 8^2, 9, 10^2, 11, 13, 21; 20:15, 19^3; 21:21, 31; 23:10, 11, 17; 26:2, 3, 6, 10, 13^2; 27:2^2, 8; 28:6, 7; 30:11, 19; 31:5, 7^2, 17, 27^2; 32:14, 19; 33:2, 4^2; 34:5^2, 9, 13^2, 35; 35:15; 36:23; 38:5^2, 25, 28^2, 29, 36^2; 39:5^2, 17^2; 41:11; 42:7

Ps 2:7; 4:3; 5:4; 6:8, 9; 7:12, 13, 14; 9:7; 10:6, 11^2, 13; 13:6; 14:1; 16:7; 18:20, 24, 35^2; 19:4; 22:24^2, 31; 24:2, 4^2; 28:6; 31:21; 33:12; 35:8, 21, 27; 36:3; 37:16; 40:3; 41:9; 44:15; 45:2, 7; 46:8; 50:1, 2; 53:1, 5^2; 54:7^2; 55:5, 18, 20^2; 60:6; 62:11; 66:14, 16, 19^2, 20; 68:10, 28; 69:7, 9, 20, 31; 71:11; 72:12; 74:3, 18; 77:9^2; 78:4, 69; 80:15; 84:3; 88:4; 91:14^2; 93:1; 98:1^2, 2^2, 3; 100:3; 101:5; 102:19; 103:10, 12, 19; 104:16; 105:5, 8; 107:2, 16; 108:7; 109:11; 110:4; 111:4, 5, 6, 9; 112:9^2; 115:3^2, 12, 16; 116:1, 2, 7; 118:18^2, 24, 27; 119:20, 50, 53, 139, 167; 120:6; 124:6; 126:2, 3; 127:5; 129:4; 132:11, 13^2; 135:4; 136:24; 138:6; 143:3^3; 146:5; 147:13^2, 20; 148:6^2; 150:6

Prv 3:19^2; 7:20, 26; 9:1^2, 2^3, 3; 10:13, 23; 12:9; 13:4, 7^2; 14:20, 21, 31, 32, 33; 15:14, 15, 23; 16:4, 22; 17:8, 16, 20^2, 21, 24, 27; 18:2, 24; 19:17^2, 23, 25; 20:12; 22:9; 23:6, 29^6; 24:29; 25:8, 28; 28:11, 22; 30:4^4, 15

Ecc 1:3, 9, 10, 13; 2:12, 21, 22^2; 3:9, 10, 11^2, 15^2, 19; 4:3^2, 8, 10; 5:4, 16^2, 17, 19^2; 6:2, 5^2, 6, 8^2, 10; 7:13, 14, 29; 8:8^2, 15; 9:9; 10:20

Song 1:4, 6; 3:8; 8:6, 8

Isa 1:2, 12, 20, 30; 5:1, 14, 25^2; 6:7; 8:18; 9:2, 8; 10:10, 12, 14, 28; 12:5; 14:4, 5, 9, 24, 27, 32; 16:13, 14; 19:12, 14, 17; 20:3; 21:4, 6, 9, 16, 17; 22:25; 23:4, 8, 9, 11; 24:3, 6; 25:8; 27:7; 28:2, 25; 29:4, 8, 10^3; 30:24, 33; 31:4; 33:5, 8^2, 14; 34:2^2, 6, 16^2, 17^2; 36:7, 12^2, 18; 37:4^2, 17, 22^3; 38:7, 15^2; 40:2, 5, 12, 13^2, 20, 21, 26; 41:4, 20^2, 26; 42:25^2; 43:27; 44:10, 18, 20, 23^2; 45:9, 18, 21^2; 47:10; 48:5^2, 13^2, 14^2, 16, 20; 49:1^2, 2^3, 10, 13, 14^2, 21^2; 50:4, 5, 10; 51:9, 10^2, 13, 18^2; 52:9^2, 10; 53:1, 2, 4, 6, 10, 12; 54:6, 10; 55:1, 5; 56:3^2; 58:14; 59:3; 60:9; 61:1^2, 9, 10^2; 62:8, 11; 63:7^2; 64:4^2; 65:20; 66:2, 8^2

Jer 2:11, 30, 37; 3:3, 6^2, 10, 11, 24; 4:17, 27; 5:23; 6:6, 24, 30; 7:29; 8:14, 21; 9:12; 10:12^3; 11:15^2, 16, 17, 18; 13:15; 14:19; 15:9^3; 16:10; 18:13^2, 15; 20:3, 13; 22:8, 21; 23:9, 17, 18^3, 28^2, 35^2, 37^2; 25:3, 4, 5, 13, 31, 36, 38; 26:11, 13, 15, 16; 27:13; 28:9, 15; 29:15, 26, 31, 32; 31:3, 11, 22; 32:31; 33:24^2; 34:14^2; 35:8, 16, 18; 36:7, 28; 38:21; 40:2, 3^2, 5, 14; 42:18, 19, 21; 43:2; 45:3; 46:10, 12^2, 17; 47:7^2; 48:8, 11^4, 36, 39, 42; 49:1^2, 16, 20^2, 24, 30^2; 50:6, 14, 15^2, 17^2, 25^2, 29^2, 43, 45^2; 51:5, 7, 10, 11, 12, 14, 15^3, 30, 34^6, 44, 49, 51, 55

Lam 1:2, 5, 8, 9, 10^2, 12, 13^4, 14^2, 15^3, 17; 2:1, 2^5, 3^2, 4, 5^4, 6^4, 7^3, 8^3, 9, 17^6, 22; 3:1, 2, 4^2, 5, 6, 7^2, 9^2, 11^2, 12, 13, 15^2, 16^2, 20, 28; 4:11^4, 16

Ezk 2:3, 5; 3:20; 4:14; 5:6; 6:9; 7:10^2; 8:12; 9:9; 12:9; 13:6; 14:9; 15:5; 16:48, 51; 17:12, 13^3, 18, 19^2, 20; 18:6^4, 7^5, 8^4, 9^2, 11, 12^5, 13^3, 14, 15^3, 16^5, 17^4, 19^3, 21, 22^2, 24^3, 26, 27, 28; 19:14^2; 21:11; 22:11^3, 13, 28; 24:12, 24; 25:12^2; 26:2; 27:26; 29:3, 9; 31:10; 33:13, 16^2, 32, 33; 36:2; 44:2, 25

Dan 1:10; 2:27, 37, 38^2, 45; 3:5, 28; 4:2; 5:26; 6:22^2, 27; 9:12^3, 14; 11:12

Hos 1:2; 2:5^2, 12; 4:1, 12, 19; 5:6; 6:1^2, 11; 7:4, 8, 12; 8:3, 5, 7, 9, 11, 14^2; 10:1; 12:2; 13:16

Joel 1:2, 4^6, 6, 7^2, 19^2, 20; 2:2, 20, 23, 25, 26, 32; 3:8

Am 3:1, 4, 6, 8^2; 4:2; 6:8; 7:1, 4, 10; 8:1, 7; 9:6

Oba 3, 18

Jna 1:9

Mic 2:4^3; 4:4; 5:1, 3; 6:2, 8, 9

Nah 1:3, 14; 2:2; 3:19

Hab 2:18

Zep 1:7^2; 3:15^2

Hag 2:19

Zec 1:2, 6, 10; 2:8, 9, 11; 3:2; 4:9, 10; 6:15; 7:7, 12; 10:3^2; 13:4

Mal 1:4, 9, 14; 2:10, 11^3, 14

Mt 3:7; 5:23, 28, 31, 33, 38, 43; 8:20; 9:6, 22; 11:11, 15, 18; 13:9, 12^3, 21, 27, 28, 43, 44^2, 54, 56; 15:13; 16:17; 19:6, 29; 20:7; 21:3; 24:45; 25:28, 29^3; 26:10, 12, 13, 65; 27:23

Mk 2:10; 3:22, 26, 29, 30; 4:9, 25^3; 5:19^2, 34; 6:2; 7:6, 37; 9:17, 22; 10:9, 29, 52; 11:3; 12:43; 13:20^2; 14:6, 8, 9; 15:14

Lk 1:25, 36, 47, 48, 49, 51^2, 52, 53^2, 54, 68, 69, 78; 2:15; 3:7, 11^3; 4:18^2; 5:24; 7:5, 16, 20, 33, 44, 45, 46, 50; 8:8, 16, 18^2, 39, 46, 48; 9:58; 10:40, 42; 11:33; 12:5^2, 44; 13:16, 25; 14:29, 33, 35; 15:5, 9, 27^2, 30; 17:19; 18:29, 42; 19:16, 18, 24, 25, 26^3, 31, 34; 20:24; 21:3, 4; 22:29, 31, 36^2; 23:22, 41; 24:34, 39

Jn 1:18^2; 2:17; 3:13, 18, 29, 32, 33^2, 34, 35, 36; 4:33, 44; 5:22, 23, 24, 26^2, 27, 30, 36^2, 37^2, 38; 6:9, 27, 29, 39^2, 44, 45^2, 46^2, 47, 54, 57; 7:29, 31, 38, 42; 8:10, 28, 29, 37, 40; 9:3, 17, 21, 30; 10:20, 21, 36; 11:39; 12:7, 38^2, 40, 48; 13:18; 14:9^2, 21, 30; 15:9, 13; 16:6, 15, 21; 17:14, 25; 18:11; 19:11; 20:21

Act 1:7; 2:24, 32, 33, 36; 3:13, 15, 16^2, 18, 21; 4:16; 5:3, 31, 32; 7:50; 9:12, 13, 14, 17; 10:15, 28; 11:8, 9, 18; 12:11^2; 13:23, 33^2, 47; 15:14, 21; 17:7, 26^2, 31^4; 19:26; 20:28^2; 21:28; 22:14; 23:9, 17, 18; 24:6; 25:25; 27:24; 28:4

Ro 1:19; 3:1, 7, 25; 4:1, 2; 5:15, 21; 6:9; 7:1, 2; 8:2, 20; 9:6, 18, 19, 21, 24, 31; 10:9, 16; 11:1, 2, 7^2, 8, 32, 34^2, 35; 12:3; 13:8; 14:3; 15:18, 26, 27; 16:2^2

1Co 1:11, 20, 27^2, 28; 2:9^2, 10, 16; 3:14; 4:9; 5:2, 3; 6:14; 7:4^2, 7, 12, 13, 15, 17^2, 25, 28, 37^2; 9:14; 10:13; 12:12, 18^2, 24, 28; 14:26^5; 15:25, 27, 38; 16:2

2Co 1:21, 22; 2:5; 3:6; 4:4, 6; 5:5^2, 10, 18^2, 19, 21; 6:14^2, 15^2, 16^2; 7:8; 8:12^2; 9:2, 9^2; 10:8, 13; 13:10

Gal 3:1^2, 13, 22; 4:6, 27^2; 5:1

Eph 1:3, 4, 6, 8, 9, 22; 2:1, 5, 6, 10, 14^2; 3:9; 4:32; 5:2^2, 5

Php 1:6; 2:9, 22; 3:4; 4:10

Col 1:12, 13^2, 21, 26; 2:12, 13, 18; 3:25; 4:13

1Th 2:12; 4:7, 8; 5:9

2Th 2:13, 16^2

1Ti 1:12; 4:3; 5:8; 6:16^2

2Ti 1:7, 9, 10^2; 2:4; 4:10, 15

Tit 1:3, 9; 2:11

Phlm 18

Heb 1:2^2, 4, 9; 2:5, 13, 18; 3:3^2; 4:10; 7:24; 8:6, 13; 9:20, 26; 10:14, 20, 29^3, 30, 35; 11:10, 16; 12:26; 13:5

Jas 1:12, 15; 2:5^2, 13, 14, 17; 3:7; 5:7

1Pt 1:3, 15; 2:9; 3:18; 4:1^3, 10; 5:10

2Pt 1:3^2, 9, 14; 3:15

1Jn 2:11, 23^2, 25, 27; 3:1, 3, 6, 15, 17, 24; 4:12, 13, 16, 18, 20^2; 5:9, 10^2, 11, 12^4, 20

2Jn 9^2

3Jn 11, 12

Jude 6

Rev 1:6; 2:7, 11, 12, 17, 18, 29; 3:1, 6, 7, 13, 22; 5:5; 9:11; 10:7; 12:6, 12; 13:18; 16:9; 17:7, 9, 17; 18:5, 6, 7, 20; 19:2^2, 7, 16; 20:6^2

HAVE

Gen 1:26, 28, 29, 30; 4:1, 20, 23; 6:7^2; 7:1, 4; 8:21; 9:3, 17; 11:6^2; 12:19; 14:22, 23, 24; 15:18; 16:5, 13; 17:5, 20^2; 18:3, 10, 12, 14, 21, 27, 31; 19:8^2, 21; 20:5, 9, 16; 21:7^3, 23, 30; 22:16; 24:19, 25, 31, 33; 26:10^2, 27, 29^3, 32; 27:19, 33^2, 37^3, 40; 28:15^2, 22; 29:34; 30:3, 8^2, 16, 18, 20, 26^2, 27^2, 29; 31:6, 12, 27, 38^3, 41, 43, 51; 32:4, 5^2, 30; 33:9, 10^2, 11; 34:30; 35:17; 37:6, 8, 9, 32; 40:8, 15; 41:15^2, 28, 41; 42:2, 36; 43:7, 21, 22; 44:4, 5, 15, 19, 20; 45:13; 46:30, 32^2; 47:1, 4, 9^2, 23, 26, 29; 48:22; 49:18, 23, 26; 50:4, 5

Ex 1:18^2; 2:20, 22; 3:7^2, 9, 12, 16, 17; 4:11, 21; 5:14, 21; 6:4, 5^2, 12; 7:1; 9:16, 27; 10:1, 2^2, 6, 16; 12:17, 31, 32; 14:5^2, 13, 18; 15:5, 17, 26; 16:3, 12, 32; 17:16; 18:3, 16; 19:4; 20:2, 3, 22^2; 21:4^2, 8, 9, 31^2; 22:3, 8; 23:13, 20; 24:12, 14; 26:2; 28:3, 7, 32; 29:35; 31:2, 3, 6^3, 11; 32:7, 8^5, 9, 13, 30, 31^2, 34; 33:13, 16; 34:9, 10, 27

Lev 4:13, 14; 6:3, 17; 7:7, 8, 10, 33, 34^2; 10:17, 18, 19^3; 11:10, 11, 13, 21, 23; 12:2; 13:2, 10, 13, 24, 29, 38, 55; 15:19, 25; 16:4, 17; 17:7, 11; 18:27; 19:23, 31, 36; 20:6, 12, 13, 24^2, 25, 26; 22:13; 23:7, 14, 24, 39; 24:22; 25:26, 31, 44; 26:9, 13, 26, 37, 40, 41^2; 27:20

Nu 3:12, 32; 4:15; 5:7, 8, 18, 19, 20, 27; 8:16, 18, 19; 9:14; 11:11, 12^2, 13, 15, 18, 20^2; 12:11^2; 13:32; 14:11, 14, 15, 20, 22^3, 27, 28, 29, 31, 35, 40; 15:22, 29; 16:15^2, 28, 30, 41; 18:6, 7, 8^2, 11, 12, 19, 20^2, 21, 23, 24^3, 26, 30, 32; 20:4, 5, 12, 15, 17, 24; 21:5, 7^2, 30^2, 34; 22:28, 34, 38; 23:4^2, 20; 24:19; 25:13, 18; 27:8, 9, 10, 11, 12, 17; 28:25, 26; 29:1, 7, 12, 35; 30:9; 31:15, 18, 49, 50; 32:4, 5, 11, 12, 17, 18, 23, 30; 33:53; 34:6, 14^2, 15; 35:3, 8^2, 13, 22, 28

Dt 1:6, 8, 28^2, 41; 2:3, 5, 9, 19, 24, 31; 3:19^2, 20^2, 21; 4:3, 5, 9, 25; 5:7, 24^2, 26, 28^4; 6:10, 11; 7:16, 24; 9:7, 8, 12^2, 13, 20, 23, 24; 10:21; 11:2^2, 7, 28; 12:21, 31^2; 13:13^2, 17; 14:9; 15:21; 17:3, 5; 18:1, 2, 8, 17^2, 20; 19:14, 19; 20:9, 18; 21:7^2, 11, 14, 15^2, 18^2, 22; 23:12, 13; 25:5, 13, 14, 15^2; 26:10, 13^4, 14^4; 28:21, 31, 36, 40, 48, 51, 64, 65, 66; 29:2, 3, 5, 6^2, 16, 17, 19, 25; 30:1, 3, 15, 19; 31:5, 13, 16, 18, 20^2, 21, 27, 29; 32:5, 21^2; 33:9^2; 34:4

Jos 1:3, 8, 9, 15^2; 2:10, 12, 13; 3:4; 5:9; 6:2; 7:11^4, 20^2; 8:1, 6, 8^2; 9:9, 19, 22, 24; 10:8; 11:20; 13:6, 8; 14:9; 17:16, 17, 18; 18:7^2; 22:2^2, 3^2, 11, 16^2, 23, 24^2, 25, 27, 31^2; 23:3, 4^2, 8, 15, 16^2; 24:7^2, 13, 22

Jdg 1:2, 7; 2:1, 2^2, 20; 3:19, 20; 5:13^2, 30^2; 6:10, 14, 17, 22; 7:9; 8:2; 9:16^4, 18^2, 19, 48^2; 10:10^2, 13, 14, 15; 11:27, 35; 13:15, 22, 23^3; 14:2, 6, 15^2, 16; 15:7, 11, 16; 16:17; 17:13; 18:9, 14, 24^2; 20:5^2, 6, 10; 21:7, 18

Ru 1:8, 12^3; 2:9^2, 10, 21; 3:3, 18; 4:9, 10

1Sa 1:15^2, 16, 20, 23, 28; 2:5, 15, 29; 3:12, 13, 14; 4:9; 5:10; 6:21; 7:6; 8:7^2, 8^2, 18, 19; 9:7, 8, 16, 24; 10:19^2; 11:9; 12:1^2, 2, 3^5, 5, 10^3, 13^2, 17, 19, 20; 13:12, 13; 14:29, 33; 15:3, 11, 13, 15^2, 20^4, 21, 24^2, 30; 16:1^2, 7, 18; 17:25, 29, 39; 18:8^3, 19; 19:4; 20:1, 3, 7, 12, 23, 29, 42; 21:2^2, 4, 5, 8, 14, 15^2; 22:8, 13, 22; 23:21, 27; 24:10, 11, 17; 25:7, 11, 21, 30^2, 31, 35^2; 26:16, 18, 19^2, 21^3; 27:5, 10; 28:9, 15, 21^2, 22; 29:3, 6, 8^2, 9, 10; 30:22

2Sa 1:10, 16; 2:5^2, 6, 7; 3:8; 4:6, 10^2, 11; 7:6^2, 7, 9^2, 11, 22; 9:9, 10; 12:8, 13, 27^2; 13:9, 28, 32; 14:15, 21, 22, 29, 31, 32; 15:7, 26, 34, 36; 16:10, 19; 17:15; 18:11, 13^2, 18; 19:5, 20, 22, 28, 29, 34, 41^2, 42, 43^2; 20:1^2; 21:4, 16; 22:22^2, 24, 30^2, 38, 39; 24:10^3, 17^3

1Ki 1:35, 44, 45^2; 2:14, 23, 42, 43; 3:12^2, 13; 5:8; 8:13, 20, 21, 27, 28, 33, 35, 43, 44, 47^3, 48, 50^3, 59; 9:3^2, 4, 6, 7^2, 9^2; 11:11, 13, 32^2, 33^3, 36^2; 12:9, 16^2; 14:15; 15:19; 17:4, 9, 12, 18; 18:9, 18^2, 36; 19:10^2, 14^2, 18^2, 20; 20:4, 5, 28, 31; 21:2, 20; 22:11, 17^2

2Ki 2:21; 3:13, 23, 27; 5:6, 13; 7:12, 17; 9:3, 5, 6, 12, 26; 10:8, 19, 24; 11:15; 13:17, 19; 17:38; 18:14, 20, 34, 35; 19:6, 11, 12^2, 17, 18^2, 20, 24^2, 25^3; 20:3^2, 5^2, 9, 15^3, 17; 21:7, 8, 15^2; 22:4, 5, 8, 9^3, 13, 17^2, 19; 23:27^2

1Ch 11:19; 15:12; 17:5^2, 6^2, 8^3, 20; 21:8^3, 17^2; 22:14^2; 28:6; 29:2, 3^4, 14, 16, 17^2, 19

2Ch 1:11, 12^3; 2:13; 6:2, 6^2, 10, 11, 18, 19, 24, 26, 33, 34, 37^3, 38^2, 39; 7:12^2, 16, 17, 18, 19, 20^2; 10:9, 16^2; 12:5^2, 7; 13:7, 9^2, 10, 11; 14:7^2, 11; 16:3, 9; 18:16^2; 20:8, 12; 21:15; 23:14; 24:20; 25:9; 28:9, 11, 13; 29:6^3, 7^2, 9, 18, 19, 31; 31:10^2; 32:13, 17; 33:7, 8^2; 34:15, 17^2, 21, 24, 25^2, 27; 35:21^2, 23

Ezr 4:3, 12, 14^2, 15, 16, 19, 20^2; 6:9, 11, 12; 7:15, 20; 9:1, 2^2, 7^2, 10, 11; 10:2^2, 10^2, 13, 14

Neh 1:6^2, 7^2, 9; 2:5, 20; 4:5; 5:3, 4, 5, 8, 14, 19; 6:13, 14; 9:33, 34, 35, 37; 10:37; 13:14, 29

Est 1:18; 3:9; 4:11; 5:4, 8; 7:3; 8:5, 7^2; 9:1, 12^2

Job 1:5, 15, 17; 3:9, 13^2; 4:4, 8; 5:3, 27; 6:8, 10^2, 15, 24; 7:20; 8:4^2, 18; 10:8, 19^2; 12:3; 13:18; 14:15, 22; 15:17, 18^2; 16:2, 3, 10^3, 15, 18; 17:13, 14; 18:17, 19; 19:3, 4, 14^2, 21^2; 20:3, 7; 21:3, 15, 29; 22:9, 15, 25, 26; 23:11, 12^2; 24:7, 19; 27:12; 28:8, 22; 30:1^3, 11, 13, 16; 31:5, 9^2, 16^2, 17, 18, 19, 20, 21, 24^2, 28, 30, 39^2; 32:13; 33:2, 8, 24, 27; 34:2, 31, 32; 35:3; 36:2, 9, 16; 38:17, 23; 39:6; 40:5; 42:3, 5, 7, 8

Ps 2:4, 6, 7; 3:6; 4:1; 5:10; 6:2; 7:3, 4^2; 8:6; 9:13; 10:2; 12:4; 13:4, 5; 14:1, 4, 6; 16:6, 8; 17:4, 6, 11^2, 14; 18:21^2, 29^2, 37, 38, 43; 19:13; 22:12^2, 16^2; 25:6, 16; 26:1^2, 3, 4, 5, 8; 27:4, 7; 30:10; 31:4, 6, 9, 13, 17; 32:5, 9; 33:21; 35:7^2, 25^2; 37:14^2, 25^2, 35; 38:8; 40:9^2, 10^3, 12^2; 41:4; 42:3; 44:1^2, 17^2, 18, 20; 45:1, 8; 48:8^2, 9; 49:14; 50:5, 8; 51:1, 4; 53:1, 4^2; 54:3; 55:9, 12^2, 19; 56:4, 11; 57:6^2; 59:8; 62:11; 63:2; 66:14; 68:13, 24; 69:7, 22, 35; 71:6, 17, 18; 72:8; 73:7, 13, 14, 25, 28; 74:7^2, 8, 18, 20; 76:5^2; 77:5; 78:3^2; 79:1^2, 2, 3, 6^2, 7, 12; 81:14, 15^2, 16^2; 82:6; 83:2, 3, 4, 5, 8; 85:10; 86:14^2, 16; 88:1, 9^2, 13, 16; 89:2, 3^2, 19^2, 20^2, 35, 51^2; 90:15; 93:3^2; 94:20; 95:10; 98:3; 102:9, 13, 27; 104:12, 33; 106:6^3; 109:2, 5; 111:2, 10; 115:5^2, 6^2, 7^2; 116:10; 118:26; 119:6, 7, 10, 11, 13, 14, 15, 22, 26, 30^2, 31, 40, 42, 43, 47, 48, 51^2, 52, 54, 55^2, 57, 61^2, 66, 67, 69, 71, 73, 74, 79, 85, 92, 94, 95, 96, 99, 101, 102, 106, 110, 111, 112, 117, 121, 126, 133, 139, 143, 152, 161, 165, 166, 168, 173, 174, 176; 123:2, 3^2; 129:1, 2^2; 130:1; 131:2; 132:14, 17; 135:16^2, 17; 140:3, 4, 5^3; 141:9; 142:3; 143:3; 146:2; 147:20; 149:9

Prv 1:14, 24^2, 25; 3:30; 4:11^2, 16; 5:12, 13; 7:14^2, 15, 16, 17, 26; 8:14; 9:5; 13:3; 14:26; 17:2^2; 19:10; 20:4, 9; 22:19, 20, 28; 23:24, 35^2; 24:23; 25:7; 27:27; 28:10, 13, 19^2, 21, 27; 29:21; 30:2, 3, 7, 20, 27; 31:11, 29

Ecc 1:14, 16^2; 2:19^3; 3:10, 19; 4:9, 11, 16; 5:13, 18; 6:1, 3; 7:12, 15, 23, 27, 28^2, 29^2; 8:9; 9:5, 6, 13; 10:5, 7; 12:1

Song 1:6, 9; 2:15; 5:1^3, 3^2; 6:5; 7:13; 8:8, 12

Isa 1:2^2, 4^2, 6, 9^2, 29^2; 2:8; 3:9, 14; 4:4^2; 5:4^2, 13, 24; 6:5, 12; 7:5, 17; 8:4, 19; 9:2, 17^2; 10:1, 11, 13^4, 14, 29; 13:3^2, 18; 14:1, 24^2; 15:7^2; 16:6, 8, 10; 17:7, 8; 18:2, 7; 19:3, 13, 14; 21:2, 3, 10^2; 22:3, 9, 10^2, 11; 23:2, 12; 24:5, 16^3; 25:9^2; 26:1, 8, 9, 13, 16, 17, 18^5; 27:11; 28:7^2, 15^4, 22; 29:13; 30:2, 7, 18, 29; 31:6, 7; 33:2, 13; 36:5, 19, 20; 37:6, 11, 12^2, 18, 19^2, 25^2, 26^3; 38:3^2, 5^2, 12; 39:4^3, 6; 40:21^3, 29; 41:8, 9^2, 25; 42:1, 4, 6, 14^2, 16, 24; 43:1^2, 4, 7^3, 8^2, 10, 12^3, 14^2, 21, 23, 27, 28^2; 44:1, 2, 8^2, 16, 18, 19^3, 21, 22^2; 45:1, 4^2, 8, 12^3, 13, 19, 20, 21, 23, 24; 46:4, 11^2; 47:6; 48:3, 5, 6, 10^2, 15^3, 16, 19; 49:4^2, 8^2, 13, 15, 16, 20, 21; 50:1^3, 2, 7, 11^2; 51:16^2, 20, 22, 23; 52:3, 5; 53:6^2; 54:7, 8, 9^2, 16^2; 55:4, 7; 56:11; 57:11, 16, 18; 58:3^2, 5, 6; 59:2^2, 3, 8, 21; 60:10; 61:7; 62:6, 9^2; 63:3, 18^2; 64:4, 5, 6; 65:2, 7, 10; 66:2, 3, 19^2, 24

Jer 1:9, 10, 16^2, 18; 2:5^2, 11, 13^2, 16, 20, 23, 25, 27, 29, 30, 31, 32, 34, 35; 3:3, 13, 18, 20, 21^2, 25^2; 4:10, 18, 22^3, 28^2, 31; 5:3^4, 5^2, 7, 11, 12, 19, 21^2, 22, 25^2, 31; 6:2, 10, 14, 19, 23, 24, 27; 7:11, 13, 14, 15, 23, 25, 30^2, 31; 8:2^5, 3, 6, 9, 11, 13, 14, 16, 19; 9:5, 13^2, 14, 16^2, 19^2; 10:11, 21, 25^2; 11:5, 10, 13, 17, 20; 12:2, 5, 6^2, 7^3, 8, 10^3, 11, 12, 13^2, 14, 15^2; 13:11, 14, 27; 14:3, 7, 10^2, 13, 14, 16, 20; 15:5, 8^2, 10^2, 15; 16:2, 5, 10, 11^6, 12, 18^2, 19; 17:4, 13, 16^2; 18:8, 15^2, 20, 22; 19:4^5, 5, 13^2, 15^2; 20:12, 17; 21:7^2, 10; 22:9, 12; 23:2^2, 3, 11, 13, 14, 17, 20^2, 21^2, 22, 25^3, 27, 36, 38; 24:5; 25:3^2, 4, 7, 8, 13, 35; 26:4, 5, 11, 12; 27:5^2, 6^2, 8, 15; 28:2, 8, 14^2; 29:4, 7^2, 9, 14, 15, 18, 19, 20, 23^4, 32; 30:2, 5, 11, 14^2, 15, 18, 24^2; 31:3^2, 18, 20, 25^2, 28, 29, 37; 32:23, 29, 30^2, 32, 33^2, 37, 42^2; 33:5^2, 8^3, 14, 21, 24^2, 25, 26; 34:5, 17, 18^2; 35:7, 8, 9, 10^2, 14, 15^3, 16, 17^5, 18; 36:2, 30, 31; 37:18^2; 38:2, 9^3, 22^2, 25; 40:3^2, 10; 41:8; 42:4, 10, 12, 14, 19, 21^2; 43:10; 44:2^2, 3, 9^2, 10, 12, 13, 14, 17, 18^2, 22, 23^3, 25^2, 26; 45:4^2; 46:5, 12, 28; 48:2, 4, 5, 29, 33, 34, 38; 49:9, 10^2, 12, 13, 14, 23, 24, 31, 37; 50:6^4, 7^2, 17, 18, 21, 24; 51:7, 9, 24, 30^3, 32, 50, 51

Lam 1:2, 8, 11, 18, 20, 21^2; 2:7, 10^2, 14^3, 16^4, 22; 3:21, 32, 42^2, 46, 53; 4:10, 12^2, 13, 14^2, 17; 5:4, 5, 6, 7^2, 8, 14, 16

Ezk 2:3; 3:6, 8, 9, 17; 4:5, 6, 14, 15; 5:5, 6^2, 7^3, 9, 11, 13^2, 15, 17; 6:8, 9, 10; 7:4, 9, 14, 20; 8:17^2, 18; 9:1, 5, 10, 11; 11:5, 6^2, 7, 8, 12^2, 15, 16^2, 17; 12:2^2, 6, 11, 22, 28; 13:3, 5, 6^2, 7^3, 8, 10, 12, 14, 15, 22^2; 14:3, 9, 22^2, 23^2; 15:6, 8; 16:5, 7, 27^2; 17:21, 24^6; 18:2, 3, 23, 31, 32; 20:27^2, 41, 43^2, 44, 48; 21:5, 15, 17, 23, 24, 25, 29, 32; 22:4, 7^3, 10^2, 12, 13, 14, 22, 25^3, 26^5, 28, 29^3, 31^3; 23:9, 34, 37^3, 38^3, 39, 40; 24:8, 13^2, 14, 21, 22; 25:15^2; 26:5, 14; 27:4, 5^2, 6^2, 11, 26; 28:10, 14, 16, 22, 25^2, 26; 29:3, 5, 6, 9, 20; 30:8, 12, 16^2, 21; 31:9, 11^2, 12^3; 32:24, 25^2, 27, 32; 33:7, 11, 29^2; 34:4^6, 12, 18^2, 19^2, 21^2, 24, 27; 35:11, 12, 13^3; 36:3, 5^2, 6^2, 7, 22, 23, 33, 36; 37:13, 14, 23, 24, 25^2; 38:8, 12, 17, 19; 39:5, 8, 15, 19, 21^2, 24, 25, 26^2, 27, 28^2, 29; 41:6; 43:8^3, 11; 44:7^2, 8^2, 12, 13, 18^2; 45:5, 10, 21; 47:13, 22; 48:11, 13, 23, 24

Dan 2:3, 9, 25, 26, 30; 3:12, 14, 15, 25, 28; 4:9, 18, 26, 30; 5:7, 14, 15, 16^2, 23^2; 6:2, 7, 22^2; 9:5^4, 6, 7, 8, 9, 10, 11^2, 15^2; 10:16; 11:5, 24, 30^2, 43; 12:7

Hos 1:6, 7; 2:4, 12, 23; 4:10^2, 12, 18; 5:1, 2, 4, 7^2, 9; 6:5^2, 7^2, 10; 7:1, 2, 5, 6, 7, 9, 13^4, 14, 15; 8:1, 4^3, 7, 10, 12; 9:9; 10:1, 3, 4, 13^3; 12:8, 10^2; 13:2, 6; 14:8^2

Joel 1:18; 3:2, 3^2, 4, 5^2, 6, 7, 19, 21

Am 1:3, 13; 2:4^3; 3:2, 4, 5, 15; 4:6^2, 7, 8, 9^2, 10^5, 11^2; 5:11^2, 14, 25, 26; 6:12, 13; 9:7, 15

Oba 1, 2, 5, 7^3, 12^3, 13^3, 14^2, 16

Jna 2:9

Mic 2:5, 9^2, 13^2; 3:4, 6; 4:6, 9; 5:2, 12, 15; 6:3^2, 12; 7:1, 9, 19

Nah 1:12; 2:2

Hab 1:14; 3:2

Zep 1:6, 17; 2:3, 8^2, 10^2; 3:4^2, 6, 19

Hag 1:6^2; 2:23

Zec **1:**4, 11, 12, 19, 21; **2:**6; **3:**4, 9; **4:**2, 9; **6:**8; **7:**3; **8:**15, 23; **9:**8, 11, 13; **10:**2^3, 6, 8^2; **12:**10; **14:**12, 18

Mal **1:**2, 6, 7, 10, 12, 13; **2:**2, 4, 8^2, 9^3, 10, 13, 17^2; **3:**7, 8^2, 9, 13^2, 14^3

Mt **2:**2, 8, 15; **3:**9, 14; **5:**13, 21, 27, 33, 38, 40, 43, 46; **6:**1, 2^2, 5, 8, 16, 32; **7:**22^2; **8:**10, 20^2, 29; **9:**13, 27; **10:**8, 23, 25; **11:**5, 17^4, 21, 23^2; **12:**3, 5, 7^2, 11, 18; **13:**12, 15, 17^3, 35, 51; **14:**4, 5, 17; **15:**6, 22, 32^2, 33, 34; **16:**7, 8; **17:**12, 15, 20; **18:**12, 26, 29, 33; **19:**4, 12, 16, 20, 21, 27^2, 28; **20:**10, 12^2, 30, 31; **21:**13, 16, 21; **22:**4, 31; **23:**23^2, 30, 37; **24:**25, 43^2; **25:**20, 22, 26, 27^2, 29, 40^2; **26:**9, 11^2, 65^2; **27:**4^2, 19^2, 43, 65; **28:**7, 20

Mk **1:**8, 24; **2:**17, 19, 25; **3:**15; **4:**15, 16, 17, 23, 40; **5:**7; **6:**18, 19, 36, 38, 48; **7:**4, 13, 16, 24; **8:**2^3, 5, 16, 17^2; **9:**1, 13, 17, 22, 50^3; **10:**20, 21, 23, 28^2, 47, 48; **11:**17, 22, 23, 24, 25; **12:**10, 26, 43; **13:**23; **14:**5^2, 7^2, 64

Lk **1:**1, 14, 62, 70; **2:**30, 44, 48; **3:**8; **4:**23, 34; **5:**5^2, 26; **6:**3, 24, 32, 33, 34; **7:**9, 22, 32^4, 39, 40; **8:**13, 14, 18, 28; **9:**3, 9, 13, 58^2; **10:**13, 24^3; **11:**5, 6, 41, 42, 52; **12:**3^2, 4, 17, 24, 30, 33, 39^2, 48, 50; **13:**26, 34; **14:**5, 10, 18^2, 19^2, 20, 28, 34; **15:**6, 9, 16, 17, 18, 21, 31; **16:**11, 12, 24, 28, 29; **17:**8, 10^2, 13; **18:**21, 22, 24, 28, 38, 39; **19:**8, 14, 17, 20, 23, 46; **21:**4; **22:**15, 28, 31, 32, 37, 71; **23:**8, 14^2, 22; **24:**17, 20, 21, 25, 26, 28, 39, 41

Jn **1:**16, 41, 45; **2:**3, 4, 10; **3:**11, 12, 15, 16; **4:**9, 10^2, 17^2, 32, 42; **5:**7, 26, 29^2, 36, 37, 38, 39, 40, 42, 46; **6:**36, 40, 53, 70; **7:**21, 23, 44, 45, 48; **8:**6, 12, 19, 26^2, 28, 38^2, 40, 41, 49, 55; **9:**27, 41; **10:**10^2, 16, 18^3, 32; **11:**34, 37^2; **12:**8^2, 28, 34, 35, 36, 48, 49; **13:**12, 14, 15^2, 18, 26, 29, 34, 35; **14:**2, 7^2, 9, 25, 26, 28, 29; **15:**3, 9, 10, 11, 12, 15^3, 16^2, 19, 20^2, 22, 24, 27; **16:**1, 3, 4, 6, 12, 22, 24, 25, 27^2, 33^4; **17:**4^2, 6^2, 7, 8^4, 12, 13, 14, 18, 22, 25^2, 26; **18:**8, 9, 20, 21, 23, 30, 35, 39; **19:**7, 10^2, 11, 15, 22^2; **20:**2^2, 13^2, 15, 25, 29^2, 31; **21:**5, 10

Act **1:**1, 4, 11, 16, 21; **2:**23^2, 36; **3:**6^2, 24^2; **4:**7, 20; **5:**9^2, 21, 26, 28; **6:**11, 14; **7:**25, 26, 34^3, 42, 52^3, 53^2; **8:**24; **9:**6, 13; **10:**10, 14, 20, 29, 47; **12:**6; **13:**2, 15, 22, 27, 33, 46, 47; **14:**13; **15:**24^2, 26, 27, 36; **16:**3, 15, 27, 36, 37^2; **17:**3, 6, 28^2; **18:**10; **19:**2^2, 21, 25, 30, 33, 37, 38; **20:**18, 20^2, 24, 25, 27, 33, 34, 35; **21:**23^2, 25; **22:**29, 30; **23:**1, 10, 14^2, 20, 21^2, 27, 28, 29; **24:**5, 6, 15, 16, 19, 20, 23, 25, 26; **25:**8, 10, 11, 15, 16^2, 24, 25, 26^3; **26:**16, 32; **27:**21^3, 29, 30, 33; **28:**6, 17, 18, 20, 27

Ro **1:**5, 10, 13^2, 32; **2:**12^2, 14; **3:**9, 13, 17, 23; **4:**17; **5:**1, 2, 11, 12; **6:**5, 14, 17, 19, 22; **8:**9, 15^2, 23; **9:**2, 9, 13^2, 15^4, 17, 18, 30; **10:**2, 3, 14^2, 16, 18, 21; **11:**3, 4^2, 11, 30^2, 31, 32; **12:**4^2; **13:**3; **14:**22; **15:**4, 15, 17, 19, 20, 21, 22, 27, 28^2, 31; **16:**4, 17, 19

1Co **2:**8, 9, 12, 16; **3:**2, 6, 10; **4:**5, 6, 8, 11, 15^3, 17; **5:**1, 2, 3, 11, 12; **6:**4, 19; **7:**2^2, 25, 28, 29, 32, 40; **8:**1; **9:**1, 4, 5, 6, 11, 12, 15^2, 16, 17, 19, 27; **10:**20; **11:**3, 10, 14, 15, 16, 22^2, 23; **12:**1, 13, 21^2, 23, 24, 25, 30; **13:**1, 2^3, 3; **15:**1, 2, 15, 19, 24^2, 31, 32, 34, 49, 54^2; **16:**1, 12, 15, 17, 18

2Co **1:**8, 12, 14, 15, 24; **2:**3, 4, 5; **3:**4, 12; **4:**1^2, 2, 7, 13; **5:**1, 12, 16; **6:**2^2; **7:**2^3, 3, 11, 14, 16; **8:**10, 11, 18, 22^3; **9:**3; **11:**2, 4^3, 6, 7^2, 9, 25; **12:**11^2, 21^3; **13:**2

Gal **1:**8, 9, 13; **2:**4, 16; **3:**4, 21^2, 27^2; **4:**9, 11, 12, 15^2; **5:**10, 13, 21, 24; **6:**4, 10, 11, 13

Eph **1:**7, 11; **2:**18; **3:**2, 12; **4:**19, 20, 21^2, 28; **5:**11; **6:**22

Php **1:**7, 12; **2:**12, 16, 20, 27; **3:**3, 4, 8, 13, 16, 17, 18; **4:**9, 11, 14, 18

Col **1:**4, 14, 18, 23; **2:**1^2, 6, 7, 23; **3:**9, 10, 13; **4:**1, 8, 11

1Th **2:**6, 8, 14^2, 15, 18; **3:**5, 6; **4:**1, 6, 12, 13^2; **5:**1

2Th **2:**15; **3:**1, 2, 4, 9, 14

1Ti **1:**6, 19, 20; **2:**4; **3:**7, 13; **5:**4, 10^5, 11, 12, 16; **6:**2, 10, 21

2Ti **1:**3, 12^2; **2:**18; **4:**7^3, 12, 20

Tit **3:**5, 8, 12

Phlm 7, 10, 12, 13^2, 19, 20

Heb **1:**5; **2:**1; **3:**10; **4:**3^2, 8, 13, 14, 15; **5:**2, 5, 11, 12^2, 14; **6:**4, 5, 10^2, 18^2, 19; **7:**5, 28; **8:**1^2, 3, 7; **9:**26; **10:**2^2, 26, 34, 36^2, 38; **11:**15^2; **12:**4, 5, 9, 17, 28; **13:**2, 5, 7^2, 9^2, 10^2, 14, 17, 18, 22, 24

Jas **1:**4; **2:**1, 3, 6, 9, 13, 14, 18; **3:**14; **4:**2^3; **5:**3, 4^2, 5^2, 6, 10, 11^2, 15

1Pt **1:**10, 12, 22; **2:**3, 10; **4:**3, 8; **5:**10, 12

2Pt **1:**1, 15, 16, 19; **2:**14, 15, 20, 21^2

1Jn **1:**1^4, 2, 3^2, 5, 6, 7, 8, 10; **2:**1, 7, 13^3, 14^4, 18, 19, 20, 21, 24^2, 26, 27, 28; **3:**14, 17, 21; **4:**3, 4, 14, 16, 17, 21; **5:**13^2, 14, 15

2Jn 1, 4, 6, 8

3Jn 4, 6, 9

Jude 11, 15^2, 22

Rev **1:**18; **2:**4, 10, 14, 20, 24^2, 25; **3:**2, 4, 8, 9, 17; **7:**3, 14; **9:**3, 4; **11:**6^2, 7; **12:**17; **13:**9; **14:**11; **16:**6; **17:**2^2, 12, 13; **18:**3^2, 5, 9; **19:**10; **21:**8; **22:**14, 16

HAVING

Gen **12:**8

Lev **7:**20; **20:**18; **22:**3, 22

Nu **24:**4, 16

Dt **10:**3

Jdg **1:**7; **19:**3

Ru **1:**13

1Sa **22:**6; **26:**2

1Ki **22:**10

1Ch **4:**42; **21:**16; **26:**12

2Ch **5:**12; **11:**12; **23:**10

Ezr **9:**5

Neh **10:**28^2; **13:**4

Est **6:**12

Ps **13:**2

Prv **6:**7; **18:**1

Isa **6:**6; **41:**15

Jer **41:**5^2

Ezk **38:**11; **40:**44; **44:**11

Dan **8:**20

Mic **1:**11

Zec **9:**9

Mt **7:**29; **8:**9; **9:**36; **15:**30; **18:**8, 9; **22:**12, 24, 25; **26:**7

Mk **6:**34; **8:**1, 18^2; **9:**43, 45, 47; **11:**13; **12:**6, 28; **14:**3, 51

Lk **1:**3; **5:**39; **7:**8; **8:**15, 43; **9:**62; **11:**36; **15:**4, 8; **17:**7; **19:**15; **20:**28; **23:**14, 46

Jn **4:**45; **5:**2; **7:**15; **13:**1, 2, 30; **18:**3, 10

Act **2:**24, 33, 47; **3:**26; **4:**37; **12:**20; **14:**19; **16:**24; **18:**18; **19:**1, 29; **22:**12; **23:**27; **24:**22; **26:**10, 22; **27:**33

Ro **2:**14; **9:**11; **12:**6; **15:**23^2

1Co **6:**1; **7:**37; **11:**4; **12:**24

2Co **2:**3; **4:**13; **6:**10; **7:**1; **9:**8; **10:**6, 15

Gal **3:**3

Eph **1:**5, 9; **2:**12, 15, 16; **4:**18; **5:**27; **6:**13, 14^2

Php **1:**23, 25, 30; **2:**2; **3:**9; **4:**18

Col **1:**20; **2:**13, 15, 19

1Th **1:**6

1Ti **1:**6, 19; **3:**4; **4:**2, 8; **5:**9, 12; **6:**8

2Ti **2:**19; **3:**5; **4:**3, 10

Tit **1:**6; **2:**8

Phlm 21

Heb **7:**3; **9:**12; **10:**1, 19, 21, 22; **11:**13^2, 39, 40

1Pt **1:**8; **2:**12; **3:**8, 16

2Pt **1:**4; **2:**14

2Jn 12

Jude 5, 16, 19

Rev **5:**6, 8; **7:**2; **8:**3; **9:**17; **12:**3, 12; **13:**1; **14:**1, 6, 14, 17; **15:**1, 2, 6^2; **17:**3, 4; **18:**1; **20:**1; **21:**11

HE

Gen **1:**5, 10, 16, 27^2, 31; **2:**2^3, 3, 8^2, 19, 21^2, 22; **3:**1, 6, 10, 11, 16^2, 17, 22, 23, 24^2; **4:**4, 5, 9, 10, 17, 20, 21, 26; **5:**1, 2, 4^2, 5, 7, 8, 10, 11, 13, 14, 16, 17, 18, 19, 20, 22, 24, 26, 27, 29, 30, 31; **6:**3, 6, 22; **8:**6, 7, 8, 9, 10^2, 12; **9:**6, 20, 21^2, 25^2, 26, 27, 29; **10:**8, 9; **11:**11, 13, 15, 17, 19, 21, 23, 25; **12:**4, 7, 8^2, 11^2, 16^3, 20; **13:**1^2, 3, 4; **14:**13, 14, 15^2, 16, 18, 19, 20; **15:**4, 5^2, 6^2, 7, 8, 9, 10^2, 13; **16:**4, 8, 12^2; **17:**12^2, 13^2, 14, 20, 22, 24, 25; **18:**1, 2^3, 7, 8^3, 9, 10, 15, 19^2, 28, 29^2, 30^2, 31^2, 32^2, 33; **19:**1, 2, 3^2, 9, 14, 16, 17, 21, 25, 27, 28, 29, 30^3, 33, 35; **20:**4, 5^2, 7^2, 13, 16^2; **21:**1^2, 13, 17, 20, 21, 30, 31; **22:**1, 2, 6, 7^2, 11, 12; **23:**8, 9^3, 13, 16; **24:**2, 7, 10, 11, 12, 15, 27, 30^4, 31, 32, 33^2, 34, 35^2, 36^2, 40, 52, 53, 54^2, 56, 62, 63, 66, 67; **25:**5, 6, 7, 17, 18, 20, 28, 29, 33^2, 34; **26:**7^3, 8, 11, 13, 14, 18, 20, 21, 22^3, 23, 25, 30, 33, 34; **27:**1^3, 2, 9, 10^2, 14, 18^2, 20, 22, 23^2, 24^2, 25^5, 27^2, 29, 31, 32, 33^2, 34, 35, 36^6, 45; **28:**5, 6^2, 9, 11^2, 12, 16, 17, 18, 19; **29:**2, 5, 6^3, 7, 9, 12^2, 13^2, 14, 20, 23^2, 25, 28, 30^2, 31, 33; **30:**2, 15, 16, 28, 29, 31, 35^2, 36, 38^2, 40, 42; **31:**1^2, 8^2, 12, 15, 18^3, 20^2, 21^3, 23, 33^2, 35, 49; **32:**2^2, 4, 6, 7, 11, 13, 14, 16, 17, 18, 19, 20^2, 22, 23^2, 25^4, 26^2, 27^2, 28, 29^2, 31^2, 32; **33:**1, 2, 3^2, 5^2, 8^2, 11^2, 12, 13, 15, 18, 19^2, 20; **34:**2, 3, 5, 7, 13, 19^2, 31; **35:**6, 7^2, 9, 10, 13, 14^3; **36:**6, 24, 43; **37:**3^2, 5, 6, 9, 10, 13, 14^3, 15, 16, 18, 21, 22, 27, 29, 30, 33, 35^2; **38:**2, 3, 5, 9^3, 10^2, 11^2, 12, 15, 16^2, 17, 18^2, 20, 21, 22, 26, 29; **39:**2^2, 3, 4^4, 5^3, 6^5, 8^3, 9, 10, 12, 13, 14^2, 15^2, 18, 20, 22, 23; **40:**3, 4, 7, 16, 20^2, 21^2, 22; **41:**1, 5, 8, 11, 12^2, 13^3, 14, 25, 28, 43^3, 45, 46, 48^2, 49, 51, 52, 55; **42:**2, 4, 6, 7^2, 9, 12, 17, 21, 23, 24, 25, 27, 28, 38^2; **43:**7, 14, 16, 18, 23^2, 24, 27^2, 28, 29^2, 30^2, 31, 34; **44:**1, 2, 5, 6^2, 10^2, 12, 14, 16, 17^2, 20, 22, 28, 31^2; **45:**1, 2, 4, 8, 14, 15, 22^2, 23, 24^2, 26^2, 27^2; **46:**1, 2, 3, 7, 28, 29; **47:**2, 17, 21, 22, 29, 30, 31^2; **48:**1, 9, 10^3, 12, 15, 17, 19^3, 20^2; **49:**4, 8, 9^2, 11, 13, 15, 19, 20, 21, 27^2, 28, 29, 33; **50:**6, 10, 12, 14^2, 16, 21, 22, 24, 26

Ex **1:**9, 16, 21; **2:**2, 10, 11^2, 12^3, 13^2, 14, 15^2, 18, 20^3, 21, 22^2; **3:**1, 2, 4^2, 5, 6^2, 12, 14, 20; **4:**2, 3^2, 4, 6^2, 7^2, 13, 14^5, 16^3, 20, 21, 23, 26, 27, 28, 31; **5:**3, 17, 23; **6:**1^2, 11; **7:**2, 13^2, 14, 15^2, 20, 22, 23; **8:**8, 10^2, 12, 15, 19, 20, 27, 31, 32; **9:**7, 12, 20, 21, 34^2, 35; **10:**6, 8, 10, 16, 17, 18, 20, 27; **11:**1^3, 8, 10; **12:**19, 23, 25, 27, 30, 31, 44, 48; **13:**5, 11, 19, 22; **14:**4, 6, 7, 8, 13; **15:**1^2, 2^2, 4, 21^2, 25^4; **16:**7, 9, 18^2, 23, 29; **17:**7, 11, 12, 16; **18:**2, 3, 4, 5, 6, 9, 11, 14^2, 24, 27; **19:**13, 15, 24; **21:**2^2, 3^3, 4, 6^2, 8^3, 9^2, 10^2, 11, 12^2, 13, 14, 15, 16^3, 17, 18, 19^3, 20^2, 21^3, 22^2, 26, 27^2, 29^2, 30, 31, 32, 35, 36; **22:**1, 2, 3^3, 4, 5, 6, 8, 9, 11^2, 12, 13, 14, 15, 16, 17, 20^2, 27^2; **23:**21, 25; **24:**1, 5, 6, 7, 11, 14, 16; **25:**39; **28:**1, 3, 4, 29, 30, 35^3; **29:**21, 30; **30:**7^2, 8, 10; **31:**15, 17, 18^2; **32:**4^2, 5, 12, 14, 17, 18, 19^3, 20, 27, 29; **33:**8, 11, 14, 15, 18, 19, 20; **34:**4, 9, 10, 28^3, 29^2, 32, 33, 34^4, 35; **35:**31, 34^3, 35; **36:**8, 10^2, 11^2, 12^2, 13, 14^2, 16, 17^2, 18, 19, 20, 22, 23, 24, 25, 27, 28, 29, 31, 33, 34, 35^2, 36^2, 37, 38; **37:**2, 3, 4, 5, 6, 7^2, 8, 10, 11, 12, 13, 15, 16, 17^2, 23, 24, 25, 26^2, 27, 28, 29; **38:**1, 2^2, 3^2, 4, 5, 6, 7^2, 8, 9, 28, 30; **39:**2, 7, 8, 22; **40:**13, 16, 19, 20, 21, 22, 23, 24, 25, 26, 27, 28, 29, 30, 33

Lev **1:**3, 4, 5, 6, 9, 10, 11, 12, 13, 14, 16, 17; **2:**1, 2^2, 8; **3:**1^2, 2, 3, 4, 6, 7^2, 8, 9^2, 10, 12, 13, 14, 15; **4:**3, 4, 8, 9, 12^2, 18, 19, 20^3, 21^2, 23^2, 24, 26, 27, 28^3, 29, 31, 32^2, 33, 35^2; **5:**1^3, 2, 3^3, 4^2, 5^3, 6^2, 7^3, 8, 9, 10^2, 11^4, 12, 13, 15, 16^2, 17^2, 18^2, 19; **6:**4^5, 5^2, 6, 7, 10^2, 11, 12, 15, 20; **7:**2, 3, 4, 8, 11, 12^2, 13, 14, 15, 16, 29, 30, 33, 35, 36, 38; **8:**7^2, 8^2, 9^2, 11, 12, 14, 15, 16, 17, 18, 19, 20, 21, 22, 23, 24, 25, 26, 27, 33, 34; **9:**2, 9, 10, 11, 12^2, 13, 14, 15, 16, 17, 18^2, 20; **10:**1, 16, 20; **11:**4^2, 5^2, 6^2, 7^3, 28, 39, 40^2; **13:**2, 6, 7^2, 9, 11, 13^2, 14, 16, 17, 33^2, 34, 36, 37, 39, 40^2, 41^3, 44^2, 45, 46^3, 51, 52, 54, 56; **14:**2, 6, 7, 8^3, 9^5, 10^2, 12, 13^2, 18, 19, 20, 21^2, 22, 23, 25, 29, 30^2, 31, 35, 37, 41, 42, 43^2, 45^2, 46, 47^2, 49, 50, 51, 52, 53; **15:**2, 4^2, 6^2, 7, 8^2, 9, 10, 11^2, 12, 13^2, 14, 16, 23^2, 24^2; **16:**2^2, 4^4, 5, 7, 12, 13^2, 14^2, 15^2, 16^2, 17^2, 18, 19, 20^2, 22, 23^2, 24, 25, 26, 28^2, 32^2, 33^3, 34; **17:**4, 13, 15^2, 16^2; **18:**5; **19:**8, 21, 22^2; **20:**2^2, 3, 4, 9, 10, 13, 14, 15, 17^2, 18, 19, 20, 21; **21:**3, 4, 7, 8^2, 10, 11, 12, 13, 14^2, 15, 17, 18^3, 21^2, 22, 23^3; **22:**3, 4^2, 5^3, 6, 7, 8, 11^2, 14, 18; **23:**11, 12, 29; **24:**4, 8, 16^4, 17, 18, 19, 20, 21^4; **25:**15, 16, 25, 27^2, 28^2, 29^2, 35^2, 40, 41^3, 48^2, 49^2, 50^2, 51^2, 52^2, 53, 54^3; **27:**8^2, 10^2, 11, 13^2, 15^2, 17, 18, 19^2, 20^2, 22, 23, 27, 28, 31, 33^3

Nu **1:**19; **3:**3, 16, 50; **5:**7^2, 14^2, 15^2, 23, 24, 27, 30; **6:**3^2, 4, 5^2, 6^2, 7, 8, 9^3, 10, 11, 12, 13, 14^2, 17, 21^2; **7:**7, 8, 9, 12, 17, 19, 23, 29, 35, 41, 47, 53, 59, 65, 71, 77, 83, 88, 89^2; **8:**3, 4; **9:**10, 13, 14; **10:**30, 31, 36; **11:**3, 30, 32, 34; **12:**1^2, 2, 6, 8, 9, 12; **14:**8, 16^2, 24^2; **15:**4, 9, 14, 27, 28, 30, 31, 36; **16:**4, 5^3, 7, 10, 26, 31, 37, 40, 47, 48; **17:**11; **19:**3, 5, 7^2, 8, 10, 11, 12^4, 13, 19, 20^2, 21^2; **20:**9, 10, 11, 13, 16, 20, 24; **21:**1, 3, 7, 8, 9^2, 14, 23, 29, 33; **22:**5, 6^2, 8, 22^2, 25, 27, 30, 31^2, 36, 41; **23:**3^2, 4, 6^3, 7, 12, 14, 15, 17^2, 18, 19^6, 20, 21^2, 22, 24^2;

24:1[2], 2, 3, 4, 7, 8[2], 9[4], 10, 15, 16, 19, 20[3], 21, 23, 24; **25:**7, 8, 11, 13[2], 15; **27:**3, 4, 9, 10, 11, 21[2], 22, 23; **30:**2[2], 5, 7, 8[2], 12, 14[4], 15[3]; **32:**10, 13, 15, 21, 40; **33:**39; **35:**6, 8, 12, 16[3], 17[4], 18[4], 19[2], 20[2], 21[4], 22, 23, 25[2], 26, 27, 28, 31, 32

Dt 1:4, 11, 27, 30[2], 36[3], 38[2]; **2:**7, 22[2], 30, 32; **3:**1, 22, 28[2]; **4:**13[3], 23, 31[2], 35, 36[3], 37[2], 39, 42; **5:**22[2], 24; **6:**10, 17, 23[3], 24, 25; **7:**8[2], 9, 10[2], 12, 13[3], 24; **8:**3[2], 10, 16[2], 18[3]; **9:**3[3], 5, 25, 28[3]; **10:**4, 6, 15, 18, 21[2]; **11:**3, 4[2], 5, 6, 7, 17, 25; **12:**10, 12, 15, 20, 31; **13:**2, 5, 10[2], 17; **14:**21, 23, 27, 29; **15:**2, 6, 8, 9, 16[3], 17, 18; **16:**16, 17[2]; **17:**6[2], 16[2], 17[2], 18[2], 19[2], 20[3]; **18:**2, 6, 7, 18, 19; **19:**4[2], 5[2], 6[2], 8[2], 11, 12, 15, 19; **20:**4, 5, 6[2], 7; **21:**16[3], 17[3], 20[2], 21, 22, 23; **22:**3, 16, 17, 19[2], 24, 27, 29[2]; **23:**1, 2, 7, 10[2], 11[2], 14, 16[2]; **24:**1, 5[4], 6, 13, 14, 15[2]; **25:**3[2], 4, 7, 8, 18[2]; **26:**5, 9, 18, 19[2]; **27:**16, 17, 18, 19, 20[2], 21, 22, 23, 24, 25, 26; **28:**8, 9, 21, 44[2], 45, 48[2], 51[2], 52[2], 54, 55[3], 60; **29:**1, 13[4], 19[2], 25[2], 26; **30:**4, 5, 9, 20; **31:**2, 3[3], 4[2], 6[2], 8[3], 11, 23; **32:**4[2], 6[2], 7, 8[2], 10[4], 13[3], 15, 19, 20, 36, 37, 39, 43, 44, 46; **33:**2[3], 3, 5, 7, 8, 9, 12[2], 13, 17, 18, 20[3], 21[4], 22[2], 23, 24, 27; **34:**6, 7

Jos 1:15, 17, 18[2]; **2:**11; **3:**1, 10; **4:**4, 21, 23; **5:**6[2], 7, 13, 14; **6:**7, 26[2]; **7:**6, 15[5], 17[3], 18, 24; **8:**4, 10, 12, 14[2], 18, 19, 26[2], 27, 29, 32[2], 33, 34; **9:**9, 10, 22, 26, 27; **10:**1[2], 7, 12, 28[4], 30[3], 32, 33, 35[2], 37[2], 39[5], 40; **11:**1, 9, 11, 12, 15, 17, 20[2]; **13:**14[2], 33; **14:**3, 10, 14; **15:**13, 15, 16, 17, 19; **17:**1[3], 4; **19:**50[2]; **20:**4[2], 5, 6[3], 9; **21:**43, 44; **22:**4, 7, 8, 18, 22[2]; **23:**3, 5, 10[2], 15, 16[2]; **24:**7, 10, 17, 18, 19[3], 20[2], 23, 27, 31

Jdg 1:7, 11, 12, 13, 19, 20, 25, 33; **2:**7, 10, 14[2], 20, 21, 23; **3:**4, 8, 10, 13, 16, 17, 18[2], 19, 20[3], 22, 24[2], 25, 27[3], 28, 31; **4:**3[2], 10, 18, 19, 20, 21[2], 22; **5:**13, 15, 25, 27[7], 31; **6:**15, 17, 18, 19[2], 20, 22, 27[3], 30[3], 31[2], 32[2], 34, 35[2], 38; **7:**5, 8, 11, 15, 16[2], 17; **8:**2, 3, 4, 5, 8, 9, 12, 14, 15, 16[2], 17, 18, 19, 20[3], 26, 30, 31, 35; **9:**3, 5[2], 7, 18, 28, 29, 31, 33, 36, 40, 43[2], 45, 48, 54[2], 56; **10:**1, 2, 4, 7, 18[2]; **11:**1, 17, 25[2], 28, 29[2], 33, 34, 35[2], 38[2], 39; **12:**5, 6[2], 9[3], 11, 14[2]; **13:**5, 6[2], 7, 11, 16, 21, 23[2]; **14:**2, 4, 6[5], 7, 8[2], 9[4], 14, 15, 16, 17, 18, 19[2], 20; **15:**1, 5[2], 6, 8[2], 10, 11, 14, 15, 17[2], 18, 19[3], 20; **16:**4, 9, 11, 12, 13, 14, 17, 18[2], 20[2], 21, 22, 25[2], 30[3], 31; **17:**2, 3, 4, 7, 8[3], 9; **18:**4, 20, 24, 26, 27, 30, 31; **19:**3, 4, 5, 7, 8, 9, 10, 13, 15[2], 16, 17[2], 18, 21, 28, 29[2]; **21:**5, 18

Ru 1:1; **2:**14, 19, 20, 21; **3:**2, 3, 4[3], 7, 9, 10, 13[2], 14, 15[2], 17[2], 18; **4:**1[2], 2, 3, 4, 8, 13, 15, 17

1Sa 1:2, 4, 5[2], 7, 22, 28[3]; **2:**6, 7, 8[2], 9, 10[2], 14, 15, 16, 23, 35; **3:**2, 4, 5[3], 6, 8, 9, 13[2], 16, 17[2], 18; **4:**13, 14, 15, 16[2], 18[5]; **5:**6, 9; **6:**5, 6, 9, 19[2], 20; **7:**3, 8, 16, 17[2]; **8:**1, 11[2], 12, 13, 14, 15, 16, 17, 21; **9:**2[3], 4[2], 6[4], 9[2], 12[3], 13[3], 16, 26, 27; **10:**9, 10, 11, 13[2], 14, 16[2], 21[2], 22, 23[2], 27; **11:**6, 7, 8, 12; **12:**5[2], 7, 9, 17, 24; **13:**1, 2, 7, 8, 9, 10[2], 13; **14:**1, 27, 33, 35, 37, 39, 40, 45[2], 47[2], 48, 52; **15:**2[2], 8, 11[2], 12, 16, 23, 27, 29[2], 30, 35; **16:**2, 5[2], 6, 8, 9, 11[3], 12[3], 16, 21[2], 22; **17:**5[2], 6, 8, 9, 12, 20, 23, 25, 26, 28[2], 30, 31, 33, 35, 36, 37, 38[2], 39[2], 40[3], 42[2], 47, 49, 54, 55; **18:**1, 3, 5, 8[2], 10, 11, 13, 15[2], 16, 27[2]; **19:**4, 5, 6, 7, 9, 10[2], 12, 14, 17[2], 18, 21, 22[2], 23[3], 24; **20:**1, 2[2], 3[2], 6, 7[2], 13, 17[3], 26[3], 29[3], 30, 31, 32[2], 34, 36[2], 42; **21:**13; **22:**2, 3, 4, 10, 12, 13, 17, 18, 19, 22, 23; **23:**6, 7, 9, 11, 13, 17, 22, 23[2], 25[2]; **24:**3, 5, 6[2], 10, 17, 19; **25:**2[2], 3, 14, 17, 21, 25, 29, 30, 36[2], 37, 38, 39; **26:**3, 10, 18; **27:**2, 3, 4, 11, 12[2]; **28:**5, 8[2], 9, 11, 14[4], 17, 20, 21, 23[3]; **29:**3, 4[3], 9; **30:**8, 9, 10, 11, 12[2], 13, 15, 16, 21, 25, 26; **31:**3, 4, 5

2Sa 1:2[2], 3, 4, 7[2], 8, 9, 10[2], 13, 15[2], 18, 21; **2:**1, 10, 19, 20, 23[2], 30; **3:**11[2], 13, 16, 21, 22[2], 23[2], 24, 25, 26, 27, 28, 30; **4:**4[2], 7; **5:**2, 4[2], 5[2], 8, 12, 13, 20, 23; **6:**7, 8, 13, 18, 19; **7:**11, 13, 14[2], 18; **8:**2[2], 3, 6, 10, 11[2], 13, 14[3]; **9:**2[2], 4[2], 6[2], 8, 11, 13; **10:**3, 5, 7, 9, 10[2], 11, 17; **11:**2, 4, 13[3], 15[2], 16[2], 20, 21; **12:**1, 3, 4, 5, 6[3], 11, 17[2], 18[2], 19, 20[3], 22, 23[2], 24, 25[2], 30[2], 31[2]; **13:**2, 4, 8, 9, 11, 13, 14, 15[2], 16, 17, 20, 21, 22, 25[2], 26, 27, 32, 36, 39[2]; **14:**7, 10, 11, 12, 14, 19[2], 26[4], 29[3], 30[2], 33[2]; **15:**2, 5, 9, 12, 14, 25, 26, 30[2], 32; **16:**3[2], 5[2], 6, 7, 13, 21, 23; **17:**2, 5, 9, 10, 12, 13, 23, 24; **18:**9, 14[2], 18[2], 23[2], 25[2], 26, 27, 28, 30, 33[2]; **19:**9[2], 14, 18[2], 21, 24, 25, 26, 27, 32[3], 39, 42; **20:**1, 3, 5[2], 6, 8[2], 10[2], 11[2], 12[2], 13, 14, 17[4], 22; **21:**1, 4, 9, 13, 16, 20, 21; **22:**2, 3, 7, 8, 10, 11[2], 12, 15, 17[3], 18, 20[3], 21, 31, 33, 34, 35, 42, 51; **23:**3, 4, 5[2], 8[2], 10, 12, 16, 17[2], 18, 19[3], 20[2], 21[2], 23[2]; **24:**1, 10, 17

1Ki 1:1, 5, 6, 7, 10, 13, 17, 19[2], 23[2], 24, 25, 26, 30, 35[2], 37, 41, 42, 51[2], 52[2], 53; **2:**1[2], 4[2], 5[2], 8, 11[2], 13, 14, 15, 17[3], 22, 24, 25[2], 27[2], 28, 29, 30[2], 31, 32, 34, 46; **3:**1, 3, 6, 15; **4:**2, 15, 19, 24[2], 31, 32, 33[2]; **5:**1, 5, 7, 12, 14; **6:**1, 4, 5[2], 6, 9, 10, 15[2], 16[2], 19, 20, 21[2], 22[3], 23, 27, 28, 29, 30, 31, 32, 33, 35, 36, 38; **7:**1, 2, 6, 7[2], 8[2], 14[3], 15, 16, 18[2], 21[3], 23, 27, 36, 37, 38, 39[2], 40, 51; **8:**12, 15, 19, 20, 21[2], 23, 42, 54, 55, 56[2], 57, 58[2], 59, 63, 64, 66; **9:**1, 2, 13[2], 24, 25[3]; **10:**3, 4, 5, 9, 15, 17, 26[2], 27; **11:**3, 8, 10[2], 14, 15, 16, 17, 19, 22, 24, 25[2], 26, 27, 28[2], 29, 31, 32, 34, 41; **12:**2, 4, 5, 6, 8, 9, 15, 18, 21, 29[2], 31, 32[5], 33[4]; **13:**2[2], 3, 4[3], 10[2], 11, 12, 13[2], 14[2], 15, 16, 18[3], 19, 21, 23[4], 24, 26[2], 27, 28, 30, 31[2], 32, 33[2]; **14:**3, 5, 6, 13, 15[2], 16, 18, 19[2], 20, 21[2], 26[3], 29; **15:**2, 3[2], 5, 7, 10, 12, 13, 15, 17, 19, 20, 21, 23[3], 26[2], 29[5], 30[3], 31, 34[2]; **16:**5, 7[2], 9, 11[4], 12, 14, 18, 19[2], 20, 23, 24[2], 26[2], 27[2], 31, 32[2], 34[2]; **17:**5[2], 6, 10[3], 11, 15, 16, 19[3], 20, 21, 22; **18:**7, 8, 9, 10[2], 12[2], 14, 17, 18, 27[5], 30, 32[2], 33, 34[2], 35, 39[2], 42, 43[2], 44[2], 46; **19:**1, 3[2], 4[3], 5, 6[2], 8, 9[2], 10, 11, 13, 14, 19[2], 20[2], 21[2]; **20:**1, 2, 7, 9, 11, 12[3], 14[3], 15[2], 16, 18, 25, 28, 31, 32[3], 33[2], 34, 36[2], 37[2], 39[3], 40, 41[2], 42; **21:**4[2], 6[2], 10, 13, 15, 18[2], 20, 26, 27, 29; **22:**4, 8, 11, 15[2], 17, 18, 19, 20, 22[2], 28, 34, 38, 39[3], 42[2], 43[2], 45[2], 46, 52, 53

2Ki 1:2, 5, 7[2], 8[2], 9[3], 11[2], 13, 15, 16, 17[2], 18; **2:**3, 4, 5, 6, 10, 12[3], 13, 14[2], 16, 17[2], 18[2], 20, 21, 22, 23[2], 24, 25[2]; **3:**2[2], 3[2], 7[2], 8[2], 16, 18, 26, 27; **4:**3, 6, 7, 8[2], 10[2], 11[2], 12[2], 13, 14, 15[2], 16, 18, 19[2], 20[2], 23, 25, 29, 30, 31, 33, 34[2], 35, 36[3], 38, 41[3], 42, 43, 44; **5:**1[2], 3, 5, 6, 7[2], 8[2], 11, 12, 13, 14[2], 15[3], 16[3], 18, 19[2], 20, 21, 22, 23, 24[3], 25[2], 26, 27; **6:**2, 3, 4, 5, 6[2], 7[2], 11, 13[3], 14, 16, 17[2], 18, 19, 21, 22, 23[2], 27, 30[3], 31, 32, 33[2]; **7:**2, 11, 17[2], 19, 20; **8:**1, 5[3], 10, 11[2], 12, 13, 14[3], 15[2], 17[3], 18[2], 19, 21, 23, 26[2], 27[2], 28, 29[2]; **9:**5[3], 6[2], 10, 11, 12[2], 14, 15, 17[2], 18, 19, 20[2], 22[2], 24, 27[2], 32, 33[2], 34[2], 36[2]; **10:**5[2], 6, 8, 9, 10, 11, 12[2], 14[2], 15[5], 16, 17[4], 19[2], 22[2], 24, 25, 31, 34; **11:**2, 3, 5, 8[3], 12, 19[2], 21; **12:**1, 18, 19, 21; **13:**2[2], 3, 4, 7, 8, 11[3], 12[2], 14, 15, 16[2], 17[4], 18[4], 21, 23, 25; **14:**2[2], 3[2], 5, 6, 7, 11, 14, 15[2], 19, 20, 22, 24[2], 25[2], 27[2], 28[3]; **15:**2[3], 3, 5, 6, 9[2], 12, 13, 15, 16[2], 18[2], 21, 24[2], 25, 26, 28[2], 31, 33[3], 34[2], 35, 36; **16:**2, 3, 4, 13, 14, 18, 19; **17:**2, 4[2], 15[2], 20, 21, 22, 23, 26, 34, 37, 39; **18:**2[3], 3, 4[2], 5, 6, 7[3], 8, 22, 27, 29, 32; **19:**1, 2, 7, 8[2], 9[3], 32, 33[2], 37; **20:**2, 7, 9, 11, 12, 15, 19, 20; **21:**1, 2, 3[2], 4, 5, 6[2], 7[2], 16[2], 17[2], 19[2], 20, 21, 22, 25, 26; **22:**1[2], 2, 4, 8, 11; **23:**2, 4, 5, 6, 7, 8, 10, 11, 14, 15, 16, 17, 18, 19, 20, 24, 28, 29[2], 31[2], 32, 33, 34, 35[2], 36[2], 37; **24:**1, 2, 3, 4[2], 5, 8[2], 9, 12, 13, 14, 15[2], 18[2], 19, 20; **25:**1, 9[2], 19, 22, 25, 27, 28, 29

1Ch 1:10; **2:**3, 21[2], 23; **3:**4[2]; **4:**10; **5:**1[2], 6, 9, 20, 26; **6:**10; **7:**23[2]; **8:**7, 8, 9, 11; **10:**3, 4, 5, 13[2], 14; **11:**2, 8, 11, 13, 19, 20[2], 21[3], 22[2], 23[2], 25; **12:**1, 18, 19[2], 20; **13:**10[3], 14; **14:**4; **15:**3, 22[2]; **16:**2, 3, 4, 12, 14, 15, 16, 21[2], 25, 33, 34, 37, 40; **17:**12, 13; **18:**2, 3, 6, 10[2], 11, 13[2]; **19:**3, 5, 8, 10, 11, 12, 17; **20:**2, 3, 6, 7; **21:**3, 6, 7, 15[2], 19, 26, 27, 28, 30; **22:**2, 6, 10[2], 11, 18[2]; **23:**1, 2, 13[2]; **25:**10, 11, 12, 13, 14, 15, 16, 17, 18, 19, 20, 21, 22, 23, 24, 25, 26, 27, 28, 29, 30, 31; **26:**10; **27:**23, 24; **28:**4[2], 5, 6[2], 7, 9[2], 12, 14, 16, 17, 20; **29:**27[3], 28

2Ch 1:4, 5, 14[2], 15; **2:**11[2], 18; **3:**2, 4, 5[2], 6, 7, 8[2], 9, 10, 14, 15, 16, 17; **4:**1, 2, 6, 7, 8[2], 9, 10, 11, 14[2], 21; **5:**1, 13; **6:**1, 4[2], 9, 10, 11, 12, 13; **7:**3, 7, 10, 11, 21, 22; **8:**4[2], 5, 11[2], 12, 14; **9:**2, 3, 4, 8, 16, 25, 26, 27, 31; **10:**2, 4, 5, 6, 8, 9, 15, 18; **11:**1[2], 6, 11, 12, 15[2], 20, 21, 22, 23[3]; **12:**1, 4, 9[2], 12[2], 13[2], 14[2]; **13:**2, 20; **14:**3, 5, 6[2], 7[2]; **15:**2[3], 4, 8[2], 9, 15, 16, 18[2]; **16:**1, 3, 5, 6, 8, 10, 12, 14; **17:**2, 3, 5, 6, 7, 8, 11, 12, 13; **18:**2[2], 3, 7, 14[2], 16, 17, 18, 19, 21, 27, 33, 34; **19:**4, 5, 9; **20:**15, 21[2], 31[3], 32, 36; **21:**2, 3[2], 4, 5[2], 6[3], 7[2], 9, 10, 11, 19, 20[3]; **22:**2[2], 3, 4, 5, 6[3], 7[2], 8, 9[3], 12; **23:**3, 7[3], 10, 19, 20; **24:**1[2], 3, 5, 15[3], 16, 19, 20, 22[2], 25; **25:**1[2], 2, 3, 4, 5, 6, 14, 15, 16, 20, 21, 24, 27; **26:**2, 3[2], 4, 5[2], 6, 8, 10[3], 15[3], 16[2], 19, 20, 21, 23; **27:**1[2], 2[2], 3[2], 4[2], 5, 6, 8[2]; **28:**1[3], 2, 3, 4, 5, 9[2], 19, 21, 22, 23[2], 24, 25; **29:**1[2], 2, 3, 4, 8, 21[2], 23, 25; **30:**6, 8, 19; **31:**3, 4, 21[2]; **32:**2, 3, 5, 6, 9, 17, 21[2], 23, 24[2], 26, 27, 29, 31; **33:**1[2], 3[2], 4, 5, 6[3], 7[2], 12[2], 13[2], 14, 15[2], 16, 19[2], 21, 22; **34:**1[2], 2, 3[3], 4[2], 5, 6, 7[2], 8[2], 19, 30, 32; **35:**2, 21[2], 22, 24[2]; **36:**2[2], 5[3], 8, 9[3], 11, 12, 13[2], 14, 15, 17[2], 18, 20, 22, 23

Ezr 1:1, 2, 3, 4; **3:**11; **5:**12, 14; **6:**17; **7:**6, 8, 9[2]; **8:**23, 31, 35; **10:**1, 6[3]

Neh 1:2; **2:**8, 18, 20; **3:**12, 14, 15; **4:**1, 2, 3[2], 18; **5:**13; **6:**10, 12, 13, 18; **7:**2; **8:**3, 5[2], 10, 18; **9:**29; **12:**8; **13:**2, 5

Est 1:3, 4, 10, 20, 22; **2:**1, 4, 7, 9[2], 17, 18; **3:**4[3], 6; **4:**4, 5, 8, 11; **5:**5, 9[2], 10[2], 11, 14; **6:**1, 4; **7:**5[2], 7, 8, 10; **8:**1, 2, 3, 5, 7, 10; **9:**25[3], 30

Job 1:10, 11[2], 12, 16, 17, 18; **2:**3, 4, 5, 6, 8[2], 10; **4:**18[2]; **5:**12, 13, 15, 18[2], 19, 20; **6:**5, 9, 14; **7:**9, 10; **8:**4, 6, 15[2], 16, 18, 20, 21; **9:**3[2], 4, 11[2], 12, 16[2], 17, 18, 19, 22, 23, 24[2], 32; **11:**6, 10, 11[3]; **12:**4, 5, 13, 14[2], 15[2], 17, 18, 19, 20, 21, 22, 23[2], 24, 25; **13:**9, 10, 15, 16, 19, 28; **14:**2[2], 5, 6[2], 10, 14, 20, 21[2]; **15:**3[2], 14[3], 15, 22[3], 23[2], 25, 26, 27, 28, 29[2], 30[2], 33; **16:**7, 9[2], 12[2], 13[2], 14[2]; **17:**3, 5, 6, 9; **18:**4, 8[2], 17, 18, 19; **19:**8[2], 9, 10[2], 11[2], 13, 16, 25; **20:**7[2], 8[2], 12, 13, 15[2], 16, 17, 18[3], 19[3], 20[3], 22, 23[2], 24; **21:**19[2], 20, 21, 22, 31, 32; **22:**2, 4[2], 8, 13, 14[2], 18, 27, 29, 30; **23:**5[2], 6[2], 8, 9[2], 10[2], 13[2], 14, 17; **24:**18[2], 20, 21, 22[2], 23; **25:**2, 4; **26:**7, 8, 9, 10, 12[2], 13; **27:**7, 8, 10[2], 16, 17, 18, 19[3], 21, 22; **28:**3, 9[2], 10, 11[2], 23, 24, 25, 26, 27[2], 28; **30:**11, 19, 24; **31:**4, 14, 15, 18, 20; **32:**1, 2, 4, 14; **33:**10[2], 11[2], 13, 16, 17, 18, 19, 24, 25, 26[4], 27, 28; **34:**9[2], 10[2], 11, 14[2], 17, 21, 23[2], 24, 25[2], 26, 28, 29[2], 33, 37[2]; **35:**7, 15[2], 16; **36:**4, 5, 6, 7[2], 9, 10, 13, 15, 16, 18, 19, 27, 30, 31[2], 32; **37:**3, 4[2], 5, 6, 7, 11[2], 12, 13, 17, 20, 23[2], 24; **39:**7[2], 8, 10, 12, 17, 21[2], 22[2], 24[2], 25[2]; **40:**2[2], 15, 17, 19[2], 21, 23[3], 24; **41:**3[2], 4, 25, 27, 29, 30, 31[2], 32, 34[2]; **42:**3, 10[2], 12, 13, 14

Ps 1:2, 3[2]; **2:**4, 5, 12; **3:**4, ttl; **7:**2, 12[3], 13[2], 14, 15[2], ttl; **9:**7, 8[2], 12[3], 16; **10:**5, 6, 8[2], 9[4], 10, 11[3], 13; **11:**6; **13:**6; **15:**2, 3, 4[2], 5[2]; **16:**8; **18:**6, 7, 9, 10[2], 11, 14[2], 16[3], 17, 19[3], 20, 30, 33, 34, 41, 48, 50, ttl; **19:**4; **20:**6; **21:**1, 4, 7; **22:**8[3], 9, 24[4], 28, 31; **23:**2[2], 3[2]; **24:**2, 4, 5, 10; **25:**8, 9[2], 12[3], 14, 15; **27:**5[3], 14; **28:**5, 6, 8; **29:**6; **31:**21, 24; **32:**1, 10; **33:**5, 7[2], 9[2], 10, 12, 13, 14, 15[2], 17, 20; **34:**4, 12[2], 20, ttl[2]; **35:**8, 14; **36:**2, 3, 4[3]; **37:**4, 5, 6, 13, 23, 24[2], 26, 33, 34, 36[3], 39, 40; **39:**6; **40:**1, 2, 3; **41:**1, 2, 5, 6[4], 8[2]; **44:**21; **45:**11; **46:**6, 8, 9[3]; **47:**2, 3, 4[2], 9; **48:**14; **49:**9, 10, 12, 15, 17[2], 18[2], 19; **50:**4[2], 9; **51:**ttl; **52:**5; **54:**5, 7; **55:**12, 17, 18, 19, 20[2], 22[2]; **56:**1; **57:**3, ttl; **58:**7, 9, 10[2], 11; **60:**12, ttl; **61:**7; **62:**2[2], 6[2]; **63:**ttl; **65:**4; **66:**5, 6, 7, 16, 17, 19; **68:**6, 20, 33, 35; **71:**6; **72:**2, 4[2], 6, 8, 12[2], 13, 14, 15[2]; **74:**5; **75:**7, 8; **76:**3, 12[2]; **77:**1, 7, 9; **78:**4, 5[2], 11, 12, 13[2], 14, 15, 16, 20[3], 23, 25, 26[2], 27, 28, 29, 33, 34, 38[2], 39, 42, 43, 45, 46, 47, 48, 49, 50[2], 53, 54, 55, 59, 60[2], 62, 66[2], 67, 68, 69[2], 70, 71, 72; **81:**5[2], 16; **82:**1; **84:**11; **85:**8; **87:**6; **89:**26, 41, 48[2]; **91:**1, 2, 3, 4, 11, 14[2], 15; **92:**12, 15; **93:**1[2]; **94:**9[4], 10[4], 14, 23; **95:**5, 7; **96:**4, 10, 13[3]; **97:**10[2]; **98:**1, 2, 3, 9[2]; **99:**1, 2, 5, 6, 7[2]; **100:**3[2]; **101:**6[2], 7[2]; **102:**16, 17, 19, 23[2], ttl; **103:**7, 9[2], 10, 12, 14[2], 15; **104:**10, 13, 14[2], 16, 19, 32[2]; **105:**5, 7, 8[2], 9, 14[2], 16[2], 17, 18, 21, 24, 25, 26[2], 28, 29, 31, 32, 33, 34, 36, 37, 39, 40, 41, 42, 43; **106:**1, 3, 8[2], 9[2], 10, 15, 23[3], 26, 33, 40, 41, 43, 44[2], 45, 46; **107:**1, 2, 6, 7, 9, 12, 13, 14, 16, 19, 20, 25, 28, 29, 30, 33, 35, 36, 38, 40, 41; **108:**13; **109:**7, 11, 15, 16[2], 17[2], 18, 19, 31; **110:**6[3], 7[2]; **111:**4, 5[2], 6[2], 9[2]; **112:**4, 5, 6, 7, 8[2], 9[2], 10; **113:**7, 8, 9; **115:**3[2], 9, 10, 11, 12[3], 13, 16; **116:**1, 2, 6; **118:**1, 18, 26, 29; **120:**1; **121:**3[2], 4, 7; **123:**2; **126:**6; **127:**2; **129:**4, 7; **130:**8; **132:**2, 11, 13; **135:**6, 7[3], 14; **136:**1; **137:**8, 9; **138:**6[2]; **142:**ttl; **143:**3[2]; **144:**2, 10; **145:**19[2], 20; **146:**4, 5, 9[2]; **147:**2, 3, 4[2], 6, 9, 10[2], 13[2], 14, 15, 16[2], 17, 18[2], 19, 20; **148:**5, 6[2], 14; **149:**4

Prv 2:7[2], 8; **3:**6, 12[2], 19, 29, 30, 33, 34[2]; **4:**4; **5:**21, 22, 23[2]; **6:**13[3], 14[2], 15, 19, 29, 30[2], 31[3], 32, 33, 34, 35[2]; **7:**8, 19, 20, 22; **8:**26, 27[2], 28[2], 29[2], 36; **9:**7[2], 8[2], 9[2], 18; **10:**3, 4, 5[2], 9[2], 10, 17[2], 18[2], 19, 22; **11:**12, 13, 15[2], 17, 19, 25, 26, 27[2], 28, 29, 30; **12:**1, 2, 8, 9[2], 11[2], 15, 17, 27; **13:**3[2], 11, 13, 18, 20, 24[2]; **14:**2[2], 17, 21[3], 29[2], 31[2]; **15:**5, 9, 10, 12, 15, 18, 24, 25, 27[2], 29, 32[2]; **16:**5, 7, 17, 20[2], 26, 30[2], 32[3]; **17:**5, 9[2], 15[2], 16, 19[2], 20[2], 21, 27, 28[2]; **18:**9, 13[2], 17, 20; **19:**1, 2, 5, 7, 8[2], 9, 16[2], 17[3], 23[2], 25, 26; **20:**4, 14[2], 19, 22; **21:**1[2], 11, 13, 17[2], 21, 26, 27, 29; **22:**5, 6[3], 8, 9[2], 11, 12, 14, 16[2], 22, 27, 29[2]; **23:**7[3], 9, 11, 13, 24, 34[2]; **24:**7, 8, 12[4], 17, 18, 24, 29; **25:**10, 13, 17, 20[2], 21, 28; **26:**5, 6, 8[2], 17, 24, 25, 27; **27:**14, 18; **28:**6[2], 7, 8[2], 9, 10, 13, 14, 16, 18, 19[2], 20, 22, 23[2], 25[2], 26[2], 27[2]; **29:**1, 3, 4, 9, 17[2], 18[2], 19[2], 21, 24, 27; **30:**5, 6, 10, 22[2], 31; **31:**11, 23, 28

APNDX

1Ti 1:12; 3:1, 5, 6, 7[2]; 5:8; 6:4, 15

2Ti 1:12, 16, 17[2], 18[2]; 2:4, 5[2], 12, 13[2], 21; 4:11, 15

Tit 1:9[2]; 2:8, 14; 3:5, 6, 11

Phlm 13, 15, 18

Heb 1:2[2], 3, 4, 5[2], 6[2], 7, 8, 13; 2:5, 8[2], 9, 11[2], 14[2], 16[2], 17, 18[2]; 3:3, 4, 17, 18; 4:3, 4, 7, 8, 10[2]; 5:1, 2, 3, 4, 5, 6, 7[2], 8[3], 9, 13; 6:13[2], 15[2]; 7:6, 8[2], 10, 13, 17, 20, 24, 25[2], 27[2]; 8:4[2], 5[2], 6[2], 8, 13[2]; 9:7, 12, 15, 19, 21, 25, 26[2], 28; 10:5[2], 8, 9[3], 12, 14, 15, 20, 23, 28, 29[2], 37; 11:4[3], 5[3], 6[3], 7, 8[4], 9, 10, 16, 17[2], 19, 21, 22, 23[2], 24, 26, 27[2], 28[2]; 12:6[2], 7, 10, 17[4], 26; 13:5, 12, 23

Jas 1:6, 7, 9, 10[2], 12[2], 13[2], 14, 18, 23, 24[2], 25; 2:5, 10, 11, 13, 14, 21, 23; 4:6[2], 7, 8, 10, 11; 5:6, 7, 15, 17, 18, 20

1Pt 1:15; 2:6, 7, 23[3]; 3:10, 13, 18, 19; 4:1, 2, 14[2]; 5:6, 7, 8

2Pt 1:9[2], 17; 2:19

1Jn 1:7, 9; 2:2, 4, 6[3], 9[2], 10, 11[2], 17, 22[2], 23, 25, 28, 29; 3:2[2], 3, 5, 7[2], 8[2], 9[2], 10, 12, 14, 16, 23, 24[4]; 4:4[2], 6[2], 8, 10, 13[2], 15, 16, 17, 18, 19, 20[5], 21; 5:5[2], 6, 9, 10[3], 12[2], 14, 15, 16[3], 18

2Jn 9[2], 11

3Jn 10[2], 11[2]

Jude 6, 9

Rev 1:1, 2, 3, 7, 16, 17, 18; 2:1, 7, 11[2], 12, 17[2], 23, 26, 27, 29; 3:1, 5, 6, 7[4], 12, 13, 20, 22; 4:3; 5:7, 8; 6:2[2], 3, 5[2], 7, 9, 12; 7:2, 14, 15; 8:1, 3; 9:2, 5; 10:2[2], 3, 7[2], 9, 11; 11:5, 15; 12:9, 12[2], 13[2], 15; 13:6, 10[2], 11[2], 12, 13[2], 14, 15, 16, 17; 14:4, 10, 16, 17; 16:15[2], 16; 17:3, 10[2], 11, 14, 15; 18:2, 22; 19:2, 9[2], 10, 11[2], 12[2], 13, 15[3], 16, 17, 20; 20:2, 3[2], 6; 21:3, 5[2], 6, 7[2], 10, 15, 16, 17; 22:1, 6, 7, 9, 10, 11[4], 20

HER

Gen 2:22; 3:6[2], 15; 4:11, 12; 8:9[3], 11; 12:15[2], 16, 19[2]; 16:2, 3[3], 4[2], 5, 6[3], 7, 9[2], 10, 11, 13; 17:15[2], 16[4]; 19:33; 20:4, 6, 7, 13; 21:10, 12, 14[2], 16[2], 17, 19; 23:2; 24:15[2], 16[2], 17, 18[2], 20, 21, 22, 28, 43, 45[3], 46[2], 47[3], 51[2], 53[2], 55[2], 57, 58, 59, 60, 61, 64, 67[2]; 25:1, 22, 23, 24[2]; 26:9; 27:6, 15[3], 17, 42[2]; 29:9, 12[2], 19[2], 20, 21, 23[2], 27, 28, 29, 31; 30:1, 3[2], 4[2], 9[2], 15, 16, 21, 22[2]; 31:19, 35; 33:2, 7; 34:2[4], 8, 11[2]; 35:17, 18, 20; 38:2[2], 8, 11, 14[3], 15[3], 16, 18[2], 19[3], 20, 22, 23[3], 24[2], 25, 26[2], 27[2]; 39:7, 10[3], 12, 13, 14, 16; 40:10; 48:7

Ex 2:5[2], 8, 9, 10; 3:22[3]; 4:25; 11:2; 15:20[2]; 18:2, 3, 6[2]; 21:4[2], 8[5], 9[2], 10[3], 11, 22[2]; 22:16[2], 17[2]

Lev 11:19; 12:2, 4[2], 5[2], 6, 7[3], 8; 15:19[3], 20, 21, 23, 24[2], 25[5], 26[4], 28, 29, 30[2], 33[3]; 18:7, 11, 15, 17[5], 18[4], 19[2], 20, 25; 19:20, 29; 20:14, 17, 18[4]; 21:3, 7, 9, 13; 22:13[3], 28; 25:19, 22; 26:4, 20, 34[2], 43

Nu 5:13[3], 15[2], 16[2], 18, 19, 24, 27[6], 29, 30, 31; 12:12, 13, 14[4]; 16:30, 32; 19:3[3], 4[2], 5[4], 8; 22:23, 25, 33; 25:8; 26:10, 59; 30:3[2], 4[8], 5[8], 6[2], 7[5], 8[6], 9[2], 10[2], 11[5], 12[6], 13[2], 14[6], 15, 16[2]; 36:8

Dt 11:6, 17; 14:18; 20:7[2]; 21:11[2], 12[3], 13[6], 14[5]; 22:13[2], 14[4], 15, 16, 17, 19, 21[4], 23[2], 25[3], 27[2], 28[2], 29[3]; 24:1[5], 3[5], 4[3]; 25:5[4], 8, 11[2], 12[2]; 28:30, 56[5], 57[3]; 32:11[4], 22

Jos 2:14, 15, 17; 6:17, 22, 23[4], 25; 8:2[2]; 10:1[2], 39; 13:17; 15:18[3], 19, 45[2], 47[4]; 17:11[6], 16; 21:13[2], 14[2], 15[2], 16[3], 17[2], 18[2], 21[2], 22[2], 23[2], 24[2], 25[2], 27[2], 28[2], 29[2], 30[2], 31[2], 32[3], 34[2], 35[2], 36[2], 37[2], 38[2], 39[2]

Jdg 1:14[3], 15, 27[5]; 4:5, 8, 18, 19, 20, 21, 22; 5:26[2], 27[2], 29[2]; 11:26[2], 34, 35, 37, 38[3], 39[2]; 13:3, 6, 9[2], 10, 13, 14[3]; 14:2, 3, 8, 16, 17[2]; 15:1, 2[6], 6[3]; 16:1, 5[2], 7, 8, 9, 11, 13, 16, 17[2], 18[2], 19; 19:2, 3[5], 25[4], 26, 27[2], 28[2], 29[3]; 20:6[2]

Ru 1:3, 5[2], 6, 7[2], 8[2], 9, 10, 14[2], 15[2], 18[2], 22[2]; 2:1, 2, 3, 10, 11, 14[2], 15[2], 16[2], 18[2], 19[3], 20[2], 22, 23; 3:1[2], 5, 6[2], 7, 15, 16[3]; 4:13[2], 16, 17

1Sa 1:4[2], 5, 6[4], 7, 8[2], 12, 13[3], 14, 18[2], 19, 22, 23[3], 24; 2:19; 4:19[4], 20[3], 21[2]; 18:17, 21; 25:19[2], 20, 23, 35[2], 39, 40, 41, 42; 28:7[2], 10, 13, 14

2Sa 3:15[2], 16[3]; 6:16, 23; 11:4[4], 26[2], 27; 12:24[2]; 13:1, 2, 5, 6, 8, 10, 11[2], 14[3], 15[4], 16, 17, 18[3], 19[5], 20[3]; 14:2, 3, 4, 5; 17:8; 20:17, 22; 21:10

1Ki 1:2[3], 3, 4, 31; 2:19[2], 20; 3:1, 17, 20[2], 26[3], 27; 9:24[2]; 10:2, 3[3], 5, 13[4]; 14:5[2], 6; 15:13[2]; 17:10, 11, 13, 15, 19[2], 20; 21:6

2Ki 4:2, 5[3], 6[2], 9, 12, 13, 14[2], 15[2], 17, 20, 22, 24, 25, 26[2], 27[4], 30, 36, 37; 5:3; 6:28, 29[2]; 8:2, 3[2], 5[3], 6; 9:10, 22, 30[2], 33[4], 34, 35[3]; 11:1, 3, 14, 15[3], 16; 19:21; 22:14

1Ch 2:18; 5:16; 6:57, 58[2], 59[2], 60[3], 67[2], 68[2], 69[2], 70[2], 71[2], 72[2], 73[2], 74[2], 75[2], 76[3], 77[2], 78[2], 79[2], 80[2], 81[2]; 7:29[4]; 15:29; 18:1

2Ch 8:11; 9:1, 2[3], 4, 12[3]; 11:20; 15:16[2]; 22:10; 23:13, 14[3], 15[2]; 34:22; 36:21

Est 1:11, 19; 2:1, 7, 9[6], 10[3], 11, 13[2], 14, 15[2], 17[2], 20[3]; 4:4[2], 5, 8[3]; 5:1, 3, 12; 8:1

Job 2:10; 5:16; 9:6; 21:10; 31:10, 18; 39:14, 16[2], 17[2], 26, 27, 29, 30

Ps 34:2; 45:13, 14[2]; 46:5[2]; 48:3, 12, 13[2]; 55:11; 58:4; 67:6; 68:13, 31; 69:15; 80:11[2], 12[2]; 84:3; 85:12; 87:5[2]; 102:13, 14; 104:17; 107:42; 123:2; 132:15[2], 16[2]; 137:5

Prv 1:20, 21; 2:4[2], 16, 17[2], 18[2], 19; 3:15, 16[2], 17[2], 18[2]; 4:6[2], 8[2], 13[2]; 5:3, 4, 5[2], 6, 8[2], 19[3]; 6:6, 8[2], 25[3], 29; 7:5, 8[2], 11[2], 21[2], 22, 25[2], 26, 27; 8:1; 9:1[2], 2[3], 3, 14, 18; 12:4; 14:1[2]; 17:12, 25; 27:8, 16; 30:20, 23, 28; 31:10, 11[2], 12, 13, 14, 15[2], 16, 17[2], 18[2], 19[2], 20[2], 21[2], 22, 23, 25, 26[2], 27, 28[4], 31[4]

Ecc 7:26[3]; 11:5

Song 2:13; 3:4; 6:9[6]; 8:5, 9[2]

Isa 1:27; 3:26; 4:5; 5:14; 7:16; 9:1[2]; 10:11[2]; 13:10, 13, 22[2]; 16:8; 21:9; 23:3, 7[2], 17, 18[3]; 24:2; 26:17[2], 21[2]; 27:2; 29:7[3]; 34:12, 13, 15[3], 16; 37:22; 40:2[4]; 49:15[2]; 51:3[3], 18[2]; 52:11; 53:7; 61:10, 11; 65:18, 19; 66:7, 8, 10[4], 11[2], 12[3]

Jer 2:23, 24[6], 32[2]; 3:1, 7, 8[3], 9, 10[2], 20; 4:17, 31[3]; 5:10[2]; 6:3[2], 4, 5, 6, 7[3]; 8:7, 19[2]; 9:20; 12:7, 9; 15:9; 17:8[2]; 19:15; 20:17; 30:18; 31:8, 15[2]; 44:17, 18, 19[4], 25; 46:21[2], 22, 23; 48:4, 15, 19, 28, 41; 49:2, 4, 14, 19[2], 22, 24[2], 26[2]; 50:2[2], 3[2], 9, 10, 13, 14, 15[6], 26[5], 27, 29[3], 30[2], 35[2], 36, 37[2], 38, 44[2]; 51:2[3], 3[2], 4, 6[2], 7, 8[2], 9[2], 27[3], 28, 30[2], 33[2], 36[2], 43, 45, 47[3], 48, 52[2], 53[2], 55[2], 56[2], 57[5], 58, 64

Lam 1:2[7], 3[2], 4[3], 5[5], 6[2], 7[7], 8[3], 9[3], 10[2], 11, 17[2]; 2:5, 7, 9[5], 16; 4:6, 7, 13[3]

Ezk 5:5, 6; 12:19; 13:16; 16:2, 32, 44, 45[2], 46[2], 48, 49[2], 53[2], 55[2], 57; 17:7[3], 9; 19:2, 3, 5[2], 11[3], 12[2], 14[2]; 22:2[2], 3, 10, 24, 25[2], 26, 27, 28; 23:4, 5[2], 7, 8[5], 9[2], 10[5], 11[5], 12, 14, 16, 17[3], 18[4], 19[2], 31, 42, 43[2], 44; 24:7[2], 8, 12[3]; 26:4[4], 6, 17; 28:22[2], 23[4]; 29:12, 19[3]; 30:4[2], 6, 7, 8, 18[5]; 31:4[2]; 32:7, 16[4], 18, 20[2], 22, 23[2], 24[2], 25[3], 26[2], 29[2]; 33:28; 34:27[2]; 36:38; 44:22

Dan 11:6[3], 7, 17

Hos 1:6; 2:2[6], 3[5], 4, 6, 7, 8[2], 9, 10[3], 11[5], 12[2], 13[4], 14[3], 15[3], 17, 23[2]; 3:1, 2, 3; 4:18, 19[2]; 9:2, 10; 10:7, 11, 14; 13:8, 16

Joel 1:8; 2:16, 22; 3:17

Am 4:3; 5:2[2]

Oba 1

Jna 1:15; 2:6

Mic 1:9; 4:6[3], 7[2], 11; 7:5, 6[2], 10[2]

Nah 2:7[2], 13; 3:4[2], 7, 8, 9, 10[3]

Zep 2:14, 15[2]; 3:1, 2, 3[3], 4[2], 19[2]

Hag 1:10; 2:3

Zec 2:5[2]; 5:11; 7:7; 8:2, 12[2]; 9:4[2], 5; 12:6; 14:10

Mal 3:11

Mt 1:6, 19[3], 20, 25[2]; 2:18; 5:28[2], 31, 32[2]; 8:15[2]; 9:18, 22, 25; 10:35[2]; 11:19; 14:4, 7, 8, 9, 11; 15:23[2], 28[2]; 19:7, 9; 20:20, 21; 21:2; 22:28; 23:37[2]; 24:29; 26:13

Mk 1:30, 31[3]; 5:23, 29[2], 32, 33, 34, 41, 43; 6:17, 23, 24, 26, 28; 7:26, 27, 29, 30[2]; 10:4, 11, 12; 12:21, 22, 23, 44[2]; 13:24, 28; 14:5, 6[2], 9; 16:11

Lk 1:5, 28, 29, 30, 35, 36[2], 38, 41, 45, 56[2], 58[4], 61; 2:7, 19, 22, 36, 51; 4:38, 39[2]; 7:12, 13[3], 35, 38, 44, 47, 48; 8:43, 44, 48, 52, 54, 55[2], 56; 10:38, 40, 41, 42; 11:27; 12:53[2]; 13:12[3], 13, 34[2]; 15:9[2]; 16:18[2]; 18:5[2]; 20:30, 31, 33; 21:4

Jn 2:4; 4:7, 10, 13, 16, 17, 21, 26, 27, 28[2]; 8:3, 7, 10, 11; 11:1, 2, 5, 23, 25, 28[2], 31[3], 33[2], 40; 12:3, 7; 16:21; 18:16; 19:27; 20:13, 15, 16, 17, 18

Act 5:8, 9, 10[4]; 7:21; 8:27; 9:37, 40, 41[3]; 12:15; 16:15, 16, 18, 19; 19:27; 21:3; 27:15, 32

Ro 7:2[2], 3[2]; 9:12, 25; 16:2[2]

1Co 7:2, 4, 10, 11[2], 12, 13[2], 34, 36, 38[2], 39[2]; 11:5[2], 6[2], 10, 15[3]; 13:5

Gal 4:25, 30

Eph 5:33

1Th 2:7

Jas 1:4; 5:18

2Pt 2:22

2Jn 1

Rev 2:21[2], 22[2], 23; 6:13; 12:1[2], 4, 5, 6, 14, 15, 16, 17; 14:8, 18; 16:19; 17:2, 4[2], 5, 6, 7, 16[3]; 18:3[3], 4[3], 5[2], 6[4], 7[2], 8[2], 9[4], 10, 11, 15[2], 18, 19, 20[2], 24; 19:2[2], 3, 8; 21:2, 11; 22:2

HERS

Dt 21:15

1Sa 25:42

2Ki 8:6

Job 39:16

HERSELF

Gen 18:12; 20:5; 24:65; 38:14

Ex 2:5

Lev 15:28; 21:9

Nu 22:25; 30:3

Jdg 5:29

Ru 2:10

1Sa 4:19; 25:23, 41

2Sa 11:2

1Ki 14:5

2Ki 4:37

Job 39:18

Ps 84:3

Prv 31:22

Isa 5:14; 34:14; 61:10

Jer 3:11; 4:31; 49:24

Ezk 22:3[2]; 23:7; 24:12

Hos 2:13

Zec 9:3

Mt 9:21

Mk 4:28

Lk 1:24; 13:11

Jn 20:14, 16

Heb 11:11

Rev 2:20; 18:7; 19:7

HIM

Gen 1:27; 2:15, 18[2], 20; 3:9, 23; 4:7, 8, 15[4], 19, 26; 5:1, 24; 6:6, 22; 7:5, 7, 16[2], 23; 8:1, 8, 9[2], 11, 12, 18; 9:8, 24; 10:21; 12:3, 4[2], 7, 20[2]; 13:1, 11, 14; 14:5, 17[2], 19, 20; 15:4, 5[2], 6, 7, 9, 10, 12; 16:1, 12, 13; 17:1, 3, 17, 19[2], 20[4], 22, 23, 27; 18:1, 2, 9, 10, 18, 19[3], 29, 30; 19:3, 5, 6, 16[3], 21, 26, 30, 32, 34[2], 35; 20:3, 6, 9, 14; 21:2, 3[2], 4, 5, 7, 16[2], 18[2], 21; 22:1, 2, 3[2], 9[2], 11, 12, 13[2]; 23:5, 14; 24:5, 6, 9, 18, 19, 24, 25, 32, 33, 35, 36, 47, 54; 25:2, 9, 21, 33; 26:2, 7, 9, 12, 14, 20, 24, 26, 31, 32[2]; 27:1[2], 12, 13, 22, 23[2], 25[2], 26, 27[2], 32, 33, 37[3], 39, 41, 42, 44, 45; 28:1[3], 6[4]; 29:5, 13[4], 14[2], 20, 23, 28, 30, 34; 30:4, 16, 20, 27, 29, 37; 31:2, 7, 14, 15, 20, 23[3], 24, 32; 32:1, 3, 6, 7, 11, 19, 20, 21, 24, 25[2], 27, 29[2], 31; 33:1, 4[3], 11, 13, 17; 34:6, 8; 35:2, 6, 7, 9, 10, 11, 13[2], 14, 15, 18, 26, 29; 36:5; 37:3, 4[3], 5, 8[2], 10[2], 11, 13, 14[2], 15[2], 18[3], 20[3], 21[2], 22[4], 23, 24[2], 27[2], 33, 35[2], 36; 38:5, 7, 10, 14, 18; 39:1[2], 3, 4[2], 5, 12[2], 15, 17, 19, 20[2], 21[2], 23; 40:7, 8, 9, 12, 23; 41:12, 13, 14, 33, 34, 42, 43[3], 45, 50; 42:4, 6, 8, 10, 16, 24, 29, 31, 37[3], 38; 43:3, 5, 7, 9[4], 19, 26[2], 32[2], 33, 34[2]; 44:7, 9, 14, 18, 20, 21[2], 24, 28, 29, 32; 45:1[2], 3, 9, 15, 26, 27[2], 28; 46:5, 6, 7[2], 20, 27, 28, 29, 31; 47:7, 18[2], 29, 31; 48:1, 10, 13, 17; 49:9, 10, 19, 23[3], 26; 50:1[2], 3[2], 7, 9, 12, 13[2], 14, 15, 17, 26

Ex 1:16; 2:2[2], 3[2], 4, 6, 10[2], 12, 13, 20, 22; 3:2, 4, 18; 4:2, 6, 11, 13, 15, 16, 18, 23, 24[2], 26, 27[2], 28[2]; 6:2, 20[2], 23[2], 25[2]; 7:16; 8:1, 20; 9:1, 13, 29; 10:1, 3, 7, 28; 12:4, 44, 48, 49; 13:14, 19; 14:6; 15:2[2], 25; 16:8; 17:10, 12; 18:7, 17; 19:3, 7, 19, 24; 20:7; 21:3, 4[2], 6[3], 10, 13, 14[2], 16, 19[2], 22, 26, 27, 29, 30[2], 31, 36; 22:2, 3[2], 7, 12, 13,

APNDX

17, 21, 25^2, 26; **23:**4, 5^3, 21^3; **24:**2, 14, 18; **28:**1, 3, 41, 43^2; **29:**5, 7, 17, 21^2, 29; **30:**21; **31:**3, 6, 18; **32:**1^2, 23, 26^2, 33; **33:**4, 15; **34:**4, 5, 6, 20, 29, 30, 31, 32, 34, 35; **35:**5, 21, 31; **36:**2, 3; **38:**23; **40:**13^2, 16

Lev 1:1, 3, 4^2; **4:**3, 12, 14, 19, 21, 26^2, 31^2, 35; **5:**2, 3, 4, 6, 10^2, 13^2, 16^2, 18^2; **6:**2, 4, 5, 7^2; **7:**18, 20; **8:**2, 4, 7^6, 8, 12^2, 30^2; **9:**9, 12, 13, 18; **13:**3^2, 4, 5^2, 6^2, 8, 10, 11^2, 12, 13, 14, 15, 17^2, 20, 21, 22, 23, 25, 26, 27^2, 28, 30, 31, 33, 34, 36, 37, 44, 46; **14:**4, 7^2, 11, 12, 14, 17, 18^2, 19, 20, 21, 25, 28, 29^2, 31, 32; **15:**7, 8, 10, 14, 15, 16, 24, 32^3, 33^2; **16:**9, 10^2, 21^2, 22; **17:**10; **18:**6; **19:**13^2, 17, 22^2, 33, 34; **20:**2, 3, 4, 5^2, 6, 9; **21:**2, 3, 8, 12, 15, 17; **22:**3, 4; **24:**9, 11, 12, 14^3, 16, 19, 20, 23^2; **25:**27, 28^2, 30, 35, 36, 37^2, 39, 41, 43, 47, 48, 49^3, 50^4, 52^2, 53^2, 54; **26:**46; **27:**8^2, 18, 19, 23, 24^2

Nu 2:5, 12, 20, 27; **3:**6, 9, 42; **4:**49; **5:**7, 8, 12, 14^2, 30; **6:**9, 11; **7:**89^3; **8:**2; **9:**7, 14; **10:**30; **11:**20, 25^2, 29, 30; **12:**6^2, 8; **13:**27, 31; **14:**24^2, 36; **15:**28^2, 29^2, 31, 33^2, 34^2, 35, 36^2; **16:**5^4, 10, 11, 25, 40; **17:**6, 11; **19:**13^2, 18, 20; **20:**9, 18, 19, 20, 21; **21:**24, 34^3, 35^2; **22:**5, 7, 16, 20, 22^2, 32, 36, 40, 41; **23:**4, 6, 9^2, 13, 14, 17^3, 21; **24:**2, 8, 9, 17^2, 19; **25:**12, 13; **26:**54; **27:**11, 18, 19^2, 20, 21^2, 22^2, 23^2; **31:**17, 18, 35; **32:**15, 16, 21; **35:**16, 17, 18, 19^2, 20^2, 21^3, 22^2, 23^2, 25, 27, 30, 32, 33

Dt 1:3, 16, 36, 38; **2:**24, 30^2, 33^2; **3:**2^3, 3^2, 28^2; **4:**7, 20, 25, 29^2, 34, 35, 42; **5:**11; **6:**13, 16; **7:**9, 10^4; **8:**6; **9:**18, 20, 23; **10:**8, 9, 12, 18, 20^2; **11:**13, 22; **13:**4^3, 8^4, 9^3, 10; **14:**27; **15:**8^2, 9, 10^2, 12, 13^2, 14^2, 18; **17:**7^2, 15, 18, 19; **18:**4, 5^2, 15, 18, 19, 20, 22; **19:**6^3, 11^3, 12^2, 13, 16, 19; **20:**5, 6, 7, 8; **21:**1, 2, 5, 15, 17, 18, 19^2, 21, 22, 23; **22:**2^2, 4, 18, 19, 26; **23:**10, 16^2; **24:**1, 7^2, 13, 15; **25:**2, 3^2, 5, 8^2, 9, 10, 11^3; **26:**3; **28:**44, 55; **29:**15^2, 20^2, 21; **30:**20; **31:**7, 14, 29; **32:**10^4, 12^2, 13^2, 15, 16^2; **33:**7^3, 9, 11^2, 12^2, 16^2, 24^2; **34:**1, 4, 6, 9^2, 11

Jos 1:18; **2:**19, 23; **4:**14; **5:**3, 13^3, 14; **6:**5, 7, 20; **7:**3, 19, 24, 25, 26; **8:**11, 14, 23; **9:**6, 9^2; **10:**7, 15, 23, 24, 29, 31, 33^2, 34, 36, 38, 43; **11:**7, 9; **13:**1; **14:**6, 7, 13; **15:**16, 17, 18^2; **19:**50; **20:**4^2, 5^2; **22:**5^2, 14, 27, 30; **24:**3^2, 14, 22, 30, 33^2

Jdg 1:3, 5, 6^2, 7, 12, 13, 14^2, 15, 24; **2:**9; **3:**10, 13, 15, 16, 19^2, 20, 23, 27, 28, 31; **4:**6, 7, 10, 13, 14, 18^2, 19^2, 21, 22^2; **5:**13, 25, 31; **6:**12^2, 13, 14, 15, 16, 17, 19, 20, 23, 25, 27, 31^5, 32^2, 34, 35; **7:**1, 3, 5, 8, 9, 19; **8:**1^2, 3, 4, 8^2, 14^2, 31; **9:**3, 4^2, 16, 19, 24, 25, 26, 28^2, 33, 34, 35, 36, 38^2, 40^2, 44, 48^3, 54^3; **10:**3, 6; **11:**2^2, 3, 11, 15, 19, 28, 34, 36; **12:**5, 6^3, 8, 11, 13; **13:**6, 10, 11, 12, 18, 23, 24, 25; **14:**3, 5, 6^2, 11^2, 13, 16, 17^2, 18, 19; **15:**1, 10, 12, 13^3, 14^2; **16:**2^3, 5^4, 8, 9, 12^2, 14, 15, 16^2, 19^4, 20, 21^3, 24, 25, 26, 31^3; **17:**9^2, 10, 11; **18:**3, 5, 15, 19, 25, 26; **19:**1, 2^2, 3^4, 4^2, 7, 9, 10^2, 12, 15, 18, 21, 22, 25, 28; **20:**23; **21:**5

Ru 2:2, 4, 10; **3:**13; **4:**1, 15

1Sa 1:11, 17, 20, 22, 23^2, 24^3, 27, 28; **2:**3, 16^2, 19^2, 25^2, 27, 28, 35, 36; **3:**7, 13, 18^4, 19; **5:**3, 4; **6:**3, 4, 8; **7:**3, 9; **8:**5, 10, 12; **9:**5, 6, 13^2, 16, 17; **10:**1, 9, 10^2, 11, 14, 16, 19, 21, 23, 24^2, 26, 27^2; **11:**3, 5; **12:**14, 24; **13:**2, 7, 8, 10^2, 14^2, 15^2; **14:**2, 7, 13^2, 17, 20, 34, 37, 39, 43, 52^2; **15:**2, 12, 13, 16, 28, 32; **16:**1, 3, 6, 7, 8, 11, 12^2, 13, 14, 15, 17, 18, 21^2, 23; **17:**7, 8, 9^2, 13, 20, 24, 25^3, 26, 27^2, 30^2, 31, 32, 33, 35^5, 38, 39, 40, 41, 42, 50, 51, 57^2, 58; **18:**1, 2^2, 3, 4, 5^2, 8, 12, 13^3, 14, 15, 17^2, 20, 21^3, 24, 27, 28; **19:**4, 7, 8, 11^3, 15^2, 18^2, 23; **20:**2, 7, 17^2, 24, 26, 30, 31, 32, 33^2, 34, 35, 36, 40; **21:**1, 5, 6, 11^2, 14; **22:**1, 2^2, 4, 6^2, 7, 10^3, 13^3, 15, 17; **23:**3, 4, 7, 9, 14^2, 17, 20, 22, 23, 25; **24:**1, 4^2, 5, 6, 8, 19; **25:**1^2, 5, 6, 12, 17, 21, 22, 25, 35, 36^2, 37^2, 39, 40; **26:**2, 3, 5, 7, 8^2, 9, 10, 19, 24; **27:**2, 4, 6, 12; **28:**3^2, 6, 7, 8^2, 9, 17, 20, 21, 23; **29:**3, 4^4, 6; **30:**4, 6, 8, 9, 11^3, 12^2, 13, 15, 16, 21; **31:**3, 5

2Sa 1:3^2, 4, 5, 6^2, 7, 8, 10^2, 11, 13, 14, 15^2, 16; **2:**1, 3, 5, 8, 9, 20, 21^2, 23^2, 32; **3:**9, 11, 16, 20^2, 22, 23^2, 24, 26, 27^3, 31, 34; **4:**4, 6, 7^3, 10^3; **5:**10, 12, 13, 14, 25; **6:**2, 7, 10, 12, 16; **7:**1, 14, 15, 23; **8:**4, 10^4, 13; **9:**1, 2^2, 3, 4, 5, 7, 9, 10; **10:**2, 9, 12, 13^2, 17; **11:**1, 4, 7^2, 8, 13^3, 15, 21, 22, 25, 27; **12:**1^2, 3^2, 4^2, 9, 17^2, 18^3, 20, 21, 23^2, 24; **13:**2, 4^2, 5^2, 6, 7, 9^2, 11, 12, 16, 17, 25^2, 26, 27^2, 28, 29, 34; **14:**3, 6, 7^2, 10, 14, 24^2, 25, 26, 29^2, 31, 32, 33; **15:**1^2, 2, 3, 4, 5^4, 9, 14, 16, 17, 18^2, 22, 24, 26^2, 30, 32; **16:**1, 10^2, 11^3, 13^2, 14, 15, 18; **17:**2^3, 6, 10, 12^4, 16, 22, 23, 24, 29; **18:**1, 9, 11^3, 15, 17^2, 19, 20, 23, 30; **19:**17^2, 23, 25, 29, 30, 31, 37^2, 38, 39, 40, 41; **20:**5, 6^2, 7, 8, 9, 10^2, 11^2, 12^2, 14, 15, 17, 21; **21:**4, 15, 17^3, 21; **22:**1, 3, 12, 13, 24, 31; **23:**9, 10, 11, 21^2, 23; **24:**2, 10, 13^3, 16, 18, 20, 22

1Ki 1:1, 2^2, 4, 5^2, 6^2, 7, 13, 17, 20, 25, 27, 33, 34, 35^2, 38, 40, 41, 42, 44^2, 45, 52^2, 53^2; **2:**8, 9^2, 16, 19, 22^2, 25, 29, 30, 31^3, 34^2, 36, 42, 46; **3:**6^2, 11, 16, 28; **4:**10, 12, 13^2, 24; **5:**1, 3, 12; **8:**5^2, 24, 25, 31^2, 32, 57, 58, 62, 65; **9:**2, 3, 12^2; **10:**1, 2; **11:**9, 10, 17, 18^3, 19, 20, 22, 23, 24, 28, 29, 30, 34; **12:**1, 3, 7, 8^3, 10^2, 13, 18^2, 20^2; **13:**4^3, 6, 11, 13, 14^2, 15, 18^3, 19, 20, 23, 24^2, 26^5, 27, 29, 30, 31, 33; **14:**3, 10^2, 11^2, 13^3, 14, 18^2, 22; **15:**3, 4^2, 5, 8, 27^2, 28, 29; **16:**4^2, 7^2, 9, 10^2, 11, 17, 18, 21, 25, 30, 31^2, 33; **17:**2, 6, 8, 17, 19^3, 21, 22, 23^2; **18:**7^2, 8, 15, 16, 17, 21^3, 24, 30, 33; **19:**5^2, 6, 7, 9^2, 13, 15, 17^2, 18, 19^3, 20, 21^2; **20:**1, 2, 7, 8^2, 9, 10, 11^2, 16, 17, 22, 23, 31, 33^4, 34^3, 35, 36^4, 37^2, 40, 41, 42; **21:**4^2, 5^2, 6, 7, 10^4, 13^4, 19^2, 21^2, 24^2; **22:**7, 8, 11, 13, 15^2, 16, 19, 21, 22^2, 26, 27, 32, 33, 53

2Ki 1:5, 6^2, 8, 9^3, 10, 11^2, 12, 13^2, 15^3, 16; **2:**2, 3, 4, 5, 6, 12, 13, 14, 15^3, 16^3, 17^2, 18, 20, 23^2; **3:**11, 12^2, 13, 15, 26^2, 27^2; **4:**1, 5, 8, 10, 12, 13, 19, 20^2, 21^2, 23, 27, 29^2, 31^2, 35, 36, 38; **5:**1, 3, 5, 6, 8, 10, 13, 15, 16, 19^2, 20^2, 21^3, 23^2, 25, 26; **6:**6, 10^2, 13^2, 15, 18, 26, 28, 29^2, 31, 32^5, 33; **7:**17^2, 20^2; **8:**6, 7, 8, 9^3, 10^2, 14, 19^2, 21^2, 29; **9:**1, 2^2, 6, 8^2, 11, 13, 15, 17, 18, 21, 25^2, 26, 27^2, 28^2, 32, 36; **10:**3, 4, 7, 8, 9, 11, 15^6, 16, 17, 18, 22, 24^2, 35; **11:**2^3, 4, 8, 12^4, 15; **12:**2, 21^2; **13:**4, 9, 14, 15^2, 19, 20, 25; **14:**19^3, 20, 21; **15:**7, 10^3, 14, 16, 19, 25^4, 30^2; **16:**5, 9; **17:**2, 3^2, 4^2, 17, 27, 36^3; **18:**5^3, 6, 7^2, 15, 21, 36^2, 37; **19:**3, 7^2, 16, 21, 37; **20:**1^2, 4, 14; **21:**6, 11, 23; **22:**18; **23:**1, 2, 17, 18, 25^4, 26, 29^3, 30^5, 33; **24:**1, 2, 12; **25:**5^2, 6^2, 7^2, 25^2, 28^2, 29, 30

1Ch 2:3^2, 4, 9, 19^2, 21, 24, 29, 35; **3:**1, 4, 5; **4:**6, 9, 10; **5:**2, 20; **7:**22; **9:**20; **10:**3, 9, 14; **11:**9, 10^2, 11, 12, 23^2, 25, 42; **12:**19, 20, 22, 23, 27; **13:**10; **14:**1, 2, 10, 14, 16, 17; **15:**1, 2, 13, 27, 29; **16:**5, 9^2, 29, 30; **17:**13^2, 14, 25; **18:**4, 10^3; **19:**2^2, 10, 14^2, 17; **20:**7; **21:**11, 12, 15, 20, 26, 28; **22:**6, 9; **23:**13; **24:**19; **26:**5, 10; **27:**7; **28:**6, 9^3; **29:**22, 23, 25^2, 30

2Ch 1:1^2, 3, 7; **2:**3^2, 4^2, 6^4, 14, 15; **5:**6; **6:**15, 16, 22^2, 23; **7:**8, 12; **8:**18; **9:**1; **10:**1, 3, 7, 8^3, 10^2, 18^2; **11:**13, 15, 18, 19, 20, 22; **12:**1, 3, 12^2; **13:**3, 5, 7, 10, 11, 19, 20; **14:**1, 5, 6, 7, 10, 13; **15:**2^4, 4, 5^2, 9^2, 15; **16:**7, 9, 10^2, 14^3; **17:**11, 14, 15^2, 16^2, 17, 18^2; **18:**2^4, 3, 6, 7, 10, 12, 14, 15, 20^2, 21, 25, 26, 30, 31^3, 32; **19:**2; **20:**30, 36; **21:**7, 9^2, 12, 17, 18, 19, 20; **22:**6, 9^4, 11^4; **23:**1, 11^4, 14, 16; **24:**3, 6, 16, 21^2, 22, 23, 25^6, 26, 27; **25:**3, 7, 10, 13, 15^2, 16^2, 23, 27^3, 28^2; **26:**1, 5, 7, 17^2, 18, 20^3, 23; **27:**5^2, 9; **28:**5^3, 16, 20^3, 21, 23^2, 24, 27^2; **29:**6, 11^3, 29; **30:**9; **31:**10, 15; **32:**3, 6, 7^2, 8, 9, 15, 17, 21, 24^2, 25^2, 29^2, 31^3, 33^2; **33:**6, 11^2, 13^3, 18, 19, 20, 24^2; **34:**26; **35:**20, 21, 22^2, 24^3; **36:**1, 3, 4, 6^3, 8, 10, 13, 17, 20, 23^3

Ezr 1:2, 3^2, 4; **4:**2, 6, 11; **5:**7, 15; **6:**11; **7:**6^2, 9, 26; **8:**3, 4, 5, 6, 7, 8, 9, 10, 11, 12, 19, 21, 22^2, 33; **10:**1

Neh 1:5, 11; **2:**1, 6^2; **3:**2, 8^2, 10, 12, 16, 17^2, 18, 19, 20, 21, 22, 23^2, 24, 25, 29, 30^2, 31; **4:**3; **6:**8, 12^2, 18, 19; **8:**4; **9:**7^2, 8; **11:**8; **13:**5, 7, 26^3, 28

Est 1:3, 12, 14, 17, 19; **2:**2, 9^2, 20; **3:**1^2, 2^2, 4, 5, 6; **4:**4, 5, 7^2, 8^3, 10, 11, 17; **5:**4, 9, 11^2, 14; **6:**3^2, 4, 5^2, 6, 9^2, 11^2, 13^4, 14; **7:**7, 9; **8:**3, 7; **10:**2

Job 1:2, 8, 10; **2:**3^3, 8, 9, 11^3, 12, 13^2; **3:**20; **4:**4; **6:**10, 14; **7:**8, 10, 17^2, 18^2; **8:**4, 18^2; **9:**3^2, 4, 11^2, 12^2, 13, 14^2, 32, 34, 35; **11:**10, 13; **12:**4, 5, 13, 16; **13:**7, 9, 15^2, 16; **14:**6, 20^2, 22^2; **15:**21, 24^2, 26, 31; **18:**6, 7, 9^2, 10^2, 11^2, 14, 20, 21; **19:**11, 16, 28; **20:**7, 9^3, 11, 14, 16, 22, 23^2, 24, 25, 26^2, 27, 29; **21:**15^2, 19, 21, 31, 33^3; **22:**3, 14, 21, 27; **23:**3, 4, 7, 8, 9^2, 13, 14, 15; **24:**1, 10, 20^2, 23; **25:**2; **26:**2, 3, 6, 14; **27:**9, 15, 20^2, 21^2, 22, 23^2; **29:**12^2, 13; **30:**25; **31:**14, 15, 29^2, 37^2; **32:**13, 14; **33:**13, 23, 24^2, 26; **34:**11, 13, 17, 19, 27, 28, 29; **35:**6^2, 7, 14^3; **36:**11, 22, 23, 26; **37:**16, 18, 19, 20, 23, 24; **39:**11^2, 12, 20, 23; **40:**2^2, 9, 11, 12, 19^2, 20, 22^2; **41:**4, 5^2, 6^2, 8, 9^2, 10, 11, 13, 22, 26^2, 28^2, 30, 32; **42:**8, 11^6

Ps 2:12; **3:**2; **4:**3^2; **5:**12; **7:**4^2, 5, 13; **8:**4^2, 5^2, 6; **10:**9; **11:**5; **12:**5^3; **13:**4; **17:**13^2; **18:**6, 11, 12, 23, 30, ttl; **20:**6; **21:**2, 3, 4, 5, 6^2; **22:**8^4, 23^3, 24^2, 25, 26, 29, 30; **24:**6; **25:**12, 14; **28:**7^2; **32:**6, 10; **33:**2, 3, 8, 18, 21; **34:**5, 6^2, 7, 8, 9, 19, 22, ttl; **35:**8^2, 10^4, 25; **37:**5, 7^2, 12, 13, 22^2, 24, 32, 33^2, 36, 40; **41:**1, 2^3, 3, 8; **42:**5, 11; **43:**5; **44:**16; **45:**11; **49:**7, 17; **50:**3^2, 18, 23; **51:**ttl; **52:**6, ttl; **53:**5; **55:**12, 20; **56:**ttl; **57:**3; **59:**ttl; **61:**7; **62:**1, 4, 5, 8^2; **63:**11; **64:**4, 10; **66:**6, 17; **67:**7; **68:**1^2, 4^2, 33; **69:**26, 30, 34; **71:**11^3; **72:**9, 11^2, 12, 15^2, 17^2; **74:**14; **76:**11^2; **78:**17, 34, 36^2, 37, 40^2, 58^2, 70, 71; **79:**10; **81:**15; **85:**9, 13; **89:**7, 20, 21, 22^2, 23, 24, 27, 28^2, 33, 41, 43, 45; **91:**2, 14^2, 15^4, 16^2; **92:**15; **94:**12, 13; **95:**2; **96:**6, 9; **97:**2, 3, 7; **98:**1; **100:**4; **101:**5^2; **103:**11, 13, 17; **104:**34; **105:**2^2, 19, 20^2, 21; **106:**7, 10, 23, 29, 31, 32, 43; **107:**32^2, 41; **109:**6, 7, 12, 17^2, 19^2, 30, 31; **111:**5; **113:**8; **116:**2; **117:**1; **119:**2, 42; **120:**6; **126:**6; **130:**7; **135:**1; **136:**4, 5, 6, 7, 10, 13, 16, 17; **140:**11; **141:**5; **142:**2^2; **144:**3^2; **145:**18^2, 19, 20; **147:**11; **148:**1, 2^2, 3^2, 4, 14; **149:**2^2, 3; **150:**1, 2^2, 3^2, 4^2, 5^2

Prv 3:6; **6:**16; **7:**10, 13^3, 20, 21^2; **8:**9, 30^3; **9:**4^3, 16^3; **10:**13^2, 24, 26; **11:**18, 26^2, 27; **12:**14; **13:**6, 18, 24^2; **14:**2, 6, 7, 31, 33, 35; **15:**9, 10, 12, 14, 21; **16:**7, 13, 22, 26, 29; **17:**8, 11, 24, 25; **18:**9, 13, 16^2, 17; **19:**6, 7^3, 17, 19; **20:**2, 7, 16, 19; **21:**25; **22:**15; **23:**6, 13, 14, 24; **24:**18^2, 24^2, 25, 29; **25:**13, 21^2; **26:**4, 12, 15, 17, 24, 25, 27; **27:**11, 13, 14, 22; **28:**8, 11, 17, 22; **29:**20, 21, 23; **30:**5; **31:**1, 6, 7, 12

Ecc 2:26; **3:**14, 22^2; **4:**10^2, 12^2, 16; **5:**12, 18, 19, 20; **6:**2, 10, 12; **7:**14; **8:**3, 4, 6, 7, 12, 15^2; **9:**2^2, 4, 17; **10:**1, 3, 8, 14^2; **11:**8

Song 1:2; **3:**1^3, 2^3, 3, 4^4, 11; **5:**4, 6^3, 8; **6:**1

Isa 3:10, 11^2; **5:**19, 23; **6:**4; **7:**4; **8:**13^2, 17; **9:**11, 13; **10:**6^2, 15^2, 20, 26; **11:**2, 3; **14:**25, 29; **15:**4, 9; **16:**3; **20:**1; **21:**6, 14^2; **22:**11, 16, 21^2, 23, 24; **24:**2; **25:**9^2, 10; **26:**3; **27:**5, 7^3; **28:**6, 26^2; **29:**12, 16^2, 21, 23; **30:**18, 32; **31:**4, 6, 8; **33:**16; **36:**3, 6, 21^2, 22; **37:**3, 7^2, 22, 38; **38:**1^2; **39:**3; **40:**3, 10^3, 13, 14^4, 17^2, 18, 20; **41:**2^3, 7; **42:**1, 25^3; **43:**7^3; **44:**3, 14, 20; **45:**1^2, 9^2, 10, 13, 24^2; **46:**7^5; **48:**14, 15^2; **49:**5, 7^2, 25; **50:**4, 8, 10; **51:**2^3; **52:**7, 15; **53:**2^3, 3^2, 4, 5, 6, 10^2, 12; **55:**4, 6, 7^2; **56:**6, 8^2; **57:**15, 17, 18^3, 19^3; **58:**5, 7, 13; **59:**15, 16^2, 19; **62:**7, 11^2; **63:**2, 11, 14; **64:**4^2, 5; **66:**2

Jer 2:3, 15, 37; **3:**1; **4:**2^2; **6:**11; **8:**6; **9:**24; **10:**25^2; **11:**19; **15:**8; **18:**18; **19:**14; **20:**2, 3, 9, 10^2, 15, 16; **21:**1, 9, 12; **22:**10^2, 12, 13^2, 14, 15, 16, 18^2; **23:**24, 28^2; **26:**8^2, 13, 19^2, 21, 22, 23^2, 24^2; **27:**6^2, 7^2, 11, 12; **28:**9, 14^2; **29:**26, 31; **30:**8, 10, 21; **31:**2, 10^2, 11^2, 20^4; **32:**3, 4, 5, 9, 10; **33:**13; **34:**2, 14; **36:**4, 8, 15, 22, 31; **37:**4, 14^2, 15^2, 17^2, 21; **38:**6, 11, 13, 14, 27^2; **39:**5^3, 7^2, 9, 12^4, 14^2; **40:**1^2, 2, 5^3, 6, 7, 14; **41:**1, 2^2, 3, 7, 11, 12, 13, 16; **42:**8, 9, 11; **43:**1; **44:**20; **45:**4; **46:**10, 25, 27; **48:**11, 12^2, 17^2, 19, 26, 27, 35^2, 39; **49:**5, 8^2, 19; **50:**16, 17^2, 32^2, 43; **51:**3^2, 44; **52:**8, 9^2, 11^3, 31, 32^2, 33, 34

Lam 1:17; **2:**19; **3:**24, 25^2, 28, 30^2

Ezk 1:3; **2:**2; **3:**18, 20^2, 27^2; **7:**15; **9:**4, 5; **10:**7; **12:**13^2, 14^2; **13:**22; **14:**4, 7^2, 8^2, 9^2, 10^2; **17:**6^2, 7^2, 12, 13^2, 15^2, 16^2, 17, 20^3; **18:**13, 20^2, 22, 32; **19:**4^2, 5, 8^2, 9^3; **21:**26^2, 27; **24:**27; **28:**9^2, 12; **29:**2, 20; **30:**11, 24; **31:**4^2, 8^2, 9^2, 11^3, 12^3, 15^3, 16, 17; **32:**2, 21^2, 22, 25, 26; **33:**2, 4, 5, 12, 16, 27; **35:**7^2; **37:**19; **38:**2, 21, 22^3; **40:**46; **43:**6; **44:**26; **45:**20; **46:**12; **47:**23

Dan 2:1, 16, 22, 24, 25, 46, 48^2; **3:**28; **4:**8, 16^2, 19, 23, 34, 35; **5:**6, 9, 11, 17, 19^2, 20, 21, 24, 29; **6:**3^2, 4, 5, 6, 14^2, 16, 18^2, 22, 23^2; **7:**10^3, 13^2, 14^2, 16, 27; **8:**4, 6, 7^5, 11, 12; **9:**4, 9, 11; **10:**16; **11:**1, 5, 11, 16^2, 17^3, 18^2, 22, 23, 25, 26, 30, 40^2, 44, 45; **12:**7

Hos 1:3, 4, 6; **4:**17; **5:**6, 14; **7:**5, 9, 10; **8:**3, 11, 12; **9:**4, 17; **11:**1, 7; **12:**2, 4^2, 14^3; **13:**11, 13; **14:**2, 4, 8^2

Joel 2:13, 14, 20

Am 1:5, 8; **2:**3; **3:**5, 14; **5:**8, 10^2, 11, 19^2; **6:**10^3; **9:**13

Oba 7

Jna 1:6^2, 8, 10, 11, 15; **3:**6^2; **4:**5, 6

Mic 1:4; **2:**7; **3:**5; **5:**5; **6:**5, 6; **7:**9, 15

Nah 1:5, 6, 7, 15

Hab 2:4, 5^2, 6^4, 9, 12, 15^3, 19, 20; **3:**5

Zep 1:6; **2:**11; **3:**9

Hag 1:12

Zec 1:8; **2:**3, 4; **3:**1, 4^3, 5; **4:**11, 12; **5:**4; **6:**12; **8:**10, 23; **9:**8^2; **10:**4^4; **12:**1, 10^2; **13:**3^4, 6

Mal 2:5^2, 12, 17; **3:**16, 17, 18^3; **4:**4

HIMSELF

HIS

Gen 1:11, 12^2, 21, 24^2, 25^2, 27; **2:**2^2, 3, 7, 21, 24^3, 25; **3:**8, 15, 20, 21, 22; **4:**1, 2, 4^2, 5^2, 7, 8^2, 17^2, 21, 23, 25^2, 26; **5:**3^3, 29; **6:**3, 5, 6, 9, 12, 20; **7:**2^2, 7^3, 13, 14^3; **8:**9, 18^3, 21^2; **9:**1, 6, 8, 21, 22^2, 24^2, 25, 26, 27; **10:**5, 10, 15, 25^2; **11:**28^2, 31^4; **12:**5^2, 8, 11, 12, 17, 20^2; **13:**1, 3^2, 10, 12, 18; **14:**12, 14^3, 15, 16^2, 17; **16:**3, 11, 12^2, 15; **17:**3, 14^2, 17^2, 19^2, 23^3, 24, 25^2, 26, 27; **18:**2, 19^2, 33^2; **19:**1, 3, 14^3, 16^3, 26, 30^2, 37, 38; **20:**2, 7, 8, 14, 17^2; **21:**2, 3, 4, 5, 7, 11, 21, 22, 32; **22:**3^3, 4, 5, 6^2, 7, 9, 10^2, 13^3, 17, 19, 21^2, 24; **23:**3, 6, 9, 10, 18, 19; **24:**2^2, 7, 9^2, 10^3, 11, 20, 21^2, 26, 27^2, 29, 30^2, 32^2, 40, 48, 59, 61, 63, 67^3; **25:**6, 8, 9, 10, 11, 17, 18, 21^2, 25, 26^3, 28, 30, 33, 34^2; **26:**7, 8, 11^2, 15^2, 17, 18^2, 25, 26^2; **27:**1^2, 5, 10, 11, 13, 14^3, 16^2, 18, 19, 20, 22, 23^2, 26, 27, 30^3, 31^3, 32, 34^2, 37, 38^2, 39, 40, 41^2; **28:**7^2, 8, 9, 11, 16, 18; **29:**1, 3, 6, 10^3, 11, 13^2, 23, 24^2, 28, 29^2, 32, 33, 34, 35; **30:**6, 8, 11, 13, 14, 18, 20, 24, 35, 40; **31:**4, 17^2, 18^4, 19, 21, 23, 25^2, 46, 53, 54, 55^3; **32:**1, 3, 13^2, 16^2, 20, 22^3, 25, 31; **33:**1, 3, 4, 5, 14, 16, 17, 18, 19; **34:**3, 4, 5^4, 13, 19, 20, 24^3, 25, 26; **35:**2, 7, 10, 18^2, 21, 22, 27, 29^2; **36:**2, 6^8, 24, 32, 33, 34, 35^2, 36, 37, 38, 39^3; **37:**1, 2^3, 3^2, 4^2, 5, 8^3, 9, 10^3, 11^2, 12, 17, 20, 22, 23^3, 26^2, 27, 29, 30, 34^3, 35^3; **38:**1, 3, 4, 5, 6, 9^3, 11^2, 12^2, 13, 16, 20^2, 28^2, 29^3, 30^3; **39:**2, 3^2, 4^3, 5, 7, 8, 9, 11, 12^2, 13, 15, 16^2, 18, 19^3, 23; **40:**1, 2, 5^2, 7, 9, 13^2, 20^2, 21; **41:**8^2, 10, 11, 12, 14, 37, 38, 42^3, 44; **42:**1, 4, 7, 8, 21, 22, 25, 27^4, 28, 35, 37, 38; **43:**8, 16, 21, 29^3, 30^3, 31, 33^2; **44:**1^2, 2, 4, 11^2, 13, 14, 19, 20^4, 22^3, 30, 33; **45:**1, 3^3, 4, 8, 14^2, 15^2, 16, 23^2, 24; **46:**1^2, 4, 6, 7^5, 8, 15^3, 18, 25, 26, 28, 29^4, 31^2; **47:**2, 3, 7, 11^2, 12^3, 20, 29; **48:**1, 9, 12^2, 13^2, 14^3, 17^3, 18^2, 19^3; **49:**1, 10, 11^4, 12^2, 13, 15, 16, 17, 20, 24^2, 26, 28, 31^2, 33^3; **50:**1, 2^2, 4, 7^2, 8^2, 10, 12, 13, 14^3, 18^2, 22, 24

Ex 1:1, 6, 9, 22; **2:**4, 7, 10, 11^2, 20, 21, 22, 24; **3:**1, 6, 13; **4:**4^2, 6^3, 7^4, 14, 15^2, 18, 20^3, 21, 25; **5:**2, 21; **6:**1, 11, 20; **7:**2, 10^2, 12, 20, 23^2; **8:**6, 15, 17^2, 24, 29^2, 31^2, 32; **9:**20^2, 21^2, 23, 33, 34^2; **10:**1^2, 13, 22, 23; **11:**2, 5, 7, 10; **12:**4^3, 9^2, 22, 29, 30, 48; **13:**10, 13; **14:**4, 5, 6^2, 9^2, 17^3, 18^2, 21, 23^2, 27^2, 31; **15:**1, 3, 4^2, 19^2, 21, 26^3; **16:**16^2, 18, 21, 29^2; **17:**11^2, 12^2, 13; **18:**1, 5^2, 7, 8, 15, 16, 24, 27^3; **20:**7, 17^4, 20; **21:**3, 4, 6^3, 7, 9, 13, 14, 15^2, 16, 17^2, 18^2, 19^2, 20^3, 21, 26^3, 27^3, 28, 29^3, 30, 34, 36^2; **22:**3, 4, 5^3, 7, 8^2, 9^2, 10, 11^2, 14, 15, 16, 27^3, 30; **23:**3, 4, 5, 6, 19, 21, 22; **24:**10^2, 11, 13; **25:**2, 31^5; **26:**19^2; **27:**2, 3^6, 11, 21; **28:**1, 4, 12, 21, 29, 30, 35, 38, 41, 43^2; **29:**4, 6, 7, 8, 9^2, 10, 14^2, 15, 16, 17^3, 19, 20^2, 21^6, 24, 27, 28, 29, 30, 31, 32, 35, 44; **30:**12, 18, 19, 21, 27^2, 28^2, 30, 33, 38; **31:**8^2, 9^2, 10, 14; **32:**11, 14, 15, 19, 27^5, 29^2; **33:**4, 8, 10, 11^2; **34:**4, 8, 15, 20, 26, 29, 30, 33, 35; **35:**11^7, 13^2, 14^2, 15, 16^4, 17, 19, 21^2, 34; **36:**4, 24^2; **37:**16^4, 17^5, 20^2, 23^3; **39:**5, 14, 21, 27, 33^6, 39^4, 40^4, 41; **40:**10, 11, 12, 14, 18^2, 31

Lev 1:3^2, 4, 6, 9^2, 10, 11, 12^3, 14^2, 15, 16^2; **2:**1, 2, 3, 10; **3:**1, 2^2, 6, 7, 8^2, 12, 13, 14; **4:**3, 4, 6, 11^5, 17, 19, 22, 23^3, 24, 25^2, 26^2, 28^4, 29, 30, 33, 34, 35; **5:**1, 4, 6^3, 7, 8^2, 10, 11, 12, 13, 15, 17, 18; **6:**2^2, 5, 6, 9, 10^3, 11, 15, 16, 20, 22^2, 25; **7:**13^2, 15, 16^2, 18^2, 20^2, 21, 25, 27, 29^3, 30, 31, 33, 34, 35; **8:**2, 6, 9^2, 11^2, 14, 15, 17^3, 18, 22, 23^2, 27, 30^6, 31^2, 36; **9:**1, 9, 22; **10:**1, 3, 6, 12; **11:**14, 15, 16, 22^4, 25, 27, 28, 29, 40^2; **12:**3; **13:**2^3, 3, 4, 5, 6, 7, 11, 12^2, 13, 23, 28, 34, 35, 37, 40, 41^3, 42^2, 43^2, 44^2, 45^3, 46, 55; **14:**2, 8^3, 9^7, 14^2, 15, 16^3, 17^3, 19, 23, 25^2, 26, 27^2, 28^3, 32, 47^2; **15:**2^2, 3^7, 5^2, 6, 7, 8, 10, 11^2, 13^4, 15, 16, 21, 22, 27; **16:**4^2, 6^2, 11, 12, 14^2, 15, 17, 19, 21, 24^3, 26^2, 28^2, 32; **17:**2, 4, 9, 10, 15, 16^2; **18:**14; **19:**3^2, 8^2, 21, 22; **20:**2, 3^2, 4, 5, 6, 9^5, 10, 11^2, 12, 17^6, 19, 20^2, 21^2; **21:**1, 2^6, 3, 4, 7, 10^3, 11^2, 12^2, 14, 15^2, 17, 20^2, 21, 22, 24; **22:**2, 3, 6, 7, 11^3, 18^4, 21, 23; **23:**29, 30, 37; **24:**9, 11, 14, 15^2, 19; **25:**10^2, 13, 25^3, 27, 28, 30, 33, 41^3, 48, 49^3, 50, 51, 52^2, 54; **27:**8, 14, 15^2, 16, 17, 18, 22, 28, 31

Nu 1:4, 44, 52^2; **2:**2, 4, 6, 8, 11, 13, 15, 17, 19, 21, 23, 26, 28, 30; **3:**7, 9, 10, 38, 48, 51; **4:**5, 9^3, 15, 19^3, 25, 27, 49^2; **5:**7, 9, 10^2, 14^2, 15, 18, 30; **6:**4, 5^3, 7^6, 8, 9^3, 11, 12^2, 13, 14, 16^2, 17^2, 18^2, 19, 21^4, 23, 25, 26; **7:**5, 11, 12, 13, 19, 25, 31, 37, 43, 49, 55, 61, 67, 73, 79; **8:**8, 13, 19, 22; **9:**2, 3, 7, 13^3; **10:**14, 18, 22, 25; **11:**1, 10, 28, 29; **12:**12; **14:**24; **15:**4, 24^2, 30, 31^2; **16:**4, 5^2, 6, 17^3, 18, 40; **17:**2, 9; **19:**3, 4, 5, 7^2, 8^2, 10, 13, 19, 21; **20:**8, 11^2, 21, 24, 25, 26^3, 28^2; **21:**23^2, 24, 26^2, 29^2, 33, 34^2, 35^3; **22:**5, 18, 21, 22^2, 23^2, 31^4; **23:**6, 7, 10, 16, 17, 18, 21; **24:**1, 2^2, 3, 4, 7^4, 8^2, 10, 13, 15, 16, 18, 20^2, 21, 23, 25^2; **25:**5, 6, 7, 13^2; **26:**54; **27:**1, 3, 4, 8^2, 9^2, 10^2, 11^4, 21^2, 23; **28:**10, 15, 24, 31; **29:**6^2, 16^2, 22^2, 25^2, 28^2, 31^2, 34^2, 38^2; **30:**2^3, 4, 7, 11, 14^2, 16^2; **31:**6; **32:**18, 21, 42; **33:**54; **35:**8^2, 21, 23^2, 25, 26, 27, 28^2, 32; **36:**2, 7, 8, 9

Dt 1:16, 31, 36, 41; **2:**12, 24, 30^2, 31^2, 32, 33^2, 34; **3:**1, 2^2, 3, 4, 11, 14, 20; **4:**13, 30, 36^3, 37^2, 40^2, 42, 47; **5:**11, 21^5, 24^3; **6:**2^2, 13, 17^2, 22; **7:**3^2, 7, 9, 10; **8:**2, 5, 6, 11^3, 18; **9:**23; **10:**6^2, 8, 9^2, 12, 13, 20; **11:**1^4, 2^3, 3^3, 14, 22; **12:**5^2, 8, 11, 21; **13:**4^2, 17, 18; **14:**13, 14, 15, 21, 23, 24; **15:**2^3, 8, 17; **16:**2, 6, 11; **17:**2, 17, 18, 19^2, 20^5; **18:**1, 5, 6, 7^2, 8, 10^2, 18; **19:**4, 5^3, 6, 9, 11, 12, 18, 19; **20:**5, 6, 7, 8^3; **21:**16, 17^2, 18^2, 19^4, 20, 21, 23; **22:**1, 3^2, 4, 19^2, 24, 26, 29^2, 30^2; **23:**1, 2, 7, 15^2; **24:**1^2, 2, 3^2, 4, 5, 7, 10^2, 12, 13, 15^3, 16; **25:**2^2, 6^2, 7^3, 8, 9^5, 10^2; **26:**2, 17^5, 18^2; **27:**10^2, 16^2, 17, 20^2, 22^3, 23, 24; **28:**1, 9, 12^2, 15^2, 40, 45^2, 54^4, 55; **29:**2^2, 12, 19, 20^2, 23^2; **30:**2, 8, 10^2, 16^4, 20; **32:**4^2, 5, 9^2, 10, 15, 19^2, 36^2, 43^5, 50; **33:**1, 2, 3, 6, 7^3, 9^4, 11^2, 12, 13, 16, 17^3, 21, 24^2, 26, 28; **34:**6, 7^2, 9, 11^2

Jos 2:19^3; **3:**15; **4:**5, 14, 18; **5:**13^3, 14^2; **6:**26^2, 27; **7:**6^2, 18, 22, 24^6, 26; **8:**1^3, 14, 18, 19, 26, 29; **9:**24; **10:**21, 33; **11:**15; **13:**27; **15:**17; **17:**3, 6, 10; **20:**4, 5^2, 6^2; **21:**12; **22:**5^2, 20, 29; **24:**3, 4, 10, 24, 28, 30, 33

Jdg 1:2, 3, 6^2, 13, 17, 25; **2:**6, 9; **3:**10^2, 16^2, 20, 21^3, 22, 24^3; **4:**7^2, 10, 11, 13, 15^4, 17, 21, 22; **5:**11, 17, 26^2, 28^2, 31; **6:**11, 13, 21^2, 27^2, 31, 32; **7:**5^2, 7, 8, 11, 13, 14^2, 21, 22; **8:**20^2, 21, 24, 25, 27^2, 29, 30, 31, 32; **9:**1^2, 3, 5^2, 7, 16^2, 17, 18^2, 19, 21, 24, 26, 28, 30, 31, 41, 48^2, 49, 53, 54^2, 55, 56^2; **10:**16; **11:**2, 3, 11, 20^2, 21, 23, 32, 34^3, 35, 39; **12:**9; **13:**2, 5, 6^2, 7, 11, 19, 20, 21, 22, 23, 24; **14:**2^2, 3^3, 4^2, 5^2, 6^3, 9^2, 10, 19^2, 20^2; **15:**1, 6^2, 14^3, 15, 17, 19; **16:**3, 5, 9, 12, 14, 16, 17, 18^2, 19^2, 20, 21, 22, 29^2, 30^3, 31^3; **17:**2^2, 3^2, 4^2, 5^2, 6, 11, 12; **18:**4, 26, 30; **19:**2, 3, 4, 5, 7, 9^3, 10, 11, 12, 13, 15, 16, 17, 21, 24, 25, 27^2, 28, 29^2; **20:**8^2; **21:**1, 21, 22, 24^3, 25

Ru 1:1^2, 2^2, 6; **2:**1, 5, 15, 20, 22; **3:**4, 7^2, 8, 14; **4:**5, 7^2, 8, 10^3, 13, 14, 17

1Sa 1:1, 3, 4, 11^2, 19, 20, 21^2, 23; **2:**9, 10^2, 11, 13, 19, 20, 22; **3:**2^2, 9, 12, 13^2, 19; **4:**10, 12^2, 13, 15, 18, 19; **5:**3^2, 4^2, 7, 11; **6:**2, 3, 5, 9^2; **7:**1, 15, 17^2; **8:**1, 2^2, 3^2, 11^3, 12^4, 14, 15^2, 16, 17, 22; **9:**2, 3, 5, 7, 10, 15, 22; **10:**1^2, 9, 14, 16, 23, 25, 27; **11:**6, 7; **12:**3, 5, 14, 22^3; **13:**2, 14^2, 16, 20^4, 22; **14:**1^2, 6, 7, 12^2, 13^4, 14, 17, 20, 26^2, 27^5, 34^3, 45, 47, 49, 50; **15:**1, 27, 34, 35; **16:**1, 4, 5, 7^2, 10, 13, 16, 17, 20, 21, 23; **17:**5, 6^2, 7^2, 13, 15, 17, 22^2, 25^2, 28, 33, 34, 35^2, 38^2, 39^2, 40^4, 43, 49^5, 51^2, 54^2, 57; **18:**1, 2, 3, 4^4, 7^2, 10, 11, 13, 14, 22^2, 26, 27^2, 30; **19:**1^2, 4^3, 5^2, 7, 9^4, 13, 16, 24; **20:**6, 17, 25, 27, 32, 33, 34, 36, 38, 40^2, 41; **21:**7, 11^2, 12, 13^3, 14; **22:**1^2, 6^3, 7, 11, 15; **23:**5, 6, 8, 11, 13, 14, 15, 16, 18, 22^2, 24, 25, 26^3; **24:**2, 3^2, 6, 7^2, 8, 16, 19, 22; **25:**1, 2, 3^2, 4, 10, 13^4, 17, 20, 24, 25^2, 36, 37^2, 39^2, 42, 43, 44; **26:**5, 7^2, 9, 10, 11, 16, 18, 19, 23^2, 25^2; **27:**1^2, 3^3, 8, 11, 12; **28:**3, 5, 7^2, 14, 18, 23, 25; **29:**2, 4^2, 5^2, 11; **30:**1, 3, 6^3, 12, 18, 22^2, 24^2, 26, 31; **31:**2, 4^2, 5^2, 6^3, 7, 8, 9^2, 10^2, 12

2Sa 1:2^2, 4, 5, 6, 10^2, 11, 12, 17; **2:**2, 3^2, 16^3, 21, 27, 29, 32^2; **3:**2, 3, 8^2, 12, 27, 29, 30, 32, 38, 39; **4:**1, 4^3, 6, 7^3, 8, 9, 10, 11^3, 12; **5:**6, 12^2, 21; **6:**6, 7, 11, 14, 17, 19, 20^2, 21; **7:**1^2, 12, 13, 14, 25, 27; **8:**3, 10, 15; **9:**3, 6, 9, 11, 13; **10:**1^2, 2^3, 3, 10; **11:**1, 2, 9^2, 10, 13^3, 27^2; **12:**3^4, 4^2, 9^2, 15, 17, 19^2, 20^2, 21, 24^2, 25, 30; **13:**2, 8, 17, 18, 22^2, 24, 28, 29, 31^2, 32, 33, 34, 36, 37; **14:**7^2, 9, 13, 14, 15, 16, 22^2, 24^2, 25^3, 26^2, 30, 31, 33; **15:**5, 12, 14, 16, 18, 22, 25, 30^2, 32^2; **16:**6^2, 9, 11, 12, 13, 18, 19, 22; **17:**6, 8, 18, 23^6; **18:**9, 14, 17, 18^2, 19, 24, 25, 28; **19:**2, 4, 8, 11^2, 17^2, 19, 24^3, 30, 39, 41; **20:**1, 3^2, 8, 10^2, 21^2, 22; **21:**1, 2, 4, 6, 12, 13, 14^2, 15, 22; **22:**1, 7^2, 9^2, 10, 14, 16, 23^2, 25, 31, 51^3; **23:**2, 8, 10^2, 18, 21^2, 23; **24:**14, 16, 20^2, 21

1Ki 1:2, 6^2, 9, 10, 21, 23, 37, 47, 49, 51; **2:**1, 3^5, 4, 5^4, 6, 9, 10, 12^2, 15, 19^2, 22, 23, 32^2, 33^4, 34, 35, 40^3; **3:**1, 3, 6, 15; **4:**7^2, 21, 25^2, 26, 27, 28, 31, 32, 34; **5:**1^2, 3^2, 10, 11; **7:**1^2, 8, 14^2, 23, 51; **8:**6, 14, 15^2, 20, 22, 28, 31, 32^3, 38^2, 39, 54^2, 56^3, 58^4, 59^2, 61^2, 66^2; **9:**11, 15, 16, 19^3, 22^5, 27; **10:**5^5, 13, 24^2, 25; **11:**3^2, 4^5, 6, 8, 9, 17, 19, 20, 21, 23, 26, 27^2, 33, 34^2, 35, 36, 41, 43^4; **12:**4, 6, 15, 18, 24, 26, 33; **13:**4^2, 11, 12, 13, 19, 24, 27, 28, 30^2, 31^2, 33; **14:**2, 4^2, 8, 18, 20^3, 21^2, 31^5; **15:**2, 3^4, 4^2, 5, 6, 8^3, 10, 11, 12, 13, 14, 15, 18, 23^3, 24^5, 26^2, 28, 29, 30, 34; **16:**3, 4, 5, 6^3, 7^2, 9^3, 10, 11^3, 13, 19^2, 20, 26, 27, 28^3, 34^3; **17:**17, 19, 23; **18:**3, 7, 42^2, 43, 46; **19:**3^2, 6, 13^2, 19; **20:**1, 11, 12, 20, 24, 31, 35, 38, 39, 41, 42^2, 43; **21:**4^3, 5, 7, 8^2, 11^2, 25, 27^2, 29^3; **22:**3, 10, 17, 19^3, 22, 31^2, 34, 35, 36^2, 38^2, 40^3, 42, 43, 45, 46, 50^5, 52^2, 53

2Ki 1:2, 8, 9, 10, 11, 12, 13^2, 16, 17; **2:**8, 12; **3:**2^3, 25, 27^2; **4:**12, 18, 19^2, 20, 25, 32, 34^6, 35, 37, 38, 39, 43; **5:**1, 3, 4, 6, 7^2, 8, 9^2, 11^2, 13, 14, 15, 20, 23, 25, 26, 27; **6:**7, 8, 11, 12, 15, 17, 24, 30^2, 32^2; **7:**12, 13; **8:**11, 14, 15^2, 18, 19^2, 20, 24^4, 26; **9:**2, 3, 6, 11^2, 13, 21^2, 23, 24^4, 25^2, 26, 28^3, 31, 32, 36; **10:**3, 10, 11^3, 15, 16, 19^2, 24, 31, 34, 35^3; **11:**2, 8^2, 9, 11^2, 18^2; **12:**1, 2, 5, 17, 18^2, 20, 21^4; **13:**8, 9^3, 12, 13^2, 14^2, 16^2, 21, 23^2, 24^2, 25; **14:**2, 3^2, 5^3, 6, 15, 16^3, 20, 21, 22, 25, 28, 29^3; **15:**2, 3, 5, 7^4, 9, 10, 14, 15, 18, 19^2, 22^3, 25^2, 30, 33, 34, 38^5; **16:**2^2, 3, 13^4, 15, 20^4; **17:**3, 15^3, 18, 20, 23^2; **18:**2, 3, 6, 12, 21, 29, 31^3, 33; **19:**1, 4, 7^2, 19, 23^2, 37^4; **20:**2, 13^5, 20, 21^3; **21:**1, 3, 6, 7, 10, 11, 12, 16, 17, 18^4, 19, 20, 21^2, 22, 23, 24^2, 26^3; **22:**1, 2, 11; **23:**3^3, 10^2, 18^2, 25^3, 26^2, 29, 30^3, 31, 32, 34^2, 35, 36, 37; **24:**1^2, 2, 3, 6^3, 7, 8, 9, 11, 12^5, 15, 17^3, 18, 20; **25:**1^2, 5, 7, 28, 29^2, 30^2

1Ch 1:13, 19^2, 43, 44, 45, 46^2, 47, 48, 49, 50^3; **2:**4, 13, 18, 35^2, 42; **3:**3, 10^3, 11^3, 12^3, 13^3, 14^2, 16^2, 17; **4:**9^3, 18, 19, 23, 25^3, 26^3, 27; **5:**1^2, 2, 4^3, 5^3, 6, 7; **6:**20^3, 21^4, 22^3, 23^3, 24^4, 26^2, 27^3, 29^3, 30^3, 39^2, 49, 50^3, 51^3, 52^3, 53^2; **7:**14, 16^3, 18, 20^4, 21^2, 22, 23^3, 24, 25^3, 26^3, 27^2, 35; **8:**1, 8, 9, 10, 30, 37^3, 39^2; **9:**5, 19^2, 36, 43^3; **10:**2, 4^2, 5, 6^2, 7, 8, 9^2, 10^2, 12, 13; **11:**10, 11, 20, 23, 25, 45; **12:**15, 19, 28; **13:**9, 10, 14; **14:**2^2, 4; **15:**3, 5, 6, 7, 8, 9, 10, 17; **16:**7, 8^2, 9, 10, 11^2, 12^3, 13^2, 14, 15, 16, 23, 24^2, 27^2, 29, 34, 37, 39, 41, 43^2; **17:**1, 11, 12, 13, 14, 21, 23, 25; **18:**3, 10^2, 14; **19:**1^2, 2^2, 3, 7, 11, 13, 15, 19; **20:**2, 8; **21:**3, 13, 16^2, 20, 21, 23, 27; **22:**5, 6, 9^3, 10^2, 17, 18; **23:**1, 13^2, 14, 25; **25:**9, 10^2, 11^2, 12^2, 13^2, 14^2, 15^2, 16^2, 17^2, 18^2, 19^2, 20^2, 21^2, 22^2, 23^2, 24^2, 25^2, 26^2, 27^2, 28^2, 29^2, 30^2, 31^2; **26:**6, 10, 14^2, 15, 22, 25^6, 26, 28, 29, 30, 31, 32; **27:**2, 4^2, 5, 6^2, 7^2, 8, 9, 10, 11, 12, 13, 14, 15; **28:**1, 2, 6, 7, 11, 19, 20; **29:**5, 23, 28^2, 30^2

2Ch 1:1^2, 8, 13; **2:**1, 11, 12, 14, 15, 17; **3:**1, 2; **4:**16; **5:**1, 7, 13; **6:**3, 4^2, 10, 12, 13^2, 19, 22, 23^3, 29^3, 30; **7:**3, 6, 10, 11; **8:**1, 6, 9^3, 14, 18; **9:**4^5, 8, 23^2, 24, 31^4; **10:**4, 6, 15, 18; **11:**4, 12, 14, 21^2, 22, 23; **12:**8, 13^2, 14, 16^3; **13:**2, 5, 6, 12, 17, 22^2; **14:**1^4, 2, 11, 13; **15:**9, 17, 18; **16:**4, 5, 12^4, 13^2, 14; **17:**1^2, 2, 3, 4^2, 5, 6, 7^2; **18:**8, 9, 16, 18^3, 21, 33, 34; **19:**1; **20:**18^2, 20, 21, 25, 30, 31, 32; **21:**1^4, 4^2, 7, 8, 9^2, 10^2, 17^3, 18, 19^4; **22:**1^2, 2, 3^2, 4^3, 9, 11; **23:**7^2, 8, 10^2, 11, 13, 17^2; **24:**1, 11, 13, 16, 22^2, 25^2, 27^3; **25:**1, 3^2, 4, 11, 14, 22, 28; **26:**1, 2, 3, 4, 8, 15, 16^3, 19^2, 20, 21^2, 23^4; **27:**1, 2, 6^2, 7^2, 9^3; **28:**1, 3, 5, 22, 25, 26^2, 27^3; **29:**1, 2, 3, 10, 19^2, 25; **30:**2, 6, 8^2, 9, 19^2, 27; **31:**1, 2, 3, 8, 10, 12, 13, 16, 20, 21^2; **32:**3^2, 9^2, 12^2, 14, 15, 16^2, 17, 21^3, 25, 26, 30, 31, 32, 33^4; **33:**3, 6, 7, 10, 12^2, 13^2, 18^2, 19^3, 20^4, 22^2, 23, 24^2, 25^2; **34:**2, 3^2, 4, 8^2, 19, 27, 31^6, 33; **35:**3, 4, 8, 9, 22, 23, 24^2, 26, 27; **36:**1, 4^3, 5, 7, 8^3, 10, 12, 13^2, 15^3, 16^3, 17, 18, 20, 22, 23^2

Ezr 1:1, 3^2, 4, 7; **2:**1, 68; **3:**2^2, 3, 9^3, 11; **4:**6; **5:**6, 15, 17; **6:**5, 7, 10, 11^2, 12; **7:**6^2, 9, 10, 11, 13, 14, 15, 23, 28; **8:**17, 18^2, 19, 22^2, 25^2; **9:**8; **10:**8, 11, 18

Neh 1:5; **2:**1, 20; **3:**1, 10, 12, 17, 23, 28, 29, 30; **4:**2, 15, 17, 18^2, 22; **5:**7, 13^2; **6:**5^2, 11, 18, 19; **7:**3^2, 6; **8:**4^2, 16; **9:**8^2, 10^2; **10:**29^2; **11:**3, 13, 17, 20; **12:**8, 36, 45, 47; **13:**10, 26, 30

Est 1:2, 3^3, 4^2, 8, 12^2, 20, 22; **2:**3, 7^2, 8, 15, 16^2, 17, 18^2; **3:**1, 10^2; **4:**1, 3, 4, 11, 17; **5:**1, 2^2, 10^2, 11^2, 14^2; **6:**6, 8, 12^2, 13^4; **7:**5, 7^2; **8:**2, 3^2, 5^2, 7, 17; **9:**1, 4, 25^3; **10:**2^2, 3^3

Job 1:3, 4^2, 10^3, 13^2, 20^2; **2:**3, 4, 5^2, 6, 7^2, 9, 10, 11, 12, 13; **3:**1^2, 19; **4:**9, 17, 18^2; **5:**3, 4, 18, 26; **6:**5, 9, 14; **7:**1, 2, 10^2; **8:**12, 15, 16^2, 17, 18, 19; **9:**5, 13, 33, 34^2; **11:**5; **12:**4, 5, 11, 16; **13:**8, 11^2; **14:**5^3, 6, 18, 20, 21, 22^2; **15:**2, 15^2, 20, 21, 23, 25, 26^2, 27^3, 29, 30^2, 31, 32^2, 33^2; **16:**9^3, 12, 13, 21; **17:**5^2, 9; **18:**4^2, 5, 6^2, 7^2, 8, 11, 12^2, 13^2, 14^2, 15^3, 16^2, 17, 19^2, 20; **19:**6, 11^2, 12; **20:**6^2, 7, 9, 10^2, 11^2, 12^2, 13, 14^2, 15, 18,

20, 21^2, 22, 23^2, 25, 26^2, 27, 28^3; 21:17, 19^2, 20^2, 21^2, 23, 24^2, 25, 31^2; 22:22^2; 23:3, 6, 11^2, 12^2, 13, 15; 24:1, 6, 15, 22, 23; 25:2, 3^2, 5; 26:8, 9^2, 11, 12^2, 13^2, 14^2; 27:1, 8, 9, 14^2, 15, 18, 19, 21, 22, 23; 28:9, 10; 29:1, 3^2, 17; 30:24^2; 31:20, 23, 30, 31; 32:1, 2, 3^2, 5, 12, 14; 33:10, 13, 17, 18^2, 19^2, 20^2, 21^2, 22^2, 23, 25^2, 26^2, 28^2, 30; 34:11, 14^3, 19, 21^2, 27, 29, 35, 36, 37^3; 35:15, 16; 36:7, 15, 18, 22, 23, 24, 26, 29, 30; 37:1, 2^2, 3, 4^2, 5, 6, 7, 11, 12, 13, 15; 38:12, 32^2, 41^2; 39:6, 8, 10, 11, 18, 19, 20, 21; 40:16^4, 17^2, 18^2, 19, 23, 24^2; 41:1, 2^2, 7^2, 12^3, 13^2, 14^2, 15^2, 18^2, 19, 20, 21^2, 22, 23, 24, 33; 42:10, 11^4, 12, 16^2

Ps 1:2^2, 3^3; 2:2, 5^2, 12; 3:4, ttl; 7:12^2, 13, 16^4, 17; 8:6; 9:7, 11, 16; 10:2, 3, 4^2, 5^3, 6, 7^2, 8, 9^2, 10, 11^2, 13, 15, 16; 11:4^3, 5, 7; 12:2; 14:1, 6, 7; 15:2, 3^3, 4, 5; 17:12; 18:6^2, 8^2, 9, 11^2, 12, 13, 14, 22^2, 24, 30, 50^3, ttl; 19:1, 5, 6^2, 12; 20:6^3; 21:2^2, 3, 5, 9; 22:24, 29, 31; 23:3; 24:3, 4, 5; 25:9, 10^2, 13^2, 14, 22; 27:4, 5^2, 6; 28:5, 8; 29:2, 9^2, 11^2; 30:4^2, 5^2; 31:21, 23; 33:4, 6, 11, 12, 14, 17, 18, 21; 34:1, 3, 6, 9, 15, 20, 22, ttl; 35:8, 9, 14, 27; 36:1, 2^2, 3, 4; 37:7, 10, 12, 13, 23, 24, 25, 26, 28, 30, 31^3, 33, 34; 38:13; 39:5, 11; 40:4; 41:2, 3^2, 5, 6, 9; 42:5, 8^2; 46:6; 47:8; 48:1; 49:7, 16, 17, 18, 19; 50:4, 6, 23; 52:7^3; 53:1, 6; 54:7; 55:20^2, 21^3; 56:4, 10^2; 57:3^2; 58:7^2, 9, 10; 59:9; 60:6; 61:6; 62:4, 12; 64:9; 65:6; 66:2^2, 5, 7^2, 8, 20; 67:1; 68:1, 4^2, 5, 21^2, 33, 34^2, 35; 69:33, 36^2; 72:7, 9, 14, 17^2, 19^2; 73:10; 76:1, 2^2; 77:8^2, 9; 78:4^2, 7, 10, 11^2, 20, 22, 26, 32, 37, 38^2, 42, 43^2, 49, 50, 52, 54^2, 56, 61^2, 62^2, 66, 69, 70, 71^2, 72^2; 79:7; 81:6^2; 85:8^2, 9, 13; 87:1; 89:23^2, 24, 25^2, 29^2, 30, 36^2, 39, 40^2, 41, 42^2, 43, 44^2, 45, 48; 91:4^3, 11, 14; 94:14^2; 95:2, 4^2, 5^2, 7^3; 96:2^2, 3^2, 6, 8^2, 13; 97:2, 3, 4, 6^2, 10, 12; 98:1^2, 2^2, 3^2; 99:5, 6^2, 7, 9; 100:2, 3^2, 4^3, 5^2; 101:5; 102:16, 19, 21, ttl; 103:1, 2, 7^2, 9, 11, 13, 15, 17, 18^2, 19^2, 20^3, 21^3, 22^2; 104:3^2, 4^2, 13, 15, 19, 23^2, 31; 105:1^2, 2, 3, 4^2, 5^3, 6^2, 7, 8, 9, 19, 21^2, 22^3, 24, 25^2, 26, 27, 28, 42^2, 43^2, 45^2; 106:1, 2, 8^2, 12^2, 13^2, 23^2, 24, 26, 33^2, 40^2, 45^2; 107:1, 8^2, 15^2, 20, 21^2, 22, 24, 31^2; 108:7; 109:6, 7, 8^2, 9^2, 10, 11, 12, 13, 14^2, 18^3, 31; 110:5; 111:3^2, 4, 5, 6^2, 7^2, 9^3, 10^2; 112:1, 2, 3^2, 5, 7, 8^3, 9^2, 10; 113:4, 8; 114:2^2; 116:2, 12, 14, 15, 18; 117:2; 118:1, 2, 3, 4, 29; 119:2, 3, 9; 125:2; 126:6; 127:2, 3, 5; 128:1; 129:7^2; 130:5, 8; 131:2; 132:1, 7^2, 13, 18^2; 133:2; 135:3, 4, 7, 9, 12, 14^2; 136:1, 2, 3, 4, 5, 6, 7, 8, 9, 10, 11, 12, 13, 14, 15^2, 16^2, 17, 18, 19, 20, 21, 22^2, 23, 24, 25, 26; 140:8; 144:4, 10; 145:3, 9^2, 12^2, 17^2, 21; 146:4^3, 5^2; 147:5, 9, 11, 15^2, 17^2, 18^2, 19^3, 20; 148:2^2, 8, 13^2, 14^2; 149:1, 3, 4, 9; 150:1^2, 2^2

Prv 2:6, 8; 3:11, 20, 31, 32; 5:21, 22^2, 23; 6:13^3, 14, 15, 27^2, 28, 29, 30, 31, 32, 33; 7:23^2; 8:22^2, 29^2, 30, 31, 36; 10:1, 9, 15, 19; 11:1, 5^2, 7, 8, 9^2, 12^2, 17^2, 19, 20, 28, 29; 12:4, 8, 10, 11, 13, 14, 15, 22, 26; 13:1, 2, 3^3, 8, 16, 22, 24^2, 25; 14:2^2, 8, 10^2, 14, 15, 20, 21, 26, 31, 32^2, 35; 15:5, 8, 20, 23, 27, 32; 16:2, 7, 9^2, 10, 11, 15, 17^2, 23^2, 26, 27, 29, 30^2, 32; 17:5, 12, 13, 18, 19, 21, 25, 27, 28^2; 18:2, 6, 7^3, 9, 11^2, 14, 17^2, 20^2; 19:1^2, 2, 3^2, 4, 7, 8, 11^2, 12, 13, 16^2, 18, 22, 24^3, 26^2; 20:2, 6, 7^2, 8, 11^2, 14, 16, 17, 19, 20^3, 24, 28; 21:2, 8, 10^2, 13, 23^3, 24, 25, 29^2; 22:5, 8, 9, 11^2, 16, 25, 29; 23:3, 6, 7^2, 14, 31; 24:7, 12, 15, 18, 26, 29; 25:5, 13, 18, 22, 28; 26:4, 5^2, 11^2, 12, 14^2, 15^3, 16, 19, 24, 25, 26; 27:8, 13, 14, 16, 17, 18, 21, 22; 28:6^2, 7, 8, 9^2, 10, 11, 13, 14, 16, 18, 19, 24^2, 25, 26, 27; 29:1, 3^2, 5^2, 10, 11, 12, 14, 15, 20, 21^2, 24, 25; 30:4^3, 6, 10, 17^2; 31:1, 7^2

Ecc 1:3, 5, 6; 2:14, 21, 22^2, 23^3, 24^2, 26; 3:11, 12, 13, 22^2; 4:4, 5^2, 8^2, 10, 14, 15; 5:14, 15^3, 17^2, 18^3, 19^2, 20^2; 6:2, 3^2, 4, 7, 12; 7:2, 15^3; 8:1^2, 3, 9, 12, 13, 15^2, 16; 9:12, 15, 16; 10:2^2, 3, 13^2; 12:5, 13

Song 1:2, 4, 12; 2:3^2, 4, 6^2, 16; 3:7, 8^2, 11^3; 4:16^2; 5:4, 11^2, 12, 13^2, 14^2, 15^2, 16; 6:2; 7:10; 8:3^2, 7, 10

Isa 1:3^2; 2:3^2, 10, 19, 20^2, 21, 22; 3:5, 6^2, 8, 11, 14; 5:1, 7, 12, 19, 25^4; 6:1, 2^2, 3, 6; 7:2^2, 14; 8:3, 7^3, 8, 17; 9:4^3, 6^2, 7^2, 11, 12^2, 17^2, 19, 20, 21^2; 10:4^2, 7^2, 12^2, 16^2, 17^3, 18^2, 19, 24, 26, 27^2, 28, 32; 11:1, 3^2, 4^2, 5^2, 8, 10, 11^2, 15^2, 16; 12:4^3; 13:5, 10, 13, 14^2; 14:17, 18, 21, 25^2, 27, 29, 31, 32; 15:4, 5; 16:6^4, 12; 17:4, 5, 7^2, 8^2, 9; 19:1, 2^2, 14; 22:21, 22, 23, 24; 23:11; 24:2, 23; 25:4, 8, 9, 11^2; 26:21; 27:1, 8, 9; 28:4, 5, 21^4, 24, 26, 28^2; 29:8^2, 22, 23; 30:4^2, 26, 27^3, 28, 30^3; 31:2, 3, 4, 7^2, 8, 9^3; 32:6; 33:6, 15^3, 16^2, 17; 34:2, 14, 16, 17; 36:6, 16^3, 18; 37:1, 4, 7^2, 20, 24^2, 38^4; 38:2, 9; 39:2^5; 40:10^3, 11^3, 12, 13, 26, 28; 41:2^3, 3, 6^2; 42:2, 4, 10, 12, 13, 21, 24^2, 25; 44:5, 6, 11, 12^2, 13, 17, 19, 20, 26^2; 45:1, 9, 10, 11, 13; 46:7^3; 47:4, 15; 48:2, 14^2, 15, 16, 19, 20; 49:2^2, 5, 7, 13^2; 50:10^2; 51:14, 15, 17, 22; 52:9, 10, 14^2; 53:5, 6, 7^2, 8, 9^3, 10^4, 11^2, 12; 54:5, 16; 55:7^2; 56:2, 3, 6, 10, 11^2; 57:2, 13, 17^2, 18^2; 58:5^2; 59:1, 2, 16^2, 17, 18^2, 19; 60:2, 22; 62:8^2, 11^2; 63:1^2, 7^2, 9^3, 10, 11^3, 12; 65:15, 20; 66:5, 6, 13, 14^3, 15^3, 16

Jer 1:2, 9, 15; 2:3, 15^2, 35; 3:1, 5; 4:7^3, 13^2, 26; 5:8, 24; 6:3, 21; 7:5, 29; 8:1, 6^2, 16^2; 9:4, 5, 8^3, 20, 23^3; 10:10^2, 12^3, 13^2, 14^2, 16^2, 23, 25; 11:19; 12:15^2; 13:23^2; 16:12; 17:5, 10^2, 11^2; 18:11, 12, 16, 18; 19:3, 9; 20:9^2; 21:2, 7, 9; 22:4^2, 7, 8, 10, 11, 13^4, 18, 28, 30^2; 23:6^2, 9, 14, 17, 18^2, 20, 27, 30, 34, 35^2, 36; 24:8; 25:4, 5, 19^3, 30^3, 38^2; 26:3, 21^2, 23; 27:7^3, 8, 12; 28:11; 29:32; 30:6^2, 8, 18, 21, 24; 31:10, 30^2, 34^2, 35; 32:4^2, 18, 19^2; 33:2, 11, 21, 26; 34:1^2, 3^2, 9^3, 10^2, 14, 15, 16^2, 17^2, 21; 35:3^2, 14, 15, 18; 36:3, 7, 14, 17, 18, 24, 30, 31^2; 37:2, 10, 17; 38:2; 39:1, 6; 40:3; 42:11; 43:10^2, 12; 44:21, 23^3, 30^4; 46:8, 10, 26; 47:3^3; 48:7^2, 10, 11^4, 12, 15, 16, 17, 25, 26, 29^4, 30^2, 35, 40; 49:1^2, 2, 3^2, 10^4, 20, 22; 50:16^2, 17, 18, 19^2, 25^2, 28, 32, 34, 43, 45; 51:3^2, 5, 6, 9, 11^2, 15^3, 16^2, 17^2, 19^2, 21^2, 23^2, 28, 31, 34, 44, 45, 59; 52:1, 3, 4^2, 8, 10, 11, 27, 31, 32, 33^2, 34^3

Lam 1:10, 12, 14, 17, 18; 2:1^3, 2, 3^2, 4^3, 5, 6^3, 7^2, 8, 17; 3:1, 3, 12, 13, 22, 27, 29, 30, 32, 34, 36, 39; 4:4, 11^2, 20

Ezk 1:15, 27^2; 3:12, 18^4, 19^3, 20^4; 7:13, 16, 20; 8:2^2, 11^2, 12; 9:1^2, 2^2, 3, 11; 10:7; 12:12^3, 14; 13:22; 14:4^5, 7^4; 16:15; 17:4, 14, 15, 17, 18, 19, 20, 21^2, 22; 18:6^2, 7^2, 8, 11, 12, 13, 14, 15^2, 16, 17^2, 18^4, 21, 22^2, 23, 24^4, 26^2, 27^2, 28, 30; 19:7, 9; 20:7, 39; 21:3, 4, 5, 21, 22, 30; 22:11^4; 25:9^2; 26:3, 9, 10, 11; 29:3, 18^2, 19, 20; 30:11, 22^2, 24; 31:2, 3, 4, 5^3, 6^3, 7^3, 8^3, 9, 10^3, 11, 12^3, 13^2, 16, 17^2, 18; 32:10, 22, 31^2, 32; 33:4^2, 5^2, 6^2, 8^3, 9^3, 11, 12^3, 13^3, 14, 16, 18, 19, 20, 26, 30; 34:12^2, 26; 35:8^2; 36:20; 37:7, 16^2, 19; 38:6^2, 21, 22; 39:11; 40:3; 43:2^2, 17; 44:27; 45:8; 46:2^2, 7, 12^3, 16^2, 17^5, 18^3; 47:3, 12, 23; 48:1

Dan 1:2^3, 3, 8, 20; 2:1^2, 2, 7, 13, 17^2, 18, 20, 32^4, 33^2, 34, 46; 3:13, 19, 20, 24, 28^2; 4:3^4, 14^4, 15^2, 16, 19, 23, 33^3, 34, 35^2, 37; 5:1, 2^4, 3^3, 6^3, 7, 9^2, 10, 20^4, 21^3, 22, 23, 29; 6:5, 10^5, 11, 13, 14, 17^2, 18^2, 22, 23, 26^2; 7:1^2, 9^3, 11, 14^2, 19^2, 20^2, 25, 26; 8:4^2, 5, 6, 7^2, 11, 21, 22, 24^2, 25^3; 9:2, 4, 10^2, 12, 14^2, 17; 10:6^6, 9^2; 11:2^2, 3, 4^4, 5^2, 6, 7, 9^2, 10^2, 11, 12, 15, 16^2, 17^3, 18^3, 19^2, 20, 21, 24^3, 25^2, 26^2, 28^3, 31, 36, 37, 38^2, 41, 42, 43, 45^2; 12:7^2

Hos 1:4, 9; 3:5; 5:5, 13^2; 6:2, 3; 7:5, 9, 10; 8:14^2; 9:8^2, 13; 10:1^2, 6, 11; 11:5, 6^2; 12:2^2, 3^2, 5, 7, 14^3; 13:12, 15^3; 14:5, 6^3, 7

Joel 2:7, 8, 11^4, 16, 18^2, 19, 20^4; 3:16^2

Am 1:2, 11^3, 15; 2:4, 7, 9^2, 14; 3:4, 7^2; 4:2, 13^2; 5:8, 19; 6:8; 7:7, 10, 17; 9:6^3, 11

Oba 3, 6, 11^2, 14^2

Jna 1:5, 7; 2:1; 3:6^2, 7, 8, 9; 4:6^2

Mic 1:2, 3, 11; 2:2^2, 7; 3:4, 8^2; 4:2^2, 4^2, 5, 12; 5:3, 4; 6:2; 7:2, 3, 6, 9, 18^2

Nah 1:2^2, 3^2, 5, 6^3, 8, 13; 2:3^2, 5, 12^4

Hab 1:11^3; 2:4^2, 5, 6, 9^2, 15, 18, 20; 3:3^2, 4^3, 5, 6, 10^2, 14^2, 16

Zep 1:7, 18; 2:3, 11, 13, 15; 3:5, 17

Hag 1:9; 2:12^2, 22

Zec 1:21; 2:1, 8, 12, 13; 3:1, 5^2, 10; 4:1, 2, 9; 5:4; 6:12, 13^2; 7:9, 10, 12; 8:4^2, 10, 16, 17; 9:7^4, 10, 14, 16^2, 17^2; 10:3^2, 12; 11:6^2, 17^4; 12:4, 10^2; 13:3^4, 4; 14:4, 9, 13^3

Mal 1:3^2, 6^2, 12, 14; 2:6^2, 7, 10, 15, 16; 3:1, 2, 5^2, 14, 16, 17; 4:2

Mt 1:2, 11, 18, 21^2, 23, 24, 25; 2:2, 11, 13, 14, 20, 21, 22; 3:3, 4^3, 7, 12^3; 4:6, 18, 21, 24; 5:1, 2, 13, 22^2, 28, 31, 32, 35, 45; 6:27, 29, 33; 7:9, 24, 26, 28; 8:3^2, 13, 14, 16, 20, 21, 23, 25; 9:1, 7, 10, 11, 19, 20, 21, 31, 37, 38; 10:1, 2^2, 10, 24^2, 25^3, 35, 36, 38, 39^2, 42; 11:1, 2, 20; 12:1, 10, 19, 21, 26, 29^2, 33^3, 46^2, 49^2; 13:19, 24, 25^2, 31, 36, 41^2, 52, 54, 55^2, 56, 57^2; 14:2, 3, 11, 12, 15, 19, 22, 31, 36; 15:5^2, 6^2, 12, 23, 32, 33, 36; 16:5, 13, 20, 21, 24^2, 25^2, 26^2, 27^3, 28; 17:1, 2^2, 10, 27; 18:6, 15, 23, 25^2, 28, 29^2, 31, 32, 34, 35; 19:3, 5, 9, 10^2, 13, 15, 23, 25, 28; 20:1, 2, 8, 28; 21:31, 34, 35, 37, 38, 41, 45; 22:2, 3, 5^2, 6, 7, 8, 15, 24^3, 25^2, 33, 45; 23:1; 24:1, 17, 18, 31^2, 32, 43, 45^2, 46, 47, 48^2, 49, 51; 25:14^2, 15^2, 18, 21, 23, 26, 31^2, 32, 33, 34, 41; 26:1, 7, 8, 23, 39, 45, 51^3, 52, 63, 65^2, 67; 27:19, 24, 25, 29^2, 31, 32, 35, 37^2, 44, 53, 60, 64; 28:3^2, 7, 8, 9, 13

Mk 1:3, 6, 16, 19, 22, 28, 41; 2:8, 15^2, 16, 23; 3:5, 7, 9, 21, 27^2, 31^2; 4:2, 34; 5:3, 15, 22, 27, 28, 31; 6:1^2, 2, 3, 4^3, 5, 14, 17, 21^2, 26, 27, 28, 29^2, 35, 41, 45, 56; 7:2, 11, 12^2, 17, 19, 25, 32^2, 33^3, 35^2; 8:1, 4, 6, 10, 12, 23^2, 25^2, 26, 27^2, 33, 34^2, 35^2, 36, 37, 38; 9:3, 14, 18, 21, 28, 31, 36, 41, 42, 50; 10:2, 7^2, 10, 11, 13, 16^2, 23, 24, 45, 46, 48, 50, 52; 11:1, 14, 18, 23; 12:6, 13, 19^4, 33, 37, 38, 43; 13:1, 15, 16, 27^2, 34^3; 14:3, 12, 13, 16, 32, 47, 51, 61, 63, 65; 15:17, 20, 21, 24, 26, 27^2; 16:7

Lk 1:5, 8, 9, 13, 14, 15, 23^2, 24, 29, 31, 32, 33, 48, 49, 50, 51, 54^2, 55, 59, 60, 62, 63, 64^2, 67, 68, 69, 70, 72, 76, 77, 80; 2:3, 5, 21, 28, 33, 34, 41, 43, 47, 48, 51; 3:1, 4, 17^3, 18, 19; 4:10, 16, 22, 24, 30, 32^2, 40; 5:12, 13, 19, 25, 29, 30; 6:1, 10, 13, 14, 17, 20^2, 40^2, 44, 45^3; 7:1, 3, 11, 12, 15, 16, 19, 38^3; 8:5, 9, 19^2, 22, 35, 39, 41, 44; 9:1, 14, 18, 23, 24^2, 26^2, 29^2, 31, 32, 42, 43, 51, 52, 53, 54, 58, 62; 10:1, 2, 7, 23, 30, 34^2, 39; 11:1^2, 6, 8^2, 18, 21^2, 22^2, 54; 12:1, 22, 25, 27, 39, 42^2, 43, 45^2, 46, 47^2; 13:6, 7, 13, 15^2, 17, 19; 14:17, 21^2, 26^2, 27, 34; 15:5, 6, 12^2, 13^2, 15, 16, 20^3, 22^3, 25, 28, 29; 16:1^2, 5, 18, 20, 21, 23^2, 24; 17:2, 16^2, 24, 31, 33^2; 18:7, 13^2, 14, 15, 39, 43; 19:13, 14, 29; 20:20, 26^2, 28^3, 44, 45; 22:4, 36^2, 39, 44, 45, 50, 51, 71; 23:11, 34, 49, 55; 24:8, 23, 26, 40^2, 47, 50

Jn 1:11^2, 12, 14, 16, 35, 41; 2:2, 5, 11^2, 12^3, 17, 21, 22, 23; 3:4, 16, 17, 20, 21, 22, 32, 33^2, 35; 4:2, 5, 6, 8, 12^2, 27, 31, 34, 41, 44, 47, 50, 51, 53; 5:9, 18, 28, 35, 37^2, 38, 43, 47; 6:2, 3, 5, 8, 12, 16, 22^3, 24, 52, 53, 60, 61, 66; 7:3, 5, 10, 16, 17, 18^2, 30, 38, 53; 8:6, 20, 44, 55; 9:1, 2^2, 3, 7, 14, 15, 18^2, 20, 21, 22, 23, 27, 28, 31; 10:3^2, 4^2, 11; 11:2, 3, 7, 8, 12, 13, 16, 32, 41, 44, 54; 12:3, 4, 16, 17, 25^2, 41, 50; 13:1^2, 3, 4, 10, 12, 16, 18, 23; 15:10, 13^2, 15, 19, 20; 16:17, 29, 32; 17:1; 18:1^2, 2, 10, 19^2, 22, 25, 26; 19:2, 17, 23^2, 25^2, 26^2, 27, 29, 30, 33, 34, 35; 20:7, 20^2, 25^2, 26, 30, 31; 21:2, 7, 14, 20, 24

Act 1:3, 7, 14, 18, 20^2, 22, 25; 2:6, 14, 29, 30^2, 31^2, 41; 3:2, 4, 7, 13, 16^2, 18, 21, 26^2; 4:26, 32; 5:1, 2, 7, 10, 31, 32, 41; 6:15; 7:4, 5^2, 6, 10^2, 13, 14^2, 20, 23^2, 25^2, 27; 8:1, 2, 28, 32^2, 33^4, 35, 39; 9:8, 12^2, 17^2, 18, 33, 41; 10:2, 7, 22, 24, 25, 34, 43; 11:13, 29; 12:1, 7^2, 10, 11, 15, 21; 13:8, 9, 13, 16, 23, 24, 25^2, 31, 36^2; 14:3, 8^2; 15:14, 18; 16:1, 3, 27^2, 32, 33, 34^2; 17:2, 16, 28; 18:2, 6, 8, 14, 18^2; 19:6, 12, 31, 33; 20:7, 10, 28, 32, 38; 21:11, 19; 22:14^2, 15, 20, 30; 23:29, 30; 24:8, 23, 24; 27:3; 28:3, 4, 8, 23, 30

Ro 1:2, 3, 5, 9, 20; 2:4, 6, 18, 26; 3:7, 20, 24, 25^2, 26; 4:5, 13, 19, 23; 5:8, 9, 10^2; 6:3, 5^2, 16; 8:3, 9, 11, 28, 29, 32; 9:19, 22^2, 23; 11:1, 2, 22, 33^2, 34; 12:20; 13:10; 14:4, 5, 13; 15:2^2, 9, 10; 16:13, 15

1Co 1:9, 29; 2:10; 3:8^2; 5:1; 6:5, 14, 18; 7:2, 4, 7, 11, 33, 36, 37^4; 9:7, 10; 10:24, 28; 11:4^2, 7, 21; 14:25^2, 30; 15:10, 23^2, 25, 27, 38; 16:12

2Co 2:11, 14; 3:7, 13; 5:10; 7:7, 12^2, 13, 15; 8:9, 17; 9:7, 9, 15; 10:10^3; 11:3, 15, 33

Gal 1:15, 16; 3:16; 4:4, 6; 5:10; 6:4, 5, 8

Eph 1:5, 6, 7^2, 9^2, 11, 12, 14, 18^2, 19^2, 20, 22, 23; 2:4, 7^2, 10, 15; 3:5, 6, 7, 16^2; 4:25, 28; 5:28, 29, 30^3, 31^2, 33; 6:10

Php 1:29; 2:4, 13, 30; 3:10^3, 21; 4:19

Col 1:9, 11, 13, 14, 20, 22^2, 24, 26, 29; 2:14, 18; 3:9; 4:15

1Th 1:10; 2:11, 12, 19; 3:13; 4:4, 6, 8

2Th 1:7, 9, 10, 11; 2:6, 8^2

1Ti 3:4^2, 5; 5:8^2, 18; 6:1, 15

2Ti 1:8, 9; 2:19, 26; 4:1^2, 8, 14, 18

Tit 1:3; 3:5, 7

Heb 1:2, 3^3, 7^2; 2:4, 8, 17; 3:2, 5, 6, 7, 15, 18; 4:1, 4, 7, 10^3, 13; 5:7; 6:10, 17; 7:10, 27; 8:11^2; 9:12; 10:13^2, 20, 30; 11:4, 5, 7, 17, 21, 22, 23; 12:10, 16; 13:12, 13, 15, 21^2

Jas 1:8, 11, 14, 18^2, 23, 24, 25, 26^2; 2:21, 22; 3:13; 4:11^2; 5:20

1Pt 1:3; **2**:9, 21, 22, 24^2; **3**:10^2, 12; **4**:2, 13; **5**:10

2Pt 1:3, 9, 16; **2**:8, 16, 22; **3**:4, 9, 13, 16

1Jn 1:3, 7, 10; **2**:3, 4, 5, 9, 10, 11^2, 12, 28; **3**:9, 10, 12^3, 14, 15, 16, 17^2, 22^2, 23^2, 24; **4**:9, 10, 12, 13, 20^2, 21; **5**:2, 3^2, 9, 10, 11, 14, 16, 20

2Jn 6, 11

3Jn 7, 10

Jude 14, 24

Rev 1:1^3, 4, 5, 6, 14^3, 15^2, 16^4, 17^2; **2**:1, 5, 18^2; **3**:5^3, 21; **6**:5, 8, 17; **7**:15; **9**:11; **10**:1^3, 2^3, 5, 7; **11**:15, 19^2; **12**:3, 4, 5, 7^2, 9, 10, 15, 16; **13**:1^2, 2^4, 3^2, 6^3, 17, 18; **14**:1, 7, 9^4, 10, 11^2, 14^2, 16, 19; **15**:2^3, 8; **16**:2^2, 3, 4, 8, 10^2, 12, 15^2, 17, 19; **17**:17; **18**:1; **19**:2^2, 5, 7, 10, 12^2, 13, 15, 16^2, 19, 20, 21; **20**:1, 4^2, 7; **21**:3, 7; **22**:3, 4^2, 6^2, 12, 14, 19

I

Gen 1:29, 30; **2**:18; **3**:10^4, 11, 12, 13, 15, 16, 17; **4**:1, 9^2, 13, 14^2, 23; **6**:7^3, 13, 17^2, 18; **7**:1, 4^3; **8**:21^3; **9**:3, 5^3, 9^2, 11, 12, 13, 14, 15, 16^2, 17; **12**:1, 2^2, 3, 7, 11, 13, 19; **13**:8, 9^3, 15, 16, 17; **14**:22, 23^3; **15**:1, 2, 7, 8^2, 14, 18; **16**:2^2, 5^2, 8, 10, 13; **17**:1, 2, 5, 6^2, 7, 8^2, 16^2, 19, 20^3, 21; **18**:3^2, 4, 5, 10, 12^2, 13, 14, 15, 17^2, 19, 21^2, 26^2, 27, 28^2, 29, 30^3, 31^2, 32^2; **19**:2, 7, 8^2, 19^2, 21^2, 22, 34; **20**:5, 6^3, 9, 11, 13, 16; **21**:7, 13, 18, 23, 24, 26^2, 30; **22**:1, 2, 5, 7, 11, 12, 16, 17^2; **23**:4^2, 8, 11^3, 13^3; **24**:2, 3^2, 5, 7, 12, 13, 14^5, 17, 19, 23, 24, 27, 31, 33^2, 34, 37, 39, 40, 42^2, 43^3, 44, 45^3, 46^2, 47^2, 48, 49, 56, 58; **25**:22, 30^2, 32; **26**:2, 3^4, 4, 9^2, 24^2; **27**:1, 2^2, 3, 4^3, 6, 7, 8, 9, 11, 12^2, 18, 19^3, 21^2, 24, 25, 32, 33, 37^4, 41, 45^2, 46; **28**:13^2, 15^4, 16, 20, 21, 22^2; **29**:18, 19^2, 21, 25, 33, 34, 35; **30**:1, 2, 3, 8^2, 13, 14, 16, 18, 20, 25, 26^2, 27^3, 28, 29, 30^2, 31^2, 32, 34; **31**:3, 5, 6, 10, 11^2, 12, 13, 27, 31^2, 35, 38^2, 39^2, 40, 41^2, 43, 44, 51, 52; **32**:4, 5^3, 9, 10^3, 11^2, 12, 20^2, 26, 29, 30; **33**:8, 9, 10^4, 11^2, 12, 14^3; **34**:8, 11, 12, 30^3; **35**:3^2, 11, 12^3; **37**:6^2, 9, 10, 13^2, 14, 16^2, 17, 30^2, 35; **38**:16, 17, 18, 22, 23, 25^2, 26^2; **39**:9^2, 14, 15, 18; **40**:8, 11^2, 14, 15^2, 16^2; **41**:9, 11, 15^2, 17, 19, 21, 22, 24, 28, 40, 41, 44; **42**:2, 14, 18, 22, 33, 34^2, 37^2; **43**:9^2, 14^2, 23; **44**:15, 17, 18, 21, 28^2, 30, 32^2, 33, 34^2; **45**:3, 4^2, 11, 18, 28^2; **46**:2, 3^2, 4^2, 30, 31; **47**:16, 23, 29^3, 30^2; **48**:4^2, 5, 7^2, 9^2, 11, 19^2, 21, 22^2; **49**:1, 7, 18, 29, 31; **50**:4^2, 5^4, 17, 19, 21, 24

Ex 2:7, 9, 10, 22; **3**:3, 4, 6, 7^2, 8, 9, 10, 11^3, 12^2, 13^2, 14^3, 16, 17^2, 19, 20^2, 21; **4**:10^2, 11, 12, 13, 14, 15, 18, 21^3, 23^2; **5**:2^3, 10, 23; **6**:1, 2, 3^2, 4, 5^2, 6^4, 7^3, 8^4, 29^2, 30; **7**:1, 2, 3, 4, 5^2, 17^2; **8**:2, 8, 9, 21, 22^2, 23, 28, 29^2; **9**:14, 15^2, 16, 18, 27^2, 28, 29^2, 30; **10**:1^2, 2^3, 4, 10, 16, 17, 29; **11**:1, 4, 8; **12**:12^3, 13^3, 17; **13**:8, 15^2; **14**:4^3, 17^3, 18^2; **15**:1, 2^2, 9^4, 26^3; **16**:4^2, 12^2, 32^2; **17**:4, 6, 9, 14; **18**:3, 6, 11, 16^2, 19; **19**:4^2, 9^2; **20**:2, 5, 22, 24^3; **21**:5^2, 13; **22**:23, 24, 27^2; **23**:7, 13, 15, 20^2, 22^2, 23, 25, 26, 27^2, 28, 29, 30, 31^2; **24**:12^2; **25**:8, 9, 16, 21, 22^3; **28**:3; **29**:35, 42, 43, 44^2, 45, 46^3; **30**:6, 36; **31**:2, 3, 6^4, 11, 13; **32**:8, 9, 10^2, 13^3, 18, 24^2, 30^2, 32, 33, 34^3; **33**:1^2, 2^2, 3^2, 5^2, 12, 13^4, 14, 16^2, 17^2, 18, 19^4, 22^2, 23; **34**:1, 9^2, 10^3, 11^2, 18, 24, 27

Lev 6:17; **7**:34; **8**:31, 35; **10**:3^2, 13, 18, 19; **11**:44^2, 45^2; **14**:34^2; **16**:2; **17**:10, 11, 12, 14; **18**:2, 3, 4, 5, 6, 21, 24, 25, 30; **19**:2, 3, 4, 10, 12, 14, 16, 18, 25, 28, 30, 31, 32, 34, 36, 37; **20**:3, 5, 6, 7, 8, 22, 23^2, 24^3, 25, 26; **21**:8, 12, 15, 23; **22**:2, 3, 8, 9, 16, 30, 31, 32^2, 33; **23**:10, 22, 30, 43^3; **24**:22; **25**:2, 17, 21, 38, 42, 55^2; **26**:1, 2, 4, 6^2, 9, 11, 12, 13^2, 16^2, 17, 18, 19^2, 21, 22, 24, 25^2, 26, 28^3, 30, 31^2, 32, 33, 36, 41, 42^3, 44^3, 45^4

Nu 3:12^2, 13^3, 41, 45; **5**:3; **6**:27; **8**:16, 17^2, 18, 19; **9**:8; **10**:10, 29, 30^2, 31; **11**:11, 12^2, 13, 14, 15^2, 17^2, 21^2; **12**:6, 8, 11, 13; **13**:2; **14**:11, 12, 17, 19, 20, 21, 22, 23, 24, 27^2, 28^2, 30, 31, 35^2; **15**:2, 18, 41^2; **16**:8, 15^2, 21, 26, 28, 45; **17**:4, 5^2; **18**:6^2, 7, 8^2, 11, 12, 19, 20, 21, 24^2, 26; **20**:12, 17, 18, 19^3, 24; **21**:2, 16, 34; **22**:6^4, 8, 11, 16, 17^3, 18, 19^2, 20, 28, 29^2, 30^3, 32, 33, 34^3, 35, 37^2, 38^3; **23**:3^2, 4^2, 8^2, 9^2, 11, 12, 13, 15, 20^2, 26^2, 27^2; **24**:10, 11, 12, 13^2, 14^2, 17^2; **25**:11, 12; **27**:12; **32**:8, 11; **33**:53, 56^2; **35**:34^2

Dt 1:8, 9^2, 12, 13, 15, 16, 17, 18, 20, 23, 29, 35, 36, 39, 42, 43; **2**:5^2, 9^2, 13, 19^2, 24, 25, 26, 27^2, 28^3, 29, 31; **3**:2, 12, 13, 15, 16, 18, 19^2, 20, 21, 23, 25; **4**:1, 2^2, 5, 8, 10, 21^2, 22^2, 26, 40; **5**:1, 5, 6, 9, 28, 31^2; **6**:2, 6; **7**:11, 17^2; **8**:1, 11, 19; **9**:9^3, 12, 13, 14^2, 15, 16, 17, 18^2, 19, 20, 21^2, 23, 24, 25^2, 26; **10**:2, 3, 5^2, 10, 11, 13; **11**:2, 8, 13, 14, 15, 22, 26, 27, 28, 32; **12**:11, 14, 20, 21, 28, 30, 32; **13**:18; **15**:5, 11, 15, 16; **17**:3, 14; **18**:16, 18^2, 19, 20; **19**:7, 9; **22**:14^3, 16, 17; **24**:8, 18, 22; **25**:8; **26**:3^2, 10, 13^3, 14^3; **27**:1, 4, 10; **28**:1, 13, 14, 15, 68; **29**:5, 6, 14, 19^2; **30**:1, 2, 8, 11, 15, 16, 18, 19^2; **31**:2^2, 5, 14, 16, 17^2, 18, 20^2, 21^3, 23^2, 27^2, 28, 29^2; **32**:1, 3, 20^2, 21^2, 23^2, 24, 26^3, 27, 39^6, 40^2, 41^2, 42, 46, 49, 52; **33**:9; **34**:4^3

Jos 1:2, 3^2, 5^3, 6, 9; **2**:4, 5, 9, 12^2; **3**:7^3; **5**:9, 14; **6**:2, 10; **7**:8, 11, 12, 19, 20^2, 21^2; **8**:1, 5, 8, 18; **10**:8; **11**:6; **13**:6^2; **14**:7^2, 8, 10, 11^2, 12; **15**:16; **17**:14; **18**:4, 6, 8; **20**:2; **22**:2; **23**:2, 4^2, 14; **24**:3, 4^2, 5^4, 6, 7, 8^3, 10^2, 11, 12, 13

Jdg 1:2, 3, 7, 12; **2**:1^4, 3^2, 20, 21, 22; **3**:19, 20; **4**:7^2, 8^2, 9, 19^2, 22; **5**:3^3, 7^2; **6**:8, 9, 10^2, 14, 15^2, 16, 17, 18^3, 22, 37^2, 39^2; **7**:4^3, 7, 9, 13, 17^2, 18^2; **8**:2, 3, 5^2, 7, 9^2, 19, 23, 24; **9**:2^2, 9, 11, 13, 29, 38, 48; **10**:11, 12, 13; **11**:9, 17, 27, 31^2, 35^2, 37^2; **12**:2^2, 3^2; **13**:4, 6, 11, 13, 14, 15, 16; **14**:2, 12^2, 16^2; **15**:1, 2^3, 3^2, 7^2, 11, 16, 18; **16**:6, 7, 10, 11, 15, 17^3, 20, 26^2, 28^3; **17**:2, 3^2, 9^3, 10, 13^2; **18**:4, 24^2; **19**:6, 8, 9, 11, 18^3, 23, 24; **20**:4^2, 6, 23, 28^3

Ru 1:12^4, 16^2, 17^2, 21; **2**:2, 7, 9, 10^2, 13, 19; **3**:1, 5, 9, 11, 12^2, 13; **4**:4^4, 6^3, 9, 10

1Sa 1:8, 11, 15^2, 16, 20, 22^2, 26, 27^2, 28; **2**:1, 16, 23, 24, 27, 28^2, 29, 30^2, 31, 33, 35^2, 36^2; **3**:4, 5^2, 6^2, 8, 11, 12^4, 13^2, 14, 16, 17; **4**:16^2; **7**:5; **8**:7, 8; **9**:8^2, 16^2, 17, 18, 19^2, 21, 23^2, 24^2, 26, 27; **10**:2, 8^2, 15, 18; **11**:2^2; **12**:1, 2^2, 3^7, 7, 17, 23^2; **13**:11, 12^3; **14**:7, 24, 29^2, 37, 40, 43^2; **15**:2, 6, 11, 13, 14, 16, 20, 24^3, 25^2, 26, 30^3; **16**:1^3, 2^2, 3^2, 5, 7, 18, 22; **17**:8, 9, 10, 28, 29, 35^2, 39^2, 43, 44, 45, 46^2, 55, 58; **18**:11, 17, 18^2, 21, 23; **19**:2, 3^4, 15, 17; **20**:1, 3, 4, 5^2, 9^2, 12^2, 13, 14^2, 20^2, 21^2, 22, 23, 29^3, 30, 36; **21**:2^3, 5, 8, 15; **22**:3^2, 9, 12, 15, 22^2; **23**:2, 4, 11, 17, 22, 23^2; **24**:4, 6, 10^2, 11^2, 17^2, 20; **25**:7, 8, 11^3, 19, 21, 22, 24, 25^2, 28, 35; **26**:6, 8^2, 11^2, 18, 19, 21^3, 23; **27**:1^3, 5^2; **28**:2, 7, 8^2, 11, 13, 15^3, 21, 22, 23; **29**:3, 6, 8^3, 9; **30**:7, 8^2, 13^2, 15

2Sa 1:3, 4, 6, 7^2, 8^2, 9, 10^3, 13, 16, 26; **2**:1^2, 6, 20, 22^2; **3**:8, 9, 13^2, 14, 18, 21, 28, 35, 39; **4**:10^2, 11; **5**:19^2; **6**:21, 22^2; **7**:2, 6^2, 7^3, 8, 9, 10, 11, 12^2, 13, 14^2, 15^2, 18, 27; **9**:1, 3, 7, 8, 9; **10**:2, 11; **11**:5, 11^2, 12; **12**:7^2, 8^2, 11^2, 12, 13, 22^2, 23^3, 27, 28; **13**:4, 5^2, 6^2, 10, 13^3, 24, 26, 28^2; **14**:2, 5, 8, 11, 12, 15^2, 18^2, 21, 22, 32^3; **15**:4^2, 7^2, 8^2, 20^3, 25, 26^2, 28, 31, 34^3; **16**:4^2, 9, 10, 18^2, 19^4; **17**:1, 2^2, 3, 11, 15; **18**:2, 4, 10, 11, 12^2, 13, 14, 18, 22, 29^2, 33; **19**:6, 7, 20^2, 22^3, 26^2, 28, 29, 33, 34^2, 35^5, 37^2, 38^2; **20**:16^2, 17^2, 19, 20, 21; **21**:3^2, 4, 6; **22**:3, 4^2, 7, 22, 23, 24, 30^2, 38^2, 39, 41, 43^2, 44, 50^2; **23**:17; **24**:2, 10^4, 12^2, 13, 14, 17^3, 24^2

1Ki 1:5, 12, 14, 21, 30^2, 35; **2**:2, 7, 8^3, 14, 15, 16, 17, 18, 20^3, 26, 30, 42^2, 43; **3**:5, 7^2, 9, 12^2, 13, 14, 17^2, 18, 21^3; **5**:5^2, 6, 8^2, 9; **6**:12^2, 13; **8**:13, 16^3, 20, 21, 26, 27, 43, 44, 48, 59; **9**:3^2, 4, 5^2, 6, 7^4; **10**:6, 7^3; **11**:11^2, 12^2, 13^2, 21, 31, 32, 34^3, 35, 36^2, 37, 38^3, 39; **12**:6, 11^2, 14^2; **13**:7, 8^2, 14, 16^2, 18, 31; **14**:2^2, 6, 7, 10; **15**:19; **16**:2, 3; **17**:1, 4, 9, 10^2, 11, 12^3, 18, 20, 21, 24; **18**:1, 8, 9, 12^4, 13^2, 15^2, 18, 22^2, 23, 24, 36^2; **19**:2, 4, 10^3, 14^3, 18, 20^3; **20**:4^2, 5, 6, 7^2, 9^2, 13^2, 28^2, 31, 32, 34^2, 35, 37, 42; **21**:2^3, 3, 4, 6^3, 7, 20, 21, 29^2; **22**:4, 5, 6^2, 8, 13, 14, 16, 17, 18, 19, 21, 22^2, 27, 30, 34

2Ki 1:2, 10, 12, 13; **2**:2^2, 3, 4^2, 5, 6^2, 9^3, 10, 18, 19, 21; **3**:7^2, 13, 14^3; **4**:2, 9, 10, 13, 22^2, 24, 26, 28^2, 30, 43; **5**:5, 6, 7^2, 11, 12, 15^2, 16^2, 17, 18^2, 20, 22; **6**:3^2, 13, 17, 18, 19, 21^2, 27, 29, 33; **7**:12, 13^2; **8**:4, 8, 9, 12; **9**:3, 5, 6, 7, 8, 9, 12, 17, 25, 26^2; **10**:9, 19, 24; **16**:7; **17**:13^2, 38; **18**:14^2, 20, 23^2, 25, 26, 32; **19**:7^2, 19, 20, 23^2, 24^2, 25^3, 27, 28^2, 34; **20**:3^2, 5^3, 6^3, 8, 15; **21**:4, 7^2, 8^3, 12, 13^2, 14; **22**:8, 16, 19^2, 20^2; **23**:17, 27^4

1Ch 4:9; **5**:3; **11**:19^2; **13**:12; **14**:10^2; **15**:12; **16**:18; **17**:1, 5^2, 6^3, 7, 8, 9, 10^3, 11^2, 12, 13^3, 14, 16; **19**:2, 12; **21**:2, 8^4, 10^2, 12, 13, 17^3, 22, 23^2, 24^2; **22**:5, 9^2, 10^2, 14^2; **23**:5; **28**:2, 6^2, 7; **29**:2, 3^4, 14, 17^3, 19

2Ch 1:7, 10, 11, 12; **2**:4, 5, 6^2, 8, 9, 10, 13; **6**:2, 5^3, 6, 10, 11, 18, 33, 34, 38, 40; **7**:12, 13^3, 14, 16, 17, 18^2, 19, 20^4; **9**:5, 6^3; **10**:11^2, 14^2; **12**:5, 7^2; **16**:3; **18**:3, 4, 5, 7, 12, 13, 14, 15, 16, 17, 18, 20, 21, 26, 29, 33; **20**:11; **25**:9, 16; **28**:23; **32**:13; **33**:7^2, 8^3; **34**:15, 24, 27, 28^2; **35**:21^3, 23

Ezr 4:19; **6**:8, 11, 12; **7**:13, 21^2, 28^2; **8**:15^2, 16, 17^2, 21, 22, 24, 26, 28; **9**:3^2, 4, 5^2, 6

Neh 1:1, 2, 4^2, 5, 6^2, 8^2, 9^2, 11^3; **2**:1^2, 2, 4, 5^2, 6, 7^2, 8, 9, 11, 12^4, 13, 14, 15, 16^3, 17, 18, 20; **4**:13^2, 14, 19, 22, 23; **5**:6^2, 7^3, 8, 9, 10^2, 11, 12, 13, 14^2, 15, 16, 18, 19; **6**:1^2, 3^4, 4, 8, 10, 11^4, 12, 13; **7**:1, 2, 3, 5, 7; **9**:8; **12**:31, 38, 40; **13**:6^3, 7, 8, 9^2, 10, 11^2, 13, 14, 15^2, 17, 19^2, 21^2, 22, 23, 25, 28, 30

Est 3:9; **4**:11, 16^4; **5**:4, 8^3, 12, 13; **7**:3, 4^2; **8**:5^2, 6^2, 7

Job 1:15, 16, 17, 19, 21^2; **3**:3, 11^3, 12, 13^3, 16, 24, 25^2, 26^3; **4**:7, 8, 16^2; **5**:3^2, 8^2; **6**:8^2, 10^3, 11^2, 22, 24^2, 28, 29; **7**:3, 4^4, 8, 11^3, 12, 13, 16^2, 19, 20^3, 21^2; **8**:8, 18; **9**:2, 11^2, 14, 15^3, 16^2, 19, 20^3, 21^3, 22, 27^3, 28^2, 29^2, 30, 32^2, 35; **10**:1^2, 2, 7, 9, 13, 14, 15^4, 18, 19^3, 20, 21^2; **11**:4; **12**:3^2, 4; **13**:2^2, 3^2, 13, 14, 15^2, 18^3, 19^2, 20, 22; **14**:14, 15; **15**:6, 17^3; **16**:2, 4^2, 5, 6^3, 12, 15, 22^2; **17**:6, 10, 13^2, 14; **19**:4, 7^3, 8, 10, 15, 16^2, 17, 18, 19, 20, 25, 26, 27; **20**:2, 3; **21**:3^2, 6^2, 27; **22**:22; **23**:3^3, 4, 5, 7, 8^2, 9^2, 10^2, 11, 12^2, 15^3, 17; **27**:5^3, 6^2, 11^2; **29**:2, 3, 4, 6, 7^2, 12, 13, 14, 15^2, 16^3, 17, 18^3, 24, 25; **30**:1^2, 9^2, 19, 20^2, 23, 25, 26^2, 28^3, 29; **31**:1^2, 5, 9, 13, 14^2, 16, 18, 19, 21^2, 23, 24, 25, 26, 28, 29, 30, 32, 33, 34^2, 36, 37^2, 39; **32**:6^2, 7, 10^2, 11^2, 12, 14, 16, 17^3, 18, 20^3, 21, 22; **33**:1, 2, 6^2, 8, 9^2, 12, 24, 27, 31, 32, 33; **34**:5, 6, 31^2, 32^3, 33; **35**:3^2, 4; **36**:2^2, 3; **37**:20; **38**:3, 4, 9, 23; **39**:6; **40**:4^3, 5^3, 7, 14, 15; **41**:11, 12; **42**:2, 3^3, 4^3, 5, 6, 8^2

Ps 2:6, 7^2, 8; **3**:4, 5^2, 6; **4**:1^2, 3, 8; **5**:2, 3, 7^2; **6**:2, 6^3; **7**:1, 3, 4^2, 17; **8**:3; **9**:1^2, 2^2, 13, 14^2; **10**:6^2; **11**:1; **12**:5^2; **13**:2, 3, 4^2, 5, 6; **16**:1, 4, 6, 7, 8^2; **17**:3, 4, 6, 15^3; **18**:1, 2, 3^2, 6, 21, 22, 23^2, 29^2, 37^2, 38, 40, 42^2, 43, 49; **19**:13^2; **20**:6; **22**:2, 6, 9, 10, 14, 17, 22^2, 25; **23**:1, 4^2, 6; **25**:1, 2, 5, 16, 20, 21; **26**:1^3, 3, 4^2, 5, 6^2, 7, 8, 11, 12; **27**:1^2, 3, 4^3, 6^3, 7, 8, 13^2, 14; **28**:1^2, 2^2, 7^2; **30**:1, 2, 3, 6^2, 7, 8^2, 9, 12; **31**:1, 5, 6^2, 7, 9, 11, 12^2, 13, 14^2, 17, 22^3; **32**:3, 5^4, 8^2; **34**:1, 4, 11; **35**:3, 11, 13, 14^2, 15, 18^2; **37**:25^2, 35, 36; **38**:6^3, 8^2, 13^2, 14, 15, 16, 17, 18^2, 20; **39**:1^4, 2^2, 3^2, 4^2, 7, 9^2, 10, 12, 13^2; **40**:1, 5, 7^2, 8, 9^2, 10^3, 12, 17; **41**:4^2, 9, 10, 11; **42**:2, 4^4, 5, 6, 9^2, 11; **43**:2, 4^2, 5; **44**:6; **45**:1^2, 17; **46**:10^3; **49**:4^2, 5; **50**:7^3, 8, 9, 11, 12^3, 13, 15, 21^3, 22, 23; **51**:3, 4, 5, 7^2, 13, 16; **52**:8^2, 9^2; **54**:6^2; **55**:2, 6^3, 7, 8, 9, 12^2, 16, 17, 23; **56**:3^2, 4^3, 9^2, 10^2, 11^2, 12, 13; **57**:1, 2, 4, 7, 8, 9^2; **59**:9, 16^2, 17; **60**:6^2, 8; **61**:2^2, 4^2, 8^2; **62**:2, 6, 11; **63**:1, 2, 4^3, 6, 7; **66**:13^2, 14, 15^2, 16, 17, 18; **68**:22^2; **69**:2^2, 3^2, 4^2, 7, 8, 10, 11^2, 12, 17, 20^3, 29, 30; **70**:5; **71**:1, 3, 6, 7, 14, 15, 16^2, 17, 18^2, 22^2, 23; **73**:3^2, 13, 14, 15^3, 16, 17^2, 21, 22^2, 23, 25^2, 28^2; **75**:2^2, 3, 4, 9^2, 10; **77**:1, 2, 3^2, 4^2, 5, 6^2, 10^2, 11^2, 12; **78**:2^2; **81**:5^2, 6, 7^3, 8, 10^2, 12, 14, 16; **82**:6; **84**:10; **85**:8; **86**:1, 2, 3, 4, 7, 11, 12^2; **87**:4; **88**:1, 4^2, 8^2, 9^2, 13, 15^3; **89**:1^2, 2, 3^2, 4, 19^2, 20^2, 23, 25, 27, 28, 29, 32, 33, 34, 35^2, 50; **91**:2^2, 14^2, 15^3, 16; **92**:4, 10; **94**:18; **95**:10, 11; **101**:1^2, 2^2, 3^2, 4, 5^2, 8^2; **102**:2^2, 4, 6^2, 7, 9, 11, 24; **104**:33^4, 34; **105**:11; **106**:5^3; **108**:1, 2, 3^2, 7^2, 9^2; **109**:4, 22, 23^2, 25, 30^2; **110**:1; **111**:1; **116**:1, 2^2, 3, 4^2, 6, 9, 10^3, 11, 12, 13, 14, 16^2, 17, 18; **118**:5, 6, 7, 10, 11, 12, 13, 17, 19^2, 21, 25^2, 28^2; **119**:6^2, 7^2, 8, 10, 11^2, 13, 14, 15, 16^2, 17, 18, 19, 22, 26, 27, 30^2, 31, 32, 33, 34^2, 35, 39, 40, 42^2, 43, 44, 45^2, 46, 47^2, 48^3, 51, 52, 55, 56^2, 57^2, 58, 59, 60, 61, 62, 63, 66, 67^3, 69, 70, 71^2, 73, 74, 75, 76, 77, 78, 80, 81, 83^2, 87, 88, 92, 93, 94^2, 95, 96, 97, 99, 100^2, 101^2, 102, 104^2, 106^3, 107, 108, 109, 110, 111, 112, 113^2, 114, 115, 116, 117^2, 119, 120, 121, 125^2, 127, 128^2, 131^2, 134, 141^2, 144, 145^2, 146^2, 147^2, 148, 152, 153, 157, 158, 159, 162, 163^2, 164, 166, 167, 168, 173, 174, 176^2; **120**:1, 5^2, 7^2; **121**:1; **122**:1, 8, 9; **123**:1; **130**:1, 5^2, 6; **131**:1, 2; **132**:3, 4, 5, 11, 12, 14^2, 15^2, 16, 17^2, 18; **135**:5; **137**:5, 6^2; **138**:1^2, 2, 3, 7; **139**:6, 7^2, 8^2, 9, 11, 14^2, 15, 18^3, 21^2, 22^2; **140**:6, 12; **141**:1^2, 10; **142**:1^2, 2^2, 3, 4, 5^2, 6^2, 7; **143**:5^3, 6, 7, 8^3, 9, 12; **144**:2, 9^2; **145**:1^2, 2^2, 5, 6; **146**:2^4

Prv 1:23^2, 24^2, 26^2, 28; **3**:28; **4**:2, 3, 11^2; **5**:12, 14; **7**:6, 7, 14^2, 15^2, 16, 17; **8**:4, 6, 12, 13, 14^2, 17, 20, 21^2, 23, 24, 25, 27, 30^2; **9**:5; **20**:9^2, 22; **22**:13, 19, 20, 21; **23**:35^4; **24**:29^2, 30, 32^2; **26**:19; **27**:11; **30**:2, 3, 7^2, 9^2, 18, 20

APNDX

21; 3:2, 15, 17; 4:1, 11^2, 12^3, 13, 15, 16^2, 18, 19, 20^2; 5:2, 3, 10, 11^3, 12, 16, 21^2; 6:11, 14^2, 17

Eph 1:15^2; 3:1, 3, 7, 8, 13, 14; 4:1, 17; 5:32; 6:19, 20^3, 21, 22

Php 1:3, 7, 8, 9, 12, 17, 18, 19, 20, 22^3, 23, 25^2, 27^2; 2:16^2, 17^2, 19^3, 20, 23^2, 24^2, 25, 27, 28^2; 3:4^2, 7, 8^3, 10, 11, 12^4, 13^2, 14, 18; 4:2, 3, 4, 10, 11^3, 12^3, 13, 15, 17^2, 18^2

Col 1:20, 23, 25, 29; 2:1^2, 4, 5^2; 4:3, 4^2, 8, 13

1Th 2:18; 3:5^2; 4:9, 13; 5:1, 23, 27

2Th 2:5^2; 3:17

1Ti 1:3^2, 12, 13^2, 15, 16, 18, 20; 2:1, 7^2, 8, 12; 3:14, 15; 4:13; 5:14, 21; 6:13

2Ti 1:3^3, 4, 5^2, 6, 11, 12^5; 2:7, 9, 10; 3:11; 4:1, 6, 7^3, 12, 13, 16, 17, 20

Tit 1:5^2; 3:8, 12^2

Phlm 4, 8, 9, 10^2, 12, 13, 14, 19^3, 21^2, 22^2

Heb 1:5^2, 13; 2:12^2, 13^2; 3:10, 11; 4:3; 5:5; 6:14^2; 7:9; 8:8, 9^3, 10^3, 12^2; 10:7^2, 9, 16^3, 17, 30; 11:32; 12:21, 26; 13:5, 6, 19^2, 22^2, 23

Jas 1:13; 2:18^2

1Pt 1:16; 2:6, 11; 5:1, 12^2

2Pt 1:12, 13^2, 14, 15, 17; 3:1^2

1Jn 2:1, 4, 7, 8, 12, 13^3, 14^2, 21, 26; 4:20; 5:13, 16

2Jn 1^2, 4^2, 5^2, 12^2

3Jn 1, 2, 3, 4, 9, 10^2, 13^2, 14^2

Jude 3, 5

Rev 1:8, 9, 10, 11, 12^2, 17^3, 18^2; 2:2, 4, 5, 6, 7, 9^2, 10, 13, 14, 15, 16, 17, 19, 20, 21, 22, 23^3, 24^2, 25, 26, 27, 28; 3:1, 2, 3^2, 5^2, 8^2, 9^3, 10, 11, 12^3, 15^2, 16, 17, 18, 19^2, 20^2, 21^2; 4:1^3, 2, 4; 5:1, 2, 4, 6, 11^2, 13; 6:1^2, 2, 3, 5^2, 6, 7, 8, 9, 12; 7:1, 2, 4, 9, 14; 8:2, 13; 9:1, 13, 16, 17; 10:1, 4^2, 5, 8, 9, 10^2; 11:3; 12:10; 13:1, 2, 3, 11; 14:1, 2^2, 6, 13, 14; 15:1, 2, 5; 16:1, 5, 7, 13, 15; 17:1, 3, 6^3, 7; 18:1, 4, 7; 19:1, 6, 10^2, 11, 17, 19; 20:1, 4^2, 11, 12; 21:1, 2, 3, 5, 6^2, 7, 9, 22; 22:7, 8^3, 9, 12, 13, 16^2, 18, 20

IF

Gen 4:7^2, 24; 8:8; 13:9^2, 16; 15:5; 18:3, 21, 26, 28, 30; 20:7; 23:8, 13; 24:8, 41, 42, 49^2; 25:22; 27:46; 28:20; 30:27, 31; 31:8^2, 50^2; 32:8; 33:10, 13; 34:15, 17, 22; 37:26; 42:19, 37, 38; 43:4, 5, 9, 11, 14; 44:22, 26, 29, 32; 47:6, 16, 29; 50:4

Ex 1:16^2; 4:8, 9, 23; 8:2, 21; 9:2; 10:4; 12:4; 13:13; 15:26; 18:23; 19:5; 20:25^2; 21:2, 3^2, 4, 5, 7, 8, 9, 10, 11, 13, 14, 16, 18, 19, 20, 21, 22, 23, 26, 27, 28, 29, 30, 32, 33^2, 35, 36; 22:1, 2, 3^2, 4, 5, 6, 7^2, 8, 10, 12, 13, 14, 15^2, 16, 17, 23, 25, 26; 23:4, 5, 22, 33; 24:14; 29:34; 32:32^2; 33:13, 15; 34:9, 20; 40:37

Lev 1:2, 3, 10, 14; 2:4, 5, 7, 14; 3:1^2, 6, 7, 12; 4:2, 3, 13, 23, 27, 28, 32; 5:1^2, 2^2, 3, 4, 7, 11, 15, 17; 6:2, 28; 7:12, 16, 18; 10:19; 11:37, 38, 39; 12:2, 5, 8; 13:4, 5, 6, 7, 8, 10, 12, 13, 16, 17, 20, 21^2, 22, 23, 24, 25, 26, 27, 28, 29, 30, 31, 32, 34, 35, 36, 37, 38, 39, 42, 43, 49, 51, 53, 55, 56, 57, 58; 14:3, 21, 37, 39, 43, 44, 48; 15:8, 16, 19, 23, 24, 25^2, 28; 17:16; 18:5; 19:5, 6, 7, 33; 20:4, 12, 13, 14, 15, 16, 17, 18, 20, 21; 21:9; 22:9, 11, 12, 13, 14; 24:19; 25:14, 20, 25^2, 26, 28, 29, 30, 33, 35, 39, 47, 49, 51, 52, 54; 26:3, 14, 15^2, 18, 21, 23, 27, 40, 41; 27:4, 5, 6, 7^2, 8, 9, 10, 11, 13, 15, 16, 17, 18, 19, 20^2, 22, 27^2, 31, 33

Nu 5:8, 12, 14, 19^2, 20^2, 27, 28; 6:9; 9:10, 14; 10:4, 9, 32; 11:15^2; 12:6, 14; 14:8, 15; 15:14, 22, 24, 27; 16:29^2, 30; 19:12; 20:19; 21:2, 9; 22:18, 20, 34; 24:13; 27:8, 9, 10, 11; 30:2, 3, 5, 6, 8, 10, 12, 14, 15; 32:5, 15, 20^2, 23, 29, 30; 33:55; 35:16, 17, 18, 20, 22, 26; 36:3

Dt 4:29^2, 30; 5:25; 6:25; 7:12, 17; 8:19; 11:13, 22, 27, 28; 12:21; 13:1, 6, 12, 14; 14:24^2; 15:5, 7, 12, 16, 21^2; 17:2, 8; 18:6, 21, 22; 19:8, 9, 11, 16, 18; 20:11, 12; 21:1, 14, 15^2, 18, 22; 22:2^2, 6, 8, 13, 20, 22, 23, 25, 28; 23:10, 22; 24:3^2, 7, 12; 25:1, 2, 3, 5, 7, 8; 28:1, 2, 9, 13, 15, 58; 30:4, 10^2, 17; 32:41

Jos 2:14, 19, 20; 8:15; 9:4; 14:12; 17:15^2; 20:5; 22:19, 22^2, 23^2, 24; 23:12; 24:15, 20

Jdg 4:8^2; 6:13, 17, 31, 36, 37; 7:10; 8:19; 9:15^2, 16^2, 19, 20, 36; 11:9, 10, 30, 36; 12:5; 13:16, 23; 14:12, 13, 18; 16:7, 11, 13, 17; 21:21

Ru 1:12^2, 17; 3:13^2; 4:4^2

1Sa 1:11; 2:16^2, 25^2; 3:9, 17; 6:3, 9^2; 7:3; 9:7; 10:22; 11:3; 12:14, 15, 25; 14:9, 10, 30; 16:2; 17:9^2; 19:11; 20:6, 7^2, 8, 9, 10, 12, 13, 21, 22, 29; 21:4, 9; 23:3, 23; 24:19; 25:22; 26:19^2; 27:5

2Sa 3:35; 7:14; 10:11^2; 11:20; 12:8, 18; 13:26; 14:32; 15:8, 25, 26, 33, 34; 16:23; 17:3, 6, 13; 18:3^2, 25; 19:6, 7, 13

1Ki 1:52^2; 2:4, 23; 3:14; 6:12; 8:31, 35, 37^4, 44, 46, 47; 9:4, 6; 11:38; 12:7, 27; 13:8; 16:31; 18:21^2; 19:2; 20:10, 39; 21:2, 6; 22:28

2Ki 1:10, 12; 2:10^2; 4:29^2; 5:13; 6:27, 31; 7:2, 4^4, 9, 19; 9:15; 10:6^2, 15, 24; 18:21, 22, 23; 20:19; 21:8

1Ch 12:17^2; 13:2; 19:12^2; 22:13; 28:7, 9^2

2Ch 6:22, 24, 26, 28^4, 32, 34, 36, 37, 38; 7:13^3, 14, 17, 19; 10:7; 15:2^2; 18:27; 20:9; 25:8; 30:9^2

Ezr 4:13, 16; 5:17

Neh 1:8, 9; 2:5^2, 7; 4:3; 9:29; 10:31; 13:21

Est 1:19; 3:9; 4:14, 16; 5:4, 8^2; 6:13; 7:3^2, 4; 8:5^2; 9:13

Job 4:2; 5:1; 6:28; 8:4, 5, 6, 18; 9:3, 13, 16, 19^2, 20^2, 23, 24, 27, 29, 30; 10:14, 15^2; 11:10, 13, 14; 13:10, 19; 14:7, 14; 16:4; 17:13; 19:5; 21:4, 15; 22:23; 24:17, 25; 27:14; 29:24; 31:5^2, 7^2, 9^2, 13, 16, 19, 20^2, 21, 24, 25, 26, 29, 31, 33, 38, 39; 33:5, 23, 27, 32, 33; 34:14^2, 16, 32; 35:3, 6^2, 7; 36:8, 11, 12; 37:20; 38:4, 5, 8, 18

Ps 7:3^2, 4, 12; 11:3; 14:2; 28:1; 40:5; 41:6; 44:20; 50:12; 53:2; 59:15; 62:10; 66:18; 73:15; 81:8; 89:30, 31; 90:10; 95:7; 124:1, 2; 130:3; 132:12; 137:5, 6^2; 139:8^2, 9, 11, 18, 24

Prv 1:10, 11; 2:1, 3, 4; 3:30; 6:1^2, 30, 31; 9:12^2; 16:31; 19:19; 22:18, 27; 23:2, 13, 15; 24:10, 11, 12; 25:21^2; 29:9, 12; 30:4, 32^2

Ecc 4:10, 11, 12; 5:8; 6:3; 10:4, 10; 11:3^2, 8

Song 1:8; 5:8; 7:12; 8:7, 9^2

Isa 1:19, 20; 5:30; 7:9; 8:20; 10:15^3; 21:12; 36:6, 7, 8; 47:12^2; 51:13; 58:9, 10, 13; 59:10; 66:3^4

Jer 2:10, 28; 3:1; 4:1^2; 5:1^2; 7:5^2, 6; 12:5^2, 16, 17; 13:17, 22; 14:18^2; 15:2, 19^2; 17:24, 27; 18:8, 10; 21:2; 22:4, 5; 23:22; 25:28; 26:3, 4, 15; 27:18^2; 31:36, 37; 33:20, 25^2; 38:15^2, 17, 18, 21, 25; 40:4^2; 42:5, 10, 13, 15; 49:9^2; 51:8

Lam 1:12; 2:6; 3:29

Ezk 3:19, 21; 10:10; 14:9, 15, 17, 19; 16:47; 18:5, 10, 14, 21; 20:11, 13, 21, 39; 21:13; 33:2, 3, 4, 6^2, 8, 9^2, 10, 13, 14, 15, 19; 43:11; 46:16, 17

Dan 2:5, 6, 9; 3:15^2, 17, 18; 4:27; 5:16

Hos 6:3; 8:7

Joel 2:14; 3:4

Am 3:4; 5:19; 6:9

Oba 5^3

Jna 1:6; 3:9

Mic 2:11; 5:8

Nah 3:12

Hag 2:12, 13

Zec 3:7^2; 6:15; 8:6; 11:12^2; 14:18

Mal 1:6^2, 8^2; 2:2^2; 3:10

Mt 4:3, 6, 9; 5:13, 23, 29, 30, 40, 46, 47; 6:14, 15, 22, 23^2, 30; 7:9, 10, 11; 8:2, 31; 9:21; 10:13^2, 25; 11:14, 21, 23; 12:7, 11, 26, 27, 28; 14:28; 15:14; 16:24, 26; 17:4, 20; 18:8, 9, 12, 13, 15^2, 16, 17^2, 19, 35; 19:10, 17, 21; 21:3, 21^2, 24, 25, 26; 22:24, 45; 23:30; 24:23, 24, 26, 43, 48; 26:24, 39, 42; 27:40, 42, 43; 28:14

Mk 1:40; 3:24, 25, 26; 4:23, 26; 5:28; 6:56; 7:11, 16; 8:3, 23, 36; 9:22, 23, 35, 43, 45, 47, 50; 10:12; 11:3, 13, 25, 26, 31, 32; 12:19; 13:21, 22; 14:21, 31, 35; 15:44; 16:18

Lk 4:3, 7, 9; 5:12, 36; 6:32, 33, 34; 7:39; 9:23, 25; 10:6^2, 13; 11:11^2, 12, 13, 18, 19, 20, 36; 12:26, 28, 38, 39, 45, 49; 13:9^2; 14:26, 34; 15:4, 8; 16:11, 12, 30, 31; 17:3^2, 4, 6; 19:8, 31, 40, 42; 20:5, 6, 28; 22:42, 67, 68; 23:31, 35, 37, 39

Jn 1:25; 3:12^2; 4:10; 5:31, 43, 47; 6:51, 62; 7:4, 17, 23, 37; 8:16, 19, 24, 31, 36, 39, 42, 46, 51, 52, 54, 55; 9:22, 31, 33, 41; 10:9, 24, 35, 37, 38; 11:9, 10, 12, 21, 32, 40, 48, 57; 12:24, 26^2, 32, 47; 13:8, 14, 17^2, 32, 35; 14:2, 3, 7, 14, 15, 23, 28; 15:6, 7, 10, 14, 18, 19, 20^2, 22, 24; 16:7^2; 18:8, 23^2, 30, 36; 19:12; 20:15; 21:22, 23, 25

Act 4:9; 5:38, 39; 8:22, 37; 9:2; 13:15; 15:29; 16:15; 17:27; 18:14, 15, 21; 19:38, 39; 20:16; 23:9; 24:19, 20; 25:5, 11^2; 26:5, 32; 27:12, 39

Ro 1:10; 2:25^2, 26, 27; 3:3, 5, 7; 4:2, 14, 24; 5:10, 15, 17; 6:5, 8; 7:2, 3^2, 16, 20; 8:9^2, 10, 11, 13^2, 17^2, 25, 31; 9:22; 10:9; 11:6^2, 12, 14, 15, 16^2, 17, 18, 21, 22, 23, 24; 12:18, 20^2; 13:4, 9; 14:15, 23; 15:24, 27

1Co 3:12, 14, 15, 17, 18; 4:7^2, 19; 5:11; 6:2, 4; 7:8, 9, 11, 12, 13, 15, 21, 28^2, 36^2, 39, 40; 8:2, 3, 8^2, 10, 13; 9:2, 11^2, 12, 16, 17^2; 10:27, 28, 30; 11:5, 6^2, 14, 15, 16, 31, 34; 12:15, 16, 17^2, 19; 14:6, 8, 11, 14, 23, 24, 27, 28, 30, 35, 37, 38; 15:2, 12, 13, 14, 15, 16, 17, 19, 29, 32^2; 16:4, 7, 10, 22

2Co 2:2, 5, 10; 3:7, 9, 11; 4:3; 5:1, 3, 14, 17; 7:14; 8:12; 9:4; 10:2, 7, 9; 11:4^2, 15, 16, 20^5, 30; 13:2^2

Gal 1:9, 10; 2:14, 17, 18, 21; 3:4, 15, 18, 21, 29; 4:7, 15; 5:2, 11, 15, 18, 25; 6:1, 3, 9

Eph 3:2; 4:21

Php 1:22; 2:1^4, 17; 3:4, 11, 12, 15; 4:8^2

Col 1:23; 2:20; 3:1, 13; 4:10

1Th 3:8; 4:14

2Th 3:10, 14

1Ti 1:8, 10; 2:15; 3:1, 5, 15; 4:4, 6; 5:4, 8, 10^5, 16; 6:3

2Ti 2:5, 11, 12^2, 13, 21, 25

Tit 1:6

Phlm 17, 18

Heb 2:2, 3; 3:6, 7, 14, 15; 4:3, 5, 7, 8; 6:3, 6; 7:11; 8:4, 7; 9:13; 10:26, 38; 11:15; 12:7, 8, 20, 25^2; 13:23

Jas 1:5, 23, 26; 2:2, 8, 9, 11^2, 15, 17; 3:2, 14; 4:11, 15; 5:15, 19

1Pt 1:6, 17; 2:3, 19, 20^2; 3:1, 13, 14, 17; 4:11^2, 14, 16, 17, 18

2Pt 1:8, 10; 2:4, 20

1Jn 1:6, 7, 8, 9, 10; 2:1, 3, 15, 19, 24, 29; 3:13, 20, 21; 4:11, 12, 20; 5:9, 14, 15, 16

2Jn 10

3Jn 6, 10

Rev 1:15; 3:3, 20; 11:5^2; 13:9; 14:9; 22:18, 19

IN

Gen 1:1, 6, 11, 12, 14, 15, 17, 20, 22^2, 26, 27^2, 29; 2:3, 4, 5, 8, 9, 17; 3:3, 5, 8^2, 10, 16, 17, 19; 4:3, 8, 12, 14, 16, 20, 22; 5:1^2, 2, 3; 6:4^3, 5, 8, 9, 14, 16^2, 17; 7:1, 7, 9, 11^2, 13, 15, 16^3, 22^2, 23; 8:1, 4, 5, 9, 11^3, 13^2, 14, 17, 21; 9:6, 7, 13, 14, 16, 27; 10:5^2, 8, 10, 20^2, 25, 31, 32^2; 11:2, 28^2, 31, 32; 12:3, 5, 6, 10^2; 13:2^3, 7, 12^2, 17^2, 18^2; 14:1, 3, 4, 5, 5^4, 6, 7, 8, 12, 13, 14; 15:1, 3, 6, 10, 13, 15^2, 16, 18; 16:2, 3, 4^2, 5, 6, 7^2, 12; 17:7, 9, 12^2, 13^2, 17, 21, 23^2, 24, 25, 26, 27; 18:1^3, 3, 9, 10, 11, 18, 26; 19:1, 2^2, 3, 5, 8, 9, 12^2, 14^2, 15, 17, 19^2, 27, 29, 30^3, 31^2, 33, 34; 20:1, 3, 5, 6^2, 8^2, 11; 21:2, 7, 11, 12^3, 14^2, 15, 18, 20, 21, 22, 33, 34; 22:3, 6, 9, 13^2, 14, 17^2, 18; 23:2^2, 6, 9, 10^2, 11, 13, 16, 17^3, 18^2, 19^2; 24:1^2, 10, 23^2, 25, 27, 31, 37, 45, 48, 54, 62, 63, 65; 25:8, 9^2, 18, 23, 24, 27; 26:1^2, 2, 3, 4, 6, 12^2, 15, 17, 18, 19, 22, 29, 31^2; 27:15, 30, 41, 45; 28:11, 14^2, 15, 16, 18, 20, 21; 29:2, 3, 21, 23^2, 25, 26, 30; 30:2, 3, 4, 14^2, 16^2, 27, 33, 35, 37^2, 38^2, 40, 41, 42; 31:10, 11, 14, 18^2, 20, 23, 24, 25^2, 28, 29, 34, 40, 41, 54, 55; 32:5, 21, 32; 33:8, 10, 15, 18; 34:5, 7^2, 11, 15, 19, 21, 28^2, 29, 30; 35:3^2, 4^2, 6, 13, 14, 17, 18, 19, 22, 26; 36:5, 6, 8, 9, 16, 17, 21, 24, 30, 31, 32, 33, 34, 35^2, 36, 37, 38, 39, 43; 37:1^2, 7, 12, 13, 15, 17, 22, 24, 29, 31, 33; 38:1, 2, 7, 8, 9, 11^2, 12, 13, 14, 16^3, 18^2, 21, 22, 24, 25, 27^2; 39:2, 3, 4, 5^3, 6, 8, 9, 12, 13, 14^2, 17, 20, 21, 22; 40:3^2, 4, 5^2, 6^2, 7, 9, 10, 11, 16, 17; 41:2, 8, 10^2, 11, 14, 16, 17, 18, 19, 22^2, 30, 31, 34, 35, 36, 37^2, 38, 40, 42, 43, 44, 47, 48^3, 52, 53, 54^2, 56, 57; 42:1, 2, 3, 5, 13, 16^2, 19, 21, 27^2, 28, 32, 34, 35, 38; 43:1, 11^2, 12^3, 15, 18^2, 21^3, 22^2, 23, 26, 28; 44:1, 2, 5^2, 8, 12, 17^2, 18, 28, 30; 45:6^2, 7, 10, 13, 16; 46:2, 5, 6, 12, 15, 20, 27, 31, 34; 47:1, 4^3, 6^2, 7, 9, 11^3, 13, 14^2, 15^3, 17, 18, 24, 25, 27^2, 28, 29^2, 30; 48:3, 5, 6, 7^3, 9, 13^2, 16, 20; 49:1, 5, 6^2, 7^2, 8, 11^2, 17, 24, 27, 29^2, 30^3; 50:4^2, 5^2, 8, 11, 13, 19, 22, 26^2

Ex 1:5, 14^{4}, 19; **2:**3, 11, 12, 15, 22, 23; **3:**1, 2, 7, 16, 20, 21, 22; **4:**2, 4, 14, 15, 17, 18^{3}, 19, 20, 21, 24, 27, 30; **5:**1^{2}, 14, 16, 19, 20, 21^{3}, 23; **6:**5, 8, 11, 28; **7:**3, 10, 11, 15^{2}, 16, 17^{3}, 18, 19^{2}, 20^{4}, 21; **8:**9, 11, 17^{2}, 20, 22^{3}, 25, 28, 29; **9:**1, 3, 5, 8, 9, 13, 14, 16^{2}, 18, 19^{2}, 21, 22, 24, 25, 26, 31; **10:**1, 2^{2}, 3, 14, 15^{2}, 16, 19, 22, 23, 28; **11:**2, 3^{4}, 5, 8, 9; **12:**1, 3, 6, 8, 11^{2}, 12, 16^{3}, 17^{2}, 18, 19^{2}, 20, 22^{3}, 23, 27, 29^{2}, 30^{2}, 33, 34, 36, 40, 42, 46, 48; **13:**3, 4, 5, 6, 7, 8, 9, 10, 14, 15, 20^{2}, 21^{2}; **14:**3^{2}, 11^{2}, 12^{2}, 23, 24, 27, 29; **15:**4, 6^{2}, 7, 8, 10, 11^{2}, 13^{2}, 17^{5}, 19^{2}, 20, 22, 26; **16:**2, 3, 4, 5, 7, 8^{2}, 10, 12, 13, 16, 25, 26, 29, 32; **17:**1, 5, 6^{2}, 8, 9, 14^{2}; **18:**1, 2, 3, 5, 6, 7, 8, 11, 12^{2}, 14, 15, 17, 23, 24, 27; **19:**1, 2, 9, 11, 16^{2}, 18; **20:**4^{3}, 7^{2}, 10, 11^{2}, 24; **21:**2, 3, 13, 16, 29^{2}, 36^{2}; **22:**4, 5^{2}, 6, 13, 21, 23, 31; **23:**2, 3, 6, 9, 10, 11, 13, 14, 15^{2}, 16^{3}, 17, 19, 20, 21, 23, 26, 29, 33; **24:**4, 6, 7, 10, 17, 18; **25:**7^{2}, 12^{3}, 15, 18, 21, 22, 26, 33^{3}, 34, 40; **26:**4^{3}, 5^{3}, 9, 10^{2}, 13, 17^{2}, 23, 28, 30, 33, 34; **27:**4, 8, 11, 19, 21; **28:**1, 3, 4, 11^{2}, 17, 20^{2}, 24, 25, 26^{2}, 29^{2}, 30^{2}, 32^{2}, 35, 38, 41, 43^{2}; **29:**1, 3, 17, 24^{2}, 29, 30^{2}, 31, 32, 39, 44; **30:**10^{2}, 30, 36; **31:**3^{4}, 4^{3}, 5^{3}, 6, 10, 15^{2}, 17; **32:**2, 3, 12, 15, 17, 20, 26, 27, 34; **33:**3^{2}, 5, 10, 12, 13^{2}, 16^{2}, 17, 22; **34:**1, 2^{3}, 4^{2}, 5, 6, 9, 10^{2}, 12, 18^{2}, 21^{2}, 23, 24, 26, 29, 32^{2}, 34, 35; **35:**15, 19^{2}, 26, 31^{4}, 32^{3}, 33^{2}, 34, 35^{4}; **36:**1, 2, 11^{3}, 12^{3}, 17, 28, 29; **37:**13, 19^{2}, 20; **38:**18, 23^{3}, 24; **39:**1, 3^{4}, 6, 10, 13^{2}, 16, 17, 18, 23, 26, 37, 41^{2}; **40:**4^{4}, 13, 15, 17^{2}, 18, 22, 23, 24, 26, 36, 38

Lev 1:7, 8, 9, 12; **2:**4, 5, 6, 7, 11; **4:**6, 7, 17, 18, 24, 29, 33; **5:**4, 5^{2}, 13, 15, 16; **6:**2^{3}, 3, 5^{2}, 7, 9, 12^{2}, 16^{2}, 18, 20^{2}, 21^{2}, 22, 25, 26^{2}, 27, 28^{2}, 30^{2}; **7:**2, 6, 9^{3}, 24^{2}, 26, 35^{2}, 36, 38^{3}; **8:**8, 21, 31, 33; **9:**9; **10:**3, 5, 13, 14, 17, 18^{2}, 19; **11:**9^{4}, 10^{4}, 11, 12, 13, 33, 34, 46; **12:**3, 4, 5^{2}; **13:**2^{2}, 3^{3}, 4^{2}, 5^{2}, 6, 7, 8, 9, 10^{2}, 11, 12, 14, 18^{2}, 19, 20, 22, 23, 24, 25^{2}, 26, 27, 28^{2}, 30^{2}, 31^{2}, 32^{3}, 34^{3}, 35, 36, 37, 38, 39^{2}, 42^{2}, 43^{3}, 44, 45, 46, 47, 48^{3}, 49^{5}, 51^{5}, 52^{3}, 53^{4}, 55, 57^{4}, 59^{2}; **14:**2, 3, 5, 6, 8, 9, 13^{2}, 16^{2}, 17, 18, 27, 28, 29, 32, 34, 35, 36^{2}, 37^{2}, 39, 40, 42, 43, 44^{2}, 47^{2}, 48^{2}, 50, 51^{2}; **15:**3, 5, 6, 7, 8, 10, 11^{2}, 12, 13, 16, 18, 19, 20, 21, 22, 27, 31; **16:**2, 4, 16^{2}, 17^{3}, 21, 22, 24, 26, 27^{3}, 28, 29, 32^{2}; **17:**3, 5, 11, 15; **18:**3, 5, 15, 18, 24^{2}; **19:**6, 15^{2}, 17^{2}, 24, 25, 28, 33, 34, 35^{4}; **20:**2, 12, 17, 23; **21:**5, 11, 13, 17, 20, 23; **22:**2, 11, 13, 18, 21, 23, 24, 25^{2}, 28; **23:**3, 4, 5, 7, 8, 14, 21, 24^{2}, 28, 29, 30, 31, 32, 39^{2}, 41^{3}, 42^{2}, 43; **24:**3^{2}, 5, 6, 8, 9, 10, 12, 16, 19, 20; **25:**1, 3, 4, 7, 9, 11^{2}, 13, 18^{2}, 19, 20, 21, 22, 24, 28^{2}, 29, 30^{2}, 31, 33, 35, 45, 53, 54^{2}; **26:**1, 3, 4, 5, 6, 16, 20, 22, 26, 28, 34, 35, 36, 39^{3}, 44, 45, 46; **27:**19, 21, 23, 24, 34

Nu 1:1^{3}, 3, 16, 19, 45; **2:**9, 16^{2}, 17^{2}, 24, 31; **3:**1^{2}, 3, 4^{3}, 13^{2}, 14, 25, 28; **4:**3, 4, 6, 8, 12^{2}, 15, 16^{2}, 19, 20, 23^{2}, 27^{3}, 28, 31, 33, 35, 37, 39, 41, 43, 47; **5:**3, 17^{2}, 18^{2}, 23; **6:**5, 9, 18; **7:**10, 84; **8:**15, 17, 19, 22^{2}, 24, 26; **9:**1^{2}, 3^{2}, 5, 7, 10, 13^{2}, 14, 17, 18, 20, 21, 22, 23; **10:**9, 10^{3}, 11, 12, 14, 29, 31, 33; **11:**1, 5, 8^{3}, 9, 10, 11, 12, 15, 18^{2}, 25, 26^{2}, 27; **12:**5^{2}, 6^{2}, 7, 8, 14^{2}, 15, 16; **13:**19^{4}, 22, 28, 29^{2}, 32, 33^{2}; **14:**2^{2}, 8, 10, 13, 14^{2}, 16, 22^{2}, 25, 28, 29, 31, 32, 33^{2}, 34, 35, 40, 45; **15:**3^{3}, 8, 13, 14, 15, 21, 26, 30, 32, 34, 38; **16:**2, 7, 13, 17, 18^{2}, 21, 26, 27, 45, 49; **17:**4, 7; **18:**10, 11, 13^{2}, 14, 15, 20, 21, 31^{2}; **19:**5, 7, 8^{2}, 9, 14^{2}, 16, 17, 18, 19; **20:**1^{2}, 5, 12, 13, 15, 16^{2}, 23, 27, 28; **21:**1, 5, 10, 11, 12, 13, 14^{3}, 20^{2}, 25^{3}, 27, 31; **22:**1, 7, 13, 21, 22, 23^{2}, 24, 26, 29, 31^{2}, 34, 36^{2}, 38; **23:**5, 12, 16, 21^{2}; **24:**2, 7, 14, 21; **25:**1, 6^{2}, 7, 9, 11, 15, 18^{3}; **26:**2, 3, 9^{2}, 19, 59, 63, 64, 65; **27:**3^{4}, 14^{4}, 17^{2}, 18, 19, 21; **28:**2, 4, 6, 7, 11, 16, 17, 18, 23, 26; **29:**1, 39; **30:**3^{2}, 5, 7, 10, 14, 16^{2}; **31:**6, 16, 35, 36; **32:**5, 13^{2}, 14, 15, 17, 26, 30, 33, 39; **33:**3^{2}, 5, 6^{2}, 8^{2}, 9, 11, 12, 13, 15, 18, 20, 22, 23, 24, 25, 28, 29, 31, 33, 36, 37^{2}, 38^{2}, 39, 40^{2}, 41, 42, 43, 44^{2}, 45, 46, 47, 48, 49, 50, 54, 55^{3}; **34:**29; **35:**1, 2, 3, 5, 12, 14, 21, 25, 28, 29, 32; **36:**8, 12, 13

Dt 1:1^{2}, 3^{3}, 4^{2}, 5, 6^{2}, 7^{4}, 8, 17, 25, 27, 30, 31^{2}, 32, 33^{4}, 37, 38, 39^{2}, 44^{2}, 46; **2:**4, 7, 8, 9, 10, 12^{2}, 14, 20, 21, 22^{2}, 23^{2}, 24, 25, 29^{2}, 37; **3:**4, 10, 11, 19, 24^{2}, 29; **4:**1, 5, 6, 7, 10, 14, 15, 17, 18, 21, 22, 25^{2}, 27, 30^{2}, 34, 37, 38, 39^{2}, 42, 43^{4}, 46^{2}; **5:**1, 2, 4, 8^{3}, 11^{2}, 14, 15, 16, 22^{2}, 29, 31, 33^{2}; **6:**1, 3, 6, 7, 16, 18^{2}, 20, 21, 23; **7:**7, 13, 17; **8:**1, 2^{2}, 5, 6, 9, 11, 16, 17; **9:**1, 4^{2}, 7, 8, 9, 10^{2}, 15, 18^{2}, 28; **10:**2^{2}, 3, 4^{2}, 5, 6^{2}, 8, 10, 11, 12, 15, 18, 19; **11:**3, 5, 6^{2}, 8, 9, 10, 14^{2}, 15, 18^{2}, 19, 21, 22, 29, 30^{2}, 31; **12:**1, 7, 8, 10^{2}, 13, 14^{2}, 15, 18^{2}, 21, 25, 28, 29, 31; **13:**5, 12, 18; **14:**9, 21^{2}, 23, 25, 29; **15:**4, 7, 8, 9, 10^{2}, 11, 12, 15, 18^{2}, 20; **16:**1, 2, 3, 4, 6, 7^{2}, 11, 12, 13, 14, 15^{3}, 16^{5}, 18; **17:**2^{2}, 4, 8, 9, 15, 18, 20^{2}; **18:**5, 7, 16^{2}, 18, 19, 20^{2}, 21, 22; **19:**1^{2}, 2, 4, 6, 9, 10, 11, 14^{2}, 15, 17; **20:**5, 6, 7, 14, 19^{2}; **21:**1^{2}, 3, 4, 5, 6, 9, 13^{2}, 14, 23; **22:**1, 3, 6^{2}, 7, 13, 15, 19, 21^{2}, 23, 24, 25, 26, 27; **23:**1, 4, 7, 8, 14^{2}, 16^{2}, 20^{2}, 21, 22, 24; **24:**1^{3}, 3, 8, 13^{2}, 14, 18, 19^{3}, 22; **25:**5, 6, 7, 9^{2}, 10, 13, 14, 15, 19; **26:**1, 2, 3, 11, 14, 17, 19^{3}; **27:**3, 4, 15, 23; **28:**3^{2}, 6, 8^{3}, 9, 11^{5}, 12, 16^{2}, 19, 20, 29^{2}, 32, 35^{2}, 38, 48^{4}, 52^{2}, 53^{2}, 55^{3}, 57^{2}, 58, 61, 62, 66, 67; **29:**1^{2}, 2, 5, 9, 11, 16, 19^{2}, 20, 21, 23^{2}, 27, 28^{3}; **30:**9^{4}, 10, 12, 14^{2}, 16^{3}, 20; **31:**2, 7, 10^{2}, 11^{2}, 13, 14^{2}, 15^{2}, 17^{2}, 18^{2}, 19, 24, 26, 28, 29^{2}, 30; **32:**10^{2}, 20, 22, 28, 34, 35, 37, 44, 47, 49, 50^{2}, 51^{2}; **33:**3, 5, 12, 16, 18^{2}, 19, 21, 24, 26^{2}, 28; **34:**5, 6^{2}, 8, 10, 11^{2}, 12^{3}

Jos 1:11, 14, 17, 18; **2:**2, 6, 11^{3}, 18, 19, 21; **3:**1, 7, 8, 13, 15, 17; **4:**3, 6, 9^{2}, 10, 11, 14, 19^{2}, 20, 21; **5:**1, 4, 5, 6, 7, 8^{2}, 10^{2}, 11, 13; **6:**1, 11, 12, 17, 18, 21, 23, 25, 26^{2}; **7:**1, 5, 13, 14, 15, 16, 21^{2}, 22; **8:**4, 9, 10, 12, 13, 14, 16, 17, 18^{2}, 22, 24^{2}, 30, 31, 32, 34; **9:**1^{3}, 9, 25, 27; **10:**6, 11, 12^{3}, 13^{2}, 16, 17, 21, 27, 30; **11:**2^{2}, 3^{2}, 4, 13, 17, 19, 20, 22^{4}; **12:**2, 5^{3}, 7, 8^{6}, 23; **13:**1^{2}, 9, 10, 12^{3}, 16, 17, 19, 21^{2}, 27, 30, 31, 32; **14:**1, 4^{2}, 6^{2}, 7, 10, 11^{2}, 12^{2}; **15:**5, 33, 48, 61; **16:**10; **17:**10^{2}, 11^{2}, 12, 15, 16; **18:**5^{2}, 8, 9, 10, 16; **19:**2, 14, 50, 51; **20:**4, 6^{2}, 7^{4}, 8^{3}; **21:**2^{2}, 6, 11, 21, 27, 32, 38, 39; **22:**2, 5, 7, 9, 10, 11, 16, 17, 19, 20^{2}, 22^{2}, 24, 25, 27^{2}, 28, 33; **23:**1, 2, 6, 12^{2}, 13^{2}, 14^{2}; **24:**2, 7^{2}, 13, 14^{3}, 15, 17^{2}, 18, 25, 26, 30^{3}, 32^{2}, 33^{2}

Jdg 1:4, 5, 9^{3}, 10, 16^{2}, 21, 27, 29^{2}, 35^{3}; **2:**3, 9^{3}, 11, 17, 19; **3:**3^{2}, 7, 12^{2}, 20, 22, 24, 27; **4:**1, 2^{2}, 5, 11, 14, 18^{3}, 20, 21, 22; **5:**6^{2}, 7^{2}, 8^{2}, 10, 11^{2}, 17^{2}, 18, 19, 20, 24, 25, 28, 31; **6:**1, 2, 10, 11, 14, 15^{2}, 17, 19^{3}, 21, 24, 26, 28, 33, 37; **7:**1, 3, 8^{2}, 11, 12, 16, 19^{2}, 20^{2}, 21, 22; **8:**2, 3, 6, 9, 10, 11, 15, 27^{2}, 28^{2}, 29, 31, 32^{3}; **9:**2, 3, 6, 7, 15^{2}, 16, 19^{2}, 24, 25^{2}, 26, 32^{2}, 33, 34, 35^{2}, 41, 43, 44^{2}, 48, 56; **10:**1^{2}, 2, 4, 5, 6, 8^{2}, 14, 17^{2}; **11:**2, 3, 4, 7, 11, 12, 17^{2}, 20, 26^{3}, 31, 39, 40; **12:**3, 7, 9, 12^{2}, 15^{3}; **13:**1, 9, 20, 25; **14:**1, 2, 6, 8, 9, 14; **15:**1^{3}, 4, 6, 8, 9^{2}, 19^{2}, 20; **16:**1, 2^{3}, 4, 9^{2}, 12^{2}, 18, 21, 30, 31; **17:**2, 4, 6^{3}, 10, 12; **18:**1^{4}, 3^{2}, 6, 7^{2}, 10, 12^{2}, 14, 17^{2}, 19, 20, 22, 28, 31; **19:**1^{2}, 4, 5^{2}, 7, 8, 9, 11^{2}, 13^{2}, 15^{4}, 16, 17, 20, 26, 27; **20:**1, 2, 6^{2}, 10, 13, 19, 20, 22^{3}, 27, 28, 29, 30, 31^{2}, 33^{2}, 36, 37^{2}, 38, 39^{2}, 42, 45, 47; **21:**1, 3^{2}, 12, 13, 15, 19^{2}, 20^{2}, 21, 22, 23, 25^{3}

Ru 1:1^{3}, 6^{3}, 7, 8, 9, 11, 14, 15^{2}, 22^{2}; **2:**2, 3, 7, 8, 10, 11, 13, 14, 17, 18, 19^{2}, 20, 22^{2}, 23; **3:**1, 2, 4, 6, 10, 13, 16, 17, 18; **4:**7^{3}, 11^{3}, 13, 14, 15, 16

1Sa 1:3, 9, 10, 13, 17, 18, 19, 24; **2:**1^{3}, 9, 13^{2}, 14, 26, 27^{2}, 29, 31, 32^{3}, 33, 34, 35^{2}, 36; **3:**1, 2, 3, 9, 11, 12, 21^{2}; **4:**1, 2^{2}, 6, 8, 14, 19^{2}, 21; **5:**3, 5, 9; **6:**1, 3, 8, 13, 18; **7:**1, 2, 6, 16^{2}; **8:**2, 3, 5, 7, 18^{2}, 21; **9:**6, 7, 9, 12, 15, 18, 19, 22; **10:**2, 25; **11:**4, 7, 8, 11^{2}, 13, 15; **12:**1, 5, 8, 17^{2}, 23, 24; **13:**2^{3}, 3, 4, 5^{2}, 6^{6}, 7, 16^{2}, 17, 22^{2}; **14:**2^{2}, 3, 7, 9, 15^{2}, 16, 19, 22^{2}, 27^{2}, 33, 34, 39, 43, 45; **15:**2, 4, 5, 12, 14, 17, 19, 21, 22^{2}, 33^{2}; **16:**12, 13, 18^{2}, 22; **17:**1, 2, 8, 12, 19, 20, 21, 22, 25, 28, 40^{4}, 45, 46, 49^{2}, 50, 54, 57; **18:**5^{2}, 10^{2}, 13, 14, 16, 18^{2}, 21^{2}, 22^{2}, 23^{2}, 26, 27^{2}; **19:**2^{2}, 3, 5, 7^{2}, 9^{2}, 11, 13, 15, 16^{2}, 18, 19, 22^{2}, 23^{2}, 24; **20:**1, 3, 5, 8, 13, 19, 24, 29^{2}, 34, 35, 42^{2}; **21:**3, 5^{2}, 6, 9^{2}, 11, 12, 13, 15; **22:**2^{2}, 4, 5, 6^{3}, 8, 11, 13^{2}, 14^{2}, 23; **23:**3, 6, 7, 14^{4}, 15^{2}, 16, 18, 19^{3}, 23, 24^{2}, 25^{2}, 29; **24:**1, 3^{2}, 10, 11^{3}, 20; **25:**1, 2^{3}, 3, 4, 5, 6, 7, 8^{2}, 9, 15, 21^{2}, 24, 28, 29, 34, 35, 36, 37; **26:**1, 2, 3^{2}, 4, 5, 7, 15^{2}, 18, 19, 20, 21, 24^{2}; **27:**1^{2}, 5^{4}, 7, 11; **28:**1, 3^{2}, 4^{2}, 20, 21, 24; **29:**1, 2, 3, 4, 5, 6^{4}, 7, 8, 9, 10^{2}, 11; **30:**6, 11, 24, 27^{3}, 28^{3}, 29^{3}, 30^{3}, 31; **31:**1, 7, 8, 9, 10

2Sa 1:1, 9, 18, 20^{2}, 23^{2}, 24, 25^{2}; **2:**3, 11, 16^{2}, 19, 23, 26, 27, 32^{2}; **3:**2, 5, 7, 17, 19^{3}, 21, 22^{3}, 23, 25, 27, 30, 32, 38; **4:**1, 7, 10, 11, 12^{3}; **5:**2^{3}, 3, 5^{2}, 6^{2}, 9, 14, 18, 22, 24; **6:**3, 11, 16, 17^{3}, 18, 20, 22^{2}; **7:**1, 2, 3, 5, 6^{3}, 7, 9, 10, 18, 19, 23, 27; **8:**6, 13, 14; **9:**4^{2}, 10, 12, 13; **10:**1, 4, 8^{3}, 9, 10, 17; **11:**2, 4, 11^{2}, 12, 14, 15^{2}, 21; **12:**1, 3, 9, 11, 16, 24, 30; **13:**5, 6, 8, 12, 13, 16, 20, 23, 30; **14:**3, 6, 13, 19^{2}, 20, 22^{2}, 25^{2}, 28, 32; **15:**4, 7, 8, 9, 10, 11, 17, 21^{2}, 25, 26, 27, 28; **16:**2, 4, 8^{2}, 19^{3}, 21, 22^{2}, 23; **17:**3, 8^{2}, 9^{2}, 11, 12, 16, 18^{2}, 23^{2}, 25, 26, 29; **18:**6, 10, 12^{2}, 14^{2}, 17, 18^{3}, 25; **19:**3, 6, 8^{2}, 10, 13, 22, 24, 27, 30, 33, 37, 43^{3}; **20:**1^{2}, 3^{3}, 8^{2}, 9, 10^{2}, 12^{2}, 15^{2}, 18, 19^{2}, 22; **21:**1, 2, 4, 5, 6, 9^{4}, 12, 14^{3}, 16, 19, 20^{2}, 22; **22:**1, 3, 7, 19, 20, 25, 31; **23:**2, 3, 5, 7, 12, 13^{2}, 14^{2}, 17, 20^{2}, 21, 39; **24:**3, 5^{2}, 9, 10, 11, 13^{2}, 14, 18

1Ki 1:1, 2, 6, 13, 14, 15, 19, 22, 23, 25, 30, 35, 41, 42, 45, 52; **2:**3^{3}, 4, 5^{2}, 6, 8, 10, 11^{2}, 26, 27, 34^{2}, 35^{2}, 36, 38, 39, 46; **3:**2, 3^{2}, 5^{2}, 6^{3}, 7, 8, 14, 17^{2}, 18^{2}, 19, 20^{2}, 21^{2}, 25, 26, 27, 28; **4:**7, 8, 9^{2}, 10, 11, 13^{3}, 15, 16^{2}, 17, 18, 19^{3}, 20, 27, 31, 33; **5:**1, 5, 9^{2}, 14, 15, 16; **6:**1^{3}, 6^{2}, 7^{3}, 8, 12^{3}, 19, 20^{4}, 27, 37^{2}, 38^{3}; **7:**3, 4^{2}, 5, 14^{2}, 19, 20, 21, 24^{2}, 35, 46^{2}, 51; **8:**1, 2, 4, 6, 8, 9, 12, 13^{2}, 17, 18^{2}, 20, 22, 23, 25, 30, 31, 32, 33, 34, 36, 37^{2}, 39, 40, 43, 45, 47^{2}, 48, 49, 52, 58, 61, 65; **9:**4^{2}, 11, 16, 18^{2}, 19^{3}, 21, 23, 25, 26^{2}, 27; **10:**2, 5, 6, 9, 11, 14, 17, 20, 21, 22, 24, 26, 27^{2}; **11:**2^{3}, 6, 7, 12, 14, 15^{2}, 16, 19, 20^{2}, 21, 22, 24, 29^{2}, 30, 33^{2}, 36, 38^{2}, 40, 41, 42, 43^{2}; **12:**2^{2}, 16^{2}, 17, 25, 26, 27, 29^{2}, 32^{4}, 33^{2}; **13:**2, 4^{2}, 8^{2}, 11^{2}, 16^{2}, 19, 22, 24, 25^{2}, 28, 30, 31, 32^{2}; **14:**5, 6^{2}, 8, 10, 11^{2}, 13^{2}, 15, 19, 20, 21^{2}, 22, 24, 25, 27, 29, 31^{2}; **15:**1, 2, 3, 4, 5^{2}, 7, 8^{2}, 9, 10, 11, 13, 15, 17, 18, 21, 23^{3}, 24^{2}, 25, 26^{3}, 28^{2}, 31, 33^{2}, 34^{3}; **16:**2, 4^{2}, 5, 6^{2}, 7^{3}, 8^{2}, 9^{3}, 10^{3}, 13, 14, 15^{2}, 16, 19^{5}, 20, 23^{2}, 25, 26^{2}, 27, 28^{2}, 29^{2}, 30, 31, 32^{2}, 34^{3}; **17:**6^{2}, 7, 10, 11, 12^{3}, 17, 24; **18:**1, 2, 4, 7, 13, 18, 23, 27, 32, 33^{2}, 36, 38, 45; **19:**8, 11^{3}, 12, 13^{3}, 16, 18; **20:**6^{2}, 12^{3}, 16, 23, 24, 25, 29^{2}, 34^{2}, 35, 37; **21:**1, 2, 8^{2}, 9, 11^{2}, 13^{2}, 18^{2}, 19, 20, 21, 24^{2}, 25, 26, 27, 29^{2}; **22:**2, 3, 10^{2}, 16, 17, 22, 23, 25, 27^{2}, 28, 35, 37, 38, 39, 40, 41, 42, 43^{3}, 45, 46, 47, 49, 50^{2}, 51, 52^{4}

2Ki 1:2^{2}, 3, 6, 13, 14, 16, 17^{2}, 18; **2:**12, 21, 24; **3:**1, 2, 18, 20, 21, 22, 24, 25, 27; **4:**2^{2}, 4, 8, 10, 15, 29, 33, 35, 36, 37, 38, 40, 41, 42; **5:**1, 3, 4, 8, 10, 12^{2}, 14, 15^{2}, 18^{4}, 19, 20, 23, 24, 25; **6:**6, 8, 12^{2}, 13, 20, 25, 32; **7:**1, 2, 3, 4, 5, 7, 12^{2}, 13^{2}, 15, 17, 18, 19, 20; **8:**2, 8, 15^{2}, 16, 17, 18^{2}, 20, 23, 24^{2}, 25, 26, 27^{3}, 28, 29^{2}; **9:**1, 2, 8, 10, 15^{2}, 16, 17, 21^{2}, 24, 25, 26, 27, 28^{3}, 29, 31, 34, 36, 37; **10:**1, 5, 7, 8^{2}, 9, 11, 12, 16, 17, 19, 24, 25, 29^{2}, 30^{3}, 31, 32^{2}, 34, 35^{2}, 36; **11:**2, 3, 4, 5, 8^{2}, 9, 10, 11, 15, 18, 20; **12:**1^{2}, 2, 3, 6, 9, 10^{3}, 18^{2}, 19, 20, 21^{2}; **13:**1^{2}, 2, 5, 6, 8, 9^{2}, 10^{2}, 11, 12, 13, 17, 20, 24; **14:**1, 2, 3, 5, 6, 7, 8, 9^{3}, 11, 14^{2}, 15, 16^{2}, 18, 19, 20, 23^{2}, 24, 28, 29; **15:**1, 2, 3, 5, 6, 7^{2}, 8^{2}, 9, 10, 11, 13^{2}, 14^{2}, 15, 17^{2}, 18, 19, 20, 21, 22, 23^{2}, 24, 25^{3}, 26, 27^{2}, 28, 29, 30^{2}, 31, 32, 33, 34, 35, 36, 37, 38^{2}; **16:**1, 2^{2}, 3, 4, 8^{2}, 18, 19, 20^{2}; **17:**1^{2}, 2, 4^{2}, 6^{4}, 8, 9, 10, 11, 14, 17, 19, 22, 24^{2}, 26, 28, 29^{2}, 31, 32; **18:**1, 2, 3, 4, 5, 9, 10, 11^{3}, 13, 15^{2}, 17, 22^{2}, 26^{3}, 28, 30; **19:**7, 10, 12, 27, 28^{2}, 29^{2}, 35^{2}, 37^{2}; **20:**1^{2}, 3^{2}, 11, 13^{3}, 15^{2}, 17^{2}, 18, 19, 20, 21; **21:**1, 2, 4^{2}, 5, 6, 7^{3}, 15, 16^{2}, 17, 18^{3}, 19, 20, 21^{2}, 22, 23, 24, 25, 26^{3}; **22:**1, 2^{2}, 3, 5, 8, 9, 14^{2}, 20; **23:**2^{2}, 3, 4, 5^{3}, 8^{2}, 9, 10, 11^{2}, 12, 14, 16, 19^{2}, 21, 22, 23^{2}, 24^{4}, 28, 29, 30^{3}, 31, 32, 33^{3}, 34, 36, 37; **24:**1, 5, 6, 8, 9, 12, 13^{2}, 17, 18, 19, 20; **25:**1^{3}, 3, 5, 8, 11, 13^{3}, 15^{2}, 19^{3}, 21, 22, 24, 25, 27^{3}, 28

1Ch 1:19, 43, 44, 45, 46^{2}, 47, 48, 49, 50; **2:**3, 4, 6, 7, 21, 22, 24; **3:**1, 4^{2}, 5; **4:**22, 38, 41^{2}; **5:**8, 9^{2}, 10^{2}, 11, 12, 16^{4}, 17^{2}, 18, 20^{2}, 22, 23; **6:**10^{2}, 31, 32, 54, 55, 62, 67, 71, 76, 78, 80; **7:**2^{2}, 5, 21, 23, 29; **8:**8, 28, 32; **9:**1, 2^{2}, 3, 9, 16, 18^{2}, 20, 22^{3}, 24, 25, 26, 28, 31, 33^{2}, 35; **10:**1, 7^{2}, 8, 10^{2}, 12; **11:**2^{2}, 3, 7, 10, 14, 15, 16, 19, 22^{2}, 23; **12:**2, 15, 17, 21, 33, 35, 36, 40; **13:**2^{2}, 3, 4, 7, 14; **14:**4, 9, 11, 13, 15; **15:**1, 29; **16:**1, 2, 10, 14, 19, 27^{2}, 29, 35, 39, 40; **17:**1^{2}, 2, 4, 5, 8, 9, 14^{2}, 17, 19, 21, 25; **18:**6, 12, 13; **19:**1, 4, 9^{2}, 10, 11, 13, 17^{2}, 18; **20:**2, 3, 8; **21:**12, 13, 16^{2}, 18, 19, 23, 28, 29^{2}; **22:**2, 3^{2}, 4, 7, 8, 9, 14^{2}, 15; **23:**11, 13, 25, 28^{3}, 29, 31^{2}, 32; **24:**3, 19, 31; **25:**5, 6, 7; **26:**12, 27, 30^{2}, 31; **27:**1^{2}, 2, 4, 5, 6, 7, 8, 9, 10, 11, 12, 13, 14, 15, 21, 24, 25^{4}, 28, 29^{2}; **28:**2, 8^{2}, 13, 19; **29:**2, 11^{2}, 12^{2}, 17^{2}, 18, 21, 25^{2}, 27^{2}, 28^{2}, 29^{3}

2Ch 1:1, 2, 3, 7, 8, 9, 10, 11, 14, 15; **2:**2, 7^{7}, 8, 9, 11, 14^{10}, 16, 17, 18; **3:**1^{3}, 2^{2}, 4, 10, 16; **4:**2, 3, 6^{3}, 7, 8, 17^{2}, 18; **5:**1, 3^{2}, 5, 7, 10, 12, 13; **6:**1, 5, 7, 8^{3}, 10, 11, 12, 13, 14^{2}, 16^{2}, 18, 22, 24, 28^{2}, 29, 31^{2}, 32, 37^{2}, 38, 40, 41; **7:**8, 9, 10, 11^{2}, 15, 18; **8:**4^{2}, 6^{2}, 8, 11, 13^{4}, 17; **9:**1^{2}, 4, 5, 8, 11, 13, 16, 19, 20, 22, 23, 25, 27^{3}, 29^{3}, 30, 31^{2}; **10:**2, 16^{2}, 17; **11:**3, 5^{2}, 10^{2}, 11, 12, 13, 17, 23; **12:**2, 5, 12, 13^{2}, 15, 16^{2}; **13:**1, 2, 3^{2}, 4, 8, 11, 20, 22; **14:**1^{3}, 2, 6^{2}, 10^{2}, 11, 14, 15; **15:**4, 5^{2}, 9, 10^{2}, 16; **16:**1^{2}, 9, 10^{2}, 11, 12^{3}, 13, 14^{3}; **17:**1, 2^{3}, 3, 4, 5^{2}, 6, 7^{2}, 9, 12, 13^{2}, 19; **18:**1, 2, 3, 9^{3}, 15, 16, 21, 22, 26^{2}, 27, 34; **19:**1, 3^{2}, 5, 6, 8, 9, 10, 11; **20:**2, 5^{2}, 6^{2}, 9^{3}, 14, 17, 20^{2}, 24, 25^{2}, 26, 27, 31, 32^{2}, 34^{2}, 36; **21:**1^{2}, 3, 5, 6^{2}, 8, 9, 11, 12^{2}, 13, 17, 18, 19, 20^{3}; **22:**1, 2, 3, 4, 6, 9, 11, 12; **23:**1, 2, 3, 5, 6, 7^{2}, 8, 9, 10, 13, 14, 17, 18^{2}, 19^{2}; **24:**1, 2, 6, 9^{2}, 10, 11, 13, 14, 16^{2}, 21, 25^{3},

27^2; **25:**1, 2, 4^2, 10, 12, 17, 18^3, 21, 24, 26, 27, 28; **26:**1, 3, 4, 5^2, 7, 8, 9, 10^5, 15, 17, 19^3, 20, 21, 23^2; **27:**1, 2, 4^2, 7, 8, 9^2; **28:**1^2, 2, 3^2, 4, 6^2, 9, 13, 22, 24^2, 25, 26, 27^3; **29:**1, 2, 3^2, 4, 6, 7, 9, 10, 16, 17^2, 18, 19^2, 25, 31, 34, 35^2; **30:**2^2, 5, 12, 13, 14, 15, 16, 17, 25, 26^2; **31:**1^2, 2, 3, 4^2, 5^2, 6^2, 7^2, 11, 12, 15^2, 16, 17, 18^2, 19^2, 21^4; **32:**5^2, 6, 10^2, 18, 21, 23, 24, 26, 29, 30, 31^3, 32^2, 33^2; **33:**1, 2, 4^2, 5, 6^2, 7^3, 12, 14^3, 15^2, 17, 18^2, 20^2, 21, 22, 24, 25; **34:**1, 2^2, 3^2, 4^2, 6, 8, 10^2, 13, 15, 17, 21^3, 22^2, 24, 28, 30^2, 31^2, 32, 33; **35:**1, 2, 3, 5, 10^2, 12, 13^3, 14, 15, 18, 19, 22, 24^2, 25^3, 26, 27; **36:**1^2, 2, 3, 5^2, 6, 7, 8^3, 9^2, 11, 12, 14, 17, 22^2, 23^2

Ezr 1:1^2, 2, 3^2, 4^2, 5, 7; **2:**42, 68, 70^2; **3:**1, 2, 8^2, 9, 10, 11; **4:**4, 6^2, 7^3, 8, 10, 15^2, 17, 23; **5:**1^2, 8^2, 13, 14, 15^2, 16^2, 17; **6:**1^2, 2^2, 3, 5, 7, 15, 18^3, 22; **7:**1, 6, 7, 8^2, 10, 13, 14, 15, 16^2, 17, 25, 27^2; **8:**1, 15, 22, 29, 31, 33; **9:**2, 7, 8^2, 9^4, 14, 15; **10:**2, 9, 13, 14, 16

Neh 1:1^3, 3^2, 11; **2:**1^3, 5, 12^2, 15, 17, 20; **3:**17, 26; **4:**2, 4, 11, 13, 16, 17, 20, 21, 22; **5:**5, 9, 14, 16, 18; **6:**2^2, 5^2, 7, 10^2, 11, 14, 15^2, 16, 17, 18^2, 19; **7:**3, 73^2; **8:**5, 7, 8^2, 14^3, 15^2, 16^4, 18; **9:**1, 3^2, 9, 12^3, 15, 17, 19^3, 21, 23, 24, 25^2, 27, 28, 29, 30, 33, 35^3, 36, 37; **10:**29, 34, 36^2, 37; **11:**1^2, 3^4, 17, 18, 20^2, 21, 24, 25^3, 27, 28, 30^2, 31, 36^2; **12:**7, 9, 12, 22, 23, 26^2, 39, 40, 46, 47^2; **13:**1^2, 6^2, 7^2, 11, 15^4, 16, 19, 23, 24^2, 27, 28, 30

Est 1:1, 2^2, 3, 5^2, 7^2, 9, 10, 12, 14, 16, 17^2, 22; **2:**3, 5, 12, 14^3, 15^2, 16^2, 17, 19, 21^2, 22, 23; **3:**2, 3, 7^2, 8, 12, 13, 14, 15; **4:**3^2, 8, 11, 13, 16^2; **5:**1^2, 2^3, 8, 9, 12, 14; **6:**4, 5^2, 6^2; **7:**3, 5, 7, 8, 9; **8:**5^3, 8^2, 9, 10, 11, 12, 13, 15, 17^2; **9:**1^3, 2, 4, 6, 11, 12^2, 13, 15, 16, 19, 20, 31, 32; **10:**2

Job 1:1, 4, 5^2, 7^2, 8, 10, 12, 13, 18, 22; **2:**2^2, 3, 6, 10; **3:**3, 20^2, 23, 26; **4:**13, 18, 19^3, 21; **5:**4, 13, 14^3, 19^2, 20^2, 23, 24, 26^3; **6:**2, 4, 6, 10, 13, 29, 30; **7:**11^2, 21^2; **8:**12, 16; **9:**4^2, 5, 29, 31, 32; **10:**1, 13; **11:**4, 14^2, 18; **12:**5, 9, 10, 12, 24, 25; **13:**14^2, 15, 27; **14:**8^2, 13, 17; **15:**9, 15^2, 21^2, 28^2, 31; **16:**4, 8, 9, 15, 17, 19; **17:**2, 3, 13, 16; **18:**3, 4, 6, 10^2, 15, 17, 19; **19:**2, 8, 15^2, 23, 24, 26, 28; **20:**11, 12, 14, 20, 22^2, 26^2, 28; **21:**7, 8, 13^2, 16, 17, 21^2, 23, 25, 26, 32, 34^2; **22:**8, 12, 14, 22, 26; **23:**6, 13; **24:**5, 6, 7, 13, 14, 16^2, 17, 18, 23; **25:**2, 5; **26:**8; **27:**3^2, 10, 15, 20; **28:**13, 14; **29:**2^2, 4, 7, 18, 20^2, 25; **30:**1, 2, 3, 6^3, 10, 14^2, 17^2, 24, 25, 28; **31:**6, 15^2, 21, 26, 32, 33; **32:**1, 5, 8, 22; **33:**2, 5, 6, 8, 9, 11, 12, 15^3; **34:**8, 20, 24^2, 25, 26; **35:**10, 14, 15^2, 16; **36:**4, 5, 8^2, 11^2, 13, 14, 15^2, 20, 31; **37:**8, 12, 16, 21, 23^3; **38:**16, 32, 33, 36, 37, 40^3; **39:**4, 10, 14^2, 16, 21^2; **40:**12, 13^2, 16^2, 21; **41:**9, 22, 23; **42:**6, 8, 11, 15

Ps 1:1^3, 2^2, 3, 5^2; **2:**4^2, 5^2, 9, 12; **3:**2; **4:**1, 4, 5, 7^2, 8^2; **5:**3^2, 4, 5, 7^2, 8, 9, 10, 11^2; **6:**1^2, 5^2; **7:**1, 2, 3, 5, 6, 8, 10; **8:**1, 9; **9:**2, 4, 8^2, 9, 10, 11, 14^2, 15^2, 16, 19, 20; **10:**1, 2^2, 4, 6^2, 8^2, 9^3, 11, 13; **11:**1, 2, 4^2; **12:**5, 6; **13:**2^2, 5^2; **14:**1, 5^2; **15:**1^2, 2, 4; **16:**1, 3^2, 6, 7, 9, 10, 11; **17:**3, 5, 7, 10, 11, 12, 14, 15; **18:**2, 6, 13, 18, 19, 24, 30, 42, ttl; **19:**4, 11, 14; **20:**1, 5^2, 7^2; **21:**1^2, 5, 7, 9^2, 13; **22:**2^2, 4, 5, 8, 14, 22, 25; **23:**2, 3, 5, 6; **24:**3, 7, 8, 9; **25:**2, 5, 8, 9, 12, 20; **26:**1^2, 3, 4, 6, 10, 11, 12^2; **27:**3, 4^2, 5^3, 6, 9, 11, 13; **28:**3, 7; **29:**2, 9; **30:**5^2, 6, 9; **31:**1^2, 6, 7^2, 8, 9, 14, 15, 17, 19, 20^2, 21, 22, 24; **32:**2, 6^2, 8, 9, 10, 11^2; **33:**1, 4, 7, 8, 18, 19, 21^2, 22; **34:**1, 2, 8, 22; **35:**7, 9^2, 15, 16, 18, 20, 25, 27; **36:**2, 4, 5, 9, 10; **37:**3^2, 4, 5, 7^2, 8, 11, 19^2, 23, 31, 33, 35, 39, 40; **38:**1^2, 2, 3^2, 7, 14, 15; **39:**6^2, 7; **40:**3^2, 5, 7, 9, 16; **41:**1, 3, 9, 12; **42:**4, 5^2, 8^2, 10, 11; **43:**5; **44:**1^2, 3, 6, 8, 17, 19; **45:**4, 5, 9, 14, 16, 17; **46:**1, 5, 8, 9^2, 10; **48:**1^2, 3, 6, 8^2, 9; **49:**5, 6^2, 12, 14^3, 20; **50:**15, 16, 21, 22; **51:**4, 5^2, 6^2, 10, 16, 18, ttl; **52:**1, 7^2, 8^2; **53:**1, 5; **54:**5; **55:**2, 3, 7, 9, 10, 11, 14, 15, 18, 21, 23; **56:**3, 4^2, 7, 8, 10^2, 11, 13, ttl; **57:**1^2, ttl; **58:**2^2, 6, 7, 9, 10, 11; **59:**3, 7, 8, 12, 13^2, 16^2; **60:**6, ttl; **61:**4^2; **62:**4, 7^2, 8, 9, 10^2; **63:**1, 2, 4, 6, 7, 11, ttl; **64:**1, 4, 5, 10^3; **65:**1, 4, 5, 8; **66:**3, 5, 6, 9, 14, 18; **68:**5, 6^2, 14^2, 16^2, 17^2, 21, 23^2, 24, 26, 30, 34; **69:**1, 2, 12, 13^3, 17, 21, 25, 35; **70:**4; **71:**1, 2, 9, 16; **72:**4, 7, 9, 14, 16, 17; **73:**4, 5, 11, 12^2, 13^2, 18, 19, 21, 25, 28; **74:**3, 4, 8^2, 12, 13, 14; **75:**8; **76:**1^2, 2^2, 7; **77:**2^2, 6, 9, 13, 18, 19^2; **78:**2, 5^2, 7, 9, 10, 12^3, 14, 15, 17, 18, 19, 22^2, 26^2, 28, 30, 33^2, 37, 40^2, 43^2, 51^2, 52, 55, 66; **79:**10; **80:**5; **81:**3^2, 5, 7^2, 9, 12, 13; **82:**1, 5; **83:**4, 12; **84:**4, 5^2, 7, 10^3, 12; **85:**6, 9, 13; **86:**2, 5, 7, 11, 15; **87:**1, 5, 7; **88:**5, 6^3, 11^2, 12^2, 13; **89:**2, 5, 6, 7^2, 10, 12, 15, 16^2, 17, 19, 24, 25^2, 30, 37, 43, 47, 49, 50; **90:**1, 4^2, 5, 6^2, 8, 9; **91:**1, 2, 6, 11, 12, 15; **92:**2, 4, 12, 13^2, 14, 15; **94:**5, 15, 17, 19, 23; **95:**4, 8^3, 10, 11; **96:**6, 9; **97:**11, 12; **98:**2; **99:**2, 4, 7; **101:**2, 6, 7; **102:**2^3, 14, 16, 21^2, 23, 24; **103:**8, 19, 20, 22; **104:**3, 22, 24, 27, 31, 34; **105:**3, 7, 12^2, 18, 23, 27, 30^2, 31, 32, 35, 36, 39, 41; **106:**5, 7, 14^2, 16, 18, 19, 21, 22, 23, 25, 26, 27, 29, 47; **107:**4^3, 5, 6, 10^3, 13, 14, 16, 19, 23^2, 24, 28, 32^2, 40; **108:**7; **109:**13, 16, 17; **110:**2, 3^2, 5, 7; **111:**1^2, 8; **112:**1, 3, 4, 6, 7; **113:**6^2; **115:**3, 8, 9, 10, 11; **116:**9, 11, 14, 15, 18, 19^2; **118:**5^2, 8^2, 9^2, 10, 11, 12, 15, 23, 24, 26; **119:**1^2, 3, 11, 14^2, 15, 16, 19, 23, 35, 37, 40, 42, 43, 47, 48, 50, 51, 54, 55, 70, 74, 75, 78, 80, 81, 83, 89, 92, 109, 114, 133, 147, 148, 161; **120:**1, 5^2; **121:**8; **123:**1; **124:**8; **125:**1, 4; **126:**4, 5^2; **127:**1^2, 4, 5; **128:**1; **129:**8; **130:**5, 7; **131:**1^2, 3; **132:**6, 11; **133:**1; **134:**1, 2; **135:**2^2, 6^3, 17, 18; **136:**10, 15, 23; **137:**2, 4, 7; **138:**3^2, 5, 7; **139:**4, 8, 9, 13, 15^2, 16^2, 18, 20, 24^2; **140:**2, 7, 11, 13; **141:**5, 6, 8; **142:**3, 5, ttl; **143:**1^2, 2, 3, 8^2; **144:**2, 12, 13, 14^2, 15; **145:**15, 17^2, 18; **146:**3^3, 4, 5; **147:**3, 10^2, 11^3, 14; **148:**1; **149:**1, 2^2, 3, 4, 5, 6^2; **150:**1^2

Prv 1:14, 15, 17^2, 20, 21^3, 22; **2:**13, 14, 15, 20, 21^2; **3:**4, 5, 6, 7, 12, 16^2, 23, 27, 33; **4:**3, 11^2, 14, 21; **5:**10, 14^2, 16, 23; **6:**8^2, 14, 18, 25, 27, 29, 34; **7:**9^3, 11, 12^2, 25; **8:**2^2, 3, 8^2, 20^2, 22, 31; **9:**4, 6, 9, 14, 16, 17, 18; **10:**5^2, 8, 13, 17, 19; **11:**4, 6, 8, 14, 20, 21, 22, 28, 31; **12:**4, 6, 15, 20, 25, 27, 28^2; **13:**6, 23; **14:**2^2, 3, 7, 13, 14, 23, 26, 28^2, 32^2, 33^2; **15:**3, 4, 6^2, 22, 23; **16:**1, 2, 5^2, 10^2, 15, 20, 21, 27, 31; **17:**8, 12, 16, 18, 24; **18:**2, 5, 9, 11, 17, 21; **19:**1^2, 20, 21, 24; **20:**4, 5, 7, 8, 20; **21:**1, 2, 9^2, 10, 14^2, 16, 19, 20, 24; **22:**5, 6, 13, 15, 18, 19, 20, 22, 29; **23:**7, 9, 17, 19, 28, 31, 34; **24:**6, 7, 10, 23, 27; **25:**5, 6^2, 7, 8, 11, 13, 19^2, 20, 24^2; **26:**1^2, 5, 7, 8, 9, 12, 13^2, 15, 16, 19, 25; **27:**10, 14, 15, 19, 22; **28:**6^2, 10^2, 11, 18, 25, 26; **29:**2, 6, 11, 20, 22, 23, 25, 27; **30:**4^2, 5, 9, 12, 19^2, 25, 26, 28, 29, 32; **31:**8, 11, 23, 25, 26, 31

Ecc 1:1, 12, 16, 18; **2:**1, 3, 5, 7^2, 9, 10, 14^2, 15^2, 16, 21^3, 23, 24, 26; **3:**9, 10, 11^2, 12^2, 17, 18, 22; **4:**14, 15, 16; **5:**2, 4, 7, 8, 14, 15, 16, 17, 19, 20; **6:**4^2, 12; **7:**4^2, 8^2, 9^2, 14^2, 15^3, 19; **8:**2, 3, 8^2, 10, 11; **9:**1^2, 3, 6, 9^2, 10, 12^3, 15, 17; **10:**1, 6^2, 16, 17, 20^2; **11:**3, 5, 6^2, 8, 9^4; **12:**1^2, 3, 4, 5, 9

Song 1:4, 9, 14; **2:**12, 14^2; **3:**2^2, 8^2, 11^2; **4:**7; **5:**4; **6:**2, 13; **7:**4, 5, 11; **8:**8, 10, 13

Isa 1:1, 6, 7, 8^2, 11, 21; **2:**2^2, 3, 5, 6, 10, 11, 17, 20, 22; **3:**7^2, 14, 18, 25; **4:**1, 2, 3^3, 6; **5:**1, 2, 4, 8, 9, 11, 12, 16^2, 21^2, 25, 30^2; **6:**1, 5, 6, 12, 13^2; **7:**1, 3, 6, 11^2, 18^3, 19^2, 20, 21, 22, 23; **8:**1, 6, 9^3, 11, 18^2, 20; **9:**1^2, 2^2, 3, 4, 5, 9, 14, 17, 18; **10:**3^2, 5, 7, 17, 20^2, 23, 24, 25, 27; **11:**3, 9, 10, 11, 15, 16; **12:**1, 4, 5, 6; **13:**3, 4, 8, 10, 13^2, 17, 20, 22^2; **14:**1, 2, 3, 6^2, 13^2, 18^2, 20, 25, 28, 30, 31, 32; **15:**1^2, 3^2, 5; **16:**3, 5^3, 10^2; **17:**4, 5, 6^3, 9, 11^3; **18:**2, 4^2, 5, 7; **19:**1, 3, 9, 10, 14^3, 16, 17, 18^2, 19^2, 20, 21, 23, 24^2; **20:**1, 6; **21:**1, 5, 8^2, 13^2; **22:**2, 3, 5, 7, 8, 12, 14, 16, 20, 23, 25^2; **23:**1, 13, 15; **24:**10, 11, 12, 13, 15^2, 18, 21, 22^2, 23^2; **25:**4, 5, 6, 7, 8, 9^2, 10, 11; **26:**1^2, 2, 3^2, 4^2, 8, 9^2, 10, 12, 16, 17^3, 18^2, 19; **27:**1^2, 2, 4^2, 8^2, 9, 12, 13^4; **28:**4, 5, 6, 7^2, 14, 16, 20, 21^2, 25^2, 29^2; **29:**15, 18, 19^2, 21, 23, 24; **30:**2^2, 3, 7, 8^2, 12, 13, 14^2, 15^3, 19, 21, 23^2, 25, 26, 28, 29, 32^2; **31:**1^2, 7, 9^2; **32:**1^2, 2^2, 13, 16^2, 18^3, 19; **33:**2, 12, 14, 17; **34:**5, 6^2, 11, 13^2; **35:**6^2, 7; **36:**1, 2, 6^2, 7, 11^3, 13, 15; **37:**7, 10, 12, 28, 29^2, 30, 36^2, 38^2; **38:**1^2, 3^2, 8, 10, 11, 15, 16, 17, 20; **39:**2^3, 4^2, 6^2, 7, 8; **40:**3^2, 11, 12^4, 14, 22, 24, 26; **41:**16^2, 18^2, 19^2; **42:**1, 2, 4, 6, 7, 12, 16, 17, 22^2, 24; **43:**4, 14, 16^2, 19^2, 20^2, 26; **44:**7, 12, 13, 16, 19^2, 20, 23; **45:**2^2, 13, 14^2, 17, 18, 19^3, 23, 24, 25; **46:**6, 7, 13; **47:**1, 8, 9^3, 10^2, 13; **48:**1^2, 10, 16; **49:**2^2, 3, 4^2, 5, 8^2, 9^3, 20, 21, 22; **50:**4, 10^2, 11^3; **51:**6, 7, 9^2, 14, 16^2, 20; **52:**6, 10; **53:**9^2, 10; **54:**6, 8, 14, 16, 17; **55:**2, 11; **56:**5, 7, 9; **57:**2^2, 5, 6, 10, 13, 15, 17; **58:**2, 3, 10, 11, 12, 14; **59:**4, 6, 7, 8, 9, 10^2, 13, 14, 19, 20, 21; **60:**10^2, 18, 22; **61:**3, 6, 7^2, 8, 10^2, 11; **62:**3^2, 4, 7, 9; **63:**1^3, 2^2, 3^2, 4, 6^2, 9^3, 13; **64:**5^2; **65:**2, 3, 4^2, 5, 8^2, 10, 16^3, 18, 19^3, 23, 25; **66:**3, 4, 8, 13, 17^2, 20^3

Jer 1:1^2, 2^2, 3^2, 5, 9; **2:**2^3, 5, 17, 18^2, 19, 23, 24^2, 27, 28, 30, 34, 37; **3:**2^2, 6, 16^2, 18, 23^2, 25; **4:**2^5, 5^3, 11, 19, 20, 30, 31; **5:**1, 6, 7, 8, 13, 14, 18, 19^2, 20^2, 24^2, 30, 31; **6:**1^2, 3, 6, 7, 10, 11, 16, 23, 24, 26, 29; **7:**2^2, 3, 4, 6, 7^2, 8, 10, 11, 12, 17^2, 22, 23, 24^2, 30^2, 31^2, 32; **8:**3, 7, 8^2, 9, 12, 16, 18, 19^3, 22; **9:**2, 4, 6, 8, 23^3, 24^3, 26^3; **10:**5, 6, 7, 13, 14^2, 15, 23^2, 24; **11:**4, 6^2, 7, 8, 12, 14, 15, 17, 21; **12:**2, 5^2, 8, 16; **13:**1, 4, 10, 17, 21, 22, 25, 27; **14:**4, 5, 6, 8^2, 9, 13, 14, 15^2, 16; **15:**4, 7, 11^2, 13, 14, 15, 17; **16:**2, 3^2, 6, 7, 9^2, 19; **17:**3, 4^2, 5, 6^3, 7, 8, 11, 13, 17, 19^3, 20, 21, 24, 25, 27^2; **18:**4, 6^2, 10, 15^3, 17, 21, 23; **19:**4, 7, 9, 10, 11, 14; **20:**1, 2^2, 6, 7, 9^3, 16; **21:**4, 5^3, 7, 9, 12, 14; **22:**2, 3, 4^2, 12, 15, 20, 21, 23^2, 30^2; **23:**5, 6, 8, 11, 12, 13^2, 14^2, 18, 19, 20, 22, 24, 25, 26, 29; **24:**8^2, 9; **25:**1, 5, 13, 23, 24, 34; **26:**1, 2^2, 4, 7, 9^2, 10, 14, 15, 16, 18, 20; **27:**1, 11, 15, 18^2, 19, 21^2; **28:**1^5, 5^3, 7^2, 11, 15, 17; **29:**5, 7, 8, 9, 10, 15, 16, 21, 22^2, 23^2, 25, 26^4, 28^2, 29, 31; **30:**2, 6, 8, 10, 11, 24; **31:**2, 4, 9, 10, 12, 13, 15, 17, 22, 23^2, 24^2, 29, 32, 33^2; **32:**1, 2^2, 7, 8^3, 9, 10, 12^3, 14, 15, 19^2, 20^2, 23^2, 34, 35, 37^3, 40, 41, 43, 44^6; **33:**1, 5^2, 10^3, 12^2, 13^6, 15^2, 16, 20; **34:**5, 6, 13, 15^3, 17, 18; **35:**1, 7^2, 8, 9, 10, 15; **36:**1, 6^4, 8^2, 9^3, 10^5, 13, 14^3, 15^2, 18, 20^3, 21^2, 22^2, 23, 28^2, 30^2, 32; **37:**1, 4, 10, 12, 13, 15^2, 17, 18, 21^2; **38:**2, 4^2, 5, 6^3, 7^3, 9^3, 13, 14, 22^2, 28; **39:**1^2, 2^2, 3^2, 5^2, 6, 9, 10, 15, 16, 17, 18; **40:**1, 6, 7^2, 9, 10^2, 11^3, 13, 15^2; **41:**1^2, 5, 8, 10^2, 12, 17, 18; **42:**10, 13, 16^2, 20, 22; **43:**4, 5, 8, 9^5, 12^2, 13; **44:**1^2, 3, 6^2, 8^2, 9^2, 10^2, 12, 13, 15^2, 16, 17^2, 21^2, 23^3, 24, 26^3, 27, 29; **45:**1^2, 3, 5; **46:**2^2, 10, 11, 14^4, 19, 21, 25, 26, 27, 28; **48:**2, 5^2, 6, 7^2, 11, 18, 20, 26^2, 28^3, 35^2, 38, 41^2, 44, 47; **49:**1, 2, 4^2, 7, 11, 16, 18^2, 21, 22, 24, 26^2, 27, 32, 33, 34, 38, 39; **50:**2^2, 4^2, 5, 9^2, 14, 16, 20^2, 22, 25, 28, 30^2, 32, 37, 39, 42, 43; **51:**1, 2, 3, 4^2, 6, 7, 10, 13, 16, 17, 18, 20, 21^2, 22^3, 23^3, 24^2, 27, 30, 39, 44, 46^3, 47, 58^2, 59, 60, 62; **52:**1, 2, 3, 4^3, 6^3, 8, 9, 10, 11^2, 12^2, 15, 17^2, 19^2, 20, 25^2, 27^2, 28, 29, 30, 31^4, 32

Lam 1:2, 4, 7^2, 9, 12, 15^2, 19, 20; **2:**1^2, 2, 3, 4, 5, 6^2, 7^2, 11, 12, 17, 19^3, 20, 21^2, 22^2; **3:**6, 10^2, 11, 20^2, 24, 27, 29, 36, 41, 45, 53, 57, 66; **4:**1, 3, 5^2, 6, 7, 8, 10, 11, 13, 14, 17, 18, 19, 20, 21; **5:**11^2

Ezk 1:1^3, 2, 3, 16, 20, 21, 28^2; **3:**3, 10, 14^2, 18, 19, 20; **4:**9, 12, 14, 16; **5:**2^2, 3^2, 4, 5, 6, 7, 8^2, 9, 10^2, 12, 13^2, 14, 15^4; **6:**6, 7, 9, 10, 13, 14; **7:**4, 7, 9, 13, 15^2, 19^2, 20; **8:**1^4, 3, 4, 5, 7, 8^2, 9, 10, 11^2, 12^2, 18^2; **9:**1^2, 2^2, 4, 5, 7, 8; **10:**1, 2^3, 3, 6, 8, 10, 13, 17, 19; **11:**2, 6, 7, 10, 11^2, 12, 15, 16, 20, 24; **12:**2, 3^2, 4^2, 5, 6^2, 7^3, 8, 10, 12, 13, 15, 22, 23, 25; **13:**4, 5^2, 9^2, 13^3, 14, 21; **14:**3, 4, 5, 7^2, 14, 16, 18, 19, 20, 23; **16:**4^2, 5^2, 6^3, 12, 15, 22^2, 24, 29, 31^4, 34^3, 38, 41, 43, 47, 49^2, 51, 52, 53, 54^2, 56, 59, 60; **17:**4, 5, 8, 9, 10, 15, 16^2, 17, 20, 23^2; **18:**3, 9, 17, 18, 22, 24^3, 26, 32; **19:**4, 8, 9^2, 10, 11, 12, 13^2; **20:**1^2, 5^2, 6, 8, 9^2, 11, 13^4, 14, 15, 16, 17, 18^2, 19, 21^3, 22^2, 23, 26^2, 27^2, 36, 40^3, 41, 43, 47^2; **21:**20, 21, 22, 23, 24^2, 30^2, 31, 32; **22:**3, 4^2, 6, 7^3, 9^3, 10^2, 11^2, 12, 13, 14, 15, 16^2, 18, 20^2, 21^2, 22^2, 24, 25^2, 27, 30; **23:**3^2, 8, 11^3, 15, 19^2, 21, 31, 32, 37, 38, 39, 43, 44^3, 45; **24:**1^3, 7, 11, 12, 13, 18^2, 25, 26, 27; **25:**4^2, 6, 10, 14; **26:**1^2, 5, 6, 8, 12, 15, 17, 18^2, 20^3; **27:**4, 8, 9^2, 10^2, 11, 12, 13, 14, 16, 17, 18^2, 19^2, 20, 21^2, 22, 24^3, 25^2, 26, 27^4, 30, 32^2, 34^3, 35; **28:**2^2, 8, 9, 12, 13^3, 14, 15^2, 18, 22^3, 23, 25^3; **29:**1^3, 3, 4, 12, 17^3, 21^2; **30:**4^2, 5, 6, 7^2, 8, 9^3, 13, 14^2, 16, 18, 19, 20^3, 24; **31:**1^3, 2, 3, 6, 7^2, 8^3, 9, 10^2, 12, 14^2, 15, 16, 17, 18^3; **32:**1^3, 2, 3, 10, 17^2, 19, 20, 23^2, 24, 25^3, 26, 27, 28, 32^2; **33:**6, 8, 9, 10, 11, 12^3, 15, 21^3, 22^2, 27^4, 30; **34:**12^2, 13, 14^3, 25^2, 26, 27, 29; **35:**5^2, 8^3; **36:**2, 3, 5, 6^2, 15, 17, 23^2, 27, 28, 31, 33^2, 34, 38; **37:**1^2, 2, 6, 8, 14^2, 17, 19^2, 20, 22, 24, 25, 26, 28; **38:**8, 12, 14, 16^2, 17^2, 18, 19^4, 23; **39:**6, 7^2, 9, 11^2, 15, 26, 27^2; **40:**1^5, 2, 3^2, 5, 25^2, 27, 29^2, 33, 39, 44; **41:**6^2; **42:**3, 6, 8, 10, 12; **43:**7^2, 8^2, 9, 11^2, 16, 17, 18, 21; **44:**2^2, 3, 5, 7^4, 8, 9^2, 11, 13, 17^2, 19, 24^3, 27^2, 28, 29, 30; **45:**1, 2^2, 3, 8^2, 16, 17^4, 18^2, 21^2, 25^3; **46:**1, 3^2, 4, 6, 8, 9^3, 10^3, 11^2, 21, 22, 23; **47:**3, 5, 19, 22, 23; **48:**8^3, 9^2, 10^5, 13^2, 15^2, 18, 21, 22, 28

Dan 1:1, 4^5, 8, 14, 15, 17^2, 18^2, 20^2; **2:**1, 4, 5, 16, 19, 22, 24^2, 25^2, 27, 28^2, 40^2, 41, 44^2, 45, 49; **3:**1^2, 13, 16, 20, 21, 24, 25, 28, 29, 30; **4:**1, 4^2, 6, 7, 8^2, 9, 10^2, 12^2, 13, 15^3, 17, 18, 21, 23^2, 25, 29, 31, 32, 35, 36, 37; **5:**2, 3, 5, 7^2, 8, 9, 11^4, 12, 13, 14^2, 15, 16, 20, 21, 23^2, 27, 29, 30; **6:**3, 4, 10, 19^2, 22, 23, 24, 25, 26, 27^2, 28^2; **7:**1, 2, 5, 7^2, 8, 13, 15^2, 19, 20, 23, 28^2; **8:**1, 2^4, 6, 7, 18, 19, 22, 23, 25^2; **9:**1, 2^2, 6, 10, 11, 13, 14, 21^2, 24, 25, 27; **10:**1, 2, 3, 4, 5, 6, 8^2, 9, 14, 17^2, 21^2; **11:**1, 2, 6^2, 7, 14, 16, 20^4, 21^2, 38, 39, 45; **12:**1, 2, 6, 7, 13

APNDX

Hos 1:1^2, 5, 10; **2:**3, 9^2, 10, 15^2, 18, 19^4, 20, 21, 23; **3:**5; **4:**1, 5^2, 16, 19; **5:**4, 5, 8^2, 9, 11, 15; **6:**2^2, 9, 10; **7:**1, 2, 5, 6^2, 16; **8:**6; **9:**2, 3^2, 5^2, 6, 8^2, 9, 10^2, 13, 15; **10:**4^2, 9, 10^2, 12^2, 13^2, 14^2, 15; **11:**9, 11; **12:**3, 4, 7, 8^2, 9^2, 11^3; **13:**1^2, 5^2, 9, 10, 11^2, 13, 16; **14:**3, 9

Joel 1:2^2, 13; **2:**1^2, 5, 8, 9^2, 15, 23^2, 26, 27, 29, 30^2, 32^3; **3:**1^2, 13, 14^2, 17, 18, 19, 21

Am 1:1^2, 14^3; **2:**7, 8, 16; **3:**4, 5, 6^2, 9^5, 10, 12^4, 13, 14; **4:**1, 6^2; **5:**6^2, 7, 10, 11, 12, 13, 15, 16^2, 17, 20, 21, 25; **6:**1^2, 6, 9, 13, 14; **7:**1, 7, 8, 10, 17^2; **8:**3^2, 9^2, 11, 13; **9:**1, 3^2, 6^2, 9, 11^2

Oba 1, 3^2, 7, 8, 11^2, 12^3, 13^3, 14^2, 18, 20

Jna 1:4, 5, 17; **2:**3, 7; **3:**6, 8; **4:**2, 5, 8, 10^2

Mic 1:1, 10^2, 11, 13; **2:**1, 4, 5, 11, 12; **3:**3, 4; **4:**1^2, 2, 5^2, 6, 7, 9^2, 10^3, 13; **5:**1, 2, 4^2, 5, 6, 7, 8^2, 10, 15; **6:**10, 12, 13^2, 14, 16; **7:**2, 5^3, 6^2, 8, 11^2, 12, 14^4, 18

Nah 1:3^3, 6, 7^2, 13; **2:**1, 3^2, 4^2, 5, 10, 12, 13; **3:**10^2, 13, 17^2, 18

Hab 1:5, 15^2; **2:**4, 13, 19, 20; **3:**2^3, 7, 11, 12^2, 16^2, 17^2, 18^2

Zep 1:1, 8, 9, 10, 12, 18^2; **2:**3, 7^2, 14^4, 15^2; **3:**2, 5, 11^2, 12^2, 13, 15, 16, 17^2, 19, 20

Hag 1:1^3, 4, 6, 8, 13, 14, 15^2; **2:**1^2, 3^3, 9, 10^2, 12, 15, 17, 19, 20, 22, 23

Zec 1:1^2, 7, 8, 16; **2:**1, 5, 10, 11^2, 12; **3:**7, 9, 10; **4:**10; **5:**4, 7, 9, 11; **6:**2^2, 3^2, 8, 14, 15; **7:**1^3, 3^2, 5, 7, 10, 12; **8:**3, 4^2, 5, 6^3, 8^3, 9^2, 10, 11, 15, 16, 17, 22, 23; **9:**1, 4, 6, 7, 16; **10:**1^2, 2, 3, 5^2, 7, 9, 11, 12^2; **11:**8, 11, 13, 16^2; **12:**2, 3^2, 4, 5^2, 6^4, 8, 9, 10^2, 11^3; **13:**1, 2, 3, 4, 6^2, 8; **14:**1, 3, 4^2, 5, 6, 8^3, 9, 10, 11, 12^2, 13, 14, 15, 20^2, 21^4

Mal 1:7, 10, 11, 12, 14; **2:**6^3, 9, 11^2, 17^2; **3:**1, 3, 4^2, 5, 8, 10, 11, 17; **4:**2, 3, 4

Mt 1:20^2; **2:**1^2, 2, 5, 6, 9, 12, 13, 16^2, 18, 19^2, 22^3, 23; **3:**1^2, 3, 6, 12, 17; **4:**6, 13^2, 16^2, 21, 23; **5:**3, 8, 12, 15, 16, 18, 19^2, 20, 21, 22^3, 25, 28, 45, 48; **6:**1, 2^2, 4^2, 5^2, 6^2, 9, 10^2, 18^2, 20, 23, 29; **7:**3^2, 4, 11, 13^2, 15, 21, 22^4; **8:**10, 11, 13, 24, 32; **9:**4, 10, 16, 25, 31, 33, 35; **10:**9, 11, 15, 16, 17, 19, 20, 23, 27^3, 28, 32, 33, 35^2, 41^2, 42^2; **11:**1, 2, 6, 8^2, 11, 16, 21^3, 23^2, 24, 26, 29; **12:**5^2, 6, 18, 19, 21, 32^2, 36, 40^2, 41, 42, 45, 50; **13:**3, 10, 13, 14, 19, 21, 24, 27, 30^2, 31, 32, 33, 34, 35, 40^2, 43, 44, 54, 57^3; **14:**2, 3, 8, 10, 11, 24, 25, 33; **15:**9, 17, 32, 33; **16:**3, 17, 19^2, 26, 27, 28; **17:**5, 22; **18:**1, 2, 4, 5, 6^2, 10^2, 14, 16, 18^2, 19, 20^2; **19:**21, 28^2; **20:**1, 3, 17, 21; **21:**8^2, 9^2, 12, 14, 15, 18, 19, 22, 24, 28, 32, 33, 41, 42^2; **22:**11, 12, 15, 16, 28, 30^3, 36, 43; **23:**2, 6, 7, 9, 13^2, 30^2, 34, 39; **24:**5, 7, 14, 15, 16, 18, 19, 20, 26^2, 30^2, 38^2, 40, 43, 44, 45, 48, 50^2; **25:**4, 10, 18, 25, 31, 35, 36, 38, 39, 43^2, 44; **26:**6^2, 12, 13, 23, 29, 55^2, 58, 61, 64, 67, 69; **27:**4, 5, 7, 19, 29, 40, 43, 44, 51, 59, 60^2; **28:**1, 18^2, 19

Mk 1:2, 3, 4, 5, 9^2, 11, 13, 14, 19, 20, 23, 35, 39, 45; **2:**1, 6, 8^2, 15, 20, 26; **3:**23, 29; **4:**1, 2, 11, 15, 17, 19, 28, 29, 31^2, 36, 38; **5:**4, 5^2, 13, 14^2, 15, 20, 27, 29, 30^2, 33, 34, 39, 40; **6:**2, 4^2, 8, 10, 11, 14, 17, 22, 25^2, 27, 28, 29, 40, 47, 48, 51, 55, 56; **7:**7, 32; **8:**1, 4, 12, 14, 26, 37, 38^2; **9:**33, 36^2, 37, 38, 39, 41, 42, 50; **10:**10, 16, 21, 24, 30^2, 32, 37, 52; **11:**4, 8^2, 9, 10^2, 15, 20, 22, 23, 25, 26, 27; **12:**4, 11, 13, 14, 23, 25^2, 26^2, 35, 38^3, 39, 41, 42, 43, 44^2; **13:**6, 8, 9, 11, 14, 16, 17, 18, 19, 24, 25, 26, 29, 32, 35; **14:**3^2, 14, 17, 20, 25, 30, 31, 49, 60, 62, 66; **15:**1, 7, 29, 38, 41, 43, 46^2; **16:**2, 5, 12, 17

Lk 1:1^2, 3, 5, 6, 7, 8, 15, 17, 18, 19, 20, 21, 22, 25, 26, 28, 29, 31, 36, 39, 41, 44^2, 47, 51, 54, 66, 69, 75, 79^2, 80^2; **2:**1, 7^3, 8^2, 11, 12^2, 14, 16, 19, 21, 23, 24, 25, 27, 28, 29, 34, 38^2, 40, 43, 44, 46^2, 51, 52^2; **3:**1, 2, 4^2, 15^2, 17, 18, 20, 22^2; **4:**2, 5, 11, 14, 15, 20, 21, 23^2, 24, 25^2, 27^2, 28, 33, 35, 44; **5:**7, 12, 18^2, 19, 22, 29, 35; **6:**1, 8, 12^2, 17, 23^3, 41^2, 42^3; **7:**1, 7, 9, 21, 23, 25^2, 28, 32, 37^2, 45, 50; **8:**10, 13, 15, 16, 23, 27^2, 29, 34^2, 35, 48, 51; **9:**12, 14, 26^2, 31, 36, 48, 49, 57; **10:**7, 12, 13^3, 20^2, 21^3, 26, 34; **11:**1, 2^3, 6, 7, 21, 26, 31, 32, 33^2, 35, 37, 43^2, 52^2; **12:**1, 3^4, 12, 15, 27, 28, 33, 38^2, 42, 45, 46^2, 52, 53^4, 58; **13:**4^2, 6, 10, 11, 14^2, 19, 21, 24^2, 26^2, 28, 29, 35; **14:**8, 10^2, 15, 21, 23; **15:**4, 7, 10, 14^2, 21, 25, 28; **16:**8, 10^4, 11, 12, 15, 19, 23^3, 24^2, 25; **17:**4^2, 6, 24, 26^2, 27, 28, 30, 31^3, 34^2, 36; **18:**2, 3, 9, 12, 17, 22, 30^2; **19:**17, 20, 30, 36, 38^3, 42, 43, 44, 47; **20:**1, 31, 33, 34, 35, 42, 45, 46^3; **21:**2, 3, 4^2, 6, 8, 11, 14, 19, 21^3, 23^2, 25^3, 27, 37^3, 38^2; **22:**6, 10, 16, 19, 20, 28, 30, 37, 44, 53, 55; **23:**4, 9, 11, 14, 19, 22, 29, 31^2, 38, 40, 43, 45, 53^3; **24:**1, 3, 4, 6, 12, 18^2, 19, 27, 29, 35^2, 36, 38, 44^3, 47, 49, 53

Jn 1:1, 2, 4, 5, 10, 18, 23, 28, 45, 47; **2:**1, 11, 14, 19, 20^2, 23^3, 25; **3:**13, 14, 15, 16, 18, 21, 23; **4:**14, 18, 20^2, 21, 23^2, 24^2, 31, 44, 53; **5:**2, 3, 4, 6, 13, 14, 26^2, 28^2, 35, 38, 39, 42, 43^2, 45; **6:**10^2, 31, 37, 45, 49, 53, 56^2, 59^2, 61; **7:**1^2, 4, 5, 9, 10, 18, 28, 37; **8:**2, 3^2, 4^2, 5, 9, 12, 17, 20^2, 21, 24^2, 31, 33, 35, 37, 44^2; **9:**3, 5, 7, 34; **10:**2, 9^2, 23^2, 25, 34, 38^2; **11:**6, 9^2, 10^3, 13, 17, 20, 24, 25, 26, 30, 31, 33, 38, 52, 56; **12:**13, 25, 35, 36, 46, 48; **13:**1, 21, 31, 32^2; **14:**1^2, 2, 10^3, 11^2, 13^2, 14, 17, 20^3, 26, 30; **15:**2, 4^4, 5^2, 6, 7^2, 9, 10^2, 11, 16, 25; **16:**21, 23^2, 24, 25^2, 26, 33^2; **17:**10, 11^2, 12^2, 13^2, 21^3, 23^3, 26^2; **18:**13, 15, 16, 20^3, 26, 38; **19:**4, 6, 13^3, 17, 18, 20, 40, 41^2; **20:**5^2, 7, 8, 12, 19, 25, 26, 30^2; **21:**2, 8

Act 1:2, 7, 8^3, 10, 11, 13, 14, 15^2, 18, 19, 20, 21; **2:**1, 6, 8, 9^3, 10^2, 11, 12, 17, 18, 19^2, 22, 26, 27, 31, 37, 38, 42^3, 46; **3:**6, 11, 13, 16^2, 22, 25, 26; **4:**3, 7, 12, 16, 17, 18, 19, 24; **5:**4^2, 7, 10, 12, 18, 20, 21, 22, 25^2, 28, 34^2, 37, 40, 42^2; **6:**1^2, 7, 15; **7:**2^2, 4, 5, 6, 7^2, 10, 12, 16, 17, 20^2, 22^3, 29, 30^3, 34, 35, 36^3, 38^3, 39, 41^2, 42^2, 44, 45, 48, 51; **8:**8, 9, 16, 21^2, 23^2, 25, 28, 33, 40; **9:**10, 11, 12^2, 17, 20, 21, 22, 25, 27^2, 28, 29, 31^2, 37^2, 42, 43; **10:**1, 3^2, 17, 23, 25, 27, 30^2, 31^2, 32, 35, 39^2, 43, 48; **11:**1, 3, 5^2, 13, 22, 26, 27, 28, 29; **12:**4, 5, 7, 14, 21; **13:**1, 5, 13, 14, 17, 18, 19, 27, 28, 29, 33^2, 35, 40, 41^2, 43; **14:**1, 3, 8, 11^2, 14, 16^2, 17, 22, 23, 25; **15:**21^2, 23, 33, 35, 36; **16:**3, 5^2, 6, 9, 12, 18, 24, 29, 32, 34, 36; **17:**2, 11^2, 16, 17^2, 21, 22^2, 24, 28, 31^3; **18:**2, 4, 5, 9, 10, 18, 21, 23, 24, 25^2, 26; **19:**5, 9, 10, 16, 21, 22, 27, 29, 30, 39, 40^2; **20:**6, 8, 9, 10, 13, 14, 16, 19, 22, 23, 29; **21:**18, 27, 29, 31, 39, 40; **22:**2, 3^3, 17^2, 19; **23:**1, 6^2, 9, 10, 11, 16, 21, 35; **24:**3, 12^3, 14^2, 18, 20, 21, 24; **25:**3, 5, 14; **26:**3, 10^2, 11, 13, 14, 16, 18, 21, 26; **27:**12, 20, 21, 27, 31, 35, 37^2, 39; **28:**7, 8, 9, 11^2, 18, 30^2

Ro 1:2, 7, 9^2, 15, 18, 19, 21, 27^2, 28, 32; **2:**7, 12, 14, 15, 16, 17, 19, 20, 28, 29^2; **3:**4, 9, 16, 20, 24, 25, 26; **4:**10^4, 12, 18, 19, 20; **5:**2, 3, 5, 6, 8, 11, 13, 17; **6:**1, 4, 5^2, 10^2, 12^2, 21; **7:**5^2, 6^2, 8, 13, 17, 18^2, 20, 22, 23^2; **8:**1, 2, 3^3, 4, 8, 9^3, 10, 11^2, 18, 20, 22, 37, 39; **9:**1^2, 2, 7, 17, 25, 26, 28, 33; **10:**6, 8^2, 9, 14^2; **11:**17, 19, 22, 23^3, 25^3, 30, 32; **12:**4, 5, 10, 11^2, 12^3, 16, 17, 18, 20; **13:**4, 9, 13^4; **14:**1, 5, 13, 17, 18, 22; **15:**12, 13^2, 15^2, 17, 23, 24, 27, 29, 30, 31; **16:**2^2, 3, 5, 7, 8, 9, 10, 11, 12^2, 13, 22

1Co 1:2^2, 5^3, 6, 7, 8, 10^2, 13, 15, 21, 29, 30, 31; **2:**3^3, 4, 5^2, 7, 11, 13; **3:**1, 16, 18, 19, 21; **4:**2, 6^2, 10, 15^2, 17^3, 20^2, 21^2; **5:**3^2, 4, 5, 9; **6:**4, 11, 19, 20^2; **7:**15, 17, 18, 20, 22, 28, 34^2, 37^2, 38^2, 39; **8:**4^2, 5^2, 6, 7, 10; **9:**1, 2, 9, 10^2, 18, 24, 25; **10:**2^2, 5, 8, 19, 25, 28, 33; **11:**2, 11, 13, 17, 18, 21, 22^2, 23, 24, 25^2, 34; **12:**6, 18, 25, 27, 28; **13:**6^2, 9^2, 10, 12; **14:**2^2, 4, 7, 10, 13, 14, 19^2, 20^3, 21, 23, 24, 25, 27, 28, 33, 34, 35, 40; **15:**2^2, 10, 17, 18, 19^2, 22^2, 23, 28, 30, 31, 41, 42^2, 43^4, 52^2, 54, 58^3; **16:**2, 11, 13, 19^2, 24

2Co 1:1, 4^2, 5, 6, 8, 9^3, 10, 12^2, 14^2, 15, 19, 20^2, 21, 22; **2:**1, 3, 5, 9, 10, 13, 14^2, 15^2, 17^2; **3:**2, 3^2, 7, 9, 10, 14^2, 18; **4:**2^2, 4, 6^2, 7, 8, 10^2, 11, 12^2; **5:**1, 2, 4, 6, 10, 11, 12^2, 17, 19, 20, 21; **6:**1, 2^2, 3, 4^5, 5^6, 12^2, 13, 16^2; **7:**1, 3, 4, 7, 9, 11^3, 12, 13, 14, 16^2; **8:**2, 6, 7^5, 18, 20, 21^2, 22^2; **9:**3^2, 4, 7, 8, 11, 14; **10:**1, 3, 6, 11^2, 14, 16^2, 17; **11:**1, 3, 6^3, 7, 9, 10^2, 17, 23^4, 25, 26^{12}, 27^5, 32, 33; **12:**2^2, 3, 5, 7, 9^2, 10^5, 11^2, 12^2, 18^2, 19; **13:**1, 3^2, 4, 5^2, 11

Gal 1:13^2, 14^2, 16, 22, 23, 24; **2:**2, 4^3, 6, 8^2, 16, 20^2, 21; **3:**3, 4^2, 8, 10^2, 11, 12, 17, 19, 26, 28; **4:**3, 9, 11, 14, 18, 19^2, 20, 25^2; **5:**1, 6, 10, 14^2, 16, 21, 25^2; **6:**1^2, 4^2, 6^2, 9^2, 12, 13, 14, 15, 17

Eph 1:1, 3^2, 4^2, 6, 7, 8, 9, 10^5, 11, 12, 13^2, 15, 16, 17, 18, 20^2, 21^2, 23; **2:**1, 2^2, 3^2, 4, 5, 6^2, 7^2, 10^2, 11^3, 12, 13, 15^3, 16, 21^2, 22; **3:**3, 4, 5, 6, 9, 10, 11, 12, 15, 16, 17^2, 20, 21; **4:**2, 3, 4, 6, 13, 14, 15^2, 16^2, 17^2, 18, 21, 23, 24; **5:**2, 5, 8, 9, 12, 19^2, 20, 21, 24, 33; **6:**1, 4, 5, 9, 10^2, 12, 13, 18, 20, 21, 24

Php 1:1, 4, 5, 6, 7^3, 8, 9^2, 13^3, 14, 18^2, 20^2, 22, 23, 24, 26, 27, 28, 29, 30^2; **2:**1, 3, 5^2, 6, 7, 8, 10^2, 12^2, 13, 15^2, 16^3, 19, 22, 24, 25, 29^2; **3:**1, 3^3, 4^2, 6, 9, 14, 15, 19, 20; **4:**1, 2, 3^2, 4, 6, 9, 10, 11^2, 12, 15, 16, 19, 21

Col 1:2, 4, 5^2, 6^3, 8, 9, 10^2, 12, 14, 16^2, 18, 19, 20^2, 21, 22^2, 23, 24^2, 27, 28^2, 29; **2:**1, 2, 3, 5^3, 6, 7^2, 9, 10, 11^2, 12, 13, 15, 16^3, 18, 20, 23^2; **3:**3, 4, 7^2, 10, 11, 15^2, 16^4, 17^2, 18, 20, 22^2; **4:**1, 2^2, 3, 5, 7, 12^2, 13^2, 15^2, 16, 17

1Th 1:1^2, 2, 3^2, 5^4, 6, 7, 8^2, 9; **2:**1^2, 2, 3, 4, 13^2, 14^2, 17^2, 19; **3:**2, 5, 7, 8, 10, 12, 13; **4:**4, 5, 6, 10, 14, 16, 17^2; **5:**2, 4, 7^2, 12, 13, 18^2

2Th 1:1, 4^3, 8, 10^3, 12^2; **2:**2, 4, 6, 10, 12, 17; **3:**4, 6, 13, 17

1Ti 1:2, 4, 13, 14, 16; **2:**2^2, 3, 6, 7^2, 9^2, 11, 12, 14, 15^2; **3:**4, 9, 11, 13^2, 15, 16^3; **4:**1, 2, 6^2, 10, 12^6, 14, 16^2; **5:**5^2, 6, 7, 17; **6:**9, 13, 15, 16, 17^3, 18, 19

2Ti 1:1, 3, 5^3, 6^2, 9, 13^2, 14, 15, 17, 18^2; **2:**1^2, 7, 10, 14, 20, 25; **3:**1, 12, 14, 15, 16; **4:**2, 5

Tit 1:2, 3, 5^3, 13, 16; **2:**2^3, 3, 7^2, 9, 10, 12; **3:**1, 3, 8, 15

Phlm 2, 4, 6^2, 7, 8, 10, 11, 13^2, 16^2, 20^2, 21, 23

Heb 1:1^2, 2, 6, 10; **2:**5, 6, 8^3, 10, 12, 13, 17^2, 18; **3:**2, 5, 8^3, 10, 11, 12^2, 15, 17, 19; **4:**2, 3, 4, 5, 6, 7, 13, 15, 16; **5:**1, 6, 7^2, 13; **6:**7, 10, 18; **7:**9, 10, 19; **8:**1, 5, 9^2, 10, 13; **9:**9, 10, 12, 23, 24, 26; **10:**3, 6, 7, 16, 22, 32, 34^3, 38; **11:**9^3, 12, 13, 18, 19, 26, 34, 37, 38^3; **12:**3, 9, 23; **13:**3^2, 4, 18, 21^3, 22

Jas 1:6, 8, 9, 10, 11, 23, 25, 27; **2:**2^3, 3, 4, 5, 10, 16; **3:**2^2, 3, 7, 14, 18; **4:**1, 5^2, 10, 16; **5:**5^2, 10, 14

1Pt 1:4, 5, 6, 8, 11, 14, 15, 17, 20, 21^2, 22; **2:**6^2, 10, 12, 22, 24; **3:**1, 4^2, 5^3, 15^2, 16, 18, 19, 20; **4:**1^2, 2, 3, 6^2, 11, 15, 19; **5:**6, 9^3, 14

2Pt 1:4, 8^2, 12^2, 13^2, 15, 17, 18, 19^2, 21; **2:**1, 5, 8, 10, 11, 12, 13, 18, 19, 22; **3:**1, 3, 5, 7, 10^2, 11, 14, 16^3, 18^2

1Jn 1:5, 6, 7^2, 8, 10; **2:**4, 5^2, 6, 8^2, 9^2, 10^2, 11^2, 14, 15^2, 16, 24^4, 27^2, 28; **3:**3, 5, 6, 9, 10, 14, 15, 17, 18^4, 22, 24^3; **4:**2, 3^2, 4^2, 9, 12^2, 13^2, 15^2, 16^3, 17^2, 18^2; **5:**7, 8^2, 10, 11, 14, 19, 20^2

2Jn 1, 2, 3, 4, 6, 7, 9^2

3Jn 1, 2, 3^2, 4

Jude 1, 4, 5, 6, 7, 10, 11^2, 12, 16, 18, 20, 21

Rev 1:4, 5, 9^3, 10, 11^2, 13, 15, 16^2, 20; **2:**1^2, 7, 8, 12, 13, 17, 18, 24; **3:**1, 4^2, 5, 7, 12, 18, 20, 21^2; **4:**1, 2^2, 3, 4, 6; **5:**1, 3^2, 6^2, 13^3; **6:**5, 6, 15^2; **7:**3, 9, 13, 14, 15, 17; **8:**1, 9; **9:**4, 6, 10, 11^2, 14, 17, 19^2; **10:**2, 7, 8, 9, 10; **11:**3, 5, 6, 8, 9, 12, 13, 15, 19^2; **12:**1, 2, 3, 7, 8, 10, 12; **13:**6^2, 8, 13, 14, 16^2; **14:**1, 5, 6, 9^2, 10^2, 13, 14, 15, 16, 17, 18, 19; **15:**1^2, 5, 6; **16:**3, 16, 19; **17:**3, 4^2, 8, 17; **18:**6, 7, 8, 10, 16, 17^2, 19^2, 22^3, 23^2, 24; **19:**1, 8, 11, 13, 14^2, 17^2; **20:**1, 4, 6, 8, 12, 13^2, 15; **21:**8, 10, 14, 23, 24, 27^2; **22:**2, 3, 4, 14, 16, 18, 19

INTO

Gen 2:7, 10, 15; **6:**18, 19; **7:**1, 7, 9, 13, 15; **8:**9^2; **9:**2; **11:**31; **12:**5^2, 10, 11, 14, 15; **13:**1; **14:**20; **16:**5; **18:**6; **19:**2, 3, 10, 23; **21:**32; **22:**2; **24:**20, 32, 67; **26:**2; **27:**17; **28:**15; **29:**1; **30:**35; **31:**33^4; **32:**7, 16; **36:**6; **37:**20, 22, 24, 28, 35, 36; **39:**4, 11, 20; **40:**3, 11^2, 13, 15, 21; **41:**57; **42:**17, 25, 37; **43:**17, 18, 24, 26, 30; **45:**4, 25; **46:**3, 4, 6, 7, 8, 26, 27, 28; **47:**14; **48:**5, 16; **49:**6, 33; **50:**13, 14

Ex 1:1, 22; **3:**18; **4:**6^2, 7^2, 19, 21, 27; **5:**3; **7:**23; **8:**3^5, 21, 24^3, 27; **9:**20; **10:**4, 19; **11:**4; **13:**5, 11; **14:**22, 28; **15:**1, 4, 5, 19, 21, 22, 25; **16:**3; **18:**5, 7, 27; **19:**1, 12; **21:**13; **23:**19, 20, 31; **24:**12, 13, 15, 18^2; **25:**14, 16; **26:**11; **27:**7; **29:**3, 30; **30:**20; **32:**24; **33:**5, 8, 9, 11; **37:**5; **38:**7; **39:**3^2; **40:**20, 21, 32, 35

Lev 1:6, 12; **6:**30; **8:**20; **9:**23; **10:**9; **11:**32; **12:**4; **13:**17; **14:**7, 8, 15, 26, 34, 36, 40, 41, 45, 46, 53; **16:**2, 3, 10, 21, 23^2, 26, 28; **19:**23; **23:**10; **25:**2; **26:**25, 32, 36, 41

Nu 4:3, 30, 35, 39, 43; **5:**17, 22, 24, 27; **7:**89; **11:**30; **13:**17; **14:**3, 4, 8, 16, 24, 25, 30, 40; **15:**2, 18; **16:**14, 30, 33, 47; **17:**8; **19:**6, 7, 14; **20:**1, 4, 12, 15, 24, 27; **21:**2, 22^2, 23, 27, 29, 34; **22:**13, 23^2, 41; **23:**14; **24:**4, 16; **25:**8; **27:**12; **31:**24, 27, 54; **32:**7, 9, 32; **33:**8, 38, 51; **34:**2; **35:**10, 28; **36:**12

Dt 1:22, 24, 27, 31, 40, 41, 43; **2:**1, 24, 29, 30; **3:**2, 3, 27; **5:**5, 30; **6:**10; **7:**1, 24, 26; **8:**7; **9:**9, 21, 28; **10:**1, 3, 22; **11:**5; **13:**16; **14:**6, 25; **17:**8; **18:**9; **19:**3, 5, 11, 12; **20:**13; **21:**10; **23:**1, 2^2, 3^2, 5, 8, 11, 18, 24,

25; 24:10; 26:5, 9; 28:25, 38, 41, 68; 29:12[2], 28; 30:5; 31:20, 21, 23; 32:26, 49

Jos 2:1, 3, 18, 19, 24; 3:11; 4:5; 6:2, 11, 14, 19, 20, 22, 24; 7:7; 8:1, 7, 13, 18, 19; 10:8, 19[2], 20, 27, 30, 32; 11:8; 13:5; 18:5, 6, 9; 20:4, 5; 21:44; 22:13; 24:4, 8[2], 11

Jdg 1:2, 3[2], 4, 16, 24, 25, 26, 34; 2:14[2], 23; 3:8, 10, 21, 28; 4:2, 7, 9, 14, 18, 21[2], 22; 5:15; 6:1, 5, 13; 7:2, 7, 9, 13, 14, 15[2], 16; 8:3, 7; 9:27[2], 42, 43, 46; 10:7[2]; 11:19, 21, 30, 32; 12:3; 13:1; 15:1, 5, 12, 13, 18[2]; 16:23, 24; 18:10, 18; 19:3, 11, 12, 15, 21, 22, 23, 29[3]; 20:4, 8, 28

Ru 1:2; 2:18; 3:14, 15; 4:11

1Sa 2:14, 36; 4:3, 5, 6, 7, 10, 13; 5:2, 5; 6:14, 19; 7:1, 13; 9:13, 14[2], 22, 25; 10:6; 11:11; 12:8, 9[3]; 14:10, 12, 21, 26, 37; 17:22, 46, 47, 49; 19:10; 20:8, 11[2], 35, 42; 21:15; 22:5[2]; 23:4, 7[2], 11, 12, 14, 16, 20, 25; 24:4, 10, 18; 26:3, 8, 10, 23; 27:1; 28:19[2]; 29:11; 30:15, 23; 31:9

2Sa 2:1; 3:8, 34; 4:6, 7; 5:8, 19[2]; 6:10[2], 12, 16; 10:2, 10, 14; 11:11, 23; 12:8, 20; 13:10[2]; 15:25, 27, 31, 37[2]; 16:8; 17:13[2], 17; 18:6, 17; 19:2, 3, 5; 20:12; 21:9; 22:7, 20; 23:11; 24:14[2]

1Ki 1:15, 28; 3:1; 6:8[2]; 8:6; 11:17, 40; 13:18; 14:12, 28[2]; 15:15, 18; 16:18, 21; 17:19, 21, 22, 23; 18:5, 9; 19:4; 20:2, 13, 28, 30[3], 33, 39; 21:4; 22:6, 12, 15, 25, 30[2], 35

2Ki 2:1, 11, 16; 3:10, 13, 18; 4:4, 11, 32, 39[2], 41; 5:18; 6:5, 20, 23; 7:4, 8[2], 12; 8:21; 9:6, 26; 10:15, 21, 23, 24; 11:4, 13, 16, 18; 12:4[3], 9[2], 11, 13, 15, 16; 13:3[2], 21; 17:6, 20; 18:21, 30; 19:1, 10, 14, 18, 23[2], 25, 28, 32, 33, 37; 20:4, 8, 17, 20; 21:14; 22:4, 5, 7, 9, 20; 23:2, 12; 24:15

1Ch 5:20; 6:15; 10:9; 11:15; 12:8; 13:13; 14:10[2], 17; 16:7; 19:2, 15; 21:13[2], 27; 22:18, 19; 23:6; 24:19

2Ch 5:7; 6:41; 7:2, 10, 11; 9:4; 12:11[2]; 13:16; 15:12, 18; 16:8; 18:5, 11, 14, 24; 20:20; 21:17[2]; 23:1, 6, 7, 12, 20; 24:10, 24; 25:20; 26:16; 27:2; 28:5[2], 9, 27; 29:4, 16[3], 31; 30:8, 9, 14, 15; 31:1, 10, 16; 32:1, 21; 33:13; 34:7, 9, 14, 17, 30; 36:17

Ezr 5:8, 12[2], 14, 15; 9:7; 10:6

Neh 2:7, 8; 5:5; 6:11; 7:5; 8:1; 9:11[2], 22, 23, 24, 27, 30; 10:29[2], 34, 38; 12:44; 13:1, 2, 15

Est 1:22[2]; 2:14, 16; 3:9, 13; 4:1, 2, 11; 6:4; 7:7, 8; 9:22

Job 3:6; 9:24; 10:9; 12:6; 14:3; 16:11; 17:12; 18:8, 18; 22:4; 30:3, 19, 31; 33:28; 34:23; 36:16; 37:8; 38:16, 22, 38; 39:12; 40:23; 41:2, 22, 28

Ps 4:2; 5:7; 7:15; 9:17; 10:9; 16:4; 18:6, 19; 22:15; 24:3; 28:1; 30:11; 31:5, 8; 32:4; 35:8, 13; 37:15, 20; 45:2, 15; 46:2; 55:15, 23; 56:8; 57:6; 60:9[2]; 63:9; 66:6, 11, 12, 13; 69:2, 27; 73:17, 18, 19; 74:7; 76:6; 78:44, 61[2]; 79:1, 12; 88:4, 18; 95:11; 96:8; 100:4[2]; 104:10; 105:23, 29; 106:15, 20, 41, 42; 107:33[2], 34, 35[2]; 108:10[2]; 109:18[2]; 114:8[2]; 115:17; 118:19, 20; 122:1; 132:3[2], 7, 8; 135:9; 136:13; 139:8; 140:10[2]; 141:10; 143:2, 7, 10

Prv 1:12; 2:10; 4:14; 6:3; 13:17; 16:29, 33; 17:10[2], 20; 18:6, 8, 10; 19:15; 23:10; 24:16; 26:9, 22; 27:10; 28:10, 14; 29:8; 30:4

Ecc 1:7; 10:8; 11:9; 12:14

Song 1:4; 3:4[2]; 4:16; 5:1; 6:2, 11; 7:11; 8:2

Isa 2:4[2], 10, 19[2], 21[2]; 3:14; 5:13, 14; 9:8, 10; 13:2, 14; 14:7, 13; 19:1, 4, 8, 23[2]; 21:4; 22:18, 21; 23:9; 24:18; 26:20; 29:17; 30:2, 6, 20, 29; 34:9[2]; 36:6, 15; 37:1, 10, 19, 24, 26, 29, 33, 34, 38; 38:18; 40:9; 44:23; 46:2; 47:5, 6; 49:13; 51:23; 52:1, 4, 9; 54:1; 55:12; 57:2; 59:5; 63:14; 65:6, 7, 17; 66:20

Jer 2:7, 21; 4:5, 29; 6:9, 25; 7:31; 8:6, 14; 9:21[2]; 10:9; 12:7; 13:16; 14:18[3]; 15:4, 14; 16:5, 8, 13, 15; 17:25; 19:5; 20:4[2], 5, 6; 21:4, 7[3], 10, 13; 22:7, 22, 25[4], 26, 28; 23:15; 24:5, 9; 26:21, 22[2], 23, 24; 27:6; 28:3, 4, 6; 29:14, 16, 21; 30:6, 16; 31:13; 32:3, 4, 18, 24, 25, 28[2], 35, 36, 43; 33:11; 34:2, 3, 10, 11, 16, 17, 20[2], 21[3]; 35:2[2], 4[2], 11; 36:5, 12[2], 20, 23; 37:4, 7, 12, 16[2], 17, 21; 38:3, 6, 9, 11[2], 14, 16, 18, 19; 39:9, 17; 40:4[2]; 41:7[2], 17; 42:14, 15, 17, 18, 19; 43:2, 3[2], 7; 44:12, 14[2], 21, 28[2], 30[3]; 46:11, 19, 24, 26[3]; 47:6; 48:7, 11, 44; 49:3, 32; 51:9, 50, 51, 59, 63; 52:12

Lam 1:3, 5, 7, 10[2], 13, 14, 18; 2:7, 9, 12; 3:2[2], 13; 4:12, 22; 5:15

Ezk 2:2; 3:22, 23, 24; 4:14; 5:4[2], 6, 10, 12; 7:11, 21, 22; 8:16; 10:7; 11:5, 9, 24; 12:4, 11; 13:5, 9; 14:19; 15:4; 16:8, 13, 39; 17:4, 15; 19:9; 20:6, 10, 15, 28, 32, 35, 37, 38, 42[2]; 21:11, 14, 30, 31; 22:19, 20; 23:9[2], 16, 17, 28[2], 31, 39; 24:3, 4; 25:3; 26:10[2], 20; 27:26, 27; 28:4, 23[2]; 29:5, 14[2]; 30:12, 17, 18, 25; 31:11, 16, 17; 32:9, 18, 24; 36:5, 24; 37:5, 10, 12, 17, 21, 22; 38:4, 8, 10; 39:23[2], 28; 40:2, 17, 32; 41:6; 42:1[2], 9, 12, 14; 43:4, 5; 44:7, 9, 12, 16, 19[2], 21, 27; 46:19, 20, 21; 47:8[3]

Dan 1:2[3], 9; 2:29, 38; 3:6, 11, 15, 20, 21, 23, 24; 5:10; 6:7, 10, 12, 16, 24; 7:25; 10:8; 11:7, 8, 9[2], 11, 28, 40, 41

Hos 2:14; 4:7; 9:4; 11:5, 9; 12:1, 12

Joel 1:14; 2:20, 31[2]; 3:2, 5, 8, 10[2]

Am 1:4, 5, 15; 2:1; 4:3; 5:5[2], 8, 19, 27; 6:12[2]; 7:12, 17; 8:10[2]; 9:2, 4

Oba 11, 13

Jna 1:3, 4, 5[2], 12, 15; 2:3, 7; 3:4

Mic 1:6, 16; 3:5; 4:3[2], 12; 5:5, 6; 7:19

Nah 3:10, 12, 14

Hab 3:16

Hag 1:6

Zec 5:4[2], 8; 6:6, 10; 10:10; 11:6[2]; 14:2

Mal 3:10

Mt 1:17[2]; 2:11, 12, 13, 14, 20, 21, 22; 3:10, 12; 4:1, 5, 8, 12[2], 18; 5:1, 20, 25, 29, 30; 6:6, 13, 26, 30; 7:19, 21; 8:5, 12, 14, 23, 28, 31, 32[2], 33; 9:1[2], 17[2], 23, 26, 28, 38; 10:5[2], 11, 12, 23; 11:7; 12:4, 9, 11, 29, 44; 13:2, 8, 20, 23, 30, 36, 42, 47, 48, 50, 54; 14:13, 15, 22, 23, 32, 34, 35; 15:11, 14, 17[2], 21, 29, 39; 16:13; 17:1, 15[2], 22, 25; 18:3, 8[2], 9[2], 12, 30; 19:1, 17, 23, 24; 20:1, 2, 4, 7; 21:2, 10, 12, 17, 18, 21, 23, 31, 33; 22:9, 10, 13; 24:16, 38; 25:14, 21, 23, 30, 41, 46[2]; 26:18, 30, 32, 41, 45, 52, 71; 27:6, 27, 53; 28:7, 10, 11, 16[2]

Mk 1:12, 14, 16, 21[2], 29, 35, 38, 45; 2:1, 11, 22[2], 26; 3:1, 13, 19, 27; 4:1, 26, 37; 5:1, 12[2], 13[2], 18; 6:1, 10, 31, 32, 36[2], 45, 46, 51, 53, 56; 7:15, 17, 18, 19[3], 24[2], 33; 8:10[2], 13, 26, 27; 9:2, 22[2], 25, 28, 31, 42, 43[3], 45[3], 47[2]; 10:1, 17, 23, 24, 25; 11:2[2], 11[2], 15, 23; 12:1, 41, 43; 13:15; 14:13, 16, 26, 28, 38, 41, 54, 68; 15:16; 16:5, 7, 12, 15, 19

Lk 1:9, 39[2], 40, 79; 2:3, 4, 15, 27, 39; 3:3, 9, 17; 4:1, 5, 14, 16, 37, 38, 42; 5:3, 4, 16, 19, 24, 37, 38; 6:4, 6, 12, 38, 39; 7:1, 11, 24, 36, 44; 8:22, 29, 30, 31, 32, 33[2], 37, 41, 51; 9:4, 10, 12, 28, 34, 44[2], 52; 10:1, 2, 5, 8, 10[2], 38[2]; 11:4; 12:5, 28, 58; 13:19; 14:1, 5, 21, 23; 15:13, 15; 16:4, 9, 16, 22, 28; 17:2, 12, 27; 18:10, 24, 25; 19:4, 12, 23, 30, 45; 20:9; 21:1, 12, 24; 22:3, 10[2], 33, 40, 46, 54, 66; 23:19, 25, 42, 46; 24:7, 26, 51

Jn 1:9, 43; 3:4, 5, 17, 19, 22, 24, 35; 4:3, 14, 28, 38, 43, 45, 46, 47, 54; 5:4, 7, 24; 6:3, 14, 15, 17, 21, 22; 7:3, 14; 8:2; 9:39; 10:1, 36, 40; 11:7, 27, 30, 54; 12:24, 46; 13:2, 3, 5, 27; 15:6; 16:13, 20, 21, 28; 17:18[2]; 18:1, 11, 15, 28, 33, 37; 19:9, 17; 20:6, 11, 25[2], 27; 21:3, 7

Act 1:11[3], 13; 2:20[2], 34; 3:1, 2, 3, 8; 5:15, 21; 7:3, 4, 6, 9, 15, 16, 23, 34, 39, 45, 55; 8:3, 38; 9:6, 8, 11, 17, 39; 10:10, 16, 22, 24; 11:8, 10, 12; 12:17; 13:14; 14:1, 20, 22, 25; 16:7, 9, 10, 15, 19, 23, 24, 34, 37, 40; 17:10; 18:7, 18, 19, 27; 19:8, 22, 29, 31; 20:1, 2, 3, 4, 9, 18; 21:3, 8, 11, 26, 28, 29, 34, 37, 38; 22:4, 10, 11, 23, 24; 23:10, 16, 20, 28; 24:27; 25:1, 23; 27:1, 2, 6, 15, 17, 30, 38, 39, 41, 43; 28:5, 17, 23

Ro 1:23, 25, 26; 5:2, 12; 6:3[2], 4; 7:23; 8:21; 10:6, 7, 18; 11:24[2]; 15:24, 28

1Co 2:9; 4:17; 9:27; 11:20; 12:13[2]; 14:9, 23

2Co 1:16; 2:13; 3:18; 7:5; 8:16; 10:5; 11:13, 14, 20; 12:4

Gal 1:6, 17, 21; 2:4; 3:27; 4:6

Eph 4:9, 15

Col 1:13; 2:18

2Th 3:5[2]

1Ti 1:3, 12, 15; 3:6, 7, 16; 5:9; 6:7, 9[2]

2Ti 3:6

Heb 1:6; 3:11, 18; 4:1, 3[2], 5, 10, 11, 14; 6:19; 8:10; 9:6, 7, 8, 12, 24[2], 25; 10:5, 16, 19, 31; 11:8; 13:11

Jas 1:2, 25; 4:13; 5:4, 12

1Pt 1:12; 2:9; 3:22

2Pt 1:11; 2:4, 6

1Jn 4:1, 9

2Jn 7, 10

Jude 4

Rev 2:10, 22[2]; 5:6; 8:5, 8; 11:11; 12:6, 9, 14[2]; 13:10[2]; 14:10, 19[2]; 15:8; 16:16, 17, 19; 17:3, 8, 11; 18:21; 19:20; 20:3, 10, 14, 15; 21:24, 26, 27; 22:14

IS

Gen 1:11, 29[2], 30; 2:9, 11[3], 12[2], 13[2], 14[3], 18, 23; 3:3, 13, 17, 22; 4:6, 9, 13; 5:1; 6:3, 13[2], 15, 17[2], 21; 7:15; 8:17, 21; 9:4, 10, 12[2], 15, 16, 17[2], 18; 10:9, 12; 11:6, 9; 12:12, 18, 19; 13:9, 18; 14:2, 3, 6, 7, 8, 15, 17, 23; 15:2, 3, 13, 16; 16:6, 14; 17:4, 10, 12[3], 13[2], 14, 17[2]; 18:9, 14, 20[2], 21; 19:8, 13, 20[3], 31[2], 37, 38; 20:2, 3, 5[2], 7, 11, 12[2], 13[2], 15, 16; 21:13, 17, 22; 22:7, 14, 17; 23:2, 9[2], 11, 15[2], 19, 20; 24:23, 35, 51, 65[2]; 25:9, 18; 26:7[2], 9[2], 10, 20, 33; 27:11, 20, 22, 27, 33, 36; 28:16, 17[3]; 29:6[2], 7[2], 19, 25; 30:15, 30, 33; 31:5, 14, 16, 29, 32, 35, 36[2], 43, 48, 50[2]; 32:2, 8, 18[2], 20, 27, 29, 30, 32; 33:11, 17, 18; 34:14, 21; 35:6[2], 10, 19, 20, 27; 36:1, 8, 19, 43; 37:10, 22, 26, 27, 30, 33[2]; 38:14, 18, 21, 24; 39:8, 9; 40:8, 12, 18; 41:15, 16, 25[2], 26, 28[2], 32[2], 38[2], 39; 42:2, 13[2], 14, 21, 22, 28[3], 30, 32[2], 36[2], 38[2]; 43:7, 27[2], 28[2], 29, 32; 44:5, 10, 15, 16, 17, 20[2], 28, 30, 31; 45:12, 20, 26[2], 28[2]; 46:33, 34; 47:3, 4, 6, 18[2], 23; 48:1, 7, 18; 49:9, 14, 21, 22, 24, 28, 29, 30[2], 32; 50:10, 11[2], 20

Ex 1:22; 2:6, 14, 18, 20[2]; 3:3, 5, 9, 13, 15[2], 16; 4:2, 14, 22; 5:2, 16[2], 22; 7:14, 17, 18; 8:10, 19, 26; 9:3[2], 4, 14, 27, 28, 29; 10:5, 7, 10; 11:5; 12:11, 19, 22[2], 27, 42[2], 43, 44, 48, 49; 13:2, 8, 14; 14:12; 15:2[3], 3[2], 6, 11[2], 26; 16:1, 15[2], 16, 23[2], 25, 26, 32, 36; 17:3, 7; 18:11, 14, 17, 18[2]; 19:5; 20:4[3], 10[2], 11, 17, 20; 21:21, 30; 22:16, 25, 27[2], 31; 23:16, 21; 25:3; 26:5, 10; 27:21; 28:8, 26; 29:1, 13[2], 14, 18[2], 21, 22[2], 23, 25, 27[4], 28, 30, 32, 34, 38; 30:6[2], 10, 13, 32; 31:7, 13, 14, 15, 17; 32:1, 5, 9, 17, 18[2], 23, 26; 33:13, 16, 21; 34:9, 10, 14[2], 19[2]; 35:4, 5; 36:25; 38:21, 26; 40:9

Lev 1:5, 8[2], 12[2], 13, 17[2]; 2:3, 6, 8[2], 9, 10[2], 15, 16; 3:3, 4[2], 5[3], 9, 10[2], 11, 14, 15[2], 16[2]; 4:3, 5, 7[2], 8, 9[2], 14, 16, 18[3], 21, 22, 24, 31, 35; 5:1, 8, 9, 11, 12, 17, 19; 6:4, 9[2], 14, 15, 17[2], 20[2], 21, 22[2], 25[3], 27, 28, 29, 30; 7:1[2], 4[3], 5, 6, 7[3], 9[2], 11, 15, 24, 35, 37; 8:5, 28, 31; 9:6; 10:3, 7, 12, 13, 17; 11:3, 4, 5, 6, 7, 10, 26, 32, 33, 36, 37, 46; 12:7; 13:3[2], 6, 8, 9, 11[2], 13[2], 15[2], 17, 18, 20, 22, 23, 24, 25[2], 27, 28[2], 30, 31, 36, 37[3], 39[2], 40[3], 41[2], 42, 44[3], 45, 46, 47, 49, 51[3], 52[2], 54, 55[3], 57[2], 59; 14:4, 7, 8, 11, 13[3], 14, 16, 17[2], 18[2], 19, 22, 25, 27, 28[2], 29[2], 31[2], 32[3], 35, 36, 40, 43, 44[2], 46, 48, 54, 57[3]; 15:2, 3, 4, 8, 13, 17, 31, 32[2], 33[2]; 16:2, 6, 11[2], 13, 15, 18; 17:2, 11[2], 14[3]; 18:6, 7, 8, 10, 11, 12, 13, 14, 15, 16, 17, 19, 22, 23, 25, 27; 19:7, 13, 20; 20:14, 17, 21, 27; 21:2[2], 3, 7[2], 10[2], 12, 19; 22:4[2], 7[2], 8, 11, 13, 24, 25, 27; 23:3[2], 5, 6, 8, 28, 36; 24:9, 16; 25:5, 12, 23, 28, 29, 30, 34, 48, 49; 27:22, 26, 28, 30[2]

Nu 1:51; 3:26, 47, 48; 4:15, 16, 24, 25, 26[2], 28, 31, 33; 5:2, 15, 17, 18, 29[2]; 6:4, 7, 8, 13, 18, 19, 20, 21; 8:24; 9:13[2]; 10:7; 11:6[2], 14, 17, 20, 23; 12:7[2], 12; 13:18, 19, 20, 27, 32; 14:7, 9[2], 18, 42; 15:25, 29; 16:3, 5, 11, 13, 40, 46[2]; 18:11[2], 13[2], 16, 19, 31; 19:2[2], 9[2], 13[2], 14[2], 15, 16, 20; 20:5[2], 13; 21:5[2], 8, 11, 13[2], 14, 16, 20, 28, 30; 22:5[2], 6[2], 11, 32, 36[2]; 23:19, 21[2], 23[2]; 24:9[2], 21; 26:9; 27:11, 14, 18; 28:3, 6, 10, 14, 16, 17, 23; 29:1; 30:1, 9; 31:20, 21; 32:4, 19; 33:6, 7, 36; 34:2, 13; 35:16, 17, 18, 21, 31, 32, 33; 36:6

Dt 1:14, 16, 17[2], 25, 28; 2:36[2]; 3:11, 12, 16, 24, 25; 4:6[2], 7[2], 8, 17, 18, 24, 31, 32, 35[2], 38, 39[2], 44, 48[2]; 5:8[3], 14[2], 21, 26; 6:4, 15, 18, 24; 7:9, 21, 25[2], 26; 8:13[2], 18[2]; 9:3, 13; 10:9, 14[2], 15, 17, 21[2]; 11:10, 11; 12:8, 12, 18, 22, 23, 25, 28; 13:6, 11, 14, 15, 18; 14:8, 10, 19, 21, 27; 15:2[2], 3, 9, 16; 16:11, 17, 20; 17:1[2], 4, 6, 15, 18; 18:2, 22; 19:4, 6[2], 16, 17; 20:1, 4, 5, 6, 7, 8[2], 11, 14, 19; 21:2, 3, 4, 6, 9, 16, 17[2], 20[2], 23[2]; 22:23, 26[2], 28[2]; 23:1, 7, 10, 11, 15, 19, 23; 24:2, 4[2], 14, 15; 25:6; 26:11, 12; 28:23[2], 43, 54, 61; 29:5, 11, 15, 23[2], 28; 30:11[2], 12, 13, 14, 20; 31:6, 8, 11, 12, 17; 32:4[3], 5, 6, 9[2], 20, 21, 22, 27, 28, 31, 32, 33, 34, 35, 36[2], 39[2], 47[2], 49[2]; 33:1, 7, 17, 22, 26, 27, 29[2]; 34:1, 4

Jos 1:2, 8, 9; 2:9, 11; 3:10, 16; 4:24; 5:4, 9, 15; 6:7; 7:2, 13, 15; 8:18, 31, 34; 9:12^2; 10:13; 11:4; 12:2^2, 9; 13:2, 3^2, 4, 9^2, 16^2, 25, 28; 14:11; 15:7^2, 8^2, 9, 10, 12, 13, 20, 25, 49, 54, 60; 16:8; 17:10, 16, 18; 18:7, 13, 14, 16, 17, 28^2; 19:8, 11, 16, 23, 31, 39, 48; 20:7; 21:11; 22:9, 16, 17, 28, 29, 31, 34; 23:3, 6, 10; 24:17, 18, 19^2, 30

Jdg 1:26; 4:11, 14^2, 20; 5:9, 28; 6:12, 13, 15, 24, 25, 31; 7:1, 3, 14; 8:2, 21^2; 9:2, 3, 18, 28^3, 32, 33^2, 38^3; 10:8, 18; 13:17, 18; 14:3, 15, 18^2; 15:2, 11, 19; 16:2^2, 3, 9, 15; 17:2; 18:6, 9, 10^2, 12, 14, 19, 24; 19:10, 12, 18, 19^4, 23, 24; 20:5, 12^2; 21:3, 5, 6, 8, 11, 12, 19^2

Ru 1:13, 15, 19; 2:5, 6, 19, 20, 22; 3:2, 12^2; 4:3, 4, 11, 15, 17^2

1Sa 1:8; 2:1^2, 2^3, 3, 5, 20, 24, 35, 36; 3:17, 18; 4:7, 16, 17^2, 21, 22^2; 5:7; 6:3, 9, 20; 9:6^2, 7^2, 9, 11, 12^3, 16, 18, 19, 20^2, 24; 10:1, 5, 7, 11^3, 12^2, 24; 11:12; 12:5^3, 6, 17^2; 13:5; 14:1, 2, 6, 7, 17; 15:7, 11, 12, 22, 23^2, 28, 29, 32; 16:6, 12, 16^2, 18^2, 19; 17:25^2, 26, 29, 46, 47, 55, 56; 18:18; 19:14, 17, 19, 22, 24; 20:1^2, 2, 3, 5, 6, 7^2, 18, 21, 26^2, 37; 21:3^2, 4^2, 5, 8, 9^3, 11, 14; 22:8^3, 14^3, 17; 23:7, 19, 22^2; 24:1, 6, 10, 11, 14, 16; 25:10^2, 17^2, 25^4, 29; 26:1, 3, 11, 15, 16^2, 17^2, 18, 20; 27:1; 28:7, 14^2, 15, 16^2; 29:1, 3, 5, 6; 30:20, 24

2Sa 1:9^2, 18, 19, 21; 2:7, 16; 3:12, 13, 23, 24^2, 29, 38; 4:10; 5:7; 6:2; 7:3^2, 18, 19, 22^2, 23, 26; 9:1^2, 2, 3^2, 4^2, 8; 11:3, 21, 24; 12:14, 18, 19^2, 21, 23; 13:16^2, 20, 23, 28, 30, 32, 33, 35; 14:5, 7^2, 13, 15, 17, 19, 20, 30; 15:2, 3, 31; 16:3, 17; 17:2, 3, 7, 8, 9^2, 10^3, 11, 14, 20, 29; 18:3, 13, 18^2, 20, 25, 27^2, 28, 29, 32^2; 19:9, 10, 11, 26, 27^2, 30, 42; 20:8, 11, 21; 21:1; 22:2, 3, 4, 31^3, 32^2, 33, 35, 48, 51; 23:5, 15, 17; 24:16, 21

1Ki 1:9, 25, 27, 41, 45; 2:3, 15^2, 22, 29, 38, 42, 44; 3:6, 8, 9, 22^4, 23^4, 27; 4:12^2, 13, 20, 29, 33; 5:4, 6; 6:1, 17, 38; 8:1, 2, 21, 23, 24, 35^2, 41, 43, 46, 60^2; 9:8, 15, 26; 11:7, 11, 33, 38; 12:24, 28, 32; 13:3, 26, 31; 14:2, 5, 10, 13, 15; 15:19; 17:3, 5, 24; 18:8, 10^2, 11, 14, 24, 27^4, 39^2, 41, 43; 19:4, 7; 20:3, 6, 28^2, 32^2; 21:2, 5, 14^2, 15, 18^3, 21; 22:3, 7, 8, 13, 16, 32

2Ki 1:3^2, 6^2, 8, 16^2; 2:14, 19^2; 3:11^2, 12, 18, 23; 4:1^2, 4, 6, 9, 13, 14^2, 23, 25, 26^4, 27, 31, 40; 5:3, 4, 6, 8, 15, 21, 22, 26; 6:1, 11, 12, 13^2, 19^2, 32, 33; 7:4, 9; 8:5^2, 7, 13; 9:8, 11, 12, 13, 17, 18, 19, 20, 22, 23, 27, 32, 34, 36, 37; 10:5, 15^3, 30, 33; 11:5; 12:4^2; 14:6; 18:10, 17, 19, 21, 22; 19:3^2, 9, 13, 21, 28, 30; 20:3, 10, 15, 17, 19^2; 22:4, 5, 13^4; 23:10, 17^2, 21; 25:4, 8

1Ch 1:27; 5:1; 6:10; 7:31; 11:4, 5, 11, 17; 12:17; 13:6^2, 11; 14:15; 16:14, 25^2, 32, 34, 40; 17:2^2, 16, 20^2, 21, 24; 19:13; 21:15, 17^2, 23, 24; 22:1^2, 5^2, 14, 16, 18^2, 19; 23:29^2; 27:6; 29:1^3, 5, 11^4, 12^2, 14, 15, 16

2Ch 1:10, 12; 2:4, 5^2, 6; 5:2, 9, 13; 6:11, 14, 15, 26^2, 32^2, 33, 36, 40; 7:3, 15, 21; 11:4; 12:6; 13:4, 6, 10, 12; 14:7, 11; 15:2; 16:3, 7, 9; 18:6, 7^2, 31; 19:2, 6, 7, 11; 20:2, 6^2, 9, 15, 34; 22:9; 23:4, 18; 25:4, 7, 9; 26:23; 28:11, 13^2, 22; 29:10; 30:9; 31:3, 10^2; 32:7, 8^2; 34:21^4; 35:12, 21; 36:23^2

Ezr 1:2, 3^4, 4, 5, 9; 2:68; 3:2, 4, 11; 4:11, 15, 19, 24; 5:2, 8^2, 15, 16^2, 17; 6:2, 5^2, 12, 18^2; 7:11, 14, 15, 16, 17, 23, 25, 27; 8:1, 22^2; 9:6, 7, 11, 13, 15; 10:2, 13^2, 23

Neh 1:3; 2:2^2, 19; 4:10^2, 14, 19; 5:5^2, 9, 14; 6:6, 7, 11; 8:9^2, 10^3, 11, 15; 9:5, 6, 10, 18, 33; 10:34, 36; 13:11, 17

Est 1:1, 19, 20; 2:7, 16; 3:7^3, 8^2, 11, 13; 4:11^2, 16; 5:3, 6^2, 7; 6:3, 4, 8; 7:2^2, 5^2, 6; 8:8, 9, 12; 9:1, 12^2, 24

Job 1:8, 10, 12, 16; 2:3, 6; 3:3, 19, 20^2, 23^2, 25^2; 4:5, 6, 19, 21; 5:4, 7, 13, 17, 27; 6:6^2, 11^2, 12^2, 13^2, 14, 16, 17, 26, 28, 29, 30; 7:1, 5^2, 7, 9, 17; 8:12, 16, 19; 9:2, 4, 19, 22, 24^2, 32, 33, 35; 10:1, 3, 7, 13, 22; 11:4, 6, 8, 9, 18; 12:4, 5^3, 10, 12, 13, 16, 24; 13:9, 19, 28; 14:1^2, 2, 7, 10, 17, 18; 15:9, 11, 14^2, 16, 20, 21, 22, 23^2, 31; 16:6, 8, 16^2, 17, 19^2; 17:1, 3, 7, 12, 13, 15, 16; 18:8, 10, 15, 21; 19:7, 17, 28, 29; 20:5, 7, 14^2, 23^2, 25, 26, 29; 21:4, 8, 9, 15, 16^2, 17, 21, 28, 30; 22:2, 3^2, 5, 12, 18, 20, 29, 30; 23:2^2, 8, 13, 14; 24:14, 17, 18^2, 22; 25:3, 4, 6^2; 26:2, 3, 6, 8, 14; 27:3^2, 8, 11, 13, 14, 19; 28:1, 2^2, 5, 7, 11, 12, 13, 14^2, 18, 20, 21, 28^2; 30:16, 18, 30, 31; 31:2, 3, 11^2, 12, 28, 35; 32:8, 19^2; 33:9, 12, 19, 21, 24; 34:4, 6, 7, 17, 18, 22, 31, 36; 35:2, 10, 14, 15; 36:4^2, 5^2, 14, 16, 18, 26; 37:1, 4, 10^2, 12, 16, 18, 21, 22, 23; 38:2, 14, 15, 19^2, 21, 24, 26^2, 30; 39:8, 11, 16^2, 20, 22, 24, 30; 40:11, 12, 16^2, 19; 41:9, 10^2, 11^2, 16, 22, 24, 33^2, 34; 42:3, 7^2, 8

Ps 1:1, 2; 2:12; 3:2, 8; 4:3; 5:9^3; 6:3, 5, 7; 7:2, 4, 8, 10, 11, 15; 8:1, 4, 9; 9:6, 15, 16^2; 10:4, 7^2, 16; 11:4^2; 12:4; 14:1^2, 3, 5, 6; 15:4; 16:3, 5, 8, 9, 11; 17:12, 13; 18:2, 3, 30^3, 31^2, 32, 34, 47; 19:3^2, 4, 5, 6^2, 7^2, 8, 9, 11^2; 21:5; 22:11^2, 14^2, 15, 28^2; 23:1; 24:1, 6, 8, 10^2; 25:8, 11, 12, 14; 26:3, 10^2; 27:1^2; 28:3, 7, 8^2; 29:3^2, 4^2; 30:5, 9; 31:9, 10, 19; 32:1^3, 2^2, 4, 6; 33:1, 4, 5, 12^2, 16^2, 17, 18, 20; 34:8^2, 9, 12, 16, 18, 20; 35:10^2; 36:1, 4, 5, 6, 7, 9; 37:13, 16, 26^2, 31, 33, 37, 39^2; 38:3^2, 7, 9^2, 10, 17, 20; 39:1, 4, 5^2, 7, 11; 40:4, 7, 8; 41:1; 42:3, 6, 10, 11; 43:5; 44:15, 17, 18, 25; 45:1^2, 2, 6^2, 11, 13^2; 46:1, 4, 5, 7^2, 11^2; 47:2^2, 5, 7, 9; 48:1, 2, 3, 10^2, 14; 49:8, 11, 12, 13, 16^2, 20^2; 50:6, 10, 12; 51:3; 52:7, 9, ttl; 53:1^2, 3^2; 54:4^2, 6; 55:4, 11, 15; 56:9; 57:4, 6, 7^2, 10; 58:4, 11^2; 59:9, 17; 60:7^4, 8, 11, 12; 61:2^2; 62:2^2, 5, 6^2, 7^2, 8; 63:1, 3; 64:6; 65:4, 9; 66:5, 10; 68:2, 5, 15, 16, 17, 20^2, 27, 34^2, 35; 69:2, 3, 13, 16; 71:11, 18, 19^2; 73:1, 4, 11, 25, 26, 28; 74:9^2, 12, 16^2; 75:1, 7, 8^3; 76:1^2, 2, 12; 77:8, 10, 13^2, 19; 79:10^2; 80:16^2; 83:8, 18; 84:5^2, 10, 11, 12; 85:9, 12; 86:8, 13; 87:1; 88:3; 89:7, 8, 10, 11, 13^2, 15, 18^2, 19, 34, 41, 47, 48; 90:4, 6, 9, 10^2, 11; 91:2, 9; 92:1, 7, 15^3; 93:1^3, 2, 4; 94:12, 22^2; 95:3, 4, 5, 7, 10; 96:4^2, 12; 97:11; 99:2^3, 3, 5, 9; 100:3^2, 5^2; 102:4, 13, ttl; 103:1, 5, 8, 11^2, 12, 16, 17; 104:13, 20, 24, 25, 26; 105:7; 106:1; 107:1, 26, 40, 43; 108:1, 4, 8^4, 9, 12, 13; 109:19, 21, 22, 27; 111:3, 4, 9, 10; 112:1, 4, 7, 8; 113:3, 4, 5; 115:2, 3, 8, 9, 10, 11; 116:5^2, 15; 117:2; 118:1, 6, 8, 9, 14^2, 15, 16, 22, 23^2, 24, 27, 29; 119:38, 50, 64, 70, 71, 72, 77, 89, 90, 96, 97, 105, 109, 118, 126, 140, 142^2, 144, 155, 160, 174; 120:5; 121:5^2; 122:3^2; 123:4; 124:7^2, 8; 125:2; 127:2, 3, 5; 128:1; 129:4; 130:4, 7^2; 131:1, 2^2; 132:14; 133:1, 2; 135:3^2, 5^2, 17, 18; 136:1; 138:5; 139:4, 6^2, 17; 140:3; 141:8; 143:4^2, 10; 144:3, 4, 8, 10, 11, 15^4; 145:3^2, 8, 9, 13, 17, 18; 146:3, 5^2, 6; 147:1^3, 5^2; 148:13^2

Prv 1:7, 17, 19; 2:7, 10; 3:13, 14, 15, 16, 18^2, 27^2, 32^2, 33; 4:7, 13, 16, 18, 19; 5:3, 4; 6:14, 23^2, 26, 30, 34; 7:11, 12, 19^2, 23, 27; 8:4, 7, 8, 11, 13, 14, 19, 34; 9:4, 10^2, 13^2, 16, 17; 10:1, 5^2, 7, 11, 13^3, 14, 15^2, 17, 18, 19, 20^2, 23, 25^2, 26, 29, 32; 11:1^2, 2, 8, 10, 11^2, 12, 13, 14^2, 15^2, 17, 22^2, 23^2, 24^3, 30^2; 12:1, 4^2, 8, 9^2, 11, 13, 15^2, 16, 18^2, 19, 20^2, 26, 27, 28^2; 13:5, 6, 7^2, 10, 12, 14, 15, 17, 19^2, 22, 23^3; 14:2, 3, 4^2, 6, 8^2, 9, 12, 13^2, 16, 17^2, 20, 21, 23, 24^2, 26, 27, 28^2, 29^3, 30, 32, 33^2, 34, 35^2; 15:4^2, 5, 6^2, 8^2, 9, 10, 13, 15, 16, 17^2, 18, 19^2, 21^2, 23, 24, 27, 29, 33^2; 16:1, 5^2, 6, 8, 10, 12^2, 14, 15^2, 16, 17, 19, 20, 22^2, 25, 27, 29, 31, 32^2, 33^2; 17:1, 3, 5, 8, 14, 16, 17, 24, 25, 26, 27, 28^2; 18:5, 7, 9^3, 10^2, 11, 12^2, 13, 17, 19, 24; 19:1^3, 2, 4, 6, 10, 11, 12^2, 13, 14, 18, 22^2, 26; 20:1^4, 2, 3, 5, 11, 14^3, 15, 16, 17, 18, 23, 25^2, 27, 28, 29^2; 21:1, 2, 3, 4, 5, 6, 8^2, 9, 11^3, 15, 19, 20, 24, 27, 30, 31^2; 22:1, 2, 6, 7, 13, 14^2, 15, 18, 22; 23:1, 5, 7^2, 11, 18, 22, 27^2, 31; 24:3^2, 5, 6, 7, 9^2, 10, 13^2, 23; 25:2^2, 3, 7, 11, 12, 13, 14, 15, 16, 18, 19, 20, 24, 25, 26, 27^2, 28^2; 26:1, 7, 8, 9, 12, 13^2, 16, 17, 19, 20^2, 21, 26; 27:3^2, 4^3, 5, 7, 8, 10^2, 13, 21; 28:3, 6^2, 7^2, 11, 12^2, 14, 15, 16, 18, 21, 24^2, 25, 26; 29:6, 9, 18^2, 20^2, 24, 27^3; 30:4^2, 5^2, 9, 11, 12^2, 13, 14, 15, 16^2, 20, 21, 22, 23^2, 28, 30, 31; 31:4^2, 6, 10, 14, 15, 18, 21, 22, 23, 26, 30^2

Ecc 1:2, 7, 8, 9^4, 10^2, 11, 14, 15^2, 17, 18; 2:1, 2, 15, 16^2, 17^3, 19, 21^3, 23, 24, 26^3; 3:1, 2, 12, 13, 15^3, 17, 19, 22^2; 4:3^2, 4^2, 6, 8, 8^6, 10, 12, 13, 14, 16^2; 5:2, 3, 5, 8, 9^2, 10, 11, 12, 13, 14, 16, 18^2, 19; 6:1^2, 2^2, 3, 7^2, 9^2, 10^4, 11, 12; 7:1, 2^2, 3^2, 4^2, 5, 6^2, 8^2, 10, 11^2, 12^3, 15^2, 18, 20, 24, 26; 8:1, 4^2, 6^2, 8^2, 9^2, 10, 11^2, 14^3, 16^2, 17; 9:1, 2^3, 3^4, 4^3, 5, 6^2, 9, 10, 11, 16^2, 18; 10:1, 2, 3^2, 5, 6, 10, 11, 13^2, 14, 16, 17, 19; 11:5^2, 7^2, 8; 12:4, 5, 8, 12^2, 13

Song 1:1, 2, 3, 13, 14, 16; 2:2, 3, 6, 9, 11^2, 12^2, 14^2, 16; 3:6, 7; 4:1, 2, 3, 4, 7, 10^2, 11, 12; 5:2^2, 9^2, 10, 11, 14, 15, 16^4; 6:1^2, 2, 3, 5, 6, 9^3, 10; 7:2^2, 4^2, 5^2, 7, 10; 8:5, 6^2, 12^2

Isa 1:5, 6, 7^2, 8, 11, 13^2, 21, 22; 2:7^4, 8, 12^2, 22^2; 3:7, 8^2, 14; 4:3^2; 5:7, 16, 25^3, 30; 6:3^2, 5, 7, 13; 7:2, 8^2, 9^2, 13, 18^2, 20, 22; 8:10, 20^2; 9:5, 6^2, 12^2, 15^2, 17^3, 19, 21^2; 10:4^2, 5, 7, 9^3, 28^2, 29^2, 31; 12:1, 2^3, 4, 5, 6; 13:6, 15^2, 22; 14:6, 7^2, 8, 9, 11^2, 16, 26^4, 27, 29; 15:1^2, 2, 6^2, 8; 16:4, 6, 9, 10, 12^2, 13; 17:1, 14^2; 18:1, 5^2; 19:11; 20:6; 21:2, 9^2; 22:5, 15, 25; 23:1^3, 3^2, 7^2, 10, 14; 24:5, 10^2, 11^3, 12^2, 13, 19^3; 25:4, 7, 9^2, 10; 26:3, 4, 7, 8, 11, 17, 19; 27:1, 4, 7, 9, 11; 28:1, 4^2, 8, 12^2, 14, 20, 27, 28, 29; 29:8^2, 11^4, 12^2, 13, 17, 20^2; 30:7, 9, 14, 18, 21, 27, 29, 33^3; 31:2, 3, 4, 9; 33:5, 6, 9^2, 17, 18^3, 22^3, 23; 34:1, 2, 6^2, 8; 36:4, 6, 7; 37:3^2, 4, 9, 13, 22, 29, 31; 38:3, 8, 12^2, 16, 22; 39:4^2, 6, 8; 40:2^2, 6^2, 7, 10, 16, 20, 22, 26, 27^2, 28^2; 41:7, 17, 24, 26^4; 42:8, 10, 19^3, 21, 22; 43:7, 9, 11, 13, 14; 44:3, 6, 8^2, 10, 12^2, 16, 19, 20, 28; 45:5^2, 6^2, 14^3, 18, 21^2, 22, 23; 46:9^2; 47:1, 4; 48:2, 4, 22; 49:4, 6, 7, 20; 50:1^3, 2^2, 4, 8^2, 9, 10; 51:5^2, 7, 13, 15, 18^2; 52:5^2, 6; 53:1, 2, 3, 7^2; 54:5^2, 9, 17^3; 55:2^2, 6; 56:1, 2; 57:1, 6, 10, 15^2, 19^2, 21; 58:5^2, 6, 7; 59:1, 5, 6, 8, 9, 11^2, 14^2, 21^2; 60:1^2; 61:1; 62:11; 63:1^2, 4^2, 11^2, 15, 16; 64:5, 7, 10, 11; 65:4, 6, 8^2; 66:1^4, 2, 3

Jer 1:13; 2:6, 8, 14^3, 19^2, 22, 25, 26^3, 34; 3:6, 23^2; 4:7^3, 8, 18^2, 20^2, 22, 31^2; 5:12, 13, 15^2, 16, 19, 27, 30; 6:6^2, 7^2, 10^2, 11, 13, 14, 16, 18, 25, 29; 7:10, 11^2, 14, 28^3, 30, 31; 8:5, 8^2, 9, 10, 11, 16, 18, 19^2, 20^2, 22^3; 9:6, 8, 12^3, 19, 21^2; 10:5, 6^2, 7, 8, 9^2, 10^2, 13, 14^4, 16^4, 19^3, 20^2, 22, 23^2; 11:5, 9, 15, 19; 12:8, 9, 11; 13:4, 10, 17, 20, 25; 14:2, 4, 17, 19^2; 15:9, 10, 14, 18; 16:10^2, 17, 19, 21; 17:1^2, 7^2, 9, 12, 15; 18:6, 12; 19:2; 20:11, 15; 21:12; 22:14, 28^3; 23:6, 9, 10^3, 15, 19, 28, 29, 33; 25:3, 13, 18, 29, 38; 26:11, 16; 28:6; 29:26, 28; 30:7^3, 12^2, 13, 15, 17, 21; 31:9, 17, 20^2, 35; 32:7^2, 8^4, 14^2, 17, 18, 24^2, 25, 27, 34, 43^2; 33:2, 5, 11, 12, 16; 34:8, 15; 36:7; 37:7, 14, 17^2; 38:5^2, 9^3, 14, 21; 40:3, 4; 41:17; 43:9, 13; 44:22, 23; 45:3; 46:7, 10, 17, 18^2, 20; 47:2, 5^2; 48:1^3, 4, 11, 15^2, 16, 17, 19, 20^3, 21, 25^2, 29, 32, 33, 38, 39, 41, 47; 49:3, 7^3, 10^2, 14, 19^3, 21, 23^2, 24, 25, 29; 50:2^3, 15, 17, 22, 23^2, 25, 27, 31, 34^2, 35, 36^2, 37^2, 38^2, 44^3, 46^2; 51:6, 8, 9^2, 11^2, 13, 16, 17^4, 19^4, 31, 33^2, 41^3, 42^2, 48, 55, 56^2, 57; 52:28

Lam 1:1^2, 3, 4, 6, 8, 9, 12^2, 14, 16, 17^2, 18, 20^2, 21, 22; 2:9, 11, 12, 13, 15, 16; 3:3, 18, 20, 22, 23, 24, 25, 26, 27, 30, 37, 47; 4:1^2, 3, 6, 8^3, 15, 18^2, 22; 5:1, 2, 4, 8, 15^2, 16, 17, 18

Ezk 1:28; 3:21; 4:14; 5:5; 6:12^3; 7:2, 3, 5, 6^3, 7^3, 10^2, 11, 12^2, 13^2, 14, 15^3, 19, 23^2; 8:17; 9:6, 9^2; 10:15, 20; 11:3^2, 7, 15, 23; 12:12, 19, 22, 27; 13:12^2, 15, 16; 15:2^2, 4^3, 5; 16:3, 7, 20, 30, 34^2, 44^2, 46^2; 17:12; 18:4, 5, 9, 10, 18, 19, 21, 25^2, 27, 29; 19:2, 10, 13, 14^2; 20:6, 15, 29^2; 21:9, 10^2, 11^2, 13, 14, 15^2, 16, 25, 26^2, 27, 28^2, 29; 22:18, 22, 24, 25; 23:4, 20^2, 22, 28, 37, 45; 24:6^2, 7, 13, 24, 27; 25:8; 26:2^3, 10, 15; 27:27, 32; 28:2, 3, 5; 29:3, 9; 30:3^2, 5, 12; 31:10, 18; 32:16, 20, 22, 23, 24, 25, 26, 29; 33:6, 14, 16, 17^2, 19, 20, 21, 24, 27, 30; 34:5, 12; 36:35; 37:11, 19; 38:8^3; 39:4, 8^3; 40:45^2, 46^2; 41:4, 22^2; 42:13, 15; 43:4, 12^2, 13; 44:3, 9, 22, 26, 31; 45:13, 14, 20; 46:11, 20; 47:16^2, 17, 18, 19, 20; 48:12, 14, 22, 29, 35

Dan 2:5, 8, 9, 10^2, 11^3, 15, 22, 28, 30, 36, 43, 45, 47^2; 3:4, 14, 15, 17, 25, 29; 4:3^2, 8, 9, 17, 18, 22^2, 24^3, 30, 31^2, 34^2, 37; 5:11^2, 14^2, 23, 25, 26, 28; 6:12, 13, 15, 20, 26; 7:14, 27, 28; 8:2, 21^3, 26; 9:11^2, 13^2, 14, 17, 18; 10:4, 14, 17, 21^2; 11:35, 36; 12:12

Hos 2:2; 4:1, 13, 17, 18; 5:1, 3^2, 4, 11; 6:3, 4, 8^2, 10^2; 7:7, 8, 11; 8:3, 5, 6, 8^2; 9:7^2, 8, 13, 15, 16^2; 10:1, 2, 5, 7, 10, 11^2, 12; 11:8, 12; 12:1, 5, 7, 11; 13:3, 4, 8, 9, 10, 12^2, 13; 14:4, 8, 9

Joel 1:5, 6, 9, 10^3, 11, 12^2, 13, 15, 16, 17^2; 2:1, 3, 4, 11^3, 13, 17; 3:13^3, 14

Am 2:11, 13^2, 15, 16; 3:5; 4:3, 13^2; 5:2^3, 8, 11, 13, 18^2, 27; 6:8, 10^2; 7:2, 5, 10, 13^2; 8:2; 9:5, 6^2, 9, 11

Oba 1, 3, 7, 15, 20

Jna 1:2, 7, 8^3, 12; 2:9; 3:8; 4:3, 8

Mic 1:2, 5^3, 9^3, 13; 2:1^2, 3, 7, 8, 10^2, 13; 3:1, 7, 11; 4:6, 9^2; 5:2; 6:8, 10, 12; 7:1^2, 2^2, 4^2, 10^2, 18

Nah 1:2^2, 3, 5, 6, 7, 11, 15; 2:1, 3, 8, 9, 10^2, 11; 3:1, 3^2, 7, 17, 18, 19^2

Hab 1:4, 13, 16; 2:3, 4^2, 5^2, 6, 13, 19^2, 20; 3:19

Zep 1:7, 14^2, 15; 2:5, 15^3; 3:1, 5, 6^2, 8, 15, 17

Hag 1:2, 4, 6, 9, 10^2; 2:3^2, 6, 8^2, 13, 14^4, 19

Zec 1:7, 11; 2:2[2], 13; 3:2; 4:1, 6; 5:2, 3, 5, 6[3], 7, 8; 6:12; 7:13; 8:23[2]; 9:9, 11, 17[2]; 10:5; 11:2[2], 3[3], 9, 16; 12:8, 10; 13:7, 9[4]; 14:4, 16

Mal 1:6[2], 7, 8[2], 10, 12[2], 13, 14; 2:1, 7, 11, 14, 17[2]; 3:2, 14[2]

Mt 1:16, 20[2], 23; 2:2[2], 5; 3:2, 3, 9, 10[2], 11, 12, 17; 4:4, 6, 7, 10, 13, 16, 17; 5:3, 10, 12, 13, 14, 16, 22, 29, 30, 32, 34, 35[2], 37, 45, 48[2]; 6:1, 6, 10, 13, 18, 21, 22, 23[2], 25, 30[2], 34; 7:3[2], 4, 6, 9, 11, 12, 13[2], 14[2], 19, 21; 8:27; 9:5, 15, 16[2], 18, 24, 37; 10:2, 7, 10, 11, 20, 24, 25, 26, 28, 32, 33, 37[2], 38; 11:6, 10[2], 11[2], 14, 16, 19, 30[2]; 12:2, 6, 8, 10, 12[2], 18, 23, 25, 26, 28, 30[2], 33, 41, 42, 43, 44, 45, 48, 50[2]; 13:11[2], 14, 15, 19, 20, 21, 22, 23, 24, 31, 32[3], 33, 37, 38, 39[2], 44, 45, 47, 52[3], 55[2], 57; 14:2[2], 4, 15[2], 26, 27; 15:5, 8, 17, 22, 26, 28; 16:2[2], 3, 7, 11, 17, 26; 17:4, 5, 12, 15; 18:1, 4, 8, 9, 10, 11, 12, 14[2], 19, 23; 19:3, 9, 10, 11, 12, 14, 17[2], 24, 26; 20:1[2], 4, 7, 14, 15[2], 23[2]; 21:9, 10, 11, 13, 20, 21, 38, 42[3]; 22:2, 8, 17, 20, 23, 32, 36, 38, 39, 42, 45; 23:8, 9[2], 10, 11, 15, 16[2], 17, 18[3], 19, 26, 38, 39; 24:6, 17, 18, 23, 26[2], 28, 32[2], 33, 45, 46, 50; 25:14, 25; 26:2[2], 8, 18, 22, 24[2], 25, 26, 28[2], 31, 38, 41[2], 45[2], 46, 48, 62, 66, 68; 27:4, 6[2], 17, 22, 33, 37, 46, 64; 28:6[2], 7, 15, 18

Mk 1:2, 15[2], 27[2]; 2:9, 16, 19, 21, 22, 24, 26, 28; 3:4, 17, 21, 29, 33, 35; 4:11, 15, 21, 22, 26, 29[2], 31[3], 32, 40, 41; 5:9[2], 35, 39, 41; 6:2[2], 3, 4, 15[2], 16[2], 18, 35[2], 50; 7:2, 6[2], 11[2], 15, 27, 29, 34; 8:16, 21; 9:5, 7, 12, 13[2], 21, 26, 31[2], 39, 40[2], 42, 43, 44, 45, 46, 47, 48, 50; 10:2, 14, 18[2], 24, 25, 27, 29, 40[2]; 11:9, 17, 21, 25, 26; 12:7, 10, 11, 14, 16, 18, 27, 28, 29[2], 30, 31[2], 32[2], 33, 35, 37; 13:11, 15, 16, 21[2], 28[2], 29, 33, 34; 14:8, 14, 19[2], 20, 21[2], 22, 24[2], 27, 34, 38[2], 41[3], 42, 44, 58, 60, 69; 15:22, 34, 42; 16:6[2], 16

Lk 1:13, 28, 36, 42, 43, 45, 49[2], 50, 61[2], 63; 2:4, 11[2], 15, 23, 24, 34, 49; 3:4, 8, 9[2], 13, 17; 4:4, 6, 8, 10, 12, 18, 21, 22, 24, 36; 5:21, 23, 34, 39; 6:2, 4, 5, 9, 20, 23, 35, 36, 40[2], 41[2], 42[3], 44, 45[2], 47, 48, 49; 7:16, 22, 23, 27[2], 28[3], 34, 35, 39[2], 47, 49; 8:10, 11[2], 17, 25[2], 26, 30, 46, 49, 52; 9:9, 19, 25, 33, 35, 38, 48, 50[2], 56, 62; 10:2, 7, 9, 11, 22[2], 26, 29, 42; 11:4, 6, 7, 8, 11, 17, 20, 23[2], 24, 26, 27, 29, 31, 32, 34[5], 35, 39, 40[2]; 12:1, 2, 6, 21[2], 23[2], 26, 28[2], 32, 34, 42, 43, 46, 48, 54, 56, 57; 13:18, 19, 21, 25, 35[2]; 14:3, 15, 22[2], 29, 32, 34, 35; 15:4, 10, 24[2], 27, 31, 32[2]; 16:2, 10[5], 12[2], 15[2], 16, 17, 18, 25, 26; 17:1, 7, 21, 30, 31, 37; 18:16, 19[2], 25, 29; 19:7, 9[2], 10, 20, 46[2]; 20:2, 14, 17[3], 22, 27, 33, 38, 41, 44; 21:9, 20, 30, 31, 37; 22:1, 11, 19[2], 20[2], 21, 22, 26[2], 27[2], 37, 38, 53, 59, 64; 23:2, 15, 33, 38; 24:6[2], 21, 29[2], 34, 39, 46

Jn 1:15, 18, 19, 27[2], 30[2], 33, 34, 38, 41, 42, 47; 2:4, 10; 3:4, 6[4], 8[2], 13, 18[2], 19[2], 29[2], 31[4], 33; 4:5, 9, 10, 11, 18, 20, 22, 23, 24, 25[2], 29, 34, 37, 42, 54; 5:2[2], 7, 10[2], 12, 24, 25[2], 27, 28, 30, 31, 32[2], 45; 6:1, 7, 9, 14, 20, 29, 31, 33, 39, 40, 42[2], 45, 46, 50, 51, 55[2], 58, 60, 63, 70; 7:4, 6[2], 8, 11, 12, 16, 18[2], 22, 25, 26, 27[2], 28, 36, 40, 41; 8:7, 13, 14, 16, 17[2], 19, 26, 29, 34, 39, 44[2], 47, 50, 52, 53, 54[3]; 9:4, 7, 8, 9[2], 11, 12, 16[2], 17, 19, 20, 21, 23, 24, 29, 30[2], 36, 37; 10:1, 2, 12, 13, 20, 29[2], 34, 38; 11:3, 4, 10, 14, 16, 28, 50; 12:13, 14, 19, 23, 27, 31, 34, 35, 50; 13:10[2], 16[2], 19, 25, 26, 31[2]; 14:21, 22, 24, 26, 28, 29; 15:1, 6[2], 8, 12, 20, 25, 26; 16:7, 8, 11, 13, 17, 18, 21[4], 32[2]; 17:1, 3, 12, 17; 18:31, 36[2], 37, 38; 19:13, 17, 30, 35, 40; 20:16, 31; 21:7, 14, 20, 22, 23, 24[2]

Act 1:7, 8, 11, 12, 19[2], 20; 2:15, 16, 25, 29[2], 34, 39; 3:2, 11, 16; 4:9, 11[2], 12[2], 16, 24, 36; 5:9, 17, 32; 6:2, 9; 7:33, 34, 37, 38, 40, 42, 49[3]; 8:10, 21, 26, 33, 36, 37; 9:5, 11, 15, 20, 21, 22, 36; 10:4, 5, 6, 14, 21, 28[2], 31, 32[2], 34, 35, 36, 42; 11:13; 12:15, 22; 13:8, 9, 11, 26, 33, 38, 40; 15:15, 16, 17, 19; 16:12; 17:3, 7, 19, 24, 25, 29; 19:4, 27, 28, 34, 35[2], 38; 20:10, 32, 35; 21:22, 28; 22:22, 25[2], 26; 23:5, 8, 19; 25:14, 16[2]; 26:14, 18; 27:8, 12, 16, 33, 34; 28:4, 22, 27, 28

Ro 1:8, 9, 12, 15, 16, 17[2], 18, 19, 25, 26, 27; 2:2, 11, 24[2], 25, 27, 28[4], 29[4]; 3:1, 4, 5, 8, 10[2], 11[2], 12, 13[2], 14, 18, 20, 21, 22[2], 24, 27[2], 28, 29[2], 30; 4:4, 5, 8, 14, 15[2], 16[4], 17; 5:5[2], 13[2], 14, 15[2], 16[2]; 6:6, 7[2], 21, 23[2]; 7:2[2], 3[2], 4, 7, 12, 13[2], 14, 16, 17, 18[3], 20, 21, 23; 8:1, 6[2], 7[2], 9, 10[2], 24[2], 27, 33, 34[4], 36, 39; 9:5, 8, 9, 13, 14, 16, 30, 33; 10:1, 4, 5, 6[2], 7, 8[2], 10, 12[2], 15, 20; 11:5, 6[4], 8, 11, 16, 23, 24, 25, 26, 27; 12:1, 2, 3, 6, 9[2], 19[2]; 13:1, 3, 4[3], 7, 9, 10, 11[2], 12[2]; 14:1, 2, 4, 11, 14[2], 17, 18, 20, 21[3], 22, 23[3]; 15:3, 9, 15, 21, 27; 16:1[2], 5[2], 19[2], 25, 26

1Co 1:2, 4, 9, 13, 18[2], 19, 20[3], 25[2], 30, 31; 2:9, 11, 12, 15[2]; 3:3, 5[2], 7, 10, 11[2], 13, 17, 19[2], 23; 4:2, 3, 4, 6, 17, 20; 5:1[3], 6, 7, 11; 6:5[2], 7, 13, 16[2], 17[2], 18, 19[2]; 7:1, 8, 9, 14[2], 15, 18[2], 19[2], 22[4], 24, 26[2], 29, 32, 33, 34[2], 35, 39[2], 40; 8:3, 4[2], 6, 7[2], 10; 9:3, 9, 10, 11, 16[2], 17, 18, 25; 10:7, 13[2], 16[2], 19[3], 25, 26, 27, 28[2], 29; 11:3[3], 5, 7[2], 8, 11, 12[2], 13, 14, 15[2], 20, 21[2], 24[2], 25; 12:3, 6, 7, 8, 12[2], 14, 15, 16; 13:4[2], 5, 10[3], 13; 14:5, 7, 9, 10, 14, 15, 17, 21, 24[2], 25, 26, 33, 34, 35; 15:12, 13, 14[2], 16, 17, 20, 26, 27[2], 36, 39[2], 40[2], 41, 42[3], 43[4], 44[4], 45, 46[3], 47[2], 48[2], 54[2], 55[2], 56[2], 58; 16:9, 15, 19

2Co 1:1, 6[3], 7, 12, 18, 21; 2:2[2], 3, 6, 16; 3:5, 11[2], 13, 14, 15[2], 17[3]; 4:3, 4, 13, 16, 17; 5:2, 5, 13[2], 17; 6:2[2], 11[2]; 7:4[2], 14, 15; 8:10, 12, 15, 18, 19, 20, 23; 9:1, 8, 9, 12; 10:6, 7[2], 10, 15[2], 18; 11:3, 10, 14, 15, 21, 29[2], 31; 12:1, 4, 9[2], 13; 13:1, 3[2], 5, 7

Gal 1:7, 11; 2:16, 17, 21; 3:10[2], 11[2], 12, 13[2], 16, 18, 20[2], 21, 25, 28[3]; 4:1, 2, 15, 18, 22, 24, 25[3], 26[3], 27, 29; 5:3[2], 4, 11, 14, 22, 23; 6:3, 6, 7, 14

Eph 1:14, 18, 19, 21[2], 23; 2:4, 8, 11, 14; 3:2, 5, 8, 9, 13, 15, 18, 20; 4:4, 6, 7, 9, 10, 15, 18, 21, 22, 24, 28, 29; 5:5, 9, 10, 12, 13, 17, 18, 23[3], 24, 32; 6:1, 2, 9[2], 17

Php 1:7, 8, 18, 21[2], 22, 23, 24, 28, 29; 2:9, 11, 13; 3:1[2], 6, 9[3], 19[3], 20, 21; 4:5

Col 1:5, 6[2], 7, 15, 17, 18[2], 23, 24[2], 25, 26, 27[2]; 2:10, 17; 3:3, 4, 5, 10, 11[2], 14, 18, 20, 25; 4:1, 7, 9, 11, 12, 15, 16

1Th 1:1, 8; 2:5, 13, 16, 19; 3:10; 4:3, 6; 5:15, 18, 21, 24

2Th 1:3, 5, 6; 2:2, 4[3], 9; 3:1, 3, 17

1Ti 1:1, 4, 5, 8, 9, 10, 14, 15, 20; 2:3, 5; 3:1, 13, 15, 16; 4:4, 5, 8[3], 9, 10, 14; 5:4, 5, 6, 8, 18; 6:3, 4, 5, 6, 7, 10, 15, 20

2Ti 1:1, 5, 6, 10, 12, 13; 2:1, 5, 9, 10, 11, 17, 18; 3:15, 16[2]; 4:6, 8, 10, 11[2]

Tit 1:1, 3, 13, 15[2]; 2:8; 3:8, 10, 11[2]

Phlm 6, 8, 12

Heb 1:8[2]; 2:6, 8, 11, 14, 18; 3:4[2], 13, 15; 4:7, 10, 12[2], 13[2], 14; 5:1, 2, 4, 13[2]; 6:4, 7, 8[3], 10, 16, 20; 7:2, 5, 6, 7, 8, 12, 14, 15, 16, 18, 25, 26, 28; 8:1[2], 3[2], 6, 10, 13; 9:2, 3, 11, 15, 16, 17[2], 20, 22, 24, 27; 10:3, 4, 7, 15, 16, 18[2], 20, 23, 25, 31; 11:1, 6[3], 7, 10, 12, 16[2], 27; 12:1, 2, 7, 13, 29; 13:4, 6, 9, 11, 15, 16, 17, 21, 23

Jas 1:6, 8, 9, 10, 11, 12[2], 13, 14[2], 15, 17[2], 21, 23, 26, 27; 2:10, 17, 19, 20, 24, 26[2]; 3:2, 5, 6[3], 7, 8, 13, 15, 16[2], 17[2], 18; 4:4[2], 12[2], 14[2], 16, 17; 5:3, 4, 11, 13[2], 14

1Pt 1:13, 15, 16, 24, 25[2]; 2:3, 6, 7[2], 15, 19, 20[2]; 3:4[2], 12, 13[2], 15, 17, 20, 22[2]; 4:5, 7, 12, 14[2], 17; 5:2, 12, 13

2Pt 1:4, 9, 17, 20; 2:17, 19[2], 20, 22[2]; 3:4, 8, 9[2], 15

1Jn 1:3, 5[3], 7, 8, 9, 10; 2:2, 4[2], 5, 7, 8[2], 9[2], 10, 11, 13, 14, 15, 16[3], 18[2], 21, 22[3], 25, 27[2], 29[2]; 3:2, 3, 4, 5, 7[2], 8, 9[2], 10, 11, 15, 20, 23; 4:2[2], 3[4], 4[3], 6, 7[2], 8, 10, 12, 15, 16, 17[2], 18[2], 20; 5:1[3], 3, 4[2], 5[2], 6[3], 9[2], 11[2], 14, 16[2], 17[2], 18[2], 20[4]

2Jn 6[2], 7[2], 11

3Jn 3, 11[3], 12

Jude 13, 24

Rev 1:3[2], 4[2], 5, 8[2], 9; 2:7, 8, 13; 3:7[2], 12; 4:8[2]; 5:2, 12, 13; 6:13, 14, 17; 7:17; 8:11; 9:11[2], 12, 13, 19; 10:8; 11:2[2], 8, 14, 18; 12:10[2], 12, 14; 13:4[2], 10, 18[3]; 14:7, 8[2], 10, 12, 15[2], 17; 15:1; 16:15, 17; 17:8[3], 9, 10[2], 11[3], 14, 18; 18:2[3], 8, 10, 17, 18, 19; 19:7, 8, 10, 13; 20:2, 5, 6, 8, 12, 14; 21:3, 6[2], 8, 16, 17, 23; 22:7, 10, 11[4], 12, 17

IT

Gen 1:4, 6, 7, 9, 10, 11, 12, 15, 18, 21, 24, 25, 28, 29, 30, 31; 2:3[2], 5[3], 10, 11, 13, 14, 15[2], 17, 18; 3:3[2], 6, 15, 17[2], 18, 19; 4:3, 8, 12, 14; 6:1, 6[2], 7, 12, 14, 15[3], 16[2], 21[2]; 7:4, 10, 17; 8:6, 13; 9:5, 13, 14, 16, 23; 10:9; 11:2, 9; 12:11, 12, 13, 14; 13:10, 15, 17[3]; 14:1; 15:6, 7, 8, 17[2]; 16:2, 6, 10, 14; 17:11; 18:6, 7[2], 8, 10, 11, 21, 28, 29, 30, 31, 32; 19:13, 17, 20[2], 29, 34; 20:13, 15; 21:12, 14[2], 16, 22, 26; 22:1, 6, 14[2], 20[2]; 23:8, 9[2], 11[2], 13[2]; 24:14, 15, 22, 30, 43, 52, 65; 25:11, 22; 26:8, 21, 22, 32, 33; 27:1, 4, 5, 10, 20[3], 25[2], 30, 31, 33, 40; 28:12[2], 13[2], 16, 18[2]; 29:2, 7[2], 10, 13, 19, 23, 25[2], 26; 30:15, 25, 28, 30[2], 33, 34, 35, 41; 31:2, 5, 10, 22, 29, 32, 35, 37, 39[2], 44, 45, 47[2], 48; 32:8, 18, 29; 33:11, 15, 20; 34:7, 21, 25; 35:8, 12, 17, 18, 22[2]; 37:5, 9, 10, 14, 21, 23, 24, 25, 26, 32[2], 33[2]; 38:1, 9[2], 13, 17, 18, 23, 24[2], 27, 28, 29; 39:5, 7, 10, 11, 13, 15, 18, 19, 22, 23; 40:1, 8, 10[2], 12, 14, 20; 41:1, 7, 8, 13[2], 15[2], 16, 21, 24, 31, 32[2], 42, 49; 42:6, 14, 27, 28, 35; 43:2, 11, 12[2], 21[2]; 44:5, 9, 10[2], 24, 31; 45:8, 12, 16, 28; 46:33; 47:18, 24, 26; 48:1, 14, 17[2], 19[2]; 49:4, 7[2], 15, 28; 50:9, 11, 20[2]

Ex 1:10, 16[2], 21; 2:3[2], 5, 6, 9[2], 11, 18, 20, 23; 3:21; 4:3[4], 4[3], 6, 7[2], 8, 9[2], 24, 25; 5:11, 19, 22; 6:8[2], 28; 7:9[2], 10; 8:10, 16, 17, 26; 9:8, 9, 10[2], 18, 24[2], 28; 10:10, 13; 11:6[2]; 12:2, 4, 5, 6[2], 7[2], 8, 9, 10[2], 11[3], 14[2], 22, 25, 26, 27, 29, 34, 39, 41[2], 42, 46, 47, 48, 51; 13:2, 5, 9, 11[2], 13, 14, 15, 16, 17; 14:2, 5, 12, 16, 20[3], 24, 27; 15:23; 16:5[2], 10, 13, 15[3], 16, 18, 19, 20[2], 21[2], 22, 24[2], 25, 26[2], 27, 31[2], 32, 33, 34; 17:6, 11, 12, 14, 15; 18:13, 18, 22[2]; 19:12, 13[3], 16, 18, 23; 20:8, 10, 11, 18, 25[3]; 21:26, 29, 31, 33, 34, 35, 36; 22:1[2], 4, 7, 9, 10[2], 11[2], 12, 13[2], 14[3], 15[4], 26, 27[2], 30[2], 31; 23:4, 11, 13, 15, 33; 24:6, 8, 10[2], 16; 25:2, 9, 11[3], 12[3], 15, 24, 25, 26, 32, 36, 37, 39; 26:6, 11, 13[2], 24[2], 31, 32; 27:2[2], 4, 5, 7, 8[3], 21[2]; 28:7[2], 8, 15[2], 16, 17, 25, 28, 32[5], 33, 35, 36, 37[3], 38[2], 43; 29:7, 12, 14, 16, 18[2], 20, 21, 22, 25, 26[2], 28[3], 34[2], 36[3], 37[2]; 30:1, 2, 3[2], 4[5], 6, 7, 8, 10[3], 16[2], 18, 21, 25[2], 32[5], 33[2], 35, 36[3], 37; 31:13, 14[2], 17; 32:4[2], 5[2], 8, 9, 13, 18[2], 19, 20[4], 24[3], 30; 33:1, 7[3], 8, 9, 16[2], 22; 34:9, 10, 12, 29; 35:5, 24; 36:2, 3, 6, 7, 13, 18, 35, 38; 37:1[3], 2[2], 3[4], 11, 13, 21, 22, 24, 25[4], 26[4], 27[3]; 38:1, 2[2], 4, 7, 8, 21, 30; 39:3[2], 4[3], 5, 9, 10, 18, 19, 20, 21, 23, 30, 31[2], 43[2]; 40:4, 9[2], 10, 11, 17, 19, 23, 29, 37, 38

Lev 1:3, 4, 6, 10, 11, 12, 13[3], 15[2], 16, 17[4]; 2:1, 2[2], 3, 4, 5, 6[2], 7, 8[2], 9[2], 10, 15[2], 16[2]; 3:1[3], 2, 4, 5[2], 6, 7, 8, 9, 10, 11[2], 12, 13[2], 15, 16, 17; 4:5, 8, 9, 10, 14, 17, 19, 20, 21, 24[2], 25, 26, 30, 31[2], 32, 33, 34, 35; 5:1[2], 2[2], 3[3], 4[3], 5, 8, 9, 10, 11[2], 12[4], 13, 16[2], 17, 18[2], 19; 6:3, 4, 5[3], 7, 9[2], 12[4], 13, 14, 15[3], 16[2], 17[3], 18[2], 20, 21[3], 22[3], 23, 25, 26[3], 27, 28[3], 29, 30; 7:1, 3, 4, 5, 6[2], 7, 9, 12, 14[2], 15[2], 16[2], 18[5], 19, 24, 25, 26, 27, 30; 8:7, 15[4], 16, 19, 21, 23[3], 28, 29[2], 30, 31[2]; 9:1, 9, 15[2], 16, 17; 10:3, 9, 12[2], 13[2], 15[2], 16, 17[2], 18[2], 19; 11:32[6], 33[2], 35, 37, 38, 40[2], 41; 12:7; 13:2, 3, 6, 8, 10, 11, 13, 15, 19, 20[3], 21[2], 22[2], 23, 25[4], 26[2], 27[2], 28[3], 30[3], 31[2], 32, 39, 42, 43, 47, 48, 49, 50, 51, 52[2], 54, 55[5], 56[2], 57[2], 58[2], 59[2]; 14:6, 9, 13, 14, 15, 25, 35[2], 36, 43, 44[2], 45, 46, 48, 53, 57[2]; 15:3, 23[2], 25; 16:12, 14, 15, 18[2], 19[3], 29, 31; 17:3, 4, 9[2], 11[2], 13, 14[3], 15; 18:8, 16, 17, 22, 23, 25, 28[2]; 19:5, 6[3], 7[3], 8, 23[2], 25; 20:14, 17, 21, 24[2]; 21:24; 22:7, 9[2], 11, 14[2], 20, 21, 23, 27[2], 28[2], 29, 30[2]; 23:3, 11, 14, 21[2], 27, 28, 29, 30, 31, 32, 36, 41[3]; 24:3[2], 7, 8, 9[3], 18, 19, 20, 21; 25:5, 10, 11[2], 12[2], 16, 21, 25, 26[2], 27, 28[3], 29[3], 30[3], 34, 50; 26:1, 16, 32, 34, 35[4], 37; 27:4, 5, 6, 7[2], 9, 10[3], 11, 12[4], 13, 14[4], 15[3], 17, 18, 19[3], 20, 21, 24, 26[3], 27[5], 30, 33[5]

Nu 1:50[2], 51[2]; 3:26; 4:5, 6, 9, 10[2], 11, 14[4], 15, 25; 5:7[2], 10, 13, 15[2], 17, 25, 26, 27; 6:9, 18; 7:1[3], 5, 10, 84, 88; 8:24; 9:3[3], 11[2], 12[3], 15, 16[2], 20, 21[2], 22[2]; 10:11, 29, 32[2], 35, 36; 11:1[2], 8[6], 9, 14, 17[2], 18, 20[2], 25[2], 31[3], 33; 12:2; 13:18, 19, 20, 23, 27[2], 30[2], 32[2]; 14:3, 7, 8, 11, 13, 14, 23, 24, 35, 41; 15:11, 19, 20, 24, 25[2], 26, 28, 34, 39[2]; 16:4, 7, 9, 13, 31, 42[2]; 17:5, 8; 18:10[3], 11, 13, 15, 19, 23, 26, 27, 29, 30[2], 31[2], 32[3]; 19:6, 9[2], 10, 12, 15, 18[2], 21, 22; 20:5, 8, 19; 21:8[3], 9[2], 14, 17, 18, 28; 22:34, 41; 23:19[2], 20, 22, 23, 27; 24:1, 8; 25:7, 13; 26:1; 27:11[2], 13; 28:6, 8, 24; 29:1, 11; 30:7[2], 8, 11, 13[2]; 31:23[3], 29[2], 54; 32:39[2], 42; 33:53, 55, 56; 34:5, 9, 12; 35:23, 25, 33[2]; 36:3

Dt 1:3, 17[2], 21, 24, 25[2], 36, 38, 39[2]; 2:16, 19, 24; 3:9, 11[2], 18, 26, 27; 4:2, 5, 14, 26[2], 32, 35, 38, 39, 40; 5:12, 14, 16, 23, 27[2], 29, 31, 33; 6:1, 3[2], 10, 18, 24, 25; 7:1, 12, 25[2], 26[4]; 8:9, 18[2], 19; 9:6, 11, 13, 21[4]; 10:15; 11:8, 10[2], 11, 12, 13, 29[2], 31; 12:1, 16, 24[2], 25[2], 28, 32[2]; 13:14, 15, 16[3]; 14:8[2], 10, 21[3], 24, 25, 28; 15:2[3], 3, 4, 9, 16, 17, 18, 20, 21[2], 22[2], 23; 16:3, 7; 17:4[3], 14, 18, 19; 18:3, 19[2], 22; 19:2, 13, 14; 20:2, 5[2], 6[2], 9, 10[2], 11[3], 12[2], 13, 19[2], 20; 21:1[2], 3, 7, 14, 16; 22:2[4], 7; 23:11, 13, 16, 20, 21[3], 22; 24:1[2], 3, 13, 15[3], 19[2], 20, 21[2]; 25:2, 6, 8, 9, 19[3]; 26:1[2], 2, 4, 10, 12; 27:2, 4, 15; 28:1, 15, 21, 24, 38, 63[2], 67[2], 68;

29:8, 19, 22, 23, 27, 28; **30:**1, 5, 11^2, 12^4, 13^4, 14, 16, 18; **31:**6, 7, 8, 9, 13, 19^2, 21^2, 22, 24, 26^2; **32:**19, 27, 47^3; **34:**4^2

Jos 1:1, 7, 11, 15; **2:**2, 5^2, 14, 19, 21; **3:**2, 3^2, 4^2, 13, 14; **4:**1, 7, 11, 18, 24; **5:**1, 8, 13; **6:**5, 8, 11, 15, 16, 17, 18, 20, 26; **7:**9, 11, 14, 15, 19, 21, 22^2; **8:**2, 5, 7, 8, 14^2, 18, 19, 24^2, 25, 28, 29, 31; **9:**1, 12^2, 16, 24, 25; **10:**1^2, 2, 4, 5, 11, 14^2, 17, 18, 20, 24, 27, 28, 30^3, 31^2, 32^2, 34^2, 35^2, 36, 37^3, 38, 39; **11:**1, 20, 23; **12:**6; **13:**6; **14:**7; **15:**3, 4, 16, 17, 18; **16:**6, 7; **17:**9, 10^2, 13, 18^3; **18:**4, 5, 8, 9, 20; **19:**14, 47^3; **21:**11, 43; **22:**12, 18, 22, 23, 24, 27, 28^2, 30, 34; **23:**1, 10, 15; **24:**4, 15, 17, 26, 27^2, 29, 32

Jdg 1:1, 8^2, 12, 13, 14, 17, 28; **2:**4, 18, 19, 22; **3:**16, 21, 27; **4:**20, 21; **6:**3, 5, 7, 11, 18, 19^2, 24^2, 25^2, 27^3, 28, 30, 31, 37, 38, 39, 40; **7:**4, 9^2, 13^3, 15, 17; **8:**27^2, 33; **9:**7, 25, 33, 42, 45, 47, 48^2, 50, 51, 52^2; **11:**4, 5, 23, 31^2, 35, 39^2; **12:**5, 6; **13:**16, 18, 19, 20^2; **14:**4, 11, 12^2, 13^2, 15^2, 16^3, 17; **15:**1, 15, 17; **16:**2^2, 4, 9, 14, 16, 25, 29; **17:**2, 3; **18:**2, 9, 10, 12, 19, 28^2; **19:**1, 5, 11, 26, 30^3; **20:**9, 28; **21:**4, 22

Ru 1:1, 13, 19; **2:**6, 11, 17, 18, 22; **3:**1, 4, 8, 12, 13, 14, 15^3; **4:**4^6, 5, 6^2, 7, 8, 16^2, 17

1Sa 1:12, 20; **2:**14, 16^2, 19, 24, 30, 36; **3:**2, 9, 11, 17, 18; **4:**3^2, 13, 18, 20; **5:**1, 2^2, 7, 9^2, 10, 11^2; **6:**2, 3^2, 8^3, 9^3, 13, 15, 16, 21; **7:**1, 2^2, 6, 7, 9, 12^2; **8:**1; **9:**20, 23, 24^4, 26; **10:**1^2, 5, 7, 9, 11, 12, 25^2; **11:**2, 7, 9, 11^2; **12:**3, 6, 15, 17, 22; **13:**3, 10, 22; **14:**1, 6, 14, 15, 19, 27, 39; **15:**11^2, 12, 27, 28; **16:**2, 6, 16, 23; **17:**25, 27, 35, 39, 48, 49, 51, 54; **18:**1, 4, 6, 10, 11, 19, 23, 26, 30; **19:**5, 13^2, 19, 21; **20:**2^2, 4, 7, 9^2, 12, 13^2, 16, 27, 33, 35; **21:**5, 6, 9^3; **22:**1, 15, 17, 22; **23:**6, 7, 13, 22, 23; **24:**1^2, 4, 5, 11, 16; **25:**11, 20, 27, 30, 37, 38; **26:**12^2, 17, 22; **27:**4; **28:**1, 14, 17, 24^2, 25; **29:**4; **30:**1^2, 3, 25^2; **31:**4, 8, 9

2Sa 1:1, 2^2, 18, 20^2; **2:**1, 23, 26^2; **3:**6, 18, 24, 26, 28, 29, 35, 36^2, 37; **4:**4, 12; **5:**9, 17, 24; **6:**3, 4, 6^2, 10, 12, 13, 17^2, 21; **7:**1, 4, 15, 25, 29^3; **8:**1; **10:**1, 3^2, 5, 7, 17; **11:**1, 2, 14^2, 16, 25; **12:**3^2, 4, 12, 15, 18, 21, 28^2, 29^2, 30; **13:**1, 2, 5^2, 8, 23, 30, 35, 36; **14:**15^2, 26^3, 30, 32; **15:**1, 2, 5, 7, 25, 32, 35^2; **16:**11, 12, 16; **17:**9^2, 13, 21, 27; **18:**3, 10, 18, 29; **19:**1, 6, 19, 25, 36; **20:**8^2, 15^2, 20^2, 22; **21:**1, 10, 11, 18; **22:**9, 48; **23:**5, 12, 16^3, 17^2; **24:**3, 12, 16^2, 24

1Ki 1:11, 18, 21, 27, 41, 48, 51; **2:**3, 15, 29, 37, 39, 41; **3:**6, 15, 18, 19, 20, 21^3, 26^3, 27; **5:**7; **6:**1, 7^3, 9, 14, 16, 17, 20, 21, 26, 38^2; **7:**3, 7, 23^2, 24^3, 25, 26^2, 27, 31^2; **8:**10, 15, 17, 18^2, 24^2, 54; **9:**1, 8, 10, 16^2, 28; **10:**6, 7, 18, 21; **11:**4, 11, 12^2, 15, 29, 30, 35, 38; **12:**2^2, 10, 20, 28; **13:**3, 4^2, 6, 9, 17, 20, 23, 24, 25, 26, 29^2, 31, 34^2; **14:**5, 6, 8, 10, 11, 25, 28; **15:**13, 21, 29; **16:**11, 18, 31^2; **17:**4, 7, 11, 12^2, 13, 17; **18:**1, 4, 6, 12, 13, 17, 23^3, 24, 25, 26, 27, 29, 33, 34^4, 36^2, 39, 44, 45; **19:**4, 10, 13^2, 14, 17; **20:**1, 6^3, 11, 12, 13, 26, 29, 33, 40; **21:**1, 2^6, 3, 6^2, 11, 15, 16^2, 18, 27; **22:**2, 3, 6, 12, 15, 32^2, 33^2, 43

2Ki 1:3, 6, 8, 16; **2:**1, 3, 5, 8, 9, 10^2, 11, 12, 20; **3:**5, 14, 15, 20, 25^3; **4:**6, 8^2, 10, 11, 18, 23^2, 25, 26^4, 27, 40, 41, 44; **5:**7, 8, 13, 16, 26; **6:**5, 6^2, 7^2, 13, 20, 24, 25, 30; **7:**2, 7, 8^2, 11, 13, 18, 19, 20; **8:**1, 3, 5, 7, 15^3; **9:**3, 12, 13, 15^2, 17, 18, 19, 22^2, 30; **10:**7, 9, 15^2, 19, 20, 25, 27; **11:**6, 18; **12:**5, 6, 7, 9^2, 10, 11, 12, 16, 17, 18; **13:**16, 17, 19, 21; **14:**5, 7, 22, 26; **15:**12, 16; **16:**8, 9^2, 10, 11, 14, 15, 17^2; **17:**5, 7, 25; **18:**1, 4^2, 9^2, 10, 16, 21^2, 25^2, 26; **19:**1^2, 4, 14^2, 25^3, 26, 32^2, 34, 35, 37; **20:**4, 7, 10, 11, 19; **21:**12, 13^2; **22:**3, 5^2, 8, 9, 10, 11; **23:**6^2, 15, 16, 17, 21, 35; **24:**2, 11, 20; **25:**1^3, 17, 24, 25, 27

1Ch 4:10; **6:**10, 55; **7:**23; **9:**32; **10:**4, 8, 13; **11:**7, 14, 18^4, 19^3; **12:**15, 17, 22; **13:**2^2, 3, 6, 13; **14:**8, 15; **15:**1, 3, 12, 13, 26, 29; **16:**1^2, 19, 30; **17:**1, 3, 11, 13, 24, 27^3; **18:**1; **19:**1, 8, 17; **20:**1^2, 2^3, 3, 4; **21:**2, 10, 15^2, 17^2, 22, 23^2, 24, 30; **22:**5, 7, 14; **23:**26; **26:**28; **27:**24; **28:**8, 10, 20; **29:**12

2Ch 1:4^2, 5, 6; **2:**4, 16^2; **3:**4^2, 8; **4:**2, 3^3, 4, 5^3, 15; **5:**9, 11, 13; **6:**7, 8^2, 11, 13^2, 15^2; **7:**20, 21, 22; **8:**1, 3, 16; **9:**5, 6, 17, 20; **10:**2^2, 10; **12:**1, 2; **13:**15; **14:**11; **15:**16^2; **16:**5^2; **18:**5, 11, 31^2, 32^2; **19:**7; **20:**1, 7, 25, 32; **21:**17, 19; **22:**8; **23:**17, 18^2; **24:**4, 5, 8, 11^3, 12, 13, 14, 22^2, 23; **25:**3, 4, 8, 14, 16, 20; **26:**2, 18^2; **28:**21; **29:**10, 16^3, 22; **30:**3, 5^2, 18; **31:**3, 21; **32:**5, 12, 30; **33:**14; **34:**4, 10^2, 11, 12, 16, 17, 18, 19, 32; **35:**3, 12; **36:**22

Ezr 1:1; **2:**68; **3:**2, 4; **4:**12, 13, 14, 19, 24; **5:**8, 16^2, 17^2; **6:**9, 12, 14, 18; **7:**10, 20, 21, 23, 24, 26; **9:**7, 11^2, 12, 15; **10:**3, 4, 9, 13

Neh 1:1, 4; **2:**1^2, 5^2, 6, 7, 10^2, 16, 19; **3:**1^3, 13, 14, 15^2; **4:**1, 7, 8, 12, 15^2, 16; **5:**5, 9; **6:**1, 3, 6^2, 7, 9, 16; **7:**1, 64; **8:**5, 15; **9:**8, 10, 23, 36, 37, 38^2; **10:**31, 34^2, 36; **11:**23; **13:**3, 8, 19

Est 1:1, 17, 19^3, 20, 22; **2:**8, 10, 22, 23^2; **3:**4, 8, 9^3, 10, 11, 12; **4:**4^2, 5^2, 8^2; **5:**1, 2, 3, 4, 6^2, 8; **6:**2, 9, 11; **7:**2^2, 3; **8:**2, 5^2, 8^2, 9, 10; **9:**1, 12^2, 13^2, 14, 17, 18, 27, 32

Job 1:5^2, 7, 19; **2:**2; **3:**3, 4^2, 5^3, 6^3, 8, 9^2, 10, 21^2; **4:**5^2, 16, 20; **5:**5, 21, 27^4; **6:**3, 9, 17, 28, 29^2; **7:**16; **8:**12^2, 15^3, 18; **9:**2, 7, 20, 22, 35; **10:**3, 16; **11:**8, 11, 14, 16; **12:**8, 14; **13:**1, 5, 9; **14:**7^2, 9, 21^2; **15:**18, 23, 32; **17:**15; **18:**2, 13, 14, 15^2; **19:**4; **20:**12, 13^3, 14, 18, 23, 25, 26; **21:**4, 19; **22:**3^2, 8, 19, 28, 30; **24:**23, 25; **25:**5; **26:**3, 9; **27:**6, 12, 14, 17^2; **28:**1, 5^3, 6^2, 8^2, 13, 14^2, 15, 16, 17^2, 19^2, 21, 27^4; **29:**11^2, 14, 24; **30:**18, 22; **31:**11, 12, 26, 36^2; **32:**19; **33:**14, 21, 27; **34:**9, 10, 18, 29, 31, 33^2; **35:**3, 13, 15^2; **36:**25^2, 30, 32, 33; **37:**3, 4, 12, 13, 20; **38:**5, 8^2, 9, 10, 13^2, 14, 18, 20, 21, 26, 29; **39:**12, 24; **40:**2, 24; **42:**7

Ps 6:7; **7:**2, 5, 12, 15; **10:**11, 13, 14^2; **17:**12; **18:**8, 32, 47; **19:**6; **21:**4; **22:**14, 30; **24:**2^2; **25:**11; **30:**9; **33:**9^2; **34:**14; **35:**9, 15, 21, 25; **37:**5, 10, 34; **38:**10; **39:**4, 9; **40:**3, 7, 14; **41:**6; **48:**5, 8, 13; **49:**8; **50:**3; **51:**16; **52:**9^2; **54:**6; **55:**10^2, 12^3, 13; **60:**2^2, 4, 12; **63:**9; **65:**9^3, 10; **68:**9, 11, 14^2, 16; **69:**18, 22, 35, 36; **73:**16, 28; **74:**11; **75:**3, 8; **78:**28; **80:**8, 9^3, 10, 13^2, 16^2; **81:**10; **84:**6; **86:**17; **87:**5; **89:**37, 39; **90:**4, 6^2, 10, 13, 17; **91:**7; **92:**1, 7; **93:**1; **94:**7, 15; **95:**5, 10; **96:**10; **99:**3; **100:**3; **101:**3; **103:**16^3; **104:**5, 6, 20, 32; **105:**12, 28; **106:**9, 32; **107:**42; **108:**13; **109:**17^2, 18, 19, 23, 27; **112:**10; **114:**3; **118:**8, 9, 23, 24; **119:**20, 33, 34, 71, 90, 97, 106, 126, 130, 140, 175; **124:**1, 2; **127:**1, 2; **128:**2; **129:**6; **132:**6^2, 11, 13, 14; **133:**1, 2; **135:**3; **136:**14; **137:**7^2; **139:**4, 6^2; **141:**5^2; **144:**10; **147:**1^2

Prv 2:21, 22; **3:**8, 14, 25, 27^3, 28; **4:**5, 15^3, 23; **6:**22^3, 32; **7:**23; **8:**11, 33; **9:**12; **10:**22^2, 23, 24; **11:**10, 11, 15, 19, 24, 26, 27; **12:**25^2; **13:**12, 19; **14:**1, 6; **15:**23; **16:**12, 14, 16, 19, 22, 26, 31; **17:**8^3, 14, 16, 21; **18:**5, 10, 13^2, 21; **19:**2, 11, 19, 23, 24; **20:**3, 5, 11, 14^2, 25; **21:**1, 9, 15, 19, 20, 27; **22:**6, 15, 18; **23:**23, 31^3, 32, 35^2; **24:**3, 12^3, 13, 14, 18^2, 23, 27, 31, 32^2; **25:**2, 7^2, 10, 16, 24, 27; **26:**15^2, 27, 28; **27:**14; **28:**8, 24; **29:**4, 7, 11, 24; **30:**15, 16, 17^2, 21; **31:**4^2, 15, 16, 24

Ecc 1:6, 8, 9, 10^2; **2:**2^2, 15^2, 18, 21, 24; **3:**10, 13, 14^4; **4:**8; **5:**4, 5, 6, 18^2; **6:**1, 2^2, 10^2; **7:**2^2, 5, 11, 12, 18, 23, 24; **8:**7, 8, 12, 13, 14^2, 17^4; **9:**10, 12, 13, 14^4, 15; **10:**8; **11:**1, 3, 7; **12:**7^2, 14^2

Song 3:4, 7, 10; **5:**2, 3; **6:**13; **8:**7^2, 13

Isa 1:6, 7^2, 13, 20, 21^2, 31; **2:**2^2; **3:**9, 10, 11, 24; **4:**3; **5:**2^5, 4^3, 5^2, 6^3, 14, 18, 19^2, 29^2; **6:**2, 7, 13^2; **7:**1^3, 2, 6^2, 7^2, 8, 11, 13, 18, 20, 21, 22, 23^2, 25; **8:**1, 10^2, 20, 21^2; **9:**7^2, 8, 18; **10:**7, 12, 13, 15^3, 17, 20, 26, 27, 30; **11:**10, 11, 15, 16; **13:**6, 9, 14, 17, 20^2; **14:**3, 9^2, 23^2, 24^2, 27^2, 32; **15:**5; **16:**2, 5, 12^2; **17:**1, 4, 5^2, 6, 10; **19:**1, 16^2, 17, 20, 21, 22; **20:**1; **21:**1, 3^2, 17; **22:**5, 7, 11, 14, 20, 25^2; **23:**1^2, 9, 13^2, 15, 17, 18; **24:**1^2, 2, 9, 13, 18, 20^2, 21; **25:**2, 8, 9; **26:**5^3, 6, 15, 18, 20; **27:**3^4, 8^2, 11, 12, 13; **28:**4^3, 15, 18, 19^4, 20^2, 28^3; **29:**2, 5, 8, 11, 16^2, 17; **30:**8^3, 14^2, 19, 21, 22, 23, 32^2, 33^3; **31:**5^2; **32:**19; **34:**1, 5, 6, 8, 10^3, 11^3, 13, 16^2, 17^2; **35:**2^2, 8^3, 9; **36:**1, 6^2, 7, 10^2, 11; **37:**1^2, 4, 9, 14^2, 26^3, 27, 33^2, 35, 38; **38:**8, 15, 17, 21; **40:**5^2, 7, 9, 19, 21, 22; **41:**4, 5, 7^3, 20, 23; **42:**5^2, 21, 25^3; **43:**9, 13, 19^2; **44:**7^2, 8, 12^2, 13^5, 14, 15^4, 17^3, 19^2, 23; **45:**8, 9, 12, 18^4, 21; **46:**6, 8, 11^4, 13; **47:**7, 10, 11^2, 14; **48:**5^3, 6, 11, 16, 20; **49:**6; **50:**1, 2; **51:**9, 10, 22, 23; **52:**6; **53:**3, 10; **54:**14; **55:**10^2, 11^4, 13; **56:**2^2, 6; **57:**1, 8, 11, 20; **58:**5^2, 7, 14; **59:**1^2, 11, 15^2, 16; **60:**22; **61:**11; **62:**9^4; **63:**5, 18; **65:**6, 8^2, 9, 24; **66:**18, 23

Jer 1:3, 12; **2:**19, 34; **3:**5, 7, 9, 16^4, 17; **4:**4, 9, 11, 18^2, 23, 28^3; **5:**1, 12, 13, 14, 15^2, 19, 20, 22^3, 31; **6:**10, 11, 19; **7:**11, 12, 20, 23, 29, 30, 31, 32; **8:**8, 16; **9:**8, 12; **10:**4^3, 5, 7, 18, 19, 23; **11:**5^2, 16^2, 18^2; **12:**8^2, 11^3, 15, 16; **13:**1^2, 2, 4, 5, 6, 7^2, 16^2, 17, 19^2, 27; **14:**5, 7; **15:**2, 8, 9, 11; **16:**10, 14; **17:**1, 9, 15, 21, 24, 27^2; **18:**4^2, 7, 9, 10^2; **19:**4, 5^2, 15; **20:**3, 4, 10; **21:**10^2, 12, 14^2; **22:**14, 15, 16, 17; **23:**18, 19, 20; **25:**12^2, 13, 15, 18, 28; **26:**8, 21; **27:**5^2, 8, 11; **28:**1, 10; **29:**7; **30:**3, 7^3, 8, 23, 24^2; **31:**10, 28, 33, 39, 40; **32:**3, 7, 8, 10, 23, 24^3, 28, 29, 31^2, 34, 35, 36, 43^2; **33:**2^2, 5, 6, 9^2; **34:**2, 22^3; **35:**11; **36:**1, 3, 7, 9, 15^2, 16, 21^2, 23^3, 28, 32; **37:**8^2, 11, 14; **38:**3, 15, 18, 20, 25; **39:**1, 4; **40:**3, 4^3, 5, 9, 15; **41:**1, 4^2, 6, 7, 9^2, 13; **42:**4^2, 6^3, 7, 16, 17, 20, 21; **43:**1; **44:**21; **46:**10, 20, 23, 26; **47:**6, 7^3; **48:**1, 2^2, 9, 20^2, 30^2, 39, 44; **49:**2, 12, 17, 18, 23, 27, 33, 39; **50:**13^2, 15, 21, 29, 32, 38, 39^2; **51:**11^2, 33, 62^3, 63^3; **52:**3, 4^3, 21^2, 22, 31

Lam 1:12, 13, 21; **2:**6, 16; **3:**22, 26, 27, 28, 37^2; **4:**4, 8^2, 11, 15; **5:**18

Ezk 1:1, 4, 13, 16, 26, 27^3, 28; **2:**10^2; **3:**3^2, 16; **4:**1^2, 2^5, 3^4, 4^2, 7, 10, 12^2; **5:**1, 2, 5, 13, 15^2, 17; **7:**6^2, 10, 19, 20^2, 21^2, 22^2; **8:**1, 17; **9:**8; **10:**1, 6, 7^2, 11, 13; **11:**3, 7^2, 13; **12:**3, 6^2, 7^2, 11, 13, 23, 25^2; **13:**7, 10, 11^3, 12^2, 13^2, 14^2, 15^2; **14:**13^3, 14, 15^2, 16, 17, 18, 19^2, 20, 21, 22, 23; **15:**3, 4^4, 5^5; **16:**14, 15, 16, 19^2, 23; **17:**4^2, 5^3, 6^2, 7, 8^4, 9^4, 10^5, 14^2, 19, 21, 22^2, 23^3, 24; **18:**4, 20; **19:**3^3; **20:**1, 9, 14, 22, 28, 42, 47, 48^2; **21:**5, 7^3, 10^4, 11^4, 12^2, 13^2, 14, 15^2, 17, 19, 23, 27^4, 28, 30, 32; **22:**3, 14^2, 20^2, 30; **23:**32, 34^3, 39, 41; **24:**3^2, 4^2, 5^3, 6^3, 7^3, 8^2, 10, 11^5, 14^3, 25, 26; **25:**3^2, 13^2, 15; **26:**1, 5^3, 14, 17; **28:**10, 18, 21; **29:**3, 9, 11^3, 15^2, 16, 17, 18, 19, 20; **30:**3, 6, 9, 12, 20, 21^3, 25; **31:**1; **32:**1, 15, 17; **33:**9, 13, 21, 33; **34:**18, 24; **35:**2, 3, 7, 10, 15^2; **36:**5, 10, 17, 18, 29, 32, 34, 36^2, 37; **37:**14^2, 16^2, 26; **38:**8, 10, 14, 16, 18; **39:**5, 8^2, 11^3, 13, 14, 15^2; **40:**22, 25, 26^2, 29^2, 31, 33, 34, 35, 36, 37, 49; **41:**15, 18, 19; **42:**15, 20^2; **43:**3, 11, 17, 18, 20^3, 21, 22, 23, 26, 27; **44:**1, 2^4, 3^2, 6, 7, 17, 24, 28, 31; **45:**3, 4, 6, 9, 17, 19; **46:**1^2, 6, 9, 13, 14, 16, 17^2, 23; **47:**5, 9, 10^2, 12, 14^2, 22^2, 23; **48:**8, 11, 14^2, 18, 19, 21, 35

Dan 1:1; **2:**7, 11^2, 40, 41, 44^2, 45, 47; **3:**1, 4, 14, 17, 18, 19; **4:**2, 12^3, 14, 15, 17^2, 21, 22, 23^2, 25, 27, 31, 32; **5:**21, 26; **6:**1, 5, 8, 17; **7:**4^2, 5^5, 6^2, 7^6, 23^2, 26; **8:**2, 8, 10^2, 12^2, 15, 22, 26, 27; **9:**13, 14, 27; **11:**12, 18, 27, 29, 35; **12:**6, 7

Hos 1:5, 10^3; **2:**7, 16, 21; **6:**4; **7:**4, 6, 9; **8:**4, 5, 6^3, 7^3, 13, 14; **9:**7; **10:**5^4, 6, 10, 12; **13:**2

Joel 1:3, 5, 7^2, 15; **2:**1, 2, 11, 28, 32; **3:**8, 18

Am 1:14; **2:**2, 5, 11; **3:**6; **4:**7^3; **5:**6^2, 13, 15, 18, 20; **6:**9; **7:**1, 2, 3, 4, 13^2; **8:**8^2, 9, 10, 12; **9:**4, 5^2, 6, 8, 11

Oba 15, 18

Jna 1:2, 3, 5, 13, 14; **2:**10; **3:**2, 7, 10; **4:**1, 3, 5, 6^2, 7^2, 8^2, 10

Mic 1:5, 7, 9, 10; **2:**1^2, 4, 10^2, 13; **3:**1, 6; **4:**1^3, 4, 8; **5:**10; **6:**9; **7:**3, 10

Nah 1:4; **3:**1, 7, 8, 9, 15

Hab 1:5, 10; **2:**2^2, 3^5, 11, 13, 18, 19^3

Zep 1:8, 10, 12, 14; **2:**3, 14; **3:**16, 18

Hag 1:4, 6, 8, 9^3; **2:**3^3, 6, 12, 13^2, 18

Zec 1:16, 21; **4:**2, 3, 7, 9; **5:**3^2, 4^4, 6, 8, 11^2; **7:**1, 13; **8:**6^2, 13, 20, 23; **9:**2, 5^2; **10:**7; **11:**9^2, 10, 11^2, 13; **12:**3^2, 9; **13:**2, 3, 4, 8, 9; **14:**4, 6, 7^3, 8^2, 10, 11, 13, 16, 17

Mal 1:8^3, 12, 13^2; **2:**2^2, 3, 13; **3:**10, 14^2, 16; **4:**1

Mt 1:22; **2:**5, 9, 15, 23; **3:**15^2; **4:**4, 6, 7, 10, 14; **5:**13^2, 15^2, 21, 27, 29^3, 30^3, 31, 33, 34, 35^2, 38, 43; **6:**10; **7:**2, 7^2, 8, 14, 25^2, 27^2, 28; **8:**9, 10, 13, 17; **9:**8, 10, 11, 16, 29, 30, 33; **10:**11, 12, 13^2, 15, 19, 20, 25, 39^2; **11:**1, 10, 12, 14, 16, 22, 23, 24, 26; **12:**2, 10, 11^3, 12, 13^2, 15, 17, 24, 32^2, 39, 41, 42, 44, 45; **13:**11^2, 19, 20, 23, 27, 32^2, 35, 40, 46, 48, 49, 53; **14:**4, 9, 11, 12, 13, 15, 26, 27, 28; **15:**5, 26^2, 28; **16:**2^2, 3, 4, 7, 11^2, 17, 18, 22, 25^2; **17:**4, 6, 20; **18:**6, 7, 8, 9^3, 13, 14, 17, 19; **19:**1, 3, 8, 9, 10, 11, 12^2, 24, 25; **20:**11, 15, 23^2, 24, 26; **21:**4, 13^2, 19^2, 20, 21, 25, 32, 33^3, 34, 42, 44^2; **22:**5, 17, 39; **23:**16, 18^2, 20, 21; **24:**23, 24, 26, 33; **25:**28, 40^2, 45^2; **26:**1, 7, 8, 10, 12, 22, 24^2, 25, 26^3, 27^2, 29, 31, 39, 42, 54, 61, 62; **27:**6^2, 24, 29, 35, 40, 48^2, 59, 60, 65; **28:**1, 2

Mk 1:2, 9, 45; **2:**1, 4, 9, 12, 15, 16, 17, 21, 23; **3:**4, 5, 21; **4:**4^2, 5^3, 6^3, 7^2, 11, 16, 19, 20, 22, 24, 30, 31^2, 32^3, 33, 37, 40; **5:**14^2, 16^2, 43; **6:**11, 15^2, 16, 18, 22, 23, 28^2, 29^2, 49, 50, 56; **7:**6, 11, 18, 19, 24, 27^2, 36; **8:**16, 17, 21, 26, 35^2, 36; **9:**5, 12, 13, 21, 22, 30, 33, 42, 43^2, 45^2, 47^2, 50; **10:**2, 14, 24, 25, 27, 40^2, 41, 43, 47; **11:**2, 13, 14^2, 17^2, 18, 30; **12:**1^2, 11, 14, 15, 16; **13:**11, 14, 22, 29; **14:**3, 5, 11, 19^2, 20, 21^2, 22, 23^2, 25, 27, 35, 41, 60, 70; **15:**2, 17, 23, 25, 29, 35, 36, 42, 45; **16:**4, 13, 18

Lk 1:3, 8, 23, 38, 41, 59; 2:1, 6, 15, 17, 18, 20, 23, 26, 43, 46, 49; 3:4, 21; 4:3, 4, 6, 8, 10, 12, 17, 20, 39, 42; 5:1, 8, 12, 17; 6:1, 4, 6, 9[2], 12, 13, 38[2], 48[2], 49; 7:8, 11, 27, 39; 8:1, 5[2], 6[3], 7[2], 10, 15, 16[3], 20, 21, 22, 29, 34, 36, 40, 50; 9:7, 11, 18, 24[2], 28, 33[2], 36, 37, 39, 45[2], 51, 57; 10:6[2], 12, 14, 21, 38; 11:1, 9[2], 10, 14[2], 25, 27, 28, 29, 32, 33, 38, 51; 12:10[2], 32, 49, 50, 54, 55, 56; 13:7[2], 8[3], 9[2], 18, 19[3], 21, 33; 14:1, 3, 18, 22, 28, 29[2], 34, 35[2]; 15:4, 5[2], 8, 9, 22, 23, 32; 16:2, 16, 17, 22; 17:1, 2, 6, 11, 14, 22, 26[2], 28, 29, 30, 31, 33[2]; 18:15, 25, 26, 35, 36, 43; 19:7, 15, 24, 29, 41, 46[2]; 20:1, 4, 7, 9, 13, 16, 18[2], 22, 24; 21:5, 13, 14, 21, 35; 22:16, 17, 19, 22, 23, 36, 38, 44, 64, 66; 23:3, 24, 26, 44, 53[3]; 24:4, 10, 15, 21, 24, 29, 30[2], 39, 43, 46[2], 51

Jn 1:5, 27, 32, 39; 2:5, 8, 9, 17, 19, 20; 3:8[3], 27; 4:6, 9, 10, 53; 5:10[2], 13, 15; 6:17, 20, 31, 39, 42, 45, 60, 61, 63, 65, 71; 7:7[2], 10, 17, 22, 51; 8:9, 17, 44, 54, 56; 9:4, 14, 27, 32, 37; 10:10, 17, 18[4], 22[2], 34; 11:2, 22, 38[2], 42, 50, 57; 12:14, 24[3], 25[2], 28[2], 29[2]; 13:19[2], 24, 25, 26[3], 30; 14:2, 8, 14, 17, 21, 22, 27, 29[2]; 15:2[2], 4, 7, 16, 18[2]; 16:7, 14, 15, 23; 17:26; 18:10, 11, 14, 18, 25, 28, 31, 34; 19:2, 11, 14, 19, 20, 24[3], 29[2], 30, 31, 35, 40; 20:1, 14, 27; 21:4, 6, 7[2], 8, 12

Act 1:7, 19, 20; 2:2, 3, 15, 17, 21, 24[2]; 3:10, 12, 17, 23; 4:3, 5, 10, 14, 16, 17, 19, 37[2]; 5:2[2], 4[4], 7, 9, 38, 39[2]; 6:2, 15; 7:5[2], 23, 31[2], 42, 44, 53; 9:5, 6, 18, 32, 37, 42, 43; 10:4, 11, 28, 42; 11:4, 5[2], 26, 30; 12:3, 9, 15[2], 18, 22; 13:17, 33, 38, 41, 46[2]; 14:1, 6; 15:5, 15, 16, 22, 25, 28, 34; 16:16, 35; 17:14; 18:14, 15[2]; 19:1, 19, 39; 20:16, 35; 21:1, 3, 20, 22, 35; 22:6, 10, 17, 22, 25; 23:5, 12, 30, 31; 24:3, 21; 25:16, 27; 26:8, 14; 27:1, 8, 14, 25[2], 28[2], 35, 39[2], 44; 28:8, 17, 19, 22, 28[2]

Ro 1:16, 17, 19; 2:24, 27; 3:4, 10, 19, 27, 30; 4:3, 10, 16[2], 17, 22, 23[2], 24; 5:16; 6:12; 7:11, 13, 16, 17[2], 20[2]; 8:3, 7, 25, 33, 34, 36; 9:12, 13, 16, 20, 26[2], 28, 32[2], 33; 10:8, 15; 11:6[3], 7, 8, 26, 35; 12:8, 18, 19; 13:9, 11; 14:6[2], 11, 14, 20, 21, 22; 15:3, 9, 21, 26, 27

1Co 1:11, 18, 19, 21, 31; 2:8, 9; 3:2, 13[3], 19; 4:2, 3, 7[2], 9, 12; 5:1; 6:5, 13; 7:1, 5, 8, 9, 21[2], 26, 29, 31; 8:7; 9:9, 10, 11, 15[2], 25, 27; 10:7, 13, 16[2], 28; 11:6, 13, 14, 15, 18, 24, 25; 12:6, 15, 16, 18, 26[2]; 13:3, 8; 14:7, 9, 10, 15, 21, 26, 27, 34, 35, 36; 15:11, 27, 32, 36, 37, 38[2], 42[2], 43[4], 44[2], 45; 16:4, 6, 15

2Co 1:6[2]; 2:10[2]; 3:16; 4:3, 13; 5:10, 13[2]; 7:8, 11, 12; 8:11, 12, 15; 9:1, 5, 9; 11:15, 17[2]; 12:1, 4, 8, 13[2], 16

Gal 1:12[2], 13, 15; 2:6; 3:4, 5, 6, 10, 11, 13, 15[2], 17, 18[2], 19[2]; 4:15, 18, 22, 27, 29

Eph 2:8; 3:5; 4:9, 29; 5:3, 12, 25, 26, 27[2], 29; 6:3

Php 1:6, 7, 20, 27, 29; 2:6, 13, 23, 25; 3:1, 21

Col 1:6[3], 9, 19; 2:14[2], 15; 3:18, 23; 4:4, 16, 17

1Th 2:1, 13[2]; 3:1, 4; 4:10; 5:24

2Th 1:3, 6; 3:1

1Ti 1:8, 13; 4:4, 5; 5:16; 6:7

2Ti 2:11; 4:16

Phlm 14, 19[2]

Heb 2:10, 17; 3:13, 15, 17; 4:1, 2, 6[2], 7; 6:4, 7[2], 17, 18; 7:8, 11, 14, 15; 8:3; 9:5, 17, 23, 27; 10:4, 7, 31; 11:2, 4, 6, 18; 12:11, 13, 17, 20; 13:9, 17

Jas 1:2, 5, 11[2], 15[2]; 2:14, 16, 17, 23; 3:6[2], 8; 4:3, 14, 17[2]; 5:3, 7, 17[2]

1Pt 1:7, 11, 12, 16; 2:6, 13, 20[4]; 3:3, 4, 11, 17; 4:4, 11, 12, 17

2Pt 1:13; 2:13, 21[2], 22

1Jn 1:2; 2:18[2], 21, 27; 3:1, 2; 4:3[2]; 5:6, 16

2Jn 6

Jude 3

Rev 1:1, 11; 2:17; 3:8; 4:1; 5:6; 6:1, 11, 14; 7:2; 8:3, 5[2], 8, 10[2], 12; 9:4, 5, 6, 7, 9; 10:1, 9[4], 10[3]; 11:2[2], 6; 12:4; 13:3, 7, 18; 14:3, 19; 15:2; 16:3, 17; 18:21; 19:6, 10, 15; 20:11, 13; 21:6, 16, 18, 21, 22, 23[2], 24[2], 25, 26, 27; 22:2, 3, 9

ITSELF

Gen 1:11, 12

Lev 7:24; 17:15; 18:25; 22:8; 25:11

Dt 14:21

1Ki 7:34

Job 10:22

Ps 41:6; 68:8

Prv 18:2; 23:31; 27:16, 25

Isa 10:15[4]; 37:30; 55:2; 60:20

Jer 31:24

Ezk 1:4; 4:14; 17:14; 29:15; 44:31

Dan 7:5

Mt 6:34; 12:25[2]

Mk 3:24, 25

Lk 11:17

Jn 15:4; 20:7; 21:25

Ro 8:16, 21, 26; 14:14

1Co 11:14; 13:4, 5

2Co 10:5

Eph 4:16

Heb 9:24

3Jn 12

LET

Gen 1:3, 6[2], 9[2], 11, 14[2], 15, 20, 22, 24, 26[2]; 11:3, 4[2], 7; 13:8; 14:24; 18:4, 30, 32; 19:8, 20, 32, 34; 21:12, 16; 24:14[3], 17, 18, 44, 45, 46, 51, 55, 60; 26:28[2]; 27:29[2], 31; 30:26; 31:32, 35, 44[2]; 32:26[2]; 33:12[2], 14, 15[2]; 34:11, 21[3], 23; 35:3; 37:17, 20, 21, 27[2]; 38:16, 23, 24; 41:33, 34[2], 35[2]; 42:16, 19; 43:9; 44:9, 10, 18[2], 33[2]; 46:30; 47:4, 6, 25; 48:16[2]; 49:21; 50:5

Ex 1:10; 3:18, 19, 20; 4:18, 21, 23[2], 26; 5:1, 2[2], 3, 4, 7, 8, 9[2], 17; 6:1, 11; 7:14, 16; 8:1, 2, 8, 20, 21, 28, 29, 32; 9:1, 2, 7, 8, 13, 17, 28, 35; 10:3, 4, 7, 10[2], 20, 24[2], 27; 11:1[2], 2, 10; 12:4, 10, 48[2]; 13:15, 17; 14:5, 12, 25; 16:19, 29; 17:11; 18:22, 27; 19:10, 22, 24; 20:19; 21:8, 26, 27; 22:7, 13; 23:11, 13; 24:14; 25:8; 32:10, 22, 24, 26; 33:12; 34:3[2], 9; 35:5; 36:6

Lev 1:3; 4:3; 10:6; 14:7, 53; 16:10, 22, 26; 18:21; 19:19; 21:17; 24:14[2]; 25:27

Nu 5:8; 6:5; 8:7[2], 8; 9:2; 10:35[2]; 11:15, 31; 12:12, 14[2]; 13:30; 14:4[2], 17; 16:38; 20:17; 21:22, 27; 22:16; 23:10[2]; 27:16; 31:3; 32:5; 33:55; 36:6

Dt 2:27, 30; 3:25, 26; 9:14; 13:2[2], 6, 13; 15:12, 13; 18:16[2]; 20:3, 5, 6, 7, 8; 21:14; 22:7; 24:1; 25:7; 32:38; 33:6[2], 7, 8, 16, 24[3]

Jos 2:15, 18; 4:22; 6:6, 7; 7:3[2]; 8:22; 9:15, 20, 21[2]; 10:28, 30; 22:23, 26; 24:28

Jdg 1:25; 2:6; 5:31[2]; 6:31[2], 32, 39[4]; 7:3, 7; 9:15, 19, 20[2]; 10:14; 11:17, 19, 37[2]; 12:5; 13:8, 12, 13, 14[2], 15; 15:5; 16:30; 18:25; 19:6, 11, 13, 20, 25, 28; 20:32

Ru 2:2, 7, 9, 13, 15, 16; 3:13, 14; 4:12

1Sa 1:18; 2:3, 16; 3:18, 19; 4:3; 5:8, 11; 6:6; 9:5, 6, 9, 10, 19; 10:7; 11:14; 13:3; 14:1, 6, 36[3]; 16:16, 22; 17:8, 32; 18:2, 17[2]; 19:4, 12, 17; 20:3, 5, 11, 16, 29[2]; 21:2, 13; 22:3, 15; 24:19; 25:8, 24[2], 25, 26, 27, 41; 26:8, 11, 19[2], 20, 22, 24[2]; 27:5; 28:22; 29:4

2Sa 1:21[2]; 2:7, 14[2]; 3:29[2]; 5:24; 7:26[2], 29[2]; 10:12; 11:12, 25; 13:5, 6, 24, 25, 26, 27, 32, 33; 14:11, 12, 18, 24[2], 32[2]; 15:7, 14, 26; 16:9, 10, 11[2]; 17:1, 5; 18:19, 22, 23; 19:19, 30, 37[2]; 20:11; 21:6; 24:14[2], 17, 22

1Ki 1:2[4], 12, 31, 34, 51; 2:6, 7, 21; 3:26; 8:26, 57, 59, 61; 11:21, 22; 17:21; 18:23[2], 24, 36, 40; 19:2, 20; 20:11, 23, 31, 32, 42; 21:7; 22:8, 13, 17, 49

2Ki 1:10, 12, 13, 14; 2:9, 16; 4:10[2], 27; 5:8, 24; 6:2[2]; 7:4, 13[2]; 9:15, 17; 10:19, 25; 11:8, 15; 12:5[2]; 13:21; 14:8; 17:27[2]; 18:29, 30; 19:10; 20:10; 22:5[2]; 23:18[3]

1Ch 13:2, 3; 16:10, 31[3], 32[2]; 17:23, 24[2], 27; 19:13[2]; 21:13[2], 17, 23

2Ch 1:9; 2:15; 6:17, 40[2], 41[2]; 14:7, 11; 15:7; 16:1, 5; 18:7, 12, 16; 19:7; 20:10; 23:6, 14; 25:7, 17; 32:15; 36:23

Ezr 1:3, 4; 4:2; 5:15, 17[2]; 6:3[2], 4, 5, 7[2], 9, 11[3], 12; 7:23, 26; 10:3[2], 14[2]

Neh 1:6, 11; 2:3, 7, 17, 18; 4:5, 22; 5:10; 6:2, 7, 10[2]; 7:3[2]; 9:32

Est 1:19[3]; 2:2, 3[2], 4; 3:9; 5:4, 8, 12, 14; 6:5, 8, 9, 10; 7:3; 8:5; 9:13[2]

Job 3:3, 4[3], 5[3], 6[3], 7[2], 8, 9[3]; 6:9, 10, 29; 7:16, 19; 9:34[2]; 10:20; 11:14; 13:13[2], 21, 22; 15:31; 16:18; 21:2; 27:6, 7; 30:11; 31:6, 8[3], 10[2], 22, 40; 32:21[2]; 34:4[2], 34[2]; 40:2

Ps 2:3; 5:10, 11[3]; 6:10[2]; 7:5[2], 9; 9:19[2]; 10:2; 17:2[2]; 18:46; 19:13, 14; 20:9; 22:8; 25:2[2], 3[2], 20, 21; 31:1, 17[3], 18; 33:8[2], 22; 34:3; 35:4[2], 5[2], 6[2], 8[3], 19[2], 24, 25[2], 26[2], 27[3]; 36:11[2]; 40:11, 14[2], 15, 16[2]; 43:3[2]; 48:11[2]; 55:15[2]; 57:5, 11; 58:7[2], 8; 59:10, 12, 13, 14[2], 15; 66:7; 67:3[2], 4, 5[2]; 68:1[3], 2, 3[3]; 69:6[2], 14[2], 15[3], 22[2], 23, 24, 25[2], 27, 28, 29, 34; 70:2[2], 3, 4[3]; 71:1, 8, 13[2]; 72:19; 74:8, 21[2]; 76:11; 78:28; 79:8, 10, 11; 80:17; 83:4, 12, 17[2]; 85:8; 88:2; 90:13, 16, 17; 95:1[2], 2, 6[2]; 96:11[3], 12; 97:1[2]; 98:7, 8[2]; 99:1[2], 3; 102:1; 104:35[2]; 105:3, 20; 106:48; 107:2, 22, 32; 109:6, 7[2], 8[2], 9, 10[2], 11[2], 12[2], 13[2], 14[2], 15, 17[2], 18, 19, 20, 28[3], 29[2]; 118:2, 3, 4; 119:10, 41, 76, 77, 78, 79, 80, 116, 122, 133, 169, 170, 173, 175[2]; 122:1; 129:5, 6; 130:2, 7; 131:3; 132:9[2]; 137:5, 6; 140:9, 10[2], 11; 141:2, 4, 5[2], 10; 145:21; 148:5, 13; 149:2[2], 3[2], 5[2], 6; 150:6

Prv 1:11[2], 12, 14; 3:1, 3, 21; 4:4, 13, 21, 25[2], 26; 5:16, 17, 18, 19[2]; 6:25; 7:18[2], 25; 9:4, 16; 17:12; 19:18; 23:17, 26; 24:17; 27:2; 28:17; 31:7, 31

Ecc 5:2[2]; 9:8[2]; 11:8, 9; 12:13

Song 1:2; 2:14[2]; 3:4; 4:16; 7:11[2], 12[2]; 8:11

Isa 1:18; 2:3, 5; 3:6; 4:1; 5:19[2]; 7:6[2]; 8:13[2]; 16:4; 19:12[2]; 21:6; 22:13; 26:10; 27:5; 29:1; 34:1; 36:14, 15; 37:10; 38:21; 41:1[4], 22[2]; 42:11[3], 12; 43:9[4], 13, 26; 44:7, 11[2]; 45:8[4], 9, 13, 21; 47:13; 50:8[2], 10; 54:2; 55:2, 7[2]; 56:3[2]; 57:13; 58:6; 66:5

Jer 2:28; 4:5; 5:24; 6:4, 5[2]; 8:14[2]; 9:18, 20, 23[3], 24; 11:19[2], 20; 12:1; 14:17[2]; 15:1, 19; 17:15, 18[4]; 18:18[3], 21[3], 22, 23; 20:12, 14, 16[2]; 23:28[2]; 27:11, 18; 29:8; 31:6; 34:9, 10[2], 11, 14[2]; 35:11; 36:19; 37:20; 38:4, 6, 11, 24; 40:1, 5, 15; 42:2; 46:6, 9, 16; 48:2; 49:11; 50:5, 26, 27, 29, 33; 51:3, 9, 10, 50

Lam 1:22; 2:18[2]; 3:40, 41

Ezk 1:24, 25; 3:27[2]; 7:12; 9:5; 11:3; 13:20; 21:14; 24:5, 6, 10; 39:7; 43:9, 10; 44:6; 45:9

Dan 1:12, 13; 2:7; 4:14, 15[2], 16[3], 19, 23[2], 27; 5:10[2], 12, 17; 9:16; 10:19

Hos 2:2; 4:4, 15, 17; 6:1; 13:2

Joel 1:3; 2:1, 16, 17[2]; 3:9[2], 10, 12

Am 4:1; 5:24

Oba 1

Jna 1:7, 14; 3:7[2], 8[2]

Mic 1:2; 4:2, 11[2]; 6:1; 7:14

Hab 2:16, 20

Zep 3:16

Zec 3:5; 7:10; 8:9, 13, 17, 21; 11:9[3]

Mal 2:15

Mt 5:16, 31, 37, 40; 6:3; 7:4; 8:22; 10:13[2]; 11:15; 13:9, 30, 43; 15:4, 14; 16:24; 17:4; 18:17; 19:6, 12; 20:26, 27; 21:19, 33, 38[2], 41; 24:15, 16, 17, 18; 26:39, 46; 27:22, 23, 42, 43, 49[2]

Mk 1:24, 38; 2:4; 4:9, 23, 35; 7:10, 16, 27; 8:34; 9:5; 10:9; 11:6; 12:1, 7; 13:14[2], 15, 16; 14:6, 42; 15:32, 36[2]

Lk 2:15; 3:11[2]; 4:34; 5:4, 5, 19; 6:42; 8:8, 22; 9:23, 33, 44, 60, 61; 12:35; 13:8; 14:4, 35; 15:23; 16:29; 17:31[2]; 20:9, 14; 21:21[3]; 22:26, 36[2], 68; 23:22, 35

Act 1:20[3]; 2:29, 36; 3:13; 4:17, 21, 23; 5:38, 40; 9:25; 10:11; 11:5; 15:33, 36; 16:35, 36, 37; 17:9; 19:38; 23:9, 22; 24:20, 23; 25:5; 27:15, 30, 32; 28:18

Ro 1:13; 3:4, 8; 6:12; 11:9, 10; 12:6, 7, 8, 9; 13:1, 12[2], 13; 14:3[2], 5, 13, 16, 19; 15:2

1Co 1:31; 3:10, 18[2], 21; 4:1; 5:8; 7:2[2], 3, 9, 10, 11[2], 12, 13, 15, 17, 18[2], 20, 24, 36[2]; 10:8, 9, 12, 24; 11:6[2], 28[2], 34; 14:13, 26, 27[2], 28[2], 29[2], 30, 34, 35, 37, 38, 40; 15:32; 16:2, 11, 14, 22

2Co 7:1; 9:7; 10:7, 11, 17; 11:16, 33

Gal 1:8, 9; 5:25, 26; 6:4, 6, 9, 10, 17

Eph 4:26, 28[2], 29, 31; 5:3, 6, 24, 33

Php 1:27; 2:3[2], 5; 3:15, 16[2]; 4:5, 6

Col 2:16, 18; 3:15, 16; 4:6

1Th 5:6[2], 8

2Th 2:3, 7

1Ti 2:11; 3:10[2], 12; 4:12; 5:4, 9, 16[2], 17; 6:1, 2, 8

2Ti 2:19

Tit 2:15; 3:14

Phlm 20

Heb 1:6; 2:1; 4:1, 11, 14, 16; 6:1; 10:22, 23, 24; 12:1^2, 13, 28; 13:1, 5, 13, 15

Jas 1:4, 5, 6, 7, 9, 13, 19; 3:13; 4:9; 5:12, 13^2, 14^2, 20

1Pt 3:3, 4, 10, 11^2; 4:11^2, 15, 16^2, 19

1Jn 2:24; 3:7, 18; 4:7

Rev 2:7, 11, 17, 29; 3:6, 13, 22; 13:9, 18; 19:7; 22:11^4, 17^3

MAY

Gen 1:20; 3:2; 8:17; 9:16; 11:4, 7; 12:13; 16:2^2; 18:19; 19:5, 32, 34; 21:30; 23:4, 9; 24:14, 49, 56; 27:4^2, 7, 10^2, 19, 21, 25, 31; 29:21; 30:3, 25; 31:37; 32:5; 42:2, 16; 43:8, 14, 18; 44:21, 26; 46:34; 47:19; 49:1

Ex 2:7, 20; 3:18; 4:5, 23; 5:1, 9; 7:4, 16, 19^2; 8:1, 8^2, 9, 16, 20, 28, 29; 9:1, 13, 15, 16, 22; 10:2, 3, 7, 12, 17, 21^2, 25; 11:7, 9; 12:16; 13:9; 14:4, 12, 26; 16:4, 32; 17:2, 6; 19:9; 20:12, 20; 21:14; 23:11, 12^2; 25:8, 14, 28, 37; 26:5, 11; 27:5; 28:1, 3^2, 4, 28, 37, 38^2, 41; 29:46; 30:16, 29, 30; 31:6, 13, 15; 32:10^2, 29; 33:5, 13^2; 35:34; 40:13, 15

Lev 7:24, 30; 10:10, 11; 11:21, 22, 34^2, 39, 47^2; 14:8; 16:13, 30; 17:5^2, 13; 19:25; 21:3; 22:5^2, 12; 23:21, 43; 24:7; 25:27, 29^2, 31, 32, 34, 35, 36, 48^2, 49^3

Nu 3:6; 4:19; 6:20; 7:5; 8:11; 9:7; 10:10; 11:13, 16, 21; 13:2; 15:39, 40; 16:21, 45; 18:2; 19:3; 22:6^2, 19; 25:4; 27:17^4, 20; 30:13^2; 31:23; 32:32; 35:6, 11, 15, 17, 18, 23; 36:8

Dt 2:6^2, 28^2; 4:1, 2, 10^2, 40; 5:1, 14, 16^2, 31, 33^3; 6:2, 3^2, 18; 7:4; 8:1, 18; 9:5, 14; 10:11; 11:8, 9, 18, 21; 12:15, 25, 28; 13:17; 14:10, 20, 21, 29; 17:19, 20; 19:3, 4, 12, 13; 21:16; 22:7, 19, 29; 23:20; 24:2, 4, 13, 19; 25:1, 3, 15; 26:12; 29:9, 13^2, 29; 30:12, 13, 19; 31:5, 12^2, 13, 14, 19, 26, 28

Jos 2:16; 3:4, 7; 4:6; 9:19; 10:4; 18:6, 8; 20:3, 4; 22:27^2, 28

Jdg 1:3; 2:22; 6:30; 9:7; 11:6, 37; 13:14, 17; 14:13, 15; 15:12; 16:5^2, 25, 26^2, 28; 17:9; 18:5, 9; 19:9, 22; 20:10, 13; 21:18

Ru 1:9, 11; 2:16; 3:1; 4:4, 14

1Sa 1:22; 2:36; 4:3; 6:8; 8:20^2; 9:16, 26, 27; 11:2, 3, 12; 12:7, 17; 14:6, 24; 15:25, 30; 17:10, 46; 18:21^2; 19:15; 20:5; 27:5; 28:7; 29:4, 8; 30:22

2Sa 3:21; 7:10, 29; 9:1, 3, 10; 11:15; 12:22; 13:5, 6, 10; 14:7, 15, 32; 15:20; 16:2, 4, 11, 12; 18:14; 19:26, 37; 20:16; 21:3; 24:2, 3, 12, 21

1Ki 1:2, 35; 2:4; 3:9; 8:29, 40, 43^2, 50, 52, 58, 60; 11:21, 36; 12:6, 9; 13:6, 16, 18; 15:19; 17:10, 12^2; 18:5, 37; 20:9; 21:2, 10; 22:8, 20

2Ki 3:11, 17; 4:22, 41, 42, 43; 5:12; 6:2, 13, 17, 20, 22, 28, 29; 7:9; 9:7; 18:27, 32; 19:4, 19; 22:4

1Ch 4:10; 13:2; 15:12; 16:35; 17:24, 27; 21:2, 10, 22^2; 23:25; 28:8

2Ch 1:10; 6:20, 31, 33^2; 7:16; 10:9; 12:8; 13:9; 16:3; 18:7, 19; 28:23; 29:10; 30:8; 35:6

Ezr 4:15; 6:10; 7:25; 9:8, 12

Neh 2:5, 7, 8; 4:22; 5:2

Est 2:3; 3:9; 4:11; 5:5, 14; 6:9; 8:8

Job 1:5; 5:11; 10:20; 13:13; 14:6; 19:29; 21:3; 22:2; 27:17; 31:6; 32:20; 33:17; 34:22, 36; 35:8^2; 36:25^2; 37:7, 12; 38:34, 35; 39:15^2

Ps 9:14, 20; 10:10, 18; 11:2; 22:17; 26:7; 27:4; 30:5, 12; 34:12; 39:4, 13; 41:10; 48:13; 50:4; 51:8; 56:13; 58:8; 59:13; 60:4, 5; 61:7, 8; 64:4; 65:4; 67:2; 68:23; 69:35; 71:3; 73:28; 76:7; 83:4, 16, 18; 84:3; 85:6, 9; 86:17; 90:12, 14; 101:6, 8; 104:9, 14; 106:5^3; 107:36, 37; 108:6; 109:15, 27; 111:6; 113:8; 119:17, 18, 73, 77, 116, 125; 124:1; 129:1; 142:7; 144:12^2, 13^2, 14

Prv 5:2; 7:5; 8:11, 21; 15:24; 18:2; 20:21; 22:19; 27:1, 11

Ecc 1:10; 2:26; 5:15; 6:10; 8:4

Song 4:16; 6:1, 13

Isa 5:8, 11, 19^2; 7:15; 10:2^2, 19; 13:2; 19:15; 24:10; 26:2; 27:5; 28:12, 21; 30:1, 8, 18^2; 36:12; 37:4, 20; 41:20, 22, 23^2, 26^2; 42:18; 43:9, 10; 44:9, 13; 45:6; 46:5; 49:15, 20; 51:14, 16, 23; 55:6, 10; 60:11^2, 21; 64:2; 65:8; 66:11^2

Jer 6:10; 7:18, 23; 9:12^2, 17^2, 18; 10:18; 11:5, 19; 13:23, 26; 16:12; 21:2; 26:3; 28:14; 29:6^2; 32:14, 39; 33:21; 35:7; 36:3^3, 7; 42:3^3, 6, 12; 44:29; 46:10; 48:9; 49:19; 50:34, 44; 51:8, 39

Lam 2:13; 3:29

Ezk 4:17; 6:6^4, 8; 11:20; 12:3, 16, 19; 14:5, 11^3, 15; 16:33, 37; 20:20; 21:5, 10, 11, 15, 19, 20, 23; 22:3; 23:48; 24:11^4; 25:10; 28:17; 34:10; 37:9; 38:16; 39:12, 17; 43:10, 11; 44:25, 30; 45:11

Dan 4:17, 27; 6:15

Hos 8:4; 13:10

Am 5:14, 15; 6:10; 8:5^2, 6; 9:1, 12

Oba 9

Jna 1:7, 11

Mic 6:5; 7:3

Hab 2:2, 9^2

Zep 2:3; 3:8, 9

Zec 11:1

Mal 3:2, 3, 10

Mt 2:8; 5:16, 45; 6:2, 4, 5, 16; 9:6, 21; 14:15; 18:16; 19:16; 20:21, 33; 23:26, 35; 26:42

Mk 1:38; 2:10; 4:12^2, 32; 5:12, 23, 28; 6:36; 7:9; 10:17, 37; 11:25; 12:15; 14:7; 15:32

Lk 2:35; 5:24; 8:16; 9:12; 11:33, 50; 12:36; 14:10, 23; 16:4, 9, 24, 28; 17:8; 18:41; 20:13, 14; 21:22, 36; 22:8, 30, 31

Jn 1:22; 3:21; 4:36; 5:20; 6:5, 7, 30, 40, 50; 7:3; 10:38; 11:11, 15, 16, 42; 12:36; 13:18, 19; 14:3, 13, 16, 31; 15:2, 16; 16:4, 24; 17:1, 11, 21^3, 22, 23^2, 24, 26; 19:4

Act 1:25; 3:19; 4:29, 30; 6:3; 8:19, 20, 22; 17:19; 19:40; 21:24^2, 37; 23:24; 25:11; 26:18

Ro 1:11^2, 12, 19; 3:8, 19^2; 6:1; 8:17; 11:10, 14, 31; 12:2; 14:2, 19; 15:6, 13, 17, 31^2, 32^2

1Co 1:8; 2:16; 3:18; 5:5, 7; 7:5, 32, 33, 34^2, 35^2; 9:18, 24; 10:13, 33; 11:19; 14:1, 5, 10, 12, 13, 31^3; 15:28, 37; 16:6^2, 10, 11

2Co 1:4, 11; 2:5; 4:7; 5:9, 10, 12; 8:11, 14^3; 9:3, 8; 10:2, 9; 11:2, 12^2, 16; 12:9

Gal 6:13

Eph 1:17, 18; 3:4, 17, 18; 4:15, 28, 29; 6:3, 11, 13, 19^2, 20, 21

Php 1:9, 10^2, 26, 27; 2:15, 16, 19, 28^2; 3:8, 10, 12, 21; 4:17

Col 1:28; 4:4, 6, 12

1Th 3:13; 4:12^2

2Th 1:5, 12; 3:1, 2, 14

1Ti 1:20; 2:2; 4:15; 5:7, 16, 20; 6:19

2Ti 1:4, 18; 2:4, 10, 26; 3:17; 4:16

Tit 1:9, 13; 2:4, 8, 10

Phlm 6

Heb 4:16; 5:1; 7:9; 10:9; 12:27, 28; 13:6, 17, 19

Jas 1:4; 2:18; 3:3; 4:3; 5:16

1Pt 2:2, 12, 15; 3:1, 16; 4:3, 11, 13; 5:6, 8

2Pt 1:15; 3:2, 14

1Jn 1:3, 4; 2:28; 4:17; 5:13^2, 20

2Jn 12

Rev 2:10; 14:13; 19:18; 22:14^2

MAYEST

Gen 2:16; 23:6; 28:3, 4; 38:16

Ex 3:10; 8:10, 22; 9:14, 29; 10:2; 18:19; 24:12; 26:33

Lev 22:23

Nu 10:2, 31; 23:13, 27

Dt 2:31; 4:40; 6:18; 7:22; 8:9; 11:14, 15; 12:15, 17, 20, 23; 14:21, 23; 15:3; 16:3, 5, 20; 17:15; 20:19; 22:3, 7; 23:20, 24, 25; 26:19; 27:3; 28:58; 30:6, 14, 16, 20^4

Jos 1:7^2, 8

Jdg 9:33; 11:8; 19:9

1Sa 20:13; 24:4; 28:15, 22

2Sa 3:21; 15:34; 22:28

1Ki 1:12; 2:3, 31; 8:29

2Ki 5:6; 8:10

1Ch 22:12, 14

2Ch 1:11; 18:33

Ezr 7:17

Neh 1:6; 6:6

Job 40:8

Ps 32:6; 45:16; 94:13; 104:27; 130:4

Prv 2:20; 5:2; 19:20

Isa 23:16; 43:26; 45:3; 47:12; 49:6, 9

Jer 4:14; 6:27; 30:13

Ezk 16:54^2, 63

Hab 2:15

Mk 14:12

Lk 12:58; 16:2

Act 8:37; 24:8, 11

1Co 7:21

Eph 6:3

1Ti 3:15

3Jn 2

Rev 3:18^3

ME

Gen 3:12^2, 13; 4:10, 14^3, 25; 6:7, 13; 7:1; 9:12, 13, 15, 17; 12:12, 13, 18^2, 19; 13:8, 9; 14:21, 24; 15:2, 3, 9; 16:2, 5, 13^2; 17:1, 2, 4, 7, 10, 11; 18:21, 27, 31; 19:8, 19^2, 20; 20:5, 6, 9^2, 11, 13^3; 21:6^2, 16, 23^3, 26, 30; 22:12; 23:4, 8^2, 9^2, 11, 13^2, 15^2; 24:5, 7^3, 12, 17, 23, 27, 30, 37, 39, 40, 43, 44, 45, 48, 49^2, 54, 56^2; 25:30, 31, 32, 33; 26:7, 27^3; 27:3, 4^2, 7^2, 9, 12^2, 13^2, 19^2, 20, 25, 26, 31, 33, 34^2, 36^2, 38^2, 46; 28:20^3, 22; 29:15^2, 19, 21, 25^2, 27, 32, 33, 34; 30:1, 6^2, 13, 14, 16, 18, 20^2, 24, 25, 26^2, 27, 28, 29, 31^2, 33^2; 31:5^2, 7^2, 9, 11, 13, 26, 27^2, 28, 29, 31, 32, 35, 36, 40, 42^2, 44, 48, 49, 50, 51, 52; 32:9, 11^2, 16, 20^2, 26^2, 29; 33:10, 11, 13, 14, 15^3; 34:4, 11^2, 12^3, 30^4; 35:3^2; 37:9, 14, 16; 38:16^3, 17; 39:7, 8, 9, 12, 14^2, 15, 17^2, 18, 19; 40:8, 9, 14^4, 15; 41:10^2, 13, 16, 24, 51, 52; 42:20, 33, 34, 36^2; 43:6, 8, 9, 16, 29; 44:21, 27, 28, 29, 34; 45:1, 4, 5^2, 7, 8^2, 9^2, 10, 18; 46:30, 31; 47:29^2, 30^2, 31; 48:3^2, 4, 7^2, 9^2, 11, 15, 16; 49:29; 50:5^4, 20

Ex 2:9, 14; 3:9, 13^2, 14, 15, 16; 4:1, 18, 23, 25; 5:1, 22; 6:7, 12^2, 30; 7:16^2; 8:1, 8, 9, 20, 28; 9:1, 13, 14; 10:3^2, 17, 28; 11:8^2; 12:32; 13:2, 8; 14:15, 17, 18; 17:2, 4; 18:4, 15, 16; 19:5, 6; 20:3, 5, 6, 23, 24, 25; 22:23, 27, 29, 30, 31; 23:14, 15, 33; 24:12; 25:2, 8, 30; 28:1, 3, 4, 41; 29:1, 44; 30:30, 31; 31:13, 17; 32:2, 10, 23, 24, 26, 32, 33; 33:12^3, 13, 15, 18, 20, 21; 34:2, 20; 40:13, 15

Lev 10:3, 19; 14:35; 20:26; 22:2; 25:23, 55; 26:14, 18, 21^2, 23^2, 27^2, 40^2

Nu 3:13, 41; 8:16^2; 11:11, 12, 13, 14, 15^3, 16; 14:11^2, 22, 23, 24, 27^2, 29, 35; 16:28, 29; 17:5, 10; 18:9; 20:12^2, 18; 21:22; 22:5, 6^2, 8, 10, 11, 13, 16, 17^2, 18, 19, 28, 29, 32, 33^3, 34^2, 37; 23:1^2, 3^2, 7^2, 10, 11, 13^2, 18, 27, 29^2; 24:12, 13; 27:14; 28:2^2; 32:11

Dt 1:14, 17, 22, 23, 37, 41, 42; 2:1, 2, 9, 17, 27, 28^2, 29, 31; 3:2, 25, 26^4; 4:5, 10^3, 14, 21; 5:7, 9, 10, 22, 23, 28^2, 29, 31; 7:4; 8:17; 9:4, 10, 11, 12, 13, 14, 19; 10:1^2, 4, 5, 10, 11; 17:14^2; 18:15, 16^2, 17; 26:10, 13, 14; 28:20; 31:2, 16, 19, 20, 28; 32:21^2, 34, 35, 39, 41, 51^2

Jos 2:4, 12^2; 7:19^2; 8:5; 10:4^2, 22; 14:6, 7, 8, 10, 11, 12^2; 15:19^3; 17:14^2; 18:4, 6, 8; 24:15

Jdg 1:3, 7, 15^3; 3:28; 4:8^2, 18, 19; 5:13; 6:17^2, 39^2; 7:2^3, 17, 18; 8:5, 15, 24; 9:7, 9, 15, 48, 54^2; 10:12, 13; 11:7^3, 9^2, 12^2, 17, 27^2, 31, 35^2, 36, 37^2; 12:2, 3^3, 5; 13:6^2, 7, 10^2, 16; 14:2, 3^2, 12, 13^2, 16^3; 15:11, 12^2; 16:6, 7, 10^3, 11, 13^3, 15^3, 17, 18, 26, 28^2, 30; 17:2, 10^2, 13; 18:4^2, 24; 19:18, 19, 20; 20:5^3

Ru 1:8, 11, 13^2, 16, 17^2, 20^3, 21^4; 2:2, 7, 10, 11, 13^2, 21; 3:5, 17^2; 4:4

1Sa 1:11, 27; 2:16, 28, 29, 30^4, 35, 36; 3:5, 6, 8, 17^2; 8:7, 8; 9:16, 18, 19^2, 21; 10:2, 8, 15; 12:1, 3, 12, 23; 13:9, 11, 12; 14:12, 33, 34, 42, 43; 15:1, 11^2, 16, 20, 25, 30^2, 32; 16:1, 2, 3, 5, 17^2, 19, 22; 17:8, 9^2, 10, 35, 37^2, 43, 44, 45; 18:8, 17; 19:15, 17^3; 20:2^2, 3, 5, 6^2, 8^3, 10, 14, 23, 28, 29^3, 31, 42; 21:2^2, 3, 8, 9, 14; 22:3, 8^5, 13^2, 15, 17, 23^2; 23:11, 12, 21, 22, 23; 24:10, 12^2, 15^2, 17, 18^3, 19, 21^2; 25:19, 21, 24^2, 32, 33, 34^2; 26:6, 8, 19^2, 24; 27:1^3, 5; 28:1, 7, 8^2, 9, 11, 12, 15^6, 16, 17, 19, 21, 22; 29:3^2, 6^2; 30:7, 13, 15^4; 31:4^3

2Sa 1:4, 7^2, 8, 9^5, 26^2; 2:7, 22; 3:8, 12, 14^2, 35, 39; 4:10; 5:20; 6:9, 21^2; 7:5^2, 7, 18; 10:2, 11^2; 11:6; 12:10, 22, 23; 13:4, 5, 6, 9, 11, 12, 13, 16^2, 17; 14:9, 10, 15, 16, 18, 19, 32^4; 15:4, 7, 8, 25^2, 26, 28, 33^2, 34,

APNDX

MIGHT

2Ch 2:12; 6:5, 6; 10:15; 11:1; 16:1; 18:6; 20:6, 12; 25:20; 31:4; 32:18, 31; 34:25; 35:12, 15, 22; 36:22

Ezr 1:1; 5:10; 8:21

Neh 5:3, 10; 6:13^{2}; 7:5; 9:24; 10:37

Est 4:2; 10:2

Job 6:8; 9:33; 16:21; 23:3^{2}, 7; 30:2; 38:13^{2}

Ps 18:40; 68:18; 76:5; 78:6, 7, 8; 105:45; 106:8; 107:7; 109:16; 118:13; 119:11, 71, 101, 148; 145:6

Prv 22:21

Ecc 2:3; 3:18^{2}; 9:10

Isa 11:2; 28:13; 33:13; 40:26, 29; 61:3^{2}; 64:1

Jer 9:1, 2, 23; 10:6; 13:11; 16:21; 17:23; 19:15; 20:17; 25:7; 26:19; 27:15^{2}; 43:3; 44:8^{2}; 49:35; 51:30

Ezk 17:7, 8^{3}, 14^{3}, 15; 20:12, 26^{2}; 24:8; 32:29, 30; 36:3; 40:4; 41:6

Dan 1:4, 5, 8; 2:20, 23; 3:28; 4:6, 30; 5:2; 6:2, 17; 8:4; 9:11, 13

Joel 3:3, 6

Am 1:13

Jna 4:5, 6

Mic 3:8; 7:16

Hab 3:16

Zec 4:6; 6:7; 8:9; 11:10, 14

Mal 2:4, 15

Mt 1:22; 2:15, 23; 4:14; 8:17, 28; 12:10, 14, 17; 13:35; 14:36; 21:4, 32, 34; 22:15; 26:4, 9, 56; 27:35

Mk 3:2, 6, 14; 5:18; 6:56; 10:51; 11:13, 18; 12:2; 14:1, 5, 11, 35; 16:1

Lk 1:74; 4:29; 5:19; 6:7, 11; 8:9, 10^{2}, 38; 11:54; 15:29; 17:6; 19:15, 23, 48; 20:20^{2}; 22:2, 4; 23:23, 26; 24:45

Jn 1:7; 3:17; 5:34, 40; 6:28; 8:6; 9:36, 39^{2}; 10:10^{2}, 17; 11:4, 57; 12:9, 10, 38; 14:29; 15:11^{2}, 25; 16:33; 17:3, 12, 13, 19; 18:9, 28, 32; 19:24, 28, 31^{2}, 35, 38; 20:31^{2}

Act 1:25; 4:21; 5:15; 7:19; 8:15; 9:2, 12, 21; 13:42; 15:17; 17:27; 20:24; 22:24; 24:26; 25:21, 26; 26:32; 27:12

Ro 1:10, 13; 3:26; 4:11^{2}, 16^{2}, 18; 5:20, 21; 6:6; 7:13^{2}; 8:4, 29; 9:11, 17^{2}, 23; 10:1; 11:14, 19, 32; 14:9; 15:4, 9, 16

1Co 2:12; 4:6, 8; 5:2; 9:19, 20^{2}, 21, 22^{2}, 23; 14:19

2Co 1:15; 2:4, 9; 4:10, 11, 15; 5:4, 21; 7:9, 12; 8:9; 9:5; 11:4, 7; 12:8

Gal 1:4, 16; 2:4, 5, 16, 19; 3:14^{2}, 22, 24; 4:5, 17

Eph 1:10, 21; 2:7, 16; 3:10, 16, 19; 4:10; 5:26, 27; 6:10, 22^{2}

Php 3:4^{2}, 11

Col 1:9, 10, 11, 18; 2:2; 4:8

1Th 2:6, 16; 3:10^{2}

2Th 2:6, 10, 12; 3:8

1Ti 1:16

2Ti 4:17^{2}

Tit 2:14; 3:8

Phlm 8, 13

Heb 2:14, 17; 6:18; 9:15; 10:36; 11:15, 35; 12:10, 18; 13:12

Jas 5:17

1Pt 1:7, 21; 3:18; 4:6

2Pt 1:4; 2:11

1Jn 2:19; 3:8; 4:9

3Jn 8

Rev 7:12; 12:14, 15; 13:17; 16:12

MIGHTEST

Dt 4:35; 6:2

Jdg 16:6, 10, 13

1Sa 17:28

Neh 9:29

Ps 8:2; 51:4

Prv 22:21

Dan 2:30

Mt 15:5

Mk 7:11

Lk 1:4

Act 9:17

Ro 3:4^{2}

1Ti 1:3, 18

MINE

Gen 14:22; 15:3; 24:33, 45; 30:25, 30; 31:10, 40, 42, 43; 41:13; 44:21; 48:5^{2}; 49:6

Ex 7:4, 5, 17; 13:2; 17:9; 18:4; 19:5; 20:26; 21:14; 23:23; 32:34; 33:23; 34:19

Lev 18:4, 30; 20:26; 22:9; 25:23

Nu 3:12, 13^{2}, 45; 8:14, 17; 10:30; 12:7; 14:28; 16:28; 18:8; 22:29; 23:11; 24:10, 13

Dt 8:17; 10:3; 26:13; 29:19; 32:22, 23, 41^{2}, 42

Jos 14:7

Jdg 6:36, 37; 7:2; 8:7; 11:30; 16:17; 17:2; 19:23

Ru 4:6

1Sa 2:1^{2}, 28, 29, 33, 35^{2}; 12:3; 14:24, 29, 43; 15:14; 17:46; 18:17; 19:17; 20:1; 21:3, 4; 23:7; 24:6, 10^{3}, 11, 12, 13; 25:33; 26:11, 18, 23, 24; 28:2

2Sa 5:19, 20; 6:22; 11:11; 14:5, 30; 16:12; 18:12^{2}, 13; 19:37; 22:4, 24, 35, 38, 41, 49

1Ki 1:33, 48; 2:15, 22; 3:26; 9:3^{2}; 10:6, 7; 11:21, 33; 14:8; 20:3^{2}; 21:20

2Ki 4:13; 5:26; 6:32; 10:6, 30^{2}; 18:34, 35^{2}; 19:28, 34; 20:6, 15; 21:14

1Ch 12:17^{3}; 14:10, 11^{2}; 16:22; 17:14, 16; 22:18; 28:2; 29:3, 17

2Ch 7:15^{2}, 16^{2}; 9:5, 6; 29:10; 32:13, 14^{2}, 15^{2}, 17^{2}

Neh 7:5

Job 3:10; 4:12, 16; 6:11; 7:7, 21; 9:20, 31; 10:6, 14, 15; 13:1^{2}, 14, 15, 23; 14:17; 16:4, 9, 17, 20; 17:2, 7, 13; 19:4, 10, 13, 15, 17, 27; 27:5, 7; 31:1, 6, 7^{3}, 9, 12, 22^{2}, 25, 33, 35; 32:6, 10, 17; 33:8; 40:4; 41:11; 42:5

Ps 3:3, 7; 5:8; 6:7^{2}, 10; 7:4, 5, 6, 8; 9:3; 13:2, 3, 4; 16:5; 17:3; 18:3, 23, 34, 37, 40, 48; 23:5; 25:2, 11, 15, 18, 19; 26:1, 3, 6, 11; 27:2, 6^{2}, 11, 12; 31:9, 10, 11^{2}, 15; 32:5, 8; 35:2, 13, 15, 19, 26; 38:4^{2}, 10, 18, 19, 20; 39:4, 5; 40:6, 12^{2}; 41:5, 9, 11, 12; 42:10; 49:4; 50:10, 11, 12; 51:2, 9; 54:4, 5, 7^{2}; 55:13^{2}; 56:2, 9; 59:1, 10; 60:7^{3}; 69:3, 4^{2}, 18, 19; 71:10; 77:4, 6; 88:8, 9, 18; 89:21; 92:11^{3}; 101:3, 6; 102:8; 105:15; 108:8^{3}; 109:20, 29; 116:8; 119:11, 18, 37, 82, 92, 98, 112, 121, 123, 136, 139, 148, 153, 157; 121:1; 123:1; 131:1; 132:4^{2}, 17; 138:7; 139:2, 22; 141:8; 143:9, 12

Prv 5:13; 8:14; 23:15

Ecc 1:16; 2:1, 3^{2}, 10; 3:17, 18; 7:25; 8:16

Song 1:6; 2:16; 6:3; 8:12

Isa 1:15, 16, 24^{2}; 5:9; 6:5; 10:5^{2}, 25; 13:3; 16:4, 11; 19:25; 22:14; 29:23; 37:29, 35; 38:12, 14; 39:4; 42:1; 43:1, 25; 45:4; 47:6; 48:5, 9, 11^{2}, 13; 49:22; 50:4, 5, 8, 11; 51:5^{2}, 16; 56:5, 7^{2}; 60:7; 63:3, 4, 5, 6; 65:9, 12, 16, 22; 66:2, 4

Jer 2:7; 3:12, 15; 7:20; 9:1; 11:15; 12:3, 7^{2}, 8, 9, 14; 13:17; 14:17; 15:14, 16; 16:17^{2}, 18, 21; 17:4; 18:6; 20:9; 23:9; 24:6; 32:8, 12, 31, 37; 33:5; 42:18; 44:6, 28; 48:31, 36^{2}; 50:11; 51:25

Lam 1:16^{2}, 19, 20, 21; 2:11, 22; 3:19, 48, 49, 51^{2}, 52, 54

Ezk 5:11, 13; 7:3, 4, 8, 9; 8:1, 3, 5, 18^{2}; 9:1, 5, 10; 11:20; 12:7; 13:9, 13; 14:13; 16:8, 18^{2}; 17:19; 18:4^{2}; 20:5^{2}, 6, 17, 22, 23, 28, 40, 42; 21:17, 31; 22:8, 13, 20, 26, 31; 23:4, 5, 39, 41^{2}; 25:7, 13, 14, 16; 29:3, 9; 35:3, 10; 36:7, 21, 22; 37:19; 43:8; 44:8, 12, 24; 47:14

Dan 4:4, 10, 34^{2}, 36; 8:3; 10:5

Hos 2:5, 10; 8:5, 13; 9:15; 11:8, 9; 13:11, 14; 14:4

Am 1:8; 9:2, 4

Jna 2:2

Mic 7:8, 10^{2}

Hab 1:12; 3:19

Zep 1:4; 3:8, 10

Hag 1:9; 2:8^{2}

Zec 1:18; 2:1, 9; 5:1, 9; 6:1; 8:6; 9:8^{2}; 10:3; 11:14; 12:4; 13:7

Mal 1:6, 7, 10; 3:7, 10, 17

Mt 7:24, 26; 20:15, 23; 25:27

Mk 9:24; 10:40

Lk 1:44; 2:30; 9:38; 11:6; 18:3; 19:23, 27

Jn 2:4; 5:30^{2}; 6:38; 7:16; 8:50; 9:11, 15, 30; 10:14; 14:24; 16:14, 15^{2}; 17:10^{2}

Act 11:6; 13:22; 21:13; 26:4

Ro 11:13; 12:19; 16:13, 23

1Co 1:15; 4:3; 9:2, 3; 10:33; 16:21

2Co 11:26, 30; 12:5

Gal 1:14; 6:11

Php 1:4; 3:9

2Th 3:17

Tit 1:4

Phlm 12, 18, 19

Rev 22:16

MY

Gen 2:23^{2}; 4:9, 13, 23^{4}; 6:3, 18; 9:9, 11, 13, 15; 12:13^{2}, 19; 13:8; 15:2, 3; 16:2, 5^{2}, 8; 17:2, 4, 7, 9, 10, 13, 14, 19, 21; 18:3, 12; 19:2, 8, 18, 19, 20, 34; 20:2, 5^{4}, 9, 11, 12^{4}, 13^{2}, 15; 21:10, 23^{2}, 30; 22:7^{2}, 8, 18; 23:4^{2}, 6, 8^{2}, 11^{2}, 13, 15; 24:2, 3, 4^{3}, 6, 7^{3}, 8^{2}, 12^{2}, 14, 18, 27^{3}, 35, 36^{2}, 37^{2}, 38^{3}, 39, 40^{3}, 41^{3}, 42^{2}, 44, 48^{3}, 49, 54, 56^{2}, 65; 26:5^{5}, 7^{2}, 9, 24; 27:1, 2, 4, 7, 8^{2}, 11, 12, 13^{2}, 18^{2}, 19, 20, 21^{2}, 24, 25^{2}, 26, 27, 31, 34, 36^{2}, 37, 38^{2}, 41^{2}, 43^{3}, 46^{2}; 28:21^{2}; 29:4, 14^{2}, 15, 21^{2}, 32^{2}, 34; 30:3^{2}, 6, 8, 15^{2}, 16, 18^{3}, 20, 23, 25, 26^{3}, 30, 32, 33^{2}; 31:5, 6, 7, 26, 28^{2}, 29, 30, 35, 36^{2}, 37^{2}, 39, 40, 41, 42^{2}, 43^{4}, 50^{2}; 32:4, 5, 9^{2}, 10, 11, 17, 18, 29, 30; 33:8, 9, 10^{2}, 11, 13, 14^{2}, 15; 34:8, 30; 35:3; 37:7^{2}, 16, 33, 35; 38:11, 26; 39:8^{2}, 15, 18; 40:9, 11, 16^{2}, 17; 41:9, 17, 22, 40^{2}, 51^{2}, 52; 42:10, 28^{2}, 36, 37^{2}, 38^{2}; 43:3, 5, 9, 14, 29; 44:2, 5, 7, 9, 10, 16^{2}, 17, 18^{2}, 19, 20, 22, 23, 24^{2}, 27^{2}, 29, 30, 32^{2}, 33, 34^{2}; 45:3, 9, 12^{2}, 13^{3}, 28; 46:31^{2}; 47:1^{2}, 6, 9^{3}, 18^{3}, 25, 29, 30; 48:9, 15^{2}, 16^{2}, 18, 19, 22^{2}; 49:3^{3}, 4, 6, 9, 26, 29^{2}; 50:5^{3}, 25

Ex 3:7, 10, 15^{2}, 20^{2}; 4:1, 10, 13, 18, 22^{2}, 23; 5:1; 6:3, 4, 5; 7:3^{2}, 4^{2}, 16; 8:1, 8, 20, 21, 22, 23; 9:1, 13, 14, 15, 16^{2}, 17, 27, 29; 10:1, 2, 3, 4, 17, 28^{2}; 11:9; 12:31; 13:15, 19; 15:2^{4}, 9^{3}; 16:4, 28^{2}; 18:4, 19; 19:5^{2}; 20:6, 24; 21:5^{3}; 22:24, 25; 23:18^{2}, 21, 27; 25:2; 29:43; 31:13; 32:10, 22, 33; 33:12, 14, 17, 19, 20, 22^{2}, 23^{2}; 34:9, 25

Lev 6:17; 15:31; 17:10; 18:4, 5^{2}, 26^{2}; 19:3, 12, 19, 30^{2}, 37^{2}; 20:3^{3}, 5, 6, 8, 22^{2}; 21:23; 22:2, 3, 31, 32; 23:2; 25:18^{2}, 21, 42, 55; 26:2^{2}, 3^{2}, 9, 11^{2}, 12, 15^{4}, 17, 25, 30, 42^{3}, 43^{2}, 44

Nu 6:27; 10:30; 11:15, 23, 28, 29; 12:6, 7, 8, 11; 14:17, 22^{3}, 24, 34; 15:40; 20:19^{2}, 24; 21:2; 22:18, 38; 23:10, 12; 24:14; 25:11^{3}, 12; 27:14; 28:2^{3}; 32:25, 27; 36:2^{2}

Dt 2:28; 4:5, 10; 5:10, 29; 8:17; 9:4, 15, 17; 11:13, 18; 18:16, 18, 19^{2}, 20; 22:16, 17; 25:7^{2}; 26:5, 14^{2}; 31:16, 17^{2}, 18, 20, 27, 29; 32:1, 2^{2}, 20, 34, 39, 40, 41, 42

Jos 1:2, 7; 2:12, 13^{4}; 5:14; 7:11, 19, 21; 9:23; 14:8^{2}, 9, 11^{2}; 15:16; 22:2; 24:15

Jdg 1:3, 7, 12; 2:1, 2, 20^{2}; 4:18; 5:9, 21; 6:10, 13, 15^{3}, 18; 8:19^{2}, 23; 9:9, 11^{2}, 13, 15, 17, 18, 29; 11:7, 12, 13, 19, 31, 35^{2}, 36, 37^{2}; 12:2, 3^{3}; 13:8, 18; 14:3, 16^{3}, 18^{2}; 15:1; 16:13, 17^{2}, 28; 17:2, 3^{2}, 13; 18:24; 19:23, 24; 20:4, 5, 6, 23, 28

Ru 1:11^{2}, 12, 13, 16^{2}; 2:2, 8^{2}, 13, 21^{2}, 22; 3:1, 10, 11^{2}, 16, 18; 4:4, 6, 10

1Sa 1:15^{2}, 16, 26^{2}, 27; 2:1^{2}, 24, 28, 29^{3}, 32, 35; 3:6, 16; 4:16; 9:5, 16^{3}, 17, 21; 10:2; 12:2^{2}, 5; 14:29, 39, 40, 42; 15:11, 25, 30; 16:22; 18:17, 18^{2}, 21; 19:2, 3^{2}; 20:1^{2}, 2^{2}, 9, 12, 13^{2}, 15, 29^{2}, 42; 21:2, 8^{2}, 15^{2}; 22:3^{2}, 8^{3}, 12, 15, 23; 23:10, 12, 17^{2}; 24:6, 8, 10, 11^{3}, 15, 16, 21^{3}; 25:5, 11^{4}, 24, 25^{2}, 26^{2}, 27^{2}, 28^{2}, 29, 30, 31^{3}, 39, 41; 26:17^{3}, 18, 19, 20, 21^{2}, 23, 24, 25; 27:12; 28:9, 21^{2}; 29:6, 8, 9; 30:13, 15, 23

2Sa 1:9, 10, 26; 2:22; 3:7, 12, 13^{2}, 14, 18^{2}, 21, 28; 4:8, 9; 5:2; 7:5, 7, 8^{2}, 10, 11, 13, 14, 15, 18; 9:7, 10, 11^{2}; 11:11^{3}; 12:28; 13:4, 5^{2}, 6^{2}, 11, 12, 13, 20, 25, 26, 32, 33; 14:7^{2}, 9^{2}, 11, 12, 15, 16, 17^{2}, 18, 19^{2}, 20, 22, 24, 31; 15:7, 15, 21^{2}; 16:3, 4, 9, 11^{3}; 18:5, 18, 22, 28, 31, 32, 33^{5}; 19:4^{3}, 12^{3}, 13^{2}, 19^{2}, 20, 26^{2}, 27^{2}, 28^{2}, 30, 35, 37^{3}; 20:9; 22:2^{3}, 3^{6}, 7^{4}, 18, 19^{2}, 21^{2}, 22, 25^{2}, 29^{2}, 30, 33^{2}, 34^{2}, 35, 37^{2}, 39, 44, 47^{2}; 23:2, 5^{3}; 24:3^{2}, 17, 21, 22, 24

1Ki 1:2^{2}, 13^{2}, 17^{2}, 18, 20^{2}, 21^{2}, 24^{2}, 27^{2}, 29, 30^{2}, 31, 33, 35^{2}, 36, 37^{2}, 48; 2:15, 20, 24, 26^{2}, 31, 32, 38, 44; 3:6, 7^{2}, 14^{3}, 17, 20^{2},

APNDX

21[2], 22[2], 23[2], 26; **5**:3, 4, 5[3], 6, 9[3]; **6**:12[4], 13; **8**:15, 16[3], 17, 18[2], 19, 20, 24, 25[2], 26, 28, 29, 59; **9**:3, 4[2], 6[2], 7[2], 13; **11**:11[2], 13, 32, 33[3], 34[3], 36[2], 38[5]; **12**:10[2], 11[2], 14[2]; **13**:6, 30, 31; **14**:7, 8[2]; **15**:19; **16**:2[2]; **17**:1, 12, 18[2], 20, 21; **18**:7, 10, 12, 13; **19**:4[2], 10, 14, 20[2]; **20**:4, 6, 7[4], 9, 32, 34[2]; **21**:2, 3, 4, 6; **22**:4[2], 49

2Ki 1:13, 14; **2**:12[2], 19; **3**:7[2]; **4**:1[2], 16, 19[2], 28, 29[2]; **5**:3, 6, 13, 18[2], 20, 22; **6**:8, 12, 15, 21, 26, 28, 29; **8**:5, 12; **9**:7, 32; **10**:6, 9, 15, 16; **13**:14[2]; **14**:9; **17**:13[3]; **18**:23, 24, 27; **19**:12, 23, 24, 28[2], 34; **20**:5, 6, 15, 19; **21**:4, 7, 8, 15; **22**:17; **23**:27[2]

1Ch 4:10; **11**:2[2], 19; **16**:22; **17**:4, 6, 7[2], 9, 10, 13[2], 14, 25; **21**:3[3], 17[2], 23; **22**:5, 7[3], 8[2], 10[2], 11, 14; **28**:2[2], 3, 4[3], 5[2], 6[3], 7[2], 9, 20; **29**:1, 2[2], 3[3], 14, 17, 19

2Ch 1:8, 9, 11; **2**:3, 4, 7, 8, 13, 14, 15; **6**:4, 5[3], 6[2], 7, 8[2], 9, 10, 15, 16[3], 19, 40; **7**:13, 14[3], 16, 17[2], 19[2], 20[3]; **8**:11; **10**:10[2], 11[2], 14[2]; **12**:7, 8; **16**:3; **18**:3, 13; **25**:16, 18; **29**:11; **32**:13, 14, 15; **33**:4, 7; **34**:25

Ezr 7:13, 28; **9**:3[4], 5[6], 6[3]; **10**:3

Neh 1:2, 6, 9[2]; **2**:3[2], 5, 8, 12[2], 18; **4**:16, 23[2]; **5**:10[2], 13, 14, 16, 17, 19; **6**:9, 14, 19; **7**:2, 5; **13**:14[3], 19, 22, 29, 31

Est 4:16; **5**:7[2], 8[2]; **7**:3[4], 4[2]; **8**:6[2]

Job 1:5, 8, 21; **2**:3; **3**:10, 24[2]; **4**:14, 15[2]; **5**:8; **6**:2[2], 3, 4, 7[2], 8, 11[2], 12[2], 13, 15, 21, 24, 29, 30[2]; **7**:5[2], 6, 7, 11[3], 13[3], 15[2], 16, 19, 21; **9**:14, 15, 16, 17, 18, 21[2], 25, 27[2], 28, 30; **10**:1[4], 6, 12, 15, 20; **11**:4; **13**:6[2], 14[3], 16, 17[2], 18, 19, 23[2], 26, 27[3]; **14**:14[2], 16[2], 17; **16**:4, 5[2], 6, 7, 8[2], 12, 13[2], 15[2], 16[2], 17, 18[2], 19[2], 20; **17**:1[2], 7, 11[3], 13, 14[3], 15[2]; **19**:2, 5, 8[2], 9[2], 12, 13, 14[2], 15, 16[2], 17[2], 19, 20[4], 21, 22, 23, 25, 26[2], 27; **20**:2, 3[2]; **21**:2, 4[2], 6; **23**:2[3], 4[2], 7, 11, 12, 16, 17; **24**:25; **27**:2[2], 3[2], 4[2], 6[2]; **29**:3, 4[2], 5, 6, 7, 14, 18[2], 19[2], 20[3], 21, 22[2], 24; **30**:1, 10, 11, 12[2], 13[2], 15[2], 16, 17[2], 18[3], 22, 25, 27, 30[2], 31[2]; **31**:4[2], 5, 7, 8, 9, 10, 13[2], 17, 18[2], 20, 21[2], 22, 24[2], 25, 27[3], 30, 31, 32, 33[2], 35, 36, 37, 38; **32**:17, 19, 20, 22; **33**:1[2], 2[3], 3[3], 7[2], 11[2]; **34**:2, 5, 6[2], 16, 36; **35**:2, 3, 10; **36**:3[2], 4; **37**:1; **38**:10; **40**:4, 8; **42**:7[2], 8[3]

Ps 2:6[2], 7; **3**:2, 3, 4, 7; **4**:1[2], 2, 7; **5**:1[2], 2[3], 3[2], 8; **6**:2, 3, 4, 6[4], 8, 9[2]; **7**:1[2], 2, 3[2], 5[2], 8, 10; **9**:1, 4[2], 13; **11**:1[2]; **13**:2[2], 3, 5; **14**:4; **16**:1, 2[3], 3, 4, 5[2], 7, 8, 9[3], 10; **17**:1[2], 2, 3, 5[2], 6, 9, 13; **18**:1, 2[8], 6[4], 17, 18[2], 20[2], 21, 24[2], 28[3], 29, 32, 33[2], 34, 36[2], 38, 46[2]; **19**:14[4]; **22**:1[3], 2, 9, 10[2], 14[3], 15[3], 16[2], 17, 18[2], 19, 20[2], 22, 25[2]; **23**:1, 3, 5[2], 6; **25**:1, 2, 5, 7[2], 15, 17[2], 18[2], 20[2]; **26**:2[2], 9[2], 12; **27**:1[3], 2[2], 3, 4, 7, 8[2], 9[2], 10[2]; **28**:1, 2[2], 6, 7[5]; **30**:1, 2, 3, 6, 7, 9, 10, 11[2], 12[2]; **31**:1, 2, 3[2], 4, 5, 7[2], 8, 9[2], 10[4], 11, 13, 14, 15, 22[2]; **32**:3[2], 4, 5[3], 7; **34**:1, 2, 4; **35**:1, 3, 4[2], 7, 9, 10, 11, 12, 13[3], 14, 17[2], 23[4], 24, 27, 28; **36**:1; **38**:3[3], 5[2], 7[2], 8, 9[2], 10[2], 11[4], 12[2], 15, 16, 17, 18, 21, 22; **39**:1[3], 2[2], 3[2], 4, 5, 7, 8, 9, 12[4]; **40**:1, 2[2], 3, 5, 8[2], 9, 10, 12, 14, 17[3]; **41**:4, 7, 9; **42**:1, 2, 3[2], 4, 5, 6[2], 8[2], 9, 10, 11[3]; **43**:1, 2, 4[2], 5[3]; **44**:4, 6[2], 15[2]; **45**:1[2]; **49**:3[2], 4, 5, 15; **50**:5, 7, 16[2], 17; **51**:1, 2, 3[2], 5, 9, 14[2], 15[2]; **53**:4; **54**:2[2], 3, 4; **55**:1[2], 2, 4, 8, 13, 17, 18; **56**:4, 5, 6[2], 8[2], 11, 13[2]; **57**:1[2], 4, 6[2], 7[2], 8; **59**:1, 3[3], 4, 9, 10[2], 11, 16[2], 17[3]; **60**:7, 8[2]; **61**:1[2], 2, 5, 8; **62**:1[2], 2[3], 5[2], 6[3], 7[4]; **63**:1[3], 3, 4, 5[2], 6, 7, 8, 9; **64**:1[3]; **66**:13, 14[2], 16, 17[2], 18, 19, 20; **68**:22, 24[2]; **69**:1, 3[3], 5[2], 6[2], 7, 8[2], 10[2], 11, 13, 18, 19[3], 20, 21[2]; **70**:2[2], 5[2]; **71**:1, 3[3], 4, 5[3], 6[2], 7, 8, 9, 10, 12[2], 13[2], 15, 17, 21, 22, 23[2], 24[2]; **73**:2[2], 13[2], 21[2], 23, 26[4], 28; **74**:12; **77**:1[2], 2[3], 3, 6[2], 10; **78**:1[3], 2; **81**:8, 11[2], 13[2], 14; **83**:13; **84**:2[3], 3[2], 8, 10; **86**:2[2], 4, 6[2], 7, 11, 12[2], 13, 14; **87**:7; **88**:1, 2[2], 3[2], 9, 13, 14, 15; **89**:1, 3[2], 20[2], 21, 24[3], 26[3], 27, 28[2], 30[2], 31[2], 33[2], 34[2], 35, 47, 50; **91**:2[3], 9, 14, 16; **92**:10, 11[2], 15; **94**:17[2], 18, 19[2], 22[3]; **95**:9, 10, 11[2]; **101**:2, 7[2]; **102**:1[2], 3[2], 4[2], 5[3], 9, 11, 23[2], 24[2]; **103**:1, 2, 22; **104**:1[2], 33[2], 34, 35; **105**:15; **108**:1[2], 8, 9[2]; **109**:1, 4[2], 5, 20, 22, 24[2], 26, 30; **110**:1[2]; **111**:1; **116**:1[2], 4, 7, 8[2], 11, 14, 16, 18; **118**:6, 7[2], 14[2], 21, 28[2]; **119**:5, 10, 13, 20, 24[2], 25, 26, 28, 32, 34, 36, 39, 43, 48, 50[2], 54[2], 57, 58, 59[2], 69, 76, 77, 80, 81, 92, 97, 99[2], 101, 103[2], 105[2], 108, 109[2], 111, 114[2], 115, 116, 120, 129, 131, 133, 139, 143, 145, 149, 154, 157, 161, 167, 168, 169, 170, 171, 172, 174, 175; **120**:1, 2, 6; **121**:1, 2; **122**:8; **129**:1, 2, 3; **130**:2[2], 5, 6; **131**:1, 2; **132**:3[2], 12[2], 14; **137**:5, 6[3]; **138**:1, 3; **139**:2[2], 3[3], 4, 8, 13[2], 14, 15, 16[2], 23[2]; **140**:4, 6[2], 7[2]; **141**:1, 2[2], 3[2], 4, 5[2], 6, 8[2]; **142**:1[3], 2[2], 3[2], 4[2], 5[2], 6[2], 7; **143**:1[2], 3[2], 4[2], 6[2], 7, 8, 10, 11, 12; **144**:1[3], 2[6]; **145**:1, 21; **146**:1, 2

Prv 1:8, 10, 15, 23[3], 24, 25[2], 30[2]; **2**:1[3]; **3**:1[3], 11, 21; **4**:2, 3[2], 4[2], 5, 10[2], 20[3]; **5**:1[3], 7, 12, 13, 20; **6**:1, 3, 20; **7**:1[3], 2[2], 4, 6[2], 14, 16, 17, 24; **8**:4, 6, 7[2], 8, 10, 19[2], 31, 32, 34[2]; **9**:5; **19**:27; **20**:9[2]; **22**:17; **23**:15[2], 16, 19, 26[2]; **24**:13, 21; **27**:11[2]; **30**:9; **31**:2[3]

Ecc 1:13, 16, 17; **2**:7, 9, 10[5], 11, 15[2], 18, 19, 20; **4**:8; **7**:15, 28; **8**:9; **9**:1; **12**:12

Song 1:6, 7, 9, 12, 13[2], 14, 15, 16; **2**:2, 3[2], 6, 7, 8, 9, 10[3], 13[2], 14, 16, 17; **3**:1[2], 2, 3, 4[2], 5; **4**:1, 7, 8, 9[4], 10[2], 11, 12[2], 16[2]; **5**:1[9], 2[8], 3[2], 4[2], 5[3], 6[3], 7, 8, 10, 16[2]; **6**:2, 3[2], 4, 9[2], 12; **7**:9, 10, 11, 12, 13; **8**:1[2], 2[2], 3, 4, 10, 12, 14

Isa 1:3, 12, 14, 25; **3**:7, 12[2], 15; **5**:1[3], 3, 4, 5, 13; **6**:7; **7**:13; **8**:4[2], 16; **10**:2, 6, 8, 10, 13[2], 14, 24; **11**:9; **12**:2[4]; **13**:3[3]; **14**:13, 25[2]; **15**:5; **16**:9, 11; **18**:4[2]; **19**:25[2]; **20**:3; **21**:3, 4[2], 8[2], 10[2]; **22**:4, 20; **24**:16[2]; **25**:1; **26**:9[2], 19, 20; **27**:5; **28**:23[2]; **29**:23; **30**:1, 2; **32**:9[2], 13, 18; **33**:13; **34**:5[2], 16; **36**:8, 9, 12, 19, 20[2]; **37**:12, 24, 25, 29[2], 35; **38**:10[2], 12, 13, 15[2], 16, 17[2], 20; **39**:4, 8; **40**:1, 27[3]; **41**:8[2], 9, 10, 25; **42**:1[3], 8[3], 14, 19[2]; **43**:4, 6[2], 7[2], 10[2], 12, 13, 20[2], 21; **44**:1, 2, 3[2], 8, 17, 20, 21[2], 28[2]; **45**:4, 11[2], 12, 13[2], 23; **46**:10[2], 11, 13[3]; **47**:6; **48**:3, 5[2], 9[2], 11[2], 12, 13, 18; **49**:1[2], 2, 3, 4[3], 5[2], 6[2], 11[2], 14, 16, 21, 22; **50**:1, 2[2], 6[3], 7; **51**:4[3], 5[2], 6[2], 7, 8[2], 16[2], 22; **52**:4, 5[2], 6[2], 13; **53**:8, 11; **54**:8, 10[2]; **55**:8[2], 9[2], 11[2]; **56**:1[2], 4[2], 5, 6, 7[2]; **57**:11, 13, 14, 21; **58**:1, 2, 13; **59**:21[3]; **60**:7, 10[2], 13[2], 21[2]; **61**:10[2]; **62**:1, 9; **63**:3[3], 4, 5, 6, 8; **65**:1, 2, 3, 5, 8, 9[2], 10, 11, 13[3], 14, 15, 19, 22, 25; **66**:1[3], 2, 5, 18, 19[3], 20

Jer 1:9[2], 12, 16; **2**:7, 11, 13, 19, 27, 31, 32; **3**:4[2], 13, 19; **4**:1, 4, 11, 19[6], 20[2], 22, 31; **5**:9, 14, 22, 26, 29, 31; **6**:8, 12, 14, 19[2], 26, 27; **7**:10, 11, 12[3], 14, 15, 20, 23[2], 25, 30[2], 31; **8**:7, 11, 18, 19, 21, 22; **9**:1[2], 2, 7, 9, 13[2]; **10**:19[2], 20[5]; **11**:4[2], 7, 10[2], 15, 20; **12**:7, 10[3], 14, 16[4]; **13**:2, 10, 17; **14**:14, 15, 17; **15**:1[2], 6, 7, 10, 15, 18[2], 19; **16**:5, 11, 17, 18, 19[3], 21[2]; **17**:3, 14, 16, 17; **18**:2, 10[2], 15, 20, 22; **19**:5, 15; **20**:9, 10[2], 11, 12, 14, 15, 17[2], 18; **21**:10, 12; **22**:18, 21, 24; **23**:1, 2[2], 3, 9, 11, 13, 22[3], 25, 27[3], 28[2], 29, 30, 32, 39; **24**:7; **25**:8, 9, 13, 15, 29; **26**:4, 5; **27**:5[2], 6, 15; **29**:9, 10, 19[2], 21, 23, 32; **30**:3, 10, 22; **31**:1, 9, 14[2], 18, 19[2], 20[2], 26, 32, 33[2]; **32**:7, 8, 9, 31[2], 34, 35, 37, 38, 40, 41[2]; **33**:5[2], 20[2], 21[3], 22, 24, 25, 26; **34**:15[2], 16, 18; **35**:13, 15; **36**:6; **37**:20[2]; **38**:9, 26; **39**:16; **42**:18[2]; **43**:10; **44**:4, 6, 10[2], 11, 26[2], 29; **45**:3[2]; **46**:27, 28; **49**:25, 37, 38; **50**:6; **51**:20, 34, 35[2], 45

Lam 1:9, 12, 13[2], 14[3], 15[2], 16[2], 18[3], 19[2], 20, 21, 22[3]; **2**:11[3], 21[2], 22; **3**:4[3], 7, 8, 9[2], 11, 13, 14, 16, 17, 18[2], 19, 20, 21, 24[2], 48, 51, 53, 56[3], 58[2], 59[2]; **4**:3, 6, 10

Ezk 1:28; **2**:2, 7; **3**:2, 3, 4, 10, 14, 17, 23, 24; **4**:14[3]; **5**:6[4], 7[2], 11, 13[3]; **6**:12, 14; **7**:8, 14, 22[2]; **8**:6; **9**:6, 8; **10**:2, 13, 19; **11**:12[2], 13, 20[2]; **12**:7[2], 13[2], 28; **13**:9, 10, 13[2], 15, 18, 19[2], 21, 23; **14**:8[2], 9[2], 11, 19, 21; **15**:7[2]; **16**:8, 14, 17[2], 19, 21, 27, 42[2], 60, 62; **17**:19, 20[2]; **18**:9[2], 17[2], 19, 21, 25, 29; **20**:8[2], 9, 11[2], 12, 13[4], 14, 15, 16[3], 19[2], 20, 21[5], 22, 24[3], 39, 44; **21**:3, 4, 5, 10, 12[2], 17, 31; **22**:8, 20, 21, 22, 26[2], 31; **23**:18[2], 25, 38[2], 39; **24**:13, 18, 21; **25**:3, 14[4], 17; **28**:25; **29**:3; **30**:15, 24, 25; **32**:3[2], 10, 32; **33**:7, 22[2], 31; **34**:6[2], 8[5], 10[2], 11, 12, 15, 17, 19, 22, 23, 24, 26, 30, 31[2]; **36**:5[2], 6[2], 8, 12, 18, 20, 23, 27[3], 28; **37**:12, 13, 14, 23, 24[3], 25[2], 26, 27[2], 28; **38**:14, 16[2], 17, 18[2], 19[2], 20, 21; **39**:7[3], 17, 19, 20, 21[3], 23, 24, 25, 29[2]; **43**:3, 7[3], 8[3]; **44**:4, 7[5], 8[2], 9, 11, 13, 15, 16[3], 23, 24[4]; **45**:8[2], 9; **46**:18; **48**:11

Dan 1:10[2]; **2**:3, 23; **3**:14, 15; **4**:4, 5[2], 8, 9, 10, 13[2], 18, 19, 24, 27, 30[2], 36[5]; **5**:13; **6**:22, 26; **7**:2, 15[3], 28[3]; **8**:17, 18; **9**:3, 4[2], 18, 19, 20[5]; **10**:3, 8, 9[2], 10[2], 15, 16[4], 17[2], 19; **12**:8

Hos 1:9, 10; **2**:2, 5[6], 7, 9[4], 12[2], 23[3]; **4**:6, 8, 12; **5**:10, 15[2]; **6**:5, 11; **7**:2, 12; **8**:1[2], 2, 12; **9**:8, 17; **10**:10; **11**:1, 7, 8; **12**:8; **13**:11

Joel 1:6, 7[2], 13; **2**:1, 25, 26, 27, 28, 29; **3**:2[3], 3, 5[3], 17

Am 2:7; **7**:8, 15; **8**:2; **9**:3, 10, 12, 14

Oba 13, 16

Jna 1:12; **2**:2, 5, 6[2], 7[2]; **4**:2[2], 3

Mic 1:9; **2**:4, 7, 8, 9[2]; **3**:3, 5; **6**:3, 5, 7[4], 16; **7**:1, 7[2], 9

Hab 1:12; **2**:1; **3**:16[3], 18, 19[3]

Zep 2:8, 9[2], 12; **3**:8[3], 10[2], 11

Hag 2:5, 23

Zec 1:6[3], 9, 16, 17; **2**:11; **3**:7[4], 8; **4**:4, 5, 6, 13; **5**:4; **6**:4, 8; **8**:7, 8; **11**:4, 8, 10[2], 12[2]; **12**:5; **13**:5, 6, 7[2], 9[3]; **14**:5

Mal 1:6[2], 11[3], 14; **2**:2, 4, 5[2], 9; **3**:1, 17; **4**:2, 4

Mt 2:6, 15; **3**:17; **5**:11; **7**:21; **8**:6, 8[2], 9, 21; **9**:18; **10**:18, 22, 32, 33, 39; **11**:10, 27, 29, 30[2]; **12**:18[4], 44, 48[2], 49[2], 50[2]; **13**:30, 35; **15**:13, 22; **16**:17, 18, 25; **17**:5, 15; **18**:5, 10, 19, 20, 21, 35; **19**:20, 29; **20**:21, 23[4]; **21**:13, 28, 37; **22**:4[3], 44[2]; **24**:5, 9, 35, 36, 48; **25**:27[2], 34, 40; **26**:12[2], 18[2], 26, 28, 29, 38, 39, 42, 53; **27**:35[2], 46[2]; **28**:10

Mk 1:2, 11; **3**:33[2], 34[2], 35[2]; **5**:9, 23, 30; **6**:23; **8**:35, 38; **9**:7, 17, 37, 39, 41; **10**:20, 29, 40[2], 51; **11**:17; **12**:6, 36[2]; **13**:6, 9, 13, 31; **14**:8, 14, 22, 24, 34; **15**:34[2]; **16**:17

Lk 1:18, 20, 25, 43, 44, 46, 47[2]; **2**:49; **3**:22; **6**:47; **7**:6, 7, 8, 27, 44[2], 45, 46[2]; **8**:21[2]; **9**:24, 26, 35, 38, 48, 59, 61; **10**:22, 29, 40; **11**:7, 24; **12**:4, 13, 17, 18[3], 19, 45; **14**:23, 24, 26, 27, 33; **15**:6, 17, 18, 24, 29; **16**:3, 5, 24, 27; **18**:21, 41; **19**:8, 23[2], 46; **20**:13, 42[2]; **21**:8, 12, 17, 33; **22**:11, 19, 20, 28, 29, 30[2], 42; **23**:46; **24**:39[2], 49

Jn 2:16; **3**:29; **4**:34, 49; **5**:17, 24, 30, 31, 43, 47; **6**:32, 51, 54[2], 55[2], 56[2], 65; **7**:6, 8, 16; **8**:14, 16, 19[2], 21, 28, 31[2], 37, 38, 43[2], 49, 51, 52, 54[2], 56; **10**:14, 15, 16, 17[2], 18, 25, 26, 27[2], 28, 29[2], 30, 32, 37; **11**:21, 32; **12**:7, 26[2], 27, 47, 48; **13**:6, 8, 9[3], 35, 37, 38; **14**:2, 7, 12, 13, 14, 15, 20, 21[2], 23[2], 24, 26, 27, 28; **15**:1, 7, 8[2], 9, 10[3], 11, 12, 14, 15, 16, 20, 21, 23, 24; **16**:5, 10, 23, 24, 26; **17**:13, 24; **18**:11, 36[4], 37; **19**:24[2]; **20**:13, 17[4], 21, 25[2], 27[2], 28[2]; **21**:15, 16, 17

Act 2:14, 17, 18[3], 25[2], 26[3], 27, 34[2]; **7**:34, 49[3], 50, 59; **9**:15, 16; **10**:30; **11**:8; **13**:22, 33; **15**:7, 17, 19; **16**:15; **20**:24[2], 25, 29, 34; **22**:1, 6; **24**:14, 17; **25**:26; **26**:4[2], 10; **28**:19

Ro 1:8, 9[3]; **2**:16; **3**:7; **7**:4, 18, 23[3]; **9**:1, 2, 3[2], 17[2], 25[2], 26; **10**:1, 21; **11**:3, 14, 27; **15**:14, 24[3], 31; **16**:3, 4, 5, 7[2], 8, 9, 11, 21[2], 25

1Co 1:4, 11; **2**:4[2]; **4**:14, 17[2]; **5**:4; **7**:25, 40; **8**:13[2]; **9**:1, 15, 17, 18[2], 27; **10**:14, 29; **11**:24, 25, 33; **13**:3[2]; **14**:14[2], 18, 19[2]; **15**:58; **16**:6, 18, 24

2Co 1:16, 23; **2**:3, 13[3]; **6**:13, 16, 18; **7**:4[2]; **8**:10, 23; **11**:1; **12**:9[3], 21

Gal 1:13, 14[2], 15; **4**:14[2], 19, 20; **6**:17

Eph 1:16; **3**:4, 13, 14; **6**:10, 19, 21

Php 1:3, 7[3], 8, 13, 14, 16, 19, 20[3], 22, 26; **2**:2, 12[3], 25[2]; **3**:1, 8; **4**:1[3], 3, 14, 16, 19

Col 1:24[2]; **2**:1; **4**:7, 10, 11, 18

1Ti 1:2, 11

2Ti 1:2, 3[2], 6, 16; **2**:1, 8; **3**:10; **4**:6, 7, 16

Phlm 4[2], 10[2], 20, 23, 24

Heb 1:5, 13; **2**:12, 13; **3**:9, 10, 11[2]; **4**:3[2], 5; **5**:5; **8**:9, 10; **10**:16, 34, 38; **12**:5; **13**:6

Jas 1:2, 16, 19; **2**:1, 3, 5, 14, 18[2]; **3**:1, 10, 12; **5**:10, 12

1Pt 5:13

2Pt 1:14, 15, 17

1Jn 2:1; **3**:13, 18

3Jn 4

Rev 1:20; **2**:3, 13[3], 16, 20, 26, 27; **3**:5, 8[2], 10, 12[5], 16, 20, 21[2]; **10**:10[2]; **11**:3; **18**:4; **21**:7; **22**:12

MYSELF

Gen 3:10; **22**:16

Ex 19:4

Nu 8:17; **12**:6

Dt 1:9, 12; **10**:5

Jdg 16:20

Ru 4:6

1Sa 13:12; **20**:5; **25**:33

2Sa 18:2; **22**:24

1Ki 18:15; **22**:30

2Ki 5:18[2]

2Ch 7:12; **18**:29

Neh 5:7

Est 5:12; **6**:6

Job 6:10; **7**:20; **9**:20, 27, 30; **10**:1; **13**:20; **19**:4, 27; **31**:17, 29; **42**:6

Ps 18:23; **35**:14; **55**:12; **57**:8; **101**:2; **108**:2; **109**:4; **119**:16, 47, 52; **131**:1, 2

Ecc 2:3, 12, 14, 19

Isa 33:10; **42**:14; **43**:21; **44**:24; **45**:23

Jer 8:18; 21:5; 22:5; 49:13

Ezk 14:7; 20:5, 9; 29:3; 35:11; 38:23^{2}

Dan 10:3

Mic 6:6

Hab 3:16

Zec 7:3

Lk 7:7; 24:39

Jn 5:31; 7:17, 28; 8:14, 18, 28, 42, 54; 10:18; 12:49; 14:3, 10, 21; 17:19

Act 10:26; 20:24; 24:10, 16; 25:22; 26:2^{2}, 9

Ro 7:25; 9:3; 11:4; 15:14; 16:2

1Co 4:4, 6; 7:7; 9:19, 27

2Co 2:1; 10:1; 11:7, 9^{2}, 16; 12:5, 13

Gal 2:18

Php 2:24; 3:13

Phlm 17

NO

Gen 8:9; 9:15; 11:30; 13:8; 15:3; 16:1; 26:29; 30:1; 31:50; 32:28; 37:22^{2}, 24, 32; 38:21, 22, 26; 40:8; 41:44; 42:11, 31, 34; 44:23; 45:1; 47:4, 13

Ex 2:12; 3:19; 5:7, 16, 18; 8:22; 9:26, 28^{2}; 10:14, 28, 29; 12:16, 19, 43, 48; 13:3, 7; 14:11, 13; 15:22; 16:4, 18, 19, 29; 17:1; 20:3; 21:8, 22; 22:2, 10; 23:8, 13, 32; 30:9, 12; 33:4, 20; 34:3, 7, 14, 17; 35:3

Lev 2:11^{2}; 5:11; 6:30; 7:23, 24, 26; 11:12; 12:4; 13:21, 26^{2}, 31, 32; 16:17, 29; 17:7, 12, 14; 19:15, 35; 20:14; 21:3, 21; 22:10, 13^{2}, 21; 23:3, 7, 8, 21, 25, 28, 31, 35, 36; 25:31, 36; 26:1, 37; 27:26, 28

Nu 1:53; 3:4; 5:8, 13, 15, 19; 6:3, 5, 6; 8:19, 25, 26; 14:18; 16:40; 18:5, 20, 23, 24, 32; 19:2, 15; 20:2, 5; 21:5; 22:26; 23:23; 26:33, 62; 27:3, 4, 8, 9, 10, 11, 17; 28:18, 25, 26; 29:1, 12, 35; 33:14; 35:31, 32

Dt 1:39; 2:5; 3:26; 4:12, 15; 5:22; 7:2, 16, 24; 8:2, 15; 10:9, 16; 11:17, 25; 12:12; 13:11; 14:27, 29; 15:4, 19; 16:3, 4, 8; 17:13, 16; 18:1, 2; 19:20; 20:12; 21:14; 22:26; 23:14, 17, 22; 24:1, 6; 25:5; 28:26, 29, 32, 65, 68^{2}; 31:2; 32:12, 20, 39; 34:6

Jos 8:20, 31; 10:14; 11:20; 14:4; 17:3; 18:7; 22:25, 27; 23:9, 13

Jdg 2:2; 4:20; 5:19; 6:4; 8:28; 10:13; 11:39; 13:5, 7, 21; 15:13; 17:6; 18:1, 7^{2}, 10, 28^{2}; 19:1, 15, 18, 19, 30; 21:12, 25

1Sa 1:2, 11, 15, 18; 2:3, 9, 24; 3:1; 6:7; 7:13; 10:14, 27; 11:3; 13:19; 14:6, 26; 15:35; 17:32, 50; 18:2; 20:15, 21, 34; 21:1, 2, 4, 6, 9; 25:31; 26:12, 21; 27:4; 28:10, 15, 20^{2}; 29:3; 30:4, 12

2Sa 1:21; 2:28; 6:23; 7:10; 12:6; 13:12, 16; 14:25; 15:3, 26; 18:13, 18, 20, 22; 20:1, 10; 21:4, 17

1Ki 1:1; 3:2, 18, 22, 26, 27; 6:18; 8:16, 23, 35, 46; 9:22; 10:5, 10, 12; 13:9, 17, 22^{2}; 17:7, 17; 18:10, 23^{2}, 25, 26; 21:4, 5; 22:17, 18, 47

2Ki 1:16, 17; 2:12; 3:9; 4:14, 41; 5:15, 25; 6:23; 7:5, 10; 9:35; 10:31; 12:7, 8; 17:4; 19:18; 22:7; 23:10, 18, 25; 25:3

1Ch 2:34; 12:17; 16:21, 22; 17:9; 22:16; 23:22, 26; 24:2, 28

2Ch 6:5, 14, 26, 36; 7:13; 8:9; 9:4; 13:9; 14:6, 11; 15:5, 19; 17:10; 18:16^{2}; 19:7; 20:12; 21:19; 22:9; 32:15; 35:18; 36:16, 17

Ezr 4:16; 9:14; 10:6

Neh 2:14, 17, 20; 6:1, 8; 13:19, 21, 26

Est 1:19; 2:14; 5:12; 8:8; 9:2

Job 3:7; 4:18; 5:19; 7:7, 8, 9, 10; 9:25; 10:18; 11:3; 12:2, 14, 24; 13:4; 14:12; 15:3, 15, 19, 28; 16:18; 18:17; 19:7, 16; 20:9, 21; 23:6; 24:7, 15, 20, 22; 26:2, 3, 6; 28:7, 18; 30:13, 17; 32:3, 5, 15, 16, 19; 34:22, 32; 36:16, 19; 38:11, 26^{2}; 40:5; 41:8, 16; 42:2, 15

Ps 3:2; 5:9; 6:5; 10:18; 14:1, 3, 4; 19:3; 22:6; 23:4; 32:2, 9; 33:16; 34:9; 36:1; 38:3, 7, 14; 39:13; 40:17; 41:8; 50:9; 53:1, 3, 4, 5; 55:19; 63:1; 69:2; 70:5; 72:12; 73:4; 74:9; 77:7; 78:64; 81:9; 83:4; 84:11; 88:4, 5; 91:10; 92:15; 101:3; 102:27; 103:16; 104:35; 105:14, 15; 107:4, 40; 119:3; 142:4^{2}; 143:2; 144:14^{2}; 146:3

Prv 1:24; 3:30; 6:7; 8:24^{2}; 10:22, 25; 11:14; 12:21, 28; 14:4; 17:16, 20, 21; 18:2; 21:10, 30; 22:24; 24:20; 25:28; 26:20^{2}; 28:1, 3, 17, 24; 29:9, 18; 30:20, 27, 31; 31:7, 11

Ecc 1:9, 11; 2:11, 16; 3:11, 12, 19; 4:1^{2}, 8, 13, 16; 5:4; 6:3, 6; 7:21; 8:5, 8^{2}, 15; 9:1, 8, 10, 15; 10:11, 20; 12:1, 12

Song 4:7; 5:6; 8:8

Isa 1:6, 13, 30; 5:6, 8, 13; 8:20; 9:7, 17, 19; 10:15, 20; 13:14, 18; 14:8; 15:6; 16:10^{2}; 19:7; 23:1^{2}, 10, 12^{2}; 24:10; 25:2; 26:21; 27:11^{2}; 28:8; 29:16; 30:7, 16, 19; 32:5; 33:8, 21; 34:16; 35:9; 37:19; 38:11; 40:20, 28, 29; 41:28^{2}; 43:10, 11, 12, 24; 44:6, 8, 12; 45:5, 9, 14, 20, 21; 47:1^{2}, 5, 6; 48:22; 50:2^{3}, 10; 51:22; 52:1, 11; 53:2^{2}, 9; 54:9, 17; 55:1; 57:1, 10, 21; 58:3; 59:8, 10, 15, 16^{2}; 60:15, 18, 19, 20; 62:4, 7, 8; 65:19, 20

Jer 2:6^{2}, 11, 13, 25^{2}, 30, 31; 3:3, 16; 4:22, 23, 25; 5:7; 6:10, 14, 23; 7:32^{2}; 8:6, 11, 13, 15, 22^{2}; 10:14; 11:19, 23; 12:11, 12; 14:3, 4, 5, 6, 19^{2}; 16:14, 19, 20; 17:21, 24^{2}; 18:12; 19:6, 11; 22:3^{2}, 10, 12, 28, 30; 23:4, 7, 17, 36; 25:6, 27, 35; 30:8, 13, 17; 31:29, 34^{2}; 33:24; 35:6^{2}, 8; 36:19; 38:6, 9, 24; 39:12; 40:15; 41:4; 42:14^{2}, 18; 44:2, 5, 17, 22, 26; 45:3; 46:25; 48:2, 8, 33, 38; 49:1^{2}, 7, 18, 33, 36; 50:14, 39, 40; 51:17, 43; 52:6

Lam 1:3, 6, 9; 2:9^{2}, 18; 4:4, 6, 15, 16, 22; 5:5

Ezk 12:23, 24, 25; 13:10, 15, 16, 21, 23; 14:11, 15; 15:5; 16:34, 41, 42; 18:32; 19:9, 14; 20:39; 21:13, 27, 32; 22:26; 24:6, 17, 27; 26:13, 14, 21; 28:3, 9, 24; 29:11, 15, 16, 18; 30:13, 14, 15, 16; 33:11, 22; 34:5, 8, 22, 28, 29; 36:12, 14, 29, 30; 37:8, 22; 39:10; 43:7; 44:2, 9, 17, 25^{2}, 28; 45:8

Dan 1:4; 2:10, 35; 3:25, 27, 29; 4:9; 6:2, 15, 22, 23; 8:4, 7; 10:3, 8^{2}, 16, 17

Hos 1:6; 2:16, 17; 4:1, 4, 6; 8:7^{2}, 8; 9:15, 16; 10:3; 13:4^{2}

Joel 1:18; 2:19; 3:17

Am 3:4, 5; 5:2, 20; 6:10; 7:14; 9:15

Mic 3:7; 4:9; 5:12, 13; 7:1

Nah 1:12, 14, 15; 2:13; 3:8, 18, 19

Hab 1:14; 2:19; 3:17^{2}

Zep 2:5; 3:5, 6, 11

Hag 2:12

Zec 1:21; 4:5, 13; 7:14; 8:10, 17; 9:8, 11; 10:2; 11:6; 13:2, 5; 14:11, 17, 18, 21

Mal 1:10

Mt 5:18, 20, 26; 6:1, 24, 25, 31, 34; 8:4, 10, 28; 9:16, 30, 36; 10:19, 42; 11:27; 12:39; 13:5, 6; 16:4, 7, 8, 20; 17:8, 9; 19:6, 18; 20:7, 13; 21:19; 22:23, 24, 25, 46; 23:9; 24:4, 21, 22, 36^{2}; 25:3, 42^{2}; 26:55

Mk 1:45; 2:2^{2}, 17, 21, 22; 3:27; 4:5, 6, 7, 17, 40; 5:3^{2}, 37, 43; 6:5, 8^{3}, 31; 7:12, 24, 36; 8:12, 16, 17, 30; 9:3, 8, 9, 25, 39; 10:8, 29; 11:14; 12:14, 18, 19, 20, 22, 34; 13:11, 20, 32^{2}; 14:25

Lk 1:7, 33; 2:7; 3:13, 14; 4:24; 5:14, 36, 37, 39; 7:9, 44, 45; 8:13, 14, 16, 27, 51, 56; 9:13, 21, 36, 62; 10:4, 22; 11:20, 29, 33, 36; 12:4, 11, 17, 22, 33; 13:11; 15:7, 16, 19, 21; 16:2, 13; 18:17, 29; 20:22, 31; 22:36, 53; 23:4, 14, 15, 22

Jn 1:18, 21, 47; 2:3; 3:2, 13, 32; 4:9, 17^{2}, 27, 38, 44; 5:7, 14, 22; 6:37, 44, 53, 65, 66; 7:4, 13, 18, 27, 30, 44, 52; 8:10, 11^{2}, 15, 20, 37, 44; 9:4, 25, 41; 10:18, 29, 41; 11:10, 54; 13:8, 28; 14:6, 19; 15:4, 13, 22; 16:10, 21, 22, 25, 29; 17:11; 18:38; 19:4, 6, 9, 11, 15; 21:5

Act 1:20; 4:17^{2}; 5:13, 23; 7:5^{2}, 11; 8:39; 9:7, 8; 10:34; 12:18; 13:28, 34, 37, 41; 15:2, 9, 24, 28; 16:28; 18:10, 15; 19:23, 24, 26, 40; 20:25, 33, 38; 21:25, 39; 23:8, 9, 22; 25:10, 11, 26; 27:20, 22; 28:2, 4, 5, 6, 18, 31

Ro 2:11; 3:9^{2}, 10, 12, 18, 20, 22; 4:15^{2}; 5:13; 6:9^{2}; 7:3, 17, 18, 20; 8:1; 10:12, 19; 11:6^{4}; 12:17; 13:1, 8, 10; 14:7, 13; 15:23

1Co 1:7, 10, 29; 2:11, 15; 3:11, 18, 21; 4:6, 11; 5:11; 6:5; 7:25, 37; 8:13; 9:10; 10:13, 24, 25, 27; 11:16; 12:3^{2}, 21^{2}, 24, 25; 13:5; 14:2, 28; 15:12, 13; 16:2, 11

2Co 2:13; 3:10; 5:16^{2}, 21; 6:3; 7:2^{3}, 5; 8:15, 20; 11:9, 10, 14, 15, 16; 13:7

Gal 2:5, 6^{2}, 16; 3:11, 15, 18, 25; 4:7, 8; 5:4, 23; 6:17

Eph 2:12, 19; 4:14, 28, 29; 5:5, 6, 11, 29

Php 2:7, 20; 3:3; 4:15

Col 2:16, 18; 3:25

1Th 3:1, 3, 5; 4:6, 13; 5:1

2Th 2:3; 3:14

1Ti 1:3; 3:3; 4:12; 5:22, 23; 6:16^{2}

2Ti 2:4, 14; 3:9; 4:16

Tit 1:7; 2:8, 15; 3:2^{2}

Heb 5:4; 6:13; 7:13; 8:7, 12; 9:17, 22; 10:2, 6, 17, 18, 26, 38; 12:11, 14, 17; 13:10, 14

Jas 1:11, 13, 17; 2:11, 13; 3:8, 12

1Pt 2:22; 3:10; 4:2

2Pt 1:20

1Jn 1:5, 8; 2:7, 19, 21, 27; 3:5, 7, 15; 4:12, 18

3Jn 4

Rev 2:17; 3:7^{2}, 8, 11, 12; 5:3, 4; 7:9, 16; 10:6; 13:17; 14:3, 5, 11; 15:8; 17:12; 18:7^{2}, 11, 14, 21, 22^{3}, 23^{2}; 19:12; 20:3, 6, 11; 21:1, 4, 22, 23, 25, 27; 22:3, 5^{2}

NOR

Gen 19:33, 35; 21:23^{2}; 45:5, 6; 49:10

Ex 4:1, 10; 10:6; 11:6; 12:9; 13:22; 20:5, 10^{5}, 17^{5}; 22:21, 28; 23:24^{2}, 26, 32; 30:9^{2}; 34:3, 10, 28; 36:6

Lev 2:11; 3:17; 10:9^{2}; 11:12, 26; 12:4; 13:34; 17:16; 18:26; 19:4, 14, 15, 18, 20, 26, 28; 20:19; 21:5, 10, 11, 12, 23; 22:22; 23:14^{2}; 25:4, 11, 20, 37; 26:1; 27:10

Nu 5:15; 6:3; 9:12; 11:19^{3}; 18:3; 20:17; 23:25

Dt 1:45; 2:19, 27, 37^{3}; 4:28^{3}, 31; 5:9, 14^{8}; 7:2, 3, 7, 25; 9:9, 18, 23, 27^{2}; 10:9, 17; 12:12, 17^{2}, 32; 13:6, 8; 14:1, 8, 27, 29; 15:7, 19; 17:11, 16; 18:1, 22; 21:4; 22:30; 23:6, 17; 24:17^{2}; 26:14; 28:36, 39, 50, 64; 29:23^{2}; 31:6^{2}; 33:9; 34:7

Jos 1:5; 6:10; 10:25; 13:13; 22:19, 26, 28; 23:7^{2}; 24:12, 19

Jdg 1:27^{4}, 30, 31^{6}, 33; 2:10, 19; 6:4^{2}; 11:15, 34; 13:4, 7, 14, 23; 14:16; 19:30

1Sa 1:15; 3:14; 5:5; 12:4, 21; 13:22; 15:29; 20:27, 31; 21:8; 22:15; 24:11; 25:31; 26:12; 27:9, 11; 28:6^{2}, 15, 18, 20; 30:12, 15, 19^{3}

2Sa 1:21; 2:19; 3:34; 13:22; 14:7; 19:6, 24^{2}; 21:4^{2}, 10

1Ki 3:8, 11, 26; 5:4; 6:7^{2}; 8:5, 57; 10:12; 12:24; 13:8, 9^{2}, 16^{2}, 17^{2}, 28; 16:11; 17:1; 18:26, 29^{2}; 20:8; 22:31

2Ki 3:14; 4:23, 31; 5:17; 6:10; 9:15; 14:6, 26^{2}; 17:35^{3}; 18:5, 12; 19:32^{3}; 20:13; 23:22^{2}

1Ch 21:24; 22:13; 23:26; 28:20^{2}

2Ch 1:11; 5:6; 6:14; 11:4; 15:5; 19:7^{2}; 20:15, 17; 21:12; 29:7; 32:7^{2}, 15; 34:2

Ezr 9:12, 14; 10:6

Neh 1:7^{2}; 2:16^{4}, 20^{2}; 4:23^{3}; 7:61; 8:9; 9:31, 34^{2}; 10:30; 13:25

Est 2:7, 10, 20; 3:2, 5; 4:16; 5:9; 9:28

Job 1:22; 3:10; 7:19; 14:12; 18:19^{2}; 24:13; 27:4; 28:8; 34:19, 22; 36:19; 41:12^{2}, 26

Ps 1:1^{2}, 5; 15:3^{2}, 5; 16:4; 19:3; 22:24; 24:4; 25:7; 26:9; 28:5; 37:25, 33; 40:4; 49:7; 50:9; 59:3; 66:20; 75:6^{2}; 78:42; 89:22, 33, 34; 91:5, 6^{2}; 103:10; 121:4, 6; 129:7; 131:1; 132:3; 144:14; 146:3

Prv 4:27; 5:13; 6:4; 8:26^{2}; 17:26; 21:30^{2}; 30:3, 8; 31:3, 4

Ecc 1:8; 3:14; 4:8; 5:10; 6:5; 8:16; 9:10^{3}, 11^{3}; 11:5; 12:1, 2

Song 2:7; 3:5; 8:4

Isa 3:7; 5:6, 27^{3}; 8:12; 11:9; 14:21^{2}; 22:2; 23:4^{2}, 18; 28:28^{2}; 30:5^{2}; 31:4; 32:5; 34:10; 35:9; 37:33^{3}; 39:2; 40:16; 42:2^{2}, 4; 43:23; 44:9, 18, 19, 20; 45:13, 17; 46:7; 47:14; 48:1, 19; 49:10^{2}; 51:14; 52:12; 53:2; 54:9; 57:11; 58:13^{2}; 59:4, 21^{2}; 60:11, 18; 62:6; 64:4; 65:17, 19, 20, 23, 25

Jer 4:11; 5:4, 12; 6:19, 20, 25; 7:16, 22, 24, 26, 28, 32; 8:2, 13; 9:16; 11:8; 13:14^{2}; 14:16^{2}; 15:10, 17; 16:5, 6^{2}, 13; 17:21, 23; 18:18^{2}; 19:4^{2}, 5, 6; 20:9; 21:7; 22:3, 10; 23:4, 32; 25:4, 33, 35; 27:9^{4}; 31:40; 35:6, 7^{3}, 8, 9^{3}, 15; 36:24^{2}; 37:2^{2}, 19; 42:14^{2}, 21; 44:3, 5, 10^{2}, 23^{3}; 46:6; 49:31, 33; 51:5, 26, 62

Lam 2:22; 3:33

Ezk 2:6; 3:18, 19; 7:11^{2}, 12; 12:24; 13:23; 14:16, 18, 20; 16:4, 47, 48; 18:17; 20:18, 44; 22:24; 23:27; 24:16, 22, 23; 28:24; 29:5, 11, 18; 31:8; 32:13; 37:23^{2}; 38:11; 43:7^{2}; 44:9, 13, 20, 22; 48:14

Dan 1:8; 2:10; 3:12, 14, 18, 27^{2}, 28; 5:8, 10, 23^{2}; 6:4, 13, 15; 10:3; 11:4, 6, 20, 24, 37^{2}

Hos 1:7^3, 10; 4:1^2, 4, 14, 15; 5:13; 7:10

Am 5:5; 8:11; 9:10

Oba 13

Jna 3:7^3

Mic 5:7

Zep 1:6, 18; 3:13

Zec 1:4; 4:6; 7:10^2, 14; 8:10; 11:16^2; 14:6, 7

Mal 4:1

Mt 5:35; 6:20^2, 25, 26; 10:9^2, 10^2, 14, 24; 11:18; 12:19; 22:29, 30; 24:21; 25:13

Mk 6:11; 8:26; 12:25

Lk 1:15; 6:44; 7:33; 9:3; 10:4^2; 12:24^2; 14:12^2, 35; 17:23; 18:4; 20:35; 21:15; 22:68; 23:15

Jn 1:13^2, 25; 4:21; 5:37; 8:19; 9:3; 11:50; 12:40; 16:3

Act 4:18; 8:21; 9:9; 13:27; 15:10; 19:37; 23:8, 12, 21; 24:12, 18; 25:8; 27:20

Ro 8:38^6, 39^3; 9:16; 14:21^2

1Co 2:6, 9; 6:9^4, 10^5; 10:32^2; 12:21

2Co 4:2; 7:12

Gal 3:28^3; 4:14; 5:6; 6:15

Eph 5:4^2, 5^2

Col 3:11^3

1Th 2:3^2, 5, 6^2; 5:5

2Th 2:2^2

1Ti 1:7; 2:12; 6:16, 17

2Ti 1:8

Heb 7:3; 9:25; 12:5, 18; 13:5

2Pt 1:8

Rev 3:15, 16; 5:3; 7:1^2, 3, 16; 9:20^2, 21^3; 14:11; 21:4

NOT

Gen 2:5^2, 17, 18, 20, 25; 3:1, 3, 4, 11, 17; 4:5, 7^2, 9, 12; 5:24; 6:3; 7:2, 8; 8:12, 21, 22; 9:4, 23; 11:7; 12:18; 13:6^2, 9; 14:23^2; 15:1, 4, 10, 13, 16; 16:10; 17:12, 14, 15; 18:3, 15, 21, 24, 25, 28, 29, 30^2, 31, 32^2; 19:7, 8, 17, 18, 20, 21, 31, 33, 35; 20:4, 5, 6, 7, 9, 11, 12; 21:10, 12, 16, 17, 23, 26; 22:12^2, 16; 24:3, 5, 6, 8^2, 21, 27, 33, 37, 39, 41, 49, 56; 26:2, 22, 24, 29; 27:1, 2, 12, 21, 23, 36^2; 28:1, 6, 8, 15, 16; 29:25, 26; 30:31, 33, 40, 42; 31:2, 5, 7, 15, 20, 24, 27, 28, 29, 32^2, 33, 34, 35^2, 38^2, 39, 52^2; 32:10, 25, 26, 32; 34:7, 17, 19, 23; 35:5, 10, 17; 36:7; 37:4, 13, 21, 27, 29, 30; 38:9, 14, 16, 20, 23, 26; 39:6, 8, 10, 23; 40:8, 23; 41:16, 21, 31, 36; 42:2, 4, 8, 13, 15, 20, 21, 22^3, 23, 32, 36^2, 37, 38; 43:3, 5^3, 8, 9, 23, 32; 44:4, 5, 15, 18, 26, 28, 30, 31, 32, 34; 45:1, 3, 5, 8, 9, 20, 24, 26; 46:3; 47:9, 18^2, 19^2, 22^2, 26, 29; 48:10, 11, 18; 49:4, 6^2, 10; 50:19, 21

Ex 1:8, 17, 19; 2:3; 3:2, 3, 5, 19^2, 21; 4:1^2, 8, 9, 10, 11, 14, 21; 5:2, 8, 9, 10, 11, 14, 19; 6:3, 9, 12; 7:4, 13, 16, 21, 24; 8:15, 18, 19, 21, 26^2, 28, 29^2, 31; 9:6, 7^2, 11, 12, 17, 18, 19, 21, 30, 32^2, 33; 10:7, 11, 15, 19, 20, 23, 26^2, 27; 11:7, 9, 10; 12:9, 13, 23, 30^2, 39^2, 45, 46; 13:13, 17, 22; 14:12, 13, 20, 28; 15:23; 16:8, 15, 20, 24, 25; 17:7; 18:17, 18; 19:12, 13^2, 15, 24; 20:4, 5, 7^2, 10, 13, 14, 15, 16, 17^2, 19, 20^2, 23, 25, 26; 21:5, 7, 8, 10, 11, 13, 18, 21, 28, 29, 33, 36; 22:8, 11^2, 13, 14, 15, 16, 18, 22, 25, 28, 29; 23:1^2, 2, 6, 7^2, 9, 18, 19, 21^2, 24, 29, 33; 24:2, 11; 25:15; 28:28, 32, 35, 43; 29:33, 34; 30:15^2, 20, 21, 32, 37; 32:1, 18, 22, 23, 32; 33:3, 11, 12, 15^2, 16, 20, 23; 34:10, 20, 25, 26, 29; 39:21, 23; 40:35, 37^2

Lev 1:17; 2:12; 4:2, 13, 22, 27; 5:1, 7, 8, 11, 17, 18; 6:12, 17, 23; 7:15, 18, 19; 8:33, 35; 10:1, 6, 7, 9, 17, 18; 11:4^2, 5, 6, 7, 8^2, 10, 11, 13, 26, 41, 42, 43, 47; 12:8; 13:4^2, 5, 6, 11, 21, 23, 28, 31, 32^2, 33, 34, 36, 53, 55^2; 14:32, 36, 48; 15:11, 31; 16:2^2, 13, 22; 17:4, 9, 16; 18:3^2, 7^2, 8, 9, 10, 11, 12, 13, 14^2, 15^2, 16, 17, 19, 20, 21, 22, 24, 26, 28, 30^2; 19:4, 7, 9, 10, 11, 12, 13^2, 14, 15, 16, 17^2, 18, 19^2, 20^3, 23, 26, 27, 28, 29, 31, 33; 20:4, 19, 22, 23, 25; 21:4, 5, 6, 7, 10, 14, 17, 18, 21, 23^2; 22:2, 4, 6, 8, 10, 12, 15, 20^2, 22, 23, 24, 25, 28; 23:22, 29; 25:5, 11, 14, 17, 20, 23, 28, 30^2, 34, 37, 39, 42, 43, 46, 53, 54; 26:11, 13, 14^2, 15, 18, 20, 21, 23, 26, 27, 31, 35, 44; 27:10, 11, 20^2, 22, 27, 33^2

Nu 1:47, 49; 2:33; 4:15, 18, 19, 20; 5:3, 14, 19, 28; 6:7; 9:6, 7, 13^2, 19, 22; 10:7, 30, 31; 11:11, 14, 15, 17, 19, 23, 25, 26; 12:2, 7, 8^2, 11, 12, 14, 15; 13:20, 31; 14:3, 9^2, 16, 22, 23, 30, 41, 42^3, 43, 44; 15:22, 34, 39; 16:12, 14^2, 15^2, 28, 29, 40^2; 17:10; 18:3, 4, 17; 19:12^2, 13^2, 20^2; 20:12^2, 17^2, 18, 20, 24; 21:22^2, 23, 34; 22:12^2, 30, 34, 37^3; 23:8^2, 9, 12, 13, 19^3, 21, 24, 26; 24:1, 12, 17^2; 25:11; 26:11, 62, 64, 65; 27:3, 17; 29:7; 30:2, 5, 11, 12; 31:18, 23, 35, 49; 32:5, 9, 11, 18, 19, 23, 30; 33:55; 35:12, 23^2, 27, 30, 33, 34; 36:7

Dt 1:9, 17^2, 21, 26, 29, 32, 35, 37, 42^2, 43, 45; 2:5^3, 9^2, 19^2, 30, 36, 37; 3:2, 4^2, 11, 22, 26, 27; 4:2, 21^2, 22, 26, 31, 42; 5:3, 5, 8, 9, 11^2, 14, 17, 32; 6:10, 11^3, 14, 16; 7:3, 7, 10, 14, 18, 21, 22, 25; 8:3^2, 4, 9, 11^2, 16, 20; 9:4, 5, 6, 7, 23, 26, 27, 28; 10:10, 17; 11:2^3, 10, 16, 17, 28^2, 30; 12:4, 8, 9, 13, 16, 17, 19, 23^2, 24, 25, 30^2, 31, 32; 13:2, 3, 6, 8, 13, 16; 14:1, 3, 7^2, 8^2, 10^2, 12, 19, 21^2, 24, 27; 15:2, 6^2, 7, 9, 10, 13, 16, 18, 21, 23; 16:5, 16, 19^2, 21; 17:1, 3, 6, 11, 12, 15^2, 16, 17, 20^2; 18:9, 10, 14, 16^2, 19, 20, 21, 22^3; 19:4, 6^2, 10, 13, 14, 15, 21; 20:1, 3^3, 5, 6, 7, 15, 18, 19^2, 20; 21:1, 3^2, 7, 8, 14^2, 16, 18^2, 20, 23^2; 22:1, 2^2, 3, 4, 5, 6, 8, 9, 10, 11, 14, 17, 19, 20, 24, 28, 29, 30; 23:1, 2^2, 3^2, 4, 5, 6, 7^2, 10^2, 15, 16, 18, 19, 20, 21, 24, 25; 24:4^2, 5, 10, 12, 14, 16, 17, 19, 20, 21; 25:3, 4, 5, 6, 7^2, 8, 9, 12, 13, 14, 18, 19; 26:13, 14; 27:5, 26; 28:12, 13^2, 14, 15, 27, 29, 30^2, 31^2, 33, 40, 41, 44, 45, 47, 49, 50, 51, 55, 56, 58, 61, 62; 29:4, 5^2, 6, 15, 20, 23, 26^2; 30:11, 12, 17, 18; 31:2, 6^2, 8^2, 13, 17^2, 21; 32:5, 6^2, 17^3, 21^2, 27^2, 31, 34, 47, 51, 52; 33:6^2, 9, 11; 34:4, 7, 10

Jos 1:5^2, 7, 8, 9^2, 18; 2:4, 5, 14, 22; 3:4^2; 5:5, 6^2, 7; 6:10; 7:3^2, 12, 13, 19; 8:1, 4, 14, 17^2, 26, 35^2; 9:14, 18, 19, 26; 10:6, 8^2, 13^2, 19^2, 25; 11:6, 11, 19; 13:13, 33; 15:63; 16:10; 17:12, 13, 16, 17; 18:2; 20:5^2, 9; 21:44, 45; 22:3, 17, 19, 20^2, 22, 24, 26, 27, 28, 31, 33; 23:6, 7, 14^2; 24:10, 12, 13^3, 19

Jdg 1:19, 21, 28, 32, 34; 2:2, 3, 10, 14, 17^2, 19, 20, 21, 22; 3:1, 22, 25, 28, 29; 4:6, 8^2, 9, 14, 16, 18; 5:23, 30^2; 6:10^2, 13, 14, 18, 23^2, 27, 39; 7:4^2; 8:1, 2, 19, 20, 23, 34; 9:15, 20, 28, 38, 41, 54; 10:6, 11; 11:2, 7, 10, 15, 17^2, 18, 20, 24, 26, 27, 28; 12:1, 2, 3, 6; 13:2, 3, 4^2, 6, 9, 14, 16^2, 23; 14:4, 6, 9, 14, 15, 16^3, 18^2; 15:1, 2, 11, 12, 13; 16:8, 9, 15^2, 17, 20; 18:1, 9, 25; 19:10, 12^2, 20, 23^2, 24, 25; 20:8, 13, 16, 34; 21:1, 5^2, 7, 8, 14, 17, 18, 22^2

Ru 1:16, 20; 2:8^2, 9^2, 11, 13, 15, 16, 20, 22; 3:1, 2, 3, 10, 11, 13, 14, 17, 18; 4:4, 10, 14

1Sa 1:7, 8^2, 11, 13, 16, 22^2; 2:3, 12, 15, 16^2, 25, 31, 32, 33; 3:2, 5, 6, 7, 13, 14, 17; 4:7, 9, 15, 20^2; 5:7, 11, 12; 6:3^2, 6, 9^2, 12; 7:8; 8:3, 5, 7^2, 18; 9:2, 4^3, 7, 13, 20^2, 21; 10:1, 16, 21; 11:7, 11, 13; 12:4, 5, 14, 15, 17, 19, 20^2, 21, 22; 13:8, 11, 12, 13, 14^2; 14:1, 3, 9, 17, 27, 30, 34, 36, 37, 39, 45^2; 15:3, 9, 11, 17, 19, 26, 29^2; 16:7^2, 10, 11; 17:8, 29, 33, 39^2, 47; 18:17, 25, 26; 19:4^2, 6, 11; 20:2^2, 3, 5, 9, 12, 14^2, 15^2, 26^3, 27, 29, 30, 31, 37, 38, 39; 21:8, 11^2; 22:5, 15, 17^2, 23; 23:14, 17^2, 19; 24:7, 10, 11^2, 12, 13, 18, 21^2; 25:7, 11, 15, 19, 25^2, 28, 34; 26:1, 8, 9, 14, 15^2, 16^2, 20, 23; 28:6, 13, 18, 23; 29:3, 4^2, 5, 6^2, 7, 8, 9; 30:2, 10, 17, 21, 22^2, 23; 31:4

2Sa 1:10, 14, 20^2, 21, 22^2, 23; 2:19, 21, 26; 3:8, 11, 13, 22, 26, 29, 34, 37, 38; 4:11; 5:6, 8, 23; 6:10; 7:6, 7, 15; 9:3, 7; 10:3; 11:3, 9, 10^3, 11, 13, 20, 21, 25; 12:13, 17, 18, 23; 13:4, 12^2, 13, 14, 16, 20, 25^2, 26, 28^2, 30, 32, 33; 14:2, 7, 10, 11^2, 13, 14, 18, 19, 24^2, 28, 29^2; 15:11, 14, 27, 35; 16:17, 19; 17:6, 7, 8, 12, 13, 16, 17, 19, 20, 22^2, 23; 18:3^2, 11, 12, 14, 20, 29; 19:7^2, 10, 13^2, 19, 21, 22, 23, 25, 43; 20:3, 10, 21; 21:2, 17; 22:22, 23, 37, 38, 39, 42, 44; 23:5^2, 16, 17^2, 19^2, 23; 24:14

1Ki 1:4, 6, 8, 10, 11^2, 13, 18, 19, 26, 27, 51, 52; 2:4, 6, 8, 9, 16, 17, 20^2, 23, 26, 28, 32, 36, 42, 43; 3:7, 11, 13^2, 21; 5:3, 6; 6:6, 13; 7:31; 8:5, 8, 11, 19, 25, 41, 46, 56, 57; 9:5, 6, 12, 20, 21; 10:3^2, 7^2, 20; 11:2, 4, 6, 10^2, 11, 12, 13, 33, 34, 39, 41; 12:15, 16, 24, 31; 13:4, 8, 10, 16, 21, 22, 28, 33; 14:2, 4, 8, 29; 15:3, 5, 7, 14, 17, 23, 29, 31; 16:5, 11, 14, 20, 27; 17:1, 12, 13, 14, 16; 18:5, 10^3, 12, 13, 18, 21, 40, 44; 19:2, 4, 11^2, 12, 18^2; 20:7, 8, 9, 11, 28, 36; 21:4, 6, 15, 29; 22:3, 7, 8^2, 17, 18, 28, 33, 39, 43^2, 45, 48, 49

2Ki 1:3^2, 4, 6^3, 15, 16^2, 18; 2:2, 4, 6, 10^2, 16, 17, 18^2, 21; 3:2, 3, 11, 14^2, 17, 26; 4:2, 3, 6, 16, 24, 27, 28^2, 29^2, 30, 31, 39, 40; 5:12^2, 13, 17, 20, 26; 6:9, 10, 11, 16, 19, 22, 27, 32; 7:2, 9, 19; 8:19, 23; 9:3, 18, 20, 37; 10:4, 5, 19, 21^2, 29, 31, 34; 11:2, 6, 15; 12:3, 6, 7, 13, 15, 16, 19; 13:2, 6, 8, 11, 12, 23; 14:3, 4, 6^2, 11, 15, 18, 24, 26, 27, 28; 15:4, 6, 9, 16, 18, 20, 21, 24, 28, 35, 36; 16:2, 5, 19; 17:2, 9, 12, 14^2, 15, 19, 22, 25, 26^2, 34, 35, 37, 38, 40; 18:6, 7, 12^2, 22, 26, 27, 29^2, 30, 31, 32^2, 36^2; 19:3, 6, 10^2, 25, 32, 33; 20:1, 13, 15, 19, 20; 21:9, 17, 22, 25; 22:2, 13, 17, 20; 23:9, 22, 26, 28, 33; 24:4, 5, 7; 25:24

1Ch 4:10, 27; 5:1; 10:4, 13, 14; 11:5, 18, 19, 21, 25; 12:19, 33; 13:3, 13; 14:14; 15:13^2; 16:22, 30; 17:4, 5, 6, 13; 19:3; 21:3, 6, 13, 17^2, 24, 30; 22:8, 13, 18^2; 23:11; 26:10; 27:23, 24; 28:3, 20^2; 29:1, 25

2Ch 1:11; 4:18; 5:6, 9, 11, 14; 6:9, 16, 32, 36, 42; 7:2, 7, 18; 8:7, 8, 11, 15; 9:2, 6^2, 19, 20, 29; 10:15, 16; 11:4; 12:7^2, 12, 14, 15; 13:5, 7, 9, 10, 12^2; 14:11, 13; 15:7, 13, 17; 16:7, 8, 12; 17:3, 4; 18:6, 7, 17^2, 27, 30, 32; 19:6, 10^2; 20:6^3, 7, 10^2, 12, 15^2, 17^2, 32, 33^2, 37; 21:7, 12, 20; 22:11; 23:8, 14; 24:5, 6, 19, 22, 25; 25:2, 4^2, 7^2, 13, 15, 16, 20, 26; 26:18; 27:2; 28:1, 10, 13, 20, 21, 27; 29:7, 11, 34; 30:3^2, 5, 7, 8, 9, 17^2, 18, 19, 26; 32:7, 11, 12, 13, 15, 17^2, 25, 26; 33:10, 23; 34:21, 25, 33; 35:3, 15, 21^2, 22^2; 36:12

Ezr 2:59, 62, 63; 3:6, 13; 4:13, 14, 21, 22; 5:5, 16; 6:8; 7:24, 25, 26; 9:1, 9, 12, 14; 10:8, 13

Neh 1:7; 2:1, 2, 3, 16; 3:5; 4:5^2, 10, 11, 14; 5:9^2, 13, 14, 15, 18; 6:1, 9, 11, 12; 7:3, 4, 61, 64, 65; 8:9, 17; 9:16, 17, 19^2, 20, 21^2, 29^2, 30, 31, 32, 35; 10:30, 31, 39; 13:1, 2, 6, 10, 14, 18^2, 19, 24, 25, 26

Est 1:15, 16, 17, 19; 2:10^2, 20; 3:2, 4, 5, 8; 4:4, 11^2, 13, 16; 5:9; 6:1, 13; 7:4; 9:10, 15, 16, 27, 28; 10:2

Job 1:10, 12, 22; 2:10^2, 12; 3:4, 6^2, 10, 11^2, 16, 18, 21, 26; 4:6, 16, 21; 5:6, 17, 24; 6:10^2, 13, 29; 7:1^2, 8, 11, 16, 19, 21^2; 8:10, 12, 15^2, 18, 20; 9:5, 7, 11^2, 13, 15, 16, 18, 21, 24, 28, 32, 34, 35^2; 10:2, 7, 10, 14, 15, 19, 20, 21; 11:2, 11, 14, 15, 20; 12:3^2, 9, 11; 13:2, 11, 16, 20^2, 21; 14:2, 4, 7, 12^2, 16, 21^2; 15:6, 9^2, 15, 18, 22, 29, 30, 31, 32; 16:6, 13, 17, 18, 22; 17:2^2, 4; 18:5, 21; 19:3, 7, 22, 27; 20:4, 8, 13, 17, 18^2, 19, 20^2, 26; 21:4, 10^2, 14, 16, 29^2; 22:5, 7, 11, 12, 14, 20; 23:8, 11, 17; 24:1^2, 12, 13, 16, 18, 21^2, 25; 25:3, 5^2; 26:8; 27:4, 5, 6^2, 11, 14, 15, 19^2, 22; 28:7, 8, 13, 14^2, 17, 19; 29:16, 22, 24^2; 30:10, 20^2, 24, 25^2, 27; 31:3, 4, 15^2, 17, 20^2, 23, 31, 32, 34; 32:6, 9, 13, 14, 16, 21, 22; 33:7, 12, 13, 14, 21, 27, 33; 34:12, 19, 23, 27, 30, 31, 32, 33; 35:13, 14, 15^2; 36:4, 5, 6, 7, 12, 13, 19, 20, 21, 26, 32; 37:4, 21, 23, 24; 39:4, 16, 22; 40:5, 23; 41:9, 12, 33; 42:3^2, 7, 8

Ps 1:1, 3, 4, 5; 3:6; 4:4; 5:4, 5; 6:1; 7:12; 9:10, 12, 18^2, 19; 10:4^2, 6, 12, 13; 14:3, 4; 15:3, 4, 5; 16:2, 4, 8, 10; 17:1, 3, 5; 18:21, 22, 36, 38, 41, 43; 19:3, 13; 21:2, 7, 11; 22:2^2, 5, 11, 19, 24; 23:1; 24:4; 25:2^2, 7, 20; 26:1, 4, 5, 9; 27:3, 9^3, 12; 28:1, 3, 5^2; 30:1, 3, 12; 31:8, 17; 32:2, 5, 6, 9; 33:16; 34:5, 10, 20; 35:11, 15^2, 19, 20, 22^2, 24, 25^2; 36:4^2, 11^2, 12; 37:1, 7, 8, 10^2, 19, 21, 24, 25, 28, 33, 36^2; 38:1, 9, 13^2, 14, 21^2; 39:1, 6, 8, 9, 12; 40:4, 6^2, 9, 10^2, 11, 12; 41:2, 11; 44:3, 6, 9, 12, 17, 18, 21, 23; 46:2, 5; 49:9, 12, 16, 17, 20; 50:3, 8, 12; 51:11^2, 16^2, 17; 52:7; 53:3, 4; 54:3, ttl; 55:1, 11, 12, 19, 23; 56:4, 8, 11, 13; 58:5, 8; 59:3, 5, 11, 13, 15; 60:10^2; 62:2, 6, 10^3; 64:4; 66:7, 9, 18, 20; 69:4, 5, 6^2, 14, 15^2, 17, 23, 27, 28, 33; 71:9^2, 12, 15, 18; 73:5; 74:9, 19^2, 21, 23; 75:4^2, 5^2; 77:2, 19; 78:4, 7, 8^3, 10, 22^2, 30, 32, 37, 38^2, 39, 42, 44, 50, 53, 56, 63, 67; 79:6^2, 8; 80:18; 81:5, 11; 82:5; 83:1^3; 85:6, 8; 86:14; 89:22, 30, 31, 33, 34, 35, 43, 48; 91:5, 7; 92:6; 94:7, 9^2, 10^2, 14; 95:8, 10, 11; 96:10; 100:3; 101:3, 4, 5, 7^2; 102:2, 17, 24; 103:2, 9, 10; 104:5, 9^2; 105:15, 28, 37; 106:7^2, 11, 13, 23, 24, 25, 34; 107:38; 108:11^2; 109:1, 14, 16, 17; 110:4; 112:6, 7, 8; 115:1^2, 5^2, 6^2, 7^2, 17; 118:6, 17, 18; 119:6, 8, 10, 11, 16, 19, 31, 36, 43, 46, 51, 60, 61, 80, 83, 85, 87, 102, 109, 110, 116, 121, 122, 133, 136, 141, 153, 155, 157, 158, 176; 121:3^2, 6; 124:1, 2, 6; 125:3; 127:5; 129:2, 7; 131:1; 132:3, 4, 10, 11; 135:16^2, 17; 137:6^2; 138:8; 139:4, 12, 15, 21^2; 140:8^2, 10, 11; 141:4^2, 5, 8; 143:2, 7; 146:3; 147:10^2, 20^2; 148:6

Prv 1:8, 10, 15, 28^2, 29; 3:1, 3, 5, 7, 11, 15, 21, 23, 24, 25, 27, 28, 29, 30, 31; 4:2, 5, 6,

1Jn 1:6, 8, 10^{2}; 2:1, 2, 4^{2}, 11, 15^{2}, 16, 19^{2}, 21^{2}, 23, 27, 28; 3:1^{2}, 2, 6^{2}, 9, 10^{3}, 12, 13, 14, 18, 21; 4:1, 3^{2}, 6^{2}, 8^{2}, 10, 18, 20^{2}; 5:3, 6, 10^{2}, 12^{2}, 16^{3}, 17, 18^{2}

2Jn 1, 5, 7, 8, 9^{2}, 10^{2}, 12

3Jn 9, 10, 11^{2}, 13

Jude 5, 6, 9, 10, 19

Rev 1:17; 2:2^{2}, 3, 9, 11, 13, 21, 24^{2}; 3:2, 3^{2}, 4, 5, 8, 9, 17, 18; 4:8; 5:5; 6:6, 10; 7:1, 3; 8:12; 9:4^{2}, 5, 6, 20^{3}; 10:4; 11:2, 6, 9; 12:8, 11; 13:8, 15; 14:4; 15:4; 16:9, 11, 18, 20; 17:8^{3}, 10, 11; 18:4^{2}; 19:10; 20:4, 5, 15; 21:25; 22:9, 10

O

Gen 17:18; 24:12, 42; 27:34, 38; 32:9; 43:20; 49:6, 18

Ex 4:10, 13; 15:6^{2}, 11, 16, 17^{2}; 32:4, 8; 34:9

Nu 10:36; 12:13; 16:22; 21:17, 29; 24:5^{2}

Dt 3:24; 4:1; 5:1, 29; 6:3, 4; 9:1, 26; 20:3; 21:8; 26:10; 27:9; 32:1^{2}, 6, 29, 43; 33:23, 29^{2}

Jos 7:7, 8, 13

Jdg 3:19; 5:3^{2}, 21, 31; 6:22; 13:8; 16:28^{2}; 21:3

1Sa 1:11; 4:9; 17:55; 20:12; 23:10, 11, 20; 26:17

2Sa 1:25; 7:18, 19^{2}, 22, 25, 27, 28, 29; 14:4, 9, 22; 15:31, 34; 16:4; 18:33^{2}; 19:4^{2}, 26; 20:1; 22:29, 50; 23:17; 24:10

1Ki 1:13, 20, 24; 3:7, 17, 26; 8:26, 28, 53; 12:16, 28; 13:2; 17:18, 20, 21; 18:26, 37; 19:4; 20:4; 21:20; 22:28

2Ki 1:11, 13; 4:40; 6:12, 26; 8:5; 9:5^{2}, 23; 13:14; 19:15, 19; 20:3

1Ch 16:13, 34, 35; 17:16, 17^{2}, 19, 20, 25, 27; 21:17; 29:11^{2}, 16, 18

2Ch 1:9; 6:14, 16, 17, 19, 41^{2}, 42; 10:16; 13:12; 14:11^{2}; 20:6, 12, 17, 20; 25:7

Ezr 9:6, 10, 15

Neh 1:5, 11; 4:4; 6:9; 13:14, 22, 29, 31

Est 7:3

Job 7:7, 20; 13:5; 14:13; 16:18, 21; 19:21; 33:31; 34:2; 37:14

Ps 2:10; 3:3, 7^{2}; 4:1, 2; 5:1, 3, 8, 10; 6:1, 2^{2}, 3, 4; 7:1, 3, 6, 8; 8:1, 9; 9:1, 2, 6, 13, 19, 20; 10:1, 12^{2}; 12:7; 13:1, 3; 16:1, 2; 17:1, 6, 7, 13, 14; 18:1, 15, 49; 19:14; 21:1; 22:2, 3, 19^{2}; 24:6, 7, 9; 25:1, 2, 4, 6, 7, 11, 17, 20, 22; 26:1, 2, 6; 27:7, 9, 11; 28:1; 29:1; 30:1, 2, 3, 4, 8, 10, 12; 31:1, 5, 9, 14, 17, 23; 33:1, 22; 34:3, 8, 9; 35:1, 22^{2}, 24; 36:5, 6, 7, 10; 38:1, 15^{2}, 21^{2}, 22; 39:12, 13; 40:5, 8, 9, 11, 13^{2}, 17; 41:10; 42:1, 5, 6, 11; 43:1^{2}, 3, 4, 5; 44:1, 4, 23; 45:3, 6, 10; 47:1; 48:9, 10; 50:7^{2}; 51:1, 10, 14, 15, 17; 52:1, 4; 54:1, 2, 6; 55:1, 9, 23; 56:1, 2, 7, 12; 57:1, 5, 7, 9, 11; 58:1^{2}, 6^{2}; 59:1, 3, 5, 8, 11, 17; 60:1^{2}, 10^{2}; 61:1, 5, 7; 62:12; 63:1; 64:1; 65:1, 2, 5; 66:8, 10; 67:3, 4, 5; 68:7, 9, 10, 24, 28, 32, 35; 69:1, 5, 6^{2}, 13^{2}, 16, 29; 70:1^{2}, 5^{2}; 71:1, 4, 5, 12^{2}, 17, 18, 19^{2}, 22^{2}; 72:1; 73:20; 74:1, 10, 18, 19, 21, 22; 75:1; 76:6; 77:13, 16; 78:1; 79:1, 8, 9, 12; 80:1, 3, 4, 7, 14, 19; 81:8^{2}; 82:8; 83:1^{2}, 13, 16; 84:1, 3, 8^{2}, 9, 12; 85:4, 7; 86:1, 2, 3, 4, 6, 8, 9, 11, 12, 14, 15, 16; 87:3; 88:1, 13; 89:5, 8, 15, 51; 90:13, 14; 92:1, 5, 9; 93:3, 5; 94:1^{2}, 5, 12, 18; 95:1, 6; 96:1, 7, 9; 97:8; 98:1; 99:8; 101:1, 2; 102:1, 12, 24; 103:1, 2, 22; 104:1^{2}, 24, 35; 105:1, 6; 106:1, 4^{2}, 47; 107:1; 108:1, 3, 5, 11^{2}; 109:1, 21, 26^{2}; 113:1; 114:5; 115:1, 9, 10; 116:4, 7, 16, 19; 117:1; 118:1, 25^{2}, 29; 119:5, 8, 10, 12, 31, 33, 41, 52, 55, 57, 64, 65, 75, 89, 97, 107, 108, 137, 145, 149, 151, 156, 159, 169, 174; 120:2; 122:2; 123:1, 3; 125:4; 126:4; 130:1, 3; 132:8; 135:1, 9, 13^{2}, 19^{2}, 20; 136:1, 2, 3, 26; 137:5, 7, 8; 138:4, 8; 139:1, 4, 17, 19, 21, 23; 140:1, 4, 6, 7, 8; 141:3, 8; 142:5; 143:1, 7, 9, 11; 144:5, 9; 145:1, 10; 146:1, 10; 147:12^{2}

Prv 4:10; 5:7; 6:9; 7:24; 8:4, 5, 32; 24:15; 30:13; 31:4

Ecc 10:16, 17; 11:9

Song 1:5, 7, 8, 9; 2:7, 14; 3:5, 11; 4:11, 16; 5:1^{2}, 8, 9, 16; 6:1, 4, 13; 7:1, 6, 13; 8:1, 4, 12

Isa 1:2^{2}; 2:5; 3:12; 5:3; 7:13; 8:8, 9; 10:5, 24, 30^{2}; 12:1; 14:12, 31^{2}; 16:9; 21:2^{2}, 10, 13; 23:4, 10, 12; 24:17; 25:1; 26:8, 13, 15, 17; 27:12; 33:2; 37:16, 17^{2}, 20; 38:3, 14, 16; 40:9^{2}, 27^{2}; 41:1; 43:1^{2}, 22^{2}; 44:1, 2, 21^{2}, 23^{2}; 45:15; 46:3, 8; 47:1^{2}, 5; 48:1, 12, 18; 49:1, 3, 13^{3}; 51:4, 9, 17; 52:1^{2}, 2^{2}; 54:1, 11; 62:6; 63:16, 17; 64:4, 8, 9, 12

Jer 2:4, 12, 28, 31; 3:14, 20; 4:1, 14, 19; 5:3, 15, 21; 6:1, 8, 18, 19, 23, 26; 7:29; 9:20; 10:1, 6, 7, 17, 23, 24; 11:5, 13, 20; 12:1, 3; 13:27; 14:7, 8, 9, 20, 22; 15:5, 15, 16; 16:19; 17:3, 13, 14; 18:6^{2}, 19; 19:3; 20:7, 12; 21:12, 13; 22:2, 23, 29; 30:10^{2}; 31:4, 7, 10, 21, 22, 23; 32:25; 34:4; 37:20; 42:19; 45:2; 46:11, 19, 27^{2}, 28; 47:6; 48:2, 19, 28, 32, 43, 46; 49:3, 4, 8, 16, 30; 50:11, 24, 31, 42; 51:13, 25, 62

Lam 1:9, 11, 20; 2:13^{2}, 18, 20; 3:55, 58, 59, 61, 64; 4:21, 22^{2}; 5:1, 19, 21

Ezk 3:25; 7:7; 8:15, 17; 10:13; 11:4, 5; 12:25; 13:4, 11; 16:35; 18:25, 29, 30, 31; 20:31, 39, 44; 23:22; 26:3; 27:3^{2}, 8; 28:16, 22; 33:7, 8, 10, 11, 20; 34:9, 17; 35:3, 15; 36:8, 22, 32; 37:3, 4, 9, 12, 13; 38:3, 16; 39:1; 44:6; 45:9

Dan 2:4, 23, 29, 31, 37; 3:4, 9, 10, 12, 14, 16, 17, 18, 24; 4:9, 18, 22, 24, 27, 31; 5:10, 18, 22; 6:7, 8, 12, 13, 15, 20, 21, 22; 8:17; 9:4, 7, 8, 15, 16, 17, 18, 19^{4}, 22; 10:11, 16, 19; 12:4, 8

Hos 5:1^{2}, 3, 8; 6:4^{2}, 11; 8:5; 9:1, 14; 10:9; 13:9, 14^{2}; 14:1

Joel 1:11^{2}, 19; 2:17, 21; 3:4, 11

Am 2:11; 3:1; 4:5, 12^{2}; 5:1, 25; 6:14; 7:2, 5, 12; 8:4, 14; 9:7

Oba 9

Jna 1:6, 14^{2}; 2:6; 4:2, 3

Mic 1:2, 13, 15; 2:7, 12; 3:1; 4:8, 10, 13; 5:1; 6:2, 3, 5, 8; 7:8

Nah 1:15; 3:18

Hab 1:2, 12^{3}; 3:2^{2}

Zep 2:1, 5; 3:14^{3}

Hag 1:4; 2:4^{2}, 23

Zec 1:9, 12; 2:7, 10, 13; 3:2, 8; 4:7; 8:13; 9:9^{2}, 13^{2}; 11:1, 2, 7; 13:7

Mal 1:6; 2:1

Mt 3:7; 6:30; 8:26; 11:25; 12:34; 14:31; 15:22, 28; 16:3, 8; 17:17; 18:32; 20:30, 31; 23:37; 26:39, 42

Mk 9:19; 12:29

Lk 3:7; 5:8; 9:41; 10:21; 12:28; 13:34; 24:25

Jn 17:5, 25

Act 1:1; 7:42; 13:10; 18:14; 25:26; 26:13, 19

Ro 2:1, 3; 7:24; 9:20; 11:33

1Co 7:16^{2}; 15:55^{2}

2Co 6:11

Gal 3:1

1Ti 6:11, 20

Heb 1:8; 10:7, 9

Jas 2:20

Rev 4:11; 6:10; 11:17; 15:4; 16:5

OF

Gen 1:2^{3}, 6, 10, 14, 15, 17, 20, 24, 25, 26^{2}, 27, 28^{2}, 29^{2}, 30^{2}; 2:1, 4^{2}, 5^{2}, 6, 7^{3}, 9^{5}, 10, 11^{2}, 12, 13^{2}, 14^{2}, 15, 16^{2}, 17^{4}, 19^{3}, 20^{2}, 21, 23^{3}; 3:1^{3}, 2^{3}, 3^{4}, 6, 7, 8^{4}, 11, 12, 14^{2}, 17^{6}, 18, 19^{2}, 20, 21, 22^{3}, 23, 24^{4}; 4:2^{2}, 3^{3}, 4^{3}, 10, 14, 16^{3}, 17^{2}, 19^{2}, 20^{2}, 21, 22^{2}, 23, 25, 26; 5:1^{3}, 4, 8, 11, 14, 17, 20, 23, 27, 29^{2}, 31; 6:1, 2^{3}, 4^{4}, 5^{3}, 7^{2}, 8, 9, 13, 14, 15^{4}, 16, 17^{2}, 19^{3}, 20^{5}, 21; 7:2^{2}, 3^{3}, 4, 6, 7^{2}, 8^{4}, 10, 11^{4}, 13^{2}, 14, 15^{2}, 16, 18, 21^{4}, 22^{2}, 23^{2}; 8:2^{2}, 3, 4^{2}, 5^{2}, 6^{2}, 8, 9^{2}, 10, 13^{3}, 14, 16, 17^{4}, 19, 20^{2}, 21; 9:2^{5}, 5^{5}, 6, 10^{6}, 11, 12, 13, 15, 16, 17, 18^{3}, 19^{2}, 21, 22^{2}, 23, 25, 26, 27, 29; 10:1^{2}, 2, 3, 4, 5, 6, 7^{2}, 10^{2}, 11, 14, 18, 19, 20, 21^{3}, 22, 23, 25, 29, 30, 31, 32^{2}; 11:1^{2}, 2, 4, 5, 8, 9^{3}, 10, 27, 28^{2}, 29^{5}, 31^{3}, 32; 12:1, 2, 3, 4, 5^{2}, 6^{2}, 8^{2}, 13, 15, 17; 13:1, 4^{2}, 7^{2}, 10^{3}, 11, 12^{2}, 13, 16^{2}, 17^{2}, 18; 14:1^{5}, 2^{5}, 3, 7, 8^{6}, 9^{4}, 10^{3}, 11, 13^{3}, 15, 17^{4}, 18^{2}, 19^{2}, 20, 21, 22^{2}, 24; 15:1, 2^{2}, 4^{2}, 7^{2}, 9^{3}, 12, 13, 16, 18; 16:2, 3, 7^{2}, 8, 9, 10, 11, 12, 13; 17:4, 5, 6^{2}, 8, 11^{2}, 12^{2}, 14, 16^{4}, 23^{2}, 24, 25, 27^{2}; 18:1^{2}, 5, 6, 10, 11, 13, 14, 18, 19^{2}, 20, 21, 25, 28^{2}; 19:1, 4^{2}, 8, 11, 12, 13^{2}, 14, 15, 16^{2}, 22, 24, 25, 26, 28^{3}, 29^{3}, 30, 31, 32, 34, 36, 37, 38^{2}; 20:2^{2}, 5^{2}, 6, 11, 12^{2}, 13, 16^{2}, 18^{3}; 21:2, 3, 9, 10, 11, 12^{2}, 13^{2}, 14^{2}, 15, 16, 17^{4}, 19, 21^{3}, 22, 25^{2}, 26, 27, 28, 30, 31, 32^{3}, 33; 22:2^{3}, 3^{2}, 6^{2}, 8, 9, 11^{2}, 13, 14^{2}, 15^{2}, 17^{2}, 18, 21; 23:1^{2}, 2, 3, 4^{2}, 5, 6^{2}, 7^{2}, 8^{2}, 9^{3}, 10^{5}, 11^{2}, 12, 13^{3}, 15, 16^{3}, 17, 18^{3}, 19^{3}, 20^{2}; 24:2, 3^{4}, 7^{2}, 9, 10^{4}, 11^{2}, 12, 13^{3}, 15^{2}, 17, 22^{3}, 24^{2}, 27^{3}, 28, 30, 31, 37^{2}, 40^{2}, 42, 43^{2}, 47, 48, 53^{2}, 60^{3}, 62; 25:3, 4^{2}, 6, 7^{2}, 8, 9^{3}, 10^{2}, 11, 12, 13^{3}, 16, 17^{2}, 18, 19, 20^{2}, 21, 22, 23, 27, 28, 34; 26:1^{2}, 2, 4^{2}, 7^{3}, 8, 9, 10, 14^{3}, 15, 17, 18^{3}, 19, 20^{2}, 21, 22, 24, 25, 26^{2}, 29, 33, 34^{2}, 35; 27:2, 9, 15, 16^{3}, 17, 19, 22, 25, 27^{3}, 28^{4}, 30^{2}, 31, 33, 34, 39^{3}, 41^{2}, 42, 45, 46^{7}; 28:1^{2}, 2^{3}, 3, 4, 5^{2}, 6^{2}, 8, 9^{2}, 11^{2}, 12^{2}, 13^{2}, 14^{2}, 15, 16, 17^{2}, 18, 19^{2}, 22; 29:1^{2}, 2^{2}, 4, 5, 10^{3}, 13, 14, 16^{2}, 22; 30:2, 14^{2}, 16, 32, 35, 36, 37^{2}, 40^{2}, 41; 31:1^{2}, 2, 3, 5, 9, 11, 13^{2}, 15, 18^{2}, 25, 29^{2}, 33, 35, 37, 38, 39^{3}, 42^{4}, 48, 53^{4}; 32:1, 2, 3^{2}, 9^{2}, 10^{3}, 11^{2}, 12, 13, 16, 20, 24, 25^{3}, 30, 32^{4}; 33:8, 10, 15^{2}, 17, 18^{2}, 19^{4}; 34:1^{2}, 2^{2}, 3, 6, 7^{2}, 8, 13, 15, 19, 20^{2}, 23, 24^{4}, 25^{2}, 26^{2}, 27, 30; 35:1, 3, 5^{2}, 6, 7, 8, 9, 11^{3}, 14, 15, 20, 21, 22, 23, 24, 25, 26^{2}, 27, 28, 29; 36:1, 2^{5}, 3, 5^{2}, 6^{3}, 7, 9^{2}, 10^{5}, 11, 12, 13^{2}, 14^{3}, 15^{4}, 16^{3}, 17^{4}, 18^{3}, 19, 20, 21^{3}, 22, 23, 24^{2}, 25^{2}, 26, 27, 28, 29, 30^{2}, 31^{2}, 32^{3}, 33^{2}, 34^{2}, 35^{3}, 36, 37, 38, 39^{4}, 40^{2}, 43^{3}; 37:1, 2^{3}, 3^{2}, 14^{2}, 20, 21, 22, 23^{2}, 25, 28^{2}, 31, 32, 36^{2}; 38:2, 7, 12^{2}, 19, 20, 21, 22, 27; 39:1^{4}, 2, 5, 11^{2}, 14, 19, 21^{2}, 22^{2}, 23; 40:1^{3}, 2^{3}, 3^{2}, 4, 5^{4}, 7, 8, 12, 14^{2}, 15^{2}, 17^{3}, 20^{2}; 41:1, 2, 3^{2}, 5, 8, 10, 11, 12, 14, 15, 16, 17, 18, 19, 25, 27, 29^{2}, 30^{2}, 31, 33, 34^{2}, 35^{2}, 36^{2}, 37^{2}, 38, 41, 42, 43, 44, 45^{3}, 46^{3}, 48^{3}, 49, 50^{3}, 51, 52^{2}, 53^{2}, 54^{2}, 55, 56^{2}; 42:5^{2}, 6, 7, 9^{2}, 12, 13^{2}, 15, 16^{2}, 19^{3}, 21, 27, 29, 30^{2}, 32^{2}, 33^{3}, 35^{2}, 36; 43:2, 7^{3}, 9, 11, 12, 14, 16, 18, 19^{2}, 21, 23, 27^{2}, 29, 34; 44:1, 2, 4, 8^{3}, 9, 16, 20^{2}, 24, 31, 33; 45:2, 8^{2}, 9, 10, 11, 12, 13^{2}, 17, 18^{3}, 19^{2}, 20^{2}, 21^{2}, 22^{4}, 23, 25^{2}, 26, 27^{2}; 46:1, 2, 3^{2}, 5, 6, 8^{2}, 9, 10^{2}, 11, 12^{3}, 13, 14, 15^{2}, 16, 17^{2}, 18, 19, 20^{3}, 21, 22, 23, 24, 25, 26, 27^{3}, 28, 31, 34; 47:1^{3}, 2, 4^{2}, 6^{4}, 9^{8}, 11^{3}, 13^{3}, 14^{2}, 15^{2}, 17, 18^{2}, 20, 21^{2}, 22^{2}, 24^{2}, 25, 26^{2}, 27^{2}, 28^{2}, 30; 48:3, 4^{2}, 5, 6, 7^{2}, 10, 16^{2}, 17, 19, 21, 22^{2}; 49:2, 3^{3}, 5, 8, 10, 11, 13^{2}, 16^{2}, 20, 24^{4}, 25^{5}, 26^{6}, 28, 29, 30^{4}, 32^{3}, 33; 50:3, 4^{3}, 5, 7^{4}, 8^{2}, 10, 11^{3}, 13^{5}, 17^{4}, 19, 23^{3}, 24, 25^{2}

Ex 1:1^{2}, 5^{2}, 7, 9^{2}, 10, 12^{2}, 13, 14, 15^{4}, 16, 17, 18; 2:1^{3}, 3, 5, 6, 7, 10, 11, 13, 15^{2}, 16, 19^{2}, 23^{5}, 25; 3:1^{4}, 2^{4}, 4^{2}, 6^{4}, 7^{2}, 8^{4}, 9^{2}, 10^{2}, 11^{2}, 12, 13^{2}, 14, 15^{5}, 16^{5}, 17^{3}, 18^{3}, 19, 21, 22^{4}; 4:5^{4}, 7, 8^{2}, 9^{3}, 10^{2}, 13, 14, 16^{2}, 20^{2}, 25, 26, 27, 28, 29^{2}, 30, 31; 5:1, 3, 4, 5, 6, 8, 10, 11, 12^{2}, 14^{2}, 15^{2}, 18, 19^{3}, 21^{2}; 6:1, 3, 4^{2}, 5^{2}, 6^{3}, 7, 9^{2}, 11^{3}, 12^{2}, 13^{5}, 14^{4}, 15^{3}, 16^{4}, 17, 18^{3}, 19^{2}, 20^{2}, 21, 22, 23^{2}, 24^{2}, 25^{4}, 26^{2}, 27^{2}, 28, 29, 30; 7:2^{2}, 3, 4^{3}, 5, 11, 16, 18^{2}, 19^{5}, 20^{2}, 21^{3}, 22, 24^{2}; 8:3, 5, 6^{2}, 7, 12, 13^{4}, 16^{2}, 17^{3}, 19, 21^{4}, 22^{3}, 24^{5}, 26^{2}, 29, 31^{2}; 9:1, 3, 4^{4}, 6^{4}, 7^{3}, 8^{3}, 9^{2}, 10, 11, 12, 13, 20^{2}, 21, 22^{3}, 23, 24, 25^{3}, 26^{2}, 29, 33, 35^{2}; 10:1, 2^{2}, 3, 5^{3}, 6^{2}, 12^{3}, 13, 14^{2}, 15^{5}, 19, 20, 21, 22, 23; 11:2^{5}, 3^{4}, 4, 5^{4}, 6, 7^{2}, 9, 10^{2}; 12:1, 2^{2}, 3^{3}, 4, 5, 6^{3}, 7^{2}, 9, 10^{2}, 12^{3}, 13, 15, 16^{2}, 17^{3}, 18^{2}, 19, 21, 22^{3}, 27^{3}, 28, 29^{4}, 31, 33, 35^{5}, 36, 37, 39^{3}, 40^{2}, 41^{3}, 42^{4}, 43, 46^{2}, 47, 50, 51^{3}; 13:2^{3}, 3^{3}, 5, 8^{2}, 9, 11, 12, 13^{2}, 14^{2}, 15^{4}, 16^{2}, 17^{2}, 18^{5}, 19^{2}, 20, 21^{2}, 22^{2}; 14:2, 3^{2}, 5^{3}, 7^{2}, 8^{4}, 9, 10^{2}, 11, 13, 15, 16^{2}, 17, 19^{3}, 20^{2}, 22^{2}, 23, 24^{4}, 25, 27, 28^{2}, 29^{2}, 30^{2}; 15:1, 3, 7, 8^{2}, 14, 15^{3}, 16, 17, 19^{4}, 20, 22, 23^{3}, 26^{2}, 27; 16:1^{6}, 2^{2}, 3^{3}, 6^{2}, 7, 9^{2}, 10^{3}, 12^{2}, 14, 15, 16^{2}, 17, 19, 20^{2}, 22, 23, 27, 29^{2}, 31^{2}, 32^{2}, 33, 35^{3}, 36; 17:1^{4}, 3, 5^{2}, 6^{3}, 7^{4}, 9^{2}, 10, 12, 13, 14^{2}, 15; 18:1^{3}, 3^{2}, 4^{3}, 5, 7, 9^{2}, 10^{5}, 12, 15, 16, 21^{6}, 24, 25^{5}; 19:1^{4}, 2, 3^{3}, 6^{2}, 7, 8, 9, 11, 12, 16, 17^{2}, 18, 19, 20^{2}, 21; 20:2^{4}, 4, 5^{2}, 6, 7, 10, 18, 22, 23^{2}, 24, 25^{2}; 21:9, 10, 19, 26^{2}, 28, 30^{2}, 32, 34^{2}, 35; 22:5^{4}, 6, 7, 8, 9^{3}, 11^{2}, 14, 17, 21, 25, 28, 29^{3}, 31; 23:5, 6, 8, 9^{2}, 11^{2}, 12, 13^{3}, 15^{2}, 16^{5}, 18^{2}, 19^{3}, 21, 25, 26, 29, 31^{2}; 24:1^{2}, 3, 4^{2}, 5^{3}, 6^{2}, 7^{2}, 8, 9^{2}, 10^{3}, 11^{2}, 12, 13, 16^{3}, 17^{5}, 18; 25:2^{2}, 3, 9^{2}, 10, 11, 12^{3}, 13, 14, 15, 17, 18^{3}, 19, 20, 22^{3}, 23, 24, 25, 26, 27, 28, 29, 31^{3}, 32^{6}, 33, 35^{4}, 36^{2}, 38, 39^{2}; 26:1^{2}, 2^{3}, 4^{4}, 5^{3}, 6, 7, 8^{3}, 9, 10^{2}, 11, 12^{3}, 13^{4}, 14^{2}, 15, 16^{2}, 17, 19, 20, 21, 22, 23, 24, 25, 26^{3}, 27^{4}, 28, 29, 31^{2}, 32^{3}, 33, 34, 35, 36^{2}, 37^{3}; 27:1, 2^{2}, 3, 4^{2}, 5^{2}, 6, 7, 9^{3}, 10^{3}, 11^{4}, 12^{2}, 13, 14^{2}, 16^{3}, 17^{2}, 18^{3}, 19^{3}, 20, 21^{3}; 28:1, 3, 6^{4}, 8^{4}, 9^{2}, 10^{2}, 11^{5}, 12^{3}, 13, 14^{2}, 15^{7}, 17^{2}, 21^{3}, 22^{2}, 23^{2}, 24^{2}, 25^{2}, 26^{3}, 27^{3}, 28^{3}, 29^{3}, 30^{3}, 31^{2}, 32^{4}, 33^{5}, 34, 36^{2}, 37, 38^{2}, 39^{3}, 43; 29:2, 4^{2}, 5^{2}, 10^{2}, 11^{2}, 12^{4}, 14, 15, 17, 19, 20^{7}, 21^{3}, 22^{2}, 23^{4}, 24^{2}, 25, 26^{2}, 27^{6}, 28^{4}, 29, 30, 31, 32^{3}, 34^{3}, 38, 40^{5}, 41, 42^{2}, 43, 44, 45, 46^{2}; 30:1, 2, 3, 4^{2}, 5, 6, 10^{3}, 12^{2}, 13^{2}, 16^{5}, 18^{3}, 20, 23^{3}, 24^{3}, 25^{2}, 26^{2}, 27, 28, 31, 32, 33, 34, 35, 36^{3}; 31:2^{4}, 3^{2}, 5^{3}, 6^{4}, 7^{3}, 8, 9, 10^{2}, 13, 15, 16, 17, 18^{4}; 32:1^{4}, 2^{3}, 4^{2}, 7^{2}, 8^{3}, 10, 11^{2}, 12^{2}, 13^{2}, 14, 15, 16^{2}, 17^{2}, 18^{3}, 19, 20^{2}, 22, 23^{3}, 26^{2}, 27, 28^{3}, 31, 32, 33, 34; 33:1^{2}, 3, 5^{2}, 6^{2}, 7^{2}, 9, 11^{2}, 16, 19, 22; 34:1, 2, 4^{2}, 5, 7, 10, 12^{2}, 15^{2}, 16, 18^{2}, 20^{2},

APNDX

17^2, 20, 22^2, 23, 25, 27^2, 28^5, 29^2, 30^2, 31, 33^3, 34, 36^4; **3:**1, 3^3, 7, 11, 14^2, 15^2, 17, 19, 20, 21; **4:**1, 2, 3^6, 4^6, 5^2, 6^4, 8^2, 10, 11^2, 12^2, 13, 14^2, 16^2, 17, 18^3, 19, 20, 21^2, 22; **5:**1, 2^2, 3^2, 4^4, 5^2, 6^2, 7^3, 8^7, 9^2, 10^4, 11^4, 12; **6:**1^2, 2, 3^2, 4^2, 5^3, 8^2, 9, 11^3, 12^3, 13, 14^2, 15^3, 16, 18^7, 19^4, 20, 21^2; **7:**1^4, 2, 3^3, 4, 6, 7^4, 8^3, 11^2, 12, 13^3, 14^2, 15; **8:**2^2, 4, 7, 8, 9, 10^2, 11, 12^2, 14, 15^2, 17, 18, 19, 21^2, 22; **9:**1^6, 2^2, 3^2, 4^3, 5, 6, 7, 8^3, 9, 10, 12, 16^4, 17, 20, 21^6, 23, 25, 26^3, 27^2; **10:**1, 2^2, 3^3, 4^2, 5^3, 6, 8, 10^2, 11, 12, 13, 16^2, 18^8, 19, 20^2, 21^3, 22, 23, 25, 26, 27; **11:**1, 3^2, 4^2, 5^3, 6, 7^4, 8^2, 9^2, 10, 11^3, 15^2; **12:**3, 4, 6^2, 7^2, 8, 9^6, 10^2, 11^2, 12^2, 14, 15^3, 17; **13:**2^3, 3^2, 4, 6, 7^2, 10, 13, 15, 16, 17^3, 18^2, 19, 22^3, 23^2; **14:**1, 2, 3^3, 4^2, 5, 6, 11^3, 12^2, 14^2, 16^2, 18^3, 19, 22, 24^2, 25, 27, 28, 29, 30^2, 36, 37^2, 38, 41, 43, 45, 47^2, 48^2, 49^4, 50^5, 51^3, 52; **15:**1^2, 2, 4, 5, 6^2, 8^2, 9^3, 10, 13^2, 14^2, 15^2, 17^2, 19^2, 20^2, 21^2, 22^2, 23^2, 24, 26, 27, 28^2, 29, 30, 32^2, 34, 35; **16:**4, 7, 10, 12, 13^3, 14, 18^3, 20; **17:**2^2, 4^3, 5^4, 6^2, 7^2, 8, 10, 11, 12^3, 13^2, 17, 18, 19^2, 22^2, 23^3, 24, 25, 26, 28, 32, 33, 34, 35, 36^2, 37^6, 38^2, 40, 42, 44^2, 45^4, 46^4, 50, 51, 52^4, 53, 54, 55, 57^2, 58; **18:**1^3, 4, 5^3, 6^4, 10, 11, 12, 15, 17, 21^2, 23, 24, 25^3, 27, 29, 30^2; **19:**3, 4, 6, 10, 13, 16, 20^3, 23; **20:**6, 8, 11, 12, 14, 15^2, 16^2, 21, 23, 27^2, 28, 30^3, 31, 33, 34, 37, 41, 42^2; **21:**1, 2, 3, 5^2, 7^3, 9^2, 10^2, 11^3, 12^2, 13, 15; **22:**3^2, 4, 5^2, 7^4, 8^3, 9^3, 10^2, 11^2, 12, 13^2, 15^3, 17^3, 19^3, 20^3, 22^2; **23:**2, 3, 4, 5, 6, 10, 11^2, 12^2, 13, 14, 15, 17, 19^2, 20, 21, 23^2, 24^2, 25^2, 26^3; **24:**1, 2^2, 3, 4^3, 6, 7, 8, 11^2, 12, 13, 14, 15, 16, 20, 21; **25:**1, 3^6, 9, 10, 14^2, 17, 18^4, 20, 21, 22^2, 24, 25^2, 28^2, 29^5, 31, 32, 34, 35, 36, 37, 39^3, 40, 41^2, 42^2, 43^2, 44^2; **26:**1, 2^3, 3, 5^2, 6, 11, 12, 13, 14, 15, 16, 19^3, 20^2, 22, 24^2; **27:**1^5, 2^2, 6, 7, 8^3, 10^3, 11; **28:**2, 3, 5, 6, 7, 9, 13, 14, 16, 17, 18, 19^3, 20^2, 22^2; **29:**2, 3^4, 4^3, 5, 6, 7, 8, 9^2, 11; **30:**5, 6^2, 12^3, 13, 14^2, 15, 16^5, 17^2, 22^3, 26^5, 29^2; **31:**1, 3, 7^3, 9^2, 10^2, 11^2, 12^3

2Sa 1:1^2, 2, 3^2, 4, 12^2, 13, 15, 18^3, 19, 20^3, 21^4, 22^4, 24^2, 25, 26, 27; **2:**1^3, 3, 4^3, 5^2, 7, 8^3, 10, 11, 12^3, 13^5, 15^4, 17^2, 18^2, 21^2, 23, 24^3, 25^2, 30, 31^3, 32^2; **3:**1^3, 2, 3^5, 4^2, 6^3, 7, 8^3, 10^2, 13, 14, 15, 17, 18^6, 19^3, 22, 23, 25, 26, 27, 28^2, 29^2, 32, 36, 37^2, 39^2; **4:**2^6, 4^3, 5^3, 6, 8^5, 9^2, 10, 11, 12^2; **5:**1, 3, 6, 7^2, 8, 9, 10, 11, 13, 14, 17, 18, 19, 20^2, 22, 23, 24^3; **6:**1, 2^4, 3^4, 4^3, 5^3, 6^2, 7^2, 8, 9^2, 10^3, 11^2, 12^6, 13, 15^3, 16^2, 17^2, 18^3, 19^4, 20^5, 21, 22^3, 23^2; **7:**2^2, 4, 6^2, 7^4, 8, 9^2, 10^2, 12, 13, 14^3, 19^2, 26^2, 27^2, 29^2; **8:**1^2, 3^2, 4, 5^3, 6, 7^2, 8, 9^2, 10^3, 11, 12^{10}, 13^2, 14, 16^2, 17^2, 18; **9:**1^2, 2^2, 3^3, 4^2, 5^3, 6^2, 7, 11, 12; **10:**1^2, 2^4, 3^2, 4, 6^6, 7^2, 8^4, 9^3, 10^3, 11, 12^2, 14^2, 16^2, 18^3, 19; **11:**1, 2, 3^2, 7, 8^2, 9^2, 11, 13, 14, 15, 17^4, 19^2, 21^2, 23, 24, 26; **12:**3^2, 4^2, 7^3, 8^2, 9^3, 10, 11^2, 14, 17, 18, 20, 25^2, 26^2, 27, 28, 30^2, 31^4; **13:**1^2, 3, 6, 10, 11, 13, 18, 19, 21, 29, 30, 32^2, 34, 36, 37^2, 39; **14:**1, 4, 7, 9, 11^2, 13, 15^2, 16^4, 17^2, 19^2, 20^3, 22, 25^2, 26, 27; **15:**2^5, 3, 6^2, 10^2, 11, 13^2, 14, 23, 24^4, 25^2, 27, 28, 29, 30, 31, 32, 34, 35; **16:**1^7, 3^2, 5^4, 6, 7, 8^3, 9, 10, 11, 15, 18, 19, 21^2, 22^2, 23^3; **17:**4, 8^2, 9, 10, 12^2, 14^4, 15, 16, 18, 20, 21, 22, 23, 24, 25^3, 26, 27^7, 29; **18:**1^2, 2^5, 3^3, 6, 7^3, 8, 9^3, 11, 12, 14^2, 17, 19^2, 22, 23, 27^3, 31, 32; **19:**5^5, 9^6, 10, 11^2, 13^4, 14^3, 16^3, 17^3, 18, 19, 20^2, 21, 22, 24, 27, 28, 29, 32, 35, 37^2, 38, 40^2, 41^2, 42^4, 43^6; **20:**1^3, 2^3, 3, 4, 5, 6, 7^2, 10, 11, 12^2, 13^2, 14, 15, 16, 17, 19^2, 21^2, 22^2, 23^2, 24; **21:**1^2, 2^6, 3, 4^2, 5^2, 6^2, 7^4, 8^5, 9^3, 10^5, 11^2, 12^4, 13^3, 14^3, 16^4, 17^3, 18^2, 19^3, 20, 21^2, 22^2; **22:**1^5, 3^2, 5^2, 6^2, 7, 8, 9^2, 11, 12, 13, 16^5, 17, 19, 21, 22, 31, 35, 36, 41, 43^2, 44^2, 46, 47^2, 51; **23:**1^5, 2, 3^3, 4^2, 6^2, 7, 8, 9^3, 11^3, 12, 13^4, 14, 15^3, 16^3, 17^2, 18^2, 19, 20^6, 21, 22, 24^4, 26, 29^5, 30^2, 32^2, 33, 34^3, 36^2, 37; **24:**1, 2^3, 3, 4^4, 5^3, 6, 7^4, 8, 9^3, 10, 11, 12, 13, 14^2, 15, 16^3, 18, 19, 21, 22, 24^3

1Ki 1:3, 5, 7, 8, 9^2, 11^2, 12, 19^2, 20^2, 25, 26, 27, 29, 30, 32, 33, 36^2, 37, 38, 39^2, 40, 41^3, 42, 44, 46, 47, 48, 50^2, 51, 52; **2:**1, 2, 3^2, 4, 5^7, 7^3, 8^2, 10, 12, 13^2, 16, 20, 22, 24, 25^2, 26^2, 27^2, 28^2, 29^2, 30, 31, 32^6, 33^2, 34, 35^2, 39^5, 43, 45, 46^2; **3:**1^5, 2, 3, 6, 7, 8, 11, 15^2, 17, 28^2; **4:**2, 3^2, 4, 5^2, 6, 8, 9, 10^2, 11^3, 12, 13^4, 14, 15, 16, 17, 18, 19^6, 21^3, 22^2, 23, 25, 26, 29, 30^3, 31, 33^6, 34^4; **5:**1^3, 3^2, 5, 6, 7, 8^2, 11^2, 13, 16, 17; **6:**1^5, 3^2, 4, 5^4, 6^2, 7^2, 8^2, 9, 10, 11, 13, 15^6, 16^2, 18, 19^2, 20, 21, 23, 24^4, 25, 26^2, 27^4, 29^2, 30, 31^3, 32^2, 33^3, 34^3, 36^2, 37^2, 38; **7:**2^3, 6, 7^2, 8, 9^2, 10^3, 11, 12^5, 13, 14^3, 15^4, 16^4, 17^3, 19^2, 21, 22^2, 23, 24, 26^2, 27^3, 28, 29, 30^2, 31^3, 32^2, 33^2, 34^2, 35^4, 36^2, 37, 38^2, 39^3, 40^2, 41^4, 42^2, 45^2, 46, 47, 48^3, 49^2, 50^5, 51^3; **8:**1^9, 2, 3, 4^2, 5, 6^4, 7, 8, 9^4, 10^2, 11^3, 14^2, 15, 16^3, 17^3, 19, 20^4, 21^3, 22^3, 23, 25^2, 26, 27, 28, 29, 30^2, 34, 36^2, 37, 38, 39^2, 41^2, 42^3, 43, 46, 47, 48, 51^3, 52^2, 53^3, 54^2, 55, 56^2, 59^2, 60, 63^3, 64^4, 65^2, 66; **9:**1^2, 4, 5^2, 7^2, 9^2, 10^2, 11^2, 13, 14, 15^3, 16, 19^2, 20^3, 21^2, 22^4, 23, 24^2, 26^3, 27^2; **10:**1^4, 2, 4, 5^4, 6^2, 9, 10^4, 11^2, 12^2, 13^2, 14^2, 15^7, 16^2, 17^4, 18, 19^2, 21^8, 22^3, 23, 25^2, 28, 29^4; **11:**1^2, 2^2, 4, 5^2, 6, 7^3, 9, 11, 12^2, 14, 15, 17, 18^3, 19^3, 20^2, 21, 23^2, 24, 25, 26^2, 27^2, 28^3, 29, 31^3, 32^2, 33^4, 34^2, 35, 39, 40^2, 41^4, 43; **12:**2^3, 3, 4, 8, 14, 15, 16, 17^2, 19, 20^2, 21^4, 22^2, 23^4, 24^3, 26, 27^4, 28^3, 31^5, 32^2, 33^3; **13:**1^3, 2^3, 4^2, 5^2, 6^3, 7, 8, 9, 11, 12, 14^2, 17, 18, 20, 21^2, 22^2, 26^3, 29^2, 31, 32^3, 33^5, 34^2; **14:**1, 2, 3^2, 4^2, 5^2, 6^2, 7, 8, 10^3, 11^2, 13^3, 14, 15, 16^2, 17, 18^2, 19^5, 21^3, 22, 24^2, 25^2, 26^4, 27^3, 28, 29^5, 31; **15:**1^2, 2, 3^2, 5^3, 6, 7^5, 8, 9^2, 10, 11, 12, 15, 16, 17^2, 18^7, 19^2, 20^3, 21, 22^2, 23^6, 24, 25^3, 26^2, 27^3, 28^2, 29^2, 30^3, 31^5, 32, 33^3, 34^2; **16:**1^2, 2^2, 3^4, 4^3, 5^5, 7^6, 8^3, 9^3, 10^2, 11^3, 12^2, 13^3, 14^5, 15^2, 16, 18, 19^2, 20^5, 21^3, 22, 23^2, 24^5, 25, 26^3, 27^5, 29^4, 30^2, 31^4, 32, 33^2, 34^2; **17:**1^3, 2, 4, 5, 6, 8, 10^2, 11, 12, 14^3, 15, 16^3, 17^2, 18, 19, 22^2, 23, 24^2; **18:**1, 3, 4, 5, 9, 10, 12, 13^2, 15, 18, 19^2, 20, 22, 24^2, 25^2, 26, 29^2, 30, 31^4, 32^2, 36^4, 38, 40^2, 41^2, 42, 44, 46^2; **19:**2^2, 6, 7, 8^2, 9, 10^2, 13, 14^2, 15, 16^3, 17^2, 19^2, 21^2; **20:**1, 2, 4, 6, 7^2, 9, 10, 11, 13, 14^2, 15^3, 17^3, 19^3, 20, 21, 22^3, 23^3, 24, 26, 27^3, 28^4, 29^2, 30, 31^3, 32, 35^3, 36, 39^2, 40, 41^2, 42, 43; **21:**1^2, 2^2, 3, 4^2, 7^2, 10, 11, 13^4, 15^2, 16^2, 17, 18^2, 19, 20, 22^4, 23^2, 24^2, 25, 26, 28; **22:**2^2, 3^4, 4, 5^2, 6^2, 7^2, 8^3, 9^2, 10^4, 11^2, 13^3, 15, 16, 18, 19^2, 22, 23, 24^2, 26^2, 27^2, 28, 29^2, 30^2, 31^2, 32^2, 33^2, 34^4, 35^2, 36, 38^2, 39^5, 41^3, 42, 43^2, 44, 45^5, 46^3, 48, 49, 50, 51^3, 52^5, 53

2Ki 1:1, 2^3, 3^5, 6^2, 7, 8, 9^3, 10^2, 11^2, 12^2, 13^4, 14, 15^2, 16^3, 17^4, 18^5; **2:**3, 5, 7^2, 9, 11^2, 12^2, 13^2, 14^2, 15^2, 16, 19^2, 21, 22, 23, 24^3; **3:**1^3, 2^2, 3^2, 4^2, 5^2, 6, 7^2, 8, 9^4, 10^2, 11^6, 12^3, 13^5, 14^3, 15, 16, 18, 19^2, 20, 24, 25^2, 26^2; **4:**1^3, 2, 3, 7^2, 9, 13, 16^2, 17, 21^2, 22^3, 25^2, 27^2, 28, 29, 30, 31, 34, 38^2, 39, 40^2, 42^4, 44; **5:**1^3, 2^2, 3, 4^2, 5^5, 6^2, 7^2, 8^2, 9^2, 11, 12^2, 14^3, 15^2, 17, 18^3, 20^3, 22^4, 23^3, 27; **6:**1, 6, 8, 9^2, 10^3, 11^4, 12^2, 15^2, 17^3, 18, 20^2, 21, 23^2, 24, 25^4, 26, 27^2, 30, 31^2, 32^2, 33; **7:**1^4, 2, 3, 4, 5^3, 6^7, 8, 9, 10^3, 12^2, 13^4, 14, 15, 16^4, 17^2, 18^4, 19; **8:**2^3, 3^2, 4^2, 6, 7^2, 8^3, 9^4, 11, 12, 16^6, 18^5, 20, 21, 22, 23^5, 24, 25^5, 26^2, 27^6, 28^2, 29^5; **9:**1^3, 2^2, 3, 5^2, 6^2, 7^5, 8, 9^5, 10, 11, 13, 14^4, 15^3, 16, 17, 20^2, 21^3, 22, 25^2, 26^4, 27^2, 28, 29^2, 30, 33, 35^2, 36^3, 37^3; **10:**1, 3, 5, 6^2, 8^2, 10^3, 11^2, 13^5, 14^2, 15, 17, 19^2, 21^3, 22, 23^6, 24^2, 25^4, 26^2, 27^2, 28, 29^2, 30^3, 31^3, 32, 33, 34^5; **11:**1, 2^3, 3, 4^3, 5^3, 6^2, 7^3, 10, 11^2, 13^3, 14, 15^3, 18^4, 19^5, 20; **12:**1^2, 2, 4^4, 5^2, 6^2, 7^3, 8^2, 9^3, 10, 11^4, 12^3, 13^6, 14, 16, 17, 18^5, 19^5, 20, 21^3; **13:**1^4, 2^3, 3^5, 4^2, 5^2, 6^2, 7^2, 8^5, 10^3, 11^3, 12^6, 13, 14^3, 16, 17^2, 18, 19, 20^2, 21^3, 22^2, 23, 24, 25^7; **14:**1^5, 2, 3, 6^3, 7^3, 8^3, 9^2, 10, 11^2, 13^6, 14^2, 15^6, 16, 17^5, 18^5, 20, 21^2, 23^5, 24^3, 25^8, 26, 27^3, 28^5, 29; **15:**1^4, 2, 3, 5^2, 6^5, 7, 8^3, 9^3, 10, 11^5, 12^2, 13^3, 14^2, 15^5, 17^3, 18^3, 19^2, 20^7, 21^5, 23^3, 24^3, 25^4, 26^5, 27^3, 28^3, 29^4, 30^4, 31^5, 32^5, 33, 34, 35^2, 36^5, 37^2, 38; **16:**1^4, 2, 3^4, 5^3, 6, 7^7, 8^3, 9^3, 10^3, 13, 14^3, 15^4, 17^2, 18^2, 19^5, 20; **17:**1^3, 2^2, 3, 4^4, 5, 6^4, 7^5, 8^4, 9^2, 14, 16^2, 17, 18^2, 19^2, 20^3, 21^2, 22^2, 23^2, 24^4, 25^2, 26^6, 27^4, 28, 29^2, 30^3, 31, 32^4, 33, 34, 36^2, 39^2; **18:**1^5, 2, 3, 4, 5^2, 7, 8, 9^5, 10^4, 11^3, 12^2, 13^3, 14^6, 15^2, 16^4, 17^3, 18^2, 19, 21^2, 23, 24^3, 26^2, 28^2, 29, 30^2, 31^4, 32^4, 33^5, 34^4, 35^3, 37^3; **19:**1, 2^2, 3^2, 4^2, 5, 6^3, 8, 9^2, 10^3, 11, 12^2, 13^5, 14^3, 15^3, 16, 17^2, 18, 19^2, 20^3, 21^2, 22, 23^5, 24^2, 25, 26^2, 29^2, 30^2, 31^4, 32, 35^2, 36, 37^2; **20:**1, 4, 5^3, 6^3, 7, 8, 9, 11, 12^2, 13^2, 16, 18^3, 19, 20^5; **21:**2^3, 3^2, 4^2, 5^3, 6, 7^4, 8^2, 9, 11, 12^2, 13^3, 14^2, 15, 16, 17^5, 18^2, 19^2, 20, 22^2, 23, 24^2, 25^5, 26; **22:**1^2, 2^2, 3^4, 4^3, 5^7, 7, 8^2, 9^3, 11^2, 12^3, 13^4, 14^4, 15, 16^2, 17, 18^3; **23:**1^2, 2^6, 3, 4^7, 5^3, 6^3, 7^2, 8^7, 9^3, 10^2, 11^5, 12^6, 13^7, 14, 15, 16^3, 17^4, 18^2, 19^3, 20, 21, 22^5, 23, 24^3, 25, 26^2, 27^2, 28^5, 29^2, 30^2, 31^2, 32, 33^4, 34^2, 35^4, 36^2, 37; **24:**1, 2^6, 3^3, 5^5, 7^5, 8^2, 9, 10^2, 11, 12^4, 13^6, 14^3, 15, 16^2, 17, 18^2, 19, 20^2; **25:**1^3, 2, 3^2, 4^2, 5^2, 6, 7^3, 8^6, 9^2, 10^3, 11^4, 12^3, 13^4, 14, 15^3, 16^2, 17^3, 18^2, 19^7, 20^2, 21^3, 22^4, 23^6, 24^2, 25^3, 26^2, 27^8, 28, 29, 30^2

1Ch 1:5, 6, 7, 8, 9^2, 12, 17, 19, 23, 28, 29, 31, 32^2, 33^2, 34, 35, 36, 37, 38, 39, 40^2, 41^2, 42^2, 43^4, 44^2, 45^2, 46^3, 47, 48, 49, 50^3, 51, 54; **2:**1, 3^5, 4, 5, 6^2, 7^2, 8, 9, 10^2, 16, 17, 18^3, 21^2, 22, 23^3, 24, 25^2, 26, 27^2, 28^2, 29^2, 30, 31^3, 32^2, 33^2, 42^5, 43, 44, 45^2, 47, 49^4, 50^4, 51^2, 52^2, 53^2, 54^3, 55^4; **3:**1^3, 2^4, 3, 5^2, 9^2, 15, 16, 17, 19^2, 21^5, 22^2, 23, 24; **4:**1, 2^2, 3^3, 4^5, 5, 6, 7, 8^2, 10, 11^2, 12^2, 13^2, 14^2, 15^3, 16, 17^2, 18^5, 19^3, 20^2, 21^8, 22, 24, 26, 27, 31, 34, 35^3, 37^5, 38, 39^2, 40^2, 41^2, 42^4, 43; **5:**1^4, 2, 3^2, 4, 6^2, 7, 8^3, 9^2, 10^2, 11^2, 13^2, 14^8, 15^4, 16, 17^4, 18^3, 20, 21^4, 22, 23^2, 24^5, 25^3, 26^6; **6:**1, 2, 3^2, 15, 16, 17^2, 18, 19^2, 20, 22, 25, 26, 28, 29, 31^2, 32^3, 33^4, 34^4, 35^4, 36^4, 37^4, 38^4, 39^2, 40^3, 41^3, 42^3, 43^3, 44^4, 45^3, 46^3, 47^4, 48^4, 49^4, 50, 54^4, 55, 56^2, 57^3, 60^2, 61^6, 62^9, 63^7, 64, 65^9, 66^6, 67^2, 70^5, 71^4, 72^2, 74^2, 76^2, 77^4, 78^3, 80^2; **7:**1, 2^5, 3^3, 4^2, 5^2, 6, 7^4, 8^2, 9^4, 10^2, 11^3, 12^2, 13^2, 14^2, 15^2, 16^2, 17^4, 19, 20, 21, 29^4, 30, 31^2, 33^2, 34, 35, 36, 38, 39, 40^5; **8:**3, 6^4, 8, 9, 10, 11, 12, 13^4, 16, 18, 21, 25, 27, 28, 29, 34, 35, 38, 39, 40^4; **9:**1^2, 3^6, 4^7, 5, 6^2, 7^5, 8^6, 9^2, 10, 11^7, 12^8, 13^5, 14^6, 15^3, 16^6, 18^2, 19^{10}, 20, 21^4, 23^4, 26^2, 27, 28^2, 29^2, 30^3, 31^2, 32^3, 33^2, 34, 35, 40, 41, 44; **10:**1, 2, 3, 7, 9, 10^2, 12^2, 13^3, 14^2; **11:**3^2, 4, 5^3, 6, 7, 8, 9, 10^2, 11^2, 12^2, 13^2, 14, 15^4, 17^3, 18^4, 19^2, 20^2, 21, 22^4, 23^2, 24, 26^4, 28, 30, 31^3, 32^2, 34^2, 35^2, 37, 38^2, 39^2, 41, 42^2, 43, 44, 45, 46; **12:**1^3, 2^3, 3^2, 7^2, 8^4, 14^4, 15, 16^2, 17, 18^3, 19^3, 20^3, 21^2, 22, 23^3, 24, 25^3, 26^2, 27, 28^2, 29^6, 30^4, 31^2, 32^4, 33^3, 34, 35, 36, 37^6, 38^3, 40^2; **13:**1, 2^3, 3^2, 4, 5^3, 6, 7^3, 9, 10, 12^2, 13^2, 14^3; **14:**1^2, 2, 4, 8, 9, 10, 11^2, 14, 15^3, 16, 17^2; **15:**1^2, 2^2, 3, 4, 5^2, 6^2, 7^2, 8^2, 9^2, 10^2, 12^4, 14^2, 15^3, 16^2, 17^6, 18, 19, 22, 24, 25^5, 26^2, 27^3, 28^3, 29^4; **16:**1^2, 2^2, 3^4, 4^3, 6^2, 7, 9, 10, 12, 13^2, 15, 16^2, 18^2, 26, 28, 29, 33^2, 35, 36, 37^2, 38, 39, 40^2, 42^2; **17:**1^3, 3, 6^3, 7, 8, 9, 11, 17^3, 18, 21^2, 24^3, 27; **18:**1^2, 3, 4, 5^3, 7^2, 8^2, 9^3, 10^3, 11, 12^3, 15^2, 16^2, 17^2; **19:**1^2, 2^4, 3^2, 6^6, 7^2, 8^2, 9^2, 10^2, 11^3, 12, 13^2, 15, 16^2, 18^2, 19^2; **20:**1^3, 2^3, 3^3, 4^2, 5^2, 6^2, 7, 8^2; **21:**2^2, 3, 5^3, 8, 10, 12^4, 13^2, 14, 15^3, 16^2, 18^2, 19^2, 21, 22, 25, 26, 28, 29^2, 30^4; **22:**1^2, 2^2, 3, 4, 5^2, 6, 7, 8, 9, 10, 11^2, 12, 13, 14^4, 15^3, 16, 17, 18, 19^5; **23:**1, 2, 3, 4^3, 6, 7, 8, 9^3, 10^2, 12, 13, 14^3, 15, 16^2, 17^2, 18^2, 19^2, 20^2, 21^2, 22, 23, 24^7, 25, 26, 27, 28^7, 29, 32^7; **24:**1^3, 3^4, 4^9, 5^7, 6^5, 19^3, 20^6, 21^2, 22^3, 23, 24^4, 25^3, 26^2, 27, 28, 29, 30^3, 31^4; **25:**1^6, 2^5, 3^3, 4^2, 5^2, 6^4, 7^2; **26:**1^5, 2, 4, 6^2, 7, 8^3, 10^2, 11, 12^2, 13, 15, 16, 19^3, 20^4, 21^3, 22^3, 23, 24^3, 26^2, 27^2, 28^5, 29, 30^5, 31^5, 32^3; **27:**1^5, 2, 3^4, 4^2, 5^2, 7, 9, 10^2, 11, 12, 13, 14^2, 15, 16^5, 17^3, 18^5, 19^4, 20^6, 21^5, 22^4, 23^2, 24^3, 25^2, 26^3, 27, 28, 29, 31, 32, 34^2; **28:**1^5, 2^4, 3, 4^6, 5^3, 8^4, 9^3, 11^7, 12^{10}, 13^6, 14^7, 15^4, 16^2, 17, 18^5, 19, 20^3, 21^5; **29:**2^8, 3^4, 4^5, 5^4, 6^6, 7^6, 8^3, 10, 12, 14^2, 16, 17, 18^5, 20, 22, 23^2, 24, 25, 26, 28, 29^4, 30

2Ch 1:1, 2^3, 3^3, 4, 5^3, 6, 9, 11, 12, 13, 16, 17^4; **2:**1, 3, 4^2, 6, 8, 10^4, 11, 12, 13, 14^6, 15, 16, 17, 18^2; **3:**1^2, 2^2, 3^2, 4^3, 6, 8, 9^2, 10, 11^4, 12^3, 13, 14, 15^3, 16, 17^2; **4:**1, 2^2, 3^2, 5^5, 7, 8, 9^2, 10, 11, 12^3, 13^2, 16^2, 17, 18, 19, 20, 21, 22^5; **5:**1^3, 2^9, 3, 4, 5, 6, 7^4, 8, 9^2, 10^2, 11, 12^5, 13^2, 14^3; **6:**2, 3^2, 4, 5^3, 7^3, 9, 10^4, 11^2, 12^3, 13^3, 14, 16^2, 17, 18, 19, 21^2, 25, 27^2, 28, 29^2, 30^2, 32, 33, 37, 38, 41, 42^2; **7:**1^2, 2^2, 3^2, 5^2, 6^2, 7^3, 8^2, 9, 10, 11^2, 12, 18, 20^2, 22^3; **8:**1^2, 2, 6^2, 7^2, 8^2, 9^5, 10, 11^6, 12, 13^4, 14^4, 15, 16^5, 17, 18^4; **9:**1^4, 3^2, 4^4, 5^2, 6^2, 9^3, 10^2, 11^3, 12, 13^2, 14^2, 15^2, 16^4, 17, 18^2, 20^9, 21^2, 22, 23^2, 24^2, 26^2, 28^2, 29^6, 31; **10:**2^3, 4, 13, 14, 15^3, 16, 17^2, 18, 19; **11:**1^2, 2^2, 3^2, 4^2, 11^2, 13, 16^4, 17^3, 18^4, 20, 21, 22, 23^2; **12:**1, 2^2, 3, 5^3, 6, 7^2, 8^2, 9^5, 10^5, 11, 12, 13^2, 15^3, 16; **13:**1, 2^2, 3^3, 5^2, 6^3, 7^2, 8^3, 9^5, 10, 11^2, 12^2, 15^2, 16, 17, 18^3, 20, 22^3; **14:**1, 2, 3, 4, 5^2, 8^4, 9, 10, 14, 15; **15:**1^2, 2, 4^2, 5, 6^2, 8^6, 9^3, 10^2, 11, 12, 13, 15, 16, 17^2, 18, 19^2; **16:**1^4, 2^5, 3, 4^3, 5, 6, 7^5, 9^2, 10^2, 11^3, 12, 13, 14^2; **17:**2^3, 3, 4^2, 6^2, 7^2, 9^3, 10^2, 11, 12, 13^3, 14^5, 16^2, 17^2; **18:**3^2, 4^2, 5^2, 6^2, 7^3, 8^3, 9^5, 10^2, 11, 12^2, 15, 17, 18^2, 19, 21, 22, 23^2, 25^2, 26^2, 28^2, 29^2, 30^3, 31^2, 32^2, 33^3, 34^2; **19:**1, 2, 3, 4, 5, 7^3, 8^6, 9, 10, 11^4; **20:**1^2, 4^3, 5^2, 6^2, 7^2, 10^3, 11, 14^8, 15^2, 16^3, 17, 18, 19^5, 20^2, 21, 22, 23^4, 25^2, 26^3, 27^2, 28, 29^3, 30, 31, 32^2, 33, 34^6, 35^2, 37^2; **21:**1, 2^3, 3^3, 4^3, 6^5, 7^2, 8, 9, 10^2, 11^2, 12^4, 13^6, 15^2, 16^2, 17, 19^5, 20^2; **22:**1^4, 2, 3^2, 4^3, 5^3, 6^5, 7^4, 8^4, 9^2, 10^3, 11^5, 12; **23:**1^6, 2^4, 3^3, 4^4, 5^3, 6^3, 9^2, 10^2, 12^2, 13^2, 14^3, 15, 17^2, 18^6, 19^2, 20^5, 21; **24:**1, 2^2, 4, 5^3, 6^8, 7^4, 8^2, 9, 11, 12^5, 13, 14^5, 15, 16, 17^2, 18^2, 20^3, 21^3, 23^5, 24^3, 25^4, 26^2, 27^5; **25:**1, 2, 4, 5, 6^3, 7^3, 9^3, 10, 11^3, 12^3, 13^3, 14^3, 15^3, 16, 17^4, 18^2, 20^3, 21^2, 23^6, 24^2, 25^5, 26^4, 28; **26:**1^2, 3, 4, 5^2, 6^3, 8, 9, 11^5, 12^4, 16^2, 17, 18^2, 19, 21^3, 22^3, 23; **27:**1, 2^2, 3^3, 4, 5^6, 7^4, 9; **28:**1, 2^2, 3^4, 5^5, 6^2, 7^2, 8^2, 9^2, 10, 11^2, 12^7, 15^2, 16, 18^3, 19^2, 20, 21^6, 22, 23^5, 24^7, 25^2, 26^4, 27^2; **29:**1, 2, 3^3, 5^3, 6^2, 7^2, 8, 10, 12^{11}, 13^4, 14^4, 15^3, 16^5, 17^5, 18^2, 19, 20^2, 21^2, 25^4, 26, 27^2, 29, 30^2, 31^2, 32, 35^3; **30:**1^2, 5^2, 6^7, 7, 8, 10, 11^2, 12^4, 13, 15^2, 16^4, 17^2, 18^2, 19^2,

APNDX

Mt 1:1^4, 3, 5^2, 6^2, 16^2, 18^2, 20^3, 22, 24; **2:**1^2, 2, 4^2, 5, 6^3, 7, 12, 13, 15^3, 16^2, 19, 20, 21, 22^3; **3:**1, 2, 3^3, 4, 6, 7^2, 9, 10, 13, 14, 16^2; **4:**1^2, 3, 4^2, 5, 6, 8^2, 13, 15^4, 16, 17, 18, 19, 21, 23^3, 25; **5:**3, 9, 10, 11, 13^2, 14, 19^3, 20^2, 21^2, 22^3, 27, 29, 30, 31, 32, 33, 35, 37, 42, 45; **6:**1^2, 2, 5^2, 8, 16, 22^2, 23, 26, 27, 28, 29, 30^2, 32, 33, 34; **7:**4, 5^2, 9, 15, 16^2, 21^2, 24, 26, 27; **8:**6, 11, 12^2, 14, 20^2, 21, 26, 27, 28^2, 29, 30, 31, 32^2, 33, 34; **9:**2^3, 3, 6^2, 9, 14, 15, 16, 20^2, 22, 27, 34, 35, 38; **10:**1^2, 2^2, 3, 5^2, 6^2, 7, 10, 14^2, 15^2, 16, 17, 20, 22, 23^2, 25^2, 29, 30, 31, 36, 37^2, 38, 41^2, 42^3; **11:**1, 2^2, 10, 11^2, 12^2, 19^3, 20, 22, 24^2, 25, 27, 29; **12:**1, 4, 8^2, 23, 24, 28^2, 31, 32, 34^3, 35^3, 36, 38^2, 39, 40^2, 41^2, 42^3, 43, 45, 50; **13:**1, 5, 11^2, 14, 15, 18, 19, 21, 22^2, 24, 27, 30, 31^2, 32^2, 33^2, 35, 36^2, 37, 38^2, 39, 40, 41^2, 42^2, 43, 44, 45, 46, 47^2, 49, 50^2, 52^2, 58; **14:**1^2, 6, 8, 13^2, 20, 24, 25, 27, 29, 31, 33^2, 34, 35^2, 36; **15:**1, 2, 3, 6^2, 7, 9, 11, 14, 18, 19, 21, 22^3, 24^2, 27, 29, 31, 37, 39; **16:**3^2, 4, 6^3, 8, 9, 10, 11^3, 12^5, 13^2, 14, 16, 18, 19^2, 21, 23^2, 27^2, 28^2; **17:**5, 9, 12^2, 13, 18, 20^2, 22^2, 25^4, 26, 27; **18:**1, 2, 3, 4, 6^2, 7, 10^2, 11, 12, 13^2, 14^2, 16, 19^2, 20, 23^2, 27, 28; **19:**1, 7, 8^2, 10, 12^2, 14^2, 23, 24^2, 28^3; **20:**1, 8, 11, 12, 13, 18, 20^2, 22^2, 23^2, 25, 28, 30, 31; **21:**1, 3, 5^2, 9^2, 11^2, 12^3, 13^2, 15, 16^2, 17, 23, 25^2, 26, 31^3, 32, 34^2, 37, 39, 40, 42, 43, 45; **22:**2, 5, 13, 16^2, 27, 28, 29, 30, 31, 32^5, 35, 42^2; **23:**4, 5^2, 7, 13, 15, 16, 22, 23^2, 25^3, 26, 27^2, 28, 29^2, 30^2, 31, 32, 33^2, 34^2, 35^3, 39; **24:**1, 3^4, 6^2, 8, 9, 12, 14, 15^2, 17, 21, 27^3, 29^2, 30^5, 31^2, 32, 36^2, 37^3, 39^2, 43, 44, 50^2, 51; **25:**1, 2, 8, 13, 14, 19, 21, 23, 30, 31^2, 34^2, 40^2, 45^2; **26:**2^2, 3^2, 6, 7, 13, 14, 15, 17^2, 21, 22, 24^3, 27, 28^2, 29^2, 30, 31^2, 33, 37, 45^2, 47^2, 51^2, 53, 56, 61, 63, 64^3, 65, 66, 67, 69, 71, 73, 75; **27:**1, 3, 5, 6, 8, 9^4, 11, 12, 19, 21, 24^2, 27^2, 29^2, 32, 33, 37, 40, 42, 43, 47, 48, 51, 52, 53, 54, 56^2, 57, 58, 60, 62; **28:**1^2, 2, 4, 11, 19^3, 20

Mk 1:1^3, 3^2, 4^2, 5^4, 6, 7, 9^2, 10, 13, 14^2, 15, 16, 17, 19, 24^2, 25, 26, 29^2, 30^2, 34; **2:**3^2, 4, 5, 6, 9, 10^2, 14^2, 17, 18^4, 19, 21, 23, 26^2, 28^2; **3:**5, 9, 11, 17^3, 18, 21, 22, 28, 29, 35; **4:**4, 5, 10, 11^2, 19^3, 26, 28, 30, 31, 32^2, 37, 38, 41; **5:**1^2, 2^2, 7, 8, 10, 11, 17, 22^2, 23, 25, 26, 27, 29^2, 30, 34, 35, 36, 37, 38^2, 40, 42^2; **6:**3^3, 6, 11, 14, 15, 21, 22^2, 23^2, 24, 25, 29, 33, 37, 43^2, 44, 47, 48, 50, 52, 53, 54, 56; **7:**1, 2, 3, 4^2, 5, 6, 7, 8^3, 9, 13^2, 14, 15, 20, 21^2, 24, 25, 26, 28, 29, 31^4, 35; **8:**3, 8, 10, 11, 15^4, 19, 20, 23, 27, 28, 30, 31^3, 33^2, 38^5; **9:**1^3, 7, 9, 12^2, 13, 17, 21, 24, 25, 26, 31^2, 35^2, 36, 37, 39, 41, 42, 47; **10:**1^2, 4, 5, 6, 10, 14^2, 15, 23, 24, 25^2, 26, 33, 35, 38^2, 39^2, 44^2, 45, 46^3, 47^2, 48, 49; **11:**1^2, 3, 5, 9, 10^2, 13, 14, 15^2, 17^3, 19, 29, 30^2, 32; **12:**2^2, 8, 9, 10, 13^2, 14^2, 22, 23, 24, 26^4, 27^2, 28^2, 29, 34, 35, 38, 44^2; **13:**1^3, 3, 7^2, 8, 13, 14^2, 15, 19, 25, 26, 27^2, 28, 32, 34, 35; **14:**1^2, 2, 3^3, 4, 9^2, 10, 12, 13^2, 14, 18, 20, 21^3, 23, 24, 25^3, 26, 27, 41^2, 43, 47^2, 54, 61, 62^3, 64, 65, 66^2, 67, 69, 70, 71; **15:**2, 3, 9, 12, 17, 18, 21^2, 22, 26^2, 32, 35, 36, 38, 39, 40^2, 43^3, 45, 46^2, 47; **16:**1, 2^2, 3, 6, 9^2, 11, 12, 14, 19

Lk 1:1, 2, 3, 4, 5^6, 6, 8, 9^2, 10^2, 11^3, 15, 16^2, 17^3, 19, 23, 26, 27^2, 29, 32^2, 33^2, 35^3, 38, 39, 40, 41, 42, 43, 44, 45, 48, 51, 52, 54, 59, 61, 65, 66^2, 68, 69^2, 70, 71, 74^2, 75, 76^2, 77^2, 78, 79^2, 80; **2:**2, 4^5, 9^2, 10, 11, 13, 21^2, 22^2, 23, 24^2, 25, 27, 31, 32, 33, 34, 35, 36^4, 37, 38, 39, 40, 41, 42, 43, 46; **3:**1^8, 2^2, 3^2, 4^4, 6, 7^2, 8^2, 9, 14, 15, 16, 23^3, 24^5, 25^5, 26^5, 27^5, 28^5, 29^5, 30^5, 31^5, 32^5, 33^5, 34^5, 35^5, 36^5, 37^5, 38^4; **4:**1, 2, 3, 4, 5^2, 6, 9^2, 14^2, 15, 17, 18^2, 19, 20, 22, 25^2, 26^2, 27^2, 29^2, 30, 31, 33, 34^2, 35^2, 37^2, 38, 40, 41^2, 43, 44; **5:**1^2, 2, 3^2, 6, 9, 10, 12, 15^2, 17^4, 19, 24^2, 27, 29^2, 33^2, 34, 36^2; **6:**1, 2, 4, 5^2, 13, 15, 16, 17^5, 19, 20, 22, 26, 30^2, 34, 35, 42, 44^2, 45^6, 49; **7:**1, 3^2, 11, 12^3, 17, 18^2, 19, 21^2, 24, 27, 28^2, 29, 30^2, 31, 34^2, 35, 36, 37, 38, 39, 42, 44; **8:**1^2, 2^2, 3^2, 4, 5, 10^2, 11, 12, 13, 14, 21, 22, 23, 24, 25, 26, 27, 28, 29^2, 32, 33, 35^2, 36, 37^2, 38, 41, 42, 43^2, 44^2, 46, 48, 49, 51; **9:**2, 5, 7^2, 8^3, 9, 11^3, 17, 19, 20, 22^2, 26^5, 27^3, 29, 31, 35, 36, 38, 43, 44^2, 45, 46, 47, 52, 55^2, 56, 58^2, 60, 62; **10:**2, 6, 7, 9, 10, 11^3, 19, 21, 22, 30, 34, 35, 36; **11:**1, 5, 6, 8, 11^2, 15^2, 16, 20^2, 24, 26, 27, 28, 29, 30, 31^4, 32^2, 34^3, 36^3, 39^2, 41, 42^2, 44, 45, 46, 47, 48, 49^2, 50^3, 51^3, 52, 53, 54; **12:**1^4, 4, 6, 7^2, 8^2, 9, 10, 13, 15^2, 16, 20, 25, 27, 28, 29, 30^2, 31, 39, 40, 42, 44, 46, 48^3, 54, 56^2, 57; **13:**1, 7, 10, 11, 14, 15, 16, 18, 19^3, 20, 21, 25, 27, 28^2, 29, 31, 33, 35; **14:**1^2, 5, 8^2, 10, 14, 15^2, 18, 19, 21^2, 24^2, 28, 32, 33; **15:**4^2, 8, 10^2, 12^2, 15, 17, 19, 26; **16:**2^2, 4, 5, 6, 7, 8^2, 9^2, 15, 16, 17, 20, 24, 28; **17:**2, 6, 7, 11, 15, 20^3, 21, 22^3, 24^2, 25, 26^3, 28, 29, 30; **18:**3, 8, 12, 16^2, 17, 24, 25, 29, 31, 34, 37, 38, 39; **19:**3, 8, 9, 10, 11, 22, 29^2, 31, 34, 37^3, 38, 39, 44, 46^2, 47; **20:**1, 4^2, 6, 10^2, 13, 15^2, 17, 20^2, 21^2, 26, 27, 32, 33, 34, 36^2, 37^3, 38^2, 39, 42, 45, 46; **21:**3, 4^3, 5, 9, 16, 17, 18, 21, 22, 24^3, 25, 26, 27, 30, 31, 34, 35, 36, 37; **22:**1, 3^2, 6, 7, 10, 11, 16, 18^3, 19, 21, 22, 23, 24, 25, 30, 39, 44, 47, 48, 50^2, 52, 53, 55, 58, 59^2, 61, 66, 69^3, 70, 71; **23:**1, 3, 6, 8^2, 11, 15, 17, 22, 23^2, 26, 27^2, 28, 35, 37, 38^2, 39, 41, 45, 51^4, 52; **24:**1, 3, 7^2, 10, 13, 14, 17, 18, 19, 22, 23, 24, 25, 31, 35^2, 36, 42^2, 44, 47, 48, 49^2

Jn 1:4, 7, 8, 12, 13^6, 14^3, 15^2, 16, 18, 19, 22, 23^2, 24, 29^2, 30, 34, 35, 36, 40, 42, 44^2, 45^3, 46, 47, 49^2, 51^2; **2:**1^2, 3, 6^3, 8, 9^2, 11^2, 14, 15^2, 16, 17, 21^2, 25; **3:**1^2, 3, 5^3, 6^2, 8, 10, 12, 13, 14, 18^2, 22, 25, 29^2, 31^2, 34, 36; **4:**5^2, 7, 9^3, 10^2, 13, 14^2, 22, 30, 32, 34, 39^3, 41, 42^2, 46, 47^2, 52, 54; **5:**1, 3^3, 4^2, 19, 25^2, 27, 29^2, 30^2, 31, 32^2, 36^2, 37, 39, 42, 44, 46; **6:**1^2, 4, 7^2, 8, 11, 13, 14, 18, 22, 25, 26, 27, 28, 29, 33, 35, 38, 39, 40, 42, 45^2, 46, 48, 51^2, 53^2, 58, 60, 62, 64, 65, 66, 68, 69, 70, 71^3; **7:**2, 7, 13^2, 14, 17^3, 18, 19, 22^2, 23, 25^2, 28, 31, 36, 37, 38^2, 39, 40^2, 41, 42^4, 43, 44, 48^2, 50, 52^2; **8:**1, 12^2, 13, 14, 17, 18^2, 23^2, 26^2, 27, 28^2, 34, 39, 40, 41^2, 42, 44^4, 46^2, 47^2, 52, 54, 59^2; **9:**3, 4, 5, 6^2, 7, 11, 16^2, 17, 18, 21, 22, 23, 31, 32, 33, 35, 40; **10:**2, 5, 7, 14, 16, 18^2, 20, 21^2, 22, 25, 26, 28, 29, 32, 35, 36^2, 37, 39, 41; **11:**1^2, 4^2, 8, 9, 11, 13^3, 19, 22, 27, 37^2, 39, 40, 42, 45, 46, 49, 51, 52, 55; **12:**2, 3^4, 4, 7, 9, 11^2, 13^3, 15, 16, 17, 21^2, 23, 24, 30, 31^2, 34^3, 36, 38^2, 41, 42^2, 43^2, 49; **13:**1^2, 2, 18, 21, 22, 23, 24, 26, 29^2, 31; **14:**10, 17, 21, 30; **15:**4, 15, 16, 19^3, 26^2; **16:**2, 4, 5, 8^3, 9, 10, 11^2, 13^2, 14, 15, 17, 19, 21, 25, 33; **17:**6, 7, 12^2, 14^2, 15, 16^2, 24; **18:**3, 5, 7, 9, 12, 15, 17, 18, 19^2, 22^2, 23, 25, 26^2, 28, 32, 33, 34^2, 36^2, 37, 39; **19:**2, 3, 5, 7, 14, 17, 19^2, 20, 21^3, 25^2, 29, 32^2, 34, 36, 38^5, 39, 40^2, 42; **20:**1, 2, 12, 19^2, 24, 25^2, 30, 31; **21:**1, 2^3, 6^2, 9, 10, 11, 12, 15, 16, 17, 24

Act 1:1, 3^3, 4^2, 6, 8, 9, 11, 13^2, 14, 15^2, 16, 17, 18, 19, 20, 21, 22^2, 24^2, 25; **2:**1, 2, 3^2, 5, 10^2, 11, 13, 14, 15, 17, 18, 19, 20, 21, 22^4, 23, 24^2, 28^2, 29, 30^2, 31^2, 33^3, 36, 37, 38^4, 42, 46; **3:**1, 2^2, 5, 6^2, 10, 12, 13^5, 15, 16, 18, 19^2, 21^3, 22, 24, 25^3, 26; **4:**1, 4^2, 6^2, 8^2, 9, 10^3, 11^2, 13^2, 15, 18, 19, 21, 22, 25, 26, 27^2, 30, 31, 32^5, 33^2, 34^2, 36^3; **5:**2, 3^2, 7, 9^2, 12, 13, 14, 15^2, 16, 17, 19, 20, 21^2, 24^2, 30, 31, 32, 34, 35, 36, 37^2, 38, 39, 40, 41; **6:**1^2, 2^2, 3^2, 4, 5^3, 7^3, 8, 9^5, 14, 15; **7:**2, 3, 4^2, 8, 10^3, 11, 16^4, 17, 22, 23, 24, 29, 30^3, 31, 32^4, 34, 35, 36, 37^2, 40^3, 41, 42^4, 43^2, 44, 45^3, 46, 49, 52^4, 53, 55^3, 56^2, 58; **8:**1, 3, 5, 7, 9, 10, 11, 12^2, 14, 16^2, 18, 20, 21, 22^2, 23^2, 24, 25^2, 26, 27^4, 32, 34^3, 37, 39^2; **9:**1, 2^2, 11^2, 13, 15, 20, 24, 26, 27, 29, 31^2, 33, 36; **10:**1, 3^2, 7^2, 12^3, 22^3, 28, 31, 32, 33, 34^2, 36^2, 38^2, 39^2, 41, 42^2, 43, 45^2, 48; **11:**1, 2, 5, 6^2, 16, 20^2, 21, 22^2, 23^2, 24^2, 28^2, 30; **12:**1, 2, 3, 4, 5, 7, 10, 11^5, 12^2, 13, 17, 18, 20, 22^2, 23^2, 24; **13:**1, 5^2, 7^2, 10^4, 11, 12, 15^3, 16, 17^4, 18, 19, 20, 21^4, 22, 23, 24^2, 25, 26^3, 27, 28, 29, 31, 34, 36, 38, 39, 40, 42, 43^2, 44, 46^2, 47^2, 48, 49, 50^2, 51; **14:**1^3, 3, 4, 5^2, 6^2, 11^2, 13, 14, 15, 19, 22^2, 26, 27; **15:**1, 2, 3, 4^2, 5^3, 6, 7, 10, 11, 14, 15, 16, 17, 18, 20, 21, 22, 23, 26, 35, 36, 40; **16:**1, 2, 3, 4, 6^2, 9, 12^2, 13, 14^4, 16, 17^2, 18^2, 19, 26, 27^2, 32, 33, 36, 39, 40^2; **17:**1, 2, 4^3, 5^2, 6, 7, 8, 9^2, 10, 11, 12^3, 13^3, 18^3, 22^2, 24, 26^4, 27, 28, 29, 30, 32^3; **18:**3, 8^2, 11, 12, 14, 15^3, 17^2, 18, 23, 25^3, 26; **19:**4, 5, 8^2, 9^2, 10^2, 11, 12, 13^2, 14^2, 16, 17, 19^3, 20, 22, 25, 27, 28^2, 29, 31^2, 33, 34^2, 35^4, 37^2, 40; **20:**4^4, 6, 7, 11, 16, 17, 19^2, 24^4, 25, 26, 27, 28, 30, 31, 32, 35, 38; **21:**5, 6, 8^3, 11, 12, 13, 14, 16^3, 20^2, 21, 26^3, 27, 28, 30, 31, 32, 35^2, 36, 39^2; **22:**3^3, 5, 8, 9, 10, 11^2, 12, 14^2, 15, 16, 18, 20^2, 30; **23:**5^2, 6^3, 9, 10, 11^2, 12, 16, 17, 20, 21, 23, 27^2, 29^4, 34^2; **24:**4, 5^3, 7, 8^2, 10, 14, 15^2, 16, 21, 22^2, 23, 25, 26; **25:**2, 8, 9, 11^2, 15, 16, 18, 19^2, 20^3, 21, 23^2, 24, 25, 26; **26:**2, 4, 5, 6^2, 7, 9^2, 10, 13, 16^2, 18^2, 20^2, 22, 25, 26^2, 31^2; **27:**1, 2^3, 5^2, 6, 8, 10^2, 11, 12, 19, 21, 22^3, 23, 25, 29, 30^2, 32, 34^2, 35, 36, 41, 42, 44; **28:**2^2, 3^2, 7^2, 8^3, 11, 15, 16, 17^3, 18, 19, 20, 21^3, 22, 23^4, 27^2, 28, 31

Ro 1:1^2, 3^2, 4^2, 6, 7, 8, 9^2, 10, 12, 16^3, 17, 18^2, 19, 20^2, 23, 24, 25, 27^2, 29, 30^2, 32^2; **2:**2, 3, 4^2, 5^3, 9^3, 11, 13^2, 15, 16, 17, 18, 19^2, 20^4, 23, 24, 25, 26, 29^3; **3:**1, 2, 3, 5, 7, 12, 13, 14, 17, 18, 20^2, 21, 22^2, 23^2, 25^2, 26, 27^2, 28, 29^3; **4:**4^2, 6, 11^4, 12^4, 13^2, 14^2, 16^5, 17, 18, 19, 20; **5:**2^2, 5, 10, 14^2, 15^2, 16, 17^3, 18^3, 19; **6:**3, 4^2, 5^2, 6, 13^2, 16^2, 17^2, 18, 19^3, 20, 21, 23^2; **7:**2, 4, 5, 6^2, 8, 22, 23^2, 24, 25^2; **8:**2^3, 3, 4, 5^2, 7, 9^3, 10^2, 11, 13, 14^2, 15^2, 16, 17, 18, 19^3, 20, 21^3, 23^2, 27^2, 29, 33, 34, 35, 39; **9:**4^2, 5, 6^2, 7, 8^3, 9, 11^3, 16^3, 21, 22, 23^2, 24^2, 26, 27^3, 29, 30, 31^2, 32, 33; **10:**2, 3^2, 4, 5, 6, 8, 13, 14, 15^3, 17, 18, 20; **11:**1^4, 2, 4^2, 5, 6^2, 8, 12^4, 13, 14, 15^3, 17^3, 20, 22, 24, 25^2, 26, 29, 33^3, 34, 36; **12:**1, 2^2, 3^2, 5, 6, 13, 16^2, 17, 20, 21; **13:**1^2, 2, 3^2, 4^2, 10, 11, 12^2; **14:**7, 9, 10, 12^2, 14, 16, 17, 18, 20, 23^2; **15:**1, 2, 3, 4, 5, 6, 7, 8^2, 12, 13^2, 14^2, 15^2, 16^3, 18^2, 19^3, 21, 26, 27, 29^3, 30, 31, 32, 33; **16:**1, 2^3, 4, 5, 7, 10, 11^2, 16, 18, 20^2, 23^2, 24, 25^3, 26^3

1Co 1:1^2, 2^2, 4, 6, 7, 8, 9, 10, 11^3, 12^5, 13, 14, 16, 17^3, 18^2, 19^2, 20^2, 21^2, 24^2, 25^2, 27^2, 28, 30^2; **2:**1^3, 4^3, 5^2, 6^3, 7, 8^3, 9, 10, 11^4, 12^3, 14^2, 15, 16^2; **3:**4^2, 10, 13, 16^2, 17^2, 19, 20; **4:**1^5, 3^2, 5^3, 6^2, 13^2, 16, 17, 19, 20, 21; **5:**4^2, 5^2, 8^2, 10^2; **6:**1, 4, 9^2, 10, 11^3, 12, 15^3, 19^2; **7:**4^2, 6, 7, 19^2, 23, 25^2, 31, 33, 34^2, 36, 40; **8:**3, 4, 6, 7, 9, 10; **9:**2, 5, 7^3, 9^2, 10, 12^2, 13^2, 14, 15, 16, 17, 18; **10:**4, 5, 7, 8, 9^2, 10^2, 11, 16^5, 17, 18^2, 21^5, 27, 29^2, 30, 31, 32, 33; **11:**1^2, 3^3, 7^2, 8^2, 10, 12^2, 16, 18, 22, 23, 24, 25, 27^3, 28^2, 32; **12:**3, 4, 5, 6, 7, 8^2, 9, 10^4, 12, 15^2, 16^2, 18, 21^2, 22, 23, 27, 28^2, 29, 30; **13:**1^2, 2, 13; **14:**10^2, 11, 12^2, 16^2, 21, 24^2, 25^2, 26, 32, 33^3, 36, 37; **15:**3, 5^2, 6^2, 7^2, 8^4, 9^2, 10^2, 12, 13, 15^2, 19, 20, 21, 32, 34, 37^2, 39^5, 40^2, 41^3, 42, 47, 49^2, 50, 52, 56^2, 58; **16:**1, 2^2, 10, 15^3, 17^2, 19, 21, 23

2Co 1:1^3, 3^3, 4, 5, 6, 7^3, 8^3, 9, 11, 12^2, 14, 16^2, 19, 20^2, 22, 24; **2:**3^2, 4^2, 6, 9, 10, 11^2, 12, 13, 14, 15, 16^2, 17^4; **3:**1^2, 2, 3^4, 5^3, 6^3, 7^4, 8, 9^2, 10, 12, 13^2, 14, 17, 18^2; **4:**2^4, 4^5, 6^5, 7^3, 10^2, 11, 13, 15^2, 17; **5:**1^2, 4, 5, 9, 10, 11, 14, 18^2, 19, 21; **6:**1, 2^2, 4, 7^3, 16^2; **7:**1^2, 4^2, 6, 10^2, 11, 12, 13, 14, 15; **8:**1^3, 2^3, 3, 4, 5, 8^3, 9, 11^2, 16, 17, 19^3, 21^2, 23^4, 24^2; **9:**2^3, 3, 4, 5^2, 7, 10, 12^2, 13^2, 14; **10:**1, 2, 4^2, 5^2, 7, 8, 12, 13^2, 14, 15^2, 16; **11:**7, 8, 10^3, 13, 14, 15, 17, 20, 22, 23, 24, 26^2, 28, 30, 31, 32; **12:**1, 2, 3, 5^2, 6^2, 7^2, 9, 11, 12, 17^2, 18, 21; **13:**1, 3, 4^2, 11^3, 14^3

Gal 1:1, 2, 4, 6, 7, 10, 11, 12^2, 13^2, 14^2, 19, 21, 22; **2:**2, 4, 5, 6, 7^2, 8, 9, 12, 14^2, 15, 16^5, 17, 20^2, 21; **3:**2^3, 5^2, 7^2, 9, 10^3, 11, 12, 13, 14^2, 15, 16^2, 17^2, 18^2, 19^2, 20, 21, 22, 26, 27; **4:**1, 2, 3, 4^2, 5, 6, 7, 9, 11, 13, 14, 15, 19, 20, 23^2, 26, 28, 30^2, 31^2; **5:**1, 4^2, 5, 8, 11, 15, 16, 18, 19, 21^2, 22, 26; **6:**1, 2, 8^2, 10^2, 12, 14, 16, 17, 18

Eph 1:1^2, 3, 4, 5^2, 6^2, 7^2, 9, 10^2, 11^2, 12, 13^3, 14^3, 15, 16, 17^4, 18^4, 19^2, 23; **2:**2^4, 3^4, 7, 8^2, 9, 12^2, 13, 14, 15^2, 19^2, 20, 22; **3:**1, 2^3, 4, 5, 6^2, 7^3, 8^2, 9^2, 10, 12, 14, 15, 16, 19^2; **4:**1^2, 3^2, 4, 6, 7^3, 9, 12^4, 13^7, 14^2, 16^3, 17, 18^3, 23, 25, 29^2, 30^2; **5:**1, 4, 5^2, 6^3, 8, 9, 11, 12^2, 17, 20, 21, 23^3, 26, 30^3, 33; **6:**4, 5, 6^2, 8, 9, 10, 11^2, 12^2, 13, 14, 15^2, 16^2, 17^3, 19

Php 1:1, 3, 4, 6^2, 7^3, 8, 10, 11^2, 12, 14, 15^2, 16, 17^2, 19^2, 22, 25, 27^3, 28^3, 29; **2:**1^2, 2^2, 3, 4, 6, 7^3, 8, 10^2, 11, 13, 15^2, 16^2, 17, 19, 22, 26, 30^2; **3:**2^3, 5^5, 8^3, 9^3, 10^2, 11, 12, 14^2, 17, 18^3; **4:**2, 3, 7, 8, 9, 10, 11, 15, 18^2, 22, 23

Col 1:1^2, 3, 4^2, 5^2, 6^2, 7^2, 9, 10^2, 12^2, 13^2, 14, 15^2, 18, 20, 22, 23, 24^2, 25^2, 27^3; **2:**2^6, 3, 5, 8^2, 9, 10, 11^3, 12^2, 13, 14^2, 15, 16^3, 17^2, 18^2, 19, 20, 22, 23^3; **3:**1, 6^2, 8, 10, 12^3, 14, 15, 16, 17, 22, 24^2, 25; **4:**3^2, 9, 11^2, 12^3, 16, 18

1Th 1:1, 2, 3^4, 4, 5, 6^3, 8, 9^2; **2:**2, 3^2, 4, 5, 6^4, 8^2, 9^2, 11, 12, 13^4, 14^4, 19^2; **3:**2^2, 6^2, 13; **4:**1, 3, 4, 5, 6, 9, 12, 15^2, 16^2; **5:**1, 2, 5^4, 8^3, 18, 22, 23^2, 28

2Th 1:1, 3^2, 4, 5^4, 8, 9^2, 11^3, 12^2; **2:**1, 2, 3^2, 4, 7^2, 8^2, 9, 10^2, 13^3, 14^2; **3:**1, 5, 6^2, 8, 16, 17, 18

1Ti 1:1^2, 5^4, 7, 9^2, 11, 14, 15^2, 20; **2:**1^2, 3, 4, 7; **3:**1, 2^2, 3, 5^2, 6, 7^2, 8, 9, 10, 12, 13, 15^3, 16^2; **4:**1, 3, 4, 5, 6^4, 8^2, 9, 10^2, 12, 14^2; **5:**8, 9, 10, 17, 18, 22, 25; **6:**1^2, 2, 3, 4, 5^3, 10^2, 11, 12, 13, 14, 15^2, 20

2Ti 1:1^3, 3, 4, 6^2, 7^4, 8^6, 10, 11, 13^2, 15, 16^2, 18; **2:**2, 3, 4, 6, 8^2, 9, 14^2, 15, 17, 18, 19^2, 20^4, 22, 24, 25, 26^2; **3:**2, 3, 4^2, 5, 6, 7, 8, 10, 11, 14^2, 16, 17; **4:**2, 5^2, 6, 8, 15, 17^2, 19

Tit 1:1^4, 2, 3, 6^2, 7, 8^2, 10, 12^2, 14; **2:**3, 5, 7, 8^2, 10, 11, 13, 14; **3:**2, 4, 5^3, 7, 11

Phlm 1, 4, 5, 6^2, 7, 9, 13, 14, 20, 25

Heb 1:2, 3^{4}, 5, 6, 7^{2}, 8^{2}, 9, 10^{2}, 13, 14; **2:**2, 4, 6^{2}, 7, 9^{2}, 10, 11, 12, 14^{3}, 15, 16^{2}, 17; **3:**1^{2}, 3, 5, 6, 8, 12^{2}, 13^{2}, 14^{2}, 16, 19; **4:**1^{3}, 3, 4, 6, 8, 9, 11, 12^{5}, 13, 14, 15, 16^{2}; **5:**2, 4, 6, 7, 9, 10^{2}, 11^{2}, 12^{4}, 13, 14^{2}; **6:**1^{4}, 2^{7}, 4^{2}, 5^{2}, 6, 9, 10, 11^{2}, 12, 16, 17^{2}, 19, 20; **7:**1^{3}, 2^{4}, 3^{3}, 4, 5^{7}, 6, 7, 8, 10, 11^{2}, 12^{2}, 13^{2}, 14^{2}, 15, 16^{2}, 17, 18, 19, 21, 22, 23, 28; **8:**1^{3}, 2^{2}, 3, 5^{2}, 6, 8^{2}, 9^{2}, 10; **9:**1, 3, 4^{2}, 5^{2}, 6, 7, 8, 10, 11^{2}, 12, 13^{4}, 14, 15^{4}, 16^{2}, 17^{2}, 19^{2}, 20, 21, 22, 23, 24^{2}, 25, 26^{3}, 28; **10:**1^{2}, 2, 3, 4^{2}, 7^{2}, 10^{2}, 12, 18, 19, 21, 22, 23, 25^{2}, 26, 27, 29^{4}, 31, 32, 33, 34^{2}, 35, 36^{2}, 39^{3}; **11:**1^{2}, 3^{2}, 4, 6, 7^{4}, 9^{2}, 11, 12^{2}, 13, 15, 18, 21^{2}, 22^{3}, 23^{2}, 24, 25^{2}, 26^{2}, 27, 28, 30, 32^{6}, 33, 34^{4}, 36^{2}, 38^{2}; **12:**1, 2^{3}, 3, 5^{2}, 9^{2}, 10, 11, 13, 15^{3}, 16, 17, 19^{2}, 22^{2}, 23^{3}, 24^{3}, 27^{2}; **13:**7^{2}, 11, 15^{2}, 20^{3}, 22, 24

Jas 1:1^{2}, 3, 5^{2}, 6, 7, 9, 10, 11^{2}, 12, 13, 14, 17^{2}, 18^{4}, 20^{2}, 21, 22, 23, 24, 25^{2}; **2:**1^{3}, 4, 5^{2}, 9, 10, 11, 12, 15, 16, 23; **3:**4, 6^{3}, 7^{5}, 8, 9, 10, 13^{2}, 17, 18^{2}; **4:**1, 4^{3}, 10, 11^{4}; **5:**3, 4^{5}, 5, 7^{2}, 8, 10^{3}, 11^{4}, 14^{2}, 15, 16, 17, 19, 20^{2}

1Pt 1:1, 2^{4}, 3^{2}, 5, 7^{3}, 8, 9^{2}, 10^{2}, 11^{3}, 13^{2}, 15, 17^{2}, 19^{2}, 20, 22, 23^{3}, 24^{2}, 25; **2:**2, 4^{2}, 7, 8^{2}, 9^{2}, 10, 12, 13, 14^{2}, 15^{2}, 16^{2}, 25; **3:**1, 3^{5}, 4^{4}, 7^{2}, 8^{2}, 12^{2}, 13, 14, 15, 16^{2}, 17, 20^{2}, 21^{4}, 22; **4:**2^{3}, 3^{3}, 4^{2}, 7, 8, 10^{2}, 11^{2}, 13, 14^{4}, 15, 17^{3}, 19^{2}; **5:**1^{3}, 2^{2}, 4, 5, 6, 10, 12, 14

2Pt 1:1^{2}, 2^{2}, 3, 4, 8, 11, 12, 16^{2}, 19, 20^{2}, 21^{2}; **2:**2^{3}, 3^{2}, 4, 5^{2}, 6, 7, 9^{2}, 10^{2}, 12, 13, 14, 15^{3}, 16, 17, 18^{2}, 19^{3}, 20^{2}, 21; **3:**1, 2^{4}, 4^{2}, 5^{4}, 7^{2}, 8, 10, 11, 12^{2}, 14, 15, 16, 17, 18

1Jn 1:1^{2}, 5, 7; **2:**2, 5, 10, 14, 15, 16^{5}, 17, 19^{3}, 21, 27^{2}, 29; **3:**1^{2}, 2, 4, 8^{3}, 9^{2}, 10^{3}, 12, 16, 17^{2}, 19, 22, 23; **4:**1, 2^{2}, 3^{2}, 4, 5^{2}, 6^{4}, 7^{2}, 9, 13, 14, 15, 17; **5:**1^{2}, 2, 3, 4, 5, 9^{4}, 10^{2}, 12, 13^{4}, 15, 18^{2}, 19, 20

2Jn 3, 4, 9^{2}, 11, 13

3Jn 3, 6, 7, 10, 11, 12^{2}

Jude 1^{2}, 3, 4^{2}, 5^{2}, 6, 7, 8, 9, 10, 11^{3}, 12^{2}, 13^{2}, 14^{2}, 15^{2}, 16, 17^{2}, 21^{2}, 22, 23, 24

Rev 1:1, 2^{5}, 3, 5^{3}, 7^{2}, 9^{3}, 10, 13^{2}, 14, 15, 16, 18^{2}, 20^{2}; **2:**1^{3}, 5, 6, 7^{4}, 8, 9^{2}, 10^{3}, 11, 12, 14^{2}, 15, 16, 17, 18^{3}, 21, 22, 23, 24, 27^{3}; **3:**1^{2}, 5^{2}, 7^{2}, 9^{2}, 10^{2}, 12^{5}, 14^{4}, 16, 17, 18^{2}; **4:**1, 4, 5^{3}, 6^{3}, 8^{2}; **5:**1, 5^{4}, 6^{4}, 7^{2}, 8^{3}, 9, 11^{3}; **6:**1^{3}, 5, 6^{3}, 7, 8^{2}, 9^{2}, 11, 12, 13^{2}, 14, 15^{2}, 16^{2}, 17; **7:**1^{2}, 2, 3, 4^{4}, 5^{6}, 6^{6}, 7^{6}, 8^{6}, 9, 13, 14^{2}, 15, 17^{2}; **8:**1, 3, 4^{3}, 5, 7, 8, 9^{2}, 10^{2}, 11^{3}, 12^{5}, 13^{5}; **9:**1, 2^{4}, 3^{2}, 4^{2}, 5, 7^{2}, 8^{2}, 9^{4}, 11, 13, 15, 16^{3}, 17^{5}, 18^{2}, 20^{5}, 21^{4}; **10:**1, 7^{3}, 8, 10; **11:**1, 4, 5, 6, 7, 8, 9, 11, 13^{3}, 15^{3}, 18, 19^{2}; **12:**1, 4^{2}, 5, 6, 10^{3}, 11^{2}, 12^{2}, 14^{2}, 15^{2}, 16, 17^{3}; **13:**1^{3}, 2^{2}, 3, 8^{2}, 10, 11, 12, 13, 14^{2}, 15^{3}, 17^{2}, 18^{2}; **14:**2^{3}, 5, 6, 7^{2}, 8^{3}, 10^{6}, 11^{2}, 12^{3}, 14, 15^{2}, 17, 18^{2}, 19^{3}, 20^{2}; **15:**1, 2^{4}, 3^{4}, 5^{2}, 6, 7^{3}, 8^{2}; **16:**1^{3}, 2, 3, 4, 5, 6, 7, 9, 10^{2}, 11^{3}, 12^{2}, 13^{6}, 14^{5}, 17^{2}, 19^{4}, 21^{4}; **17:**1^{2}, 2^{3}, 3^{2}, 4^{2}, 5^{2}, 6^{3}, 7^{2}, 8^{3}, 11, 14^{2}, 17, 18; **18:**2^{3}, 3^{6}, 4^{3}, 9^{2}, 10, 11, 12^{5}, 13, 15^{2}, 18, 19, 22^{4}, 23^{4}, 24^{3}; **19:**1, 2, 5, 6^{3}, 7, 8, 9^{2}, 10^{4}, 12, 13, 15^{4}, 16^{2}, 17^{2}, 18^{6}, 19, 20^{2}, 21^{2}; **20:**1, 4^{3}, 5, 6^{2}, 7, 8^{3}, 9^{3}, 10, 12^{2}, 14, 15^{2}; **21:**2, 3^{2}, 6^{3}, 9^{2}, 10, 11, 12^{3}, 14^{3}, 16, 17^{2}, 18^{3}, 19^{3}, 21^{2}, 22, 23^{3}, 24^{3}, 25, 26, 27; **22:**1^{5}, 2^{7}, 3^{2}, 5, 6, 7^{2}, 8, 9^{3}, 10^{2}, 14, 16, 17, 18^{2}, 19^{5}, 21

ON

Gen 2:2^{2}; **4:**15, 16; **6:**1, 6; **8:**4, 5, 9, 14, 20; **12:**8^{3}, 9; **13:**3, 4; **14:**15; **17:**3; **18:**5, 16; **19:**2, 34; **20:**9^{2}; **21:**14, 33; **22:**4, 9; **24:**33, 45; **25:**26; **28:**12^{2}, 20; **29:**1; **31:**22; **32:**1, 19; **33:**4, 14, 16; **34:**25; **37:**23; **38:**9, 19; **40:**14, 16, 19; **41:**45, 50; **43:**31, 32; **44:**14, 34; **46:**20, 29^{2}; **48:**16; **49:**26^{2}

Ex 1:10; **2:**6, 11; **4:**3^{2}; **6:**28; **8:**4; **9:**6; **12:**7^{2}, 11, 18, 23, 29, 37; **14:**16, 22^{2}, 29^{2}; **15:**14, 19; **16:**1, 5, 14, 22, 26, 27, 29^{2}, 30; **17:**5, 9, 12^{2}; **18:**13; **19:**4, 16, 18, 20; **21:**30; **22:**30; **23:**12; **24:**6, 8, 17; **25:**19^{3}, 20, 26; **26:**10, 13^{4}, 18, 20, 35^{2}; **27:**12, 13, 15, 21; **28:**9, 10^{2}, 23, 24, 25, 27, 37; **29:**9, 30; **31:**17; **32:**6, 15^{3}, 22, 26, 30; **33:**4, 19; **34:**21, 33; **35:**2; **36:**11; **37:**7, 8^{5}, 9; **38:**2, 7, 9, 15; **39:**7, 17, 18, 19^{2}, 20, 31; **40:**2, 17, 20, 24, 38

Lev 1:8, 9, 11, 12^{2}, 15, 16; **2:**12; **3:**4, 5^{2}; **4:**12; **5:**12; **6:**10^{2}, 11, 12; **7:**4, 16, 17, 18; **8:**26, 28; **9:**1, 14, 24; **11:**2, 27, 34; **13:**3^{2}, 5, 6, 21, 26, 31, 32, 34, 36, 51^{2}, 55; **14:**9, 10, 23, 37; **15:**6, 14, 23^{2}, 29; **16:**4^{2}, 10, 23, 24, 29, 30, 32; **19:**6, 7; **20:**25; **21:**10; **22:**30; **23:**6, 11, 21, 27, 35, 36, 39^{2}, 40; **24:**6, 7; **25:**9

Nu 1:1, 18; **2:**3, 10, 18, 25; **3:**10, 13, 29, 35; **4:**12; **6:**9, 10, 23; **7:**1, 11, 18, 24, 30, 36, 42, 48, 54, 60, 66, 72, 78; **8:**17; **9:**5, 6^{2}, 15; **10:**5, 6, 11; **11:**31^{2}; **14:**5; **16:**1, 27, 41, 46, 47; **17:**8; **19:**12^{2}, 19^{3}; **20:**19; **21:**13; **22:**1, 24^{2}, 31, 41; **23:**2, 14, 30; **24:**20, 21; **28:**9, 25; **29:**1, 7, 12, 17, 20, 23, 26, 29, 32, 35; **30:**8, 12; **31:**19^{2}, 24; **32:**19^{2}, 32; **33:**3^{2}; **34:**4^{3}, 9, 11, 15; **35:**5^{4}, 14

Dt 1:1, 3, 5, 41; **2:**28; **3:**8; **4:**15, 17, 18, 41, 46, 47, 49; **6:**9; **7:**25; **9:**10; **10:**2, 4; **11:**30; **16:**8; **21:**19, 22; **22:**5, 6, 28; **23:**11; **26:**7; **27:**2; **28:**1, 2; **30:**7; **32:**11, 13, 22, 41; **33:**26

Jos 1:14, 15; **2:**10, 19; **3:**17^{2}; **4:**14, 19, 22; **5:**1, 10, 11, 12, 14; **6:**7^{2}, 8, 9, 13^{2}, 15^{2}; **7:**2, 7; **8:**8, 9, 11, 12, 13^{2}, 19, 22^{2}, 24, 29, 33^{2}; **9:**1, 12, 17; **10:**26, 32, 35; **11:**2^{2}, 3^{2}; **12:**1^{2}, 3^{2}, 7^{2}; **13:**16, 27, 32; **14:**3, 9; **15:**3, 7, 10^{2}; **16:**1, 5, 6^{2}; **17:**5, 7, 8, 9, 10^{2}; **18:**5^{2}, 7, 12^{2}, 13, 15, 16^{2}, 20; **19:**13^{2}, 14, 27, 34^{2}; **20:**8; **22:**4, 7, 20; **24:**2, 8, 14, 15, 30

Jdg 1:8; **2:**9; **3:**25; **4:**15, 17, 23; **5:**1, 10, 15, 17, 30; **6:**32, 37, 38, 40; **7:**1, 17, 18, 25; **8:**11, 21, 26, 34; **9:**8, 42, 48, 49; **10:**4, 8; **11:**18; **12:**14; **13:**5, 19, 20^{2}; **14:**9, 15, 17, 18; **15:**5, 18; **16:**29; **19:**1, 5, 8, 9, 14, 29; **20:**30, 48; **21:**4, 19^{3}

Ru 1:7; **2:**3, 9, 10; **3:**15

1Sa 1:11; **2:**26, 34; **5:**3, 4, 5; **6:**4^{2}, 7, 15; **7:**6, 10; **9:**20^{4}, 27^{2}; **10:**3; **11:**2, 7, 11; **12:**11; **13:**5; **14:**1, 4^{2}, 16, 19, 24, 32, 40^{2}, 47; **15:**12, 16, 18; **16:**6, 7^{4}, 16; **17:**3^{4}, 41; **18:**10, 24; **19:**23; **20:**20, 21, 27, 41; **21:**13; **22:**18; **23:**19, 21, 24, 26^{2}; **24:**7; **25:**13^{3}, 14, 18, 19, 20, 23, 41; **26:**13, 25; **27:**11; **28:**8, 20, 22; **29:**2^{2}; **30:**1, 2; **31:**7^{2}, 8

2Sa 1:2, 10, 11, 24; **2:**13^{2}, 21, 25; **3:**12, 29^{4}; **4:**5, 7; **5:**8, 10; **6:**5^{6}; **8:**7; **9:**3, 6, 13; **11:**13; **12:**18, 30; **13:**5, 19^{4}, 31; **14:**2, 3, 4, 9^{2}, 12, 14, 22, 26, 30^{2}, 31, 33; **15:**6, 18^{2}, 33; **16:**2, 6^{2}, 12, 13; **17:**12; **19:**40^{2}; **20:**8, 13; **21:**10, 20^{2}; **22:**4, 49; **23:**1; **24:**5, 20^{2}

1Ki 1:20, 27, 46, 48, 50, 51; **2:**4, 5, 14, 15, 16, 19^{2}, 20, 24, 28, 37, 42; **3:**6; **4:**24^{3}, 29; **5:**3, 4; **6:**10, 15, 16; **7:**3, 9, 28, 29, 35, 36^{2}, 39^{3}, 41, 43, 49^{2}; **8:**20, 23, 25, 27, 50, 54, 66; **9:**26; **10:**9, 19^{2}, 20^{2}; **11:**30; **12:**32; **13:**4; **14:**23; **16:**11, 24; **18:**7, 23^{2}, 24^{2}, 25, 26, 33^{3}, 39, 46; **19:**6, 15; **20:**11, 20, 31, 32^{2}; **21:**9, 12; **22:**10^{2}, 19^{3}, 20^{2}, 24, 30

2Ki 1:4, 6, 9, 13, 16; **2:**6, 8, 11, 15, 24; **3:**11, 21, 22, 25; **4:**8, 10, 11, 18, 20, 21, 31, 38; **5:**2, 11, 18; **6:**29, 31; **7:**2, 17; **8:**12, 15^{2}; **9:**3, 6, 13, 17, 18, 19, 32, 33^{2}; **10:**3, 15, 30; **11:**5, 7, 9^{2}, 16, 19; **12:**9, 15; **13:**21, 23; **14:**4, 20; **15:**4, 12; **16:**4, 14; **18:**14, 20, 21^{2}, 23, 24, 26, 27; **19:**22, 26; **20:**5, 7; **23:**8, 12, 13; **25:**3, 8, 27

1Ch 4:10; **6:**32, 39, 44, 49, 78^{2}; **10:**5, 8; **12:**18, 37, 40^{4}; **13:**6; **14:**2; **15:**20, 21; **16:**7; **18:**7; **20:**6^{2}; **21:**17^{3}; **22:**18; **23:**28, 31; **26:**30; **29:**15, 21, 22, 23, 25

2Ch 2:4^{3}; **3:**7, 13, 15, 16^{2}, 17^{4}; **4:**6^{2}, 7^{2}, 8^{2}, 10, 12^{2}, 13^{2}; **6:**10, 18; **7:**6, 10, 22; **8:**12, 13^{3}; **9:**8, 18, 19^{2}; **10:**12^{2}; **11:**12; **14:**7, 11; **16:**7^{2}, 8; **17:**19; **18:**9, 18^{2}, 24, 29; **20:**2, 19, 26, 29; **23:**4, 8^{2}, 15; **24:**25; **26:**15; **27:**3; **28:**4; **29:**17^{2}, 21, 22; **30:**15; **32:**15, 17, 18, 22; **33:**14; **34:**4; **35:**1; **36:**15^{2}

Ezr 4:10, 11, 16; **5:**3, 6^{2}, 8; **6:**13, 15; **7:**9; **8:**31, 33, 36; **10:**9

Neh 2:14; **3:**7, 13; **4:**13, 17, 22; **6:**14; **8:**4^{2}, 13, 18; **9:**10^{2}, 11, 32^{6}; **10:**31^{3}; **12:**31; **13:**1, 15^{2}, 16, 19, 21^{2}

Est 1:2, 10, 11; **2:**14, 21, 23; **3:**6, 12; **4:**1; **5:**1^{2}; **6:**1, 2, 4, 9, 11; **7:**2, 10; **8:**1, 9, 10^{2}, 13, 14; **9:**1, 2, 10, 11, 15^{2}, 16, 17^{2}, 18^{3}, 25

Job 1:10; **4:**13; **5:**11; **9:**11; **13:**13; **15:**26, 27; **16:**16, 19; **17:**9; **18:**11; **19:**10; **21:**3, 6; **23:**9^{2}; **24:**20; **27:**17, 20; **29:**9, 14, 24; **31:**2; **36:**2, 7, 16, 17; **37:**6; **38:**26^{2}; **39:**18, 21, 27, 28; **40:**12

Ps 4:ttl; **6:**ttl; **7:**7; **12:**8; **21:**3; **22:**8; **25:**3, 5, 21; **27:**14^{2}; **31:**13; **35:**17; **37:**34; **48:**2; **49:**14; **52:**9; **54:**ttl; **55:**ttl; **57:**4; **63:**6; **65:**12; **66:**6; **67:**ttl; **68:**18, 21, 25; **69:**6, 29; **71:**21; **75:**5; **76:**ttl; **78:**53; **79:**1; **81:**3; **82:**5; **83:**14; **87:**7; **91:**14; **92:**11; **93:**4; **104:**32; **107:**41; **113:**5; **118:**6; **119:**59, 84, 143; **124:**1, 2; **142:**4; **143:**5^{2}

Prv 4:25; **5:**5; **9:**14, 15; **14:**21, 31; **15:**14; **20:**22; **22:**3; **27:**12, 18

Ecc 2:3, 11^{2}; **4:**1

Song 2:12; **3:**1; **5:**3

Isa 7:25; **9:**17, 20^{2}; **10:**12; **11:**8^{2}; **13:**18; **14:**1; **15:**2, 3; **16:**12; **18:**3^{2}; **22:**16; **24:**18, 21; **25:**6^{2}; **26:**3, 5; **27:**11^{2}; **28:**1, 4, 20; **30:**17; **31:**1, 4; **32:**15, 19; **33:**5, 16; **36:**5, 6, 8, 9, 11; **37:**23, 27; **40:**26; **42:**25; **44:**20; **47:**1; **48:**14^{2}; **49:**10, 15, 18; **51:**5, 9; **52:**1^{2}; **53:**6; **54:**3^{2}, 8, 10; **56:**2; **57:**17; **58:**4, 13; **59:**17^{2}; **60:**7, 10; **63:**7^{2}

Jer 4:7; **5:**9, 29; **6:**23, 25; **7:**29; **8:**13^{2}, 21; **9:**9; **10:**25; **11:**20; **12:**15; **13:**2, 27; **15:**10^{2}; **17:**11, 21, 22, 24, 25, 27; **18:**3; **20:**3, 10^{2}, 12; **22:**4; **23:**12; **25:**29, 30; **30:**6, 18; **31:**29, 30; **32:**29; **33:**26; **36:**22, 23^{2}; **38:**22; **43:**3, 12; **46:**4; **48:**11; **49:**23, 24, 29; **50:**6, 19; **52:**23

Lam 1:2; **2:**21; **4:**6

Ezk 1:8, 10^{2}, 23^{2}; **3:**23; **4:**6; **7:**16; **10:**3; **11:**23; **16:**11, 12, 15, 33; **18:**2; **19:**8; **21:**16^{2}; **23:**5^{2}, 7, 22; **24:**3^{2}, 10, 17; **25:**9; **26:**17; **28:**23; **31:**4; **33:**32; **36:**3; **37:**21; **39:**6, 9, 11, 17; **40:**2, 5, 10^{4}, 12^{4}, 21^{2}, 26^{2}, 34^{2}, 37^{2}, 39^{2}, 40, 41^{2}, 48^{4}, 49^{2}; **41:**1^{2}, 2^{2}, 5, 10, 15^{2}, 16, 19^{2}, 20, 25^{2}, 26^{3}; **42:**7, 9, 14; **43:**20^{2}, 22; **44:**19; **45:**7^{2}; **46:**1, 12, 19; **47:**2, 7^{2}, 12^{2}; **48:**16, 21^{2}, 30

Dan 3:27; **6:**14; **7:**5; **8:**5, 18; **10:**9; **11:**17, 31; **12:**5^{2}

Hos 4:8; **5:**1; **6:**3; **10:**5, 8^{2}; **11:**4, 6; **12:**1, 6

Joel 2:5, 7, 32

Am 1:7, 10; **2:**7; **5:**19

Oba 11, 12, 13^{2}, 21

Jna 3:5; **4:**5, 10

Mic 2:13

Nah 1:2

Hab 1:13; **2:**9, 15, 16; **3:**10, 19

Zep 1:9, 12

Zec 1:12^{2}; **5:**3^{2}; **10:**5; **12:**6^{2}; **13:**9; **14:**4, 13

Mal 1:10

Mt 1:18, 20; **4:**5, 21; **5:**14, 15, 28, 39, 45^{4}; **6:**25; **9:**2, 6, 27, 36; **10:**29, 34; **12:**1, 5, 10, 11^{2}, 12; **13:**2; **14:**3, 13, 19, 25, 26, 28, 29; **15:**22, 32, 35; **16:**19^{2}; **17:**6, 15; **18:**18^{2}, 19, 28, 33^{2}; **19:**13, 15; **20:**21^{2}, 23^{2}, 30, 31, 34; **21:**7, 19, 38, 44^{2}, 46; **22:**11, 40, 44; **23:**4; **24:**17, 20; **25:**33^{2}, 34, 41; **26:**5, 7, 12, 39, 45, 50, 55, 57, 64; **27:**19, 25^{2}, 28, 30, 31, 38^{2}, 48

Mk 1:21; **2:**10, 12, 21, 23, 24; **3:**2, 4, 5, 9, 21, 34; **4:**1, 5, 8, 16, 20, 21, 38; **5:**19, 23; **6:**9, 21, 47; **8:**2, 6, 23, 33; **9:**3, 20, 22, 40; **10:**37^{2}, 40^{2}, 47, 48; **11:**7, 12; **12:**12, 36; **13:**15; **14:**2, 3, 6, 35, 41, 46, 51, 62, 65; **15:**19, 20, 27^{2}, 29, 36, 40; **16:**5, 18, 19

Lk 1:11, 25, 50, 59, 65, 78; **2:**14; **4:**9, 16, 20, 31, 40; **5:**12, 17; **6:**1, 2, 6, 7, 9, 20, 29, 48; **7:**13, 16, 40; **8:**8, 13, 15, 16, 22, 23, 32; **9:**37; **10:**11, 19, 31, 32^{2}, 33, 34, 35, 37; **11:**33; **12:**22, 49, 51; **13:**7, 10, 13, 14^{2}, 15, 16; **14:**1, 3, 5; **15:**5, 20, 22^{3}; **16:**24; **17:**13, 16; **18:**8, 32, 38, 39; **19:**43; **20:**1, 18, 19, 42; **21:**12, 26, 35^{2}; **22:**21, 30, 64, 69; **23:**26, 30, 33^{2}, 39, 54; **24:**49

Jn 1:12, 33; **2:**11; **3:**18, 36^{2}; **4:**6, 35, 39; **5:**9, 16, 24; **6:**2, 19, 22, 25, 29, 35, 40, 47; **7:**22, 23^{2}, 30, 31, 38, 39, 44, 48; **8:**6, 8, 20, 30, 31; **9:**6, 35, 36; **10:**42; **11:**45, 48; **12:**11, 12, 15, 37, 42, 44^{3}, 46; **13:**22, 23, 25; **14:**12; **16:**9; **17:**4, 20; **19:**2^{2}, 18, 19, 31, 37; **20:**22; **21:**1, 4, 6, 20

Act 2:18^{2}, 21, 25, 30, 34; **3:**4, 12; **4:**3, 5, 22; **5:**5, 15, 18, 30; **6:**6, 15; **7:**5, 6, 54, 55, 56; **8:**17, 18, 19, 36, 39; **9:**12, 14, 17, 21; **10:**4, 7, 9^{2}, 19, 23, 39, 44, 45; **11:**15^{2}, 17; **12:**7, 8, 10; **13:**3, 9, 11, 14, 15, 34, 36; **14:**10, 23; **15:**3; **16:**13, 31; **17:**5, 26; **18:**8, 10; **19:**4^{2}, 6, 16, 17; **20:**7, 10, 37; **21:**3, 5^{2}, 23, 27, 40; **22:**16, 19, 30; **23:**2, 24, 32; **25:**6, 17^{2}, 23; **27:**20, 33, 44^{2}; **28:**3^{2}, 4, 8

Ro 4:5, 24; **9:**15^{2}, 18, 23, 33; **10:**6, 11, 14; **11:**22; **12:**7^{2}, 8, 20; **13:**12, 14; **15:**3, 24; **16:**6, 19

1Co 1:4; **11:**10; **14:**25; **15:**53^{2}, 54^{2}; **16:**6, 17

2Co 1:11, 16; **4:**8; **5:**12; **6:**7^{2}; **7:**5; **8:**1, 24; **10:**7; **11:**20

Gal 3:13, 14, 27; **6:**16

Eph 1:10; **4:**8, 24; **6:**3, 11, 14

Php 1:29; **2:**4^{2}, 27^{3}; **4:**8

Col 3:1, 2^{3}, 6, 10, 12, 14

1Th 5:8

2Th 1:8

1Ti 1:16, 18; **3:**16; **4:**14; **5:**22; **6:**12, 19

2Ti 1:6; **2:**22

Tit 3:6, 13

Phlm 18

Heb 1:3[2], 13; 2:16[2]; 4:4; 5:2[2]; 6:1, 2; 8:1, 4; 9:10; 10:12; 11:13; 12:25

Jas 3:6[2]; 4:14; 5:5, 17

1Pt 1:17; 2:6, 24; 3:3, 22; 4:14[2], 16

2Pt 3:12

1Jn 3:23; 5:10, 13[2]

3Jn 6

Jude 20

Rev 1:10; 3:3; 4:2, 4, 9, 10; 5:1[2], 10, 13; 6:2, 5, 8, 10[2], 16[2]; 7:1[4], 11, 15, 16; 9:7, 17; 10:2; 11:10, 16; 13:13, 14[2]; 14:1, 6, 14, 15, 16[2]; 15:2; 17:8, 9; 18:19, 20; 19:4, 12, 16[2], 18, 19; 20:2, 6, 9, 11; 21:13[4]; 22:2

OR

Gen 13:9; 17:12; 24:21, 49, 50; 26:11; 27:21; 30:1; 31:14, 24, 29, 39, 43, 50; 37:8, 32; 39:10; 41:44; 42:16; 44:8, 16, 19

Ex 4:11[4]; 5:3; 10:15; 11:7; 12:5, 19; 16:4; 17:7; 19:12, 13[2]; 20:4[3]; 21:4, 6, 15, 16, 17, 18, 20, 21, 26, 27, 28, 29, 31, 32, 33[2], 36; 22:1[2], 4[2], 5, 6[2], 7, 9, 10[5], 14, 22; 23:4; 28:43; 29:34; 30:20, 33; 34:19

Lev 1:10, 14; 2:4; 3:1, 6; 4:23, 28; 5:1, 2[3], 3, 4[2], 6, 7, 11; 6:2[3], 3, 4[3], 5; 7:16, 21[2], 23[2], 26; 11:4, 32[3], 35, 36, 42; 12:6[2], 7, 8; 13:2[2], 16, 19, 24[2], 29[2], 30, 38, 42[2], 43, 47, 48[3], 49[4], 51[3], 52[3], 53[2], 55, 56[3], 57[2], 58[2], 59[4]; 14:22, 30, 37; 15:3, 14, 23, 25, 29; 16:29; 17:3[3], 8[2], 10, 13[2], 15[2]; 18:7, 9[2], 10, 17; 19:35; 20:2, 9[2], 17, 25[2], 27[2]; 21:7, 11, 14[3], 18[3], 19[2], 20[6]; 22:4[2], 5[2], 8, 10, 13, 16, 18, 19, 21[2], 22[5], 23[2], 24[3], 27[2], 28; 25:14, 35, 36, 47[3], 49[3]; 26:15; 27:10, 12, 14, 20, 26, 27, 28, 30, 32, 33

Nu 5:6, 14, 30; 6:2, 3[2], 7[2], 10; 9:10[2], 21, 22[3]; 11:8, 22, 23; 13:18[2], 19[2], 20[2]; 14:2; 15:3[4], 5, 6, 8[2], 11[3], 14, 30; 16:14, 29; 18:15, 17[2]; 19:16[3], 18[3]; 20:5[3], 17; 21:22; 22:18, 26; 23:8, 19; 24:13; 30:2, 5, 6, 10, 12, 13, 14; 32:19; 35:18, 20, 21, 22, 23

Dt 3:24; 4:16, 23, 25, 32, 34; 5:8[3], 21[4], 32; 7:14[2], 25; 8:2; 9:5; 12:17[5]; 13:1[2], 2, 3, 5, 6[4], 7; 14:7, 21, 24, 26[4]; 15:2, 12, 21[2]; 17:1[2], 2, 3[2], 5[2], 6, 12, 20; 18:3, 10[5], 11[4], 20; 19:15[2]; 21:18; 22:1, 2, 4, 6[3]; 23:1, 3, 18; 24:3, 6, 7, 14; 27:15, 16, 22; 28:14, 51[3]; 29:6, 18[3]; 32:36

Jos 1:7; 5:13; 7:3; 8:17, 20, 22; 10:14; 19:2; 22:22, 23[3], 28, 29; 23:6; 24:15

Jdg 2:22; 5:8, 30; 9:2; 11:25; 13:14; 14:3, 6; 18:19; 19:13; 20:28; 21:22

Ru 1:16; 3:10

1Sa 2:14[3]; 6:12; 12:3[3]; 13:19; 14:6, 52; 16:7; 18:18; 20:2, 10, 12; 21:3, 8; 22:8, 15; 25:31, 36; 26:10[2], 18; 29:3; 30:2

2Sa 2:21; 3:29[4], 35; 14:19; 15:4, 21; 17:9; 19:35, 42; 20:20; 24:13[2]

1Ki 3:7; 8:23, 37, 38, 46; 9:6; 15:17; 18:10, 27[3]; 20:18, 39; 21:2, 6; 22:6, 15

2Ki 2:16, 21; 4:13; 6:27; 9:32; 12:13; 13:19; 17:34[2]; 20:9; 22:2; 23:10

1Ch 21:12[2]

2Ch 1:11; 6:28[3], 29[2], 36; 7:13[2]; 8:15; 14:11; 15:13[2]; 16:1; 18:5, 14, 30; 20:9[2]; 32:15; 36:17[2]

Ezr 7:24[2], 26[3]; 9:12; 10:13

Neh 2:16; 5:8; 10:31[2]; 13:20, 25

Est 4:11, 16; 8:6; 9:12

Job 3:12, 15, 16; 4:7; 6:5, 6, 12, 22, 23[2]; 7:12; 8:3; 10:4; 11:10; 12:8; 13:9, 22; 15:3, 7; 16:3; 22:3, 11; 25:4; 28:16, 18; 31:5, 9, 13, 16, 17, 19, 24, 26, 27, 29, 34, 38, 39; 32:12; 34:13, 29, 33; 35:6, 7; 36:23, 29; 37:13[2]; 38:5, 6, 8, 16, 17, 21, 22, 25, 28, 31, 32, 36, 37, 39; 39:1, 2, 5, 9, 10, 11, 13, 15; 40:9; 41:1, 2, 5, 7, 13, 20

Ps 18:31; 24:3; 32:9; 35:14; 44:20; 50:8, 13, 16; 66:ttl; 67:ttl; 68:ttl; 69:31; 75:ttl; 76:ttl; 83:ttl; 87:ttl; 88:11, ttl; 89:8; 90:2; 92:ttl; 94:16; 108:ttl; 120:3; 131:1; 132:4; 139:7; 144:3

Prv 6:7; 7:22; 8:8, 23; 20:20; 22:26; 23:34; 28:24; 29:9; 30:4, 9, 32

Ecc 2:19, 25; 5:12; 9:1; 11:3, 6[2]; 12:2[3], 6[4], 14

Song 2:9, 17; 6:12; 8:14

Isa 1:11[2]; 7:11; 10:14[2], 15[2]; 17:6[2], 8; 19:15[2]; 27:5, 7; 29:8, 16; 30:14; 38:14; 40:13, 18, 25; 41:22, 23; 42:19; 43:9; 44:10; 45:9, 10; 49:24; 50:1, 2; 57:11; 66:8

Jer 2:18, 32; 7:22; 11:14, 19; 13:23; 14:22; 15:5[2]; 16:2, 7, 10[2]; 18:14; 20:17; 21:13; 22:18[2]; 23:33[2]; 32:43; 34:9; 36:23; 37:18[2]; 40:5; 42:6, 17; 44:14, 28; 48:24

Ezk 2:5, 7; 3:11; 4:14; 14:7, 17, 19; 15:2, 3; 17:9, 15; 21:16[2]; 22:14; 34:6; 44:22, 25[4], 31[2]; 46:12

Dan 2:10[2]; 4:19, 35; 6:4, 7, 12, 24; 11:29

Joel 1:2

Am 3:12; 4:8; 5:19; 6:2

Mic 6:7

Hag 2:12[4]

Zec 8:10

Mal 1:8; 2:13, 17

Mt 5:17, 18, 36; 6:24, 25, 31[2]; 7:4, 9, 10, 16; 9:5; 10:11, 14, 19, 37[2]; 11:3; 12:5, 25, 29, 33; 13:21; 15:4, 5, 6; 16:14, 26; 17:25[2]; 18:8[3], 16[2], 20; 19:29[7]; 21:25; 22:17; 23:17, 19; 24:23; 25:37, 38, 39[2], 44[5]; 27:17

Mk 2:9; 3:4[2], 33; 4:17, 21, 30; 6:15, 56[2]; 7:10, 11, 12; 8:37; 10:29[7]; 11:30; 12:14, 15; 13:21, 35[3]

Lk 2:24; 3:15; 5:23; 6:9[2]; 7:19, 20; 8:16; 9:25; 11:11, 12; 12:11[2], 14, 29, 38, 41; 13:4, 15; 14:5, 12, 31, 32; 16:13; 17:7, 21, 23; 18:11, 29[4]; 20:2, 4, 22; 22:27

Jn 2:6; 4:27; 6:19; 7:17, 48; 9:2, 21, 25; 13:29; 14:11; 18:34

Act 1:7; 3:12[2]; 4:7, 34; 5:38; 7:49; 8:34; 9:2; 10:14, 28[2]; 11:8; 17:21, 29[2]; 18:14; 19:12; 20:33[2]; 23:9, 15, 29; 24:20, 23; 25:11; 26:31; 28:6, 17, 21

Ro 2:4, 15; 3:1; 4:9, 10, 13; 6:16; 8:35[6]; 9:11; 10:7; 11:34, 35; 12:7[2], 8; 14:4, 8, 10, 13, 21[2]

1Co 1:13; 2:1; 3:22[7]; 4:3, 21; 5:10[3], 11[5]; 7:11, 15, 16; 8:5; 9:6, 7, 8, 10; 10:19, 31[2]; 11:4, 5, 6, 22; 12:13[2], 26; 13:1; 14:6[3], 7[2], 23, 24, 27, 29, 36, 37; 15:11, 37

2Co 1:6, 13, 17; 3:1[2]; 5:9, 10, 13; 6:15; 8:23; 9:7; 10:12; 11:4[2]; 12:2, 3, 6; 13:1

Gal 1:8, 10[2]; 2:2; 3:2, 5, 15; 4:9

Eph 3:20; 5:3, 27[2]; 6:8

Php 1:18, 20, 27; 2:3

Col 1:16[3], 20; 2:16[4]; 3:17

1Th 2:19[2]; 5:10

2Th 2:2, 4, 15

1Ti 2:9[3]; 5:4, 16, 19

Tit 1:6; 3:12

Phlm 18

Heb 2:6; 10:28; 12:16, 20

Jas 2:3, 15; 4:13, 15

1Pt 1:11; 2:14; 3:3, 9; 4:15[3]

Rev 2:5, 16; 3:15; 13:16, 17[3]; 14:9; 20:4; 21:27

OUR

Gen 1:26[2]; 5:29[2]; 19:31, 32[2], 34; 23:6; 24:60; 29:26; 31:1[2], 14, 15, 16[2], 32; 33:12; 34:9, 14, 16, 17, 21, 31; 37:26, 27[3]; 41:12; 42:13, 21, 32[2]; 43:4, 7[2], 8, 18[2], 21[3], 22[3], 28; 44:8, 25, 26[2], 31; 46:34[2]; 47:3, 18[4], 19[3], 25

Ex 1:10; 3:18; 5:3, 8, 21; 8:10, 26, 27; 10:9[6], 25, 26[2]; 12:27; 17:3[2]; 34:9[2]

Lev 25:20

Nu 11:6[2]; 13:33; 14:3[2]; 20:3, 4, 15[2], 16; 21:5; 27:3, 4[2]; 31:49, 50; 32:16[2], 17, 18, 19, 26[4], 32; 36:2, 3[2], 4

Dt 1:6, 19, 20, 25, 28[2], 41; 2:1, 8, 29, 33, 36, 37; 3:3[2]; 4:7; 5:2, 3, 24, 25, 27[2]; 6:4, 20, 22, 23, 24[2], 25[2]; 21:7[2], 20[2]; 26:3, 7[5], 15; 29:15, 18, 29[2]; 31:17; 32:3, 27, 31[2]

Jos 2:11, 13, 14[2], 19, 20, 24; 5:13; 7:9; 9:11[2], 12[3], 13[2], 24; 17:4; 18:6; 21:2; 22:19, 24, 25, 27[5], 28[2], 29; 24:17[3], 18, 24

Jdg 6:13; 9:3; 10:10; 11:2, 6, 8, 24; 13:23; 16:23[3], 24[4]; 18:5; 19:19; 21:7, 18, 22

Ru 2:20; 3:2; 4:3

1Sa 2:2; 4:3; 5:7, 10, 11; 7:8; 8:20[2]; 9:6, 7, 8; 12:10, 19; 14:9, 10; 16:16; 17:9, 47; 20:29; 23:20; 25:14, 17; 30:23

2Sa 7:22; 10:12[2]; 12:18; 18:12; 19:9, 41, 43[2]; 22:32

1Ki 1:11, 43, 47; 8:21, 40, 53, 57[2], 58[2], 59, 61, 65; 12:4, 10; 20:31[2]

2Ki 7:9; 18:22; 19:19; 22:13

1Ch 12:17, 19; 13:2[2], 3; 15:13; 16:14, 35; 17:20; 19:13[2]; 28:2, 8; 29:10, 13, 15[2], 16, 18

2Ch 2:4, 5; 6:31; 10:4, 10; 13:10, 11, 12; 14:7, 11[2]; 19:7; 20:6, 7, 9, 12[2]; 28:13[3]; 29:6[2], 9[4]; 32:8[2], 11; 34:21

Ezr 4:3; 5:12; 7:27; 8:17, 18, 21[3], 22, 23, 25, 30, 31, 33; 9:6[3], 7[4], 8[4], 9[3], 10, 13[4], 15; 10:2, 3[2], 14[3]

Neh 4:4, 9[2], 11, 15, 20, 23; 5:2[2], 3, 4, 5[8], 8[2], 9[2]; 6:1, 16[2]; 8:10; 9:9, 16, 32[6], 34[4], 36, 37[3], 38; 10:29, 30[2], 32, 33, 34[3], 35, 36[6], 37[5], 38, 39; 13:2, 4, 18, 27

Job 8:9; 17:16; 22:20; 28:22; 37:19

Ps 8:1, 9; 12:4[3]; 17:11; 18:31; 20:5[2], 7; 22:4; 33:20[3], 21; 35:21; 40:3; 44:1[2], 5, 7, 9, 13, 18[2], 20[2], 24[2], 25[2], 26; 46:1, 7, 11; 47:3, 4, 6; 48:1, 8, 14[2]; 50:3; 59:11; 60:10, 12; 65:3, 5; 66:8, 9[2], 11, 12; 67:6; 68:19, 20; 74:9; 77:13; 78:3, 5; 79:4, 9[2], 10, 12; 80:6[2]; 81:1, 3; 84:9; 85:4, 9, 12; 89:17, 18[2]; 90:1, 8[2], 9[2], 10, 12[2], 14, 17[3]; 92:13; 94:23; 95:1, 6, 7; 98:3; 99:5, 8, 9[2]; 103:10[2], 12, 14; 105:7; 106:6, 7, 47; 108:11, 13; 113:5; 115:3; 116:5; 118:23; 122:2, 9; 123:2[2], 4; 124:1, 2, 4, 5, 7, 8; 126:2[2], 4; 135:2, 5; 136:23, 24; 137:2; 141:7; 144:12[2], 13[3], 14[2]; 147:1, 5, 7

Prv 1:13; 7:18

Song 1:16, 17[2]; 2:9, 12, 15; 7:13; 8:8

Isa 1:10; 3:6; 4:1[3]; 20:6; 25:9; 26:8, 12, 13; 28:15; 33:2, 20, 22[3]; 35:2; 36:7; 37:20; 38:20; 40:3, 8; 42:17; 47:4; 52:10; 53:1, 3, 4[2], 5[3]; 55:7; 58:3; 59:12[4], 13; 61:2, 6; 63:16[3], 17, 18; 64:6[2], 7, 8[2], 11[4]

Jer 3:22, 23, 24[2], 25[6]; 5:19, 24; 6:24; 8:14; 9:18[2], 19, 21[2]; 11:21; 12:4; 14:7[2], 20[2], 22; 16:10[3], 19; 17:12; 18:12; 20:10; 21:13; 23:6, 36; 26:16, 19; 31:6; 33:16; 35:6, 8[5], 10; 36:15; 37:3; 42:2, 6[2], 20[2]; 43:2; 44:17[4], 19, 25; 46:16[2]; 50:28; 51:10[2], 51

Lam 3:40, 41[2], 44, 46; 4:17[3], 18[5], 19, 20; 5:1, 2[2], 3, 4[2], 5, 7, 9[2], 10, 15[2], 16, 17[2], 21

Ezk 33:10[2], 21; 37:11[3]; 40:1

Dan 1:13; 3:17; 9:6[3], 8[3], 9, 10, 12, 13[3], 14, 15, 16[2], 17, 18[3]

Hos 7:5; 14:2, 3[2]

Joel 1:16[2]

Am 6:13

Mic 2:4; 4:5, 11; 5:5[2], 6[2]; 7:17, 19, 20

Zec 1:6[2]; 9:7

Mal 2:10

Mt 3:9; 6:9, 11, 12[2]; 8:17[2]; 20:33; 21:42; 23:30; 25:8; 27:25

Mk 9:40; 11:10; 12:11, 29

Lk 1:55, 71, 72, 73, 74, 75, 78, 79; 3:8; 7:5; 11:2, 3, 4; 13:26; 17:5, 10; 23:41; 24:20, 22, 32

Jn 3:11; 4:12, 20; 6:31; 7:51; 8:39, 53; 9:20; 11:11, 48; 12:38; 14:23; 19:7

Act 2:8, 11, 39; 3:12, 13, 25; 5:30; 7:2, 11, 12, 15, 19[2], 38, 39, 44, 45[2]; 13:17; 14:17; 15:10, 25, 26, 36; 16:20; 17:20, 28; 19:25, 27; 20:21; 21:5[2], 6, 7, 15; 22:14; 24:6, 7; 26:5, 6, 7; 27:10, 19; 28:17, 25

Ro 1:3, 7; 3:5; 4:1, 12, 24, 25[2]; 5:1, 5, 11, 21; 6:6, 11, 23; 7:5, 25; 8:16, 23, 26, 39; 9:10; 10:16; 12:7; 13:11; 15:4, 6; 16:1, 9, 18, 20, 24

1Co 1:1, 2, 3, 7, 8, 9, 10; 2:7; 4:12; 5:4[2], 7; 6:11; 9:1, 10[2]; 10:1, 6, 11; 12:23, 24; 15:3, 14, 31, 57; 16:12, 23

2Co 1:1, 2, 3, 4, 5, 7, 8, 11, 12[3], 18, 22; 3:2[2], 5; 4:3, 6, 10, 11, 16, 17; 5:1, 2, 12; 6:11[2]; 7:3, 4, 5, 12, 14; 8:9, 22, 23, 24; 9:3; 10:4, 8, 13, 14, 15[2], 16; 11:31

Gal 1:3, 4[2]; 2:4; 3:24; 6:14, 18

Eph 1:2, 3, 14, 17; 2:3[2], 14; 3:11, 14; 5:20; 6:22, 24

Php 1:2; 3:20, 21; 4:20, 23

Col 1:1, 2, 3, 7; 3:4

1Th 1:1, 2, 3[2], 5; 2:1, 2, 3, 4, 8, 9, 19[2], 20; 3:2[2], 5, 7, 9, 11[3], 13[2]; 5:9, 23, 28

2Th 1:1, 2, 8, 10, 11, 12[2]; 2:1[2], 14[2], 15, 16[2]; 3:6, 12, 14, 18

1Ti 1:1[2], 2[2], 12, 14; 2:3; 6:3, 14

2Ti 1:2, 8, 9, 10; 4:15

Tit 1:3, 4; 2:10, 13; 3:4, 6

Phlm 1[2], 2[2], 3, 25

Heb 1:3; 3:1, 14; 4:14, 15; 7:14; 10:22[2], 23; 12:2, 9, 10, 29; 13:15, 20, 23

Jas 2:1, 21; 3:6

1Pt 1:3; 2:24; 4:3

2Pt 1:1, 2, 8, 11, 14, 16; 3:15^{2}, 18

1Jn 1:1^{2}, 3, 9^{2}; 2:2; 3:5, 16, 19, 20^{2}, 21; 4:10, 17; 5:4

2Jn 12

3Jn 12, 14

Jude 4^{2}, 17, 21, 25

Rev 1:5; 5:10; 6:10; 7:3, 10, 12; 11:8, 15; 12:10^{3}; 19:1, 5; 22:21

OURS

Gen 26:20; 31:16; 34:23

Nu 32:32

1Ki 22:3

Ezk 36:2

Mk 12:7

Lk 20:14

1Co 1:2

2Co 1:14

Tit 3:14

1Jn 2:2

OURSELVES

Gen 37:10; 44:16

Nu 32:17

Dt 2:35; 3:7

1Sa 14:8

1Ch 19:13

Ezr 4:3; 8:21

Neh 10:32

Job 34:4

Ps 83:12; 100:3

Prv 7:18

Isa 28:15; 56:12

Jer 50:5

Lk 22:71

Jn 4:42

Act 6:4; 23:14

Ro 8:23^{3}; 15:1

1Co 11:31

2Co 1:4, 9^{2}; 3:1, 5^{2}; 4:2, 5^{2}; 5:12, 13; 6:4; 7:1; 10:12^{2}, 14; 12:19

Gal 2:17

1Th 2:10

2Th 1:4; 3:7, 9

Tit 3:3

Heb 10:25

1Jn 1:8

OUT

Gen 2:9, 10, 19, 23; 3:19, 24; 4:14, 16; 8:10, 19; 9:10; 10:11, 14; 12:1, 4; 13:1; 14:8, 17; 15:4, 7, 14; 17:6; 19:5, 6, 8, 12, 14^{2}, 24, 29, 30; 21:10, 17, 21; 22:11, 15; 23:4, 8; 24:11, 13, 15, 29, 44, 63; 25:25, 26; 26:8; 27:3, 30; 28:10, 16; 29:2; 30:16^{2}; 31:13, 33; 32:25; 34:1, 6, 7, 24^{2}, 26^{2}; 35:9, 11; 37:14, 21, 22, 23, 28; 38:28^{2}, 29, 30; 39:12, 15, 18; 40:14, 15, 17; 41:2, 3, 14, 18, 33, 45, 46; 43:2, 23, 31; 44:4, 8^{2}, 16, 28; 45:1, 19, 24, 25; 46:26; 47:1, 10, 30; 48:12, 14, 22; 49:20; 50:24

Ex 1:5, 10^{2}; 2:10, 11, 13, 19; 3:2, 4, 8^{2}, 10, 11, 12, 17, 20; 4:6, 7, 9; 5:10; 6:1, 6^{3}, 7, 11, 13, 26, 27; 7:2, 4, 5, 15, 19; 8:6, 12, 13^{3}, 16, 17, 29, 30; 9:15, 29, 33; 10:5, 6, 11, 12, 18, 21; 11:1, 4, 8^{3}, 10; 12:5, 15, 17, 21, 22, 33, 39^{2}, 41, 42, 46, 51; 13:3^{3}, 4, 8, 9, 14, 16, 18; 14:8, 10, 11, 16, 21, 26, 30; 15:12, 20, 22; 16:1, 4, 6, 27, 29; 17:3, 6, 9^{2}, 14; 18:1, 7, 9, 10^{2}, 21, 25; 19:1, 3, 17; 20:2^{2}; 21:2, 3^{2}, 4, 5, 7, 11, 27; 22:6, 7; 23:13, 15, 16, 28, 29, 30, 31; 24:16; 25:32^{3}, 33, 35; 28:35; 29:23, 46; 32:1^{2}, 4, 7, 8^{2}, 11, 12, 19, 23, 24, 27, 32, 33; 33:1, 2, 7, 8, 11; 34:11, 18, 24, 34^{2}; 37:7, 8, 9, 18^{3}, 19, 21

Lev 1:1, 15; 2:14; 4:12^{2}, 18, 25, 30, 34; 5:9, 15, 18; 6:6, 12, 13; 7:14, 35; 8:26, 33; 9:9, 23, 24; 10:2, 4, 5, 7, 14; 11:45; 13:12, 20, 25, 56^{4}; 14:3, 8, 38, 41, 43, 45, 53; 15:2, 16, 25; 16:17, 18; 17:3, 13; 18:24, 25, 28^{2}; 19:36; 20:22, 23; 21:12; 22:33; 23:17, 43; 24:10, 23; 25:12, 28, 30, 31, 33, 38, 42, 51, 54, 55; 26:6, 13, 33, 45; 27:21

Nu 1:1; 3:9; 5:2, 3, 4, 23, 25; 6:19; 9:1; 10:12, 33, 34; 11:15, 20^{2}, 24, 26; 12:4^{2}, 12, 14, 15; 13:16, 17; 14:44; 15:41; 16:13, 14, 27, 35, 37, 46; 17:9; 18:29^{2}; 20:5, 8, 10, 11, 16, 18, 20; 21:5, 13, 23, 26, 28, 32^{2}, 33; 22:5, 6, 11^{2}, 23, 32, 36; 23:7, 22; 24:7, 8, 17^{2}, 19; 26:4; 27:17^{2}, 21; 28:26; 30:2, 6, 12; 31:5, 27, 28, 36; 32:11, 21, 23, 24; 33:1, 2^{2}, 3, 12, 38, 52, 55; 34:5, 7, 8, 9, 10, 12; 35:25

Dt 1:22, 24, 27, 33, 44; 2:14, 23, 26, 32; 3:1, 8; 4:12, 15, 20^{2}, 33, 34, 36^{2}, 37^{2}, 38, 45, 46; 5:4, 6, 15^{2}, 22, 23, 24, 26; 6:12, 19, 21, 23; 7:1, 8^{2}, 19^{2}, 22; 8:3, 7, 9, 14, 15; 9:3, 4^{2}, 5, 7, 10, 12^{2}, 14, 16, 17, 21, 26, 28^{2}, 29^{2}; 10:4; 11:2, 10, 23, 28; 12:3, 5, 27; 13:5^{3}, 10, 13; 15:11, 13, 14^{3}; 16:1, 3^{2}, 6; 17:18; 18:5, 6, 12; 20:1^{2}; 21:19; 22:21, 24; 23:4, 10, 23; 24:1, 2, 3, 5, 9, 11; 25:4, 6, 11, 17, 19; 26:4, 8, 13; 27:18; 28:6, 7, 19, 25, 38, 57; 29:7, 20, 21, 25, 28; 30:4; 31:2, 21; 32:13^{2}, 39; 33:18, 27

Jos 1:8; 2:1, 2, 3, 5, 7, 10, 19; 3:10, 12^{2}; 4:2^{2}, 3^{2}, 4, 8, 16, 17, 18, 19, 20; 5:4^{2}, 5^{2}, 6; 6:1, 10, 22^{2}, 23^{2}, 25; 7:23^{2}; 8:3, 5, 6, 14, 17, 18^{2}, 19^{2}, 22, 26; 9:12, 26; 10:22^{2}, 23, 24; 11:4; 13:6, 12; 14:7, 11, 12; 15:3, 4^{2}, 7, 9, 11^{3}, 63; 16:2, 3, 6, 7, 8^{2}, 10; 17:12, 13, 18; 18:4, 12, 14, 15^{2}; 19:9, 12, 13, 17, 24, 27, 32, 34, 40, 47; 20:2, 8^{3}; 21:3, 4^{4}, 5^{3}, 6^{4}, 7^{3}, 9^{2}, 16, 17, 20, 23, 25, 27, 28, 30, 32, 34, 36, 38; 22:9, 31, 32; 23:5, 9, 13; 24:5, 6, 10, 12, 17, 18, 32

Jdg 1:16, 19^{2}, 21, 24, 27, 28, 29, 30, 31, 32, 33; 2:1, 3, 12, 15, 16, 17, 18, 21, 23; 3:10, 19, 20, 22^{2}, 24; 4:6, 14, 18, 22; 5:4^{2}, 14^{3}, 28; 6:8, 9^{3}, 19, 20, 21^{2}, 30, 38; 7:23^{3}; 8:34; 9:4, 15, 17, 20^{2}, 27, 29, 33, 35, 38, 39, 41, 42, 43; 10:12; 11:2, 3, 5, 7, 13, 24, 34, 36; 12:2; 13:5; 14:9, 12, 14^{2}, 18; 15:17; 16:14, 20^{2}, 21, 25; 17:7, 8; 18:2, 11^{2}, 14, 17; 19:1, 16, 23, 24, 27, 30; 20:1, 10, 14^{2}, 15, 20, 21, 25, 28, 31, 33^{3}, 34, 38, 40, 42; 21:16, 17, 21^{2}, 24

Ru 1:7, 13, 21, 22; 2:6, 17, 22; 4:3

1Sa 1:3, 15, 16; 2:3, 5, 8, 10, 28; 3:3; 4:1, 3^{2}, 8, 12, 13, 16^{2}; 5:10; 7:3, 6, 8, 11, 14; 8:8, 18, 20; 9:11, 14, 16^{2}, 26; 10:18^{3}, 19; 11:2, 3, 5, 7, 10; 12:6, 8, 10, 11; 13:10, 17, 23; 14:11, 48; 15:6; 16:16; 17:4^{2}, 8, 23, 34, 35^{2}, 37^{3}, 40, 51; 18:5, 6, 11, 13, 16; 19:3, 8, 10; 20:11^{2}, 21, 35, 36, 41; 21:5; 23:13, 15, 23; 24:2, 7, 8, 14, 15, 21; 25:5, 14, 29^{2}, 37; 26:4, 19, 20, 24; 27:1; 28:1, 3, 9, 13, 17; 29:6; 30:16^{2}

2Sa 1:2, 3; 2:12, 13, 23; 3:18^{2}, 25, 26; 4:4, 9; 5:2, 13, 24; 6:3, 4, 20; 7:6, 9, 12; 8:1; 9:5; 10:3, 8, 16; 11:8, 13, 17, 23; 12:7, 11; 13:9^{3}, 17, 18; 14:16^{2}; 15:11, 24, 35; 16:5, 7^{2}; 17:1, 21; 18:3, 4, 6; 19:9^{3}, 19; 20:7^{2}, 8, 10, 12, 13, 16, 22; 21:10, 17; 22:1^{2}, 7, 9^{2}, 15, 17, 46; 23:4, 16^{2}, 21, 29; 24:4, 7, 16, 20

1Ki 1:29, 39; 2:27, 37, 42, 46; 3:7; 4:23, 33; 5:6, 13; 6:1, 8; 7:13, 47; 8:1, 8^{2}, 9, 10, 16^{2}, 19, 21, 41, 42, 44, 51, 53; 9:7^{2}, 9, 12, 24; 10:28, 29^{2}; 11:12, 18^{2}, 29, 31, 32, 34, 35; 12:25, 28; 13:1, 3, 5; 14:15, 21, 24; 15:12, 17; 16:2; 17:19, 23; 18:28, 44; 19:13; 20:16, 17^{3}, 18^{2}, 19, 21, 24, 31, 39, 42; 21:10, 13, 26; 22:3, 32, 34, 35, 46

2Ki 2:23, 24; 3:6; 4:4, 5, 18, 21, 37, 39, 40^{2}, 41; 5:2^{2}, 11, 27; 6:7, 27^{2}; 7:12^{2}, 16, 20; 8:3; 9:2, 15, 19, 21^{2}, 24, 30, 32; 10:3, 9, 25, 26, 28; 11:8, 9; 12:11, 12; 13:5, 25^{2}; 14:27; 16:3, 7^{2}; 17:7, 8, 18, 20, 23^{2}, 36^{2}, 39; 18:18, 29, 31, 33, 34, 35^{2}; 19:9, 19, 27, 31^{2}, 35; 20:4, 6; 21:2, 7, 8, 15; 23:4, 6, 8, 16, 18, 27; 24:3, 7, 12, 13, 20; 25:7, 19, 21, 27

1Ch 5:18; 6:60, 61^{2}, 62^{4}, 63^{3}, 65^{3}, 66, 70, 71, 72, 74, 76, 77, 78, 80; 7:11; 9:28; 11:2, 18^{2}, 23; 12:2, 17; 13:7; 14:8, 15, 17; 15:25, 29; 16:33; 17:21^{2}; 18:1; 19:3, 6^{3}, 9, 10; 20:1, 2, 3; 21:16, 21; 26:14, 27; 27:1; 28:18

2Ch 1:10, 16, 17^{2}; 2:2, 8, 14, 16; 4:18; 5:2, 9, 10, 11; 6:5, 9, 32, 34; 7:20^{2}, 22; 8:11; 9:28^{2}; 10:2; 11:13, 16; 12:3, 7, 13; 13:9; 14:5, 8^{2}, 9, 10; 15:2, 5, 8^{2}, 9^{3}, 17; 16:1, 2^{2}, 7; 17:6; 18:20, 21^{2}, 31, 33; 19:2, 3, 4; 20:4, 7, 10, 11, 17, 21; 21:15, 19; 22:7; 23:2, 7, 8, 11, 14; 24:5, 6^{2}; 25:6, 10, 15; 26:11, 18, 20^{2}; 28:3, 9, 21^{2}; 29:5, 7, 16^{2}; 30:6, 25^{2}; 31:1^{2}; 32:11, 13, 14^{2}, 15^{3}, 17^{2}; 33:2, 8, 15^{2}; 34:14, 21, 25, 33; 35:20, 24

Ezr 1:7; 2:1; 3:8; 5:14^{2}; 6:4, 5, 21; 7:20, 28; 8:35; 9:5; 10:1

Neh 1:9; 2:13; 3:25, 26, 27; 4:2, 5; 5:13^{2}; 6:8; 7:6; 8:17; 9:7, 15, 18, 27; 12:27, 28, 29, 44; 13:8, 14

Est 2:9, 13, 23; 3:15; 4:1, 11; 5:2; 7:8^{2}; 8:4, 14, 15; 9:4

Job 1:17, 21; 3:11, 24; 5:5, 6; 6:17; 8:10, 19; 9:6, 8, 10, 14; 10:7, 10, 18; 11:7^{2}, 13; 12:15, 22^{2}; 13:9; 14:4, 12, 18, 19; 15:13, 22, 25, 30; 16:13, 20; 18:4, 5, 6, 14, 18; 19:7; 20:15, 25^{2}; 21:17; 22:16; 24:4, 12^{2}, 24; 26:7; 27:21, 22, 23; 28:2^{2}, 3, 4, 5, 10, 27; 29:6, 7, 16, 17, 19, 25; 30:16, 24; 31:7, 8, 12, 34; 32:11, 13; 33:6, 21; 35:9; 36:16, 26; 37:1, 2, 9^{2}, 18, 22, 23; 38:1, 8, 13, 29; 39:3, 5; 40:6; 41:1, 19^{2}, 20^{2}, 21

Ps 3:4; 5:10; 8:2; 9:5; 10:5, 15, 16; 14:7; 15:5; 17:1; 18:6, 8^{2}, 14^{2}, 16, 42, 45; 19:4, 5; 20:2; 21:8^{2}; 22:7, 9, 14^{2}; 25:15, 17, 22; 27:12; 31:4, 12; 34:6, 17, 19; 35:3; 37:14; 40:2^{2}; 42:4; 43:3; 44:2^{2}, 20, 21; 45:8; 50:2, 9^{2}; 51:1, 9; 52:5^{2}; 53:6; 54:7; 55:23; 58:6; 59:7; 60:6, 8, 10; 62:8; 64:6; 66:12; 68:6, 31^{2}, 33, 35; 69:14^{2}, 24, 28; 71:4^{2}, 6; 73:7, 10; 74:11; 75:8^{2}; 77:17^{2}; 78:15, 16, 20, 55, 65; 79:6; 80:8^{2}, 11, 13; 81:5, 10, 16; 82:4, 5; 84:2; 85:5, 11; 88:9; 89:19, 34; 94:12; 97:10; 102:ttl; 104:2, 14, 35; 105:41; 107:3, 6, 13, 14, 19, 28; 108:7, 9; 109:10, 13, 14; 110:2; 111:2; 113:7^{2}; 114:1; 118:26; 119:18, 43; 121:8; 124:7; 128:5; 130:1; 132:5; 134:3; 135:7, 21; 136:6, 11, 12; 142:2, 7; 143:11; 144:6, 7, 14; 147:18

Prv 1:23, 24; 2:6, 22; 3:10; 4:23; 5:15^{2}; 6:9; 8:12; 9:1; 10:31; 11:8; 12:13; 13:9; 15:2, 28; 17:14, 23; 20:5, 20; 21:16; 22:10^{2}; 24:20; 25:1, 2, 19; 26:20; 28:11; 30:17; 31:18, 20

Ecc 1:13; 3:11; 4:14; 7:24, 25, 27, 29; 8:3, 17^{2}; 12:3, 9, 10

Song 3:6; 4:16; 8:11

Isa 2:3; 5:2, 25; 8:8; 9:12, 17, 21; 10:4; 11:1^{2}, 16; 12:3, 6; 13:9, 13; 14:19, 26, 27, 29; 15:4, 5; 16:2, 4, 8, 10^{2}; 18:2, 7; 19:23; 21:11; 22:16^{2}; 23:11; 24:18; 26:16, 17, 19, 21; 28:7^{2}, 27; 29:4^{4}, 9, 10, 18^{2}; 30:11^{2}, 13, 14; 31:3; 34:3^{2}, 11, 16; 35:6; 36:16, 18, 19, 20^{2}; 37:28, 32^{2}; 38:6; 40:12, 22^{2}, 26; 42:5^{2}, 7^{2}; 43:13, 25; 44:13^{3}, 22; 45:12, 23; 46:6, 7; 48:1, 3, 21^{2}; 51:17, 22; 52:11^{2}, 12; 53:2, 8, 12; 55:11, 12; 57:4, 14; 58:7, 10; 59:5, 21^{3}; 62:10, 12; 63:11; 65:2, 9^{2}; 66:5, 11, 20

Jer 1:5, 10, 14; 2:6, 13; 3:18; 4:1, 16; 5:6^{2}; 6:1^{2}, 4, 7^{2}, 11, 12; 7:15^{2}, 18, 20, 22, 25; 8:1^{2}; 9:8, 18, 19^{2}; 10:3, 12, 13, 17, 18, 22, 25; 11:4, 7; 12:3, 8, 14^{2}, 15; 14:16; 15:1, 6, 21^{2}; 16:9, 13, 14, 16; 17:8, 16, 19, 22; 18:21, 23; 19:13; 20:3, 8, 18; 21:9, 12^{2}; 22:3, 11, 14, 26, 28; 23:3, 7, 8, 16, 39; 24:5; 26:23; 27:10, 15; 30:7, 19; 31:32, 37; 32:4, 17, 21^{2}, 29, 37; 34:3, 13^{2}; 36:6, 11, 21, 30; 37:4, 5, 12, 17, 21; 38:8, 10, 13, 18, 23^{2}; 39:4^{2}, 7, 14; 40:12; 44:7, 17^{2}, 18, 19^{2}, 25, 28; 46:20; 47:2; 48:15, 31, 44, 45; 49:5, 20; 50:3, 8^{2}, 28, 45; 51:6, 15, 16, 25, 34, 44, 45, 55; 52:3, 7, 11, 25, 27, 31

Lam 1:10; 2:4, 8, 12, 19^{2}; 3:7, 8, 38, 55; 4:1, 3, 11; 5:8

Ezk 1:4^{3}, 5, 13; 3:25; 4:12; 5:2, 12; 6:14; 7:8; 9:8; 10:7, 19; 11:7, 9, 17, 19; 12:5, 12, 14; 13:2, 17, 21, 23; 14:9, 13, 19; 15:7; 16:5, 15, 27, 36; 19:14; 20:8, 9, 10, 13, 14, 21, 28, 33^{2}, 34^{4}, 38^{2}, 41^{2}; 21:3, 4, 5, 19, 31; 22:15, 22, 31; 23:26, 34, 48; 24:6^{2}, 12; 25:7^{2}, 13, 16; 27:6, 33; 28:16; 29:4, 8; 30:13, 22, 25; 31:4, 11; 32:3, 7, 21; 33:21; 34:11, 12^{3}, 13, 25, 27; 35:3, 7, 11; 36:5, 20, 24, 26; 37:1, 12, 13, 23; 38:8^{2}, 12, 15; 39:3^{2}, 10^{2}, 14, 27, 29; 42:11, 14; 43:6, 11, 23, 25; 44:3; 45:14, 15^{3}; 46:9, 18^{2}, 20; 47:1, 2^{2}, 8, 12; 48:19, 30

Dan 2:34, 45; 3:15, 17; 5:2, 3, 13; 6:23^{2}; 7:17, 24, 25; 8:4, 7, 9, 22; 9:15; 11:7, 41, 44^{2}

Hos 1:11; 2:2, 10, 15, 17, 18; 4:2; 5:10; 7:5; 9:15; 10:11; 11:1, 11^{2}; 12:8, 13; 13:3^{2}

Joel 2:16, 28, 29; 3:7, 16

Am 3:4, 12^{2}; 4:3, 11; 5:3, 6, 8; 6:4^{2}, 10^{2}; 7:11; 8:8; 9:3, 6, 7, 15

Oba 6, 8^{2}

Jna 1:4; 2:1, 2, 4, 10; 4:5

Mic 1:3; 2:9, 13; 4:6, 9, 10; 5:2, 10, 12, 13, 14; 6:4^{2}; 7:2, 15, 17

Nah 1:6, 11, 14; 2:2, 9

Hab 1:2; 2:11^{2}; 3:4, 13, 14

Zep 1:4, 17; 2:4, 13; 3:11, 15, 19

Hag 2:5, 16^{2}

OVER

SHALL

APNDX

14, 15[2]; **11:**2, 3, 4, 8[2], 9[2], 10, 11[3], 12, 13[2], 20, 23, 24[2], 25, 26, 27, 28, 29, 31, 32[3], 33[2], 34[2], 35[3], 36[2], 37, 38, 39, 40[2], 41[2], 42, 43[2], 44[3], 45; **12:**2[2], 3, 4[2], 5[2], 6, 7[2], 8[3]; **13:**2[2], 3[2], 4, 5[2], 6[3], 7, 8, 9, 10, 11[2], 13[2], 14, 15, 16, 17[2], 20, 21, 22, 23, 25[2], 26, 27[2], 28, 30[2], 31, 32, 33[3], 34[3], 36[2], 37, 39, 43, 44, 45[3], 46[4], 49, 50, 51, 52[2], 53, 54[2], 55, 56, 58[2]; **14:**2[2], 3[2], 4, 5, 6[2], 7[3], 8[3], 9[6], 10, 11, 12, 13[2], 14[2], 15, 16[2], 17, 18[2], 19[2], 20[3], 21, 22, 23, 24[2], 25[2], 26, 27, 28, 29, 30, 31, 35, 36[2], 37, 38, 39[2], 40[2], 41[2], 42[3], 44, 45[2], 46, 47[2], 48[2], 49, 50, 51, 52, 53[2]; **15:**3, 4, 5, 6, 7, 8, 9, 10[2], 11, 12[2], 13[2], 14, 15[2], 16, 17, 18[2], 19[2], 20[2], 21, 22, 23, 24[2], 25[2], 26[2], 27[2], 28[2], 29, 30[2], 31; **16:**3, 4[5], 5, 6, 7, 8, 9, 10, 11[3], 12, 13, 14[2], 15, 16[2], 17, 18[2], 19, 20, 21[2], 22[2], 23[3], 24, 25, 26, 27[2], 28[2], 29[2], 30, 31[2], 32[4], 33[3], 34; **17:**4[2], 6, 7[2], 9, 12[2], 13, 14[2], 15[2], 16; **18:**3[3], 4, 5[2], 6, 23, 26[2], 29[2], 30; **19:**2, 3, 5, 6[2], 7, 8[2], 11, 12, 13, 15, 19[2], 20[2], 21, 22[2], 23[5], 24, 25, 26[2], 27, 28, 30, 33, 34, 35, 36, 37; **20:**2[2], 8, 9[2], 10, 11[2], 12[2], 13[2], 14, 15[2], 16[2], 17[3], 18[3], 19, 20[3], 21[2], 22, 23, 24, 25[2], 26, 27[3]; **21:**1, 4, 5[2], 6[2], 7[2], 8, 9, 10, 11, 12, 13, 14[2], 15, 18, 21[2], 22, 23; **22:**3, 4, 6[2], 7[2], 8, 9, 10[2], 11[2], 13[2], 14[2], 15, 19, 20[2], 21[2], 22, 23, 24[2], 25[2], 27[2], 28, 30[2], 31, 32; **23:**2, 3[2], 4, 7[2], 8[2], 10[2], 11[2], 12, 13[2], 14[2], 15[2], 16[2], 17[3], 18[2], 19, 20[2], 21[3], 24, 25[2], 27[3], 28, 29[2], 31[2], 32[3], 34, 35[2], 36[4], 37, 39[3], 40[2], 41[3], 42[2]; **24:**3[2], 4, 5, 8, 9[2], 15, 16[3], 17, 18, 19, 20, 21[2], 22; **25:**2, 4, 6, 7, 8, 9, 10[4], 11[2], 12[2], 13, 14, 15, 17, 18[2], 19[2], 20[3], 21, 22[2], 23, 24, 25, 28[3], 30[2], 31[2], 33, 40[2], 41[3], 42, 44[2], 45[2], 46[3], 50[3], 51, 52[2], 53[2], 54; **26:**1[2], 2, 4[2], 5[3], 6[3], 7[2], 8[3], 10, 11, 12, 15, 16[3], 17[3], 20[3], 22[2], 25[2], 26[3], 29[2], 30, 32, 33, 34[2], 35, 36[3], 37[2], 38[2], 39[2], 40, 43[3]; **27:**2[2], 3[2], 4, 5, 6[2], 7, 8[3], 9, 10[3], 11, 12[2], 13, 14[4], 15[2], 16[3], 17, 18[2], 19[2], 20, 21[2], 23[2], 24, 25[2], 26, 27[3], 28[2], 29[3], 31, 32, 33[4]

Nu 1:3, 4, 5, 50[3], 51[3], 52, 53[2]; **2:**2[2], 3[2], 5[2], 7, 9, 10[2], 12[2], 14, 16, 17[2], 18[2], 20[2], 22, 24, 25[2], 27[2], 29, 31; **3:**7, 8, 10[2], 12, 13, 23, 24, 25, 29, 30, 31, 32, 35, 36, 38[2], 45; **4:**4, 5[2], 6[3], 7[2], 8[2], 9, 10[2], 11[2], 12[2], 13, 14[2], 15[2], 19, 20, 25, 26, 27[2], 28, 32; **5:**3[2], 6, 7[2], 8, 9, 10[2], 15[3], 16, 17[2], 18[2], 19, 21[2], 22[2], 23[2], 24[2], 25[2], 26[2], 27[5], 28[2], 30[2], 31[2]; **6:**2, 3[3], 4, 5[3], 6, 7, 9[2], 10, 11[2], 12[3], 13, 14, 16[2], 17[2], 18[2], 19[2], 20, 21, 23, 27; **7:**11; **8:**2, 10, 11, 12, 14, 15, 24, 25[2], 26[2]; **9:**3[2], 10[2], 11, 12[2], 13[2], 14[3]; **10:**3[2], 4, 5, 6[2], 7[2], 8[2], 9[3], 10, 32[3]; **11:**4, 17, 18[3], 19, 22[2], 23; **12:**8; **13:**2; **14:**13, 21, 23[2], 24, 27, 29, 30, 31, 32, 33, 34[2], 35[2], 41, 43; **15:**4, 9, 11, 12[2], 13, 14, 15[2], 16, 19[2], 20[2], 21, 24[2], 25[3], 26, 27, 28[2], 29, 30, 31[2], 35[2], 39; **16:**7[2], 22, 28, 30, 38; **17:**3, 5[3], 13[2]; **18:**1[2], 2, 3[2], 4[2], 5, 7[3], 9[3], 10[2], 11, 12, 13[3], 14, 15, 18, 23[3], 24, 26, 27, 28[2], 29, 30, 31, 32[2]; **19:**3[2], 4, 5[2], 6, 7[4], 8[2], 9[2], 10[2], 11, 12[3], 13[2], 14, 16, 17[2], 18, 19[3], 20[3], 21[3], 22[2]; **20:**8, 12, 24[2], 26[2]; **21:**8[2]; **22:**4, 6, 8, 11, 20, 35, 38; **23:**8[2], 9[2], 19[2], 23, 24[2]; **24:**7[4], 8[2], 9, 14, 17[5], 18[3], 19[3], 20, 22[2], 23, 24[4]; **25:**13; **26:**53, 54, 55[2], 56, 65; **27:**8, 9, 10, 11[3], 21[4]; **28:**2, 3, 7, 11, 14, 15, 17, 18[2], 19[2], 20[2], 23, 24[2], 25[2], 26[2], 27, 31[2]; **29:**1[2], 2, 3, 7[3], 8[2], 9, 12[3], 13[2], 14, 17, 18, 21, 24, 27, 30, 33, 35[2], 36, 37, 39; **30:**2[2], 4[3], 5[2], 7[2], 8[2], 9, 11[2], 12[2], 15[2]; **31:**4, 23[4], 24[3]; **32:**6[2], 11, 15, 17, 22[2], 26, 29[2], 30; **33:**52, 53, 54[5], 55[3], 56[2]; **34:**2, 3[2], 4[3], 5[2], 6[2], 7[2], 8[2], 9[3], 10, 11[3], 12[3], 13, 17, 18; **35:**2, 3[2], 4[2], 5[3], 6[4], 7[3], 8[5], 11, 12, 13[2], 14[3], 15, 16, 17, 18, 19[2], 21[2], 24, 25[3], 26, 27, 28, 29, 30[2], 31[2], 32, 33, 34; **36:**3[3], 4[3], 6, 7[2], 8, 9[2]

Dt 1:17[3], 22[2], 28, 30, 35, 36, 38[2], 39[2]; **2:**4, 6[2], 25[2], 29; **3:**18, 19, 20, 21, 22[2], 28[2]; **4:**2[2], 6, 10, 22, 25[3], 26[3], 27[3], 28; **5:**25, 27[2], 32[2], 33[2]; **6:**6, 8, 10[2], 14, 16, 17, 25; **7:**1, 2, 5[2], 12[2], 14, 16[2], 19, 23[2], 24[2], 25; **8:**1, 19[2], 20; **9:**3[2]; **11:**8, 13[2], 18, 19, 22, 23, 24[3], 25[3], 29, 31[2], 32; **12:**1, 2[2], 3[2], 4, 5[2], 6, 7[2], 8, 11[3], 12, 14, 16[2], 18, 20, 22, 26, 27, 29; **13:**4[2], 5, 8, 9, 11[2], 16[2], 17; **14:**1, 4, 6, 7, 8, 9[2], 11, 12, 19, 21, 23, 24, 25, 29[2]; **15:**2[2], 3, 4[2], 6, 10[2], 11, 16, 17, 18[2], 20, 22; **16:**2, 4[2], 6, 7, 8, 15[2], 16[3], 17, 18; **17:**6[2], 7, 8, 9[2], 10[2], 11[3], 12, 13, 15, 16[2], 17[2], 18[2], 19[2]; **18:**1[2], 2, 3[2], 6, 7, 8, 10, 15, 18[2], 19[2], 20[3], 21; **19:**4, 5, 12, 13, 15[2], 17[2], 18, 19, 20[2], 21[2]; **20:**2[2], 3, 5, 8[2], 9[2], 11[4]; **21:**2[2], 3[2], 4[2], 5[2], 6, 7, 8, 12, 13[3], 14, 16, 17, 19, 20, 21[2], 23; **22:**2, 5[2], 15, 16, 17, 18, 19[2], 21[2], 22, 24[2], 25, 29[2], 30; **23:**1, 2[2], 3[2], 8, 10[2], 11[3], 13, 14, 16[2], 17, 22; **24:**5[4], 6, 7, 8[2], 11, 13, 15, 16[3], 19, 20, 21; **25:**1, 2[2], 5[2], 6[2], 8, 9[3], 10, 12, 19; **26:**1, 2, 3, 4; **27:**2[2], 4[2], 12, 13, 14, 15, 16, 17, 18, 19, 20, 21, 22, 23, 24, 25, 26; **28:**1, 2, 4, 5, 7[2], 8[2], 9, 10[2], 11, 12, 13, 15[2], 17, 18, 20, 21, 22[2], 23[2], 24[2], 25, 26[2], 28, 29, 30, 31[4], 32[3], 33, 35, 36, 37, 38, 39, 40, 41, 42, 43, 44[2], 45[2], 46, 48[2], 49, 50, 51[2], 52[2], 53, 54[2], 55[2], 56, 57[3], 60, 62, 63[2], 64, 65[2], 66, 68[3]; **29:**19, 20[3], 21, 22[3], 24, 25; **30:**1, 12, 13, 16, 18[2]; **31:**3, 4, 5, 11, 17[3], 18, 20[2], 21[3]; **32:**2[2], 20, 22[2], 24, 25, 35[2], 36, 37, 42, 46, 47; **33:**3, 10[2], 12[3], 17, 19[3], 22, 25[2], 27[2], 28[3], 29

Jos 1:3, 4, 5, 8, 11, 14[2], 15, 18; **2:**5, 14, 19[5]; **3:**3, 4, 8, 10, 13[4]; **4:**3[2], 7[2], 21, 22; **6:**3, 4[3], 5[4], 10[3], 17[2], 19, 26[2]; **7:**8, 9[2], 14[7], 15[2], 25; **8:**2, 4, 5, 7, 8[3]; **9:**7, 23; **10:**8, 25; **14:**9, 12; **15:**4; **17:**18[2]; **18:**4[2], 5[3], 6; **20:**3, 4[3], 5, 6[3]; **22:**22, 25, 28, 34; **23:**5[2], 10, 12, 13, 15[2], 16[2]; **24:**27[2]

Jdg 1:1, 2; **2:**2[2], 3[2]; **4:**9[2], 20; **5:**11[2], 24[2]; **6:**15, 37; **7:**4[5], 11, 17[2]; **8:**23[2]; **9:**33; **10:**18; **11:**9, 24, 31[2]; **13:**5[3], 7, 8[2], 12[2], 15, 22; **14:**13, 16; **15:**3, 18; **16:**2, 7, 11, 17; **18:**5, 10; **20:**9, 18[2], 23, 28[2]; **21:**1, 5, 7, 11[2], 16, 22

Ru 1:16; **2:**2, 9; **3:**1, 3, 4[2], 13; **4:**12, 15

1Sa 1:11, 28; **2:**9[2], 10[4], 25[2], 30, 31, 32[2], 33[3], 34[3], 35[2], 36[3]; **3:**9, 11, 14; **4:**8; **5:**7, 8; **6:**2[2], 3[2], 4[2], 5[2], 9, 20; **8:**9, 11[2], 17, 18[2]; **9:**7, 13[2], 17, 19; **10:**2, 3, 5[2], 27; **11:**7, 9[2], 10, 12, 13; **12:**12, 14, 15, 17, 25[2]; **13:**14; **14:**10, 37, 39, 45[2]; **15:**33; **16:**16[2]; **17:**9, 25, 26, 27, 36, 47; **18:**25; **19:**6; **20:**7, 10, 31, 32; **21:**15; **23:**2, 17[2], 20, 23; **24:**4, 12, 13, 20; **25:**6, 11, 29[2], 30[3], 31[2]; **26:**10[3]; **27:**1[3], 12; **28:**8, 10, 11, 15, 19; **29:**9; **30:**8[2], 23, 24[2]

2Sa 2:1[2], 26[2]; **3:**12, 39; **4:**11; **5:**8[2], 19, 24; **6:**9, 22; **7:**10, 12, 13, 14, 15, 16[2]; **9:**10[2], 11[2]; **11:**11; **12:**5, 6, 10, 11, 14, 23[2]; **13:**13; **14:**7[2], 10, 11, 17, 18; **15:**8, 10, 14, 15, 21, 25, 35, 36; **16:**3, 10, 20, 21[2]; **17:**2, 3, 6, 10, 12[3], 13; **19:**21, 22, 37, 38[2]; **20:**6, 18, 21; **21:**3[2], 4; **22:**4, 44, 45[2], 46[2]; **23:**4, 6, 7[2]; **24:**13[2]

1Ki 1:13[2], 17[2], 20, 21[3], 24[2], 30[2], 35[2], 52[3]; **2:**4, 24, 32, 33[2], 37[2], 44, 45[2]; **3:**5, 12, 13; **5:**5, 6, 9; **8:**19[2], 25, 29[2], 30, 33, 38, 42[2], 44, 47, 59; **9:**3, 5, 6, 7, 8[3], 9; **11:**2[2], 32, 38; **12:**10, 24, 26, 27[2]; **13:**2[3], 3[2], 22, 32; **14:**3[2], 5[2], 11[2], 12, 13[2], 14[2], 15[3], 16; **16:**4[2]; **17:**1, 4, 14[2]; **18:**12[3], 14, 31; **19:**17[3]; **20:**6[3], 10, 14, 23, 25, 28, 36, 39, 40, 42; **21:**19, 23, 24[2]; **22:**6[3], 12, 15[3], 16, 20

2Ki 1:2; **2:**9, 10[2], 16, 21; **3:**8, 17[3], 19[2]; **4:**2, 10[2], 23, 43[2]; **5:**8, 10, 17, 27; **6:**8, 15, 21[2], 27, 31; **7:**1, 4[3], 12, 18; **8:**1, 8, 9, 10; **9:**8, 10[2], 36, 37[2]; **10:**4, 10, 18, 19[2], 24, 30; **11:**5[2], 6[2], 7, 8; **12:**5; **14:**6[2]; **15:**12; **16:**15; **17:**12, 35, 36[3], 37[2], 38[2], 39[2]; **18:**22, 29, 30; **19:**6, 7[2], 10[2], 29[2], 30, 31[2], 32, 33[2]; **20:**8[2], 9, 17[2], 18[3]; **21:**12, 14; **22:**17[2], 18, 20; **23:**27; **25:**24

1Ch 11:6, 19; **12:**17; **13:**12; **14:**10, 15; **16:**30, 33; **17:**9[3], 11[2], 12, 13, 14, 27; **21:**12; **22:**9[3], 10[2]; **23:**26; **28:**6, 21[2]

2Ch 1:7, 12; **2:**8, 9, 14; **6:**9[2], 16, 21, 24, 29[3]; **7:**14, 15, 16, 18, 19, 21[2], 22; **8:**11; **10:**10; **11:**4; **12:**7, 8; **13:**12; **15:**7; **18:**5[2], 11, 14[3], 15, 19; **19:**9, 10[3], 11[2]; **20:**16, 17, 20[2]; **23:**3, 4[2], 5[2], 6[2], 7[2]; **25:**4[3], 8, 9; **26:**18; **28:**13; **30:**9[2]; **32:**11, 12, 15, 17; **33:**4; **34:**25[2], 26, 28; **35:**3

Ezr 4:21; **6:**8, 11, 12; **7:**18, 20, 21, 24; **9:**10

Neh 2:6, 8; **4:**3, 11, 12, 20; **5:**8; **6:**7, 9; **9:**29; **10:**38[2], 39; **13:**25, 27

Est 1:15, 17[3], 18[2], 20[3]; **4:**11[2], 14[2]; **5:**3, 6[2], 8; **6:**6, 9, 11; **7:**2[2]; **8:**6; **9:**12[2]

Job 1:21; **2:**10[2]; **4:**17[2]; **5:**19[2], 20, 23, 24, 25; **7:**4, 7, 8, 9, 10[2], 13[2], 20, 21[2]; **8:**2, 10, 13, 14[2], 15[4], 18, 19, 22[2]; **9:**14, 19, 20[2], 31; **10:**21; **11:**3, 17, 19[2], 20[3]; **12:**2, 7[2], 8[2]; **13:**11, 16[2], 18, 19; **14:**6, 12, 14, 22[2]; **15:**21, 22, 24[2], 29[3], 30[3], 31, 32[2], 33[2], 34[2]; **16:**3, 22[2]; **17:**5, 8[2], 9[2], 15, 16; **18:**4[2], 5[2], 6[2], 7[2], 9[2], 11[2], 12[2], 13[2], 14[2], 15[2], 16[2], 17[2], 18, 19, 20; **19:**25, 26, 27[2]; **20:**7[2], 8[3], 9[2], 10[2], 11, 15[2], 16[2], 17, 18[4], 20[2], 21[2], 22[2], 23[2], 24[2], 26[3], 27[2], 28[2]; **21:**19, 20[2], 22, 26[2], 30, 31[2], 32[2], 33[2]; **22:**21, 25, 27, 28[2], 29, 30; **23:**10; **24:**15, 20[4]; **27:**4, 6, 13, 14, 15[2], 17[2], 19[2], 22, 23[2]; **28:**12, 15, 17, 18, 19[2]; **29:**18[2]; **31:**14[2]; **33:**3[2], 7[2], 25[2], 26[2], 28, 33; **34:**11, 15[2], 17, 20[3], 24; **35:**3; **36:**4, 11, 12[2]; **37:**19, 20[2]; **38:**11, 15; **40:**2, 4; **41:**6[2], 9; **42:**8

Ps 1:3[3], 5, 6; **2:**4[2], 5, 8; **5:**4, 5; **6:**5; **7:**7, 8, 16[2]; **9:**3, 7, 8[2], 17, 18[2]; **10:**6[2]; **11:**6[2]; **12:**3; **13:**2[2], 5; **14:**7[2]; **15:**1[2], 5; **16:**4, 8, 9; **17:**3, 15; **18:**3, 43, 44[2], 45; **19:**13[2]; **21:**1[2], 7, 8[2], 9[2]; **22:**25, 26[3], 27[2], 29[2], 30[2], 31[3]; **23:**1, 6; **24:**3[2], 5, 7, 9; **25:**12[2], 13[2], 15; **26:**1; **27:**1[2], 3, 5[3], 6, 14; **28:**5; **30:**6, 9[2]; **31:**24; **32:**6[2], 10[2]; **33:**17, 21; **34:**1, 2[2], 10, 21[2], 22; **35:**9[2], 10, 28; **36:**8, 9, 12; **37:**2, 4, 5, 6, 9[2], 10[2], 11[2], 13, 15[2], 17, 18, 19[2], 20[4], 22[2], 24, 28, 29, 31, 34, 38[2], 40[2]; **39:**6; **40:**3[2]; **41:**2, 5, 8; **42:**2, 5, 8, 11; **43:**5; **44:**6, 21; **45:**4, 11, 12[2], 14[2], 15[2], 16, 17; **46:**4, 5[2]; **47:**3, 4; **49:**3[2], 5, 11, 14[3], 15, 17[2], 19[2]; **50:**3[4], 4, 6; **51:**7[2], 13, 14, 15, 19; **52:**5[2], 6[2]; **53:**6[2]; **54:**5; **55:**16, 17, 19, 22[2], 23; **56:**7, 9; **57:**3[2]; **58:**9, 10[2], 11; **59:**10[2]; **60:**12[2]; **61:**7; **62:**2, 3[2], 6; **63:**3, 5[2], 9, 10[2], 11[3]; **64:**5, 7[2], 8[2], 9[3], 10[3]; **65:**1, 2, 4; **66:**3, 4[3]; **67:**6[2], 7[2]; **68:**13, 21, 29, 31[2]; **69:**31, 32[2], 36[2]; **71:**6, 15, 23, 24; **72:**2, 3, 4[3], 5, 6, 7, 8, 9[2], 10[2], 11[2], 12, 13[2], 14[2], 15[4], 16[3], 17[4]; **73:**27; **74:**10[2]; **75:**2, 8, 10; **76:**10, 12; **79:**5; **80:**3, 7, 19; **81:**9; **82:**7; **85:**11[2], 12[2], 13[2]; **86:**9[2]; **87:**5[2], 6, 7; **88:**10, 11, 12, 13; **89:**2, 5, 12, 14, 15, 16[2], 17, 21[2], 22, 24[2], 26, 28, 36, 37, 46, 48[2]; **91:**1, 3, 4[2], 7[2], 10[2], 11, 12, 15; **92:**7, 9[2], 10, 11[2], 12[2], 13, 14[2]; **94:**3[2], 4, 7[2], 9[2], 10[2], 15[2], 20, 23[3]; **96:**10[3], 12, 13; **98:**9; **101:**3, 4, 6[2], 7[2]; **102:**15, 16[2], 18[3], 26[3], 27, 28[2]; **103:**16; **104:**12, 31[2], 34; **107:**42[2], 43; **108:**13[2]; **109:**7, 31; **110:**2, 3, 5, 6[3], 7[2]; **112:**2[2], 3, 6[2], 7, 8, 9, 10[3]; **115:**14; **116:**12; **118:**7, 17, 20; **119:**6, 7, 9, 27, 33, 34[2], 42, 44, 88, 117, 144, 146, 165, 171, 172, 175; **120:**3[2]; **121:**4, 6, 7[2], 8; **122:**2, 6; **125:**1, 3, 5[2]; **126:**5, 6; **127:**5[2]; **128:**2, 3, 4, 5; **130:**3, 8; **132:**12[2], 16, 18; **137:**4, 8, 9; **138:**4, 5, 7; **139:**7[2], 10[2], 11[2]; **140:**11, 13[2]; **141:**5[4], 6; **142:**7; **143:**2; **144:**5; **145:**4[2], 6, 7[2], 10[2], 11, 21; **146:**10; **148:**6

Prv 1:5, 9, 13[2], 28[3], 31, 32[2], 33[2]; **2:**11[2], 21[2], 22[2]; **3:**2, 6, 8, 10[2], 22, 23, 24, 26[2], 35[2]; **4:**6[2], 8[2], 9[2], 10, 12; **5:**22[2], 23[2]; **6:**11, 15[2], 22[3], 29, 31[2], 33[2]; **8:**6, 7, 17, 35; **9:**11[2]; **10:**7, 8, 9, 10, 24[2], 27, 28[2], 29, 30[2], 31; **11:**3[2], 5[2], 6[2], 7, 9, 15, 18, 21[2], 25[2], 26[2], 27, 28[2], 29[2], 31; **12:**3[2], 6, 7, 8[2], 11, 13, 14[2], 19, 21[2], 24[2]; **13:**2[2], 3, 4, 9, 11[2], 13[2], 18[2], 20[2], 21, 25; **14:**3, 11[2], 14[2], 22, 26; **15:**10, 27; **16:**3, 5, 20, 21; **17:**2[2], 5, 11, 13; **18:**20[2], 21; **19:**5[2], 8, 9[2], 15, 16, 19, 21, 23[2]; **20:**4, 17, 20, 21, 22; **21:**7, 13[2], 15, 16, 17[2], 18, 28; **22:**5, 8[2], 9, 10[2], 11, 13, 14, 15, 16, 18, 29[2]; **23:**11, 13, 15, 16, 18, 21[2], 24[2], 25[2], 33[2], 35; **24:**4, 8, 12, 14[3], 16, 20[2], 22, 24[2], 25[2], 26, 34; **25:**4, 5, 22; **26:**2, 26, 27; **27:**14, 18[2]; **28:**2, 8, 9, 10[2], 13[2], 14, 16, 17, 18[2], 19[2], 20[2], 22, 23, 25, 26, 27[2]; **29:**1, 14, 16, 17[2], 21, 23[2], 25; **30:**17[2]; **31:**11, 25, 30

Ecc 1:9[2], 11[2]; **2:**16, 18, 19[2], 21; **3:**14, 17, 22[2]; **4:**12, 15, 16; **5:**10, 15[2], 16, 20; **6:**4, 12; **7:**18, 26[2]; **8:**1, 5, 7[2], 8, 12, 13[2], 15, 17[2]; **9:**5; **10:**8[2], 9[2], 14[2], 20[2]; **11:**2, 3, 4[2], 6[2], 8; **12:**3[2], 4[3], 5[5], 7[2], 14

Song 1:13; **5:**3[2]; **7:**8; **8:**8[2]

Isa 1:18[2], 19, 20, 27, 28[2], 29[2], 30, 31[3]; **2:**2[4], 3[2], 4[5], 11[3], 12[2], 17[3], 18, 19, 20; **3:**4, 5[2], 6, 7, 10[2], 11[2], 24[2], 25, 26[2]; **4:**1, 2[2], 3[2], 4[2], 5, 6; **5:**5[2], 6[2], 9, 10[2], 14, 15[3], 16[2], 17[2], 24[2], 26, 27[3], 28, 29[5], 30; **6:**8, 13[4]; **7:**7[2], 8, 9, 14[3], 15, 16[2], 17, 18[2], 19[2], 20[2], 21[2], 22[4], 23[3], 24[2], 25[3]; **8:**4[2], 7, 8[4], 9[3], 10[2], 12, 14, 15, 19, 21[4], 22[2]; **9:**1, 5, 6[2], 7, 9, 11, 12, 17[2], 18[3], 19[2], 20[4], 21; **10:**3, 4[2], 11, 12, 15[2], 16[2], 17[2], 18[2], 19, 20[3], 21, 22[2], 23, 24[2], 25, 26[2], 27[3], 32[2], 33[3], 34[2]; **11:**1[2], 2, 3[2], 4[3], 5, 6[3], 7[3], 8[2], 9[2], 10[4], 11[3], 12[2], 13[4], 14[4], 15[3], 16[2]; **12:**3, 4; **13:**6, 7[2], 8[5], 9, 10[3], 13, 14[2], 15[2], 16[2], 17[2], 18[3], 19, 20[4], 21[4], 22[2]; **14:**1[2], 2[4], 3[2], 10, 16, 20, 24[2], 25, 27[2], 29[2], 30[3], 31[2], 32[2]; **15:**2[2], 3[2], 4[4], 5[4], 6, 7, 9; **16:**2[2], 5[2], 6, 7[3], 10[3], 11, 12[3], 14[2]; **17:**1, 2[3], 3[2], 4[3], 5[2], 6, 7[2], 8[2], 9[2], 11, 13[4]; **18:**5, 6[3], 7; **19:**1[3], 2, 3[2], 4, 5[2], 6[3], 7, 8[3], 9, 10, 15, 16[2], 17[2], 18[2], 19, 20[4], 21[4], 22[5], 23[3], 24, 25; **20:**4, 5, 6[2]; **21:**13, 16, 17; **22:**7[3], 13, 14, 18, 19, 20, 21, 22[4], 23, 24, 25[2]; **23:**5, 7, 15[3], 17[3], 18[3]; **24:**2, 3, 9[2], 13[2], 14[3], 18[3], 20[4], 21[2], 22[3], 23[2]; **25:**2, 3[2], 5, 6, 8, 9, 10[2], 11[2], 12; **26:**1, 6, 11[2], 14[2], 19[3], 21[2]; **27:**1[2], 5, 6[2], 9[2], 10[3], 11, 12[3], 13[4]; **28:**2, 3, 4, 5, 9[2], 15[2], 16, 17[2], 18[4], 19[3], 21[2]; **29:**2[2], 4[3], 5[3], 7, 8[2], 14[2], 16[3], 17[2], 18[2], 19[2], 22[2], 23[2], 24[2]; **30:**3, 6, 7, 13, 14[3], 15[2], 16[2], 17[2], 19[2], 20[2], 21, 22, 23[3], 24, 25, 26[2], 28[2], 29, 30[2], 31, 32[3]; **31:**3[4], 4, 7, 8[4], 9[2]; **32:**1[2], 2, 3[2], 4[2], 5, 8, 10[3], 12, 13, 14[3], 16, 17, 18, 19[2]; **33:**1, 4[2], 6, 7[2], 11[3], 12[2], 14[2], 16[4], 17[2], 18, 20[4], 21[2], 24[2]; **34:**3[3], 4[3], 5[2], 7[2], 9[2], 10[4], 11[3], 12[3], 13[2], 14[3], 15[2], 16[2], 17[2]; **35:**1[2], 2[3], 5[2], 6[2], 7[2], 8[5], 9[4], 10[3]; **36:**7, 14, 15; **37:**6, 7, 10[2], 30[2], 31, 32[2], 33, 34[2]; **38:**7, 10, 11[2], 15[2], 19[2], 21, 22; **39:**6[2], 7[3], 8; **40:**4[3], 5[2], 6, 8, 10, 11[3], 20, 24[6], 25, 30[2], 31[4]; **41:**11[3], 12, 16[2], 22, 25[3], 27; **42:**1, 2, 3[3], 4[2], 13[4], 17[2]; **43:**2[2], 10, 13, 17[2], 19[2], 20, 21; **44:**4, 5[3], 7[3], 9, 11[3], 15, 19[2], 26, 28[2]; **45:**1, 9, 13[2], 14[6], 16[2], 17[2], 23[3], 24[3], 25[2]; **46:**7[2], 10, 13[2]; **47:**3[2], 7, 8[2], 9[2], 11[3], 13, 14[4], 15[3]; **48:**14, 15; **49:**5[2], 7[3], 9[2], 10[4], 11, 12, 17[2], 19[2], 20,

22[2], 23[3], 24, 25[2], 26[2]; 50:7[2], 9[3], 11[2]; 51:3[2], 4, 5[3], 6[5], 8[3], 11[4], 12[2], 19[2]; 52:1, 3, 6[2], 8[4], 10, 12, 13[2], 15[4]; 53:2[2], 8, 10[3], 11[4], 12; 54:3, 5, 10[3], 13[2], 14, 15[3], 17[2]; 55:3, 5, 11[4], 12[3], 13[4]; 56:5, 7[2], 12; 57:2[2], 12, 13[4], 14; 58:4, 8[4], 9[2], 10, 11, 12[2]; 59:6[2], 8, 19[3], 20, 21; 60:2[3], 3, 4[2], 5[3], 6[4], 7[3], 9, 10[2], 11[2], 12[2], 13, 14[3], 18, 19[3], 20[4], 21[2], 22; 61:4[3], 5[2], 6[4], 7[4], 9[2], 10; 62:2[2], 4[2], 5[2], 6, 8, 9[2], 12; 63:3; 64:5; 65:9[2], 10, 12, 13[6], 14[3], 15[2], 16[2], 17, 19, 20[3], 21[2], 22[3], 23, 24, 25[4]; 66:5[2], 8[2], 9[2], 12[2], 13, 14[3], 16, 17, 18[2], 19, 20, 22[2], 23[2], 24[4]

Jer 1:7, 14, 15[2], 19[2]; 2:3[2], 19[2], 24, 35; 3:1[2], 15, 16[6], 17[3], 18[2], 19; 4:2[2], 7, 9[4], 10, 11, 12, 13[2], 14, 21, 27, 28, 29[3]; 5:6[4], 7, 9[2], 12[2], 13[2], 14, 17[4], 19[3], 29[2]; 6:3[3], 9, 10, 11, 12, 15[2], 16, 21[2], 22, 23, 26, 30; 7:20[3], 23, 32[2], 33[2], 34; 8:1, 2[3], 3, 4[2], 10, 12[2], 13[3], 17; 9:7, 9[2], 22[2]; 10:10[2], 11[2], 15, 21[2]; 11:4, 11[2], 12[2], 22[2], 23; 12:4[2], 12[2], 13[3], 15, 16[2]; 13:10, 12[3], 17[2], 18, 19[4], 21[2], 27; 14:13[2], 15[2], 16[2]; 15:2[2], 5[3], 11, 12, 14, 20[2]; 16:4[6], 6[3], 7[2], 10[2], 13, 14, 16[2], 19[2], 20, 21; 17:4, 6[3], 8[5], 11[2], 13[2], 14[2], 24, 25[2], 26, 27[2]; 18:7, 9, 14, 16, 18, 20; 19:2, 3, 6, 8, 9[2], 11, 13; 20:4[4], 5, 6, 10[2], 11[5]; 21:3, 6, 7[2], 9[3], 10[2], 13[2], 14; 22:4, 5, 7, 8[2], 9, 10, 11, 12[2], 18[2], 19, 22[2], 26, 27, 30[2]; 23:3, 4[3], 5[2], 6[3], 7, 8, 12[2], 17[2], 19, 20[2], 24, 26, 32, 33, 34, 35, 36[2], 38, 40; 24:7[2], 9; 25:11[2], 12, 14, 16, 26, 28[2], 29, 30[3], 31, 32[2], 33[3], 34, 35, 36; 26:9[2], 15, 18[2]; 27:4, 7[2], 8, 9, 11, 14, 16, 22[2]; 28:9[2], 14; 29:7, 12[2], 13[2], 21, 22, 32[2]; 30:3, 7, 8[2], 9, 10[3], 16[3], 18[2], 19[3], 20[2], 21[3], 22, 23, 24[2]; 31:1, 5[2], 6[2], 8, 9[2], 12[4], 13, 14, 16[2], 17, 18, 22, 23[2], 24, 28, 29, 30[2], 33[2], 34[2], 36, 38, 39[2], 40[2]; 32:3, 4[4], 5[3], 7, 15, 28, 29, 36, 38, 40, 43, 44; 33:9[3], 10[2], 11[2], 12, 13, 15, 16[3], 17, 18; 34:2, 3[2], 5, 20, 22; 35:6, 7[2], 15, 19; 36:29[2], 30[2]; 37:7[2], 8, 9[2], 19; 38:2[4], 3[2], 17[2], 18[2], 20[3], 22[2], 23; 39:12, 16, 18; 40:9, 15; 42:4[2], 5, 14, 16[4], 17[3], 18[4], 20, 22; 43:10, 11, 12[3], 13[2]; 44:12[4], 14[3], 26, 27, 28[3], 29[2]; 46:6, 10[2], 14, 18, 19, 22[2], 23, 24[2], 26, 27[2]; 47:2[4], 3; 48:2[2], 3, 5, 7, 8[4], 9, 12[2], 13, 18[2], 26[2], 30[2], 31, 33[2], 34, 36[2], 37[2], 38, 39[2], 40[2], 41, 42, 43, 44[2], 45[2]; 49:2[3], 3, 4, 5[2], 10, 12, 13[2], 17[3], 18[2], 19, 20[2], 22[2], 26[2], 27, 28, 29[3], 32, 33[2], 36[2], 39; 50:3[4], 4[2], 5[2], 9[4], 10[2], 12[3], 13[3], 16[2], 19[2], 20[3], 30[2], 32[3], 34, 36[2], 37[2], 38, 39[4], 40[2], 41[2], 42[3], 44, 45[2]; 51:2[3], 4, 14, 18, 26, 29[2], 31, 33, 35[2], 37, 38[2], 44[2], 46[3], 47[2], 48[2], 49, 52, 53, 56, 57, 58[4], 62[2], 63, 64[3]

Lam 1:21; 2:13[3], 20[2]; 4:15, 20, 21; 5:21

Ezk 2:5; 3:10, 18, 19, 20[3], 21, 25[2]; 4:3[2], 7, 10, 13, 16[2]; 5:4, 10[2], 11, 12[3], 13[2], 15[2], 16[2], 17[2]; 6:4[2], 6[2], 7[2], 8[2], 9[3], 10, 11, 12[3], 13[2], 14; 7:4[3], 9[2], 11[2], 13[3], 15[2], 16[2], 17[2], 18[3], 19[4], 21, 22[2], 24[2], 25[2], 26[4], 27[4]; 8:18; 9:10; 11:10[2], 11[2], 12, 16, 18[2], 20; 12:11[2], 12[4], 13[3], 15[2], 16, 19, 20[3], 23, 24, 25[3], 28[2]; 13:9[5], 11[4], 12, 13, 14[4], 21[2], 23[2]; 14:8, 10[2], 16[3], 18[2], 20[2], 22[5], 23[2]; 15:3, 5, 7[3]; 16:16[2], 39[4], 40[2], 41, 42, 44, 53, 55[3]; 17:9[3], 10[3], 15[3], 16, 17, 18, 20, 21[3], 23[3], 24; 18:3, 4, 9, 13[4], 17[2], 18, 19, 20[5], 21[2], 22[2], 24[3], 26, 27, 28[2], 30; 19:14; 20:11, 13, 20, 21, 31, 32, 38[2], 40, 42[2], 43[2], 44, 47[3], 48[2]; 21:4, 5, 7[6], 12[3], 13, 19, 23, 24, 25, 26, 27, 29, 30, 32; 22:5, 14, 21, 22[2]; 23:24[3], 25[5], 26, 29[4], 45, 47[2], 49[3]; 24:12, 14[2], 16, 21, 22[2], 23[3], 24[2], 25, 26, 27[2]; 25:4[3], 5, 11, 13, 14[2], 17[2]; 26:2, 4, 5[2], 6[2], 8[2], 9[2], 10[3], 11[3], 12[3], 13, 15, 16[4], 17, 18[2], 19[3], 20[3]; 27:27, 28, 29[2], 30[4], 31[2], 32, 34, 35[3], 36; 28:7[2], 8, 18, 19, 22[3], 23[2], 24[2], 25[3], 26[4]; 29:4, 6, 9[2], 11[3], 12, 14, 15[3], 16[3], 19[2], 21; 30:3, 4[5], 5, 6[3], 7[2], 8[2], 9[2], 11[2], 13, 16[3], 17[2], 18[5], 19, 21, 24, 25[4], 26; 31:11, 13[2], 16; 32:3, 6, 7[2], 9, 10[3], 11, 12[2], 13, 15[4], 16[3], 20, 21, 27[2], 29, 31[2], 32; 33:4, 5[2], 8, 9, 12[3], 13[4], 15[2], 16[2], 18, 19, 25, 26, 27[2], 28[3], 29, 33; 34:10, 14[3], 22, 23[3], 25, 26, 27[4], 28[4], 29, 30; 35:6[2], 8, 9[2], 10, 15; 36:7, 8, 9, 10[2], 11[2], 12, 23[2], 25, 27, 28[2], 30, 31[2], 33[2], 34, 35, 36, 38[2]; 37:5, 6[2], 13, 14[4], 17, 18, 19, 20, 22[3], 23[2], 24[3], 25[3], 26, 27[2], 28[2]; 38:8, 10[2], 13, 16[2], 18[3], 19, 20[4], 21, 23; 39:6, 7, 9[3], 10[3], 11[4], 12, 13[3], 14[2], 15, 16[2], 18, 19, 20, 21, 22, 23, 28; 40:4; 42:13[2], 14[4]; 43:7, 12, 13[3], 14[2], 15[2], 16, 17[4], 18, 21, 22, 24[2], 25, 26[2], 27[2]; 44:2[4], 3[3], 9, 10, 11[3], 12, 13[2], 14, 15[2], 16[3], 17[3], 18[3], 19[3], 20[2], 21, 22[2], 23, 24[4], 25, 26, 27, 28[2], 29[2], 30[2], 31; 45:1[5], 2, 3, 4[3], 5, 6[2], 7[2], 8[3], 10, 11[2], 12[2], 13[2], 14, 16, 17[2], 19, 20, 21[2], 22, 23, 24, 25; 46:1[3], 2[6], 3, 4[2], 5[2], 6[2], 7[2], 8[3], 9[5], 10[2], 11, 12[5], 15, 16[2], 17[3], 18[2], 20[2], 24; 47:8, 9[7], 10[4], 11[2], 12[5], 13[3], 14[2], 15, 17, 18, 20, 21, 22[5], 23[2]; 48:8[3], 9[2], 10[2], 11, 12, 13[2], 14, 15[2], 16, 17, 18[3], 19, 20[2], 21[3], 22, 23, 24, 28, 29, 31, 35

Dan 1:10; 2:5[2], 6, 9, 28, 29, 30, 39[2], 40[2], 41[2], 42, 43[2], 44[5], 45; 3:6, 10[2], 15[2], 29[2]; 4:25[5], 26, 32[4]; 5:7[3]; 6:5, 7[2], 12[2], 26[2]; 7:14[2], 17, 18, 23[4], 24[4], 25[3], 26[2], 27[2]; 8:13, 14, 17, 19[2], 22, 23, 24[4], 25[5], 26; 9:25[2], 26[4], 27[4]; 10:14, 20; 11:2[3], 3[2], 4[5], 5[3], 6[5], 7[5], 8[2], 9[2], 10[4], 11[4], 12[3], 13[3], 14[3], 15[3], 16[4], 17[4], 18[4], 19[2], 20[2], 21[3], 22[3], 23[3], 24[4], 25[4], 26[3], 27[4], 28[3], 29[2], 30[4], 31[4], 32[3], 33[2], 34[3], 35, 36[5], 37[2], 38[2], 39[4], 40[4], 41[3], 42[2], 43[2], 44[2], 45[3]; 12:1[4], 2, 3, 4[2], 6, 7[3], 8, 10[4], 11[2]

Hos 1:5, 10[3], 11[3]; 2:6, 7[5], 10, 12, 15, 16, 17, 21[2], 22[2], 23; 3:4, 5[2]; 4:3[3], 5, 9, 10[3], 13[2], 14, 19; 5:5[2], 6[2], 7, 9[2], 14; 6:2, 3[2], 4[2]; 7:12, 16[2]; 8:1, 2, 3, 6, 7[3], 8, 10, 11, 13, 14; 9:2[2], 3[3], 4[5], 6[4], 7, 11, 12, 13, 16, 17; 10:2[3], 3, 5[2], 6[3], 8[3], 10[2], 11[2], 14[2], 15[2]; 11:5[2], 6[2], 8[4], 10[4], 11; 12:8, 14[2]; 13:3, 8, 13, 14, 15[5], 16[4]; 14:3, 5, 6[2], 7[3], 8, 9[4]

Joel 1:15; 2:2, 3, 4, 5, 6[2], 7[4], 8[3], 9[4], 10[4], 11, 19, 20[2], 24[2], 26[2], 27[2], 28[4], 31, 32[5]; 3:1, 8, 15[2], 16[2], 17[3], 18[6], 19[2], 20

Am 1:2[2], 4, 5, 7, 8, 10, 12, 14, 15; 2:2[2], 5, 14[3], 15[3], 16; 3:5, 6[2], 11[3], 12, 14[2], 15[2]; 4:2, 3[2]; 5:2, 3[2], 4, 5[2], 6, 9, 11[2], 13, 14, 16[3], 17, 20; 6:7[2], 9[2], 10[4], 12, 14; 7:2, 3, 5, 6, 9[2], 11[2], 17[4]; 8:3[3], 8[3], 9, 12[3], 13, 14; 9:1[2], 2, 3, 4, 5[4], 9, 10[2], 13[3], 14[3], 15

Oba 3, 8, 9, 10, 15[2], 16[4], 17[3], 18[3], 19[3], 20[2], 21[2]

Jna 1:11, 12; 3:4

Mic 1:4[2], 7[3], 11, 14, 15; 2:3[2], 4, 5, 6[2], 10, 11, 12, 13; 3:4, 6[6], 7[2], 12[2]; 4:1[4], 2[2], 3[4], 4[2], 7, 8[2], 10, 12; 5:1, 2, 3, 4[3], 5[4], 6[2], 7, 8, 9[2], 10; 6:6[2], 7, 9, 11, 14, 16; 7:4, 8[2], 9, 10[4], 11, 12, 13, 16[3], 17[4]

Nah 1:8, 9, 10, 12[2], 15; 2:3[2], 4[4], 5[4], 6[2], 7[3], 8[3], 13[2]; 3:7[3], 12[2], 13[2], 15[3], 18, 19

Hab 1:2, 6, 7, 8[3], 9[3], 10[4], 11[2], 12, 17; 2:1, 3, 4, 6, 7[3], 8, 11[2], 13[2], 14, 16[2], 17, 19; 3:17[6]

Zep 1:8, 10[2], 12, 13[3], 14, 17[2], 18[3]; 2:3, 4[3], 5, 6, 7[4], 9[3], 10, 11, 12, 14[5], 15; 3:8, 10, 12, 13[4], 16

Hag 2:7, 9, 12, 13[2], 22

Zec 1:16[2], 17[3]; 2:4, 9[2], 11[2], 12[2]; 3:9, 10; 4:7, 9, 10[2]; 5:3[2], 4[3], 11; 6:12[2], 13[5], 14, 15[3]; 8:3, 4, 5, 8[2], 12[4], 13[2], 16, 19, 20[2], 21, 22, 23[3]; 9:1[2], 2, 4, 5[5], 6, 7[2], 8, 10[3], 14[4], 15[4], 16[2], 17; 10:1, 5[3], 6, 7[4], 8, 9[2], 10, 11[5], 12; 11:6, 16[3], 17[3]; 12:2, 3, 5[2], 6[2], 7, 8[3], 9, 10[3], 11, 12; 13:1, 2[2], 3[4], 4[3], 5, 6[2], 7, 8[3], 9[2]; 14:1, 2[3], 3, 4[4], 5[4], 6[2], 7[4], 8[3], 9[2], 10[2], 11[3], 12[4], 13[4], 14[2], 15[2], 16[2], 17[2], 18, 19, 20[2], 21[3]

Mal 1:4[2], 5[2], 11[3]; 2:3, 4; 3:1[3], 2, 3[2], 4, 7, 10, 11[2], 12[2], 17, 18; 4:1[4], 2[2], 3[3], 6

Mt 1:21[2], 23[3]; 2:6[2], 23; 3:11; 4:4, 6[2]; 5:4, 5, 6, 7, 8, 9, 11[2], 13, 18, 19[5], 20[2], 21[2], 22[5], 31, 32[2], 39, 41; 6:4, 6, 7, 18, 22, 23, 25[3], 30, 31[3], 33, 34; 7:2[2], 7[3], 8, 11, 16, 20, 21, 26; 8:8, 11[2], 12[2]; 9:15[2], 18, 21; 10:11, 14, 15, 18, 19[3], 21[2], 22[2], 23, 25, 26[2], 29, 32, 33, 36, 39[2], 41[2], 42[2]; 11:6, 10, 16, 22, 24, 29; 12:11[2], 18, 19[2], 20[2], 21, 25, 26, 27, 31[2], 32[2], 36[2], 39, 40, 41[2], 42[2], 45, 50; 13:12[3], 14[4], 40, 41[2], 42[2], 43, 49[2], 50[2]; 15:5, 6, 13, 14; 16:4, 18, 19[2], 22, 25[2], 26[2], 27[2], 28; 17:11, 12, 17[2], 20[3], 22, 23[2]; 18:3, 4, 5, 6, 15[2], 17, 18[4], 19[3], 21, 35; 19:5[3], 9[2], 16, 23, 27, 28[2], 29[2], 30[2]; 20:7, 16, 18[2], 19[2], 22, 23[2], 26, 32; 21:2, 3, 13, 21[3], 22[2], 25, 26, 41, 43, 44[3]; 22:9, 13, 24, 28; 23:11, 12[4], 14, 16[2], 18, 20, 21, 22, 34[2], 36, 39[2]; 24:2[2], 3[2], 5[2], 6, 7[2], 9[3], 10[3], 11[2], 12[2], 13[2], 14[2], 15, 21[2], 22, 23, 24[3], 26, 27, 29[4], 30[3], 31[2], 33, 34, 35[2], 37, 39, 40[2], 41[2], 46, 47, 48, 49, 50, 51[2]; 25:1, 29[3], 30, 31[2], 32[2], 33, 34, 37, 40, 41, 44, 45, 46; 26:13[2], 21, 23, 31[2], 33, 48, 52, 53, 54, 64; 27:22, 64; 28:7, 10

Mk 1:2, 8; 2:20[2]; 3:28[2], 29, 35; 4:22, 24[2], 25[2], 30[2]; 5:23, 28; 6:11[2], 24, 37; 7:11[2]; 8:12, 35[3], 36[2], 37, 38[2]; 9:1, 19[2], 31[2], 35, 37[2], 39, 41[2], 42, 43, 45, 49[2]; 10:7, 8, 11, 12, 15[2], 17, 23, 30, 31, 33[3], 34[5], 35, 39[2], 40, 43[2], 44; 11:2, 17, 23[5], 24, 31, 32; 12:7, 9, 15[2], 23[2], 25, 40; 13:2[2], 4[3], 6[2], 7[2], 8[3], 9[3], 11[3], 12[3], 13[3], 14, 19[2], 21, 22[2], 24[2], 25[2], 26, 27[2], 29, 30, 31[2]; 14:9[2], 13, 14[2], 18, 27[2], 29, 32, 44, 62; 15:12; 16:3, 7, 16[2], 17[3], 18[4]

Lk 1:13, 14, 15[3], 16, 17, 18, 20[2], 32[3], 33[2], 34, 35[4], 37, 45, 48, 60, 66; 2:10, 12[2], 23, 34, 35; 3:5[4], 6, 10, 12, 14, 16; 4:4, 7, 10, 11; 5:35[2], 37; 6:21[2], 22[3], 25[2], 26, 35[2], 37[3], 38[3], 39, 40; 7:7, 23, 27, 31; 8:17[2], 18[2], 50; 9:24[2], 26[3], 27, 41, 44, 48[3]; 10:6[2], 12, 14, 19, 25, 42; 11:5[2], 7, 9[3], 10, 11, 12, 13, 18, 19, 22, 29, 30, 31, 32[2], 36, 49, 51; 12:2[2], 3[2], 5, 8[2], 9, 10[3], 11[2], 12, 17, 20[2], 22[2], 29[2], 31, 37[2], 38, 42, 43, 45, 47, 48[2], 52, 53; 13:3, 5, 8, 18, 20, 24, 25, 26, 27, 28[2], 29[2], 30[2], 32, 35[2]; 14:5, 11[2], 15, 24, 34; 15:7; 16:3, 12; 17:10, 21, 22[2], 23, 24, 26, 30, 31, 33[4], 34[3], 35[2], 36[2]; 18:7, 8, 14[2], 17[2], 18, 24, 30, 31, 32[2], 33[2], 41; 19:26[2], 30, 31, 43[2], 44[2]; 20:5, 13, 15, 16[2], 18[3], 35, 47; 21:6[2], 7[2], 8, 9, 10, 11[2], 12, 13, 14, 15, 16[2], 17, 18, 20, 23, 24[3], 25, 26, 27, 32, 33[2], 35, 36; 22:10, 11[2], 12, 18, 26, 34, 49, 69; 23:29, 30, 31

Jn 1:51; 3:12, 36; 4:13, 14[4], 21, 23; 5:24, 25[2], 28, 29, 43, 47; 6:5, 27, 28, 35[2], 37, 45, 51, 57, 58, 62, 68; 7:17, 34[2], 35, 36[2], 38, 41; 8:12[2], 21[2], 24[2], 28, 32[2], 33, 36[2], 51, 52, 55; 9:21; 10:9[2], 16[2], 28[2]; 11:12, 23, 24, 25, 26, 48; 12:25[2], 26, 27, 31, 48; 13:21, 26, 32[2], 33, 35, 38; 14:12[2], 13, 14, 16, 17, 19, 20, 21, 26; 15:7[2], 8, 10, 16, 26, 27; 16:2, 4, 13[3], 14[3], 15[2], 16[2], 17[2], 19[2], 20[4], 22, 23[2], 24, 25[2], 26, 32[2], 33; 17:20; 18:11; 19:15, 24, 36, 37; 20:25; 21:6, 18, 21, 23

Act 1:5, 8[2], 11; 2:17[4], 18, 20, 21[3], 26, 37, 38, 39; 3:19, 20, 22[3], 23[2], 25; 4:16; 5:9; 6:14[2]; 7:3, 7[2], 37[2]; 8:33; 9:6; 10:6, 32, 43; 11:14[2], 16; 13:22, 41; 15:11, 27, 29; 18:10; 19:39; 20:22, 25, 29, 30; 21:11[2]; 22:10[2]; 23:3; 24:15, 22; 26:2; 27:22, 25, 34; 28:26[3]

Ro 1:17; 2:12[2], 13, 16, 26, 27; 3:3, 5, 6, 20, 30; 4:1, 18, 24; 5:9, 10, 17, 19; 6:1[2], 2, 5, 8, 14, 15; 7:3, 7, 24; 8:11, 13[2], 18, 21, 31, 32, 33, 35[2], 39; 9:7, 9, 12, 14, 20, 26[2], 27, 30, 33; 10:5, 6, 7, 11, 13[2], 14[3], 15; 11:15, 23, 24, 26[3], 27, 35; 13:2; 14:4, 10, 11[2], 12; 15:12[3], 21[2], 29; 16:20

1Co 1:8; 3:8, 13[4], 14, 15[3], 17; 4:5, 17, 21; 6:2[2], 3, 5, 9, 10, 13, 15, 16; 7:28; 8:10, 11; 9:11; 11:22[2], 27[2]; 12:15, 16; 13:8[3], 10, 12; 14:6[2], 7, 8, 9[2], 11[2], 16; 15:22, 24[2], 26, 28[2], 29, 37, 49, 51[2], 52[3], 54[3]; 16:3, 4, 5, 12

2Co 1:7, 13; 3:8, 16[2]; 4:14[2]; 5:3; 6:16, 18; 9:6[2]; 10:15; 11:10, 15; 12:6, 20[2], 21; 13:1, 4, 6, 11

Gal 2:16; 3:8, 11, 12; 4:30; 5:2, 10, 16, 21; 6:4, 5, 7, 8[2], 9

Eph 5:14, 31[3]; 6:8, 16, 21

Php 1:19, 20[2], 22, 25; 2:23, 24; 3:15, 21; 4:7, 9, 19

Col 3:4[2], 24, 25; 4:7, 9

1Th 4:15, 16[2], 17[2]; 5:3[2]

2Th 1:7, 9, 10; 2:3, 8[3], 11; 3:3

1Ti 2:15; 3:5; 4:1; 6:15

2Ti 2:2, 11, 12, 21; 3:1, 2, 9[2], 12, 13; 4:1, 3, 4[2], 8, 18

Tit 3:12

Phlm 22

Heb 1:5, 11[2], 12[2], 14; 2:3; 3:11; 4:3, 5; 6:6; 8:10, 11[2]; 9:14, 28; 10:27, 29, 30, 37, 38[2]; 11:18, 32; 12:9, 14, 20, 25; 13:6

Jas 1:5, 7, 10, 11, 12, 25; 2:10, 12, 13; 3:1; 4:10, 14, 15; 5:1, 3[2], 15[3], 20[2]

1Pt 2:6, 12, 20; 4:5, 8, 13, 17, 18; 5:1, 4[2]

2Pt 1:8, 10, 11; 2:1[2], 2[2], 3, 12, 13; 3:3, 10[3], 11, 12[2]

1Jn 2:18, 24[2], 27, 28; 3:2[4], 19; 4:15; 5:16[3]

2Jn 2

3Jn 14[2]

Rev 1:7[2], 19; 2:10[2], 11, 23, 27[2]; 3:4, 5, 10, 12; 5:10; 6:17; 7:15, 16[2], 17[3]; 9:6[4]; 10:7, 9[2]; 11:2, 3, 7[3], 8, 9[2], 10[2], 15; 13:8, 10; 14:10[2]; 15:4[2]; 17:8[2], 13, 14[2], 16[3], 17; 18:7, 8[2], 9[2], 11, 15, 21[2], 22[3], 23[2]; 19:15; 20:6[2], 7, 8, 10; 21:3[3], 4[3], 7[2], 8, 24, 25[2], 26, 27; 22:3[3], 4[2], 5[2], 12, 18[2], 19[2]

SHALT

Gen 2:17[2]; 3:14[2], 15, 16, 17[2], 18, 19[2]; 4:7[2], 12; 6:14[2], 15, 16[4], 18, 19, 21; 7:2; 12:2; 15:15[2]; 16:11[2]; 17:4, 9, 15, 19; 20:7[2], 13; 21:23, 30; 24:3, 4, 7, 8, 37, 38, 40, 41[2]; 27:10, 40[4]; 28:1, 6, 14, 22; 29:27; 30:31; 31:50[2], 52; 32:18; 35:17; 37:8[2]; 40:13; 41:40; 43:9; 45:10[2]; 47:30; 49:4; 50:5

Ex 3:14, 15, 18; 4:9, 12, 15, 16, 17[2], 22; 6:1; 7:2, 9, 15[2], 16, 17; 9:15; 10:28; 12:46; 13:5, 6, 8, 10, 12, 13[3], 14; 15:17; 17:6; 18:20[2], 21, 23[2]; 19:3, 6, 12, 24; 20:3, 4, 5, 7, 9, 10, 13, 14, 15, 16, 17[2], 22, 24[2], 25, 26; 21:1, 14, 23; 22:18, 21, 25[2], 26, 28, 29[2], 30[2]; 23:1, 2[2], 3, 4, 5, 6, 8, 9, 10[2], 11[2], 12[2], 14, 15[2], 18, 19[2], 22, 24[2], 27, 31, 32;

25:11^3, 12, 13, 14, 16, 17, 18^2, 21^2, 23, 24, 25^2, 26, 28, 29^2, 30, 31, 37; 26:1^2, 4^2, 5^2, 6, 7^2, 9^2, 10, 11, 14, 15, 17, 18, 19, 22, 23, 26, 29^2, 30, 31, 32, 33, 34, 35^2, 36, 37^2; 27:1, 2^2, 3^2, 4^2, 5, 6, 8, 9, 20; 28:2, 3, 9, 11^2, 12, 13, 14, 15^3, 17, 22, 23^2, 24, 25, 26^2, 27^2, 30, 31, 33, 36, 37, 39^3, 40^3, 41^2, 42; 29:1, 2, 3, 4^2, 5, 6, 7, 8, 9^2, 10, 11, 12, 13, 14, 15, 16^2, 17, 18, 19, 20, 21, 22, 24^2, 25, 26, 27, 31, 34, 35^2, 36^3, 37, 38, 39^2, 41^2; 30:1^2, 3^2, 4^2, 5, 6, 16^2, 18^3, 25, 26, 29, 30, 31, 35, 36, 37; 33:21, 23; 34:14, 17, 18^2, 20^3, 21^3, 22, 24, 25, 26^2; 40:2, 3, 4^2, 5, 6, 7^2, 8, 9^2, 10, 11, 12, 13, 14, 15

Lev 2:6, 8, 13^3, 14, 15; 6:21^2, 27; 9:3; 13:55, 57, 58; 17:8; 18:7^2, 8, 9, 10, 11, 12, 13, 14^2, 15^2, 16, 17^2, 18, 19, 20, 21^2, 22, 23; 19:9^2, 10^3, 12, 13, 14^2, 15^2, 16^2, 17^2, 18^2, 19^2, 27, 32, 34; 20:2, 16, 19; 21:8; 23:22^3; 24:5, 6, 7, 15; 25:3^2, 4, 5, 8, 9, 15, 16^2, 17, 35, 37, 39, 43^2, 44

Nu 1:49, 50; 3:9, 10, 15, 41, 47^2, 48; 4:23, 29, 30; 7:5; 8:7, 8, 9^2, 10, 12, 13, 14, 15, 26; 10:2; 11:23; 14:15; 15:5, 6, 7, 10; 17:3, 4, 10; 18:10, 15^2, 16, 17^3, 20^2, 30; 20:8^2, 18, 20; 21:34; 22:12^2, 20, 35; 23:5, 13^2; 26:54^2; 27:7^2, 8, 13, 20; 28:3, 4^2, 7, 8^2, 21; 31:2, 30

Dt 1:37; 2:28; 3:2, 27, 28; 4:25, 29^2, 30, 40; 5:7, 8, 9, 11, 13, 14, 17, 18, 19, 20, 21^2, 31; 6:5, 7^2, 8, 9, 11, 13^2, 18, 21; 7:2^2, 3^3, 11, 14, 16^2, 17, 18^2, 21, 24, 25, 26^3; 8:2, 5, 6, 9^2, 10, 18; 9:3; 10:2, 20^3; 11:1, 20, 29; 12:5, 14^2, 18, 20, 21^2, 22, 24^2, 25^2, 26, 27^2, 31, 32; 13:3, 5, 8^3, 9, 10, 12, 14, 15, 16^2, 18; 14:3, 21^2, 22, 23, 25^2, 26^3, 27, 28^2; 15:1, 6^3, 7, 8^2, 10, 11, 12, 13, 14^2, 15, 17^2, 19^2, 20, 21, 22, 23^2; 16:2, 3^2, 6, 7^2, 8^2, 9, 10^2, 11, 12^2, 13, 14, 15^2, 18, 19^2, 20, 21^2, 22; 17:1, 5^2, 7, 8, 9, 10^2, 11^2, 12, 14^3, 15^2; 18:4, 9, 13, 14, 22; 19:2, 3, 7, 9^2, 13, 14^2, 19; 20:12, 13, 14^2, 15, 16, 17, 19^3, 20^2; 21:9^2, 12, 13, 14^3, 21, 23; 22:1^2, 2^2, 3^3, 4^2, 6, 7, 8, 9, 10, 11, 12, 21, 22, 24, 26; 23:6, 7^2, 12^2, 13^3, 15, 16, 18, 19, 20, 21^2, 22, 23, 24, 25; 24:4, 7, 10, 11, 12, 13, 14, 15, 17, 18, 19, 20, 21, 22; 25:4, 12, 13, 14, 15^2, 19^2; 26:2^4, 3, 5, 10, 11, 13, 16; 27:2, 3, 4, 5^2, 6^2, 7^2, 8, 10; 28:1, 2, 3^2, 6^2, 9, 12^2, 13^2, 14, 16^2, 19^2, 25^2, 29^3, 30^5, 31^2, 33, 34^2, 36^2, 37, 38^2, 39^2, 40^2, 41^2, 43, 44^2, 48, 49, 53, 64, 65, 66^2, 67^4, 68; 30:1, 2^2, 5, 8, 10, 17; 31:2, 3, 7, 11, 16, 23; 32:52^2; 33:29; 34:4

Jos 1:6, 8^3; 2:18^2; 3:8; 6:3; 8:2; 11:6; 17:17, 18^2

Jdg 4:20; 6:14, 16, 23, 26; 7:5, 11; 9:33^2; 11:2, 30; 13:3, 5, 7

Ru 2:21; 3:4^3

1Sa 2:16, 32; 3:9; 9:16; 10:2, 3^2, 4, 5^2, 6^2, 8^3; 14:44; 16:3^2, 16; 18:21; 19:11; 20:2, 8, 14, 15, 18, 19^2, 31; 22:16, 23; 23:17; 24:20; 26:25^2; 28:1, 2, 19; 30:8

2Sa 3:13; 5:2^2, 6, 23, 24; 7:5, 8, 12; 9:7, 10; 10:11; 11:25; 12:13; 13:13; 15:33, 35^2; 18:3, 20^3; 19:23, 38; 21:4, 17

1Ki 2:37^2, 42; 5:6, 9^3; 8:19, 44; 11:37^2; 12:10^2; 13:17; 14:5; 17:4; 19:16^2; 20:5, 13, 34, 39; 21:19^2; 22:11, 22, 25^2

2Ki 1:4^2, 6^2, 16^2; 4:4^3, 16; 5:10; 6:22; 7:2^2, 19^2; 8:13; 9:7; 10:5; 13:17, 19; 19:11; 20:1, 5, 9, 18; 22:20

1Ch 11:2^2, 5; 14:15^2; 17:4, 7; 19:12; 21:22; 22:8, 13; 28:3

2Ch 2:16^2; 6:9, 34; 7:17; 10:10^2; 16:9; 18:10, 21^2, 24^2; 21:15; 34:28

Ezr 4:13, 15, 16; 7:20

Est 4:13; 6:13^2

Job 5:21^2, 22^2, 23, 24^3, 25, 26; 7:21; 9:31; 11:15^3, 16, 17^2, 18^3, 19; 14:15; 17:4; 22:23^2, 24, 25, 26^2, 27^2, 28, 29; 35:14; 38:11

Ps 2:9^2; 5:3, 6; 12:7^2; 17:3; 21:9, 10, 12^2; 31:20^2; 32:7^2, 8; 36:8; 37:3^2, 10, 34; 50:15; 51:6, 19; 55:23; 59:8^2; 65:3; 67:4; 71:20^2, 21; 73:20, 24; 76:10; 81:9; 82:8; 89:2; 91:4, 5, 8, 13^2; 92:10; 102:12, 13, 26^2; 119:32; 128:2^2, 5, 6; 138:7; 142:7

Prv 2:5, 9; 3:4, 23, 24^2; 4:12; 9:12^2; 20:13; 22:24; 23:8, 14^2, 34, 35; 24:6; 25:22; 27:27

Ecc 11:1; 12:1

Isa 1:26; 12:1; 14:4, 15, 20; 17:10^2, 11^2; 22:18; 23:12^2; 25:5; 29:4^2, 6; 30:19, 22^2, 23; 33:1^3, 19; 37:11; 38:1; 39:7; 41:12^2, 15^2, 16^3; 43:2; 44:21, 26, 28; 47:1, 5, 11^3, 12; 49:18, 20, 21, 23; 51:22; 53:10; 54:3, 4^4, 14^3, 17; 55:5; 58:9^2, 11, 12^2, 13, 14; 60:5, 16^3, 18; 62:2, 3, 4^2, 12

Jer 1:7^2; 2:36, 37^2; 3:19^2; 4:1, 2, 30; 5:19; 7:27^2, 28; 8:4; 13:12, 13; 14:17; 15:2, 19^2; 16:2^2, 8, 10, 11; 17:4; 18:22; 19:10, 11; 20:6^3; 21:8; 22:15, 22, 23; 23:33, 37; 25:27, 28; 26:4, 8; 28:13, 16; 29:24; 31:4^3, 5; 34:3^3, 4, 5, 14; 36:6, 29; 37:17; 38:17, 18, 23^3, 24, 26; 39:17, 18; 40:16; 45:4; 46:11^2; 48:2, 7; 49:12^2; 51:26, 61^2, 62, 63, 64

Lam 4:21^2

Ezk 2:4, 7; 3:18, 25, 26^2, 27; 4:3, 4^2, 5, 6, 7^2, 8, 9^2, 10^2, 11^2, 12^2, 15; 5:2^3, 3; 8:6, 13, 15; 12:3, 4^2, 6^2; 16:41, 43, 61^2, 62; 21:7, 32^2; 22:2, 16^2; 23:27, 32^2, 33, 34^2; 24:13, 16, 27^2; 25:7; 26:14^2, 21^2; 27:34, 36^2; 28:8, 9, 10, 19^2; 29:5^2; 31:18^2; 32:28^2; 33:7, 8, 14; 35:4^2, 12, 15; 36:12^2, 14, 15^2; 38:8^2, 9^2, 10, 11, 14, 15, 16; 39:4, 5; 43:19, 20^2, 21, 22, 23, 24, 25; 44:6; 45:3, 18, 20; 46:13^2, 14

Dan 4:26; 5:16^2; 12:13

Hos 2:16^2, 20; 3:3^3; 4:5, 6; 13:4

Am 7:17

Oba 10

Mic 1:14; 2:5; 4:10^4, 13; 5:12, 13; 6:14^3, 15^5

Nah 3:11^3

Hab 2:7

Zep 3:11^2, 15

Zec 2:11; 3:7^2; 4:7, 9; 13:3

Mt 1:21; 4:7, 10^2; 5:21, 26, 27, 33^2, 36, 43; 6:5; 7:5; 11:23; 12:37^2; 16:19^2; 17:27; 19:18^4, 19, 21; 22:37, 39; 26:34, 75

Mk 6:23; 10:21; 12:30, 31; 14:30, 72

Lk 1:13, 14, 20, 31^2, 76^2; 4:8^2, 12; 5:10; 6:42; 10:15, 27, 28; 12:59; 13:9; 14:10, 14^2; 17:4, 8; 18:22; 22:34, 61; 23:43

Jn 1:33, 42, 50; 13:7, 8, 36; 21:18^2

Act 2:28; 13:11, 35; 16:31; 22:15; 23:5; 25:12, 22

Ro 2:3; 7:7; 10:9^3; 11:22; 12:20; 13:3, 9^6

1Co 7:16^2; 9:9; 14:16

Gal 5:14

1Ti 4:6, 16; 5:18

Heb 1:12

Jas 2:8

3Jn 6

Rev 2:10; 3:3^2; 16:5; 18:14

SHE

Gen 2:23^2; 3:6, 12, 20; 4:1, 2, 17, 22, 25^2; 8:9; 11:30; 12:14, 16, 18, 19; 15:9; 16:1, 4^3, 5^2, 6, 8, 13^2; 17:16; 18:15; 19:26, 33^2, 35^2, 38; 20:2, 3, 5^3, 12^3, 16; 21:7, 9, 10, 14, 15, 16^3, 19^2; 22:20, 24; 24:14^2, 16, 18^2, 19^2, 20, 24^2, 25, 36, 44, 45, 46^2, 47, 55, 58, 64^2, 65^2, 67; 25:2, 21, 22^2, 26; 26:7^3, 9^2; 27:16, 17^2, 42; 29:9, 12, 32^2, 33^2, 34, 35^3; 30:1, 3^2, 4, 6, 8, 9^2, 11, 13, 15, 17, 18, 20, 21, 23, 24, 35; 31:35, 38; 32:14, 15; 34:1; 35:8, 16, 17, 18^2; 36:12, 14; 38:3, 4^2, 5^2, 14^3, 15, 16^2, 17, 18^2, 19, 24, 25^3, 26, 28, 29; 39:7, 10, 12, 13, 14, 16, 17, 19; 45:23; 46:15, 18, 25

Ex 1:16; 2:2^2, 3^3, 5^2, 6^3, 7, 10^3, 22; 4:26; 6:20, 23, 25; 21:4, 7, 8, 11

Lev 12:2^2, 4^2, 5^3, 6, 7, 8^3; 15:19, 20^2, 22, 23, 25, 26^2, 28^3, 29; 18:7, 9, 11, 12, 13, 14, 15, 19; 19:20^2; 20:17, 18; 21:9^3; 22:12, 13; 26:43

Nu 5:13^2, 14^2, 27, 28; 12:10, 14; 15:27; 22:25, 27, 28, 33; 26:59; 30:4^2, 5, 6^3, 7, 8^3, 10, 11

Dt 21:12, 13^2, 14; 22:19, 21^2, 24, 29; 24:1, 2^2, 4; 25:6; 28:57^2

Jos 2:6^2, 8, 9, 15^2, 16, 21^3; 6:17^2, 22, 23, 25^3; 15:18^3

Jdg 1:14^3, 15; 4:4, 5, 6, 9, 18, 19; 5:24, 25^2, 26^4, 29; 8:31; 11:34, 36, 37, 38, 39^2; 13:9, 14; 14:3, 7, 17^3; 15:2; 16:8, 9, 14, 15, 16, 18, 19^4, 20; 19:3; 20:5

Ru 1:3, 6^3, 7^2, 9, 15, 18^3, 20; 2:2, 3, 7^3, 10, 13, 14^2, 15, 16, 17^2, 18^5, 19^2, 23; 3:5, 6, 7, 9, 14^2, 15^2, 16^3, 17, 18; 4:13^2

1Sa 1:7^3, 10, 11, 12, 13^2, 18, 20, 22, 23, 24^2, 26; 2:5, 19, 21; 4:19^2, 20^2, 21, 22; 18:19, 21; 19:14; 25:3, 19^2, 20^3, 23, 35, 36, 41, 42; 28:12, 14, 24, 25

2Sa 4:4; 6:16; 11:4^3, 26, 27; 12:24; 13:2, 8, 9, 10, 11, 12, 14, 16, 18; 14:4, 5, 11, 27; 20:17, 18; 21:8^2

1Ki 1:17, 22, 28; 2:13, 14, 16, 19, 20, 21; 3:19, 20, 26, 27; 10:1, 2^3, 6, 10, 13^3; 14:5^2, 6, 17; 15:13; 17:11, 12, 15^2, 18; 21:8, 9, 11

2Ki 2:24; 4:2, 5^2, 6, 7, 8, 9, 12, 13, 14, 15, 16, 21, 22, 23, 24, 25, 26, 27^2, 28, 36, 37; 5:2, 3; 6:28, 29; 8:2, 3, 6^2; 9:30, 31, 34; 11:1, 13, 14, 16^2; 22:14, 15

1Ch 1:32; 2:21, 26, 29, 35, 49; 4:17; 7:14, 16, 23; 15:29

2Ch 9:1^3, 5, 9, 12^4; 15:16; 22:10, 11^2; 23:12, 13, 15; 34:22, 23; 36:21^2

Est 1:11, 15, 17, 19; 2:1, 7, 9, 10, 12, 13, 14^4, 15, 17, 20; 4:4, 8; 5:2, 12

Job 1:3; 39:16, 18^2, 28, 29, 30; 42:12

Ps 45:14; 46:5; 68:12; 80:11; 84:3

Prv 1:20, 21^2; 3:15, 18; 4:6^2, 8^2, 9^2, 13; 7:11, 12, 13, 21^2, 26; 8:2, 3; 9:1, 2^3, 3^2, 4, 13, 14, 16; 12:4; 23:22, 25, 28; 30:20, 23; 31:12, 13, 14^2, 15, 16^2, 17, 18, 19, 20^2, 21, 22, 24, 25, 26, 27, 30

Song 6:9^2, 10; 8:5, 8^2, 9^2

Isa 3:26; 8:3; 23:3, 17; 40:2; 49:15; 51:18^2; 66:7^3, 8

Jer 3:1, 6, 7^2, 9; 4:17; 6:6, 7; 11:15; 15:9^3; 33:16; 46:24; 50:9, 12, 14, 15^2, 29^2; 51:8, 9, 42, 53

Lam 1:1^3, 2^2, 3^2, 4, 7, 8^2, 9^3, 10

Ezk 5:6; 16:46, 48, 49; 19:2^2, 3, 5^3, 10, 11^2, 12^2, 13, 14; 23:5^2, 7^3, 8, 9, 10, 11^2, 12, 13, 14^2, 16^2, 17, 18, 19^2, 20, 43; 24:7^2, 12; 26:2^3, 17; 32:20

Dan 11:6^2, 17

Hos 1:6, 8^2; 2:2, 3, 5^2, 6, 7^4, 8, 12, 13^3, 15^2; 13:16

Am 5:2^2

Mic 1:7, 13; 5:3; 7:10^2

Nah 2:7, 10; 3:10^2

Zep 2:15; 3:2^4

Zec 9:4

Mal 2:14

Mt 1:18, 21, 25; 8:15; 9:18, 21; 12:42; 14:7, 8, 11; 15:23, 25, 27; 20:21; 22:28; 26:10, 12^2

Mk 1:31; 5:23^2, 26, 27, 28, 29^2, 42; 6:19, 24^2, 25; 7:26, 28, 30^2; 10:12; 12:23, 42, 44^2; 14:3, 6, 8^3, 9, 67^2; 16:10

Lk 1:29^2, 36, 42, 45, 57^2; 2:6, 7, 36, 37, 38; 4:39; 7:12, 37, 39, 44, 47; 8:42, 47^5, 50, 52, 53, 55; 10:39, 40; 11:31; 13:13; 15:8^2, 9^2; 18:3, 5; 20:33; 21:4^2

Jn 8:11; 11:20, 27, 28^2, 29^2, 31^2, 32; 12:7; 16:21^3; 20:2, 11^2, 13, 14^2, 15, 16, 18

Act 5:8, 10; 9:36, 37, 39, 40^3; 12:14^2, 15; 16:14, 15^3, 18

Ro 7:2, 3^5; 16:2^2

1Co 7:11, 12, 28, 34^3, 36, 39^2, 40^2; 11:5

Gal 4:27

Eph 5:33

1Ti 2:15; 5:5, 6^2, 10^5

Heb 11:11^2, 31

Jas 2:25

Rev 2:21; 6:13; 12:2, 5, 6, 14^2; 14:8; 18:6^2, 7^2, 8, 19; 19:8

SHOULD

Gen 2:18; 4:15; 18:25; 21:7; 23:8; 26:7; 27:45; 29:7, 19; 30:38; 33:13; 34:31; 38:9^2; 40:15; 43:25; 44:7, 8, 17, 22; 47:15, 26

Ex 3:11^2; 5:2; 14:12; 22:3; 32:12; 35:1; 39:7, 23

Lev 4:13, 22; 9:6; 10:18, 19; 11:43; 20:26; 24:23; 26:13; 27:26

Nu 7:9; 9:4; 11:13; 12:14; 14:3, 31; 15:34; 20:4; 23:19^2; 27:4; 32:9; 35:28, 32

Dt 1:18, 33, 39; 4:5, 21^2, 42; 5:25; 17:16; 20:18; 25:3^2; 29:18^2; 32:27^2, 30

Jos 8:29, 33; 9:27; 11:20; 22:28, 29; 24:16

Jdg 8:6, 15; 9:9, 11, 13, 28^2, 38, 41; 20:38; 21:3, 22

Ru 1:12^3

1Sa 2:30; 8:7; 9:6; 10:22; 12:21, 23; 15:21, 29; 17:26; 18:18, 19; 19:1, 17; 20:2, 5; 22:13; 24:6; 26:11; 27:1, 5, 11; 29:4^2

2Sa 2:22[2]; 12:23; 13:26; 15:20; 16:9, 19[2]; 18:12, 13; 19:19, 22, 34, 35, 36, 43; 20:20; 21:5; 23:17

1Ki 1:27; 2:1, 15; 6:6; 8:36; 11:10; 14:2; 21:3

2Ki 3:27; 4:43; 6:33; 7:19; 8:13; 11:9, 17; 17:15, 28; 18:35; 22:19

1Ch 9:28; 11:19; 16:42; 21:17, 18; 23:13, 32; 25:1; 29:14

2Ch 2:6; 4:20; 6:27; 15:13; 20:21; 23:16, 19; 25:13; 29:11, 24; 30:1, 5; 32:4, 14

Ezr 2:63; 4:22; 7:23; 8:17[2]; 9:14[2]; 10:5, 7, 8

Neh 2:3; 5:12; 6:3, 11, 13; 7:65; 8:14, 15; 9:12, 15, 19, 23; 10:37; 11:23; 13:1, 2, 19[3], 22[2]

Est 1:8, 22[2]; 2:10, 11; 3:14; 4:8; 8:13; 9:21, 22, 25[2], 27, 28[2]

Job 3:12, 13[2]; 6:10, 11[2], 14; 8:7; 9:2, 32[2]; 10:19[2]; 11:2[2], 3; 13:5, 9; 15:2, 3, 14[2]; 16:5; 19:28; 21:4, 15[2]; 23:7; 27:5; 31:1, 28; 32:7[2], 13; 34:6, 9, 10[2], 23, 33; 36:16[2]; 41:11

Ps 27:3[2]; 30:3; 38:16; 49:5, 9; 69:22; 73:15; 78:5, 6[2]; 79:10; 81:14, 15[2], 16[2]; 95:11; 104:5; 106:23; 115:2; 119:92; 139:18; 143:8

Prv 8:29; 22:6, 27

Ecc 2:3, 18, 24[2]; 3:13, 14, 22; 5:6; 7:14

Song 1:7; 8:1[2], 3[2]

Isa 1:5, 9[2]; 5:2, 4; 8:11, 19; 10:15[2]; 36:20; 41:7; 48:11, 19; 49:15; 50:4; 51:14[2]; 53:2; 54:9; 57:6, 16; 63:13

Jer 5:17; 20:18; 23:22; 25:29; 26:24; 27:10[2], 17; 29:26; 32:31, 35; 33:20, 21, 24; 34:9[2], 10[2]; 37:10, 21[2]; 39:14; 40:15[2]; 44:14; 46:13; 51:53[2], 60

Lam 1:10, 16, 17; 3:26, 44; 4:12

Ezk 8:6; 13:19[2], 22; 14:3, 14; 18:23[2]; 19:9; 20:9, 14, 22, 25; 21:10; 22:30[2]; 24:8; 33:10; 34:2

Dan 1:3, 10, 16, 18; 2:13, 18, 29, 46; 3:11, 19; 5:15, 29; 6:1, 2, 23; 7:14

Hos 10:3, 10; 13:13

Joel 2:17[2]

Jna 4:11

Mic 6:16

Zep 3:7

Hag 1:2

Zec 7:3, 7, 11, 12; 8:6

Mal 1:13; 2:7[2]

Mt 2:4, 12; 5:29[2], 30[2]; 7:12; 11:3; 12:16; 13:15[4]; 15:33; 16:11, 20; 17:27; 18:14, 30, 34; 19:13; 20:10, 31; 24:22[2]; 25:27; 26:35; 27:20

Mk 3:9[2], 12, 14; 4:12[2], 22, 26, 27[2]; 5:43[2]; 6:8, 12; 7:36; 8:30; 9:9, 10, 18, 30, 34; 10:13, 32, 36, 48, 51; 11:16; 12:19; 13:20; 14:31; 15:11, 24

Lk 1:29, 43, 57, 71; 2:1, 6, 26; 4:42; 5:7; 6:31; 7:4, 19, 20; 8:12, 56; 9:13, 31, 46, 51; 15:32; 17:2, 6, 20; 18:39; 19:11, 27, 40; 20:10, 20, 28; 22:23, 24; 23:24; 24:16, 21, 47

Jn 1:31; 2:25; 3:15, 16, 20; 5:23; 6:14, 39[2], 64, 71; 7:23, 39; 8:5, 19, 55; 9:3, 22, 41; 11:27, 37, 50, 51, 52, 57; 12:4, 23, 33, 40[2], 42, 46, 49[2]; 13:1, 11, 15, 24[2], 29; 14:7; 15:16[2]; 16:1, 30; 17:2; 18:4, 14, 28, 32, 36, 37, 39; 19:31, 36; 21:19, 23, 25[2]

Act 1:4; 2:24, 25, 47; 3:18; 5:26, 28, 40; 6:2; 7:6[2], 44; 8:31; 10:17, 28, 47; 11:22, 28; 12:19; 13:28, 46; 14:15; 15:2, 7; 17:27; 18:14; 19:4[2], 27[2]; 20:38; 21:4, 16, 26; 22:22, 24, 29; 23:10, 27; 24:23, 26; 25:4; 26:8[2], 20, 22, 23[4]; 27:1, 17, 20, 21, 29, 42, 43; 28:6, 27[3]

Ro 2:21, 22; 4:13; 6:4, 6, 12; 7:4[2], 6; 8:26; 11:8[2], 11, 25[2]; 15:16, 20

1Co 1:15, 17, 29; 2:5; 4:3; 5:1; 9:10[2], 12, 14, 15[2], 27; 10:1, 6, 20; 11:31, 32; 12:25[2]

2Co 1:9, 17; 2:3, 4, 7, 11; 4:4; 5:15; 8:20; 9:3, 4; 10:8[2]; 11:3; 12:6, 7[2]; 13:7[2], 10

Gal 1:10; 2:2, 9, 10; 3:1, 17, 19, 21, 23; 5:7; 6:12, 14

Eph 1:4, 12; 2:9, 10; 3:6, 8; 5:27

Php 1:12; 2:10, 11, 27

Col 1:19; 2:4

1Th 3:3, 4; 4:3, 4; 5:4, 10

2Th 2:11; 3:10

1Ti 1:16

Tit 2:12; 3:7

Phlm 14

Heb 2:1, 9; 3:18; 4:1; 7:11; 8:4, 7; 9:23, 25; 10:2, 4; 11:5, 8, 28, 40; 12:19

Jas 1:18

1Pt 1:10, 11; 2:9, 21, 24; 3:9; 4:2

2Pt 2:6; 3:9[2]

1Jn 3:1, 11, 23; 4:3

2Jn 6

Jude 3, 18[2]

Rev 6:4, 11[3]; 7:1; 8:3; 9:4, 5[2], 20; 10:6, 7; 11:18; 12:6; 13:14, 15[2]; 19:8, 15; 20:3[2]

SHOULDEST

Gen 3:11; 14:23; 26:10; 29:15

Nu 11:12

Dt 4:19; 26:18; 29:12; 30:12, 13

Jdg 11:23

Ru 2:10

1Sa 20:8

2Sa 9:8

1Ki 1:20

2Ki 8:14; 13:19; 14:10[2]; 19:25

1Ch 17:7

2Ch 19:2; 25:16, 19[2]

Job 7:17[2], 18; 10:3[2]; 38:20[2]

Ps 50:16; 130:3

Prv 5:6; 25:7; 27:22

Ecc 5:5[2]; 7:16, 17, 18

Isa 37:26; 48:5, 7, 17; 49:6; 51:12

Jer 14:8, 9; 29:26; 49:16

Oba 12[3], 13[2], 14[2]

Mt 8:8; 18:33

Mk 10:35

Lk 7:6

Jn 11:40; 17:15[2]

Act 13:47; 22:14[2]

Tit 1:5

Phlm 15

Rev 11:18[2]

SO

Gen 1:7, 9, 11, 15, 24, 27, 30; 3:24; 6:22; 8:11; 11:8; 12:4, 19; 13:6, 16; 15:5; 18:5; 19:7, 11, 18; 20:17; 21:6; 22:8, 19; 24:46; 25:22; 27:1, 20, 23; 28:21; 29:26, 28; 30:33, 42; 31:21, 28, 36; 32:19, 21; 33:16; 34:12; 35:6; 37:14; 40:7; 41:4, 13, 21, 39, 57; 42:20[2], 34; 43:6, 11, 34; 44:5, 17; 45:8, 21, 24; 47:13, 20, 28; 48:10, 18; 49:17; 50:3, 17, 26

Ex 1:10; 2:18; 4:26; 5:12, 22; 6:9; 7:6, 10, 20, 22; 8:7, 17, 18[2], 24, 26; 9:24; 10:10, 11, 15, 20; 11:10; 12:28, 36, 50; 14:4, 20, 25, 28; 15:22; 16:17, 30, 34; 17:6, 10; 18:22, 23, 24; 19:16, 25; 21:12, 22; 22:6; 25:9, 33; 27:8; 28:7; 30:21, 23; 32:21, 24; 33:16; 36:6, 13; 37:19; 39:32, 42, 43; 40:16, 33

Lev 4:20; 7:7; 8:34, 35, 36; 10:5, 13; 11:32; 14:13, 21; 16:4, 16; 24:19, 20; 26:15; 27:12, 14

Nu 1:19, 45, 54; 2:17, 34[2]; 4:26; 5:4[2]; 6:21; 8:3, 4, 7, 20, 22; 9:5, 14, 16, 20, 21; 12:7; 13:21, 33; 14:28; 15:12, 14, 15, 20; 16:27; 17:11[2]; 20:8; 21:35; 22:30, 35; 25:8; 31:5; 32:23, 28, 31; 35:7, 16, 29, 33; 36:3, 4, 7, 10

Dt 1:11, 15, 43, 46; 2:5, 16; 3:3, 21, 29; 4:5, 7[2], 8[2]; 7:4, 19; 8:5, 20; 9:3, 8, 15; 12:4, 10, 22, 30, 31; 13:5; 14:24; 17:7; 18:14; 19:10, 19; 20:18; 21:9, 21; 22:3, 5, 21, 22, 24, 26; 24:8; 25:9; 28:34, 54, 55, 63; 29:22; 30:17; 31:17; 32:12; 33:25; 34:5, 8

Jos 1:5, 17; 2:21, 23; 3:7; 4:8; 5:15; 6:11, 14, 20[2], 27; 7:4, 16, 22, 26; 8:3, 22[2], 25; 9:26; 10:1, 7, 13, 23, 39, 40; 11:7, 15[2], 16, 23; 14:5, 11, 12; 15:7; 16:4; 19:51; 21:40; 22:6, 25, 28; 23:15; 24:10, 25, 28

Jdg 1:3, 7, 35; 2:14, 17; 3:14, 22, 30; 4:14, 15, 21, 23; 5:28, 31; 6:3, 20, 27, 38, 40; 7:1, 5, 8, 15, 17, 19; 8:18, 21, 28; 9:49; 10:9; 11:5, 10, 21, 23, 24, 32; 12:5; 13:19; 14:10[2], 15; 15:11; 16:9, 16, 30; 17:10; 18:21; 19:4, 21, 23, 24, 25, 30; 20:11, 36, 46; 21:14, 23

Ru 1:17, 19, 22; 2:7, 17, 23; 4:8, 13

1Sa 1:7[2], 9, 18, 23; 2:3, 5, 14, 21; 3:9, 17; 4:4, 5; 5:7, 9, 11; 6:10; 7:13; 8:8; 9:10, 21, 24; 10:9; 11:7, 11[2]; 12:18; 13:22; 14:15, 23, 24, 44, 45, 47; 15:6, 31, 33; 16:13, 23; 17:27, 50; 18:30; 19:12, 17, 18; 20:2, 13, 16, 24, 34; 21:6; 22:14; 23:5[2]; 24:7; 25:12, 20, 21, 22, 25, 35; 26:7, 12, 24, 25; 27:1, 11[2]; 28:23; 29:8, 11; 30:3, 9, 10, 21, 23, 24, 25; 31:6

2Sa 1:2, 10; 2:2, 16, 28, 31; 3:9[2], 20, 30, 34, 35; 5:3, 9, 25; 6:10, 12, 13, 15, 19; 7:8, 17; 8:2; 9:11, 13; 10:14, 19; 11:12, 20[2], 22; 12:31; 13:2, 6, 8, 15, 20, 35, 38; 14:3, 7, 17, 23, 24, 25, 28, 33; 15:2, 5, 6, 9, 34, 37; 16:10[2], 19, 22, 23; 17:3, 12[2], 26; 18:6; 19:13, 14, 15; 20:2, 3, 5, 10[2], 18, 21; 22:4, 35, 37; 23:5; 24:8, 13, 15, 24, 25

1Ki 1:3, 6, 30, 36, 37, 38, 40, 45, 53; 2:7, 10, 23, 27, 34, 38, 46; 3:9, 12, 13; 4:1; 5:4, 10, 18; 6:7, 9, 14, 20, 21, 26, 27, 33, 38; 7:9, 18, 22, 40, 51; 8:11, 25, 46, 48, 54, 63; 9:25; 10:13, 23, 29; 11:19; 12:12, 16[2], 19, 32, 33; 13:4, 9, 10, 13, 19; 14:4, 6, 28; 15:20; 16:6, 22, 28; 17:5, 10, 17; 18:4, 6, 12, 16, 20, 42; 19:2, 13, 19; 20:10, 19, 25, 29, 32, 34, 37, 38, 40; 21:5, 8; 22:8, 12, 15, 22, 29, 37, 40

2Ki 1:17; 2:2, 4, 8, 10[2], 22; 3:9, 12, 24; 4:5, 8, 25, 36, 40, 44; 5:8, 9, 12, 19, 21; 6:4, 23, 29, 31; 7:10, 16, 20; 8:6, 9, 14, 15, 21; 9:4, 14, 16, 18, 22[2], 27, 33, 37; 10:11, 16, 21; 11:2, 6; 12:6, 10; 13:5, 24; 15:5, 7, 12, 20; 16:7, 11; 17:4, 7, 23, 25, 32, 41[2]; 18:5, 21; 19:5, 8, 36; 22:14; 23:18; 24:6; 25:6, 21

1Ch 9:1, 23; 10:4, 6, 13; 11:6, 9; 13:4, 5, 13; 14:11; 15:14, 17, 19, 25; 16:1, 37; 17:15; 18:14; 19:2, 7, 14, 17; 20:3; 21:3, 11, 14, 25; 22:5; 23:1; 25:7; 29:14

2Ch 1:3, 10, 17; 2:3; 5:14; 6:16, 31; 7:5, 21; 8:14, 16; 9:12; 10:3, 12, 15, 16; 11:17; 12:9, 13; 13:9, 13, 17; 14:1, 7, 12; 15:10; 17:10; 18:7, 11, 21, 28, 29; 19:10; 20:6, 20[2], 25, 30; 21:10, 17, 19; 22:1, 9, 11[2]; 23:8, 15; 24:13, 24; 25:21; 26:23; 27:5, 6; 28:14; 29:17, 22, 25, 34, 35; 30:5, 6, 9, 10, 26; 32:4, 17, 21, 23, 26; 33:8, 9, 20; 34:6, 26, 28; 35:6, 10, 12, 16

Ezr 2:70; 3:13; 4:13, 15, 24; 5:17; 6:13; 8:23, 30; 9:2, 14; 10:12, 16

Neh 2:4, 6, 11, 15, 18; 4:6, 10, 18, 21, 23; 5:12, 13, 15; 6:3, 13, 15; 7:73; 8:8, 11, 16, 17; 9:10, 11, 21, 22, 24, 25, 28; 12:40, 43; 13:20, 21

Est 1:8, 13, 17; 2:4, 8, 12, 16, 17; 3:2; 4:4, 6, 16, 17; 5:2[2], 5, 13; 6:6, 10; 7:1, 5, 10; 8:4, 14; 9:14, 27

Job 1:3, 5, 12; 2:7, 13; 5:12, 16, 27; 7:3, 9, 15, 20; 8:13; 9:2, 30, 35; 13:9; 14:12; 21:4; 23:7; 24:19, 25; 27:6; 32:1, 22; 33:20; 34:25, 28; 35:15; 36:16; 41:10, 16; 42:7, 9, 12, 15, 17

Ps 1:4; 7:7; 18:3, 34; 21:13; 22:1; 26:6; 35:25; 37:3; 40:12; 42:1; 45:11; 48:5, 8, 10; 58:5, 11; 61:8; 63:2; 64:8; 65:9; 68:2[2]; 72:7; 73:20, 22; 77:4, 13; 78:21, 29, 53, 60, 72; 79:13; 80:12, 18; 81:12; 83:15; 90:11, 12; 102:4, 15; 103:5, 11, 12, 13, 15; 104:25; 106:9, 30, 32, 33; 107:2, 29, 30, 38; 109:17[2], 18; 115:8; 119:27, 42, 44, 88, 134; 123:2; 125:2; 127:2, 4; 135:18; 147:20

Prv 1:19; 2:2; 3:4, 10, 22; 6:11, 29; 7:13; 10:25, 26; 11:19, 22; 15:7; 19:24; 20:30; 23:7; 24:14, 29, 34; 25:12, 13, 16, 17, 20, 23, 25, 27; 26:1, 2, 7, 8, 9, 11, 14, 19, 20, 21; 27:8, 9, 17, 18, 19, 20, 21; 28:15; 30:33; 31:11

Ecc 2:9, 15; 3:11, 19[2]; 4:1; 5:16; 6:2, 3; 7:6; 8:10[2]; 9:2, 12; 10:1; 11:5

Song 2:2, 3; 5:9

Isa 5:24; 6:13; 10:7[2], 11, 26; 14:24[2]; 16:2, 6; 18:4; 20:2, 4; 21:1; 22:22; 23:1, 5; 24:2[6]; 26:17; 28:8; 29:8; 30:14; 31:4, 5; 36:6; 37:5, 8, 37; 38:8, 13, 14, 16; 40:20; 41:7; 47:7, 12[2]; 52:14, 15; 53:7; 54:9; 55:9, 11; 59:19; 60:15; 61:11; 62:5[2]; 63:8, 14; 65:8; 66:13, 22

Jer 2:26, 36; 3:20; 5:19, 27, 31; 6:7; 9:10; 10:18; 11:4, 5; 13:2, 5, 11; 17:11; 18:4, 6; 19:11; 21:2; 24:2, 3, 5, 8[2]; 26:3, 7; 28:6, 11, 17; 29:17; 30:7; 31:28; 32:8, 11, 42; 33:22, 26; 34:5; 35:11; 36:14, 15, 21; 37:14; 38:6, 11, 12, 13, 16, 20, 23, 27, 28; 39:13, 14; 40:5; 41:7, 8, 14; 42:17, 18, 20; 43:4, 7; 44:14, 22; 46:18; 48:30[2], 39; 50:40; 51:8, 49, 60; 52:5, 6, 26

Lam 2:22; 3:29; 4:14; 5:20

Ezk 1:18, 28; 3:2, 14; 4:5; 5:15, 17; 6:14; 8:5, 10; 11:24; 12:7, 11; 13:14[2]; 14:15, 17; 15:6; 16:16, 42, 44; 17:6; 18:4, 30; 19:14; 20:36; 21:24; 22:20, 22; 23:18, 27, 44; 24:18, 19; 28:14; 31:9; 33:7; 34:12; 35:15; 36:38; 37:7, 10, 23; 38:20; 39:7, 10, 22, 23; 40:5, 47; 41:4, 7, 13, 18, 19; 43:5, 15, 27; 45:20[2]; 47:21

Dan 1:5, 14; 2:2, 15, 42; 3:17; 5:6; 6:23, 28; 7:16; 8:4, 17; 10:7; 11:9, 15, 30

Hos 1:3; 3:2, 3; 4:7; 6:9; 8:7; 10:15; 11:2; 13:6; 14:2

Joel 2:4; 3:17

Am 3:12; 4:8; 5:9, 14

Oba 16

Jna 1:3, 4, 6[2], 7, 12, 15; 3:3, 5; 4:5, 6

Mic 2:2; 5:14; 7:3

Zep 3:6, 7

Hag 2:5, 14[3]

Zec 1:6, 14, 21; 3:5; 4:4; 6:7; 7:3, 13; 8:13, 15; 10:1; 11:11, 12; 14:15

Mal 3:13

Mt 1:17; 3:15; 5:12, 16, 19, 47; 6:30; 7:12, 17; 8:10, 13, 28, 31; 9:19, 33; 11:26[2]; 12:40, 45; 13:2, 27, 32, 40, 49; 15:33[2]; 18:13, 14, 31, 35; 19:8, 10, 12; 20:8, 16, 26, 34; 22:10; 23:28; 24:27, 33, 37, 39, 46; 25:9, 20; 27:64, 66; 28:15

Mk 2:2, 8; 3:20[2]; 4:1, 17, 26, 32, 37, 40; 6:31; 7:18, 36; 8:8; 9:3; 10:8, 43; 13:29; 14:59; 15:5, 15, 39; 16:19

Lk 1:21, 60; 2:6, 21; 5:7, 10, 15; 6:3, 10, 26; 7:9; 9:15; 10:21[2]; 11:2, 30; 12:21, 28, 38, 43, 54; 14:21, 33; 16:5, 26; 17:10, 24, 26; 18:13, 39; 20:15, 20; 21:31, 34; 22:26; 24:24

Jn 3:8, 14, 16; 4:40, 46, 53; 5:21, 26; 6:9, 10, 19, 57; 7:43; 8:7, 59; 10:15; 11:28; 12:37, 50; 13:12, 13, 33; 14:2, 9, 31; 15:8, 9; 17:18; 18:15, 22; 20:4, 20, 21; 21:11, 15

Act 1:11; 3:12, 18; 4:21; 5:8[2], 32; 7:1, 5, 8, 15, 19, 51; 8:32; 10:14; 11:8; 12:8, 15; 13:4, 8, 47; 14:1; 15:30, 39[2]; 16:5, 26; 17:11, 33; 19:2, 10, 12, 14, 16, 20, 22, 27; 20:11, 13, 24, 35; 21:11, 35; 22:24; 23:7, 11, 18, 22; 24:9, 14; 27:17, 44; 28:9, 14

Ro 1:15, 20; 4:18; 5:3, 11, 12, 15, 16, 18, 19, 21; 6:3, 4, 19; 7:2, 3[2], 25; 8:8, 9, 17; 9:16; 10:17; 11:5, 16, 26, 31; 12:5, 20; 14:12; 15:19, 20

1Co 1:7; 2:11; 3:7, 15; 4:1; 5:1, 3; 6:5; 7:17[2], 26, 36, 37, 38, 40; 8:12; 9:14, 15, 24, 26[2]; 11:12, 28; 12:12; 13:2; 14:9, 10, 12, 25; 15:11[2], 15, 22, 42, 45, 54; 16:1

2Co 1:5, 7, 10; 2:7; 3:7; 4:12; 5:3; 7:7, 14; 8:6, 11; 9:7; 10:7; 11:3, 9, 22[3]; 12:16

Gal 1:6, 9; 3:3, 4, 9; 4:3, 29, 31; 5:17; 6:2

Eph 2:15; 4:20, 21; 5:24, 28, 33

Php 1:13, 20; 2:23; 3:17; 4:1

Col 2:6; 3:13

1Th 1:7, 8; 2:4, 8; 4:1, 14, 17; 5:2

2Th 1:4; 2:4; 3:17

1Ti 1:4; 3:11; 6:20

2Ti 3:8

Heb 1:4; 2:3; 3:11, 19; 4:7; 5:3, 5; 6:15; 7:9, 22; 9:28; 10:25, 33; 11:3, 12; 12:1[2], 20, 21; 13:6

Jas 1:11; 2:12[2], 17, 26; 3:4, 5, 6, 10, 12

1Pt 1:15; 2:3, 15; 3:17; 4:10; 5:13

2Pt 1:11

1Jn 2:6; 4:11, 17

Rev 1:7; 2:15; 3:16; 8:12; 13:13; 16:7, 18[2]; 17:3; 18:7, 17; 22:20

THAN

Gen 3:1; 4:13; 19:9; 25:23; 26:16; 29:19, 30; 34:19; 36:7; 37:3, 4; 38:26; 39:9; 41:40; 48:19

Ex 1:9; 14:12; 18:11; 30:15; 36:5

Lev 13:3, 4, 20, 21, 25, 26, 30, 31, 32, 34; 14:37; 27:8

Nu 3:46; 13:31; 14:12; 22:15; 24:7

Dt 1:28; 4:38; 7:1, 7, 17; 9:1, 14; 11:23; 20:1

Jos 10:2, 11

Jdg 2:19; 8:2; 11:25; 14:18[2]; 15:2, 3; 16:30

Ru 3:10, 12; 4:15

1Sa 1:8; 9:2[2]; 10:23; 15:22[2], 28; 18:30; 24:17; 27:1

2Sa 1:23[2]; 6:22; 13:14, 15, 16; 17:14; 18:8; 19:7, 43[2]; 20:5, 6; 23:23

1Ki 1:37, 47[2]; 2:32; 4:31[2]; 12:10; 16:25, 33; 19:4; 20:23[2], 25; 21:2

2Ki 5:12; 6:16; 9:35; 21:9

1Ch 4:9; 11:21; 24:4

2Ch 10:10; 20:25; 21:13; 25:9; 29:34; 30:18; 32:7; 33:9

Ezr 9:13

Est 1:19; 2:17; 4:13; 6:6

Job 3:21; 4:17[2]; 6:3; 7:6, 15; 9:25; 11:6, 8, 9[2], 17; 15:10; 23:2, 12; 30:1, 8; 32:2, 4; 33:12, 25; 34:19, 23; 35:2, 5, 11[2]; 36:21; 42:12

Ps 4:7; 8:5; 19:10[3]; 37:16; 40:5, 12; 45:2; 51:7; 52:3[2]; 55:21[2]; 61:2; 62:9; 63:3; 69:4, 31; 73:7; 76:4; 84:10[2]; 87:2; 89:27; 93:4[2]; 105:24; 118:8, 9; 119:72, 98, 99, 100, 103; 130:6[2]; 139:18; 142:6

Prv 3:14[2], 15; 5:3; 8:10, 11, 19[3]; 11:24; 12:9, 26; 15:16, 17; 16:8, 16[2], 19, 32[2]; 17:1, 10, 12; 18:19, 24; 19:1, 22; 21:3, 9, 19; 22:1[2]; 25:7, 24; 26:12, 16; 27:3, 5, 10; 28:6, 23; 29:20; 30:2

Ecc 1:16; 2:9, 16, 24, 25; 3:22; 4:2, 3, 6, 9, 13; 5:1, 5, 8[2]; 6:3, 5, 8, 9, 10; 7:1[2], 2, 3, 5, 8[2], 10, 19, 26; 8:15; 9:4, 16, 17, 18

Song 1:2, 4; 4:10[2]; 5:9[2]

Isa 13:12[2]; 28:20[2]; 33:19; 40:17; 52:14[2]; 54:1; 55:9[3]; 56:5; 57:8; 65:5

Jer 3:11; 4:13; 5:3; 7:26; 8:3; 16:12; 20:7; 31:11; 46:23

Lam 4:6, 7[3], 8, 9, 19

Ezk 3:9; 5:6[2], 7; 6:14; 8:15; 15:2[2]; 16:47, 51, 52[2]; 23:11[2]; 28:3; 36:11; 42:5[3], 6

Dan 1:10, 15, 20; 2:30; 3:19; 7:20; 8:3; 11:2, 8, 13

Hos 2:7; 6:6

Am 6:2[2]

Jna 4:3, 8, 11

Mic 7:4

Nah 3:8

Hab 1:8[2], 13[2]

Hag 2:9

Mt 3:11; 5:37, 47; 6:25[2], 26; 10:15, 31, 37[2]; 11:9, 11[2], 22, 24; 12:6, 12, 41, 42, 45[2]; 18:8, 9, 13; 19:24; 21:36; 23:15; 26:53; 27:64

Mk 1:7; 4:31, 32; 6:11; 8:14; 9:43, 45, 47; 10:25; 12:31, 33, 43; 14:5

Lk 3:13, 16; 7:26, 28[2]; 10:12, 14; 11:22, 26[2], 31, 32; 12:7, 23[2], 24; 14:8; 15:7; 16:8, 17; 17:2; 18:14, 25; 21:3

Jn 1:50; 3:19; 4:1, 12; 5:20, 36; 7:31; 8:53; 10:29; 12:43; 13:16[2]; 14:12, 28; 15:13, 20; 21:15

Act 4:19; 5:29; 15:28; 17:11; 20:35; 23:13, 21; 25:6; 26:22; 27:11

Ro 1:25; 3:9; 8:37; 12:3; 13:11

1Co 1:25[2]; 3:11; 7:9; 9:15; 10:22; 14:5, 18, 19; 15:10

2Co 1:13

Gal 1:8, 9; 4:27

Eph 3:8

Php 2:3

1Ti 1:4; 5:8

2Ti 3:4

Phlm 21

Heb 1:4[2]; 2:7, 9; 3:3[2]; 4:12; 7:26; 9:23; 11:4, 25, 26; 12:24

1Pt 1:7; 3:17

2Pt 2:20, 21

1Jn 3:20; 4:4

3Jn 4

Rev 2:19

THAT

Gen 1:4, 10, 12, 18, 20[2], 21[2], 25[2], 26, 28, 30, 31; 2:3, 4, 9, 11, 12, 13, 14, 17, 18, 19; 3:5, 6[2], 7, 11[2], 13; 4:3, 8, 14[2]; 5:1, 5; 6:2[2], 3, 4, 5[2], 6, 7, 17, 21, 22; 7:2, 4, 5, 8[2], 10, 14, 16, 19, 21[2], 22, 23; 8:1, 6, 11, 17[3]; 9:2, 3, 10[2], 12, 14, 16[2], 17, 18; 10:11; 11:2, 7; 12:1, 3[2], 5[2], 11[2], 12, 13, 14[2], 18[2], 20; 13:1, 6[2], 10, 14, 16; 14:2, 5, 7, 10, 13, 14, 17, 23[3], 24; 15:4, 7, 8, 13[2], 14, 17[2]; 16:2, 4, 5, 10, 13[2]; 17:12[2], 13[2], 14, 17[2], 18, 23[2]; 18:5, 17, 18, 19[3], 24, 25[3]; 19:5, 11[2], 14, 17, 21, 25, 29, 32, 33, 34[2], 35; 20:6, 7[2], 9[2], 10, 13, 16; 21:3, 6[2], 7, 8, 12, 22[3], 23[2], 30[2], 31; 22:1, 12, 14, 17, 20; 23:4, 6, 8, 9, 10, 11, 15, 17[2], 18, 20; 24:2[2], 3, 6, 7, 9, 11, 14[4], 15, 22, 30, 32, 36, 43, 49, 52, 54, 55, 56, 65, 66; 25:5, 11, 18, 26, 30; 26:1, 5, 8, 11, 12, 21, 22, 28, 29, 32; 27:1[2], 4[2], 7, 8, 10[2], 19, 20, 21, 25, 29[2], 30, 31, 33, 40, 45; 28:3, 4, 6[2], 7, 8, 11[2], 15, 18, 19[2], 20, 21, 22; 29:2, 7, 10, 12[2], 13, 19[2], 21, 23, 25, 31, 33; 30:1, 3, 9, 15, 16, 25[2], 27, 33[2], 35[4], 38, 41[2]; 31:1[2], 5, 6, 10[2], 12, 16, 19, 20[2], 21, 22, 24, 26, 27, 29, 32, 35, 36, 37, 39, 43, 52[2]; 32:2, 5, 7, 13[2], 19, 20, 21, 22, 23, 25, 29, 32; 33:9, 11, 13, 14, 15, 16; 34:5, 14[2], 15, 24[2], 25, 28[2], 29; 35:1, 2[2], 5, 6[2], 17, 18, 20, 22[2]; 36:7, 16, 17, 18, 24[2], 29, 30, 31, 40; 37:4, 10, 22[2], 23[2]; 38:1[2], 9[3], 14, 16[2], 18, 21[2], 22, 24, 26, 27, 28, 29, 30; 39:3[3], 4, 5[4], 6, 7, 8, 10, 11, 13, 14, 15[2], 18, 19, 22, 23[2]; 40:1, 7, 15, 16, 20; 41:1, 8[2], 15[2], 21, 24, 27, 31, 32, 35, 36[2], 53, 57; 42:1, 2[2], 5, 6, 14[2], 16, 21, 23, 28, 29, 33, 34[2], 35; 43:7, 8, 12, 14, 15, 18[2], 21, 25, 32; 44:2, 7, 15[2], 17, 21, 27, 30, 31[2], 34; 45:1, 5, 8, 10, 11, 12[2], 13, 15, 24; 46:1, 26, 32, 34[2]; 47:1, 13, 14, 17, 18[2], 19[2], 24, 26, 29; 48:1, 10, 17, 20; 49:1[2], 15[2], 17[2], 25, 26, 28, 29, 30, 32; 50:14, 15

Ex 1:5, 6, 10, 21, 22; 2:2, 7, 11, 12[2], 13, 18, 20[2], 23; 3:4, 8, 10, 11[2], 12, 14, 16, 18, 19, 20, 21, 22; 4:2, 5[2], 8, 9, 14, 21[2], 23, 24, 31[2]; 5:1, 2, 9, 19, 22; 6:7, 11, 26, 27, 29[2]; 7:2[2], 4, 5, 13, 16, 17[2], 18, 19[2], 20[2], 21, 25; 8:1, 8[2], 9, 10[2], 15, 16, 20, 22[3], 28, 29; 9:1, 4, 6, 13, 14[2], 15, 16, 17, 19, 20, 21, 22, 25, 28, 29[2], 30, 34; 10:1, 2[3], 3, 5[2], 6, 7[2], 8, 11[2], 12[2], 13[2], 15, 17, 20, 21, 25, 28; 11:5[2], 7[2], 8[2], 9, 10; 12:8, 10, 15, 16[2], 19[2], 22[2], 25, 27, 29[3], 33, 36, 37, 41, 42, 44, 48, 49[2], 51; 13:5, 8[2], 9, 12[3], 14, 15[2], 17[2]; 14:2, 4[3], 5[2], 12[3], 15, 18, 20, 21, 24, 25[2], 26, 28, 30, 31; 15:7, 26[2]; 16:4, 5[2], 6, 7[2], 8, 10, 12, 13, 14, 18[2], 22, 23[4], 25, 27, 29, 32; 17:2, 3, 6, 11, 16; 18:1[2], 8[2], 11, 13, 14[2], 17, 18, 19, 20, 22, 24; 19:8, 9, 12, 16[3]; 20:4[3], 5, 6, 7, 10, 11, 12, 17, 20[2], 22, 26; 21:12[2], 14, 15, 16, 17, 19, 22, 26, 28, 29, 35, 36; 22:2, 6[2], 11, 13, 16, 20, 25, 26, 27[2], 31; 23:5, 11, 12, 13, 22; 24:7, 12; 25:2[2], 8, 9, 14, 21, 26, 28, 33, 35, 37, 40; 26:5[2], 10, 11, 12[2], 13[2], 33; 27:5, 20; 28:1, 3[3], 4, 28[2], 32, 35, 37, 38[2], 41, 43; 29:1, 13[3], 21, 22[2], 23, 27[2], 30[2], 32, 38, 46[3]; 30:6[2], 12, 13[2], 14[2], 16, 20, 21, 29, 30, 38; 31:6[3], 7, 11, 13[3], 14[2]; 32:1[2], 10[2], 13, 18[3], 19, 21, 22, 23, 25, 28, 29, 30; 33:5, 7, 8, 13[3], 16[3], 17, 22; 34:1, 3, 7, 10, 11, 19[2], 29[2], 32, 34, 35; 35:1, 10, 22, 24, 25[2], 34, 35[2]; 36:1, 4, 8, 18, 19; 37:8, 13; 38:15, 22, 24, 25, 26[2]; 39:5, 7, 21[2], 23, 32, 42; 40:4, 9, 13, 15, 16, 17, 37

Lev 1:5, 8, 12, 17; 2:8, 10; 3:3[2], 4, 5, 9[2], 10, 14[2], 15, 17; 4:3, 5, 8[2], 9, 16, 18, 35; 5:3, 4, 5[3], 8, 11, 13, 16; 6:2, 3[2], 4[3], 5, 7, 18, 22, 26, 27; 7:3, 4[2], 7, 8, 9[3], 14, 15, 16, 18[2], 19[2], 20[3], 21[2], 24[2], 25, 27[2], 29, 30, 33, 36, 38; 8:10, 16, 25, 26, 31, 32, 35; 9:1, 5, 6, 19; 10:3[2], 10, 11, 12[2], 20; 11:2, 3, 4[2], 9, 10[2], 12, 20, 21, 26, 27, 28, 29, 31, 34[2], 36, 39, 40[2], 41, 42, 43[2], 44, 45, 46[2], 47[2]; 12:7; 13:4, 7, 8, 12, 13, 17, 24, 31[2], 33, 37, 39, 41, 47, 50, 51, 52, 54, 55, 57; 14:4, 5, 6, 7, 8[3], 9, 11[2], 14, 16, 17[2], 18[2], 19, 25, 27, 28[2], 29[2], 31, 32, 35, 36[3], 40, 41, 43, 46[2], 47[2]; 15:4, 6[2], 7[2], 8[2], 9, 10[2], 11, 12, 13, 20[2], 22, 28, 31[2], 32, 33[4]; 16:2[2], 13[3], 15[2], 16, 18, 26, 28, 29[2], 30[2]; 17:3[2], 4[2], 5[2], 8, 9, 10[4], 11, 12, 13[2], 15[3]; 18:6, 26, 28[2], 29, 30[2]; 19:8[2], 13, 20, 25, 31, 34; 20:2[2], 3, 5[2], 6[2], 9, 10[2], 11, 14, 22, 24, 25, 26, 27[2]; 21:2[2], 3, 7, 10[2], 17, 18[2], 19, 20, 21, 23; 22:2[2], 3[2], 4, 8, 11, 18, 20, 23[2], 24, 33; 23:12, 14, 15, 21, 28, 29[2], 30[2], 42, 43[2]; 24:2, 7, 12, 14[2], 16[2], 17, 18, 21[2], 23[2]; 25:5, 6, 7, 11[2], 25, 27, 28[2], 30[2], 33, 35, 36, 39, 44, 45[2], 47, 48, 49, 50[2], 51; 26:13, 15[2], 16, 17, 25, 36, 39, 40, 41, 44, 45; 27:8, 9, 15, 18, 19, 23, 28[2]

Nu 1:3, 5, 20, 21, 22[2], 23, 24, 25, 26, 27, 28, 29, 30, 31, 32, 33, 34, 35, 36, 37, 38, 39, 40, 41, 42, 43, 44, 45[2], 46, 50, 51, 53, 54; 2:4, 5, 6, 8, 9, 11, 13, 15, 16, 19, 21, 23, 24, 26, 27, 28, 30, 31, 32, 34; 3:1, 6, 10, 12, 13, 22[2], 32, 34, 36, 38[2], 39, 43, 46, 49[2], 51; 4:3, 15, 16, 19, 23, 25, 26, 30, 35, 36, 37[2], 38, 39, 40, 41[2], 42, 43, 44, 45, 46, 47, 48; 5:2[2], 3, 6[2], 17, 18, 19, 22, 24[2], 27[3]; 6:4, 6, 11[2], 12, 20, 21[2]; 7:1, 2[2], 5, 9, 10, 12, 88, 89; 8:11, 15, 17, 19, 20, 22, 24; 9:4, 5, 6[3], 7, 13[2], 14, 15, 17, 21[2], 22; 10:2, 5, 6, 9, 10, 11, 32, 35[2]; 11:1, 4, 11, 12, 13, 16, 17, 20, 21, 25[2], 26, 29[2], 32[3], 34[2]; 12:14; 13:2, 18, 19[2], 28, 31, 32[2]; 14:1, 2,

3, 6, 14^4, 23, 29, 35, 37, 38, 42, 45; **15:**4, 12, 13, 15, 16, 19, 23^2, 24, 26, 28, 29^3, 30^2, 31, 32, 33, 38^2, 39^2, 40; **16:**7, 9, 11, 13^2, 14, 21, 28, 30^2, 31^2, 32, 33, 34, 35, 37, 39, 40^2, 42, 45, 49^2; **17:**5, 8, 10; **18:**2, 3, 5, 7, 11, 13, 15, 16, 23; **19:**2, 3, 8, 9, 10^2, 11, 13^2, 14^2, 16, 18^2, 20^2, 21^3, 22; **20:**3, 4, 14, 29; **21:**1, 7, 8^2, 9, 13, 15, 16, 20, 27, 29, 32; **22:**2, 4^2, 6^3, 19, 20, 24, 28, 34, 35^2, 36, 38^2, 40, 41^2; **23:**12, 19^2, 26^2, 27, 28; **24:**1, 9^2, 13, 19^2, 20; **25:**4, 5, 9, 11, 14^2, 15; **26:**1, 2, 7, 9, 10, 18, 22, 25, 27, 34, 37, 41, 43, 47, 50, 54, 57, 62, 63; **27:**3, 11, 14, 17, 20; **29:**40; **30:**2, 5, 7, 8^2, 9, 14, 15; **31:**8, 17, 18, 20, 23^2, 26, 27, 35, 36, 42, 43, 52; **32:**1, 9, 11, 13, 24, 32; **33:**55, 56; **34:**2; **35:**2, 6, 8^2, 11, 12, 15^2, 16, 20, 21^2, 23, 32^2, 33^2; **36:**8^2

Dt **1:**3^2, 9, 16^2, 17, 18, 19, 30, 31^2, 35, 36, 39, 41, 44, 46; **2:**6^2, 17, 20, 25, 28^2, 30, 31, 34, 36; **3:**4, 8^2, 12, 18^2, 19, 21^2, 23, 24, 25^2; **4:**1, 2, 3, 4, 5, 7, 8, 10^4, 14^2, 15, 17^2, 18^2, 21^3, 22, 26, 32^2, 34, 35^2, 36, 39, 40^2, 42^2; **5:**1, 5, 8^3, 9, 10, 11, 14^2, 15^2, 16^2, 21, 23, 24, 26, 27^2, 28, 29^3, 31, 33^3; **6:**1, 2^2, 3^3, 18^3, 23, 24; **7:**4, 6, 9^2, 10^2, 12, 15, 16, 20, 25; **8:**1, 3^3, 5, 7, 11, 13, 15, 16^2, 18^2, 19; **9:**3, 4, 5, 6, 7, 8, 11, 14, 19, 21, 24; **10:**1, 2, 8, 10, 11, 14, 21; **11:**6, 8, 9^2, 14^2, 15, 16, 17^2, 18, 21, 25, 29; **12:**1, 3, 7, 8, 10, 11, 12, 13^2, 14, 18^2, 19, 23, 25^2, 28^2, 30^3; **13:**3^2, 5^2, 10, 14, 15^2, 17, 18; **14:**2, 6^2, 7^2, 9^2, 19, 21^3, 22, 23, 24, 26, 27, 29; **15:**2, 3, 8, 9, 10^2, 14, 15, 18, 19; **16:**3, 6, 11^2, 12, 13, 14, 20^2; **17:**1, 2, 4, 5^5, 6, 9, 10^2, 12^3, 14, 16^2, 17, 18^2, 19, 20^3; **18:**3, 8, 10^2, 12, 16^2, 17, 18, 19, 20^2, 22; **19:**3, 4, 5, 10, 11, 12, 13, 14, 15, 16; **20:**2, 4, 5, 6, 7, 8, 9, 11^2, 14, 16, 18, 20^2; **21:**2, 3^2, 4, 6^3, 9, 11, 13, 15, 16^2, 17, 18, 21, 23^3; **22:**5^2, 7^2, 8, 18^2, 21, 22, 23, 24^2, 25, 28, 29; **23:**1, 8, 10^2, 13, 14, 16, 19, 20^2, 23; **24:**1, 4^2, 7, 8^2, 9, 13, 14^2, 18, 19, 22; **25:**1, 2, 6^2, 9^2, 10, 11, 15, 16^2, 18, 19; **26:**2^2, 3^2, 9, 11, 12, 14, 15, 18, 19; **27:**2, 3^2, 4, 15, 16, 17, 18, 19, 20, 21, 22, 23, 24, 25, 26; **28:**1, 7, 8, 10, 13, 15, 20, 23^2, 34, 35, 43, 54^2, 55, 57, 58^2, 63; **29:**2, 6^2, 9^2, 11, 12, 13^2, 15^2, 18, 19, 20^2, 21, 22^4, 23^2, 27, 29; **30:**2, 3, 6, 7, 12^2, 13^2, 14, 16^2, 17, 18^2, 19^2, 20^4; **31:**5, 6, 8, 12^3, 13, 14^2, 17^3, 18^2, 19, 20, 21, 25, 26, 28, 29; **32:**6, 13, 17, 18^2, 21, 27, 29^3, 35, 36, 39^2, 41, 42, 48, 49; **33:**11^3, 13, 16^2, 20; **34:**1, 12

Jos **1:**1, 3^2, 7^2, 8^2, 16, 18^2; **2:**3, 5, 9^3, 10, 12, 13^2, 14, 19, 23; **3:**2, 4, 7^2, 8, 10^2, 13^3, 15^2, 16^3, 17; **4:**1, 6^2, 7, 10^2, 11, 14, 16^2, 18^2, 24^3; **5:**1^2, 2, 4^2, 5^2, 6^4, 8, 12, 13; **6:**5, 7, 8, 9, 15^2, 17^3, 20^2, 21, 22^2, 23^2, 24, 25, 26^2; **7:**14, 15^3, 24, 26; **8:**5^2, 8, 9, 11, 13^2, 14^2, 16, 17, 18^2, 20^2, 21^2, 22^2, 24, 25^3, 27, 29^2, 33^3, 34, 35^2; **9:**2, 9, 10^2, 16^3, 24, 26, 27; **10:**2, 4, 6, 10, 11, 14^2, 20, 24, 27, 28^2, 30, 32^2, 35^4, 37^3, 39, 40; **11:**1, 2, 4, 10, 11, 13^2, 15, 16, 17, 19, 20^4, 21, 23; **12:**4, 7; **13:**2, 4, 9^2, 16^2, 17, 22, 25; **14:**6, 8, 9, 11, 12^3, 14; **15:**2, 4, 7, 8, 16, 18, 46; **16:**1, 10; **17:**7, 12, 13, 16; **18:**6, 8^2, 13, 14, 16; **19:**8, 11; **20:**3^2, 4^3, 6^2, 9^2; **21:**26, 44; **22:**2^2, 10, 16^3, 18^2, 20, 23, 27^3, 28^2, 29^2, 30, 31, 34; **23:**1^2, 3^2, 4^2, 6^2, 7^2, 10, 11, 12, 13, 14, 15; **24:**5, 8, 15, 16, 17, 20, 22, 25, 26, 29, 31^2, 33

Jdg **1:**1, 3, 9, 10, 12, 14, 17, 21, 27, 28, 29, 35; **2:**4, 5, 7^2, 10, 12, 14^2, 16, 18, 19, 20, 22; **3:**2, 3, 18, 19^2, 22, 24, 27, 29, 30; **4:**2, 4, 9, 12, 13, 15, 20. 23; **5:**1, 5, 7^2, 9, 10^2, 11, 13, 14, 18, 21, 30, 31; **6:**3, 8, 9, 11, 17, 21, 22, 25^3, 27^2, 28^2, 30^2, 31^2, 32, 37, 40; **7:**1^2, 2, 4, 5^2, 6, 7, 9, 11, 13^3, 15, 17, 18, 19^2; **8:**1, 3, 4, 5, 6, 10^2, 11, 15^2, 21, 24, 26^3, 28, 31, 33; **9:**2^3, 6, 7, 16, 24, 25^2, 28, 32, 33^2, 34, 35, 38^2, 41, 42, 44^2, 45^2, 46, 47, 48^2, 49, 54, 55; **10:**4, 8^2, 9, 18; **11:**4, 5, 6, 8, 12, 21, 24, 26^2, 31, 35^2, 36, 37, 39, 40; **12:**3, 5^2, 6, 14; **13:**8, 10, 11, 13, 14^2, 16, 17, 20, 21; **14:**3, 4^3, 9, 11, 13, 15^3, 17; **15:**1, 2, 7, 11^2, 12^2, 14^2, 17^2, 19; **16:**3, 4, 5, 7, 11, 16, 17, 18, 20, 25^2, 26^3, 27, 28, 30; **17:**2, 6, 13; **18:**1, 5, 7^2, 9, 10, 12, 14^2, 17^2, 19, 22, 23, 24, 26, 27, 28, 31; **19:**1, 5, 9^2, 10, 12, 15, 18, 22^2, 23, 30^3; **20:**2, 3, 4^2, 5, 10^2, 12, 13, 15^2, 17, 21, 26, 34, 35, 36, 38, 41, 46^3, 48^2; **21:**3, 4, 5^2, 7^2, 8, 11^2, 12, 13, 14, 15, 16, 17^2, 18, 19, 22^2, 23, 24, 25

Ru **1:**1, 6^2, 9, 11, 13, 18, 19; **2:**5, 6^2, 7, 9^3, 10, 11, 13^2, 16, 17, 18, 19, 22^2; **3:**1, 4, 5, 6, 8, 11^2, 12, 13, 14, 15, 16; **4:**3, 4, 9^3, 10, 11^2, 14

1Sa **1:**4, 12, 17, 20, 22, 26; **2:**4, 5^4, 13, 14^2, 15, 21, 22^2, 24, 30^3, 31^2, 34, 35^2, 36^3; **3:**2^2, 4, 8, 9, 11, 12, 13, 14, 17^2, 20; **4:**3, 4, 5, 6, 8, 9, 15, 16, 18, 19^2, 20; **5:**5, 7, 9, 10, 11, 12; **6:**5, 8, 9^3, 15; **7:**2, 6, 7, 8, 10; **8:**1, 7^2, 8, 9, 10, 11, 18^2, 20^2; **9:**5, 6^2, 8, 9, 13, 16, 19, 20, 22, 24^3, 26^2, 27; **10:**5^2, 7, 9^2, 11^3, 14, 16, 18, 24; **11:**2, 3, 5, 9^2, 10, 11^3, 12^2; **12:**1, 5, 6^2, 7, 12, 14, 17^2, 18, 19, 23; **13:**3, 4^2, 6, 8, 10^2, 11^3, 14, 15, 16, 17, 18, 22^2; **14:**1^3, 2, 3, 6^2, 7, 14, 17, 18, 19^2, 20, 21^3, 22, 23, 24^3, 27, 28, 31, 33, 34, 35, 37, 39, 43, 45, 48; **15:**2, 3, 7, 9^3, 11, 25, 28, 29, 30, 35; **16:**4, 6, 13, 16, 17, 18, 23; **17:**10, 12, 13, 25^2, 26^3, 27, 28, 37, 41, 43, 46^2, 47, 48, 49; **18:**1, 2, 4, 6, 9, 10, 15, 18, 19, 21^2, 23, 27, 28^2, 30^2; **19:**1, 3, 10, 15, 17, 18, 22, 24^2; **20:**1, 2, 3, 5, 6, 7, 9, 13, 14, 26, 27, 30, 33, 35; **21:**6, 7^2, 9^3, 10, 15; **22:**2^3, 4, 6^2, 7, 8^5, 11, 13^2, 17, 18^2, 21, 22^2, 23; **23:**6, 7^2, 9, 10, 13, 15, 17, 22, 23, 25, 26, 28; **24:**1, 4, 5, 6, 10, 11^2, 16, 18, 19, 20^2, 21^2; **25:**4, 6^2, 7, 10, 11, 17, 20, 21^3, 22^2, 26, 27, 30, 31^3, 34, 35, 37, 38^2, 39^2, 42; **26:**3, 4, 11^2, 14, 16^2; **27:**1, 2, 4, 5, 6, 7; **28:**1^2, 3, 7^3, 9, 14, 15, 21, 22, 25; **29:**4, 7, 8, 9, 10; **30:**1, 2, 4, 9^2, 10, 15, 16, 18, 19, 21^2, 22^3, 23^2, 24^2, 25^2; **31:**5, 6, 7^4, 8, 11

2Sa **1:**2^2, 4, 5^2, 6, 10^4, 11, 13, 15; **2:**1, 3, 4^2, 5, 11, 16, 17, 23^2, 24, 26, 29, 31; **3:**6, 8, 13, 19^2, 20, 21^3, 23, 24, 25^2, 27, 29^5, 31, 37^2, 38; **4:**1, 2, 4^2, 10; **5:**2, 8^2, 12^2, 14, 17, 20, 24; **6:**2^2, 3, 9, 12, 13^2, 17; **7:**2, 3, 4^2, 6, 9, 10, 11^2, 18, 22, 25, 28, 29; **8:**1, 7, 9, 11; **9:**1^2, 3, 8, 9, 10, 11, 12; **10:**1, 3^2, 6, 9, 10, 12, 13, 14, 15, 16, 19^2; **11:**1, 2, 12, 14, 15, 16^2, 20^2, 21, 22, 26, 27; **12:**4^2, 5, 8, 14, 15, 18^3, 19^2, 21, 22, 31; **13:**1, 2, 5, 6, 10, 15, 16, 17, 18, 19, 23, 27, 30, 32^2, 33, 34, 36; **14:**1, 2, 7^2, 11, 13, 14, 15^2, 16, 18, 19, 20, 22^2, 26, 32; **15:**1, 2^2, 4^2, 5, 6, 7, 11, 14, 17, 22, 30, 32, 35, 36; **16:**2, 4^2, 12^2, 14, 16, 21^2; **17:**2, 7, 8, 9^2, 10^2, 11^3, 12, 13, 14, 16, 21, 22^2, 23, 25, 27, 29; **18:**1, 3, 7, 8, 9, 11, 12, 15, 19, 22, 28, 31, 32^2; **19:**2^2, 3, 6^3, 7^2, 14, 19^3, 20, 22^2, 25, 26, 28, 34, 37, 38^2, 43; **20:**8, 10, 11^2, 12^3, 15, 16, 19, 20; **21:**3, 4, 5^3, 7, 13, 14^2, 17, 18, 20; **22:**1, 18, 28, 31, 35, 37, 39, 40, 41^2, 48^2, 49^2; **23:**3, 7, 8, 9, 10, 15, 16, 17^2; **24:**2, 3, 5, 9, 10^2, 12, 13^2, 16, 17, 18, 21, 24

1Ki **1:**2, 11, 12, 20, 21, 29, 35, 40, 41, 45^2, 49, 51; **2:**1, 3^2, 4, 5^2, 7, 11, 15^3, 17, 25, 27, 29, 31, 37^2, 39, 41, 42^2, 43, 44, 46; **3:**4^2, 6, 8, 9, 10, 12, 13^2, 16, 18^2, 23, 28; **4:**12, 27, 29, 33^2; **5:**1, 3, 4, 6^4, 7, 9, 15, 16; **6:**1, 6, 7, 17, 22, 27; **7:**3, 18, 19, 29, 40, 41, 42, 48, 51; **8:**1, 4, 5^2, 8, 10, 11, 12, 16^2, 18, 19, 20, 23, 24, 25^3, 27, 29^2, 36, 40^2, 41, 43^4, 44, 46^2, 47, 50^2, 52^2, 54, 56^2, 58, 59, 60^3, 64^2, 65, 66; **9:**2, 3, 4, 8, 11, 16, 19^2, 20, 21, 23^2, 25, 27; **10:**2^2, 4, 6, 8, 11, 13, 14, 15, 27; **11:**4, 7, 10^2, 17, 19, 21^3, 22, 25, 27, 28, 29^2, 30, 33^2, 36, 37, 38^3, 41, 42; **12:**3, 6^2, 8, 9, 10^2, 13, 15, 16, 18, 20^3, 32^2; **13:**2, 3, 4^2, 6, 9, 10, 11^2, 14, 17, 18, 20^2, 21, 23, 26, 31; **14:**1, 2^2, 5, 6, 8, 9, 10^2, 11^2, 14, 22, 25, 28, 29; **15:**5^2, 7, 11, 12, 17, 18^2, 19, 21, 23, 29^2, 31; **16:**4^2, 7, 11^2, 14, 16^2, 18^2, 20, 22^2, 25, 27, 30, 31, 33; **17:**3, 4, 5, 7, 10, 12^2, 14, 17^2, 24^2; **18:**1, 4, 5, 7, 9, 10, 12, 17^2, 18, 24, 26, 27, 29^2, 30, 36^4, 37^3, 38, 44^2, 45; **19:**1, 3, 4, 8, 13, 17^3; **20:**4, 6, 9, 10, 11^2, 12, 13, 16, 25, 26, 28, 29, 30, 31, 37, 41; **21:**1, 2, 3, 5, 8, 10, 13, 15^2, 16^2, 21^2, 24^2, 27; **22:**2, 3, 7, 13^2, 14, 16^2, 17, 18, 20^2, 25, 31, 32, 33^2, 35, 39^2, 43, 45, 53

2Ki **1:**2, 3, 4, 6^3, 16; **2:**1, 3^2, 5^2, 8, 9, 11, 13, 14; **3:**2, 5, 9, 10, 11, 14, 15, 17^2, 20, 21^2, 24, 26^2, 27; **4:**1, 4, 6, 8^2, 9, 10, 11, 17^2, 18, 22, 25^2, 40, 41, 42, 43; **5:**3, 4, 6, 7^2, 8^3, 15, 18, 20; **6:**9, 12^2, 13, 16^2, 17, 20^2, 22, 24, 28, 29, 30; **7:**9, 12, 13^3, 19; **8:**3, 4, 5, 6^2, 10, 12, 13^2, 14, 15^2, 23; **9:**7, 8^2, 22, 25, 37; **10:**1, 5^4, 7, 9, 10^2, 11, 17, 19, 21^2, 22, 23, 24, 25, 29^2, 30^2, 34, 36; **11:**1, 2, 5^2, 6, 7, 8, 9^3, 10, 15, 17; **12:**2, 4^4, 6, 9^2, 10^3, 11^3, 12, 13, 14, 18^2, 19; **13:**2, 5, 8, 11, 12, 21; **14:**3, 5, 6, 9^3, 10, 14, 22, 24, 26, 27, 28; **15:**3^2, 4, 5, 6, 9, 16^2, 18, 19, 21, 24, 26, 28, 31, 34^2, 36; **16:**2, 6, 8, 10, 11, 16, 17, 18; **17:**2^2, 7, 9, 14, 15^3, 25, 38; **18:**1, 3^2, 4, 5^2, 9, 10, 12, 14, 15, 16, 20, 21, 22, 26, 27, 32, 35^2; **19:**1, 4, 8, 19^2, 20, 21, 25^2, 29, 30, 31, 33, 35^2, 37; **20:**3, 4, 8^2, 9^2, 12^2, 13^2, 15^2, 17^3, 18; **21:**2, 7, 8^2, 11, 12, 15, 16, 17^2, 20, 21^2, 24; **22:**2, 3, 4, 5, 7, 9^3, 11, 13^3, 15, 17, 19; **23:**3, 4, 5, 7, 8, 10, 11, 12, 13, 15^2, 16, 17^3, 18, 19^2, 20, 22, 24^3, 25, 26, 28, 32^2, 33, 37^2; **24:**3, 4, 5, 7, 9^2, 10, 16, 19^2, 20; **25:**1, 10, 11^2, 13^2, 19^3, 22, 23, 25^3, 27^2, 28

1Ch **1:**43; **2:**9, 24, 55; **4:**10^5, 21, 23, 33, 41, 43; **5:**18, 20; **6:**10^2, 31, 33, 49, 61; **7:**21^2, 40; **9:**2, 16, 28, 31, 33; **10:**5, 7^3, 8, 11, 13; **11:**2, 14, 17^2, 18, 19^2, 31; **12:**1, 8, 15, 20, 22, 23, 24, 32, 38, 40; **13:**2^3, 4, 6^2, 11, 12, 14; **14:**2, 8, 11, 15; **15:**12^2, 13, 26^2, 27, 29; **16:**1, 7, 10, 12, 30, 32, 35, 39, 40, 41, 42; **17:**1, 2, 3, 5, 7, 8, 10^2, 11^2, 13, 16, 20, 23, 24, 25, 27; **18:**1, 7, 11; **19:**1, 3^2, 6, 9, 10, 13, 14, 15, 16^2, 19; **20:**1^2, 3, 4^2; **21:**2, 5^2, 10, 12^2, 15, 17^3, 18, 22^2, 23, 24, 28^2, 29; **22:**2, 5, 12, 19; **23:**13, 24, 25, 29^2, 32; **25:**7^2; **26:**6, 28; **27:**1, 6, 26, 28, 29^2; **28:**1, 8, 12, 18; **29:**3, 9, 11, 14, 16, 17, 21, 22, 27, 30

2Ch **1:**3, 5, 7, 10^2, 11, 12, 13, 15; **2:**6, 7^2, 8, 10, 12^2, 17; **3:**1, 4, 15, 17^2; **4:**11, 19, 20, 21; **5:**1^2, 5, 6, 9, 11, 13, 14; **6:**1, 4, 5^2, 6, 8, 10, 11, 14, 15, 16^2, 20^2, 31, 33^3, 34, 40; **7:**7, 10, 11, 13, 15, 16, 17, 21^2; **8:**2, 6^2, 7, 10, 11, 18; **9:**1^2, 3, 6, 12, 13, 14, 23, 27; **10:**2, 4, 6, 8^2, 9^2, 10^2, 15, 16, 17, 18^2; **11:**1, 13; **12:**2, 3, 5, 7, 8, 10, 12; **13:**5, 9^2, 15, 18; **14:**2, 8^2, 11, 13^2; **15:**5^2, 8, 9, 13, 18^2; **16:**1, 2, 3, 5, 7; **17:**10^2; **18:**2, 6, 12, 13, 15, 16, 17, 19^2, 24, 30, 31, 32^2, 33, 34; **19:**2, 3, 10^2; **20:**1, 2, 6, 12, 21, 29, 32, 37; **21:**6, 7, 16, 17^2, 19; **22:**1, 8^2, 10, 11^2; **23:**4, 6, 8^3, 9, 14, 16, 19, 21; **24:**2, 4, 5, 7, 9, 11^2, 20, 23, 26; **25:**2, 3^2, 5, 10, 12, 13, 14^2, 16^2, 18^3, 19, 20, 24, 27; **26:**2, 4^2, 7, 11, 13, 17, 18; **27:**2^2; **28:**1, 7, 9^2, 12, 15, 16, 22, 23; **29:**2^2, 6, 10, 11, 16, 24, 29, 34, 36; **30:**1, 3, 5, 6, 8, 9^2, 14, 17^2, 19, 21, 22, 25^3; **31:**1, 4^2, 6, 10, 16, 19^2, 20, 21; **32:**2^2, 4, 5, 7, 9, 10, 14^3, 18^2, 21, 23, 26, 31^3; **33:**2, 8^2, 13, 15, 18, 22, 25; **34:**2, 4^2, 9^2, 10^2, 12, 13, 14, 16, 17, 19, 21^4, 22^2, 23, 24, 25, 28, 30, 32, 33^2; **35:**3, 6, 7, 12, 17^2, 18^2, 21, 22, 24^2, 26; **36:**5, 8, 9, 12, 17, 20, 22^2

Ezr **1:**1^2, 4, 6^2, 11; **2:**1, 62, 63; **3:**5^2, 7, 8, 12, 13; **4:**1, 10, 11, 12, 13, 15^3, 16, 17, 19^2, 21, 22; **5:**1, 4, 5, 6, 8, 10^2, 11, 12, 14, 15, 16, 17; **6:**2, 8^2, 9, 10, 11, 12^2, 13; **7:**11, 13, 16, 17, 18, 19, 21, 24, 25^3; **8:**1, 15, 17, 21, 22^2, 34, 35; **9:**2, 4^2, 8, 12, 13^2, 14; **10:**3, 5, 6, 7, 8^2, 13, 17, 18, 19

Neh **1:**2^2, 3, 4, 5^2, 6, 8, 9; **2:**1, 5^2, 7, 8^2, 10, 12, 14, 16, 17^2, 18, 19; **3:**15, 16, 25, 26, 27; **4:**1^2, 3, 7^3, 10, 12, 15^2, 16^2, 17^2, 18, 22, 23; **5:**2^2, 3^2, 4^2, 9, 11, 12, 13, 14^2, 15, 17^2, 18, 19; **6:**1^3, 2, 3, 6^2, 9, 11, 12^2, 13^3, 14, 16^3; **7:**2, 5, 6^2, 64, 65, 72; **8:**1, 2, 3^2, 9, 12, 14, 15, 17^2; **9:**6^2, 10, 11, 15, 17, 18, 21, 23, 24, 28, 29, 32, 33, 35, 36; **10:**1, 28, 30, 31^2, 36, 37^2, 39; **11:**2, 3, 6, 12, 19, 23; **12:**1, 31, 38, 40, 43^2, 44^2; **13:**1^2, 2, 3, 7, 10^2, 14, 17, 19^4, 21, 22^2, 23

Est **1:**2, 5, 8, 10, 13, 16, 17, 19^3, 22^2; **2:**2, 3, 7, 8, 10, 12, 14, 15, 17; **3:**1, 2, 4^2, 5, 6, 7^3, 9^2, 12^2, 14^2; **4:**1, 7^2, 8^2, 11^2, 13, 16, 17; **5:**1, 2^2, 4, 5^2, 8, 9^2, 12, 14; **6:**1, 2, 3, 4, 8, 9, 10^2, 13, 14; **7:**5, 7, 10; **8:**1, 3, 6, 9^3, 11, 13^2, 14; **9:**1^4, 5, 11^2, 15, 16, 18, 19, 20, 21, 22, 24, 25^2, 26, 27, 28^2

Job **1:**1^2, 3, 5^2, 8^2, 10, 11, 12; **2:**3^2, 4, 11, 13; **3:**4, 6, 7, 8, 12, 15, 20, 25; **4:**4, 8, 19; **5:**1, 11^2, 12, 24, 25; **6:**2, 6, 7, 8^3, 9^2, 11^2, 14, 26; **7:**7, 8, 9, 12, 15, 17^2, 18, 20; **8:**13, 22; **9:**16, 26, 28, 32, 33; **10:**3^2, 6, 7^2, 9, 13, 18, 20; **11:**5, 6^4, 16; **12:**5^2, 6, 9; **13:**5, 9, 13, 18, 19, 28; **14:**1, 5, 6, 7^2, 13^3; **15:**7, 9, 13, 14^2, 17, 22, 23, 31; **16:**3, 21; **17:**3, 5, 9; **18:**20^2, 21; **19:**3, 4, 6, 8, 15, 23^2, 24, 25^2, 29; **20:**5, 18, 20, 26; **21:**3^2, 15, 18, 22, 29, 30; **22:**2, 3^2, 11, 14; **23:**3^2, 9, 10, 13, 14; **24:**1, 7, 13, 21; **25:**4, 6; **26:**2^2, 3; **27:**5, 7, 11, 15, 18; **28:**11, 28; **29:**2, 12^2, 13, 25; **30:**1, 23, 25, 31; **31:**6, 12, 15, 28, 29, 31, 34, 35^3, 38; **32:**5, 12^2, 20; **33:**12, 17, 20, 21^2, 27; **34:**2, 9, 10^2, 17^2, 19, 23, 25, 28, 30, 32, 36; **35:**2; **36:**2, 4, 9, 10, 16, 24, 32; **37:**2, 7, 12, 20, 24; **38:**2, 13^2, 20^2, 34, 35; **39:**2, 12, 15^2, 24; **40:**2^2, 8, 11, 12, 14, 19, 23; **41:**10, 11, 16, 17, 26; **42:**2^2, 3^2, 7^2, 8, 11^2

Ps **1:**1, 3; **2:**4, 12; **3:**1^2, 6; **4:**3^2, 6, 7; **5:**4, 6, 11^2; **7:**1, 4^2, 6, 8; **8:**2, 4^2; **9:**10^2, 13^2, 14, 15, 17, 20; **10:**2, 10, 18; **11:**2, 5; **12:**3, 5; **13:**4; **14:**1, 2, 3, 7; **15:**2, 3, 4^2, 5^2; **16:**3, 4; **17:**1, 2, 3, 5, 7^2, 9, 12; **18:**12, 30, 32, 34, 36, 38, 39, 40^2, 47, 48, ttl; **20:**6; **21:**8; **22:**3, 7, 8, 9, 23, 25, 26, 29^2, 31^2; **24:**1, 4, 6^2; **25:**3, 12^2, 14; **26:**7; **27:**4^2; **28:**1; **30:**3, 12; **31:**4, 6, 11, 15, 19^2, 24; **32:**6, 10, 11; **33:**18^2; **34:**7, 8^2, 9, 10, 12^2, 16, 18, 21, 22; **35:**1^2, 3, 4^2, 8^2, 10^2, 11, 14, 19^2, 20, 26^2, 27; **36:**1, 4, 10; **37:**9, 13, 16, 22, 37; **38:**12^2, 13, 14, 19, 20^2; **39:**1, 4, 13; **40:**4^2, 12, 14^2, 15, 16; **41:**1, 7, 8, 10, 11; **42:**4; **44:**5, 7, 13, 16; **45:**14; **46:**5, 10; **48:**13; **49:**6, 9, 10, 11, 12, 20^2; **50:**4, 5, 16, 21, 22, 23; **51:**4, 8; **52:**7; **53:**1, 2^2, 3, 5, 6; **54:**4; **55:**6, 12^3, 18, 19; **56:**2, 13; **57:**2, 3, 4; **58:**4, 8, 11^2; **59:**1, 13^2; **60:**4^2, 5, 12; **61:**2, 5, 8; **62:**11; **63:**9, 11^2; **64:**4, 8; **65:**2, 4, 5, 8; **66:**16; **67:**2; **68:**1, 4, 11, 12, 18,

APNDX

20, 23, 28, 30, 33^2, 35; **69:**4^3, 6^2, 9, 10, 12, 14, 22, 23, 31, 32, 34, 35, 36; **70:**2^2, 3, 4; **71:**6, 10, 13^2, 18, 24; **72:**6, 9, 12; **73:**25, 27^2, 28; **74:**3, 9, 18^2, 23; **75:**1; **76:**11^2; **77:**4, 14; **78:**4, 5, 6, 7, 8, 11, 20, 35, 39^2, 44, 53, 60, 65; **79:**4, 6^2, 11; **80:**1^2, 12, 15; **81:**5, 13; **83:**2, 4, 16, 18^2; **84:**4, 11, 12; **85:**6, 9^2, 12; **86:**2, 5, 17; **87:**4, 5, 6; **88:**4^2, 5; **89:**7, 10, 15, 19, 23, 34, 35, 41, 48; **90:**9, 12, 14; **91:**1, 5, 6^2; **92:**7, 11, 13, 15; **93:**1; **94:**9^2, 10^2, 11, 13; **95:**10, 11; **96:**10^2, 12; **97:**7^2, 10; **98:**7; **99:**6, 7, 8; **100:**3^2; **101:**3, 5, 6^2, 7^2, 8; **102:**4, 8, 11, 20; **103:**1, 5, 6, 11, 13, 14, 17, 18, 20^2, 21; **104:**5, 9^2, 14, 15, 26, 27, 28; **105:**3, 5, 19, 34, 45; **106:**3^2, 4, 5^3, 8, 10, 20, 23, 31, 32, 33, 40, 41, 46; **107:**7, 8, 15, 21, 23^2, 29, 31, 34, 36, 38; **108:**6, 13; **109:**11, 15, 16^2, 20, 27^3, 31; **111:**2, 5, 6, 10; **112:**1^2; **113:**6, 8; **114:**5^2, 6; **115:**8^2, 11, 13, 17; **118:**2, 3, 4^2, 7^2, 13, 26; **119:**2^2, 5, 11, 17, 18, 20, 21, 42, 53, 57, 63^2, 71^2, 73, 74, 75^2, 77, 79^2, 80, 84, 101, 106, 116, 118, 125, 132, 138, 148, 150, 152, 162; **120:**5^2, 6; **121:**3, 4; **122:**3, 6; **123:**1, 2, 4; **125:**1, 4^2; **126:**1, 5, 6; **127:**1, 5; **128:**1^2, 4^2; **129:**5, 7; **130:**4, 6^2; **131:**2; **132:**12; **133:**2^2, 3; **134:**3; **135:**2, 5^2, 6, 18^2, 20; **136:**5, 6, 7, 10; **137:**3^2, 8, 9; **138:**8; **139:**14, 21^2; **140:**9, 10, 12; **141:**4, 10; **142:**4, 7; **143:**3, 7, 12; **144:**3^2, 4, 10, 12^2, 13^2, 14^3, 15^3; **145:**14^2, 18^2, 19, 20; **146:**4, 5, 6, 8; **147:**11^2; **148:**4; **149:**2; **150:**6

Prv 1:12, 19, 29; **2:**2, 7, 12, 19, 20; **3:**13^2, 18^2; **4:**18, 22; **5:**2^2, 6, 13; **6:**11, 17, 18^2, 19^2, 29, 32; **7:**5, 23; **8:**9^2, 11, 17^2, 21^2, 29, 32, 34, 36^2; **9:**4, 7^2, 16, 18^2; **10:**4, 5^3, 9^2, 10, 13^2, 17^2, 18^2, 19, 26; **11:**12, 13, 15^2, 17, 18, 19, 20, 24^2, 25, 26^2, 27^2, 28, 29, 30; **12:**1, 4, 8, 9^2, 11^2, 15, 17, 18, 20, 22, 27; **13:**3^2, 6, 7^2, 11, 13, 18^2, 20, 23, 24^2; **14:**2^2, 6, 13, 17, 21^2, 22^2, 29^2, 31^2, 33^2, 35; **15:**5, 9, 10^2, 12, 14, 15, 18, 21, 24, 27^2, 31, 32^2; **16:**5, 13, 17, 20, 22, 25, 26, 29, 32^3; **17:**2, 5, 8, 9^2, 15^2, 19^2, 20^2, 21, 24, 25, 27, 28; **18:**2, 9^2, 13, 17, 21, 24^2; **19:**1^2, 2^2, 5, 6, 8^2, 9, 16^2, 17^2, 20, 21, 23, 25, 26^2, 27; **20:**8, 16, 19^2, 25; **21:**5, 6, 16, 17^2, 21, 28; **22:**5, 8, 9, 11, 14, 16^2, 19, 21^3, 23, 26^2; **23:**5, 6, 22, 24, 25, 30^2, 34^2; **24:**8, 11^2, 12^2, 21, 24, 25, 26, 34; **25:**7^2, 10, 13, 18, 20^2, 28^2; **26:**6, 8^2, 10, 16, 17^2, 19, 24, 27, 28; **27:**8^2, 10, 11^2, 13, 14, 18; **28:**3, 4, 5, 6^2, 7, 8^2, 9, 11, 13, 14^2, 16^2, 17, 18, 19^2, 20, 21, 22^2, 23^2, 25^2, 26, 27^2; **29:**1^2, 3, 4, 5, 14, 18, 20, 21, 27; **30:**5, 11, 12, 15, 16^2, 17, 23; **31:**1, 3, 6^2, 11, 18, 30

Ecc 1:9^4, 11^2, 13, 14, 15^2, 16, 17, 18; **2:**3, 6, 7, 8, 9, 11^2, 12^2, 13, 14, 15, 16, 17, 18, 21, 24^3, 26^3; **3:**2, 9^2, 11^2, 12, 13, 14^2, 15^3, 16^2, 18^3, 19^2, 21^2, 22^3; **4:**1, 3, 4, 10, 14, 15, 16^2; **5:**1, 4, 5^2, 6, 8, 10^2, 11, 16^2, 18^2; **6:**2^2, 3^3, 8, 10^3, 11; **7:**2, 10, 11, 12^2, 13, 14, 15^2, 18^2, 20, 21, 22, 24, 29; **8:**2, 7, 8^3, 9, 12^2, 14^2, 15, 16^2, 17^2; **9:**1^2, 2^4, 3^3, 4, 5, 6, 9, 11, 12^2, 15, 17; **10:**1, 3^2, 8, 9, 20; **11:**4^2, 5, 6, 8, 9; **12:**3, 5, 10

Song 1:7; **2:**7, 14, 15; **3:**3, 4^2, 5, 6; **4:**1, 2, 5, 16; **5:**2, 7, 8^2, 9; **6:**1, 5, 9, 10, 13; **7:**3, 9^2; **8:**1^2, 4, 5^2, 10, 12, 13

Isa 1:4, 28, 29, 30; **2:**1, 2, 8, 11, 12^2, 13, 14, 17, 20; **3:**7, 10, 15, 18, 24; **4:**1, 2^2, 3^4; **5:**2, 4^2, 6, 8^3, 11^3, 14, 16, 18, 19^3, 20^3, 21, 22, 30; **6:**1, 4; **7:**1, 8, 15, 16, 17^2, 18^4, 20, 21^2, 22^2, 23^2, 25; **8:**6, 11, 17, 19^3, 21; **9:**2^2, 9, 13, 15, 16; **10:**1^2, 2^2, 12, 14^2, 15^3, 19, 20^3, 24, 27^2, 32; **11:**10, 11^2, 16; **12:**1, 4^2; **13:**2, 3, 8, 14, 15^2; **14:**3, 4, 6, 16^3, 17^2, 19^2, 21, 25, 26^2, 28, 29, 32; **15:**7, 9; **16:**2, 3, 12^2, 13^2, 14; **17:**4^2, 5, 7, 8, 9, 12, 14^2; **18:**2, 7; **19:**3, 8^2, 9^2, 10, 13, 16, 17, 18, 19, 21, 23, 24; **20:**1, 6; **21:**3, 10, 14^2; **22:**1, 2, 3, 7, 8, 9, 11, 12, 16^3, 20^2, 25^3; **23:**1, 2, 13, 15^2, 16^2, 17, 18; **24:**6, 8, 9, 10, 18^2, 21^3; **25:**7, 9, 11; **26:**1, 2, 5, 17, 19; **27:**1^3, 2, 5, 6, 7^2, 9, 11^2, 12^2, 13^2; **28:**1, 4, 5, 6^2, 8, 9, 13, 14, 16, 19, 20^2, 21; **29:**4, 5, 7^3, 8, 11^2, 12, 15, 16^2, 18, 20, 21^2, 24^2; **30:**1^3, 2, 5, 6, 8, 9^2, 14^2, 16, 18^3, 23^2, 24, 26; **31:**1, 2, 3^2, 7; **32:**3^2, 9, 11, 20^2; **33:**1, 13^2, 15^4, 17, 18, 19, 20, 24; **34:**1^2; **35:**4; **36:**1, 5, 6, 11, 12^2, 20^2, 22; **37:**1, 4, 6, 8, 16, 20^2, 26^2, 30, 31, 32, 34, 38; **38:**3, 7^2, 13, 18, 22; **39:**1^2, 2^2, 4^2, 6^3, 7; **40:**2^2, 3, 9^2, 11, 20^4, 22^2, 23, 26^2, 28, 29, 31; **41:**3, 7^3, 11^2, 12^2, 20^2, 22, 23^4, 24, 26^5, 27, 28; **42:**5^5, 7, 8, 10^2, 11, 16^2, 17^2, 18, 19^2; **43:**1^2, 7, 8^2, 9, 10^2, 12, 13, 25, 26; **44:**2, 3, 7, 8, 9^2, 10, 13, 18^2, 20, 24^4, 25^2, 26^2, 27, 28; **45:**3^2, 6^2, 9^2, 10, 15, 16, 18^2, 19, 20^3, 21, 23, 24; **46:**5, 10, 11, 12; **47:**7, 8^3, 13; **48:**4, 8^3, 9, 16, 17, 18; **49:**5, 6^2, 7, 9^2, 10, 15, 17, 19, 20, 23^2, 25, 26^2; **50:**2, 4^2, 6, 7, 8, 9, 10^3, 11^3; **51:**1^2, 2, 6, 7, 9, 10, 12^3, 13, 14^3, 15, 16, 18^2, 22, 23^3; **52:**5^2, 6^3, 7^5, 11, 15^2; **53:**2; **54:**1^2, 9^2, 10, 16^2, 17^2; **55:**1^2, 2^3, 5^2, 10, 11^2, 13; **56:**2^3, 3, 4^2, 5, 6^2, 8, 11; **57:**1, 11, 13, 15^2, 19^2; **58:**2, 5, 6^2, 7^4, 12; **59:**1^2, 2, 5^2, 15^2, 16^2, 20, 21; **60:**8, 11^2, 12, 14^2, 15, 16, 21; **61:**1, 2, 3^3, 9^2, 11; **62:**1, 6, 9^2; **63:**1^3, 2, 5, 7, 8, 11^2, 12, 13^2; **64:**1^3, 2, 4, 5^2, 7^2; **65:**1^3, 2, 3^2, 5, 8, 10, 11^6, 12, 16^2, 18, 20, 24; **66:**1, 2, 3^4, 4, 5^3, 6, 10^2, 11^2, 17, 18, 19^3, 23, 24

Jer 1:1, 7, 17; **2:**2, 3, 5, 6^3, 8^2, 11, 13, 17, 19^3, 24^2, 28; **3:**1, 6, 9, 13, 16, 17, 18; **4:**4, 9^2, 11, 14, 16, 31^3; **5:**1^2, 6, 7, 19, 22, 24, 26; **6:**10, 11, 15^2, 27; **7:**1, 2, 7, 8, 18, 22, 23^2, 25, 28, 32; **8:**1, 3, 10, 12, 13, 16^2, 19; **9:**1^2, 2^2, 10, 12^3, 17^2, 18, 24^3, 25, 26^2; **10:**4, 11, 18, 23^2, 25^2; **11:**1, 3, 4, 5, 7, 13, 14, 17, 19^3, 20^2, 21^2; **12:**1, 4, 14, 15, 17; **13:**4, 6, 11, 12, 13, 20^2, 23, 24, 26; **14:**1, 8, 9, 15, 18^2, 22; **15:**4, 9, 10, 13, 15, 18; **16:**3^3, 10, 12, 13, 14^2, 15^2, 21; **17:**4, 5, 7, 8, 11, 13^2, 16, 18, 20, 23; **18:**4, 8^2, 10, 14, 16, 19, 20; **19:**2, 6, 7, 8, 9, 10, 11, 15^2; **20:**1, 2, 3, 6, 12, 16, 17, 18; **21:**2^2, 4, 7, 9^3, 12^2; **22:**2^2, 5, 10, 13^2, 14, 21, 23, 25, 26, 30; **23:**1, 2, 5, 7, 14, 16, 17^2, 24, 25, 26, 28^2, 29, 30, 31, 32, 34^2, 39; **24:**1, 2, 3, 5, 7, 8^2, 10; **25:**1^2, 3, 5, 7, 12^2, 13^2, 16, 23, 24, 30, 31, 33; **26:**2, 3, 8^2, 12, 13, 15, 20, 24; **27:**5, 8^3, 10, 11, 13, 14, 15^3, 16, 18, 19, 21, 22; **28:**1, 3, 4, 5, 6, 7, 8, 9, 12, 14; **29:**1, 2, 4, 6^2, 8, 10, 11, 16^4, 17, 25, 26^3, 31, 32; **30:**1, 2, 3^2, 4, 7^2, 8^2, 13, 16^3, 19, 20, 21; **31:**4, 6, 8, 10, 11, 17, 19^2, 24, 27, 28, 30, 31, 32^2, 33, 37, 38; **32:**1, 7, 8^2, 9, 11^2, 12^2, 14, 23, 24, 29, 31^2, 35, 39, 40^2, 42; **33:**2, 9^2, 10, 11^2, 13, 14^2, 15, 20, 21, 22, 24, 26; **34:**7, 8^2, 9^2, 10^2, 13, 18, 20, 21; **35:**7, 8, 10, 11, 14, 17, 18; **36:**1, 2, 3^3, 6, 7, 8, 9^2, 13, 23^3, 24, 25, 27, 28, 31; **37:**5, 7, 10, 11, 15, 18, 20, 21^2; **38:**1, 2^2, 4, 5, 6, 7, 9, 14, 16^2, 19, 21, 22, 25, 26, 27, 28; **39:**4, 9^4, 14, 16, 17; **40:**1^3, 6, 7^2, 10, 11^4, 13, 14, 15; **41:**1, 2, 3^2, 5, 7^2, 8, 9, 10^2, 11^2, 12, 13^2, 14, 16^2; **42:**3^2, 4, 6, 7, 10, 12, 16, 17^2, 19, 20, 22; **43:**1, 3, 5, 6, 10, 13; **44:**1, 2, 3, 4, 8^3, 10, 12, 13, 14^2, 15^3, 16, 20, 21, 22, 24, 25, 26^2, 27, 28^2, 29^3, 30^2; **45:**1, 4^2; **46:**7, 9^2, 10, 13, 25, 26; **47:**1^2, 2^2, 4^2; **48:**9, 10^2, 12^2, 17^2, 18, 19^2, 20, 28^2, 35^2, 36, 41, 44^2, 45; **49:**2^2, 4, 5^2, 8, 12, 13, 16^2, 17, 19^3, 20^2, 22, 26, 31, 32, 34, 37, 39; **50:**1, 4, 5, 7, 10, 12, 13, 14, 16, 20, 21, 28, 29^2, 30, 31, 33, 34, 37, 44^3, 45^2; **51:**1^2, 2, 3^2, 4, 7, 12, 13, 24, 31, 32, 39, 44, 46^2, 47, 48, 50, 52, 60^2, 62^2, 63, 64; **52:**2^2, 3, 4, 6, 14, 15^3, 17^2, 19^2, 20, 25^2, 31, 32

Lam 1:1^2, 6, 7, 8, 10^2, 12, 16, 17, 21^3; **2:**4, 13, 15^2, 16, 17^2, 19, 22^2; **3:**1, 6, 7, 22, 25^2, 26, 27, 30, 37, 44, 57, 62; **4:**5^2, 6, 9^2, 12, 13, 14, 17, 18, 21; **5:**8, 16

Ezk 1:1, 18, 23, 25, 26, 28^2; **2:**2^2, 3, 5, 8^2; **3:**1, 2, 3, 10, 13, 15, 16, 21, 26, 27^2; **4:**4, 9, 12, 14, 17; **5:**5, 6, 7^2, 9, 13, 14^2, 15; **6:**6, 7, 8^2, 9, 10^3, 12^3, 13, 14; **7:**4, 7, 9^3, 13, 15^2, 16, 27; **8:**1, 3, 4, 6^2, 9, 13, 17; **9:**1, 4^3, 8; **10:**1, 6, 7^2, 12, 15, 20^2; **11:**2, 5, 10, 12^2, 13, 20, 24, 25; **12:**4, 6, 10, 12^2, 14, 15, 16^2, 19^3, 20^2, 22^2, 25, 27^2; **13:**2^2, 3, 6, 9^3, 11, 14^3, 15^2, 18^2, 19^3, 20, 21, 22, 23; **14:**4^2, 5, 7, 8^2, 9, 10, 11^2, 15^2, 17^2, 19, 22^3, 23^2; **15:**7; **16:**5, 15, 21, 24, 25, 27, 31^2, 32, 33, 34, 37^3, 38, 44, 45, 46^2, 47, 52^2, 54^3, 57, 62, 63^2; **17:**7, 8^3, 9, 14^3, 15^2, 16, 19^2, 20, 21^2, 24; **18:**2, 4, 5, 8^2, 10^2, 11, 14, 15, 17^2, 18, 19, 20, 21^2, 22^2, 23^2, 24^4, 26, 27^2, 28, 32; **19:**5, 9, 11, 14; **20:**1, 6^2, 9, 12^3, 14, 15, 20^2, 22, 23, 25, 26^5, 27, 32^2, 38^2, 42, 43, 44, 48; **21:**4, 5^2, 7, 10, 11, 14, 15, 19, 20, 23^2, 24^3, 26^2, 29; **22:**3, 4, 5^2, 9, 10, 14, 16, 22, 24, 30^2; **23:**7, 13^2, 14, 27, 37, 40, 43, 44, 45, 48, 49; **24:**8^2, 11^3, 19, 21, 24^2, 25, 26^3, 27^2; **25:**5, 7, 8, 10, 11, 12, 17; **26:**1, 2^2, 6, 17^2, 18, 19, 20^3; **27:**3, 7^2, 8, 27, 29; **28:**3, 8, 9^2, 13, 14, 15, 17, 18, 19, 22, 23, 24^3, 25, 26^2; **29:**3, 6, 9, 12^2, 15, 16, 18, 21^2; **30:**5, 6, 7^2, 8, 9, 12, 19, 20, 22, 25, 26; **31:**1, 9^2, 14^3, 16^2, 17^3, 18; **32:**1, 15^3, 17, 18, 20, 21, 24, 25^2, 27, 28, 29^2, 30^2, 32; **33:**5, 8, 11, 12^2, 13^2, 14, 15, 16^2, 19, 21^2, 22, 24, 27^3, 28, 29, 30, 32, 33; **34:**2, 3, 4^4, 10, 12^2, 16^4, 19^2, 27^2, 30^2; **35:**4, 5, 7^2, 8, 9, 12^2, 15; **36:**3, 4^2, 7, 11, 18, 23, 28, 30, 31, 33, 34, 35, 36^4, 38; **37:**6, 9, 13, 14, 25, 28; **38:**7, 8, 10, 11^2, 12^3, 14, 16, 17, 18, 19, 20^3, 22, 23; **39:**4, 6^2, 7, 9, 10^3, 11^2, 12, 13, 14, 15, 17^2, 21^2, 22^2, 23, 26, 28; **40:**1, 4^3, 10^2, 12^2, 20, 21, 22, 24, 26, 34, 37, 39, 41, 47, 48^2, 49; **41:**6, 9^2, 11^2, 12, 17, 18, 19, 22; **42:**1, 7, 8, 12, 13; **43:**1, 3^2, 8, 10, 11^2, 19, 27; **44:**3, 5, 7, 9, 10, 14, 15, 17, 18, 22^2, 25, 27, 30, 31; **45:**11, 13, 20^2, 22; **46:**1, 2, 4, 8, 9^2, 12, 18, 20, 24; **47:**2, 3, 5^2, 9^2, 10, 12, 22^2, 23; **48:**9, 11, 12, 15, 18, 19, 22, 35

Dan 1:3, 5, 8^2, 13, 16, 18, 20^2; **2:**8, 9, 10^2, 11^2, 13, 16^2, 18^2, 21, 25, 28, 29, 30^3, 34^2, 35^2, 40, 45^2, 46, 47; **3:**3^2, 5^2, 7^2, 8, 10^2, 11, 15^3, 18, 19, 20, 22, 28^2, 29^2; **4:**1, 2, 6, 9^2, 17^2, 19, 20, 22, 25^2, 26^2, 30, 32, 34, 37; **5:**2, 3, 5, 6, 13, 14^2, 15, 16, 19, 21^2, 25, 29, 30; **6:**2, 7, 8, 10, 12^2, 13^2, 15^2, 17, 22, 23, 25, 26^2; **7:**7, 14^2, 16, 20^4, 22, 24; **8:**1, 2, 4^2, 6, 7, 13, 21, 22; **9:**2, 4^2, 7^3, 11^2, 12, 13, 15, 16, 17, 25, 26, 27; **10:**7^2, 11, 12, 16, 21^2; **11:**3, 6^3, 16, 24, 26, 30, 31, 32, 33, 36^2; **12:**1^4, 2, 3^2, 5, 7^2, 11^2, 12

Hos 1:1, 5^2, 10; **2:**3, 5^2, 6, 8, 12, 16^2, 18, 21, 23; **4:**3, 4, 6, 14; **5:**9, 10; **6:**5, 8; **7:**2, 7; **8:**3, 4; **9:**4, 10, 12; **10:**5, 10, 11; **11:**3, 4; **12:**8, 9; **13:**2, 3^2, 8, 10; **14:**7

Joel 1:1, 4^3; **2:**5, 11, 16, 17, 25, 26, 27^2, 28, 32; **3:**1, 3, 6, 17, 18^2, 21

Am 1:5, 8, 13; **2:**7, 13, 15^3, 16^2; **3:**1, 12, 14^2; **4:**1, 2^2, 3, 13^2; **5:**3^2, 8^2, 9^2, 10^2, 13, 14, 15, 18; **6:**1, 3, 4, 5, 6, 7^2, 8, 9, 10^2; **7:**2; **8:**3, 4, 5^2, 6, 8, 9^2, 11, 13, 14; **9:**1^3, 5^2, 6^2, 8, 11^2, 12^2, 13^2

Oba 3^2, 7^2, 8, 9, 11^2, 12, 14^2, 20

Jna 1:2, 4, 5, 6^2, 7, 10, 11, 12; **2:**8, 9^2; **3:**2^2, 8, 9, 10^3; **4:**2, 6, 7, 8^2, 11^2

Mic 1:1, 2, 4; **2:**1, 4, 5, 6^2, 7^2, 8; **3:**4, 5^3, 6^2, 9; **4:**1, 6^4, 7^2, 11; **5:**2, 3, 7, 10^2; **6:**5, 10, 14, 16; **7:**3, 5, 10, 11^2, 12, 13, 18

Nah 1:5, 7, 11, 14, 15^2; **2:**1; **3:**4, 7^2, 8^2, 19

Hab 1:3, 6^2, 8, 13^2, 14; **2:**2^2, 6^3, 7^2, 8, 9^3, 12, 13, 15^3, 17, 18^2, 19; **3:**8, 16

Zep 1:5^4, 6^2, 8, 9, 10^2, 11, 12^4, 15, 17, 18; **2:**5, 15^3; **3:**1, 6^3, 8^2, 9, 11^2, 16, 18, 19^4, 20^2

Hag 1:2, 6, 9, 11; **2:**3, 5, 13, 14, 18, 22, 23

Zec 1:8, 9, 10, 11, 13, 14, 15, 19, 21; **2:**3, 7, 8, 9, 11^2; **3:**2, 4, 7, 8, 9^2, 10; **4:**1^2, 4, 5, 9, 14; **5:**3^4, 4, 5^2, 6, 7, 10; **6:**4, 7, 8, 15^2; **7:**1, 11, 13, 14; **8:**9^3, 10, 13, 16, 17, 20, 23^3; **9:**7, 8^2, 12, 16; **11:**1, 5, 9^4, 10, 11^3, 13, 14, 16^5, 17; **12:**3^2, 4, 6, 7, 8^3, 9^3, 10, 11, 14; **13:**1, 2^2, 3^3, 4^2, 7, 8; **14:**4, 6^2, 7, 8^2, 9, 12, 13^2, 15, 16^2, 17, 18^2, 19, 20, 21^2

Mal 1:6, 7, 9, 10, 12, 13; **2:**4^2, 12^2, 13, 15, 16^2, 17; **3:**3, 5^2, 10^2, 14^2, 15^2, 16^3, 17^2, 18^2; **4:**1^4, 2, 3

Mt 1:6, 20, 22; **2:**2, 6, 8, 12, 15, 16^2, 17, 22, 23; **3:**3, 9, 11; **4:**3, 4, 12, 14, 17, 24^2; **5:**4, 14, 15, 16, 17, 20, 21, 22, 23, 27, 28, 29^2, 30^2, 32^2, 33, 38, 39, 42^2, 43, 44^2, 45; **6:**1, 2, 4, 5, 7, 16, 18, 23^2, 29, 32; **7:**1, 3^2, 6, 8^3, 11, 12, 13, 14, 19, 21^2, 22, 23, 25, 26, 27; **8:**4, 8, 10, 11, 16^2, 17, 24, 27, 28^2, 33, 34; **9:**6^2, 12^3, 13, 16, 22, 26, 28, 30, 31, 38; **10:**14, 15, 19, 20, 22, 25, 26^2, 27^2, 34, 37^2, 38, 39^2, 40^3, 41^2; **11:**3, 8, 11^2, 15, 24, 25, 28; **12:**1, 2, 3, 5, 6, 10, 11, 16, 17, 22, 30^2, 36^2, 45, 48; **13:**2, 12, 17, 19, 20^2, 22^2, 23^2, 28, 32, 35, 37, 39, 41, 44^2, 46, 47, 52, 53, 54; **14:**1, 15, 20, 21, 33, 35^3, 36; **15:**4, 11^2, 12, 17, 28, 30, 31, 37, 38; **16:**1, 11^3, 12, 13, 14, 15, 18, 20^2, 21^2, 23^2; **17:**10, 12, 13, 18, 24, 27^2; **18:**6^2, 7^2, 10^2, 11, 12, 13^2, 14, 16, 19^2, 25, 27, 28, 31, 32^2, 34; **19:**1, 4, 12, 13, 16, 17, 21, 22, 23, 28, 29, 30; **20:**1, 7, 9, 10, 14, 21, 22^2, 23, 25^2, 30, 32, 33; **21:**4, 9^3, 12^2, 15, 31, 32, 34, 45; **22:**3, 16, 21, 23, 31, 34, 46; **23:**3, 11, 12, 13, 17, 18, 19, 21, 22^2, 26^2, 31, 35, 37, 39; **24:**2, 4, 6, 13, 19^2, 20, 24, 32, 33, 36, 38^2, 43, 46, 47, 48, 50^2; **25:**3, 9, 10, 16, 17, 18, 20, 22, 24, 25, 26, 29^3; **26:**2, 4, 12, 13, 16, 17, 21, 23, 24^2, 29, 34, 41, 46, 48^2, 52, 53, 54, 55, 56, 57, 63, 68, 71, 73; **27:**3, 4^3, 8, 9^2, 14, 15, 17, 18, 19, 20, 21, 24^2, 31, 33, 35, 39, 40, 46, 47^2, 54^2, 62, 63^2, 64; **28:**5, 7, 10, 11

Mk 1:9, 14, 22, 27, 32^2, 34, 36, 38, 45; **2:**1, 2, 8, 10^2, 12, 15, 16, 17^2, 21, 23, 24, 25; **3:**2, 9, 10, 12, 14^2, 20, 24, 25, 29; **4:**1, 8, 9, 10, 11, 12, 15, 22, 24, 25^3, 28, 31, 32, 37, 38, 40, 41; **5:**4, 7, 10, 12, 14^2, 15, 16^2, 18^2, 23, 26, 29^2, 30, 32, 36, 38, 40, 43^2; **6:**2, 5, 8, 10, 11, 12, 13, 14, 15^2, 20, 21, 22, 25, 36, 44, 55^2, 56; **7:**2, 9, 11, 15^2, 18, 20^2, 26, 32, 34, 36; **8:**8, 9, 21, 25, 27, 29, 30, 31, 32, 33^2; **9:**1^2, 7, 9, 10, 11, 12, 13, 18, 23, 25, 26, 30, 31, 32, 33, 37, 39, 40, 42^2, 43, 45; **10:**13^2, 17, 18, 22, 23, 24, 29, 31, 35, 36, 37, 38^2, 39^2, 42, 47, 48, 51^2; **11:**3, 5, 9^3, 10, 15^2, 16, 23^2, 24, 25, 32; **12:**2, 12, 14, 15, 17^2, 19, 26, 28, 34^2, 35, 41, 43, 44; **13:**2, 11^3, 13, 14^2, 16, 17^2, 18, 20, 24, 25, 28, 29, 30, 32^2; **14:**4, 9, 12^2, 20, 21^2, 25^2, 28, 30, 35, 42, 44^2, 47, 58, 69, 70, 72; **15:**5, 6, 7, 9, 10, 11, 12, 29^2, 32^2, 35, 39, 42; **16:**1, 4, 7, 10, 11, 12, 16^2, 17

Lk 1:4, 7, 8, 19, 20, 21, 22, 23, 28, 35, 41, 43, 45, 49, 50, 57, 59, 61, 65, 66, 71^2, 74^2, 79;

2:1[2], 6[2], 18, 20, 23, 24, 26, 35, 38[2], 46, 47, 49[2]; **3:**7, 8, 11[3], 13, 20, 21; **4:**3, 4, 6, 18, 20, 26, 29, 40, 41, 42; **5:**1, 3, 7[2], 9, 17, 24[2], 25, 29, 31[2], 36; **6:**1, 2, 4, 5, 6, 7, 12, 18, 21[2], 23, 24, 25[2], 28, 29[2], 30[2], 31, 32, 38, 40, 41[2], 42[3], 45[2], 48, 49[3]; **7:**3, 4, 6, 9, 10[2], 11, 14, 15, 16[2], 19, 20, 21[2], 22, 28[2], 29, 36, 37, 39, 43, 49[2]; **8:**1, 8, 10, 12, 14, 15, 16, 17[2], 18, 22, 31, 32, 34, 36, 38, 40, 41, 45, 46, 47, 53, 56; **9:**5, 7[3], 8[2], 10, 11, 12, 17, 18, 19, 20, 21, 32[2], 37, 39, 45[2], 48[2], 50, 51, 54, 57; **10:**2, 9, 11, 12[3], 16[4], 20, 21[2], 23, 24, 31, 36, 37, 38, 40[2], 42; **11:**1, 4, 10[3], 11, 13, 18, 23[2], 26, 27, 28, 33, 35, 38, 40[3], 44, 48, 50, 52, 54; **12:**1, 2[2], 3, 4[3], 9, 10, 13, 21, 26, 27, 30, 33[2], 36[2], 37, 39, 42, 43, 44[2], 45, 46, 47, 48, 51, 56, 58; **13:**1[2], 2, 4[2], 9, 14, 17, 23, 32, 33, 34, 35; **14:**1, 9, 10[3], 11, 12, 15[2], 17, 21, 23, 24, 29, 31, 33[2], 35; **15:**4, 7[2], 10, 12, 14, 15, 16, 29, 31, 32; **16:**1, 2, 4, 9, 10[3], 12[2], 15, 16, 18, 22, 24, 25, 26[2], 27, 28; **17:**1, 2[2], 9[2], 10, 11, 12, 14, 15, 18, 24, 27, 29, 31[2], 34; **18:**1, 3, 8, 9, 11, 12, 14[2], 15, 19, 22, 24[2], 26, 29, 31, 35, 37, 39, 41[2]; **19:**4, 7[2], 10, 11, 15[2], 21[2], 22[3], 23, 24[2], 26[3], 27, 32, 37, 38, 40, 43, 45[2]; **20:**1, 2, 6, 7, 10, 14, 17, 18, 19, 20[2], 21, 27, 28, 35, 37, 40, 41; **21:**3, 4, 6, 8, 20, 21, 22, 23[2], 30, 31, 34, 35, 36[2], 37; **22:**8, 9, 21, 22, 23, 25, 26[3], 27[4], 30, 31, 32, 34[2], 36[2], 37[2], 40, 47, 63, 64, 70; **23:**2, 7[2], 14, 23, 24, 25, 26, 29, 48[2], 49, 53, 54; **24:**10, 12, 13, 15, 16, 17, 21, 23[2], 25, 33, 37, 39, 44, 45, 47

Jn 1:3, 7, 8[2], 9[2], 12, 15, 21, 22[2], 25[2], 31, 33, 34, 39, 48; **2:**9, 10, 14, 16, 17, 18, 22, 25; **3:**2[2], 6[2], 7, 8, 11[2], 13, 15, 16[2], 17, 18[2], 19, 20, 21[3], 26, 28[2], 29, 31[3], 32, 33[2], 36[2]; **4:**1, 5, 9, 10, 11, 14[2], 15, 18, 19, 20, 24, 25, 26, 27, 29, 32, 34, 36[4], 37, 38, 39[2], 40, 42, 44, 45, 47[2], 50, 53, 54; **5:**6[2], 10, 11, 12, 13[2], 15, 18, 20[2], 23[2], 24[2], 25, 28, 29[2], 32[2], 34, 36[3], 40, 42, 44, 45[2]; **6:**2, 5, 7, 11, 12[2], 13, 14[3], 15, 18, 22[4], 23, 24, 27, 28, 29, 30, 32, 35[2], 36, 37[2], 38, 39, 40[2], 42, 45, 46, 47, 48, 50, 51, 56, 57, 58[2], 61, 63[2], 64[2], 65, 66, 69[2], 71; **7:**3[2], 4, 7, 16, 18[3], 23, 26, 28, 32, 33, 35, 36, 37, 38, 39[2], 42, 50; **8:**5, 6, 7, 12, 16, 17, 18[2], 24[2], 25, 26, 27, 28[2], 29[2], 37, 38[2], 40, 47, 48, 50, 52, 54[2]; **9:**2, 3, 4, 8[2], 11, 13, 16, 17, 18[2], 20[2], 22[2], 24[2], 25, 29, 30, 31, 32[2], 35, 36, 37, 39[2]; **10:**1, 2, 8, 10[2], 12, 17, 21, 25, 33, 38[2], 41; **11:**2, 4[2], 6, 7, 11[2], 13, 15, 16, 17, 20, 22, 24, 25, 27, 29, 30, 31, 37, 39, 40, 41, 42[3], 44, 49, 50[3], 51[3], 52[3], 53, 56, 57[2]; **12:**2, 6, 9[2], 10, 11, 12[2], 13, 16[2], 17, 18[2], 20, 23, 25[2], 29[2], 34, 35, 36, 38, 39, 40, 44[2], 45[2], 46, 48[3], 50; **13:**1[2], 3[2], 5, 10, 15, 16[2], 18[2], 19[2], 20[3], 21, 24, 27, 29[3], 34[2], 35; **14:**3, 9, 10[3], 11, 12[2], 13[2], 16, 20[2], 21[3], 22, 24, 29, 31[2]; **15:**2[3], 5, 8, 11[2], 12, 13, 15, 16[3], 17, 18, 20, 21, 23, 25[2]; **16:**1, 2[2], 4[2], 5, 7, 13, 15[2], 17, 18, 19[2], 20, 21, 23, 24, 26[2], 27, 30[3], 32, 33; **17:**1, 2, 3, 7, 8[2], 11, 12[2], 13, 15[2], 19, 21[4], 22, 23[3], 24[2], 25, 26; **18:**4, 8, 9, 13, 14[2], 15, 16[2], 17, 28, 32, 36, 37[3], 39[2]; **19:**4[2], 8, 10, 11, 13[2], 21, 24, 27[2], 28[2], 31[4], 33, 35[3], 36, 38; **20:**3, 7, 8, 9, 14, 18[2], 29, 31[3]; **21:**3, 4, 7[2], 12, 14[2], 15, 16, 17, 20, 22[2], 23[4], 24, 25[2]

Act 1:1, 2, 4, 8, 16, 19[2], 21, 22[2], 25[2]; **2:**6, 14, 16, 20, 21, 24, 25, 29, 30[2], 31, 36[2], 39, 41, 44; **3:**2, 10[2], 11, 17, 18, 19, 23[2], 24; **4:**2, 5, 10, 13[2], 16[2], 17[2], 21, 23, 24[2], 29, 30, 32[2], 34[2]; **5:**5, 9, 15[2], 17, 21[2], 28, 32, 33, 40, 41; **6:**2, 14, 15; **7:**5, 6[2], 7, 12, 16, 19, 24, 25, 27, 36, 37, 38, 44[2], 45; **8:**1, 4, 7[2], 8, 9, 11, 14, 15, 18, 19, 20, 23, 24, 26, 31, 37, 39; **9:**2, 12, 14, 17[2], 20, 21[4], 22, 23, 26, 27, 35, 37, 38[2], 43; **10:**2, 7, 14, 15, 22, 27, 28[3], 33[2], 34, 35, 37, 38, 42, 43, 45, 47; **11:**1[2], 2, 9, 16, 17, 19, 22, 23, 26, 28; **12:**1, 9, 10, 11, 15, 19; **13:**1[2], 16, 20, 25, 27, 28, 29, 32, 33, 34, 38, 39, 40, 42, 46, 47; **14:**1[2], 6, 9, 15[2], 17, 18, 21, 22, 27; **15:**2, 4, 5, 7[2], 11, 17, 19, 20[2], 21, 24, 26, 29, 39; **16:**2, 3, 4, 10, 12[2], 14, 19, 26, 27, 32, 38; **17:**3[2], 6, 7, 11, 13, 15, 17, 22, 24[2], 27, 29, 31[2]; **18:**2, 5, 7, 14, 21, 28[2]; **19:**1, 4[2], 9, 10, 12, 16[2], 18, 22, 23, 25, 26[2], 27[2], 31, 34, 35[2], 36; **20:**18, 20, 22, 23[2], 24, 25, 26, 29, 31, 34[2], 35, 38; **21:**1, 4, 8, 11, 12, 21[2], 22, 23, 24[3], 25[2], 26, 28, 29, 31, 35, 38[2]; **22:**2, 6, 9[2], 11[2], 14[2], 17, 19[2], 20, 22, 24[2], 25[2], 26, 29; **23:**2, 4, 5, 6, 8, 9, 12, 14, 15, 19, 20, 21, 22, 24, 27, 30, 34; **24:**2[2], 4[2], 9, 10[2], 11[2], 14, 15, 21, 22, 23, 26[2]; **25:**3, 4[2], 16, 24, 25[2], 26; **26:**5, 8, 9, 18[2], 20, 23[3], 26, 27, 29[2], 30; **27:**1, 10, 13, 20, 24, 25, 27, 33, 43, 44; **28:**1, 6, 8, 16, 17, 19, 20, 21, 22, 25, 28[2], 30

Ro 1:7, 8, 9, 11, 12[2], 13[2], 15, 16, 19, 20[2], 21, 26, 27[2], 32[2]; **2:**1[2], 2, 3[2], 4, 8, 9, 10, 18, 19, 21, 22[2], 23, 28, 29; **3:**2, 4, 8[2], 9, 11[2], 12, 19[2], 22, 24, 25, 26, 28; **4:**1, 4, 5[2], 9, 11[3], 12, 13, 16[3], 18[2], 21, 23, 24; **5:**3, 8, 12, 14[2], 16, 20, 21; **6:**1, 2, 3, 4, 6[3], 7, 8, 9, 10[2], 12, 13, 16, 17[2]; **7:**1[2], 3[2], 4[2], 6[2], 13[4], 14, 15[3], 16[2], 17[2], 18[3], 19[2], 20[3], 21, 24; **8:**3, 4, 5[2], 8, 9, 11[3], 16, 17[2], 18, 22, 24, 25, 27, 28[2], 29, 32, 33, 34[3], 37, 38; **9:**2, 3, 8, 11[2], 16[3], 17[2], 20[2], 23, 26, 30, 32; **10:**1, 2, 4, 5, 6, 7, 8, 9[2], 12, 15, 19, 20[2]; **11:**7, 8[2], 10, 11, 19, 25[2], 31, 32; **12:**1, 2[2], 3, 6, 7, 8[4], 9[2], 15[2]; **13:**1, 2, 3, 4[2], 8, 11[2]; **14:**1, 2, 3[3], 4, 6[4], 9, 13, 14[2], 18, 20, 22[2], 23; **15:**1, 3, 4, 6, 8, 9, 12, 13, 14, 15, 16[2], 19, 21, 29, 30, 31[3], 32; **16:**2[2], 5, 11, 18, 19, 25

1Co 1:2[2], 5, 7, 8, 10[3], 11, 12, 14, 15, 18, 21[2], 26, 28, 29, 31[2]; **2:**5, 6[2], 9, 12[2], 15, 16; **3:**7[3], 8[2], 11, 16[2], 18, 20; **4:**2, 3, 4, 6[3], 7, 8, 9; **5:**1[2], 2[2], 3, 5, 6, 7, 11, 12[2], 13[2]; **6:**2, 3[2], 5[2], 6, 8, 9, 15, 16, 17, 18[2], 19; **7:**5[2], 7[2], 12, 13, 22[2], 25, 26[2], 29[2], 30[3], 31, 32[2], 33[2], 34[2], 35[3], 36, 37[2], 38[2], 40; **8:**1, 2, 4[3], 5, 7, 9; **9:**3, 9, 10[4], 13, 14, 15[2], 18[2], 19, 20[4], 21[3], 22[2], 23, 24[2], 25, 26, 27; **10:**1[2], 4[3], 12, 13[2], 17, 19[2], 20[2], 25, 27, 28, 30, 33; **11:**2, 3, 5[2], 13, 14, 17[2], 18, 19, 22, 23[2], 28[2], 29, 32, 34; **12:**2, 3[3], 11, 12, 24, 25[2], 28; **13:**2, 10[2]; **14:**1, 2, 3, 4[2], 5[5], 11[2], 12, 13[2], 16, 19, 21, 22[3], 23[2], 24, 25, 27, 30, 31, 37[2]; **15:**3[2], 4[2], 5, 6, 7, 9, 12[2], 15[2], 20, 23, 26, 27, 28[2], 36, 37[3], 46[3], 48[2], 50, 54, 58; **16:**2, 4, 6[2], 10, 11, 15[2], 16[2], 17, 18, 19

2Co 1:4, 7, 8[2], 9, 10, 11, 12, 14, 15, 17[2], 23, 24; **2:**1, 2, 3, 4[2], 5, 7, 8, 9, 15[2]; **3:**5, 7, 10[2], 11[2], 12, 13[2], 17; **4:**3, 7, 10, 11, 14, 15; **5:**1, 3, 4[3], 5, 6, 9, 10[2], 12, 14, 15[2], 19, 21; **6:**1, 3, 15; **7:**3, 6[2], 7, 8, 9[3], 11, 12[3], 16; **8:**2, 4, 6[2], 7, 9[2], 11[2], 12[2], 13, 14[3], 15[2], 19, 20; **9:**2, 3, 4, 5[2], 8, 10; **10:**2[2], 5, 7[2], 9, 11, 12, 15[2], 17, 18; **11:**2, 3, 4, 7, 9, 12[3], 16, 17, 18, 28[2], 31; **12:**4, 6[2], 8, 9, 13, 19, 20, 21; **13:**2, 5, 6[2], 7[4]

Gal 1:4, 6[2], 7, 8, 9, 11, 13, 16, 23; **2:**2, 4[2], 5, 7, 8, 9[2], 10, 12, 13, 14, 16[2], 19; **3:**1, 5, 7, 8, 10, 11, 12, 13, 14[2], 17[3], 22[2], 24, 25; **4:**1, 5[2], 9, 15, 17, 21, 22, 27[2], 29[2]; **5:**2, 3[2], 7, 8, 10[2], 15, 17[2], 21, 24; **6:**6[2], 7, 8[2], 13, 14

Eph 1:4, 10, 12, 13[3], 17, 18, 21[2], 23; **2:**2, 7, 8, 10, 11[2], 12[2], 16, 17; **3:**3, 6, 8, 10, 13, 16, 17[2], 19, 20[3]; **4:**1, 9[2], 10[3], 14, 16, 17, 18, 21, 22, 24, 28[3], 29[2]; **5:**5, 13, 14, 15, 26, 27[2], 28, 33; **6:**3, 5, 8, 9, 11, 13, 19[2], 20, 21, 22[2], 24

Php 1:6, 9, 10[3], 12, 13, 17, 19, 20[2], 25, 26, 27[2], 28; **2:**2, 10, 11[2], 15, 16[2], 19, 22, 24, 25, 26[2], 28[2]; **3:**4, 8, 9, 10, 12[2], 18, 21; **4:**2, 10, 11, 14, 15, 17, 22

Col 1:9, 10, 16[2], 18, 19, 21, 24, 28; **2:**1, 2, 14; **3:**9, 10, 24, 25; **4:**1[2], 3, 4, 5, 6, 8, 12, 13[2], 16[2], 17

1Th 1:7[2], 8; **2:**1, 2, 10, 12, 13, 16; **3:**3[2], 4, 6, 10[2]; **4:**1, 3, 4, 6[2], 8, 9, 10, 11, 12[3], 13, 14, 15; **5:**1, 2, 4[2], 7[2], 10, 14, 15[2], 21, 24, 27

2Th 1:3, 4[2], 5, 6, 8[2], 10[2], 11, 12; **2:**2[2], 3[2], 4[4], 5, 6, 8, 10[2], 11, 12; **3:**1, 2, 4, 6[2], 8, 10, 11, 12[2], 14[2]

1Ti 1:3[2], 8, 9, 10[2], 12, 15, 16, 18, 20; **2:**1, 2[2], 8, 9; **3:**4, 13, 15; **4:**1, 8[2], 10, 14, 15, 16; **5:**3, 4, 5, 6, 7, 14, 16[3], 17, 18, 20[2], 21, 25; **6:**1, 2, 5, 9, 14, 17[2], 18[2], 19, 20

2Ti 1:3, 4, 5[2], 6, 12[3], 14, 15, 18[2]; **2:**1, 2, 4[2], 6, 8, 10, 14, 15, 18, 19[2], 22, 23, 25, 26; **3:**1, 3, 12, 15, 17; **4:**8[2], 13, 16, 17[2]

Tit 1:2, 5[2], 9, 13, 14, 15, 16; **2:**2, 3, 4, 5, 8[3], 10, 11, 12, 13, 14; **3:**4, 7, 8[2], 10, 11[2], 13, 14, 15[2]

Phlm 6, 8, 12, 13, 14, 15, 18, 21, 22

Heb 2:3, 6[2], 8[2], 9, 11, 14[3], 17, 18[2]; **3:**2, 4, 10, 16, 17, 18[2], 19; **4:**2, 6, 10, 11, 13, 14[2], 16; **5:**1, 2[2], 4, 5, 7[2], 9, 12, 13, 14; **6:**7, 8, 9, 10, 11, 12, 18, 19; **7:**2, 5[2], 6, 8[2], 11, 14, 15, 21, 25; **8:**3, 4[2], 5, 7, 9, 10, 13[2]; **9:**4[2], 8, 9[2], 11, 15[2], 23, 25, 28; **10:**2, 4, 9, 14, 15, 16, 20, 23, 26, 28, 30, 33, 34, 36, 37, 39; **11:**3[2], 4, 5[2], 6[4], 13, 14[2], 15, 16, 17, 18, 19, 28, 31, 35, 40; **12:**1, 2, 3, 10, 13, 17, 18[2], 19[2], 20, 21, 24[2], 25[4], 27[3]; **13:**3, 6, 9[2], 12, 15, 17[4], 19, 20[2], 21, 23, 24

Jas 1:3, 4, 5, 6, 7[2], 9, 10, 12[2], 18; **2:**3, 5, 7, 11, 12, 13, 19, 20, 24; **3:**1, 3, 6, 17, 18; **4:**1, 3, 4, 5[2], 11, 12, 13, 14, 15[2], 17; **5:**1, 11, 16, 17, 20

1Pt 1:4, 7[2], 10, 11, 12[2], 13, 18, 21[2], 22; **2:**2, 3, 6, 9, 12, 14[2], 15, 21, 23, 24; **3:**1, 3, 4, 7, 9[2], 10[2], 12, 13[2], 15[2], 16[2], 17, 18, 20; **4:**1, 2, 4, 5, 6[2], 11, 13, 17[2], 19; **5:**1, 4, 6, 9[2], 10, 12, 13, 14

2Pt 1:1, 3[2], 4[2], 8, 9[2], 14, 15, 19[2], 20; **2:**1, 4, 6, 8, 10, 12, 13, 14, 17, 18, 22; **3:**2, 3, 5, 6, 8, 9[2], 10, 11, 14[2], 15, 16

1Jn 1:1, 2, 3[2], 4, 5, 6, 8, 10; **2:**1, 3, 4, 5, 6, 9, 10, 11[2], 13, 14, 15, 16, 17, 18[2], 19[2], 21, 22[3], 23, 24[2], 25, 26, 27, 28, 29[3]; **3:**1, 2, 3, 5, 7, 8[2], 10, 11[2], 12, 14[2], 15, 19, 22, 23, 24[2]; **4:**2[2], 3[4], 4[2], 6[2], 7, 8, 9[2], 10[2], 13, 14, 15, 16[2], 17, 18, 20, 21; **5:**1[4], 2, 3, 4, 5[3], 6[2], 7, 8, 10[3], 11, 12[2], 13[4], 14[2], 15[3], 16[2], 18[3], 19, 20[4]

2Jn 1, 4, 5[2], 6[2], 7, 8[2], 9, 11, 12

3Jn 2, 3, 4, 7, 8, 10, 11[4], 12

Jude 1, 3, 5[2], 15, 18, 24

Rev 1:2, 3[2], 5, 9, 12, 18; **2:**1, 6, 7[2], 10, 11[2], 14, 15, 17[3], 20, 22, 23, 25, 26, 29; **3:**1[3], 2, 5, 6, 7[4], 9, 10, 11[2], 12, 13, 15, 17, 18[4], 21, 22; **4:**3, 9, 10[2]; **5:**1, 7, 12, 13[2], 14; **6:**2, 4[3], 5, 8, 9, 10, 11[2], 16; **7:**1, 15; **8:**3; **9:**4, 5[2], 17, 20; **10:**6[4]; **11:**1, 6, 7, 10[2], 18[3]; **12:**6, 9, 12[2], 13, 14, 15; **13:**6, 8, 10[2], 13, 14[3], 15[2], 17[2], 18; **14:**3, 6, 7, 8, 12, 13, 15, 16, 18; **15:**2, 5; **16:**12, 14, 15; **17:**1, 7, 8[3], 11, 14, 18; **18:**4[2], 10[2], 14, 16[2], 19[2], 21, 24; **19:**4, 5, 8, 10, 11, 12, 15, 17, 18[2], 19, 20[3], 21; **20:**2, 3[2], 4, 6, 10, 11; **21:**5, 6, 7, 10, 15, 17, 27; **22:**7, 11[3], 14[2], 17[2], 18[2]

THE

Gen 1:1[3], 2[6], 4[3], 5[5], 6[4], 7[5], 8[4], 9[3], 10[3], 11[4], 12[2], 13[3], 14[4], 15[3], 16[5], 17[3], 18[4], 19[3], 20[4], 21, 22[3], 23[3], 24[3], 25[3], 26[7], 27, 28[6], 29[4], 30[3], 31[3]; **2:**1[3], 2[2], 3, 4[7], 5[6], 6[3], 7[4], 8[2], 9[7], 10, 11[3], 12[2], 13[4], 14[4], 15[3], 16[3], 17[3], 18[2], 19[5], 20[3], 21[2], 22[3], 25; **3:**1[5], 2[5], 3[4], 4[2], 5, 6[4], 7, 8[9], 9, 10, 11, 12[3], 13[4], 14[4], 15, 16, 17[4], 18[2], 19[2], 20, 21, 22[3], 23[3], 24[5]; **4:**1, 2, 3[3], 4[3], 6, 7, 8, 9, 10[2], 11, 12[2], 13, 14[3], 15[2], 16[4], 17[3], 19[4], 20, 21[2], 22, 26[2]; **5:**1[4], 2, 4, 5, 8, 11, 14, 17, 20, 23, 27, 29[2], 31; **6:**1[2], 2[2], 3, 4[4], 5[3], 6[2], 7[6], 8[2], 9, 11[2], 12[2], 13[3], 14, 15[5], 16[4], 17[3], 18, 19, 20; **7:**1[2], 2[2], 3[5], 4[3], 5, 6[2], 7[3], 8, 9[3], 10[3], 11[8], 12[2], 13[4], 14[2], 15[2], 16, 17[5], 18[5], 19[4], 20[2], 21[2], 22[2], 23[7], 24[2]; **8:**1[4], 2[4], 3[5], 4[5], 5[7], 6[3], 7[2], 8[3], 9[7], 10[2], 11[4], 12, 13[10], 14[4], 16, 17[3], 19[2], 20[2], 21[4], 22; **9:**1, 2[7], 3, 4[2], 5[4], 6, 7, 10[5], 11[2], 12[2], 13[2], 14[3], 15, 16[4], 17[3], 18[3], 19[2], 21, 22[2], 23, 26, 27, 28, 29; **10:**1[3], 2, 3, 4, 5[2], 6, 7[2], 8, 9[3], 10[2], 11, 12, 16[3], 17[3], 18[5], 19[2], 20, 21[4], 22, 23, 25[2], 29, 30, 31, 32[5]; **11:**1, 2[2], 4[2], 5[4], 6[2], 8[4], 9[7], 10[2], 27, 28[2], 29[5], 31[3], 32; **12:**1, 3, 4, 5[3], 6[5], 7[2], 8[6], 9, 10[3], 12, 14[2], 15[2], 17; **13:**1, 3[3], 4[5], 6, 7[5], 9[5], 10[5], 11[3], 12[3], 13[2], 14[2], 15, 16[4], 17[3], 18[2]; **14:**1, 2, 3[2], 4, 5[5], 6[2], 7[3], 8[7], 9, 10[3], 11, 13[3], 15, 16[3], 17[5], 18[2], 19, 20, 21[3], 22[4], 24[3]; **15:**1[2], 2, 4[2], 5, 6, 7[2], 10[2], 11[2], 12, 16[3], 17, 18[5], 19[3], 20[3], 21[4]; **16:**2[2], 3[2], 5, 7[5], 8, 9[2], 10[2], 11[3], 12, 13[2], 14; **17:**1[2], 8[2], 11[2], 12, 14, 21, 23[3], 24, 25, 26, 27[3]; **18:**1[5], 2[2], 4, 6[2], 7, 8[2], 9, 10[2], 11, 13, 14[3], 16[2], 17, 18[2], 19[3], 20[2], 21, 22[2], 23[2], 24[3], 25[6], 26[3], 27, 28[2], 30, 31, 32, 33; **19:**1[2], 2, 4[5], 5, 6[2], 8, 9[2], 10[3], 11[4], 12[2], 13[4], 14, 15[4], 16[5], 17[2], 19, 21, 22[2], 23[2], 24[2], 25[4], 27[3], 28[5], 29[6], 30, 31[5], 33, 34[3], 35, 36, 37[4], 38[4]; **20:**1, 3, 5, 6, 7, 8[2], 11, 12[2], 16, 18[3]; **21:**1[2], 2, 3, 8[2], 9[2], 10, 11, 12, 13[2], 14[3], 15[4], 16[2], 17[5], 18, 19[2], 20[2], 21[2], 22, 23[2], 28, 32[3], 33[3], 34; **22:**2[2], 3[4], 4[2], 5[2], 6[3], 7[3], 9[4], 10, 11[2], 12, 13[2], 14[3], 15[3], 16, 17[5], 18[2], 21; **23:**1[2], 2[2], 3, 5, 6, 7[3], 8, 9[2], 10[5], 11[4], 12[2], 13[4], 15, 16[4], 17[6], 18[3], 19[4], 20[3]; **24:**1, 3[6], 5[3], 7[2], 8, 9[2], 10[4], 11[4], 13[4], 14[2], 15, 16[2], 17, 20[2], 21[2], 22[2], 24[2], 26[2], 27[4], 28, 29[2], 30[6], 31[3], 32[4], 35, 37[2], 39, 40, 42, 43[2], 44[3], 45, 46, 47[3], 48[3], 49[2], 50[2], 51, 52[2], 53, 54[2], 55[2], 56, 57, 60[2], 61[3], 62[3], 63[3], 64, 65[3], 66; **25:**3, 4[2], 6[3], 7[2], 8, 9[4], 10[2], 11[2], 12[2], 13[3], 16, 17[3], 18, 19, 20[4], 21[2], 22[2], 23[5], 25, 27[2], 29, 32; **26:**1[4], 2[2], 3, 4[3], 7[4], 8, 10, 12[2], 13, 14, 15[3], 17, 18[5], 19, 20[4], 21, 22[3], 24[3], 25[2], 26, 28, 29[2], 31, 32[2], 33[2], 34[4]; **27:**2, 3, 5, 7, 9[2], 15, 16[4], 17[3], 20, 22[3], 27[4], 28[3], 30, 34, 39[3], 40, 41[2], 46[4]; **28:**1, 2[2], 4[2], 5[2], 6, 8, 9[3], 11[2], 12[3], 13[4], 14[8], 16, 17[2], 18[3], 19[3], 21, 22; **29:**1[3], 2[3], 3[6], 5, 6, 7[2], 8[4], 10[5], 13, 14, 16[4], 20, 22[2], 23, 25, 26[2], 27, 31, 32, 33, 35; **30:**2[2], 13, 14[2], 16[2], 17, 19, 24, 27, 30, 32[5], 33[2], 35[5], 36, 37[3], 38[5], 39[2], 40[6], 41[6], 42[3], 43; **31:**1, 2, 3[2], 4, 5, 8[4], 9, 10[4], 11, 12[2], 13[3], 16, 18[2], 19, 20, 21[2], 22, 23, 24, 25[2], 26, 29[2], 33, 34[3], 35[2], 38, 39, 40[3], 42[4], 46, 48, 49, 53[4], 54[2], 55; **32:**1, 2, 3[2], 6, 7[3], 8[2], 9, 10[3], 11[4], 12[2], 16, 17, 19[3], 20, 21[2], 22, 23, 24[2], 25[2], 26, 30[2], 31, 32[6]; **33:**1[2], 2, 3, 5[3], 6, 8, 10, 13[3], 14[2], 15[2], 17[2], 18[2], 19[2]; **34:**1[3], 2[3], 3[3], 5, 6, 7[3], 8, 10, 12, 13, 19[3], 20[2], 21[2], 22, 24[2], 25[4], 26[2], 27[3], 28[2], 29, 30[4]; **35:**1, 2, 3[2], 4[2], 5[3], 6[2], 7[2], 8, 12[2], 13, 14, 15[2], 17, 19, 20, 21, 22, 23, 24,

APNDX

25, 26[2], 27, 28, 29; **36:**1, 2[6], 5[2], 6[4], 7, 9[3], 10[5], 11, 12, 13[2], 14[3], 15[3], 16[3], 17[4], 18[3], 19, 20[3], 21[4], 22, 23, 24[4], 25[2], 26, 27, 28, 29[2], 30[2], 31[3], 32[2], 33, 34, 35[3], 37, 38, 39[4], 40[2], 43[4]; **37:**1[2], 2[5], 3, 5, 7, 8, 9[3], 10, 11, 13, 14[2], 15[2], 17, 22, 24, 27, 28[2], 29[2], 30, 31[3], 32, 35, 36[2]; **38:**7[3], 9[2], 10[2], 12[2], 14, 16, 17, 19, 20[4], 21[3], 22[2], 24, 25[2], 27, 28[2], 30; **39:**1[3], 2[3], 3[2], 5[7], 6, 8, 11[3], 14, 17, 19, 20[3], 21[4], 22[5], 23[4]; **40:**1[3], 2[4], 3[5], 4[2], 5[5], 6, 7, 9, 10[2], 11[2], 12[2], 13, 15[3], 16[2], 17[3], 18[2], 19, 20[4], 21[2], 22, 23; **41:**1[2], 2, 3[4], 4[2], 5, 6, 7[2], 8[3], 9, 10[3], 11, 12[2], 14, 17[2], 18, 19, 20[3], 21, 23, 24[3], 25, 26[3], 27[3], 28, 29, 30[4], 31[2], 32[2], 33, 34[4], 35[3], 36[5], 37[3], 38, 40, 41, 43[3], 44, 45[2], 46[2], 47[2], 48[8], 49[2], 50[2], 51[2], 52[3], 53[2], 54[3], 55[3], 56[7], 57; **42:**5[3], 6[5], 7, 9[3], 12[2], 13[3], 15, 16, 18, 19[2], 21, 22, 25, 26, 27, 29, 30[4], 32[2], 33[4], 34, 35, 38[3]; **43:**1[2], 2, 3, 5, 6, 7[2], 8, 9, 11[3], 12[2], 13, 14, 15, 16, 17[3], 18[3], 19[3], 20, 21[2], 23, 24[2], 25, 26[3], 27, 32[4], 33[3]; **44:**1[2], 2[4], 3[2], 4[2], 8[2], 11, 12[3], 13, 14, 16[2], 17[2], 22, 24, 26, 28, 29, 30[2], 31[3], 32[2], 33[2], 34[2]; **45:**2[2], 6[3], 7, 8, 10, 12, 16, 17, 18[4], 19, 20[2], 21[3], 23[2], 24, 25, 26, 27[3]; **46:**1, 2[2], 3, 5[2], 6, 8[2], 9, 10[2], 11, 12[3], 13, 14, 15[2], 16, 17[2], 18, 19, 20[2], 21, 22[2], 23, 24, 25[2], 26[2], 27[3], 28, 31, 32, 34[2]; **47:**1[2], 4[4], 6[4], 9[8], 11[4], 13[5], 14[5], 15[4], 17[4], 18[2], 19, 20[4], 21[3], 22[3], 23[2], 24[3], 25, 26[4], 27[2], 28[2], 29, 31; **48:**2, 3, 5, 6, 7[4], 10, 12, 14[2], 15, 16[5], 17, 18, 21, 22[2]; **49:**1, 3[3], 8, 9, 10[3], 11[3], 13[2], 15, 16, 17[3], 19, 22, 23, 24[5], 25[5], 26[7], 27[3], 28, 29[3], 30[5], 32[4], 33[2]; **50:**2[2], 3[2], 4[3], 5, 7[4], 8[2], 10, 11[7], 13[5], 15, 17[4], 19, 23[3], 24, 25

Ex 1:1[2], 5[2], 7[2], 9[2], 10, 12[3], 13[2], 14, 15[6], 16[3], 17[3], 18[3], 19[4], 20[2], 21, 22; **2:**1, 2, 3[3], 5[5], 6[3], 7[2], 8[2], 9[2], 10[2], 12[2], 13[3], 14, 15[2], 16[2], 17, 19[3], 20, 21, 23[4], 25; **3:**1[6], 2[5], 3, 4[3], 5, 6[4], 7[2], 8[9], 9[4], 10, 11, 12, 13[2], 14, 15[5], 16[3], 17[8], 18[6], 19, 20, 21[2], 22; **4:**1, 2, 3[2], 4[2], 5[4], 6, 8[4], 9[6], 10, 11[5], 13, 14[3], 16, 19[2], 20[2], 21[2], 22, 24[3], 25, 26, 27[3], 28[3], 29[2], 30[5], 31[3]; **5:**1[2], 2[2], 3[5], 4[2], 5[2], 6[3], 7, 8[2], 9, 10[3], 12[2], 13, 14[2], 15[2], 16, 17, 18, 19[2], 20, 21[3], 22; **6:**1, 2, 3, 4[2], 5[3], 6[4], 7[3], 8[3], 9, 10, 11, 12[2], 13[4], 14[4], 15[3], 16[4], 17, 18[3], 19[2], 20[2], 21, 22, 24[3], 25[4], 26[3], 27, 28[3], 29[2], 30; **7:**1, 2, 3, 4[2], 5[3], 6, 8, 10, 11[3], 13, 14[2], 15[4], 16[3], 17[5], 18[6], 19[3], 20[8], 21[7], 22[2], 24[4], 25[2]; **8:**1[2], 3[2], 4, 5[5], 6[3], 7[2], 8[4], 9[2], 10, 11[2], 12[2], 13[6], 14, 15, 16[4], 17[5], 18, 19[3], 20[4], 21[3], 22[5], 24[5], 25, 26[5], 27[2], 28[2], 29[4], 30, 31[3], 32; **9:**1[3], 3[8], 4[4], 5[3], 6[5], 7[4], 8[4], 9[2], 10, 11[5], 12[3], 13[4], 14, 15, 16, 18, 19[3], 20[4], 21[3], 22[4], 23[5], 24[2], 25[6], 26[2], 27, 28, 29[5], 30, 31[5], 32[2], 33[5], 34[3], 35[3]; **10:**1[2], 2[2], 3[2], 4, 5[6], 6[5], 7[2], 8, 9, 10, 11, 12[6], 13[5], 14[3], 15[11], 16, 17, 18, 19[4], 20[2], 21[2], 22, 23, 24, 25, 26[2], 27; **11:**1, 2[2], 3[9], 4[2], 5[7], 6, 7[3], 8, 9[2], 10[2]; **12:**1[2], 2[3], 3[3], 4[5], 5[3], 6[5], 7[4], 8, 9, 10[2], 11, 12[5], 13[5], 14, 15[3], 16[2], 17[2], 18[5], 19[2], 21[2], 22[8], 23[8], 25[2], 27[7], 28[2], 29[8], 30[2], 31[2], 33[3], 34, 35[3], 36[5], 37, 39, 40[2], 41[6], 42[4], 43[3], 46[2], 47, 48[3], 49, 50[2], 51[4]; **13:**1, 2[3], 3[3], 4, 5[7], 6[2], 8, 9[2], 11[3], 12[4], 13, 14[2], 15[8], 16, 17[5], 18[6], 19[2], 20[2], 21[2], 22[4]; **14:**1, 2[3], 3[3], 4[2], 5[4], 7, 8[4], 9[3], 10[4], 11, 12[4], 13[4], 14, 15[2], 16[4], 17[2], 18[2], 19[4], 20[6], 21[5], 22[5], 23[3], 24[8], 25[4], 26[4], 27[8], 28[5], 29[4], 30[5], 31[5]; **15:**1[5], 2, 3[2], 4[2], 5[2], 6, 7, 8[6], 9[2], 10[2], 11, 12, 13, 14[2], 15[3], 16[2], 17[3], 18, 19[8], 20[3], 21[3], 22[3], 23[2], 24, 25[4], 26[4], 27; **16:**1[6], 2[3], 3[6], 4[2], 5, 6[3], 7[4], 8[6], 9[3], 10[6], 11, 12[4], 13[5], 14[5], 15[3], 16[3], 17, 19, 20, 21, 22[3], 23[5], 24, 25[2], 26[2], 27[2], 28, 29[5], 30[2], 31[3], 32[5], 33, 34[2], 35[3], 36; **17:**1[6], 2[2], 3[2], 4, 5[4], 6[5], 7[6], 9[3], 10[2], 12[6], 13[2], 14[3], 15, 16[2]; **18:**1[2], 3[2], 4[4], 5[2], 7, 8[5], 9[4], 10[7], 11[2], 12, 13[5], 14[3], 15, 16, 17, 19[2], 20[2], 21, 22[2], 24, 25, 26[2]; **19:**1[5], 2[3], 3[4], 4, 5, 6[2], 7[3], 8[5], 9[5], 10[2], 11[5], 12[4], 13[2], 14[3], 15[2], 16[7], 17[4], 18[4], 19[2], 20[6], 21[3], 22[3], 23[3], 24[4], 25; **20:**2[3], 4[3], 5[5], 7[3], 8, 10[3], 11[5], 12[2], 18[7], 20, 21[2], 22[2]; **21:**1, 2, 4, 5, 6[3], 7, 9, 19, 22[2], 26[2], 28[3], 29[2], 30, 32[2], 34[4], 35[3], 36[2]; **22:**3, 4, 5[2], 6[4], 7[2], 8[4], 9[3], 11[2], 12, 14, 15, 17, 20, 21, 24, 26, 28[2], 29[2], 30, 31[2]; **23:**1, 5, 6, 7[2], 8[4], 9[2], 10, 11[4], 12[3], 13, 14, 15[3], 16[7], 17[2], 18[3], 19[4], 20[2], 23[6], 25[2], 26, 27, 28[3], 29[3], 30, 31[7]; **24:**1[2], 2[2], 3[7], 4[5], 5[2], 6[3], 7[5], 8[5], 9, 10[2], 11[2], 12[2], 13, 14, 15[2], 16[6], 17[7], 18[4]; **25:**1, 2, 3, 6, 7[2], 9[4], 10[3], 12[3], 14[5], 15[3], 16[2], 17[2], 18[2], 19[6], 20[5], 21[4], 22[5], 23[3], 25, 26[3], 27[4], 28[2], 29, 30, 31[2], 32[5], 33[3], 34, 35[5], 36, 37[2], 38[2], 40; **26:**1, 2[3], 3, 4[7], 5[6], 6[2], 7, 8[3], 9[3], 10[6], 11[3], 12[6], 13[7], 14, 15, 16[2], 17[2], 18[3], 19, 20[3], 22[2], 23[3], 24[2], 26[3], 27[7], 28[3], 29[3], 30[3], 32, 33[8], 34[4], 35[9], 36[2], 37; **27:**1[2], 2[3], 3, 4[2], 5[5], 6, 7[5], 8, 9[4], 10[3], 11[3], 12[3], 13[3], 14[2], 15, 16[2], 17[2], 18[4], 19[6], 20[3], 21[7]; **28:**1[2], 3[2], 4[2], 6, 7[2], 8[4], 9[2], 10[3], 11[5], 12[5], 14[3], 15[3], 16[2], 17[2], 18, 19, 20, 21[5], 22[2], 23[4], 24[4], 25[5], 26[5], 27[6], 28[8], 29[5], 30[7], 31[2], 32[4], 33[2], 34[2], 35[2], 36[2], 37[3], 38[4], 39[3], 41, 42[2], 43[4]; **29:**1[2], 3[3], 4[3], 5[8], 6[3], 7, 9[2], 10[4], 11[5], 12[7], 13[7], 14[3], 15[2], 16[2], 17[2], 18[4], 19[3], 20[9], 21[4], 22[10], 23[3], 24[3], 25[3], 26[3], 27[6], 28[4], 29, 30[3], 31[3], 32[7], 33, 34[5], 36, 37[2], 38[2], 39[3], 40[3], 41[5], 42[4], 43[2], 44[4], 45, 46[3]; **30:**2[5], 3[3], 4[4], 5, 6[5], 7, 8[2], 10[5], 11, 12[3], 13[4], 14, 15[3], 16[7], 17, 18[3], 20[4], 22, 24[2], 25[2], 26[4], 27[3], 28[2], 30, 31, 32, 34, 35[2], 36[3], 37[3]; **31:**1, 2[3], 3, 6[3], 7[7], 8[3], 9[2], 10[5], 11[2], 12, 13[2], 14, 15[4], 16[3], 17[3], 18; **32:**1[5], 2[2], 3[2], 4, 5, 6[2], 7[2], 8[2], 9, 11[2], 12[4], 13, 14[2], 15[6], 16[5], 17[3], 18[3], 19[5], 20[4], 22[2], 23[2], 24, 25, 26[4], 27[2], 28[3], 29, 30[3], 31, 33, 34[3], 35[3]; **33:**1[4], 2[6], 3[2], 4, 5[3], 6[2], 7[9], 8[3], 9[5], 10[4], 11[4], 12, 16[3], 17, 19[2], 21, 22; **34:**1[4], 2[4], 3[2], 4[4], 5[4], 6[3], 7[7], 8, 10[4], 11[6], 12[3], 14, 15[2], 18[4], 19, 20[2], 21, 22[4], 23[3], 24[3], 25[5], 26[4], 27[2], 28[5], 29[3], 30[2], 31[2], 32[2], 34[3], 35[4]; **35:**1[4], 2[2], 3, 4[4], 5[2], 8[2], 9[2], 10, 11, 12[5], 13[2], 14[4], 15[7], 16[2], 17[5], 18[4], 19[6], 20[3], 21[5], 22, 24[2], 25, 26, 27[3], 28[3], 29[4], 30[5], 31, 33, 34[2], 35[4]; **36:**1[4], 2[2], 3[5], 4[3], 5[4], 6[4], 7[2], 8[2], 9[3], 10[2], 11[6], 12[5], 13[2], 14[2], 15[3], 17[6], 18, 19, 20, 21[2], 22[2], 23[2], 24, 25[3], 27[2], 28[3], 29[2], 31[3], 32[6], 33[4], 34[3], 37, 38; **37:**1[4], 3[3], 5[5], 6[3], 7[2], 8[5], 9[5], 10[4], 12, 13[3], 14[5], 15[2], 16[2], 17[3], 18[5], 19[3], 20, 21[4], 22, 24, 25[6], 26[3], 27[4], 28, 29[4]; **38:**1[4], 2[4], 3[8], 4[3], 5[3], 6, 7[5], 8[7], 9[4], 10[2], 11[4], 12[3], 13, 14[3], 15[2], 16[2], 17[7], 18[8], 19, 20[3], 21[8], 22[4], 23, 24[8], 25[4], 26[2], 27[6], 28[2], 29[2], 30[8], 31[8]; **39:**1[4], 2, 3[5], 4, 5[4], 6[2], 7[4], 8[3], 9[3], 10[2], 11, 12, 13, 14[5], 15[2], 16[3], 17[4], 18[5], 19[5], 20[6], 21[8], 22[2], 23[4], 24[2], 25[5], 26[3], 29, 30[4], 31[2], 32[6], 33[2], 34[4], 35[4], 36[3], 37[5], 38[5], 39[2], 40[9], 41[5], 42[3], 43[2]; **40:**1, 2[5], 3[4], 4[4], 5[7], 6[6], 7[4], 8[3], 9[3], 10[3], 11, 12[3], 13[2], 15, 16, 17[5], 18[3], 19[5], 20[6], 21[7], 22[6], 23[3], 24[6], 25[3], 26[4], 27, 28[3], 29[8], 30[4], 32[4], 33[6], 34[5], 35[6], 36[3], 37[2], 38[5]

Lev 1:1[3], 2[5], 3[5], 4[2], 5[9], 6, 7[5], 8[7], 9[3], 10[3], 11[5], 12[4], 13[5], 14[2], 15[6], 16[4], 17[6]; **2:**1, 2[8], 3[4], 4, 7, 8[4], 9[4], 10[3], 11[2], 12[4], 13[2], 14[3], 16[6]; **3:**1[2], 2[7], 3[7], 4[6], 5[5], 6[2], 7, 8[5], 9[10], 10[6], 11[5], 12, 13[6], 14[5], 15[6], 16[6]; **4:**1, 2[3], 3[4], 4[8], 5[4], 6[6], 7[15], 8[7], 9[6], 10[5], 11[2], 12[5], 13[6], 14[5], 15[7], 16[4], 17[4], 18[13], 19, 20[3], 21[4], 22[2], 23, 24[5], 25[7], 26[4], 27[3], 28, 29[5], 30[7], 31[7], 33[4], 34[8], 35[10]; **5:**1, 2, 3, 6[4], 7[2], 8[2], 9[8], 10[3], 11, 12[5], 13[3], 14, 15[6], 16[7], 17[2], 18[3], 19; **6:**1, 2, 4[2], 5[3], 6[3], 7[2], 8, 9[8], 10[6], 11[2], 12[6], 13[2], 14[5], 15[8], 16[5], 17[2], 18[4], 19, 20[5], 21[3], 22[2], 23, 24, 25[6], 26[5], 27[3], 28, 29[2], 30[5]; **7:**1[2], 2[5], 3[4], 4[6], 5[3], 6[2], 7[3], 8[4], 9[5], 10, 11[3], 12, 13[2], 14[5], 15[4], 16[4], 17[4], 18[4], 19[2], 20[4], 21[5], 22, 23, 24[3], 25[4], 28, 29[5], 30[6], 31[4], 32[3], 33[5], 34[6], 35[8], 36[3], 37[8], 38[5]; **8:**1, 2[3], 3[4], 4[5], 5[3], 7[6], 8[4], 9[5], 10[2], 11[3], 12, 13, 14[5], 15[7], 16[6], 17[3], 18[4], 19[2], 20[4], 21[6], 22[4], 23[4], 24[6], 25[8], 26[4], 27, 28[3], 29[4], 30[3], 31[6], 32[2], 33[4], 34, 35[5], 36[2]; **9:**1[2], 2, 3[3], 4[2], 5[4], 6[4], 7[5], 8[3], 9[8], 10[7], 11[3], 12[3], 13[4], 14[4], 15[5], 16[2], 17[4], 18[5], 19[8], 20[4], 21[3], 22[3], 23[6], 24[5]; **10:**1[2], 2[2], 3[2], 4[4], 5, 6[4], 7[6], 8, 9[2], 11[4], 12[4], 13[3], 14[3], 15[6], 16[3], 17[5], 18[3], 19[4]; **11:**1, 2[4], 3[3], 4[5], 5[3], 6[3], 7[3], 9[4], 10[4], 12, 13[4], 14[2], 16[4], 17[3], 18[3], 19[4], 21, 22[4], 24[2], 25[2], 26[3], 27, 28[2], 29[5], 30[5], 31, 32, 38, 39[2], 40[4], 41, 42[2], 44[2], 45[2], 46[5], 47[4]; **12:**1, 2[3], 3[2], 4[3], 5, 6[6], 7[3], 8[4]; **13:**1, 2[5], 3[9], 4[6], 5[6], 6[6], 7[4], 8[4], 9[2], 10[5], 11[2], 12[5], 13[3], 15[3], 16[2], 17[4], 18[2], 19[3], 20[5], 21[3], 22[2], 23[2], 24[2], 25[7], 26[4], 27[5], 28[5], 29[2], 30[5], 31[7], 32[6], 33[3], 34[7], 35[2], 36[4], 37[3], 38, 39[4], 40, 41, 42, 43[6], 44, 45[2], 46[3], 47[2], 48, 49[6], 50[3], 51[7], 52[2], 53[5], 54[3], 55[5], 56[7], 57[4], 58[3], 59[3]; **14:**1, 2[4], 3[5], 4, 5[2], 6[8], 7[3], 8, 9, 10[2], 11[6], 12[3], 13[8], 14[8], 15[3], 16[4], 17[9], 18[6], 19[3], 20[5], 22[2], 23[6], 24[6], 25[9], 26[3], 27[3], 28[9], 29[5], 30[3], 31[5], 32[2], 33, 34[3], 35[3], 36[7], 37[5], 38[5], 39[5], 40[4], 41[3], 42[2], 43[4], 44[4], 45[6], 46[3], 47[2], 48[7], 49, 50[2], 51[8], 52[8], 53[4], 54, 55, 57; **15:**1, 2, 4, 5, 6[2], 7[3], 8[2], 9, 10[2], 11[2], 12[2], 14[6], 15[5], 16, 17[2], 18[2], 19, 21, 22, 23, 24, 25[5], 26[3], 27, 29[5], 30[6], 31, 32, 33[2]; **16:**1[4], 2[7], 3, 4[3], 5[3], 6, 7[5], 8[4], 9[2], 10[5], 11[4], 12[3], 13[7], 14[5], 15[8], 16[6], 17[4], 18[8], 19[3], 20[5], 21[8], 22[3], 23[4], 24[4], 25[3], 26[3], 27[7], 28, 29[3], 30[2], 32[5], 33[7], 34[2]; **17:**1, 2[3], 3[3], 4[6], 5[9], 6[9], 8[2], 9[4], 10[2], 11[6], 12, 13[3], 14[7], 15; **18:**1, 2[2], 3[4], 4, 5, 6, 7[2], 8, 9[2], 10, 11, 12, 13, 14, 15, 16, 17, 18, 21[3], 24, 25[3], 27[3], 28[2], 29, 30; **19:**1, 2[3], 3, 4, 5, 6[4], 7, 8[2], 9[3], 10[2], 12[2], 13[2], 14[3], 15[4], 16[2], 18[2], 21[4], 22[5], 23[2], 24[3], 25[4], 26, 27[2], 28[2], 29[2], 30, 31, 32[4], 34[3], 36[2], 37; **20:**1, 2[5], 4[3], 6, 7, 8, 10[3], 11, 15, 16[2], 17, 18, 19, 22, 23[2], 24, 25, 26; **21:**1[4], 5, 6[4], 8[2], 9[2], 10[3], 12[5], 15, 16, 17, 21[5], 22[3], 23[3], 24; **22:**1, 2[3], 3[4], 4[3], 6[2], 7[2], 8, 9, 10[3], 11, 12[2], 13, 14[4], 15[3], 16[2], 17, 18[4], 19[3], 21, 22[3], 24, 25, 26, 27[3], 29, 30[3], 31, 32[2], 33[2]; **23:**1, 2[3], 3[4], 4[2], 5[3], 6[4], 7, 8[2], 9, 10[5], 11[5], 12[3], 13[4], 14, 15[5], 16[3], 17[2], 18[4], 19[2], 20[7], 21, 22[5], 23, 24[4], 25, 26, 27[2], 28, 30, 32[2], 33, 34[4], 35, 36[3], 37[3], 38[3], 39[7], 40[5], 41[3], 43[3], 44[3]; **24:**1, 2[3], 3[7], 4[3], 6[2], 7[2], 8[2], 9[3], 10[4], 11[5], 12[2], 13, 14[2], 15, 16[7], 22[2], 23[4]; **25:**1, 2[4], 3, 4[3], 5[2], 6[2], 7[2], 8[2], 9[6], 10[3], 11, 12[3], 13, 15[4], 16[7], 17, 18, 19, 20, 21, 22[3], 23[2], 24[2], 26, 27[4], 28[3], 30[4], 31[5], 32[5], 33[8], 34[2], 38[3], 40, 41, 42, 44, 45[2], 46, 47[3], 50[5], 51[2], 52[2], 53, 54, 55[3]; **26:**1, 2, 4[3], 5[4], 6[3], 7, 8, 10[2], 13[3], 16[2], 19, 20[2], 25[4], 26, 29[2], 30, 31, 32, 33, 34[2], 36[2], 38[2], 39, 40, 41[2], 42, 43[2], 44[2], 45[5], 46[4]; **27:**1, 2[3], 3[3], 5[2], 6[2], 7, 8[3], 9[2], 10, 11[3], 12[2], 14[3], 15[2], 16[2], 17, 18[6], 19[3], 20[2], 21[5], 22[2], 23[5], 24[5], 25[3], 26[4], 28[3], 30[8], 31, 32[6], 33, 34[3]

Nu 1:1[8], 2[5], 4, 5[4], 6, 7, 8, 9, 10[3], 11, 12, 13, 14, 15, 16[3], 18[6], 19[2], 20[4], 21, 22[4], 23, 24[4], 25, 26[4], 27, 28[4], 29, 30[4], 31, 32[5], 33, 34[4], 35, 36[4], 37, 38[4], 39, 40[4], 41, 42[4], 43, 44[2], 45[2], 47[2], 48, 49[3], 50[6], 51[5], 52, 53[7], 54[2]; **2:**1, 2[4], 3[7], 5[3], 7[3], 9, 10[6], 12[4], 14[4], 16[2], 17[6], 18[6], 20[4], 22[4], 24[2], 25[6], 27[4], 29[4], 31, 32[3], 33[3], 34[3]; **3:**1[3], 2[3], 3[4], 4[5], 5, 6[2], 7[6], 8[7], 9[2], 10, 11, 12[6], 13[6], 14[2], 15[2], 16[2], 17, 18[2], 19, 20[4], 21[6], 22[2], 23[3], 24[5], 25[11], 26[9], 27[10], 28[4], 29[4], 30[6], 31[8], 32[7], 33[5], 34[2], 35[7], 36[8], 37[2], 38[9], 39[4], 40[5], 41[9], 42[3], 43[2], 44, 45[7], 46[4], 47[4], 48[2], 49[2], 50[5], 51[4]; **4:**1, 2[4], 3[4], 4[5], 5[3], 6[2], 7[5], 8[2], 9[3], 10, 11[2], 12[2], 13[2], 14[8], 15[9], 16[12], 17, 18[4], 19, 20, 21, 22[3], 23[4], 24[3], 25[10], 26[9], 27[4], 28[8], 29[2], 30[4], 31[7], 32[4], 33[8], 34[5], 35[4], 37[7], 38[2], 39[4], 40, 41[6], 42[3], 43[4], 45[5], 46[3], 47[6], 49[4]; **5:**1, 2[3], 3[2], 4[4], 5, 6[2], 7[2], 8[7], 9[3], 10, 11, 12, 13[2], 14[2], 15[3], 16[2], 17[6], 18[9], 19[3], 21[6], 22[2], 23[2], 24[5], 25[6], 26[6], 27[4], 28, 29, 30[4], 31; **6:**1, 2[2], 4[4], 5[7], 6[2], 7, 8[2], 9[3], 10[5], 11[4], 12[4], 13[6], 14[3], 16[2], 17[4], 18[10], 19[7], 20[5], 21[5], 22, 23, 24, 25, 26, 27; **7:**1[5], 2[4], 3[3], 4, 5[4], 6[3], 7, 8[4], 9[3], 10[5], 11[3], 12[3], 13[3], 15, 16, 17[3], 18[2], 19[3], 21, 22, 23[3], 24[3], 25[3], 27, 28, 29[3], 30[3], 31[3], 33, 34, 35[3], 36[3], 37[3], 39, 40, 41[3], 42[3], 43[3], 45, 46, 47[3], 48[3], 49[3], 51, 52, 53[3], 54[3], 55[3], 57, 58, 59[3], 60[3], 61[3], 63, 64, 65[3], 66[3], 67[3], 69, 70, 71[3], 72[3], 73[3], 75, 76, 77[3], 78[3], 79[3], 81, 82, 83[3], 84[4], 85[3], 86[5], 87[7], 88[9], 89[6]; **8:**1, 2[3], 3[3], 4[6], 5, 6[2], 9[5], 10[4], 11[5], 12[7], 13[2], 14[3], 15[4], 16[3], 17[4], 18[3], 19[10], 20[6], 21[2], 22[5], 23, 24[4], 25[2], 26[4]; **9:**1[5], 2[2], 3[3], 4[2], 5[6], 6[2], 7[3], 8, 9, 10[3], 11[2], 12[3], 13[5], 14[7], 15[9], 16[2], 17[6], 18[7], 19[5], 20[6], 21[5], 22[3], 23[10]; **10:**1, 2[4], 3[4], 4[2], 5[2], 6[3], 7, 8[3], 9[3], 10[5], 11[6], 12[4], 13[3], 14[5], 15[4], 16[4], 17[4], 18[3], 19[4], 20[4], 21[4], 22[4], 23[4], 24[4], 25[6], 26[4], 27[4], 28[2], 29[5], 31, 32[2], 33[6], 34[3], 35, 36; **11:**1[7], 2[3], 3[4], 4[2], 5[6], 7[3], 8[3], 9[4], 10[4], 11[2], 12[2], 16[6], 17[3], 18[4], 20, 21, 22[4], 23[2], 24[7], 25[4], 26[9], 27, 28[2], 29[2], 30[2], 31[7], 32[4], 33[6], 34[2], 35; **12:**1, 2[2], 3[4], 4[3], 5[5], 6, 8[2], 9[2], 10[2], 11, 12, 13, 14[2], 15[2], 16[2]; **13:**1, 2[2], 3[4], 4[2], 5[2], 6[2], 7[2], 8[2], 9[2], 10[2], 11[3], 12[2], 13[2], 14[2], 15[2], 16[4], 17[2], 18[2], 19, 20[6], 21[2], 22[2], 23[3], 24[4], 25, 26[6], 27[2], 28[4], 29[10], 30, 31[2], 32[5], 33[3]; **14:**1[2], 2[3], 3[2], 5[3], 6[3], 7[3], 8, 9[4], 10[6], 11[2], 12, 13[2], 14, 15[2], 16[3], 17, 18[6], 19[2], 20, 21[3], 22, 23, 24, 25[6], 26, 27[2], 28, 30[3], 31, 33[2], 34[3], 35, 36[4], 37[4], 38[4], 39[2], 40[5], 41[2], 42, 43[5], 44[5], 45[2]; **15:**1, 2[2], 3[4], 4[2], 5[2], 6, 7[2], 8, 10, 12, 13[2], 14, 15[4], 16, 17, 18[2], 19[3], 20[3], 21[2], 22, 23[4], 24[6], 25[5], 26[4], 27, 28[3], 29[2], 30[4], 31[2], 32[3], 33, 35[4], 36[3], 37, 38[4], 39[2], 41[3]; **16:**1[5], 2[3], 3[4], 5, 7[3], 9[6], 10[2], 11, 12, 13, 14, 15, 16, 17, 18[3], 19[7], 20, 22[3], 23, 24[2], 25, 26[2], 27[2], 28, 29[3], 30[4], 31, 32[2], 33[3], 34[2], 35[2], 36, 37[5], 38[4], 39[3], 40[5], 41[5], 42[6], 43[2], 44, 46[4], 47[5], 48[3], 49[2], 50[4]; **17:**1, 2[3], 3[3], 4[3], 5[3], 6[2], 7[3], 8[4], 9[3], 10[3], 11, 12, 13[2]; **18:**1[4], 2[3], 3[5], 4[5], 5[5], 6[6], 7[3], 8[5], 9[2], 10, 11[3], 12[7], 13[2], 15[4], 16[3], 17[5], 18[3], 19[5], 20[2], 21[5], 22[3], 23[5], 24[5], 25, 26[5], 27[4], 28[4], 29[3], 30[6], 31[2], 32[3]; **19:**1, 2[4], 3[2], 4[3], 5, 6[4], 7[4], 8, 9[5], 10[5], 11, 12[4], 13[4], 14[3], 16, 17[2], 18[4], 19[5], 20[5], 21[2], 22[2]; **20:**1[5], 2, 3[2], 4[2], 6[7], 7, 8[5], 9[2], 10[2], 11[3], 12[4], 13[3], 14[2], 15, 16[2], 17[7], 18, 19[2], 22[2], 23[3], 24[3], 27[3], 28[3], 29[2]; **21:**1[4], 2, 3[5], 4[6], 5[2], 6[3], 7[5], 8, 9, 10, 11[2], 12, 13[6], 14[5], 15[4], 16[3], 18[7], 20[3], 21, 22[5], 23, 24[5], 25[3], 26[4], 27, 28[3], 29, 31[2], 32[2], 33[3], 34[2]; **22:**1[2], 2[2], 3[2], 4[6], 5[6], 6, 7[4], 8[2], 10, 11[2], 12, 13[3], 14, 16, 18[3], 19, 20[2], 21[2], 22[3], 23[9], 24[3], 25[5], 26[4], 27[4], 28[3], 29, 30, 31[5], 32[2], 33, 34[3], 35[5], 36[2], 38, 40, 41[4]; **23:**3, 5, 6, 7[3], 8, 9[5], 10[5], 12, 13, 14[2], 15, 16, 17[2], 19, 21[2], 22, 24[4], 26, 28; **24:**1[2], 2, 3[2], 4[3], 6[5], 7, 8[2], 11, 13[3], 14, 15[2], 16[5], 17[2], 19, 20[2], 21, 22, 24; **25:**1[2], 2[3], 3[2], 4[7], 5, 6[8], 7[4], 8[6], 9, 10, 11[5], 13[2], 14[5], 15[3], 16, 17, 18[5]; **26:**1[4], 2[3], 3[2], 4[5], 5[6], 6[4], 7[2], 8, 9[4], 10[2], 11, 12[7], 13[4], 14[2], 15[7], 16[4], 17[4], 18[2], 19[2], 20[7], 21[5], 22, 23[5], 24[4], 25, 26[7], 27[2], 28, 29[5], 30[5], 31[4], 32[4], 33[3], 34, 35[7], 36[3], 37[3], 38[7], 39[4], 40[5], 41, 42[4], 43[2], 44[7], 45[5], 46[2], 47[2], 48[5], 49[4], 50, 51[2], 52, 53[2], 54[2], 55[3], 56[2], 57[7], 58[12], 59[2], 61, 62[2], 63[3], 64[3], 65[4]; **27:**1[8], 2[6], 3[4], 4[2], 5, 6, 7[2], 8, 11[2], 12[3], 14[6], 15, 16[4], 17[2], 18[3], 19[2], 20[2], 21[5], 22[3], 23[2]; **28:**1, 2, 3[3], 4[3], 5, 6, 7[6], 8[5], 9[3], 10[2], 11[3], 13, 14[4], 15[3], 16[4], 17[2], 18, 19[2], 21, 23[2], 24[5], 25, 26[3], 27[3], 29, 30, 31; **29:**1[4], 2[2], 4, 5, 6[4], 7, 8[2], 10, 11[4], 12[3], 13[2], 14[2], 15, 16[2], 17[2], 18[4], 19[3], 20[2], 21[4], 22, 23[2], 24[4], 25[2], 26[2], 27[4], 28, 29[2], 30[4], 31, 32[2], 33[4], 34, 35, 36[2], 37[4], 38, 39, 40[2]; **30:**1[5], 2, 3, 5[2], 7, 8[2], 12[3], 13, 14, 16[3]; **31:**1, 2[2], 3[4], 4[2], 5, 6[6], 7[3], 8[4], 9[3], 11[2], 12[8], 13[4], 14[4], 15, 16[6], 17, 18, 19[3],

APNDX

9, 10[3], 12[3], 13[2], 14[3], 15[3], 16[3], 17[2], 18[4], 19[3], 21[4], 22[2], 23[7], 24[6], 25[5], 27[4], 28[2], 29, 30[2], 31[2], 32[3], 34[2], 35[3], 37; **16:**1[3], 2[7], 3[4], 4, 5[3], 6[3], 8[6], 9[3], 10[2], 11, 12[2], 13[2], 14[2], 15[2], 16[3], 18[2], 19, 21[2], 22[3], 23[3]; **17:**2[2], 3[3], 4[2], 5, 7, 8[2], 9[2], 10, 11[2], 12[3], 13, 14[8], 15[2], 16[4], 17, 19[3], 20[4], 21[2], 22[2], 23, 24, 25[2], 26, 27[4], 29[3]; **18:**1, 2[8], 3[2], 4[5], 5[5], 6[4], 7[2], 8[5], 9[7], 11[2], 12[4], 13, 14[3], 16[3], 17, 18[2], 19[3], 20, 21, 22, 23[2], 24[5], 25[3], 26[4], 27[6], 28[6], 29[3], 30, 31[2], 32[4], 33[3]; **19:**1, 2[4], 3[2], 4[2], 5[6], 7[2], 8[7], 9[7], 10, 11[6], 12[2], 13[2], 14[4], 15[3], 16[2], 17[3], 18[3], 19[4], 20[3], 21[2], 23[2], 24[5], 25[2], 26, 27[2], 28[2], 29[2], 30[2], 31[2], 32, 33, 34[2], 35[2], 36[2], 37[2], 38, 39[3], 40[4], 41[5], 42[4], 43[7]; **20:**1[2], 2[2], 3[4], 4[2], 5[2], 6, 7[4], 8[2], 9[2], 10[4], 12[6], 13[3], 14[2], 15[4], 16, 17[2], 18, 19[2], 21[6], 22[6], 23[4], 24[2], 25, 26; **21:**1[4], 2[8], 3[4], 4, 5[3], 6[3], 7[5], 8[7], 9[7], 10[7], 11[2], 12[6], 13[3], 14[5], 15[2], 16[3], 17[4], 18[4], 19[5], 20, 21[2], 22[3]; **22:**1[6], 2, 3[2], 4, 5[2], 6[2], 7, 8[2], 10, 11[2], 12, 13, 14[2], 16[8], 19[2], 21[2], 22[2], 25, 26[2], 27[2], 28[2], 29, 31[2], 32, 36, 41, 42, 43[4], 44[2], 47[3], 48, 49, 50, 51; **23:**1[6], 2[2], 3[3], 4[5], 6, 7[3], 8[7], 9[5], 10[4], 11[5], 12[4], 13[6], 14[2], 15[3], 16[6], 17[2], 18[3], 19, 20[3], 21[3], 22[2], 23[2], 24[3], 25[2], 26[3], 27[2], 28[2], 29[3], 30[2], 31[2], 32[2], 33[3], 34[5], 35[2], 36[2], 37[3], 39; **24:**1[2], 2[7], 3[6], 4[8], 5[4], 6, 7[5], 8[2], 9[6], 10[3], 11[4], 12, 14[3], 15[4], 16[9], 17[3], 18[3], 19[2], 20[3], 21[5], 22[2], 23[3], 24[4], 25[4]

1Ki 1:2[3], 3[2], 4[3], 5, 7[2], 8[4], 9[4], 10[2], 11[2], 12, 14, 15[5], 16[2], 17, 18, 19[5], 20[3], 21, 22[2], 23[5], 25[4], 26[2], 27[3], 28[2], 29[2], 30, 31[2], 32[4], 33[2], 34[3], 36[4], 37[3], 38[5], 39[4], 40[4], 41[4], 42[4], 44[7], 45[4], 46[2], 47[4], 48[2], 49, 50[2], 51[3], 52, 53; **2:**1, 2[2], 3[3], 4[2], 5[7], 6, 7[2], 8[4], 9, 10, 11, 12, 13[2], 15[3], 17[2], 18, 19[2], 20, 21, 22[4], 23, 24[2], 25[2], 26[4], 27[4], 28[4], 29[4], 30[4], 31[3], 32[6], 33[3], 34[2], 35[6], 36, 37[2], 38[3], 39[2], 42[4], 43[3], 44[3], 45[2], 46[4]; **3:**1[4], 2[3], 3[2], 4[2], 5, 8, 10[2], 11, 13, 15[3], 16, 17[2], 18[3], 19, 21[2], 22[6], 23[6], 24[2], 25[4], 26[5], 27[3], 28[4]; **4:**2[3], 3[3], 4[3], 5[4], 6[3], 7, 8, 9, 10[2], 11[3], 12[2], 13[4], 14, 15, 16, 17, 18, 19[6], 20[2], 21[5], 23, 24[4], 25, 28[3], 29[2], 30[4], 31[2], 33[3], 34[2]; **5:**1, 3[5], 4, 5[3], 6, 7[2], 8, 9[2], 12, 13, 14, 15, 16[4], 17[3], 18[2]; **6:**1[8], 2[5], 3[8], 4, 5[6], 6[8], 7[2], 8[7], 9[2], 10[2], 11[2], 13, 14, 15[8], 16[6], 17[2], 18[2], 19[5], 20[4], 21[3], 22[4], 23, 24[8], 25[2], 26[3], 27[12], 28, 29[2], 30[2], 31[4], 32[3], 33[3], 34[5], 35, 36, 37[5], 38[6]; **7:**2[6], 3, 5[2], 6[5], 7[4], 8[2], 9[5], 10, 11, 12[6], 14, 16[6], 17[5], 18[5], 19[4], 20[6], 21[7], 22[4], 23[2], 24[3], 25[5], 26[2], 27[3], 28[4], 29[4], 30[3], 31[6], 32[5], 33[3], 34[3], 35[7], 36[4], 37, 38, 39[8], 40[6], 41[10], 42[4], 43[2], 44, 45[5], 46[3], 47[3], 48[6], 49[7], 50[12], 51[10]; **8:**1[10], 2[4], 3[3], 4[8], 5[2], 6[9], 7[6], 8[5], 9[5], 10[5], 11[6], 12[2], 14[3], 15, 16[2], 17[3], 18, 19[2], 20[6], 21[4], 22[4], 25, 27[2], 28[3], 29[2], 30, 31, 32[2], 33, 34[2], 36[2], 37[2], 38, 39[2], 40[2], 43[2], 44[3], 46[3], 47[2], 48[3], 51[2], 52[2], 53[3], 54[3], 55, 56[2], 57, 59[5], 60[3], 61, 62[2], 63[5], 64[13], 65[3], 66[5]; **9:**1[4], 2[2], 3, 5[2], 7, 8, 9[3], 10[5], 11[2], 12, 13, 14, 15[5], 16[2], 17, 18[2], 19[2], 20[3], 21[2], 22, 23[4], 24, 25[5], 26[3], 27[3]; **10:**1[4], 3, 4[2], 5[5], 6, 7[3], 9[3], 10[2], 11, 12[5], 13, 14, 15[6], 17[3], 18[2], 19[6], 20[4], 21[4], 22[3], 23[2], 24, 26[2], 27[3], 28[2], 29[3]; **11:**1[2], 2[3], 4[2], 5[4], 6[3], 7[4], 9[2], 10, 11[2], 12, 13, 14[3], 15[3], 19[4], 20[2], 21[2], 23, 25[2], 26[2], 27[4], 28[4], 29[4], 30, 31[4], 32[3], 33[6], 34[2], 35, 36, 39, 40, 41[4], 42, 43; **12:**2[2], 3, 4, 5, 6, 8[3], 9, 10, 12[4], 13[3], 14[2], 15[7], 16[4], 17[2], 18, 19, 20[3], 21[5], 22[2], 23[4], 24[6], 26[2], 27[3], 28[2], 29[2], 30[2], 31[3], 32[8], 33[6]; **13:**1[3], 2[7], 3[5], 4[4], 5[7], 6[7], 7[2], 8[2], 9[3], 10, 11[4], 12, 13[2], 14[2], 17[3], 18[2], 20[4], 21[6], 22[4], 23[2], 24[5], 25[6], 26[9], 27, 28[7], 29[6], 31[2], 32[7], 33[5], 34[3]; **14:**1, 2[2], 3, 4, 5[2], 6[2], 7[2], 8[2], 10[4], 11[6], 12[2], 13[3], 14[2], 15[4], 16, 17[3], 18[4], 19[5], 20, 21[4], 22[2], 24[5], 25, 26[6], 27[5], 28[5], 29[5], 31; **15:**1[2], 2, 3[3], 4, 5[5], 6, 7[5], 8, 9, 10, 11[2], 12[3], 13, 14[2], 15[4], 18[10], 20[4], 22[2], 23[7], 24, 25[2], 26[3], 27[3], 28, 29[4], 30[2], 31[5], 33[2], 34[3]; **16:**1[3], 2, 3[4], 4[5], 5[5], 7[10], 8[2], 9, 10, 11, 12[4], 13[3], 14[5], 15[3], 16[5], 18[4], 19[3], 20[5], 21[3], 22[3], 23, 24[6], 25[2], 26[3], 27[5], 29[3], 30[3], 31[4], 32, 33[2], 34[6]; **17:**1[3], 2[2], 3, 4[2], 5[3], 6[4], 7[2], 8[2], 10[3], 12, 14[6], 15, 16[4], 17[4], 20[2], 21[2], 22[4], 23[3], 24[3]; **18:**1[4], 3[2], 4[2], 5[3], 6, 7, 9, 10[2], 12[3], 13[3], 15, 18[2], 19[3], 20[2], 21[3], 22[2], 23, 24[5], 25[2], 26[3], 28, 29[3], 30[4], 31[5], 32[4], 33[5], 34[4], 35[3], 36[4], 37, 38[8], 39[5], 40[2], 42[2], 43, 44[3], 45[2], 46[3]; **19:**1[2], 2[2], 4, 6, 7[4], 8[2], 9[2], 10[3], 11[11], 12[4], 13[2], 14[3], 15[2], 16[2], 17[2], 18, 19[2], 20, 21[3]; **20:**1, 2, 3, 4, 5, 6, 7[3], 8[2], 9[4], 10[3], 11, 12[3], 13[2], 14[5], 15[5], 16[3], 17[3], 19[4], 20[3], 21[3], 22[5], 23[4], 24, 25[2], 26[3], 27[4], 28[7], 29[5], 30[4], 31[3], 32, 33[2], 34, 35[5], 36[2], 37, 38[3], 39[4], 40, 41[3], 42, 43; **21:**1[2], 2, 3[2], 4[3], 6, 7[3], 8[3], 9[2], 10, 11[5], 12, 13[5], 15[2], 16[2], 17[3], 18, 19[4], 20[2], 21, 22[5], 23[3], 24[5], 25[2], 26[3], 28[3], 29[2]; **22:**2[3], 3[3], 4, 5[3], 6[5], 7, 8[4], 9[2], 10[5], 11[3], 12[3], 13[5], 14[2], 15[5], 16[3], 17[2], 18, 19[4], 20, 21, 22[2], 23[3], 24[4], 26[4], 27[2], 28, 29[2], 30[4], 31[2], 32[3], 33[3], 34[5], 35[7], 36[3], 37[2], 38[5], 39[7], 41[2], 42, 43[6], 44, 45[5], 46[4], 48, 49[2], 50, 51[2], 52[6], 53

2Ki 1:1, 2, 3[6], 4, 5, 6[3], 8, 9[3], 10, 11, 12, 13[3], 14[2], 15[3], 16[2], 17[4], 18[5]; **2:**1, 2[2], 3[3], 4[2], 5[3], 6[2], 7[2], 8, 12[2], 13[2], 14[4], 15[4], 16[2], 19[5], 21[4], 22[2], 23[2], 24[3]; **3:**1[2], 2[3], 3[2], 4[2], 5[2], 6, 7[2], 8[2], 9[5], 10[3], 11[5], 12[4], 13[6], 14[3], 15[3], 16, 17, 18[3], 20[4], 21[3], 22[6], 23[2], 24[4], 25[5], 26[3], 27; **4:**1[5], 2[2], 4, 5[2], 6[2], 7[3], 10, 11, 13[3], 15, 16, 17[2], 18[2], 21[3], 22[3], 25[2], 26, 27[5], 29[2], 30[3], 31[4], 32[2], 33[2], 34[4], 35[3], 37, 38[6], 39[2], 40[3], 41[3], 42[4], 43[2], 44[2]; **5:**1[3], 2[2], 3, 4[2], 5[2], 6[2], 7[2], 8[3], 9[2], 11[4], 12, 13, 14[3], 15[2], 16, 17, 18[5], 20[3], 21, 22[2], 24[3], 26, 27; **6:**1[3], 5[2], 6[3], 8, 9[3], 10[3], 11[3], 12[3], 14, 15[3], 17[4], 18[2], 19[3], 20[3], 21, 23[2], 25, 26[2], 27[3], 28, 29, 30[5], 31[2], 32[8], 33[3]; **7:**1[4], 2[3], 3[2], 4[5], 5[5], 6[9], 7[2], 8[2], 9[2], 10[5], 11[2], 12[7], 13[5], 14[3], 15[4], 16[5], 17[8], 18[3], 19[2], 20[2]; **8:**1[3], 2[5], 3[5], 4[4], 5[4], 6[7], 7[2], 8[3], 10, 11, 12[3], 13, 15, 16[3], 18[6], 19, 20, 21[5], 22[3], 23[5], 24, 25[3], 26, 27[7], 28[3], 29[4]; **9:**1[3], 2[2], 3[3], 4[3], 5[2], 6[5], 7[7], 8[2], 9[5], 10[3], 11[2], 12, 13[2], 14[2], 15[3], 17[2], 18[3], 19, 20[4], 21[2], 22, 24, 25[4], 26[7], 27[5], 28, 29[2], 31, 32, 33[2], 35[3], 36[5], 37[4]; **10:**1[2], 3, 5[5], 6[6], 7[2], 8[5], 9[2], 10[6], 11, 12[2], 13[6], 14[2], 15[2], 16, 17[2], 18, 19[3], 21[3], 22[2], 23[6], 24[2], 25[9], 26[2], 27[2], 29[3], 30[4], 31[3], 32[2], 33[5], 34[5], 36; **11:**1[2], 2[4], 3[3], 4[9], 5[4], 6[5], 7[5], 8[3], 9[6], 10[4], 11[8], 12[4], 13[6], 14[7], 15[10], 16[4], 17[6], 18[8], 19[14], 20[5]; **12:**1, 2[3], 3[3], 4[11], 5[3], 6[4], 7[6], 8[4], 9[11], 10[6], 11[9], 12[4], 13[5], 14[3], 15[2], 16[4], 18[6], 19[5], 20, 21[3]; **13:**1[3], 2[4], 3[5], 4[4], 5[4], 6[3], 7[3], 8[5], 10[2], 11[4], 12[5], 13, 14[3], 16[3], 17[5], 18[3], 19, 20[5], 21[4], 22, 23, 25[6]; **14:**1[2], 3[2], 4[3], 5[2], 6[9], 7[2], 8[2], 9[4], 11, 12, 13[5], 14[6], 15[5], 16, 17[2], 18[5], 20, 21, 22, 23[3], 24[4], 25[9], 26[2], 27[4], 28[5], 29; **15:**1, 3[2], 4[3], 5[7], 6[5], 7, 8[2], 9[4], 10[2], 11[5], 12[4], 13[2], 14[2], 15[5], 16[2], 17[2], 18[4], 19[3], 20[5], 21[5], 23[2], 24[4], 25[4], 26[5], 27[2], 28[4], 29[2], 30[4], 31[5], 32[3], 33, 34[2], 35[6], 36[5], 37[3], 38; **16:**1[3], 2[2], 3[7], 4[2], 6[2], 7[4], 8[6], 9[3], 10[5], 11[2], 12[5], 13[2], 14[8], 15[13], 16, 17[5], 18[7], 19[5], 20; **17:**1[2], 2[3], 4[3], 5[2], 6[5], 7[4], 8[5], 9[5], 11[4], 12, 13[5], 14[2], 15[2], 16[3], 17[3], 18[2], 19[3], 20[3], 21[3], 22[2], 23[2], 24[2], 25[3], 26[9], 27[5], 28[2], 29[3], 30[3], 31[3], 32[5], 33[3], 34[5], 35, 36[2], 37[4], 38, 39[2], 41; **18:**1[2], 2, 3[2], 4[5], 5[2], 6[2], 7[2], 8[5], 9[2], 10[3], 11[4], 12[4], 13[2], 14[2], 15[5], 16[6], 17[5], 18[6], 19[2], 20, 21, 22, 23, 24[2], 25[2], 26[6], 27[2], 28[4], 29, 30[4], 31[2], 32, 33[4], 34[2], 35[3], 36[2], 37[6]; **19:**1[2], 2[6], 3[2], 4[7], 5, 6[4], 7, 8, 10[2], 11, 12[3], 13[4], 14[6], 15[5], 16[2], 17[2], 18[2], 19[3], 20[2], 21[5], 22, 23[9], 24[2], 26[5], 28, 29[4], 30[2], 31[2], 32[2], 33[3], 35[5], 37[3]; **20:**1[3], 2[2], 4[3], 5[6], 6[2], 7, 8[5], 9[4], 10[2], 11[4], 12, 13[6], 14, 15, 16[2], 17[2], 18[2], 19[2], 20[6]; **21:**2[6], 3[2], 4[3], 5[4], 6[3], 7[3], 8[3], 9[3], 10[2], 11, 12, 13[3], 14[2], 15, 16[2], 17[5], 18[2], 19, 20[2], 21[2], 22[3], 23[2], 24[4], 25[5], 26; **22:**1, 2[5], 3[7], 4[7], 5[12], 6, 7, 8[7], 9[10], 10[4], 11[4], 12[6], 13[6], 14[7], 15[2], 16[5], 17, 18[4], 19[3], 20[2]; **23:**1[2], 2[13], 3[6], 4[13], 5[9], 6[9], 7[6], 8[12], 9[5], 10[3], 11[11], 12[11], 13[11], 14[3], 15[6], 16[8], 17[5], 18[2], 19[6], 20[3], 21[5], 22[5], 23[2], 24[12], 25[2], 26[3], 27[2], 28[5], 29[2], 30[3], 31, 32[2], 33[2], 34[2], 35[9], 36, 37[2]; **24:**2[8], 3[3], 4[2], 5[5], 7[5], 8, 9[2], 10[2], 11, 12[4], 13[9], 14[6], 15[4], 16[2], 17, 18, 19[2], 20[3]; **25:**1[4], 2[2], 3[6], 4[10], 5[4], 6[2], 7[2], 8[6], 9[4], 10[5], 11[9], 12[4], 13[9], 14[5], 15[4], 16[5], 17[8], 18[6], 19[11], 20[2], 21[2], 22[4], 23[8], 24[4], 25[6], 26[4], 27[7], 28[2], 29, 30[2]

1Ch 1:5, 6, 7, 8, 9[2], 10, 12, 14[3], 15[3], 16[3], 17, 19[3], 23, 27, 28, 29, 31, 32[2], 33[2], 34, 35, 36, 37, 38, 39, 40[2], 41[2], 42[2], 43[5], 44, 45[2], 46[3], 48, 49, 50[3], 51, 54; **2:**1, 3[6], 4, 5, 6, 7[3], 8, 9, 10, 13[2], 14[2], 15[2], 16, 17[2], 18, 21[2], 22, 23[4], 24, 25[3], 26, 27[2], 28[2], 29[2], 30, 31[3], 32[2], 33[2], 42[5], 43, 44, 45[2], 47, 49[4], 50[4], 51[2], 52[2], 53[7], 54[5], 55[7]; **3:**1[5], 2[5], 3[2], 5, 9[3], 15[5], 16, 17, 19[2], 21[5], 22[2], 23, 24; **4:**1, 2[3], 3[2], 4[5], 5, 6, 7, 8[2], 10, 11[2], 12[2], 13[2], 14[2], 15[3], 16, 17[2], 18[5], 19[5], 20[2], 21[7], 22[2], 23[2], 24, 26, 27, 31, 33, 34, 35[3], 37[5], 38, 39[3], 40, 41[2], 42[2], 43[2]; **5:**1[7], 2[2], 3[2], 4, 6, 7[2], 8[3], 9[4], 10[3], 11[2], 12[2], 13, 14[8], 15[3], 16, 17[2], 18[4], 19, 20[2], 22[2], 23[3], 24[3], 25[4], 26[7]; **6:**1, 2, 3[2], 10[2], 15[2], 16, 17[2], 18, 19[3], 22, 25, 26, 28[2], 29, 31[4], 32[5], 33[4], 34[4], 35[4], 36[4], 37[4], 38[4], 39[2], 40[3], 41[3], 42[3], 43[3], 44[5], 45[3], 46[3], 47[4], 48[3], 49[6], 50, 54[4], 55[2], 56[4], 57[3], 60, 61[4], 62[5], 63[4], 64[2], 65[6], 66[4], 67, 70[4], 71[3], 72, 74, 76, 77[3], 78[4], 80; **7:**1, 2[2], 3[2], 4, 5, 6, 7[2], 8[2], 9[2], 10[2], 11[2], 12[2], 13[2], 14[3], 15[3], 16[2], 17[4], 19, 20, 21, 24[2], 28[4], 29[4], 30, 31[2], 33[2], 34, 35, 36, 38, 39, 40[5]; **8:**1[2], 2[2], 3, 6[4], 8, 10, 12[2], 13[3], 16, 18, 21, 25, 27, 28, 29, 34, 35, 38, 39[3], 40[2]; **9:**1[2], 2[4], 3[3], 4[6], 5[2], 6, 7[4], 8[6], 9[2], 10, 11[7], 12[8], 13[4], 14[5], 15[3], 16[7], 17[2], 18[3], 19[12], 20[3], 21[4], 22[2], 23[6], 24[2], 26[3], 27[3], 28[2], 29[8], 30[4], 31[6], 32[3], 33[4], 34, 35, 40, 41, 44; **10:**1[3], 2[3], 3[3], 5, 7[3], 8[3], 9[3], 10[2], 11, 12[4], 13[3], 14[3]; **11:**2, 3[5], 4[3], 5[3], 6[2], 7[2], 8[3], 9, 10[4], 11[4], 12[3], 13[3], 14[3], 15[6], 16[2], 17[3], 18[6], 19[2], 20[3], 21[3], 22[2], 23[3], 24[3], 25[2], 26[4], 27[2], 28[3], 29[2], 30[3], 31[3], 32[3], 33[2], 34[4], 35[3], 36[2], 37[2], 38[2], 39[4], 40[2], 41[2], 42[3], 43[2], 44[3], 45[2], 46[3], 47; **12:**1[3], 2[2], 3[5], 4[4], 5, 6, 7, 8[7], 9[3], 10[2], 11[2], 12[2], 13[2], 14[4], 15[4], 16[2], 17, 18[3], 19[4], 20, 21[3], 22, 23[6], 24[2], 25[2], 26, 27[2], 29[5], 30[2], 31, 32[3], 35, 37[5], 38; **13:**1, 2[4], 3[2], 4[4], 5[2], 6[3], 7[3], 9[3], 10[3], 11, 12, 13[4], 14[4]; **14:**2, 4, 8[2], 9[2], 10[2], 11[2], 13[2], 14, 15[4], 16[2], 17[3]; **15:**1[2], 2[4], 3[2], 4[2], 5[2], 6[2], 7[2], 8[2], 9[2], 10[2], 11[2], 12[6], 13[3], 14[4], 15[6], 16[4], 17[5], 18[2], 19, 21, 22[2], 23, 24[4], 25[6], 26[4], 27[6], 28[4], 29[5]; **16:**1[3], 2[5], 4[4], 5, 6[3], 7[2], 8[2], 10[2], 11, 12, 14[2], 15, 16, 17, 18[2], 23[2], 24, 25, 26[4], 28[3], 29[4], 30[2], 31[4], 32[3], 33[5], 34, 35, 36[3], 37[4], 38, 39[5], 40[5], 41[2], 42, 43; **17:**1[4], 3[2], 4, 5, 6, 7[3], 8[3], 9[2], 10[2], 16[2], 17, 18, 21, 23, 24[3], 27; **18:**1[3], 2, 3, 4, 5[2], 6[2], 7[2], 8[3], 9, 11[5], 12[3], 13[2], 15[3], 16[3], 17[5]; **19:**1[2], 2[4], 3[3], 4, 5[3], 6[2], 7[2], 8[2], 9[6], 10[3], 11[4], 12[2], 13[2], 14[3], 15[3], 16[6], 17[3], 18[4], 19[4]; **20:**1[6], 2[2], 3[4], 4[4], 5[4], 6[2], 7, 8[3]; **21:**2[3], 3[2], 4, 5[3], 6, 8, 9, 10, 11, 12[8], 13[3], 14, 15[7], 16[5], 17, 18[5], 19[3], 20, 21[2], 22[5], 23[5], 24[2], 25, 26[3], 27[3], 28[3], 29[6], 30[3]; **22:**1[4], 2[3], 3[4], 4, 5[2], 6, 7[2], 8[3], 10, 11[3], 12[3], 13[2], 14[2], 16[5], 17, 18[5], 19[10]; **23:**2[3], 3[2], 4[3], 5[2], 6, 7, 8[2], 9[3], 10[2], 11[2], 12, 13[3], 14[2], 15, 16[2], 17[3], 18[2], 19[5], 20[3], 21[2], 22, 23, 24[9], 25, 26[3], 27[2], 28[10], 29[4], 30, 31[6], 32[10]; **24:**1[3], 2, 3[2], 4[6], 5[5], 6[10], 7[2], 8[2], 9[2], 10[2], 11[2], 12[2], 13[2], 14[2], 15[2], 16[2], 17[2], 18[2], 19[4], 20[4], 21[2], 22[2], 23[5], 24[2], 25[2], 26[2], 27, 29, 30[4], 31[7]; **25:**1[6], 2[5], 3[3], 4, 5[4], 6[6], 7[3], 8[4], 9[2], 10, 11, 12, 13, 14, 15, 16, 17, 18, 19, 20, 21, 22, 23, 24, 25, 26, 27, 28, 29, 30, 31; **26:**1[5], 2[5], 3[3], 4[6], 5[3], 6, 7, 8[2], 10[4], 11[4], 12[5], 13[3], 14, 15, 16[4], 18, 19[4], 20[5], 21[4], 22[4], 23[4], 24[3], 26[7], 27[3], 28[5], 29[2], 30[5], 31[6], 32[4]; **27:**1[6], 2[3], 3[5], 4[3], 5[4], 6[2], 7[3], 8[3], 9[4], 10[4], 11[4], 12[4], 13[4], 14[4], 15[3], 16[6], 17[3], 18[2], 19[2], 20[4], 21[3], 22[3], 23[4], 24[4], 25[8], 26[4], 27[6], 28[5], 29[5], 30[4], 31[4], 32[2], 33[3], 34[3]; **28:**1[15], 2[6], 4[6], 5[4], 8[6], 9[4], 10[2], 11[8], 12[10], 13[10], 15[7], 16[2], 17[4], 18[7], 19[2], 20[5], 21[7]; **29:**1[5], 2[5], 3[3], 4[3], 5[4], 6[6], 7[2], 8[5], 9[3], 10[2], 11[8], 15, 17[2], 18[3], 19[2], 20[6], 21[3], 22[5], 23[2], 24[4], 25[2], 26, 27, 29[8], 30[3]

2Ch 1:1[2], 2[4], 3[7], 4[2], 5[6], 6[4], 9[2], 11, 12[2], 13[3], 14[2], 15[3], 16[2], 17[3]; **2:**1[2], 2, 3, 4[8], 5, 6, 7, 9, 10, 11[2], 12[3], 14[3], 15[4], 17[3], 18[2]; **3:**1[6], 2[3], 3[6], 4[7], 5, 6[2], 7[6], 8[5], 9[3], 10, 11[8], 12[6], 13, 14, 15[3], 16[4], 17[9]; **4:**1[3], 2, 3[2], 4[5], 5[4], 6[5], 7[3], 8[3], 9[5], 10[4], 11[5], 12[10], 13[4], 14, 16[5], 17[3], 18[2], 19[5], 20[3], 21[3], 22[11]; **5:**1[9], 2[10], 3[4], 4[3], 5[7], 6[2], 7[9], 8[6], 9[6], 10[4], 11[3], 12[4], 13[7], 14[5]; **6:**1[2], 3[3], 4, 5[3], 7[3], 8, 9[2], 10[7], 11[4], 12[4], 13[3], 14[2], 16, 18[2], 19[3], 20[2], 21, 22, 23[2], 24[2], 25[3], 26, 27[2], 28[2], 30[2], 31, 32, 33[3], 34[2], 35, 37[2], 38[3], 39, 40, 41, 42[2]; **7:**1[6], 2[6], 3[8], 4[3], 5[3], 6[6], 7[10], 8[4], 9[4], 10[5], 11[5], 12, 13[2], 15, 18, 20, 21, 22[2]; **8:**1[3], 2[2], 4[2], 5[2], 6[5], 7[6], 8[2], 9, 10[2], 11[7], 12[4], 13[8], 14[8], 15[4], 16[7], 17[2], 18[3]; **9:**1[2], 3[3], 4[5], 5, 6[3], 8[2], 9[2], 10[2], 11[6], 12[2], 13, 14[2], 16[3], 17, 18[4], 19[4], 20[5], 21[3], 22[2], 23[3], 25[2], 26[5], 27[3], 29[3], 31; **10:**2[3], 4, 5, 6, 8[3], 9, 10[2], 12[4], 13[3], 14[2], 15[7], 16[4], 17[2], 18[2], 19; **11:**1[2], 2[3], 3, 4[3], 11, 13[2], 14[3], 15[3], 16[3], 17[3], 18[4], 20, 21, 22[2], 23; **12:**1[3], 2[2], 3[4], 4, 5[4], 6[3], 7[4], 8[3], 9[6], 10[5], 11[5], 12[2], 13[3], 14, 15[4], 16; **13:**1, 2, 3[2], 5[2], 6[3], 7[2], 8[4], 9[7], 10[5], 11[7], 12, 13, 14[4], 15[2], 16, 18[3], 19[3], 20[2], 22[4]; **14:**1[2], 2[2], 3[5], 4[3], 5[4], 6[2], 7[2], 9, 10[2], 11, 12[3], 13[3], 14[4], 15; **15:**1[2], 2, 3, 4, 5[2], 8[9], 9[2], 10[3], 11[3], 12, 13, 14, 15[2], 16[3], 17[2], 18[2], 19[2]; **16:**1[3], 2[4], 4[3], 6[3], 7[5], 8[3], 9[4], 10[3], 11[3], 12[3], 13, 14[3]; **17:**2[3], 3[2], 4[2], 5[2], 6[3], 7[2], 9[5], 10[4], 11[2], 13[2], 14[4], 15, 16[2], 18, 19[3]; **18:**2, 3, 4[3], 5[2], 6, 7[5], 8[2], 9[4], 10[2], 11[4], 12[4], 13, 14[2], 15[4], 16[2], 17, 18[4], 19, 20[2], 21[2], 22[3], 23[4], 25[4], 26[2], 27, 28[2], 29[4], 30[4], 31[4], 32[3], 33[4], 34[6]; **19:**1, 2[5], 3[2], 4[2], 5[2], 6[3], 7[3], 8[6], 9[2], 10, 11[9]; **20:**1[3], 2, 3, 4[3], 5[4], 6[2], 7[2], 9, 10[2], 13, 14[9], 15[2], 16[4], 17[3], 18[4], 19[6], 20[3], 21[5], 22[2], 23[3], 24[4], 25[3], 26[6], 27[2], 28[2], 29[4], 30, 31, 32[3], 33[3], 34[6], 36, 37[3]; **21:**1, 2, 3[2], 4[3], 6[6], 7[3], 8[2], 9[3], 10[4], 11[2], 12[4], 13[5], 14, 15, 16[5], 17[3], 18, 19[2], 20[3]; **22:**1[6], 2, 3[2], 4[4], 5[2], 6[3], 7[4], 8[4], 9[4], 10[3], 11[8], 12[2]; **23:**1[7], 2[4], 3[6], 4[5], 5[7], 6[7], 7[4], 8[6], 9[3], 10[8], 11[4], 12[6], 13[8], 14[8], 15[3], 16[3], 17[4], 18[11], 19[4], 20[14], 21[4]; **24:**2[4], 4[2], 5[6], 6[9], 7[5], 8[4], 9[4], 10[3], 11[7], 12[9], 13[3], 14[8], 16[2], 17[4], 18[2], 19, 20[7], 21[5], 22[3], 23[8], 24[4], 25[6], 26[2], 27[7]; **25:**2[2], 3[2], 4[7], 5, 7[3], 8[2], 9[5], 10, 11[2], 12[5], 13[3], 14[4], 15[4], 16[3], 17[3], 18[3], 19, 20[2], 21[2], 22, 23[6], 24[7], 25[2], 26[4], 27[2], 28; **26:**1[2], 2, 4[2], 5[3], 6[5], 7[3], 8[2], 9[4], 10[4], 11[6], 12[4], 13[2], 14, 15[2], 16[4], 17[2], 18[6], 19[6], 20[3], 21[7], 22[4], 23[3]; **27:**1, 2[5], 3[4], 4[2], 5[7], 6, 7[4], 9; **28:**1[2], 2[2], 3[7], 4[2], 5[5], 6[2], 7[4], 8[2], 9[3], 10[2], 11[3], 12[7], 13[2], 14[5], 15[5], 16, 17, 18[7], 19[2], 21[6], 22[2], 23[4], 24[7], 25, 26[3], 27[3]; **29:**1, 2[2], 3[5], 4[3], 5[4], 6[4], 7[5], 8[2], 9, 10, 11, 12[11], 13[2], 14[2], 15[6], 16[12], 17[10], 18[7], 19[3], 20[5], 21[6], 22[10], 23[4], 24[5], 25[8], 26[4], 27[7], 28[4], 29, 30[6], 31[4], 32[4], 33, 34[7], 35[7], 36[3]; **30:**1[4], 2[4], 3[2], 4[3], 5[2], 6[9], 7, 8[3], 9[2], 10[2], 12[6], 13[2], 14[3], 15[8], 16[6], 17[6], 18[3], 19[3], 20[2], 21[6], 22[5], 23, 24[3], 25[6], 26[3], 27[3]; **31:**1[6], 2[7], 3[9], 4[6], 5[6], 6[5], 7[4], 8[3], 9[3], 10[7], 11[2], 12[5], 13[5], 14[8], 15[4], 16[2], 17[4], 18[2], 19[8], 20, 21[4]; **32:**1[2], 3[3], 4[5], 5[3], 6[4], 7[2], 8[3], 10, 11[3], 12, 13[3], 14, 15, 16, 17[4], 18[4], 19[6], 20[3], 21[7], 22[5], 23[2], 24[2], 25, 26[5], 28, 30[3], 31[5], 32[7], 33[4]; **33:**2[6], 3[2], 4[3], 5[4], 6[5], 7[3], 8[6], 9[4], 10, 11[5], 12[2], 13, 14[6], 15[9], 16[3], 17[3], 18[8], 19[3], 22[3], 23, 25[4]; **34:**2[5], 3[7], 4[6], 5[2], 6, 7[5], 8[10], 9[7], 10[9], 11[3], 12[8], 13[3], 14[6],

15[6], 16[3], 17[7], 18[4], 19[3], 20[5], 21[7], 22[7], 23[2],
24[5], 25, 26[4], 27[2], 28[4], 29[2], 30[13], 31[5], 32[3],
33[6]; **35:1**[4], 2[4], 3[6], 4[3], 5[8], 6[4], 7[5], 8[6], 9[2], 10[4],
11[4], 12[7], 13[4], 14[7], 15[6], 16[7], 17[3], 18[6], 19[2],
20, 21, 22[3], 23[2], 24[2], 25[3], 26[4], 27[2]; **36:1**[3],
3[2], 4, 5[2], 7[3], 8[4], 9[2], 10[4], 12[5], 13, 14[7], 15,
16[3], 17[4], 18[7], 19[4], 20[3], 21[4], 22[6], 23[4]

Ezr 1:1[6], 2[3], 3[3], 4[3], 5[6], 7[5], 8[3], 9, 11[2]; **2:1**[4], 2[3],
3, 4, 5, 6[2], 7, 8, 9, 10, 11, 12, 13, 14, 15,
16, 17, 18, 19, 20, 21, 22, 23, 24, 25, 26,
27, 28, 29, 30, 31[2], 32, 33, 34, 35, 36[3], 37,
38, 39, 40[3], 41[2], 42[8], 43[4], 44[3], 45[3], 46[3],
47[3], 48[3], 49[3], 50[3], 51[3], 52[3], 53[3], 54[2], 55[4],
56[3], 57[4], 58[2], 60[3], 61[7], 62, 63[2], 64, 68[5],
69[2], 70[6]; **3:1**[4], 2[7], 3[3], 4[4], 5[5], 6[6], 7[4], 8[13], 9[5],
10[9], 11[6], 12[4], 13[8]; **4:1**[5], 2[3], 3[5], 4[4], 5[2], 6[3],
7[6], 8[3], 9[12], 10[6], 11[5], 12[6], 13[4], 14[3], 15[5], 16[3],
17[6], 18, 20, 22[2], 23[3], 24[4]; **5:1**[6], 2[4], 3[2], 4[2],
5[4], 6[6], 7, 8[5], 10[3], 11[3], 12[5], 13[3], 14[6], 15[2],
16[3], 17[4]; **6:1**[4], 2[3], 3[10], 4[2], 5[5], 6[3], 7[5], 8[5], 9[4],
10[3], 12, 13[2], 14[8], 15[6], 16[7], 17[3], 18[4], 19[5],
20[6], 21[5], 22[7]; **7:1**[4], 2[3], 3[3], 4[3], 5[5], 6[5], 7[8], 8[3],
9[5], 10[2], 11[8], 12[3], 13, 14[2], 15[3], 16[6], 17[2],
18[4], 19[4], 20[2], 21[7], 23[5], 24, 25[4], 26[3], 27[4],
28[4]; **8:1**[4], 2[3], 3[3], 4[2], 5[2], 6[2], 7[2], 8[2], 9[2], 10[2],
11[2], 12[2], 13, 14, 15[4], 17[5], 18[4], 19, 20[4], 21,
22[5], 24[2], 25[6], 28[5], 29[7], 30[7], 31[7], 33[11], 34,
35[4], 36[6]; **9:1**[14], 2[4], 3, 4[4], 5[2], 6, 7[5], 8, 9[4],
11[5], 12[2], 14; **10:1**[2], 2[4], 3[4], 5[2], 6[4], 7[2], 8[4], 9[8],
10[2], 11[4], 12, 13, 14[4], 15[3], 16[8], 17[3], 18[4],
19, 20, 21, 22, 23[2], 24[2], 25, 26, 27, 28, 29,
30, 31, 33, 34, 43

Neh 1:1[5], 2[2], 3[5], 4, 5, 6[4], 7[3], 8[2], 9[3], 11[4]; **2:1**[5],
2, 3[5], 4[2], 5[3], 6[3], 7[4], 8[10], 9[5], 10[5], 12[3], 13[6],
14[4], 15[5], 16[7], 17[3], 18[2], 19[5], 20; **3:1**[6], 2[2],
3[6], 4[5], 5[2], 6[7], 7[6], 8[5], 9[3], 10[2], 11[5], 12[3], 13[7],
14[6], 15[12], 16[8], 17[4], 18[3], 19[6], 20[7], 21[6], 22[3],
23[2], 24[5], 25[8], 26[5], 27[3], 28[2], 29[4], 30[3], 31[7],
32[5]; **4:1**[2], 2[4], 3, 4, 5, 6[4], 7[5], 10[3], 11[2], 12,
13[4], 14[5], 15, 16[9], 17[3], 18[2], 19[6], 20[2], 21[5],
22[4], 23[2]; **5:1**[2], 3, 4, 5, 7[2], 8[2], 9[3], 11[5], 12,
13[3], 14[7], 15[4], 16[2], 17[2], 18[3]; **6:1**[5], 2[2], 3, 4,
5, 6[3], 7, 9, 10[8], 11, 14[3], 15[3], 16, 17[2], 18[4];
7:1[5], 2[2], 3[4], 4[3], 5[5], 6[4], 7[3], 8, 9, 10, 11[2], 12,
13, 14, 15, 16, 17, 18, 19, 20, 21, 22, 23,
24, 25, 26, 27, 28, 29, 30, 31, 32, 33[2], 34[2],
35, 36, 37, 38, 39[3], 40, 41, 42, 43[3], 44[2],
45[7], 46[4], 47[3], 48[3], 49[3], 50[3], 51[3], 52[3], 53[3],
54[3], 55[3], 56[2], 57[4], 58[3], 59[4], 60[2], 62[3], 63[6],
64, 65[2], 66, 70[5], 71[4], 72[2], 73[6]; **8:1**[7], 2[5], 3[9],
4[2], 5[5], 6[5], 7[4], 8[4], 9[10], 10[4], 11[3], 12[2], 13[9],
14[5], 15, 16[8], 17[6], 18[7]; **9:1**[2], 2[2], 3[5], 4[3], 5[2],
6[4], 7[4], 8[7], 9[2], 10, 11[6], 12[3], 14, 15[2], 19[6], 21,
22[4], 23[2], 24[7], 27[3], 28[2], 29, 30[3], 32[6], 35,
36[3], 37; **10:1**[2], 8, 9[3], 14[2], 28[10], 29[3], 30[2],
31[7], 32[3], 33[10], 34[10], 35[4], 36[6], 37[10], 38[10],
39[13]; **11:1**[5], 2[2], 3[7], 4[9], 5[7], 6, 7[8], 9[3], 10[2],
11[7], 12[8], 13[5], 14[2], 15[5], 16[5], 17[9], 18[2], 19[2],
20[4], 21[2], 22[10], 23[2], 24[5], 25[5], 27, 28, 30[3],
31, 35, 36; **12:1**[3], 7[3], 8[2], 9, 12[3], 22[6], 23[7],
24[5], 25[3], 26[7], 27[4], 28[4], 29[3], 30[5], 31[5], 32,
35[7], 36[3], 37[7], 38[7], 39[7], 40[4], 41, 42, 43[3],
44[12], 45[6], 46[2], 47[8]; **13:1**[6], 2[2], 3[2], 4[4], 5[12],
6[3], 7[3], 8[2], 9[5], 10[5], 11[2], 12[5], 13[6], 14[2], 15[3],
16[2], 17[2], 18, 19[6], 20, 21[2], 22[4], 24[3], 28[4],
29[4], 30[3], 31[2]

Est 1:1, 2[3], 3[4], 4[2], 5[6], 6, 7[3], 8[4], 9[3], 10[6], 11[5],
12[3], 13[4], 14[5], 15[4], 16[8], 17[3], 18[4], 19[5], 20[2],
21[5], 22[3]; **2:1**, 2[2], 3[9], 4[4], 5[4], 6[2], 7, 8[6], 9[5],
11[2], 12[5], 13[4], 14[9], 15[8], 16[3], 17[4], 18[4], 19[3],
20, 21[4], 22[3], 23[4]; **3:1**[3], 2[3], 3[3], 6[4], 7[6], 8[4], 9[5],
10[4], 11[3], 12[9], 13[6], 14[2], 15[6]; **4:1**[2], 2[2], 3[2], 4,
5, 6[3], 7[4], 8[4], 9, 11[8], 13[2], 14[2], 16[3]; **5:1**[8], 2[7],
3[3], 4[3], 5[3], 6[4], 8[6], 9, 11[6], 12[4], 13[2], 14[5]; **6:1**[4],
2[4], 3[2], 4[6], 5[3], 6[4], 7[3], 8[5], 9[8], 10[5], 11[6], 12,
13[2], 14[2]; **7:1**[2], 2[5], 3[2], 4[2], 5[2], 6[3], 7[5], 8[10], 9[6],
10[2]; **8:1**[5], 2[2], 3[4], 4[3], 5[8], 6[2], 7[6], 8[6], 9[10], 10[2],
11[5], 12[4], 13[3], 14[4], 15[3], 16, 17[6]; **9:1**[10], 2[4],
3[7], 4[2], 5[3], 6[2], 10[5], 11[3], 12[7], 13[3], 14[2], 15[4],
16[3], 17[4], 18[5], 19[5], 20[3], 21[4], 22[4], 23, 24[6],
25[3], 26[2], 27, 28[2], 29[3], 30[4], 31[4], 32[2]; **10:1**[4],
2[7], 3[4]

Job 1:1, 3[3], 5[3], 6[2], 7[3], 8[2], 9, 10[2], 12[3], 14[2], 15[4],
16[3], 17[5], 19[4], 20, 21[4]; **2:1**[3], 2[3], 3[2], 4, 6, 7[3],
8, 10[2], 11[3], 13; **3:3**[2], 4, 5[3], 6[4], 8, 9[4], 10,
11[3], 12[2], 14, 17[2], 18[3], 19[2], 20, 22, 24, 25;
4:1, 3, 4, 6, 7, 8, 9[2], 10[6], 11[2], 13[2], 15, 16,
19[2]; **5:1**, 2[2], 3, 4, 5[3], 6[2], 7, 10[2], 12[2], 13[3],
14[3], 15[4], 16, 17[3], 20[2], 21[2], 22[2], 23[4], 25[2];
6:2, 3[2], 4[4], 5[2], 6, 7, 8, 10[2], 12, 14[2], 15, 16[2],
18, 19[2], 23[3], 26, 27; **7:1**, 2[2], 4[3], 8, 9[2], 11[2],
21[2]; **8:1**, 2, 3, 5, 6, 8[2], 11[2], 13[2], 16, 17[2],
19[2], 20, 22[2]; **9:5**, 6[2], 7[2], 8[3], 9[2], 13, 22[2],
23[3], 24[5], 26[3], 31; **10:1**, 3[3], 5, 9, 18[2], 19[2],
21[2], 22[2]; **11:1**, 2, 6, 7, 9[3], 17[2], 20[4]; **12:2**,
4, 5, 6, 7[3], 8[3], 9[2], 10[2], 11[2], 12, 15[2], 16[2], 17,
18, 19, 20[4], 21[2], 22, 23[2], 24[4], 25; **13:2**, 3,
6, 19, 25, 26, 27[2]; **14:5**, 7, 8[4], 9, 10, 11[3],
12, 13, 14, 15, 18[2], 19[6]; **15:1**, 2, 5[2], 7[2], 8,
10, 11, 15, 19, 20[3], 21, 22, 23, 24, 25, 26,
29[2], 30[2], 33[2], 34[2]; **16:5**, 10, 11[3], 13, 15,
16, 22; **17:1**, 5, 6, 8[2], 9, 11, 12[2], 13[2], 14,
16[3]; **18:1**, 4[2], 5[3], 6, 7, 9[3], 10[3], 13[2], 14, 17[2],
18, 21[3]; **19:9**, 17, 20, 21, 24, 25[2], 28[2],
29[3]; **20:1**, 3[2], 5[4], 6[2], 8, 9, 10, 11[2], 14, 16[2],
17[3], 18, 19, 22[2], 23, 24[2], 25[2], 27[2], 28[2],
29[2]; **21:7**, 9, 12[3], 13, 14, 15, 16[2], 17[2], 18[2],
20[2], 21[2], 25, 26[2], 27, 28[4], 29, 30[3], 32[2],
33[2]; **22:1**, 3, 6, 7[2], 8[3], 9[2], 12[3], 13, 14, 15,
17, 18[2], 19[2], 20[2], 22, 23, 24[3], 25, 26, 28,
29, 30[3]; **23:5**, 7, 9[2], 10, 12[2], 14, 16, 17[2];
24:1, 2, 3[3], 4[4], 5[2], 6[3], 7[2], 8[3], 9[3], 10[2], 12[3],
13[3], 14[4], 15[3], 16[3], 17[4], 18[4], 19[2], 20[2], 21[2],
22, 24[3]; **25:1**, 5[2], 6; **26:2**, 3, 5[2], 7[3], 8[2], 9,
10[2], 11, 12[2], 13[2], 14; **27:2**, 3[2], 7[2], 8[2], 10,
11[2], 13[3], 14, 16[2], 17[3], 18, 19, 20, 21; **28:1**,
2[2], 3[2], 4[4], 5, 6[2], 7, 8[2], 9[3], 10, 11[2], 12, 13[3],
14[2], 15, 16[3], 17[3], 18, 19, 20, 21[3], 22, 23[2],
24[3], 25[3], 26[3], 28[2]; **29:2**, 4[2], 5, 6, 7[3], 8[2], 9,
10[2], 11[2], 12[2], 13[2], 15[2], 16[2], 17[3], 18, 19[2],
23[2], 24, 25[2]; **30:1**, 2, 3, 4, 6[4], 7[2], 8, 11,
12[2], 14, 15, 16, 17, 18[2], 19, 22, 23, 24, 25,
27, 28[2], 31; **31:2**, 3[2], 7, 11, 13, 15[2], 16[3],
17, 20, 21[2], 22, 24, 26[2], 28[2], 29, 31, 32[3],
34[2], 35, 37, 38, 39[2], 40; **32:2**[4], 5, 6[2], 8[2], 9,
18; **33:3**, 4[3], 6, 8, 11, 15[2], 16, 18[2], 19, 22[2],
24, 25, 28[2], 30[2]; **34:3**[2], 8, 10, 11, 12, 13[2],
16, 19[4], 20[2], 21, 22, 25, 26, 28[4], 30[2], 36;
35:5[2], 8, 9[4], 10, 11[3], 12, 13; **36:6**[3], 7[2], 12,
13, 14, 15, 16, 17[2], 19, 20, 26, 27[2], 28,
29[3], 30[2], 31, 32[2], 33[3]; **37:2**[2], 3[3], 4, 6[4], 7, 8,
9[3], 10[3], 11, 12[3], 14, 15, 16[3], 17[2], 18, 21[3],
22, 23; **38:1**[2], 4[2], 5[2], 6[2], 7[2], 8[2], 9[2], 12[2],
13[3], 14, 15[2], 16[4], 17[3], 18[2], 19[2], 20[3], 21,
22[4], 23[2], 24[3], 25[2], 26[2], 27[3], 28[2], 29[2], 30[3],
31[2], 33[3], 34, 36[2], 37[2], 38[2], 39[4], 40, 41;
39:1[4], 2[2], 5[3], 6[2], 7[4], 8[2], 9, 10[3], 13[3], 14,
15[2], 18, 19, 20, 21[2], 22, 23[3], 24[3], 25[5], 26[2],
27, 28[4], 29, 30; **40:1**, 2, 3, 6[2], 11, 12, 13,
16, 17, 19[2], 20[3], 21[3], 22[3]; **41:6**[2], 8, 9[2], 11,
13, 14, 18[2], 23, 24, 25, 26[4], 28, 29, 30,
31[2], 32, 34; **42:1**, 5[2], 7[4], 8, 9[5], 10[3], 11[2],
12[2], 14[6], 15[2]

Ps 1:1[6], 2[2], 3, 4[3], 5[4], 6[5]; **2:1**[2], 2[4], 4[2], 7[2], 8[3], 10,
11, 12[2]; **3:3**, 4, 5, 7[3], 8; **4:3**[2], 5[2], 6, 7, ttl;
5:2, 3[2], 5, 6[2], 7, 10, 12, ttl; **6:5**, 6, 8[2], 9[2],
ttl; **7:5**[3], 6[2], 7[2], 8[2], 9[5], 10, 11[2], 13[2], 15,
17[3], ttl[3]; **8:1**[2], 2[3], 3[3], 4, 5, 6, 7[2], 8[6], 9, ttl;
9:4, 5[2], 7, 8[2], 9[2], 11[2], 12[2], 13, 14[2], 15[3],
16[4], 17[2], 18[3], 19, 20, ttl; **10:2**[3], 3[3], 4[2], 8[5],
9[2], 10, 12, 13, 14[3], 15[3], 16[2], 17[2], 18[4];
11:1, 2[3], 3[2], 4[3], 5[3], 6[2], 7[2], ttl; **12:1**[3], 3[2], 5[5],
6[2], 8[2], ttl; **13:3**, 6, ttl; **14:1**, 2[2], 4[2], 5[2], 6[2],
7[3], ttl; **15:2**, 4, 5; **16:2**, 3[3], 5[2], 6, 7[2], 8, 11;
17:1, 2, 3, 4[3], 8[3], 9, 11, 13, 14[2]; **18:2**[2], 3,
4[2], 5[2], 6, 7[3], 9, 10[2], 11, 12, 13[3], 15[5], 18[2],
20[2], 21[2], 24[2], 25, 26[2], 27, 28, 30[2], 31, 35,
39, 40, 41, 42[4], 43[4], 44, 45, 46[2], 47, 48,
49, ttl[9]; **19:1**[3], 4[4], 6[4], 7[6], 8[6], 9[4], 10, 13,
14[2], ttl; **20:1**[4], 2, 5[2], 6[2], 7[2], 9, ttl; **21:1**, 2,
3, 7[4], 9[3], 10[2], 12, ttl; **22:1**, 2[2], 3, 6, 7[2], 8, 9,
10, 14, 15, 16[2], 20[3], 21[3], 22[2], 23[3], 24[2], 25,
26[2], 27[5], 28[4], 29, 30, ttl; **23:1**, 2, 3, 4[2], 5,
6[3]; **24:1**[4], 2[2], 3[2], 5[3], 6, 7, 8[2], 9, 10[2]; **25:5**[2],
7, 8[2], 9[2], 10[2], 12[2], 13, 14[2], 15[2], 17; **26:1**,
5[2], 7, 8[2], 12[2]; **27:1**[3], 2, 4[6], 5[2], 6, 10, 12,
13[4], 14[2]; **28:1**, 2, 3[2], 4[2], 5[3], 6[2], 7, 8[2];
29:1[2], 2[4], 3[5], 4[4], 5[5], 7[3], 8[5], 9[4], 10[3], 11[2];
30:3[2], 4[2], 5, 8, 9[2], 12, ttl[2]; **31:4**, 6, 8[2], 13,
15, 17[2], 18[2], 19, 20[3], 21, 22, 23[4], 24, ttl;
32:2[2], 3, 4, 5[2], 6, 8, 9[2], 10[2], 11; **33:1**[2], 2[2],
4[2], 5[3], 6[5], 7[3], 8[4], 10[5], 11[3], 12[3], 13[2], 14[3],
16, 18[2], 20; **34:1**, 2[2], 3, 4, 6, 7[2], 8[2], 9, 10[2],
11[2], 15[3], 16[4], 17[2], 18, 19[3], 21[2], 22[2]; **35:3**[2],
5[3], 6[2], 9, 10[3], 12, 15, 17, 18, 19, 20, 27[2],
28; **36:1**[2], 3, 5[2], 6, 7[2], 8[2], 9, 10, 11[3], 12,
ttl[3]; **37:1**, 2[2], 3[2], 4[2], 5, 6[2], 7[2], 9[2], 10, 11[3],
12[2], 13, 14[3], 16, 17[4], 18[3], 19[2], 20[4], 21[2],
22, 23[2], 24, 25, 28[3], 29[2], 30[2], 31, 32[3], 33,
34[3], 35, 37[3], 38[3], 39[4], 40[2]; **38:6**, 8, 10, 12,
20; **39:1**, 3, 4, 8[2], 10, ttl; **40:1**, 2, 3, 4[2], 7[2],
9, 10, 12, 16, 17, ttl; **41:1**[2], 2[3], 3[2], 13, ttl;
42:1[2], 2, 4[3], 5, 6[3], 7, 8[4], 9[2], 11, ttl[2]; **43:1**,
2[3], 4[2], 5; **44:1**, 2[2], 3[2], 8, 10, 11, 14[3], 15,
16[2], 19[2], 20, 21[2], 22[2], 25[2], ttl[2]; **45:1**[3], 2,
5[3], 6, 7, 8, 9, 11, 12[3], 13, 14[2], 15, 16, 17,
ttl[2]; **46:2**[4], 3[3], 4[5], 5, 6[3], 7[2], 8[3], 9[6], 10[2], 11[2],
ttl[2]; **47:1**, 2[2], 3[2], 4, 5[2], 7[2], 8[2], 9[6], ttl[2];
48:1[3], 2[6], 4, 7, 8[3], 9, 10[2], 11, 12, 13, ttl;
49:1, 3, 4, 5[2], 6, 8, 10[2], 12, 14[4], 15[2], 16,
19, 20, ttl[2]; **50:1**[6], 2, 4[2], 6, 10[2], 11[4], 12[2],
13[2], 14, 15, 16, 23; **51:1**, 6[2], 8, 12, 17, 18,
19, ttl[2]; **52:1**, 5[2], 6, 7[2], 8[2], ttl[3]; **53:1**, 2, 4,
5, 6[2], ttl; **54:2**, 4, ttl[2]; **55:3**[4], 4, 7, 8, 9, 10[2],
11, 14, 16, 18, 21, 22[3], 23, ttl; **56:7**, 10,
13[2], ttl[2]; **57:1**, 3, 4, 5[2], 6, 9[2], 10[2], 11[2], ttl[2];
58:2[2], 3[2], 4[2], 5, 6[2], 8[2], 9, 10[4], 11[2], ttl;
59:2, 3, 5[2], 6, 8, 10, 12[2], 13[2], 14, 16[2], 17,
ttl[2]; **60:2**[2], 3, 4, 6, 7, 9, 11, ttl[2]; **61:2**[3], 3, 4,
5, 6, ttl; **62:7**, 9, ttl; **63:2**, 6, 7, 9[2], 10, 11[2],
ttl; **64:1**, 2[4], 4, 6[2], 9, 10[3], ttl; **65:1**, 4[2], 5[4],
6, 7[5], 8[3], 9[2], 10[3], 11, 12[3], 13[2], ttl; **66:2**, 3,
4, 5[2], 6[2], 7[2], 8, 11, 15, 18, 19, ttl; **67:3**[2],
4[3], 5[2], 6, 7[2], ttl; **68:2**[3], 3, 4, 5[2], 6[2], 7, 8[5],
10, 11[3], 12, 13[2], 14, 15[3], 16[2], 17[3], 18[2],
19[2], 20[3], 21[2], 22[3], 23[3], 24[2], 25[3], 26[3], 27[3],
30[6], 32[2], 33, 34, 35, ttl; **69:1**, 2, 4, 9[2], 12[3],
13[2], 14[2], 15[3], 16, 26, 28[3], 30, 31, 32, 33[2],
34[2], 35, 36, ttl; **70:ttl**; **71:4**[4], 6, 8, 9, 15[2],
16[2], 20[2], 22[2], 24; **72:1**[2], 3[3], 4[5], 5, 6[2], 7[2],
8[3], 9[2], 10[3], 12[2], 13[3], 15, 16[6], 17, 18[2], 19,
20[2]; **73:3**[3], 9[2], 11, 12[2], 14, 15, 17, 26, 28;
74:1, 2, 3[3], 4, 5, 6, 7[2], 8[2], 10[2], 12[2], 13[4],
14[3], 15[2], 16[4], 17[2], 18[2], 19[4], 20[4], 21[2], 22,
23[2]; **75:2**, 3[3], 4[3], 6[3], 7, 8[7], 9, 10[4], ttl;
76:3[5], 4, 5[2], 6, 8, 9[2], 10[2], 11, 12[3], ttl;
77:2[3], 5[2], 6, 7, 10[3], 11[2], 13, 14[2], 15, 16[3],
17[2], 18[5], 19[2], 20, ttl; **78:1**, 4[3], 6[2], 7, 9[2], 10,
12[3], 13[2], 14[2], 15[3], 16, 17[2], 19, 20[3], 21,
23[2], 24, 25, 26[2], 27[2], 28, 31[3], 35, 40[2], 41,
42[2], 43, 46[2], 48, 49, 50, 51, 52, 53, 54,
55[2], 56, 60[2], 61, 62, 63, 64, 65, 66, 67[2],
68[2], 69, 70, 71, 72[2]; **79:1**, 2[6], 6[2], 9, 10[4],
11[3]; **80:1**, 4, 5, 8, 9, 10[4], 11[2], 12, 13[4], 15[2],
16, 17[2], ttl; **81:1**, 2[3], 3[3], 4, 5, 6[2], 7[2], 10[2],
15[2], 16[3], ttl; **82:1**[3], 2[2], 3[2], 4[3], 5[2], 6, 7, 8;
83:2, 4, 6[3], 7[2], 8, 9[2], 10, 12, 13[2], 14[3], 18[2];
84:2[3], 3[2], 5[2], 6[3], 9, 10[2], 11[2], 12, ttl[2]; **85:1**,
2, 3, 8, 11, 12, 13, ttl[2]; **86:4**, 6, 7, 8, 13,
14[2], 16; **87:1**, 2[3], 5, 6[2], 7[2], ttl; **88:3**, 4, 5[3],
6[2], 10[2], 11, 12[2], 13, ttl[3]; **89:1**[2], 2, 5[3], 6[5],
7[2], 9[3], 11[4], 12[2], 14, 15[3], 16, 17, 18[2], 19,
22[2], 25[2], 26, 27[2], 29, 32, 34, 36, 37, 39[2],
41, 42, 43[2], 44, 45, 48[2], 50[3], 51, 52, ttl;
90:2[3], 4, 5, 6[2], 8, 10, 11, 15[2], 17[4], ttl;
91:1[4], 2, 3[3], 5[2], 6[2], 8[2], 9[2], 13[3]; **92:1**, 2, 3[2],
4, 7[3], 9, 10, 11, 12[2], 13[3], 15, ttl; **93:1**[3], 3[3],
4[4]; **94:2**[2], 3[2], 4, 6[3], 7[2], 8, 9[2], 10, 11[2], 12,
13[3], 14, 15, 16[2], 17, 19, 20, 21[3], 22[2], 23;
95:1[2], 3, 4[4], 5[2], 6, 7[2], 8[3]; **96:1**[3], 2, 3, 4, 5[4],
7[3], 8[2], 9[3], 10[4], 11[4], 12[3], 13[4]; **97:1**[3], 2, 4[2],
5[6], 6[2], 8, 9, 10[4], 11[2], 12[2]; **98:1**[2], 2[3], 3[4], 4[2],
5[4], 6[2], 7[3], 8[2], 9[4]; **99:1**[4], 2[2], 4, 5, 6, 7[2], 9[2];
100:1, 2, 3[2], 5; **101:3**, 6[2], 8[4]; **102:2**[2], 5,
6[2], 7, 8, 13[2], 14, 15[5], 16, 17[2], 18[3], 19[3],
20[2], 21[2], 22[3], 23, 24, 25[4], 27, 28, ttl[2];
103:1, 2, 5, 6, 7, 8, 11[2], 12[2], 13, 15, 16[2],
17[2], 19[2], 20[2], 21, 22[2]; **104:1**, 2, 3[5], 5[2], 6[3],
7, 8[3], 9, 10[3], 11[2], 12[3], 13[3], 14[3], 15, 16[3],
17[3], 18[4], 19[2], 20[2], 21, 22, 23, 24, 26, 30[2],
31[3], 32[3], 33, 34, 35[5]; **105:1**[2], 3[2], 4, 5, 7[2],
8, 10, 11[2], 16[2], 19[3], 20[3], 23, 27, 30, 33,
34, 35[2], 36[2], 38, 39, 40[2], 41[3], 44[4], 45;
106:1[2], 2[2], 4, 5[2], 7[3], 9[3], 10[3], 11, 14[2], 16[3],
17[2], 18[2], 19, 20, 22[2], 23, 24, 25[2], 26, 27[2],
28[2], 29, 30, 32, 34[2], 35, 38[3], 40[2], 41[2], 45,
47, 48[3]; **107:1**, 2[4], 3[5], 4, 6, 7, 8[2], 9[2], 10,
11[3], 13, 14, 15[2], 16[2], 18, 19, 21[2], 22, 23,
24[3], 25[2], 26[2], 28, 29[2], 31[2], 32[4], 33, 34, 35,
36, 37, 40, 41, 42, 43[2]; **108:3**[2], 4[2], 5[2], 7, 8,
10, 12; **109:2**[4], 11[2], 13, 14[3], 15[3], 16[2], 19,
20[2], 21, 23[2], 30[2], 31[2], ttl; **110:1**, 2[3], 3[5], 4[2],
5[2], 6[4], 7[3]; **111:1**[5], 2[2], 4, 6[3], 7, 10[3]; **112:1**[3],
2[2], 4[2], 6, 7, 9, 10[3]; **113:1**[4], 2[2], 3[5], 4[2], 5, 6[2],
7[4], 8, 9[2]; **114:1**, 3, 4[2], 7[4], 8[2]; **115:2**, 3, 4,
9, 10, 11[2], 12[3], 13, 14, 15, 16[5], 17[2], 18[2];
116:1, 3[2], 4[2], 5, 6[2], 7, 9[3], 12, 13[3], 14[2], 15[3],
16, 17[3], 18[2], 19[4]; **117:1**, 2[3]; **118:1**, 3, 4,
5[2], 6, 7, 8, 9, 10, 11[2], 12[3], 13, 14, 15[5],
16[4], 17[2], 18, 19[2], 20[2], 22[4], 23, 24[2], 26[4],
27[4], 29; **119:1**[4], 2, 13, 14, 19, 20, 21, 25,
27, 29, 30, 32, 33[2], 35, 43, 49, 51, 53, 54,
55, 61[2], 64, 69, 72, 78, 83, 84, 85, 88, 90,
95, 97, 100, 108, 110, 111, 112, 115,
119[2], 122, 123, 130[2], 134, 142, 144, 147[2],
148, 155, 158, 160; **120:1**, 4, 5; **121:1**, 2,
5[2], 6[2], 7, 8; **122:1**[2], 4[6], 5[2], 6, 9[2]; **123:1**, 2[5],
4[3]; **124:1**, 2, 4[2], 5, 6, 7[3], 8[2]; **125:1**, 2[2], 3[5],
5[2]; **126:1**[2], 2[2], 3, 4[2]; **127:1**[5], 2, 3[3], 4[2], 5[3];
128:1, 2, 3, 4[2], 5[3]; **129:3**, 4[3], 6[2], 7, 8[4];
130:1, 2, 5, 6[3], 7[2]; **131:3**; **132:2**[2], 3, 5[2],
6[2], 8, 10, 11[2], 13, 17; **133:2**[4], 3[5]; **134:1**[4],
2[2], 3; **135:1**[4], 2[4], 3[2], 4, 5, 6[2], 7[5], 8, 9, 11[2],
14, 15[3], 19[2], 20[3], 21[2]; **136:1**, 2, 3, 5, 6[2], 8,
9, 13, 14, 15, 16, 19, 20, 26; **137:1**, 2[2], 3,
4, 6, 7[3], 9; **138:1**, 3, 4[3], 5[4], 6[3], 7[2], 8[2];
139:9[4], 11[2], 12[5], 15[2], 17, 18, 19, 24, ttl;
140:1[2], 4[3], 5[2], 6[2], 7[3], 8[2], 9[2], 10, 11[2], 12[5],
13[2], ttl; **141:2**[2], 3, 5, 7[2], 8, 9[3], 10; **142:1**[2],
3, 5[2], 7, ttl; **143:3**[2], 5[2], 7, 8[2], 10; **144:1**, 3,
5, 7, 10, 11, 12, 15; **145:3**, 5, 6, 7, 8, 9, 11,
12[2], 14, 15, 16, 17, 18, 19, 20[2], 21[2];
146:1[2], 2, 3, 5[2], 6, 7[4], 8[6], 9[5], 10[2]; **147:1**,
2[2], 3, 4[2], 6[4], 7[2], 8[3], 9[2], 10[3], 11, 12, 13, 14[2],
16, 18, 20; **148:1**[4], 4, 5[2], 7[2], 11[2], 13[3], 14[4];
149:1[3], 2, 3[2], 4[2], 5, 6, 7[2], 9[2]; **150:1**[2], 3[3], 4,
5[2], 6[2]

Prv 1:1[2], 2, 3, 4[2], 6[3], 7[3], 8[2], 11, 12[2], 15, 17[2],
19[3], 20, 21[4], 22, 29[2], 31, 32[3]; **2:5**[3], 6, 7,
8[2], 12[3], 13[2], 14[2], 16[2], 17[2], 18, 19, 20[3], 21[3],
22[3]; **3:3**, 4, 5, 7, 9[2], 11[2], 12[2], 13[2], 14[3], 15,
19[3], 20[3], 25[2], 26, 27, 31, 32[3], 33[6], 34[2],
35[2]; **4:1**, 3, 5, 7, 10, 11, 14[3], 17[2], 18[4], 19[2],
21, 23, 26, 27[2]; **5:3**, 6, 7, 8, 9, 10, 11, 13,
14[2], 16, 18, 19, 20, 21[3], 22[2], 23; **6:2**[2], 3,
5[4], 6, 8[2], 10, 16, 20, 23[3], 24[3], 26[2], 31, 34[2];
7:2, 3, 5[2], 6, 7[2], 8[2], 9[3], 10, 12, 18, 19, 20,
21, 22[3], 23, 24, 27[2]; **8:2**[4], 3[5], 4, 6, 8, 11,
13[4], 16[2], 20[3], 22[2], 23[2], 25[2], 26[5], 27[3], 28[3],
29[4], 31[2], 34[2], 35; **9:3**[2], 5, 6[2], 10[5], 11, 14[3],
18[2]; **10:1**[2], 3[5], 4[2], 6[4], 7[4], 8, 10, 11[3], 13[2],
14[2], 15[3], 16[4], 17, 19, 20[4], 21[2], 22[2], 24[4],
25[3], 26[3], 27[4], 28[4], 29[4], 30[3], 31[3], 32[4]; **11:1**,
2, 3[3], 4, 5[3], 6[2], 7, 8[2], 9, 10[3], 11[5], 13, 14[2],

17, 18, 20, 21^3, 23^4, 25, 26^2, 28, 29^3, 30^2, 31^4; **12:**2, 3^2, 5^4, 6^4, 7^3, 10^3, 12^4, 13^3, 14^2, 15, 18^3, 19, 20^2, 21^2, 22, 23, 24^3, 25, 26^3, 27^2, 28^2; **13:**2^3, 4^4, 6^2, 8^2, 9^4, 10, 12^2, 13^2, 14^3, 15, 19^2, 21, 22^3, 23^2, 25^4; **14:**1, 2, 3^4, 4^3, 7^2, 8^3, 9, 10, 11^4, 12^2, 13^2, 14, 15^2, 16, 18^2, 19^5, 20^2, 21, 23^2, 24^3, 26^2, 27^3, 28^5, 30^4, 31^2, 32^2, 33^2, 35; **15:**2^3, 3^4, 4, 6^4, 7^4, 8^5, 9^3, 10, 11^3, 12, 13^2, 14^2, 15^2, 16^2, 19^4, 22, 23, 24^2, 25^5, 26^5, 28^4, 29^4, 30^4, 31^3, 33^3; **16:**1^5, 2^3, 3, 4^3, 5, 6^2, 7, 9, 10^2, 11^3, 12, 13, 14, 15^3, 17^2, 19^3, 20, 21^3, 22, 23^2, 24^2, 25^2, 29, 31^2, 32, 33^4; **17:**2^2, 3^4, 5, 6^2, 8, 14, 15^3, 16, 18, 21, 22, 23^2, 24^3, 26; **18:**3, 4^2, 5^3, 7, 8^3, 10^3, 11, 12, 14, 15^4, 18^2, 19, 20^2, 21^3, 22, 23^2; **19:**1, 2, 3^2, 4, 6^2, 7^2, 11, 12^3, 13^2, 14^2, 16, 17^2, 21^2, 22, 23^2, 25, 27^2, 28^2, 29; **20:**2^2, 4^2, 5, 7, 8, 10, 12^3, 14, 15, 21^2, 22, 23, 24, 25, 26^2, 27^5, 28, 29^3, 30^3; **21:**1^4, 2^2, 3, 4^2, 5^2, 6, 7^2, 8^2, 9, 10^2, 11^3, 12^4, 13^2, 14, 15^2, 16^4, 18^4, 19, 20^2, 22^4, 25^2, 26^2, 27^2, 28, 29, 30, 31^3; **22:**2^3, 3^2, 4^2, 5^2, 6, 7^4, 8, 9, 10, 11^2, 12^4, 13^2, 14^2, 15^2, 16^2, 17^2, 19, 21^3, 22^3, 23^2, 28; **23:**6, 8, 9^2, 10^3, 12, 13^2, 14, 17^3, 19, 21^2, 23, 24^2, 28, 30, 31^2, 32, 34^3; **24:**4, 7, 9^2, 10, 12, 13, 14, 15^2, 16, 18, 19, 20^3, 21^2, 22, 23, 24^2, 27, 29, 30^4, 31^2, 33; **25:**1, 2^2, 3^3, 4^3, 5^2, 6^3, 7^2, 8, 13^3, 15, 22, 23, 24^2, 26; **26:**2^3, 3^3, 6^2, 7^3, 9^2, 10^2, 13^3, 14^2, 15, 16, 17, 19, 20^2, 22^3, 26; **27:**3, 6^2, 7^2, 9^2, 10, 12^2, 14, 16^2, 17, 18^2, 19, 20, 21^2, 23, 24, 25^3, 26^4, 27^2; **28:**1^2, 2^3, 3, 4^3, 5, 6, 7, 8, 9, 10^2, 11^2, 12, 14, 15, 16, 17^2, 23, 24^2, 25, 27, 28^2; **29:**2^4, 4^2, 6^2, 7^4, 10^3, 13^3, 14^2, 15, 16^2, 18^2, 21, 23, 25^2, 26^2, 27^3; **30:**1^4, 2, 3^2, 4^4, 9^2, 14^3, 15, 16^4, 17^4, 19^7, 20, 21, 24, 25^2, 26^2, 27, 28, 33^4; **31:**1^2, 2^2, 5^3, 8^2, 9^2, 11, 12, 14, 16, 19^2, 20^2, 21, 23^3, 24, 26, 27^2, 30, 31^2

Ecc 1:1^3, 2, 3, 4, 5^2, 6^4, 7^5, 8^2, 9^2, 12, 13, 14^2; **2:**3^3, 6, 8^4, 11^3, 12^2, 14^2, 15, 16^5, 17^2, 18^2, 19, 20^2, 22^2, 23, 24, 26; **3:**1, 10^2, 11^4, 13^2, 16^3, 17^2, 18^2, 19^3, 20, 21^4; **4:**1^4, 2^2, 3^2, 5, 6, 7, 10, 15^3, 16; **5:**1^2, 3, 6^2, 7, 8^4, 9^4, 11^2, 12^3, 13^2, 16, 18^3, 19, 20^2; **6:**1, 3, 5^2, 7^2, 8^4, 9^4, 11, 12^2; **7:**1^2, 2^4, 3^3, 4^5, 5^3, 6^3, 7, 8^4, 9, 10^2, 11, 12, 13, 14^5, 15, 19^2, 25^2, 26^2, 27^2; **8:**1^3, 2^2, 4, 5, 6, 8^3, 9, 10^4, 11^2, 13, 14^5, 15^3, 16^2, 17^3; **9:**1^3, 2^7, 3^4, 4, 5^3, 6, 9^6, 10, 11^6, 12^4, 13, 15, 16, 17^2; **10:**1^2, 3, 4^2, 5^2, 6, 7, 10^2, 11, 12^2, 13^3, 15^3, 16, 17, 18^3, 20^5; **11:**1, 2, 3^7, 4^2, 5^5, 6^2, 7^3, 8, 9^3; **12:**1^3, 2^6, 3^6, 4^7, 5^5, 6^6, 7^3, 8, 9^2, 10, 11^3, 12, 13^3

Song 1:1, 2, 3^2, 4^2, 5^2, 6^3, 7, 8^3, 12^2, 14, 17; **2:**1^3, 2^2, 3^4, 4, 7^3, 8^3, 9^2, 11^2, 12^6, 13^3, 14^4, 15^3, 16, 17^3; **3:**2^3, 3^2, 4, 5^3, 6^2, 7, 8, 9, 10^5, 11^4; **4:**2, 4, 5, 6^4, 8^5, 10, 11^3, 14, 16; **5:**2^3, 4^2, 5^2, 7^4, 10, 11, 12^2, 14, 15; **6:**2^2, 3, 6, 9^5, 10^3, 11^5, 12, 13^2; **7:**1^3, 4^3, 5^3, 8^4, 9^3, 11^2, 12^4, 13; **8:**1, 2, 5^2, 6^2, 7^2, 8, 11^2, 12, 13^2, 14

Isa 1:1^3, 2, 3^2, 4^2, 5^2, 6^3, 8, 9, 10^3, 11^5, 13^3, 16, 17^3, 18, 19^2, 20^3, 21, 23^3, 24^3, 26^4, 28^4, 29^2, 31^2; **2:**1^2, 2^6, 3^7, 4, 5^2, 6^4, 8, 9^2, 10^4, 11^3, 12^2, 13^2, 14^2, 16, 17^3, 18, 19^7, 20^2, 21^7; **3:**1^6, 2^6, 3^5, 5^5, 6, 7, 8^2, 9, 10^2, 11^2, 12, 13^2, 14^6, 15^3, 16^2, 17^5, 18^3, 19^3, 20^6, 21, 22^4, 23^4, 25^2, 26; **4:**2^4, 3, 4^7, 5^3, 6^2; **5:**2^3, 5^2, 6, 7^4, 8^2, 9, 10, 11, 12^6, 15^4, 16, 17^3, 19^2, 23^3, 24^8, 25^5, 26^3, 27^2, 29, 30^5; **6:**1^3, 2, 3^2, 4^4, 5^3, 6^3, 8^2, 10, 11^3, 12^3, 13^2; **7:**1^5, 2^5, 3^6, 4^3, 5, 6^2, 7, 8^2, 9^2, 10, 11^3, 12, 14, 15^2, 16^4, 17^3, 18^6, 19^3, 20^8, 22^2, 24, 25^4; **8:**1, 2^2, 3^2, 4^4, 5, 6, 7^4, 8^3, 10, 11^2, 13, 14^2, 16^2, 17^2, 18^3, 19^2, 20^2, 22; **9:**1^7, 2^4, 3^4, 4^4, 5, 6^4, 7^4, 8, 9^3, 10^2, 11^2, 12^2, 13^2, 14, 15^4, 16, 17, 18^5, 19^6, 20^3; **10:**2^4, 3^2, 4^2, 5^2, 6^5, 10^2, 12^5, 13^4, 14^5, 15^4, 16^3, 17, 18, 19^2, 20^4, 21^3, 22^3, 23^3, 24^3, 25, 26^5, 27^2, 29, 31, 32^3, 33^5, 34^2; **11:**1, 2^7, 3^4, 4^7, 5^2, 6^7, 7^4, 8^5, 9^5, 10^2, 11^5, 12^5, 13^2, 14^5, 15^5, 16^3; **12:**2, 3, 4^2, 5^2, 6^2; **13:**1^2, 2^5, 4^6, 5^4, 6^3, 9^4, 10^4, 11^6, 12, 13^5, 14, 15, 17, 18^3, 19^3, 20^2, 21, 22^2; **14:**1^3, 2^4, 3^3, 4^3, 5^5, 6^2, 7, 8^2, 9^5, 11^4, 12^3, 13^5, 14^3, 15^2, 16^2, 17^3, 18^2, 19^3, 20, 21^4, 22^3, 23^3, 24, 25, 26^4, 27, 28, 29^2, 30^3, 31, 32^4; **15:**1^3, 2, 3, 4, 5^2, 6^3, 7^3, 8^4, 9^3; **16:**1^6, 2^3, 3^4, 4^6, 5^2, 6, 7, 8^7, 9^3, 10^3, 12, 13^2, 14^4; **17:**1, 2, 3^6, 4^2, 5^4, 6^5, 7, 8^4, 9, 10^2, 11^4, 12^5, 13^6, 14^3; **18:**1^2, 2^3, 3^3, 4^2, 5^6, 6^7, 7^7; **19:**1^5, 2^2, 3^6, 4^4, 5^3, 6^3, 7^5, 8^3, 10, 11^6, 12, 13^4, 14^2, 15, 16^3, 17^3, 18^4, 19^5, 20^4, 21^4, 22^2, 23^4, 24^3, 25^2; **20:**1^2, 2^4, 3, 4^4, 6^2; **21:**1^5, 2^3, 3^3, 4, 5^3, 6, 8^2, 9^2, 10^3, 11^3, 12^3, 13^2, 14^2, 15^4, 16^3, 17^5; **22:**1^3, 2, 3, 4^2, 5^4, 6^2, 7^2, 8^4, 9^4, 10^3, 11^4, 12, 14^2, 15^2, 17, 18^2, 20, 21^2, 22^2, 24^5, 25^5; **23:**1^2, 2^3, 3^3, 4^3, 5^2, 6, 8^3, 9^4, 11^5, 13^6, 15^2, 16, 17^6, 18^2; **24:**1^3, 2^{10}, 3^2, 4^4, 5^5, 6^4, 7^3, 8^4, 10, 11^3, 12^2, 13^6, 14^3, 15^6, 16^5, 17^3, 18^9, 19^3, 20^2, 21^6, 22^2, 23^3; **25:**3^3, 4^7, 5^6, 6^3, 7^3, 8^4, 9, 10^3, 11^2, 12^4; **26:**1, 2^3, 4^2, 5^3, 6^5, 7^4, 8^3, 9^4, 10^4, 11^2, 15^4, 17, 18^3, 19^3, 20, 21^4; **27:**1^4, 3, 4, 6^2, 7, 8^2, 9^5, 10^4, 11^2, 12^4, 13^6; **28:**1^4, 2^3, 3^2, 4^5, 5^2, 6^2, 7^4, 9^2, 12^3, 13^2, 14^2, 15, 16, 17^6, 18, 19^2, 20^2, 21^2, 22^2, 24^2, 25^6, 27^4, 28, 29; **29:**1, 4^4, 5^3, 6^2, 7^2, 8^2, 10^4, 11^2, 12, 13^2, 14^2, 15^2, 16^3, 17, 18^5, 19^4, 20^2, 21^2, 22^2, 23^4; **30:**1^2, 2^2, 3^3, 6^8, 7, 8, 9^2, 10^2, 11^3, 12, 14^5, 15^2, 16, 17^3, 18^2, 19^2, 20^3, 21^3, 22^2, 23^4, 24^5, 25^3, 26^{11}, 27^3, 28^6, 29^4, 30^4, 31^3, 32^2, 33^4; **31:**1^2, 2^3, 3^2, 4^6, 5, 6, 8^4, 9^2; **32:**2^3, 3^2, 4^4, 5^2, 6^6, 7^4, 8, 10^2, 12^3, 13^3, 14^4, 15^3, 16^2, 17^2, 19^2, 20^3; **33:**2, 3^5, 4^3, 5, 6^3, 7, 8^4, 9, 10, 12^3, 14^3, 15, 16, 17^2, 18^3, 20^3, 21, 22^3, 23^4, 24^2; **34:**1^2, 2^3, 3, 4^5, 5, 6^7, 7^3, 8^4, 9^3, 10, 11^6, 12^2, 13, 14^6, 15^2, 16^2, 17; **35:**1^4, 2^5, 3^2, 5^4, 6^5, 7^3, 8^3, 9, 10^2; **36:**1^2, 2^5, 3^3, 4^2, 6, 7, 8, 9^2, 10^2, 11^5, 12^2, 13^4, 14, 15^4, 16^2, 18^5, 19^2, 20^2, 21, 22^6; **37:**1^2, 2^6, 3^2, 4^7, 5, 6^4, 7, 8, 10^2, 11, 12^3, 13^4, 14^6, 15, 16^4, 17^2, 18^2, 19^2, 20^3, 21^2, 22^5, 23, 24^9, 25^3, 27^5, 29, 30^4, 31^2, 32^2, 33^2, 34^3, 36^5, 38^3; **38:**1^3, 2^2, 4^2, 5^2, 6^2, 7^2, 8^4, 9, 10^4, 11^6, 15, 16, 17, 18^2, 19^4, 20^5, 21, 22^3; **39:**1, 2^6, 3, 5^2, 6^2, 7^2, 8^2; **40:**2, 3^5, 4^2, 5^4, 6^4, 7^5, 8^3, 9^2, 10, 11, 12^7, 13^2, 14^2, 15^4, 16, 19^2, 21^3, 22^4, 23^3, 24^2, 25, 26, 27, 28^5, 29, 30^2, 31; **41:**1, 2^4, 3, 4^5, 5^3, 7^5, 8, 9^3, 10, 13, 14^2, 15^2, 16^4, 17^3, 18^4, 19^9, 20^3, 21^2, 22^2, 23, 25^4, 26, 27; **42:**1, 2, 3, 4^2, 5^4, 6^3, 7^4, 8, 9, 10^6, 11^7, 12^2, 13, 15^2, 16, 17, 19, 20, 21^2, 23, 24^2, 25^2; **43:**1, 2^4, 3^2, 5^2, 6^4, 8^2, 9^2, 10, 11, 12, 13, 14^4, 15^2, 16^3, 17^3, 18^2, 19^2, 20^6, 23, 24, 28^3; **44:**2^2, 3, 4^2, 5^4, 6^5, 7^2, 11, 12^4, 13^5, 14^5, 16^2, 17, 19^4, 23^3, 24^5, 25^2, 26^4, 27, 28; **45:**1^4, 2^3, 3^3, 5, 6^4, 7^2, 8^3, 9^4, 10, 11^3, 12^2, 13, 14^3, 15, 17, 18^4, 19^3, 20^2, 21, 22^2, 23, 24, 25^2; **46:**1^3, 2, 3^4, 6^2, 7, 9, 10^3, 11^2; **47:**1^3, 2^4, 4^2, 5^2, 6, 7, 8, 9^3, 12, 13^4, 14^3; **48:**1^5, 2^3, 3^2, 5, 7^2, 8, 10, 12^2, 13^3, 14^2, 16^3, 17^4, 18^2, 19^3, 20^4, 21^5, 22^2; **49:**1^3, 2, 4, 5^4, 6^5, 7^5, 8^4, 9^2, 10^2, 12^3, 13, 14, 15, 16, 18, 19^2, 20^3, 22^3, 23^3, 24^3, 25^5, 26^2; **50:**1^2, 2^2, 3, 4^4, 5, 6^2, 7, 9^2, 10^4, 11^2; **51:**1^4, 3^4, 4, 5^2, 6^4, 7^2, 8^2, 9^4, 10^6, 11^2, 12, 13^8, 14^2, 15^3, 16^4, 17^5, 18^3, 19^2, 20^5, 22^5, 23^3; **52:**1^3, 2^2, 3, 4^2, 5^2, 7^2, 8^3, 9, 10^6, 11^3, 12^2, 14, 15; **53:**1^2, 5, 6^2, 7, 8^3, 9^2, 10^3, 11, 12^6; **54:**1^5, 2^2, 3^4, 4^2, 5^4, 6, 8, 9^3, 10^4, 13^2, 16^4, 17^4; **55:**1, 3, 4^2, 5^2, 6, 7^3, 8, 9^2, 10^5, 11, 12^4, 13^5; **56:**1, 2^3, 3^5, 4^3, 6^6, 8^2, 9^2; **57:**1^3, 3^4, 4, 5^4, 6^2, 8^2, 9, 10^2, 13^2, 14^3, 15^6, 16^2, 17^2, 19^3, 20^2, 21; **58:**1, 2^2, 3, 4, 5, 6^4, 7^3, 8^3, 9^5, 10^3, 11, 12^5, 13^4, 14^6; **59:**1, 5, 6, 8, 10^3, 13^2, 14, 15, 17, 18, 19^8, 20^2, 21^4; **60:**1^2, 2^4, 3^2, 5^4, 6^4, 7^3, 8, 9^5, 10, 11^2, 12, 13^6, 14^6, 16^5, 19^3, 20^2, 21^3, 22; **61:**1^8, 2^3, 3^5, 4^4, 5^2, 6^5, 7, 8, 9^4, 10^3, 11^5; **62:**1^2, 2^3, 3^3, 4, 5^2, 6, 7, 8^5, 9^2, 10^6, 11^4, 12^3; **63:**1, 2, 3^2, 4^2, 6^2, 7^8, 9^2, 11^3, 12^2, 13^2, 14^3, 15^2, 17, 18; **64:**1^2, 2^4, 3, 4^4, 6, 8^2; **65:**2, 4^2, 5, 7^4, 8^3, 10^2, 11^2, 12^2, 13, 15, 16^5, 17, 19^2, 20^2, 21, 22^3, 23^3, 25^6; **66:**1^5, 2, 5^3, 6^3, 8, 9^3, 11^2, 12^3, 14^2, 15, 16^3, 17^5, 19^4, 20^5, 21, 22^3, 23, 24^2

Jer 1:1^4, 2^5, 3^7, 4^2, 5^3, 7, 8, 9^2, 10^2, 11^2, 12, 13^5, 14^4, 15^8, 16, 18^6, 19; **2:**1^2, 2^5, 3^3, 4^4, 5, 6^4, 7^2, 8^5, 9, 10, 12, 13, 15, 16^2, 17^2, 18^5, 19^2, 20, 21, 22, 23, 24^2, 26^2, 27, 28^2, 29, 31^2, 33, 34^3, 37; **3:**1^2, 2^5, 3, 4, 5, 6^4, 8^2, 9^2, 10, 11^2, 12^3, 13^3, 14, 16^5, 17^6, 18^5, 19^2, 20, 21^3, 22, 23^4, 24, 25^3; **4:**1, 2^2, 3^2, 4^3, 5^3, 6^2, 7^3, 8^2, 9^7, 10^2, 11^3, 16^2, 17, 19^3, 20, 21^3, 23^2, 24^2, 25^2, 26^4, 27^2, 28^2, 29^4, 31^3; **5:**1^3, 2, 3, 4^3, 5^6, 6^2, 7^2, 8, 9, 10, 11^3, 12, 13^2, 14, 15, 17, 18, 19, 20, 22^5, 24^5, 28^7, 29, 30, 31^3; **6:**1^3, 2, 3, 4^3, 6^3, 9^3, 10^2, 11^7, 12^3, 13^4, 14^2, 15^2, 16^4, 17^2, 19, 20, 21^4, 22^4, 23, 24, 25^4, 26, 29^5, 30; **7:**1^2, 2^5, 3^2, 4^6, 6^3, 7, 11, 12^2, 13, 14, 15, 17^2, 18^5, 19^2, 20^5, 21^2, 22^2, 23, 24^2, 25^3, 28^2, 29^2, 30^3, 31^4, 32^5, 33^5, 34^9; **8:**1^{10}, 2^5, 3^3, 4, 6^2, 7^8, 8^4, 9^3, 10^4, 11^2, 12^2, 13^5, 14^3, 16^6, 17, 19^4, 20^2, 21^2, 22^2; **9:**1^2, 2, 3^3, 5, 6^2, 7^2, 9, 10^8, 11, 12^4, 13, 14, 15^2, 16, 17^2, 19, 20^3, 21^3, 22^5, 23^4, 24^3, 25^3, 26^5; **10:**1^2, 2^5, 3^7, 5, 7^2, 8, 9^5, 10^5, 11^4, 12^3, 13^5, 14, 15^2, 16^4, 17^2, 18^3, 21^2, 22^4, 23, 25^2; **11:**1^2, 2^3, 3^3, 4^3, 5, 6^4, 7^2, 8^2, 9^3, 10^3, 11, 12^3, 13^3, 14, 15, 16^3, 17^4, 18, 19^5, 20^2, 21^4, 22^3, 23^2; **12:**1^2, 3^2, 4^5, 5^3, 6, 7^2, 8, 9^3, 11, 12^8, 13^2, 14^3, 16^3, 17; **13:**1, 2^2, 3^3, 4^2, 5, 6^2, 7^3, 8^2, 9^3, 10, 11^5, 12, 13^6, 14^3, 15, 16^3, 17, 18^3, 19^2, 20^2, 22, 23^2, 24^3, 25^2, 27^3; **14:**1^3, 2^3, 3^2, 4^3, 5^2, 6^3, 8^3, 9, 10^2, 11, 12^3, 13^2, 14^3, 15^2, 16^4, 17, 18^6, 19, 20, 21, 22^3; **15:**1, 2^7, 3^7, 4^2, 6, 7^2, 8^5, 9^4, 10, 11^4, 12^2, 13, 16, 17^2, 19^3, 20, 21^4; **16:**1^2, 3^3, 4^6, 5^3, 6^2, 7^2, 8, 9^8, 10^2, 11, 12, 14^5, 15^5, 16^3, 18, 19^4, 21; **17:**1^4, 2^2, 3^2, 4, 5^3, 6^4, 7^3, 8^3, 9, 10^4, 11^2, 12^2, 13^4, 15^2, 16, 17, 18, 19^7, 20^3, 21^3, 22^2, 24^4, 25^4, 26^8, 27^5; **18:**1^2, 2, 3^2, 4^4, 5^2, 6^3, 8, 10, 11^3, 12, 13^3, 14^4, 15, 17^4, 18^6, 19, 21^4, 23; **19:**1^5, 2^5, 3^5, 4^2, 5, 6^5, 7^7, 8, 9^4, 10^3, 11, 12^2, 13^6, 14^4, 15^3; **20:**1^4, 2^5, 3^3, 4^5, 5^6, 8^2, 10, 11, 12^3, 13^5, 14^2, 15, 16^5, 17, 18; **21:**1^5, 2^2, 4^6, 6, 7^{10}, 8^3, 9^4, 10^3, 11^4, 12^5, 13^3, 14^3; **22:**1^3, 2^3, 3^7, 4^2, 5, 6^3, 7, 8, 9^2, 10, 11^2, 12, 16^3, 18^2, 19^2, 20, 22, 23^2, 24^3, 25^5, 27, 29^2, 30^2; **23:**1^3, 2^4, 3, 4, 5^3, 6, 7^5, 8^4, 9^3, 10^4, 11, 12^3, 13, 14^3, 15^5, 16^5, 17^2, 18^2, 19^3, 20^4, 22, 23, 24^2, 25, 26^3, 28^4, 29^2, 30^2, 31^2, 32^2, 33^4, 34^5, 35^2, 36^5, 37^3, 38^7, 39; **24:**1^6, 2^2, 3^3, 4^2, 5^4, 7, 8^5, 9^2, 10^4; **25:**1^5, 2^4, 3^5, 4^2, 5^3, 6, 7^2, 8, 9^5, 10^{10}, 11, 12^4, 13, 14, 15^3, 16, 17^4, 18^3, 20^7, 21, 22^5, 23, 24^4, 25^4, 26^7, 27^3, 28^2, 29^4, 30^4, 31^6, 32^3, 33^6, 34^3, 35^3, 36^5, 37^3, 38^3; **26:**1^4, 2^6, 3^2, 4, 5^2, 6^2, 7^5, 8^5, 9^5, 10^7, 11^4, 12^4, 13^4, 15^2, 16^6, 17^4, 18^7, 19^4, 20^4, 21^3, 22^2, 23^4, 24^4; **27:**1^4, 2, 3^8, 4^2, 5^4, 6^4, 7, 8^9, 9, 11^4, 12^2, 13^6, 14^3, 15^2, 16^5, 17, 18^8, 19^6, 20^2, 21^7, 22^2; **28:**1^{12}, 2^4, 3^2, 4^5, 5^8, 6^5, 7^2, 8, 9^5, 10^3, 11^7, 12^7, 13^2, 14^5, 15^3, 16^4, 17^3; **29:**1^8, 2^6, 3^3, 4^2, 5, 7^4, 8^3, 9, 10, 11^2, 14^5, 15, 16^4, 17^4, 18^6, 19^3, 20^3, 21^5, 22^4, 23, 24, 25^6, 26^6, 28, 29^3, 30^2, 31^3, 32^5; **30:**1^2, 2^2, 3^5, 4^2, 5, 7, 8, 9, 10^2, 11, 12, 14^3, 15, 17, 18^5, 19, 21^2, 23^4, 24^4; **31:**1^4, 2^4, 3, 4, 5^2, 6^3, 7^4, 8^6, 9, 10^3, 11^2, 12^6, 13^2, 14^3, 15, 16^4, 17, 18^2, 19, 20, 21^2, 22^2, 23^5, 24, 25, 27^6, 28, 29^2, 30, 31^4, 32^5, 33^3, 34^4, 35^8, 36^2, 37^5, 38^7, 39^2, 40^9; **32:**1^4, 2^5, 3^3, 4^4, 5^2, 6^2, 7^2, 8^9, 9^2, 10^3, 11^3, 12^{12}, 14^3, 15^2, 16^4, 17^2, 18^6, 19^3, 20, 21, 24^8, 25^4, 26^2, 27^2, 28^4, 29^2, 30^5, 31, 32^5, 33^2, 34, 35^4, 36^7, 39, 42^2, 43^2, 44^{10}; **33:**1^5, 2^4, 4^7, 5^2, 6, 7^3, 9^5, 10^3, 11^{16}, 12^2, 13^{12}, 14^4, 15^2, 16^2, 17^3, 18^2, 19^2, 20^3, 21^2, 22^5, 23^2, 24^2, 25^2, 26^2; **34:**1^6, 2^5, 3^2, 4^4, 5^4, 6, 7^3, 8^4, 10^3, 11^2, 12^3, 13^5, 14, 15, 17^7, 18^5, 19^8, 20^6, 21^4, 22^2; **35:**1^4, 2^5, 3^4, 4^{11}, 5^3, 6, 7, 8^2, 11^5, 12^2, 13^5, 14^2, 15^2, 16^3, 17^4, 18^5, 19^3; **36:**1^3, 2^4, 3^2, 4^4, 5^2, 6^8, 7^4, 8^6, 9^7, 10^{13}, 11^5, 12^9, 13^4, 14^9, 16^2, 18, 19, 20^8, 21^8, 22^4, 23^6, 24, 25^2, 26^7, 27^6, 28^3, 29^2, 30^6, 31^3, 32^6; **37:**1^3, 2^5, 3^6, 4, 5, 6^3, 7^3, 8, 9^2, 10^2, 11^2, 12^3, 13^6, 14^2, 15^4, 16^2, 17^5, 19, 20^3, 21^8; **38:**1^6, 2^5, 3^3, 4^8, 5^2, 6^6, 7^6, 8^2, 9^5, 10^4, 11^5, 12^2, 13^3, 14^6, 16^3, 17^4, 18^3, 19^3, 20^2, 21^2, 22^4, 23^3, 25^3, 26, 27^3, 28^3; **39:**1^2, 2^5, 3^6, 4^9, 5^3, 6^4, 8^5, 9^7, 10^6, 11^2, 13^3, 14^5, 15^4, 16^3, 17^3, 18^2; **40:**1^4, 2^3, 3^2, 4^2, 5^7, 6^3, 7^8, 8^6, 9^5, 10, 11^6, 12^2, 13^4, 14^4, 15^4, 16^2; **41:**1^7, 2^7, 3^3, 4, 5^2, 6^2, 7^6, 8, 9^5, 10^9, 11^5, 12^3, 13^4, 14^2, 15^2, 16^{10}, 17, 18^5; **42:**1^7, 2^2, 3^3, 4^3, 5^3, 6^4, 7^2, 8^6, 9^2, 10, 11^2, 13^2, 14^3, 15^4, 16^3, 17^5, 18^3, 19, 20^3, 21^3, 22^4; **43:**1^4, 2^4, 3^3, 4^7, 5^5, 6^7, 7^3, 8^2, 9^5, 10^3, 11^3, 12^3, 13^5; **44:**1^4, 2^4, 4, 6^2, 7^3, 8^4, 9^7, 11^2, 12^9, 13^4, 14^4, 15^4, 16^3, 17^3, 18^3, 19, 20^4, 21^6, 22^3, 23^3, 24^5, 25^3, 26^7, 27^4, 28^5, 29, 30^4; **45:**1^6, 2^2, 3, 4, 5; **46:**1^4, 2^4, 3, 4^3, 5, 6^4, 7, 8^4, 9^6, 10^6, 11, 12^4, 13^4, 14, 15, 16^2, 17, 18^4, 20, 21^3, 22, 23^2, 24^4, 25^3, 26^5, 27, 28^2; **47:**1^4, 2^7, 3^6, 4^6, 5, 6, 7^2; **48:**1^2, 2, 5^3, 6^2, 8^4, 9, 10^2, 12^2, 13, 14, 15^3, 16, 17^2, 18, 19, 21, 24^2, 25^2, 26, 28^5, 29^2, 30, 31, 32^4, 33^3, 34^2, 35^2, 36^2, 37^2, 38^3, 39, 40, 41^3, 42, 43^3, 44^6, 45^7, 46, 47^4; **49:**1^2, 2^4, 3, 4, 5, 6^3, 7^2, 8^2, 12^2, 13^2, 14^3, 15, 16^7, 17, 18^3, 19^4, 20^5, 21^5, 22^4, 23, 25^2, 26^2, 27^2, 28^4, 30, 31^2, 32^3, 34^5, 35^3, 36^3, 37^2, 38^3, 39^3; **50:**1^5, 2, 3, 4^4, 5^2, 6, 7^4, 8^5, 9, 10, 11, 12^2, 13^2, 14^2, 15^2, 16^4, 17^2, 18^4, 20^3, 21^3, 22, 23^3, 24, 25^6, 26, 27^2, 28^5, 29^4, 30^2, 31^2, 32, 33^3, 34^3, 35^3, 36, 37^2, 38, 39^5, 40^2, 41^3, 42^4, 43^2, 44^4, 45^6, 46^5; **51:**1^2, 2, 3, 4^3, 5^2, 6^3, 7^4, 9, 10^3, 11^9, 12^7, 13, 14, 15^3, 16^5, 17, 18^2, 19^4, 20, 21^2, 22^2, 23^2, 24^2, 25^3, 26, 27^7, 28^6, 29^3, 30, 31, 32^3, 33^4, 34, 35^3, 36, 39, 40, 41^3, 42^3, 44^2, 45^3, 46^3, 47^3, 48^5, 49^3, 50^2, 51^2, 52^3, 53^2, 54^2, 55^2, 56^2, 57^2, 58^5, 59^6, 60, 63, 64^2; **52:**1, 2^2, 3^3, 4^4, 5^2, 6^7, 7^{11}, 8^4, 9^3, 10^3, 11^3, 12^6, 13^6, 14^5, 15^{10}, 16^4, 17^9, 18^6, 19^9, 20^5, 21^3, 22^4, 23^2, 24^6, 25^{13}, 26^3, 27^2, 28^2, 29, 30^5, 31^7, 32^2, 33, 34^3

Lam 1:1^3, 2, 3^2, 4^2, 5^4, 6^2, 7^5, 9, 10^2, 11, 12^2, 13, 14^2, 15^5, 16^2, 17, 18, 19^2, 20, 21; **2:**1^5, 2^7, 3^2, 4^3, 5^2, 6^6, 7^7, 8^5, 9^4, 10^5, 11^7, 12^3, 13, 15^5, 16^2, 17^3, 18^3, 19^7, 20^5, 21^6, 22^2; **3:**1^2, 3, 12, 13, 14, 18, 19^2, 22, 24, 25^2, 26^2, 27, 29, 31, 32, 33, 34^2, 35^3, 36, 37, 38^2, 39, 40, 41, 45^3, 48^2, 50, 51, 53, 55, 57, 58, 62^2, 64, 66^2; **4:**1^5, 2^4, 3^5, 4^4, 5, 6^5, 8, 9^3, 10^4, 11^2, 12^7, 13^5, 14, 15, 16^5, 19^4, 20^4, 21^2, 22; **5:**6^3, 9^3, 10, 11^3, 12, 13^3, 14^3, 15, 16, 18^2

Ezk 1:1^7, 2^3, 3^9, 4^5, 5^3, 7^3, 8, 10^7, 12, 13^6, 14^2, 15^3, 16^4, 19^5, 20^5, 21^5, 22^6, 23^3, 24^6, 25, 26^7, 27^5, 28^{10}; **2:**2, 3, 4; **3:**1, 4, 5, 7^2, 11^3, 12^3, 13^5, 14^4, 15^2. 16^3, 17^2, 18^3, 19, 21^2, 22^3, 23^5, 24, 26, 27; **4:**1, 2, 3^2, 4^4, 5^5, 6^2, 7, 8, 9^2, 11, 13^3, 16; **5:**1, 2^5, 4^4, 5^3, 6^2, 7^4, 8^4, 9, 10^6, 11, 12^4, 13, 14^2, 15^2, 16^2, 17^2; **6:**1^2, 2, 3^7, 5^2, 6^2, 7^3, 8^3, 9^2, 10, 11^6, 12^3, 13^4, 14^3; **7:**1^2, 2^5, 3, 4^2, 5, 6, 7^6, 9^2, 10^3, 12^5, 13^4, 14^3, 15^6, 16^2, 19^5, 20^2, 21^4, 22, 23^2, 24^4, 26^4, 27^6; **8:**1^7, 2^4, 3^{10}, 4^4, 5^7, 6^2, 7^3, 8^2, 9, 10^3, 11^4, 12^7, 14^4, 16^{12}, 17^4; **9:**1, 2^4,

APNDX

17^3, 18, 19^2, 20^2, 21, 23, 24, 26^2, 27^3, 28^3,
29, 30^2, 31^4, 33, 35, 36^2, 37^2; **8:**1, 2, 3, 4,
6^4, 8, 10, 11, 13^2, 14^2, 15^3, 19, 20, 23^3,
26^2, 27^2, 28^2, 29, 31^3, 33^2, 34, 35^2, 36,
38^3; **9:**1, 7, 9^3, 10^2, 11, 12, 14, 15, 16, 17,
20^2, 22^2, 24^2, 25^2, 26, 27, 28, 31^3, 33^2,
34^2, 35^2, 36, 42, 43, 44, 45, 46, 47, 48, 50;
10:1^3, 2, 5, 6^2, 10^2, 14^2, 15, 17, 19, 21^2,
23, 24^2, 25^2, 29, 30, 31, 32^3, 33^4, 34, 35,
37, 38^2, 39^2, 41, 42, 44, 45, 46^2, 48, 49,
51, 52; **11:**1, 2, 3, 4^2, 5, 7, 8^3, 9^2, 10^4, 11^3,
12, 13, 15^5, 16, 17, 18^2, 19, 20^3, 21, 23,
27^4, 30, 32; **12:**1, 2^5, 4, 7^2, 8, 9^4, 10^4, 11,
12^2, 13^2, 14^2, 17^2, 18, 20, 21^2, 22^2, 23^2,
24^2, 25^2, 26^6, 27^4, 28^2, 29^3, 30^2, 31, 32^2,
33^4, 34, 35^3, 36^2, 37, 38^2, 39^3, 41^3, 43;
13:1, 3^2, 4, 7, 8, 9, 10, 11, 12^4, 13^2, 14^3,
15^2, 16, 18, 19^2, 20^3, 22, 24^2, 25^2, 26^2,
27^4, 28, 29, 32^3, 33, 34^2, 35^4; **14:**1^4, 2^2, 3^3,
4, 5, 7, 8, 9, 10^2, 12^3, 13, 14^5, 16^2, 17^2,
20^2, 21^2, 23, 24, 25^3, 26, 27^2, 30, 31, 35^2,
38^2, 39, 41^4, 43^4, 47, 49^2, 51, 52, 53^4, 54^4,
55^2, 60^2, 61^4, 62^3, 63, 64, 65^2, 66^3, 68^2,
72^4; **15:**1^4, 2^2, 3, 7, 8, 9^2, 10, 11^2, 12^2, 14,
15, 16^3, 18, 19, 20, 21^2, 22^2, 25, 26^3, 27^2,
28^2, 29, 30, 31^2, 32^2, 33^3, 34, 37, 38^4, 39^3,
40^2, 42^4, 43^2, 44, 45^2, 46^3, 47; **16:**1^2, 2^6,
3^3, 4, 5^2, 6, 8, 9^2, 12, 13, 14, 15^2, 18, 19^2,
20^2

Lk 1:2^2, 3, 4, 5^4, 6^2, 8^2, 9^4, 10^3, 11^3, 13, 15^3,
16^2, 17^8, 18, 19^2, 20, 21^2, 22, 23, 25^2, 26^2,
27^2, 28^2, 30, 32^4, 33, 34, 35^5, 36, 38^3, 39,
40, 41^3, 42, 43, 44^2, 45, 46, 48, 51^2, 52,
53^2, 58, 59^3, 65, 66^2, 67, 68, 69, 70^2, 71,
72, 73, 74, 75, 76^4, 77, 78^2, 79^2, 80^3; **2:**1,
4^3, 6, 7, 8^2, 9^4, 10, 11^2, 12, 13^2, 14, 15^3,
16, 17, 18, 20^2, 21^4, 22^3, 23^4, 24^2, 25^3,
26^2, 27^6, 31, 32^2, 34, 35, 36^2, 37, 38, 39^2,
40^2, 41^2, 42^2, 43^2, 44, 46^3, 50; **3:**1^4, 2^4, 3^3,
4^7, 5^2, 6, 7^2, 9^4, 10, 14, 15^2, 16^2, 17^2, 18,
19^2, 21^2, 22, 23^2, 24^5, 25^5, 26^5, 27^5, 28^5,
29^5, 30^5, 31^5, 32^5, 33^5, 34^5, 35^5, 36^5, 37^5,
38^4; **4:**1^3, 2, 3^2, 5^3, 6^2, 8, 9^2, 12, 13^2, 14^3,
16^2, 17^4, 18^7, 19^2, 20^4, 22, 25^3, 27^3, 28,
29^3, 30, 31, 33, 34, 35^2, 36, 37^2, 38, 39,
40, 41, 42, 43, 44; **5:**1^3, 2^2, 3^4, 4, 5^2, 7^2, 9^2,
10, 13, 14, 15, 16, 17^3, 19^4, 21^2, 24^3, 27,
32, 33^3, 34^3, 35^2, 36^4, 37^3, 39; **6:**1^4, 2^2, 4^3,
5^2, 6, 7^2, 8^3, 9, 10^2, 15, 16^2, 17^3, 19, 20,
22, 23^2, 26, 29^2, 33, 35^4, 38, 39^3, 40, 41^2,
42^4, 45^4, 46, 48^3, 49^3; **7:**1^2, 3^2, 6^2, 9, 10^2,
11, 12^4, 13, 14, 17, 18, 20, 22^7, 24^2, 28^2,
29^3, 30^2, 31^2, 32, 33, 34, 36^2, 37^2, 38^2, 39,
41^2, 44^2, 45, 47, 50; **8:**1^3, 3, 5^3, 7, 10^2,
11^3, 12^3, 13^2, 15^2, 16, 19, 21, 22^2, 23, 24^3,
25, 26^2, 27^2, 29^5, 31, 32, 33^5, 34^2, 35^3, 36,
37^4, 38^2, 39, 40, 41, 42, 44, 45, 47^2, 49^3,
51^4, 54; **9:**2^2, 5, 6^2, 7^2, 8, 10^2, 11^2, 12^4,
16^4, 18, 19^2, 20, 22^3, 24, 25, 26^2, 27, 29,
32, 34, 35, 36, 37^2, 38, 42^3, 43, 44^2, 47,
48, 51, 52, 56, 57, 58^2, 60^2, 62^2; **10:**1, 2^4,
4, 6, 7^2, 9^2, 10^2, 11^2, 13, 14, 17^2, 19^2, 20,
21, 22^5, 23^2, 26, 27, 31, 32^2, 35^2, 36; **11:**7,
13, 14^3, 15^2, 20^2, 24, 26^2, 27^3, 28, 29^3,
30^2, 31^7, 32^3, 33, 34^3, 35, 36^2, 38, 39^4,
42^2, 43^3, 44, 45, 46, 47^2, 48, 49, 50^4, 51^4,
52, 53^2; **12:**1^3, 3^3, 4, 7, 8^2, 9, 10^2, 11, 12^2,
13^2, 15^2, 16, 22, 23^2, 24^2, 26, 27, 28^3, 30^2,
31, 32, 33, 36, 37, 38^2, 39^3, 40, 42, 45,
46^2, 48, 49, 53^{10}, 54^2, 55, 56^3, 58^6, 59;
13:1, 2, 4, 7^2, 10^2, 14^5, 15^3, 16, 17^2, 18,
19^3, 20, 21, 22, 24, 25^4, 28^2, 29^5, 31^2, 32,
33, 34, 35^3; **14:**1^3, 2, 3^2, 5, 7, 8, 9, 10^2,
13^4, 14^2, 15, 18, 21^8, 22, 23^3, 28, 29, 32,
34, 35^2; **15:**1, 2, 4^2, 8, 9, 10^2, 12^2, 13, 16^2,
21, 22^2, 23, 25^2, 26, 27, 30; **16:**1, 3^2, 4, 5,
8^4, 9, 10, 11^2, 13^4, 14, 15, 16^3, 17, 21^3,
22^3, 24, 29, 30, 31^2; **17:**1, 2, 5^2, 6^3, 7, 9,
11, 14, 17, 20^3, 21, 22^4, 24^4, 26^3, 27^3, 28,
29, 30^2, 31^3, 34^2, 35^2, 36^3, 37^2; **18:**6^2, 8^2,
10^3, 11, 12, 13, 14, 16, 17, 20, 22, 24, 25,
27, 29, 30, 31^3, 32, 33, 34, 35, 36, 39, 43;
19:2^2, 3, 5, 8^3, 10, 11, 15^2, 16, 18, 23, 24,
29^2, 30^2, 31, 33^3, 34, 35, 36, 37^5, 38^4, 39^2,
40, 41, 42, 43, 44^2, 45, 46, 47^5, 48; **20:**1^6,
4, 6, 9, 10^5, 13^2, 14^3, 15^3, 16, 17^5, 19^4,
20^2, 21^2, 25^2, 26, 27, 29, 30, 31^2, 32, 33,
34, 35^2, 36^4, 37^6, 38^2, 39, 42^2, 45^2, 46^5,
47; **21:**1^2, 4^2, 5, 6^2, 8, 9, 12, 20, 21^3, 22,
23, 24^5, 25^6, 26^2, 27, 29^2, 31, 35^2, 36, 37^4,
38^3; **22:**1^2, 2^2, 3^2, 4, 6^2, 7^2, 8, 10^2, 11^5, 13,
14^2, 16, 17, 18^3, 20^2, 21^2, 22, 24, 25^2, 26,
30, 31, 34, 37^2, 39, 40, 44, 47, 48, 49, 50^2,
52^3, 53^2, 54, 55^2, 56, 59, 60, 61^4, 63, 64,
66^4, 67, 69^3, 70; **23:**1, 2, 3^2, 4^2, 5^2, 6, 10,
12, 13^3, 14, 17, 19, 22, 23^2, 26^2, 29^5, 30^2,
31, 33^5, 35^3, 36, 37^2, 38^2, 39, 40^2, 41, 44^3,
45^4, 46, 47, 48^2, 49, 51^4, 52, 54^2, 55^2, 56^2;
24:1^5, 2^2, 3^2, 5^3, 7^3, 9^3, 10^2, 12^2, 18^2, 19,
20, 21, 22, 24^2, 25, 27^3, 28, 29, 32^2, 33^2,
34, 35, 36, 44^4, 45, 46^2, 49^2, 53

Jn 1:1^4, 2^2, 4^2, 5^2, 7^2, 9^2, 10^3, 12, 13^3, 14^4, 17,
18^3, 19^2, 20, 23^5, 24, 29^4, 32, 33^4, 34, 35,
36, 37, 39, 40, 41^2, 42, 43, 44, 45^3, 48,
49^2, 50, 51^2; **2:**1^2, 2, 3, 5, 6^3, 7^2, 8^2, 9^8,
10^2, 13, 14^2, 15^5, 17, 18, 20, 21, 22^3, 23^3;
3:1^2, 2, 3, 4, 5^2, 6^2, 8^3, 13, 14^3, 16, 17^3,
18^2, 19^2, 20^2, 21, 22, 25, 26, 28, 29^5, 31^2,
34^2, 35^2, 36^3; **4:**1^2, 5, 6^2, 8, 9^3, 10, 11^2, 12,
14^2, 15, 17, 19, 20, 21^2, 22, 23^4, 25, 27,
28^3, 29, 30, 31, 33, 34, 35, 39^3, 40, 42^4,
45^4, 46, 47, 49, 50^2, 52^3, 53^3, 54; **5:**1, 2^2,
3^2, 4^4, 7^3, 9^3, 10^2, 11, 14, 15^2, 16^2, 18^3,
19^3, 20^2, 21^3, 22^3, 23^4, 25^4, 26^2, 27, 28^3,
29^2, 30^2, 32, 33, 36^4, 37, 39, 42, 44, 45;
6:1^2, 4^2, 10^3, 11^4, 12, 13^2, 14^2, 16, 17, 18,
19^2, 21^3, 22^5, 23^2, 24, 25^2, 26^2, 27^3, 28,
29, 31, 32, 33^2, 35, 37, 38, 39^2, 40^3, 41^2,
42, 44^2, 45^2, 46^2, 49, 50, 51^4, 52, 53^2, 54,
57^2, 59, 62, 63^3, 64, 67, 68, 69^2, 71^2; **7:**1,
2, 3, 4, 7^2, 10, 11^2, 12^2, 13, 14^3, 15, 17, 18,
19^2, 20, 22^2, 23^3, 24, 26^2, 28, 31, 32^4, 35^4,
37^2, 38, 39^2, 40^2, 41, 42^3, 43, 45^2, 46, 47,
48^2, 49; **8:**1, 2^3, 3^2, 4, 5, 6, 8, 9^4, 10, 12^3,
13, 15, 16, 17, 18, 20^2, 22, 25^2, 26, 27, 28,
29, 32^2, 34, 35^3, 36, 39, 40, 41, 44^5, 45,
46, 48, 52^2, 53, 57, 59^2; **9:**3, 4^2, 5^3, 6^5, 7,
8, 11, 13, 14^2, 15, 16^2, 17, 18^2, 22^3, 24^2,
30, 32^2, 35, 40; **10:**1^3, 2^3, 3^2, 4, 5, 7^2, 8, 9,
10, 11^3, 12^6, 13^2, 14, 15^3, 19, 21^3, 22^3, 23,
24^2, 25, 31, 33, 35^2, 36^3, 37, 38^2, 40; **11:**1,
2, 4^2, 6, 8, 9^3, 10, 15, 17, 19, 20, 24^2, 25^2,
27^3, 28, 30, 31^3, 33^2, 36, 37^2, 38, 39^2, 40,
41^3, 42, 45^2, 46, 47^2, 48, 49, 50^2, 52, 54^2,
55^3, 56^2, 57^2; **12:**1^2, 2, 3^4, 5, 6^2, 7, 8, 9^2,
10, 11, 12^2, 13^3, 16, 17^2, 18, 19^2, 20, 21,
23^2, 24, 29, 31^2, 32, 34^3, 35^2, 36^2, 38^4,
42^3, 43^2, 46, 47^2, 48^3, 49, 50; **13:**1^5, 2^2, 3,
5^2, 16, 18, 22, 26^2, 27, 28, 29^3, 30, 31, 33,
38; **14:**4, 5, 6^4, 8, 9^2, 10^5, 11^3, 12, 13^2, 16,
17^2, 19, 22, 24^2, 26^3, 27, 28, 30, 31^3;
15:1^2, 3, 4^2, 5^3, 6, 9, 15, 16, 18, 19^5, 20^2,
24, 25, 26^4, 27; **16:**2^2, 3, 4^2, 7^2, 8, 11, 13,
15, 16, 17, 20, 21^3, 23, 25^2, 26, 27, 28^4,
32^3, 33^2; **17:**1, 3, 4^2, 5^2, 6^2, 8, 9, 11^2, 12^3,
13, 14^3, 15^2, 16^2, 18^2, 19, 21, 22, 23, 24^2,
25, 26; **18:**1^2, 2, 3, 6, 9, 10^2, 11^2, 12^3, 13,
14^2, 15^3, 16^3, 17^2, 18, 19, 20^4, 22^3, 23, 24,
26^3, 27, 28^3, 31, 32, 33^3, 35, 36, 37^3, 38,
39^3; **19:**2, 3, 5^3, 6, 7^2, 8, 9, 11, 12, 13^3,
14^4, 15, 17^2, 18, 19^4, 20^3, 21^5, 23^3, 24^2,
25^2, 26, 27, 28, 30^2, 31^5, 32^4, 34, 36, 38^3,
39, 40^4, 41^2, 42^2; **20:**1^5, 2^3, 3, 4^2, 5, 6^2, 7^2,
8, 9^2, 10, 11^2, 12^5, 15, 18^2, 19^7, 20^2, 22, 24,
25^6, 26^2, 30, 31^2; **21:**1^2, 2, 4^3, 6^4, 7^3, 8^2,
10, 11^2, 12^2, 14^2, 16, 17^2, 20, 23, 24, 25^3

Act 1:1, 2^3, 3^2, 4^2, 5, 6, 7^3, 8^3, 12, 13^2, 14^2,
15^3, 16^2, 18^2, 19^2, 20, 21^2, 22, 24, 26^2;
2:1, 2, 4^2, 6, 9, 10, 11, 14, 15^2, 16, 17, 19,
20^3, 21^2, 22, 23, 24, 25, 28, 29, 30^2, 31,
33^4, 34^2, 36, 37^2, 38^4, 39^2, 41, 42, 43, 46,
47^3; **3:**1^3, 2^3, 3, 6, 7, 8, 9, 10^2, 11^3, 12, 13^3,
14^2, 15^2, 16^2, 18, 19^3, 21^4, 22^2, 23, 24,
25^5; **4:**1^5, 2^3, 3, 4^3, 5, 6^3, 7, 8^2, 9^2, 10^3, 11^3,
13, 14, 15, 17, 18, 19, 20, 21, 22, 23, 24,
25^3, 26^4, 27^2, 30, 31^3, 32^3, 33^3, 34^2, 35,
36^3, 37^2; **5:**2^2, 3^3, 5, 6, 7, 8, 9^4, 10^2, 11,
12^3, 13^2, 14^2, 15^4, 16, 17^3, 18^2, 19^3, 20^3,
21^7, 22^2, 23^3, 24^4, 25^3, 26^3, 27^2, 29, 30,
32, 33, 34^4, 37^2, 40^2, 41^2, 42; **6:**1^5, 2^4, 3,
4^2, 5^3, 6, 7^5, 8, 9^3, 10^2, 12^4, 13, 14, 15^2;
7:1, 2, 3, 4^2, 7, 8^3, 9, 10, 11, 13, 16^3, 17^3,
19^2, 22^2, 23, 24, 26, 28, 29, 30^2, 31^3, 32^4,
33^2, 34, 35^4, 36^3, 37^2, 38^5, 40, 41^2, 42^5,
43^2, 44^3, 45^4, 46, 48^2, 49^2, 51, 52^4, 53^2,
54, 55^3, 56^3, 58^2; **8:**1^3, 3, 4, 5, 6^2, 9^2, 10^3,
12^3, 13, 14^2, 15, 16^2, 17, 18^2, 19, 20, 21,
22, 23^2, 24, 25^4, 26^4, 27^2, 28, 29, 30, 32^3,
33, 34^2, 35, 36, 37, 38^3, 39^4, 40; **9:**1^3, 2, 4,
5^2, 6^2, 7, 8^2, 10, 11^3, 14, 15^3, 17^4, 19, 20^2,
21, 22^2, 23, 24, 25^2, 26, 27^4, 29^3, 30, 31^5,
32, 33, 35, 38, 39^3, 40, 41, 42; **10:**1^2, 2,
3^2, 6, 7, 9^4, 11^2, 12^2, 15^2, 16, 17^2, 19^2, 21^2,
22^3, 23, 24, 30, 31, 32^2, 36^2, 37, 38^2, 39^2,
40, 41^2, 42^2, 43, 44^2, 45^4, 47, 48^2; **11:**1^3,
2, 4^2, 5, 6^3, 9, 11, 12^2, 15^2, 16^3, 17^2, 18,
19^3, 20^2, 21^3, 22^3, 23^2, 24^2, 26^2, 28^3, 29^2,
30^2; **12:**1^2, 2^2, 3^2, 4, 5, 6^4, 7^4, 8, 9, 10^5,
11^5, 12^3, 13^2, 14^2, 16, 17^4, 18, 19, 20^2,
22^2, 23^4, 24; **13:**1^2, 2^3, 4, 5^3, 6, 7^3, 8^3, 9,
10^3, 11^4, 12^3, 14^2, 15^6, 17^3, 18^2, 19, 20^2,
21^3, 22, 24^2, 26^2, 27^2, 29, 30, 31, 32^3, 33^2,
34^2, 36, 38, 39, 40, 42^4, 43^4, 44^3, 45^2, 46^2,
47^4, 48^3, 49^3, 50^4, 51, 52^2; **14:**1^4, 2^3, 3^2,
4^4, 5^2, 6, 7, 9, 11^4, 12, 13^3, 14^2, 15^2, 18,
19^2, 20^3, 21, 22^4, 23, 25, 26^2, 27^3, 28;
15:1^2, 2, 3^4, 4^2, 5^3, 6, 7^3, 8^2, 10^2, 11^2, 12^2,
14^2, 15^2, 16^2, 17^4, 18^2, 19, 21, 22^3, 23^3,
24, 26, 27, 28, 30^2, 31, 32, 33^2, 35^2, 36^2,
38, 39^2, 40^2, 41; **16:**1, 2, 3, 4^3, 5^2, 6^3, 7, 9,
10^3, 11, 12, 13^3, 14^3, 15, 17^4, 18^3, 19^3, 20,
22^2, 23, 24^2, 25, 26^3, 27^4, 31, 32^3, 33^2,
35^2, 36^3, 38^2, 39, 40^3; **17:**1, 2, 3, 4^2, 5^5, 6^3,
7, 8^3, 9, 10^3, 11^2, 13^3, 14^2, 16, 17^4, 18^3,
21, 22, 23, 24, 26^4, 27, 29^2, 30, 31^3, 32^2,
34^2; **18:**3, 4^3, 5^2, 6, 7, 8^4, 9^2, 11, 12^3, 13,
14, 16, 17^4, 18, 19^2, 22, 23^2, 24, 25^6, 26^2,
27^2, 28^2; **19:**1, 2, 4^2, 5^2, 6, 7, 8^4, 9^3, 10^3,
11, 12^3, 13^3, 14, 15, 16^2, 17^3, 19, 20, 21,
23, 24, 25, 27^3, 28, 29^2, 30^2, 31^2, 32^2, 33^4,
34^2, 35^6, 38^2, 41; **20:**1^2, 3, 4, 6, 7^4, 8, 9,
12, 15^3, 16^2, 17^2, 18, 19^3, 21^2, 22^2, 23,
24^4, 25, 26, 27, 28^4, 29, 31, 32, 35^3, 38^2;
21:1, 3^2, 4, 5^2, 7, 8^4, 9, 11^5, 13^2, 14^2, 16,
17, 18^2, 19, 20^2, 21^3, 22, 24, 25, 26^5, 27^4,
28^4, 29^2, 30^4, 31^2, 32^2, 33, 34^4, 35^4, 36^2,
37^2, 38, 39, 40^4; **22:**2^2, 3^4, 4, 5^4, 7, 9^2, 10,
11^2, 12^2, 13, 14^2, 16^2, 17, 20^2, 21, 22, 23,
24^2, 25, 26^2, 27, 28, 29, 30^4; **23:**1, 2^2, 3^2,
5^2, 6^6, 7^3, 8^2, 9^2, 10^3, 11^2, 12, 14, 15^2, 16,
17^2, 18^2, 19^2, 20^2, 22^2, 23^2, 24, 26, 27, 28,
30^2, 31, 32^3, 33^2, 34^2; **24:**1^3, 5^4, 6, 7, 9,
10^2, 12^4, 13, 14^4, 15^2, 18, 20, 21^2, 22^2, 24,
26, 27; **25:**1, 2^3, 3, 6^2, 7, 8^3, 9, 10, 12, 14,
15^3, 16^4, 17^3, 18, 21, 22, 23^4, 24^2, 27;
26:1, 2^2, 3, 4^2, 5^2, 6^2, 7, 8, 9, 10^2, 12, 13^3,
14^3, 16, 17^2, 18, 19, 20^2, 21^2, 22, 23^4, 25,
26, 27, 30^2; **27:**2, 3, 4, 5, 6, 7, 8^2, 9, 10,
11^4, 12^3, 13, 15^2, 16, 17^2, 18^2, 19^3, 21, 22,
23, 27^2, 29^2, 30^5, 31^3, 32^3, 33^2, 34, 37,
38^3, 39^3, 40^5, 41^5, 42^2, 43^2, 44^2; **28:**1, 2^3,
3^2, 4^3, 5^2, 7^3, 8, 9, 11, 13^2, 15^2, 16^4, 17^5,
19, 20, 21, 23^3, 24, 25^2, 27, 28^2, 29, 31^2

Ro 1:1, 2, 3^2, 4^4, 5, 6, 7, 8, 9, 10, 11, 12, 14^4,
15, 16^4, 17^2, 18^2, 20^4, 23^2, 24, 25^3, 26,
27^3, 32^2; **2:**1, 2, 3^2, 4^2, 5^2, 8, 9^2, 10^2, 12^2,
13^4, 14^5, 15^3, 16^2, 17, 18^2, 19, 20^4, 23^2,
24^2, 25^2, 26^3, 27^3, 28, 29^3; **3:**1, 2, 3, 5, 6,
7, 12, 13, 17, 19^3, 20^4, 21^4, 22, 23, 24,
25^2, 26, 27, 28^2, 29^4, 30, 31^2; **4:**1, 3, 4, 5,
6^2, 8^2, 9^2, 11^4, 12^3, 13^5, 14^2, 15, 16^6, 17,
18, 19, 20, 24; **5:**2, 5^2, 6, 10, 11, 12, 13^2,
14^2, 15^5, 16^3, 17, 18^3, 19, 20^2; **6:**4^3, 5^2, 6,
9, 12, 13, 14, 15, 17^2, 18, 19^2, 20, 21, 22,
23^2; **7:**1^2, 2^4, 4^3, 5^3, 6^3, 7^3, 8^2, 9^2, 10, 11,
12^2, 13, 14, 16, 19^2, 22^2, 23^2, 24, 25^4;
8:1^2, 2^3, 3^4, 4^4, 5^6, 7^2, 8, 9^4, 10^2, 11^3, 12^2,
13^4, 14^2, 15^2, 16^2, 18^2, 19^4, 20^2, 21^4, 22,
23^4, 26^2, 27^5, 28, 29^2, 33, 34, 35, 36^2, 39;
9:1^2, 3, 4^7, 5^2, 6, 7, 8^6, 9, 11^2, 12^2, 17^2, 20,
21^3, 22, 23^2, 24^2, 26^3, 27^4, 28^3, 29, 30^2,
31^2, 32^2; **10:**3, 4^2, 5^3, 6, 7^2, 8^2, 9^2, 10^2, 11,
12^3, 13^2, 15^2, 16, 17, 18^3; **11:**1^2, 2, 4^3, 5,
7^2, 8, 11, 12^6, 13^2, 15^5, 16^4, 17^3, 18^3, 19,
21, 22, 24^2, 25^2, 26, 28^3, 29, 33^3, 34^2;
12:1, 2, 3^2, 4, 6^2, 11, 13, 16, 17, 19; **13:**1^2,
2^2, 3^3, 4^3, 8, 10^2, 11, 12^4, 13, 14^3; **14:**1, 6^6,
8^3, 9, 10, 11, 14, 17^2, 19, 20; **15:**1^2, 3, 4, 5,
6, 7, 8^4, 9^2, 11, 12^2, 13^3, 15^2, 16^6, 18, 19^3,
20, 25, 26, 27, 29^3, 30^3, 31, 32, 33; **16:**1,
2, 4^2, 5^2, 7, 8, 11^2, 12^3, 13, 14, 15, 16, 17,
18^2, 20^2, 22, 23^3, 24, 25^4, 26^5

1Co 1:1, 2^2, 3, 4, 6, 7, 8^2, 9, 10^4, 11, 13, 16,
17^2, 18^3, 19^4, 20^4, 21^3, 22^2, 23^2, 24^2, 25^2,
26, 27^6, 28, 31; **2:**1, 4, 5^2, 6^2, 7^3, 8^2, 9^2,
10^2, 11^4, 12^4, 13^2, 14^3, 16^3; **3:**5, 6, 7, 10^2,
13^2, 16^2, 17^2, 19^2, 20^3, 22; **4:**1^2, 4, 5^5, 9^2,
13^3, 15, 17, 19^3, 20, 21; **5:**1, 4^2, 5^5, 6, 7,
8^3, 10^3; **6:**1^2, 2^4, 4, 6, 9^2, 10, 11^3, 12, 13^6,
14, 15^3, 17, 18, 19^2; **7:**1, 3^4, 4^4, 5, 8, 10^3,
11, 12^2, 13, 14^4, 15, 17, 19^2, 20, 22^2, 23,
25^2, 26, 28, 29, 31, 32^3, 33^2, 34^5, 35, 36,
39^3, 40; **8:**3, 4^2, 6, 7, 8^2, 10^2, 11, 12, 13;
9:1, 2^2, 5^2, 7^3, 8^2, 9^4, 12, 13^4, 14^3, 16^2, 17,
18^3, 19, 20^5, 21, 22^2, 23, 24, 25, 26; **10:**1^2,
2^2, 3, 4, 5, 6, 7, 10, 11^2, 13, 16^6, 18^3, 19,
20^2, 21^5, 22, 25, 26^3, 28^3, 29, 31, 32^3, 33;
11:2, 3^5, 6, 7^4, 8^4, 9^4, 10^2, 11^5, 12^4, 16,
17^2, 18, 20, 22, 23^3, 25^3, 26, 27^3, 29, 32^2,
34; **12:**3^3, 4, 5, 6, 7^2, 8^4, 9^3, 10^2, 11, 12^2,
14, 15^4, 16^4, 17^4, 18^2, 19, 21^4, 22, 23, 24,
25^3, 26^2, 27, 28, 30, 31; **13:**1, 2, 3, 6, 13;
14:2, 4, 5, 7, 8^2, 9^2, 10, 11^2, 12^2, 15^4, 16^3,
17, 19, 21^2, 23, 25, 27, 28, 29^2, 30, 32^3,
33^2, 34^2, 35, 36, 37^3; **15:**1, 3, 4^2, 5, 6, 7,
9^3, 10^2, 12^2, 13, 15, 16, 20^2, 21^2, 23, 24^3,
26, 28, 29^3, 32^2, 34, 35, 39, 40^4, 41^3, 42^2,
45^2, 47^4, 48^2, 49^4, 50, 52^4, 54, 56^3, 57,
58^3; **16:**1^3, 2^2, 7^2, 10^2, 11, 12, 13, 15^4, 17,
19^3, 20, 21, 22, 23

2Co 1:1^3, 2, 3^3, 4, 5, 6^2, 7^2, 9^2, 11^2, 12^3, 13,
14^2, 17^2, 19, 20^2, 22^2; **2:**2, 3, 4, 9, 10, 12,
14, 16^4, 17^2; **3:**3^4, 6^5, 7^4, 8^2, 9^2, 10, 13^2,
14^3, 15, 16, 17^3, 18^5; **4:**2^4, 4^5, 5, 6^5, 7^2,
10^4, 11, 13, 14, 15^3, 16, 18^4; **5:**1, 5^3, 6^2,
8^2, 10^2, 11^2, 14, 16^2, 18, 19^2, 21; **6:**1, 2^3,
3, 4, 6, 7^5, 13, 16^3, 17^2, 18; **7:**1^2, 6, 7^2, 8,
10^2, 12^2, 13^2, 15; **8:**1^2, 2^2, 4^2, 5^2, 6, 8^2, 9,
11, 16^2, 17, 18^3, 19^3, 21^3, 22, 23^2, 24^2;
9:1^2, 2, 3, 5^2, 9, 10^2, 12^3, 13^2, 14; **10:**1, 2,
3^2, 4^2, 5^2, 7, 8, 12, 13^2, 14, 16^2, 17, 18;
11:3^2, 5, 7, 9, 10^2, 13, 15, 17, 18, 20, 22,
24, 25, 26^4, 28^2, 30, 31, 32^4, 33; **12:**1, 2^3,
3^2, 6, 7^4, 8, 9, 11, 12, 14^5, 15^2, 18^2, 21;
13:1^2, 2, 4^2, 5, 8^2, 10^2, 11, 13, 14^5

Gal 1:1^2, 2^2, 3, 4, 6, 7, 10, 11, 12, 13^2, 14^2,
16, 19^2, 20, 21, 22, 23; **2:**2, 5^2, 7^4, 8^4, 9^4,
10^2, 11, 12^2, 13, 14^6, 15, 16^8, 17, 18, 19^2,
20^4, 21^2; **3:**1, 2^4, 3^2, 5^4, 7^2, 8^3, 10^5, 11^3,
12^3, 13^2, 14^4, 15, 16, 17^3, 18^2, 19^4, 21^3,
22^2, 23^2, 24, 26, 29; **4:**1, 2^2, 3^2, 4^3, 5^2, 6, 9,
13^3, 15, 16, 21^2, 22^2, 23^3, 24^3, 26, 27, 28,
29^2, 30^6, 31^2; **5:**1^2, 3, 4, 5^2, 7, 9, 10, 11^2,

THEE

73:22, 23, 25^{2}, 27^{2}; **74**:22, 23; **75**:1^{2}; **76**:10; **77**:16^{2}; **79**:6, 11, 12, 13; **80**:14, 18; **81**:7^{3}, 8, 9, 10, 16; **83**:2, 5; **84**:4, 5, 12; **85**:6; **86**:2, 3, 4, 5, 7, 8, 9, 12, 14; **87**:3, 7; **88**:1, 2, 9^{2}, 10, 13^{2}; **89**:8^{2}; **90**:8, 13; **91**:3, 4, 7, 10, 11^{2}, 12; **94**:20; **101**:1; **102**:1, 28; **103**:4; **104**:27; **105**:11; **108**:3^{2}; **114**:5; **116**:4, 7, 17, 19; **118**:21, 25^{2}, 28^{2}; **119**:7, 10, 11, 62, 63, 74, 76, 79, 108, 120, 126, 146, 164, 168, 169, 170, 175; **120**:3^{2}; **121**:3, 6, 7; **122**:6, 8; **123**:1; **128**:2, 5; **130**:1, 4; **134**:3; **135**:9; **137**:5, 6, 8; **138**:1^{2}, 4; **139**:12^{2}, 14, 15, 18, 20, 21^{2}; **141**:1^{2}, 2, 8^{2}; **142**:5; **143**:6^{2}, 8^{2}, 9; **144**:9^{2}; **145**:1, 2, 10^{2}, 15; **147**:13, 14

Prv 1:10; **2**:1, 11^{2}, 12, 16; **3**:2, 3, 28, 29, 30; **4**:6^{2}, 8^{2}, 9, 11^{2}, 24^{2}, 25; **5**:17, 19; **6**:22^{3}, 24, 25; **7**:1, 5, 15^{2}; **9**:8^{2}; **20**:22; **22**:18, 19^{2}, 20, 21^{2}, 27; **23**:1, 7^{2}, 11, 22, 25; **25**:7, 8, 10, 16, 17^{2}, 22; **27**:2; **29**:17; **30**:6, 7, 9, 10

Ecc 2:1; **7**:21; **8**:2; **9**:9; **10**:4, 16; **11**:9^{2}

Song 1:3, 4^{3}, 9, 11; **4**:7; **6**:1, 13; **7**:5, 12, 13; **8**:1^{2}, 2^{3}, 5^{4}

Isa 1:25; **2**:10; **3**:12^{2}; **7**:5, 11, 17; **8**:1; **9**:3; **10**:24^{2}; **12**:1, 6; **14**:3, 8, 9^{3}, 10, 11^{2}, 16^{3}, 29; **16**:4, 9; **19**:12; **22**:1, 3, 15, 16, 17^{2}, 18, 19^{2}; **24**:17; **25**:1, 3^{2}; **26**:3^{2}, 8^{2}, 9^{2}, 13^{2}, 16, 20; **29**:3^{3}, 11, 12; **30**:19^{2}, 21, 22; **33**:1^{3}, 2; **36**:8^{2}, 11, 12; **37**:9, 10, 22^{3}, 29, 30; **38**:3^{2}, 6, 7, 18^{2}, 19; **39**:3, 7; **40**:9; **41**:9^{4}, 10^{4}, 11^{2}, 12^{2}, 13^{2}, 14, 15; **42**:6^{3}; **43**:1^{4}, 2^{3}, 3, 4^{2}, 5^{2}, 23^{2}; **44**:2^{3}, 8, 21, 22, 24; **45**:2, 3^{2}, 4^{2}, 5, 14^{5}; **47**:3, 5, 9^{2}, 10, 11^{3}, 13^{2}, 15^{2}; **48**:5^{2}, 6, 9^{2}, 10^{2}, 17^{2}; **49**:6, 7, 8^{4}, 15, 16, 17^{2}, 18^{3}, 19, 23, 25, 26; **51**:16, 19^{3}, 23; **52**:1, 14; **54**:6, 7^{2}, 8^{2}, 9^{2}, 10^{2}, 14, 15, 17^{2}; **55**:5^{3}; **57**:8, 12, 13; **58**:8, 9, 11, 12, 14^{2}; **59**:12, 21; **60**:1, 2^{2}, 4, 5^{2}, 6, 7^{2}, 9, 10^{3}, 11, 12, 13, 14^{4}, 15^{2}, 19^{2}; **62**:4, 5^{2}; **64**:4, 5, 7, 9, 11; **65**:15

Jer 1:5^{4}, 7^{2}, 8^{2}, 10, 17^{2}, 18, 19^{4}; **2**:2, 17, 19^{3}, 21, 22^{2}, 28^{2}, 31, 35; **3**:19^{2}, 22; **4**:14, 18, 30^{2}; **5**:7; **6**:8^{2}, 23, 26^{2}, 27; **7**:16, 27^{2}; **10**:6, 7^{3}, 25; **11**:15, 17^{2}, 20; **12**:1^{2}, 3, 5^{2}, 6^{3}; **13**:1, 6, 12, 20, 21^{3}, 27; **14**:7, 20, 22; **15**:2, 5^{2}, 6^{2}, 11, 14, 19^{2}, 20^{6}, 21^{2}; **16**:2, 10, 19; **17**:4^{2}, 13, 16^{2}; **18**:2, 20, 23; **19**:2, 10; **20**:4, 12, 15; **21**:2, 13; **22**:6, 7, 21, 23, 24, 25, 26^{2}; **23**:33, 37; **25**:15; **26**:2; **27**:2; **28**:8, 15, 16; **29**:22, 26; **30**:2^{2}, 10, 11^{6}, 14^{3}, 15, 16^{3}, 17^{3}; **31**:3^{2}, 4, 21^{2}, 23; **32**:7^{2}, 8, 17, 20, 25; **33**:3^{2}; **34**:3, 4, 5^{3}, 14^{3}; **36**:2^{3}, 19, 28; **37**:18, 20^{3}; **38**:4, 10, 14, 15^{2}, 16^{2}, 20^{4}, 22^{2}, 25^{5}; **39**:12, 16, 17, 18^{2}; **40**:4^{6}, 5, 14, 15^{3}; **42**:2^{2}, 5, 6; **43**:2, 3; **44**:16; **45**:2, 5; **46**:14^{2}, 27, 28^{5}; **48**:2, 18, 27, 32, 43, 46; **49**:5^{2}, 9, 15, 16^{2}; **50**:21, 24, 31^{2}, 42; **51**:14^{2}, 20^{2}, 21^{2}, 22^{3}, 23^{3}, 25^{4}, 26, 36

Lam 1:22; **2**:13^{5}, 14^{2}, 15, 16, 17; **3**:57; **4**:21, 22; **5**:21

Ezk 2:1, 3, 4, 6, 8^{2}; **3**:3, 4, 6^{2}, 7, 10, 11, 17, 22, 25^{2}, 27; **4**:1^{2}, 3^{2}, 5, 6, 8^{2}, 9^{2}, 15; **5**:1^{3}, 8^{2}, 9, 10^{3}, 11, 12^{3}, 14^{2}, 15^{2}, 17^{3}; **7**:3^{4}, 4^{3}, 6, 7, 8^{4}, 9^{2}; **8**:6, 13, 15; **12**:3, 6, 9; **16**:4, 5^{3}, 6^{4}, 7, 8^{5}, 9^{3}, 10^{4}, 11, 14, 17, 19^{2}, 23, 24^{2}, 27^{3}, 33, 34^{3}, 37, 38^{2}, 39^{3}, 40^{3}, 41^{2}, 42^{2}, 44, 57, 59, 60^{2}, 61, 62, 63; **20**:47^{2}; **21**:3^{2}, 4, 7, 16, 19, 29^{3}, 30, 31^{3}; **22**:4, 5^{2}, 6, 7^{3}, 9^{3}, 10^{2}, 11, 12, 13, 14, 15^{3}; **23**:22^{2}, 24^{3}, 25^{2}, 26, 27, 28, 29^{2}, 30; **24**:2, 13^{2}, 14, 16, 17, 26^{2}; **25**:4^{3}, 7^{5}; **26**:3^{2}, 8^{3}, 10, 14, 15, 16, 17^{2}, 19^{3}, 20^{2}, 21; **27**:5, 7, 8, 9^{2}, 10, 15, 21, 25, 26^{2}, 27^{2}, 30, 31^{2}, 32^{2}, 34, 35, 36; **28**:3, 4, 7, 8, 9^{2}, 13, 14, 15, 16^{3}, 17^{3}, 18^{4}, 19^{2}, 22^{2}; **29**:3, 4, 5^{3}, 7^{2}, 8^{2}, 10, 21; **32**:3^{2}, 4^{4}, 6, 7, 8, 10^{2}, 11; **33**:7, 30, 31^{2}; **35**:3^{3}, 6^{3}, 9, 11, 14, 15; **36**:12, 15; **37**:16, 18; **38**:3, 4^{2}, 6, 7, 9, 13, 15, 16^{2}, 17; **39**:1, 2^{4}, 4^{2}; **40**:4^{2}; **44**:5

Dan 1:12, 13; **2**:23^{3}, 29^{2}, 31, 37, 38, 39^{2}; **3**:12, 16, 18; **4**:9^{2}, 18, 19^{2}, 25^{4}, 26, 27, 31^{2}, 32^{3}; **5**:10, 14^{3}, 16, 23; **6**:7, 12, 13, 16, 20, 22; **8**:19; **9**:7^{2}, 8, 15, 16, 18, 22, 23; **10**:11^{2}, 14, 19, 20, 21; **11**:2

Hos 1:2; **2**:19^{2}, 20; **3**:3; **4**:5, 6; **5**:8; **6**:4^{2}, 11; **8**:2, 5; **11**:8^{4}, 9; **12**:9; **13**:5, 10, 11; **14**:3

Joel 1:19, 20

Am 3:11; **4**:12^{2}; **5**:17; **6**:10; **7**:2, 5, 10, 12

Oba 2, 3, 4, 5^{2}, 7^{5}, 10, 15

Jna 1:8, 11, 14^{3}; **2**:7, 9; **3**:2; **4**:2^{2}, 3

Mic 1:13, 15, 16^{3}; **2**:11, 12; **4**:8, 9^{2}, 10, 11; **5**:2, 10, 13, 14; **6**:3^{2}, 4^{3}, 8^{2}, 13^{3}, 14, 15, 16; **7**:12, 17, 18

Nah 1:11, 12^{2}, 13, 14, 15; **2**:13; **3**:5, 6^{3}, 7^{3}, 13, 14, 15^{3}, 19^{2}

Hab 1:2; **2**:7^{2}, 8, 16, 17; **3**:10

Zep 2:5; **3**:11, 12, 15, 17^{3}, 18, 19

Hag 2:23^{3}

Zec 1:9; **2**:10, 11^{2}; **3**:2^{2}, 4^{2}, 7, 8; **9**:9, 11, 12, 13; **11**:15; **14**:1, 5

Mal 1:7, 8; **2**:14; **3**:8, 13

Mt 1:20; **2**:6, 13; **3**:14; **4**:6^{2}, 9, 10; **5**:23, 25^{2}, 26, 29^{3}, 30^{3}, 39, 40, 41, 42^{2}; **6**:2, 4, 6, 18, 23; **8**:13, 19, 29; **9**:2, 5, 22; **11**:10, 21^{2}, 23, 24, 25; **12**:38, 47; **14**:4, 28; **15**:28; **16**:17, 18, 19, 22^{2}, 23; **17**:4, 27; **18**:8^{3}, 9^{3}, 15^{3}, 16^{2}, 17, 22, 26, 29, 32, 33; **19**:27; **20**:13, 14; **21**:5, 19, 23; **23**:37; **25**:21, 23, 24, 37^{3}, 38^{3}, 39^{2}, 44^{2}; **26**:17, 33, 34, 35^{2}, 62, 63, 68, 73; **27**:13

Mk 1:2, 24^{2}, 37; **2**:5, 9, 11; **3**:32; **5**:7^{2}, 19^{2}, 23, 31, 34, 41; **6**:18, 22, 23; **8**:33; **9**:5, 17, 25, 43^{2}, 45^{2}, 47^{2}; **10**:28, 49, 51, 52; **11**:14, 28; **14**:30, 31^{2}, 36, 60; **15**:4

Lk 1:3, 13, 19^{2}, 28, 35^{3}; **2**:48; **3**:22; **4**:6, 8, 10^{2}, 11, 34^{2}; **5**:20, 23, 24; **6**:29, 30; **7**:7, 14, 20, 27, 40, 47, 50; **8**:20, 28^{2}, 39, 45^{2}, 48; **9**:33, 38, 57, 61; **10**:13^{2}, 21, 35; **11**:7, 27, 35, 36; **12**:20, 58^{3}, 59; **13**:31^{2}, 34; **14**:9^{2}, 10^{3}, 12^{2}, 14, 18, 19; **15**:18, 29; **16**:2, 27; **17**:3, 4^{2}, 19; **18**:11, 28, 41, 42; **19**:21, 22, 43^{4}, 44^{3}; **20**:2; **22**:11, 32, 33, 34, 64; **23**:43

Jn 1:48^{2}, 50^{2}; **2**:4; **3**:3, 5, 7, 11, 26; **4**:10^{2}, 26; **5**:10, 12, 14; **6**:30; **7**:20; **8**:10, 11; **9**:26, 37; **10**:33; **11**:8, 22, 28, 40, 41; **13**:8, 37, 38; **16**:30; **17**:1, 3, 4, 5, 7, 8, 11, 13, 21, 25^{2}; **18**:26, 30, 34, 35; **19**:10^{2}, 11^{2}; **21**:3, 15, 16, 17, 18^{3}, 20, 22, 23

Act 3:6; **5**:9; **7**:3^{2}, 27, 34, 35; **8**:20, 22, 34; **9**:5, 6, 17, 34; **10**:6, 19, 20, 22^{2}, 32, 33^{2}; **11**:14; **12**:8; **13**:11, 33, 47; **16**:18; **17**:32; **18**:10^{3}; **21**:21, 23, 24, 37, 39; **22**:10^{2}, 14, 18, 19, 21; **23**:3, 18^{2}, 20, 21, 30^{2}, 35; **24**:2, 4^{2}, 8, 14, 19, 25; **25**:26; **26**:2, 3^{2}, 14, 16^{3}, 17^{2}, 24; **27**:24^{2}; **28**:21^{2}, 22

Ro 2:4, 27; **4**:17; **9**:17^{2}; **10**:8; **11**:18, 21, 22; **13**:4; **15**:3, 9

1Co 4:7; **8**:10; **12**:21

2Co 6:2^{2}; **12**:9

Gal 3:8

Eph 5:14; **6**:3

Php 4:3

1Ti 1:3, 18^{2}; **3**:14^{2}; **4**:14^{2}, 16; **5**:21; **6**:13, 21

2Ti 1:3, 4, 5^{2}, 6^{2}, 14; **2**:7; **3**:15; **4**:1, 11, 13, 21

Tit 1:5^{2}; **2**:15; **3**:12, 15

Phlm 4, 7, 8, 9, 10, 11^{2}, 16, 18^{2}, 19, 20, 21, 23

Heb 1:5, 9; **2**:12; **5**:5; **6**:14^{2}; **8**:5; **13**:5^{2}

Jas 2:18

2Jn 5^{2}, 13

3Jn 3, 13, 14^{3}

Jude 9

Rev 2:4, 5, 10, 14, 16, 20; **3**:3^{2}, 8, 9, 10, 16, 18; **4**:1; **11**:17^{2}; **14**:15; **15**:4^{2}; **17**:1, 7; **18**:14^{2}, 22^{3}, 23^{2}; **21**:9

THEIR

Gen 1:21, 25; **5**:2; **6**:20^{2}; **7**:14; **8**:19; **9**:23^{4}; **10**:5^{3}, 20^{4}, 30, 31^{4}, 32^{2}; **11**:7; **12**:5; **13**:6; **14**:6, 11^{2}, 24; **17**:7, 8, 9, 23; **18**:20, 22, 26; **19**:10, 33, 35, 36; **20**:8; **24**:52, 59; **25**:13^{2}, 16^{4}; **26**:18; **31**:38, 43, 53; **32**:15; **33**:2, 6; **34**:13, 18, 20^{2}, 21, 23^{2}, 27, 28^{3}, 29^{3}; **35**:4^{3}; **36**:7^{2}, 19, 30, 40^{3}, 43^{2}; **37**:2, 4, 12, 16, 21, 22, 25^{2}, 32; **40**:1; **42**:6, 24, 25, 26, 28, 29, 35^{2}, 36; **43**:2, 11, 15, 24^{2}, 26, 27, 28; **44**:3, 13; **45**:25, 27; **46**:5^{3}, 6^{2}, 17, 32^{3}; **47**:1^{2}, 4, 9, 12, 17^{2}, 22^{2}, 30; **48**:6^{2}; **49**:5, 6^{4}, 7^{2}, 28; **50**:8^{3}, 15, 17

Ex 1:11, 14^{2}; **2**:11, 16, 17, 18, 23, 24; **3**:7^{3}; **4**:5, 31^{2}; **5**:4, 5, 6, 10, 21; **6**:4, 6, 14, 16, 17, 19, 25, 26; **7**:11, 12, 19^{4}, 22; **8**:7, 18, 26; **10**:7, 23; **12**:3, 34^{4}, 42, 51; **13**:20; **14**:10, 19, 22^{2}, 25, 26^{2}, 29^{2}; **16**:1^{2}; **17**:1; **18**:7, 23; **19**:7, 10, 14; **21**:32; **22**:23; **23**:24^{3}, 26, 27, 32, 33; **25**:20^{3}, 34^{2}, 36^{2}, 40; **26**:21, 25, 29, 32, 37; **27**:10^{2}, 11^{2}, 12^{2}, 14^{2}, 15^{2}, 16^{2}, 17^{2}, 18, 21; **28**:10^{2}, 12, 20, 21, 38, 42; **29**:10, 15, 19, 20^{2}, 25, 28^{2}, 45, 46^{2}; **30**:12, 19^{2}, 21^{3}; **31**:16; **32**:3, 4, 15, 25^{2}, 32, 34; **33**:6; **34**:13^{3}, 15^{2}, 16^{4}; **35**:17, 18, 25; **36**:26, 30, 34, 36, 38^{4}; **37**:9^{3}, 22^{2}; **38**:10^{3}, 11^{3}, 12^{3}, 14^{2}, 15^{2}, 17^{2}, 19^{5}, 28; **39**:13, 14; **40**:15^{3}, 31^{2}, 36, 38

Lev 4:15; **6**:17; **7**:34, 36, 38; **8**:14, 16, 18, 22, 24^{3}, 25, 28; **9**:24; **10**:5, 19^{2}; **11**:8^{2}, 11^{2}, 21, 27, 35, 36, 37, 38; **13**:38, 39; **15**:31^{2}; **16**:16^{3}, 21^{2}, 22, 27^{3}, 34; **17**:5, 7^{2}; **18**:3, 6, 9, 10, 29; **20**:4, 5, 11, 12, 13, 16, 17, 18, 19, 20, 24, 27; **21**:5^{3}, 6^{3}, 17; **22**:16, 25; **23**:4, 18^{2}; **24**:14; **25**:32, 33, 34^{2}, 45; **26**:4, 13, 20, 36^{2}, 39^{2}, 40^{3}, 41^{3}, 43^{2}, 44^{2}, 45^{3}

Nu 1:2^{4}, 3, 16, 17, 18^{4}, 20^{4}, 22^{4}, 24^{3}, 26^{3}, 28^{3}, 30^{3}, 32^{3}, 34^{3}, 36^{3}, 38^{3}, 40^{3}, 42^{3}, 45, 47, 52^{2}; **2**:2, 3, 9, 10, 16, 17, 18, 24, 25, 31, 32^{2}, 34^{3}; **3**:4, 10, 15^{2}, 17, 18, 19, 20^{2}, 31, 37^{3}, 39, 40, 45; **4**:2^{2}, 22^{2}, 26^{2}, 27^{3}, 28, 29^{2}, 31^{2}, 32^{6}, 33, 34^{2}, 36, 38^{2}, 40^{2}, 42^{2}, 44, 46^{2}; **5**:3, 7; **6**:15^{2}; **7**:2, 3, 7, 8, 9, 10, 11, 87; **8**:7^{2}, 10, 12, 21, 22, 26^{2}; **9**:17, 18, 20, 22; **10**:6^{2}, 12, 13, 14, 18, 22, 25, 28; **11**:10, 12, 33; **13**:2, 4, 33; **14**:1, 5, 6, 9, 23; **15**:12, 25^{3}, 38^{2}; **16**:15, 22, 26, 27^{4}, 32^{2}, 38, 45; **17**:2^{3}, 3, 6^{3}, 10; **18**:11, 17^{2}, 20, 21, 23; **20**:6, 8^{2}, 11; **21**:2, 3, 18; **22**:7; **24**:2, 8; **25**:2^{2}, 18^{2}; **26**:2, 12, 15, 20, 23, 26, 28, 35, 37, 38, 41, 42^{2}, 44, 48, 50, 55, 57, 59; **27**:5, 7^{2}, 14, 19; **28**:2, 14, 20, 28, 31; **29**:3, 6^{2}, 9, 11, 14, 18^{3}, 19, 21^{3}, 24^{3}, 27^{3}, 30^{3}, 33^{3}, 37^{3}; **30**:9; **31**:9^{4}, 10^{2}, 29; **32**:17, 38; **33**:1, 2^{4}, 4^{2}, 12, 52^{3}; **34**:14^{4}, 15; **35**:2, 3^{3}, 7; **36**:3, 4^{2}, 6, 11, 12^{2}

Dt 1:8, 25; **2**:5, 9, 12, 21, 22, 23; **4**:10, 37, 38; **5**:29; **7**:5^{4}, 10, 16, 24^{2}, 25; **9**:5, 14, 27^{2}; **10**:6, 11, 15; **11**:4^{2}, 6^{3}, 9; **12**:2, 3^{4}, 29, 30^{2}, 31^{4}; **13**:13; **14**:8^{2}; **18**:2^{2}, 18; **19**:1^{2}; **20**:18^{2}; **21**:5, 6; **23**:3, 6^{2}, 8; **29**:8, 17^{2}, 25, 28; **31**:7, 11, 13, 19, 20, 21^{2}, 28; **32**:5, 8, 20, 21, 27, 29, 30, 31, 32^{3}, 33, 35^{2}, 36, 37^{2}, 38^{2}; **33**:29

Jos 1:6; **3**:14; **4**:6, 18, 21; **5**:1, 6, 7^{2}, 8; **7**:6, 8^{2}, 11, 12^{3}, 16; **8**:13, 19, 33^{2}; **9**:4, 5^{2}, 14, 16, 17^{2}; **10**:5, 13, 19, 24, 40, 42; **11**:4, 6^{2}, 9^{2}, 13, 17, 20, 21, 23^{2}; **12**:1, 7; **13**:8, 14, 15, 16, 23, 24, 25, 28^{2}, 29, 30, 31, 33; **14**:2, 4^{3}; **15**:1, 2, 5, 12, 20, 32, 36, 41, 44, 46, 51, 54, 57, 59, 60, 62; **16**:4, 5^{2}, 8, 9; **17**:2^{2}, 4; **18**:2, 5^{2}, 7^{2}, 10, 11^{2}, 12, 20, 21, 24, 28^{2}; **19**:1^{2}, 2, 6, 7, 8, 9, 10^{2}, 11, 15, 16^{2}, 17, 18, 22^{2}, 23^{2}, 24, 25, 30, 31^{2}, 32, 33, 38, 39^{2}, 40, 41, 47, 48^{2}, 49; **21**:3^{2}, 7, 8, 19, 20, 26, 33^{2}, 40^{2}, 41, 42, 43, 44^{4}; **22**:6, 7^{2}, 9, 14; **23**:1, 2^{4}, 5, 7; **24**:1^{3}, 8

Jdg 1:4, 7^{3}; **2**:2, 3, 4, 10, 12, 14^{2}, 17^{2}, 18^{2}, 19^{3}, 20, 22; **3**:4, 6^{5}, 7, 25; **5**:18, 20, 22; **6**:5^{3}, 9; **7**:2, 6^{3}, 8^{2}, 12, 19, 20^{2}; **8**:3, 10, 21, 26, 28, 33, 34^{2}; **9**:3, 24^{2}, 26, 27^{2}, 57; **10**:12; **12**:2; **13**:20; **14**:17, 19; **15**:13; **16**:18, 23, 24, 25; **18**:1, 2^{2}, 8^{2}, 14, 16, 23, 26, 29; **19**:14, 21, 22; **20**:13, 22, 33^{2}, 42; **21**:2, 6, 22^{2}, 23^{2}

Ru 1:9, 14

1Sa 1:19; **2**:20, 25, 33; **5**:9; **6**:6, 7, 10, 11, 13^{2}; **8**:9, 22; **9**:16; **10**:4, 12, 21; **11**:4; **12**:9; **14**:30, 46; **15**:24; **17**:1, 18^{2}, 51, 53; **18**:27; **21**:13; **22**:17^{2}; **23**:5; **25**:12; **28**:1, 23; **29**:1; **30**:2, 3^{3}, 4; **31**:9, 13

2Sa 1:23^{2}; **2**:26; **3**:18, 30; **4**:12^{2}; **5**:21; **7**:10, 23, 24; **10**:3, 4^{3}, 18; **12**:30; **13**:31, 36; **15**:11, 36; **17**:8; **18**:28; **20**:2, 3; **22**:46; **23**:17, 19

1Ki 2:4^{3}, 15, 33; **4**:8; **6**:27; **7**:25, 31, 33^{4}; **8**:7, 23, 25, 34, 35, 37^{2}, 44, 45^{3}, 48^{5}, 49^{3}, 50, 66; **9**:9^{2}, 21; **10**:5, 29; **11**:2, 8; **12**:16, 27; **13**:11, 12; **14**:15^{2}, 22^{2}, 27, 30; **15**:16, 32; **16**:2, 13, 26; **18**:28, 37, 39; **19**:21; **20**:6, 23, 24, 25, 32^{2}; **22**:10

2Ki 1:14; **3**:24, 27; **5**:24; **6**:20, 22, 23; **7**:7^{4}, 15; **8**:12^{4}, 21; **10**:7; **11**:12; **13**:3, 5; **14**:12; **16**:15^{2}; **17**:7, 9^{2}, 14^{3}, 15, 16, 17^{2}, 19, 23, 25, 29^{2}, 31, 33, 34^{2}, 40, 41^{4}; **18**:12, 27^{2}, 35, 36, 37; **19**:17, 18, 26; **21**:8, 14^{2}, 15; **22**:7, 17; **23**:2, 3^{2}, 9, 14; **25**:21, 23^{2}, 24

1Ch 1:29; **3**:9, 19; **4**:3, 27, 31, 32, 33^{3}, 38^{3}, 39, 41^{3}, 42; **5**:7^{2}, 9, 10^{2}, 13^{2}, 15, 16, 20^{2}, 21^{2}, 22, 24^{2}, 25; **6**:19, 32^{2}, 33, 44, 48, 54^{3}, 57, 60^{2}, 62, 63, 64, 65, 66; **7**:2^{2}, 4^{2}, 5^{2}, 7^{2}, 9^{3}, 11, 21, 22, 28, 30, 32, 40; **8**:28, 32; **9**:1, 2^{2}, 6, 9^{3}, 13^{2}, 17, 19, 22^{3}, 23, 25^{2}, 26, 32, 34, 38^{2}; **10**:7, 9, 10, 12; **11**:19^{2}, 21; **12**:30, 32^{2}, 39; **13**:2, 8; **14**:12; **15**:15, 16, 17, 18; **16**:21, 38; **17**:9, 22; **19**:4^{2}, 7; **20**:2; **21**:16; **23**:3^{2}, 11, 22, 24^{2}, 28, 32; **24**:2, 3^{2}, 4^{2}, 19^{3}, 30, 31^{2}; **25**:1, 3, 6, 7; **26**:6, 8^{2}, 13; **27**:1^{2}; **28**:15, 18; **29**:18, 20^{2}, 21

2Ch 1:17; **3**:13^{2}; **4**:4, 7, 16, 20; **5**:8, 12^{2}, 13; **6**:14, 16, 25, 26, 28^{2}, 34, 35^{3}, 36, 37, 38^{5}, 39^{3}; **7**:3, 6^{2}, 10, 14^{3}, 22; **8**:8, 14^{3}; **9**:4^{2}, 6; **10**:16; **11**:13, 14^{2}, 16^{2}; **13**:10, 16, 18; **14**:4; **15**:4, 12^{3}, 15^{2}; **17**:14; **18**:9; **19**:4, 10; **20**:13^{3}, 27, 33^{2}; **21**:3; **22**:5; **24**:18^{2}, 24^{2}; **25**:4, 5, 10, 15, 20; **26**:11, 13; **28**:6, 8, 15; **29**:6^{2}, 15, 23, 24, 30, 34; **30**:7, 16^{2}, 22, 27^{2}; **31**:1, 2, 6, 15^{2}, 16^{4}, 17^{3}, 18^{5}, 19; **32**:13, 17; **33**:17; **34**:5, 6, 25, 30, 32, 33^{2}; **35**:2, 10^{2}, 11, 15^{3}, 25; **36**:15, 17^{2}

Ezr 1:6; **2**:59^{2}, 61, 62, 65^{2}, 66^{2}, 67^{2}, 69, 70^{2}; **3**:8^{2}, 9^{2}, 10, 12; **4**:5, 7, 9, 17, 23; **5**:3, 5, 8,

10; 6:12, 13, 18^2, 20, 22; 7:13, 16, 17^2; 8:1, 19, 24, 26; 9:1, 2^2, 11^2, 12^4; 10:16^2, 19^3

Neh 2:18; 3:5^3, 18, 23; 4:3, 4^2, 5^2, 13^4, 15; 5:1^2, 5, 6, 8, 11^4, 14, 15; 6:6, 9, 14, 16; 7:61^2, 63, 64, 67^2, 68^2, 69, 73^2; 8:6^3, 7, 12, 15, 16; 9:2^2, 3^3, 4, 6, 9, 11, 15^2, 16, 17^3, 20^2, 21^2, 23^2, 24^2, 26, 27^3, 28, 29, 35^2, 37; 10:10, 28^3, 29^2, 30; 11:3, 9, 12, 14^2, 19, 25, 30, 31; 12:7, 9, 24, 27, 42, 45; 13:11, 13^2, 24, 25^3

Est 1:17^2, 20, 22; 2:3, 12; 3:8, 12; 8:9^3, 11, 13; 9:2^2, 5, 10, 15, 16^4, 22, 27^3, 28, 31^3

Job 1:4^2, 5^2, 13, 18; 2:12^3; 3:8, 15; 4:21; 5:5, 12^2, 13, 15; 6:17, 18; 8:4, 8, 10; 11:3, 20; 12:18; 14:12; 15:18, 35; 16:10; 17:2, 4; 19:12, 15; 20:10; 21:8^4, 9, 10^2, 11^2, 13, 16^2, 17, 29; 22:6, 18; 24:5^2, 11^2, 18, 23; 27:23; 29:9^2, 10^3, 23, 25; 30:2, 4, 9^2, 12; 31:16, 39; 33:16; 34:24, 25; 36:9^2, 10, 11^2, 14, 15, 20; 37:8; 38:15, 40; 39:3^2, 4; 40:12, 13, 22; 42:15^2

Ps 2:3^2, 12; 4:7^2; 5:9^4, 10^2, 11; 7:7; 9:5, 6, 10, 15; 10:17; 11:2^2, 6; 16:4^3; 17:7, 10^2, 11, 14^3; 18:45; 19:3, 4^2; 21:10^2, 12; 22:13; 26:10; 28:3^2, 4^4, 8; 33:15^2, 19; 34:5, 15, 17; 35:6, 7, 16, 17, 21, 25; 36:7; 37:14, 15^3, 18, 39; 40:15; 44:1, 3^2, 12; 49:6^2, 8, 10, 11^5, 13^4, 14^2; 55:9, 15, 23; 56:5; 57:4; 58:4, 6^2; 59:7^2, 12^3; 62:4; 64:3^3, 8; 65:7; 68:27^2; 69:22^2, 23^2, 25^2, 27; 70:3; 72:14^2; 73:4^2, 7, 9^2, 17, 20; 74:4, 8; 76:5^2; 78:4, 5, 6, 7, 8^2, 12, 18^2, 28^2, 29, 30^3, 33^2, 35^2, 36^2, 37, 38, 44^2, 46^2, 47^2, 48^2, 50^2, 51, 53, 55, 57, 58^2, 63^2, 64^2; 79:3, 10, 12^2; 81:12^2, 14^2, 15; 83:11^2, 16; 85:2; 89:17, 32^2; 90:10, 16; 91:12; 93:3^2; 94:23^2; 95:10; 98:8; 99:8; 102:17, 28; 104:11, 12, 17, 21^2, 22, 27, 29^2; 105:14, 24, 25, 29^2, 30^2, 31, 32, 33^3, 35^2, 36^2, 37; 106:11, 15^2, 18, 20, 21, 25, 27, 29, 32, 35, 36, 37^2, 38^2, 39^2, 42^2, 43^2, 44^2; 107:5, 6^2, 12, 13^2, 14, 17^2, 18, 19^2, 20, 26, 27, 28^2, 30, 38; 109:10^2, 13, 25, 29; 115:2, 4, 7, 9^2, 10^2, 11^2; 119:70, 118; 123:2; 124:3, 6; 125:3, 4, 5; 129:3; 132:12; 135:12, 17; 136:10, 21; 140:2, 3^2, 9; 141:4, 5, 6, 10; 144:8, 11, 12; 145:15, 19; 147:3, 4; 149:2, 5, 6^2, 8^2

Prv 1:6, 15, 16, 18^2, 22, 31^2; 2:15; 4:16, 22; 8:21; 9:15; 10:15; 11:6, 20; 14:24; 17:6; 18:19; 20:29; 21:12; 22:23; 23:11^2; 24:2^2, 22; 25:27; 29:13, 16; 30:5, 11^2, 12^2, 13^2, 14, 25, 26

Ecc 2:3; 3:11; 4:1, 9; 5:11, 13; 9:1, 3, 6^3

Isa 2:4^2, 7^4, 8^3; 3:4, 8^2, 9^3, 10, 12, 16, 17, 18^4; 5:12, 13^2, 14^3, 17, 21^2, 24^2, 25, 27^2, 28^3, 29; 6:10^5, 13; 8:12, 19, 21^2; 9:17^2; 10:2, 5, 13, 25, 29; 11:7, 14; 13:8, 10, 11^2, 16^4, 18^2, 20, 21, 22^2; 14:1, 2^2, 9, 21, 25; 15:2, 3^3, 4; 16:10^2; 18:2, 7; 20:4, 5^2; 21:14; 24:14; 25:11^2; 26:11, 14, 21; 28:25; 29:13^4, 14^2, 15^2, 19; 30:6^2, 7, 26; 31:3, 4; 33:2, 7, 9, 23, 24; 34:2, 3^4, 4, 7^2; 35:10; 36:12^2, 20, 21, 22; 37:18, 19, 27; 40:24, 26, 31; 41:1, 17, 29^2; 42:11, 15; 43:9, 14; 44:9^2, 18^2, 25; 45:12, 20; 46:1; 47:9; 49:9, 22^2, 23^2, 26^2; 50:2, 3; 51:7, 11; 52:15; 53:11; 54:17; 55:12; 56:7^2, 11; 57:2, 8; 58:1^2, 2; 59:5, 6^4, 7^3, 8, 18; 60:8, 9^2, 10, 11; 61:6, 7^2, 8, 9^2; 62:6; 63:3, 6, 8, 9, 10; 65:2, 4, 6, 7^2, 22, 23; 66:3^3, 4^2, 18^2, 24^2

Jer 1:8, 16^2, 17; 2:11^2, 26^4, 27^3; 3:17, 21^2, 24^4; 4:16; 5:3, 4, 5, 6^3, 16, 24, 27, 31; 6:3^2, 10, 12^2, 19, 23, 27; 7:18, 19, 24^2, 26^3, 28^2, 30, 31^2; 8:1, 7, 10^2, 12, 19; 9:3^2, 5, 8, 14^2, 16; 10:7, 9, 15, 21; 11:8^2, 10^2, 12, 14, 18, 22^2, 23; 12:2^2, 14; 13:10; 14:3^4, 4, 6, 10^3, 11, 12, 14, 16^4; 15:7, 8, 9; 16:3^2, 4, 7^2, 15^2, 17^2, 18^3; 17:1, 2^3, 23^2, 25; 18:8, 15, 16, 17, 21^6, 22, 23^3; 19:4, 5, 7^3, 9^4, 15; 20:4, 5, 11; 21:7^2; 22:9; 23:3, 8, 10^2, 11, 12^2, 16, 22^2, 26, 27^2, 31, 32^2; 24:5, 7^2, 9, 10; 25:12, 14^2, 36, 38; 26:3; 27:4, 8, 11^2; 29:23; 30:3, 9^2, 10, 20^2, 21^2; 31:12, 13^2, 17, 23, 32, 33^3, 34^2; 32:18, 22, 30^2, 32^4, 34, 35^2, 38, 39, 40, 44; 33:8^2, 12, 20, 26; 34:14, 16, 20^3, 21^2; 35:14, 16; 36:3^2, 6, 7, 15, 24, 31; 37:7; 38:18, 19, 23; 40:7, 8, 9; 41:5^3, 8; 42:17; 43:1^2; 44:3, 5^2, 9, 12, 15; 46:5, 10, 21^2, 25^2, 26, 27; 47:3, 5; 48:12, 13, 33, 34, 44; 49:1, 3, 7, 20, 21, 29^5, 32^3, 35, 37^2; 50:4, 5, 6^2, 7^2, 9, 27^2, 34^2, 37^2, 38, 42, 45; 51:5, 18, 24, 30^2, 39^2, 55, 56

Lam 1:11, 14, 19^2, 22; 2:10^2, 12^3, 15^2, 16, 18, 20; 3:14, 46, 60^2, 61^2, 62, 63^3, 64; 4:3, 7, 8^3, 10^2, 14, 20; 5:7, 8, 12, 14

Ezk 1:5, 7^2, 8^4, 9, 10, 11^3, 13, 16^3, 17, 18^2, 20, 22, 23^2, 24^2, 25^2, 26; 2:3, 6^3; 3:8^2, 9; 4:4, 5, 12, 13, 17; 5:10, 16; 6:5, 9^4, 13^4, 14; 7:11, 18, 19^7, 20^2, 24^2, 27^2; 8:16^2, 17; 9:10^2; 10:8, 10, 11, 12^4, 16, 19, 21, 22^2; 11:19, 20, 21^4, 22; 12:3^2, 4^2, 5, 6, 7, 16, 19^2; 13:2, 3, 17; 14:3^4, 5^2, 10, 11^2, 14^2, 20^2, 22^2, 23^2; 16:39, 40, 45^2, 47^2, 53, 55^2; 19:4, 7^2, 8^2; 20:4, 8, 16^2, 18^3, 24^2, 26, 28^4, 30; 21:6, 14, 15^3, 23, 28, 29; 22:6, 10, 26, 31^2; 23:3^3, 4, 7, 8, 15^3, 17, 20, 24, 30, 36, 37^3, 39^2, 42^2, 45, 47^4; 24:25^6; 25:4^2; 26:10, 16^3, 17; 27:9, 11, 29, 30^2, 32, 35^2; 28:7, 25, 26; 29:7^2, 14, 16; 30:11, 13; 31:6^2, 14^4; 32:2, 10, 14^2, 24^2, 25^2, 26, 27^5, 29, 30^3; 33:2^2, 17, 29, 31^3; 34:10^2, 13, 14, 23, 24, 27^2, 30; 35:5^2; 36:5^2, 7, 12, 17^4, 18, 19^2, 23; 37:10, 20, 21, 23^5, 25^3, 27; 38:16; 39:22, 23^2, 24^2, 26^3, 27, 28^2; 40:16, 22^3, 41, 44; 41:16; 42:4, 11^3, 14; 43:7^4, 8^4, 9^2, 10, 11; 44:10^2, 12^2, 13^2, 18^2, 19^2, 20^3, 22, 28^2; 45:4, 8; 46:16, 18; 47:10^2, 12; 48:29, 34

Dan 1:15, 16; 2:30; 3:21^4, 27^2, 28^2, 29; 4:21; 6:24^3; 7:12^2; 8:23; 9:7; 11:8^3, 32

Hos 1:7; 2:5, 17; 3:5^2; 4:7, 8^2, 9^2, 12^3, 18, 19; 5:4^2, 5, 6^2, 7, 15^2; 7:2^3, 3^2, 6^2, 7^2, 10, 12, 14^2, 15, 16^3; 8:4^2, 13^2; 9:4^3, 6^2, 9^2, 10, 11, 12, 15^3, 16^2; 10:2^3, 8, 10; 11:3, 4, 6, 11; 12:11; 13:2^2, 6^2, 8, 16^2; 14:4

Joel 1:3^2, 17; 2:6, 7, 10, 17, 22; 3:6, 13, 15, 19, 21

Am 1:13, 15; 2:4^2, 8; 3:10; 4:1; 5:12; 6:2, 4; 7:11; 8:7; 9:4, 15^2

Oba 12, 13^5, 17

Jna 1:2; 2:8; 3:8, 10^2; 4:11^2

Mic 2:1^2, 9^2, 12, 13; 3:2^3, 3^2, 4, 5^2, 7; 4:3^2, 13^2; 6:12^2, 16; 7:4, 13, 16^4, 17, 19

Nah 2:2, 5, 7; 3:3^2, 17

Hab 1:7^2, 8^3, 9, 15^2, 16^4, 17; 2:15; 3:11, 14

Zep 1:9, 12^2, 13^2, 17^2, 18^2; 2:7^2, 8, 10, 14; 3:6^3, 7^2, 13

Hag 1:12^2, 14; 2:14, 22

Zec 1:21; 2:9; 5:6, 9; 7:2, 11, 12; 8:8, 12; 9:16; 10:2, 5, 6, 7^3, 9; 11:3, 5, 6, 8, 16; 12:5^2, 12^2, 13^2, 14; 14:12^6

Mal 4:6

Mt 1:21; 2:11, 12; 3:6; 4:6, 20, 21^2, 22, 23; 6:2, 5, 7, 14, 15, 16^2; 7:6, 16, 20; 8:22, 33, 34; 9:2, 4, 29, 30, 35; 10:17, 21; 11:1, 5, 16; 12:9, 25; 13:15^5, 43, 54, 58; 14:14; 15:2, 8^3, 27; 17:6, 8, 25; 18:10, 31, 35; 19:12; 20:4, 8, 31, 34^2; 21:7, 8, 41; 22:5, 7, 16, 18, 22; 23:3, 4, 5^3; 25:1, 3, 4^2, 7; 26:43, 67; 27:39

Mk 1:5, 18, 19, 20, 23, 39; 2:5, 6; 3:4, 5; 4:12, 15; 5:17; 6:6, 8^2, 26, 52; 7:3, 6^2; 8:3; 9:34, 44, 46, 48; 10:42; 11:4, 7, 8; 12:12, 15, 44; 13:12; 14:40, 46, 56, 59, 65; 15:19, 29; 16:14

Lk 1:16, 20, 51, 52, 66, 77; 2:8, 39, 44; 3:15; 4:11, 15, 29; 5:2, 6, 7, 11, 15, 20, 22, 30; 6:1, 8, 17, 22, 23, 26; 7:21; 8:3, 12; 9:47, 60; 11:17, 48; 12:36, 42; 13:1; 14:4; 16:4, 8; 17:13; 19:32, 35, 36, 40; 20:23, 26; 21:1, 4, 12; 22:66; 23:25, 48; 24:5, 11, 16, 31^2, 45

Jn 3:19; 4:38; 8:9; 10:39; 11:19, 46; 12:40^4; 13:12; 15:22, 25; 17:19, 20; 18:8; 19:3, 31; 20:10

Act 1:9, 19, 26; 2:37, 45, 46; 4:5, 23, 24, 29; 5:18; 6:1, 6; 7:19, 34, 39, 41, 54, 57, 58, 60; 8:17, 36; 9:24; 10:9; 11:18; 12:17, 20^2, 25; 13:3, 5, 18, 19, 22, 27, 33, 50, 51; 14:2, 3, 5, 11, 13, 14, 16; 15:3, 9, 13, 22, 26; 16:19, 22, 24, 33; 17:21, 26; 18:3; 19:18, 19; 21:21, 24; 22:22, 23, 30; 23:16, 28, 29; 25:19; 26:18; 27:13, 43; 28:6, 27^5

Ro 1:21^2, 24^2, 26, 27^2, 28; 2:15^3; 3:3, 13^3, 15, 16, 18; 10:3, 18^2; 11:9, 10^2, 11, 12, 24, 27, 30; 13:7; 15:27^3; 16:4, 5, 18

1Co 3:19; 8:7, 12; 14:35; 16:19

2Co 3:14, 15; 5:19; 6:16; 8:2^3, 3^2, 5, 14^2; 9:14; 11:15

Gal 2:13

Eph 4:17, 18; 5:24, 28^2

Php 2:21; 3:19^2

Col 2:2

1Th 2:15, 16; 5:13

2Th 3:12

1Ti 3:11, 12^2; 4:2; 5:4, 12; 6:1

2Ti 2:17; 3:2, 9; 4:3, 4, 16

Tit 1:12, 15; 2:4^2, 5, 9; 3:13

Heb 2:10, 15; 3:10; 5:14; 7:5; 8:9, 10^2, 12^3; 10:16^2, 17; 11:16, 35; 12:10; 13:7

Jas 1:27; 3:3

1Pt 3:5, 12, 14; 4:14, 19

2Pt 2:2, 3, 8, 12, 13; 3:3, 16

3Jn 6

Jude 6^2, 13, 15^2, 16^2, 18

Rev 2:22; 3:4; 4:4, 10; 6:11^2, 14; 7:3, 9, 11, 14, 17; 9:4, 5, 7^2, 8, 9, 10^2, 17, 18, 19^4, 20, 21^4; 10:3, 4; 11:5^2, 6, 7, 8, 9^2, 11, 12, 16^2; 12:8, 11^2; 13:16^2; 14:1, 2, 5, 11, 13^2; 15:6; 16:10, 11^3; 17:13, 17^2; 18:11, 19; 19:19, 21; 20:4^2, 12, 13; 21:3, 4, 8, 24; 22:4

THEM

Gen 1:14, 15, 17, 22, 26, 27, 28^2; 2:1, 19^2; 3:7, 21; 5:2^2; 6:1, 2, 4, 7, 13^2, 19, 20, 21; 7:13; 9:1, 19; 10:1; 11:3, 6, 8, 9, 29, 31; 12:3; 13:6; 14:8, 14, 15^3, 24; 15:5, 10, 11, 13^2; 18:2^2, 8^2, 16^2; 19:1^2, 3^2, 5^2, 6, 8^2, 9, 10, 12, 13, 17, 18; 20:14; 21:27^2, 31; 22:6, 8; 23:8; 24:28, 53, 56, 60; 25:6, 26; 26:15^2, 18^2, 27, 30, 31; 27:9, 13, 14, 15; 28:11; 29:4, 5, 6, 7, 9^2; 30:14, 35, 37, 40, 42; 31:5, 9, 32, 33, 34^3, 55; 32:2, 4, 16, 23^2; 33:3, 13; 34:8, 14, 21^3, 23; 35:4, 5; 36:7; 37:6, 13, 17^2, 18, 22; 38:26; 39:14; 40:3, 4^2, 5, 6^2, 8^2, 11, 17, 22; 41:3, 6, 8^2, 19, 21^2, 23, 27, 30, 35^2; 42:7^4, 9^2, 12, 14, 17, 18, 22, 23^2, 24^4, 25^2, 27, 28, 29, 36; 43:2, 11, 16, 23, 24, 27, 32, 34; 44:4^2, 6^2, 15; 45:1, 15, 21^2, 22, 24, 26, 27; 47:2, 6^3, 11, 17^2, 20, 21, 22^2, 24; 48:6, 9^2, 10^3, 12, 13^2, 16^2, 20; 49:7^2, 28^3, 29^2; 50:12, 19, 21^2

Ex 1:7, 10^2, 11^2, 12, 14, 16, 17, 18, 19, 21; 2:17^2, 25; 3:8^2, 9, 13^2, 16, 22; 4:20; 5:4, 5, 7, 8, 9, 13, 14, 21; 6:1^2, 3, 4^2, 13; 7:5, 6, 13, 22; 8:2, 14, 15, 19; 9:2^2, 12, 17, 19, 27; 10:2, 8, 10, 14^2, 19, 27; 12:3, 16, 21, 33, 36, 38, 42; 13:17, 21^3; 14:3, 4, 7, 9^2, 10, 13, 17, 19^2, 20, 22, 23, 25^2, 28^2, 29; 15:5, 7^2, 9^2, 10, 12, 13, 15, 16, 17^2, 19, 21, 25^2; 16:3, 4, 12, 15, 16, 20^2, 23; 17:2; 18:8^2, 11, 16, 20^2, 21, 22, 25; 19:10^2, 21, 22, 24, 25; 20:5^3, 6, 11; 21:1, 34; 22:11, 23; 23:23, 24^2, 29, 30, 31, 32; 24:12, 14; 25:3, 8^2, 12, 13, 14, 18, 28^2, 29, 40; 26:1, 24, 37^2; 27:6; 28:9, 11, 14, 25, 26, 27, 33, 40^2, 41^4, 42; 29:1^2, 2, 3^2, 4, 8, 9^2, 13^2, 17, 22, 24, 25^2, 29, 30, 33, 35, 46^2; 30:5, 12^3, 13, 14, 21, 29^2, 30; 31:5; 32:2^2, 3, 4, 8^2, 10^2, 12^3, 13, 18^3, 19, 21, 24^2, 25, 27, 31, 34; 34:31^2, 32, 33; 35:1^2, 23, 26, 29, 33, 35^2; 36:8^2, 14, 29, 36^2; 37:4, 7, 15, 28; 38:6, 25, 28; 39:7, 18, 19, 20, 43; 40:12, 14, 15

Lev 1:2, 12; 2:12; 3:4, 10, 15, 16; 4:2, 9, 10, 20^2, 35; 5:8; 6:10, 17, 18; 7:4, 5, 7, 34, 35, 36^2; 8:6, 10, 11, 13^3, 26, 27, 28^2; 9:2, 7, 13, 14, 22; 10:1^2, 2, 3, 4, 5, 11, 17; 11:1, 4^2, 9, 22, 24, 25, 26, 28, 31, 32, 33, 42, 43; 13:58; 14:6, 12, 23, 24, 40, 42, 45, 51; 15:2, 14, 15, 29, 31; 16:4, 7, 16, 21, 23, 28; 17:2, 5^2, 7, 8, 16; 18:2, 5, 29; 19:2, 10, 31^2, 37; 20:6, 8, 11^2, 12^2, 13^2, 16, 18, 22, 23, 27^2; 21:1, 23; 22:3, 9, 16^2, 18, 22, 25^2, 31; 23:2, 10, 20, 22, 43; 24:6, 12; 25:2, 18, 31, 44, 45, 46^2, 51; 26:3, 36^2, 39, 41^2, 43^2, 44^4; 27:2

Nu 1:3, 19, 21, 22, 23, 25, 27, 29, 31, 33, 35, 37, 39, 41, 43, 47, 49; 2:4, 13, 15, 19, 21, 23, 26, 28, 30; 3:6, 15, 16, 22^2, 32, 34, 43, 47, 48, 49^2, 51; 4:8, 12^3, 19^2, 23, 26, 27, 29, 30, 36, 40, 44, 48; 5:3, 4, 12, 23; 6:2, 16, 19, 20, 23, 27; 7:1^2, 2, 3, 5^2, 6, 9, 13, 19, 25, 31, 37, 43, 49, 55, 61, 67, 73, 79; 8:6, 7^5, 8, 13, 15^2, 16, 17, 20, 21^3, 22; 9:8; 10:2^2, 3, 33^2, 34, 35; 11:1^2, 3, 4, 12^2, 16^2, 17, 21, 22^4, 24, 25, 26^2, 28, 29, 31, 32; 12:9; 13:2, 3, 17^2, 26^2; 14:2, 6, 9^2, 10, 11, 12^2, 13, 14^2, 16^2, 23, 28, 31, 40, 45^2; 15:2, 18, 25, 26, 29, 38^2, 39; 16:3^3, 7, 9, 15^2, 17, 18, 19, 21, 28, 30^2, 31, 32, 33^2, 34^2, 38^3, 45, 46, 49; 17:2, 4; 18:8, 11, 12^2, 18, 20, 24, 26^2, 30; 19:9, 10, 21; 20:6, 8, 10, 12, 13, 25, 26, 28; 21:1, 3, 16, 30^2, 33; 22:6^2, 8, 11^3, 12, 20; 23:11, 13^4, 21, 22, 25^2, 27; 24:8, 10; 25:4, 8, 11, 17; 26:3, 7, 10, 18, 22, 25, 27, 34, 37, 41, 43, 47, 50, 62^2, 64, 65^2; 27:3, 7^2, 17^4; 28:2, 3, 31; 30:12^3, 14^2, 15^2; 31:3, 6^2, 8, 13, 15, 27^2, 30, 36, 47, 51; 32:7, 8, 9, 13, 15, 17, 19, 20, 28, 29^2, 33, 41; 33:4, 51, 55, 56; 34:2; 35:2, 3, 5, 6, 7, 8^2, 10, 15; 36:6

Dt 1:3, 8^2, 13, 15, 29, 39, 42; 2:5, 6^2, 9, 11, 12^4, 14, 15^2, 19^2, 20, 21^3, 22^2, 23; 3:4, 6, 14, 20, 22, 28; 4:1, 3, 6, 7, 9, 10, 13, 14, 19^2, 31, 37; 5:1^3, 9^3, 10, 22^2, 29^2, 30, 31^3; 6:1, 7^2, 8, 9; 7:2^5, 3, 5, 9, 10^2, 11, 12, 15^2, 16, 17, 18, 20, 21, 22, 23^2, 24, 25; 8:19^2; 9:3^4, 4^2, 5, 10, 12^2, 14, 17^2, 28^5; 10:2, 4, 11, 15^2; 11:4^2, 6, 9, 16, 18, 19^2, 20, 21,

12, 13, 17, 23^2, 25^3, 31, 32, 34; **21**:2^3, 3^2, 6, 7, 8, 12^2, 13, 14, 16, 17, 21, 24, 27, 31^2, 36, 37, 42, 45; **22**:1, 3, 4, 6^2, 20, 21, 29, 35, 41, 43; **23**:4^2, 13, 26, 30, 31, 34^3, 37; **24**:2, 4, 16, 19^2, 39, 45; **25**:2, 3, 9, 14, 16, 19, 20, 22, 32, 34, 40, 41, 45; **26**:10, 15, 19, 22, 27, 31, 36, 38, 40, 43, 44, 45, 48, 51, 70, 71, 73; **27**:6, 7, 10, 17, 21, 22, 26, 35, 47, 48, 65; **28**:9, 10, 16, 18, 19, 20

Mk 1:17, 20, 22, 31, 32, 38, 44; **2**:2^2, 8, 12, 13, 17, 19^3, 20, 25, 26, 27; **3**:4, 5, 12, 14, 17, 23^2, 33, 34; **4**:2^2, 9, 11^2, 12, 13, 21, 24, 33, 34, 35, 40; **5**:10, 12, 13, 16, 19, 38, 39, 40^2, 43; **6**:4, 5, 7^2, 8, 10, 11, 13, 22, 31, 33^2, 34^2, 36, 37^3, 38, 39, 41^3, 46, 48^4, 50^2, 51; **7**:6, 9, 14, 18, 36^2; **8**:1, 3^2, 5, 6^2, 7^2, 9, 13, 14, 15, 17, 21, 27, 29, 30, 31, 34; **9**:1^2, 2^2, 3, 4, 7, 9, 12, 14^2, 16, 29, 31, 33, 35, 36^2; **10**:1, 3, 5, 6, 11, 13^2, 14^2, 16^3, 24^2, 27, 32^2, 36, 38, 39, 40, 42^4; **11**:2, 5^2, 6^2, 8, 15^2, 17, 22, 24^2, 29, 33; **12**:1, 4, 6, 12, 15, 16, 17, 23, 24, 28^2, 38, 43; **13**:5, 9, 12, 14, 17^2; **14**:7, 10, 13, 16, 20, 22, 23, 24, 27, 34, 37, 40, 41, 44, 47, 48, 52, 69^2, 70; **15**:6, 7, 8, 9, 11, 12, 14, 15, 24, 35; **16**:6, 10, 12, 13, 14^2, 15, 17, 18, 19, 20

Lk 1:2, 22^2, 50, 52, 65, 66^2, 79; **2**:7, 9^2, 10, 15, 17, 18, 19, 20, 34, 38, 46^2, 49, 50, 51^2; **3**:11, 13, 14, 16; **4**:6, 18, 20, 21, 23, 26, 27, 30, 31, 39, 40^3, 41^2, 42, 43; **5**:2, 7, 14, 17, 22, 25, 29, 31, 34^2, 35, 36; **6**:1, 2, 3, 4, 5, 9, 10, 13, 17, 19, 27, 28^2, 30, 31, 32^2, 33, 34, 39, 47; **7**:6, 19, 22, 38^2, 42^2, 44; **8**:21, 22, 25, 31, 32^3, 34, 36, 37, 54, 56; **9**:1, 2, 3, 5, 10, 11^3, 13^2, 14, 15, 16, 17, 18, 20, 21^2, 23, 34, 45, 46^2, 48, 54, 55, 56, 61; **10**:1, 2, 9, 18, 21, 24^2, 35; **11**:2, 5, 13, 15, 17, 19, 31, 44^2, 47, 48, 49^2, 52, 53; **12**:4, 6, 15, 16, 24, 37^2, 38, 42; **13**:2, 4, 14, 23, 32, 34; **14**:5, 7, 10, 15, 17, 19, 23, 25; **15**:2, 3, 4, 6, 12^2; **16**:15, 28, 29^2, 30; **17**:14^2, 15, 20, 23^2, 27, 29, 37; **18**:1, 7, 8, 15^2, 16^2, 29, 31, 34; **19**:13^2, 24, 27^2, 32, 33, 40, 45^2, 46; **20**:3, 8, 15, 17, 19, 23, 25, 33, 34, 41; **21**:8, 10, 21^3, 23^2, 26, 29, 35; **22**:4, 6, 10, 13, 15, 19, 23, 24^2, 25^3, 35, 36, 38, 40, 41, 45, 46, 47, 50, 55, 58, 67, 70; **23**:1, 14, 17, 20, 22, 23, 25, 28, 34, 35, 51; **24**:1, 4, 5, 10, 11^2, 13, 15, 17, 18, 19, 24, 25, 27, 29, 30^2, 33^2, 35, 36^2, 38, 40, 41, 43, 44, 46, 50^2, 51^2

Jn 1:12^2, 22, 26, 38^2, 39; **2**:7^2, 8, 15, 16, 19, 22, 24; **3**:22; **4**:32, 34, 40, 52; **5**:11, 17, 19, 21, 39; **6**:2, 7^2, 11, 13^2, 17, 20, 26, 29, 31, 32, 35, 43, 53, 61, 70; **7**:6, 9, 16, 21, 25, 33, 44, 45, 47, 50^2; **8**:2, 6, 7, 12, 14, 21, 23, 25, 27, 28, 34, 39, 42, 47, 58, 59; **9**:15, 16, 19, 20, 27, 30, 41; **10**:3, 4, 6^2, 7, 8, 12, 16, 20, 25, 27, 28^2, 29^2, 32, 34, 35; **11**:11, 14, 19, 37, 44, 46^2, 49^2; **12**:2, 20, 23, 35, 36, 37, 40; **13**:1, 5, 12, 17, 29; **14**:21; **15**:6^2, 22, 24; **16**:4, 12, 19, 31; **17**:6, 8^2, 9^2, 10, 12^3, 14^2, 15^2, 17, 18, 20, 22, 23^2, 26^3; **18**:4, 5^2, 6, 7, 9, 18, 21^2, 29, 31, 38; **19**:4, 5, 6, 15, 16, 24; **20**:2, 13, 17, 19, 20, 21, 22^2, 23, 24, 25, 26; **21**:3, 5, 6, 10, 12, 13

Act 1:3, 4^2, 7, 10, 16; **2**:3^2, 4, 6, 11, 14, 38, 41, 45; **3**:2, 5^2, 8, 11; **4**:1, 3^2, 4, 7, 8, 13, 14, 15, 16^2, 17, 18^2, 19, 21^3, 23, 24, 32^2, 33, 34^2, 35; **5**:5, 9, 13^2, 15^2, 16, 18, 19, 21, 22, 24, 25, 26, 27^3, 32, 33, 35, 38, 40^2; **6**:2, 6, 9; **7**:6^2, 24, 25, 26^2, 34, 36, 39, 42, 43, 52; **8**:3, 5, 7, 11, 14, 15, 16, 17, 18; **9**:2, 21^2, 27, 28, 38, 39^2, 40; **10**:7, 8^2, 20^2, 23^3, 24, 28, 44, 46, 48; **11**:3, 4, 12, 15, 17, 20, 21, 23, 28; **12**:10, 17^2, 20, 21, 25; **13**:2, 3^2, 8, 13, 15, 17, 19, 20, 21, 22, 27, 31, 42, 43^2, 50, 51; **14**:5^2, 18, 22, 23^2, 27; **15**:2^2, 4, 5^2, 7, 8^2, 9, 12, 14, 19, 20, 21, 23, 32, 37, 38^3, 39; **16**:4, 7, 10, 19, 20, 22^2, 23^3, 24, 25, 30, 33, 34^2, 37^2, 39^3, 40; **17**:2^2, 4, 5^2, 6, 9, 12, 16, 17, 18, 33, 34; **18**:2, 3, 6, 11, 16, 19, 20, 21, 26, 27; **19**:2, 3, 6^2, 9, 12^2, 13^2, 16^3, 17, 19^3, 22, 38; **20**:1, 2, 6, 7, 18, 30, 32, 34, 36; **21**:1, 7, 16, 19, 23, 24^3, 26^2, 32, 40; **22**:2, 5, 11, 19, 20, 30; **23**:2, 10^2, 21^2, 24, 27, 31; **24**:21, 22; **25**:5, 6, 11; **26**:10, 11^4, 13, 18^2, 20, 30; **27**:9, 10, 21, 24, 33, 35, 42, 43; **28**:3, 14, 17, 23, 27

Ro 1:19^2, 24, 26, 28, 32^2; **2**:2, 3, 7, 8, 19; **3**:2, 19, 22; **4**:11^2, 12; **5**:14; **7**:1; **8**:1, 28^2, 30^3; **9**:25, 26; **10**:2, 5, 15, 19, 20^2; **11**:8, 9, 11, 12^2, 14^2, 15^2, 17^2, 22, 23, 27, 32; **12**:14, 15^2; **15**:3, 26, 27^2, 28, 31; **16**:10, 11, 14, 15, 17^2

1Co 1:2, 11, 18, 21, 24; **2**:6, 9, 10, 14; **4**:19; **5**:12^2, 13; **6**:4, 13, 15; **7**:8, 9, 36; **8**:9; **9**:3, 20^2, 21^2; **10**:4, 5, 7, 8, 9, 10, 11, 27; **11**:2, 22; **12**:18; **14**:10, 22^4, 34, 35; **15**:20; **16**:3, 18

2Co 1:4; **2**:3, 13, 15^2; **4**:3, 4^2; **5**:12, 15, 19; **6**:16^2, 17; **8**:22, 24; **9**:2, 13; **11**:8, 12; **12**:17; **13**:2

Gal 1:17; **2**:2^2, 12, 14; **3**:10, 12^2, 22; **4**:5, 8, 15, 17; **6**:10, 16

Eph 2:10, 17; **4**:18; **5**:7, 11, 12; **6**:4, 5, 9, 24

Php 1:28; **3**:8, 17

Col 2:1, 15^2; **3**:7, 19; **4**:5, 13^2

1Th 2:16; **4**:12, 13, 14, 15, 17; **5**:3, 12, 13, 14

2Th 1:6, 8, 10; **2**:10, 11; **3**:12

1Ti 1:10, 16, 18; **3**:7, 10; **4**:3, 15, 16^2; **5**:4, 16^3, 20; **6**:2^3, 17

2Ti 2:14^2, 19, 22, 25; **3**:11, 14; **4**:8

Tit 1:13, 15; **2**:9; **3**:1, 13, 15

Heb 1:12, 14; **2**:1, 3, 4, 11, 15, 18; **3**:17, 18; **4**:2^3, 8; **5**:2, 9, 14; **6**:6, 7, 12, 16; **7**:6, 8, 25^2; **8**:8, 9^3, 10^2; **9**:10, 28; **10**:14, 16^2, 33, 39^2; **11**:6, 13^3, 16, 28, 31; **12**:9, 11, 19; **13**:3^3, 7, 9, 17, 24

Jas 1:12; **2**:5, 16^2, 25; **3**:18; **5**:3, 4, 11, 14

1Pt 1:11, 12; **2**:7, 8, 14^2; **3**:7, 12; **4**:4, 6, 17, 19

2Pt 1:1, 12; **2**:1, 4^2, 6^2, 8, 10, 11, 18, 19, 20, 21^2, 22; **3**:16

1Jn 2:26; **4**:4, 5; **5**:16

3Jn 9, 10^2

Jude 1, 5, 7, 11, 15, 23

Rev 2:2^3, 9, 14, 15, 16, 22, 27; **3**:9^2, 10; **4**:8; **5**:8, 11, 13; **6**:8, 9, 10, 11^2; **7**:4, 14, 15, 16, 17^2; **8**:2, 12; **9**:3, 4, 5^2, 6, 11, 16, 17^2, 19; **10**:4; **11**:1, 5^2, 6, 7^3, 10^2, 11^3, 12^2, 18^2; **12**:4, 10, 12; **13**:6, 7, 12, 14^2; **14**:6, 9, 13; **15**:1, 2; **16**:2, 6, 14, 16; **17**:14; **18**:14; **19**:15, 18^2, 20^2; **20**:4^3, 8, 9, 10, 11, 13; **21**:3^2, 14, 24; **22**:5, 8, 9

THEMSELVES

Gen 3:7, 8; **13**:11; **19**:11; **21**:28, 29; **30**:40; **32**:16; **33**:6, 7^2; **34**:30; **42**:6; **43**:26, 32^2

Ex 5:7; **11**:8; **12**:39; **18**:26; **19**:22; **26**:9^2; **32**:1, 7, 26; **33**:6; **36**:16^2

Lev 15:18; **22**:2

Nu 6:2^2; **8**:7; **10**:3, 4; **11**:32; **16**:3; **20**:2; **27**:3

Dt 7:20; **9**:12; **31**:14, 20; **32**:5, 27, 31

Jos 8:27; **9**:2; **10**:5, 13, 16; **11**:14; **22**:12; **24**:1

Jdg 2:12, 17, 19; **5**:2, 9; **7**:2, 23, 24; **10**:17; **12**:1; **15**:9; **20**:2, 14, 20, 22^2, 30, 33, 37

1Sa 2:5; **3**:13; **4**:2; **8**:4; **13**:5, 6, 11; **14**:11^2, 20, 22; **21**:4; **22**:2; **28**:4

2Sa 2:25; **5**:18, 22; **10**:8, 15, 17; **16**:14; **22**:45

1Ki 8:2, 47; **18**:23, 28; **20**:12

2Ki 2:15; **7**:12; **8**:20; **17**:17, 32; **19**:29

1Ch 11:1, 10, 14; **12**:8; **13**:2; **14**:9, 13; **15**:14; **19**:6, 7, 9, 11; **21**:20; **29**:24

2Ch 3:13; **5**:3; **6**:37; **7**:3, 14; **12**:6, 7^2; **13**:7; **14**:13; **15**:10; **20**:4, 25, 26; **21**:8; **29**:15, 29, 34^2; **30**:3^2, 11, 15, 18, 24; **31**:18; **32**:8; **35**:14^2

Ezr 3:1; **6**:20, 21; **9**:1, 2^2; **10**:7, 9

Neh 4:2; **8**:1, 16; **9**:2, 25; **10**:28; **11**:2; **12**:28, 30; **13**:22

Est 8:11, 13; **9**:2, 15, 16, 27, 31

Job 1:6; **2**:1; **3**:14; **6**:4; **16**:10; **24**:4, 16; **29**:8; **30**:14; **34**:22; **39**:3; **41**:23, 25

Ps 2:2; **3**:6; **9**:20; **18**:44; **35**:15^2, 26; **37**:11; **38**:16; **44**:10; **49**:6; **56**:6^2; **57**:6; **59**:4; **64**:5, 8; **66**:3, 7; **80**:6; **81**:15; **94**:4, 21; **97**:7; **104**:22; **106**:28; **109**:29; **140**:8

Prv 23:5; **28**:28

Ecc 3:18; **11**:3; **12**:3

Isa 2:6; **3**:9; **8**:21; **10**:31; **15**:3; **22**:7; **30**:2; **46**:2; **47**:14; **48**:2^2; **49**:18; **56**:6; **59**:6; **60**:4, 14; **66**:17^2

Jer 2:24; **4**:2; **5**:7, 22; **7**:19; **9**:5; **11**:17; **12**:13; **16**:6^2, 7; **25**:14; **27**:7; **30**:8, 21; **34**:10; **41**:5; **49**:29; **50**:9

Lam 2:10; **4**:14

Ezk 6:9; **7**:18; **10**:17, 22; **14**:18; **26**:16; **27**:30, 31; **31**:14; **34**:2, 8, 10, 27; **37**:23; **43**:26; **44**:18, 25^2; **45**:5

Dan 2:43; **10**:7; **11**:6, 14

Hos 1:11; **4**:14; **7**:14; **9**:9, 10; **10**:10

Am 2:8; **6**:4, 5, 6, 7; **9**:3

Mic 3:4

Hab 1:7, 8; **2**:13

Zep 2:8, 10

Zec 4:12; **11**:5; **12**:3, 7

Mt 9:3; **14**:2, 15; **16**:7; **19**:12; **21**:25, 38; **23**:4

Mk 1:27; **2**:8; **4**:17; **6**:14, 30, 36, 51; **8**:16; **9**:2, 8, 10, 34; **10**:26; **11**:31; **12**:7; **14**:4; **15**:31; **16**:3

Lk 4:36; **7**:30, 49; **18**:9; **20**:5, 14, 20; **22**:23; **23**:12; **24**:12

Jn 6:52; **7**:35; **11**:55, 56; **12**:19; **16**:17; **17**:13; **18**:18, 28; **19**:24

Act 4:15; **5**:36; **11**:26; **15**:32; **16**:37; **18**:6; **21**:25; **23**:12, 21; **24**:15; **26**:31; **27**:40, 43; **28**:4, 25, 29

Ro 1:22, 24, 27; **2**:14; **10**:3; **13**:2

1Co 6:9; **16**:15

2Co 5:15; **8**:3; **10**:12^5; **11**:13

Gal 6:13

Eph 4:19

Php 2:3

1Th 1:9

1Ti 1:10; **2**:9; **3**:13; **6**:10, 19

2Ti 2:25, 26; **4**:3

Tit 1:12

Heb 6:6; **9**:23

1Pt 1:12; **3**:5

2Pt 2:1, 13, 19

Jude 7, 10, 12, 19

Rev 6:15; **8**:6

THEN

Gen 3:5; **4**:26; **8**:9; **12**:6; **13**:7, 9^2, 11, 16, 18; **17**:17; **18**:15, 26; **19**:15, 24; **20**:9; **21**:32; **22**:4; **24**:8, 41, 50; **25**:1, 8, 34; **26**:12, 26; **27**:41, 45; **28**:9, 21; **29**:1, 8, 25; **30**:14; **31**:8^2, 16, 17, 25, 33, 54; **32**:7, 8, 18; **33**:6, 10; **34**:16, 17; **35**:2; **37**:28; **38**:11, 21; **39**:9; **41**:9, 14; **42**:25, 34, 38; **43**:9; **44**:8, 11, 13, 18, 26, 32; **45**:1; **47**:1, 6, 23; **49**:4

Ex 1:16^2; **2**:7; **4**:25, 26, 31; **5**:15; **6**:1, 12; **7**:9, 11; **8**:8, 19; **9**:1; **10**:16; **12**:21, 44, 48; **13**:13; **15**:1, 15; **16**:4, 6, 7; **17**:8; **18**:2, 23; **19**:5; **21**:3, 6, 8, 11, 13, 19, 23, 28, 30, 35; **22**:3, 8, 11, 13; **23**:22; **24**:9; **29**:7, 20, 34; **30**:12; **32**:24, 26; **34**:20; **36**:1; **40**:34, 37

Lev 1:14; **3**:7, 12; **4**:3, 14, 28; **5**:1, 3, 4, 7, 11, 12, 15; **6**:4; **7**:12; **10**:3; **12**:2, 4, 5, 8; **13**:2, 4, 5, 8, 9, 13, 17, 21, 22, 25, 26, 27, 30^2, 31, 34, 36, 39, 43, 54, 56, 58; **14**:4, 21, 36, 38, 40, 44, 48; **15**:8, 13, 16, 28; **16**:15; **17**:15, 16; **19**:23; **20**:5; **22**:14, 27; **23**:10, 19; **25**:2, 9, 21, 25, 27, 28, 29, 30, 33, 35, 41, 52, 54; **26**:4, 18, 24, 28, 34^2, 41^2, 42; **27**:4, 5, 6, 7, 8, 10, 11, 13, 14, 15, 16, 18, 19, 23, 27^2, 33

Nu 2:7, 14, 17, 22, 29; **5**:7, 15, 21, 25, 27, 28, 31; **6**:9; **7**:89; **8**:8; **9**:17, 19, 21; **10**:4, 5, 6, 9; **11**:10; **12**:8; **14**:5, 8, 13, 15, 45; **15**:4, 9, 19, 24, 27; **16**:3, 29, 30; **18**:26, 30; **19**:7, 12; **20**:1, 19; **21**:1, 2, 17; **22**:31; **27**:1, 8, 9, 10, 11; **30**:4, 7, 8, 11, 12, 14, 15; **32**:22, 29; **33**:52, 55; **34**:3; **35**:11, 24; **36**:3, 4

Dt 1:29, 41; **2**:1, 32; **3**:1, 20; **4**:41; **5**:25; **6**:12, 21; **8**:10, 14; **9**:9, 23; **11**:17, 23; **12**:11, 21; **13**:14; **14**:25; **15**:12, 17; **17**:5, 8; **18**:7; **19**:9, 12, 17, 19; **20**:10, 11, 12; **21**:2, 12, 14, 16, 19; **22**:2, 8, 15, 21, 22, 24, 25, 29; **23**:9, 10, 24, 25; **24**:1, 7; **25**:1, 3, 7, 8, 9, 12; **26**:13; **28**:59; **29**:20, 25; **30**:3; **31**:17, 20; **32**:15; **33**:28

Jos 1:8^2, 10, 15; **2**:15, 20; **3**:3; **4**:4, 7, 22; **6**:10; **7**:21; **8**:7, 21, 30; **10**:12, 22, 29, 33; **14**:6, 11, 12; **15**:1; **17**:15; **19**:12, 29, 34; **20**:5, 6; **21**:1; **22**:1, 7, 19, 21; **23**:16; **24**:9, 20

Jdg 2:18; **3**:23; **4**:8^2, 21; **5**:1, 8, 11, 13, 19, 22; **6**:13, 17, 21^2, 24, 27, 30, 33, 37; **7**:1, 11, 18, 24; **8**:3, 7, 18, 21, 22; **9**:12, 14, 15, 19^2, 23, 29, 33, 38, 50, 54; **10**:17; **11**:3, 11, 17, 18, 29, 31; **12**:3, 4, 6^2, 7, 10; **13**:6, 8, 21; **14**:3, 5, 12, 13; **15**:6, 9, 11; **16**:1, 7, 8, 11, 17, 18, 23, 31; **17**:13; **18**:7, 14, 18; **19**:26, 28; **20**:1, 3, 26; **21**:16, 19, 21

Ru 1:6, 9, 18, 21; **2**:5, 8, 10, 13; **3**:1, 13, 18; **4**:1, 4, 5

1Sa 1:8, 11, 17, 22; **2**:16^2; **3**:10, 16; **6**:3, 4, 6, 9^2; **7**:3, 4, 12; **8**:4; **9**:4, 7, 10, 18, 21; **10**:1, 2, 3, 11, 25; **11**:1, 3, 4, 14; **12**:8, 14, 15, 21; **13**:6; **14**:8, 9, 10, 17, 28, 29, 33, 36, 40, 43, 46; **15**:10, 14, 16, 19, 30, 32, 34; **16**:8, 9, 13, 18; **17**:9^2, 45; **18**:3, 30; **19**:5,

22; **20:**4, 6, 7, 9, 10, 12, 13, 18, 19, 21, 30; **21:**1, 14^2; **22:**5, 7, 9, 11, 14, 15; **23:**1, 3, 4, 10, 12, 13, 19; **24:**2, 4; **25:**11, 18, 31; **26:**2, 6, 8, 13, 14, 15, 21, 25; **27:**6; **28:**7, 9, 11, 16^2, 20, 25; **29:**3, 6; **30:**4, 22, 23; **31:**4

2Sa 1:11; **2:**15, 20, 22, 26^2, 27; **3:**8, 16, 18, 24; **5:**1, 24^2; **6:**20; **7:**18; **8:**6, 10; **9:**5, 9, 11; **10:**2, 5, 11^2, 14; **11:**10, 11, 18, 21, 25; **12:**18, 20^2, 21; **13:**7, 15, 17, 18, 26, 28, 29, 31; **14:**11, 12, 13, 17, 18, 31; **15:**2, 8, 10, 19, 33, 34; **16:**4, 9, 10, 20, 21; **17:**5, 13, 15, 22, 24; **18:**14, 19, 21, 22, 23; **19:**6, 8, 12, 35, 40, 42, 43; **20:**4, 16, 17, 18, 22; **21:**1, 17, 18; **22:**8, 43; **23:**14^2; **24:**6

1Ki 1:5, 13, 28, 31, 35; **2:**12, 20, 23, 28, 29, 43; **3:**14, 16, 23, 26, 27; **6:**10, 12; **7:**7, 38; **8:**1, 12, 32, 34, 36, 39, 45, 49; **9:**5, 7, 11, 24; **11:**7, 22; **12:**5, 7, 18, 25, 27; **13:**15, 31; **15:**18, 22; **16:**1, 21; **18:**21, 22, 38; **19:**2, 5, 20, 21; **20:**7, 14, 15, 33^2, 34, 36, 37, 39; **21:**10, 13, 14; **22:**6, 9, 47, 49

2Ki 1:1, 9, 10; **3:**27; **4:**3, 7, 14, 20, 24, 28, 29, 35, 37, 41; **5:**13, 14, 17; **6:**8, 31; **7:**1, 2, 4, 9; **8:**1, 16, 22; **9:**3^2, 11, 13, 15, 19, 25; **10:**4, 6; **12:**7, 17; **13:**17, 19; **14:**8; **15:**16; **16:**5; **17:**5, 27, 28; **18:**24, 26, 28, 31, 37; **19:**20; **20:**2, 14, 19; **23:**17; **24:**1

1Ch 1:29; **2:**24; **6:**32; **9:**36; **10:**4, 7; **11:**1, 16^2; **12:**3, 18^2; **14:**11, 15; **15:**2; **16:**7, 33; **17:**2; **18:**6; **19:**5^2, 12^2, 15; **21:**3, 16, 18, 22, 28; **22:**1, 6, 13; **26:**14; **28:**2, 11; **29:**5, 6, 9, 23

2Ch 1:2, 13; **2:**6, 11; **3:**1; **5:**2, 11, 13; **6:**1, 17, 23, 25, 27, 29, 30, 33, 35, 39; **7:**4, 14, 18, 20; **8:**12, 17; **10:**18; **12:**5; **13:**15; **14:**10; **16:**2, 6, 10; **18:**16, 20, 23, 25, 27; **20:**2, 9, 14, 27, 37; **21:**9; **23:**11, 13, 14, 17; **24:**17; **25:**10, 16, 17; **26:**1, 19; **28:**12, 15; **29:**12, 18, 20, 31; **30:**15, 27; **31:**1, 9, 11; **32:**18; **33:**13; **34:**18, 29; **36:**1

Ezr 1:5; **3:**2, 9; **4:**2, 4, 9, 13, 17, 24; **5:**1, 2, 4, 5, 9, 16; **6:**1, 13; **8:**16, 21, 24, 31; **9:**4; **10:**5, 6, 9, 12

Neh 2:2, 4, 9, 14, 15, 17, 18, 20; **3:**1; **4:**7; **5:**7, 8, 12^2; **6:**5, 8; **8:**10; **9:**4, 5; **12:**31; **13:**9, 11, 12, 17, 21, 27

Est 1:13; **2:**2, 13, 18, 19; **3:**3, 5, 12; **4:**4, 5, 13, 14, 15; **5:**3, 5, 7, 9, 14^2; **6:**3, 10, 11, 13; **7:**3, 5, 6, 8^2, 9, 10; **8:**4, 7, 9; **9:**13, 29

Job 1:7, 9, 20; **2:**9; **3:**13; **4:**1, 15; **6:**10; **7:**14; **8:**1, 18; **9:**1, 29, 35; **10:**14, 18, 20; **11:**1, 10, 11, 15; **13:**20, 22; **15:**1; **16:**1, 22; **18:**1; **19:**1; **20:**1; **21:**34; **22:**1, 24, 26, 29; **23:**1; **25:**1, 4; **27:**12; **28:**20, 27; **29:**11, 18; **30:**26; **31:**1, 8, 10, 14, 22; **32:**2, 5; **33:**16, 24; **34:**29^2; **36:**9, 18; **37:**8; **38:**1, 21; **40:**3, 6, 14; **41:**10; **42:**1, 11

Ps 2:5; **18:**7, 15, 42; **19:**13; **27:**10; **39:**3; **40:**7; **43:**4; **50:**18; **51:**13, 19^2; **55:**6, 7, 12^2; **56:**9; **67:**6; **69:**4; **73:**17; **78:**34, 65; **80:**12; **89:**19, 32; **96:**12; **106:**12, 30; **107:**6, 13, 19, 28, 30; **116:**4; **119:**6, 92; **124:**3, 4, 5; **126:**2^2; **142:**3

Prv 1:28; **2:**5, 9; **3:**23; **8:**30; **11:**2; **15:**11; **18:**3; **20:**14, 24; **24:**14, 32

Ecc 2:11, 13, 15^3; **4:**7, 11; **8:**15, 17; **9:**16; **10:**10; **12:**7

Song 8:10

Isa 5:17; **6:**5, 6, 8, 11; **7:**3; **8:**3; **14:**25, 32; **24:**23; **28:**18; **30:**23; **31:**8; **32:**16; **33:**23; **35:**5, 6; **36:**3, 9, 11, 13, 22; **37:**21, 36; **38:**2, 4; **39:**3, 4, 5, 8; **40:**18, 25; **41:**1; **44:**15; **48:**18; **49:**4, 21; **58:**8, 9, 10, 14; **60:**5; **63:**11; **66:**12

Jer 1:4, 6, 9, 12, 14; **2:**21; **4:**1, 10; **5:**7, 19; **7:**7, 34; **8:**5, 22; **11:**5, 6, 12, 15, 18; **12:**5^2, 16; **13:**7, 8, 13, 23; **14:**11, 13, 14, 18^2; **15:**1, 2, 19; **16:**11; **17:**25, 27; **18:**3, 5, 10, 18; **19:**10, 14; **20:**2, 3, 9; **21:**3; **22:**4, 9, 15, 16, 22; **23:**22, 33; **24:**3; **25:**17, 28; **26:**6, 10, 11, 12, 16, 17; **27:**7, 22; **28:**5, 9, 10, 12, 15; **29:**12, 30; **31:**13, 36; **32:**2, 8, 26; **33:**21, 26; **34:**6, 10; **35:**3, 12; **36:**4, 10, 12, 13, 18, 19, 27, 32; **37:**5, 6, 12, 14, 17, 21; **38:**1, 5, 6, 7, 10, 14, 15, 17^2, 18, 24, 26, 27; **39:**4, 6, 9; **40:**6, 8, 15; **41:**2, 10, 12, 13, 16; **42:**1, 4, 5, 8, 10, 16; **43:**2, 8; **44:**15, 17, 20; **47:**2; **49:**1, 2; **51:**48, 62; **52:**7, 9, 11, 15

Lam 3:54

Ezk 3:3, 12, 15, 23, 24; **4:**14, 15; **5:**1, 4; **6:**13; **7:**26; **8:**2, 5, 8, 12, 14, 15, 17; **9:**6, 9; **10:**1, 4, 6, 18; **11:**2, 13, 22, 25; **12:**4; **14:**1, 13; **16:**9, 53, 55, 61; **18:**13; **19:**5, 8; **20:**2, 7, 8, 13, 21, 28, 29, 49; **21:**4, 10; **22:**3; **23:**13, 18, 39, 43; **24:**11, 20; **26:**16; **28:**25; **32:**4, 14, 15; **33:**4, 10, 23, 29, 33; **36:**25, 31, 36; **37:**9, 11, 14, 16; **39:**15, 28; **40:**6, 9, 13, 17, 19; **41:**3; **42:**1, 13, 14; **44:**1, 2, 4; **46:**2, 12^2, 17, 20, 21, 24; **47:**2, 6, 8

Dan 1:10, 11, 13, 18; **2:**2, 4, 14, 15, 16, 17, 19^2, 25, 35, 46, 48, 49; **3:**2, 3, 4, 13^2, 19, 21, 24, 26^2, 28, 30; **4:**7, 19; **5:**3, 6, 8, 9, 13, 17, 24, 29; **6:**3, 4, 5, 6, 11, 12, 13, 14, 15, 16, 18, 19, 21, 23, 25; **7:**1, 11, 19; **8:**3, 13, 14, 15; **10:**5, 9, 12, 16, 18, 20; **11:**10, 19, 20, 28; **12:**5, 8

Hos 1:9, 11; **2:**7^2; **3:**1; **5:**13; **6:**3; **7:**1; **10:**3; **11:**1, 10

Joel 2:18, 23; **3:**17

Am 6:2, 10; **7:**2, 5, 8, 10, 14; **8:**2

Jna 1:5, 8, 10, 11, 16; **2:**1, 4; **4:**4, 10

Mic 3:4, 7; **5:**3, 5; **7:**10

Hab 1:11

Zep 3:9, 11

Hag 1:3, 12, 13; **2:**13, 14

Zec 1:9, 12, 18, 21; **2:**2; **3:**7; **4:**5, 6, 11, 14; **5:**1, 3, 5, 9, 10; **6:**4, 8, 11; **7:**4; **11:**9, 14; **13:**3, 6; **14:**3

Mal 1:6; **3:**4, 16, 18

Mt 1:19, 24; **2:**7, 16, 17; **3:**5, 13, 15; **4:**1, 5, 10, 11; **5:**24; **7:**5, 11, 23; **8:**26; **9:**6, 14, 15, 29, 37; **11:**20; **12:**12, 13, 14, 22, 26, 28, 29, 38, 44, 45, 47; **13:**19, 26, 27, 28, 36, 43, 52, 56; **14:**33; **15:**1, 12, 15, 21, 25, 28, 32; **16:**6, 12, 20, 22, 24, 27; **17:**4, 10, 13, 17, 19, 26; **18:**16, 21, 27, 32; **19:**7, 13, 23, 25, 27; **20:**20; **21:**1, 25; **22:**8, 13, 15, 21, 35, 43, 45; **23:**1, 32; **24:**9, 10, 14, 16, 21, 23, 30^2, 40, 45; **25:**1, 7, 16, 24, 27, 31, 34, 37, 41, 44, 45; **26:**3, 14, 25, 31, 36, 38, 45, 50, 52, 54, 56, 65, 67, 74; **27:**3, 9, 13, 16, 22, 25, 26, 27, 38, 58; **28:**10, 16

Mk 2:20; **3:**27, 31; **4:**13, 28; **7:**1, 5; **10:**8, 21, 26, 28; **11:**31; **12:**18, 37; **13:**14, 21, 26, 27; **14:**63; **15:**12, 14; **16:**19

Lk 1:34; **2:**28; **3:**7, 10, 12; **5:**35, 36; **6:**9, 42; **7:**6, 22, 31; **8:**12, 19, 24, 33, 35, 37; **9:**1, 12, 16, 46; **10:**37; **11:**13, 26, 45; **12:**20, 26, 28, 41, 42; **13:**7, 9, 15, 18, 23, 26; **14:**10, 12, 16, 21; **15:**1; **16:**3, 7, 27; **17:**1; **18:**26, 28, 31; **19:**15, 16, 23; **20:**5, 9, 13, 17, 27, 39, 44, 45; **21:**10, 20, 21, 27, 28; **22:**3, 7, 36, 52, 54, 70^2; **23:**4, 9, 30, 34; **24:**12, 25, 45

Jn 1:21, 22, 25, 38; **2:**10, 18, 20; **3:**25; **4:**5, 9, 11, 28, 30, 35, 45, 48, 52; **5:**4, 12, 19; **6:**5, 14, 21, 28, 30, 32, 34, 41, 42, 53, 67, 68; **7:**6, 10, 11, 25, 28, 30, 33^2, 35, 45, 47; **8:**12, 19, 21, 22, 25, 28^2, 31^2, 41, 48, 52, 57, 59; **9:**12, 15, 19, 24, 26, 28; **10:**7, 24, 31; **11:**7, 12, 14, 16, 17, 20, 21, 31, 32, 36, 41, 45, 47, 53, 56; **12:**1, 3, 4, 7, 16, 28, 35; **13:**6, 14, 22, 25, 27, 30; **14:**9; **16:**17; **18:**3, 6, 7, 10, 11, 12, 16, 17, 19, 27, 28, 29, 31, 33, 36, 37, 40; **19:**1, 5, 10, 16, 20, 21, 23, 27, 32, 40; **20:**2, 6, 8, 10, 19, 20, 21, 26, 27; **21:**5, 9, 13, 20, 23

Act 1:12; **2:**38, 41; **3:**6; **4:**8; **5:**9, 10, 17, 25, 26, 29, 34; **6:**2, 9, 11; **7:**1, 4, 14, 29, 32, 33, 42, 57; **8:**5, 13, 17, 24, 29, 35; **9:**13, 19, 25, 31, 39; **10:**21, 23, 34, 46, 48; **11:**16, 17, 18, 22, 25, 29; **12:**3, 15; **13:**9, 12, 16, 46; **14:**13; **15:**12, 22; **16:**1, 29; **17:**14, 18, 22, 29; **18:**9, 17, 18; **19:**3, 4, 13, 36; **21:**13, 26, 33; **22:**22, 27, 29; **23:**3, 5, 17, 19, 22, 27, 31; **24:**10; **25:**2, 10, 12, 22; **26:**1^2, 20, 28, 32; **27:**20, 29, 32, 36; **28:**1

Ro 3:1, 6, 9, 27, 31; **4:**1, 9, 10; **5:**9; **6:**1, 15, 18, 21; **7:**3, 7, 13, 16, 17, 21, 25; **8:**8, 17, 25, 31; **9:**14, 16, 19, 30; **10:**14, 17; **11:**1, 5, 6^2, 7, 11, 19; **12:**6; **13:**3; **14:**12, 16; **15:**1

1Co 3:5, 7; **4:**5; **5:**10; **6:**4, 15; **7:**38; **9:**18; **10:**19; **12:**28; **13:**10, 12^2; **14:**15, 26; **15:**5, 7, 13, 14, 16, 18, 24, 28, 29, 54

2Co 2:2; **3:**12; **4:**12; **5:**14, 20; **6:**1; **12:**10

Gal 1:18; **2:**1, 21; **3:**9, 19, 21, 29; **4:**7, 8, 15, 29, 31; **5:**11, 16; **6:**4

Eph 5:15

Php 1:18

Col 3:1, 4

1Th 4:1, 17; **5:**3

2Th 2:8

1Ti 2:13; **3:**2, 10

Heb 2:14; **4:**8, 14; **7:**27; **8:**7; **9:**1, 9, 26; **10:**2, 7, 9; **12:**8, 26

Jas 1:15; **2:**4, 24; **3:**17; **4:**14

1Pt 4:1

2Pt 3:6, 11

1Jn 1:5; **3:**21

Rev 3:16; **22:**9

THERE

Gen 1:3^2, 6, 14, 30; **2:**5, 6, 8, 11, 12, 20; **4:**26; **6:**4; **7:**9; **9:**11; **11:**2, 7, 9, 31; **12:**7, 8, 10^2; **13:**4^2, 7, 8, 18; **14:**8, 10, 13; **18:**24, 28^2, 29^2, 30^3, 31^2, 32; **19:**1, 31; **21:**31, 33; **22:**2, 9; **23:**13; **24:**23, 33; **25:**10, 24; **26:**1, 8, 17, 19, 25^3, 28; **28:**11; **29:**2; **31:**14, 46; **32:**4, 13, 24, 29; **33:**20; **35:**1^2, 3, 7^2, 16; **36:**31; **37:**24, 28; **38:**2, 21, 22; **39:**9, 11^2, 20, 22; **40:**8, 17; **41:**2, 8, 12^2, 15, 18, 24, 29, 30, 39, 54; **42:**1, 2, 16; **43:**25, 30; **44:**14; **45:**1, 6^2, 11^2; **46:**3; **47:**13, 18; **48:**7^2; **49:**31^3; **50:**5, 9, 10

Ex 1:8, 10; **2:**1, 12; **5:**9, 13, 16, 18; **7:**19, 21; **8:**10, 15, 18, 22, 24, 31; **9:**3, 4, 7, 14, 22, 24^2, 26, 28, 29; **10:**14, 15, 19, 21, 22, 26; **11:**6^2; **12:**16^2, 19, 30^3, 43; **13:**3, 7^2; **14:**11, 28; **15:**25^2, 27; **16:**14, 24, 26, 27; **17:**1, 3, 6^2; **19:**2, 13, 16; **21:**30; **22:**2, 3; **23:**26; **24:**10, 12; **25:**22, 35; **26:**17, 20; **27:**9, 11; **28:**32; **29:**42, 43; **30:**12, 34; **32:**17, 24, 28; **33:**20, 21; **34:**2, 5, 28; **35:**2; **36:**30; **39:**23; **40:**30

Lev 6:27; **7:**7; **8:**31; **9:**24; **10:**2; **11:**36; **13:**10, 19, 21, 24^2, 26, 30, 31, 32, 37, 42; **14:**35; **16:**17, 23; **17:**3, 8, 10, 13; **20:**14; **21:**1; **22:**10, 13, 21; **23:**27; **25:**51, 52

Nu 1:4, 53; **5:**13; **6:**5; **8:**19; **9:**6, 15, 17; **11:**6, 16, 17, 26, 27, 31, 34; **12:**6; **13:**20, 28, 33; **14:**35, 43; **16:**35, 46; **18:**5; **19:**18; **20:**1^2, 2, 4, 5, 26, 28; **21:**5^2, 28, 32, 35; **22:**5, 11, 29; **23:**23^2; **24:**17; **26:**62, 64, 65; **31:**5, 16, 49; **32:**26; **33:**9, 38; **35:**6

Dt 1:2, 28, 35, 46; **2:**36; **3:**4, 24; **4:**7, 8, 28, 32, 35, 39; **5:**26, 29; **7:**14, 24; **8:**15; **10:**5, 6^2; **11:**17, 25; **12:**5, 7, 11^2, 14^2, 21; **13:**1, 12, 17; **14:**23, 24, 26; **15:**4, 7, 9, 21; **16:**2, 4^2, 6, 11; **17:**2, 8, 12; **18:**7, 10; **20:**5, 7, 8; **21:**4; **22:**26, 27; **23:**10, 17; **25:**1; **26:**2, 5^2; **27:**5, 7; **28:**32, 36, 64, 65, 68; **29:**18^2; **31:**26; **32:**12, 28, 36, 39^2; **33:**19, 21, 26; **34:**5, 10

Jos 1:5; **2:**1, 2, 4, 11, 16, 22; **3:**1, 4; **4:**8, 9; **5:**1, 13; **7:**4, 13; **8:**11, 14, 17, 32, 35; **9:**23; **10:**8, 14; **11:**11, 19, 22^2; **13:**1; **14:**12; **17:**1, 2, 5, 15; **18:**1, 2, 10; **21:**44, 45; **22:**10, 17; **24:**26

Jdg 1:7; **2:**5, 10; **3:**29; **4:**16, 17, 20; **5:**8, 11, 14, 15, 16, 27; **6:**11, 21, 24, 39, 40; **7:**3^2, 4, 13; **8:**10; **9:**21, 36, 37, 51; **10:**1; **11:**3; **12:**6; **13:**2; **14:**3, 8, 10; **15:**19; **16:**1, 9, 12, 17, 27^2; **17:**1, 6, 7^2; **18:**1, 2, 7, 10, 11, 14, 28; **19:**1^2, 2, 4, 7, 10, 15, 16, 18, 19^3, 30; **20:**16, 26, 27, 34, 38, 44; **21:**1, 2, 3, 4, 5, 6, 8^2, 9^2, 17, 19, 25

Ru 1:1, 2, 4, 11, 17; **3:**12; **4:**1, 4, 17

1Sa 1:1, 3, 11, 22, 28; **2:**2^3, 27, 31, 32; **3:**1; **4:**4, 7, 10^2, 12, 16, 17; **5:**11^2; **6:**7, 14^2; **7:**6, 14, 17^3; **9:**1, 2, 4, 6, 7, 12; **10:**3, 24, 26; **11:**3, 13, 14, 15^3; **13:**19, 22^2; **14:**4, 6, 15, 17, 20, 25, 30, 34, 39, 45, 52; **16:**11; **17:**3, 4, 23, 29, 34, 46, 50; **18:**10; **19:**8, 16; **20:**3, 6^2, 8, 12, 21, 29; **21:**3, 4^2, 6^2, 7, 8, 9^2; **22:**2, 8^2, 22; **23:**22, 27; **24:**11; **25:**2, 7, 10, 13, 34; **26:**15; **27:**1, 5; **28:**7, 10, 20; **30:**17, 19; **31:**12

2Sa 1:21^3; **2:**4, 15, 17, 18^2, 23, 30; **3:**1, 6, 27, 29, 38; **4:**3; **5:**13, 20, 21; **6:**7^2; **7:**22^2; **9:**1, 2, 3; **10:**18; **11:**8, 17; **12:**1, 4; **13:**16, 30, 34, 38; **14:**6, 11, 25^2, 27, 30, 32^2; **15:**3, 13, 21, 28, 29, 35, 36; **16:**14; **17:**9, 12, 13^2, 22; **18:**7^2, 8, 11, 13, 25; **19:**7, 17, 18, 22; **20:**1^2, 7; **21:**1, 18, 19, 20; **22:**9, 42; **23:**9; **24:**9, 13, 15, 25

1Ki 1:2, 14, 34, 52; **2:**4, 33, 36; **3:**2, 4, 12, 13, 16, 18; **4:**34; **5:**4, 6, 9, 12; **6:**7, 18, 19; **7:**4, 24, 29, 34, 35; **8:**8, 9^2, 21, 23, 25, 29, 35, 37^4, 46, 56, 60, 64; **9:**3^2, 5; **10:**3, 5, 10, 12, 19, 20^2; **11:**16, 36; **12:**20; **13:**1, 11, 17; **14:**2, 13, 21, 24, 30; **15:**6, 7, 16, 19, 32; **17:**1, 4, 7, 9^2, 10, 17; **18:**2, 10^2, 26, 29, 40, 41, 43, 44, 45; **19:**3, 6, 9, 13; **20:**1, 13, 17, 28, 30, 40; **21:**13, 25; **22:**7, 8, 21, 36, 47

2Ki 1:3, 6^2, 10, 14, 16; **2:**11, 16, 21^2, 23, 24; **3:**9, 11, 20, 27; **4:**1, 6, 10, 11, 31, 38, 40, 41, 42; **5:**8, 15, 17, 18, 22; **6:**2, 10, 25, 26; **7:**3, 4, 5^2, 10^2; **9:**2, 10, 16, 17, 18, 23, 27, 32; **10:**2, 8, 10, 21, 23; **11:**16; **12:**10, 13; **13:**6; **14:**9, 19, 26; **15:**20; **16:**6; **17:**11, 18, 25, 27; **18:**18; **19:**3, 32; **20:**13, 15; **22:**7; **23:**16, 20, 22, 25^2, 27, 34; **25:**3, 23

1Ch 3:4; **4:**23, 40, 41^3, 43; **5:**22; **11:**13; **12:**8, 16, 17, 19, 20, 22, 39, 40; **13:**10; **14:**11,

12; 16:37; 17:20^2; 19:5; 20:2, 4, 5, 6; 21:14, 26, 28; 22:15, 16; 24:4^2; 26:31; 27:24; 28:21; 29:15

2Ch 1:3, 12; 5:9, 10; 6:5, 6, 14, 16, 20, 26, 28^4, 36; 7:7, 13, 16^2, 18; 8:2; 9:2, 4, 9, 11, 18, 19^2; 12:13, 15; 13:2, 7, 8, 17; 14:9, 14; 15:5, 19; 16:3^2; 18:6, 7, 20; 19:3, 7; 20:2^2, 6, 26; 21:12, 17; 23:15; 24:11; 25:7, 18, 27; 28:9, 10, 13, 18; 30:13, 17, 26^2; 32:4, 7, 14, 21, 25; 34:13; 35:18; 36:16, 23

Ezr 1:3; 2:63, 65^2; 4:20; 5:17^2; 6:2, 12; 7:7, 23; 8:15^2, 21, 25, 32; 9:14; 10:1, 2, 18

Neh 1:3, 9^2; 2:10, 11, 12, 14; 4:10; 5:1, 2, 3, 4, 17; 6:1, 7, 8, 11, 18; 7:65, 67; 8:17; 12:46; 13:16, 19, 26

Est 1:18, 19; 2:2, 5; 3:8, 12; 4:3, 11, 14; 6:3; 7:7

Job 1:1, 2, 6, 8, 13, 14, 16, 17, 18, 19; 2:1, 3; 3:3, 17^2, 18, 19; 4:16; 5:1, 4, 19; 6:6, 30; 7:1; 9:33; 10:7; 11:18; 12:14, 24; 14:7; 15:11; 17:2; 19:7, 29; 20:21; 21:33, 34; 22:29; 23:7, 8; 25:3; 28:1, 7; 30:26; 31:2; 32:5, 8, 12; 33:9, 23; 34:22; 35:12; 36:16, 18; 38:26; 39:30; 41:33; 42:11

Ps 3:2^2; 4:6; 5:9; 6:5; 7:2, 3; 14:1^2, 2, 3, 5; 16:11; 18:8, 41; 19:3, 6, 11; 22:11; 30:9; 32:2; 33:16; 34:9; 36:1, 12; 38:3^2, 7; 45:12; 46:4; 48:6; 50:22; 53:1^2, 2, 3, 5; 55:18; 58:11; 66:6; 68:27; 69:2, 20, 35; 71:11; 72:16; 73:4, 11, 25; 74:9^2; 75:8; 76:3; 79:3; 81:9; 86:8^2; 87:4, 6, 7; 91:10; 92:15; 104:26^2; 105:31, 37; 106:11; 107:12, 36, 40; 109:12^2; 112:4; 122:5; 130:4, 7; 132:17; 133:3; 135:17; 137:1, 3; 139:4, 8^2, 10, 16, 24; 142:4; 144:14^2; 146:3

Prv 7:10; 8:8, 24^2, 27; 9:18; 10:19; 11:10, 14, 24^2; 12:18, 21, 28; 13:7^2, 23; 14:9, 12, 23; 16:25, 27; 17:16; 18:24; 19:18, 21; 20:15; 21:20, 30; 22:13; 23:18; 24:6, 14, 20; 25:4; 26:12, 13, 20^2, 25; 28:12; 29:6, 9, 18, 20; 30:11, 12, 13, 14, 15, 18, 24, 29, 31

Ecc 1:9, 10, 11^2; 2:11, 16, 21, 24; 3:1, 12, 16^2, 17^2, 22; 4:1, 8^3, 16; 5:7, 8, 11, 13, 14; 6:1, 11; 7:11, 15^2, 20; 8:4, 6, 8^2, 9, 14^3, 16; 9:2, 3, 4, 10, 14^2, 15; 10:5; 11:3; 12:12

Song 4:4, 7; 6:6, 8; 7:12; 8:5^2

Isa 1:6; 2:7^2; 3:24; 4:6; 5:6, 8; 6:12; 7:23, 25; 8:20; 9:7; 10:14; 11:1, 10, 16; 13:20^2, 21^3; 14:31; 15:6; 16:10^2; 17:9; 19:15, 19, 23; 22:18^2; 23:1, 10, 12; 24:11, 13; 27:10^2; 28:8, 10, 13; 29:2; 30:14, 25, 28; 33:21; 34:12, 14, 15^2; 35:8, 9^3; 37:3, 33; 39:2, 4, 8; 40:28; 41:17, 26^3, 28^2; 43:10^2, 11, 12, 13; 44:6, 8^2, 19, 20; 45:5^2, 6^2, 14^2, 18, 21^2, 22; 46:9^2; 47:1, 14; 48:16, 22; 50:2^3; 51:18^2; 52:1, 4; 53:2; 57:10, 21; 59:8, 11, 15, 16^2; 63:3, 5^2; 64:7; 65:9, 20

Jer 2:10, 25; 3:3, 6; 4:25; 5:1; 6:14, 20; 7:2, 32; 8:11, 13, 14, 22^3; 10:6, 7, 13, 14, 20; 11:23; 13:4, 6; 14:4, 5, 6, 19^2, 22; 16:13, 19; 17:25; 18:2, 12; 19:2, 11; 20:6^2; 22:1, 4, 26; 26:20; 27:22; 29:6; 30:13; 31:6, 17, 24; 32:5, 17, 27; 33:10, 20; 36:12, 22, 32; 37:10, 13, 16, 17^2, 20; 38:6, 9, 26, 28; 41:1, 3, 5; 42:14, 15, 16^3, 17; 43:2; 44:12, 14^2, 27, 28; 46:17; 47:7; 48:2, 38; 49:18, 23, 33^2, 36; 50:3, 20, 39, 40; 51:16, 17; 52:6, 23, 34

Lam 1:12, 17, 20, 21; 3:29; 4:15; 5:8

Ezk 1:3, 25; 2:5, 10; 3:15, 22^2, 23; 4:14; 7:11, 25; 8:1, 4, 11, 14; 10:1, 8; 12:13, 24, 28; 13:10, 11, 13, 16, 20; 17:7, 20; 20:28^4, 35, 40^3, 43; 22:20, 25; 23:2, 3^2; 28:3, 24; 29:14; 30:13, 18; 32:22, 24, 26, 29, 30; 34:5, 8, 14, 26; 35:10; 37:2, 7, 8; 38:19; 39:11^2, 28; 40:3, 16, 17, 25, 26, 27, 29, 33, 49; 41:7, 25^2, 26; 42:13, 14; 45:2; 46:19, 21, 22, 23; 47:2, 9, 23; 48:35

Dan 2:9, 10^2, 11, 28, 41; 3:12, 29; 4:31; 5:11; 6:4; 7:8^2, 14; 8:3, 4, 7^2, 15; 10:8, 13, 17^2, 18, 21; 11:2, 14, 15; 12:1^2, 5, 11

Hos 1:10; 2:15; 4:1, 9; 6:7, 10; 7:7, 9; 9:12, 15; 10:9; 12:4, 11; 13:4, 8

Joel 2:2; 3:2, 12, 17

Am 3:6, 11; 4:7; 5:2, 6; 6:9, 10, 12; 7:12^2; 8:3

Oba 7, 17, 18

Jna 1:4; 4:5

Mic 3:7; 4:9, 10^2; 6:10; 7:1, 2

Nah 1:11; 2:9; 3:3^2, 15, 19

Hab 1:3; 2:19; 3:4, 17

Zep 1:10, 14; 2:5, 15; 3:6^2

Hag 1:6; 2:14, 16^2

Zec 1:8; 5:7, 9, 11; 6:1; 8:4, 10^2, 20; 10:2; 11:3; 12:11; 13:1; 14:4, 9, 11, 18, 20, 21

Mal 1:10; 3:10^2

Mt 2:1, 13, 15, 18; 4:25; 5:23, 24; 6:21; 7:9, 13, 14; 8:2, 5, 12, 24, 26, 28, 30; 9:18; 10:11, 26; 11:11; 12:10, 11, 39, 45; 13:42, 50, 58; 14:23; 15:29; 16:4, 28; 17:3, 14; 18:20; 19:2, 12^3, 13, 17; 21:17, 33; 22:11, 13, 23, 25; 24:2, 7, 22, 23, 24, 28, 51; 25:6, 9, 25, 30; 26:5, 7, 13, 71; 27:36, 38, 45, 47, 55, 57, 61; 28:2, 7, 10

Mk 1:5, 7, 11, 13, 23, 35, 38, 40; 2:2, 6^2, 15; 3:1^2, 31; 4:1, 3, 22, 36, 37, 39; 5:2, 11^2, 22, 35; 6:5, 10, 31; 7:4, 15; 8:12; 9:1, 4, 7, 39; 10:17, 18, 29; 11:5, 27; 12:18, 20, 31, 32^2, 42; 13:2, 8^2, 21; 14:2, 3, 4, 13, 15, 51, 57, 66; 15:7, 33, 40; 16:7

Lk 1:5, 11, 33, 45, 61; 2:1, 6, 7, 8, 13, 25, 36; 4:14, 17, 33; 5:15, 17, 29; 6:6, 19; 7:12, 16, 28, 41; 8:23, 24, 27, 32^2, 41, 49; 9:4, 17, 27, 30, 34, 35, 46; 10:6, 31; 11:26, 29; 12:1, 2, 18, 34, 52, 54, 55; 13:1, 11, 14, 23, 28, 30^2, 31; 14:2, 22, 25; 15:10, 13, 14; 16:1, 19, 20, 26; 17:12, 17, 18, 21, 23, 34; 18:2, 3, 29; 19:2; 20:27, 29; 21:6, 7, 11, 18, 23, 25; 22:10, 12, 24, 43; 23:27, 32, 33, 44, 50; 24:18

Jn 1:6, 26, 46; 2:1^2, 6^2, 12; 3:1, 22, 23^2, 25; 4:6, 7, 35, 40, 46; 5:1, 2, 5, 32, 45; 6:3, 9, 10, 22^2, 23, 24, 64; 7:4, 12, 43; 8:44, 50; 9:16; 10:16, 19, 40, 42; 11:9, 10, 15, 31, 54; 12:2, 9, 20, 26, 28; 13:23; 14:3; 18:18; 19:25, 29, 34, 39, 41, 42; 21:2, 9, 11, 25

Act 2:2, 3, 5, 41; 4:12^2, 34; 5:16, 34; 6:1, 9; 7:11, 12, 30; 8:1, 8, 9; 9:3, 10, 18, 33, 36, 38; 10:1, 13, 18; 11:11, 28^2; 12:18, 19; 13:1, 11, 25; 14:5, 7, 8, 19, 28; 15:5, 7, 33, 34; 16:1, 9, 15, 26; 17:7, 14, 21; 18:11, 18, 19, 23; 19:2, 14, 21, 23, 35, 38, 40; 20:3, 4, 8, 9, 13, 22; 21:3, 4, 10^2, 16, 20, 40; 22:5, 6, 10, 12; 23:7, 8, 9, 10, 21; 24:11, 15; 25:5, 9, 11, 14^2, 20; 27:6, 12, 14, 22, 23, 34; 28:3, 12, 18, 23

Ro 2:11; 3:1, 10, 11^2, 12, 18, 20, 22; 4:15; 5:13; 8:1; 9:14, 26; 10:12; 11:5, 26; 13:1, 9; 14:14; 15:12

1Co 1:10, 11; 3:3; 5:1; 6:5, 7; 7:34; 8:4, 5^2, 6, 7; 10:13; 11:18, 19; 12:4, 5, 6, 25; 13:8^3; 14:10, 23, 24, 28; 15:12, 13, 39, 40, 41, 44^2; 16:2, 9

2Co 1:17; 3:17; 8:11^2, 12, 14; 12:7, 20

Gal 1:7; 3:21, 28^3; 5:23

Eph 4:4; 6:9

Php 2:1; 4:8^2

Col 3:11, 25

2Th 2:3; 3:11

1Ti 1:10; 2:5

2Ti 2:20; 4:8

Tit 1:10; 3:12

Phlm 23

Heb 3:12; 4:9, 13; 7:8, 11, 12, 15, 18; 8:4; 9:2, 16; 10:3, 18, 26; 11:12; 12:16

Jas 2:2^2, 3, 19; 3:16; 4:12, 13

2Pt 1:17; 2:1^2; 3:3

1Jn 2:10, 18; 4:18; 5:7, 8, 16, 17

2Jn 10

Jude 4, 18

Rev 2:14; 4:3, 5, 6; 6:4^2, 12; 7:4; 8:1, 3, 5, 7, 10; 9:2, 3, 10, 12; 10:6; 11:1, 13, 15, 19^2; 12:1, 3, 6, 7; 13:5; 14:8; 16:2, 17, 18^2, 21; 17:1, 10; 20:11; 21:1, 4^2, 9, 25^2, 27; 22:2, 3, 5^2

THEREFORE

Gen 2:24; 3:23; 4:15; 11:9; 12:12, 19; 17:9; 18:5, 12; 19:8, 22; 20:6, 7, 8; 21:23; 23:15; 24:65; 25:30; 26:33; 27:3, 8, 28, 43; 29:15, 32, 33, 34, 35; 30:6, 15; 31:44, 48; 32:32; 33:10, 17; 34:21; 37:20; 38:29; 41:33; 42:21, 22; 44:30, 33; 45:5; 47:4; 50:5, 21

Ex 1:11, 20; 3:9, 10; 4:12; 5:8, 17, 18; 9:19; 10:17; 12:17; 13:10, 15; 15:23; 16:29; 19:5; 31:14; 32:10, 34; 33:5, 13

Lev 8:35; 9:8; 11:44, 45; 13:52; 16:4; 17:12, 14; 18:5, 25, 26, 30; 19:8, 37; 20:7, 22, 23, 25; 21:6, 8; 22:9^2, 31; 25:17

Nu 3:12; 11:18; 14:16, 43; 16:38; 18:7, 24, 30; 20:12; 21:7; 22:5, 6, 17, 19, 34; 24:11, 14; 27:4; 31:17, 50; 35:34

Dt 2:4; 4:1, 6, 15, 37, 39, 40; 5:15, 25, 32; 6:3; 7:9, 11; 8:6; 9:3, 6, 26; 10:16, 19; 11:1, 8, 18; 14:7; 15:11, 15; 16:2, 15; 18:2; 23:14; 24:18, 22; 25:19; 26:16; 27:4, 10; 28:48; 29:9; 30:19; 31:19, 22

Jos 1:2; 2:12; 3:12; 4:17; 7:12, 14; 8:6, 9; 9:6, 11, 19, 23, 24; 10:5, 9; 13:7; 14:4, 12, 14; 17:1, 4; 18:6; 19:9, 47; 22:4, 26, 28; 23:6, 11, 15; 24:10, 14, 18, 23, 27

Jdg 2:23; 3:8, 25; 6:32; 7:3; 8:7; 9:16, 32; 11:8, 13, 26; 13:4; 14:2; 15:2; 16:12; 17:3; 18:14; 19:7; 20:13, 42; 21:20

Ru 3:3, 9; 4:8

1Sa 1:7, 13, 28; 3:9, 14; 5:5, 8, 10; 6:7; 8:9; 9:13; 10:12, 19, 22; 11:10; 12:7, 13, 16; 13:12^2; 14:41; 15:1, 25; 17:51; 18:13, 22; 19:2; 20:8, 29; 21:3; 22:1; 23:2, 20, 23, 28; 24:15, 21; 25:17, 26; 26:4, 8, 19, 20; 27:12; 28:2, 15, 18, 22; 31:4

2Sa 2:7; 4:11; 5:20; 6:21, 23; 7:8, 27, 29; 9:10; 12:10, 16, 19, 28; 13:13, 33; 14:15, 17, 21, 26, 29, 30, 32; 15:29, 35; 17:11, 16; 18:3; 19:7, 10, 20, 23, 27, 28; 22:25, 50; 23:17, 19

1Ki 1:12; 2:2, 6, 9, 19, 24, 33, 44; 3:9; 5:6; 8:25, 61; 9:9; 10:9; 11:40; 12:4, 18, 24; 13:26; 14:10, 12; 18:19, 23; 20:23, 28, 42; 22:19, 23

2Ki 1:4, 6, 14, 16; 2:17; 3:23; 4:33; 5:15, 27; 6:7, 11, 14; 7:4, 9, 12, 14; 9:26; 10:19; 12:7; 14:11; 15:16; 17:4, 18, 25, 26; 18:23; 19:18, 19, 26, 28, 32; 21:12; 22:17, 20

1Ch 10:14; 11:3, 7, 19; 14:11, 14, 16; 17:7, 23, 25, 27; 21:7, 12; 22:5, 16, 19; 23:11; 24:2; 28:8; 29:13

2Ch 2:7, 15; 6:10, 16, 19, 21, 41; 7:22; 9:8; 10:4; 12:5, 7; 14:7; 15:7; 16:7, 9; 17:5; 18:5, 12, 16, 18, 22, 31, 33; 19:2; 20:26; 28:11, 23; 30:7, 17; 32:15, 25; 34:25; 35:14, 24; 36:17

Ezr 2:62; 4:14; 5:17; 6:6; 9:12; 10:3, 11

Neh 2:20; 4:13, 20; 5:2; 6:7, 9, 13; 7:64; 9:27, 28, 30, 32; 13:8, 28

Est 1:12; 2:23; 3:8; 9:19, 26

Job 5:17; 6:3, 28; 7:11; 9:22; 10:15; 11:6; 17:4; 20:2, 21; 21:14; 22:10; 23:15; 32:10; 34:10, 25, 33; 35:14, 16; 37:24; 42:3, 8

Ps 1:5; 2:10; 7:7; 16:9; 18:24, 49; 21:12; 25:8; 26:1; 27:6; 28:7; 31:3; 36:7; 40:12; 42:6; 45:2, 7, 17; 46:2; 55:19; 59:5; 63:7; 73:6, 10; 78:21, 33; 91:14; 106:23, 26, 40; 107:12; 110:7; 116:2, 10; 118:7; 119:104, 119, 127, 128, 129, 140; 139:19; 143:4

Prv 1:31; 4:7; 5:7; 6:15, 34; 7:15, 24; 8:32; 17:11, 14; 20:4, 19

Ecc 2:1, 17, 20; 5:2; 8:6, 11; 11:10

Song 1:3

Isa 1:24; 2:6, 9; 3:17; 5:13, 14, 24, 25; 7:14; 8:7; 9:11, 14, 17; 10:16, 24; 12:3; 13:7, 13; 15:4, 7; 16:7, 9; 17:10; 21:3; 22:4; 24:6^2; 25:3; 26:14; 27:9, 11; 28:16, 22; 29:14, 22; 30:3, 7, 13, 16^2, 18^2; 36:8; 37:19, 20, 27, 29, 33; 38:20; 42:25; 43:4, 12, 28; 47:8, 11; 50:7^2; 51:11, 21; 52:5, 6^2; 53:12; 57:10; 59:9, 16; 60:11; 61:7; 63:5, 10; 65:7, 12, 13

Jer 1:17; 2:19, 33; 3:3; 5:4, 27; 6:11, 15, 18, 21; 7:14, 16, 20, 27, 32; 8:10, 12; 9:7, 15; 10:21; 11:8, 11, 14, 21, 22; 12:8; 13:12, 24, 26; 14:10, 15, 17, 22; 15:6, 19; 16:13, 14, 21; 18:11, 13, 21; 19:6; 20:11; 22:18; 23:2, 7, 15, 30, 32, 38, 39; 25:8, 27, 30; 26:13; 27:9, 14; 28:16; 29:20, 27, 28, 32; 30:10, 16; 31:3, 12, 20; 32:23, 28, 36; 34:12, 17; 35:17, 19; 36:6, 14, 30; 37:20; 38:4; 40:3; 42:15, 22; 44:7, 11, 22, 23, 26; 48:11, 12, 31, 36; 49:2, 20, 26; 50:18, 30, 39, 45; 51:7, 36, 47

Lam 1:8, 9; 2:8; 3:21, 24

Ezk 3:17; 4:7; 5:7, 8, 10, 11; 7:20; 8:18; 11:4, 7, 16, 17; 12:3, 23, 28; 13:8^2, 13, 23; 14:4, 6; 15:6; 16:27, 34, 37, 43, 50; 17:19; 18:30; 20:27; 21:4, 6, 12, 14, 24; 22:4, 13, 19^2, 31; 23:22, 31, 35^2; 24:9; 25:4, 7, 9, 13, 16; 26:3; 28:6, 7, 16, 18; 29:8, 10, 19; 30:22; 31:5, 10, 11; 32:3; 33:7, 10, 12; 34:7, 9, 20, 22; 35:6, 11; 36:3, 4, 5, 6, 7, 14, 22; 37:12; 38:14; 39:1, 23, 25; 41:7; 42:6; 44:2, 12

Dan 1:8, 19; 2:6, 9, 10, 24; 3:7, 19, 22, 29; 4:6; 8:8; 9:11, 14, 17, 23, 25; 10:8; 11:30, 44

Hos 2:2, 6, 9, 14; 4:3, 5, 7, 13, 14; 5:5, 10, 12; 6:5; 8:6; 9:9; 10:14; 12:6, 14; 13:3, 6, 7

Joel 2:12

Am 2:14; 3:2, 11; 4:12; 5:11, 13, 16, 27; 6:7, 8; 7:16, 17

Jna 4:2, 3

Mic 1:6, 8, 14; 2:3, 5; 3:6, 12; 5:3; 6:13, 16; 7:7

Hab 1:4^{2}, 15, 16, 17

Zep 1:13; 2:9; 3:8

Hag 1:5, 10

Zec 1:3, 16; 7:12, 13; 8:19; 10:2

Mal 2:9, 15, 16; 3:6

Mt 3:8, 10; 5:19, 23, 48; 6:2, 8, 9, 22, 23, 25, 31, 34; 7:12, 24; 9:38; 10:16, 26, 31, 32; 12:27; 13:13, 18, 40, 52; 14:2; 18:4, 23, 26; 19:6, 27; 21:40, 43; 22:9, 17, 21, 28; 23:3, 14, 20; 24:15, 42, 44; 25:13, 27, 28; 27:17, 64; 28:19

Mk 1:38; 2:28; 6:14, 19; 8:38; 10:9; 11:24; 12:6, 9, 23, 24, 27, 37; 13:35

Lk 1:35; 3:8, 9; 4:7, 43; 6:36; 7:42; 8:18; 10:2^{2}, 40; 11:19, 34, 35, 36, 49; 12:3, 7, 22, 40; 13:14; 14:20; 15:28; 16:11, 27; 19:12; 20:15, 25, 29, 33, 44; 21:8, 14, 36; 23:16, 20, 22

Jn 1:31; 2:22; 3:29; 4:1, 6, 33; 5:10, 16, 18; 6:13, 15, 24, 30, 43, 45, 52, 60, 65; 7:3, 22, 40; 8:13, 24, 36, 47; 9:7, 8, 10, 16, 23, 41; 10:17, 19, 39; 11:3, 6, 33, 38, 54; 12:9, 17, 19, 21, 29, 39, 50; 13:11, 24, 31; 15:19; 16:15, 18, 22; 18:4, 8, 25, 31, 37, 39; 19:1, 4, 6, 8, 11, 13, 16, 24^{2}, 26, 30, 31, 38, 42; 20:3, 25; 21:6, 7

Act 1:6; 2:26, 30, 33, 36; 3:19; 8:4, 22; 10:20, 29^{2}, 32, 33^{2}; 12:5; 13:38, 40; 14:3; 15:2, 10, 27; 16:11, 36; 17:12, 17, 20, 23; 19:32; 20:11, 28, 31; 21:22, 23; 23:15; 25:5, 17; 26:22; 28:20, 28

Ro 2:1, 21, 26; 3:20, 28; 4:16, 22; 5:1, 18; 6:4, 12; 8:1, 12; 9:18; 11:22; 12:1, 20; 13:2, 7, 10, 12; 14:8, 13, 19; 15:17, 28; 16:19

1Co 3:21; 4:5; 5:7, 8, 13; 6:7, 20; 7:8, 26; 8:4; 9:26; 10:31; 11:20; 12:15, 16; 14:11, 23; 15:11, 58; 16:11, 18

2Co 1:17; 4:1, 13^{2}; 5:6, 11, 17; 7:1, 13, 16; 8:7, 11; 9:5; 11:15; 12:9, 10; 13:10

Gal 2:17; 3:5, 7; 4:16; 5:1; 6:10

Eph 2:19; 4:1, 17; 5:1, 7, 24; 6:14

Php 2:1, 23, 28, 29; 3:15; 4:1

Col 2:6, 16; 3:5, 12

1Th 3:7; 4:8; 5:6

2Th 2:15

1Ti 2:1, 8; 4:10; 5:14

2Ti 1:8; 2:1, 3, 10, 21; 4:1

Phlm 12, 15, 17

Heb 1:9; 2:1; 4:1, 6, 9, 11, 16; 6:1; 7:11; 9:23; 10:19, 35; 11:12; 13:13, 15

Jas 4:4, 7, 17; 5:7

1Pt 2:7; 4:7; 5:6

2Pt 3:17

1Jn 2:24; 3:1; 4:5

3Jn 8

Jude 5

Rev 2:5; 3:3^{2}, 19; 7:15; 12:12; 18:8

THEREOF

Gen 2:17, 19, 21; 3:5, 6; 4:4; 6:16; 9:4^{2}; 40:10, 18; 41:8; 45:16; 47:21

Ex 3:20; 5:8; 9:18; 10:26; 12:9, 43, 44, 45, 46, 48; 16:31; 19:18; 22:11, 12, 14, 15; 23:10; 25:9, 10^{3}, 12, 17^{2}, 19, 23^{3}, 25, 26, 29^{4}, 37^{2}, 38^{2}; 26:30; 27:1, 2, 3, 4, 10, 19^{2}; 28:7^{2}, 8, 16^{2}, 26, 27^{2}, 28, 32, 33; 29:33, 41; 30:2^{4}, 3^{3}, 4, 37; 35:12; 36:29; 37:6^{2}, 8, 10^{3}, 12, 13, 18^{3}, 24, 25, 26, 27^{2}; 38:1^{3}, 2^{2}, 3, 4; 39:5, 9^{2}, 20, 35, 36, 37^{2}; 40:4, 9, 18^{2}

Lev 1:15, 17; 2:2^{3}, 9, 16^{3}; 3:8, 9, 13, 14; 4:30^{2}, 31, 34, 35; 5:12; 6:15, 16, 20, 27^{2}, 29; 7:2, 3, 6, 19; 8:11; 9:13, 17; 11:39; 13:4, 18, 20; 14:45; 17:13, 14^{2}; 18:25; 19:23, 24, 25^{2}; 22:13, 14, 24; 23:10, 13^{2}; 24:5; 25:3, 7, 10, 12, 16, 27; 27:10, 13, 16, 21, 31, 33

Nu 1:50^{2}; 2:6, 8, 11; 3:25, 26, 31, 36^{4}; 4:6, 8, 9, 10, 11, 14, 16, 31^{3}; 5:7^{2}, 26; 7:1^{2}, 13; 8:3, 4^{2}, 25; 9:3, 14; 11:7; 13:32; 18:28, 29^{2}, 30; 21:25, 32; 26:56; 28:7, 8, 9; 29:19; 32:33, 41, 42; 34:2, 4, 12

Dt 3:11, 12, 17; 9:21; 12:15; 13:15, 16^{2}; 15:23; 20:13, 14, 19; 26:14^{3}; 28:30, 31; 29:23; 33:16

Jos 6:2, 26; 7:14; 8:2^{2}; 9:1; 10:2, 28, 30^{2}, 37^{2}, 39^{3}; 11:10; 13:23^{2}; 15:7, 12, 47; 16:3, 8; 18:12, 14, 20; 19:14, 29, 33; 21:2, 11, 12; 22:7; 23:14

Jdg 1:18^{3}, 26^{2}; 3:2; 5:23; 7:15; 8:14, 27; 14:9; 15:19; 17:4

1Sa 5:6; 6:8; 7:14; 17:51; 20:20; 28:24

2Sa 20:8; 23:16

1Ki 2:32; 3:27; 6:2^{3}, 3^{2}, 20, 38; 7:2^{3}, 6^{2}, 21^{2}, 26, 27, 30, 31, 35^{2}, 36^{2}; 8:7; 13:26; 15:21, 22; 16:34^{2}; 17:13

2Ki 2:12; 3:25; 4:39, 40, 42, 43, 44; 7:2, 19; 13:14; 15:16; 16:10; 17:24; 18:8; 19:23^{2}, 29; 22:16, 19; 23:6

1Ch 2:23; 6:55, 56; 7:28^{4}; 8:12; 9:27; 16:32; 21:27; 23:26; 28:11^{4}, 15^{2}

2Ch 3:7^{2}, 8; 4:1^{3}, 2, 22; 5:8; 13:11, 19^{3}; 16:6; 28:18^{3}; 29:18^{2}; 32:1; 34:24, 27; 36:19^{2}

Ezr 4:12, 16; 6:3^{3}; 9:9; 10:14

Neh 1:3; 2:3, 13, 17; 3:3^{4}, 6^{4}, 13^{3}, 14^{3}, 15^{3}; 4:6; 6:16; 9:36^{2}; 11:25^{3}, 27, 28, 30^{2}; 13:14

Est 1:22; 2:22; 3:12; 8:9^{2}; 9:18^{2}

Job 3:9; 4:12, 16; 9:6, 24; 11:9; 14:7, 8^{2}; 15:29; 24:2, 13^{2}; 26:5; 28:13, 15, 22, 23^{2}; 31:17, 38, 39^{2}; 36:27, 33; 38:5, 6^{2}, 9, 19, 20^{2}, 33

Ps 19:6; 24:1; 34:2; 46:3^{2}; 48:12; 50:1, 12; 55:10, 11; 60:2; 65:10^{3}; 71:15; 72:16; 74:6; 75:3, 8; 80:10; 89:9, 11; 96:11; 97:1; 98:7; 102:14; 103:16; 107:25, 29; 137:2, 7

Prv 1:19; 3:14; 12:28; 14:12; 16:25, 33; 18:21; 20:21; 21:22; 24:31^{2}; 25:8; 27:18; 28:2^{2}

Ecc 5:11, 13, 19; 6:2; 7:8

Song 1:12; 3:10^{3}; 4:16; 7:8; 8:6, 11, 12

Isa 3:14; 4:4; 5:2, 5^{2}, 30; 6:13; 13:9, 10; 14:17; 15:8^{2}; 16:8; 17:6; 19:3^{2}, 10, 13, 14^{2}, 17, 19; 21:2; 22:11; 23:11, 13^{2}; 24:1, 5, 20; 27:10, 11; 28:25; 30:27, 33; 31:4; 33:20^{2}; 34:9^{3}, 10, 12, 13; 37:24^{2}, 30; 40:6, 16, 22; 41:9; 42:10, 11; 44:15, 16^{2}, 17, 19^{2}, 26; 48:19; 62:1^{2}

Jer 1:13, 15, 18^{2}; 2:7^{2}; 4:26; 5:1, 22, 31; 6:24; 11:19; 14:2, 8; 17:27; 19:8, 12; 20:5^{2}; 21:14; 23:14; 25:9, 18^{2}; 26:15; 29:7; 30:18; 31:23, 24, 35; 33:2, 12; 34:1, 18; 46:8, 22; 48:9, 38; 49:13, 17, 18, 21, 32; 50:29, 40; 51:28^{2}, 42; 52:21

Lam 2:2; 4:11

Ezk 1:4, 5; 4:9^{2}; 5:3, 4; 7:12, 13, 14; 9:4; 10:7; 11:6, 9, 11, 18^{2}; 13:14^{2}; 14:13; 15:3; 17:6, 9^{3}, 12^{2}, 23; 19:7; 20:29; 22:21, 22, 25^{2}, 27; 23:34; 24:4, 11; 27:9; 31:15; 32:7, 12, 13; 38:13; 40:6, 9, 20^{2}, 21^{4}, 22, 24^{2}, 25, 26^{2}, 29^{4}, 31^{2}, 33^{4}, 34^{2}, 36^{3}, 37^{2}, 38; 41:2, 4, 12, 13, 15, 22^{4}; 42:7; 43:11^{9}, 12, 13^{2}, 16, 17^{2}, 20; 44:5, 14; 45:1, 2, 11; 46:8, 16; 47:11^{2}, 12^{4}; 48:10, 15, 16, 18, 21

Dan 1:5; 2:5, 6^{2}, 9, 26, 31, 36, 45; 3:1; 4:7, 9, 10, 11^{2}, 12^{3}, 18, 19^{2}, 20, 21, 23; 5:7, 8, 15, 16; 7:4; 9:26

Hos 2:9^{2}; 4:13; 8:14; 9:4; 10:5^{3}; 14:7

Joel 1:7

Am 1:3, 6, 7, 9, 10, 11, 13, 14; 2:1, 3^{2}, 4, 6; 3:9^{2}; 8:10; 9:11, 14

Jna 1:3

Mic 1:6^{2}, 7^{3}; 3:11^{3}; 5:6; 6:12^{2}, 16

Nah 1:8; 2:5

Hab 2:18

Zep 1:13; 3:5

Zec 2:2^{2}; 3:9; 4:2, 3, 7, 11; 5:2^{2}, 4^{2}, 8; 7:7; 8:5; 9:1; 14:4

Mal 1:12

Mt 2:16; 6:34; 12:36; 13:32, 44; 14:13; 21:43; 22:7; 27:34

Mk 6:16

Lk 19:33; 21:20; 22:16

Jn 3:8; 4:12; 6:50; 7:7

Act 15:16

Ro 6:12; 13:14

1Co 9:7, 23; 10:26, 28

2Ti 3:5

Heb 7:18

Jas 1:11

1Pt 1:24; 5:2

1Jn 2:17

Rev 5:2, 5, 9; 16:12, 21; 21:15^{2}, 17, 23

THESE

Gen 2:4; 6:9; 9:19; 10:1, 5, 20, 29, 31, 32^{2}; 11:10, 27; 14:2, 3, 13; 15:1, 10; 19:8; 20:8; 21:29, 30; 22:1, 20, 23; 23:1; 24:28; 25:4, 7, 12, 13, 16^{2}, 17, 19; 26:3, 4; 27:36, 42, 46; 29:13; 31:43^{4}; 32:17; 33:8; 34:21; 35:26; 36:1, 5, 9, 10, 12, 13^{2}, 14, 15, 16^{2}, 17^{3}, 18^{2}, 19^{2}, 20, 21, 23, 24, 25, 26, 27, 28, 29, 30, 31, 40, 43; 37:2; 38:25^{2}; 39:7, 17; 40:1; 42:36; 43:7, 16^{2}; 44:6, 7; 45:6; 46:8, 15, 18^{2}, 22, 25^{2}; 48:1, 8; 49:28

Ex 1:1; 4:9; 6:14^{2}, 15, 16, 19, 24, 25, 26, 27^{2}; 10:1; 11:8, 10; 14:20; 15:26; 19:6, 7; 20:1; 21:1, 11; 24:8; 25:39; 28:4; 30:34; 32:4, 8; 33:4; 34:1, 27^{2}; 35:1

Lev 2:8; 5:4, 5, 13, 17; 6:3; 11:2, 4, 9, 13, 21, 22, 24, 29, 31; 16:4; 18:24^{2}, 26, 27, 29, 30; 20:23; 21:14; 22:22, 25; 23:2, 4, 37; 25:54; 26:14, 23, 46; 27:34

Nu 1:5, 16, 17, 44; 2:9, 32; 3:1, 2, 3, 17, 18, 20, 21, 27, 33, 35; 4:15, 37, 41, 45; 5:23; 13:4, 16; 14:22, 39; 15:13, 22; 16:14, 26, 28, 29, 30, 31, 38; 21:25; 22:9, 28, 32, 33; 24:10; 26:7, 14, 18, 22, 25, 27, 30, 34, 35, 36, 37^{2}, 41, 42^{2}, 47, 50, 51, 53, 57, 58, 63, 64; 27:1; 28:23; 29:39; 30:16; 31:16; 33:1, 2; 34:17, 19, 29; 35:13, 15, 24, 29; 36:13

Dt 1:1, 35; 2:7; 3:5, 21; 4:6, 30, 42, 45; 5:22; 6:1, 6, 24, 25; 7:12, 17; 8:2, 4; 9:4, 5; 10:21; 11:18, 22, 23; 12:1, 28, 30; 14:4, 7, 9, 12; 15:5; 16:12; 17:19; 18:12^{2}, 14; 19:9^{2}, 11; 20:15, 16; 22:17; 23:18; 25:3; 26:16; 27:4, 12, 13; 28:2, 15, 45, 65; 29:1, 18; 30:1, 7; 31:1, 3, 17, 28; 32:45

Jos 2:11; 4:6, 7, 21; 9:13^{2}; 10:16, 24, 42; 11:5, 14; 12:1, 7; 13:12, 32; 14:1, 10; 17:2, 3, 9; 19:8, 16, 31, 48, 51; 20:9; 21:3, 8, 9, 42^{2}; 22:3; 23:3, 4, 7^{2}, 12^{2}, 13; 24:26, 29

Jdg 2:4; 3:1; 9:3; 13:23^{2}; 16:15; 18:14, 18; 19:13; 20:17, 25, 35, 44, 46

Ru 3:17; 4:18

1Sa 4:8^{2}; 6:17; 10:7; 14:6, 8, 49; 16:10; 17:17, 18, 39; 18:26; 21:5, 12; 23:2; 24:7, 16; 25:37; 29:3^{3}, 4; 31:4

2Sa 3:5, 39; 5:14; 7:17, 21; 13:21; 14:19; 16:2; 21:22; 23:1, 8, 17^{2}, 22; 24:17, 23

1Ki 4:2, 8; 7:9, 45; 8:59; 9:13, 23; 10:8, 10; 11:2; 17:1, 17; 18:36; 20:19; 21:1; 22:11, 17, 23

2Ki 1:7, 13; 2:21; 3:10, 13; 6:20; 7:8; 10:9; 17:41; 18:27; 20:14; 21:11; 23:16, 17; 25:16, 17, 20

1Ch 1:23, 29, 31, 33, 43, 54; 2:1, 18, 23, 33, 50, 55; 3:1, 4, 5, 9; 4:2, 3, 4, 6, 12, 18, 22, 23, 31, 33, 38, 41; 5:14, 17, 24; 6:17, 19, 31, 33, 50, 54, 64, 65; 7:8, 11, 17, 29, 33, 40; 8:6^{2}, 10, 28^{2}, 32, 38^{2}, 40; 9:9, 22^{2}, 26, 33, 34^{2}, 44^{2}; 10:4; 11:10, 19^{3}, 24; 12:1, 14, 15, 23, 38; 14:4; 17:15, 19; 18:11; 20:8; 21:17; 23:9, 10, 24; 24:1, 19, 20, 30, 31; 25:5, 6; 26:8, 12, 19; 27:22, 31; 29:17, 19

2Ch 3:3, 13; 4:18; 5:5; 8:10; 9:7; 14:7, 8; 15:8; 17:14, 19; 18:10, 16, 22; 21:2; 24:26; 29:32; 32:1; 35:7; 36:18

Ezr 1:11; 2:1, 59, 62; 4:21; 5:9, 11, 15; 6:8^{2}; 7:1; 8:1, 13; 9:1, 14; 10:44

Neh 1:4, 10; 4:2; 5:6; 6:6, 7, 14, 16; 7:6, 61, 64; 10:8; 11:3, 7; 12:1, 7, 26; 13:26

Est 1:5; 2:1; 3:1; 4:11; 9:20, 26, 27, 28^{2}, 31, 32

Job 8:2; 10:13; 12:3, 9; 19:3; 26:14; 32:1, 5; 33:29; 42:7

Ps 15:5; 42:4; 50:21; 57:1; 73:12; 104:27; 107:24, 43

Prv 6:16; 24:23; 25:1

Ecc 7:10; 11:9; 12:12

Isa 7:4; 34:16; 36:12, 20; 38:16^{2}; 39:3; 40:26; 42:16; 44:21; 45:7; 47:7, 9, 13; 48:14; 49:12^{3}, 18, 21^{3}; 51:19; 57:6; 60:8; 64:12; 65:5

Jer 2:34; 3:7, 12; 4:18; 5:4, 5, 9, 19, 25, 29; 7:2, 4, 10, 13, 27; 9:9, 24, 26; 10:11; 11:6; 13:22; 14:22; 16:10; 17:20; 20:1; 22:2, 5; 23:21; 24:5; 25:9, 11, 30; 26:7,

10, 15; 27:6, 12; 28:14; 29:1; 30:4, 15; 31:21; 32:14; 34:6, 7; 36:16, 17, 18, 24; 38:9, 12, 16, 24, 27; 43:1, 10; 45:1; 51:60, 61; 52:20, 22

Lam 1:16; 4:9; 5:17

Ezk 1:21^{2}; 8:15; 10:17^{2}; 11:2; 14:3, 14, 16, 18; 16:5, 20, 30, 43; 17:12, 18; 18:10, 13; 23:10, 30; 24:19; 27:21, 24; 30:17; 35:10^{2}; 36:20; 37:3, 4, 5, 9, 11, 18; 40:24, 28, 29, 32, 33, 35, 46; 42:5, 9; 43:13, 18, 27; 46:22, 24; 47:8, 9; 48:1^{2}, 16, 29, 30

Dan 1:6, 17; 2:28, 40, 44^{2}; 3:12, 13, 21, 23, 27; 6:2, 5, 6, 11, 14, 15; 7:17; 10:21; 11:6, 27, 41; 12:6, 7, 8

Hos 2:12; 14:9

Am 6:2

Mic 2:7

Hab 2:6

Hag 2:13

Zec 1:9^{2}, 10, 12, 19^{2}, 21^{3}; 3:7; 4:4, 5, 11, 12, 13, 14; 5:10; 6:4, 5, 8; 7:3; 8:6, 9^{2}, 10, 12, 15, 16, 17; 13:6; 14:15

Mt 1:20; 2:3; 3:9; 4:3, 9; 5:19, 37; 6:29, 32^{2}, 33; 7:24, 26, 28; 9:18; 10:2, 5, 42; 11:25; 13:34, 51, 53, 54, 56; 15:20; 18:6, 10, 14; 19:1, 20; 20:12, 21; 21:16, 23, 24, 27; 22:22, 40; 23:23, 36; 24:2, 3, 6, 8, 33, 34; 25:40, 45, 46; 26:1, 62

Mk 2:8; 4:11, 15, 16, 18, 20; 6:2; 7:23; 8:4; 9:42; 10:20; 11:28^{2}, 29, 33; 12:31, 40; 13:2, 4^{2}, 8, 29, 30; 14:60; 16:17

Lk 1:19, 20, 65; 2:19, 51; 3:8; 4:28; 5:27; 7:9, 18; 8:8, 13, 21; 9:28, 44; 10:1, 21, 36; 11:27, 42, 53; 12:27, 30^{2}, 31; 13:2, 7, 16, 17; 14:6, 15, 21; 15:26, 29; 16:14; 17:2; 18:21, 22, 34; 19:11, 15, 40; 20:2, 8, 16; 21:4, 6, 7^{2}, 9, 12, 22, 28, 31, 36; 23:31, 49; 24:9, 10, 14, 17, 18, 21, 26, 44, 48

Jn 1:28, 50; 2:16, 18; 3:2, 9, 10, 22; 5:3, 16, 19, 20, 34; 6:1, 5, 59; 7:1, 4, 9, 31; 8:20, 28, 30; 9:22, 40; 10:19, 21; 11:11; 12:16^{3}, 36, 41; 13:17; 14:12, 25; 15:11, 17, 21; 16:1, 3, 4^{2}, 6, 25, 33; 17:1, 11, 13, 20, 25; 18:1, 8; 19:24, 36; 20:18, 31; 21:1, 15, 24^{2}

Act 1:9, 14, 21, 24; 2:7, 13, 15, 22; 3:24; 4:16; 5:5^{2}, 11, 24, 32, 35, 36, 38; 7:1, 50, 54; 8:24; 10:8, 44, 47; 11:12, 18, 22, 27; 12:17; 13:42; 14:15^{2}, 18; 15:17, 28; 16:17, 20, 38; 17:6, 7, 8, 11, 20; 18:1; 19:21, 28, 36, 37; 20:5, 24, 34; 21:12, 38; 23:22; 24:8, 9, 20, 22; 25:9, 11^{2}, 20; 26:16, 21, 26^{2}, 29; 27:31; 28:29

Ro 2:14; 8:31, 37; 9:8; 11:24, 31; 14:18; 15:23^{2}

1Co 4:6, 14; 9:8, 15^{2}; 10:6, 11; 12:2, 11, 23; 13:13^{2}

2Co 2:16; 7:1; 13:10

Gal 2:6; 4:24; 5:17, 19

Eph 5:6

Php 4:8

Col 3:8, 14; 4:11

1Th 3:3; 4:18

2Th 2:5

1Ti 3:10, 14; 4:6, 11, 15; 5:7, 21; 6:2, 11

2Ti 1:12; 2:14, 21; 3:8

Tit 2:15; 3:8^{2}

Heb 1:2; 7:13; 9:6, 23^{2}; 10:18; 11:13, 39

Jas 3:10

1Pt 1:20

2Pt 1:4, 8, 9, 10, 12, 15; 2:12, 17; 3:11, 16, 17

1Jn 1:4; 2:1, 26; 5:7, 8, 13

Jude 8, 10, 12, 14, 16, 19

Rev 2:1, 8, 12, 18; 3:1, 7, 14; 7:1, 13, 14; 9:18, 20; 11:4, 6, 10; 14:4^{3}; 16:9; 17:13, 14, 16; 18:1, 15; 19:1, 9, 20; 21:5; 22:6, 8^{2}, 16, 18, 20

THEY

Gen 2:4, 24, 25; 3:7^{3}, 8; 4:8; 5:2; 6:2^{3}, 4, 19; 7:14, 15, 16, 23^{2}; 8:17; 9:2, 23; 11:2^{3}, 3^{3}, 4, 6^{3}, 7, 8, 31^{2}; 12:5^{4}, 12^{3}, 20; 13:6^{2}, 11; 14:4^{2}, 7, 8, 10, 11, 12; 15:13, 14^{2}, 16; 18:5, 8, 9, 19, 21; 19:2, 3^{2}, 4, 5, 8, 9^{3}, 11^{2}, 16, 17, 33, 35; 20:11, 17; 21:30, 31, 32^{2}; 22:6, 8, 9, 19; 24:19, 41, 54^{2}, 57, 58, 59, 60, 61; 25:18, 25; 26:18, 20, 21, 22, 28, 30, 31^{2}, 32; 29:2, 3, 4, 5, 6, 8^{2}, 20; 30:38^{2}, 41; 31:23, 37, 43, 46^{2}, 54; 32:18; 33:4, 6^{2}, 7; 34:5, 7^{2}, 14, 22, 23, 25, 26, 27, 28, 29, 30, 31; 35:4, 5^{2}, 16; 36:7^{2}; 37:4, 5, 8, 16, 17, 18^{2}, 19, 23, 24, 25^{2}, 28^{2}, 31, 32^{2}; 38:21; 39:22; 40:4, 5, 6, 8, 15; 41:2, 14, 18, 21^{3}, 43; 42:7, 8, 10, 13, 20, 21, 23, 26, 28, 29, 35^{3}; 43:2^{2}, 7, 15, 18^{2}, 19^{2}, 24, 25^{3}, 26, 28^{2}, 32, 33, 34; 44:1, 3, 4, 7, 11, 13, 14; 45:3, 4, 24, 25, 27; 46:6^{2}, 28, 32^{2}; 47:1^{2}, 3, 4, 14, 17, 18, 22, 25, 27; 48:5, 9; 49:6^{2}, 26, 31^{2}; 50:8, 10^{2}, 11, 15, 16, 17^{2}, 18, 26

Ex 1:10^{2}, 11^{2}, 12^{3}, 14^{2}, 19; 2:16, 18, 19, 23; 3:13, 18; 4:1^{2}, 5, 8^{2}, 9, 18, 31^{2}; 5:1, 3, 8^{3}, 9, 10, 16, 19, 20^{2}, 21; 6:4, 9, 27; 7:6, 7, 10, 11, 12^{2}, 16, 17, 19, 24; 8:1, 8, 9, 11, 14, 17, 18, 20, 21, 26; 9:1, 10, 13, 19, 32; 10:3, 5^{2}, 6^{2}, 7, 8, 11, 12, 14^{2}, 15^{2}, 23; 12:3, 7^{2}, 8^{2}, 28, 33^{2}, 35, 36^{3}, 39^{4}, 50; 13:17^{2}, 20; 14:2, 3, 4, 5, 10, 11, 15, 17, 25; 15:5, 10, 16, 22^{2}, 23^{3}, 27^{2}; 16:1, 4, 5^{3}, 10, 15^{2}, 18^{2}, 20, 21, 22, 24, 27, 32, 35^{3}; 17:4, 7, 12; 18:7^{2}, 11, 16^{2}, 20^{2}, 22^{3}, 26^{3}; 19:1, 2, 13, 14, 17, 21; 20:18, 19; 21:28, 35^{2}; 22:23; 23:11, 33^{2}; 24:2, 7, 10, 11; 25:2, 10, 15, 37^{2}; 26:24^{3}, 25; 27:8, 20; 28:3, 4^{2}, 5, 6, 20, 21, 28, 30, 38, 41, 42, 43^{4}; 29:33^{2}, 46; 30:4, 12, 13, 15, 20^{4}, 21^{2}, 29, 30; 31:6, 11; 32:4, 6, 8^{2}, 13, 15, 17, 20, 22, 23, 24, 35; 33:4; 34:15, 30; 35:21^{2}, 22, 25; 36:3^{2}, 4, 5, 6, 7, 29; 39:1, 3, 4, 6, 7, 9, 10, 13, 15, 16, 17, 18, 19, 20, 21, 24, 25, 27, 30, 31, 32, 33, 43^{2}; 40:15, 32^{3}, 37

Lev 2:12; 4:13, 14, 24, 33; 6:16, 20; 7:2^{2}; 8:28; 9:5, 13, 20, 24; 10:2, 5, 7, 14, 15, 19; 11:8, 10, 11, 13^{3}, 28, 31, 32, 35^{2}, 42; 13:54; 14:36, 40^{2}, 41^{2}, 42; 15:18, 31^{2}; 16:1, 27; 17:5^{2}, 7^{2}; 18:17; 19:20; 20:12, 13, 14^{2}, 16, 17, 19, 20^{2}, 21, 23, 27; 21:5^{2}, 6^{3}, 7^{2}; 22:2^{3}, 9^{3}, 11, 15^{2}, 16, 18, 25; 23:17^{3}, 18, 20; 24:2, 9, 11, 12, 23; 25:31^{2}, 42^{2}, 45^{2}, 46, 55; 26:7, 17, 26, 36^{2}, 37, 39^{2}, 40^{3}, 41, 43^{2}, 44; 27:11

Nu 1:1, 18^{2}, 46, 50^{2}, 54; 2:2, 3, 16, 17^{2}, 24, 31^{2}, 34^{2}; 3:4^{2}, 6, 7, 8, 9, 10, 13, 31; 4:5, 7, 8, 9^{2}, 10, 11, 12^{2}, 13, 14^{3}, 15^{2}, 19^{2}, 20^{2}, 25, 26, 37, 41, 49^{2}; 5:2, 3, 7^{2}, 9; 6:7, 27; 7:3^{2}, 5, 9, 11; 8:11, 16, 21, 22, 24, 25; 9:1, 4, 5, 6^{2}, 11, 12^{2}, 18^{2}, 20^{2}, 21^{2}, 22, 23^{3}; 10:3, 4, 6, 8, 10, 13, 21, 28, 33, 34; 11:13, 16, 17, 21, 25, 26^{2}, 32^{2}, 34; 12:2, 4, 5; 13:2, 18, 19^{3}, 21, 22, 23^{3}, 25, 26, 27, 31, 32^{2}; 14:4, 7, 9, 11, 12, 14^{2}, 23, 27, 31, 32, 35^{2}, 40, 44; 15:25, 32, 33, 34, 38^{2}; 16:2, 3, 16, 18, 22, 27, 29, 30, 33^{2}, 34, 37, 38^{3}, 39^{2}, 42, 45, 49; 17:5, 9, 10; 18:2, 3^{3}, 4, 6, 9, 12, 13, 15, 17, 21, 22, 23^{2}, 24^{2}; 19:2, 17; 20:2, 6, 27, 29; 21:3, 4, 6, 11, 12, 13, 16, 18, 27, 32, 33, 35^{2}; 22:3, 5^{2}, 6, 7, 12, 14, 15, 16, 39; 24:6; 25:2, 18^{2}; 26:7, 9, 10, 41, 50, 55, 57, 61, 62, 63, 64, 65; 27:2, 21^{2}; 28:19, 31; 29:8, 13; 30:9; 31:7^{2}, 8^{2}, 10^{2}, 11, 12, 49, 52; 32:1, 5, 9^{3}, 11, 12, 16, 30^{2}, 38; 33:3, 6, 7^{2}, 8, 9^{2}, 10, 11, 12, 13, 14, 15, 16, 17, 18, 19, 20, 21, 22, 23, 24, 25, 26, 27, 28, 29, 30, 31, 32, 33, 34, 35, 36, 37, 41, 42, 43, 44, 45, 46, 47, 48, 49; 34:29; 35:2, 3, 12; 36:2, 3^{2}, 4, 6^{2}, 12

Dt 1:22, 24, 25, 39^{2}; 2:4, 12, 15, 21, 22; 3:20; 4:9, 10^{3}, 45, 46, 47; 5:28^{3}, 29, 31; 6:8; 7:4^{2}, 20, 23; 9:12^{2}, 14, 29; 10:5, 7, 11; 11:4, 18, 30; 12:30, 31^{2}; 14:7^{2}, 12, 19; 15:6; 16:16, 18; 17:5, 9, 10^{2}, 11^{3}; 18:1, 2, 3, 8, 17^{2}; 19:14; 20:8, 9, 11, 18^{2}, 20; 21:2, 7, 15, 18, 20; 22:6, 17, 19, 21, 22, 24, 28; 23:3, 4^{2}; 25:1^{2}; 26:12; 28:7, 10, 22, 41, 46, 60; 29:22, 25, 26^{2}; 31:12^{2}, 16, 17^{2}, 18^{2}, 20^{2}, 21, 24, 30; 32:5^{2}, 7, 16^{2}, 17^{2}, 20, 21^{2}, 24, 27, 28, 29^{3}, 37; 33:3, 9, 10^{2}, 11, 17^{2}, 19^{3}

Jos 1:15, 16; 2:1, 3, 4, 7^{2}, 8, 13, 21, 22, 24; 3:1^{2}, 3, 6, 7, 13, 15; 4:8, 9, 14^{2}, 16, 18, 20; 5:4, 5^{2}, 6, 7^{2}, 8^{3}, 11, 12^{2}; 6:5, 11, 14^{2}, 15^{2}, 19, 20, 21, 23, 24^{2}; 7:3^{2}, 4, 5, 11^{3}, 12, 21, 22, 23, 24, 25, 26; 8:5, 6^{3}, 9, 13, 14, 15, 16, 17, 19^{2}, 20^{2}, 21, 22^{3}, 23, 24^{3}, 29, 31, 33; 9:2, 4^{2}, 6, 8, 9, 13, 16^{4}, 24, 26; 10:2, 5, 11^{4}, 20, 23, 24^{2}, 26, 27^{2}, 34, 35, 36, 37, 39; 11:4^{2}, 5, 7, 8^{2}, 11, 14^{3}, 19, 20^{2}; 14:4, 5; 16:10; 17:4, 10, 13, 16^{2}, 18^{2}; 18:4^{2}, 5; 19:2, 49, 50, 51; 20:3, 4, 5, 7, 8; 21:2, 9, 11, 12, 13, 20, 21, 27, 43; 22:6, 9, 10, 15^{2}, 28; 23:12, 13; 24:1, 2, 7, 8, 22, 30, 32, 33

Jdg 1:4, 5^{3}, 6, 7, 10, 16, 17, 19, 20, 22, 24, 25^{2}, 28, 32, 34, 35; 2:3, 5^{2}, 9, 12, 13, 14, 15^{2}, 17^{4}, 19^{2}, 22; 3:4^{2}, 6, 12, 24^{2}, 25^{3}, 26, 28, 29; 4:12, 24; 5:7, 8, 11^{2}, 14, 19, 20, 23, 30^{2}; 6:3, 4, 5^{4}, 29^{3}, 35; 7:11, 19^{2}, 20, 21, 25^{3}; 8:1, 5, 18^{3}, 19, 24^{2}, 25^{2}, 28, 35; 9:3, 4, 7, 8, 9, 25, 27, 31, 34, 36, 41, 42, 46, 51, 55; 10:4, 8, 16; 11:2, 6, 13, 17, 18, 21, 22; 12:4, 6^{2}; 14:9, 11^{2}, 13, 14, 15; 15:6, 10, 11, 12, 13^{2}; 16:2, 7, 11, 23, 24^{2}, 25^{3}, 30; 17:4; 18:2^{3}, 3^{3}, 5, 7^{2}, 8, 9, 12^{2}, 13, 15, 19, 21, 22, 23^{2}, 26, 27^{2}, 28^{2}, 29, 31; 19:4, 5, 6, 8^{2}, 11, 14^{2}, 15, 21, 22, 25^{2}; 20:5, 6, 10^{3}, 22, 31, 32, 34, 36^{3}, 38, 39^{2}, 41, 42^{2}, 43, 45^{2}, 48^{2}; 21:5, 8, 12^{2}, 14^{3}, 17, 19, 20, 23^{2}, 24

Ru 1:2, 4^{2}, 7, 9, 10, 11, 13, 14, 19^{4}, 22; 2:4, 9^{2}, 21, 22; 4:2, 17

1Sa 1:9^{2}, 19, 25; 2:4, 5^{2}, 12, 14, 15, 20, 22, 25, 27, 30, 34; 4:2^{2}, 4, 6^{2}, 7^{2}, 9, 10; 5:2, 3^{2}, 4, 7, 8^{3}, 9^{2}, 10^{2}, 11; 6:3, 4^{2}, 6^{2}, 11, 12, 13^{2}, 14, 16, 18, 19, 21; 7:6, 7, 10, 11, 13; 8:2, 6, 7^{3}, 8^{3}, 19; 9:4^{4}, 5, 10, 11^{2}, 12, 13, 14^{2}, 20, 25, 26^{2}, 27; 10:2, 4, 5, 10, 14, 21, 22, 23, 27; 11:5^{2}, 7, 9^{2}, 11^{2}, 15^{2}; 12:4, 5, 9^{2}, 10, 21; 13:5, 6, 21; 14:9, 10, 11, 13, 15, 16, 17, 20, 21, 22^{2}, 25, 30, 31, 33^{2}, 36; 15:3, 6, 9, 15, 18; 16:6; 17:11, 19, 24, 31, 51, 53; 18:6, 7, 8^{2}, 20, 27, 30; 19:1, 8, 20^{2}, 21^{2}, 22, 24; 20:11, 41; 21:11; 22:1, 4, 11, 17; 23:1^{2}, 12, 13, 18, 24, 25, 28; 25:7, 8, 9, 11, 13, 16, 26, 40, 43; 26:12^{2}, 19^{3}; 27:11; 28:4, 8, 25^{2}; 29:5; 30:2, 4, 10, 11^{2}, 12, 16^{2}, 19, 20, 21^{3}, 22^{2}, 24; 31:7^{2}, 8, 9, 10^{2}, 13

2Sa 1:12^{2}, 23^{3}; 2:3, 4^{3}, 13, 16^{2}, 24, 28, 29, 32^{2}; 3:21, 23, 32; 4:6^{3}, 7^{2}, 8, 12^{2}; 5:3, 8, 11, 17, 21; 6:3, 4, 6, 13, 17; 7:10; 8:14; 9:2; 10:5, 6, 13, 14, 15^{2}, 16, 19^{2}; 11:1, 10, 20; 12:18, 19, 20; 13:9, 30, 32; 14:6, 7^{2}, 11; 15:11^{2}, 24, 29, 30^{2}, 36; 16:22; 17:8^{2}, 10, 17^{2}, 18^{2}, 20^{4}, 21^{2}, 22, 29; 18:3^{2}, 17; 19:3, 8, 14, 17; 20:3, 7, 8, 14, 15^{2}, 18^{3}, 22^{2}; 21:5, 9^{2}, 13, 14^{2}; 22:18, 19, 39^{2}, 42, 45^{2}, 46; 23:6, 7, 9; 24:3, 5, 6^{2}, 7, 8^{2}, 13, 17

1Ki 1:1, 3, 7, 23, 25, 32, 39, 41, 44, 45, 53; 2:7, 39; 3:22, 24, 28^{2}; 4:21, 27, 28; 5:1, 6, 12, 14, 17, 18; 6:8, 10, 27; 7:28, 47; 8:1, 4, 8^{3}, 9, 25, 30, 33, 35^{2}, 36, 40^{2}, 42, 43, 46^{2}, 47^{2}, 50^{2}, 51, 52, 66; 9:8, 9^{2}, 12, 22, 28; 10:25, 29; 11:2^{2}, 18^{3}, 24, 29, 33, 41; 12:3, 7^{2}, 8, 13, 20, 24, 27; 13:11, 13, 20, 25, 27, 30; 14:15, 18, 19, 22^{2}, 23, 24, 29; 15:7, 8, 22, 23, 31; 16:5, 13^{2}, 14, 17, 20, 27; 18:6, 10^{2}, 26^{3}, 28, 29, 34^{2}, 39^{2}, 40; 19:10, 14, 21; 20:6^{2}, 12, 15, 16, 17, 18^{2}, 20, 23^{2}, 25, 29, 32, 33; 21:12, 13, 14; 22:1, 6, 32^{2}, 33, 37, 38, 39, 45, 48

2Ki 1:6, 8, 18; 2:2, 4, 6, 7, 8^{2}, 9, 11, 14, 15^{2}, 16, 17^{3}, 18, 20; 3:9, 21, 22, 23^{2}, 24^{3}, 25^{3}, 26, 27; 4:39, 40^{4}, 41, 42, 43^{2}, 44; 5:23, 24; 6:4^{2}, 14, 16^{2}, 18, 20^{4}, 22, 23^{2}, 25; 7:3, 4^{2}, 5^{2}, 6, 7, 8, 9, 10^{3}, 11, 12^{3}, 13^{2}, 14, 15; 8:23; 9:12, 13, 21, 27, 33, 35^{2}, 36, 37; 10:4, 7, 8, 13, 14, 16, 20, 21, 24, 25, 26, 27, 34, 35; 11:2, 7, 9, 12^{2}, 16, 17, 18, 19, 20; 12:10^{2}, 11^{2}, 14, 15^{3}, 19, 21; 13:5, 6, 8, 9, 12, 20, 21^{3}; 14:12, 15, 18, 19^{2}, 20, 28; 15:6, 7, 11, 15, 16, 21, 26, 31, 36; 16:5, 18, 19; 17:8, 9, 10, 11, 12, 14, 15^{3}, 16, 17, 19, 21, 22, 24, 25, 26^{3}, 28^{2}, 29, 32, 33^{2}, 34^{3}, 40^{2}, 41; 18:10, 12, 17^{3}, 18, 20, 27, 34, 35; 19:3, 18^{2}, 26^{2}, 31, 35^{2}, 37; 20:7, 14^{2}, 15^{2}, 18^{2}, 20; 21:8, 9, 14, 15, 17, 25; 22:7, 14, 17^{2}, 19, 20; 23:1, 9, 18, 28; 24:5; 25:1, 6^{2}, 7, 14^{2}, 23^{2}, 26

1Ch 4:14, 23, 28, 39, 40^{2}, 43; 5:10^{2}, 16, 19, 20^{3}, 21, 22, 23, 25; 6:31, 32^{2}, 33, 55, 56, 57, 65, 67^{2}; 7:2, 4, 21; 8:6; 9:1, 18, 23, 27, 28, 33, 38; 10:7^{2}, 8, 9^{2}, 10, 12; 11:3, 7, 14, 19; 12:1^{2}, 2, 15^{2}, 19, 21^{2}, 33, 39, 40; 13:2, 4, 7, 9; 14:11^{2}, 12^{2}, 16; 15:26; 16:1^{2}, 20; 17:9; 19:6, 7, 11, 14, 15, 16^{2}, 17, 19^{2}; 20:4, 8; 21:3^{2}, 5, 17^{2}; 22:4; 23:11, 24, 25, 26, 32; 24:4, 5; 25:8; 26:6, 8, 13, 14, 27, 31; 28:21; 29:8, 9^{2}, 21, 22, 29

2Ch 1:17^{2}; 2:17; 3:13; 4:6^{2}, 20; 5:5, 9^{2}, 10, 13; 6:21, 24, 26^{2}, 27, 31^{2}, 32, 34, 36^{2}, 37^{2}, 38^{2}; 7:3, 9^{2}, 22; 8:9, 15, 18; 9:24, 28, 29; 10:3, 7^{2}; 11:4, 17^{2}; 12:2, 6, 7^{2}, 8^{2}, 15; 13:11^{2}, 13, 14, 18; 14:1, 7, 10, 13^{3}, 14^{2}, 15; 15:4, 9^{2}, 10, 11^{2}, 12, 14, 15; 16:4, 6, 11, 14^{2}; 17:9, 10; 18:5, 9, 10, 14, 29, 31^{2}, 32; 19:8, 10; 20:2, 4, 8, 10^{2}, 11, 16, 20^{2}, 21, 22^{2}, 23, 24^{2}, 25^{4}, 26^{2}, 27, 28, 29, 34, 36, 37; 21:17, 20; 22:4, 9^{4}; 23:2^{2}, 6^{3}, 11, 15^{2}, 16, 20, 21; 24:7, 8, 9, 10, 11^{2}, 13, 14^{3}, 16, 18, 19^{2}, 21, 23, 24^{2}, 25^{4}, 26, 27; 25:10, 12, 13, 20, 21, 22, 26, 27^{2}, 28; 26:18, 20, 23^{2}; 27:7, 9; 28:5, 6, 15, 18, 23^{2}, 26, 27^{2}; 29:7, 15, 16, 17^{4}, 18, 19, 21, 22^{5}, 23^{2}, 24, 29, 30^{2}, 34; 30:1, 3, 5^{3}, 9, 10, 14^{2}, 15, 16^{2}, 18, 22, 23; 31:1, 4, 5, 6, 7, 8, 11, 18; 32:3, 18^{2}, 19, 21, 32, 33; 33:8, 10, 18, 19, 20; 34:4, 9^{3}, 10^{2}, 11, 13, 14, 16, 17, 22^{2}, 24, 25^{2}, 28, 33; 35:1, 6, 11, 12^{3}, 13^{2}, 14, 15, 24, 25, 27; 36:8, 16, 19, 20

Ezr 1:6; 2:59^{3}, 62^{2}, 63, 68, 69; 3:3^{2}, 4, 6, 7^{2}, 8, 10, 11^{2}; 4:2, 6, 11, 13, 15, 23; 5:5^{2}, 7,

APNDX

30, 37[2], 38, 39; 10:9, 10, 22, 24, 39, 45, 46, 48; 11:2, 18[2], 19, 20, 22, 23, 26, 30; 12:10[3], 15[2], 16[2], 19, 20, 25; 13:2, 3[2], 4[2], 5[3], 6[2], 13, 14[2], 17, 21, 27[3], 28[2], 29[2], 45, 48, 51; 14:1, 3, 6, 7, 11, 12, 14, 18[2], 21[2], 23[3], 24[2], 25[2], 26[2], 27[2], 28; 15:2, 3[2], 4[3], 11, 13, 20, 23, 30[4], 31[2], 33[2], 36, 39; 16:3, 4[2], 6, 7[2], 8, 19, 23[2], 31, 32, 37[2], 38[3], 39, 40[3]; 17:1[2], 6[2], 8[2], 9[2], 11, 13, 15[2], 19, 27[2], 32; 18:3, 6, 20, 26; 19:2, 3, 4, 5[2], 6, 10, 16, 19, 26, 28[2], 29, 32, 33, 34; 20:8, 12, 18, 37, 38[2]; 21:5, 6, 12, 20[3], 21[2], 22, 24[2], 25[2], 27, 29[2], 30, 31, 32[2]; 22:2[2], 9[2], 18, 19, 22, 23, 24, 25, 29; 23:4, 12[2], 13, 14, 20, 21[3], 24, 28, 30, 32, 33; 24:12, 13[2], 14, 15, 19, 20; 25:7, 14, 17, 18; 26:5, 10, 18, 20, 30, 31[2]; 27:1, 12, 13[2], 17[3], 18, 27, 28[2], 29, 30[2], 36[2], 38[2], 39[3], 40[2], 41, 43, 44; 28:1[2], 2, 4, 6[3], 10, 15, 17, 18, 21, 23, 25[2], 27[2], 28

Ro 1:20, 21[2], 22, 28, 32; 3:9[2], 12[2], 13, 17; 4:7, 11, 14, 17; 5:17; 8:5[2], 8, 14, 23; 9:6, 7[2], 8, 26, 32[2]; 10:1, 2, 3, 14[5], 15[2], 16, 18; 11:3[2], 8[2], 10, 11[2], 20, 23[2], 28[2], 31; 13:2, 6; 15:21[2], 27; 16:18

1Co 2:8[2], 14[2]; 3:20; 7:8, 9, 14, 29[2], 30[6], 31; 9:13[2], 14, 24, 25; 10:4, 5, 6, 11, 18, 20, 33; 11:19; 12:19, 20; 13:8[2]; 14:7, 21, 23, 34, 35; 15:10, 11, 18, 23, 29[2], 35, 48[2]; 16:4, 15, 17, 18

2Co 5:15; 6:16; 8:3, 5, 23; 9:4, 5, 13; 10:10, 12; 11:12[2], 22[3], 23; 12:21

Gal 1:23, 24; 2:4, 6[2], 7, 9[2], 10, 12, 14; 3:7, 9; 4:17[2]; 5:12, 21, 24; 6:12[2], 13[2]

Eph 4:14; 5:31

Php 3:18; 4:2, 22

Col 1:16, 20; 3:21; 4:9

1Th 1:9; 2:14, 15, 16; 5:3[2], 7[2]

2Th 2:10[2], 11, 12; 3:12

1Ti 1:3, 7[2], 20; 2:15; 3:13; 5:7, 11[2], 12, 13[2], 17, 24, 25; 6:2[3], 9, 10, 17, 18[2], 19

2Ti 1:15; 2:10, 14, 16, 23, 26; 3:6, 9; 4:3[2], 4

Tit 1:10, 11, 13, 16[3]; 2:3, 4, 10; 3:8, 9, 14

Heb 1:4, 11[2], 12, 14; 2:11; 3:10[2], 11, 16, 18, 19; 4:3, 5, 6; 6:6[2]; 7:5[2], 23[2]; 8:9, 10, 11; 9:15; 10:1, 2; 11:13, 14[2], 15[3], 16, 23[2], 29, 30, 35, 37[3], 38, 40; 12:10, 19, 20, 25; 13:10, 17[3], 24

Jas 2:7, 12; 3:3, 4[2]; 4:1; 5:15

1Pt 1:12; 2:8, 12[3]; 3:1, 2, 10, 16[2]; 4:4, 6

2Pt 1:8, 21; 2:3, 10[2], 12, 13[3], 14, 18[2], 19[2], 20[2], 21; 3:4, 5, 16[2]

1Jn 2:19[7]; 4:1, 5[2]

2Jn 1

3Jn 7

Jude 10[3], 11, 12[2], 15, 18, 19

Rev 1:3, 7, 15; 2:2, 9, 22, 24, 27; 3:4[2], 9; 4:4, 8[2], 11; 5:9; 6:4, 9, 10, 11[2]; 7:13, 14, 15, 16; 8:7, 11; 9:4, 5[2], 8, 9, 10, 11, 19, 20, 21; 11:2, 3, 6, 7, 9, 10, 11, 12[2], 18; 12:6, 11[2]; 13:4[2], 14; 14:3, 4[3], 5, 11, 12, 13; 15:3; 16:4, 6[2], 9, 10, 14, 15; 17:8[2], 14; 18:9, 18, 19; 19:3, 9; 20:4[2], 6, 9, 13; 21:3, 26, 27; 22:4, 5[2], 14[2]

THINE

Gen 13:14; 14:20, 23; 15:4[3]; 20:7; 21:18; 22:2, 12[2], 16; 30:27; 31:12, 32; 38:18; 40:13; 44:18; 46:4; 47:19; 48:6; 49:8

Ex 4:2, 4, 6, 7, 17, 21; 5:16; 7:15, 19; 8:3[2], 5; 9:14, 22; 10:12, 21; 13:9[2], 16[2]; 14:16, 26; 15:7, 16, 17; 17:5; 20:24; 22:30; 23:1, 4, 12[2], 22[2], 27; 32:13; 34:9

Lev 2:13; 10:15; 18:10, 14; 19:17; 27:23, 27

Nu 5:20; 10:35; 18:9, 11, 13[2], 14, 15, 16, 18[2], 20; 22:30[2], 32; 27:18, 20

Dt 2:24; 3:21, 27[2]; 4:9, 19, 39; 5:14[2]; 6:5, 6, 7, 8[2], 19; 7:13, 16, 17, 19, 24, 26; 8:2, 5, 14, 17; 9:4, 5, 26, 29; 10:21; 11:14, 19, 20; 12:17, 18; 13:6, 8, 9, 17; 14:23, 25, 26, 28, 29; 15:3[2], 7[2], 8, 9, 10[2], 11, 16; 16:10, 15[2]; 18:4, 21; 19:13, 14, 21; 20:1, 13, 14; 21:10[2], 12, 13; 22:2, 8; 23:9, 14, 20, 24, 25; 24:19[2], 20; 25:12, 14, 19; 26:4, 11, 12, 16; 28:7, 8, 12, 20, 25, 31[4], 32[2], 34, 40, 48, 53[2], 55, 57, 67[2]; 29:3; 30:2, 4, 6[2], 7, 9, 10, 17; 33:10, 29; 34:4

Jos 2:3, 17, 20; 6:2; 7:13; 8:18; 9:25; 10:8; 14:9; 17:18[2]

Jdg 4:7, 9, 14; 5:31; 6:39; 7:7, 9, 11; 8:6[2], 15; 9:29; 11:36; 12:1; 16:15; 18:19; 19:5, 6, 8, 9, 22; 20:28

Ru 2:9, 10, 11, 13[2]; 3:9[2]; 4:11, 15

1Sa 1:11[3], 16, 18; 2:31[2], 32, 33[4], 36; 9:19, 20; 14:7, 19; 15:17, 28; 16:1; 17:28, 46; 20:3, 29, 30; 21:3, 8; 22:14; 23:4; 24:4[2], 10, 15, 18, 20; 25:6, 8[2], 24[3], 25, 26[2], 27, 28, 29, 31, 35, 41; 26:8[2], 21; 27:5; 28:16, 17, 21, 22

2Sa 1:14, 25; 3:21; 4:8; 5:19; 7:3, 9, 11, 16, 21; 11:10; 12:10, 11[2]; 13:10; 14:7, 8, 12, 17, 19; 16:4; 17:11; 19:6, 27, 28; 20:17; 22:28; 24:13, 16, 17

1Ki 1:12, 13, 17, 53; 2:26, 37, 44[2]; 3:11, 20, 26; 8:18[2], 24, 29, 31, 51, 52, 53; 11:22; 12:16; 13:8, 18; 14:12; 17:11; 19:10, 14; 20:4, 6[2], 13, 28; 21:7, 19, 22; 22:34

2Ki 4:2, 16, 29; 7:2, 19; 8:1, 8; 9:1; 10:5, 15[2]; 13:16; 14:10; 19:16[2], 22; 20:1, 15, 17; 22:19, 20

1Ch 4:10; 12:18[2]; 14:10; 17:2, 8, 10, 17, 19, 22; 21:12, 15, 17, 24; 29:11[3], 12[2], 14, 16[3]

2Ch 1:11[2]; 6:8[2], 15, 20, 22, 40[2], 42; 9:5; 10:16; 16:7, 8; 18:33; 19:3; 20:6; 25:15, 19[2]; 26:18; 34:27, 28

Ezr 7:14, 25

Neh 1:6[2], 11; 6:8

Job 1:11, 12; 2:5, 6, 9; 5:25; 7:8, 17; 10:3, 7, 8, 13, 17; 11:4, 6, 13[2], 14, 17; 13:21, 24; 14:3, 15; 15:5, 6[2], 12; 22:5, 22, 30; 35:7; 40:14; 41:8

Ps 2:8; 6:1; 7:6; 8:2; 10:12, 17; 16:10; 17:2, 6; 20:4; 21:8[2], 9, 12, 13; 26:6, 8; 27:14; 28:9; 31:2, 5, 22; 37:4; 38:2, 3; 39:10; 44:3; 45:5, 10[2]; 50:20, 21; 51:19; 56:7; 66:3; 68:9, 23; 69:9, 24; 71:2, 16; 74:1, 2, 4, 16[2], 22, 23; 77:15, 17; 79:1; 83:2; 84:3, 9; 85:3, 4, 5; 86:1, 16; 88:2; 89:10, 11[2], 38, 51[2]; 90:7, 11; 91:8; 92:9[2]; 93:5; 94:5; 102:2, 10; 103:3; 104:28; 106:5; 110:1, 2; 116:16; 119:91, 94, 173; 128:2, 3; 130:2; 132:10; 138:7, 8; 139:5, 16, 20; 144:6, 7; 145:16

Prv 2:2[2], 10; 3:1, 3, 5[2], 7, 9, 21, 27; 4:4, 9, 20, 21[2], 25[2]; 5:1, 9, 15[2], 17; 6:4[2], 21, 25; 7:2, 3, 25; 20:13; 22:17[2]; 23:4, 5, 12[2], 15, 17, 18, 19, 26[2], 33[2]; 24:17[2], 27; 25:7, 10, 21; 27:2[2], 10; 30:32

Ecc 5:2, 6; 7:18, 22; 11:6, 9[2]

Song 4:9, 10; 6:5; 7:4, 5[2]; 8:6[2]

Isa 6:7; 12:1; 14:13; 26:11; 30:20, 21; 33:17, 18, 20; 37:17[2], 23; 38:1; 39:4, 6; 42:6; 43:24; 44:3; 45:14; 47:6, 8, 9, 10, 12; 48:8; 49:18, 20, 21; 51:22; 54:2, 5; 57:10; 58:7, 8, 13[3]; 60:4, 5, 17, 20; 62:8; 63:2, 17, 19; 64:2

Jer 2:2, 19, 22, 37[2]; 3:2, 13; 4:1, 14, 18; 5:3, 17[2]; 6:9; 7:29; 9:6; 10:24; 13:22[2], 27[2]; 15:14; 17:4[2]; 18:23; 20:4, 6; 22:17[2]; 25:28; 28:7; 30:14, 15[2], 16; 31:16, 17, 21; 32:7[2], 8[2], 19; 34:3; 36:14; 38:12, 17; 40:4; 42:2; 43:9; 49:16; 51:13

Lam 2:14, 16, 17[2], 18, 19, 21; 3:56; 4:22[2]

Ezk 3:10[2], 18, 20, 24; 4:7; 5:1, 9, 11; 6:11; 7:3, 4, 8, 9; 8:5; 10:2; 16:6, 7, 12[2], 15, 22, 27, 30, 31[2], 39, 41, 43[2], 46, 51[2], 52, 54, 58, 61; 21:14; 22:4, 14[2], 16; 23:25, 27, 31, 34; 24:16, 17, 26; 25:6; 27:6, 10, 11, 15; 28:2[2], 4, 5, 6, 17, 18; 33:8; 35:11[2]; 37:17, 20; 38:4, 12; 39:3; 40:4[3]; 44:5[2], 30

Dan 2:38; 3:17; 4:19, 27; 5:22; 9:16, 18[2], 19; 10:12

Hos 9:7; 13:9; 14:1

Joel 2:17

Oba 3, 15

Jna 1:8; 2:7

Mic 4:10, 13; 5:9[3], 12, 13; 7:14

Nah 3:13

Hab 3:8[2], 11, 13, 15

Zep 3:15, 16

Zec 3:4; 5:5; 13:6

Mt 5:25, 33, 43; 6:2, 4, 13, 17, 22, 23; 7:3, 4[2], 5; 9:6; 12:13; 18:9; 20:14, 15; 22:44; 25:25

Mk 2:11; 3:5; 9:47; 12:36

Lk 4:7; 5:24, 33; 6:41, 42[3]; 7:44; 8:39; 11:34[2]; 12:19, 58; 13:12; 15:31; 19:22, 42, 43; 20:43; 22:42

Jn 2:17; 8:10; 9:10, 17, 26; 17:5, 6, 9, 10[2], 11; 18:35

Act 2:27; 4:30; 5:3, 4[2]; 8:22, 37; 10:4, 31; 13:35; 23:35

Ro 10:6, 9; 11:3; 12:20

1Co 10:29

1Ti 5:23

Phlm 19

Heb 1:10, 13

Rev 3:18

THIS

Gen 2:23; 3:13, 14; 4:14; 5:1, 29; 6:15; 7:1; 9:12, 17; 11:6; 12:7, 12, 18; 15:2, 4, 7, 18; 17:10, 21; 18:25, 32; 19:5, 9, 12, 13, 14[2], 20, 21[2], 34, 37, 38; 20:5, 6, 10, 11, 13; 21:10[2], 26, 30; 22:14, 16; 23:19; 24:5, 7, 8, 12, 41, 42, 58, 65; 25:31, 32, 33; 26:3, 10, 11, 33; 28:15, 16, 17[3], 20, 22; 29:25, 27, 33, 34; 30:31; 31:1, 13, 38, 43, 48[2], 51[2], 52[5]; 32:2, 10, 19, 32; 33:8; 34:4, 14, 15; 35:17, 20; 36:24; 37:6, 10, 19, 22, 32; 38:21, 22, 23, 28, 29; 39:9[2], 11, 19; 40:12, 14, 18; 41:9, 24, 28, 34, 38, 39; 42:13, 18, 21, 28, 32; 43:10, 11, 29; 44:5, 7, 15, 29; 45:17, 19, 23; 47:23, 26; 48:4, 9, 15, 18; 49:28; 50:11, 20, 24

Ex 1:18; 2:6, 9, 12, 14, 15; 3:3, 12[2], 15[2], 21; 4:17; 5:22, 23; 7:17, 23; 8:19, 23, 32; 9:5, 14, 16, 18, 27; 10:6, 7, 17[2]; 12:2, 3, 12, 14, 17[2], 24, 25, 26, 42, 43; 13:3[2], 4, 5[2], 8, 10, 14; 14:5, 12; 15:1; 16:3[2], 8, 15, 16, 23, 32; 17:3, 4, 14; 18:14, 18[2], 23[2]; 21:31; 25:3; 26:13; 28:17; 29:1, 38, 42; 30:13, 31; 32:1, 9, 12, 13, 21, 23, 24, 29, 31; 33:12, 13, 17; 34:11; 35:4; 37:8; 38:15, 21; 39:10

Lev 4:20; 6:9, 14, 20, 25; 7:1, 11, 35, 37; 8:5, 34; 9:6; 10:3, 19; 11:46; 12:7; 13:59; 14:2, 32, 54, 57; 15:3, 32; 16:29, 34; 17:2, 7; 23:27, 34; 24:10; 25:13; 26:16, 18, 27

Nu 4:4, 24, 28, 31, 33; 5:19, 22, 29, 30, 31; 6:13, 20, 21, 23; 7:17, 23, 29, 35, 41, 47, 53, 59, 65, 71, 77, 83, 84, 88; 8:4, 24; 9:3; 11:6, 11, 12, 13, 14, 31; 13:17, 27; 14:2, 3, 8, 11, 13, 14[2], 15, 16, 19[2], 27, 29, 32, 35[2]; 15:13; 16:6, 21, 45; 18:9, 11, 27; 19:2, 14; 20:4, 5, 10, 12, 13; 21:2, 5, 17; 22:1, 4, 6, 8, 17, 19, 24, 30; 23:23; 24:14, 23; 26:9; 27:12; 28:3, 10, 14, 17, 24; 29:7; 30:1; 31:21; 32:5, 15, 19, 20, 22, 32; 34:2, 6, 7, 9, 12, 13, 15; 35:5, 14; 36:6

Dt 1:1, 5[2], 6, 10, 31, 32, 35; 2:3, 7, 18, 22, 25, 30; 3:8, 12, 14, 18, 26, 27, 28; 4:4, 6[2], 8[2], 20, 22, 26, 32, 38, 39, 40, 41, 44, 46, 47, 49; 5:1, 3[2], 24, 25, 28; 6:6, 24; 7:11; 8:1, 11, 17, 18, 19; 9:1, 3, 4, 6, 7, 13, 27; 10:8, 13, 15; 11:2, 4, 5, 8, 13, 26, 27, 28, 32; 12:8; 13:11, 18; 15:2, 5, 10, 15; 17:18, 19; 18:3, 16; 19:4, 9; 20:3; 21:7, 20; 22:14, 16, 20, 26; 24:18, 22; 26:3, 9[2], 16, 17, 18; 27:1, 3, 4, 8, 9, 10, 26; 28:1, 13, 14, 15, 58[3], 61; 29:4, 7, 9, 10, 12, 14[2], 15[2], 18, 19, 20, 21, 24[2], 27[2], 28, 29; 30:2, 8, 10, 11[2], 15, 16, 18, 19; 31:2[2], 7, 9, 11, 12, 16, 19[2], 21, 22, 24, 26, 27, 30; 32:27, 29, 34, 44, 46[2], 47, 49; 33:1, 7; 34:4, 6

Jos 1:2[2], 4, 6, 8, 11, 13, 14, 15; 2:14, 17, 18, 20; 3:4, 7; 4:3, 6, 9, 22; 5:4, 9[2]; 6:25, 26; 7:7, 25, 26[2]; 8:20, 22, 28, 29, 33; 9:1, 12, 20, 24, 27; 10:13, 27; 11:6; 12:7; 13:2, 7, 13, 23, 28, 29; 14:10[2], 11, 12, 14; 15:1, 4, 12, 20, 63; 16:8, 10; 18:14, 19, 20, 28; 19:8, 16, 23, 31, 39, 48; 22:3, 7, 16[3], 17, 18, 22, 24, 29, 31[2]; 23:8, 9, 13, 14, 15; 24:15, 27

Jdg 1:21, 26; 2:2[2], 20; 4:14; 6:13, 14, 20, 24, 26, 29[2], 39[2]; 7:4[2], 14; 8:9; 9:18, 19, 29, 38; 10:4, 15; 11:27, 37; 12:3; 13:23; 15:6, 7, 11, 18, 19; 16:18, 28; 18:3, 12, 24; 19:11, 23[2], 24, 30; 20:3, 9, 12, 16; 21:3, 6, 11, 22

Ru 1:19; 2:5; 3:13, 18; 4:7[2], 9, 10, 12, 14

1Sa 1:3, 27; 2:20, 23, 34; 4:6, 14; 5:5; 6:9, 18, 20; 8:8, 11; 9:6, 13, 16, 17, 24; 10:11, 19, 27; 11:2, 13; 12:2, 5, 8, 16, 19, 20; 14:10, 28, 29, 33, 38[2], 45[2]; 15:14, 16, 28; 16:8, 9, 12; 17:10, 17, 25, 26[2], 27, 32, 33, 36, 37, 46[2], 47, 55; 18:21, 24; 20:2, 3, 21; 21:5, 11, 15[2]; 22:8, 13, 15; 23:26; 24:6, 10, 16, 18, 19; 25:21, 24, 25, 27, 31, 32, 33; 26:8, 16, 17, 19, 21, 24; 27:6; 28:10, 18[2]; 29:3[2], 4, 5, 6, 8; 30:8, 15[2], 20, 24, 25

2Sa 1:17; 2:1, 5, 6[2]; 3:8[2], 38, 39; 4:3, 8; 6:8; 7:6, 17, 19[2], 27, 28; 8:1; 10:1; 11:3, 11, 25; 12:5, 6, 11, 12, 14, 21; 13:1, 12, 16, 17, 20, 32; 14:3, 13, 15, 19, 20[2], 21; 15:1, 6, 20; 16:9, 11, 12, 17, 18; 17:1, 6, 7, 16; 18:18, 20[2], 31; 19:5[2], 6[3], 7, 14, 20, 21, 22[3], 35, 42; 21:18; 22:1; 23:5, 17[2]; 24:3

1Ki 1:25, 27, 30, 41, 45, 48; 2:23, 24, 26; 3:6[2], 9, 10, 11, 17, 18, 19, 22, 23; 4:24[2]; 5:7[2]; 6:12; 7:8, 28, 37; 8:8, 24, 27, 29[2],

30, 31, 33, 35, 38, 42, 43, 54, 61; 9:3, 7, 8^3, 9, 13, 15, 21; 10:12; 11:10, 11, 27, 39; 12:6, 7^2, 9, 10, 19, 24, 27^2, 30; 13:3, 8, 16, 33, 34; 14:2, 15; 17:21, 24; 18:36, 37; 19:2; 20:6, 7, 9, 12, 13^2, 24, 28, 34, 39; 22:20, 27

2Ki 1:2; 2:19, 22; 3:16, 18, 23; 4:9, 12, 13, 16, 36, 43; 5:6, 7, 18^2, 20; 6:11, 18, 19^2, 24, 28, 31, 32, 33; 7:1, 2, 9, 18; 8:5^2, 8, 9, 13, 22; 9:1, 11, 25, 26, 27, 34, 36, 37; 10:2, 6, 27; 11:5; 14:7, 10; 15:12; 16:6; 17:12, 23, 34, 41; 18:19, 21, 22, 25^2, 30; 19:3, 21, 29^2, 31, 32, 33, 34; 20:6^2, 9, 17; 21:7, 15; 22:13^2, 16, 17, 19, 20; 23:3^2, 21, 23, 27; 24:3

1Ch 4:41, 43; 5:26; 11:11, 19; 13:11; 16:7; 17:5, 15, 17, 19, 26; 18:1; 19:1; 20:4; 21:3, 7, 8, 22; 22:1^2; 26:30; 27:6; 28:7, 8, 19^2; 29:5, 14, 16, 18

2Ch 1:10^2, 11; 2:4; 5:9; 6:15, 18, 20^2, 21, 22, 24, 26, 29, 32, 33, 34, 40; 7:12, 15, 16, 20, 21^3, 22; 8:8; 10:6, 7, 9, 19; 11:4; 14:11; 16:10; 18:19, 26; 19:10; 20:1, 2, 7, 9^2, 12, 15, 17, 26, 35; 21:10, 18; 23:4; 24:4, 18; 25:9, 16; 28:22; 29:9, 28; 30:9; 31:1, 10; 32:9, 15, 20, 30; 33:7, 14; 34:21, 24, 25, 27, 28, 31; 35:19, 20, 21, 25

Ezr 1:9; 3:12; 4:8, 10, 11^2, 13, 15^2, 16^3, 19, 21, 22; 5:3^3, 4^2, 5, 6^2, 8, 9, 12, 13, 17^2; 6:7^2, 8, 11^2, 12, 13, 15, 16, 17; 7:6, 11, 17, 24, 27; 8:1, 23, 35, 36; 9:2, 3, 7^2, 10, 13, 15^2; 10:2, 4, 5, 9, 13^2, 14, 15

Neh 1:11^2; 2:2, 18, 19; 3:7; 5:10, 11, 12, 13^2, 16, 18^2, 19; 6:4, 12, 16; 7:7; 8:9, 10; 9:1, 10, 18, 32, 36, 38; 13:4, 6, 14, 17, 18^2, 22, 27

Est 1:1, 17, 18; 4:14^2, 15; 5:4, 13; 6:3, 9; 7:6; 9:4, 13, 21, 26^2, 29

Job 1:3, 22; 2:10, 11; 3:1; 4:6; 5:27; 8:19; 9:22; 10:13; 12:9; 13:1; 17:8; 18:21; 19:26; 20:2, 4, 29; 21:2; 27:13; 31:11, 28; 33:12; 34:16; 35:2; 36:21; 37:1, 14; 38:2; 42:16

Ps 2:7; 7:3; 11:6; 12:7; 17:14; 18:ttl; 22:31; 24:6, 8, 10; 27:3; 32:6; 34:6; 35:22; 41:11; 44:17, 21; 48:14; 49:1, 13; 50:22; 51:4; 52:7; 56:9; 62:11; 68:16; 69:31, 32; 71:18; 73:16; 74:2, 18; 77:10; 78:21, 32, 54, 59; 80:14; 81:4, 5; 87:4, 5, 6; 92:6; 95:10; 102:18; 104:25; 109:20, 27; 113:2; 115:18; 118:20, 23, 24; 119:50, 56, 91; 121:8; 132:14; 149:9

Prv 6:3; 7:14; 22:19

Ecc 1:10, 13, 17; 2:1, 10, 15, 19, 21, 23, 24, 26; 4:4^2, 8, 16; 5:10, 16, 19; 6:2, 5, 9, 12; 7:6, 10, 18^2, 23, 27, 29; 8:9, 10, 14; 9:1^2, 3, 9, 13; 11:6; 12:13

Song 3:6; 5:16^2; 7:7; 8:5

Isa 1:12; 3:6; 5:25; 6:7, 9, 10; 8:6, 11, 12, 20; 9:5, 7, 12, 16, 17, 21; 10:4; 12:5; 14:4, 16, 26^2, 28; 16:13; 17:14; 20:6; 22:14, 15; 23:7, 8, 13; 24:3; 25:6, 7, 9^2, 10; 26:1; 27:9^2; 28:11, 12^2, 14, 29; 29:11, 12, 13, 14; 30:7, 9, 12, 13, 21; 36:4, 6, 7, 10^2, 15; 37:3, 22, 30^2, 32, 33, 34, 35; 38:6^2, 7^2, 19; 39:6; 41:20; 42:22, 23; 43:9, 21; 45:21; 46:8; 47:8; 48:1, 6^2, 16, 20; 50:11; 51:21; 54:9, 17; 56:2, 12; 58:4, 5, 6; 59:21; 63:1^2; 66:2, 14

Jer 1:10, 18; 2:12, 17; 3:4, 10, 25; 4:8, 10, 11, 18, 28; 5:7, 9, 14^2, 20, 21, 23, 29; 6:6, 19, 21; 7:2, 3, 6, 7, 10, 11, 14, 16, 20, 23, 25, 28, 33; 8:3, 5; 9:9, 12, 15, 24; 10:18, 19; 11:2, 3, 5, 6, 7, 8, 14; 13:9, 10^2, 12, 13, 25; 14:10, 11, 13, 15, 17; 15:1, 20; 16:2, 3^2, 5, 6, 9, 10^2, 13, 21; 17:24, 25^2; 18:6; 19:3, 4^2, 6, 7, 8, 11^2, 12^2, 15; 20:5; 21:4, 6, 7, 8, 9, 10; 22:1, 3, 4^2, 5, 8^2, 11, 12, 16, 21, 28, 30; 23:6, 26, 32, 33, 38; 24:5, 6, 8; 25:3, 9, 11, 13, 15, 18; 26:1, 6^2, 9^2, 11^2, 12^2, 15, 16, 20^2; 27:1, 16, 17, 19, 22; 28:3^2, 4, 6, 7, 15, 16; 29:10, 16, 28, 29, 32; 30:17, 21; 31:23, 26, 33; 32:3, 8, 14^2, 15, 20^2, 22, 23, 28, 29^2, 31^2, 35, 36, 37, 41, 42^2, 43; 33:4, 5, 10, 12, 16, 24; 34:2, 8, 22; 35:14, 16; 36:1, 2, 7, 29^2; 37:8, 10, 18, 19; 38:2, 3, 4^4, 16, 17, 18, 21, 23; 39:16; 40:2^2, 3, 4, 16; 42:2, 10, 13, 18, 19, 21; 44:2, 4, 6, 7, 10, 22, 23^2, 29^2; 45:4; 46:7, 10; 50:17, 25; 51:6, 59, 62, 63; 52:28

Lam 2:15, 16, 20; 3:21; 5:17

Ezk 1:5, 23, 28; 2:3; 3:1, 3; 4:3; 5:5; 6:10; 8:5, 15, 17; 10:15, 20; 11:2, 3, 6, 7, 11, 15; 12:10, 23; 16:20, 43, 44, 49; 17:7; 18:2, 3; 19:14; 20:27, 29, 31; 21:11, 26; 23:11, 38; 24:2^2, 24; 31:18; 32:16; 33:33; 36:22, 32, 35, 37; 39:8; 40:10^2, 12^2, 21, 26, 34, 37, 39, 41, 45, 48^2, 49; 41:4, 22; 43:12^2, 13; 44:2; 45:1, 2, 3, 13, 16; 46:3, 20; 47:6, 12, 13, 14, 15, 17, 18, 19, 20, 21; 48:10, 12, 29

Dan 1:14; 2:12, 18, 30, 31, 32, 36, 38, 47; 3:16, 29; 4:17, 18, 24^2, 28, 30; 5:7, 15, 22, 24, 25, 26; 6:3, 5, 28; 7:6, 7, 8, 16, 24; 8:16; 9:7, 13, 15; 10:8, 11, 17^2; 11:18; 12:5

Hos 5:1; 7:10, 16

Joel 1:2^2; 3:9

Am 3:1; 4:1, 5, 12; 5:1; 7:3, 6^2; 8:4, 8; 9:12

Oba 20

Jna 1:7, 8, 10, 12, 14; 4:2

Mic 1:5; 2:3^2, 10, 11; 3:9; 5:5

Hab 1:11

Zep 1:4; 2:10, 15

Hag 1:2, 4; 2:3, 7, 9^2, 14^2, 15, 18, 19

Zec 2:4; 3:2; 4:6, 9; 5:3^2, 5, 6^2, 7, 8; 6:15; 8:6, 11, 12; 14:12, 15, 19

Mal 1:9, 13; 2:1, 4, 12, 13; 3:9; 4:3

Mt 1:18, 22; 3:3, 17; 6:9, 11; 7:12; 8:9^2, 27; 9:3, 28; 10:23; 11:10, 14, 16, 23; 12:6, 7, 23, 24, 32, 41, 42, 45; 13:15, 19, 22, 28, 40, 54^2, 55, 56; 14:2, 15; 15:8, 11, 12, 15; 16:18, 22; 17:5, 20, 21; 18:4; 19:5, 11, 26; 20:14; 21:4, 10, 11, 21^2, 23, 38, 42, 44; 22:20, 33, 38; 23:36; 24:14, 21, 34, 43; 26:8, 9, 12, 13^3, 26, 28, 29, 31, 34, 39, 42, 56, 61, 71; 27:8, 19, 24, 37, 47, 54; 28:14, 15^2

Mk 1:27^2; 2:7, 12; 4:13, 19, 41; 5:32, 39; 6:2^2, 3, 35; 7:6, 29; 8:12^2, 38; 9:7, 21, 29; 10:5, 7, 30; 11:3, 23, 28; 12:7, 10, 11, 16, 30, 31, 43; 13:19, 30; 14:4, 9^2, 22, 24, 27, 30^2, 36, 58, 69, 71; 15:39

Lk 1:18, 29, 34, 36, 43, 61, 66; 2:2, 11, 12, 15, 17, 34; 3:20; 4:3, 6, 21^2, 22, 23, 36; 5:6, 21; 6:3; 7:4, 8, 17, 27, 31, 39^2, 44, 45, 46, 49; 8:9, 11, 14, 25; 9:9, 13, 35, 45, 48, 54; 10:5, 11, 20, 28; 11:29, 30, 31, 32, 50, 51; 12:18, 20, 39, 41, 56; 13:6, 7, 8, 16^2; 14:9, 30; 15:2, 3, 24, 30, 32; 16:2, 8, 24, 26, 28; 17:6, 18, 25; 18:1, 5, 9, 11, 14, 23, 30, 34; 19:9^2, 14, 42; 20:2, 9, 14, 17, 19, 34; 21:3, 23, 32, 34; 22:15, 17, 19^2, 20, 23, 34, 37, 42, 53, 56, 59; 23:2, 4, 5, 14^2, 18, 38, 41, 47, 52; 24:21

Jn 1:15, 19, 30, 34; 2:11, 12, 19, 20, 22; 3:19, 29; 4:13, 15, 20, 21, 27, 29, 42, 54; 5:1, 28; 6:6, 14, 29, 34, 39, 40, 42, 50, 51, 52, 58^2, 60^2, 61; 7:8^2, 15, 25, 26, 27, 31, 36, 39, 40^2, 41, 46, 49; 8:4, 6, 23^2, 40; 9:2, 3, 8, 9, 16, 19, 20, 24, 29, 33, 39; 10:6, 16, 18, 41; 11:4, 9, 26, 37^2, 39, 47, 51; 12:5, 6, 7, 18^2, 25, 27^3, 30, 31^2, 33, 34; 13:1, 28, 35; 14:30; 15:12, 13, 25; 16:11, 17, 18, 30; 17:3; 18:17, 29, 34, 36^2, 37^2, 38, 40; 19:12, 20, 28, 38; 20:22, 30; 21:1, 14, 19^2, 21, 23, 24

Act 1:6, 11, 16, 17, 18, 25; 2:6, 12, 14, 16, 29, 31, 32, 33, 37, 40; 3:12^2, 16^2; 4:7, 9, 10, 11, 17, 22; 5:4, 20, 24, 28^2, 37, 38^2; 6:3, 13^2, 14^2; 7:4, 6, 7, 29, 35, 37, 38, 40, 60^2; 8:10, 19, 21, 22, 29, 32, 34; 9:2, 13, 21^2, 22, 36; 10:16, 17, 30; 11:10; 13:17, 23, 26, 33, 34, 38, 48; 15:2, 6, 15, 16, 23; 16:18, 36; 17:3, 18, 19, 23, 30, 32; 18:10, 13, 18, 21, 25; 19:5, 10, 17, 25, 26, 27, 40^2; 20:26, 29; 21:11, 23, 28^3; 22:3^2, 4, 22, 26, 28; 23:1, 9, 13, 17, 18, 25, 27; 24:2, 5, 10, 14, 21^2, 25; 25:5, 24; 26:2, 16, 22, 26, 29, 31, 32; 27:10, 21, 23, 33, 34; 28:4, 9, 20^2, 22, 26, 27

Ro 1:26; 2:3; 3:26; 4:9; 5:2; 6:6; 7:24; 8:18; 9:9^2, 10, 17; 10:6; 11:5, 8, 25, 27; 12:2; 13:6^2, 9^2; 14:9, 13; 15:9, 28^2; 16:22

1Co 1:12, 20^2; 2:6^2, 8; 3:12, 18, 19; 4:11, 13, 17; 5:2, 3, 10; 6:3, 4; 7:6, 7, 26, 29, 31^2, 35; 8:7, 9; 9:3, 10, 12^2, 17, 23; 10:28; 11:10, 17, 20, 22, 24^2, 25^2, 26^2, 27^2, 30; 14:21; 15:6, 19, 34, 50, 53^2, 54^2; 16:12

2Co 1:12, 15; 2:1, 3, 6, 9; 3:10, 14, 15; 4:1, 4, 7; 5:1, 2, 4; 7:3, 11^2; 8:5, 7, 10, 14, 19, 20^2; 9:3, 4, 6, 12, 13; 10:7, 11; 11:10, 17; 12:8, 13; 13:1, 9

Gal 1:4; 3:2, 17; 4:25; 5:8, 14, 16; 6:16

Eph 1:21; 2:2; 3:1, 8, 14; 4:17; 5:5, 31, 32; 6:1, 12

Php 1:6, 7, 9, 19, 22, 25; 2:5; 3:13, 15

Col 1:9, 27; 2:4; 3:20; 4:16

1Th 2:13; 3:5; 4:3, 15; 5:18, 27

2Th 1:11; 2:11; 3:10, 14

1Ti 1:9, 15, 16, 18; 2:3; 3:1; 4:9, 16; 6:7, 14, 17

2Ti 1:15; 2:4, 19; 3:1, 6; 4:10

Tit 1:5, 13; 2:12; 3:8

Heb 1:5; 3:3; 4:4, 5; 5:4; 6:3; 7:1, 4, 21, 24, 27; 8:1, 3, 10; 9:8, 11, 15, 20, 27; 10:12, 16; 11:5; 12:27; 13:19

Jas 1:3, 25, 26, 27; 2:5; 3:15; 4:15

1Pt 1:25; 2:19, 20; 3:5; 4:6, 16; 5:12

2Pt 1:5, 13, 14, 17, 18, 20; 3:1, 3, 5, 8

1Jn 1:5; 2:25; 3:3, 8, 10, 11, 17, 23; 4:3, 9, 17, 21; 5:2, 3, 4, 6, 9, 11^2, 14, 20

2Jn 6^2, 7, 10

Jude 4, 5

Rev 1:3; 2:6, 24; 4:1; 7:9; 11:5, 15; 18:18; 20:5, 14; 22:7, 9, 10, 18^2, 19^2

THOU

Gen 2:16, 17^3; 3:9, 11^3, 12, 13, 14^4, 15, 16, 17^3, 18, 19^5; 4:6, 7^4, 10, 11, 12^2, 14; 6:14, 15, 16^4, 18^2, 19, 21^2; 7:1, 2; 8:16; 10:19^2, 30; 12:2, 11, 13, 18^2, 19; 13:9^2, 10, 14, 15; 14:23; 15:2, 3, 5, 15^2; 16:8^2, 11, 13; 17:1, 4, 8, 9^2, 15, 19; 18:5, 15, 23, 24, 28; 19:12^2, 15, 17^2, 19^2, 21, 22, 34; 20:3^2, 4, 6, 7^5, 9^3, 10^2, 13; 21:22, 23^3, 26, 29, 30; 22:2, 12^3, 16, 18; 23:6^2, 13; 24:3, 4, 5, 6^2, 7, 8, 14^2, 23, 31^2, 37, 38, 40, 41^3, 42, 44, 47, 58, 60^2; 25:18; 26:9, 10^2, 16, 29^2; 27:10, 18, 19, 20, 21, 24, 32, 33, 36, 38, 40^3, 43, 45; 28:1, 3, 4^2, 6, 13, 14, 15, 22; 29:14, 15^2, 25^2, 27; 30:15^2, 16, 26, 29, 30, 31^2; 31:13^2, 24, 26^2, 27, 28, 29^2, 30^3, 31, 32^2, 36, 37^2, 39, 41, 42, 43, 44^2, 50^2, 52; 32:10, 12, 17^2, 18, 26, 28, 29; 33:8, 9, 10; 35:1, 17; 37:8^2, 10, 15; 38:16^2, 17^2, 23, 29; 39:9, 17; 40:13^2; 41:15, 39, 40^2; 43:4, 5, 8, 9; 44:4, 18, 21, 23; 45:10^4, 11^2, 19; 46:30; 47:6, 8, 25, 30^2; 48:6; 49:3, 4^3, 6^2, 8, 9; 50:5

Ex 2:13, 14^2; 3:5, 10, 12, 14, 15, 18^2; 4:9^2, 10, 12, 13, 15, 16, 17^2, 21^2, 22, 23, 25, 26; 5:15, 22^2, 23; 6:1, 29; 7:2, 9, 15^2, 16^2, 17; 8:2, 10, 21, 22; 9:2, 14, 15, 17^2, 19, 29; 10:2, 3, 4, 7, 25, 28^2, 29; 12:44, 46; 13:5, 6, 8, 10, 12^3, 13^4, 14; 14:11^2, 15, 16; 15:7^2, 10, 12, 13^3, 16, 17^2, 26; 17:3, 5, 6; 18:14^2, 17, 18^3, 19^2, 20, 21, 23^2; 19:3, 6, 12, 23, 24^2; 20:3, 4, 5, 7, 9, 10^2, 13, 14, 15, 16, 17^2, 19, 22, 24, 25^4, 26; 21:1, 2, 14, 23; 22:18, 21, 23, 25^3, 26^2, 28, 29^2, 30^2; 23:1, 2^2, 3, 4^2, 5^2, 6, 7, 8, 9, 10, 11^2, 12^2, 14, 15^3, 16^2, 18, 19^2, 22, 24^2, 27, 30, 31, 32, 33; 24:1, 12; 25:11^2, 12, 13, 14, 16, 17, 18^2, 21^2, 23, 24, 25^2, 26, 28, 29^2, 30, 31, 37, 40; 26:1^2, 4^2, 5^2, 6, 7^2, 9, 10, 11, 14, 15, 17, 18, 19, 22, 23, 26, 29^2, 30, 31, 32, 33^2, 34, 35^2, 36, 37^2; 27:1, 2^2, 3^2, 4^2, 5, 6, 8, 9, 20; 28:1, 2, 3, 9, 11^2, 12, 13, 14, 15^3, 17, 22, 23, 24, 25, 26^2, 27, 30, 31, 33, 36, 37, 39^3, 40^3, 41, 42; 29:1, 2, 3, 4, 5, 6, 7, 8, 9^2, 10, 11, 12, 13, 14, 15, 16^2, 17, 18, 19, 20, 21, 22, 24, 25, 26, 27, 31, 34, 35^2, 36^4, 37, 38, 39^2, 41; 30:1^2, 3^2, 4^2, 5, 6, 12^3, 16, 18^3, 23, 25, 26, 29, 30, 31, 35, 36, 37; 31:13; 32:7, 11, 13, 21, 22, 32^2; 33:1^2, 3, 12^5, 16, 17^2, 20, 21, 23; 34:1, 10, 11, 12^2, 14, 15^2, 16, 17, 18^3, 20^4, 21^3, 22, 24, 25, 26^2, 27; 40:2, 3, 4^2, 5, 6, 7, 8, 9, 10, 11, 12, 13, 14, 15^2

Lev 2:4, 6, 8, 13^3, 14^2, 15; 6:21^2, 27; 8:3; 9:3; 10:9, 14; 13:55, 57, 58; 17:8; 18:7^2, 8, 9, 10, 11, 12, 13, 14^2, 15^2, 16, 17^2, 18, 19, 20, 21^2, 22, 23; 19:9^2, 10^3, 12, 13, 14, 15^2, 16^2, 17^2, 18^2, 19^2, 27, 32, 34; 20:2, 16, 19; 21:8; 22:23; 23:22^4; 24:5, 6, 7, 15; 25:3^2, 4, 5, 8, 9, 14, 15, 16^2, 17, 35, 36, 37, 39, 43, 44; 27:12

Nu 1:3, 49, 50; 3:9, 10, 15, 41, 47^2, 48; 4:23, 29, 30; 5:19^2, 20^2; 7:5; 8:2, 7, 8, 9^2, 10, 12, 13, 14, 15, 26; 10:2^2, 29, 31^2, 32; 11:11^2, 12^2, 15, 16, 17, 18, 21, 23, 29; 13:2, 27; 14:13, 14^3, 15, 17, 19; 15:5, 6, 7, 8, 10; 16:11, 13^2, 14^2, 15, 16^2, 17, 22, 37; 17:2, 3, 4, 10; 18:1^2, 2^2, 7, 10, 15^2, 16, 17^2, 20^2, 30; 20:8^4, 14, 18, 20; 21:2, 29, 34^2; 22:6^2, 12^2, 17, 20, 28, 29, 30, 32, 34, 35, 37; 23:5, 11^2, 13^2, 18, 27; 24:10, 11, 12, 21; 26:54^2; 27:7^2, 8, 13^2, 20; 28:3, 4^2, 7, 8^2, 21; 31:2, 26, 30

Dt 1:14, 31, 37; 2:4, 7, 18, 19, 28, 31, 37; 3:2^2, 21, 24, 27, 28; 4:9, 10, 19^2, 25, 29^3, 30^2, 33, 35, 36, 38, 40^2; 5:7, 8, 9, 11, 13, 14^3, 15, 17, 18, 19, 20, 21^2, 27^2, 31^2; 6:2^2, 5, 7^5, 8, 9, 10, 11^4, 12, 13, 18^2, 21; 7:1^2, 2^2, 3^3, 6, 11, 14, 15, 16^2, 17, 18, 19, 21, 22, 24^2, 25^2, 26^4; 8:2^2, 3, 5, 6, 9^3, 10^2, 11, 12, 13, 14, 17, 18, 19; 9:1, 2^2, 3, 4, 5, 6, 7^2, 12, 26^2, 28, 29; 10:2^2, 20^3; 11:1, 10^2, 14, 15, 19^4, 20, 29^2; 12:5, 13^2, 14^2, 15, 17^2, 18^4, 19^2, 20^2, 21^2, 22, 23^2, 24^2, 25^2, 26^2, 27^2, 28, 29^2, 30^2, 31, 32; 13:2, 3, 5,

6^{2}, 8^{3}, 9, 10, 12, 14, 15, 16, 18; **14**:2, 3, 21^{4}, 22, 23^{2}, 24, 25, 26^{4}, 27, 28, 29; **15**:1, 3, 5, 6^{3}, 7, 8, 9, 10^{3}, 11, 12, 13^{2}, 14^{2}, 15^{2}, 17^{2}, 18^{2}, 19^{2}, 20^{2}, 21, 22, 23^{2}; **16**:2, 3^{5}, 4, 5, 6^{2}, 7^{2}, 8^{2}, 9^{2}, 10^{2}, 11^{2}, 12^{3}, 13^{2}, 14^{2}, 15^{2}, 18, 19^{2}, 20^{2}, 21^{2}, 22; **17**:1, 4, 5, 7, 8, 9, 10^{2}, 11^{2}, 12, 14, 15^{3}; **18**:4, 9^{2}, 13, 14, 16, 21, 22; **19**:1, 2, 3, 7, 9^{2}, 13, 14^{2}, 19; **20**:1^{2}, 10, 12, 13, 14^{2}, 15, 16, 17, 19^{4}, 20^{3}; **21**:8, 9^{2}, 10^{2}, 11, 12, 13, 14^{5}, 21, 22, 23; **22**:1^{2}, 2^{3}, 3^{5}, 4^{2}, 6, 7^{2}, 8^{3}, 9^{2}, 10, 11, 12^{2}, 21, 22, 24, 26; **23**:6, 7^{3}, 12^{2}, 13^{3}, 15, 16, 18, 19, 20^{4}, 21^{2}, 22, 23^{3}, 24^{3}, 25^{3}; **24**:4, 7, 8, 10^{2}, 11^{2}, 12, 13, 14, 15, 17, 18^{2}, 19^{2}, 20^{2}, 21^{2}, 22^{2}; **25**:4, 12, 13, 14, 15^{2}, 18, 19^{2}; **26**:1, 2^{2}, 3, 5, 10^{2}, 11^{2}, 12, 13^{2}, 14, 15^{2}, 16, 17, 18, 19; **27**:2, 3^{3}, 4, 5^{2}, 6^{2}, 7, 8, 9, 10; **28**:1, 2, 3^{2}, 6^{4}, 8, 9, 10, 12^{2}, 13^{3}, 14, 15, 16^{2}, 19^{4}, 20^{4}, 21, 22, 24, 25, 27, 29^{3}, 30^{4}, 31^{2}, 33^{2}, 34^{2}, 36^{3}, 37, 38, 39, 40^{2}, 41^{2}, 43, 44^{2}, 45^{2}, 47, 48, 49, 51, 52, 53, 58^{2}, 60, 61, 62, 63, 64^{2}, 65, 66, 67^{4}, 68; **29**:12; **30**:1, 2, 5, 6, 8, 10^{2}, 12, 13, 14, 16^{2}, 17, 18, 19, 20^{4}; **31**:2, 3, 7^{2}, 11, 14, 16, 23; **32**:14, 15^{3}, 18, 50, 52^{2}; **33**:7, 8^{2}, 23, 29^{2}; **34**:4

Jos 1:2, 6, 7^{4}, 8^{4}, 9^{2}, 16^{2}, 18; **2**:17, 18^{3}, 20^{2}; **3**:8; **5**:13, 15; **6**:3; **7**:7, 9, 10, 13, 19, 25; **8**:1, 2^{2}; **10**:12^{2}; **11**:6; **13**:1, 6; **14**:6, 9, 12; **15**:18, 19; **17**:14, 15, 17^{2}, 18^{2}

Jdg 1:14, 15; **4**:8^{2}, 9, 20, 22; **5**:4^{2}, 12, 16, 21; **6**:4, 12, 14, 16, 17, 18, 23, 26, 36^{2}, 37^{2}; **7**:5, 10^{2}, 11; **8**:1^{3}, 18, 21, 22^{3}; **9**:8, 10, 12, 14, 32, 33^{3}, 36, 38^{2}; **10**:15; **11**:2^{2}, 8, 12^{2}, 23, 24, 25, 27, 30, 33, 35^{2}, 36; **12**:1, 5; **13**:3^{2}, 5, 7, 8, 11, 16^{3}, 18; **14**:3, 16^{2}; **15**:2, 11^{2}, 18; **16**:6, 10^{2}, 13^{3}, 15^{2}; **17**:2^{2}, 9; **18**:3^{2}, 19, 23, 25; **19**:9, 17^{2}

Ru 1:15, 16^{2}, 17; **2**:8, 9^{2}, 10, 11^{3}, 12, 13^{2}, 14, 19^{2}, 21, 22; **3**:2, 4^{3}, 5, 9^{2}, 10^{3}, 11^{2}, 15, 16, 18; **4**:4^{2}, 5^{2}, 6, 11

1Sa 1:8^{2}, 11, 14, 17, 23; **2**:16, 32; **3**:5, 6, 8, 9, 17; **4**:20; **8**:5; **9**:16, 21, 27; **10**:2^{3}, 3^{2}, 4, 5^{3}, 6, 7, 8^{3}; **12**:4^{2}; **13**:11^{2}, 13^{2}, 14; **14**:37, 43, 44; **15**:1, 7, 13, 17^{2}, 19, 23, 26, 28; **16**:1, 3^{2}, 4, 16; **17**:28^{4}, 33^{2}, 43, 45^{2}, 52, 56, 58^{2}; **18**:17, 21; **19**:3, 5^{2}, 11^{2}, 17; **20**:2, 8^{3}, 13, 14, 15, 18, 19^{3}, 21, 23, 30^{2}, 31; **21**:1, 9^{2}; **22**:12, 13^{2}, 16^{2}, 18, 23^{2}; **23**:17; **24**:4, 9, 11^{2}, 14, 17^{2}, 18^{3}, 19, 20, 21^{2}; **25**:6, 7, 17, 25, 31, 33, 34; **26**:11, 14^{2}, 15^{2}, 16, 25^{2}; **27**:8; **28**:1^{3}, 2, 9^{2}, 12^{2}, 13, 15^{2}, 16, 18, 19, 21, 22^{3}; **29**:4, 6, 7, 8, 9; **30**:8, 13^{2}, 15^{2}

2Sa 1:3, 5, 8, 13, 14, 25, 26; **2**:20, 26^{2}, 27; **3**:7, 8, 13^{3}, 21, 24^{2}, 25^{2}, 34; **5**:2^{3}, 6^{2}, 19, 23, 24^{2}, 25; **6**:22; **7**:5, 8, 9, 12, 18, 19, 20, 21, 22, 23, 24^{2}, 25^{2}, 27, 28^{2}, 29; **9**:2, 7, 8, 10^{2}; **10**:3, 11; **11**:10^{2}, 11, 19, 21, 25^{2}; **12**:7, 9^{2}, 10, 12, 13, 14, 21^{3}; **13**:4^{2}, 12, 13, 16; **14**:11, 13; **15**:2, 19^{2}, 20^{2}, 27, 33^{2}, 34^{2}, 35^{3}; **16**:2, 7^{2}, 8^{3}, 10, 17, 21; **17**:3, 6, 8, 11; **18**:3^{3}, 11^{2}, 13, 20^{3}, 21, 22^{2}; **19**:5, 6^{3}, 7, 13^{2}, 14, 19, 23, 25, 28, 29^{2}, 33, 38; **20**:4, 6, 9, 17, 19^{2}; **21**:4, 17^{2}; **22**:3, 26^{2}, 27^{2}, 28^{2}, 29, 36, 37, 40^{2}, 41, 44^{2}, 49^{2}; **24**:13

1Ki 1:6, 11, 12, 13, 14, 16, 17, 18, 20^{2}, 24, 27, 42; **2**:2, 3^{3}, 5, 8, 9^{3}, 13, 15, 22, 26^{3}, 31, 37^{3}, 42^{3}, 43, 44^{2}; **3**:6^{3}, 7, 8, 11, 13, 14; **5**:3, 6^{3}, 8, 9^{3}; **6**:12^{2}; **8**:18, 19, 24^{2}, 25^{2}, 26, 28, 29^{2}, 30^{3}, 32, 34^{2}, 35, 36^{3}, 39^{4}, 40, 43, 44^{2}, 45, 46, 48^{2}, 49, 51, 53^{3}; **9**:3^{2}, 4, 13; **11**:11, 22^{2}, 37, 38; **12**:4, 7, 10^{3}; **13**:8, 9, 14, 17^{2}, 18, 21; **14**:2, 5, 6^{2}, 8, 9, 12; **16**:2; **17**:4, 13, 18^{2}, 20, 24; **18**:7, 9, 11, 14, 17, 18^{2}, 36, 37^{2}; **19**:9, 13, 15, 16^{2}; **20**:5, 9, 13^{2}, 14, 22, 25, 34, 36^{2}, 39, 42; **21**:5, 7, 10, 19^{3}, 20^{2}, 22, 29; **22**:4^{2}, 11^{2}, 16, 19, 22, 25^{2}, 28, 30

2Ki 1:4^{2}, 6^{3}, 9, 16^{3}; **2**:3, 5, 10^{2}, 23^{2}; **3**:7^{2}; **4**:1, 2, 4^{3}, 7, 13^{2}, 16^{2}, 23, 29, 40; **5**:6, 8, 10, 13, 25; **6**:9, 12, 22^{3}; **7**:2, 19; **8**:1^{2}, 10, 12^{3}, 13, 14; **9**:2, 7, 18, 19, 25; **10**:5^{2}, 30; **13**:17^{2}, 19^{4}; **14**:10^{4}; **17**:26; **18**:14, 19, 20^{3}, 21, 23, 24; **19**:6, 10, 11^{2}, 15^{3}, 19^{3}, 20, 22^{2}, 23, 25^{2}, 28; **20**:1, 5, 9, 18, 19; **22**:18, 19^{2}, 20; **23**:17

1Ch 4:10^{2}; **11**:2^{3}, 5; **12**:18; **14**:10, 15^{2}; **17**:4, 7^{2}, 8, 11, 16, 17, 18, 19, 21, 22^{2}, 23^{2}, 25^{2}, 26, 27; **19**:3, 12; **21**:22; **22**:8^{3}, 11, 12, 13^{2}, 14; **28**:3^{2}, 9^{4}, 20; **29**:10, 11, 12, 17

2Ch 1:8, 9, 11^{2}; **2**:3, 16^{2}; **6**:8, 9, 15^{2}, 16^{2}, 17, 20^{2}, 21^{2}, 23, 25^{2}, 26, 27^{3}, 30^{3}, 31, 33, 34^{2}, 35, 36, 38^{2}, 39, 41; **7**:17; **9**:6; **10**:4, 7, 10^{3}; **13**:4; **14**:11; **16**:7, 8, 9^{2}; **18**:3^{2}, 10, 12, 15, 21^{2}, 24^{2}, 27, 29, 33; **19**:2, 3; **20**:6^{2}, 7, 9, 10, 11, 12, 15, 37; **21**:12, 15; **24**:6; **25**:8, 15, 16^{3}, 19^{5}; **26**:18; **34**:26, 27^{2}, 28; **35**:21

Ezr 4:13, 15, 16; **7**:14, 16, 17, 19, 20, 25; **9**:11, 13, 14^{2}, 15; **10**:12

Neh 1:6, 7, 8, 10; **2**:2, 4, 5, 6; **5**:12; **6**:6^{3}, 7, 8^{2}, 14; **9**:6^{4}, 7, 8, 10^{2}, 11^{2}, 12, 13, 15, 17^{2}, 19, 20, 21, 22, 23^{2}, 24, 27^{3}, 28^{3}, 29, 30^{2}, 31^{2}, 33^{2}, 34, 35^{2}, 36, 37

Est 3:3; **4**:13, 14^{3}; **5**:3, 14^{2}; **6**:10^{2}, 13^{2}

Job 1:7, 8, 10^{2}; **2**:2, 3^{2}, 9, 10; **4**:2, 3^{2}, 4, 5^{2}; **5**:1, 17, 21^{2}, 22^{2}, 23, 24^{2}, 25, 26, 27; **7**:12, 14, 17^{2}, 18, 19, 20^{2}, 21^{2}; **8**:2, 5, 6; **9**:12, 28, 31; **10**:2, 3^{2}, 4^{2}, 6, 7, 8, 9^{2}, 10, 11, 12, 13, 14^{2}, 15, 16^{2}, 17, 18; **11**:3, 4, 7^{2}, 8^{2}, 13, 15^{2}, 16, 17^{2}, 18^{3}, 19; **13**:22^{2}, 24, 25^{2}, 26, 27^{2}; **14**:3, 5, 13^{3}, 15^{2}, 16^{2}, 17, 19^{2}, 20^{2}; **15**:4, 5, 7^{2}, 8^{2}, 9^{2}, 13; **16**:3, 7, 8, 18; **17**:4^{2}, 14^{2}; **20**:4; **22**:3^{2}, 6, 7^{2}, 9, 11, 13, 15, 23^{3}, 24, 25, 26, 27^{2}, 28, 29; **26**:2^{2}, 3^{2}, 4; **30**:20^{2}, 21^{2}, 22^{2}, 23; **31**:24; **33**:5, 8, 12, 13, 32; **34**:16, 17, 18, 32, 33^{3}; **35**:2^{2}, 3, 5, 6^{3}, 7^{2}, 8, 14^{3}; **36**:17, 21, 23, 24; **37**:6, 15, 16, 18; **38**:3, 4^{2}, 5, 11, 12, 16^{2}, 17, 18^{2}, 20^{2}, 21^{2}, 22^{2}, 31, 32^{2}, 33^{2}, 34, 35, 39; **39**:1^{2}, 2^{2}, 10, 11^{2}, 12, 13, 19^{2}, 20; **40**:7, 8^{3}, 9^{2}; **41**:1^{2}, 2, 4, 5^{2}, 7; **42**:2, 4

Ps 2:7, 9^{2}; **3**:3, 7^{2}; **4**:1, 6, 7, 8; **5**:3, 4, 5, 6, 10, 11, 12^{2}; **6**:3; **7**:6, 7; **8**:2^{2}, 3, 4^{2}, 5, 6^{2}; **9**:2, 4^{2}, 5^{3}, 6^{2}, 10, 13; **10**:1^{2}, 13, 14^{3}, 15^{2}, 17^{3}; **12**:7^{2}; **13**:1^{2}; **16**:2^{2}, 5, 10^{2}, 11; **17**:3^{3}, 6, 7, 14; **18**:25^{2}, 26^{2}, 27, 28, 35, 36, 39^{2}, 40, 43^{2}, 48^{2}; **19**:12; **21**:2, 3^{2}, 4, 5, 6^{2}, 9, 10, 12^{2}, 13; **22**:1^{2}, 2, 3^{2}, 4, 9^{2}, 10, 15, 19, 21; **23**:4, 5^{2}; **25**:5, 7, 17; **27**:8, 9; **28**:1; **30**:1, 2, 3^{2}, 7^{2}, 10, 11^{2}; **31**:2, 3, 4, 5, 7^{2}, 8, 14, 19^{2}, 20^{2}, 22; **32**:5, 6, 7^{3}, 8; **35**:17, 22; **36**:6, 8; **37**:1, 3^{2}, 10, 34; **38**:15; **39**:5, 9, 11^{2}; **40**:5, 6^{3}, 9, 11, 17; **41**:2, 3, 10, 11, 12; **42**:5^{3}, 9, 11^{3}; **43**:2^{2}, 5^{2}; **44**:1, 2^{2}, 3, 4, 7, 9, 10, 11, 12, 13, 14, 19, 23, 24; **45**:2, 7, 11, 16; **48**:7; **49**:16, 18; **50**:15, 16^{2}, 17, 18^{2}, 19, 20^{2}, 21^{2}; **51**:4^{3}, 6^{2}, 8, 14, 15, 16^{2}, 17, 18, 19; **52**:1, 3, 4^{2}, 9; **53**:5; **55**:13, 23; **56**:2, 8^{2}, 13^{2}; **57**:5, 11; **59**:5, 8^{2}, 16; **60**:1^{3}, 2^{2}, 3^{2}, 4, 8, 10^{2}; **61**:3, 5^{2}, 6; **62**:5, 12; **63**:1, 7; **65**:2, 3, 4, 5, 8, 9^{4}, 10^{4}, 11; **66**:3, 10^{2}, 11^{2}, 12^{2}; **67**:4; **68**:7^{2}, 9^{2}, 10, 18^{3}, 28, 30, 35; **69**:5, 19, 26^{2}; **70**:5; **71**:3^{3}, 5^{2}, 6, 7, 17, 20, 21, 22, 23; **73**:18^{2}, 20^{2}, 23, 24, 27; **74**:1, 2^{3}, 11, 13^{2}, 14, 15^{2}, 16, 17^{2}; **76**:4, 7^{3}, 8, 10; **77**:4, 14^{2}, 15, 20; **79**:5, 11; **80**:1^{2}, 4, 5, 6, 8^{2}, 9, 12, 15, 17; **81**:7, 8, 9; **82**:8; **83**:1, 18; **85**:1^{2}, 2^{2}, 3^{2}, 5^{2}, 6; **86**:2, 5, 7, 9, 10^{2}, 13, 15, 17; **88**:5, 6, 7, 8^{2}, 10, 14^{2}, 18; **89**:2, 9^{2}, 10^{2}, 11, 12, 13, 17, 19, 26, 38^{2}, 39^{2}, 40^{2}, 42^{2}, 43, 44, 45^{2}, 46, 47, 49; **90**:1, 2^{2}, 3, 5, 8, 15, 17^{2}; **91**:4, 5, 8, 9, 12, 13^{2}; **92**:4, 8, 10; **93**:2; **94**:2, 12, 13; **97**:9^{2}; **99**:4^{2}, 8^{3}; **101**:2; **102**:10, 12, 13, 25, 26^{2}, 27; **104**:1^{2}, 6, 8, 9, 20, 24, 26, 27, 28^{2}, 29^{2}, 30^{2}, 35; **106**:4; **108**:5, 11^{2}; **109**:6, 21^{2}, 27, 28; **110**:1, 2, 3, 4; **114**:5^{4}, 7; **115**:9; **116**:8, 16; **118**:13, 21, 28^{2}; **119**:4, 12, 18, 21, 25, 26, 28, 32, 37, 49, 57, 65, 68, 75, 82, 84, 86, 90, 93, 98, 102, 114, 117, 118, 119, 132^{2}, 137, 138, 151, 152, 171; **120**:3; **123**:1; **128**:2^{2}, 5, 6; **130**:3, 4; **132**:8; **137**:8; **138**:2, 3, 7^{2}; **139**:1, 2^{2}, 3, 4, 5, 8^{2}, 13^{2}, 19; **140**:6, 7; **142**:3, 5, 7; **143**:10; **144**:3^{2}; **145**:15, 16

Prv 1:10, 15; **2**:1, 2, 3, 4, 5, 9, 20; **3**:4, 15, 23, 24^{3}, 28, 31; **4**:8, 12^{3}; **5**:2, 6^{2}, 9, 11, 19, 20; **6**:1^{2}, 2^{2}, 3, 6, 9^{2}, 22^{3}, 35; **7**:4; **9**:12^{4}; **14**:7; **19**:19^{2}, 20; **20**:13^{2}, 22; **22**:18, 21, 24, 25, 26, 27, 29; **23**:1, 2, 5, 6^{2}, 8^{2}, 13, 14, 17, 19, 31, 34, 35; **24**:1, 6, 10, 11, 12, 13, 14, 19, 21, 24; **25**:7, 8, 16^{2}, 22; **26**:4, 12; **27**:1, 22, 23, 27; **29**:20; **30**:4, 6^{2}, 10, 32^{2}; **31**:29

Ecc 5:1, 2, 4^{2}, 5^{2}, 6, 7, 8; **7**:10^{2}, 16, 17^{2}, 18, 21, 22; **8**:4; **9**:9^{2}, 10; **10**:17; **11**:1, 2, 5^{2}, 6, 9; **12**:1

Song 1:7^{3}, 8^{2}, 15^{3}, 16; **2**:17; **4**:1^{3}, 7, 9^{2}, 16; **5**:9^{2}; **6**:1, 4; **7**:6; **8**:1, 12, 13, 14

Isa 1:26; **2**:6; **3**:6^{2}; **7**:3, 16; **9**:3, 4; **12**:1^{3}, 6; **14**:3, 4, 8, 10^{2}, 12^{2}, 13, 15, 19, 20^{2}, 29, 31; **16**:4; **17**:10^{2}, 11^{2}; **22**:1, 2, 8, 16^{3}, 18; **23**:2, 4, 12^{3}, 16^{2}; **25**:1^{2}, 2, 4, 5; **26**:3, 7, 12^{2}, 14, 15^{4}, 20; **27**:8; **29**:4, 6; **30**:19, 22^{2}, 23; **33**:1^{4}, 2, 19^{3}; **36**:4, 5^{3}, 6, 7, 8, 9; **37**:6, 10, 11^{2}, 16^{3}, 20^{2}, 21, 23^{2}, 24, 26^{2}, 29; **38**:1, 12, 13, 16, 17^{2}; **39**:7, 8; **40**:27, 28^{2}; **41**:8, 9^{2}, 10, 12, 14, 15, 16^{2}; **42**:20; **43**:1, 2^{3}, 4^{2}, 22^{2}, 23^{2}, 24^{4}, 26^{2}; **44**:2, 17, 21^{3}, 26, 28; **45**:3, 4, 5, 9, 10^{2}, 15; **47**:1, 5^{2}, 6^{2}, 7^{2}, 8, 10^{3}, 11^{3}, 12^{3}, 13, 15; **48**:4, 5, 6^{2}, 7^{2}, 8^{3}, 17, 18; **49**:3, 6^{2}, 9, 18, 20^{2}, 21, 23; **51**:9, 10, 12^{2}, 16, 17, 21, 22, 23; **53**:10; **54**:1^{2}, 3, 4^{4}, 6, 11, 14^{3}, 17; **55**:5^{2}; **57**:6^{2}, 7^{2}, 8^{5}, 9, 10^{4}, 11^{3}, 13; **58**:3^{2}, 5, 7^{4}, 9^{3}, 10, 11, 12^{2}, 13, 14; **60**:5, 15, 16^{2}, 18; **62**:2, 3, 4^{2}, 8, 12; **63**:2, 14, 16^{2}, 17, 19; **64**:1^{2}, 3^{2}, 5^{2}, 7, 8^{2}, 12^{2}; **65**:5

Jer 1:5, 7^{2}, 11, 12, 13, 17; **2**:2, 17^{2}, 18^{2}, 19, 20^{2}, 21, 22, 23^{3}, 25, 27^{2}, 28, 33^{2}, 35^{2}, 36^{3}, 37^{2}; **3**:1, 2^{3}, 3^{2}, 4^{2}, 5^{2}, 6, 7, 12, 13, 19, 22; **4**:1^{3}, 2, 10, 14, 19, 30^{6}; **5**:3^{2}, 15, 17, 19; **6**:8, 27; **7**:16, 17, 27^{2}, 28; **8**:4; **10**:6, 24; **11**:3, 14, 15^{2}, 18, 21; **12**:1, 2^{2}, 3^{2}, 5^{4}; **13**:4, 12, 13, 21^{2}, 22, 25, 27; **14**:7, 8, 9^{2}, 17, 19^{2}, 22^{2}; **15**:2, 5, 6^{2}, 10, 14, 15, 17, 18, 19^{5}; **16**:2^{2}, 8, 10, 11; **17**:4^{2}, 14, 16, 17; **18**:22, 23; **19**:10; **20**:6^{5}, 7^{2}; **21**:8; **22**:2, 6, 15^{2}, 21^{2}, 22, 23, 25; **23**:33, 37; **24**:3; **25**:27, 28, 30; **26**:4, 8, 9; **27**:13; **28**:6, 7, 13^{2}, 15, 16^{2}; **29**:24, 25, 26, 27; **30**:10, 13^{2}, 15; **31**:4^{2}, 5, 18^{3}, 21, 22^{2}; **32**:3, 17, 18, 22, 23^{2}, 24^{2}, 25; **33**:3, 24; **34**:3^{2}, 4, 5, 14; **36**:6^{3}, 14, 17, 19, 29^{3}; **37**:13, 17, 20; **38**:15^{2}, 17^{2}, 18^{2}, 21, 23^{2}, 24, 25, 26; **39**:17^{2}, 18^{2}; **40**:14, 16^{2}; **43**:2; **44**:16; **45**:3, 4, 5^{2}; **46**:11^{2}, 19, 27, 28; **47**:5, 6^{2}; **48**:2, 7^{2}, 18, 27^{2}; **49**:4, 12^{3}, 16^{2}; **50**:24^{4}, 31; **51**:13, 20, 26, 61, 62^{2}, 63^{2}, 64

Lam 1:10, 21^{3}, 22; **2**:20, 21^{2}, 22; **3**:17, 42, 43^{3}, 44, 45, 56, 57^{2}, 58^{2}, 59^{2}, 60, 61; **4**:21; **5**:19, 20, 21, 22^{2}

Ezk 2:4, 6^{2}, 7, 8^{2}; **3**:1, 5, 6, 18^{2}, 19^{2}, 20, 21^{2}, 25^{2}, 26, 27; **4**:1, 3^{2}, 4^{3}, 5, 6^{2}, 7^{2}, 8^{2}, 9^{3}, 10^{2}, 11^{2}, 12^{2}, 15; **5**:1, 2^{3}, 3, 11; **7**:2, 7; **8**:6^{2}, 12, 13, 15^{2}, 17; **9**:8, 11; **11**:13; **12**:2, 3^{2}, 4^{2}, 5, 6^{3}, 9, 10; **13**:2, 17^{2}; **16**:4^{3}, 5^{2}, 6^{2}, 7^{3}, 8, 13^{4}, 15, 16, 17, 18, 19, 20^{3}, 21, 22^{2}, 24, 25, 26, 28^{3}, 29^{2}, 30, 31^{2}, 33, 34^{2}, 36, 37^{3}, 41, 43^{2}, 45^{2}, 47^{2}, 48^{2}, 51^{2}, 52^{5}, 54^{3}, 55, 58, 59, 61^{2}, 62, 63^{2}; **17**:9; **19**:1; **20**:4^{2}; **21**:6, 7^{2}, 14, 19^{2}, 25, 28^{2}, 30, 32^{2}; **22**:2^{4}, 3, 4^{4}, 8, 12^{2}, 13, 16^{2}, 24; **23**:21, 27, 28, 30^{2}, 31, 32^{2}, 33, 34^{2}, 35^{2}, 36, 40, 41; **24**:13^{2}, 16, 19^{2}, 25, 27^{2}; **25**:3, 6, 7; **26**:14^{2}, 17, 20, 21^{3}; **27**:2, 3^{2}, 7, 25, 33^{2}, 34, 36; **28**:2^{3}, 3, 4, 5, 6, 8, 9^{2}, 10, 12, 13^{2}, 14^{3}, 15^{2}, 16, 17, 18, 19^{2}; **29**:5^{2}, 7^{2}; **31**:2, 10, 18^{3}; **32**:2^{3}, 6, 9, 19^{2}, 28; **33**:7^{2}, 8^{2}, 9^{2}, 10, 12, 14, 27, 30, 32; **35**:4^{2}, 5, 6, 10, 11, 12^{2}, 15^{2}; **36**:1, 12^{2}, 13, 14, 15^{2}; **37**:3, 16, 18^{2}, 20; **38**:7^{3}, 8^{2}, 9^{3}, 10, 11, 13^{2}, 14, 15^{2}, 16, 17; **39**:1, 4^{2}, 5, 17; **40**:4^{2}; **43**:10, 19, 20^{2}, 21, 22, 23^{2}, 24, 25; **44**:6; **45**:3, 18, 20; **46**:13^{2}, 14; **47**:6

Dan 1:13; **2**:23^{2}, 26, 30, 31, 34, 37, 38, 41^{2}, 43, 45, 47; **3**:10, 12^{2}, 18; **4**:18^{2}, 20, 22, 25, 26, 32, 35; **5**:13, 16^{3}, 18, 22^{2}, 23^{3}, 27; **6**:12, 13, 16, 20; **8**:20, 26; **9**:7, 23; **10**:12, 19, 20; **12**:4, 13^{2}

Hos 2:16, 20, 23^{2}; **3**:3^{3}; **4**:5, 6^{3}, 15; **5**:3; **9**:1^{2}, 14; **10**:9, 13; **12**:6; **13**:4, 9, 10; **14**:1

Am 5:23; **7**:8, 12, 16^{2}, 17; **8**:2

Oba 2, 3, 4^{2}, 5, 10, 11^{2}, 12^{3}, 13^{2}, 14^{2}, 15

Jna 1:6, 8^{2}, 10, 14; **2**:2, 3, 6; **4**:2, 4, 9, 10^{2}

Mic 1:11, 13, 14; **2**:5, 7; **4**:8, 9, 10^{4}, 13; **5**:2^{2}, 12, 13; **6**:1, 14^{3}, 15^{4}; **7**:19, 20^{2}

Nah 1:14; **3**:8, 11^{3}, 16

Hab 1:2^{2}, 3, 12^{3}, 13^{2}; **2**:7, 8, 10, 15, 16^{2}; **3**:8, 9, 12^{2}, 13^{2}, 14, 15

Zep 3:7^{2}, 11^{3}, 15, 16

Zec 1:3, 12^{2}, 14; **2**:2, 11; **3**:7^{3}, 8; **4**:2, 5, 7^{2}, 9, 13; **5**:2; **6**:10; **13**:3^{2}

Mal 1:2; **2**:14

Mt 1:20, 21; **2**:6, 13; **3**:14; **4**:3, 6^{2}, 7, 9, 10^{2}; **5**:21, 22, 23, 25^{2}, 26^{2}, 27, 33, 36^{2}, 42, 43; **6**:2, 3, 5^{2}, 6^{3}, 17^{2}, 18; **7**:3, 4, 5^{2}; **8**:2^{2}, 3, 4, 8, 13, 19, 29^{2}, 31; **9**:27; **11**:3, 23, 25; **12**:37^{2}; **13**:10, 27, 28; **14**:28, 31^{2}, 33; **15**:5, 12, 22, 28; **16**:14, 16, 17, 18, 19^{2}, 23^{2}; **17**:4, 25, 27^{3}; **18**:15, 28, 32^{2}, 33; **19**:17^{2}, 18^{4}, 19, 21^{3}; **20**:12, 13, 21, 30, 31; **21**:16^{2}, 21^{2}, 23; **22**:12, 16^{3}, 17, 37, 39, 44; **23**:26, 37; **25**:20, 21^{3}, 22, 23^{2}, 24^{3}, 25, 26^{2}, 27; **26**:17, 25, 34, 39, 50, 53, 62, 63^{2}, 64, 68, 69, 70, 73, 75; **27**:4, 11^{2}, 13, 19, 40^{2}, 46

Mk 1:11, 24^{3}, 40^{2}, 41, 44; **3**:11; **4**:38; **5**:7^{2}, 8, 31^{2}, 35; **6**:22, 23, 25; **7**:11; **8**:29, 33; **9**:22, 23, 24, 25; **10**:18, 19, 21^{3}, 35, 47, 48, 51; **11**:21, 23^{2}, 28; **12**:14^{2}, 30, 31, 32, 34, 36; **13**:2; **14**:12^{2}, 30, 36, 37^{2}, 60, 61, 67, 68, 70^{2}, 72; **15**:2^{2}, 4, 29, 34

Lk 1:4^{2}, 13, 14, 20^{2}, 28^{2}, 30, 31, 42, 76^{2}; **2**:29, 31, 48; **3**:22; **4**:3, 7, 8^{2}, 9, 11, 12, 34^{3}, 41; **5**:10, 12^{2}, 13; **6**:41, 42^{4}; **7**:6, 19, 20, 43, 44^{2}, 45, 46; **8**:28, 45; **9**:54, 57, 60; **10**:15, 21, 26, 27, 28^{2}, 35, 36, 37, 40, 41; **11**:27, 45; **12**:19, 20^{2}, 41, 58^{3}, 59^{2}; **13**:9, 12, 15, 26; **14**:8^{2}, 9, 10^{2}, 12, 13, 14^{2}, 22; **15**:29, 30, 31; **16**:2, 5, 7, 25^{2}, 27; **17**:4, 6^{2}, 8; **18**:19, 20, 22^{3}, 38, 39, 41; **19**:17^{3}, 19, 21^{4}, 22^{2}, 23, 42^{2}, 44; **20**:2, 21^{2}, 39, 42; **22**:9, 32, 34^{2}, 42, 48, 58, 60, 61, 67, 70; **23**:3^{2}, 37, 39, 40^{2}, 42, 43; **24**:18

Jn 1:19, 21^{2}, 22^{2}, 25^{2}, 33, 38, 42^{2}, 48^{2}, 49^{2}, 50^{2}; **2**:10, 18^{2}, 20; **3**:2^{2}, 8, 10, 26; **4**:9, 10^{2}, 11^{2}, 12, 17, 18^{3}, 19, 27^{2}; **5**:6, 14; **6**:25, 30^{2}, 68, 69; **7**:3, 4, 20, 52; **8**:5, 13, 25, 33, 48, 52^{2}, 53^{2}, 57^{2}; **9**:17, 28, 34^{2}, 35, 37; **10**:24^{2}, 33, 36; **11**:3, 8, 21, 22, 26, 27, 32, 40^{2}, 41, 42^{2}; **12**:34; **13**:6, 7^{2}, 8^{2}, 27, 36^{3}, 38^{2}; **14**:5, 9^{2}, 10, 22; **16**:5, 29, 30^{2};

17:2^2, 3, 4, 5, 6^2, 7, 8^2, 9, 11, 12, 15^2, 18, 21^2, 22, 23^3, 24^3, 25, 26; **18:**9, 17, 21, 22, 23, 25, 33, 34, 35, 37^2; **19:**9, 10^2, 11, 12^2; **20:**13, 15^4, 29^2; **21:**12, 15^2, 16^2, 17^4, 18^6, 22

Act 1:6, 24^2; **2:**27^2, 28^2, 34; **4:**24, 27; **5:**4^2; **7:**28^2, 33; **8:**20, 21, 23, 30^2, 37^2; **9:**4, 5^2, 6^2, 17^2; **10:**6, 15, 33^2; **11:**3, 9, 14; **12:**15; **13:**10^3, 11, 33, 35, 47; **16:**31; **17:**19, 20; **21:**20, 21, 22, 24, 37, 38; **22:**7, 8^2, 14, 15^2, 16, 26, 27; **23:**3^2, 4, 5, 11^2, 19, 20, 21, 22^2; **24:**4, 10, 11; **25:**9, 10, 12^2, 22; **26:**1, 14, 15^2, 16, 24, 27^2, 28, 29; **27:**24; **28:**22

Ro 2:1^5, 3^2, 4, 17, 19, 21^4, 22^4, 23^2, 25^2; **3:**4^2; 7:7; **9:**19, 20^2; **10:**9^2; **11:**17, 18^2, 19, 20, 22^2, 24; **12:**20; **13:**3^2, 4, 9^6; **14:**4, 10^2, 15, 22

1Co 4:7^5; **7:**16^4, 21^2, 27^2, 28^2; **9:**9; **14:**16^2, 17; **15:**36^2, 37^2

Gal 2:14^2; **4:**7, 27^2; **5:**14; **6:**1

Eph 5:14; **6:**3

Col 4:17^2

1Ti 1:3, 18; **3:**15^2; **4:**6^3, 12, 16; **5:**18, 21; **6:**11, 12, 14

2Ti 1:6, 8^2, 13, 15, 18; **2:**1, 2^2, 3; **3:**10, 14^3, 15; **4:**5, 13, 15

Tit 1:5; **2:**1; **3:**8

Phlm 5, 12, 15, 17, 19, 21

Heb 1:5, 9, 10, 11, 12^2; **2:**6^2, 7^2, 8; **5:**5, 6; **7:**17, 21; **8:**5; **10:**5^2, 6, 8; **12:**5^2

Jas 2:3^2, 8, 11^3, 18, 19^2, 20, 22; **4:**11^2, 12

3Jn 2, 3, 5^2, 6^2

Rev 1:11, 19, 20^2; **2:**2^2, 4, 5^2, 6^2, 9, 10^2, 13^2, 14, 15, 20; **3:**1^2, 3^3, 4, 8, 10, 11, 15^2, 16, 17^2, 18^3; **4:**11^2; **5:**9^2; **6:**6, 10; **7:**14; **10:**11; **11:**17, 18; **15:**3, 4; **16:**5^2, 6; **17:**7, 8, 12, 15, 16, 18; **18:**14, 20; **19:**10; **22:**9

THY

Gen 3:10, 14^2, 15^2, 16^4, 17^3, 19; **4:**6, 9, 10, 11^2, 14; **6:**18^3; **7:**1; **8:**16^3; **12:**1^3, 2, 7, 13, 18, 19^2; **13:**8, 15, 16^2; **14:**20; **15:**1^2, 5, 13, 15, 18; **16:**5, 6^2, 9, 10, 11; **17:**5^2, 7^2, 8, 9, 10, 12, 13^2, 15, 19; **18:**3^2, 9, 10; **19:**12^2, 15^2, 17, 19^3; **20:**6, 13, 16; **21:**12^3, 13; **22:**2, 12, 16, 17^2, 18, 20; **23:**6^2, 11, 15; **24:**2, 5, 7, 14^3, 17, 19, 23, 40, 43, 44, 46, 51, 60; **25:**23^2, 31; **26:**3^2, 4^3, 9, 10, 24^2; **27:**3^3, 6^2, 9, 10, 13, 19^2, 20, 29^2, 31, 32^2, 35^2, 37, 39, 40^3, 42, 44, 45; **28:**2^2, 4, 13^2, 14^2; **29:**15, 18; **30:**14, 15, 27, 28, 29, 31, 32, 33, 34; **31:**3^2, 8^2, 13, 30, 31, 32, 37^2, 38^3, 41^3; **32:**4, 5, 6, 9^2, 10, 12, 18, 20, 27, 28, 29; **33:**5, 10^2; **35:**1, 10^3, 11, 12; **37:**10^2, 13, 14, 32; **38:**8^2, 11, 13, 18^3, 24; **39:**19; **40:**13, 19^2; **41:**40; **42:**10, 11, 13; **43:**28; **44:**7, 8, 9, 16, 18^2, 21, 23, 24, 27, 30, 31^2, 32, 33; **45:**9, 10^4, 11, 17; **46:**3, 30, 34; **47:**3, 4^2, 5^2, 6, 15, 29^2; **48:**1, 2, 4, 5, 6, 11^2, 18, 22; **49:**4, 8^3, 18, 25, 26; **50:**6, 16, 17^2, 18

Ex 2:9, 13; **3:**5^2, 6, 18; **4:**6, 7, 9, 10, 12, 14, 15, 16, 19, 23^2; **5:**15, 16^2, 23^2; **7:**1^2, 2, 9, 19; **8:**2, 3^5, 4^2, 5, 9^3, 10, 11^3, 16, 21^3, 23; **9:**3, 14^2, 15, 19, 30; **10:**2^2, 4, 6^4, 29; **11:**8; **12:**24; **13:**5, 7, 8, 9, 11, 13, 14; **14:**16; **15:**6^2, 7, 8, 10, 12, 13^3, 16, 17, 26; **17:**5; **18:**6^2; **20:**2, 5, 7, 9, 10^8, 12^4, 16, 17^3, 24^3, 25, 26; **22:**26, 28, 29^3, 30; **23:**6, 10, 11^3, 12^2, 13, 16^2, 17, 19^2, 25^2, 26^2, 31, 33; **28:**1, 2, 4, 41; **29:**12, 26; **32:**4, 7, 8, 11^2, 12^2, 13, 32; **33:**1, 5, 13^4, 15, 16^3, 18; **34:**9, 10, 16^2, 19, 20, 24^3, 26^2

Lev 2:5, 7, 13^3, 14^2; **5:**15, 18; **6:**6; **9:**7^2; **10:**9, 13^2, 14^4, 15; **16:**2; **18:**7^3, 8^2, 9^3, 10^2, 11^3, 12^2, 13^2, 14, 15^2, 16^2, 20, 21^2; **19:**9^2, 10^2, 12, 13, 14, 15, 16^2, 17^2, 18^2, 19^2, 27, 29, 32; **20:**19^2; **21:**8, 17; **23:**22^2; **25:**3^2, 4^2, 5^2, 6^4, 7^2, 11, 14^2, 15, 17, 25, 35, 36^2, 37^2, 39, 43, 44^2, 47, 53; **27:**2, 3^2, 4, 5, 6^2, 7, 8, 13, 15, 16, 17, 18, 19, 23, 25, 27

Nu 5:19, 20, 21^3, 22^3; **11:**11^2, 12, 15; **14:**13, 14, 19, 20; **16:**10, 11, 16; **18:**1^3, 2^3, 3, 7, 8, 9, 11^3, 19^3, 20; **20:**8, 14, 16, 17^2, 19; **21:**22^2, 34; **22:**32; **23:**3, 15; **24:**5^2, 11, 12, 14, 21^2; **27:**13^2; **31:**2, 49; **32:**4, 5^2, 25, 27, 31

Dt 1:21^2, 31; **2:**7^4, 27, 30^2; **3:**2, 24^5; **4:**3, 9^5, 10, 19, 21, 23, 24, 25, 29^3, 30, 31^2, 37, 40^3; **5:**6, 9, 11, 12, 13, 14^{10}, 15^2, 16^5, 20, 21^3; **6:**2^5, 3, 5^3, 7, 9^2, 10^2, 13, 15^2, 18, 20, 21; **7:**1, 2, 3^2, 4, 6^2, 9, 12^2, 13^7, 16, 18, 19^2, 20, 21, 22, 23, 25; **8:**2, 3, 4^2, 5, 6, 7, 10, 11, 13^4, 14, 16^2, 18^2, 19; **9:**3^2, 4, 5^3, 6^2, 7, 12, 26^2, 27, 29^3; **10:**9, 11, 12^5, 13, 14, 15, 20, 21^2, 22^2; **11:**1, 10^2, 12^2, 14^2, 15^2, 20, 29; **12:**1, 7, 13, 14^2, 15^3, 17^8, 18^8, 20^4, 21^5, 25, 26^2, 27^4, 28^2, 29, 31; **13:**5, 6^7, 10, 12^2, 16, 17, 18^2; **14:**2, 21^2, 22, 23^6, 24^2, 25, 26^3, 27, 28, 29^2; **15:**3, 4, 5, 6, 7^5, 9^2, 10^2, 11^4, 12, 14^4, 15, 17^2, 18, 19^5, 20^2, 21, 22; **16:**1^2, 2, 3, 4, 5^2, 6, 7^2, 8, 10^3, 11^7, 13^2, 14^6, 15^2, 16^2, 17, 18^3, 20, 21, 22; **17:**1^2, 2^3, 5, 8^2, 12, 14, 15^3; **18:**4^3, 5^2, 6, 9, 12, 13, 14, 15^2, 16; **19:**1^2, 2^2, 3^2, 8^4, 9, 10^2, 14^2; **20:**1, 13, 14, 16, 17; **21:**1, 2^2, 5, 8^2, 10, 11, 13, 23^2; **22:**1^2, 2^2, 3, 4, 5, 7, 8, 9^3, 12, 17; **23:**5^3, 6, 7, 13, 14^3, 16, 18^2, 19, 20^2, 21^2, 23^3, 24^3, 25^2; **24:**4, 9, 10, 13, 14^4, 18, 19^2, 21; **25:**3, 13, 15^2, 16, 19^2; **26:**1, 2^3, 3, 4, 5, 10^2, 11, 12, 13^3, 15^2, 16^2, 17, 19; **27:**2, 3^2, 5, 6^2, 7, 9, 10; **28:**1^2, 2, 4^5, 5^2, 7, 8^2, 9, 11^4, 12, 13, 15, 17^2, 18^4, 20, 23^2, 24, 26, 29, 31^2, 32^2, 33^2, 35^2, 36^2, 40, 42^2, 45, 46, 47, 48, 51^4, 52^6, 53^3, 55, 57, 58, 59^2, 62, 64, 65, 66^2; **29:**5^2, 11^4, 12^2, 13; **30:**1, 2^3, 3^3, 4, 5^3, 6^4, 7, 9^5, 10^3, 14^2, 16^2, 19, 20^4; **31:**3, 6, 11, 12^2, 14, 16, 27^2; **32:**6, 7^2, 50^2; **33:**3^3, 8^3, 9^2, 10^2, 18^2, 25^3, 26, 27, 29^2; **34:**4

Jos 1:5, 8^2, 9, 17, 18^2; **2:**18^4, 19; **5:**15^2; **7:**9, 10; **8:**1, 18; **9:**8, 9^2, 24^2; **10:**6^2; **14:**9^2; **24:**12^2

Jdg 1:3; **5:**12, 14; **6:**14, 17, 25^2, 26, 30; **7:**10; **8:**15, 22^2; **9:**38, 54; **11:**10, 17, 19, 24, 36^2; **13:**12, 16, 17^2; **14:**3, 13, 15^2; **15:**2, 18; **16:**6, 15; **17:**10; **18:**19^2, 25^3; **19:**19^2, 20

Ru 1:10, 15^2, 16^2; **2:**11^4, 12, 13, 14; **3:**3, 9, 12, 17; **4:**12, 15^2

1Sa 1:8, 14, 17, 18, 26; **2:**1, 16, 27, 28, 29, 30^2, 31, 34; **3:**9, 10; **4:**17; **8:**5^2; **9:**20^2; **10:**2; **12:**19^2; **13:**13^2, 14; **14:**7, 28; **15:**15, 21, 24, 30, 33^2; **16:**11, 16, 19; **17:**17^2, 18, 28, 32, 34, 36, 44, 55, 58; **19:**11; **20:**1, 3^2, 4, 6, 7, 8^3, 10, 15, 18, 22, 30, 31, 42; **22:**14^2, 15, 16, 22, 23; **23:**10, 11^2, 20; **24:**9, 11^2, 16; **25:**7, 8^3, 26, 28, 29^2, 33, 35^2; **26:**15^2, 17, 24; **27:**5; **28:**1, 2, 17, 19, 21^2, 22; **29:**6^3, 8, 10; **31:**4

2Sa 1:16^3, 19, 26; **2:**21^2, 22; **3:**8, 12, 25^2, 34^2; **4:**8; **5:**1^2; **6:**21; **7:**9, 12^4, 16^2, 19^2, 20, 21^2, 23^3, 24, 25, 26^2, 27^2, 28^2, 29^3; **9:**2, 6, 7^2, 8, 9, 10^4, 11; **10:**3; **11:**8^2, 10, 11, 21, 24^2, 25; **12:**8^3, 9, 10, 11^3, 13; **13:**5^2, 7, 20^3, 24^2, 35; **14:**6, 11^2, 15, 17, 19^2, 20, 22^2, 31; **15:**2, 3, 8, 15, 19, 20, 21, 27, 34^3; **16:**3, 4, 8^2, 17^3, 19^2, 21^2; **17:**8^2, 10; **18:**28, 29; **19:**5^6, 6, 7^2, 14, 19, 20, 26^2, 27, 28, 29, 35^2, 36, 37^2; **20:**6; **22:**36^2, 50; **24:**3, 10, 13^2, 23

1Ki 1:2, 12, 13, 14, 17^2, 19, 26^2, 27, 30, 47^2; **2:**3, 4, 6, 7^2, 21, 37, 38, 39, 44; **3:**6, 7, 8^2, 9^3, 12, 13, 14^2, 22^2, 23^2; **5:**5^3, 6^2, 8; **6:**12; **8:**19^2, 23, 24^2, 25^2, 26^2, 28^2, 29, 30^3, 32, 33^2, 34, 35, 36^4, 38, 39, 41^2, 42^3, 43^4, 44^2, 48, 49, 50, 51, 52^2, 53; **9:**3^2, 4, 5^2; **10:**6^2, 7, 8^3, 9; **11:**11, 12^3, 13, 37; **12:**4^2, 7, 9, 10, 28; **13:**6, 21, 22^2; **14:**9, 12; **15:**19^2; **16:**3; **17:**12, 13, 19, 23, 24; **18:**8, 9, 10, 11, 12, 14, 18, 31, 36^2, 44; **19:**2, 10^2, 14^2, 15, 16; **20:**3^4, 4, 5^4, 6, 9, 31, 32, 33, 34, 39^2, 40^2, 42^3; **21:**2, 5, 6, 19, 21; **22:**4^2, 13, 23, 30, 49

2Ki 1:10, 12, 13^2, 14; **2:**2, 3^2, 4, 5^2, 6, 9, 16^2; **3:**7^2, 13^2; **4:**1^2, 3, 4, 7^2, 24, 26, 29^2, 30, 36; **5:**8, 10, 15, 17^2, 18^2, 25, 27; **6:**3, 12, 22^2, 28, 29; **8:**9, 13; **9:**1, 7, 22; **10:**5, 15, 30; **14:**9, 10; **15:**12; **16:**7^2; **18:**23, 24, 26, 27; **19:**4^3, 10, 22, 23, 27^4, 28^4; **20:**3, 5^3, 6, 17, 18; **22:**9, 19, 20^2

1Ch 10:4; **11:**1^2, 2; **12:**18^2; **16:**35^2; **17:**11^4, 17, 18^2, 19, 21^2, 22, 23, 24^2, 25^2, 26, 27; **19:**3; **21:**8, 12, 17; **22:**11, 12; **28:**6, 9, 21; **29:**13, 17, 18, 19^3

2Ch 1:9, 10; **2:**8^2, 10, 14^2; **6:**2, 9^2, 14, 15^2, 16^2, 17^2, 19^2, 20^2, 21^3, 23, 24^2, 25, 26, 27^4, 29, 30, 31, 32^4, 33^4, 34^2, 38, 39^2, 41^4, 42; **7:**12, 17, 18^2; **9:**5, 6, 7^3, 8^3; **10:**4^2, 7, 9, 10; **14:**11; **16:**3^2, 7; **18:**3, 12, 22, 29; **20:**7^2, 8, 9^2, 11, 37; **21:**12^2, 13^2, 14^4, 15^2; **25:**18; **34:**16, 27, 28^2

Ezr 4:11, 15; **7:**14, 18, 19, 20, 25^2, 26; **9:**10, 11, 14

Neh 1:6^2, 7, 8, 10^4, 11^4; **2:**2, 5^2, 6; **9:**5, 8, 14^2, 16, 17, 18, 19, 20^2, 25, 26^2, 27, 28, 29^3, 30^2, 31, 32, 34^3, 35; **13:**22

Est 3:8; **4:**14^2; **5:**3, 6^2; **7:**2^2, 3; **9:**12^2

Job 1:11, 12, 18^2; **2:**5; **4:**4, 6^4; **5:**24^2, 25, 26, 27; **8:**2, 4, 5, 6, 7^2, 21^2; **10:**5^2, 12, 17; **11:**3, 14, 15, 16, 18; **13:**21, 24; **14:**13; **15:**5, 10, 12, 13^2; **21:**14; **22:**3, 5, 6, 23, 25, 26^2, 27^2, 28; **30:**21; **33:**5, 6, 8, 31, 33; **34:**33; **35:**4, 6, 8^2; **36:**16, 19; **37:**17; **38:**3, 11, 12, 21, 34; **39:**9, 11, 12^2, 26, 27; **40:**7, 11; **41:**5; **42:**7

Ps 2:8; **3:**8^2; **4:**6; **5:**5, 7^4, 8^2, 11; **6:**1, 4; **8:**1^2, 3^2, 6, 9; **9:**1, 2, 3, 10, 14^2, 19; **10:**5, 14; **13:**1, 5^2; **15:**1^2; **16:**11^2; **17:**2, 4, 5, 7^2, 8, 13, 14^2, 15^2; **18:**15^2, 35^3, 49; **19:**11, 13, 14; **20:**3^2, 4, 5^2; **21:**1^2, 5, 6, 8, 12, 13; **22:**22; **23:**4^2; **24:**6; **25:**4^2, 5, 6^2, 7^2, 11; **26:**3^2, 7, 8; **27:**8, 9^2, 11; **28:**2, 9; **30:**7^2, 9; **31:**1, 3, 7, 15, 16^3, 19, 20; **32:**4; **33:**22; **34:**13^2; **35:**3, 24, 28^2; **36:**5^2, 6^2, 7^2, 8^2, 9, 10^2; **37:**5, 6^2; **38:**1^2, 2; **39:**10, 12; **40:**5^2, 8^2, 10^5, 11^3, 16; **41:**12; **42:**3, 7^3, 10; **43:**3^4; **44:**2, 3^2, 5, 8, 12^2, 17, 18, 22, 24, 26; **45:**2, 3^4, 4^2, 6^2, 7^2, 8, 9^2, 10, 11^2, 12, 16^2, 17; **48:**9^2, 10^3, 11; **50:**7, 8^2, 9^2, 14, 16, 19^2, 20; **51:**1^2, 4, 9, 11^2, 12^2, 13, 14, 15, 18; **52:**2, 5, 9^2; **54:**1^2, 5, 6; **55:**22; **56:**8^2, 12; **57:**1, 5, 10^2, 11; **59:**11, 16^2; **60:**3, 5^2; **61:**4^2, 5, 8; **63:**2^2, 3, 4, 7, 8; **65:**4^3, 8, 11^2; **66:**3^2, 4, 13; **67:**2^2; **68:**7, 10^2, 23^2, 24, 28^2, 29, 35; **69:**7, 13^2, 16^2, 17^2, 24, 27, 29; **70:**4; **71:**2, 8^2, 15^2, 16, 17, 18^2, 19, 22, 24; **72:**1^2, 2^2; **73:**15, 24, 28; **74:**1, 2, 3, 4, 7^2, 10, 11^3, 13, 18, 19^2, 21; **75:**1^2; **76:**6, 7; **77:**11, 12^2, 13, 14, 15, 18, 19^3, 20; **79:**1, 2^2, 5, 6^2, 8, 9^2, 10, 11, 13^3; **80:**2, 3, 4, 7, 15, 16, 17^2, 18, 19; **81:**10^2; **83:**1, 3^2, 15^2, 16; **84:**1, 4, 10; **85:**1, 2, 3, 6, 7^2; **86:**2, 4, 8, 9, 11^3, 12, 13, 16^2; **88:**5, 7^2, 11^2, 12^2, 14, 15, 16^2; **89:**1, 2, 4^2, 5^2, 8, 10, 12, 13^2, 14^2, 15, 16^2, 17, 19, 39, 46, 49^2, 50; **90:**4, 7, 8, 9, 11^2, 13, 14, 16^3; **91:**4, 7^2, 9, 10, 11, 12; **92:**1, 2^2, 4^2, 5^2; **93:**2, 5; **94:**5, 12, 18, 19; **97:**8; **99:**3; **102:**2, 10, 12, 14, 15, 24, 25, 27, 28; **103:**3, 4, 5^2; **104:**7^2, 13, 24^2, 29, 30; **106:**4^2, 5^2, 7^2, 47^2; **108:**4^2, 5, 6^2; **109:**1, 21^2, 26, 27, 28; **110:**1, 2, 3^3, 5; **115:**1^3; **116:**7, 16^2; **119:**4, 5, 6, 7, 8, 9, 10, 11, 12, 13, 14, 15^2, 16^2, 17^2, 18, 19, 20, 21, 22, 23^2, 24, 25, 26, 27^2, 28, 29, 30, 31, 32, 33, 34, 35, 36, 37, 38^3, 39, 40^2, 41^3, 42, 43, 44, 45, 46, 47, 48^2, 49, 50, 51, 52, 53, 54, 55^2, 56, 57, 58^2, 59, 60, 61, 62, 63, 64^2, 65^2, 66, 67, 68, 69, 70, 71, 72, 73^2, 74, 75, 76^3, 77^2, 78, 79, 80, 81^2, 82, 83, 84, 85, 86, 87, 88^2, 89, 90, 91, 92, 93, 94, 95, 96, 97, 98, 99, 100, 101, 102, 103, 104, 105, 106, 107, 108, 109, 110, 111, 112, 113, 114, 116, 117, 118, 119, 120, 122, 123^2, 124^3, 125^2, 126, 127, 128, 129, 130, 131, 132, 133, 134, 135^3, 136, 137, 138, 139, 140^2, 141, 142^2, 143, 144, 145, 146, 147, 148, 149^2, 150, 151, 152, 153, 154, 155, 156^2, 157, 158, 159^2, 160^2, 161, 162, 163, 164, 165, 166^2, 167, 168^2, 169, 170, 171, 172^2, 173, 174^2, 175, 176^2; **121:**3, 5^3, 7, 8^2; **122:**2, 7^2, 9; **128:**3^3, 5, 6; **132:**8^2, 9^2, 10, 11^2, 12^2; **135:**13^2; **137:**9; **138:**2^6, 4, 7, 8; **139:**7^2, 10^2, 14, 16, 17, 20; **140:**13^2; **142:**7; **143:**1^2, 2^2, 5^2, 7, 8, 10^2, 11^2, 12^2; **144:**5; **145:**1, 2, 4^2, 5^2, 6^2, 7^2, 10^2, 11^2, 13^2; **146:**10; **147:**12, 13^2, 14

Prv 1:8^2, 9^2, 14, 15; **2:**3, 10; **3:**3, 6^2, 8^2, 9, 10^2, 22^2, 23^2, 24, 26^2, 28, 29; **4:**7, 10, 12, 13, 23, 26^2, 27; **5:**2, 8, 9, 10^2, 11^2, 16, 18^2; **6:**1^2, 2^2, 3^2, 9, 11^2, 20^2, 21; **7:**3, 4, 15; **9:**11^2; **16:**3^2; **19:**18^2, 20; **22:**18, 19, 25, 27, 28; **23:**2, 8, 9, 16, 22^2, 25^2; **24:**6, 10, 12, 13, 14^2, 27, 28^2, 34^2; **25:**8, 9^2, 17^2; **27:**10^3, 23^2, 26, 27^3; **29:**17^2; **30:**32; **31:**3^2, 8, 9

Ecc 5:1, 2^2, 6^3; **7:**9, 17, 21; **9:**7^4, 8^2, 9^4, 10^2; **10:**4, 16^2, 17^2, 20^2; **11:**1, 6, 9^3, 10^2; **12:**1^2

Song 1:2, 3^2, 4, 7^2, 8^2, 10^2; **2:**14^4; **4:**1^2, 2, 3^4, 4, 5, 9, 10^2, 11^3, 13; **5:**9^2; **6:**1^2, 5, 6, 7^2; **7:**1^2, 2^2, 3, 4^2, 7^2, 8^2, 9; **8:**5, 13

Isa 1:22^2, 23, 25^2, 26^2; **2:**6; **3:**6, 12, 25^2; **4:**1; **6:**7^2; **7:**3, 11, 17^2; **8:**8; **10:**22, 27^2, 30; **14:**3^2, 9, 11^2, 19, 20^2, 30^2; **16:**3, 9^2; **17:**10^2, 11^2; **19:**12; **20:**2^3; **22:**2, 3, 7, 18^2, 19^2, 21^3; **23:**10; **25:**1^2, 12; **26:**8^2, 9, 11, 13, 16, 17, 19^2, 20^2; **29:**4^3, 5; **30:**19, 20^2, 22^2, 23^2; **33:**6, 23; **36:**8, 9, 11, 12; **37:**4^3, 10, 23, 24, 28^4, 29^4; **38:**3, 5^4, 17, 18, 19; **39:**6, 7; **40:**9; **41:**10, 13^2, 14; **43:**1, 3^3, 4, 5, 23^2, 24^2, 25^2, 27^2; **44:**3, 22^2, 24, 27, 28; **45:**3, 4, 9; **47:**2, 3^2, 6, 7, 9, 10^3, 12^2, 13, 15^2; **48:**4^2, 17^2, 18^2, 19^2; **49:**16, 17^2, 19^3, 22^2, 23^3, 25, 26^2; **51:**13, 15, 16, 20^2, 22^2, 23^2; **52:**1^2, 2, 7, 8; **54:**2^3, 3, 4^2, 5^2, 6, 8, 11^2, 12^3, 13^2, 15; **55:**5; **57:**6^2, 7, 8^2, 9^2, 10, 11, 12^2, 13; **58:**1, 7^2, 8^3, 10^3, 11^2, 13^2, 14; **59:**21^4; **60:**1, 3^2, 4^3, 9^2, 10, 11, 14, 16^2, 17, 18^4, 19^3, 20^3, 21; **62:**2^2, 3, 4^3, 5^2, 6, 8^2, 11; **63:**2, 14, 15^6, 16, 17^3, 18^2, 19; **64:**1, 2^2, 3, 5, 7^2, 8, 9, 10, 12; **66:**9

Jer 1:9, 17; **2:**2, 16, 17, 19^2, 20^2, 23, 25^2, 28^4, 33^2, 34, 36, 37; **3:**2^2, 13^2; **4:**7^2, 14, 18^3, 30^3; **5:**7, 14, 17^7; **10:**6, 17, 25^2; **11:**13^2, 16, 20, 21; **12:**1, 6^2; **13:**1, 4, 20, 22^2, 25^2, 26^3, 27^2; **14:**7, 9, 19, 21^3; **15:**11, 13^4, 15^2, 16^3, 17; **17:**3^4; **18:**20, 23; **20:**3, 4, 6, 12; **22:**2^2, 7, 15, 17, 20^2, 21^3, 22^3, 23, 25, 26;

27:2, 13; **28:**6; **29:**25; **30:**8^2, 10, 12^2, 13, 14^2, 15^2, 17; **31:**4, 7, 16^2, 17, 21; **32:**17, 21, 23^2; **34:**5; **37:**18; **38:**16, 17, 20, 22^2, 23^2; **39:**18^2; **40:**2; **42:**2, 3, 5; **45:**5; **46:**12^2, 15, 27; **47:**6; **48:**7^2, 18^2, 32^3, 46^2; **49:**4, 11^2, 16^2; **50:**31; **51:**13, 36

Lam 1:10; **2:**13, 14^2, 19^2; **3:**23, 55, 65; **4:**22; **5:**19

Ezk 2:1, 8; **3:**3^2, 8^2, 9, 11, 19, 21, 26^2, 27; **4:**3, 4, 6, 7, 8, 9, 10, 15; **5:**1, 3, 11; **6:**2, 11; **7:**3, 4, 8, 9; **9:**8^2; **11:**15^3; **12:**3, 4, 6^2, 18^2; **13:**4, 17^2; **16:**3^4, 4^2, 5, 6^2, 7, 8^2, 9, 11^2, 12, 13, 14^2, 15^2, 16^2, 17, 18, 20^3, 22^3, 23, 25^4, 26^2, 27, 29, 33^3, 34, 36^6, 37^3, 39^3, 43^2, 45^2, 46^3, 47, 48^2, 49, 51^2, 52^4, 53, 55^2, 56^3, 57^2, 58, 60, 61^4, 63^2; **19:**2, 10^2; **20:**46^2; **21:**2^2, 6, 12, 16, 30, 32; **22:**4^3, 12, 13^2, 15; **23:**21^3, 22^2, 25^5, 26^2, 27^2, 28, 29^4, 31, 32, 33, 35^3, 40; **24:**13^2, 14^2, 16, 17^3, 27; **25:**2, 4^2, 6; **26:**8, 9^2, 10^2, 11^3, 12^7, 13^2, 15, 18^2; **27:**4^3, 5, 6, 7, 8^3, 9^2, 10^2, 11^4, 12^2, 13^2, 14, 15, 16^3, 17^2, 18^2, 19^2, 20, 21, 22^2, 23, 24^2, 25, 26, 27^{10}, 28, 33^3, 34^2; **28:**4^2, 5^4, 7^2, 13^3, 15, 16, 17^3, 18^2, 21; **29:**2, 4^6, 5, 7, 10; **31:**2; **32:**2^2, 5^2, 6, 8, 9, 10, 12; **33:**2, 9, 12, 17, 30, 31, 32; **35:**2, 4, 8^3, 9, 11, 12; **36:**13, 14, 15; **37:**18; **38:**2, 4, 7, 9, 10, 13, 15; **39:**3^3, 4

Dan 1:12, 13; **2:**4, 28^3, 29^3, 30; **3:**12, 18; **4:**22^2, 25, 26, 27^2, 32; **5:**10^2, 11^4, 16, 17^2, 18, 23^5, 26, 28; **6:**16, 20; **9:**5^2, 6^2, 11^2, 13, 15, 16^5, 17^3, 18^2, 19^3, 23, 24^2; **10:**12^3, 14; **11:**14; **12:**1^2, 9, 13^2

Hos 2:6; **4:**4, 5, 6^2; **6:**5; **8:**1, 5; **9:**1; **10:**13^2, 14^2; **12:**6^2, 9; **13:**4, 10^3, 14^2; **14:**1, 8

Joel 2:17; **3:**11

Am 3:11^2; **4:**12; **5:**23^2; **6:**10; **7:**16, 17^4; **8:**14; **9:**15

Oba 4, 7^2, 9, 10^2, 12, 15

Jna 1:6, 8; **2:**3^2, 4^2

Mic 1:11, 16^2; **4:**9, 13; **5:**10^2, 11^2, 13^2, 14^2; **6:**1, 8, 9, 13, 14; **7:**4^2, 5^2, 10, 11, 14^2, 15

Nah 1:13, 14^3, 15^2; **2:**1^3, 13^3; **3:**5^4, 9, 12, 13^3, 14, 16, 17^2, 18^3, 19^3

Hab 1:13; **2:**10^2, 15, 16^2; **3:**2^2, 8^2, 9^2, 11, 13

Zep 1:7; **3:**11^2, 15, 17

Zec 3:8; **9:**9, 11^2, 13^2; **11:**1^2; **14:**1

Mal 1:6, 8^2; **2:**14^3

Mt 1:20; **4:**6, 7, 10; **5:**23^2, 24^4, 29^3, 30^3, 36, 39, 40^2, 43; **6:**3^2, 4, 6^4, 9, 10^2, 17, 18^2, 22, 23; **7:**3, 4, 5, 22^3; **8:**4, 13; **9:**2, 5, 6, 14, 18, 22; **11:**10^2, 26; **12:**2, 37^2, 47^2; **13:**27; **15:**2, 4, 28; **17:**16; **18:**8^2, 15^2, 33; **19:**19^3; **20:**14, 21^2; **21:**5; **22:**37^4, 39, 44; **23:**37; **24:**3; **25:**21, 23, 25; **26:**18, 42, 52, 73

Mk 1:2^2, 25, 44^2; **2:**5, 9^2, 11^2, 18; **3:**32^2; **5:**9, 19, 23, 34^2, 35; **6:**18; **7:**5, 10^2, 29^2; **9:**18, 38, 43, 45; **10:**19, 21, 37^3, 52^2; **12:**30^5, 31, 36; **14:**70

Lk 1:13^2, 31, 36, 38, 42, 44, 61; **2:**29^2, 30, 32, 35, 48; **4:**8, 11, 12, 23, 35; **5:**5, 14, 20, 23, 24; **6:**10, 29^2, 30, 41, 42^2; **7:**27^2, 48, 50; **8:**20^2, 30, 48, 49; **9:**40, 41, 49; **10:**17, 21, 27^6; **11:**2^3, 34^2, 36; **12:**20; **13:**26, 34; **14:**12^4; **15:**19^2, 21^2, 27^2, 29, 30^2, 32; **16:**2, 6, 7, 25^2; **17:**3, 19^2; **18:**20^2, 42^2; **19:**5, 16, 18, 20, 39, 42^2, 44^2; **20:**43; **22:**32^2; **23:**42, 46

Jn 4:16, 18, 42, 50^2, 51, 53; **5:**8, 10, 11, 12; **7:**3; **8:**13, 19; **11:**23; **12:**15, 28; **13:**37, 38; **17:**1^2, 6^2, 12, 14, 17^2, 26; **18:**11; **19:**26, 27; **20:**27^2; **21:**18

Act 2:28, 35^2; **3:**25; **4:**25, 27, 28^2, 29^2, 30; **5:**9; **7:**3^2, 32, 33^2; **8:**20, 21, 22; **9:**13, 14, 15, 17, 34; **10:**4, 31; **11:**14; **12:**8^2; **14:**10; **16:**31; **18:**9; **22:**13, 16, 18, 20; **23:**5; **24:**2, 4, 25; **26:**16

Ro 2:5, 17, 23, 25; **3:**4; **4:**18; **8:**36; **9:**7; **10:**8^2, 9; **11:**3; **13:**9; **14:**10^2, 15^3, 21; **15:**9

1Co 7:16^2; **8:**11; **14:**16; **15:**55^2

Gal 3:16; **5:**14

Eph 6:2

1Ti 4:12, 15; **5:**23; **6:**20

2Ti 1:4, 5^2; **4:**5, 9, 21, 22

Phlm 2, 5, 6, 7, 13, 14^2, 21

Heb 1:8^2, 9^2, 12, 13; **2:**7, 12; **10:**7, 9; **11:**18

Jas 2:8, 18^2

2Jn 4, 13

3Jn 2, 6

Rev 2:2^3, 4, 5, 9, 13, 19^3; **3:**1, 2, 8, 9, 11, 15, 18; **4:**11; **5:**9; **10:**9^2; **11:**17, 18^3; **14:**15, 18; **15:**3^2, 4^2; **16:**7; **18:**10, 14, 23^2; **19:**10^2; **22:**9^2

THYSELF

Gen 13:9; **14:**21; **16:**9; **33:**9

Ex 9:17; **10:**3, 28; **18:**14, 18, 22; **20:**5; **34:**2, 12

Lev 9:7; **18:**20, 23; **19:**18, 34

Nu 11:17; **16:**13

Dt 4:9; **5:**9; **9:**1; **12:**13, 19, 30; **20:**14; **22:**1, 3, 4, 12; **23:**13; **28:**40

Jos 17:15

Ru 3:3^2; **4:**6

1Sa 19:2^2; **20:**8, 19; **25:**26

2Sa 5:24; **7:**24; **13:**5; **14:**2^2; **18:**13^2; **22:**26^2, 27^2

1Ki 2:2, 3; **3:**11^3; **13:**7; **14:**2, 6; **17:**3; **18:**1; **20:**22, 40; **21:**20; **22:**25

2Ki 22:19

1Ch 21:12

2Ch 1:11; **18:**24; **20:**37; **21:**13; **34:**27^2

Est 4:13

Job 8:8; **10:**16; **15:**8; **22:**21; **30:**21; **40:**10^2

Ps 7:6; **10:**1; **18:**25^2, 26^2; **35:**23; **37:**1, 4, 7, 8; **49:**18; **50:**21; **52:**1; **55:**1; **60:**1; **80:**15, 17; **85:**3; **89:**46; **94:**1, 2; **104:**2

Prv 6:3^2, 5; **9:**12; **24:**19, 27; **25:**6; **27:**1; **30:**32

Ecc 7:16^2, 22

Isa 26:20; **33:**3; **45:**15; **52:**2^2; **57:**8, 9; **58:**7, 14; **63:**14; **64:**12; **65:**5

Jer 2:17; **4:**30^2; **6:**26; **17:**4; **20:**4; **22:**15; **32:**8; **45:**5; **46:**19; **47:**5, 6

Lam 2:18; **3:**44; **4:**21

Ezk 3:24; **16:**17; **22:**4, 16; **23:**40^2; **31:**10; **38:**7

Dan 5:17, 23; **10:**12

Hos 13:9

Oba 4

Mic 1:10; **5:**1

Nah 3:15^2

Zec 2:7

Mt 4:6; **5:**33; **8:**4; **19:**19; **22:**39; **27:**40

Mk 1:44; **12:**31; **15:**30

Lk 4:9, 23; **5:**14; **6:**42; **7:**6; **10:**27; **17:**8; **23:**37, 39

Jn 1:22; **7:**4; **8:**13, 53; **10:**33; **14:**22; **18:**34; **21:**18

Act 8:29; **12:**8; **16:**28; **21:**24^2; **24:**8; **26:**1, 24

Ro 2:1, 5, 19, 21; **13:**9; **14:**22

Gal 5:14; **6:**1

1Ti 3:15; **4:**7, 15, 16^2; **5:**22; **6:**5

2Ti 2:15

Tit 2:7

Jas 2:8

TO

Gen 1:14, 15, 16^2, 17, 18^2, 29, 30^3; **2:**5^2, 9^2, 10, 15^2, 19, 20^3, 21; **3:**6^3, 12, 16, 18, 21, 22, 23, 24; **4:**3, 4, 5, 8, 11, 14, 23^2, 26^3; **6:**1^2, 4, 16, 17, 19, 20, 21, 22; **7:**2, 3, 4, 10; **8:**1, 6, 7, 8, 11, 13; **9:**8, 10, 11, 14, 15, 20; **10:**8, 19, 21; **11:**2, 3^2, 4, 5, 6^2, 7, 8, 31; **12:**5, 10, 11^3, 12, 14, 19^2; **13:**3, 6, 9^3, 15^2; **14:**1, 7, 10, 17, 21, 22, 23; **15:**3, 5, 6, 7^2, 15, 17; **16:**2, 3^2, 6, 7, 9, 16; **17:**1, 7^2, 8; **18:**2, 5, 7, 10, 11, 14, 16, 19, 21, 25^2, 27, 31; **19:**1^2, 5, 8, 9^2, 10^2, 11, 13, 17^2, 19, 20, 27, 29, 30, 31, 34; **20:**3^2, 6, 9, 13^2, 16; **21:**2, 3, 6, 17, 22, 23^2, 26; **22:**1, 5, 9, 10, 14, 19, 20, 23; **23:**2^2, 7^2, 8, 16; **24:**4, 5, 8, 9, 10, 11^2, 13, 14^2, 15^2, 16^2, 17, 20, 21, 22, 23, 25, 27, 30, 32, 33, 36, 37, 38, 41, 43^4, 44, 48, 49^2, 52^2, 53^3, 56, 63, 65; **25:**8, 11, 13, 16, 20^2, 22, 24, 30, 32^2, 33; **26:**4, 7^2, 8, 11, 23, 26, 27, 31, 32, 34, 35; **27:**1, 3, 4, 5^4, 8, 9, 10, 11, 12, 14, 20, 25^2, 29^2, 30, 37, 40, 42^2, 43^2, 45, 46; **28:**2^2, 4^2, 5, 6^2, 7, 9, 11, 12, 13^2, 14^4, 15, 20^2, 21; **29:**10, 13^3, 14, 19^2, 20, 23^2, 25^2, 26, 28, 29^2; **30:**4, 9, 14, 15, 16, 18, 22, 24, 25^2, 32, 33, 34, 38^2, 41; **31:**3, 4, 7, 9, 10, 18^2, 19, 20, 24^2, 26^2, 28, 29^2, 31, 32, 35, 36, 51, 52, 54; **32:**3, 5, 6^3, 8, 9, 13, 30; **33:**3^2, 4, 8, 11, 14, 17, 18; **34:**1, 4, 6, 7, 8, 12, 14^2, 16, 17, 19, 21, 22^2, 25, 30^3; **35:**1, 2, 3, 6, 12^2, 16^2, 17, 18, 19, 22, 26; **36:**4, 12^2, 14, 40, 43; **37:**7, 8, 9, 10^5, 12, 13, 14^2, 17, 18, 19, 22^2, 23, 25^3, 27, 28, 32, 35^2; **38:**1^2, 8, 9^2, 11, 12, 13^2, 14^2, 15, 16, 20, 22, 23, 24, 25, 26, 27, 28, 29; **39:**1, 3, 5, 7, 8, 10^4, 11^2, 13, 14^2, 15, 17^2, 18, 19^2, 22, 23^2; **40:**1, 5, 7, 8, 9^2, 20, 22; **41:**1, 8, 11, 12^4, 13^2, 15, 24, 25, 28, 32, 36, 43, 45, 52, 54, 55^2, 57^2; **42:**3, 5, 6^2, 7, 9, 10, 12, 21, 24, 25^3, 27, 28, 30, 35, 37^2, 38; **43:**2, 6, 7, 15, 16, 19, 20, 21^2, 22, 23, 26^2, 30, 33^2; **44:**2, 7, 11, 13, 14, 24, 29, 30, 31^2, 32, 33, 34; **45:**1, 4, 5, 7^2, 8, 9, 11, 21, 22^2, 23, 27; **46:**1, 3, 5, 18, 22, 28, 29^2, 32, 33; **47:**4, 6, 12, 21^2, 24; **48:**1, 4, 7, 11, 12, 17, 22; **49:**4^2, 15, 28, 29; **50:**2, 7, 10, 11, 14, 20^3, 24^3

Ex 1:10, 11, 13, 15, 16, 21; **2:**1, 4^2, 5^2, 7^2, 8, 11, 13, 14, 15, 16, 18^2, 21, 23; **3:**1^3, 4, 6, 8^2, 13, 16, 18^2, 21; **4:**8^2, 9, 14, 16^2, 18^2, 20, 21, 23, 24^2, 25, 27^2; **5:**2, 7, 8, 10, 12, 14, 16, 17, 21^3, 23^3; **6:**1, 3, 4, 7^2, 8^4, 13, 16, 17, 19, 20, 23, 25^2, 26^2, 27^2, 28; **7:**1, 14, 15, 17, 18, 20, 23, 24; **8:**2, 5, 9, 10^2, 13, 18, 20, 22, 23, 25, 26^2, 27, 28, 29^3, 31; **9:**2, 5, 8, 16, 18^2; **10:**3, 4^2, 5, 10, 26, 28; **12:**2, 3^2, 4^2, 13^2, 14, 16, 21, 23^3, 24^2, 25^2, 26, 29, 35, 37, 41^2, 42^2, 48, 49, 51; **13:**5, 6, 10, 11, 14, 15^2, 17^2, 21^3; **14:**11^2, 12, 13^3, 20^2, 21, 23, 24, 27; **15:**17, 21, 23, 26^2, 27; **16:**3^3, 5, 8^2, 10, 13, 15^2, 16^2, 18, 21, 22, 23^3, 25^3, 27^2, 28, 32, 33, 34, 35; **17:**1^2, 3, 4, 9, 10^2, 11, 16; **18:**7, 8, 9, 12, 13^2, 14^2, 15, 18, 19, 21, 23^2, 24; **19:**2, 3, 10^2, 12^2, 13, 16, 17, 20, 21, 22, 23, 24; **20:**5, 8, 20; **21:**6, 7, 8^2, 12, 14, 15, 16, 17, 19, 29^3, 31, 36; **22:**5, 7, 8, 9, 10, 16, 17^2, 18, 19, 25^2, 26, 27, 29, 31; **23:**1, 2^3, 4, 5, 20^2, 24, 27; **24:**4, 12, 14; **25:**7, 9, 20, 25, 27, 29, 35; **26:**3^2, 7, 13, 28, 30; **27:**3, 5, 7, 20^2, 21; **28:**3, 8, 10, 11, 14, 21^2, 35, 36, 42, 43; **29:**1^2, 10, 29^2, 30, 33^2, 35^2, 36, 41^2, 42, 44^2; **30:**1, 4^2, 15, 16, 18, 20^3, 21^3, 37^2, 38; **31:**4^2, 5^2, 10, 11, 14, 15^2, 16; **32:**1, 5^2, 6^3, 12^2, 13, 14, 19, 20, 27, 28, 29^2, 30; **33:**1^2, 5, 7, 8, 9, 11, 19, 22; **34:**2, 7, 12, 24, 29, 30, 34, 35; **35:**2^3, 9, 19^2, 21, 27, 29^2, 32^2, 33^2, 35; **36:**1^3, 2^2, 3, 5, 6, 7, 12, 18, 29^2, 33^2, 34; **37:**2, 3, 5, 9^2, 14, 15, 16, 21, 27^2, 29; **38:**5, 7, 18, 21^2, 26, 30; **39:**1, 3, 4, 5, 7, 14^3, 26, 30^2, 31, 32, 37, 41^2, 42; **40:**4, 5, 16, 17, 30, 35

Lev 1:4, 9, 14; **2:**2^2, 13; **4:**2, 3, 5, 16, 23, 27, 28, 35; **5:**4^2, 7, 10, 11, 12^2, 17; **6:**2, 4, 5, 25, 30; **7:**8, 35, 36, 38; **8:**5, 11, 12, 15, 31, 34^2; **9:**1, 4^2, 16; **10:**7, 15, 17^2, 19; **11:**1, 7, 8, 21, 31, 37, 45, 47; **12:**2, 8; **13:**12, 15, 19, 59^2; **14:**4^2, 7, 8, 11, 14, 17, 18, 19, 21^2, 22, 25, 28, 29^2, 31^2, 32^2, 34, 35, 36^2, 38, 41, 49, 57; **15:**1, 13, 14, 28, 29; **16:**10^3, 17, 27, 30, 32, 34; **17:**4, 5, 9, 11^2; **18:**4, 6^3, 14, 17, 18^3, 19, 20, 21, 23^2; **19:**4, 11, 20^2, 24, 29^3, 31; **20:**2^2, 3^2, 5, 6, 9, 10, 11, 12, 13, 15, 16, 22, 24, 27; **21:**4, 10, 11, 14, 17, 21^2, 24; **22:**2, 8, 16, 18, 21^2, 33; **23:**2, 11, 20, 22, 28, 37^2, 43; **24:**2^2, 16^2, 17, 19, 20, 21, 23; **25:**9, 15, 16^3, 25, 26^2, 27, 28^2, 30, 38^2, 39, 46, 47, 50^2; **26:**1, 5, 8, 21, 37, 44^2; **27:**8, 14, 16, 17, 18, 19, 20, 24^2, 25, 27^2, 29

Nu 1:3^2, 18, 20^3, 22^3, 24^3, 26^3, 28^3, 30^3, 32^3, 34^3, 36^3, 38^3, 40^3, 42^3, 45^2, 50, 51^2, 54; **2:**10, 18, 34^2; **3:**3, 7, 8, 9, 10, 16, 20, 22, 34, 38, 46, 48^2, 51^2; **4:**3, 7, 11, 14, 15^2, 16, 19^2, 20, 23^2, 24, 30, 31, 33, 37, 41, 45, 47, 49^3; **5:**6, 8^2, 15, 19, 20, 21^2, 22^3, 24, 26, 27^2, 29; **6:**2^2, 4, 10^2, 21; **7:**1, 5^3, 7, 89; **8:**7, 12, 15, 19^4, 20, 21, 22, 24, 26; **9:**3^2, 5, 12, 13, 14^2, 20^2; **10:**3, 7, 8, 9, 10, 11, 13, 14, 18, 22, 28, 30^2, 31^2, 33, 35; **11:**4, 13, 14, 16, 18^2, 22^2, 23, 25; **12:**8^2; **13:**16, 17, 21, 26^4, 30, 31, 32; **14:**3^2, 4, 7, 14^2, 16, 20, 22, 25, 28, 29, 30, 36^2, 38, 44; **15:**3, 12^3, 24, 28, 34, 35, 39, 41; **16:**5^3, 7, 9^5, 10, 12, 13, 16, 28, 31, 33, 40^3, 42; **17:**2^2, 5^2, 6, 8, 10; **18:**6^2, 7, 8, 11^2, 16^2, 19, 24^2, 28; **20:**5^3, 8, 12, 17^2, 21; **21:**3, 4, 5, 7, 8, 9, 15, 16, 18, 19^2, 20, 23^2, 29, 32, 33, 34; **22:**2, 5^2, 11, 13^2, 14, 16^2, 18, 20, 23, 26^3, 30, 32, 36, 37^3, 38, 40^2, 41; **23:**3^2, 11, 12, 14, 17, 20, 23; **24:**1^2, 2, 10, 11^2, 12, 13, 14, 25; **25:**1, 2; **26:**1, 2^2, 18, 22, 25, 27, 37, 43, 47, 50, 53, 54^4, 55, 56, 59; **27:**7, 8, 11, 14; **28:**2, 7, 22, 30; **29:**5, 9^2, 14, 15, 18, 21, 24, 27, 30, 33, 37, 40; **30:**2^2, 13, 14; **31:**4, 6^3, 13, 16, 21, 27, 28, 36, 50, 52; **32:**2, 6^2, 8, 14, 19, 20, 27, 29, 33^2, 39; **33:**2^2, 14, 53, 54^3, 55, 56^2; **34:**4^5, 8, 9, 10, 11, 12, 13^2, 14^2, 18, 29; **35:**2, 3, 5, 6, 7, 8, 11, 16, 17, 18, 21, 24, 25, 30^3, 31, 32^2; **36:**2^3, 3^2, 5, 6^2, 7^2, 9^2

Dt 1:3, 5, 7^2, 8^2, 9, 14, 19, 27^2, 28, 30, 33^3, 35, 36^2, 38, 41^2, 45; **2:**4, 15, 16, 18, 22, 24, 25, 27, 31^2, 32, 34; **3:**1^2, 3, 7, 12, 18, 24^3, 28; **4:**1, 5, 9, 10, 13, 14^2, 19, 20, 25^2, 26^2, 30, 34^2, 36, 38^3; **5:**4, 5, 12, 15, 23, 30, 31, 32^3; **6:**1^2, 2, 3, 10^4, 19, 20, 23, 24^2, 25; **7:**1, 6, 9, 10^4, 11, 12^2, 13, 24, 25; **8:**1, 2^3, 3, 6^2, 16, 18; **9:**1^4, 4, 5, 6, 7, 8^2, 9, 10,

11, 18^2, 19, 20, 22, 23, 27^2, 28^2; **10:**4, 6, 7, 8^4, 10, 11, 12^4, 13, 15, 20; **11:**4^2, 8, 9^2, 10, 11, 13^3, 16, 21, 22^4, 25, 28, 29^2, 31^2, 32; **12:**1^2, 5, 9^2, 10, 11^2, 13, 15, 19, 20, 21, 29, 30, 31^2, 32; **13:**2, 3, 5^4, 9^2, 10, 12, 17, 18^3; **14:**2, 23^2, 24^2; **15:**4, 5^2, 11^2, 15, 18; **16:**2, 6, 8, 9^3, 11, 17; **17:**6^2, 7^2, 10^3, 11^4, 12, 16^4, 17^2, 19^3, 20^3; **18:**5^2, 8, 9, 10, 14, 16, 19, 20^2, 22; **19:**2, 3, 5^2, 8, 9^3, 14, 16, 19; **20:**1, 4^2, 5, 9, 10, 18, 19^2; **21:**1, 5^2, 10, 11, 12, 16, 22^2; **22:**2, 4, 6, 7, 14, 16, 21^2, 22, 27; **23:**2, 3, 4, 14^2, 19, 20^2, 21, 22; **24:**1, 3, 4^2, 5, 6^2, 8^2, 10, 11, 16^3, 17, 18, 19, 22; **25:**2^4, 5^2, 7^3, 8^2, 11, 19; **26:**2, 3, 5, 13^3, 14^2, 16, 17^4, 18, 19; **27:**12, 13, 18, 25, 26; **28:**1^3, 7, 11, 12^2, 13^2, 14^4, 15^3, 20, 21, 25, 31^2, 44^2, 45, 50, 55, 56, 58, 63^7; **29:**1, 4^3, 8^2, 13^4, 18, 19^3, 21, 22, 27, 29; **30:**1^2, 2, 6, 10, 12, 16^4, 18^2, 19, 20^4; **31:**4^2, 7^2, 11, 12, 13^2, 16, 21, 24, 28, 29^2; **32:**8^2, 13, 16^2, 17^3, 21^4, 26, 30, 35, 40, 41, 43^2, 45, 46^2, 47; **33:**7, 9, 17, 24; **34:**1, 4, 5, 10, 11^4

Jos 1:1, 2^2, 5, 6, 7^4, 8^2, 11^3, 12^3, 18; **2:**1, 2^2, 3^2, 5, 6, 7, 16, 20, 23; **3:**1, 2, 5, 7, 8, 13, 14^2; **4:**1, 6, 8, 10^2, 11, 13, 18, 21, 23; **5:**1, 8, 13, 14; **6:**5, 8, 15, 16, 17, 20, 25; **7:**2, 3^2, 6, 7^3, 13, 14^2, 19; **8:**1, 2, 3, 5, 8, 9, 10, 12, 14^2, 16, 20^3, 23, 24, 34; **9:**1, 2, 3, 6^2, 10^3, 11^2, 12, 15, 16, 20, 24^2, 25; **10:**1^3, 6^3, 10^2, 11^2, 12, 13, 15, 18, 19, 20, 21^2, 24, 25, 27, 28, 32^2, 33, 35^2, 37^2, 38, 39^5, 43; **11:**1^4, 2, 3^3, 5, 6, 11, 14, 17, 20, 23^2; **12:**3^2, 7^2; **13:**1, 3, 4, 15, 24, 31; **14:**1, 4, 7, 11^2, 12; **15:**1, 3^6, 6^2, 7, 8, 9^2, 10^2, 11^2, 12^2, 13^2, 15, 16^2, 17, 18^2, 20; **16:**1, 2^2, 3^2, 5, 6^2, 7^3; **17:**1, 4^2, 5, 7, 8, 13^2, 14, 15, 17^2; **18:**3^2, 4^2, 6, 8^2, 9^2, 10, 11, 12, 13^2, 15, 16^4, 17^2, 19, 20, 21, 28; **19:**1^2, 8^2, 10, 11^2, 12^2, 13^4, 14, 16, 17^2, 22, 23, 24, 26^2, 27^4, 29^4, 31, 32^2, 33, 34^5, 39, 40, 47, 48, 49, 50; **20:**2; **21:**2^2, 12, 13^2, 21, 27, 32, 33, 38, 43, 44, 45; **22:**5^6, 7, 9^3, 10^2, 12^2, 13^2, 15^2, 16, 18^2, 23^3, 24^2, 26, 27^2, 28^3, 29, 31^2, 32, 33^2; **23:**1, 4, 6^4, 7, 9, 12, 14, 15, 16; **24:**1, 4, 5, 9, 15, 16, 22, 29, 33

Jdg 1:1^2, 7, 9, 12^2, 13, 14^3, 23, 28^2, 34^2, 36; **2:**1^2, 4, 6, 12, 19^3, 22; **3:**1, 2, 4^2, 6^2, 9, 10, 18, 27, 28; **4:**5, 7, 9, 10, 12, 17, 18^2, 19, 22; **5:**3, 11, 16, 23^2, 26^2, 29, 30^2; **6:**5, 7, 11, 22, 25, 29, 31, 35; **7:**2, 3, 5, 6^2, 9, 10^2, 11, 17, 20, 22^2, 25; **8:**1, 3, 4, 8, 27, 33, 35^2; **9:**1, 3, 7, 8, 9, 10, 11, 13, 16, 21, 24, 26, 29^2, 31, 33, 36, 42, 48, 49, 50, 51^2, 52, 53; **10:**1, 9, 12, 18^2; **11:**3, 4, 5, 8, 9, 10, 12^2, 16, 20, 24, 27, 31, 32, 33, 34^2, 35, 36^2, 39^2, 40; **12:**1^2, 3, 6; **13:**5, 7^2, 9, 11, 12, 17, 20^2, 21^2, 23, 25; **14:**1, 2, 3, 5^2, 8^2, 9, 10, 11^2, 15^2, 17^2, 19^2, 20; **15:**1^3, 2, 4, 6, 10^4, 11^2, 12, 17; **16:**1, 3, 4, 5, 6^2, 8, 16, 19^2, 21, 22, 23^2, 25; **17:**3^2, 4, 8^3, 9, 11, 13; **18:**1, 2^4, 7^2, 8, 9^3, 10, 14^2, 15, 17, 19^2, 22, 30; **19:**1^2, 2, 3^3, 5^2, 7, 8, 9^3, 12, 13^2, 14, 15^3, 18^3, 22, 25^2, 27; **20:**1, 3, 4^2, 5, 8, 9, 10^3, 13^2, 14^2, 18^2, 20^2, 21, 23, 25, 28^2, 31^3, 36, 39, 40^2, 47, 48^2; **21:**1, 2, 3^2, 4, 5^3, 7, 8^4, 12, 13^3, 18, 19, 21^2, 22^2, 23, 24^3

Ru 1:1^2, 7, 8, 12^2, 16^2, 17, 18, 19^3, 22; **2:**2, 3, 8, 10, 12, 15, 18, 19^2, 20^2, 23; **3:**2, 3, 6, 7, 8, 11, 13^2, 16^2, 17; **4:**1, 4^2, 5, 6, 7^2, 10^2, 15, 17

1Sa 1:3^2, 4^2, 6, 7, 8^2, 12, 19^2, 20, 21, 25, 28^2; **2:**6, 8^2, 10, 11^2, 15^2, 16, 19^3, 20, 24, 28^4, 29, 33^2, 35, 36^2; **3:**2^2, 3, 6, 8, 11, 15, 17, 19, 20^2, 21; **4:**1^2, 3, 4, 9, 12, 16, 18, 19; **5:**3, 4^2, 10^5, 11, 12; **6:**2^2, 3, 4^2, 7, 9^2, 10, 12^3, 13, 16, 18^2, 20^2, 21^2; **7:**1, 2, 5, 6, 7, 8^2, 10, 14, 16^2, 17; **8:**1, 4, 5, 6, 8, 11, 12^3, 13^3, 14, 15^2, 16, 19, 22; **9:**3, 5^2, 6, 7^3, 8^2, 9^2, 10, 11^2, 12^3, 13^2, 14^2, 16^2, 17, 18, 19^2, 21, 26^2, 27^2; **10:**1, 2^2, 3^3, 5^3, 8^4, 9^2, 10, 11^2, 13, 14^3, 17, 20, 21, 24, 25, 26; **11:**3^2, 4, 9^2, 10, 11, 12, 13^2, 14^2, 15; **12:**3, 7^2, 17, 19, 22, 23; **13:**2, 4, 5, 7, 8^2, 9, 10^2, 12, 13, 14, 17, 18^3, 20^2, 21, 22, 23; **14:**1^2, 4, 6^3, 7, 9, 12, 19, 20, 21, 25, 26, 27, 30, 31, 43, 45, 46; **15:**1^2, 2, 5, 6, 7, 11, 12^3, 13, 15, 16, 21, 22^2, 27, 28, 32, 34^3, 35; **16:**1, 2^2, 3, 4, 5^3, 6, 9, 10, 12^2, 13, 16^2, 17, 21, 22, 23; **17:**1^2, 8^3, 9^2, 13^2, 15, 17^2, 20^2, 23, 25, 26^2, 27, 32, 33^3, 39, 40, 43, 44^3, 45^3, 46, 48^3, 49, 52^3, 54, 58; **18:**1, 2, 4^4, 6^2, 8, 10, 11, 17^2, 18, 19^3, 21^2, 23^2, 25^3, 26, 27^2, 30; **19:**1^2, 2^2, 4, 5, 7, 10^2, 11^4, 14, 15^2, 18^3, 20, 22^2, 23^2; **20:**5^2, 6, 8, 9, 10, 12, 13^2, 17, 18^2, 19, 21, 24, 27^3, 28^2, 29, 30, 33^2, 35, 37, 38, 40, 41, 42; **21:**1^2, 2, 6, 7, 10, 11, 14, 15; **22:**1^2, 3, 8, 9^2, 11^2, 13, 15^2, 17^2, 18; **23:**3, 4, 5, 6^3, 7, 8^4, 9, 10^3, 13, 15, 16, 18, 19^2, 20^3, 23^2, 24, 25, 26^2; **24:**1, 2, 3^2, 4, 5, 6, 7, 8, 9, 10, 11, 16, 17; **25:**1, 5^2, 6^3, 8^2, 9^2, 14, 17, 22, 23, 26^2, 29^2, 30^3, 32^2, 33, 34, 35^2, 36, 37, 38, 39^3, 40^5, 41^2, 44; **26:**1, 2^2, 5, 6^5, 7, 8^2, 9, 10, 13, 14^3, 15^3, 16, 20^2, 23^2, 25^2; **27:**1, 4, 8, 9, 10, 11^2, 12; **28:**1^3, 2^2, 7^2, 8, 9^2, 10^2, 12, 14, 15^2, 17^3, 19; **29:**1, 4^3, 5, 9^2, 11^3; **30:**1^2, 3, 4, 7^2, 9, 11, 12, 13^2, 14, 15^3, 19^2, 21^5, 22, 24, 26^2, 27^3, 28^3, 29^3, 30^3, 31^3; **31:**8^2, 9, 10, 11, 12

2Sa 1:1, 2^3, 14^2, 26; **2:**1, 8, 10, 12, 14, 15, 19^2, 21^3, 22^3, 23^3, 24, 26, 29, 32; **3:**5, 6, 7, 8^3, 9^3, 10^3, 12^2, 13, 14^2, 16, 17, 19^3, 20^2, 23, 24, 25^3, 27^2, 31^2, 35^3, 37, 39; **4:**2, 3, 4^2, 5, 8^2, 10; **5:**1, 2, 3^2, 4, 6, 8, 11, 13, 17^2, 19, 20, 24, 25; **6:**2, 6^2, 8, 9, 19^3, 20^4, 21; **7:**1, 3, 4, 5, 6, 7, 8, 11^2, 17^2, 19, 21^2, 22, 23^5, 24^2, 27^2, 29; **8:**1, 2^4, 3, 5, 6, 7, 10^2; **9:**9^3, 10, 11; **10:**1, 2, 3^3, 4, 5, 14, 16, 17, 19^2; **11:**1^2, 2^2, 6^2, 8^2, 9, 11^3, 12^3, 13^2, 14^2, 16, 27; **12:**4^3, 5, 7, 9^2, 10, 14^2, 17^2, 18^2, 20, 22, 23^2, 27, 29; **13:**1, 2^2, 4, 5, 6, 7^2, 8, 9, 10, 11, 12, 13, 23, 24, 25, 30^2, 33^2, 36, 37, 38, 39; **14:**2^2, 3, 4^2, 6, 7, 8, 10, 11^2, 15, 16, 17, 19^2, 20^3, 22^2, 23^2, 24^2, 25^2, 29^3, 31, 32^3, 33^3; **15:**1^2, 2, 3, 5^2, 6^2, 7, 8, 9, 13, 14, 15, 16, 19^2, 22, 26, 28, 29, 32^3, 34, 35; **16:**2^2, 3, 4, 5, 10, 11^2, 15, 16, 17^2, 20, 21; **17:**6, 9, 11^2, 13, 14^2, 15, 17, 18, 20^3, 21, 23^2, 24, 25^2, 27^2, 29; **18:**11, 17, 18, 21, 22, 24, 28, 32, 33; **19:**5, 8, 11^6, 12, 13^2, 15^5, 16, 18^2, 19, 20^2, 21, 22^2, 24, 25^3, 26, 28, 31, 34, 37, 38, 40, 41, 42; **20:**1^2, 2, 3^2, 4, 5, 6, 7, 9^2, 10^2, 13, 14, 15, 18, 19, 21, 22^3; **21:**2^2, 9, 10, 16, 17, 18, 20, 22; **22:**4, 7, 21^2, 25^2, 31, 35, 40, 42, 44, 51^2; **23:**3, 5, 9, 10, 13, 16, 21, 23, 37; **24:**1, 2^2, 4, 6^4, 7^4, 8, 13^2, 15^2, 16^2, 18, 19, 21^3

1Ki 1:3, 4, 5, 8, 21, 23, 31^2, 33^2, 35, 38^2, 43, 44, 47, 48, 51, 52, 53^2; **2:**3^2, 4^2, 5^2, 6^2, 7, 8^4, 9^2, 13, 14, 17, 19^3, 21^2, 23, 24, 26^2, 28, 30, 32, 39, 40^3, 41, 42, 44^3; **3:**4^2, 5, 6, 7, 9^2, 11, 12, 14, 15^2, 18, 21, 25^2, 28; **4:**10, 11, 12^2, 13^2, 15, 24, 25, 28, 34; **5:**2, 5, 6^2, 7, 8^2, 9, 10, 11^2, 14, 17, 18; **6:**1^2, 3, 11, 12, 19, 38; **7:**7, 8, 9, 14^2, 16, 18, 23, 32, 34, 36, 41, 42, 45, 50; **8:**6, 10, 11, 13^2, 16^2, 17, 18, 25^2, 28^4, 30, 31^2, 32^3, 33, 36, 39^2, 43^3, 44, 46, 52, 53, 54, 56, 58^2, 61^2, 64; **9:**1^2, 2, 3, 4^2, 5, 8, 10, 11, 12, 14, 15, 19, 21, 28^2; **10:**1, 2^2, 6, 9^2, 10, 13, 14, 16, 17, 24^2, 27^2; **11:**2, 4, 11, 13, 15^2, 17, 18^2, 19, 21^2, 22^2, 24, 25, 29, 31^2, 33^2, 36, 37, 38, 40; **12:**1^3, 2, 5, 7, 9, 11, 12^2, 14^2, 16^2, 18^4, 20, 21^4, 23, 24^4, 26, 27^2, 28^2, 30; **13:**1, 4^2, 5, 10, 11, 17^2, 20, 22, 23^2, 26, 27, 29^3, 31^2, 32, 34^2; **14:**2^3, 3, 4^2, 5^2, 6^2, 8, 9^2, 12, 13, 15^2, 16, 17^2, 18, 21^2, 22, 24, 25; **15:**4^2, 17^2, 18, 21, 25, 26, 27^2, 29^2, 30, 33, 34; **16:**1, 2^3, 7, 8, 11^2, 12, 13^2, 15, 18, 19^2, 21, 23, 26^3, 29, 31^3, 33^2, 34; **17:**1, 4, 7, 9^3, 10^3, 11^2, 15, 16, 17, 18^4, 24; **18:**1^2, 2, 5, 6, 9, 10, 12, 15, 16^2, 17, 19, 27, 29^2, 31, 36, 40, 42^3, 43, 44, 45^2, 46; **19:**2^2, 3^2, 9, 10, 14, 15^2, 16^2, 17, 20; **20:**2, 4, 6, 9, 12, 22, 26^3, 30, 31, 32, 33^2, 35, 42, 43^2; **21:**1, 2, 3, 4, 5, 8, 10, 14, 15^3, 16^4, 17, 18^2, 20^2, 22^2, 25, 26, 27, 28; **22:**2^2, 4^3, 5, 6, 12, 13, 15^2, 17, 24, 25, 26, 29, 32^2, 33, 36^2, 37, 41, 42, 48^2, 51, 52, 53^2

2Ki 1:3^3, 6^2, 7, 9, 10, 16^2, 17; **2:**1, 2^2, 3^2, 4^2, 5^2, 6, 7, 9, 11, 15^3, 18, 20, 22, 25^2; **3:**1, 3, 5, 7^2, 10, 12, 13^4, 15, 20, 21^2, 23, 24, 26, 27; **4:**1^2, 5, 6, 8^3, 10, 12, 13^3, 14, 16, 17, 18^2, 19^2, 20, 22, 23^2, 24, 25^3, 26, 27^3, 29, 31, 35, 37, 38, 39, 40^2, 44; **5:**5, 6^2, 7^4, 8^2, 10, 11, 13, 14, 15, 16, 17, 18, 21, 22, 24, 26^3; **6:**4, 7, 10, 18^2, 19^2, 20, 22, 23, 24, 28^2, 30, 31, 32^3; **7:**1, 3, 5^2, 6^3, 8, 9, 10, 11, 12^2, 16, 17^2, 18^3; **8:**1, 3^2, 5^5, 7, 9^2, 14^3, 15, 16, 17, 19^2, 21, 25, 26, 28, 29^2; **9:**1, 2, 4, 5^2, 10, 11^2, 12, 15^3, 16^2, 17, 18^3, 19^2, 22, 23, 25, 26, 27^2, 28, 29, 30, 32^2, 35; **10:**1^3, 2, 5, 6^4, 7^3, 9^2, 12, 13, 15^3, 17^3, 19^3, 21, 24, 25^4, 29^2, 30, 31^2, 32; **11:**4, 9^3, 10, 11, 13, 19, 21; **12:**1, 4^2, 5, 8^2, 11, 12^4, 14, 15, 17^2, 18, 20; **13:**1, 2, 7, 10, 16, 21; **14:**2, 3, 5, 6^3, 8, 9^4, 10, 11, 12^2, 13, 14, 19^2, 22, 23, 24, 25, 28; **15:**1, 2, 3, 9, 12, 13, 14, 16, 17, 18, 19, 20^2, 23, 24, 27, 28, 29, 32, 33, 34, 37; **16:**1, 2, 3^2, 5^2, 6^2, 7, 8, 9, 10^4, 11, 12, 15, 16; **17:**1, 4^2, 5, 9, 11^2, 13^2, 14, 17^4, 23, 26, 31, 35^2, 36, 37; **18:**1^2, 2, 3, 4, 6, 8, 9, 14^2, 16, 17^2, 18^2, 19, 22, 23^2, 25^2, 26, 27^4, 29, 31^2, 32, 37; **19:**1, 2, 3^2, 4, 5, 6, 7^2, 9, 10, 11, 16, 20^2, 21, 23^2, 25^2, 34, 35, 37; **20:**1, 2, 4^2, 10; **21:**1, 6^2, 7^2, 8^3, 9, 11, 14, 15, 16^2, 19; **22:**1, 2^2, 3^2, 4, 5^2, 6^2, 8, 9, 11, 13, 15, 17, 18^3; **23:**3^4, 4, 5^5, 6, 8, 9, 10^2, 11, 15^2, 16, 19^4, 20, 23, 25^2, 29, 30, 31, 32, 33, 34^2, 35^5, 36, 37; **24:**2^2, 3^2, 7, 8, 9, 12, 15^2, 16, 17, 18, 19, 20; **25:**1, 6^2, 7, 11, 12, 13, 20^2, 23^2, 24^3, 25, 26, 27^2, 28

1Ch 1:10; **2:**21, 23, 35^2; **4:**27, 39^2, 42; **5:**1, 18^3, 20, 26; **6:**19, 32, 49^2, 56, 57, 62, 64; **7:**2, 11, 15, 21, 22, 23, 40^2; **8:**6; **9:**1, 9, 22, 25^2, 27, 29, 32; **10:**4, 8^2, 9^2, 11, 12, 13; **11:**1, 3^3, 4, 5, 10^2, 13, 15^2, 18^2, 21, 23, 25, 31; **12:**1^2, 8, 15, 16, 17^4, 18, 19^4, 20^2, 22^2, 23^6, 24, 31, 32^2, 33, 36, 38^3; **13:**2, 3, 5, 6^4, 9, 10, 11, 12, 13^2; **14:**1^2, 8, 11, 15^2, 16; **15:**2^3, 3^2, 14, 15, 16^3, 19, 21, 25, 26, 29^2; **16:**3^2, 4^3, 5, 7, 15, 17^2, 20^2, 21, 23, 25^2, 33, 35, 37, 38, 40^3, 41^2, 43^2; **17:**1^2, 3^2, 4, 5^2, 6^2, 10, 11^2, 15^2, 17^2, 18, 19, 20, 21^3, 24, 25, 27; **18:**1, 3, 5, 7, 10^3; **19:**1, 2^4, 3^4, 5, 6^2, 7, 15, 16, 19; **20:**1^2, 2, 3, 4; **21:**1, 2^4, 3, 4, 6, 11, 12^2, 15^2, 17, 18^2, 21^3, 22, 23, 24, 25, 30; **22:**2^3, 4, 5, 6, 7^2, 8, 9, 13, 17, 19^4; **23:**4, 5, 11, 13^3, 28, 30^2, 31^2; **24:**3, 4, 7^2, 8^2, 9^2, 10^2, 11^2, 12^2, 13^2, 14^2, 15^2, 16^2, 17^2, 18^2, 19^2; **25:**1^2, 2, 3^2, 5^2, 6^2, 9^2, 10, 11, 12, 13, 14, 15, 16, 17, 18, 19, 20, 21, 22, 23, 24, 25, 26, 27, 28, 29, 30, 31; **26:**12, 13, 14, 15^2, 16, 27, 31, 32; **27:**1, 23, 24; **28:**1, 2, 4^3, 5, 6, 7, 10, 11, 15, 20; **29:**2^2, 3^2, 4, 5^2, 8, 9, 12^2, 14, 16, 17, 19^3, 20, 22^2

2Ch 1:2^3, 3, 4, 6, 8, 11, 13^2; **2:**1, 2^3, 3^3, 4^5, 6^2, 7^2, 8, 9^2, 10, 11, 12, 14^4, 16^3, 18^3; **3:**1, 2, 4, 8^2, 11^2, 12^2; **4:**2, 6^2, 7, 11, 12^2, 13, 16; **5:**2, 7, 11, 13^3, 14; **6:**4, 5^2, 6, 7, 8^2, 16^3, 19^3, 20, 22, 23, 24, 25^2, 31, 33^2, 34, 38; **7:**3, 6, 7, 10^2, 11, 12^2, 13, 17, 18, 20, 21; **8:**1, 2^2, 3, 6, 8, 13, 14^4, 17^2, 18^2; **9:**1^2, 5, 8^4, 11^2, 12^2, 13, 14, 15, 16, 18^2, 21, 23, 26; **10:**1^3, 2, 3, 6^2, 7^2, 9^2, 11, 12^2, 15, 16^3, 18^4; **11:**1^3, 2, 3, 4, 13, 14, 16^3, 18, 22^2; **12:**1, 2, 4^2, 5^3, 7, 10, 13^2, 14; **13:**1, 5^4, 8, 9, 11, 12, 13, 15; **14:**4^2, 11, 15; **15:**2, 5^2, 9, 12, 13; **16:**1^2, 2, 5, 7, 9^2, 12^2; **17:**4, 5, 7^2, 14, 15; **18:**2^4, 3, 4, 5^2, 11, 12^3, 14^3, 15^2, 16, 17, 23, 24, 25^2, 28, 29^2, 31^3, 32, 33; **19:**1^2, 2^2, 3, 4, 6, 8, 10; **20:**1^2, 3, 4^2, 6, 7, 11^3, 12, 16, 17^2, 18, 19, 21, 22^2, 23^2, 24, 25, 27^3, 28, 31, 36^3, 37^2; **21:**3, 4, 5, 6, 7^3, 11, 12, 13^2, 19, 20; **22:**1, 2, 3, 4, 5, 6^2, 7^2, 8^2, 9^2; **23:**2, 7, 8^3, 9, 10, 12, 13, 15, 17, 18; **24:**1, 4^2, 5^3, 6^2, 9^2, 11^2, 12^3, 14^2, 17, 19^2, 22, 23^2; **25:**1, 3^2, 5^3, 7^2, 8^2, 9^3, 10^3, 11, 13, 14^2, 16^2, 17, 18^4, 19^2, 21, 22^2, 23^2, 24, 27^2; **26:**2, 3, 4, 5, 8^2, 11^2, 13, 14, 15^2, 16^2, 18^3, 19, 20, 23; **27:**1, 2, 8; **28:**1, 5, 7, 8, 9, 10, 13^3, 15^5, 16, 23, 25^2; **29:**1, 2, 8^3, 10, 11^2, 15^2, 16^2, 17^2, 18, 20, 21, 24, 25, 27, 30, 32, 34; **30:**1^4, 2, 3, 5^3, 6^2, 7, 10^2, 11, 12^2, 13, 16, 17, 19^2, 20, 22, 23, 24^2, 27; **31:**1^2, 2^4, 3, 4, 7, 10^2, 11, 14, 15^4, 16, 17, 18, 19^3, 21; **32:**1, 2, 3, 5, 6^2, 8^2, 9, 11^2, 13, 14, 15, 17^2, 18^2, 20, 21, 23^2, 24, 25, 30, 31^2; **33:**1, 6^3, 7^2, 8^2, 9^2, 10^2, 11, 13, 14, 16, 18, 21; **34:**1, 2^2, 3^2, 7, 8, 9^2, 10^2, 11^3, 12, 15^2, 16^2, 17, 19, 21, 22^3, 23, 25, 26, 28^2, 31^3, 32^3, 33^2; **35:**2, 4^2, 5, 6, 7^2, 8^2, 10, 12^2, 13, 15, 16^3, 18, 20, 21^3, 22, 23, 24, 25, 26; **36:**2, 4^2, 5, 6^2, 7, 9, 10, 11, 15, 18, 20^2, 21^2, 23

Ezr 1:2, 3, 5^2; **2:**68^2; **3:**1, 2, 4, 6, 7^5, 8, 9, 10; **4:**2^2, 3^2, 5, 8, 12, 14, 17^2, 21^2, 22^2, 23^2; **5:**2, 3^3, 5^2, 8, 9^2, 10, 13, 17^3; **6:**5, 8, 9, 12^4, 13, 14^2, 17, 21, 22; **7:**6, 8, 9^3, 10^3, 11, 13^2, 14^2, 15, 18^3, 20, 21, 22^3, 24, 26^3, 27, 28; **8:**15^2, 17, 21, 22^2, 30^2, 31, 32, 36; **9:**1^2, 6^2, 7^4, 8^3, 9^4, 11^2, 12; **10:**3^3, 5^2, 8, 10, 13, 16

Neh 1:1, 4, 9, 11^3; **2:**1, 4, 6, 7, 8^3, 9, 10, 11, 12, 13, 14^3, 16^5, 19; **3:**2, 5, 16, 19^2, 21, 31; **4:**1, 5, 6, 7^2, 8^3, 10, 11, 12, 14^2, 15^3, 16, 19^2, 22; **5:**5^2, 8, 9, 11, 12, 13, 14, 19; **6:**1, 2, 3, 6^2, 7^3, 10^2, 11, 14, 16, 19^2; **7:**1, 3, 5, 6^2, 63, 70, 71; **8:**1^2, 6, 7, 8, 12^4, 13, 15; **9:**8^3, 12, 15^2, 16, 17^5, 19^2, 20, 23^2, 26^2, 27, 28, 36; **10:**29^3, 31, 32, 33, 34^2, 35, 36^2, 37, 38; **11:**1^3, 2, 3, 17; **12:**22, 24^3, 27^3, 44, 45; **13:**3, 5^2, 7, 10, 13^2, 19^2, 22^2, 24, 26, 27^2, 28

Est 1:1, 6, 7, 8^3, 9, 11^3, 12, 13, 15, 16^3, 17, 20^2, 21, 22^3; **2:**3, 8^3, 9^2, 11, 12^4, 13, 14, 15, 18^2, 21, 22; **3:**4^2, 6^2, 7^3, 8, 9^2, 11^3, 12^5, 13^5, 14, 15; **4:**4^2, 5^3, 6, 7^3, 8^6, 11^4, 12, 13, 14^2, 16, 17; **5:**1, 2, 3, 5^2, 6, 8^4, 12, 14^2; **6:**1, 2, 3, 4^2, 6^4, 7, 8, 9^4, 10^2, 11, 12^2, 13, 14; **7:**1, 2, 4^3, 5, 7^2; **8:**3, 5^2, 6^2, 7, 9^6, 11^7, 13^2; **9:**1^3, 2, 13^3, 14, 19, 21, 22^3, 23, 24^3, 27^2, 29, 30, 31; **10:**3

Job 1:4^2, 5, 6, 7, 11, 15, 16, 17, 19; **2:**1^2, 2, 3, 5, 8, 11^3; **3:**8, 20, 23; **4:**2, 12, 14, 20; **5:**1, 4, 11^2, 26; **6:**7, 9, 14, 18, 24, 26; **7:**1, 3^2, 4, 9, 10, 20; **8:**5, 8, 22; **9:**14, 15, 18, 19, 26; **10:**19, 21; **11:**6; **12:**3, 4, 5, 8, 22, 24, 25; **13:**3^2, 6, 12, 23, 25, 26; **14:**15, 18, 21; **15:**8, 20, 24, 28; **16:**8, 11, 12; **17:**5, 14^2, 16; **18:**11, 14; **19:**3, 17, 20^2; **20:**2, 3, 6, 10, 18, 23; **21:**4, 13, 30^2, 31, 32; **22:**3^2, 7^2, 14, 19, 23; **23:**2, 3; **24:**5, 7, 10, 12, 17, 21, 23; **25:**5; **26:**4, 10; **28:**3, 11, 24, 25, 28; **29:**7, 10, 11, 12, 13^2, 15^2, 16; **30:**1, 6, 10, 21, 22^2, 23^2, 24, 29^2, 31; **31:**3^2, 5, 7, 11, 12, 16, 23, 24, 28, 30^2, 32, 36, 39; **32:**1, 10, 11^2, 19, 22; **33:**1, 6, 22, 23, 24, 25, 30^2, 32^2; **34:**4, 11^2, 16, 18^3, 19, 28, 31, 33; **35:**2, 9; **36:**2, 3, 6, 10, 27, 32; **37:**6^3, 13, 15; **38:**12, 14, 20^2, 26^2, 27^3, 34, 36,

40; **39**:9, 11, 17, 21; **40**:19; **41**:10, 13, 16, 17, 31, 32[2]; **42**:7, 8

Ps 4:ttl; **5**:1, ttl; **6**:6, ttl; **7**:2, 6, 8[2], 9, 17[2]; **8**:6, ttl; **9**:2, 6, 8, 11, 20, ttl; **10**:9, 14, 17, 18; **11**:1[2], ttl; **12**:ttl; **13**:ttl; **14**:2, ttl; **15**:3, 4, 5; **16**:2, 3[2], 10; **17**:11, 14; **18**:3, 20[2], 24[2], 30, 34, 38, 41, 50[4], ttl; **19**:4, 5, 10, ttl; **20**:4, ttl; **21**:11, ttl; **22**:7, 11, 15, 19, 29, 30, ttl; **23**:2; **25**:7; **27**:2, 4[2], 13; **28**:1[2], 3, 4[3]; **29**:6, 9; **30**:1, 3, 7, 8, 9, 12[2]; **31**:2[2], 11, 13, 16, 18, ttl; **32**:10; **33**:10, 11, 19[2]; **34**:9, 16; **35**:4[2], 11, 12, 23, 24, 26; **36**:2, 3[2], 10, 12, ttl; **37**:5, 7, 8, 14[2], 32, 34; **38**:17, 22, ttl[2]; **39**:1, 4, 11, ttl[2]; **40**:4, 5, 8, 12, 13[2], 14[2], ttl; **41**:6[2], 13, ttl; **42**:4, ttl; **43**:3; **44**:7, 9, 10, 13[2], 20, 25, ttl; **45**:17, ttl; **46**:9, ttl; **47**:6, ttl; **48**:1, 10, 13; **49**:4, 7, 10, 11, 18, 19, ttl; **50**:4[2], 8, 16[2], 19, 22, 23; **51**:1, 6, 8, ttl[2]; **52**:3, ttl[2]; **53**:2, 5, ttl; **54**:2, ttl[2]; **55**:1, 22, ttl; **56**:ttl; **57**:ttl; **58**:5, 7, ttl; **59**:4, 5[2], ttl[2]; **60**:1, 2, 3, 4, ttl[2]; **61**:2, ttl; **62**:4, 9, 12[2], ttl[2]; **63**:2, 9; **64**:3, 8, ttl; **65**:4, 8, ttl; **66**:4, 8, 9, 12, 19, ttl; **67**:1, ttl; **68**:4, 16, 33, ttl; **69**:10, 11, 16, 20, 21, 23, 26, ttl; **70**:1[2], 2, ttl[3]; **71**:1, 2, 3, 11, 13, 18[2]; **72**:3, 8, 15; **73**:1[2], 10, 16, 24, 28[2]; **74**:7, 14[2]; **75**:4, 9, ttl; **76**:7, 8, 9[2], 11, 12, ttl; **77**:2, 6, 9, ttl[2]; **78**:1[2], 4[2], 5, 6[2], 10, 13[2], 16, 24, 25, 26, 48[2], 50[2], 52, 54[2], 55, 58[2], 63, 66, 71, 72; **79**:2, 3, 4[2], 11[2], 13; **80**:3, 5, 7, 9, 19, ttl; **81**:11, ttl; **82**:3; **83**:9[2], 12, 17; **84**:7, 10, ttl; **85**:4, 5, 8[2], ttl; **86**:5, 6, 11; **87**:4; **88**:10, 15, ttl; **89**:1, 4, 7[2], 8, 19, 29, 33, 39, 40, 41, 42, 43, 44[2]; **90**:2, 3, 11, 12, 15; **91**:11; **92**:1[2], 2, 15; **94**:1[2], 2; **95**:1, 7; **96**:2, 4[2], 13; **98**:9; **100**:5; **101**:3; **102**:4, 5, 13, 18, 20[3], 21, 22; **103**:8, 10, 17, 18[3]; **104**:9, 11, 14, 15[2], 23, 26, 29, 33; **105**:8, 10, 13[2], 14, 22, 25[2], 39; **106**:8, 23, 26, 27[2], 29, 45, 46, 47[2], 48; **107**:4, 7, 8, 12, 15, 21, 23, 26[2], 27, 31, 36, 38, 40; **109**:12[2], 16, 26, 31, ttl; **111**:4; **112**:9; **113**:3, 6, 9[2]; **115**:16; **116**:17; **118**:8[2], 9[2], 19; **119**:4, 5, 9, 25, 27, 31, 35, 36, 38, 41, 42, 49, 58, 60, 62, 76, 91, 95, 103, 112, 121, 126, 128, 132, 135, 149, 154, 156, 159, 169, 170; **121**:3; **122**:4; **124**:6; **125**:4; **127**:2[3]; **130**:2; **132**:4[2], 17; **133**:1, 2; **135**:7; **136**:3, 4, 5, 6, 7, 8, 9, 10, 13, 14, 16, 17, 25; **137**:6, 7, 8; **139**:12, ttl; **140**:4, 11, ttl; **141**:4[2]; **143**:1, 3[2], 8[2], 9, 10; **144**:1[2], 4, 14; **145**:3, 4, 8, 9, 12[2], 18; **146**:4, 7; **147**:1, 6, 8, 9[2], 18; **149**:7, 8, 9; **150**:2

Prv 1:2[2], 3, 4[3], 6, 16[2]; **2**:2, 7, 12, 13, 14, 16; **3**:2, 8[2], 15, 18, 22, 27[2], 28, 32; **4**:1, 8, 9[2], 16, 20, 22, 27[2]; **5**:1, 5, 13; **6**:4[2], 6, 10, 18, 24, 26, 29, 30; **7**:8, 15[2], 21, 22[2], 23, 24, 25, 27[2]; **8**:4, 7, 9[2], 11[2], 13, 21, 29; **9**:4, 7, 9, 15, 16; **10**:3, 16[2], 23[2], 26[3], 29[2]; **11**:1, 17, 18, 19[2], 20, 24, 29; **12**:4, 6, 8, 20, 21, 22; **13**:5, 14, 18, 19[3], 21, 22, 25; **14**:8, 15, 22, 23, 27, 29, 34; **15**:8, 18, 21, 24, 26, 28; **16**:5, 7, 12[2], 16[3], 17, 19[2], 23, 24[2], 30[2], 32; **17**:4[2], 15, 16[2], 21, 23, 25[2], 26[2]; **18**:5[2], 9, 18, 19; **19**:6, 7, 10, 11, 23, 24, 27[2]; **20**:2, 3, 10, 13, 17, 25[2]; **21**:3[2], 5[2], 6, 7, 9, 15[3], 19, 20, 25; **22**:1, 7, 9, 16[3], 19[2], 20, 21, 25, 27; **23**:1, 2[2], 4, 7, 12, 21, 30; **24**:1, 8, 9, 11[2], 12[2], 13, 20, 21, 23[2], 25, 29[4], 33; **25**:2[2], 8[3], 9, 10, 13, 20, 21[2], 24, 25, 27[2]; **26**:4, 5, 8, 11[2], 15[2], 17, 21[3]; **27**:1, 4, 7, 14, 19[2], 21, 23[2], 24; **28**:10, 17[2], 20, 21, 22; **29**:7, 12, 15[2], 27[2]; **30**:14, 17, 23; **31**:3, 4, 6, 8, 15[2], 19, 20[2], 25, 27

Ecc 1:5, 6, 11, 13[3], 16, 17[2]; **2**:1, 3[2], 6, 11, 12, 14, 15[2], 16, 20[2], 21, 26[5]; **3**:1[2], 2[4], 3[4], 4[4], 5[4], 6[4], 7[4], 8[2], 10[2], 11, 12[2], 14, 15, 20, 21, 22; **4**:10[2], 14; **5**:1[3], 2, 4, 6[2], 11, 12, 13, 15, 18[3], 19[4]; **6**:2[2], 6, 8; **7**:2[5], 5[2], 9, 11, 12, 14, 25[4], 27; **8**:1, 2, 3, 6, 8[2], 9, 11, 14[3], 15[3], 16[2], 17[3]; **9**:1, 2[8], 3, 4[2], 10, 11[6]; **10**:1, 3, 10[2], 15[2], 16; **11**:2[2], 7; **12**:5, 7, 10

Song 1:7, 9; **2**:3, 4; **3**:3; **4**:6[2]; **5**:2, 5[2], 6; **6**:2[3], 11[2]; **7**:7[2], 8, 9, 12; **8**:2, 11, 13[2], 14[2]

Isa 1:11, 12[2], 14, 16, 17; **2**:2, 3[2], 19, 20[3], 21[2], 22; **3**:4, 8, 10, 12, 13[2], 15, 24; **4**:1, 3; **5**:1, 4, 5[2], 8[2], 22[2], 26; **7**:1[2], 3, 7, 13, 15, 16, 18, 21, 22, 23; **8**:2, 3, 4, 8, 10, 11, 12[2], 14[2], 19, 20[3], 21, 22; **9**:3, 7[2], 16; **10**:2[2], 3, 6[3], 7, 11, 12, 20, 26, 27, 28[2], 30, 31; **11**:10, 11[2], 16; **13**:5, 9, 10, 11, 14, 16, 18, 20, 22; **14**:1, 2, 3[2], 9, 11, 12, 15[2], 16, 19, 24; **15**:1[2], 2[3], 7; **16**:1[2], 4, 10, 12[3]; **17**:4, 7[2], 8, 11[2], 12[2]; **18**:1, 2[2], 6, 7; **19**:3[4], 14, 18, 19[2], 21, 22, 23; **20**:4, 6; **21**:2, 11, 14, 16; **22**:1, 4, 5, 7, 8, 10, 12[4], 13, 20, 21[2], 23, 24; **23**:1, 6, 7, 9[2], 11, 12, 13, 15[2], 17[2], 18[2]; **24**:2, 9, 16, 18, 20, 21; **25**:2, 4[2], 11, 12[2]; **26**:5[2], 8[2], 10, 14, 21; **27**:6, 7, 9, 12, 13[2]; **28**:1[2], 2, 6[3], 9, 11, 12[2], 17[2], 19, 21, 24, 26; **29**:1[3], 11, 12, 14, 15, 20, 24; **30**:1[2], 2[3], 4, 6, 7[2], 8, 10[2], 11, 13[2], 14[2], 21[2], 28[3], 29[2], 30; **31**:1[2], 4, 9; **32**:4, 5, 6[4], 7; **33**:1[3], 4; **34**:1, 2, 5, 10, 12, 14, 17; **35**:4, 10; **36**:1, 2, 4, 6, 7[3], 8[2], 10, 11, 12[4], 14, 16[2], 17, 22; **37**:1, 3[2], 4, 5, 7[2], 9[2], 10, 11, 17, 21, 22, 24[2], 26[2], 35, 38; **38**:4, 5, 10, 12, 13, 16, 17, 19, 20[2], 22; **39**:1, 5, 6, 8; **40**:2, 14, 16, 17, 18, 20, 22, 23, 25, 29[2]; **41**:1, 2[3], 6, 22, 23, 27[2]; **42**:1, 2, 5, 7[2], 8[2], 9, 10, 17, 23[2], 24, 25; **43**:6[2], 14, 20[2], 23, 24, 28[2]; **44**:13, 15, 19[2], 26[2], 27, 28[2]; **45**:1[4], 9, 10, 11, 16, 18, 24; **46**:1, 4[2], 5, 8, 11; **47**:7, 8, 9, 11, 12, 14[2], 15; **48**:3, 5[2], 17, 18, 20, 21; **49**:5[3], 6[3], 7[3], 8[3], 9[2], 18, 20, 21, 22[2], 23; **50**:1, 2[2], 4[3], 6[2], 8; **51**:1[2], 4, 6, 8, 10, 13, 18, 23[2]; **52**:4, 5, 8; **53**:1, 6, 7, 10[2]; **54**:3, 4, 16; **55**:1, 4[2], 7, 10[2], 13; **56**:1[2], 3, 6[4], 7, 8, 9, 10, 11, 12; **57**:1[2], 6, 7, 8, 9, 11, 15[2], 18, 19[2], 21; **58**:2[2], 4[3], 5[4], 6[3], 7[3], 10, 12, 14; **59**:7[2], 18[4], 20; **60**:3[2], 4, 8, 9[2], 13; **61**:1[5], 2[2], 3[2], 11[2]; **62**:8, 11; **63**:1, 5[2], 6, 7[3], 10, 12, 14[2], 17; **64**:2[3], 7; **65**:3[2], 5, 10, 12[2], 24; **66**:2[2], 5, 6, 8, 9[3], 12, 15, 19[3], 20, 23[4]

Jer 1:2, 7, 8, 10[6], 12, 19; **2**:1, 7, 18[4], 24, 27[2], 28, 33, 36; **3**:1, 3, 5, 9, 12, 13, 14, 15, 16[2], 17[2], 18; **4**:3, 4, 7, 9, 11[4], 16, 22[2]; **5**:1, 3[2], 7, 19, 31; **6**:1, 2, 6, 10, 13, 17, 19, 20[2]; **7**:1, 2, 3, 6, 7[2], 10, 12, 14[3], 16, 18[4], 19[2], 27, 30, 31, 34; **8**:5, 6, 10[2], 14[2], 19; **9**:3, 5[2], 6, 8, 12, 15, 21; **10**:5, 7, 10, 13, 20[2], 22, 23, 24; **11**:1, 2, 4, 5, 8, 10[3], 11, 13[4], 15, 17[2], 19; **12**:9, 11, 12, 13, 14, 15[3], 16[3]; **13**:2, 4, 6[3], 7, 10[3], 11[2], 16, 18, 21, 23; **14**:1, 3[2], 8, 10, 16[2]; **15**:2[5], 3[3], 4, 5, 8[2], 9, 10[2], 11, 13, 14, 18, 20[2]; **16**:5, 7[2], 8[3], 9, 10, 21[2]; **17**:3, 4, 10[3], 16, 21, 24[3], 27[2]; **18**:1, 2[2], 3, 4[2], 5, 7[3], 8, 9[2], 11[3], 15[3], 16, 18, 19[2], 20[2], 21[2], 22, 23; **19**:5, 7[2], 9, 11, 12, 14[2]; **20**:3, 4[2], 5, 6[2], 15, 17, 18; **21**:2, 3, 9, 14; **22**:1, 3, 8, 16, 17[2], 20, 27[2]; **23**:3, 13, 21, 22, 27[3], 28, 32, 35[2], 37; **24**:1, 6, 7, 9[2], 10; **25**:1, 2, 4, 5, 6[3], 7[2], 12, 14[2], 15[2], 17, 18[2], 28[2], 29, 31[2], 32, 35[2]; **26**:2[2], 3, 4[2], 5[2], 6, 8[2], 11[2], 12[2], 15[2], 16[3], 17, 18, 19, 20, 21[2], 24[2]; **27**:2, 3[6], 4, 6, 8, 9[5], 10, 12[2], 16[3], 18[2], 20, 22[2]; **28**:1, 3, 4, 6, 9, 15; **29**:1[4], 3, 4, 6, 7, 8[2], 10[2], 11, 14, 18[3], 19, 20, 24, 25[2], 27, 31[2], 32; **30**:1, 3[3], 8, 11, 13, 21[2]; **31**:2[2], 6, 9[2], 12, 15, 17, 18, 21, 28[8], 32[2], 38, 39; **32**:1, 4, 5, 7, 8[2], 11, 19[3], 22[2], 23[2], 24[2], 29[2], 30, 31, 32[2], 33, 34, 35[4], 37, 40, 41, 44; **33**:2, 5[2], 7, 9, 11, 12, 14, 15, 17, 18[3], 21, 23, 26[2]; **34**:2, 3[2], 8, 9, 11, 12, 15, 16[2], 17[6], 20, 22[2]; **35**:2, 8, 9[2], 10, 11[2], 13[2], 14, 15[3], 19; **36**:1, 3, 8, 9[3], 16, 20, 21, 23, 25, 26, 27, 29[2], 30[3], 32; **37**:3, 7[4], 11, 12[2], 13, 14[3], 20[2]; **38**:2, 4, 8, 9[2], 11, 15, 16, 18, 19, 21, 22, 23[2], 25, 26[3], 27; **39**:4, 5[2], 7[2], 9, 11, 12, 16; **40**:1, 4[3], 5[2], 6, 7, 8[2], 9[2], 10, 12[2], 13[2], 14, 15; **41**:1[2], 4, 5[2], 6[3], 10[3], 12, 13, 15, 17[2]; **42**:4[2], 5[3], 6, 7, 8, 9, 11[2], 12[2], 15[2], 16, 17[2], 21, 22[2]; **43**:1[2], 2[2], 3[2], 4, 5, 7, 11[3]; **44**:1, 3[4], 5[2], 7[3], 8, 11, 12[2], 14[4], 17[2], 18[3], 19[2], 20[3], 24, 25[3], 28; **45**:3; **46**:1, 3, 13, 16[3], 19; **47**:1, 3, 4[2]; **48**:4, 9, 11, 12, 15, 16, 32, 33, 35[2], 39; **49**:2, 3, 9, 10, 12, 14, 24, 28, 29, 34, 37, 39; **50**:5[2], 6[2], 9, 16[2], 19, 21, 27, 28, 29[2], 33, 34, 39, 42; **51**:9, 11, 16, 24, 27, 29, 30, 31[3], 33, 35[2], 40, 49, 53, 61[2], 62, 63; **52**:1, 2, 3, 4, 9, 11, 15, 17, 26[2], 27, 31

Lam 1:2, 4, 11, 12, 14[2], 15, 17, 19, 21; **2**:2, 4, 6, 8[2], 10, 12, 13[3], 14, 17, 20; **3**:13, 14, 21, 25, 30, 32, 34, 35, 36, 37, 40, 64; **4**:2, 3, 4, 8; **5**:2[2], 6[3], 13, 19

Ezk 1:1, 9, 11, 12, 20[2]; **2**:3[2]; **3**:2, 3, 5[2], 6[2], 11, 15, 16, 18[2], 26[2]; **4**:3, 4, 5, 8, 9, 10, 11; **5**:1[2], 7, 13, 16; **6**:3[4], 13; **7**:3, 8, 9, 13, 14[2], 19, 21, 24, 27; **8**:1, 3[3], 4, 7, 14, 17[4]; **9**:1, 3[2], 5, 8; **10**:5, 6, 11, 16; **11**:13, 16, 24; **12**:2[2], 3, 12, 13[2], 14, 17, 23, 25, 26, 27; **13**:5, 6, 13, 14, 16, 18[3], 19[3], 20[2], 21; **14**:4[2], 7[2], 12, 15, 19, 21; **15**:3[2], 6; **16**:2, 4, 5[3], 7[2], 17, 20, 21[2], 23, 25[2], 26[2], 33[2], 34, 41, 42, 55[3]; **17**:9, 12[3], 17, 20, 24; **18**:3, 6[2], 7[2], 9, 10, 12, 15, 16, 24, 30; **19**:3, 6, 9, 12, 14[2]; **20**:1[2], 3, 4, 6, 8, 10, 12, 13, 21[2], 26[2], 28[2], 31, 32, 35, 37, 42[2], 44[2], 47[2]; **21**:3, 4, 7, 10, 11[2], 17, 19, 20[2], 21, 22[6], 23[2], 24[2], 28, 29, 30, 31, 32; **22**:3, 4[2], 6[2], 9, 12, 18, 20[2], 27[3]; **23**:15[2], 17, 19, 21, 24, 27, 32, 37[2], 39[2], 40, 46, 48[2]; **24**:6[2], 7, 8[2], 9, 13, 14[3], 17, 19, 24, 26[2], 27; **25**:4, 7[2], 14[2], 15; **26**:1, 3[2], 5, 11, 13, 14, 15, 17[2], 20; **27**:5, 7, 9, 19, 30; **28**:8, 17, 18, 25; **29**:4, 5[2], 6, 7, 14, 16, 17, 18, 21; **30**:9, 10, 11, 13, 20, 21[5], 22; **31**:1, 2, 14[3], 15[2], 16[2], 18; **32**:1, 4, 6, 12, 14, 17, 20, 21, 24, 25, 27, 29, 30; **33**:2, 8, 9, 12, 13[2], 21, 22, 27[2], 30[2], 33; **34**:2, 5, 8, 10, 13, 15, 18[2], 25, 26, 28; **35**:11[2], 12; **36**:4[7], 5, 6[3], 8[2], 12, 15[2], 19[2], 20, 27, 28, 33, 37; **37**:2, 5, 7, 9, 12, 17, 22; **38**:9, 10, 11[2], 12[3], 13[5], 16, 18, 20; **39**:2, 3, 4[2], 11, 13, 14[2], 17[2], 24[2], 28; **40**:4[2], 13, 16[3], 23, 24, 26[2], 27, 28[2], 29, 31, 32, 33, 34, 35[2], 36, 37, 39, 40, 46[2], 48, 49; **41**:1, 7[2], 16, 17; **42**:11[2], 12, 14, 19, 20; **43**:1, 3[3], 10, 14[2], 18[2], 19[2]; **44**:3, 6[2], 7[2], 11[2], 12, 13[3], 15[3], 16[2], 17, 19, 20, 23, 24, 25, 27, 30; **45**:4, 8[2], 15, 17[2], 23, 25[4]; **46**:5[2], 7, 9, 11[5], 14, 17[3], 18, 20, 21; **47**:3, 4[2], 5, 6[2], 9, 10[3], 11, 12, 13, 14, 15, 19[2], 21, 22[2], 23; **48**:1[3], 28

Dan 1:2, 4, 7[3], 10, 11, 12[2], 14; **2**:2[2], 3, 4, 5, 9, 12, 13, 14[2], 15[2], 17[2], 21, 24, 26[2], 28, 29[3], 30[2], 34, 35, 39, 43, 44, 45[2]; **3**:2[3], 4, 9, 13, 16[2], 17, 19, 20[2], 26; **4**:2, 3, 6, 8, 11, 17[2], 18, 19[2], 20, 22, 25[2], 26, 27, 31, 32[2], 34, 35, 37; **5**:1, 2, 7[2], 8, 16, 17[3], 28; **6**:1, 3, 4, 6, 7[2], 8, 12, 14[2], 18, 20[3]; **7**:4, 5, 6, 11, 13, 22, 25, 26[2], 27; **8**:2, 4, 6, 7[2], 10[2], 11, 12, 13[2], 15, 16, 23, 25; **9**:2, 3, 4[2], 6[2], 7[2], 8[4], 9, 10, 16[2], 17, 21, 22, 23, 24[6], 25[2], 27; **10**:6, 7, 12[2], 13, 14, 20; **11**:1[2], 3, 4[2], 6[2], 10, 14, 15, 16, 17, 18[2], 21, 25, 27, 28, 34, 35[4], 36, 39, 44[2], 45; **12**:1, 2[2], 3, 4[2], 6[2], 7, 12

Hos 1:2, 4, 5, 10; **2**:1, 7, 9, 11, 13, 18, 21, 23; **3**:1[2], 2; **4**:6, 10[2], 12, 15, 17; **5**:2, 4, 5, 6, 12, 13[2], 14, 15; **6**:3; **7**:10[2], 11[2], 16; **8**:1, 5, 9, 11[2], 12, 13; **9**:3, 4, 10, 12, 13; **10**:1[2], 3, 6, 8[2], 11[2], 12[2]; **11**:2, 3, 4, 5, 7[2], 9; **12**:2[2], 6, 7, 9, 14; **13**:2, 6; **14**:2, 3, 8

Joel 1:1, 19; **2**:2, 9, 12, 13, 17, 23, 25, 28, 32; **3**:4, 8[2], 11, 12[2], 18, 20

Am 1:6[2], 9; **2**:4, 7, 8, 10, 12; **3**:10, 14; **4**:1, 4, 7[3], 8, 10, 12; **5**:2, 3, 5[2], 6, 7, 16[2], 18, 26, 27; **6**:1[2], 2[2], 3, 5[2], 9, 10, 13; **7**:2, 4, 10[2], 14; **8**:4[2], 9[2], 12[4]; **9**:2

Oba 3, 5[2], 7, 9, 14, 21

Jna 1:2, 3[4], 4, 5, 6, 7, 13[2], 17; **2**:5, 6; **3**:3, 4, 5, 7; **4**:2, 3[2], 4, 6[2], 8[4], 9[3]

Mic 1:1, 7[2], 9, 13[2], 14[2]; **2**:1, 6[2], 7; **3**:1, 8[2]; **4**:1, 2[2], 8, 10[2]; **5**:2, 10; **6**:8[3], 14; **7**:1, 9, 11, 12[4], 15, 20[2]

Nah 1:3; **2**:5; **3**:1, 7

Hab 1:3, 6, 8, 13, 17; **2**:1, 6[2], 9[2], 10, 12, 15, 18, 19[2]; **3**:9, 14[2], 19[2]

Zep 1:8, 10, 12, 18; **2**:15; **3**:1[2], 2, 4, 5, 8[3], 9[2], 16[2], 18, 19

Hag 1:1, 4, 6, 8, 9; **2**:2[3], 5, 16[3], 17, 21

Zec 1:6[3], 10[2], 11, 16, 21[4]; **2**:2[2], 3, 4, 9, 11; **3**:1, 4, 7; **4**:2, 4, 10; **5**:3[2], 10, 11; **6**:7[4], 14[4], 15; **7**:1, 2, 3[2], 5[2], 9, 11, 13; **8**:1, 10, 12, 13, 14[2], 15[2], 16, 19, 20, 21[3], 22[2], 23; **9**:10[2], 12[2]; **10**:1, 6; **11**:9, 13, 17; **12**:9[2]; **13**:1[2], 2[2], 3, 4[2], 5, 8; **14**:2, 5, 6, 7[2], 10, 13, 16[4], 17, 18, 19

Mal 1:1; **2**:2[3], 5, 8, 15, 16; **3**:1, 5[2], 10, 14, 16; **4**:6[2]

Mt 1:11, 12, 17, 18, 19[2], 20; **2**:1, 2, 8, 12, 13[2], 16, 19, 22; **3**:5, 7[3], 9[3], 11, 13[2], 14[2], 15[2]; **4**:1, 3, 16, 17[2]; **5**:13[2], 17[3], 22, 23, 24, 25[2], 28, 32, 39, 41, 42, 44, 45; **6**:1, 5, 6, 16, 18, 24, 30[2]; **7**:2, 4, 5, 8, 11[2], 12[2], 13, 15, 22, 28; **8**:4, 9[3], 10, 18, 20, 21, 25, 28, 29[2], 31, 33, 34; **9**:2, 5[2], 6[2], 7, 10, 13[2], 14, 16, 24, 28[2], 29, 32; **10**:1[2], 6, 13, 17, 21[3], 22, 28[2], 34[2], 35, 42; **11**:1[3], 5, 7[2], 8, 9, 14, 15, 20, 23, 27; **12**:1[2], 2, 4, 10, 12, 13, 18, 25, 32, 39, 42, 46[2], 47; **13**:3, 9, 11[2], 12, 13, 17[2], 30[2], 31, 43, 48, 53; **14**:4, 5, 7, 9, 11[2], 15, 16, 18, 19[4], 22[2], 23, 29[2], 30; **15**:1, 5, 20, 26[3], 31[4], 32, 33, 35, 36[2]; **16**:3, 5[2], 11, 21, 22, 27; **17**:4, 9, 14[3], 16, 17, 19, 20, 24[2], 27; **18**:7, 8[2], 9[2], 11, 17[2], 21, 24, 25[3], 34; **19**:1, 3, 5, 7[2], 8, 10, 11, 12, 14, 21, 24[2]; **20**:1, 15, 17, 18[2], 19[4], 20, 22[2], 23[3], 28[3]; **21**:1, 9, 14, 15, 19, 21, 28[2], 30, 33, 34, 43, 44, 46; **22**:3[2], 5[2], 8, 9, 11, 13, 17, 23, 34, 46; **23**:1[2], 4, 5, 7, 13, 15, 23[2], 34; **24**:1[2], 6, 9, 17, 18, 19, 21, 31, 43, 45, 49[2]; **25**:1, 6, 9, 10[2], 11, 15[4], 27[2], 45[2]; **26**:1, 2, 8, 9, 16, 17[2], 18, 22, 26, 27, 37, 45, 49, 53, 55[2], 57, 58, 59[2], 61[2], 73, 74[2]; **27**:1[2], 2, 3, 4[2], 6, 7, 14, 15, 19, 24, 26, 31, 32, 33, 34, 46, 48, 49, 51, 58[2], 60; **28**:1[2], 8, 9, 14, 20

Mk 1:7, 9, 17, 24[2], 34, 40[2], 44[2], 45[3]; **2**:2, 9[3], 10[2], 15, 17[2], 18, 23[2], 26[2]; **3**:4[4], 7, 9, 10, 14, 15[3], 21; **4**:1, 3, 4, 9, 11, 21[2], 23, 24, 25, 33, 34, 41; **5**:7, 14, 15, 16, 17[2], 19, 20, 32, 37, 38, 40, 43; **6**:2, 7, 18, 21, 27, 28[2], 31, 34, 36, 37[2], 39, 41[3], 45[3], 46, 53, 55; **7**:2, 4, 5, 11[2], 12, 16, 27[2], 30, 32, 34, 37[2]; **8**:1, 2, 3, 6[3], 7, 11, 13, 14, 22[2], 26[2], 31, 32; **9**:5[2], 6, 14, 15, 18, 22, 23, 32, 33, 35, 41[2], 43[2], 45[2], 47[2]; **10**:2[2], 4[2], 7, 12, 13, 14, 17, 21, 24, 25[2], 28, 30, 32[2], 33[3], 40[3], 41, 42[2], 45[3], 46, 47, 49, 50; **11**:1, 7, 13, 15[2], 21, 23, 27[2], 28; **12**:1[2], 2, 12, 13, 14[2], 17[2], 23, 33[2], 36, 38; **13**:5, 9[2], 12[3], 14, 15, 16, 17[2], 21, 22, 27, 29, 34[3]; **14**:1, 5, 8[2], 10, 11, 14, 19[2], 21, 22, 23, 32[2], 33[2], 40, 45, 48, 53, 55[2], 64, 65[4], 69[2], 70, 71[2], 72; **15**:1, 8[2], 15[2], 18, 20, 21, 23, 36[2], 38, 45; **16**:8, 9, 15

Lk 1:1, 3[2], 8, 9[2], 16, 17[4], 19[2], 20, 23[2], 25, 27[2], 38, 41, 43[2], 49, 50, 55[3], 56, 59[2], 62, 72[3],

APNDX

73, 76, 77, 79^3; **2:**1, 3, 5, 10, 14, 15^3, 22^4, 23, 24^2, 27, 29, 32, 38, 39^2, 41, 42, 44, 45, 46, 51; **3:**7^4, 8^3, 11, 12, 14, 16, 21, 23; **4:**6, 9, 10, 16^2, 18^7, 19, 20, 21, 31, 34^2, 41, 43; **5:**1^2, 7, 11, 12, 14^2, 15^2, 17^2, 18^2, 21, 23^2, 24, 25, 26, 32^2; **6:**1, 2, 4^2, 6, 8, 9^4, 11, 12^3, 17^2, 19, 26, 27, 29, 30, 31^2, 33^2, 34^4, 35, 38, 42^2, 47^2; **7:**2, 4, 6, 7, 8^2, 10, 11, 12, 15^2, 19, 22, 24^2, 25, 26, 31, 32^2, 36, 38, 40, 42, 43, 44, 45, 47, 49, 50; **8:**1, 4, 5, 8, 10^2, 14, 18^2, 19, 20, 22, 24, 25, 27, 28, 29, 31, 32, 35^2, 37, 39, 40, 49, 51, 53, 55; **9:**1, 2^2, 9, 10, 12, 13, 14, 16^3, 17, 18, 21, 23, 28^2, 33^2, 37, 40, 42, 45, 51^3, 52, 53, 54, 56^3, 57, 58, 59, 62; **10:**5, 6, 7, 15^2, 19, 22^2, 24^2, 25, 29, 30, 34^2, 35, 38, 40^2; **11:**1^2, 4, 6^2, 10, 13^2, 14, 17, 26, 27, 29, 30, 31, 37^2, 42^2, 46, 53^3, 54; **12:**1, 5, 12, 13, 17, 19, 25, 26, 28^2, 32, 37^2, 39, 41, 42, 45^3, 47, 48, 49, 50, 51, 54, 55, 58^3; **13:**12, 14, 15, 24^2, 25^3, 26, 32^2, 33^2; **14:**1^2, 3, 6, 7, 8, 9^2, 12, 17^2, 18, 19, 21, 23, 26, 28^2, 29^2, 30^2, 31^2, 35; **15:**1, 12^2, 14, 15^2, 17^2, 18, 19, 20, 21, 22, 24, 25, 29; **16:**3, 4, 7, 9, 11, 13, 17^2, 21, 22, 26^2, 27; **17:**3, 4, 7, 10, 11^2, 14, 18^2, 22, 23, 31, 33; **18:**1^3, 10, 13, 14, 16, 18, 25^2, 30, 31, 33, 35, 40; **19:**3, 4^2, 5^2, 7, 8, 9, 10^2, 11, 12^2, 14, 15^3, 19, 24, 28, 29^2, 35, 37, 45, 47, 48; **20:**1, 9^3, 10, 16, 18, 19, 22, 27, 30, 33, 35, 46; **21:**7, 9, 12, 13, 14, 15, 16^2, 21, 23, 28^2, 29, 31, 34, 36^3, 38^2; **22:**5, 6, 15, 23, 31, 33^2, 39, 44, 45, 47, 52; **23:**2^3, 4^2, 5, 7, 8^2, 11, 15, 20^2, 25, 30^3, 32^2, 33, 36, 43, 48, 51, 56; **24:**4, 5, 9, 11, 12, 13, 15, 17, 18, 20^2, 21, 24, 25, 26^2, 29, 30^2, 32^2, 33, 34, 46^2, 50, 51, 52

Jn 1:7, 8, 12^3, 19, 22, 27, 31, 33, 38, 42, 47; **2:**2, 4, 7, 12, 13; **3:**2, 13, 17, 20, 21, 23, 26^2, 33; **4:**5^3, 7^2, 8, 10^2, 11, 15, 20, 23, 28, 32, 33^2, 34^2, 35, 38, 52; **5:**1, 7, 10, 16, 18, 26^2, 27, 35, 36, 40, 45; **6:**6, 11^2, 15, 17, 24, 31, 35, 37^2, 38, 44, 52, 68; **7:**1, 4^2, 19, 20, 24, 25, 30, 32, 45, 50; **8:**6, 26^3, 27, 31, 33, 37, 40, 41, 56, 59; **9:**11, 13, 26^2; **10:**3, 10^3, 18^2, 24, 29, 31, 39; **11:**7, 8, 15, 19^2, 31, 38, 45, 46, 53^2, 54, 55^2, 56; **12:**1, 5, 10, 12^2, 13, 20, 21, 29, 38, 47^2; **13:**2, 3, 5^2, 6, 10^2, 12, 14, 15, 19, 24, 26^2, 29, 33, 35; **14:**2, 18, 21, 26, 29^2; **15:**25; **16:**5, 10, 12, 13, 16, 17, 19, 28, 32; **17:**1, 2, 4, 11, 13; **18:**6, 13^2, 14, 20, 31^3, 36, 37; **19:**4, 7, 10^2, 12, 16, 20, 21, 23, 27, 29, 33, 39, 40; **20:**2^2, 3, 4, 8, 15, 16, 17^3, 21, 27; **21:**1, 6, 9, 11, 14, 15, 16, 21, 22, 23

Act 1:1, 3^2, 6, 7, 16, 19, 22, 25; **2:**4, 7, 12, 14, 17, 21, 27, 28, 30^3, 37, 39^2, 45, 46, 47; **3:**2, 3, 5, 12, 13, 14, 23, 26; **4:**5, 9, 10, 15, 16^2, 17, 18, 19, 23, 24, 28^2, 30; **5:**2, 3^3, 9, 13, 14, 20, 21^2, 28, 29, 31^3, 32, 33^2, 34, 35^2, 36^3, 38, 39, 40, 41, 42; **6:**4^2, 7, 10, 12, 13; **7:**5^3, 7, 13, 14, 17, 19, 23, 26, 30, 31, 33, 34, 35^2, 38^2, 39, 40, 42^2, 43, 44, 46, 54, 60; **8:**2, 3, 5, 10^2, 11, 24, 25, 27^2, 29, 30, 32, 36, 38, 40; **9:**2^2, 4, 5, 6, 10, 13, 14, 15, 23, 24, 26^3, 27^2, 29, 30^2, 32^2, 35, 37, 38^3, 40, 43; **10:**2^2, 3, 5, 6, 8, 9, 11, 13, 21, 22^2, 28, 32, 33^2, 41^2, 42^3, 43, 48^2; **11:**2, 3, 5, 13, 15, 18, 19, 20, 25^2, 26, 28, 29^2, 30; **12:**1, 3, 4^4, 10, 11, 12, 13, 17^2, 19^2, 20; **13:**2, 4, 5, 7, 8, 10, 11, 13^2, 14, 19, 22^2, 23, 24, 25, 26, 31, 34^2, 35, 42, 43^2, 44, 46^2, 47, 48; **14:**1, 3, 5^2, 9, 11, 16, 20, 21^3, 22, 23, 24, 26^2; **15:**2, 4, 5^3, 6, 10^2, 12, 14, 15, 19, 22^2, 24, 25, 28^3, 29, 30, 34, 37, 38^2; **16:**1, 3, 4, 6, 7^2, 8, 9, 10^2, 11^2, 12, 13, 15^2, 16^2, 18^2, 20, 21^2, 22, 23, 30, 32, 36^2, 39; **17:**1, 5^2, 7, 14^2, 15^2, 16, 18, 20, 21^2, 23, 25, 26, 29, 30; **18:**1, 2, 5, 7, 9, 10, 12, 13^2, 14, 15, 19, 20, 22, 24, 26, 27^2; **19:**1^2, 13, 17, 21^2, 27, 36^2, 40; **20:**1, 3^2, 6, 7^2, 13^3, 14, 15, 16^2, 17, 18, 20, 21^2, 24, 26, 27, 28^2, 30, 31, 32^4, 34, 35^4; **21:**1, 3, 4^2, 7, 12^2, 13^4, 15, 17, 21^3, 23, 25, 26, 31, 33, 34, 37, 39; **22:**2, 3, 5^3, 6, 9, 10, 12, 17^2, 24, 25, 30; **23:**2, 3^3, 9, 10^3, 14, 15^3, 17, 18^3, 19, 20^2, 22, 23^2, 29^3, 30^3, 31, 32^2, 33^2, 35; **24:**2, 6^2, 8, 10, 11^2, 16, 17^2, 19, 23^3, 25, 27; **25:**1, 3^2, 6, 9^2, 10^2, 11, 13, 15, 16^5, 17, 19, 20, 21^3, 22, 24, 25^2, 26^2, 27^3; **26:**1, 3^2, 7, 9^2, 10, 11, 12, 14^2, 16, 18^3, 20^2, 21, 22, 23, 28, 29; **27:**2, 3^2, 5, 12^4, 16, 21, 22, 27, 30, 31^2, 33, 34, 35^2, 39, 40, 42, 43^2, 44^2; **28:**4, 6, 8^2, 13^2, 14, 15, 16^3, 17, 19^2, 20^2, 22, 23^2

Ro 1:1, 3, 4^2, 5, 7^3, 10, 11^2, 13, 14^4, 15^2, 16^3, 17, 22, 23^2, 24^2, 28^3, 30; **2:**2, 4, 6^2, 7, 10^3, 16; **3:**15, 19, 25^2, 26; **4:**1, 2, 4, 5, 8, 9, 12, 13^2, 16^4, 18, 20, 21, 22, 23, 24; **5:**7, 10, 14^2, 16, 18; **6:**2, 11, 16^3, 19^3, 22; **7:**1, 2, 3^2, 4^3, 5, 10^2, 18^2, 23; **8:**1, 6^2, 7, 12^2, 15, 18, 20, 23, 27, 28^3, 29^2, 31, 33, 38, 39; **9:**3, 4, 11, 15, 20, 21, 22^3, 26, 30, 31; **10:**1, 2, 3, 4, 6, 7, 19, 21; **11:**2, 4^2, 5, 11^2, 13, 14, 23, 24, 25, 35, 36^2; **12:**2, 3^5, 6^3, 9, 10, 13^2, 16, 17; **13:**2, 3^2, 4^2, 7^5, 8, 10, 11, 14; **14:**1, 4^2, 6^3, 7^2, 9, 11^2, 12, 13, 14^3, 18, 21^2, 22; **15:**1^2, 2, 5^2, 7, 8, 9, 12, 14, 15, 16, 17, 18^2, 20, 21, 22, 23, 24^3, 25, 26, 27, 28, 30; **16:**17, 25^4, 26^2, 27

1Co 1:1, 2^2, 17^2, 18, 19, 21, 27^2, 28^2; **2:**1, 2, 6, 12; **3:**2, 5, 8, 10, 18, 22; **4:**5, 6^3, 7, 8, 9^3, 14, 18, 19; **5:**5, 9, 11^2, 12^2; **6:**1, 2, 3, 4^2, 5^2, 6, 7^2, 16; **7:**1, 2, 5, 8, 9^2, 11, 12^2, 13, 15, 17, 25, 26, 27, 32, 39^2; **8:**2, 6, 8, 9, 10^2, 13^2; **9:**2, 3, 4^2, 5, 6, 15, 16, 20, 21^3, 22^2, 25, 27; **10:**6, 7^2, 13^4, 15, 19, 20^2, 22, 27^2, 31, 32^3; **11:**2, 6, 7, 10, 15, 16, 20, 22^3, 29, 33; **12:**3, 7^2, 8^2, 9^2, 10^5, 11, 13, 21, 22, 23, 24; **13:**3^2, 12; **14:**3, 6, 8, 9, 12, 22^2, 28^2, 30, 32, 34^2, 35, 37, 39^2; **15:**3, 4, 9, 24, 32, 34^2, 38, 54, 57; **16:**1, 3, 7, 12^2, 15, 16

2Co 1:2, 4, 8, 12, 13, 15, 16^3, 17, 23; **2:**1, 3, 6, 7, 9, 10^2, 12^2, 14, 16^2; **3:**1^2, 3, 4, 5, 7, 13, 16, 18; **4:**2, 3, 6^2, 15; **5:**2, 8^2, 10, 12^2, 13, 18^2, 19, 20, 21; **7:**3^2, 9, 10^2, 11, 14^2; **8:**1, 3, 4, 5, 7, 8, 10^2, 11, 12^2, 16, 19^2, 24; **9:**1^3, 2, 5, 8^2, 9, 10, 11^2; **10:**2^2, 4, 5, 6, 7, 13^3, 14, 15, 16^3; **11:**1, 2^2, 7, 8, 9^2, 15, 32; **12:**1^2, 2, 4, 6^2, 7^2, 11, 13^2, 14^4; **13:**1, 2^2, 3, 7, 10^3

Gal 1:3, 4, 5, 10, 16, 17^2, 18^2; **2:**1, 2, 3, 4, 5, 6^4, 8, 9^2, 10, 11^3, 14^2, 17, 19; **3:**5, 6, 10, 16^3, 18, 19, 22, 24, 29; **4:**5, 9^2, 15, 18, 20^2, 21, 24, 25; **5:**3^2, 13, 17; **6:**3, 8^2, 12^2, 13, 16

Eph 1:1^2, 2, 5^2, 6, 7, 9, 11, 12, 16, 19^2, 21, 22^2; **2:**2^2, 7, 15, 17^2; **3:**2, 7, 9, 10, 11, 16^2, 18, 19, 20^2; **4:**3, 7, 14^2, 16, 19, 22, 27, 28^2, 29, 32; **5:**2, 12, 19^2, 21, 24, 27, 28; **6:**4, 5^2, 7^2, 11, 13^2, 16, 19, 20, 21, 23

Php 1:1, 7, 14, 16^2, 19, 20, 21^3, 23^2, 24, 26, 28^2, 29^2, 30; **2:**6, 11, 13^2, 19, 23, 25^3, 30; **3:**1^3, 7, 13, 21^2; **4:**11, 12^6, 17, 18, 19

Col 1:2, 3, 4, 9^2, 11, 12, 20, 22, 23, 25^3, 26, 27, 29; **2:**2, 14^2, 17, 20, 22, 23; **3:**9, 15, 16, 17, 21, 22, 23; **4:**3, 4, 6, 10, 17^2

1Th 1:2, 7, 8^2, 9^2, 10^2; **2:**2, 4, 8, 15, 16^4, 17; **3:**1, 2^2, 4, 5, 6^2, 9, 12, 13; **4:**1^2, 4, 9, 11^3, 13, 17; **5:**9^2, 12, 13, 15

2Th 1:3, 6^2, 7, 10^2, 12; **2:**13^3, 14; **3:**7, 8, 9^2

1Ti 1:3, 4, 7, 10, 11^2, 15, 16^2, 18, 20; **2:**4^2, 6, 12^3; **3:**2^2, 3, 5, 8, 13, 14, 15; **4:**1, 3^3, 4, 8, 13^3, 15^2; **5:**4^2, 11, 13^2, 14^2, 24; **6:**3^3, 16, 17, 18^2, 19, 20

2Ti 1:1, 2, 4, 5, 8, 9^2, 10, 12; **2:**2^2, 4, 8, 14^2, 15^2, 20^2, 24, 25; **3:**2, 7^2, 15; **4:**3, 6, 8, 9, 10, 11, 12, 14, 16, 18, 21

Tit 1:1, 3, 4, 7^2, 9^2, 14; **2:**3, 4^3, 5^2, 6, 8, 9^2, 11; **3:**1^5, 2^2, 5, 7, 8, 12^3, 14

Phlm 2^2, 3, 8, 11^3, 16, 19

Heb 1:5^2, 13, 14; **2:**1^2, 3, 4, 5, 10, 11, 15, 17^3, 18; **3:**2, 5, 7, 13, 15, 18^2; **4:**1, 6, 7^2, 9, 11, 12, 13, 16; **5:**1, 3, 5^2, 7, 11^2, 12, 14^2; **6:**5, 6^3, 8, 10^2, 11, 13, 16, 17, 18^2; **7:**2, 5^2, 13, 23, 25^3, 27; **8:**3^2, 4, 5^3, 9^2, 10^2, 11, 12, 13; **9:**9, 11^2, 13, 14^2, 19^2, 24, 26, 27, 28; **10:**1, 2, 7, 9, 15, 19, 20, 24^2, 31, 32, 39; **11:**6^2, 7, 8, 11, 15, 16, 19, 20, 24^2, 25^2, 29, 32, 34, 35; **12:**11, 19, 22, 23^3, 24^2; **13:**2, 8, 10, 14, 15^2, 16^2, 18, 19^2, 21^2

Jas 1:1, 5, 12, 19^3, 21, 26, 27^2; **2:**3^2, 5, 8, 9, 16; **3:**2, 10, 17; **4:**2, 5, 7, 8^2, 9^2, 12^2, 13^3, 15, 17^3; **5:**1, 16, 17

1Pt 1:1, 2, 3, 4, 5, 12, 13^2, 14, 17; **2:**4, 5^2, 8, 13^2, 15, 18^3, 23, 24; **3:**1, 7, 15^2, 18^2; **4:**2^2, 3, 4, 5^2, 6^3, 9, 10, 11, 12, 19^2; **5:**3, 5^2, 11

2Pt 1:1, 3, 5^2, 6^3, 7^2, 10, 12, 13, 15, 17; **2:**4^2, 8, 9^3, 10, 12, 13, 17, 21^2, 22^3; **3:**9^2, 11, 13, 15, 16, 18

1Jn 1:9^2; **2:**6; **3:**5, 16; **4:**10, 11, 14, 16; **5:**11, 14

2Jn 8, 12^3

3Jn 4, 5^2, 8^2, 9, 13, 14^2

Jude 1, 3^2, 4, 7, 13, 15^2, 24^2, 25

Rev 1:1^2, 4^2, 6, 8, 12, 13; **2:**7^2, 12, 14^3, 17^2, 19, 20^4, 21, 23, 26, 27; **3:**2, 7, 9^2, 10, 18, 20, 21^2; **4:**3, 8, 9, 11; **5:**2^2, 3^2, 4^3, 5^2, 9^3, 12; **6:**2, 4^2, 8, 16, 17; **7:**2^3, 10, 14; **8:**2, 6, 13^2; **9:**1, 5, 6, 9, 10, 14, 15; **10:**4, 5, 7^2; **11:**6^4, 9, 10, 12, 13, 17^2, 18; **12:**2, 4^3, 5^2, 12, 14, 15, 17; **13:**3, 4, 5, 6, 7^2, 12, 14^3, 15, 16; **14:**4, 6^2, 7, 15^2, 18; **15:**8; **16:**1, 6, 8, 9, 14^2, 19; **17:**17^2; **18:**6^2, 17; **19:**7, 8, 10, 17, 19; **20:**8^3, 12, 13; **21:**10, 15, 17, 23; **22:**6, 8, 12, 14, 16

UNDER

Gen 1:7, 9; **6:**17; **7:**19; **16:**9; **18:**4, 8; **19:**8; **21:**15; **24:**2, 9; **35:**4, 8; **39:**23; **41:**35; **47:**29; **49:**25

Ex 6:6, 7; **17:**12, 14; **18:**10; **20:**4; **21:**20; **23:**5; **24:**4, 10; **25:**35^3; **26:**19^3, 21^2, 25^2, 33; **27:**5; **30:**4; **36:**24^3, 26^2, 30; **37:**21^3, 27; **38:**4

Lev 15:10; **22:**27; **27:**32

Nu 3:36; **4:**28, 33; **6:**18; **7:**8; **16:**31; **22:**27; **31:**49; **33:**1

Dt 2:25; **3:**17; **4:**11, 19, 49; **7:**24; **9:**14; **12:**2; **25:**19; **28:**23; **29:**20

Jos 7:21, 22; **11:**3, 17; **12:**3; **13:**5; **16:**10; **24:**26

Jdg 1:7; **3:**16, 30; **4:**5; **6:**11, 19; **9:**29

Ru 2:12

1Sa 7:11; **14:**2; **21:**3, 4, 8; **22:**6; **31:**13

2Sa 2:23; **3:**27; **4:**6; **12:**31^3; **18:**2^3, 9^2; **22:**10, 37, 39, 40, 48

1Ki 4:25^2; **5:**3; **7:**24, 30, 32, 44; **8:**6; **13:**14; **14:**23; **18:**23^2, 25; **19:**4, 5

2Ki 8:20, 22; **9:**13, 33; **13:**5; **14:**27; **16:**4, 17; **17:**7, 10

1Ch 10:12; **17:**1; **24:**19; **25:**2, 3, 6; **26:**28; **27:**23

2Ch 4:3, 15; **5:**7; **13:**18; **21:**8, 10^2; **26:**11, 13; **28:**4, 10; **31:**13

Neh 2:14; **8:**17

Job 9:13; **20:**12; **26:**5, 8; **28:**5, 24; **30:**7; **37:**3; **40:**21; **41:**11, 30

Ps 8:6; **10:**7; **17:**8; **18:**9, 36, 38, 39, 47; **36:**7; **44:**5; **45:**5; **47:**3^2; **91:**1, 4, 13; **106:**42; **140:**3; **144:**2

Prv 12:24; **22:**27

Ecc 1:3, 9, 13, 14; **2:**3, 11, 17, 18, 19, 20, 22; **3:**1, 16; **4:**1, 3, 7, 15; **5:**13, 18; **6:**1, 12; **7:**6; **8:**9, 15^2, 17; **9:**3, 6, 9^2, 11, 13; **10:**5

Song 2:3, 6; **4:**11; **8:**3, 5

Isa 3:6; **10:**4^2, 16; **14:**11, 19, 25; **18:**7; **24:**5; **25:**10; **28:**3, 15; **34:**15; **57:**5^2; **58:**5

Jer 2:20; **3:**6, 13; **10:**11; **12:**10; **27:**8, 11, 12; **33:**13; **38:**11, 12^2; **48:**45; **52:**20

Lam 1:15; **3:**34, 66; **4:**20; **5:**5, 13

Ezk 1:8, 23; **6:**13^2; **10:**2, 8, 20, 21; **17:**6, 23; **20:**37; **24:**5; **31:**6^2, 17; **32:**27; **42:**9; **46:**23; **47:**1^2

Dan 4:12, 14, 21; **7:**27; **8:**13; **9:**12

Hos 4:12, 13; **14:**7

Joel 1:17

Am 2:13

Oba 7

Jna 4:5

Mic 1:4; **4:**4^2

Zec 3:10^2

Mal 4:3

Mt 2:16; **5:**13, 15; **7:**6; **8:**8, 9^2; **23:**37

Mk 4:21^2, 32; **6:**11; **7:**28

Lk 7:6, 8^2; **8:**16; **11:**33; **13:**34; **17:**24^2

Jn 1:48, 50

Act 2:5; **4:**12; **8:**27; **23:**12, 14; **27:**4, 7, 16, 30

Ro 3:9, 13, 19; **6:**14^2, 15^2; **7:**14; **16:**20

1Co 6:12; **7:**15; **9:**20^3, 21, 27; **10:**1; **14:**34; **15:**25, 27^3, 28

2Co 11:32

Gal 3:10, 22, 23, 25; **4:**2, 3, 4, 5, 21; **5:**18

Eph 1:22

Php 2:10

Col 1:23

1Ti 5:9; **6:**1

Heb 2:8^4; **7:**11; **9:**15; **10:**28, 29

Jas 2:3

1Pt 5:6

Jude 6

Rev 5:3, 13; **6:**9; **11:**2; **12:**1

UNTIL

Gen 8:5, 7; **24:**19, 33; **26:**13; **27:**44, 45; **28:**15; **29:**8; **32:**4, 24; **33:**3, 14; **34:**5; **39:**16; **41:**49; **46:**34; **49:**10

Ex 9:18; **10:**26; **12:**6, 10^2, 15, 18, 22; **16:**20, 23, 35^2; **17:**12; **23:**18, 30; **24:**14; **33:**8; **34:**34, 35

Lev 7:15; **8:**33; **11:**24, 25, 27, 28, 31, 32, 39, 40^2; **12:**4; **14:**46; **15:**5, 6, 7, 8, 10^2, 11, 16,

17, 18, 19, 21, 22, 23, 27; **16:**17; **17:**15; **19:**6, 13; **22:**4, 6, 30; **23:**14; **25:**22^2, 28

Nu 4:3, 23; **6:**5; **9:**15; **11:**20; **14:**19, 33; **19:**7, 8, 10, 21, 22; **20:**17; **21:**22, 35; **23:**24; **24:**22; **32:**13, 17, 18, 21; **35:**12, 28, 32

Dt 1:31; **2:**14^2, 15, 29; **3:**3, 20^2; **7:**20, 23, 24; **9:**7, 21; **11:**5; **16:**4; **20:**20; **22:**2; **28:**20^2, 21, 22, 24, 48, 51^2, 52, 61; **31:**24, 30

Jos 1:15; **2:**16, 22; **3:**17; **4:**10, 23^2; **5:**1; **6:**10; **7:**6, 13; **8:**24, 26, 29; **10:**13, 26, 27, 33; **11:**8, 14; **13:**13; **20:**6^2, 9; **22:**17; **23:**13, 15

Jdg 4:24; **5:**7; **6:**18^2; **13:**15; **18:**30; **19:**8, 25; **20:**23, 26

Ru 1:19; **2:**7, 17, 21; **3:**3, 13, 14, 18^2

1Sa 1:22, 23^2; **3:**15; **7:**11; **9:**13; **11:**11; **14:**9, 24, 36; **15:**7, 18, 35; **17:**52; **19:**2, 23; **20:**41; **25:**36; **30:**4

2Sa 1:12; **4:**3; **5:**25; **10:**5; **15:**24, 28; **17:**13; **19:**7, 24; **21:**10; **22:**38; **23:**10

1Ki 3:1, 2; **5:**3; **6:**22; **10:**7; **11:**16, 40; **15:**29; **17:**14; **18:**26, 29; **22:**11, 27

2Ki 6:25; **7:**3; **8:**6, 11; **10:**8, 11; **17:**20, 23; **18:**32; **24:**20

1Ch 5:22; **6:**32; **12:**22; **19:**5; **28:**20

2Ch 8:8, 16; **9:**6; **16:**12; **18:**10, 26, 34; **21:**15; **24:**10; **29:**28, 34; **31:**1; **35:**14; **36:**16, 20, 21

Ezr 4:5, 21; **5:**16; **8:**29; **9:**4; **10:**14

Neh 7:3; **8:**3; **12:**23

Job 14:13; **26:**10

Ps 36:2; **57:**1; **71:**18; **73:**17; **94:**13; **104:**23; **105:**19; **110:**1; **112:**8; **123:**2; **132:**5

Prv 7:18

Song 2:17; **3:**4; **4:**6; **8:**4

Isa 5:11; **6:**11; **26:**20; **32:**15; **36:**17; **39:**6; **62:**1

Jer 23:20; **27:**7, 8, 22; **30:**24^2; **32:**5; **36:**23; **37:**21; **38:**28; **44:**27; **52:**34

Ezk 21:27; **33:**22; **46:**2

Dan 4:32; **7:**22, 25; **9:**27

Hos 7:4

Mic 5:3; **7:**9

Zep 3:8

Mt 1:17; **2:**13, 15; **11:**12, 13, 23; **13:**30; **17:**9; **18:**22^2; **24:**38, 39; **26:**29; **27:**64; **28:**15

Mk 14:25; **15:**33

Lk 1:20; **13:**35; **15:**4; **16:**16; **17:**27; **21:**24; **22:**16, 18; **23:**44; **24:**49

Jn 2:10; **9:**18

Act 1:2; **2:**35; **3:**21; **10:**30; **13:**20; **20:**7; **21:**26; **23:**1, 14

Ro 5:13; **8:**22; **11:**25

1Co 4:5; **16:**8

2Co 3:14

Gal 4:2, 19

Eph 1:14

Php 1:5, 6

2Th 2:7

1Ti 6:14

Heb 1:13; **9:**10

Jas 5:7

2Pt 1:19

1Jn 2:9

Rev 6:11; **17:**17; **20:**5

UNTO

Gen 1:9, 28; **2:**19, 22, 24; **3:**1, 2, 4, 6, 9^2, 13, 14, 16, 17^2, 19^2, 21; **4:**3, 4, 5, 6, 7, 9, 10, 12, 13, 15, 18, 19, 23^2; **6:**1, 4, 13, 20, 21; **7:**1, 5, 9, 15; **8:**9^2, 12, 15, 20; **9:**1, 8, 17, 24, 25; **10:**1, 19^3, 21, 25, 30; **11:**4, 31; **12:**1^2, 4, 6^2, 7^4, 8^2, 11, 18; **13:**3, 4, 8, 10, 14, 17, 18; **14:**6, 14, 15, 21, 22; **15:**1, 4, 5, 7, 9, 10, 13, 18^2; **16:**2^2, 4, 5, 6, 9, 10, 11, 13; **17:**1, 7, 8, 9, 15, 17, 18, 21, 23; **18:**1, 6, 7^2, 9, 10, 13, 14, 21, 27, 29, 30, 31, 33; **19:**3, 5^3, 6, 8^2, 12, 14^2, 16, 18, 19, 20, 21, 31^2, 34, 37, 38; **20:**5, 6, 9^3, 10, 13^2, 14, 16^2, 17; **21:**1, 3, 5, 7, 9, 10, 12^3, 14, 17, 22, 23^3, 27, 29, 30; **22:**1, 3, 5, 7, 11, 12, 15, 19, 20; **23:**3, 5, 13, 14, 15, 16, 18, 20; **24:**2, 3, 4^2, 5^3, 6, 7^4, 10, 12, 14, 20, 24^2, 25, 29^2, 30^2, 36, 38^2, 39, 40, 42, 45^2, 47, 48, 50, 54, 56, 58, 60, 65; **25:**5, 6^2, 12, 17, 18, 23, 33^2; **26:**1^2, 2, 3^3, 4, 9, 10, 16, 24, 27, 29, 32, 33, 35; **27:**1^2, 6^2, 13, 18, 19, 20, 21, 22, 26, 31^2, 32, 34, 37^2, 38, 39, 42; **28:**1, 4, 5, 9^2, 22; **29:**4, 5, 6, 15, 20, 21^2, 23, 24, 25, 30, 34; **30:**1, 3, 4, 14, 15, 16, 17, 25^2, 27, 29, 30, 40; **31:**3^2, 4, 5, 11, 12, 13^2, 14, 16, 24, 29, 39, 43^3, 46, 52, 55; **32:**3, 4, 9^2, 10, 16, 18, 19, 27, 32; **33:**1^3, 9, 13, 14^2, 16; **34:**1, 3^2, 4, 6, 9^2, 11^3, 12, 14^2, 15, 16, 17, 20, 22, 23, 24^2; **35:**1^3, 2, 3, 4, 7, 9, 10, 11, 17, 20, 27^3, 29; **36:**5; **37:**2, 4, 6, 10, 13^2, 18, 22, 23, 26, 29, 30, 35, 36; **38:**2, 8^2, 9, 12, 14, 16^3, 18; **39:**8, 10, 14^4, 17^3, 19; **40:**6, 8^2, 12, 13, 14^2, 16, 20, 21; **41:**8, 9, 13, 14, 15, 17, 24, 25, 28^2, 32, 38, 39, 40, 41, 44, 50^2, 55^2, 56; **42:**1, 7^3, 9, 10, 12, 14^2, 18, 20, 22, 23, 25, 28^2, 29^3, 31, 33, 34, 36, 37; **43:**2, 3^2, 5, 8, 9, 11, 13, 23, 29^2, 32, 34; **44:**4^2, 6, 7, 8, 10, 15, 16, 17, 18, 20, 21^2, 22, 23, 24, 27, 32^2; **45:**1, 3, 4, 9^2, 10, 12, 17^3, 18, 24, 25, 27; **46:**1, 2, 15, 18, 20^2, 25^2, 28^2, 29, 30, 31^4, 34; **47:**2, 3^2, 4, 5^2, 8, 9^2, 15, 17, 18^2, 19, 23, 24, 26, 29, 31^2; **48:**2, 3^2, 4, 5^2, 7, 9^2, 10, 11, 13, 15, 17, 18, 21^2; **49:**1, 2, 6, 10, 11^2, 13, 15, 26, 28, 29^2, 33; **50:**4, 12, 15, 16, 17^3, 19, 20, 21, 24^2

Ex 1:9, 10, 18, 19^2; **2:**9, 10, 11, 20, 23, 25; **3:**2, 4, 8^3, 9, 10, 11^2, 12, 13^5, 14^3, 15^4, 16^2, 17^2, 18^2; **4:**1^2, 2, 4, 5, 6, 9, 10^2, 11, 15, 16, 18^2, 19, 21, 22, 23, 30; **5:**1, 3, 4^2, 15, 16, 21, 22; **6:**1, 2^2, 3^3, 6, 8, 9^2, 10, 11, 12, 13^4, 28, 29^3, 30; **7:**1, 2, 4, 7, 8^2, 9^2, 10, 13, 14, 15^2, 16^2, 19^2, 22; **8:**1^3, 5^2, 8, 9, 10, 12, 15, 16^2, 19^2, 20^2; **9:**1^2, 8^2, 12^2, 13^2, 22, 27, 29^2, 33; **10:**1^2, 3^2, 5, 6, 7^2, 8^2, 9, 10, 12, 21, 24, 25, 28; **11:**1, 5, 8^2, 9^2; **12:**1, 2, 3, 4, 14, 21, 23, 26, 29, 36, 42, 43, 49; **13:**1, 2, 3, 5, 8, 9, 11, 12, 14; **14:**1, 2, 10, 11, 13, 15^3, 22, 24, 26, 29; **15:**1^2, 11, 13, 25; **16:**1, 3, 4, 6, 9^2, 10, 11, 12, 15, 20, 23^2, 25, 28, 33, 35; **17:**2, 4^2, 5, 9, 14; **18:**5, 6^2, 8, 13, 14, 15^2, 16, 17, 19^2, 22, 26; **19:**3^2, 4^2, 5, 6^2, 8, 9^3, 10^2, 12, 14, 15, 21^2, 23, 24^2, 25^2; **20:**4, 5, 6, 19, 20, 21, 22^2, 23, 24^2, 26; **21:**6^2, 8, 9, 11, 31, 32, 34; **22:**7, 8^2, 9, 10, 11, 12, 17, 20^2, 23, 26, 27, 29, 31; **23:**13, 14, 22^2, 23, 27, 31^2, 33; **24:**1^2, 5, 12, 14^3, 16; **25:**1, 2, 22, 25, 33, 34; **26:**24, 33; **27:**21; **28:**1^2, 3^2, 4, 12, 28, 29, 35, 41, 42, 43^3; **29:**1^2, 4, 17^2, 18^2, 25, 28, 34, 35, 41, 42; **30:**3, 10, 11, 12, 14, 15, 16, 17, 20, 22, 23, 30, 31^2, 32, 34^2, 36, 37, 38; **31:**1, 12, 13, 14, 18; **32:**1^2, 2^2, 3, 7, 9, 13^2, 14, 17, 19, 21^2, 23, 24, 25, 26^2, 27, 30^2, 31, 33, 34^2; **33:**1^4, 3, 5^3, 7, 8, 11^2, 12^2, 15, 17; **34:**1^2, 2, 4^2, 7, 15, 16, 25, 26, 27, 31^2, 34; **35:**1, 4, 5, 22, 29, 30; **36:**2, 3, 5, 10^2, 13; **37:**26; **38:**4; **39:**21, 31, 33; **40:**1, 12, 13, 15, 32

Lev 1:1^2, 2^3, 9, 13, 15, 17; **2:**1, 2, 8^3, 9, 11, 12, 14, 16; **3:**3, 5, 6, 9, 11, 14; **4:**1, 2, 3, 4, 12, 31, 35; **5:**6, 7, 8, 12, 14, 15, 16, 18; **6:**1, 2, 5, 6^2, 8, 9, 11, 15, 17, 19, 20, 21, 22, 24, 25; **7:**5, 11, 14, 18, 20, 21, 22, 23, 25, 28, 29^3, 32, 34^2, 35, 38; **8:**1, 3, 4, 5, 7, 21, 28, 31; **9:**2, 3, 4, 6, 7^2, 8, 9, 12, 13, 18, 23; **10:**3, 4, 6^3, 8, 11, 12^3, 19; **11:**1^2, 2, 4, 5, 6, 10, 11, 12, 20, 23, 26, 27, 28, 29, 35, 38; **12:**1, 2, 6^2; **13:**1, 2^2, 9, 16^2, 49; **14:**1, 2, 23^2, 33^2; **15:**1, 2^2, 14^2, 26, 29^2; **16:**1, 2^2, 18, 22, 29, 31, 34; **17:**1, 2^4, 4^3, 5^4, 6, 7^2, 8, 9^2, 12, 14; **18:**1, 2^2, 19; **19:**1, 2^2, 4, 5, 21^2, 23, 25, 34; **20:**1, 2, 3, 4, 16, 24^2, 26; **21:**1^3, 2, 3, 6, 7, 8, 16, 17, 23^2, 24^2; **22:**1, 2^2, 3^3, 12, 13, 14^2, 15, 17, 18^4, 21, 22^2, 24, 26, 27, 29; **23:**1, 2^2, 6, 8, 9, 10^4, 12, 13, 14, 15, 16^2, 17, 18^2, 21, 22, 23, 24, 25, 26, 27^2, 32^2, 33, 34^2, 36^3, 37, 38, 39, 41, 44; **24:**1, 2, 3, 7, 9, 11, 13, 15; **25:**1, 2^3, 4, 5, 8^2, 10^4, 11, 12, 13, 14, 15^2, 16, 27^2, 28, 39, 40, 41^2, 47, 49, 50^2, 51, 52^2, 55; **26:**1, 5^2, 9, 14, 16, 18, 21^2, 23, 24, 27^2, 28, 31, 40, 41; **27:**1, 2^2, 3, 5, 6, 9^2, 11, 13, 14, 15, 16, 18^2, 19, 21, 22, 23^3, 24, 28^2, 30, 32

Nu 1:1, 48, 50; **2:**1^2, 5; **3:**5, 6, 9^2, 11, 13, 14, 40, 44, 48, 51; **4:**1^2, 9, 17^2, 19^2, 21, 27, 30, 35, 39, 43, 47; **5:**1, 4, 5, 6, 7^2, 8^2, 9, 11, 12^2, 15, 19, 21; **6:**1, 2^3, 5, 6, 8, 12, 13, 14, 17, 21, 22, 23^3, 25; **7:**4, 5, 6, 7, 8^2, 9^2, 11, 89^2; **8:**1, 2^2, 4^3, 5, 7, 12, 13, 16^2, 19, 20^2, 22, 23, 24, 26; **9:**1, 4, 7, 8, 9, 10^2, 12, 14, 21; **10:**1, 4, 29^2, 30, 32^2, 36; **11:**2^2, 11, 12^3, 13^2, 16^3, 18, 20, 23^2, 25^2, 26, 29, 35; **12:**4^4, 6^2, 11, 13, 14; **13:**1, 2, 17, 21, 22, 23, 26^3, 27, 32; **14:**2, 3, 7, 11, 13, 16, 18, 19, 23, 26^2, 28, 35, 39, 40, 44, 45; **15:**1, 2^3, 3^2, 4, 7, 8, 10, 13, 14, 17, 18^2, 19, 21, 22, 24, 25, 33^2, 35, 37, 38, 39, 40; **16:**3, 5^4, 8, 9^2, 15, 16, 19^2, 20^2, 23, 24, 25, 26, 30, 32, 36, 37, 38, 40, 44, 46^2, 50^2; **17:**1, 2, 6, 9, 10, 12, 13; **18:**1, 2^2, 4^2, 7, 8^2, 9, 10, 11, 12, 13, 15, 17, 19^2, 20, 24^2, 25, 26^2, 27, 28, 30^2; **19:**1^2, 2, 3, 10^2, 21; **20:**5, 6^2, 7, 8, 10, 12, 14, 16, 18, 19, 22, 23, 24^2, 25, 26; **21:**2, 7, 8, 16, 17, 21, 24^2, 26, 29, 30^3, 34^2; **22:**4, 5, 7^2, 8^2, 9, 10^2, 12, 13, 14, 16, 17^2, 18, 19, 20^3, 25, 28^2, 29, 30^3, 32, 34, 35^2, 36, 37^3, 38^2, 39; **23:**1, 3, 4, 5, 6, 11^2, 13^2, 15, 16, 17, 18, 25, 26, 27^2, 28, 29; **24:**10, 11, 12^2, 14; **25:**2, 3, 4, 5^2, 6, 10, 12, 16; **26:**1^2, 52, 53, 59, 60; **27:**4, 6, 7, 8^2, 9, 10, 11^2, 12^2, 13, 15, 18; **28:**1, 2^3, 3^2, 6, 7, 8, 11, 13^2, 14^3, 15, 19^2, 24, 26, 27, 28^2, 29, 31; **29:**1, 2, 6^2, 8^2, 12, 13, 14, 36, 39; **30:**1, 2, 3; **31:**1, 2, 3^2, 12^3, 15, 21, 25, 28, 29, 30, 41, 43, 47, 48, 49; **32:**2^2, 5, 6, 9, 11^3, 16, 17, 18, 20, 25, 29, 31, 33^2, 38, 40; **33:**7, 9, 49, 50, 51^2, 56^2; **34:**1, 2^2, 5, 8, 11, 13, 16, 17, 29; **35:**1, 2^2, 4, 6, 8, 9, 10^2, 12, 25, 29; **36:**2, 4, 8, 11, 13

Dt 1:1, 2, 3^3, 6, 7^3, 8^2, 9, 17, 20^3, 21, 22, 24, 25, 29, 35, 39, 41, 42^2, 43, 44, 45, 46; **2:**1, 2, 4, 5, 9^2, 12^2, 14, 17, 19, 22, 23, 26, 27, 29, 31, 35, 36^2, 37^4; **3:**2^3, 6, 8, 10, 12, 13, 14^2, 15, 16^4, 17, 20^3, 21^2, 26^2; **4:**1^2, 2, 4, 7, 10, 11, 12, 13, 15^2, 19^2, 20, 21, 23, 30, 31, 32, 35, 42, 45, 48, 49; **5:**1, 9^2, 10, 22^2, 23, 27^2, 28^3, 31; **6:**7, 10, 18, 21, 23; **7:**2, 3^2, 6^2, 8, 12^2, 13, 16, 18^2, 19, 23, 25; **8:**1, 18, 20; **9:**3, 5, 7, 10, 12, 13, 19, 26, 27; **10:**1^3, 3, 4^2, 7, 8^2, 10, 11^3; **11:**3^2, 4^3, 5, 6, 9^2, 12, 13, 21, 22, 24, 25, 29; **12:**4, 5^2, 7, 11, 18, 26, 31^2; **13:**2, 3, 4, 7^2, 8^2, 17; **14:**2^2, 7, 8, 10, 19, 21^3, 25; **15:**2, 5, 6, 8, 9^2, 10^2, 11, 12, 14, 16, 17^2, 18, 19, 21; **16:**1, 2, 7, 9, 10^2, 15, 21; **17:**1^2, 5, 9^2, 12^2, 14, 16; **18:**2, 3, 6, 12, 14^2, 15^3, 17, 18^2, 19; **19:**5, 8^2, 19^2; **20:**2^2, 3^2, 5, 6, 7, 8^2, 9, 10^2, 11^2, 14, 15, 18; **21:**2, 3, 4, 5, 6, 8^2, 11, 13, 18, 19^2, 20; **22:**1, 2^2, 5^2, 13, 15, 16^2, 19, 23, 24, 26, 29; **23:**5^2, 15^2, 18, 20^2, 21, 23, 25; **24:**9, 11, 13, 15^2; **25:**1, 3, 5^3, 7^2, 8, 9^2, 16, 17; **26:**1, 2, 3^5, 7, 11^2, 12, 13^2, 15, 17, 19; **27:**2, 3, 5, 6, 9, 14, 15; **28:**1, 2, 8, 9^2, 11, 12^3, 13, 15, 20, 21, 26^2, 31, 32, 35, 36, 45, 60, 64, 68^2; **29:**2^5, 4, 7^2, 8, 11, 13^4, 21, 24, 26, 29^2; **30:**2, 4, 10^2, 12, 13, 14, 18, 20^2; **31:**1, 2^2, 4^2, 5^2, 7^4, 9^2, 14, 16, 18, 20^2, 23, 28; **32:**3, 17, 22, 43, 46^2, 48, 49^2, 50^2, 52; **33:**2, 7, 9, 19, 26, 29^2; **34:**1^2, 2, 3, 4^5, 6, 9, 10

Jos 1:1, 2, 3^2, 4^2, 6^2, 15, 17^2, 18; **2:**3, 4, 7, 8, 9, 10, 12^2, 16, 17, 18, 21, 22, 24; **3:**4, 5, 6, 7, 9, 15; **4:**1, 5^2, 7, 8^2, 9, 10, 12, 13, 15, 18^2, 21; **5:**2, 6^2, 9^2, 13^2, 14^2, 15; **6:**2, 6, 7, 8, 16, 19, 22^2, 25; **7:**2, 3, 5, 9, 10, 19^2, 22, 23^2, 24, 26^2; **8:**1, 2^2, 5, 18, 24, 27^2, 28, 29, 30, 31; **9:**3, 6^2, 7, 8^2, 9, 11, 12, 15, 17, 18, 19^2, 20, 21^2, 22, 25^2, 26, 27; **10:**3^4, 4, 6, 8, 9, 10, 11, 14, 15, 22, 23, 24^2, 25, 28, 29, 30^2, 31, 34, 36, 41^2, 43; **11:**6, 8^3, 9, 14, 17, 23^2; **12:**1, 2, 3, 5, 6, 7^2; **13:**1, 3, 4, 5, 6^2, 7, 9, 10, 11, 14^2, 15, 24^2, 25, 26^2, 27, 29, 31, 33^2; **14:**3, 4, 6^3, 10, 13, 14; **15:**3, 4, 5, 8, 9, 10^2, 11^2, 13, 18^2, 46, 47, 63; **16:**1, 2, 3, 5, 6, 8, 10; **17:**7, 9, 14, 17; **18:**3, 10, 18; **19:**10, 12, 28, 33; **20:**1, 2, 4^2, 6^3; **21:**1^3, 2, 3, 8, 27, 34, 43^2, 44, 45; **22:**2, 3, 4^3, 5, 6, 7^2, 8^2, 9, 10, 13, 15^2, 19, 21, 24, 31, 32; **23:**1, 2, 3, 4^2, 5, 7, 8^2, 9, 11, 12^2, 13, 14, 16; **24:**2, 4^2, 6^2, 7, 10, 11, 15, 19, 21, 22, 23, 24, 27^4, 28

Jdg 1:3, 14, 15, 20, 21, 24, 26, 33; **2:**1^2, 3, 4, 5, 6, 10, 12, 15, 17^2, 19, 20; **3:**3, 4, 9, 13, 15^2, 17, 19, 20^2, 26, 28; **4:**3, 6, 7, 8, 11, 13, 14, 16, 18^2, 19, 20, 21, 22; **5:**3, 18; **6:**4, 6, 7, 8^2, 10, 11, 12^2, 13, 15, 16, 17, 18, 19, 20, 23^2, 24^2, 25, 26, 27, 30, 31, 35^3, 36, 39; **7:**2, 4^4, 5^2, 7^2, 8, 9^2, 11^2, 13^2, 17, 19, 22, 24^2; **8:**1, 2, 5^2, 6, 8, 9, 14, 15^2, 18, 20, 22, 23, 24, 27, 35; **9:**1, 5, 7^3, 8, 9, 11, 12, 13, 14, 15, 16, 31, 36, 38, 40, 48, 52^2, 54^2, 55, 56; **10:**4, 10, 11, 14, 15^3; **11:**2, 6, 7^2, 8, 9, 10, 12, 13^3, 14, 15, 16, 17^2, 19^2, 22^2, 28, 29, 30, 32, 33, 34, 35, 36^2, 37, 39; **12:**1, 2, 3, 5, 6; **13:**3^2, 5, 6, 7, 8^2, 9, 10^3, 11^2, 12, 13^2, 15, 16^2, 17, 18, 19, 22, 23; **14:**3^2, 10, 12^2, 13, 14, 15^2, 16^2, 18^2, 19; **15:**7, 11^4, 12^3, 13, 14, 19; **16:**1, 5^2, 7, 9, 10, 11, 12, 13^2, 14, 15, 16, 17^2, 18, 23, 26, 28; **17:**2, 3^2, 4, 9^2, 10^2, 11; **18:**1^2, 2, 3, 4, 5, 6, 8^2, 10, 12, 13^2, 14, 15, 18, 19^3, 23^2, 24, 25, 26, 27^2, 29; **19:**2, 3, 5, 6, 9, 11, 12, 13, 18, 21, 23^2, 24^2, 25, 28^2, 30; **20:**1, 14, 26, 32, 36, 42, 45^2, 47; **21:**1, 5, 12, 13, 22^4, 23

Ru 1:7, 8, 10^2, 14, 15^2, 18, 20; **2:**2^2, 3, 4, 5, 8, 9, 10, 11^3, 13^2, 14, 19, 20^3, 21, 22, 23; **3:**1, 3, 5^2, 6, 13, 17; **4:**1, 3, 8, 9^2, 12, 13, 14, 15, 16

1Sa 1:3, 5, 10, 11^2, 14, 21, 22, 23, 24, 26; **2:**10, 11, 14, 16, 20, 22, 23, 25, 27^3, 28, 34; **3:**1, 5, 7, 9, 14, 17^2; **4:**3, 7, 8, 9, 16, 20; **5:**1, 5, 8^2; **6:**5, 12, 14, 15, 17, 18^2; **7:**3^3, 5, 8, 9^2, 14, 17; **8:**4, 5, 6, 7^3, 8^2, 9^2, 10, 22^3; **9:**6, 10, 11, 16, 17, 19, 23^2, 24; **10:**2, 7, 8, 11, 14, 15, 16, 17, 18, 19; **11:**1, 3^2, 7, 9^2, 10^2, 12; **12:**1^3, 2, 5, 6, 8, 10, 12, 17, 18, 19^3, 20; **13:**12, 15, 17^2; **14:**1, 4, 6, 7, 8^2, 9^2, 10^2, 11, 12, 17, 18, 19^2, 23, 33, 34, 35^2, 36^2, 40^3, 41, 45, 52; **15:**1^2, 6, 10, 11, 13, 15, 16^2, 20, 21, 24, 26, 28, 32;

APNDX

16:1, 3^2, 5, 7, 10, 11^2, 15, 17, 19, 20; **17:**8^2, 13, 17, 18, 28, 34, 37, 39, 41, 43, 44, 46, 52^2, 55; **18:**1, 8, 18, 19; **19:**4^2, 6, 11, 17^2; **20:**2, 4, 5^2, 11, 12^2, 21, 22, 27, 29, 30^2, 31, 32, 36, 40^2; **21:**1, 2^2, 5, 8, 11, 14; **22:**2, 3, 5, 7, 8, 13, 15, 17, 22; **23:**2, 3, 17^2, 27; **24:**4^3, 6^2, 16, 19, 21, 22^2; **25:**5, 6, 7, 8, 11, 13, 15, 16, 19, 21, 22, 27^2, 31^2, 34, 35, 40^2; **26:**1; **27:**2, 5, 6^2, 8; **28:**1, 7, 8^2, 9, 11, 13^2, 14, 15, 18, 21^4, 22, 23; **29:**3^3, 4^2, 6^3, 8^2; **30:**13, 15, 17, 24, 25, 26; **31:**4

2Sa 1:3^2, 4, 5, 7, 8, 9, 10, 13, 14, 16, 26; **2:**1^2, 5^4, 6; **3:**2, 7, 8, 12, 16, 21^2, 24, 38; **4:**8, 9; **5:**1, 6^2, 14, 19; **6:**10, 12, 21, 23; **7:**2, 4, 8, 9, 17, 20, 24, 27, 28; **8:**10, 11, 15; **9:**2^2, 3^2, 4^2, 6, 7, 9^2, 11, 12; **10:**2^2, 3^3, 5, 13; **11:**4^2, 7, 10^3, 11, 16, 19, 20^2, 23^3, 25^2; **12:**1^3, 3, 4^2, 8, 11, 13^2, 14, 15^2, 18^2, 19, 21, 24, 31^2; **13:**4^2, 5^2, 6, 10, 11^2, 13, 14, 15, 16^3, 17, 20, 22, 25, 26, 28, 29, 35, 39; **14:**2, 3, 5, 8, 9, 10, 12, 15^2, 18, 21, 27, 30, 31^2, 32; **15:**2, 3, 4, 7^2, 9, 14, 15, 25, 26, 27, 33^2, 34, 36; **16:**2, 3, 4, 9, 10, 16^2, 18, 21^2, 22; **17:**1, 3, 6, 7, 11, 15, 20, 21; **18:**2, 4, 11, 12, 18, 20, 21, 23, 24, 26, 28, 30, 32; **19:**2, 7^2, 8, 11, 14, 19^2, 22, 23^2, 25, 27, 28, 29, 30^2, 33, 34^2, 35, 37, 38, 39, 41; **20:**2, 3^2, 8, 14, 16, 17^2, 21, 22^2; **21:**2^2, 3, 4, 6^2, 8, 17; **22:**1, 42, 45^2, 50^2, 51; **23:**10, 13, 16, 19; **24:**3^2, 9, 10, 11, 12^2, 13^2, 14, 17, 18^2, 21, 22^2, 23^2, 24^2, 25

1Ki 1:2, 11, 13^3, 15^2, 16, 17^2, 27, 30, 33, 42, 51, 53; **2:**5^2, 7, 9, 14, 16, 17, 18, 19^3, 20, 22, 26^2, 27, 28, 29, 30, 31, 36, 38, 39, 42^3; **3:**2, 6, 11, 12, 13, 16, 26; **4:**12, 21^2, 27, 28, 33; **5:**1, 3, 5^3, 6^2, 7, 9^2; **6:**12, 24; **7:**8, 9, 48; **8:**1, 2, 5, 6, 8, 15, 18^2, 19, 26, 28^2, 29, 33, 34^2, 40, 44, 46, 47, 48^3, 52^4, 54, 56, 58, 59, 63, 65, 66; **9:**2, 3, 8, 13, 16, 21, 24, 25; **10:**5, 12, 13; **11:**2^3, 8, 9, 11, 14, 18, 22, 24, 35, 36, 38^2, 40; **12:**3, 5, 7^2, 9, 10^5, 15^2, 16^2, 19, 20, 22, 23^2, 27^2, 28, 30, 32^2, 33; **13:**1, 2, 6, 7, 8, 11, 12, 13, 14, 15, 18^3, 20, 21, 22, 26^3, 34; **14:**5^2, 27; **15:**19, 20, 29; **17:**1, 2, 5, 8, 13^2, 18^2, 19, 20, 21, 23; **18:**1, 2, 5^3, 15, 17, 19, 20^2, 21, 22, 25, 30^3, 31, 40, 41, 44; **19:**2, 5, 8, 9^2, 13, 15, 18, 20, 21^2; **20:**2, 5, 6, 7, 8^2, 9, 10^2, 12, 13, 22, 23, 25, 28, 31, 34, 35, 36, 39^2, 40, 42; **21:**2^2, 3, 5, 6^3, 7, 8, 11^2, 19^2, 25; **22:**3, 4, 5, 6, 8, 13^2, 14, 15, 16, 18, 22, 24, 26, 30, 34, 38, 49

2Ki 1:2, 3, 5^2, 6^4, 7, 9^2, 11^2, 12, 13, 15^2, 16; **2:**2^2, 3, 4, 5, 6, 9, 10, 16, 18^2, 19, 21, 22, 23^2; **3:**3, 4, 13^2, 26; **4:**1^2, 2, 6^2, 9, 13^2, 16, 17, 19, 22, 25, 26, 33, 36, 38, 42; **5:**1, 3, 5, 6, 7, 10, 13, 14, 17^2, 19, 25, 26, 27^2; **6:**1, 2, 9, 11, 15, 18, 19, 21, 26, 28^2, 29, 33; **7:**4, 5, 10, 12, 15, 20; **8:**1, 3, 6, 8, 10^2, 12, 22; **9:**1, 5, 6, 11^2, 20; **10:**1, 6, 10, 17, 18, 19, 22, 23, 27, 30^2; **11:**15; **12:**7; **13:**4, 14, 15^2, 18, 23^2; **14:**6, 7, 13, 25; **15:**5, 12^2; **16:**6, 9; **17:**12, 23, 32, 34, 41; **18:**4, 8, 11, 14, 19, 21, 22, 26, 27, 32; **19:**3, 6, 9, 29; **20:**1^2, 2, 5, 6, 8, 11, 12, 13, 14^3, 16, 17, 19; **21:**15; **22:**6, 8, 13^2, 14, 15, 17, 20; **23:**1, 4, 5, 6, 21, 25, 35; **24:**7; **25:**2, 8, 17, 24

1Ch 1:19; **2:**3, 9, 19; **3:**1, 4, 5; **4:**31, 33, 39, 41, 43; **5:**1, 8, 9, 11, 23^2, 26^2; **6:**48, 61, 63, 67, 71, 77; **7:**28; **10:**9, 14; **11:**1, 2; **12:**8, 16, 17^3, 18, 40; **13:**2^4, 5, 9; **14:**10, 14; **15:**2, 3, 12^2; **16:**8, 9^2, 16, 18, 23, 28^2, 29^2, 34, 40; **17:**2, 5, 7, 15, 26; **18:**3, 11; **19:**2, 3^2, 11, 14; **20:**8; **21:**5, 8, 9, 10, 11, 13, 15, 17, 18, 22, 23, 26; **22:**7, 8, 9; **23:**13, 25, 26, 31^2; **26:**6; **28:**1, 3, 6; **29:**1, 5, 12, 17, 18, 19, 21^2, 22, 24

2Ch 1:2, 5, 7^2, 8^2, 9, 12; **2:**15; **3:**1; **5:**2, 3, 6, 7, 9; **6:**14, 17, 19, 20, 21, 25, 27, 30^2, 31, 34, 36, 37, 38, 40; **7:**8, 10, 12, 15, 21^2; **8:**11, 12, 15, 16; **9:**12, 26, 28; **10:**5^2, 7, 9, 10^3, 15, 16, 19; **11:**3, 14, 16, 23; **12:**5; **13:**7, 10, 11, 14; **14:**7, 9, 11, 13; **15:**2, 4, 11, 14, 19; **16:**4, 7; **17:**3, 16; **18:**3, 4, 5, 7^2, 14, 17, 20, 23, 29; **19:**4; **20:**9, 15, 21, 24, 26, 28, 33; **21:**10; **23:**3, 14; **24:**5, 6, 11, 17, 19, 20, 23; **25:**12, 13, 14, 15^2, 16^2; **26:**18^3, 21; **27:**5; **28:**9^2, 10, 13, 16, 20, 21, 23, 25; **29:**5, 7, 11, 30, 31; **30:**1, 5, 6, 8, 9^2, 10, 17, 21, 22, 27; **31:**6, 16; **32:**9^2, 13, 18, 23, 24^2, 25, 31; **33:**2, 13, 17, 18, 22; **34:**4, 6, 25, 26; **35:**1, 3^2, 8^2, 9, 12, 22; **36:**13

Ezr 1:8, 11; **2:**1^3, 63, 69; **3:**3, 5, 6, 7^2, 8^2, 11; **4:**1, 2^2, 3^3, 6, 7, 11^2, 12^2, 13, 15, 17^2, 18, 20, 23, 24; **5:**1^2, 3, 4, 6, 7^2, 8, 9, 12, 14, 15; **6:**5^2, 8, 10, 21, 22; **7:**7, 11, 12, 15, 22, 26, 28; **8:**17^3, 22, 25, 26, 28^3, 30, 31, 35^2, 36; **9:**4, 5, 6, 7, 9, 11, 12^2; **10:**1, 2, 4, 7^2, 9, 10, 11

Neh 1:3, 9^3; **2:**1, 2, 3, 4, 5^3, 6, 7, 8, 17, 18, 20; **3:**1^2, 2, 4^3, 5, 7^2, 8^3, 9, 10^2, 12, 13, 15, 16^2, 17, 20, 24^2, 26, 27, 31, 32; **4:**6, 9, 12^2, 14, 15^2, 19, 20, 22; **5:**5, 7, 8^3, 14, 15, 16, 17; **6:**2, 3, 4, 5, 8, 10, 17^2, 18; **7:**3, 6, 65, 70; **8:**1, 3, 9^2, 10^3, 12, 13, 15, 17, 18^2; **9:**4, 14, 27, 28, 29^2, 32, 34, 36, 37, 38; **10:**28, 30, 35, 36, 37^2, 38, 39; **11:**30; **12:**37, 38, 39, 46, 47^2; **13:**4, 6, 12, 13, 16, 17, 21, 25^2, 27

Est 1:1, 3, 5^2, 14, 15, 17, 18, 19; **2:**2, 3^2, 8^2, 9, 13^2, 14, 15, 16, 18, 22; **3:**3, 4^2, 8, 10, 11, 12, 14; **4:**6, 7, 8^4, 10^2, 11^2, 16; **5:**3, 4^2, 6, 12^2, 14^3; **6:**3, 4, 5, 6^2, 11, 13, 14; **7:**2, 5; **8:**1^2, 2, 6, 7, 9^4, 13; **9:**5, 12, 13, 20, 22, 23, 26, 27, 30; **10:**3

Job 1:2, 7, 8, 12, 14; **2:**2, 3, 6, 7, 9, 10, 13; **3:**6, 20, 25; **5:**7, 8^2; **6:**22, 28; **7:**4, 20; **8:**5; **9:**12, 16; **10:**2, 3, 15; **11:**7, 19; **12:**8; **13:**2, 12, 20, 27; **15:**19; **16:**20; **19:**11; **20:**6, 29; **21:**14, 15, 33; **22:**2^2, 17, 21, 26, 27, 28; **23:**5; **28:**28; **29:**21; **30:**20, 26; **31:**10, 37^2; **32:**12, 21; **33:**22, 23, 24, 26^3, 31, 33; **34:**2, 10, 11, 14, 15, 28, 31, 34, 36, 37; **35:**3, 5, 6; **37:**3, 14, 19; **38:**17, 35, 41; **39:**4, 13^2; **40:**6, 7, 14, 19; **41:**3^2; **42:**4, 7, 8, 11

Ps 2:5, 7; **3:**4, 8; **4:**3; **5:**2^2, 3; **7:**4, ttl; **10:**14; **13:**6; **16:**2, 6; **17:**1^2, 6; **18:**6, 39, 41, 44, 49^2, ttl; **19:**2^2, 6; **22:**5, 22, 24, 27, 31; **24:**4; **25:**1, 10, 16; **26:**11; **27:**6, 8, 12; **28:**1, 2; **29:**1^2, 2^2, 11; **30:**2, 4, 8, 12; **31:**22; **32:**2, 5^2, 6^2, 9; **33:**2, 3; **34:**5, 11, 15, 18; **35:**3, 10, 23; **36:**5, 10; **37:**5; **39:**12; **40:**1, 3, 5, 15; **41:**2, 4, 8, 10; **42:**3, 7, 8, 9, 10; **43:**3, 4^2; **44:**3, 25; **45:**14^2; **46:**9; **47:**1, 6, 9; **48:**10, 14; **50:**1, 5, 14^2, 16; **51:**1, 12, 13, 18, ttl; **52:**ttl; **54:**5, 6; **55:**2, 14; **56:**1, 4, 9, 11, 12; **57:**1^2, 2^2, 9, 10^2; **59:**13, 17; **61:**1, 2, 8; **62:**11, 12; **65:**1, 2, 4; **66:**1, 3^2, 4, 15, 17; **67:**1; **68:**4, 20, 29, 31, 32^2, 34, 35; **69:**1, 8^2, 13, 16, 18, 27; **70:**5; **71:**2, 7, 18, 19, 22, 23, 24; **72:**1, 8; **74:**3, 19, 20; **75:**1^2, 4; **76:**11^2; **77:**1^3; **78:**36, 46^2, 62; **79:**2^2, 12; **80:**6, 11^2; **81:**1^2, 8^2, 12, 13, 15; **83:**9^2; **85:**1, 8; **86:**3^2, 4, 5, 6, 8^2, 16^2; **88:**2, 3, 8, 9, 13; **89:**3, 6^2, 8, 26, 35, 49; **90:**12, 16^2; **92:**1^2; **94:**15; **95:**1, 2, 11; **96:**1^2, 2, 7^2, 8^2; **98:**1, 4, 5; **99:**7; **100:**1, 4; **101:**1, 2; **102:**1, 2, 12; **103:**7^2, 17, 20; **104:**8, 23, 33; **105:**1, 2^2, 9, 10, 11; **106:**1, 4, 25, 28, 31^2, 36, 37, 38, 47; **107:**1, 6, 13, 18, 19, 28, 30; **108:**3, 4; **109:**4, 12, 17, 19, 25; **110:**1; **111:**5, 9; **112:**4; **113:**3, 5; **115:**1^3, 8; **116:**2, 7, 12, 14, 18; **118:**1, 6, 18, 27, 29; **119:**6, 15, 20, 25, 28, 31, 33, 36, 38, 41, 48, 49, 58, 59, 62, 65, 72, 76, 77, 79, 90, 103, 105^2, 107, 112, 116, 117, 124, 130, 132^2, 146, 149; **120:**1, 3^2; **121:**1; **122:**1, 4^2; **123:**1, 2^2; **125:**3, 4, 5; **130:**1; **132:**2^2, 11; **135:**3, 4, 12, 18; **136:**1, 2, 22, 26; **138:**1, 6; **139:**6, 17; **140:**6, 13; **141:**1^4, 8; **142:**1^2, 5, 6; **143:**6, 7, 8, 9; **144:**9^2, 10; **145:**18; **146:**2, 10; **147:**1, 7^2, 19^2; **148:**14; **149:**1, 3

Prv 1:5, 9, 23^2, 33; **2:**2, 10, 18^2, 19; **3:**5, 15, 22, 28, 34; **4:**4, 18, 20, 22; **5:**1, 9^2; **6:**16; **7:**4, 13, 24; **8:**4, 32; **11:**27; **12:**14, 15; **14:**6, 12; **15:**9, 10, 12; **16:**3, 22, 25; **18:**13; **19:**17; **20:**23; **22:**17, 21; **23:**12, 22; **24:**11, 14, 24; **25:**7; **26:**4; **28:**27; **29:**17; **30:**1^2, 5, 6, 10; **31:**3, 6^2, 24

Ecc 1:6, 7; **2:**3, 17, 18; **3:**20; **5:**4; **7:**21; **8:**4, 9, 14; **9:**3, 13; **12:**7

Song 1:13, 14; **2:**10; **8:**11

Isa 1:4, 6, 9^2, 10, 11, 13, 14, 23; **2:**2; **3:**9^2, 11; **5:**8, 11, 18, 20, 21, 22, 26, 30; **6:**3, 6; **7:**3, 4, 10; **8:**1, 2, 3, 5, 19^4, 22; **9:**6^2, 13; **10:**1, 11, 21, 30; **12:**5; **13:**2, 15; **14:**10^2; **15:**4^2, 5, 8^2; **16:**1, 8; **18:**4, 6, 7; **19:**11, 16, 17, 20^2, 21; **20:**1; **21:**2, 4, 6, 9, 10, 16; **22:**11^2, 15^2; **24:**16; **25:**6; **26:**15; **27:**2, 12; **28:**5, 13, 15; **29:**2, 11, 15; **30:**10^2, 18, 19, 22; **31:**1, 4, 6, 7; **32:**9; **33:**2, 21; **34:**17; **35:**2; **36:**2, 3, 4, 10, 11^2; **37:**2, 3, 6^2, 14, 15, 21, 30; **38:**1^3, 2, 5, 7, 15; **39:**3^4; **40:**2, 9, 18, 20; **41:**9, 13; **42:**3, 5, 10, 12, 16, 24; **44:**5, 7, 17^2, 22; **45:**9, 10^2, 14^3, 19, 20, 22, 23; **46:**3, 7, 12; **47:**15; **48:**11, 12, 13, 16, 22; **49:**1, 3, 6; **51:**1, 2^2, 4^2, 7, 11, 16, 19; **52:**7; **53:**12; **54:**9; **55:**2, 3, 5, 7, 11; **56:**4, 5, 8; **57:**9, 18; **59:**16, 20; **60:**5^2, 7^2, 9, 10, 11, 13, 14, 19^2; **61:**1, 3^2, 7; **62:**11; **63:**5; **65:**1, 2, 11, 15; **66:**1, 19, 20, 24

Jer 1:3^2, 4, 5, 7, 9, 11, 12, 13, 14, 16, 17; **2:**3, 10, 17, 21, 27, 31^2; **3:**1, 2, 4, 6, 7, 10, 11, 14, 17, 18, 22, 25; **4:**1, 10, 12, 13, 18^2; **5:**5^2, 13, 19, 24; **6:**3, 4, 10, 12, 13^2, 19, 20; **7:**9, 12, 13, 14^2, 18, 21, 22, 23, 25^2, 26, 27^2, 28; **8:**4, 10^3; **10:**1, 6, 7, 11; **11:**2, 3, 5, 6, 7^2, 9, 11^2, 12^2, 13, 14, 17, 20; **12:**6, 8, 9, 11; **13:**1, 3, 6, 8, 11^2, 12^2, 13, 18, 27; **14:**2, 10, 11, 13, 14^3, 17; **15:**1, 2, 16, 18, 19^2, 20; **16:**1, 10, 11, 12, 15, 19, 20; **17:**15, 17, 19, 20, 24, 26, 27; **18:**8; **19:**2, 4, 5, 11, 12, 13^2; **20:**3, 8, 12, 13, 15; **21:**1^2, 3, 8, 9; **22:**6^2, 8, 13, 21; **23:**1, 5, 12, 14, 16^2, 17^2, 33, 38; **24:**3, 4, 7, 10; **25:**2, 3^3, 4, 5, 7, 15, 17, 27, 28, 30, 33; **26:**2^2, 3, 4, 5, 8, 10, 11, 12, 14, 15, 16, 23; **27:**1, 3, 4^2, 5^2, 9, 10, 14^3, 15, 16^2, 17; **28:**1, 5, 12, 15; **29:**1, 3, 4^2, 7, 9, 12^2, 19, 21, 25, 28, 30, 31; **30:**2, 9, 15, 17, 21^2; **31:**3, 6, 26, 32, 34, 38, 40^3; **32:**6, 7, 8, 12, 16^2, 18, 20, 24, 25, 26, 29^2, 31, 33, 35, 37; **33:**1, 3, 6, 9^2, 14, 15, 19, 22; **34:**1, 6, 8^2, 14^2, 16, 17, 20; **35:**1, 2^2, 5, 12, 14^3, 15^2, 16, 17^2, 18^2; **36:**1, 2^3, 3, 4, 9, 13, 14^2, 15, 16, 18, 19, 32; **37:**2, 3, 6, 7, 18, 19; **38:**1, 4^2, 12, 14^2, 15^3, 16, 17^2, 19, 20^2, 24, 25^5, 26, 27; **39:**12^4, 14, 15, 18; **40:**1, 2, 4^3, 5, 6, 7, 9, 10, 12, 14, 15, 16; **41:**1, 6, 8, 14; **42:**1, 2^2, 4^3, 7, 9^2, 10, 12, 20^4, 21; **43:**1, 2, 8, 10; **44:**4, 5, 8^2, 10, 12, 15, 16^2, 17^2, 18, 19^2, 20, 23, 24, 25, 29; **45:**1, 2, 4, 5; **48:**1, 9, 12, 27, 34^3, 46; **49:**2, 4, 14, 29, 31; **50:**15, 27, 29, 44; **51:**2, 6, 9, 24, 44, 48, 53; **52:**5, 9, 22, 32

Lam 1:12^2, 21, 22^2; **2:**1, 18; **3:**10, 25, 41, 64, 65; **4:**4, 15, 21; **5:**4, 16, 21

Ezk 1:3, 16; **2:**1^2, 2^2, 3^2, 4^2, 7, 8, 9; **3:**1^2, 3, 4^3, 6, 7^2, 10^2, 11^2, 16, 17, 18, 22, 24, 27; **4:**3, 9, 15, 16; **5:**15; **6:**1, 10; **7:**1, 2, 7, 27; **8:**5, 6, 8, 9, 12, 13, 15, 17; **9:**4, 7, 9; **10:**2, 7, 13; **11:**1, 2, 5, 14, 15^2, 25; **12:**1, 6, 8, 9, 10, 11, 19, 21, 23, 28; **13:**1, 2, 3, 11, 12, 15, 18; **14:**1, 2, 4^2, 6, 10, 22; **15:**1; **16:**1, 3, 5, 6^2, 8, 20^2, 23, 24, 27, 29, 33, 34, 36, 37, 54, 60, 61; **17:**1, 2, 3, 11; **18:**1, 22; **19:**4; **20:**2, 3^2, 5^4, 6, 7, 8, 9, 15, 18, 23, 27^2, 29^2, 30, 31, 39, 45; **21:**1, 7, 8, 18, 23, 29^2; **22:**1, 4^2, 17, 23, 24, 28; **23:**1, 16, 27, 30, 36^2, 37, 38, 40, 43, 44^4; **24:**1, 3^2, 15, 18, 19, 20, 21, 24, 26, 27; **25:**1, 3, 8, 10; **26:**1, 2; **27:**1, 3; **28:**1, 2, 11, 12, 20, 24; **29:**1, 4^2, 10, 17, 19; **30:**1, 20; **31:**1, 2, 4, 8, 14, 17, 18; **32:**1, 2, 17, 18; **33:**1, 2, 7, 8, 10, 11, 12, 14, 16, 21, 23, 25, 27, 31, 32; **34:**1, 2^2, 18, 20; **35:**1, 3, 6, 15; **36:**1, 3, 6, 9, 11, 13, 16, 20, 22, 32; **37:**3, 4^2, 5, 9^2, 11, 12, 15, 18, 19, 21, 25; **38:**1, 7^2, 13, 14; **39:**4, 11, 17, 24, 28; **40:**4^2, 6, 14, 15, 19, 22, 45, 46; **41:**4, 17, 20, 22; **42:**13^2; **43:**6, 7, 18, 19^2, 24; **44:**2, 5^2, 11, 12, 13^2, 15^2, 16, 26, 27, 28, 30; **45:**1, 4, 7; **46:**4, 7, 12, 13, 14, 16, 20, 24; **47:**1, 2, 6, 8, 10, 14^2, 18, 21, 22^2; **48:**2, 3, 4, 5, 6, 7, 8^2, 9, 12, 14, 18, 23, 24, 25, 26, 27, 28, 29

Dan 1:1, 3, 7^2, 10, 21; **2:**3, 5, 9, 19, 21, 23^2, 24^3, 25^2, 26, 27, 46, 47; **3:**3, 14, 18, 24^2; **4:**1^2, 6, 7, 11, 16, 18, 20, 22, 26, 27, 34^2, 35, 36^4; **5:**13, 15, 17; **6:**2, 6, 15^2, 16, 19, 20, 21, 25^2, 26; **7:**5, 10, 16, 26; **8:**1^3, 6, 7, 13, 14^2, 17; **9:**3, 4, 6, 7^3, 25, 26; **10:**1, 11^4, 12, 15, 16, 19^2, 20; **11:**18; **12:**7

Hos 1:1, 2, 4, 6, 10^2; **2:**1, 14, 19^2, 20, 23; **3:**1, 3; **4:**12, 15; **5:**4, 12, 14; **6:**1, 3^2, 4^2; **7:**7, 13^2, 14; **8:**2, 11; **9:**4^2, 10, 17; **10:**1, 6, 15; **11:**2, 4; **12:**4, 14; **13:**7; **14:**1, 2, 5

Joel 1:14, 20; **2:**13, 14, 19; **3:**6

Am 1:5; **2:**7; **3:**7; **4:**6, 8^2, 9, 10^2, 11, 12^2, 13; **5:**4, 15, 18, 25; **6:**2, 10, 14; **7:**1, 4, 8, 12, 15^2; **8:**1, 2; **9:**7

Oba 15, 20

Jna 1:1, 3^2, 5, 6, 8, 9, 10, 11^3, 12^2, 14, 16; **2:**1, 2, 7, 9, 10; **3:**1, 2^2, 3, 6, 8, 10; **4:**2^2, 9

Mic 1:9^2, 12, 15^2; **2:**11; **3:**4, 6^2, 8; **4:**1, 8, 13^2; **5:**2, 3, 4; **6:**3, 5, 9; **7:**7, 8, 10, 15, 18, 20

Nah 3:13

Hab 1:2, 10, 11, 16^2; **2:**1, 5^2, 7, 15, 16, 19; **3:**13, 16

Zep 1:1; **2:**5, 11

Hag 1:1, 9, 13; **2:**20

Zec 1:1, 3^3, 4^2, 6, 7, 9, 14, 19; **2:**2, 4, 5, 8, 11; **3:**2, 4^2, 6; **4:**2, 5, 6^2, 7, 8, 9, 11, 12; **5:**2, 3, 5, 11; **6:**4, 5, 8, 9, 12, 15; **7:**1, 2, 3, 4, 5^2, 8; **8:**3, 11, 15, 18; **9:**9, 10, 12; **11:**7, 12, 13^2, 15^2; **12:**2; **13:**3, 6; **14:**5, 10^3, 17, 20, 21

Mal 1:6, 8, 9, 11^2, 14; **2:**2, 4, 12; **3:**3, 4, 7^2; **4:**2, 4

Mt 1:17, 20^2, 24; **2:**5, 11; **3:**7, 9^2, 10, 11, 13, 15, 16; **4:**6, 7, 9, 10, 11, 19, 24; **5:**1, 15, 18, 20, 22, 26, 28, 32, 33, 34, 39, 44; **6:**2, 5, 8, 16^2, 18^2, 25, 27, 29, 33, 34; **7:**6, 7, 11, 14, 21, 23, 24, 26; **8:**4^2, 5, 7, 10, 11, 13^2, 15, 16, 18, 19, 20, 21, 22, 26, 32; **9:**2, 6, 8, 9, 11, 12, 15, 16, 18, 24, 28^2, 29, 37; **10:**1, 15, 23, 42^2; **11:**3, 4, 7, 9, 11, 16^2, 17^2, 21^2, 22, 23, 24, 25, 27, 28, 29; **12:**2, 3, 6, 11, 20, 22, 25, 28, 31^3, 36, 39, 45, 47, 48; **13:**2, 3, 10^2, 11^2, 17, 24^2, 27, 28^2, 31, 33^2, 34^2, 36^2, 37, 44, 45, 47, 51^2, 52^3, 57;

14:2, 4, 16, 17, 22, 25, 27, 28, 31, 35; **15:**3, 8, 10, 12, 15^2, 22, 24, 28^2, 29, 30, 32, 33, 34; **16:**2, 4, 6, 8, 15, 17^2, 18, 19, 21^2, 22, 23^2, 24, 28; **17:**3, 4, 11, 12^2, 13, 20^4, 22, 26^2, 27; **18:**1, 2, 3, 7, 10, 13, 17^2, 18, 19, 22^2, 23, 24, 31, 32, 34, 35; **19:**3^2, 4, 7, 8, 9, 10, 11, 13, 14, 16, 17, 18, 20, 21, 23^2, 24, 26, 27, 28^2; **20:**1, 4, 6, 7^2, 8^2, 12, 14^2, 17, 18^2, 21^2, 22, 23, 25, 28, 32, 33; **21:**1^2, 2^2, 3, 5, 13, 16^2, 19, 21^3, 23, 24, 25, 27, 31^3, 32, 36, 37, 40, 41^2, 42, 43; **22:**1, 2, 4, 12, 16, 17, 19, 20, 21^4, 24, 25, 26, 29, 31, 37, 39, 42, 43, 44; **23:**13, 14, 15, 16, 23, 25, 27^2, 28, 29, 31, 34, 35, 36, 37, 38, 39; **24:**2^2, 3, 4, 13, 14, 19, 23, 26, 27, 34, 47; **25:**1, 8, 12, 14, 15, 20, 21, 22, 23, 26, 28, 29, 34, 36, 39, 40^4, 41, 44, 45; **26:**1, 3, 7, 10, 13, 14, 15^2, 17, 18, 21, 22, 24, 25, 29, 31, 33, 34^2, 35, 36^2, 38^2, 40^2, 45, 50, 52, 58, 62, 63, 64^2, 68, 69, 71, 73, 75; **27:**8, 11, 13, 15, 17^2, 19, 21^2, 22^2, 26, 27, 33, 45, 53, 55, 62, 64, 65; **28:**5, 10, 11, 12, 18^2, 20

Mk 1:5, 13, 17, 31, 32, 37, 38, 40, 41, 44^2; **2:**2, 3, 4, 5, 8, 11, 13, 14, 16, 17, 18, 19, 24, 25, 27; **3:**3, 4, 5, 8, 13^2, 23^2, 28^2, 31, 32; **4:**1, 2, 9, 11^3, 13, 21, 24^2, 33, 34, 35^2, 38, 39, 40; **5:**1, 8, 11, 19, 21^3, 31, 34, 36, 39, 41^2; **6:**2, 4, 7, 10, 11, 18, 22, 23^2, 24, 25, 30, 31, 33, 35, 37^2, 38, 45, 48^2, 50, 51; **7:**1, 6, 9, 14^3, 18, 27^2, 28, 29, 31, 32, 34; **8:**1^2, 12^2, 17, 19, 21, 22, 27, 29^2, 34^2; **9:**1^2, 4, 13^2, 17, 19, 20, 21, 23, 25, 29, 31, 35, 36, 41; **10:**1, 3, 5, 11, 14^2, 15, 18, 20, 21, 23, 24, 28, 29, 32, 33^2, 35, 36, 37^2, 38, 39^2, 42, 45, 49, 51^3, 52; **11:**1, 2, 3, 5, 6, 11, 14, 17, 21, 22, 23^2, 24, 28, 29, 33^2; **12:**1, 4, 6, 9, 13, 14, 15, 16^2, 17, 18, 19^2, 24, 26, 32, 34, 38, 43^3; **13:**1, 2, 13, 19, 30, 37^2; **14:**9, 10^2, 12, 13, 16, 18, 19, 20, 24, 25, 27, 29, 30^2, 34^2, 36, 37, 41, 48, 61, 65, 72; **15:**2, 6, 8, 9, 11, 12^2, 14, 15, 22, 41^2, 43, 44, 46; **16:**2, 6, 7, 12, 13, 14, 15, 19

Lk 1:2, 3, 11, 13, 18, 19^2, 22^2, 26, 28, 30, 32, 34, 35, 38, 61, 74, 77, 80; **2:**4, 10, 11, 12, 15^2, 20, 26, 34, 38, 48, 49, 50, 51; **3:**2, 8^2, 9, 11, 12, 13, 14, 16, 18; **4:**3, 5, 6^2, 8, 9, 12, 17, 21, 23^2, 24, 26^3, 29, 39, 40, 42, 43; **5:**4, 5, 7, 10, 14, 20, 22, 24^2, 27, 31, 33, 34, 36; **6:**2, 5, 9, 10, 13, 23, 24, 25^2, 26, 27, 29, 35, 38, 39; **7:**2, 3, 6, 7, 8, 9^2, 13, 14, 19, 20^2, 21, 22, 24, 26, 28, 32^2, 40^2, 43, 44, 47, 48; **8:**3, 10, 21, 22^2, 25, 39^2, 47, 48; **9:**3, 11, 12, 13, 20, 33, 43, 48, 50, 57, 58, 59, 60, 62; **10:**2, 9^2, 11, 12, 13^2, 17, 18, 19, 20, 21, 23, 26, 28, 29, 35, 36, 37, 41; **11:**1, 2, 5^3, 8, 9^2, 13, 17, 24, 27, 30, 39, 41, 42, 43, 44, 45, 46, 47, 51^2, 52, 53; **12:**1, 4, 5, 8, 10, 11^2, 13, 14, 15, 16, 20, 22^2, 27, 31, 36^2, 37, 41^2, 44, 48; **13:**2, 7, 8, 12, 14, 18, 23^2, 24, 25^2, 31, 32, 34, 35^2; **14:**3, 7, 10, 15, 16, 18, 23, 24, 25; **15:**1, 3, 6, 7, 10, 12, 16, 18, 21, 27, 31; **16:**1^2, 2, 5^3, 6, 7, 9, 15, 28, 29, 30, 31; **17:**1^2, 5, 6, 7, 8, 14^2, 19, 22, 24, 37^2; **18:**1, 3, 7, 9, 13, 15, 16^2, 17, 19, 22^2, 29^2, 31^2, 32, 35, 40, 41, 42, 43; **19:**5, 8, 9, 13, 15, 17, 22, 24, 25, 26^2, 31, 32, 33, 39, 40, 42, 46; **20:**2, 3, 8, 15, 20, 22, 23, 25^3, 28^2, 34, 36, 38, 41, 42, 45; **21:**3, 4, 10, 23, 32; **22:**4, 6, 9, 10, 11^2, 13, 15, 16, 18, 19, 22, 25, 29^2, 33, 35, 36, 37, 38, 40, 43, 46, 47, 48, 49, 52, 61, 67, 70; **23:**1, 7, 14^2, 15, 17, 18, 22, 25, 28, 42, 43^2, 52; **24:**1, 5, 6, 9, 10, 12, 17, 18, 19^2, 25, 27, 28, 36^2, 38, 41, 44^2, 46

Jn 1:11, 22, 25, 29, 33, 38^2, 39, 41, 43, 45, 46^2, 48^2, 49, 50^2, 51^2; **2:**3, 4, 5^2, 7, 8^2, 10, 16, 18^2, 19, 22, 24; **3:**2, 3^2, 4, 5, 7, 9, 10, 11, 26^2, 34; **4:**7, 8, 9, 10, 11, 13, 15, 16, 17, 19, 21, 25, 26^2, 30, 32, 34, 35, 36, 40, 42, 45, 47, 48, 49, 50^2, 52, 53; **5:**6, 8, 10, 11, 12, 14^2, 19^2, 22, 24^2, 25, 29^2, 33^2; **6:**5^2, 8, 12, 13, 16, 19, 20, 23, 25, 26, 27^2, 28, 29, 30, 32^2, 33, 34, 35, 36, 43, 45, 47, 53^2, 61, 63, 65^3, 67; **7:**3, 6, 8^2, 9, 10, 21, 22, 26, 33^2, 35, 37, 45, 50, 52, 53; **8:**1, 2, 3, 4, 7, 9, 10, 11, 12, 13, 14, 19, 21, 23, 24, 25^3, 28, 34, 39^2, 42, 48, 51, 52, 55, 57, 58^2; **9:**7, 10, 11, 12, 15, 17, 24, 29, 30, 34, 35, 37, 40, 41; **10:**1, 6^2, 7^2, 24, 26, 28, 35, 41; **11:**3, 4, 8, 11, 14, 15, 16, 18, 21, 23, 24, 25, 27, 29, 31, 32, 34, 39, 40^2, 44, 49, 54; **12:**16, 24, 25, 27, 32, 35, 50; **13:**1^2, 6, 7, 8, 9, 12, 16, 20, 21, 25, 27, 28, 29, 33, 34, 36, 37, 38; **14:**3, 5, 6^2, 8, 9, 10, 12^2, 22^3, 23^2, 25, 26, 27^2, 28^3; **15:**3, 7, 11, 15, 20, 21, 22, 26; **16:**1, 3, 4, 6, 7^2, 12, 14, 15, 17, 19, 20, 23, 25^2, 26, 29, 33; **17:**6, 8, 26; **18:**4, 5, 6, 11, 15, 16^2, 17, 21, 24, 25, 28, 29, 30^2, 31^2, 33, 35, 37^2, 38^3, 39^2; **19:**4, 5, 6, 9, 10^2, 11, 14, 15, 16, 26, 27; **20:**1, 2, 10, 13^2, 15^2, 16^2, 17^3, 18, 19^2, 20, 21, 22, 23, 25^2, 26, 28, 29; **21:**3^2, 5, 6, 7^2, 10, 12, 15^2, 16^2, 17^4, 18, 19, 22, 23

Act 1:2, 7, 8^2, 12, 19, 22; **2:**3, 14^2, 29^2, 34, 37, 38, 39, 41; **3:**5, 10, 11, 12, 14, 20, 22^4, 25, 26; **4:**1, 3, 8, 10, 19^3, 23, 29, 35; **5:**4^2, 8, 9, 16, 35, 38; **6:**2; **7:**2, 3, 13, 26, 31, 37^3, 38, 40, 41, 44, 45; **8:**1, 5, 6, 14, 20, 26^3, 29, 35, 36; **9:**1, 2, 4, 6, 11, 15^2, 17, 21, 27, 34, 38; **10:**3, 4, 7, 8, 9, 11, 15, 19, 21, 28^2, 29, 32, 36, 41, 42; **11:**4, 7, 11^2, 13, 17, 18, 19, 20, 21, 22, 23, 24, 26, 27, 29; **12:**5, 8^2, 10^2, 15, 17^3, 21; **13:**4, 6, 15, 20, 21, 22, 23, 31, 32^2, 33, 36, 38^2, 41, 47, 51; **14:**3, 6^2, 13, 15^2, 18, 27; **15:**2, 3, 7, 8, 13, 18, 20, 23, 25^2, 33, 36, 39, 40; **16:**10, 13, 14, 17, 19, 25, 32, 37, 38; **17:**2, 3, 5, 6, 10, 15^2, 18, 19, 23, 29, 31, 34; **18:**2, 6^2, 14, 21, 26^2; **19:**2^2, 3^3, 4, 12, 22, 24, 30, 31, 33; **20:**1, 6, 7, 13, 18, 20, 22, 24, 27, 28, 34, 38; **21:**1^3, 2, 8, 11, 18, 20, 31, 32, 37^2, 39, 40^2; **22:**1, 4, 5^2, 6, 7^2, 8, 10, 13^2, 15, 18, 20, 21^2, 22, 25, 27; **23:**3, 15, 17^2, 18^3, 21, 23, 24, 26; **24:**2, 4, 8, 10^2, 14, 23; **25:**6, 11^2, 12^2, 13, 14, 21, 22, 26; **26:**1, 6, 7, 11, 14, 16^2, 17, 18, 19, 20, 22, 23, 28, 32^2; **27:**1, 3, 8, 10, 21, 40; **28:**17, 19, 21, 25, 26, 28^2, 30

Ro 1:1, 10, 11, 13, 16, 19, 26; **2:**5, 8, 14; **3:**2, 7, 22; **4:**3, 6, 11; **5:**5, 15, 16, 18, 21^2; **6:**10^2, 11^2, 13^3, 16^2, 19^2, 22; **7:**4, 5, 10, 13, 16; **9:**12, 17, 19, 21^2, 23, 26, 29; **10:**3, 10^2, 12, 18, 20, 21; **11:**4, 8, 9, 11, 27, 35; **12:**1, 3, 19; **13:**1; **14:**6, 8^2; **15:**8, 9, 15, 19, 23, 25^2, 27, 29, 32; **16:**1, 4, 5, 19^2

1Co 1:2, 3, 8, 9, 11, 18, 23^2, 24, 30; **2:**1, 7, 10, 14; **3:**1^4, 10; **4:**9, 11, 13, 17, 21; **5:**5, 9, 11; **6:**12, 17; **7:**1, 3^2, 10, 27; **8:**1, 4, 7^2; **9:**2, 11, 15, 16, 17, 19, 20; **10:**2, 11, 28^2; **11:**13, 14, 17, 23, 34; **12:**2, 21, 31; **14:**2^2, 3, 6, 11^2, 21, 26, 34, 36, 37; **15:**1^2, 2, 3, 6, 28^2; **16:**3, 5, 9, 11, 12, 16

2Co 1:1, 13, 15, 16, 20, 23; **2:**3, 4^2, 12, 14, 15, 16^2; **3:**15; **4:**4, 11; **5:**5, 11, 12, 15^2, 19^3; **6:**11, 13, 18; **7:**12^2; **8:**2, 5, 17; **9:**5, 12, 13^3, 15; **10:**13, 14; **11:**9; **12:**9, 17, 19, 20

Gal 1:2, 6, 8^2, 9, 17, 20, 22; **2:**2, 7^2, 9^3, 14, 19; **3:**8, 23, 24; **4:**8, 13; **5:**2, 4, 13; **6:**6, 10^2, 11, 14^2

Eph 1:5, 9, 14, 15, 17; **2:**10, 16, 18, 21; **3:**3, 5^2, 7, 8, 10, 14, 20, 21; **4:**7, 8, 13^2, 16, 19, 29, 30; **5:**10, 20, 22^2, 24, 31; **6:**5, 9, 13, 19, 22

Php 1:2, 11, 12^2, 29; **2:**8, 19, 27, 30; **3:**10, 11, 13, 15, 21^2; **4:**5, 6, 16, 20

Col 1:2, 6, 8, 10, 11, 12, 20; **2:**2; **3:**18, 20, 23; **4:**1, 3, 7, 8, 9, 10, 11^2

1Th 1:1^2, 5, 9; **2:**1, 2, 8^2, 9^2, 12, 18; **3:**6, 11; **4:**7^2, 8, 9, 15^2; **5:**1, 15, 23, 27

2Th 1:1, 2; **2:**1; **3:**9

1Ti 1:2, 6, 17, 18, 20; **2:**4; **3:**14^2, 16; **4:**7, 8, 16^2; **6:**16

2Ti 1:12, 14, 16, 18^2; **2:**9, 15, 16, 21^2, 24; **3:**9, 11, 15, 17; **4:**4, 8, 9, 10^2, 18

Tit 1:3, 15^2, 16; **2:**9, 14; **3:**2, 8, 12^2, 13

Phlm 1, 13, 16, 19, 21, 22

Heb 1:1, 2, 5, 8; **2:**3, 5, 10, 12^2, 17; **3:**6, 14; **4:**2^2, 13, 16; **5:**4, 5, 7, 9; **6:**1, 6, 8, 11, 17; **7:**3, 4, 19, 21, 25; **8:**5; **9:**20, 27, 28^2; **10:**24, 29, 30, 39; **11:**4, 26; **12:**2, 4, 5^2, 9, 11, 18^2, 22^2; **13:**6, 7, 13, 22

Jas 1:23; **2:**2, 3, 16, 23; **4:**6; **5:**7

1Pt 1:2^2, 3, 5, 7, 10, 12^5, 13, 22, 25; **2:**4, 7^2, 14^2, 24, 25; **3:**5, 7^2, 12, 19, 22; **4:**7, 12, 19; **5:**5, 10, 12

2Pt 1:2, 3^2, 4, 11, 16, 19; **2:**4, 6, 9, 21, 22; **3:**1, 7, 12, 15^2, 16

1Jn 1:2^2, 3, 4, 5; **2:**1, 7, 8, 12, 13^3, 14^2, 21, 26; **3:**14; **5:**13, 16^3, 17

2Jn 1, 5, 10, 12^2

3Jn 1, 9, 13

Jude 2, 3^3, 6, 11, 21, 24

Rev 1:1^3, 4, 5, 6, 11^8, 13, 15, 17; **2:**1, 5, 7, 8, 10, 11, 14, 16, 17, 18^2, 20, 23, 24^2, 26, 29; **3:**1, 6, 13, 14, 22; **4:**3, 6; **5:**5, 10, 13^2; **6:**2, 4, 8, 11^2, 13; **7:**10, 12, 13, 14, 17; **8:**3; **9:**1, 3, 7^2, 10, 19; **10:**4, 8, 9^3, 11; **11:**1, 2, 3, 12, 18; **12:**5, 11, 12, 13; **13:**2, 4^2, 5^2, 7, 15; **14:**4, 6, 13, 14, 20; **15:**7; **16:**8, 14, 19; **17:**1^2, 7, 13, 15, 17; **18:**5, 6, 18; **19:**1, 9^3, 10, 17; **20:**4; **21:**5, 6^2, 9, 11, 18; **22:**6^2, 9, 10, 16, 18^3

UP

Gen 2:6, 21; **4:**8; **7:**11, 17^2; **8:**7, 13; **13:**1, 10, 14; **14:**22; **17:**22; **18:**2, 16; **19:**1, 2, 14, 27, 28, 30; **20:**18; **21:**14, 16, 18, 32; **22:**3^2, 4, 13^2, 19; **23:**3, 7; **24:**16, 54, 63, 64; **25:**8, 17, 34; **26:**23, 31; **27:**38; **28:**12, 18^2; **29:**11; **31:**10, 12, 17, 21, 35, 45, 55; **32:**22; **33:**1, 5; **35:**1, 3, 13, 14, 29; **37:**25, 28, 35; **38:**8, 12, 13; **39:**15, 16, 18; **40:**13, 19, 20; **41:**2, 3, 4, 5, 6, 18, 19, 20, 21, 22, 23, 27, 34, 35, 44, 48^3; **43:**2, 15, 29; **44:**4, 17, 24, 30, 33, 34; **45:**9, 25; **46:**4, 5, 29, 31; **47:**14; **48:**17; **49:**4^2, 9^2, 33^2; **50:**5, 6, 7^2, 9, 14, 23, 25

Ex 1:8, 10; **2:**17, 23; **3:**8, 17; **7:**12, 20; **8:**3, 4, 5, 6, 7, 20; **9:**10, 13, 16, 32; **10:**12, 14; **12:**6, 30, 31, 34, 38; **13:**18, 19; **14:**10, 16; **15:**7; **16:**13, 14, 23, 24, 33, 34; **17:**3, 10, 11, 12; **19:**3, 12, 13, 20^2, 23, 24^2; **20:**25, 26; **22:**2; **24:**1, 2, 4, 9, 12, 13^2, 15, 18; **26:**15, 30, 33; **29:**27; **32:**1^2, 4, 6^2, 8, 23, 30; **33:**1^2, 3, 5, 8, 10, 12, 15; **34:**2, 3, 4^2, 24; **35:**21, 26; **36:**2, 20; **40:**2, 8^2, 17, 18^3, 21, 28, 33^2, 36, 37^2

Lev 6:10; **9:**22; **11:**45; **13:**4, 5, 11, 21, 26, 31, 33, 37, 42, 50, 54; **14:**38, 46; **19:**16, 32; **22:**30; **26:**1^2, 38

Nu 1:51; **6:**26; **7:**1; **9:**15, 17, 21^2, 22; **10:**11, 21, 35; **11:**32; **13:**17^2, 21, 30, 31^2, 32^2; **14:**1, 13, 36, 37, 40^3, 42, 44; **15:**19, 20; **16:**2, 3, 12, 13, 14, 24, 25, 27, 30, 32, 34, 37, 45; **17:**4, 7; **18:**26; **19:**9^2; **20:**4, 5, 11, 25, 27; **21:**3, 5, 17, 33; **22:**4^2, 13, 14, 20, 21, 41; **23:**7, 18^2, 24^2; **24:**2, 3, 8, 9, 15, 20, 21, 23, 25; **25:**4, 7; **26:**10; **27:**12; **31:**52; **32:**9, 11, 14; **33:**38

Dt 1:21, 22, 24, 26, 28^2, 41^2, 42, 43; **2:**13, 24; **3:**1, 27^2; **4:**19; **5:**5; **6:**7; **8:**14; **9:**1, 9, 23; **10:**1, 3; **11:**6, 17, 18, 19; **14:**25, 28; **16:**22; **17:**8, 20; **18:**15, 18; **19:**11, 15, 16; **20:**1; **22:**4, 14, 19; **23:**14; **24:**5; **25:**7^2, 9; **27:**2, 4, 5; **28:**7, 33, 43; **29:**22; **30:**12; **31:**5, 16; **32:**11, 17, 30, 34^2, 36, 38, 40, 49, 50; **33:**2; **34:**1

Jos 2:6, 8, 10; **3:**6^2, 16; **4:**5, 8, 9, 16, 17, 18^2, 19, 23^2; **5:**1, 7, 13; **6:**1, 5, 6, 12, 20, 26^2; **7:**2^2, 3^2, 4, 10, 13, 16; **8:**1, 3, 7, 10^2, 11, 14, 20, 31; **9:**4; **10:**4, 5, 6, 9, 10, 12, 33, 36; **11:**6, 17; **12:**7; **14:**8; **15:**3^2, 6^2, 7^2, 8^2, 15; **16:**1; **17:**15; **18:**1, 11, 12^2, 17; **19:**10, 11, 12, 47; **20:**5; **22:**12, 33; **24:**17, 26, 32

Jdg 1:1, 2, 3, 4, 16, 22, 36; **2:**1^2, 4, 16, 18; **3:**9, 15; **4:**5, 10^2, 12, 14; **6:**3^2, 5, 8, 13, 21, 35, 38; **7:**1; **8:**8, 11, 13, 20, 28; **9:**7, 18, 32, 33, 34, 35, 43, 48, 51; **11:**2, 13, 16, 31, 37; **12:**3; **13:**20; **14:**2, 19; **15:**5, 6, 9, 10^2, 13; **16:**3, 5, 8, 18^2, 29, 31; **18:**9, 12, 17, 30, 31; **19:**5, 7, 9, 10, 17, 27, 28^3, 30; **20:**3, 9, 18^3, 19, 23^3, 26, 28, 30, 31, 33, 38, 40^2; **21:**2, 5^2, 8, 19

Ru 1:9, 14; **2:**15, 18; **3:**14; **4:**1, 5, 10

1Sa 1:3, 5, 6, 7, 9, 19, 21, 22^2, 24; **2:**6, 7, 8^2, 14, 19, 35; **5:**12; **6:**9, 10, 13, 20, 21; **7:**1, 7, 10; **8:**8; **9:**11, 13^2, 14^2, 19, 24, 26; **10:**3, 18, 25; **11:**1, 4; **12:**6; **13:**5, 15; **14:**9, 10^2, 12^2, 13, 21, 46; **15:**2, 6, 11, 12, 34; **16:**13; **17:**20, 23, 25^2; **19:**15; **20:**38; **21:**12; **22:**8; **23:**11, 12, 19, 29; **24:**7, 16, 22; **25:**5, 13, 35; **26:**19; **27:**8; **28:**8, 11^2, 14, 15, 25; **29:**9, 10^2, 11^2; **30:**4

2Sa 2:1^3, 2, 3, 22, 27, 32; **3:**10, 32; **4:**4, 12; **5:**8, 17, 19^2, 22, 23; **6:**2, 12, 15; **7:**6, 12; **12:**3^2, 11, 17; **13:**29, 34, 36; **14:**14; **15:**2, 20, 24, 30^4; **17:**16, 21; **18:**9, 18, 24^2, 28^2, 31, 33; **19:**34; **20:**2, 3, 15, 19, 20, 21; **21:**6, 8, 13; **22:**9, 40, 49^2; **23:**1, 8, 18; **24:**9, 11, 18, 19, 22

1Ki 1:35, 40, 45, 49; **2:**19, 34; **3:**15; **6:**8; **7:**21^3; **8:**1, 3, 4^2, 20, 35, 54; **9:**16, 24; **10:**5, 29; **11:**14, 15, 23, 26, 27; **12:**8, 10, 18, 24, 27, 28^2; **13:**4, 29; **14:**10, 14, 15, 16, 25; **15:**4, 17; **16:**17, 32, 34; **17:**7, 19; **18:**38, 41, 42^2, 43^2, 44, 46; **20:**1, 22, 26, 33; **21:**16, 21, 25; **22:**6, 12, 20, 29, 35, 38

2Ki 1:3, 4, 6^2, 7, 9, 13, 14, 16; **2:**1, 11, 13, 16, 23^4; **3:**7, 8, 21, 22, 24; **4:**21, 29, 34, 35, 36, 37; **6:**7, 24; **7:**5; **8:**12; **9:**1, 2, 8, 25, 27, 32; **10:**1, 5, 6, 15; **12:**10^2, 17^2; **13:**21; **14:**10, 11, 26; **15:**14, 16; **16:**5, 7^2, 9; **17:**3, 4, 5^2, 7, 10, 36; **18:**9, 13, 17^2, 25^2; **19:**4, 14, 22, 23, 24, 26, 28; **20:**5, 8, 17; **21:**3^2; **22:**4; **23:**2, 9, 29; **24:**1, 10; **25:**4, 6, 27

1Ch 5:26; **11:**6, 11, 20; **13:**6^2; **14:**2, 8, 10^2, 11, 14; **15:**3, 12, 14, 16, 25, 28; **17:**5, 11; **21:**1, 16, 18^2, 19, 27; **25:**5; **26:**16; **28:**2

2Ch 1:4, 6, 17; **2:**16; **3:**17; **5:**2, 4, 5^2, 13; **6:**10, 26; **7:**13, 20; **8:**11; **9:**4; **10:**8, 10, 18; **11:**4; **12:**2, 9; **13:**4, 6; **16:**1; **17:**6; **18:**2, 5, 11, 14, 19, 28, 34; **20:**16, 19, 23; **21:**4, 9, 16, 17; **24:**7, 23; **25:**14, 19, 21; **26:**16, 19; **28:**9, 12, 15, 24; **29:**7, 20;

30:7, 27; **32**:5^2, 25; **33**:3, 14, 19; **34**:30; **35**:20; **36**:6, 15, 22, 23

Ezr 1:1, 3, 5^2, 11^2; **2**:1, 59, 63, 68; **3**:2; **4**:2, 12^2, 13, 16, 23; **5**:2, 3, 9, 11; **6**:1, 11; **7**:6, 7, 9, 13, 28; **8**:1; **9**:5, 6^2, 9; **10**:6, 10

Neh 2:1, 15, 17, 18; **3**:1^2, 3, 6, 13, 14, 15, 19, 31, 32; **4**:3, 7, 14; **5**:2; **6**:1, 10; **7**:1, 5, 6, 61, 65; **8**:5, 6; **9**:3, 4, 5, 18; **10**:38; **12**:1, 31, 37^2

Est 2:7, 20; **5**:9; **7**:7

Job 1:5, 7, 16; **2**:2, 12^2; **3**:8, 10, 11; **4**:15; **5**:5^2, 11, 18; **6**:3, 4; **7**:9; **8**:11; **9**:7; **10**:15, 18; **11**:10, 15, 20; **12**:14, 15; **13**:19; **14**:10, 11, 17^2; **15**:30; **16**:4, 8, 12; **17**:8; **18**:16; **19**:8, 12; **20**:6, 15, 27; **21**:19; **22**:22, 23, 24, 26, 29; **24**:22; **26**:8; **27**:7, 16; **28**:4, 5; **29**:8; **30**:4, 12, 20, 22, 28; **31**:14, 18, 21, 29; **33**:5; **34**:7; **36**:13; **37**:7, 20; **38**:3, 8, 10, 34; **39**:4, 18, 27, 30; **40**:7, 23^2; **41**:10, 15, 25; **42**:8

Ps 3:1, 3; **4**:6; **5**:3; **7**:6; **9**:13; **10**:12; **14**:4; **15**:3; **16**:4; **17**:5, 7; **18**:8, 35, 39, 48^2; **20**:5; **21**:9; **22**:15; **24**:4, 7^2, 9^2; **25**:1; **27**:2, 5, 6, 10, 12; **28**:2, 5, 9; **30**:1, 3; **31**:8, 19; **33**:7; **35**:2, 11, 23, 25; **39**:6; **40**:2, 5, 12; **41**:8, 9, 10; **44**:5; **47**:5; **53**:4; **54**:3; **56**:1, 2; **57**:3, 8; **59**:1, 15; **63**:4; **69**:9, 15, 29; **71**:6, 20; **74**:3, 4, 5, 8, 15, 23; **75**:3, 4, 5, 7; **77**:9; **78**:21, 38, 48; **80**:2; **81**:3, 12; **83**:2; **86**:4; **87**:6; **88**:8, 15; **89**:2, 4, 42; **90**:5, 6; **91**:12; **92**:11; **93**:3^3; **94**:2, 16^2, 18; **97**:3; **102**:10, 16; **104**:8; **105**:35; **106**:9, 17, 18, 26, 30; **107**:25, 26; **109**:23; **110**:7; **113**:7; **119**:48, 117; **121**:1; **122**:4; **123**:1; **124**:2, 3; **127**:2^2; **129**:6; **132**:3; **134**:2; **139**:8, 21; **140**:10; **141**:2; **143**:8; **144**:12; **145**:14; **147**:2, 3, 6

Prv 1:12; **2**:3, 7; **3**:20; **7**:1; **8**:23, 30; **10**:12, 14; **13**:22; **15**:1, 18; **16**:27; **21**:20; **22**:6; **23**:8; **24**:16; **25**:7; **26**:9, 24; **28**:25; **29**:21, 22; **30**:4, 13, 31, 32; **31**:28

Ecc 2:26; **3**:2, 3; **4**:10^2, 15; **10**:4, 12; **12**:4

Song 2:7, 10; **3**:5; **4**:2, 12; **5**:5; **6**:6; **7**:8, 12, 13; **8**:4, 5^2

Isa 1:2, 6; **2**:3, 4, 12, 13, 14; **3**:13, 14; **5**:5, 6, 11, 13, 24, 26; **6**:1; **7**:1, 6; **8**:7^2, 16; **9**:11, 18^2; **10**:15^2, 24, 26^2, 28, 29, 30; **11**:12, 16; **13**:2, 14, 17; **14**:4, 8, 9^2, 22; **15**:2, 5^3, 7; **18**:3; **19**:5, 6; **21**:2; **22**:1; **23**:4^2, 13^2, 18; **24**:10, 14, 18, 22; **25**:8; **26**:11; **27**:9; **28**:4, 7, 21; **30**:26; **32**:9, 13; **33**:3, 10, 12; **34**:3, 10, 13; **35**:9; **36**:1, 10^2; **37**:4, 14, 23, 24, 25, 27, 29; **38**:22; **39**:6; **40**:9^3, 15, 26, 31; **41**:2, 25; **42**:2, 11, 13, 15^2; **43**:6; **44**:4, 11, 26, 27; **45**:8, 13, 20; **47**:13; **48**:13; **49**:6, 18, 19, 21, 22^2, 23; **50**:2, 9; **51**:6, 8, 17, 18; **52**:8; **53**:2; **55**:13^2; **57**:7, 8^2, 14^3, 20; **58**:1, 12; **59**:19; **60**:4, 7, 10; **61**:1, 4; **62**:10^3; **63**:11; **64**:7, 11

Jer 1:17; **2**:6, 24; **3**:2, 6; **4**:3, 6, 7, 13, 29; **5**:10, 17^3; **6**:1, 4; **7**:13, 16, 25, 29; **9**:10^2, 12, 18, 21; **10**:17, 20, 25; **11**:7, 13, 14; **12**:17; **13**:19, 20; **14**:2, 6; **15**:9; **16**:14, 15; **18**:7, 15, 21; **20**:9; **21**:2; **22**:20^2, 22; **23**:4, 7, 8, 10; **24**:6; **25**:32; **26**:5, 10, 17; **27**:22; **29**:15, 19, 22; **30**:9, 13; **31**:6, 21, 28, 40; **32**:2, 3, 33; **33**:1, 15; **34**:21; **35**:11, 15; **36**:5, 20; **37**:10, 11; **38**:10, 13^2; **39**:2, 5, 15; **42**:10; **45**:4; **46**:4, 7, 8^2, 9, 11; **47**:2, 6; **48**:5^2, 15, 44; **49**:5, 14, 19, 22, 28, 31; **50**:2, 3, 9, 21, 26, 32, 38, 41, 44; **51**:1^2, 3, 9, 11, 12^2, 14, 27^2, 34, 36, 42, 44, 53; **52**:7, 9, 31

Lam 1:14^2, 19; **2**:2, 5^2, 7, 10, 16, 17, 19, 22; **3**:41, 62, 63; **4**:5; **5**:12

Ezk 1:13, 19^2, 20, 21^2; **3**:12, 14; **4**:14; **7**:11; **8**:3, 5^2, 11; **9**:3; **10**:4, 15, 16^2, 17^2, 19^2; **11**:1, 22, 23, 24^2; **13**:5^2, 10; **14**:3, 4, 7; **16**:40; **17**:9^2, 14, 17, 24; **18**:6, 12, 15; **19**:1, 3, 6, 12^2; **20**:5^2, 6, 15, 23, 28, 42; **21**:15, 22; **22**:30; **23**:22, 27, 46, 47; **24**:8; **26**:3^2, 8, 17, 19; **27**:2, 30, 32; **28**:2, 5, 12^2, 14, 17; **29**:4; **30**:21; **31**:4, 10^3, 14^2; **32**:2, 3; **33**:25; **34**:4, 16, 18, 23, 29; **36**:3^2, 7, 13; **37**:6, 8, 10, 12, 13; **38**:11, 16, 18; **39**:2, 15; **40**:6, 22, 26, 31, 34, 37, 40, 49; **41**:16; **43**:5, 24; **44**:12; **47**:14

Dan 2:21, 44; **3**:1, 2, 3^2, 5, 7, 12, 14, 18, 22, 24; **4**:17, 34; **5**:19, 20, 23; **6**:23^2; **7**:3, 4, 5, 8^2, 20; **8**:3^2, 8, 22^2, 23, 25, 26, 27; **9**:24; **10**:5; **11**:2^2, 3, 4^2, 6, 7, 10^2, 12, 14, 15, 20, 21, 23, 25^2; **12**:1, 4, 7, 9, 11

Hos 1:11; **2**:6, 15; **4**:8, 15, 19; **6**:1, 2; **8**:4, 7, 8, 9; **9**:6, 12, 16; **10**:4, 8, 12; **11**:8; **13**:12, 15^2, 16

Joel 1:6, 10, 12, 20; **2**:9, 20^2; **3**:9^2, 12

Am 1:6, 9, 13; **2**:10, 11; **3**:1, 5, 10; **4**:10; **5**:1, 2; **6**:8, 10, 14; **7**:1, 4; **8**:4, 8, 10, 14; **9**:2, 5, 7, 11^3, 15

Oba 1, 6, 14, 21

Jna 1:2, 3, 12, 15, 17; **2**:6; **4**:6, 10

Mic 2:4, 8, 13^2; **3**:10; **4**:2, 3; **5**:3, 9, 14; **6**:4, 14; **7**:3, 6

Nah 1:4, 9; **2**:1, 7; **3**:3, 15

Hab 1:3, 6, 9, 15; **2**:4, 6, 7; **3**:10, 16

Zep 2:4; **3**:8

Hag 1:8, 14

Zec 1:18, 21^2; **2**:1, 13; **5**:1, 5, 7, 9^2; **6**:1, 12; **9**:3, 13, 16; **10**:11, 12; **11**:16, 17; **14**:10, 13, 16, 17, 18^2, 19

Mal 3:15, 17; **4**:1, 2

Mt 3:9, 12, 16; **4**:1, 5, 6, 8, 16; **5**:1; **6**:19, 20; **9**:6, 16; **10**:17, 19, 21^2; **11**:5; **12**:42; **13**:4, 5, 6, 7, 26, 28, 29^2; **14**:12, 19, 20, 23; **15**:13, 29, 37; **16**:9, 10, 24; **17**:1, 8, 27^2; **19**:20; **20**:17, 18; **22**:7, 24; **23**:13, 32; **24**:9, 43; **26**:52; **27**:37, 50

Mk 1:10, 31, 35; **2**:4, 9, 11, 12, 21; **3**:13, 26; **4**:4, 5, 6, 7, 8, 27, 32; **5**:29; **6**:29, 41, 43, 51; **7**:34; **8**:8, 19, 20, 24, 25, 34; **9**:2, 27; **10**:16, 21, 32, 33; **11**:20; **12**:19; **13**:9, 11, 12, 16; **14**:42, 60; **15**:37, 39, 41; **16**:18, 19

Lk 1:66, 69; **2**:4, 28, 42; **3**:8, 20; **4**:5, 11, 16^2, 25, 29; **5**:23, 24, 25^2, 28; **6**:8, 20; **7**:15, 16; **8**:6, 7, 8, 37; **9**:16, 17, 23, 28, 51; **10**:25, 34; **11**:27, 31, 32; **12**:19, 21; **13**:11, 25; **14**:10; **16**:23; **17**:6, 13; **18**:10, 13, 21, 31; **19**:4, 5, 20, 21, 22, 28; **20**:28; **21**:1, 12, 28^2; **22**:45; **23**:5, 46; **24**:33, 50, 51

Jn 2:7, 13, 17, 19, 20; **3**:13, 14^2; **4**:14, 35; **5**:1, 8, 9, 11, 12, 21; **6**:3, 5, 12, 39, 40, 44, 54, 62; **7**:8^2, 10^2, 14; **8**:7, 10, 28, 59; **10**:1, 31; **11**:31, 41, 55; **12**:20, 32, 34; **13**:18; **17**:1; **18**:11, 30; **19**:30; **21**:11

Act 1:2, 9, 10, 11^2, 13, 15, 22; **2**:14^2, 24, 30, 32; **3**:1, 6, 7, 8, 13, 22, 26; **4**:24, 26; **5**:5, 6, 10, 17, 30, 34, 36, 37; **6**:12, 13; **7**:20, 21, 37, 42, 43, 55; **8**:31, 39; **9**:40, 41; **10**:4, 9, 16, 26^2, 40; **11**:2, 10, 28; **12**:7^2, 23; **13**:1, 16, 22, 31, 33, 34, 43, 50; **14**:2, 11, 20; **15**:2, 5, 7, 16; **16**:22; **17**:13; **18**:22; **20**:9, 11, 32; **21**:4, 12, 15^2, 27; **22**:3, 13, 22; **24**:11, 12; **25**:9, 18; **26**:10, 30; **27**:15, 17, 27, 40^2

Ro 1:24, 26; **2**:5; **4**:24; **6**:4; **8**:11^2, 32; **9**:17; **10**:7; **14**:4; **15**:16

1Co 4:6, 18, 19; **5**:2; **6**:14^2; **8**:1; **10**:7; **13**:4; **15**:15^2, 24, 35, 54

2Co 2:7; **4**:14^2; **5**:4; **9**:5; **12**:2, 4, 14

Gal 1:17, 18; **2**:1, 2; **3**:23

Eph 2:6; **4**:8, 10, 15; **6**:4

Col 1:5, 24; **2**:7, 18

1Th 2:16; **4**:17

1Ti 2:8; **3**:6, 16; **4**:6; **5**:10; **6**:19

2Ti 1:6; **4**:8

Heb 1:12; **5**:7; **7**:27^2; **11**:17^2, 19; **12**:12, 15

Jas 4:10; **5**:15

1Pt 1:13, 21; **2**:5^2

2Pt 1:13; **3**:1, 10

1Jn 3:17

Jude 12, 20

Rev 4:1; **8**:4, 7^2; **10**:4, 5, 9, 10; **11**:12^2; **12**:5, 16; **13**:1, 11; **14**:11; **15**:1; **16**:12; **18**:21; **19**:3; **20**:3, 9, 13^2

UPON

Gen 1:2^2, 11, 15, 17, 25, 26, 28, 29, 30; **2**:5, 21; **3**:14; **4**:15, 26; **6**:12^2, 17; **7**:3, 4, 6, 8, 10, 12, 14, 17, 18^2, 19, 21^2, 23, 24; **8**:4, 17^2, 19; **9**:2^5, 16^2, 17, 23; **11**:4, 8, 9; **12**:8, 11; **15**:11, 12^2; **16**:5; **17**:17; **18**:6, 19, 27, 31; **19**:3, 9, 16^3, 23, 24^2, 25; **22**:2, 6, 9, 12, 17; **24**:15, 16, 18, 30, 47^2, 61; **26**:7, 10, 25; **27**:12, 13, 15, 16^2; **28**:11, 18; **29**:2, 3, 32; **30**:3; **31**:10, 12, 17, 34, 35, 46, 54; **32**:31^2, 32; **34**:25, 27; **35**:5, 20; **37**:22, 27, 34; **38**:28, 29, 30; **39**:5, 7; **40**:6, 17; **41**:3, 5, 17, 42; **42**:1, 21; **43**:18, 30; **44**:21; **45**:14^2, 15; **46**:4; **47**:31; **48**:2, 14^2, 17, 18; **50**:1^2, 23

Ex 1:16; **2**:25; **3**:6, 12, 22^2; **4**:9^2, 20, 31; **5**:3, 8, 9, 21; **7**:4, 5, 17, 19^5; **8**:3^2, 4^2, 5, 7, 14, 18^2, 21^3; **9**:3^6, 9^2, 10^2, 11^2, 14^3, 19^2, 22^3, 23^2, 33; **10**:6, 12, 13; **11**:1^2, 5; **12**:13^2, 23, 33, 34; **13**:9, 16; **14**:4^2, 17^4, 18^3, 22, 26^3, 29, 30, 31; **15**:9, 15, 16, 19, 26^2; **16**:14; **17**:6; **18**:8; **19**:11, 16, 18, 20, 22, 24; **20**:5, 12, 25; **21**:14, 19, 22, 30; **22**:3, 25; **24**:11, 16; **25**:11, 21, 22, 30; **26**:4, 7, 32^2, 34; **27**:2, 4, 7; **28**:8, 12^2, 22, 23, 26, 29, 30^2, 33, 34, 35, 36, 37^2, 38^2, 41, 43^2; **29**:5, 6^2, 7, 8, 10, 12, 13^2, 15, 16, 18, 19, 20^5, 21^5, 22, 25, 38; **30**:1, 4, 7, 8, 10^2, 32, 33; **31**:18; **32**:16, 20, 21, 29^3, 34; **33**:16, 21; **34**:1, 7^2, 28, 35; **35**:3; **36**:17^2; **37**:3^2, 13, 16, 27; **39**:5, 15, 19, 24, 25, 30, 31, 43; **40**:4, 13, 19, 20, 22, 23, 29, 38

Lev 1:4, 5, 7^2, 8^2, 11, 12, 13, 17^3; **2**:1, 2, 9, 15; **3**:2^2, 3, 5^2, 8^2, 9, 10, 11, 13^2, 14, 15, 16; **4**:4, 7, 8, 9, 10, 15, 18, 19, 24, 25, 26, 29, 30, 31, 33, 34, 35; **5**:9, 11; **6**:9, 10, 12^2, 13, 15^2, 27; **7**:2, 5, 20, 31; **8**:7^2, 8, 9^3, 11, 12, 13^2, 14, 15^2, 16^2, 18, 19, 21, 22, 23^3, 24^4, 25, 26, 27^2, 28, 30^5; **9**:9, 10, 12, 13, 14, 17, 18, 20^2, 24; **10**:6, 7; **11**:20, 21^2, 27, 29, 32, 37, 38, 41, 42^3, 44, 46; **13**:25, 27, 29, 30, 43, 45, 50; **14**:7, 14^3, 17^4, 18, 20, 25^3, 28^4, 29, 48; **15**:8, 9, 20^2, 22, 24, 26; **16**:2^2, 4, 8, 9, 13^2, 14, 15, 18, 19, 21^2, 22, 25; **17**:6, 11; **18**:25; **19**:17, 19, 28; **20**:9, 11, 12, 13, 16, 27; **21**:5, 10, 12; **22**:3, 22; **23**:37; **24**:4, 6, 7, 14; **25**:21, 37; **26**:21, 25, 30, 35, 36, 37

Nu 1:53; **4**:7, 8, 10, 11, 14^2, 25; **5**:14^2, 15, 25, 26, 30^2; **6**:5, 7, 19, 25, 26, 27; **7**:9, 89; **8**:7, 10, 12, 24, 25; **9**:15, 18, 19, 20, 22; **10**:34; **11**:9^2, 11, 17^2, 25^2, 26, 29, 31; **12**:3, 10, 11; **13**:23; **14**:18, 36, 37; **15**:31, 32, 38, 39; **16**:3, 4, 7, 22, 33, 45; **17**:2, 3; **18**:5, 17; **19**:2, 13^2, 15, 18^4, 19, 20; **20**:6, 26, 28; **21**:8^2, 9, 15; **22**:22, 30; **23**:4; **24**:2; **27**:18, 20, 23; **30**:14; **31**:27; **33**:4; **35**:22, 23

Dt 1:36; **2**:25; **4**:7, 10, 13, 26, 30, 32, 36, 39, 40; **5**:9; **6**:8, 9, 22^3; **7**:6, 7, 15^2, 16, 22; **8**:4; **11**:12, 18, 20^2, 21, 25^2, 29^2; **12**:1, 2^2, 16, 19, 24, 27^2; **13**:9, 17; **14**:2; **15**:23; **17**:7, 18; **19**:5, 10; **21**:23; **22**:6^2, 8, 12, 14, 19; **23**:13, 19^2, 20^2; **24**:15^2; **26**:6; **27**:3, 5, 8, 12, 13; **28**:8, 15, 20, 24, 45, 46^2, 48, 56, 60, 61; **29**:5^2, 20, 22, 27; **30**:1, 3, 7, 18; **31**:17; **32**:2^2, 23^2, 24, 35, 42; **33**:10, 16^2, 26, 28, 29; **34**:9

Jos 1:3; **2**:6, 8, 9, 15^2, 19^2; **3**:13, 16; **4**:5; **7**:6^2, 10; **8**:7, 20, 32; **9**:4, 5^2, 20; **10**:11, 12, 13, 18, 24^2, 26; **11**:4, 7; **12**:2; **13**:9; **19**:34; **20**:8; **23**:15^2; **24**:7

Jdg 3:10, 16, 22, 23; **4**:16; **6**:14, 20, 26, 28, 34, 37, 39^2, 40; **7**:5, 6, 25; **8**:21; **9**:5, 18, 24^2, 33, 44, 49, 53, 57^2; **11**:29, 37, 38; **12**:1; **13**:19; **14**:6, 17, 19; **15**:12, 14^2, 16; **16**:3, 9, 12, 14, 17, 19, 20, 26, 27, 29, 30^2; **18**:19, 25; **19**:14, 20, 27, 28; **20**:5, 37, 41, 48

Ru 3:3, 15; **4**:5, 10

1Sa 1:9, 11; **2**:8, 10, 28, 34; **4**:12, 13, 19; **5**:3, 4^2, 6, 7^2; **6**:8, 11; **7**:10; **9**:16, 24, 25; **10**:1, 6, 10; **11**:2, 6; **13**:12, 13; **14**:1, 13^2, 25, 32; **15**:19, 27; **16**:13, 16, 23; **17**:5, 6, 38, 39, 49, 51; **18**:4, 10, 17^2; **19**:9, 20, 23; **20**:9, 25^2, 31; **21**:13; **22**:17, 18^2; **24**:2, 12, 13; **25**:24^2, 39, 42; **26**:12; **28**:18, 23; **30**:14^3, 16, 17; **31**:2^2, 4, 5

2Sa 1:2, 6^2, 9^2, 10^2, 15, 16, 19, 21, 24; **4**:11; **5**:20, 23; **6**:3, 8; **9**:8; **11**:2^2, 21, 23, 24; **12**:16; **13**:18, 29; **14**:7; **15**:14, 32; **16**:1, 8, 22; **17**:2, 12^2, 14; **18**:9, 17, 28; **20**:8^2, 12; **21**:10^2; **22**:7, 11^2, 28, 34; **24**:15, 16, 20

1Ki 1:13, 17, 20, 24, 30, 33, 35, 38, 44, 47; **2**:5, 12, 25, 29, 31, 32^2, 33^6, 34, 37, 44, 46; **3**:4, 26; **5**:5; **6**:32^3, 35; **7**:2^2, 3, 16, 17, 18^2, 19, 20^2, 22, 25^2, 29, 31, 38, 41, 42; **8**:31, 32, 36; **9**:5^2, 9^2, 21, 25^2; **10**:20; **12**:4, 9, 32, 33^2; **13**:2^3, 3, 29; **14**:10; **17**:14, 19, 20, 21; **18**:1, 26, 28, 42; **19**:11, 19; **20**:30, 31, 38; **21**:4, 21, 27, 29; **22**:17

2Ki 2:9, 16; **3**:15, 22, 27; **4**:4^2, 5^2, 21, 29, 31, 32, 33, 34^5, 35; **5**:23; **6**:26, 30^2; **7**:6, 9, 17, 20; **8**:1; **9**:25, 37; **11**:12; **12**:11; **13**:13, 16^3, 18; **16**:13, 15^2, 17; **18**:21^2, 23; **19**:7; **21**:12; **22**:16^2, 20; **23**:6, 16, 20^2; **24**:3; **25**:6, 17^2

1Ch 1:10; **5**:16; **6**:49; **9**:27; **10**:4; **12**:8, 18, 19; **13**:11; **14**:11, 14, 17; **15**:13, 15, 27; **16**:8, 40; **19**:17; **20**:2; **21**:14, 16, 26^2; **22**:8; **28**:2, 5, 19; **29**:25

2Ch 1:6; **4**:4^2, 13, 14; **6**:13^2, 16, 20^2, 22, 23, 27; **7**:3^2, 22; **9**:19; **10**:4, 9, 11; **12**:7; **13**:4, 10, 11, 18; **14**:14; **15**:1, 5; **17**:10; **18**:16, 18, 23; **19**:2, 7, 10^2; **20**:9, 12, 14; **22**:8; **23**:11, 20; **24**:7, 9, 18, 20, 22, 27; **25**:13, 28; **26**:15, 16, 20; **28**:11, 15; **29**:8, 22^2, 23, 24, 27; **32**:8, 12, 25^2, 26; **33**:11; **34**:4, 5, 21, 24^2, 25, 28^2; **35**:3, 16; **36**:17^2

Ezr 3:3^2; **5**:5; **6**:19; **7**:6, 9^2, 17, 24, 26, 28; **8**:18, 22, 31; **9**:5, 13

Neh 2:8, 12, 18; 4:4, 12, 19; 5:4, 18, 19; 6:1, 14; 8:2, 4, 16; 9:1, 4, 10, 13, 32, 33; 10:34; 12:31^{2}, 38; 13:18^{3}

Est 1:6; 2:15, 17; 3:13; 4:5; 5:1; 6:8^{2}; 7:8; 8:7^{2}, 12^{2}, 14, 17; 9:2, 3, 13, 25, 27^{3}; 10:1^{2}

Job 1:12, 15, 17, 19, 20; 2:11, 12, 13; 3:4, 5, 6, 25; 4:5, 14; 5:10^{2}; 6:28; 7:1, 8, 17; 8:9, 15; 9:8, 33; 10:1, 3, 16, 17; 12:4, 21; 13:11, 27; 14:3, 22; 15:21, 26^{2}, 29; 16:9^{2}, 10^{2}, 13, 14^{2}, 15; 18:8, 15; 19:21^{2}, 25; 20:4, 22, 23^{2}, 25; 21:5, 9, 17; 22:28; 24:23; 25:3; 26:7, 9; 27:9, 10, 22; 28:9; 29:3, 4, 13, 19, 22; 30:12, 14^{2}, 15, 16^{2}, 22, 30; 31:1, 10, 36; 33:7, 15^{2}, 19, 27; 34:14, 21, 23; 36:28, 30; 37:12; 38:5, 24; 39:28; 40:4; 41:8, 30, 33; 42:11

Ps 2:6; 3:7, 8; 4:1, 4, 6; 5:ttl; 6:2, ttl; 7:5, 16^{2}; 8:ttl; 9:13, ttl; 11:2, 6; 12:ttl; 14:2, 4; 17:6; 18:3, 6, 10^{2}, 33; 21:5, 12; 22:9, 10, 13, 17, 18, 29, ttl; 24:2^{2}; 25:16, 18; 27:2, 5, 7; 29:3^{2}, 10; 30:10; 31:9, 16, 17; 32:4; 33:14, 18^{2}, 22; 34:15; 35:8, 16; 36:4; 37:9, 12; 40:2, 12, 17; 41:2, 3; 43:4; 44:17; 45:3, 9, ttl; 46:ttl; 47:8; 48:6; 49:4; 50:10, 15; 51:1, 19; 53:2, 4, ttl; 54:7; 55:3, 4, 5, 10, 15, 16, 22; 56:12, ttl; 59:9, 10; 60:ttl; 61:ttl; 62:1, 5, 10; 63:6; 64:8; 65:5, 12; 66:11; 67:1, 2, 4; 68:4, 33; 69:9, 15, 24, ttl; 72:6, 16; 73:25; 74:5; 78:24, 27, 31, 49; 79:6^{3}; 80:17^{2}, 18, ttl; 81:ttl; 84:9, ttl; 86:5, 7, 16; 88:7, 9, ttl; 89:19, 22; 90:17^{2}; 91:13, 14, 15; 92:3^{3}; 94:23; 99:6^{2}; 101:6; 102:7, 13; 103:17; 104:3, 27; 105:1, 16, 38; 106:29; 107:40; 109:25; 112:2, 8; 116:2, 3, 4, 13, 17; 118:5, 7; 119:49, 53, 87, 132, 135; 121:5; 123:2^{2}, 3^{2}; 125:3, 5; 128:6; 129:3, 6, 8; 132:11, 12, 18; 133:2^{2}, 3; 135:9^{2}; 137:2; 139:5; 140:10; 141:7; 144:9; 145:15, 18^{2}; 147:7, 8, 15; 149:5, 7^{2}, 9; 150:5^{2}

Prv 1:27, 28; 3:3, 18; 6:21, 28; 7:3^{2}; 8:27; 9:3; 10:6, 24; 11:26; 19:12, 17; 23:5, 31, 34; 24:25, 32; 25:12, 20, 22; 26:14^{2}, 27; 28:22; 30:19, 24, 32

Ecc 5:2; 7:20; 8:6, 14, 16; 9:12; 10:7^{2}; 11:1, 2, 3

Song 1:6^{2}; 2:8^{2}, 17; 3:8; 4:16; 5:5, 15; 6:13; 7:5; 8:5, 6^{2}, 9, 14

Isa 1:25; 2:12^{2}, 13^{2}, 14^{2}, 15^{2}, 16^{2}; 3:26; 4:5^{3}; 5:6; 6:1, 7; 7:17^{3}, 19^{2}; 8:7, 17; 9:2, 6, 7^{2}, 8; 10:12, 20^{2}, 26; 11:2, 14^{2}; 12:4; 13:2; 14:13, 16, 25, 26^{2}; 15:9^{3}; 16:5; 18:2, 4, 6^{2}; 19:1, 8, 12; 20:3^{2}; 21:3, 8, 13; 22:22, 24, 25; 23:17; 24:17, 20, 21; 26:16; 28:4, 10^{4}, 13^{4}, 22, 27; 29:10; 30:6^{2}, 16^{2}, 17, 18, 25^{2}, 32; 32:11, 13^{2}, 15; 33:4, 20; 34:2^{2}, 5^{2}, 11; 35:10; 36:8, 12; 37:7; 38:21; 40:7, 22, 24, 31; 41:25^{3}; 42:1, 5, 25; 43:2, 22; 44:3^{4}, 19; 45:12; 46:1^{2}, 7; 47:6, 9, 11^{3}, 13; 48:2; 49:13, 16, 22; 50:10; 51:5, 6, 11; 52:7; 53:5; 55:6, 7; 56:7; 57:7; 58:14; 59:17, 21; 60:1, 2^{2}; 61:1; 62:6; 63:3; 64:7; 65:3, 7^{2}; 66:4, 12^{2}, 20^{3}, 24

Jer 1:14; 2:3, 15, 20, 34, 37; 3:6, 12, 21; 4:20, 29; 5:3, 10, 12, 15; 6:11^{2}, 12, 19, 21, 23, 26; 7:20^{5}; 8:2; 9:3, 22; 10:25^{2}; 11:8, 11, 16, 23; 12:12; 13:1, 4, 13, 16, 22, 26; 14:16, 22; 15:5, 8^{3}, 14; 16:4, 17; 17:1^{2}, 2, 18, 25; 18:22; 19:3, 13, 15^{2}; 22:2, 4, 23, 24, 30; 23:2, 12, 17, 19, 40; 24:6; 25:13, 26, 29, 30, 33; 26:15^{3}; 27:2, 5; 28:14; 29:12, 16, 17; 30:16, 18, 23; 31:5, 6, 19, 20, 26, 39; 32:19, 23, 29, 42^{2}; 33:17, 21; 35:17^{2}; 36:4, 6, 30, 31^{3}; 39:5, 16; 40:2, 3, 4; 42:12, 17, 18^{2}; 43:10; 44:2^{2}; 45:5; 46:16, 21; 47:5; 48:8, 18, 21^{4}, 22^{3}, 23^{3}, 24^{3}, 32^{2}, 37^{2}, 38, 43, 44^{2}; 49:5, 8, 36, 37; 50:15, 19, 35^{4}, 36^{2}, 37^{4}, 38^{2}, 42; 51:12, 13, 25, 35^{2}, 42, 47, 52, 56^{2}, 60, 64; 52:9, 22^{2}, 23

Lam 1:10, 14; 2:10^{2}, 11; 3:28, 47, 53, 55, 57; 4:19; 5:1, 18

Ezk 1:3, 15, 17, 22, 26^{2}, 28; 2:1, 2; 3:14, 22, 24, 25; 4:1, 4^{3}, 5, 8, 9; 5:1^{2}, 13, 16^{2}, 17^{2}; 6:3, 12, 13, 14; 7:2, 3^{3}, 4, 8^{2}, 12, 14, 18^{2}, 26^{2}; 8:1, 10; 9:4, 6, 8^{2}, 10; 10:11; 11:5, 8, 13, 21, 23; 12:6, 7, 12, 13; 13:9, 15^{2}, 18; 14:9, 13^{2}, 17, 19, 21, 22^{2}; 16:5, 8, 11, 12, 14, 41, 43; 17:19, 20, 22; 18:6, 8, 11, 13^{2}, 15, 20^{2}; 19:9; 20:8, 13, 21; 21:12^{4}, 29, 31; 22:9, 20, 21, 22, 24, 31^{2}; 23:6, 8, 9, 10, 12^{2}, 14, 15^{2}, 16, 20, 23, 41, 42^{2}, 46, 49; 24:6, 7^{2}, 8, 11, 13, 17^{2}, 23^{2}; 25:7, 11, 12, 13, 14, 16, 17^{2}; 26:7, 14, 16, 19; 27:11^{2}, 29, 30; 28:7, 12, 14, 18, 23, 26; 29:5, 7, 8; 30:4, 9, 15, 25; 31:12, 13^{2}; 32:4^{3}, 5, 8, 11, 27; 33:2, 3, 4, 5, 10, 22, 26; 34:6^{2}, 13, 14^{2}; 36:10, 11, 12, 18^{2}, 25, 29; 37:1, 4, 6^{2}, 8, 9, 10, 16^{2}, 22; 38:12^{2}, 15, 20^{2}, 22^{3}; 39:2, 4, 5, 14, 17, 21, 25, 29; 40:1, 2, 4, 16, 17, 26, 31, 34, 37, 43; 41:25^{2}, 26; 43:3, 12, 14, 20, 24, 27^{2}; 44:4, 17, 18^{2}; 45:19^{3}, 22; 47:10, 12

Dan 1:13; 2:10, 28, 29, 34, 46; 3:27; 4:5, 13, 21, 24, 28, 33; 5:5; 6:10, 17, 23; 7:1, 2, 4, 6, 23; 8:7, 10, 17; 9:11, 12^{2}, 13, 14^{2}, 17, 24^{2}, 27; 10:7, 10^{2}, 16; 11:18, 24, 42; 12:6, 7

Hos 1:4, 6, 7; 2:4, 13, 23; 4:13^{2}; 5:1, 10; 7:9, 12, 14; 8:14; 9:1; 10:7, 11, 12, 14; 12:14; 13:13; 14:3

Joel 1:6; 2:2, 8, 9^{2}, 28, 29^{2}; 3:4, 7

Am 1:12; 2:2, 5, 8; 3:5, 9, 14; 4:2, 7^{3}, 13; 5:2, 8, 11; 6:4^{2}, 12; 7:7; 8:2, 10^{2}; 9:1, 4, 6, 8, 9, 15

Oba 11, 15^{2}, 16, 17

Jna 1:6^{2}, 7^{2}, 8, 12, 14; 2:10; 4:8

Mic 1:3; 2:1; 3:11^{2}; 4:11; 5:1, 7, 9, 15; 7:16, 19

Nah 1:15; 2:7; 3:3, 5, 6, 7, 18, 19

Hab 1:13; 2:1^{2}, 2; 3:1, 8, 19

Zep 1:4^{2}, 5, 17; 2:2^{2}; 3:8^{2}, 9

Hag 1:9, 11^{9}; 2:15

Zec 1:7, 8, 16; 2:9; 3:5^{2}, 9; 4:2^{2}, 3^{2}, 11^{2}; 5:8, 11; 6:8, 11, 13^{2}; 9:9^{2}, 16; 10:6; 11:11, 17^{2}; 12:4, 10^{3}; 13:7; 14:4, 12, 17, 20

Mal 1:7; 2:2, 3; 3:16

Mt 3:16; 4:13; 6:19; 7:24, 25^{2}, 26, 27; 9:18; 10:13, 27; 11:29; 12:2, 18; 13:5; 16:18; 19:28; 20:25; 21:5; 23:9, 18, 35^{2}, 36; 24:2, 3; 25:31; 26:10; 27:29, 30, 35; 28:2

Mk 1:10; 3:10; 6:5, 17, 39, 48, 49; 7:30, 32; 8:23, 25; 10:16, 27, 34, 42; 11:7, 11; 13:2, 3; 14:67; 15:19, 24

Lk 1:12, 35, 58; 2:9, 25, 40; 3:22; 4:18; 5:1, 19, 24, 36; 6:10, 48^{2}, 49; 8:6, 43; 9:38; 10:6; 11:20, 22; 12:1, 3; 13:4; 17:31; 18:13; 19:35, 43, 44; 20:1, 18; 21:6, 23, 25, 34; 22:25, 56, 61; 23:26; 24:1, 49

Jn 1:32, 33, 36, 51; 4:27; 9:15; 11:38; 12:35; 18:4; 19:29, 31

Act 1:8, 26; 2:3, 17, 43; 3:4; 4:1, 33; 5:11^{2}, 28; 6:12; 7:57, 59; 8:16, 24; 10:9; 11:6, 19; 12:7, 21^{2}; 13:11, 40; 15:10, 17, 28; 16:23; 18:6; 19:6, 13; 20:7; 21:35; 22:13; 24:7; 26:16; 27:26, 29

Ro 2:9; 3:22; 4:9^{2}; 5:12, 18^{2}; 9:28; 10:12, 13; 11:32; 13:4, 6; 15:20

1Co 1:2; 3:12; 7:35^{2}; 9:16; 10:11; 12:23; 15:10; 16:2

2Co 1:11, 23; 3:15; 5:2, 4; 8:4, 22; 11:28; 12:9

Gal 4:11; 6:16

Eph 2:20; 4:26; 5:6

Php 1:3; 2:7, 17, 27

Col 3:5

1Th 2:16; 5:3^{2}

1Ti 4:15

Heb 6:7, 18; 8:6; 11:21

Jas 2:21; 4:3; 5:1

1Pt 4:14; 5:7

2Pt 2:1, 5

1Jn 1:1; 3:1

Jude 15

Rev 1:17; 2:24; 3:3, 10^{2}, 12^{2}; 4:3, 4; 5:7, 13; 7:10; 8:3, 7, 10^{2}; 9:3; 10:1, 2, 5^{2}, 8^{2}; 11:10, 11^{2}, 16; 12:1, 3; 13:1^{3}, 8; 14:14; 16:1, 2^{3}, 3, 4, 8, 10, 12, 18, 21; 17:1, 3, 5, 16; 18:24; 19:11, 14, 21; 20:3, 4^{2}; 21:5

US

Gen 1:26; 3:22; 5:29; 11:3, 4^{4}, 7; 19:5, 13, 31, 32, 34; 20:9; 23:6^{3}; 24:23, 55, 65; 26:10^{2}, 16, 22, 28^{3}, 29; 31:14, 15, 37, 44, 50, 53; 32:18, 20; 33:12^{2}; 34:9^{2}, 10, 14, 16, 17, 21^{4}, 22^{3}, 23^{2}; 35:3; 37:8^{2}, 17, 20, 21, 27; 39:14^{2}, 17; 41:12^{2}, 13; 42:2, 21^{2}, 28, 30^{2}, 33; 43:2, 3, 4, 5, 7, 18^{3}; 44:25, 26^{2}, 27, 30, 31; 47:15, 19^{2}, 25; 50:15^{2}

Ex 1:10^{2}; 2:14, 19^{2}; 3:18^{2}; 5:3^{3}, 8, 16, 17, 21; 8:26, 27; 10:7, 25, 26; 13:14, 15, 16; 14:5, 11^{3}, 12^{2}, 25; 16:3, 7, 8; 17:2, 3^{2}, 7, 9; 19:23; 20:19^{2}; 24:14; 32:1^{3}, 23^{3}; 33:15, 16; 34:9^{2}

Nu 10:29, 31^{2}, 32^{2}; 11:4, 13, 18^{2}; 12:2, 11; 13:27, 30; 14:3^{2}, 4^{2}, 8^{3}, 9^{2}; 16:13^{3}, 14^{2}, 34; 20:5^{2}, 14, 15, 16, 17; 21:5, 7; 22:4, 14; 27:4; 31:49; 32:5, 19

Dt 1:6, 14, 19, 20, 22^{3}, 25^{3}, 27^{4}, 41; 2:29, 30, 32, 33, 36^{2}, 37; 3:1; 5:2, 3^{3}, 24, 25, 27; 6:21, 23^{3}, 24^{2}, 25; 9:28; 13:2^{2}, 6, 13; 26:3, 6^{3}, 8, 9^{2}, 15; 29:7, 15^{2}, 29; 30:12^{2}, 13^{2}; 31:17^{2}; 33:4

Jos 1:16^{2}; 2:9, 14, 17, 18, 20, 24; 4:23; 5:6, 13; 7:7^{2}, 9, 25; 8:5, 6^{2}; 9:6, 7, 11^{2}, 20, 22^{2}, 25; 10:6^{4}; 17:4, 16; 21:2; 22:17, 19^{2}, 22, 23, 25, 26^{2}, 27^{2}, 28^{2}, 31, 34; 24:17^{2}, 18, 27^{2}

Jdg 1:1, 24; 6:13^{6}; 8:1^{2}, 21, 22^{2}; 9:8, 10, 12, 14; 10:15^{2}; 11:8, 10, 19, 24; 12:1; 13:8^{2}, 15, 23^{3}; 14:15^{2}; 15:10^{2}, 11^{2}; 16:5, 24, 25; 18:19^{2}, 25; 19:11, 13, 28; 20:3, 8^{2}, 13, 18, 32^{2}, 39; 21:1, 22

Ru 2:20

1Sa 4:3^{5}, 7, 8^{2}; 5:7^{2}, 10^{2}, 11; 6:2, 9^{3}, 20; 7:8^{2}, 12; 8:5^{2}, 6^{2}, 19, 20^{2}; 9:5^{2}, 6^{2}, 8, 9, 10, 27; 10:16, 19, 27; 11:1, 3^{2}, 10, 12, 14; 12:4^{2}, 10, 12, 19; 14:1, 6^{2}, 9, 10^{2}, 12, 17, 36^{3}; 17:9; 20:11, 42; 21:5; 23:19; 25:7, 15, 16, 40; 26:11; 27:11; 29:4^{2}, 9; 30:22, 23^{3}

2Sa 2:14; 5:2; 10:12; 11:23^{2}; 13:25, 26; 15:14^{3}, 19, 20; 17:5; 18:3^{5}; 19:9^{2}, 10, 42^{2}, 43; 20:6^{2}; 21:4, 5^{2}, 6, 17; 24:14

1Ki 3:18; 5:6; 8:57^{3}; 12:4, 9, 10; 18:23, 26; 20:23, 31

2Ki 1:6^{2}; 4:9, 10^{3}, 13; 6:1, 2^{3}, 11, 16; 7:4^{3}, 6^{2}, 9, 12, 13; 9:5, 12; 10:5; 14:8; 18:26, 30, 32; 19:19; 22:13^{2}

1Ch 13:2^{2}, 3^{2}; 15:13; 16:35^{3}; 19:13

2Ch 10:4, 9, 10; 13:10, 12; 14:7^{3}, 11; 20:9, 11^{3}, 12; 25:17; 29:10; 32:7, 8^{2}, 11; 34:21

Ezr 4:2^{2}, 3^{2}, 12, 14, 18; 5:11, 17; 8:17, 18^{2}, 21, 22, 23, 31^{2}; 9:8^{3}, 9^{4}, 13^{3}, 14^{2}; 10:3, 14

Neh 2:17, 18, 19^{2}, 20; 4:12^{2}, 15^{2}, 20^{2}, 22, 23; 5:8, 10, 17^{2}; 6:2, 7, 9, 10^{2}, 16; 9:32, 33, 37; 10:32; 13:18

Job 9:33^{2}; 15:9, 10; 21:14; 22:17; 31:15; 34:4^{3}, 37; 35:11^{2}; 37:19

Ps 2:3^{2}; 4:6^{2}; 12:4; 17:11; 20:9; 33:22; 34:3; 44:1, 5, 7^{2}, 9, 10^{2}, 11^{2}, 13^{2}, 14, 17, 19^{2}, 23, 26; 46:7, 11; 47:3, 4; 54:ttl; 60:1^{3}, 3, 10, 11; 62:8; 65:5; 66:10^{2}, 11, 12; 67:1^{3}, 6, 7; 68:19, 28; 74:1, 8, 9; 78:3; 79:4, 8^{2}, 9^{2}; 80:2, 3, 6, 7, 18, 19; 83:4, 12; 85:4^{2}, 5, 6, 7^{2}, 13; 90:12, 14, 15^{2}, 17^{2}; 95:1^{2}, 2, 6^{2}; 100:3; 103:10^{2}, 12; 106:47^{2}; 108:11, 12; 115:1^{2}, 12^{2}; 117:2; 118:27; 119:4; 122:1; 123:2, 3^{2}; 124:2, 3^{2}, 4, 6; 126:3; 136:23, 24; 137:3^{5}, 8

Prv 1:11^{3}, 12, 14^{2}; 7:18^{2}

Ecc 1:10; 12:13

Song 2:15; 5:9; 7:11^{2}, 12^{2}

Isa 1:9, 18; 2:3^{2}, 5; 4:1; 6:8; 7:6^{3}; 8:10; 9:6^{2}; 14:8, 10; 17:14^{2}; 22:13; 25:9; 26:12^{2}, 13; 28:15; 29:15^{2}; 30:10^{2}, 11; 32:15; 33:2, 14^{2}, 21, 22; 36:11, 15, 18; 37:20; 41:1, 22^{2}; 43:9, 26; 50:8; 53:6; 59:9^{2}, 11, 12^{2}; 63:7, 16^{2}, 17; 64:6, 7^{2}, 12

Jer 2:6^{2}, 27; 3:25; 4:5, 8, 13; 5:12, 19, 24^{2}; 6:4^{2}, 5^{2}, 24, 26; 8:8, 14^{4}; 9:18, 19; 11:19^{2}; 14:7, 9^{2}, 19^{2}, 21^{2}; 16:10; 18:18^{3}; 21:2^{4}, 13; 26:16; 29:15, 28; 31:6; 35:6, 8, 9, 10, 11; 36:17; 37:3, 9; 38:16, 25^{2}; 40:10; 41:8; 42:2^{2}, 3, 5^{2}, 6, 20^{2}; 43:3^{4}; 44:16; 46:16; 48:2; 50:5; 51:9, 10

Lam 3:40, 41, 43, 45, 46, 47; 4:17^{2}, 19^{2}; 5:1, 4, 8^{2}, 16, 20^{2}, 21, 22^{2}

Ezk 8:12; 11:3, 15; 24:19^{2}; 33:10, 24; 35:12; 37:18

Dan 1:12; 2:23; 3:17^{2}; 9:7, 8, 10, 11, 12^{3}, 13, 14, 16

Hos 6:1^{3}, 2^{2}, 3; 10:3, 8^{2}; 12:4; 14:2, 3

Am 4:1; 6:13; 9:10

Oba 1

Jna 1:6, 7^{2}, 8^{2}, 11, 14^{2}

Mic 3:11^{2}; 4:2^{2}; 5:1, 6; 7:19

Zec 1:6^{2}; 8:21

Mal 1:2, 9; 2:10

Mt 1:23; 3:15; 6:11, 12, 13^{2}; 8:25, 29, 31^{2}; 9:27; 13:36, 56; 15:15, 23; 17:4^{2}; 20:7, 12, 30, 31; 21:25, 38^{2}; 22:17, 25; 24:3; 25:8, 9, 11; 26:46, 63, 68; 27:4, 25, 49

Mk 1:24^{2}, 38; 4:35; 5:12; 6:3; 9:5^{2}, 22^{2}, 38^{2}, 40; 10:35, 37; 12:7, 19; 13:4; 14:15, 42; 15:36; 16:3

Lk 1:1, 2, 69, 71, 74, 78; 2:15^{2}, 48; 4:34^{2}; 7:5, 16, 20; 8:22; 9:33^{2}, 49, 50^{2}; 10:11, 17; 11:1, 3, 4^{4}, 45; 12:41; 13:25; 15:23; 16:26^{2}; 17:13; 19:14; 20:2, 6, 14, 22, 28; 22:8, 67; 23:18, 30^{2}, 39; 24:22, 24, 29, 32^{3}

Jn 1:14, 22; 2:18; 4:12, 25; 6:34, 52; 8:5; 9:34; 10:24^{2}; 11:7, 15, 16, 50; 14:8^{2}, 9, 22, 31; 16:17; 17:21; 18:31; 19:24

Act 1:17, 21^2, 22^2; 2:29; 3:4, 12; 4:17; 5:28; 6:14; 7:27, 38, 40^3; 10:41, 42; 11:13, 15, 17; 13:33, 47; 14:11, 17; 15:7, 8, 9, 24, 25, 28, 36; 16:9, 10, 14, 15^2, 16, 17^2, 21, 37^4; 17:27; 20:5, 14; 21:5, 11, 16, 17, 18; 23:9; 24:4, 7; 25:24; 27:2, 6, 7, 20; 28:2^2, 7^2, 10^2, 15^2

Ro 3:8; 4:16, 24; 5:5, 8^2; 6:3; 8:4, 18, 26, 31^2, 32^2, 34, 35, 37, 39; 9:24, 29; 12:6^2, 7; 13:12^2, 13; 14:7, 12, 13, 19; 15:2, 7; 16:6

1Co 1:18, 30; 2:10, 12; 4:1, 6, 8, 9; 5:7, 8; 6:14; 7:15; 8:6, 8; 10:8, 9; 15:32, 57; 16:16

2Co 1:4, 5, 8, 10^2, 11^2, 14, 19, 20, 21^2, 22; 2:11, 14^2; 3:3, 6; 4:7, 12, 14^2, 17; 5:5^2, 14, 18^2, 19, 20, 21; 6:12; 7:1, 2, 6, 7, 9; 8:4^2, 5, 7, 19^2, 20^2; 9:11; 10:2, 8, 13

Gal 1:4, 23; 2:4; 3:13^2, 24; 4:26; 5:1, 25, 26; 6:9, 10

Eph 1:3, 4, 5, 6, 8, 9; 2:4, 5, 6^2, 7, 14; 3:20; 4:7; 5:2^2

Php 3:15, 16^2, 17

Col 1:8, 12, 13^2; 2:14^2; 4:3^2

1Th 1:6, 9, 10; 2:8, 13, 15, 16, 18; 3:6^4; 4:1, 7, 8; 5:6^2, 8, 9, 10, 25

2Th 1:7; 2:2, 16^2; 3:1, 6, 7, 9

1Ti 6:8, 17

2Ti 1:7, 9^3, 14; 2:12

Tit 2:12, 14^2; 3:5, 6, 15

Heb 1:2; 2:3; 4:1^2, 2, 11, 14, 16; 6:1, 18, 20; 7:26; 9:12, 24; 10:15, 20, 22, 23, 24; 11:40^2; 12:1^4, 9, 10, 28; 13:13, 15, 18

Jas 1:18; 3:3; 4:5

1Pt 1:3, 12; 2:21^2; 3:18, 21; 4:1, 3, 17; 5:10

2Pt 1:1, 3^2, 4; 3:2

1Jn 1:2, 3, 7, 8, 9^2, 10; 2:19^5, 25; 3:1^2, 16, 18, 20, 21, 23, 24^2; 4:6^2, 7, 9, 10, 11, 12^2, 13^2, 16, 19; 5:11, 14, 15, 20

2Jn 2^2

3Jn 9, 10

Rev 1:5^2, 6; 5:9, 10; 6:16^2; 19:7

WAS

Gen 1:2^2, 3, 4, 7, 9, 10, 11, 12^2, 15, 18, 21, 24, 25, 30, 31; 2:5^2, 10, 19, 20, 23; 3:1, 6^2, 10^2, 20, 23; 4:2^2, 5, 18, 19, 20, 21^2, 22, 26; 5:24, 32; 6:5^2, 9, 11^2, 12; 7:6^2, 12, 17^2, 22^2, 23^2; 8:1, 2, 11, 13, 14; 9:19, 21^2; 10:9, 10, 19, 25^3, 30; 11:1, 10, 29, 30; 12:4, 6, 10^2, 11, 14^2, 15, 18; 13:2, 6^2, 7, 10, 14; 14:10, 14, 18; 15:12, 17; 16:1, 4, 5, 14, 16; 17:1, 24^2, 25^2, 26; 18:10, 15; 19:22, 23; 20:16; 21:3, 5^2, 8^2, 11, 15, 20; 22:20, 24; 23:1, 17^3; 24:1, 15, 16, 29, 33, 36, 67; 25:1, 8, 10, 17, 20, 21^2, 26^2, 27^2, 29, 30; 26:1^2, 7, 8, 28, 34; 27:1, 30; 28:7, 11, 17, 19; 29:2, 12^2, 16^2, 17^2, 25, 31^2, 33, 34; 30:2, 29, 30, 37; 31:1^2, 2, 22^2, 31, 36, 39, 40, 48; 32:7^2, 24, 25; 34:19, 24, 28^2, 29; 35:3, 4, 5, 8^2, 16, 17, 18, 19, 29; 36:12, 22, 24, 32, 35, 39^2; 37:1, 2^2, 3, 15, 23^2, 24^2, 29; 38:1, 2, 5, 6, 7, 12, 13, 14^2, 16, 21^2, 22, 24, 25, 29, 30; 39:1, 2^3, 3, 5, 6, 11, 13, 19, 20, 21, 22, 23^2; 40:2, 3, 9, 10, 11, 15, 16^2, 17, 20; 41:7, 8^2, 10, 12, 13, 24, 32, 37, 46, 48, 49, 53, 54^2, 55, 56, 57; 42:1, 5, 6^2, 27, 35; 43:1, 12^2, 18, 21, 26, 34; 44:3, 12, 14; 45:8, 16; 47:13^2, 14, 18, 28; 48:7, 14^2; 49:7^2, 15^2, 26, 32, 33; 50:9, 11, 15, 26

Ex 1:5, 7, 14, 15; 2:2, 11, 12, 21; 3:2, 6; 4:6, 7, 14; 5:13, 19; 6:3; 7:7, 15, 21^2, 22; 8:15, 19, 24; 9:7^2, 11, 24^2, 25, 26, 31^3, 33, 35; 10:13, 15, 22; 11:3, 6; 12:29, 30^3, 34, 39, 40; 13:17; 14:5^2, 20; 15:23; 16:14, 15, 20, 24, 31^2; 17:1; 18:3, 4^2, 11; 19:16, 18; 20:21; 22:13; 24:10, 17, 18; 25:40; 26:30; 27:8; 29:33; 31:17; 32:16; 33:7, 8; 34:28, 34; 35:23, 24; 36:7, 9, 12, 15^2, 21; 37:1, 6, 10, 22, 25^3; 38:1^2, 18^3, 21, 23, 24^2, 25, 29; 39:4, 5^2, 9^2, 10^2, 19, 23, 32; 40:17, 35, 36, 37, 38^2

Lev 4:10; 6:2, 3, 4, 27; 8:4, 10, 16, 21, 25, 26, 29, 30; 9:8, 15, 18; 10:16^2, 18, 20; 13:18; 14:6, 48; 15:10; 16:27; 17:15; 19:20; 21:10; 24:10, 11; 25:33, 50, 51; 27:24

Nu 1:44; 3:16, 21, 27, 33, 35; 6:12; 7:9, 10, 12, 13^2, 17, 19, 23, 25^2, 29, 31, 35, 37^2, 41, 43, 47, 49^2, 53, 55, 59, 61^2, 65, 67^2, 71, 73^2, 77, 79^2, 83, 84^2, 86, 88^2, 89^2; 8:4^2; 9:14, 15^2, 16, 17, 20^2, 21^4, 22; 10:11, 14, 15, 16, 17, 18, 19, 20, 22, 23, 24, 25^2, 26, 27, 34; 11:1, 2, 4, 7, 8, 10^2, 18, 25, 26, 33^2; 12:3, 9, 10, 15^2; 13:20, 22, 24; 14:16; 15:34; 16:15, 31, 42, 47, 48, 50; 17:6, 8; 19:13; 20:1, 2, 13, 29; 21:4, 24, 26, 35; 22:3^2, 4, 22^2, 26, 27, 30^2, 36; 24:10, 20; 25:3, 8, 11, 13, 14^3, 15^3, 18; 26:46, 59, 60, 62, 64, 65; 27:3, 13; 28:6; 31:14, 16, 26, 32, 36^2, 37, 38, 39, 40, 41, 43, 52; 32:1, 10, 13^2, 39; 33:14, 39; 35:23, 25^2, 26; 36:2

Dt 1:34, 37; 2:14, 15, 20, 36; 3:3, 4, 8, 11^2, 13, 26; 4:21, 35; 8:2, 15; 9:8, 9, 10, 19^2, 20, 21, 28; 10:6; 11:6; 19:6; 21:15; 22:27; 26:5; 29:27; 32:12, 50; 33:5, 16, 21; 34:7^2, 9

Jos 1:5, 17; 2:2, 5, 15; 3:7; 4:10; 5:1, 13; 6:1, 21, 24, 27^2; 7:1, 16, 17, 18, 22, 26; 8:11, 13, 17, 25, 29, 33, 35; 9:5, 10, 24; 10:2^2, 14, 17; 11:10, 11, 19, 20, 22; 12:4; 13:1, 16, 23^2, 25, 29, 30, 33; 14:2, 7^2, 11^2, 15^2; 15:1^2, 2, 5^2, 9^2, 11, 12, 15; 16:5^2; 17:1^3, 2, 7, 9, 10^2; 18:1, 12, 14^2, 15, 17, 19, 20^2; 19:1, 9^2, 10, 18, 25, 33, 41; 21:10; 22:14, 17; 24:26, 33

Jdg 1:10, 11, 17, 19, 22, 23, 28, 36; 2:14, 15, 18, 19, 20; 3:8, 17, 20, 24, 25, 27, 30, 31; 4:1, 2, 11, 12, 16, 17, 21, 22; 5:8^2, 14, 15; 6:3, 6, 11, 21, 22, 27, 28^5, 30, 34, 35, 38, 40^2; 7:8, 13^2, 15; 8:3^2, 11, 13, 20, 26^2, 28^2, 31, 32, 33; 9:5, 6, 25, 30, 44, 45, 47, 51, 55; 10:2, 5, 7, 9, 16; 11:1^2, 5, 18, 34, 39; 12:5, 7, 10, 12, 15; 13:2^3, 6^2, 9, 16, 21; 14:4, 8, 19, 20; 15:14, 18, 19; 16:2, 4, 9, 16, 20, 22, 27, 29; 17:1^2, 6^2, 7^2, 11^2, 12; 18:1, 7, 20, 28^3, 29^2, 31; 19:1^2, 2, 10, 11, 15, 16, 26^2, 27, 29, 30^2; 20:1, 3, 4, 27, 34^2, 38, 41; 21:25^2

Ru 1:1, 2, 3, 4, 5, 7, 18, 19; 2:1, 3^2, 5, 6, 14, 15, 17, 18; 3:7, 8; 4:3, 7^2, 9^2, 13

1Sa 1:1^2, 2, 4, 10, 13, 18, 20, 24; 2:13^2, 17, 22, 26; 3:1^2, 2, 3^2, 7, 19, 20; 4:2, 6, 10^2, 11, 15, 18, 19^2, 21; 5:3, 4^2, 6, 7, 9^2, 11^2; 6:1, 4, 9, 14, 15; 7:2^2, 10, 13, 14, 17^2; 8:1, 2; 9:1^2, 2^3, 5, 9, 10, 24; 10:9, 20, 21^2, 23; 11:6, 11; 12:8, 12, 15; 13:3, 4, 7, 19, 22^2; 14:3, 4^2, 5, 14, 15^2, 18, 19, 20^2, 25, 27, 35, 39, 42, 43, 50^2, 51^2, 52; 15:9^2, 12; 16:12, 23^3; 17:3, 4, 5^2, 7, 12^2, 14, 20, 28, 40, 42, 50, 51; 18:1, 4, 5, 6, 8, 10, 12^3, 14, 15, 19, 28, 29, 30; 19:7, 8, 9, 16, 19, 20, 21, 23; 20:19, 24, 25, 27^2, 30, 33, 34, 37, 41; 21:1, 6^3, 7^2, 12; 22:2^3, 4, 6, 9, 22; 23:7^2, 13^2, 15^2; 24:1^2, 3; 25:2^3, 3^4, 7, 20, 21, 36^2, 37, 39, 44; 26:4, 12, 16, 21, 24; 27:4^2, 7; 28:3, 5, 14, 20^2, 21; 30:3, 6^2, 19, 25; 31:3, 4, 5

2Sa 1:1, 2, 10^4, 26; 2:10, 11^2, 16, 17^2, 18, 32; 3:1, 2, 6, 7, 8, 22^2, 23, 26, 27, 35, 37; 4:1, 2^2, 4^3; 5:2, 4, 10, 13; 6:3, 4, 7, 8, 9, 12, 13, 14, 20, 21; 7:9, 19; 8:16^2, 17, 18; 9:2^2, 6, 12, 13; 10:9, 17; 11:1, 2, 4, 7, 26, 27; 12:3, 4^2, 5, 15, 18^2, 19, 21^2, 22, 30^2; 13:1, 2^2, 3^2, 6, 8, 15, 19, 21, 38, 39^2; 14:1, 6, 25^2, 26^2, 27^2; 15:2, 5, 12, 17, 30, 32; 16:1, 5, 16, 23^2; 17:6, 19, 22, 23^2, 25^2, 27; 18:6, 7, 8, 9^2, 14, 29, 33; 19:1, 2^2, 16, 18, 25, 32^2, 39; 20:1, 8, 10, 13, 17, 23^2, 24^2, 25, 26; 21:1, 7, 11, 14, 16, 18^2, 19^2, 20^3; 22:8, 10, 11, 19, 24, 42; 23:1, 2, 8, 9, 10, 11^2, 14^2, 16, 18, 19^2, 23, 24; 24:1, 2, 11, 16, 25^2

1Ki 1:1, 4, 6, 15, 23, 51; 2:5, 10, 12, 15^2, 26, 29^2, 34, 41^2, 46; 3:2, 4, 12, 15, 17, 18^3, 21^2, 26, 28; 4:1, 4, 5^2, 6^2, 15, 16, 19^3, 22, 31^2; 5:1, 12, 13, 14; 6:2, 3^2, 6^3, 7^5, 8, 17, 18^3, 20^2, 22, 24, 25, 26^2, 37, 38^2; 7:1, 2, 3, 4, 5, 6^2, 7, 8, 10, 12, 14^3, 16^2, 20, 22^2, 23^2, 24, 25, 26^2, 27, 28, 29, 31^2, 32, 33, 35, 38, 47, 48, 51; 8:9, 17, 18^2, 54, 57, 64^3; 9:1, 25; 10:2^2, 3, 5, 6, 7, 14, 19, 20, 21; 11:4^3, 9^2, 14, 15^2, 20, 21, 25, 26, 27, 28^2, 30, 40, 42, 43; 12:2^2, 15, 18, 20^2, 21; 13:5, 6^2, 9, 17, 24^2, 26; 14:6, 8, 21^2, 28, 30, 31^2; 15:2, 3, 5, 6, 7, 10, 11, 14, 16, 22, 23, 24, 32; 16:6, 9, 18, 28; 17:1, 10, 11, 17^2; 18:2, 3, 4, 7, 13, 26^3, 29^2, 30, 38, 45^2, 46; 19:6, 11^2, 12, 13, 19; 20:12, 16, 29^2, 36, 40^2, 41; 21:1, 11, 15^2, 16, 25; 22:13, 33, 35, 37, 42^2, 43, 47^2, 50

2Ki 1:2^2, 7, 8; 2:17, 23; 3:4, 5, 9, 20^2, 26, 27; 4:8^2, 18, 31, 32^2, 36, 38, 41; 5:1^3, 8, 11, 14; 6:5^2, 11, 13, 15, 17, 25^2, 26; 7:5, 7, 10, 15, 16; 8:5, 6, 7^2, 11, 17, 18, 24, 26^2, 27, 29; 9:15, 16, 21, 30, 33, 34; 10:5^2, 12, 15, 21^2, 22, 30, 36; 11:1, 2, 3, 14, 16, 20, 21; 12:1, 2, 6, 9, 10^3, 12, 13, 16^2, 18; 13:2, 3, 11, 13, 14, 19, 21, 23; 14:2^2, 3, 5, 9^3, 12, 16, 20, 21, 24, 25, 26^2; 15:2^2, 3, 5^2, 9, 12, 18, 24, 28, 33^2, 34, 38; 16:2^2, 8, 10, 12, 14, 20; 17:2, 7, 18^2, 23, 25; 18:2^3, 3, 5, 7, 9, 10, 15, 18, 36, 37; 19:2, 8, 37; 20:1, 4, 13^2; 21:1^2, 2, 15, 16, 18, 19^2, 20, 26; 22:1^2, 2, 7^2, 9, 19; 23:2, 11, 15, 22, 23, 25, 26, 31^2, 32, 36^2, 37; 24:8^2, 9, 10, 18^2, 19; 25:2, 3, 4, 13, 16, 17^2, 19, 21, 30

1Ch 1:19^3, 39, 43, 44, 45, 46^2, 47, 48, 49, 50^3; 2:3, 17, 19, 21, 24, 26^2, 29, 34, 42, 45^2, 49; 3:10; 4:3, 9, 11, 40, 41; 5:1^2, 2, 6, 7, 20, 22; 6:54; 7:2, 9, 15^2, 16, 24, 25, 40; 8:29, 34, 37; 9:17, 20^2, 21, 27, 31, 35, 40; 10:3, 4, 5; 11:2, 6, 9, 12^2, 13^2, 16^2, 18, 20, 21^2, 23, 25; 12:3, 14, 18, 22, 27, 40; 13:4, 10, 11, 12; 14:2, 8; 15:22^2, 27; 16:39; 17:13, 17; 18:15, 16, 17; 19:10, 17; 20:1, 2, 4, 5^2, 6^3; 21:5, 6, 7, 15, 20, 30; 22:7; 23:1, 3, 8, 11, 13, 16, 28; 24:21, 25, 29; 25:1, 7; 26:1, 10, 20, 24, 28, 31; 27:2, 3, 4^2, 5, 6^2, 7, 8, 9, 10, 11, 12, 13, 14, 15, 16, 24, 25^2, 26, 27^2, 28^2, 29^2, 30^2, 31^2, 32^2, 33^2, 34^2; 29:27

2Ch 1:1^2, 3^2, 6, 11, 13; 2:14; 3:3^2, 4^3, 6, 8, 9, 11^2, 12^2, 15^2; 4:3^2, 4, 5, 6, 11, 19; 5:1, 3, 10, 13; 6:7, 8^2; 7:7^2; 8:16^3; 9:1^2, 2, 4, 5, 6, 9, 13, 19, 20, 31; 10:2, 15, 18; 11:1; 12:13^2, 16; 13:2^2, 7, 13, 14; 14:1, 2, 5, 14; 15:4, 5, 6, 8, 9, 15, 17, 19; 16:3, 6, 10^2, 12^2, 14; 17:3, 6, 15, 16, 18; 18:14, 32; 20:25, 26, 29, 30, 31^2, 32; 21:1, 3, 4, 5, 6, 17^2, 20; 22:2^2, 3, 6, 7^2, 8, 9, 10, 11, 12; 23:15, 18, 19, 21; 24:1^2, 2, 4, 11^2, 13, 15^2; 25:1^2, 2, 3, 10^2, 14, 15, 18^3, 22; 26:1, 3^2, 4, 13, 15^2, 16^2, 19^2, 20, 21^3; 27:1^2, 2, 8; 28:1^2, 5, 7, 9^3; 29:1^2, 2, 6, 8, 25, 28, 32, 34, 35, 36; 30:5, 12, 17, 18, 26^2, 27; 31:1, 12^2, 14, 20; 32:2^2, 4, 5, 14, 15, 21, 23, 24, 25^2, 31^2; 33:1, 2, 12, 13^2, 19^2, 21, 22; 34:1, 2, 3, 9, 14, 16, 17, 27, 30; 35:10, 16, 18, 19, 24, 26; 36:2, 5^2, 8, 9^2, 10, 11, 12, 16

Ezr 1:6; 2:61, 64; 3:1, 3, 6, 11, 12, 13; 4:7, 14, 15, 20, 23; 5:5, 7, 11, 14^2, 17; 6:1, 2^2, 15^2; 7:6, 8, 28^2; 8:22, 23, 31, 33^3, 34, 35; 10:9

Neh 1:1, 11; 2:1, 2, 10, 11, 12, 14^2, 18; 3:16, 25; 4:1, 3, 6, 15, 18; 5:1, 6, 14, 18^3; 6:1, 6, 10, 13, 15, 16, 18; 7:1, 2, 4, 7, 63, 64, 66, 72; 8:1, 3, 5, 17, 18; 10:29; 11:9^2, 11, 14, 17, 22, 23, 24; 12:8, 37, 43; 13:1, 4, 5, 6, 13^2, 26^2, 28

Est 1:2, 8, 10, 11, 12, 13, 14; 2:1^2, 5^2, 7, 8^2, 12, 13, 15, 16, 20, 22, 23^3; 3:4, 5, 12^2, 14, 15^2; 4:1, 3, 4, 5^2, 6, 8; 5:2^2, 9; 6:2, 4; 7:6, 7, 8^2, 10; 8:1, 9, 13, 14, 15; 9:1, 4, 11, 14, 22, 32; 10:3

Job 1:1^3, 3^2, 5, 6, 13, 16, 17, 18; 2:1, 11, 13; 3:3^2, 25, 26^2; 4:4, 12, 16^2; 8:7; 15:7, 19; 16:12; 17:6; 20:4; 22:16; 23:17; 29:4^2, 5, 13, 14, 15^2, 16, 19, 20^2; 30:2, 25^2; 31:18, 23, 25; 32:1, 2^2, 3, 5^2, 6, 12; 33:27; 42:7

Ps 4:1; 7:4; 18:7, 9, 12, 18, 23, 41; 22:9, 10; 30:7; 31:11, 13; 32:4; 33:9; 35:13; 37:36; 38:13, 14; 39:2^2, 3^2, 9; 50:21; 51:5; 53:5; 55:12^2, 13, 18, 21; 63:ttl; 66:14, 17; 68:8, 9, 11, 14; 69:10, 12, 20; 73:3, 16, 21^2, 22^2; 74:5; 76:8; 77:3^2, 18; 78:8, 21^2, 30, 35, 37, 59, 62; 79:3; 81:4; 87:4, 5, 6; 95:10; 97:8; 105:17, 18, 37, 38; 106:9, 11, 18, 30, 31, 38, 40; 107:12; 114:2, 3; 116:6, 10; 119:67, 158; 122:1; 124:1, 2, 3; 126:2; 139:15^2, 16; 142:3, 4, ttl

Prv 4:3; 5:14; 8:23^2, 24, 25, 27, 30^2; 23:35; 24:31^2

Ecc 1:10, 12; 2:3, 9, 10, 11^2, 15, 24; 3:16^2; 4:1; 5:6; 7:23; 9:14, 15; 12:7, 9, 10^2

Song 2:3, 4; 3:4; 5:6; 6:12; 8:10, 11

Isa 1:21; 6:4; 7:2^2; 9:1; 10:14, 26; 11:16; 14:28; 21:3^2, 14; 22:14, 25; 23:13; 26:16; 28:13; 36:3, 21, 22; 37:2, 8, 38; 38:1, 8, 9, 20; 39:1, 2^3; 41:28^2; 43:10, 12, 13; 47:6; 48:8, 16; 49:21; 50:2^2, 5; 52:14; 53:3, 5^3, 7^2, 8^3, 9, 12; 57:17^2; 59:15, 16^2, 17; 63:3, 5^2, 8, 9, 10; 65:1, 2; 66:7

Jer 2:2, 3; 3:21; 4:23, 25, 26; 7:12; 8:16; 11:19; 13:7^2, 20; 14:4, 5, 6; 15:9, 16; 17:16; 18:4; 20:1, 2, 7, 8, 9^2, 14; 22:15, 16^2; 25:1; 26:20, 21, 24; 28:1; 31:11, 15, 18, 19^3, 26, 32; 32:1, 2^2, 8, 9, 11^2; 33:1; 35:4^2; 36:22, 23^3; 37:5, 11, 13^3, 16; 38:6^2, 7, 27, 28^3; 39:2, 15; 40:5; 41:7, 9; 44:6^2; 46:2, 5, 21; 48:13, 27^2; 49:12, 21; 51:5, 59; 52:1^2, 2, 5, 6^2, 7^2, 8, 12, 17, 19^2, 20, 21^3, 22^2, 27, 34

Lam 1:1^2; 2:5, 12; 3:10, 14; 4:6, 7, 20; 5:10

Ezk 1:1, 2, 3, 4, 5, 7, 12, 13^2, 16^2, 20^3, 21, 22, 25^2, 26^3, 28^2; 2:9^2, 10^2; 3:3, 14, 22; 8:3, 4, 14; 9:2, 3^2, 8; 10:1, 4^2, 5, 7^2, 9, 13, 14^2, 17, 19, 21, 22; 11:22; 12:7; 13:10; 15:5^2; 16:3, 4, 8, 13, 14, 15, 19, 36, 45, 49^2, 56, 57; 17:7, 8; 19:4, 5, 7, 8, 10, 11, 12^2; 21:22; 22:10; 23:5, 11, 13, 17^2, 18^2, 40, 42, 43; 24:18; 25:3^2; 26:2; 27:7^2, 12, 16, 18, 20; 28:13^2, 15, 17; 29:18^2; 30:22; 31:3^2, 5, 7^2, 8; 32:15, 25; 33:22^4, 24; 34:4^4, 6, 8, 16^4; 35:10, 15; 36:17, 23, 35,

WE

2Co 1:4[2], 6[3], 8[3], 9[2], 10, 12, 13, 14, 24; 2:11, 15, 16, 17[2]; 3:1[2], 4, 5, 12[2], 18; 4:1[3], 5, 7, 8[2], 11, 13[2], 16, 18; 5:1[2], 2, 3, 4[2], 6[3], 7, 8, 9[2], 10, 11[2], 12, 13[2], 14, 16[3], 20[2], 21; 6:1, 9; 7:2[3], 5[2], 13[2], 14; 8:1, 4, 5, 6, 18, 22[2]; 9:4[2]; 10:2, 3[2], 7, 11[4], 12, 13, 14[3], 15; 11:4, 6, 12, 21; 12:18[2], 19[3]; 13:4[2], 6, 7[2], 8, 9[3]

Gal 1:8[2], 9; 2:4, 5, 9, 10, 15, 16[2], 17[2]; 3:14, 23, 24, 25; 4:3[2], 5, 28, 31; 5:5, 25; 6:9[2], 10

Eph 1:4, 7, 11, 12; 2:3, 5, 10[2], 18; 3:12, 20; 4:13, 14, 25; 5:30; 6:12

Php 3:3, 16, 20

Col 1:3, 4, 9[2], 14, 28[2]

1Th 1:2, 5, 8, 9; 2:2[2], 4[2], 5, 6[2], 7, 8, 9[2], 10, 11, 13, 17, 18; 3:1[2], 3, 4[3], 6, 7, 8, 9[2], 10, 12; 4:1, 2, 6, 10, 11, 14, 15[2], 17[2]; 5:5, 10[2], 12, 14

2Th 1:3, 4, 11; 2:1, 13; 3:2, 4[2], 6, 7, 8[2], 9, 10[2], 11, 12

1Ti 1:8; 2:2; 4:10[2]; 6:7[2]

2Ti 2:11[2], 12[3], 13

Tit 2:12; 3:3, 5, 7

Phlm 7

Heb 2:1[3], 3[2], 5, 8, 9; 3:6[2], 14[2], 19; 4:3, 13, 14, 15[2], 16; 5:11; 6:3, 9[2], 11, 18, 19; 7:19; 8:1[2]; 9:5; 10:10, 26[2], 30, 39; 11:3; 12:1, 9[3], 10, 25[2], 28[2]; 13:6, 10, 14[2], 18[2]

Jas 1:18; 3:1, 2, 3[2], 9[2]; 4:13, 15; 5:11, 17

1Pt 2:24; 4:3

2Pt 1:16[2], 18[2], 19; 3:13

1Jn 1:1[3], 2, 3[2], 4, 5, 6[3], 7[2], 8[3], 9, 10[3]; 2:1, 3[3], 5[2], 18, 28; 3:1, 2[5], 11, 14[3], 16[2], 19[2], 21, 22[3], 23, 24; 4:6[2], 9, 10, 11, 12, 13[2], 14, 16, 17[2], 19, 21; 5:2[3], 3, 9, 14[2], 15[5], 18, 19[2], 20[3]

2Jn 4, 5[2], 6, 8[3]

3Jn 8[2], 12, 14

Rev 5:10; 7:3; 11:17

WERE

Gen 1:5, 7[2], 8, 13, 19, 23, 31; 2:1, 4, 25[2]; 3:7[2]; 4:8; 5:2, 4, 5, 8, 11, 14, 17, 20, 23, 27, 31; 6:1, 2, 4[2]; 7:10, 11[2], 18, 19[2], 20, 23[2]; 8:2, 3, 5, 7, 8, 9, 11, 13; 9:18, 23, 29; 10:1, 5, 18, 21, 25, 29, 32; 11:32; 13:13; 14:3, 5, 13, 17; 17:23[2], 27; 18:11; 19:11, 36; 20:8; 21:16; 23:1, 17[3], 20; 24:10, 32, 54, 63; 25:3, 4, 24[2]; 26:35; 27:1, 15, 23, 42; 29:2, 3; 30:35[2], 42[2]; 31:10, 19; 34:5[2], 7[2], 14, 25; 35:2, 4[2], 5, 6, 22, 26, 28; 36:5, 7[2], 11, 12, 13, 14, 15, 16, 18, 22, 23, 25; 37:7, 27; 38:27; 39:20, 22; 40:5, 6, 7, 10; 41:21, 48, 50, 53; 42:28, 35; 43:18[2], 34; 44:3, 4; 45:3; 46:12, 15, 20, 21, 22[2], 25, 26, 27[3], 31; 48:5, 10; 49:24; 50:3, 4, 23

Ex 1:5, 7, 12; 5:12, 14, 19; 6:4, 16, 18, 20; 7:20[3], 25; 8:18; 9:26, 32[2], 34; 10:6, 8, 11, 14[2]; 12:33, 37, 39; 14:10, 11, 21, 22, 29; 15:8[2], 23, 25, 27; 17:12[2]; 19:1, 2[2], 16; 21:3, 29; 22:21; 23:9; 24:10[2]; 28:32; 32:3, 15[3], 16, 25; 34:1, 30; 35:22, 25; 36:6, 9, 15, 29, 30[2], 36, 38; 37:9, 13, 14, 16, 17, 20, 22, 25; 38:2, 9, 10[2], 11[2], 12, 14, 15, 16, 17[2], 19, 20, 25, 27; 39:13, 14; 40:37

Lev 8:28; 10:12, 16; 14:35; 18:27, 28, 30; 19:34; 26:37

Nu 1:1, 16, 20, 21[2], 22[2], 23[2], 24, 25[2], 26, 27[2], 28, 29[2], 30, 31[2], 32, 33[2], 34, 35[2], 36, 37[2], 38, 39[2], 40, 41[2], 42, 43[2], 44, 45[3], 46[2], 47; 2:4[2], 6[2], 8[2], 9[2], 11[2], 13[2], 15[2], 16[2], 19[2], 21[2], 23[2], 24[2], 26[2], 28[2], 30[2], 31[2], 32[3], 33; 3:3, 17, 22[3], 28, 34[2], 39[2], 43[2], 49[2], 51; 4:36[2], 37[2], 38, 40[2], 41, 42, 44[2], 45, 46, 48[2], 49[2]; 6:12; 7:2[3], 13, 86, 87, 88; 8:21; 9:1, 6[2], 15, 22; 10:28; 11:1, 26[2], 29, 31[3]; 12:3, 8; 13:3, 4, 22, 33[2]; 14:3, 6, 29, 38; 15:26, 32; 16:34, 39[2], 49; 18:27; 19:18; 21:32; 22:3, 22, 29, 40; 23:22; 24:8; 25:5, 6, 9; 26:7[2], 9, 18, 19, 20, 21, 22, 25, 27, 28, 33, 34, 37, 40, 41[2], 43[2], 47[2], 50[2], 51, 54, 57, 62[3], 63; 31:5, 8, 38, 39, 40, 48; 33:9, 38; 36:11, 12

Dt 1:41; 2:11, 14[2], 15, 16; 3:5; 4:32, 46, 47; 5:5, 29; 6:21; 7:7[2]; 8:15; 9:15; 10:2, 19; 24:9; 25:17, 18; 28:62, 67[2]; 29:17; 31:24, 30; 32:27, 29; 33:5; 34:8

Jos 2:4, 7, 8, 10, 22; 3:15[2], 16, 17; 4:1, 7[2], 11, 18[2], 23[2]; 5:1[3], 4, 5[2], 6[2], 7, 8; 6:23; 7:12; 8:11, 14, 15, 16[3], 22, 24[2], 25, 35; 9:1, 10, 13, 16, 17, 24; 10:1, 2, 11[2], 20, 26, 28, 30, 32, 35, 37[2], 39; 11:2, 5, 11; 13:21, 22, 31; 14:4, 12[2]; 15:4, 7, 11, 21; 16:8, 9; 17:2, 5, 9, 13; 18:12, 14, 19, 21; 19:8, 22, 33; 20:9; 21:4, 10, 19, 26, 33, 40[2], 41, 42[2]; 22:9, 30; 24:15

Jdg 2:10, 12, 15; 3:4, 19, 24, 25; 4:13; 5:6, 15[2], 16, 18, 22; 6:5, 33; 7:1[2], 6, 11, 12, 19[2]; 8:4, 10[2], 18[2], 19, 21, 24, 26; 9:29, 34, 35, 36, 40, 43, 44, 47, 48[2]; 10:8, 17; 11:3, 33; 12:2, 5; 13:23; 15:14; 16:2, 7, 9, 11, 12, 25, 27[2], 30[2]; 17:2, 4; 18:3, 7[2], 16, 17, 22[3], 26, 27, 30; 19:10, 11, 14, 16, 22, 27; 20:3, 11, 15[2], 16, 17[2], 31, 36, 41, 44, 46[2]; 21:9[2], 13

Ru 1:13, 19; 4:11

1Sa 1:3; 2:5[2], 12, 27; 4:3, 4, 7, 11, 15, 19; 5:4, 12; 6:13, 15; 7:7[2], 10, 13, 14; 8:2; 9:3, 4, 5, 14, 20, 22[2], 25, 27; 10:14, 16; 11:8, 9, 11[2]; 13:2[2], 4, 6[2], 8, 11, 15, 16, 22; 14:2[2], 14, 17[2], 20, 21[2], 24, 26, 27, 28, 31, 41, 49[2]; 16:6; 17:1, 2, 11, 13, 19, 24, 31; 18:26; 19:16; 20:9; 21:5; 22:2, 6[2], 11; 23:13, 24; 25:1, 2, 7[2], 15[4], 16[2], 40, 43; 26:12; 27:2, 8; 29:4; 30:1, 2, 3, 4, 5, 9[2], 10, 16, 21[2], 27[3], 28[3], 29[3], 30[3], 31[2]; 31:7[3]

2Sa 1:11, 12, 23[4]; 2:3, 4, 18, 24; 3:2, 5, 20, 23, 31, 34; 4:1[2], 2, 3; 5:13, 14; 6:2; 8:7, 17, 18; 9:12; 10:5, 8, 13, 14, 15, 16, 19[2]; 11:16, 23; 12:1, 31; 13:18[2], 30; 14:27; 15:4, 11, 14, 16, 22, 24; 16:6, 14; 17:21, 22, 29; 18:1, 7; 19:9, 17, 28, 43; 20:3, 8, 14, 15, 18, 25; 21:2, 9, 13, 22; 22:9, 13, 16, 18, 23; 23:9[2], 11; 24:9[2]

1Ki 1:8, 41, 49[2]; 2:5, 11; 3:16, 18; 4:2, 4, 20, 28, 32; 5:3, 14, 16; 6:1, 24, 25, 31, 32, 34[3]; 7:4, 5, 6, 9, 11, 17, 18, 19[2], 20, 24[2], 25, 28, 29[3], 30, 31, 32[2], 33, 34[2], 35, 41[2], 42, 45, 47; 8:4, 5[2], 8[2], 10, 47; 9:20[2], 21[2], 22, 23[2]; 10:12, 19, 21[3]; 11:29; 12:1, 8, 10, 21, 31; 14:4, 9, 20, 24; 15:14, 18; 16:15, 16, 21, 25, 30, 33; 20:1, 15, 23, 27[2], 30; 21:8, 11; 22:43, 48

2Ki 2:3, 5, 8, 9, 15, 22; 3:14, 21[2]; 4:6, 38, 40; 5:3; 6:20[2]; 7:3, 5, 10; 9:5; 10:4, 6, 29[2]; 11:2, 9, 10; 12:3, 13; 13:21; 14:4, 14; 15:4, 16[2], 35; 16:17; 17:2, 9, 15; 18:5, 17; 19:12, 18, 26[3], 35; 21:11; 23:3, 4, 7, 8[2], 12, 13[2], 16, 19, 20, 24[2]; 24:16; 25:4, 5, 10, 11, 13, 15, 19[3], 25, 26, 28

1Ch 1:19, 23, 51; 2:3, 4, 9, 16, 25, 27, 28, 33, 42, 50; 3:1[2], 4, 5, 9, 15, 19, 24; 4:3, 6, 7, 14, 17, 20[2], 21, 23, 24, 31, 32, 33[2], 38, 41, 43; 5:3, 7, 9, 13, 17, 18, 20[3], 24; 6:18, 48, 49, 60, 61[2], 63, 71, 77, 78; 7:1, 2, 4, 5, 7, 11, 16, 17, 19, 21, 28, 40[2]; 8:3, 8, 10, 13, 28, 35, 38, 39, 40; 9:1[3], 2, 9, 17, 18, 19[2], 22[3], 24, 25[2], 26[2], 29, 31, 32, 33[2], 34, 41, 44; 10:7[2]; 11:4, 13, 26; 12:1, 2, 8[2], 14, 20, 21[2], 23, 24, 27, 31, 32[3], 33, 38, 39, 40; 14:12; 15:19, 23, 24; 16:19, 41[2], 42; 18:7, 16, 17; 19:5[2], 9[2], 14, 15, 16[2], 19; 20:2, 3, 4, 6, 8; 21:5, 16, 29; 22:2; 23:3, 4[2], 5, 7, 9, 10[2], 11, 14, 15, 17[2], 24[2], 27; 24:4[3], 5[2], 19, 20, 26, 30; 25:5, 6, 7[2], 9, 10, 11, 12, 13, 14, 15, 16, 17, 18, 19, 20, 21, 22, 23, 24, 25, 26, 27, 28, 29, 30, 31; 26:2, 4, 6[2], 7, 8, 11, 12, 17, 21, 22, 26, 29, 30, 31[2], 32; 27:1, 2, 4, 5, 7, 8, 9, 10, 11, 12, 13, 14, 15, 22, 28, 29, 31; 29:8, 15

2Ch 2:17[2]; 3:11, 13; 4:3, 4, 12[2], 13, 19, 22; 5:5, 6, 9[2], 11[3], 12, 13; 8:7[2], 8, 9, 10; 9:11, 18[2], 20[3]; 10:1, 8, 10; 11:1, 13; 12:3, 5, 15; 13:13, 18; 14:8, 13[3]; 15:5, 17; 16:8; 17:10, 13; 18:30; 20:22[2], 24, 25, 33, 37[2]; 21:2, 13, 16; 22:4, 6, 11; 23:8[2], 9, 14; 24:14, 25; 25:12, 24; 26:12, 17; 28:6, 15[2], 23; 29:29, 31, 32, 33, 34[2], 35; 30:8, 14, 15, 17[2], 21; 31:1, 6, 13, 15, 19[3]; 32:3, 9, 13, 18, 19; 34:4, 12, 13[3], 32, 33; 35:3, 7[2], 14, 15, 17, 18; 36:20

Ezr 1:6, 11[2]; 2:58, 59[2], 62[3], 65[2], 66; 3:1, 5, 8, 12; 5:1, 2, 6, 10, 14; 6:1, 20[2], 21; 8:3, 20, 35; 9:1, 4, 9; 10:15, 16, 18

Neh 1:2, 9; 2:13[2]; 4:7[2], 16; 5:2, 3, 4, 8, 15, 16, 17, 18; 6:16[2], 18; 7:1, 4[2], 60, 61[2], 64[2], 67, 73; 8:3, 12, 13, 17; 9:1, 17, 25, 26; 10:1, 8; 11:6, 12, 18, 19, 20, 21, 22, 36; 12:7, 9, 12, 22, 23, 25, 26, 44, 46; 13:10, 13

Est 1:5[2], 6[2]; 2:7, 8, 9, 12, 14, 19, 21, 23; 3:1, 2, 3, 6, 12[2], 13; 6:1, 14; 8:9, 11; 9:11, 15, 16, 18, 20

Job 1:2, 5, 13, 14, 18; 4:7; 6:2, 20[2]; 9:15, 21; 16:4; 18:20; 19:23[2], 24; 21:4; 22:16; 28:5; 29:2, 5; 30:3, 5, 7, 8[2]; 31:20, 28; 32:4, 15; 33:21; 34:35; 39:16; 42:15

Ps 14:2, 5, 7; 17:12; 18:7, 8, 11, 15[2], 17, 22, 37, 38; 22:5[2]; 33:6; 34:5[2]; 35:13; 39:12; 45:9; 46:6; 48:4, 5; 50:12; 53:2, 5, 6; 55:18, 21[3]; 68:25, 33; 73:2; 77:16[2]; 78:29, 30, 37, 39, 57, 63; 80:10[2]; 81:6; 90:2; 105:12; 106:35, 36, 39, 42, 43; 119:5; 126:1; 139:16[2]; 148:5

Prv 8:24[2], 25, 31

Ecc 2:7, 9; 4:1; 7:10; 8:10

Song 1:6; 5:4; 6:13

Isa 5:18, 25; 7:23; 10:15; 14:2; 26:18, 20; 27:13; 30:4, 5; 33:3; 37:12, 19, 27[3], 36; 41:5, 11; 42:24; 46:1[2]; 51:13; 52:14; 53:3; 63:19

Jer 1:1; 4:25, 26; 5:8; 6:15[2]; 8:12[2]; 9:1; 11:13; 14:3, 4; 15:16; 20:2; 22:24, 26; 24:1, 2; 26:9; 29:1, 2; 30:14, 15; 31:2, 15; 34:5, 7, 8, 15; 36:16, 24, 28, 32; 37:15, 21; 40:1[2], 4, 6, 7[2], 11[2], 12, 13; 41:2, 3[2], 7, 8, 9, 10, 11, 13[3], 16, 18; 42:8, 16; 43:5; 44:17; 49:2; 50:11, 33; 52:7, 14, 17, 20, 22, 23[2], 25[3], 30, 32

Lam 2:4, 6; 4:5, 7[3], 10; 5:12

Ezk 1:1, 7, 9, 11[3], 16, 18[3], 19[2], 20, 21[2], 23, 27; 7:13; 8:16; 9:6, 8; 10:1, 12, 15, 17, 19, 20; 14:14, 16, 18, 20; 16:47, 50; 17:6; 19:12; 20:9, 24, 25; 22:6; 23:2, 3, 4[3], 6, 7, 42; 27:8[3], 9[2], 10, 11[2], 13, 15[2], 17, 19, 21, 22, 23, 24; 29:13; 31:5, 8[2], 9, 15, 17; 32:27, 29; 34:5[2]; 36:19, 31; 37:2[2]; 40:7, 10[2], 12, 15, 16[3], 17[2], 21[2], 22[2], 25, 26[2], 29, 30, 31[2], 33[2], 34[2], 37[2], 38, 39, 40[2], 41, 42, 43, 44, 49; 41:2, 6, 8, 9, 11, 16, 20, 21, 22, 25[3], 26; 42:3, 5[2], 6, 8[2], 10, 11[2], 12; 43:3; 46:22[2]; 47:3, 4[2], 5, 7

Dan 1:6, 20; 2:34, 42; 3:3, 20, 21[2], 27; 4:10, 12, 21, 33; 5:3, 6, 9, 12; 6:18; 7:4, 7, 8[2], 9, 10, 12, 19, 20; 8:3; 10:3, 5, 7, 12

Hos 2:23; 4:7; 5:10; 8:12; 9:10; 12:8; 13:6[2]

Am 4:7, 8, 11

Oba 7

Jna 1:5[2], 10; 2:5

Mic 1:13

Nah 3:9[2], 10[2]

Hab 3:6

Hag 2:16[3]

Zec 1:8[2]; 6:1, 2; 7:3; 8:9, 13; 10:2

Mt 1:11, 12; 2:11, 13, 16; 3:6, 16; 4:18, 24[3]; 5:12; 7:28; 8:16[2], 32; 9:25, 30, 31, 36; 11:20, 21; 12:1, 3, 4, 23; 13:2, 6, 54, 57; 14:20, 21, 26, 32, 33, 34, 35, 36; 15:1, 12, 30, 37, 38; 16:5; 17:6, 14, 23, 24; 18:6[3], 31; 19:12[2], 13, 25; 20:9, 24; 21:1, 15; 22:3, 8[2], 25, 33, 34, 41; 24:24, 37, 38[2]; 25:2[2], 3, 10; 26:22, 26, 43, 51, 57, 71; 27:17, 33, 38, 44, 52, 54[2], 55; 28:11[2], 12, 15

Mk 1:5, 16, 19, 22, 27, 29, 32[2], 34, 36; 2:2, 6, 12, 15, 25, 26; 4:10, 33, 34, 36; 5:13[2], 15, 40, 42; 6:2, 3, 13, 31, 34, 42, 44, 50, 51, 54, 55, 56[2]; 7:35, 37; 8:8, 9; 9:4, 6, 9, 15, 32, 42[2]; 10:24, 26, 32[3]; 11:12; 12:14, 20, 41; 13:22; 14:4, 11, 21, 35, 40, 53; 15:32, 40, 44; 16:5, 8[2]

Lk 1:2, 6, 7, 10, 23, 45, 65; 2:6[2], 8, 9, 15, 18, 21, 22, 33, 47, 48; 3:15[2], 21; 4:2, 20[2], 25, 27, 28, 32, 36; 5:2[2], 7, 9, 10, 17[2], 26[2]; 6:3, 4, 11, 18[2]; 7:10, 20, 21, 24, 39; 8:1, 4[2], 23[2], 30, 33, 35[2], 37, 38, 40, 45, 56; 9:10, 14, 17, 18, 30, 32[3], 37, 43; 11:29, 52; 12:1; 13:1, 2, 4, 17[2]; 14:7, 17, 24; 16:14, 16; 17:2[2], 9, 12, 14, 17, 27; 18:9, 34; 19:32, 33, 48; 20:29; 22:5, 44, 49, 52, 55; 23:5, 6, 12[2], 23, 32, 33, 39, 48; 24:4, 5, 10, 16, 21, 22, 24, 31, 33, 35, 37, 44, 53

Jn 1:3, 13, 24[2], 28; 2:6; 3:19, 23; 4:8, 40; 5:35; 6:2, 11, 12, 19, 22[2], 26, 64, 65; 7:10[2]; 8:33, 39, 42; 9:10, 33, 40, 41; 10:6, 41; 11:25, 31, 52, 57; 12:12, 16, 20; 13:1; 14:2; 15:19; 16:19; 17:6; 18:30, 36; 19:11, 28, 36; 20:19[2], 20, 26; 21:2, 6, 8[2], 9, 11

Act 1:6, 13, 15; 2:1, 2, 4, 5, 6, 7, 8, 12[2], 37, 41[2], 43, 44; 3:10; 4:6[2], 13, 26, 27, 31[2], 32, 34[2]; 5:12[2], 14, 16[2], 17[2], 21, 33, 36, 37, 41; 6:1, 7, 10; 7:16, 30, 54; 8:1, 4, 7[3], 12, 13, 14, 15, 16, 39; 9:2, 8, 19, 21, 23, 26, 31[2]; 10:12, 17, 18, 21, 27, 38, 45; 11:1, 2, 10, 11, 19, 20[2], 26; 12:3, 10, 12, 16; 13:1, 5, 42, 45[2], 48[2], 52; 14:6, 27; 15:4[2], 10, 30, 33; 16:2, 3, 4[2], 5, 6, 7, 12, 14, 26[3], 32, 38; 17:11[2], 12, 14, 21; 18:3, 5, 8, 14; 19:3, 5, 7, 9, 12, 14, 21, 28, 31, 32; 20:8[2], 12, 16, 18, 34; 21:1, 5, 8, 17, 18, 24, 27[2], 30, 38; 22:5, 9[2], 11; 23:6, 9, 13; 24:9; 25:17; 26:10, 14, 29, 31; 27:4, 7, 11, 17, 27, 30, 36, 37, 39[2]; 28:1, 7, 9, 10, 14, 17, 24

Ro 1:21; 3:2; 4:2, 17; 5:6, 8, 10[2], 19; 6:3[2], 17, 20[2]; 7:5[2], 6; 9:3, 25, 32; 11:7, 19, 20; 15:4[2]; 16:7

1Co 1:9, 13; 3:2; 4:9; 5:3; 6:11; 7:7, 14; 9:15; 10:1, 2, 5, 6, 7, 9, 10; 11:5; 12:2[2], 17[4], 19[2]; 15:11

APNDX

2Co 1:8; 3:14; 5:1, 14; 7:5^{4}, 8, 9^{2}, 13; 8:3; 11:17; 12:12, 13; 13:2

Gal 1:17, 22; 2:2, 6, 12^{2}; 3:16, 23; 4:3^{2}, 5; 5:12

Eph 1:13; 2:1, 3, 5, 12, 13, 17^{2}; 5:8

Php 3:7, 12; 4:10, 18

Col 1:16^{2}, 21

1Th 1:5, 7; 2:2^{2}, 4, 7, 8^{2}; 3:4, 7

2Th 3:10

Tit 3:3

Phlm 14

Heb 2:15; 3:5; 4:3; 5:8; 6:4^{2}; 7:11, 21, 23^{2}; 8:4; 9:6, 9, 15; 10:32, 33^{2}; 11:3^{2}, 13^{2}, 23, 29, 30, 34, 35, 37^{4}

Jas 5:3

1Pt 1:18; 2:8, 10, 21, 24, 25; 3:20^{2}

2Pt 1:16, 18, 21; 2:1, 18; 3:2, 4, 5

1Jn 2:19^{2}; 3:12

Jude 4, 17

Rev 1:14^{2}; 4:1, 4, 5, 6, 8, 11; 6:1, 9, 11^{2}, 14; 7:4^{2}, 5^{3}, 6^{3}, 7^{3}, 8^{3}; 8:2, 5, 7, 8, 9^{2}, 10, 11; 9:2, 7^{4}, 8, 9, 10, 15^{2}, 16, 17, 19, 20; 10:1; 11:13^{2}, 15, 18, 19; 12:9, 14; 13:2, 3; 14:3^{2}, 4^{2}; 15:2, 8; 16:9, 18^{2}, 20; 17:8; 18:14, 15, 19, 23^{2}, 24; 19:6, 12^{2}, 14, 20, 21^{2}; 20:4, 5, 12^{3}, 13^{3}, 14; 21:1, 19, 21^{2}; 22:2

WHEN

Gen 2:4; 3:6; 4:8, 12; 5:2; 6:1, 4; 7:6; 9:14; 12:4, 11, 12, 14; 14:14; 15:11, 12, 17; 16:4, 5, 6, 16; 17:1, 24, 25; 18:2; 19:15, 17, 23, 29^{2}, 33^{2}, 35^{2}; 20:13; 21:5; 24:19, 30^{2}, 36, 41, 43, 52, 64; 25:20, 24, 26; 26:8, 34; 27:1, 5, 34, 40; 28:6; 29:10, 13, 31; 30:1, 9, 25, 30, 33, 38^{2}, 42; 31:49; 32:2, 17, 19, 25; 33:18; 34:2, 7, 25; 35:1, 7, 9, 17, 22; 37:4, 18, 23; 38:5, 9, 15, 25, 28; 39:13, 15, 19; 40:13, 14, 16; 41:21, 46, 55; 42:1, 21, 35; 43:2, 16, 21, 26; 44:4^{2}, 24, 30, 31; 45:27; 46:33; 47:15, 18; 48:7^{2}, 17; 49:33; 50:4, 11, 15, 17

Ex 1:10, 16; 2:2, 3, 5, 6, 11, 12, 13, 15, 18; 3:4, 12, 13, 21; 4:6, 14, 21, 31; 5:13; 6:28; 7:5, 7, 9; 8:9, 15; 9:34; 10:13; 11:1; 12:13^{2}, 23, 25, 26, 27, 44, 48; 13:5, 8, 11, 14, 15, 17^{2}; 14:10, 18, 27; 15:23, 25; 16:3^{2}, 8, 14, 15, 18, 21, 32; 17:11^{2}; 18:1, 14, 16; 19:1, 9, 13, 19; 20:18; 22:27; 23:16; 28:29, 30, 35^{2}, 43^{2}; 29:30, 36; 30:7, 8, 12^{3}, 15, 20^{2}; 31:18; 32:1, 5, 17, 25, 34; 33:4, 8; 34:24, 29^{2}, 30, 34; 40:32^{2}, 36

Lev 2:1, 8; 4:14, 22; 5:3, 4, 5; 6:20, 21, 27; 7:35; 9:24; 10:9, 20; 11:31, 32; 12:6; 13:2, 3, 9, 14, 20; 14:34, 57^{2}; 15:2, 13, 23, 31; 16:1, 17, 20, 23; 18:28; 19:9, 23; 20:4; 22:7, 16, 27, 29; 23:10, 12, 22^{2}, 39, 43; 24:16; 25:2; 26:17, 25, 26, 35, 36, 37, 44; 27:2, 14, 21

Nu 1:51^{2}; 3:4; 4:5, 15, 19, 20; 5:6, 21, 27, 29, 30; 6:2, 7, 13; 7:84, 89; 8:2, 19; 9:17, 19, 20, 21, 22; 10:3, 5, 6, 7, 28, 34, 35, 36; 11:1, 2, 9, 25; 12:12; 15:2, 8, 18, 19, 28; 16:4, 42; 18:26, 30, 32; 19:14; 20:3, 16, 29; 21:1, 8, 9; 22:25, 27, 36; 23:17; 24:1, 20, 23; 25:7; 26:9, 10, 61, 64; 27:13; 28:26; 30:6; 32:1, 8, 9; 33:39, 51; 34:2; 35:10, 19, 21; 36:4

Dt 1:19, 41; 2:8, 12, 16, 19, 22; 4:10, 19, 25, 30; 5:23, 28; 6:7^{4}, 10, 11, 20; 7:1, 2; 8:10, 12, 13; 9:9, 23; 11:19^{4}, 29; 12:10^{2}, 20, 25, 28, 29; 13:18; 14:24; 15:4, 10, 13, 18; 16:3; 17:14, 18; 18:9, 22; 19:1, 5; 20:1, 2, 9, 10, 13, 19; 21:9, 10, 16, 18; 22:8, 14, 26; 23:4, 9, 11^{2}, 13, 21, 24, 25; 24:1, 2, 5, 10, 13, 19, 20, 21; 25:4, 11, 17, 18, 19; 26:1, 7, 12; 27:2, 3, 4, 12; 28:6^{2}, 19^{2}; 29:7, 19, 22, 25; 30:1; 31:11, 20, 21, 24; 32:8^{2}, 19, 36; 33:5; 34:7

Jos 2:5, 10, 14, 18; 3:3, 8, 14; 4:1, 6, 7, 11, 18, 21; 5:1, 8, 13; 6:5^{2}, 8, 16, 18, 20^{2}; 7:8, 21; 8:5, 8, 13, 14, 20, 21, 24^{2}; 9:1, 3, 22; 10:1, 12, 20, 24; 11:1, 5; 14:7; 17:13; 19:49; 20:4; 22:7, 10, 12, 28, 30; 23:16; 24:7

Jdg 1:14, 25, 28; 2:4, 6, 18, 19, 21; 3:9, 15, 18, 24^{2}, 27; 4:1, 18, 20, 22; 5:2, 4^{2}, 26, 31; 6:3, 7, 22, 28, 29; 7:13, 15, 17, 18; 8:1, 3, 7, 9, 12; 9:7, 22, 30, 33, 36, 46, 55; 11:5, 7, 13, 16, 31, 35; 12:2, 3, 5; 13:17, 20; 14:11; 15:5, 14, 17, 19; 16:2, 9, 15, 16, 18, 24, 25; 17:3; 18:2, 3, 10, 22, 26; 19:1, 3, 5, 7, 9, 11, 14, 15, 17, 25, 29; 20:10, 39, 40, 41; 21:22

Ru 1:1, 18, 19; 2:9, 15; 3:4, 7, 15, 16; 4:13

1Sa 1:4, 7, 20, 24; 2:13, 19, 27; 3:2, 12; 4:2, 3^{2}, 5, 6, 13^{2}, 14, 18, 19; 5:2, 3, 4, 7; 6:6, 16; 7:7^{2}; 8:1, 6; 9:5, 9, 14, 17, 25; 10:2, 5, 7, 9, 10, 11, 13, 14, 20, 21^{2}, 23; 11:6, 8; 12:8, 9, 12^{2}; 13:1, 6; 14:17, 22, 26, 27, 52; 15:2, 6, 12, 17; 16:6, 16, 23; 17:11, 24, 28, 31, 35, 42, 48, 51, 55; 18:1, 6, 15, 19, 26; 19:14, 16, 20, 21; 20:12, 15, 19^{2}, 24, 37; 21:6; 22:1, 6, 17, 22; 23:6, 25; 24:1, 8, 16, 18; 25:9, 15, 23, 30, 31, 37, 39, 40; 26:20; 28:5, 6, 12, 22; 30:1, 12, 16, 21, 26; 31:5, 7, 8, 11

2Sa 1:1, 2, 7; 2:10, 24, 30; 3:13, 23, 26, 27, 28, 35; 4:1, 4, 7, 10, 11; 5:2, 4, 17, 23, 24; 6:6, 13; 7:1, 12; 8:5, 9, 13; 9:2, 6; 10:5, 6, 7, 9, 14, 15, 17, 19; 11:1, 7, 10, 13, 16, 19, 20, 26, 27; 12:19, 20, 21; 13:5, 6, 11, 21, 28^{2}; 14:4, 26, 29, 33; 15:2, 5, 32; 16:1, 5, 7, 16; 17:6, 9, 20^{2}, 23, 27; 18:5, 29; 19:3, 25, 39; 20:8, 12^{2}, 13, 17; 21:12, 21; 22:5; 23:4, 9; 24:8, 11, 16, 17

1Ki 1:21, 23, 41; 2:7, 8; 3:21^{2}; 5:7; 6:7; 7:24; 8:9^{2}, 10, 21, 30^{2}, 33, 35^{2}, 42, 53, 54; 9:1, 10; 10:1, 2, 4; 11:4, 15, 21, 24, 29; 12:2, 16, 20, 21; 13:4, 24, 26, 31; 14:5, 6, 12, 17, 21, 28; 15:21, 29; 16:11, 18; 17:10; 18:4, 10, 12, 13, 17, 29, 39; 19:3, 13, 15; 20:12; 21:15, 16, 27; 22:25, 32, 33, 42

2Ki 1:5; 2:1, 9, 10, 14, 15, 17, 18; 3:5, 15, 20, 21, 24, 26; 4:4, 6, 10, 12, 15, 18, 20, 25, 27, 32, 36; 5:6, 7, 8, 13, 18^{2}, 21, 24, 26; 6:4, 15, 18, 20, 21, 23, 30, 32; 7:5, 8, 12, 17; 8:6, 17, 26, 29; 9:2, 5, 15, 22, 25, 27, 30, 34; 10:7, 15, 17, 24; 11:1, 13, 14, 21; 12:10; 13:21; 14:2; 15:2, 33; 16:2, 12; 18:2, 17, 18, 32; 19:1, 9, 35; 21:1, 19; 22:1, 11, 19; 23:29, 31, 36; 24:8, 18; 25:23

1Ch 1:44, 45, 46, 47, 48, 49, 50; 2:19, 21; 5:7; 6:15; 7:23; 10:5, 7, 8, 9, 11; 11:2; 12:15, 19; 13:9; 14:8, 12, 15; 15:26; 16:2, 19, 20; 17:11; 18:5, 9; 19:6, 8, 10, 15, 16, 17, 19; 20:7; 21:28; 23:1

2Ch 4:3; 5:10^{2}, 11, 13; 6:21, 26^{2}, 27, 29; 7:1, 3, 6; 9:1^{2}, 3; 10:2, 16; 11:1; 12:1, 7, 11, 12, 13; 13:7, 14; 15:4, 8, 9; 16:5; 18:14, 24, 31, 32; 19:8; 20:9, 10, 21, 22, 23, 24, 25, 29, 31; 21:4, 5, 20; 22:2, 6, 7, 8, 9, 10; 23:7^{2}, 12, 15; 24:1, 11, 14, 15^{2}, 22, 25; 25:1, 3; 26:3, 16; 27:1, 8; 28:1; 29:1, 22, 27, 29; 31:1, 8; 32:2, 21; 33:1, 12, 21; 34:1, 7, 8, 9, 14, 19, 27; 35:20; 36:2, 5, 9, 10, 11

Ezr 2:68; 3:1, 10, 11, 12; 4:1, 23; 9:1, 3; 10:1^{2}, 6

Neh 1:4; 2:3, 6, 10, 19; 4:1, 7, 12, 15; 5:6; 6:1, 16; 7:1, 73; 8:5, 9; 9:18, 27, 28; 10:38; 13:3, 19

Est 1:2, 4, 5, 10, 17, 20; 2:1, 7, 8^{2}, 12, 15, 19, 20, 23; 3:4, 5; 4:1; 5:2, 9, 10; 9:1, 25

Job 1:5, 6, 13; 2:1, 11, 12; 3:11, 22; 4:13; 5:21; 6:5, 17; 7:4^{2}, 13; 11:3; 16:22; 17:16; 20:23; 21:6, 21; 22:29; 23:10, 15; 27:8, 9; 28:26; 29:2, 3^{2}, 4, 5^{2}, 6, 7^{2}, 11^{2}; 30:26^{2}; 31:13, 14^{2}, 21, 26, 29; 32:5, 16; 33:15; 34:29^{2}; 36:13, 20; 37:4, 15, 17; 38:4, 7, 8, 9, 38, 40, 41; 39:1^{2}, 2; 41:25; 42:10

Ps 2:12; 3:ttl; 4:1^{2}, 3; 8:3; 9:3, 12; 10:9; 12:8; 13:4; 14:7; 17:15; 20:9; 21:12; 22:9, 24; 27:2, 7, 8, 10; 28:2^{2}; 30:9; 31:22; 32:3, 6; 34:ttl; 35:13; 37:33, 34; 38:16; 39:11; 41:5, 6; 42:2, 4; 49:5, 16^{2}, 17, 18; 50:18; 51:4^{2}, ttl; 52:ttl; 53:6; 54:ttl; 56:6, 9, ttl; 57:ttl; 58:7, 10; 59:ttl; 60:ttl^{2}; 61:2; 63:6, ttl; 65:9; 66:14; 68:7^{2}, 9, 14; 69:10; 71:9, 18, 23; 72:12; 73:3, 16, 20^{2}; 75:2; 76:7, 9; 78:34, 42, 59; 81:5; 87:6; 89:9; 90:4; 92:7^{2}; 94:8, 18; 95:9; 101:2; 102:2^{2}, 16, 22, ttl; 105:12, 13, 38; 106:44; 109:7, 23, 25, 28; 114:1; 119:6, 7, 32, 74, 82, 84, 171; 120:7; 122:1; 124:2, 3; 126:1; 137:1; 138:3, 4; 139:15, 16, 18; 141:1, 6, 7; 142:3, ttl

Prv 1:26, 27^{2}; 2:10; 3:24, 25, 27, 28; 4:8, 12^{2}; 5:11; 6:3, 9, 22^{3}, 30; 8:24^{2}, 27^{2}, 28^{2}, 29^{2}; 11:2, 7, 10^{2}; 13:12; 14:7; 16:7; 17:14, 28; 18:3; 20:14; 21:11^{2}, 27; 22:6; 23:1, 16, 22, 31^{3}, 35; 24:14, 17^{2}; 25:8; 26:25; 28:1, 12^{2}, 28^{2}; 29:2^{2}, 16; 30:22^{2}, 23; 31:23

Ecc 4:10; 5:1, 4, 11; 8:7, 16; 9:12; 10:3, 16, 17; 12:1, 3, 4, 5

Song 5:6; 8:1, 8

Isa 1:12, 15^{2}; 2:19, 21; 3:6; 4:4; 5:4; 6:13; 8:19, 21; 9:1, 3; 10:12, 18; 13:19; 16:12; 17:5; 18:3^{2}, 5; 20:1; 24:13^{2}, 23; 25:4; 26:9, 11, 16; 27:8, 9, 11; 28:4, 15, 18, 25; 29:8^{2}, 23; 30:19, 21^{2}, 25, 29^{2}; 31:3, 4; 32:7, 19; 33:1^{2}; 37:1, 9, 36; 38:9; 41:17, 28; 43:2^{2}, 12; 48:7, 13, 21; 50:2^{2}; 52:8; 53:2, 10; 54:6; 57:13, 20; 58:7; 59:19; 64:2, 3; 65:12^{2}; 66:4^{2}, 14

Jer 2:2, 7, 17, 20, 26; 3:8, 16; 4:30; 5:7, 19; 6:14, 15; 8:11, 12, 18; 10:13; 11:15; 12:1; 13:21, 27; 14:12^{2}; 16:10; 17:6, 8; 18:22; 21:1; 22:23; 23:33; 25:12; 26:8, 10, 21^{2}; 27:20; 28:9; 29:13; 31:2, 23, 35; 32:16; 34:1, 7, 10, 14, 18; 35:11; 36:11, 13, 16, 23; 37:5, 11, 13, 16; 38:7, 28; 39:4, 5; 40:1, 7, 11; 41:7, 11, 13; 42:6, 18, 20; 43:1, 11; 44:19; 45:1; 51:16, 55, 59, 61, 63; 52:1

Lam 1:7; 2:12^{2}; 3:8, 37; 4:15

Ezk 1:9, 12, 17^{2}, 19^{2}, 21^{3}, 24^{2}, 25, 28; 2:2, 9; 3:18, 20, 27; 4:6; 5:2, 13, 15, 16; 6:8, 13; 8:7, 8; 10:3, 5, 6, 9, 11, 16^{2}, 17^{2}, 19; 11:13; 12:15; 13:12; 14:9, 13, 21, 23; 15:5^{2}, 7; 16:6^{3}, 8, 22, 53, 55, 61, 63; 17:10, 18; 18:19, 24, 26, 27; 19:5; 20:5^{2}, 28, 31^{2}, 41, 42, 44; 21:7, 25, 29; 22:28; 23:5, 11, 14, 39; 24:24, 25; 25:3^{3}, 17; 26:10, 15^{2}, 19^{2}, 20; 27:33, 34; 28:22, 25, 26; 29:7^{2}, 16; 30:4, 8^{2}, 18, 25; 31:5, 15, 16; 32:7, 9, 10, 15^{2}; 33:2, 3, 8, 13, 14, 18, 29, 33; 34:5, 27; 35:11, 14; 36:17, 20^{2}, 23; 37:8, 13, 18, 28; 38:14, 16, 18; 39:15, 26, 27; 42:14, 15; 43:3, 18, 23, 27; 44:7, 10, 15, 17, 19, 21; 45:1; 46:8, 9, 10^{2}, 12; 47:3, 7; 48:11

Dan 3:7; 5:20; 6:10, 14, 20; 8:2, 8, 15, 17, 23; 10:9, 11, 15, 19, 20; 11:4, 12, 34; 12:7^{2}

Hos 1:8; 2:15; 4:14^{2}; 5:13; 6:11; 7:1, 12, 14; 9:12; 10:10; 11:1, 10; 13:1^{2}

Joel 2:8; 3:1

Am 3:4; 4:7, 9; 7:2; 8:5

Jna 2:7; 4:2, 7, 8

Mic 2:1; 5:5^{2}, 6^{2}; 7:1, 8^{2}

Nah 1:12; 3:17

Hab 1:13; 2:1; 3:16^{2}

Zep 3:20

Hag 1:9; 2:5, 16^{2}

Zec 7:2, 5, 6^{2}, 7^{2}; 8:14; 9:1, 13; 12:2; 13:3^{2}, 4; 14:3

Mal 2:17; 3:2, 17

Mt 1:18; 2:1, 3, 4, 7, 8, 9, 10, 11^{2}, 13, 14, 16, 19, 22; 3:7, 16; 4:2, 3, 12; 5:1, 11; 6:2, 3, 5, 6^{2}, 7, 16, 17; 7:28; 8:1, 5, 10, 14, 16, 18, 23, 28, 32, 34; 9:8, 11, 12, 15, 22, 23, 25, 27, 28, 31, 33, 36; 10:1, 12, 14, 19, 23; 11:1, 2; 12:2, 3, 9, 15, 24, 43, 44; 13:4, 6, 19, 21, 26, 32, 44, 46, 48, 53, 54; 14:5, 6, 13^{2}, 15, 23^{2}, 26, 29, 30, 32, 34, 35; 15:2, 31; 16:2, 5, 8, 13; 17:6, 8, 14, 24, 25, 27; 18:24, 31; 19:1, 22, 25, 28; 20:2, 8, 9, 10, 11, 24, 30; 21:1, 10, 15, 19, 20, 23, 32, 34, 38, 40, 45, 46; 22:7, 11, 22, 25, 33, 34; 23:15; 24:3, 15, 32, 33, 46, 50; 25:31, 37, 38, 39, 44; 26:1, 6, 8, 10, 20, 29, 30, 71; 27:1, 2, 3, 12, 17, 19, 24, 26, 29, 33, 34, 47, 50, 54, 57, 59; 28:11, 12, 17

Mk 1:19, 26, 29, 32, 37; 2:4^{2}, 5, 8, 16, 17, 20, 25; 3:5, 8, 11, 21; 4:6, 10, 15, 16, 17, 29, 31, 32, 34, 35, 36; 5:2, 6, 18, 21, 22, 27, 39, 40; 6:2, 11, 16, 20, 21, 22, 29, 34, 35, 38, 41, 46, 47, 49, 53, 54; 7:2, 4, 14, 17, 30; 8:17, 19, 20, 23, 33, 34, 38; 9:8, 14, 15, 20, 25, 28, 36; 10:14, 17, 41, 47; 11:1, 11, 12, 13, 19, 24, 25; 12:14, 23, 25, 34; 13:4^{2}, 7, 11, 14, 28, 29, 33, 35; 14:11, 12, 23, 26, 40, 67, 72; 15:15, 20, 24, 33, 35, 39, 41, 42, 45; 16:1, 4, 9, 11

Lk 1:9, 12, 22, 29, 41; 2:2, 17, 21, 22, 27, 39, 42, 43, 45, 48; 3:21; 4:2, 13, 17, 25^{2}, 28, 35, 40, 42; 5:4, 6, 8, 11, 12, 19, 20, 22, 35; 6:3, 13, 22^{2}, 26, 42, 48; 7:1, 3, 4, 6, 9, 12, 13, 20, 24, 37, 39, 42; 8:4, 8, 13, 14, 16, 27, 28, 34, 40, 45, 47, 50, 51; 9:5, 10, 11, 12, 26, 32, 36, 37, 51, 54; 10:31, 32, 33, 35^{2}; 11:1, 2, 14, 21, 22, 24, 25, 29, 33, 34^{2}, 36, 38; 12:1, 11, 36^{2}, 37, 40, 43, 46^{2}, 54, 55, 58; 13:12, 17, 25, 28, 35; 14:7, 8, 10^{2}, 12, 13, 15; 15:5, 6, 9, 14, 17, 20; 16:4, 9; 17:7, 10, 14, 15, 20^{2}, 22, 30; 18:8, 15, 22, 23, 24, 40, 43; 19:5, 7, 15, 28, 29, 37, 41; 20:13, 14, 16, 37; 21:7^{2}, 9, 20, 28, 30, 31; 22:7, 10, 14, 32, 35, 40, 45, 49, 53, 55, 64; 23:6, 8, 13, 33, 42, 46, 47; 24:6, 23, 40

Jn 1:19, 42, 48; 2:3, 9, 10, 15, 22, 23^{2}; 3:4; 4:1, 21, 23, 25, 40, 45, 47, 52, 54; 5:6, 7, 25; 6:5, 11, 12, 14, 15, 16, 19, 22, 24, 25^{2}, 60, 61; 7:9, 10, 27, 31, 40; 8:3, 7, 10, 28, 44; 9:4, 6, 14, 35; 10:4; 11:4, 6, 17, 28, 31, 32, 33, 43; 12:12, 14, 16, 17, 41; 13:1,

19, 21, 26^2, 31; 14:29; 15:26; 16:4, 8, 13, 21, 25; 18:1, 22, 38; 19:6, 8, 13, 23, 26, 30, 33; 20:1, 14, 19, 20^2, 22, 24; 21:4, 7, 15, 18^2, 19

Act 1:6, 9, 13; 2:1, 6, 37; 3:12, 13, 19; 4:7, 13, 15, 21, 24, 31; 5:7, 21, 22, 23, 24, 27, 33, 40; 6:1, 6; 7:2, 4, 5, 12, 17, 21, 23, 30, 31, 54, 60; 8:12, 13, 14, 15, 18, 25, 39; 9:8, 19, 26, 30, 37, 39, 40, 41; 10:4, 7, 8, 32; 11:2, 6, 18, 20, 23, 26; 12:4, 6, 10, 11, 12, 14, 16, 19, 25; 13:3, 5, 6, 12, 13, 14, 17, 19, 22, 24, 29, 42, 43, 45, 48; 14:5, 11, 14, 21, 23, 25, 27; 15:2, 4, 7, 30^2, 31; 16:6, 15, 19, 23, 34, 35, 38, 40; 17:1, 6, 8, 9, 13, 16, 32; 18:5, 6, 12, 14, 20, 22, 26, 27^2; 19:5, 6, 9, 21, 28, 30, 34, 35, 41; 20:2, 3, 7, 11, 14, 18, 36; 21:3, 5, 6, 7, 11, 12, 14, 17, 19, 20, 27^2, 32, 34, 35, 40^2; 22:2, 11, 17, 20, 26; 23:6, 7, 10, 12, 16, 28, 30, 33, 34^2, 35; 24:2, 22^2, 24, 25; 25:1, 6, 7, 12, 14, 15, 17, 18, 21, 23, 25; 26:10, 14, 30, 31; 27:1, 4, 5, 7, 9^2, 13, 15, 17, 20, 27, 28, 30, 35^2, 38, 39, 40; 28:1, 3, 4, 6, 9, 10, 15^2, 16, 17, 18, 19, 23, 25, 29

Ro 1:21; 2:14, 16; 3:4; 4:10, 19; 5:6, 10, 13; 6:20; 7:5, 9, 21; 9:10; 11:27; 13:11; 15:28, 29

1Co 2:1; 5:4; 8:12; 9:18, 27; 11:18, 20, 24, 25, 32, 33, 34; 13:10, 11^2; 14:16, 26; 15:24^2, 27, 28, 54; 16:2, 3, 5, 12

2Co 1:17; 2:3, 12; 3:15, 16; 7:5, 7; 10:2, 6, 11^2, 15; 11:9; 12:10, 20, 21; 13:9

Gal 1:15; 2:7, 9, 11, 12, 14; 4:3, 4, 8, 18; 6:3

Eph 1:20; 2:5; 3:4; 4:8

Php 2:19, 28; 4:15

Col 3:4, 7; 4:16

1Th 2:6, 13; 3:1, 4, 5, 6; 5:3

2Th 1:7, 10; 2:5; 3:10

1Ti 1:3; 5:11

2Ti 1:5, 17; 4:3, 13

Tit 3:12

Heb 1:3, 6; 3:9, 16; 5:7, 12; 6:13; 7:10, 27; 8:5, 8, 9; 9:6, 19; 10:5, 8; 11:8, 11, 17, 21, 22, 23, 24, 31; 12:5, 17

Jas 1:2, 12, 13, 14, 15^2; 2:21, 25

1Pt 1:11; 2:20^2, 23^2; 3:20; 4:3, 13; 5:4

2Pt 1:16, 17, 18; 2:18

1Jn 2:28; 3:2; 5:2

3Jn 3

Jude 3, 9, 12

Rev 1:17; 4:9; 5:8; 6:1, 3, 5, 7, 9, 12, 13, 14; 8:1; 9:5; 10:3^2, 4, 7; 11:7; 12:13; 17:6, 8, 10; 18:9, 18; 20:7; 22:8

WHICH

Gen 1:7^2, 21, 29^2; 2:2^2, 3, 11, 14, 22; 3:1, 3, 17, 24; 4:11; 5:29; 6:2, 4, 15; 7:23; 8:6, 7, 12; 9:4, 12, 15, 17; 11:5, 6; 13:4, 5, 15, 18; 14:2, 3, 6, 7, 15, 17, 20, 24^2; 16:15; 17:10, 12, 21; 18:8, 10, 13, 17, 19, 21, 27; 19:5, 8, 14, 15, 19, 21, 25, 29; 20:3, 13; 21:2, 9, 25, 29; 22:2, 3, 9, 17; 23:9^2, 16, 17^3; 24:7^2, 24, 42, 48, 60; 25:6, 7, 9, 10; 26:2, 3, 15, 18^2, 32, 35; 27:8, 15, 17, 27, 45, 46; 28:4, 9, 15, 22; 29:27; 30:26, 30, 37, 38; 31:1, 10, 12, 16, 18^2, 39, 43, 51; 32:8, 9, 10, 12, 13, 32^2; 33:5, 8, 18; 34:1, 7, 28^2; 35:3, 4^3, 6, 12, 19, 26, 27; 36:5, 6; 37:6; 38:10, 14; 39:1, 6, 17, 19, 23; 40:5, 20; 41:28, 36, 43, 48^2, 50; 42:9, 38; 43:2, 26, 32; 44:5, 8; 45:6, 27^2; 46:5, 6, 8, 15, 20, 22, 25, 26, 27^2, 31; 47:14, 22, 26; 48:5, 6, 15, 16, 22; 49:1, 30^2; 50:3, 5, 10, 11, 13, 15, 24

Ex 1:1, 8, 15; 3:7, 16, 20; 4:9, 18, 19, 21, 28, 30; 5:8, 14; 6:7, 8, 27; 7:15, 17; 8:3, 12, 22; 9:3, 19; 10:2, 5^3, 6, 15, 19, 21; 12:10, 16, 19, 25, 39; 13:3, 5, 8, 12; 14:13, 19, 31; 15:7, 13, 16, 17^2, 25, 26^2; 16:1, 5, 8, 15, 16^2, 23^3, 26, 32; 18:3, 9; 19:6, 7, 22; 20:2, 12; 21:1; 22:9, 13; 23:16^2, 20, 28; 24:3, 5, 8, 12; 25:3, 16, 22^2, 40; 26:10, 13, 30; 27:21; 28:4, 8, 24, 26, 38; 29:27^4, 35, 38; 30:37; 32:1, 2, 3, 4, 7, 8^2, 11, 14, 20, 23, 32, 34, 35; 33:1^2, 7^2; 34:1, 10, 11, 34; 35:1, 4, 25, 29; 36:3, 4, 5, 12, 17, 25; 37:16; 38:8; 39:19

Lev 1:8, 12; 2:10, 11; 3:4, 5, 10, 15; 4:2, 3, 7^2, 9, 13, 14, 18^2, 22, 27, 28^2; 5:6, 7, 8, 10, 17; 6:2, 3, 4^4, 5, 10, 15, 20; 7:4, 8, 11, 21, 24, 25, 36, 38; 8:5, 30, 32, 36; 9:5, 6, 8, 12, 15, 18^2, 19, 24; 10:1, 6, 11, 14, 16; 11:2, 10, 13, 21, 23, 26, 34^2, 36, 37, 39; 13:18, 58; 14:32, 34, 37, 40; 15:12; 16:2, 6, 9, 10, 11^2, 23; 17:2, 5, 8, 13, 15^2; 18:5, 24, 27, 30; 19:22^2, 36; 20:8, 23, 24, 25; 21:3, 8; 22:2, 3, 6, 8, 15, 18, 24, 32; 23:2, 4, 10, 37, 38; 25:2, 5, 11, 25, 28, 31, 38, 42, 44, 45; 26:13, 22, 32, 40, 46; 27:11, 22^2, 26, 29, 34

Nu 1:17, 44; 2:12, 32; 3:3, 26, 39, 46; 4:26, 37; 5:7, 9, 18; 6:5, 18, 21; 8:4; 10:4, 25, 29; 11:5, 12, 17, 20; 12:3; 13:2, 16, 24, 32^2, 33; 14:6, 7, 8, 11, 15, 16, 22^2, 23, 27^2, 29, 30, 31^2, 34, 36, 38, 40, 45; 15:2, 22, 39, 41; 16:11, 12, 40; 18:9, 12, 13, 15, 16, 19, 21, 24, 26, 28; 19:2^2, 15; 20:12, 24; 21:1, 11, 13, 20, 30, 34; 22:5, 11, 20, 30, 36^2; 23:12; 24:4^2, 6, 12, 16^2; 25:18; 26:4, 9; 27:12, 17^5; 28:3, 6, 23; 30:1, 8^2, 14, 16; 31:12, 14, 21^2, 28, 30, 32, 36, 38, 39, 40, 41, 42, 47, 48, 49; 32:4, 7, 9, 11, 24, 38, 39; 33:1, 4, 6, 7, 36, 40, 55; 34:13^2, 17; 35:4, 6^2, 7, 8^2, 11, 13, 14, 25, 31, 34; 36:6, 13

Dt 1:1, 4^2, 8, 14, 18, 19, 20, 25, 30, 35, 38, 39^2, 44; 2:4, 8, 11, 12, 14, 22, 23^2, 29^3, 35, 36; 3:2, 4, 9, 12^2, 13, 16, 19, 20^2, 28; 4:1^2, 2^2, 6, 8, 9, 13, 19, 21, 23^2, 28, 31, 32, 40^2, 42, 44, 45, 47, 48^2; 5:1, 6, 16, 28, 31^2, 33^2; 6:1, 2, 6, 10^2, 11^3, 12, 14, 17, 18^2, 20, 23; 7:8, 9, 11, 12, 13, 15, 16, 19; 8:1^2, 2, 3, 10, 11, 14, 16, 18, 20; 9:3, 5, 9, 10, 12^2, 16, 18, 21, 23, 26^2, 28, 29; 10:2, 4, 5, 11, 13, 17, 21; 11:2^2, 3, 7, 8, 9, 12, 13, 17, 21, 22, 27, 28^2, 30, 31, 32; 12:1^2, 2, 5, 9, 10, 11^2, 14, 15, 17, 18, 21^2, 25, 26^2, 28^2, 31; 13:2, 5^2, 6^2, 7, 10, 12, 13, 18^2; 14:4, 12, 23, 24, 25, 29^2; 15:3, 4, 5, 7, 8, 20; 16:2, 4, 5, 6, 7, 10, 11, 15, 16, 17, 18, 20^2, 21, 22; 17:2, 3, 5, 8, 10^2, 11^3, 14, 15, 18; 18:6, 7, 8, 9, 14, 17, 19, 20^2, 21, 22; 19:2, 3, 4, 8, 9, 10, 14^2, 16, 17, 20; 20:1, 14, 15^2, 16, 18, 20; 21:1, 2, 3^3, 4, 9, 16^2, 18, 23; 22:3, 5, 9, 28; 23:13, 15, 16, 23^2; 24:3, 4^2, 5; 25:6^2, 15, 19; 26:1, 2^2, 3, 10, 11, 12, 13, 15, 19; 27:1, 2, 3, 4, 10; 28:1, 8, 11, 13, 14, 15, 33, 34, 36^2, 45, 48, 50, 51, 52, 53, 54, 56, 57, 60, 61, 64, 67; 29:1^2, 3, 12, 16, 17, 22, 23, 25, 29; 30:1, 5, 7, 8, 10, 11, 20; 31:5, 7, 9, 11, 13, 16, 18, 20, 21^2, 23, 25, 29; 32:15, 21^2, 38, 46^2, 49^2, 52; 34:4, 11, 12

Jos 1:2, 6, 7, 11, 13, 14, 15^2; 2:3, 6, 7, 17, 18, 20; 3:4, 16; 4:9, 10, 20, 23; 5:1^2, 6^2; 6:25; 7:2, 11, 14^3; 8:27, 31, 32, 33, 35; 9:1, 10, 13, 20, 27; 10:11, 20, 24, 27, 32; 12:1, 2^2, 4, 7^2, 9; 13:3^2, 8, 10, 12, 21^2, 30, 32; 14:1^2, 15; 15:7, 8, 9, 10, 13, 25, 49, 54, 60; 17:5; 18:2, 3, 7, 13, 14, 16, 17, 28; 19:50, 51; 20:7; 21:4, 9, 10, 11, 20, 40, 43, 45; 22:4, 5, 9, 17, 28, 30; 23:13, 14, 15^2, 16^2; 24:5, 8, 12, 13^3, 14, 15, 17, 18, 23, 27, 30, 31, 32^2, 33

Jdg 1:16, 26; 2:1, 10^2, 12, 16, 17, 20, 21; 3:1, 4, 16, 20, 31; 4:2, 11^2, 14; 6:2, 8, 11, 13, 26; 8:27, 35; 9:2, 4, 13, 24^2, 56; 10:4^2, 8, 14; 11:24, 28, 36, 39; 12:5; 13:8; 14:19; 15:19; 16:8, 24, 29^2, 30^2; 17:2, 6; 18:5, 16, 24, 27^2, 31; 19:10, 14, 16, 19; 20:9, 13, 15, 18, 31, 36, 42, 46; 21:12, 14, 19, 25

Ru 1:22; 2:9, 11; 4:3, 11, 12, 14, 15^2

1Sa 1:27; 2:20, 29, 32, 35; 3:11, 12, 13; 4:4; 6:4, 7, 8, 17, 18; 7:14; 8:8, 18; 9:22, 23^2, 24^2; 10:2, 4; 11:11; 12:7, 8, 16, 17, 21; 13:5, 13, 14; 14:2, 4, 14^2, 21, 22, 30, 39; 15:2, 14, 20, 21; 16:4, 16, 19; 17:1, 31, 40; 20:23, 27, 36, 37; 22:9, 14; 23:13, 19; 24:4; 25:7, 27, 32, 33, 34, 35, 44; 26:1, 3; 28:21; 29:1, 3, 4; 30:10, 14, 17, 20, 21, 23, 27^3, 28^3, 29^3, 30^3, 31; 31:11

2Sa 2:15, 16, 32; 3:8, 14, 26; 4:8; 5:6; 6:4, 21, 22; 7:12, 23; 8:11^2; 9:3; 10:12; 12:3; 13:10, 23; 14:7, 13, 14; 15:4, 7, 16, 18; 16:11, 21, 23; 17:10, 18, 25; 18:18, 28; 19:5, 16, 19, 38; 20:5, 8; 21:12, 16, 18; 22:44; 23:15; 24:2, 24

1Ki 1:8, 9, 48; 2:4, 8, 24, 27, 31, 44, 46; 3:8, 13, 21, 28; 4:2, 7, 11, 12, 13^2, 19, 20, 34; 5:3, 7, 8, 16^2; 6:1, 2, 12^2, 20, 38; 7:8, 17, 20, 41, 45, 51; 8:1, 2, 9, 15, 21, 26, 28, 29^2, 34, 36, 38, 40, 43, 44, 48^4, 51, 56, 58, 63; 9:1, 3, 6, 7^2, 8, 12, 13, 15, 19, 20, 23, 24, 25, 26; 10:3, 5, 7, 8, 9, 10, 13, 24; 11:2, 8, 9, 10, 11, 13, 18, 23, 32, 33, 36; 12:4, 8^2, 9, 15, 17, 21, 28, 31, 32, 33^2; 13:3, 4^2, 5, 11, 12, 21, 22, 26^2, 32^2; 14:2, 8, 15, 18, 20, 21, 22, 24, 26, 27; 15:3, 5, 11, 15^2, 20, 23, 27, 29, 30^2; 16:12, 13^2, 15, 19^2, 24, 27, 32, 34; 17:9, 16; 18:3, 19, 26^2; 19:3, 18^2; 20:19, 34; 21:1, 4, 11, 15, 18, 25; 22:13, 16, 24, 38, 39, 43, 46

2Ki 1:4, 6, 7, 16, 17, 18; 2:15, 22; 3:3, 8, 11; 4:4, 9; 5:20; 6:10, 11; 7:13, 15; 8:21, 29; 9:5, 15, 19, 27, 36; 10:5, 6, 10^2, 17, 30, 31, 33; 11:2, 16; 12:2, 20; 13:2^2, 11, 25; 14:3, 5, 6, 11, 15, 21, 24, 25^2, 28; 15:3, 9, 12, 15, 18, 24, 28, 34; 16:2, 7, 14, 19; 17:2, 7, 8, 13^2, 15, 19, 22, 25, 26, 29, 32, 34, 37; 18:3, 6, 9, 14, 16, 17, 18, 21, 27, 37; 19:2, 4, 6^2, 12^2, 15, 16, 20, 28, 29; 20:3, 11, 17, 18, 19; 21:2, 3, 4, 7^2, 8, 11, 15, 16, 20, 25; 22:2, 4^2, 5, 13, 16, 18^2, 20; 23:2, 8, 10, 11, 12^2, 13^2, 15, 16, 17, 19, 24, 27^2, 32, 37; 24:2, 4, 9, 13, 19; 25:4, 8, 16, 19^2

1Ch 1:46; 2:3, 19, 42, 55; 3:1; 4:10, 11, 18; 6:61, 65; 9:22, 25; 10:13^2; 11:4, 5; 12:31, 32, 33; 13:2, 6; 14:4; 15:3; 16:15, 16, 40; 17:11; 19:13, 18; 20:4; 21:19, 23, 24, 29; 22:13; 23:4, 5, 29^2; 25:2; 26:22, 26^2; 27:1, 31; 29:3, 17, 19

2Ch 1:3, 4, 6, 14; 2:5, 9, 11, 14, 15; 3:5; 4:3, 12^2, 13; 5:2, 3, 6, 10, 12; 6:4, 9, 14, 15^2, 16, 17, 18, 19, 20, 21, 25, 27, 31, 32, 33, 34^2, 36, 38^3, 39; 7:6, 7, 14, 19, 20^2, 21, 22; 8:2, 4, 7, 12; 9:2, 4, 5, 7, 8, 10, 12, 14, 18; 10:8, 9, 15; 11:1, 10, 15, 19, 20; 12:4, 9, 10, 13; 13:4, 8, 10; 14:2; 15:8, 11; 16:14^2; 17:2; 18:23; 20:2, 11, 22, 25, 32; 21:6, 9, 13; 22:6; 23:9, 19; 24:2, 20, 22; 25:2, 9, 13, 15^2, 21; 26:4, 23; 27:2; 28:1, 6, 11, 15, 23; 29:2, 6, 19, 32; 30:7, 8, 16; 31:6, 10, 12, 19, 20; 32:3, 19, 21; 33:2, 3, 7^3, 8, 11, 22^2; 34:2, 9, 11, 24, 26, 31; 35:3^2, 26; 36:5, 8^2, 9, 12, 14, 23

Ezr 1:2, 3^2, 5, 7; 2:1, 2, 59, 61, 68; 4:2, 12, 15, 18, 20, 24; 5:2, 6, 8, 11, 14, 16, 17; 6:5^3, 6, 9^2, 12, 13, 15, 18, 21; 7:6, 8, 13, 14, 15, 16, 17, 20, 21, 25, 27^2; 8:25, 35; 9:11^3; 10:14

Neh 1:2, 6^2, 7; 2:8, 13, 18; 3:25; 4:2, 3, 12, 14, 17, 23; 5:8, 18; 6:6; 7:5, 61, 63, 72; 8:1, 4, 9, 14; 9:5, 15, 23, 26, 29, 35; 10:29; 12:8, 37; 13:5, 15, 16

Est 1:1, 2, 9, 13, 14^2, 18, 20; 2:4, 6, 9, 14, 16, 21; 3:3, 13; 4:6, 16; 6:8^2; 7:9; 8:2, 5^2, 8, 9, 11, 12; 9:13, 22, 25, 26^2

Job 3:3, 14, 16, 21, 22, 25^2; 4:14, 19, 21; 5:1, 9, 11; 6:16, 19, 26; 9:5^2, 6, 7, 8, 9, 10; 11:6; 14:19; 15:9, 14, 16, 17, 18, 28^2; 16:8; 20:7, 9, 11, 18, 19, 20; 21:27; 22:15, 16, 17; 23:5; 24:11, 16, 19; 25:6; 27:11, 13; 28:7^2; 29:16; 32:19; 33:27; 34:8, 32; 35:5; 36:16, 24, 28; 37:5, 16, 18, 21; 38:23, 24; 39:14; 40:15; 41:1; 42:3, 8

Ps 1:4; 3:2; 7:10, 15, ttl; 8:3; 9:11, 13, 15, 16; 17:7, 13, 14^2; 18:17; 19:5; 21:11; 25:3; 28:3; 31:18, 19^2; 32:8, 9; 35:7, 10, 27; 40:5^2; 41:9; 44:10; 45:1; 51:8; 58:5, 7, 8; 59:12; 60:10^2; 61:7; 65:6, 7, 9; 66:9, 14, 20; 68:6, 16, 28, 33; 69:4, 22; 71:20, 23; 74:2^2; 78:3, 5, 6, 45^2, 54, 60, 68, 69; 79:10; 80:12, 15; 81:10; 83:10; 85:12; 86:17; 89:49; 90:5; 91:9; 94:20; 102:18; 104:8, 10, 12, 15, 16; 105:8, 9; 106:21, 36; 107:25, 37; 109:19; 114:8; 115:15; 118:20, 22, 24, 27; 119:21, 39, 47, 48, 49, 85, 165; 121:2; 125:1; 129:6, 8; 134:1; 135:21; 136:13, 16, 17; 138:8; 139:16; 140:2; 141:5, 9; 144:1; 146:6^2, 7^2; 147:9; 148:6

Prv 1:19; 2:16, 17; 6:7; 7:5; 9:5; 11:22; 12:27; 14:12, 33; 19:17; 20:25; 22:28; 23:5, 8; 24:13; 25:1; 27:16; 28:3; 30:18^2, 21, 24, 29, 30; 31:3

Ecc 1:3, 9^3, 10, 15^2; 2:3, 12, 16, 18, 20; 3:2, 10, 15^3, 19; 4:2^2, 3, 15; 5:4, 13, 15, 18^2; 6:1, 10, 12; 7:13, 19, 24, 28; 8:7, 12, 13, 14, 15; 9:9^2; 10:5^2, 20; 12:5, 10, 11

Song 1:1; 3:7; 4:2, 5; 6:6; 7:2, 4, 13; 8:6, 12

Isa 1:1, 29; 2:8, 20; 3:12; 5:23; 6:6; 8:18; 10:1, 3; 11:10, 11, 16; 13:1, 17; 14:12; 15:7; 17:2, 8, 9, 12; 18:1; 19:15, 16, 17; 21:10; 22:3, 15; 26:2; 27:13; 28:1, 2, 4^2, 14, 29; 29:11; 30:10, 24, 31, 32; 31:7; 36:3; 37:4, 12^2, 17, 22, 29, 30; 38:3, 8^2; 39:6, 7, 8; 42:5; 43:16, 17; 44:2, 14; 45:3; 46:3^2; 47:11; 48:1^2, 14, 17^2; 49:20; 50:1; 51:10, 12, 17, 23; 52:15^2; 55:2^3, 11; 56:8, 11; 57:16; 59:5, 21; 61:9; 62:2, 6, 8; 63:7; 64:3; 65:2, 4^2, 5, 7, 18; 66:4, 22

Jer 2:11^2; 3:6, 15; 5:17, 21^2, 22; 7:10, 11, 12, 14^2, 30, 31^2; 8:3, 17; 9:13, 14, 24, 25; 10:1; 11:4^2, 5, 8, 10^2, 11, 17; 12:14; 13:4, 6, 10^3; 15:4, 14^2, 18; 17:4^2, 16, 19; 18:1, 14; 19:2, 3, 5; 20:2, 5, 16; 21:1, 4, 13; 22:6, 11^2, 28; 23:4, 7, 8^2, 27^2, 40; 24:2, 8; 25:2, 13^2, 22, 26, 27, 29; 26:2, 3, 4, 19; 27:3, 8, 9, 18, 20; 28:1, 6, 9; 29:1, 8, 19, 21, 22, 23, 27; 31:2, 21, 32, 35^2; 32:1, 2, 8, 11^2, 14^2, 20, 22, 32, 34, 35^2; 33:3, 4, 9, 10, 12, 14, 24; 34:1, 5, 8, 10, 14, 15, 18^2, 19, 21; 35:1, 4^2, 15, 16; 36:3, 4, 6, 21, 27, 28, 32; 37:2, 7, 19; 38:3, 7, 20; 39:10; 40:1, 4, 7, 10, 15; 41:9, 13, 17; 42:5, 8,

16, 21; 43:1, 9; 44:1^2, 3, 9, 14^2, 15, 20, 22; 45:4^2; 46:1, 2^2; 49:28, 31^2; 50:3; 51:12, 25, 44, 59; 52:2, 7, 12^2, 19^2, 20, 25^2

Lam 1:12; 2:3, 17; 5:18

Ezk 1:2, 23^2; 3:20, 23; 4:10, 14; 5:9, 16^2; 6:9^3; 7:13^2; 8:3, 14, 17; 9:2, 3, 6, 11; 10:22; 11:1, 3, 23; 12:2, 28; 13:11, 16^2, 17; 14:7; 15:2, 6; 16:14, 17, 19, 27, 32, 36, 45, 51, 52, 57, 59; 17:3; 18:5, 14, 18, 19, 21, 27; 19:14; 20:6, 11, 13, 15^2, 21, 28, 32, 42; 21:14; 22:4, 5, 13^2; 23:6, 24, 42; 24:21, 27; 25:9; 26:6, 17^2; 27:3, 7^2, 27; 29:3, 16; 30:22; 32:9, 23, 24^2, 27, 29, 30; 33:14, 16, 19, 29; 34:4^4, 16^4, 19^2; 35:11, 12; 36:4, 5, 21, 22, 23^2; 37:1, 19; 38:8, 12, 17; 39:19, 28; 40:2, 6^3, 40, 44, 46; 41:1, 6, 9^2, 15; 42:1, 3^2, 11, 13, 14; 43:3, 19; 44:1, 10, 13; 45:4, 14; 46:19^2; 47:8, 9, 14, 16^2, 22; 48:8, 11^2, 22, 29

Dan 1:2, 5, 8, 10, 15; 2:14, 26, 27, 34, 39, 44; 3:2, 12, 14, 15, 18, 29; 4:5, 20, 21, 24; 5:2^2, 3, 13, 23; 6:1, 8, 12, 13, 15, 24, 26; 7:6, 11, 14^2, 17^2, 19^2, 20, 23; 8:1, 2, 3, 6, 9, 13, 16, 20, 26; 9:1, 6, 10, 12, 14, 18; 10:4, 10, 21; 11:4, 7, 16, 24; 12:1, 6, 7

Hos 1:3, 10; 2:8, 23; 5:9

Joel 1:4^3; 2:25

Am 1:1, 4, 7, 10, 12; 2:4; 3:1; 4:1^3, 3; 5:1, 3, 26; 6:1, 13^2; 9:10, 12, 15

Oba 20

Jna 1:9; 4:10^2

Mic 1:1; 2:3; 5:3; 6:14; 7:10, 14, 20

Nah 3:17

Hab 1:1, 5, 6; 2:4, 6, 17

Zep 1:1, 9; 2:3

Hag 1:11; 2:14

Zec 1:6, 7, 12, 19, 21^2; 2:8; 4:2, 10, 12; 6:5, 6, 10; 7:3, 7, 12; 8:9; 10:5; 11:10, 16; 12:1; 13:6; 14:4, 7, 16

Mal 1:13, 14; 2:11; 4:4

Mt 1:20, 22, 23; 2:9, 15, 16, 17, 20, 23; 3:10; 4:13, 14, 16^2, 24^2; 5:6, 10, 12, 16, 44, 45, 46, 48; 6:1, 4, 6^2, 9, 18^2, 27, 30; 7:6, 11, 13, 14, 15, 21, 24, 26; 8:17; 9:8, 16, 20; 10:20, 28^2, 32, 33; 11:4, 10, 14, 21, 23^2; 12:2, 4^2, 10, 17, 50; 13:14, 17^2, 19^2, 23, 24, 31, 32, 33, 35^2, 41, 44, 48, 52^2; 14:9; 15:1, 11^2, 13, 18, 20, 27; 16:8, 17, 28; 17:5; 18:6, 10, 11, 12, 13, 14, 19, 23, 24, 28; 19:4, 9, 12^3, 18, 28; 20:1, 12; 21:4, 21, 24, 33, 41, 42; 22:2, 4, 8, 11, 21, 23, 31, 35, 36; 23:9, 16, 24, 26, 27, 31, 37; 24:16, 17, 18; 25:1, 24, 28, 29; 26:25, 28, 51, 62, 75; 27:3, 9, 17, 22, 35, 44, 52, 55, 56, 60; 28:5

Mk 1:2, 44; 2:3, 24, 26^2; 3:1, 3, 17, 19, 22, 34; 4:16, 18, 20, 22, 25, 31; 5:25, 35, 41; 6:2, 26; 7:1, 4, 13, 15, 20; 9:1, 17, 39; 10:42; 11:21, 23, 25, 26; 12:10, 18, 25, 28, 38, 40, 42, 43; 13:19, 32; 14:18, 24, 32, 60; 15:7, 22, 28, 34, 39, 41, 43, 46; 16:6, 14

Lk 1:1, 2, 20, 35, 45, 70, 73; 2:4, 10, 11, 15^2, 17, 18, 21, 24, 31, 33, 34, 37, 50; 3:9, 13, 19, 22, 23, 24^5, 25^5, 26^5, 27^5, 28^5, 29^5, 30^5, 31^5, 32^5, 33^5, 34^5, 35^5, 36^5, 37^5, 38^4; 4:22, 33; 5:3, 7, 9, 10, 17, 18, 21; 6:2, 3, 4, 8, 16, 17, 27^2, 28, 32, 33, 45^2, 46, 48, 49; 7:25, 27, 37, 39, 41, 42, 47; 8:2, 3, 13^2, 14^2, 15, 16, 18, 20, 21, 26, 27, 36, 43; 9:27, 30, 31, 36, 43, 46, 61; 10:11, 13, 15, 23, 24^2, 30, 36, 39, 42; 11:2, 5, 27, 33, 35, 40^2, 44, 50, 51; 12:1, 3, 5, 15, 20, 24, 25, 26, 28, 33, 47; 13:11, 14, 19, 21, 30^2, 34; 14:2, 5, 7, 24, 28; 15:4, 6, 7, 9, 30; 16:1, 10, 12^2, 15^2, 19, 20, 21, 26; 17:7, 10^2, 12, 31; 18:2, 7, 9, 27, 34, 39; 19:2, 10, 20, 26, 27, 30, 42; 20:17, 20, 25^2, 27, 35, 46, 47; 21:6^2, 15, 21^2, 22, 26; 22:1, 19, 20, 23, 24, 28, 49, 52; 23:27, 29^2, 33, 39, 48, 55; 24:1, 10, 12, 13, 14, 18, 19, 21, 22, 23, 24, 44^2

Jn 1:9, 13, 18, 24, 29, 30, 33, 38, 40, 41, 42; 2:9, 10, 22, 23; 3:6^2, 13, 29; 4:5, 9, 12, 25, 29, 39, 53; 5:2, 5, 12, 15, 23, 28, 30, 32, 36, 37, 39, 44; 6:1, 2, 9, 13, 22, 27^3, 33, 39^2, 40, 41, 44, 46, 50, 51^2, 58; 7:31, 39; 8:9, 26, 31, 38^2, 40, 46, 53; 9:1, 7, 8, 39^2, 40; 10:6, 16, 29, 32; 11:2, 16, 27, 31, 33, 37, 42, 45^2; 12:1, 4, 21, 38, 49; 13:1; 14:24^2, 26; 15:3, 24, 26; 17:4, 5, 6, 8, 9, 20, 22, 24; 18:1, 2, 5, 9^2, 11, 13, 14, 16, 21, 22, 32; 19:17, 24, 32, 39; 20:8, 16, 30; 21:10, 20^2, 24, 25^2

Act 1:2, 4, 7, 11^2, 12, 16^2, 21, 24, 25; 2:7, 16, 22, 33; 3:2, 10^2, 11, 16, 18, 20, 21, 23, 25; 4:4, 11^2, 14, 20, 21, 24, 32, 36; 5:9, 16, 17; 6:9, 10, 11, 13, 14; 7:3, 17, 18, 20, 34, 35, 37, 38, 40, 43, 45, 52^2; 8:1, 6^2, 9, 13, 14, 24, 26, 32; 9:7, 11, 19, 21, 22, 30, 32, 33, 36^2, 39; 10:2, 7, 17^2, 18, 21, 36, 37^2, 39, 42, 44, 45, 47; 11:6, 13, 19, 20, 22, 28, 29, 30; 12:9, 10; 13:1, 7, 22, 27, 31, 32, 39, 40, 41, 45; 14:3, 13, 14, 15, 26; 15:1, 5, 8, 10, 16, 19, 23, 24, 29, 31; 16:1, 2, 3, 4, 12, 13, 14^2, 16, 17, 21; 17:5, 12, 21, 31, 34; 18:27; 19:4, 10, 13, 14, 19, 24, 26, 31, 35, 37, 38; 20:19, 24, 28^2, 32^2, 38; 21:8, 9, 20, 21, 23, 25, 27, 38, 39; 22:1, 3, 5, 10, 12, 29; 23:13, 21; 24:14^2, 15, 24; 25:5, 7^2, 16, 19, 24; 26:3, 4, 5, 7^2, 10, 13, 16^2, 18, 22; 27:8, 11, 12, 16, 17, 39, 43; 28:9, 11, 24, 31

Ro 1:2, 3, 19, 26, 27^2, 28, 32; 2:2, 3, 14, 15, 19, 20, 21, 27, 28^2, 29; 3:22, 26, 30; 4:11, 12, 14, 16^2, 17, 18; 5:5, 15, 17; 6:17; 7:2, 5, 10, 13^2, 15, 16, 18, 19, 23; 8:1, 18, 23, 26, 39; 9:6, 8, 23, 25^2, 30^2, 31; 10:5^2, 6, 8; 11:2, 7, 14, 22, 24^2; 12:1, 9^2, 14; 13:3, 4; 14:3, 19, 22; 15:17, 18, 22, 26, 31; 16:1^2, 10, 11, 12, 14, 15, 17^2, 19, 25

1Co 1:2, 4, 11, 18, 24, 27, 28^2; 2:7, 8, 9, 11, 12, 13^3; 3:10, 11, 14, 17; 4:6, 17, 19; 6:16, 19^2, 20; 7:13, 35; 8:10^3; 9:13^2, 14, 24; 10:16^2, 18, 19, 20, 30; 11:19, 23^2, 24; 12:6, 22, 23, 24; 13:10^2; 14:22; 15:1^2, 2, 3, 10^2, 18, 27, 29, 31, 36, 37, 46^3, 57; 16:17

2Co 1:1^2, 4, 6^2, 8, 9, 21; 2:2, 4, 6, 14, 17; 3:7, 10, 11^2, 13^2, 14; 4:4, 11, 14, 16, 17, 18^4; 5:2, 12, 15^2; 7:14; 8:11, 16, 19, 20, 22; 9:2, 6^2, 11, 14; 10:2, 8, 13; 11:4^2, 9^2, 12, 17, 28, 30, 31; 12:4, 6, 21^2; 13:2, 3, 7, 10

Gal 1:2, 7, 8, 11, 17, 20, 22, 23^2; 2:2^2, 4, 10, 12, 18, 20; 3:7, 9, 10, 16, 17, 21, 23; 4:8, 14, 24^3, 25, 26^2, 27; 5:6, 12, 19, 21^2; 6:1

Eph 1:1, 9, 10^2, 14, 20, 21, 23; 2:10, 11, 17; 3:2, 5, 9, 11, 13, 19; 4:15, 16, 22, 24, 28, 29; 5:4, 12; 6:2, 17, 20

Php 1:1, 6, 11, 12, 23, 28, 30; 2:5, 9, 13, 21; 3:3, 6, 9^3, 12, 13^2, 17; 4:3, 7, 9, 13, 18, 21

Col 1:2, 4, 5, 6, 12, 23^3, 24^2, 25, 26, 27, 29; 2:10, 14, 17, 18, 19, 22, 23; 3:1, 5^2, 6, 7, 10, 14, 15, 25; 4:1, 3, 9, 11^2, 15^2, 17

1Th 1:1, 10; 2:4, 13^2, 14; 3:10; 4:5, 10, 13^2, 14, 15^2, 17; 5:12, 15, 21

2Th 1:5^2; 2:15, 16; 3:4, 6, 11, 17

1Ti 1:1, 4^2, 6, 11, 14, 16, 18, 19; 2:10; 3:7, 13, 15; 4:3^2, 8, 14; 5:13; 6:3, 9, 10, 15, 16, 20, 21

2Ti 1:1, 5, 6, 9, 12^2, 13^2, 14^2, 15; 2:10; 3:6, 11, 14, 15^2; 4:8

Tit 1:1, 2, 3, 11; 2:1; 3:5, 6, 8

Phlm 5, 6, 8, 11

Heb 1:5, 13; 2:1, 3, 11, 13; 3:5; 4:3, 15; 5:8, 12; 6:7, 8, 10, 18, 19^2; 7:2, 13, 14, 19, 28^2; 8:1, 2, 6, 13; 9:2, 3, 4, 5, 7, 9^2, 10, 15, 20, 24; 10:1, 8, 10, 11, 20, 27, 32, 35; 11:3^2, 4, 7^2, 8, 10, 12, 29; 12:1, 5, 9, 11, 12, 13, 14, 19, 20, 23, 27, 28; 13:3, 7, 9, 10, 21

Jas 1:1, 12, 21; 2:5, 7, 16, 23; 3:4, 9; 5:4^2, 11, 20

1Pt 1:3, 10, 11, 12^2, 15, 23, 25; 2:7^3, 8, 10^2, 11, 12; 3:4^2, 13, 19, 20; 4:11, 12; 5:1, 2

2Pt 1:18; 2:11, 15; 3:1, 2, 7, 10, 16^2

1Jn 1:1^4, 2, 3, 5; 2:7^2, 8, 24^2, 27; 3:24; 5:9, 16

2Jn 2, 5, 8

3Jn 6, 10, 11^2

Jude 3, 6, 10, 15^2, 17

Rev 1:1^2, 3, 4^5, 7, 8^3, 11, 19^3, 20^2; 2:2^2, 6, 7, 8, 9, 10, 12, 15, 17, 20, 23, 24, 25; 3:2, 4, 9, 10, 11, 12^2; 4:1^3, 5, 8; 5:6, 8, 13; 6:9; 7:4, 9, 10, 13, 14, 17; 8:2, 3, 4, 6, 9, 13; 9:4, 11, 13, 14^2, 15, 18, 20^2; 10:4, 5, 6, 8^3; 11:2, 8, 11, 16, 17, 18; 12:4, 9, 10, 13, 16, 17; 13:2, 4, 12, 14^2; 14:3, 4^2, 10, 13, 17, 18; 16:2^2, 5, 9, 14; 17:1, 7, 9^2, 12^2, 15, 16, 18^2; 18:6, 14, 15; 19:2, 9, 14, 20, 21; 20:2, 4, 8, 12^2, 13^2; 21:8^2, 9, 12, 24, 27; 22:2, 6, 8, 9, 11, 19, 20

WHO

Gen 3:11; 12:7; 14:12; 21:7, 26; 24:15, 27; 27:18, 32, 33; 30:2; 33:5; 35:3; 36:1, 19, 20, 35; 42:30; 43:22; 48:8, 14; 49:9, 25^2

Ex 2:14; 3:11; 4:11^2, 28; 5:2, 20; 6:12; 10:8; 12:27, 40; 15:11^2; 18:10^2; 21:8; 32:26

Lev 5:8; 12:7; 27:12

Nu 6:21; 7:2; 9:6; 11:4, 18; 12:7; 14:36; 16:5^2; 21:26; 23:10; 24:9, 23; 25:6; 26:9, 47, 63; 27:21; 31:27

Dt 1:33; 2:25; 4:7, 46; 5:3, 26; 8:15^2, 16; 9:2; 21:1; 30:12, 13; 33:9, 26, 29^2

Jos 9:8; 11:8; 12:2; 13:12; 15:19; 17:16^2; 21:10

Jdg 1:1; 2:7; 3:9, 19; 6:29, 35; 7:1; 8:34; 9:28^2, 38; 11:39; 15:6; 17:4, 5, 7; 18:2, 3, 29; 19:1; 21:5

Ru 2:3, 20; 3:9, 16

1Sa 2:25; 4:8; 6:20; 10:12, 19; 11:12; 14:17, 45; 16:16; 17:25, 26; 18:18; 20:10; 22:14; 23:22; 25:10^2; 26:6, 9, 14, 15; 30:23, 24

2Sa 1:8, 24^2; 4:5, 9, 10; 6:20; 7:18; 10:18; 11:21; 12:22; 16:10; 22:4, 32^2; 23:1, 20

1Ki 1:20, 27; 2:24, 32; 3:9; 8:23, 24, 50; 9:9; 12:2, 9, 18; 13:26; 14:8^2, 14, 16^2; 17:1; 19:19; 20:14; 21:11; 22:20, 52

2Ki 4:5; 7:17; 8:14; 9:31, 32^2; 10:9, 13, 29; 13:6, 11; 14:24; 15:9, 18, 24, 28; 17:36; 18:35; 23:15, 16

1Ch 2:7, 22; 4:22; 5:8, 10; 6:39; 7:24, 31; 8:12, 13^2; 9:1, 18, 31, 33; 11:10, 12, 22; 12:18; 16:41; 17:16; 19:7; 21:16; 22:9; 24:28; 25:1, 3, 9; 27:6; 29:5, 14

2Ch 1:10; 2:6^2, 12; 6:4; 8:8; 10:2; 17:16; 18:19; 19:6; 20:7, 34, 35; 22:9; 26:1, 5; 28:5; 30:7; 32:4, 14, 31; 34:26; 35:21; 36:13, 17, 23

Ezr 1:3; 3:12; 5:3, 9, 12

Neh 1:11; 3:3; 6:10, 11; 7:7; 9:7, 27^2, 32; 13:26

Est 2:6, 15, 22; 4:11, 14; 6:2, 4; 7:5, 9

Job 3:8, 15; 4:2, 7; 5:10; 9:4, 12^2, 19, 24; 11:10; 12:3, 4, 9; 13:19; 14:4; 16:9; 17:3, 15; 21:31^2; 23:13; 24:25; 26:14; 27:2^2; 30:4; 34:7, 13^2, 29^2; 35:10, 11; 36:22, 23^2; 38:2, 5^2, 6, 8, 25, 28, 29, 36^2, 37^2, 41; 39:5^2; 41:10, 11, 13^2, 14, 33; 42:3

Ps 4:6; 6:5; 8:1; 12:4^2; 14:4; 15:1^2; 16:7; 17:9; 18:3, 31^2, ttl; 19:12; 24:3^2, 4, 8, 10; 34:ttl; 35:10; 37:7^2; 39:6; 42:11; 43:5; 53:4; 59:7; 60:9^2; 64:3, 5; 65:5; 68:19; 71:19^2; 72:18; 73:12; 76:7; 77:13; 78:6; 83:12; 84:6; 89:6^2, 8; 90:11; 94:16^2; 103:3^2, 4^2, 5; 104:2^2, 3^3, 4, 5; 105:17; 106:2^2; 108:10^2, 11; 113:5^2, 6; 119:1, 38; 124:1, 2, 6, 8; 130:3; 135:8, 9, 10; 136:4, 23, 25; 137:7, 8; 140:4; 144:2, 10; 147:8^3, 17

Prv 2:13, 14; 9:15; 18:14; 20:6, 9, 25; 21:24; 23:29^6; 24:22; 26:18; 27:4; 30:4^4, 9; 31:10

Ecc 2:19, 25^2; 3:21, 22; 4:3, 13; 6:12^2; 7:13, 24; 8:1^2, 4, 7, 10; 10:14; 11:5; 12:7

Song 3:6; 6:10; 8:2, 5

Isa 1:12; 6:8; 14:6, 27^2; 23:8; 24:18; 27:4; 29:15^2, 22; 33:14^2; 36:20; 37:2; 40:12, 13, 14, 26; 41:2, 4, 26; 42:19^2, 23^2, 24; 43:9, 13; 44:7, 10; 45:21^2; 49:21^2; 50:8^2, 9, 10; 51:12, 19; 53:1, 8; 60:8; 63:1; 65:16; 66:8^2

Jer 1:16; 2:24; 9:12^2; 10:7; 15:5^3; 17:9; 18:13; 20:1, 15; 21:13^2; 23:18^2; 26:20, 23; 30:21; 36:32; 46:7; 49:4, 19^4; 50:44^4; 52:25

Lam 2:13; 3:37

Ezk 10:7

Dan 1:10; 2:23; 3:15, 28; 6:27

Hos 3:1; 7:4; 14:9

Joel 2:11, 14

Am 1:1; 3:8^2, 10; 5:7

Oba 3

Jna 3:9

Mic 3:2^2, 3; 5:8; 6:9; 7:18

Nah 1:6^2; 3:7

Hab 2:5

Zep 3:18

Hag 2:3

Zec 4:7, 10

Mal 1:10; 3:2^2

Mt 1:16; 3:7; 10:2, 4, 11; 12:48^2; 13:9, 43, 46; 18:1; 19:25; 21:10, 23; 24:45; 25:14; 26:3, 68; 27:57

Mk 1:19, 24; 2:7; 3:33; 4:16; 5:3, 30, 31; 9:34; 10:26; 11:28; 13:34; 15:7, 21, 41; 16:3

Lk 1:36; 3:7; 4:34; 5:12, 21^2; 7:2, 39, 49; 8:45^2; 9:9, 31; 10:22^2, 29; 12:14, 42; 16:11, 12, 14; 18:26, 30; 19:3; 20:2; 22:64; 23:7, 19, 51

Jn 1:19, 22, 27; 4:10; 5:13; 6:60, 64^2; 7:20, 49; 8:25; 9:2, 19, 21, 36; 12:34, 38; 13:11, 24, 25; 18:18; 21:12

Act 1:23; 3:3; 4:25, 36; 5:36; 7:27, 35, 38, 46, 53; 8:15, 27, 33; 9:5; 10:32, 38, 41; 11:14, 17, 23; 13:7, 9, 31, 43; 14:8, 9, 16, 19; 15:17, 27, 38; 16:24; 17:10; 18:27; 19:15; 21:4, 32, 33, 37; 22:8; 23:18, 33; 24:1, 6, 19; 26:15; 28:7, 10, 18

Ro 1:18, 25^2, 32; 2:6, 7, 27; 3:5, 19; 4:12^2, 16, 17, 18, 25; 5:14; 7:4, 24; 8:1, 4, 20, 28, 31, 33, 34^3, 35; 9:4, 5, 19, 20; 10:6, 7, 16; 11:4, 34^2, 35; 14:2, 4, 20; 16:4, 5, 6, 7^2, 12, 22

1Co 1:8, 30; 2:16; 3:5^2; 4:5, 7, 17^2; 6:4; 9:7^3; 10:13; 14:8

2Co 1:4, 10, 19, 22; 2:2, 16; 3:6; 4:4, 6; 5:5, 18, 21; 8:10, 19; 10:1; 11:29^2

Gal 1:1, 4, 15; 2:3, 4, 6^2, 9, 15, 20; 3:1; 4:23; 5:7; 6:10, 13

Eph 1:3, 11, 12, 19; 2:1, 4, 11, 13, 14; 3:8, 9; 4:6, 19; 5:5

Php 2:6, 20; 3:19, 21

Col 1:7, 8, 13, 15, 18, 24; 2:12; 3:4; 4:7, 9, 11, 12

1Th 2:12, 15; 4:8; 5:8, 10, 24

2Th 1:7, 9; 2:4, 7, 12; 3:3

1Ti 1:12, 13; 2:4, 6; 4:10; 5:17; 6:13^2, 15, 16, 17

2Ti 1:9, 10; 2:2, 4, 18, 26; 4:1

Tit 1:11; 2:14

Heb 1:1, 3, 7, 14; 2:9, 11, 15; 3:2, 3; 5:2, 7, 14; 6:4, 12, 18; 7:1, 5, 9, 16, 26, 27, 28; 8:1, 5; 9:14; 10:29, 39; 11:11, 27, 33; 12:2, 16, 25; 13:7

Jas 3:13; 4:12^2; 5:4, 10

1Pt 1:5, 10, 17, 20, 21; 2:9, 22, 23, 24; 3:5, 13, 22; 4:5; 5:1, 10

2Pt 2:1, 15, 18

1Jn 2:22; 3:12; 4:21; 5:5

2Jn 7

3Jn 9

Jude 4, 18, 19

Rev 1:2, 5, 9; 2:1, 13, 14, 18; 4:9; 5:2; 6:17; 10:6; 12:5; 13:4^2; 14:11; 15:4, 7; 18:8, 9

WHOM

Gen 2:8; 3:12; 4:25; 6:7; 10:14; 15:14; 21:3; 22:2; 24:3, 14, 40, 44, 47; 25:12; 30:26; 41:38; 43:27, 29; 44:10, 16; 45:4; 46:18; 48:9, 15; 49:8

Ex 4:13; 6:5, 26; 14:13; 18:9; 22:9; 23:27; 28:3; 32:13; 33:12, 19^2; 35:21, 23, 24; 36:1

Lev 6:5; 13:45; 14:32; 15:18; 16:32^2; 17:7; 22:5; 25:27, 55; 26:45; 27:24^2

Nu 3:3; 4:41, 45, 46; 5:7; 11:16, 21; 12:1, 12; 16:5, 7; 17:5; 22:6^2; 23:8^2; 26:5, 59, 64; 27:18; 34:29; 36:6

Dt 4:46; 7:19; 9:2^2; 17:15; 19:4, 17; 21:8; 24:11; 28:55; 29:26^2; 31:4; 32:17^2, 20, 37; 33:8^2; 34:10

Jos 2:10; 4:4; 5:6, 7; 10:11, 25; 13:8, 21; 24:15, 17

Jdg 4:22; 7:4; 8:15, 18; 12:9; 14:20; 21:23

Ru 2:19^2; 4:1^2, 12

1Sa 2:33; 6:20; 9:17, 20; 10:24; 12:3^2, 13^2; 16:3; 17:28, 45; 21:9; 24:14^2; 25:11, 25; 28:8, 11; 29:5; 30:13, 21

2Sa 7:7, 15, 23; 14:7; 15:33; 16:18, 19; 17:3; 19:10; 20:3; 21:6, 8^2; 23:8^2

1Ki 2:5; 5:5; 7:8; 9:21; 10:26; 11:20, 34; 13:23; 17:1, 20; 18:15, 31; 20:14, 42; 21:25, 26; 22:8

2Ki 3:14; 5:16; 6:19, 22; 8:5; 10:24; 16:3; 17:8, 11, 15, 27, 28, 33, 34, 35; 18:20; 19:4, 10, 22^2; 21:2, 9; 23:5; 25:22

1Ch 1:12; 2:21; 5:6, 25; 6:31; 7:14, 21; 9:22; 11:10, 11; 17:6, 21^2; 26:32; 29:1, 8

2Ch 1:11; 2:7; 8:8; 9:25; 17:19; 18:7; 20:10; 22:7; 23:18; 28:3; 33:2, 9

Ezr 2:1, 65; 4:10; 5:14; 8:20; 10:44

Neh 1:10; 7:6, 67; 8:10; 9:37

Est 2:6, 7; 4:5, 11; 6:6^2, 7, 9^2, 11, 13

Job 3:23; 5:17; 9:15; 15:19; 19:19, 27; 25:3; 26:4; 30:2

Ps 10:3; 16:3; 18:2, 43; 27:1^2; 32:2; 33:12; 41:9; 45:16; 47:4; 65:4; 69:26^2; 73:25; 80:17; 86:9; 88:5; 89:21; 94:1^2, 12; 95:11; 104:26; 105:26; 106:34, 38; 107:2; 144:2; 146:3

Prv 3:12^2, 27; 25:7; 30:31

Ecc 4:8; 5:19; 6:2; 8:14^2; 9:9

Song 1:7; 3:1, 2, 3^2, 4

Isa 6:8; 8:12, 18; 10:3; 19:25; 22:16; 23:2; 28:9^2, 12; 31:6; 36:5; 37:4, 10, 23^2; 40:14, 18, 25; 41:8, 9; 42:1^2, 24; 43:10; 44:1, 2; 46:5; 47:15; 49:3, 7^2; 50:1^2; 51:18, 19; 53:1; 57:4^2, 11; 66:13

Jer 1:2; 6:10; 7:9; 8:2^5; 9:12, 16; 11:12; 14:16; 18:8; 19:4; 20:6; 23:9; 24:5; 25:15, 17; 26:5; 27:5; 29:1, 3, 4, 20, 22; 30:9, 17; 33:5; 34:11, 16; 37:1; 38:9; 39:17; 40:5; 41:2, 9, 10, 16^2, 18; 42:6, 9, 11; 44:3; 50:20; 52:28

Lam 1:10, 14; 2:20; 4:20

Ezk 9:6; 11:1, 7, 15; 13:22; 16:20, 37; 20:9; 23:7, 9, 22, 28^2, 37, 40^2; 24:21; 28:25; 31:2, 18; 32:19; 38:17

Dan 1:4^2, 7, 11; 2:24; 3:12, 17; 4:8; 5:11^2, 12, 13, 19^4; 6:2, 16, 20; 7:8, 20; 9:21; 11:21, 38, 39

Hos 13:10

Joel 2:32; 3:2

Am 6:1; 7:2, 5

Nah 3:19

Zep 3:18

Zec 1:4, 10; 7:14; 12:10

Mal 1:4; 2:14; 3:1^2

Mt 1:16; 3:17; 7:9; 11:10; 12:18^2, 27; 16:13, 15; 17:5, 25; 18:7; 19:11; 20:23; 23:35; 24:45, 46; 26:24; 27:9, 15, 17

Mk 1:11; 3:13; 6:16; 8:27, 29; 10:40; 13:20; 14:21, 71; 15:12, 40; 16:9

Lk 6:13, 14, 34, 47; 7:4, 27, 43, 47; 8:2, 35, 38; 9:9, 18, 20; 10:22; 11:19; 12:5, 37, 42, 43, 48; 13:4, 16; 17:1; 19:15; 22:22; 23:25

Jn 1:15, 26, 30, 33, 45, 47; 3:26, 34; 4:18; 5:21, 38, 45; 6:29, 68; 7:25, 28; 8:53, 54; 10:35, 36; 11:3; 12:1, 9, 38; 13:18, 22, 23, 24, 26; 14:17, 26; 15:26; 17:3, 11, 24; 18:4, 7; 19:26, 37; 20:2, 15; 21:7, 20

Act 1:2, 3; 2:24, 36; 3:2, 13, 15, 16, 21; 4:10^2, 22, 27; 5:25, 30, 32, 36; 6:3, 6; 7:7, 35, 39, 45, 52; 8:10, 34; 9:5, 37; 10:21, 39; 13:22, 25, 37; 14:23; 15:17, 24; 17:3, 7, 23, 31; 18:26; 19:13, 16, 25, 27; 20:25; 21:16, 29; 22:5, 8; 23:29; 24:6, 8; 25:15, 16, 18, 19, 24, 26; 26:15, 17, 26; 27:23; 28:4, 8, 15, 23

Ro 1:5, 6, 9; 3:25; 4:6, 8, 17, 24; 5:2, 11; 6:16^2; 8:29, 30^3; 9:4, 5, 15^2, 18^2, 24; 10:14^2; 11:36; 13:7^4; 14:15; 15:21; 16:4

1Co 1:9; 3:5; 7:39; 8:6^2, 11; 10:11; 15:6, 15

2Co 1:10; 2:3, 10^2; 4:4; 8:22; 10:18; 11:4; 12:17

Gal 1:5; 2:5; 3:19; 4:19; 6:14

Eph 1:7, 11, 13^2; 2:3, 21, 22; 3:12, 15; 4:16; 6:22

Php 2:15; 3:8, 18

Col 1:14, 27, 28; 2:3, 11; 4:8, 10

1Th 1:10

2Th 2:8

1Ti 1:15, 20^2; 6:16^2

2Ti 1:3, 12, 15; 2:17; 3:14; 4:15, 18

Phlm 10, 12, 13

Heb 1:2^2; 2:10^2; 3:17, 18; 4:6, 13; 5:11; 6:7; 7:2, 4, 8, 13; 11:18, 38; 12:6^2, 7; 13:21, 23

Jas 1:17

1Pt 1:8^2, 12; 2:4; 4:11; 5:8, 9

2Pt 1:17; 2:2, 17, 19

1Jn 4:20^2

2Jn 1

3Jn 1, 6

Jude 13

Rev 7:2; 17:2; 20:8

WHOSE

Gen 1:11, 12; 7:22; 11:4; 16:1; 17:14; 22:24; 24:23, 37, 47; 32:17^2; 38:1, 2, 6, 25^2; 44:17; 49:22

Ex 34:14; 35:21, 26, 29; 36:2^2

Lev 13:40; 14:32; 15:32; 16:27; 21:10; 22:4; 24:10

Nu 24:3, 15

Dt 8:9^2; 19:1; 28:49; 29:18

Jos 24:15

Jdg 4:2; 6:10; 8:31; 13:2; 16:4; 17:1

Ru 2:2, 5, 12; 3:2

1Sa 9:1, 2; 10:26; 12:3^3; 17:4, 12, 55, 56, 58; 25:2

2Sa 3:7, 12; 6:2; 9:2, 12; 13:1, 3; 14:27; 16:5, 8; 17:10, 25; 20:1; 21:16, 19

1Ki 3:26; 8:39; 11:26

2Ki 7:2, 17; 8:1, 5; 12:15; 18:22^2

1Ch 2:16, 26, 34; 7:2, 15; 8:29, 38; 9:35, 44; 12:8; 13:6; 20:5, 6; 26:7

2Ch 6:30; 16:9; 28:9

Ezr 1:5; 5:14; 7:15; 8:13

Est 2:5

Job 1:1; 3:23; 4:19; 5:5; 8:14^2; 12:6, 10; 22:16; 26:4; 30:1; 38:29; 39:6

Ps 15:4; 17:14; 26:10; 32:1^2, 2, 9; 33:12; 38:14; 57:4; 78:8; 83:18; 84:5^2; 105:18; 144:8, 11, 15; 146:5

Prv 2:15; 26:26; 30:14

Ecc 2:21; 7:26

Isa 1:30; 2:22; 5:28; 6:13; 10:10; 14:2; 18:2, 7; 23:7, 8^2; 26:3; 28:1; 30:13; 31:9; 36:7^2; 43:14; 45:1; 51:7, 15; 57:15, 20; 58:11

Jer 5:15; 17:5, 7; 19:13; 22:25; 32:29; 33:5; 37:13; 44:28; 46:7, 18; 48:15; 49:12; 51:57

Ezk 3:6; 11:21; 17:6, 16^2; 20:9, 14, 22; 21:25, 27, 29; 23:20^2; 24:6^2; 32:23; 40:3, 45, 46; 42:15; 43:4; 47:12

Dan 2:11, 26, 31; 3:1, 27; 4:8, 19, 20, 21^2, 34, 37; 5:23^2; 7:9, 19, 20, 27; 10:1, 5

Joel 1:6

Am 2:9; 5:27

Oba 3

Jna 1:7, 8

Mic 5:2

Nah 3:8

Zec 6:12; 11:5

Mt 3:11, 12; 10:3; 22:20, 28, 42

Mk 1:7; 7:25; 12:16, 23

Lk 1:27; 2:25; 3:16, 17; 6:6; 12:20; 13:1; 20:24, 33; 24:18

Jn 1:6, 27; 4:46; 6:42; 10:12; 11:2; 18:26; 19:24; 20:23^2

Act 7:58; 10:5, 6, 32; 11:13; 12:12, 25; 13:6, 25; 15:37; 16:14; 18:7; 27:23; 28:7, 11

Ro 2:29; 3:8, 14; 4:7^2; 9:5

2Co 8:18; 11:15

Gal 3:1

Php 3:19^3; 4:3

2Th 2:9

Tit 1:11

Heb 3:6, 17; 6:8; 7:6; 11:10; 12:26; 13:7, 11

1Pt 2:24; 3:3, 6

2Pt 2:3

Jude 12

Rev 9:11; 13:8, 12; 17:8; 20:11

WITH

Gen 3:6, 12; 4:8; 5:22, 24; 6:3, 9, 11, 13^2, 14, 16, 18^2, 19; 7:7, 13, 23; 8:1, 16, 17^2, 18; 9:4, 8, 9^2, 10^3, 11, 12; 11:31; 12:4, 13, 17; 13:1, 5; 14:2^2, 5, 8, 9^3, 13, 17, 24; 15:14, 18; 16:6, 11; 17:3, 4, 12, 13, 19^2, 21, 22, 23, 27^2; 18:11, 16, 23, 25, 33; 19:1, 9^2, 11, 30, 32, 33, 34^2, 35, 36; 20:16^2; 21:6, 10^2, 19, 20, 22, 23^3; 22:3, 5; 23:4^2, 8, 16; 24:15, 32, 40, 45, 49, 54, 55, 58; 25:30; 26:3, 8, 10, 15, 20^2, 24, 28^2; 27:15, 34, 35, 37, 44; 28:4, 15, 20; 29:6, 9^2, 14, 19, 25, 27, 30; 30:8^2, 15, 16^2, 20^2, 29, 33; 31:3, 5, 6, 21, 23, 25, 26, 27^4, 32^2, 36, 38, 42, 50; 32:4, 6, 7, 9, 10, 11, 15, 20, 24, 25, 28^2; 33:1, 5, 7, 10, 11, 13^2, 15^2; 34:2, 5, 6, 7, 8, 9, 10, 16, 20, 21, 22, 23, 26, 31^2; 35:2, 3, 6, 13, 14, 15, 22; 37:2^3, 14^2, 25; 38:14, 24, 25; 39:2, 3, 7, 8, 10, 12, 14^2, 15, 18, 21, 23; 40:4, 7, 14; 41:6, 10, 12, 23, 27; 42:4, 6, 13, 24, 25, 26, 32, 33, 38^2; 43:3, 4, 5, 6, 8, 16^2, 19, 32^2, 34; 44:1, 9, 10, 16, 23, 26^2, 29, 30, 31^2, 33, 34; 45:1, 5, 15, 23^2; 46:1, 4, 6, 7^2, 15, 26; 47:12, 17, 29, 30; 48:1, 12, 21, 22^2; 49:12^2, 25, 29, 30; 50:7, 9, 10, 13, 14

Ex 1:1, 7, 10, 11, 13, 14[2], 20; 2:3[2], 21, 24[3]; 3:2, 8, 12, 17, 18, 20; 4:12, 15[2]; 5:3[3], 15; 6:1[2], 4, 6[2]; 7:11, 17, 22; 8:2, 5, 7, 17, 18; 9:9, 10, 15, 24; 10:9[6], 10, 24, 26[2]; 12:8[2], 9[4], 10, 11, 22, 38, 48; 13:5, 7[2], 9, 13, 19[2]; 14:6, 8, 11; 15:8, 10, 19[2], 20[2]; 16:3, 12, 18, 20, 31; 17:2[2], 3, 5, 8, 9[2], 10, 13, 16; 18:5, 6, 12, 18, 19, 22; 19:9, 17, 24; 20:19[2], 22, 23; 21:3, 6, 8, 9, 14, 18[2], 20, 22, 29; 22:14, 15, 16, 19, 24, 30[3]; 23:1, 5, 11[2], 18, 32[2]; 24:2, 3, 8, 14; 25:2, 11, 13, 14, 20, 22[2], 24, 28[2], 33[2], 34, 39; 26:1[2], 6, 29[2], 31, 32, 36, 37; 27:2, 6, 8, 16, 17; 28:1, 3, 6, 11[2], 15, 21[2], 28, 41; 29:2[2], 3, 4, 5, 9, 12, 14, 21[2], 34, 40[2], 43; 30:3, 5, 6, 10, 20, 28, 34, 36; 31:3, 6, 8, 9, 18[2]; 32:4, 11[2]; 33:3, 9, 12, 14, 15, 16, 22; 34:3, 5, 10, 12, 15, 20, 25, 27[2], 28, 29[2], 31, 32, 33, 34, 35; 35:12, 14, 16, 23, 24, 25, 31, 35; 36:8, 13, 34[2], 35, 36, 38[2]; 37:2, 4, 9[2], 11, 15, 26, 28; 38:2, 6, 7, 17, 23; 39:3, 6, 14, 21, 23, 37[2]; 40:3, 12, 14

Lev 1:12, 13, 16, 17; 2:2, 4[2], 5, 7, 11, 13[2], 16; 3:4, 10, 15; 4:9, 11[2], 12, 20[3], 25, 30, 34; 5:4[2], 15, 16, 18; 6:6, 10, 16, 17, 21; 7:4, 10, 12[4], 13, 17, 19, 24, 30; 8:2, 6, 7[3], 13, 15, 17, 30[2], 31, 32; 9:4, 11, 13; 10:9, 14, 15[2], 16; 11:43[2], 44; 13:57; 14:10, 16, 21, 27, 31, 37, 52[6]; 15:3, 17, 18[2], 24, 33; 16:3, 4[2], 10, 14[2], 15[2], 19, 24; 17:13, 15; 18:20[2], 22[2], 23; 19:13, 19[2], 20, 22, 26, 33, 34; 20:2, 5, 10[2], 11, 12, 13[2], 14, 15, 18, 20, 24, 27; 21:9; 22:6, 8, 11, 14; 23:13, 17, 18[2], 20[2]; 24:23; 25:6, 23, 35[2], 36, 40, 41, 43, 45, 46, 50[2], 52, 53[2], 54; 26:9, 39, 40, 42[3], 44

Nu 1:2, 4, 5; 2:2, 17, 31; 3:1; 4:5, 8, 11, 12, 32[2]; 5:7, 13[2], 19[2], 20, 21, 23; 6:15[2], 17, 20; 7:13, 19, 25, 31, 37, 43, 49, 55, 61, 67, 73, 79, 87, 89; 8:8[2], 26; 9:11; 10:3, 4, 8, 9, 10, 29, 32; 11:15, 16, 17[2], 18, 33; 12:8; 13:23, 27, 31; 14:8, 9, 10, 12, 21, 24, 27, 43; 15:4, 5, 6, 9[2], 14, 15, 16, 24, 35, 36; 16:2, 10, 13, 14, 18, 22, 30; 17:4, 13; 18:1[2], 2[2], 7, 11[2], 19[2]; 19:4, 5, 12, 16; 20:3, 11, 13, 18, 20[2]; 21:18, 24; 22:7, 8, 9, 12, 13, 14, 20, 21, 22, 27, 35[2], 39, 40; 23:13, 17, 21; 24:8; 25:1, 14, 18; 26:3, 10; 27:21; 28:5, 9, 12[2], 13, 20, 28; 29:3, 9, 14; 30:2, 8, 10; 31:6, 8, 10, 14[2], 17, 18, 23, 35; 32:19, 29, 30, 33; 33:1, 3; 34:2, 12; 35:7, 16, 17, 18, 21, 23, 25

Dt 1:16, 37; 2:5, 7, 9, 19, 24, 26; 3:5, 13, 26, 27; 4:11[2], 21, 23, 29[2], 37, 40[2]; 5:2, 3[2], 4, 16, 22, 23, 24, 29[2], 33; 6:3[2], 5[3], 18, 21; 7:2, 3, 5[2], 8, 9, 23, 25; 8:3, 16; 9:8, 9, 10[2], 15, 20, 21, 26; 10:9, 12[2], 14, 22; 11:2, 9, 10, 13[2]; 12:3, 12, 23, 25[2], 28[2]; 13:3[2], 10, 15[2], 16; 14:27, 29; 15:3, 16, 19; 16:3, 4, 10, 18; 17:5, 19; 18:1, 6, 11, 13; 19:5[2], 13; 20:1, 4, 12, 13, 20; 21:3, 21; 22:2, 3[3], 6, 7, 9, 10, 21, 22[2], 23, 24, 25[2], 28, 29; 23:4[2], 11, 16, 23, 25; 24:5, 12; 25:3, 11; 26:5, 8[5], 9, 15, 16[2]; 27:1, 2, 3, 4, 14, 20, 21, 22, 23; 28:22[7], 27[4], 28, 30, 32, 35, 40, 47[2], 68; 29:1[2], 10, 12[2], 14, 15[4], 25; 30:2[2], 6[2], 10[2]; 31:6, 7, 8, 16[2], 20, 23, 27; 32:12, 14[2], 15, 16[2], 21[4], 22, 24[4], 25, 34, 39, 42[2], 43; 33:2, 8[2], 17, 20, 21[2], 23[2], 24; 34:4

Jos 1:5[2], 9, 17[2]; 2:6, 14, 19; 3:7[2]; 4:3, 8; 5:6, 13; 6:4, 5[2], 8, 9[2], 10, 13[2], 16, 17, 20[2], 21, 24, 27; 7:12, 15[2], 24, 25[3]; 8:1, 5, 11, 24, 35; 9:2[3], 6, 7, 11[2], 15[2], 16; 10:1, 4[2], 7, 10, 11[2], 15, 20, 24, 28, 29, 30, 31, 32, 34, 35, 36, 37, 38, 39, 43; 11:4[2], 6, 7, 9, 10, 11[2], 12, 14, 18, 19, 21; 13:8, 21, 22; 14:4, 8, 12; 15:32, 36, 41, 44, 45, 46, 47[2], 51, 54, 57, 59, 60, 62, 63; 16:9; 18:24, 28; 19:15, 16, 22, 30, 31, 38, 46, 47, 48; 21:2, 8, 11, 13[2], 14[2], 15[2], 16[3], 17[2], 18[2], 19, 21[2], 22[2], 23[2], 24[2], 25[2], 26, 27[2], 28[2], 29[2], 30[2], 31[2], 32[3], 33, 34[2], 35[2], 36[2], 37[2], 38[2], 39[2], 41, 42; 22:5[2], 8[8], 14, 15, 18, 24, 27[3], 30; 23:4, 12; 24:6, 8, 12[2], 25

Jdg 1:3[3], 8, 16, 17, 18[3], 19, 21, 22, 25; 2:1, 2, 18; 3:27, 31; 4:6, 7, 8[2], 9[2], 10[2], 13, 15, 18; 5:15, 26; 6:5, 12, 13, 16, 17, 26, 39; 7:1, 2, 4[3], 5, 10, 11, 16, 18[2], 19; 8:1[2], 4, 7[2], 10, 15, 16; 9:1[2], 16, 19[2], 23, 26, 32, 33, 34, 35, 38, 39, 44, 45, 48[2], 52; 11:3, 6, 8, 11, 12, 33, 34[2], 38, 39; 12:1[2], 2, 4; 13:9, 19; 14:7, 11, 15, 18; 15:1, 5, 6, 8, 13, 14, 16[2]; 16:3, 7, 8, 9, 11, 13, 14[3], 15, 16, 21, 29[2], 30[2]; 17:2, 10, 11; 18:4, 7, 11, 16, 17[2], 19, 23, 25, 27[2], 28; 19:3, 4, 5, 10[2], 19, 20, 24, 29; 20:1, 37, 38, 40, 43, 48; 21:5, 10[2], 12

Ru 1:6, 7, 8[3], 10, 11, 18, 20, 22; 2:4, 6, 19[2], 22, 23; 3:1, 2

1Sa 1:24[2]; 2:4, 13[2], 18, 19, 22, 26[2], 29; 3:14, 19; 4:4, 5, 8, 12[2], 19; 5:6, 7, 8, 9, 12; 6:11, 15, 19; 7:3, 10; 9:3, 5, 19, 24, 25; 10:5, 6, 7, 26; 11:1, 2, 7, 10; 12:2, 7, 20, 24; 13:2[2], 4, 5, 15, 16, 22[3]; 14:2, 7, 17, 18, 20, 21[4], 27, 28, 32, 33, 34[2], 43, 45; 15:6, 8, 25, 26, 30; 16:1, 2, 5, 16, 18, 19, 20, 23; 17:5, 9, 19, 20, 23, 25, 28, 32, 33, 37, 38[2], 39, 43, 45[3], 47, 50[2], 57; 18:1, 6[3], 10, 11, 12, 14, 22, 28; 19:3, 8[2], 9[2], 10, 13, 16; 20:5, 8[2], 13[2], 16, 35[2], 41; 21:1, 8; 22:2, 3, 4, 6, 8, 17, 19[2], 23[2]; 23:5[2], 6, 19, 23[2]; 24:7, 8, 18; 25:7, 15, 16, 25, 26, 29, 31, 33, 39, 42; 26:2, 6[2], 8; 27:2[2], 3[3], 5; 28:1[2], 8, 12, 14[2], 19[2], 23; 29:2, 3, 4[3], 6, 8, 9, 10[2]; 30:1, 3, 4, 9, 14, 21, 22[2], 23; 31:5

2Sa 1:2, 11, 17, 21, 24; 2:3[2], 23; 3:8, 12[2], 13, 16, 17, 20[2], 21, 22[2], 23, 27, 31[2]; 5:3, 10; 6:2[2], 12, 14[2], 15[2]; 7:3, 7[2], 9, 12, 14[2], 22, 29; 8:2[3], 10[2], 11; 10:13, 17, 19; 11:1, 4, 5, 9, 11, 13, 17; 12:3[2], 9[2], 11, 17, 24, 30; 13:11, 14, 18, 20, 24, 26[2], 27, 28, 31; 14:2, 17, 19; 15:11, 12, 14[2], 19[2], 20[2], 22, 23, 24, 27, 30, 31, 32, 33, 35, 36; 16:1, 10, 14, 15, 17, 18, 21, 23[2]; 17:2, 8, 10, 12, 16, 22, 24, 29; 18:1, 2, 5[2], 14, 27; 19:4, 7, 16, 17[2], 22, 25, 31, 33[2], 34, 36[2], 37, 38, 40, 41; 20:8, 9, 15, 16; 21:15[2], 16, 17, 18, 19; 22:26[2], 27[2], 40; 23:5[2], 6, 7[2], 9, 21[2]; 24:2

1Ki 1:1, 7[2], 8, 14, 21, 22, 23, 31, 33, 34, 37[2], 40[3], 41, 44, 49, 51; 2:4[2], 8[3], 9, 10, 32, 43; 3:1, 6, 17, 18; 4:13; 5:6; 6:8, 9, 10, 12, 15[3], 16, 18, 20, 21[2], 22[2], 28, 29, 30, 32, 35, 36; 7:2, 3, 5, 7, 9, 12, 14, 18, 26, 31, 49; 8:5, 9, 15[2], 21, 23[2], 24[3], 25, 46, 48[2], 54, 55, 57[2], 61, 62, 65; 9:11[2], 16, 27; 10:1, 2[3], 18, 22, 26; 11:1, 4, 9, 16, 17, 18, 21, 22, 29, 38, 43; 12:6, 8[2], 10, 11[3], 14[2], 18, 21; 13:7, 8, 15, 16[3], 18, 19; 14:3, 6, 8, 20, 22, 31[2]; 15:3, 8, 14, 19, 20, 22, 24[2]; 16:2, 6, 7, 13, 17, 18, 26, 28; 17:18, 20; 18:4, 13, 28, 32, 33, 35, 45; 19:1, 10, 14, 19[2], 21; 20:1, 20, 21, 34[2], 38; 21:8[2], 13; 22:4, 11, 13, 27[2], 31[2], 40, 44, 49, 50[2]

2Ki 1:8, 9, 11, 13, 14, 15[2]; 2:1, 16; 3:4, 7, 12, 13, 17, 19, 20, 26; 4:13, 26[3]; 5:1, 3, 5, 9[2], 23, 26; 6:1, 3, 4, 8, 15, 16[2], 18[2], 22[2], 32, 33; 7:2, 19; 8:2, 4, 9, 12[2], 21, 24[2], 28; 9:13, 15, 18, 19, 24, 28; 10:2[2], 6, 13, 15, 16, 23, 25, 31, 35; 11:3, 4[2], 8[2], 9, 11, 14, 15, 20; 12:15, 21; 13:9, 13[2], 19, 23; 14:10, 15, 16[2], 20, 22, 29[2]; 15:7[2], 16, 19, 22, 25[2], 38[2]; 16:15, 20[2]; 17:15, 18, 35, 36, 38; 18:7, 17, 26, 27, 28, 31, 37; 19:1, 2, 6, 23, 24, 32, 37; 20:3, 21; 21:6, 11, 18; 22:7, 14, 17; 23:2, 3, 11, 14, 18, 24, 25[3]; 24:4, 6; 25:7, 9, 10, 11, 17, 24, 25[2], 28

1Ch 2:23[2]; 4:9, 10, 23; 5:10, 18, 19[2], 20; 6:32, 33, 57[2], 58[2], 59[2], 60[3], 64, 67[2], 68[2], 69[2], 70[2], 71[2], 72[2], 73[2], 74[2], 75[2], 76[3], 77[2], 78[2], 79[2], 80[2], 81[2]; 7:4, 23, 28; 8:12, 32; 9:20, 25, 38; 11:3, 9, 10[2], 13, 19, 23[2], 42; 12:2, 19, 27, 33, 34[2], 37, 38, 39; 13:1[2], 2, 8[7], 14; 14:1, 12; 15:15, 16[2], 18, 19, 20, 21, 24, 25, 27[2], 28[5]; 16:5[3], 6, 16, 38, 41, 42[3]; 17:2, 6, 8, 11, 20; 18:10[2], 11; 19:14, 17, 19; 20:3[4], 4, 5; 21:7, 20, 21; 22:11, 13, 15, 16, 18; 23:2, 5; 24:5; 25:1[3], 3, 6, 7, 9; 26:16; 27:32; 28:1[3], 9[2], 20, 21[2]; 29:2, 6, 8, 9[2], 17, 21, 22, 30

2Ch 1:1, 3, 14; 2:3[2], 7[2], 8, 12, 13, 14[2]; 3:4, 5[2], 6, 7, 8, 9, 10; 4:5, 9, 20; 5:10, 12[3], 13[2]; 6:4[2], 11, 14, 15[3], 16, 18, 36, 38[2], 41; 7:3, 6, 8, 18; 8:5, 18; 9:1[3], 17, 18, 21, 25, 31; 10:6, 8[2], 10, 11[2], 14[2], 18; 12:1, 3[2], 16; 13:3[2], 8, 9, 11, 12[2], 14, 17, 19[3]; 14:1, 9, 11[3], 13; 15:2[2], 6, 9[2], 12[2], 14[4], 15[2]; 16:3, 8, 10[2], 13, 14; 17:3, 8[2], 9, 14, 15, 16, 17[2], 18; 18:1, 2[2], 3[2], 10, 12, 26[2], 30[3]; 19:6, 7, 9, 11; 20:1, 13, 17[2], 18, 19, 21, 25, 27, 28, 35, 36, 37; 21:1[2], 3, 4, 7, 9[2], 14, 18; 22:1, 5, 6, 7, 9, 12; 23:1, 3, 7[2], 8, 13[2], 14, 18[2], 21; 24:21, 24; 25:2, 7[3], 13, 16, 19, 24, 28; 26:2, 13, 17, 19, 23[2]; 27:5, 9; 28:5, 9, 10[2], 15, 18[2], 27; 29:8, 10, 18[2], 24, 25[3], 26[2], 27[2], 29, 30[2], 35; 30:6, 21[2], 23, 25; 31:9, 21; 32:3, 7[3], 8[2], 9, 18, 21[2], 33; 33:6[2], 11, 20; 34:6, 25, 31[2]; 35:12, 13, 21[3], 22; 36:10, 17, 19, 23

Ezr 1:3, 4[4], 5, 6[5], 11; 2:2, 63[2]; 3:9[2], 10[2], 11, 12, 13; 4:2, 3; 5:2, 8; 6:4, 12, 16, 22; 7:13, 16, 17[2], 18, 28; 8:1, 3, 4, 5, 6, 7, 8, 9, 10, 11, 12, 13, 14, 17, 18, 19, 24, 33[2]; 9:2, 11[3], 14[2]; 10:3, 4, 12, 14, 16, 17

Neh 1:3; 2:3, 9, 12[2], 13, 17; 3:1; 4:13, 17[3], 22; 5:7; 6:5; 7:7, 65; 8:2, 6[2]; 9:1[2], 4, 6, 8, 13, 24[2]; 10:32, 38; 11:25; 12:1, 24, 27[5], 35, 36, 40, 41, 42, 43; 13:2[2], 9, 11, 17, 25

Est 1:6, 10, 11; 2:6[2], 9, 12[3], 13, 20; 3:1, 11, 12; 4:1[2], 2, 13; 5:9, 12[2], 14; 6:14; 7:1; 8:3, 8[2], 10, 15[2]; 9:5, 29, 30

Job 1:4, 15, 17; 2:7, 10, 11, 13; 3:14, 15[2]; 4:2, 18; 5:14, 23[2]; 7:5, 14; 8:21[2], 22; 9:2, 3, 14, 17, 18, 30, 35; 10:2, 11[2], 13; 12:2, 5, 12, 13, 16, 18; 13:3, 17, 19; 14:3, 5; 15:2, 3[2], 10, 11[2], 20, 27; 16:5, 8, 9, 10, 14, 16, 21; 17:2, 3[2]; 18:6; 19:2, 4, 6, 16, 20, 22, 24; 20:11, 26; 21:8, 24, 25; 22:4, 16, 18, 21; 23:4, 6, 7, 14; 24:8, 14, 22; 25:2, 4; 26:10, 12; 27:11, 13, 14; 28:14, 16[2], 19, 22; 29:5, 6; 30:1, 21, 30; 31:1, 5, 13, 18[2], 20; 32:14; 33:19[2], 23, 26, 29, 30; 34:8[2], 9, 23; 35:4; 36:4, 7, 18, 32; 37:4, 5, 18, 22; 38:8, 30, 32; 39:4, 10, 19, 24; 40:2, 9, 10[2], 15, 22, 24; 41:1[2], 2, 4, 5[2], 7[2], 13, 15, 28; 42:8, 11

Ps 2:9, 11[2]; 3:4; 4:4; 5:4, 9, 12[2]; 6:6[2]; 7:4, 11, 14; 8:5; 9:1, 6; 10:14; 12:2[3], 4; 13:6; 15:3; 17:10, 14, 15; 18:25[2], 26[2], 32, 39; 20:6; 21:3, 6; 22:13; 23:4, 5; 25:14, 19; 26:4[2], 5, 7, 9[2]; 27:7; 28:3[2], 7; 29:11; 30:11; 31:9, 10[2]; 32:7, 8, 9; 33:2[2], 3; 34:3; 35:1[2], 13, 16[2], 19, 26; 36:8, 9; 37:12, 24; 38:7; 39:1[2], 2, 3, 11, 12; 42:4[4], 8, 10; 44:1, 2, 9, 19; 45:3, 7, 12, 15; 46:3, 7, 11; 47:1, 5[2], 7; 48:7; 50:5, 18[2]; 51:7, 12, 19[2]; 54:4, ttl; 55:18, 20; 58:9; 59:7; 60:5, 10, ttl[2]; 62:4; 63:5[2]; 64:7; 65:4, 6, 9, 10, 11, 13[2]; 66:13, 15[2], 17[2]; 68:6, 13[2], 19, 25, 27, 30[2]; 69:10, 28, 30[2]; 71:8[2], 13, 22[2]; 72:2[2], 19; 73:7, 19, 23, 24; 74:6; 75:5; 77:1[2], 6, 15; 78:8, 14[2], 36[2], 37, 47[2], 58[2], 62, 71; 80:5, 10, 16; 81:2, 16[2]; 83:5, 7, 8, 15[2], 16; 85:5; 86:12; 87:4; 88:4, 7; 89:1, 3, 10, 20, 21, 24, 28, 32[2], 38, 45; 90:5, 14; 91:4, 8, 15, 16; 92:3, 10; 93:1[2]; 94:20; 95:2[2], 10; 96:13[2]; 98:5[2], 6, 9[2]; 100:2[2], 4[2]; 101:2, 6; 102:9; 103:4, 5, 10; 104:1, 2[2], 6[2], 13, 28; 105:9, 18, 25, 37, 40, 43[2]; 106:4[2], 5, 6, 29, 32, 33, 38, 39[2], 43; 107:9, 12, 22; 108:1, 6, 11; 109:2, 3, 14, 18[2], 29[3], 30; 110:6; 111:1; 112:5, 9, 10; 113:8[2]; 116:7; 118:7, 27; 119:2, 7, 10, 13, 17, 34, 58, 65, 69, 78, 93, 98, 124, 145; 120:4, 6; 123:3, 4[2]; 125:5; 126:2[2], 6[2]; 127:5; 128:2; 130:4, 7[2]; 132:9, 15, 16, 18; 136:12[2]; 138:1, 3; 139:3, 18, 21, 22; 141:4; 142:1[2], 7; 143:2; 147:7, 8, 14, 20; 149:3, 4, 8[2]; 150:3[2], 4[2]

Prv 1:11, 13, 15, 31; 2:1, 16; 3:5, 9[2], 10[2], 30, 32; 4:7, 23; 5:10, 17, 18, 19, 20, 22; 6:1, 2[2], 12, 13[3], 22, 25, 32; 7:1, 5, 10, 13, 14, 16[3], 17, 18, 20, 21[2]; 8:12, 18, 24, 30, 31; 10:4, 10, 18, 22; 11:2, 9, 10; 12:11, 14, 21; 13:10, 16, 20; 14:1, 10, 14, 18; 15:16; 16:7, 8, 19[2]; 17:1, 14; 18:1, 3, 20[2]; 19:2, 7, 23; 20:8, 13, 17, 18, 19[2]; 21:9, 19, 27; 22:24[2]; 23:1, 7, 11, 13, 14, 21; 24:1, 4, 21, 28, 31; 25:9, 24; 26:17, 23, 24; 27:14, 22; 28:4, 20, 23; 29:3, 9, 24; 30:8, 16, 19, 22, 28; 31:13, 16, 17, 21, 26

Ecc 1:8[2], 11, 16; 2:1, 3, 9; 4:6[2], 8, 15; 5:2, 10[2], 11, 17; 6:3, 4[2], 10; 7:11; 8:12, 13, 15, 16; 9:7[2], 9, 10; 11:5; 12:14

Song 1:2, 6, 10[2], 11; 2:3, 5[2], 13; 3:6[2], 10, 11; 4:8[2], 9[2], 13[2], 14[2]; 5:1[3], 2[2], 5[2], 12, 14[2]; 6:1, 4, 10; 7:1, 2; 8:9

Isa 1:4, 6, 7, 13, 20, 22, 27[2]; 3:10, 11, 14, 16[2], 17; 5:2, 13, 18[2], 26; 6:2[3], 4, 6, 10[3]; 7:2[2], 4, 20, 24[2], 25; 8:1, 10, 11; 9:5[2], 7[2], 10, 12; 10:22, 24, 33, 34; 11:4[4], 6[2], 15; 12:1, 3; 13:9; 14:1, 6, 19, 20, 21, 23, 30; 15:3, 5; 16:4, 9[2], 14; 17:5, 10; 18:1, 5; 19:23, 24[2]; 20:4; 21:3, 7[2], 9, 14; 22:2, 6, 12, 17, 21[2]; 23:17; 24:2[12], 9, 12; 25:5, 11; 26:9[2], 17, 18, 19; 27:1, 5[2], 6, 8; 28:1, 2, 11, 15[2], 18[2], 27[3], 28[2]; 29:3, 6[3], 9[2], 13[2]; 30:1, 24[2], 27, 28, 29, 30[3], 31, 32[2]; 31:8; 32:7; 33:1[2], 5, 14[2], 21; 34:3, 6[4], 7[4], 14, 15; 35:2, 4[2], 7, 10; 36:2, 12, 13, 16, 22; 37:1, 2, 9, 25, 33, 38; 38:3, 11, 12, 14; 40:9, 10[2], 11[2], 12, 14, 19, 31; 41:3, 4, 7[2], 10[2], 11, 12; 43:2, 5, 23[3], 24[4]; 44:5, 12[3], 13[3], 16; 45:9[2], 17; 47:6, 12[2], 15; 48:10, 20; 49:4[2], 18[2], 23, 25[2], 26[3]; 50:3, 8, 11; 51:11, 21; 52:8, 12; 53:3, 5, 9[2], 12[3]; 54:1, 7, 8, 9, 11[3]; 55:3, 12[2]; 56:12; 57:5, 8, 9, 15; 58:4, 14; 59:3[2], 6, 12, 17, 21; 60:7, 9; 61:8, 10[4]; 62:11; 63:1, 3, 11, 12; 64:11; 65:23; 66:10[3], 11[2], 15[4], 16

Jer 1:8, 19; 2:9[2], 22, 29, 35; 3:1, 2[3], 9[2], 10, 15, 18, 20; 4:8, 30[3]; 5:17, 18; 6:3, 11[3], 12, 26, 28; 8:8, 19[2]; 9:4, 8, 15, 18[2], 25; 10:3, 4[2], 13, 24; 11:5, 10, 15, 16, 19; 12:1[2], 5[2], 6; 13:12[2], 13, 17; 14:3, 17[3], 18[2], 21; 15:6, 7, 11, 14, 17, 20; 16:8, 18; 17:1[2], 18; 18:6, 17, 18, 19, 23; 19:4, 5, 10; 20:4, 9, 11, 17, 18; 21:2, 5[2], 7, 10; 22:7, 14[2], 15, 16, 19; 23:15; 24:1, 7; 25:6, 7, 26, 31[2]; 26:11, 14, 21, 22, 23, 24; 27:8[3], 18; 28:4; 29:13, 16, 18[3], 23; 30:6[2], 11, 14[2], 23[2]; 31:3[2], 4, 7, 8[3], 9[2], 14[2], 24, 27[2], 31[2], 32, 33; 32:4, 5, 21[5], 22, 29, 30, 40, 41[2]; 33:5[2], 21[2], 25; 34:2, 3, 5, 8, 13, 22; 36:18[2], 23; 37:8, 10, 15; 38:6, 10, 11, 13, 17, 18, 23, 25, 27; 39:3, 7, 8, 9; 40:4[2], 5, 6, 9; 41:1, 2[2], 3[2], 5, 7, 9, 11, 12, 13[2], 15, 16; 42:6, 8, 11, 17; 43:6, 12, 13; 44:8, 25[2]; 46:4, 10, 22[2], 25, 28; 47:5; 48:7, 32, 33, 39; 49:2,

3, 20; 50:5, 39, 45; 51:5, 14[2], 16, 20[2], 21[2], 22[3], 23[3], 28, 32, 34, 40, 42, 58, 59; 52:13, 14, 22, 32

Lam 1:2, 16; 2:1, 4, 10, 11; 3:5, 9, 15[2], 16[2], 30, 41, 43, 44, 48; 4:9[2], 14; 5:6, 9

Ezk 1:15; 2:6; 3:3, 4, 10, 22, 24, 25, 27; 4:12, 16[2], 17; 5:2[2], 11[2], 12[2]; 6:9[2], 11[2]; 7:15, 18, 27; 8:11, 16, 17, 18; 9:1[2], 2[2], 3, 7, 11; 10:2[2], 4, 6, 7; 11:6, 13; 12:7, 12, 18[3], 19[2]; 13:10, 11, 13, 14, 15, 22; 14:11; 16:8, 9[2], 10[4], 11, 13, 16, 17, 26, 28[2], 36[2], 37[2], 40[2], 41, 59, 60, 62; 17:3, 7, 12, 13, 16, 17, 20, 21; 18:7, 16; 19:4, 11; 20:6, 7, 15, 18, 31, 33[3], 34[3], 35, 36[2], 39[2], 40, 41, 44; 21:6[2], 21, 22, 24; 22:7, 11, 14, 28, 31; 23:6, 7[4], 8, 10, 14, 15, 16, 17[2], 23, 24[2], 25, 29, 30, 33[3], 37, 40, 42[2], 43[2], 47[3]; 24:4, 7, 12, 16, 26; 25:6[2], 10, 15, 17; 26:7[3], 8, 9, 11, 16, 20[3]; 27:7, 9, 11, 12, 14, 16, 21, 22[2], 24, 31[2], 33; 28:4[2], 16, 26; 30:5, 11[2], 24; 31:3[2], 4, 11, 14, 16, 17[2], 18[2]; 32:2[2], 3, 4, 5, 6, 7, 18, 19, 21, 24, 25[2], 27[2], 28[2], 29[3], 30[4], 32[2]; 33:25, 31; 34:3, 4[2], 16, 18[2], 19[2], 21[3], 25, 29, 30; 35:8[2], 13; 36:5[2], 37, 38; 37:6, 19[2], 23[3], 26[2], 27; 38:4[2], 5[2], 6, 9, 13, 15, 22[3]; 39:4, 9, 10, 14, 20[3]; 40:3, 4[2]; 41:13, 15, 16, 18; 42:16[2], 17, 18, 19; 43:2, 22; 44:5[3], 17, 18, 19; 45:2; 46:14, 23; 47:22; 48:20, 34

Dan 1:2, 8[2], 9, 13, 19; 2:5, 11, 14, 18, 22, 41, 43[3]; 4:15[3], 23[3], 25[2], 32, 33; 5:7, 16, 21[3], 29; 6:14, 17[2], 20; 7:7, 13, 19, 21; 8:7, 18; 9:3, 15, 22, 26, 27; 10:5, 7, 13, 17, 20, 21; 11:3, 7, 8[2], 11[3], 13[2], 17[2], 22, 23[2], 25[2], 28, 30, 34[2], 38[2], 39[2], 40[3], 44

Hos 2:2, 3, 6, 7, 13, 18[3]; 4:1, 3[2], 4, 5, 14[2], 18; 5:5, 6[2], 7; 6:8; 7:3[2], 5[2], 14; 9:8; 11:4[2], 12[4]; 12:1, 2, 3, 4; 13:3, 16; 14:2, 8

Joel 1:8; 2:12[4], 20, 24, 26; 3:2, 4, 18[2]

Am 1:3, 11, 13, 14[2]; 2:2[3], 3; 3:15; 4:2[2], 5, 9, 10; 5:8, 14; 6:6, 7, 8, 10, 11[2], 12; 7:7, 9; 8:3; 9:1

Oba 7

Jna 1:3; 2:6, 9; 3:6, 8

Mic 1:7; 2:4, 8, 10; 3:5, 10[2]; 5:1, 6; 6:2[2], 6[2], 7[2], 8, 11[2], 15; 7:2, 3, 14

Nah 1:8; 2:3, 7, 12[2]; 3:12

Hab 1:15; 2:6, 12, 14, 16, 19; 3:9, 13, 14, 15, 16

Zep 1:3, 4, 8, 9, 12; 3:8, 9, 14, 17[2]

Hag 1:6[2], 12, 13; 2:4, 5, 7, 12, 17[3]

Zec 1:2, 6, 9, 13[2], 14[2], 15, 16, 19; 2:1, 3, 7; 3:3, 4, 5; 4:1, 2, 4, 5, 7, 10; 5:4, 5, 10; 6:4; 7:14; 8:2[2], 4, 23[2]; 9:4, 8, 13, 14, 15; 10:5, 9, 11; 11:10; 12:3, 4[3]; 13:6; 14:5

Mal 1:8; 2:3, 4, 5, 6, 13[4], 16, 17; 3:9; 4:2, 4, 6

Mt 1:18, 23[2]; 2:3, 10, 11; 3:11[3], 12; 4:21, 24[2]; 5:22, 25[2], 28, 41; 7:2[2]; 8:11, 16[2], 24, 28, 29; 9:10, 11, 15, 20, 32, 36; 11:7; 12:3, 4, 22, 30[2], 41, 42, 45, 46, 47; 13:15[3], 20, 29, 56; 14:7, 9, 14, 24; 15:8[2], 20, 22, 30, 32; 16:1, 27; 17:3, 17; 18:9, 16, 26, 27, 29; 19:10, 26[2]; 20:2, 13, 15, 20, 22[2], 23[2], 24; 21:2, 25; 22:10, 16, 25, 37[3]; 23:4, 30; 24:19, 30, 31, 49, 51; 25:3, 4, 10, 16, 19, 27, 31; 26:11, 15, 18, 20, 23, 29, 35, 36, 37, 38, 40, 47[2], 51, 52, 55[2], 58, 67, 69, 71, 72; 27:7, 19, 22, 34, 38, 41, 44, 46, 48, 50, 54; 28:8, 12, 20

Mk 1:6[2], 8[2], 13, 20, 23, 24, 26, 27, 29, 32, 36, 41; 2:15, 16[2], 19[2], 25, 26; 3:5, 6, 7, 14; 4:10, 16, 24, 30, 33, 36; 5:2, 3, 4, 5, 7[2], 15, 16, 18[2], 24, 40, 42; 6:3, 9, 13, 22, 25, 26, 34, 50; 7:2[2], 5, 6; 8:2, 4, 10, 11, 14, 34, 38; 9:1, 2, 4[2], 8, 10[2], 14, 16, 18, 19, 24, 47, 49[2], 50; 10:27[3], 30, 38[2], 39, 41, 46; 11:11, 31; 12:30[4], 33[4]; 13:17, 26; 14:7, 14, 17, 18, 20, 31, 33, 43[2], 48[2], 49, 53, 54, 58, 65, 67; 15:1, 7[2], 17, 19, 23, 27, 28, 31, 32, 34, 37, 41; 16:10, 14, 17, 20[2]

Lk 1:15, 25, 28, 30, 36, 37, 39, 41, 42, 51, 53, 56, 58, 66, 67; 2:5[2], 13, 16, 36, 37, 40, 48, 51, 52; 3:14, 16[3], 17; 4:28, 32, 33, 34, 36, 38, 40; 5:9, 10, 18, 19, 26, 29, 30, 34, 36; 6:3, 4, 11[2], 17, 18, 38; 7:6, 11, 12, 24, 29, 36, 38[3], 44[2], 46[2], 49; 8:1, 7, 13, 14, 15, 16, 22, 23, 28[2], 29, 37, 38, 45; 9:18, 30, 32[3], 41, 49; 10:17, 27[4]; 11:7, 20, 23[2], 31, 32, 37, 46[2]; 12:13, 25, 46, 47, 48, 50, 58; 13:1, 14; 14:9, 10, 15, 18, 25, 31[2]; 15:2, 6, 9, 13, 16, 17, 29, 30, 31; 16:21; 17:15, 20; 18:7, 11, 27[2]; 19:7, 23, 37, 44; 20:1, 5; 21:5, 20, 23, 25, 27, 34; 22:4, 11, 14, 15[2], 21, 28, 33, 48, 49, 52, 53, 56, 59; 23:9, 11, 18, 23, 32, 35, 43, 46, 55; 24:1, 10, 15, 24, 29[2], 30, 32, 33, 44, 49, 52

Jn 1:1, 2, 26, 31, 33[2], 39; 2:4, 7; 3:2, 22, 26; 4:6, 9, 11, 27[2], 40; 5:18; 6:3, 13, 22, 66; 7:33; 8:6, 29, 38[2]; 9:6, 37, 40; 11:2[2], 16, 31, 33, 43, 44[2], 54; 12:2, 3[2], 8, 17, 35, 40[2]; 13:5, 8, 18, 33; 14:9, 16, 17, 23, 25, 27, 30; 15:27; 16:4, 32; 17:5[3], 12, 24; 18:1, 2, 3, 5, 15, 18, 22, 26; 19:3, 15[2], 18, 29, 32, 34, 40; 20:7, 24, 26; 21:3, 8

Act 1:4, 5[2], 14[3], 17, 18, 21, 22, 26; 2:1, 4[2], 14, 28, 29, 30, 40, 46[2], 47; 3:4, 8, 10, 25; 4:8, 13, 14, 24, 27, 29, 31[2], 33; 5:1, 12, 16, 17[2], 21, 23, 26, 28, 31; 6:9; 7:9[2], 19, 38[2], 45, 48, 54, 57[2], 60; 8:6, 7[3], 11, 13, 20[2], 31, 37; 9:7, 17, 19, 28, 39[2], 43; 10:2, 6, 20, 23, 27, 35, 38[3], 41, 45, 46; 11:2, 3, 12, 16[2], 21, 23, 26; 12:2, 6, 17, 20[2], 25; 13:1, 7, 9, 16, 17, 31, 45, 52[2]; 14:4[2], 5, 10, 13, 15, 17, 18, 20, 23, 27, 28; 15:2, 4, 22[2], 24, 25[2], 32, 35, 37, 38[2]; 16:3, 11, 16, 28, 34; 17:2, 4, 5, 11, 15, 17[4], 23, 24, 25, 34; 18:2, 3, 8, 10, 12, 14, 18, 19, 20; 19:4, 6, 25, 26, 29[2], 33, 34, 38; 20:9, 14, 18, 19[2], 24, 28, 31, 34, 36; 21:1, 5, 7, 8, 16[3], 18, 24[2], 26, 29, 33, 36, 40; 22:9, 11, 22, 25, 28; 23:15, 19, 21, 27, 32; 24:1[2], 3, 7, 12, 18[2], 24, 26; 25:5, 12, 23[2], 24[2]; 26:8, 9, 12, 13, 24, 30; 27:2, 10, 18, 19, 24, 39, 41; 28:10[2], 14, 16, 20[2], 27[3], 31

Ro 1:4, 9, 12, 27, 29; 2:11; 3:13; 5:1; 6:4, 6, 8[2]; 7:18, 21, 25[2]; 8:16, 17[2], 18, 25, 26, 32; 9:14, 22; 10:9, 10[2]; 11:17; 12:8[3], 10, 15[2], 18, 21; 14:15[2], 20; 15:6, 10, 13, 14, 24, 30, 32[2], 33; 16:14, 15, 16, 20, 24

1Co 1:2, 17; 2:1, 3, 4, 13; 3:2[2], 9, 19; 4:3, 8, 12, 21; 5:4, 8[3], 9, 10[3], 11; 6:6, 7, 9, 20; 7:5, 12, 13, 23, 24; 8:7; 9:13, 23; 10:5, 13, 20; 11:5, 32; 12:26[2], 30; 13:1; 14:5[2], 6, 15[4], 16, 18, 19, 21, 23, 39; 15:10, 32, 35; 16:4, 6, 7, 10, 11, 12, 14, 16, 19, 20, 21, 23, 24

2Co 1:1, 12, 17, 21; 2:1, 4, 7; 3:3[2], 18; 4:14; 5:1, 2, 8; 6:1, 14[3], 15[2], 16; 7:3, 4, 8, 15; 8:4, 18, 19[2], 22; 9:4; 10:2, 12; 11:1[2], 2, 4, 9, 25, 32; 12:16, 18; 13:4, 11, 12, 14

Gal 1:2, 16, 18; 2:1[2], 3, 5, 12, 13[2], 20; 3:9; 4:18, 20, 25, 30; 5:1, 24; 6:11, 18

Eph 1:3, 13; 2:5, 19; 3:12, 16, 18, 19; 4:2[2], 14, 19, 25, 28, 31; 5:6, 7, 11, 18[2], 26; 6:2, 3, 5, 6, 7, 9, 14, 15, 18[2], 23, 24

Php 1:1, 4, 11, 20, 23, 25, 27; 2:6, 12, 17, 18, 22[2], 23, 29; 4:3[3], 6, 9, 14, 15, 21, 23

Col 1:9, 11[2]; 2:4, 5, 7, 11, 12[2], 13, 19, 20, 22; 3:1, 3, 4, 9, 16, 22; 4:2, 6[2], 9, 18

1Th 1:6; 2:2, 4, 17; 3:4, 13; 4:11, 14, 16[3], 17[2], 18; 5:3, 10, 26, 28

2Th 1:6, 7[2], 9, 11; 2:5, 8[2], 9, 10; 3:1, 8, 10, 12, 14, 16, 17, 18

1Ti 1:10, 14; 2:9[2], 10, 11, 15; 3:4, 6; 4:2, 3, 4, 14; 5:2; 6:6, 10, 21

2Ti 1:3, 4, 9; 2:4, 10, 11[2], 12, 22; 3:6[2]; 4:2, 11[2], 13[2], 16, 17, 22[2]

Tit 2:15; 3:15[2]

Phlm 13, 19, 25

Heb 1:9; 2:4[2], 7, 9; 3:10, 17[2]; 4:2, 13, 15; 5:2, 7; 7:21; 8:8[3], 9, 10; 9:4, 11, 19, 21, 22, 23[2], 24, 25; 10:1, 16, 22[2]; 11:7, 9[2], 25, 31[2], 37; 12:1[2], 7[2], 14, 17, 18, 20, 28; 13:3, 5, 9[3], 12, 16, 17[2], 23, 25

Jas 1:6, 11, 13, 17, 18, 21; 2:1, 2, 22; 3:4, 13[2]; 4:4; 5:14

1Pt 1:7, 8, 12, 18, 19, 22; 2:15, 18, 20; 3:2, 6, 7, 15; 4:1, 4, 13; 5:5, 13, 14[2]

2Pt 1:1, 18; 2:3, 6, 7, 8, 13[2], 14, 16, 17, 20; 3:6, 8, 10[2], 12, 17

1Jn 1:1, 2, 3[3], 6, 7; 2:1, 19

2Jn 2, 3, 12

3Jn 10, 13

Jude 9, 12, 14, 23, 24

Rev 1:7, 12, 13[2]; 2:12, 16, 22, 23, 27; 3:4, 17, 18, 20[2], 21[2]; 4:1; 5:1, 2, 12; 6:8[5], 10; 7:2, 9, 10; 8:3, 4, 5, 7, 8, 13; 9:19; 10:1, 3; 11:6; 12:1, 2, 5, 9, 17[2]; 13:4, 7, 10[2]; 14:1, 2, 4, 7, 9, 10, 15, 18; 15:2, 6, 8; 16:8, 9; 17:1, 2[2], 4, 6[3], 12, 14[2], 16; 18:1, 2, 3, 8, 9, 16, 21; 19:2, 13, 15[2], 17, 20[3], 21[2]; 20:4, 6; 21:3[3], 8, 9, 15, 16, 19; 22:12, 21

WITHOUT

Gen 1:2; 6:14; 9:22; 19:16; 24:11, 31; 37:33; 41:44, 49

Ex 12:5; 21:11; 25:11; 26:35; 27:21; 29:1, 14; 33:7[2]; 37:2; 40:22

Lev 1:3, 10; 3:1, 6; 4:3, 12, 21, 23, 28, 32; 5:15, 18; 6:6, 11; 8:17; 9:2, 3, 11; 10:12; 13:46, 55; 14:10[2], 40, 41; 16:27; 22:19; 23:12, 18; 24:3, 14; 26:43

Nu 5:3, 4; 6:14[3]; 15:24, 35, 36; 19:2, 3, 9; 20:19; 28:3, 9, 11, 19, 31; 29:2, 8, 13, 17, 20, 23, 26, 29, 32, 36; 31:13, 19; 35:5, 22[2], 26, 27

Dt 8:9; 23:12; 25:5; 32:4, 25

Jos 3:10; 6:23

Jdg 2:23; 6:5; 7:12; 11:30

Ru 4:14

1Sa 19:5; 30:8

2Sa 23:4

1Ki 6:6, 29, 30; 7:9; 8:8; 22:1

2Ki 10:24; 11:15; 16:18; 18:25; 23:4, 6; 25:16

1Ch 2:30, 32; 21:24; 22:3, 14

2Ch 5:9; 12:3; 15:3[3]; 21:20; 24:8; 32:3, 5; 33:14

Ezr 6:9; 7:22; 10:13

Neh 13:20

Job 2:3; 4:20, 21; 5:9; 6:6; 7:6; 8:11[2]; 9:10, 17; 10:22; 11:15; 12:25; 24:7, 10; 26:2; 30:28; 31:19, 39; 33:9; 34:6, 20, 24, 35[2]; 35:16; 36:12; 38:2; 39:16; 41:33; 42:3

Ps 7:4; 25:3; 31:11; 35:7[2], 19; 59:4; 69:4; 105:34; 109:3; 119:78, 161

Prv 1:11, 20; 3:30; 5:23; 6:15; 7:12; 11:22; 15:22; 16:8; 19:2; 22:13; 23:29; 24:27, 28; 25:14, 28; 29:1

Ecc 10:11

Song 6:8; 8:1

Isa 5:9, 14; 6:11[2]; 10:4; 33:7; 36:10; 45:17; 52:3, 4; 55:1[2]

Jer 2:15, 32; 4:7, 23; 5:21; 9:11, 21; 15:13; 21:4; 22:13; 26:9; 32:43; 33:10[5], 12[2]; 34:22; 44:19, 22; 46:19; 48:9; 49:31; 51:29, 37; 52:20

Lam 1:6; 3:49, 52

Ezk 2:10; 7:15; 14:23; 17:9; 33:15; 38:11; 40:19, 40, 44; 41:9, 17[2], 25; 42:7; 43:21, 22, 23[2], 25; 45:18, 23; 46:2, 4[2], 6[2], 13; 47:2

Dan 2:34, 45; 8:25; 11:18

Hos 3:4[6]; 7:1, 11

Joel 1:6

Zec 2:4

Mt 5:22; 10:29; 12:46, 47; 13:34, 57; 15:16; 26:69

Mk 1:45; 3:31, 32; 4:11, 34; 6:4; 7:15, 18[2]; 11:4; 14:58

Lk 1:10, 74; 6:49; 8:20; 11:40; 13:25; 20:28, 29; 22:35

Jn 1:3; 8:7; 15:5, 25; 18:16; 19:23; 20:11

Act 5:23, 26; 9:9; 10:29; 12:5; 14:17; 25:17

Ro 1:9, 20, 31[2]; 2:12[2]; 3:3, 21, 28; 4:6; 5:6; 7:8, 9; 10:14; 11:29; 12:9

1Co 4:8; 5:12, 13; 6:18; 7:32, 35; 9:18, 21[4]; 11:11[2]; 14:7, 10; 16:10

2Co 7:5; 10:13, 15; 11:28

Eph 1:4; 2:12[2]; 3:21; 5:27

Php 1:10, 14; 2:14, 15

Col 2:11; 4:5

1Th 1:3; 2:13; 4:12; 5:17

1Ti 2:8; 3:7, 16; 5:21; 6:14

2Ti 1:3; 3:3

Phlm 14

Heb 4:15; 7:3[3], 7, 20, 21; 9:7, 14, 18, 22, 28; 10:23, 28; 11:6, 40; 12:8, 14; 13:5, 11, 12, 13

Jas 2:13, 18, 20, 26[2]; 3:17[2]

1Pt 1:17, 19[2]; 3:1; 4:9

2Pt 2:17; 3:14

Jude 12[3]

Rev 11:2; 14:5, 10, 20; 22:15

WOULD

Gen 2:19; 21:7; 30:34; 42:21, 22; 43:7; 44:22

Ex 2:4; 8:32; 9:35; 10:20, 27; 11:10; 13:15; 16:3

Nu 11:29[2]; 14:2[2]; 20:3; 21:23; 22:18, 29[2]; 24:13

Dt 1:26, 43, 45; 2:30; 3:26; 5:29; 7:8; 8:20; 9:25; 10:10; 23:5, 21; 28:56, 67[2]; 32:26[2], 29

Jos 5:6[2]; 7:7; 17:12; 24:10

Jdg 1:27, 34, 35; 2:17; 3:4; 8:19, 24[2]; 9:29[2]; 11:17[2]; 13:23[3]; 14:6; 15:1; 19:10, 25; 20:13

Ru 1:13[2]

1Sa 2:16, 25; 13:13; 15:9; 18:2; 20:9; 22:17, 22; 26:23; 31:4

2Sa 2:21; 4:6, 10; 6:10; 11:20; 12:8, 17, 18; 13:14, 16, 25; 14:16, 29[2]; 15:4; 18:11, 12, 33; 23:15, 16, 17

1Ki 8:12; 13:33; 18:32; 20:33; 21:4; 22:18, 49

2Ki 2:1; 3:14; 5:3[2]; 7:2; 8:19; 13:23; 14:11, 27; 17:14; 18:12; 24:4

1Ch 10:4; 11:17, 18, 19; 13:4; 19:19; 27:23

2Ch 6:1; 10:16; 12:12; 15:13; 18:17; 21:7; 24:19; 25:20; 33:10; 35:22

Ezr 10:8, 19

Neh 6:11, 14; 9:24, 29, 30; 10:30, 31[2]

Est 3:4; 6:6; 8:11; 9:5, 27

Job 5:8[2]; 6:3, 8, 9[2], 10; 7:16; 8:6; 9:15[2], 16, 21[2], 35; 11:5, 6, 12; 13:3, 5; 16:5; 23:4, 5[3], 6; 27:22; 30:1; 31:12, 35[2], 36, 37[2]; 32:22; 34:27; 36:16; 41:32

Ps 22:8; 35:25; 40:5; 50:12; 51:16; 55:6, 7, 8, 12; 56:1, 2; 57:3; 69:4; 81:11[2]; 106:23; 107:8, 15, 21, 31; 119:57; 142:4

Prv 1:25, 30

Song 3:4; 8:1, 2[3], 7[2]

Isa 27:4[3]; 28:12; 30:15; 42:24; 54:9

Jer 8:18; 10:7; 13:11; 18:10; 22:24; 29:19; 36:25[2]; 38:26; 49:9; 51:9

Lam 4:12

Ezk 3:6; 6:10; 13:6; 20:8, 13, 15, 21, 23; 38:17

Dan 1:8; 2:8, 16[2], 18; 5:19[4]; 7:19; 9:2

Hos 7:1; 11:7

Oba 5[2]

Jna 3:10; 4:5

Zec 7:13[2]

Mal 1:10

Mt 2:18; 5:42; 7:12; 8:34; 11:21, 23; 12:7, 38; 14:5, 7; 16:1; 18:23, 30; 22:3; 23:30, 37[2]; 24:43[3]; 27:15, 34

Mk 3:2, 13; 5:10; 6:19, 26, 48; 7:24, 26; 9:30; 10:35, 36; 11:16

Lk 1:62, 74; 5:3; 6:7, 31; 7:3, 36, 39; 8:31, 32, 41; 9:53; 10:1, 2; 12:39[2]; 13:34[2]; 15:16, 28; 16:26[2]; 18:4, 13, 15; 19:27, 40; 22:49; 24:28

Jn 1:43; 4:10, 40, 47; 5:46; 6:6, 11, 15; 7:1, 44; 8:39, 42; 9:27; 12:21; 14:2, 28; 15:19; 18:30, 36

Act 2:30; 5:24; 7:5, 25[2], 26, 39; 8:31; 9:38; 10:10; 11:23; 12:6; 14:13; 16:3, 27; 17:20; 18:14; 19:30, 31, 33; 20:16; 21:14; 22:30; 23:12, 15, 20, 28; 24:6; 25:3, 4, 20, 22; 26:5, 29; 27:30; 28:18

Ro 1:13; 5:7; 7:15, 16, 19[2], 20, 21; 11:25; 16:19

1Co 2:8; 4:8, 18; 7:7, 32; 10:1, 20; 11:3, 31; 12:1; 14:5

2Co 1:8; 2:1, 8; 5:4; 8:4, 6; 9:5; 10:9; 11:1; 12:6, 20[2]

Gal 1:7; 2:10; 3:2, 8; 4:15, 17; 5:12, 17

Eph 3:16

Php 1:12

Col 1:27; 2:1; 4:3

1Th 2:9, 12, 18; 4:1, 13

2Th 1:11; 3:10

Phlm 13, 14

Heb 4:8; 10:2; 11:32; 12:17

1Jn 2:19

2Jn 12

3Jn 10

Rev 3:15; 13:15

WOULDEST

Gen 30:15; 31:30, 31

Ex 7:16; 23:5

Dt 8:2; 21:11; 28:62

Jos 15:18

2Sa 14:11; 18:13

1Ki 1:16; 18:9

2Ki 4:13; 5:13; 6:22

1Ch 4:10[2]

2Ch 6:20; 20:10

Ezr 9:14

Neh 2:5

Job 8:5; 14:13[3]

Isa 48:8; 64:1[2]

Lk 16:27

Jn 4:10; 11:40; 21:18[2]

Act 23:20; 24:4

Heb 10:5, 8

YE

Gen 3:1, 3[3], 4, 5[2]; 4:23; 9:4, 7; 17:10, 11; 18:5[3]; 19:2, 8; 22:5; 24:49; 26:27[2]; 29:4, 5, 7; 31:6; 32:4, 19[2], 20; 34:9, 10[2], 11, 12, 15, 17, 30; 40:7; 42:1, 7, 9[2], 12, 14, 15[2], 16[2], 19[2], 20, 22, 33, 34[3], 36[2], 38[2]; 43:3, 5, 6[2], 7, 27, 29; 44:4, 5, 10, 15[2], 19, 23, 27, 29[2]; 45:4, 5, 9, 13[3], 17, 18, 19, 24; 46:34[2]; 47:23, 24; 49:2; 50:17, 20, 21, 25

Ex 1:16[2], 18, 22[2]; 2:18, 20; 3:12, 18, 21[2], 22[2]; 4:15; 5:4, 5, 7, 8[2], 11[2], 14, 17[3], 18, 19, 21; 6:7; 8:25, 28[2]; 9:28, 30; 10:2, 11[2], 24; 11:7; 12:3, 5, 6, 10[2], 11[2], 13, 14[2], 15[2], 17[2], 18, 20[2], 22, 24, 25[2], 26, 27, 31[2], 32, 46; 13:3, 4, 19; 14:2, 13[3], 14; 15:21; 16:3, 6, 7[2], 8, 12[3], 16, 23[2], 25, 26, 28, 29; 17:2[2]; 19:4, 5[2], 6, 12; 20:20, 22, 23[2]; 22:21, 22, 31[3]; 23:9[2], 25; 24:1, 14; 25:2, 3, 9, 19; 30:9[2], 32, 37; 31:13[2], 14; 32:30; 33:5; 34:13; 35:1, 3, 5

Lev 1:2; 2:11[2], 12; 3:17; 7:23, 24, 26, 32; 8:32, 33, 35[2]; 9:3, 6; 10:6, 7[2], 9[2], 10, 11, 13, 14, 17, 18; 11:2, 3, 4, 8[2], 9[2], 11[2], 13, 21, 22, 24, 33, 39, 42, 43[3], 44[3], 45; 14:34; 15:31; 16:29, 30, 31; 17:14; 18:3[4], 4, 5, 24, 26, 28, 30[3]; 19:2, 3, 4, 5[2], 6, 9, 11, 12, 15, 19, 23[2], 25, 26[2], 27, 28, 30, 33, 34, 35, 36, 37; 20:7, 8, 15, 22, 23, 24, 25[2], 26[2]; 22:19, 20, 22, 24[2], 25, 28, 29, 30, 31, 32; 23:2, 3, 4, 6, 7[2], 8[2], 10[2], 12[2], 14[2], 15[2], 16[2], 17, 18, 19, 21[2], 22, 24, 25[2], 27, 28, 31, 32[2], 35, 36[3], 37, 38, 39[2], 40[2], 41[2], 42; 24:22; 25:2, 9, 10[3], 11, 12, 13, 14, 17, 18[2], 19, 20, 22[2], 23, 24, 44, 45, 46[2]; 26:1[2], 2, 3, 5, 6, 7, 10, 12, 13, 14, 15[3], 16, 17[2], 18, 21, 23, 25[2], 26, 27, 29[2], 34, 35, 37, 38

Nu 1:2; 4:18, 27, 32; 5:3[2]; 6:23; 9:3[2], 14; 10:5, 6, 7[2], 9[4], 10; 11:18[3], 19, 20; 12:4, 8; 13:2, 20; 14:9[2], 28, 30, 31[2], 34[3], 41, 42, 43[2]; 15:2, 12[2], 14, 15, 18, 19[2], 20[3], 21, 22, 29, 39[3], 40; 16:3[2], 7[2], 8, 10, 11, 17, 26, 28, 30, 41; 18:3, 5, 7, 26[2], 28[3], 29, 30, 31[2], 32[4]; 19:3; 20:4, 5, 8, 10, 12[2], 24; 21:5, 17; 22:19; 25:5; 27:8, 9, 10, 11, 14; 28:2, 3, 11, 18, 19, 20, 23, 24, 25[2], 26[3], 27, 31; 29:1[2], 2, 7[3], 8, 12[3], 13, 17, 35[2], 36, 39; 31:4, 15, 19, 23[2], 24[3]; 32:6, 7, 14, 15[2], 20[2], 22, 23[2], 29; 33:51, 52, 53, 54[4], 55[3]; 34:2, 6, 7, 8, 10, 13, 18; 35:2, 4, 5, 6[3], 7[2], 8[3], 10, 11, 13[2], 14[2], 31, 32, 33[2], 34

Dt 1:6, 10, 11, 14, 17[3], 18, 19, 20, 22, 26, 27, 31[2], 32, 33, 39, 41[3], 42, 43, 45, 46[2]; 2:3, 4[2], 6[4], 24; 3:18, 19, 20, 22; 4:1, 2[3], 4, 5[2], 11, 12[2], 14[2], 15[2], 16, 20, 22, 23, 25, 26[3], 27, 28; 5:1, 5, 23[2], 24, 28, 32[2], 33[4]; 6:1[2], 3, 14, 16[2], 17; 7:5[2], 7[2], 12, 25; 8:1[2], 19, 20[2]; 9:7[2], 8, 16[2], 18, 21, 22, 23[2], 24; 10:19[2]; 11:2, 5, 8[3], 9, 10, 11, 13, 16, 17, 18, 19, 22, 23, 25, 27, 28[2], 31[2], 32; 12:1[2], 2[2], 3[2], 4, 5, 6, 7[4], 8, 9, 10[2], 11[2], 12[2], 16[2]; 13:3, 4[2], 13; 14:1[2], 4, 6, 7, 8, 9[2], 10, 11, 12, 20, 21; 17:16; 18:15; 19:19; 20:2, 3[2], 18; 22:24[2]; 23:4; 24:8, 9; 25:17; 27:2, 4[2], 12; 28:62[2], 63, 68; 29:2, 6[3], 7, 9[2], 10, 16[2], 17; 30:18[2]; 31:5, 13[2], 19, 27, 29[2]; 32:1, 3, 6, 43, 46, 47[2], 51[2]

Jos 1:11, 14, 15; 2:5, 10[3], 12, 13, 14, 16; 3:3[2], 4[3], 8[2], 10; 4:3[3], 5, 6, 7, 17, 22, 23, 24; 6:3[2], 4, 5, 10[2], 18[3], 22; 7:12, 13, 14; 8:2, 4[2], 7, 8[3]; 9:6, 7, 8[2], 11, 22[2], 23; 10:19, 25; 18:3, 6; 22:2, 3, 4, 16[3], 18[2], 19, 24, 25[2], 27, 31[2]; 23:3, 5, 6[2], 7, 8, 11, 12, 13, 14, 16[2]; 24:6, 7, 8, 11, 13[5], 14, 15[2], 19, 20, 22[2], 27

Jdg 2:2[4]; 5:2, 3[2], 9, 10[2], 23[2]; 6:10[2], 31[2]; 7:17, 18; 8:15, 18, 19, 24; 9:7, 15, 16[3], 18, 19[2], 48; 10:12, 13, 14; 11:7[3], 9, 26; 12:2, 3[2], 4; 14:12, 13[2], 15, 18[2]; 15:7, 10, 12; 18:6, 8, 9, 10[2], 14[2], 18, 24[3]; 19:24; 20:7; 21:11[2], 21, 22[2]

Ru 1:8, 9, 11, 13[2], 21; 4:2, 9, 10

1Sa 2:23, 24, 29; 4:9[2]; 6:3[2], 5[2], 6, 8, 21; 7:3; 8:17, 18[2], 22; 9:13[3], 19; 10:14, 19[2], 24; 11:9[2], 10; 12:1, 5, 11, 12[2], 13[2], 14[2], 15, 17[2], 20, 21[2], 25[3]; 14:33, 38, 40; 15:6, 32; 17:8[2], 9, 25; 18:25; 21:14[2], 15; 22:7, 13; 23:21[2], 23; 25:6, 13; 26:16[2]; 27:10; 29:10; 30:23

2Sa 1:21, 24; 2:5[2], 6, 7; 3:17, 38; 7:7; 11:15[2], 20[3], 21; 13:28; 15:10[2], 36[2]; 16:10; 19:10, 11, 12[3], 13, 22[2], 42, 43[2]; 21:3, 4; 24:2

1Ki 1:34, 35, 45; 9:6[2]; 11:2; 12:6, 9, 24; 18:18, 21, 24, 25; 20:28, 33; 22:3

2Ki 1:3, 5; 2:3, 5, 16; 3:17[4], 19; 6:2, 11, 19, 32; 7:1; 9:11; 10:6[3], 8, 9, 13; 11:5, 6, 8[2]; 12:7; 17:12, 13, 27, 35, 36[3], 37[2], 38[2], 39; 18:19, 22[2], 31[2], 32; 19:6, 10, 29[2]; 22:13, 18

1Ch 12:17[2]; 15:12[3], 13; 16:9, 10, 13[2], 15, 19, 28, 35; 17:6; 22:19; 28:8

2Ch 7:19; 10:6, 9; 11:4; 12:5; 13:5, 8[2], 9, 11, 12[2]; 15:2[4], 7; 18:14, 25, 27, 30; 19:6[2], 9, 10[2]; 20:15[2], 16[2], 17[2], 20[3]; 23:4, 7; 24:5, 20[3]; 28:9, 10, 11, 13[2]; 29:5, 8, 11, 31; 30:6, 7[2], 8, 9[2]; 32:10[2], 12, 13; 34:23, 26

Ezr 4:2, 3, 18, 21, 22; 6:6, 8; 7:25; 8:28, 29[2]; 9:11, 12; 10:10

Neh 1:8, 9; 2:17, 19[2], 20; 4:12, 14, 20[2]; 5:7, 8, 9[2], 11; 8:10, 11; 13:17, 18, 21[2], 25

Est 4:16; 8:8

Job 6:21[2], 26, 27[2]; 12:2; 13:2, 4[2], 5, 7, 8[2], 9, 10; 16:2, 4; 17:10; 18:2; 19:2, 3[3], 5, 21, 22, 28, 29[2]; 21:27, 28, 29[2], 34; 27:12[2]; 32:6, 11, 13; 34:2[2], 10, 18; 42:7, 8

Ps 2:10[2], 12; 4:2[3]; 6:8; 11:1; 14:6; 22:23[3]; 24:7[3], 9[2]; 27:8; 29:1; 30:4; 31:23, 24; 32:9, 11[2]; 33:1; 34:9, 11; 47:1, 7; 48:13[2]; 49:1[2]; 50:22; 58:1[3], 2[2]; 62:3[3], 8; 66:1, 8, 16; 68:13[2], 16[2], 26, 32, 34; 82:2, 6, 7; 90:3; 94:8[3]; 95:7; 96:7; 97:7, 10, 12; 99:5; 100:1, 3; 103:20, 21[3]; 104:35; 105:2, 3, 6[2], 45; 106:1, 48; 111:1; 112:1; 113:1[2], 9; 114:6[3]; 115:11, 15; 116:19; 117:1[2], 2; 119:115; 134:1[2]; 135:1[3], 2, 20, 21; 139:19; 146:1, 10; 147:1, 20; 148:1[2], 2[2], 3[2], 4[2], 7, 14; 149:1, 9; 150:1, 6

Prv 1:22[2], 24, 25; 4:1, 2; 5:7; 7:24; 8:5[3], 32

Song 1:5; 2:7[2]; 3:3, 5[2], 11; 5:8[2]; 6:13; 8:4

Isa 1:5[2], 10[2], 12, 15[2], 19[2], 20[2], 29[3], 30; 2:3, 5, 22; 3:10, 14, 15[2]; 6:9[2]; 7:9[2], 13[2]; 8:9[5], 12[2]; 10:3[3]; 12:3, 4; 13:2, 6; 16:1, 7; 18:2, 3[3]; 19:11; 21:5, 12[2], 13[2]; 22:9[2], 10[2], 11[2], 14; 23:1, 2, 6[2], 14; 24:15; 26:2, 4, 19; 27:2, 12[2]; 28:12, 14, 15, 18, 22, 23; 29:1, 9; 30:12, 15[2], 16[2], 17[2], 21[3], 22, 29; 31:6; 32:9[2], 10[2], 11[2], 20; 33:11[2], 13[2]; 34:1[2], 16; 35:3; 36:4, 7, 13, 16[2]; 37:6, 10, 30[2]; 40:1[2], 2, 3, 18[2], 21[3], 25; 41:14, 23, 24; 42:10, 17, 18[3]; 43:10[2], 12, 18, 19; 44:8[2], 23[3], 26; 45:8, 11, 17, 19, 20, 21, 22; 46:5, 8, 12; 48:1, 6, 14, 16[2], 20[4]; 49:1; 50:1, 11[4]; 51:1[4], 7[3]; 52:3[2], 9, 11[5], 12; 55:1[2], 2[2], 6[2], 12; 56:1, 9[2], 12; 57:3, 4[3], 14[2]; 58:3, 4[3], 6; 61:6[3], 7; 62:6, 10, 11; 65:11, 12[3], 13[3], 14, 15, 18; 66:1, 5, 10[3], 11[2], 12[2], 13, 14

Jer 2:4, 7[2], 12[2], 29[2], 31; 3:13, 16, 20, 22; 4:4, 5[2], 10, 16; 5:1[2], 10, 14, 19[3], 22[2], 31; 6:1, 4, 6, 16[2], 18; 7:2, 4, 5[2], 6, 8, 9[2], 12, 13[3], 14, 23[2]; 8:8; 9:4[2], 17, 20; 10:1, 11; 11:2, 4, 6, 13; 12:9; 13:15, 16, 17, 23; 14:13[2]; 16:12[2], 13[3]; 17:4, 20[2], 22[2], 24, 27; 18:6, 11, 13; 19:3; 20:13; 21:3, 4, 11; 22:3, 4, 5, 10, 26[2], 30; 23:2, 17, 20, 35, 36[2], 38[3]; 25:3, 4, 5, 7[2], 8, 27, 28, 29[2], 34[3]; 26:4, 5, 11, 12, 15[3]; 27:4, 9[2], 10, 13, 14, 15[2]; 29:5, 6[2], 7, 8, 12[2], 13[2], 15, 19, 20[2], 26, 28; 30:6, 22, 24; 31:6, 7[2], 10; 32:5[2], 36, 43; 33:10, 20; 34:14, 15[2], 16[2], 17; 35:5, 6[2], 7[4], 13, 14, 15[3], 18; 36:19; 37:7, 10, 18; 40:3, 10[3]; 42:9, 10, 11, 13, 15[2], 16[3], 18[3], 19[2], 20[2], 21, 22[2]; 44:2, 3, 7, 8[4], 9, 21[2], 22, 23[2], 25[2], 26, 29; 46:3, 4, 9[2], 14[2]; 48:14, 17[2], 20, 26, 28; 49:3, 5, 8, 14, 28, 30; 50:2, 11[4], 14, 29, 45; 51:3[2], 27, 45[2], 46, 50

Lam 1:12; 4:15

Ezk 5:7; 6:3, 7, 8[2], 13; 7:4, 9; 9:5[2], 7; 11:5, 6[2], 7, 8, 10[2], 11, 12[2], 17; 12:20, 22; 13:2, 5, 7[3], 8, 9, 11, 12, 14[3], 18[2], 19, 20[2], 21, 22, 23[2]; 14:8, 22[2], 23[2]; 15:7; 17:12, 21; 18:2[2], 3, 19, 25, 31[2], 32; 20:3, 7, 18, 20, 29, 30[2], 31[3], 32, 34, 38, 39[4], 41, 42, 43[4], 44[2]; 21:24[3]; 22:19, 21, 22[2]; 23:40, 49[2]; 24:21, 22[2], 23[2], 24[2]; 25:5; 30:2; 33:10, 11[3], 20[2], 25[2], 26[4]; 34:3[4], 4[6], 7, 9, 18[2], 19[2], 21[2], 31; 35:9, 13; 36:1, 3[2], 4, 6, 8[2], 9, 11, 22[2], 23, 25, 27, 28[2], 30, 31; 37:4, 5, 6[2], 13, 14[2]; 39:17, 18, 19[3], 20; 44:6, 7[2], 8[2], 28, 30; 45:1[2], 6, 10, 13[2], 14, 20, 21; 47:13, 14, 18, 21, 22, 23; 48:8, 9, 20, 29

Dan 1:10; 2:5[2], 6[2], 8[2], 9[3]; 3:5[2], 14, 15[5], 26

Hos 1:9, 10[2]; 2:1; 4:1, 15[2], 18; 5:1[4], 8; 9:5; 10:13[3]; 14:3

Joel 1:2[2], 3, 5[2], 11[3], 13[3], 14; 2:1, 12, 19, 22, 23, 26, 27; 3:4[3], 5, 6[2], 7, 9, 11, 13, 17

Am 2:11, 12; 3:13; 4:1, 3^{2}, 5, 6, 8, 9, 10, 11^{2}; 5:1, 4^{2}, 6, 7, 11^{5}, 14^{2}, 22, 25, 26^{2}; 6:2^{2}, 3, 12, 13; 8:4; 9:7

Oba 1, 16

Mic 1:2, 10^{2}, 11; 2:3^{2}, 6, 8, 9^{2}, 10; 3:1, 6^{2}, 9; 6:1, 2^{2}, 5, 9, 16^{2}; 7:5^{2}

Nah 1:9; 2:9

Hab 1:5^{2}

Zep 1:11; 2:3^{3}, 12^{2}; 3:8

Hag 1:4, 6^{6}, 9^{3}; 2:3, 4, 5^{2}, 17

Zec 1:3, 4^{2}; 2:9; 3:10; 6:15^{2}; 7:5^{2}, 6^{3}, 7; 8:9, 13^{2}, 15, 16^{2}; 9:12; 10:1; 11:2, 12; 14:5^{3}

Mal 1:2, 5, 6, 7^{3}, 8^{2}, 10, 12^{2}, 13^{4}; 2:1, 2^{3}, 4, 8^{3}, 9, 13, 14, 16, 17^{3}; 3:1^{2}, 6, 7^{2}, 8^{2}, 9^{2}, 10, 12, 13, 14, 18; 4:2, 3, 4

Mt 2:8; 3:2, 3; 5:11, 13, 14, 20, 21, 27, 33, 38, 39, 43, 45, 46^{2}, 47^{2}, 48; 6:1^{2}, 7, 8^{3}, 9, 14, 15, 16, 24, 25^{3}, 26, 28, 30, 32, 33; 7:1, 2^{3}, 6, 7, 11, 12^{2}, 13, 16, 20, 23; 8:26^{2}; 9:4, 6, 13, 28, 38; 10:5, 7, 8, 11^{2}, 12, 14, 16, 18, 19^{2}, 20, 22, 23^{2}, 27^{3}, 31^{2}; 11:4, 7, 8, 9, 14, 17^{2}, 28, 29; 12:3, 5, 7^{2}, 34; 13:14^{2}, 17^{2}, 18, 29^{2}, 30, 51; 14:16; 15:3, 5, 6, 7, 16, 17, 34; 16:2, 3^{3}, 8^{3}, 9^{2}, 10, 11^{2}, 15; 17:5, 20^{2}; 18:3^{2}, 10, 12, 18^{2}, 35; 19:4, 28^{2}; 20:4, 6, 7^{2}, 22^{3}, 23, 25, 32; 21:2, 3, 5, 13, 16, 21^{3}, 22^{2}, 24, 25, 28, 32^{4}, 42; 22:9^{2}, 18^{2}, 29, 31, 42; 23:3, 8^{2}, 10, 13^{3}, 14^{2}, 15^{2}, 16, 17, 19, 23^{2}, 24, 25, 27, 28^{2}, 29, 31^{2}, 32, 33^{3}, 34^{2}, 35, 37, 39^{2}; 24:2, 6^{2}, 9, 15, 20, 32, 33^{2}, 42, 44^{2}; 25:6, 9, 13, 30, 34, 35^{3}, 36^{3}, 40^{2}, 41, 42^{2}, 43^{3}, 45^{2}; 26:2, 10, 11^{2}, 15, 27, 31, 36, 38, 40, 41, 55^{2}, 64, 65, 66; 27:17, 21, 24, 65^{2}; 28:5^{2}, 7, 13, 19

Mk 1:3, 15, 17; 2:8, 10, 25; 4:13^{2}, 24^{2}, 40^{2}; 5:39; 6:10^{2}, 11, 31, 37, 38; 7:8^{2}, 9^{2}, 11, 12, 13^{2}, 18^{2}; 8:5, 17^{4}, 18^{3}, 19, 20, 21, 29; 9:16, 33, 41, 50; 10:36, 38^{3}, 39^{2}, 42; 11:2^{2}, 3^{2}, 5, 17, 24^{4}, 25^{2}, 26, 31; 12:10, 15, 24^{2}, 26, 27; 13:7^{2}, 9^{2}, 11^{4}, 13, 14, 18, 23, 28, 29^{2}, 33^{2}, 35^{2}; 14:6, 7^{4}, 13, 14, 27, 32, 34, 38^{2}, 48, 49, 62, 64^{2}, 71; 15:9, 12^{2}; 16:6, 7, 15

Lk 2:12, 49^{2}; 3:4; 4:23; 5:22, 24, 30, 34; 6:2, 3, 20, 21^{4}, 22, 23, 24, 25^{2}, 31^{2}, 32^{2}, 33^{2}, 34^{3}, 35^{2}, 36, 37^{3}, 38, 46; 7:22, 24, 25, 26, 32^{2}, 33, 34; 8:18; 9:4, 5, 13, 20, 55^{2}; 10:2, 5, 8, 10, 11, 23, 24^{2}; 11:2, 9, 13, 18, 39, 40, 41, 42^{2}, 43, 44, 46^{3}, 47, 48^{3}, 52^{3}; 12:1, 3^{2}, 5, 7, 11^{3}, 12, 22^{2}, 24, 26^{2}, 28, 29^{4}, 30, 31, 33, 36, 40^{2}, 51, 54^{2}, 55^{2}, 56^{3}, 57; 13:2, 3^{2}, 4, 5^{2}, 25^{2}, 26, 27^{2}, 28, 32, 34, 35^{2}; 16:9, 11, 12, 13, 15; 17:6^{2}, 10^{2}, 22^{2}; 19:30^{2}, 31^{2}, 33, 46; 20:5, 23; 21:6, 8^{2}, 9, 14, 16, 17, 19, 20, 30, 31^{3}, 36^{2}; 22:10, 11, 26, 28, 30, 35, 40, 46^{2}, 51, 52, 53, 67, 68, 70; 23:14^{2}; 24:5, 17^{2}, 38, 39, 41, 48, 49^{2}

Jn 1:26, 38, 51; 3:7, 11, 12^{2}, 28; 4:20, 21, 22^{2}, 32, 35, 38^{2}, 48^{2}; 5:20, 33, 34, 35, 37, 38^{2}, 39^{2}, 40^{2}, 42, 43^{2}, 44, 45, 46^{2}, 47^{2}; 6:26^{3}, 29, 36, 53^{2}, 62, 67; 7:8, 19, 21, 22, 23, 28^{3}, 34^{2}, 36^{2}, 45, 47; 8:14, 15, 19^{3}, 21^{2}, 22, 23^{2}, 24^{3}, 28^{2}, 31^{2}, 32, 33, 36, 37^{2}, 38^{2}, 39^{2}, 40, 41, 42, 43^{2}, 44^{2}, 45, 46, 47^{2}, 49, 54, 55; 9:19, 27^{3}, 30, 41^{3}; 10:20, 25, 26^{2}, 32, 34, 36, 38^{2}; 11:15, 34, 39, 49, 56; 12:8^{2}, 19^{2}, 35, 36^{2}; 13:10, 11, 12, 13^{2}, 14, 15, 17^{3}, 19, 33^{2}, 34^{2}, 35^{2}; 14:1, 3, 4^{2}, 7^{3}, 13, 14, 15, 17, 19^{2}, 20^{2}, 24, 28^{3}, 29; 15:3, 4^{2}, 5^{2}, 7^{3}, 8^{2}, 9, 10^{2}, 12, 14^{2}, 16^{3}, 17, 18, 19^{2}, 27^{2}; 16:1, 4, 10, 12, 16^{2}, 17^{2}, 19^{3}, 20^{2}, 22, 23^{2}, 24^{2}, 26, 27, 31, 32, 33^{2}; 18:4, 7, 8, 29, 31, 39^{2}; 19:4, 6, 35; 20:22, 23^{2}, 31^{2}; 21:5, 6, 10

Act 1:4, 5, 8^{2}, 11^{3}; 2:14^{2}, 15, 22^{2}, 23, 33, 36, 38; 3:12^{3}, 13, 14, 16, 17, 19, 22, 25; 4:7, 8, 10, 19; 5:8, 9, 25, 28^{2}, 30, 35^{2}, 39^{2}; 6:3; 7:4, 26^{2}, 37, 42^{2}, 43^{2}, 49, 51^{3}, 52; 8:24^{2}; 10:21^{2}, 28, 29, 37; 11:16; 13:15^{2}, 16, 25, 39, 41^{2}, 46; 14:15^{2}; 15:1^{2}, 7, 10, 24, 29^{4}; 16:15; 17:22^{2}, 23; 18:14, 15; 19:2^{2}, 3, 15, 25, 26, 35, 36, 37, 39; 20:18, 25, 34, 35; 21:13; 22:1, 3; 23:15^{2}; 25:24; 27:21, 31, 33; 28:26^{2}

Ro 1:6, 11; 6:3, 11, 12, 13, 14, 16^{4}, 17^{2}, 18, 19, 20^{2}, 21^{2}, 22; 7:1, 4^{2}; 8:9, 13^{4}, 15^{2}; 9:26; 11:2, 25^{2}, 30; 12:1, 2^{2}; 13:5, 6, 14; 14:1; 15:6, 7, 10, 11^{2}, 13, 14, 30; 16:2^{2}, 17

1Co 1:5, 7, 8, 9, 10^{2}, 13, 26, 30; 3:2^{2}, 3^{2}, 4, 5, 9^{2}, 16^{2}, 17, 23; 4:6, 8^{4}, 10^{3}, 15^{2}, 16, 21; 5:2, 4, 6, 7^{2}, 10, 12; 6:2^{2}, 3, 4, 7^{3}, 8, 9, 11^{3}, 15, 16, 19^{3}, 20; 7:1, 5^{2}, 23^{2}, 35; 8:12^{2}; 9:1, 2, 13, 24^{2}; 10:1, 7, 10, 13^{2}, 15, 20, 21^{2}, 27, 31^{2}; 11:1, 2, 17, 18, 20, 22^{2}, 25^{2}, 26^{2}, 33, 34; 12:2^{3}, 27; 14:1, 5^{2}, 9^{3}, 12^{3}, 18, 20, 23, 26, 31; 15:1^{2}, 2^{3}, 11, 17, 58^{2}; 16:1, 3, 6, 13, 15, 16, 18, 20

2Co 1:7^{2}, 11, 13^{2}, 14^{2}, 15, 24; 2:4^{2}, 7, 8, 9, 10; 3:2, 3; 5:12, 20; 6:1, 11, 12^{2}, 13, 14, 16, 17, 18; 7:3, 9^{4}, 11^{2}, 15; 8:7^{2}, 9^{2}, 11, 13, 24; 9:3, 4, 5, 8; 10:7; 11:1, 4^{4}, 7, 19^{2}, 20; 12:11, 13, 19, 20; 13:3, 5^{3}, 6, 7^{2}, 9

Gal 1:6, 9, 13; 3:1, 2, 3^{2}, 4, 7, 26, 28, 29^{2}; 4:6, 8^{2}, 9^{3}, 10, 12^{2}, 13, 14, 15^{2}, 17, 21^{2}; 5:2, 4, 7^{2}, 10, 13, 15^{2}, 16, 17^{2}, 18^{2}; 6:1, 2, 11

Eph 1:13^{4}, 18; 2:2, 5, 8, 11, 12, 13, 19, 22; 3:2, 4^{2}, 13, 17, 19; 4:1^{2}, 4, 17, 20, 21, 22, 24, 26, 30, 32; 5:1, 5, 7, 8^{2}, 15, 17; 6:4, 9, 11, 13, 16, 21, 22

Php 1:7, 10^{2}, 12, 27, 30; 2:2^{2}, 12, 15^{2}, 18, 22, 26, 28^{2}; 3:15, 17; 4:9, 10^{2}, 14^{2}, 15^{2}, 16

Col 1:4, 5, 6, 7, 9, 10, 23^{2}; 2:1, 6^{2}, 7, 10, 11, 12, 20^{2}; 3:1, 3, 4, 7^{2}, 8, 9, 13, 15^{2}, 17, 23, 24^{2}; 4:1, 6^{2}, 10, 12, 16

1Th 1:5, 6, 7, 9; 2:2, 5, 8, 9, 10, 11, 12, 13^{3}, 14^{2}, 19, 20; 3:4, 6, 8; 4:1^{3}, 2, 3, 9^{2}, 10^{2}, 11, 12^{2}, 13; 5:1, 4, 5, 11

2Th 1:4, 5^{2}, 12; 2:2, 5, 6, 15; 3:4, 6, 7, 13

Heb 3:7, 15; 4:7; 5:11, 12^{2}; 6:10^{2}, 12; 10:25, 29, 32^{2}, 33^{2}, 34^{2}, 36^{3}; 12:3, 4, 5, 7, 8^{2}, 17, 18, 22, 25; 13:5, 23

Jas 1:2, 4, 22; 2:3, 4, 6, 7, 8^{2}, 9^{2}, 12, 16^{2}, 24; 3:14; 4:2^{5}, 3^{3}, 4^{2}, 5, 8^{2}, 13, 14, 15, 16; 5:1, 3, 5^{2}, 6, 8, 9, 11, 12, 16

1Pt 1:6^{2}, 8^{3}, 15, 16, 17, 18^{2}, 22^{2}; 2:2, 3, 5, 9^{2}, 15, 20^{4}, 21^{2}, 24, 25; 3:1, 6^{2}, 7, 8, 9^{2}, 13, 14^{2}, 17; 4:4, 7, 13^{2}, 14^{2}; 5:4, 5, 10, 12, 14

2Pt 1:4, 8, 10^{2}, 12, 15, 19^{2}; 3:2, 11, 14^{2}, 17^{3}

1Jn 1:3; 2:1, 7^{2}, 13^{3}, 14^{3}, 18, 20^{2}, 21^{2}, 24^{3}, 27^{3}, 29^{2}; 3:5, 11, 15; 4:2, 3, 4; 5:13^{3}

2Jn 6^{2}

3Jn 12

Jude 3, 5, 17, 20

Rev 2:10^{2}, 25; 12:12^{2}; 18:4^{2}, 20; 19:5^{2}, 18

YEA

Gen 3:1; 17:16; 20:6; 27:33

Lev 25:35

Nu 10:32

Dt 33:3

Jdg 5:29

1Sa 15:20; 21:5; 24:11

2Sa 19:30; 22:39

2Ki 2:3, 5; 16:3

1Ch 16:21

2Ch 26:20

Ezr 9:2

Neh 5:15, 16; 6:10; 9:18, 21

Est 5:12

Job 1:15, 17; 2:4; 5:19; 6:10, 27, 29; 9:10; 11:15, 18, 19; 12:3; 14:10; 15:4, 6, 15; 18:5; 19:18; 20:8, 25; 21:7; 22:25; 25:5; 28:27; 30:2, 8, 9; 31:8, 11; 32:12; 33:14, 22; 34:12; 36:7; 40:5; 41:24

Ps 7:4, 5; 8:7; 16:6; 18:10, 14, 48; 19:10; 23:4; 25:3; 27:6; 29:5, 10; 31:9; 35:10, 15, 21, 27; 37:10, 36; 40:8; 41:9; 43:4; 44:22; 57:1; 58:2; 59:16; 68:3, 16, 18; 72:11; 78:19, 38, 41; 83:11, 17; 84:2, 3; 85:12; 90:17; 93:4; 94:23; 102:13, 26; 105:12, 14; 106:24, 37; 109:30; 116:5; 118:11; 119:34, 103, 127; 128:6; 137:1; 138:5; 139:12; 144:15

Prv 2:3, 9; 3:24; 6:16; 7:26; 8:18, 19; 16:4; 22:10; 23:16, 34; 24:5; 29:17; 30:15, 18, 29; 31:20

Ecc 1:16; 2:18, 23; 3:19; 4:3, 8^{2}; 6:6; 7:18; 8:17; 9:3; 10:3; 12:9

Song 1:16; 5:1, 16; 6:9; 8:1

Isa 1:15; 5:10, 29; 14:8; 19:21; 24:16; 26:8, 9, 11; 29:5; 30:33; 32:13; 40:24^{3}; 41:10^{2}, 23, 26^{3}; 42:13; 43:7, 13; 44:8, 12, 15^{2}, 16, 19; 45:21; 46:6, 7, 11; 47:3; 48:8^{3}, 15; 49:15; 55:1; 56:9, 11; 59:15; 60:12; 66:3

Jer 2:37; 5:28; 8:7; 12:2^{2}, 6; 14:5, 18; 23:11, 26; 27:21; 31:3, 19; 32:41; 46:16; 51:44

Lam 1:8

Ezk 6:14; 16:6, 8, 9, 28, 52; 17:10; 22:2, 21, 29; 23:36; 26:18; 28:26; 32:10, 28; 34:6; 36:12; 37:27; 39:13

Dan 8:11; 9:11, 21; 10:19; 11:22, 24, 26

Hos 2:19; 4:3; 7:9; 8:10; 9:12, 16; 12:4, 11

Joel 1:16, 18; 2:3, 19; 3:4

Am 8:6

Oba 13, 16

Jna 3:8

Mic 3:7

Nah 1:5

Hab 2:5

Zep 2:1

Hag 2:19

Zec 7:12; 8:22; 10:7; 14:5, 21

Mal 2:2; 3:15^{2}; 4:1

Mt 5:37^{2}; 9:28; 11:9; 13:51; 21:16; 26:60

Lk 2:35; 7:26; 11:28; 12:5, 57; 14:26; 24:22

Jn 11:27; 16:2, 32; 21:15, 16

Act 3:16, 24; 5:8; 7:43; 20:34; 22:27

Ro 3:4, 31; 8:34; 14:4; 15:20

1Co 1:28; 2:10; 4:3; 9:16; 15:15; 16:6

2Co 1:17^{2}, 18, 19^{2}, 20; 5:16; 7:11^{6}, 13; 8:3

Gal 4:17

Php 1:18; 2:17; 3:8

2Ti 3:12

Phlm 20

Heb 11:36

Jas 2:18; 5:12^{2}

1Pt 5:5

2Pt 1:13

3Jn 12

Rev 14:13

YET

Gen 6:3; 7:4; 8:10, 12; 15:16; 18:22, 29, 32; 20:12; 21:26; 25:6; 27:30; 29:7, 9, 27, 30; 31:14, 30; 37:5, 8, 9; 38:5; 40:13, 19, 23; 43:6, 7, 27, 28; 44:4, 14; 45:3, 6, 11, 26, 28; 46:30; 48:7

Ex 4:18; 5:11, 18; 9:17, 30, 34; 10:7; 11:1; 21:22; 32:32; 33:12; 36:3

Lev 5:17; 11:7, 21; 13:40, 41; 25:22, 51; 26:18, 24, 44

Nu 9:10; 11:33; 19:13; 22:15, 20; 30:16; 32:14, 15

Dt 1:32; 9:29; 12:9; 14:8; 20:6; 22:17; 29:4; 31:27; 32:52

Jos 3:4; 13:1, 2; 14:11; 17:12, 13; 18:2

Jdg 1:35; 2:10, 17; 6:24, 31; 7:4; 8:4, 20; 9:5; 10:13; 15:7; 17:4; 19:19; 20:28; 21:14

Ru 1:11

1Sa 3:6, 7^{2}; 8:9; 10:22; 12:20; 13:7, 21; 15:30; 16:11; 18:29; 20:14; 23:4, 22; 24:11; 25:29

2Sa 1:9; 3:35; 5:13, 22; 6:22; 7:19; 9:1, 3^{2}; 12:18, 22; 14:14; 18:12, 14, 22; 19:28^{2}, 35; 21:15, 20; 23:5

1Ki 1:14, 22, 42; 8:28, 47; 11:17; 12:2, 5, 6; 14:8; 19:18; 20:6, 32; 22:8, 43

2Ki 3:17; 4:6; 6:33; 8:19, 22; 13:23; 14:3, 4; 17:13; 19:30

1Ch 12:1; 14:13; 17:17; 20:6; 26:10; 29:1

2Ch 1:11; 6:16, 26, 37; 10:6; 13:6; 14:7; 16:8, 12; 18:7; 20:33; 24:19; 27:2; 28:22; 30:18; 32:15, 16; 33:17; 34:3

Ezr 3:6; 5:16; 9:9, 15; 10:2

Neh 1:9; 2:16; 5:5, 18; 6:4; 9:19, 28, 29, 30^{2}; 13:18, 26

Est 2:20; 5:13; 6:14; 8:3

Job 1:16, 17, 18; 3:26; 5:7; 6:10; 8:7, 12; 9:15, 16, 21, 31; 10:8, 15; 13:15; 14:9; 19:26; 20:7, 14; 21:32; 22:18; 24:12, 23; 29:5; 32:3; 33:14; 35:14, 15; 36:2

Ps 2:6; 37:10, 25, 36; 40:17; 42:5, 8, 11; 43:5; 44:17; 49:13; 55:21; 68:13; 71:14; 78:17, 30, 56; 90:10; 94:7; 107:41; 119:51, 83, 109, 110, 141, 143, 157; 129:2; 138:6; 139:16^{2}; 141:5

Prv 6:10; 8:26; 9:9; 11:24; 13:7^{2}; 19:7, 19; 23:35; 24:33; 27:22; 30:12, 25, 26, 27; 31:15

Ecc 1:7; 2:3, 19, 21; 4:2, 3, 8; 6:2, 6, 7; 7:28; 8:12, 17^{2}; 9:11^{3}, 15; 11:8

Isa 6:13; 10:22, 25, 32; 14:1, 15; 17:6; 26:10; 27:10; 28:4, 12; 29:2, 17; 30:20; 31:2; 42:25^{2}; 44:1, 11; 46:7, 10; 49:4, 5, 15; 53:4, 7, 10; 56:8; 57:10; 58:2; 65:24

Jer 2:9, 11, 21, 22, 32, 35; 3:1, 8, 10; 4:27; 5:22^{2}, 28; 7:26; 9:20; 11:8; 12:1; 14:9, 15; 15:1, 9, 10; 18:23; 22:6, 24; 23:21^{2}, 32; 25:7; 27:15; 30:11; 31:5, 23, 39; 32:33; 33:1; 34:4; 36:24; 37:10; 40:5; 44:28; 46:28; 48:47; 51:33, 53

Lam 3:32; 4:17

YOU

Jas 1:5, 26; 2:6^2, 16; 3:13; 4:1, 7, 8, 10; 5:1, 3, 4, 6, 13, 14, 19

1Pt 1:2, 4, 10, 12^2, 13, 15, 20, 25; 2:7, 9, 11, 12; 3:13, 15^2, 16; 4:4, 12^2, 14, 15; 5:1, 2, 5, 6, 7, 10^2, 12, 13^2, 14

2Pt 1:2, 8^2, 11, 12, 13^2, 16; 2:1, 3, 13; 3:1, 15

1Jn 1:2, 3, 4, 5; 2:1, 7, 8^2, 12^2, 13^3, 14^3, 21, 24^2, 26^2, 27^4; 3:7, 13; 4:4; 5:13

2Jn 3, 10, 12^2

Jude 2, 3^3, 5, 12, 18, 24^2

Rev 1:4; 2:10, 13, 23, 24^2; 12:12; 18:6, 20; 22:16, 21

YOUR

Gen 3:5; 9:2, 5^2, 9; 17:11, 12, 13; 18:4, 5^2; 19:2^3, 8; 23:8; 31:5, 6, 7, 9, 29; 34:8, 9, 11, 16; 35:2; 37:7; 42:15, 16^2, 19^3, 20^2, 33^2, 34^2; 43:3, 5, 7^2, 11, 12^3, 13, 14, 23^4, 27, 29; 44:10, 17, 23; 45:4, 7, 12, 17, 18^2, 19^3, 20; 46:33; 47:3, 16^2, 23, 24^4; 48:21; 49:2; 50:4, 21

Ex 3:13, 15, 16, 22^2; 5:4, 11, 13^2, 14, 19^2; 6:7; 8:25, 28; 10:8, 10, 16, 17, 24^3; 12:4, 5, 11^5, 14, 15, 17^2, 19, 20, 21, 23, 26, 32^2; 14:14; 16:7, 8^2, 9, 12, 16, 32, 33; 19:15; 20:20; 22:24^2; 23:21, 25, 31; 29:42; 30:8, 10, 15, 16, 31; 31:13; 32:2^3, 13^2, 30; 34:23; 35:3

Lev 1:2; 3:17^2; 6:18; 7:26, 32; 8:33; 10:4, 6^3, 9; 11:44, 45; 14:34; 16:29^2, 30, 31; 17:11, 15; 18:2, 4, 26, 30; 19:2, 3, 4, 5, 9, 10, 25, 27, 28, 31, 33, 34, 36; 20:7, 24, 25; 22:3^2, 19, 24, 25, 29, 33; 23:3, 10, 14^3, 17, 21^2, 22^2, 27, 28, 31^2, 32^2, 38^3, 40, 41, 43^2; 24:3, 22^2; 25:9, 17, 19, 24, 38^2, 45^2, 46^3, 55; 26:1^2, 5^3, 6, 7, 8, 12, 13^2, 15, 16^2, 17, 18, 19^3, 20^2, 21, 22^3, 24, 25, 26^3, 28, 29^2, 30^4, 31^3, 32, 33^2, 34, 35, 37, 38, 39

Nu 9:10; 10:8, 9^3, 10^7; 11:20; 14:29^2, 31, 32, 33^3, 34, 42; 15:2, 3, 14, 15, 20, 21^2, 23, 39^2, 40, 41^3; 18:1, 6, 7^2, 23, 26, 27, 28, 29, 31^3; 22:13; 28:11, 26; 29:7, 39^7; 31:19, 20, 24; 32:6, 8, 14, 22, 23, 24^3; 33:54^2, 55^2; 34:3^2, 4, 6, 7, 8, 9, 10, 12; 35:29^2

Dt 1:7, 8, 10, 11, 12^3, 13, 15^2, 16^2, 26, 27, 30^2, 32, 33, 34, 35, 37, 39^2, 40, 42, 45; 2:4, 24; 3:18^2, 19^4, 20^2, 21, 22, 26; 4:1, 2, 3, 4, 6^2, 21, 23, 26, 34^2; 5:1, 22, 23^2, 28, 30, 32, 33^2; 6:1, 16, 17; 7:8, 14; 8:1, 20^2; 9:16, 17, 18, 21, 23; 10:16, 17; 11:2^2, 7, 9^2, 13^3, 14, 16, 18^4, 19, 21^3, 22, 24^2, 25, 27, 28, 31; 12:4, 5^2, 6^8, 7^3, 9, 10^2, 11^6, 12^6; 13:3^4, 4, 5; 14:1^2; 20:3^2, 4^2, 18; 28:68; 29:2, 5, 6, 10^5, 11^2, 22; 30:18; 31:5, 12, 13, 26, 28^2, 29; 32:17, 38, 46^2, 47^2

Jos 1:3, 4, 11, 13, 14^4, 15^3; 2:9, 11, 16, 21; 3:3^2, 9; 4:5, 6, 21, 22, 23^2, 24; 6:10^2; 7:14; 8:7^2; 9:11; 10:19^3, 24, 25; 15:4; 18:3; 20:3; 22:3^2, 4^4, 5^3, 8^3, 19, 24, 25, 27; 23:3^2, 4, 5^3, 8, 10, 11, 13^4, 14^3, 15^2, 16; 24:2, 3, 6^2, 7, 8, 11, 14, 15, 19^2, 23, 27

Jdg 2:1, 3; 3:28^2; 6:10; 7:15; 8:3, 7; 9:2^2, 15, 18; 10:14; 11:9; 18:6, 10; 19:5, 9, 30; 20:7

Ru 1:11, 12, 13

1Sa 2:3, 23; 6:4, 5^4, 6; 7:3^2; 8:11, 13, 14^3, 15^2, 16^4, 17, 18; 10:19^5; 11:2; 12:1, 6, 7, 8^2, 11, 12^2, 14, 15, 16, 17, 20, 24, 25; 17:8, 9; 26:16

2Sa 1:24; 2:5, 7^2; 3:31; 4:11; 10:5; 15:27

1Ki 1:33; 8:61; 9:6; 11:2; 12:11, 14^2, 16, 24; 18:24, 25

2Ki 2:3, 5; 3:17^2, 18; 9:15; 10:2, 3^2, 6, 24; 12:7; 17:13^2, 39^2; 18:32; 19:6; 23:21

1Ch 15:12; 16:18; 19:5; 22:18, 19^3; 28:8^2; 29:20

2Ch 10:11, 14, 16; 11:4; 13:12; 15:7^2; 18:14; 19:10^2; 20:20; 24:5; 28:9^2, 10, 11; 29:5, 8; 30:7^2, 8^2, 9^3; 32:14, 15; 33:8; 35:3^2, 4^2, 5, 6

Ezr 4:2; 6:6; 7:17, 18; 8:28; 9:12^3; 10:11

Neh 4:14^5; 5:8; 8:9, 10^2, 11; 9:5; 13:18, 25^2

Job 6:22, 25, 27; 13:5^2, 12^2, 13, 17; 16:4, 5; 18:3; 21:2, 5^2, 27, 34; 32:11^2, 14; 42:8

Ps 4:4^2, 5; 11:1; 22:26; 24:7, 9; 31:24; 47:1; 58:2, 9; 62:8, 10; 69:32; 75:5; 76:11; 78:1; 95:8, 9; 105:11; 115:14; 134:2; 146:3

Prv 1:26^2, 27^2

Isa 1:7^4, 11, 12, 14^2, 15^2, 16, 18; 3:14; 8:13^2; 10:3; 23:7, 14; 28:18^2, 22; 29:10^2, 16; 30:3^2, 15; 31:7; 32:11; 33:4, 11; 35:4; 36:17; 37:6; 40:1, 9, 26; 41:21^2, 24, 26; 43:14^2, 15^2; 46:1, 4; 50:1^4, 11; 51:2, 6; 52:12; 55:2^2, 3^2, 8^2, 9^2; 58:3^2, 4; 59:2^3, 3^4; 61:5^3, 7; 65:7^2, 15; 66:5^2, 14^2, 20, 22^2

Jer 2:5, 9, 30^3; 3:18, 22; 4:3, 4^2; 5:19, 25^2; 6:16, 20^2; 7:3^2, 5^2, 6, 7, 11, 14, 15, 21^2, 22, 23, 25; 9:20^2; 11:4^2, 5, 7; 12:13; 13:16^2, 17, 18^2, 20; 16:9^2, 11, 12, 13; 17:1, 22^2; 18:11^2; 21:4, 12, 14; 23:2, 39; 25:4, 5^2, 6, 7^2, 34^2; 26:11, 13^3, 14, 15; 27:4, 9^5, 10, 12, 16; 29:6^2, 8^3, 13, 14, 16, 21; 30:22; 34:13, 14; 35:6, 7, 15^3, 18; 37:19; 38:5; 40:10^2; 42:4^2, 9, 12, 13, 15, 20^2, 21; 44:3, 7, 8, 9^3, 10, 21^3, 22^2, 25^5; 46:4; 48:6; 50:12; 51:24, 46, 50

Ezk 5:16; 6:3, 4^3, 5^2, 6^5; 9:5; 11:5, 6, 7, 11; 12:11, 25; 13:19^2, 20^2, 21^3, 23; 14:6^3; 16:45^2, 55; 18:25, 29, 30^2, 31; 20:5, 7, 18, 19, 20, 27, 30, 31^3, 32, 36, 39^2, 40^3, 41, 42, 43^4, 44^2; 21:24^4; 23:48, 49^2; 24:21^5, 22, 23^5; 33:11, 25^2, 26; 34:18^3, 19^2, 21, 31; 35:13^2; 36:8^2, 11^2, 22, 24, 25^2, 26, 28^2, 29, 31^5, 32^2, 33; 37:12^2, 13^2, 14, 25; 43:27^2; 44:6, 7, 30^2; 45:9, 12; 47:14

Dan 1:10^4; 2:5, 47; 10:21

Hos 1:9; 2:1^2, 2; 4:13^2, 14^2; 5:13; 6:4; 9:10; 10:12, 15

Joel 1:2^2, 3^2, 5, 13, 14; 2:12, 13^3, 14, 23, 26, 27, 28^4; 3:4^2, 5, 7^2, 8^2, 10^2, 17

Am 2:11^2; 3:2; 4:2, 4^2, 6^2, 9^4, 10^4; 5:11, 12^2, 21^2, 22^2, 26^3; 6:2; 8:10^2

Mic 2:3, 10; 3:12

Hab 1:5

Zep 3:20^2

Hag 1:4, 5, 7; 2:3, 17

Zec 1:2, 4^3, 5, 6; 6:15; 7:10; 8:9, 13, 14, 16, 17

Mal 1:5, 9^2, 10, 13; 2:2, 3^3, 13, 15, 16, 17; 3:7, 11^3, 13; 4:3

Mt 5:12, 16^3, 20, 37, 44, 45, 47, 48; 6:1^2, 8, 14, 15^2, 21^2, 25^2, 26, 32; 7:6, 11^2; 9:4, 11, 29; 10:9, 10, 13^2, 14^2, 20, 29, 30; 11:29; 12:27^2; 13:16^2; 15:3, 6; 17:20, 24; 18:14, 35; 19:8^2; 20:26, 27; 23:8, 9^2, 10, 11, 32, 34, 38; 24:20, 42; 25:8; 26:45; 27:65

Mk 2:8; 6:11; 7:9, 13; 8:17; 10:5, 43; 11:2, 25^2, 26^2; 13:18; 14:41; 16:7

Lk 3:14; 4:21; 5:4, 22; 6:22, 23, 24, 27, 35^2, 36, 38; 7:22; 8:25; 9:3, 5, 44; 10:3, 6, 10, 11, 20; 11:13^2, 19^2, 39, 46, 47, 48; 12:7, 22, 30, 32, 34^2, 35^2; 13:35; 16:11, 12, 15; 19:30; 21:14, 15, 18, 19^2, 28^2, 30, 34; 22:53; 23:28; 24:38

Jn 4:35; 6:49, 58; 7:6; 8:17, 21, 24^2, 38, 41, 42, 44^2, 54, 56; 9:19, 41; 10:34; 11:15; 12:30; 13:14^2; 14:1, 26, 27; 15:11, 16; 16:6, 20, 22^2, 24; 18:31; 19:14, 15; 20:17^2

Act 2:17^4, 39; 3:17, 19, 22^2; 5:28; 7:37^2, 43, 51, 52; 13:41; 15:24; 17:23, 28; 18:6^2, 15; 19:37; 20:30; 24:22; 27:34

Ro 1:8; 6:12, 13^2, 19^3, 22; 8:11; 11:25, 28, 31; 12:1^2, 2, 16; 14:16; 15:24, 30; 16:19^2, 20

1Co 1:4, 26; 2:5; 4:6; 5:6; 6:5, 8, 15, 19^2, 20^2; 7:5, 14, 35; 9:11; 14:34; 15:14, 17^2, 31, 34, 58; 16:3^2, 14, 17

2Co 1:6^2, 14, 24^2; 2:8, 10; 4:5, 15; 5:11, 13; 6:12; 7:7^3, 13; 8:7, 8, 9, 14^2, 19, 24^2; 9:2^2, 5, 10^3, 13^2; 10:6, 8, 15; 11:3; 12:19; 13:5^2, 9

Gal 4:6, 15, 16; 6:13, 18

Eph 1:13, 15, 18; 3:13, 17; 4:4, 23, 26, 29; 5:19, 22, 25; 6:1, 4, 5^2, 9, 14, 15, 22

Php 1:5, 9, 19, 25, 26, 27^2, 28; 2:12, 17, 19, 20, 25, 30; 4:5, 6, 7, 10, 17, 19

Col 1:4, 8, 21; 2:5^2, 13^2, 18; 3:2, 3, 5, 8, 15, 16, 18, 19, 20, 21, 22; 4:1, 6, 8^2

1Th 1:3, 4, 5, 8; 2:14, 17; 3:2, 5, 6, 7, 9, 10^2, 13; 4:3, 11^2; 5:23

2Th 1:3, 4^2; 2:17; 3:5

Phlm 22, 25

Heb 3:8, 9, 15; 4:7; 6:10; 9:14; 10:34, 35; 12:3, 13; 13:5, 17

Jas 1:3, 21, 22; 2:2; 3:14; 4:1^2, 3, 8^2, 9^2, 14, 16; 5:1, 2^2, 3^2, 4, 5, 8, 12^2, 16

1Pt 1:7, 9^2, 13, 14, 17, 18^2, 21, 22; 2:12^2, 16, 18, 20, 25; 3:1, 2, 7, 15, 16; 4:14; 5:7, 8, 9

2Pt 1:5, 10, 19; 3:1, 17

1Jn 1:4; 2:12

2Jn 10

Jude 12, 20

Rev 1:9; 2:23; 16:1

YOURS

Gen 45:20

Dt 11:24

Jos 2:14

2Ch 20:15

Jer 5:19

Lk 6:20

Jn 15:20

1Co 3:21, 22; 8:9; 16:18

2Co 12:14

YOURSELVES

Gen 18:4; 45:5; 49:1, 2

Ex 19:12; 30:37; 32:29

Lev 11:43^2, 44^2; 18:24, 30; 19:4; 20:7

Nu 11:18; 16:3, 21; 31:3, 18, 19

Dt 2:4; 4:15, 16, 23, 25; 11:16, 23; 14:1; 31:14, 29

Jos 2:16; 3:5; 6:18^2; 7:13; 8:2; 23:7, 11, 16; 24:22

Jdg 15:12

1Sa 2:29; 4:9^2; 10:19; 14:34; 16:5

1Ki 18:25; 20:12

2Ki 17:35

1Ch 15:12

2Ch 20:17; 29:5, 31; 30:8; 32:11; 35:4, 6

Ezr 10:11

Neh 13:25

Job 19:3, 5; 27:12; 42:8

Isa 8:9^3; 29:9; 45:20; 46:8; 48:14; 49:9; 50:1, 11; 52:3; 57:4, 5; 61:6

Jer 4:4, 5; 6:1; 8:14; 13:18; 17:21; 25:34; 26:15; 37:9; 44:8; 50:14

Ezk 14:6; 18:30, 32; 20:7, 18, 31, 43; 36:31; 39:17^2; 44:8

Hos 10:12

Joel 1:13; 3:11^2

Am 3:9; 5:26

Zep 2:1

Zec 7:6^2

Mt 3:9; 6:19, 20; 16:8; 23:13, 15, 31; 25:9

Mk 6:31; 9:33, 50; 13:9

Lk 3:8; 11:46, 52; 12:33, 36, 57; 13:28; 16:9, 15; 17:3, 14; 21:34; 22:17; 23:28

Jn 3:28; 6:43; 16:19

Act 2:22, 40; 5:35; 13:46; 15:29; 20:10, 28, 34

Ro 6:11, 13, 16; 12:19

1Co 5:13; 6:7; 7:5; 11:13; 16:16

2Co 7:11^2; 11:19; 13:5

Eph 2:8; 5:19, 21, 22

Col 3:18

1Th 2:1; 3:3; 4:9; 5:2, 11, 13, 15

2Th 3:6, 7

Heb 10:34; 13:3, 17

Jas 2:4; 4:7, 10

1Pt 1:14; 2:13; 4:1, 8; 5:5, 6

1Jn 5:21

2Jn 8

Jude 20, 21

Rev 19:17

Dictionary of Hebrew and Aramaic Words

Dictionary Features

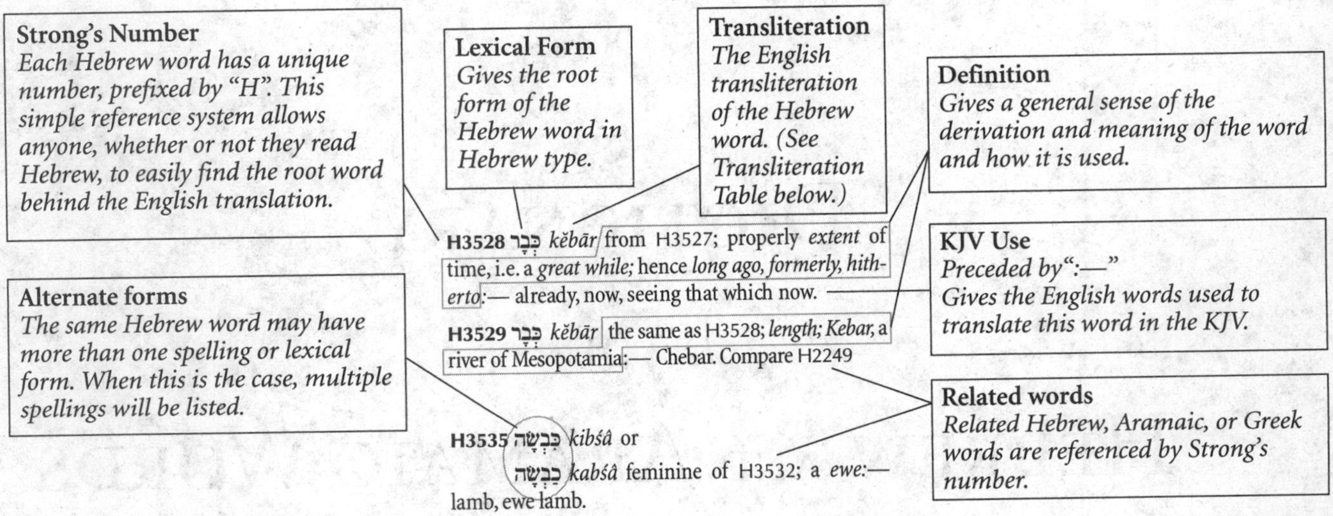

Strong's Number
Each Hebrew word has a unique number, prefixed by "H". This simple reference system allows anyone, whether or not they read Hebrew, to easily find the root word behind the English translation.

Lexical Form
Gives the root form of the Hebrew word in Hebrew type.

Transliteration
The English transliteration of the Hebrew word. (See Transliteration Table below.)

Definition
Gives a general sense of the derivation and meaning of the word and how it is used.

H3528 כְּבָר *kĕbār* from H3527; properly *extent* of time, i.e. a *great while;* hence *long ago, formerly, hitherto:*— already, now, seeing that which now.

H3529 כְּבָר *kĕbār* the same as H3528; *length; Kebar,* a river of Mesopotamia:— Chebar. Compare H2249

H3535 כִּבְשָׂה *kibśâ* or
כַּבְשָׂה *kabśâ* feminine of H3532; a *ewe:*— lamb, ewe lamb.

KJV Use
Preceded by ":—"
Gives the English words used to translate this word in the KJV.

Alternate forms
The same Hebrew word may have more than one spelling or lexical form. When this is the case, multiple spellings will be listed.

Related words
Related Hebrew, Aramaic, or Greek words are referenced by Strong's number.

Hebrew Transliteration Table

Consonants

Character		*Transliteration*
א	*ʾālep*	ʾ
ב	*bêt*	*b*
ג	*gîmel*	*g*
ד	*dālet*	*d*
ה	*hê*	*h*
ו	*wāw*	*w*
ז	*zayin*	*z*
ח	*ḥêt*	*ḥ*
ט	*ṭêt*	*ṭ*
י	*yôd*	*y*
ך, כ	*kāp*	*k*
ל	*lāmed*	*l*
ם, מ	*mêm*	*m*
ן, נ	*nûn*	*n*
ס	*sāmek*	*s*
ע	*ʿayin*	ʿ
ף, פ	*pê*	*p*
ץ, צ	*ṣādê*	*ṣ*
ק	*qôp*	*q*
ר	*rêš*	*r*
שׂ	*śîn*	*ś*
שׁ	*šîn*	*š*
ת	*tāw*	*t*

Vowels

Character		*Transliteration*
◌ַ	*pataḥ*	*a*
◌ַ	furtive *pataḥ*	*a*
◌ָ	*qāmeṣ*	*ā*
◌ָה	final *qāmeṣ hê*	*â*
◌ָיו	3d masc. sg. suf.	*āyw*
◌ֶ	*sēgōl*	*e*
◌ֵ	*ṣērê*	*ē*
◌ֵי	*ṣērê yôd*	*ê* (ֵי = *êy*)
◌ֶי	*sēgōl yôd*	*ê* (ֶי = *êy*)
◌ִ	short *ḥîreq*	*i*
◌ִ	long *ḥîreq*	*ī*
◌ִי	*ḥîreq yôd*	*î* (ִי = *îy*)
◌ָ	*qāmeṣ ḥāṭûp*	*o*
◌ֹ	*ḥōlem*	*ō*
וֹ	full *ḥōlem*	*ô*
◌ֻ	short *qibbûṣ*	*u*
◌ֻ	long *qibbûṣ*	*ū*
וּ	*šûreq*	*û*
◌ֳ	*ḥāṭēp qāmeṣ*	*ŏ*
◌ֲ	*ḥāṭēp pataḥ*	*ă*
◌ֱ	*ḥāṭēp sēgōl*	*ĕ*
◌ְ	vocal *šĕwāʾ*	*ĕ*

Dictionary of Hebrew and Aramaic Words

The almost 8,700 entries in this dictionary provide the user with a listing of the Hebrew and Aramaic words translated into the English of the King James Version. James Strong treated Hebrew and Aramaic ("Chaldee" as it was referred to in his day) as one language, so all of the words from either language are listed in alphabetical order and numbered for ease of reference. See the diagram of features on the facing page for an explanation of the entries. See the section "Exploring the original languages" in the Introduction (beginning on page x) for ideas on how to use this in Bible study.

Grammatical information is included in the entries that can be helpful in using this book. For additional clarity, some of those grammatical terms are defined here.

denominative(ly): A verb or a noun derived from another (usually more primitive or earlier) noun.

inceptive: The beginning of an action, as to ascend the throne thereby beginning to rule.

in the margin: The translators of the King James Version used an ancient Jewish text called the Masoretic Text to translate the Old Testament scriptures. The ancient Masoretes (Jewish biblical scholars) had a careful, honored oral tradition of interpretation of the Old Testament texts. This oral tradition was eventually written alongside of the biblical texts. Because of their reverence for the original text, and their desire to preserve every "jot and tittle" of the ancient texts, when the oral tradition deviated, even minutely, from the written word, these devoted scholars and scribes would not change the written text by presuming that the oral tradition was superior. Rather, they would note in the margin of the text the way in which the oral tradition read the word.

From time to time the King James translators found that the oral tradition seemed to make more sense in the context of a verse and thus they chose to follow it instead of the written text. In this work, Strong preserved the original Hebrew spelling in the text, and indicated that the translation that was used in the King James version was "in the margin."

orthography: As in English, there are sometimes cases in Hebrew or Aramaic where the same word is spelled more than one way, e.g., honor, honour. When there is a difference in spelling and it has no effect on the meaning of the words, this is noted as an othrographical variant.

patrial: A rarely used, but descriptive term for a person who is named after a place or country, e.g., Israeli named as a citizen of the modern State of Israel.

patronymic(ally): The descriptive term for a person who is named for another person (in the Old Testament, a father). Thus a person from Ephraim's family could be called an Ephramite. (This word might also refer to a person from the tribal area of Ephraim, in which case the word is better referred to as "patrial," above.)

permutation: Frequently, especially with foreign names which contain sounds that are unfamiliar to the native Hebrew or Aramaic speaker, the spelling of a name is varied—it has permutations. An example is entry H783.

pronominal: Some nouns that used repeatedly with a pronoun attached as a suffix become names in their own right. When this occurs, the reader is informed that this name is simply another noun with a pronoun attached. An example is entry H3818.

reduplicated: In many languages, including Hebrew and Aramaic, new words are made, or old words strengthened, by repeating a sound in a word. A very modern English word of this sort is "bling-bling."

א

H1 אָב *ʾāb* a primitive word; *father* (in a literal and immediate, or figurative and remote application):— chief, father, forefather, fatherless, patrimony, principal. Compare names in "Abi-"

H2 אַב *ʾab* (Aramaic) corresponding to H1:— father.

H3 אֵב *ʾēb* from the same as H24; a *green* plant:— greenness, fruit.

H4 אֵב *ʾēb* (Aramaic) corresponding to H3:— fruit.

H5 אֲבַגְתָא *ʾăbagtāʾ* of foreign origin; *Abagtha,* a eunuch of Xerxes:— Abagtha.

H6 אָבַד *ʾābad* a primitive root; properly to *wander* away, i.e. *lose* oneself; by implication to *perish* (causative *destroy*):— break, destroy, destruction, not escape, fail, lose, perish, cause to perish, make perish, spend, and surely, take, be undone, utterly, be void of, have no way to flee.

H7 אֲבַד *ʾăbad* corresponding to H6:— destroy, perish.

H8 אֹבֵד *ʾōbēd* active participle of H6; (concrete) *wretched* or (abstract) *destruction:*— perish.

H9 אֲבֵדָה *ʾăbēdâ* from H6; concretely something *lost;* abstractly *destruction,* i.e. Hades:— lost. Compare H10

H10 אֲבַדֹּה *ʾăbaddōh* the same as H9, miswritten for H11; a *perishing:*— destruction.

H11 אֲבַדּוֹן *ʾăbaddôn* intensive from H6; abstractly, a *perishing;* concretely, Hades:— destruction.

H12 אַבְדָן *ʾabdān* from H6; a *perishing:*— destruction.

H13 אָבְדָן *ʾobdān* from H6; a *perishing:*— destruction.

H14 אָבָה *ʾābâ* a primitive root; to *breathe* after, i.e. (figuratively) to *be acquiescent:*— consent, rest content, will, be willing.

H15 אָבֶה *ʾābeh* from H14; *longing:*— desire.

H16 אֵבֶה *ʾēbeh* from H14 (in the sense of *bending* towards); the *papyrus:*— swift.

H17 אֲבוֹי *ʾăbôy* from H14 (in the sense of *desiring*); *want:*— sorrow.

H18 אֵבוּס *ʾēbûs* from H75; a *manger* or *staff:*— crib.

H19 אִבְחָה *ʾibḥâ* from an unused root (apparently meaning to *turn*); *brandishing* of a sword:— point.

H20 אֲבַטִּיחַ *ʾăbaṭṭiaḥ* of uncertain derivation; a *melon* (only plural):— melon.

H21 אֲבִי *ʾăbî* from H1; *fatherly; Abi,* Hezekiah's mother:— Abi.

H22 אֲבִיאֵל *ʾăbîʾēl* from H1 and H410; *father* (i.e. *possessor*) *of God; Abiel,* the name of two Israelites:— Abiel.

H23 אֲבִיאָסָף *ʾăbîʾāsāp* from H1 and H622; *father of gathering* (i.e. *gatherer*); *Abiasaph,* an Israelite:— Abiasaph.

H24 אָבִיב *ʾābîb* from an unused root (meaning to *be tender*); *reen,* i.e. a young *ear* of grain; hence the name of the month *Abib* or Nisan:— Abib, ear, green ears of corn.

H25 אֲבִי גִבְעוֹן *ʾăbî gibʿôn* from H1 and H1391; *father* (i.e. *founder*) *of Gibon; Abi-Gibon,* perhaps an Israelite:— father of Gibeon.

H26 אֲבִיגַיִל *ʾăbîgayil* or shorter

אֲבִיגַל *ʾăbîgal* from H1 and H1524; *father* (i.e. *source*) *of joy; Abigail* or *Abigal,* the name of two Israelitesses:— Abigal.

H27 אֲבִידָן *ʾăbîdān* from H1 and H1777; *father of judgment* (i.e. *judge*); *Abidan,* an Israelite:— Abidan.

H28 אֲבִידָע *ʾăbîdāʿ* from H1 and H3045; *father of knowledge* (i.e. *knowing*); *Abida,* a son of Abraham by Keturah:— Abida, Abidah.

H29 אֲבִיָּה *ʾăbîyâ* or prolonged

אֲבִיָּהוּ *ʾăbîyāhû* from H1 and H3050; *father* (i.e. *worshipper*) *of Jah; Abijah,* the name of several Israelite men and two Israelitesses:— Abiah, Abijah.

H30 אֲבִיהוּא *ʾăbîhûʾ* from H1 and H1931; *father* (i.e. *worshipper*) of *Him* (i.e. *God*); *Abihu,* a son of Aaron:— Abihu.

H31 אֲבִיהוּד *ʾăbîhûd* from H1 and H1935; *father* (i.e. *possessor*) *of renown; Abihud,* the name of two Israelites:— Abihud.

H32 אֲבִיהַיִל *ʾăbîhayil* or (more correctly)

אֲבִיחַיִל *ʾăbîḥayil* from H1 and H2428; *father* (i.e. *possessor*) *of might: Abihail* or *Abichail,* the name of three Israelites and two Israelitesses:— Abihail.

H33 אֲבִי הָעֶזְרִי *ʾăbî hāʿezrî* from H44 with the article inserted; *father of the Ezrite;* an *Abiezrite* or descendant of Abiezer:— Abiezrite.

H34 אֶבְיוֹן *ʾebyôn* from H14, in the sense of *want* (especially in feeling); *destitute:*— beggar, needy, poor, poor man.

H35 אֲבִיּוֹנָה *ʾăbîyônâ* from H14; provocative of *desire;* the *caper* berry (from its *stimulative* taste):— desire.

H36 אֲבִיטוּב *ʾăbîṭûb* from H1 and H2898; *father of goodness* (i.e. *good*); *Abitub,* an Israelite:— Abitub.

H37 אֲבִיטַל *ʾăbîṭal* from H1 and H2919; *father of dew* (i.e. *fresh*); *Abital,* a wife of King David:— Abital.

H38 אֲבִיָּם *ʾăbîyām* from H1 and H3220; *father of* (the) *sea* (i.e. *seaman*); *Abijam* (or Abijah), a king of Judah:— Abijam.

H39 אֲבִימָאֵל *ʾăbîmāʾēl* from H1 and an elsewhere unused (probably foreign) word; *father of Mael* (apparently some Arab tribe); *Abimael,* a son of Joktan:— Abimael.

H40 אֲבִימֶלֶךְ *ʾăbîmelek* from H1 and H4428; *father of* (the) *king; Abimelek,* the name of two Philistine kings and of two Israelites:— Abimelech.

H41 אֲבִינָדָב *ʾăbînādāb* from H1 and H5068; *father of generosity* (i.e. *liberal*); *Abinadab,* the name of four Israelites:— Abinadab.

H42 אֲבִינֹעַם *ʾăbînōʿam* from H1 and H5278; *father of pleasantness* (i.e. *gracious*); *Abinoam,* an Israelite:— Abinoam.

H43 אֶבְיָסָף *ʾebyāsāp* contracted from H23; *Ebjasaph,* an Israelite:— Abiasaph.

H44 אֲבִיעֶזֶר *ʾăbîʿezer* from H1 and H5829; *father of help* (i.e. *helpful*); *Abiezer,* the name of two Israelites:— Abiezer.

H45 אֲבִי-עַלְבוֹן *ʾăbî-ʿalbôn* from H1 and an unused root of uncertain derivation; probably *father of strength* (i.e. *valiant*); *Abialbon,* an Israelite:— Abialbon.

H46 אָבִיר *ʾābîr* from H82; *mighty* (spoken of God) :— mighty, mighty one.

H47 אַבִּיר *ʾabbîr* for H46:— angel, bull, chiefest, mighty, mighty one, stouthearted, strong, strong one, valiant.

H48 אֲבִירָם *ʾăbîrām* from H1 and H7311; *father of height* (i.e. *lofty*); *Abiram,* the name of two Israelites:— Abiram.

H49 אֲבִישַׁג *ʾăbîšag* from H1 and H7686; *father of error* (i.e. *blundering*); *Abishag,* a concubine of David:— Abishag.

H50 אֲבִישׁוּעַ *ʾăbîšûaʿ* from H1 and H7771; *father of plenty* (i.e. *prosperous*); *Abishua,* the name of two Israelites:— Abishua.

H51 אֲבִישׁוּר *ʾăbîšûr* from H1 and H7791; *father of* (the) *wall* (i.e. perhaps *mason*); *Abishur,* an Israelite:— Abishur.

H52 אֲבִישַׁי *ʾăbîšay* or (shorter)

אַבְשַׁי *ʾabšay* from H1 and H7862; *father of a gift* (i.e. probably *generous*); *Abishai,* an Israelite:— Abishai.

H53 אֲבִישָׁלוֹם *ʾăbîšālôm* or (shortened)

אַבְשָׁלוֹם *ʾabšālôm* from H1 and H7965; *father of peace* (i.e. *friendly*); *Abshalom,* a son of David; also (the fuller form) a later Israelite:— Abishalom, Absalom.

H54 אֶבְיָתָר *ʾebyātār* contracted from H1 and H3498; *father of abundance* (i.e. *liberal*); *Ebjathar,* an Israelite:— Abiathar.

H55 אָבַךְ *ʾābak* a primitive root; probably to *coil* upward:— mount up.

H56 אָבַל *ʾābal* a primitive root; to *bewail:*— lament, mourn.

H57 אָבֵל *ʾābēl* from H56; *lamenting:*— mourn, mourner, mourning.

H58 אָבֵל *ʾābēl* from an unused root (meaning to *be grassy*); a *meadow:*— plain. Compare also the proper names beginning with Abel-

H59 אָבֵל *ʾābēl* from H58; a *meadow; Abel,* the name of two places in Palestine:— Abel.

H60 אֵבֶל *ʾēbel* from H56; *lamentation:*— mourning.

H61 אֲבָל *ʾăbāl* apparently from H56 through the idea of *negation; nay,* i.e. *truly* or *yet:*— but, indeed, nevertheless, verily.

H62 אָבֵל בֵּית-מַעֲכָה *ʾābēl bêt-măʿakâ* from H58 and H1004 and H4601; *meadow of Beth-Maakah; Abel of Beth-maakah,* a place in Palestine:— Abel-beth-maachah, Abel of Beth-maachah.

H63 אָבֵל הַשִּׁטִּים *ʾābēl haššiṭṭîm* from H58 and the plural of H7848, with the article inserted; *meadow of the acacias; Abel hash-Shittim,* a place in Palestine:— Abel-shittim.

H64 אָבֵל כְּרָמִים *ʾābēl kĕrāmîm* from H58 and the plural of H3754; *meadow of vineyards; Abel-Keramim,* a place in Palestine:— plain of the vineyards.

H65 אָבֵל מְחוֹלָה *ʾābēl mĕḥôlâ* from H58 and H4246; *meadow of dancing; Abel-Mecholah,* a place in Palestine:— Abel-meholah.

H66 אָבֵל מַיִם *ʾabēl mayim* from H58 and H4325; *meadow of water; Abel-Majim,* a place in Palestine:— Abel-maim.

H67 אָבֵל מִצְרַיִם *ʾābēl miṣrayim* from H58 and H4714; *meadow of Egypt; Abel-Mitsrajim,* a place in Palestine:— Abel-mizraim.

H68 אֶבֶן *ʾeben* from the root of H1129 through the meaning to *build;* a *stone:*— carbuncle, mason, plummet, stone, chalkstone, hailstone, headstone, slingstone, stony, weight, divers weights.

H69 אֶבֶן *ʾeben* (Aramaic) corresponding to H68:— stone.

H70 אֹבֶן *ʾōben* from the same as H68; a *pair of stones* (only dual); a potter's *wheel* or a midwife's *stool* (consisting alike of two horizontal disks with a support between):— wheel, stool.

H71 אֲבָנָה *ʾăbānâ* perhaps feminine of H68; *stony; Abanah,* a river near Damascus:— Abana. Compare H549

H72 אֶבֶן הָעֵזֶר *ʾeben hāʿēzer* from H68 and H5828 with the article inserted; *stone of the help; Eben-ha-Ezer,* a place in Palestine:— Ebenezer.

H73 אַבְנֵט *ʾabnēṭ* of uncertain derivation; a *belt:*— girdle.

H74 אַבְנֵר *ʾabnēr* or (fully)

אֲבִינֵר *ʾăbînēr* from H1 and H5216; *father of light* (i.e. *enlightening*); *Abner,* an Israelite:— Abner.

H75 אָבַס *ʾābas* a primitive root; to *fodder:*— fatted, stalled.

H76 אֲבַעְבֻּעָה *ʾăbaʿbuʿâ* (by reduplication) from an unused root (meaning to *belch* forth); an inflammatory *pustule* (as *eruption*):— blains.

H77 אֶבֶץ *ʾebeṣ* from an unused root probably meaning to *gleam; conspicuous; Ebets,* a place in Palestine:— Abez.

H78 אִבְצָן *ʾibṣān* from the same as H76; *splendid; Ibtsan,* an Israelite:— Ibzan.

H79 אָבַק *ʾābaq* a primitive root; probably to *float* away (as vapor), but used only as denominative from H80; to *make dusty,* i.e. *grapple:*— wrestle.

H80 אָבָק *ʾābāq* from root of H79; light *particles* (as *volatile*):— dust, small dust, powder.

H81 אֲבָקָה *ʾăbāqâ* feminine of H80:— powder.

H82 אָבַר *ʾābar* a primitive root; to *soar:*— fly.

H83 אֵבֶר *ʾēber* from H82; a *pinion:*— longwinged.

H84 אֶבְרָה *ʾebrâ* feminine of H83:— feather, wing.

H85 אַבְרָהָם *ʾabrāhām* contracted from H1 and an unused root (probably meaning to *be populous*); *father of a multitude; Abraham,* the later name of Abram:— Abraham.

H86 אַבְרֵךְ *ʾabrēk* probably an Egyptian word meaning *kneel:*— bow the knee.

H87 אַבְרָם *ʾabrām* contracted from H48; *high father; Abram,* the original name of Abraham:— Abram.

H88 אֹבֹת *ʾōbōt* plural of H178; water-*skins; Oboth,* a place in the Desert:— Oboth.

H89 אָגֵא *ʾāgēʾ* of uncertain derivation [compare H90]; *Agè,* an Israelite:— Agee.

H90 אֲגַג *ʾăgag* or

אֲגָג *ʾăgāg* of uncertain derivation [compare H89]; *flame; Agag,* a title of Amalekitish kings:— Agag.

H91 אֲגָגִי *ʾăgāgî* patrial or patronymic from H90; an *Agagite* or descendant (subject) of Agag:— Agagite.

H92 אֲגֻדָּה *ʾăguddâ* feminine passive participle of an unused root (meaning to *bind*); a *band, bundle, knot,* or *arch:*— bunch, burden, troop.

H93 אֱגוֹז *ʾĕgôz* probably of Persian origin; a *nut:*— nut.

H94 אָגוּר *ʾāgûr* passive participle of H103; *gathered* (i.e. *received* among the sages); *Agur,* a fanciful name for Solomon:— Agur.

H95 אֲגוֹרָה *ʾăgôrâ* from the same as H94; properly something *gathered,* i.e. perhaps a *grain* or *berry;* used only of a small (silver) *coin:*— piece of silver.

H96 אֶגֶל *ʾegel* from an unused root (meaning to *flow* down or together as drops); a *reservoir:*— drop.

H97 אֶגְלַיִם *ʾeglayim* dual of H96; a *double pond; Eglajim,* a place in Moab:— Eglaim.

H98 אֲגַם *ʾăgam* from an unused root (meaning to *collect* as water); a *marsh;* hence a *rush* (as growing in swamps); hence a *stockade* of reeds:— pond, pool, standing water.

H99 אָגֵם *ʾāgēm* probably from the same as H98 (in the sense of *stagnant* water); figuratively *sad:*— pond.

H100 אַגְמוֹן *ʾagmôn* from the same as H98; a marshy *pool* [others from a different root, a *kettle];* by implication a *rush* (as growing there); collectively a *rope* of rushes:— bulrush, caldron, hook, rush.

H101 אַגָּן *ʾaggān* probably from H5059; a *bowl* (as *pounded* out hollow):— basin, cup, goblet.

H102 אַגָּף *ʾaggāp* probably from H5062 (through the idea of *impending*); a *cover* or *heap;* i.e. (only plural) *wings* or an army, or *crowds* of troops:— bands.

H103 אָגַר *ʾāgar* a primitive root; to *harvest:*— gather.

H104 אִגְּרָא *ʾiggĕrāʾ* (Aramaic) of Persian origin; an *epistle* (as carried by a state courier or postman):— letter.

H105 אֲגַרְטָל *ʾăgarṭāl* of uncertain derivation; a *basin:*— charger.

H106 אֶגְרֹף *ʾegrōp* from H1640 (in the sense of *grasping*); the *clenched* hand:— fist.

H107 אִגֶּרֶת *ʾiggeret* feminine of H104; an *epistle:* — letter.

H108 אֵד *ʾēd* from the same as H181 (in the sense of *enveloping*); a *fog:*— mist, vapor.

H109 אָדַב *ʾādab* a primitive root; to *languish:*— grieve.

H110 אַדְבְּאֵל *ʾadbĕʾēl* probably from H109 (in the sense of *chastisement*) and H410; *disciplined of God; Adbeël,* a son of Ishmael:— Adbeel.

H111 אֲדַד *ʾădad* probably an orthographical variation for H2301; *Adad* (or Hadad), an Edomite:— Hadad.

H112 אִדּוֹ *ʾiddô* of uncertain derivation; *Iddo,* an Israelite:— Iddo.

H113 אָדוֹן *ʾādôn* or (shortened)

אָדֹן *ʾādōn* from an unused root (meaning to *rule*); *sovereign,* i.e. *controller* (human or divine):— lord, master, owner. Compare also names beginning with "Adoni-"

H114 אַדּוֹן *ʾaddôn* probably intensive for H113; *powerful; Addon,* apparently an Israelite:— Addon.

H115 אֲדוֹרַיִם *ʾădôrayim* dual from H142 (in the sense of *eminence*); *double mound; Adorajim,* a place in Palestine:— Adoraim.

H116 אֱדַיִן *ʾĕdayin* (Aramaic) of uncertain derivation; *then* (of time):— now, that time, then.

H117 אַדִּיר *ʾaddîr* from H142; *wide* or (generally) *large;* figuratively *powerful:*— excellent, famous, gallant, glorious, goodly, lordly, mighty, mighty one, mightier, noble, principal, worthy.

H118 אֲדַלְיָא *ʾădalyāʾ* of Persian derivation; *Adalja,* a son of Haman:— Adalia.

H119 אָדַם *ʾādam;* to *show blood* (in the face), i.e. *flush* or turn rosy:— be red, dyed red, made red, ruddy.

H120 אָדָם *ʾādām* from H119; *ruddy,* i.e. a *human being* (an individual or the species, *mankind,* etc.) :— another, hypocrite, common sort, low, man, mean man, man of low degree, person.

H121 אָדָם *ʾādām* the same as H120; *Adam,* the name of the first man, also of a place in Palestine:— Adam.

H122 אָדֹם *ʾādōm* from H119; *rosy:*— red, ruddy.

H123 אֱדֹם *ʾĕdōm* or (fully)

אֱדוֹם *ʾĕdôm* from H122; *red* [see Gen 25:25]; *Edom,* the elder twin-brother of Jacob; hence the region (Idumaea) occupied by him:— Edom, Edomites, Idumea.

H124 אֹדֶם *ʾōdem* from H119; *redness,* i.e. the *ruby, garnet,* or some other red gem:— sardius.

H125 אֲדַמְדָּם *ʾădamdām* reduplicated from H119; *reddish:*— (somewhat) reddish.

H126 אַדְמָה *ʾadmâ* contraction for H127; *earthy; Admah,* a place near the Dead Sea:— Admah.

H127 אֲדָמָה *ʾădāmâ* from H119; *soil* (from its general *redness*):— country, earth, ground, husbandman, husbandry, land.

H128 אֲדָמָה *ʾădāmâ* the same as H127; *Adamah,* a place in Palestine:— Adamah.

H129 אֲדָמִי *ʾădāmî* from H127; *earthy; Adami,* a place in Palestine:— Adami.

H130 אֱדֹמִי *ʾĕdōmî* or (fully)

אֱדוֹמִי *ʾĕdômî* patronymically from H123; an *Edomite,* or descendant from (or inhabitant of) Edom:— Edomite. See H726

H131 אֲדֻמִּים *ʾădummîm* plural of H121; *red* spots; *Adummim,* a pass in Palestine:— Adummim.

H132 אַדְמֹנִי *ʾadmōnî* or (fully)

אַדְמוֹנִי *ʾadmônî* from H119; *reddish* (of the hair or the complexion):— red, ruddy.

H133 אַדְמָתָא *ʾadmātāʾ* probably of Persian derivation; *Admatha,* a Persian nobleman:— Admatha.

H134 אֶדֶן *ʾeden* from the same as H113 (in the sense of *strength*); a *basis* (of a building, a column, etc.):— foundation, socket.

H135 אַדָּן *ʾaddān* intensive from the same as H134; *firm; Addan,* an Israelite:— Adan.

H136 אֲדֹנָי *ʾădōnāy* an emphatic form of H113; the *Lord* (used as a proper name of God only):— Lord, my Lord.

H137 אֲדֹנִי־בֶזֶק *ʾădōnî-bezeq* from H113 and H966; *lord of Bezek; Adoni-Bezek,* a Canaanitish king:— Adoni-bezek.

H138 אֲדֹנִיָּה *ʾădōnîyâ* or (prolonged)

אֲדֹנִיָּהוּ *ʾădōnîyāhû* from H113 and H3050; *lord* (i.e. worshipper) of Jah; *Adonijah,* the name of three Israelites:— Adonijah.

H139 אֲדֹנִי־צֶדֶק *ʾădōnî-ṣedeq* from H113 and H6664; *lord of justice; Adoni-Tsedek,* a Canaanitish king:— Adoni-zedek.

H140 אֲדֹנִיקָם *ʾădōnîqām* from H113 and H6965; *lord of rising* (i.e. *high*); *Adonikam,* the name of one or two Israelites:— Adonikam.

H141 אֲדֹנִירָם *ʾădōnîrām* from H113 and H7311; *lord of height; Adoniram,* an Israelite:— Adoniram.

H142 אָדַר *ʾādar* a primitive root; to *expand,* i.e. *be great* or (figuratively) *magnificent:*— glorious, become glorious, honourable.

H143 אֲדָר *ʾădār* probably of foreign derivation; perhaps meaning *fire; Adar,* the 12th Hebrew month:— Adar.

H144 אֲדָר *ʾădār* (Aramaic) corresponding to H143 :— Adar.

H145 אֶדֶר *ʾeder* from H142; *amplitude,* i.e. (concretely) a *mantle;* also (figuratively) *splendor:*— goodly, robe.

H146 אַדָּר *ʾaddār* intensively from H142; *ample; Addar,* a place in Palestine; also an Israelite:— Addar.

H147 אִדַּר *ʾiddar* (Aramaic) intensively from a root corresponding to H142; *ample,* i.e. a threshing-*floor:*— threshingfloor.

H148 אֲדַרְגָּזֵר *ʾădargāzēr* (Aramaic) from the same as H147, and H1505; a *chief diviner,* or *astrologer:*— judge.

H149 אַדְרַזְדָּא *ʾadrazdāʾ* (Aramaic) probably of Persian origin; *quickly* or *carefully:*— diligently.

H150 אֲדַרְכֹּן *ʾădarkōn* of Persian origin; a *daric* or Persian coin:— dram.

H151 אֲדֹרָם *ʾădōrām* contraction for H141; *Adoram* (or Adoniram), an Israelite:— Adoram.

H152 אַדְרַמֶּלֶךְ *ʾadrammelek* from H142 and H4428; *splendor of* (the) *king; Adrammelek,* the name of an Assyrian idol, also of a son of Sennacherib:— Adrammelech.

H153 אֶדְרָע *ʾedrāʿ* (Aramaic) an orthographical variation for H1872; an *arm,* i.e. (figuratively) *power:*— force.

H154 אֶדְרֶעִי *ʾedreʿî* from the equivalent of H153; *mighty; Edrei,* the name of two places in Palestine:— Edrei.

H155 אַדֶּרֶת *ʾadderet* feminine of H117; something *ample* (as a *large* vine, a *wide* dress); also the same as H145:— garment, glory, goodly, mantle, robe.

H156 אָדַשׁ *ʾādaš* a primitive root; to *tread* our (grain):— thresh.

H157 אָהַב *ʾāhab* or

אָהֵב *ʾāhēb* a primitive root; to *have affection* for (sexually or otherwise):— love, loved, lovely, lover, beloved, like, friend.

H158 אַהַב *ʾahab* from H157; *affection* (in a good or a bad sense):— love, lover.

H159 אֹהַב *ʾōhab* from H156; meaning the same as H158:— love.

H160 אַהֲבָה *ʾahăbâ* feminine of H158 and meaning the same:— love.

H161 אֹהַד *ʾōhad* from an unused root meaning to *be united; unity; Ohad,* an Israelite:— Ohad.

H162 אֲהָהּ *ʾăhāh* apparently a primitive word expressing *pain* as an exclamation; *Oh!:*— ah, alas.

H163 אַהֲוָא *ʾahăwāʾ* probably of foreign origin; *Ahava,* a river of Babylonia:— Ahava.

H164 אֵהוּד *ʾēhûd* from the same as H161; *united; Ehud,* the name of two or three Israelites:— Ehud.

H165 אֱהִי *ʾěhî* apparently an orthographical variation for H346; *where:*— I will be (Hos 13:10, 14) *[which is often the rendering of the same Hebrew form from H1961].*

H166 אָהַל *ʾāhal* a primitive root; to *be clear:*— shine.

H167 אָהַל *ʾāhal* a denominative from H168; to *tent:*— pitch a tent, remove a tent.

H168 אֹהֶל *ʾōhel* from H166; a *tent* (as *clearly* conspicuous from a distance):— covering, dwelling, place, home, tabernacle, tent.

H169 אֹהֶל *ʾōhel* the same as H168; *Ohel,* an Israelite:— Ohel.

H170 אָהֳלָה *Ohŏlâ* in form a feminine of H168, but in fact for

אָהֳלָהּ *Ohŏlāh; her tent* (i.e. idolatrous *sanctuary*); *Oholah,* a symbolic name for Samaria:— Aholah.

H171 אָהֳלִיאָב *Ohŏlîʾāb* from H168 and H1; *tent of* (his) *father; Oholiab,* an Israelite:— Aholiab.

H172 אָהֳלִיבָה *Ohŏlîbâ* (similarly with H170) for

אָהֳלִיבָהּ *Ohŏlîbāh* from H168; *my tent* (is) *in her; Oholibah,* a symbolic name for Judah:— Aholibah.

H173 אָהֳלִיבָמָה *Ohŏlîbāmâ* from H168 and H1116; *tent of* (the) *height: Oholibamah,* a wife of Esau:— Aholibamah.

H174 אֲהָלִים *ʾăhālîm* or (feminine)

אֲהָלוֹת *ʾăhālôt* only used thus in the plural; of foreign origin; *aloe* wood (i.e. sticks):— aloes, tree of lign-aloes.

H175 אַהֲרוֹן *ʾahărôn* of uncertain derivation; *Aharon,* the brother of Moses:— Aaron.

H176 אוֹ *ʾô* presumed to be the "construct" or genitival form of

אַו *ʾaw* shortened for H185; *desire* (and so probably in Prov 31:4); hence (by way of alternative) *or,* also *if:*— also, and, either, if, at the least, nor, or, otherwise, then, whether.

H177 אוּאֵל *ʾûʾēl* from H176 and H410; *wish of God; Uel,* an Israelite:— Uel.

H178 אוֹב *ʾôb* from the same as H1 (apparently through the idea of *prattling* a father's name); properly a *mumble,* i.e. a water-skin (from its hollow sound); hence a *necromancer* (ventriloquist, as from a jar):— bottle, familiar spirit.

H179 אוֹבִיל *ʾôbîl* probably from H56; *mournful; Obil,* an Ishmaelite:— Obil.

H180 אוּבָל *ʾûbāl* or (shortened)

אֻבָל *ʾūbāl* from H2986 (in the sense of H2988); a *stream:*— river.

H181 אוּד *ʾûd* from an unused root meaning to *rake* together; a *poker* (for *turning* or *gathering* embers):— brand, firebrand.

H182 אוֹדוֹת *ʾôdôt* or (shortened)

אֹדוֹת *ʾōdôt* only thus in the plural; from the same as H181; *turnings* (i.e. *occasions*); (adverbially) on *account* of:— cause, because, concerning, sake.

H183 אָוָה *ʾāwâ* a primitive root; to *wish* for:— covet, desire, greatly desire, be desirous, long, lust, lust after.

H184 אָוָה *ʾāwâ* a primitive root; to *extend* or *mark* out:— point out.

H185 אַוָּה *ʾawwâ* from H183; *longing:*— desire, lust after, pleasure.

H186 אוּזַי *ʾûzay* perhaps by permutation for H5813, *strong; Uzai,* an Israelite:— Uzai.

H187 אוּזָל *ʾûzāl* of uncertain derivation; *Uzal,* a son of Joktan:— Uzal.

H188 אוֹי *ʾôy* probably from H183 (in the sense of *crying* out after); *lamentation;* also as an interjection *Oh!:*— alas, woe.

H189 אֱוִי *ʾěwî* probably from H183; *desirous; Evi,* a Midianitish chief:— Evi.

H190 אוֹיָה *ʾôyâ* feminine of H188:— woe.

H191 אֱוִיל *ʾěwîl* from an unused root (meaning to be *perverse*); (figuratively) *silly:*— fool, foolish, foolish man.

H192 אֱוִיל מְרֹדַךְ *ʾěwîl měrōdak* of Aramaic derivation and probably meaning *soldier of Merodak; Evil-Merodak,* a Babylonian king:— Evil-merodach.

H193 אוּל *ʾûl* from an unused root meaning to *twist,* i.e. (by implication) *be strong;* the *body* (as being *rolled* together); also *powerful:*— mighty, strength.

H194 אוּלַי *ʾûlay* or (shortened)

אֻלַי *ʾūlay* from H176; *if not;* hence *perhaps:* — if so be, may be, peradventure, unless.

H195 אוּלַי *ʾûlay* of Persian derivation; the *Ulai* (or Eulaeus), a river of Persia:— Ulai.

H196 אֱוִלִי *ʾěwīlî* from H191; *silly, foolish;* hence (morally) *impious:*— foolish.

H197 אוּלָם *ʾûlām* or (shortened)

אֻלָם *ʾūlām* from H481 (in the sense of *tying*); a *vestibule* (as *bound* to the building):— porch.

H198 אוּלָם *ʾûlām* apparently from H481 (in the sense of *dumbness*); *solitary; Ulam,* the name of two Israelites:— Ulam.

H199 אוּלָם *ʾûlām* apparently a variation of H194; *however* or *on the contrary:*— as for, but, howbeit, in very deed, surely, truly, wherefore.

H200 אִוֶּלֶת *ʾiwwelet* from the same as H191; *silliness:*— folly, foolishly, foolishness.

H201 אוֹמָר *ʾômār* from H559; *talkative; Omar,* a grandson of Esau:— Omar.

H202 אוֹן *ʾôn* probably from the same as H205 (in the sense of *effort,* but successful); *ability, power,* (figuratively) *wealth:*— force, goods, might, strength, substance.

H203 אוֹן *ʾôn* the same as H202; *On,* an Israelite:— On.

H204 אוֹן *ʾôn* or (shortened)

אֹן *ʾōn* of Egyptian derivation; *On,* a city of Egypt:— On.

H205 אָוֶן *ʾāwen* from an unused root perhaps meaning properly to *pant* (hence to *exert* oneself, usually in vain; to *come to naught*); strictly *nothingness;* also *trouble, vanity, wickedness;* specifically an *idol:*— affliction, evil, false, idol, iniquity, mischief, mourners, mourning, naught, sorrow, unjust, unrighteous, vain, vanity, wicked, wickedness. Compare H369

H206 אָוֶן *ʾāwen* the same as H205; *idolatry; Aven,* the contemptuous synonym of three places, one in Coele-Syria, one in Egypt (On), and one in Palestine (Bethel):— Aven. See also H204, H1007

H207 אוֹנוֹ *ʾônô* or (shortened)

אֹנוֹ *ʾōnô* prolonged from H202; *strong; Ono,* a place in Palestine:— Ono.

H208 אוֹנָם *ʾônām* a variation of H209; *strong; Onam,* the name of an Edomite and of an Israelite:— Onam.

H209 אוֹנָן *ʾônān* a variation of H207; *strong; Onan,* a son of Judah:— Onan.

H210 אוּפָז *ʾûpāz* perhaps a corruption of H211; *Uphaz,* a famous gold region:— Uphaz.

H211 אוֹפִיר *ʾôpîr* or (shortened)

אֹפִיר *ʾōpîr* and

אוֹפִר *ʾôpīr* of uncertain derivation; *Ophir,* the name of a son of Joktan, and of a gold region in the East:— Ophir.

H212 אוֹפָן *ʾôpān* or (shortened)

אֹפָן *ʾōpān* from an unused root meaning to *revolve;* a *wheel:*— wheel.

H213 אוּץ *ʾûṣ* a primitive root; to *press;* (by implication) to *be close, hurry, withdraw:*— haste, hasten, hasty, make haste, labor, be narrow.

H214 אוֹצָר *ʾôṣār* from H686; a *depository:*— armory, cellar, garner, store, storehouse, treasure, treasure house, treasury.

H215 אוֹר *ʾôr* a primitive root; *to be* (causatively *make*) *luminous* (literally and metaphorically):— break of day, glorious, kindle, light, lighten, enlighten, enlightened, be enlightened, set on fire, shine.

H216 אוֹר *ʾôr* from H215; *illumination* or (concrete) *luminary* (in every sense, including *lightning, happiness,* etc.):— bright, clear, day, light, lightning, morning, sun.

H217 אוּר *ʾûr* from H215; *flame,* hence (in the plural) the *East* (as being the region of light):— fire, light. See also H224

H218 אוּר *ʾûr* the same as H217; *Ur,* a place in Chaldaea; also an Israelite:— Ur.

H219 אוֹרָה *ʾôrâ* feminine of H216; *luminousness,* i.e. (figurative) *prosperity;* also a plant (as being *bright*):— herb, light.

H220 אֲוֵרָה *ʾăwērâ* by transposition for H723; a *stall:*— cote.

H221 אוּרִי *ʾûrî* from H217; *fiery; Uri,* the name of three Israelites:— Uri.

H222 אוּרִיאֵל *ʾûrîʾēl* from H217 and H410; *flame of God; Uriel,* the name of two Israelites:— Uriel.

H223 אוּרִיָּה *ʾûrîyâ* or (prolonged)

אוּרִיָּהוּ *ʾûrîyāhû* from H217 and H3050; *flame of Jah; Urijah,* the name of one Hittite and five Israelites:— Uriah, Urijah.

H224 אוּרִים *ʾûrîm* plural of H217; *lights; Urim,* the oracular brilliancy of the figures in the high-priest's breastplate:— Urim.

H225 אוּת *ʾût* a primitive root; properly to *come,* i.e. (implied) to *assent:*— consent.

H226 אוֹת *ʾôt* probably from H225 (in the sense of *appearing*); a *signal* (literal or figurative), as a *flag, beacon, monument, omen, prodigy, evidence,* etc:— mark, miracle, sign, ensign, token.

H227 אָז *ʾāz* a demonstrative adverb; *at that time* or *place;* also as a conjunction, *therefore:*— beginning, for, from, hitherto, now, of old, once, since, then, at which time, yet.

H228 אֲזָא *ʾăzāʾ* or

אֲזָה *ʾăzâ* (Aramaic) to *kindle;* (by implication) to *heat:*— heat, hot.

H229 אֶזְבַּי *ʾezbay* probably from H231; *hyssop-like; Ezbai,* an Israelite:— Ezbai.

H230 אֲזָד *ʾăzād* (Aramaic) of uncertain derivation; *firm:*— be gone.

H231 אֵזוֹב *ʾēzôb* probably of foreign derivation; *hyssop:*— hyssop.

H232 אֵזוֹר *ʾēzôr* from H246; something *girt;* a *belt,* also a *band:*— girdle.

H233 אֲזַי *ʾăzay* probably from H227; *at that time* :— then.

H234 אַזְכָּרָה *ʾazkārâ* from H2142; a *reminder;* specifically *remembrance-offering:*— memorial.

H235 אָזַל *ʾāzal* a primitive root; to *go away,* hence to *disappear:*— fail, gad about, go to and fro *[but in Ezek 27:19 the word is rendered* by *many* "from Uzal," *by others* "yarn"], be gone, be spent.

H236 אֲזַל *ʾăzal* (Aramaic) the same as H235; to *depart:*— go, go up.

H237 אֶזֶל *ʾezel* from H235; *departure; Ezel,* a memorial stone in Palestine:— Ezel.

H238 אָזַן *ʾāzan* a primitive root; probably to *expand;* but used only as a denominative from H241; to *broaden out the ear* (with the hand), i.e. (by implication) to *listen:*— give ear, perceive by the ear, hear, hearken. See H239

H239 אָזַן *ʾāzan* a primitive root [rather identical with H238 through the idea of *scales* as if two ears]; to *weigh,* i.e. (figuratively) *ponder:*— give good heed.

H240 אָזֵן *ʾāzēn* from H238; a *spade* or *paddle* (as having a *broad* end):— weapon.

H241 אֹזֶן *ʾōzen* from H238; *broadness,* i.e. (concretely) the *ear* (from its form in man):— advertise, audience, displease, ear, hearing, show.

H242 אֻזֵּן שֶׁאֱרָה *ʾuzzēn šeʾĕrâ* from H238 and H7609; *plat of Sheerah* (i.e. settled by him); *Uzzen-Sheërah,* a place in Palestine:— Uzzen-sherah.

H243 אַזְנוֹת תָּבוֹר *ʾaznôt tābôr* from H238 and H8396; *flats* (i.e. *tops*) *of Tabor* (i.e. situated on it); *Aznoth-Tabor,* a place in Palestine:— Aznoth-tabor.

H244 אׇזְנִי *ʾoznî* from H241; *having* (quick) *ears; Ozni,* an Israelite; also an *Oznite* (collectively), his descendants:— Ozni, Oznites.

H245 אֲזַנְיָה *ʾăzanyâ* from H238 and H3050; *heard* by *Jah; Azanjah,* an Israelite:— Azaniah.

H246 אֲזִקִּים *ʾăziqqîm* a variation for H213; *manacles:*— chains.

H247 אָזַר *ʾāzar* a primitive root; to *belt:*— bind about, compass about, gird, gird up, gird with.

H248 אֶזְרוֹעַ *ʾezrôaʿ* a variation for H2220; the *arm:*— arm.

H249 אֶזְרָח *ʾezrāḥ* from H2224 (in the sense of *springing up*); a spontaneous *growth,* i.e. *native* (tree or persons):— bay tree, born, born in the land, born in the country, born of the country, homeborn, of the country, of one's own country, of one's own nation.

H250 אֶזְרָחִי *ʾezrāḥî* patronymically from H2246; an *Ezrachite* or descendant of Zerach:— Ezrahite.

H251 אָח *ʾāḥ* a primitive word; a *brother* (used in the widest sense of literal relationship and metaphorical affinity or resemblance [like H1]):— another, brother, brotherly, kindred, like, other. Compare also the proper names beginning with "Ah-" or "Ahi-"

H252 אַח *ʾaḥ* (Aramaic) corresponding to H251 :— brother.

H253 אָח *ʾāḥ* a variation for H162; *Oh!* (expressive of grief or surprise):— ah, alas.

H254 אָח *ʾāḥ* of uncertain derivation; a fire-*pot* or chafing-dish:— hearth.

H255 אֹחַ *ʾōaḥ* probably from H253; a *howler* or lonesome wild animal:— doleful creature.

H256 אַחְאָב *ʾaḥʾāb* once (by contraction) (Jer. 29:22)

אֶחָב *ʾeḥāb* from H251 and H1; *brother* [i.e. *friend] of* (his) *father; Achab,* the name of a king of Israel and of a prophet at Babylon:— Ahab.

H257 אַחְבָּן *ʾaḥbān* from H251 and H995; *brother* (i.e. *possessor*) *of understanding; Achban,* an Israelite:— Ahban.

H258 אָחַד *ʾāḥad* perhaps a primitive root; to *unify,* i.e. (figuratively) *collect* (one's thoughts):— go one way or other.

H259 אֶחָד *ʾeḥād* a numeral from H258; properly *united,* i.e. *one;* or (as an ordinal) *first:*— a, alike, alone, altogether, and, any, anything, apiece, a certain, -ly (e.g., daily), each, each one, eleven, every, few, first, highway, a man, once, one, only, other some, together.

H260 אָחוּ *ʾāḥû* of uncertain (perhaps Egyptian) derivation; a *bulrush* or any marshy grass (particularly that along the Nile):— flag, meadow.

H261 אֵחוּד *ʾēḥûd* from H258; *united; Echud,* the name of three Israelites:— Ehud.

H262 אַחְוָה *ʾoḥwâ* from H2331 (in the sense of H2324); an *utterance:*— declaration.

H263 אַחֲוָה *ʾaḥăwâ* (Aramaic) corresponding to H262; *solution* (of riddles):— showing.

H264 אַחֲוָה *ʾaḥăwâ* from H251; *fraternity:*— brotherhood.

H265 אֲחוֹחַ *ʾăḥôaḥ* by reduplicated from H251; *brotherly; Achoach,* an Israelite:— Ahoah.

H266 אֲחוֹחִי *ʾăḥôḥî* patronymically from H264; an *Achochite* or descendant of Achoach:— Ahohite.

H267 אֲחוּמַי *ʾăḥûmay* perhaps from H251 and H4325; *brother* (i.e. *neighbour*) *of water; Achumai,* an Israelite:— Ahumai.

H268 אָחוֹר *ʾāḥôr* or (shortened)

אָחֹר *ʾāḥōr* from H299; the *hinder* part; hence (adverbially) *behind, backward;* also (as facing north) the *West:*— after, afterward, back, backpart, backside, backward, hereafter, hind, behind, hinder part, time to come, without.

H269 אָחוֹת *ʾāḥôt* irregular feminine of H251; a *sister* (used very widely [like H250], literally and figuratively):— other, another, sister, together.

H270 אָחַז *ʾāḥaz* a primitive root; to *seize* (often with the accessory idea of holding in possession):— be affrighted, bar, hold, catch hold, lay hold, take hold, hold back, come upon, fasten, handle, portion, possess, get possession, have or take possession.

H271 אָחָז *ʾāḥāz* from H270; *possessor; Achaz,* the name of a Jewish king and of an Israelite:— Ahaz.

H272 אֲחֻזָּה *ʾăḥuzzâ* feminine passive participle from H270; something *seized,* i.e. a *possession* (especially of land):— possession.

H273 אַחְזַי *ʾaḥzay* from H270; *seizer; Achzai,* an Israelite:— Ahasai.

H274 אֲחַזְיָה *ʾăḥazyâ* from H270 and H3050; *Jah has seized; Achazjah,* the name of a Jewish and an Israelite king:— Ahaziah.

H275 אֲחֻזָּם *ʾăḥuzzām* from H270; *seizure; Achuzzam,* an Israelite:— Ahuzam.

H276 אֲחֻזַּת *ʾăḥuzzat* a variation of H272; *possession; Achuzzath,* a Philistine:— Ahuzzath.

H277 אֲחִי *ʾăḥî* from H251; *brotherly; Achi,* the name of two Israelites:— Ahi.

H278 אֵחִי *ʾēḥî* probably the same as H277; *Echi,* an Israelite:— Ahi.

H279 אֲחִיאָם *ʾăḥîʾām* from H251 and H517; *brother of the mother* (i.e. *uncle*); *Achiam,* an Israelite:— Ahiam.

H280 אֲחִידָה *ʾăḥîdâ* (Aramaic) corresponding to H2420, an *enigma:*— hard sentence.

H281 אֲחִיָּה *ʾăḥîyâ* or (prolonged)

אֲחִיָּהוּ *ʾăḥîyāhû* from H251 and H3050; *brother* (i.e. *worshipper*) *of Jah; Achijah,* the name of nine Israelites:— Ahiah, Ahijah.

H282 אֲחִיהוּד *ʾăḥîhûd* from H251 and H1935; *brother* (i.e. *possessor*) *of renown; Achihud,* an Israelite:— Ahihud.

H283 אַחְיוֹ *ʾaḥyô* prolonged from H251; *brotherly; Achio,* the name of three Israelites:— Ahio.

H284 אֲחִיחֻד *ʾăḥîḥūd* from H251 and H2330; *brother of a riddle* (i.e. *mysterious*); *Achichud,* an Israelite:— Ahihud.

H285 אֲחִיטוּב *ʾăḥîṭûb* from H251 and H2898; *brother of goodness; Achitub,* the name of several priests:— Ahitub.

H286 אֲחִילוּד *ʾăḥîlûd* from H251 and H3205; *brother of one born; Achilud,* an Israelite:— Ahilud.

H287 אֲחִימוֹת *ʾăḥîmôt* from H251 and H4191; *brother of death; Achimoth,* an Israelite:— Ahimoth.

H288 אֲחִימֶלֶךְ *ʾăḥîmelek* from H251 and H4428; *brother of* (the) *king; Achimelek,* the name of an Israelite and of a Hittite:— Ahimelech.

H289 אֲחִימַן *ʾăḥîman* or

אֲחִימָן *ʾḥîmān* from H251 and H4480; *brother of a portion* (i.e. *gift*); *Achiman,* the name of an Anakite and of an Israelite:— Ahiman.

H290 אֲחִימַעַץ *ʾăḥîmaʿaṣ* from H251 and the equivalent of H4619; *brother of anger; Achimaats,* the name of three Israelites:— Ahimaaz.

H291 אַחְיָן *ʾaḥyān* from H251; *brotherly; Achjan,* an Israelite:— Ahian.

H292 אֲחִינָדָב *ʾăḥînādāb* from H251 and H5068; *brother of liberality; Achinadab,* an Israelite:— Ahinadab.

H293 אֲחִינֹעַם *ʾăḥînōʿam* from H251 and H5278; *brother of pleasantness; Achinoam,* the name of two Israelitesses:— Ahinoam.

H294 אֲחִיסָמָךְ *ʾăḥîsāmāk* from H251 and H5564; *brother of support; Achisamak,* an Israelite:— Ahisamach.

H295 אֲחִיעֶזֶר *ʾăḥîʿezer* from H251 and H5828; *brother of help: Achiezer,* the name of two Israelites:— Ahiezer.

H296 אֲחִיקָם *ʾăḥîqām* from H251 and H6965; *brother of rising* (i.e. *high*); *Achikam,* an Israelite:— Ahikam.

H297 אֲחִירָם *ʾăḥîrām* from H251 and H7311; *brother of height* (i.e. *high*); *Achiram,* an Israelite:— Ahiram.

H298 אֲחִירָמִי *ʾăḥîrāmî* patronymic from H297; an *Achiramite* or descendants (collectively) of Achiram :— Ahiramites.

H299 אֲחִירַע *ʾăḥîraʿ* from H251 and H7451; *brother of wrong; Achira,* an Israelite:— Ahira.

H300 אֲחִישַׁחַר *ʾăḥîšaḥar* from H251 and H7837; *brother of* (the) *dawn; Achishachar,* an Israelite:— Ahishar.

H301 אֲחִישָׁר *ʾăḥîšār* from H251 and H7891; *brother of* (the) *singer; Achishar,* an Israelite:— Ahishar.

H302 אֲחִיתֹפֶל *ʾăḥîtōpel* from H251 and H8602; *brother of folly; Achithophel,* an Israelite:— Ahithophel.

H303 אַחְלָב *ʾaḥlāb* from the same root as H2459; *fatness* (i.e. *fertile*); *Achlab,* a place in Palestine:— Ahiab.

H304 אַחְלַי *ʾaḥlay* the same as H305; *wishful; Achlai,* the name of an Israelitess and of an Israelite:— Ahlai.

H305 אַחֲלַי *ʾaḥălay* or

אַחֲלֵי *ʾaḥălê* probably from H253 and a variation of H3868; *would that!:*— O that, would God.

H306 אַחְלָמָה *ʾaḥlāmâ* perhaps from H2492 (and thus *dream-stone*); a gem, probably the *amethyst:*— amethyst.

H307 אַחְמְתָא *ʾaḥmĕtāʾ* of Persian derivation; *Achmetha* (i.e. *Ecbatana*), the summer capital of Persia:— Achmetha.

H308 אֲחַסְבַּי *ʾăḥasbay* of uncertain derivation; *Achasbai,* an Israelite:— Ahasbai.

H309 אָחַר *ʾāḥar* a primitive root; to *loiter* (i.e. *be behind*); by implication to *procrastinate:*— continue, defer, delay, hinder, be late, be slack, stay, stay there, tarry, tarry longer.

H310 אַחַר *ʾaḥar* from H209; properly the *hind* part; generally used as an adverb or conjunction, *after* (in various senses):— after, after that, afterward, again, at, away from, back, back from, backside, behind, beside, by, follow, follow after, following, forasmuch, from, hereafter, hinder end, outlive, overlive, persecute, posterity, pursuing, remnant, seeing, since, thenceforth, when, with.

H311 אַחַר *ʾaḥar* (Aramaic) corresponding to H310; *after:*— after, hereafter.

H312 אַחֵר *ʾaḥēr* from H309; properly *hinder;* generally *next, other,* etc:— other, other man, another, another man, following, next, strange.

H313 אַחֵר *ʾaḥēr* the same as H312; *Acher,* an Israelite:— Aher.

H314 אַחֲרוֹן *ʾaḥărôn* or (shortened)

אַחֲרֹן *ʾaḥărōn* from H309; *hinder;* generally *late* or *last;* specifically (as facing the east) *western:*— after, afterward, to come, following, hind, hinder, hindermost, hindmost, last, latter, rearward, utmost, uttermost.

H315 אַחְרַח *ʾaḥraḥ* from H310 and H251; *after* (his) *brother; Achrach,* an Israelite:— Aharah.

H316 אֲחַרְחֵל *ʾăḥarḥēl* from H310 and H2426; *behind* (the) *intrenchment* (i.e. *safe*); *Acharchel,* an Israelite:— Aharhel.

H317 אָחֳרִי *ʾoḥŏrî* (Aramaic) from H311; *other:*— other, another.

H318 אָחֳרֵין *ʾoḥŏrên* or (shortened)

אָחֳרֵן *ʾoḥŏrēn* (Aramaic) from H317; *last:*— at last.

H319 אַחֲרִית *ʾaḥărît* from H310; the *last* or *end,* hence the *future;* also *posterity:*— end, last end, latter, latter end, end time, hindermost, uttermost, length, posterity, remnant, residue, reward.

H320 אַחֲרִית *ʾaḥărît* (Aramaic) from H311; the same as H319; *later:*— latter.

H321 אָחֳרָן *ʾoḥŏrān* (Aramaic) from H311; the same as H317; *other:*— other, another.

H322 אֲחֹרַנִּית *ʾăḥōrannît* prolonged from H268; *backwards:*— back, backward, back again.

H323 אֲחַשְׁדַּרְפַּן *ʾăḥašdarpan* of Persian derivation; a *satrap* or governor of a main province (of Persia):— lieutenant.

H324 אֲחַשְׁדַּרְפַּן *ʾăḥašdarpan* (Aramaic) corresponding to H323:— prince.

H325 אֲחַשְׁוֵרוֹשׁ *ʾăḥašwērôš* or (shortened) (Esth 10:1)

אַחַשְׁרֹשׁ *ʾaḥašrōš* of Persian origin; *Achashverosh* (i.e. Ahasuerus or Artaxerxes, but in this case Xerxes), the title (rather than name) of a Persian king:— Ahasuerus.

H326 אֲחַשְׁתָּרִי *ʾăḥaštārî* probably of Persian derivation; an *achastarite* (i.e. courier); the designation (rather than name) of an Israelite:— Haakashtari *[including the article].*

H327 אֲחַשְׁתְּרָן *ʾăḥaštārān* of Persian origin; a *mule* :— camel.

H328 אַט *ʾaṭ* from an unused root perhaps meaning to *move softly;* (as a noun) a *necromancer* (from their soft incantations), (as an adverb) *gently:*— charmer, gently, secret, softly.

H329 אָטָד *ʾāṭād* from an unused root probably meaning to *pierce* or *make fast;* a *thorn*-tree (especially the *buckthorn*):— Atad, bramble, thorn.

H330 אֵטוּן *ʾēṭûn* from an unused root (probably meaning to *bind*); properly *twisted* (yarn), i.e. *tapestry:*— fine linen.

H331 אָטַם *ʾāṭam* a primitive root; to *close* (the lips or ears); by analogy to *contract* (a window by bevelled jambs):— narrow, shut, stop.

H332 אָטַר *ʾāṭar* a primitive root; to *close* up:— shut.

H333 אָטֵר *ʾāṭēr* from H332; *maimed; Ater,* the name of three Israelites:— Ater.

H334 אִטֵּר *ʾiṭṭēr* from H332; *shut* up, i.e. *impeded* (as to the use of the right hand):— left-handed.

H335 אַי *ʾay* perhaps from H370; *where?* hence *how?* :— how, what, whence, where, whether, which, which way.

H336 אִי *ʾî* probably identical with H335 (through the idea of a *query*); *not:*— island (Job 22:30).

H337 אִי *ʾî* shortened from H188; *alas!:*— woe.

H338 אִי *ʾî* probably identical with H337 (through the idea of a *doleful* sound); a *howler* (used only in the plural), i.e. any solitary wild creature:— wild beast of the islands.

H339 אִי *ʾî* from H183; properly a *habitable* spot (as *desirable*); dry *land,* a *coast,* an *island:*— country, isle, island.

H340 אָיַב *ʾāyab* a primitive root; to *hate* (as one of an opposite tribe or party); hence to *be hostile:*— be an enemy.

H341 אֹיֵב *ʾōyēb* or (fully)

אוֹיֵב *ʾôyēb* active participle of H340; *hating;* an *adversary:*— enemy, foe.

H342 אֵיבָה *ʾêbâ* from H340; *hostility:*— enmity, hatred.

H343 אֵיד *ʾêd* from the same as H181 (in the sense of *bending* down); *oppression;* by implication *misfortune, ruin:*— calamity, destruction.

H344 אַיָּה *ʾayyâ* perhaps from H337; the *screamer,* i.e. a *hawk:*— kite, vulture.

H345 אַיָּה *ʾayyâ* the same as H344; *Ajah,* the name of two Israelites:— Aiah, Ajah.

H346 אַיֵּה *ʾayyēh* prolonged from H335; *where?:*— where.

H347 אִיּוֹב *ʾiyôb* from H340; *hated* (i.e. *persecuted*); *Ijob,* the patriarch famous for his patience:— Job.

H348 אִיזֶבֶל *ʾîzebel* from H336 and H2083; *chaste; Izebel,* the wife of king Ahab:— Jezebel.

H349 אֵיךְ *ʾêk* also

אֵיכָה *ʾêkâ* and

אֵיכָכָה *ʾêkākâ* prolonged from H335; *how?* or *how!;* also *where:*— how, what.

H350 אִי־כָבוֹד *ʾî-kābôd* from H336 and H3519; (there is) *no glory,* i.e. *inglorious; Ikabod,* a son of Phineas:— I-chabod.

H351 אֵיכֹה *ʾêkōh* probably a variation for H349, but not as an interrogative; *where:*— where.

H352 אַיִל *ʾayil* from the same as H193; properly *strength;* hence anything *strong;* specifically a *chief* (politically); also a *ram* (from his strength); a *pilaster* (as a strong support); an *oak* or other strong tree:— mighty, mighty man, lintel, oak, post, ram, tree.

H353 אֱיָל *ʾĕyāl* a variation of H352; *strength:*— strength.

H354 אַיָּל *ʾayyāl* an intensive form of H352 (in the sense of *ram*); a *stag* or male deer:— hart.

H355 אַיָּלָה *ʾayyālâ* feminine of H354; a *doe* or female deer:— hind.

H356 אֵילוֹן *ʾêlôn* or (shortened)

אֵלוֹן *ʾēlôn* or

אֵילֹן *ʾêlōn* from H352; *oak-grove; Elon,* the name of a place in Palestine, and also of one Hittite, two Israelites:— Elon.

H357 אַיָּלוֹן *ʾayyālôn* from H354; *deer-field; Ajalon,* the name of five places in Palestine:— Aijalon, Ajalon.

H358 אֵילוֹן בֵּית חָנָן *ʾêlôn bêt ḥānān* from H356, H1004, and H2608; *oak-grove of* (the) *house of favor; Elon of Beth-chanan,* a place in Palestine:— Elon-beth-hanan.

H359 אֵילוֹת *ʾêlôt* or

אֵילַת *ʾêlat* from H352; *trees* or a *grove* (i.e. palms); *Eloth* or *Elath,* a place on the Red Sea:— Elath, Eloth.

H360 אֱיָלוּת *ʾĕyālût* feminine of H353; *power;* by implication *protection:*— strength.

H361 אֵילָם *ʾêlām* or (shortened)

אֵלָם *ʾēlām* or (feminine)

אֵלַמָּה *ʾēlammâ* probably from H352; a *pillar-space* (or colonnade), i.e. an *enclosure* (or portico):— arch.

H362 אֵילִם *ʾêlīm* plural of H352; palm-*trees; Elim,* a place in the Desert:— Elim.

H363 אִילָן *ʾîlān* (Aramaic) corresponding to H356; a *tree:*— tree.

H364 אֵיל פָּארָן *ʾêl pāʾrān* from H352 and H6290; *oak of Paran; El-Paran,* a portion of the district of Paran:— El-paran.

H365 אַיֶּלֶת *ʾayyelet* the same as H355; a *doe:*— hind, Aijeleth.

H366 אָיֹם *ʾāyōm* from an unused root (meaning to *frighten*); *frightful:*— terrible.

H367 אֵימָה *ʾêmâ* or (shortened)

אֵמָה *ʾēmâ* from the same as H355; *fright;* concretely an *idol* (as a bugbear):— dread, fear, horror, idol, terrible, terror.

H368 אֵימִים *ʾêmîm* plural of H367; *terrors; Emim,* an early Canaanitish (or Moabitish) tribe:— Emims.

H369 אַיִן *ʾayin* as if from a primitive root meaning to *be nothing* or *not exist;* a *non-entity;* generally used as a negative particle:— else, except, fail, fatherless, be gone, incurable, neither, never, no, nowhere, none, nor, nor any, nor any thing, not, nothing, to nought, past, unsearchable, well-nigh, without. Compare H370

H370 אַיִן *ʾayin* probably identical with H369 in the sense of *query* (compare H336); *where?* (only in connection with prepositional prefix, *whence*):— whence, where.

H371 אִין *ʾîn* apparently a shortened form of H369; but (like H370) interrogative; is it *not?:*— not.

H372 אִיעֶזֶר *ʾîʿezer* from H336 and H5828; *helpless; Iezer,* an Israelite:— Jeezer.

H373 אִיעֶזְרִי *ʾîʿezrî* patronymic from H372; an *Iezrite* or descendants of Iezer:— Jezerite.

H374 אֵיפָה *ʾêpâ* or (shortened)

אֵפָה *ʾēpâ* of Egyptian derivation; an *ephah* or measure for grain; hence a *measure* in general:— ephah, measure, divers measures.

H375 אֵיפֹה *ʾêpōh* from H335 and H6311; *what place?;* also (of time) *when?;* or (of means) *how?:*— what manner, where.

H376 אִישׁ *ʾîš* contraction for H582 [or perhaps rather from an unused root meaning to *be extant*]; a *man* as an individual or a male person; often used as an adjunct to a more definite term (and in such cases frequently not expressed in translation):— also, another, any, any man, a certain, champion, consent, each, every, every one, fellow, man, footman, husbandman, goodman, great man, mighty man, he, high, high degree, him, him that is, husband, mankind, none, one, people, person, steward, what man, whatsoever man, whoso, whosoever, worthy. Compare H802

H377 אִישׁ *ʾîš* denominative from H376; to *be a man,* i.e. act in a manly way:— show (one) self a man.

H378 אִישׁ־בֹּשֶׁת *ʾîš-bōšet* from H376 and H1322; *man of shame; Ish-Bosheth,* a son of King Saul:— Ish-bosheth.

H379 אִישְׁהוֹד *ʾîšĕhôd* from H376 and H1935; *man of renown; Ishod,* an Israelite:— Ishod.

H380 אִישׁוֹן *ʾîšôn* dimin. from H376; the *little man* of the eye; the *pupil* or *ball;* hence the *middle* (of night):— apple of the eye, black, obscure.

H381 אִישׁ־חַיִל *ʾîš-ḥayil* from H376 and H2428, *man of might;* by defective transcription (2 Sam. 23:20)

אִישׁ־חַי *ʾîš-hay* as if from H376 and H2416, *living man; Ish-chail* (or *Ish-chai*), an Israelite:— a valiant man.

H382 אִישׁ־טוֹב *ʾîš-ṭôb* from H376 and H2897; *man of Tob; Ish-Tob,* a place in Palestine:— Ish-tob.

H383 אִיתַי *ʾîtay* (Aramaic) corresponding to H3426; properly *entity;* used only as a particle of affirmation, there *is:*— art thou, can, do ye, have, it be, there is, there are, we will not.

H384 אִיתִיאֵל *ʾîtîʾēl* perhaps from H837 and H410; *God has arrived; Ithiel,* the name of an Israelites, also of a symbolic person:— Ithiel.

H385 אִיתָמָר *ʾîtāmār* from H339 and H8558; *coast of the palm*-tree; *Ithamar,* a son of Aaron:— Ithamar.

H386 אֵיתָן *ʾêtān* or (shortened)

אֵתָן *ʾētān* from an unused root (meaning to *continue*); *permanence;* hence (concretely) *permanent;* specifically a *chieftain:*— hard, mighty, rough, strength, strong.

H387 אֵיתָן *ʾêtān* the same as H386; *permanent; Ethan,* the name of four Israelites:— Ethan.

H388 אֵיתָנִים *ʾêtānîm* plural of H386; always with the article; the *permanent* brooks; *Ethanim,* the name of a month:— Ethanim.

H389 אַךְ *ʾak* akin to H408; a particle of affirmation, *surely;* hence (by limitation) *only:*— also, in any wise, at least, but certainly, even, howbeit, nevertheless, notwithstanding, only, save, surely, of a surety, truly, verily, wherefore, yet, yet but.

H390 אַכַּד *ʾakkad* from an unused root probably meaning to *strengthen;* a *fortress; Accad,* a place in Babylonia:— Accad.

H391 אַכְזָב *ʾakzāb* from H3576; *falsehood;* by implication *treachery:*— liar, lie.

H392 אַכְזִיב *ʾakzîb* from H391; *deceitful* (in the sense of a winter-torrent which *fails* in summer); *Akzib,* the name of two places in Palestine:— Achzib.

H393 אַכְזָר *ʾakzār* from an unused root (apparently meaning to *act harshly*); *violent;* by implication *deadly;* also (in a good sense) *brave:*— cruel, fierce.

H394 אַכְזָרִי *ʾakzārî* from H398; *terrible:*— cruel, cruel one.

H395 אַכְזְרִיּוּת *ʾakzĕriyût* from H394; *fierceness:*— cruel.

H396 אֲכִילָה *ʾăkîlâ* feminine from H398; something *eatable,* i.e. *food:*— meat.

H397 אָכִישׁ *ʾākîš* of uncertain derivation; *Akish,* a Philistine king:— Achish.

H398 אָכַל *ʾākal* a primitive root; to *eat* (literally or figuratively):— at all, burn up, consume, devour, devourer, devour up, dine, eat, eater, eat up, feed, feed with, food, freely, in . . . wise, indeed, in plenty, meat, lay meat, quite.

H399 אֲכַל *ʾăkal* (Aramaic) corresponding to H398 :— accuse, devour, eat.

H400 אֹכֶל *ʾōkel* from H398; *food:*— eating, food, mealtime, meat, prey, victuals.

H401 אֻכָל *ʾukāl* or

אֻכָּל *ʾukkāl* apparently from H398; *devoured; Ucal,* a fancy name:— Ucal.

H402 אָכְלָה *ʾoklâ* feminine of H401; *food:*— consume, devour, eat, food, meat.

H403 אָכֵן *ʾākēn* from H3559 [compare H3651]; *firmly;* figuratively *surely;* also (adversatively) *but:*— but, certainly, nevertheless, surely, truly, verily.

H404 אָכַף *ʾākap* a primitive root; apparently meaning to *curve* (as with a burden); to *urge:*— crave.

H405 אֶכֶף *ʾekep* from H404; a *load;* by implication a *stroke* (others *dignity*):— hand.

H406 אִכָּר *ʾikkār* from an unused root meaning to *dig;* a *farmer:*— husbandman, ploughman.

H407 אַכְשָׁף *ʾakšāp* from H3784; *fascination; Acshaph,* a place in Palestine:— Achshaph.

H408 אַל *ʾal* a negative particle [akin to H3808]; *not* (the qualified negation, used as a deprecative); once (Job 24:25) as a noun, *nothing:*— nay, neither, never, no, nor, not, nothing worth, rather than.

H409 אַל *ʾal* (Aramaic) corresponding to H408:— not.

H410 אֵל *ʾēl* shortened from H352; *strength;* as adjective *mighty;* especially the *Almighty* (but used also of any *deity*):— God, god, goodly, great, idol, might, mighty one, power, strong. Compare names in "-el"

H411 אֵל *ʾēl;* a demonstrative particle (but only in a plural sense) *these* or *those:*— these, those. Compare H428

H412 אֵל *ʾēl* (Aramaic) corresponding to H411:— these.

H413 אֵל *ʾēl* but used only in this shortened construct form

אֶל *ʾel* a primitive particle; properly denoting motion *towards,* but occasionally used of a quiescent position, i.e. *near, with* or *among;* often in general, *to:*— about, according to, after, against, among, as for, at, because, before, beside, both . . . and, by, concerning, for, from, hath, in, into, near, of, out of, over, through, to, toward, under, unto, upon, whether, with, within.

H414 אֵלָא *ʾēlāʾ* a variation of H424; *oak; Ela,* an Israelite:— Elah.

H415 אֵל אֱלֹהֵי יִשְׂרָאֵל *ʾēl ʾĕlōhê yiśrāʾēl* from H410 and H430 and H3478; the *mighty God of Jisrael; El-Elohi-Jisrael,* the title given to a consecrated spot by Jacob:— El-elohe-israel.

H416 אֵל בֵּית־אֵל *ʾēl bêt-ʾēl* from H410 and H1008; the *God of Bethel; El-Bethel,* the title given to a consecrated spot by Jacob:— El-beth-el.

H417 אֶלְגָּבִישׁ *ʾelgābîš* from H410 and H1378; *hail* (as if a *great pearl*):— great hailstones.

H418 אַלְגּוּמִּים *ʾalgûmmîm* by transposition for H484; sticks of *algum* wood:— algum trees.

H419 אֶלְדָּד *ʾeldād* from H410 and H1780; *God has loved; Eldad,* an Israelite:— Eldad.

H420 אֶלְדָּעָה *ʾeldāʿâ* from H410 and H3045; *God of knowledge; Eldaah,* a son of Midian:— Eldaah.

H421 אָלָה *ʾālâ* a primitive root [rather identical with H422 through the idea of *invocation*]; to *bewail:*— lament.

H422 אָלָה *ʾālâ* a primitive root; properly to *adjure,* i.e. (usually in a bad sense) *imprecate:*— adjure, curse, swear.

H423 אָלָה *ʾālâ* from H422; an *imprecation:*— curse, cursing, execration, oath, swearing.

H424 אֵלָה *ʾēlâ* feminine of H352; an *oak* or other strong tree:— elm, oak, teil tree.

H425 אֵלָה *ʾēlâ* the same as H424; *Elah,* the name of an Edomite, of four Israelites, and also of a place in Palestine:— Elah.

H426 אֱלָהּ *ʾĕlāh* (Aramaic) corresponding to H433; *God:*— God, god.

H427 אַלָּה *ʾallâ* a variation of H424:— oak.

H428 אֵלֶּה *ʾēlleh* prolonged from H411; *these* or *those:*— another, the other, one sort, so, some, such, them, these, these same, they, this, those, thus, which, who, whom.

H429 אֵלֶּה *ʾēlleh* (Aramaic) corresponding to H428 :— these.

H430 אֱלֹהִים *ʾĕlōhîm* plural of H433; *gods* in the ordinary sense; but specifically used (in the plural thus, especially with the article) of the supreme *God;* occasionally applied by way of deference to *magistrates;* and sometimes as a superlative:— angels, exceeding, God, gods, godess, godly, great, very great, judges, mighty.

H431 אֲלוּ *ʾălû* (Aramaic) probably prolonged from H412; *lo!:*— behold.

H432 אִלּוּ *ʾillû* probably from H408; *nay,* i.e. (softened) *if:*— but if, yea though.

H433 אֱלוֹהַּ *ʾĕlôah* probably prolonged (emphatically) from H410; a *deity* or the *Deity:*— God, god. See H430

H434 אֱלוּל *ʾĕlûl* for H457; good for *nothing:*— thing of nought.

H435 אֱלוּל *ʾĕlûl* probably of foreign derivation; *Elul,* the sixth Jewish month:— Elul.

H436 אֵלוֹן *ʾēlôn* prolonged from H352; an *oak* or other strong tree:— plain. See also H356

H437 אַלּוֹן *ʾallôn* a variation of H436:— oak.

H438 אַלּוֹן *ʾallôn* the same as H437; *Allon,* an Israelite, also a place in Palestine:— Allon.

H439 אַלּוֹן בָּכוּת *ʾallôn bākût* from H437 and a variation of H1068; *oak of weeping; Allon-Bakuth,* a monumental tree:— Allon-bachuth.

H440 אֵלוֹנִי *ʾēlônî* or rather (shortened)

אֵלֹנִי *ʾēlōnî* patronymic from H438; an *Alonite* or descendants (collectively) of Alon:— Elonites.

H441 אַלּוּף *ʾallûp* or (shortened)

אַלֻּף *ʾallup* from H502; *familiar; a friend,* also *gentle;* hence a *bullock* (as being tame; applied, although masculine, to a *cow*); and so a *chieftain* (as notable like neat cattle):— captain, duke, friend, chief friend, governor, guide, ox.

H442 אָלוּשׁ *ʾālûš* of uncertain derivation; *Alush,* a place in the Desert:— Alush.

H443 אֶלְזָבָד *ʾelzābād* from H410 and H2064; *God has bestowed; Elzabad,* the name of two Israelites:— Elzabad.

H444 אָלַח *ʾālaḥ* a primitive root; to *muddle,* i.e. (figuratively and intransitively) to *turn* (morally) *corrupt:*— become filthy.

H445 אֶלְחָנָן *ʾelḥānān* from H410 and H2603; *God* (is) *gracious; Elchanan,* an Israelite:— Elkanan.

H446 אֱלִיאָב *ʾĕlîʾāb* from H410 and H1; *God of* (his) *father; Eliab,* the name of six Israelites:— Eliab.

H447 אֱלִיאֵל *ʾĕlîʾēl* from H410 repeated; *God of* (his) *God; Eliel,* the name of nine Israelites:— Eliel.

H448 אֱלִיאָתָה *ʾĕlîʾātâ* or (contracted)

אֱלִיָּתָה *ʾlîyātâ* from H410 and H225; *God of* (his) *consent; Eliathah,* an Israelite:— Eliathah.

H449 אֱלִידָד *ʾĕlîdād* from the same as H419; *God of* (his) *love; Elidad,* an Israelite:— Elidad.

H450 אֶלְיָדָע *ʾelyādāʿ* from H410 and H3045; *God* (is) *knowing; Eljada,* the name of two Israelites and of an Aramaean leader:— Eliada.

H451 אַלְיָה *ʾalyâ* from H422 (in the original sense of *strength*); the *stout* part, i.e. the fat *tail* of the Oriental sheep:— rump.

H452 אֵלִיָּה *ʾēlîyâ* or (prolonged)

אֵלִיָּהוּ *ʾēlîyāhû* from H410 and H3050; *God of Jehovah; Elijah,* the name of the famous prophet and of two other Israelites:— Elijah, Eliah.

H453 אֱלִיהוּ *ʾĕlîhû* or (fully)

אֱלִיהוּא *ʾĕlîhûʾ* from H410 and H1931; *God of him; Elihu,* the name of one of Job's friends, and of three Israelites:— Elihu.

H454 אֶלְיְהוֹעֵינַי *ʾelyĕhôʿênay* or (shortened)

אֶלְיוֹעֵינַי *ʾelyôʿênay* from H413 and H3068 and H5869; *towards Jehovah* (are) *my eyes; Eljehoenai* or *Eljoenai,* the name of seven Israelites:— Elihoenai, Elionai.

H455 אֶלְיַחְבָּא *ʾelyaḥbāʾ* from H410 and H2244; *God will hide; Eljachba,* an Israelite:— Eliahbah.

H456 אֱלִיחֹרֶף *ʾĕlîḥōrep* from H410 and H2779; *God of autumn; Elichoreph,* an Israelite:— Elihoreph.

H457 אֱלִיל *ʾĕlîl* apparently from H408; good for *nothing,* by analogy *vain* or *vanity;* specifically an *idol:*— idol, no value, thing of nought.

H458 אֱלִימֶלֶךְ *ʾĕlîmelek* from H410 and H4428; *God of* (the) *king; Elimelek,* an Israelite:— Elimelech.

H459 אִלֵּין *ʾillên* or shorter

אִלֵּן *ʾillēn* (Aramaic) prolonged from H412; *these:*— the, these.

H460 אֶלְיָסָף *ʾelyāsāp* from H410 and H3254; *God* (is) *gatherer; Eljasaph,* the name of two Israelites:— Eliasaph.

H461 אֱלִיעֶזֶר *ʾĕlîʿezer* from H410 and H5828; *God of help; Eliezer,* the name of a Damascene and of ten Israelites:— Eliezer.

H462 אֱלִיעֵינַי *ʾĕlîʿênay* probably contracted for H454; *Elienai,* an Israelite:— Elienai.

H463 אֱלִיעָם *ʾĕlîʿām* from H410 and H5971; *God of* (the) *people; Eliam,* an Israelite:— Eliam.

H464 אֱלִיפַז *ʾĕlîpaz* from H410 and H6337; *God of gold; Eliphaz,* the name of one of Job's friends, and of a son of Esau:— Eliphaz.

H465 אֱלִיפָל *ʾĕlîpāl* from H410 and H6337; *God of judgment; Eliphal,* an Israelite:— Eliphal.

H466 אֱלִיפְלֵהוּ *ʾĕlîpĕlēhû* from H410 and H6395; *God of his distinction; Eliphelehu,* an Israelite:— Elipheleh.

H467 אֱלִיפֶלֶט *ʾĕlîpeleṭ* or (shortened)

אֶלְפֶּלֶט *ʾelpeleṭ* from H410 and H6405; *God of deliverance; Eliphelet* or *Elpelet,* the name of six Israelites:— Eliphalet, Eliphelet, Elpalet.

H468 אֱלִיצוּר *ʾĕlîṣûr* from H410 and H6697; *God of* (the) *rock; Elitsur,* an Israelite:— Elizur.

H469 אֱלִיצָפָן *ʾĕlîṣāpān* or (shortened)

אֶלְצָפָן *ʾelṣāpān* from H410 and H6845; *God of treasure; Elitsaphan* or *Eltsaphan,* an Israelite:— Elizaphan, Elzaphan.

H470 אֱלִיקָא *ʾĕlîqāʾ* from H410 and H6958; *God of rejection; Elika,* an Israelite:— Elika.

H471 אֶלְיָקִים *ʾelyāqîm* from H410 and H6965; *God of raising; Eljakim,* the name of four Israelites:— Eliakim.

H472 אֱלִישֶׁבַע *ʾĕlîšebaʿ* from H410 and H7651 (in the sense of H7650); *God of* (the) *oath; Elisheba,* the wife of Aaron:— Elisheba.

H473 אֱלִישָׁה *ʾĕlîšâ* probably of foreign derivation; *Elishah,* a son of Javan:— Elishah.

H474 אֱלִישׁוּעַ *ʾĕlîšûaʿ* from H410 and H7769; *God of supplication* (or *of riches*); *Elishua,* a son of King David:— Elishua.

H475 אֶלְיָשִׁיב *ʾelyāšîb* from H410 and H7725; *God will restore; Eljashib,* the name of six Israelites:— Eliashib.

H476 אֱלִישָׁמָע *ʾĕlîšāmāʿ* from H410 and H7725; *God of hearing; Elishama,* the name of seven Israelites:— Elishama.

H477 אֱלִישָׁע *ʾĕlîšāʿ* contracted for H474; *Elisha,* the famous prophet:— Elisha.

H478 אֱלִישָׁפָט *ʾĕlîšāpāṭ* from H410 and H8199; *God of judgment; Elishaphat,* an Israelite:— Elishaphat.

H479 אִלֵּךְ *ʾillēk* (Aramaic) prolonged from H412; *these:*— these, those.

H480 אַלְלַי *ʾallay* by reduplication from H421; *alas!* :— woe.

H481 אָלַם *ʾālam* a primitive root; to *tie* fast; hence (of the mouth) to be *tongue-tied:*— bind, be dumb, put to silence.

H482 אֵלֶם *ʾēlem* from H481; *silence* (i.e. mute justice):— congregation. Compare H3128

H483 אִלֵּם *ʾillēm* from H481; *speechless:*— dumb, dumb man.

H484 אַלְמֻגִּים *ʾalmuggîm* probably of foreign derivation (used thus only in the plural); *almug* (i.e. probably sandal-wood) sticks:— almug trees. Compare H418

H485 אֲלֻמָּה *ʾălummâ* or (masculine)
אָלֻם *ʾālum* passive participle of H481; something *bound;* a *sheaf:*— sheaf.

H486 אַלְמוֹדָד *ʾalmôdād* probably of foreign derivation; *Almodad,* a son of Joktan:— Almodad.

H487 אַלַּמֶּלֶךְ *ʾallammelek* from H427 and H4428; *oak of* (the) *king; Allammelek,* a place in Palestine:— Alammelech.

H488 אַלְמָן *ʾalmān* prolonged from H481 in the sense of *bereavement; discarded* (as a divorced person):— forsaken.

H489 אַלְמֹן *ʾalmōn* from H481 as in H488; *bereavement:*— widowhood.

H490 אַלְמָנָה *ʾalmānâ* feminine of H488; a *widow;* also a *desolate* place:— desolate house, desolate place, widow.

H491 אַלְמָנוּת *ʾalmānût* feminine of H488; concretely a *widow;* abstractly *widowhood:*— widow, widowhood.

H492 אַלְמֹנִי *ʾalmōnî* from H489 in the sense of *concealment; some* one (i.e. *so and so,* without giving the name of the person or place):— one, and such.

H493 אֶלְנַעַם *ʾelnaʿam* from H410 and H5276; *God* (is his) *delight; Elnaam,* an Israelite:— Elnaam.

H494 אֶלְנָתָן *ʾelnātān* from H410 and H5414; *God* (is the) *giver; Elnathan,* the name of four Israelites:— Elnathan.

H495 אֶלָּסָר *ʾellāsār* probably of foreign derivation; *Ellasar,* an early country of Asia:— Ellasar.

H496 אֶלְעָד *ʾelʿād* from H410 and H5749; *God has testified; Elad,* an Israelite:— Elead.

H497 אֶלְעָדָה *ʾelʿādâ* from H410 and H5710; *God has decked; Eladah,* an Israelite:— Eladah.

H498 אֶלְעוּזַי *ʾelʿûzay* from H410 and H5756 (in the sense of H5797); *God* (is) *defensive; Eluzai,* an Israelite:— Eluzai.

H499 אֶלְעָזָר *ʾelʿāzār* from H410 and H5826; *God* (is) *helper; Elazar,* the name of seven Israelites:— Eleazar.

H500 אֶלְעָלֵא *ʾelʿālēʾ* or (more properly)
אֶלְעָלֵה *ʾelʿālēh* from H410 and H5927; *God* (is) *going up; Elale* or *Elaleh,* a place east of the Jordan:— Elealeh.

H501 אֶלְעָשָׂה *ʾelʿāśâ* from H410 and H6213; *God has made; Elasah,* the name of four Israelites:— Elasah, Eleasah.

H502 אָלַף *ʾālap* a primitive root, to *associate* with; hence to *learn* (and causative to *teach*):— learn, teach, utter.

H503 אָלַף *ʾālap* denominative from H505; causative to *make a thousandfold:*— bring forth thousands.

H504 אֶלֶף *ʾelep* from H502; a *family;* also (from the sense of *yoking* or *taming*) an *ox* or *cow:*— family, kine, oxen.

H505 אֶלֶף *ʾelep* properly the same as H504; hence (an ox's head being the first letter of the alphabet, and this eventually used as a numeral) a *thousand:*— thousand.

H506 אֲלַף *ʾălap* or
אֶלֶף *ʾelep* (Aramaic) corresponding to H505 :— thousand.

H507 אֶלֶף *ʾelep* the same as H505; *Eleph,* a place in Palestine:— Eleph.

H508 אֶלְפַּעַל *ʾelpaʿal* from H410 and H6466; *God* (is) *act; Elpaal,* an Israelite:— Elpaal.

H509 אָלַץ *ʾālaṣ* a primitive root; to *press:*— urge.

H510 אַלְקוּם *ʾalqûm* probably from H408 and H6965; a *non-rising* (i.e. *inability to resist*):— no rising up.

H511 אֶלְקָנָה *ʾelqānâ* from H410 and H7069; *God has obtained; Elkanah,* the name of seven Israelites:— Elkanah.

H512 אֶלְקֹשִׁי *ʾelqōšî* patrial from a name of uncertain derivation; an *Elkoshite* or native of Elkosh:— Elkoshite.

H513 אֶלְתּוֹלַד *ʾeltôlad* probably from H410 and a masculine form of H8435 [compare H8434]; *God* (is) *generator; Eltolad,* a place in Palestine:— Eltolad.

H514 אֶלְתְּקֵא *ʾeltĕqēʾ* or (more properly)
אֶלְתְּקֵה *ʾeltĕqēh* of uncertain derivation; *Eltekeh* or *Elteke,* a place in Palestine:— Eltekeh.

H515 אֶלְתְּקֹן *ʾeltĕqōn* from H410 and H8626; *God* (is) *straight; Eltekon,* a place in Palestine:— Eltekon.

H516 אַל תַּשְׁחֵת *ʾal tašḥēt* from H408 and H7843; *Thou must not destroy;* probably the opening words of a popular song:— Al-taschith.

H517 אֵם *ʾēm* a primitive word; a *mother* (as the *bond* of the family); in a wide sense (both literally and figuratively) [like H1]:— dam, mother, parting.

H518 אִם *ʾim* a primitive particle; used very widely as demonstrative, *lo!;* interrogative, *whether?;* or conditional, *if, although;* also *Oh that!, when;* hence as a negative, *not:*— and, and not, cannot, doubtless not, if, if not, that not, not, but, either, except, more, moreover if, more than, neither, nevertheless, nor, oh that, or, save, save only, saving, seeing, since, sith, surely, surely no more, surely none, surely not, though, of a truth, unless, verily, when, whereas, whether, while, yet.

H519 אָמָה *ʾāmâ* apparently a primitive word; a *maid-servant* or female slave:— handmaid, bondmaid, bondwoman, maid, maidservant.

H520 אַמָּה *ʾammâ* prolonged from H517; properly a *mother* (i.e. *unit*) of measure, of the *fore-arm* (below the elbow), i.e. a *cubit;* also a door-*base* (as a *bond* of the entrance):— cubit, hundred *[by exchange for H3967],* measure, post.

H521 אַמָּה *ʾammâ* (Aramaic) corresponding to H520:— cubit.

H522 אַמָּה *ʾammâ* the same as H520; *Ammah,* a hill in Palestine:— Ammah.

H523 אֻמָּה *ʾummah* from the same as H517; a *collection,* i.e. community of persons:— nation, people.

H524 אֻמָּה *ʾummâ* (Aramaic) corresponding to H523:— nation.

H525 אָמוֹן *ʾāmôn* from H539, probably in the sense of *training; skilled,* i.e. an architect [like H542]:— one brought up.

H526 אָמוֹן *ʾāmôn* the same as H525; *Amon,* the name of three Israelites:— Amon.

H527 אָמוֹן *ʾāmôn* a variation for H1995; a *throng* of people:— multitude.

H528 אָמוֹן *ʾāmôn* of Egyptian derivation; *Amon* (i.e. Ammon or Amn), a deity of Egypt (used only as an adjunct of H4996):— multitude, populous.

H529 אֵמוּן *ʾēmûn* from H539; *established,* i.e. (figuratively) *trusty;* also (abstractly) *trustworthiness:*— faith, faithful, truth.

H530 אֱמוּנָה *ʾĕmûnâ* or (shortened)
אֱמֻנָה *ʾĕmūnâ* feminine of H529; literally *firmness;* figuaratively *security;* morally *fidelity:*— faith, faithful, faithfully, faithfulness, faithful man, set office, stability, steady, truly, truth, verily.

H531 אָמוֹץ *ʾāmôṣ* from H553; *strong; Amots,* an Israelite:— Amos.

H532 אָמִי *ʾāmî* an abbreviation for H526; *Ami,* an Israelite:— Ami.

H533 אַמִּיץ *ʾammîṣ* or (shortened)
אַמִּץ *ʾammiṣ* from H553; *strong* or (abstractly) *strength:*— courageous, mighty, strong, strong one.

H534 אָמִיר *ʾāmîr* apparently from H559 (in the sense of *self-exaltation*); a *summit* (of a tree or mountain):— bough, branch.

H535 אָמַל *ʾāmal* a primitive root; to *droop;* by implication to *be sick,* to *mourn:*— languish, be weak, wax feeble.

H536 אֻמְלַל *ʾumlal* from H535; *sick:*— weak.

H537 אֲמֵלָל *ʾămēlāl* from H535; *languid:*— feeble.

H538 אֲמָם *ʾămām* from H517; *gathering*-spot; *Amam,* a place in Palestine:— Amam.

H539 אָמַן *ʾāman* a primitive root; properly to *build up* or *support;* to *foster* as a parent or nurse; figuratively to *render* (or *be*) *firm* or faithful, to *trust* or believe, to be *permanent* or quiet; morally to *be true* or certain; once (Isa 30:21; by interchange for H541) to *go to the right hand:*— hence assurance, believe, bring up, establish, fail, be faithful, be of long continuance, be stedfast, be sure, surely, trusty, verified, nurse, nursing father, trust, put trust, turn to the right.

H540 אֲמַן *ʾăman* (Aramaic) corresponding to H539 :— believe, faithful, sure.

H541 אָמַן *ʾāman* denominative from H3225; to take the *right hand* road:— turn to the right. See H539

H542 אָמָן *ʾāmān* from H539 (in the sense of *training*); an *expert:*— cunning workman.

H543 אָמֵן *ʾāmēn* from H539; *sure;* abstractly *faithfulness;* adverb *truly:*— Amen, so be it, truth.

H544 אֹמֶן *ʾōmen* from H539; *verity:*— truth.

H545 אָמְנָה *ʾomnâ* feminine of H544 (in the specific sense of *training*); *tutelage:*— brought up.

H546 אָמְנָה *ʾomnâ* feminine of H544 (in its usual sense); adverb *surely:*— indeed.

H547 אֹמְנָה *ʾōmĕnâ* feminine active participle of H544 (in the original sense of *supporting*); a *column:*— pillar.

H548 אֲמָנָה *ʾămānâ* feminine of H543; something *fixed,* i.e. a *covenant,* an *allowance:*— certain portion, sure.

H549 אֲמָנָה *ʾămānâ* the same as H548; *Amanah,* a mountain near Damascus:— Amana.

H550 אַמְנוֹן *ʾamnôn* or

אֲמִינוֹן *ʾămînôn* from H539; *faithful; Amnon* (or Aminon), a son of David:— Amnon.

H551 אָמְנָם *ʾomnām* adverb from H544; *verily:*— indeed, no doubt, surely, true, truly, it is true, of a truth.

H552 אֻמְנָם *ʾumnām* an orthographic variation of H551:— in deed, in very deed; of a surety.

H553 אָמַץ *ʾāmaṣ* a primitive root; to *be alert,* physically (on foot) or mentally (in courage):— confirm, be courageous, be of good courage, be stedfastly minded, be strong, be stronger, establish, fortify, harden, increase, prevail, strengthen, strengthen self, make strong, make obstinate, make speed.

H554 אָמֹץ *ʾāmōṣ* probably from H553; of a *strong* color, i.e. *red* (others *fleet*):— bay.

H555 אֹמֶץ *ʾōmeṣ* from H553; *strength:*— stronger.

H556 אַמְצָה *ʾomṣâ* from H553; *force:*— strength.

H557 אַמְצִי *ʾamṣî* from H553; *strong; Amtsi,* an Israelite:— Amzi.

H558 אֲמַצְיָה *ʾămaṣyâ* or

אֲמַצְיָהוּ *ʾămaṣyāhû* from H553 and H3050; *strength of Jah; Amatsjah,* the name of four Israelites:— Amaziah.

H559 אָמַר *ʾāmar* a primitive root; to *say* (used with great latitude):— answer, appoint, avouch, bid, boast self, call, certify, challenge, charge, command, at the commandment, give commandment, commune, consider, declare, demand, desire, determine, expressly, indeed, intend, name, plainly, promise, publish, report, require, say, speak, speak against, speak of, still, suppose, talk, tell, term, that is, think, use speech, utter, verily, yet.

H560 אֲמַר *ʾămar* (Aramaic) corresponding to H559 :— command, declare, say, speak, tell.

H561 אֵמֶר *ʾēmer* from H559; something *said:*— answer, appointed unto him, saying, speech, word.

H562 אֹמֶר *ʾōmer* the same as H561:— promise, speech, thing, word.

H563 אִמַּר *ʾimmar* (Aramaic) perhaps from H560 (in the sense of *bringing forth*); a *lamb:*— lamb.

H564 אִמֵּר *ʾimmēr* from H559; *talkative; Immer,* the name of five Israelites:— Immer.

H565 אִמְרָה *ʾimrâ* or

אֶמְרָה *ʾemrâ* feminine of H561, and meaning the same:— commandment, speech, word.

H566 אִמְרִי *ʾimrî* from H564; *wordy; Imri,* the name of two Israelites:— Imri.

H567 אֱמֹרִי *ʾĕmōrî* probably a patronymic from an unused name derived from H559 in the sense of *publicity,* i.e. prominence; thus a *mountaineer;* an *Emorite,* one of the Canaanitish tribes:— Amorite.

H568 אֲמַרְיָה *ʾămaryâ* or (prolonged)

אֲמַרְיָהוּ *ʾămaryāhû* from H559 and H3050; *Jah has said* (i.e. promised); *Amarjah,* the name of nine Israelites:— Amariah.

H569 אַמְרָפֶל *ʾamrāpel* of uncertain (perhaps foreign) derivation; *Amraphel,* a king of Shinar:— Amraphel.

H570 אֶמֶשׁ *ʾemeš;* time *past,* i.e. *yesterday* or *last night:*— former time, yesterday, yesternight.

H571 אֱמֶת *ʾemet* contracted from H539; *stability;* figuratively *certainty, truth, trustworthiness:*— assured, assuredly, establishment, faithful, right, sure, true, truly, truth, verity.

H572 אַמְתַּחַת *ʾamtaḥat* from H4969; properly something *expansive,* i.e. a *bag:*— sack.

H573 אֲמִתַּי *ʾămittay* from H571; *veracious; Amittai,* an Israelite:— Amittai.

H574 אֵמְתָנִי *ʾēmettānî* (Aramaic) from a root corresponding to that of H4975; well-*loined* (i.e. burly) or *mighty:*— terrible.

H575 אָן *ʾān* or

אָנָה *ʾānâ* contracted from H370; *where?;* hence *whither?, when?;* also *hither* and *thither:*— whither, any whither, no whither, whithersoever, now, where.

H576 אֲנָא *ʾănāʾ* or

אֲנָה *ʾănâ* (Aramaic) corresponding to H589; *I:*— I, as for me.

H577 אָנָּא *ʾonnāʾ* or

אָנָּה *ʾonnâ* apparently contracted from H160 and H4994; *oh now!:*— I beseech thee, O; I pray thee, O.

H578 אָנָה *ʾānâ* a primitive root; to *groan:*— lament, mourn.

H579 אָנָה *ʾānâ* a primitive root [perhaps rather identical with H578 through the idea of *contraction* in anguish]; to *approach;* hence to *meet* in various senses:— befall, deliver, happen, seek a quarrel.

H580 אֲנוּ *ʾănû* contracted for H587; *we:*— we.

H581 אִנּוּן *ʾinnûn* or (feminine)

אִנִּין *ʾinnîn* (Aramaic) corresponding to H1992; *they:*— are, them, these.

H582 אֱנוֹשׁ *ʾĕnôš* from H605; properly a *mortal* (and thus differing from the more dignified H120); hence a *man* in general (singly or collectively):— another, bloodthirsty, certain, chapman, divers, fellow, in the flower of their age, husband, man, certain man, mortal man, people, person, servant, some, some of them, stranger, those, their trade. It is often unexpressed in the English Version, especially when used in apposition with another word. Compare H376

H583 אֱנוֹשׁ *ʾĕnôš* the same as H582; *Enosh,* a son of Seth:— Enos.

H584 אָנַח *ʾānaḥ* a primitive root; to *sigh:*— groan, mourn, sigh.

H585 אֲנָחָה *ʾănāḥâ* from H585; *sighing:*— groaning, mourning, sighing.

H586 אֲנַחְנָא *ʾănaḥnāʾ* or

אֲנַחְנָה *ʾănaḥnâ* (Aramaic) corresponding to H587; *we:*— we.

H587 אֲנַחְנוּ *ʾănaḥnû* apparently from H595; *we:*— ourselves, us, we.

H588 אֲנָחֲרָת *ʾănāḥărāt* probably from the same root as H5170; a *forge* or narrow pass; *Anacharath,* a place in Palestine:— Anaharath.

H589 אֲנִי *ʾănî* contracted from H595; *I:*— I, me, as for me, mine, myself, we, which, who.

H590 אֳנִי *ʾŏnî* probably from H579 (in the sense of *conveyance*); a *ship* or (collectively) a *fleet:*— galley, navy, navy of ships.

H591 אֳנִיָּה *ʾŏnîyâ* feminine of H590; a *ship:*— ship, shipmen.

H592 אֲנִיָּה *ʾănîyâ* from H578; *groaning:*— lamentation, sorrow.

H593 אֲנִיעָם *ʾănîʿām* from H578 and H5971; *groaning* of (the) *people; Aniam,* an Israelite:— Aniam.

H594 אֲנָךְ *ʾănāk* probably from an unused root meaning to *be narrow;* according to most a *plumbline,* and to others a *hook:*— plumbline.

H595 אָנֹכִי *ʾānōkî* a primitive pronoun; *I:*— I, me, which.

H596 אָנַן *ʾānan* a primitive root; to *mourn,* i.e. *complain:*— complain.

H597 אָנַס *ʾānas* to *insist:*— compel.

H598 אֲנַס *ʾănas* (Aramaic) corresponding to H597; figuratively to *distress:*— trouble.

H599 אָנַף *ʾānap* a primitive root; to *breathe* hard, i.e. *be enraged:*— be angry, be displeased.

H600 אֲנַף *ʾănap* (Aramaic) corresponding to H639 (only in the plural as a singular); the *face:*— face, visage.

H601 אֲנָפָה *ʾănāpâ* from H599; an unclean bird, perhaps the *parrot* (from its *irascibility*):— heron.

H602 אָנַק *ʾānaq* a primitive root; to *shriek:*— cry, groan.

H603 אֲנָקָה *ʾănāqâ* from H602; *shrieking:*— crying out, groaning, sighing.

H604 אֲנָקָה *ʾănāqâ* the same as H603; some kind of lizard, probably the *gecko* (from its *wail*):— ferret.

H605 אָנַשׁ *ʾānaš* a primitive root; to *be frail, feeble,* or (figuratively) *melancholy:*— desperate, desperately wicked, incurable, sick, woeful.

H606 אֱנָשׁ *ʾĕnāš* or

אֱנַשׁ *ʾĕnaš* (Aramaic) corresponding to H582; a *man:*— man, whosoever.

H607 אַנְתָּה *ʾantâ* (Aramaic) corresponding to H859; *thou:*— as for thee, thou.

H608 אַנְתּוּן *ʾantûn* (Aramaic) plural of H607; *ye* :— ye.

H609 אָסָא *ʾāsāʾ* of uncertain derivation; *Asa,* the name of a king and of a Levite:— Asa.

HEB

H610 אָסוּךְ *ʾāsûk* from H5480; *anointed,* i.e. an oil-*flask:*— pot.

H611 אָסוֹן *ʾāsôn* of uncertain derivation; *hurt:*— mischief.

H612 אֵסוּר *ʾēsûr* from H631; a *bond* (especially *manacles* of a prisoner):— band, prison.

H613 אֱסוּר *ʾĕsûr* (Aramaic) corresponding to H612 :— band, imprisonment.

H614 אָסִיף *ʾāsîp* or

אָסִף *ʾāsîp* from H622; *gathered,* i.e. (abstractly) a *gathering* in of crops:— ingathering.

H615 אָסִיר *ʾāsîr* from H631; *bound,* i.e. a *captive:*— bound, those which are bound, prisoner.

H616 אַסִּיר *ʾassîr* for H615:— prisoner.

H617 אַסִּיר *ʾassîr* the same as H616; *prisoner; Assir,* the name of two Israelites:— Assir.

H618 אָסָם *ʾāsām* from an unused root meaning to *heap* together; a *storehouse* (only in the plural):— barn, storehouse.

H619 אַסְנָה *ʾasnâ* of uncertain derivation; *Asnah,* one of the Nethinim:— Asnah.

H620 אָסְנַפַּר *ʾosnappar* of foreign derivation; *Osnappar,* an Assyrian king:— Asnapper.

H621 אָסְנַת *ʾāsĕnat* of Egyptian derivation; *Asenath,* the wife of Joseph:— Asenath.

H622 אָסַף *ʾāsap* a primitive root; to *gather* for any purpose; hence to *receive, take away,* i.e. remove (destroy, leave behind, put up, restore, etc.):— assemble, bring, consume, destroy, fetch, gather, gather in, gather together, gather up again, generally, get, get him, lose, put all together, receive, recover another from leprosy, rearward, be rearward, surely, take, take away, take into, take up, utterly, withdraw.

H623 אָסָף *ʾāsāp* from H622; *collector; Asaph,* the name of three Israelites, and of the family of the first:— Asaph.

H624 אָסֻף *ʾāsūp* passive participle of H622; *collected* (only in the plural), i.e. a *collection* (of offerings):— threshold, Asuppim.

H625 אֹסֶף *ʾōsep* from H622; a *collection* (of fruits) :— gathering.

H626 אֲסֵפָה *ʾăsēpâ* from H622; a *collection* of people (only adverbially):— together.

H627 אֲסֻפָּה *ʾăsūpâ* feminine of H624; a *collection* of (learned) men (only in the plural):— assembly.

H628 אַסְפְּסֻף *ʾaspĕsūp* by reduplication from H624; *gathered up together,* i.e. a promiscuous *assemblage* (of people):— mixt multitude.

H629 אָסְפַּרְנָא *ʾosparnāʾ* (Aramaic) of Persian derivation; *diligently:*— fast, forthwith, speed, speedily.

H630 אַסְפָּתָא *ʾaspātāʾ* of Persian derivation; *Aspatha,* a son of Haman:— Aspatha.

H631 אָסַר *ʾāsar* a primitive root; to *yoke* or *hitch;* by analogy to *fasten* in any sense, to *join* battle:— bind, fast, gird, harness, hold, keep, make ready, order, prepare, prison, prisoner, put in bonds, set in array, tie.

H632 אֱסָר *ʾĕsār* or

אִסָּר *ʾissār* from H631; an *obligation* or *vow* (of abstinence):— binding, bond.

H633 אֱסָר *ʾĕsār* (Aramaic) corresponding to H632 in a legal sense; an *interdict:*— decree.

H634 אֵסַר־חַדּוֹן *ʾēsar-ḥaddôn* of foreign derivation; *Esar-chaddon,* an Assyrian king:— Esar-haddon.

H635 אֶסְתֵּר *ʾestēr* of Persian derivation; *Ester,* the Jewish heroine:— Esther.

H636 אָע *ʾāʿ* (Aramaic) corresponding to H6086; a *tree* or *wood:*— timber, wood.

H637 אַף *ʾap* a primitive particle; meaning *accession* (used as an adverb or conjunction); *also* or *yea;* adversatively *though:*— also, although, and, and furthermore, and yet, but, even, how much less, +how much more, moreover, with, yea.

H638 אַף *ʾap* (Aramaic) corresponding to H637 :— also.

H639 אַף *ʾap* from H599; properly the *nose* or *nostril;* hence the *face,* and occasionally a *person;* also (from the rapid breathing in passion) *ire:*— anger, angry, before, countenance, face, forbearing, forehead, longsuffering, nose, nostril, snout, worthy, wrath.

H640 אָפַד *ʾāpad* a primitive root [rather a denominative from H646]; to *gird* on (the ephod):— bind, gird.

H641 אֵפֹד *ʾēpōd* the same as H646 shortened; *Ephod,* an Israelite:— Ephod.

H642 אֵפֻדָּה *ʾēpuddâ* feminine of H646; a *girding* on (of the ephod); hence generally a *plating* (of metal):— ephod, ornament.

H643 אַפֶּדֶן *ʾappeden* apparently of foreign derivation; a *pavilion* or palace-tent:— palace.

H644 אָפָה *ʾāpâ* a primitive root; to *cook,* especially to *bake:*— bake, baker, bakemeats.

H645 אֵפוֹ *ʾēpô* or

אֵפוֹא *ʾēpôʾ* from H6311; strictly a demonstrative particle, *here;* but used of time, *now* or *then:*— here, now, where?.

H646 אֵפוֹד *ʾēpôd* rarely

אֵפֹד *ʾēpōd* probably of foreign derivation; a *girdle;* specifically the *ephod* or high-priest's shoulder-piece; also generally an *image:*— ephod.

H647 אֲפִיחַ *ʾăpîaḥ* perhaps from H6315; *breeze; Aphiach,* an Israelite:— Aphiah.

H648 אָפִיל *ʾapîl* from the same as H651 (in the sense of *weakness*); *unripe:*— not grown up.

H649 אַפַּיִם *ʾappayim* dual of H639; *two nostrils; Appajim,* an Israelite:— Appaim.

H650 אָפִיק *ʾāpîq* from H622; properly *containing,* i.e. a *tube;* also a *bed* or *valley* of a stream; also a *strong* thing or a *hero:*— brook, channel, mighty, river, scale, stream, strong piece.

H651 אָפֵל *ʾāpēl* from an unused root meaning to *set* as the sun; *dusky:*— very dark.

H652 אֹפֶל *ʾōpel* from the same as H651; *dusk:*— darkness, obscurity, privily.

H653 אֲפֵלָה *ʾăpēlâ* feminine of H651; *duskiness,* figuratively *misfortune;* concretely *concealment:*— dark, darkness, gloominess, thick.

H654 אֶפְלָל *ʾeplāl* from H6419; *judge; Ephlah,* an Israelite:— Ephlal.

H655 אֹפֶן *ʾōpen* from an unused root meaning to *revolve;* a *turn,* i.e. a *season:*— fitly.

H656 אָפֵס *ʾāpēs* a primitive root; to *disappear,* i.e. *cease:*— be clean gone, be at an end, be brought to nought, fail.

H657 אֶפֶס *ʾepes* from H656; *cessation,* i.e. an *end* (especially of the earth); often used adverbially *no further,* also (like H6466) the *ankle* (in the dual), as being the extremity of the leg or foot:— ankle, but, but only, end, howbeit, less than nothing, nevertheless, no, nowhere, none, none beside, not, not any, notwithstanding, thing of nought, save, saving, there, uttermost part, want, without, without cause.

H658 אֶפֶס דַּמִּים *ʾepes dommîm* from H657 and the plural of H1818; *boundary of blood*-drops; *Ephes-Dammim,* a place in Palestine:— Ephes-dammim.

H659 אֵפַע *ʾēpaʿ* from an unused root probably meaning to *breathe;* properly a *breath,* i.e. *nothing:*— of nought.

H660 אֶפְעֶה *ʾepʿeh* from H659 (in the sense of *hissing*); an *asp* or other venomous serpent:— viper.

H661 אָפַף *ʾāpap* a primitive root; to *surround:*— compass.

H662 אָפַק *ʾāpaq* a primitive root; to *contain,* i.e. (reflexively) *abstain:*— force, force oneself, restrain.

H663 אֲפֵק *ʾăpēq* or

אֲפִיק *ʾăpîq* from H662 (in the sense of *strength*); *fortress; Aphek* (or *Aphik*), the name of three places in Palestine:— Aphek, Aphik.

H664 אֲפֵקָה *ʾăpēqâ* feminine of H663; *fortress: Aphekah,* a place in Palestine:— Aphekah.

H665 אֵפֶר *ʾēper* from an unused root meaning to *bestrew; ashes:*— ashes.

H666 אֲפֵר *ʾăpēr* from the same as H665 (in the sense of *covering*); a *turban:*— ashes.

H667 אֶפְרֹחַ *ʾeprōaḥ* from H6524 (in the sense of *bursting* the shell); the *brood* of a bird:— young, young one.

H668 אַפִּרְיוֹן *ʾappiryôn* probably of Egyptian derivation; a *palanquin:*— chariot.

H669 אֶפְרַיִם *ʾeprayim* dual of a masculine form of H672; *double fruit; Ephrajim,* a son of Joseph; also the tribe descended from him, and its territory:— Ephraim, Ephraimites.

H670 אֲפָרְסַי *ʾăpārĕsay* (Aramaic) of foreign origin (only in the plural); an *Apharesite* or inhabitant of an unknown region of Assyria:— Apharsite.

H671 אֲפַרְסְכַי *ʾăparsĕkay* or

אֲפַרְסַתְכַי *ʾăparsatkay* (Aramaic) of foreign origin (only in the plural); an *Apharsekite* or *Apharsathkite,* an unknown Assyrian tribe:— Apharsachites, Apharsathchites.

H672 אֶפְרָת *ʾeprāt* or

אֶפְרָתָה *ʾeprātâ* from H6509; *fruitfulness; Ephrath,* another name for Bethlehem; once (Ps 132:6) perhaps for *Ephraim;* also of an Israelitish woman:— Ephrath, Ephratah.

H673 אֶפְרָתִי *ʾeprātî* patrial from H672; an *Ephrathite* or an *Ephraimite:*— Ephraimite, Ephrathite.

H674 אַפְּתֹם *ʾappĕtōm* (Aramaic) of Persian origin; *revenue;* others *at the last:*— revenue.

H675 אֶצְבּוֹן *ʾeṣbôn* or

אֶצְבֹּן *ʾeṣbōn* of uncertain derivation; *Etsbon,* the name of two Israelites:— Ezbon.

H676 אֶצְבַּע *ʾeṣbaʿ* from the same as H6648 (in the sense of *grasping*); something to *seize* with, i.e. a *finger;* by analogy a *toe:*— finger, toe.

H677 אֶצְבַּע *ʾeṣbaʿ* (Aramaic) corresponding to H676 :— finger, toe.

H678 אָצִיל *ʾāṣîl* from H680 (in its secondary sense of *separation*); an *extremity* (Isa 41:9), also a *noble* :— chief man, noble.

H679 אַצִּיל *ʾaṣṣîl* from H680 (in its primary sense of *uniting*); a *joint* of the hand (i.e. *knuckle*); also (according to some) a *party-wall* (Ezek 41:8):— armhole, great.

H680 אָצַל *ʾāṣal* a primitive root; properly to *join;* used only as a denominative from H681; to *separate;* hence to *select, refuse, contract:*— keep, reserve, straiten, take.

H681 אֵצֶל *ʾēṣel* from H680 (in the sense of *joining*); a *side;* (as a preposition) *near:*— at, by, hard by, from, from beside, beside, near, near unto, toward, with. See also H1018

H682 אָצֵל *ʾāṣēl* from H680; *noble; Atsel,* the name of an Israelite, and of a place in Palestine:— Azal, Azel.

H683 אֲצַלְיָהוּ *ʾăṣalyāhû* from H680 and H3050 prolonged; *Jah has reserved; Atsaljah,* an Israelite:— Azaliah.

H684 אֹצֶם *ʾōṣem* from an unused root probably meaning to *be strong; strength* (i.e. *strong*); *Otsem,* the name of two Israelites:— Ozem.

H685 אֶצְעָדָה *ʾesʿādâ* a variation from H6807; properly a *step-chain;* by analogy a *bracelet:*— bracelet, chain.

H686 אָצַר *ʾāṣar* a primitive root; to *store* up:— store, lay up in store, treasure, make treasurer.

H687 אֵצֶר *ʾēṣer* from H686; *treasure; Etser,* an Idumaean:— Ezer.

H688 אֶקְדָּח *ʾeqdāḥ* from H6916; *burning,* i.e. a *carbuncle* or other fiery gem:— carbuncle.

H689 אַקּוֹ *ʾaqqô* probably from H602; *slender,* i.e. the *ibex:*— wild goat.

H690 אֲרָא *ʾărāʾ* probably for H738; *lion; Ara,* an Israelite:— Ara.

H691 אֶרְאֵל *ʾerʾēl* probably for H739; a *hero* (collectively):— valiant one.

H692 אַרְאֵלִי *ʾarʾēlî* from H691; *heroic, Areli* (or an *Arelite,* collectively), an Israelite and his descendants:— Areli, Arelites.

H693 אָרַב *ʾārab* a primitive root; to *lurk:*— ambush, lie in ambush, ambushment, lay wait, lie in wait.

H694 אֲרָב *ʾărāb* from H693; *ambush; Arab,* a place in Palestine:— Arab.

H695 אֶרֶב *ʾereb* from H693; *ambuscade:*— den, lie in wait.

H696 אֹרֶב *ʾōreb* the same as H695:— wait.

H697 אַרְבֶּה *ʾarbeh* from H7235; a *locust* (from its rapid *increase*):— grasshopper, locust.

H698 אָרֳבָה *orŏbâ* feminine of H696 (only in the plural); *ambuscades:*— spoils.

H699 אֲרֻבָּה *ʾărubbâ* feminine participle passive of H693 (as if for *lurking*); a *lattice;* (by implication) a *window, dove-cot* (because of the pigeon-holes), *chimney* (with its apertures for smoke), *sluice* (with openings for water):— chimney, window.

H700 אֲרֻבּוֹת *ʾărubbôt* plural of H699; *Arubboth,* a place in Palestine:— Aruboth.

H701 אַרְבִּי *ʾarbî* patrial from H634; an *Arbite* or native of Arab:— Arbite.

H702 אַרְבַּע *ʾarbaʿ* masculine

אַרְבָּעָה *ʾarbāʿâ* from H7251; *four:*— four.

H703 אַרְבַּע *ʾarbaʿ* (Aramaic) corresponding to H702 :— four.

H704 אַרְבַּע *ʾarbaʿ* the same as H702; *Arba,* one of the Anakim:— Arba.

H705 אַרְבָּעִים *ʾarbāʿîm* multiple of H702; *forty:*— forty.

H706 אַרְבַּעְתַּיִם *ʾarbaʿtayim* dual of H702; *fourfold:*— fourfold.

H707 אָרַג *ʾārag* a primitive root; to *plait* or *weave* :— weave, weaver.

H708 אֶרֶג *ʾereg* from H707; a *weaving;* a *braid;* also a *shuttle:*— beam, weaver's shuttle.

H709 אַרְגֹּב *ʾargōb* from the same as H7263; *stony; Argob,* a district of Palestine:— Argob.

H710 אַרְגְּוָן *ʾargĕwān* a variation for H713; *purple:*— purple.

H711 אַרְגְּוָן *ʾargĕwān* (Aramaic) corresponding to H710:— purple.

H712 אַרְגָּז *ʾargāz* perhaps from H7264 (in the sense of being *suspended*); a *box* (as a pannier):— coffer.

H713 אַרְגָּמָן *ʾargāmān* of foreign origin; *purple* (the color or the dyed stuff):— purple.

H714 אַרְדְּ *ʾard* from an unused root probably meaning to *wander; fugitive; Ard,* the name of two Israelites:— Ard.

H715 אַרְדּוֹן *ʾardôn* from the same as H714; *roaming; Ardon,* an Israelite:— Ardon.

H716 אַרְדִּי *ʾardî* patronymic from H714; an *Ardite* (collectively) or descendant of Ard:— Ardites.

H717 אָרָה *ʾārâ* a primitive root; to *pluck:*— gather, pluck.

H718 אֲרוּ *ʾărû* (Aramaic) probably akin to H431; *lo!:*— behold, lo.

H719 אַרְוַד *ʾarwad* probably from H7300; a refuge for the *roving; Arvad,* an island-city of Palestine:— Arvad.

H720 אֲרוֹד *ʾărôd* an orthographical variation of H719; *fugitive; Arod,* an Israelite:— Arod.

H721 אַרְוָדִי *ʾarwādî* patrial from H719; an *Arvadite* or citizen of Arvad:— Arvadite.

H722 אֲרוֹדִי *ʾărôdî* patronymic from H721; an *Arodite* or descendant of Arod:— Arodi, Arodites.

H723 אֻרְוָה *ʾurwâ* or

אֲרָיָה *ʾărāyâ* from H717 (in the sense of *feeding*); a *herding-place* for an animal:— stall.

H724 אֲרוּכָה *ʾărûkâ* or

אֲרֻכָה *ʾărūkâ* feminine passive participle of H748 (in the sense of *restoring* to soundness); *wholeness* (literal or figurative):— health, made up, perfected.

H725 אֲרוּמָה *ʾărûmâ* a variation of H7316; *height; Arumah,* a place in Palestine:— Arumah.

H726 אֲרוֹמִי *ʾărômî* a clerical error for H130; an *Edomite* (as in the margin):— Syrian.

H727 אָרוֹן *ʾārôn* or

אָרֹן *ʾārōn* from H717 (in the sense of *gathering*); a *box:*— ark, chest, coffin.

H728 אֲרַוְנָה *ʾărawnâ* or (by transposition)

אוֹרְנָה *ʾôrĕnâ* or

אַרְנִיָּה *ʾarnîyâ* all by orthographical variation for H771; *Aravnah* (or *Arnijah* or *Ornah*), a Jebusite:— Araunah.

H729 אָרַז *ʾāraz* a primitive root; to be *firm;* used only in the passive participle as a denominative from H730; of *cedar:*— made of cedar.

H730 אֶרֶז *ʾerez* from H729; a *cedar* tree (from the tenacity of its roots):— cedar (tree).

H731 אַרְזָה *ʾarzâ* feminine of H730; *cedar* wainscoting:— cedar work.

H732 אָרַח *ʾāraḥ* a primitive root; to *travel:*— go, wayfaring, wayfaring man.

H733 אָרַח *ʾāraḥ* from H732; *way-faring; Arach,* the name of three Israelites:— Arah.

H734 אֹרַח *ʾōraḥ* from H732; a well trodden *road* (literal or figurative); also a *caravan:*— manner, path, race, rank, traveller, troop, byway, highway, way.

H735 אֹרַח *ʾōraḥ* (Aramaic) corresponding to H734; a *road:*— way.

H736 אֹרְחָה *ʾōrĕḥâ* feminine active participle of H732; a *caravan:*— company, travelling company.

H737 אֲרֻחָה *ʾărūḥâ* feminine passive participle of H732 (in the sense of *appointing*); a *ration* of food:— allowance, diet, dinner, victuals.

H738 אֲרִי *ʾărî* or (prolonged)

אַרְיֵה *ʾaryēh* from H717 (in the sense of *violence*); a *lion:*— lion, young lion, pierce *[from the margin].*

H739 אֲרִיאֵל *ʾărîʾēl* or

אֲרִאֵל *ʾărīʾēl* from H738 and H410; *lion of God,* i.e. *heroic:*— lionlike men.

H740 אֲרִיאֵל *ʾărîʾēl* the same as H739; *Ariel,* a symbolic name for Jerusalem, also the name of an Israelite:— Ariel.

H741 אֲרִאֵיל *ʾărīʾēl* either by transposition for H739 or, more probably, an orthographical variation for H2025; the *altar* of the Temple:— altar.

H742 אֲרִידַי *ʾărîday* of Persian origin; *Aridai,* a son of Haman:— Aridai.

H743 אֲרִידָתָא *ʾărîdātāʾ* of Persian origin; *Aridatha,* a son of Haman:— Aridatha.

H744 אַרְיֵה *ʾaryēh* (Aramaic) corresponding to H738 :— *lion.*

H745 אַרְיֵה *ʾaryēh* the same as H738; *lion; Arjeh,* an Israelite:— Arieh.

H746 אֲרְיוֹךְ *ʾăryôk* of foreign origin; *Arjok,* the name of two Babylonians:— Arioch.

H747 אֲרִיסַי *ʾărîsay* of Persian origin; *Arisai,* a son of Haman:— Arisai.

H748 אָרַךְ *ʾārak* a primitive root; to *be* (causatively *make*) *long* (literally or figuratively):— defer, draw out, lengthen, be long, become long, make long, prolong, outlive, overlive, tarry, tarry long.

H749 אֲרַךְ *ʾărak* (Aramaic) properly corresponding to H748, but used only in the sense of *reaching* to a given point; to *suit:*— be meet.

H750 אָרֵךְ *ʾārēk* from H748; *long:*— longsuffering, longwinged, patient, slow to anger.

H751 אֶרֶךְ *ʾerek* from H748; *length; Erek,* a place in Babylonia:— Erech.

H752 אָרֹךְ *ʾārōk* from H748; *long:*— long.

H753 אֹרֶךְ *ʾōrek* from H748; *length:*— for ever, length, long.

H754 אַרְכָּא *ʾarkāʾ* or

אַרְכָּה *ʾarkâ* (Aramaic) from H749; *length:*— lengthening, prolonged.

H755 אַרְכֻבָּה *ʾarkūbâ* (Aramaic) from an unused root corresponding to H7392 (in the sense of *bending* the knee); the *knee:*— knee.

H756 אַרְכְּוַי *ʾarkĕway* (Aramaic) patrial from H751; an *Arkevite* (collectively) or native of Erek:— Archevite.

H757 אַרְכִּי *ʾarkî* patrial from another place (in Palestine) of similar name with H751; an *Arkite* or native of Erek:— Archi, Archite.

H758 אֲרָם *ʾărām* from the same as H759; the *highland; Aram* or Syria, and its inhabitants; also the name of a son of Shem, a grandson of Nahor, and of an Israelite:— Aram, Mesopotamia, Syria, Syrians.

H759 אַרְמוֹן *ʾarmôn* from an unused root (meaning to *be elevated*); a *citadel* (from its *height*):— castle, palace. Compare H2038

H760 אֲרַם צוֹבָה *ʾăram ṣôbâ* from H758 and H6678; *Aram of Tsoba* (or Coele-Syria):— Aram-zobah.

H761 אֲרַמִּי *ʾărammî* patrial from H758; an *Aramite* or Aramaean:— Syrian, Aramitess.

H762 אֲרָמִית *ʾărāmît* feminine of H761; (only adverbially) *in Aramaean:*— in the Syrian language, in the Syrian tongue, in Syriack.

H763 אֲרַם נַהֲרַיִם *ʾăram nahărayim* from H758 and the dual of H5104; *Aram of* (the) *two rivers* (Euphrates and Tigris) or Mesopotamia:— Aram-naharaim, Mesopotamia.

H764 אַרְמֹנִי *ʾarmōnî* from H759; *palatial; Armoni,* an Israelite:— Armoni.

H765 אֲרָן *ʾărān* from H7422; *stridulous; Aran,* an Edomite:— Aran.

H766 אֹרֶן *ʾōren* from the same as H765 (in the sense of *strength*); the *ash* tree (from its toughness):— ash.

H767 אֹרֶן *ʾōren* the same as H766; *Oren,* an Israelite:— Oren.

H768 אַרְנֶבֶת *ʾarnebet* of uncertain derivation; the *hare:*— hare.

H769 אַרְנוֹן *ʾarnôn* or

אַרְנֹן *ʾarnōn* from H7422; a *brawling* stream; the *Arnon,* a river east of the Jordan; also its territory:— Arnon.

H770 אַרְנָן *ʾarnān* probably from the same as H769; *noisy; Arnan,* an Israelite:— Arnan.

H771 אׇרְנָן *ʾornān* probably from H766; *strong; Ornan,* a Jebusite:— Ornan. See H728

H772 אֲרַע *ʾăraʿ* (Aramaic) corresponding to H776; the *earth;* by implication (figuratively) *low:*— earth, interior.

H773 אַרְעִית *ʾarʿît* (Aramaic) feminine of H772; the *bottom:*— bottom.

H774 אַרְפָּד *ʾarpād* from H7502; *spread* out; *Arpad,* a place in Syria:— Arpad, Arphad.

H775 אַרְפַּכְשַׁד *ʾarpakšad* probably of foreign origin; *Arpakshad,* a son of Noah; also the region settled by him:— Arphaxad.

H776 אֶרֶץ *ʾereṣ* from an unused root probably meaning to *be firm;* the *earth* (at large, or partitively a *land*):— common, country, earth, field, ground, land, nations, way, wilderness, world.

H777 אַרְצָא *ʾarṣāʾ* from H776; *earthiness; Artsa,* an Israelite:— Arza.

H778 אֲרַק *ʾăraq* (Aramaic) by transmutation for H772; the *earth:*— earth.

H779 אָרַר *ʾārar* a primitive root; to *execrate:*— bitterly curse.

H780 אֲרָרַט *ʾărāraṭ* of foreign origin; *Ararat* (or rather Armenia):— Ararat, Armenia.

H781 אָרַשׂ *ʾāraś* a primitive root; to *engage* for matrimony:— betroth, espouse.

H782 אֲרֶשֶׁת *ʾărešet* from H781 (in the sense of *desiring* to possess); a *longing* for:— request.

H783 אַרְתַּחְשַׁשְׁתָּא *ʾartaḥšaštāʾ* or

אַרְתַּחְשַׁשְׁתְּא *ʾartaḥšaštĕʾ* or by permutation

אַרְתַּחְשַׁסְתְּא *ʾartaḥšastĕʾ* of foreign origin; *Artachshasta* (or Artaxerxes), a title (rather than name) of several Persian kings:— Artaxerxes.

H784 אֵשׁ *ʾēš* a primitive word; *fire* (literal or figurative):— burning, fiery, fire, flaming, hot.

H785 אֵשׁ *ʾēš* (Aramaic) corresponding to H784 :— flame.

H786 אִשׁ *ʾîš* identical (in origin and formation) with H784; *entity;* used only adverbially, there *is* or *are:*— are there, none can. Compare H3426

H787 אֹשׁ *ʾōš* (Aramaic) corresponding (by transposition and abbreviation) to H803; a *foundation:*— foundation.

H788 אַשְׁבֵּל *ʾašbēl* probably from the same as H7640; *flowing; Ashbel,* an Israelite:— Ashbel.

H789 אַשְׁבֵּלִי *ʾašbēlî* patronymic from H788; an *Ashbelite* (collectively) or descendant of Ashbel :— Ashbelites.

H790 אֶשְׁבָּן *ʾeššĕbbān* probably from the same as H7644; *vigorous; Eshban,* an Idumaean:— Eshban.

H791 אַשְׁבֵּעַ *ʾašbēaʿ* from H7650; *adjurer; Asbeä,* an Israelite:— Ashbea.

H792 אֶשְׁבַּעַל *ʾešbaʿal* from H376 and H1168; *man of Baal; Eshbaal* (or Ishbosheth), a son of King Saul:— Eshbaal.

H793 אֶשֶׁד *ʾešed* from an unused root meaning to *pour;* an *outpouring:*— stream.

H794 אֲשֵׁדָה *ʾăšēdâ* feminine of H793; a *ravine:*— springs.

H795 אַשְׁדּוֹד *ʾašdôd* from H7703; *ravager: Ashdod,* a place in Palestine:— Ashdod.

H796 אַשְׁדּוֹדִי *ʾašdôdî* patrial from H795; an *Ashdodite* (often collectively) or inhabitant of Ashdod :— Ashdodites, of Ashdod.

H797 אַשְׁדּוֹדִית *ʾašdôdît* feminine of H796; (only adverbially) *in the language of Ashdod:*— in the speech of Ashdod.

H798 אַשְׁדּוֹת הַפִּסְגָּה *ʾašdôt happisgâ* from the plural of H794 and H6449 with the article interposed; *ravines of the Pisgah; Ashdoth-Pisgah,* a place east of the Jordan:— Ashdoth-pisgah.

H799 אֶשְׁדָּת *ʾešdāt* from H784 and H1881; a *fire-law:*— fiery law.

H800 אֶשָּׁה *ʾeššâ* feminine of H784; *fire:*— fire.

H801 אִשֶּׁה *ʾiššâ* the same as H800, but used in a liturgical sense; properly a *burnt-offering;* but occasionally of any *sacrifice:*— offering by fire, offering made by fire, sacrifice, made by fire.

H802 אִשָּׁה *ʾiššâ* feminine of H376 or H582 irregular plural

נָשִׁים *nāšîm;* a *woman* (used in the same wide sense as H582):— adulteress, each, every, female, many, none, one, together, wife, woman. Often unexpressed in English.

H803 אֲשׁוּיָה *ʾăšûyâ* feminine passive participle from an unused root meaning to *found; foundation:*— foundation.

H804 אַשּׁוּר *ʾaššûr* or

אַשֻּׁר *ʾaššūr* apparently from H833 (in the sense of *successful*); *Ashshur,* the second son of Shem; also his descendants and the country occupied by them (i.e. Assyria), its region and its empire:— Asshur, Assur, Assyria, Assyrians. See H838

H805 אֲשׁוּרִי *ʾăšûrî* or

אַשּׁוּרִי *ʾaššûrî* from a patrial word of the same form as H804; an *Ashurite* (collectively) or inhabitant of Ashur, a district in Palestine:— Asshurim, Ashurites.

H806 אַשְׁחוּר *ʾašḥûr* probably from H7835; *black: Ashchur,* an Israelite:— Ashur.

H807 אֲשִׁימָא *ʾăšîmāʾ* of foreign origin; *Ashima,* a deity of Hamath:— Ashima.

H808 אָשִׁישׁ *ʾāšîš* from the same as H784 (in the sense of *pressing* down firmly; compare H803); a (ruined) *foundation:*— foundation.

H809 אֲשִׁישָׁה *ʾăšîšâ* feminine of H808; something closely *pressed* together, i.e. a *cake* of raisins or other comfits:— flagon.

H810 אֶשֶׁךְ *ʾešek* from an unused root (probably meaning to *bunch* together); a *testicle* (as a *lump*):— stone.

H811 אֶשְׁכּוֹל *ʾeškôl* or

אֶשְׁכֹּל *ʾeškōl* probably prolonged from H810; a *bunch of grapes* or other fruit:— cluster, cluster of grapes.

H812 אֶשְׁכֹּל *ʾeškōl* the same as H811; *Eshcol,* the name of an Amorite, also of a valley in Palestine:— Eshcol.

H813 אַשְׁכְּנַז *ʾaškĕnaz* of foreign origin; *Ashkenaz,* a Japhethite, also his descendants:— Ashkenaz.

H814 אֶשְׁכָּר *ʾeškār* for H7939; a *gratuity:*— gift, present.

H815 אֵשֶׁל *ʾēšel* from a root of uncertain signification; a *tamarisk* tree; by extension a *grove* of any kind:— grove, tree.

H816 אָשַׁם *ʾāšam* or

אָשֵׁם *ʾāšēm* a primitive root; to *be guilty;* by implication to *be punished* or *perish:*— certainly, be desolate, become desolate, be made desolate, destroy, greatly, be guilty, become guilty, be found guilty, hold guilty, offend, acknowledge offence, trespass.

H817 אָשָׁם *ʾāšām* from H816; *guilt;* by implication a *fault;* also a *sin-offering:*— guiltiness, sin, offering for sin, trespass, trespass offering.

H818 אָשֵׁם *ʾāšēm* from H816; *guilty;* hence *presenting a sin-offering:*— one which is faulty, guilty.

H819 אַשְׁמָה *ʾašmâ* feminine of H817; *guiltiness,* a *fault,* the *presentation of a sin-offering:*— offend, sin, trespass offering, cause of trespass, trespassing.

H820 אַשְׁמָן *ʾašmān* probably from H8081; a *fat* field:— desolate place.

H821 אַשְׁמֻרָה *ʾašmūrâ* or

אַשְׁמוּרָה *ʾašmûrâ* or

אַשְׁמֹרֶת *ʾašmōret* (feminine) from H8104; a night *watch:*— watch.

H822 אֶשְׁנָב *ʾešnāb* apparently from an unused root (probably meaning to *leave interstices*); a latticed *window:*— casement, lattice.

H823 אַשְׁנָה *ʾašnâ* probably a variation for H3466; *Ashnah,* the name of two places in Palestine:— Ashnah.

H824 אֶשְׁעָן *ʾešʿān* from H8172; *support; Eshan,* a place in Palestine:— Eshean.

H825 אַשָּׁף *ʾaššāp* from an unused root (probably meaning to *lisp,* i.e. *practise enchantment*); a *conjurer:*— astrologer.

H826 אַשָּׁף *ʾaššāp* (Aramaic) corresponding to H825 :— astrologer.

H827 אַשְׁפָּה *ʾašpâ* perhaps (feminine) from the same as H825 (in the sense of *covering*); a *quiver* or arrow-case:— quiver.

H828 אַשְׁפְּנַז *ʾašpĕnaz* of foreign origin; *Ashpenaz,* a Babylonian eunuch:— Ashpenaz.

H829 אֶשְׁפָּר *ʾešpār* of uncertain derivation; a measured *portion:*— good piece, good piece of flesh.

H830 אַשְׁפֹּת *ʾašpōt* or

אַשְׁפּוֹת *ʾašpôt* or (contracted)

שְׁפֹת *šĕpōt* plural of a noun of the same form as H827, from H8192 (in the sense of *scraping*); a heap of *rubbish* or *filth:*— dung, dung hill.

H831 אַשְׁקְלוֹן *ʾašqĕlôn* probably from H8254 in the sense of *weighing*-place (i.e. *mart*); *Ashkelon,* a place in Palestine:— Ashkelon, Askalon.

H832 אֶשְׁקְלוֹנִי *ʾešqĕlônî* patrial from H831; an *Ashkelonite* (collectively) or inhabitant of Ashkelon:— Eshkalonites.

H833 אָשַׁר *ʾāšar* or

אָשֵׁר *ʾāšēr* a primitive root; to *be straight* (used in the widest sense, especially to *be level, right, happy*); figuratively to *go forward, be honest, prosper:*— bless, call blessed, be blessed, happy, call happy, go, guide, lead, relieve.

H834 אֲשֶׁר *ʾăšer* a primitive relative pronoun (of every gender and number); *who, which, what, that;* also (as adverbially and conjunctionally) *when, where, how, because, in order that,* etc:— after, alike, as, as soon as, because, every, for, forasmuch, from whence, how, howsoever, if, that, so that, that thing, that thing which, that wherein, through, until, whatsoever, when, where, whereas, wherein, whereof, whereon, wheresoever, wherewith, which, whilst, whither, whithersoever, who, whom, whosoever, whose. As it is indeclinable, it is often accompanied by the personal pronoun expletively, used to show the connection.

H835 אֶשֶׁר *ʾešer* from H833; *happiness;* only in masculine plural construct as interjection, how *happy!:*— blessed, happy.

H836 אָשֵׁר *ʾāšēr* from H833; *happy; Asher,* a son of Jacob, and the tribe descended from him, with its territory; also a place in Palestine:— Asher.

H837 אֹשֶׁר *ʾōšer* from H833; *happiness:*— happy.

H838 אָשֻׁר *ʾāšur* or

אַשֻּׁר *ʾaššūr* from H833 in the sense of *going;* a *step:*— going, step.

H839 אֲשֻׁר *ʾăšūr* contracted for H8391; the *cedar* tree or some other light elastic wood:— Ashurite.

H840 אֲשַׂרְאֵל *ʾăśarʾēl* by orthographical variation from H833 and H410; *right of God; Asarel,* an Israelite:— Asareel.

H841 אֲשַׂרְאֵלָה *ʾăśarʾēlâ* from the same as H840; *right towards God; Asarelah,* an Israelite:— Asarelah. Compare H3480

H842 אֲשֵׁרָה *ʾăšērâ* or

אֲשֵׁירָה *ʾăšêrâ* from H833; *happy; Asherah* (or Astarte) a Phoenician goddess; also an *image* of the same:— grove. Compare H6253

H843 אָשֵׁרִי *ʾāšērî* patronymic from H836; an *Asherite* (collectively) or descendant of Asher:— Asherites.

H844 אַשְׂרִיאֵל *ʾaśrîʾēl* an orthographical variation for H840; *Asriel,* the name of two Israelites:— Ashriel, Asriel.

H845 אַשְׂרִאֵלִי *ʾaśriʾēlî* patronymic from H844; an *Asrielite* (collectively) or descendant of Asriel:— Asrielites.

H846 אֻשַּׁרְנָא *ʾuššarnāʾ* (Aramaic) from a root corresponding to H833; a *wall* (from its uprightness):— wall.

H847 אֶשְׁתָּאֹל *ʾeštāʾōl* or

אֶשְׁתָּאוֹל *ʾeštāʾôl* probably from H7592; *intreaty; Eshtaol,* a place in Palestine:— Eshtaol.

H848 אֶשְׁתָּאֻלִי *ʾeštāʾūlî* patrial from H847; an *Eshtaolite* (collectively) or inhabitant of Eshtaol:— Eshtaulites.

H849 אֶשְׁתַּדּוּר *ʾeštaddûr* (Aramaic) from H7712 (in a bad sense); *rebellion:*— sedition.

H850 אֶשְׁתּוֹן *ʾeštôn* probably from the same as H7764; *restful; Eshton,* an Israelite:— Eshton.

H851 אֶשְׁתְּמֹעַ *ʾeštĕmōaʿ* or

אֶשְׁתְּמוֹעַ *ʾeštĕmôaʿ* or

אֶשְׁתְּמֹה *ʾeštĕmōh* from H8085 (in the sense of *obedience*); *Eshtemoa* or *Eshtemoh,* a place in Palestine:— Eshtemoa, Eshtemoh.

H852 אָת *ʾāt* (Aramaic) corresponding to H226; a *portent:*— sign.

H853 אֵת *ʾēt* apparently contracted from H226 in the demonstrative sense of *entity;* properly *self* (but generally used to point out more definitely the object of a verb or preposition, *even* or *namely*):— *[as such unrepresented in English].*

H854 אֵת *ʾēt* probably from H579; properly *nearness* (used only as a preposition or adverb), *near;* hence generally *with, by, at, among,* etc:— against, among, before, by, for, from, in, into, of, out of, with. Often with another preposition prefixed.

H855 אֵת *ʾēt* of uncertain derivation; a *hoe* or other digging implement:— coulter, plowshare.

H856 אֶתְבַּעַל *ʾetbaʿal* from H854 and H1168; *with Baal; Ethbaal,* a Phoenician king:— Ethbaal.

H857 אָתָה *ʾātâ* or

אָתָא *ʾātāʾ* a primitive root [collateral to H225 contracted]; to *arrive:*— come, become, things to come, come upon, bring.

H858 אָתָה *ʾātâ* or

אָתָא *ʾātāʾ* (Aramaic) corresponding to H857 :— come, become, bring.

H859 אַתָּה *ʾattâ* or (shortened)

אַתָּ *ʾattā* or

אַת *ʾat* or feminine (irregular) sometimes

אַתִּי *ʾattî* or plural masculine

אַתֶּם *ʾattem* feminine

אַתֵּן *ʾatten* or

אַתֵּנָה *ʾattēnâ* or

אַתֵּנָּה *ʾattēnnâ* a primitive pronoun of the second person; *thou* and *thee,* or (plural) *ye* and *you:*— thee, thou, ye, you.

H860 אָתוֹן *ʾātôn* probably from the same as H386 (in the sense of *patience*); a female *ass* (from its docility):— ass, she ass.

H861 אַתּוּן *ʾattûn* (Aramaic) probably from a root corresponding to H784; probably a *fire-place,* i.e. *furnace:*— furnace.

H862 אַתּוּק *ʾattûq* or

אַתִּיק *ʾattîq* from H5423 in the sense of *decreasing;* a *ledge* or offset in a building:— gallery.

H863 אִתַּי *ʾittay* or

אִיתַי *ʾîtay* from H854; *near; Ittai* or *Ithai,* the name of a Gittite and of an Israelite:— Ithai, Ittai.

H864 אֵתָם *ʾētām* of Egyptian derivation; *Etham,* a place in the Desert:— Etham.

H865 אֶתְמוֹל *ʾetmôl* or

אִתְמוֹל *ʾitmôl* or

אֶתְמוּל *ʾetmûl* probably from H853 or H854 and H4136; *heretofore;* definitely *yesterday:*— beforetime, before that time, heretofore, of late, of old, times past, yesterday.

H866 אֶתְנָה *ʾetnâ* from H8566; a *present* (as the price of harlotry):— reward.

H867 אֶתְנִי *ʾetnî* perhaps from H866; *munificence; Ethni,* an Israelite:— Ethni.

H868 אֶתְנַן *ʾetnan* the same as H866; a *gift* (as the price of harlotry or idolatry):— hire, reward.

H869 אֶתְנַן *ʾetnan* the same as H868 in the sense of H867; *Ethnan,* an Israelite:— Ethnan.

H870 אֲתַר *ʾătar* (Aramaic) from a root corresponding to that of H871; a *place;* (adverbially) *after:*— after, place.

H871 אֲתָרִים *ʾătārîm* plural from an unused root (probably meaning to *step*); *places; Atharim,* a place near Palestine:— spies.

ב

H872 בִּאָה *biʾâ* from H935; an *entrance* to a building:— entry.

H873 בִּאוּשׁ *biʾûš* (Aramaic) from H888; *wicked:*— bad.

H874 בָּאַר *bāʾar* a primitive root; to *dig;* by analogy to *engrace;* figuratively to *explain:*— declare, make plain, plainly.

H875 בְּאֵר *bĕʾēr* from H874; a *pit;* especially a *well:*— pit, well.

H876 בְּאֵר *bĕʾēr* the same as H875; *Beër,* a place in the Desert, also one in Palestine:— Beer.

H877 בֹּאר *bōʾr* from H874; a *cistern:*— cistern.

H878 בְּאֵרָא *bĕʾērāʾ* from H875; a *well; Beëra,* an Israelite:— Beera.

H879 בְּאֵר אֵלִים *bĕʾēr ʾēlîm* from H875 and the plural of H410; *well of heroes; Beër-Elim,* a place in the Desert:— Beer-elim.

H880 בְּאֵרָה *bĕʾērâ* the same as H878; *Beërah,* an Israelite:— Beerah.

HEB

H881 בְּאֵרוֹת *bĕʾērôt* feminine plural of H875; *wells; Beëroth,* a place in Palestine:— Beeroth.

H882 בְּאֵרִי *bĕʾērî* from H875; *fountained; Beëri,* the name of a Hittite and of an Israelite:— Beeri.

H883 בְּאֵר לַחַי רֹאִי *bĕʾēr lāḥāy rōʾî* from H875 and H2416 (with prefix) and H7203; *well of a living* (one) *my Seer; Beër-Lachai-Roï,* a place in the Desert:— Beer-lahai-roi.

H884 בְּאֵר שֶׁבַע *bĕʾēr šebaʿ* from H875 and H7651 (in the sense of H7650); *well of an oath; Beër-Sheba,* a place in Palestine:— Beer-shebah.

H885 בְּאֵרֹת בְּנֵי־יַעֲקַן *bĕʾērōt bĕnê-yaʿăqan* from the feminine plural of H875, and the plural contracted of H1121, and H3292; *wells of* (the) *sons of Jaakan; Beeroth-Bene-Jaakan,* a place in the Desert:— Beeroth of the children of Jaakan.

H886 בְּאֵרֹתִי *bĕʾērōtî* patrial from H881; a *Beërothite* or inhabitant of Beëroth:— Beerothite.

H887 בָּאַשׁ *bāʾaš* a primitive root; to *smell* bad; figuratively to *be offensive* morally:— be abhorred, make to be abhorred, be had in abomination, be loathsome, make selves odious, stink, cause a stinking savour, make to stink, utterly.

H888 בְּאֵשׁ *bĕʾēš* corresponding to H887:— displease.

H889 בְּאֹשׁ *bĕʾōš* from H887; a *stench:*— stink.

H890 בָּאְשָׁה *boʾšâ* feminine of H889; *stink-weed* or any other noxious or useless plant:— cockle.

H891 בְּאֻשִׁים *bĕʾūšîm* plural of H889; *poison-berries:*— wild grapes.

H892 בָּבָה *bābâ* feminine active participle of an unused root meaning to *hollow* out; something *hollowed* (as a *gate*), i.e. the *pupil* of the eye:— apple of the eye.

H893 בֵּבַי *bēbay* probably of foreign origin; *Bebai,* an Israelite:— Bebai.

H894 בָּבֶל *bābel* from H1101; *confusion; Babel* (i.e. Babylon), including Babylonia and the Babylonian empire:— Babel, Babylon.

H895 בָּבֶל *bābel* (Aramaic) corresponding to H894 :— Babylon.

H896 בַּבְלִי *bablî* (Aramaic) patrial from H895; a *Babylonian:*— Babylonia.

H897 בַּג *bag* a Persian word; *food:*— spoil *[from the margin for H957].*

H898 בָּגַד *bāgad* a primitive root; to *cover* (with a garment); figuratively to *act covertly;* by implication to *pillage:*— deal deceitfully, deal treacherously, deal unfaithfully, offend, transgress, transgressor, depart treacherously, treacherous dealer, treacherous man, unfaithfully, unfaithful man, very.

H899 בֶּגֶד *beged* from H898; a *covering,* i.e. clothing; also *treachery* or *pillage:*— apparel, cloth, clothes, clothing, garment, lap, rag, raiment, robe, very treacherously, vesture, wardrobe.

H900 בֹּגְדוֹת *bōgĕdôt* feminine plural active participle of H898; *treacheries:*— treacherous.

H901 בָּגוֹד *bāgôd* from H898; *treacherous:*— treacherous.

H902 בִּגְוַי *bigway* probably of foreign origin; *Bigvai,* an Israelite:— Bigvai.

H903 בִּגְתָא *bigtāʾ* of Persian derivation; *Bigtha,* a eunuch of Xerxes:— Bigtha.

H904 בִּגְתָן *bigtān* or

בִּגְתָנָא *bigtānāʾ* of similar derivation to H903; *Bigthan* or *Bigthana,* a eunuch of Xerxes:— Bigthan, Bigthana.

H905 בַּד *bad* from H909; properly *separation;* by implication a *part* of the body, *branch* of a tree, *bar* for carrying; figuratively *chief* of a city; especially (with preposition prefixed) as adverb, *apart, only, besides:*— alone, apart, bar, besides, branch, by self, of each alike, except, only, part, staff, strength.

H906 בַּד *bad* perhaps from H909 (in the sense of *divided* fibres); flaxen *thread* or yarn; hence a *linen* garment:— linen.

H907 בַּד *bad* from H908; a *brag* or *lie;* also a *liar:*— liar, lie.

H908 בָּדָא *bādāʾ* a primitive root; (figuratively) to *invent:*— devise, feign.

H909 בָּדַד *bādad* a primitive root; to *divide,* i.e. (reflexively) *be solitary:*— alone.

H910 בָּדָד *bādād* from H909; *separate;* adverbially *separately:*— alone, desolate, only, solitary.

H911 בְּדַד *bĕdad* from H909; *separation; Bedad,* an Edomite:— Bedad.

H912 בֵּדְיָה *bēdĕyâ* probably shortened for H5662; *servant of Jehovah; Bedejah,* an Israelite:— Bedeiah.

H913 בְּדִיל *bĕdîl* from H914; *alloy* (because *removed* by smelting); by analogy *tin:*— plummet, tin.

H914 בָּדַל *bādal* a primitive root; to *divide* (in various senses literally or figuratively, *separate, distinguish, differ, select,* etc.):— make difference, put difference, divide, divide asunder, seperate, make separation, seperate self, sever, sever out, utterly.

H915 בָּדָל *bādāl* from H914; a *part:*— piece.

H916 בְּדֹלַח *bĕdōlaḥ* probably from H914; something in *pieces,* i.e. *bdellium,* a (fragrant) gum (perhaps *amber*); others a *pearl:*— bdellium.

H917 בְּדָן *bĕdān* probably short for H5658; *servile: Bedan,* the name of two Israelites:— Bedan.

H918 בָּדַק *bādaq* a primitive root; to *gap* open; used only as a denominative from H919; to *mend* a breach:— repair.

H919 בֶּדֶק *bedeq* from H918; a *gap* or *leak* (in a building or a ship):— breach, calker.

H920 בִּדְקַר *bidqar* probably from H1856 with preposition prefixed; *by stabbing,* i.e. *assassin; Bidkar,* an Israelite:— Bidkar.

H921 בְּדַר *bĕdar* (Aramaic) corresponding (by transposition) to H6504; to *scatter:*— scatter.

H922 בֹּהוּ *bōhû* from an unused root (meaning to *be empty*); a *vacuity,* i.e. (superficially) an undistinguishable *ruin:*— emptiness, void.

H923 בַּהַט *bahaṭ* from an unused root (probably meaning to *glisten*); white *marble* or perhaps *alabaster:*— red marble.

H924 בְּהִילוּ *bĕhîlû* (Aramaic) from H927; a *hurry;* only adverbially *hastily:*— in haste.

H925 בָּהִיר *bāhîr* from an unused root (meaning to *be bright*); *shining:*— bright.

H926 בָּהַל *bāhal* a primitive root; to *tremble* inwardly (or *palpitate*), i.e. (figuratively) *be* (causatively *make*) (suddenly) *alarmed* or *agitated;* by implication to *hasten* anxiously:— be afraid, be affrighted, make afraid, be amazed, be dismayed, be rash, haste, be hasty, get hastily, make haste, hasten, speedy, give speedily, thrust out, trouble, vex.

H927 בְּהַל *bĕhal* (Aramaic) corresponding to H926; to *terrify, hasten:*— in haste, trouble.

H928 בֶּהָלָה *behālâ* from H926; *panic, destruction* :— terror, trouble.

H929 בְּהֵמָה *bĕhēmâ* from an unused root (probably meaning to be *mute*); properly a *dumb* beast; especially any large quadruped or *animal* (often collectively):— beast, cattle.

H930 בְּהֵמוֹת *bĕhēmôt* in form a plural of H929, but really a singular of Egyptian derivation; a *water-ox,* i.e. the *hippopotamus* or Nile-horse:— Behemoth.

H931 בֹּהֶן *bōhen* from an unused root apparently meaning to *be thick;* the *thumb* of the hand or *great toe* of the foot:— thumb, great toe.

H932 בֹּהַן *bōhan* an orthographical variation of H931; *thumb; Bohan,* an Israelite:— Bohan.

H933 בֹּהַק *bōhaq* from an unused root meaning to *be pale;* white *scurf:*— freckled spot.

H934 בַּהֶרֶת *baheret* feminine active participle of the same as H925; a *whitish* spot on the skin:— bright spot.

H935 בּוֹא *bôʾ* a primitive root; to *go* or *come* (in a wide variety of applications):— abide, apply, attain, be, befall, besiege, bring, bring forth, bring in, bring into, bring to pass, call, carry, certainly, come, cause to come, let to come, thing for to come, come against, come in, come out, come upon, come to pass, depart, doubtless again, eat, employ, enter, cause to enter, enter in, enter into, entering, entrance, entry, be fallen, fetch, follow, get, give, go, go down, go in, go to war, grant, have, indeed, invade, lead, lift up, mention, pull in, put, resort, run, run down, send, set, stricken in age, well stricken in age, surely, take, take in, way.

H936 בּוּז *bûz* a primitive root; to *disrespect:*— contemn, despise utterly.

H937 בּוּז *bûz* from H936; *disrespect:*— contempt, contemptuously, despised, shamed.

H938 בּוּז *bûz* the same as H937; *Buz,* the name of a son of Nahor, and of an Israelite:— Buz.

H939 בּוּזָה *bûzâ* feminine passive participle of H936; something *scorned;* an object of *contempt:*— despised.

H940 בּוּזִי *bûzî* patronymic from H938; a *Buzite* or descendant of Buz:— Buzite.

H941 בּוּזִי *bûzî* the same as H940, *Buzi,* an Israelite:— Buzi.

H942 בַּוַּי *bawway* probably of Persian origin; *Bavvai,* an Israelite:— Bavai.

H943 בּוּךְ *bûk* a primitive root; to *involve* (literally or figuratively):— be entangled, be perplexed.

H944 בּוּל *bûl* for H2981; *produce* (of the earth, etc.):— food, stock.

H945 בּוּל *bûl* the same as H944 (in the sense of *rain*); *Bul,* the eighth Hebrew month:— Bul.

H946 בּוּנָה *bûnâ* from H995; *discretion; Bunah,* an Israelite:— Bunah.

H947 בּוּס *bûs* a primitive root; to *trample* (literally or figuratively):— loath, tread, tread down, tread under, tread under foot, be polluted.

H948 בּוּץ *bûṣ* from an unused root (of the same form) meaning to *bleach,* i.e. (intransitively) *be* *white;* probably *cotton* (of some sort):— fine linen, white linen.

H949 בּוֹצֵץ *bôṣēṣ* from the same as H948; *shining; Botsets,* a rock near Michmash:— Bozez.

H950 בּוּקָה *bûqâ* feminine passive participle of an unused root (meaning to *be hollow*); *emptiness* (as adjective):— empty.

H951 בּוֹקֵר *bôqēr* properly active participle from H1239 as denominative from H1241; a *cattle-tender:*— herdman.

H952 בּוּר *bûr* a primitive root; to *bore,* i.e. (figuratively) *examine:*— declare.

H953 בּוֹר *bôr* from H952 (in the sense of H877); a pit *hole* (especially one used as a *cistern or prison*):— cistern, dungeon, fountain, pit, well.

H954 בּוֹשׁ *bôš* a primitive root; properly to *pale,* i.e. by implication to *be ashamed;* also (by implication) to *be disappointed,* or *delayed:*— shame, be ashamed, make ashamed, bring to shame, cause shame, put to shame, with shame, ashamed, be condounded, put to confusion, become dry, delay, be long.

H955 בּוּשָׁה *bûšâ* feminine participle passive of H954; *shame:*— shame.

H956 בּוּת *bût* (Aramaic) apparently denominative from H1005; to *lodge* over night:— pass the night.

H957 בַּז *baz* from H962; *plunder:*— booty, prey, spoil, spoiled.

H958 בָּזָא *bāzāʾ* a primitive root; probably to *cleave* :— spoil.

H959 בָּזָה *bāzâ* a primitive root; to *disesteem:*— despise, disdain, contemn, contemptible, think to scorn, vile person.

H960 בָּזֹה *bāzōh* from H959; *scorned:*— despise.

H961 בִּזָּה *bizzâ* feminine of H957; *booty:*— prey, spoil.

H962 בָּזַז *bāzaz* a primitive root; to *plunder:*— catch, gather, for a prey, take for a prey, rob, robber, spoil, take, take away, take spoil, utterly.

H963 בִּזָּיוֹן *bizzāyôn* from H959; *disesteem:*— contempt.

H964 בִּזְיוֹתְיָה *bizyôtĕyâ* from H959 and H3050; *contempts of Jah; Bizjothjah,* a place in Palestine:— Bizjothjah.

H965 בָּזָק *bāzāq* from an unused root meaning to *lighten;* a *flash* of lightning:— flash of lightning.

H966 בֶּזֶק *bezeq* from H965; *lightning; Bezek,* a place in Palestine:— Bezek.

H967 בָּזַר *bāzar* a primitive root; to *disperse:*— scatter.

H968 בִּזְתָא *biztāʾ* of Persian origin; *Biztha,* a eunuch of Xerxes:— Biztha.

H969 בָּחוֹן *bāḥôn* from H974; an *assayer* of metals:— tower.

H970 בָּחוּר *bāḥûr* or

בָּחֻר *bāḥūr* participle passive of H977; properly *selected,* i.e. a *youth* (often collectively):— young, young man, choice young man, chosen, hole.

H971 בַּחִין *baḥîn* another form of H975; a watch-*tower* of besiegers:— tower.

H972 בָּחִיר *bāḥîr* from H977; *select:*— choose, chosen one, elect.

H973 בָּחַל *bāḥal* a primitive root; to *loathe:*— abhor, get hastily *[from the margin for H926].*

H974 בָּחַן *bāḥan* a primitive root; to *test* (especially metals); generally and figuratively to *investigate:*— examine, prove, tempt, try, trial.

H975 בַּחַן *baḥan* from H974 (in the sense of keeping a *look-out*); a watch-*tower:*— tower.

H976 בֹּחַן *bōḥan* from H974; *trial:*— tried.

H977 בָּחַר *bāḥar* a primitive root; properly to *try,* i.e. (by implication) *select:*— acceptable, appoint, choose, choice, excellent, join, be rather, require.

H978 בַּחֲרוּמִי *baḥărûmî* patrial from H980 (by transposition); a *Bacharumite* or inhabitant of Bachurim:— Baharumite.

H979 בְּחֻרוֹת *bĕḥūrôt* or

בְּחוּרוֹת *bĕḥûrôt* feminine plural of H970 also (masculine plural)

בְּחֻרִים *bĕḥūrîm; youth* (collectively and abstractly):— young men, youth.

H980 בַּחֻרִים *baḥūrîm* or

בַּחוּרִים *baḥûrîm; young men; Bachurim,* a place in Palestine:— Bahurim.

H981 בָּטָא *bāṭāʾ* or

בָּטָה *bāṭâ* a primitive root; to *babble;* hence to *vociferate* angrily:— pronounce, speak unadvisedly.

H982 בָּטַח *bāṭaḥ* a primitive root; properly to *hie* for refuge [but not so *precipitately* as H2620]; figuratively to *trust,* be *confident* or *sure:*— be bold, be confident, be secure, be sure, careless, careless one, careless woman, put confidence, hope, make to hope, trust, put trust, make to trust.

H983 בֶּטַח *beṭaḥ* from H982; properly a place of *refuge;* abstractly *safety,* both the fact *(security)* and the feeling *(trust)*; often (adverbially with or without preposition) *safely:*— assurance, boldly, without care, careless, confidence, hope, safe, safely, safety, secure, surely.

H984 בֶּטַח *beṭaḥ* the same as H983; *Betach,* a place in Syria:— Betah.

H985 בִּטְחָה *biṭḥâ* feminine of H984; *trust:*— confidence.

H986 בִּטָּחוֹן *biṭṭāḥôn* from H982; *trust:*— confidence, hope.

H987 בַּטֻּחוֹת *baṭṭūḥôt* feminine plural from H982; *security:*— secure.

H988 בָּטַל *bāṭal* a primitive root; to *desist* from labor:— cease.

H989 בְּטֵל *bĕṭēl* (Aramaic) corresponding to H988; to *stop:*— cease, cause to cease, make to cease, hinder.

H990 בֶּטֶן *beṭen* from an unused root probably meaning to *be hollow;* the *belly,* especially the *womb;* also the *bosom* or *body* of anything:— belly, body, as they be born, within, womb.

H991 בֶּטֶן *beṭen* the same as H990; *Beten,* a place in Palestine:— Beten.

H992 בֹּטֶן *bōṭen* from H990; (only in plural) a *pistachio*-nut (from its form):— nut.

H993 בְּטֹנִים *bĕṭōnîm* probably plural from H992; *hollows: Betonim,* a place in Palestine:— Betonim.

H994 בִּי *bî* perhaps from H1158 (in the sense of *asking*); properly a *request;* used only adverbially (always with "my Lord"); *Oh that!; with leave,* or *if it please:*— alas, O, oh.

H995 בִּין *bîn* a primitive root; to *separate* mentally (or *distinguish*), i.e. (generally) *understand:*— attend, consider, be cunning, diligently, direct, discern, eloquent, feel, inform, instruct, have intelligence, know, look well to, mark, perceive, be prudent, regard, skilfull, can skill, teach, think, understand, make to understand, understanding, cause understanding, get understanding, give understanding, have understanding, view, wise, wise man, deal wisely.

H996 בֵּין *bên* sometimes in the plural masculine or feminine; properly the construct contracted form of an otherwise unused noun from H995; a *distinction;* but used only as a preposition, *between* (repeated before each noun, often with other particles); also as a conjunction, *either . . . or:*— among, asunder, at, between, betwixt . . . and, from, from the midst, in, out of, whether, whether it be . . . or, within.

H997 בֵּין *bên* (Aramaic) corresponding to H996 :— among, between.

H998 בִּינָה *bînah* from H995; *understanding:*— knowledge, meaning, perfectly, understanding, wisdom.

H999 בִּינָה *bînâ* (Aramaic) corresponding to H998 :— knowledge.

H1000 בֵּיצָה *bêṣâ* from the same as H948; an *egg* (from its whiteness):— egg.

H1001 בִּירָא *bîrāʾ* (Aramaic) corresponding to H1002; a *palace:*— palace.

H1002 בִּירָה *bîrâ* of foreign origin; a *castle* or *palace:*— palace.

H1003 בִּירָנִית *bîrānît* from H1002; a *fortress:*— castle.

H1004 בַּיִת *bayit* probably from H1129 abbreviated; a *house* (in the greatest variation of applications, especially *family,* etc.):— court, daughter, door, dungeon, family, forth of, great as would contain, hangings, home, home born, house, winter house, household, inside, inward, palace, place, prison, steward, tablet, temple, web, within, without.

H1005 בַּיִת *bayit* (Aramaic) corresponding to H1004 :— house.

H1006 בַּיִת *bayit* the same as H1004; *Bajith,* a place in Palestine:— Bajith.

H1007 בֵּית אָוֶן *bêt ʾāwen* from H1004 and H205; *house of vanity; Beth-Aven,* a place in Palestine:— Beth-aven.

H1008 בֵּית־אֵל *bêt-ʾēl* from H1004 and H410; *house of God; Beth-El,* a place in Palestine:— Beth-el.

H1009 בֵּית אַרְבֵּאל *bêt ʾarbēʾl* from H1004 and H695 and H410; *house of God's ambush; Beth-Arbel,* a place in Palestine:— Beth-Arbel.

H1010 בֵּית בַּעַל מְעוֹן *bêt baʿal mĕʿôn* from H1004 and H1168 and H4583, *house of Baal of* (the) *habitation of* [apparently by transposition] or (shorter)

בֵּית מְעוֹן *bêt mĕʿôn house of habitation of* (Baal); *Beth-Baal-Meön,* a place in Palestine:— Beth-baal-meon. Compare H1186 and H1194

H1011 בֵּית בִּרְאִי *bêt birʾî* from H1004 and H1254; *house of a creative* one; *Beth-Biri,* a place in Palestine:— Beth-birei.

H1012 בֵּית בָּרָה *bêt bārâ* probably from H1004 and H5679; *house of* (the) *ford; Beth-Barah,* a place in Palestine:— Beth-barah.

H1013 בֵּית־גָּדֵר *bêt-gādēr* from H1004 and H1447; *house of* (the) *wall; Beth-Gader,* a place in Palestine:— Beth-gader.

H1014 בֵּית גָּמוּל *bêt gāmûl* from H1004 and the passive participle of H1576; *house of* (the) *weaned; Beth-Gamul,* a place east of the Jordan:— Beth-gamul.

H1015 בֵּית דִּבְלָתַיִם *bêt diblātayim* from H1004 and the dual of H1690; *house of* (the) *two fig-cakes; Beth-Diblathajim,* a place east of the Jordan:— Beth-diblathaim.

H1016 בֵּית־דָּגוֹן *bêt-dāgôn* from H1004 and H1712; *house of Dagon; Beth-Dagon,* the name of two places in Palestine:— Beth-dagon.

H1017 בֵּית הָאֱלִי *bêt hāʾĕlî* patrial from H1008 with the article interposed; a *Beth-elite,* or inhabitant of Bethel:— Bethelite.

H1018 בֵּית הָאֵצֶל *bêt hāʾēṣel* from H1004 and H681 with the article interposed; *house of the side; Beth-ha-Etsel,* a place in Palestine:— Beth-ezel.

H1019 בֵּית הַגִּלְגָּל *bêt haggilgāl* from H1004 and H1537 with the article interposed; *house of the Gilgal* (or *rolling*); *Beth-hag-Gilgal,* a place in Palestine:— Beth-gilgal.

H1020 בֵּית הַיְשִׁימוֹת *bêt hayšîmôt* from H1004 and the plural of H3451 with the article interposed; *house of the deserts; Beth-ha-Jeshimoth,* a town east of the Jordan:— Beth-jeshimoth.

H1021 בֵּית הַכֶּרֶם *bêt hakkerem* from H1004 and H3754 with the article interposed; *house of the vineyard; Beth-hak-Kerem,* a place in Palestine:— Beth-haccerem.

H1022 בֵּית הַלַּחְמִי *bêt hallaḥmî* patrial from H1035 with the article inserted; a *Beth-lechemite,* or native of Bethlechem:— Bethlehemite.

H1023 בֵּית הַמֶּרְחָק *bêt hammerḥāq* from H1004 and H4801 with the article interposed; *house of the breadth; Beth-ham-Merchak,* a place in Palestine:— place that was far off.

H1024 בֵּית הַמַּרְכָּבוֹת *bêt hammarkābôt* or (shortened)

בֵּית מַרְכָּבוֹת *bêt markābôt* from H1004 and the plural of H4818 (with or without the article interposed); *place of* (the) *chariots; Beth-ham-Markaboth* or *Beth-Markaboth,* a place in Palestine:— Beth-marcaboth.

H1025 בֵּית הָעֵמֶק *bêt hāʿēmeq* from H1004 and H6010 with the article interposed; *house of the valley; Beth-ha-Emek,* a place in Palestine:— Beth-emek.

H1026 בֵּית הָעֲרָבָה *bêt hāʿărābâ* from H1004 and H6160 with the article interposed; *house of the Desert; Beth-ha-Arabah,* a place in Palestine:— Beth-arabah.

H1027 בֵּית הָרָם *bêt hārām* probably for H1027; *Beth-ha-Ram,* a place east of the Jordan:— Beth-aram.

H1028 בֵּית הָרָן *bêt hārān* probably for H1027; *Beth-ha-Ran,* a place east of the Jordan:— Beth-haran.

H1029 בֵּית הַשִּׁטָּה *bêt haššiṭṭâ* from H1004 and H7848 with the article interposed; *house of the acacia; Beth-hash-Shittah,* a place in Palestine:— Beth-shittah.

H1030 בֵּית הַשִּׁמְשִׁי *bêt haššimšî* patrial from H1053 with the article inserted; a *Beth-shimshite,* or inhabitant of Bethshemesh:— Bethshemite.

H1031 בֵּית חָגְלָה *bêt ḥoglâ* from H1004 and the same as H2295; *house of a partridge; Beth-Choglah,* a place in Palestine:— Beth-hoglah.

H1032 בֵּית חוֹרוֹן *bêt ḥôrôn* from H1004 and H2356; *house of hollowness; Beth-Choron,* the name of two adjoining places in Palestine:— Beth-horon.

H1033 בֵּית כַּר *bêt kar* from H1004 and H3733; *house of pasture; Beth-Car,* a place in Palestine:— Beth-car.

H1034 בֵּית לְבָאוֹת *bêt lĕbāʾôt* from H1004 and the plural of H3833; *house of lionesses; Beth-Lebaoth,* a place in Palestine:— Beth-lebaoth. Compare H3822

H1035 בֵּית לֶחֶם *bêt leḥem* from H1004 and H3899; *house of bread; Beth-Lechem,* a place in Palestine:— Beth-lehem.

H1036 בֵּית לְעַפְרָה *bêt lĕʿaprâ* from H1004 and the feminine of H6083 (with preposition interposed); *house to* (i.e. *of*) *dust; Beth-le-Aphrah,* a place in Palestine:— house of Aphrah.

H1037 בֵּית מִלּוֹא *bêt millôʾ* or

בֵּית מִלֹּא *bêt millōʾ* from H1004 and H4407; *house of* (the) *rampart; Beth-Millo,* the name of two citadels:— house of Millo.

H1038 בֵּית מַעֲכָה *bêt maʿăkâ* from H1004 and H4601; *house of Maakah; Beth-Maakah,* a place in Palestine:— Beth-maachah.

H1039 בֵּית נִמְרָה *bêt nimrâ* from H1004 and the feminine of H5246; *house of* (the) *leopard; Beth-Nimrah,* a place east of the Jordan:— Beth-nimrah. Compare H5247

H1040 בֵּית עֵדֶן *bêt ʿēden* from H1004 and H5730; *house of pleasure; Beth-Eden,* a place in Syria:— Beth-eden.

H1041 בֵּית עַזְמָוֶת *bêt ʿazmāwet* from H1004 and H5820; *house of Azmaveth,* a place in Palestine:— Beth-azmaveth. Compare H5820

H1042 בֵּית עֲנוֹת *bêt ʿănôt* from H1004 and a plural from H6030; *house of replies; Beth-Anoth,* a place in Palestine:— Beth-anoth.

H1043 בֵּית עֲנָת *bêt ʿănāt* an orthographical variation for H1042; *Beth-Anath,* a place in Palestine:— Beth-anath.

H1044 בֵּית עֵקֶד *bêt ʿēqed* from H1004 and a derivative of H6123; *house of* (the) *binding* (for sheep-shearing); *beth-Eked,* a place in Palestine:— shearing-house.

H1045 בֵּית עַשְׁתָּרוֹת *bêt ʿaštārôt* from H1004 and H6252; *house of Ashtoreths; Beth-Ashtaroth,* a place in Palestine:— house of Ashtaroth. Compare H1203, H6252

H1046 בֵּית פֶּלֶט *bêt peleṭ* from H1004 and H6412; *house of escape; Beth-Palet,* a place in Palestine:— Beth-palet.

H1047 בֵּית פְּעוֹר *bêt pĕʿôr* from H1004 and H6465; *house of Peor; Beth-Peor,* a place east of the Jordan:— Beth-peor.

H1048 בֵּית פַּצֵּץ *bêt paṣṣēṣ* from H1004 and a derivative from H6327; *house of dispersion; Beth-Patstsets,* a place in Palestine:— Beth-pazzez.

H1049 בֵּית צוּר *bêt ṣûr* from H1004 and H6697; *house of* (the) *rock; Beth-Tsur,* a place in Palestine:— Beth-zur.

H1050 בֵּית רְחוֹב *bêt rĕḥôb* from H1004 and H7339; *house of* (the) *street; Beth-Rechob,* a place in Palestine:— Beth-rehob.

H1051 בֵּית רָפָא *bêt rāpāʾ* from H1004 and H7497; *house of* (the) *giant; Beth-Rapha,* an Israelite:— Beth-rapha.

H1052 בֵּית שְׁאָן *bêt šĕʾān* or

בֵּית שָׁן *bêt šān* from H1004 and H7599; *house of ease; Beth-Shean* or *Beth-Shan,* a place in Palestine:— Beth-shean, Beth-Shan.

H1053 בֵּית שֶׁמֶשׁ *bêt šemeš* from H1004 and H8121; *house of* (the) *sun; Beth-Shemesh,* a place in Palestine:— Beth-shemesh.

H1054 בֵּית תַּפּוּחַ *bêt tappûaḥ* from H1004 and H8598; *house of* (the) *apple; Beth-Tappuach,* a place in Palestine:— Beth-tappuah.

H1055 בִּיתָן *bîtān* probably from H1004; a *palace* (i.e. *large house*):— palace.

H1056 בָּכָא *bākāʾ* from H1058; *weeping; Baca,* a valley in Palestine:— Baca.

H1057 בָּכָא *bākāʾ* the same as H1056; the *weeping* tree (some gum-distilling tree, perhaps the *balsam*):— mulberry tree.

H1058 בָּכָה *bākâ* a primitive root; to *weep;* generally to *bemoan:*— at all, bewail, complain, make lamentation, more, mourn, sore, with tears, weep.

H1059 בֶּכֶה *bekeh* from H1058; a *weeping:*— sore.

H1060 בְּכוֹר *bĕkôr* from H1069; *firstborn;* hence *chief:*— eldest, eldest son, firstborn, firstling.

H1061 בִּכּוּר *bikkûr* from H1069; the *first-fruits* of the crop:— first fruit, firstripe, hasty fruit.

H1062 בְּכוֹרָה *bĕkôrâ* or (shortened)

בְּכֹרָה *bĕkōrâ* feminine of H1060; the *firstling* of man or beast; abstractly *primogeniture:*— birthright, firstborn, firstling.

H1063 בִּכּוּרָה *bikkûrâ* feminine of H1061; the *early* fig:— firstripe, firstripe fruit.

H1064 בְּכוֹרַת *bĕkôrat* feminine of H1062; *primogeniture; Bekorath,* an Israelite:— Bechorath.

H1065 בְּכִי *bĕkî* from H1058; a *weeping;* by analogy, a *dripping:*— overflowing, sore, weeping, continual weeping, wept.

H1066 בֹּכִים *bōkîm* plural active participle of H1058; (with the article) the *weepers; Bokim,* a place in Palestine:— Bochim.

H1067 בְּכִירָה *bĕkîrâ* feminine from H1069; the *eldest* daughter:— firstborn.

H1068 בְּכִית *bĕkît* from H1058; a *weeping:*— mourning.

H1069 בָּכַר *bākar* a primitive root; properly to *burst* the womb, i.e. (causatively) *bear* or *make early fruit* (of woman or tree); also (as denominative from H1061) to *give the birthright:*— make firstborn, be firstling, bring forth first child, bring forth new fruit.

H1070 בֶּכֶר *beker* from H1069 (in the sense of *youth*); a young *camel:*— dromedary.

H1071 בֶּכֶר *beker* the same as H1070; *Beker,* the name of two Israelites:— Becher.

H1072 בִּכְרָה *bikrâ* feminine of H1070; a young *she-camel:*— dromedary.

H1073 בַּכֻּרָה *bakkūrâ* by orthographical variation for H1063; a *first-ripe* fig:— first-ripe.

H1074 בֹּכְרוּ *bōkĕrû* from H1069; *first-born; Bokeru,* an Israelite:— Bocheru.

H1075 בִּכְרִי *bikrî* from H1069; *youthful; Bikri,* an Israelite:— Bichri.

H1076 בַּכְרִי *bakrî* patronymic from H1071; a *Bakrite* (collectively) or descendants of Beker:— Bachrites.

H1077 בַּל *bal* from H1086; properly a *failure;* by implication *nothing;* usually (adverbially) *not* at all; also *lest:*— lest, neither, no, none, none that . . ., not, not any, nothing.

H1078 בֵּל *bēl* by contraction for H1168; *Bel,* the Baal of the Babylonians:— Bel.

H1079 בָּל *bāl* (Aramaic) from H1080; properly *anxiety,* i.e. (by implication) the *heart* (as its seat):— heart.

H1080 בְּלָא *bĕlāʾ* (Aramaic) corresponding to H1086 (but used only in a mental sense); to *afflict:*— wear out.

H1081 בַּלְאֲדָן *balʾădān* from H1078 and H113 (contracted); *Bel* (is his) *lord; Baladan,* the name of a Babylonian prince:— Baladan.

H1082 בָּלַג *bālag* a primitive root; to *break off* or *loose* (in a favorable or unfavorable sense), i.e. *desist* (from grief) or *invade* (with destruction):— comfort, recover strength, strengthen.

H1083 בִּלְגָּה *bilgâ* from H1082; *desistance; Bilgah,* the name of two Israelites:— Bilgah.

H1084 בִּלְגַּי *bilgay* from H1082; *desistant; Bilgai,* an Israelite:— Bilgai.

H1085 בִּלְדַּד *bildad* of uncertain derivation; *Bildad,* one of Job's friends:— Bildad.

H1086 בָּלָה *bālâ* a primitive root; to *fail;* by implication to *wear out, decay* (causatively *consume, spend*) :— consume, enjoy long, become old, make old, wax old, spend, waste.

H1087 בָּלֶה *bāleh* from H1086; *worn out:*— old.

H1088 בָּלָה *bālâ* feminine of H1087; *failure; Balah,* a place in Palestine:— Balah.

H1089 בָּלַה *bālah* a primitive root [rather by transposition for H926]; to *palpitate;* hence (causatively) to *terrify:*— trouble.

H1090 בִּלְהָה *bilhâ* from H1089; *timid; Bilhah,* the name of one of Jacob's concubines; also of a place in Palestine:— Bilhah.

H1091 בַּלָּהָה *balāhâ* from H1089; *alarm;* hence *destruction:*— terror, trouble.

H1092 בִּלְהָן *bilhān* from H1089; *timid; Bilhan,* the name of an Edomite and of an Israelite:— Bilhan.

H1093 בְּלוֹ *bĕlô* (Aramaic) from a root corresponding to H1086; *excise* (on articles consumed):— tribute.

H1094 בְּלוֹא *bĕlôʾ* or (fully)

בְּלוֹי *blôy* from H1086; (only in plural construct) *rags:*— old.

H1095 בֵּלְטְשַׁאצַּר *bēlṭĕšaʾṣṣar* of foreign derivation; *Belteshatstsar,* the Babylonian name of Daniel:— Belteshazzar.

H1096 בֵּלְטְשַׁאצַּר *bēlṭĕšaʾṣṣar* (Aramaic) corresponding to H1095:— Belteshazzar.

H1097 בְּלִי *bĕlî* from H1086; properly *failure,* i.e. *nothing* or *destruction;* usually (with preposition) *without, not yet, because not, as long as,* etc:— corruption, ignorantly, for lack of, where no . . . is, so that no, none, not, unawares, without.

H1098 בְּלִיל *bĕlîl* from H1101; *mixed,* i.e. (specifically) *feed* (for cattle):— corn, fodder, provender.

H1099 בְּלִימָה *bĕlîmâ* from H1097 and H4100; (as indefinite) *nothing whatever:*— nothing.

H1100 בְּלִיַּעַל *bĕlîyaʿal* from H1097 and H3276; *without profit, worthlessness;* by extension *destruction, wickedness* (often in connection with H376, 802, H1121, etc.):— Belial, evil, naughty, ungodly, ungodly men, wicked.

H1101 בָּלַל *bālal* a primitive root; to *overflow* (specifically with oil); by implication to *mix;* also (denominatively from H1098) to *fodder:*— anoint, confound, fade, mingle, mix self, give provender, temper.

H1102 בָּלַם *bālam* a primitive root; to *muzzle:*— be held in.

H1103 בָּלַס *bālas* a primitive root; to *pinch* sycamore figs (a process necessary to ripen them):— gatherer.

H1104 בָּלַע *bālaʿ* a primitive root; to *make away with* (specifically by *swallowing*); generally to *destroy:*— cover, destroy, devour, eat up, be at end, spend up, swallow down, swallow up.

H1105 בֶּלַע *belaʿ* from H1104; a *gulp;* figuratively *destruction:*— devouring, that which he hath swallowed up.

H1106 בֶּלַע *belaʿ* the same as H1105; *Bela,* the name of a place, also of an Edomite and of two Israelites:— Bela.

H1107 בִּלְעֲדֵי *bilʿădê* or

בַּלְעֲדֵי *balʿădê* construct plural from H1077 and H5703; *not till,* i.e. (as preposition or adverb) *except, without, besides:*— beside, not, not in, save, without.

H1108 בַּלְעִי *balʿî* patronym. from H1106; a *Belaite* (collectively) or descendants of Bela:— Belaites.

H1109 בִּלְעָם *bilʿām* probably from H1077 and H5971; *not* (of the) *people,* i.e. *foreigner; Bilam,* a Mesopotamian prophet; also a place in Palestine:— Balaam, Bileam.

H1110 בָּלַק *bālaq* a primitive root; to *annihilate:*— waste, make waste.

H1111 בָּלָק *bālāq* from H1110; *waster; Balak,* a Moabitish king:— Balak.

H1112 בֵּלְשַׁאצַּר *bēlĕšaʾṣṣar* or

בֵּלְאשַׁצַּר *bēlĕʾšaṣṣar* of foreign origin (compare H1095); *Belshatstsar,* a Babylonian king:— Belshazzar.

H1113 בֵּלְשַׁאצַּר *bēlĕšaʾṣṣar* (Aramaic) corresponding to H1112:— Belshazzar.

H1114 בִּלְשָׁן *bilšān* of uncertain derivation; *Bilshan,* an Israelite:— Bilshan.

H1115 בִּלְתִּי *biltî* construct feminine of H1086 (equivalent to H1097); properly a *failure of,* i.e. (used only as a negative particle, usually with prepositional prefix) *not, except, without, unless, besides, because not, until,* etc:— because unsatiable, beside, but, continual, except, from, lest, neither, no more, none, not, nothing, save, that no, without.

H1116 בָּמָה *bāmâ* from an unused root (meaning *to be high*); an *elevation:*— height, high place, wave.

H1117 בָּמָה *bāmâ* the same as H1116; *Bamah,* a place in Palestine:— Bamah. See also H1120

H1118 בִּמְהָל *bimhāl* probably from H4107 with prepositional prefix; *with pruning; Bimhal,* an Israelite:— Bimhal.

H1119 בְּמוֹ *bĕmô* prolonged for prepositional prefix; *in, with, by,* etc:— for, in, into, through.

H1120 בָּמוֹת *bāmôt* plural of H1116, *heights,* or (fully)

בָּמוֹת בַּעַל *bāmôt baʿal* from H1116 and H1168; *heights of Baal; Bamoth* or *Bamoth-Baal,* a place east of the Jordan:— Bamoth, Bamoth-baal.

H1121 בֵּן *bēn* from H1129; a *son* (as a *builder* of the family name), in the widest sense (of literal and figurative relationship, including *grandson, subject, nation, quality* or *condition,* etc. [like H1, H251, etc.]):— afflicted, age, Ahohite, Ammonite, Hachmonite, Levite, anointed one, appointed to, arrow, arrow, Assyrian, Babylonian, Egyptian, Grecian, one born, bough, branch, breed, bullock, young bullock, calf, young calf, came up in, child, colt, common, corn, daughter, of first, firstborn, foal, very fruitful, postage, in, kid, lamb, man, man, meet, mighty, nephew, old, people, people, rebel, robber, servant born, soldier, son, spark, steward, stranger, surely, them of, tumultuous one, valiantest, whelp, worthy, young, young one, youth.

H1122 בֵּן *bēn* the same as H1121; *Ben,* an Israelite:— Ben.

H1123 בֵּן *bēn* (Aramaic) corresponding to H1121 :— child, son, young.

H1124 בְּנָא *bĕnāʾ* or

בְּנָה *bĕnâ* (Aramaic) corresponding to H1129; to *build:*— build, make.

H1125 בֶּן־אֲבִינָדָב *ben-ʾăbînādāb* from H1121 and H40; (the) *son of Abinadab; Ben-Abinadab,* an Israelite:— the son of Abinadab.

H1126 בֶּן־אוֹנִי *ben-ʾônî* from H1121 and H205; *son of my sorrow; Ben-Oni,* the original name of Benjamin:— Ben-oni.

H1127 בֶּן־גֶּבֶר *ben-geber* from H1121 and H1397; *son of* (the) *hero; Ben-Geber,* an Israelite:— the son of Geber.

H1128 בֶּן־דֶּקֶר *ben-deqer* from H1121 and a derivative of H1856; *son of piercing* (or *of a lance*); *Ben-Deker,* an Israelite:— the son of Dekar.

H1129 בָּנָה *bānâ* a primitive root; to *build* (literally and figuratively):— build, begin to build, builder, obtain children, make, repair, set, set up, surely.

H1130 בֶּן־הֲדַד *bin-hădad* from H1121 and H1908; *son of Hadad; Ben-Hadad,* the name of several Syrian kings:— Ben-hadad.

H1131 בִּנּוּי *binnûy* from H1129; *built up; Binnui,* an Israelite:— Binnui.

H1132 בֶּן־זוֹחֵת *bēn-zôḥēt* from H1121 and H2105; *son of Zocheth; Ben-Zocheth,* an Israelite:— Benzoketh.

H1133 בֶּן־חוּר *ben-ḥûr* from H1121 and H2354; *son of Chur; Ben-Chur,* an Israelite:— the son of Hur.

H1134 בֶּן־חַיִל *ben-ḥayil* from H1121 and H2428; *son of might; Ben-Chail,* an Israelite:— Ben-hail.

H1135 בֶּן־חָנָן *ben-ḥānān* from H1121 and H2605; *son of Chanan; Ben-Chanan,* an Israelite:— Benhanan.

H1136 בֶּן־חֶסֶד *ben-ḥesed* from H1121 and H2617; *son of kindness: Ben-Chesed,* an Israelite:— the son of Hesed.

H1137 בָּנִי *bānî* from H1129; *built; Bani,* the name of five Israelites:— Bani.

H1138 בֻּנִּי *bunnî* or (fuller)

בּוּנִי *bûnî* from H1129; *built; Bunni* or *Buni,* an Israelite:— Bunni.

H1139 בְּנֵי־בְרַק *bĕnê-bĕraq* from the plural construct of H1121 and H1300; *sons of lightning, Bene-berak,* a place in Palestine:— Bene-barak.

H1140 בִּנְיָה *binyâ* feminine from H1129; a *structure:*— building.

H1141 בְּנָיָה *bĕnāyâ* or (prolonged)

בְּנָיָהוּ *bĕnāyāhû* from H1129 and H3050; *Jah has built; Benajah,* the name of twelve Israelites:— Benaiah.

H1142 בְּנֵי יַעֲקָן *bĕnê yaʿăqān* from the plural of H1121 and H3292; *sons of Yaakan; Bene-Jaakan,* a place in the Desert:— Bene-jaakan.

H1143 בֵּנַיִם *bēnayim* dual of H996; a *double interval,* i.e. the space between two armies:— champion.

H1144 בִּנְיָמִין *binyāmîn* from H1121 and H3225; *son of* (the) *right hand; Binjamin,* youngest son of Jacob; also the tribe descended from him, and its territory:— Benjamin.

H1145 בֶּן־יְמִינִי *ben-yĕmînî* sometimes (with the article inserted)

בֶּן־הַיְמִינִי *bēn-hayyĕmînî* with H376 inserted (1 Sam. 9:1)

בֶּן־אִישׁ יְמִינִי *ben-ʾîš yĕmînî son of a man of Jemini,* or shortened (1 Sam. 9:4; Esth. 2:5)

אִישׁ יְמִינִי *ʾîš yĕmînî a man of Jemini,* (1 Sam. 20:1) simply

יְמִינִי *yĕmînî a Jeminite,* plural

בְּנֵי יְמִינִי *bĕnê yĕmînî* patronymic from H1144; a *Benjaminite,* or descendant of Benjamin:— Benjamite, of Benjamin.

H1146 בִּנְיָן *binyān* from H1129; an *edifice:*— building.

H1147 בִּנְיָן *binyān* (Aramaic) corresponding to H1146:— building.

H1148 בְּנִינוּ *bĕnînû* probably from H1121 with pronominal suffix; *our son; Beninu,* an Israelite:— Beninu.

H1149 בְּנַס *bĕnas* (Aramaic) of uncertain affinity; to *be enraged:*— be angry.

H1150 בִּנְעָא *binʿāʾ* or

בִּנְעָה *binʿâ* of uncertain derivation; *Bina* or *Binah,* an Israelite:— Binea, Bineah.

H1151 בֶּן־עַמִּי *ben-ʿammî* from H1121 and H5971 with pronominal suffix; *son of my people; Ben-Ammi,* a son of Lot:— Ben-ammi.

H1152 בְּסוֹדְיָה *bĕsôdĕyâ* from H5475 and H3050 with prepositional prefix; *in* (the) *counsel of Jehovah; Besodejah,* an Israelite:— Besodeiah.

H1153 בְּסַי *bĕsay* from H947; *domineering; Besai,* one of the Nethinim:— Besai.

H1154 בֶּסֶר *beser* from an unused root meaning to *be sour;* an *immature* grape:— unripe grape.

H1155 בֹּסֶר *bōser* from the same as H1154:— sour grape.

H1156 בְּעָא *bĕʿāʾ* or

בְּעָה *bĕʿâ* (Aramaic) corresponding to H1158; to *seek* or *ask:*— ask, desire, make petition, pray, request, seek.

H1157 בְּעַד *bĕʿad* from H5704 with prepositional prefix; *in up to* or *over against;* generally *at, beside, among, behind, for,* etc:— about, at, by, by means of, for, over, through, up, upon, within.

H1158 בָּעָה *bāʿâ* a primitive root; to *gush* over, i.e. to *swell;* (figuratively) to *desire* earnestly; by implication to *ask:*— cause, inquire, seek up, swell out.

H1159 בָּעוּ *bāʿû* (Aramaic) from H1156; a *request* :— petition.

H1160 בְּעוֹר *bĕʿôr* from H1197 (in the sense of *burning*); a *lamp; Beör,* the name of the father of an Edomitish king; also of that of Balaam:— Beor.

H1161 בִּעוּתִים *biʿûtîm* masculine plural from H1204; *alarms:*— terrors.

H1162 בֹּעַז *bōʿaz* from an unused root of uncertain meaning; *Boaz,* the ancestor of David; also the name of a pillar in front of the temple:— Boaz.

H1163 בָּעַט *bāʿat* a primitive root; to *trample* down, i.e. (figuratively) *despise:*— kick.

H1164 בְּעִי *bĕʿî* from H1158; a *prayer:*— grave.

H1165 בְּעִיר *bĕʿîr* from H1197 (in the sense of *eating*); cattle:— beast, cattle.

H1166 בָּעַל *bāʿal* a primitive root; to *be master;* hence (as denominative from H1167) to *marry:*— have dominion, have dominion over, be husband, marry, married, wife.

H1167 בַּעַל *baʿal* from H1166; a *master;* hence a *husband,* or (figuratively) *owner* (often used with another noun in modifications of this latter sense) :— archer, babbler, bird, captain, chief man, confederate, have to do, dreamer, those to whom it is due, furious, those that are given to it, great, hairy, he that hath it, have, horseman, husband, lord, man, married, master, person, sworn, they of.

H1168 בַּעַל *baʿal* the same as H1167; *Baal,* a Phoenician deity:— Baal, *[plural]* Baalim.

H1169 בְּעֵל *bĕʿēl* (Aramaic) corresponding to H1167 :— chancellor.

H1170 בַּעַל בְּרִית *baʿal bĕrît* from H1168 and H1285; *Baal of* (the) *covenant; Baal-Berith,* a special deity of the Shechemites:— Baal-berith.

H1171 בַּעַל גָּד *baʿal gād* from H1168 and H1409; *Baal of Fortune; Baal-Gad,* a place in Syria:— Baal-gad.

H1172 בַּעֲלָה *baʿălâ* feminine of H1167; a *mistress* :— that hath, mistress.

H1173 בַּעֲלָה *baʿălâ* the same as H1172; *Baalah,* the name of three places in Palestine:— Baalah.

H1174 בַּעַל הָמוֹן *baʿal hāmôn* from H1167 and H1995; *possessor of a multitude; Baal-Hamon,* a place in Palestine:— Baal-hamon.

H1175 בְּעָלוֹת *bĕʿālôt* plural of H1172; *mistresses; Beäloth,* a place in Palestine:— Bealoth, in Aloth *[by mistake for a plural from H5927 with prepositional prefix].*

H1176 בַּעַל זְבוּב *baʿal zĕbûb* from H1168 and H2070; *Baal of* (the) *Fly; Baal-Zebub,* a special deity of the Ekronites:— Baal-zebub.

H1177 בַּעַל חָנָן *baʿal ḥānān* from H1167 and H2603; *possessor of grace; Baal-Chanan,* the name of an Edomite, also of an Israelite:— Baal-hanan.

H1178 בַּעַל חָצוֹר *baʿal ḥāṣôr* from H1167 and a modification of H2691; *possessor of a village; Baal-Chatsor,* a place in Palestine:— Baal-hazor.

H1179 בַּעַל חֶרְמוֹן *baʿal ḥermôn* from H1167 and H2768; *possessor of Hermon; Baal-Chermon,* a place in Palestine:— Baal-hermon.

H1180 בַּעֲלִי *baʿălî* from H1167 with pronominal suffix; *my master; Baali,* a symbolical name for Jehovah:— Baali.

H1181 בַּעֲלֵי בָּמוֹת *baʿălê bāmôt* from the plural of H1168 and the plural of H1116; *Baals of* (the) *heights; Baale-Bamoth,* a place east of the Jordan:— lords of the high places.

H1182 בְּעֶלְיָדָע *bĕʿelyādāʿ* from H1168 and H3045; *Baal has known; Beëljada,* an Israelite:— Beeliada.

H1183 בְּעַלְיָה *bĕʿalyâ* from H1167 and H3050; *Jah* (is) *master; Bealjah,* an Israelite:— Bealiah.

H1184 בַּעֲלֵי יְהוּדָה *baʿălê yĕhûdâ* from the plural of H1167 and H3063; *masters of Judah; Baale-Jehudah,* a place in Palestine:— Baale of Judah.

H1185 בַּעֲלִיס *baʿălîs* probably from a derivative of H5965 with prepositional prefix; *in exultation; Baalis,* an Ammonitish king:— Baalis.

H1186 בַּעַל מְעוֹן *baʿal mĕʿôn* from H1168 and H4583; *Baal of* (the) *habitation* (of) [compare H1010]; *Baal-Meön,* a place east of the Jordan:— Baal-meon.

H1187 בַּעַל פְּעוֹר *baʿal pĕʿôr* from H1168 and H6465; *Baal of Peor; Baal-Peör,* a Moabitish deity:— Baal-peor.

H1188 בַּעַל פְּרָצִים *baʿal pĕrāṣîm* from H1167 and the plural of H6556; *possessor of breaches; Baal-Peratsim,* a place in Palestine:— Baal-perazim.

H1189 בַּעַל צְפוֹן *baʿal ṣĕpôn* from H1168 and H6828 (in the sense of *cold*) [according to others an Egyptian form of *Typhon,* the destroyer]; *Baal of winter; Baal-Tsephon,* a place in Egypt:— Baal-zephon.

H1190 בַּעַל שָׁלִשָׁה *baʿal šālišâ* from H1168 and H8031; *Baal of Shalishah, Baal-Shalishah,* a place in Palestine:— Baal-shalisha.

H1191 בַּעֲלָת *baʿălāt* a modification of H1172; *mistressship; Baalath,* a place in Palestine:— Baalath.

H1192 בַּעֲלַת בְּאֵר *baʿălāt bĕʾēr* from H1172 and H875; *mistress of a well; Baalath-Beër,* a place in Palestine:— Baalath-beer.

H1193 בַּעַל תָּמָר *baʿal tāmār* from H1167 and H8558; *possessor of* (the) *palm-tree; Baal-Tamar,* a place in Palestine:— Baal-tamar.

H1194 בְּעֹן *bĕʿōn* probably a contraction of H1010; *Beön,* a place east of the Jordan:— Beon.

H1195 בַּעֲנָא *baʿănāʾ* the same as H1196; *Baana,* the name of four Israelites:— Baana, Baanah.

H1196 בַּעֲנָה *baʿănâ* from a derivative of H6031 with prepositional prefix; *in affliction; Baanah,* the name of four Israelites:— Baanah.

H1197 בָּעַר *bāʿar* a primitive root; to *kindle,* i.e. *consume* (by fire or by eating); also (as denominative from H1198) to *be (-come) brutish:*— be brutish, bring away, put away, take away, burn, eat, eat up, cause to eat, feed, heat, kindle, set, set on fire, waste.

H1198 בַּעַר *baʿar* from H1197; properly *food* (as *consumed*); i.e. (by extension) of cattle *brutishness;* (concretely) *stupid:*— brutish, brutish person, foolish.

H1199 בָּעֲרָא *bāʿărāʾ* from H1198; *brutish; Baara,* an Israelitish woman:— Baara.

H1200 בְּעֵרָה *bĕʿērâ* from H1197; a *burning:*— fire.

H1201 בַּעְשָׁא *baʿšāʾ* from an unused root meaning to *stink; offensiveness:-Basha,* a king of Israel:— Baasha.

H1202 בַּעֲשֵׂיָה *baʿăśēâ* from H6213 and H3050 with prepositional prefix; *in* (the) *work of Jah; Baasejah,* an Israelite:— Baaseiah.

H1203 בְּעֶשְׁתְּרָה *bĕʿeštĕrâ* from H6251 (as singular of H6252) with prepositional prefix; *with Ashtoreth; Beështerah,* a place east of the Jordan:— Beeshterah.

H1204 בָּעַת *bāʿat* a primitive root; to *fear:*— affright, be afraid, make afraid, terrify, trouble.

H1205 בְּעָתָה *bĕʿātâ* from H1204; *fear:*— trouble.

H1206 בֹּץ *bōṣ* probably the same as H948; *mud* (as *whitish* clay):— mire.

H1207 בִּצָּה *biṣṣâ* intensively from H1206; a *swamp* :— fen, mire, miry place.

H1208 בָּצוֹר *bāṣôr* from H1219; *inaccessible,* i.e. *lofty* :— vintage *[by confusion with H1210].*

H1209 בֵּצַי *bēṣay* perhaps the same as H1153; *Betsai,* the name of two Israelites:— Bezai.

H1210 בָּצִיר *bāṣîr* from H1219; *clipped,* i.e. the *grape crop:*— vintage.

H1211 בֶּצֶל *beṣel* from an unused root apparently meaning to *peel;* an *onion:*— onion.

H1212 בְּצַלְאֵל *bĕṣalʾēl* probably from H6738 and H410 with prepositional prefix; *in* (the) *shadow* (i.e. protection) *of God; Betsalel;* the name of two Israelites:— Bezaleel.

H1213 בַּצְלוּת *baṣlût* or

בַּצְלִית *baṣlît* from the same as H1211; a *peeling; Batsluth* or *Batslith;* an Israelite:— Bazlith, Bazluth.

H1214 בָּצַע *bāṣaʿ* a primitive root to *break* off, i.e. (usually) *plunder;* figuratively to *finish,* or (intransitively) *stop:*— covet, be covetous, cut, cut off, finish, fulfill, gain, gain greedily, get, be given to covetousness, greedy, perform, be wounded.

H1215 בֶּצַע *beṣaʿ* from H1214; *plunder;* by extension *gain* (usually unjust):— covetousness, gain, dishonest gain, lucre, profit.

H1216 בָּצֵק *bāṣēq* a primitive root; perhaps to *swell* up, i.e. *blister:*— swell.

H1217 בָּצֵק *bāṣēq* from H1216; *dough* (as *swelling* by fermentation):— dough, flour.

H1218 בָּצְקַת *boṣqat* from H1216; a *swell* of ground; *Botscath,* a place in Palestine:— Bozcath, Boskath.

H1219 בָּצַר *bāṣar* a primitive root; to *clip* off; specifically (as denominative from H1210) to *gather* grapes; also to *be isolated* (i.e. *inaccessible* by height or fortification):— cut off, fenced, defenced, fortify, gather, grape gatherer, mighty things, restrain, strong, wall, wall up, withhold.

H1220 בֶּצֶר *beṣer* from H1219; strictly a *clipping,* i.e. *gold* (as *dug* out):— gold defence.

H1221 בֶּצֶר *beṣer* from same as H1220; an *inaccessible* spot; *Betser,* a place in Palestine; also an Israelite:— Bezer.

H1222 בְּצַר *bĕṣar* another form for H1220; *gold:*— gold.

H1223 בָּצְרָה *boṣrâ* feminine from H1219; an *enclosure,* i.e. *sheep-fold:*— Bozrah.

H1224 בָּצְרָה *boṣrâ* the same as H1223; *Botsrah,* a place in Edom:— Bozrah.

H1225 בִּצָּרוֹן *biṣṣārôn* masculine intensive from H1219; a *fortress:*— stronghold.

H1226 בַּצֹּרֶת *baṣṣōret* feminine intensive from H1219; *restraint* (of rain), i.e. *drought:*— dearth, drought.

H1227 בַּקְבּוּק *baqbûq* the same as H1228; *Bakbuk,* one of the *Nethinim:*— Bakbuk.

H1228 בַּקְבֻּק *baqbūq* from H1238; a *bottle* (from the gurgling in *emptying*):— bottle, cruse.

H1229 בַּקְבֻּקְיָה *baqbuqyâ* from H1228 and H3050; *emptying* (i.e. *wasting*) *of Jah; Bakbukjah,* an Israelite:— Bakbukiah.

H1230 בַּקְבַּקַּר *baqbaqqar* reduplicated from H1239; *searcher; Bakbakkar,* an Israelite:— Bakbakkar.

H1231 בֻּקִּי *būqqî* from H1238; *wasteful; Bukki,* the name of two Israelites:— Bukki.

H1232 בֻּקִּיָּה *buqqîyâ* from H1238 and H3050; *wasting of Jah; Bukkijah,* an Israelite:— Bukkiah.

H1233 בְּקִיעַ *bĕqîaʿ* from H1234; a *fissure:*— breach, cleft.

H1234 בָּקַע *bāqaʿ* a primitive root; to *cleave;* gen to *rend, break, rip* or *open:*— make a breach, break forth, break into, break out, break in pieces, break through, break up, be ready to burst, cleave, cleave asunder, cut out, divide, hatch, rend, rend asunder, rip up, tear, win.

H1235 בֶּקַע *beqaʿ* from H1234; a *section* (half) of a shekel, i.e. a *beka* (a weight and a coin):— bekah, half a shekel.

H1236 בִּקְעָא *biqʿāʾ* (Aramaic) corresponding to H1237:— plain.

H1237 בִּקְעָה *biqʿâ* from H1234; properly a *split,* i.e. a wide level *valley* between mountains:— plain, valley.

H1238 בָּקַק *bāqaq* a primitive root; to *pour* out, i.e. to *empty,* figuratively to *depopulate;* by analogy to *spread* out (as a fruitful vine):— empty, make empty, empty out, fail, utterly, make void.

H1239 בָּקַר *bāqar* a primitive root; properly to *plough,* or (generally) *break* forth, i.e. (figuratively) to *inspect, admire, care for, consider:*— inquire, make inquiry, search, make search, seek out.

H1240 בְּקַר *bĕqar* (Aramaic) corresponding to H1239:— inquire, make search.

H1241 בָּקָר *bāqār* from H1239; a *beeve* or animal of the ox kind of either gender (as used for *ploughing*); collectively a *herd:*— beeve, bull, bullock, calf, cow, great cattle, heifer, herd, kine, ox.

H1242 בֹּקֶר *bōqer* from H1239; properly *dawn* (as the *break* of day); generally *morning:*— day, day, early, morning, morrow.

H1243 בַּקָּרָה *baqqārâ* intensive from H1239; a *looking after:*— seek out.

H1244 בִּקֹּרֶת *biqqōret* from H1239; properly *examination,* i.e. (by implication) *punishment:*— scourged.

H1245 בָּקַשׁ *bāqaš* a primitive root; to *search* out (by any method, specifically in worship or prayer); by implication to *strive after:*— ask, beg, beseech, desire, enquire, get, make inquisition, procure, request, make request, require, seek, seek for.

H1246 בַּקָּשָׁה *baqqāšâ* from H1245; a *petition:*— request.

H1247 בַּר *bar* (Aramaic) corresponding to H1121; a *son, grandson,* etc:— old, son.

H1248 בַּר *bar* borrowed (as a title) from H1247; the *heir* (apparent to the throne):— son.

H1249 בַּר *bar* from H1305 (in its various senses); *beloved;* also *pure, empty:*— choice, clean, clear, pure.

H1250 בָּר *bār* or

בַּר *bar* from H1305 (in the sense of *winnowing*); *grain* of any kind (even while standing in the field); by extension the open *country:*— corn, wheat.

H1251 בַּר *bar* (Aramaic) corresponding to H1250; a *field:*— field.

H1252 בֹּר *bōr* from H1305; *purity:*— cleanness, pureness.

H1253 בֹּר *bōr* the same as H1252; vegetable *lye* (from its *cleansing*); used as a *soap* for washing, or a *flux* for metals:— never so, purely.

H1254 בָּרָא *bārāʾ* a primitive root; (absolutely) to *create;* (qualified) to *cut* down (a wood), *select, feed* (as formative processes):— choose, create, creator, cut down, dispatch, do, make, make fat.

H1255 בְּרֹאדַךְ בַּלְאֲדָן *bĕrōʾdak balʾădān* a variation of H4757; *Berodak-Baladan,* a Babylonian king:— Berodach-baladan.

H1256 בְּרָאיָה *bĕrāʾyâ* from H1254 and H3050; *Jah has created; Berajah,* an Israelite:— Beraiah.

H1257 בַּרְבֻּר *barbūr* by reduplicated from H1250; a *fowl* (as fattened on *grain*):— fowl.

H1258 בָּרַד *bārad* a primitive root, to *hail:*— hail.

H1259 בָּרָד *bārād* from H1258; *hail:*— hail, hail stones.

H1260 בֶּרֶד *bered* from H1258; *hail; Bered,* the name of a place south of Palestine, also of an Israelite:— Bered.

H1261 בָּרֹד *bārōd* from H1258; *spotted* (as if with *hail*):— grisled.

H1262 בָּרָה *bārâ* a primitive root; to *select;* also (as denominative from H1250) to *feed;* also (as equivalent to H1305) to *render clear* (Eccl 3:18):— choose, eat, cause to eat, manifest, meat, give meat.

H1263 בָּרוּךְ *bārûk* passive participle from H1288; *blessed; Baruk,* the name of three Israelites:— Baruch.

H1264 בְּרוֹם *bĕrôm* probably of foreign origin; *damask* (stuff of variegated thread):— rich apparel.

H1265 בְּרוֹשׁ *bĕrôš* of uncertain derivation; a *cypress* (?) tree; hence a *lance* or a *musical* instrument (as made of that wood):— fir, fir tree.

H1266 בְּרוֹת *bĕrôt* a variation of H1265; the *cypress* (or some elastic tree):— fir.

H1267 בָּרוּת *bārût* from H1262; *food:*— meat.

H1268 בֵּרוֹתָה *bērôtâ* or

בֵּרֹתַי *bērōtay* probably from H1266; *cypress* or *cypress-like; Berothah* or *Berothai,* a place north of Palestine:— Berothah, Berothai.

H1269 בִּרְזוֹת *birzôt* probably feminine plural from an unused root (apparently meaning to *pierce*); *holes; Birzoth,* an Israelite:— Birzavith *[from the margin].*

H1270 בַּרְזֶל *barzel* perhaps from the root of H1269; *iron* (as *cutting*); by extension an iron *implement:*— head, ax head, iron.

H1271 בַּרְזִלַּי *barzillay* from H1270; *iron* hearted; *Barzillai,* the name of three Israelites:— Barzillai.

H1272 בָּרַח *bāraḥ* a primitive root; to *bolt,* i.e. figuratively to *flee* suddenly:— chase, chase away; drive away, fain, flee, flee away, put to flight, make haste, reach, run away, shoot.

H1273 בַּרְחֻמִי *barhūmî* by transposition for H978; a *Barchumite*, or native of *Bachurim:*— Barhumite.

H1274 בְּרִי *bĕrî* from H1262; *fat:*— fat.

H1275 בֵּרִי *bērî* probably by contraction from H882; *Beri*, an Israelite:— Beri.

H1276 בֵּרִי *bērî* of uncertain derivation; (only in the plural and with the article) the *Berites*, a place in Palestine:— Berites.

H1277 בָּרִיא *bārî᾽* from H1254 (in the sense of H1262); *fatted* or *plump:*— fat, fat fleshed, fatter, fed, firm, plenteous, rank.

H1278 בְּרִיאָה *bĕrî᾽â* feminine from H1254; a *creation*, i.e. a *novelty:*— new thing.

H1279 בִּרְיָה *biryâ* feminine from H1262; *food:*— meat.

H1280 בְּרִיחַ *bĕrîaḥ* from H1272; a *bolt:*— bar, fugitive.

H1281 בָּרִיחַ *bārîaḥ* or (shortened)

בָּרִחַ *bārīaḥ* from H1272; a *fugitive*, i.e. the *serpent* (as *fleeing*), and the constellation by that name:— crooked, noble, piercing.

H1282 בָּרִיחַ *bārîaḥ* the same as H1281; *Bariach*, an Israelite:— Bariah.

H1283 בְּרִיעָה *bĕrî*ʿ*â* apparently from the feminine of H7451 with prepositional prefix; *in trouble; Beriah*, the name of four Israelites:— Beriah.

H1284 בְּרִיעִי *bĕrî*ʿ*î* patronymic from H1283; a *Berite* (collectively) or descendants of Beriah:— Beerites.

H1285 בְּרִית *bĕrît* from H1262 (in the sense of *cutting* [like H1254]); a *compact* (because made by passing between *pieces* of flesh):— confederacy, confederate, covenant, league.

H1286 בְּרִית *bĕrît* the same as H1285; *Berith*, a Shechemitish deity:— Berith.

H1287 בֹּרִית *bōrît* feminine of H1253; vegetable *alkali:*— sope.

H1288 בָּרַךְ *bārak* a primitive root; to *kneel;* by implication to *bless* God (as an act of adoration), and (vice-versa) man (as a benefit); also (by euphemism) to *curse* (God or the king, as treason):— abundantly, altogether, at all, blaspheme, bless, congratulate, curse, greatly, indeed, kneel, kneel down, praise, salute, still, thank.

H1289 בְּרַךְ *bĕrak* (Aramaic) corresponding to H1288 :— bless, kneel.

H1290 בֶּרֶךְ *berek* from H1288; a *knee:*— knee.

H1291 בֶּרֶךְ *berek* (Aramaic) corresponding to H1290 :— knee.

H1292 בָּרַכְאֵל *bārak᾽ēl* from H1288 and H410, *God has blessed; Barakel*, the father of one of Job's friends:— Barachel.

H1293 בְּרָכָה *bĕrākâ* from H1288; *benediction;* by implication *prosperity:*— blessing, liberal, pool, present.

H1294 בְּרָכָה *bĕrākâ* the same as H1293; *Berakah*, the name of an Israelite, and also of a valley in Palestine:— Berachah.

H1295 בְּרֵכָה *bĕrēkâ* from H1288; a *reservoir* (at which camels *kneel* as a resting-place):— pool, fishpool.

H1296 בֶּרֶכְיָה *berekyâ* or

בֶּרֶכְיָהוּ *berekyāhû* from H1290 and H3050; *knee* (i.e. *blessing*) of *Jah; Berekjah*, the name of six Israelites:— Berachiah, Berechiah.

H1297 בְּרַם *bĕram* (Aramaic) perhaps from H7313 with prepositional prefix; properly *highly*, i.e. *surely;* but used adversatively, *however:*— but, nevertheless, yet.

H1298 בֶּרַע *bera*ʿ of uncertain derivation; *Bera*, a Sodomitish king:— Bera.

H1299 בָּרַק *bāraq* a primitive root; to *lighten* (lightning):— cast forth.

H1300 בָּרָק *bārāq* from H1299; *lightning;* by analogy a *gleam;* concretely a *flashing* sword:— bright, glitter, glittering, glittering sword, lightning.

H1301 בָּרָק *bārāq* the same as H1300; *Barak*, an Israelite:— Barak.

H1302 בַּרְקוֹס *barqôs* of uncertain derivation; *Barkos*, one of the Nethinim:— Barkos.

H1303 בַּרְקָן *barqān* from H1300; a *thorn* (perhaps as burning *brightly*):— brier.

H1304 בָּרֶקֶת *bārĕqat* or

בָּרְקַת *borqat* from H1300; a gem (as *flashing*), perhaps the *emerald:*— carbuncle.

H1305 בָּרַר *bārar* a primitive root; to *clarify* (i.e. *brighten*), *examine, select:*— make bright, choice, chosen, cleanse (be clean), clearly, polished, pure, purify, shew self pure, purge, purge out.

H1306 בִּרְשַׁע *birša*ʿ probably from H7562 with prepositional prefix; *with wickedness; Birsha*, a king of Gomorrah:— Birsha.

H1307 בֵּרֹתִי *bērōtî* patrial from H1268; a *Berothite*, or inhabitant of Berothai:— Berothite.

H1308 בְּשׂוֹר *bĕśôr* from H1810; *cheerful; Besor*, a stream of Palestine:— Besor.

H1309 בְּשׂוֹרָה *bĕśôrâ* or (shortened)

בְּשֹׂרָה *bĕśōrâ* feminine from H1310; glad *tidings;* by implication *reward for good news:*— reward for tidings.

H1310 בָּשַׁל *bāšal* a primitive root; properly to *boil* up; hence to *be done* in cooking; figuratively to *ripen:*— bake, boil, bring forth, roast, seethe, sod, be sodden.

H1311 בָּשֵׁל *bāšēl* from H1310; *boiled:*— at all, sodden.

H1312 בִּשְׁלָם *bišlām* of foreign derivation; *Bishlam*, a Persian:— Bishlam.

H1313 בָּשָׂם *bāśām* from an unused root meaning to *be fragrant;* [compare H5561] the *balsam* plant:— spice.

H1314 בֶּשֶׂם *bešem* or

בֹּשֶׂם *bōśem* from the same as H1313; *fragrance;* by implication *spicery;* also the *balsam* plant:— smell, spice, sweet, sweet odour.

H1315 בָּשְׂמַת *bośmat* feminine of H1314 (the second form); *fragrance; Bosmath*, the name of a wife of Esau, and of a daughter of Solomon:— Bashemath, Basmath.

H1316 בָּשָׁן *bāšān* of uncertain derivation; *Bashan* (often with the article), a region east of the Jordan:— Bashan.

H1317 בָּשְׁנָה *bošnâ* feminine from H954; *shamefulness:*— shame.

H1318 בָּשַׁס *bāšas* a primitive root; to *trample* down :— tread.

H1319 בָּשַׂר *bāśar* a primitive root; properly to *be fresh*, i.e. *full (rosy*, figuratively *cheerful*); to *announce* (glad news):— messenger, preach, publish, shew forth, tidings, bear tidings, bring tidings, carry tidings, good tidings, tell good tidings, preach good tidings.

H1320 בָּשָׂר *bāśār* from H1319; *flesh* (from its *freshness*); by extension *body, person;* also (by euphemism) the *pudenda* of a man:— body, flesh, fat fleshed, lean fleshed, kin, mankind, nakedness, self, skin.

H1321 בְּשַׂר *bĕśar* (Aramaic) corresponding to H1320:— flesh.

H1322 בֹּשֶׁת *bōšet* from H954; *shame* (the feeling and the condition, as well as its cause); by implication (specifically) an *idol:*— ashamed, confusion, greatly, shame, put to shame, shameful thing.

H1323 בַּת *bat* from H1129 (as feminine of H1121); a *daughter* (used in the same wide sense as other terms of relationship, literally and figuratively):— apple of the eye, branch, company, daughter, first, old, owl, town, village.

H1324 בַּת *bat* probably from the same as H1327; a *bath* or Hebrew measure (as a means of *division*) of liquids:— bath.

H1325 בַּת *bat* (Aramaic) corresponding to H1324 :— bath.

H1326 בָּתָה *bātâ* probably an orthographical variation for H1327; *desolation:*— waste.

H1327 בַּתָּה *battâ* feminine from an unused root (meaning to *break* in pieces); *desolation:*— desolate.

H1328 בְּתוּאֵל *bĕtû᾽ēl* apparently from the same as H1326 and H410; *destroyed of God; Bethuel*, the name of a nephew of Abraham, and of a place in Palestine:— Bethuel. Compare H1329

H1329 בְּתוּל *bĕtûl* for H1328; *Bethul* (i.e. *Bethuel*), a place in Palestine:— Bethuel.

H1330 בְּתוּלָה *bĕtûlâ* feminine passive participle of an unused root meaning to *separate;* a *virgin* (from her *privacy*); sometimes (by continuation) a *bride;* also (figuratively) a *city* or *state:*— maid, virgin.

H1331 בְּתוּלִים *bĕtûlîm* masculine plural of the same as H1330; (collectively and abstractly) *virginity;* by implication and concretely the *tokens* of it:— maid, virginity.

H1332 בִּתְיָה *bityâ* from H1323 and H3050; *daughter* (i.e. worshipper) *of Jah; Bithjah*, an Egyptian woman:— Bithiah.

H1333 בָּתַק *bātaq* a primitive root; to *cut* in pieces :— thrust through.

H1334 בָּתַר *bātar* a primitive root, to *chop* up:— divide.

H1335 בֶּתֶר *beter* from H1334; a *section:*— part, piece.

H1336 בֶּתֶר *beter* the same as H1335; *Bether*, a (craggy) place in Palestine:— Bether.

H1337 בַּת רַבִּים *bat rabbîm* from H1323 and a masculine plural from H7227; the *daughter* (i.e. *city*) *of Rabbah:*— Bath-rabbim.

H1338 בִּתְרוֹן *bitrôn* from H1334; (with the article) the *craggy* spot; *Bithron*, a place east of the Jordan:— Bithron.

H1339 בַּת־שֶׁבַע *bat-šeba*ʿ from H1323 and H7651 (in the sense of H7650); *daughter of an oath; Bath-Sheba*, the mother of Solomon:— Bath-sheba.

H1340 בַּת־שׁוּעַ *bat-šûa*ʿ from H1323 and H7771; *daughter of wealth; Bath-shuä*, the same as H1339 :— Bath-shua.

ג

H1341 גֵּא *gē*ᵓ for H1343; *haughty:*— proud.

H1342 גָּאָה *gāᵓâ* a primitive root; to *mount* up; hence in general to *rise,* (figuratively) be *majestic:*— gloriously, grow up, increase, be risen, triumph.

H1343 גֵּאֶה *gēᵓeh* from H1342; *lofty;* figuratively *arrogant:*— proud.

H1344 גֵּאָה *gēᵓâ* feminine from H1342; *arrogance* :— pride.

H1345 גְּאוּאֵל *gĕᵓûᵓēl* from H1342 and H410; *majesty of God; Geüel,* an Israelite:— Geuel.

H1346 גַּאֲוָה *gaᵓăwâ* from H1342; *arrogance* or *majesty;* by implication (concretely) *ornament:*— excellency, haughtiness, highness, pride, proudly, swelling.

H1347 גָּאוֹן *gāᵓôn* from H1342; the same as H1346 :— arrogancy, excellency, excellent, majesty, pomp, pride, proud, swelling.

H1348 גֵּאוּת *gēᵓût* from H1342; the same as H1346 :— excellent things, lifting up, majesty, pride, proudly, raging.

H1349 גַּאֲיוֹן *gaᵓăyôn* from H1342; *haughty:*— proud.

H1350 גָּאַל *gāᵓal* a primitive root, to *redeem* (according to the Oriental law of kinship), i.e. to *be the next of kin* (and as such to *buy back* a relative's property, *marry* his widow, etc.):— in any wise, at all, avenger, deliver, kinsfolk, kinsman, near kinsman, do the part of a kinsman, perform the part of a kinsman, do the kinsman's part, next kinsman, purchase, ransom, redeem, redeemer, revenger.

H1351 גָּאַל *gāᵓal* a primitive root, [rather identical with H1350, through the idea of *freeing,* i.e. *repudiating];* to *soil* or (figuratively) *desecrate:*— defile, pollute, stain.

H1352 גֹּאֶל *gōᵓel* from H1351; *profanation:*— defile.

H1353 גְּאֻלָּה *gĕᵓullâ* feminine passive participle of H1350; *redemption* (including the right and the object); by implication *relationship:*— kindred, redeem, redemption, right.

H1354 גַּב *gab* from an unused root meaning to *hollow* or *curve;* the *back* (as *rounded* [compare H1460 and H1479]); by analogy the *top* or *rim,* a *boss,* a *vault, arch* of eye, *bulwarks,* etc:— back, body, boss, eminent place, higher place, eyebrows, nave, ring.

H1355 גַּב *gab* (Aramaic) corresponding to H1354 :— back.

H1356 גֵּב *gēb* from H1461; a *log* (as *cut* out); also *well* or *cistern* as *dug*):— beam, ditch, pit.

H1357 גֵּב *gēb* probably from H1461 [compare H1462]; a *locust* (from its *cutting*):— locust.

H1358 גֹּב *gōb* (Aramaic) from a root corresponding to H1461; a *pit* (for wild animals) (as *cut* out):— den.

H1359 גֹּב *gōb* or (fully)

גּוֹב *gôb* from H1461; *pit; Gob,* a place in Palestine:— Gob.

H1360 גֶּבֶה *gebeh* from an unused root meaning probably to *collect;* a *reservoir;* by analogy a *march:*— marish, pit.

H1361 גָּבַהּ *gābah* a primitive root; to *soar,* i.e. *be lofty;* figuratively to *be haughty:*— exalt, be haughty, be high, be higher, make high, lift up, mount up, be proud, raise up great height, upward.

H1362 גָּבָהּ *gābāh* from H1361; *lofty* (literally or figuratively):— high, proud.

H1363 גֹּבַהּ *gōbah* from H1361; *elation, grandeur, arrogance:*— excellency, haughty, height, high, loftiness, pride.

H1364 גָּבֹהַּ *gābōah* or (fully)

גָּבוֹהַּ *gābôah* from H1361; *elevated* (or *elated*), *powerful, arrogant:*— haughty, height, high, higher, lofty, proud, exceeding proudly.

H1365 גַּבְהוּת *gabhût* from H1361; *pride:*— loftiness, lofty.

H1366 גְּבוּל *gĕbûl* or (shortened)

גְּבֻל *gĕbūl* from H1379; properly a *cord* (as *twisted*), i.e. (by implication) a *boundary;* by extension the *territory* inclosed:— border, bound, coast, great, landmark, limit, quarter, space.

H1367 גְּבוּלָה *gĕbûlâ* or (shortened)

גְּבֻלָה *gĕbūlâ* feminine of H1366; a *boundary, region:*— border, bound, coast, landmark, place.

H1368 גִּבּוֹר *gibbôr* or (shortened)

גִּבֹּר *gibbōr* intensive from the same as H1397; *powerful;* by implication *warrior, tyrant:*— champion, chief, excel, giant, man, mighty, mighty man, mighty one, strong, strong man, valiant man.

H1369 גְּבוּרָה *gĕbûrâ* feminine passive participle from the same as H1368; *force* (literal or figurative); by implication *valor, victory:*— force, mastery, might, mighty, mighty act, mighty power, power, strength.

H1370 גְּבוּרָה *gĕbûrâ* (Aramaic) corresponding to H1369; *power:*— might.

H1371 גִּבֵּחַ *gibbēaḥ* from an unused root meaning to *be high* (in the forehead); *bald* in the forehead:— forehead bald.

H1372 גַּבַּחַת *gabbahat* from the same as H1371; *baldness* in the forehead; by analogy a *bare spot* on the right side of cloth:— bald forehead, without.

H1373 גַּבַּי *gabbay* from the same as H1354; *collective; Gabbai,* an Israelite:— Gabbai.

H1374 גֵּבִים *gēbîm* plural of H1356; *cisterns; Gebim,* a place in Palestine:— Gebim.

H1375 גְּבִיעַ *gĕbiaᶜ* from an unused root (meaning to *be convex*); a *goblet;* by analogy the *calyx* of a flower:— house, cup, pot.

H1376 גְּבִיר *gĕbîr* from H1396; a *master:*— lord.

H1377 גְּבִירָה *gĕbîrâ* feminine of H1376; a *mistress:*— queen.

H1378 גָּבִישׁ *gābîš* from an unused root (probably meaning to *freeze*); *crystal* (from its resemblance to *ice*):— pearl.

H1379 גָּבַל *gābal* a primitive root; properly to *twist* as a rope; only (as a denominative from H1366) to *bound* (as by a line):— be border, set bounds about.

H1380 גְּבַל *gĕbal* from H1379 (in the sense of a *chain* of hills); a *mountain; Gebal,* a place in Phoenicia:— Gebal.

H1381 גְּבָל *gĕbāl* the same as H1380; *Gebal,* a region in Idumaea:— Gebal.

H1382 גִּבְלִי *giblî* patrial from H1380; a *Gebalite,* or inhabitant of Gebal:— Giblites, stone-squarer.

H1383 גַּבְלֻת *gablūt* from H1379; a twisted *chain* or *lace:*— end.

H1384 גִּבֵּן *gibbēn* from an unused root meaning to be *arched* or *contracted; hunch-backed:*— crookbackt.

H1385 גְּבִינָה *gĕbînâ* feminine from the same as H1384; *curdled* milk:— cheese.

H1386 גַּבְנֹן *gabnōn* from the same as H1384; a *hump* or *peak* of hills:— high.

H1387 גֶּבַע *gebaᶜ* from the same as H1375, a *hillock; Geba,* a place in Palestine:— Gaba, Geba, Gibeah.

H1388 גִּבְעָא *gibᶜāᵓ* by permutation for H1389; a *hill; Giba,* a place in Palestine:— Gibeah.

H1389 גִּבְעָה *gibᶜâ* feminine from the same as H1387; a *hillock:*— hill, little hill.

H1390 גִּבְעָה *gibᶜâ* the same as H1389; *Gibah;* the name of three places in Palestine:— Gibeah, the hill.

H1391 גִּבְעוֹן *gibᶜôn* from the same as H1387; *hilly; Gibon,* a place in Palestine:— Gibeon.

H1392 גִּבְעֹל *gōbĕᶜōl* prolonged from H1375; the *calyx* of a flower:— bolled.

H1393 גִּבְעֹנִי *gibᶜōnî* patrial from H1391; a *Gibonite,* or inhabitant of Gibon:— Gibeonite.

H1394 גִּבְעַת *gibᶜat* from the same as H1375; *hilliness; Gibath:*— Gibeath.

H1395 גִּבְעָתִי *gibᶜātî* patrial from H1390; a *Gibathite,* or inhabitant of Gibath:— Gibeathite.

H1396 גָּבַר *gābar* a primitive root; to *be strong;* by implication to *prevail, act insolently:*— exceed, confirm, be great, be mighty, prevail, put to more strength, strengthen, be stronger, be valiant.

H1397 גֶּבֶר *geber* from H1396; properly a *valiant* man or *warrior;* generally a *person* simply:— every one, man, mighty.

H1398 גֶּבֶר *geber* the same as H1397; *Geber,* the name of two Israelites:— Geber.

H1399 גְּבַר *gĕbar* from H1396; the same as H1397; a person:— man.

H1400 גְּבַר *gĕbar* corresponding to H1399:— certain, man.

H1401 גִּבָּר *gībār* (Aramaic) intensive of H1400; *valiant,* or *warrior:*— mighty.

H1402 גִּבָּר *gibbār* intensive of H1399; *Gibbar,* an Israelite:— Gibbar.

H1403 גַּבְרִיאֵל *gabrîᵓēl* from H1397 and H410; *man of God; Gabriel,* an archangel:— Gabriel.

H1404 גְּבֶרֶת *gĕberet* feminine of H1376; *mistress* :— lady, mistress.

H1405 גִּבְּתוֹן *gibbĕtôn* intensively from H1389; a *hilly* spot; *Gibbethon,* a place in Palestine:— Gibbethon.

H1406 גָּג *gāg* probably by reduplication from H1342; a *roof;* by analogy the *top* of an altar:— roof, roof of the house, top, top of the house, housetop.

H1407 גַּד *gad* from H1413 (in the sense of *cutting*); *coriander* seed (from its furrows):— coriander.

H1408 גַּד *gad* a variation of H1409; *Fortune,* a Babylonian deity:— that troop.

H1409 גָּד *gād* from H1464 (in the sense of *distributing*); *fortune:*— troop.

H1410 גָּד *gād* from H1464; *Gad,* a son of Jacob, including his tribe and its territory; also a prophet:— Gad.

H1411 גְּדָבָר *gĕdābār* (Aramaic) corresponding to H1489; a *treasurer:*— treasurer.

H1412 גֻּדְגֹּדָה *gudgōdâ* by reduplication from H1413 (in the sense of *cutting*) *cleft; Gudgodah,* a place in the Desert:— Gudgodah.

H1413 גָּדַד *gādad* a primitive root [compare H1464]; to *crowd;* also to *gash* (as if by *pressing* into):— assemble selves by troops, gather selves together, gather self in troops, cut selves.

H1414 גְּדַד *gĕdad* (Aramaic) corresponding to H1413; to *cut* down:— hew down.

H1415 גָּדָה *gādâ* from an unused root (meaning to *cut* off); a *border* of a river (as *cut* into by the stream):— bank.

H1416 גְּדוּד *gĕdûd* from H1413; a *crowd* (especially of soldiers):— army, band, band of men, company, troop, troop of robbers.

H1417 גְּדוּד *gĕdûd* or (feminine)

גְּדֻדָה *gĕdūdâ* from H1413; a *furrow* (as *cut*):— furrow.

H1418 גְּדוּדָה *gĕdûdâ* feminine participle passive of H1413; an *incision:*— cutting.

H1419 גָּדוֹל *gādôl* or (shortened)

גָּדֹל *gādōl* from H1431; *great* (in any sense); hence *older;* also *insolent:*— aloud, elder, eldest, exceeding, +exceedingly, far, great, great man, great matter, great thing, greater, greatness, man of great, high, long, loud, mighty, more, much, noble, proud thing, sore, very, very.

H1420 גְּדוּלָה *gĕdûlâ* or (shortened)

גְּדֻלָּה *gĕdullâ* or (less accurately)

גְּדוּלָּה *gĕdûllâ* feminine of H1419; *greatness;* (concretely) *mighty acts:*— dignity, great things, greatness, majesty.

H1421 גִּדּוּף *giddûp* or (shortened)

גִּדֻּף *giddūp* and (feminine)

גִּדּוּפָה *giddûpâ* or

גִּדֻּפָה *giddūpâ* from H1422; *vilification:*— reproach, reviling.

H1422 גְּדוּפָה *gĕdûpâ* feminine passive participle of H1422; a *revilement:*— taunt.

H1423 גְּדִי *gĕdî* from the same as H1415; a young *goat* (from *browsing*):— kid.

H1424 גָּדִי *gādî* from H1409; *fortunate; Gadi,* an Israelite:— Gadi.

H1425 גָּדִי *gādî* patronymic from H1410; a *Gadite* (collectively) or descendants of Gad:— Gadites, children of God.

H1426 גַּדִּי *gaddî* intensive for H1424; *Gaddi,* an Israelite:— Gaddi.

H1427 גַּדִּיאֵל *gaddîʾēl* from H1409 and H410; *fortune of God; Gaddiel,* an Israelite:— Gaddiel.

H1428 גִּדְיָה *gidyâ* or

גַּדְיָה *gadyâ* the same as H1415; a river *brink:*— bank.

H1429 גְּדִיָּה *gĕdîyâ* feminine of H1423; a young female *goat:*— kid.

H1430 גָּדִישׁ *gādîš* from an unused root (meaning to *heap* up); a *stack* of sheaves; by analogy a *tomb:*— shock of corn, stack of corn, tomb.

H1431 גָּדַל *gādal* a primitive root; properly to *twist* [compare H1434], i.e. to *be* (causatively *make*) *large* (in various senses, as in body, mind, estate or honor, also in pride):— advance, boast, bring up, exceed, excellent, be great, become great, do great things, give great, make great, wax great, be greater, be come to great estate, grow, grow up, increased, left up, magnify, magnifical, be much set by, nourish, nourish up, pass, promote, proudly spoken, tower.

H1432 גָּדֵל *gādēl* from H1431; *large* (literally or figuratively):— great, grew.

H1433 גֹּדֶל *gōdel* from H1431; *magnitude* (literal or figurative):— greatness, stout, stoutness.

H1434 גְּדִל *gĕdīl* from H1431 (in the sense of *twisting*); *thread,* i.e. a *tassel* or *festoon:*— fringe, wreath.

H1435 גִּדֵּל *giddēl* from H1431; *stout; Giddel,* the name of one of the Nethinim, also of one of "Solomon's servants":— Giddel.

H1436 גְּדַלְיָה *gĕdalyâ* or (prolonged)

גְּדַלְיָהוּ *gĕdalyāhû* from H1431 and H3050; *Jah has become great; Gedaljah,* the name of five Israelites:— Gedaliah.

H1437 גִּדַּלְתִּי *giddaltî* from H1431; *I have made great; Giddalti,* an Israelite:— Giddalti.

H1438 גָּדַע *gādaᶜ* a primitive root; to *fell* a tree; generally to *destroy* anything:— cut, cut asunder, cut in sunder, cut down, cut off, hew down.

H1439 גִּדְעוֹן *gidᶜôn* from H1438; *feller* (i.e. *warrior*): *Gidon,* an Israelite:— Gideon.

H1440 גִּדְעֹנִי *gidᶜōny* from H1438; a *cutting* (i.e. *desolation*); *Gidom,* a place in Palestine:— Gidom.

H1441 גִּדְעֹנִי *gidᶜōnî* from H1438; *warlike* [compare H1439]; *Gidoni,* an Israelite:— Gideoni.

H1442 גָּדַף *gādap* a primitive root; to *hack* (with words), i.e. *revile:*— blaspheme, reproach.

H1443 גָּדַר *gādar* a primitive root; to *wall* in or around:— close up, fence up, hedge, inclose, make up a wall, mason, repairer.

H1444 גֶּדֶר *geder* from H1443; a *circumvallation:*— wall.

H1445 גֶּדֶר *geder* the same as H1444; *Geder,* a place in Palestine:— Geder.

H1446 גְּדֹר *gĕdōr* or (fully)

גְּדוֹר *gĕdôr* from H1443; *inclosure; Gedor,* a place in Palestine; also the name of three Israelites:— Gedor.

H1447 גָּדֵר *gādēr* from H1443; a *circumvallation;* by implication an *inclosure:*— fence, hedge, wall.

H1448 גְּדֵרָה *gĕdērâ* feminine of H1447; *inclosure* (especially for flocks):— sheepcote, fold, hedge, wall.

H1449 גְּדֵרָה *gĕdērâ* the same as H1448; (with the article) *Gederah,* a place in Palestine:— Gederah, hedges.

H1450 גְּדֵרוֹת *gĕdērôt* plural of H1448; *walls; Gederoth,* a place in Palestine:— Gederoth.

H1451 גְּדֵרִי *gĕdērî* patrial from H1445; a *Gederite,* or inhabitant of Geder:— Gederite.

H1452 גְּדֵרָתִי *gĕdērātî* patrial from H1449; a *Gederathite,* or inhabitant of Gederah:— Gederathite.

H1453 גְּדֵרֹתַיִם *gĕdērōtayim* dual of H1448; *double wall; Gederothajim,* a place in Palestine:— Gederothaim.

H1454 גֵּה *gēh* probably a clerical error for H2088; *this:*— this.

H1455 גָּהָה *gāhâ* a primitive root; to *remove* (a bandage from a wound, i.e., *heal* it):— cure.

H1456 גֵּהָה *gēhâ* from H1455; a *cure:*— medicine.

H1457 גָּהַר *gāhar* a primitive root; to *prostrate* oneself:— cast self down, stretch self.

H1458 גַּו *gaw* another form for H1460; the *back:*— back.

H1459 גַּו *gaw* (Aramaic) corresponding to H1460; the *middle:*— midst, same, therein, wherein.

H1460 גֵּו *gēw* from H1342 [corresponding to H1354]; the *back;* by analogy the *middle:*— among, back, body.

H1461 גּוּב *gûb* a primitive root; to *dig:*— husbandman.

H1462 גּוֹב *gôb* from H1461; the *locust* (from its *grubbing* as a larve):— grasshopper, great.

H1463 גּוֹג *gôg* of uncertain derivation; *Gog,* the name of an Israelite, also of some northern nation:— Gog.

H1464 גּוּד *gûd* a primitive root [akin to H1413]; to *crowd* upon, i.e. *attack:*— invade, overcome.

H1465 גֵּוָה *gēwâ* feminine of H1460; the *back,* i.e. (by extension) the *person:*— body.

H1466 גֵּוָה *gēwâ* the same as H1465; *exaltation;* (figuratively) *arrogance:*— lifting up, pride.

H1467 גֵּוָה *gēwâ* (Aramaic) corresponding to H1466 :— pride.

H1468 גּוּז *gûz* a primitive root [compare H1494]; properly to *shear* off; but used only in the (figurative) sense of *passing* rapidly:— bring, cut off.

H1469 גּוֹזָל *gôzāl* or (shortened)

גֹּזָל *gōzāl* from H1497; a *nestling* (as being comparatively *nude* of feathers):— young, young pigeon.

H1470 גּוֹזָן *gôzān* probably from H1468; a *quarry* (as a place of *cutting* stones); *Gozan,* a province of Assyria:— Gozan.

H1471 גּוֹי *gôy* rarely (shortened)

גֹּי *gōy* apparently from the same root as H1465 (in the sense of *massing*); a foreign *nation;* hence a *Gentile;* also (figuratively) a *troop* of animals, or a *flight* of locusts:— Gentile, heathen, nation, people.

H1472 גְּוִיָּה *gĕwîyâ* prolonged for H1465; a *body,* whether alive or dead:— body, dead body, carcase, corpse.

H1473 גּוֹלָה *gôlâ* or (shortened)

גֹּלָה *gōlâ* active participle feminine of H1540; *exile;* concretely and collectively *exiles:*— carried away, captive, captivity, removing.

H1474 גּוֹלָן *gôlān* from H1478; *captive; Golan,* a place east of the Jordan:— Golan.

H1475 גּוּמָּץ *gûmmāṣ* of uncertain derivation; a *pit* :— pit.

H1476 גּוּנִי *gûnî* probably from H1598; *protected; Guni,* the name of two Israelites:— Guni.

H1477 גּוּנִי *gûnî* patronymic from H1476; a *Gunite* (collectively with article prefixed) or descendant of Guni:— Gunites.

H1478 גָּוַע *gāwaᶜ* a primitive root; to *breathe* out, i.e. (by implication) *expire:*— die, be dead, give up the ghost, perish.

H1479 גּוּף *gûp* a primitive root; properly to *hollow* or *arch,* i.e. (figuratively) *close;* to *shut:*— shut.

H1480 גּוּפָה *gûpâ* from H1479; a *corpse* (as *closed* to sense):— body.

H1481 גּוּר *gûr* a primitive root; properly to *turn* aside from the road (for a lodging or any other purpose), i.e. *sojourn* (as a guest); also to *shrink, fear* (as in a *strange* place); also to *gather* for hostility (as *afraid*):— abide, assemble, be afraid, dwell, fear, gather, gather together, inhabitant, remain, sojourn, stand in awe, stranger, be)stranger, surely.

H1482 גּוּר *gûr* or (shortened)

גֻּר *gūr* perhaps from H1481; a *cub* (as still *abiding* in the lair), especially of the lion:— whelp, young one.

H1483 גּוּר *gûr* the same as H1482; *Gur,* a place in Palestine:— Gur.

H1484 גּוֹר *gôr* or (feminine)

גֹּרָה *gōrâ* a variation of H1482:— whelp.

H1485 גּוּר־בַּעַל *gûr-ba*ᶜ*al* from H1481 and H1168; *dwelling of Baal; Gur-Baal,* a place in Arabia:— Gurbaal.

H1486 גּוֹרָל *gôrâl* or (shortened)

גֹּרָל *gōrāl* from an unused root meaning to *be rough* (as stone); properly a *pebble,* i.e. a *lot* (small stones being used for that purpose); figuratively a *portion* or *destiny* (as if determined by lot):— lot.

H1487 גּוּשׁ *gûš* or rather (by permutation)

גִּישׁ *gîš* of uncertain derivation; a *mass* of earth:— clod.

H1488 גֵּז *gēz* from H1494; a *fleece* (as *shorn*); also mown *grass:*— fleece, mowing, mown grass.

H1489 גִּזְבָּר *gizzĕbbār* of foreign derivation; *treasurer:*— treasurer.

H1490 גִּזְבָּר *gizbār* (Aramaic) corresponding to H1489:— treasurer.

H1491 גָּזָה *gāzâ* a primitive root [akin to H1468]; to *cut* off, i.e. *portion* out:— take.

H1492 גִּזָּה *gizzâ* feminine from H1494; a *fleece:*— fleece.

H1493 גִּזוֹנִי *gizônî* patrial from the unused name of a place apparently in Palestine; a *Gizonite* or inhabitant of Gizoh:— Gizonite.

H1494 גָּזַז *gāzaz* a primitive root [akin to H1468]; to *cut* off; specifically to *shear* a flock, or *shave* the hair; figuratively to *destroy* an enemy:— cut off, cut down, poll, shave, shear, shearer, sheepshearer.

H1495 גָּזֵז *gāzēz* from H1494; *shearer; Gazez,* the name of two Israelites:— Gazez.

H1496 גָּזִית *gāzît* from H1491; something *cut,* i.e. *dressed* stone:— hewed, hewn stone, wrought.

H1497 גָּזַל *gāzal* a primitive root; to *pluck* off; specifically to *flay, strip* or *rob:*— catch, consume, exercise robbery, pluck, pluck off, rob, spoil, take away, take away by force, take away by violence, tear.

H1498 גָּזֵל *gāzēl* from H1497; *robbery,* or (concretely) *plunder:*— robbery, thing taken away by violence.

H1499 גֵּזֶל *gēzel* from H1497; *plunder,* i.e. *violence* :— violence, violent perverting.

H1500 גְּזֵלָה *gĕzēlâ* feminine of H1498 and meaning the same:— that he had robbed, that which he took violently away, spoil, violence.

H1501 גָּזָם *gāzām* from an unused root meaning to *devour;* a kind of *locust:*— palmer-worm.

H1502 גַּזָּם *gazzām* from the same as H1501; *devourer; Gazzam,* one of the Nethinim:— Gazzam.

H1503 גֶּזַע *geza*ᶜ from an unused root meaning to *cut* down (trees); the *trunk* or *stump* of a tree (as felled or as planted):— stem, stock.

H1504 גָּזַר *gāzar* a primitive root; to *cut* down or off; (figuratively) to *destroy, divide, exclude* or *decide:*— cut down, cut off, decree, divide, snatch.

H1505 גְּזַר *gĕzar* (Aramaic) corresponding to H1504; to *quarry; determine:*— cut out, soothsayer.

H1506 גֶּזֶר *gezer* from H1504; something *cut* off; a *portion:*— part, piece.

H1507 גֶּזֶר *gezer* the same as H1506; *Gezer,* a place in Palestine:— Gazer, Gezer.

H1508 גִּזְרָה *gizrâ* feminine of H1506; the *figure* or person (as if *cut* out); also an *inclosure* (as *separated*):— polishing, separate place.

H1509 גְּזֵרָה *gĕzērâ* from H1504; a *desert* (as *separated*):— not inhabited.

H1510 גְּזֵרָה *gĕzērâ* (Aramaic) from H1505 (as H1504); a *decree:*— decree.

H1511 גִּזְרִי *gizrî* (in the margin), patrial from H1507; a *Gezerite* (collectively) or inhabitant of Gezerp; better (as in the text) by transposition

גִּרְזִי *girzî* patrial of H1630; a *Girzite* (collectively) or member of a native tribe in Palestine:— Gezrites.

H1512 גָּחוֹן *gāḥôn* probably from H1518; the external *abdomen, belly* (as the *source* of the foetus [compare H1521]):— belly.

H1513 גֶּחֶל *geḥel* or (feminine)

גַּחֶלֶת *gaḥelet* from an unused root meaning to *glow* or *kindle;* an *ember:*— coal, burning coal.

H1514 גַּחַם *gaḥam* from an unused root meaning to *burn; flame; Bacham,* a son of Nahor:— Gaham.

H1515 גַּחַר *gaḥar* from an unused root meaning to *hide; lurker; Gachar,* one of the Nethinim:— Gahar.

H1516 גַּיְא *gay*ᵓ or (shortened)

גַּי *gay* probably (by transmutation) from the same root as H1466 (abbreviated); a *gorge* (from its *lofty* sides; hence narrow, but not a gully or winter-torrent):— valley.

H1517 גִּיד *gîd* probably from H1464; a *thong* (as *compressing*); by analogy a *tendon:*— sinew.

H1518 גִּיחַ *gîaḥ* or (shortened)

גֹּחַ *gōaḥ* a primitive root; to *gush* forth (as water), generally to *issue:*— break forth, labor to bring forth, come forth, draw up, take out.

H1519 גִּיחַ *gîaḥ* or (shortened)

גּוּחַ *gûaḥ* (Aramaic) corresponding to H1518; to *rush* forth:— strive.

H1520 גִּיחַ *gîaḥ* from H1518; a *fountain; Giach,* a place in Palestine:— Giah.

H1521 גִּיחוֹן *gîḥôn* or (shortened)

גִּחֹן *gīḥôn* from H1518; *stream; Gichon,* a river of Paradise; also a valley (or pool) near Jerusalem:— Gihon.

H1522 גֵּיחֲזִי *gêḥăzî* or

גֵּחֲזִי *gēḥăzî* apparently from H1516 and H2372; *valley of a visionary; Gechazi,* the servant of Elisha:— Gehazi.

H1523 גִּיל *gîl* or (by permutation)

גּוּל *gûl* a primitive root; properly to *spin* round (under the influence of any violent emotion), i.e. usually *rejoice,* or (as *cringing*) *fear:*— be glad, joy, be joyful, rejoice.

H1524 גִּיל *gîl* from H1523; a *revolution* (of time, i.e. an *age*); also *joy:*— exceedingly, gladness, greatly, joy, rejoice, rejoicing, sort.

H1525 גִּילָה *gîlâ* or

גִּילַת *gîlat* feminine of H1524; *joy:*— joy, rejoicing.

H1526 גִּילֹנִי *gîlōnî* patrial from H1542; a *Gilonite* or inhabitant of Giloh:— Gilonite.

H1527 גִּינַת *gînat* of uncertain derivation; *Ginath,* an Israelite:— Ginath.

H1528 גִּיר *gîr* (Aramaic) corresponding to H1615; *lime:*— plaster.

H1529 גֵּישָׁן *gêšān* from the same as H1487; *lumpish; Geshan,* an Israelite:— Geshan.

H1530 גַּל *gal* from H1556; something *rolled,* i.e. a *heap* of stone or dung (plural *ruins*), by analogy a *spring* of water (plural *waves*):— billow, heap, spring, wave.

H1531 גֹּל *gōl* from H1556; a *cup* for oil (as *round*) :— bowl.

H1532 גַּלָּב *gallāb* from an unused root meaning to *shave;* a *barber:*— barber.

H1533 גִּלְבֹּעַ *gilbōa*ᶜ from H1530 and H1158; *fountain of ebullation; Gilboa,* a mountain of Palestine:— Gilboa.

H1534 גַּלְגַּל *galgal* by reduplication from H1556; a *wheel;* by analogy a *whirlwind;* also *dust* (as *whirled*):— heaven, rolling thing, wheel.

H1535 גַּלְגַּל *galgal* (Aramaic) corresponding to H1534; a *wheel:*— wheel.

H1536 גִּלְגָּל *gilgāl* a variation of H1534:— wheel.

H1537 גִּלְגָּל *gilgāl* the same as H1536 (with the article as a proper noun); *Gilgal,* the name of three places in Palestine:— Gilgal. See also H1019

H1538 גֻּלְגֹּלֶת *gulgōlet* by reduplication from H1556; a *skull* (as *round*); by implication a *head* (in enumeration of persons):— head, every man, poll, skull.

H1539 גֶּלֶד *geled* from an unused root probably meaning to *polish;* the (human) *skin* (as *smooth*):— skin.

H1540 גָּלָה *gālâ* a primitive root; to *denude* (especially in a disgraceful sense); by implication to *exile* (captives being usually *stripped*); figuratively to *reveal:*— advertise, appear, bewray, bring, carry captive, lead captive, go captive, go into captivity, carry into captivity, depart, disclose, discover, exile, be gone, open, plainly, publish, remove, reveal, shamelessly, shew, surely, tell, uncover.

H1541 גְּלָה *gĕlâ* or

גְּלָא *gĕlā*ᵓ (Aramaic) corresponding to H1540 :— bring over, carry away, reveal.

H1542 גִּלֹה *gilōh* or (fully)

גִּילֹה *gîlōh* from H1540; *open; Giloh,* a place in Palestine:— Giloh.

H1543 גֻּלָּה *gullâ* feminine from H1556; a *fountain, bowl* or *globe* (all as *round*):— bowl, pommel, spring.

H1544 גִּלּוּל *gillûl* or (shortened)

גִּלֻּל *gillūl* from H1556; properly a *log* (as *round*); by implication an *idol:*— idol.

H1545 גְּלוֹם *gĕlôm* from H1563; *clothing* (as *wrapped*):— clothes.

H1546 גָּלוּת *gālût* feminine from H1540; *captivity;* concretely *exiles* (collectively):— captives, they that are carried away captives, captivity.

H1547 גָּלוּת *gālût* (Aramaic) corresponding to H1546:— captivity.

H1548 גָּלַח *gālaḥ* a primitive root; properly to *be bald,* i.e. (causatively) to *shave;* figuratively to *lay waste:*— poll, shave, shave off.

H1549 גִּלָּיוֹן *gillāyôn* or

גִּלְיוֹן *gilyôn* from H1540; a *tablet* for writing (as *bare*); by analogy a *mirror* (as a *plate*):— glass, roll.

H1550 גָּלִיל *gālîl* from H1556; a *valve* of a folding door (as *turning*); also a *ring* (as *round*):— folding, ring.

H1551 גָּלִיל *gālîl* or (prolonged)

גָּלִילָה *gālîlâ* the same as H1550; a *circle* (with the article); *Galil* (as a special *circuit*) in the North of Palestine:— Galilee.

H1552 גְּלִילָה *gĕlîlâ* feminine of H1550; a *circuit* or *region:*— border, coast, country.

H1553 גְּלִילוֹת *gĕlîlôt* plural of H1552; *circles; Geliloth,* a place in Palestine:— Geliloth.

H1554 גַּלִּים *gallîm* plur of H1530; *springs; Gallim,* a place in Palestine:— Gallim.

H1555 גָּלְיַת *golyat* perhaps from H1540; *exile; Goljath,* a Philistine:— Goliath.

H1556 גָּלַל *gālal* a primitive root; to *roll* (literally or figuratively):— commit, remove, roll, roll away, roll down, roll together, run down, seek occasion, trust, wallow.

H1557 גָּלָל *gālāl* from H1556; *dung* (as in *balls*):— dung.

H1558 גָּלָל *gālāl* from H1556; a *circumstance* (as *rolled* around); only used adverbially, on *account* of:— because, of, for, for sake.

H1559 גָּלָל *gālāl* from H1556, in the sense of H1560; *great; Galal,* the name of two Israelites:— Galal.

H1560 גְּלָל *gĕlāl* (Aramaic) from a root corresponding to H1556; *weight* or *size* (as if *rolled*):— great.

H1561 גֵּלֶל *gēlel* a variation of H1557; *dung* (plural *balls* of dung):— dung.

H1562 גִּלֲלַי *gilălay* from H1561; *dungy; Gilalai,* an Israelite:— Gilalai.

H1563 גָּלַם *gālam* a primitive root; to *fold:*— wrap together.

H1564 גֹּלֶם *gōlem* from H1563; a *wrapped* (and unformed *mass,* i.e. as the *embryo*):— substance yet being unperfect.

H1565 גַּלְמוּד *galmûd* probably by prolongation from H1563; *sterile* (as *wrapped* up too hard); figuratively *desolate:*— desolate, solitary.

H1566 גָּלַע *gālaᶜ* a primitive root; to *be obstinate* :— meddle, meddle with, intermeddle with.

H1567 גַּלְעֵד *galᶜēd* from H1530 and H5707; *heap of testimony; Galed,* a memorial cairn east of the Jordan:— Galeed.

H1568 גִּלְעָד *gilᶜād* probably from H1567; *Gilad,* a region east of the Jordan; also the name of three Israelites:— Gilead, Gileadite.

H1569 גִּלְעָדִי *gilᶜādî* patronymic from H1568; a *Giladite* or descendant of Gilad:— Gileadite.

H1570 גָּלַשׁ *gālaš* a primitive root; probably to *caper* (as a goat):— appear.

H1571 גַּם *gam* by contraction from an unused root meaning to *gather;* properly *assemblage;* used only adverbially *also, even, yea, though:* often repeated as correlative *both . . . and:*— again, alike, also, as, so much as, as soon, both . . . and, so . . . and, but, either . . . or, even, for all, likewise, in like manner, moreover, nay . . . neither, one, then, therefore, though, what, with, yea.

H1572 גָּמָא *gāmāᵓ* a primitive root (literally or figuratively) to *absorb:*— swallow, drink.

H1573 גֹּמֶא *gōmeᵓ* from H1572; properly an *absorbent,* i.e. the *bulrush* (from its *porosity*); specifically the *papyrus:*— rush, bulrush.

H1574 גֹּמֶד *gōmed* from an unused root apparently meaning to *grasp;* properly a *span:*— cubit.

H1575 גַּמָּד *gammād* from the same as H1574; a *warrior* (as *grasping* weapons):— Gammadims.

H1576 גְּמוּל *gĕmûl* from H1580; *treatment,* i.e. an *act* (of good or ill); by implication *service* or *requital:*— as hast served, benefit, desert, deserving, that which he hath given, recompense, reward.

H1577 גָּמוּל *gāmûl* passive participle of H1580; *rewarded; Gamul,* an Israelite:— Gamul. See also H1014

H1578 גְּמוּלָה *gĕmûlâ* feminine of H1576; meaning the same:— deed, recompense, such a reward.

H1579 גִּמְזוֹ *gimzô* of uncertain derivation; Gimzo, a place in Palestine:— Gimzo.

H1580 גָּמַל *gāmal* a primitive root; to *treat* a person (well or ill), i.e. *benefit* or *require;* by implication (of *toil*) to *ripen,* i.e. (specifically) to *wean:*— bestow on, deal bountifully, do, do good, recompense, requite, reward, ripen serve, mean, yield.

H1581 גָּמָל *gāmāl* apparently from H1580 (in the sense of *labor* or *burden-bearing*); a *camel:*— camel.

H1582 גְּמַלִּי *gĕmallî* probably from H1581; *camel-driver; Gemalli,* an Israelite:— Gemalli.

H1583 גַּמְלִיאֵל *gamlîᵓēl* from H1580 and H410; *reward of God; Gamliel,* an Israelite:— Gamaliel.

H1584 גָּמַר *gāmar* a primitive root; to *end* (in the sense of *completion* or *failure*):— cease, come to an end, fail, perfect, perform.

H1585 גְּמַר *gĕmar* (Aramaic) corresponding to H1584:— perfect.

H1586 גֹּמֶר *gōmer* from H1584; *completion; Gomer,* the name of a son of Japheth and of his descendants; also of a Hebrewess:— Gomer.

H1587 גְּמַרְיָה *gĕmaryâ* or

גְּמַרְיָהוּ *gĕmaryāhû* from H1584 and H3050; *Jah has perfected; Gemarjah,* the name of two Israelites:— Gemariah.

H1588 גַּן *gan* from H1598; a *garden* (as *fenced*):— garden.

H1589 גָּנַב *gānab* a primitive root; to *thieve* (literally or figuratively); by implication to *deceive:*— carry away, indeed, secretly bring, steal, steal away, get by stealth.

H1590 גַּנָּב *gannāb* from H1589; a *stealer:*— thief.

H1591 גְּנֵבָה *gĕnēbâ* from H1589; *stealing,* i.e. (concretely) something *stolen:*— theft.

H1592 גְּנֻבַת *gĕnūbat* from H1589; *theft; Genubath,* an Edomitish prince:— Genubath.

H1593 גַּנָּה *gannâ* feminine of H1588; a *garden:*— garden.

H1594 גִּנָּה *ginnâ* another form for H1593:— garden.

H1595 גֶּנֶז *genez* from an unused root meaning to *store; treasure;* by implication a *coffer:*— chest, treasury.

H1596 גְּנַז *gĕnaz* (Aramaic) corresponding to H1595; *treasure:*— treasure.

H1597 גִּנְזַךְ *ganzak* prolonged from H1595; a *treasury:*— treasury.

H1598 גָּנַן *gānan* a primitive root; to *hedge* about, i.e. (generally) *protect:*— defend.

H1599 גִּנְּתוֹן *ginnĕtôn* or

גִּנְּתוֹ *ginnĕtô* from H1598; *gardener; Ginnethon* or *Ginnetho,* an Israelite:— Ginnetho, Ginnethon.

H1600 גָּעָה *gāᶜâ* a primitive root; to *bellow* (as cattle):— low.

H1601 גֹּעָה *gōᶜâ* feminine active participle of H1600; *lowing; Goah,* a place near Jerus:— Goath.

H1602 גָּעַל *gāᶜal* a primitive root; to *detest;* by implication to *reject:*— abhor, fail, lothe, vilely cast away.

H1603 גַּעַל *gaᶜal* from H1602; *loathing; Gaal,* an Israelite:— Gaal.

H1604 גֹּעַל *gōᶜal* from H1602; *abhorrence:*— loathing.

H1605 גָּעַר *gāᶜar* a primitive root; to *chide:*— corrupt, rebuke, reprove.

H1606 גְּעָרָה *gĕᶜārâ* from H1605; a *chiding:*— rebuke, rebuking, reproof.

H1607 גָּעַשׁ *gāᶜaš* a primitive root; to *agitate* violently:— move, shake, toss, trouble.

H1608 גַּעַשׁ *gaᶜaš* from H1607; a *quaking; Gaash,* a hill in Palestine:— Gaash.

H1609 גַּעְתָּם *gaᶜtām* of uncertain derivation; *Gatam,* an Edomite:— Gatam.

H1610 גַּף *gap* from an unused root meaning to *arch;* the *back,* by extension the *body* or self:— highest places, himself.

H1611 גַּף *gap* (Aramaic) corresponding to H1610; a *wing:*— wing.

H1612 גֶּפֶן *gepen* from an unused root meaning to *bend;* a *vine* (as *twining*), especially the grape:— vine, tree.

H1613 גֹּפֶר *gōper* from an unused root, probably meaning to *house in;* a kind of tree or wood (as used for *building*), apparently the *cypress:*— gopher.

H1614 גָּפְרִית *goprît* probably feminine of H1613; properly cypress-*resin;* by analogy *sulphur* (as equally inflammable):— brimstone.

H1615 גִּר *gîr* perhaps from H3564; *lime* (from being *burned* in a kiln):— chalkstone.

H1616 גֵּר *gēr* or (fully)

גֵּיר *gêr* from H1481; properly a *guest;* by implication a *foreigner:*— alien, sojourner, stranger.

H1617 גֵּרָא *gērāᵓ* perhaps from H1626; a *grain; Gera,* the name of six Israelites:— Gera.

H1618 גָּרָב *gārāb* from an unused root meaning to *scratch; scurf* (from *itching*):— scab, scurvy.

H1619 גָּרֵב *gārēb* from the same as H1618; *scabby; Gareb,* the name of an Israelite, also of a hill near Jerusalem:— Gareb.

H1620 גַּרְגַּר *gargar* by reduplication from H1641; a *berry* (as if a pellet of *rumination*):— berry.

H1621 גַּרְגְּרוֹת *gargĕrôt* feminine plural from H1641; the *throat* (as used in *rumination*):— neck.

H1622 גִּרְגָּשִׁי *girgāšî* patrial from an unused name [of uncertain derivation]; a *Girgashite,* one of the native tribes of Canaan:— Girgashite, Girgasite.

H1623 גָּרַד *gārad* a primitive root; to *abrade:*— scrape.

H1624 גָּרָה *gārâ* a primitive root; properly to *grate,* i.e. (figuratively) to *anger:*— contend, meddle, stir up, strive.

H1625 גֵּרָה *gērâ* from H1641; the *cud* (as *scraping* the throat):— cud.

H1626 גֵּרָה *gērâ* from H1641 (as in H1625); properly (like H1620) a *kernel* (round as if *scraped*), i.e. a *gerah* or small weight (and coin):— gerah.

H1627 גָּרוֹן *gārôn* or (shortened)

גָּרֹן *gārōn* from H1641; the *throat* [compare H1621] (as *roughened* by swallowing):— aloud, mouth, neck, throat.

H1628 גֵּרוּת *gērût* from H1481; a (temporary) *residence:*— habitation.

H1629 גָּרַז *gāraz* a primitive root; to *cut* off:— cut off.

H1630 גְּרִזִים *gĕrîzîm* plural of an unused noun from H1629 [compare H1511], *cut up* (i.e. *rocky*); *Gerizim,* a mountain of Palestine:— Gerizim.

H1631 גַּרְזֶן *garzen* from H1629; an *axe:*— ax.

H1632 גָּרֹל *gārōl* from the same as H1486; *harsh* :— man of great *[as in the margin which reads H1419].*

H1633 גָּרַם *gāram* a primitive root; to *be spare* or *skeleton-like;* used only as a denominative from H1634; (causatively) to *bone,* i.e. *denude* (by extension *crunch*) the bones:— gnaw the bones, break.

H1634 גֶּרֶם *gerem* from H1633; a *bone* (as the *skeleton* of the body); hence *self,* i.e. (figuratively) *very:*— bone, strong, top.

H1635 גְּרַם *gerem* (Aramaic) corresponding to H1634; a *bone:*— bone.

H1636 גַּרְמִי *garmî* from H1634; *bony,* i.e. *strong:*— Garmite.

H1637 גֹּרֶן *gōren* from an unused root meaning to *smooth;* a threshing-*floor* (as made *even*); by analogy any open *area:*— floor, barnfloor, cornfloor, threshingfloor, threshingplace, void place.

H1638 גָּרַס *gāras* a primitive root; to *crush;* also (intransitively and figuratively) to *dissolve:*— break.

H1639 גָּרַע *gāraᶜ* a primitive root; to *scrape* off; by implication to *shave, remove, lessen* or *withhold:*— abate, clip, minish, diminish, do away, take away, keep back, restrain, make small, withdraw.

H1640 גָּרַף *gārap* a primitive root; to *bear* off violently:— sweep away.

H1641 גָּרַר *gārar* a primitive root; to *drag* off roughly; by implication to *bring up* the cud (i.e. *ruminate*); by analogy to *saw:*— catch, chew, continuing, destroy, saw.

H1642 גְּרָר *gĕrār* probably from H1641; a *rolling* country; *Gerar,* a Philistine city:— Gerar.

H1643 גֶּרֶשׂ *gereś* from an unused root meaning to *husk;* a *kernel* (collectively), i.e. *grain:*— beaten corn.

H1644 גָּרַשׁ *gāraš* a primitive root; to *drive* out from a possession; especially to *expatriate* or *divorce:*— cast up, cast out, divorced, divorced woman, drive away, drive forth, drive out, expel, surely put away, trouble, thrust out.

H1645 גֶּרֶשׁ *gereš* from H1644; *produce* (as if *expelled*):— put forth.

H1646 גְּרֻשָׁה *gĕrūšâ* feminine passive participle of H1644; (abstractly) *dispossession:*— exaction.

H1647 גֵּרְשֹׁם *gērĕšōm* for H1648; *Gereshom,* the name of four Israelites:— Gershom.

H1648 גֵּרְשׁוֹן *gērĕšôn* or

גֵּרְשׁוֹם *gērĕšōm* from H1644; a *refugee; Gereshon* or *Gereshom,* an Israelite:— Gershon, Gershom.

H1649 גֵּרְשֻׁנִּי *gērĕšunnî* patronymic from H1648; a *Gereshonite* or descendant of Gereshon:— Gershonite, sons of Gershon.

H1650 גְּשׁוּר *gĕšûr* from an unused root (meaning to *join*); *bridge; Geshur,* a district of Syria:— Geshur, Geshurite.

H1651 גְּשׁוּרִי *gĕšûrî* patrial from H1650; a *Geshurite* (also collectively) or inhabitant of Geshur:— Geshuri, Geshurites.

H1652 גָּשַׁם *gāšam* a primitive root; to *shower* violently:— rain, cause to rain.

H1653 גֶּשֶׁם *gešem* from H1652; a *shower:*— rain, shower.

H1654 גֶּשֶׁם *gešem* or (prolonged)

גַּשְׁמוּ *gašmû* the same as H1653; *Geshem* or *Gashmu,* an Arabian:— Geshem, Gashmu.

H1655 גֶּשֶׁם *gešem* (Aramaic) apparently the same as H1653; used in a peculiar sense, the *body* (probably for the [figurative] idea of a *hard* rain):— body.

H1656 גֹּשֶׁם *gōšem* from H1652; equivalent to H1653:— rained upon.

H1657 גֹּשֶׁן *gōšen* probably of Egyptian origin; *Goshen,* the residence of the Israelites in Egypt; also a place in Palestine:— Goshen.

H1658 גִּשְׁפָּא *gišpāᵓ* of uncertain derivation; *Gishpa,* an Israelite:— Gispa.

H1659 גָּשַׁשׁ *gāšaš* a primitive root; apparently to *feel* about:— grope.

H1660 גַּת *gat* probably from H5059 (in the sense of *treading* out grapes); a wine-*press* (or vat for holding the grapes in pressing them):— press, winepress, winefat.

H1661 גַּת *gat* the same as H1660; *Gath,* a Philistine city:— Gath.

H1662 גַּת־הַחֵפֶר *gat-haḥēper* or (abridged)

גִּתָּה־חֵפֶר *gittoh-ḥēper* from H1660 and H2658 with the article inserted; *wine-press of (the) well; Gath-Chepher,* a place in Palestine:— Gath-kephr, Gittah-kephr.

H1663 גִּתִּי *gittî* patrial from H1661; a *Gittite* or inhabitant of Gath:— Gittite.

H1664 גִּתַּיִם *gittayim* dual of H1660; *double winepress; Gittajim,* a place in Palestine:— Gittaim.

H1665 גִּתִּית *gittît* feminine of H1663; a *Gittite* harp :— Gittith.

H1666 גֶּתֶר *geter* of uncertain derivation; *Gether,* a son of Aram, and the region settled by him:— Gether.

H1667 גַּת־רִמּוֹן *gat-rimmôn* from H1660 and H7416; *wine-press of* (the) *pomegranate; Gath-Rimmon,* a place in Palestine:— Gath-rimmon.

ד

H1668 דָּא *dāᵓ* (Aramaic) corresponding to H2088; *this:*— one . . . another, this.

H1669 דָּאַב *dāᵓab* a primitive root; to *pine:*— mourn, sorrow, sorrowful.

H1670 דְּאָבָה *dĕᵓābâ* from H1669; properly *pining;* by analogy *fear:*— sorrow.

H1671 דְּאָבוֹן *dĕᵓābôn* from H1669; *pining:*— sorrow.

H1672 דָּאַג *dāᵓag* a primitive root; *be anxious:*— be afraid, be careful, be sorry, sorrow, take thought.

H1673 דֹּאֵג *dōᵓēg* or (fully)

דּוֹאֵג *dôᵓēg* active participle of H1672; *anxious; Doëg,* an Edomite:— Doeg.

H1674 דְּאָגָה *dĕᵓāgâ* from H1672; *anxiety:*— care, carefulness, fear, heaviness, sorrow.

H1675 דָּאָה *dāᵓâ* a primitive root; to *dart,* i.e. *fly* rapidly:— fly.

H1676 דָּאָה *dāᵓâ* from H1675; the *kite* (from its rapid *flight*):— vulture. See H7201

H1677 דֹּב *dōb* or (fully)

דּוֹב *dôb* from H1680; the *bear* (as slow):— bear.

H1678 דֹּב *dōb* (Aramaic) corresponding to H1677 :— bear.

H1679 דֹּבֶא *dōbeᵓ* from an unused root (compare H1680) (probably meaning to *be sluggish,* i.e. *restful*); *quiet:*— strength.

H1680 דָּבַב *dābab* a primitive root (compare H1679); to *move* slowly, i.e. *glide:*— cause to speak.

H1681 דִּבָּה *dibbâ* from H1680 (in the sense of *furtive* motion); *slander:*— defaming, evil report, infamy, slander.

H1682 דְּבוֹרָה *dĕbôrâ* or (shortened)

דְּבֹרָה *dĕbōrâ* from H1696 (in the sense of *orderly* motion); the *bee* (from its *systematic* instincts):— bee.

H1683 דְּבוֹרָה *dĕbôrâ* or (shortened)

דְּבֹרָה *dĕbōrâ* the same as H1682; *Deborah,* the name of two Hebrewesses:— Deborah.

H1684 דְּבַח *dĕbaḥ* (Aramaic) corresponding to H2076; to *sacrifice* (an animal):— offer sacrifice.

H1685 דְּבַח *dĕbaḥ* (Aramaic) from H1684; a *sacrifice:*— sacrifice.

H1686 דִּבְיוֹן *dibyôn* in the margin for the textual reading

חֶרְיוֹן *ḥeryôn* both (in the plural only and) of uncertain derivation; probably some cheap vegetable, perhaps a bulbous root:— dove's dung.

H1687 דְּבִיר *dĕbîr* or (shortened)

דְּבִר *dĕbīr* from H1696 (apparently in the sense of *oracle*); the *shrine* or innermost part of the sanctuary:— oracle.

H1688 דְּבִיר *dĕbîr* or (shortened)

דְּבִר *dĕbīr* (Josh 13:26 [but see H3810]), the same as H1687; *Debir,* the name of an Amoritish king and of two places in Palestine:— Debir.

H1689 דִּבְלָה *diblâ* probably an orthographical error for H7247; *Diblah,* a place in Syria:— Diblath.

H1690 דְּבֵלָה *dĕbēlâ* from an unused root (akin to H2082) probably meaning to *press* together; a *cake* of pressed figs:— cake of figs, lump of figs.

H1691 דִּבְלַיִם *diblayim* dual from the masculine of H1690; *two cakes; Diblajim,* a symbolic name:— Diblaim.

H1692 דָּבַק *dābaq* a primitive root; properly to *impinge,* i.e. *cling* or *adhere;* figuratively to *catch* by pursuit:— abide fast, cleave, cleave fast together, follow close, follow hard, follow hard after, be joined, be joined together, keep, keep fast, overtake, pursue hard, stick, take.

H1693 דְּבַק *dĕbaq* (Aramaic) corresponding to H1692; to *stick* to:— cleave.

H1694 דֶּבֶק *debeq* from H1692; a *joint;* by implication *solder:*— joint, solder.

H1695 דָּבֵק *dābēq* from H1692; *adhering:*— cleave, joining, stick closer.

H1696 דָּבַר *dābar* a primitive root; perhaps properly to *arrange;* but used figuratively (of words) to *speak;* rarely (in a destructive sense) to *subdue:*— answer, appoint, bid, command, commune, declare, destroy, give, name, promise, pronounce, rehearse, say, speak, be spokesman, subdue, talk, teach, tell, think, use entreaties, utter, well, work.

H1697 דָּבָר *dābār* from H1696; a *word;* by implication a *matter* (as *spoken* of) or *thing;* adverbially a *cause:*— act, advice, affair, answer, any such, any thing, because of, book, business, care, case, cause, certain rate, chronicles, commandment, commune, communication, concern, concerning, confer, counsel, dearth, decree, deed, disease, due, duty, effect, eloquent, errand, evilfavouredness, glory, harm, hurt, iniquity, judgment, language, lying, manner, matter, message, [no] thing, oracle, ought, parts, pertaining, please, portion, power, promise, provision, purpose, question, rate, reason, report, request, said, as hast said, sake, saying, sentence, sign, so, some uncleanness, somewhat to say, song, speech, spoken, talk, task, that, there done, thing, thing concerning, thought, thus, tidings, what, whatsoever, wherewith, which, word, work.

H1698 דֶּבֶר *deber* from H1696 (in the sense of *destroying*); a *pestilence:*— murrain, pestilence, plague.

H1699 דֹּבֶר *dōber* from H1696 (in its original sense); a *pasture* (from its *arrangement* of the flock):— fold, manner.

H1699' דִּבֵּר *dibbēr* for H1697:— word.

H1700 דִּבְרָה *dibrâ* feminine of H1697; a *reason, suit* or *style:*— cause, end, estate, order, regard.

H1701 דִּבְרָה *dibrâ* (Aramaic) corresponding to H1700:— intent, sake.

H1702 דֹּבְרָה *dōbĕrâ* feminine active participle of H1696 in the sense of *driving* [compare H1699]; a *raft:*— float.

H1703 דַּבָּרָה *dabbārâ* intensive from H1696; a *word* :— word.

H1704 דִּבְרִי *dibrî* from H1697; *wordy; Dibri,* an Israelite:— Dibri.

H1705 דָּבְרַת *dābĕrat* from H1697 (perhaps in the sense of H1699); *Daberath,* a place in Palestine:— Dabareh, Daberath.

H1706 דְּבַשׁ *dĕbaš* from an unused root meaning to *be gummy; honey* (from its *stickiness*); by analogy *syrup:*— honey, honeycomb.

H1707 דַּבֶּשֶׁת *dobbĕšĕt* intensive from the same as H1706; a sticky *mass,* i.e. the *hump* of a camel:— bunch of a camel.

H1708 דַּבֶּשֶׁת *dabbešet* the same as H1707; *Dabbesheth,* a place in Palestine:— Dabbesheth.

H1709 דָּג *dāg* or (fully)

דָּאג *dā'g* Neh 13:16 from H1711; a *fish* (as *prolific*); or perhaps rather from H1672 (as *timid*); but still better from H1672 (in the sense of *squirming,* i.e. moving by the vibratory action of the tail); a *fish* (often used collectively):— fish.

H1710 דָּגָה *dāgâ* feminine of H1709, and meaning the same:— fish.

H1711 דָּגָה *dāgâ* a primitive root; to *move rapidly;* used only as a denominative from H1709; to *spawn,* i.e. *become numerous:*— grow.

H1712 דָּגוֹן *dāgôn* from H1709; the *fish-god; Dagon,* a Philistine deity:— Dagon.

H1713 דָּגַל *dāgal* a primitive root; to *flaunt,* i.e. *raise a flag;* figuratively to *be conspicuous:*— set up banners, with banners, chiefest.

H1714 דֶּגֶל *degel* from H1713; a *flag:*— banner, standard.

H1715 דָּגָן *dāgān* from H1711; properly *increase,* i.e. *grain:*— corn, cornfloor, wheat.

H1716 דָּגַר *dāgar* a primitive root; to *brood* over eggs or young:— gather, sit.

H1717 דַּד *dad* apparently from the same as H1730; the *breast* (as the seat of *love,* or from its shape):— breast, teat.

H1718 דָּדָה *dādâ* a doubtful root; to *walk gently:*— go softly, go with.

H1719 דְּדָן *dĕdān* or (prolonged)

דְּדָנֶה *dĕdāneh* (Ezek 25:13), of uncertain derivation; *Dedan,* the name of two Cushites and of their territory:— Dedan.

H1720 דְּדָנִים *dĕdānîm* plural of H1719 (as patrial); *Dedanites,* the descendants or inhabitants of Dedan:— Dedanim.

H1721 דֹּדָנִים *dōdānîm* or by orthographical error

רֹדָנִים *rōdānîm* (1 Chron 1:7), a plural of uncertain derivation; *Dodanites,* or descendants of a son of Javan:— Dodanim.

H1722 דְּהַב *dĕhab* (Aramaic) corresponding to H2091; *gold:*— gold, golden.

H1723 דַּהֲוָא *dahăwā'* (Aramaic) of uncertain derivation; *Dahava,* a people colonized in Samaria:— Dehavites.

H1724 דָּהַם *dāham* a primitive root (compare H1740); to *be dumb,* i.e. (figuratively) *dumbfounded:*— be astonished.

H1725 דָּהַר *dāhar* a primitive root; to *curvet* or move irregularly:— pause.

H1726 דַּהֲהַר *dahăhar* by reduplication from H1725; a *gallop:*— pransing.

H1727 דּוּב *dûb* a primitive root; to *mope,* i.e. (figuratively) *pine:*— sorrow.

H1728 דַּוָּג *dawwāg* an orthographical variation of H1709 as a denominative [H1771]; a *fisherman:*— fisher.

H1729 דּוּגָה *dûggâ* feminine from the same as H1728; properly *fishery,* i.e. a *hook* for fishing:— fishhook.

H1730 דּוֹד *dôd* or (shortened)

דֹּד *dōd* from an unused root meaning properly to *boil,* i.e. (figuratively) to *love;* by implication a *love-token, lover, friend;* specifically an *uncle:*— beloved, wellbeloved, father's brother, love, uncle.

H1731 דּוּד *dûd* from the same as H1730; a *pot* (for *boiling*); also (by resemblance of shape) a *basket:*— basket, caldron, kettle, pot, seething pot.

H1732 דָּוִד *dāwīd* rarely (fully)

דָּוִיד *dāwîd* from the same as H1730; *loving; David,* the youngest son of Jesse:— David.

H1733 דּוֹדָה *dôdâ* feminine of H1730; an *aunt:*— aunt, father's sister, uncle's wife.

H1734 דּוֹדוֹ *dôdô* from H1730; *loving; Dodo,* the name of three Israelites:— Dodo.

H1735 דּוֹדָוָהוּ *dôdāwāhû* from H1730 and H3050; *love of Jah; Dodavah,* an Israelite:— Dodavah.

H1736 דּוּדַי *dûday* from H1731; a *boiler* or *basket;* also the *mandrake* (as *aphrodisiac*):— basket, mandrake.

H1737 דּוֹדַי *dôday* formed like H1736; *amatory; Dodai,* an Israelite:— Dodai.

H1738 דָּוָה *dāwâ* a primitive root; to *be sick* (as if in menstruation):— infirmity.

H1739 דָּוֶה *dāweh* from H1738; *sick* (especially in menstruation):— faint, menstruous cloth, she that is sick, having sickness.

H1740 דּוּחַ *dûaḥ* a primitive root; to *thrust* away; figuratively to *cleanse:*— cast out, purge, wash.

H1741 דְּוַי *dĕway* from H1739; *sickness;* figuratively *loathing:*— languishing, sorrowful.

H1742 דַּוָּי *dawwāy* from H1739; *sick;* figuratively *troubled:*— faint.

H1743 דּוּךְ *dûk* a primitive root; to *bruise* in a mortar:— beat.

H1744 דּוּכִיפַת *dûkîpat* of uncertain derivation; the *hoopoe* or else the *grouse:*— lapwing.

H1745 דּוּמָה *dûmâ* from an unused root meaning to *be dumb* (compare H1820); *silence;* figuratively *death:*— silence.

H1746 דּוּמָה *dûmâ* the same as H1745; *Dumah,* a tribe and region of Arabia:— Dumah.

H1747 דּוּמִיָּה *dûmîyâ* from H1820; *stillness;* adverbially *silently;* abstractly *quiet, trust:*— silence, silent, waiteth.

H1748 דּוּמָם *dûmām* from H1826; *still;* adverbially *silently:*— dumb, silent, quietly wait.

H1749 דּוֹנַג *dônag* of uncertain derivation; *wax:*— wax.

H1750 דּוּץ *dûṣ* a primitive root; to *leap:*— be turned.

H1751 דּוּק *dûq* (Aramaic) corresponding to H1854; to *crumble:*— be broken to pieces.

H1752 דּוּר *dûr* a primitive root; properly to *gyrate* (or move in a circle), i.e. to *remain:*— dwell.

H1753 דּוּר *dûr* (Aramaic) corresponding to H1752; to *reside:*— dwell.

H1754 דּוּר *dûr* from H1752; a *circle, ball* or *pile:*— ball, turn, round about.

H1755 דּוֹר *dôr* or (shortened)

דֹּר *dōr* from H1752; properly a *revolution* of time, i.e. an *age* or generation; also a *dwelling:*— age, evermore, generation, ever, never, posterity.

H1756 דּוֹר *dôr* or (by permutation)

דֹּאר *dōʾr* (Josh 17:11; 1 Kings 4:11), from H1755; *dwelling; Dor,* a place in Palestine:— Dor.

H1757 דּוּרָא *dûrāʾ* (Aramaic) probably from H1753; *circle* or *dwelling; Dura,* a place in Babylonia:— Dura.

H1758 דּוּשׁ *dûš* or

דּוֹשׁ *dôš* or

דִּישׁ *dîš* a primitive root; to *trample* or *thresh* :— break, tear, thresh, tread out, tread down, at grass [Jer 50:11, *by mistake for H1877].*

H1759 דּוּשׁ *dûš* (Aramaic) corresponding to H1758; to *trample:*— tread down.

H1760 דָּחָה *dāḥâ* or

דָּחַח *dāḥaḥ* (Jer 23:12), a primitive root; to *push* down:— chase, drive away, drive on, overthrow, outcast, sore, thrust, totter.

H1761 דַּחֲוָה *daḥăwâ* (Aramaic) from the equivalent of H1760; probably a musical *instrument* (as being *struck*):— instrument of music.

H1762 דְּחִי *dĕḥî* from H1760; a *push,* i.e. (by implication) a *fall:*— falling.

H1763 דְּחַל *dĕḥal* (Aramaic) corresponding to H2199; to *slink,* i.e. (by implication) to *fear,* or (causatively) *be formidable:*— make afraid, dreadful, fear, terrible.

H1764 דֹּחַן *dōḥan* of uncertain derivation; *millet* :— millet.

H1765 דָּחַף *dāḥap* a primitive root; to *urge,* i.e. *hasten:*— haste, be hastened, pressed on.

H1766 דָּחַק *dāḥaq* a primitive root; to *press,* i.e. *oppress:*— thrust, vex.

H1767 דַּי *day* of uncertain derivation; *enough* (as noun or adverb), used chiefly with prepositions in phrases:— able, according to, after, after ability, among, as, as oft as, enough, more than enough, from, in, since, sufficient, much as is sufficient, sufficiently, too much, very, when.

H1768 דִּי *dî* (Aramaic) apparently for H1668; *that,* used as relative, conjunction, and especially (with preposition) in adverbial phrases; also as a preposition *of:*— as, but, for, forasmuch, now, of, seeing, than, that, therefore, until, what, whatsoever, when, which, whom, whose.

H1769 דִּיבוֹן *dîbôn* or (shortened)

דִּיבֹן *dîbōn* from H1727; *pining; Dibon,* the name of three places in Palestine:— Dibon, *[Also, with H1410 added,* Dibon-gad.].

H1770 דִּיג *dîg* denominative from H1709; to *fish* :— fish.

H1771 דַּיָּג *dayyāg* from H1770; a *fisherman:*— fisher.

H1772 דַּיָּה *dayyâ* intensive from H1675; a *falcon* (from its *rapid* flight):— vulture.

H1773 דְּיוֹ *dĕyô* of uncertain derivation; *ink:*— ink.

H1774 דִּי זָהָב *dî zāhāb* as if from H1768 and H2091; *of gold; Dizahab,* a place in the Desert:— Dizahab.

H1775 דִּימוֹן *dîmôn* perhaps for H1769; *Dimon,* a place in Palestine:— Dimon.

H1776 דִּימוֹנָה *dîmônâ* feminine of H1775; *Dimonah,* a place in Palestine:— Dimonah.

H1777 דִּין *dîn* or (Gen. 6:3)

דּוּן *dûn* a primitive root [compare H113]; to *rule;* by implication to *judge* (as umpire); also to *strive* (as at law):— contend, execute judgment, judge, minister judgment, plead, plead the cause, at strife, strive.

H1778 דִּין *dîn* (Aramaic) corresponding to H1777; to *judge:*— judge.

H1779 דִּין *dîn* or (Job 19:29)

דּוּן *dûn* from H1777; *judgment* (the suit, justice, sentence or tribunal); by implication also *strife:*— cause, judgment, plea, strife.

H1780 דִּין *dîn* (Aramaic) corresponding to H1779 :— judgment.

H1781 דַּיָּן *dayyān* from H1777; a *judge* or *advocate:*— judge.

H1782 דַּיָּן *dayyān* (Aramaic) corresponding to H1781 :— judge.

H1783 דִּינָה *dînâ* feminine of H1779; *justice; Dinah,* the daughter of Jacob:— Dinah.

H1784 דִּינַי *dînay* (Aramaic) patrial from an uncertain primitive; a *Dinaite* or inhabitant of some unknown Assyrian province:— Dinaite.

H1785 דָּיֵק *dāyēq* from a root corresponding to H1751; a *battering*-tower:— fort.

H1786 דַּיִשׁ *dayiš* from H1758; *threshing* time:— threshing.

H1787 דִּישׁוֹן *dîšôn*

דִּישֹׁן *dîšōn*

דִּשׁוֹן *dîšôn* or

דִּשֹׁן *dîšōn* the same as H1788; *Dishon,* the name of two Edomites:— Dishon.

H1788 דִּישֹׁן *dîšōn* from H1758; the *leaper,* i.e. an *antelope:*— pygarg.

H1789 דִּישָׁן *dîšān* another form of H1787; *Dishan,* an Edomite:— Dishan, Dishon.

H1790 דַּךְ *dak* from an unused root (compare, H1794); *crushed,* i.e. (figuratively) *injured:*— afflicted, oppressed.

H1791 דֵּךְ *dēk* or

דָּךְ *dāk* (Aramaic) prolonged from H1668; *this:*— the same, this.

H1792 דָּכָא *dākāʾ* a primitive root (compare H1794); to *crumble;* transitively to *bruise* (literally or figuratively):— beat to pieces, break, break in pieces, bruise, contrite, crush, destroy, humble, oppress, smite.

H1793 דַּכָּא *dakkāʾ* from H1792; *crushed* (literally *powder,* or figuratively *contrite*):— contrite, destruction.

H1794 דָּכָה *dākâ* a primitive root (compare H1790, H1792); to *collapse* (physically or mentally):— break, break sore, contrite, crouch.

H1795 דַּכָּה *dakkâ* from H1794 like H1793; *mutilated:*— wounded.

H1796 דֳּכִי *dŏkî* from H1794; a *dashing* of surf:— wave.

H1797 דִּכֵּן *dikkēn* (Aramaic) prolonged from H1791; *this:*— same, that, this.

H1798 דְּכַר *dĕkar* (Aramaic) corresponding to H2145; properly a *male,* i.e. of sheep:— ram.

H1799 דִּכְרוֹן *dikrôn* or

דָּכְרָן *dokrān* (Aramaic) corresponding to H2146; a *register:*— record.

H1800 דַּל *dal* from H1809; properly *dangling,* i.e. (by implication) *weak* or *thin:*— lean, needy, poor, poor man, weaker.

H1801 דָּלַג *dālag* a primitive root; to *spring:*— leap.

H1802 דָּלָה *dālâ* a primitive root (compare H1809); properly to *dangle,* i.e. to *let down* a bucket (for *drawing* out water); figuratively to *deliver:*— draw, draw out, enough, lift up.

H1803 דַּלָּה *dallâ* from H1802; properly something *dangling,* i.e. a loose *thread* or *hair;* figuratively *indigent:*— hair, pining sickness, poor, poorest sort.

H1804 דָּלַח *dālaḥ* a primitive root; to *roil* water:— trouble.

H1805 דְּלִי *dĕlî* or

דֳּלִי *dŏlî* from H1802; a *pail* or *jar* (for *drawing* water):— bucket.

H1806 דְּלָיָה *dĕlāyâ* or (prolonged)

דְּלָיָהוּ *dĕlāyāhû* from H1802 and H3050; *Jah has delivered; Delajah,* the name of five Israelites:— Dalaiah, Delaiah.

H1807 דְּלִילָה *dĕlîlâ* from H1809; *languishing; Delilah,* a Philistine woman:— Delilah.

H1808 דָּלִיָּה *dālîyâ* from H1802; something *dangling,* i.e. a *bough:*— branch.

H1809 דָּלַל *dālal* a primitive root (compare H1802); to *slacken* or *be feeble;* figuratively to *be oppressed:*— bring low, dry up, be emptied, be not equal, fail, be impoverished, be made thin.

H1810 דִּלְעָן *dilʿān* of uncertain derivation; *Dilan,* a place in Palestine:— Dilean.

H1811 דָּלַף *dālap* a primitive root; to *drip;* by implication to *weep:*— drop through, melt, pour out.

H1812 דֶּלֶף *delep* from H1811; a *dripping:*— dropping.

H1813 דַּלְפוֹן *dalpôn* from H1811; *dripping; Dalphon,* a son of Haman:— Dalphon.

H1814 דָּלַק *dālaq* a primitive root; to *flame* (literally or figuratively):— burning, chase, inflame, kindle, persecute, persecutor, pursue hotly.

H1815 דְּלַק *dĕlaq* (Aramaic) corresponding to H1814 :— burn.

H1816 דַּלֶּקֶת *dalleqet* from H1814; a *burning* fever :— inflammation.

H1817 דֶּלֶת *delet* from H1802; something *swinging,* i.e. the *valve* of a door:— door, gate, two-leaved gate, leaf, lid. [In Ps 141:3, *dâl,* irregular].

H1818 דָּם *dām* from H1826 (compare H119); *blood* (as that which when shed causes *death*) of man or an animal; by analogy the *juice* of the grape; figuratively (especially in the plural) *bloodshed* (i.e. *drops* of blood):— blood, bloody, bloodguiltiness, bloodthirsty, innocent.

H1819 דָּמָה *dāmâ* a primitive root; to *compare;* by implication to *resemble, liken, consider:*— compare, devise, be like, liken, mean, think, use similitudes.

H1820 **דָּמָה** *dāmâ* a primitive root; to *be dumb* or *silent;* hence to *fail* or *perish;* transitively to *destroy:*— cease, be cut down, be cut off, destroy, be brought to silence, be undone, utterly.

H1821 **דְּמָה** *dĕmâ* (Aramaic) corresponding to H1918; to *resemble:*— be like.

H1822 **דֻּמָּה** *dummâ* from H1820; *desolation;* concretely *desolate:*— destroy.

H1823 **דְּמוּת** *dĕmût* from H1819; *resemblance;* concretely *model, shape;* adverbially *like:*— fashion, like, likeness, like as, manner, similitude.

H1824 **דְּמִי** *dĕmî* or

דֳּמִי *dŏmî* from H1820; *quiet:*— cutting off, rest, silence.

H1825 **דִּמְיוֹן** *dimyôn* from H1819; *resemblance:*— like.

H1826 **דָּמַם** *dāmam* a primitive root [compare H1724, H1820]; to *be dumb;* by implication to *be astonished,* to *stop;* also to *perish:*— cease, be cut down, be cut off, forbear, hold peace, quiet self, rest, be silent, keep silence, put to silence, be still, stand still, tarry, wait.

H1827 **דְּמָמָה** *dĕmāmâ* feminine from H1826; *quiet* :— calm, silence, still.

H1828 **דֹּמֶן** *dōmen* of uncertain derivation; *manure* :— dung.

H1829 **דִּמְנָה** *dimnâ* feminine from the same as H1828; a *dung-heap; Dimnah,* a place in Palestine:— Dimnah.

H1830 **דָּמַע** *dāmaᶜ* a primitive root; to *weep:*— sore, weep.

H1831 **דֶּמַע** *demaᶜ* from H1830; a *tear;* figuratively *juice:*— liquor.

H1832 **דִּמְעָה** *dimᶜâ* feminine of H1831; *weeping* :— tears.

H1833 **דְּמֶשֶׁק** *dĕmešeq* by orthographical variation from H1834; *damask* (as a fabric of Damascus):— in Damascus.

H1834 **דַּמֶּשֶׂק** *dammeśeq* or

דּוּמֶשֶׂק *dûmeśeq* or

דַּרְמֶשֶׂק *darmeśeq* of foreign origin; *Damascus,* a city of Syria:— Damascus.

H1835 **דָּן** *dān* from H1777; *judge; Dan,* one of the sons of Jacob; also the tribe descended from him, and its territory; likewise a place in Palestine colonized by them:— Dan.

H1836 **דֵּן** *dēn* (Aramaic) an orthographical variation of H1791; *this:*— aforetime, after this manner, hereafter, one . . . another, such, therefore, these, this, this matter, thus, wherefore, which.

H1837 **דַּנָּה** *dannâ* of uncertain derivation; *Dannah,* a place in Palestine:— Dannah.

H1838 **דִּנְהָבָה** *dinhābâ* of uncertain derivation; *Dinhabah,* an Edomitish town:— Dinhaban.

H1839 **דָּנִי** *dānî* patronymic from H1835; a *Danite* (often collectively) or descendant (or inhabitant) of Dan:— Danites, of Dan.

H1840 **דָּנִיֵּאל** *dānîyēʾl* in Ezekiel

דָּנִאֵל *dānīʾēl* from H1835 and H410; *judge of God; Daniel* or *Danijel,* the name of two Israelites:— Daniel.

H1841 **דָּנִיֵּאל** *dānîyēʾl* (Aramaic) corresponding to H1840; *Danijel,* the Hebrew prophet:— Daniel.

H1842 **דָּן יַעַן** *dān yaᶜan* from H1835 and (apparently) H3282; *judge of purpose; Dan-Jaan,* a place in Palestine:— Dan-jaan.

H1843 **דֵּעַ** *dēaᶜ* from H3045; *knowledge:*— knowledge, opinion.

H1844 **דֵּעָה** *dēᶜâ* feminine of H1843; *knowledge:*— knowledge.

H1845 **דְּעוּאֵל** *dĕᶜûʾēl* from H3045 and H410; *known of God; Deüel,* an Israelite:— Deuel.

H1846 **דָּעַךְ** *dāᶜak* a primitive root; to *be extinguished;* figuratively to *expire* or *be dried up:*— be extinct, consumed, put out, quenched.

H1847 **דַּעַת** *daᶜat* from H3045; *knowledge:*— cunning, ignorantly, know, knowledge, unawares, wittingly.

H1848 **דָּפִי** *dāpî* from an unused root (meaning to *push* over); a *stumbling*-block:— slanderest.

H1849 **דָּפַק** *dāpaq* a primitive root; to *knock;* by analogy to *press* severely:— beat, knock, overdrive.

H1850 **דָּפְקָה** *dopqâ* from H1849; a *knock; Dophkah,* a place in the Desert:— Dophkah.

H1851 **דַּק** *daq* from H1854; *crushed,* i.e. (by implication) *small* or *thin:*— dwarf, leanfleshed, very little thing, small, thin.

H1852 **דֹּק** *dōq* from H1854; something *crumbling,* i.e. *fine* (as a *thin* cloth):— curtain.

H1853 **דִּקְלָה** *diqlâ* of foreign origin; *Diklah,* a region of Arabia:— Diklah.

H1854 **דָּקַק** *dāqaq* a primitive root [compare H1915]; to *crush* (or intransitively) *crumble:*— beat in pieces, beat small, bruise, make dust, powder, into powder, be small, very small, stamp, stamp small.

H1855 **דְּקַק** *dĕqaq* (Aramaic) corresponding to H1854; to *crumble* or (transitively) *crush:*— break to pieces.

H1856 **דָּקַר** *dāqar* a primitive root; to *stab;* by analogy to *starve;* figuratively to *revile:*— pierce, strike through, thrust through, wound.

H1857 **דֶּקֶר** *deqer* from H1856; a *stab; Deker,* an Israelite:— Dekar.

H1858 **דַּר** *dar* apparently from the same as H1865; properly a *pearl* (from its sheen as rapidly *turned*); by analogy *pearl-stone,* i.e. mother-of-pearl or alabaster:— white.

H1859 **דָּר** *dār* (Aramaic) corresponding to H1755; an *age:*— generation.

H1860 **דְּרָאוֹן** *dĕrāʾôn* or

דֵּרָאוֹן *dērāʾôn* from an unused root (meaning to *repulse*); an object of *aversion:*— abhorring, contempt.

H1861 **דָּרְבוֹן** *dorbôn* [also

דָּרְבָן *dorbān*]; of uncertain derivation; a *goad:*— goad.

H1862 **דַּרְדַּע** *dardaᶜ* apparently from H1858 and H1843; *pearl of knowledge; Darda,* an Israelite:— Darda.

H1863 **דַּרְדַּר** *dardar* of uncertain derivation; a *thorn* :— thistle.

H1864 **דָּרוֹם** *dārôm* of uncertain derivation; the *south* poet, the *south wind:*— south.

H1865 **דְּרוֹר** *dĕrôr* from an unused root (meaning to *move rapidly*); *freedom;* hence *spontaneity* of outflow, and so *clear:*— liberty, pure.

H1866 **דְּרוֹר** *dĕrôr* the same as H1865, applied to a bird; the *swift,* a kind of swallow:— swallow.

H1867 **דָּרְיָוֶשׁ** *dārĕyāwēš* of Persian origin; *Darejavesh,* a title (rather than name) of several Persian kings:— Darius.

H1868 **דָּרְיָוֶשׁ** *dārĕyāwēš* (Aramaic) corresponding to H1867:— Darius.

H1869 **דָּרַךְ** *dārak* a primitive root; to *tread;* by implication to *walk;* also to *string* a bow (by treading on it in bending):— archer, bend, come, draw, go, go over, guide, lead, lead forth, thresh, tread, tread down, walk.

H1870 **דֶּרֶךְ** *derek* from H1869; a *road* (as *trodden*); figuratively a *course* of life or *mode* of action, often adverbially:— along, away, because of, by, conversation, custom, [east-]ward, journey, manner, passenger, through, toward, way, highway, pathway, wayside, whither, whithersoever.

H1871 **דַּרְכְּמוֹן** *darkĕmôn* of Persian origin; a *"drachma,"* or coin:— dram.

H1872 **דְּרָע** *dĕrāᶜ* (Aramaic) corresponding to H2220; an *arm:*— arm.

H1873 **דָּרַע** *dāraᶜ* probably contracted from H1862; *Dara,* an Israelite:— Dara.

H1874 **דַּרְקוֹן** *darqôn* of uncertain derivation; *Darkon,* one of "Solomon's servants":— Darkon.

H1875 **דָּרַשׁ** *dāraš* a primitive root; properly to *tread* or *frequent;* usually to *follow* (for pursuit or search); by implication to *seek* or *ask;* specifically to *worship:*— ask, at all, care for, diligently, inquire, make inquisition, necromancer, question, require, search, seek, seek for, seek out, surely.

H1876 **דָּשָׁא** *dāšāʾ* a primitive root; to *sprout:*— bring forth, spring.

H1877 **דֶּשֶׁא** *dešeʾ* from H1876; a *sprout;* by analogy *grass:*— grass, tender grass, green, herb, tender herb.

H1878 **דָּשֵׁן** *dāšēn* a primitive root; to *be fat;* transitively to *fatten* (or regard as fat); specifically to *anoint;* figuratively to *satisfy;* denominatively (from H1880) to *remove* (fat) *ashes* (of sacrifices):— accept, anoint, take away the ashes, take away the ashes from, receive ashes, make fat, wax fat.

H1879 **דָּשֵׁן** *dāšēn* from H1878; *fat;* figuratively *rich, fertile:*— fat.

H1880 **דֶּשֶׁן** *dešen* from H1878; the *fat;* abstractly *fatness,* i.e. (figuratively) *abundance;* specifically the (fatty) *ashes* of sacrifices:— ashes, fatness.

H1881 **דָּת** *dāt* of uncertain (perhaps foreign) derivation; a royal *edict* or statute:— commandment, commission, decree, law, manner.

H1882 **דָּת** *dāt* (Aramaic) corresponding to H1881 :— decree, law.

H1883 **דֶּתֶא** *dētēʾ* corresponding to H1877:— tender grass.

H1884 **דְּתָבָר** *dĕtābār* (Aramaic) of Persian origin; meaning one *skilled in law;* a *judge:*— counsellor.

H1885 **דָּתָן** *dātān* of uncertain derivation; *Dathan,* an Israelite:— Dathan.

H1886 **דֹּתָן** *dōtān* or

דֹּתַיִן *dōtayin* (Gen 37:17), an Aramaic dual form of uncertain derivation; *Dothan,* a place in Palestine:— Dothan.

ה

H1887 הֵא *hēʾ* a primitive particle; *lo!:*— behold, lo.

H1888 הֵא *hēʾ* or

הָא *hāʾ* (Aramaic) corresponding to H1887 :— even, lo.

H1889 הֶאָח *heʾāḥ* from H1887 and H253; *aha!:*— ah, aha, ha.

H1890 הַבְהָב *habhāb* by reduplication from H3051; *gift* (in sacrifice), i.e. *holocaust:*— offering.

H1891 הָבַל *hābal* a primitive root; to *be vain* in act, word, or expectation; specifically to *lead astray:*— be vain, become vain, make vain.

H1892 הֶבֶל *hebel* or (rarely in the absolute)

הֲבֵל *hăbēl* from H1891; *emptiness* or *vanity;* figuratively something *transitory* and *unsatisfactory;* often used as an adverb:— altogether, vain, vanity.

H1893 הֶבֶל *hebel* the same as H1892; *Hebel,* the son of Adam:— Abel.

H1894 הֹבֶן *hōben* only in plural, from an unused root meaning to *be hard; ebony:*— ebony.

H1895 הָבַר *hābar* a primitive root of uncertain (perhaps foreign) derivation; to *be a horoscopist:*— astrologer.

H1896 הֵגֵא *hēgēʾ* or (by permutation)

הֵגַי *hēgay* probably of Persian origin; *Hege* or *Hegai,* a eunuch of Xerxes:— Hegai, Hege.

H1897 הָגָה *hāgâ* a primitive root [compare H1901]; to *murmur* (in pleasure or anger); by implication to *ponder:*— imagine, meditate, mourn, mutter, roar, sore, speak, study, talk, utter.

H1898 הָגָה *hāgâ* a primitive root; to *remove:*— stay, take away.

H1899 הֶגֶה *hegeh* from H1897; a *muttering* (in sighing, thought, or as thunder):— mourning, sound, tale.

H1900 הָגוּת *hāgût* from H1897; *musing:*— meditation.

H1901 הָגִיג *hāgîg* from an unused root akin to H1897; properly a *murmur,* i.e. *complaint:*— meditation, musing.

H1902 הִגָּיוֹן *higgāyôn* intensive from H1897; a *murmuring* sound, i.e. a musical notation (probably similar to the modern *affetuoso* to indicate solemnity of movement); by implication a *machination:*— device, Higgaion, meditation, solemn sound.

H1903 הָגִין *hāgîn* of uncertain derivation; perhaps *suitable* or *turning:*— directly.

H1904 הָגָר *hāgār* of uncertain (perhaps foreign) derivation; *Hagar,* the mother of Ishmael:— Hagar.

H1905 הַגְרִי *hagrî* or (prolonged)

הַגְרִיא *hagrîʾ* perhaps patronymic from H1904; a *Hagrite* or member of a certain Arabian clan:— Hagarene, Hagarite, Haggeri.

H1906 הֵד *hēd* for H1959; a *shout:*— sounding again.

H1907 הַדָּבָר *haddābār* (Aramaic) probably of foreign origin; a *vizier:*— counsellor.

H1908 הֲדַד *hădad* probably of foreign origin [compare H111]; *Hadad,* the name of an idol, and of several kings of Edom:— Hadad.

H1909 הֲדַדְעֶזֶר *hădadʿezer* from H1908 and H5828; *Hadad* (is his) *help; Hadadezer,* a Syrian king:— Hadadezer. Compare H1928

H1910 הֲדַדְרִמּוֹן *hădadrimmôn* from H1908 and H7417; *Hadad-Rimmon,* a place in Palestine:— Hadad-rimmon.

H1911 הָדָה *hādâ* a primitive root [compare H3034]; to *stretch forth* the hand:— put.

H1912 הֹדוּ *hōdû* of foreign origin; *Hodu* (i.e. Hindûstan):— India.

H1913 הֲדוֹרָם *hădôrām* or

הֲדֹרָם *hădōrām* probably of foreign derivation; *Hadoram,* a son of Joktan, and the tribe descended from him:— Hadoram.

H1914 הִדַּי *hidday* of uncertain derivation; *Hiddai,* an Israelite:— Hiddai.

H1915 הָדַךְ *hādak* a primitive root [compare H1854]; to *crush* with the foot:— tread down.

H1916 הֲדֹם *hădōm* from an unused root meaning to *stamp* upon; a foot-*stool:*— footstool.

H1917 הַדָּם *haddām* (Aramaic) from a root corresponding to that of H1916; something *stamped* to pieces, i.e. a *bit:*— piece.

H1918 הֲדַס *hădas* of uncertain derivation; the *myrtle:*— myrtle, myrtle tree.

H1919 הֲדַסָּה *hădassâ* feminine of H1918; *Hadassah* (or Esther):— Hadassah.

H1920 הָדַף *hādap* a primitive root; to *push* away or down:— cast away, cast out, drive, expel, thrust, thrust away.

H1921 הָדַר *hādar* a primitive root; to *swell* up (literally or figuratively, active or passive); by implication to *favor* or *honour, be high* or *proud:*— countenance, crooked place, glorious, honour, put forth.

H1922 הֲדַר *hăddar* (Aramaic) corresponding to H1921; to *magnify* (figuratively):— glorify, honour.

H1923 הֲדַר *hădar* (Aramaic) from H1922; *magnificence:*— honour, majesty.

H1924 הֲדַר *hădar* the same as H1926; *Hadar,* an Edomite:— Hadar.

H1925 הֶדֶר *heder* from H1921; *honour;* used (figuratively) for the *capital* city (Jerusalem):— glory.

H1926 הָדָר *hādār* from H1921; *magnificence,* i.e. ornament or splendor:— beauty, comeliness, excellency, glorious, glory, goodly, honour, majesty.

H1927 הֲדָרָה *hădārâ* feminine of H1926; *decoration:*— beauty, honour.

H1928 הֲדַרְעֶזֶר *hădarʿezer* from H1924 and H5828; *Hadar* (i.e. *Hadad,* H1908) is his *help; Hadarezer* (i.e. Hadadezer, H1909), a Syrian king:— Hadarezer.

H1929 הָהּ *hāh* a shortened form of H162; *ah!* expressing grief:— woe worth.

H1930 הוֹ *hô* by permutation from H1929; *oh!:*— alas.

H1931 הוּא *hûʾ* of which the feminine (beyond the Pentateuch) is

הִיא *hîʾ* a primitive word; the third person pronoun singular, *he* (*she* or *it*) only expressed when emphatic or without a verb; also (intensively) *self,* or (especially with the article) the *same:* sometimes (as demonstrative) *this* or *that;* occasionally (instead of copula) *as* or *are:*— he, as for her, him, himself, it, the same, she, herself, such, that, that . . . it, these, they this, those, which, which is, who.

H1932 הוּא *hûʾ* or (feminine)

הִיא *hîʾ* (Aramaic) corresponding to H1931 :— are, it, this.

H1933 הָוָא *hāwāʾ* or

הָוָה *hāwâ* a primitive root [compare H183, H1961] supposed to mean properly to *breathe;* to *be* (in the sense of existence):— be, have.

H1934 הֲוָא *hăwāʾ* or

הֲוָה *hăwâ* (Aramaic) corresponding to H1933; to *exist;* used in a great variety of applications (especially in connection with other words):— be, become, behold, came, came to pass, cease, cleave, consider, do, give, have, judge, keep, labour, mingle, mingle self, put, see, seek, set, slay, take heed, tremble, walk, would.

HEB

H1935 הוֹד *hôd* from an unused root; *grandeur* (i.e. an imposing form and appearance):— beauty, comeliness, excellency, glorious, glory, goodly, honour, majesty.

H1936 הוֹד *hôd* the same as H1935; *Hod,* an Israelite:— Hod.

H1937 הוֹדְוָה *hôdĕwâ* a form of H1938; *Hodevah* (or Hodevjah), an Israelite:— Hodevah.

H1938 הוֹדַוְיָה *hôdawyâ* from H1935 and H3050; *majesty of Jah; Hodavjah,* the name of three Israelites:— Hodaviah.

H1939 הוֹדַיְוָהוּ *hôdaywāhû* a form of H1938; *Hodajvah,* an Israelite:— Hodaiah.

H1940 הוֹדִיָּה *hôdîyâ* a form for the feminine of H3064; a *Jewess:*— Hodiah.

H1941 הוֹדִיָּה *hôdîyâ* a form of H1938; *Hodijah,* the name of three Israelites:— Hodijah.

H1942 הַוָּה *hawwâ* from H1933 (in the sense of eagerly *coveting* and *rushing* upon by implication of *falling*); *desire;* also *ruin:*— calamity, iniquity, mischief, mischievous, mischievous thing, naughtiness, naughty, noisome, perverse thing, substance, very wickedness.

H1943 הֹוָה *hōwâ* another form for H1942; *ruin:*— mischief.

H1944 הוֹהָם *hôhām* of uncertain derivation; *Hoham,* a Canaanitish king:— Hoham.

H1945 הוֹי *hôy* a prolonged form of H1930 [akin to H188]; *oh!:*— ah, alas, ho, O, woe.

H1946 הוּךְ *hûk* (Aramaic) corresponding to H1981; to *go;* causatively to *bring:*— bring again, come, go, go up.

H1947 הוֹלֵלָה *hôlēlâ* feminine active participle of H1984; *folly:*— madness.

H1948 הוֹלֵלוּת *hôlēlût* from active participle of H1984; *folly:*— madness.

H1949 הוּם *hûm* a primitive root [compare H2000]; to *make an uproar,* or *agitate* greatly:— destroy, move, make a noise, put, ring again.

H1950 הוֹמָם *hômām* from H2000; *raging; Homam,* an Edomitish chieftain:— Homam. Compare H1967

H1951 הוּן *hûn* a primitive root; properly to *be naught,* i.e. (figuratively) to *be* (causatively *act*) *light:*— be ready.

H1952 הוֹן *hôn* from the same as H1951 in the sense of H202; *wealth;* by implication *enough:*— enough, for nought, riches, substance, wealth.

H1953 הוֹשָׁמָע *hôšāmāʿ* from H3068 and H8085; *Jehovah has heard; Hoshama,* an Israelite:— Hoshama.

H1954 הוֹשֵׁעַ *hôšēa*[c] from H3467; *deliverer; Hosheä,* the name of five Israelites:— Hosea, Hoshea, Oshea.

H1955 הוֹשַׁעְיָה *hôša*[c]*ih* from H3467 and H3050; *Jah has saved; Hoshajah,* the name of two Israelites:— Hoshaiah.

H1956 הוֹתִיר *hôtîr* from H3498; *he has caused to remain; Hothir,* an Israelite:— Hothir.

H1957 הָזָה *hāzâ* a primitive root [compare H2372]; to *dream:*— sleep.

H1958 הִי *hî* for H5092; *lamentation:*— woe.

H1959 הֵידָד *hêdād* from an unused root (meaning to *shout*); *acclamation:*— shout, shouting.

H1960 הֻיְּדָה *huyyĕdâ* from the same as H1959; properly an *acclaim,* i.e. a *choir* of singers:— thanksgiving.

H1961 הָיָה *hāyâ* a primitive root [compare H1933]; to *exist,* i.e. *be* or *become, come to pass* (always emphatic, and not a mere copula or auxiliary):— beacon, altogether, be, become, be accomplished, be committed, be like, break, cause, come, come to pass, do, faint, fall, follow, happen, have, last, pertain, quit self, quit oneself, require, use.

H1962 הַיָּה *hayyâ* another form for H1943; *ruin:*— calamity.

H1963 הֵיךְ *hêk* another form for H349; *how?:*— how.

H1964 הֵיכָל *hêkāl* probably from H3201 (in the sense of *capacity*); a large public building, such as a *palace* or *temple:*— palace, temple.

H1965 הֵיכַל *hêkal* (Aramaic) corresponding to H1964:— palace, temple.

H1966 הֵילֵל *hêlēl* from H1984 (in the sense of *brightness*); the *morning-star:*— lucifer.

H1967 הֵימָם *hêmām* another form for H1950; *Hemam,* an Idumaean:— Hemam.

H1968 הֵימָן *hêmān* probably from H539; *faithful; Heman,* the name of at least two Israelites:— Heman.

H1969 הִין *hîn* probably of Egyptian origin; a *hin* or liquid measure:— hin.

H1970 הָכַר *hākar* a primitive root; apparently to *injure:*— make self strange.

H1971 הַכָּרָה *hakkārâ* from H5234; *respect,* i.e. partiality:— shew.

H1972 הָלָא *hālā*ʾ probably denominative from H1973; to *remove* or be *remote:*— cast far off.

H1973 הָלְאָה *hol*ʾ*â* from the primitive form of the article

הַל *hal; to the distance,* i.e. *far away;* also (of time) *thus far:*— back, beyond, forward, henceforward, hitherto, thenceforth, yonder.

H1974 הִלּוּל *hillûl* from H1984 (in the sense of *rejoicing*); a *celebration* of thanksgiving for harvest:— merry, praise.

H1975 הַלָּז *hollāz* from H1976; *this* or *that:*— side, that, this.

H1976 הַלָּזֶה *hollāzeh* from the article [see H1973] and H2088; *this very:*— this.

H1977 הַלֵּזוּ *hallēzû* another form of H1976; *that* :— this.

H1978 הָלִיךְ *hālîk* from H1980; a *walk,* i.e. (by implication) a *step:*— step.

H1979 הֲלִיכָה *hălîkâ* feminine of H1978; a *walking;* by implication a *procession* or *march,* a *caravan:*— company, going, walk, way.

H1980 הָלַךְ *hālak* akin to H3212; a primitive root; to *walk* (in a great variety of applications, literally and figuratively):— along, all along, apace, behave, behave self, come, continually, on continually, be conversant, depart, be eased, enter, exercise, exercise self, follow, forth, forward, get, go, go about, go abroad, go along, go away, go forward, go on, go out, go up and down, greater, grow, be wont to haunt, lead, march, more and more, move, move self, needs, on, pass, pass away, be at the point, quite, run, run along, send, speedily, spread, still, surely, tale-bearer, travel, traveller, walk, walk abroad, walk, on, walk to and fro, walk up and down, walk to places, wander, wax, wayfaring man, be weak, whirl.

H1981 הֲלַךְ *hălak* (Aramaic) corresponding to H1980 [compare H1946]; to *walk:*— walk.

H1982 הֵלֶךְ *hēlek* from H1980; properly a *journey,* i.e. (by implication) a *wayfarer;* also a *flowing:*— dropped, traveller.

H1983 הֲלָךְ *hălāk* (Aramaic) from H1981; properly a *journey,* i.e. (by implication) *toll* on goods at a road:— custom.

H1984 הָלַל *hālal* a primitive root; to *be clear* (originally of sound, but usually of color); to *shine;* hence to *make a show,* to *boast;* and thus to *be* (clamourously) *foolish;* to *rave;* causatively to *celebrate;* also to *stultify:*— boast, make boast, boast self, celebrate, commend, fool, foolish, foolishly, deal foolishly, make fool, glory, give light, be mad, be mad against, make mad, feign self mad, give in marriage, be praised, sing praise, be worthy of praise, rage, renowned, shine.

H1985 הִלֵּל *hillēl* from H1984; *praising* (namely God); *Hillel,* an Israelite:— Hillel.

H1986 הָלַם *hālam* a primitive root; to *strike* down; by implication to *hammer, stamp, conquer, disband:*— beat, beat down, break, break down, overcome, smite, smite with the hammer.

H1987 הֶלֶם *helem* from H1986; *smiter; Helem,* the name of two Israelites:— Helem.

H1988 הֲלֹם *hălōm* from the article [see H1973]; *hither:*— here, hither, hitherto, thither.

H1989 הַלְמוּת *halmût* from H1986; a *hammer* (or *mallet*):— hammer.

H1990 הָם *hām* of uncertain derivation; *Ham,* a region of Palestine:— Ham.

H1991 הֵם *hēm* from H1993; *abundance,* i.e. *wealth* :— any of theirs.

H1992 הֵם *hēm* or (prolonged)

הֵמָּה *hēmmâ* masculine plural from H1931; *they* (only used when emphatic):— it, like, how many soever they be, so many more as they, same, the same, so, such, their, them, these, they, those, which, who, whom, withal, ye.

H1993 הָמָה *hāmâ* a primitive root [compare H1949]; to *make a loud sound* (like English "hum"); by implication to *be in great commotion* or *tumult,* to *rage, war, moan, clamor:*— clamorous, concourse, cry aloud, be disquieted, loud, mourn, be moved, make a noise, rage, roar, sound, be troubled, make a tumult, tumultuous, be in an uproar.

H1994 הִמּוֹ *himmô* or (prolonged)

הִמּוֹן *himmôn* (Aramaic) corresponding to H1992; *they:*— are, them, those.

H1995 הָמוֹן *hāmôn* or

הָמֹן *hāmōn* (Ezek 5:7), from H1993; a *noise, tumult, crowd;* also *disquietude, wealth:*— abundance, company, many, multitude, multiply, noise, riches, rumbling, sounding, store, tumult.

H1996 הֲמוֹן גּוֹג *hămôn gôg* from H1995 and H1463; the *multitude of Gog;* the fanciful name of an emblematic place in Palestine:— Hamon-gog.

H1997 הֲמוֹנָה *hămônâ* feminine of H1995; *multitude; Hamonah,* the same as H1996:— Hamonah.

H1998 הֶמְיָה *hemyâ* from H1993; *sound:*— noise.

H1999 הֲמֻלָּה *hămullâ* or (too fully)

הֲמוּלָּה *hămûllâ* (Jer 11:16), feminine passive participle of an unused root meaning to *rush* (as rain with a windy roar); a *sound:*— speech, tumult.

H2000 הָמַם *hāmam* a primitive root [compare H1949, H1993]; properly to *put in commotion;* by implication to *disturb, drive, destroy:*— break, consume, crush, destroy, discomfit, trouble, vex.

H2001 הָמָן *hāmān* of foreign derivation; *Haman,* a Persian vizier:— Haman.

H2002 הַמְנִיךְ *hamnîk* (Aramaic), the text is

הֲמוּנֵךְ *hămûnēk* of foreign origin; a *necklace:*— chain.

H2003 הָמָס *hāmās* from an unused root apparently meaning to *crackle;* a dry *twig* or *brushwood:*— melting.

H2004 הֵן *hēn* feminine plural from H1931; *they* (only used when emphatic):— in, such like, them, with them, thereby, therein, they, more than they, wherein, in which, whom, withal.

H2005 הֵן *hēn* a primitive particle; *lo!;* also (as expressing surprise) *if:*— behold, if, lo, though.

H2006 הֵן *hēn* (Aramaic) corresponding to H2005; *lo!* also *there[-fore], [un-]less, whether, but, if:*— if, that if, or, whether.

H2007 הֵנָּה *hēnnâ* prolonged for H2004; *themselves* (often used emphatically for the copula, also in indirect relation):— in, such, such and such things, their, them, into them, thence, therein, these, they, they had, on this side, those, wherein.

H2008 הֵנָּה *hēnnâ* from H2004; *hither* or *thither* (but used both of place and time):— here, hither, hitherto, now, on this side, on that side, since, this way, that way, thitherward, thus far, to . . . fro, yet.

H2009 הִנֵּה *hinnēh* prolonged for H2005; *lo!:*— behold, lo, see.

H2010 הֲנָחָה *hănāḥâ* from H5117; *permission* of rest, i.e. *quiet:*— release.

H2011 הִנֹּם *hinnōm* probably of foreign origin; *Hinnom,* apparently a Jebusite:— Hinnom.

H2012 הֵנַע *hēna*[c] probably of foreign derivation; *Hena,* a place apparently in Mesopotamia:— Hena.

H2013 הָסָה *hāsâ* a primitive root; to *hush:*— hold peace, hold tongue, silence, keep silence, be silent, still.

H2014 הֲפֻגָה *hăpūgâ* from H6313; *relaxation:*— intermission.

H2015 הָפַךְ *hāpak* a primitive root; to *turn* about or over; by implication to *change, overturn, return, pervert:*— become, change, come, be converted, give, make a bed, overthrow, overturn, perverse, retire, tumble, turn, turn again, turn aside, turn back, turn to the contrary, turn every way.

H2016 הֶפֶךְ *hepek* or

הֵפֶךְ *hēpek* from H2015; a *turn,* i.e. the *reverse:*— contrary.

H2017 הֹפֶךְ *hōpek* from H2015; an *upset,* i.e. (abstractly) *perversity:*— turning of things upside down.

H2018 הֲפֵכָה *hăpēkâ* feminine of H2016; *destruction:*— overthrow.

H2019 הֲפַכְפַּךְ *hăpakpak* by reduplication from H2015; *very perverse:*— froward.

H2020 הַצָּלָה *haṣṣālâ* from H5337; *rescue:*— deliverance.

H2021 הֹצֶן *hōṣen* from an unused root meaning apparently to *be sharp* or *strong;* a *weapon* of war:— chariot.

H2022 הַר *har* a shortened form of H2042; a *mountain* or *range* of hills (sometimes used figuratively):— hill, hill country, mount, mountain, promotion.

H2023 הֹר *hōr* another form for H2022; *mountain; Hor,* the name of a peak in Idumaea and of one in Syria:— Hor.

H2024 הָרָא *hārā*ʾ perhaps from H2022; *mountainousness; Hara,* a region of Media:— Hara.

H2025 הַרְאֵל *harʾēl* from H2022 and H410; *mount of God;* figuratively the *altar* of burnt-offering:— altar. Compare H739

H2026 הָרַג *hārag* a primitive root; to *smite* with deadly intent:— destroy, out of hand, kill, murder, murderer, put to death, make slaughter, slay, slayer, surely.

H2027 הֶרֶג *hereg* from H2026; *slaughter:*— be slain, slaughter.

H2028 הֲרֵגָה *hărēgâ* feminine of H2027; *slaughter* :— slaughter.

H2029 הָרָה *hārâ* a primitive root; to *be* (or *become*) *pregnant, conceive* (literally or figuratively):— bear, be with child, conceive, progenitor.

H2030 הָרֶה *hāreh* or

הָרִי *hārî* (Hos 14:1), from H2029; *pregnant* :— with child, be with child, woman with child, conceive, great.

H2031 הַרְהֹר *harhōr* (Aramaic) from a root corresponding to H2029; a mental *conception:*— thought.

H2032 הֵרוֹן *hērôn* or

הֵרָיוֹן *hērāyôn* from H2029; *pregnancy:*— conception.

H2033 הֲרוֹרִי *hărôrî* another form for H2043; a *Harorite* or mountaineer:— Harorite.

H2034 הֲרִיסָה *hărîsâ* from H2040; something *demolished:*— ruin.

H2035 הֲרִיסוּת *hărîsût* from H2040; *demolition:*— destruction.

H2036 הֹרָם *hōrām* from an unused root (meaning to *tower* up); *high; Horam,* a Canaanitish king:— Horam.

H2037 הָרֻם *hārūm* passive participle of the same as H2036; *high; Harum,* an Israelite:— Harum.

H2038 הַרְמוֹן *harmôn* from the same as H2036; a *castle* (from its height):— palace.

H2039 הָרָן *hārān* perhaps from H2022; *mountaineer; Haran,* the name of two men:— Haran.

H2040 הָרַס *hāras* a primitive root; to *pull* down or in pieces, *break, destroy:*— beat down, break, break down, break through, destroy, overthrow, pluck down, pull down, ruin, throw down, utterly.

H2041 הֶרֶס *heres* from H2040; *demolition:*— destruction.

H2042 הָרָר *hārār* from an unused root meaning to *loom* up; a *mountain:*— hill, mount, mountain.

H2043 הֲרָרִי *hărārî* or

הָרָרִי *hārārî* (2 Sam. 23:11) or

הָאֲרָרִי *hāʾrārî* (2 Sam 23:34, last clause), apparently from H2042; a *mountaineer:*— Hararite.

H2044 הָשֵׁם *hāšēm* perhaps from the same as H2828; *wealthy; Hashem,* an Israelite:— Hashem.

H2045 הַשְׁמָעוּת *hašmāʿût* from H8085; *announcement:*— to cause to hear.

H2046 הִתּוּךְ *hittûk* from H5413; a *melting:*— is melted.

H2047 הֲתָךְ *hătāk* probably of foreign origin; *Hathak,* a Persian eunuch:— Hatach.

H2048 הָתַל *hātal* a primitive root; to *deride;* by implication to *cheat:*— deal deceitfully, deceive, mock.

H2049 הָתֹל *hātōl* from H2048 (only in plural collectively); a *derision:*— mocker.

H2050 הָתַת *hātat* a primitive root; properly to *break* in upon, i.e. to *assail:*— imagine mischief.

ו

H2051 וְדָן *wĕdān* perhaps for H5730; *Vedan* (or Aden), a place in Arabia:— Dan also.

H2052 וָהֵב *wāhēb* of uncertain derivation; *Vaheb,* a place in Moab:— what he did.

H2053 וָו *wāw* probably a *hook* (the name of the sixth Hebrew letter):— hook.

H2054 וָזָר *wāzār* presumed to be from an unused root meaning to *bear* guilt; *crime:*— strange.

H2055 וַיְזָתָא *wayzātā*ʾ of foreign origin; *Vajezatha,* a son of Haman:— Vajezatha.

H2056 וָלָד *wālād* for H3206; a *boy:*— child.

H2057 וַנְיָה *wanyâ* perhaps for H6043; *Vanjah,* an Israelite:— Vaniah.

H2058 וָפְסִי *wopsî* probably from H3254; *additional; Vophsi,* an Israelite:— Vophsi.

H2059 וַשְׁנִי *wašnî* probably from H3461; *weak; Vashni,* an Israelite:— Vashni.

H2060 וַשְׁתִּי *waštî* of Persian origin; *Vashti,* the queen of Xerxes:— Vashti.

ז

H2061 זְאֵב *zĕʾēb* from an unused root meaning to *be yellow;* a *wolf:*— wolf.

H2062 זְאֵב *zĕʾēb* the same as H2061; *Zeëb,* a Midianitish prince:— Zeeb.

H2063 זֹאת *zōʾt* irregular feminine of H2089; *this* (often used adverbially):— hereby, herein, herewith, it, likewise, the one, the other, the same, she, so, so much, such, such deed, that, therefore, these, this, this thing, thus.

H2064 זָבַד *zābad* a primitive root; to *confer:*— endue.

H2065 זֶבֶד *zebed* from H2064; a *gift:*— dowry.

H2066 זָבָד *zābād* from H2064; *giver; Zabad,* the name of seven Israelites:— Zabad.

H2067 זַבְדִּי *zobdî* from H2065; *giving; Zabdi,* the name of four Israelites:— Zabdi.

H2068 זַבְדִּיאֵל *zobdîʾēl* from H2065 and H410; *gift of God; Zabdiel,* the name of two Israelites:— Zabdiel.

H2069 זְבַדְיָה *zĕbadîâ* or

זְבַדְיָהוּ *zĕbadyāhû* from H2064 and H3050; *Jah has given; Zebadjah,* the name of nine Israelites:— Zebadiah.

H2070 זְבוּב *zĕbûb* from an unused root (meaning to *flit*); a *fly* (especially one of a stinging nature):— fly.

H2071 זָבוּד *zābûd* from H2064; *given; Zabud,* an Israelite:— Zabud.

H2072 זַבּוּד *zabbûd* a form of H2071; *given; Zabbud,* an Israelite:— Zabbud.

H2073 זְבוּל *zĕbûl* or

זְבֻל *zĕbūl* from H2082; a *residence:*— dwell in, dwelling, habitation.

H2074 זְבוּלוּן *zĕbûlûn* or

זְבֻלוּן *zĕbūlûn* or

זְבוּלֻן *zĕbûlūn* from H2082; *habitation; Zebulon,* a son of Jacob; also his territory and tribe:— Zebulun.

H2075 זְבוּלֹנִי *zĕbûlōnî* patronymic from H2074; a *Zebulonite* or descendant of Zebulun:— Zebulonite.

H2076 זָבַח *zābaḥ* a primitive root; to *slaughter* an animal (usually in sacrifice):— kill, offer, sacrifice, do sacrifice, slay.

H2077 זֶבַח *zebaḥ* from H2076; properly a *slaughter,* i.e. the *flesh* of an animal; by implication a *sacrifice* (the victim or the act):— offer, offering, sacrifice.

H2078 זֶבַח *zebaḥ* the same as H2077; *sacrifice; Zebach,* a Midianitish prince:— Zebah.

H2079 זַבַּי *zabby* probably by orthographical error for H2140; *Zabbai* (or Zaccai), an Israelite:— Zabbai.

H2080 זְבִידָה *zĕbîdâ* feminine from H2064; *giving; Zebidah,* an Israelitess:— Zebudah.

H2081 זְבִינָא *zĕbînā*ʾ from an unused root (meaning to *purchase*); *gainfulness; Zebina,* an Israelite:— Zebina.

H2082 זָבַל *zābal* a primitive root; apparently properly to *inclose,* i.e. to *reside:*— dwell with.

H2083 זְבֻל *zĕbūl* the same as H2073; *dwelling; Zebul,* an Israelite:— Zebul. Compare H2073

H2084 זְבַן *zĕban* (Aramaic) corresponding to the root of H2081; to *acquire* by purchase:— gain.

H2085 זָג *zāg* from an unused root probably meaning to *inclose;* the *skin* of a grape:— husk.

H2086 זֵד *zēd* from H2102; *arrogant:*— presumptuous, proud.

H2087 זָדוֹן *zādôn* from H2102; *arrogance:*— presumptuously, pride, proud, proud man.

H2088 זֶה *zeh* a primitive word; the masculine demonstrative pronoun, *this* or *that:*— he, hence, here, it, itself, now, of him the one . . . the other, than the other, the same, the self same, out of the same, such, such an one, that, these, this, this hath, this man, on this side . . . on that side, thus, very, which. Compare H2063, H2090, H2097, H2098

H2089 זֶה *zeh* (1 Sam. 17:34), by permutation for H7716; a *sheep:*— lamb.

H2090 זֹה *zōh* for H2088; *this* or *that:*— as well as another, it, this, that, thus and thus.

H2091 זָהָב *zāhāb* from an unused root meaning to *shimmer; gold;* figuratively something *gold-colored* (i.e. *yellow*), as *oil,* a *clear sky:*— gold, golden, fair weather.

H2092 זָהַם *zāham* a primitive root; to *be rancid,* i.e. (transitively) to *loathe:*— abhor.

H2093 זַהַם *zaham* from H2092; *loathing; Zaham,* an Israelite:— Zaham.

H2094 זָהַר *zāhar* a primitive root; to *gleam;* figuratively to *enlighten* (by caution):— admonish, shine, teach, warn, give warning.

H2095 זְהַר *zĕhar* (Aramaic) corresponding to H2094; (passive) *be admonished:*— take heed.

H2096 זֹהַר *zōhar* from H2094; *brilliancy:*— brightness.

H2097 זוֹ *zô* for H2088; *this* or *that:*— that, this.

H2098 זוּ *zû* for H2088; *this* or *that:*— that this, wherein, which, whom.

H2099 זִו *zīw* probably from an unused root meaning to *be prominent;* properly *brightness* [compare H2122], i.e. (figuratively) the month of *flowers; Ziv* (corresponding to Ijar or May):— Zif.

H2100 זוּב *zûb* a primitive root; to *flow* freely (as water), i.e. (specifically) to *have* a (sexual) *flux;* figuratively to *waste* away; also to *overflow:*— flow, gush out, have an issue, have a running issue, pine away, run.

H2101 זוֹב *zôb* from H2100; a seminal or menstrual *flux:*— issue.

H2102 זוּד *zûd* or (by permutation)

זִיד *zîd* a primitive root; to *seethe;* figuratively to *be insolent:*— be proud, deal proudly, presume, presumptuously, come presumptuously, sod.

H2103 זוּד *zûd* (Aramaic) corresponding to H2102; to *be proud:*— in pride.

H2104 זוּזִים *zûzîm* plural probably from the same as H2123; *prominent; Zuzites,* an aboriginal tribe of Palestine:— Zuzims.

H2105 זוֹחֵת *zôḥēt* of uncertain origin; *Zocheth,* an Israelite:— Zoheth.

H2106 זָוִית *zāwît* apparently from the same root as H2099 (in the sense of *prominence*); an *angle* (as *projecting*), i.e. (by implication) a *corner-column* (or *anta*):— corner, corner stone.

H2107 זוּל *zûl* a primitive root [compare H2151]; probably to *shake* out, i.e. (by implication) to *scatter* profusely; figuratively to *treat lightly:*— lavish, despise.

H2108 זוּלָה *zûlâ* from H2107; properly *scattering,* i.e. *removal;* used adverbially *except:*— beside, but, only, save.

H2109 זוּן *zûn* a primitive root; perhaps properly to *be plump,* i.e. (transitively) to *nourish:*— feed.

H2110 זוּן *zûn* (Aramaic) corresponding to H2109 :— feed.

H2111 זוּעַ *zûaᶜ* a primitive root; properly to *shake* off, i.e. (figuratively) to *agitate* (as with fear):— move, tremble, vex.

H2112 זוּעַ *zûaᶜ* (Aramaic) corresponding to H2111; to *shake* (with fear):— tremble.

H2113 זְוָעָה *zĕwāᶜâ* from H2111; *agitation, fear:*— be removed, trouble, vexation. Compare H2189

H2114 זוּר *zûr* a primitive root; to *turn* aside (especially for lodging); hence to *be a foreigner, strange, profane;* specifically (active participle) to *commit adultery:*— another, another man, come from another place, fanner, go away, strange, stranger, strange thing, strange woman, estrange.

H2115 זוּר *zûr* a primitive root [compare H6695]; to *press* together, *tighten:*— close, crush, thrust together.

H2116 זוּרֶה *zĕreh* from H2115; *trodden* on:— that which is crushed.

H2117 זָזָא *zāzāᵓ* probably from the root of H2123; *prominent; Zaza,* an Israelite:— Zaza.

H2118 זָחַח *zāḥaḥ* a primitive root; to *shove* or *displace:*— loose.

H2119 זָחַל *zāḥal* a primitive root; to *crawl;* by implication to *fear:*— be afraid, serpent, worm.

H2120 זֹחֶלֶת *zōḥelet* feminine active participle of H2119; *crawling* (i.e. *serpent*); *Zocheleth,* a boundary stone in Palestine:— Zoheleth.

H2121 זֵידוֹן *zêdôn* from H2102; *boiling* of water, i.e. *wave:*— proud.

H2122 זִיו *zîw* (Aramaic) corresponding to H2099; (figuratively) *cheerfulness:*— brightness, countenance.

H2123 זִיז *zîz* from an unused root apparently meaning to *be conspicuous; fulness* of the breast; also a moving *creature:*— abundance, wild beast.

H2124 זִיזָא *zîzāᵓ* apparently from the same as H2123; *prominence; Ziza,* the name of two Israelites:— Ziza.

H2125 זִיזָה *zîzâ* another form for H2124; *Zizah,* an Israelite:— Zizah.

H2126 זִינָא *zînāᵓ* from H2109; well *fed;* or perhaps an orthographical error for H2124; *Zina,* an Israelite:— Zina.

H2127 זִיעַ *zîaᶜ* from H2111; *agitation; Zia,* an Israelite:— Zia.

H2128 זִיף *zîp* from the same as H2203; *flowing; Ziph,* the name of a place in Palestine; also of an Israelite:— Ziph.

H2129 זִיפָה *zîpâ* feminine of H2128; a *flowing; Ziphah,* an Israelite:— Ziphah.

H2130 זִיפִי *zîpî* patrial from H2128; a *Ziphite* or inhabitant of Ziph:— Ziphim, Ziphite.

H2131 זִיקָה *zîqâ* (Isa. 50:11) (feminine)

זִק *zīq* or

זֵק *zēq* from H2187; properly what *leaps* forth, i.e. *flash* of fire, or a burning *arrow;* also (from the original sense of the root) a *bond:*— chain, fetter, firebrand, spark.

H2132 זַיִת *zayit* probably from an unused root [akin to H2099]; an *olive* (as yielding *illuminating* oil), the tree, the branch or the berry:— olive, olive tree, oliveyard, Olivet.

H2133 זֵיתָן *zêtān* from H2132; *olive* grove; *Zethan,* an Israelite:— Zethan.

H2134 זַךְ *zak* from H2141; *clear:*— clean, pure.

H2135 זָכָה *zākâ* a primitive root [compare H2141]; to *be translucent;* figuratively to *be innocent:*— be clean, make clean, cleanse, be clear, count pure.

H2136 זָכוּ *zākû* (Aramaic) from a root corresponding to H2135; *purity:*— innocency.

H2137 זְכוּכִית *zĕkûkît* from H2135; properly *transparency,* i.e. *glass:*— crystal.

H2138 זָכוּר *zākûr* properly passive participle of H2142, but used for H2145; a *male* (of man or animals):— males, men-children.

H2139 זַכּוּר *zakkûr* from H2142; *mindful; Zakkur,* the name of seven Israelites:— Zaccur, Zacchur.

H2140 זַכַּי *zakkay* from H2141; *pure; Zakkai,* an Israelite:— Zaccai.

H2141 זָכַךְ *zākak* a primitive root [compare H2135]; to *be transparent* or *clean* (physically or morally):— be clean, make clean, be pure, be purer.

H2142 זָכַר *zākar* a primitive root; properly to *mark* (so as to be recognized), i.e. to *remember;* by implication to *mention;* also (as denominative from H2145) to *be male:*— burn incense, earnestly, be male, mention, make mention, make mention of, be mindful, recount, record, recorder, remember, make to be remembered, bring to remembrance, call to remembrance, come to remembrance, keep in remembrance, put in remembrance, still, think on, well.

H2143 זֵכֶר *zēker* or

זֶכֶר *zeker* from H2142; a *momento,* abstractly *recollection* (rarely if ever); by implication *commemoration:*— memorial, memory, remembrance, scent.

H2144 זֶכֶר *zeker* the same as H2143; *Zeker,* an Israelite:— Zeker.

H2145 זָכָר *zākār* from H2142; properly *remembered,* i.e. a *male* (of man or animals, as being the most noteworthy sex):— him, male, man, man child, mankind.

H2146 זִכָּרוֹן *zikārôn* from H2142; a *momento* (or memorable thing, day or writing):— memorial, record.

H2147 זִכְרִי *zikrî* from H2142; *memorable; Zicri,* the name of twelve Israelites:— Zichri.

H2148 זְכַרְיָה *zĕkaryâ* or

זְכַרְיָהוּ *zĕkaryāhû* from H2142 and H3050; *Jah has remembered; Zecarjah,* the name of twenty-nine Israelites:— Zachariah, Zechariah.

H2149 זֻלּוּת *zullût* from H2151; properly a *shaking,* i.e. perhaps a *tempest:*— vilest.

H2150 זַלְזַל *zalzal* by reduplication from H2151; *tremulous,* i.e. a *twig:*— sprig.

H2151 זָלַל *zālal* a primitive root [compare H2107]; to *shake* (as in the wind), i.e. to *quake;* figuratively to *be loose* morally, *worthless* or *prodigal:*— blow down, glutton, riotous, riotous eater, vile.

H2152 זַלְעָפָה *zalᶜāpâ* or

זִלְעָפָה *zilᶜāpâ* from H2196; a *glow* (of wind or anger); also a *famine* (as *consuming*):— horrible, horror, terrible.

H2153 זִלְפָּה *zilpâ* from an unused root apparently meaning to *trickle,* as myrrh; fragrant *dropping; Zilpah,* Leah's maid:— Zilpah.

H2154 זִמָּה *zimmâ* or

זַמָּה *zammâ* from H2161; a *plan,* especially a bad one:— heinous crime, lewd, lewdly, lewdness, mischief, purpose, thought, wicked device, wicked mind, wickedness.

H2155 זִמָּה *zimmâ* the same as H2154; *Zimmah,* the name of two Israelites:— Zimmah.

H2156 זְמוֹרָה *zĕmôrâ* or

זְמֹרָה *zĕmōrâ* (feminine) and

זְמֹר *zĕmōr* masculine from H2168; a *twig* (as *pruned*):— vine, branch, slip.

H2157 זַמְזֹם *zamzōm* from H2161; *intriguing;* a *Zamzumite,* or native tribe of Palestine:— Zamzummim.

H2158 זָמִיר *zāmîr* or

זָמִר *zāmīr* and (feminine)

זְמִרָה *zĕmīrâ* from H2167; a *song* to be accompanied with instrumental music:— psalm, psalmist, singing, song.

H2159 זָמִיר *zāmîr* from H2168; a *twig* (as *pruned*) :— branch.

H2160 זְמִירָה *zĕmîrâ* feminine of H2158; *song: Zemirah,* an Israelite:— Zemira.

H2161 זָמַם *zāmam* a primitive root; to *plan,* usually in a bad sense:— consider, devise, imagine, plot, purpose, think, think evil.

H2162 זָמָם *zāmām* from H2161; a *plot:*— wicked device.

H2163 זָמַן *zāman* a primitive root; to *fix* (a time) :— appoint.

H2164 זְמַן *zĕman* (Aramaic) corresponding to H2163; to *agree* (on a time and place):— prepare.

H2165 זְמָן *zĕmān* from H2163; an *appointed* occasion:— season, time.

H2166 זְמָן *zĕmān* (Aramaic) from H2165; the same as H2165:— season, time.

H2167 זָמַר *zāmar* a primitive root [perhaps identical with H2168 through the idea of *striking* with the fingers]; properly to *touch* the strings or parts of a musical instrument, i.e. *play* upon it; to make *music,* accompanied by the voice; hence to *celebrate* in song and music:— give praise, sing forth praises, psalms.

H2168 זָמַר *zāmar* a primitive root [compare H2167, H5568, H6785]; to *trim* (a vine):— prune.

H2169 זֶמֶר *zemer* apparently from H2167 or H2168; a *gazelle* (from its lightly *touching* the ground):— chamois.

H2170 זְמָר *zĕmār* (Aramaic) from a root corresponding to H2167; instrumental *music:*— music.

H2171 זַמָּר *zommār* (Aramaic) from the same as H2170; an instrumental *musician:*— singer.

H2172 זִמְרָה *zimrâ* from H2167; a *musical* piece or *song* to be accompanied by an instrument:— melody, psalm.

H2173 זִמְרָה *zimrâ* from H2168; *pruned* (i.e. *choice*) fruit:— best fruit.

H2174 זִמְרִי *zimrî* from H2167; *musical; Zimri,* the name of five Israelites, and of an Arabian tribe:— Zimri.

H2175 זִמְרָן *zimrān* from H2167; *musical; Zimran,* a son of Abraham by Keturah:— Zimran.

H2176 זִמְרָת *zimrāt* from H2167; instrumental *music;* by implication*praise:*— song.

H2177 זַן *zan* from H2109; properly *nourished* (or fully *developed*), i.e. a *form* or *sort:*— divers kinds, all manner of store.

H2178 זַן *zan* (Aramaic) corresponding to H2177; *sort:*— kind.

H2179 זָנַב *zānab* a primitive root meaning to *wag;* used only as a denominative from H2180; to *curtail,* i.e. *cut* off the rear:— smite the hindmost.

H2180 זָנָב *zānāb* from H2179 (in the original sense of *flapping*); the *tail* (literally or figuratively):— tail.

H2181 זָנָה *zānâ* a primitive root [highly *fed* and therefore *wanton];* to *commit adultery* (usually of the female, and less often of simple fornication, rarely of involuntary ravishment); figuratively to *commit idolatry* (the Jewish people being regarded as the spouse of Jehovah):— commit fornication, cause to commit fornication, continually, great, harlot, be an harlot, play the harlot, whore, cause to be a whore, play the whore, whoredom, commit whoredom, fall to whoredom, go a-whoring, cause to go a-whoring, whorish.

H2182 זָנוֹחַ *zānôaḥ* from H2186; *rejected; Zanoach,* the name of two places in Palestine:— Zanoah.

H2183 זָנוּן *zānûn* from H2181; *adultery;* figuratively *idolatry:*— whoredom.

H2184 זְנוּת *zĕnût* from H2181; *adultery,* i.e. (figuratively) *infidelity, idolatry:*— whoredom.

H2185 זֹנוֹת *zōnôt* regarded by some as if from H2109 or an unused root, and applied to military *equipments;* but evidently the feminine plural active participle of H2181; *harlots:*— armour.

H2186 זָנַח *zānaḥ* a primitive root; to *push* aside, i.e. *reject, forsake, fail:*— cast away, cast off, remove far away, remove far off.

H2187 זָנַק *zānaq* a primitive root; properly to *draw together* the feet (as an animal about to dart upon its prey), i.e. to *spring* forward:— leap.

H2188 זֵעָה *zēʿâ* from H2111 (in the sense of H3154); *perspiration:*— sweat.

H2189 זַעֲוָה *zaʿăwâ* by transposition for H2113; *agitation, maltreatment:*— removed, trouble.

H2190 זַעֲוָן *zāʿăwān* from H2111; *disquiet; Zaavan,* an Idumaean:— Zaavan.

H2191 זְעֵיר *zĕʿēr* from an unused root [akin (by permutation) to H6819], meaning to *dwindle; small* :— little.

H2192 זְעֵיר *zĕʿêr* (Aramaic) corresponding to H2191 :— *little.*

H2193 זָעַךְ *zāʿak* a primitive root; to *extinguish:*— be extinct.

H2194 זָעַם *zāʿam* a primitive root; properly to *foam* at the mouth, i.e. to *be enraged:*— abhor, abominable, angry, be angry, defy, indignation, have indignation.

H2195 זַעַם *zaʿam* from H2194; strictly *froth* at the mouth, i.e. (figuratively) *fury* (especially of God's displeasure with sin):— angry, indignation, rage.

H2196 זָעַף *zāʿap* a primitive root; properly to *boil* up, i.e. (figuratively) to *be peevish* or *angry:*— fret, sad, worse liking, be wroth.

H2197 זַעַף *zaʿap* from H2196; *anger:*— indignation, rage, raging, wrath.

H2198 זָעֵף *zāʿēp* from H2196; *angry:*— displeased.

H2199 זָעַק *zāʿaq* a privitive root; to *shriek* (from anguish or danger); by analogy (as a herald) to *announce* or *convene* publicly:— assemble, call (together), (make a) cry (out), come with such a company, gather (together), cause to be proclaim.

H2200 זְעִק *zĕʿīq* (Aramaic) corresponding to H2199; to *make an outcry:*— cry.

H2201 זַעַק *zaʿaq* and (feminine)

זְעָקָה *zĕʿāqâ* from H2199; a *shriek* or *outcry:*— cry, crying.

H2202 זִפְרֹן *ziprōn* from an unused root (meaning to *be fragrant*); *Ziphron,* a place in Palestine:— Ziphron.

H2203 זֶפֶת *zepet* from an unused root (meaning to *liquify*); *asphalt* (from its tendency to *soften* in the sun):— pitch.

H2204 זָקֵן *zāqēn* a primitive root; to *be old:*— aged man, old, be old, wax old, old man.

H2205 זָקֵן *zāqēn* from H2204; *old:*— aged, ancient, ancient man, elder, eldest, old, old man, old men and . . . women), senator.

H2206 זָקָן *zāqān* from H2204; the *beard* (as indicating *age*):— beard.

H2207 זֹקֶן *zōqen* from H2204; old *age:*— age.

H2208 זָקֻן *zāqūn* properly passive participle of H2204 (used only in the plural as a noun); *old* age:— old age.

H2209 זִקְנָה *ziqnâ* feminine of H2205; old *age:*— old (age).

H2210 זָקַף *zāqap* a primitive root; to *lift,* i.e. (figuratively) *comfort:*— raise, raise up.

H2211 זְקַף *zĕqap* (Aramaic) corresponding to H2210; to *hang,* i.e. *impale:*— set up.

H2212 זָקַק *zāqaq* a primitive root; to *strain,* (figuratively) *extract, clarify:*— fine, pour down, purge, purify, refine.

H2213 זֵר *zēr* from H2237 (in the sense of *scattering*); a *chaplet* (as *spread* around the top), i.e. (specifically) a border *moulding:*— crown.

H2214 זָרָא *zārāʾ* from H2114 (in the sense of *estrangement*) [compare H2219]; *disgust:*— loathsome.

H2215 זָרַב *zārab* a primitive root; to *flow* away:— wax warm.

H2216 זְרֻבָּבֶל *zĕrubbābel* from H2215 and H894; *descended of* (i.e. from) *Babylon,* i.e. born there; *Zerubbabel,* an Israelite:— Zerubbabel.

H2217 זְרֻבָּבֶל *zĕrubbābel* (Aramaic) corresponding to H2216:— Zerubbabel.

H2218 זֶרֶד *zered* from an unused root meaning to *be exuberant* in growth; lined with *shrubbery; Zered,* a brook east of the Dead Sea:— Zared, Zered.

H2219 זָרָה *zārâ* a primitive root [compare H2114]; to *toss* about; by implication to *diffuse, winnow:*— cast away, compass, disperse, fan, scatter, scatter away, spread, strew, winnow.

H2220 זְרוֹעַ *zĕrôaʿ* or (shortened)

זְרֹעַ *zĕrōaʿ* and (feminine)

זְרוֹעָה *zĕrôʿâ* or

זְרֹעָה *zĕrōʿâ* from H2232; the *arm* (as *stretched* out), or (of animals) the *foreleg;* figuratively *force:*— arm, help, mighty, power, shoulder, strength.

H2221 זֵרוּעַ *zērûaʿ* from H2232; something *sown,* i.e. a *plant:*— sowing, thing that is sown.

H2222 זַרְזִיף *zarzîp* by reduplication from an unused root meaning to *flow;* a *pouring rain:*— water.

H2223 זַרְזִיר *zarzîr* by reduplication from H2115; properly tightly *girt,* i.e. probably a *racer,* or some fleet animal (as being *slender* in the waist):— greyhound.

H2224 זָרַח *zāraḥ* a primitive root; properly to *irradiate* (or shoot forth beams), i.e. to *rise* (as the sun); specifically to *appear* (as a symptom of leprosy):— raise, rise, rise up, as soon as it is up.

H2225 זֶרַח *zeraḥ* from H2224; a *rising* of light:— rising.

H2226 זֶרַח *zeraḥ* the same as H2225; *Zerach,* the name of three Israelites, also of an Idumaean and an Ethiopian prince:— Zarah, Zerah.

H2227 זַרְחִי *zarḥî* patronymic from H2226; a *Zarchite* or descendant of Zerach:— Zarchite.

H2228 זְרַחְיָה *zĕraḥyâ* from H2225 and H3050; *Jah has risen; Zerachjah,* the name of two Israelites:— Zerahiah.

H2229 זָרַם *zāram* a primitive root; to *gush* (as water) :— carry away as with a flood, pour out.

H2230 זֶרֶם *zerem* from H2229; a *gush* of water:— flood, overflowing, shower, storm, tempest.

H2231 זִרְמָה *zirmâ* feminine of H2230; a *gushing* of fluid (semen):— issue.

H2232 זָרַע *zāra*ᶜ a primitive root; to *sow;* figuratively to *disseminate, plant, fructify:*— bear, conceive seed, set with, sow, sower, yield.

H2233 זֶרַע *zera*ᶜ from H2232; *seed;* figuratively *fruit, plant, sowing-time, posterity:*— carnally, child, fruitful, seed, seedtime, sowing-time.

H2234 זְרַע *zĕra*ᶜ (Aramaic) corresponding to H2233; *posterity:*— seed.

H2235 זֵרֹעַ *zērōa*ᶜ or

זֵרְעֹן *zērᶜōn* from H2232; something *sown* (only in the plural), i.e. a *vegetable* (as food):— pulse.

H2236 זָרַק *zāraq* a primitive root; to *sprinkle* (fluid or solid particles):— be here and there, scatter, sprinkle, strew.

H2237 זָרַר *zārar* a primitive root [compare H2114]; perhaps to *diffuse,* i.e. (specifically) to *sneeze:*— sneeze.

H2238 זֶרֶשׁ *zereš* of Persian origin; *Zeresh,* Haman's wife:— Zeresh.

H2239 זֶרֶת *zeret* from H2219; the *spread* of the fingers, i.e. a *span:*— span.

H2240 זַתּוּא *zottû*ᵓ of uncertain derivation; *Zattu,* an Israelite:— Zattu.

H2241 זֵתָם *zētām* apparently a variation for H2133; *Zetham,* an Israelite:— Zetham.

H2242 זֵתַר *zētar* of Persian origin; *Zethar,* a eunuch of Xerxes:— Zethar.

ח

H2243 חֹב *ḥōb* by contraction from H2245; properly a *cherisher,* i.e. the *bosom:*— bosom.

H2244 חָבָא *ḥābā*ᵓ a primitive root [compare H2245]; to *secrete:*— held, hide, hide self, do secretly.

H2245 חָבַב *ḥābab* a primitive root [compare H2244, H2247]; properly to *hide* (as in the bosom), i.e. to *cherish* (with affection):— love.

H2246 חֹבָב *ḥōbāb* from H2245; *cherished; Chobab,* father-in-law of Moses:— Hobab.

H2247 חָבָה *ḥābâ* a primitive root [compare H2245]; to *secrete:*— hide, hide self.

H2248 חֲבוּלָה *ḥăbûlâ* (Aramaic) from H2255; properly *overthrown,* i.e. (morally) *crime:*— hurt.

H2249 חָבוֹר *ḥābôr* from H2266; *united; Chabor,* a river of Assyria:— Habor.

H2250 חַבּוּרָה *ḥabbûrâ* or

חַבֻּרָה *ḥabbūrâ* or

חֲבֻרָה *ḥăbūrâ* from H2266; properly *bound* (with stripes), i.e. a *weal* (or black-and-blue mark itself):— blueness, bruise, hurt, stripe, wound.

H2251 חָבַט *ḥābaṭ* a primitive root; to *knock* out or off:— beat, beat off, beat out, thresh.

H2252 חֲבַיָּה *ḥăbayyâ* or

חֲבָיָה *ḥăbāyâ* from H2247 and H3050; *Jah has hidden; Chabajah,* an Israelite:— Habaiah.

H2253 חֶבְיוֹן *ḥebyôn* from H2247; a *concealment* :— hiding.

H2254 חָבַל *ḥābal* a primitive root; to *wind* tightly (as a rope), i.e. to *bind;* specifically by a *pledge;* figuratively to *pervert, destroy;* also to *writhe* in pain (especially of parturition):— at all, band, bring forth, corrupt, deal corruptly, destroy, offend, lay to pledge, take a pledge, spoil, travail, very, withhold.

H2255 חֲבַל *ḥăbal* (Aramaic) corresponding to H2254; to *ruin:*— destroy, hurt.

H2256 חֶבֶל *ḥebel* or

חֵבֶל *ḥēbel* from H2254; a *rope* (as *twisted*), especially a measuring *line;* by implication a *district* or *inheritance* (as *measured*); or a *noose* (as of *cords*); figuratively a *company* (as if *tied* together); also a *throe* (especially of parturition); also *ruin:*— band, coast, company, cord, country, destruction, line, lot, pain, pang, portion, region, rope, snare, sorrow, tackling.

H2257 חֲבַל *ḥăbal* (Aramaic) from H2255; *harm* (personal or pecuniary):— damage, hurt.

H2258 חֲבֹל *ḥăbōl* or (feminine)

חֲבֹלָה *ḥăbōlâ* from H2254; a *pawn* (as security for debt):— pledge.

H2259 חֹבֵל *ḥōbēl* active participle from H2254 (in the sense of handling *ropes*); a *sailor:*— pilot, shipmaster.

H2260 חִבֵּל *ḥibbēl* from H2254 (in the sense of furnished with *ropes*); a *mast:*— mast.

H2261 חֲבַצֶּלֶת *ḥăbaṣṣelet* of uncertain derivation; probably *meadow-saffron:*— rose.

H2262 חֲבַצַּנְיָה *ḥăbaṣṣanyâ* of uncertain derivation; *Chabatstsanjah,* a Rechabite:— Habazaniah.

H2263 חָבַק *ḥābaq* a primitive root; to *clasp* (the hands or in embrace):— embrace, fold.

H2264 חִבֻּק *ḥibbūq* from H2263; a *clasping* of the hands (in idleness):— fold.

H2265 חֲבַקּוּק *ḥăbaqqûq* by reduplication from H2263; *embrace; Chabakkuk,* the prophet:— Habakkuk.

H2266 חָבַר *ḥābar* a primitive root; to *join* (literally or figuratively); specifically (by means of spells) to *fascinate:*— charm, charmer, be compact, couple, couple together, have fellowship with, heap up, join, join self, join together, join self together, league.

H2267 חֶבֶר *ḥeber* from H2266; a *society;* also a *spell:*— charmer, charminging, company, enchantment, wide.

H2268 חֶבֶר *ḥeber* the same as H2267; *community; Cheber,* the name of a Kenite and of three Israelites:— Heber.

H2269 חֲבַר *ḥăbar* (Aramaic) from a root corresponding to H2266; an *associate:*— companion, fellow.

H2270 חָבֵר *ḥābēr* from H2266; an *associate:*— companion, fellow, knit together.

H2271 חַבָּר *ḥabbār* from H2266; a *partner:*— companion.

H2272 חֲבַרְבֻּרָה *ḥăbarbūrâ* by reduplication from H2266; a *streak* (like a *line*), as on the tiger:— spot.

H2273 חַבְרָה *ḥabrâ* (Aramaic) feminine of H2269; an *associate:*—other.

H2274 חֶבְרָה *ḥebrâ* feminine of H2267; *association* :—company.

H2275 חֶבְרוֹן *ḥebrôn* from H2267; seat of *association; Chebron,* a place in Palestine, also the name of two Israelites:—Hebron.

H2276 חֶבְרוֹנִי *ḥebrônî* or

חֶבְרֹנִי *ḥebrōnî* patronymic from H2275; *Chebronite* (collectively), an inhabitant of Chebron:—Hebronites.

H2277 חֶבְרִי *ḥebrî* patronymic from H2268; a *Chebrite* (collectively) or descendant of Cheber:—Heberites.

H2278 חֲבֶרֶת *ḥăberet* feminine of H2270; a *consort:*—companion.

H2279 חֹבֶרֶת *ḥōberet* feminine active participle of H2266; a *joint:*—which coupleth, coupling.

H2280 חָבַשׁ *ḥābaš* a primitive root; to *wrap* firmly (especially a turban, compress, or *saddle*); figuratively to *stop,* to *rule:*—bind, bind up, gird about, govern, healer, put, saddle, wrap about.

H2281 חָבֵת *ḥābēt* from an unused root probably meaning to *cook* [compare H4227]; something *fried,* probably a griddle-*cake:*—pan.

H2282 חַג *ḥag* or

חָג *ḥāg* from H2287; a *festival,* or a *victim* therefor:—feast, feast day, solemn feast, sacrifice, solemnity.

H2283 חָגָּא *ḥāgā*ᵓ from an unused root meaning to *revolve* [compare H2287]; properly *vertigo,* i.e. (figuratively) *fear:*—terror.

H2284 חָגָב *ḥāgāb* of uncertain derivation; a *locust* :—locust.

H2285 חָגָב *ḥāgāb* the same as H2284; *locust; Chagab,* one of the Nethinim:— Hagab.

H2286 חֲגָבָא *ḥăgābā*ᵓ or

חֲגָבָה *ḥăgābâ* feminine of H2285; *locust; Chagaba* or *Chagabah,* one of the Nethinim:— Hagaba, Hagabah.

H2287 חָגַג *ḥāgag* a primitive root [compare H2283, H2328; properly to move in a *circle,* i.e. (specifically) to *march* in a sacred procession, to *observe* a festival; by implication to *be giddy:*— celebrate, dance, keep a feast, hold a feast, keep a solemn feast, keep holyday, reel to and fro.

H2288 חֲגָו *ḥăgāw* from an unused root meaning to take *refuge;* a *rift* in rocks:— cleft.

H2289 חָגוֹר *ḥāgôr* from H2296; *belted:*— girded with.

H2290 חֲגוֹר *ḥăgôr* or

חֲגֹר *ḥăgōr* and (feminine)

חֲגוֹרָה *ḥăgôrâ* or

חֲגֹרָה *ḥăgōrâ* from H2296; a *belt* (for the waist):— apron, armour, gird, girdle.

H2291 חַגִּי *ḥaggî* from H2287; *festive; Chaggi,* an Israelite; also (patronymically) a *Chaggite,* or descendant of the same:— Haggi, Haggites.

H2292 חַגַּי *ḥaggay* from H2282; *festive; Chaggai,* a Hebrew prophet:— Haggai.

H2293 חַגִּיָּה *ḥaggîyâ* from H2282 and H3050; *festival of Jah; Chaggijah,* an Israelite:— Haggiah.

H2294 חַגִּית *ḥaggît* feminine of H2291; *festive; Chaggith,* a wife of David:— Haggith.

H2295 חָגְלָה *ḥoglâ* of uncertain derivation; probably a *partridge; Choglah,* an Israelitess:— Hoglah. See also H1031

H2296 חָגַר *ḥāgar* a primitive root; to *gird* on (as a belt, armor, etc.):— be able to put on, be afraid, appointed, gird, restrain, on every side.

H2297 חַד *ḥad* abridged from H259; *one:*— one.

H2298 חַד *ḥad* (Aramaic) corresponding to H2297; as cardinal *one;* as article *single;* as ordinal *first;* adverbially *at once:*— a, first, one, together.

H2299 חַד *ḥad* from H2300; *sharp:*— sharp.

H2300 חָדַד *ḥādad* a primitive root; to *be* (causatively *make*) *sharp* or (figuratively) *severe:*— be fierce, sharpen.

H2301 חֲדַד *ḥădad* from H2300; *fierce; Chadad,* an Ishmaelite:— Hadad.

H2302 חָדָה *ḥādâ* a primitive root; to *rejoice:*— make glad, be joined, rejoice.

H2303 חַדּוּד *ḥaddûd* from H2300; a *point:*— sharp.

H2304 חֶדְוָה *ḥedwâ* from H2302; *rejoicing:*— gladness, joy.

H2305 חֶדְוָה *ḥedwâ* (Aramaic) corresponding to H2304:— *joy.*

H2306 חֲדִי *ḥădî* (Aramaic) corresponding to H2373; a *breast:*— breast.

H2307 חָדִיד *ḥādîd* from H2300; a *peak; Chadid,* a place in Palestine:— Hadid.

H2308 חָדַל *ḥādal* a primitive root; properly to *be flabby,* i.e. (by implication) *desist;* (figuratively) *be lacking* or *idle:*— cease, end, fail, forbear, forsake, leave, leave off, let alone, rest, be unoccupied, want.

H2309 חֶדֶל *ḥedel* from H2308; *rest,* i.e. the state of the *dead:*— world.

H2310 חָדֵל *ḥādēl* from H2308; *vacant,* i.e. *ceasing* or *destitute:*— he that forbeareth, frail, rejected.

H2311 חַדְלָי *ḥadlay* from H2309; *idle; Chadlai,* an Israelite:— Hadlai.

H2312 חֵדֶק *ḥēdeq* from an unused root meaning to *sting;* a *prickly* plant:— brier, thorn.

H2313 חִדֶּקֶל *ḥiddeqel* probably of foreign origin; the *Chiddekel* (or Tigris) river:— Hiddekel.

H2314 חָדַר *ḥādar* a primitive root; properly to *inclose* (as a room), i.e. (by analogy) to *beset* (as in a siege):— enter a privy chamber.

H2315 חֶדֶר *ḥeder* from H2314; an *apartment* (usually literally):— chamber, bed chamber, inner chamber, innermost part, inward part, parlour, south, within.

H2316 חֲדַר *ḥădar* another form for H2315; *chamber; Chadar,* an Ishmaelite:— Hadar.

H2317 חַדְרָךְ *ḥadrāk* of uncertain derivation; *Chadrak,* a Syrian deity:— Hadrach.

H2318 חָדַשׁ *ḥādaš* a primitive root; to *be new;* causatively to *rebuild:*— renew, repair.

H2319 חָדָשׁ *ḥādāš* from H2318; *new:*— fresh, new thing.

H2320 חֹדֶשׁ *ḥōdeš* from H2318; the *new* moon; by implication a *month:*— month, monthly, new moon.

H2321 חֹדֶשׁ *ḥōdeš* the same as H2320; *Chodesh,* an Israelitess:— Hodesh.

H2322 חֲדָשָׁה *ḥădāšâ* feminine of H2319; *new; Chadashah,* a place in Palestine:— Hadashah.

H2323 חֲדַת *ḥădāt* (Aramaic) corresponding to H2319; *new:*— new.

H2324 חֲוָא *ḥăwāʾ* (Aramaic) corresponding to H2331; to *show:*— shew.

H2325 חוּב *ḥûb* also

חָיַב *ḥāyab* a primitive root; properly perhaps to *tie,* i.e. (figuratively and reflexively) to *owe,* or (by implication) to *forfeit:*— make endanger.

H2326 חוֹב *ḥôb* from H2325; *debt:*— debtor.

H2327 חוֹבָה *ḥôbâ* feminine active participle of H2247; *hiding* place; *Chobah,* a place in Syria:— Hobah.

H2328 חוּג *ḥûg* a primitive root [compare H2287]; to describe a *circle:*— compass.

H2329 חוּג *ḥûg* from H2328; a *circle:*— circle, circuit, compass.

H2330 חוּד *ḥûd* a primitive root; properly to *tie* a knot, i.e. (figuratively) to *propound* a riddle:— put forth.

H2331 חָוָה *ḥāwâ* a primitive root; [compare H2324, H2421]; properly to *live;* by implication (intensively) to *declare* or *show:*— show.

H2332 חַוָּה *ḥawwâ* causative from H2331; *life-giver; Chavvah* (or Eve), the first woman:— Eve.

H2333 חַוָּה *ḥawwâ* properly the same as H2332 *(life-giving,* i.e. *living-place);* by implication an encampment or *village:*— town, small town.

H2334 חַוּוֹת יָאִיר *ḥawwôt yāʾîr* from the plural of H2333 and a modification of H3265; *hamlets of Jair,* a region of Palestine:— Havoth-jair, Bashan-Havoth-jair.

H2335 חוֹזַי *ḥôzay* from H2374; *visionary; Chozai,* an Israelite:— the seers.

H2336 חוֹחַ *ḥôaḥ* from an unused root apparently meaning to *pierce;* a *thorn;* by analogy a *ring* for the nose:— bramble, thistle, thorn.

H2337 חָוָח *ḥāwāḥ* perhaps the same as H2336; a *dell* or *crevice* (as if *pierced* in the earth):— thicket.

H2338 חוּט *ḥûṭ* (Aramaic) corresponding to the root of H2339, perhaps as a denominative; to *string* together, i.e. (figuratively) to *repair:*— join.

H2339 חוּט *ḥûṭ* from an unused root probably meaning to *sew;* a *string;* by implication a measuring *tape:*— cord, fillet, line, thread.

H2340 חִוִּי *ḥiwwî* perhaps from H2333; a *villager;* a *Chivvite,* one of the aboriginal tribes of Palestine:— Hivite.

H2341 חֲוִילָה *ḥawîlâ* probably from H2342; *circular; Chavilah,* the name of two or three eastern regions; also perhaps of two men:— Havilah.

H2342 חוּל *ḥûl* or

חִיל *ḥîl* a primitive root; properly to *twist* or *whirl* (in a circular or spiral manner), i.e. (specifically) to *dance,* to *writhe* in pain (especially of parturition) or fear; figuratively to *wait,* to *pervert:*— bear, bring forth, make to bring forth, calve, make to calve, dance, drive away, fall grievously, fall with pain, fear, form, great, grieve, grievous, be grievous, hope, look, make, be in pain, be much pained, be sore pained, rest, shake, shapen, sorrow, be sorrowful, stay, tarry, travail, travail with pain, tremble, trust, wait carefully, wait patiently, be wounded.

H2343 חוּל *ḥûl* from H2342; a *circle; Chul,* a son of Aram; also the region settled by him:— Hul.

H2344 חוֹל *ḥôl* from H2342; *sand* (as *round* or whirling particles):— sand.

H2345 חוּם *ḥûm* from an unused root meaning to *be warm;* (by implication) *sunburnt* or *swarthy* (blackish):— brown.

H2346 חוֹמָה *ḥômâ* feminine active participle of an unused root apparently meaning to *join;* a *wall* of protection:— wall, walled.

HEB

H2347 חוּס *ḥûs* a primitive root; properly to *cover,* i.e. (figuratively) to be *compassionate:*— pity, regard, spare.

H2348 חוֹף *ḥôp* from an unused root meaning to *cover;* a *cove* (as a *sheltered* bay):— coast of the sea, haven, shore, sea side.

H2349 חוּפָם *ḥûpām* from the same as H2348; *protection; Chupham,* an Israelite:— Hupham.

H2350 חוּפָמִי *ḥûpāmî* patronymic from H2349; a *Chuphamite* or descendant of Chupham:— Huphamites.

H2351 חוּץ *ḥûṣ* or (shortened)

חֻץ *ḥuṣ* (both forms feminine in the plural); from an unused root meaning to *sever;* properly *separate* by a wall, i.e. *outside, outdoors:*— abroad, field, forth, highway, more, out, outside, outward, street, without.

H2352 חוּר *ḥûr* or (shortened)

חֻר *ḥur* from an unused root probably meaning to *bore;* the *crevice* of a serpent; the *cell* of a prison:— hole.

H2353 חוּר *ḥûr* from H2357; *white* linen:— white.

H2354 חוּר *ḥûr* the same as H2353 or H2352; *Chur,* the name of four Israelites and one Midianite:— Hur.

H2355 חוֹר *ḥôr* the same as H2353; *white* linen:— network. Compare H2715

H2356 חוֹר *ḥôr* or (shortened)

חֹר *ḥōr* the same as H2352; a *cavity, socket, den:*— cave, hole.

H2357 חָוַר *ḥāwar* a primitive root; to *blanch* (as with shame):— wax pale.

H2358 חִוָּר *ḥiwwār* (Aramaic) from a root corresponding to H2357; *white:*— white.

H2359 חוּרִי *ḥûrî* probably from H2353; *linen-worker: Churi,* an Israelite:— Huri.

H2360 חוּרַי *ḥûray* probably an orthographical variation for H2359; *Churai,* an Israelite:— Hurai.

H2361 חוּרָם *ḥûrām* probably from H2353; *whiteness,* i.e. noble; *Churam,* the name of an Israelite and two Syrians:— Huram. Compare H2438

H2362 חַוְרָן *ḥawrān* apparently from H2357 (in the sense of H2352); *cavernous; Chavran,* a region east of the Jordan:— Hauran.

H2363 חוּשׁ *ḥûš* a primitive root; to *hurry;* figuratively to *be eager* with excitement or enjoyment:— haste, make haste, hasten, ready.

H2364 חוּשָׁה *ḥûšâ* from H2363; *haste; Chushah*, an Israelite:— Hushah.

H2365 חוּשַׁי *ḥûšay* from H2363; *hasty; Chushai*, an Israelite:— Hushai.

H2366 חוּשִׁים *ḥûšîm* or

חֻשִׁים *ḥušîm* or

חֻשִׁם *ḥušim* plural from H2363; *hasters; Chushim*, the name of three Israelites:— Hushim.

H2367 חוּשָׁם *ḥûšām* or

חֻשָׁם *ḥušām* from H2363; *hastily; Chusham*, an Idumaean:— Husham.

H2368 חוֹתָם *ḥôtām* or

חֹתָם *ḥōtām* from H2856; a *signature*-ring:— seal, signet.

H2369 חוֹתָם *ḥôtām* the same as H2368; *seal; Chotham*, the name of two Israelites:— Hotham, Hothan.

H2370 חֲזָא *ḥăzāʾ* or

חֲזָה *ḥăzâ* (Aramaic) corresponding to H2372; to *gaze* upon; mentally to *dream, be usual* (i.e. *seem*):— behold, have a dream, see, be wont.

H2371 חֲזָאֵל *ḥăzāʾēl* or

חֲזָהאֵל *ḥăzāhʾēl* from H2372 and H410; *God has seen; Chazaël*, a king of Syria:— Hazael.

H2372 חָזָה *ḥāzâ* a primitive root; to *gaze* at; mentally to *perceive, contemplate* (with pleasure); specifically to *have a vision of*:— behold, look, prophesy, provide, see.

H2373 חָזֶה *ḥāzeh* from H2372; the *breast* (as most *seen* in front):— breast.

H2374 חֹזֶה *ḥōzeh* active participle of H2372; a *beholder* in vision; also a *compact* (as *looked upon* with approval):— agreement, prophet, see that, seer, stargazer.

H2375 חֲזוֹ *ḥăzô* from H2372; *seer; Chazo*, a nephew of Abraham:— Hazo.

H2376 חֵזֵו *ḥēzēw* (Aramaic) from H2370; a *sight* :— look, vision.

H2377 חָזוֹן *ḥāzôn* from H2372; a *sight* (mentally), i.e. a *dream, revelation*, or *oracle*:— vision.

H2378 חָזוֹת *ḥāzôt* from H2372; a *revelation*:— vision.

H2379 חֲזוֹת *ḥăzôt* (Aramaic) from H2370; a *view* :— sight.

H2380 חָזוּת *ḥāzût* from H2372; a *look;* hence (figuratively) striking *appearance, revelation*, or (by implication) *compact*:— agreement, notable, notable one, vision.

H2381 חֲזִיאֵל *ḥăzîʾēl* from H2372 and H410; *seen of God; Chaziel*, a Levite:— Haziel.

H2382 חֲזָיָה *ḥăzāyâ* from H2372 and H3050; *Jah has seen; Chazajah*, an Israelite:— Hazaiah.

H2383 חֶזְיוֹן *ḥezyôn* from H2372; *vision; Chezjon*, a Syrian:— Hezion.

H2384 חִזָּיוֹן *ḥizzāyôn* from H2372; a *revelation*, especially by *dream*:— vision.

H2385 חֲזִיז *ḥăzîz* from an unused root meaning to *glare;* a *flash* of lightning:— bright cloud, lightning.

H2386 חֲזִיר *ḥăzîr* from an unused root probably meaning to *enclose;* a *hog* (perhaps as *penned*):— boar, swine.

H2387 חֵזִיר *ḥēzîr* from the same as H2386; perhaps *protected; Chezir*, the name of two Israelites:— Hezir.

H2388 חָזַק *ḥāzaq* a primitive root; to *fasten* upon; hence to *seize, be strong* (figuratively *courageous*, causatively *strengthen, cure, help, repair, fortify*), *obstinate;* to *bind, restrain, conquer*:— aid, amend, calker, catch, cleave, confirm, be constant, constrain, continue, be of good courage, take courage, be courageous, courageously, encourage, encourage self, be established, fasten, force, fortify, make hard, harden, help, hold, lay hold, hold fast, lean, maintain, play the man, mend, become mighty, wax mighty, prevail, be recovered, repair, retain, seize, be sore, wax sore, strengthen, strengthen self, be stout, be strong, make strong, shew self strong, wax strong, be stronger, be sure, take, take hold, be urgent, behave self valiantly, withstand.

H2389 חָזָק *ḥāzāq* from H2388; *strong* (usually in a bad sense, *hard, bold, violent*):— harder, hottest, impudent, loud, mighty, sore, stiffhearted, strong, stronger.

H2390 חָזֵק *ḥāzēq* from H2388; *powerful*:— wax louder, stronger.

H2391 חֵזֶק *ḥēzeq* from H2388; *help*:— strength.

H2392 חֹזֶק *ḥōzeq* from H2388; *power*:— strength.

H2393 חֶזְקָה *ḥezqâ* feminine of H2391; prevailing *power*:— strength, strengthen self, strong, was strong.

H2394 חׇזְקָה *ḥozqâ* feminine of H2392; *vehemence* (usually in a bad sense):— force, mightily, repair, sharply.

H2395 חִזְקִי *ḥizqî* from H2388; *strong; Chizki*, an Israelite:— Hezeki.

H2396 חִזְקִיָּה *ḥizqîyâ* or

חִזְקִיָּהוּ *ḥizqîyāhû* also

יְחִזְקִיָּה *yĕḥizqîyâ* or

יְחִזְקִיָּהוּ *yĕḥizqîyāhû* from H2388 and H3050; *strengthened of Jah; Chizkijah*, a king of Judah, also the name of two other Israelites:— Hezekiah, Hizkiah, Hizkijah. Compare H3169

H2397 חָח *ḥāh* once (Ezek. 29:4)

חָחִי *ḥāḥî* from the same as H2336; a *ring* for the nose (or lips):— bracelet, chain, hook.

H2398 חָטָא *ḥāṭāʾ* a primitive root; properly to *miss;* hence (figuratively and generally) to *sin;* by inference to *forfeit, lack, expiate, repent*, (causatively) *lead astray, condemn*:— bear the blame, cleanse, commit sin, by fault, harm he hath done, loss, miss, offend, make an offender, offer for sin, purge, purify, purify self, make reconciliation, sin, cause to sin, make to sin, sinful, sinner, trespass.

H2399 חֵטְא *ḥēṭĕʾ* from H2398; a *crime* or its *penalty*:— fault, grievously, offence, sin, punishment of sin.

H2400 חַטָּא *ḥaṭṭāʾ* intensive from H2398; a *criminal*, or one accounted *guilty*:— offender, sinful, sinner.

H2401 חֲטָאָה *ḥăṭāʾâ* feminine of H2399; an *offence*, or a *sacrifice* for it:— sin, sin offering.

H2402 חַטָּאָה *ḥaṭṭāʾâ* (Aramaic) corresponding to H2401; an *offence*, and the *penalty* or *sacrifice* for it:— sin (offering).

H2403 חַטָּאָה *ḥaṭṭāʾâ* or

חַטָּאת *ḥaṭṭāʾt* from H2398; an *offence* (sometimes habitual *sinfulness*), and its penalty, occasion, sacrifice, or expiation; also (concretely) an *offender*:— punishment, punnishment of sin, purifying, purification for sin, sin, sinner, offering.

H2404 חָטַב *ḥāṭab* a primitive root; to *chop* or *carve* wood:— cut down, hew, hewer, polish.

H2405 חֲטֻבָה *ḥăṭūbâ* feminine passive participle of H2404; properly a *carving;* hence a *tapestry* (as figured):— carved.

H2406 חִטָּה *ḥiṭṭâ* of uncertain derivation; *wheat*, whether the grain or the plant:— wheat, wheaten.

H2407 חַטּוּשׁ *ḥaṭṭûš* from an unused root of uncertain signification; *Chattush*, the name of four or five Israelites:— Hattush.

H2408 חֲטִי *ḥăṭāy* (Aramaic) from a root corresponding to H2398; an *offence*:— sin.

H2409 חַטָּיָא *ḥaṭṭāyāʾ* (Aramaic) from the same as H2408; an *expiation*:— sin offering.

H2410 חֲטִיטָא *ḥăṭîṭāʾ* from an unused root apparently meaning to *dig* out; *explorer; Chatita*, a temple porter:— Hatita.

H2411 חַטִּיל *ḥaṭṭîl* from an unused root apparently meaning to *wave; fluctuating; Chattil*, one of "Solomon's servants":— Hattil.

H2412 חֲטִיפָא *ḥaṭîpāʾ* from H2414; *robber; Chatipha*, one of the Nethinim:— Hatipha.

H2413 חָטַם *ḥāṭam* a primitive root; to *stop*:— refrain.

H2414 חָטַף *ḥāṭap* a primitive root; to *clutch;* hence to *seize* as a prisoner:— catch.

H2415 חֹטֶר *ḥōṭer* from an unused root of uncertain signification; a *twig*:— rod.

H2416 חַי *ḥay* from H2421; *alive;* hence *raw* (flesh); *fresh* (plant, water, year), *strong;* also (as noun, especially in the feminine singular and masculine plural) *life* (or living thing), whether literally or figuratively:— age, alive, appetite, beast, wild beast, company, congregation, life, lifetime, live, lively, living, living creature, living thing, maintenance, merry, multitude, be old, old, quick, raw, running, springing, troop.

H2417 חַי *ḥay* (Aramaic) from H2418; *alive;* also (as noun in plural) *life*:— life, that liveth, living.

H2418 חֲיָא *ḥăyāʾ* or

חֲיָה *ḥăyâ* (Aramaic) corresponding to H2421; to *live*:— live, keep alive.

H2419 חִיאֵל *ḥîʾēl* from H2416 and H410; *living of God; Chiel*, an Israelite:— Hiel.

H2420 חִידָה *ḥîdâ* from H2330; a *puzzle;* hence a *trick, conundrum*, sententious *maxim*:— dark saying, dark sentence, dark speech, hard question, proverb, riddle.

H2421 חָיָה *ḥāyâ* a primitive root [compare H2331, H2421]; to *live*, whether literally or figuratively; causatively to *revive*:— keep alive, leave alive, make alive, certainly, give life, promise life, let live, suffer to live, nourish up, preserve, preserve alive, quicken, recover, repair, restore, restore to life, revive, save, save alive, save life, save lives, God save, surely, be whole.

H2422 חָיֶה *ḥāyeh* from H2421; *vigorous*:— lively.

H2423 חֵיוָא *ḥêwāʾ* (Aramaic) from H2418; an *animal*:— beast.

H2424 חַיּוּת *ḥayyût* from H2421; *life*:— living.

H2425 חָיַי *ḥāyay* a primitive root [compare H2421] to *live;* causatively to *revive*:— live, save life.

H2426 חֵיל *ḥêl* or (shortened)

חֵל *ḥēl* a collateral form of H2428; an *army;* also (by analogy) an *intrenchment*:— army, bulwark, host, poor, rampart, trench, wall.

H2427 חִיל *ḥîl* and (feminine)

חִילָה *ḥîlâ* from H2342; a *throe* (especially of childbirth):— pain, pang, sorrow.

H2428 חַיִל *ḥayil* from H2342; probably a *force,* whether of men, means or other resources; an *army, wealth, virtue, valor, strength:*— able, activity, army, army, band of men, band of soldiers, company, forces, great forces, goods, host, might, power, riches, strength, strong, substance, train, valiant, valiant, valiantly, valour, virtuous, virtuously, war, worthy, worthily.

H2429 חַיִל *ḥayil* (Aramaic) corresponding to H2428; an *army,* or *strength:*— aloud, army, most mighty, power.

H2430 חֵילָה *ḥêlâ* feminine of H2428; an *intrenchment:*— bulwark.

H2431 חֵילָם *ḥêlām* or

חֵלָאם *ḥēlāʾm* from H2428; *fortress; Chelam,* a place east of Palestine:— Helam.

H2432 חִיֵן *ḥîēn* from H2428; *fortress; Chilen,* a place in Palestine:— Hilen.

H2433 חִין *ḥîn* another form for H2580; *beauty:*— comely.

H2434 חַיִץ *ḥayiṣ* another form for H2351; a *wall* :— wall.

H2435 חִיצוֹן *ḥîṣôn* from H2434; properly the (outer) *wall side;* hence *exterior;* figuratively *secular* (as opposed to sacred):— outer, outward, utter, without.

H2436 חֵיק *ḥêq* or

חֵק *ḥēq* and

חוֹק *ḥôq* from an unused root, apparently meaning to *enclose;* the *bosom* (literally or figuratively):— bosom, bottom, lap, midst, within.

H2437 חִירָה *ḥîrâ* from H2357 in the sense of *splendor; Chirah,* an Adulammite:— Hirah.

H2438 חִירָם *ḥîrām* or

חִירוֹם *ḥîrōm* another form of H2361; *Chiram* or *Chirom,* the name of two Tyrians:— Hiram, Huram.

H2439 חִישׁ *ḥîš* another form for H2363; to *hurry* :— make haste.

H2440 חִישׁ *ḥîš* from H2439; properly a *hurry;* hence (adverb) *quickly:*— soon.

H2441 חֵךְ *ḥēk* probably from H2596 in the sense of *tasting;* properly the *palate* or inside of the mouth; hence the *mouth* itself (as the organ of speech, taste and kissing):— mouth, roof of the mouth, taste.

H2442 חָכָה *ḥākâ* a primitive root [apparently akin to H2707 through the idea of *piercing*]; properly to *adhere* to; hence to await:— long, tarry, wait.

H2443 חַכָּה *ḥakkâ* probably from H2442; a *hook* (as *adhering*):— angle, hook.

H2444 חֲכִילָה *ḥăkîlâ* from the same as H2447; *dark; Chakilah,* a hill in Palestine:— Hachilah.

H2445 חַכִּים *ḥakkîm* (Aramaic) from a root corresponding to H2449; *wise,* i.e. a *Magian:*— wise.

H2446 חֲכַלְיָה *ḥăkalyâ* from the base of H2447 and H3050; *darkness of Jah; Chakaljah,* an Israelite:— Hachaliah.

H2447 חַכְלִיל *ḥaklîl* by reduplication from an unused root apparently meaning to *be dark;* darkly *flashing* (only of the eyes); in a good sense, *brilliant* (as stimulated by wine):— red.

H2448 חַכְלִלוּת *ḥaklîlût* from H2447; *flash* (of the eyes); in a bad sense, *bleariness:*— redness.

H2449 חָכַם *ḥākam* a primitive root, to *be wise* (in mind, word or act):— exceeding, teach wisdom, be wise, make self wise, shew self wise, deal wisely, never so wisely, make wiser.

H2450 חָכָם *ḥākām* from H2449; *wise,* (i.e. intelligent, skilful or artful):— cunning, cunning man, subtil, wise, wise hearted, wise man, unwise.

H2451 חָכְמָה *ḥokmâ* from H2449; *wisdom* (in a good sense):— skilful, wisdom, wisely, wit.

H2452 חָכְמָה *ḥokmâ* (Aramaic) corresponding to H2451; *wisdom:*— wisdom.

H2453 חַכְמוֹנִי *ḥakmônî* from H2449; *skilful; Chakmoni,* an Israelite:— Hachmoni, Hachmonite.

H2454 חָכְמוֹת *ḥokmôt* or

חַכְמוֹת *ḥakmôt* collateral forms of H2451; *wisdom:*— wisdom, every wise woman.

H2455 חֹל *ḥōl* from H2490; properly *exposed;* hence *profane:*— common, profane, profane place, unholy.

H2456 חָלָא *ḥālāʾ* a primitive root [compare H2470]; to *be sick:*— be diseased.

H2457 חֶלְאָה *helʾâ* from H2456; properly *disease;* hence *rust:*— scum.

H2458 חֶלְאָה *helʾâ* the same as H2457; *Chelah,* an Israelitess:— Helah.

H2459 חֶלֶב *ḥeleb* or

חֵלֶב *ḥēleb* from an unused root meaning to *be fat; fat,* whether literally or figuratively; hence the *richest* or *choice* part:— best, fat, fatness, finest, grease, marrow.

H2460 חֵלֶב *ḥēleb* the same as H2459; *fatness; Cheleb,* an Israelite:— Heleb.

H2461 חָלָב *ḥālāb* from the same as H2459; *milk* (as the *richness* of kine):— cheese, milk, sucking.

H2462 חֶלְבָּה *ḥelbâ* feminine of H2459; *fertility; Chelbah,* a place in Palestine:— Helbah.

H2463 חֶלְבּוֹן *ḥelbôn* from H2459; *fruitful; Chelbon,* a place in Syria:— Helbon.

H2464 חֶלְבְּנָה *ḥelbĕnâ* from H2459; *galbanam,* an odorous gum (as if *fatty*):— galbanum.

H2465 חֶלֶד *ḥeled* from an unused root apparently meaning to *glide* swiftly; *life* (as a *fleeting* portion of time); hence the *world* (as *transient*):— age, short time, world.

H2466 חֵלֶד *ḥēled* the same as H2465; *Cheled,* an Israelite:— Heled.

H2467 חֹלֶד *ḥōled* from the same as H2465; a *weasel* (from its *gliding* motion):— weasel.

H2468 חֻלְדָּה *ḥuldâ* feminine of H2467; *Chuldah,* an Israelitess:— Huldah.

H2469 חֶלְדַּי *ḥelday* from H2466; *worldliness; Cheldai,* the name of two Israelites:— Heldai.

H2470 חָלָה *ḥālâ* a primitive root [compare H2342, H2470, H2490]; properly to *be rubbed* or *worn;* hence (figuratively) to *be weak, sick, afflicted;* or (causatively) to *grieve, make sick;* also to *stroke* (in flattering), *entreat:*— beseech, diseased, be diseased, grief, put to grief, be grieved, grievous, be grievous, infirmity, intreat, lay to, put to pain, pray, make prayer, be sick, fall sick, make sick, sore, be sorry, make suit, make supplication, woman in travail, be weak, become weak, be wounded.

H2471 חַלָּה *ḥallâ* from H2490; a *cake* (as usually *punctured*):— cake.

H2472 חֲלוֹם *ḥălôm* or (shortened)

חֲלֹם *ḥălōm* from H2492; a *dream:*— dream, dreamer.

H2473 חֹלוּן *ḥōlûn* or (shortened)

חֹלֹן *ḥōlōn* probably from H2344; *sandy; Cholon,* the name of two places in Palestine:— Holon.

H2474 חַלּוֹן *ḥallôn*; a *window* (as *perforated*):— window.

H2475 חֲלוֹף *ḥălôp* from H2498; properly *surviving;* by implication (collectively) *orphans:*— destruction.

H2476 חֲלוּשָׁה *ḥălûšâ* feminine passive participle of H2522; *defeat:*— being overcome.

H2477 חֲלַח *ḥălaḥ* probably of foreign origin; *Chalach,* a region of Assyria:— Halah.

H2478 חַלְחוּל *ḥalḥûl* by reduplication from H2342; *contorted; Chalchul,* a place in Palestine:— Halhul.

H2479 חַלְחָלָה *ḥalḥālâ* feminine from the same as H2478; *writhing* (in childbirth); by implication *terror:*— pain, great pain, much pain.

H2480 חָלַט *ḥālaṭ* a primitive root; to *snatch* at:— catch.

H2481 חֲלִי *ḥălî* from H2470; a *trinket* (as *polished*) :— jewel, ornament.

H2482 חֲלִי *ḥălî* the same as H2481; *Chali,* a place in Palestine:— Hali.

H2483 חֳלִי *ḥŏlî* from H2470; *malady, anxiety, calamity:*— disease, grief, is sick, sickness.

H2484 חֶלְיָה *ḥelyâ* feminine of H2481; a *trinket:*— jewel.

H2485 חָלִיל *ḥālîl* from H2490; a *flute* (as *perforated*):— pipe.

H2486 חָלִילָה *ḥālîlâ* or

חָלִלָה *ḥālîlâ* a directive from H2490; literally *for a profaned* thing; used (interjectionally) *far be it!:*— be far, forbid, God forbid.

H2487 חֲלִיפָה *ḥălîpâ* from H2498; *alternation:*— change, course.

H2488 חֲלִיצָה *ḥălîṣâ* from H2503; *spoil:*— armour.

H2489 חֵלְכָא *ḥēlĕkāʾ* or

חֵלְכָה *ḥēlĕkâ* apparently from an unused root probably meaning to *be dark* or (figuratively) *unhappy;* a *wretch,* i.e. unfortunate:— poor.

H2490 חָלַל *ḥālal* a primitive root [compare H2470]; properly to *bore,* i.e. (by implication) to *wound,* to *dissolve;* figuratively to *profane* (a person, place or thing), to *break* (one's word), to *begin* (as if by an "opening wedge"); denominatively (from H2485) to *play* (the flute):— begin, men began, defile, break, defile, eat, eat as common things, first, gather the grape thereof, take inheritance, pipe, player on instruments, pollute, profane, cast as profane, profane self, prostitute, slay, slain, sorrow, stain, wound.

H2491 חָלָל *ḥālāl* from H2490; *pierced* (especially to death); figuratively *polluted:*— kill, profane, slain, slain man, slew, wounded, deadly wounded.

H2492 חָלַם *ḥālam* a primitive root; properly to *bind* firmly, i.e. (by implication) to *be* (causatively to *make*) *plump;* also (through the figurative sense of *dumbness*) to *dream:*— dream, cause to dream, dreamer, be in good liking, recover.

HEB

H2493 חֵלֶם *ḥēlem* (Aramaic) from a root corresponding to H2492; a *dream:*— dream.

H2494 חֵלֶם *ḥēlem* from H2492; a *dream; Chelem,* an Israelite:— Helem. Compare H2469

H2495 חַלָּמוּת *ḥallāmût* from H2492 (in the sense of *insipidity*); probably *purslain:*— egg.

H2496 חַלָּמִישׁ *ḥallāmîš* probably from H2492 (in the sense of *hardness*); *flint:*— flint, flinty, rock.

H2497 חֵלֹן *ḥēlōn* from H2428; *strong; Chelon,* an Israelite:— Helon.

H2498 חָלַף *ḥālap* a primitive root; properly to *slide* by, i.e. (by implication) to *hasten* away, *pass* on, *spring* up, *pierce* or *change:*— abolish, alter, change, cut off, go on forward, grow up, be over, pass, pass away, pass on, pass through, renew, sprout, strike through.

H2499 חֲלַף *ḥălāp* (Aramaic) corresponding to H2498; to *pass* on (of time):— passive.

H2500 חֵלֶף *ḥēlep* from H2498; properly *exchange;* hence (as preposition) *instead of:*— for.

H2501 חֶלֶף *ḥelep* the same as H2500; *change; Cheleph,* a place in Palestine:— Heleph.

H2502 חָלַץ *ḥālaṣ* a primitive root; to *pull* off; hence (intensively) to *strip,* (reflexively) to *depart;* by implication to *deliver, equip* (for fight); *present, strengthen:*— arm, arm self, armed, go armed, ready armed, armed man, armed soldier, deliver, draw out, make fat, loose, prepared, ready prepared, put off, take away, withdraw self.

H2503 חֶלֶץ *ḥeleṣ* or

חֵלֶץ *ḥēleṣ* from H2502; perhaps *strength; Chelets,* the name of two Israelites:— Helez.

H2504 חָלָץ *ḥālāṣ* from H2502 (in the sense of *strength*); only in the dual; the *loins* (as the seat of vigor):— loins, reins.

H2505 חָלַק *ḥālaq* a primitive root; to *be smooth* (figuratively); by implication (as smooth stones were used for *lots*) to *apportion* or *separate:*— deal, distribute, divide, flatter, give, part, have part, impart, partner, take away a portion, receive, separate self, smooth, be smooth, be smoother.

H2506 חֵלֶק *ḥēleq* from H2505; properly *smoothness* (of the tongue); also an *allotment:*— flattery, inheritance, part, partake, portion.

H2507 חֵלֶק *ḥēleq* the same as H2506; *portion; Chelek,* an Israelite:— Helek.

H2508 חֲלָק *ḥălāq* (Aramaic) from a root corresponding to H2505; a *part:*— portion.

H2509 חָלָק *ḥālāq* from H2505; *smooth* (especially of tongue):— flattering, smooth.

H2510 חָלָק *ḥālāq* the same as H2509; *bare; Chalak,* a mountain of Idumaea:— Halak.

H2511 חַלָּק *ḥallāq* from H2505; *smooth:*— smooth.

H2512 חַלֻּק *ḥallūq* from H2505; *smooth:*— smooth.

H2513 חֶלְקָה *ḥelqâ* feminine of H2506; properly *smoothness;* figuratively *flattery;* also an *allotment* :— field, flattering, flattery, ground, parcel, part, piece of land, piece of ground, plat, portion, slippery place, smooth, smooth thing.

H2514 חֲלַקָּה *ḥălaqqâ* feminine from H2505; *flattery:*— flattery.

H2515 חֲלֻקָּה *ḥăluqqâ* feminine of H2512; a *distribution:*— division.

H2516 חֶלְקִי *ḥelqî* patronymic from H2507; a *Chelkite* or descendant of Chelek:— Helkites.

H2517 חֶלְקַי *ḥelqay* from H2505; *apportioned; Chelkai,* an Israelite:— Helkai.

H2518 חִלְקִיָּה *ḥilqîyâ* or

חִלְקִיָּהוּ *ḥilqîyāhû* from H2506 and H3050; *portion of Jah; Chilhijah,* the name of eight Israelites:— Hilkiah.

H2519 חֲלַקְלַקָּה *ḥălaqlaqqâ* by reduplication from H2505; properly something *very smooth;* i.e. a *treacherous* spot; figuratively *blandishment:*— flattery, slippery.

H2520 חֶלְקַת *ḥelqat* a form of H2513; *smoothness; Chelkath,* a place in Palestine:— Helkath.

H2521 חֶלְקַת הַצֻּרִים *ḥelqat haṣṣūrîm* from H2520 and the plural of H6697, with the article inserted; *smoothness of the rocks; Chelkath Hats-tsurim,* a place in Palestine:— Helkath-hazzurim.

H2522 חָלַשׁ *ḥālaš* a primitive root; to *prostrate;* by implication to *overthrow, decay:*— discomfit, waste away, weaken.

H2523 חַלָּשׁ *ḥallāš* from H2522; *frail:*— weak.

H2524 חָם *ḥām* from the same as H2346; a *father-in-law* (as in *affinity*):— father in law.

H2525 חָם *ḥām* from H2552; *hot:*— hot, warm.

H2526 חָם *ḥām* the same as H2525; *hot* (from the tropical habitat); *Cham,* a son of Noah; also (as a patronymic) his descendants or their country:— Ham.

H2527 חֹם *ḥōm* from H2552; *heat:*— heat, to be hot, to be warm.

H2528 חֱמָא *ḥĕmāʾ* or

חֲמָה *ḥămâ* (Aramaic) corresponding to H2534; *anger:*— fury.

H2529 חֶמְאָה *ḥemʾâ* or (shortened)

חֵמָה *ḥēmâ* from the same root as H2346; curdled *milk* or *cheese:*— butter.

H2530 חָמַד *ḥāmad* a primitive root; to *delight* in :— beauty, greatly beloved, covet, delectable thing, delight, great delight, desire, goodly, lust, pleasant, be pleasant, pleasant thing, precious, precious thing.

H2531 חֶמֶד *ḥemed* from H2530; *delight:*— desirable, pleasant.

H2532 חֶמְדָּה *ḥemdâ* feminine of H2531; *delight:*— desire, goodly, pleasant, precious.

H2533 חֶמְדָּן *ḥemdān* from H2531; *pleasant; Chemdan,* an Idumaean:— Hemdan.

H2534 חֵמָה *ḥēmâ* or (Dan. 11:44)

חֵמָא *ḥēmāʾ* from H3179; *heat;* figuratively *anger, poison* (from its *fever*):— anger, bottles, hot displeasure, furious, furiously, fury, heat, indignation, poison, rage, wrath, wrathful. See H2529

H2535 חַמָּה *ḥammâ* from H2525; *heat;* by implication the *sun:*— heat, sun.

H2536 חַמּוּאֵל *ḥammûʾēl* from H2535 and H410; *anger of God; Chammuel,* an Israelite:— Hamuel.

H2537 חֲמוּטַל *ḥămûṭal* or

חֲמִיטַל *ḥămîṭal* from H2524 and H2919; *father-in-law of dew; Chamutal* or *Chamital,* an Israelitess:— Hamutal.

H2538 חָמוּל *ḥāmûl* from H2550; *pitied; Chamul,* an Israelite:— Hamul.

H2539 חָמוּלִי *ḥāmûlî* patronymic from H2538; a *Chamulite* (collectively) or descendant of Chamul :— Hamulites.

H2540 חַמּוֹן *ḥammôn* from H2552; *warm* spring; *Chammon,* the name of two places in Palestine:— Hammon.

H2541 חָמוֹץ *ḥāmôṣ* from H2556; properly *violent;* by implication a *robber:*— oppressed.

H2542 חַמּוּק *ḥammûq* from H2559; a *wrapping,* i.e. *drawers:*— joints.

H2543 חֲמוֹר *ḥămôr* or (shortened)

חֲמֹר *ḥămōr* from H2560; a male *ass* (from its dun *red*):— ass, he ass.

H2544 חֲמוֹר *ḥămôr* the same as H2543; *ass; Chamor,* a Canaanite:— Hamor.

H2545 חֲמוֹת *ḥămôt* or (shortened)

חֲמֹת *ḥămōt* feminine of H2524; a *mother-in-law:*— mother in law.

H2546 חֹמֶט *ḥōmeṭ* from an unused root probably meaning to *lie low;* a *lizard* (as *creeping*):— snail.

H2547 חֻמְטָה *ḥumṭâ* feminine of H2546; *low; Chumtah,* a place in Palestine:— Humtah.

H2548 חָמִיץ *ḥāmîṣ* from H2556; *seasoned,* i.e. *salt* provender:— clean.

H2549 חֲמִישִׁי *ḥămîšî* or

חֲמִשִּׁי *ḥămiššî* ordinal from H2568; *fifth;* also a *fifth:*— fifth, fifth part.

H2550 חָמַל *ḥāmal* a primitive root; to *commiserate;* by implication to *spare:*— have compassion, pity, have pity, spare.

H2551 חֶמְלָה *ḥemlâ* from H2550; *commiseration:*— merciful, pity.

H2552 חָמַם *ḥāmam* a primitive root; to *be hot* (literally or figuratively):— enflame self, get heat, have heat, be hot, wax hot, warm, be warm, wax warm, warm self, warm at.

H2553 חַמָּן *ḥammān* from H2535; a *sun*-pillar:— idol, image.

H2554 חָמַס *ḥāmas* a primitive root; to *be violent;* by implication to *maltreat:*— make bare, shake off, violate, do violence, take away violently, wrong, imagine wrongfully.

H2555 חָמָס *ḥāmās* from H2554; *violence;* by implication *wrong;* by metonymy unjust *gain:*— cruel, cruelty, damage, false, injustice, oppressor, unrighteous, violence, violence against, violence done, violent, violent dealing, wrong.

H2556 חָמֵץ *ḥāmēṣ* a primitive root; to *be pungent;* i.e. in taste *(sour,* i.e. literally *fermented,* or figuratively *harsh*), in color *(dazzling)*:— cruel, cruel man, dyed, be grieved, leavened.

H2557 חָמֵץ *ḥāmēṣ* from H2556; *ferment,* (figuratively) *extortion:*— leaven, leavened, leavend bread.

H2558 חֹמֶץ *ḥōmeṣ* from H2556; *vinegar:*— vinegar.

H2559 חָמַק *ḥāmaq* a primitive root; properly to *enwrap;* hence to *depart* (i.e. turn about):— go about, withdraw self.

H2560 חָמַר *ḥāmar* a primitive root; properly to *boil* up; hence to *ferment* (with scum); to *glow* (with redness); as denominative (from H2564) to *smear* with pitch:— daub, befoul, be red, trouble.

H2561 חֶמֶר *ḥemer* from H2560; *wine* (as *fermenting*):— pure, red wine.

H2562 חֲמַר *ḥămar* (Aramaic) corresponding to H2561; *wine:*— wine.

H2563 חֹמֶר *ḥōmer* from H2560; properly a *bubbling* up, i.e. of water, a *wave;* of earth, *mire* or *clay* (cement); also a *heap;* hence a *chomer* or dry measure:— clay, heap, homer, mire, motion.

H2564 חֵמָר *ḥēmār* from H2560; *bitumen* (as *rising* to the surface):— slime, slimepit.

H2565 חֲמֹרָה *ḥămōrâ* from H2560 [compare H2563]; a *heap:*— heap.

H2566 חַמְרָן *ḥamrān* from H2560; *red; Chamran,* an Idumaean:— Amran.

H2567 חָמַשׁ *ḥāmaš* a denominative from H2568; to *tax a fifth:*— take up the fifth part.

H2568 חָמֵשׁ *ḥāmēš* masculine

חֲמִשָּׁה *ḥămiššâ* a primitive numeral; *five:*— fifteen, fifth, five, five apiece.

H2569 חֹמֶשׁ *ḥōmeš* from H2567; a *fifth* tax:— fifth part.

H2570 חֹמֶשׁ *ḥōmeš* from an unused root probably meaning to *be stout;* the *abdomen* (as *obese*):— fifth rib.

H2571 חָמֻשׁ *ḥāmūš* passive participle of the same as H2570; *staunch,* i.e. able-bodied *soldiers:*— armed, armed men, harnessed.

H2572 חֲמִשִּׁים *ḥămiššîm* multiple of H2568; *fifty* :— fifty.

H2573 חֵמֶת *ḥēmet* from the same as H2346; a skin *bottle* (as *tied* up):— bottle.

H2574 חֲמָת *ḥămāt* from the same as H2346; *walled; Chamath,* a place in Syria:— Hamath, Hemath.

H2575 חַמַּת *ḥammat* a variation for the first part of H2576; *hot* springs; *Chammath,* a place in Palestine:— Hammath.

H2576 חַמֹּת דֹּאר *ḥammōt dōʾr* from the plural of H2535 and H1756; *hot springs of Dor; Chammath-Dor,* a place in Palestine:— Hamath-Dor.

H2577 חֲמָתִי *ḥămātî* patrial from H2574; a *Chamathite* or native of *Chamath:*— Hamathite.

H2578 חֲמַת צוֹבָה *ḥămat ṣôbâ* from H2574 and H6678; *Chamath of Tsobah; Chamath-Tsobah;* probably the same as H2574:— Hamath-Zobah.

H2579 חֲמַת רַבָּה *ḥămat rabbâ* from H2574 and H7237; *Chamath of Rabbah; Chamath-Rabbah,* probably the same as H2574.

H2580 חֵן *ḥēn* from H2603; *graciousness,* i.e. subjective *(kindness, favor)* or objective *(beauty)*:— favour, grace, gracious, pleasant, precious, wellfavoured.

H2581 חֵן *ḥēn* the same as H2580; *grace; Chen,* a figurative name for an Israelite:— Hen.

H2582 חֵנָדָד *ḥēnādād* probably from H2580 and H1908; *favor of Hadad; Chenadad,* an Israelite:— Henadad.

H2583 חָנָה *ḥānâ* a primitive root [compare H2603]; properly to *incline;* by implication to *decline* (of the slanting rays of evening); specifically to *pitch* a tent; generally to *encamp* (for abode or siege):— abide, abide in tents, camp, dwell, encamp, grow to an end, lie, pitch, pitch tent, rest in tent.

H2584 חַנָּה *ḥannâ* from H2603; *favored; Channah,* an Israelitess:— Hannah.

H2585 חֲנוֹךְ *ḥănôk* from H2596; *initiated; Chanok,* an antediluvian patriarch:— Enoch.

H2586 חָנוּן *ḥānûn* from H2603; *favored; Chanun,* the name of an Ammonite and of two Israelites:— Hanun.

H2587 חַנּוּן *ḥannûn* from H2603; *gracious:*— gracious.

H2588 חָנוּת *ḥānût* from H2583; properly a *vault* or *cell* (with an arch); by implication a *prison:*— cabin.

H2589 חַנּוֹת *hannôt* from H2603 (in the sense of *prayer*); *supplication:*— be gracious, intreated.

H2590 חָנַט *ḥānaṭ* a primitive root; to *spice;* by implication to *embalm;* also to *ripen:*— embalm, put forth.

H2591 חִנְטָה *ḥinṭâ* (Aramaic) corresponding to H2406; *wheat:*— wheat.

H2592 חַנִּיאֵל *ḥannîʾēl* from H2603 and H410; *favor of God; Channiel,* the name of two Israelites:— Hanniel.

H2593 חָנִיךְ *ḥānîk* from H2596; *initiated;* i.e. *practised:*— trained.

H2594 חֲנִינָה *ḥănînâ* from H2603; *graciousness:*— favour.

H2595 חֲנִית *ḥănît* from H2583; a *lance* (for *thrusting,* like *pitching* a tent):— javelin, spear.

H2596 חָנַךְ *ḥānak* a primitive root; properly to *narrow* [compare H2614]; figuratively to *initiate* or *discipline:*— dedicate, train up.

H2597 חֲנֻכָּא *ḥănukkāʾ* (Aramaic) corresponding to H2598; *consecration:*— dedication.

H2598 חֲנֻכָּה *ḥănukkâ* from H2596; *initiation,* i.e. *consecration:*— dedicating, dedication.

H2599 חֲנֹכִי *ḥănōkî* patronymic from H2585; a *Chanokite* (collectively) or descendant of Chanok:— Hanochites.

H2600 חִנָּם *ḥinnām* from H2580; *gratis,* i.e. devoid of cost, reason or advantage:— without a cause, without cost, without wages, causeless, to cost nothing, free, freely, innocent, for nothing, for nought, in vain.

H2601 חֲנַמְאֵל *ḥănamʾēl* probably by orthographical variation for H2606; *Chanamel,* an Israelite:— Hanameel.

H2602 חֲנָמָל *ḥănāmāl* of uncertain derivation; perhaps the *aphis* or plant-louse:— frost.

H2603 חָנַן *ḥānan* a primitive root [compare H2583]; properly to *bend* or stoop in kindness to an inferior; to *favor, bestow;* causatively to *implore* (i.e. move to favor by petition):— beseech, fair, favour, find favour, shew favour, be favourable, be gracious, deal graciously, give graciously, grant graciously, intreat, merciful, be merciful, have mercy on, have mercy upon, shew mercy, have pity upon, pray, make supplication, very.

H2604 חֲנַן *ḥănan* (Aramaic) corresponding to H2608; to *favor* or (causatively) to *entreat:*— shew mercy, make supplication.

H2605 חָנָן *ḥānān* from H2603; *favor; Chanan,* the name of seven Israelites:— Canan.

H2606 חֲנַנְאֵל *ḥănanʾēl* from H2603 and H410; *God has favored; Chananel,* probably an Israelite, from whom a tower of Jerusalem was named:— Hananeel.

H2607 חֲנָנִי *ḥănānî* from H2603; *gracious; Chanani,* the name of six Israelites:— Hanani.

H2608 חֲנַנְיָה *ḥănanyâ* or

חֲנַנְיָהוּ *ḥănanyāhû* from H2603 and H3050; *Jah has favored; Chananjah,* the name of thirteen Israelites:— Hananiah.

H2609 חָנֵס *ḥānēs* of Egyptian derivation; *Chanes,* a place in Egypt:— Hanes.

H2610 חָנֵף *ḥānēp* a primitive root; to *soil,* especially in a moral sense:— corrupt, defile, greatly, pollute, profane.

H2611 חָנֵף *ḥānēp* from H2610; *soiled* (i.e. with sin), *impious:*— hypocrite, hypocritical.

H2612 חֹנֶף *ḥōnep* from H2610; moral *filth,* i.e. *wickedness:*— hypocrisy.

H2613 חֲנֻפָּה *ḥănūpâ* feminine from H2610; *impiety:*— profaneness.

H2614 חָנַק *ḥānaq* a primitive root [compare H2596]; to *be narrow;* by implication to *throttle,* or (reflexively) to *choke* oneself to death (by a rope):— hang self, strangle.

H2615 חַנָּתֹן *ḥannātōn* probably from H2603; *favored; Channathon,* a place in Palestine:— Hannathon.

H2616 חָסַד *ḥāsad* a primitive root; properly perhaps to *bow* (the neck only [compare H2603] in courtesy to an equal), i.e. to *be kind;* also (by euphemism [compare H1288], but rarely) to *reprove:*— shew self merciful, put to shame.

H2617 חֶסֶד *ḥesed* from H2616; *kindness;* by implication (towards God) *piety;* rarely (by opposition) *reproof,* or (subjectively) *beauty:*— favour, good deed, goodliness, goodness, kindly, kindness, lovingkindness, merciful, merciful kindness, mercy, pity, reproach, wicked thing.

H2618 חֶסֶד *ḥesed* the same as H2617; *favor; Chesed,* an Israelite:— Hesed.

H2619 חֲסַדְיָה *ḥăsadyâ* from H2617 and H3050; *Jah has favored; Chasadjah,* an Israelite:— Hasadiah.

H2620 חָסָה *ḥāsâ* a primitive root; to *flee* for protection [compare H982]; figuratively to *confide* in:— have hope, make refuge, trust, put trust.

H2621 חֹסָה *ḥōsâ* from H2620; *hopeful; Chosah,* an Israelite; also a place in Palestine:— Hosah.

H2622 חָסוּת *ḥāsût* from H2620; *confidence:*— trust.

H2623 חָסִיד *ḥāsîd* from H2616; properly *kind,* i.e. (religiously) *pious* (a saint):— godly, godly man, good, holy, holy one, merciful, saint, ungodly.

H2624 חֲסִידָה *ḥăsîdâ* feminine of H2623; the *kind* (maternal) bird, i.e. a *stork:*— feather, stork.

H2625 חָסִיל *ḥāsîl* from H2628; the *ravager,* i.e. a *locust:*— caterpillar.

H2626 חֲסִין *ḥăsîn* from H2630; properly *firm,* i.e. (by implication) *mighty:*— strong.

H2627 חַסִּיר *ḥassîr* (Aramaic) from a root corresponding to H2637; *deficient:*— wanting.

H2628 חָסַל *ḥāsal* a primitive root; to *eat* off:— consume.

H2629 חָסַם *ḥāsam* a primitive root; to *muzzle;* by analogy to *stop* the nose:— muzzle, stop.

H2630 חָסַן *ḥāsan* a primitive root; properly to *(be) compact;* by implication to *hoard:*— lay up.

H2631 חֲסַן *ḥăsan* (Aramaic) corresponding to H2630; to *hold* in occupancy:— possess.

H2632 חֵסֶן *ḥēsen* (Aramaic) from H2631; *strength* :— power.

H2633 חֹסֶן *ḥōsen* from H2630; *wealth:*— riches, strength, treasure.

H2634 חָסֹן *ḥāsōn* from H2630; *powerful:*— strong.

H2635 חֲסַף *ḥăsap* (Aramaic) from a root corresponding to that of H2636; a *clod:*— clay.

H2636 חַסְפַּס *haspas* reduplicated from an unused root meaning apparently to *peel;* a *shred* or *scale:*— round thing.

H2637 חָסֵר *ḥāsēr* a primitive root; to *lack;* by implication to *fail, want, lessen:*— be abated, bereave, decrease, fail, cause to fail, lack, have lack, make lower, want.

H2638 חָסֵר *ḥāsēr* from H2637; *lacking;* hence *without:*— destitute, fail, lack, have need, void, want.

H2639 חֶסֶר *ḥeser* from H2637; *lack;* hence *destitution:*— poverty, want.

H2640 חֹסֶר *ḥōser* from H2637; *poverty:*— in want of.

H2641 חַסְרָה *ḥasrâ* from H2637; *want;* Chasrah, an Israelite:— Hasrah.

H2642 חֶסְרוֹן *ḥesrôn* from H2637; *deficiency:*— wanting.

H2643 חַף *ḥap* from H2653 (in the moral sense of *covered* from soil); *pure:*— innocent.

H2644 חָפָא *ḥāpāʾ* an orthographical variation of H2645; properly to *cover,* i.e. (in a sinister sense) to *act covertly:*— do secretly.

H2645 חָפָה *ḥāpâ* a primitive root [compare H2644, H2653]; to *cover;* by implication to *veil,* to *incase, protect:*— ceil, cover, overlay.

H2646 חֻפָּה *ḥuppâ* from H2645; a *canopy:*— chamber, closet, defence.

H2647 חֻפָּה *ḥuppâ* the same as H2646; *Chuppah,* an Israelite:— Huppah.

H2648 חָפַז *ḥāpaz* a primitive root; properly to *start* up suddenly, i.e. (by implication) to *hasten* away, to *fear:*— haste, make haste, haste away, tremble.

H2649 חִפָּזוֹן *ḥippāzôn* from H2468; *hasty flight:*— haste.

H2650 חֻפִּים *ḥuppîm* plural of H2646 [compare H2349]; *Chuppim,* an Israelite:— Huppim.

H2651 חֹפֶן *ḥōpen* from an unused root of uncertain signification; a *fist* (only in the dual):— fists, hands, both hands, handful.

H2652 חָפְנִי *ḥopnî* from H2651; perhaps *pugilist; Chophni,* an Israelite:— Hophni.

H2653 חָפַף *ḥāpap* a primitive root [compare H2645, H3182]; to *cover* (in protection):— cover.

H2654 חָפֵץ *ḥāpēṣ* a primitive root; properly to *incline* to; by implication (literally but rarely) to *bend;* figuratively to *be pleased* with, *desire:*— any at all, delight, have delight, take delight, desire, favour, like, move, be pleased, be well pleased, have pleasure, will, would.

H2655 חָפֵץ *ḥāpēṣ* from H2654; *pleased* with:— delight in, desire, favour, please, have pleasure, whosoever would, willing, wish.

H2656 חֵפֶץ *ḥēpeṣ* from H2654; *pleasure;* hence (abstractly) *desire;* concretely a *valuable* thing; hence (by extension) a *matter* (as something in mind):— acceptable, delight, delightsome, desire, things desired, matter, pleasant, pleasure, purpose, willingly.

H2657 חֶפְצִי בָהּ *ḥepṣî bāh* from H2656 with suffixes; *my delight* (is) *in her; Cheptsi-bah,* a fanciful name for Palestine:— Hephzi-bah.

H2658 חָפַר *ḥāpar* a primitive root; properly to *pry* into; by implication to *delve,* to *explore:*— dig, paw, search out, seek.

H2659 חָפֵר *ḥāpēr* a primitive root [perhaps rather the same as H2658 through the idea of *detection*]; to *blush;* figuratively to *be ashamed, disappointed;* causatively to *shame, reproach:*— be ashamed, be confounded, be brought to confusion, be brousht unto shame, come to shame, be put to shame, bring reproach.

H2660 חֵפֶר *ḥēper* from H2658 or H2659; a *pit* or *shame; Chepher,* a place in Palestine; also the name of three Israelites:— Hepher.

H2661 חֲפֹר *ḥăpōr* from H2658 only in connection with H6512, a *hole,* which ought rather to be joined as one word, thus

חֲפַרְפֵּרָה *ḥaparpērâ* by reduplication from H2658; a *burrower,* i.e. probably a *rat:*— mole.

H2662 חֶפְרִי *ḥeprî* patronymic from H2660; a *Chephrite* (collectively) or descendant of *Chepher* :— Hepherites.

H2663 חֲפָרַיִם *ḥăpārayim* dual of H2660; *double pit; Chapharajim,* a place in Palestine:— Haphraim.

H2664 חָפַשׂ *ḥāpaś* a primitive root; to *seek;* causatively to *conceal* oneself (i.e. let be sought), or *mask:*— change, diligent, make diligent search, disguise self, hide, search, search for, search out.

H2665 חֵפֶשׂ *ḥēpeś* from H2664; something *covert,* i.e. a *trick:*— search.

H2666 חָפַשׁ *ḥāpaš* a primitive root; to *spread* loose, figuratively to *manumit:*— be free.

H2667 חֹפֶשׁ *ḥōpeš* from H2666; something *spread* loosely, i.e. a *carpet:*— precious.

H2668 חֻפְשָׁה *ḥupšâ* from H2666; *liberty* (from slavery):— freedom.

H2669 חָפְשׁוּת *ḥopšût* and

חָפְשִׁית *ḥopšît* from H2666; *prostration* by sickness (with H1004, a *hospital*):— several.

H2670 חָפְשִׁי *ḥopšî* from H2666; *exempt* (from bondage, tax or care):— free, liberty.

H2671 חֵץ *ḥēṣ* from H2686; properly a *piercer,* i.e. an *arrow;* by implication a *wound;* figuratively (of God) thunder-*bolt;* (by interchange for H6086) the *shaft* of a spear:— archer, arrow, dart, shaft, staff, wound.

H2672 חָצַב *ḥāṣab* or

חָצֵב *ḥāṣēb* a primitive root; to *cut* or carve (wood, stone or other material); by implication to *hew, split, square, quarry, engrave:*— cut, dig, divide, grave, hew, hew out, hewer, make, mason.

H2673 חָצָה *ḥāṣâ* a primitive root [compare H2686]; to *cut* or *split* in two; to *halve:*— divide, live out half, reach to the midst, part.

H2674 חָצוֹר *ḥāṣôr* a collective form of H2691; *village; Chatsor,* the name (thus simply) of two places in Palestine and of one in Arabia:— Hazor.

H2675 חָצוֹר חֲדַתָּה *ḥāṣôr ḥădattâ* from H2674 and an Aramaic form of the feminine of H2319 [compare H2323]; *new Chatsor,* a place in Palestine:— Hazor, Hadattah *[as if two places].*

H2676 חֲצוֹת *ḥăṣôt* from H2673; the *middle* (of the night):— midnight.

H2677 חֵצִי *ḥēṣî* from H2673; the *half* or *middle:*— half, middle, midnight, midst, part, two parts.

H2678 חִצִּי *ḥiṣṣî* or

חֵצִי *ḥēṣî* prolonged from H2671; an *arrow* :— arrow.

H2679 חֲצִי הַמְּנֻחוֹת *ḥăṣî hammĕnūḥôt* from H2677 and the plural of H4496, with the article interposed; *midst of the resting-places; Chatsi-ham-Menuchoth,* an Israelite:— half of the Manahethites.

H2680 חֲצִי הַמְּנַחְתִּי *ḥăṣî hammĕnaḥtî* patronymic from H2679; a *Chatsi-ham-Menachtite* or descendant of Chatsi-ham-Menuchoth:— half of the Manahethites.

H2681 חָצִיר *ḥāṣîr* a collateral form of H2691; a *court* or *abode:*— court.

H2682 חָצִיר *ḥāṣîr* perhaps originally the same as H2681, from the *greenness* of a court-yard; *grass;* also a *leek* (collectively):— grass, hay, herb, leek.

H2683 חֵצֶן *ḥēṣen* from an unused root meaning to hold *firmly;* the *bosom* (as *comprised* between the arms):— bosom.

H2684 חֹצֶן *ḥōṣen* a collateral form of H2683, and meaning the same:— arm, lap.

H2685 חֲצַף *ḥăṣap* (Aramaic) a primitive root; properly to *shear* or cut close; figuratively to *be severe:*— hasty, be urgent.

H2686 חָצַץ *ḥāṣaṣ* a primitive root [compare H2678]; properly to *chop* into, pierce or sever; hence to *curtail,* to *distribute* (into ranks); as denominative from H2671, to *shoot* an arrow:— archer, bands, cut off in the midst.

H2687 חָצָץ *ḥāṣāṣ* from H2687; properly something *cutting;* hence *gravel* (as *grit*); also (like H2671) an *arrow:*— arrow, gravel, gravel stone.

H2688 חַצְצוֹן תָּמָר *ḥaṣṣôn tāmār* or

חַצֲצוֹן תָּמָר *ḥaṣăṣôn tāmār* from H2686 and H8558; *division* [i.e. perhaps *row*] *of* (the) *palm-tree; Chatsetson-tamar,* a place in Palestine:— Hazezon-tamar.

H2689 חֲצֹצְרָה *ḥăṣōṣĕrâ* by reduplication from H2690; a *trumpet* (from its *sundered* or quavering note):— trumpet, trumpeter.

H2690 חָצַר *ḥāṣar* a primitive root, properly to *surround* with a stockade, and thus *separate* from the open country; but used only in this reduplicated form:

חֲצֹצֵר *ḥăṣōṣēr* or (2 Chron. 5:12)

חֲצֹרֵר *ḥăṣōrēr* as derived from H2689; to *trumpet,* i.e. blow on that instrument:— blow, sound, trumpeter.

H2691 חָצֵר *ḥāṣēr* masculine and feminine; from H2690 in its original sense; a *yard* (as *inclosed* by a fence); also a *hamlet* (as similarly *surrounded* with walls):— court, tower, village.

H2692 חֲצַר אַדָּר *ḥăṣar ʾaddār* from H2691 and H146; (the) *village of Addar; Chatsar-Addar,* a place in Palestine:— Hazar-addar.

H2693 חֲצַר גַּדָּה *ḥăṣar gaddâ* from H2691 and a feminine of H1408; (the) *village of* (female) *Fortune; Chatsar-Gaddah,* a place in Palestine:— Hazar-gaddah.

H2694 חֲצַר הַתִּיכוֹן *ḥăṣar hattîkôn* from H2691 and H8484 with the article interposed; *village of the middle; Chatsar-hat-Tikon,* a place in Palestine:— Hazar-hatticon.

H2695 חֶצְרוֹ *ḥeṣrô* by an orthographical variation for H2696; *inclosure; Chetsro,* an Israelite:— Hezro, Hezrai.

H2696 חֶצְרוֹן *ḥeṣrôn* from H2691; *court-yard; Chetsron,* the name of a place in Palestine; also of two Israelites:— Hezron.

H2697 חֶצְרוֹנִי *ḥeṣrônî* patronymic from H2696; a *Chetsronite* or (collectively) descendants of Chetsron :— Hezronites.

H2698 חֲצֵרוֹת *ḥăṣērôt* feminine plural of H2691; *yards; Chatseroth,* a place in Palestine:— Hazeroth.

H2699 חֲצֵרִים *ḥăṣērîm* plural masculine of H2691; *yards; Chatserim,* a place in Palestine:— Hazerim.

H2700 חֲצַרְמָוֶת *ḥăṣarmāwet* from H2691 and H4194; *village of death; Chatsarmaveth,* a place in Arabia:— Hazarmaveth.

H2701 חֲצַר סוּסָה *ḥăṣar sûsâ* from H2691 and H5484; *village of cavalry; Chatsar-Susah,* a place in Palestine:— Hazar-susah.

H2702 חֲצַר סוּסִים *ḥăṣar sûsîm* from H2691 and the plur of H5483; *village of horses; Chatsar-Susim,* a place in Palestine:— Hazar-susim.

H2703 חֲצַר עֵינוֹן *ḥăṣar ʿênôn* from H2691 and a derivative of H5869; *village of springs; Chatsar-Enon,* a place in Palestine:— Hazar-enon.

H2704 חֲצַר עֵינָן *ḥăṣar ʿênān* from H2691 and the same as H5881; *village of springs; Chatsar-Enan,* a place in Palestine:— Hazar-enan.

H2705 חֲצַר שׁוּעָל *ḥăṣar šûʿāl* from H2691 and H7776; *village of* (the) *fox; Chatsar-Shual,* a place in Palestine:— Hazar-shual.

H2706 חֹק *ḥōq* from H2710; an *enactment;* hence an *appointment* (of time, space, quantity, labor or usage):— appointed, bound, commandment, convenient, custom, decree, decreed, due, law, measure, necessary, ordinance, ordinary, portion, set time, statute, task.

H2707 חָקָה *ḥāqâ* a primitive root; to *carve;* by implication to *delineate;* also to *intrench:*— carved work, portrayed, set a print.

H2708 חֻקָּה *ḥuqqâ* feminine of H2706, and meaning substantially the same:— appointed, custom, manner, ordinance, site, statute.

H2709 חֲקוּפָא *ḥăqûpāʾ* from an unused root probably meaning to *bend; crooked; Chakupha,* one of the Nethinim:— Hakupha.

H2710 חָקַק *ḥāqaq* a primitive root; properly to *hack,* i.e. *engrave* (Judg 5:14, to *be a scribe* simply); by implication to *enact* (laws being *cut* in stone or metal tablets in primitive times) or (generally) *prescribe:*— appoint, decree, governor, grave, lawgiver, note, pourtray, print, set.

H2711 חֵקֶק *ḥēqeq* from H2710; an *enactment,* a *resolution:*— decree, thought.

H2712 חֻקֹּק *ḥuqqōq* or (fully)

חוּקֹק *ḥûqōq* from H2710; *appointed; Chukkok* or *Chukok,* a place in Palestine:— Hukkok, Hukok.

H2713 חָקַר *ḥāqar* a primitive root; properly to *penetrate;* hence to *examine* intimately:— find out, search, make search, search out, seek, seek out, sound, try.

H2714 חֵקֶר *ḥēqer* from H2713; *examination, enumeration, deliberation:*— finding out, number, search, searched, search out, searching, unsearchable.

H2715 חֹר *ḥōr* or (fully)

חוֹר *ḥôr* from H2787; properly *white* or *pure* (from the *cleansing* or *shining* power of fire [compare H2751]); hence (figuratively) *noble* (in rank) :— noble.

H2716 חֶרֶא *ḥereʾ* also

חֲרִי *ḥărî* from an unused (and vulgar) root probably meaning to *evacuate* the bowels; *excrement:*— dung.

H2717 חָרַב *ḥārab* or

חָרֵב *ḥārēb* a primitive root; to *parch* (through drought), i.e. (by analogy) to *desolate, destroy, kill:*— decay, desolate, be desolate, destroy, destroyer, be dry, dry up, slay, surely, waste, lay waste, lie waste, make waste.

H2718 חֲרַב *ḥărab* (Aramaic) a root corresponding to H2717; to *demolish:*— destroy.

H2719 חֶרֶב *ḥereb* from H2717; *drought;* also a *cutting* instrument (from its *destructive* effect), as a *knife, sword,* or other sharp implement:— axe, dagger, knife, mattock, sword, tool.

H2720 חָרֵב *ḥārēb* from H2717; *parched* or *ruined* :— desolate, dry, waste.

H2721 חֹרֶב *ḥōreb* a collateral form of H2719; *drought* or *desolation:*— desolation, drought, dry, heat, utterly, waste.

H2722 חֹרֵב *ḥōrēb* from H2717; *desolate; Choreb,* a (generical) name for the Sinaitic mountains:— Horeb.

H2723 חָרְבָּה *ḥorbâ* feminine of H2721; properly *drought,* i.e. (by implication) a *desolation:*— decayed place, desolate, desolate place, desolation, destruction, waste, laid waste, waste place.

H2724 חָרָבָה *ḥārābâ* feminine of H2720; a *desert* :— dry, dry ground, dry land.

H2725 חֲרָבוֹן *ḥărābôn* from H2717; parching *heat* :— drought.

H2726 חַרְבוֹנָא *harbônāʾ* or

חַרְבוֹנָה *ḥarbônâ* of Persian origin; *Charbona* or *Charbonah,* a eunuch of Xerxes:— Harbona, Harbonah.

H2727 חָרַג *ḥārag* a primitive root; properly to *leap* suddenly, i.e. (by implication) to *be dismayed:*— be afraid.

H2728 חָרְגֹּל *ḥorgōl* from H2727; the *leaping* insect, i.e. a *locust:*— beetle.

H2729 חָרַד *ḥārad* a primitive root; to *shudder* with terror; hence to *fear;* also to *hasten* (with anxiety):— be afraid, make afraid, be careful, discomfit, fray, fray away, quake, tremble.

H2730 חָרֵד *ḥārēd* from H2729; *fearful;* also *reverential:*— afraid, trembling.

H2731 חֲרָדָה *ḥărādâ* feminine of H2730; *fear, anxiety:*— care, exceedingly, fear, quaking, trembling.

H2732 חֲרָדָה *ḥărādâ* the same as H2731; *Charadah,* a place in the Desert:— Haradah.

H2733 חֲרֹדִי *ḥărōdî* patrial from a derivative of H2729 [compare H5878]; a *Charodite,* or inhabitant of *Charod:*— Harodite.

H2734 חָרָה *ḥārâ* a primitive root [compare H2787]; to *glow* or grow warm; figuratively (usually) to *blaze* up, of anger, zeal, jealousy:— be angry, burn, be displeased, earnestly, fret self, grieve, be hot, wax hot, be incensed, kindle, very, be wroth. See H8474

H2735 חֹר הַגִּדְגָּד *ḥōr haggidgād* from H2356 and a collateral (masculine) form of H1412, with the article interposed; *hole of the cleft; Chor-hag-Gidgad,* a place in the Desert:— Hor-hagidgad.

H2736 חַרְהֲיָה *ḥarhăyâ* from H2734 and H3050; *fearing Jah; Charhajah,* an Israelite:— Harhaiah.

H2737 חָרוּז *ḥārûz* from an unused root meaning to *perforate;* properly *pierced,* i.e. a *bead* of pearl, gems or jewels (as strung):— chain.

H2738 חָרוּל *ḥārûl* or (shortened)

חָרֻל *ḥārūl* apparently passive participle of an unused root probably meaning to *be prickly;* properly *pointed,* i.e. a *bramble* or other thorny weed:— nettle.

H2739 חֲרוּמַף *ḥărûmap* from passive participle of H2763 and H639; *snubnosed; Charumaph,* an Israelite:— Harumaph.

H2740 חָרוֹן *ḥārôn* or (shortened)

חָרֹן *ḥārōn* from H2734; a *burning* of anger :— sore displeasure, fierce, fierceness, fury, wrath, fierce wrath, wrathful.

H2741 חֲרוּפִי *ḥărûpî* a patrial from (probably) a collateral form of H2756; a *Charuphite* or inhabitant of Charuph (or Chariph):— Haruphite.

H2742 חָרוּץ *ḥārûṣ* or

חָרֻץ *ḥārūṣ* passive participle of H2782; properly *incised* or (actively) *incisive;* hence (as noun masculine or feminine) a *trench* (as dug), *gold* (as mined), a *threshing-sledge* (having sharp teeth); (figuratively) *determination;* also *eager:*— decision, diligent, gold, fine gold, pointed things, sharp, threshing instrument, wall.

H2743 חָרוּץ *ḥārûṣ* the same as H2742; *earnest; Charuts,* an Israelite:— Haruz.

H2744 חַרְחוּר *ḥarḥûr* a fuller form of H2746; *inflammation; Charchur,* one of the Nethinim:— Harhur.

H2745 חַרְחַס *ḥarḥas* from the same as H2775; perhaps *shining; Charchas,* an Israelite:— Harhas.

H2746 חַרְחֻר *ḥarḥūr* from H2787; *fever* (as *hot*):— extreme burning.

H2747 חֶרֶט *ḥereṭ* from a primitive root meaning to *engrave;* a *chisel* or *graver;* also a *style* for writing:— graving tool, pen.

H2748 חַרְטֹם *ḥarṭōm* from the same as H2747; a *horoscopist* (as *drawing* magical lines or circles):— magician.

H2749 חַרְטֹם *ḥarṭōm* (Aramaic) the same as H2748 :— magician.

H2750 חֳרִי *ḥŏrî* from H2734; a *burning* (i.e. intense) anger:— fierce, great, heat.

H2751 חֹרִי *ḥōrî* from the same as H2353; *white* bread:— white.

H2752 חֹרִי *ḥōrî* from H2356; *cavedweller* or troglodyte; a *Chorite* or aboriginal Idumaean:— Horims, Horites.

H2753 חֹרִי *ḥōrî* or

חוֹרִי *ḥôrî* the same as H2752; *Chori,* the name of two men:— Hori.

H2754 חָרִיט *ḥārîṭ* from the same as H2747; properly *cut* out (or *hollow*), i.e. (by implication) a *pocket:*— bag, crisping pin.

H2755 חֲרֵי־יוֹנִים *ḥărê-yônîm* from the plural of H2716 and the plural of H3123; or perhaps rather the plural of a single word

חֲרָאיוֹן *ḥărāʾyôn* of similar or uncertain derivation; *excrements of doves,* probably a kind of vegetable:— doves' dung.

HEB

H2756 חָרִיף *ḥārîp* from H2778; *autumnal; Chariph,* the name of two Israelites:— Hariph.

H2757 חָרִיץ *ḥārîṣ* or

חָרִץ *ḥāriṣ* from H2872; properly *incisure* or (passive) *incised* [compare H2742]; hence a *threshing-sledge* (with *sharp* teeth): also a *slice* (as cut):— cheese, harrow.

H2758 חָרִישׁ *ḥārîš* from H2790; *ploughing* or its season:— earing, earing time, ground.

H2759 חֲרִישִׁי *ḥărîšî* from H2790 in the sense of *silence; quiet,* i.e. *sultry* (as noun feminine the *sirocco* or hot east wind):— vehement.

H2760 חָרַךְ *ḥārak* a primitive root; to *braid* (i.e. to *entangle* or snare) or *catch* (game) in a net:— roast.

H2761 חֲרַךְ *ḥărak* (Aramaic) a root probably allied to the equivalent of H2787; to *scorch:*— singe.

H2762 חֶרֶךְ *ḥerek* from H2760; properly a *net,* i.e. (by analogy) *lattice:*— lattice.

H2763 חָרַם *ḥāram* a primitive root; to *seclude;* specifically (by a ban) to *devote* to religious uses (especially destruction); physically and reflexively to be *blunt* as to the nose:— make accursed, consecrate, destroy, utterly destroy, devote, forfeit, have a flat nose, utterly, utterly slay, utterly make away.

H2764 חֵרֶם *ḥērem* or (Zech. 14:11)

חֶרֶם *ḥerem* from H2763; physically (as *shutting in*) a *net* (either literally or figuratively); usually a *doomed* object; abstractly *extermination:*— curse, cursed thing, accursed, accursed thing, dedicated thing, things which should have been utterly destroyed, utter destruction, appointed to utter destruction, devoted, devoted thing, net.

H2765 חֳרֵם *ḥŏrēm* from H2763; *devoted; Chorem,* a place in Palestine:— Horem.

H2766 חָרִם *ḥārim* from H2763; *snub-nosed; Charim,* an Israelite:— Harim.

H2767 חָרְמָה *ḥormâ* from H2763; *devoted; Chormah,* a place in Palestine:— Hormah.

H2768 חֶרְמוֹן *ḥermôn* from H2763; *abrupt; Chermon,* a mount of Palestine:— Hermon.

H2769 חֶרְמוֹנִים *ḥermônîm* plural of H2768; *Hermons,* i.e. its peaks:— the Hermonites.

H2770 חֶרְמֵשׁ *ḥermēš* from H2763; a *sickle* (as *cutting*):— sickle.

H2771 חָרָן *ḥārān* from H2787; *parched; Charan,* the name of a man and also of a place:— Haran.

H2772 חֹרֹנִי *ḥōrōnî* patrial from H2773; a *Choronite* or inhabitant of Choronaim:— Horonite.

H2773 חֹרֹנַיִם *ḥōrōnayim* dual of a derivative from H2356; *double cave-town; Choronajim,* a place in Moab:— Horonaim.

H2774 חַרְנֶפֶר *ḥarneper* of uncertain derivation; *Charnepher,* an Israelite:— Harnepher.

H2775 חֶרֶס *ḥeres* or (with a directive enclitic)

חַרְסָה *ḥarsâ* from an unused root meaning to *scrape;* the *itch;* also [perhaps from the mediating idea of H2777] the *sun:*— itch, sun.

H2776 חֶרֶס *ḥeres* the same as H2775; *shining; Cheres,* a mountain in Palestine:— Heres.

H2777 חַרְסוּת *ḥarsût* from H2775 (apparently in the sense of a red *tile* used for scraping); a *potsherd,* i.e. (by implication) a *pottery;* the name of a gate at Jerusalem:— east.

H2778 חָרַף *ḥārap* a primitive root; to *pull* off, i.e. (by implication) to *expose* (as by *stripping*); specifically to *betroth* (as if a surrender); figuratively to carp at, i.e. *defame;* denominatively (from H2779) to spend the *winter:*— betroth, blaspheme, defy, jeopard, rail, reproach, upbraid.

H2779 חֹרֶף *ḥōrep* from H2778; properly the *crop* gathered, i.e. (by implication) the *autumn* (and winter) season; figuratively *ripeness* of age:— cold, winter, winterhouse, youth.

H2780 חָרֵף *ḥārēp* from H2778; *reproachful; Chareph,* an Israelite:— Hareph.

H2781 חֶרְפָּה *ḥerpâ* from H2778; *contumely, disgrace,* the *pudenda:*— rebuke, reproach, reproachfully, shame.

H2782 חָרַץ *ḥāraṣ* a primitive root; properly to *point* sharply, i.e. (literally) to *wound;* figuratively to *be alert,* to *decide:*— bestir self, decide, decree, determine, maim, move.

H2783 חֲרַץ *ḥăraṣ* (Aramaic) from a root corresponding to H2782 in the sense of *vigor;* the *loin* (as the seat of strength):— loin.

H2784 חַרְצֻבָּה *ḥarṣubbâ* of uncertain derivation; a *fetter;* figuratively a *pain:*— band.

H2785 חַרְצַן *ḥarṣan* from H2782; a *sour* grape (as *sharp* in taste):— kernel.

H2786 חָרַק *ḥāraq* a primitive root; to *grate* the teeth:— gnash.

H2787 חָרַר *ḥārar* a primitive root; to *glow,* i.e. literally (to *melt, burn, dry* up) or figuratively (to *show* or *incite passion*):— by angry, burn, dry, kindle.

H2788 חָרֵר *ḥārēr* from H2787; *arid:*— parched place.

H2789 חֶרֶשׂ *ḥereś* a collateral form mediating between H2775 and H2791; a piece of *pottery:*— earth, earthen, sherd, potsherd, stone.

H2790 חָרַשׁ *ḥāraš* a primitive root; to *scratch,* i.e. (by implication) to *engrave, plough;* hence (from the use of tools) to *fabricate* (of any material); figuratively to *devise* (in a bad sense); hence (from the idea of secrecy) to be *silent,* to *let alone;* hence (by implication) to *be deaf* (as an accompaniment of dumbness):— altogether, cease, conceal, be deaf, devise, ear, graven, imagine, leave off speaking, hold peace, plow, plower, plowman, be quiet, rest, practise secretly, keep silence, be silent, speak not a word, be still, hold tongue, worker.

H2791 חֶרֶשׁ *ḥereš* from H2790; magical *craft;* also *silence:*— cunning, secretly.

H2792 חֶרֶשׁ *ḥereš* the same as H2791; *Cheresh,* a Levite:— Heresh.

H2793 חֹרֶשׁ *ḥōreš* from H2790; a *forest* (perhaps as furnishing the material for fabric):— bough, forest, shroud, wood.

H2794 חֹרֵשׁ *ḥōrēš* active participle of H2790; a *fabricator* or mechanic:— artificer.

H2795 חֵרֵשׁ *ḥērēš* from H2790; *deaf* (whether literally or spiritually):— deaf.

H2796 חָרָשׁ *ḥārāš* from H2790; a *fabricator* of any material:— artificer, carpenter, carpenter, craftsman, engraver, maker, mason, skilful, smith, smith, worker, workman, such as wrought.

H2797 חַרְשָׁא *ḥaršāʾ* from H2792; *magician; Charsha,* one of the Nethinim:— Harsha.

H2798 חֲרָשִׁים *ḥărāšîm* plural of H2796; *mechanics,* the name of a valley in Jerusalem:— Charashim, craftsmen.

H2799 חֲרֹשֶׁת *ḥărōšet* from H2790; mechanical *work:*— carving, cutting.

H2800 חֲרֹשֶׁת *ḥărōšet* the same as H2799; *Charosheth,* a place in Palestine:— Harosheth.

H2801 חָרַת *ḥārat* a primitive root; to *engrave:*— graven.

H2802 חֶרֶת *ḥeret* from H2801 [but equivalent to H2793]; *forest; Chereth,* a thicket in Palestine:— Hereth.

H2803 חָשַׁב *ḥāšab* a primitive root; properly to *plait* or interpenetrate, i.e. (literally) to *weave* or (generally) to *fabricate;* figuratively to *plot* or contrive (usually in a malicious sense); hence (from the mental effort) to *think, regard, value, compute:*— account, make account of, conceive, consider, count, cunning, cunning man, cunning work, cunning workman, devise, esteem, find out, forecast, hold, imagine, impute, invent, be like, mean, purpose, reckon, reckoning be made, regard, think.

H2804 חֲשַׁב *ḥăšab* (Aramaic) corresponding to H2803; to *regard:*— repute.

H2805 חֵשֶׁב *ḥēšeb* from H2803; a *belt* or strap (as being interlaced):— curious girdle.

H2806 חַשְׁבַּדָּנָה *ḥašbaddānâ* from H2803 and H1777; *considerate judge; Chasbaddanah,* an Israelite:— Hasbadana.

H2807 חֲשֻׁבָה *ḥăšūbâ* from H2803; *estimation; Chashubah,* an Israelite:— Hashubah.

H2808 חֶשְׁבּוֹן *ḥešbôn* from H2803; properly *contrivance;* by implication *intelligence:*— account, device, reason.

H2809 חֶשְׁבּוֹן *ḥešbôn* the same as H2808; *Cheshbon,* a place east of the Jordan:— Heshbon.

H2810 חִשָּׁבוֹן *ḥiššobbôn* from H2803; a *contrivance,* i.e. actual (a warlike *machine*) or mental (a *machination*):— engine, invention.

H2811 חֲשַׁבְיָה *ḥăšabyâ* or

חֲשַׁבְיָהוּ *ḥăšabyāhû* from H2803 and H3050; *Jah has regarded; Chashabjah,* the name of nine Israelites:— Hashabiah.

H2812 חֲשַׁבְנָה *ḥăšabnâ* feminine of H2808; *inventiveness; Chashnah,* an Israelite:— Hashabnah.

H2813 חֲשַׁבְנְיָה *ḥăšabnēyâ* from H2808 and H3050; *thought of Jah; Chashabnejah,* the name of two Israelites:— Hashabniah.

H2814 חָשָׁה *ḥāšâ* a primitive root; to *hush* or keep quiet:— hold peace, keep silence, be silent, still, be still.

H2815 חַשּׁוּב *ḥaššēwwb* from H2803; *intelligent; Chashshub,* the name of two or three Israelites:— Hashub, Hasshub.

H2816 חֲשׁוֹךְ *ḥăšôk* (Aramaic) from a root corresponding to H2821; the *dark:*— darkness.

H2817 חֲשׂוּפָא *ḥăśûpāʾ* or

חֲשֻׂפָא *ḥăśūpāʾ* from H2834; *nakedness; Chasupha,* one of the Nethinim:— Hashupha, Hasupha.

H2818 חֲשַׁח *ḥăšaḥ* (Aramaic) a collateral root to one corresponding to H2363 in the sense of *readiness;* to *be necessary* (from the idea of *convenience*) or (transitively) to *need:*— careful, have need of.

H2819 חַשְׁחוּת *ḥašḥût* from a root corresponding to H2818; *necessity:*— be needful.

H2820 חָשַׂךְ *ḥāśak* a primitive root; to *restrain* or (reflexively) *refrain;* by implication to *refuse, spare, preserve;* also (by interchange with H2821) to *observe:*— assuage, darken, forbear, hinder, hold back, keep, keep back, punish, refrain, reserve, spare, withhold.

H2821 חָשַׁךְ *ḥāšak* a primitive root; to *be dark* (as *withholding* light); transitively to *darken:*— be black, be dark, make dark, darken, cause darkness, be dim, hide.

H2822 חֹשֶׁךְ *ḥōšek* from H2821; the *dark;* hence (literally) *darkness;* figuratively *misery, destruction, death, ignorance, sorrow, wickedness:*— dark, darkness, night, obscurity.

H2823 חָשֹׁךְ *ḥāšōk* from H2821; *dark* (figuratively i.e. *obscure*):— mean.

H2824 חֶשְׁכָה *ḥeškâ* from H2821; *darkness:*— dark.

H2825 חֲשֵׁכָה *ḥăšēkâ* or

חֲשֵׁיכָה *ḥăšēkâ* from H2821; *darkness;* figuratively *misery:*— darkness.

H2826 חָשַׁל *ḥāšal* a primitive root; to *make* (intransitively *be*) *unsteady,* i.e. *weak:*— feeble.

H2827 חֲשַׁל *ḥăšal* (Aramaic) a root corresponding to H2826; to *weaken,* i.e. *crush:*— subdue.

H2828 חָשֻׁם *ḥāšūm* from the same as H2831; *enriched; Chashum,* the name of two or three Israelites:— Hashum.

H2829 חֶשְׁמוֹן *ḥešmôn* the same as H2831; *opulent; Cheshmon,* a place in Palestine:— Heshmon.

H2830 חַשְׁמַל *ḥašmal* of uncertain derivation; probably *bronze* or polished spectrum metal:— amber.

H2831 חַשְׁמַן *ḥašman* from an unused root (probably meaning *firm* or *capacious* in resources); apparently *wealthy:*— princes.

H2832 חַשְׁמֹנָה *ḥašmōnâ* feminine of H2831; *fertile; Chasmonah,* a place in the Desert:— Hashmonah.

H2833 חֹשֶׁן *ḥōšen* from an unused root probably meaning to *contain* or *sparkle;* perhaps a *pocket* (as holding the Urim and Thummim), or *rich* (as containing gems), used only of the *gorget* of the highpriest:— breastplate.

H2834 חָשַׂף *ḥāśap* a primitive root; to *strip* off, i.e. generally to *make naked* (for exertion or in disgrace), to *drain* away or *bail* up (a liquid):— make bare, clean, discover, draw out, take, uncover.

H2835 חָשִׂף *ḥāśīp* from H2834; properly *drawn off,* i.e. separated; hence a small *company* (as divided from the rest):— little flock.

H2836 חָשַׁק *ḥāšaq* a primitive root; to *cling,* i.e. *join,* (figuratively) to *love, delight* in; elliptically (or by interchange for H2820) to *deliver:*— have a delight, desire, have a desire, fillet, long, set love, in love.

H2837 חֵשֶׁק *ḥēšeq* from H2836; *delight:*— desire, pleasure.

H2838 חָשֻׁק *ḥāšūq* or

חָשׁוּק *ḥāšûq* passive participle of H2836; *attached,* i.e. a fence-*rail* or rod connecting the posts or pillars:— fillet.

H2839 חִשֻּׁק *ḥiššūq* from H2836; *conjoined,* i.e. a wheel-*spoke* or rod connecting the hub with the rim:— felloe.

H2840 חִשֻּׁר *ḥiššūr* from an unused root meaning to *bind* together; *combined,* i.e. the *nave* or hub of a wheel (as holding the spokes together):— spoke.

H2841 חַשְׁרָה *ḥašrâ* from the same as H2840; properly a *combination* or gathering, i.e. of watery *clouds:*— dark.

H2842 חָשַׁשׁ *ḥāšaš* by variation for H7179; dry *grass:*— chaff.

H2843 חֻשָׁתִי *ḥūšātî* patronymic from H2364; a *Chushathite* or descendant of Chushah:— Hushathite.

H2844 חַת *ḥat* from H2865; concretely *crushed;* also *afraid;* abstractly *terror:*— broken, dismayed, dread, fear.

H2845 חֵת *ḥēt* from H2865; *terror; Cheth,* an aboriginal Canaanite:— Heth.

H2846 חָתָה *ḥātâ* a primitive root; to lay *hold* of; especially to *pick* up fire:— heap, take, take away.

H2847 חִתָּה *ḥittâ* from H2865; *fear:*— terror.

H2848 חִתּוּל *ḥittûl* from H2853; *swathed,* i.e. a *bandage:*— roller.

H2849 חַתְחַת *ḥatḥat* from H2844; *terror:*— fear.

H2850 חִתִּי *ḥittî* patronymic from H2845; a *Chittite,* or descendant of Cheth:— Hittite, Hittites.

H2851 חִתִּית *ḥittît* from H2865; *fear:*— terror.

H2852 חָתַךְ *ḥātak* a primitive root; properly to *cut* off, i.e. (figuratively) to *decree:*— determine.

H2853 חָתַל *ḥātal* a primitive root; to *swathe:*— at all, swaddle.

H2854 חֲתֻלָּה *ḥătullâ* from H2853; a *swathing* cloth (figuratively):— swaddling band.

H2855 חֶתְלֹן *ḥetlōn* from H2853; *enswathed; Chethlon,* a place in Palestine:— Hethlon.

H2856 חָתַם *ḥātam* a primitive root; to *close* up; especially to *seal:*— make an end, mark, seal, seal up, stop.

H2857 חֲתַם *ḥătam* (Aramaic) a root corresponding to H2856; to *seal:*— seal.

H2858 חֹתֶמֶת *ḥōtemet* feminine active participle of H2856; a *seal:*— signet.

H2859 חָתַן *ḥātan* a primitive root; to *give* (a daughter) *away* in marriage; hence (generally) to *contract affinity* by marriage:— join in affinity, father in law, make marriages, mother in law, son in law.

H2860 חָתָן *ḥātān* from H2859; a *relative* by marriage (especially through the bride); figuratively a *circumcised* child (as a species of religious espousal):— bridegroom, husband, son in law.

H2861 חֲתֻנָּה *ḥătunnâ* from H2859; a *wedding:*— espousal.

H2862 חָתַף *ḥātap* a primitive root; to *clutch:*— take away.

H2863 חֶתֶף *ḥetep* from H2862; properly *rapine;* figuratively *robbery:*— prey.

H2864 חָתַר *ḥātar* a primitive root; to *force* a passage, as by burglary; figuratively with oars:— dig, dig through, row.

H2865 חָתַת *ḥātat* a primitive root; properly to *prostrate;* hence to *break* down, either (literally) by violence, or (figuratively) by confusion and fear:— abolish, affright, be afraid, make afraid, amaze, beat down, discourage, dismay, cause to dismay, go down, scare, terrify.

H2866 חֲתַת *ḥătat* from H2865; *dismay:*— casting down.

H2867 חֲתַת *ḥătat* the same as H2866; *Chathath,* an Israelite:— Hathath.

ט

H2868 טְאֵב *ṭĕʾēb* (Aramaic) a primitive root; to *rejoice:*— be glad.

H2869 טָב *ṭāb* (Aramaic) from H2868; the same as H2896; *good:*— fine, good.

H2870 טָבְאֵל *ṭābĕʾēl* from H2895 and H410; *pleasing* (to) *God; Tabeël,* the name of a Syrian and of a Persian:— Tabeal, Tabeel.

H2871 טָבוּל *ṭābûl* passive participle of H2881; properly *dyed,* i.e. a *turban* (probably as of *colored* stuff):— dyed attire.

H2872 טַבּוּר *ṭabbûr* from an unused root meaning to *pile* up; properly *accumulated;* i.e. (by implication) a *summit:*— middle, midst.

H2873 טָבַח *ṭābaḥ* a primitive root; to *slaughter* (animals of men):— kill, slaughter, make slaughter, slay.

H2874 טֶבַח *ṭebaḥ* from H2873; properly something *slaughtered;* hence a *beast* (or *meat,* as butchered); abstractly *butchery* (or concretely a place of slaughter):— beast, slaughter, slay, sore.

H2875 טֶבַח *ṭebaḥ* the same as H2874; *massacre; Tebach,* the name of a Mesopotamian and of an Israelite:— Tebah.

H2876 טַבָּח *ṭabbāḥ* from H2873; properly a *butcher;* hence a *lifeguardsman* (because acting as executioner); also a *cook* (as usually slaughtering the animal for food):— cook, guard.

H2877 טַבָּח *ṭabbāḥ* (Aramaic) the same as H2876; a *lifeguardsman:*— guard.

H2878 טִבְחָה *ṭibḥâ* feminine of H2874 and meaning the same:— flesh, slaughter.

H2879 טַבָּחָה *ṭabbāḥâ* feminine of H2876; a female *cook:*— cook.

H2880 טִבְחַת *ṭibḥat* from H2878; *slaughter; Tibchath,* a place in Syria:— Tibhath.

H2881 טָבַל *ṭābal* a primitive root; to *dip:*— dip, plunge.

H2882 טְבַלְיָהוּ *ṭĕbalyāhû* from H2881 and H3050; *Jah has dipped; Tebaljah,* an Israelite:— Tebaliah.

H2883 טָבַע *ṭābaᶜ* a primitive root; to *sink:*— drown, fasten, settle, sink.

H2884 טַבָּעוֹת *ṭabbāᶜôt* plural of H2885; *rings; Tabbaoth,* one of the Nethinim:— Tabbaoth.

H2885 טַבַּעַת *ṭabbaᶜat* from H2883; properly a *seal* (as *sunk* into the wax), i.e. *signet* (for sealing); hence (generally) a *ring* of any kind:— ring.

H2886 טַבְרִמּוֹן *ṭabrimmôn* from H2895 and H7417; *pleasing* (to) *Rimmon; Tabrimmon,* a Syrian:— Tabrimmon.

H2887 טֵבֵת *ṭēbet* probably of foreign derivation; *Tebeth,* the tenth Hebrew month:— Tebeth.

H2888 טַבַּת *ṭabbat* of uncertain derivation; *Tabbath,* a place east of the Jordan:— Tabbath.

H2889 טָהוֹר *ṭāhôr* or

טָהֹר *ṭāhōr* from H2891; *pure* (in a physical, chemical, ceremonial, or moral sense):— clean, fair, pure, pureness.

H2890 טְהוֹר *ṭĕhôr* from H2891; *purity:*— pureness.

H2891 טָהֵר *ṭāhēr* a primitive root; properly to *be bright;* i.e. (by implication) to *be pure* (physically *sound, clear, unadulterated;* Levitically *uncontaminated;* morally *innocent* or *holy*):— be clean, make clean, make self clean, pronounce clean, cleanse, cleanse self, purge, purify, purifier, purify self.

H2892 טֹהַר *ṭōhar* from H2891; literally *brightness;* ceremonially *purification:*— clearness, glory, purifying.

H2893 טָהֳרָה *ṭohŏrâ* feminine of H2892; ceremonial *purification;* moral *purity:*— is cleansed, cleansing, purification, purifying.

H2894 טוּא *ṭûʾ* a primitive root; to *sweep away:*— sweep.

H2895 טוֹב *ṭôb* a primitive root; to *be* (transitive *do* or *make*) good (or *well*) in the widest sense:— be better, cheer, be good, do good, seem good, goodly, make goodly, please, well, be well, do well, go well, play well.

H2896 טוֹב *ṭôb* from H2895; *good* (as an adjective) in the widest sense; used likewise as a noun, both in the masculine and the feminine, the singular and the plural *(good,* a *good* or *good* thing, a *good* man or woman; the *good, goods* or *good* things, *good* men or women), also as an adverb *(well)*:— beautiful, best, better, bountiful, cheerful, at ease, fair, fair word, favour, be in favour, fine, glad, good, good deed, goodlier, goodliest, goodly, goodness, goods, graciously, joyful, kindly, kindness, liketh, liketh best, loving, merry, most, pleasant, pleaseth, pleasure, precious, prosperity, ready, sweet, wealth, welfare, well, be well, wellfavoured.

H2897 טוֹב *ṭôb* the same as H2896; *good; Tob,* a region apparently east of the Jordan:— Tob.

H2898 טוּב *ṭûb* from H2895; *good* (as a noun), in the widest sense, especially *goodness* (superlative concretely the *best*), *beauty, gladness, welfare:*— fair, gladness, good, goodness, good thing, goods, joy, go well with.

H2899 טוֹב אֲדֹנִיָּהוּ *ṭôb ʾădōnîyāhû* from H2896 and H138; *pleasing* (to) *Adonijah; Tob-Adonijah,* an Israelite:— Tob-adonijah.

H2900 טוֹבִיָּה *ṭôbîyâ* or

טוֹבִיָּהוּ *ṭôbîyāhû* from H2896 and H3050; *goodness of Jehovah; Tobijah,* the name of three Israelites and of one Samaritan:— Tobiah, Tobijah.

H2901 טָוָה *ṭāwâ* a primitive root; to *spin:*— spin.

H2902 טוּחַ *ṭûaḥ* a primitive root; to *smear,* especially with lime:— daub, overlay, plaister, smut.

H2903 טוֹטָפָה *ṭôṭāpâ* from an unused root meaning to *go around* or *bind;* a *fillet* for the forehead:— frontlet.

H2904 טוּל *ṭûl* a primitive root; to *pitch* over or *reel;* hence (transitively) to *cast* down or out:— carry away, cast, cast down, cast forth, cast out, be utterly cast down, send out.

H2905 טוּר *ṭûr* from an unused root meaning to *range* in a regular manner; a *row;* hence a *wall:*— row.

H2906 טוּר *ṭûr* (Aramaic) corresponding to H6697; a *rock* or hill:— mountain.

H2907 טוּשׂ *ṭûś* a primitive root; to *pounce* as a bird of prey:— haste.

H2908 טְוָת *ṭĕwāt* (Aramaic) from a root corresponding to H2901; *hunger* (as *twisting*):— fasting.

H2909 טָחָה *ṭāḥâ* a primitive root; to *stretch* a bow, as an *archer:*— shot, bowshot.

H2910 טֻחָה *ṭūḥâ* from H2909 (or H2902) in the sense of *overlaying;* (in the plural only) the *kidneys* (as being *covered*); hence (figuratively) the inmost *thought:*— inward parts.

H2911 טְחוֹן *ṭĕḥôn* from H2912; a hand *mill;* hence a *millstone:*— to grind.

H2912 טָחַן *ṭāḥan* a primitive root; to *grind* meal; hence to *be a concubine* (that being their employment):— grind, grinder.

H2913 טַחֲנָה *ṭaḥănâ* from H2912; a hand *mill;* hence (figuratively) *chewing:*— grinding.

H2914 טְחֹר *ṭĕḥōr* from an unused root meaning to *burn;* a *boil* or ulcer (from the inflammation), especially a tumor in the anus or pudenda (the piles):— emerod.

H2915 טִיחַ *ṭîaḥ* from (the equivalent of) H2902; mortar or *plaster:*— daubing.

H2916 טִיט *ṭîṭ* from an unused root meaning apparently to *be sticky* [rather perhaps a denominative from H2894, through the idea of dirt to be *swept* away]; *mud* or *clay;* figuratively *calamity:*— clay, dirt, mire.

H2917 טִין *ṭîn* (Aramaic) perhaps by interchange for a word corresponding to H2916; *clay:*— miry.

H2918 טִירָה *ṭîrâ* feminine of (an equivalent to) H2905; a *wall;* hence a *fortress* or a *hamlet:*— castkem goodly castle, habitation, palace, row.

H2919 טַל *ṭal* from H2926; *dew* (as *covering* vegetation):— dew.

H2920 טַל *ṭal* (Aramaic) the same as H2919:— dew.

H2921 טָלָא *ṭālāʾ* a primitive root; properly to *cover* with pieces; i.e. (by implication) to *spot* or *variegate* (as tapestry):— clouted, with divers colours, spotted.

H2922 טְלָא *ṭĕlāʾ* apparently from H2921 in the (original) sense of *covering* (for protection); a *lamb* [compare H2924]:— lamb.

H2923 טְלָאִים *ṭĕlāʾîm* from the plural of H2922; *lambs; Telaim,* a place in Palestine:— Telaim.

H2924 טָלֶה *ṭāleh* by variation for H2922; a *lamb* :— lamb.

H2925 טַלְטֵלָה *ṭalṭēlâ* from H2904; *overthrow* or *rejection:*— captivity.

H2926 טָלַל *ṭālal* a primitive root; properly to *strew* over, i.e. (by implication) to *cover* in or *plate* (with beams):— cover.

H2927 טְלַל *ṭĕlal* (Aramaic) corresponding to H2926; to *cover* with shade:— have a shadow.

H2928 טֶלֶם *ṭelem* from an unused root meaning to *break* up or treat violently; *oppression; Telem,* the name of a place in Idumaea, also of a temple doorkeeper:— Telem.

H2929 טַלְמוֹן *ṭalmôn* from the same as H2728; *oppressive; Talmon,* a temple doorkeeper:— Talmon.

H2930 טָמֵא *ṭāmēʾ* a primitive root; to *be foul,* especially in a ceremonial or moral sense (*contaminated*):— defile, defile self, pollute, pollute self, be unclean, make unclean, make self unclean, pronounce unclean, utterly.

H2931 טָמֵא *ṭāmēʾ* from H2930; *foul* in a religious sense:— defiled, infamous, polluted, pollution, unclean.

H2932 טֻמְאָה *ṭumʾâ* from H2930; religious *impurity:*— filthiness, unclean, uncleanness.

H2933 טָמָה *ṭāmâ* a collateral form of H2930; to *be impure* in a religious sense:— be defiled, be reputed vile.

H2934 טָמַן *ṭāman* a primitive root; to *hide* (by *covering* over):— hide, lay privily, in secret.

H2935 טֶנֶא *ṭeneʾ* from an unused root probably meaning to *weave;* a *basket* (of interlaced osiers):— basket.

H2936 טָנַף *ṭānap* a primitive root; to *soil:*— defile.

H2937 טָעָה *ṭāʿâ* a primitive root; to *wander;* causatively to *lead astray:*— seduce.

H2938 טָעַם *ṭāʿam* a primitive root; to *taste;* figuratively to *perceive:*— but, perceive, taste.

H2939 טְעֵם *ṭĕʿam* (Aramaic) corresponding to H2938; to *taste;* causatively to *feed:*— make to eat, feed.

H2940 טַעַם *ṭaʿam* from H2938; properly a *taste,* i.e. (figuratively) *perception;* by implication *intelligence;* transitively a *mandate:*— advice, behaviour, decree, discretion, judgment, reason, taste, understanding.

H2941 טַעַם *ṭaʿam* (Aramaic) from H2939; properly a *taste,* i.e. (as in H2940) a judicial *sentence:*— account, to be commanded, commandment, matter.

H2942 טְעֵם *ṭĕʿēm* (Aramaic) from H2939, and equivalent to H2941; properly *flavor;* figuratively *judgment* (both subjectively and objectively); hence *account* (both subjective and objective):— chancellor, command, commandment, decree, regard, taste, wisdom.

H2943 טָעַן *ṭāʿan* a primitive root; to *load* a beast :— lade.

H2944 טָעַן *ṭāʿan* a primitive root; to *stab:*— thrust through.

H2945 טַף *ṭap* from H2952 (perhaps referring to the *tripping* gait of children); a *family* (mostly used collectively in the singular):— children, little children, little ones, families.

H2946 טָפַח *ṭāpaḥ* a primitive root; to *flatten* out or *extend* (as a tent); figuratively to *nurse* a child (as *promotive* of growth); or perhaps a denominative from H2947, from *dandling* on the palms:— span, swaddle.

H2947 טֶפַח *ṭepaḥ* from H2946; a *spread* of the hand, i.e. a *palm-breadth* (not "span" of the fingers); architecturally a *corbel* (as a supporting palm):— coping, hand-breadth.

H2948 טֹפַח *ṭōpaḥ* from H2946 (the same as H2947):— hand-breadth (broad).

H2949 טִפֻּח *ṭippūḥ* from H2946; *nursing:*— span long.

H2950 טָפַל *ṭāpal* a primitive root; properly to *stick* on as a patch; figuratively to *impute* falsely:— forge, forger, sew up.

H2951 טִפְסַר *ṭipsar* of foreign derivation; a military *governor:*— captain.

H2952 טָפַף *ṭāpap* a primitive root; apparently to *trip* (with short steps) coquetishly:— mince.

H2953 טְפַר *ṭĕpar* (Aramaic) from a root corresponding to H6852, and meaning the same as H6856; a finger-*nail;* also a *hoof* or *claw:*— nail.

H2954 טָפַשׁ *ṭāpaš* a primitive root; properly apparently to *be thick;* figuratively to *be stupid:*— be fat.

H2955 טָפַת *ṭāpat* probably from H5197; a *dropping* (of ointment); *Taphath,* an Israelitess:— Taphath.

H2956 טָרַד *ṭārad* a primitive root; to *drive* on; figuratively to *follow* close:— continual.

H2957 טְרַד *ṭĕrad* (Aramaic) corresponding to H2956; to *expel:*— drive.

H2958 טְרוֹם *ṭĕrôm* a variation of H2962; *not yet:*— before.

H2959 טָרַח *ṭāraḥ* a primitive root; to *overburden* :— weary.

H2960 טֹרַח *ṭōraḥ* from H2959; a *burden:*— cumbrance, trouble.

H2961 טָרִי *ṭārî* from an unused root apparently meaning to *be moist;* properly *dripping;* hence *fresh* (i.e. recently made such):— new, putrefying.

H2962 טֶרֶם *ṭerem* from an unused root apparently meaning to *interrupt* or *suspend;* properly *non-occurrence;* used adverbially *not yet* or *before:*— before, ere, not yet.

H2963 טָרַף *ṭārap* a primitive root; to *pluck* off or *pull* to pieces; causatively to *supply* with food (as in morsels):— catch, without doubt, feed, ravin, rend in pieces, surely, tear, tear in pieces.

H2964 טֶרֶף *ṭerep* from H2963; something *torn,* i.e. a fragment, e.g. a *fresh* leaf, *prey, food:*— leaf, meat, prey, spoil.

H2965 טָרָף *ṭārāp* from H2963; recently *torn* off, i.e. *fresh:*— pluckt off.

H2966 טְרֵפָה *ṭĕrēpâ* feminine (collective) of H2964; *prey,* i.e. flocks devoured by animals:— ravin, torn, torn of beasts, torn in pieces, that which was torn.

H2967 טַרְפְּלָי *ṭarpĕlay* (Aramaic) from a name of foreign derivation; a *Tarpelite* (collectively) or inhabitant of Tarpel, a place in Assyria:— Tarpelites.

י

H2968 יָאַב *yāʾab* a primitive root; to *desire:*— long.

H2969 יָאָה *yāʾâ* a primitive root; to *be suitable:*— appertain.

H2970 יַאֲזַנְיָה *yaʾăzanyâ* or

יַאֲזַנְיָהוּ *yaʾăzanyāhû* from H238 and H3050; *heard of Jah; Jaazanjah,* the name of four Israelites:— Jaazaniah. Compare H3153

H2971 יָאִיר *yāʾîr* from H215; *enlightener; Jaïr,* the name of four Israelites:— Jair.

H2972 יָאִרִי *yāʾîrî* patronymic from H2971; a *Jaïrite* or descendant of Jair:— Jairite.

H2973 יָאַל *yāʾal* a primitive root; properly to *be slack,* i.e. (figuratively) to *be foolish:*— dote, be foolish, do foolishly, become fools.

H2974 יָאַל *yāʾal* a primitive root [probably rather the same as H2973 through the idea of mental *weakness*]; properly to *yield,* especially *assent;* hence (positively) to *undertake* as an act of volition:— assay, begin, be content, please, take upon, willingly, would.

H2975 יְאֹר *yĕʾōr* of Egyptian origin; a *channel,* e.g. a fosse, canal, shaft; specifically the *Nile,* as the one river of Egypt, including its collateral trenches, also the *Tigris,* as the main river of Assyria:— brook, flood, river, stream.

H2976 יָאַשׁ *yāʾaš* a primitive root; to *desist,* i.e. (figuratively) to *despond:*— despair, cause to despair, one that is desperate, be no hope.

H2977 יֹאשִׁיָּה *yōʾšîyâ* or

יֹאשִׁיָּהוּ *yōʾšîyāhû* from the same root as H803 and H3050; *founded of Jah; Joshijah,* the name of two Israelites:— Josiah.

H2978 יְאִתוֹן *yĕʾîtôn* from H857; an *entry:*— entrance.

H2979 יְאָתְרַי *yĕʾāteray* from the same as H871; *stepping; Jeätherai,* an Israelite:— Jeaterai.

H2980 יָבַב *yābab* a primitive root; to *bawl:*— cry out.

H2981 יְבוּל *yĕbûl* from H2986; *produce,* i.e. a *crop* or (figuratively) *wealth:*— fruit, increase.

H2982 יְבוּס *yĕbûs* from H947; *trodden,* i.e. threshing-place; *Jebus,* the aboriginal name of Jerusalem:— Jebus.

H2983 יְבוּסִי *yĕbûsî* patrial from H2982; a *Jebusite* or inhabitant of Jebus:— Jebusite, Jebusites.

H2984 יִבְחַר *yibḥar* from H977; *choice; Jibchar,* an Israelite:— Ibhar.

H2985 יָבִין *yābîn* from H995; *intelligent; Jabin,* the name of two Canaanitish kings:— Jabin.

H2986 יָבַל *yābal* a primitive root; properly to *flow;* causatively to *bring* (especially with pomp):— bring, bring forth, carry, lead, lead forth.

H2987 יְבַל *yĕbal* (Aramaic) corresponding to H2986; to *bring:*— bring, carry.

H2988 יָבָל *yābāl* from H2986; a *stream:*— course, watercourse, stream.

H2989 יָבָל *yābāl* the same as H2988; *Jabal,* an antediluvian:— Jabal.

H2990 יַבֵּל *yabbāl* from H2986; having *running* sores:— wen.

H2991 יִבְלְעָם *yiblĕʿām* from H1104 and H5971; *devouring people; Jibleäm,* a place in Palestine:— Ibleam.

H2992 יָבַם *yābam* a primitive root of doubtful meaning; used only as a denominative from H2993; to *marry* a (deceased) brother's widow :— perform the duty of a husband's brother, marry.

H2993 יָבָם *yābām* from (the original of) H2992; a *brother-in-law:*— husband's brother.

H2994 יְבֵמֶת *yĕbēmet* feminine participle of H2992; a *sister-in-law:*— brother's wife, sister in law.

H2995 יַבְנְאֵל *yabnĕʾēl* from H1129 and H410; *built of God; Jabneël,* the name of two places in Palestine:— Jabneel.

H2996 יַבְנֶה *yabneh* from H1129; a *building; Jabneh,* a place in Palestine:— Jabneh.

H2997 יִבְנְיָה *yibnĕyâ* from H1129 and H3050; *built of Jah; Jibnejah,* an Israelite:— Ibneiah.

H2998 יִבְנִיָּה *yibnîyâ* from H1129 and H3050; *building of Jah; Jibnijah,* an Israelite:— Ibnijah.

H2999 יַבֹּק *yabbōq* probably from H1238; *pouring* forth; Jabbok, a river east of the Jordan:— Jabbok.

H3000 יְבֶרֶכְיָהוּ *yĕberekyāhû* from H1288 and H3050; *blessed of Jah; Jeberekjah,* an Israelite:— Jeberechiah.

H3001 יָבֵשׁ *yābēš* a primitive root; to *be ashamed, confused* or *disappointed;* also (as failing) to *dry* up (as water) or *wither* (as herbage):— be ashamed, clean, be confounded, dry, make dry, dry up, shame, do shamefully, utterly, wither, wither away.

H3002 יָבֵשׁ *yābēš* from H3001; *dry:*— dried, dried away, dry.

H3003 יָבֵשׁ *yābēš* also

יָבִישׁ *yābēš* the same as H3002 often with the addition of H1568, i.e. *Jabesh of Gilad; Jabesh,* the name of an Israelite and of a place in Palestine:— Jabesh, Jabesh-Gilead.

H3004 יַבָּשָׁה *yabbāšâ* from H3001; *dry* ground:— dry, dry ground, dry land.

H3005 יִבְשָׂם *yibśām* from the same as H1314; *fragrant: Jibsam,* an Israelite:— Jibsam.

H3006 יַבֶּשֶׁת *yabbešet* a variation of H3004; *dry* ground:— dry land.

H3007 יַבֶּשֶׁת *yabbešet* (Aramaic) corresponding to H3006; *dry* land:— earth.

H3008 יִגְאָל *yigʾāl* from H1450; *avenger; Jigal,* the name of three Israelites:— Igal, Igeal.

H3009 יָגַב *yāgab* a primitive root; to *dig* or plough :— husbandman.

H3010 יָגֵב *yāgēb* from H2009; a ploughed *field:*— field.

H3011 יָגְבְּהָה *yogbĕhâ* feminine from H1361; *hillock; Jogbehah,* a place east of the Jordan:— Jogbehah.

H3012 יִגְדַּלְיָהוּ *yigdalyāhû* from H1431 and H3050; *magnified of Jah; Jigdaljah,* an Israelite:— Igdaliah.

H3013 יָגָה *yāgâ* a primitive root; to *grieve:*— afflict, cause grief, grieve, sorrowful, vex.

H3014 יָגָה *yāgâ* a primitive root [probably rather the same as H3013 through the common idea of *dissatisfaction*]; to *push* away:— be removed.

H3015 יָגוֹן *yāgôn* from H3013; *affliction:*— grief, sorrow.

H3016 יָגוֹר *yāgôr* from H3025; *fearful:*— afraid, fearest.

H3017 יָגוּר *yāgûr* probably from H1481; a *lodging; Jagur,* a place in Palestine:— Jagur.

H3018 יְגִיעַ *yĕgîaʿ* from H3021; *toil;* hence a *work, produce, property* (as the result of labor):— labour, work.

H3019 יָגִיעַ *yāgîaʿ* from H3021; *tired:*— weary.

H3020 יָגְלִי *yoglî* from H1540; *exiled; Jogli,* an Israelite:— Jogli.

H3021 יָגַע *yāgaʿ* a primitive root; properly to *gasp;* hence to *be exhausted,* to *tire,* to *toil:*— faint, labour, make to labour, weary, be weary.

H3022 יָגָע *yāgāʿ* from H3021; *earnings* (as the product of toil):— that which he laboured for.

H3023 יָגֵעַ *yāgēaʿ* from H3021; *tired;* hence (transitively) *tiresome:*— full of labour, weary.

H3024 יְגִיעָה *yĕgîʿâ* feminine of H3019; *fatigue:*— weariness.

H3025 יָגֹר *yāgōr* a primitive root; to *fear:*— be afraid, fear.

H3026 יְגַר שַׂהֲדוּתָא *yĕgar śahădûtāʾ* (Aramaic) from a word derived from an unused root (meaning to *gather*) and a derivative of a root corresponding to H7717; *heap of the testimony: Jegar-Sahadutha,* a cairn east of the Jordan:— Jegar-Sahadutha.

H3027 יָד *yād* a primitive word; a *hand* (the *open* one [indicating *power, means, direction,* etc.], in distinction from H3709, the *closed* one); used (as noun, adverb, etc.) in a great variety of applications, both literally and figuratively, both proximate and remote [as follow]:— be able, be able, about, armholes, at, axletree, because of, beside, border, bounty, broad, brokenhanded, by, charge, coast, consecrate, creditor, custody, debt, dominion, enough, fellowship, force, from, hand, handstaves, handy work, he, himself, in, labour, large, ledge, lefthanded, means, mine, ministry, near, of, order, ordinance, our, parts, pain, power, presumptuously, service, side, sore, state, stay, draw with strength, stroke, swear, terror, thee, by them, themselves, thine own, thou, through, throwing, thumb, times, to, under, us, wait on, side, wayside, where, wide, with, with him, with me, with you, work, yield, yourselves.

H3028 יַד *yad* (Aramaic) corresponding to H3027 :— hand, power.

H3029 יְדָא *yĕdāᵓ* (Aramaic) corresponding to H3034; to *praise:*— thank, give thanks.

H3030 יִדְאֲלָה *yidᵓălâ* of uncertain derivation; *Jidalah,* a place in Palestine:— Idalah.

H3031 יִדְבָּשׁ *yidbāš* from the same as H1706; perhaps *honeyed; Jidbash,* an Israelite:— Idbash.

H3032 יָדַד *yādad* a primitive root; properly to *handle* [compare H3034], i.e. to *throw,* e.g. lots:— cast.

H3033 יְדִדוּת *yĕdîdût* from H3039; properly *affection;* concretely a *darling* object:— dearly beloved.

H3034 יָדָה *yādâ* a primitive root; used only as denominative from H3027; literally to *use* (i.e. hold out) *the hand;* physically to *throw* (a stone, an arrow) at or away; especially to *revere* or *worship* (with extended hands); intensively to *bemoan* (by wringing the hands):— cast, cast out, confess, make confession, praise, shoot, thank, give thanks, be thankful, thanksgiving.

H3035 יִדּוֹ *yiddô* from H3034; *praised; Jiddo,* an Israelite:— Iddo.

H3036 יָדוֹן *yādôn* from H3034; *thankful; Jadon,* an Israelite:— Jadon.

H3037 יַדּוּעַ *yaddûaᶜ* from H3045; *knowing; Jadduä,* the name of two Israelites:— Jaddua.

H3038 יְדוּתוּן *yĕdûtûn* or

יְדֻתוּן *yĕdūtûn* or

יְדִיתוּן *yĕdîtûn* probably from H3034; *laudatory; Jeduthun,* an Israelite:— Jeduthun.

H3039 יְדִיד *yĕdîd* from the same as H1730; *loved* :— amiable, beloved, wellbeloved, loves.

H3040 יְדִידָה *yĕdîdâ* feminine of H3039; *beloved; Jedidah,* an Israelitess:— Jedidah.

H3041 יְדִידְיָה *yĕdîdĕyâ* from H3039 and H3050; *beloved of Jah; Jedidejah,* a name of Solomon:— Jedidiah.

H3042 יְדָיָה *yĕdāyâ* from H3034 and H3050; *praised of Jah; Jedajah,* the name of two Israelites:— Jedaiah.

H3043 יְדִיעֲאֵל *yĕdîᶜăᵓēl* from H3045 and H410; *knowing God; Jediaël,* the name of three Israelites:— Jediael.

H3044 יִדְלָף *yidlāp* from H1811; *tearful; Jidlaph,* a Mesopotamian:— Jidlaph.

H3045 יָדַע *yādaᶜ* a primitive root; to *know* (properly to ascertain by *seeing*); used in a great variety of senses, figurative, literal, euphemistic and inferential (including *observation, care, recognition;* and causatively *instruction, designation, punishment,* etc.) [as follow]:— acknowledge, acquaintance, acquainted with, advise, answer, appoint, assuredly, be aware, be aware, unawares, cannot, certainly, for a certainty, comprehend, consider, could they, cunning, declare, be diligent, discern, can discern, cause to discern, discover, endued with, familiar friend, famous, feel, can have, be ignorant, instruct, kinsfolk, kinsman, know, cause to know, let know, make know, knowledge, come to give knowledge, have knowledge, take knowledge, have knowledge, be known, make known, make to be known, make self known, be learned, lie by man, mark, perceive, privy to, prognosticator, regard, have respect, skilful, shew, can skill, man of skill, be sure, of a surety, teach, tell, can tell, understand, have understanding, will be, wist, wit, wot.

H3046 יְדַע *yĕdaᶜ* (Aramaic) corresponding to H3045:— certify, know, make known, teach.

H3047 יָדָע *yādāᶜ* from H3045; *knowing; Jada,* an Israelite:— Jada.

H3048 יְדַעְיָה *yĕdaᶜyâ* from H3045 and H3050; *Jah has known; Jedajah,* the name of two Israelites:— Jedaiah.

H3049 יִדְּעֹנִי *yiddĕᶜōnî* from H3045; properly a *knowing* one; specifically a *conjurer;* (by implication) a *ghost:*— wizard.

H3050 יָהּ *yāh* contracted for H3068, and meaning the same; *Jah,* the sacred name:— Jah, the Lord, most vehement. Compare names in "-iah," "-jah."

H3051 יָהַב *yāhab* a primitive root; to *give* (whether literally or figuratively); generally to *put;* imperative (reflexively) *come:*— ascribe, bring, come on, give, go, set, take.

H3052 יְהַב *yĕhab* (Aramaic) corresponding to H3051 :— deliver, give, lay, prolong, pay, yield.

H3053 יְהָב *yĕhāb* from H3051; properly what is *given* (by Providence), i.e. a *lot:*— burden.

H3054 יָהַד *yāhad* denominative from a form corresponding to H3061; to *Judaize,* i.e. become Jewish:— become Jews.

H3055 יְהֻד *yĕhūd* a briefer form of one corresponding to H3061; *Jehud,* a place in Palestine:— Jehud.

H3056 יֶהְדַּי *yehday* perhaps from a form corresponding to H3061; *Judaistic; Jehdai,* an Israelite:— Jehdai.

H3057 יְהֻדִיָּה *yĕhūdîyâ* feminine of H3064; *Jehudijah,* a Jewess:— Jehudijah.

H3058 יֵהוּא *yēhûᵓ* from H3068 and H1931; *Jehovah* (is) *He; Jehu,* the name of five Israelites:— Jehu.

H3059 יְהוֹאָחָז *yĕhôᵓāḥāz* from H3068 and H270; *Jehovah-seized; Jehoächaz,* the name of three Israelites:— Jehoahaz. Compare H3099

H3060 יְהוֹאָשׁ *yĕhôᵓāš* from H3068 and (perhaps) H784; *Jehovah-fired; Jehoäsh,* the name of two Israelites kings:— Jehoash. Compare H3101

H3061 יְהוּד *yĕhûd* (Aramaic) contracted from a form corresponding to H3063; properly *Judah,* hence *Judaea:*— Jewry, Judah, Judea.

H3062 יְהוּדָאִי *yĕhûdāᵓî* (Aramaic) patrial from H3061; a *Jehudaïte* (or Judaite), i.e. Jew:— Jew.

H3063 יְהוּדָה *yĕhûdâ* from H3034; *celebrated; Jehudah* (or Judah), the name of five Israelites; also of the tribe descended from the first, and of its territory:— Judah.

H3064 יְהוּדִי *yĕhûdî* patronymic from H3063; a *Jehudite* (i.e. Judaite or Jew), or descendant of Jehudah (i.e. Judah):— Jew.

H3065 יְהוּדִי *yĕhûdî* the same as H3064; *Jehudi,* an Israelite:— Jehudi.

H3066 יְהוּדִית *yĕhûdît* feminine of H3064; the *Jewish* (used adverbially) language:— in the Jews' language.

H3067 יְהוּדִית *yĕhûdît* the same as H3066; *Jewess; Jehudith,* a Canaanitess:— Judith.

H3068 יְהֹוָה *YHWH* from H1961; (the) self-*Existent* or Eternal; *Jehovah,* Jewish national name of God:— Jehovah, the Lord. Compare H3050, H3069

H3069 יְהֹוִה *YHWH* a variation of H3068 [used after H136, and pronounced by Jews as H430, in order to prevent the repetition of the same sound, since they elsewhere pronounce H3068 as H136]:— God.

H3070 יְהֹוָה יִרְאֶה *YHWH yirᵓeh* from H3068 and H7200; *Jehovah will see* (to it); *Jehovah-Jireh,* a symbolical name for Mount Moriah:— Jehovah-jireh.

H3071 יְהֹוָה נִסִּי *YHWH nissî* from H3068 and H5251 with pronominal suffix; *Jehovah* (is) *my banner; Jehovah-Nissi,* a symbolical name of an altar in the Desert:— Jehovah-nissi.

H3072 יְהֹוָה צִדְקֵנוּ *YHWH ṣidqēnû* from H3068 and H6664 with pronominal suffix; *Jehovah* (is) *our right; Jehovah-Tsidkenu,* a symbolical epithet of the Messiah and of Jerus:— the Lord our righteousness.

H3073 יְהֹוָה שָׁלוֹם *YHWH šālôm* from H3068 and H7965; *Jehovah* (is) *peace; Jehovah-Shalom,* a symbolical name of an altar in Palestine:— Jehovah-shalom.

H3074 יְהֹוָה שָׁמָּה *YHWH šommâ* from H3068 and H8033 with directive enclitic; *Jehovah* (is) *thither; Jehovah-Shammah,* a symbolical title of Jerusalem:— Jehovah-shammah.

H3075 יְהוֹזָבָד *yĕhôzābād* from H3068 and H2064; *Jehovah-endowed; Jehozabad,* the name of three Israelites:— Jehozabad. Compare H3107

H3076 יְהוֹחָנָן *yĕhôḥānān* from H3068 and H2603; *Jehovah-favored; Jehochanan,* the name of eight Israelites:— Jehohanan, Johanan. Compare H3110

H3077 יְהוֹיָדָע *yĕhôyādāᶜ* from H3068 and H3045; *Jehovah-known; Jehojada,* the name of three Israelites:— Jehoiada. Compare H3111

H3078 יְהוֹיָכִין *yĕhôyākîn* from H3068 and H3559; *Jehovah will establish; Jehojakin,* a Jewish king:— Jehoiachin. Compare H3112

H3079 יְהוֹיָקִים *yĕhôyāqîm* from H3068 abbreviated and H6965; *Jehovah will raise; Jehojakim,* a Jewish king:— Jehoiakim. Compare H3113

H3080 יְהוֹיָרִיב *yĕhôyārîb* from H3068 and H7378; *Jehovah will contend; Jehojarib,* the name of two Israelites:— Jehoiarib. Compare H3114

H3081 יְהוּכַל *yĕhûkal* from H3201; *potent; Jehukal,* an Israelite:— Jehucal. Compare H3116

H3082 יְהוֹנָדָב *yĕhônādāb* from H3068 and H5068; *Jehovah-largessed; Jehonadab,* the name of an Israelite and of an Arab:— Jehonadab, Jonadab. Compare H3122

H3083 יְהוֹנָתָן *yĕhônātān* from H3068 and H5414; *Jehovah-given; Jehonathan,* the name of four Israelites:— Jonathan. Compare H3129

H3084 יְהוֹסֵף *yĕhôsēp* a fuller form of H3130; *Joseph* (i.e. Joseph), a son of Jacob:— Joseph.

H3085 יְהוֹעַדָּה *yĕhôᶜaddâ* from H3068 and H5710; *Jehovah-adorned; Jehoäddah,* an Israelite:— Jehoada.

H3086 יְהוֹעַדִּין *yĕhôᶜaddîn* or

יְהוֹעַדָּן *yĕhôᶜaddān* from H3068 and H5727; *Jehovah-pleased; Jehoäddin* or *Jehoäddan,* an Israelitess:— Jehoaddan.

H3087 יְהוֹצָדָק *yĕhôṣādāq* from H3068 and H6663; *Jehovah-righted; Jehotsadak,* an Israelite:— Jehozadek, Josedech. Compare H3136

H3088 יְהוֹרָם *yĕhôrām* from H3068 and H7311; *Jehovah-raised; Jehoram,* the name of a Syrian and of three Israelites:— Jehoram, Joram. Compare H3141

H3089 יְהוֹשֶׁבַע *yĕhôšebaᶜ* from H3068 and H7650; *Jehovah-sworn; Jehosheba,* an Israelitess:— Jehosheba. Compare H3090

H3090 יְהוֹשַׁבְעַת *yĕhûšabᶜat* a form of H3089; *Jehoshabath,* an Israelitess:— Jehoshabeath.

H3091 יְהוֹשׁוּעַ *yĕhôšûaᶜ* or

יְהוֹשֻׁעַ *yĕhôšūaᶜ* from H3068 and H3467; *Jehovah-saved; Jehoshuä* (i.e. Joshua), the Jewish leader:— Jehoshua, Jehoshuah, Joshua. Compare H1954, H3442

H3092 יְהוֹשָׁפָט *yĕhôšāpāṭ* from H3068 and H8199; *Jehovah-judged; Jehoshaphat,* the name of six Israelites; also of a valley near Jerusalem:— Jehoshaphat. Compare H3146

H3093 יָהִיר *yāhîr* probably from the same as H2022; *elated;* hence *arrogant:*— haughty, proud.

H3094 יְהַלֶּלְאֵל *yĕhallelʾēl* from H1984 and H410; *praising God; Jehallelel,* the name of two Israelites:— Jehaleleel, Jehalelel.

H3095 יַהֲלֹם *yahălōm* from H1986 (in the sense of *hardness*); a precious stone, probably *onyx:*— diamond.

H3096 יַהַץ *yahaṣ* or

יַהְצָה *yahṣâ* or (feminine)

יַהְצָה *yahṣâ* from an unused root meaning to *stamp;* perhaps *threshing*-floor; *Jahats* or *Jahtsah,* a place east of the Jordan:— Jahaz, Jahazah, Jahzah.

H3097 יוֹאָב *yôʾāb* from H3068 and H1; *Jehovah-fathered; Joäb,* the name of three Israelites:— Joab.

H3098 יוֹאָח *yôʾāḥ* from H3068 and H251; *Jehovah-brothered; Joach,* the name of four Israelites:— Joah.

H3099 יוֹאָחָז *yôʾāḥāz* a form of H3059; *Joächaz,* the name of two Israelites:— Jehoahaz, Joahaz.

H3100 יוֹאֵל *yôʾēl* from H3068 and H410; *Jehovah* (is his) *God; Joël,* the name of twelve Israelites:— Joel.

H3101 יוֹאָשׁ *yôʾāš* or

יֹאָשׁ *yōʾāš* (2 Chron. 24:1), a form of H3060; *Joäsh,* the name of six Israelites:— Joash.

H3102 יוֹב *yôb* perhaps a form of H3103, but more probably by erroneous transcription for H3437; *Job,* an Israelite:— Job.

H3103 יוֹבָב *yôbāb* from H2980; *howler; Jobab,* the name of two Israelites and of three foreigners:— Jobab.

H3104 יוֹבֵל *yôbēl* or

יֹבֵל *yōbēl* apparently from H2986; the *blast* of a horn (from its *continuous* sound); specifically the *signal* of the silver trumpets; hence the instrument itself and the festival thus introduced:— jubile, ram's horn, trumpet.

H3105 יוּבַל *yûbal* from H2986; a *stream:*— river.

H3106 יוּבָל *yûbāl* from H2986; *stream; Jubal,* an antediluvian:— Jubal.

H3107 יוֹזָבָד *yôzābād* a form of H3075; *Jozabad,* the name of ten Israelites:— Josabad, Jozabad.

H3108 יוֹזָכָר *yôzākār* from H3068 and H2142; *Jehovah-remembered; Jozacar,* an Israelite:— Jozachar.

H3109 יוֹחָא *yôḥāʾ* probably from H3068 and a variation of H2421; *Jehovah-revived; Jocha,* the name of two Israelites:— Joha.

H3110 יוֹחָנָן *yôḥānān* a form of H3076; *Jochanan,* the name of nine Israelites:— Johanan.

H3111 יוֹיָדָע *yôyādāᶜ* a form of H3077; *Jojada,* the name of two Israelites:— Jehoiada, Joiada.

H3112 יוֹיָכִין *yôyākîn* a form of H3078; *Jojakin,* an Israelite king:— Jehoiachin.

H3113 יוֹיָקִים *yôyāqîm* a form of H3079; *Jojakim,* an Israelite:— Joiakim. Compare H3137

H3114 יוֹיָרִיב *yôyārîb* a form of H3080; *Jojarib,* the name of four Israelites:— Joiarib.

H3115 יוֹכֶבֶד *yôkebed* from H3068 contracted and H3513; *Jehovah-gloried; Jokebed,* the mother of Moses :— Jochebed.

H3116 יוּכַל *yûkal* a form of H3081; *Jukal,* an Israelite:— Jucal.

H3117 יוֹם *yôm* from an unused root meaning to *be hot;* a *dry* (as the *warm* hours), whether literally (from sunrise to sunset, or from one sunset to the next), or figuratively (a space of time defined by an associated term), [often used adverbially]:— age, always, chronicles, continually, continuance, daily, day, birthday, each day, today, now a days, two days, days agone, elder, end, evening, ever, everlasting, evermore, forever, full, life, as long as, so long as . . . live, now, even now, old, outlived, perpetually, presently, remaineth, required, season, since, space, then, time, process of time, as at other times, in trouble, weather, when, as when, a while, the while, within a while, while that, whole, whole age, year, full year, yearly, younger.

H3118 יוֹם *yôm* (Aramaic) corresponding to H3117; a *day:*— day (by day), time.

H3119 יוֹמָם *yûmām* from H3117; *daily:*— daily, day, by day, in the day, daytime, in the daytime.

H3120 יָוָן *yāwān* probably from the same as H3196; *effervescing* (i.e. hot and active); *Javan,* the name of a son of Joktan, and of the race *(Ionians,* i.e. Greeks) descended from him, with their territory; also of a place in Arabia:— Javan.

H3121 יָוֵן *yāwēn* from the same as H3196; properly *dregs* (as *effervescing*); hence *mud:*— mire, miry.

H3122 יוֹנָדָב *yônādāb* a form of H3082; *Jonadab,* the name of an Israelite and of a Rechabite:— Jonadab.

H3123 יוֹנָה *yônâ* probably from the same as H3196; a *dove* (apparently from the *warmth* of their mating):— dove, pigeon.

H3124 יוֹנָה *yônâ* the same as H3123; *Jonah,* an Israelite:— Jonah.

H3125 יְוָנִי *yĕwānî* patronymic from H3121; a *Jevanite,* or descendant of Javan:— Grecian.

H3126 יוֹנֵק *yônēq* active participle of H3243; a *sucker;* hence a *twig* (of a tree felled and sprouting):— tender plant.

H3127 יוֹנֶקֶת *yôneqet* feminine of H3126; a *sprout* :— branch, tender branch, young twig.

H3128 יוֹנַת אֵלֶם רְחֹקִים *yônat ʾēlem rĕḥōqîm* from H3123 and H482 and the plural of H7350; *dove of* (the) *silence* (i.e. *dumb* Israel) *of* (i.e. among) *distances* (i.e. strangers); the title of a ditty (used for a name of its melody):— Jonath-elem-rechokim.

H3129 יוֹנָתָן *yônātān* a form of H3083; *Jonathan,* the name of ten Israelites:— Jonathan.

H3130 יוֹסֵף *yôsēp* future of H3254; *let him add* (or perhaps simply active participle *adding*); *Joseph,* the name of seven Israelites:— Joseph. Compare H3084

H3131 יוֹסִפְיָה *yôsipyâ* from active participle of H3254 and H3050; *Jah* (is) *adding; Josiphjah,* an Israelite:— Josiphiah.

H3132 יוֹעֵאלָה *yôᶜēʾlâ* perhaps feminine active participle of H3276; *furthermore; Joelah,* an Israelite:— Joelah.

H3133 יוֹעֵד *yôᶜēd* apparently active participle of H3259; *appointer; Joed,* an Israelite:— Joed.

H3134 יוֹעֶזֶר *yôᶜezer* from H3068 and H5828; *Jehovah* (is his) *help; Joezer,* an Israelite:— Joezer.

H3135 יוֹעָשׁ *yôᶜāš* from H3068 and H5789; *Jehovah-hastened; Joash,* the name of two Israelites:— Joash.

H3136 יוֹצָדָק *yôṣādāq* a form of H3087; *Jotsadak,* an Israelite:— Jozadak.

H3137 יוֹקִים *yôqîm* a form of H3113; *Jokim,* an Israelite:— Jokim.

H3138 יוֹרֶה *yôreh* active participle of H3384; *sprinkling;* hence a *sprinkling* (or autumnal showers):— first rain, former rain.

H3139 יוֹרָה *yôrâ* from H3384; *rainy; Jorah,* an Israelite:— Jorah.

H3140 יוֹרַי *yôray* from H3384; *rainy; Jorai,* an Israelite:— Jorai.

H3141 יוֹרָם *yôrām* a form of H3088; *Joram,* the name of three Israelites and one Syrian:— Joram.

H3142 יוּשַׁב חֶסֶד *yûšab ḥesed* from H7725 and H2617; *kindness will be returned; Jushab-Chesed,* an Israelite:— Jushab-hesed.

H3143 יוֹשִׁבְיָה *yôšibyâ* from H3427 and H3050; *Jehovah will cause to dwell; Joshibjah,* an Israelite:— Josibiah.

H3144 יוֹשָׁה *yôšâ* probably a form of H3145; *Joshah,* an Israelite:— Joshah.

H3145 יוֹשַׁוְיָה *yôšawyâ* from H3068 and H7737; *Jehovah-set; Joshavjah,* an Israelite:— Joshaviah. Compare H3144

H3146 יוֹשָׁפָט *yôšāpāṭ* a form of H3092; *Joshaphat,* an Israelite:— Joshaphat.

H3147 יוֹתָם *yôtām* from H3068 and H8535; *Jehovah* (is) *perfect; Jotham,* the name of three Israelites:— Jotham.

H3148 יוֹתֵר *yôtēr* active participle of H3498; properly *redundant;* hence *over and above,* as adjective, noun, adverb or conjunction [as follows]:— better, more, moreover, over, profit.

H3149 יְזוּאֵל *yĕzawʾēl* from an unused root (meaning to *sprinkle*) and H410; *sprinkled of God; Jezavel,* an Israelite:— Jeziel *[from the margin].*

H3150 יִזִּיָּה *yizzîyâ* from the same as the first part of H3149 and H3050; *sprinkled of Jah; Jizzijah,* an Israelite:— Jeziah.

H3151 יָזִיז *yāzîz* from the same as H2123; *he will make promiment; Jaziz,* an Israelite:— Jaziz.

H3152 יִזְלִיאָה *yizlîʾâ* perhaps from an unused root (meaning to *draw up*); *he will draw out; Jizliah,* an Israelite:— Jezliah.

H3153 יְזַנְיָה *yĕzanyâ* or

יְזַנְיָהוּ *yuzonyāhû* probably for H2970; *Jezanjah,* an Israelite:— Jezaniah.

H3154 יֶזַע *yezaᶜ* from an unused root meaning to *ooze; sweat,* i.e. (by implication) a *sweating* dress:— any thing that causeth sweat.

H3155 יִזְרָח *yizrāḥ* a variation for H250; a *Jizrach* (i.e. Ezrachite or Zarchite) or descendant of Zerach :— Izrahite.

H3156 יִזְרַחְיָה *yizraḥyâ* from H2224 and H3050; *Jah will shine; Jizrachjah,* the name of two Israelites:— Izrahiah, Jezrahiah.

H3157 יִזְרְעֶאל *yizrĕᶜēʾl* from H2232 and H410; *God will sow; Jizreël,* the name of two places in Palestine and of two Israelites:— Jezreel.

H3158 יִזְרְעֵאלִי *yizrĕᶜēʾlî* patronymic from H3157; a *Jizreëlite* or native of Jizreel:— Jezreelite.

H3159 יִזְרְעֵאלִית *yizrĕᶜēʾlît* feminine of H3158; a *Jezreëlitess:*— Jezreelitess.

H3160 יְחֻבָּה *yĕḥubbâ* from H2247; *hidden; Jechubbah,* an Israelite:— Jehubbah.

H3161 יָחַד *yāḥad* a primitive root; to *be* (or become) *one:*— join, unite.

H3162 יַחַד *yaḥad* from H3161; properly a *unit,* i.e. (adverbially) *unitedly:*— alike, at all, at once, both, likewise, only, altogether, together, withal.

H3163 יַחְדּוֹ *yaḥdô* from H3162 with pronominal suffix; *his unity,* i.e. (adverbially) *together; Jachdo,* an Israelite:— Jahdo.

H3164 יַחְדִּיאֵל *yaḥdîʾēl* from H3162 and H410; *unity of God; Jachdiël,* an Israelite:— Jahdiel.

H3165 יֶחְדִּיָּהוּ *yeḥdîyāhû* from H3162 and H3050; *unity of Jah; Jechdijah,* the name of two Israelites:— Jehdeiah.

H3166 יַחֲזִיאֵל *yaḥăzîʾēl* from H2372 and H410; *beheld of God; Jachaziël,* the name of five Israelites:— Jahaziel, Jahziel.

H3167 יַחְזְיָה *yaḥzĕyâ* from H2372 and H3050; *Jah will behold; Jachzejah,* an Israelite:— Jahaziah.

H3168 יְחֶזְקֵאל *yĕḥezqēʾl* from H2388 and H410; *God will strengthen; Jechezkel,* the name of two Israelites:— Ezekiel, Jehezekel.

H3169 יְחִזְקִיָּה *yĕḥizqîyâ* or

יְחִזְקִיָּהוּ *yĕḥizqîyāhû* from H3388 and H3050; *strengthened of Jah; Jechizkijah,* the name of five Israelites:— Hezekiah, Jehizkiah. Compare H2396

H3170 יַחְזֵרָה *yaḥzērâ* from the same as H2386; perhaps *protection; Jachzerah,* an Israelite:— Jahzerah.

H3171 יְחִיאֵל *yĕḥîʾēl* or (2 Chron. 29:14)

יְחוּאֵל *yĕḥawʾēl* from H2421 and H410; *God will live; Jechiël* (or *Jechavel*), the name of eight Israelites:— Jehiel.

H3172 יְחִיאֵלִי *yĕḥîʾēlî* patronymic from H3171; a *Jechiëlite* or descendant of Jechiel:— Jehieli.

H3173 יָחִיד *yāḥîd* from H3161; properly *united,* i.e. *sole;* by implication *beloved;* also *lonely;* (feminine) the *life* (as not to be replaced):— darling, desolate, only, only child, only son, solitary.

H3174 יְחִיָּה *yĕḥîyâ* from H2421 and H3050; *Jah will live; Jechijah,* an Israelite:— Jehiah.

H3175 יָחִיל *yāḥîl* from H3176; *expectant:*— should hope.

H3176 יָחַל *yāḥal* a primitive root; to *wait;* by implication to *be patient, hope:*— hope, cause to hope, have hope, make to hope, be pained, stay, tarry, trust, wait.

H3177 יַחְלְאֵל *yaḥlĕʾēl* from H3176 and H410; *expectant of God; Jachleël,* an Israelite:— Jahleel.

H3178 יַחְלְאֵלִי *yaḥlĕʾēlî* patronymic from H3177; a *Jachleëlite* or descendant of Jachleel:— Jahleelites.

H3179 יָחַם *yāḥam* a primitive root; probably to *be hot;* figuratively to *conceive:*— get heat, be hot, conceive, be warm.

H3180 יַחְמוּר *yaḥmûr* from H2560; a kind of *deer* (from the color; compare H2543):— fallow deer.

H3181 יַחְמַי *yaḥmay* probably from H3179; *hot; Jachmai,* an Israelite:— Jahmai.

H3182 יָחֵף *yāḥēp* from an unused root meaning to *take off the shoes; unsandalled:*— barefoot, being unshod.

H3183 יַחְצְאֵל *yaḥṣĕʾēl* from H2673 and H410; *God will allot; Jachtseël,* an Israelite:— Jahzeel. Compare H3185

H3184 יַחְצְאֵלִי *yaḥṣĕʾēlî* patronymic from H3183; a *Jachtseëlite* (collectively) or descendant of Jachtseel:— Jahzeelites.

H3185 יַחְצִיאֵל *yaḥṣîʾēl* from H2673 and H410; *allotted of God; Jachtsiël,* an Israelite:— Jahziel. Compare H3183

H3186 יָחַר *yāḥar* a primitive root; to *delay:*— tarry longer.

H3187 יָחַשׂ *yāḥaś* a primitive root; to *sprout;* used only as denominative from H3188; to *enroll* by pedigree:— geneology, number after geneology, number throughout the genealogy, geneology to be reckoned, be reckoned by genealogies.

H3188 יַחַשׂ *yaḥaś* from H3187; a *pedigree* or family list (as *growing* spontaneously):— genealogy.

H3189 יַחַת *yaḥat* from H3161; *unity; Jachath,* the name of four Israelites:— Jahath.

H3190 יָטַב *yāṭab* a primitive root; to *be* (causatively) *make well,* literally *(sound, beautiful)* or figuratively *(happy, successful, right):*— be accepted, amend, use aright, benefit, be better, make better, seem best, make cheerful, be comely, be content, diligent, diligently, dress, earnestly, find favour, give, be glad, do good, be good, make good, do goodness, be merry, make merry, please, please well, shew more kindness, skilfully, very small, surely, make sweet, thoroughly, tire, trim, very, be well, can well, deal well, entreat well, go well, have well said, have well seen.

H3191 יְטַב *yĕṭab* (Aramaic) corresponding to H3190 :— seem good.

H3192 יָטְבָה *yoṭbâ* from H3190; *pleasantness; Jotbah,* a place in Palestine:— Jotbah.

H3193 יָטְבָתָה *yoṭbātâ* from H3192; *Jotbathah,* a place in the Desert:— Jotbath, Jotbathah.

H3194 יֻטָּה *yuṭṭâ* or

יוּטָה *yûṭâ* from H5186; *extended; Juttah* (or *Jutah*), a place in Palestine:— Juttah.

H3195 יְטוּר *yĕṭûr* probably from the same as H2905; *encircled* (i.e. inclosed); *Jetur,* a son of Ishmael:— Jetur.

H3196 יַיִן *yayin* from an unused root meaning to *effervesce; wine* (as fermented); by implication *intoxication:*— banqueting, wine, winebibber.

H3197 יַךְ *yak* by erroneous transcription for H3027; a *hand* or *side:*— side, wayside.

H3198 יָכַח *yākaḥ* a primitive root; to *be right* (i.e. correct); reciprocally to *argue;* causatively to *decide, justify* or *convict:*— appoint, argue, chasten, convince, correct, correction, daysman, dispute, judge, maintain, plead, reason, reason together, rebuke, reprove, repover, surely, in any wise.

H3199 יָכִין *yākîn* from H3559; *he* (or *it*) *will establish; Jakin,* the name of three Israelites and of a temple pillar:— Jachin.

H3200 יָכִינִי *yākînî* patronymic from H3199; a *Jakinite* (collectively) or descendant of Jakin:— Jachinites.

H3201 יָכֹל *yākōl* or (fuller)

יָכוֹל *yākôl* a primitive root; to *be able,* literally *(can , could)* or morally *(may, might):*— be able, any at all, any ways, attain, can, can away with, cannot, could, endure, might, overcome, have power, prevail, still, suffer.

H3202 יְכֵל *yĕkēl* or

יְכִיל *yĕkîl* (Aramaic) corresponding to H3201 :— be able, can, couldest, prevail.

H3203 יְכָלְיָה *yĕkolyâ* and

יְכָלְיָהוּ *yĕkolyāhû* or (2 Chron. 26:3)

יְכִילְיָה *yĕkîlĕyâ* from H3201 and H3050; *Jah will enable; Jekoljah* or *Jekiljah,* an Israelitess:— Jecholiah, Jecoliah.

H3204 יְכָנְיָה *yĕkonyâ* and

יְכָנְיָהוּ *yĕkonyāhû* or (Jer. 27:20)

יְכוֹנְיָה *yĕkônĕyâ* from H3559 and H3050; *Jah will establish; Jekonjah,* a Jewish king:— Jeconiah. Compare H3659

H3205 יָלַד *yālad* a primitive root; to *bear* young; causatively to *beget;* medially to *act as midwife;* specifically to *show lineage:*— bear, beget, birth, birthday, born, bring forth, bring forth children, bring forth young, make to bring forth, bring up, calve, child, come, be delivered, be delivered of a child, time of delivery, gender, hatch, labour, midwife, do the office of a midwife, declare pedigrees, be the son of, traviail, woman in travail, travailing woman, woman that travaileth.

H3206 יֶלֶד *yeled* from H3205; something *born,* i.e. a *lad* or *offspring:*— boy, child, fruit, son, young man, young one.

H3207 יַלְדָּה *yaldâ* feminine of H3206; a *lass:*— damsel, girl.

H3208 יַלְדוּת *yaldût* abstractly from H3206; *boyhood* (or *girlhood*):— childhood, youth.

H3209 יִלּוֹד *yillôd* passive from H3205; *born:*— born.

H3210 יָלוֹן *yālôn* from H3885; *lodging; Jalon,* an Israelite:— Jalon.

H3211 יָלִיד *yālîd* from H3205; *born:*— born, homeborn, child, son.

H3212 יָלַךְ *yālak* a primitive root [compare H1980]; to *walk* (literally or figuratively); causatively to *carry* (in various senses):— again, away, bear, bring, carry, carry away, come, come away, depart, flow, follow, following, get, get away, get hence, get him, go, cause to go, make go, go away, going, gone, go one's way, go out, grow, lead, lead forth, let down, march, prosper, pursue, cause to run, spread, take away, take journey, vanish, walk, cause to walk, walking, wax, be weak.

H3213 יָלַל *yālal* a primitive root; to *howl* (with a wailing tone) or *yell* (with a boisterous one):— howl, make to howl, be howling.

H3214 יְלֵל *yĕlēl* from H3213; a *howl;*:— howling.

H3215 יְלָלָה *yĕlālâ* feminine of H3214; a *howling* :— howling.

H3216 יָלַע *yālaʿ* a primitive root; to *blurt* or utter inconsiderately:— devour.

H3217 יַלֶּפֶת *yallepet* from an unused root apparently meaning to *stick* or *scrape; scurf* or *tetter:*— scabbed.

H3218 יֶלֶק *yeleq* from an unused root meaning to *lick* up; a *devourer;* specifically the young *locust:*— cankerworm, caterpillar.

H3219 יַלְקוּט *yalqûṭ* from H3950; a travelling *pouch* (as if for gleanings):— scrip.

H3220 יָם *yām* from an unused root meaning to *roar;* a *sea* (as breaking in *noisy* surf) or large body of water; specifically (with the article) the *Mediterranean;* sometimes a large *river,* or an artificial *basin;* locally, the *west,* or (rarely) the *south:*— sea, seafaring man, seashore, south, west, western, side, westward.

H3221 יָם *yām* (Aramaic) corresponding to H3220 :— sea.

H3222 יֵם *yēm* from the same as H3117; a *warm* spring:— mule.

H3223 יְמוּאֵל *yĕmûʾēl* from H3117 and H410; *day of God; Jemuel,* an Israelite:— Jemuel.

H3224 יְמִימָה *yĕmîmâ* perhaps from the same as H3117; properly *warm,* i.e. *affectionate;* hence *dove* [compare H3123]; *Jemimah,* one of Job's daughters:— Jemimah.

H3225 יָמִין *yāmîn* from H3231; the *right* hand or side (leg, eye) of a person or other object (as the *stronger* and more dexterous); locally, the *south:*— left-handed, right, right hand, right side, south.

H3226 יָמִין *yāmîn* the same as H3225; *Jamin,* the name of three Israelites:— Jamin. See also H1144

H3227 יְמִינִי *yĕmînî* for H3225; *right:*— right, on the right hand.

H3228 יְמִינִי *yĕmînî* patronymic from H3226; a *Jeminite* (collectively) or descendant of Jamin:— Jaminites. See also H1145

H3229 יִמְלָא *yimlāʾ* or

יִמְלָה *yimlâ* from H4390; *full; Jimla* or *Jimlah,* an Israelite:— Imla, Imlah.

H3230 יַמְלֵךְ *yamlēk* from H4427; *he will make king; Jamlek,* an Israelite:— Jamlech.

H3231 יָמַן *yāman* a primitive root; to *be* (physically) *right* (i.e. firm); but used only as denominative from H3225 and transitively, to *be right-handed* or *take the right-hand* side:— go to the right, go on the right hand, turn to the right hand, use the right hand.

H3232 יִמְנָה *yimnâ* from H3231; *prosperity* (as betokened by the *right* hand); *Jimnah,* the name of two Israelites; also (with the article) of the posterity of one of them:— Imna, Imnah, Jimnah, Jimnites.

H3233 יְמָנִי *yĕmānî* from H3231; *right* (i.e. at the right hand):— right, on the right hand.

H3234 יִמְנָע *yimnāʿ* from H4513; *he will restrain; Jimna,* an Israelite:— Imna.

H3235 יָמַר *yāmar* a primitive root; to *exchange;* by implication to *change places:*— boast selves, change.

H3236 יִמְרָה *yimrâ* probably from H3235; *interchange; Jimrah,* an Israelite:— Imrah.

H3237 יָמַשׁ *yāmaš* a primitive root; to *touch:*— feel.

H3238 יָנָה *yānâ* a primitive root; to *rage* or *be violent;* by implication to *suppress,* to *maltreat:*— destroy, oppress, thrust out by oppression, oppressing, oppresor, proud, vex, do violence.

H3239 יָנוֹחַ *yānôaḥ* or (with enclitic)

יָנוֹחָה *yānôḥâ* from H3240; *quiet; Janoäch* or *Janochah,* a place in Palestine:— Janoah, Janohah.

H3240 יָנַח *yānaḥ* a primitive root; to *deposit;* by implication to *allow to stay:*— bestow, cast down, lay, lay down, lay up, leave, leave off, let alone, let remain, pacify, place, put, set, set down, suffer, withdraw, withhold. (The Hiphil forms with the *dagesh* are here referred to, in accordance with the older grammarians; but if any distinction of the kind is to be made, these should rather be referred to H5117, and the others here.).

H3241 יָנִים *yānîm* from H5123; *asleep; Janim,* a place in Palestine:— Janum *[from the margin].*

H3242 יְנִיקָה *yĕnîqâ* from H3243; a *sucker* or sapling:— young twig.

H3243 יָנַק *yānaq* a primitive root; to *suck;* causatively to *give milk:*— milch, nurse, nursing mother, suck, give suck, make to suck, sucking child, suckling.

H3244 יַנְשׁוּף *yanšûp* or

יַנְשֹׁוף *yanšôp* apparently from H5398; an unclean (aquatic) bird; probably the *heron* (perhaps from its *blowing* cry, or because the *night*-heron is meant [compare H5399]):— owl, great owl.

H3245 יָסַד *yāsad* a primitive root; to *set* (literally or figuratively); intensively to *found;* reflexively to *sit* down together, i.e. *settle, consult:*— appoint, take counsel, establish, found, lay the foundation, lay for a foundation, foundation, instruct, lay, ordain, set, sure.

H3246 יְסֻד *yĕsūd* from H3245; a *foundation* (figuratively, i.e. *beginning*):— began.

H3247 יְסוֹד *yĕsôd* from H3245; a *foundation* (literally or figuratively):— bottom, foundation, repairing.

H3248 יְסוּדָה *yĕsûdâ* feminine of H3246; a *foundation:*— foundation.

H3249 יָסוּר *yāsûr* from H5493; *departing:*— they that depart.

H3250 יִסּוֹר *yissôr* from H3256; a *reprover:*— instruct.

H3251 יָסַךְ *yāsak* a primitive root; to *pour* (intransitively):— be poured.

H3252 יִסְכָּה *yiskâ* from an unused root meaning to *watch; observant; Jiskah,* sister of Lot:— Iscah.

H3253 יִסְמַכְיָהוּ *yismakyāhû* from H5564 and H3050; *Jah will sustain; Jismakjah,* an Israelite:— Ismachiah.

H3254 יָסַף *yāsap* a primitive root; to *add* or *augment* (often adverbially to *continue* to do a thing):— add, again, any more, cease, come more, conceive again, continue, exceed, further, gather together, get more, give moreover, henceforth, increase, increase more and more, join, longer, longer bring, longer do, longer make, longer much, longer put, more, the more, much more, yet more, more and more, proceed, proceed further, prolong, put, be stronger, yet, yield.

H3255 יְסַף *yĕsap* (Aramaic) corresponding to H3254 :— add.

H3256 יָסַר *yāsar* a primitive root; to *chastise,* literally (with blows) or figuratively (with words); hence to *instruct:*— bind, chasten, chastise, correct, instruct, punish, reform, reprove, sore, teach.

H3257 יָע *yāʿ* from H3261; a *shovel:*— shovel.

H3258 יַעְבֵּץ *yaʿbēṣ* from an unused root probably meaning to *grieve; sorrowful; Jabets,* the name of an Israelite, and also of a place in Palestine:— Jabez.

H3259 יָעַד *yāʿad* a primitive root; to *fix* upon (by agreement or appointment); by implication to *meet* (at a stated time), to *summon* (to trial), to *direct* (in a certain quarter or position), to *engage* (for marriage):— agree, appoint, make an appointment, appoint a time, assemble, assemble selves, betroth, gather selves, gather together, meet, meet together, set, set a time.

H3260 יֶעְדִּי *yeʿdî* from H3259; *appointed; Jedi,* an Israelite:— Iddo *[from the margin].* See H3035

H3261 יָעָה *yāʿâ* a primitive root; apparently to *brush* aside:— sweep away.

H3262 יְעוּאֵל *yĕʿûʾēl* from H3261 and H410; *carried away of God; Jeüel,* the name of four Israelites:— Jehiel, Jeiel, Jeuel. Compare H3273

H3263 יְעוּץ *yĕʿûṣ* from H5779; *counsellor; Jeüts,* an Israelite:— Jeuz.

H3264 יָעוֹר *yāʿôr* a variation of H3293; a *forest:*— wood.

H3265 יָעוּר *yāʿûr* apparently passive participle of the same as H3293; *wooded; Jaür,* an Israelite:— Jair *[from the margin].*

H3266 יְעוּשׁ *yĕʿûš* from H5789; *hasty; Jeüsh,* the name of an Edomite and of four Israelites:— Jehush, Jeush. Compare H3274

H3267 יָעַז *yāʿaz* a primitive root; to be *bold* or *obstinate:*— fierce.

H3268 יַעֲזִיאֵל *yaʿăzîʾēl* from H3267 and H410; *emboldened of God; Jaaziël,* an Israelite:— Jaaziel.

H3269 יַעֲזִיָּהוּ *yaʿăzîyāhû* from H3267 and H3050; *emboldened of Jah; Jaazijah,* an Israelite:— Jaaziah.

H3270 יַעֲזֵיר *yaʿăzêr* or

יַעְזֵר *yaʿzēr* from H5826; *helpful; Jaazer* or *Jazer,* a place east of the Jordan:— Jaazer, Jazer.

H3271 יָעַט *yāʿaṭ* a primitive root; to *clothe:*— cover.

H3272 יְעַט *yĕʿaṭ* (Aramaic) corresponding to H3289; to *counsel;* reflexively to *consult:*— counsellor, consult together.

H3273 יְעִיאֵל *yĕʿîʾēl* from H3261 and H410; *carried away of God; Jeïel,* the name of six Israelites:— Jeiel, Jehiel. Compare H3262

H3274 יְעִישׁ *yĕʿîš* from H5789; *hasty; Jeish,* the name of an Edomite and of an Israelite:— Jeush *[from the margin].* Compare H3266

H3275 יַעְכָּן *yaʿkān* from the same as H5912; *troublesome; Jakan,* an Israelite:— Jachan.

H3276 יָעַל *yāʿal* a primitive root; properly to *ascend;* figuratively to *be valuable* (objectively *useful,* subjectively *benefited*):— at all, set forward, can do good, profit, have profit, be profitable.

H3277 יָעֵל *yāʿēl* from H3276; an *ibex* (as *climbing*):— wild goat.

H3278 יָעֵל *yāʿēl* the same as H3277; *Jaël,* a Canaanite:— Jael.

H3279 יַעֲלָא *yaʿălāʾ* or
יַעֲלָה *yaʿălâ* the same as H3280 or direct from H3276; *Jaala* or *Jaalah,* one of the Nethinim:— Jaala, Jaalah.

H3280 יַעֲלָה *yaʿălâ* feminine of H3277:— roe.

H3281 יַעְלָם *yaʿlām* from H5956; *occult; Jalam,* an Edomite:— Jalam.

H3282 יַעַן *yaʿan* from an unused root meaning to *pay attention;* properly *heed;* by implication *purpose* (sake or account); used adverbially to indicate the *reason* or cause:— because, because that, forasmuch, forasmuch as, seeing then, that, whereas, why.

H3283 יָעֵן *yāʿēn* from the same as H3282; the *ostrich* (probably from its *answering* cry):— ostrich.

H3284 יַעֲנָה *yaʿănâ* feminine of H3283, and meaning the same:— owl.

H3285 יַעֲנַי *yaʿănay* from the same as H3283; *responsive; Jaanai,* an Israelite:— Jaanai.

H3286 יָעַף *yāʿap* a primitive root; to *tire* (as if from wearisome *flight*):— faint, cause to fly, be weary, weary self.

H3287 יָעֵף *yāʿēp* from H3286; *fatigued;* figuratively *exhausted:*— faint, weary.

H3288 יְעָף *yĕʿāp* from H3286; *fatigue* (adverbially, utterly *exhausted*):— swiftly.

H3289 יָעַץ *yāʿaṣ* a primitive root; to *advise;* reflexively to *deliberate* or *resolve:*— advertise, take advice, advise, advise well, consult, counsel, give counsel, take counsel, counsellor, determine, devise, guide purpose.

H3290 יַעֲקֹב *yaʿăqōb* from H6117; *heel-catcher* (i.e. supplanter); *Jaakob,* the Israelitish patriarch:— Jacob.

H3291 יַעֲקֹבָה *yaʿăqōbâ* from H3290; *Jaakobah,* an Israelite:— Jaakobah.

H3292 יַעֲקָן *yaʿăqān* from the same as H6130; *Jaakan,* an Idumaean:— Jaakan. Compare H1142

H3293 יַעַר *yaʿar* from an unused root probably meaning to *thicken* with verdure; a *copse* of bushes; hence a *forest;* hence *honey* in the *comb* (as hived in trees):— honeycomb, forest, wood.

H3294 יַעְרָה *yaʿrâ* a form of H3295; *Jarah,* an Israelite:— Jarah.

H3295 יַעֲרָה *yaʿărâ* feminine of H3293, and meaning the same:— honeycomb, forest.

H3296 יַעֲרֵי אֹרְגִים *yaʿărê ʾōrĕgîm* from the plural of H3293 and the masculine plural participle active of H707; *woods of weavers; Jaare-Oregim,* an Israelite:— Jaare-oregim.

H3297 יְעָרִים *yĕʿārîm* plural of H3293; *forests; Jeärim,* a place in Palestine:— Jearim. Compare H7157

H3298 יַעֲרֶשְׁיָה *yaʿărešyâ* from an unused root of uncertain signification and H3050; *Jaareshjah,* an Israelite:— Jaresiah.

H3299 יַעֲשׂוּ *yaʿăśû* from H6213; *they will do; Jaasu,* an Israelite:— Jaasau.

H3300 יַעֲשִׂיאֵל *yaʿăśîʾēl* from H6213 and H410; *made of God; Jaasiel,* an Israelite:— Jaasiel, Jasiel.

H3301 יִפְדְּיָה *yipdĕyâ* from H6299 and H3050; *Jah will liberate; Jiphdejah,* an Israelite:— Iphedeiah.

H3302 יָפָה *yāpâ* a primitive root; properly to *be bright,* i.e. (by implication) *beautiful:*— be beautiful, be fair, be fairer, make self fair, deck.

H3303 יָפֶה *yāpēh* from H3302; *beautiful* (literally or figuratively):— beautiful, beauty, comely, fair, fairest, fair one, goodly, pleasant, well.

H3304 יְפֵה־פִיָּה *yĕpēh-pîyâ* from H3302 by reduplication; *very beautiful:*— very fair.

H3305 יָפוֹ *yāpô* or
יָפוֹא *yāpôʾ* (Ezra 3:7), from H3302; *beautiful; Japho,* a place in Palestine:— Japha, Joppa.

H3306 יָפַח *yāpaḥ* a primitive root; properly to *breathe* hard, i.e. (by implication) to *sigh:*— bewail self.

H3307 יָפֵחַ *yāpēaḥ* from H3306; properly *puffing,* i.e. (figuratively) *meditating:*— such as breathe out.

H3308 יֳפִי *yŏpî* from H3302; *beauty:*— beauty.

H3309 יָפִיעַ *yāpîaʿ* from H3313; *bright; Japhia,* the name of a Canaanite, an Israelite, and a place in Palestine:— Japhia.

H3310 יַפְלֵט *yaplēṭ* from H6403; *he will deliver; Japhlet,* an Israelite:— Japhlet.

H3311 יַפְלֵטִי *yaplēṭî* patronymic from H3310; a *Japhletite* or descendant of Japhlet:— Japhleti.

H3312 יְפֻנֶּה *yĕpunneh* from H6437; *he will be prepared; Jephunneh,* the name of two Israelites:— Jephunneh.

H3313 יָפַע *yāpaʿ* a primitive root; to *shine:*— be light, shew self, shine, cause to shine, shine forth.

H3314 יִפְעָה *yipʿâ* from H3313; *splendor* or (figuratively) *beauty:*— brightness.

H3315 יֶפֶת *yepet* from H6601; *expansion; Jepheth,* a son of Noah; also his posterity:— Japheth.

H3316 יִפְתָּח *yiptāḥ* from H6605; *he will open; Jiphtach,* an Israelite; also a place in Palestine:— Jephthah, Jiphtah.

H3317 יִפְתַּח־אֵל *yiptaḥ-ʾēl* from H6605 and H410; *God will open; Jiphtach-el,* a place in Palestine:— Jiphthah-el.

H3318 יָצָא *yāṣāʾ* a primitive root; to *go* (causatively bring) out, in a great variety of applications, literally and figuratively, direct and proximal:— after, appear, assuredly, bear out, begotten, break out, bring forth, bring out, bring up, carry out, come, come abroad, come out, come thereat, come without, be condemned, depart, departing, departure, draw forth, in the end, escape, exact, fail, fall, fall out, fetch forth, fetch out, get away, get forth, get hence, get out, able to go, able to go forth, cause to go forth, cause to go out, let go out, go abroad, go forth, go on out, going out, grow, have forth, have out, issue out, lay out, lie out, lead out, pluck out, proceed, pull out, put away, be risen, scarce, send with commandment, shoot forth, spread, spring out, stand out, still, surely, take forth, take out, at any time, to and fro, utter.

H3319 יְצָא *yĕṣāʾ* (Aramaic) corresponding to H3318 :— finish.

H3320 יָצַב *yāṣab* a primitive root; to *place* (any thing so as to stay); reflexively to *station, offer, continue:*— present selves, remaining, resort, set, set selves, stand, be able to stand, can stand, withstand, stand fast, stand forth, standing, stand still, stand up.

H3321 יְצֵב *yĕṣēb* (Aramaic) corresponding to H3320, to *be firm;* hence to *speak surely:*— truth.

H3322 יָצַג *yāṣag* a primitive root; to *place* permanently:— establish, leave, make, present, put, set, stay.

H3323 יִצְהָר *yiṣhār* from H6671; *oil* (as producing *light*); figuratively *anointing:*— anointed, oil.

H3324 יִצְהָר *yiṣhār* the same as H3323; *Jitshar,* an Israelite:— Izhar.

H3325 יִצְהָרִי *yiṣhārî* patronymic from H3324; a *Jitsharite* or descendant of Jitshar:— Izeharites, Izharites.

H3326 יָצוּעַ *yāṣûaʿ* passive participle of H3331; *spread,* i.e. a *bed;* (architecturally) an *extension,* i.e. *wing* or *lean-to* (a single story or collectively):— bed, chamber, couch.

H3327 יִצְחָק *yiṣḥāq* from H6711; *laughter* (i.e. *mockery*); *Jitschak* (or Isaac), son of Abraham:— Isaac. Compare H3446

H3328 יִצְחַר *yiṣḥar* from the same as H6713; *he will shine; Jitschar,* an Israelite:— and Zehoar *[from the margin].*

H3329 יָצִיא *yāṣîʾ* from H3318; *issue,* i.e. offspring :— those that came forth.

H3330 יַצִּיב *yaṣṣîb* (Aramaic) from H3321; *fixed, sure;* concretely *certainty:*— certain (-ty), true, truth.

H3331 יָצַע *yāṣaʿ* a primitive root; to *strew* as a surface:— make [one's] bed, lie, spread.

H3332 יָצַק *yāṣaq* a primitive root; properly to *pour* out (transitively or intransitively); by implication to *melt* or *cast* as metal; by extension to *place* firmly, to *stiffen* or grow hard:— cast, cleave fast, be firm, be as firm, grow, be hard, lay out, molten, overflow, pour, pour out, run out, set down, stedfast.

H3333 יְצֻקָה *yĕṣūqâ* passive participle feminine of H3332; *poured* out, i.e. *run* into a mould:— when it was cast.

H3334 יָצַר *yāṣar* a primitive root; to *press* (intransitively), i.e. *be narrow;* figuratively *be in distress:*— be distressed, be narrow, be straitened, be in straits, be vexed.

H3335 יָצַר *yāṣar* probably identical with H3334 (through the *squeezing* into shape); ([compare H3331]); to *mould* into a form; especially as a *potter;* figuratively to *determine* (i.e. form a resolution):— earthen, fashion, form, frame, make, maker, potter, purpose.

H3336 יֵצֶר *yēṣer* from H3335; a *form;* figuratively *conception* (i.e. purpose):— frame, thing framed, imagination, mind, work.

H3337 יֵצֶר *yēṣer* the same as H3336; *Jetser,* an Israelite:— Jezer.

H3338 יָצֻר *yāṣūr* passive participle of H3335; *structure,* i.e. limb or part:— member.

H3339 יִצְרִי *yiṣrî* from H3335; *formative; Jitsri,* an Israelite:— Isri.

H3340 יִצְרִי *yiṣrî* patronymic from H3337; a *Jitsrite* (collectively) or descendant of Jetser:— Jezerites.

H3341 יָצַת *yāṣat* a primitive root; to *burn* or *set on fire;* figuratively to *desolate:*— burn (up), be desolate, set (on) fire ([fire]), kindle.

H3342 יֶקֶב *yeqeb* from an unused root meaning to *excavate;* a *trough* (as dug out); specifically a wine-*vat* (whether the lower one, into which the juice drains; or the upper, in which the grapes are crushed):— fats, presses, press-fat, wine, winepress.

H3343 יְקַבְצְאֵל *yĕqabṣĕʾēl* from H6908 and H410; *God will gather; Jekabtseël,* a place in Palestine:— Jekabzeel. Compare H6909

H3344 יָקַד *yāqad* a primitive root; to *burn:*— burn, be burning, from the hearth, kindle.

H3345 יְקַד *yĕqad* (Aramaic) corresponding to H3344:— burning.

H3346 יְקֵדָא *yĕqēdāʾ* (Aramaic) from H3345; a *conflagration:*— burning.

H3347 יָקְדְעָם *yoqdĕʿām* from H3344 and H5971; *burning of* (the) *people; Jokdeäm,* a place in Palestine:— Jokdeam.

H3348 יָקֶה *yāqeh* from an unused root probably meaning to *obey; obedient; Jakeh,* a symbolical name (for Solomon):— Jakeh.

H3349 יִקָּהָה *yiqqāhâ* from the same as H3348; *obedience:*— gathering, to obey.

H3350 יְקוֹד *yĕqôd* from H3344; a *burning:*— burning.

H3351 יְקוּם *yĕqûm* from H6965; properly *standing* (extant), i.e. by implication a *living thing:*— substance, living substance.

H3352 יָקוֹשׁ *yāqôš* from H3369; properly *entangling;* hence a *snarer:*— fowler.

H3353 יָקוּשׁ *yāqûš* passive participle of H3369; properly *entangled,* i.e. by implication (intransitively) a *snare,* or (transitively) a *snarer:*— fowler, snare.

H3354 יְקוּתִיאֵל *yĕqûtîʾēl* from the same as H3348 and H410; *obedience of God; Jekuthiël,* an Israelite:— Jekuthiel.

H3355 יָקְטָן *yoqṭān* from H6994; *he will be made little; Joktan,* an Arabian patriarch:— Joktan.

H3356 יָקִים *yāqîm* from H6965; *he will raise; Jakim,* the name of two Israelites:— Jakim. Compare H3079

H3357 יַקִּיר *yaqqîr* from H3365; *precious:*— dear.

H3358 יַקִּיר *yaqqîr* (Aramaic) corresponding to H3357:— noble, rare.

H3359 יְקַמְיָה *yĕqamyâ* from H6965 and H3050; *Jah will rise; Jekamjah,* the name of two Israelites:— Jekamiah. Compare H3079

H3360 יְקַמְעָם *yĕqamʿām* from H6965 and H5971; (the) *people will rise; Jekamam,* an Israelite:— Jekameam. Compare H3079, H3361

H3361 יָקְמְעָם *yoqmĕʿām* from H6965 and H5971; (the) *people will be raised; Jokmeäm,* a place in Palestine:— Jokmeam. Compare H3360, H3362

H3362 יָקְנְעָם *yoqnĕʿām* from H6969 and H5971; (the) *people will be lamented; Jokneäm,* a place in Palestine:— Jokneam.

H3363 יָקַע *yāqaʿ* a primitive root; properly to *sever* oneself, i.e. (by implication) to *be dislocated;* figuratively to *abandon;* causatively to *impale* (and thus allow to drop to pieces by *rotting*):— be alienated, depart, hang, hang up, be out of joint.

H3364 יָקַץ *yāqaṣ* a primitive root; to *awake* (intransitively):— awake, be awaked.

H3365 יָקַר *yāqar* a primitive root; properly apparently to *be heavy,* i.e. (figuratively) *valuable;* causatively to *make rare* (figuratively to *inhibit*):— be precious, make precious, be prized, be set by, withdraw.

H3366 יְקָר *yĕqār* from H3365; *value,* i.e. (concretely) *wealth;* abstractly *costliness, dignity:*— honour, precious, precious things, price.

H3367 יְקָר *yĕqār* (Aramaic) corresponding to H3366 :— glory, honour.

H3368 יָקָר *yāqār* from H3365; *valuable* (objectively or subjectively):— brightness, clear, costly, excellent, fat, honourable women, precious, reputation.

H3369 יָקֹשׁ *yāqōš* a primitive root; to *ensnare* (literally or figuratively):— fowler, snare, lay snare, lay a snare.

H3370 יָקְשָׁן *yoqšān* from H3369; *insidious; Jokshan,* an Arabian patriarch:— Jokshan.

H3371 יָקְתְאֵל *yoqtĕʾēl* probably from the same as H3348 and H410; *veneration of God* [compare H3354]; *Joktheël,* the name of a place in Palestine, and of one in Idumaea:— Joktheel.

H3372 יָרֵא *yārēʾ* a primitive root; to *fear;* morally to *revere;* causatively to *frighten:*— affright, be afraid, make afraid, dread, dreadful, fear, put in fear, fearful, fearfully, fearing, reverence, be had in reverence, reverend, see, terrible, terrible act, terribleness, terrible thing.

H3373 יָרֵא *yārēʾ* from H3372; *fearing;* morally *reverent:*— afraid, fear, fearful.

H3374 יִרְאָה *yirʾâ* feminine of H3373; *fear* (also used as infinitive); morally *reverence:*— dreadful, exceedingly, fear, fearfulness.

H3375 יִרְאוֹן *yirʾôn* from H3372; *fearfulness; Jiron,* a place in Palestine:— Iron.

H3376 יִרְאִיָּיה *yirʾîyāyh* from H3373 and H3050; *fearful of Jah; Jirijah,* an Israelite:— Irijah.

H3377 יָרֵב *yārēb* from H7378; *he will contend; Jareb,* a symbolical name for Assyria:— Jareb. Compare H3402

H3378 יְרֻבַּעַל *yĕrubbaʿal* from H7378 and H1168; *Baal will contend; Jerubbaal,* a symbolic name of Gideon:— Jerubbaal.

H3379 יָרָבְעָם *yārobʿām* from H7378 and H5971; (the) *people will contend; Jarobam,* the name of two Israelites kings:— Jeroboam.

H3380 יְרֻבֶּשֶׁת *yĕrubbešet* from H7378 and H1322; *shame* (i.e. the idol) *will contend; Jerubbesheth,* a symbolic name for Gideon:— Jerubbesheth.

H3381 יָרַד *yārad* a primitive root; to *descend* (literally to *go downwards;* or conventionally to a lower region, as the shore, a boundary, the enemy, etc.; or figuratively to *fall*); causatively to *bring down* (in all the above applications):— abundantly, bring down, carry down, cast down, come down, cause to come down, coming down, fall, fall down, get down, go down, going down, go downward, hang down, indeed, let down, light, light down, put down, put off, run down, cause to run down, let run down, sink, subdue, take down.

H3382 יֶרֶד *yered* from H3381; a *descent; Jered,* the name of an antediluvian, and of an Israelite:— Jared.

H3383 יַרְדֵּן *yardēn* from H3381; a *descender; Jarden,* the principal river of Palestine:— Jordan.

H3384 יָרָה *yārâ* or (2 Chron. 26:15)

יָרָא *yārāʾ* a primitive root; properly to *flow* as water (i.e. to *rain*); trans to *lay* or *throw* (especially an arrow, i.e. to *shoot*); figuratively to *point* out (as if by *aiming* the finger), to *teach:*— archer, archer, cast, direct, inform, instruct, lay, shew, shoot, teach, teacher, teaching, through.

H3385 יְרוּאֵל *yĕrûʾēl* from H3384 and H410; *founded of God; Jeruel,* a place in Palestine:— Jeruel.

H3386 יָרוֹחַ *yārôaḥ* perhaps denominative from H3394; (born at the) new *moon; Jaroäch,* an Israelite:— Jaroah.

H3387 יָרוֹק *yārôq* from H3417; *green,* i.e. an herb :— green thing.

H3388 יְרוּשָׁא *yĕrûšāʾ* or

יְרוּשָׁה *yĕrûšâ* feminine passive participle of H3423; *possessed; Jerusha* or *Jerushah,* an Israelitess:— Jerusha, Jerushah.

H3389 יְרוּשָׁלַםִ *yĕrûšālaim* rarely

יְרוּשָׁלַיִם *yĕrûšālayim* a dual (in allusion to its two main hills [the true pointing, at least of the former reading, seems to be that of H3390]); probably from (the passive participle of) H3384 and H7999; *founded peaceful; Jerushalaïm* or *Jerushalem,* the capital city of Palestine:— Jerusalem.

H3390 יְרוּשְׁלֵם *yĕrûšālēm* (Aramaic) corresponding to H3389:— Jerusalem.

H3391 יֶרַח *yeraḥ* from an unused root of uncertain signification; a *lunation,* i.e. *month:*— month, moon.

H3392 יֶרַח *yeraḥ* the same as H3391; *Jerach,* an Arabian patriarch:— Jerah.

H3393 יְרַח *yĕraḥ* (Aramaic) corresponding to H3391; a *month:*— month.

H3394 יָרֵחַ *yārēaḥ* from the same as H3391; the *moon:*— moon.

H3395 יְרֹחָם *yĕrōḥām* from H7355; *compassionate; Jerocham,* the name of seven or eight Israelites:— Jeroham.

H3396 יְרַחְמְאֵל *yĕraḥmĕʾēl* from H7355 and H410; *God will compassionate; Jerachmeël,* the name of three Israelites:— Jerahmeel.

H3397 יְרַחְמְאֵלִי *yĕraḥmĕʾēlî* patronymic from H3396; a *Jerachmeëlite* or descendant of Jerachmeel:— Jerahmeelites.

H3398 יַרְחָע *yarḥāʿ* probably of Egyptian origin; *Jarcha,* an Egyptian:— Jarha.

H3399 יָרַט *yāraṭ* a primitive root; to *precipitate* or *hurl (rush)* headlong; (intransitively) to *be rash:*— be perverse, turn over.

H3400 יְרִיאֵל *yĕrîʾēl* from H3384 and H410; *thrown of God; Jeriël,* an Israelite:— Jeriel. Compare H3385

H3401 יָרִיב *yārîb* from H7378; literally *he will contend;* properly adjectivally *contentious;* used as noun, an *adversary:*— that contend, that contendeth, that strive.

H3402 יָרִיב *yārîb* the same as H3401; *Jarib,* the name of three Israelites:— Jarib.

H3403 יְרִיבַי *yĕrîbay* from H3401; *contentious; Jeribai,* an Israelite:— Jeribai.

HEB

H3404 יְרִיָּה *yĕrîyâ* or

יְרִיָּהוּ *yĕrîyāhû* from H3384 and H3050; *Jah will throw; Jerijah,* an Israelite:— Jeriah, Jerijah.

H3405 יְרִיחוֹ *yĕrîḥô* or

יְרֵחוֹ *yĕrēḥô* or variation (1 Kings 16:34)

יְרִיחֹה *yĕrîḥōh* perhaps from H3394; *its month;* or else from H7306; *fragrant; Jericho* or *Jerecho,* a place in Palestine:— Jericho.

H3406 יְרִימוֹת *yĕrîmôt* or

יְרֵימוֹת *yĕrêmôt* or

יְרֵמוֹת *yĕrēmôt* feminine plural from H7311; *elevations; Jerimoth* or *Jeremoth,* the name of twelve Israelites:— Jeremoth, Jerimoth, and Ramoth *[from the margin].*

H3407 יְרִיעָה *yĕrîʿâ* from H3415; a *hanging* (as *tremulous*):— curtain.

H3408 יְרִיעוֹת *yĕrîʿôt* plural of H3407; *curtains; Jerioth,* an Israelitess:— Jerioth.

H3409 יָרֵךְ *yārēk* from an unused root meaning to *be soft;* the *thigh* (from its fleshy *softness*); by euphemism the *generative parts;* figuratively a *shank, flank, side:*— body, loins, shaft, side, thigh.

H3410 יַרְכָא *yarkāʾ* (Aramaic) corresponding to H3411; a *thigh:*— thigh.

H3411 יְרֵכָה *yĕrēkâ* feminine of H3409; properly the *flank;* but used only figuratively, the *rear* or *recess:*— border, coast, part, quarter, side.

H3412 יַרְמוּת *yarmût* from H7311; *elevation; Jarmuth,* the name of two places in Palestine:— Jarmuth.

H3413 יְרֵמַי *yĕrēmay* from H7311; *elevated; Jeremai,* an Israelite:— Jeremai.

H3414 יִרְמְיָה *yirmĕyâ* or

יִרְמְיָהוּ *yirmĕyāhû* from H7311 and H3050; *Jah will rise; Jirmejah,* the name of eight or nine Israelites:— Jeremiah.

H3415 יָרַע *yāraʿ* a primitive root; properly to *be broken* up (with any violent action), i.e. (figuratively) to *fear:*— be grievous *[only Isa 15:4; the rest belong* to H7489].

H3416 יִרְפְּאֵל *yirpĕʾēl* from H7495 and H410; *God will heal; Jirpeël,* a place in Palestine:— Irpeel.

H3417 יָרַק *yāraq* a primitive root; to *spit:*— but, spit.

H3418 יֶרֶק *yereq* from H3417 (in the sense of *vacuity* of color); properly *pallor,* i.e. hence the yellowish *green* of young and sickly vegetation; concretely *verdure,* i.e. grass or vegetation:— grass, green, green thing.

H3419 יָרָק *yārāq* from the same as H3418; properly *green;* concretely a *vegetable:*— green, herbs.

H3420 יֵרָקוֹן *yērāqôn* from H3418; *paleness,* whether of persons (from fright), or of plants (from drought) :— greenish, yellow, mildew.

H3421 יָרְקְעָם *yorqĕʿām* from H7324 and H5971; *people will be poured forth; Jorkeäm,* a place in Palestine:— Jorkeam.

H3422 יְרַקְרַק *yĕraqraq* from the same as H3418; *yellowishness:*— greenish, yellow.

H3423 יָרַשׁ *yāraš* or

יָרֵשׁ *yārēš* a primitive root; to *occupy* (by *driving* out previous tenants, and *possessing* in their place); by implication to *seize,* to *rob,* to *inherit;* also to *expel,* to *impoverish,* to *ruin:*— cast out, consume, destroy, disinherit, dispossess, drive, driving out, enjoy, expel, without fail, inherit, give to inherit, leave for an inheritance, inheritor, magistrate, be poor, make poor, come to poverty, possess, give to possess, make to possess, get in possession, have in possession, take possession, seize upon, succeed, utterly.

H3424 יְרֵשָׁה *yĕrēšâ* from H3423; *occupancy:*— possession.

H3425 יְרֻשָּׁה *yĕruššâ* from H3423; something *occupied;* a *conquest;* also a *patrimony:*— heritage, inheritance, possession.

H3426 יֵשׁ *yēš* perhaps from an unused root meaning to *stand* out, or *exist; entity:* used adverbially or as a copula for the substantive verb (H1961); there *is* or *are* (or any other form of the verb to *be,* as may suit the connection):— are, there are, be, he be, it be, shall be, there be, there may be, there shall be, there should be, thou do, had, hast, hath, which hath, have, I have, shalt have, that have, is, he is, it is, there is, substance, it was, there was, were, there were, ye will, thou wilt, wouldest.

H3427 יָשַׁב *yāšab* a primitive root; properly to *sit* down (specifically as judge, in ambush, in quiet); by implication to *dwell,* to *remain;* causatively to *settle,* to *marry:*— abide, make to abide, abiding, continue, dwell, cause to dwell, make to dwell, dwelling, ease self, endure, establish, fail, habitation, haunt, inhabit, make to inhabit, inhabitant, make to keep house, lurking, marry, marrying, place, bring again to place, remain, return, eat, set, settle, sit, downsitting, sit down, sit still, sitting down, sitting place, situate, take, tarry.

H3428 יֶשֶׁבְאָב *yešebʾāb* from H3427 and H1; *seat of* (his) *father; Jeshebab,* an Israelite:— Jeshebeab.

H3429 יֹשֵׁב בַּשֶּׁבֶת *yōšēb baššebet* from the active participle of H3427 and H7674, with a preposition and the article interposed; *sitting in the seat; Josheb-bash-Shebeth,* an Israelite:— that sat in the seat.

H3430 יִשְׁבּוֹ בְּנֹב *yišbô bĕnōb* from H3427 and H5011, with a pronominal suffix and a preposition interposed; *his dwelling* (is) *in Nob; Jishbo-be-Nob,* a Philistine:— Ishbi-benob *[from the margin].*

H3431 יִשְׁבַּח *yišbaḥ* from H7623; *he will praise; Jishbach,* an Israelite:— Ishbah.

H3432 יָשֻׁבִי *yāšūbî* patronymic from H3437; a *Jashubite,* or descendant of Jashub:— Jashubites.

H3433 יָשֻׁבִי לֶחֶם *yāšūbî leḥem* from H7725 and H3899; probably the text should be pointed

יֹשְׁבֵי לֶחֶם *yōššĕbê leḥem* and rendered "(they were) inhabitants of Lechem," i.e. of Bethlehem (by contraction). Compare H3902.; *returner of bread; Jashubi-Lechem,* an Israelite:— Jashubi-lehem.

H3434 יָשָׁבְעָם *yāšobʿām* from H7725 and H5971; *people will return; Jashobam,* the name of two or three Israelites:— Jashobeam.

H3435 יִשְׁבָּק *yišbāq* from an unused root corresponding to H7662; *he will leave; Jishbak,* a son of Abraham:— Ishbak.

H3436 יָשְׁבְּקָשָׁה *yošbĕqāšâ* from H3427 and H7186; a *hard seat; Joshbekashah,* an Israelite:— Joshbekashah.

H3437 יָשׁוּב *yāšûb* or

יָשִׁיב *yāšib* from H7725; *he will return; Jashub,* the name of two Israelites:— Jashub.

H3438 יִשְׁוָה *yišwâ* from H7737; *he will level; Jishvah,* an Israelite:— Ishvah, Isvah.

H3439 יְשׁוֹחָיָה *yĕšôḥāyâ* from the same as H3445 and H3050; *Jah will empty; Jeshochajah,* an Israelite:— Jeshoaiah.

H3440 יִשְׁוִי *yišwî* from H7737; *level; Jishvi,* the name of two Israelites:— Ishuai, Ishvi, Isui, Jesui.

H3441 יִשְׁוִי *yišwî* patronymic from H3440; a *Jishvite* (collectively) or descendant of jishvi:— Jesuites.

H3442 יֵשׁוּעַ *yēšûaʿ* for H3091; *he will save; Jeshua,* the name of ten Israelites, also of a place in Palestine:— Jeshua.

H3443 יֵשׁוּעַ *yēšûaʿ* (Aramaic) corresponding to H3442:— Jeshua.

H3444 יְשׁוּעָה *yĕšûʿâ* feminine passive participle of H3467; something *saved,* i.e. (abstractly) *deliverance;* hence *aid, victory, prosperity:*— deliverance, health, help, helping, salvation, save, saving, saving health, welfare.

H3445 יֶשַׁח *yešaḥ* from an unused root meaning to *gape* (as the empty stomach); *hunger:*— casting down.

H3446 יִשְׂחָק *yiśḥāq* from H7831; *he will laugh; Jischak,* the heir of Abraham:— Isaac. Compare H3327

H3447 יָשַׁט *yāšaṭ* a primitive root; to *extend:*— hold out.

H3448 יִשַׁי *yīšay* by Aramaic

אִישַׁי *ʾîšay* from the same as H3426; *extant; Jishai,* David's father:— Jesse.

H3449 יִשִּׁיָּה *yiššîyâ* or

יִשִּׁיָּהוּ *yiššîyāhû* from H5383 and H3050; *Jah will lend; Jishshijah,* the name of five Israelites:— Ishiah, Ishiah, Ishijah, Jesiah.

H3450 יְשִׂימָאֵל *yĕśîmāʾēl* from H7760 and H410; *God will place; Jesimaël,* an Israelite:— Jesimael.

H3451 יְשִׁימָה *yĕšîmah* from H3456; *desolation:*— let death seize *[from the margin].*

H3452 יְשִׁימוֹן *yĕšîmôn* from H3456; a *desolation:*— desert, Jeshimon, solitary, wilderness.

H3453 יָשִׁישׁ *yāšîš* from H3486; an *old* man:— aged, very aged man, ancient, very old.

H3454 יְשִׁישַׁי *yĕšîšāy* from H3453; *aged; Jeshishai,* an Israelite:— Jeshishai.

H3455 יָשַׂם *yāśam* a primitive root; to *place;* intransitively to *be placed:*— be put, be set.

H3456 יָשַׁם *yāšam* a primitive root; to *lie waste:*— be desolate.

H3457 יִשְׁמָא *yišmāʾ* from H3456; *desolate; Jishma,* an Israelite:— Ishma.

H3458 יִשְׁמָעֵאל *yišmāʿēʾl* from H8085 and H410; *God will hear; Jishmaël,* the name of Abraham's oldest son, and of five Israelites:— Ishmael.

H3459 יִשְׁמָעֵאלִי *yišmāʿēʾlî* patronymic from H3458; a *Jishmaëlite* or descendant of Jishmael:— Ishmaelite.

H3460 יִשְׁמַעְיָה *yišmaʿyâ* or

יִשְׁמַעְיָהוּ *yšĕmaʿyāhû* from H8085 and H3050; *Jah will hear; Jishmajah,* the name of two Israelites:— Ishmaiah.

H3461 יִשְׁמְרַי *yišmĕray* from H8104; *preservative; Jishmerai,* an Israelite:— Ishmerai.

H3462 יָשֵׁן *yāšan* a primitive root; properly to *be slack* or *languid,* i.e. (by implication) *sleep* (figuratively to *die*); also to *grow old, stale* or *inveterate*:— old, old store, remain long, sleep, make to sleep.

H3463 יָשֵׁן *yāšan* from H3462; *sleepy*:— asleep, sleep, one out of sleep, sleepeth, sleeping, slept.

H3464 יָשֵׁן *yāšēn* the same as H3463; *Jashen*, an Israelite:— Jashen.

H3465 יָשָׁן *yāšān* from H3462; *old*:— old.

H3466 יְשָׁנָה *yĕšānâ* feminine of H3465; *Jeshanah*, a place in Palestine:— Jeshanah.

H3467 יָשַׁע *yāšaᶜ* a primitive root; properly to *be open, wide* or *free*, i.e. (by implication) to *be safe*; causatively to *free* or *succor*:— at all, avenging, defend, deliver, deliverer, help, preserve, rescue, be safe, bring salvation, having salvation, save, saviour, get victory.

H3468 יֶשַׁע *yešaᶜ* or

יֵשַׁע *yēšaᶜ* from H3467; *liberty, deliverance, prosperity*:— safety, salvation, saving.

H3469 יִשְׁעִי *yišᶜî* from H3467; *saving; Jishi*, the name of four Israelites:— Ishi.

H3470 יְשַׁעְיָה *yĕšaᶜyâ* or

יְשַׁעְיָהוּ *yĕšaᶜyāhû* from H3467 and H3050; *Jah has saved; Jeshajah*, the name of seven Israelites:— Isaiah, Jesaiah, Jeshaiah.

H3471 יָשְׁפֵה *yāšĕpēh* from an unused root meaning to *polish*; a gem supposed to be *jasper* (from the resemblance in name):— jasper.

H3472 יִשְׁפָּה *yišpâ* perhaps from H8192; *he will scratch; Jishpah*, an Israelite:— Ispah.

H3473 יִשְׁפָּן *yišpān* probably from the same as H8227; *he will hide; Jishpan*, an Israelite:— Ishpan.

H3474 יָשַׁר *yāšar* a primitive root; to *be straight* or *even*; figuratively to *be* (causatively to *make*) *right, pleasant, prosperous*:— direct, fit, seem good, seem meet, please, please well, be right, esteem right, go right on, bring straight, look straight, make straight, take the straight way, be upright, uprightly.

H3475 יֵשֶׁר *yēšer* from H3474; the *right; Jesher*, an Israelite:— Jesher.

H3476 יֹשֶׁר *yōšer* from H3474; the *right*:— equity, meet, right, upright, uprightness.

H3477 יָשָׁר *yāšār* from H3474; *straight* (literally or figuratively):— convenient, equity, Jasher, just, meet, meetest, pleased well, right, righteous, straight, upright, most upright, uprightly, uprightness.

H3478 יִשְׂרָאֵל *yiśrāʾēl* from H8280 and H410; *he will rule as God; Jisraël*, a symbolical name of Jacob; also (typically) of his posterity:— Israel.

H3479 יִשְׂרָאֵל *yiśrāʾēl* (Aramaic) corresponding to H3478:— Israel.

H3480 יְשַׂרְאֵלָה *yĕśarʾēlâ* by variation from H3477 and H410 with directive enclitic; *right towards God; Jesarelah*, an Israelite:— Jesharelah. Compare H841

H3481 יִשְׂרְאֵלִי *yiśrĕʾēlî* patronymic from H3478; a *Jisreëlite* or descendant of Jisrael:— of Israel, Israelite.

H3482 יִשְׂרְאֵלִית *yiśrĕʾēlît* feminine of H3481; a *Jisreëlitess* or female descendant of Jisrael:— Israelitish.

H3483 יִשְׁרָה *yišrâ* feminine of H3477; *rectitude*:— uprightness.

H3484 יְשֻׁרוּן *yĕšūrûn* from H3474; *upright; Jeshurun*, a symbolic name for Israel:— Jeshurun.

H3485 יִשָּׂשכָר *yiśśāskār* from H5375 and H7939; *he will bring a reward; Jissaskar*, a son of Jacob:— Issachar.

H3486 יָשֵׁשׁ *yāšēš* from an unused root meaning to *blanch; gray*-haired, i.e. an *aged* man:— stoop for age.

H3487 יַת *yat* (Aramaic) corresponding to H853; a sign of the object of a verb:— whom.

H3488 יְתִב *yĕtīb* (Aramaic) corresponding to H3427; to *sit* or *dwell*:— dwell, set, be set, sit.

H3489 יָתֵד *yātēd* from an unused root meaning to *pin* through or fast; a *peg*:— nail, paddle, pin, stake.

H3490 יָתוֹם *yātôm* from an unused root meaning to *be lonely*; a *bereaved* person:— fatherless, fatherless child, orphan.

H3491 יָתוּר *yātûr* passive participle of H3498; properly what is *left*, i.e. (by implication) a *gleaning*:— range.

H3492 יַתִּיר *yattîr* from H3498; *redundant; Jattir*, a place in Palestine:— Jattir.

H3493 יַתִּיר *yattîr* (Aramaic) corresponding to H3492; *preeminent*; adverbially *very*:— exceeding, exceedingly, excellent.

H3494 יִתְלָה *yitlâ* probably from H8518; it *will hang*, i.e. be high: *Jithlah*, a place in Palestine:— Jethlah.

H3495 יִתְמָה *yitmâ* from the same as H3490; *orphanage; Jithmah*, an Israelite:— Ithmah.

H3496 יַתְנִיאֵל *yatnîʾēl* from an unused root meaning to *endure*, and H410; *continued of God; Jathniël*, an Israelite:— Jathniel.

H3497 יִתְנָן *yitnān* from the same as H8577; *extensive; Jithnan*, a place in Palestine:— Ithnan.

H3498 יָתַר *yātar* a primitive root; to *jut* over or *exceed*; by implication to *excel*; (intransitively) to *remain* or *be left*; causatively to *leave, cause to abound, preserve*:— excel, leave, leave a remnant, left behind, too much, make plenteous, preserve, remain, be remaining, let remain, remainder, remnant, reserve, residue, rest.

H3499 יֶתֶר *yeter* from H3498; properly an *overhanging*, i.e. (by implication) an *excess, superiority, remainder*; also a small *rope* (as hanging free):— abundant, cord, exceeding, excellency, excellent, what they leave, that hath left, plentifully, remnant, residue, rest, string, with.

H3500 יֶתֶר *yeter* the same as H3499; *Jether*, the name of five or six Israelites and of one Midianite:— Jether, Jethro. Compare H3503

H3501 יִתְרָא *yitrāʾ* by variation for H3502; *Jithra*, an Israelite (or Ishmaelite):— Ithra.

H3502 יִתְרָה *yitrâ* feminine of H3499; properly *excellence*, i.e. (by implication) *wealth*:— abundance, riches.

H3503 יִתְרוֹ *yitrô* from H3499 with pronominal suffix; *his excellence; Jethro*, Moses' father-in-law:— Jethro. Compare H3500

H3504 יִתְרוֹן *yitrôn* from H3498; *preeminence, gain*:— better, excellency, excelleth, profit, profitable.

H3505 יִתְרִי *yitrî* patronymic from H3500; a *Jithrite* or descendant of Jether:— Ithrite.

H3506 יִתְרָן *yitrān* from H3498; *excellent; Jithran*, the name of an Edomite and of an Israelite:— Ithran.

H3507 יִתְרְעָם *yitrĕᶜām* from H3499 and H5971; *excellence of people; Jithreäm*, a son of David:— Ithream.

H3508 יֹתֶרֶת *yōteret* feminine active participle of H3498; the *lobe* or *flap* of the liver (as if redundant or outhanging):— caul.

H3509 יְתֵת *yĕtēt* of uncertain derivation; *Jetheth*, an Edomite:— Jetheth.

כ

H3510 כָּאַב *kāʾab* a primitive root; properly to feel *pain*; by implication to *grieve*; figuratively to *spoil*:— grieving, mar, have pain, make sad, make sore, sorrowful, be sorrowful.

H3511 כְּאֵב *kĕʾēb* from H3510; *suffering* (physical or mental), *adversity*:— grief, pain, sorrow.

H3512 כָּאָה *kāʾâ* a primitive root; to *despond*: causatively to *deject*:— broken, be grieved, make sad.

H3513 כָּבַד *kābad* or

כָּבֵד *kābēd* a primitive root; to *be heavy*, i.e. in a bad sense *(burdensome, severe, dull)* or in a good sense *(numerous, rich, honorable)*; causatively to *make weighty* (in the same two senses):— abounding with, more grievously afflict, boast, be chargeable, be dim, glorify, be glorious, make glorious, glorious things, glory, great, very great, be grievous, harden, be heavy, make heavy, be heavier, lay heavily, honour, bring to honour, come to honour, do honour, get honour, be had in honour, honour self, honourable, be honourable, honourable man, lade, more be laid, make self many, nobles, prevail, promote, promote to honour, be rich, be sore, go sore, stop.

H3514 כֹּבֶד *kōbed* from H3513; *weight, multitude, vehemence*:— grievousness, heavy, great number.

H3515 כָּבֵד *kābēd* from H3513; *heavy*; figuratively in a good sense *(numerous)* or in a bad sense *(severe, difficult, stupid)*:— great, so great, grievous, hard, hardened, heary, too heavy, heavier, laden, much, slow, sore, thick.

H3516 כָּבֵד *kābēd* the same as H3515; the *liver* (as the *heaviest* of the viscera):— liver.

H3517 כְּבֵדֻת *kĕbēdūt* feminine of H3515; *difficulty*:— heavily.

H3518 כָּבָה *kābâ* a primitive root; to *expire* or (causatively) to *extinguish* (fire, light, anger):— go out, put out, quench.

H3519 כָּבוֹד *kābôd* rarely

כָּבֹד *kābōd* from H3513; properly *weight*; but only figuratively in a good sense, *splendor* or *copiousness*:— glorious, gloriously, glory, honour, honourable.

H3520 כְּבוּדָּה *kbĕwwddâ* irregular feminine passive participle of H3513; *weightiness*, i.e. *magnificence, wealth*:— carriage, all glorious, stately.

H3521 כָּבוּל *kābûl* from the same as H3525 in the sense of *limitation; sterile; Cabul*, the name of two places in Palestine:— Cabul.

H3522 כַּבּוֹן *kabbôn* from an unused root meaning to *heap* up; *hilly; Cabbon*, a place in Palestine:— Cabbon.

H3523 כְּבִיר *kĕbîr* from H3527 in the original sense of *plaiting*; a *matrass* (or intertwined materials):— pillow.

H3524 כַּבִּיר *kabbîr* from H3527; *vast*, whether in extent (figuratively of power, *mighty*; of time, *aged*),

HEB

or in number, *many:*— feeble, mighty, most, much, strong, valiant.

H3525 כֶּבֶל *kebel* from an unused root meaning to *twine* or braid together; a *fetter:*— fetter.

H3526 כָּבַס *kābas* a primitive root; to *trample;* hence to *wash* (properly by stamping with the feet), whether literally (including the *fulling* process) or figuratively:— fuller, wash, washing.

H3527 כָּבַר *kābar* a primitive root; properly to *plait* together, i.e. (figuratively) to *augment* (especially in number or quantity, to *accumulate*):— in abundance, multiply.

H3528 כְּבָר *kĕbār* from H3527; properly *extent* of time, i.e. a *great while;* hence *long ago, formerly, hitherto:*— already, now, seeing that which now.

H3529 כְּבָר *kĕbār* the same as H3528; *length; Kebar,* a river of Mesopotamia:— Chebar. Compare H2249

H3530 כִּבְרָה *kibrâ* feminine of H3528; properly *length,* i.e. a *measure* (of uncertain dimension):— little.

H3531 כְּבָרָה *kĕbārâ* from H3527 in its original sense. a *sieve* (as netted):— sieve.

H3532 כֶּבֶשׂ *kebeś* from an unused root meaning to *dominate;* a *ram* (just old enough to *butt*):— lamb, sheep.

H3533 כָּבַשׁ *kābaš* a primitive root; to *tread* down; hence negatively to *disregard;* positively to *conquer, subjugate, violate:*— bring into bondage, force, keep under, subdue, bring into subjection.

H3534 כֶּבֶשׁ *kebeš* from H3533; a *footstool* (as trodden upon):— footstool.

H3535 כִּבְשָׂה *kibśâ* or

כַּבְשָׂה *kabśâ* feminine of H3532; a *ewe:*— lamb, ewe lamb.

H3536 כִּבְשָׁן *kibšān* from H3533; a smelting *furnace* (as *reducing* metals):— furnace.

H3537 כַּד *kad* from an unused root meaning to *deepen;* properly a *pail;* but generally of earthenware; a *jar* for domestic purposes:— barrel, pitcher.

H3538 כְּדַב *kĕdab* (Aramaic) from a root corresponding to H3576; *false:*— lying.

H3539 כַּדְכֹּד *kadkōd* from the same as H3537 in the sense of *striking fire* from a metal forged; a *sparkling* gem, probably the ruby:— agate.

H3540 כְּדָרְלָעֹמֶר *kĕdorlāᶜōmer* of foreign origin; *Kedorlaomer,* an early Persian king:— Chedorlaomer.

H3541 כֹּה *kōh* from the prefix *k* and H1931; properly *like this,* i.e. by implication (of manner) *thus* (or *so*); also (of place) *here* (or *hither*); or (of time) *now:*— also, here, hitherto, like, on the other side, so, so and much, such, on that manner, thhis, on this manner, on this side, on this way, this way and that way, meanwhile, yonder.

H3542 כָּה *kâ* (Aramaic) corresponding to H3541 :— hitherto.

H3543 כָּהָה *kāhâ* a primitive root; to *be weak,* i.e. (figuratively) to *despond* (causatively *rebuke*), or (of light, the eye) to *grow dull:*— darken, be dim, fail, faint, restrain, utterly.

H3544 כֵּהֶה *kēheh* from H3543; *feeble, obscure:*— somewhat dark, darkish, wax dim, heaviness, smoking.

H3545 כֵּהָה *kēhâ* feminine of H3544; properly a *weakening;* figuratively *alleviation,* i.e. cure:— healing.

H3546 כְּהַל *kĕhal* (Aramaic) a root corresponding to H3201 and H3557; to *be able:*— be able, could.

H3547 כָּהַן *kāhan* a primitive root, apparently meaning to *mediate* in religious services; but used only as denominative from H3548; to *officiate* as a priest; figuratively to *put on regalia:*— deck, be priest, do the office of a priest, execute the priest's office, minister in the priest's office.

H3548 כֹּהֵן *kōhēn* active participle of H3547; literally one *officiating,* a *priest;* also (by courtesy) an *acting priest* (although a layman):— chief ruler, own, priest, prince, principal officer.

H3549 כָּהֵן *kāhēn* (Aramaic) corresponding to H3548 :— priest.

H3550 כְּהֻנָּה *kĕhunnâ* from H3547; *priesthood:*— priesthood, priest's office.

H3551 כַּו *kaw* (Aramaic) from a root corresponding to H3854 in the sense of *piercing;* a *window* (as a performation):— window.

H3552 כּוּב *kûb* of foreign derivation; *Kub,* a country near Egypt:— Chub.

H3553 כּוֹבַע *kôbaᶜ* from an unused root meaning to be *high* or *rounded;* a *helmet* (as *arched*):— helmet. Compare H6959

H3554 כָּוָה *kāwâ* a primitive root; properly to *prick* or *penetrate;* hence to *blister* (as smarting or eating into):— burn.

H3555 כְּוִיָּה *kĕwîyâ* from H3554; a *branding:*— burning.

H3556 כּוֹכָב *kôkāb* probably from the same as H3522 (in the sense of *rolling*) or H3554 (in the sense of *blazing*); a *star* (as *round* or as *shining*); figuratively a *prince:*— star, stargazer.

H3557 כּוּל *kûl* a primitive root; properly to *keep in;* hence to *measure;* figuratively to *maintain* (in various senses):— abide, be able to abide, can abide, bear, comprehend, contain, feed, forbearing, guide, hold, holding in, nourish, nourisher, be present, make provision, receive, sustain, provide sustenance, provide victuals.

H3558 כּוּמָז *kûmāz* from an unused root meaning to *store* away; a *jewel* (probably gold beads):— tablet.

H3559 כּוּן *kûn* a primitive root; properly to *be erect* (i.e. stand perpendicular); hence (causatively) to *set up,* in a great variety of applications, whether literally *(establish, fix, prepare, apply),* or figuratively *(appoint, render sure, proper* or *prosperous):*— certain, certainty, confirm, direct, faithfulness, fashion, fasten, firm, be fitted, be fixed, frame, be meet, ordain, order, perfect, preparation, make preparation, prepare, prepare self, provide, make provision, ready, be ready, make ready, right, set, set aright, set fast, set forth, be stable, stablish, establish, stand, tarry, very deed.

H3560 כּוּן *kûn* probably from H3559; *established; Kun,* a place in Syria:— Chun.

H3561 כַּוָּן *kawwān* from H3559; something *prepared,* i.e. a sacrificial *wafer:*— cake.

H3562 כּוֹנַנְיָהוּ *kônanyāhû* from H3559 and H3050; *Jah has sustained; Conanjah,* the name of two Israelites:— Conaniah, Cononiah. Compare H3663

H3563 כּוֹס *kôs* from an unused root meaning to *hold* together; a *cup* (as a container), often figuratively a *lot* (as if a potion); also some unclean bird, probably an *owl* (perhaps from the cup-like cavity of its eye):— cup, owl, small owl. Compare H3599

H3564 כּוּר *kûr* from an unused root meaning properly to *dig* through; a *pot* or *furnace* (as if excavated):— furnace. Compare H3600

H3565 כּוֹר עָשָׁן *kôr ᶜāšān* from H3564 and H6227; *furnace of smoke; Cor-Ashan,* a place in Palestine:— Chor-ashan.

H3566 כּוֹרֶשׁ *kôreš* or (Ezra 1:1 [last time], 2)

כֹּרֶשׁ *kōreš* from the Persian; *Koresh* (or Cyrus), the Persian king:— Cyrus.

H3567 כּוֹרֶשׁ *kôreš* (Aramaic) corresponding to H3566 :— Cyrus.

H3568 כּוּשׁ *kûš* probably of foreign origin; *Cush* (or Ethiopia), the name of a son of Ham, and of his territory; also of an Israelite:— Chush, Cush, Ethiopia.

H3569 כּוּשִׁי *kûšî* patronymic from H3568; a *Cushite,* or descendant of Cush:— Cushi, Cushite, Ethiopian, Ethiopians.

H3570 כּוּשִׁי *kûšî* the same as H3569; *Cushi,* the name of two Israelites:— Cushi.

H3571 כּוּשִׁית *kûšît* feminine of H3569; a *Cushite woman:*— Ethiopian.

H3572 כּוּשָׁן *kûšān* perhaps from H3569; *Cushan,* a region of Arabia:— Cushan.

H3573 כּוּשַׁן רִשְׁעָתַיִם *kûšan riš ᶜātayim* apparently from H3572 and the dual of H7564; *Cushan of double wickedness; Cushan-Rishathajim,* a Mesopotamian king:— Chushan-rishathayim.

H3574 כּוֹשָׁרָה *kôšārâ* from H3787; *prosperity;* in plural *freedom:*— chain.

H3575 כּוּת *kût* or (feminine)

כּוּתָה *kûtâ* of foreign origin; *Cuth* or *Cuthath,* a province of Assyria:— Cuth.

H3576 כָּזַב *kāzab* a primitive root; to *lie* (i.e. *deceive*), literally and figuratively:— fail, liar, be found a liar, make a liar, lie, lying, be in vain.

H3577 כָּזָב *kāzāb* from H3576; *falsehood;* literally *(untruth)* or figuratively *(idol)*:— deceitful, false, leasing, liar, lie, lying.

H3578 כֹּזֵבָא *kōzēbāʾ* from H3576; *fallacious; Cozeba,* a place in Palestine:— Choseba.

H3579 כָּזְבִּי *kozbî* from H3576; *false; Cozbi,* a Midianitess:— Cozbi.

H3580 כְּזִיב *kĕzib* from H3576; *falsified; Kezib,* a place in Palestine:— Chezib.

H3581 כֹּחַ *kōaḥ* or (Dan. 11:6)

כּוֹחַ *kôaḥ* from an unused root meaning to *be firm; vigor,* literally *(force,* in a good or a bad sense) or figuratively *(capacity, means, produce)*; also (from its hardiness) a large *lizard:*— ability, able, chameleon, force, fruits, might, power, powerful, strength, substance, wealth.

H3582 כָּחַד *kāḥad* a primitive root; to *secrete,* by act or word; hence (intensively) to *destroy:*— conceal, cut down, cut off, desolate, hide.

H3583 כָּחַל *kāḥal* a primitive root; to *paint* (with stibium):— paint.

H3584 כָּחַשׁ *kāḥaš* a primitive root; to *be untrue,* in word (to *lie, feign, disown*) or deed (to *disappoint,* fail, cringe):— deceive, deny, dissemble, fail, deal falsely, be found liars, lie, belie, lying, submit selves.

H3585 כַּחַשׁ *kaḥaš* from H3584; literally a *failure* of flesh, i.e. *emaciation; figuratively hypocrisy:*— leanness, lies, lying.

H3586 כֶּחָשׁ *keḥāš* from H3584; *faithless:*— lying.

H3587 כִּי *kî* from H3554; a *brand* or *scar:*— burning.

H3588 כִּי *kî* a primitive particle [the full form of the prepositional prefix] indicating *causal* relations of all kinds, antecedent or consequent; (by implication) very widely used as a relative conjunction or adverb [as below]; often largely modified by other particles annexed:— and, as, forasmuch as, inasmuch as, whereas, assured, assuredly, but, certainly, doubtless, else, even, except, for, how, that because that, in that, so that, than that, nevertheless, now, rightly, seeing, since, surely, then, therefore, though, although, till, truly, until, when, whether, while, whom, yea, yet.

H3589 כִּיד *kîd* from a primitive root meaning to *strike;* a *crushing;* figuratively *calamity:*— destruction.

H3590 כִּידוֹד *kîdôd* from the same as H3589 [compare H3539]; properly something *struck* off, i.e. a *spark* (as struck):— spark.

H3591 כִּידוֹן *kîdôn* from the same as H3589; properly something to *strike* with, i.e. a *dart* (perhaps smaller than H2595):— lance, shield, spear, target.

H3592 כִּידוֹן *kîdôn* the same as H3591; *Kidon,* a place in Palestine:— Chidon.

H3593 כִּידוֹר *kîdôr* of uncertain derivation; perhaps *tumult:*— battle.

H3594 כִּיּוּן *kîyûn* from H3559; properly a *statue,* i.e. idol; but used (by euphemism) for some heathen deity (perhaps corresponding to Priapus or Baalpeor):— Chiun.

H3595 כִּיּוֹר *kîyôr* or

כִּיֹּר *kîyōr* from the same as H3564; properly something *round* (as *excavated* or *bored*), i.e. a chafing-*dish* for coals or a *caldron* for cooking; hence (from similarity of form) a *wash-bowl;* also (for the same reason) a *pulpit* or platform:— hearth, laver, pan, scaffold.

H3596 כִּילַי *kîlay* or

כֵּלַי *kēlay* from H3557 in the sense of *withholding; niggardly:*— churl.

H3597 כֵּילַף *kêlap* from an unused root meaning to *clap* or strike with noise; a *club* or sledge-hammer:— hammer.

H3598 כִּימָה *kîmâ* from the same as H3558; a *cluster* of stars, i.e. the *Pleiades:*— Pleiades, seven stars.

H3599 כִּיס *kîs* a form for H3563; a *cup;* also a *bag* for money or weights:— bag, cup, purse.

H3600 כִּיר *kîr* a form for H3564 (only in the dual); a cooking *range* (consisting of two parallel stones, across which the boiler is set):— ranges for pots.

H3601 כִּישׁוֹר *kîšôr* from H3787; literally a *director,* i.e. the *spindle* or shank of a distaff (H6418), by which it is twirled:— spindle.

H3602 כָּכָה *kākâ* from H3541; *just so,* referring to the previous or following context:— after that manner, after this manner, this matter, so, even so, in such a case, thus.

H3603 כִּכָּר *kikkār* from H3769; a *circle,* i.e. (by implication) a circumjacent *tract* or region, especially the *Ghôr* or valley of the Jordan; also a (round) *loaf;* also a *talent* (or large [round] coin):— loaf, morsel, piece, plain, talent.

H3604 כִּכַּר *kikkēr* (Aramaic) corresponding to H3603; a *talent:*— talent.

H3605 כֹּל *kōl* or (Jer. 33:8)

כּוֹל *kôl* from H3634; properly the *whole;* hence *all, any* or *every* (in the singular only, but often in a plural sense):— all, in all, all manner, all [ye], altogether, any, any manner, enough, every, every one, every place, every thing, howsoever, as many as, nothing, ought, whatsoever, whole, the whole, whoso, whosoever.

H3606 כֹּל *kōl* (Aramaic) corresponding to H3605 :— all, any, as, forasmuch as, because, for this cause, every, no manner, none, therefore, wherefore, though, whatsoever, wheresoever, whosoever, whole, the whole.

H3607 כָּלָא *kālāʾ* a primitive root; to *restrict,* by act *(hold* back or in) or word *(prohibit*):— finish, forbid, keep, keep back, refrain, restrain, retain, shut up, be stayed, withhold.

H3608 כֶּלֶא *keleʾ* from H3607; a *prison:*— prison. Compare H3610, H3628

H3609 כִּלְאָב *kilʾāb* apparently from H3607 and H1; *restraint of* (his) *father; Kilab,* an Israelite:— Chileab.

H3610 כִּלְאַיִם *kilʾayim* dual of H3608 in the original sense of *separation; two heterogeneities:*— divers seeds, diverse kinds, mingled, mingled seed.

H3611 כֶּלֶב *keleb* from an unused root meaning to *yelp,* or else to *attack;* a *dog;* hence (by euphemism) a male *prostitute:*— dog.

H3612 כָּלֵב *kālēb* perhaps a form of H3611, or else from the same root in the sense of *forcible; Caleb,* the name of three Israelites:— Caleb.

H3613 כָּלֵב אֶפְרָתָה *kālēb ʾeprātâ* from H3612 and H672; *Caleb-Ephrathah,* a place in Egypt (if the text is correct):— Caleb-ephrathah.

H3614 כָּלִבּוֹ *kālibbô* probably by erroneous transcription for

כָּלֵבִי *kālēbî* patronymic from H3612; a *Calebite* or descendant of Caleb:— of the house of Caleb.

H3615 כָּלָה *kālâ* a primitive root; to *end,* whether intransitively (to *cease, be finished, perish*) or transitively (to *complete, prepare, consume*):— accomplish, cease, consume, consume away, determine, destroy, destroy utterly, be done, when . . . were done, end, be an end of, expire, fail, cause to fail, faint, finish, fulfil, fully, have, leave, leave off, long, bring to pass, wholly reap, make clean riddance, spend, quite take away, waste.

H3616 כָּלֶה *kāleh* from H3615; *pining:*— fail.

H3617 כָּלָה *kālâ* from H3615; a *completion;* adverbially *completely;* also *destruction:*— altogether, consume, be consumed, utterly consume, consummation, consumption, was determined, end, full end, utter end, riddance.

H3618 כַּלָּה *kallâ* from H3634; a *bride* (as if *perfect*); hence a *son's wife:*— bride, daughter-in-law, spouse.

H3619 כְּלוּב *kēlûb* from the same as H3611; a bird-*trap* (as furnished with a *clap*-stick or treadle to spring it); hence a *basket* (as resembling a wicker cage):— basket, cage.

H3620 כְּלוּב *kēlûb* the same as H3619; *Kelub,* the name of two Israelites:— Chelub.

H3621 כְּלוּבַי *kēlûbay* a form of H3612; *Kelubai,* an Israelite:— Chelubai.

H3622 כְּלוּהַי *kēlûhay* from H3615; *completed; Keluhai,* an Israelite:— Chelluh.

H3623 כְּלוּלָה *kēlûlâ* denominative passive participle from H3618; *bridehood* (only in the plural):— espousal.

H3624 כֶּלַח *kelaḥ* from an unused root meaning to *be complete; maturity:*— full age, old age.

H3625 כֶּלַח *kelaḥ* the same as H3624; *Kelach,* a place in Assyria:— Calah.

H3626 כָּל־חֹזֶה *kol-ḥōzeh* from H3605 and H2374; *every seer; Col-Chozeh,* an Israelite:— Col-hozeh.

H3627 כְּלִי *kēlî* from H3615; something *prepared,* i.e. any *apparatus* (as an implement, utensil, dress, vessel or weapon):— armour, armourbearer, artillery, bag, carriage, furnish, furniture, instrument, jewel, that is made of, one from another, that which pertaineth, pot, psaltery, sack, stuff, thing, tool, vessel, ware, weapon, whatsoever.

H3628 כְּלִיא *kēlîʾ* or

כְּלוּא *kēlûʾ* from H3607 [compare H3608]; a *prison:*— prison.

H3629 כִּלְיָה *kilyâ* feminine of H3627 (only in the plural); a *kidney* (as an essential *organ*); figuratively the *mind* (as the interior self):— kidneys, reins.

H3630 כִּלְיוֹן *kilyôn* a form of H3631; *Kiljon,* an Israelite:— Chilion.

H3631 כִּלָּיוֹן *killāyôn* from H3615; *pining, destruction:*— consumption, failing.

H3632 כָּלִיל *kālîl* from H3634; *complete;* as noun, the *whole* (specifically a sacrifice *entirely consumed*); as adverb *fully:*— all, every whit, flame, perfect, perfection, utterly, whole burnt offering, whole burnt sacrifice, wholly.

H3633 כַּלְכֹּל *kalkōl* from H3557; *sustenance; Calcol,* an Israelite:— Calcol, Chalcol.

H3634 כָּלַל *kālal* a primitive root; to *complete:*— perfect, make perfect.

H3635 כְּלַל *kēlal* (Aramaic) corresponding to H3634; to *complete:*— finish, make up, set up.

H3636 כְּלָל *kēlāl* from H3634; *complete; Kelal,* an Israelite:— Chelal.

H3637 כָּלַם *kālam* a primitive root; properly to *wound;* but only figuratively, to *taunt* or *insult:*— be ashamed, make ashamed, blush, be confounded, be put to confusion, hurt, reproach, shame, do shame, put to shame.

H3638 כִּלְמָד *kilmād* of foreign derivation; *Kilmad,* a place apparently in the Assyrian empire:— Chilmad.

H3639 כְּלִמָּה *kēlimmâ* from H3637; *disgrace:*— confusion, dishonour, reproach, shame.

H3640 כְּלִמּוּת *kēlimmût* from H3639; *disgrace:*— shame.

H3641 כַּלְנֶה *kalneh* or

כַּלְנֵה *kalnēh* also

כַּלְנוֹ *kalnô* of foreign derivation; *Calneh* or *Calno,* a place in the Assyrian empire:— Calneh, Calno. Compare H3656

H3642 כָּמַהּ *kāmah* a primitive root; to *pine* after :— long.

H3643 כִּמְהָם *kimhām* from H3642; *pining; Kimham,* an Israelite:— Chimham.

H3644 כְּמוֹ *kĕmô* or

כָּמוֹ *kāmô* a form of the prefix *k*, but used separately [compare H3651]; *as, thus, so:*— according to, as, such as, as it were, as well as, in comparison of, like, like as, like to, like unto, thus, when, worth.

H3645 כְּמוֹשׁ *kĕmôš* or (Jer. 48:7)

כְּמִישׁ *kĕmîš* from an unused root meaning to *subdue;* the *powerful; Kemosh,* the god of the Moabites:— Chemosh.

H3646 כַּמֹּן *kammōn* from an unused root meaning to *store* up or *preserve; "cummin"* (from its use as a *condiment*):— cummin.

H3647 כָּמַס *kāmas* a primitive root; to *store* away, i.e. (figuratively) in the memory:— lay up in store.

H3648 כְּמַר *kĕmar* a primitive root; properly to *intertwine* or *contract,* i.e. (by implication) to *shrivel* (as with heat); figuratively to *be* deeply *affected* with passion (love or pity):— be black, be kindled, yearn.

H3649 כָּמָר *kāmār* from H3648; properly an *ascetic* (as if *shrunk* with self-maceration), i.e. an idolatrous *priest* (only in plural):— Chemarims, priests, idolatrous priests.

H3650 כִּמְרִיר *kimrîr* reduplicated from H3648; *obscuration* (as if from *shrinkage* of light), i.e. an *eclipse* (only in plural):— blackness.

H3651 כֵּן *kēn* from H3559; properly *set* upright; hence (figuratively as adjective) *just;* but usually (as adverb or conjunction) *rightly* or *so* (in various applications to manner, time and relation; often with other particles):— after that, after this, afterward, afterwards, as . . . as, forasmuch, as yet, because, for which cause, following, howbeit, in like manner, the like, likewise, the more, right, so, even so, state, straightway, such, such thing, surely, therefore, wherefore, this, thus, true, well, you.

H3652 כֵּן *kēn* (Aramaic) corresponding to H3651; *so:*— thus.

H3653 כֵּן *kēn* the same as H3651, used as a noun; a *stand,* i.e. pedestal or station:— base, estate, foot, office, place, well.

H3654 כֵּן *kēn* from H3661 in the sense of *fastening;* a *gnat* (from infixing its sting; used only in plural [and irregular in Exod 8:17, 18; Hebrew 13:14]):— lice, manner.

H3655 כָּנָה *kānâ* a primitive root; to *address* by an additional name; hence, to *eulogize:*— give flattering titles, surname, surname himself.

H3656 כַּנֶּה *kanneh* for H3641; *Canneh,* a place in Assyria:— Canneh.

H3657 כַּנָּה *kannâ* from H3661; a *plant* (as *set*):— vineyard.

H3658 כִּנּוֹר *kinnôr* from an unused root meaning to *twang;* a *harp:*— harp.

H3659 כָּנְיָהוּ *konyāhû* for H3204; *Conjah,* an Israelite king:— Coniah.

H3660 כְּנֵמָא *kĕnēmāʾ* (Aramaic) corresponding to H3644; *so* or *thus:*— so, this manner, in this sort, thus.

H3661 כָּנַן *kānan* a primitive root; to *set* out, i.e. *plant:*— vineyard.

H3662 כְּנָנִי *kĕnānî* from H3661; *planted; Kenani,* an Israelite:— Chenani.

H3663 כְּנַנְיָה *kĕnanyâ* or

כְּנַנְיָהוּ *kĕnanyāhû* from H3661 and H3050; *Jah has planted; Kenanjah,* an Israelite:— Chenaniah.

H3664 כָּנַס *kānas* a primitive root; to *collect;* hence, to *enfold:*— gather, gather together, heap up, wrap self.

H3665 כָּנַע *kānaᶜ* a primitive root; properly to *bend* the knee; hence to *humiliate, vanquish:*— bring down, bring low, bring into subjection, bring under, humble, humble self, subdue.

H3666 כִּנְעָה *kinᶜâ* from H3665 in the sense of *folding* [compare H3664]; a *package:*— wares.

H3667 כְּנַעַן *kĕnaᶜan* from H3665; *humiliated; Kenaan,* a son of Ham; also the country inhabited by him:— Canaan, merchant, traffick.

H3668 כְּנַעֲנָה *kĕnaᶜănâ* feminine of H3667; *Kenaanah,* the name of two Israelites:— Chenaanah.

H3669 כְּנַעֲנִי *kĕnaᶜanî* patrial from H3667; a *Kenaanite* or inhabitant of Kenaan; by implication a *pedlar* (the Canaanites standing for their neighbors the Ishmaelites, who conducted mercantile caravans):— Canaanite, merchant, trafficker.

H3670 כָּנַף *kānap* a primitive root; properly to *project* laterally, i.e. probably (reflexively) to *withdraw:*— be removed.

H3671 כָּנָף *kānāp* from H3670; an *edge* or *extremity;* specifically (of a bird or army) a *wing,* (of a garment or bed-clothing) a *flap,* (of the earth) a *quarter,* (of a building) a *pinnacle:*— bird, border, corner, end, feather, feathered, flying, other, one another, overspreading, quarters, skirt, sort, uttermost part, wing, winged.

H3672 כִּנְּרוֹת *kinnĕrôt* or

כִּנֶּרֶת *kinneret* respectively plural and singular feminine from the same as H3658; perhaps *harp*-shaped; *Kinneroth* or *Kinnereth,* a place in Palestine:— Chinnereth, Chinneroth, Cinneroth.

H3673 כָּנַשׁ *kānaš* (Aramaic) corresponding to H3664; to *assemble:*— gather together.

H3674 כְּנָת *kĕnāt* from H3655; a *colleague* (as having the same title):— companion.

H3675 כְּנָת *kĕnāt* (Aramaic) corresponding to H3674 :— companion.

H3676 כֵּס *kēs* apparently a contraction for H3678, but probably by erroneous transcription for H5251 :— sworn.

H3677 כֶּסֶא *keseʾ* or

כֶּסֶה *keseh* apparently from H3680; properly *fulness* or the *full moon,* i.e. its festival:— appointed, time appointed.

H3678 כִּסֵּא *kisseʾ* or

כִּסֵּה *kissēh* from H3680; properly *covered,* i.e. a *throne* (as *canopied*):— seat, stool, throne.

H3679 כַּסְדַּי *kasday* for H3778:— Aramaic.

H3680 כָּסָה *kāsâ* a primitive root; properly to *plump,* i.e. *fill up* hollows; by implication to *cover* (for clothing or secrecy):— clad self, close, clothe, conceal, cover, cover self, hide, flee to hide, overwhelm. Compare H3780

H3681 כָּסוּי *kāsûy* passive participle of H3680; properly *covered,* i.e. (as noun) a *covering:*— covering.

H3682 כְּסוּת *kĕsût* from H3680; a *cover* (garment); figuratively a *veiling:*— covering, raiment, vesture.

H3683 כָּסַח *kāsaḥ* a primitive root; to *cut off:*— cut down, cut up.

H3684 כְּסִיל *kĕsîl* from H3688; properly *fat,* i.e. (figuratively) stupid or *silly:*— fool, foolish.

H3685 כְּסִיל *kĕsîl* the same as H3684; any notable *constellation;* specifically *Orion* (as if a *burly* one):— constellation, Orion.

H3686 כְּסִיל *kĕsîl* the same as H3684; *Kesil,* a place in Palestine:— Chesil.

H3687 כְּסִילוּת *kĕsîlût* from H3684; *silliness:*— foolish.

H3688 כָּסַל *kāsal* a primitive root; properly to *be fat,* i.e. (figuratively) *silly:*— be foolish.

H3689 כֶּסֶל *kesel* from H3688; properly *fatness,* i.e. by implication (literally) the *loin* (as the seat of the leaf *fat*) or (generally) the *viscera;* also (figuratively) *silliness* or (in a good sense) *trust:*— confidence, flank, folly, hope, loin.

H3690 כִּסְלָה *kislâ* feminine of H3689; in a good sense, *trust;* in a bad one, *silliness:*— confidence, folly.

H3691 כִּסְלֵו *kislēw* probably of foreign origin; *Kisleu,* the 9th Hebrew month:— Chisleu.

H3692 כִּסְלוֹן *kislôn* from H3688; *hopeful; Kislon,* an Israelite:— Chislon.

H3693 כְּסָלוֹן *kĕsālôn* from H3688; *fertile; Kesalon,* a place in Palestine:— Chesalon.

H3694 כְּסֻלּוֹת *kĕsullôt* feminine plural of passive participle of H3688; *fattened, Kesulloth,* a place in Palestine:— Chesulloth.

H3695 כַּסְלֻחִים *kaslūḥîm* a plural probably of foreign derivation; *Casluchim,* a people cognate to the Egyptians:— Casluhim.

H3696 כִּסְלֹת תָּבֹר *kislōt tābōr* from the feminine plural of H3689 and H8396; *flanks of Tabor; Kisloth-Tabor,* a place in Palestine:— Chisloth-tabor.

H3697 כָּסַם *kāsam* a primitive root; to *shear:*— only, poll. Compare H3765

H3698 כֻּסֶּמֶת *kussemet* from H3697; *spelt* (from its bristliness as if just *shorn*):— fitches, rie.

H3699 כָּסַס *kāsas* a primitive root; to *estimate:*— make count.

H3700 כָּסַף *kāsap* a primitive root; properly to become *pale,* i.e. (by implication) to *pine* after; also to *fear:*— desire, have desire, be greedy, long, sore.

H3701 כֶּסֶף *kesep* from H3700; *silver* (from its *pale* color); by implication *money:*— money, price, silver, silverling.

H3702 כְּסַף *kĕsap* (Aramaic) corresponding to H3701:— money, silver.

H3703 כָּסִפְיָא *kāsipyāʾ* perhaps from H3701; *silvery; Casiphja,* a place in Babylonia:— Casiphia.

H3704 כֶּסֶת *keset* from H3680; a *cushion* or pillow (as *covering* a seat or bed):— pillow.

H3705 כְּעַן *kĕᶜan* (Aramaic) probably from H3652; *now:*— now.

H3706 כְּעֶנֶת *kĕᶜenet* or

כְּעֶת *kĕᶜet* (Aramaic) feminine of H3705; *thus* (only in the formula "and *so forth*"):— at such a time.

H3707 כָּעַס *kaᶜas* a primitive root; to *trouble;* by implication to *grieve, rage, be indignant:*— be angry, be grieved, take indignation, provoke, provoke to anger, provoke unto wrath, have sorrow, vex, be wroth.

H3708 כַּעַס *ka*ᶜ*as* or (in Job)

כַּעַשׂ *ka*ᶜ*aś* from H3707; *vexation:*— anger, angry, grief, indignation, provocation, provoking, sore, sorrow, spite, wrath.

H3709 כַּף *kap* from H3721; the hollow *hand* or palm (so of the *paw* of an animal, of the *sole*, and even of the *bowl* of a dish or sling, the *handle* of a bolt, the *leaves* of a palm-tree); figuratively *power:*— branch, foot, hand, handful, handle, handled, hollow, middle, palm, paw, power, sole, spoon.

H3710 כֵּף *kēp* from H3721; a hollow *rock:*— rock.

H3711 כָּפָה *kāpâ* a primitive root; properly to *bend*, i.e. (figuratively) to *tame* or subdue:— pacify.

H3712 כִּפָּה *kippâ* feminine of H3709; a *leaf* of a palm-tree:— branch.

H3713 כְּפוֹר *kĕpôr* from H3722; properly a *cover*, i.e. (by implication) a *tankard* (or *covered* goblet); also white *frost* (as *covering* the ground):— bason, hoar-frost, hoary frost.

H3714 כָּפִיס *kāpîs* from an unused root meaning to *connect;* a *girder:*— beam.

H3715 כְּפִיר *kĕpîr* from H3722; a *village* (as *covered* in by walls); also a young *lion* (perhaps as *covered* with a mane):— lion, young lion, village. Compare H3723

H3716 כְּפִירָה *kĕpîrâ* feminine of H3715; the *village* (always with the article); *Kephirah*, a place in Palestine:— Chephirah.

H3717 כָּפַל *kāpal* a primitive root; to *fold* together; figuratively to *repeat:*— double.

H3718 כֶּפֶל *kepel* from H3717; a *duplicate:*— double.

H3719 כָּפַן *kāpan* a primitive root; to *bend:*— bend.

H3720 כָּפָן *kāpān* from H3719; *hunger* (as making to *stoop* with emptiness and pain):— famine.

H3721 כָּפַף *kāpap* a primitive root; to *curve:*— bow down, bow self.

H3722 כָּפַר *kāpar* a primitive root; to *cover* (specifically with bitumen); figuratively to *expiate* or *condone*, to *placate* or *cancel:*— appease, make atonement, make an atonement, cleanse, disannul, forgive, be merciful, pacify, pardon, purge, purge away, put off, reconcile, make reconciliation.

H3723 כָּפָר *kāpār* from H3722; a *village* (as *protected* by walls):— village. Compare H3715

H3724 כֹּפֶר *kōper* from H3722; properly a *cover*, i.e. (literally) a *village* (as *covered* in); (specifically) *bitumen* (as used for *coating*), and the *henna* plant (as used for *dyeing*); figuratively a *redemption*-price:— bribe, camphire, pitch, ransom, satisfaction, sum of money, village.

H3725 כִּפֻּר *kippūr* from H3722; *expiation* (only in plural):— atonement.

H3726 כְּפַר הָעַמּוֹנִי *kĕpar hā*ᶜ*ammônî* from H3723 and H5984, with the article interposed; *village of the Ammonite; Kefar-ha-Ammoni*, a place in Palestine:— Chefar-haamonai.

H3727 כַּפֹּרֶת *kappōreh* from H3722; a *lid* (used only of the *cover* of the sacred Ark):— mercy seat.

H3728 כָּפַשׁ *kāpaš* a primitive root; to *tread* down; figuratively to *humiliate:*— cover.

H3729 כְּפַת *kĕpat* (Aramaic) a root of uncertain correspondence; to *fetter:*— bind.

H3730 כַּפְתֹּר *kaptōr* or (Amos 9:1)

כַּפְתּוֹר *kaptôr* probably from an unused root meaning to *encircle;* a *chaplet;* but used only in an architectonic sense, i.e. the *capital* of a column, or a wreath-like *button* or *disk* on the candelabrum:— knop, lintel, upper lintel.

H3731 כַּפְתֹּר *kaptōr* or (Amos 9:7)

כַּפְתּוֹר *kaptôr* apparently the same as H3730; *Caphtor* (i.e. a *wreath*-shaped island), the original seat of the Philistines:— Caphtor.

H3732 כַּפְתֹּרִי *kaptōrî* patrial from H3731; a *Caphtorite* (collectively) or native of Caphtor:— Caphthoriam, Caphtorim, Caphtorims.

H3733 כַּר *kar* from H3769 in the sense of *plumpness;* a *ram* (as *full-grown* and *fat*), including a *battering-ram* (as *butting*); hence a *meadow* (as *for sheep*); also a *pad* or camel's saddle (as *puffed out*):— captain, furniture, lamb, pasture, large pasture, ram. See also H1033, H3746

H3734 כֹּר *kōr* from the same as H3564; properly a deep round *vessel*, i.e. (specifically) a *cor* or measure for things dry:— cor, measure. Aramaic the same

H3735 כְּרָא *kĕrā*ʾ (Aramaic) probably corresponding to H3738 in the sense of *piercing* (figuratively); to *grieve:*— be grieved.

H3736 כַּרְבֵּל *karbēl* from the same as H3525; to *gird* or *clothe:*— clothed.

H3737 כַּרְבְּלָא *karbĕlā*ʾ (Aramaic) from a verb corresponding to that of H3736; a *mantle:*— hat.

H3738 כָּרָה *kārâ* a primitive root; properly to *dig;* figuratively to *plot;* generally to *bore* or open:— dig, make, make a banquet, open.

H3739 כָּרָה *kārâ* usually assigned as a primitive root, but probably only a special application of H3738 (through the common idea of *planning* implied in a bargain); to *purchase:*— buy, prepare.

H3740 כֵּרָה *kērâ* from H3739; a *purchase:*— provision.

H3741 כָּרָה *kārâ* feminine of H3733; a *meadow:*— cottage.

H3742 כְּרוּב *kĕrûb* of uncertain derivation; a *cherub* or imaginary figure:— cherub, *[plural]* cherubims.

H3743 כְּרוּב *kĕrûb* the same as H3742; *Kerub*, a place in Babylonia:— Cherub.

H3744 כָּרוֹז *kārôz* (Aramaic) from H3745; a *herald:*— herald.

H3745 כְּרַז *kĕraz* (Aramaic) probably of Greek origin (**κηρύσσω** *kērysso*); to *proclaim:*— make a proclamation.

H3746 כָּרִי *kārî* perhaps an abridged plural of H3733 in the sense of *leader* (of the flock); a *life-guardsman:*— captains, Cherethites *[from the margin]*.

H3747 כְּרִית *kĕrît* from H3772; a *cut; Kerith*, a brook of Palestine:— Cherith.

H3748 כְּרִיתוּת *kĕrîtût* from H3772; a *cutting* (of the matrimonial bond), i.e. *divorce:*— divorce, divorcement.

H3749 כַּרְכֹּב *karkōb* expanded from the same as H3522; a *rim* or top margin:— compass.

H3750 כַּרְכֹּם *karkōm* probably of foreign origin; the *crocus:*— saffron.

H3751 כַּרְכְּמִישׁ *karkĕmîš* of foreign derivation; *Karkemish*, a place in Syria:— Carchemish.

H3752 כַּרְכַּס *karkas* of Persian origin; *Karkas*, a eunuch of Xerxes:— Carcas.

H3753 כַּרְכָּרָה *karkārâ* from H3769; a *dromedary* (from its *rapid* motion as if dancing):— swift beast.

H3754 כֶּרֶם *kerem* from an unused root of uncertain meaning; a *garden* or *vineyard:*— vines, vineyard, increase of the vineyards, vintage. See also H1021

H3755 כֹּרֵם *kōrēm* active participle of an imaginary denominative from H3754; a *vinedresser:*— vine dresser *[as one or two words]*.

H3756 כַּרְמִי *karmî* from H3754; *gardener; Karmi*, the name of three Israelites:— Carmi.

H3757 כַּרְמִי *karmî* patronymic from H3756; a *Karmite* or descendant of *Karmi:*— Carmites.

H3758 כַּרְמִיל *karmîl* probably of foreign origin; *carmine*, a deep red:— crimson.

H3759 כַּרְמֶל *karmel* from H3754; a planted *field* (garden, orchard, vineyard or park); by implication garden *produce:*— full ears, full ears of corn, green ears, fruitful field, fruitful place, plentiful, plentiful field.

H3760 כַּרְמֶל *karmel* the same as H3759; *Karmel*, the name of a hill and of a town in Palestine:— Carmel, fruitful field, fruitful place, plentiful, plentiful field.

H3761 כַּרְמְלִי *karmĕlî* patronymic from H3760; a *Karmelite* or inhabitant of Karmel (the town):— Carmelite.

H3762 כַּרְמְלִית *karmĕlît* feminine of H3761; a *Karmelitess* or female inhabitant of Karmel:— Carmelitess.

H3763 כְּרָן *kĕrān* of uncertain derivation; *Keran*, an aboriginal Idumaean:— Cheran.

H3764 כָּרְסֵא *korsē*ʾ (Aramaic) corresponding to H3678; a *throne:*— throne.

H3765 כִּרְסֵם *kirsēm* from H3697; to *lay waste:*— waste.

H3766 כָּרַע *kāra*ᶜ a primitive root; to *bend* the knee; by implication to *sink*, to *prostrate:*— bow, bow down, bow self, bring down, bring low, cast down, couch, fall, feeble, kneeling, sink, smite down, stoop down, subdue, very.

H3767 כְּרָע *kārā*ᶜ from H3766; the *leg* (from the knee to the ankle) of men or locusts (only in the dual):— leg.

H3768 כַּרְפַּס *karpas* of foreign origin; *byssus* or fine vegetable wool:— green.

H3769 כָּרַר *kārar* a primitive root; to *dance* (i.e. *whirl*):— dance, dancing.

H3770 כְּרֵשׂ *kĕrēś* by variation from H7164; the *paunch* or belly (as *swelling* out):— belly.

H3771 כַּרְשְׁנָא *karšĕnā*ʾ of foreign origin; *Karshena*, a courtier of Xerxes:— Carshena.

H3772 כָּרַת *kārat* a primitive root; to *cut* (off, down or asunder); by implication to *destroy* or *consume;* specifically to *covenant* (i.e. make an alliance or bargain, originally by cutting flesh and passing between the pieces):— be chewed, be confederate, covenant, cut, cut down, cut off, destroy, fail, feller, be freed, hew, hew down, make a league, make a covenant, lose, perish, utterly, want.

H3773 כָּרֻתָה *kārūtâ* passive participle feminine of H3772; something *cut*, i.e. a hewn *timber:*— beam.

H3774 כְּרֵתִי *kĕrētî* probably from H3772 in the sense of *executioner;* a *Kerethite* or *life-guardsman* [compare H2876] (only collectively in the singular as plural):— Cherethims, Cherethites.

H3775 כֶּשֶׂב *keśeb* apparently by transposition for H3532; a young *sheep:*— lamb.

H3776 כִּשְׂבָּה *kiśbâ* feminine of H3775; a young *ewe:*— lamb.

H3777 כֶּשֶׂד *keśed* from an unused root of uncertain meaning; *Kesed,* a relative of Abraham:— Chesed.

H3778 כַּשְׂדִּי *kaśdî* occasionally (with enclitic)

כַּשְׂדִּימָה *kaśdîmâ towards* the *Kasdites,* into Chaldea), patronymic from H3777 (only in the plural); a *Kasdite,* or descendant of Kesed; by implication a *Chaldaean* (as if so descended); also an *astrologer* (as if proverbial of that people):— Chaldeans, Chaldees, inhabitants of Chaldea.

H3779 כַּשְׂדַּי *kaśday* (Aramaic) corresponding to H3778; a *Chaldaean* (as if so descended); also an *astrologer* (as if proverbial of that people):— Chaldeans, Chaldees, inhabitants of Chaldea.

H3780 כָּשָׂה *kāśâ* a primitive root; to *grow fat* (i.e. be *covered* with flesh):— be covered. Compare H3680

H3781 כַּשִּׁיל *kaššîl* from H3782; properly a *feller,* i.e. an *axe:*— ax.

H3782 כָּשַׁל *kāšal* a primitive root; to *totter* or *waver* (through weakness of the legs, especially the ankle); by implication to *falter, stumble,* faint or fall:— bereave *[from the margin],* cast down, be decayed, fail, cause to fail, fall, cause to fall, make to fall, fall down, falling, feeble, be ruined, be the ruin of, overthrown, be overthrown, stumble, cause to stumble, utterly, be weak.

H3783 כִּשָּׁלוֹן *kiššālôn* from H3782; properly a *tottering,* i.e. *ruin:*— fall.

H3784 כָּשַׁף *kāšap* a primitive root; properly to *whisper* a spell, i.e. to *inchant* or practise magic:— sorcerer, witch, use witchcraft.

H3785 כֶּשֶׁף *kešep* from H3784; *magic:*— sorcery, witchcraft.

H3786 כַּשָּׁף *kaššāp* from H3784; a *magician:*— sorcerer.

H3787 כָּשֵׁר *kāšēr* a primitive root; properly to be *straight* or *right;* by implication to *be acceptable;* also to *succeed* or prosper:— direct, be right, prosper.

H3788 כִּשְׁרוֹן *kišrôn* from H3787; *success, advantage:*— equity, good, right.

H3789 כָּתַב *kātab* a primitive root; to *grave;* by implication to *write* (describe, inscribe, prescribe, subscribe):— describe, record, prescribe, subscribe, write, writing, written.

H3790 כְּתַב *kĕtab* (Aramaic) corresponding to H3789:— write, written.

H3791 כְּתָב *kĕtāb* from H3789; something *written,* i.e. a *writing, record* or *book:*— register, scripture, writing.

H3792 כְּתָב *kĕtāb* (Aramaic) corresponding to H3791:— prescribing, writing, written.

H3793 כְּתֹבֶת *kĕtōbet* from H3789; a *letter* or other *mark* branded on the skin:— any mark.

H3794 כִּתִּי *kittî* or

כִּתִּיִּי *kittîyî* patrial from an unused name denoting Cyprus (only in the plural); a *Kittite* or Cypriote; hence an *islander* in general, i.e. the Greeks or Romans on the shores opposite Palestine:— Chittim, Kittim.

H3795 כָּתִית *kātît* from H3807; *beaten,* i.e. pure (oil) :— beaten.

H3796 כֹּתֶל *kōtel* from an unused root meaning to *compact;* a *wall* (as *gathering* inmates):— wall.

H3797 כְּתַל *kĕtal* (Aramaic) corresponding to H3796:— wall.

H3798 כִּתְלִישׁ *kĕtlîš* from H3796 and H376; *wall of a man; Kithlish,* a place in Palestine:— Kithlish.

H3799 כָּתַם *kātam* a primitive root; properly to *carve* or *engrave,* i.e. (by implication) to *inscribe* indelibly:— mark.

H3800 כֶּתֶם *ketem* from H3799; properly something *carved* out, i.e. *ore;* hence *gold* (pure as originally mined):— gold, fine gold, most fine gold, pure gold, golden wedge.

H3801 כְּתֹנֶת *kĕtōnet* or

כֻּתֹּנֶת *kuttōnet* from an unused root meaning to *cover* [compare H3802]; a *shirt:*— coat, garment, robe.

H3802 כָּתֵף *kātēp* from an unused root meaning to *clothe;* the *shoulder* (proper, i.e. upper end of the arm; as being the spot where the garments hang); figuratively *side-piece* or lateral projection of anything:— arm, corner, shoulder, shoulderpiece, side, undersetter.

H3803 כָּתַר *kātar* a primitive root; to *enclose;* hence (in a friendly sense) to *crown,* (in a hostile one) to *besiege;* also to *wait* (as restraining oneself):— beset round, compass about, be crowned, inclose round, suffer.

H3804 כֶּתֶר *keter* from H3803; properly a *circlet,* i.e. a *diadem:*— crown.

H3805 כֹּתֶרֶת *kōteret* feminine active participle of H3803; the *capital* of a column:— chapiter.

H3806 כָּתַשׁ *kātaš* a primitive root; to *butt* or *pound* :— bray.

H3807 כָּתַת *kātat* a primitive root; to *bruise* or violently *strike:*— beat, beat down, beat to pieces, break in pieces, crushed, destroy, discomfit, smite, stamp.

ל

H3808 לֹא *lō'* or

לוֹא *lô'* or

לֹה *lōh* (Deut 3:11), a primitive particle; *not* (the simple or absolute negation); by implication *no;* often used with other particles (as follows):— before, or else, ere, except, ignorant, much, less, nay, neither, never, no, none, nor, nothing, not, as though . . . not, cannot, for not, not out of, of nought, otherwise, out of, surely, as truly as, of a truth, verily, for want, whether, without.

H3809 לָא *lā'* or

לָה *lâ* (Dan 4:32), (Aramaic) corresponding to H3808:— or even, neither, no, none, nor, cannot, as nothing, without.

H3810 לֹא דְבַר *lō' dĕbar* or

לוֹ דְבַר *lô dĕbar* (2 Sam. 9:4, 5) or

לִדְבִר *lidbir* (Josh 13:26) probably rather

לֹדְבַר *lōdĕbar* from H3808 and H1699; *pastureless; Lo-Debar,* a place in Palestine:— Debir, Lodebar.

H3811 לָאָה *lā'â* a primitive root; to *tire;* (figuratively) to *be* (or *make*) *disgusted:*— faint, grieve, lothe, weary, be weary, make weary, weary selves.

H3812 לֵאָה *lē'â* from H3811; *weary; Leah,* a wife of Jacob:— Leah.

H3813 לָאַט *lā'aṭ* a primitive root; to *muffle:*— cover.

H3814 לָאט *lā't* from H3813 (or perhaps for active participle of H3874); properly *muffled,* i.e. *silently* :— softly.

H3815 לָאֵל *lā'ēl* from the prepositional prefix and H410; (belonging) *to God; Laël* an Israelite:— Lael.

H3816 לְאֹם *lĕ'ōm* or

לְאוֹם *lĕ'ôm* from an unused root meaning to *gather;* a *community:*— nation, people.

H3817 לְאֻמִּים *lĕ'ummîm* plural of H3816; *communities; Leümmim,* an Arabian:— Leummim.

H3818 לֹא עַמִּי *lō' 'ammî* from H3808 and H5971 with pronominal suffix; *not my people; Lo-Ammi,* the symbolic name of a son of Hosea:— Lo-ammi.

H3819 לֹא רֻחָמָה *lō' ruḥāmâ* from H3808 and H7355; *not pitied; Lo-Ruchamah,* the symbolic name of a son of Hosea:— Lo-ruhamah.

H3820 לֵב *lēb* a form of H3824; the *heart;* also used (figuratively) very widely for the feelings, the will and even the intellect; likewise for the *centre* of anything:— care for, comfortably, consent, considered, courageous, friendly, heart, brokenhearted, hardhearted, merryhearted, stiffhearted, stouthearted, double heart, hearted, heed, I, kindly, midst, mind, minded, regarded, themselves, unawares, understanding, well, willingly, wisdom.

H3821 לֵב *lēb* (Aramaic) corresponding to H3820 :— heart.

H3822 לְבָאוֹת *lĕbā'ôt* plural of H3833; *lionesses; Lebaoth,* a place in Palestine:— Lebaoth. See also H1034

H3823 לָבַב *lābab* a primitive root; properly to *be enclosed* (as if with *fat*); by implication (as denominative from H3824) to *unheart,* i.e. (in a good sense) *transport* (with love), or (in a bad sense) *stultify;* also (as denominatively from H3834) to *make cakes:*— make cakes, ravish, be wise.

H3824 לֵבָב *lēbāb* from H3823; the *heart* (as the most interior organ); used also like H3820:— bethink themselves, breast, comfortably, courage, heart, fainthearted, tenderhearted, midst, mind, unawares, understanding.

H3825 לְבַב *lĕbab* (Aramaic) corresponding to H3824 :— heart.

H3826 לִבָּה *libbâ* feminine of H3820; the *heart:*— heart.

H3827 לַבָּה *labbâ* for H3852; *flame:*— flame.

H3828 לְבוֹנָה *lĕbônâ* or

לְבֹנָה *lĕbônâ* from H3836; *frankincense* (from its *whiteness* or perhaps that of its smoke):— incense, frankincense.

H3829 לְבוֹנָה *lĕbônâ* the same as H3828; *Lebonah,* a place in Palestine:— Lebonah.

H3830 לְבוּשׁ *lĕbûš* or

לְבֻשׁ *lĕbûš* from H3847; a *garment* (literally or figuratively); by implication (euphemisticly) a *wife:*— apparel, clothed with, clothing, garment, raiment, vestment, vesture.

H3831 לְבוּשׁ *lĕbûš* (Aramaic) corresponding to H3830 :— garment.

H3832 לָבַט *lābaṭ* a primitive root; to *overthrow;* intransitively to *fall:*— fall.

H3833 לָבִיא *lābîʾ* or (Ezek. 19:2)

לְבִיָא *lĕbîyāʾ* irregular masculine plural

לְבָאִים *lĕbāʾîm* irregular feminine plural

לְבָאוֹת *lĕbāʾôt* from an unused root meaning to *roar;* a *lion* (properly a lion*ess* as the fiercer [although not a *roarer;* compare H738]):— lion, great lion, old lion, stout lion, lioness, young lion.

H3834 לָבִיבָה *lābîbâ* or rather

לְבִבָה *lĕbībâ* from H3823 in its original sense of *fatness* (or perhaps of *folding*); a *cake* (either as *fried* or *turned*):— cake.

H3835 לָבַן *lāban* a primitive root; to *be* (or become) *white;* also (as denominative from H3843) to *make bricks:*— make brick, be white, be made white, make white, be whiter.

H3836 לָבָן *lābān* or (Gen. 49:12)

לָבֵן *lābēn* from H3835; *white:*— white.

H3837 לָבָן *lābān* the same as H3836; *Laban,* a Mesopotamian; also a place in the Desert:— Laban.

H3838 לְבָנָא *lĕbānāʾ* or

לְבָנָה *lĕbānâ* the same as H3842; *Lebana* or *Lebanah,* one of the Nethinim:— Lebana, Lebanah.

H3839 לִבְנֶה *libneh* from H3835; some sort of *whitish* tree, perhaps the *storax:*— poplar.

H3840 לִבְנָה *libnâ* from H3835; properly *whiteness,* i.e. (by implication) *transparency:*— paved.

H3841 לִבְנָה *libnâ* the same as H3839; *Libnah,* a place in the Desert and one in Palestine:— Libnah.

H3842 לְבָנָה *lĕbānâ* from H3835; properly (the) *white,* i.e. the *moon:*— moon. See also H3838

H3843 לְבֵנָה *lĕbēnâ* from H3835; a *brick* (from the *whiteness* of the clay):— brick, altar of brick, tile.

H3844 לְבָנוֹן *lĕbānôn* from H3825; (the) *white* mountain (from its snow); *Lebanon,* a mountain range in Palestine:— Lebanon.

H3845 לִבְנִי *libnî* from H3835; *white; Libni,* an Israelite:— Libni.

H3846 לִבְנִי *libnî* patronymic from H3845; a *Libnite* or descendant of Libni (collectively):— Libnites.

H3847 לָבַשׁ *lābaš* or

לָבֵשׁ *lābēš* a primitive root; properly *wrap* around, i.e. (by implication) to *put on* a garment or *clothe* (oneself, or another), literally or figuratively:— apparel, in apparel, arm, array, array self, clothe, clothe self, come upon, put, put on, put upon, wear.

H3848 לְבַשׁ *lĕbaš* (Aramaic) corresponding to H3847 :— clothe.

H3849 לֹג *lōg* from an unused root apparently meaning to *deepen* or *hollow* [like H3537]; a *log* or measure for liquids:— log of oil.

H3850 לֹד *lōd* from an unused root of uncertain signification; *Lod,* a place in Palestine:— Lod.

H3851 לַהַב *lahab* from an unused root meaning to *gleam;* a *flash;* figuratively a sharply polished *blade* or *point* of a weapon:— blade, bright, flame, glittering.

H3852 לֶהָבָה *lehābâ* or

לַהֶבֶת *lahebet* feminine of H3851, and meaning the same:— flame, flaming, head of a spear.

H3853 לְהָבִים *lehābîm* plural of H3851; *flames; Lehabim,* a son of Mizrain, and his descendants :— Lehabim.

H3854 לַהַג *lahag* from an unused root meaning to *be eager;* intense mental *application:*— study.

H3855 לַהַד *lahad* from an unused root meaning to *glow* [compare H3851] or else to *be earnest* [compare H3854]; *Lahad,* an Israelite:— Lahad.

H3856 לָהַהּ *lāhah* a primitive root meaning properly to *burn,* i.e. (by implication) to *be rabid* (figuratively *insane*); also (from the *exhaustion* of frenzy) to *languish:*— faint, mad.

H3857 לָהַט *lāhaṭ* a primitive root; properly to *lick,* i.e. (by implication) to *blaze:*— burn, burn up, set on fire, flaming, kindle.

H3858 לַהַט *lahaṭ* from H3857; a *blaze;* also (from the idea of *enwrapping*) *magic* (as *covert*):— flaming, enchantment.

H3859 לָהַם *lāham* a primitive root; properly to *burn* in, i.e. (figuratively) to *rankle:*— wound.

H3860 לָהֵן *lāhēn* from the prefixed preposition meaning *to* or *for* and H2005; properly *for if;* hence *therefore:*— for them *[by mistake for prepositional suffix]*.

H3861 לָהֵן *lāhēn* (Aramaic) corresponding to H3860; *therefore;* also *except:*— but, except, save, therefore, wherefore.

H3862 לַהֲקָה *lahăqâ* probably from an unused root meaning to *gather;* an *assembly:*— company.

H3863 לוּא *lûʾ* or

לֻא *lūʾ* or

לוּ *lû* a conditional particle; *if;* by implication (interjectionally as a wish) *would that!:*— if, if haply, peradventure, I pray thee, though, I would, would God, would God that.

H3864 לוּבִי *lûbî* or

לֻבִּי *lubbî* (Dan 11:43), patrial from a name probably derived from an unused root meaning to *thirst,* i.e. a *dry* region; apparently a *Libyan* or inhabitant of interior Africa (only in plural):— Lubim, Lubims, Libyans.

H3865 לוּד *lûd* probably of foreign derivation; *Lud,* the name of two nations:— Lud, Lydia.

H3866 לוּדִי *lûdî* or

לוּדִיִּי *lûdîyî* patrial from H3865; a *Ludite* or inhabitant of Lud (only in plural):— Ludim, Lydians.

H3867 לָוָה *lāwâ* a primitive root; properly to *twine,* i.e. (by implication) to *unite,* to *remain;* also to *borrow* (as a form of *obligation*) or (causatively) to *lend:*— abide with, borrow, borrower, cleave, join, join self, lend, lender.

H3868 לוּז *lûz* a primitive root; to *turn* aside [compare H3867, H3874 and H3885], i.e. (literally) to *depart,* (figuratively) *be perverse:*— depart, froward, perverse, perverseness.

H3869 לוּז *lûz* probably of foreign origin; some kind of *nut*-tree, perhaps the *almond:*— hazel.

H3870 לוּז *lûz* probably from H3869 (as growing there); *Luz,* the name of two places in Palestine:— Luz.

H3871 לוּחַ *lûaḥ* or

לֻחַ *lūaḥ* from a primitive root; probably meaning to *glisten;* a *tablet* (as *polished*), of stone, wood or metal:— board, plate, table.

H3872 לוּחִית *lûḥît* or

לֻחוֹת *lūḥôt* (Jer 48:5), from the same as H3871; *floored; Luchith,* a place east of the Jordan:— Luhith.

H3873 לוֹחֵשׁ *lôḥēš* active participle of H3907; (the) *enchanter; Lochesh,* an Israelite:— Hallohesh, Haloshesh *[including the article]*.

H3874 לוּט *lûṭ* a primitive root; to *wrap* up:— cast, wrap.

H3875 לוֹט *lôṭ* from H3874; a *veil:*— covering.

H3876 לוֹט *lôṭ* the same as H3875; *Lot,* Abraham's nephew:— Lot.

H3877 לוֹטָן *lôṭān* from H3875; *covering; Lotan,* an Idumaean:— Lotan.

H3878 לֵוִי *lēwî* from H3867; *attached; Levi,* a son of Jacob:— Levi. See also H3879, H3881

H3879 לֵוִי *lēwî* (Aramaic) corresponding to H3880 :— Levite.

H3880 לִוְיָה *liwyâ* from H3867; something *attached,* i.e. a *wreath:*— ornament.

H3881 לֵוִיִּי *lēwîyî* or

לֵוִי *lēwî* patronymic from H3878; a *Levite* or descendant of Levi:— Levite.

H3882 לִוְיָתָן *liwyātān* from H3867; a *wreathed* animal, i.e. a *serpent* (especially the *crocodile* or some other large sea-monster); figuratively the constellation of the *dragon;* also as a symbol of *Babylon:*— leviathan, mourning.

H3883 לוּל *lûl* from an unused root meaning to *fold* back; a *spiral* step:— winding stair. Compare H3924

H3884 לוּלֵא *lûlēʾ* or

לוּלֵי *lûlê* from H3863 and H3808; *if not:*— except, had not, if, if . . . not, unless, were it not that.

H3885 לוּן *lûn* or

לִין *lîn* a primitive root; to *stop* (usually over night); by implication to *stay* permanently; hence (in a bad sense) to be *obstinate* (especially in words, to *complain*):— abide, abide all night, continue, dwell, endure, grudge, be left, lie all night, lodge, cause to lodge, lodge all night, lodge in, lodging, lodge this night, murmer, make to murmur, remain, tarry, tarry all night, tarry that night.

H3886 לוּעַ *lûaʿ* a primitive root; to *gulp;* figuratively to *be rash:*— swallow down, swallow up.

H3887 לוּץ *lûṣ* a primitive root; properly to *make mouths* at, i.e. to *scoff:* hence (from the effort to pronounce a foreign language) to *interpret,* or (generally) *intercede:*— ambassador, have in derision, interpreter, make a mock, mocker, scorn, scorner, scornful, teacher.

H3888 לוּשׁ *lûš* a primitive root; to *knead:*— knead.

H3889 לוּשׁ *lûš* from H3888; *kneading; Lush,* a place in Palestine:— Laish *[from the margin]*. Compare H3919

H3890 לְוָת *lĕwāt* (Aramaic) from a root corresponding to H3867; properly *adhesion,* i.e. (as preposition) *with:*— thee.

H3891 לְזוּת *lĕzût* from H3868; *perverseness:*— perverse.

HEB

H3892 לַח *laḥ* from an unused root meaning to *be new; fresh,* i.e. unused or undried:— green, moist.

H3893 לֵחַ *lēaḥ* from the same as H3892; *freshness,* i.e. vigor:— natural force.

H3894 לָחוּם *lāḥûm* or

לָחֻם *lāḥūm* passive participle of H3898; properly *eaten,* i.e. *food;* also *flesh,* i.e. *body:*— while . . . is eating, flesh.

H3895 לְחִי *lĕḥî* from an unused root meaning to *be soft;* the *cheek* (from its *fleshiness*); hence the *jaw-bone:*— cheek, cheek bone, jaw, jaw bone.

H3896 לֶחִי *leḥî* a form of H3895; *Lechi,* a place in Palestine:— Lehi. Compare also H7437

H3897 לָחַךְ *lāḥak* a primitive root; to *lick:*— lick, lick up.

H3898 לָחַם *lāḥam* a primitive root; to *feed* on; figuratively to *consume;* by implication to *battle* (as *destruction*):— devour, eat, ever, fight, fighting, overcome, prevail, war, make war, warring.

H3899 לֶחֶם *leḥem* from H3898; *food* (for man or beast), especially *bread,* or *grain* (for making it):— bread, shewbread, eat, food, fruit, loaf, meat, victuals. See also H1036

H3900 לְחֶם *lĕḥem* (Aramaic) corresponding to H3899 :— feast.

H3901 לָחֶם *lāḥem* from H3898, *battle:*— war.

H3902 לַחְמִי *laḥmî* from H3899; *foodful; Lachmi,* an Israelite; or rather probably a brief form (or perhaps erroneous transcription) for H1022:— Lahmi. See also H3433

H3903 לַחְמָס *laḥmās* probably by erroneous transcription for

לַחְמָם *laḥmām;* from H3899; *food-like; Lachmam* or *Lachmas,* a place in Palestine:— Lahmam.

H3904 לְחֵנָה *lĕḥēnâ* (Aramaic) from an unused root of uncertain meaning; a *concubine:*— concubine.

H3905 לָחַץ *lāḥaṣ* a primitive root; properly to *press,* i.e. (figuratively) to *distress:*— afflict, crush, force, hold fast, oppress, oppressor, thrust self.

H3906 לַחַץ *laḥaṣ* from H3905; *distress:*— affliction, oppression.

H3907 לָחַשׁ *lāḥaš* a primitive root; to *whisper;* by implication to *mumble* a spell (as a magician):— charmer, whisper, whisper together.

H3908 לַחַשׁ *laḥaš* from H3907; properly a *whisper,* by implication (in a good sense) a private *prayer,* (in a bad one) an *incantation;* concretely an *amulet:*— charmed, earring, enchantment, orator, prayer.

H3909 לָט *lāṭ* a form of H3814 or else participle from H3874; properly *covered,* i.e. *secret;* by implication *incantation;* also *secrecy* or (adverbially) *covertly:*— enchantment, privily, secretly, softly.

H3910 לֹט *lōṭ* probably from H3874; a gum (from its *sticky* nature), probably *Ladanum:*— myrrh.

H3911 לְטָאָה *lĕṭāʾâ* from an unused root meaning to *hide;* a kind of *lizard* (from its *covert* habits):— lizard.

H3912 לְטוּשִׁם *lĕṭûšim* masculine plural of passive participle of H3913; *hammered* (i.e. *oppressed*) ones; *Letushim,* an Arabian tribe:— Letushim.

H3913 לָטַשׁ *lāṭaš* a primitive root; properly to *hammer* out (an edge), i.e. to *sharpen:*— instructer, sharp, sharpen, whet.

H3914 לֹיָה *lōyâ* a form of H3880; a *wreath:*— addition.

H3915 לַיִל *layil* or (Isa. 21:11)

לֵיל *lêl* also

לַיְלָה *laylâ* from the same as H3883; properly a *twist* (away of the light), i.e. *night;* figuratively *adversity:*— night, midnight, night season.

H3916 לֵילְיָא *lêlĕyāʾ* (Aramaic) corresponding to H3915:— night.

H3917 לִילִית *lîlît* from H3915; a *night* spectre:— screech owl.

H3918 לַיִשׁ *layiš* from H3888 in the sense of *crushing;* a lion (from his destructive *blows*):— lion, old lion.

H3919 לַיִשׁ *layiš* the same as H3918; *Laïsh,* the name of two places in Palestine:— Laish. Compare H3889

H3920 לָכַד *lākad* a primitive root; to *catch* (in a net, trap or pit); generally to *capture* or occupy; also to *choose* (by lot); figuratively to *cohere:*— at all, catch, catch self, be frozen, be holden, stick together, take.

H3921 לֶכֶד *leked* from H3920; something to *capture* with, i.e. a *noose:*— being taken.

H3922 לֵכָה *lēkâ* from H3212; a *journey; Lekah,* a place in Palestine:— Lecah.

H3923 לָכִישׁ *lākîš* from an unused root of uncertain meaning; *Lakish,* a place in Palestine:— Lachish.

H3924 לֻלָאָה *lulāʾâ* from the same as H3883; a *loop:*— loop.

H3925 לָמַד *lāmad* a primitive root; properly to *goad,* i.e. (by implication) to *teach* (the rod being an Oriental *incentive*):— unaccustomed, diligently, expert, instruct, learn, skilful, teach, teacher, teaching.

H3926 לְמוֹ *lĕmô* a prolonged and separable form of the prefixed preposition; *to* or *for:*— at, for, to, upon.

H3927 לְמוּאֵל *lĕmûʾēl* or

לְמוֹאֵל *lĕmôʾēl* from H3926 and H410; (belonging) *to God; Lemuël* or *Lemoël,* a symbolic name of Solomon:— Lemuel.

H3928 לִמּוּד *limmûd* or

לִמֻּד *limmūd* from H3925; *instructed:*— accustomed, disciple, learned, taught, used.

H3929 לֶמֶךְ *lemek* from an unused root of uncertain meaning; *Lemek,* the name of two antediluvian patriarchs:— Lamech.

H3930 לֹעַ *lōaʿ* from H3886; the *gullet:*— throat.

H3931 לָעַב *lāʿab* a primitive root; to *deride:*— mock.

H3932 לָעַג *lāʿag* a primitive root; to *deride;* by implication (as if imitating a foreigner) to *speak unintelligibly:*— have in derision, laugh, laugh to scorn, mock, mock on, stammering.

H3933 לַעַג *laʿag* from H3932; *derision, scoffing:*— derision, scorn, scorning.

H3934 לָעֵג *lāʿēg* from H3932; a *buffoon;* also a *foreigner:*— mocker, stammering.

H3935 לַעְדָּה *laʿdâ* from an unused root of uncertain meaning; *Ladah,* an Israelite:— Laadah.

H3936 לַעְדָּן *laʿdān* from the same as H3935; *Ladan,* the name of two Israelites:— Laadan.

H3937 לָעַז *lāʿaz* a primitive root; to *speak in a foreign tongue:*— strange language.

H3938 לָעַט *lāʿaṭ* a primitive root; to *swallow* greedily; causatively to *feed:*— feed.

H3939 לַעֲנָה *laʿănâ* from an unused root supposed to mean to *curse; wormwood* (regarded as *poisonous,* and therefore *accursed*):— hemlock, wormwood.

H3940 לַפִּיד *lappîd* or

לַפִּד *lappīd* from an unused root probably meaning to *shine;* a *flambeau, lamp* or *flame:*— brand, firebrand, lamp, burning lamp, lightning, torch.

H3941 לַפִּידוֹת *lappîdôt* feminine plural of H3940; *Lappidoth,* the husband of Deborah:— Lappidoth.

H3942 לִפְנָי *lipnāy* from the prefixed preposition *(to* or *for)* and H6440; *anterior:*— before.

H3943 לָפַת *lāpat* a primitive root; properly to *bend,* i.e. (by implication) to *clasp;* also (reflexively) to *turn* around or aside:— take hold, turn aside, turn self.

H3944 לָצוֹן *lāṣôn* from H3887; *derision:*— scornful, scorning.

H3945 לָצַץ *lāṣaṣ* a primitive root; to *deride:*— scorn.

H3946 לַקּוּם *laqqûm* from an unused root thought to mean to *stop* up by a barricade; perhaps *fortification; Lakkum,* a place in Palestine:— Lakum.

H3947 לָקַח *lāqaḥ* a primitive root; to *take* (in the widest variety of applications):— accept, bring, buy, carry away, drawn, fetch, get, infold, many, mingle, place, receive, receiving, reserve, seize, send for, take, take away, taking, taking up, use, win.

H3948 לֶקַח *leqaḥ* from H3947; properly something *received,* i.e. (mentally) *instruction* (whether on the part of the teacher or hearer); also (in an active and sinister sense) *inveiglement:*— doctrine, learning, fair speech.

H3949 לִקְחִי *liqḥî* from H3947; *learned; Likchi,* an Israelite:— Likhi.

H3950 לָקַט *lāqaṭ* a primitive root; properly to *pick* up, i.e. (generally) to *gather;* specifically to *glean:*— gather, gather up, glean.

H3951 לֶקֶט *leqeṭ* from H3950; the *gleaning:*— gleaning.

H3952 לָקַק *lāqaq* a primitive root; to *lick* or *lap:*— lap, lick.

H3953 לָקַשׁ *lāqaš* a primitive root; to *gather* the *after* crop:— gather.

H3954 לֶקֶשׁ *leqeš* from H3953; the *after crop:*— latter growth.

H3955 לְשַׁד *lĕšad* from an unused root of uncertain meaning; apparently *juice,* i.e. (figuratively) *vigor;* also a sweet or fat *cake:*— fresh, moisture.

H3956 לָשׁוֹן *lāšôn* or

לָשֹׁן *lāšōn* also (in plural) feminine

לְשֹׁנָה *lĕšōnâ* from H3960; the *tongue* (or man or animals), used literally (as the instrument of licking, eating, or speech), and figuratively (speech, an ingot, a fork of flame, a cove of water):— babbler, bay, evil speaker, language, talker, tongue, wedge.

H3957 לִשְׁכָּה *liškâ* from an unused root of uncertain meaning; a *room* in a building (whether for storage, eating, or lodging):— chamber, parlour. Compare H5393

H3958 לֶשֶׁם *lešem* from an unused root of uncertain meaning; a *gem,* perhaps the *jacinth:*— ligure.

H3959 לֶשֶׁם *lešem* the same as H3958; *Leshem,* a place in Palestine:— Leshem.

H3960 לָשַׁן *lāšan* a primitive root; properly to *lick;* but used only as a denominative from H3956; to *wag the tongue,* i.e. to *calumniate:*— accuse, slander.

H3961 לִשָּׁן *liššān* (Aramaic) corresponding to H3956; *speech,* i.e. a *nation:*— language.

H3962 לֶשַׁע *lešaᶜ* from an unused root thought to mean to *break* through; a boiling *spring; Lesha,* a place probably east of the Jordan:— Lasha.

H3963 לֶתֶךְ *letek* from an unused root of uncertain meaning; a *measure* for things dry:— half homer.

מ

H3964 מָא *māʾ* (Aramaic) corresponding to H4100; (as indefinite) *that:*— what.

H3965 מַאֲבוּס *maʾăbûs* from H75; a *granary:*— storehouse.

H3966 מְאֹד *mĕʾōd* from the same as H181; properly *vehemence,* i.e. (with or without preposition) *vehemently;* by implication *wholly, speedily,* etc. (often with other words as an intensive or superlative; especially when repeated):— diligently, especially, exceeding, exceedingly, far, fast, good, great, greatly, louder and louder, might, mightily, mighty, much, so much, quickly, sore, so sore, utterly, very, very much, very sore, well.

H3967 מֵאָה *mēʾâ* or

מֵאיָה *mēʾyâ* probably a primitive numeral; a *hundred;* also as a multiplicative and a fraction:— hundred, hundredfold, hundredth, sixscore.

H3968 מֵאָה *mēʾâ* the same as H3967; *Meäh,* a tower in Jerusalem:— Meah.

H3969 מְאָה *mĕʾâ* (Aramaic) corresponding to H3967 :— hundred.

H3970 מַאֲוַי *maʾăway* from H183; a *desire:*— desire.

H3971 מאוּם *mʾûm* usually

מוּם *mûm* as if passive participle from an unused root probably meaning to *stain;* a *blemish* (physical or moral):— blemish, blot, spot.

H3972 מְאוּמָה *mĕʾûmâ* apparently a form of H3971; properly a *speck* or *point,* i.e. (by implication) *something;* with negative *nothing:*— fault, no, nought, ought, somewhat, any thing, nothing.

H3973 מָאוֹס *māʾôs* from H3988; *refuse:*— refuse.

H3974 מָאוֹר *māʾôr* or

מָאֹר *māʾōr* also (in plural) feminine

מְאוֹרָה *mĕʾôrâ* or

מְאֹרָה *mĕʾōrâ* from H215; properly a *luminous* body or *luminary,* i.e. (abstractly) *light* (as an element); figuratively *brightness,* i.e. *cheerfulness;* specifically a *chandelier:*— bright, light.

H3975 מְאוּרָה *mĕʾûrâ* feminine passive participle of H215; something *lighted,* i.e. an *aperture;* by implication a *crevice* or *hole* (of a serpent):— den.

H3976 מֹאזֵן *mōʾzēn* from H239; (only in the dual) a pair of *scales:*— balances.

H3977 מֹאזֵן *mōʾzēn* (Aramaic) corresponding to H3976:— balances.

H3978 מַאֲכָל *maʾăkāl* from H398; an *eatable* (including provender, flesh and fruit):— food, fruit, meat, bakemeats, victual.

H3979 מַאֲכֶלֶת *maʾăkelet* from H398; something to *eat* with, i.e. a *knife:*— knife.

H3980 מַא־כֹלֶת *maʾ-kōlet* from H398; something *eaten* (by fire), i.e. *fuel:*— fuel.

H3981 מַאֲמָץ *maʾămāṣ* from H553; *strength,* i.e. (plural) *resources:*— force.

H3982 מַאֲמַר *maʾămar* from H559; something (authoritatively) *said,* i.e. an *edict:*— commandment, decree.

H3983 מֵאמַר *mēʾmar* (Aramaic) corresponding to H3982:— appointment, word.

H3984 מָאן *māʾn* (Aramaic) probably from a root corresponding to H579 in the sense of an *inclosure* by sides; a *utensil:*— vessel.

H3985 מָאֵן *māʾēn* a primitive root; to *refuse:*— refuse, utterly.

H3986 מָאֵן *māʾēn* from H3985; *unwilling:*— refuse.

H3987 מֵאֵן *mēʾēn* from H3985; *refractory:*— refuse.

H3988 מָאַס *māʾas* a primitive root; to *spurn;* also (intransitively) to *disappear:*— abhor, cast away, cast off, contemn, despise, disdain, loathe, become loathesome, melt away, refuse, reject, reprobate, utterly, vile person.

H3989 מַאֲפֶה *maʾăpeh* from H644; something *baked,* i.e. a *batch:*— baken.

H3990 מַאֲפֵל *maʾăpēl* from the same as H651; something *opaque:*— darkness.

H3991 מַאְפֵלְיָה *maʾăpēlyâ* prolonged feminine of H3990; *opaqueness:*— darkness.

H3992 מָאַר *māʾar* a primitive root; to *be bitter* of (causatively) to *embitter,* i.e. *be painful:*— fretting, picking.

H3993 מַאֲרָב *maʾărāb* from H693; an *ambuscade* :— lie in ambush, ambushment, lurking place, lying in wait.

H3994 מְאֵרָה *mĕʾērâ* from H779; an *execration:*— curse.

H3995 מִבְדָּלָה *mibdālâ* from H914; a *separation,* i.e. (concretely) a *separate* place:— separate.

H3996 מָבוֹא *mābôʾ* from H935; an *entrance* (the place or the act); specifically (with or without H8121) *sunset* or the *west;* also (adverbially with preposition) *towards:*— by which came, as cometh, in coming, as men enter into, entering, entrance into, entry, where goeth, going down, westward. Compare H4126

H3997 מְבוֹאָה *mĕbôʾâ* feminine of H3996; a *haven* :— entry.

H3998 מְבוּכָה *mĕbûkâ* from H943; *perplexity:*— perplexity.

H3999 מַבּוּל *mabbûl* from H2986 in the sense of *flowing;* a *deluge:*— flood.

H4000 מָבוֹן *mābôn* from H995; *instructing:*— taught.

H4001 מְבוּסָה *mĕbûsâ* from H947; a *trampling:*— treading down, trodden down, trodden under foot.

H4002 מַבּוּעַ *mabbûaᶜ* from H5042; a *fountain:*— fountain, spring.

H4003 מְבוּקָה *mĕbûqâ* from the same as H950; *emptiness:*— void.

H4004 מִבְחוֹר *mibḥôr* from H977; *select,* i.e. well fortified:— choice.

H4005 מִבְחָר *mibḥār* from H977; *select,* i.e. best:— choice, choicest, chosen.

H4006 מִבְחָר *mibḥār* the same as H4005; *Mibchar,* an Israelite:— Mibhar.

H4007 מַבָּט *mabbāṭ* or

מֶבָּט *mebāṭ* from H5027; something *expected,* i.e. (abstractly) *expectation:*— expectation.

H4008 מִבְטָא *mibṭāʾ* from H981; a rash *utterance* (hasty vow):— that which . . . uttered, uttered out of.

H4009 מִבְטָח *mibṭāḥ* from H982; properly a *refuge,* i.e. (objectively) *security,* or (subjectively) *assurance:*— confidence, hope, sure, trust.

H4010 מַבְלִיגִית *mablîgît* from H1082; *desistance* (or rather *desolation*):— comfort self.

H4011 מִבְנֶה *mibneh* from H1129; a *building:*— frame.

H4012 מְבֻנַּי *mĕbunnay* from H1129; *built* up; *Mebunnai,* an Israelite:— Mebunnai.

H4013 מִבְצָר *mibṣār* also (in plural) feminine (Dan. 11:15)

מִבְצָרָה *mibṣārâ* from H1219; a *fortification, castle,* or *fortified* city; figuratively a *defender:*— fenced, defenced, most fenced, fortress, strong, most strong, strong hold.

H4014 מִבְצָר *mibṣār* the same as H4013; *Mibtsar,* an Idumaean:— Mibzar.

H4015 מִבְרָח *mibrāḥ* from H1272; a *refugee:*— fugitive.

H4016 מָבֻשׁ *mābûš* from H954; (plural) the (male) *pudenda:*— secrets.

H4017 מִבְשָׂם *mibśām* from the same as H1314; *fragrant; Mibsam,* the name of an Ishmaelite and of an Israelite:— Mibsam.

H4018 מְבַשְּׁלָה *mĕbaššĕlâ* from H1310; a cooking *hearth:*— boiling-place.

H4019 מַגְבִּישׁ *magbîš* from the same as H1378; *stiffening; Magbish,* an Israelite, or a place in Palestine:— Magbish.

H4020 מִגְבָּלָה *migbālâ* from H1379; a *border:*— end.

H4021 מִגְבָּעָה *migbāᶜâ* from the same as H1389; a *cap* (as *hemispherical*):— bonnet.

H4022 מֶגֶד *meged* from an unused root properly meaning to *be eminent;* properly a *distinguished* thing; hence something *valuable,* as a product or fruit:— pleasant, precious fruit, precious thing.

H4023 מְגִדּוֹן *mĕgiddôn* (Zech. 12:11) or

מְגִדּוֹ *mĕgiddô* from H1413; *rendezvous; Megiddon* or *Megiddo,* a place in Palestine:— Megiddo, Megiddon.

H4024 מִגְדּוֹל *migdôl* or

מִגְדֹּל *migdōl* probably of Egyptian origin; *Migdol,* a place in Egypt:— Migdol, tower.

H4025 מַגְדִּיאֵל *magdîʾēl* from H4022 and H410; *preciousness of God; Magdiël,* an Idumaean:— Magdiel.

H4026 מִגְדָּל *migdāl* also (in plural) feminine

מִגְדָּלָה *migdālâ* from H1431; a *tower* (from its size or height); by analogy a *rostrum;* figuratively a (pyramidal) *bed* of flowers:— castle, flower, tower. Compare the names following

H4027 מִגְדַּל־אֵל *migdal-ʾēl* from H4026 and H410; *tower of God; Migdal-El,* a place in Palestine:— Migdal-el.

H4028 מִגְדַּל־גָּד *migdal-gād* from H4026 and H1408; *tower of Fortune; Migdal-Gad,* a place in Palestine:— Migdal-gad.

H4029 מִגְדַּל־עֵדֶר *migdal-ᶜēder* from H4026 and H5739; *tower of a flock; Migdal-Eder,* a place in Palestine:— Migdal-eder, tower of the flock.

H4030 מִגְדָּנָה *migdānâ* from the same as H4022; *preciousness,* i.e. a *gem:*— precious thing, present.

H4031 מָגוֹג *māgôg* from H1463; *Magog,* a son of Japheth; also a barbarous northern region:— Magog.

H4032 מָגוֹר *māgôr* or (Lam. 2:22)

מָגוּר *māgûr* from H1481 in the sense of *fearing;* a *fright* (objectively or subjectively):— fear, terror. Compare H4036

H4033 מָגוּר *māgûr* or

מָגֻר *māgūr* from H1481 in the sense of *lodging;* a temporary *abode;* by extension a permanent *residence:*— dwelling, pilgrimage, where sojourn, be a stranger. Compare H4032

H4034 מְגוֹרָה *mĕgôrah* feminine of H4032; *affright* :— fear.

H4035 מְגוּרָה *mĕgûrâ* feminine of H4032 or of H4033; a *fright;* also a *granary:*— barn, fear.

H4036 מָגוֹר מִסָּבִיב *māgôr missābîb* from H4032 and H5439 with the preposition inserted; *affright from around; Magor-mis-Sabib,* a symbolic name of Pashur :— Magor-missabib.

H4037 מַגְזֵרָה *magzērâ* from H1504; a *cutting* implement, i.e. a *blade:*— axe.

H4038 מַגָּל *maggāl* from an unused root meaning to *reap;* a *sickle:*— sickle.

H4039 מְגִלָּה *mĕgillâ* from H1556; a *roll:*— roll, volume.

H4040 מְגִלָּה *mĕgillâ* (Aramaic) corresponding to H4039:— roll.

H4041 מְגַמָּה *mĕgammâ* from the same as H1571; properly *accumulation,* i.e. *impulse* or *direction:*— sup up.

H4042 מָגַן *māgan* a denominative from H4043; properly to *shield; encompass* with; figuratively to *rescue,* to *hand* safely *over* (i.e. *surrender*):— deliver.

H4043 מָגֵן *māgēn* also (in plural) feminine

מְגִנָּה *mĕginnâ* from H1598; a *shield* (i.e. the small one or *buckler*); figuratively a *protector;* also the scaly *hide* of the crocodile:— armed, buckler, defence, ruler, scale, shield.

H4044 מְגִנָּה *mĕginnâ* from H4042; a *covering* (in a bad sense), i.e. *blindness* or obduracy:— sorrow. See also H4043

H4045 מִגְעֶרֶת *migᶜeret* from H1605; *reproof* (i.e. curse):— rebuke.

H4046 מַגֵּפָה *maggēpâ* from H5062; a *pestilence;* by analogy *defeat:*— plague, be plagued, slaughter, stroke.

H4047 מַגְפִּיעָשׁ *magpîᶜāš* apparently from H1479 or H5062 and H6211; *exterminator of* (the) *moth; Magpiash,* an Israelite:— Magpiash.

H4048 מָגַר *māgar* a primitive root; to *yield up;* intensively to *precipitate:*— cast down, terror.

H4049 מְגַר *mĕgar* (Aramaic) corresponding to H4048; to *overthrow:*— destroy.

H4050 מְגֵרָה *mĕgērâ* from H1641; a *saw:*— axe, saw.

H4051 מִגְרוֹן *migrôn* from H4048; *precipice; Migron,* a place in Palestine:— Migron.

H4052 מִגְרָעָה *migrāᶜâ* from H1639; a *ledge* or offset:— narrowed rest.

H4053 מִגְרָפָה *megrāpâ* from H1640; something *thrown off* (by the spade), i.e. a *clod:*— clod.

H4054 מִגְרָשׁ *migrāš* also (in plural) feminine (Ezek. 27:28).

מִגְרָשָׁה *migrāšâ* from H1644; a *suburb* (i.e. open country whither flocks are *driven* for pasture); hence the *area* around a building, or the *margin* of the sea:— cast out, suburb.

H4055 מַד *mad* or

מֵד *mēd* from H4058; properly *extent,* i.e. *height;* also a *measure; by implication a vesture* (as measured); also a *carpet:*— armour, clothes, garment, judgment, measure, raiment, stature.

H4056 מַדְבַּח *madbaḥ* (Aramaic) from H1684; a sacrificial *altar:*— altar.

H4057 מִדְבָּר *midbār* from H1696 in the sense of *driving;* a *pasture* (i.e. open field, whither cattle are driven); by implication a *desert;* also *speech* (including its organs):— desert, south, speech, wilderness.

H4058 מָדַד *mādad* a primitive root; properly to *stretch;* by implication to *measure* (as if by *stretching* a line); figuratively to *be extended:*— measure, mete, stretch self.

H4059 מִדַּד *middad* from H5074; *flight:*— be gone.

H4060 מִדָּה *middâ* feminine of H4055; properly *extension,* i.e. height or breadth; also a *measure* (including its standard); hence a *portion* (as measured) or a *vestment;* specifically *tribute* (as measured):— garment, measure, measuring, meteyard, piece, size, stature, great stature, tribute, wide.

H4061 מִדָּה *middâ* or

מִנְדָּה *mindâ* (Aramaic) corresponding to H4060; *tribute* in money:— toll, tribute.

H4062 מַדְהֵבָה *madhēbâ* perhaps from the equivalent of H1722; *gold-making,* i.e. *exactress:*— golden city.

H4063 מֶדֶו *medew* from an unused root meaning to *stretch;* properly *extent,* i.e. *measure;* by implication a *dress* (as measured):— garment.

H4064 מַדְוֶה *madweh* from H1738; *sickness:*— disease.

H4065 מַדּוּחַ *maddûaḥ* from H5080; *seduction:*— cause of banishment.

H4066 מָדוֹן *mādôn* from H1777; a *contest* or quarrel:— brawling, contention, contentious, discord, strife. Compare H4079, H4090

H4067 מָדוֹן *mādôn* from the same as H4063; *extensiveness,* i.e. height:— stature.

H4068 מָדוֹן *mādôn* the same as H4067; *Madon,* a place in Palestine:— Madon.

H4069 מַדּוּעַ *maddûaᶜ* or

מַדֻּעַ *maddūaᶜ* from H4100 and the passive participle of H3045; *what* (is) *known?;* i.e. (by implication) (adverbially) *why?:*— how, wherefore, why.

H4070 מְדוֹר *mĕdôr* or

מְדֹר *mĕdōr* or

מְדָר *mĕdār* (Aramaic) from H1753; a *dwelling:*— dwelling.

H4071 מְדוּרָה *mĕdûrâ* or

מְדֻרָה *mĕdūrâ* from H1752 in the sense of *accumulation;* a *pile* of fuel:— pile, pile for fire.

H4072 מִדְחֶה *midḥeh* from H1760; *overthrow:*— ruin.

H4073 מְדַחְפָה *mĕdaḥpâ* from H1765; a *push,* i.e. ruin:— overthrow.

H4074 מָדַי *māday* of foreign derivation; *Madai,* a country of central Asia:— Madai, Medes, Media.

H4075 מָדַי *māday* patrial from H4074; a *Madian* or native of Madai:— Mede.

H4076 מָדַי *māday* (Aramaic) corresponding to H4074:— Mede, Medes.

H4077 מָדַי *māday* (Aramaic) corresponding to H4075:— Median.

H4078 מַדַּי *madday* from H4100 and H1767; *what* (is) *enough,* i.e. *sufficiently:*— sufficiently.

H4079 מִדְיָן *midyān* a variation for H4066:— brawling, contention, contentious.

H4080 מִדְיָן *midyān* the same as H4079; *Midjan,* a son of Abraham; also his country and (collectively) his descendants:— Midian, Midianite.

H4081 מִדִּין *middîn* a variation for H4080:— Middin.

H4082 מְדִינָה *mĕdînâ* from H1777; properly a *judgeship,* i.e. *jurisdiction;* by implication a *district* (as ruled by a judge); generally a *region:*— province, every province.

H4083 מְדִינָה *mĕdînâ* (Aramaic) corresponding to H4082:— province.

H4084 מִדְיָנִי *midyānî* patronymic or patrial from H4080; a *Midjanite* or descendant (native) of Midjan:— Midianite. Compare H4092

H4085 מְדֹכָה *mĕdōkâ* from H1743; a *mortar:*— mortar.

H4086 מַדְמֵן *madmēn* from the same as H1828; *dunghill; Madmen,* a place in Palestine:— Madmen.

H4087 מַדְמֵנָה *madmēnâ* feminine from the same as H1828; a *dunghill:*— dunghill.

H4088 מַדְמֵנָה *madmēnâ* the same as H4087; *Madmenah,* a place in Palestine:— Madmenah.

H4089 מַדְמַנָּה *madmannâ* a variation for H4087; *Madmannah,* a place in Palestine:— Madmannah.

H4090 מְדָן *mĕdān* a form of H4066:— discord, strife.

H4091 מְדָן *mĕdān* the same as H4090; *Medan,* a son of Abraham:— Medan.

H4092 מְדָנִי *mĕdānî* a variation of H4084:— Midianite.

H4093 מַדָּע *maddāᶜ* or

מַדַּע *maddaᶜ* from H3045; *intelligence* or *consciousness:*— knowledge, science, thought.

H4094 מַדְקָרָה *madqārâ* from H1856; a *wound:*— piercing.

H4095 מַדְרֵגָה *madrēgâ* from an unused root meaning to *step;* properly a *step;* by implication a *steep* or inaccessible place:— stair, steep place.

H4096 מִדְרָךְ *midrāk* from H1869; a *treading,* i.e. a place for stepping on:— foot breadth.

H4097 מִדְרָשׁ *midrāš* from H1875; properly an *investigation,* i.e. (by implication) a *treatise* or elaborate compilation:— story.

H4098 מְדֻשָּׁה *mĕduššâ* from H1758; a *threshing,* i.e. (concretely and figuratively) *down-trodden* people:— threshing.

H4099 מְדָתָא *mĕdātāʾ* of Persian origin; *Medatha,* the father of Haman:— Hammedatha *[including the article].*

H4100 מָה *mâ* or

מָה *mah* or

מָ־ *mā-* or

מַ־ *ma-* also

מֶה *meh* a primitive particle; properly interrogative *what?* (including *how? why? when?*); but also exclamatory *what!* (including *how!*), or indefinitely *what* (including *whatever,* and even relatively *that which*); often used with prefixes in various adverbial or conjunctional senses:— how, how long, how oft, howsoever, nothing, what, what end, what good, what purpose, what thing, whereby, wherefore, wherein, whereto wherewith, why, for why.

H4101 מָה *mâ* (Aramaic) corresponding to H4100 :— how great, how mighty, that which, what, whatsoever, why.

H4102 מָהַהּ *māhah* apparently a denominative from H4100; properly to *question* or hesitate, i.e. (by implication) to *be reluctant:*— delay, linger, stay selves, tarry.

H4103 מְהוּמָה *mĕhûmâ* from H1949; *confusion* or uproar:— destruction, discomfiture, trouble, tumult, vexation, vexed.

H4104 מְהוּמָן *mĕhûmān* of Persian origin; *Mehuman,* a eunuch of Xerxes:— Mehuman.

H4105 מְהֵיטַבְאֵל *mĕhêṭabʾēl* from H3190 (augmented) and H410; *bettered of God; Jehetabel,* the name of an Edomitish man and woman:— Mehetabeel, Mehetabel.

H4106 מָהִיר *māhîr* or

מָהִר *māhīr* from H4116; *quick;* hence *skilful:*— diligent, hasty, ready.

H4107 מָהַל *māhal* a primitive root; properly to *cut down* or *reduce,* i.e. by implication to *adulterate:*— mixed.

H4108 מַהְלֵךְ *mahlēk* from H1980; a *walking* (plural collective), i.e. *access:*— place to walk.

H4109 מַהֲלָךְ *mahălāk* from H1980; a *walk,* i.e. a *passage* or a *distance:*— journey, walk.

H4110 מַהֲלָל *mahălāl* from H1984; *fame:*— praise.

H4111 מַהֲלַלְאֵל *mahălalʾēl* from H4110 and H410; *praise of God; Mahalalel,* the name of an antediluvian patriarch and of an Israelite:— Mahalaleel.

H4112 מַהֲלֻמָּה *mahălummâ* from H1986; a *blow:*— stripe, stroke.

H4113 מַהֲמֹרָה *mahămōrâ* from an unused root of uncertain meaning; perhaps an *abyss:*— deep pit.

H4114 מַהְפֵּכָה *mahpēkâ* from H2015; a *destruction* :— when . . . overthrew, overthrow, overthrown.

H4115 מַהְפֶּכֶת *mahpeket* from H2015; a *wrench,* i.e. the *stocks:*— prison, stocks.

H4116 מָהַר *māhar* a primitive root; properly to *be liquid* or *flow* easily, i.e. (by implication), to *hurry* (in a good or a bad sense); often used (with another verb) adverbially *promptly:*— be carried headlong, fearful, haste, cause to make haste, in haste, make haste, hasten, hastily, hasty, be hasty, quickly, fetch quickly, make ready quickly, rash, shortly, soon, be so soon, make speed, speedily, straightway, suddenly, swift.

H4117 מָהַר *māhar* a primitive root (perhaps rather the same as H4116 through the idea of *readiness* in assent); to *bargain* (for a wife), i.e. to *wed:*— endow, surely.

H4118 מַהֵר *mahēr* from H4116; properly *hurrying;* hence (adverbially) *in a hurry:*— hasteth, hastily, at once, quickly, soon, speedily, suddenly.

H4119 מֹהַר *mōhar* from H4117; a *price* (for a wife) :— dowry.

H4120 מְהֵרָה *mĕhērâ* feminine of H4118; properly a *hurry;* hence (adverbially) *promptly:*— hastily, quickly, shortly, soon, make speed, with speed, speedily, swiftly.

H4121 מַהֲרַי *mahăray* from H4116; *hasty; Maharai,* an Israelite:— Maharai.

H4122 מַהֵר שָׁלָל חָשׁ בַּז *mahēr šālāl ḥāš baz* from H4118 and H7998 and H2363 and H957; *hasting* (is he [the enemy] to the) *booty, swift* (to the) *prey; Maher-Shalal-Chash-Baz;* the symbolic name of the son of Isaiah:— Maher-shalal-hash-baz.

H4123 מַהֲתַלָּה *mahătallâ* from H2048; a *delusion* :— deceit.

H4124 מוֹאָב *môʾāb* from a prolonged form of the prepositional prefix *m-* and H1; *from* (her [the mother's]) *father; Moäb,* an incestuous son of Lot; also his territory and descendants:— Joab.

H4125 מוֹאָבִי *môʾābî* feminine

מוֹאָבִיָּה *môʾābiyâ* or

מוֹאָבִית *môʾābît* patronymic from H4124; a *Moäbite* or *Moäbitess,* i.e. a descendant from Moab:— of Moab, woman of Moab, Moabite, Moabitish, Moabitess.

H4126 מוֹבָא *môbāʾ* by transposition for H3996; an *entrance:*— coming.

H4127 מוּג *mûg* a primitive root; to *melt,* i.e. literally (to *soften,* flow down, *disappear*), or figuratively (to *fear, faint*):— consume, dissolve, faint, be faint-hearted, melt, melt away, make soft.

H4128 מוּד *mûd* a primitive root; to *shake:*— measure.

H4129 מוֹדַע *môdāʿ* or rather

מֹדַע *mōdāʿ* from H3045; an *acquaintance* :— kinswoman.

H4130 מוֹדַעַת *môdaʿat* from H3045; *acquaintance* :— kindred.

H4131 מוֹט *môṭ* a primitive root; to *waver;* by implication to *slip, shake, fall:*— be carried, cast, be out of course, be fallen in decay, exceedingly, fall, falling down, be moved, be removed, be ready, shake, slide, slip.

H4132 מוֹט *môṭ* from H4131; a *wavering,* i.e. *fall;* by implication a *pole* (as shaking); hence a *yoke* (as essentially a bent pole):— bar, be moved, staff, yoke.

H4133 מוֹטָה *môṭâ* feminine of H4132; a *pole;* by implication an ox-*bow;* hence a *yoke* (either literally or figuratively):— bands, heavy, staves, yoke.

H4134 מוּךְ *mûk* a primitive root; to *become thin,* i.e. (figuratively) *be impoverished:*— be waxen poor, be poorer.

H4135 מוּל *mûl* a primitive root; to *cut* short, i.e. *curtail* (specifically the prepuce, i.e. to *circumcise*); by implication to *blunt;* figuratively to *destroy:*— circumcise, circumcising, circumcise selves, cut down, cut in pieces, destroy, must needs.

H4136 מוּל *mûl* or

מוֹל *môl* (Deut. 1:1), or

מוֹאל *môʾl* (Neh. 12:38), or

מֻל *mūl* (Num 22:5), from H4135; properly *abrupt,* i.e. a *precipice;* by implication the *front;* used only adverbially (with prepositional prefix) *opposite:*— against, over against, before, forefront, from, Godward, toward, with.

H4137 מוֹלָדָה *môlādâ* from H3205; *birth; Moladah,* a place in Palestine:— Moladah.

H4138 מוֹלֶדֶת *môledet* from H3205; *nativity* (plural *birth-place*); by implication *lineage, native country;* also *offspring, family:*— begotten, born, issue, kindred, native, nativity.

H4139 מוּלָה *mûlâ* from H4135; *circumcision:*— circumcision.

H4140 מוֹלִיד *môlîd* from H3205; *genitor; Molid,* an Israelite:— Molid.

H4141 מוּסָב *mûsāb* from H5437; a *turn,* i.e. *circuit* (of a building):— winding about.

H4142 מוּסַבָּה *mûsobbâ* or

מֻסַבָּה *musabbâ* feminine of H4141; a *reversal,* i.e. the *backside* (of a gem), *fold* (of a double-leaved door), *transmutation* (of a name):— being changed, inclosed, be set, turning.

H4143 מוּסָד *mûsād* from H3245; a *foundation:*— foundation.

H4144 מוֹסָד *môsād* from H3245; a *foundation:*— foundation.

H4145 מוּסָדָה *mûsādâ* feminine of H4143; a *foundation;* figuratively an *appointment:*— foundation, grounded. Compare H4328

H4146 מוֹסָדָה *môsādâ* or

מֹסָדָה *mōsādâ* feminine of H4144; a *foundation:*— foundation.

H4147 מוֹסֵר *môsēr* also (in plural) feminine

מוֹסֵרָה *môsērâ* or

מֹסְרָה *mōsērâ* from H3256; properly *chastisement,* i.e. (by implication) a *halter;* figuratively *restraint:*— band, bond.

H4148 מוּסָר *mûsār* from H3256; properly *chastisement;* figuratively *reproof, warning* or *instruction;* also *restraint:*— bond, chastening, chasteneth, chastisement, check, correction, discipline, doctrine, instruction, rebuke.

H4149 מוֹסֵרָה *môsērâ* or (plural)

מֹסֵרוֹת *mōsērôt* feminine of H4147; *correction* or *corrections; Moserah* or *Moseroth,* a place in the Desert:— Mosera, Moseroth.

H4150 מוֹעֵד *môʿēd* or

מֹעֵד *mōʿēd* or (feminine)

מוֹעָדָה *môʿādâ* (2 Chron 8:13), from H3259; properly an *appointment,* i.e. a fixed *time* or season; specifically a *festival;* conventionally a *year;* by implication, an *assembly* (as convened for a definite purpose); technically the *congregation;* by extension, the *place of meeting;* also a *signal* (as appointed beforehand):— appointed, appointed sign, appointed time, assembly, place of assembly, solemn assembly, congregation, feast, set feast, solemn feast, season, appointed season, due season, solemn, solemnity, synagogue, time, set time, time appointed.

H4151 מוֹעֵד *môʿād* from H3259; properly an *assembly* [as in H4150]; figuratively a *troop:*— appointed time.

H4152 מוּעָדָה *mûʿādâ* from H3259; an *appointed* place, i.e. *asylum:*— appointed.

H4153 מוֹעַדְיָה *môʿadyâ* from H4151 and H3050; *assembly of Jah; Moädjah,* an Israelite:— Moadiah. Compare H4573

H4154 מוּעֶדֶת *mûʿedet* feminine passive participle of H4571; properly *made to slip,* i.e. *dislocated:*— out of joint.

H4155 מוּעָף *mûʿāp* from H5774; properly *covered,* i.e. *dark;* abstractly *obscurity,* i.e. *distress:*— dimness.

H4156 מוֹעֵצָה *môʿēṣâ* from H3289; a *purpose:*— counsel, device.

H4157 מוּעָקָה *mûʿāqâ* from H5781; *pressure,* i.e. (figuratively) *distress:*— affliction.

H4158 מוֹפַעַת *môpaʿat* (Jer. 48:21), or

מֵיפַעַת *mêpaʿat* or

מֵפַעַת *mēpaʿat* from H3313; *illuminative; Mophaath* or *Mephaath,* a place in Palestine:— Mephaath.

H4159 מוֹפֵת *môpēt* or

מֹפֵת *mōpēt* from H3302 in the sense of *conspicuousness;* a *miracle;* by implication a *token* or *omen:*— miracle, sign, wonder, wondered at.

H4160 מוּץ *mûṣ* a primitive root; to *press,* i.e. (figuratively) to *oppress:*— extortioner.

H4161 מוֹצָא *môṣāʾ* or

מֹצָא *mōṣāʾ* from H3318; a *going forth,* i.e. (the act) an *egress,* or (the place) an *exit;* hence a *source* or *product;* specifically *dawn,* the *rising* of the sun (the *East*), *exportation, utterance,* a *gate,* a *fountain,* a *mine,* a *meadow* (as producing grass):— brought out, bud, that which came out, east, going forth, goings out, that which is gone out, thing that is gone out, outgoing, proceeded out, spring, vein, watercourse, watersprings, spring.

H4162 מוֹצָא *môṣāʾ* the same as H4161; *Motsa,* the name of two Israelites:— Moza.

H4163 מוֹצָאָה *môṣāʾâ* feminine of H4161; a family *descent;* also a *sewer* [margin; compare H6675]:— draught house; going forth.

H4164 מוּצַק *mûṣaq* or

מוּצָק *mûṣāq* from H3332; *narrowness;* figuratively *distress:*— anguish, is straitened, straitness.

H4165 מוּצָק *mûṣāq* from H5694; properly *fusion,* i.e. literally a *casting* (of metal); figuratively a *mass* (of clay):— casting, hardness.

H4166 מוּצָקָה *mûṣāqâ* or

מֻצָקָה *muṣāqâ* from H3332; properly something *poured* out, i.e. a *casting* (of metal); by implication a *tube* (as cast):— when it was cast, pipe.

H4167 מוּק *mûq* a primitive root; to *jeer,* i.e. (intensively) *blaspheme:*— be corrupt.

H4168 מוֹקֵד *môqēd* from H3344; a *fire* or *fuel;* abstractly a *conflagration:*— burning, hearth.

H4169 מוֹקְדָה *môqědâ* feminine of H4168; *fuel:*— burning.

H4170 מוֹקֵשׁ *môqēš* or

מֹקֵשׁ *mōqēš* from H3369; a *noose* (for catching animals) (literally or figuratively); by implication a *hook* (for the nose):— be ensnared, gin, snare, is snared, trap.

H4171 מוּר *mûr* a primitive root; to *alter;* by implication to *barter,* to *dispose of:*— at all, change, exchange, remove.

H4172 מוֹרָא *môrāʾ* or

מֹרָא *mōrāʾ* or

מוֹרָה *môrâ* (Ps 9:20), from H3372; *fear;* by implication a *fearful* thing or deed:— dread, fear, that ought to be feared, terribleness, terror.

H4173 מוֹרַג *môrag* or

מֹרַג *mōrag* from an unused root meaning to *triturate;* a threshing *sledge:*— threshing instrument.

H4174 מוֹרָד *môrād* from H3381; a *descent;* architecturally an ornamental *appendage,* perhaps a *festoon:*— going down, steep place, thin work.

H4175 מוֹרֶה *môreh* from H3384; an *archer;* also *teacher* or *teaching;* also the *early rain* [see H3138] :— rain, early rain.

H4176 מוֹרֶה *môreh* or

מֹרֶה *mōreh* the same as H4175; *Moreh,* a Canaanite; also a hill (perhaps named from him):— Moreh.

H4177 מוֹרָה *môrâ* from H4171 in the sense of *shearing;* a *razor:*— razor.

H4178 מוֹרָט *môrāṭ* from H3399; *obstinate,* i.e. independent:— peeled.

H4179 מוֹרִיָּה *môrîyâ* or

מֹרִיָּה *mōrîyâ* from H7200 and H3050; *seen of Jah; Morijah,* a hill in Palestine:— Moriah.

H4180 מוֹרָשׁ *môrāš* from H3423; a *possession;* figuratively *delight:*— possession, thought.

H4181 מוֹרָשָׁה *môrāšâ* feminine of H4180; a *possession:*— heritage, inheritance, possession.

H4182 מוֹרֶשֶׁת גַּת *môrešet gat* from H3423 and H1661; *possession of Gath; Moresheth-Gath,* a place in Palestine:— Moresheth-gath.

H4183 מוֹרַשְׁתִּי *môraštî* patrial from H4182; a *Morashtite* or inhabitant of Moresheth-Gath:— Morashthite.

H4184 מוּשׁ *mûš* a primitive root; to *touch:*— feel, handle.

H4185 מוּשׁ *mûš* a primitive root [perhaps rather the same as H4184 through the idea of receding by *contact*]; to *withdraw* (both literally and figuratively, whether intransitively or transitively):— cease, depart, go back, remove, take away.

H4186 מוֹשָׁב *môšāb* or

מֹשָׁב *mōšāb* from H3427; a *seat;* figuratively a *site;* abstractly a *session;* by extension an *abode* (the place or the time); by implication *population:*— assembly, dwell in, dwelling, dwellingplace, wherein dwelt, that dwelt in, inhabited place, seat, sitting, situation, sojourning.

H4187 מוּשִׁי *mûšî* or

מֻשִּׁי *muššî* from H4184; *sensitive; Mushi,* a Levite:— Mushi.

H4188 מוּשִׁי *mûšî* patronymic from H4187; a *Mushite* (collectively) or descendant of Mushi:— Mushites.

H4189 מוֹשְׁכָה *môšěkâ* act participle feminine of H4900; something *drawing,* i.e. (figuratively) a *cord:*— band.

H4190 מוֹשָׁעָה *môšāʿâ* from H3467; *deliverance:*— salvation.

H4191 מוּת *mût* a primitive root; to *die* (literally or figuratively); causatively to *kill:*— at all, crying, dead, be dead, dead body, dead man, dead one, death, put to death, worthy of death, destroy, destroyer, die, cause to die, be like to die, must die, kill, necromancer, must needs, slay, surely, very suddenly, in no wise.

H4192 מוּת *mût* (Ps. 48:14), or

מוּת לַבֵּן *mût labbēn* from H4191 and H1121 with the preposition and article interposed; *"To die for the son",* probably the title of a popular song:— death, Muth-labben.

H4193 מוֹת *môt* (Aramaic) corresponding to H4194; *death:*— death.

H4194 מָוֶת *māwet* from H4191; *death* (natural or violent); concretely the *dead,* their place or state *(hades)*; figuratively *pestilence, ruin:*— dead, be dead, deadly, death, die, died.

H4195 מוֹתָר *môtār* from H3498; literally *gain;* figuratively *superiority:*— plenteousness, preeminence, profit.

H4196 מִזְבֵּחַ *mizbēaḥ* from H2076; an *altar:*— altar.

H4197 מֶזֶג *mezeg* from an unused root meaning to *mingle* (water with wine); *tempered* wine:— liquor.

H4198 מָזֶה *māzeh* from an unused root meaning to *suck* out; *exhausted:*— burnt.

H4199 מִזָּה *mizzâ* probably from an unused root meaning to *faint* with fear; *terror; Mizzah,* an Edomite:— Mizzah.

H4200 מֶזֶו *mezew* probably from an unused root meaning to *gather* in; a *granary:*— garner.

H4201 מְזוּזָה *mězûzâ* or

מְזֻזָה *mězūzâ* from the same as H2123; a *door-post* (as *prominent*):— post, door post, side post.

H4202 מָזוֹן *māzôn* from H2109; *food:*— meat, victual.

H4203 מָזוֹן *māzôn* (Aramaic) corresponding to H4202:— meat.

H4204 מָזוֹר *māzôr* from H2114 in the sense of *turning aside* from truth; *treachery,* i.e. a *plot:*— wound.

H4205 מָזוֹר *māzôr* or

מָזֹר *māzōr* from H2115 in the sense of *binding* up; a *bandage,* i.e. remedy; hence a *sore* (as needing a compress):— bound up, wound.

H4206 מָזִיחַ *māzîaḥ* or

מֵזַח *mēzaḥ* from H2118; a *belt* (as movable):— girdle, strength.

H4207 מַזְלֵג *mazlēg* or (feminine)

מִזְלָגָה *mizlāgâ* from an unused root meaning to draw up; a *fork:*— fleshhook.

H4208 מַזָּלָה *mazzālâ* apparently from H5140 in the sense of *raining;* a *constellation,* i.e. Zodiacal sign (perhaps as affecting the weather):— planet. Compare H4216

H4209 מְזִמָּה *mězimmâ* from H2161; a *plan,* usually evil *(machination),* sometimes good *(sagacity)*:— device, wicked device, discretion, intent, witty invention, lewdness, mischievous, mischievous device, thought, wickedly.

H4210 מִזְמוֹר *mizmôr* from H2167; properly instrumental *music;* by implication a *poem* set to notes:— psalm.

H4211 מַזְמֵרָה *mazmērâ* from H2168; a *pruning-knife:*— pruning-hook.

H4212 מְזַמְּרָה *mězammĕrâ* from H2168; a *tweezer* (only in the plural):— snuffers.

H4213 מִזְעָר *mizᶜār* from the same as H2191; *fewness;* by implication as superlative *diminutiveness:*— few, very.

H4214 מִזְרֶה *mizreh* from H2219; a winnowing *shovel* (as scattering the chaff):— fan.

H4215 מְזָרֶה *mĕzāreh* apparently from H2219; properly a *scatterer,* i.e. the north *wind* (as dispersing clouds; only in plural):— north.

H4216 מַזָּרָה *mazzārâ* apparently from H5144 in the sense of *distinction;* some noted *constellation* (only in the plural), perhaps collectively the *zodiac:*— Mazzoroth. Compare H4208

H4217 מִזְרָח *mizrāḥ* from H2224; *sunrise,* i.e. the *east:*— east, east side, eastward, rising, sunrising, rising of the sun.

H4218 מִזְרָע *mizrāᶜ* from H2232; a planted *field:*— thing sown.

H4219 מִזְרָק *mizrāq* from H2236; a *bowl* (as if for sprinkling):— bason, bowl.

H4220 מֵחַ *mēaḥ* from H4229 in the sense of *greasing; fat;* figuratively *rich:*— fatling, fatling one.

H4221 מֹחַ *mōaḥ* from the same as H4220; *fat,* i.e. marrow:— marrow.

H4222 מָחָא *māḥāˀ* a primitive root; to *rub* or *strike* the hands together (in exultation):— clap.

H4223 מְחָא *mĕḥāˀ* (Aramaic) corresponding to H4222; to *strike* in pieces; also to *arrest;* specifically to *impale:*— hang, smite, stay.

H4224 מַחֲבֵא *maḥăbēˀ* or

מַחֲבֹא *maḥăbōˀ* from H2244; a *refuge:*— hiding place, lurking place.

H4225 מַחְבֶּרֶת *maḥberet* from H2266; a *junction,* i.e. seam or sewed piece:— coupling.

H4226 מְחַבְּרָה *mĕḥabbĕrâ* from H2266; a *joiner,* i.e. brace or cramp:— coupling, joining.

H4227 מַחֲבַת *maḥăbat* from the same as H2281; a *pan* for baking in:— pan.

H4228 מַחֲגֹרֶת *maḥăgōret* from H2296; a *girdle:*— girding.

H4229 מָחָה *māḥâ* a primitive root; properly to *stroke* or *rub;* by implication to *erase;* also to *smooth* (as if with oil), i.e. *grease* or make fat; also to *touch,* i.e. reach to:— abolish, blot out, destroy, full of marrow, put out, reach unto, utterly, wipe, wipe away, wipe out.

H4230 מְחוּגָה *mĕḥûgâ* from H2328; an instrument for marking a circle, i.e. *compasses:*— compass.

H4231 מָחוֹז *māḥôz* from an unused root meaning to *enclose;* a *harbor* (as *shut* in by the shore):— haven.

H4232 מְחוּיָאֵל *mĕḥûyāˀēl* or

מְחִיָּיאֵל *mĕḥîyyāˀēl* from H4229 and H410; *smitten of God; Mechujael* or *Mechijael,* an antediluvian patriarch:— Mehujael.

H4233 מַחֲוִים *maḥăwîm* apparently a patrial, but from an unknown place (in the plural only for a singular); a *Machavite* or inhabitant of some place named Machaveh:— Mahavite.

H4234 מָחוֹל *māḥôl* from H2342; a (round) *dance* :— dance, dancing.

H4235 מָחוֹל *māḥôl* the same as H4234; *dancing; Machol,* an Israelite:— Mahol.

H4236 מַחֲזֶה *maḥăzeh* from H2372; a *vision:*— vision.

H4237 מֶחֱזָה *meḥĕzâ* from H2372; a *window:*— light.

H4238 מַחֲזִיאוֹת *maḥăzîˀôt* feminine plural from H2372; *visions; Machazioth,* an Israelite:— Mahazioth.

H4239 מְחִי *mĕḥî* from H4229; a *stroke,* i.e. battering-*ram:*— engines.

H4240 מְחִידָא *mĕḥîdāˀ* from H2330; *junction; Mechida,* one of the Nethinim:— Mehida.

H4241 מִחְיָה *miḥyâ* from H2421; *preservation of life;* hence *sustenance;* also the live flesh, i.e. the *quick:*— preserve life, quick, recover selves, reviving, sustenance, victuals.

H4242 מְחִיר *mĕḥîr* from an unused root meaning to *buy; price, payment, wages:*— gain, hire, price, sold, worth.

H4243 מְחִיר *mĕḥîr* the same as H4242; *price; Mechir,* an Israelite:— Mehir.

H4244 מַחְלָה *maḥlâ* from H2470; *sickness; Machlah,* the name apparently of two Israelitesses:— Mahlah.

H4245 מַחֲלֶה *maḥăleh* or (feminine)

מַחֲלָה *maḥălâ* from H2470; *sickness:*— disease, infirmity, sickness.

H4246 מְחֹלָה *mĕḥōlâ* feminine of H4234; a *dance* :— company, dances, dancing.

H4247 מְחִלָּה *mĕḥillâ* from H2490; a *cavern* (as if excavated):— cave.

H4248 מַחְלוֹן *maḥlôn* from H2470; *sick; Machlon,* an Israelite:— Mahlon.

H4249 מַחְלִי *maḥlî* from H2470; *sick; Machli,* the name of two Israelites:— Mahli.

H4250 מַחְלִי *maḥlî* patronymic from H4249; a *Machlite* or (collectively) descendant of Machli:— Mahlites.

H4251 מַחְלֻי *maḥlūy* from H2470; a *disease:*— disease.

H4252 מַחֲלָף *maḥălāp* from H2498; a (sacrificial) *knife* (as *gliding* through the flesh):— knife.

H4253 מַחְלָפָה *maḥlāpâ* from H2498; a *ringlet* of hair (as *gliding* over each other):— lock.

H4254 מַחֲלָצָה *maḥălāṣâ* from H2502; a *mantle* (as easily *drawn off*):— changeable suit of apparel, change of raiment.

H4255 מַחְלְקָה *maḥlĕqâ* (Aramaic) corresponding to H4256; a *section* (of the Levites):— course.

H4256 מַחֲלֹקֶת *maḥălōqet* from H2505; a *section* (of Levites, people or soldiers):— company, course, division, portion. See also H5555

H4257 מַחֲלַת *maḥălat* from H2470; *sickness; Machalath,* probably the title (initial word) of a popular song:— Mahalath.

H4258 מַחֲלַת *maḥălat* the same as H4257; *sickness; Machalath,* the name of an Ishmaelitess and of an Israelitess:— Mahalath.

H4259 מְחֹלָתִי *mĕḥōlātî* patrial from H65; a *Mecholathite* or inhabitant of Abel-Mecholah:— Mecholathite.

H4260 מַחֲמָאָה *maḥămāˀâ* a denominative from H2529; something *buttery* (i.e. unctuous and pleasant), as (figuratively) *flattery:*— than butter.

H4261 מַחְמָד *maḥmād* from H2530; *delightful;* hence a *delight,* i.e. object of affection or desire:— beloved, desire, goodly, lovely, pleasant, pleasant thing.

H4262 מַחְמֻד *maḥmūd* or

מַחְמוּד *maḥmûd* from H2530; *desired;* hence a *valuable:*— pleasant thing.

H4263 מַחְמָל *maḥmāl* from H2550; properly *sympathy;* (by paronomasia with H4261) *delight:*— pitieth.

H4264 מַחֲנֶה *maḥăneh* from H2583; an *encampment* (of travellers or troops); hence an *army,* whether literally (of soldiers) or figuratively (of dancers, angels, cattle, locusts, stars; or even the sacred courts):— army, band, battle, camp, company, drove, host, tents.

H4265 מַחֲנֵה־דָן *maḥănēh-dān* from H4264 and H1835; *camp of Dan; Machaneh-Dan,* a place in Palestine:— Mahaneh-dan.

H4266 מַחֲנַיִם *maḥănayim* dual of H4264; *double camp; Machanajim,* a place in Palestine:— Mahanaim.

H4267 מַחֲנָק *maḥănaq* from H2614; *choking:*— strangling.

H4268 מַחֲסֶה *maḥăseh* or

מַחְסֶה *maḥseh* from H2620; a *shelter* (literally or figuratively):— hope, refuge, place of refuge, shelter, trust.

H4269 מַחְסוֹם *maḥsôm* from H2629; a *muzzle:*— bridle.

H4270 מַחְסוֹר *maḥsôr* or

מַחְסֹר *maḥsōr* from H2637; *deficiency;* hence *impoverishment:*— lack, need, penury, poor, poverty, want.

H4271 מַחְסֵיָה *maḥsêâ* from H4268 and H3050; *refuge of* (i.e. *in*) *Jah; Machsejah,* an Israelite:— Maaseiah.

H4272 מָחַץ *māḥaṣ* a primitive root; to *dash* asunder; by implication to *crush, smash* or violently *plunge;* figuratively to *subdue* or *destroy:*— dip, pierce, pierce through, smite, smite through, strike through, wound.

H4273 מַחַץ *maḥaṣ* from H4272; a *confusion:*— stroke.

H4274 מַחְצֵב *maḥṣēb* from H2672; properly a *hewing;* concretely a *quarry:*— hewed, hewn.

H4275 מֶחֱצָה *meḥĕṣâ* from H2673; a *halving:*— half.

H4276 מַחֲצִית *maḥăṣît* from H2673; a *halving* or the *middle:*— half, half so much, midday.

H4277 מָחַק *māḥaq* a primitive root; to *crush:*— smite off.

H4278 מֶחְקָר *meḥqār* from H2713; properly *scrutinized,* i.e. (by implication) a *recess:*— deep place.

H4279 מָחָר *māḥār* probably from H309; properly *deferred,* i.e. the *morrow;* usually (adverbially) *tomorrow;* indefinitely *hereafter:*— time to come, tomorrow.

H4280 מַחֲרָאָה *maḥărāˀâ* from the same as H2716; a *sink:*— draught house.

H4281 מַחֲרֵשָׁה *maḥărēšâ* from H2790; probably a *pick*-axe:— mattock.

H4282 מַחֲרֶשֶׁת *maḥărešet* from H2790; probably a *hoe:*— share.

H4283 מָחֳרָת *moḥŏrāt* or

מָחֳרָתָם *moḥŏrātām* (1 Sam 30:17), feminine from the same as H4279; the *morrow* or (adverbially) *tomorrow:*— morrow, next day.

H4284 מַחֲשָׁבָה *maḥăšābâ* or

מַחֲשֶׁבֶת *maḥăšebet* from H2803; a *contrivance,* i.e. (concretely) a *texture, machine,* or (abstractly) *intention, plan* (whether bad, a *plot;* or good, *advice*):— cunning, cunning work, curious work, device, devised, imagination, invented, means, purpose, thought.

H4285 מַחְשָׁךְ *maḥšāk* from H2821; *darkness;* concretely a *dark place:*— dark, darkness, dark place.

H4286 מַחְשֹׂף *maḥśōp* from H2834; a *peeling:*— made appear.

H4287 מַחַת *maḥat* probably from H4229; *erasure; Machath,* the name of two Israelites:— Mahath.

H4288 מְחִתָּה *mĕḥittâ* from H2846; properly a *dissolution;* concretely a *ruin,* or (abstractly) *consternation:*— destruction, dismaying, ruin, terror.

H4289 מַחְתָּה *maḥtâ* the same as H4288 in the sense of *removal;* a *pan* for live coals:— censer, firepan, snuffdish.

H4290 מַחְתֶּרֶת *maḥteret* from H2864; a *burglary;* figuratively *unexpected examination:*— breaking up, secret search.

H4291 מְטָא *mĕṭāʾ* or

מְטָה *mĕṭâ* (Aramaic) apparently corresponding to H4672 in the intransitive sense of being found *present;* to *arrive, extend* or *happen:*— come, reach.

H4292 מַטְאֲטֵא *maṭʾăṭēʾ* apparently a denominative from H2916; a *broom* (as removing *dirt* [compare English "to dust", i.e. remove dust]):— besom.

H4293 מַטְבֵּחַ *maṭbēaḥ* from H2873; *slaughter:*— slaughter.

H4294 מַטֶּה *maṭṭeh* or (feminine)

מַטָּה *maṭṭâ* from H5186; a *branch* (as *extending*); figuratively a *tribe;* also a *rod,* whether for chastising (figuratively *correction*), ruling (a *sceptre*), throwing (a *lance*), or walking (a *staff;* figuratively a *support* of life, e.g. bread):— rod, staff, tribe.

H4295 מַטָּה *maṭṭâ* from H5786 with directive enclitic appended; *downward, below* or *beneath;* often adverbially with or without prefixes:— beneath, down, downward, less, very low, under, underneath.

H4296 מִטָּה *miṭṭâ* from H5186; a *bed* (as *extended*) for sleeping or eating; by analogy a *sofa, litter* or *bier:*— bed, bedchamber, bier.

H4297 מֻטֶּה *muṭṭeh* from H5186; a *stretching,* i.e. *distortion* (figuratively *iniquity*):— perverseness.

H4298 מֻטָּה *muṭṭâ* from H5186; *expansion:*— stretching out.

H4299 מַטְוֶה *maṭweh* from H2901; something *spun* :— spun.

H4300 מְטִיל *mĕṭîl* from H2904 in the sense of *hammering* out; an iron *bar* (as *forged*):— bar.

H4301 מַטְמוֹן *maṭmôn* or

מַטְמֹן *maṭmōn* or

מַטְמֻן *maṭmūn* from H2934; a *secret* storehouse; hence a *secreted* valuable (buried); generally *money:*— hidden riches, treasure, hid treasures.

H4302 מַטָּע *maṭṭāʿ* from H5193; something *planted,* i.e. the place (a *garden* or vineyard), or the thing (a *plant,* figuratively of men); by implication the act, *planting:*— plant, plantation, planting.

H4303 מַטְעַם *maṭʿam* or (feminine)

מַטְעַמָּה *maṭʿammâ* from H2938; a *delicacy* :— dainty, dainty meat, savoury meat.

H4304 מִטְפַּחַת *mitpaḥat* from H2946; a wide *cloak* (for a woman):— vail, wimple.

H4305 מָטַר *māṭar* a primitive root; to *rain:*— rain, cause to rain, rain upon.

H4306 מָטָר *māṭār* from H4305; *rain:*— rain.

H4307 מַטָּרָא *maṭṭārāʾ* or

מַטָּרָה *maṭṭārâ* from H5201; a *jail* (as a *guardhouse*); also an *aim* (as being closely *watched*):— mark, prison.

H4308 מַטְרֵד *maṭrēd* from H2956; *propulsive; Matred,* an Edomitess:— Matred.

H4309 מַטְרִי *maṭrî* from H4305; *rainy; Matri,* an Israelite:— Matri.

H4310 מִי *mî* an interrogative pronoun of persons, as H4100 is of things, *who?* (occasionally, by a peculiar idiom, of things); also (indefinitely) *whoever;* often used in oblique construction with prefix or suffix:— any, any man, he, him, O that! what, which, who, whom, whose, whosoever, would to God.

H4311 מֵידְבָא *mêdĕbāʾ* from H4325 and H1679; *water of quiet; Medeba,* a place in Palestine:— Medeba.

H4312 מֵידָד *mêdād* from H3032 in the sense of *loving; affectionate; Medad,* an Israelite:— Medad.

H4313 מֵי הַיַּרְקוֹן *mê hayyarqôn* from H4325 and H3420 with the article interposed; *water of the yellowness; Me-haj-Jarkon,* a place in Palestine:— Me-jarkon.

H4314 מֵי זָהָב *mê zāhāb* from H4325 and H2091, *water of gold; Me-Zahab,* an Edomite:— Mezahab.

H4315 מֵיטָב *mêṭāb* from H3190; the *best* part:— best.

H4316 מִיכָא *mîkāʾ* a variation for H4318; *Mica,* the name of two Israelites:— Micha.

H4317 מִיכָאֵל *mîkāʾēl* from H4310 and (the prefix derived from) H3588 and H410; *who* (is) *like God?; Mikael,* the name of an archangel and of nine Israelites:— Michael.

H4318 מִיכָה *mîkâ* an abbreviation of H4320; *Micah,* the name of seven Israelites:— Micha, Micaiah, Michah.

H4319 מִיכָהוּ *mîkāhû* a contraction for H4321; *Mikehu,* an Israelite prophet:— Micaiah (2 Chron 18:8).

H4320 מִיכָיָה *mîkāyâ* from H4310 and (the prefix derived from) H3588 and H3050; *who* (is) *like Jah?; Micajah,* the name of two Israelites:— Micah, Michaiah. Compare H4318

H4321 מִיכָיְהוּ *mîkāyĕhû* or

מִכָיְהוּ *mîkāyĕhû* (Jer 36:11), abbreviated for H4322; *Mikajah,* the name of three Israelites:— Micah, Micaiah, Michaiah.

H4322 מִיכָיָהוּ *mîkāyāhû* for H4320; *Mikajah,* the name of an Israelite and an Israelitess:— Michaiah.

H4323 מִיכָל *mîkāl* from H3201; properly a *container,* i.e. a *streamlet:*— brook.

H4324 מִיכָל *mîkāl* apparently the same as H4323; *rivulet; Mikal,* Saul's daughter:— Michal.

H4325 מַיִם *mayim* dual of a primitive noun (but used in a singular sense); *water;* figuratively *juice;* by euphemism *urine, semen:*— piss, wasting, water, watering, watercourse, waterflood, waterspring.

H4326 מִיָּמִן *mîyāmīn* a form for H4509; *Mijamin,* the name of three Israelites:— Miamin, Mijamin.

H4327 מִין *mîn* from an unused root meaning to *portion* out; a *sort,* i.e. *species:*— kind. Compare H4480

H4328 מְיֻסָּדָה *mĕyussādâ* properly feminine passive participle of H3245; something *founded,* i.e. a *foundation:*— foundation.

H4329 מֵיסָךְ *mêsāk* from H5526; a *portico* (as *covered*):— covert.

H4330 מִיץ *mîṣ* from H4160; *pressure:*— churning, forcing, wringing.

H4331 מֵישָׁא *mêšāʾ* from H4185; *departure; Mesha,* a place in Arabia; also an Israelite:— Mesha.

H4332 מִישָׁאֵל *mîšāʾēl* from H4310 and H410 with the abbreviated inseparable relative [see H834] interposed; *who* (is) *what God* (is)?; *Mishaël,* the name of three Israelites:— Mishael.

H4333 מִישָׁאֵל *mîšāʾēl* (Aramaic) corresponding to H4332; *Mishaël,* an Israelite:— Mishael.

H4334 מִישׁוֹר *mîšôr* or

מִישֹׁר *mîšōr* from H3474; a *level,* i.e. a *plain* (often used [with the article prefixed] as a proper name of certain districts); figuratively *concord:* also *straightness,* i.e. (figuratively) *justice* (sometimes adverbially *justly*):— equity, even place, plain, right, righteously, straight, made straight, uprightness.

H4335 מֵישַׁךְ *mêšak* borrowed from H4336; *Meshak,* an Israelite:— Meshak.

H4336 מֵישַׁךְ *mêšak* (Aramaic) of foreign origin and doubtful signification; *Meshak,* the Babylonian name of H4333:— Meshak.

H4337 מֵישָׁע *mêšāʿ* from H3467; *safety; Mesha,* an Israelite:— Mesha.

H4338 מֵישַׁע *mêšaʿ* a variation for H4337; *safety; Mesha,* a Moabite:— Mesha.

H4339 מֵישָׁר *mêšār* from H3474; *evenness,* i.e. (figuratively) *prosperity* or *concord;* also *straightness,* i.e. (figuratively) *rectitude* (only in plural with singular sense; often adverbially):— agreement, aright, that are equal, equity, right, things that are right, righteously, right things, sweetly, upright, uprightly, uprightness.

H4340 מֵיתָר *mêtār* from H3498; a *cord* (of a tent) [compare H3499] or the *string* (of a bow):— cord, string.

H4341 מַכְאֹב *makʾōb* sometimes

מַכְאוֹב *makʾôb* also (feminine, Isa. 53:3)

מַכְאֹבָה *makʾōbâ* from H3510; *anguish* or (figuratively) *affliction:*— grief, pain, sorrow.

H4342 מַכְבִּיר *makbîr* transitive participle of H3527; *plenty:*— abundance.

H4343 מַכְבֵּנָא *makbēnāʾ* from the same as H3522; *knoll; Macbena,* a place in Palestine settled by him:— Machbenah.

H4344 מַכְבַּנַּי *makbannay* patrial from H4343; a *Macbannite* or native of Macbena:— Machbanai.

H4345 מִכְבָּר *mikbār* from H3527 in the sense of *covering* [compare H3531]; a *grate:*— grate.

H4346 מַכְבֵּר *makbēr* from H3527 in the sense of *covering;* a cloth (as *netted* [compare H4345]):— thick cloth.

H4347 מַכָּה *makkâ* or (masculine)

מַכֶּה *makkeh* (plural only) from H5221; a *blow* (in 2 Chron 2:10, of the flail); by implication a *wound;* figuratively *carnage,* also *pestilence:*— beaten, blow, plague, slaughter, smote, sore, stripe, stroke, wound, wounded.

H4348 מִכְוָה *mikwâ* from H3554; a *burn:*— that burneth, burning.

H4349 מָכוֹן *mākôn* from H3559; properly a *fixture,* i.e. a *basis;* generally a *place,* especially as an *abode:*— foundation, habitation, place, dwelling-place, settled place.

H4350 מְכוֹנָה *mĕkônâ* or

מְכֹנָה *mĕkōnâ* feminine of H4349; a *pedestal,* also a *spot:*— base.

H4351 מְכוּרָה *mĕkûrâ* or

מְכֹרָה *mĕkōrâ* from the same as H3564 in the sense of *digging; origin* (as if a mine):— birth, habitation, nativity.

H4352 מָכִי *mākî* probably from H4134; *pining; Maki,* an Israelite:— Machi.

H4353 מָכִיר *mākîr* from H4376; *salesman; Makir,* an Israelite:— Machir.

H4354 מָכִירִי *mākîrî* patronymic from H4353; a *Makirite* or descendant of Makir:— of Machir.

H4355 מָכַךְ *mākak* a primitive root; to *tumble* (in ruins); figuratively to *perish:*— be brought low, decay.

H4356 מִכְלָאָה *miklāʾâ* or

מִכְלָה *miklâ* from H3607; a *pen* (for flocks) :— fold, sheepfold. Compare H4357

H4357 מִכְלָה *miklâ* from H3615; *completion* (in plural concretely adverbially *wholly*):— perfect. Compare H4356

H4358 מִכְלוֹל *miklôl* from H3634; *perfection* (i.e. concretely adverbially *splendidly*):— most gorgeously, all sorts.

H4359 מִכְלָל *miklāl* from H3634; *perfection* (of beauty):— perfection.

H4360 מִכְלֻל *miklūl* from H3634; something *perfect,* i.e. a splendid *garment:*— all sorts.

H4361 מַכֹּלֶת *makkōlet* from H398; *nourishment:*— food.

H4362 מִכְמָן *mikman* from the same as H3646 in the sense of *hiding; treasure* (as *hidden*):— treasure.

H4363 מִכְמָס *mikmās* (Ezra 2:27; Neh. 7:31), or

מִכְמָשׁ *mikmāš* or

מִכְמַשׂ *mikmaś* (Neh. 11:31), from H3647; *hidden; Mikmas* or *Mikmash,* a place in Palestine:— Mikmas, Mikmash.

H4364 מַכְמָר *makmār* or

מִכְמֹר *mikmōr* from H3648 in the sense of *blackening* by heat; a (hunter's) *net* (as *dark* from concealment):— net.

H4365 מִכְמֶרֶת *mikmeret* or

מִכְמֹרֶת *mikmōret* feminine of H4364; a (fisher's) *net:*— drag, net.

H4366 מִכְמְתָת *mikmĕtāt* apparently from an unused root meaning to *hide; concealment; Mikmethath,* a place in Palestine:— Michmethath.

H4367 מַכְנַדְבַי *maknadbay* from H4100 and H5068 with a particle interposed; *what* (is) *like* (a) *liberal* (man)?; *Maknadbai,* an Israelite:— Machnadebai.

H4368 מְכֹנָה *mĕkōnâ* the same as H4350; a *base; Mekonah,* a place in Palestine:— Mekonah.

H4369 מְכֻנָה *mĕkūnâ* the same as H4350; a *spot:*— base.

H4370 מִכְנָס *miknās* from H3647 in the sense of *hiding;* (only in dual) *drawers* (from *concealing* the private parts):— breeches.

H4371 מֶכֶס *mekes* probably from an unused root meaning to *enumerate;* an *assessment* (as based upon a *cencus*):— tribute.

H4372 מִכְסֶה *mikseh* from H3680; a *covering,* i.e. weather-*boarding:*— covering.

H4373 מִכְסָה *miksâ* feminine of H4371; an *enumeration;* by implication a *valuation:*— number, worth.

H4374 מְכַסֶּה *mĕkasseh* from H3680; a *covering,* i.e. *garment;* specifically a *coverlet* (for a bed), an *awning* (from the sun); also the *omentum* (as covering the intestines):— clothing, to cover, that which covereth.

H4375 מַכְפֵּלָה *makpēlâ* from H3717; a *fold; Makpelah,* a place in Palestine:— Machpelah.

H4376 מָכַר *mākar* a primitive root; to *sell,* literally (as merchandise, a daughter in marriage, into slavery), or figuratively (to *surrender*):— at all, sell, sell away, seller, sell self.

H4377 מֶכֶר *meker* from H4376; *merchandise;* also *value:*— pay, price, ware.

H4378 מַכָּר *makkār* from H5234; an *acquaintance* :— acquaintance.

H4379 מִכְרֶה *mikreh* from H3738; a *pit* (for salt):— saltpit.

H4380 מְכֵרָה *mĕkērâ* probably from the same as H3564 in the sense of *stabbing;* a *sword:*— habitation.

H4381 מִכְרִי *mikrî* from H4376; *salesman; Mikri,* an Israelite:— Michri.

H4382 מְכֵרָתִי *mĕkarātî* patrial from an unused name (the same as H4380) of a place in Palestine; a *Mekerathite,* or inhabitant of Mekerah:— Mecherathite.

H4383 מִכְשׁוֹל *mikšôl* or

מִכְשֹׁל *mikšōl* masculine from H3782; a *stumbling-block,* literally or figuratively *(obstacle, enticement* [specifically an idol], *scruple*):— caused to fall, offence, nothing offered, ruin, stumbling-block.

H4384 מַכְשֵׁלָה *makšēlâ* feminine from H3782; a *stumbling-block,* but only figuratively *(fall, enticement* [idol]):— ruin, stumbling-block.

H4385 מִכְתָּב *miktāb* from H3789; a thing *written,* the *characters,* or a *document* (letter, copy, edict, poem):— writing.

H4386 מְכִתָּה *mĕkittâ* from H3807; a *fracture:*— bursting.

H4387 מִכְתָּם *miktām* from H3799; an *engraving,* i.e. (technically) a *poem:*— Michtam.

H4388 מַכְתֵּשׁ *maktēš* from H3806; a *mortar;* by analogy a *socket* (of a tooth):— hollow place, mortar.

H4389 מַכְתֵּשׁ *maktēš* the same as H4388; *dell;* the *Maktesh,* a place in Jerusalem:— Maktesh.

H4390 מָלֵא *mālēʾ* or

מָלָא *mālāʾ* (Esth 7:5), a primitive root, to *fill* or (intransitively) *be full* of, in a wide application (literally and figuratively):— accomplish, confirm, consecrate, be at an end, be expired, be fenced, fill, fulfil, be full, become full, draw full, give in full, go fully, fully set, give in full tale, overflow, fulness, furnish, gather, gather selves, gather together, presume, replenish, satisfy, set space, take a handfull, have wholly.

H4391 מְלָא *mĕlāʾ* (Aramaic) corresponding to H4390; to *fill:*— fill, be full.

H4392 מָלֵא *mālēʾ* from H4390; *full* (literally or figuratively) or *filling* (literally); also (concretely) *fulness;* adverbially *fully:*— she that was with child, fill, filled, filled with, full, fully, multitude, as is worth.

H4393 מְלֹא *mĕlōʾ* rarely

מְלוֹא *mĕlôʾ* or

מְלוֹ *mĕlô* (Ezek 41:8), from H4390; *fulness* (literally or figuratively):— all along, all that is in, all that is therein, fill, full, that whereof . . . was full, fulness, handful, multitude.

H4394 מִלֻּא *millūʾ* from H4390; a *fulfilling* (only in plural), i.e. (literally) a *setting* (of gems), or (technically) *consecration* (also concretely a dedicatory *sacrifice*):— consecration, be set.

H4395 מְלֵאָה *mĕlēʾâ* feminine of H4392; something *fulfilled,* i.e. *abundance* (of produce):— fruit, first of ripe fruit, fulness.

H4396 מִלֻּאָה *millūʾâ* feminine of H4394; a *filling,* i.e. *setting* (of gems):— inclosing, setting.

H4397 מַלְאָךְ *malʾāk* from an unused root meaning to *despatch* as a deputy; a *messenger;* specifically of God, i.e. an *angel* (also a prophet, priest or teacher):— ambassador, angel, king, messenger.

H4398 מַלְאַךְ *malʾak* (Aramaic) corresponding to H4397; an *angel:*— angel.

H4399 מְלָאכָה *mĕlāʾkâ* from the same as H4397; properly *deputyship,* i.e. ministry; generally *employment* (never servile) or work (abstractly or concretely); also *property* (as the result of *labor*):— business, cattle, industrious, occupation, occupied, officer, stuff, thing, thing made, use, work, workmanship, manner of workmanship, workman.

H4400 מַלְאֲכוּת *malʾăkût* from the same as H4397; a *message:*— message.

H4401 מַלְאָכִי *malʾākî* from the same as H4397; *ministrative; Malaki,* a prophet:— Malachi.

H4402 מִלֵּאת *millēʾt* from H4390; *fulness,* i.e. (concretely) a *plump* socket (of the eye):— fitly.

H4403 מַלְבּוּשׁ *malbûš* or

מַלְבֻּשׁ *malbūš* from H3847; a *garment,* or (collectively) *clothing:*— apparel, raiment, vestment.

H4404 מַלְבֵּן *malbēn* from H3835 (denominatively); a *brick-kiln:*— brickkiln.

H4405 מִלָּה *millâ* from H4448 (plural masculine as if from

מִלֶּה *milleh*); a *word;* collectively a *discourse;* figuratively a *topic:*— answer, byword, matter, any thing to say, what to say, to speak, speaking, speech, talking, word.

H4406 מִלָּה *millâ* (Aramaic) corresponding to H4405; a *word, command, discourse,* or *subject:*— commandment, matter, thing, word.

H4407 מִלּוֹא *millôʾ* or

מִלֹּא *millōʾ* (2 Kings 12:20), from H4390; a *rampart* (as *filled* in), i.e. the *citadel:*— Millo. See also H1037

H4408 מָלוּחַ *malûaḥ* from H4414; *sea-purslain* (from its *saltness*):— mallows.

H4409 מַלּוּךְ *mallûk* or

מַלּוּכִי *mallûkî* (Neh 12:14), from H4427; *regnant; Malluk*, the name of five Israelites:— Malluch, Melichu *[from the margin]*.

H4410 מְלוּכָה *mělûkâ* feminine passive participle of H4427; something *ruled*, i.e. a *realm*:— kingdom, king's, royal.

H4411 מָלוֹן *mālôn* from H3885; a *lodgment*, i.e. *caravanserai* or *encampment*:— inn, place where . . . lodge, lodging, lodging place.

H4412 מְלוּנָה *mělûnâ* feminine from H3885; a *hut*, a *hammock*:— cottage, lodge.

H4413 מַלּוֹתִי *mallôtî* apparently from H4448; *I have talked* (i.e. *loquacious*); *Mallothi*, an Israelite:— Mallothi.

H4414 מָלַח *mālaḥ* a primitive root; properly to *rub* to pieces or pulverize; intransitively to *disappear* as dust; also (as denominative from H4417) to *salt* whether internally (to *season* with salt) or externally (to *rub* with salt):— at all, salt, season, temper together, vanish away.

H4415 מְלַח *mělaḥ* (Aramaic) corresponding to H4414; to *eat* salt, i.e. (generally) *subsist*:— have maintenance.

H4416 מְלַח *mělaḥ* (Aramaic) from H4415; *salt*:— maintenance, salt.

H4417 מֶלַח *melaḥ* from H4414; properly *powder*, i.e. (specifically) *salt* (as easily pulverized and dissolved):— salt, saltpit.

H4418 מָלָח *mālāḥ* from H4414 in its original sense; a *rag* or old garment:— rotten rag.

H4419 מַלָּח *mallāḥ* from H4414 in its secondary sense; a *sailor* (as following "the salt"):— mariner.

H4420 מְלֵחָה *mělēḥâ* from H4414 (in its denominative sense); properly *salted* (i.e. land [H776 being understood]), i.e. a *desert*:— barren land, barrenness, salt land.

H4421 מִלְחָמָה *milḥāmâ* from H3898 (in the sense of *fighting*); a *battle* (i.e. the *engagement*); generally *war* (i.e. *warfare*):— battle, fight, fighting, war, warrior.

H4422 מָלַט *mālaṭ* a primitive root; properly to *be smooth*, i.e. (by implication) to *escape* (as if by *slipperiness*); causatively to *release* or *rescue;* specifically to *bring forth* young, *emit* sparks:— deliver, deliver self, escape, lay, leap out, let alone, let go, preserve, save, speedily, surely.

H4423 מֶלֶט *meleṭ* from H4422, *cement* (from its plastic *smoothness*):— clay.

H4424 מְלַטְיָה *mělaṭyâ* from H4423 and H3050; (whom) *Jah has delivered; Melatjah*, a Gibeonite:— Melatiah.

H4425 מְלִילָה *mělîlâ* from H4449 (in the sense of *cropping* [compare H4135]); a *head* of grain (as *cut* off):— ear.

H4426 מְלִיצָה *mělîṣâ* from H3887; an *aphorism;* also a *satire*:— interpretation, taunting.

H4427 מָלַךְ *mālak* a primitive root; to *reign;* inceptively to *ascend the throne;* causatively to *induct* into royalty; hence (by implication) to *take counsel*:— consult, indeed, be king, make king, set a king, set up king, be queen, make queen, reign, begin to reign, make to reign, reigning, rule, surely.

H4428 מֶלֶךְ *melek* from H4427; a *king*:— king, royal.

H4429 מֶלֶךְ *melek* the same as H4428; *king; Melek*, the name of two Israelites:— Melech, Hammelech *[by including the article]*.

H4430 מֶלֶךְ *melek* (Aramaic) corresponding to H4428; a *king*:— king, royal.

H4431 מְלַךְ *mělak* (Aramaic) from a root corresponding to H4427 in the sense of *consultation; advice*:— counsel.

H4432 מֹלֶךְ *mōlek* from H4427; *Molek* (i.e. king), the chief deity of the Ammonites:— Molech. Compare H4445

H4433 מַלְכָּא *malkā*ʾ (Aramaic) corresponding to H4436; a *queen*:— queen.

H4434 מַלְכֹּדֶת *malkōdet* from H3920; a *snare*:— trap.

H4435 מִלְכֹּדֶת *milkōdet* a form of H4436; *queen; Milcah*, the name of a Hebrewess and of an Israelite:— Milcah.

H4436 מַלְכָּה *malkâ* feminine of H4428; a *queen*:— queen.

H4437 מַלְכוּ *malkû* (Aramaic) corresponding to H4438; *dominion* (abstractly or concretely):— kingdom, kingly, realm, reign.

H4438 מַלְכוּת *malkût* or

מַלְכֻת *malkūt* or (in plural)

מַלְכֻיָּה *malkuyyâ* from H4427; a *rule;* concretely a *dominion*:— empire, kingdom, realm, reign, royal.

H4439 מַלְכִּיאֵל *malkîʾēl* from H4428 and H410; *king of* (i.e. appointed by) *God; Malkiël*, an Israelite:— Malchiel.

H4440 מַלְכִּיאֵלִי *malkîʾēlî* patronymic from H4439; a *Malkiëlite* or descendant of Malkiel:— Malchielite.

H4441 מַלְכִּיָּה *malkîyâ* or

מַלְכִּיָּהוּ *malkîâhû* (Jer 38:6), from H4428 and H3050; *king of* (i.e. appointed by) *Jah; Malkijah*, the name of ten Israelites:— Malchiah, Malchijah.

H4442 מַלְכִּי־צֶדֶק *malkî-ṣedeq* from H4428 and H6664; *king of right; Malki-Tsedek*, an early king in Palestine:— Melchizedek.

H4443 מַלְכִּירָם *malkîrām* from H4428 and H7311; *king of a high* one (i.e. of exaltation); *Malkiram*, an Israelite:— Malchiram.

H4444 מַלְכִּישׁוּעַ *malkîšûa*ʿ from H4428 and H7769; *king of wealth; Malkishua*, an Israelite:— Malchishua.

H4445 מַלְכָּם *malkām* or

מִלְכּוֹם *milkôm* from H4428 for H4432; *Malcam* or *Milcom*, the national idol of the Ammonites:— Malcham, Milcom.

H4446 מְלֶכֶת *mělеket* from H4427; a *queen*:— queen.

H4447 מֹלֶכֶת *mōleket* feminine active participle of H4427; *queen; Moleketh*, an Israelitess:— Hammoleketh *[including the article]*.

H4448 מָלַל *mālal* a primitive root; to *speak* (mostly poetically) or *say*:— say, speak, utter.

H4449 מְלַל *mělal* (Aramaic) corresponding to H4448; to *speak*:— say, speak, speaking.

H4450 מִלֲלַי *milălay* from H4448; *talkative; Milalai*, an Israelite:— Milalai.

H4451 מַלְמָד *malmād* from H3925; a *goad* for oxen :— goad.

H4452 מָלַץ *mālaṣ* a primitive root; to *be smooth*, i.e. (figuratively) *pleasant*:— be sweet.

H4453 מֶלְצָר *melṣār* of Persian derivation; the *butler* or other officer in the Babylonian court:— Melzar.

H4454 מָלַק *mālaq* a primitive root; to *crack* a joint; by implication to *wring* the neck of a fowl (without separating it):— wring off.

H4455 מַלְקוֹחַ *malqûaḥ* from H3947; transitive (in dual) the *jaws* (as taking food); intransitive *spoil* [and captives] (as taken):— booty, jaws, prey.

H4456 מַלְקוֹשׁ *malqôš* from H3953; the spring *rain* (compare H3954); figuratively *eloquence*:— latter rain.

H4457 מֶלְקָח *melqāḥ* or

מַלְקָח *malqāḥ* from H3947; (only in dual) *tweezers*:— snuffers, tongs.

H4458 מֶלְתָּחָה *meltāḥâ* from an unused root meaning to *spread* out; a *wardrobe* (i.e. room where clothing is *spread*):— vestry.

H4459 מַלְתָּעָה *maltāʿâ* transposed for H4973; a *grinder*, i.e. back *tooth*:— great tooth.

H4460 מַמְּגֻרָה *mammĕgūrâ* from H4048 (in the sense of *depositing*); a *granary*:— barn.

H4461 מֵמַד *mēmad* from H4058; a *measure*:— measure.

H4462 מְמוּכָן *měmûkān* or transposed

מוֹמֻכָן *mômūkān* (Esth 1:16), of Persian derivation; *Memucan* or *Momucan*, a Persian satrap:— Memucan.

H4463 מָמוֹת *māmôt* from H4191; a mortal *disease;* concretely a *corpse*:— death.

H4464 מַמְזֵר *mamzēr* from an unused root meaning to *alienate;* a *mongrel*, i.e. born of a Jewish father and a heathen mother:— bastard.

H4465 מִמְכָּר *mimkār* from H4376; *merchandise;* abstractly a *selling*:— ought, sale, that which cometh of sale, that which . . . sold, ware.

H4466 מִמְכֶּרֶת *mimkeret* feminine of H4465; a *sale* :— sold as.

H4467 מַמְלָכָה *mamlākâ* from H4427; *domination*, i.e. (abstractly) the estate *(rule)* or (concretely) the country *(realm)*:— kingdom, king's, reign, royal.

H4468 מַמְלָכוּת *mamlākût* a form of H4467 and equivalent to it:— kingdom, reign.

H4469 מַמְסָךְ *mamsāk* from H4537; *mixture*, i.e. (specifically) wine *mixed* (with water or spices):— drink-offering, mixed wine.

H4470 מֶמֶר *memer* from an unused root meaning to *grieve; sorrow*:— bitterness.

H4471 מַמְרֵא *mamrē*ʾ from H4754 (in the sense of *vigor*); *lusty; Mamre*, an Amorite:— Mamre.

H4472 מַמְרֹר *mamrōr* from H4843; a *bitterness*, i.e. (figuratively) calamity:— bitterness.

H4473 מִמְשַׁח *mimšaḥ* from H4886, in the sense of *expansion; outspread* (i.e. with outstretched wings) :— anointed.

H4474 מִמְשָׁל *mimšāl* from H4910; a *ruler* or (abstractly) *rule*:— dominion, that ruled.

H4475 מֶמְשָׁלָה *memšālâ* feminine of H4474; *rule;* also (concretely in plural) a *realm* or a *ruler*:— dominion, government, power, to rule.

H4476 מִמְשָׁק *mimšāq* from the same as H4943; a *possession:*— breeding.

H4477 מַמְתַּק *mamtaq* from H4985; something *sweet* (literally or figuratively):— sweet, most sweet.

H4478 מָן *mān* from H4100; literally a *whatness* (so to speak), i.e. *manna* (so called from the question about it):— manna.

H4479 מָן *mān* (Aramaic) from H4101; *who* or *what* (properly interrogative, hence also indefinite and relative):— what, who, whomsoever, whoso.

H4480 מִן *min* or

מִנִּי *minnî* or

מִנֵּי *minnê* construct plural (Isa. 30:11) for H4482; properly a *part* of; hence (prepositionally), *from* or *out of* in many senses (as follows):— above, after, among, at, because of, by, by reason of, from, from among, in, neither, nor, of, out of, over, since, then, through, whether, with.

H4481 מִן *min* (Aramaic) corresponding to H4480 :— according, after, because, before, by, for, from, him, more than, of, out of, part, since, these, to, upon, when.

H4482 מֵן *mēn* from an unused root meaning to *apportion;* a *part;* hence a musical *chord* (as parted into strings):— in [the same] (Ps 68:23), stringed instrument (Ps 150:4), whereby (Ps 45:8 *[defective plural]*).

H4483 מְנָא *měnāʾ* or

מְנָה *měnâ* (Aramaic) corresponding to H4487; to *count; appoint:*— number, ordain, set.

H4484 מְנֵא *měnēʾ* (Aramaic) passive participle of H4483; *numbered:*— Mene.

H4485 מַנְגִּינָה *mangînâ* from H5059; a *satire:*— music.

H4486 מַנְדַּע *mandaᶜ* (Aramaic) corresponding to H4093; *wisdom* or *intelligence:*— knowledge, reason, understanding.

H4487 מָנָה *mānâ* a primitive root; properly to *weigh* out; by implication to *allot* or constitute officially; also to *enumerate* or enroll:— appoint, count, number, prepare, set, tell.

H4488 מָנֶה *māneh* from H4487; properly a fixed *weight* or measured amount, i.e. (technically) a *maneh* or mina:— maneh, pound.

H4489 מֹנֶה *mōneh* from H4487; properly something *weighed* out, i.e. (figuratively) a *portion* of time, i.e. an *instance:*— time.

H4490 מָנָה *mānâ* from H4487; properly something *weighted* out, i.e. (generally) a *division;* specifically (of food) a *ration;* also a *lot:*— such things as belonged, part, portion.

H4491 מִנְהָג *minhāg* from H5090; the *driving* (of a chariot):— driving.

H4492 מִנְהָרָה *minhārâ* from H5102; properly a *channel* or fissure, i.e. (by implication) a *cavern:*— den.

H4493 מָנוֹד *mānôd* from H5110; a *nodding* or *toss* (of the head in derision):— shaking.

H4494 מָנוֹחַ *mānôaḥ* from H5117; *quiet,* i.e. (concretely) a *settled spot,* or (figuratively) a *home:*— rest, place of rest.

H4495 מָנוֹחַ *mānôaḥ* the same as H4494; *rest; Manoäch,* an Israelite:— Manoah.

H4496 מְנוּחָה *měnûḥâ* or

מְנֻחָה *měnûḥâ* feminine of H4495; *repose* or (adverbially) *peacefully;* figuratively *consolation* (specifically *matrimony*); hence (concretely) an *abode:*— comfortable, ease, quiet, rest, resting place, still.

H4497 מָנוֹן *mānôn* from H5125; a *continuator,* i.e. *heir:*— son.

H4498 מָנוֹס *mānôs* from H5127; a *retreat* (literally or figuratively); abstractly a *fleeing:*— apace, escape, way to flee, flight, refuge.

H4499 מְנוּסָה *měnûsâ* or

מְנֻסָה *měnūsâ* feminine of H4498; *retreat:*— fleeing, flight.

H4500 מָנוֹר *mānôr* from H5214; a *yoke* (properly for *ploughing*), i.e. the *frame* of a loom:— beam.

H4501 מְנוֹרָה *měnôrâ* or

מְנֹרָה *měnōrâ* feminine of H4500 (in the original sense of H5216); a *chandelier:*— candlestick.

H4502 מִנְּזָר *minnězār* from H5144; a *prince:*— crowned.

H4503 מִנְחָה *minḥâ* from an unused root meaning to *apportion,* i.e. *bestow;* a *donation;* euphemistically *tribute;* specifically a sacrificial *offering* (usually bloodless and voluntary):— gift, oblation, offering, meat offering, present, sacrifice.

H4504 מִנְחָה *minḥâ* (Aramaic) corresponding to H4503; a sacrificial *offering:*— oblation, meat offering.

H4505 מְנַחֵם *měnaḥēm* from H5162; *comforter; Menachem,* an Israelite:— Menahem.

H4506 מָנַחַת *mānaḥat* from H5117; *rest; Manachath,* the name of an Edomite and of a place in Moab:— Manahath.

H4507 מְנִי *měnî* from H4487; the *Apportioner,* i.e. Fate (as an idol):— number.

H4508 מִנִּי *minnî* of foreign derivation; *Minni,* an Armenian province:— Minni.

H4509 מִנְיָמִין *minyāmîn* from H4480 and H3225; *from* (the) *right hand; Minjamin,* the name of two Israelites:— Miniamin. Compare H4326

H4510 מִנְיָן *minyān* (Aramaic) from H4483; *enumeration:*— number.

H4511 מִנִּית *minnît* from the same as H4482; *enumeration; Minnith,* a place east of the Jordan:— Minnith.

H4512 מִנְלֶה *minleh* from H5239; *completion,* i.e. (in produce) *wealth:*— perfection.

H4513 מָנַע *mānaᶜ* a primitive root; to *debar* (negatively or positively) from benefit or injury:— deny, keep, keep back, refrain, restrain, withhold.

H4514 מַנְעוּל *manᶜûl* or

מַנְעֻל *manᶜūl* from H5274; a *bolt:*— lock.

H4515 מִנְעָל *minᶜāl* from H5274; a *bolt:*— shoe.

H4516 מַנְעַם *manᶜam* from H5276; a *delicacy:*— dainty.

H4517 מְנַעְנַע *měnaᶜnaᶜ* from H5128; a *sistrum* (so called from its *rattling* sound):— cornet.

H4518 מְנַקִּית *měnaqqît* from H5352; a *sacrificial basin* (for holding blood):— bowl.

H4519 מְנַשֶּׁה *měnaššeh* from H5382; *causing to forget; Menashsheh,* a grandson of Jacob, also the tribe descendant from him, and its territory:— Manasseh.

H4520 מְנַשִּׁי *měnaššî* from H4519; a *Menashshite* or descendant from him, and its territory:— Manasseh.

H4521 מְנָת *měnāt* from H4487; an *allotment* (by courtesy, law or providence):— portion.

H4522 מַס *mas* or

מִס *mîs* from H4549; properly a *burden* (as causing to *faint*), i.e. a *tax* in the form of forced *labor:*— discomfited, levy, taskmaster, tribute, tributary.

H4523 מָס *mās* from H4549; *fainting,* i.e. (figuratively) *disconsolate:*— is afflicted.

H4524 מֵסַב *mēsab* plural masculine

מְסִבִּים *měsibbîm* or plural feminine

מְסִבּוֹת *měsibbôt* from H5437; a *divan* (as *enclosing* the room); abstractly (adverbially) *around:*— that compass about, round about, place round about, at table.

H4525 מַסְגֵּר *masgēr* from H5462; a *fastener,* i.e. (of a person) a *smith,* (of a thing) a *prison:*— prison, smith.

H4526 מִסְגֶּרֶת *misgeret* from H5462; something *enclosing,* i.e. a *margin* (of a region, of a panel); concretely a *stronghold:*— border, close place, hole.

H4527 מַסַּד *massad* from H3245; a *foundation:*— foundation.

H4528 מִסְדְּרוֹן *misděrôn* from the same as H5468; a *colonnade* or internal portico (from its *rows* of pillars):— porch.

H4529 מָסָה *māsâ* a primitive root; to *dissolve:*— make to consume away, melt, make to melt, water.

H4530 מִסָּה *missâ* from H4549 (in the sense of *flowing*); *abundance,* i.e. (adverbially) *liberally:*— tribute.

H4531 מַסָּה *massâ* from H5254; a *testing,* of men (judicial) or of God (querulous):— temptation, trial.

H4532 מַסָּה *massâ* the same as H4531; *Massah,* a place in the Desert:— Massah.

H4533 מַסְוֶה *masweh* apparently from an unused root meaning to *cover;* a *veil:*— vail.

H4534 מְסוּכָה *měsûkâ* for H4881; a *hedge:*— thorn hedge.

H4535 מַסָּח *massāḥ* from H5255 in the sense of *staving* off; a *cordon,* (adverbially) or (as a) military *barrier:*— broken down.

H4536 מִסְחָר *misḥār* from H5503; *trade:*— traffic.

H4537 מָסַךְ *māsak* a primitive root; to *mix,* especially wine (with spices):— mingle.

H4538 מֶסֶךְ *mesek* from H4537; a *mixture,* i.e. of wine with spices:— mixture.

H4539 מָסָךְ *māsāk* from H5526; a *cover,* i.e. *veil:*— covering, curtain, hanging.

H4540 מְסֻכָּה *měsukkâ* from H5526; a *covering,* i.e. garniture:— covering.

H4541 מַסֵּכָה *massēkâ* from H5258; properly a *pouring* over, i.e. *fusion* of metal (especially a *cast* image); by implication a *libation,* i.e. league; concretely a *coverlet* (as if *poured* out):— covering, molten, molten image, vail.

H4542 מִסְכֵּן *miskēn* from H5531; *indigent:*— poor, poor man.

H4543 מִסְכְּנָה *miskěnâ* by transposition from H3664; a *magazine:*— store, storehouse, treasure.

H4544 מִסְכֵּנֻת *miskēnūt* from H4542; *indigence:*— scarceness.

H4545 מַסֶּכֶת *masseket* from H5259 in the sense of *spreading* out; something *expanded,* i.e. the *warp* in a loom (as *stretched* out to receive the woof):— web.

H4546 מְסִלָּה *mĕsillâ* from H5549; a *thoroughfare* (as *turnpiked*), literally or figuratively; specifically a *viaduct,* a *staircase:*— causeway, course, highway, path, terrace.

H4547 מַסְלוּל *maslûl* from H5549; a *thoroughfare* (as turnpiked):— highway.

H4548 מַסְמֵר *masmēr* or

מִסְמֵר *mismēr* also (feminine)

מַסְמְרָה *masmĕrâ* or

מִסְמְרָה *mismĕrâ* or even

מַשְׂמְרָה *maśmĕrâ* (Eccl 12:11), from H5568; a *peg* (as *bristling* from the surface):— nail.

H4549 מָסַס *māsas* a primitive root; to *liquefy;* figuratively to *waste* (with disease), to *faint* (with fatigue, fear or grief):— discourage, faint, be loosed, melt, melt away, refuse, utterly.

H4550 מַסַּע *massaᶜ* from H5265; a *departure* (from *striking* the tents), i.e. march (not necessarily a single day's travel); by implication a *station* (or point of *departure*):— journey, journeying.

H4551 מַסָּע *massāᶜ* from H5265 in the sense of *projecting;* a *missile* (spear or arrow); also a *quarry* (whence stones are, as it were, *ejected*):— before it was brought, dart.

H4552 מִסְעָד *misᶜād* from H5582; a *balustrade* (for stairs):— pillar.

H4553 מִסְפֵּד *mispēd* from H5594; a *lamentation:*— lamentation, one mourneth, mourning, wailing.

H4554 מִסְפּוֹא *mispôʾ* from an unused root meaning to *collect; fodder:*— provender.

H4555 מִסְפָּחָה *mispāḥâ* from H5596; a *veil* (as *spread* out):— kerchief.

H4556 מִסְפַּחַת *mispaḥat* from H5596; *scurf* (as *spreading* over the surface):— scab.

H4557 מִסְפָּר *mispār* from H5608; a *number,* definitely (arithmetical) or indefinitely (large, *innumerable;* small, a *few*); also (abstractly) *narration:*— abundance, account, all, few, infinite, number, certain number, numbered, tale, telling, time.

H4558 מִסְפָּר *mispār* the same as H4457; *number; Mispar,* an Israelite:— Mizpar. Compare H4559

H4559 מִסְפֶּרֶת *misperet* feminine of H4457; *enumeration; Mispereth,* an Israelite:— Mispereth. Compare H4458

H4560 מָסַר *māsar* a primitive root; to *sunder,* i.e. (transitively) *set apart,* or (reflexively) *apostatize:*— commit, deliver.

H4561 מֹסָר *mōsār* from H3256; *admonition:*— instruction.

H4562 מָסֹרֶת *māsōret* from H631; a *band:*— bond.

H4563 מִסְתּוֹר *mistôr* from H5641; a *refuge:*— covert.

H4564 מַסְתֵּר *mastēr* from H5641; properly a *hider,* i.e. (abstractly) a hiding, i.e. *aversion:*— hid.

H4565 מִסְתָּר *mistār* from H5641; properly a *concealer,* i.e. a *covert:*— secret, secretly, secret place.

H4566 מַעְבָּד *maᶜbād* from H5647; an *act:*— work.

H4567 מַעְבָד *maᶜbād* (Aramaic) corresponding to H4566; an *act:*— work.

H4568 מַעֲבֶה *maᶜăbeh* from H5666; properly *compact* (part of soil), i.e. *loam:*— clay.

H4569 מַעֲבָר *maᶜăbār* or feminine

מַעֲבָרָה *maᶜăbārâ* from H5674; a *crossing-place* (of a river, a *ford;* of a mountain, a *pass*); abstractly a *transit,* i.e. (figuratively) *overwhelming:*— ford, place where . . . pass, passage.

H4570 מַעְגָּל *maᶜgāl* or feminine

מַעְגָּלָה *maᶜgālâ* from the same as H5696; a *track* (literally or figuratively); also a *rampart* (as *circular*):— going, path, trench, way, wayside.

H4571 מָעַד *māᶜad* a primitive root; to *waver:*— make to shake, slide, slip.

H4572 מַעֲדַי *maᶜăday* from H5710; *ornamental; Maadai,* an Israelite:— Maadai.

H4573 מַעַדְיָה *maᶜadyâ* from H5710 and H3050; *ornament of Jah; Maadjah,* an Israelite:— Maadiah. Compare H4153

H4574 מַעֲדָן *maᶜădān* or feminine

מַעֲדַנָּה *maᶜădannâ* from H5727; a *delicacy* or (abstractly) *pleasure* (adverbially *cheerfully*):— dainty, delicately, delight.

H4575 מַעֲדַנָּה *maᶜădannâ* by transposition from H6029; a *bond,* i.e. *groups:*— influence.

H4576 מַעְדֵּר *maᶜdēr* from H5737; a (weeding) *hoe* :— mattock.

H4577 מְעָה *mĕᶜâ* or

מְעָא *mĕᶜāʾ* (Aramaic) corresponding to H4578; only in plural the *bowels:*— belly.

H4578 מֵעֶה *mēᶜeh* from an unused root probably meaning to *be soft;* used only in plural the *intestines,* or (collectively) the *abdomen,* figuratively *sympathy;* by implication a *vest;* by extension the *stomach,* the *uterus* (or of men, the seat of generation), the *heart* (figuratively):— belly, bowels, heart, womb.

H4579 מֵעָה *mēᶜâ* feminine of H4578; the *belly,* i.e. (figuratively) interior:— gravel.

H4580 מָעוֹג *māᶜôg* from H5746; a *cake* of bread (with H3934 a *table-buffoon,* i.e. *parasite*):— cake, feast.

H4581 מָעוֹז *māᶜôz* also

מָעוּז *māᶜûz* or

מָעֹז *māᶜōz* also

מָעֻז *māᶜūz* from H5810; a *fortified* place; figuratively, a *defense:*— force, fort, fortress, rock, strength, strengthen, strong, most strong, strong hold.

H4582 מָעוֹךְ *māᶜôk* from H4600; *oppressed; Maok,* a Philistine:— Maoch.

H4583 מָעוֹן *māᶜôn* or

מָעִין *māᶜîn* (1 Chron. 4:41), from the same as H5772; an *abode,* of God (the Tabernacle or the Temple), men (their home) or animals (their lair); hence a *retreat* (asylum):— den, dwelling, dwelling place, dwellingplace, habitation.

H4584 מָעוֹן *māᶜôn* the same as H4583; a *residence; Maon,* the name of an Israelite and of a place in Palestine:— Maon, Maonites. Compare H1010, H4586

H4585 מְעוֹנָה *mĕᶜônâ* or

מְעֹנָה *mĕᶜōnâ* feminine of H4583, and meaning the same:— den, habitation, place, dwelling place, refuge.

H4586 מְעוּנִי *mĕᶜûnāy* or

מְעִינִי *mĕᶜînî* probably patrial from H4584; a *Meünite,* or inhabitant of Maon (only in plural):— Mehunim, Mehunims, Meunim.

H4587 מְעוֹנֹתַי *mĕᶜônōtay* plural of H4585; *habitative; Meonothai,* an Israelite:— Meonothai.

H4588 מָעוּף *māᶜûp* from H5774 in the sense of *covering* with shade [compare H4155]; *darkness:*— dimness.

H4589 מָעוֹר *māᶜôr* from H5783; *nakedness,* i.e. (in plural) the *pudenda:*— nakedness.

H4590 מַעַזְיָה *maᶜazyâ* or

מַעַזְיָהוּ *maᶜazyāhû* probably from H5756 (in the sense of *protection*) and H3050; *rescue of Jah; Maazjah,* the name of two Israelites:— Maaziah.

H4591 מָעַט *māᶜaṭ* a primitive root; properly to *pare* off, i.e. *lessen;* intransitively to *be* (or causatively to *make*) *small* or *few* (or figuratively *ineffective*):— suffer to decrease, diminish, be few, borrow a few, give few, make few in number, fewness, gather least, gather little, be little, seem little, less, give the less, be minished, bring to nothing.

H4592 מְעַט *mĕᶜaṭ* or

מְעָט *mĕᶜāṭ* from H4591; a *little* or *few* (often adverbially or comparatively):— almost, few, some few, very few, fewer, fewest, lightly, little, little while, small, very small, small matter, small thing, some, soon, very.

H4593 מָעֹט *māᶜōṭ* passive adjective of H4591; *thinned* (as to the edge), i.e. *sharp:*— wrapped up.

H4594 מַעֲטֶה *maᶜăṭeh* from H5844; a *vestment:*— garment.

H4595 מַעֲטָפָה *maᶜăṭāpâ* from H5848; a *cloak:*— mantle.

H4596 מְעִי *mĕᶜî* from H5753; a *pile* of rubbish (as *contorted*), i.e. a *ruin* (compare H5856):— heap.

H4597 מָעַי *māᶜay* probably from H4578; *sympathetic; Maai,* an Israelite:— Maai.

H4598 מְעִיל *mĕᶜîl* from H4603 in the sense of *covering;* a *robe* (i.e. upper and outer *garment*):— cloke, coat, mantle, robe.

H4599 מַעְיָן *maᶜyān* or

מַעְיְנוֹ *maᶜyĕnô* (Ps. 114:8), or (feminine)

מַעְיָנָה *maᶜyānâ* from H5869 (as a denominative in the sense of a *spring*); a *fountain* (also collectively), figuratively a *source* (of satisfaction):— fountain, spring, well.

H4600 מָעַךְ *māᶜak* a primitive root; to *press,* i.e. to *pierce, emasculate, handle:*— bruised, stuck, be pressed.

H4601 מַעֲכָה *maᶜăkâ* or

מַעֲכָת *maᶜăkāt* (Josh 13:13), from H4600; *depression; Maakah* (or *Maakath*), the name of a place in Syria, also of a Mesopotamian, of three Israelites, and of four Israelitesses and one Syrian woman:— Maachah, Maachathites. See also H1038

H4602 מַעֲכָתִי *maᶜăkātî* patrial from H4601; a *Maakathite,* or inhabitant of Maakah:— Maachathite.

H4603 מָעַל *māᶜal* a primitive root; properly to *cover* up; used only figuratively to *act covertly,* i.e. *treacherously:*— transgress, trespass, commit trespass, do a trespass, trespassing.

H4604 מַעַל *maᶜal* from H4603; *treachery,* i.e. sin :— falsehood, grievously, sore, transgression, trespass, very.

H4605 מַעַל *maʿal* from H5927; properly the *upper* part, used only adverbially with prefix *upward, above, overhead, from the top,* etc:— above, exceeding, exceedingly, forward, on high, very high, over, up, upon, upward, very.

H4606 מֵעָל *mēʿāl* (Aramaic) from H5954; (only in plural as singular) the *setting* (of the sun):— going down.

H4607 מֹעַל *mōʿal* from H5927; a *raising* (of the hands):— lifting up.

H4608 מַעֲלֶה *maʿăleh* from H5927; an *elevation,* i.e. (concretely) *acclivity* or *platform;* abstractly (the relation or state) a *rise* or (figuratively) *priority:*— ascent, before, chiefest, cliff, that goeth up, going up, hill, mounting up, stairs.

H4609 מַעֲלָה *maʿălâ* feminine of H4608; *elevation,* i.e. the act (literally a *journey* to a higher place, figuratively a *thought* arising), or (concretely) the condition (literally a *step* or *grade*-mark, figuratively a *superiority* of station); specifically a climactic *progression* (in certain Psalms):— things that come up, degree, high degree, deal, go up, stair, step, story.

H4610 מַעֲלֵה עַקְרַבִּים *maʿălēh ʿaqrabbîm* from H4608 and (the plural of) H6137; *Steep of Scorpions,* a place in the Desert:— Maaleh-accrabim, the ascent of Akrabbim, going up of Akrabbim.

H4611 מַעֲלָל *maʿălāl* from H5953; an *act* (good or bad):— doing, endeavour, invention, work.

H4612 מַעֲמָד *maʿămād* from H5975; (figuratively) a *position:*— attendance, office, place, state.

H4613 מׇעֳמָד *moʿŏmād* from H5975; literally a *foothold:*— standing.

H4614 מַעֲמָסָה *maʿămāsâ* from H6006; *burdensomeness:*— burdensome.

H4615 מַעֲמָק *maʿămāq* from H6009; a *deep:*— deep, depth.

H4616 מַעַן *maʿan* from H6030; properly *heed,* i.e. *purpose;* used only adverbially, *on account of* (as a motive or an aim), teleologically *in order that:*— because of, to the end that, to the intent that, for, for to, for . . . 's sake, lest, that, to.

H4617 מַעֲנֶה *maʿăneh* from H6030; a *reply* (favorable or contradictory):— answer, himself.

H4618 מַעֲנָה *maʿănâ* from H6031, in the sense of *depression* or *tilling;* a *furrow:*— acre, furrow.

H4619 מַעַץ *maʿaṣ* from H6095; *closure; Maats,* an Israelite:— Maaz.

H4620 מַעֲצֵבָה *maʿăṣēbâ* from H6087; *anguish:*— sorrow.

H4621 מַעֲצָד *maʿăṣād* from an unused root meaning to *hew;* an *axe:*— ax, tongs.

H4622 מַעְצוֹר *maʿṣôr* from H6113; objectively a *hindrance:*— restraint.

H4623 מַעְצָר *maʿṣār* from H6113; subjectively *control:*— rule.

H4624 מַעֲקֶה *maʿăqeh* from an unused root meaning to *repress;* a *parapet:*— battlement.

H4625 מַעֲקָשׁ *maʿăqāš* from H6140; a *crook* (in a road):— crooked thing.

H4626 מַעַר *maʿar* from H6168; a *nude* place, i.e. (literally) the *pudenda,* or (figuratively) a vacant *space:*— nakedness, proportion.

H4627 מַעֲרָב *maʿărāb* from H6148, in the sense of *trading; traffic;* by implication mercantile *goods:*— market, merchandise.

H4628 מַעֲרָב *maʿărāb* or (feminine)

מַעֲרָבָה *maʿărābâ* from H6150, in the sense of *shading;* the *west* (as the region of the *evening* sun):— west.

H4629 מַעֲרֶה *maʿăreh* from H6168; a *nude* place, i.e. a *common:*— meadows.

H4630 מַעֲרָה *maʿărâ* feminine of H4629; an *open* spot:— army *[from the margin].*

H4631 מְעָרָה *mĕʿārâ* from H5783; a *cavern* (as dark) :— cave, den, hole.

H4632 מְעָרָה *mĕʿārâ* the same as H4631; *cave; Meărah,* a place in Palestine:— Mearah.

H4633 מַעֲרָךְ *maʿărāk* from H6186; an *arrangement,* i.e. (figuratively) mental *disposition:*— preparation.

H4634 מַעֲרָכָה *maʿărākâ* feminine of H4683; an *arrangement;* concretely a *pile;* specifically a military *array:*— army, fight, be set in order, ordered place, rank, row.

H4635 מַעֲרֶכֶת *maʿăreket* from H6186; an *arrangement,* i.e. (concretely) a *pile* (of loaves):— row, shewbread.

H4636 מַעֲרֹם *maʿărōm* from H6191, in the sense of *stripping; bare:*— naked.

H4637 מַעֲרָצָה *maʿărāṣâ* from H6206; *violence:*— terror.

H4638 מַעֲרָת *maʿărāt* a form of H4630; *waste; Maarath,* a place in Palestine:— Maarath.

H4639 מַעֲשֶׂה *maʿăśeh* from H6213; an *action* (good or bad); generally a *transaction;* abstractly *activity;* by implication a *product* (specifically a *poem*) or (generally) *property:*— act, art, bakemeat, business, deed, do, doing, labour, thing made, ware of making, occupation, thing offered, operation, possession, well, work, handywork, needlework, network, working, workmanship, wrought.

H4640 מַעֲשַׂי *maʿăśay* from H6213; *operative; Maasai,* an Israelite:— Maasiai.

H4641 מַעֲשֵׂיָה *maʿăśêâ* or

מַעֲשֵׂיָהוּ *maʿăśēāhû* from H4639 and H3050; *work of Jah; Maasejah,* the name of sixteen Israelites:— Maaseiah.

H4642 מַעֲשַׁקָּה *maʿăšaqqâ* from H6231; *oppression* :— oppression, oppressor.

H4643 מַעֲשֵׂר *maʿăśēr* or

מַעֲשַׂר *maʿăśar* and (in plural) feminine

מַעַשְׂרָה *maʿaśrâ* from H6240; a *tenth;* especially a *tithe:*— tenth, tenth part, tithe, tithing.

H4644 מֹף *mōp* of Egyptian origin; *Moph,* the capital of Lower Egypt:— Memphis. Compare H5297

H4645 מִפְגָּע *mipgāʿ* from H6293; an *object of attack:*— mark.

H4646 מַפָּח *mappāḥ* from H5301; a *breathing out* (of life), i.e. expiring:— giving up.

H4647 מַפֻּחַ *mappuăḥ* from H5301; the *bellows* (i.e. *blower*) of a forge:— bellows.

H4648 מְפִיבֹשֶׁת *mĕpîbōšet* or

מְפִבֹשֶׁת *mĕpibōšet* probably from H6284 and H1322; *dispeller of shame* (i.e. of Baal); *Mephibosheth,* the name of two Israelites:— Mephibosheth.

H4649 מֻפִּים *muppîm* a plural apparently from H5130; *wavings; Muppim,* an Israelite:— Muppim. Compare H8206

H4650 מֵפִיץ *mēpîṣ* from H6327; a *breaker,* i.e. mallet:— maul.

H4651 מַפָּל *mappāl* from H5307; a *falling* off, i.e. chaff; also something *pendulous,* i.e. a flap:— flake, refuse.

H4652 מִפְלָאָה *miplāʾâ* from H6381; a *miracle:*— wondrous work.

H4653 מִפְלַגָּה *miplaggâ* from H6385; a *classification:*— division.

H4654 מַפָּלָה *mappālâ* or

מַפֵּלָה *mappēlâ* from H5307; something *fallen,* i.e. a *ruin:*— ruin, ruinous.

H4655 מִפְלָט *miplāṭ* from H6403; an *escape:*— escape.

H4656 מִפְלֶצֶת *mipleṣet* from H6426; a *terror,* i.e. an idol:— idol.

H4657 מִפְלָשׂ *miplāś* from an unused root meaning to *balance;* a *poising:*— balancing.

H4658 מַפֶּלֶת *mappelet* from H5307; *fall,* i.e. *decadence;* concretely a *ruin;* specifically a *carcase:*— carcase, fall, ruin.

H4659 מִפְעָל *mipʿal* or (feminine)

מִפְעָלָה *mipʿālâ* from H6466; a *performance* :— work.

H4660 מַפָּץ *mappāṣ* from H5310; a *smiting* to pieces :— slaughter.

H4661 מַפֵּץ *mappēṣ* from H5310; a *smiter,* i.e. a war *club:*— battle ax.

H4662 מִפְקָד *mipqād* from H6485; an *appointment,* i.e. *mandate;* concretely a designated *spot;* specifically a *census:*— appointed place, commandment, number.

H4663 מִפְקָד *mipqād* the same as H4662; *assignment; Miphkad,* the name of a gate in Jerusalem:— Miphkad.

H4664 מִפְרָץ *miprāṣ* from H6555; a *break* (in the shore), i.e. a *haven:*— breach.

H4665 מִפְרֶקֶת *mipreqet* from H6561; properly a *fracture,* i.e. *joint (vertebra)* of the neck:— neck.

H4666 מִפְרָשׂ *miprāś* from H6566; an *expansion:*— that which . . . spreadest forth, spreading.

H4667 מִפְשָׂעָה *mipśāʿâ* from H6585; a *stride,* i.e. (by euphemism) the *crotch:*— buttocks.

H4668 מַפְתֵּחַ *maptēaḥ* from H6605; an *opener,* i.e. a *key:*— key.

H4669 מִפְתָּח *miptāḥ* from H6605; an *aperture,* i.e. (figuratively) *utterance:*— opening.

H4670 מִפְתָּן *miptān* from the same as H6620; a *stretcher,* i.e. a *sill:*— threshold.

H4671 מֹץ *mōṣ* or

מוֹץ *môṣ* (Zeph 2:2), from H4160; *chaff* (as *pressed* out, i.e. *winnowed* or [rather] threshed loose):— chaff.

H4672 מָצָא *māṣāʾ* a primitive root; properly to *come* forth to, i.e. *appear* or *exist;* transitively to *attain,* i.e. *find* or *acquire;* figuratively to *occur, meet* or *be present:*— be able, befall, being, catch, certainly, cause to come, come on, come to, come to hand, deliver, be enough, find, cause to find, finding, find occasion, find out, get, get hold upon, have, have here, be here, hit, be left, light on, light upon, meet, meet with, occasion serve, present, be present, ready, speed, suffice, take hold on.

H4673 מַצָּב *maṣṣāb* from H5324; a fixed *spot;* figuratively an *office,* a military *post:*— garrison, station, place where . . . stood.

H4674 מֻצָּב *muṣṣāb* from H5324; a *station,* i.e. military *post:*— mountain.

H4675 מַצָּבָה *maṣṣābâ* or

מִצָּבָה *miṣṣābâ* feminine of H4673; a military *guard:*— army, garrison.

H4676 מַצֵּבָה *maṣṣēbâ* feminine (causative) participle of H5324; something *stationed,* i.e. a *column* or (memorial *stone*); by analogy an *idol:*— garrison, image, standing image, pillar.

H4677 מְצֹבָיָה *mĕṣōbāyâ* apparently from H4672 and H3050; *found of Jah; Metsobajah,* a place in Palestine:— Mesobaite.

H4678 מַצֶּבֶת *maṣṣebet* from H5324; something *stationary,* i.e. a monumental *stone;* also the *stock* of a tree:— pillar, substance.

H4679 מְצַד *mĕṣad* or

מְצָד *mĕṣād* or (feminine)

מְצָדָה *mĕṣādâ* from H6679; a *fastness* (as a *covert* of ambush):— castle, fort, hold, strong hold, munition.

H4680 מָצָה *māṣâ* a primitive root; to *suck* out; by implication to *drain,* to *squeeze* out:— suck, wring, wring out.

H4681 מֹצָה *mōṣâ* active participle feminine of H4680; *drained; Motsah,* a place in Palestine:— Mozah.

H4682 מַצָּה *maṣṣâ* from H4711 in the sense of *greedily* devouring for sweetness; properly *sweetness;* concretely *sweet* (i.e. not soured or bittered with yeast); specifically an *unfermented cake* or loaf, or (elliptically) the festival of *Passover* (because no leaven was then used):— unleavened, unleavened bread, unleavened cake, without leaven.

H4683 מַצָּה *maṣṣâ* from H5327; a *quarrel:*— contention, debate, strife.

H4684 מַצְהָלָה *mashālâ* from H6670; a *whinnying* (through impatience for battle or lust):— neighing.

H4685 מָצוֹד *māṣôd* or (feminine)

מְצוֹדָה *mĕṣôdâ* or

מְצֹדָה *mĕṣōdâ* from H6679; a *net* (for *capturing* animals or fishes); also (by interchange for H4679) a *fastness* or (besieging) *tower:*— bulwark, hold, munition, net, snare.

H4686 מָצוּד *māṣûd* or (feminine)

מְצוּדָה *mĕṣûdâ* or

מְצֻדָה *mĕṣūdâ* for H4685; a *net,* or (abstractly) *capture;* also a *fastness:*— castle, defence, fort, fortress, hold, strong hold, be hunted, net, snare, strong place.

H4687 מִצְוָה *miṣwâ* from H6680; a *command,* whether human or divine (collectively the *Law*) :— commanded, which was commanded, commandment, law, ordinance, precept.

H4688 מְצוֹלָה *mĕṣôlâ* or

מְצֹלָה *mĕṣōlā* also

מְצוּלָה *mĕṣûlâ* or

מְצֻלָה *mĕṣūlâ* from the same as H6683; a *deep* place (of water or mud):— bottom, deep, depth.

H4689 מָצוֹק *māṣôq* from H6693; a *narrow* place, i.e. (abstractly and figuratively) *confinement* or *disability:*— anguish, distress, straitness.

H4690 מָצוּק *māṣûq* or

מָצֻק *māṣuq* from H6693; something *narrow,* i.e. a *column* or *hill*-top:— pillar, situate.

H4691 מְצוּקָה *mĕṣûqâ* or

מְצֻקָה *mĕṣūqâ* feminine of H4690; *narrowness,* i.e. (figuratively) *trouble:*— anguish, distress.

H4692 מָצוֹר *māṣôr* or

מָצוּר *māṣûr* from H6696; something *hemming* in, i.e. (objectively) a *mound* (of besiegers), (abstractly) a *siege,* (figuratively) *distress;* or (subjectively) a *fastness:*— besieged, bulwark, defence, fenced, fortress, siege, hold, strong hold, tower.

H4693 מָצוֹר *māṣôr* the same as H4692 in the sense of a *limit; Egypt* (as the *border* of Palestine):— besieged places, defence, fortified.

H4694 מְצוּרָה *mĕṣûrâ* or

מְצֻרָה *mĕṣūrâ* feminine of H4692; a *hemming* in, i.e. (objectively) a *mound* (of siege), or (subjectively) a *rampart* (of protection), (abstractly) *fortification:*— fenced, fenced city, fort, munition, strong hold.

H4695 מַצּוּת *maṣṣût* from H5327; a *quarrel:*— that contended.

H4696 מֵצַח *mēṣaḥ* from an unused root meaning to be *clear,* i.e. *conspicuous;* the *forehead* (as *open* and *prominent*):— brow, forehead, impudent.

H4697 מִצְחָה *misḥâ* from the same as H4696; a *shin-piece* of armor (as *prominent*), only plural:— greaves.

H4698 מְצִלָּה *mĕṣillâ* from H6750; a *tinkler,* i.e. a *bell:*— bell.

H4699 מְצֻלָּה *mĕṣullâ* from H6751; *shade:*— bottom.

H4700 מְצֵלֶת *mĕṣēlet* from H6750; (only dual) double *tinklers,* i.e. cymbals:— cymbals.

H4701 מִצְנֶפֶת *miṣnepet* from H6801; a *tiara,* i.e. official *turban* (of a king or high priest):— diadem, mitre.

H4702 מַצָּע *maṣṣāᶜ* from H3331; a *couch:*— bed.

H4703 מִצְעָד *miṣᶜād* from H6805; a *step;* figuratively *companionship:*— going, step.

H4704 מִצְּעִירָה *miṣṣĕᶜîrâ* feminine of H4705; properly *littleness;* concretely *diminutive:*— little.

H4705 מִצְעָר *miṣᶜār* from H6819; *petty* (in size or number); adverbially a *short* (time):— little one, little while, small.

H4706 מִצְעָר *miṣᶜār* the same as H4705; *Mitsar,* a peak of Lebanon:— Mizar.

H4707 מִצְפֶּה *miṣpeh* from H6822; an *observatory,* especially for military purposes:— watch tower.

H4708 מִצְפֶּה *miṣpeh* the same as H4707; *Mitspeh,* the name of five places in Palestine:— Mizpeh, watch tower. Compare H4709

H4709 מִצְפָּה *miṣpâ* feminine of H4708. [This seems rather to be only an orthographical variation of H4708 when "in pause".]; *Mitspah,* the name of two places in Palestine:— Mitspah.

H4710 מִצְפֻּן *miṣpūn* from H6845; a *secret* (place or thing, perhaps *treasure*):— hidden thing.

H4711 מָצַץ *māṣaṣ* a primitive root; to *suck:*— milk.

H4712 מֵצַר *mēṣar* from H6896; something *tight,* i.e. (figuratively) *trouble:*— distress, pain, strait.

H4713 מִצְרִי *miṣrî* from H4714; a *Mitsrite,* or inhabitant of Mitsrajim:— Egyptian, of Egypt.

H4714 מִצְרַיִם *miṣrayim* dual of H4693; *Mitsrajim,* i.e. Upper and Lower Egypt:— Egypt, Egyptians, Mizraim.

H4715 מִצְרֵף *miṣrēp* from H6884; a *crucible:*— fining pot.

H4716 מַק *maq* from H4743; properly a *melting,* i.e. *putridity:*— rottenness, stink.

H4717 מַקָּבָה *maqqābâ* from H5344; properly a *perforatrix,* i.e. a *hammer* (as *piercing*):— hammer.

H4718 מַקֶּבֶת *maqqebet* from H5344; properly a *perforator,* i.e. *hammer* (as *piercing*); also (intransitively) a *perforation,* i.e. a *quarry:*— hammer, hole.

H4719 מַקֵּדָה *maqqēdâ* from the same as H5348 in the denominative sense of *herding* (compare H5349); *fold; Makkedah,* a place in Palestine:— Makkedah.

H4720 מִקְדָּשׁ *miqdāš* or

מִקְּדָשׁ *miqqĕdāš* (Exod 15:17), from H6942; a *consecrated* thing or place, especially a *palace, sanctuary* (whether of Jehovah or of idols) or *asylum:*— chapel, hallowed part, holy place, sanctuary.

H4721 מַקְהֵל *maqhēl* or (feminine)

מַקְהֵלָה *maqhēlâ* from H6950; an *assembly* :— congregation.

H4722 מַקְהֵלֹת *maqhēlōt* plural of H4721 (feminine); *assemblies; Makheloth,* a place in the Desert :— Makheloth.

H4723 מִקְוֶה *miqweh* or

מִקְוֵה *miqwēh* (1 Kings 10:28), or

מִקְוֵא *miqwēᵓ* (2 Chron 1:16), from H6960; something *waited* for, i.e. *confidence* (objectively or subjectively); also a *collection,* i.e. (of water) a *pond,* or (of men and horses) a *caravan* or *drove:*— abiding, gathering together, hope, linen yarn, plenty of water, pool.

H4724 מִקְוָה *miqwâ* feminine of H4723; a *collection,* i.e. (of water) a *reservoir:*— ditch.

H4725 מָקוֹם *māqôm* or

מָקֹם *māqōm* also (feminine)

מְקוֹמָה *mĕqômâ* or

מְקֹמָה *mĕqōmâ* from H6965; properly a *standing,* i.e. a *spot;* but used widely of a *locality* (generally or specifically); also (figuratively) of a *condition* (of body or mind):— country, home, open, place, room, space, whithersoever.

H4726 מָקוֹר *māqôr* or

מָקֹר *māqōr* from H6979; properly something *dug,* i.e. a (general) *source* (of water, even when naturally flowing; also of tears, blood [by euphemism of the female *pudenda*]; figuratively of happiness, wisdom, progeny):— fountain, issue, spring, well, wellspring.

H4727 מִקָּח *miqqāḥ* from H3947; *reception:*— taking.

H4728 מַקָּחָה *maqqāḥâ* from H3947; something *received,* i.e. *merchandise* (purchased):— ware.

H4729 מִקְטָר *miqṭār* from H6999; something to *fume* (incense) on, i.e. a *hearth* place:— to burn . . . upon.

H4730 מִקְטֶרֶת *miqṭeret* feminine of H4729; something to *fume* (incense) in, i.e. a *coal-pan:*— censer.

H4731 מַקֵּל *maqqēl* or (feminine)

מַקְּלָה *maqqělâ* from an unused root meaning apparently to *germinate;* a *shoot,* i.e. *stick* (with leaves on, or for walking, striking, guiding, divining):— rod, staff, handstaff.

H4732 מִקְלוֹת *miqlôt* plural of (feminine) H4731; *rods; Mikloth,* a place in the Desert:— Mikloth.

H4733 מִקְלָט *miqlāṭ* from H7038 in the sense of *taking* in; an *asylum* (as a *receptacle*):— refuge.

H4734 מִקְלַעַת *miqlaᶜat* from H7049; a *sculpture* (probably in bass-relief):— carved, carved figure, carving, graving.

H4735 מִקְנֶה *miqneh* from H7069; something *bought,* i.e. *property,* but only live *stock;* abstractly *acquisition:*— cattle, flock, herd, possession, purchase, substance.

H4736 מִקְנָה *miqnâ* feminine of H4735; properly a *buying,* i.e. *acquisition;* concretely a piece of *property* (land or living); also the *sum* paid:— bought, he that is bought, possession, piece, purchase.

H4737 מִקְנֵיָהוּ *miqnêāhû* from H4735 and H3050; *possession of Jah; Miknejah,* an Israelite:— Mikneiah.

H4738 מִקְסָם *miqsām* from H7080; an *augury:*— divination.

H4739 מָקַץ *māqaṣ* from H7112; *end; Makats,* a place in Palestine:— Makaz.

H4740 מַקְצוֹעַ *maqṣôaᶜ* or

מַקְצֹעַ *maqṣōaᶜ* or (feminine)

מַקְצֹעָה *maqṣōᶜâ* from H7106 in the denominative sense of *bending;* an *angle* or recess:— corner, turning.

H4741 מַקְצֻעָה *maqṣūᶜâ* from H7106; a *scraper,* i.e. a carving *chisel:*— plane.

H4742 מְקֻצְעָה *měquṣᶜâ* from H7106 in the denominative sense of *bending;* an *angle:*— corner.

H4743 מָקַק *māqaq* a primitive root; to *melt;* figuratively to *flow, dwindle, vanish:*— consume away, be corrupt, dissolve, pine away.

H4744 מִקְרָא *miqrāᵓ* from H7121; something *called* out, i.e. a public *meeting* (the act, the persons, or the place); also a *rehearsal:*— assembly, calling, convocation, reading.

H4745 מִקְרֶה *miqreh* from H7136; something *met* with, i.e. an *accident* or *fortune:*— something befallen, befalleth, chance, event, hap, happeneth.

H4746 מְקָרֶה *měqāreh* from H7136; properly something *meeting,* i.e. a *frame* (of timbers):— building.

H4747 מְקֵרָה *měqērâ* from the same as H7119; a *cooling* off:— summer.

H4748 מִקְשֶׁה *miqšeh* from H7185 in the sense of *knotting* up round and hard; something *turned* (rounded), i.e. a *curl* (of tresses):— well set hair.

H4749 מִקְשָׁה *miqšâ* feminine of H4748; *rounded* work, i.e. mounded by *hammering (repoussé):*— beaten, beaten out of one piece, beaten work, upright, whole piece.

H4750 מִקְשָׁה *miqšâ* denominative from H7180; literally a *cucumbered* field, i.e. a *cucumber* patch:— garden of cucumbers.

H4751 מַר *mar* or (feminine)

מָרָה *mārâ* from H4843; *bitter* (literally or figuratively); also (as noun) *bitterness,* or (adverbially) *bitterly:*— angry, bitter, betterly, bitterness, chafed, discontented, great, heavy.

H4752 מַר *mar* from H4843 in its original sense of *distillation;* a *drop:*— drop.

H4753 מֹר *mōr* or

מוֹר *môr* from H4843; *myrrh* (as *distilling* in drops, and also as *bitter*):— myrrh.

H4754 מָרָא *mārāᵓ* a primitive root; to *rebel;* hence (through the idea of *maltreating*) to *whip,* i.e. *lash* (self with wings, as the ostrich in running):— be filthy, lift up self.

H4755 מָרָא *mārāᵓ* for H4751 feminine; *bitter; Mara,* a symbolic name of Naomi:— Mara.

H4756 מָרֵא *mārēᵓ* (Aramaic) from a root corresponding to H4754 in the sense of *domineering;* a *master:*— lord, Lord.

H4757 מְרֹאדַךְ בַּלְאֲדָן *měrōᵓdak balᵓădān* of foreign derivation; *Merodak-Baladan,* a Babylonian king:— Merodach-baladan. Compare H4781

H4758 מַרְאֶה *marᵓeh* from H7200; a *view* (the act of seeing); also an *appearance* (the thing seen), whether (real) a *shape* (especially if handsome, *comeliness;* often plural the *looks*), or (mental) a *vision:*— apparently, appearance, appeareth, as soon as, beautiful, beauty, countenance, fair, favoured, form, goodly, to look on, to look to, to look upon, looketh, pattern, to see, seem, sight, visage, vision.

H4759 מַרְאָה *marᵓâ* feminine of H4758; a *vision;* also (causatively) a *mirror:*— looking glass, vision.

H4760 מֻרְאָה *murᵓâ* apparently feminine passive causative participle of H7200; something *conspicuous,* i.e. the *craw* of a bird (from its *prominence*):— crop.

H4761 מַרְאָשָׁה *marᵓāšâ* denominative from H7218; properly *headship,* i.e. (plural for collective) *dominion:*— principality.

H4762 מַרְאֵשָׁה *marᵓēšâ* or

מָרֵשָׁה *marēšâ* formed like H4761; *summit; Mareshah,* the name of two Israelites and of a place in Palestine:— Mareshah.

H4763 מְרַאֲשָׁה *měraᵓăšâ* formed like H4761; properly a *headpiece,* i.e. (plural for adverb) *at* (or *as*) the *head-rest* (or pillow):— bolster, head, pillow. Compare H4772

H4764 מֵרָב *mērāb* from H7231; *increase; Merab,* a daughter of Saul:— Merab.

H4765 מַרְבַד *marbad* from H7234; a *coverlet:*— covering of tapestry.

H4766 מַרְבֶה *marbeh* from H7235; properly *increasing;* as noun, *greatness,* or (adverbially) *greatly:*— great, increase.

H4767 מִרְבָּה *mirbâ* from H7235; *abundance,* i.e. a great quantity:— much.

H4768 מַרְבִּית *marbît* from H7235; a *multitude;* also *offspring;* specifically *interest* (on capital):— greatest part, greatness, increase, multitude.

H4769 מַרְבֵּץ *marbēṣ* a *reclining* place, i.e. *fold* (for flocks):— couching place, place to lie down.

H4770 מַרְבֵּק *marbēq* from an unused root meaning to *tie* up; a *stall* (for cattle):— fat, fatted, stall.

H4771 מַרְגּוֹעַ *margôaᶜ* from H7280; a *resting* place :— rest.

H4772 מַרְגְּלָה *margělâ* denominative from H7272; (plural for collective) a *footpiece,* i.e. (adverbially) *at the foot,* or (directly) the *foot* itself:— feet. Compare H4763

H4773 מַרְגֵּמָה *margēmâ* from H7275; a *stone*-heap :— sling.

H4774 מַרְגֵּעָה *margēᶜâ* from H7280; *rest:*— refreshing.

H4775 מָרַד *mārad* a primitive root; to *rebel:*— rebel, rebellious.

H4776 מְרַד *měrad* (Aramaic) from a root corresponding to H4775; *rebellion:*— rebellion.

H4777 מֶרֶד *mered* from H4775; *rebellion:*— rebellion.

H4778 מֶרֶד *mered* the same as H4777; *Mered,* an Israelite:— Mered.

H4779 מָרָד *mārād* (Aramaic) from the same as H4776; *rebellious:*— rebellious.

H4780 מַרְדּוּת *mardût* from H4775; *rebelliousness* :— rebellious.

H4781 מְרֹדָךְ *měrōdāk* of foreign derivation; *Merodak,* a Babylonian idol:— Merodach. Compare H4757

H4782 מָרְדְּכַי *morděkay* of foreign derivation; *Mordecai,* an Israelite:— Mordecai.

H4783 מֻרְדָּף *murdāp* from H7291; *persecuted:*— persecuted.

H4784 מָרָה *mārâ* a primitive root; to *be* (causatively *make*) *bitter* (or unpleasant); (figuratively) to *rebel* (or resist; causatively to *provoke*):— bitter, change, be disobedient, disobey, grievously, provocation, provoke, provoking, rebel, rebel against, rebellious, be rebellious.

H4785 מָרָה *mārâ* the same as H4751 feminine; *bitter; Marah,* a place in the Desert:— Marah.

H4786 מֹרָה *mōrâ* from H4843; *bitterness,* i.e. (figuratively) *trouble:*— grief.

H4787 מָרָה *mārâ* a form of H4786; *trouble:*— bitterness.

H4788 מָרוּד *mārûd* from H7300 in the sense of *maltreatment;* an *outcast;* (abstractly) *destitution:*— cast out, misery.

H4789 מֵרוֹז *mērôz* of uncertain derivation; *Meroz,* a place in Palestine:— Meroz.

H4790 מְרוֹחַ *měrôaḥ* from H4799; *bruised,* i.e. *emasculated:*— broken.

H4791 מָרוֹם *mārôm* from H7311; *altitude,* i.e. concretely (an *elevated place*), abstractly *(elevation),* figuratively *(elation),* or adverbially *(aloft):*— above, far above, dignity, haughty, height, high, most high, on high, high one, high place, loftily, upward.

H4792 מֵרוֹם *mērôm* formed like H4791; *height; Merom,* a lake in Palestine:— Merom.

H4793 מֵרוֹץ *mērôṣ* from H7323; a *run* (the trial of speed):— race.

H4794 מְרוּצָה *měrûṣâ* or

מְרֻצָה *měruṣâ* feminine of H4793; a *race* (the act), whether the manner or the progress:— course, running. Compare H4835

H4795 מָרוּק *mārûq* from H4838; properly *rubbed;* but used abstractly, a *rubbing* (with perfumery):— purification.

H4796 מָרוֹת *mārôt* plural of H4751 feminine; *bitter springs; Maroth,* a place in Palestine:— Maroth.

H4797 מִרְזַח *mirzaḥ* from an unused root meaning to *scream;* a *cry,* i.e. (of joy), a *revel:*— banquet.

H4798 מַרְזֵחַ *marzēaḥ* formed like H4797; a *cry,* i.e. (of grief) a *lamentation:*— mourning.

H4799 מָרַח *mārah* a primitive root; properly to *soften* by rubbing or pressure; hence (medicinally) to *apply* as an emollient:— lay for a plaister.

H4800 מֶרְחָב *merhāb* from H7337; *enlargement,* either literally (an *open space,* usually in a good sense), or figuratively *(liberty)*:— breadth, large place, large room.

H4801 מֶרְחָק *merhāq* from H7368; *remoteness,* i.e. (concretely) a *distant* place; often (adverbially) *from afar:*— far, afar off, dwell in far, very far off, far country, far off. See also H1023

H4802 מַרְחֶשֶׁת *marhešet* from H7370; a *stew-pan* :— fryingpan.

H4803 מָרַט *māraṭ* a primitive root; to *polish;* by implication to *make bald* (the head), to *gall* (the shoulder); also, to *sharpen:*— bright, furbish, have his hair fallen off, hair be fallen off, peeled, pluck off, pluck off hair.

H4804 מְרַט *mĕraṭ* (Aramaic) corresponding to H4803; to *pull* off:— be plucked.

H4805 מְרִי *mĕrî* from H4784; *bitterness,* i.e. (figuratively) *rebellion;* concretely *bitter,* or *rebellious:*— bitter, rebel, most rebellious, rebellion, rebellious.

H4806 מְרִיא *mĕrî*ʾ from H4754 in the sense of *grossness,* through the idea of *domineering* (compare H4756); *stall-fed;* often (as noun) a *beeve:*— fat beast, fat cattle, fatling, fed beast.

H4807 מְרִיב בַּעַל *mĕrîb baʿal* from H7378 and H1168; *quarreller of Baal; Merib-Baal,* an epithet of Gideon:— Merib-baal. Compare H4810

H4808 מְרִיבָה *mĕrîbâ* from H7378; *quarrel:*— provocation, strife.

H4809 מְרִיבָה *mĕrîbâ* the same as H4808; *Meribah,* the name of two places in the Desert:— Meribah.

H4810 מְרִי בַעַל *mĕrî baʿal* from H4805 and H1168; *rebellion of* (i.e. *against*) *Baal; Meri-Baal,* an epithet of Gideon:— Meri-baal. Compare H4807

H4811 מְרָיָה *mĕrāyâ* from H4784; *rebellion; Merajah,* an Israelite:— Meraiah. Compare H3236

H4812 מְרָיוֹת *mĕrāyôt* plural of H4811; *rebellious; Merajoth,* the name of two Israelites:— Meraioth.

H4813 מִרְיָם *miryām* from H4805; *rebelliously; Mirjam,* the name of two Israelitesses:— Miriam.

H4814 מְרִירוּת *mĕrîrût* from H4843; *bitterness,* i.e. (figuratively) *grief:*— bitterness.

H4815 מְרִירִי *mĕrîrî* from H4843; *bitter,* i.e. *poisonous:*— bitter.

H4816 מֹרֶךְ *mōrek* perhaps from H7401; *softness,* i.e. (figuratively) *fear:*— faintness.

H4817 מֶרְכָּב *merkāb* from H7392; a *chariot;* also a *seat* (in a vehicle):— chariot, covering, saddle.

H4818 מֶרְכָּבָה *merkābâ* feminine of H4817; a *chariot:*— chariot. See also H1024

H4819 מַרְכֹּלֶת *markōlet* from H7402; a *mart:*— merchandise.

H4820 מִרְמָה *mirmâ* from H7411 in the sense of *deceiving; fraud:*— craft, deceit, deceitful, deceitfully, false, feigned, guile, subtilly, treachery.

H4821 מִרְמָה *mirmâ* the same as H4820; *Mirmah,* an Israelite:— Mirma.

H4822 מְרֵמוֹת *mĕrēmôt* plural from H7311; *heights; Meremoth,* the name of two Israelites:— Meremoth.

H4823 מִרְמָס *mirmās* from H7429; *abasement* (the act or the thing):— tread down, treading, trodden down, to be trodden under foot.

H4824 מֵרֹנֹתִי *mērōnōtî* patrial from an unused noun; a *Meronothite,* or inhabitant of some (otherwise unknown) Meronoth:— Meronothite.

H4825 מֶרֶס *meres* of foreign derivation; *Meres,* a Persian:— Meres.

H4826 מַרְסְנָא *marsĕnā*ʾ of foreign derivation; *Marsena,* a Persian:— Marsena.

H4827 מֵרַע *mēraʿ* from H7489; used as (abstractly) noun, *wickedness:*— do mischief.

H4828 מֵרֵעַ *mērēaʿ* from H7462 in the sense of *companionship;* a *friend:*— companion, friend.

H4829 מִרְעֶה *mirʿeh* from H7462 in the sense of *feeding; pasture* (the place or the act); also the *haunt* of wild animals:— feeding place, pasture.

H4830 מִרְעִית *mirʿît* from H7462 in the sense of *feeding; pasturage;* concretely a *flock:*— flock, pasture.

H4831 מַרְעֲלָה *marʿălâ* from H7477; perhaps *earthquake; Maralah,* a place in Palestine:— Maralah.

H4832 מַרְפֵּא *marpē*ʾ from H7495; properly *curative,* i.e. literally (concretely) a *medicine,* or (abstractly) a *cure;* figuratively (concretely) *deliverance,* or (abstractly) *placidity:*— cure, incurable, healing, health, remedy, sound, wholesome, yielding.

H4833 מִרְפָּשׂ *mirpāś* from H7515; *muddled* water :— that which . . . have fouled.

H4834 מָרַץ *māraṣ* a primitive root; properly to *press,* i.e. (figuratively) to be *pungent* or vehement; to *irritate:*— embolden, be forcible, grievous, sore.

H4835 מְרֻצָה *mĕrūṣâ* from H7533; *oppression:*— violence. See also H4794

H4836 מַרְצֵעַ *marṣēaʿ* from H7527; an *awl:*— aul.

H4837 מַרְצֶפֶת *marṣepet* from H7528; a *pavement* :— pavement.

H4838 מָרַק *māraq* a primitive root; to *polish;* by implication to *sharpen;* also to *rinse:*— bright, furbish, scour.

H4839 מָרָק *mārāq* from H4838; *soup* (as if a *rinsing*):— broth. See also H6564

H4840 מֶרְקָח *merqāh* from H7543; a *spicy* herb:— sweet.

H4841 מֶרְקָחָה *merqāhâ* feminine of H4840; abstractly a *seasoning* (with spicery); concretely an *unguent-kettle* (for preparing spiced oil):— pot of ointment, well.

H4842 מִרְקַחַת *mirqahat* from H7543; an aromatic *unguent;* also an *unguent-pot:*— prepared by the apothecaries' art, compound, ointment.

H4843 מָרַר *mārar* a primitive root; properly to *trickle* [see H4752]; but used only as a denominative from H4751; to *be* (causatively *make*) *bitter* (literally or figuratively):— be bitter, be in bitterness, deal bitterly, have bitterness, make bitter, bitterly, be moved with choler, be grieved, have sorely grieved, it grieveth, provoke, vex.

H4844 מְרֹר *mĕrōr* or

מְרוֹר *mĕrôr* from H4843; a *bitter* herb:— bitter, bitterness.

H4845 מְרֵרָה *mĕrērâ* from H4843; *bile* (from its bitterness):— gall.

H4846 מְרֹרָה *mĕrōrâ* or

מְרוֹרָה *mĕrôrâ* from H4843; properly *bitterness;* concretely a *bitter thing;* specifically *bile;* also *venom* (of a serpent):— bitter, bitter thing, gall.

H4847 מְרָרִי *mĕrārî* from H4843; *bitter; Merari,* an Israelite:— Merari. See also H4848

H4848 מְרָרִי *mĕrārî* from H4847; a *Merarite* (collectively), or descendant of Merari:— Merarites.

H4849 מִרְשַׁעַת *miršaʿat* from H7561; a female *wicked doer:*— wicked woman.

H4850 מְרָתַיִם *mĕrātayim* dual of H4751 feminine; *double bitterness; Merathajim,* an epithet of Babylon:— Merathaim.

H4851 מַשׁ *maš* of foreign derivation; *Mash,* a son of Aram, and the people descendant from him:— Mash.

H4852 מֵשָׁא *mēšā*ʾ of foreign derivation; *Mesha,* a place in Arabia:— Mesha.

H4853 מַשָּׂא *maśśā*ʾ from H5375; a *burden;* specifically *tribute,* or (abstractly) *porterage;* figuratively an *utterance,* chiefly a *doom,* especially *singing;* mental, *desire:*— burden, carry away, prophecy, they set, song, tribute.

H4854 מַשָּׂא *maśśā*ʾ the same as H4853; *burden; Massa,* a son of Ishmael:— Massa.

H4855 מַשָּׁא *maššā*ʾ from H5383; a *loan;* by implication *interest* on a debt:— exaction, usury.

H4856 מַשֹּׂא *maśśō*ʾ from H5375; *partiality* (as a *lifting* up):— respect.

H4857 מַשְׁאָב *mašʾāb* from H7579; a *trough* for cattle to drink from:— place of drawing water.

H4858 מַשָּׂאָה *maśśāʾâ* from H5375; a *conflagration* (from the *rising* of smoke):— burden.

H4859 מַשָּׁאָה *maššāʾâ* feminine of H4855; a *loan* :— anything, debt.

H4860 מַשָּׁאוֹן *maššāʾôn* from H5377; *dissimulation* :— deceit.

H4861 מִשְׁאָל *mišʾāl* from H7592; *request; Mishal,* a place in Palestine:— Mishal, Misheal. Compare H4913

H4862 מִשְׁאָלָה *mišʾālâ* from H7592; a *request:*— desire, petition.

H4863 מִשְׁאֶרֶת *mišʾeret* from H7604 in the original sense of *swelling;* a *kneading-trough* (in which the dough *rises*):— kneading trough, store.

H4864 מַשְׂאֵת *maśʾēt* from H5375; properly (abstractly) a *raising* (as of the hands in prayer), or *rising* (of flame); figuratively an *utterance;* concretely a *beacon* (as *raised*); a *present* (as taken), *mess,* or *tribute;* figuratively a *reproach* (as a burden):— burden, collection, sign of fire, flame, great flame, gift, lifting up, mess, oblation, reward.

H4865 מִשְׁבְּצָה *mišbĕṣâ* from H7660; a *brocade;* by analogy a (reticulated) *setting* of a gem:— ouch, wrought.

H4866 מִשְׁבֵּר *mišbēr* from H7665; the *orifice* of the womb (from which the foetus *breaks* forth):— birth, breaking forth.

H4867 מִשְׁבָּר *mišbār* from H7665; a *breaker* (of the sea):— billow, wave.

H4868 מִשְׁבָּת *mišbāt* from H7673; *cessation,* i.e. destruction:— sabbath.

H4869 מִשְׂגָּב *miśgāb* from H7682; properly a *cliff* (or other *lofty* or *inaccessible* place); abstractly *altitude;*

figuratively a *refuge:*— defence, high fort, high tower, refuge.

H4870 מִשְׂגָּב *miśgāb* from H4869; *Misgab,* a place in Moab:— Misgab.

H4870'מִשְׁגֶּה *mišgeh* from H7686; an *error:*— oversight.

H4871 מָשָׁה *māšâ* a primitive root; to *pull* out (literally or figuratively):— draw, draw out.

H4872 מֹשֶׁה *mōšeh* from H4871; *drawing* out (of the water), i.e. *rescued; Mosheh,* the Israelite lawgiver:— Moses.

H4873 מֹשֶׁה *mōšeh* (Aramaic) corresponding to H4872:— Moses.

H4874 מַשֶּׁה *maššeh* from H5383; a *debt:*— creditor.

H4875 מְשׁוֹאָה *mĕšôʾâ* or

מְשֹׁאָה *mĕšōʾâ* from the same as H7722; (a) *ruin,* abstractly (the act) or concretely (the wreck):— desolation, waste.

H4876 מַשּׁוּאָה *maššûʾâ* or

מַשֻּׁאָה *maššūʾâ* for H4875; *ruin:*— desolation, destruction.

H4877 מְשׁוֹבָב *mĕšôbāb* from H7725; *returned; Meshobab,* an Israelite:— Meshobab.

H4878 מְשׁוּבָה *mĕšûbâ* or

מְשֻׁבָה *mĕšūbâ* from H7725; *apostasy:*— backsliding, turning away.

H4879 מְשׁוּגָה *mĕšûgâ* from an unused root meaning to *stray; mistake:*— error.

H4880 מָשׁוֹט *māšôṭ* or

מִשּׁוֹט *miššôṭ* from H7751; an *oar:*— oar.

H4881 מְשׂוּכָה *mĕśûkâ* or

מְשֻׂכָה *mĕśūkâ* from H7753; a *hedge:*— hedge.

H4882 מְשׁוּסָה *mĕšûsâ* from an unused root meaning to *plunder; spoliation:*— spoil.

H4883 מַשּׂוֹר *maśśôr* from an unused root meaning to *rasp;* a *saw:*— saw.

H4884 מְשׂוּרָה *mĕśûrâ* from an unused root meaning apparently to *divide;* a *measure* (for liquids):— measure.

H4885 מָשׂוֹשׂ *māśôś* from H7797; *delight,* concretely (the cause or object) or abstractly (the feeling):— joy, mirth, rejoice.

H4886 מָשַׁח *māšaḥ* a primitive root; to *rub* with oil, i.e. to *anoint;* by implication to *consecrate;* also to *paint:*— anoint, paint.

H4887 מְשַׁח *mĕšaḥ* (Aramaic) from a root corresponding to H4886; *oil:*— oil.

H4888 מִשְׁחָה *mišḥâ* or

מָשְׁחָה *mošḥâ* from H4886; *unction* (the act); by implication a consecratory *gift:*— to be anointed, anointing, ointment.

H4889 מַשְׁחִית *mašḥît* from H7843; *destructive,* i.e. (as noun) *destruction,* literally (specifically a *snare*) or figuratively *(corruption):*— corruption, to destroy, destroying, destruction, trap. utterly.

H4890 מִשְׂחָק *miśḥāq* from H7831; a *laughing-stock* :— scorn.

H4891 מִשְׁחָר *mišḥār* from H7836 in the sense of day *breaking; dawn:*— morning.

H4892 מַשְׁחֵת *mašḥēt* for H4889; *destruction:*— destroying.

H4893 מִשְׁחָת *mišḥāt* or

מָשְׁחָת *mošḥāt* from H7843; *disfigurement* :— corruption, marred.

H4894 מִשְׁטוֹחַ *mišṭôaḥ* from H7849; a *spreading-place:*— to spread forth, spreading, to spread upon.

H4895 מַשְׂטֵמָה *maśṭēmâ* from the same as H7850; *enmity:*— hatred.

H4896 מִשְׁטָר *mišṭār* from H7860; *jurisdiction:*— dominion.

H4897 מֶשִׁי *mešî* from H4871; *silk* (as *drawn* from the cocoon):— silk.

H4898 מְשֵׁיזַבְאֵל *mĕšêzabʾēl* from an equivalent to H7804 and H410; *delivered of God; Meshezabel,* an Israelite:— Meshezabeel.

H4899 מָשִׁיחַ *māšîaḥ* from H4886; *anointed;* usually a *consecrated* person (as a king, priest, or saint); specifically the *Messiah:*— anointed, Messiah.

H4900 מָשַׁךְ *māšak* a primitive root; to *draw,* used in a great variety of applications (including to *sow,* to *sound,* to *prolong,* to *develop,* to *march,* to *remove,* to *delay,* to *be tall,* etc.):— draw, draw along, draw out, continue, defer, extend, forbear, give, handle, make long, prolong, sound long, sow, scatter, stretch out.

H4901 מֶשֶׁךְ *mešek* from H4900; a *sowing;* also a *possession:*— precious, price.

H4902 מֶשֶׁךְ *mešek* the same in form as H4901, but probably of foreign derivation; *Meshek,* a son of Japheth, and the people descendant from him:— Mesech, Meshech.

H4903 מִשְׁכַּב *miškab* (Aramaic) corresponding to H4904; a *bed:*— bed.

H4904 מִשְׁכָּב *miškāb* from H7901; a *bed* (figuratively a *bier*); abstractly *sleep;* by euphemism carnal *intercourse:*— bed, bedchamber, couch, lieth with, lying with.

H4905 מַשְׂכִּיל *maśkîl* from H7919; *instructive,* i.e. a *didactic* poem:— Maschil.

H4906 מַשְׂכִּית *maśkît* from the same as H7906; a *figure* (carved on stone, the wall, or any object); figuratively *imagination:*— conceit, image, imagery, picture, wish.

H4907 מִשְׁכַּן *miškan* (Aramaic) corresponding to H4908; *residence:*— habitation.

H4908 מִשְׁכָּן *miškān* from H7931; a *residence* (including a shepherd's *hut,* the *lair* of animals, figuratively the *grave;* also the *Temple*); specifically the *Tabernacle* (properly its wooden walls):— dwelleth, dwelling, dwelling place, habitation, tabernacle, tent.

H4909 מַשְׂכֹּרֶת *maśkōret* from H7936; *wages* or a *reward:*— reward, wages.

H4910 מָשַׁל *māšal* a primitive root; to *rule:*— dominion, have dominion, make to have dominion, governor, indeed, reign, rule, bear rule, cause to rule, have rule, ruling, ruler, have power.

H4911 מָשַׁל *māšal* denominatively from H4912; to *liken,* i.e. (transitively) to use figurative language (an allegory, adage, song or the like); intransitively to *resemble:*— be like, become like, compare, use prover, use as a proverb, speak, speak in proverbs, utter.

H4912 מָשָׁל *māšāl* apparently from H4910 in some original sense of *superiority* in mental action; properly a pithy *maxim,* usually of a metaphorical nature; hence a *simile* (as an adage, poem, discourse):— byword, like, parable, proverb.

H4913 מָשָׁל *māšāl* for H4861; *Mashal,* a place in Palestine:— Mashal.

H4914 מְשֹׁל *mĕšōl* from H4911; a *satire:*— byword.

H4915 מֹשֶׁל *mōšel* (1) from H4910; *empire;* (2) from H4911; a *parallel:*— dominion, like.

H4916 מִשְׁלוֹחַ *mišlôaḥ* or

מִשְׁלַח *mišlāḥ* from H7971; a *sending* out, i.e. (abstractly) *presentation* (favorable), or *seizure* (unfavorable); also (concretely) a place of *dismissal,* or a *business* to be discharged:— to lay, to put, sending, sending forth, to set.

H4917 מִשְׁלַחַת *mišlaḥat* feminine of H4916; a *mission,* i.e. (abstract and favorable) *release,* or (concrete and unfavorable) an *army:*— discharge, sending.

H4918 מְשֻׁלָּם *mĕšullām* from H7999; *allied; Meshullam,* the name of seventeen Israelites:— Meshullam.

H4919 מְשִׁלֵּמוֹת *mĕšillēmôt* plural from H7999; *reconciliations; Meshillemoth,* an Israelite:— Meshillemoth. Compare H4921

H4920 מְשֶׁלֶמְיָה *mĕšelemyâ* or

מְשֶׁלֶמְיָהוּ *mĕšelemyāhû* from H7999 and H3050; *ally of Jah; Meshelemjah,* an Israelite:— Meshelemiah.

H4921 מְשִׁלֵּמִית *mĕšillēmît* from H7999; *reconciliation; Meshillemith,* an Israelite:— Meshillemith. Compare H4919

H4922 מְשֻׁלֶּמֶת *mĕšullemet* feminine of H4918; *Meshullemeth,* an Israelitess:— Meshullemeth.

H4923 מְשַׁמָּה *mĕšammâ* from H8074; a *waste* or *amazement:*— astonishment, desolate.

H4924 מַשְׁמָן *mašmān* from H8080; *fat,* i.e. (literally and abstractly) *fatness;* but usually (figuratively and concretely) a *rich* dish, a *fertile* field, a *robust* man:— fat one, fatness, fattest, fattest place.

H4925 מִשְׁמַנָּה *mišmannâ* from H8080; *fatness; Mashmannah,* an Israelite:— Mishmannah.

H4926 מִשְׁמָע *mišmāᶜ* from H8085; a *report:*— hearing.

H4927 מִשְׁמָע *mišmāᶜ* the same as H4926; *Mishma,* the name of a son of Ishmael, and of an Israelite:— Mishma.

H4928 מִשְׁמַעַת *mišmaᶜat* feminine of H4926; *audience,* i.e. the royal *court;* also *obedience,* i.e. (concretely) a *subject:*— bidding, guard, obey.

H4929 מִשְׁמָר *mišmār* from H8104; a *guard* (the man, the post, or the *prison*); figuratively a *deposit;* also (as observed) a *usage* (abstractly), or an *example* (concretely):— diligence, guard, office, prison, ward, watch.

H4930 מַשְׂמְרָה *maśmĕrâ* for H4548 feminine; a *peg* :— nail.

H4931 מִשְׁמֶרֶת *mišmeret* feminine of H4929; *watch,* i.e. the act *(custody)* or (concretely) the *sentry,* the *post;* objectively *preservation,* or (concretely) *safe;* figuratively *observance,* i.e. (abstractly) *duty,* or (objectively) a *usage* or *party:*— charge, keep, to be kept, office, ordinance, safeguard, ward, watch.

H4932 מִשְׁנֶה *mišneh* from H8138; properly a *repetition,* i.e. a *duplicate (copy* of a document), or a *double* (in amount); by implication a *second* (in order, rank, age, quality or location):— college, copy, double, fatlings, next, second, second order, twice as much.

H4933 מְשִׁסָּה *mᵉšissâ* from H8155; *plunder:*— booty, spoil.

H4934 מִשְׁעוֹל *miš*ʿ*ôl* from the same as H8168; a *hollow*, i.e. a narrow passage:— path.

H4935 מִשְׁעִי *miš*ʿ*î* probably from H8159; *inspection:*— to supple.

H4936 מִשְׁעָם *miš*ʿ*ām* apparently from H8159; *inspection; Misham*, an Israelite:— Misham.

H4937 מִשְׁעֵן *miš*ʿ*ēn* or

מִשְׁעָן *miš*ʿ*ān* from H8172; a *support* (concretely), i.e. (figuratively) a *protector* or *sustenance* :— stay.

H4938 מִשְׁעֵנָה *miš*ʿ*ēnâ* or

מִשְׁעֶנֶת *miš*ʿ*enet* feminine of H4937; *support* (abstractly), i.e. (figuratively) *sustenance* or (concretely) a *walking-stick:*— staff.

H4939 מִשְׂפָּח *miśpāḥ* from H5596; *slaughter:*— oppression.

H4940 מִשְׁפָּחָה *mišpāḥâ* from H8192 [compare H8198]; a *family*, i.e. circle of relatives; figuratively a *class* (of persons), a *species* (of animals) or *sort* (of things); by extension a *tribe* or *people:*— family, kind, kindred.

H4941 מִשְׁפָּט *mišpāṭ* from H8199; properly a *verdict* (favorable or unfavorable) pronounced judicially, especially a *sentence* or formal decree (human or [particularly] divine *law*, individual or collective), including the act, the place, the suit, the crime, and the penalty; abstractly *justice*, including a particular *right*, or *privilege* (statutory or customary), or even a *style:*— adversary, ceremony, charge, crime, custom, desert, determination, discretion, disposing, due, fashion, form, to be judged, judgment, just, justice, justly, law, manner of law, lawful, manner, measure, order, due order, ordinance, right, sentence, usest, worthy, wrong.

H4942 מִשְׁפָּת *mišpāt* from H8192; a *stall* for cattle (only dual):— burden, sheepfold.

H4943 מֶשֶׁק *mešeq* from an unused root meaning to *hold; possession:*— steward.

H4944 מַשָּׁק *maššāq* from H8264; a *traversing*, i.e. rapid *motion:*— running to and fro.

H4945 מַשְׁקֶה *mašqeh* from H8248; properly *causing to drink*, i.e. a *butler;* by implication (intransitively) *drink* (itself); figuratively a *well-watered* region:— butler, butlership, cupbearer, drink, drinking, fat pasture, watered.

H4946 מִשְׁקוֹל *mišqôl* from H8254; *weight:*— weight.

H4947 מַשְׁקוֹף *mašqôp* from H8259 in its original sense of *overhanging;* a *lintel:*— lintel.

H4948 מִשְׁקָל *mišqāl* from H8254; *weight* (numerically estimated); hence, *weighing* (the act):— weight, full weight.

H4949 מִשְׁקֶלֶת *mišqelet* or

מִשְׁקֹלֶת *mišqōlet* feminine of H4948 or H4947; a *weight*, i.e. a *plummet* (with line attached):— plummet.

H4950 מִשְׁקָע *mišqāʿ* from H8257; a *settling* place (of water), i.e. a pond:— deep.

H4951 מִשְׂרָה *miśrâ* from H8280; *empire:*— government.

H4952 מִשְׁרָה *mišrâ* from H8281 in the sense of *loosening; maceration*, i.e. steeped *juice:*— liquor.

H4953 מַשְׁרוֹקִי *mašrôqî* (Aramaic) from a root corresponding to H8319; a (musical) *pipe* (from its *whistling* sound):— flute.

H4954 מִשְׁרָעִי *mišrāʿî* patrial from an unused noun from an unused root; probably meaning to *stretch* out; *extension;* a *Mishraite*, or inhabitant (collectively) of Mishra:— Mishraites.

H4955 מִשְׂרָפָה *miśrāpâ* from H8313; *combustion*, i.e. *cremation* (of a corpse), or *calcination* (of lime):— burning.

H4956 מִשְׂרְפוֹת מַיִם *miśrᵉpôt mayim* from the plural of H4955 and H4325; *burnings of water; Misrephoth-Majim*, a place in Palestine:— Misrephoth-mayim.

H4957 מַשְׂרֵקָה *maśrēqâ* a form for H7796 used denominatively; *vineyard; Masrekah*, a place in Idumaea:— Masrekah.

H4958 מַשְׂרֵת *maśrēt* apparently from an unused root meaning to *perforate*, i.e. hollow out; a *pan:*— pan.

H4959 מָשַׁשׁ *māšaš* a primitive root; to *feel* of; by implication to *grope:*— feel, grope, search.

H4960 מִשְׁתֶּה *mišteh* from H8354; *drink;* by implication *drinking* (the act); also (by implication), a *banquet* or (generally) feast:— banquet, drank, drink, feast, feasted, feasting.

H4961 מִשְׁתֶּה *mišteh* (Aramaic) corresponding to H4960; a *banquet:*— banquet.

H4962 מַת *mat* from the same as H4970; properly an *adult* (as of full length); by implication a *man* (only in the plural):— few, friends, men, persons, small.

H4963 מַתְבֵּן *matbēn* denominative from H8401; *straw* in the heap:— straw.

H4964 מֶתֶג *meteg* from an unused root meaning to *curb;* a *bit:*— bit, bridle.

H4965 מֶתֶג הָאַמָּה *meteg hāʾammâ* from H4964 and H520 with the article interposed; *bit of the metropolis; Metheg-ha-Ammah*, an epithet of Gath:— Metheg-ammah.

H4966 מָתוֹק *mātôq* or

מָתוּק *mātûq* from H4985; *sweet:*— sweet, sweeter, sweetness.

H4967 מְתוּשָׁאֵל *mᵉtûšāʾēl* from H4962 and H410, with the relative interposed; *man who* (is) *of God; Methushaël*, an antediluvian patriarch:— Methusael.

H4968 מְתוּשֶׁלַח *mᵉtûšelaḥ* from H4962 and H7973; *man of a dart; Methushelach*, an antediluvian patriarch:— Methuselah.

H4969 מָתַח *mātaḥ* a primitive root; to *stretch* out :— spread out.

H4970 מָתַי *mātay* from an unused root meaning to *extend;* properly *extent* (of time); but used only adverbially (especially with other particles prefixed), *when* (either relative or interrogative):— long, when.

H4971 מַתְכֹּנֶת *matkōnet* from H8505 in the transferred sense of *measuring; proportion* (in size, number or ingredients):— composition, measure, state, tale.

H4972 מַתְּלָאָה *mattᵉlāʾâ* from H4100 and H8513; *what a trouble!:*— what a weariness.

H4973 מְתַלְּעָה *mᵉtallᵉʿâ* contracted from H3216; properly a *biter*, i.e. a *tooth:*— cheek tooth, jaw tooth, jaw.

H4974 מְתֹם *mᵉtōm* from H8552; *wholesomeness;* also (adverbially) *completely:*— men *[by reading* H4962], soundness.

H4975 מֹתֶן *mōten* from an unused root meaning to *be slender;* properly the *waist* or small of the back; only in plural the *loins:*— greyhound, loins, side.

H4976 מַתָּן *mattān* from H5414; a *present:*— gift, to give, reward.

H4977 מַתָּן *mattān* the same as H4976; *Mattan*, the name of a priest of Baal, and of an Israelite:— Mattan.

H4978 מַתְּנָא *mattᵉnāʾ* (Aramaic) corresponding to H4979:— gift.

H4979 מַתָּנָה *mattānâ* feminine of H4976; a *present;* specifically (in a good sense) a sacrificial *offering*, (in a bad sense) a *bribe:*— gift.

H4980 מַתָּנָה *mattānâ* the same as H4979; *Mattanah*, a place in the Desert:— Mattanah.

H4981 מִתְנִי *mitnî* probably patrial from an unused noun meaning *slenderness;* a *Mithnite*, or inhabitant of Methen:— Mithnite.

H4982 מַתְּנַי *mattᵉnay* from H4976; *liberal; Mattenai*, the name of three Israelites:— Mattenai.

H4983 מַתַּנְיָה *mattanyâ* or

מַתַּנְיָהוּ *mattanyāhû* from H4976 and H3050; *gift of Jah; Mattanjah*, the name of ten Israelites:— Mattaniah.

H4984 מִתְנַשֵּׂא *mitnaśśēʾ* from H5375; (used as abstract) supreme *exaltation:*— exalted.

H4985 מָתַק *mātaq* a primitive root; to *suck;* by implication to *relish*, or (intransitive) *be sweet:*— be sweet, be made sweet, take sweet.

H4986 מֶתֶק *meteq* from H4985; figuratively *pleasantness* (of discourse):— sweetness.

H4987 מֹתֶק *mōteq* from H4985; *sweetness:*— sweetness.

H4988 מָתָק *mātāq* from H4985; a *dainty*, i.e. (generally) *food:*— feed sweetly.

H4989 מִתְקָה *mitqâ* feminine of H4987; *sweetness; Mithkah*, a place in the Desert:— Mithcah.

H4990 מִתְרְדָת *mitrᵉdāt* of Persian origin; *Mithredath*, the name of two Persians:— Mithredath.

H4991 מַתָּת *mattāt* feminine of H4976 abbreviated; a *present:*— gift.

H4992 מַתַּתָּה *mattattâ* for H4993; *gift of Jah; Mattattah*, an Israelite:— Mattathah.

H4993 מַתִּתְיָה *mattityâ* or

מַתִּתְיָהוּ *mattityāhû* from H4991 and H3050; *gift of Jah; Mattithjah*, the name of four Israelites:— Mattithiah.

נ

H4994 נָא *nāʾ* a primitive particle of incitement and entreaty, which may usually be rendered *I pray, now* or *then;* added mostly to verbs (in the imperative or future), or to interjections, occasionally to an adverb or conjunction:— I beseech thee, I pray, I pray thee, I pray you, go to, now, oh.

H4995 נָא *nāʾ* apparently from H5106 in the sense of *harshness* from refusal; properly *tough*, i.e. *uncooked* (flesh):— raw.

H4996 נֹא *nōʾ* of Egyptian origin; *No* (i.e. *Thebes*), the capital of Upper Egypt:— No. Compare H528

H4997 נֹאד *nōʾd* or

נֹאוד *nōʾwd* also (feminine)

נֹאדָה *nōʾdâ* from an unused root of uncertain signification; a (skin or leather) *bag* (for fluids):— bottle.

H4998 נָאָה *nāʾâ* a primitive root; properly to *be at home,* i.e. (by implication) to be *pleasant* (or *suitable*), i.e. *beautiful:*— be beautiful, become, be comely.

H4999 נָאָה *nāʾâ* from H4998; a *home;* figuratively a *pasture:*— habitation, house, pasture, pleasant place.

H5000 נָאוֶה *nāʾweh* from H4998 or H5116; *suitable,* or *beautiful:*— becometh, comely, seemly.

H5001 נָאַם *nāʾam* a primitive root; properly to *whisper,* i.e. (by implication) to *utter* as an oracle:— say.

H5002 נְאֻם *nĕʾūm* from H5001; an *oracle:*— said, hath said, saith.

H5003 נָאַף *nāʾap* a primitive root; to *commit adultery;* figuratively to *apostatize:*— adulterer, adulteress, commit adultery, commiting adultery, woman that breaketh wedlock.

H5004 נִאֻף *nīʾūp* from H5003; *adultery:*— adultery.

H5005 נַאֲפוּף *naʾăpûp* from H5003; *adultery:*— adultery.

H5006 נָאַץ *nāʾaṣ* a primitive root; to *scorn;* or (Eccl 12:5) by interchange for H5132, to *bloom:*— abhor, blaspheme, give occasion to blaspheme, contemn, despise, flourish, great, provoke.

H5007 נְאָצָה *nĕʾāṣâ* or

נֶאָצָה *neʾāṣâ* from H5006; *scorn:*— blasphemy.

H5008 נָאַק *nāʾaq* a primitive root; to *groan:*— groan.

H5009 נְאָקָה *nĕʾāqâ* from H5008; a *groan:*— *groaning.*

H5010 נָאַר *nāʾar* a primitive root; to *reject:*— abhor, make void.

H5011 נֹב *nōb* the same as H5108; *fruit; Nob,* a place in Palestine:— Nob.

H5012 נָבָא *nābāʾ* a primitive root; to *prophesy,* i.e. speak (or sing) by inspiration (in prediction or simple discourse):— prophesy, prophesying, make self a prophet.

H5013 נְבָא *nĕbāʾ* (Aramaic) corresponding to H5012:— prophesy.

H5014 נָבַב *nābab* a primitive root; to *pierce;* to *be hollow,* or (figuratively) *foolish:*— hollow, vain.

H5015 נְבוֹ *nĕbô* probably of foreign derivation; *Nebo,* the name of a Babylonian deity, also of a mountain in Moab, and of a place in Palestine:— Nebo.

H5016 נְבוּאָה *nĕbûʾâ* from H5012; a *prediction* (spoken or written):— prophecy.

H5017 נְבוּאָה *nĕbûʾâ* (Aramaic) corresponding to H5016; inspired *teaching:*— prophesying.

H5018 נְבוּזַרְאֲדָן *nĕbûzarʾădān* of foreign origin; *Nebuzaradan,* a Babylonian general:— Nebuzaradan.

H5019 נְבוּכַדְנֶאצַּר *nĕbûkadneʾṣṣar* or

נְבֻכַדְנֶאצַּר *nĕbûkadneʾṣṣar* (2 Kings 24:1, 10), or

נְבוּכַדְנֶצַּר *nĕbûkadneṣṣar* (Est. 2:6; Dan. 1:18), or

נְבוּכַדְרֶאצַּר *nĕbûkadreʾṣṣar* or

נְבוּכַדְרֶאצּוֹר *nĕbûkadreʾṣṣôr* (Ezra 2:1; Jer 49:28), of foreign derivation; *Nebukadnetstsar* (or *-retstsar,* or *-retstsor*), king of Babylon:— Nebuchadnezzar, Nebuchadrezzar.

H5020 נְבוּכַדְנֶצַּר *nĕbûkadneṣṣar* (Aramaic) corresponding to H5019:— Nebuchadnezzar.

H5021 נְבוּשַׁזְבָּן *nĕbûšazbān* of foreign derivation; *Nebushazban,* Nebuchadnezzar's chief eunuch:— Nebushazban.

H5022 נָבוֹת *nābôt* feminine plural from the same as H5011; *fruits; Naboth,* an Israelite:— Naboth.

H5023 נְבִזְבָּה *nĕbizbâ* (Aramaic) of uncertain derivation; a *largess:*— reward.

H5024 נָבַח *nābaḥ* a primitive root; to *bark* (as a dog):— bark.

H5025 נֹבַח *nōbaḥ* from H5024; a *bark; Nobach,* the name of an Israelite, and of a place east of the Jordan:— Nobah.

H5026 נִבְחַז *nibḥaz* of foreign origin; *Nibchaz,* a deity of the Avites:— Nibhaz.

H5027 נָבַט *nābaṭ* a primitive root; to *scan,* i.e. look intently at; by implication to *regard* with pleasure, favor or care:— behold, cause to behold, consider, look, look down, regard, have respect, see.

H5028 נְבָט *nĕbāṭ* from H5027; *regard; Nebat,* the father of Jeroboam I:— Nebat.

H5029 נְבִיא *nĕbîʾ* (Aramaic) corresponding to H5030; a *prophet:*— prophet.

H5030 נָבִיא *nābîʾ* from H5012; a *prophet* or (generally) *inspired* man:— prophecy, that prophesy, prophet.

H5031 נְבִיאָה *nĕbîʾâ* feminine of H5030; a *prophetess* or (generally) *inspired* woman; by implication a *poetess;* by association a *prophet's wife:*— prophetess.

H5032 נְבָיוֹת *nĕbāyôt* or

נְבָיֹת *nĕbāyōt* feminine plural from H5107; *fruitfulnesses; Nebajoth,* a son of Ishmael, and the country settled by him:— Nebaioth, Nebajoth.

H5033 נֵבֶךְ *nēbek* from an unused root meaning to *burst* forth; a *fountain:*— spring.

H5034 נָבֵל *nābēl* a primitive root; to *wilt;* generally to *fall* away, *fail, faint;* figuratively to *be foolish* or (morally) *wicked;* causatively to *despise, disgrace:*— disgrace, dishonour, lightly esteem, fade, fade away, fading, fall down, falling, fall off, do foolishly, come to nought, surely, make vile, wither.

H5035 נֶבֶל *nebel* or

נֵבֶל *nēbel* from H5034; a skin-*bag* for liquids (from *collapsing* when empty); hence, a *vase* (as similar in shape when full); also a *lyre* (as having a body of like form):— bottle, pitcher, psaltery, vessel, viol.

H5036 נָבָל *nābāl* from H5034; *stupid; wicked* (especially *impious*):— fool, foolish, foolish man, foolish woman, vile person.

H5037 נָבָל *nābāl* the same as H5036; *dolt; Nabal,* an Israelite:— Nabal.

H5038 נְבֵלָה *nĕbēlâ* from H5034; a *flabby* thing, i.e. a *carcase* or *carrion* (human or bestial, often collectively); figuratively an *idol:*— body, dead body, carcase, dead carcase, dead of itself, which died, beast that dieth of itself, which dieth of itself.

H5039 נְבָלָה *nĕbālâ* feminine of H5036; *foolishness,* i.e. (morally) *wickedness;* concretely a *crime;* by extension *punishment:*— folly, vile, villany.

H5040 נַבְלוּת *nablût* from H5036; properly *disgrace,* i.e. the (female) *pudenda:*— lewdness.

H5041 נְבַלָּט *nĕballāṭ* apparently from H5036 and H3909; *foolish secrecy; Neballat,* a place in Palestine:— Neballat.

H5042 נָבַע *nābaᶜ* a primitive root; to *gush* forth; figuratively to *utter* (good or bad words); specifically to *emit* (a foul odor):— belch out, flowing, pour out, send forth, utter, utter abundantly.

H5043 נֶבְרְשָׁא *nebraštāʾ* (Aramaic) from an unused root meaning to *shine;* a *light;* plural (collectively) a *chandelier:*— candlestick.

H5044 נִבְשָׁן *nibšān* of uncertain derivation; *Nibshan,* a place in Palestine:— Nibshan.

H5045 נֶגֶב *negeb* from an unused root meaning to *be parched;* the *south* (from its drought); specifically the *Negeb* or southern district of Judah, occasionally, *Egypt* (as south to Palestine):— south, south country, south side, southward.

H5046 נָגַד *nāgad* a primitive root; properly to *front,* i.e. stand boldly out opposite; by implication (causatively), to *manifest;* figuratively to *announce* (always by word of mouth to one present); specifically to *expose, predict, explain, praise:*— bewray, certainly, certify, declare, declaring, denounce, expound, fully, messenger, plainly, profess, rehearse, report, shew, shew forth, speak, surely, tell, utter.

H5047 נְגַד *nĕgad* (Aramaic) corresponding to H5046; to *flow* (through the idea of *clearing* the way):— issue.

H5048 נֶגֶד *neged* from H5046; a *front,* i.e. part opposite; specifically a *counterpart,* or mate; usually (adverbially, especially with preposition) *over against* or *before:*— about, against, over against, aloof, far, far off, from, over, presence, other side, sight, to view.

H5049 נֶגֶד *neged* (Aramaic) corresponding to H5048; *opposite:*— toward.

H5050 נָגַהּ *nāgah* a primitive root; to *glitter;* causatively to *illuminate:*— lighten, enlighten, shine, cause to shine.

H5051 נֹגַהּ *nōgah* the same as H5051; *Nogah,* a son of David:— Nogah.

H5052 נֹגַהּ *nōgah* the same as H5051; *Nogah,* a son of David:— Nogah.

H5053 נֹגַהּ *nōgah* (Aramaic) corresponding to H5051; *dawn:*— morning.

H5054 נְגֹהָה *nĕgōhâ* feminine of H5051; *splendor* :— brightness.

H5055 נָגַח *nāgaḥ* a primitive root; to *but* with the horns; figuratively to *war* against:— gore, push, push down, pushing.

H5056 נַגָּח *naggāḥ* from H5055; *butting,* i.e. *vicious* :— used to push, wont to push.

H5057 נָגִיד *nāgîd* or

נָגִד *nāgîd* from H5046; a *commander* (as occupying the *front*), civil, military or religious; generally (abstract plural), *honorable* themes:— captain, chief, excellent thing, governor, chief governor, leader, noble, prince, ruler, chief ruler.

H5058 נְגִינָה *nĕgînâ* or

נְגִינַת *nĕgînat* (Ps 61:title), from H5059; properly instrumental *music;* by implication a stringed *instrument;* by extension a *poem* set to music; specifically an *epigram:*— stringed instrument, musick, Neginoth *[plural]*, song.

H5059 נָגַן *nāgan* a primitive root; properly to *thrum*, i.e. *beat* a tune with the fingers; especially to *play* on a stringed instrument; hence (generally) to *make music* :— player on instruments, sing to the stringed instruments, melody, minstrel, play, player, playing.

H5060 נָגַע *nāgaᶜ* a primitive root; properly to *touch*, i.e. *lay the hand upon* (for any purpose; euphemistically, to *lie with* a woman); by implication to *reach* (figuratively to *arrive, acquire*); violently, to *strike* (punish, defeat, destroy, etc.):— beat, bring, be able to bring, bring down, cast, come, come nigh, draw near, draw nigh, get up, happen, join, near, plague, reach, reach up, smite, strike, touch.

H5061 נֶגַע *negaᶜ* from H5060; a *blow* (figuratively *infliction*); also (by implication) a *spot* (concretely a *leprous* person or dress):— plague, sore, stricken, stripe, stroke, wound.

H5062 נָגַף *nāgap* a primitive root; to *push, gore, defeat, stub* (the toe), *inflict* (a disease):— beat, dash, hurt, plague, slay, smite, smite down, strike, stumble, surely, put to the worse.

H5063 נֶגֶף *negep* from H5062; a *trip* (of the foot); figuratively an *infliction* (of disease):— plague, stumbling.

H5064 נָגַר *nāgar* a primitive root; to *flow;* figuratively to *stretch* out; causatively to *pour* out or down; figuratively to *deliver* over:— fall, flow away, pour down, pour out, run, shed, spilt, trickle down.

H5065 נָגַשׂ *nāgaś* a primitive root; to *drive* (an animal, a workman, a debtor, an army); by implication to *tax, harass, tyrannize:*— distress, driver, exact, exactor, oppress, oppressor, raiser of taxes, taskmaster.

H5066 נָגַשׁ *nāgaš* a primitive root; to *be* or *come* (causatively *bring*) *near* (for any purpose); euphemistically to *lie with* a woman; as an enemy, to *attack;* religiously to *worship;* causatively to *present;* figuratively to *adduce* an argument; by reversal, to *stand back:*— approach, make to approach, approach nigh, bring, bring forth, bring hither, bring near, come, cause to come near, come hither, come near, come nigh, give place, go hard, go up, be near, draw near, go near, draw nigh, offer, overtake, present, put, stand.

H5067 נֵד *nēd* from H5110 in the sense of *piling* up; a *mound*, i.e. *wave:*— heap.

H5068 נָדַב *nādab* a primitive root; to *impel;* hence to *volunteer* (as a soldier), to *present* spontaneously:— offer freely, be willing, give willingly, make willing, offer self willingly.

H5069 נְדַב *nědab* (Aramaic) corresponding to H5068; *be* (or *give*) *liberal (-ly)*:— be minded of . . . own freewill, freewill offering, offer freely, offer willingly.

H5070 נָדָב *nādāb* from H5068; *liberal; Nadab*, the name of four Israelites:— Nadab.

H5071 נְדָבָה *nědābâ* from H5068; properly (abstractly) *spontaneity*, or (adjectivally) *spontaneous;* also (concretely) a *spontaneous* or (by inference, in plural) *abundant* gift:— free offering, freewill offering, freely, plentiful, voluntary, voluntarily, voluntary offering, willing, willingly, willing offering.

H5072 נְדַבְיָה *nědabyâ* from H5068 and H3050; *largess of Jah; Nedabjah*, an Israelite:— Nedabiah.

H5073 נִדְבָּךְ *nidbāk* (Aramaic) from a root meaning to *stick;* a *layer* (of building materials):— row.

H5074 נָדַד *nādad* a primitive root; properly to *wave* to and fro (rarely to *flap* up and down); figuratively to *rove, flee*, or (causatively) to *drive* away:— chase, chase away, could not, depart, flee, flee apace, flee away, move, remove, thrust away, wander, wander abroad, wanderer, wandering.

H5075 נְדַד *nědad* (Aramaic) corresponding to H5074; to *depart:*— go from.

H5076 נָדֻד *nādūd* passive participle of H5074; properly *tossed;* abstractly a *rolling* (on the bed) :— tossing to and fro.

H5077 נָדָה *nādâ* or

נָדָא *nādāʾ* (2 Kings 17:21), a primitive root; properly to *toss;* figuratively to *exclude*, i.e. banish, postpone, prohibit:— cast out, drive, put far away.

H5078 נֵדֶה *nēdeh* from H5077 in the sense of freely *flinging* money; a *bounty* (for prostitution):— gifts.

H5079 נִדָּה *niddâ* from H5074; properly *rejection;* by implication *impurity*, especially personal (menstruation) or moral (idolatry, incest):— far, filthiness, flowers, menstruous, menstruous woman, put apart, removed, removed woman, separation, set apart, uncleanness, unclean thing, unclean with filthiness.

H5080 נָדַח *nādaḥ* a primitive root; to *push* off; used in a great variety of applications, literally and figuratively (to expel, mislead, strike, inflict, etc.):— banish, bring, cast down, cast out, chase, compel, draw away, drive, drive away, drive out, drive quite, fetch a stroke, force, go away, outcast, thrust away, thrust out, withdraw.

H5081 נָדִיב *nādîb* from H5068; properly *voluntary*, i.e. generous; hence, *magnanimous;* as noun, a *grandee* (sometimes a *tyrant*):— free, liberal, liberal things, noble, prince, willing, willinghearted.

H5082 נְדִיבָה *nědîbâ* feminine of H5081; properly *nobility*, i.e. reputation:— soul.

H5083 נָדָן *nādān* probably from an unused root meaning to *give;* a *present* (for prostitution):— gift.

H5084 נָדָן *nādān* of uncertain derivation; a *sheath* (of a sword):— sheath.

H5085 נִדְנֶה *nidneh* (Aramaic) from the same as H5084; a *sheath;* figuratively the *body* (as the receptacle of the soul):— body.

H5086 נָדַף *nādap* a primitive root; to *shove* asunder, i.e. *disperse:*— drive, drive away, drive to and fro, thrust down, shaken, tossed to and fro.

H5087 נָדַר *nādar* a primitive root; to *promise* (positively, to do or give something to God):— vow, make a vow.

H5088 נֶדֶר *neder* or

נֵדֶר *nēder* from H5087; a *promise* (to God); also (concretely) a thing *promised:*— vow, vowed.

H5089 נֹהַּ *nōah* from an unused root meaning to *lament; lamentation:*— wailing.

H5090 נָהַג *nāhag* a primitive root; to *drive* forth (a person, an animal or chariot), i.e. *lead, carry away;* reflexively to *proceed* (i.e. impel or guide oneself); also (from the *panting* induced by effort), to *sigh:*— acquaint, bring, bring away, carry away, drive, drive away, lead, lead away, lead forth, guide, be guide.

H5091 נָהָה *nāhâ* a primitive root; to *groan*, i.e. *bewail;* hence (through the idea of *crying* aloud) to *assemble* (as if on proclamation):— lament, wail.

H5092 נְהִי *něhî* from H5091; an *elegy:*— lamentation, wailing.

H5093 נִהְיָה *nihyâ* feminine of H5092; *lamentation* :— doleful.

H5094 נְהִיר *něhîr* (Aramaic) from the same as H5105; *illumination*, i.e. (figuratively) wisdom:— light.

H5095 נָהַל *nāhal* a primitive root; properly to run with a *sparkle*, i.e. *flow;* hence (transitively) to *conduct*, and (by inference) to *protect, sustain:*— carry, feed, guide, lead, lead gently, lead on.

H5096 נַהֲלָל *nahălāl* or

נַהֲלֹל *nahălōl* the same as H5097; *Nahalal* or *Nahalol*, a place in Palestine:— Nahalal, Nahallal, Nahalol.

H5097 נַהֲלֹל *nahălōl* from H5095; *pasture:*— bush.

H5098 נָהַם *nāham* a primitive root; to *growl:*— mourn, roar, roaring.

H5099 נַהַם *naham* from H5098; a *snarl:*— roaring.

H5100 נְהָמָה *něhāmâ* feminine of H5099; *snarling* :— disquietness, roaring.

H5101 נָהַק *nāhaq* a primitive root; to *bray* (as an ass), *scream* (from hunger):— bray.

H5102 נָהַר *nāhar* a primitive root; to *sparkle*, i.e. (figuratively) *be cheerful;* hence (from the *sheen* of a running stream) to *flow*, i.e. (figuratively) *assemble:*— flow, flow together, be lightened.

H5103 נְהַר *něhar* (Aramaic) from a root corresponding to H5102; a *river*, especially the Euphrates:— river, stream.

H5104 נָהָר *nāhār* from H5102; a *stream* (including the *sea;* especially the Nile, Euphrates, etc.); figuratively, *prosperity:*— flood, river.

H5105 נְהָרָה *něhārâ* from H5102 in its original sense; *daylight:*— light.

H5106 נוּא *nûʾ* a primitive root; to *refuse, forbid, dissuade*, or *neutralize:*— break, disallow, discourage, make of none effect.

H5107 נוּב *nûb* a primitive root; to *germinate*, i.e. (figuratively) to (causatively *make*) *flourish;* also (of words), to *utter:*— bring forth, bring forth fruit, make cheerful, increase.

H5108 נוֹב *nôb* or

נֵיב *nêb* from H5107; *produce*, literally or figuratively:— fruit.

H5109 נוֹבַי *nôbay* from H5108; *fruitful; Nobai*, an Israelite:— Nebai *[from the margin]*.

H5110 נוּד *nûd* a primitive root; to *nod*, i.e. waver; figuratively to *wander, flee, disappear;* also (from *shaking* the head in sympathy), to *console, deplore*, or (from *tossing* the head in scorn) *taunt:*— bemoan, flee, get, mourn, make to move, take pity, remove, shake, skip for joy, be sorry, vagabond, way, wandering.

H5111 נוּד *nûd* (Aramaic) corresponding to H5116; to *flee:*— get away.

H5112 נוֹד *nôdd* only defectively

נֹד *nōd* from H5110; *exile:*— wandering.

H5113 נוֹד *nôd* the same as H5112; *vagrancy; Nod*, the land of Cain:— Nod.

H5114 נוֹדָב *nôdāb* from H5068; *noble; Nodab*, an Arab tribe:— Nodab.

H5115 נָוָה *nāḥâ* a primitive root; to *rest* (as at home); causatively (through the implied idea of *beauty* [comparative H5116]), to *celebrate* (with praises):— keep at home, prepare an habitation.

H5116 נָוֶה *nāweh* or (feminine)

נָוָה *nāwâ* from H5115; (adjectivally) *at home;* hence (by implication of satisfaction) *lovely;* also (noun) a *home,* of God (temple), men (residence), flocks (pasture), or wild animals *(den)*:— comely, dwelling, dwellingplace, fold, habitation, pleasant place, sheepcote, stable, tarried.

H5117 נוּחַ *nûaḥ* a primitive root; to *rest,* i.e. *settle* down; used in a great variety of applications, literally and figuratively, intransitively, transitively and causatively (to *dwell, stay, let fall, place, let alone, withdraw, give comfort,* etc.):— cease, be confederate, lay, let down, quiet, be quiet, remain, rest, cause to rest, be at rest, give rest, have rest, make to rest, set down. Compare H3241

H5118 נוּחַ *nûaḥ* or

נוֹחַ *nôaḥ* from H5117; *quiet:*— rest, rested, resting place.

H5119 נוֹחָה *nôḥâ* feminine of H5118; *quietude; Nochah,* an Israelite:— Nohah.

H5120 נוּט *nûṭ* to *quake*:— be moved.

H5121 נָוִית *nawît* from H5115; *residence; Navith,* a place in Palestine:— Naioth *[from the margin]*.

H5122 נְוָלוּ *nĕwālû* or

נְוָלִי *nĕwālî* (Aramaic) from an unused root probably meaning to be *foul;* a *sink:*— dunghill.

H5123 נוּם *nûm* a primitive root; to *slumber* (from drowsiness):— sleep, slumber.

H5124 נוּמָה *nûmâ* from H5123; *sleepiness:*— drowsiness.

H5125 נוּן *nûn* a primitive root; to *resprout,* i.e. propagate by shoots; figuratively, to *be perpetual:*— be continued.

H5126 נוּן *nûn* or

נוֹן *nôn* (1 Chron 7:27), from H5125; *perpetuity; Nun* or *Non,* the father of Joshua:— Non, Nun.

H5127 נוּס *nûs* a primitive root; to *flit,* i.e. *vanish* away (subside, escape; causatively chase, impel, deliver):— abate, away, be displayed, flee, make to flee, flee away, fleeing, put to flight, hide, lift up a standard.

H5128 נוּעַ *nûa*ᶜ a primitive root; to *waver,* in a great variety of applications, literally and figuratively (as subjoined):— continually, fugitive, make to go up and down, be gone away, move, be moveable, be moved, be promoted, reel, remove, scatter, set, shake, sift, stagger, to and fro, be vagabond, wag, wander, make wander, wander up and down.

H5129 נוֹעַדְיָה *nô*ᶜ*adyâ* from H3259 and H3050; *convened of Jah; Noädjah,* the name of an Israelite, and a false prophetess:— Noadiah.

H5130 נוּף *nûp* a primitive root; to *quiver* (i.e. *vibrate* up and down, or *rock* to and fro); used in a great variety of applications (including sprinkling, beckoning, rubbing, bastinadoing, sawing, waving, etc.):— lift up, move, offer, perfume, send, shake, sift, strike, wave.

H5131 נוֹף *nôp* from H5130; *elevation:*— situation. Compare H5297

H5132 נוּץ *nûṣ* a primitive root; properly to *flash;* hence, to *blossom* (from the brilliancy of color); also, to *fly* away (from the quickness of motion):— flee away, bud, bud forth.

H5133 נוֹצָה *nôṣâ* or

נֹצָה *nōṣâ* feminine active participle of H5327 in the sense of *flying;* a *pinion* (or wing feather); often (collectively) *plumage:*— feather, feathers, ostrich.

H5134 נוּק *nûq* a primitive root; to *suckle:*— nurse.

H5135 נוּר *nûr* (Aramaic) from an unused root (corresponding to that of H5216) meaning to *shine; fire:*— fiery, fire.

H5136 נוּשׁ *nûš* a primitive root; to *be sick,* i.e. (figuratively) *distressed:*— be full of heaviness.

H5137 נָזָה *nāzâ* a primitive root; to *spirt,* i.e. *besprinkle* (especially in expiation):— sprinkle.

H5138 נָזִיד *nāzîd* from H2102; something *boiled,* i.e. *soup:*— pottage.

H5139 נָזִיר *nāzîr* or

נָזִר *nāzīr* from H5144; *separate,* i.e. consecrated (as *prince, a Nazirite); hence (figuratively from the latter) an unpruned vine (like an unshorn Nazirite):— Nazarite [by a false alliteration with Nazareth], separate, seperated, vine undressed.*

H5140 נָזַל *nāzal* a primitive root; to *drip,* or *shed* by trickling:— distil, drop, flood, flow, cause to flow, flowing, gush out, melt, pour, pour down, running water, stream.

H5141 נֶזֶם *nezem* from an unused root of uncertain meaning; a nose-*ring:*— earring, jewel.

H5142 נְזַק *nĕzaq* (Aramaic) corresponding to the root of H5143; to *suffer* (causatively *inflict*) *loss:*— have damage, endamage, hurt, hurtful.

H5143 נֵזֶק *nēzeq* from an unused root meaning to *injure; loss:*— damage.

H5144 נָזַר *nāzar* a primitive root; to *hold aloof,* i.e. (intransitively) *abstain* (from food and drink, from impurity, and even from divine worship [i.e. *apostatize*]); specifically to *set apart* (to sacred purposes), i.e. *devote:*— consecrate, separate, seperating, self.

H5145 נֶזֶר *nezer* or

נֵזֶר *nēzer* from H5144; properly something *set apart,* i.e. (abstractly) *dedication* (of a priest or Nazirite); hence (concretely) unshorn *locks;* also (by implication) a *chaplet* (especially of royalty):— consecration, crown, hair, separation.

H5146 נֹחַ *nōaḥ* the same as H5118; *rest; Noäch,* the patriarch of the flood:— Noah.

H5147 נַחְבִּי *naḥbî* from H2247; *occult; Nachbi,* an Israelite:— Nakbi.

H5148 נָחָה *nāḥâ* a primitive root; to *guide;* by implication to *transport* (into exile, or as colonists):— bestow, bring, govern, guide, lead, lead forth, put, straiten.

H5149 נְחוּם *nĕḥûm* from H5162; *comforted; Nechum,* an Israelite:— Nehum.

H5150 נִחוּם *niḥûm* or

נִחֻם *niḥūm* from H5162; properly *consoled;* abstractly *solace:*— comfort, comfortable, repenting.

H5151 נַחוּם *naḥûm* from H5162; *comfortable; Nachum,* an Israelite prophet:— Nahum.

H5152 נָחוֹר *nāḥôr* from the same as H5170; *snorer; Nachor,* the name of the grandfather and a brother of Abraham:— Nahor.

H5153 נָחוּשׁ *nāḥûš* apparently passive participle of H5172 (perhaps in the sense of *ringing,* i.e. bell-metal; or from the *red* color of the throat of a serpent [H5175, as denominative] when hissing); *coppery,* i.e. (figuratively) hard:— of brass.

H5154 נְחוּשָׁה *nĕḥûšâ* or

נְחֻשָׁה *nĕḥūšâ* feminine of H5153; *copper:*— brass, steel. Compare H5176

H5155 נְחִילָה *nĕḥîlâ* probably denominative from H2485; a *flute:*— *[plural]* Nehiloth.

H5156 נְחִיר *nĕḥîr* from the same as H5170; a *nostril:*— *[dual]* nostrils.

H5157 נָחַל *nāḥal* a primitive root; to *inherit* (as a [figuratively] mode of descent), or (generally) to *occupy;* causatively to *bequeath,* or (generally) *distribute, instate:*— divide, have, have inheritance, take as an heritage, inherit, cause to inherit, give to inherit, make to inherit, distribute for inheritance, divide inheritance, divide for inheritance, divide for an inheritance, divide by inheritance, give for inheritance, have inheritance, leave for inheritance, take inheritance, take for inheritance, possess, have in possession, cause to possess, be made to possess.

H5158 נַחַל *naḥal* or (feminine)

נַחְלָה *naḥălâ* (Ezek 47:19; 48:28), from H5157 in its original sense; a *stream,* especially a winter *torrent;* (by implication) a (narrow) *valley* (in which a brook runs); also a *shaft* (of a mine):— brook, flood, river, stream, valley.

H5159 נַחֲלָה *naḥălâ* from H5157 (in its usual sense); properly something *inherited,* i.e. (abstractly) *occupancy,* or (concretely) an *heirloom;* generally an *estate, patrimony* or *portion:*— heritage, to inherit, inheritance, possession. Compare H5158

H5160 נַחֲלִיאֵל *naḥălî*ᵓ*ēl* from H5158 and H410; *valley of God; Nachaliël,* a place in the Desert:— Nahaliel.

H5161 נֶחֱלָמִי *neḥĕlāmî* apparently a patronymic from an unused name (apparently passive participle of H2492); *dreamed;* a *Nechelamite,* or descendant of Nechlam:— Nehelamite.

H5162 נָחַם *nāḥam* a primitive root; properly to *sigh,* i.e. *breathe* strongly; by implication to *be sorry,* i.e. (in a favorable sense) to *pity, console* or (reflexively) *rue;* or (unfavorably) to *avenge* (oneself):— comfort, comfort self, ease one's self, repent, repenter, repenting, repent self.

H5163 נַחַם *naḥam* from H5162; *consolation; Nacham,* an Israelite:— Naham.

H5164 נֹחַם *nōḥam* from H5162; *ruefulness,* i.e. desistance:— repentance.

H5165 נֶחָמָה *neḥāmâ* from H5162; *consolation:*— comfort.

H5166 נְחֶמְיָה *nĕḥemyâ* from H5162 and H3050; *consolation of Jah; Nechemjah,* the name of three Israelites:— Nehemiah.

H5167 נַחֲמָנִי *naḥămānî* from H5162; *consolatory; Nachamani,* an Israelite:— Nahamani.

H5168 נַחְנוּ *naḥnû* for H587; *we:*— we.

H5169 נָחַץ *nāḥaṣ* a primitive root; to *be urgent:*— require haste.

H5170 נַחַר *naḥar* and (feminine)

נַחֲרָה *naḥărâ* from an unused root meaning to *snort* or *snore;* a *snorting:*— nostrils, snorting.

H5171 נַחֲרַי *naḥăray* or

נַחְרַי *naḥray* from the same as H5170; *snorer; Nacharai* or *Nachrai,* an Israelite:— Naharai, Nahari.

H5172 נָחַשׁ *nāḥaš* a primitive root; properly to *hiss,* i.e. *whisper* a (magic) spell; generally to *prognosticate:*— certainly, divine, enchanter, enchantment, use enchantment, learn by experience, indeed, diligently observe.

H5173 נַחַשׁ *naḥaš* from H5172; an *incantation* or *augury:*— enchantment.

H5174 נְחָשׁ *nĕḥāš* (Aramaic) corresponding to H5154; *copper:*— brass.

H5175 נָחָשׁ *nāḥāš* from H5172; a *snake* (from its *hiss*):— serpent.

H5176 נָחָשׁ *nāḥāš* the same as H5175; *Nachash,* the name of two persons apparently non-Israelites:— Nahash.

H5177 נַחְשׁוֹן *naḥšôn* from H5172; *enchanter; Nachshon,* an Israelite:— Naashon, Nahshon.

H5178 נְחֹשֶׁת *nĕḥōšet* for H5154; *copper;* hence, something made of that metal, i.e. *coin,* a *fetter;* figuratively *base* (as compared with gold or silver):— brasen, brass, chain, copper, fetter, fetter of brass, filthiness, steel.

H5179 נְחֻשְׁתָּא *nĕḥuštā*ʾ from H5178; *copper; Nechushta,* an Israelitess:— Nehushta.

H5180 נְחֻשְׁתָּן *nĕḥuštān* from H5178; something made of *copper,* i.e. the copper *serpent* of the Desert:— Nehushtan.

H5181 נָחַת *nāḥat* a primitive root; to *sink,* i.e. *descend;* causatively, to *press* or *lead* down:— be broken, come down, cause to come down, enter, go down, press sore, settle, stick fast.

H5182 נְחַת *nĕḥat* (Aramaic) corresponding to H5181; to *descend;* causatively, to *bring away, deposit, depose:*— carry, come down, depose, lay up, place.

H5183 נַחַת *naḥat* from H5182; a *descent,* i.e. imposition, unfavorable *(punishment)* or favorable *(food)*; also (intransitively; perhaps from H5117), *restfulness:*— lighting down, quiet, quietness, to rest, be set on.

H5184 נַחַת *naḥat* the same as H5183; *quiet; Nachath,* the name of an Edomite and of two Israelites:— Nahath.

H5185 נָחֵת *nāḥēt* from H5181; *descending:*— come down.

H5186 נָטָה *nāṭâ* a primitive root; to *stretch* or spread out; by implication to *bend* away (including moral deflection); used in a great variety of application (as follows):— afternoon, apply, bow, bow down, bowing, carry aside, decline, deliver, extend, go down, be gone, incline, intend, lay, let down, offer, outstretched, overthrown, pervert, pitch, prolong, put away, shew, spread, spread out, stretch, stretch forth, stretch out, take, take aside, turn turn aside, turn away, wrest, cause to yield.

H5187 נְטִיל *nĕṭîl* from H5190; *laden:*— that bear.

H5188 נְטִיפָה *nĕṭîpâ* from H5197; a *pendant* for the ears (especially of pearls):— chain, collar.

H5189 נְטִישָׁה *nĕṭîšâ* from H5203; a *tendril* (as an offshoot):— battlement, branch, plant.

H5190 נָטַל *nāṭal* a primitive root; to *lift;* by implication to *impose:*— bear, offer, take up.

H5191 נְטַל *nĕṭal* (Aramaic) corresponding to H5190; to *raise:*— take up.

H5192 נֵטֶל *nēṭel* from H5190; a *burden:*— weighty.

H5193 נָטַע *nāṭa*ᶜ a primitive root; properly to *strike* in, i.e. *fix;* specifically to *plant* (literally or figuratively):— fastened, plant, planter.

H5194 נֶטַע *neṭa*ᶜ from H5193; a *plant;* collectively, a *plantation;* abstractly, a *planting:*— plant.

H5195 נָטִיעַ *nāṭîa*ᶜ from H5193; a *plant:*— plant.

H5196 נְטָעִים *nĕṭā*ᶜ*îm* plural of H5194; *Netaïm,* a place in Palestine:— plants.

H5197 נָטַף *nāṭap* a primitive root; to *ooze,* i.e. *distil* gradually; by implication to *fall in drops;* figuratively to *speak* by inspiration:— drop, dropping, prophesy, prophet.

H5198 נָטָף *nāṭāp* from H5197; a *drop;* specifically, an aromatic *gum* (probably *stacte*):— drop, stacte.

H5199 נְטֹפָה *nĕṭōpâ* from H5197; *distillation; Netophah,* a place in Palestine:— Netophah.

H5200 נְטֹפָתִי *nĕṭōpātî* patronymic from H5199; a *Netophathite,* or inhabitant of Netophah:— Netophathite.

H5201 נָטַר *nāṭar* a primitive root; to *guard;* figuratively to *cherish* (anger):— bear grudge, keep, keeper, reserve.

H5202 נְטַר *nĕṭar* (Aramaic) corresponding to H5201; to *retain:*— keep.

H5203 נָטַשׁ *nāṭaš* a primitive root; properly to *pound,* i.e. *smite;* by implication (as if beating out, and thus expanding) to *disperse;* also, to *thrust* off, down, out or upon (including *reject, let alone, permit, remit,* etc.):— cast off, drawn, let fall, forsake, join battle, leave, leave off, lie still, loose, spread self, spread abroad, stretch out, suffer.

H5204 נִי *nî* a doubtful word; apparently from H5091; *lamentation:*— wailing.

H5205 נִיד *nîd* from H5110; *motion* (of the lips in speech):— moving.

H5206 נִידָה *nîdâ* feminine of H5205; *removal,* i.e. exile:— removed.

H5207 נִיחוֹחַ *nîḥôaḥ* or

נִיחֹחַ *nîḥōaḥ* from H5117; properly *restful,* i.e. *pleasant;* abstractly *delight:*— sweet, sweet odour.

H5208 נִיחוֹחַ *nîḥôaḥ* or (shorter)

נִיחֹחַ *nîḥōaḥ* (Aramaic) corresponding to H5207; *pleasure:*— sweet odour, sweet savour.

H5209 נִין *nîn* from H5125; *progeny:*— son.

H5210 נִינְוֵה *nînĕwēh* of foreign origin; *Nineveh,* the capital of Assyria:— Nineveh.

H5211 נִיס *nîs* from H5127; *fugitive:*— that fleeth.

H5212 נִיסָן *nîsān* probably of foreign origin; *Nisan,* the first month of the Jewish sacred year:— Nisan.

H5213 נִיצוֹץ *nîṣôṣ* from H5340; a *spark:*— spark.

H5214 נִיר *nîr* a root probably identical with that of H5216, through the idea of the *gleam* of a fresh furrow; to *till* the soil:— break up.

H5215 נִיר *nîr* or

נִר *nīr* from H5214; properly *ploughing,* i.e. (concretely) freshly *ploughed* land:— fallow ground, ploughing, tillage.

H5216 נִיר *nîr* or

נִר *nīr* also

נֵיר *nêr* or

נֵר *nēr* or (feminine)

נֵרָה *nērâ* from a primitive root [see H5214; H5135] properly meaning to *glisten;* a *lamp* (i.e. the burner) or *light* (literally or figuratively):— candle, lamp, light.

H5217 נָכָא *nākā*ʾ a primitive root; to *smite,* i.e. *drive* away:— be viler.

H5218 נָכֵא *nākē*ʾ or

נָכָא *nākā*ʾ from H5217; *smitten,* i.e. (figuratively) *afflicted:*— broken, stricken, wounded.

H5219 נְכֹאת *nĕkōʾt* from H5218; properly a *smiting,* i.e. (concretely) an aromatic *gum* [perhaps *styrax]* (as *powdered*):— spicery, spices.

H5220 נֶכֶד *neked* from an unused root meaning to *propagate; offspring:*— nephew, son's son.

H5221 נָכָה *nākâ* a primitive root; to *strike* (lightly or severely, literally or figuratively):— beat, cast forth, clap, give wounds, go forward, indeed, kill, make slaughter, murderer, punish, slaughter, slay, slayer, slaying, smite, smiter, smiting, strike, be stricken, stripes, give stripes, surely, wound.

H5222 נֵכֶה *nēkeh* from H5221; a *smiter,* i.e. (figuratively) *traducer:*— abject.

H5223 נָכֶה *nākeh smitten;* i.e. (literally) maimed, or (figuratively) dejected:— contrite, lame.

H5224 נְכוֹ *nĕkô* probably of Egyptian origin; *Neko* an Egyptian king:— Necho. Compare H6549

H5225 נָכוֹן *nākôn* from H3559; *prepared; Nakon,* probably an Israelite:— Nachon.

H5226 נֵכַח *nēkaḥ* from an unused root meaning to *be straightforward;* properly the *fore* part; used adverbially, *opposite:*— before, over against.

H5227 נֹכַח *nōkaḥ* from the same as H5226; properly, the *front* part; used adverbially (especially with preposition), *opposite, in front of, forward, in behalf of:*— against, over against, before, directly, for, right, right on.

H5228 נָכֹחַ *nākōaḥ* from the same as H5226; *straightforward,* i.e. (figuratively), *equitable, correct,* or (abstractly), *integrity:*— plain, right, uprightness.

H5229 נְכֹחָה *nĕkōḥâ* feminine of H5228; properly *straightforwardness,* i.e. (figuratively) *integrity,* or (concretely) *a truth:*— equity, right, right thing, uprightness.

H5230 נָכַל *nākal* a primitive root; to *defraud,* i.e. *act treacherously:*— beguile, conspire, deceiver, deal subtilly.

H5231 נֵכֶל *nēkel* from H5230; *deceit:*— wile.

H5232 נְכַס *nĕkas* (Aramaic) corresponding to H5233 :— goods.

H5233 נֶכֶס *nekes* from an unused root meaning to *accumulate; treasure:*— riches, wealth.

H5234 נָכַר *nākar* a primitive root; properly to *scrutinize,* i.e. look intently at; hence (with *recognition* implied), to *acknowledge, be acquainted with, care for, respect, revere,* or (with *suspicion* implied), to *disregard, ignore, be strange* toward, *reject, resign, dissimulate* (as if ignorant or disowning):— acknowledge, could, deliver, discern, dissemble, estrange, feign self to be another, know, take knowledge, take notice, perceive, regard, respect, have respect, behave self strangely, make self strange.

H5235 נֶכֶר *neker* or

נֹכֶר *nōker* from H5234; something *strange,* i.e. unexpected *calamity:*— strange.

H5236 נֵכָר *nēkār* from H5234; *foreign,* or (concretely) a *foreigner,* or (abstractly) *heathendom:*— alien, strange, stranger.

H5237 נָכְרִי *nokrî* from H5235 (second form); *strange,* in a variety of degrees and applications *(foreign, non-relative, adulterous, different, wonderful):*— alien, foreigner, outlandish, strange, stranger, strange woman.

H5238 נְכֹת *někōt* probably for H5219; *spicery,* i.e. (generally) *valuables:*— precious things.

H5239 נָלָה *nālâ* apparently a primitive root; to *complete:*— make an end.

H5240 נְמִבְזֶה *němibzeh* from H959; *despised:*— vile.

H5241 נְמוּאֵל *němûʾēl* apparently for H3223; *Nemuel,* the name of two Israelites:— Nemuel.

H5242 נְמוּאֵלִי *němûʾēlî* from H5241; a *Nemuelite,* or descendant of Nemuel:— Nemuelite.

H5243 נָמַל *nāmal* a primitive root; to *become clipped* or (specifically) *circumcised:*— branch to be cut off, be cut down, be cut off, circumcise.

H5244 נְמָלָה *němālâ* feminine from H5243; an *ant* (probably from its almost *bisected* form):— ant.

H5245 נְמַר *němar* (Aramaic) corresponding to H5246 :— leopard.

H5246 נָמֵר *nāmēr* from an unused root meaning properly to *filtrate,* i.e. *be limpid* [compare H5247 and H5249]; and thus to *spot* or *stain* as if by dripping; a *leopard* (from its stripes):— leopard.

H5247 נִמְרָה *nimrâ* from the same as H5246; *clear* water; *Nimrah,* a place east of the Jordan:— Nimrah. See also H1039, H5249

H5248 נִמְרוֹד *nimrôd* or

נִמְרֹד *nimrōd* probably of foreign origin; *Nimrod,* a son of Cush:— Nimrod.

H5249 נִמְרִים *nimrîm* plural of a masculine corresponding to H5247; *clear* waters; *Nimrim,* a place east of the Jordan:— Nimrim. Compare H1039

H5250 נִמְשִׁי *nimšî* probably from H4871; *extricated; Nimshi,* the (grand-) father of Jehu:— Nimshi.

H5251 נֵס *nēs* from H5264; a *flag;* also a *sail;* by implication a *flagstaff;* generally a *signal;* figuratively a *token:*— banner, pole, sail, sign, ensign, standard.

H5252 נְסִבָּה *někibbâ* feminine participle passive of H5437; properly an *environment,* i.e. *circumstance* or *turn* of affairs:— cause.

H5253 נָסַג *nāsag* a primitive root; to *retreat:*— departing away, remove, take, take hold, turn away.

H5254 נָסָה *nāsâ* a primitive root; to *test;* by implication to *attempt:*— adventure, assay, prove, tempt, try.

H5255 נָסַח *nāsaḥ* a primitive root; to *tear* away:— destroy, pluck, root.

H5256 נְסַח *něsāḥ* (Aramaic) corresponding to H5255 :— pull down.

H5257 נְסִיךְ *něsîk* from H5258; properly something *poured* out, i.e. a *libation;* also a molten *image;* by implication a *prince* (as *anointed*):— drink offering, duke, prince, principal.

H5258 נָסַךְ *nāsak* a primitive root; to *pour* out, especially a libation, or to *cast* (metal); by analogy to *anoint* a king:— cover, melt, offer, pour, cause to pour, pour out, set, set up.

H5259 נָסַךְ *nāsak* a primitive root [probably identical with H5258 through the idea of fusion]; to *interweave,* i.e. (figuratively) to *overspread:*— that is spread.

H5260 נְסַךְ *něsak* (Aramaic) corresponding to H5258; to *pour* out a libation:— offer.

H5261 נְסַךְ *něsak* (Aramaic) corresponding to H5262; a *libation:*— drink offering.

H5262 נֶסֶךְ *nesek* or

נֵסֶךְ *nēsek* from H5258; a *libation;* also a *cast idol:*— cover, drink offering, molten image.

H5263 נָסַס *nāsas* a primitive root; to *wane,* i.e. *be sick:*— faint.

H5264 נָסַס *nāsas* a primitive root; to *gleam* from afar, i.e. to *be conspicuous* as a signal; or rather perhaps a denominative from H5251 [and identical with H5263, through the idea of a flag as *fluttering* in the wind]; to *raise a beacon:*— lift up as an ensign.

H5265 נָסַע *nāsaʿ* a primitive root; properly to *pull* up, especially the tent-pins, i.e. *start* on a journey:— cause to blow, bring, get, go, make to go forth, go away, go forth, go forward, go onward, go out, journey, take journey, march, remove, set aside, set forward, still, be on his way, go their way.

H5266 נָסַק *nāsaq* a primitive root; to *go up:*— ascend.

H5267 נְסַק *něsaq* (Aramaic) corresponding to H5266 :— take up.

H5268 נִסְרֹךְ *nisrōk* of foreign origin; *Nisrok,* a Babylonian idol:— Nisroch.

H5269 נֵעָה *nēʿâ* from H5128; *motion; Neäh,* a place in Palestine:— Neah.

H5270 נֹעָה *nōʿâ* from H5128; *movement; Noäh,* an Israelitess:— Noah.

H5271 נָעוּר *nāʿûr* or

נָעֻר *nāʿūr* and (feminine)

נְעֻרָה *něʿūrâ* properly passive participle from H5288 as denominative; (only in plural collectively or emphatically) *youth,* the state *(juvenility)* or the persons *(young* people):— childhood, youth.

H5272 נְעִיאֵל *něʿîʾēl* from H5128 and H410; *moved of God; Neïel,* a place in Palestine:— Neiel.

H5273 נָעִים *nāʿîm* from H5276; *delightful* (objectively or subjectively, literally or figuratively):— pleasant, pleasure, sweet.

H5274 נָעַל *nāʿal* a primitive root; properly to *fasten* up, i.e. with a bar or cord; hence (denominatively from H5275), to *sandal,* i.e. furnish with slippers:— bolt, inclose, lock, shoe, shut up.

H5275 נַעַל *naʿal* or (feminine)

נַעֲלָה *naʿălâ* from H5274; properly a sandal *tongue;* by extension a *sandal* or slipper (sometimes as a symbol of occupancy, a refusal to marry, or of something valueless):— dryshod, shoe, pair of shoes, shoelatchet.

H5276 נָעֵם *nāʿēm* a primitive root; to *be agreeable* (literally or figuratively):— pass in beauty, be delight, be pleasant, be sweet.

H5277 נַעַם *naʿam* from H5276; *pleasure; Naam,* an Israelite:— Naam.

H5278 נֹעַם *nōʿam* from H5276; *agreeableness,* i.e. *delight, suitableness, splendor* or *grace:*— beauty, pleasant, pleasantness.

H5279 נַעֲמָה *naʿămâ* feminine of H5277; *pleasantness; Naamah,* the name of an antediluvian woman, or an Ammonitess, and of a place in Palestine:— Naamah.

H5280 נַעֲמִי *naʿămî* patronymic from H5283; a *Naamanite,* or descendant of Naaman (collectively):— Naamites.

H5281 נָעֳמִי *noʿŏmî* patronymic from H5278; *pleasant; Noömi,* an Israelitess:— Naomi.

H5282 נַעֲמָן *naʿămān* from H5276; *pleasantness* (plural as concrete):— pleasant.

H5283 נַעֲמָן *naʿămān* the same as H5282; *Naaman,* the name of an Israelite and of a Damascene:— Naaman.

H5284 נַעֲמָתִי *naʿămātî* patrial from a place corresponding in name (but not identical) with H5279; a *Naamathite,* or inhabitant of Naamah:— Naamathite.

H5285 נַעֲצוּץ *naʿăṣûṣ* from an unused root meaning to *prick;* probably a *brier;* by implication a *thicket* of thorny bushes:— thorn.

H5286 נָעַר *nāʿar* a primitive root; to *growl:*— yell.

H5287 נָעַר *nāʿar* a primitive root [probably identical with H5286, through the idea of the *rustling* of mane, which usually accompanies the lion's roar]; to *tumble* about:— shake, shake off, shake out, shake self, overthrow, toss up and down.

H5288 נַעַר *naʿar* from H5287; (concretely) a *boy* (as active), from the age of infancy to adolescence; by implication a *servant;* also (by interchange of sex), a *girl* (of similar latitude in age):— babe, boy, child, damsel *[from the margin],* lad, servant, young, young man.

H5289 נַעַר *naʿar* from H5287 in its derivative sense of *tossing* about; a *wanderer:*— young one.

H5290 נֹעַר *nōʿar* from H5287; (abstractly) *boyhood* [compare H5288]:— child, youth.

H5291 נַעֲרָה *naʿărâ* feminine of H5288; a *girl* (from infancy to adolescence):— damsel, maid, maiden, young, young woman.

H5292 נַעֲרָה *naʿărâ* the same as H5291; *Naarah,* the name of an Israelitess, and of a place in Palestine:— Naarah, Naarath.

H5293 נַעֲרַי *naʿăray* from H5288; *youthful; Naarai,* an Israelite:— Naarai.

H5294 נְעַרְיָה *něʿaryâ* from H5288 and H3050; *servant of Jah; Neärjah,* the name of two Israelites:— Neariah.

H5295 נַעֲרָן *naʿărān* from H5288; *juvenile; Naaran,* a place in Palestine:— Naaran.

H5296 נְעֹרֶת *něʿōret* from H5287; something *shaken* out, i.e. *tow* (as the refuse of flax):— tow.

H5297 נֹף *nōp* a variation of H4644; *Noph,* the capital of Upper Egypt:— Noph.

H5298 נֶפֶג *nepeg* from an unused root probably meaning to *spring* forth; a *sprout; Nepheg,* the name of two Israelites:— Nepheg.

H5299 נָפָה *nāpâ* from H5130 in the sense of *lifting;* a *height;* also a *sieve:*— border, coast, region, sieve.

H5300 נְפוּשְׁסִים *něpûšěsîm* for H5304; *Nephushesim,* a Temple-servant:— Nephisesim *[from the margin].*

H5301 נָפַח *nāpaḥ* a primitive root; to *puff,* in various applications (literally, to *inflate, blow* hard, *scatter, kindle, expire;* figuratively, to *disesteem*):— blow, breath, give up, cause to lose life, seething, snuff.

H5302 נֹפַח *nōpaḥ* from H5301; a *gust; Nophach,* a place in Moab:— Nophah.

H5303 נְפִיל *nĕpîl* or

נְפִל *nĕpîl* from H5307; properly, a *feller,* i.e. a *bully* or *tyrant:*— giant.

H5304 נְפִיסִים *nĕpîsîm* plural from an unused root meaning to *scatter; expansions; Nephisim,* a Temple-servant:— Nephusim *[from the margin].*

H5305 נָפִישׁ *nāpîš* from H5314; *refreshed; Naphish,* a son of Ishmael, and his posterity:— Naphish.

H5306 נֹפֶךְ *nōpek* from an unused root meaning to *glisten; shining;* a gem, probably the *garnet:*— emerald.

H5307 נָפַל *nāpal* a primitive root; to *fall,* in a great variety of applications (intransitively or causatively, literally or figuratively):— be accepted, cast, cast down, cast self, cast lots, cast out, cease, die, divide, divide by lot, fail, let fail, fall, cause to fall, let fall, make fall, ready to fall, fall away, fall down, fallen, falling, fell, felling, fugitive, have inheritance, inferior, be judged *[by mistake for* H6419*],* lay, lay along, lie down, cause to lie down, light, light down, be lost, hast lost, lying, overthrow, overwhelm, perish, present, presented, presenting, rot, make to rot, slay, smite out, surely, throw down.

H5308 נְפַל *nĕpal* (Aramaic) corresponding to H5307 :— fall, fall down, have occasion.

H5309 נֵפֶל *nepel* or

נֵפֶל *nēpel* from H5307; something *fallen,* i.e. an *abortion:*— untimely birth.

H5310 נָפַץ *nāpaṣ* a primitive root; to *dash* to pieces, or *scatter:*— be beaten in sunder, break, break in pieces, broken, dash, dash in pieces, cause to be discharged, dispersed, be overspread, scatter.

H5311 נֶפֶץ *nepeṣ* from H5310; a *storm* (as dispersing):— scattering.

H5312 נְפַק *nĕpaq* (Aramaic) a primitive root; to *issue;* causatively, to *bring out:*— come forth, go forth, take forth, take out.

H5313 נִפְקָא *nipqāʾ* (Aramaic) from H5312; an *outgo,* i.e. expense:— expense.

H5314 נָפַשׁ *nāpaš* a primitive root; to *breathe;* passive, to *be breathed* upon, i.e. (figuratively) *refreshed* (as if by a current of air):— be refreshed, refresh selves.

H5315 נֶפֶשׁ *nepeš* from H5314; properly a *breathing* creature, i.e. *animal* or (abstractly) *vitality;* used very widely in a literal, accommodated or figurative sense (bodily or mental):— any, appetite, beast, body, breath, creature, dead, deadly, desire, discontented, fish, ghost, greedy, he, heart, hearty, life, hath life, jeopardy of life, life in jeopardy, lust, man, me, mind, mortally, one, own, person, pleasure, self, herself, himself, myself, thyself, themselves, yourselves, slay, soul, tablet, they, thing, will, she will, would have it.

H5316 נֶפֶת *nepet* for H5299; a *height:*— country.

H5317 נֹפֶת *nōpet* from H5130 in the sense of *shaking* to pieces; a *dripping* i.e. of *honey* (from the comb):— honeycomb.

H5318 נֶפְתּוֹחַ *neptôah* from H6605; *opened,* i.e. a *spring; Nephtoäch,* a place in Palestine:— Neptoah.

H5319 נַפְתּוּל *naptûl* from H6617; properly *wrestled;* but used (in the plural) transitively, a *struggle:*— wrestling.

H5320 נַפְתֻּחִים *naptūḥîm* plural of foreign origin; *Naphtuchim,* an Egyptian tribe:— Naptuhim.

H5321 נַפְתָּלִי *naptālî* from H6617; *my wrestling; Naphtali,* a son of Jacob, with the tribe descended from him, and its territory:— Naphtali.

H5322 נֵץ *nēṣ* from H5340; a *flower* (from its *brilliancy*); also a *hawk* (from its *flashing* speed):— blossom, hawk.

H5323 נָצָא *nāṣāʾ* a primitive root; to *go away:*— flee.

H5324 נָצַב *nāṣab* a primitive root; to *station,* in various applications (literally or figuratively):— appointed, deputy, erect, establish, Huzzah *[by mistake for a proper name],* lay, officer, pillar, present, rear up, set, set over, set up, settle, sharpen, stablish, stand, make to stand, standing, stand still, stand up, stand upright, best state.

H5325 נִצָּב *niṣṣāb* passive participle of H5324; *fixed,* i.e. a *handle:*— haft.

H5326 נִצְבָּה *niṣbâ* (Aramaic) from a root corresponding to H5324; *fixedness,* i.e. *firmness:*— strength.

H5327 נָצָה *nāṣâ* a primitive root; properly to *go forth,* i.e. (by implication) to *be expelled,* and (consequently) *desolate;* causatively to *lay waste;* also (specifically), to *quarrel:*— be laid waste, ruinous, strive, strive together.

H5328 נִצָּה *niṣṣâ* feminine of H5322; a *blossom:*— flower.

H5329 נָצַח *nāṣaḥ* a primitive root; properly to *glitter* from afar, i.e. to be *eminent* (as a superintendent, especially of the Temple services and its music); also (as denominative from H5331), to *be permanent:*— excel, chief musician, chief singer, oversee, overseer, set forward.

H5330 נְצַח *nĕṣaḥ* (Aramaic) corresponding to H5329; to *become chief:*— be preferred.

H5331 נֶצַח *neṣaḥ* or

נֵצַח *nēṣaḥ* from H5329; properly a *goal,* i.e. the bright object at a distance travelled towards; hence (figuratively), *splendor,* or (subjectively) *truthfulness,* or (objectively) *confidence;* but usually (adverbially), *continually* (i.e. to the most distant point of view):— alway, always, constantly, end, ever, never, evermore, perpetual, strength, victory.

H5332 נֵצַח *nēṣaḥ* probably identical with H5331, through the idea of *brilliancy* of color; *juice* of the grape (as blood red):— blood, strength.

H5333 נְצִיב *nĕṣîb* or

נְצִב *nĕṣib* from H5324; something *stationary,* i.e. a *prefect,* a military *post,* a *statue:*— garrison, officer, pillar.

H5334 נְצִיב *nĕṣîb* the same as H5333; *station; Netsib,* a place in Palestine:— Nezib.

H5335 נְצִיחַ *nĕṣîah* from H5329; *conspicuous; Netsiach,* a Temple-servant:— Neziah.

H5336 נָצִיר *nāṣîr* from H5341; properly *conservative;* but used passively, *delivered:*— preserved.

H5337 נָצַל *nāṣal* a primitive root; to *snatch* away, whether in a good or a bad sense:— at all, defend, deliver, deliver self, escape, without fail, part, pluck, preserve, recover, rescue, rid, save, spoil, strip, surely, take, take out.

H5338 נְצַל *nĕṣal* (Aramaic) corresponding to H5337; to *extricate:*— deliver, rescue.

H5339 נִצָּן *niṣṣān* from H5322; a *blossom:*— flower.

H5340 נָצַץ *nāṣaṣ* a primitive root; to *glare,* i.e. *be bright*-colored:— sparkle.

H5341 נָצַר *nāṣar* a primitive root; to *guard,* in a good sense (to *protect, maintain, obey,* etc.) or a bad one (to *conceal,* etc.):— besieged, hidden thing, keep, keeper, keeping, monument, observe, preserve, preserver, subtil, watcher, watchman.

H5342 נֵצֶר *nēṣer* from H5341 in the sense of *greenness* as a striking color; a *shoot;* figuratively, a *descendant:*— branch.

H5343 נְקֵא *nĕqēʾ* (Aramaic) from a root corresponding to H5352; *clean:*— pure.

H5344 נָקַב *nāqab* a primitive root; to *puncture,* literally (to *perforate,* with more or less violence) or figuratively (to *specify, designate, libel*):— appoint, blaspheme, bore, curse, express, with holes, name, pierce, strike through.

H5345 נֶקֶב *neqeb* a *bezel* (for a gem):— pipe.

H5346 נֶקֶב *neqeb* the same as H5345; *dell; Nekeb,* a place in Palestine:— Nekeb.

H5347 נְקֵבָה *nĕqēbâ* from H5344; *female* (from the sexual form):— female.

H5348 נָקֹד *nāqōd* from an unused root meaning to *mark* (by *puncturing* or *branding*); *spotted:*— speckled.

H5349 נֹקֵד *nōqēd* active participle from the same as H5348; a *spotter* (of sheep or cattle), i.e. the owner or tender (who thus marks them):— herdman, sheepmaster.

H5350 נִקֻּד *niqqūd* from the same as H5348; a *crumb* (as *broken* to spots); also a *biscuit* (as *pricked*):— cracknel, mouldy.

H5351 נְקֻדָּה *nĕquddâ* feminine of H5348; a *boss* :— stud.

H5352 נָקָה *nāqâ* a primitive root; to *be* (or *make*) *clean* (literally or figuratively); by implication (in an adverse sense) to *be bare,* i.e. *extirpated:*— acquit at all, altogether, be blameless, cleanse, clear, be clear, clearing, cut off, be desolate, be free, be guiltless, hold guiltless, be innocent, hold innocent, by no means, be quit, be unpunished, leave unpunished, utterly, wholly.

H5353 נְקוֹדָא *nĕqôdāʾ* feminine of H5348 (in the figurative sense of *marked*); *distinction; Nekoda,* a Temple-servant:— Nekoda.

H5354 נָקַט *nāqaṭ* a primitive root; to *loathe:*— weary.

H5355 נָקִי *nāqî* or

נָקִיא *nāqîʾ* (Joel 4:19; Jonah 1:14), from H5352; *innocent:*— blameless, clean, clear, exempted, free, guiltless, innocent, quit.

H5356 נִקָּיוֹן *niqqāyôn* or

נִקָּיֹן *niqqāyōn* from H5352; *clearness* (literal or figurative):— cleanness, innocency.

H5357 נָקִיק *nāqîq* from an unused root meaning to *bore; a cleft:*— hole.

H5358 נָקַם *nāqam* a primitive root; to *grudge,* i.e. *avenge* or *punish:*— avenge, avenger, avenge self, punish, revenge, revenge self, surely, take vengeance.

H5359 נָקָם *nāqām* from H5358; *revenge:*— avenged, quarrel, vengeance.

H5360 נְקָמָה *nĕqāmâ* feminine of H5359; *avengement,* whether the act or the passion:— avenge, revenge, revenging, vengeance.

H5361 נָקַע *nāqaᶜ* a primitive root; to *feel aversion:*— be alienated.

H5362 נָקַף *nāqap* a primitive root; to *strike* with more or less violence *(beat, fell, corrode)*; by implication (of attack) to *knock together,* i.e. *surround* or *circulate:*— compass, compass about, compassing, cut down, destroy, go round, go round about, go about, inclose, round.

H5363 נֹקֶף *nōqep* from H5362; a *threshing* (of olives):— shaking.

H5364 נִקְפָּה *niqpâ* from H5362; probably a *rope* (as *encircling*):— rent.

H5365 נָקַר *nāqar* a primitive root; to *bore (penetrate, quarry)*:— dig, pick out, pierce, put out, thrust out.

H5366 נְקָרָה *nĕqārâ* from H5365; a *fissure:*— cleft, clift.

H5367 נָקַשׁ *nāqaš* a primitive root; to *entrap* (with a noose), literally or figuratively:— catch, snare, lay a snare.

H5368 נְקַשׁ *nĕqaš* (Aramaic) corresponding to H5367; but used in the sense of H5362; to *knock:*— smote.

H5369 נֵר *nēr* the same as H5216; *lamp; Ner,* an Israelite:— Ner.

H5370 נֵרְגַל *nērĕgal* of foreign origin; *Nergal,* a Cuthite deity:— Nergal.

H5371 נֵרְגַל שַׂרְאֶצֶר *nērĕgal śar*ᵓ*eṣer* from H5370 and H8272; *Nergal-Sharetser,* the name of two Babylonians:— Nergal-sharezer.

H5372 נִרְגָּן *nirgān* from an unused root meaning to *roll* to pieces; a *slanderer:*— talebearer, whisperer.

H5373 נֵרְדְּ *nērd* of foreign origin; *nard,* an aromatic:— spikenard.

H5374 נֵרִיָּה *nērîyâ* or

נֵרִיָּהוּ *nērōyyāhû* from H5216 and H3050; *light of Jah; Nerijah,* an Israelite:— Neriah.

H5375 נָשָׂא *nāśā*ᵓ or

נָסָה *nāsâ* (Ps 4:6 [7]), a primitive root; to *lift,* in a great variety of applications, literally and figuratively, absolutely and relatively (as follows):— accept, advance, arise, bear, able to bear, armourbearer, suffer to bear, bear up, bring, bring forth, burn, carry, carry away, cast, contain, desire, ease, exact, exalt, exalt self, extol, fetch, forgive, furnish, further, give, go on, help, high, hold up, honourable, +honourable man, lade, lay, lift up, lift self up, lofty, marry, magnify, needs, obtain, pardon, raise, raise up, receive, regard, respect, set, set up, spare, stir up, swear, take, take away, take up, utterly, wear, yield.

H5376 נְשָׂא *nĕśā*ᵓ (Aramaic) corresponding to H5375 :— carry away, make insurrection, take.

H5377 נָשָׁא *nāšā*ᵓ a primitive root; to *lead astray,* i.e. (mentally) to *delude,* or (morally) to *seduce:*— beguile, deceive, greatly, utterly.

H5378 נָשָׁא *nāšā*ᵓ a primitive root [perhaps identical with H5377, through the idea of *imposition];* to *lend* on interest; by implication to *dun* for debt:— debt, exact, giver of usury.

H5379 נִשֵּׂאת *niśśē*ᵓ*t* passive participle feminine of H5375; something *taken,* i.e. a *present:*— gift.

H5380 נָשַׁב *nāšab* a primitive root; to *blow;* by implication to *disperse:*— blow, cause to blow, drive away.

H5381 נָשַׂג *nāśag* a primitive root; to *reach* (literally or figuratively):— ability, be able, attain, attain unto, get, be able to get, can get, lay at, put, reach, remove, wax rich, surely, take, overtake, take hold of, takeon, take upon.

H5382 נָשָׁה *nāšâ* a primitive root; to *forget;* figuratively, to *neglect;* causatively, to *remit, remove:*— forget, deprive, exact.

H5383 נָשָׁה *nāšâ* a primitive root [rather identical with H5382, in the sense of H5378]; to *lend* or (by reciprocity) *borrow* on security or interest:— creditor, exact, extortioner, lend, usurer, lend on usury, taker of usury.

H5384 נָשֶׁה *nāšeh* from H5382, in the sense of *failure; rheumatic* or *crippled* (from the incident to Jacob):— which shrank.

H5385 נְשׂוּאָה *nĕśû*ᵓ*â* or rather

נְשֻׂאָה *nĕśû*ᵓ*â* feminine passive participle of H5375; something *borne,* i.e. a *load:*— carriage.

H5386 נְשִׁי *nĕšî* from H5383; a *debt:*— debt.

H5387 נָשִׂיא *nāśî*ᵓ or

נָשִׂא *nāśî*ᵓ from H5375; properly an *exalted* one, i.e. a *king* or *sheik;* also a rising *mist:*— captain, chief, cloud, governor, prince, ruler, vapour.

H5388 נְשִׁיָּה *nĕšîyâ* from H5382; *oblivion:*— forgetfulness.

H5389 נָשִׁין *nāšîn* (Aramaic) irregular plural feminine of H606:— women.

H5390 נְשִׁיקָה *nĕšîqâ* from H5401; a *kiss:*— kiss.

H5391 נָשַׁךְ *nāšak* a primitive root; to *strike* with a sting (as a serpent); figuratively, to *oppress* with interest on a loan:— bite, lend upon usury.

H5392 נֶשֶׁךְ *nešek* from H5391; *interest* on a debt :— usury.

H5393 נִשְׁכָּה *niškâ* for H3957; a *cell:*— chamber.

H5394 נָשַׁל *nāšal* a primitive root; to *pluck* off, i.e. *divest, eject,* or *drop:*— cast, cast out, drive, loose, put off, put out, slip.

H5395 נָשַׁם *nāšam* a primitive root; properly to *blow* away, i.e. *destroy:*— destroy.

H5396 נִשְׁמָא *nišmā*ᵓ (Aramaic) corresponding to H5397; vital *breath:*— breath.

H5397 נְשָׁמָה *nĕšāmâ* from H5395; a *puff,* i.e. *wind,* angry or vital *breath,* divine *inspiration, intellect.* or (concretely) an *animal:*— blast, breath, that breatheth, inspiration, soul, spirit.

H5398 נָשַׁף *nāšap* a primitive root; to *breeze,* i.e. *blow* up fresh (as the wind):— blow.

H5399 נֶשֶׁף *nešep* from H5398; properly a *breeze,* i.e. (by implication) *dusk* (when the evening breeze prevails):— dark, dawning of the day, dawning of the morning, night, twilight.

H5400 נָשַׂק *nāśaq* a primitive root; to *catch* fire:— burn, kindle.

H5401 נָשַׁק *nāšaq* a primitive root [identical with H5400, through the idea of *fastening* up; compare H2388, H2836]; to *kiss,* literally or figuratively *(touch)*; also (as a mode of *attachment*), to *equip* with weapons:— armed, armed men, rule, kiss, that touched.

H5402 נֶשֶׁק *nešeq* or

נֵשֶׁק *nēšeq* from H5401; military *equipment,* i.e. (collectively) *arms* (offensive of defensive), or (concretely) an *arsenal:*— armed men, armour, armoury, battle, harness, weapon.

H5403 נְשַׁר *nĕšar* (Aramaic) corresponding to H5404; an *eagle:*— eagle.

H5404 נֶשֶׁר *nešer* from an unused root meaning to *lacerate;* the *eagle* (or other large bird of prey):— eagle.

H5405 נָשַׁת *nāšat* a primitive root; properly to *eliminate,* i.e. (intransitively) to *dry* up:— fail.

H5406 נִשְׁתְּוָן *ništĕwān* probably of Persian origin; an *epistle:*— letter.

H5407 נִשְׁתְּוָן *ništĕwān* (Aramaic) corresponding to H5406:— letter.

H5408 נָתַח *nātaḥ* a primitive root; to *dismember* :— cut, cut in pieces, divide, hew in pieces.

H5409 נֵתַח *nētaḥ* from H5408; a *fragment:*— part, piece.

H5410 נָתִיב *nātîb* or (feminine)

נְתִיבָה *nĕtîbâ* or

נְתִבָה *nĕtībâ* (Jer 6:16), from an unused root meaning to *tramp;* a (beaten) *track:*— path, pathway, traveller, way.

H5411 נָתִין *nātîn* or

נָתוּן *nātûn* (Ezra 8:17; the proper form, as passive participle) from H5414; one *given,* i.e. (in the plural only) the *Nethinim,* or Temple-servants (as *given* up to that duty):— Nethinims.

H5412 נְתִין *nĕtîn* (Aramaic) corresponding to H5411 :— Nethinims.

H5413 נָתַךְ *nātak* a primitive root; to *flow* forth (literally or figuratively); by implication to *liquefy:*— drop, gather, gather together, melt, pour, pour forth, pour out.

H5414 נָתַן *nātan* a primitive root; to *give,* used with great latitude of application *(put, make, etc.)*:— add, apply, appoint, ascribe, assign, avenge, be, be healed, bestow, bring, bring forth, bring hither, cast, cause, charge, come, commit, consider, count, cry, deliver, deliver up, direct, distribute, do, doubtless, without fail, fasten, frame, get, give, give forth, give over, give up, grant, hang, hang up, have, indeed, lay, lay unto charge, lay up, leave, give leave, lend, let, let out, lie, lift up, make, O that, occupy, offer, ordain, pay, perform, place, pour, print, pull, put, put forth, recompense, render, requite, restore, send, send out, set, set forth, shew, shoot forth, shoot up, sing, slander, strike, submit, suffer, surely, take, thrust, trade, turn, utter, weep, willingly, withdraw, would God, would to God, yield.

H5415 נְתַן *nĕtan* (Aramaic) corresponding to H5414; *give:*— bestow, give, pay.

H5416 נָתָן *nātān* from H5414; *given; Nathan,* the name of five Israelites:— Nathan.

H5417 נְתַנְאֵל *nĕtan*ᵓ*ēl* from H5414 and H410; *given of God; Nethanel,* the name of ten Israelites:— Nethaneel.

H5418 נְתַנְיָה *nĕtanyâ* or

נְתַנְיָהוּ *nĕtanyāhû* from H5414 and H3050; *given of Jah; Nethanjah,* the name of four Israelites:— Nethaniah.

H5419 נְתַן־מֶלֶךְ *nĕtan-melek* from H5414 and H4428; *given of* (the) *king; Nethan-Melek,* an Israelite:— Nathan-melech.

H5420 נָתַס *nātas* a primitive root; to *tear* up:— mar.

H5421 נָתַע *nātaᶜ* for H5422; to *tear* out:— break.

H5422 נָתַץ *nātaṣ* a primitive root; to *tear* down:— beat down, break down, break out, cast down, destroy, overthrow, pull down, throw down.

H5423 נָתַק *nātaq* a primitive root; to *tear* off:— break, break off, burst, draw, draw away, lift up, pluck away, pluck off, pull, pull out, root out.

H5424 נֶתֶק *neteq* from H5423; *scurf:*— scall, dry scall.

H5425 נָתַר *nātar* a primitive root; to *jump,* i.e. *be* violently *agitated;* causatively to *terrify, shake* off, *untie:*— drive asunder, leap, loose, let loose, make, move, undo.

H5426 נְתַר *nĕtar* (Aramaic) corresponding to H5425 :— shake off.

H5427 נֶתֶר *neter* from H5425; mineral *potash* (so called from *effervescing* with acid):— nitre.

H5428 נָתַשׁ *nātaš* a primitive root; to *tear* away:— destroy, forsake, pluck, pluck out, pluck up, pluck up by the roots, pull up, root out, root up, utterly.

ס

H5429 סְאָה *sĕʾâ* from an unused root meaning to *define;* a *seäh,* or certain measure (as *determinative*) for grain:— measure.

H5430 סְאוֹן *sĕʾôn* from H5431; perhaps a military *boot* (as a protection from *mud*):— battle.

H5431 סָאַן *sāʾan* a primitive root; to *be miry;* used only as denominative from H5430; to *shoe,* i.e. (active participle) a *soldier* shod:— warrior.

H5432 סַאסְּאָה *saʾsĕʾâ* for H5429; *measurement,* i.e. *moderation:*— measure.

H5433 סָבָא *sābāʾ* a primitive root; to *quaff* to satiety, i.e. *become tipsy:*— drunkard, fill self, Sabean, winebibber.

H5434 סְבָא *sĕbāʾ* of foreign origin; *Seba,* a son of Cush, and the country settled by him:— Seba.

H5435 סֹבֶא *sōbeʾ* from H5433; *potation,* concretely *(wine),* or abstractly *(carousal):*— drink, drunken, wine.

H5436 סְבָאִי *sĕbāʾî* patrial from H5434; a *Sebaite,* or inhabitant of Seba:— Sabean.

H5437 סָבַב *sābab* a primitive root; to *revolve, surround* or *border;* used in various applications, literally and figuratively (as follows):— bring, cast, fetch, lead, make, walk, whirl, round about, be about on every side, apply, avoid, beset, beset about, besiege, bring again, carry, carry about, change, cause to come about, circuit, compass, fetch a compass, compass about, compass round, drive, environ, on every side, beset, beset about, beset round about, close round about, cause to come about, go about, go round about, stand round about, inclose, remove, return, set, sit down, turn, turn about, turn self about, turn aside, turn away, turn back.

H5438 סִבָּה *sibbâ* from H5437; a (providential) *turn* (of affairs):— cause.

H5439 סָבִיב *sābîb* or (feminine)

סְבִיבָה *sĕbîbâ* from H5437; (as noun) a *circle, neighbor,* or *environs;* but chiefly (as adverb, with or without preposition) *around:*— about, place about, round about, circuit, compass, on every side.

H5440 סָבַךְ *sābak* a primitive root; to *entwine:*— fold together, wrap.

H5441 סֹבֶךְ *sōbek* from H5440; a *copse:*— thicket.

H5442 סְבָךְ *sĕbāk* from H5440; a *copse:*— thick, thicket.

H5443 סַבְּכָא *sabbĕkāʾ* or

שַׂבְּכָא *śabbĕkāʾ* (Aramaic) from a root corresponding to H5440; a *lyre:*— sackbut.

H5444 סִבְּכַי *sibkay* from H5440; *copse-like; Sibbecau,* an Israelite:— Sibbecai, Sibbechai.

H5445 סָבַל *sābal* a primitive root; to *carry* (literally or figuratively), or (reflexively) *be burdensome;* specifically to *be gravid:*— bear, be a burden, carry, strong to labour.

H5446 סְבַל *sĕbal* (Aramaic) corresponding to H5445; to *erect:*— strongly laid.

H5447 סֵבֶל *sēbel* from H5445; a *load* (literal or figurative):— burden, charge.

H5448 סֹבֶל *sōbel* only in the form

סֻבָּל *subbāl* from H5445; a *load* (figurative) :— burden.

H5449 סַבָּל *sabbāl* from H5445; a *porter:*— burden, to bear burdens, bearer of burdens.

H5450 סְבָלָה *sĕbālâ* from H5447; *porterage:*— burden.

H5451 סִבֹּלֶת *sibbōlet* for H7641; an *ear* of grain:— Sibboleth.

H5452 סְבַר *sĕbar* (Aramaic) a primitive root; to *bear in mind,* i.e. *hope:*— think.

H5453 סִבְרַיִם *sibrayim* dual from a root corresponding to H5452; *double hope; Sibrajim,* a place in Syria:— Sibraim.

H5454 סַבְתָּא *sabtāʾ* or

סַבְתָּה *sabtâ* probably of foreign derivation; *Sabta* or *Sabtah,* the name of a son of Cush, and the country occupied by his posterity:— Sabta, Sabtah.

H5455 סַבְתְּכָא *sabtĕkāʾ* probably of foreign derivation; *Sabteca,* the name of a son of Cush, and the region settled by him:— Sabtecha, Sabtechah.

H5456 סָגַד *sāgad* a primitive root; to *prostrate* oneself (in homage):— fall down.

H5457 סְגִד *sĕgīd* (Aramaic) corresponding to H5456 :— worship.

H5458 סְגוֹר *sĕgôr* from H5462; properly *shut up,* i.e. the *breast* (as inclosing the heart); also *gold* (as generally *shut* up safely):— caul, gold.

H5459 סְגֻלָּה *sĕgullâ* feminine passive participle of an unused root meaning to *shut* up; *wealth* (as closely *shut* up):— jewel, peculiar, peculiar treasure, proper good, special.

H5460 סְגַן *sĕgan* (Aramaic) corresponding to H5461 :— governor.

H5461 סָגָן *sāgān* from an unused root meaning to *superintend;* a *praefect* of a province:— prince, ruler.

H5462 סָגַר *sāgar* a primitive root; to *shut* up; figuratively to *surrender:*— close up, deliver, deliver up, give over, give up, inclose, pure, repair, shut, shut in, shut self, shut out, shut up, shut up together, stop, straitly.

H5463 סְגַר *sĕgar* (Aramaic) corresponding to H5462 :— shut up.

H5464 סַגְרִיר *sagrîr* probably from H5462 in the sense of *sweeping* away; a pouring rain:— very rainy.

H5465 סַד *sad* from an unused root meaning to *stop;* the *stocks:*— stocks.

H5466 סָדִין *sādîn* from an unused root meaning to *envelop;* a *wrapper,* i.e. *shirt:*— fine linen, sheet.

H5467 סְדֹם *sĕdōm* from an unused root meaning to *scorch; burnt* (i.e. *volcanic* or *bituminous*) district; *Sedom,* a place near the Dead Sea:— Sodom.

H5468 סֶדֶר *seder* from an unused root meaning to *arrange; order:*— order.

H5469 סַהַר *sahar* from an unused root meaning to *be round; roundness:*— round.

H5470 סֹהַר *sōhar* from the same as H5469; a *dungeon* (as *surrounded* by walls):— prison.

H5471 סוֹא *sôʾ* of foreign derivation; *So,* an Egyptian king:— So.

H5472 סוּג *sûg* a primitive root; properly to *flinch,* i.e. (by implication) to *go back,* literally (to *retreat*) or figuratively (to *apostatize*):— backslider, drive, go back, turn, turn away, turn back.

H5473 סוּג *sûg* a primitive root [probably rather identical with H5472 through the idea of *shrinking* from a hedge; compare H7735]; to *hem* in, i.e. *bind:*— set about.

H5474 סוּגַר *sûgar* from H5462; an *inclosure,* i.e. *cage* (for an animal):— ward.

H5475 סוֹד *sôd* from H3245; a *session,* i.e. *company* of persons (in close deliberation); by implication *intimacy, consultation,* a *secret:*— assembly, counsel, inward, secret, secret counsel.

H5476 סוֹדִי *sôdî* from H5475; a *confidant; Sodi,* an Israelite:— Sodi.

H5477 סוּחַ *sûaḥ* from an unused root meaning to *wipe* away; *sweeping; Suäch,* an Israelite:— Suah.

H5478 סוּחָה *sûḥâ* from the same as H5477; something *swept* away, i.e. *filth:*— torn.

H5479 סוֹטַי *sôṭay* from H7750; *roving; Sotai,* one of the Nethinim:— Sotai.

H5480 סוּךְ *sûk* a primitive root; properly to *smear* over (with oil), i.e. *anoint:*— anoint, anoint self, at all.

H5481 סוּמְפּוֹנְיָה *sûmĕpōnĕyâ* or

סוּמְפֹּנְיָה *sûmĕpōnĕyâ* or

סִיפֹּנְיָא *sîpōnĕyāʾ* (Dan 3:10), (Aramaic) of Greek origin (**συμφωνία** *symphōnia*); a *bagpipe* (with a double pipe):— dulcimer.

H5482 סְוֵנֵה *sĕwēnēh* rather to be written

סְוֵנָה *sĕwēnâ* for

סְוֵן *sĕwēn;* of Egyptian derivation; *Seven,* a place in Upper Egypt:— Syene.

H5483 סוּס *sûs* or

סֻס *sūs* from an unused root meaning to *skip* (properly for joy); a *horse* (as leaping); also a *swallow* (from its rapid *flight*):— crane, horse, horseback, horsehoof. Compare H6571

H5484 סוּסָה *sûsâ* feminine of H5483; a *mare:*— company of horses.

H5485 סוּסִי *sûsî* from H5483; *horselike; Susi,* an Israelite:— Susi.

H5486 סוּף *sûp* a primitive root; to *snatch* away, i.e. *terminate:*— consume, have an end, perish, be utterly.

H5487 סוּף *sûp* (Aramaic) corresponding to H5486; to *come to an end:*— consume, fulfil.

H5488 סוּף *sûp* probably of Egyptian origin; a *reed,* especially the *papyrus:*— flag, Red sea, weed. Compare H5489

H5489 סוּף *sûp* for H5488 (by ellipsis of H3220); the *Reed (Sea):*— Red sea.

H5490 סוֹף *sôp* from H5486; a *termination:*— conclusion, end, hinder part.

H5491 סוֹף *sôp* (Aramaic) corresponding to H5490 :— end.

H5492 סוּפָה *sûpâ* from H5486; a *hurricane:*— Red Sea, storm, tempest, whirlwind, Red sea.

H5493 סוּר *sûr* or

שׂוּר *śûr* (Hos 9:12), a primitive root; to *turn* off (literally or figuratively):— behead, bring, call back, decline, depart, eschew, get you, go, go aside, grievous, lay away, lay by, leave undone, be past, pluck away, put, put away, put down, rebel, remove, remove to and fro, revolt, be sour, take, take away, take off, turn, turn aside, turn away, turn in, withdraw, be without.

H5494 סוּר *sûr* probably passive participle of H5493; *turned* off, i.e. *deteriorated:*— degenerate.

H5495 סוּר *sûr* the same as H5494; *Sur,* a gate of the Temple:— Sur.

H5496 סוּת *sût* perhaps denominative from H7898; properly to *prick,* i.e. (figuratively) stimulate; by implication to *seduce:*— entice, move, persuade, provoke, remove, set on, stir up, take away.

H5497 סוּת *sût* probably from the same root as H4533; *covering,* i.e. *clothing:*— clothes.

H5498 סָחַב *sāḥab* a primitive root; to *trail* along:— draw, draw out, tear.

H5499 סְחָבָה *sĕḥābâ* from H5498; a *rag:*— cast clout.

H5500 סָחָה *sāḥâ* a primitive root; to *sweep* away :— scrape.

H5501 סְחִי *sĕḥî* from H5500; *refuse* (as *swept* off) :— offscouring.

H5502 סָחַף *sāḥap* a primitive root; to *scrape* off:— sweep, sweep away.

H5503 סָחַר *sāḥar* a primitive root; to *travel* round (specifically as a *pedlar*); intensively to *palpitate:*— go about, merchant, merchantman, occupy with, pant, trade, traffick.

H5504 סַחַר *saḥar* from H5503; *profit* (from trade) :— merchandise.

H5505 סָחַר *sāḥar* from H5503; an *emporium;* abstractly *profit* (from trade):— mart, merchandise.

H5506 סְחֹרָה *sĕḥōrâ* from H5503; *traffic:*— merchandise.

H5507 סֹחֵרָה *sōḥērâ* properly active participle feminine of H5503; something *surrounding* the person, i.e. a *shield:*— buckler.

H5508 סֹחֶרֶת *sōḥeret* similar to H5507; probably a (black) *tile* (or *tessara*) for laying borders with:— black marble.

H5509 סִיג *sîg* or

סוּג *sûg* (Ezek 22:18), from H5472 in the sense of *refuse; scoria:*— dross.

H5510 סִיוָן *sîwān* probably of Persian origin; *Sivan,* the third Hebrew month:— Sivan.

H5511 סִיחוֹן *sîḥôn* or

סִיחֹן *sîḥōn* from the same as H5477; *tempestuous; Sichon,* an Amoritish king:— Sihon.

H5512 סִין *sîn* of uncertain derivation; *Sin,* the name of an Egyptian town and (probably) desert adjoining:— Sin.

H5513 סִינִי *sînî* from an otherwise unknown name of a man; a *Sinite,* or descendant of one of the sons of Canaan:— Sinite.

H5514 סִינַי *sînay* of uncertain derivation; *Sinai,* a mountain of Arabia:— Sinai.

H5515 סִינִים *sînîm* plural of an otherwise unknown name; *Sinim,* a distant Oriental region:— Sinim.

H5516 סִיסְרָא *sîsĕrāʾ* of uncertain derivation; *Sisera,* the name of a Canaanitish king and of one of the Nethinim:— Sisera.

H5517 סִיעָא *sîʿāʾ* or

סִיעֲהָא *sîʿăhāʾ* from an unused root meaning to *converse; congregation; Sia,* or *Siaha,* one of the Nethinim:— Sia, Siaha.

H5518 סִיר *sîr* or (feminine)

סִירָה *sîrâ* or

סִרָה *sīrâ* (Jer 52:18), from a primitive root meaning to *boil* up; a *pot;* also a *thorn* (as springing up rapidly); by implication a *hook:*— caldron, fishhook, pan, pot, washpot, thorn.

H5519 סָךְ *sāk* from H5526; properly a *thicket* of men, i.e. a *crowd:*— multitude.

H5520 סֹךְ *sōk* from H5526; a *hut* (as of *entwined* boughs); also a *lair:*— covert, den, pavilion, tabernacle.

H5521 סֻכָּה *sukkâ* feminine of H5520; a *hut* or *lair:*— booth, cottage, covert, pavilion, tabernacle, tent.

H5522 סִכּוּת *sikkût* feminine of H5519; an (idolatrous) *booth:*— tabernacle.

H5523 סֻכּוֹת *sukkôt* or

סֻכֹּת *sukkōt* plural of H5521; *booths; Succoth,* the name of a place in Egypt and of three in Palestine:— Succoth.

H5524 סֻכּוֹת בְּנוֹת *sukkôt bĕnôt* from H5523 and the (irregular) plural of H1323; *booths of (the) daughters; brothels,* i.e. idolatrous *tents* for impure purposes:— Succoth-benoth.

H5525 סֻכִּי *sukkî* patrial from an unknown name (perhaps H5520); a *Sukkite,* or inhabitant of some place near Egypt (i.e. *hut-dwellers*):— Sukkims.

H5526 סָכַךְ *sākak* or

שָׂכַךְ *śākak* (Exod 33:22), a primitive root; properly to *entwine* as a screen; by implication to *fence* in, *cover* over, (figuratively) *protect:*— cover, defence, defend, hedge in, join together, set, shut up.

H5527 סְכָכָה *sĕkākâ* from H5526; *inclosure; Secacah,* a place in Palestine:— Secacah.

H5528 סָכַל *sākal* for H3688; to *be silly:*— do foolishly, make foolish, play the fool, turn into foolishness.

H5529 סֶכֶל *sekel* from H5528; *silliness;* concretely and collectively *dolts:*— folly.

H5530 סָכָל *sākāl* from H5528; *silly:*— fool, foolish, sottish.

H5531 סִכְלוּת *siklût* or

שִׂכְלוּת *śiklût* (Eccl 1:17), from H5528; *silliness:*— folly, foolishness.

H5532 סָכַן *sākan* a primitive root; to *be familiar* with; by implication to *minister* to, *be serviceable* to, be *customary:*— acquaint, acquaint self, be advantage, ever, profit, be profitable, unprofitable, treasurer, be wont.

H5533 סָכַן *sākan* probably a denominative from H7915; properly *to cut,* i.e. *damage;* also to *grow* (causatively *make*) *poor:*— endanger, impoverish.

H5534 סָכַר *sākar* a primitive root; to *shut* up; by implication to *surrender:*— stop, give over. See also H5462; H7936

H5535 סָכַת *sākat* a primitive root; to *be silent;* by implication to *observe* quietly:— take heed.

H5536 סַל *sal* from H5549; properly a willow *twig* (as *pendulous*), i.e. an *osier;* but only as woven into a *basket:*— basket.

H5537 סָלָא *sālāʾ* a primitive root; to *suspend* in a balance, i.e. *weigh:*— compare.

H5538 סִלָּא *sillāʾ* from H5549; an *embankment; Silla,* a place in Jerusalem:— Silla.

H5539 סָלַד *sālad* a primitive root; probably to *leap* (with joy), i.e. *exult:*— harden self.

H5540 סֶלֶד *seled* from H5539; *exultation; Seled,* an Israelit:— Seled.

H5541 סָלָה *sālâ* a primitive root; to *hang* up, i.e. *weigh,* or (figuratively) *contemn:*— tread down, tread under foot, value.

H5542 סֶלָה *selâ* from H5541; *suspension* (of music), i.e. *pause:*— Selah.

H5543 סַלּוּ *sallû* or

סַלּוּא *salûʾ* or

סָלוּא *sālûʾ* or

סַלַּי *salay* from H5541; *weighed; Sallu* or *Sallai,* the name of two Israelites:— Sallai, Sallu, Salu.

H5544 סִלּוֹן *sillôn* or

סַלּוֹן *sallôn* from H5541; a *prickle* (as if *pendulous*):— brier, thorn.

H5545 סָלַח *sālaḥ* a primitive root; to *forgive:*— forgive, pardon, spare.

H5546 סַלָּח *sallāḥ* from H5545; *placable:*— ready to forgive.

H5547 סְלִיחָה *sĕlîḥâ* from H5545; *pardon:*— forgiveness, pardon.

H5548 סַלְכָה *salkâ* from an unused root meaning to *walk; walking; Salcah,* a place east of the Jordan:— Salcah, Salchah.

H5549 סָלַל *sālal* a primitive root; to *mound* up (especially a turnpike); figuratively to *exalt;* reflexively, to *oppose* (as by a dam):— cast up, exalt, exalt self, extol, make plain, raise up.

H5550 סֹלְלָה *sōlĕlâ* or

סוֹלְלָה *sôlĕlâ* active participle feminine of H5549, but used passively; a military *mound,* i.e. *rampart* of besiegers:— bank, mount.

H5551 סֻלָּם *sĕllām* from H5549; a *stair-case:*— ladder.

H5552 סַלְסִלָּה *salsillâ* from H5541; a *twig* (as *pendulous*):— basket.

H5553 סֶלַע *sĕlaʿ* from an unused root meaning to be *lofty;* a craggy *rock,* literal or figurative (a *fortress*):— rock, ragged rock, stone, stony, strong hold.

H5554 סֶלַע *sĕlaʿ* the same as H5553; *Sela,* the rock-city of Idumaea:— rock, Sela, Selah.

H5555 סֶלַע הַמַּחְלְקוֹת *selaᶜ hammaḥlĕqôt* from H5553 and the plural of H4256 with the article interposed; *rock of the divisions; Sela-ham-Machlekoth,* a place in Palestine:— Sela-hammalekoth.

H5556 סָלְעָם *solᶜām* apparently from the same as H5553 in the sense of *crushing* as with a rock, i.e. consuming; a kind of *locust* (from its *destructiveness*):— bald locust.

H5557 סָלַף *sālap* a primitive root; properly to *wrench,* i.e. (figuratively) to *subvert:*— overthrow, pervert.

H5558 סֶלֶף *selep* from H5557; *distortion,* i.e. (figuratively) *viciousness:*— perverseness.

H5559 סְלִק *sĕlīq* (Aramaic) a primitive root; to *ascend:*— come, come up.

H5560 סֹלֶת *sōlet* from an unused root meaning to *strip; flour* (as *chipped* off):— flour, fine flour, meal.

H5561 סַם *sam* from an unused root meaning to *smell* sweet; an *aroma:*— sweet, sweet spice.

H5562 סַמְגַּר נְבוֹ *samgar nĕbô* of foreign origin; *Samgar-Nebo,* a Babylonian general:— Samgar-nebo.

H5563 סְמָדַר *sĕmādar* of uncertain derivation; a vine *blossom;* used also adverbially *abloom:*— tender grape.

H5564 סָמַךְ *sāmak* a primitive root; to *prop* (literally or figuratively); reflexive to *lean* upon or *take hold* of (in a favorable or unfavorable sense):— bear up, establish, hold, uphold, lay, lean, like hard, put, rest self, set self, stand fast, stay, stay self, sustain.

H5565 סְמַכְיָהוּ *sĕmakyāhû* from H5564 and H3050; *supported of Jah; Semakjah,* an Israelite:— Semachiah.

H5566 סֶמֶל *semel* or

סֵמֶל *sēmel* from an unused root meaning to *resemble;* a *likeness:*— figure, idol, image.

H5567 סָמַן *sāman* a primitive root; to *designate:*— appointed.

H5568 סָמַר *sāmar* a primitive root; to *be erect,* i.e. *bristle* as hair:— stand up, tremble.

H5569 סָמָר *sāmār* from H5568; *bristling,* i.e. *shaggy* :— rough.

H5570 סְנָאָה *sĕnāʾâ* from an unused root meaning to *prick; thorny; Senaah,* a place in Palestine:— Senaah, Nassenaah [with the article].

H5571 סַנְבַלַּט *sanballaṭ* of foreign origin; *Sanballat,* a Persian satrap of Samaria:— Sanballat.

H5572 סְנֶה *sĕneh* from an unused root meaning to *prick;* a *bramble:*— bush.

H5573 סֶנֶה *seneh* the same as H5572; *thorn; Seneh,* a crag in Palestine:— Seneh.

H5574 סְנוּאָה *sĕnûʾâ* or

סְנֻאָה *sĕnūʾâ* from the same as H5570; *pointed;* (used with the article as a proper name) *Senuah,* the name of two Israelites:— Hasemuah *[including the article],* Senuah.

H5575 סַנְוֵר *sanwēr* of uncertain derivation; (in plural) *blindness:*— blindness.

H5576 סַנְחֵרִיב *sanḥērîb* of foreign origin; *Sancherib,* an Assyrian king:— Sennacherib.

H5577 סַנְסִן *sansīn* from an unused root meaning to be *pointed;* a *twig* (as *tapering*):— bough.

H5578 סַנְסַנָּה *sansannâ* feminine of a form of H5577; a *bough; Sansannah,* a place in Palestine:— Sansannah.

H5579 סְנַפִּיר *sĕnappîr* of uncertain derivation; a *fin* (collectively):— fins.

H5580 סָס *sās* from the same as H5483; a *moth* (from the *agility* of the fly):— worm.

H5581 סִסְמַי *sismay* of uncertain derivation; *Sismai,* an Israelite:— Sisamai.

H5582 סָעַד *sāᶜad* a primitive root; to *support* (mostly figuratively):— comfort, establish, hold up, refresh self, strengthen, be upholden.

H5583 סְעַד *sĕᶜad* (Aramaic) corresponding to H5582; to *aid:*— helping.

H5584 סָעָה *sāᶜâ* a primitive root; to *rush:*— storm.

H5585 סָעִיף *sāᶜîp* from H5586; a *fissure* (of rocks); also a *bough* (as *subdivided*):— branch, outmost branch, clift, top.

H5586 סָעַף *sāᶜap* a primitive root; properly to *divide* up; but used only as denominative from H5585, to *disbranch* (a tree):— top.

H5587 סָעִף *sāᶜip* or

שָׂעִף *śāᶜip* from H5586; *divided* (in mind), i.e. (abstractly) a *sentiment:*— opinion.

H5588 סֵעֵף *sēᶜēp* from H5586; *divided* (in mind), i.e. (concretely) a *skeptic:*— thought.

H5589 סְעַפָּה *sĕᶜappâ* feminine of H5585; a *twig:*— bough, branch. Compare H5634

H5590 סָעַר *sāᶜar* a primitive root; to *rush* upon; by implication to *toss* (transitive or intransitive, literally or figuratively):— be tempestuous, toss with tempest, be sore troubled, come out as a whirlwind, drive with the whirlwind, scatter with a whirlwind.

H5591 סַעַר *saᶜar* or (feminine)

סְעָרָה *sĕᶜārâ* from H5590; a *hurricane:*— storm, stormy, tempest, whirlwind.

H5592 סַף *sap* from H5605, in its original sense of *containing;* a *vestibule* (as a *limit*); also a *dish* (for holding blood or wine):— bason, bowl, cup, door, door post, gate, post, threshold.

H5593 סַף *sap* the same as H5592; *Saph,* a Philistine:— Saph. Compare H5598

H5594 סָפַד *sāpad* a primitive root; properly to *tear* the hair and *beat* the breasts (as Orientals do in grief); generally to *lament;* by implication to *wail:*— lament, mourn, mourner, wail.

H5595 סָפָה *sāpâ* a primitive root; properly to *scrape* (literally to *shave;* but usually figuratively) together (i.e. to *accumulate* or *increase*) or away (i.e. to *scatter, remove* or *ruin;* intransitive to *perish*):— add, augment, consume, destroy, heap, join, perish, put.

H5596 סָפַח *sāpaḥ* or

שָׂפַח *śāpaḥ* (Isa 3:17), a primitive root; properly to *scrape* out, but in certain peculiar senses (of *removal* or *association*):— abiding, gather together, cleave, smite with the scab.

H5597 סַפַּחַת *sappaḥat* from H5596; the *mange* (as making the hair fall off):— scab.

H5598 סִפַּי *sippay* from H5592; *bason-like; Sippai,* a Philistine:— Sippai. Compare H5593

H5599 סָפִיחַ *sāpîaḥ* from H5596; something (spontaneously) *falling* off, i.e. a *self-sown* crop; figuratively a *freshet:*— such things as grow of themselves, things which grow, which groweth of its own accord, which groweth of itself.

H5600 סְפִינָה *sĕpînâ* from H5603; a (sea-going) *vessel* (as *ceiled* with a deck):— ship.

H5601 סַפִּיר *sappîr* from H5608; a *gem* (perhaps as used for *scratching* other substances), probably the *sapphire:*— sapphire.

H5602 סֵפֶל *sēpel* from an unused root meaning to *depress;* a *basin* (as *deepened* out):— bowl, dish.

H5603 סָפַן *sāpan* a primitive root; to *hide* by covering; specifically to *roof* (passive pariticiple as noun, a *roof*) or *wainscot;* figuratively to *reserve:*— ceiled, cover, seated.

H5604 סִפֻּן *sippūn* from H5603; a *wainscot:*— ceiling.

H5605 סָפַף *sāpap* a primitive root; properly to *snatch* away, i.e. *terminate;* but used only as denominative from H5592 (in the sense of a *vestibule*), to *wait at* the *threshold:*— be a door-keeper.

H5606 סָפַק *sāpaq* or

שָׂפַק *śāpaq* (1 Kings 20:10; Job 27:23; Isa 2:6), a primitive root; to *clap* the hands (in token of compact, derision, grief, indignation or punishment); by implication of satisfaction, to *be enough;* by implication of excess, to *vomit:*— clap, smite, strike, suffice, wallow.

H5607 סֵפֶק *sēpeq* or

שֶׂפֶק *śepeq* (Job 20:22; 36:18), from H5606; *chastisement;* also *satiety:*— stroke, sufficiency.

H5608 סָפַר *sāpar* a primitive root; properly to *score* with a mark as a tally or record, i.e. (by implication) to *inscribe,* and also to *enumerate;* intensively to *recount,* i.e. *celebrate:*— commune, count, account, declare, number, penknife, reckon, scribe, shew forth, speak, talk, tell, tell out, writer.

H5609 סְפַר *sĕpar* (Aramaic) from a root corresponding to H5608; a *book:*— book, roll.

H5610 סְפָר *sĕpār* from H5608; a *census:*— numbering.

H5611 סְפָר *sĕpār* the same as H5610; *Sephar,* a place in Arabia:— Sephar.

H5612 סֵפֶר *sēper* or (feminine)

סִפְרָה *siprâ* (Ps. 56:8 [9]), from H5608; properly *writing* (the art or a document); by implication a *book:*— bill, book, evidence, learned, learning, letter, register, scroll.

H5613 סָפֵר *sāpēr* (Aramaic) from the same as H5609; a *scribe* (secular or sacred):— scribe.

H5614 סְפָרָד *sĕpārād* of foreign derivation; *Sepharad,* a region of Assyria:— Sepharad.

H5615 סְפֹרָה *sĕpōrâ* from H5608; a *numeration:*— number.

H5616 סְפַרְוִי *sĕparwî* patrial from H5617; a *Sepharvite* or inhabitant of Sepharvain:— Sepharvite.

H5617 סְפַרְוַיִם *sĕparwayim* (dual), or

סְפָרִים *sĕpārîm* (plural) of foreign derivation; *Sepharvajim* or *Sepharim,* a place in Assyria:— Sepharvaim.

H5618 סֹפֶרֶת *sōperet* feminine active participle of H5608; a *scribe* (properly female); *Sophereth,* a temple servant:— Sophereth.

H5619 סָקַל *sāqal* a primitive root; properly to *be weighty;* but used only in the sense of *lapidation* or its contrary (as if a *de*lapidation):— stone, cast stones, gather out stones, throw stones, surely.

H5620 סַר *sar* from H5637 contracted; *peevish:*— heavy, sad.

H5621 סָרָב *sārāb* from an unused root meaning to *sting;* a thistle:— brier.

H5622 סַרְבַּל *sarbal* (Aramaic) of uncertain derivation a *cloak:*— coat.

H5623 סַרְגּוֹן *sargôn* of foreign derivation; *Sargon,* an Assyrian king:— Sargon.

H5624 סֶרֶד *sered* from a primitive root meaning to *tremble; trembling; Sered,* an Israelite:— Sered.

H5625 סַרְדִּי *sardî* patronymic from H5624; a *Seredite* (collectively) or descendant of Sered:— Sardites.

H5626 סִרָה *sîrâ* from H5493; *departure; Sirah,* a cistern so-called:— Sirah. See also H5518

H5627 סָרָה *sārâ* from H5493; *apostasy, crime;* figuratively *remission:*— continual, rebellion, revolt, revolted, turn away, wrong.

H5628 סָרַח *sāraḥ* a primitive root; to *extend* (even to *excess*):— exceeding, hand, spread, stretch self, banish.

H5629 סֶרַח *seraḥ* from H5628; a *redundancy:*— remnant.

H5630 סִרְיֹן *siryōn* for H8302; a coat of *mail:*— brigandine.

H5631 סָרִיס *sārîs* or

סָרִס *sārīs* from an unused root meaning to *castrate;* a *eunuch;* by implication *valet* (especially of the female apartments), and thus a *minister* of state:— chamberlain, eunuch, officer. Compare H7249

H5632 סָרֵךְ *sārēk* (Aramaic) of foreign origin; an *emir:*— president.

H5633 סֶרֶן *seren* from an unused root of uncertain meaning; an *axle;* figuratively a *peer:*— lord, plate.

H5634 סַרְעַפָּה *sarʿappâ* for H5589; a *twig:*— bough.

H5635 סָרַף *sārap* a primitive root; to *cremate,* i.e. to *be* (near) *of kin* (such being privileged to kindle the pyre):— burn.

H5636 סַרְפָּד *sarpād* from H5635; a *nettle* (as stinging like a *burn*):— brier.

H5637 סָרַר *sārar* a primitive root; to *turn* away, i.e. (morally) *be refractory:*— away, backsliding, rebellious, revolter, revolting, slide back, stubborn, withdrew.

H5638 סְתָו *sĕtāw* from an unused root meaning to *hide; winter* (as the dark season):— winter.

H5639 סְתוּר *sĕtûr* from H5641; *hidden; Sethur,* an Israelite:— Sethur.

H5640 סָתַם *sātam* or

שָׂתַם *śātam* (Num. 24:15), a primitive root; to *stop* up; by implication to *repair;* figuratively to *keep secret:*— closed up, hidden, secret, shut out, shut up, stop.

H5641 סָתַר *sātar* a primitive root; to *hide* (by covering), literally or figuratively:— be absent, keep close, conceal, hide, hide self, secret, keep secret, surely.

H5642 סְתַר *sĕtar* (Aramaic) corresponding to H5641; to *conceal;* figuratively to *demolish:*— destroy, secret thing.

H5643 סֵתֶר *sēter* or (feminine)

סִתְרָה *sitrâ* (Deut. 32:38), from H5641; a *cover* (in a good or a bad, a literal or a figurative sense):— backbiting, covering, covert, disguiseth, hiding place, privily, protection, secret, secretly, secret place.

H5644 סִתְרִי *sitrî* from H5643; *protective; Sithri,* an Israelite:— Zithri.

ע

H5645 עָב *ʿāb* masculine and feminine; from H5743; properly an *envelope,* i.e. *darkness* (or *density,* 2 Chron 4:17); specifically a (scud) *cloud;* also a *copse:*— clay, cloud, thick cloud, thick, thicket. Compare H5672

H5646 עָב *ʿāb* or

עֹב *ʿōb* from an unused root meaning to *cover;* properly equivalent to H5645; but used only as an architectural term, an *architrave* (as *shading* the pillars):— thick, thick beam, thick plant.

H5647 עָבַד *ʿābad* a primitive root; to *work* (in any sense); by implication to *serve, till,* (causative) *enslave,* etc:— be, keep in bondage, be bondmen, bond-service, compel, do, dress, ear, execute, husbandman, keep, labour, labouring man, bring to pass, serve, cause to serve, make to serve, serving, serve self, servant, be servants, become servants, do service, use service, till, tiller, transgress *[from margin],* work, set a work, be wrought, worshipper.

H5648 עֲבַד *ʿăbad* (Aramaic) corresponding to H5647; to *do, make, prepare, keep,* etc:— cut, do, execute, go on, make, move work.

H5649 עֲבַד *ʿăbad* (Aramaic) from H5648; a *servant:*— servant.

H5650 עֶבֶד *ʿebed* from H5647; a *servant:*— bondage, bondman, servant, bondservant, manservant.

H5651 עֶבֶד *ʿebed* the same as H5650; *Ebed,* the name of two Israelites:— Ebed.

H5652 עֲבָד *ʿăbād* from H5647; a *deed:*— work.

H5653 עַבְדָּא *ʿabdāʾ* from H5647; *work; Abda,* the name of two Israelites:— Abda.

H5654 עֹבֵד אֱדוֹם *ʿōbēd ʾĕdôm* from the active participle of H5647 and H123; *worker of Edom; Obed-Edom,* the name of five Israelites:— Obed-edom.

H5655 עַבְדְּאֵל *ʿabdĕʾēl* from H5647 and H410; *serving God; Abdeël,* an Israelite:— Abdeel. Compare H5661

H5656 עֲבֹדָה *ʿăbōdâ* or

עֲבוֹדָה *ʿăbôdâ* from H5647; *work* of any kind :— act, bondage, bondservant, effect, labour, ministering, ministry, office, service, servile, servitude, tillage, use, work, wrought.

H5657 עֲבֻדָּה *ʿăbuddâ* passive participle of H5647; something *wrought,* i.e. (concretely) *service:*— household, store of servants.

H5658 עַבְדּוֹן *ʿabdôn* from H5647; *servitude; Abdon,* the name of a place in Palestine and of four Israelites:— Abdon. Compare H5683

H5659 עַבְדוּת *ʿabdût* from H5647; *servitude:*— bondage.

H5660 עַבְדִּי *ʿabdî* from H5647; *serviceable; Abdi,* the name of two Israelites:— Abdi.

H5661 עַבְדִיאֵל *ʿabdîʾēl* from H5650 and H410; *servant of God; Abdiël,* an Israelite:— Abdiel. Compare H5655

H5662 עֹבַדְיָה *ʿōbadyâ* or

עֹבַדְיָהוּ *ʿōbadyāhû* active participle of H5647 and H3050; *serving Jah; Obadjah,* the name of thirteen Israelites:— Obadiah.

H5663 עֶבֶד מֶלֶךְ *ʿebed melek* from H5650 and H4428; *servant of a king; Ebed-Melek,* a eunuch of king Zedekeah:— Ebed-melech.

H5664 עֲבֵד נְגוֹ *ʿăbēd nĕgô* the same as H5665; *Abed-Nego,* the Babylonian name of one of Daniel's companions:— Abed-nego.

H5665 עֲבֵד נְגוֹא *ʿăbēd nĕgôʾ* (Aramaic) of foreign origin; *Abed-Nego,* the name of Azariah:— Abednego.

H5666 עָבָה *ʿābâ* a primitive root; to *be dense:*— be thicker, grow thick.

H5667 עֲבוֹט *ʿăbôṭ* or

עֲבֹט *ʿăbōṭ* from H5670; a *pawn:*— pledge.

H5668 עָבוּר *ʿābûr* or

עָבֻר *ʿābūr* passive participle of H5674; properly *crossed,* i.e. (abstractly) *transit;* used only adverbially on *account* of, in *order* that:— because of, for, for . . . 's sake, that, intent that, to.

H5669 עָבוּר *ʿābûr* the same as H5668; *passed,* i.e. *kept* over; used only of *stored* grain:— old corn.

H5670 עָבַט *ʿābaṭ* a primitive root; to *pawn;* causatively to *lend* (on security); figuratively to *entangle:*— borrow, break *[ranks],* fetch *[a pledge],* lend, surely.

H5671 עַבְטִיט *ʿabṭîṭ* from H5670; something *pledged,* i.e. (collectively) *pawned* goods:— thick clay *[by a false etymology].*

H5672 עֲבִי *ʿăbî* or

עֳבִי *ʿŏbî* from H5666; *density,* i.e. *depth* or *width:*— thick, thickness. Compare H5645

H5673 עֲבִידָה *ʿăbîdâ* (Aramaic) from H5648; *labor* or *business:*— affairs, service, work.

H5674 עָבַר *ʿābar* a primitive root; to *cross* over; used very widely of any *transition* (literal or figurative; transitive, intransitive, intensive or causative); specifically to *cover* (in copulation):— alienate, alter, at all, beyond, bring, bring over, bring through, carry over, come, overcome, come on, come over, conduct, conduct over, convey over, current, deliver, do away, enter, escape, fail, gender, get over, go, make go, go away, go beyond, go by, go forth, go his way, go in, go on, go over, go through, have away, have more, lay, meddle, overrun, make partition, pass, cause to pass, cause to pass through, give passage, make pass, make to pass, overpass, pass along, pass away, pass beyond, pass by, passenger, pass on, pass out, pass over, pass through, proclaim, cause to proclaim, make proclamation, perish, provoke to anger, put away, rage, raiser of taxes, remove, send over, set apart, shave, cause to sound, make sound, speedily, sweet smelling, take, take away, transgress, make to transgress, transgressor, translate, turn away, wayfaring man, be wrath.

H5675 עֲבַר *ʿăbar* (Aramaic) corresponding to H5676 :— beyond, this side.

H5676 עֵבֶר *ʿēber* from H5674; properly a region *across;* but used only adverbially (with or without a preposition) on the *opposite* side (especially of the Jordan; usually meaning the *east*):— against, beyond, by, from, over, passage, quarter, side, other side, this side, straight.

H5677 עֵבֶר *ʿēbēr* the same as H5676; *Eber,* the name of two patriarchs and four Israelites:— Eber, Heber.

H5678 עֶבְרָה *ʿebrâ* feminine of H5676; an *outburst* of passion:— anger, rage, wrath.

H5679 עֲבָרָה *ʿăbārâ* from H5674; a *crossing*-place :— ferry, plain *[from the margin].*

H5680 עִבְרִי *ʿibrî* patronymic from H5677; an *Eberite* (i.e. Hebrew) or descendant of Eber:— Hebrew, Hebrewess, Hebrew woman.

H5681 עִבְרִי *ʿibrî* the same as H5680; *Ibri,* an Israelite:— Ibri.

H5682 עֲבָרִים *ʿăbārîm* plural of H5676; regions *beyond; Abarim,* a place in Palestine:— Abarim, passages.

H5683 עֶבְרֹן *ʿebrōn* from H5676; *transitional; Ebron,* a place in Palestine:— Hebron. Perhaps a clerical error for H5658.

H5684 עֶבְרֹנָה *ʿebrōnâ* feminine of H5683; *Ebronah,* a place in the Desert:— Ebronah.

H5685 עָבַשׁ *ʿābaš* a primitive root; to *dry* up:— be rotten.

H5686 עָבַת *ʿābat* a primitive root; to *interlace,* i.e. (figuratively) to *pervert:*— wrap up.

H5687 עָבֹת *ʿābōt* or

עָבוֹת *ʿābôt* from H5686; *intwined,* i.e. *dense* :— thick.

H5688 עֲבֹת *ʿăbōt* or

עֲבוֹת *ʿăbôt* or (feminine)

עֲבֹתָה *ʿăbōtâ* the same as H5687; something *intwined,* i.e. a *string, wreath* or *foliage:*— band, cord, rope, thick bough, thick branch, wreathen, wreathen chain.

H5689 עָגַב *ʿāgab* a primitive root; to *breathe* after, i.e. to *love* (sensually):— dote, lover.

H5690 עֶגֶב *ʿegeb* from H5689; *love* (concretely), i.e. *amative* words:— much love, very lovely.

H5691 עֲגָבָה *ʿăgābâ* from H5689; *love* (abstractly), i.e. *amorousness:*— inordinate love.

H5692 עֻגָּה *ʿuggâ* from H5746; an *ashcake* (as *round*):— cake, cake upon the hearth.

H5693 עָגוּר *ʿāgûr* passive participle [but with active sense] of an unused root meaning to *twitter;* probably the *swallow:*— swallow.

H5694 עָגִיל *ʿāgîl* from the same as H5696; something *round,* i.e. a *ring* (for the ears):— earring.

H5695 עֵגֶל *ʿēgel* from the same as H5696; a (male) *calf* (as *frisking* round), especially one nearly grown (i.e. a *steer*):— bullock, calf.

H5696 עָגֹל *ʿāgōl* or

עָגוֹל *ʿāgôl* from an unused root meaning to *revolve, circular:*— round.

H5697 עֶגְלָה *ʿeglâ* feminine of H5695; a (female) *calf,* especially one nearly grown (i.e. a *heifer*):— calf, cow, heifer.

H5698 עֶגְלָה *ʿeglâ* the same as H5697; *Eglah,* a wife of David:— Eglah.

H5699 עֲגָלָה *ʿăgālâ* from the same as H5696; something *revolving,* i.e. a wheeled *vehicle:*— cart, chariot, wagon.

H5700 עֶגְלוֹן *ʿeglôn* from H5695; *vituline; Eglon,* the name of a place in Palestine and of a Moabitish king:— Eglon.

H5701 עָגַם *ʿāgam* a primitive root; to *be sad:*— grieve.

H5702 עָגַן *ʿāgan* a primitive root; to *debar,* i.e. from marriage:— stay.

H5703 עַד *ʿad* from H5710; properly a (peremptory) *terminus,* i.e. (by implication) *duration,* in the sense of *advance* or *perpetuity* (substantially as a noun, either with or without a preposition):— eternity, ever, everlasting, evermore, old, perpetually, world without end.

H5704 עַד *ʿad* properly the same as H5703 (used as a preposition, adverb or conjunction; especially with a preposition); *as far* (or *long,* or *much*) *as,* whether of space *(even unto)* or time *(during, while, until)* or degree *(equally with)*:— against, and, as, at, before, by, by that, even, even to, for, forasmuch as, hitherto, how long, into, so long as, so much as, that, so that, till, toward, until, when, while, yet, as yet.

H5705 עַד *ʿad* (Aramaic) corresponding to H5704 :— and, at, for, hitherto, on, till, to, unto, until, within.

H5706 עַד *ʿad* the same as H5703 in the sense of the *aim* of an attack; *booty:*— prey.

H5707 עֵד *ʿēd* from H5749 contracted; concretely *a witness;* abstractly *testimony;* specifically a *recorder,* i.e. *prince:*— witness.

H5708 עֵד *ʿēd* from an unused root meaning to *set* a period [compare H5710, H5749]; the *menstrual* flux (as periodical); by implication (in plural) *soiling:*— filthy.

H5709 עֲדָא *ʿădāʾ* or

עֲדָה *ʿădâ* (Aramaic) corresponding to H5710 :— alter, depart, pass, pass away, remove, take, take away.

H5710 עָדָה *ʿādâ* a primitive root; to *advance,* i.e. *pass* on or *continue;* causatively to *remove;* specifically to *bedeck* (i.e. bring an ornament upon):— adorn, deck, deck self, pass by, take away.

H5711 עָדָה *ʿādâ* from H5710; *ornament; Adah,* the name of two women:— Adah.

H5712 עֵדָה *ʿēdâ* feminine of H5707 in the original sense of *fixture;* a stated *assemblage* (specifically a *concourse,* or generally a *family* or *crowd*):— assembly, company, congregation, multitude, people, swarm. Compare H5713

H5713 עֵדָה *ʿēdâ* feminine of H5707 in its technical sense; *testimony:*— testimony, witness. Compare H5712

H5714 עִדּוֹ *ʿiddô* or

עִדּוֹא *ʿiddôʾ* or

עִדִּיא *ʿiddîʾ* from H5710; *timely; Iddo* (or *Iddi*), the name of five Israelites:— Iddo. Compare H3035, H3260

H5715 עֵדוּת *ʿēdût* feminine of H5707; *testimony* :— testimony, witness.

H5716 עֲדִי *ʿădî* from H5710 in the sense of *trappings; finery;* generally an *outfit;* specifically a *headstall:*— excellent, mouth, ornament.

H5717 עֲדִיאֵל *ʿădîʾēl* from H5716 and H410; *ornament of God; Adiel,* the name of three Israelites:— Adiel.

H5718 עֲדָיָה *ʿădāyâ* or

עֲדָיָהוּ *ʿădāyāhû* from H5710 and H3050; *Jah has adorned; Adajah,* the name of eight Israelites:— Adaiah.

H5719 עָדִין *ʿādîn* from H5727; *voluptuous:*— given to pleasures.

H5720 עָדִין *ʿādîn* the same as H5719; *Adin,* the name of two Israelites:— Adin.

H5721 עֲדִינָא *ʿădōynāʾ* from H5719; *effeminacy; Adina,* an Israelite:— Adina.

H5722 עֲדִינוֹ *ʿădînô* probably from H5719 in the original sense of *slender* (i.e. a *spear*); *his spear:*— Adino.

H5723 עֲדִיתַיִם *ʿădîtayim* dual of a feminine of H5706; *double prey; Adithajim,* a place in Palestine:— Adithaim.

H5724 עַדְלַי *ʿadlay* probably from an unused root of uncertain meaning; *Adlai,* an Israelite:— Adlai.

H5725 עֲדֻלָּם *ʿădullām* probably from the passive participle of the same as H5724; *Adullam,* a place in Palestine:— Adullam.

H5726 עֲדֻלָּמִי *ʿădullāmî* patrial from H5725; an *Adullamite* or native of Adullam:— Adullamite.

H5727 עָדַן *ʿādan* a primitive root; to be *soft* or *pleasant;* figuratively and reflexively to *live voluptuously:*— delight self.

H5728 עֲדֶן *ʿăden* or

עֲדֶנָּה *ʿădennâ* from H5704 and H2004; *till now:*— yet.

H5729 עֶדֶן *ʿeden* from H5727; *pleasure; Eden,* a place in Mesopotamia:— Eden.

H5730 עֵדֶן *ʿēden* or (feminine)

עֶדְנָה *ʿednâ* from H5727; *pleasure:*— delicate, delight, pleasure. See also H1040

H5731 עֵדֶן *ʿēden* the same as H5730 (masculine); *Eden,* the region of Adam's home:— Eden.

H5732 עִדָּן *ʿiddān* (Aramaic) from a root corresponding to that of H5708; a set *time;* technically a *year:*— time.

H5733 עַדְנָא *ʿadnāʾ* from H5727; *pleasure; Adna,* the name of two Israelites:— Adna.

H5734 עַדְנָה *ʿadnâ* from H5727; *pleasure; Adnah,* the name of two Israelites:— Adnah.

H5735 עֲדְעָדָה *ʿădʿādâ* from H5712; *festival; Adadah,* a place in Palestine:— Adadah.

H5736 עָדַף *ʿādap* a primitive root; to *be* (causatively *have*) *redundant:*— be more, odd number, be over and above, have over, overplus, remain.

H5737 עָדַר *ʿādar* a primitive root; to *arrange,* as a battle, a vineyard (to *hoe*); hence to *muster,* and so to *miss* (or find *wanting*):— dig, fall, keep, keep rank, lack.

H5738 עֶדֶר *ʿeder* from H5737; an *arrangement* (i.e. drove); *Eder,* an Israelite:— Ader.

H5739 עֵדֶר *ʿēder* from H5737; an *arrangement,* i.e. *muster* (of animals):— drove, flock, herd.

H5740 עֵדֶר *ʿēder* the same as H5739; *Eder,* the name of an Israelite and of two places in Palestine:— Edar, Eder.

H5741 עַדְרִיאֵל *ʿadrîʾēl* from H5739 and H410; *flock of God; Adriel,* an Israelite:— Adriel.

H5742 עָדָשׁ *ʿādāš* from an unused root of uncertain meaning; a *lentil:*— lentile.

H5743 עוּב *ʿûb* a primitive root; to be *dense* or *dark,* i.e. to *becloud:*— cover with a cloud.

H5744 עוֹבֵד *ʿôbēd* active participle of H5647; *serving; Obed,* the name of five Israelites:— Obed.

H5745 עוֹבָל *ʿôbāl* of foreign derivation; *Obal,* a son of Joktan:— Obal.

H5746 עוּג *ʿûg* a primitive root; properly to *gyrate;* but used only as denominative from H5692, to *bake* (round cakes on the hearth):— bake.

H5747 עוֹג *ʿôg* probably from H5746; *round; Og,* a king of Bashan:— Og.

H5748 עוּגָב *ʿûgāb* or

עֻגָּב *ʿuggāb* from H5689 in the original sense of *breathing;* a *reed*-instrument of music:— organ.

H5749 עוּד *ʿûd* a primitive root; to *duplicate* or *repeat;* by implication to *protest, testify* (as by reiteration); intensively to *encompass, restore* (as a sort of reduplication):— admonish, charge, earnestly, lift up, protest, call to record, take to record, relieve, rob, solemnly, stand upright, testify, give warning, witness, bear witness, call to witness, give witness, take to witness.

H5750 עוֹד *ʿôd* or

עֹד *ʿōd* from H5749; properly *iteration* or *continuance;* used only adverbially (with or without preposition), *again, repeatedly, still, more:*— again, all life long, at all, besides, but, else, further, furthermore, henceforth, longer, any longer, more, any more, moreover, once, since, still, be still, when, good while, the while, while having being, yet, as yet, because yet, whether yet, while yet, yet within.

H5751 עוֹד *ʿôd* (Aramaic) corresponding to H5750 :— while.

H5752 עוֹדֵד *ʿôdēd* or

עֹדֵד *ʿōdēd* from H5749; *reiteration; Oded,* the name of two Israelites:— Oded.

H5753 עָוָה *ʿāwâ* a primitive root; to *crook,* literally or figuratively (as follows):— do amiss, bow down, make crooked, commit iniquity, pervert, perverse, do perversely, trouble, turn, do wickedly, do wrong.

H5754 עַוָּה *ʿawwâ* intensively from H5753 abbreviated; *overthrow:*— overturn.

H5755 עִוָּה *ʿiwwâ* or

עַוָּא *ʿawwāʾ* (2 Kings 17:24), for H5754; *Ivvah* or *Avva,* a region of Assyria:— Ava, Ivah.

H5756 עוּז *ʿûz* a primitive root; to *be strong;* causatively to *strengthen,* i.e. (figuratively) to *save* (by flight):— gather, gather self, gather self to flee, retire.

H5757 עַוִּי *ʿawwî* patrial from H5755; an *Avvite* or native of Avvah (only plural):— Avims, Avites.

H5758 עִוְיָא *ʿiwyāʾ* (Aramaic) from a root corresponding to H5753; *perverseness:*— iniquity.

H5759 עֲוִיל *ʿăwîl* from H5764; a *babe:*— young child, little one.

H5760 עֲוִיל *ʿăwîl* from H5765; *perverse* (morally) :— ungodly.

H5761 עַוִּים *ʿawwîm* plural of H5757; *Avvim* (as inhabited by Avvites), a place in Palestine (with the article prefixed):— Avim.

H5762 עֲוִית *ʿăwît* or perhaps

עַיּוֹת *ʿayyôt* as if plural of H5857

עַיּוּת *ʿayût* from H5753; *ruin; Avvith* (or *Avvoth*), a place in Palestine:— Avith.

H5763 עוּל *ʿûl* a primitive root; to *suckle,* i.e. *give milk:*— milch, with young, ewe great with young.

H5764 עוּל *ʿûl* from H5763; a *babe:*— sucking child, infant.

H5765 עָוַל *ʿāwal* a primitive root; to *distort* (morally):— deal unjustly, unrighteous.

H5766 עֶוֶל *ʿewel* or

עָוֶל *ʿāwel* and (feminine)

עַוְלָה *ʿawlâ* or

עוֹלָה *ʿôlâ* or

עֹלָה *ʿōlâ* from H5765; (moral) *evil:*— iniquity, perverseness, unjust, unjustly, unrighteousness, unrighteously, wicked, wickedness.

H5767 עַוָּל *ʿawwāl* intensive from H5765; *evil* (morally):— unjust, unrighteous, wicked.

H5768 עוֹלֵל *ʿôlēl* or

עֹלָל *ʿōlāl* from H5763; a *suckling:*— babe, child, young child, infant, little one.

H5769 עוֹלָם *ʿôlām* or

עֹלָם *ʿōlām* from H5956; properly *concealed,* i.e. the *vanishing* point; generally time *out of mind* (past or future), i.e. (practically) *eternity;* frequently adverbially (especially with preposition prefixed) *always:*— alway, always, ancient, ancient time, any more, continuance, eternal, ever, for ever, never, everlasting, evermore, ever of old, lasting, long, long time, old, of old, of old time, perpetual, at any time, world, beginning of the world, world without end. Compare H5331, H5703

H5770 עָוַן *ʿāwan* denominative from H5869; to *watch* (with jealousy):— eye.

H5771 עָוֹן *ʿāwōn* or

עָווֹן *ʿāwôn* (2 Kings 7:9; Ps 51:5 [7]), from H5753; *perversity,* i.e. (moral) *evil:*— fault, iniquity, mischief, punishment, punishment of iniquity, sin.

H5772 עוֹנָה *ʿônâ* from an unused root apparently meaning to *dwell* together; (sexual) *cohabitation:*— duty of marriage.

H5773 עַוְעֶה *ʿawʿeh* from H5753; *perversity:*— perverse.

H5774 עוּף *ʿûp* a primitive root; to *cover* (with wings or obscurity); hence (as denominative from H5775) to *fly;* also (by implication of dimness) to *faint* (from the darkness of swooning):— brandish, be faint, wax faint, flee away, fly, fly away, set, shine forth, weary.

H5775 עוֹף *ʿôp* from H5774; a *bird* (as *covered* with feathers, or rather as *covering* with wings), often collectively:— bird, that flieth, flying, fowl.

H5776 עוֹף *ʿôp* (Aramaic) corresponding to H5775 :— fowl.

H5777 עוֹפֶרֶת *ʿôperet* or

עֹפֶרֶת *ʿōperet* feminine participle active of H6080; *lead* (from its *dusty* color):— lead.

H5778 עוֹפַי *ʿôpay* from H5775; *birdlike; Ephai,* an Israelite:— Ephai *[from margin].*

H5779 עוּץ *ʿûṣ* a prim .root; to *consult:*— take advice, take counsel together.

H5780 עוּץ *ʿûṣ* apparently from H5779; *consultation; Uts,* a son of Aram, also a Seirite, and the regions settled by them:— Uz.

H5781 עוּק *ʿûq* a primitive root; to *pack:*— be pressed.

H5782 עוּר *ʿûr* a primitive root [rather identical with H5783 through the idea of *opening* the eyes]; to *wake* (literally or figuratively):— awake, waken, wake up, lift up, lift up self, master, raise, raise up, stir up, stir up self.

H5783 עוּר *ʿûr* a primitive root; to *(be) bare:*— be made naked.

H5784 עוּר *ʿûr* (Aramaic) *chaff* (as the *naked* husk) :— chaff.

H5785 עוֹר *ʿôr* from H5783; *skin* (as *naked*); by implication *hide, leather:*— hide, leather, skin.

H5786 עָוַר *ʿāwar* a primitive root [rather denominatively from H5785 through the idea of a *film* over the eyes]; to *blind:*— blind, put out. See also H5895

H5787 עִוֵּר *ʿēwwēr* intensive from H5786; *blind* (literally or figuratively):— blind, blind men, blind people.

H5788 עִוָּרוֹן *ʿiwwārôn* and (feminine)

עַוֶּרֶת *ʿawweret* from H5787; *blindness:*— blind, blindness.

H5789 עוּשׁ *ʿûš* a primitive root; to *hasten:*— assemble self.

H5790 עוּת *ʿût* for H5789; to *hasten,* i.e. *succor:*— speak in season.

H5791 עָוַת *ʿāwat* a primitive root; to *wrest:*— bow self, crooked, make crooked, falsifying, overthrow, deal perversely, pervert, subvert, turn upside down.

H5792 עַוָּתָה *ʿawwātâ* from H5791; *oppression:*— wrong.

H5793 עוּתַי *ʿûtay* from H5790; *succoring; Uthai,* the name of two Israelites:— Uthai.

H5794 עַז *ʿaz* from H5810; *strong, vehement, harsh* :— fierce, greedy, mighty, power, roughly, strong.

H5795 עֵז *ʿēz* from H5810; a she-*goat* (as *strong*), but masculine in plural (which also is used elliptically for *goats' hair*):— goat, she goat, kid.

H5796 עֵז *ʿēz* (Aramaic) corresponding to H5795 :— goat.

H5797 עֹז *ʿōz* or (fully)

עוֹז *ʿôz* from H5810; *strength* in various applications *(force, security, majesty, praise)*:— boldness, loud, might, power, strength, strong.

H5798 עֻזָּא *ʿuzzāʾ* or

עֻזָּה *ʿuzzâ* feminine of H5797; *strength; Uzza* or *Uzzah,* the name of five Israelites:— Uzza, Uzzah.

H5799 עֲזָאזֵל *ʿăzāʾzēl* from H5795 and H235; *goat of departure;* the *scapegoat:*— scapegoat.

H5800 עָזַב *ʿāzab* a primitive root; to *loosen,* i.e. *relinquish, permit,* etc:— commit self, fail, forsake, fortify, help, leave, leave destitute, leave off, refuse, surely.

H5801 עִזָּבוֹן *ʿizzābôn* from H5800 in the sense of *letting go* (for a price, i.e. *selling*); *trade,* i.e. the place *(mart)* or the payment *(revenue)*:— fair, ware.

H5802 עַזְבּוּק *ʿazbûq* from H5794 and the root of H950; *stern depopulator; Azbuk,* an Israelite:— Azbuk.

H5803 עַזְגָּד *ʿazgād* from H5794 and H1409; *stern troop; Azgad,* an Israelite:— Azgad.

H5804 עַזָּה *ʿazzâ* feminine of H5794; *strong; Azzah,* a place in Palestine:— Azzah, Gaza.

H5805 עֲזוּבָה *ʿăzûbâ* feminine passive participle of H5800; *desertion* (of inhabitants):— forsaking.

H5806 עֲזוּבָה *ʿăzûbâ* the same as H5805; *Azubah,* the name of two Israelitesses:— Azubah.

H5807 עֱזוּז *ʿĕzûz* from H5810; *forcibleness:*— might, strength.

H5808 עִזּוּז *ʿizzûz* from H5810; *forcible;* collectively and concretely an *army:*— power, strong.

H5809 עַזּוּר *ʿazzûr* or

עַזֻּר *ʿazzūr* from H5826; *helpful; Azzur,* the name of three Israelites:— Azur, Azzur.

H5810 עָזַז ʿ*āzaz* a primitive root; to *be stout* (literally or figuratively):— harden, impudent, prevail, strengthen, strengthen self, be strong.

H5811 עָזָז ʿ*āzāz* from H5810; *strong; Azaz,* an Israelite:— Azaz.

H5812 עֲזַזְיָהוּ ʿ*ăzazyāhû* from H5810 and H3050; *Jah has strengthened; Azazjah,* the name of three Israelites:— Azaziah.

H5813 עֻזִּי ʿ*uzzî* from H5810; *forceful; Uzzi,* the name of six Israelites:— Uzzi.

H5814 עֻזִּיָּא ʿ*uzzîyāʾ* perhaps for H5818; *Uzzija,* an Israelite:— Uzzia.

H5815 עֲזִיאֵל ʿ*ăzîʾēl* from H5756 and H410; *strengthened of God; Aziël,* an Israelite:— Aziel. Compare H3268

H5816 עֻזִּיאֵל ʿ*uzzîʾēl* from H5797 and H410; *strength of God; Uzziël,* the name of six Israelites:— Uzziel.

H5817 עָזִּיאֵלִי ʿ*ozzîʾēlî* patronymic from H5816; an *Uzziëlite* (collectively) or descendant of Uzziel :— Uzzielites.

H5818 עֻזִּיָּה ʿ*uzzîyâ* or

עֻזִּיָּהוּ ʿ*uzzîyāhû* from H5797 and H3050; *strength of Jah; Uzzijah,* the name of five Israelites:— Uzziah.

H5819 עֲזִיזָא ʿ*ăzîzāʾ* from H5756; *strengthfulness; Aziza,* an Israelite:— Aziza.

H5820 עַזְמָוֶת ʿ*azmāwet* from H5794 and H4194; *strong* one *of death; Azmaveth,* the name of three Israelites and of a place in Palestine:— Azmaveth. See also H1041

H5821 עַזָּן ʿ*azzān* from H5794; *strong* one; *Azzan,* an Israelite:— Azzan.

H5822 עָזְנִיָּה ʿ*oznîyâ* probably feminine of H5797; probably the *sea-eagle* (from its *strength*):— ospray.

H5823 עָזַק ʿ*āzaq* a primitive root; to *grub* over:— fence about.

H5824 עִזְקָא ʿ*izqāʾ* (Aramaic) from a root corresponding to H5823; a *signet*-ring (as engraved):— signet.

H5825 עֲזֵקָה ʿ*ăzēqâ* from H5823; *tilled; Azekah,* a place in Palestine:— Azekah.

H5826 עָזַר ʿ*āzar* a primitive root; to *surround,* i.e. *protect* or *aid:*— help, succour.

H5827 עֶזֶר ʿ*ezer* from H5826; *help; Ezer,* the name of two Israelites:— Ezer. Compare H5829

H5828 עֵזֶר ʿ*ēzer* from H5826; *aid:*— help.

H5829 עֵזֶר ʿ*ēzer* the same as H5828; *Ezer,* the name of four Israelites:— Ezer. Compare H5827

H5830 עֶזְרָא ʿ*ezrāʾ* a variation of H5833; *Ezra,* an Israelite:— Ezra.

H5831 עֶזְרָא ʿ*ezrāʾ* (Aramaic) corresponding to H5830; *Ezra,* an Israelite:— Ezra.

H5832 עֲזַרְאֵל ʿ*ăzarʾēl* from H5826 and H410; *God has helped; Azarel,* the name of five Israelites:— Azarael, Azareel.

H5833 עֶזְרָה ʿ*ezrâ* or

עֶזְרָת ʿ*ezrāt* (Ps. 60:11 [13]; 108:12 [13]), feminine of H5828; *aid:*— help, helped, helper.

H5834 עֶזְרָה ʿ*ezrâ* the same as H5833; *Ezrah,* an Israelite:— Ezrah.

H5835 עֲזָרָה ʿ*ăzārâ* from H5826 in its original meaning of *surrounding;* an *inclosure;* also a *border:*— court, settle.

H5836 עֶזְרִי ʿ*ezrî* from H5828; *helpful; Ezri,* an Israelite:— Ezri.

H5837 עַזְרִיאֵל ʿ*azrîʾēl* from H5828 and H410; *help of God; Azriël,* the name of three Israelites:— Azriel.

H5838 עֲזַרְיָה ʿ*ăzaryâ* or

עֲזַרְיָהוּ ʿ*ăzaryāhû* from H5826 and H3050; *Jah has helped; Azarjah,* the name of nineteen Israelites:— Azariah.

H5839 עֲזַרְיָה ʿ*ăzaryâ* (Aramaic) corresponding to H5838; *Azarjah,* one of Daniel's companions:— Azariah.

H5840 עַזְרִיקָם ʿ*azrîqām* from H5828 and active participle of H6965; *help of an enemy; Azrikam,* the name of four Israelites:— Azrikam.

H5841 עַזָּתִי ʿ*azzātî* patrial from H5804; an *Azzathite* or inhabitant of Azzah:— Gazathite, Gazite.

H5842 עֵט ʿ*ēṭ* from H5860 (contracted) in the sense of *swooping,* i.e. *side-long stroke;* a *stylus* or marking stick:— pen.

H5843 עֵטָא ʿ*ēṭāʾ* (Aramaic) from H3272; *prudence* :— counsel.

H5844 עָטָה ʿ*āṭâ* a primitive root; to *wrap,* i.e. *cover, veil, clothe* or *roll:*— array self, be clad, cover, put a covering, cover self, fill, put on, surely, turn aside.

H5845 עֲטִין ʿ*ăṭîn* from an unused root meaning apparently to *contain;* a *receptacle* (for milk, i.e. *pail;* figuratively *breast*):— breast.

H5846 עֲטִישָׁה ʿ*ăṭîšâ* from an unused root meaning to *sneeze; sneezing:*— sneezing.

H5847 עֲטַלֵּף ʿ*ăṭallēp* of uncertain derivation; a *bat* :— bat.

H5848 עָטַף ʿ*āṭap* a primitive root; to *shroud,* i.e. *clothe* (whether transitively or reflexively); hence (from the idea of *darkness*) to *languish:*— cover, cover over, fall, faint, feebler, hide self, be overwhelmed, swoon.

H5849 עָטַר ʿ*āṭar* a primitive root; to *encircle* (for attack or protection); especially to *crown* (literally or figuratively):— compass, crown.

H5850 עֲטָרָה ʿ*ăṭārâ* from H5849; a *crown:*— crown.

H5851 עֲטָרָה ʿ*ăṭārâ* the same as H5850; *Atarah,* an Israelitess:— Atarah.

H5852 עֲטָרוֹת ʿ*ăṭārôt* or

עֲטָרֹת ʿ*ăṭārōt* plural of H5850; *Ataroth,* the name (thus simply) of two places in Palestine:— Ataroth.

H5853 עַטְרוֹת אַדָּר ʿ*aṭrôt ʾaddār* from the same as H5852 and H146; *crowns of Addar; Atroth-Addar,* a place in Palestine:— Ataroth-adar, Ataroth-addar.

H5854 עַטְרוֹת בֵּית יוֹאָב ʿ*aṭrôt bêt yôʾāb* from the same as H5852 and H1004 and H3097; *crowns of the house of Joäb; Atroth-beth-Joäb,* a place in Palestine:— Ataroth the house of Joab.

H5855 עַטְרוֹת שׁוֹפָן ʿ*aṭrôt šôpān* from the same as H5852 and a name otherwise unused [being from the same as H8226] meaning *hidden; crowns of Shophan; Atroth-Shophan,* a place in Palestine:— Atroth, Shophan *[as if two places].*

H5856 עִי ʿ*î* from H5753; a *ruin* (as if overturned) :— heap.

H5857 עַי ʿ*ay* or (feminine)

עַיָּא ʿ*ayyāʾ* (Neh. 11:31), or

עַיָּת ʿ*ayyāt* (Isa. 10:28), for H5856; *Ai, Aja* or *Ajath,* a place in Palestine:— Ai, Aija, Aijath, Hai.

H5858 עֵיבָל ʿ*êbāl* perhaps from an unused root probably meaning to be *bald; bare; Ebal,* a mountain of Palestine:— Ebal.

H5859 עִיּוֹן ʿ*îyôn* from H5856; *ruin; Ijon,* a place in Palestine:— Ijon.

H5860 עִיט ʿ*îṭ* a primitive root; to *swoop* down upon (literally or figuratively):— fly, rail.

H5861 עַיִט ʿ*ayiṭ* from H5680; a *hawk* or other bird of prey:— bird, fowl, ravenous, ravenous bird.

H5862 עֵיטָם ʿ*êṭām* from H5861; *hawk-ground; Etam,* a place in Palestine:— Etam.

H5863 עִיֵּי הָעֲבָרִים ʿ*îyê hāʿăbārîm* from the plural of H5856 and the plural of the active participle of H5674 with the article interposed; *ruins of the passers; Ije-ha-Abarim,* a place near Palestine:— Ije-abarim.

H5864 עִיִּים ʿ*îyîm* plural of H5856; *ruins; Ijim,* a place in the Desert:— Iim.

H5865 עֵילוֹם ʿ*êlôm* for H5769:— ever.

H5866 עִילַי ʿ*îlay* from H5927; *elevated; Ilai,* an Israelite:— Ilai.

H5867 עֵילָם ʿ*êlām* or

עוֹלָם ʿ*ôlām* (Ezra 10:2; Jer 49:36), probably from H5956; *hidden,* i.e. *distant; Elam,* a son of Shem, and his descendants, with their country; also of six Israelites:— Elam.

H5868 עֲיָם ʿ*ăyām* of doubtful origin and authenticity; probably meaning *strength:*— mighty.

H5869 עַיִן ʿ*ayin* probably a primitive word; an *eye* (literal or figurative); by analogy a *fountain* (as the *eye* of the landscape):— affliction, outward appearance, before, think best, colour, conceit, be content, countenance, displease, eye, eyebrow, eyed, eyesight, face, favour, fountain, furrow *[from the margin],* him, humble, knowledge, look, look well, me, open, openly, please, not please, presence, regard, resemblance, sight, thee, them, think, us, well, you, yourselves.

H5870 עַיִן ʿ*ayin* (Aramaic) corresponding to H5869; an *eye:*— eye.

H5871 עַיִן ʿ*ayin* the same as H5869; *fountain; Ajin,* the name (thus simply) of two places in Palestine:— Ain.

H5872 עֵין גֶּדִי ʿ*ên gedî* from H5869 and H1423; *fountain of a kid; En-Gedi,* a place in Palestine:— En-gedi.

H5873 עֵין גַּנִּים ʿ*ên gannîm* from H5869 and the plural of H1588; *fountain of gardens; En-Gannim,* a place in Palestine:— En-gannim.

H5874 עֵין־דֹּאר ʿ*ên-dʾōr* or

עֵין דּוֹר ʿ*ên dôr* or

עֵין־דֹּר ʿ*ên-dōr* from H5869 and H1755; *fountain of dwelling; En-Dor,* a place in Palestine:— En-dor.

H5875 עֵין הַקּוֹרֵא ʿ*ên haqqôrēʾ* from H5869 and the active participle of H7121; *fountain of One calling; En-hak-Korè,* a place near Palestine:— En-hakhore.

H5876 עֵין חַדָּה ʿ*ên ḥaddâ* from H5869 and the feminine of a derivative from H2300; *fountain of sharpness; En-Chaddah,* a place in Palestine:— En-haddah.

H5877 עֵין חָצוֹר ʿên ḥāṣôr from H5869 and the same as H2674; *fountain of a village; En-Chatsor,* a place in Palestine:— En-hazor.

H5878 עֵין חֲרֹד ʿên ḥărōd from H5869 and a derivative of H2729; *fountain of trembling; En-Charod,* a place in Palestine:— well of Harod.

H5879 עֵינַיִם ʿênayim or

עֵינָם ʿênām dual of H5869; *double fountain; Enajim* or *Enam,* a place in Palestine:— Enaim, openly (Gen 38:21).

H5880 עֵין מִשְׁפָּט ʿên mišpāṭ from H5869 and H4941; *fountain of judgment; En-Mishpat,* a place near Palestine:— En-mishpat.

H5881 עֵינָן ʿênān from H5869; *having eyes; Enan,* an Israelite:— Enan. Compare H2704

H5882 עֵין עֶגְלַיִם ʿên ʿeglayim from H5869 and the dual of H5695; *fountain of two calves; En-Eglajim,* a place in Palestine:— En-eglaim.

H5883 עֵין רֹגֵל ʿên rōgēl from H5869 and the active participle of H7270; *fountain of a traveller; En-Rogel,* a place near Jerusalem:— En-rogel.

H5884 עֵין רִמּוֹן ʿên rimmôn from H5869 and H7416; *fountain of a pomegranate; En-Rimmon,* a place in Palestine:— En-rimmon.

H5885 עֵין שֶׁמֶשׁ ʿên šemeš from H5869 and H8121; *fountain of the sun; En-Shemesh,* a place in Palestine:— En-shemesh.

H5886 עֵין תַּנִּים ʿên tannîm from H5869 and the plural of H8565; *fountain of jackals; En-Tannim,* a pool near Jerusalem:— dragon well.

H5887 עֵין תַּפּוּחַ ʿên tappûaḥ from H5869 and H8598; *fountain of an apple-tree; En-Tappuäch,* a place in Palestine:— En-tappuah.

H5888 עָיֵף ʿāyēp a primitive root; to *languish:*— be wearied.

H5889 עָיֵף ʿāyēp from H5888; *languid:*— faint, thirsty, weary.

H5890 עֵיפָה ʿêpâ feminine from H5774; *obscurity* (as if from *covering*):— darkness.

H5891 עֵיפָה ʿêpâ the same as H5890; *Ephah,* the name of a son of Midian, and of the region settled by him; also of an Israelite and of an Isrealitess:— Ephah.

H5892 עִיר ʿîr or (in the plural)

עָר ʿār or

עָיַר ʿāyar (Judg. 10:4), from H5782 a *city* (a place guarded by *waking* or a watch) in the widest sense (even of a mere *encampment* or *post*):— Ai *[from margin],* city, court *[from margin],* town.

H5893 עִיר ʿîr the same as H5892; *Ir,* an Israelite:— Ir.

H5894 עִיר ʿîr (Aramaic) from a root corresponding to H5782; a *watcher,* i.e. an *angel* (as guardian):— watcher.

H5895 עַיִר ʿayîr from H5782 in the sense of *raising* (i.e. *bearing* a burden); properly a young *ass* (as just broken to a load); hence an ass-*colt:*— colt, ass colt, foal, young ass.

H5896 עִירָא ʿîrāʾ from H5782; *wakefulness; Ira,* the name of three Israelites:— Ira.

H5897 עִירָד ʿîrād from the same as H6166; *fugitive; Irad,* an antediluvian:— Irad.

H5898 עִיר הַמֶּלַח ʿîr hammelaḥ from H5892 and H4417 with the article of substance interposed; *city of (the) salt; Ir-ham-Melach,* a place near Palestine:— the city of salt.

H5899 עִיר הַתְּמָרִים ʿîr hattĕmārîm from H5892 and the plural of H8558 with the article interposed; *city of the palmtrees; Ir-hat-Temarim,* a place in Palestine:— the city of palmtrees.

H5900 עִירוּ ʿîrû from H5892; a *citizen; Iru,* an Israelite:— Iru.

H5901 עִירִי ʿîrî from H5892; *urbane; Iri,* an Israelite:— Iri.

H5902 עִירָם ʿîrām from H5892; *city-wise; Iram,* an Idumaean:— Iram.

H5903 עֵירֹם ʿêrōm or

עֵרֹם ʿērōm from H6191; *nudity:*— naked, nakedness.

H5904 עִיר נָחָשׁ ʿîr nāḥāš from H5892 and H5175; *city of a serpent; Ir-Nachash,* a place in Palestine:— Ir-nahash.

H5905 עִיר שֶׁמֶשׁ ʿîr šemeš from H5892 and H8121; *city of the sun; Ir-Shemesh,* a place in Palestine:— Ir-shemesh.

H5906 עַיִשׁ ʿayiš or

עָשׁ ʿāš from H5789; the constellation of the Great *Bear* (perhaps from its *migration* through the heavens):— Arcturus.

H5907 עַכְבּוֹר ʿakbôr probably for H5909; *Akbor,* the name of an Idumaean and two Israelites:— Achbor.

H5908 עַכָּבִישׁ ʿakkābîš probably from an unused root in the literal sense of *entangling;* a *spider* (as *weaving* a network):— spider.

H5909 עַכְבָּר ʿakbār probably from the same as H5908 in the secondary sense of *attacking;* a *mouse* (as *nibbling*):— mouse.

H5910 עַכּוֹ ʿakkô apparently from an unused root meaning to *hem* in; *Akko* (from its situation on a *bay*):— Accho.

H5911 עָכוֹר ʿākôr from H5916; *troubled; Akor,* the name of a place in Palestine:— Achor.

H5912 עָכָן ʿākān from an unused root meaning to *trouble; troublesome; Akan,* an Israelite:— Achan. Compare H5917

H5913 עָכַס ʿākas a primitive root; properly to *tie,* specifically with fetters; but used only as a denominative from H5914; to *put on anklets:*— make a tinkling ornament.

H5914 עֶכֶס ʿekes from H5913; a *fetter;* hence an *anklet:*— stocks, tinkling ornament.

H5915 עַכְסָה ʿaksâ feminine of H5914; *anklet; Aksah,* an Israelitess:— Achsah.

H5916 עָכַר ʿākar a primitive root; properly to *roil* water; figuratively to *disturb* or *afflict:*— trouble, stir.

H5917 עָכָר ʿākār from H5916; *troublesome; Akar,* an Israelite:— Achar. Compare H5912

H5918 עָכְרָן ʿokrān from H5916; *muddler; Okran,* an Israelite:— Ocran.

H5919 עַכְשׁוּב ʿakšûb probably from an unused root meaning to *coil;* an *asp* (from lurking *coiled* up):— adder.

H5920 עַל ʿal from H5927; properly the *top;* specifically the *Highest* (i.e. *God*); also (adverbially) *aloft, to Jehovah:*— above, high, most High.

H5921 עַל ʿal properly the same as H5920 used as a preposition (in the singular or plural, often with prefix, or as conjunction with a particle following); *above, over, upon,* or *against* (yet always in this last relation with a downward aspect) in a great variety of applications (as follow):— above, according to, accordingly, after, against, as against, among, and, as, at, because of, beside, beside the rest of, between, beyond the time, both and, by, by reason of, had the charge of, concerning for, in, in that, of, forth of, out of, from, from off, on, upon, over, than, through, throughout, to, touching, with.

H5922 עַל ʿal (Aramaic) corresponding to H5921 :— about, against, concerning, for, therefore, from, in, more, of, on, thereon, upon, to, unto, why with.

HEB

H5923 עֹל ʿōl or

עוֹל ʿôl from H5953; a *yoke* (as *imposed* on the neck), literally or figuratively:— yoke.

H5924 עֵלָּא ʿēllāʾ (Aramaic) from H5922; *above* :— over.

H5925 עֻלָּא ʿullāʾ feminine of H5923; *burden; Ulla,* an Israelite:— Ulla.

H5926 עִלֵּג ʿillēg from an unused root meaning to *stutter; stuttering:*— stammerer.

H5927 עָלָה ʿālâ a primitive root; to *ascend,* intransitively *(be high)* or actively *(Mount)*; used in a great variety of senses, primary and secondary, literally and figuratively (as follow):— arise, arise up, ascend up, cause to ascend, at once, break *[the day],* break up, bring, bring up, burn, cause to burn, carry up, cast up, shew, climb, climb up, come, cause to come up, make to come up, come up, cut off, dawn, depart, exalt, excel, fall, fetch up, get up, go, make to go up, go away, go up, grow, grow over, increase, lay, leap, levy, lift up, lift self up, light, make up, mention, mount up, offer, make to pay, perfect, prefer, put, put on, raise, recover, restore, rise, make to rise up, rise up, scale, set, set up, shoot forth, shoot up, spring, begin to spring, spring up, stir up, take away, take up, work.

H5928 עֲלָה ʿălâ (Aramaic) corresponding to H5930; a *holocaust:*— burnt offering.

H5929 עָלֶה ʿāleh from H5927; a *leaf* (as *coming up* on a tree); collectively *foliage:*— branch, leaf.

H5930 עֹלָה ʿōlâ or

עוֹלָה ʿôlâ feminine active participle of H5927; a *step* or (collectively *stairs, as ascending*); usually a *holocaust* (as *going up* in smoke):— ascent, burnt offering, burnt sacrifice, go up to. See also H5766

H5931 עִלָּה ʿillâ (Aramaic) feminine from a root corresponding to H5927; a *pretext* (as *arising* artificially):— occasion.

H5932 עַלְוָה ʿalwâ for H5766; moral *perverseness* :— iniquity.

H5933 עַלְוָה ʿalwâ or

עַלְיָה ʿalyâ the same as H5932; *Alvah* or *Aljah,* an Idumaean:— Aliah, Alvah.

H5934 עָלוּם ʿālûm passive participle of H5956 in the denominative sense of H5958; (only in plural as abstract) *adolescence;* figuratively *vigor:*— youth.

H5935 עַלְוָן ʿalwān or

עַלְיָן ʿalyān from H5927; *lofty; Alvan* or *Aljan,* an Idumaean:— Alian, Alvan.

H5936 עֲלוּקָה ʿălûqâ feminine passive participle of an unused root meaning to *suck;* the *leech:*— horse-leech.

H5937 עָלַז ʿālaz a primitive root; to *jump* for joy, i.e. *exult:*— be joyful, rejoice, triumph.

H5938 עָלֵז *ʿālēz* from H5937; *exultant:*— that rejoiceth.

H5939 עֲלָטָה *ʿălāṭâ* feminine from an unused root meaning to *cover; dusk:*— dark, twilight.

H5940 עֱלִי *ʿĕlî* from H5927; a *pestle* (as *lifted*):— pestle.

H5941 עֵלִי *ʿēlî* from H5927; *lofty; Eli,* an Israelite high-priest:— Eli.

H5942 עִלִּי *ʿillî* from H5927; *high,* i.e. comparatively :— upper.

H5943 עִלַּי *ʿillay* (Aramaic) corresponding to H5942; *supreme* (i.e. *God*):— high, most high.

H5944 עֲלִיָּה *ʿălîyâ* feminine from H5927; something *lofty,* i.e. a *stair-way;* also a *second-story* room (or even one on the roof); figuratively the *sky:*— ascent, chamber, upper chamber, going up, loft, parlour.

H5945 עֶלְיוֹן *ʿelyôn* from H5927; an *elevation,* i.e. (adjectivally) *lofty* (comparatively); as title, the *Supreme:*— high, Most high, on high, higher, highest, upper, uppermost.

H5946 עֶלְיוֹן *ʿelyôn* (Aramaic) corresponding to H5945; the *Supreme:*— Most high.

H5947 עַלִּיז *ʿallîz* from H5937; *exultant:*— joyous, that rejoice, rejoicing.

H5948 עֲלִיל *ʿălîl* from H5953 in the sense of *completing;* probably a *crucible* (as *working* over the metal):— furnace.

H5949 עֲלִילָה *ʿălîlâ* or

עֲלִלָה *ʿălīlâ* from H5953 in the sense of *effecting;* an *exploit* (of God), or a *performance* (of man, often in a bad sense); by implication an *opportunity:*— act, action, deed, doing, invention, occasion, work.

H5950 עֲלִילִיָּה *ʿălîlîyâ* for H5949; (miraculous) *execution:*— work.

H5951 עֲלִיצוּת *ʿălîṣût* from H5970; *exultation:*— rejoicing.

H5952 עַלִּי *ʿallî* (Aramaic) from H5927; a *second-story* room:— chamber. Compare H5944

H5953 עָלַל *ʿālal* a primitive root; to *effect* thoroughly; specifically to *glean* (also figuratively); by implication (in a bad sense) to *overdo,* i.e. maltreat, be saucy to, pain, impose (also literally):— abuse, affect, child, defile, do, glean, mock, practise, throughly, work, work wonderfully.

H5954 עֲלַל *ʿălal* (Aramaic) corresponding to H5953 (in the sense of *thrusting* oneself in), to *enter;* causatively to *introduce:*— bring in, come in, go in.

H5955 עֹלֵלָה *ʿōlēlâ* feminine active participle of H5953; only in plural *gleanings;* by extension *gleaning-time:*— grapes, gleaning grapes, gleaning of the grapes, grapegleanings.

H5956 עָלַם *ʿālam* a primitive root; to *veil* from sight, i.e. *conceal* (literally or figuratively):— any ways, blind, dissembler, hide, hide self, secret, secret thing.

H5957 עָלַם *ʿālam* (Aramaic) corresponding to H5769; *remote* time, i.e. the *future* or *past* indefinitely; often adverbially *forever:*— for ever, never, everlasting, old.

H5958 עֶלֶם *ʿelem* from H5956; properly something *kept out of sight* [compare H5959], i.e. a *lad:*— young man, stripling.

H5959 עַלְמָה *ʿalmâ* feminine of H5958; a *lass* (as *veiled* or private):— damsel, maid, virgin.

H5960 עַלְמוֹן *ʿalmôn* from H5956; *hidden; Almon,* a place in Palestine. See also H5963

H5961 עֲלָמוֹת *ʿălāmôt* plural of H5959; properly *girls,* i.e. the *soprano* or female voice, perhaps *falsetto:*— Alamoth.

H5962 עַלְמִי *ʿalmî* (Aramaic) patrial from a name corresponding to H5867 contracted; an *Elamite* or inhabitant of Elam:— Elamite.

H5963 עַלְמֹן דִּבְלָתָיְמָה *ʿalmôn diblātāyĕmâ* from the same as H5960 and the dual of H1690 [compare H1015] with enclitic of direction; *Almon towards Diblathajim; Almon-Diblathajemah,* a place in Moab :— Almon-diblathaim.

H5964 עָלֶמֶת *ʿālemet* from H5956; a *covering; Alemeth,* the name of a place in Palestine and of two Israelites:— Alameth, Alemeth.

H5965 עָלַס *ʿālas* a primitive root; to *leap* for joy, i.e. *exult, wave* joyously:— peacock, rejoice, solace self.

H5966 עָלַע *ʿālaʿ* a primitive root; to *sip* up:— suck up.

H5967 עֲלַע *ʿălaʿ* (Aramaic) corresponding to H6763; a *rib:*— rib.

H5968 עָלַף *ʿālap* a primitive root; to *veil* or *cover;* figuratively to *be languid:*— faint, overlaid, wrap self.

H5969 עֻלְפֶּה *ʿulpeh* from H5968; an *envelope,* i.e. (figuratively) *mourning:*— fainted.

H5970 עָלַץ *ʿālaṣ* a primitive root; to *jump* for joy, i.e. *exult:*— be joyful, rejoice, triumph.

H5971 עַם *ʿam* from H6004; a *people* (as a congregated *unit*); specifically a *tribe* (as those of Israel); hence (collectively) *troops* or *attendants;* figuratively a *flock:*— folk, men, nation, people.

H5972 עַם *ʿam* (Aramaic) corresponding to H5971 :— people.

H5973 עִם *ʿim* from H6004; adverbially or prepositionally, *with* (i.e. in *conjunction* with), in varied applications; specifically *equally with;* often with preposition prefixed (and then usually unrepresented in English):— accompanying, against, and, as, as long as, before, beside, by, by reason of, for all, from, from among, from between, in, like, more than, of, to, unto, with, withal.

H5974 עִם *ʿim* Aramaic corresponding to H5973 :— by, from, like, to, toward, with.

H5975 עָמַד *ʿāmad* a primitive root; to *stand,* in various relations (literally and figuratively, intransitively and transitively):— abide, abide behind, appoint, arise, cease, confirm, continue, dwell, be employed, endure, establish, leave, make, ordain, be over, place, present, be present, present self, raise up, remain, repair, serve, set, set forth, set over, settle, set up, stand, make to stand, make to be at a stand, withstand, stand by, stand fast, stand firm, stand still, stand up, stay, be at a stay, stay up, tarry.

H5976 עָמַד *ʿāmad* for H4571; to *shake:*— be at a stand.

H5977 עֹמֶד *ʿōmed* from H5975; a *spot* (as being *fixed*):— place, stood, where stood, upright.

H5978 עִמָּד *ʿimmād* prolonged for H5973; along *with:*— against, by, from, in, me, mine, of, that I take, unto, upon, with, within.

H5979 עֶמְדָּה *ʿemdâ* from H5975; a *station,* i.e. domicile:— standing.

H5980 עֻמָּה *ʿummâ* from H6004; *conjunction,* i.e. *society;* mostly adverbially or prepositionally (with preposition prefixed), *near, beside, along with:*— against, over against, at, beside, hard by, in points.

H5981 עֻמָּה *ʿummâ* the same as H5980; *association; Ummah,* a place in Palestine:— Ummah.

H5982 עַמּוּד *ʿammûd* or

עַמֻּד *ʿammūd* from H5975; a *column* (as *standing*); also a *stand,* i.e. platform:— apiece, pillar.

H5983 עַמּוֹן *ʿammôn* from H5971; *tribal,* i.e. *inbred; Ammon,* a son of Lot; also his posterity and their country:— Ammon, Ammonites.

H5984 עַמּוֹנִי *ʿammônî* patronymic from H5983; an *Ammonite* or (adjectivally) *Ammonitish:*— Ammonite, Ammonites.

H5985 עַמּוֹנִית *ʿammônît* feminine of H5984; an *Ammonitess:*— Ammonite, Ammonitess.

H5986 עָמוֹס *ʿāmôs* from H6006; *burdensome; Amos,* an Israelite prophet:— Amos.

H5987 עָמוֹק *ʿāmôq* from H6009; *deep; Amok,* an Israelite:— Amok.

H5988 עַמִּיאֵל *ʿammîʾēl* from H5971 and H410; *people of God; Ammiël,* the name of three or four Israelites:— Ammiel.

H5989 עַמִּיהוּד *ʿammîhûd* from H5971 and H1935; *people of splendor; Ammihud,* the name of three Israelites:— Ammihud.

H5990 עַמִּיזָבָד *ʿammîzābād* from H5971 and H2064; *people of endowment; Ammizabad,* an Israelite:— Ammizabad.

H5991 עַמִּיחוּר *ʿammîḥûr* from H5971 and H2353; *people of nobility; Ammichur,* a Syrian prince:— Ammihud *[from the margin].*

H5992 עַמִּינָדָב *ʿammînādāb* from H5971 and H5068; *people of liberality; Amminidab,* the name of four Israelites:— Amminidab.

H5993 עַמִּי נָדִיב *ʿammî nādîb* from H5971 and H5081; *my people* (is) *liberal; Ammi-Nadib,* probably an Israelite:— Amminadib.

H5994 עֲמִיק *ʿămîq* (Aramaic) corresponding to H6012; *profound,* i.e. unsearchable:— deep.

H5995 עָמִיר *ʿāmîr* from H6014; a *bunch* of grain:— handful, sheaf.

H5996 עַמִּישַׁדַּי *ʿammîšadday* from H5971 and H7706; *people of* (the) *Almighty; Ammishaddai,* an Israelite:— Ammishaddai.

H5997 עָמִית *ʿāmît* from a primitive root meaning to *associate; companionship;* hence (concretely) a *comrade* or kindred man:— another, fellow, neighbour.

H5998 עָמַל *ʿāmal* a primitive root; to *toil,* i.e. *work severely* and with irksomeness:— labour, take labour, labour in.

H5999 עָמָל *ʿāmāl* from H5998; *toil,* i.e. *wearing effort;* hence *worry,* whether of body or mind:— grievance, grievousness, iniquity, labour, mischief, miserable, misery, pain, painful, perverseness, sorrow, toil, travail, trouble, wearisome, wickedness.

H6000 עָמָל *ʿāmāl* the same as H5999; *Amal,* an Israelite:— Amal.

H6001 עָמֵל ʿ*āmēl* from H5998; *toiling;* concretely a *laborer;* figuratively *sorrowful:*— that laboureth, that is a misery, had taken labour, wicked, workman.

H6002 עֲמָלֵק ʿ*ămālēq* probably of foreign origin; *Amalek,* a descendant of Esau; also his posterity and their country:— Amalek.

H6003 עֲמָלֵקִי ʿ*ămālēqî* patronymic from H6002; an *Amalekite* (or collectively the *Amalekites*) or descendants of Amalek:— Amalekite, Amalekites.

H6004 עָמַם ʿ*āmam* a primitive root; to *associate;* by implication to *overshadow* (by *huddling* together):— become dim, hide.

H6005 עִמָּנוּאֵל ʿ*immānûʾēl* from H5973 and H410 with suffixed pronoun inserted; *with us* (is) *God; Immanuel,* a typological name of Isaiah's son:— Immanuel.

H6006 עָמַס ʿ*āmas* or

עָמַשׂ ʿ*āmaś* a primitive root; to *load,* i.e. *impose* a burden (or figuratively infliction):— be borne, heavy burden, burden self, lade, load, put.

H6007 עֲמַסְיָה ʿ*ămasyâ* from H6006 and H3050; *Jah has loaded; Amasjah,* an Israelite:— Amasiah.

H6008 עַמְעָד ʿ*amʿād* from H5971 and H5703; *people of time; Amad,* a place in Palestine:— Amad.

H6009 עָמַק ʿ*āmaq* a primitive root; to *be* (causatively *make*) *deep* (literally or figuratively):— deep, be deep, have deeply, make deep, seek deep, depth, be profound.

H6010 עֵמֶק ʿ*ēmeq* from H6009; a *vale* (i.e. broad *depression*):— dale, vale, valley *[often used as a part of proper names].* See also H1025

H6011 עֹמֶק ʿ*ōmeq* from H6009; *depth:*— depth.

H6012 עָמֵק ʿ*āmēq* from H6009; *deep* (literally or figuratively):— deeper, depth, strange.

H6013 עָמֹק ʿ*āmōq* from H6009; *deep* (literally or figuratively):— deep, exceeding deep, deep thing.

H6014 עָמַר ʿ*āmar* a primitive root; properly apparently to *heap;* figuratively to *chastise* (as if *piling* blows); specifically (as denominative from H6016) to *gather* grain:— bind sheaves, make merchandise of.

H6015 עֲמַר ʿ*ămar* (Aramaic) corresponding to H6785; *wool:*— wool.

H6016 עֹמֶר ʿ*ōmer* from H6014; properly a *heap,* i.e. a *sheaf;* also an *omer,* as a dry measure:— omer, sheaf.

H6017 עֲמֹרָה ʿ*ămōrâ* from H6014; a (ruined) *heap; Amorah,* a place in Palestine:— Ghomorrah.

H6018 עָמְרִי ʿ*omrî* from H6014; *heaping; Omri,* an Israelite:— Omri.

H6019 עַמְרָם ʿ*amrām* probably from H5971 and H7311; *high people; Amram,* the name of two Israelites:— Amram.

H6020 עַמְרָמִי ʿ*amrāmî* patronymic from H6019; an *Amramite* or descendant of Amram:— Amramite.

H6021 עֲמָשָׂא ʿ*ămāśāʾ* from H6006; *burden; Amasa,* the name of two Israelites:— Amasa.

H6022 עֲמָשַׂי ʿ*ămāśay* from H6006; *burdensome; Amasai,* the name of three Israelites:— Amasai.

H6023 עֲמַשְׁסַי ʿ*ămašsay* probably from H6006; *burdensome; Amashsay,* an Israelite:— Amashai.

H6024 עֲנָב ʿ*ănāb* from the same as H6025; *fruit; Anab,* a place in Palestine:— Anab.

H6025 עֵנָב ʿ*ēnāb* from an unused root probably meaning to *bear* fruit; a *grape:*— grape, ripe grape, wine.

H6026 עָנַג ʿ*ānag* a primitive root; to be *soft* or pliable, i.e. (figuratively) *effeminate* or luxurious:— delicate, delicateness, delight, have delight, delight self, sport self.

H6027 עֹנֶג ʿ*ōneg* from H6026; *luxury:*— delight, pleasant.

H6028 עָנֹג ʿ*ānōg* from H6026; *luxurious:*— delicate.

H6029 עָנַד ʿ*ānad* a primitive root; to *lace* fast:— bind, tie.

H6030 עָנָה ʿ*ānâ* a primitive root; properly to *eye* or (generally) to *heed,* i.e. *pay attention;* by implication to *respond;* by extension to *begin* to speak; specifically to *sing, shout, testify, announce:*— give account, afflict *[by mistake for H6031],* answer, cause to answer, give answer, bring low *[by mistake for H6031],* cry, hear, Leannoth, lift up, say, scholar, shout, give a shout, sing, sing together by course, speak, testify, utter, witness, bear witness. See also H1042, H1043

H6031 עָנָה ʿ*ānâ* a primitive root [possibly rather identical with H6030 through the idea of *looking* down or *browbeating];* to *depress* literally or figuratively, transitively or intransitively (in various applications, as follow):— abase self, afflict, affliction, afflict self, answer *[by mistake for H6030],* chasten self, deal hardly with, defile, exercise, force, gentleness, humble, humble self, hurt, ravish, sing *[by mistake for H6030],* speak *[by mistake for H6030],* submit self, weaken, in any wise.

H6032 עֲנָה ʿ*ănâ* (Aramaic) corresponding to H6030 :— answer, speak.

H6033 עֲנָה ʿ*ănâ* (Aramaic) corresponding to H6031 :— poor.

H6034 עֲנָה ʿ*ănâ* probably from H6030; an *answer; Anah,* the name of two Edomites and one Edomitess:— Anah.

H6035 עָנָו ʿ*ānāw* or [by intermixture with H6041]

עָנָיו ʿ*ānāyw* from H6031; *depressed* (figuratively), in mind *(gentle)* or circumstances *(needy,* especially *saintly)*:— humble, lowly, meek, poor. Compare H6041

H6036 עָנוּב ʿ*ānûb* passive participle from the same as H6025; *borne* (as fruit); *Anub,* an Israelite:— Anub.

H6037 עַנְוָה ʿ*anwâ* feminine of H6035; *mildness* (royal); also (concretely) *oppressed:*— gentleness, meekness.

H6038 עֲנָוָה ʿ*ănāwâ* from H6035; *condescension,* human and subjective *(modesty),* or divine and objective *(clemency)*:— gentleness, humility, meekness.

H6039 ענות ʿ*ĕnût* from H6031; *affliction:*— affliction.

H6040 עֳנִי ʿ*ŏnî* from H6031; *depression,* i.e. misery:— afflicted, affliction, trouble.

H6041 עָנִי ʿ*ānî* from H6031; *depressed,* in mind or circumstances [practically the same as H6035, although the margin constantly disputes this, making H6035 subjective and H6041 objective]:— afflicted, humble, lowly, needy, poor.

H6042 עֻנִּי ʿ*unnî* from H6031; *afflicted; Unni,* the name of two Israelites:— Unni.

H6043 עֲנָיָה ʿ*ănāyâ* from H6030; *Jah has answered; Anajah,* the name of two Israelites:— Anaiah.

H6044 עָנִים ʿ*ānîm* for plural of H5869; *fountains; Anim,* a place in Palestine:— Anim.

H6045 עִנְיָן ʿ*inyān* from H6031; *ado,* i.e. (generally) *employment* or (specifically) an *affair:*— business, travail.

H6046 עָנֵם ʿ*ānēm* from the dual of H5869; *two fountains; Anem,* a place in Palestine:— Anem.

H6047 עֲנָמִים ʿ*ănāmîm* as if plural of some Egyptian word; *Anamim,* a son of Mizraim and his descendants, with their country:— Anamim.

H6048 עֲנַמֶּלֶךְ ʿ*ănammelek* of foreign origin; *Anammelek,* an Assyrian deity:— Anammelech.

H6049 עָנַן ʿ*ānan* a primitive root; to *cover;* used only as denominative from H6051, to *cloud* over; figuratively to *act covertly,* i.e. practise magic:— bring, enchanter, Meonemin, observe times, observer of times, soothsayer, sorcerer.

H6050 עֲנַן ʿ*ănan* (Aramaic) corresponding to H6051 :— cloud.

H6051 עָנָן ʿ*ānān* from H6049; a *cloud* (as *covering* the sky), i.e. the *nimbus* or thunder-cloud:— cloud, cloudy.

H6052 עָנָן ʿ*ānān* the same as H6051; *cloud; Anan,* an Israelite:— Anan.

H6053 עֲנָנָה ʿ*ănānâ* feminine of H6051; *cloudiness* :— cloud.

H6054 עֲנָנִי ʿ*ănānî* from H6051; *cloudy; Anani,* an Israelite:— Anani.

H6055 עֲנַנְיָה ʿ*ănanyâ* from H6049 and H3050; *Jah has covered; Ananjah,* the name of an Israelite and of a place in Palestine:— Ananiah.

H6056 עֲנַף ʿ*ănap* or

עֶנֶף ʿ*enep* (Aramaic) corresponding to H6057 :— bough, branch.

H6057 עָנָף ʿ*ānāp* from an unused root meaning to *cover;* a *twig* (as *covering* the limbs):— bough, branch.

H6058 עָנֵף ʿ*ānēp* from the same as H6057; *branching:*— full of branches.

H6059 עָנַק ʿ*ānaq* a primitive root; properly to *choke;* used only as denominative from H6060, to *collar,* i.e. adorn with a necklace; figuratively to *fit out* with supplies:— compass about as a chain, furnish, liberally.

H6060 עָנָק ʿ*ānāq* from H6059; a *necklace* (as if *strangling*):— chain.

H6061 עָנָק ʿ*ānāq* the same as H6060; *Anak,* a Canaanite:— Anak.

H6062 עֲנָקִי ʿ*ănāqî* patronymic from H6061; an *Anakite* or descendant of Anak:— Anakim.

H6063 עָנֵר ʿ*ānēr* probably for H5288; *Aner,* an Amorite, also a place in Palestine:— Aner.

H6064 עָנַשׁ ʿ*ānaš* a primitive root; properly to *urge;* by implication to *inflict* a penalty, specifically to *fine:*— amerce, condemn, punish, surely.

H6065 עֲנַשׁ ʿ*ănaš* (Aramaic) corresponding to H6066; a *mulct:*— confiscation.

H6066 עֹנֶשׁ ʿ*ōneš* from H6064; a *fine:*— punishment, tribute.

H6067 עֲנָת ʿ*ănāt* from H6030; *answer; Anath,* an Israelite:— Anath.

HEB

H6068 עֲנָתוֹת *ʿănātôt* plural of H6067; *Anathoth,* the name of two Israelites, also of a place in Palestine:— Anathoth.

H6069 עַנְתֹתִי *ʿantōtî* or

עַנְּתֹתִי *ʿannĕtôtî* patrial from H6068; an *Antothite* or inhabitant of Anathoth:— of Anathoth, Anethothite, Anetothite, Antothite.

H6070 עַנְתֹתִיָּה *ʿantōtîyâ* from the same as H6068 and H3050; *answers of Jah; Anthothijah,* an Israelite:— Antothijah.

H6071 עָסִיס *ʿāsîs* from H6072; *just* or fresh grape-juice (as just *trodden* out):— juice, new wine, sweet wine.

H6072 עָסַס *ʿāsas* a primitive root; to *squeeze* out juice; figuratively to *trample:*— tread down.

H6073 עֳפֶא *ʿŏpeʾ* from an unused root meaning to *cover;* a *bough* (as covering the tree):— branch.

H6074 עֳפִי *ʿŏpî* (Aramaic) corresponding to H6073; a *twig;* bough, i.e. (collectively) *foliage:*— leaves.

H6075 עָפַל *ʿāpal* a primitive root; to *swell;* figuratively *be elated:*— be lifted up, presume.

H6076 עֹפֶל *ʿōpel* from H6075; a *tumor;* also a *mound,* i.e. fortress:— emerod, fort, strong hold, tower.

H6077 עֹפֶל *ʿōpel* the same as H6076; *Ophel,* a ridge in Jerusalem:— Ophel.

H6078 עָפְנִי *ʿopnî* from an unused noun [denoting a place in Palestine; from an unused root of uncertain meaning]; an *Ophnite* (collectively) or inhabitant of Ophen:— Ophni.

H6079 עַפְעַף *ʿapʿap* from H5774; an *eyelash* (as *fluttering*); figuratively morning *ray:*— dawning, eye-lid.

H6080 עָפַר *ʿāpar* a primitive root; meaning either to *be gray* or perhaps rather to *pulverize;* used only as denominative from H6083, to *be dust:*— cast dust.

H6081 עֵפֶר *ʿēper* probably a variation of H6082; *gazelle; Epher,* the name of an Arabian and of two Israelites:— Epher.

H6082 עֹפֶר *ʿōper* from H6080; a *fawn* (from the *dusty* color):— young roe, young hart.

H6083 עָפָר *ʿāpār* from H6080; *dust* (as *powdered* or *gray*); hence *clay, earth, mud:*— ashes, dust, earth, ground, morter, powder, rubbish.

H6084 עָפְרָה *ʿoprâ* feminine of H6082; *female fawn; Ophrah,* the name of an Israelite and of two places in Palestine:— Ophrah.

H6085 עֶפְרוֹן *ʿeprôn* from the same as H6081; *fawn-like; Ephron,* the name of a Canaanite and of two places in Palestine:— Ephron, Ephrain *[from the margin].*

H6086 עֵץ *ʿēṣ* from H6095; a *tree* (from its *firmness*); hence *wood* (plural *sticks*):— carpenter, gallows, helve, pine, plank, staff, stalk, stick, stock, timber, tree, wood.

H6087 עָצַב *ʿāṣab* a primitive root; properly to *carve,* i.e. *fabricate* or *fashion;* hence (in a bad sense) to *worry, pain* or *anger:*— displease, grieve, hurt, make, be sorry, vex, worship, wrest.

H6088 עֲצַב *ʿăṣab* (Aramaic) corresponding to H6087; to *afflict:*— lamentable.

H6089 עֶצֶב *ʿeṣeb* from H6087; an earthen *vessel;* usually (painful) *toil;* also a *pang* (whether of body or mind):— grievous, idol, labor, sorrow.

H6090 עֹצֶב *ʿōṣeb* a variation of H6089; an *idol* (as fashioned); also *pain* (bodily or mental):— idol, sorrow, wicked.

H6091 עָצָב *ʿāṣāb* from H6087; an (idolatrous) *image* :— idol, image.

H6092 עָצֵב *ʿāṣēb* from H6087; a (hired) *workman* :— labour.

H6093 עִצָּבוֹן *ʿiṣṣābôn* from H6087; *worrisomeness,* i.e. *labor* or *pain:*— sorrow, toil.

H6094 עַצֶּבֶת *ʿaṣṣebet* from H6087; an *idol;* also a *pain* or *wound:*— sorrow, wound.

H6095 עָצָה *ʿāṣâ* a primitive root; properly to *fasten* (or *make firm*), i.e. to *close* (the eyes):— shut.

H6096 עָצֶה *ʿāṣeh* from H6095; the *spine* (as giving *firmness* to the body):— back bone.

H6097 עֵצָה *ʿēṣâ* feminine of H6086; *timber:*— trees.

H6098 עֵצָה *ʿēṣâ* from H3289; *advice;* by implication *plan;* also *prudence:*— advice, advisement, counsel, counsellor, purpose.

H6099 עָצוּם *ʿāṣûm* or

עָצֻם *ʿāṣūm* passive participle of H6105; *powerful* (specifically a *paw*); by implication *numerous:*— feeble, great, mighty, must, strong.

H6100 עֶצְיוֹן גֶּבֶר *ʿeṣyôn geḇer* (shorter)

עֶצְיֹן *ʿeṣyōn* from H6096 and H1397; *backbone-like of a man; Etsjon-Geber,* a place on the Red Sea:— Ezion-gaber, Ezion-geber.

H6101 עָצַל *ʿāṣal* a primitive root; to *lean* idly, i.e. to be *indolent* or *slack:*— be slothful.

H6102 עָצֵל *ʿāṣēl* from H6101; *indolent:*— slothful, sluggard.

H6103 עַצְלָה *ʿaṣlâ* feminine of H6102; (as abstract) *indolence:*— slothfulness.

H6104 עַצְלוּת *ʿaṣlût* from H6101; *indolence:*— idleness.

H6105 עָצַם *ʿāṣam* a primitive root; to *bind* fast, i.e. *close* (the eyes); intransitively to *be* (causatively *make*) *powerful* or *numerous;* denominatively (from H6106) to *craunch* the bones:— break the bones, close, be great, be increased, be mighty, wax mighty, be mightier, be more, shut, be strong, become strong, make stronger.

H6106 עֶצֶם *ʿeṣem* from H6105; a *bone* (as *strong*); by extension the *body;* figuratively the *substance,* i.e. (as pronoun) *selfsame:*— body, bone, life, same, selfsame, strength, very.

H6107 עֶצֶם *ʿeṣem* the same as H6106; *bone; Etsem,* a place in Palestine:— Azem, Ezem.

H6108 עֹצֶם *ʿōṣem* from H6105; *power;* hence *body* :— might, strong, substance.

H6109 עָצְמָה *ʿoṣmâ* feminine of H6108; *powerfulness;* by extension *numerousness:*— abundance, strength.

H6110 עַצֻּמָה *ʿaṣṣūmâ* feminine of H6099; a *bulwark,* i.e. (figuratively) *argument:*— strong.

H6111 עַצְמוֹן *ʿaṣmôn* or

עַצְמֹן *ʿaṣmōn* from H6107; *bone-like; Atsmon,* a place near Palestine:— Azmon.

H6112 עֵצֶן *ʿēṣen* from an unused root meaning to *be sharp* or *strong;* a *spear:*— Eznite *[from the margin].*

H6113 עָצַר *ʿāṣar* a primitive root; to *inclose;* by analogy to *hold back;* also to *maintain, rule, assemble:*— be able, close up, detain, fast, keep, keep self close, keep till, prevail, recover, refrain, reign, restrain, retain, shut, shut up, slack, stay, stop, withhold, withhold self.

H6114 עֶצֶר *ʿeṣer* from H6113; *restraint:*— magistrate.

H6115 עֹצֶר *ʿōṣer* from H6113; *closure;* also *constraint:*— barren, oppression, prison.

H6116 עֲצָרָה *ʿăṣārâ* or

עֲצֶרֶת *ʿăṣeret* from H6113; an *assembly,* especially on a *festival* or *holiday:*— assembly, solemn assembly, solemn meeting.

H6117 עָקַב *ʿāqab* a primitive root; properly to *swell* out or up; used only as denominative from H6119, to *seize by the heel;* figuratively to *circumvent* (as if *tripping* up the heels); also to *restrain* (as if holding by the heel):— take by the heel, stay, supplant, utterly.

H6118 עֵקֶב *ʿēqeb* from H6117 in the sense of H6119; a *heel,* i.e. (figuratively) the *last* of anything (used adverbially *for ever*); also *result,* i.e. *compensation;* and so (adverbially with preposition or relative) on *account* of:— because, by, end, for, if, reward.

H6119 עָקֵב *ʿāqēb* or (feminine)

עִקְּבָה *ʿiqqēbâ* from H6117; a *heel* (as *protuberant*); hence a *track;* figuratively the *rear* (of an army):— heel, horsehoof, last, lier in wait *[by mistake for H6120],* step, footstep.

H6120 עָקֵב *ʿāqēb* from H6117 in its denominative sense; a *lier in wait:*— heel *[by mistake for H6119].*

H6121 עָקֹב *ʿāqōb* from H6117; in the original sense, a *knoll* (as *swelling up*); in the denominative sense (transitively) *fraudulent* or (intransitively) *tracked:*— crooked, deceitful, polluted.

H6122 עָקְבָה *ʿoqbâ* feminine of an unused form from H6117 meaning a *trick; trickery:*— subtilty.

H6123 עָקַד *ʿāqad* a primitive root; to *tie* with thongs :— bind.

H6124 עָקֹד *ʿāqōd* from H6123; *striped* (with *bands*) :— ring straked.

H6125 עָקָה *ʿāqâ* from H5781; *constraint:*— oppression.

H6126 עַקּוּב *ʿaqqûb* from H6117; *insidious; Akkub,* the name of five Israelites:— Akkub.

H6127 עָקַל *ʿāqal* a primitive root; to *wrest:*— wrong.

H6128 עֲקַלְקַל *ʿăqalqal* from H6127; *winding:*— byway, crooked way.

H6129 עֲקַלָּתוֹן *ʿăqallātôn* from H6127; *tortuous:*— crooked.

H6130 עָקָן *ʿāqān* from an unused root meaning to *twist; tortuous; Akan,* an Idumaean:— Akan. Compare H3292

H6131 עָקַר *ʿāqar* a primitive root; to *pluck* up (especially by the roots); specifically to *hamstring;* figuratively to *exterminate:*— dig down, hough, pluck up, root up.

H6132 עֲקַר *ʿăqar* (Aramaic) corresponding to H6131 :— pluck up by the roots.

H6133 עֵקֶר *ʿēqer* from H6131; figuratively a *transplanted* person, i.e. naturalized citizen:— stock.

H6134 עֵקֶר *ʿēqer* the same as H6133; *Eker,* an Israelite:— Eker.

H6135 עָקָר *ʿāqār* from H6131; *sterile* (as if *extirpated* in the generative organs):— barren, male or female barren, barren woman.

H6136 עִקַּר *ʿiqqar* (Aramaic) from H6132; a *stock* :— stump.

H6137 עַקְרָב *ʿaqrāb* of uncertain derivation; a *scorpion;* figuratively a *scourge* or knotted whip:— scorpion.

H6138 עֶקְרוֹן *ʿeqrôn* from H6131; *eradication; Ekron,* a place in Palestine:— Ekron.

H6139 עֶקְרוֹנִי *ʿeqrônî* or

עֶקְרֹנִי *ʿeqrônî* patrial from H6138; an *Ekronite* or inhabitant of Ekron:— Ekronite.

H6140 עָקַשׁ *ʿāqaš* a primitive root; to *knot* or *distort;* figuratively to *pervert* (act or declare perverse):— make crooked, prove perverse, that is perverse, pervert.

H6141 עִקֵּשׁ *ʿiqqēš* from H6140; *distorted;* hence *false* :— crooked, froward, perverse.

H6142 עִקֵּשׁ *ʿiqqēš* the same as H6141; *perverse; Ikkesh,* an Israelite:— Ikkesh.

H6143 עִקְּשׁוּת *ʿiqqĕšût* from H6141; *perversity:*— froward.

H6144 עָר *ʿār* the same as H5892; a *city; Ar,* a place in Moab:— Ar.

H6145 עָר *ʿār* from H5782; a *foe* (as *watchful* for mischief):— enemy.

H6146 עָר *ʿār* (Aramaic) corresponding to H6145 :— enemy.

H6147 עֵר *ʿēr* from H5782; *watchful; Er,* the name of two Israelites:— Er.

H6148 עָרַב *ʿārab* a primitive root; to *braid,* i.e. *intermix;* technically to *traffic* (as if by barter); also to *give* or *be security* (as a kind of exchange):— engage, intermeddle, meddle with, mingle, mingle self, mortgage, occupy, give pledges, be surety, become surety, put in surety, undertake.

H6149 עָרֵב *ʿārēb* a primitive root [rather identical with H6148 through the idea of close *association];* to be *agreeable:*— be pleasant, be pleasing, take pleasure in, be sweet.

H6150 עָרַב *ʿārab* a primitive root [rather identical with H6148 through the idea of *covering* with a texture]; to *grow dusky* at sundown:— be darkened, evening, toward evening.

H6151 עֲרַב *ʿărab* (Aramaic) corresponding to H6148; to *commingle:*— mingle, mingle self, mix.

H6152 עֲרָב *ʿărāb* or

עֲרַב *ʿărab* from H6150 in the figurative sense of *sterility; Arab* (i.e. *Arabia*), a country east of Palestine:— Arabia.

H6153 עֶרֶב *ʿereb* from H6150; *dusk:*— day, even, evening, eveningtide, even tide, night.

H6154 עֵרֶב *ʿēreb* or

עֶרֶב *ʿereb* (1 Kings 10:15; with the article prefixed), from H6148; the *web* (or transverse threads of cloth); also a *mixture,* (or *mongrel* race) :— Arabia, mingled people, mixed, mixed multitude, woof.

H6155 עָרָב *ʿārāb* from H6148; a *willow* (from the use of osiers as wattles):— willow.

H6156 עָרֵב *ʿārēb* from H6149; *pleasant:*— sweet.

H6157 עָרֹב *ʿārōb* from H6148; a *mosquito* (from its *swarming*):— divers sorts of flies, swarm.

H6158 עֹרֵב *ʿōrēb* or

עוֹרֵב *ʿôrēb* from H6150; a *raven* (from its *dusky* hue):— raven.

H6159 עֹרֵב *ʿōrēb* or

עוֹרֵב *ʿôrēb* the same as H6158; *Oreb,* the name of a Midianite and of a cliff near the Jordan:— Oreb.

H6160 עֲרָבָה *ʿărābâ* from H6150 (in the sense of *sterility*); a *desert;* especially (with the article prefixed) the (generally) sterile valley of the Jordan and its continuation to the Red Sea:— Arabah, champaign, desert, evening, heaven, plain, wilderness. See also H1026

H6161 עֲרֻבָּה *ʿărubbâ* feminine passive participle of H6048 in the sense of a *bargain* or *exchange;* something given as *security,* i.e. (literally) a *token* (of safety) or (metaphorically) a *bondsman:*— pledge, surety.

H6162 עֲרָבוֹן *ʿărābôn* from H6148 (in the sense of *exchange*); a *pawn* (given as security):— pledge.

H6163 עֲרָבִי *ʿărābî* or

עַרְבִי *ʿarbî* patrial from H6152; an *Arabian* or inhabitant of Arab (i.e. Arabia):— Arabian.

H6164 עַרְבָתִי *ʿarbātî* patrial from H1026; an *Arbathite* or inhabitant of (Beth-) Arabah:— Arbathite.

H6165 עָרַג *ʿārag* a primitive root; to *long* for:— cry, pant.

H6166 עֲרָד *ʿărād* from an unused root meaning to *sequester* itself; *fugitive; Arad,* the name of a place near Palestine, also of a Canaanite and an Israelite:— Arad.

H6167 עֲרָד *ʿărād* (Aramaic) corresponding to H6171; an *onager:*— wild ass.

H6168 עָרָה *ʿārâ* a primitive root; to *be* (causatively *make*) *bare;* hence to *empty, pour* out, *demolish:*— leave destitute, discover, empty, make naked, pour, pour out, rase, spread self, uncover.

H6169 עָרָה *ʿārâ* feminine from H6168; a *naked* (i.e. level) plot:— paper reed.

H6170 עֲרוּגָה *ʿărûgâ* or

עֲרֻגָה *ʿărūgâ* feminine passive participle of H6165; something *piled* up (as if [figuratively] *raised* by mental aspiration), i.e. a *parterre:*— bed, furrow.

H6171 עָרוֹד *ʿārôd* from the same as H6166; an *onager* (from his *lonesome* habits):— wild ass.

H6172 עֶרְוָה *ʿerwâ* from H6168; *nudity,* literally (especially the *pudenda*) or figuratively *(disgrace, blemish)*:— nakedness, shame, unclean, uncleanness.

H6173 עַרְוָה *ʿarwâ* (Aramaic) corresponding to H6172; *nakedness,* i.e. (figuratively) *impoverishment:*— dishonour.

H6174 עָרוֹם *ʿārôm* or

עָרֹם *ʿārōm* from H6191 (in its original sense); *nude,* either partially or totally:— naked.

H6175 עָרוּם *ʿārûm* passive participle of H6191; *cunning* (usually in a bad sense):— crafty, prudent, subtil.

H6176 עֲרוֹעֵר *ʿărôʿēr* or

עַרְעָר *ʿarʿār* from H6209 reduplicated; a *juniper* (from its *nudity* of situation):— heath.

H6177 עֲרוֹעֵר *ʿărôʿēr* or

עֲרֹעֵר *ʿărōʿēr* or

עַרְעוֹר *ʿarʿôr* the same as H6176; *nudity* of situation; *Aroër,* the name of three places in or near Palestine:— Aroer.

H6178 עָרוּץ *ʿārûṣ* passive participle of H6206; *feared,* i.e. (concretely) a *horrible* place or *chasm* :— cliffs.

H6179 עֵרִי *ʿērî* from H5782; *watchful; Eri,* an Israelite:— Eri.

H6180 עֵרִי *ʿērî* patronymic of H6179; an *Erite* (collectively) or descendant of Eri:— Erites.

H6181 עֶרְיָה *ʿeryâ* for H6172; *nudity:*— bare, naked, quite.

H6182 עֲרִיסָה *ʿărîsâ* from an unused root meaning to *comminute; meal:*— dough.

H6183 עָרִיף *ʿārîp* from H6201; the *sky* (as *drooping* at the horizon):— heaven.

H6184 עָרִיץ *ʿārîṣ* from H6206; *fearful,* i.e. *powerful* or *tyrannical:*— mighty, oppressor, in great power, strong, terrible, violent.

H6185 עֲרִירִי *ʿărîrî* from H6209; *bare,* i.e. destitute (of children):— childless.

H6186 עָרַךְ *ʿārak* a primitive root; to set in a *row,* i.e. *arrange,* put in *order* (in a very wide variety of applications):— put in array, set in array, put the battle in array, put self in array, set self in array, compare, direct, equal, esteem, estimate, expert in war, furnish, handle, join battle, ordain, order, lay in order, put in order, reckon up in order, set in order, prepare, tax, value.

H6187 עֵרֶךְ *ʿērek* from H6186; a *pile, equipment, estimate:*— equal, estimation, order, things that are set in order, price, proportion, set at, suit, taxation, valuest.

H6188 עָרֵל *ʿārēl* a primitive root; properly to *strip;* but used only as denominative from H6189; to *expose* or *remove* the *prepuce,* whether literally (to *go naked*) or figuratively (to *refrain* from using):— count uncircumcised, foreskin to be uncovered.

H6189 עָרֵל *ʿārēl* from H6188; properly *exposed,* i.e. projecting loose (as to the prepuce); used only technically *uncircumcised* (i.e. still having the prepuce uncurtailed):— uncircumcised, uncircumcised person.

H6190 עָרְלָה *ʿorlâ* feminine of H6189; the *prepuce* :— foreskin, uncircumcised.

H6191 עָרַם *ʿāram* a primitive root; properly to *be* (or *make*) *bare;* but used only in the derivative sense (through the idea perhaps of *smoothness*) to *be cunning* (usually in a bad sense):— very, beware, take crafty counsel, be prudent, deal subtilly.

H6192 עָרַם *ʿāram* a primitive root; to *pile* up:— gather together.

H6193 עֹרֶם *ʿōrem* from H6191; a *stratagem:*— craftiness.

H6194 עָרֵם *ʿārēm* (Jer. 50:26), or (feminine)

עֲרֵמָה *ʿărēmâ* from H6192; a *heap;* specifically a *sheaf:*— heap, heap of corn, sheaf.

H6195 עָרְמָה *ʿormâ* feminine of H6193; *trickery;* or (in a good sense) *discretion:*— guile, prudence, subtilty, wilily, wisdom.

H6196 עַרְמוֹן *ʿarmôn* probably from H6191; the *plane* tree (from its *smooth* and shed bark):— chestnut tree.

H6197 עֵרָן *ʿērān* probably from H5782; *watchful; Eran,* an Israelite:— Eran.

H6198 עֵרָנִי *ʿērānî* patronymic from H6197; an *Eranite* or descendant (collectively) of Eran:— Eranites.

H6199 עַרְעָר *ʿarʿār* from H6209; *naked,* i.e. (figuratively) *poor:*— destitute. See also H6176

H6200 עֲרֹעֵרִי *ʿărōʿērî* patronymic from H6177; an *Aroërite* or inhabitant of Aroër:— Aroerite.

H6201 עָרַף *ʿārap* a primitive root; to *droop;* hence to *drip:*— drop, drop down.

H6202 עָרַף *ʿārap* a primitive root [rather identical with H6201 through the idea of *slopping];* properly to *bend* downward; but used only as a denominative from H6203, to *break the neck;* hence (figuratively) to *destroy:*— that is beheaded, break down, break neck, cut off neck, strike off neck.

H6203 עֹרֶף *ʿōrep* from H6202; the *nape* or back of the neck (as *declining*); hence the *back* generally (whether literally or figuratively):— back, neck, stiffnecked.

H6204 עָרְפָּה *ʿorpâ* feminine of H6203; *mane; Orpah,* Moabitess:— Orpah.

H6205 עֲרָפֶל *ʿărāpel* probably from H6201; *gloom* (as if a *lowering* sky):— dark, dark cloud, darkness, gross darkness, thick darkness.

H6206 עָרַץ *ʿāraṣ* a primitive root; to *awe* or (intransitively) to *dread;* hence to *harass:*— be affrighted, be afraid, be dread, be feared, be terrified, break, dread, fear, oppress, prevail, shake terribly.

H6207 עָרַק *ʿāraq* a primitive root; to *gnaw,* i.e. (figuratively) *eat* (by hyperbole); also (participle) a *pain:*— fleeing, sinew.

H6208 עַרְקִי *ʿarqî* patrial from an unused name meaning a *tush;* an *Arkite* or inhabitant of Erek:— Arkite.

H6209 עָרַר *ʿārar* a primitive root; to *bare;* figuratively to *demolish:*— make bare, break, raise up [perhaps by clerical error for *raze*], utterly.

H6210 עֶרֶשׂ *ʿereś* from an unused root meaning perhaps to *arch;* a *couch* (properly with a *canopy*):— bed, bedstead, couch.

H6211 עָשׁ *ʿāš* from H6244; a *moth:*— moth. See also H5906

H6212 עֶשֶׂב *ʿéseb* from an unused root meaning to *glisten* (or *be green*); *grass* (or any tender shoot):— grass, herb.

H6213 עָשָׂה *ʿāśâ* a primitive root; to *do* or *make,* in the broadest sense and widest application (as follows):— accomplish, advance, appoint, apt, be at, become, bear, bestow, bring forth, bruise, by busy, certainly, have the charge of, commit, deal, deal with, deck, displease, do, dress, ready dressed, execute, put in execution, exercise, fashion, feast, fighting man, finish, fit, fly, follow, fulfil, furnish, gather, get, go about, govern, grant, great, hinder, hold, hold a feast, indeed, be industrious, journey, keep, labour, maintain, make, be meet, observe, be occupied, offer, officer, pare, bring to pass, come to pass, perform, practise, prepare, procure, provide, put, requite, sacrifice, serve, set, show, sin, spend, surely, take, thoroughly, trim, very, vex, be warrior, work, workman, yield, use.

H6214 עֲשָׂהאֵל *ʿăśāhʾēl* from H6213 and H410; *God has made; Asahel,* the name of four Israelites:— Asahel.

H6215 עֵשָׂו *ʿēśāw* apparently a form of the passive participle of H6213 in the original sense of *handling; rough* (i.e. sensibly *felt*); *Esau,* a son of Isaac, including his posterity:— Esau.

H6216 עָשׁוֹק *ʿāšôq* from H6231; *oppressive* (as noun, a *tyrant*):— oppressor.

H6217 עָשׁוּק *ʿāšûq* or

עָשֻׁק *ʿāšuq* passive participle of H6231; used in plural masculine as abstract *tyranny:*— oppressed, oppression. *[Doubtful.]*.

H6218 עָשׂוֹר *ʿāśôr* or

עָשֹׂר *ʿāśōr* from H6235; *ten;* by abbreviation ten *strings,* and so a *decachord:*— ten, instrument of ten strings, tenth.

H6219 עָשׁוֹת *ʿāšôt* from H6245; *shining,* i.e. polished:— bright.

H6220 עַשְׁוָת *ʿašwāt* for H6219; *bright; Ashvath,* an Israelite:— Ashvath.

H6221 עֲשִׂיאֵל *ʿăśîʾēl* from H6213 and H410; *made of God; Asiël,* an Israelite:— Asiel.

H6222 עֲשָׂיָה *ʿăśāyâ* from H6213 and H3050; *Jah has made; Asajah,* the name of three or four Israelites:— Asaiah.

H6223 עָשִׁיר *ʿāšîr* from H6238; *rich,* whether literally or figuratively *(noble*):— rich, rich man.

H6224 עֲשִׂירִי *ʿăśîrî* from H6235; *tenth;* by abbreviation *tenth month* or (feminine) *part:*— tenth, tenth part.

H6225 עָשַׁן *ʿāšan* a primitive root; to *smoke,* whether literally or figuratively:— be angry, smoke, be on a smoke.

H6226 עָשֵׁן *ʿāšan* from H6225; *smoky:*— smoking.

H6227 עָשָׁן *ʿāšān* from H6225; *smoke,* literal or figurative *(vapor, dust, anger*):— smoke, smoking.

H6228 עָשָׁן *ʿāšān* the same as H6227; *Ashan,* a place in Palestine:— Ashan.

H6229 עָשַׂק *ʿāśaq* a primitive root (identical with H6231); to *press upon,* i.e. *quarrel:*— strive with.

H6230 עֵשֶׂק *ʿēśeq* from H6229; *strife:*— Esek.

H6231 עָשַׁק *ʿāšaq* a primitive root (compare H6229); to *press* upon, i.e. *oppress, defraud, violate, overflow:*— get deceitfully, deceive, defraud, drink up, oppress, use oppression, oppressor, do violence, do wrong.

H6232 עֵשֶׁק *ʿēšeq* from H6231; *oppression; Eshek,* an Israelite:— Eshek.

H6233 עֹשֶׁק *ʿōšeq* from H6231; *injury, fraud,* (subjectively) *distress,* (concretely) *unjust gain:*— cruelly, extortion, oppression, thing deceitfully gotten.

H6234 עָשְׁקָה *ʿošqâ* feminine of H6233; *anguish:*— oppressed.

H6235 עֶשֶׂר *ʿeśer* masculine

עֲשָׂרָה *ʿăśārâ* from H6237; *ten* (as an *accumulation* to the extent of the digits):— ten, fifteen, seventeen.

H6236 עֲשַׂר *ʿăśar* masculine

עַשְׂרָה *ʿăśrâ* (Aramaic) corresponding to H6235; *ten:*— ten, twelve.

H6237 עָשַׂר *ʿāśar* a primitive root (identical with H6238); to *accumulate;* but used only as denominative from H6235; to *tithe,* i.e. take or give a tenth:— surely, give the tenth, take the tenth, tithe, have tithes, take tithes, tithing, truly.

H6238 עָשַׁר *ʿāšar* a primitive root; properly to *accumulate;* chiefly (specifically) to *grow* (causatively *make*) *rich:*— be rich, become rich, enrich, make rich, make self rich, wax rich, make [1 Kings 22:48 *margin*]. See H6240

H6239 עֹשֶׁר *ʿōšer* from H6238; *wealth:*— far richer, riches.

H6240 עָשָׂר *ʿāśār* for H6235; *ten* (only in combination), i.e. *-teen;* also (ordinal) *-teenth:*— eighteen, eighteenth, fifteen, fifteenth, fourteen, fourteenth, nineteen, nineteenth, seventeen, seventeenth, sixteen, sixteenth, thirteen, thirteenth, eleven, eleventh, sixscore thousand, twelve, twelfth.

H6241 עִשָּׂרוֹן *ʿiśśārôn* or

עִשָּׂרֹן *ʿiśśārōn* from H6235; (fractional) a *tenth* part:— tenth deal.

H6242 עֶשְׂרִים *ʿeśrîm* from H6235; *twenty;* also (ordinal) *twentieth:*— sixscore, twenty, twentieth.

H6243 עֶשְׂרִין *ʿeśrîn* (Aramaic) corresponding to H6242:— twenty.

H6244 עָשֵׁשׁ *ʿāšēš* a primitive root; probably to *shrink,* i.e. *fail:*— be consumed.

H6245 עָשַׁת *ʿāšat* a primitive root; probably to be *sleek,* i.e. *glossy;* hence (through the idea of *polishing*) to *excogitate* (as if *forming* in the mind):— shine, think.

H6246 עֲשִׁת *ʿăšit* (Aramaic) corresponding to H6245; to *purpose:*— think.

H6247 עֶשֶׁת *ʿešet* from H6245; a *fabric:*— bright.

H6248 עַשְׁתּוּת *ʿaštût* from H6245; *cogitation:*— thought.

H6249 עַשְׁתֵּי *ʿaštê* apparently masculine plural construct of H6247 in the sense of an *afterthought;* (used only in connection with H6240 in lieu of H259) *eleven* or (ordinal) *eleventh:*— eleven, eleventh.

H6250 עֶשְׁתֹּנָה *ʿeštōnâ* from H6245; *thinking:*— thought.

H6251 עַשְׁתְּרָה *ʿaštĕrâ* probably from H6238; *increase:*— flock.

H6252 עַשְׁתָּרוֹת *ʿaštārôt* or

עַשְׁתָּרֹת *ʿaštārōt* plural of H6251; *Ashtaroth,* the name of a Sidonian deity, and of a place east of the Jordan:— Ashtaroth, Astaroth. See also H1045, H6253, H6255

H6253 עַשְׁתֹּרֶת *ʿaštōret* probably for H6251; *Ashtoreth,* the Phoenician goddess of love (and *increase*):— Ashtoreth.

H6254 עַשְׁתְּרָתִי *ʿaštĕrātî* patrial from H6252; an *Ashterathite* or inhabitant of Ashtaroth:— Ashterathite.

H6255 עַשְׁתְּרֹת קַרְנַיִם *ʿaštĕrōt qarnayim* from H6252 and the dual of H7161; *Ashtaroth of* (the) *double horns* (a symbol of the deity); *Ashteroth-Karnaïm,* a place east of the Jordan:— Ashtoreth Karnaim.

H6256 עֵת *ʿēt* from H5703; *time,* especially (adverbially with preposition) *now, when,* etc:— after, always, certain, continually, evening, long, season, due season, so long as, eventide, eveningtide, noontide, time, mealtime, what time, when.

H6257 עָתַד *ʿātad* a primitive root; to *prepare:*— make fit, be ready to become.

H6258 עַתָּה *ʿattâ* from H6256; at *this time,* whether adverb, conjunction or expletive:— henceforth, now, straightway, this time, whereas.

H6259 עָתוּד *ʿātûd* passive participle of H6257; *prepared:*— ready.

H6260 עַתּוּד *ʿattûd* or

עַתֻּד *ʿattūd* from H6257; *prepared,* i.e. *full grown;* spoken only (in plural) of *he-goats,* or (figuratively) *leaders* of the people:— chief one, goat, he goat, ram.

H6261 עִתִּי *ʿittî* from H6256; *timely:*— fit.

H6262 עַתַּי *ʿattay* for H6261; *Attai,* the name of three Israelites:— Attai.

H6263 עֲתִיד *ʿătîd* (Aramaic) corresponding to H6264; *prepared:*— ready.

H6264 עָתִיד *ʿātîd* from H6257; *prepared;* by implication *skilful;* feminine plural the *future;* also *treasure:*— things that shall come, ready, treasures.

H6265 עֲתָיָה *ʿătāyâ* from H5790 and H3050; *Jah has helped; Athajah,* an Israelite:— Athaiah.

H6266 עָתִיק *ʿātîq* from H6275; properly *antique,* i.e. *venerable* or *splendid:*— durable.

H6267 עַתִּיק *ʿattîq* from H6275; *removed,* i.e. *weaned;* also *antique:*— ancient, drawn.

H6268 עַתִּיק *ʿattîq* (Aramaic) corresponding to H6267; *venerable:*— ancient.

H6269 עֲתָךְ *ʿătāk* from an unused root meaning to *sojourn; lodging; Athak,* a place in Palestine:— Athach.

H6270 עַתְלַי *ʿatlay* from an unused root meaning to *compress; constringent; Athlai,* an Israelite:— Athlai.

H6271 עֲתַלְיָה *ʿătalyâ* or

עֲתַלְיָהוּ *ʿătalyāhû* from the same as H6270 and H3050; *Jah has constrained; Athaljah,* the name of an Israelitess and two Israelites:— Athaliah.

H6272 עָתַם *ʿātam* a primitive root; probably to *glow,* i.e. (figuratively) *be desolated:*— be darkened.

H6273 עָתְנִי *ʿotnî* from an unused root meaning to *force; forcible; Othni,* an Israelite:— Othni.

H6274 עָתְנִיאֵל *ʿotnîʾēl* from the same as H6273 and H410; *force of God; Othniël,* an Israelite:— Othniel.

H6275 עָתַק *ʿātaq* a primitive root; to *remove* (intransitively or transitively); figuratively to *grow old;* specifically to *transcribe:*— copy out, leave off, become old, wax old, remove.

H6276 עָתֵק *ʿātēq* from H6275; *antique,* i.e. *valued:*— durable.

H6277 עָתָק *ʿātāq* from H6275 in the sense of *license; impudent:*— arrogancy, grievous, grievous hard, things, stiff.

H6278 עֵת קָצִין *ʿēt qāṣîn* from H6256 and H7011; *time of a judge; Eth-Katsin,* a place in Palestine:— Ittah-kazin *[by including directive enclitic].*

H6279 עָתַר *ʿātar* a primitive root [rather denominative from H6281]; to burn *incense* in worship, i.e. *intercede* (reciprocally *listen* to prayer):— intreat, pray, make prayer.

H6280 עָתַר *ʿātar* a primitive root; to *be* (causatively *make*) *abundant:*— deceitful, multiply.

H6281 עֶתֶר *ʿeter* from H6280; *abundance; Ether,* a place in Palestine:— Ether.

H6282 עָתָר *ʿātār* from H6280; *incense* (as increasing to a *volume* of smoke); hence (from H6279) a *worshipper:*— suppliant, thick.

H6283 עֲתֶרֶת *ʿăteret* from H6280; *copiousness:*— abundance.

פ

H6284 פָּאָה *pāʾâ* a primitive root; to *puff,* i.e. *blow away:*— scatter into corners.

H6285 פֵּאָה *pēʾâ* feminine of H6311; properly *mouth* in a figurative sense, i.e. *direction, region, extremity:*— corner, end, quarter, side.

H6286 פָּאַר *pāʾar* a primitive root; to *gleam,* i.e. (causatively) *embellish;* figuratively to *boast;* also to *explain* (i.e. make clear) oneself; denominative from H6288, to *shake* a tree:— beautify, boast self, go over the boughs, glorify, glorify self, glory, vaunt self.

H6287 פְּאֵר *pěʾēr* from H6286; an *embellishment,* i.e. fancy *head-dress:*— beauty, bonnet, goodly, ornament, tire.

H6288 פְּאֹרָה *pěʾōrâ* or

פֹּרָאה *pōrāʾh* or

פֻּארָה *puʾrâ* from H6286; properly *ornamentation,* i.e. (plural) *foliage* (including the limbs) as *bright* green:— bough, branch, sprig.

H6289 פָּארוּר *pāʾrûr* from H6286; properly *illuminated,* i.e. a *glow;* as noun, a *flush* (of anxiety):— blackness.

H6290 פָּארָן *pāʾrān* from H6286; *ornamental; Paran,* a desert of Arabia:— Paran.

H6291 פַּג *pag* from an unused root meaning to *be torpid,* i.e. *crude;* an *unripe* figuratively:— green fig.

H6292 פִּגּוּל *piggûl* or

פִּגֻּל *piggūl* from an unused root meaning to *stink;* properly *fetid,* i.e. (figuratively) *unclean* (ceremonially):— abominable, abomination, abominable thing.

H6293 פָּגַע *pāgaʿ* a primitive root; to *impinge,* by accident or violence, or (figuratively) by importunity:— come, come betwixt, cause to entreat, fall, fall upon, make intercession, intercessor, intreat, lay, light upon, meet, meet together, pray, reach, run.

H6294 פֶּגַע *pegaʿ* from H6293; *impact* (casual):— chance, occurrent.

H6295 פַּגְעִיאֵל *pagʿîʾēl* from H6294 and H410; *accident of God; Pagiël,* an Israelite:— Pagiel.

H6296 פָּגַר *pāgar* a primitive root; to *relax,* i.e. become *exhausted:*— be faint.

H6297 פֶּגֶר *peger* from H6296; a *carcase* (as *limp*), whether of man or beast; figuratively an idolatrous *image:*— carcase, corpse, dead body.

H6298 פָּגַשׁ *pāgaš* a primitive root; to *come in contact with,* whether by accident or violence; figuratively to *concur:*— meet, meet with, meet together.

H6299 פָּדָה *pādâ* a primitive root; to *sever,* i.e. *ransom;* generally to *release, preserve:*— at all, deliver, by any means, ransom, redeem, that are to be redeemed, let be redeemed, rescue, surely.

H6300 פְּדַהְאֵל *pědahʾēl* from H6299 and H410; *God has ransomed; Pedahel,* an Israelite:— Pedahel.

H6301 פְּדָהצוּר *pědāhṣûr* from H6299 and H6697; a *rock* (i.e. God) *has ransomed; Pedahtsur,* an Israelite:— Pedahzur.

H6302 פָּדוּי *pādûy* passive participle of H6299; *ransomed* (and so occurring under H6299); as abstract (in plural masculine) a *ransom:*— to be redeemed, that are to be redeemed, that were redeemed.

H6303 פָּדוֹן *pādôn* from H6299; *ransom; Padon,* one of the Nethinim:— Padon.

H6304 פְּדוּת *pědût* or

פְּדֻת *pědūt* from H6929; *distinction;* also *deliverance:*— division, redeem, redemption.

H6305 פְּדָיָה *pědāyâ* or

פְּדָיָהוּ *pědāyāhû* from H6299 and H3050; *Jah has ransomed; Pedajah,* the name of six Israelites:— Pedaiah.

H6306 פִּדְיוֹם *pidyôm* or

פִּדְיֹם *pidyōm* also

פִּדְיוֹן *pidyôn* or

פִּדְיֹן *pidyōn* from H6299; a *ransom:*— ransom, that were redeemed, redemption.

H6307 פַּדָּן *paddān* from an unused root meaning to *extend;* a *plateau;* or

פַּדַּן אֲרָם *paddan ʾărām* from the same and H758; the *table-land of Aram: Paddan* or *Paddan-Aram,* a region of Syria:— Padan, Padan-aram.

H6308 פָּדַע *pādaʿ* a primitive root; to *retrieve:*— deliver.

H6309 פֶּדֶר *peder* from an unused root meaning to *be greasy; suet:*— fat.

H6310 פֶּה *peh* from H6284; the *mouth* (as the means of *blowing*), whether literally or figuratively (particularly *speech*); specifically *edge, portion* or *side;* adverbially (with preposition) *according to:*— accord, according as, according to, after, appointment, assent, collar, command, commandment, eat, edge, end, entry, file, hole, in, mind, mouth, part, portion, say, should say, saying, sentence, skirt, sound, speech, spoken, talk, tenor, to, two-edged, wish, word.

H6311 פֹּה *pōh* or

פֹּא *pōʾ* (Job 38:11), or

פּוֹ *pô* probably from a primitive inseparable particle [HEB]P (of demonstrative force) and H1931; *this place* (French *içi*), i.e. *here* or *hence:*— here, hither, the one side, the other side, this side, that side.

H6312 פּוּאָה *pûʾâ* or

פֻּוָּה *puwwâ* from H6284; a *blast; Puäh* or *Puvvah,* the name of two Israelites:— Phuvah, Pua, Puah.

H6313 פּוּג *pûg* a primitive root; to *be sluggish:*— cease, be feeble, faint, be slacked.

H6314 פּוּגָה *pûgâ* from H6313; *intermission:*— rest.

H6315 פּוּחַ *pûaḥ* a primitive root; to *puff,* i.e. blow with the breath or air; hence to *fan* (as a breeze), to *utter,* to *kindle* (a fire), to *scoff:*— blow, blow upon, break, puff, bring into a snare, speak, utter.

H6316 פּוּט *pûṭ Put,* a son of Ham, also the name of his descendants or their region, and of a Persian tribe:— Phut, Put.

H6317 פּוּטִיאֵל *pûṭîʾēl* from an unused root (probably meaning to *disparage*) and H410; *contempt of God; Putiël,* an Israelite:— Putiel.

H6318 פּוֹטִיפַר *pôṭîpar* of Egyptian derivation; *Potiphar,* an Egyptian:— Potiphar.

H6319 פּוֹטִי פֶרַע *pôṭî peraʿ* of Egyptian derivation; *Poti-Phera,* an Egyptian:— Poti-pherah.

H6320 פּוּךְ *pûk* from an unused root meaning to *paint; dye* (specifically *stibium* for the eyes):— fair colours, glistering, painted, painting.

H6321 פּוֹל *pôl* from an unused root meaning to *be thick;* a *bean* (as *plump*):— beans.

H6322 פּוּל *pûl* of foreign origin; *Pul,* the name of an Assyrian king and of an Ethiopian tribe:— Pul.

H6323 פּוּן *pûn* a primitive root meaning to *turn,* i.e. *be perplexed:*— be distracted.

HEB

H6324 פּוּנִי *pûnî* patronymic from an unused name meaning a *turn;* a *Punite* (collectively) or descendant of an unknown Pun:— Punites.

H6325 פּוּנֹן *pûnōn* from H6323; *perplexity; Punon,* a place in the Desert:— Punon.

H6326 פּוּעָה *pûʿâ* from an unused root meaning to *glitter; brilliancy; Puäh,* an Israelitess:— Puah.

H6327 פּוּץ *pûṣ* a primitive root; to *dash* in pieces, literally or figuratively (especially to *disperse*):— break in pieces, dash in pieces, shake to pieces, cast, cast abroad, disperse, disperse selves, drive, retire, scatter, scatter abroad, spread abroad.

H6328 פּוּק *pûq* a primitive root; to *waver:*— stumble, move.

H6329 פּוּק *pûq* a primitive root [rather identical with H6328 through the idea of *dropping* out; compare H5312]; to *issue,* i.e. *furnish;* causatively to *secure;* figuratively to *succeed:*— afford, draw out, further, get, obtain.

H6330 פּוּקָה *pûqâ* from H6328; a *stumbling-block* :— grief.

H6331 פּוּר *pûr* a primitive root; to *crush:*— break, bring to nought, utterly take.

H6332 פּוּר *pûr* also (plural)

פּוּרִים *pûrîm* or

פֻּרִים *pūrîm* from H6331; a *lot* (as by means of a *broken* piece):— Pur, Purim.

H6333 פּוּרָה *pûrâ* from H6331; a *wine-press* (as *crushing* the grapes):— winepress.

H6334 פּוֹרָתָא *pôrātāʾ* of Persian origin; *Poratha,* a son of Haman:— Poratha.

H6335 פּוּשׁ *pûš* a primitive root; to *spread;* figuratively *act proudly:*— grow up, be grown fat, spread selves, be scattered.

H6336 פּוּתִי *pûtî* patronymic from an unused name meaning a *hinge;* a *Puthite* (collectively) or descendant of an unknown Puth:— Puhites *[as if from H6312].*

H6337 פָּז *pāz* from H6388; *pure* (gold); hence *gold* itself (as refined):— fine gold, pure gold.

H6338 פָּזַז *pāzaz* a primitive root; to *refine* (gold) :— best [gold].

H6339 פָּזַז *pāzaz* a primitive root [rather identical with H6338]; to *solidify* (as if by *refining*); also to *spring* (as if *separating* the limbs):— leap, be made strong.

H6340 פָּזַר *pāzar* a primitive root; to *scatter,* whether in enmity or bounty:— disperse, scatter, scatter abroad.

H6341 פַּח *paḥ* from H6351; a (metallic) *sheet* (as *pounded* thin); also a spring *net* (as spread out like a *lamina*):— gin, plate, thin plate, snare.

H6342 פָּחַד *pāḥad* a primitive root; to *be startled* (by a sudden alarm); hence to *fear* in general:— be afraid, stand in awe, fear, be in fear, make to shake.

H6343 פַּחַד *paḥad* from H6342; a (sudden) *alarm* (properly the object feared, by implication the feeling):— dread, dreadful, fear, great fear, thing greatly feared, terror.

H6344 פַּחַד *paḥad* the same as H6343; a *testicle* (as a cause of *shame* akin to fear):— stone.

H6345 פַּחְדָּה *paḥdâ* feminine of H6343; *alarm* (i.e. *awe*):— fear.

H6346 פֶּחָה *peḥâ* of foreign origin; a *prefect* (of a city or small district):— captain, deputy, governor.

H6347 פֶּחָה *peḥâ* (Aramaic) corresponding to H6346 :— captain, governor.

H6348 פָּחַז *pāḥaz* a primitive root; to *bubble* up or *froth* (as boiling water), i.e. (figuratively) to *be unimportant:*— light.

H6349 פַּחַז *paḥaz* from H6348; *ebullition,* i.e. froth (figuratively lust):— unstable.

H6350 פַּחֲזוּת *paḥăzût* from H6348; *frivolity:*— lightness.

H6351 פָּחַח *pāḥaḥ* a primitive root; to *batter* out; but used only as denominative from H6341, to *spread a net:*— be snared.

H6352 פֶּחָם *peḥām* perhaps from an unused root probably meaning to *be black;* a *coal,* whether charred or live:— coals.

H6353 פֶּחָר *peḥār* (Aramaic) from an unused root probably meaning to *fashion;* a *potter:*— potter.

H6354 פַּחַת *paḥat* probably from an unused root apparently meaning to *dig;* a *pit,* especially for catching animals:— hole, pit, snare.

H6355 פַּחַת מוֹאָב *paḥat môʾāb* from H6354 and H4124; *pit of Moäb; Pachath-Moäb,* an Israelite:— Pahath-moab.

H6356 פְּחֶתֶת *pĕḥetet* from the same as H6354; a *hole* (by mildew in a garment):— fret inward.

H6357 פִּטְדָה *piṭdâ* of foreign derivation; a *gem,* probably the *topaz:*— topaz.

H6358 פָּטוּר *pāṭûr* passive participle of H6362; *opened,* i.e. (as noun) a *bud:*— open.

H6359 פָּטִיר *pāṭîr* from H6362; *open,* i.e. *unoccupied:*— free.

H6360 פַּטִּישׁ *paṭṭîš* intensive from an unused root meaning to *pound;* a *hammer:*— hammer.

H6361 פַּטִּישׁ *paṭṭîš* (Aramaic) from a root corresponding to that of H6360; a *gown* (as if *hammered* out wide):— hose.

H6362 פָּטַר *pāṭar* a primitive root; to *cleave* or burst through, i.e. (causatively) to *emit,* whether literally or figuratively *(gape)*:— dismiss, free, let out, shoot out, slip away.

H6363 פֶּטֶר *peter* or

פִּטְרָה *piṭrâ* from H6362; a *fissure,* i.e. (concretely) *firstling* (as *opening* the matrix):— firstling, openeth, such as open.

H6364 פִּי־בֶסֶת *pî-beset* of Egyptian origin; *Pi-Beseth,* a place in Egypt:— Pi-beseth.

H6365 פִּיד *pîd* from an unused root probably meaning to *pierce;* (figuratively) *misfortune:*— destruction, ruin.

H6366 פֵּיָה *pêâ* or

פִּיָּה *pîyâ* feminine of H6310; an *edge:*— edge, two-edged.

H6367 פִּי הַחִרֹת *pî hahîrōt* from H6310 and the feminine plural of a noun (from the same root as H2356), with the article interp; *mouth of the gorges; Pi-ha-Chiroth,* a place in Egypt:— Pi-hahiroth. [In Num 14:19 without Pi-.].

H6368 פִּיחַ *pîaḥ* from H6315; a *powder* (as easily *puffed* away), i.e. *ashes* or *dust:*— ashes.

H6369 פִּיכֹל *pîkōl* apparently from H6310 and H3605; *mouth of all; Picol,* a Philistine:— Phichol.

H6370 פִּילֶגֶשׁ *pîlegeš* or

פִּלֶגֶשׁ *pīlegeš* of uncertain derivation; a *concubine;* also (masculine) a *paramour:*— concubine, paramour.

H6371 פִּימָה *pîmâ* probably from an unused root meaning to *be plump; obesity:*— collops.

H6372 פִּינְחָס *pînĕḥās* apparently from H6310 and a variation of H5175; *mouth of a serpent; Pinechas,* the name of three Israelites:— Phinehas.

H6373 פִּינֹן *pînōn* probably the same as H6325; *Pinon,* an Idumaean:— Pinon.

H6374 פִּיפִיָּה *pîpîyâ* for H6366; an *edge* or *tooth:*— tooth, two-edged.

H6375 פִּיק *pîq* from H6329; a *tottering:*— smite together.

H6376 פִּישׁוֹן *pîšôn* from H6335; *dispersive; Pishon,* a river of Eden:— Pison.

H6377 פִּיתוֹן *pîtôn* probably from the same as H6596; *expansive; Pithon,* an Israelite:— Pithon.

H6378 פַּךְ *pak* from H6379; a *flask* (from which a liquid may *flow*):— box, vial.

H6379 פָּכָה *pākâ* a primitive root; to *pour:*— run out.

H6380 פֹּכֶרֶת צְבָיִים *pōkeret ṣĕbāyîm* from the active participle (of the same form as the first word) feminine of an unused root (meaning to *entrap*) and plural of H6643; *trap of gazelles; Pokereth-Tsebajim,* one of the "servants of Solomon":— Pochereth of Zebaim.

H6381 פָּלָא *pālāʾ* a primitive root; properly perhaps to *separate,* i.e. *distinguish* (literally or figuratively); by implication to *be* (causatively *make*) *great, difficult, wonderful:*— accomplish, hard, arise . . . too hard, be too hard, hidden, things too high, marvellous, be marvellous, be marvellously, do a marvellous work, shew marvellous, shew self marvellous, marvellous thing, marvellous work, marvellously, marvels, miracles, perform, separate, make singular, wonderful, be wonderful, great wonders, make wonderful, wonderful things, wonderful works, wondrous wonders, wonderfully, wondrous things, wondrous works, wondrously.

H6382 פֶּלֶא *peleʾ* from H6381; a *miracle:*— marvellous thing, wonder, wonderful, wonderfully.

H6383 פִּלְאִי *pilʾî* or

פָּלִיא *pālîʾ* from H6381; *remarkable:*— secret, wonderful.

H6384 פַּלֻּאִי *paluʾî* patronymic from H6396; a *Palluite* (collectively) or descendant of Pallu:— Palluites.

H6385 פָּלַג *pālag* a primitive root; to *split* (literally or figuratively):— divide.

H6386 פְּלַג *pĕlag* (Aramaic) corresponding to H6385 :— divided.

H6387 פְּלַג *pĕlag* (Aramaic) from H6386; a *half:*— dividing.

H6388 פֶּלֶג *peleg* from H6385; a *rill* (i.e. small *channel* of water, as in irrigation):— river, stream.

H6389 פֶּלֶג *peleg* the same as H6388; *earthquake; Peleg,* a son of Shem:— Peleg.

H6390 פְּלַגָּה *pĕlaggâ* from H6385; a *runlet,* i.e. *gully* :— division, river.

H6391 פְּלֻגָּה *pĕluggâ* from H6385; a *section:*— division.

H6392 פְּלֻגָּה *pĕluggâ* (Aramaic) corresponding to H6391: — division.

H6393 פְּלָדָה *pĕlādâ* from an unused root meaning to *divide;* a *cleaver,* i.e. iron *armature* (of a chariot):— torch.

H6394 פִּלְדָּשׁ *pildāš* of uncertain derivation; *Pildash,* a relative of Abraham:— Pildash.

H6395 פָּלָה *pālâ* a primitive root; to *distinguish* (literally or figuratively):— put a difference, show marvellous, separate, set apart, sever, make wonderfully.

H6396 פַּלּוּא *pallû*ʾ from H6395; *distinguished; Pallu,* an Israelite:— Pallu, Phallu.

H6397 פְּלוֹנִי *pĕlônî* patronymic from an unused name (from H6395) meaning *separate;* a *Pelonite* or inhabitant of an unknown Palon:— Pelonite.

H6398 פָּלַח *pālaḥ* a primitive root; to *slice,* i.e. *break* open or *pierce:*— bring forth, cleave, cut, shred, strike through.

H6399 פְּלַח *pĕlaḥ* (Aramaic) corresponding to H6398; to *serve* or worship:— minister, serve.

H6400 פֶּלַח *pelaḥ* from H6398; a *slice:*— piece.

H6401 פִּלְחָא *pilḥā*ʾ from H6400; *slicing; Pilcha,* an Israelite:— Pilcha.

H6402 פָּלְחָן *polḥān* (Aramaic) from H6399; *worship:*— service.

H6403 פָּלַט *pālaṭ* a primitive root; to *slip* out, i.e. *escape;* causatively to *deliver:*— calve, carry away safe, deliver, escape, cause to escape.

H6404 פֶּלֶט *peleṭ* from H6403; *escape; Pelet,* the name of two Israelites:— Pelet. See also H1046

H6405 פַּלֵּט *pallēṭ* from H6403; *escape:*— deliverance, escape.

H6406 פַּלְטִי *palṭî* from H6403; *delivered; Palti,* the name of two Israelites:— Palti, Phalti.

H6407 פַּלְטִי *palṭî* patronymic from H6406; a *Paltite* or descendant of Palti:— Paltite.

H6408 פִּלְטַי *pilṭay* for H6407; *Piltai,* an Israelite:— Piltai.

H6409 פַּלְטִיאֵל *palṭîʾēl* from the same as H6404 and H410; *deliverance of God; Paltiël,* the name of two Israelites:— Paltiel, Phatliel.

H6410 פְּלַטְיָה *pĕlaṭyâ* or

פְּלַטְיָהוּ *pĕlaṭyāhû* from H6403 and H3050; *Jah has delivered; Pelatjah,* the name of four Israelites:— Pelatiah.

H6411 פְּלָיָה *pĕlāyâ* or

פְּלָאיָה *pĕlāʾyâ* from H6381 and H3050; *Jah has distinguished; Pelajah,* the name of three Israelites:— Pelaiah.

H6412 פָּלִיט *pālîṭ* or

פָּלֵיט *pālêṭ* or

פָּלֵט *pālēṭ* from H6403; a *refugee:*— escape, that have escaped, escapeth, fugitive.

H6413 פְּלֵיטָה *pĕlêṭâ* or

פְּלֵטָה *pĕlēṭâ* feminine of H6412; *deliverance;* concretely an *escaped* portion:— deliverance, escape, that is escaped, remnant.

H6414 פָּלִיל *pālîl* from H6419; a *magistrate:*— judge.

H6415 פְּלִילָה *pĕlîlâ* feminine of H6414; *justice:*— judgment.

H6416 פְּלִילִי *pĕlîlî* from H6414; *judicial:*— judge.

H6417 פְּלִילִיָּה *pĕlîlîyâ* feminine of H6416; *judicature:*— judgment.

H6418 פֶּלֶךְ *pelek* from an unused root meaning to *be round;* a *circuit* (i.e. *district*); also a *spindle* (as *whirled*); hence a *crutch:*— staff, distaff, part.

H6419 פָּלַל *pālal* a primitive root; to *judge* (officially or mentally); by extension to *intercede, pray:*— intreat, judge, judgement, pray, make prayer, praying, make supplication.

H6420 פָּלָל *pālāl* from H6419; *judge; Palal,* an Israelite:— Palal.

H6421 פְּלַלְיָה *pĕlalyâ* from H6419 and H3050; *Jah has judged; Pelaljah,* an Israelite:— Pelaliah.

H6422 פַּלְמוֹנִי *palmônî* probably for H6423; a *certain* one, i.e. so-and-so:— certain.

H6423 פְּלֹנִי *pĕlōnî* from H6395; *such* a one, i.e. a specified *person:*— such.

H6424 פָּלַס *pālas* a primitive root; properly to *roll* flat, i.e. *prepare* (a road); also to *revolve,* i.e. *weigh* (mentally):— make, ponder, weigh.

H6425 פֶּלֶס *peles* from H6424; a *balance:*— scales, weight.

H6426 פָּלַץ *pālaṣ* a primitive root; properly perhaps to *rend,* i.e. (by implication) to *quiver:*— tremble.

H6427 פַּלָּצוּת *pallāṣût* from H6426; *affright:*— fearfulness, horror, trembling.

H6428 פָּלַשׁ *pālaš* a primitive root; to *roll* (in dust) :— roll self, wallow self.

H6429 פְּלֶשֶׁת *pĕlešet* from H6428; *rolling,* i.e. *migratory; Pelesheth,* a region of Syria:— Palestina, Palestine, Philistia, Philistines.

H6430 פְּלִשְׁתִּי *pĕlištî* patrial from H6429; a *Pelishtite* or inhabitant of Pelesheth:— Philistine.

H6431 פֶּלֶת *pelet* from an unused root meaning to *flee; swiftness; Peleth,* the name of two Israelites:— Peleth.

H6432 פְּלֵתִי *pĕlētōy* from the same form as H6431; a *courier* (collectively) or official *messenger:*— Pelethites.

H6433 פֻּם *pūm* (Aramaic) probably for H6310; the *mouth* (literally or figuratively):— mouth.

H6434 פֵּן *pēn* from an unused root meaning to *turn;* an *angle* (of a street or wall):— corner.

H6435 פֵּן *pēn* from H6437; properly *removal;* used only (in the construct) adverbially as conjunction *lest:*— lest, lest peradventure, peradventure, that . . . not.

H6436 פַּנַּג *pannag* of uncertain derivation; probably *pastry:*— Pannag.

H6437 פָּנָה *pānâ* a primitive root; to *turn;* by implication to *face,* i.e. *appear, look,* etc:— appear, at eventide, behold, cast out, come on, corner, dawning, empty, go away, lie, look, mark, pass away, prepare, regard, respect, have respect to, turn, return, turn aside, turn away, turn back, turn face, turn self, right early.

H6438 פִּנָּה *pinnâ* feminine of H6434; an *angle;* by implication a *pinnacle;* figuratively a *chieftain:*— bulwark, chief, corner, stay, tower.

H6439 פְּנוּאֵל *pĕnûʾēl* or (more properly)

פְּנִיאֵל *pĕnîʾēl* from H6437 and H410; *face of God; Penuël* or *Peniël,* a place east of Jordan; also (as Penuel) the name of two Israelites:— Peniel, Penuel.

H6440 פָּנִים *pānîm* plural (but always as singular) of an unused noun

פָּנֶה *pāneh* from H6437; the *face* (as the part that *turns*); used in a great variety of applications (literally and figuratively); also (with preposition prefixed) as a preposition *(before,* etc.):— accept, afore, before, aforetime, beforetime, against, anger, as, as long as, at, battle, because, because of, beseech, countenance, edge, employ, endure, enquire, face, favour, fear of, for, forefront, forepart, form, former time, forward, from, front, heaviness, him, himself, honourable, impudent, in, it, looks, looketh, me, meet, more than, mouth, of, off, of old, old time, on, open, out of, over against, the partial, person, please, presence, prospect, was purposed, by reason of, regard, right forth, serve, shewbread, sight, state, straight, street, thee, them, themselves, through, throughout, till, time past, times past, to, unto, toward, upon, upside, upside down, with, within, withstand, ye, you.

HEB

H6441 פְּנִימָה *pĕnîmâ* from H6440 with directive enclitic; *faceward,* i.e. *indoors:*— in, within, inner part, inward.

H6442 פְּנִימִי *pĕnîmî* from H6440; *interior:*— within, inner, inward.

H6443 פָּנִין *pānîn* or

פָּנִי *pānî* from the same as H6434; probably a *pearl* (as *round*):— ruby.

H6444 פְּנִנָּה *pĕninnâ* probably feminine from H6443 contracted; *Peninnah,* an Israelitess:— Peninnah.

H6445 פָּנַק *pānaq* a primitive root; to *enervate:*— bring up.

H6446 פַּס *pas* from H6461; properly the *palm* (of the hand) or *sole* (of the foot) [compare H6447]; by implication (plural) a *long and sleeved* tunic (perhaps simply a *side* one; from the original sense of the root, i.e. of *many breadths*):— colours, divers colours.

H6447 פַּס *pas* (Aramaic) from a root corresponding to H6461; the *palm* (of the hand, as being *spread* out):— part.

H6448 פָּסַג *pāsag* a primitive root; to *cut up,* i.e. (figuratively) *contemplate:*— consider.

H6449 פִּסְגָּה *pisgâ* from H6448; a *cleft; Pisgah,* a mountian east of Jordan:— Pisgah.

H6450 פַּס דַּמִּים *pas dammîm* from H6446 and the plural of H1818; *palm* (i.e. *dell*) *of bloodshed; Pas-Dammim,* a place in Palestine:— Pas-dammim. Compare H658

H6451 פִּסָּה *pissâ* from H6461; *expansion,* i.e. *abundance:*— handful.

H6452 פָּסַח *pāsaḥ* a primitive root; to *hop,* i.e. (figuratively) *skip* over (or *spare*); by implication to *hesitate;* also (literally) to *limp,* to *dance:*— halt, become lame, leap, pass over.

H6453 פֶּסַח *pesaḥ* from H6452; a *pretermission,* i.e. *exemption;* used only technically of the Jewish *Passover* (the festival or the victim):— passover, passover offering.

H6454 פָּסֵחַ *pāsēaḥ* from H6452; *limping; Paseäch,* the name of two Israelites:— Paseah, Phaseah.

H6455 פִּסֵּחַ *pissēaḥ* from H6452; *lame:*— lame.

H6456 פְּסִיל *pĕsîl* from H6458; an *idol:*— carved image, graven image, quarry.

H6457 פָּסַךְ *pāsak* from an unused root meaning to *divide; divider; Pasak,* an Israelite:— Pasach.

H6458 פָּסַל *pāsal* a primitive root; to *carve,* whether wood or stone:— grave, hew.

H6459 פֶּסֶל *pesel* from H6458; an *idol:*— carved image, graven image.

H6460 פְּסַנְטֵרִין *pĕsanṭērîn* (Aramaic), or

פְּסַנְתֵּרִין *pĕsantērîn* a transliteration of the Greek **ψαλτήριον** *psalmtērion;* a *lyre:*— psaltery.

H6461 פָּסַס *pāsas* a primitive root; probably to *disperse,* i.e. (intransitively) *disappear:*— cease.

H6462 פִּסְפָּה *pispâ* perhaps from H6461; *dispersion* ; *Pispah,* an Israelite:— Pispah.

H6463 פָּעָה *pāᶜâ* a primitive root; to *scream:*— cry.

H6464 פָּעוּ *pāᶜû* or

פָּעִי *pāᶜî* from H6463; *screaming; Paü* or *Paï,* a place in Edom:— Pai, Pau.

H6465 פְּעוֹר *pĕᶜôr* from H6473; a *gap; Peör,* a mountain east of Jordan; also (for H1187) a deity worshipped there:— Peor. See also H1047

H6466 פָּעַל *pāᶜal* a primitive root; to *do* or *make* (systematically and habitually), especially to *practise:*— commit, do, doer, evildoer, make, maker, ordain, work, worker.

H6467 פֹּעַל *pōᶜal* from H6466; an *act* or *work* (concrete):— act, deed, do, getting, maker, work.

H6468 פְּעֻלָּה *pĕᶜullâ* feminine passive participle of H6466; (abstractly) *work:*— labour, reward, wages, work.

H6469 פְּעֻלְּתַי *pĕᶜullĕtay* from H6468; *laborious; Peüllethai,* an Israelite:— Peulthai.

H6470 פָּעַם *pāᶜam* a primitive root; to *tap,* i.e. beat regularly; hence (generally) to *impel* or *agitate:*— move, trouble.

H6471 פַּעַם *paᶜam* or (feminine)

פַּעֲמָה *paᶜămâ* from H6470; a *stroke,* literal or figurative (in various applications, as follow):— anvil, corner, foot, footstep, going, hundredfold, now, this once, once, order, rank, step, thrice, time, oftentimes, second time, this time, two times, twice, wheel.

H6472 פַּעֲמֹן *paᶜămōn* from H6471; a *bell* (as *struck*) :— bell.

H6473 פָּעַר *pāᶜar* a primitive root; to *yawn,* i.e. *open* wide (literally or figuratively):— gape, open, open wide.

H6474 פַּעֲרַי *paᶜăray* from H6473; *yawning; Paarai,* an Israelite:— Paarai.

H6475 פָּצָה *pāṣâ* a primitive root; to *rend,* i.e. *open* (especially the mouth):— deliver, gape, open, rid, utter.

H6476 פָּצַח *pāṣaḥ* a primitive root; to *break* out (in joyful sound):— break, break forth, break forth into joy, make a loud noise.

H6477 פְּצִירָה *pĕṣîrâ* from H6484; *bluntness:*— file.

H6478 פָּצַל *pāṣal* a primitive root; to *peel:*— pill.

H6479 פְּצָלָה *pĕṣālâ* from H6478; a *peeling:*— strake.

H6480 פָּצַם *pāṣam* a primitive root; to *rend* (by earthquake):— break.

H6481 פָּצַע *pāṣaᶜ* a primitive root; to *split,* i.e. *wound* :— *wound.*

H6482 פֶּצַע *peṣaᶜ* from H6481; a *wound:*— wound, wounding.

H6483 פִּצֵּץ *piṣṣēṣ* from an unused root meaning to *dissever; dispersive; Pitstsets,* a priest:— Apses *[including the article].*

H6484 פָּצַר *pāṣar* a primitive root; to *peck* at, i.e. (figuratively) *stun* or *dull:*— press, urge, stubbornness.

H6485 פָּקַד *pāqad* a primitive root; to *visit* (with friendly or hostile intent); by analogy to *oversee, muster, charge, care for, miss, deposit,* etc:— appoint, at all, avenge, bestow, charge, appoint to have the charge, give a charge, commit, count, deliver to keep, be empty, enjoin, go see, hurt, do judgment, lack, lay up, look, make, by any means, miss, number, officer, overseer, make overseer, have oversight, have the oversight, punish, reckon, remember, call to remembrance, set, set over, sum, surely, visit, want.

H6486 פְּקֻדָּה *pĕquddâ* feminine passive participle of H6485; *visitation* (in many senses, chiefly official):— account, charge, that have the charge, custody, that which . . . laid up, numbers, office, officer, ordering, oversight, prison, reckoning, visitation.

H6487 פִּקָּדוֹן *piqqādôn* from H6485; a *deposit:*— that which was delivered, that which was delivered to keep, store.

H6488 פְּקִדֻת *pĕqidūt* from H6496; *supervision:*— ward.

H6489 פְּקוֹד *pĕqôd* from H6485; *punishment; Pekod,* a symbolic name for Babylon:— Pekod.

H6490 פִּקּוּד *piqqûd* or

פִּקֻּד *piqqūd* from H6485; properly *appointed,* i.e. a *mandate* (of God; plural only, collectively for the *Law*):— commandment, precept, statute.

H6491 פָּקַח *pāqaḥ* a primitive root; to *open* (the senses, especially the eyes); figuratively to *be observant:*— open.

H6492 פֶּקַח *peqaḥ* from H6491; *watch; Pekach,* an Israelite king:— Pekah.

H6493 פִּקֵּחַ *piqqēaḥ* from H6491; *clear-sighted;* figuratively *intelligent:*— seeing, wise.

H6494 פְּקַחְיָה *pĕqaḥyâ* from H6491 and H3050; *Jah has observed; Pekachjah,* an Israelite king:— Pekahiah.

H6495 פְּקַח־קוֹחַ *pĕqaḥ-qôaḥ* from H6491 redoubled; *opening* (of a dungeon), i.e. *jail-delivery* (figuratively *salvation* from sin):— opening of the prison.

H6496 פָּקִיד *pāqîd* from H6485; a *superintendent* (civil, military or religious):— which had the charge, governor, office, overseer, that was set.

H6497 פֶּקַע *peqaᶜ* from an unused root meaning to *burst;* only used as an architectural term of an ornament similar to H6498, a *semi-globe:*— knop.

H6498 פַּקֻּעָה *paqqūᶜâ* from the same as H6497; the *wild cucumber* (from *splitting* open to shed its seeds):— gourd.

H6499 פַּר *par* or

פָּר *pār* from H6565; a *bullock* (apparently as *breaking* forth in wild strength, or perhaps as *dividing* the hoof):— bull, young bullock, bullock, calf, ox.

H6500 פָּרָא *pārā᾿* a primitive root; to *bear fruit:*— be fruitful.

H6501 פֶּרֶא *pere᾿* or

פֶּרֶה *pereh* (Jer 2:24), from H6500 in the secondary sense of *running* wild; the *onager:*— wild, wild ass.

H6502 פִּרְאָם *pir᾿ām* from H6501; *wildly; Piram,* a Canaanite:— Piram.

H6503 פַּרְבָּר *parbār* or

פַּרְוָר *parwār* of foreign origin; *Parbar* or *Parvar,* a quarter of Jerusalem:— Parbar, suburb.

H6504 פָּרַד *pārad* a primitive root; to *break* through, i.e. *spread* or *separate* (oneself):— disperse, divide, be out of joint, part, scatter, scatter abroad, separate, seperate self, sever self, stretch, sunder.

H6505 פֶּרֶד *pered* from H6504; a *mule* (perhaps from his *lonely* habits):— mule.

H6506 פִּרְדָּה *pirdâ* feminine of H6505; a *she-mule* :— mule.

H6507 פְּרֻדָה *pĕrūdâ* feminine passive participle of H6504; something *separated,* i.e. a *kernel:*— seed.

H6508 פַּרְדֵּס *pardēs* of foreign origin; a *park:*— forest, orchard.

H6509 פָּרָה *pārâ* a primitive root; to *bear fruit* (literally or figuratively):— bear, bring forth, bring forth fruit, fruitful, be fruitful, cause to be fruitful, make fruitful, grow, increase.

H6510 פָּרָה *pārâ* feminine of H6499; a *heifer:*— cow, heifer, kine.

H6511 פָּרָה *pārâ* the same as H6510; *Parah,* a place in Palestine:— Parah.

H6512 פֵּרָה *pērâ* from H6331; a *hole* (as *broken,* i.e. dug):— mole. Compare H2661

H6513 פֻּרָה *pūrâ* for H6288; *foliage; Purah,* an Israelite:— Phurah.

H6514 פְּרוּדָא *pĕrûdā᾿* or

פְּרִידָא *pĕrîdā᾿* from H6504; *dispersion; Peruda* or *Perida,* one of "Solomon's servants":— Perida, Peruda.

H6515 פָּרוּחַ *pārûaḥ* passive participle of H6524; *blossomed; Paruăch,* an Israelite:— Paruah.

H6516 פַּרְוַיִם *parwayim* of foreign origin; *Parvajim,* an Oriental region:— Parvaim.

H6517 פָּרוּר *pārûr* passive participle of H6565 in the sense of *spreading* out [compare H6524]; a *skillet* (as *flat* or *deep*):— pan, pot.

H6518 פָּרָז *pārāz* from an unused root meaning to *separate,* i.e. *decide;* a *chieftain:*— village.

H6519 פְּרָזָה *pĕrāzâ* from the same as H6518; an *open* country:— unwalled town, town without walls, unwalled village.

H6520 פְּרָזוֹן *pĕrāzôn* from the same as H6518; *magistracy,* i.e. *leadership* (also concretely *chieftains*):— village.

H6521 פְּרָזִי *pĕrāzî* or

פְּרוֹזִי *pĕrôzî* from H6519; a *rustic:*— village.

H6522 פְּרִזִּי *pĕrizzî* for H6521; inhabitant *of the open country;* a *Perizzite,* one of the Canaanitish tribes:— Perizzite.

H6523 פַּרְזֶל *parzel* (Aramaic) corresponding to H1270; *iron:*— iron.

H6524 פָּרַח *pāraḥ* a primitive root; to *break* forth as a bud, i.e. *bloom;* generally to *spread;* specifically to *fly* (as extending the wings); figuratively to *flourish:*— abroad, abundantly, blossom, break forth, break out, bud, flourish, make fly, grow, spread, spring, spring up.

H6525 פֶּרַח *peraḥ* from H6524; a *calyx* (natural or artificial); generally *bloom:*— blossom, bud, flower.

H6526 פִּרְחַח *pirḥaḥ* from H6524; *progeny,* i.e. a *brood:*— youth.

H6527 פָּרַט *pāraṭ* a primitive root; to *scatter* words, i.e. *prate* (or *hum*):— chant.

H6528 פֶּרֶט *pereṭ* from H6527; a *stray* or *single* berry:— grape.

H6529 פְּרִי *pĕrî* from H6509; *fruit* (literal or figurative):— bough, fruit, firstfruit, fruitful, reward.

H6530 פְּרִיץ *pĕrîṣ* from H6555; *violent,* i.e. a *tyrant:*— destroyer, ravenous, robber.

H6531 פֶּרֶךְ *perek* from an unused root meaning to *break* apart; *fracture,* i.e. *severity:*— cruelty, rigour.

H6532 פֹּרֶכֶת *pōreket* feminine active participle of the same as H6531; a *separatrix,* i.e. (the sacred) *screen:*— vail.

H6533 פָּרַם *pāram* a primitive root; to *tear:*— rend.

H6534 פַּרְמַשְׁתָּא *parmaštāʾ* of Persian origin; *Parmashta,* a son of Haman:— Parmasta.

H6535 פַּרְנַךְ *parnak* of uncertain derivation; *Parnak,* an Israelite:— Parnach.

H6536 פָּרַס *pāras* a primitive root; to *break* in pieces, i.e. (usually without violence) to *split, distribute:*— deal, divide, have hoofs, part, tear.

H6537 פְּרַס *pĕras* (Aramaic) corresponding to H6536; to *split* up:— divide, Upharsin.

H6538 פֶּרֶס *peres* from H6536; a *claw;* also a kind of *eagle:*— claw, ossifrage.

H6539 פָּרַס *pāras* of foreign origin; *Paras* (i.e. *Persia*), an Eastern country, including its inhabitants:— Persia, Persians.

H6540 פָּרַס *pāras* (Aramaic) corresponding to H6539 :— Persia, Persians.

H6541 פַּרְסָה *parsâ* feminine of H6538; a *claw* or split *hoof:*— claw, clovenfooted, hoof.

H6542 פַּרְסִי *parsî* patrial from H6539; a *Parsite* (i.e. *Persian*), or inhabitant of Peres:— Persian.

H6543 פַּרְסִי *parsî* (Aramaic) corresponding to H6542 :— Persian.

H6544 פָּרַע *pāraʿ* a primitive root; to *loosen;* by implication to *expose, dismiss;* figuratively *absolve, begin:*— avenge, avoid, bare, go back, let, naked, make naked, set at nought, perish, refuse, uncover.

H6545 פֶּרַע *peraʿ* from H6544; the *hair* (as *dishevelled*):— locks.

H6546 פַּרְעָה *parʿâ* feminine of H6545 (in the sense of *beginning*); *leadership* (plural concretely *leaders*):— avenging, revenge.

H6547 פַּרְעֹה *parʿōh* of Egyptian derivation; *Paroh,* a generical title of Egyptian kings:— Pharaoh.

H6548 פַּרְעֹה חָפְרַע *parʿōh ḥopraʿ* of Egyptian derivation; *Paroh-Chophra,* an Egyptian king:— Pharaoh-hophra.

H6549 פַּרְעֹה נְכֹה *parʿōh nĕkōh* or

פַּרְעֹה נְכוֹ *parʿōh nĕkô* of Egyptian derivation; *Paroh-Nekoh* (or *-Neko*), an Egyptian king:— Pharaoh-necho, Pharaoh-nechoh.

H6550 פַּרְעֹשׁ *parʿōš* probably from H6544 and H6211; a *flea* (as the *isolated insect*):— flea.

H6551 פַּרְעֹשׁ *parʿōš* the same as H6550; *Parosh,* the name of four Israelites:— Parosh, Pharosh.

H6552 פִּרְעָתוֹן *pirʿātôn* from H6546; *chieftaincy; Pirathon,* a place in Palestine:— Pirathon.

H6553 פִּרְעָתוֹנִי *pirʿātônî* or

פִּרְעָתֹנִי *pirʿātônî* patrial from H6552; a *Pirathonite* or inhabitant of Pirathon:— Pirathonite.

H6554 פַּרְפַּר *parpar* probably from H6565 in the sense of *rushing; rapid; Parpar,* a river of Syria:— Pharpar.

H6555 פָּרַץ *pāraṣ* a primitive root; to *break* out (in many applications, direct and indirect, literal and figurative):— abroad, breach, make a breach, break, break away, break down, breaker, break forth, break in, break up, burst out, come abroad, spread abroad, compel, disperse, grow, increase, open, press, scatter, urge.

H6556 פֶּרֶץ *pereṣ* from H6555; a *break* (literal or figurative):— breach, breaking forth, breaking in, forth, gap.

H6557 פֶּרֶץ *pereṣ* the same as H6556; *Perets,* the name of two Israelites:— Perez, Pharez.

H6558 פַּרְצִי *parṣî* patronymic from H6557; a *Partsite* (collectively) or descendant of Perets:— Pharzites.

H6559 פְּרָצִים *pĕrāṣîm* plural of H6556; *breaks; Peratsim,* a mountain in Palestine:— Perazim.

H6560 פֶּרֶץ עֻזָּא *pereṣ ʿuzzāʾ* from H6556 and H5798; *break of Uzza; Perets-Uzza,* a place in Palestine:— Perez-uzza.

H6561 פָּרַק *pāraq* a primitive root; to *break* off or *craunch;* figuratively to *deliver:*— break, break off, deliver, redeem, rend, rend in pieces, tear in pieces.

H6562 פְּרַק *pĕraq* (Aramaic) corresponding to H6561; to *discontinue:*— break off.

H6563 פֶּרֶק *pereq* from H6561; *rapine;* also a *fork* (in roads):— crossway, robbery.

H6564 פָּרָק *pārāq* from H6561; *soup* (as full of *crumbed* meat):— broth. See also H4832

H6565 פָּרַר *pārar* a primitive root; to *break* up (usually figuratively, i.e. to *violate, frustrate*):— any ways, break, break asunder, cast off, cause to cease, clean, defeat, disannul, disappoint, dissolve, divide, make of none effect, fail, frustrate, bring to nought, come to nought, utterly, make void.

H6566 פָּרַשׂ *pāraś* a primitive root; to *break* apart, *disperse,* etc:— break, chop in pieces, lay open, scatter, spread, spread abroad, spread forth, spread selves, spread out, stretch, stretch forth, stretch out.

H6567 פָּרָשׁ *pārāš* a primitive root; to *separate,* literally (to *disperse*) or figuratively (to *specify*); also (by implication) to *wound:*— scatter, declare, distinctly, shew, sting.

H6568 פְּרַשׁ *pĕraš* (Aramaic) corresponding to H6567; to *specify:*— distinctly.

H6569 פֶּרֶשׁ *pereš* from H6567; *excrement* (as *eliminated*):— dung.

H6570 פֶּרֶשׁ *pereš* the same as H6569; *Peresh,* an Israelite:— Peresh.

H6571 פָּרָשׁ *pārāš* from H6567; a *steed* (as *stretched* out to a vehicle, not single nor for mounting [compare H5483]); also (by implication) a *driver* (in a chariot), i.e. (collectively) cavalry:— horseman.

H6572 פַּרְשֶׁגֶן *paršegen* or

פַּתְשֶׁגֶן *patšegen* of foreign origin; a *transcript:*— copy.

H6573 פַּרְשֶׁגֶן *paršegen* (Aramaic) corresponding to H6572:— copy.

H6574 פַּרְשְׁדֹן *paršĕdōn* perhaps by compounding H6567 and H6504 (in the sense of *straddling*) [compare H6576]; the *crotch* (or *anus*):— dirt.

H6575 פָּרָשָׁה *pārāšâ* from H6567; *exposition:*— declaration, sum.

H6576 פַּרְשֵׁז *paršēz* a root apparently formed by compounding H6567 and that of H6518 [compare H6574]; to *expand:*— spread.

H6577 פַּרְשַׁנְדָּתָא *paršandātāʾ* of Persian origin; *Parshandatha,* a son of Haman:— Parshandatha.

H6578 פְּרָת *pĕrāt* from an unused root meaning to *break* forth; *rushing; Perath* (i.e. *Euphrates*), a river of the East:— Euphrates.

H6579 פַּרְתַּם *partam* of Persian origin; a *grandee* :— noble, most noble, prince.

H6580 פַּשׁ *paš* probably from an unused root meaning to *disintegrate; stupidity* (as a result of *grossness* or of *degeneracy*):— extremity.

H6581 פָּשָׂה *pāśâ* a primitive root; to *spread:*— spread.

H6582 פָּשַׁח *pāšaḥ* a primitive root; to *tear* in pieces :— pull in pieces.

H6583 פַּשְׁחוּר *pašḥûr* probably from H6582; *liberation; Pashchur,* the name of four Israelites:— Pashur.

H6584 פָּשַׁט *pāšaṭ* a primitive root; to *spread* out (i.e. *deploy* in hostile array); by analogy to *strip* (i.e. *unclothe, plunder, flay,* etc.):— fall upon, flay, invade, make an invasion, pull off, put off, make a road, run upon, rush, set, spoil, spread selves, spread selves abroad, strip, strip off, strip self.

H6585 פָּשַׂע *pāśaʿ* a primitive root; to *stride* (from *spreading* the legs), i.e. *rush* upon:— go.

H6586 פָּשַׁע *pāšaʿ* a primitive root [rather identical with H6585 through the idea of *expansion];* to *break* away (from just authority), i.e. *trespass, apostatize, quarrel:*— offend, rebel, revolt, transgress, transgression, transgressor.

H6587 פֶּשַׂע *peśaʿ* from H6585; a *stride:*— step.

H6588 פֶּשַׁע *pešaʿ* from H6586; a *revolt* (national moral or religious):— rebellion, sin, transgression, trespass.

H6589 פָּשַׂק *pāśaq* a primitive root; to *dispart* (the feet or lips), i.e. *become licentious:*— open, open wide.

H6590 פְּשַׁר *pĕšar* (Aramaic) corresponding to H6622; to *interpret:*— make interpretations, interpreting.

H6591 פְּשַׁר *pĕšar* (Aramaic) from H6590; an *interpretation:*— interpretation.

H6592 פֵּשֶׁר *pēšer* corresponding to H6591:— interpretation.

H6593 פִּשְׁתֶּה *pišteh* from the same as H6580 as in the sense of *comminuting; linen* (i.e. the thread, as *carded*):— flax, linen.

H6594 פִּשְׁתָּה *pištâ* feminine of H6593; *flax;* by implication a *wick:*— flax, tow.

H6595 פַּת *pat* from H6626; a *bit:*— meat, morsel, piece.

H6596 פֹּת *pōt* or

פֹּתָה *pōtâ* (Ezek 13:19), from an unused root meaning to *open;* a *hole,* i.e. *hinge* or the female *pudenda:*— hinge, secret part.

H6597 פִּתְאוֹם *pitʾôm* or

פִּתְאֹם *pitʾōm* from H6621; *instantly:*— straightway, sudden, suddenly.

H6598 פַּתְבַּג *patbag* of Persian origin; a *dainty:*— portion of meat, provision of meat.

HEB

H6599 פִּתְגָם *pitgām* of Persian origin; a (judicial) *sentence:*— decree, sentence.

H6600 פִּתְגָם *pitgām* (Aramaic) corresponding to H6599; a *word, answer, letter* or *decree:*— answer, letter, matter, word.

H6601 פָּתָה *pātâ* a primitive root; to *open,* i.e. *be* (causatively *make*) *roomy;* usually figuratively (in a mental or moral sense) to *be* (causatively *make*) *simple* or (in a sinister way) *delude:*— allure, deceive, enlarge, entice, flatter, persuade, silly, silly one.

H6602 פְּתוּאֵל *pĕtû*ʾ*ēl* from H6601 and H410; *enlarged of God; Pethuël,* an Israelite:— Pethuel.

H6603 פִּתּוּחַ *pittûaḥ* or

פִּתֻּחַ *pittūaḥ* passive participle of H6605; *sculpture* (in low or high relief or even intaglio):— carved, carved work, grave, are graven, graving, engraving.

H6604 פְּתוֹר *pĕtôr* of foreign origin; *Pethor,* a place in Mesopotamia:— Pethor.

H6605 פָּתַח *pātaḥ* a primitive root; to *open* wide (literally or figuratively); specifically to *loosen, begin, plough, carve:*— appear, break forth, draw, draw out, let go free, grave, engrave, graven, loose, loose self, open, be open, be set open, opening, put off, ungird, unstop, have vent.

H6606 פְּתַח *pĕtaḥ* (Aramaic) corresponding to H6605; to *open:*— open.

H6607 פֶּתַח *petaḥ* from H6605; an *opening* (literally), i.e. *door (gate)* or *entrance* way:— door, entering, entering in, entrance, entry, gate, opening, place.

H6608 פֵּתַח *pētaḥ* from H6605; *opening* (figuratively) i.e. *disclosure:*— entrance.

H6609 פְּתִחָה *pĕtīḥâ* from H6605; something *opened,* i.e. a *drawn* sword:— drawn sword.

H6610 פִּתְחוֹן *pitḥôn* from H6605; *opening* (the act) :— open, opening.

H6611 פְּתַחְיָה *pĕtaḥyâ* from H6605 and H3050; *Jah has opened; Pethachjah,* the name of four Israelites:— Pethakiah.

H6612 פְּתִי *pĕtî* or

פֶּתִי *petî* or

פְּתָאִי *pĕtā*ʾ*î* from H6601; *silly* (i.e. *seducible*) :— foolish, simple, simplicity, simple one.

H6613 פְּתַי *pĕtay* (Aramaic) from a root corresponding to H6601; *open,* i.e. (as noun) *width:*— breadth.

H6614 פְּתִיגִיל *pĕtīgîl* of uncertain derivation; probably a figured *mantle* for holidays:— stomacher.

H6615 פְּתַיּוּת *pĕtayyût* from H6612; *silliness* (i.e. *seducibility*):— simple.

H6616 פָּתִיל *pātîl* from H6617; *twine:*— bound, bracelet, lace, line, ribband, thread, wire.

H6617 פָּתַל *pātal* a primitive root; to *twine,* i.e. (literally) to *struggle* or (figuratively) *be* (morally) *tortuous:*— froward, shew self froward, shew self unsavoury, wrestle.

H6618 פְּתַלְתֹּל *pĕtaltōl* from H6617; *tortuous* (i.e. crafty):— crooked.

H6619 פִּתֹם *pītōm* of Egyptian derivation; *Pithom,* a place in Egypt:— Pithom.

H6620 פֶּתֶן *peten* from an unused root meaning to *twist;* an *asp* (from its *contortions*):— adder.

H6621 פֶּתַע *petaᶜ* from an unused root meaning to *open* (the eyes); a *wink,* i.e. *moment* [compare H6597] (used only [with or without preposition] adverbially *quickly* or *unexpectedly*):— at an instant suddenly, very.

H6622 פָּתַר *pātar* a primitive root; to *open* up, i.e. (figuratively) *interpret* (a dream):— interpret, interpretation, interpreter.

H6623 פִּתְרוֹן *pitrôn* or

פִּתְרֹן *pitrōn* from H6622; *interpretation* (of a dream):— interpretation.

H6624 פַּתְרוֹס *patrôs* of Egyptian derivation; *Pathros,* a part of Egypt:— Pathros.

H6625 פַּתְרֻסִי *patrūsî* patrial from H6624; a *Pathrusite,* or inhabitant of Pathros:— Pathrusim.

H6626 פָּתַת *pātat* a primitive root; to *open,* i.e. *break:*— part.

צ

H6627 צָאָה *ṣāʾâ* from H3318; *issue,* i.e. (human) *excrement:*— that which cometh from, that cometh out.

H6628 צֶאֶל *ṣeʾel* from an unused root meaning to *be slender;* the *lotus* tree:— shady tree.

H6629 צֹאן *ṣōʾn* or

צְאוֹן *ṣĕʾôn* (Ps 144:13), from an unused root meaning to *migrate;* a collective name for a *flock* (of sheep or goats); also figuratively (of men):— cattle, small cattle, flock, flocks, lamb, lambs, sheep, sheepcote, sheepfold, sheepshearer, shepherds.

H6630 צַאֲנָן *ṣaʾănān* from the same as H6629 used denominatively; *sheep* pasture; *Zaanan,* a place in Palestine:— Zaanan.

H6631 צֶאֱצָא *ṣeʾĕṣāʾ* from H3318; *issue,* i.e. *produce, children:*— that which cometh out, that come forth, offspring.

H6632 צָב *ṣāb* from an unused root meaning to *establish;* a *palanquin* or *canopy* (as a *fixture*); also a species of *lizard* (probably as clinging *fast*):— covered, litter, tortoise.

H6633 צָבָא *ṣābāʾ* a primitive root; to *mass* (an army or servants):— assemble, fight, perform, muster, wait upon, war.

H6634 צְבָא *ṣĕbāʾ* (Aramaic) corresponding to H6633 in the figurative sense of *summoning* one's wishes; to *please:*— will, would.

H6635 צָבָא *ṣābāʾ* or (feminine)

צְבָאָה *ṣĕbāʾâ* from H6633; a *mass* of persons (or figuratively things), especially regularly organized for war (an *army*); by implication a *campaign,* literally or figuratively (specifically *hardship, worship*):— appointed time, army, army, battle, battle, company, host, service, soldiers, waiting upon, war, warfare.

H6636 צְבֹאִים *ṣĕbōʾîm* or (more correctly)

צְבִיִּים *ṣĕbîyîm* or

צְבִיִם *ṣĕbîyīm* plural of H6643; *gazelles; Tseboïm* or *Tsebijim,* a place in Palestine:— Zeboiim, Zeboim.

H6637 צֹבֵבָה *ṣōbēbâ* feminine active participle of the same as H6632; the *canopier* (with the article); *Tsobebah,* an Israelitess:— Zobebah.

H6638 צָבָה *ṣābâ* a primitive root; to *amass,* i.e. *grow turgid;* specifically to *array* an army against:— fight, swell.

H6639 צָבֶה *ṣābeh* from H6638; *turgid:*— swell.

H6640 צְבוּ *ṣĕbû* (Aramaic) from H6634; properly *will;* concretely an *affair* (as a matter of *determination*):— purpose.

H6641 צָבוּעַ *ṣābûaᶜ* passive participle of the same as H6648; *dyed* (in stripes), i.e. the *hyena:*— speckled.

H6642 צָבַט *ṣābaṭ* a primitive root; to *grasp,* i.e. *hand* out:— reach.

H6643 צְבִי *ṣĕbî* from H6638 in the sense of *prominence; splendor* (as *conspicuous*); also a *gazelle* (as *beautiful*):— beautiful, beauty, glorious, glory, goodly, pleasant, roe, roebuck.

H6644 צִבְיָא *ṣibyāʾ* for H6645; *Tsibja,* an Israelite :— Zibia.

H6645 צִבְיָה *ṣibyâ* for H6646; *Tsibjah,* an Israelitess :— Zibiah.

H6646 צְבִיָּה *ṣĕbîyâ* feminine of H6643; a *female* gazelle:— roe.

H6647 צְבַע *ṣĕbaᶜ* (Aramaic) a root corresponding to that of H6648; to *dip:*— wet.

H6648 צֶבַע *ṣebaᶜ* from an unused root meaning to *dip* (into coloring fluid); a *dye:*— divers, colours.

H6649 צִבְעוֹן *ṣibᶜôn* from the same as H6648; *variegated; Tsibon,* an Idumaean:— Zibeon.

H6650 צְבֹעִים *ṣĕbōᶜîm* plural of H6641; *hyenas; Tseboïm,* a place in Palestine:— Zeboim.

H6651 צָבַר *ṣābar* a primitive root; to *aggregate:*— gather, gather together, heap, heap up, lay up.

H6652 צִבֻּר *ṣibbūr* from H6551; a *pile:*— heap.

H6653 צֶבֶת *ṣebet* from an unused root apparently meaning to *grip;* a *lock* of stalks:— handful.

H6654 צַד *ṣad* contracted from an unused root meaning to *sidle* off; a *side;* figuratively an *adversary:*— side, beside.

H6655 צַד *ṣad* (Aramaic) corresponding to H6654; used adverbially (with preposition) at or upon the *side* of:— against, concerning.

H6656 צְדָא *ṣĕdāʾ* (Aramaic) from an unused root corresponding to H6658 in the sense of *intentness;* a (sinister) *design:*— true.

H6657 צְדָד *ṣĕdād* from the same as H6654; a *siding; Tsedad,* a place near Palestine:— Zedad.

H6658 צָדָה *ṣādâ* a primitive root; to *chase;* by implication to *desolate:*— destroy, hunt, lie in wait.

H6659 צָדוֹק *ṣādôq* from H6663; *just; Tsadok,* the name of eight or nine Israelites:— Zadok.

H6660 צְדִיָּה *ṣĕdîyâ* from H6658; *design* [compare H6656]:— lying in wait.

H6661 צִדִּים *ṣiddîm* plural of H6654; *sides; Tsiddim* (with the article), a place in Palestine:— Ziddim.

H6662 צַדִּיק *ṣadîq* from H6663; *just:*— just, lawful, righteous, righteous man.

H6663 צָדַק *ṣādaq* a primitive root; to *be* (causatively *make*) *right* (in a moral or forensic sense):— cleanse, clear self, be just, do justice, justify, justify self, be righteous, turn to righteousness.

H6664 צֶדֶק *ṣedeq* from H6663; the *right* (natural, morally or legal); also (abstract) *equity* or (figurative) *prosperity:*— even, just, that which is altogether just, justice, right, unrighteousness, righteous, righteous cause, righteously, righteousness.

H6665 צִדְקָה *ṣidqâ* (Aramaic) corresponding to H6666; *beneficence:*— righteousness.

H6666 צְדָקָה *ṣĕdāqâ* from H6663; *rightness* (abstract), subjective *(rectitude)*, objective *(justice)*, moral *(virtue)* or figurative *(prosperity)*:— justice, moderately, right, righteous act, righteously, righteousness.

H6667 צִדְקִיָּה *ṣidqîyâ* or

צִדְקִיָּהוּ *ṣidqîyāhû* from H6664 and H3050; *right of Jah; Tsidkijah,* the name of six Israelites:— Zedekiah, Zidkijah.

H6668 צָהַב *ṣāhab* a primitive root; to *glitter,* i.e. *be golden* in color:— fine.

H6669 צָהֹב *ṣāhōb* from H6668; *golden* in color:— yellow.

H6670 צָהַל *ṣāhal* a primitive root; to *gleam,* i.e. (figuratively) *be cheerful;* by transference to *sound* clear (of various animal or human expressions):— bellow, cry aloud, cry out, lift up, neigh, rejoice, make to shine, shout.

H6671 צָהַר *ṣāhar* a primitive root; to *glisten;* used only as denominative from H3323, to *press* out *oil:*— make oil.

H6672 צֹהַר *ṣōhar* from H6671; a *light* (i.e. *window*); dual *double light,* i.e. *noon:*— midday, noon, noonday, noontide, window.

H6673 צַו *ṣaw* or

צָו *ṣāw* from H6680; an *injunction:*— commandment, precept.

H6674 צוֹא *ṣôʾ* or

צֹא *ṣōʾ* from an unused root meaning to *issue; soiled* (as if *excrementitious*):— filthy.

H6675 צוֹאָה *ṣôʾâ* or

צֹאָה *ṣōʾâ* feminine of H6674; *excrement;* generally *dirt;* figuratively *pollution:*— dung, filth, filthiness. Margin for H2716.

H6676 צַוַּאר *ṣawwaʾr* (Aramaic) corresponding to H6677:— neck.

H6677 צַוָּאר *ṣawwāʾr* or

צַוָּר *ṣawwār* (Neh. 3:5), or

צַוָּרֹן *ṣawwārōn* (Cant. 4:9), or (feminine)

צַוָּארָה *ṣawwāʾrâ* (Mic 2:3), intensive from H6696 in the sense of *binding;* the back of the *neck* (as that on which burdens are *bound*):— neck.

H6678 צוֹבָא *ṣôbāʾ* or

צוֹבָה *ṣôbâ* or

צֹבָה *ṣōbâ* from an unused root meaning to *station;* a *station; Zoba* or *Zobah,* a region of Syria:— Zoba, Zobah.

H6679 צוּד *ṣûd* a primitive root; to *lie* alongside (i.e. in wait); by implication to *catch* an animal (figuratively men); (denominative from H6718) to *victual* (for a journey):— chase, hunt, sore, take, take provision.

H6680 צָוָה *ṣāwâ* a primitive root; (intensively) to *constitute, enjoin:*— appoint, bid, forbid, charge, give a charge, command, give a commandment, give in commandment, send with commandment, commander, send a messenger, put in order, set in order.

H6681 צָוַח *ṣāwaḥ* a primitive root; to *screech* (exultingly):— shout.

H6682 צְוָחָה *ṣĕwāḥâ* from H6681; a *screech* (of anguish):— cry, crying.

H6683 צוּלָה *ṣûlâ* from an unused root meaning to *sink;* an *abyss* (of the sea):— deep.

H6684 צוּם *ṣûm* a primitive root; to *cover* over (the mouth), i.e. to *fast:*— at all, fast.

H6685 צוֹם *ṣôm* or

צֹם *ṣōm* from H6684; a *fast:*— fast, fasting.

H6686 צוּעָר *ṣûʿār* from H6819; *small; Tsuär,* an Israelite:— Zuar.

H6687 צוּף *ṣûp* a primitive root; to *overflow:*— flow, make to overflow, swim.

H6688 צוּף *ṣûp* from H6687; *comb* of honey (from *dripping*):— honeycomb.

H6689 צוּף *ṣûp* or

צוֹפַי *ṣôpay* or

צִיף *ṣîp* from H6688; *honey-comb; Tsuph* or *Tsophai* or *Tsiph,* the name of an Israelite and of a place in Palestine:— Zophai, Zuph.

H6690 צוֹפַח *ṣôpaḥ* from an unused root meaning to *expand, breadth; Tsophach,* an Israelite:— Zophah.

H6691 צוֹפַר *ṣôpar* from H6852; *departing; Tsophar,* a friend of Job:— Zophar.

H6692 צוּץ *ṣûṣ* a primitive root; to *twinkle,* i.e. *glance;* by analogy to *blossom* (figuratively *flourish*):— bloom, blossom, flourish, shew self.

H6693 צוּק *ṣûq* a primitive root; to *compress,* i.e. (figuratively) *oppress, distress:*— constrain, distress, lie sore, press, oppressor, straiten.

H6694 צוּק *ṣûq* a primitive root [rather identical with H6693 through the idea of *narrowness* (of orifice)]; to *pour* out, i.e. (figuratively) *smelt, utter:*— be molten, pour.

H6695 צוֹק *ṣôq* or (feminine)

צוּקָה *ṣûqâ* from H6693; a *strait,* i.e. (figuratively) *distress:*— anguish, troublous.

H6696 צוּר *ṣûr* a primitive root; to *cramp,* i.e. *confine* (in many applications, literal and figurative, formative or hostile):— adversary, assault, beset, besiege, bind, bind up, cast, distress, fashion, fortify, inclose, lay siege, put up in bags.

H6697 צוּר *ṣûr* or

צֻר *ṣūr* from H6696; properly a *cliff* (or sharp rock, as *compressed*); generally a *rock* or *boulder;* figuratively a *refuge;* also an *edge* (as *precipitous*):— edge, God, mighty God, mighty one, rock, sharp, stone, strength, strong. See also H1049

H6698 צוּר *ṣûr* the same as H6697; *rock; Tsur,* the name of a Midianite and of an Israelite:— Zur.

H6699 צוּרָה *ṣûrâ* feminine of H6697; a *rock* (Job 28:10); also a *form* (as if *pressed* out):— form, rock.

H6700 צוּרִיאֵל *ṣûrîʾēl* from H6697 and H410; *rock of God; Tsuriël,* an Israelite:— Zuriel.

H6701 צוּרִישַׁדַּי *ṣûrîšadday* from H6697 and H7706; *rock of* (the) *Almighty; Tsurishaddai,* an Israelite:— Zurishaddai.

H6702 צוּת *ṣût* a primitive root; to *blaze:*— burn.

H6703 צַח *ṣaḥ* from H6705; *dazzling,* i.e. *sunny, bright,* (figuratively) *evident:*— clear, dry, plainly, white.

H6704 צִחֶה *ṣîḥeh* from an unused root meaning to *glow; parched:*— dried up.

H6705 צָחַח *ṣāḥaḥ* a primitive root; to *glare,* i.e. *be dazzling* white:— be whiter.

H6706 צְחִיחַ *ṣĕḥîaḥ* from H6705; *glaring,* i.e. *exposed* to the bright sun:— higher place, top.

H6707 צְחִיחָה *ṣĕḥîḥâ* feminine of H6706; a *parched* region, i.e. the *desert:*— dry land.

H6708 צְחִיחִי *ṣĕḥîḥî* from H6706; *bare* spot, i.e. in the *glaring* sun:— higher place.

H6709 צַחֲנָה *ṣaḥănâ* from an unused root meaning to *putrefy; stench:*— ill savour.

H6710 צַחְצָחָה *ṣaḥṣāḥâ* from H6705; a *dry* place, i.e. *desert:*— drought.

H6711 צָחַק *ṣāḥaq* a primitive root; to *laugh* outright (in merriment or scorn); by implication to *sport:*— laugh, mock, play, make sport.

H6712 צְחֹק *ṣĕḥōq* from H6711; *laughter* (in pleasure or derision):— laugh, laughed to scorn.

H6713 צַחַר *ṣaḥar* from an unused root meaning to *dazzle; sheen,* i.e. *whiteness:*— white.

H6714 צֹחַר *ṣōḥar* from the same as H6713; *whiteness; Tsochar,* the name of a Hittite and of an Israelite:— Zohar. Compare H3328

H6715 צָחֹר *ṣāḥōr* from the same as H6713; *white* :— white.

H6716 צִי *ṣî* from H6680; a *ship* (as a *fixture*):— ship.

H6717 צִיבָא *ṣîbāʾ* from the same as H6678; *station; Tsiba,* an Israelite:— Ziba.

H6718 צַיִד *ṣayid* from a form of H6679 and meaning the same; the *chase;* also *game* (thus taken); (generally) *lunch* (especially for a journey):— catcheth, food, hunter, hunting, that which he took in hunting, venison, victuals.

H6719 צַיָּד *ṣayyād* from the same as H6718; a *huntsman:*— hunter.

H6720 צֵידָה *ṣêdâ* or

צֵדָה *ṣēdâ* feminine of H6718; *food:*— meat, provision, venison, victuals.

H6721 צִידוֹן *ṣîdôn* or

צִידֹן *ṣîdōn* from H6679 in the sense of *catching* fish; *fishery; Tsidon,* the name of a son of Canaan, and of a place in Palestine:— Sidon, Zidon.

H6722 צִידֹנִי *ṣîdōnî* (or

צִדֹנִי) *ṣîdōnî* patrial from H6721; a *Tsidonian* or inhabitant of Tsidon:— Sidonian, of Sidon, Zidonian.

H6723 צִיּוּן *ṣîwwn* from an unused root meaning to *parch; aridity;* concretely a *desert:*— barren, drought, dry, dry land, dry place, solitary place, wilderness.

H6724 צִיוֹן *ṣîôn* from the same as H6723; a *desert* :— dry place.

H6725 צִיּוּן *ṣîwwn* from the same as H6723 in the sense of *conspicuousness* [compare H5329]; a monumental or guiding *pillar:*— sign, title, waymark.

H6726 צִיּוֹן *ṣîyôn* the same (regularly) as H6725; *Tsijon* (as a permanent *capital*), a mountain of Jerusalem:— Zion.

H6727 צִיחָא *ṣîḥāʾ* or

צִחָא *ṣîḥāʾ* as if feminine of H6704; *drought; Tsicha,* the name of two Nethinim:— Ziha.

H6728 צִיִּי *ṣîyî* from the same as H6723; a *desert-dweller,* i.e. *nomad* or wild *beast:*— wild beast of the desert, that dwell in the wilderness, inhabiting the wilderness.

H6729 צִינֹק *ṣînōq* from an unused root meaning to *confine;* the *pillory:*— stocks.

HEB

H6730 צִיעֹר *ṣîᶜōr* from H6819; *small; Tsior,* a place in Palestine:— Zior.

H6731 צִיץ *ṣîṣ* or

צִץ *ṣîṣ* from H6692; properly *glistening,* i.e. a burnished *plate;* also a *flower* (as *bright* colored); a *wing* (as *gleaming* in the air):— blossom, flower, plate, wing.

H6732 צִיץ *ṣîṣ* the same as H6731; *bloom; Tsits,* a place in Palestine:— Ziz.

H6733 צִיצָה *ṣîṣâ* feminine of H6731; a *flower:*— flower.

H6734 צִיצִת *ṣîṣît* feminine of H6731; a *floral* or *wing*-like projection, i.e. a *fore-lock* of hair, a *tassel:*— fringe, lock.

H6735 צִיר *ṣîr* from H6696; a *hinge* (as *pressed* in turning); also a *throe* (as a physical or mental *pressure*); also a *herald* or errand-doer (as *constrained* by the principal):— ambassador, hinge, messenger, pain, pang, sorrow. Compare H6736

H6736 צִיר *ṣîr* the same as H6735; a *form* (of beauty; as if *pressed* out, i.e. carved); hence an (idolatrous) *image:*— beauty, idol.

H6737 צִיר *ṣāyar* a denominative from H6735 in the sense of *ambassador;* to *make an errand,* i.e. *betake* oneself:— make as if . . . had been ambassador.

H6738 צֵל *ṣēl* from H6751; *shade,* whether literal or figurative:— defence, shade, shadow.

H6739 צְלָא *ṣēlāᵓ* (Aramaic) probably corresponding to H6760 in the sense of *bowing; pray:*— pray.

H6740 צָלָה *ṣālâ* a primitive root; to *roast:*— roast.

H6741 צִלָּה *ṣillâ* feminine of H6738; *Tsillah,* an antediluvian woman:— Zillah.

H6742 צְלוּל *ṣēlûl* from H6749 in the sense of *rolling;* a (round or flattened) *cake:*— cake.

H6743 צָלַח *ṣālaḥ* or

צָלֵחַ *ṣālēaḥ* a primitive root; to *push* forward, in various senses (literal or figurative, transitive or intransitive):— break out, come, come mightily, go over, be good, be meet, be profitable, prosper, cause to prosper, effect prosperously, make to prosper, send prosperity, prosperous, make prosperous, prosperously.

H6744 צְלַח *ṣēlaḥ* (Aramaic) corresponding to H6743; to *advance* (transitively or intransitively):— promote, prosper.

H6745 צֵלָחָה *ṣēlāḥâ* from H6743; something *protracted* or flattened out, i.e. a *platter:*— pan.

H6746 צְלֹחִית *ṣēlōḥît* from H6743; something *prolonged* or tall, i.e. a *vial* or salt-*cellar:*— cruse.

H6747 צַלַּחַת *ṣallahat* from H6743; something *advanced* or deep, i.e. a *bowl;* figuratively the *bosom:*— bosom, dish.

H6748 צָלִי *ṣālî* passive participle of H6740; *roasted* :— roast.

H6749 צָלַל *ṣālal* a primitive root; properly to *tumble* down, i.e. *settle* by a waving motion:— sink. Compare H6750, H6751

H6750 צָלַל *ṣālal* a primitive root [rather identical with H6749 through the idea of *vibration];* to *tinkle,* i.e. *rattle* together (as the ears in *reddening* with shame, or the teeth in *chattering* with fear):— quiver, tingle.

H6751 צָלַל *ṣālal* a primitive root [rather identical with H6749 through the idea of *hovering* over (compare H6754)]; to *shade,* as twilight or an opaque object:— begin to be dark, shadowing.

H6752 צֵלֶל *ṣēlel* from H6751; *shade:*— shadow.

H6753 צְלֶלְפּוֹנִי *ṣēlelpônî* from H6752 and the active participle of H6437; *shade-facing; Tselelponi,* an Israelitess:— Hazelelponi *[including the article].*

H6754 צֶלֶם *ṣelem* from an unused root meaning to *shade;* a *phantom,* i.e. (figuratively) *illusion, resemblance;* hence a representative *figure,* especially an *idol:*— image, vain shew.

H6755 צֶלֶם *ṣelem* or

צְלֵם *ṣēlem* (Aramaic) corresponding to H6754; an idolatrous *figure:*— form, image.

H6756 צַלְמוֹן *ṣalmôn* from H6754; *shady; Tsalmon,* the name of a place in Palestine and of an Israelite:— Zalmon.

H6757 צַלְמָוֶת *ṣalmāwet* from H6738 and H4194; *shade of death,* i.e. the *grave* (figuratively *calamity*):— shadow of death.

H6758 צַלְמֹנָה *ṣalmōnâ* feminine of H6757; *shadiness; Tsalmonah,* a place in the Desert:— Zalmonah.

H6759 צַלְמֻנָּע *ṣalmunnāᶜ* from H6738 and H4513; *shade has been denied; Tsalmunna,* a Midianite:— Zalmunna.

H6760 צָלַע *ṣālaᶜ* a primitive root; probably to *curve;* used only as denominative from H6763, to *limp* (as if *one-sided*):— halt.

H6761 צֶלַע *ṣelaᶜ* from H6760; a *limping* or *fall* (figurative):— adversity, halt, halting.

H6762 צֶלַע *ṣelaᶜ* the same as H6761; *Tsela,* a place in Palestine:— Zelah.

H6763 צֵלָע *ṣēlāᶜ* or (feminine)

צַלְעָה *salᶜâ* from H6760; a *rib* (as *curved*), literally (of the body) or figuratively (of a door, i.e. *leaf*); hence a *side,* literally (of a person) or figuratively (of an object or the sky, i.e. *quarter*); architecturally a (especially floor or ceiling) *timber* or *plank* (single or collect, i.e. a *flooring*):— beam, board, chamber, corner, leaf, plank, rib, side, side chamber.

H6764 צָלָף *ṣālāp* from an unused root of unknown meaning; *Tsalaph,* an Israelite:— Zalaph.

H6765 צְלָפְחָד *ṣēlophād* from the same as H6764 and H259; *Tselophchad,* an Israelite:— Zelophehad.

H6766 צֶלְצַח *ṣelṣah* from H6738 and H6703; *clear shade; Tseltsach,* a place in Palestine:— Zelzah.

H6767 צְלָצַל *ṣēlāṣal* from H6750 reduplicated; a *clatter,* i.e. (abstractly) *whirring* (of wings); (concretely) a *cricket;* also a *harpoon* (as *rattling*), a *cymbal* (as *clanging*):— cymbal, locust, shadowing, spear.

H6768 צֶלֶק *ṣeleq* from an unused root meaning to *split; fissure; Tselek,* an Israelite:— Zelek.

H6769 צִלְּתַי *ṣillětay* from the feminine of H6738; *shady; Tsillethai,* the name of two Israelites:— Zilthai.

H6770 צָמֵא *ṣāmēᵓ* a primitive root; to *thirst* (literally or figuratively):— thirst, be athirst, suffer thirst, be thirsty.

H6771 צָמֵא *ṣāmēᵓ* from H6770; *thirsty* (literally or figuratively):— thirst, that thirsteth, thirsty.

H6772 צָמָא *ṣāmāᵓ* from H6770; *thirst* (literal or figurative):— thirst, thirsty.

H6773 צִמְאָה *simᵓâ* feminine of H6772; *thirst* (figuratively of *libidinousnes*):— thirst.

H6774 צִמָּאוֹן *ṣimmāᵓôn* from H6771; a *thirsty* place, i.e. *desert:*— drought, dry ground, thirsty land.

H6775 צָמַד *ṣāmad* a primitive root; to *link,* i.e. *gird;* figuratively to *serve,* (mentally) *contrive:*— fasten, frame, join, join self.

H6776 צֶמֶד *ṣemed* a *yoke* or *team* (i.e. pair); hence an *acre* (i.e. day's task for a yoke of cattle to plough):— acre, couple, together, two asses, yoke, yoke of oxen.

H6777 צַמָּה *ṣammâ* from an unused root meaning to *fasten* on; a *veil:*— locks.

H6778 צִמּוּק *ṣammûq* from H6784; a cake of *dried* grapes:— bunch of raisins, cluster of raisins.

H6779 צָמַח *ṣāmāḥ* a primitive root; to *sprout* (transitively or intransitively, literally or figuratively):— bear, bring forth, bud, cause to bud forth, make to bud, grow, cause to grow, make to grow, grow again, grow up, spring, cause to spring forth, spring forth, spring up.

H6780 צֶמַח *semaḥ* from H6779; a *sprout* (usually concrete), literal or figurative:— branch, bud, that which grew upon, where grew, spring, springing.

H6781 צָמִיד *ṣāmîd* or

צָמִד *ṣēmîd* from H6775; a *bracelet* or *arm-clasp;* generally a *lid:*— bracelet, covering.

H6782 צַמִּים *ṣammîm* from the same as H6777; a *noose* (as *fastening*); figuratively *destruction:*— robber.

H6783 צְמִיתֻת *ṣēmîtūt* or

צְמִתֻת *ṣēmîtūt* from H6789; *excision,* i.e. *destruction;* used only (adverbially) with preposition prefixed *to extinction,* i.e. *perpetually:*— ever.

H6784 צָמַק *ṣāmaq* a primitive root; to *dry* up:— dry.

H6785 צֶמֶר *ṣemer* from an unused root probably meaning to *be shaggy; wool:*— wool, woollen.

H6786 צְמָרִי *ṣēmārî* patrial from an unused name of a place in Palestine; a *Tsemarite* or branch of the Canaanites:— Zemarite.

H6787 צְמָרַיִם *ṣēmārayim* dual of H6785; *double fleece; Tsemarajim,* a place in Palestine:— Zemaraim.

H6788 צַמֶּרֶת *ṣammeret* from the same as H6785; *fleeciness,* i.e. *foliage:*— highest branch, top.

H6789 צָמַת *ṣāmat* a primitive root; to *extirpate* (literally or figuratively):— consume, cut off, destroy, vanish.

H6790 צִן *ṣin* from an unused root meaning to *prick;* a *crag; Tsin,* a part of the Desert:— Zin.

H6791 צֵן *ṣēn* from an unused root meaning to *be prickly;* a *thorn;* hence a cactus-*hedge:*— thorn.

H6792 צֹנֵא *ṣōnēᵓ* or

צֹנֶה *ṣōneh* for H6629; a *flock:*— sheep.

H6793 צִנָּה *ṣinnâ* feminine of H6791; a *hook* (as *pointed*); also a (large) *shield* (as if guarding by *prickliness*); also a *cold* (as *piercing*):— buckler, cold, hook, shield, target.

H6794 צִנּוּר *ṣinnûr* from an unused root perhaps meaning to *be hollow;* a *culvert:*— gutter, water-spout.

H6795 צָנַח *ṣānaḥ* a primitive root; to *alight;* (transitively) to *cause to descend,* i.e. *drive* down:— fasten, light from off.

H6796 צָנִין *ṣānîn* or

צָנִן *ṣānîn* from the same as H6791; a *thorn* :— thorn.

H6797 צָנִיף *ṣānîp* or

צָנוֹף *ṣānôp* or feminine

צָנִיפָה *ṣānîpâ* from H6801; a *head-dress* (i.e. piece of cloth *wrapped* around):— diadem, hood, mitre.

H6798 צָנַם *ṣānam* a primitive root; to *blast* or *shrink* :— withered.

H6799 צְנָן *ṣĕnān* probably for H6630; *Tsenan,* a place near Palestine:— Zenan.

H6800 צָנַע *ṣānaᶜ* a primitive root; to *humiliate:*— humbly, lowly.

H6801 צָנַף *ṣānap* a primitive root; to *wrap,* i.e. *roll* or *dress:*— be attired, surely, violently turn.

H6802 צְנֵפָה *ṣĕnēpâ* from H6801; a *ball:*— toss.

H6803 צִנְצֶנֶת *ṣinṣenet* from the same as H6791; a *vase* (probably a vial *tapering* at the top):— pot.

H6804 צַנְתָּרָה *ṣantārâ* probably from the same as H6794; a *tube:*— pipe.

H6805 צָעַד *ṣāᶜad* a primitive root; to *pace,* i.e. *step* regularly; (upward) to *mount;* (along) to *march;* (down and causatively) to *hurl:*— bring, go, march, march through, run over.

H6806 צַעַד *ṣaᶜad* from H6804; a *pace* or regular *step:*— pace, step.

H6807 צְעָדָה *ṣĕᶜādâ* feminine of H6806; a *march;* (concretely) an (ornamental) *ankle-chain:*— going, ornament of the legs.

H6808 צָעָה *ṣāᶜâ* a primitive root; to *tip* over (for the purpose of *spilling* or *pouring* out), i.e. (figuratively) *depopulate;* by implication to *imprison* or *conquer;* (reflexively) to *lie down* (for coition):— captive exile, travelling, wander, cause to wander, wanderer.

H6809 צָעִיף *ṣāᶜîp* from an unused root meaning to *wrap* over; a *veil:*— vail.

H6810 צָעִיר *ṣāᶜîr* or

צָעוֹר *ṣāᶜôr* from H6819; *little;* (in number) *few;* (in age) *young,* (in value) *ignoble:*— least, little, little one, small, small one, young, younger, youngest.

H6811 צָעִיר *ṣāᶜîr* the same as H6810; *Tsaïr,* a place in Idumaea:— Zair.

H6812 צְעִירָה *ṣĕᶜîrâ* feminine of H6810; *smallness* (of age), i.e. *juvenility:*— youth.

H6813 צָעַן *ṣāᶜan* a primitive root; to *load* up (beasts), i.e. to *migrate:*— be taken down.

H6814 צֹעַן *ṣōᶜan* of Egyptian derivation; *Tsoän,* a place in Egypt:— Zoan.

H6815 צַעֲנַנִּים *ṣaᶜănannîm* or (dual)

צַעֲנַיִם *ṣaᶜănayim* plural from H6813; *removals; Tsaanannim* or *Tsaanajim,* a place in Palestine:— Zaannannim, Zaanaim.

H6816 צַעְצֻעַ *ṣaᶜṣūaᶜ* from an unused root meaning to *bestrew* with carvings; *sculpture:*— image work.

H6817 צָעַק *ṣāᶜaq* a primitive root; to *shriek;* (by implication) to *proclaim* (an assembly):— at all, call together, cry, cry out, gather, gather selves together, gather together.

H6818 צְעָקָה *ṣaᶜăqâ* from H6817; a *shriek:*— cry, crying.

H6819 צָעַר *ṣāᶜar* a primitive root; to *be small,* i.e. (figuratively) *ignoble:*— be brought low, little one, be small.

H6820 צֹעַר *ṣōᶜar* from H6819; *little; Tsoär,* a place east of the Jordan:— Zoar.

H6821 צָפַד *ṣāpad* a primitive root; to *adhere:*— cleave.

H6822 צָפָה *ṣāpâ* a primitive root; properly to *lean* forward, i.e. to *peer* into the distance; by implication to *observe, await:*— behold, espy, look up, look well, wait for, watch, keep the watch, watchman.

H6823 צָפָה *ṣāpâ* a primitive root [probably rather identical with H6822 through the idea of *expansion* in outlook transfered to act]; to *sheet* over (especially with metal):— cover, overlay.

H6824 צָפָה *ṣāpâ* from H6823; an *inundation* (as *covering*):— swimmest.

H6825 צְפוֹ *ṣĕpô* or

צְפִי *ṣĕpî* from H6822; *observant; Tsepho* or *Tsephi,* an Idumaean:— Zephi, Zepho.

H6826 צִפּוּי *ṣippûy* from H6823; *encasement* (with metal):— covering, overlaying.

H6827 צְפוֹן *ṣĕpôn* probably for H6837; *Tsephon,* an Israelite:— Zephon.

H6828 צָפוֹן *ṣāpôn* or

צָפֹן *ṣāpōn* from H6845; properly *hidden,* i.e. *dark;* used only of the *north* as a quarter *(gloomy* and *unknown)*:— north, northern, north side, northward, north wind.

H6829 צָפוֹן *ṣāpôn* the same as H6828; *boreal; Tsaphon,* a place in Palestine:— Zaphon.

H6830 צְפוֹנִי *ṣĕpônî* from H6828; *northern:*— northern.

H6831 צְפוֹנִי *ṣĕpônî* patronymic from H6827; a *Tsephonite,* or (collectively) descendant of Tsephon :— Zephonites.

H6832 צְפוּעַ *ṣĕpûaᶜ* from the same as H6848; *excrement* (as *protruded*):— dung.

H6833 צִפּוֹר *ṣippôr* or

צִפֹּר *ṣippōr* from H6852; a little *bird* (as *hopping*):— bird, fowl, sparrow.

H6834 צִפּוֹר *ṣippôr* the same as H6833; *Tsippor,* a Moabite:— Zippor.

H6835 צַפַּחַת *ṣappaḥat* from an unused root meaning to *expand;* a *saucer* (as *flat*):— cruse.

H6836 צְפִיָּה *ṣĕpîyâ* from H6822; *watchfulness:*— watching.

H6837 צִפְיוֹן *ṣipyôn* from H6822; *watch*-tower; *Tsiphjon,* an Israelite:— Ziphion. Compare H6827

H6838 צַפִּיחִת *ṣappîḥit* from the same as H6835; a flat thin *cake:*— wafer.

H6839 צֹפִים *ṣōpîm* plural of active participle of H6822; *watchers; Tsophim,* a place east of the Jordan:— Zophim.

H6840 צָפִין *ṣāpîn* from H6845; a *treasure* (as *hidden*):— hid.

H6841 צְפִיר *ṣĕpîr* (Aramaic) corresponding to H6842; a he-*goat:*— he goat.

H6842 צָפִיר *ṣāpîr* from H6852; a male *goat* (as *prancing*):— goat, he goat.

H6843 צְפִירָה *ṣĕpîrâ* feminine formed like H6842; a *crown* (as *encircling* the head); also a *turn* of affairs (i.e. *mishap*):— diadem, morning.

H6844 צָפִית *ṣāpît* from H6822; a *sentry:*— watchtower.

H6845 צָפַן *ṣāpan* a primitive root; to *hide* (by *covering* over); by implication to *hoard* or *reserve;* figuratively to *deny;* specifically (favorably) to *protect,* (unfavorably) to *lurk:*— esteem, hide, hidden one, hide self, lay up, lurk privily, be set privily, secret, keep secretly, secret place.

H6846 צְפַנְיָה *ṣĕpanyâ* or

צְפַנְיָהוּ *ṣĕpanyāhû* from H6845 and H3050; *Jah has secreted; Tsephanjah,* the name of four Israelites:— Zephaniah.

H6847 צָפְנַת פַּעְנֵחַ *ṣopnat paᶜnēaḥ* of Egyptian derivation; *Tsophnath-Paneäch,* Joseph's Egyptian name :— Zaphnath-paaneah.

H6848 צֶפַע *ṣepaᶜ* or

צִפְעֹנִי *ṣipᶜōnî* from an unused root meaning to *extrude;* a *viper* (as *thrusting* out the tongue, i.e. *hissing*):— adder, cockatrice.

H6849 צְפִעָה *ṣĕpīᶜâ* feminine from the same as H6848; an *outcast* thing:— issue.

H6850 צָפַף *ṣāpap* a primitive root; to *coo* or *chirp* (as a bird):— chatter, peep, whisper.

H6851 צַפְצָפָה *ṣapṣāpâ* from H6687; a *willow* (as growing in *overflowed* places):— willow tree.

H6852 צָפַר *ṣāpar* a primitive root; to *skip* about, i.e. *return:*— depart early.

H6853 צְפַר *ṣĕpar* (Aramaic) corresponding to H6833; a *bird:*— bird.

H6854 צְפַרְדֵּעַ *ṣĕpardēaᶜ* from H6852 and a word elsewhere unused meaning a *swamp;* a *marsh-leaper,* i.e. *frog:*— frog.

H6855 צִפֹּרָה *ṣippōrâ* feminine of H6833; *bird; Tsipporah,* Moses' wife:— Zipporah.

H6856 צִפֹּרֶן *ṣippōren* from H6852 (in the denominative sense [from H6833] of *scratching*); properly a *claw,* i.e. (human) *nail;* also the *point* of a style (or pen, tipped with adamant):— nail, point.

H6857 צְפַת *ṣĕpat* from H6822; *watch*-tower; *Tsephath,* a place in Palestine:— Zephath.

H6858 צֶפֶת *ṣepet* from an unused root meaning to *encircle;* a *capital* of a column:— chapiter.

H6859 צְפָתָה *ṣĕpātâ* the same as H6857; *Tsephathah,* a place in Palestine:— Zephathah.

H6860 צִקְלַג *ṣiqlag* or

צִיקְלַג *ṣîqĕlag* (1 Chron. 12:1, 20), of uncertain derivation; *Tsiklag* or *Tsikelag,* a place in Palestine:— Ziklag.

H6861 צִקְלֹן *ṣiqlōn* from an unused root meaning to *wind;* a *sack* (as *tied* at the mouth):— husk.

H6862 צַר *ṣar* or

צָר *ṣār* from H6887; *narrow;* (as a noun) a *tight* place (usually figuratively, i.e. *trouble*); also a *pebble* (as in H6864); (transitively) an *opponent* (as *crowding*):— adversary, afflicted, affliction, anguish, close, distress, enemy, flint, foe, narrow, small, sorrow, strait, tribulation, trouble.

H6863 צֵר *ṣēr* from H6887; *rock; Tser,* a place in Palestine:— Zer.

H6864 צֹר *ṣōr* from H6696; a *stone* (as if *pressed* hard or to a point); (by implication of use) a *knife:*— flint, sharp stone.

H6865 צֹר *ṣōr* or

צוֹר *ṣôr* the same as H6864; a *rock; Tsor,* a place in Palestine:— Tyre, Tyrus.

H6866 צָרַב *ṣārab* a primitive root; to *burn:*— burn.

H6867 צָרֶבֶת *ṣārebet* from H6686; *conflagration* (of fire or disease):— burning, inflammation.

H6868 צְרֵדָה *ṣĕrēdâ* or

צְרֵדָתָה *ṣĕrēdātâ* apparently from an unused root meaning to *pierce; puncture; Tseredah,* a place in Palestine:— Zereda, Zeredathah.

H6869 צָרָה *ṣārâ* feminine of H6862; *tightness* (i.e. figuratively *trouble*); transitive a female *rival:*— adversary, adversity, affliction, anguish, distress, tribulation, trouble.

H6870 צְרוּיָה *ṣĕrûyâ* feminine participle passive from the same as H6875; *wounded; Tserujah,* an Israelitess:— Zeruiah.

H6871 צְרוּעָה *ṣĕrûᶜâ* feminine passive participle of H6879; *leprous; Tseruäh,* an Israelitess:— Zeruah.

H6872 צְרוֹר *ṣĕrôr* or (shorter)

צְרֹר *ṣĕrōr* from H6887; a *parcel* (as *packed* up); also a *kernel* or *particle* (as if a *package*):— bag, bendeth, bundle, least grain, small stone.

H6873 צָרַח *ṣāraḥ* a primitive root; to *be clear* (in tone, i.e. *shrill*), i.e. to *whoop:*— cry, roar.

H6874 צְרִי *ṣĕrî* the same as H6875; *Tseri,* an Israelite:— Zeri. Compare H3340

H6875 צְרִי *ṣĕrî* or

צֳרִי *ṣŏrî* from an unused root meaning to *crack* [as by *pressure],* hence to *leak; distillation,* i.e. *balsam:*— balm.

H6876 צֹרִי *ṣōrî* patrial from H6865; a *Tsorite* or inhabitant of Tsor (i.e. *Syrian*):— of Tyre, man of Tyre.

H6877 צְרִיחַ *ṣĕrîaḥ* from H6873 in the sense of *clearness* of vision; a *citadel:*— high place, hold.

H6878 צֹרֶךְ *ṣōrek* from an unused root meaning to *need; need:*— need.

H6879 צָרַע *ṣāraᶜ* a primitive root; to *scourge,* i.e. (intransitively and figuratively) to *be stricken with leprosy:*— leper, leprous.

H6880 צִרְעָה *ṣirᶜâ* from H6879; a *wasp* (as *stinging*):— hornet.

H6881 צָרְעָה *ṣorᶜâ* apparently another form for H6880; *Tsorah,* a place in Palestine:— Zareah, Zorah, Zoreah.

H6882 צָרְעִי *ṣorᶜî* or

צָרְעָתִי *ṣorᶜātî* patrial from H6881; a *Tsorite* or *Tsorathite,* i.e. inhabitant of Tsorah:— Zorites, Zareathites, Zorathites.

H6883 צָרַעַת *ṣāraᶜat* from H6879; *leprosy:*— leprosy.

H6884 צָרַף *ṣārap* a primitive root; to *fuse* (metal), i.e. *refine* (literally or figuratively):— cast, finer, refine, refiner, founder, goldsmith, melt, pure, purge away, try.

H6885 צֹרְפִי *ṣōrĕpî* from H6884; *refiner; Tsorephi* (with the article), an Israelite:— goldsmith's.

H6886 צָרְפַת *ṣārĕpat* from H6884; *refinement; Tsarephath,* a place in Palestine:— Zarephath.

H6887 צָרַר *ṣārar* a primitive root; to *cramp,* literally or figuratively, transitively or intransitively (as follows):— adversary, afflict, be in affliction, besiege, bind, bind up, distress, be in distress, bring distress, enemy, narrower, oppress, pangs, shut up, be in a strait, be in trouble, vex.

H6888 צְרֵרָה *ṣĕrērâ* apparently by erroneous transcription for H6868; *Tsererah* for *Tseredah:*— Zererath.

H6889 צֶרֶת *ṣeret* perhaps from H6671; *splendor; Tsereth,* an Israelite:— Zereth.

H6890 צֶרֶת הַשַּׁחַר *ṣeret haššaḥar* from the same as H6889 and H7837 with the article interposed; *splendor of the dawn; Tsereth-hash-Shachar,* a place in Palestine:— Zareth-shahar.

H6891 צָרְתָן *ṣārĕtān* perhaps for H6868; *Tsarethan,* a place in Palestine:— Zarthan.

ק

H6892 קֵא *qēʾ* or

קִיא *qîʾ* from H6958; *vomit:*— vomit.

H6893 קָאַת *qāʾat* from H6958; probably the *pelican* (from *vomiting*):— cormorant.

H6894 קַב *qab* from H6895; a *hollow,* i.e. vessel used as a (dry) *measure:*— cab.

H6895 קָבַב *qābab* a primitive root; to *scoop* out, i.e. (figuratively) to *malign* or *execrate* (i.e. *stab* with words):— at all, curse.

H6896 קֵבָה *qēbâ* from H6895; the *paunch* (as a *cavity*) or first stomach of ruminants:— maw.

H6897 קֹבָה *qōbâ* from H6895; the *abdomen* (as a cavity):— belly.

H6898 קֻבָּה *qubbâ* from H6895; a *pavilion* (as a domed *cavity*):— tent.

H6899 קִבּוּץ *qibbûṣ* from H6908; a *throng:*— company.

H6900 קְבוּרָה *qĕbûrâ* or

קְבֻרָה *qĕbūrâ* feminine passive participle of H6912; *sepulture;* (concretely) a *sepulchre:*— burial, burying place, grave, sepulchre.

H6901 קָבַל *qābal* a primitive root; to *admit,* i.e. *take* (literally or figuratively):— choose, hold, take hold, receive, take, undertake.

H6902 קְבַל *qĕbal* (Aramaic) corresponding to H6901; to *acquire:*— receive, take.

H6903 קְבֵל *qĕbēl* or

קֳבֵל *qŏbēl* (Aramaic) corresponding to H6905; (adverbially) *in front of;* usually (with other particles) *on account of, so as, since, hence:*— according to, as, because, before, for this cause, forasmuch as, by this means, over against, by reason of, that, therefore, though, wherefore.

H6904 קֹבֶל *qōbel* from H6901 in the sense of *confronting* (as standing *opposite* in order to receive); a *battering*-ram:— war.

H6905 זָבָל *zābāl* from H6901 in the sense of *opposite* [see H6904]; the *presence,* i.e. (adverbially) *in front of:*— before.

H6906 קָבַע *qābaᶜ* a primitive root; to *cover,* i.e. (figuratively) *defraud:*— rob, spoil.

H6907 קֻבַּעַת *qubbaᶜat* from H6906; a *goblet* (as deep like a *cover*):— dregs.

H6908 קָבַץ *qābaṣ* a primitive root; to *grasp,* i.e. *collect:*— assemble, assemble selves, gather, gather together, gather together, gather selves together, gather up, bring together, heap, resort, surely, take up.

H6909 קַבְצְאֵל *qabṣĕʾēl* from H6908 and H410; *God has gathered; Kabtseël,* a place in Palestine:— Kabzeel. Compare H3343

H6910 קְבֻצָה *qĕbūṣâ* feminine passive participle of H6908; a *hoard:*— gather.

H6911 קִבְצַיִם *qibṣayim* dual from H6908; a *double heap; Kibtsajim,* a place in Palestine:— Kibzaim.

H6912 קָבַר *qābar* a primitive root; to *inter:*— in any wise, bury, burier.

H6913 קֶבֶר *qeber* or (feminine)

קִבְרָה *qibrâ* from H6912; a *sepulchre:*— burying place, grave, sepulchre.

H6914 קִבְרוֹת הַתַּאֲוָה *qibrôt hattaʾăwâ* from the feminine plural of H6913 and H8378 with the article interposed; *graves of the longing; Kidbroth-hat-Taavh,* a place in the Desert:— Kibroth-hattaavah.

H6915 קָדַד *qādad* a primitive root; to *shrivel* up, i.e. *contract* or *bend* the body (or neck) in deference:— bow the head, bow down the head, stoop.

H6916 קִדָּה *qiddâ* from H6915; *cassia* bark (as in *shrivelled* rolls):— cassia.

H6917 קָדוּם *qādûm* passive participle of H6923; a *pristine* hero:— ancient.

H6918 קָדוֹשׁ *qādôš* or

קָדֹשׁ *qādōš* from H6942; *sacred* (ceremonially or morally); (as noun) *God* (by eminence), an *angel,* a *saint,* a *sanctuary:*— holy, holy One, saint.

H6919 קָדַח *qādaḥ* a primitive root to *inflame:*— burn, kindle.

H6920 קַדַּחַת *qaddaḥat* from H6919; *inflammation,* i.e. febrile disease:— burning ague, fever.

H6921 קָדִים *qādîm* or

קָדִם *qādīm* from H6923; the *fore* or front part; hence (by orientation) the *East* (often adverbially *eastward,* for brevity the *east wind*):— east, eastward, east wind.

H6922 קַדִּישׁ *qaddîš* (Aramaic) corresponding to H6918:— holy, holy one, saint.

H6923 קָדַם *qādam* a primitive root; to *project* (one self), i.e. *precede;* hence to *anticipate, hasten, meet* (usually for help):— come before, go before, flee before, disappoint, meet, prevent.

H6924 קֶדֶם *qedem* or

קֵדְמָה *qēdĕmâ* from H6923; the *front,* of place (absolutely the *fore part,* relatively the *East*) or time *(antiquity*); often used adverbially *(before, anciently, eastward*):— aforetime, ancient, ancient time, before, east, east end, east part, east side, eastward, eternal, ever, everlasting, forward, old, past. Compare H6926

H6925 קֳדָם *qŏdām* or

קְדָם *qĕdām* (Aramaic) (Dan. 7:13), corresponding to H6924; *before:*— before, from, I, I thought, me, of, it pleased, presence.

H6926 קִדְמָה *qidmâ* feminine of H6924; the *forward* part (or relatively) *East* (often adverbially *on* the *east* or *in front*):— east, eastward.

H6927 קַדְמָה *qadmâ* from H6923; *priority* (in time); also used adverbially *(before)*:— afore, antiquity, former estate, old estate.

H6928 קַדְמָה *qadmâ* (Aramaic) corresponding to H6927; *former* time:— aforetime, ago.

H6929 קֵדְמָה *qēdmâ* from H6923; *precedence; Kedemah,* a son of Ishmael:— Kedemah.

H6930 קַדְמוֹן *qadmôn* from H6923; *eastern:*— east.

H6931 קַדְמוֹנִי *qadmônî* or

קַדְמֹנִי *qadmōnî* from H6930; (of time) *anterior* or (of place) *oriental:*— ancient, they that went before, east, old, thing of old.

H6932 קְדֵמוֹת *qĕdēmôt* from H6923; *beginnings; Kedemoth,* a place in eastern Palestine:— Kedemoth.

H6933 קַדְמַי *qadmay* (Aramaic) from a root corresponding to H6923; *first:*— first.

H6934 קַדְמִיאֵל *qadmî'ēl* from H6924 and H410; *presence of God; Kadmiël,* the name of three Israelites:— Kadmiel.

H6935 קַדְמֹנִי *qadmōnî* the same as H6931; *ancient,* i.e. aboriginal; *Kadmonite* (collectively), the name of a tribe in Palestine:— Kadmonites.

H6936 קׇדְקֹד *qodqōd* from H6915; the *crown* of the head (as the part most *bowed*):— crown, crown of the head, pate, scalp, top of the head.

H6937 קָדַר *qādar* a primitive root; to *be ashy,* i.e. *dark*-colored; by implication to *mourn* (in sackcloth or sordid garments):— be black, be blackish, be dark, make dark, darken, heavily, mourn, cause to mourn.

H6938 קֵדָר *qēdār* from H6937; *dusky* (of the skin or the tent); *Kedar,* a son of Ishmael; also (collectively) *bedawin* (as his descendants or representatives):— Kedar.

H6939 קִדְרוֹן *qidrôn* from H6937; *dusky* place; *Kidron,* a brook near Jerusalem:— Kidron.

H6940 קַדְרוּת *qadrût* from H6937; *duskiness:*— blackness.

H6941 קְדֹרַנִּית *qĕdōrannît* adverbially from H6937; *blackish ones* (i.e. *in sackcloth*); used adverbially in *mourning* weeds:— mournfully.

H6942 קָדַשׁ *qādaš* a primitive root; to *be* (causatively *make, pronounce* or *observe* as) *clean* (ceremonially or morally):— appoint, bid, consecrate, dedicate, defile, hallow, be holy, keep holy, be holier, holy place, keep, prepare, proclaim, purify, sanctify, sanctified one, sanctify self, wholly.

H6943 קֶדֶשׁ *qedeš* from H6942; a *sanctum; Kedesh,* the name of four places in Palestine:— Kedesh.

H6944 קֹדֶשׁ *qōdeš* from H6942; a *sacred* place or thing; rarely abstract *sanctity:*— consecrated, consecrated thing, dedicated, dedicated thing, hallowed, hallowed thing, holiness, holy, most holy, holy day, holy portion, holy thing, most holy thing, saint, sanctuary.

H6945 קָדֵשׁ *qādēš* from H6942; a (quasi) *sacred* person, i.e. (technically) a (male) *devotee* (by prostitution) to licentious idolatry:— sodomite, unclean.

H6946 קָדֵשׁ *qādēš* the same as H6945; *sanctuary; Kadesh,* a place in the Desert:— Kadesh. Compare H6947

H6947 קָדֵשׁ בַּרְנֵעַ *qādēš barnēa*ᶜ from the same as H6946 and an otherwise unused word (apparently compounded of a correspondent to H1251 and a derivative of H5128) meaning *desert of a fugitive; Kadesh of* (the) *Wilderness of Wandering; Kadesh-Barneä,* a place in the Desert:— Kadesh-barnea.

H6948 קְדֵשָׁה *qĕdēšâ* feminine of H6945; a female *devotee* (i.e. *prostitute*):— harlot, whore.

H6949 קָהָה *qāhâ* a primitive root; to be *dull:*— be set on edge, be blunt.

H6950 קָהַל *qāhal* a primitive root; to *convoke:*— assemble, assemble selves, assemble together, gather, gather selves, gather together.

H6951 קָהָל *qāhāl* from H6950; *assemblage* (usually concrete):— assembly, company, congregation, multitude.

H6952 קְהִלָּה *qĕhillâ* from H6950; an *assemblage:*— assembly, congregation.

H6953 קֹהֶלֶת *qōhelet* feminine of active participle from H6950; a (female) *assembler* (i.e. lecturer); abstract *preaching* (used as a "nom de plume," *Koheleth*):— preacher.

H6954 קְהֵלָתָה *qĕhēlātâ* from H6950; *convocation; Kehelathah,* a place in the Desert:— Kehelathah.

H6955 קְהָת *qĕhāt* from an unused root meaning to *ally* oneself; *allied; Kehath,* an Israelite:— Kohath.

H6956 קֳהָתִי *qŏhātî* patronymic from H6955; a *Kohathite* (collectively) or descendant of Kehath:— Kohathites.

H6957 קַו *qaw* or

קָו *qāw* from H6960 [compare H6961]; a *cord* (as *connecting*), especially for measuring; figuratively a *rule;* also a *rim,* a musical *string* or *accord:*— line. Compare H6978

H6958 קוֹא *qô'* or

קָיָה *qāyâ* (Jer 25:27) ,a primitive root; to *vomit:*— spue, spue out, vomit, vomit out, vomit up, vomit up again.

H6959 קוֹבַע *qôba*ᶜ a form collateral to H3553; a *helmet:*— helmet.

H6960 קָוָה *qāwâ* a primitive root; to *bind* together (perhaps by *twisting*), i.e. *collect;* (figuratively) to *expect:*— gather, gather together, look, patiently, tarry, wait, wait for, wait on, wait upon.

H6961 קָוֶה *qāweh* from H6960; a (measuring) *cord* (as if for *binding*):— line.

H6962 קוּט *qûṭ* a primitive root; properly to *cut off,* i.e. (figuratively) *detest:*— be grieved, lothe self.

H6963 קוֹל *qûl* or

קֹל *qōl* from an unused root meaning to *call* aloud; a *voice* or *sound:*— aloud, bleating, crackling, cry, cry out, fame, lightness, lowing, noise, hold peace, proclaim, proclamation, sing, sound, spark, thunder, thundering, voice, yell.

H6964 קוֹלָיָה *qôlāyâ* from H6963 and H3050; *voice of Jah; Kolajah,* the name of two Israelites:— Kolaiah.

H6965 קוּם *qûm* a primitive root; to *rise* (in various applications, literal, figurative, intensive and causative):— abide, accomplish, be clearer, confirm, continue, decree, be dim, endure, enemy, enjoin, get up, make good, help, hold, lift up, help to lift up again, make, but newly, ordain, perform, pitch, raise, raise up, rear, rear up, remain, rise, arise, rise up, rise up again, rise up against, rouse up, set, set up, stablish, establish, stand, make to stand, stand up, stir up, strengthen, succeed, sure, assure, make sure, surely, up, be up, uphold, be uprising.

H6966 קוּם *qûm* (Aramaic) corresponding to H6965 :— appoint, establish, make, raise up self, arise, rise up, stand, make to stand, set, set up.

H6967 קוֹמָה *qômâ* from H6965; *height:*— along, height, high, stature, tall.

H6968 קוֹמְמִיּוּת *qôměmîyût* from H6965; *elevation,* i.e. (adverbially) *erectly* (figuratively):— upright.

H6969 קוּן *qûn* a primitive root; to *strike* a musical note, i.e. *chant* or *wail* (at a funeral):— lament, mourning woman.

H6970 קוֹעַ *qôa*ᶜ probably from H6972 in the original sense of *cutting* off; *curtailment; Koä,* region of Babylonia:— Koa.

H6971 קוֹף *qôp* or

קֹף *qōp* probably of foreign origin; a *monkey:*— ape.

H6972 קוּץ *qûṣ* a primitive root; to *clip* off; used only as denominative from H7019; to *spend the harvest* season:— summer.

H6973 קוּץ *qûṣ* a primitive root [rather identical with H6972 through the idea of *severing* oneself from (compare H6962)]; to be (causatively *make*) *disgusted* or *anxious:*— abhor, be distressed, be grieved, loathe, vex, be weary.

H6974 קוּץ *qûṣ* a primitive root [rather identical with H6972 through the idea of *abruptness* in starting up from sleep (compare H3364)]; to *awake* (literally or figuratively):— arise, wake, awake, be awake, watch.

H6975 קוֹץ *qôṣ* or

קֹץ *qōṣ* from H6972 (in the sense of *pricking*); a *thorn:*— thorn.

H6976 קוֹץ *qôṣ* the same as H6975; *Kots,* the name of two Israelites:— Koz, Hakkoz *[including the article].*

H6977 קְוֻצָּה *qĕwuṣṣâ* feminine passive participle of H6972 in its original sense; a *forelock* (as *shorn*):— lock.

H6978 קַו־קַו *qaw-qaw* from H6957 (in the sense of a *fastening*); *stalwart:*— meted out.

H6979 קוּר *qûr* a primitive root; to *trench;* by implication to *throw forth;* also (denominatively from H7023) to *wall up,* whether literally (to *build* a wall) or figuratively (to *stop*):— break down, cast out, destroy, dig.

H6980 קוּר *qûr* from H6979; (only plural) *trenches,* i.e. a *web* (as if so formed):— web.

H6981 קוֹרֵא *qôrē'* or

קֹרֵא *qōrē'* (1 Chron. 26:1), active participle of H7121; *crier; Korè,* the name of two Israelites:— Kore.

H6982 קוֹרָה *qôrâ* or

קֹרָה *qōrâ* from H6979; a *rafter* (forming *trenches* as it were); by implication a *roof:*— beam, roof.

H6983 קוֹשׁ *qôš* a primitive root; to *bend;* used only as denominative for H3369, to *set a trap:*— lay a snare.

H6984 קוּשָׁיָהוּ *qûšāyāhû* from the passive participle of H6983 and H3050; *entrapped of Jah; Kushajah,* an Israelite:— Kushaiah.

H6985 קַט *qaṭ* from H6990 in the sense of *abbreviation;* a *little,* i.e. (adverbially) *merely:*— very.

H6986 קֶטֶב *qeṭeb* from an unused root meaning to *cut* off; *ruin:*— destroying, destruction.

H6987 קֹטֶב *qōṭeb* from the same as H6986; *extermination:*— destruction.

H6988 קְטוֹרָה *qĕṭôrâ* from H6999; *perfume:*— incense.

H6989 קְטוּרָה *qĕṭûrâ* feminine passive participle of H6999; *perfumed; Keturah,* a wife of Abraham:— Keturah.

H6990 קָטַט *qāṭaṭ* a primitive root; to *clip* off, i.e. (figuratively) *destroy:*— be cut off.

H6991 קָטַל *qāṭal* a primitive root; properly to *cut* off, i.e. (figuratively) *put to death:*— kill, slay.

H6992 קְטַל *qĕṭal* (Aramaic) corresponding to H6991; to *kill:*— slay.

H6993 קֶטֶל *qeṭel* from H6991; a violent *death:*— slaughter.

H6994 קָטֹן *qāṭōn* a primitive root [rather denominatively from H6996]; to *diminish,* i.e. *be* (causatively *make*) *diminutive* or (figuratively) *of no account:*— be a small thing, make small, be not worthy.

H6995 קֹטֶן *qōṭen* from H6994; a *pettiness,* i.e. the *little finger:*— little finger.

H6996 קָטָן *qāṭān* or

קָטֹן *qāṭōn* from H6962; *abbreviated,* i.e. *diminutive,* literally (in quantity, size or number) or figuratively (in age or importance):— least, less, lesser, little, little one, small, smallest, small one, small quantity, small thing, young, younger, youngest.

H6997 קָטָן *qāṭān* the same as H6996; *small; Katan,* an Israelite:— Hakkatan *[including the article].*

H6998 קָטַף *qāṭap* a primitive root; to *strip* off:— crop off, cut down, cut up, pluck.

H6999 קָטַר *qāṭar* a primitive root [rather identical with H7000 through the idea of fumigation in a *close* place and perhaps thus *driving* out the occupants]; to *smoke,* i.e. turn into fragrance by fire (especially as an act of worship):— burn, burn incense, burn sacrifice, burn incense upon, incense, altar for incense, kindle, offer, offer incense, offer a sacrifice.

H7000 קָטַר *qāṭar* a primitive root; to *inclose:*— join.

H7001 קְטַר *qĕṭar* (Aramaic) from a root corresponding to H7000; a *knot* (as *tied* up), i.e. (figuratively) a *riddle;* also a *vertebra* (as if a knot):— doubt, joint.

H7002 קִטֵּר *qiṭṭēr* from H6999; *perfume:*— incense.

H7003 קִטְרוֹן *qiṭrôn* from H6999; *fumigative; Kitron,* a place in Palestine:— Kitron.

H7004 קְטֹרֶת *qĕṭōret* from H6999; a *fumigation:*— incense, sweet incense, perfume.

H7005 קַטָּת *qaṭṭāt* from H6996; *littleness, Kattath,* a place in Palestine:— Kattath.

H7006 קָיָה *qāyâ* a primitive root; to *vomit:*— spue.

H7007 קַיִט *qayiṭ* (Aramaic) corresponding to H7019; *harvest:*— summer.

H7008 קִיטוֹר *qîṭôr* or

קִיטֹר *qîṭōr* from H6999; a *fume,* i.e. *cloud:*— smoke, vapour.

H7009 קִים *qîm* from H6965; an *opponent* (as *rising* against one), i.e. (collectively) enemies:— substance.

H7010 קְיָם *qĕyām* (Aramaic) from H6966; an *edict* (as *arising* in law):— decree, statute.

H7011 קַיָּם *qayyām* (Aramaic) from H6966; *permanent* (as *rising* firmly):— stedfast, sure.

H7012 קִימָה *qîmâ* from H6965; an *arising:*— rising up.

H7013 קַיִן *qayin* from H6969 in the original sense of *fixity;* a *lance* (as *striking fast*):— spear.

H7014 קַיִן *qayin* the same as H7013 (with a play upon the affinity to H7069); *Kajin,* the name of the first child, also of a place in Palestine, and of an Oriental tribe:— Cain, Kenite, Kenites.

H7015 קִינָה *qînâ* from H6969; a *dirge* (as accompanied by *beating* the breasts or on instruments):— lamentation.

H7016 קִינָה *qînâ* the same as H7015; *Kinah,* a place in Palestine:— Kinah.

H7017 קֵינִי *qênî* or

קִינִי *qînî* (1 Chron. 2:55), patronymic from H7014; a *Kenite* or member of the tribe of Kajin:— Kenite.

H7018 קֵינָן *qênān* from the same as H7064; *fixed; Kenan,* an antediluvian:— Cainan, Kenan.

H7019 קַיִץ *qayōṣ* from H6972; *harvest* (as the *crop*), whether the produce (grain or fruit) or the (dry) season:— summer, summer fruit, summer house.

H7020 קִיצוֹן *qîṣôn* from H6972; *terminal:*— outmost, uttermost.

H7021 קִיקָיוֹן *qîqāyôn* perhaps from H7006; the *gourd* (as *nauseous*):— gourd.

H7022 קִיקָלוֹן *qîqālôn* from H7036; intense *disgrace* :— shameful spewing.

H7023 קִיר *qîr* or

קִר *qir* (Isa. 22:5), or (feminine)

קִירָה *qîrâ* from H6979; a *wall* (as built in a *trench*):— mason, side, town, very, wall.

H7024 קִיר *qîr* the same as H7023; *fortress; Kir,* a place in Assyria; also one in Moab:— Kir. Compare H7025

H7025 קִיר חֶרֶשׂ *qîr ḥereś* or (feminine of the latter word)

קִיר חֲרֶשֶׂת *qîr ḥăreśet* from H7023 and H2789; *fortress of earthenware; Kir-Cheres* or *Kir-Chareseth,* a place in Moab:— Kir-haraseth, Kir-hareseth, Kir-haresh, Kir-heres.

H7026 קֵירֹס *qêrōs* or

קֵרֹס *qērōs* from the same as H7166; *ankled; Keros,* one of the Nethinim:— Keros.

H7027 קִישׁ *qîš* from H6983; a *bow; Kish,* the name of five Israelites:— Kish.

H7028 קִישׁוֹן *qîšôn* from H6983; *winding; Kishon,* a river of Palestine:— Kishon, Kison.

H7029 קִישִׁי *qîšî* from H6983; *bowed; Kishi,* an Israelite:— Kishi.

H7030 קִיתָרֹס *qîtārōs* (Aramaic) of Greek origin (**κίθαρις** *kitharis*); a *lyre:*— harp.

H7031 קַל *qal* contracted from H7043; *light;* (by implication) *rapid* (also adverbially):— light, swift, swiftly.

H7032 קָל *qāl* (Aramaic) corresponding to H6963 :— sound, voice.

H7033 קָלָה *qālâ* a primitive root [rather identical with H7034 through the idea of *shrinkage* by heat]; to *toast,* i.e. *scorch* partially or slowly:— dried, loathsome, parch, roast.

H7034 קָלָה *qālâ* a primitive root; to *be light* (as implied in *rapid* motion), but figuratively only *(be* [causatively *hold] in contempt*):— base, contemn, despise, lightly esteem, set light, seem vile.

H7035 קָלַהּ *qālah* for H6950; to *assemble:*— gather together.

H7036 קָלוֹן *qālôn* from H7034; *disgrace;* (by implication) the *pudenda:*— confusion, dishonour, ignominy, reproach, shame.

H7037 קַלַּחַת *qallaḥat* apparently but a form for H6747; a *kettle:*— caldron.

H7038 קָלַט *qālaṭ* a primitive root; to *maim:*— lacking in his parts.

H7039 קָלִי *qālî* or

קָלִיא *qālî*ʾ from H7033; *roasted* ears of grain :— parched corn.

H7040 קַלַּי *qallay* from H7043; *frivolous; Kallai,* an Israelite:— Kallai.

H7041 קֵלָיָה *qēlāyâ* from H7034; *insignificance; Kelajah,* an Israelite:— Kelaiah.

H7042 קְלִיטָא *qĕlîṭā*ʾ from H7038; *maiming; Kelita,* the name of three Israelites:— Kelita.

H7043 קָלַל *qālal* a primitive root; to *be* (causatively *make*) *light,* literally *(swift, small, sharp,* etc.) or figuratively *(easy, trifling, vile,* etc.):— abate, make bright, bring into contempt, curse, accurse, despise, ease, be easy, be easier, be a light thing, make lighter, make somewhat lighter, move lightly, seem a light thing, set light, lighten, lightly afflict, lightly esteem, slightly, be swift, be swifter, be vile, be more vile, make vile, revile, whet.

H7044 קָלָל *qālāl* from H7043; *brightened* (as if *sharpened*):— burnished, polished.

H7045 קְלָלָה *qĕlālâ* from H7043; *vilification:*— curse, accursed, cursing.

H7046 קָלַס *qālas* a primitive root; to *disparage,* i.e. ridicule:— mock, scoff, scorn.

H7047 קֶלֶס *qeles* from H7046; a *laughing-stock:*— derision.

H7048 קַלָּסָה *qallāsâ* intensive from H7046; *ridicule:*— mocking.

H7049 קָלַע *qālaᶜ* a primitive root; to *sling;* also to *carve* (as if a *circular* motion, or into *light* forms):— carve, sling, sling out.

H7050 קֶלַע *qelaᶜ* from H7049; a *sling;* also a (door) *screen* (as if *slung* across), or the *valve* (of the door) itself:— hanging, leaf, sling.

H7051 קַלָּע *qallāᶜ* intensive from H7049; a *slinger* :— slinger.

H7052 קְלֹקֵל *qĕlōqēl* from H7043; *insubstantial:*— light.

H7053 קִלְּשׁוֹן *qillĕšôn* from an unused root meaning to *prick;* a *prong,* i.e. hay-fork:— fork.

H7054 קָמָה *qāmâ* feminine of active participle of H6965; something that *rises,* i.e. a *stalk* of grain:— corn, standing corn, grown up, talk.

H7055 קְמוּאֵל *qĕmûʾēl* from H6965 and H410; *raised of God; Kemuël,* the name of a relative of Abraham, and of two Israelites:— Kemuel.

H7056 קָמוֹן *qāmôn* from H6965; an *elevation; Kamon,* a place east of the Jordan:— Camon.

H7057 קִמּוֹשׁ *qimmôš* or

קִימוֹשׁ *qîmôš* from an unused root meaning to *sting;* a *prickly* plant:— nettle. Compare H7063

H7058 קֶמַח *qemaḥ* from an unused root probably meaning to *grind; flour:*— flour, meal.

H7059 קָמַט *qāmaṭ* a primitive root; to *pluck,* i.e. destroy:— cut down, fill with wrinkles.

H7060 קָמַל *qāmal* a primitive root; to *wither:*— hew down, wither.

H7061 קָמַץ *qāmaṣ* a primitive root; to *grasp* with the hand:— take an handful.

H7062 קֹמֶץ *qōmeṣ* from H7061; a *grasp,* i.e. *handful:*— handful.

H7063 קִמָּשׁוֹן *qimmāšôn* from the same as H7057; a *prickly* plant:— thorn.

H7064 קֵן *qēn* contracted from H7077; a *nest* (as *fixed*), sometimes including the *nestlings;* figuratively a *chamber* or *dwelling:*— nest, room.

H7065 קָנָא *qānā'* a primitive root; to *be* (causatively *make*) *zealous,* i.e. (in a bad sense) *jealous* or *envious:*— envy, be envyious, be jealous, move to jealousy, provoke to jealousy, very, zeal, be zealous.

H7066 קְנָא *qĕnā'* (Aramaic) corresponding to H7069; to *purchase:*— buy.

H7067 קַנָּא *qonnā'* from H7065; *jealous:*— jealous. Compare H7072

H7068 קִנְאָה *qin'â* from H7065; *jealousy* or *envy* :— envy, envied, jealousy, sake, zeal.

H7069 קָנָה *qānâ* a primitive root; to *erect,* i.e. *create;* by extension to *procure,* especially by purchase (causatively *sell*); by implication to *own:*— attain, buy, buyer, teach to keep cattle, get, provoke to jealousy, possess, possessor, purchase, recover, redeem, surely, verily.

H7070 קָנֶה *qāneh* from H7069; a *reed* (as *erect*); by resemblance a *rod* (especially for measuring), *shaft, tube, stem,* the *radius* (of the arm), *beam* (of a steelyard):— balance, bone, branch, calamus, cane, reed, spearman, stalk.

H7071 קָנָה *qānâ* feminine of H7070; *reediness; Kanah,* the name of a stream and of a place in Palestine:— Kanah.

H7072 קַנּוֹא *qannô'* for H7067; *jealous* or *angry:*— jealous.

H7073 קְנַז *qĕnaz* probably from an unused root meaning to *hunt; hunter; Kenaz,* the name of an Edomite and of two Israelites:— Kenaz.

H7074 קְנִזִּי *qĕnizzî* patronymic from H7073, a *Kenizzite* or descendant of Kenaz:— Kenezite, Kenizzites.

H7075 קִנְיָן *qinyān* from H7069; *creation,* i.e. (concretely) *creatures;* also *acquisition, purchase, wealth:*— getting, goods, with money, riches, substance.

H7076 קִנָּמוֹן *qinnāmôn* from an unused root (meaning to *erect*); *cinnamon* bark (as in *upright* rolls):— cinnamon.

H7077 קָנַן *qānan* a primitive root; to *erect;* but used only as denominative from H7064; to *nestle,* i.e. *build* or *occupy* as a nest:— make . . . nest.

H7078 קֶנֶץ *qenes* from an unused root probably meaning to *wrench; perversion:*— end.

H7079 קְנָת *qĕnāt* from H7069; *possession; Kenath,* a place east of the Jordan:— Kenath.

H7080 קָסַם *qāsam* a primitive root; properly to *distribute,* i.e. *determine* by lot or magical scroll; by implication to *divine:*— divine, diviner, divination, prudent, soothsayer, use divination.

H7081 קֶסֶם *qesem* from H7080; a *lot;* also *divination* (including its *fee*), *oracle:*— divination, reward of divination, divine sentence, witchcraft.

H7082 קָסַס *qāsas* a primitive root; to *lop* off:— cut off.

H7083 קֶסֶת *qeset* from the same as H3563 (or as H7185); properly a *cup,* i.e. an *ink-stand:*— inkhorn.

H7084 קְעִילָה *qĕ'îlâ* perhaps from H7049 in the sense of *inclosing; citadel; Keïlah,* a place in Palestine:— Keilah.

H7085 קַעֲקַע *qa'ăqa'* from the same as H6970; an *incision* or gash:— mark.

H7086 קְעָרָה *qĕ'ārâ* probably from H7167; a *bowl* (as *cut* out hollow):— charger, dish.

H7087 קָפָא *qāpā'* a primitive root; to *shrink,* i.e. *thicken* (as unracked wine, curdled milk, clouded sky, frozen water):— congeal, curdle, dark, settle.

H7088 קָפַד *qāpad* a primitive root; to *contract,* i.e. roll together:— cut off.

H7089 קְפָדָה *qĕpādâ* from H7088; *shrinking,* i.e. terror:— destruction.

H7090 קִפּוֹד *qippôd* or

קִפֹּד *qippōd* from H7088; a species of bird, perhaps the *bittern* (from its *contracted* form):— bittern.

H7091 קִפּוֹז *qippôz* from an unused root mean to *contract,* i.e. *spring* forward; an *arrow-snake* (as *darting* on its prey):— great owl.

H7092 קָפַץ *qāpas* a primitive root; to *draw together,* i.e. close; by implication to *leap* (by *contracting* the limbs); specifically to *die* (from *gathering* up the feet):— shut, shut up, skip, stop, take out of the way.

H7093 קֵץ *qēs* contracted from H7112; an *extremity;* adverbially (with preposition prefixed) *after:*— after, border, utmost border, end, infinite, process.

H7094 קָצַב *qāsab* a primitive root; to *clip,* or (generally) *chop:*— cut down, shorn.

H7095 קֶצֶב *qeseb* from H7094; *shape* (as if *cut* out); *base* (as if there *cut* off):— bottom, size.

H7096 קָצָה *qāsâ* a primitive root; to *cut* off; (figuratively) to *destroy;* (partially) to *scrape* off:— cut off, cut short, scrape, scrape off.

H7097 קָצֶה *qāseh* or (negatively only)

קֵצֶה *qēseh* from H7096; an *extremity* (used in a great variety of applications and idioms; compare H7093):— after, border, brim, brink, edge, end, infinite, frontier, outmost coast, quarter, shore, side, outside, some, utmost, utmost part, uttermost, uttermost part.

H7098 קָצָה *qāsâ* feminine of H7097; a *termination* (used like H7097):— coast, corner, edge, selvedge, lowest, part, uttermost part.

H7099 קֶצֶו *qesew* and (feminine)

קִצְוָה *qiswâ* from H7096; a *limit* (used like H7097, but with less variety):— end, edge, uttermost part.

H7100 קֶצַח *qesah* from an unused root apparently meaning to *incise; fennel-flower* (from its *pungency*):— fitches.

H7101 קָצִין *qāsîn* from H7096 in the sense of *determining;* a *magistrate* (as *deciding*) or other *leader:*— captain, guide, prince, ruler. Compare H6278

H7102 קְצִיעָה *qĕsî'â* from H7106; *cassia* (as *peeled;* plural the *bark*):— cassia.

H7103 קְצִיעָה *qĕsî'â* the same as H7102; *Ketsiah,* a daughter of Job:— Kezia.

H7104 קְצִיץ *qĕsîs* from H7112; *abrupt; Keziz,* a valley in Palestine:— Keziz.

H7105 קָצִיר *qāsîr* from H7114; *severed,* i.e. *harvest* (as *reaped*), the crop, the time, the reaper, or figuratively; also a *limb* (of a tree, or simply *foliage*):— bough, branch, harvest, harvest man.

H7106 קָצַע *qāsa'* a primitive root; to *strip* off, i.e. (partially) *scrape;* by implication to *segregate* (as an angle):— cause to scrape, corner.

H7107 קָצַף *qāsap* a primitive root; to *crack* off, i.e. (figuratively) *burst* out in rage:— anger, be angry, displease, fret self, provoke to wrath, wrath come, be wroth.

H7108 קְצַף *qĕsap* (Aramaic) corresponding to H7107; to *become enraged:*— be furious.

H7109 קְצַף *qĕsap* (Aramaic) from H7108; *rage:*— wrath.

H7110 קֶצֶף *qesep* from H7107; a *splinter* (as *chipped* off); figuratively *rage* or *strife:*— foam, indignation, sore, wrath.

H7111 קְצָפָה *qĕsāpâ* from H7107; a *fragment:*— barked.

H7112 קָצַץ *qāsas* a primitive root; to *chop* off (literally or figuratively):— cut, cut asunder, cut in pieces, cut in sunder, cut off, utmost.

H7113 קְצַץ *qĕsas* (Aramaic) corresponding to H7112 :— cut off.

H7114 קָצַר *qāsar* a primitive root; to *dock* off, i.e. *curtail* (transitively or intransitively, literally or figuratively); especially to *harvest* (grass or grain):— at all, cut down, much discouraged, grieve, harvestman, lothe, mourn, reap, reaper, be shorter, wax short, shorten, shorter, straiten, trouble, vex.

H7115 קֹצֶר *qōser* from H7114; *shortness* (of spirit), i.e. impatience:— anguish.

H7116 קָצֵר *qāsēr* from H7114; *short* (whether in size, number, life, strength or temper):— few, hasty, small, soon.

H7117 קְצָת *qĕsāt* from H7096; a *termination* (literal or figurative); also (by implication) a *portion;* adverbially (with preposition prefixed) *after:*— end, part, some.

H7118 קְצָת *qĕsāt* (Aramaic) corresponding to H7117 :— end, partly.

H7119 קַר *qar* contracted from an unused root meaning to *chill; cool;* figuratively *quiet:*— cold, excellent *[from the margin]*.

H7120 קֹר *qōr* from the same as H7119; *cold:*— cold.

H7121 קָרָא *qārā'* a primitive root [rather identical with H7122 through the idea of *accosting* a person met]; to *call* out to (i.e. properly *address* by name, but used in a wide variety of applications):— bewray self, that are bidden, call, call for, call forth, call self, call upon, cry, cry unto, famous, be famous, guest, invite, mention, name, give name, preach, proclaim, make proclamation, pronounce, publish, read, renowned, say.

H7122 קָרָא *qārā'* a primitive root; to *encounter,* whether accidentally or in a hostile manner:— befall, chance, by chance, come, cause to come, come upon, fall out, happen, meet.

H7123 קְרָא *qĕrā'* (Aramaic) corresponding to H7121 :— call, cry, read.

H7124 קֹרֵא *qōrē'* properly active participle of H7121; a *caller,* i.e. *partridge* (from its *cry*):— partridge. See also H6981

H7125 קִרְאָה *qer'â* from H7122; an *encountering,* accidental, friendly or hostile (also adverbially *opposite*):— against, against he come, help, meet, seek, to, in the way.

H7126 קָרַב *qārab* a primitive root; to *approach* (causatively *bring near*) for whatever purpose:— approach, cause to approach, bring, cause to bring, bring forth, bring near, come, cause to come near, come near, come nigh, draw near, cause to draw near, draw nigh, go, go near, be at hand, join, be near, offer, present, produce, make ready, stand, take.

H7127 קְרֵב *qĕrēb* (Aramaic) corresponding to H7126 :— approach, come, come near, come nigh, draw near.

H7128 קְרָב *qĕrāb* from H7126; hostile *encounter* :— battle, war.

H7129 קְרָב *qĕrāb* (Aramaic) corresponding to H7128 :— war.

H7130 קֶרֶב *qereb* from H7126; properly the *nearest* part, i.e. the *centre,* whether literally, figuratively or adverbially (especially with preposition):— among, before, bowels, unto charge, eat, eat up, heart, him, in, inward, inwardly, inward part, inwards, inward thought, midst, out of, purtenance, therein, through, within self.

H7131 קָרֵב *qārēb* from H7126; *near:*— approach, come, come near, come nigh, draw near.

H7132 קְרָבָה *qĕrābâ* from H7126; *approach:*— approaching, draw near.

H7133 קׇרְבָּן *qorbān* or

קֻרְבָּן *qurbān* from H7126; something *brought near* the altar, i.e. a sacrificial *present:*— oblation, that is offered, offering.

H7134 קַרְדֹּם *qardōm* perhaps from H6923 in the sense of *striking* upon; an *axe:*— ax.

H7135 קָרָה *qārâ* feminine of H7119; *coolness:*— cold.

H7136 קָרָה *qārâ* a primitive root; to *light upon* (chiefly by accident); causatively to *bring about;* specifically to *impose* timbers (for roof or floor):— appoint, lay beams, make beams, befall, bring, come, come to pass unto, floor, hap was, happen, happen unto, meet, send good speed.

H7137 קָרֶה *qāreh* from H7136; an (unfortunate) *occurrence,* i.e. some accidental (ceremonial) *disqualification:*— uncleanness that chanceth.

H7138 קָרוֹב *qārôb* or

קָרֹב *qārōb* from H7126; *near* (in place, kindred or time):— allied, approach, at hand, any of kin, kinsfolk, kinsman, near, that is near, near of kin, neighbour, next, that is next, nigh, nigh, them that come nigh, nigh at hand, more ready, short, shortly.

H7139 קָרַח *qāraḥ* a primitive root; to *depilate:*— make bald, make self bald.

H7140 קֶרַח *qeraḥ* or

קֹרַח *qōraḥ* from H7139; *ice* (as if bald, i.e. *smooth*); hence, *hail;* by resemblance, rock *crystal:*— crystal, frost, ice.

H7141 קֹרַח *qōraḥ* from H7139; *ice; Korach,* the name of two Edomites and three Israelites:— Korah.

H7142 קֵרֵחַ *qērēaḥ* from H7139; *bald* (on the back of the head):— bald, bald head.

H7143 קָרֵחַ *qārēaḥ* from H7139; *bald; Kareäch,* an Israelite:— Careach, Kareah.

H7144 קׇרְחָה *qorḥâ* or

קׇרְחָא *qorḥā'* (Ezek 27:31), from H7139; *baldness:*— bald, baldness, utterly.

H7145 קׇרְחִי *qorḥî* patronymic from H7141; a *Korchite* (collectively) or descendant of Korach:— Korahite, Korathite, sons of Kore, Korhite.

H7146 קָרַחַת *qāraḥat* from H7139; a *bald* spot (on the back of the head); figuratively a *threadbare* spot (on the back side of the cloth):— bald head, bare within.

H7147 קְרִי *qĕrî* from H7136; hostile *encounter:*— contrary.

H7148 קָרִיא *qārî'* from H7121; *called,* i.e. *select:*— famous, renowned.

H7149 קִרְיָא *qiryā'* or

קִרְיָה *qiryâ* (Aramaic) corresponding to H7151 :— city.

H7150 קְרִיאָה *qĕrî'â* from H7121; a *proclamation* :— preaching.

H7151 קִרְיָה *qeryâ* from H7136 in the sense of *flooring,* i.e. building; a *city:*— city.

H7152 קְרִיּוֹת *qĕrîyôt* plural of H7151; *buildings; Kerioth,* the name of two places in Palestine:— Kerioth, Kirioth.

H7153 קִרְיַת אַרְבַּע *qiryat 'arba*ᶜ or (with the article interposed)

קִרְיַת הָאַרְבַּע *qiryat hā'arba*ᶜ (Neh. 11:25), from H7151 and H704 or H702; *city of Arba,* or *city of the four* (giants); *Kirjath-Arba* or *Kirjath-ha-Arba,* a place in Palestine:— Kirjath-arba.

H7154 קִרְיַת בַּעַל *qiryat ba*ᶜ*al* from H7151 and H1168; *city of Baal; Kirjath-Baal,* a place in Palestine:— Kirjath-baal.

H7155 קִרְיַת חֻצוֹת *qiryat ḥûṣôt* from H7151 and the feminine plural of H2351; *city of streets; Kirjath-Chutsoth,* a place in Moab:— Kirjath-huzoth.

H7156 קִרְיָתַיִם *qiryātayim* dual of H7151; *double city; Kirjathaïm,* the name of two places in Palestine:— Kiriathaim, Kirjathaim.

H7157 קִרְיַת יְעָרִים *qiryat yĕ*ᶜ*ārîm* or (Jer. 26:20) with the article interposed; or (Josh. 18:28) simply the former part of the word; or

קִרְיַת עָרִים *qiryat* ᶜ*ārîm* from H7151 and the plural of H3293 or H5892; *city of forests,* or *city of towns; Kirjath-Jeärim* or *Kirjath-Arim,* a place in Palestine:— Kirjath, Kirjath-jearim, Kirjath-arim.

H7158 קִרְיַת סַנָּה *qiryat sannâ* or

קִרְיַת סֵפֶר *qiryat sēper* from H7151 and a simpler feminine from the same as H5577, or (for the latter name) H5612; *city of branches,* or *of a book; Kirjath-Sannah* or *Kirjath-Sepher,* a place in Palestine:— Kirjath-sannah, Kirjath-sepher.

H7159 קָרַם *qāram* a primitive root; to *cover:*— cover.

H7160 קָרַן *qāran* a primitive root; to *push* or gore; used only as denominative from H7161, to *shoot out horns;* figuratively *rays:*— have horns, shine.

H7161 קֶרֶן *qeren* from H7160; a *horn* (as *projecting*); by implication a *flask, cornet;* by resemblance an elephant's *tooth* (i.e. *ivory*), a *corner* (of the altar), a *peak* (of a mountain), a *ray* (of light); figuratively *power:*— hill, horn.

H7162 קֶרֶן *qeren* (Aramaic) corresponding to H7161; a *horn* (literally or for sound):— horn, cornet.

H7163 קֶרֶן הַפּוּךְ *qeren happûk* from H7161 and H6320; *horn of cosmetic; Keren-hap-Puk,* one of Job's daughters:— Keren-happuch.

H7164 קָרַס *qāras* a primitive root; properly to *protrude;* used only as denominative from H7165 (for alliteration with H7167), to *hunch,* i.e. be humpbacked:— stoop.

H7165 קֶרֶס *qeres* from H7164; a *knob* or belaying-pin (from its swelling form):— tache.

H7166 קַרְסֹל *qarsōl* from H7164; an *ankle* (as a *protuberance* or joint):— foot.

H7167 קָרַע *qāra*ᶜ a primitive root; to *rend,* literally or figuratively *(revile, paint* the eyes, as if enlarging them):— cut out, rend, surely, tear.

H7168 קֶרַע *qera*ᶜ from H7167; a *rag:*— piece, rag.

H7169 קָרַץ *qāraṣ* a primitive root; to *pinch,* i.e. (partially) to *bite* the lips, *blink* the eyes (as a gesture of malice), or (fully) to *squeeze* off (a piece of clay in order to mould a vessel from it):— form, move, wink.

H7170 קְרַץ *qĕraṣ* (Aramaic) corresponding to H7171 in the sense of a *bit* (to "eat the *morsels* of" any one, i.e. *chew* him up [figuratively] by *slander*):— accuse.

H7171 קֶרֶץ *qereṣ* from H7169; *extirpation* (as if by *constriction*):— destruction.

H7172 קַרְקַע *qarqa*ᶜ from H7167; *floor* (as if a pavement of pieces or *tesserae*), of a building or the sea:— bottom, floor, one side of the floor.

H7173 קַרְקַע *qarqa*ᶜ the same as H7172; *ground-floor; Karka* (with the article prefixed), a place in Palestine:— Karkaa.

H7174 קַרְקֹר *qarqōr* from H6979; *foundation; Karkor,* a place east of the Jordan:— Karkor.

H7175 קֶרֶשׁ *qereš* from an unused root meaning to *split* off; a *slab* or plank; by implication a *deck* of a ship:— bench, board.

H7176 קֶרֶת *qeret* from H7136 in the sense of building; a *city:*— city.

H7177 קַרְתָּה *qarttâ* from H7176; *city; Kartah,* a place in Palestine:— Kartah.

H7178 קַרְתָּן *qartān* from H7176; *city-plot; Kartan,* a place in Palestine:— Kartan.

H7179 קַשׁ *qaš* from H7197; *straw* (as *dry*):— stubble.

H7180 קִשֻּׁא *qiššū'* from an unused root (meaning to be *hard*); a *cucumber* (from the difficulty of *digestion*):— cucumber.

H7181 קָשַׁב *qāšab* a primitive root; to *prick up* the ears, i.e. *hearken:*— attend, cause to hear, hearken, give heed, incline, mark, mark well, regard.

H7182 קֶשֶׁב *qešeb* from H7181; a *hearkening:*— diligently, hearing, much heed, that regarded.

H7183 קַשָּׁב *qaššāb* or

קַשֻּׁב *qaššūb* from H7181; *hearkening:*— attent, attentive.

H7184 קָשָׂה *qāśâ* or

קַשְׂוָה *qaśwâ* from an unused root meaning to be *round;* a *jug* (from its shape):— cover, cup.

H7185 קָשָׁה *qāšâ* a primitive root; properly to *be dense,* i.e. tough or *severe* (in various applications):— be cruel, be fiercer, make grievous, be hard, ask a hard thing, be in hard labour, have hard labour, seem hard, would hardly, harden, be sore, be stiffnecked, make stiff, stiffen.

H7186 קָשֶׁה *qāšeh* from H7185; *severe* (in various applications):— churlish, cruel, grievous, hard, hard-hearted, hard thing, heavy, impudent, obstinate, prevailed, rough, roughly, sore, sorrowful, stiff, stiffnecked, stubborn, in trouble.

H7187 קְשׁוֹט *qĕšôṭ* or

קְשֹׁט *qĕšōṭ* (Aramaic) corresponding to H7189; *fidelity:*— truth.

H7188 קָשַׁח *qāšaḥ* a primitive root; to *be* (causatively *make*) *unfeeling:*— harden.

H7189 קֹשֶׁט *qōšeṭ* or

קֹשְׁטְ *qōšṭ* from an unused root meaning to *balance; equity* (as evenly *weighed*), i.e. *reality:*— truth.

H7190 קְשִׁי *qĕšî* from H7185; *obstinacy:*— stubbornness.

H7191 קִשְׁיוֹן *qišyôn* from H7190; *hard ground; Kishjon,* a place in Palestine:— Kishion, Keshon.

H7192 קְשִׂיטָה *qĕśîṭâ* from an unused root (probably meaning to *weigh* out); an *ingot* (as definitely *estimated* and stamped for a coin):— piece of money, piece of silver.

H7193 קַשְׂקֶשֶׂת *qaśqeśet* by reduplication from an unused root meaning to *shale* off as bark; a *scale* (of a fish); hence a coat of *mail* (as composed of or covered with jointed *plates* of metal):— mail, scale.

H7194 קָשַׁר *qāšar* a primitive root; to *tie,* physically *(gird, confine, compact)* or mentally (in *love, league*) :— bind, bind up, conspire, make a conspiracy, conspirator, join together, knit, stronger, work treason.

H7195 קֶשֶׁר *qešer* from H7194; an (unlawful) *alliance:*— confederacy, conspiracy, treason.

H7196 קִשֻּׁר *qiššūr* from H7194; an (ornamental) *girdle* (for women):— attire, headband.

H7197 קָשַׁשׁ *qāšaš* a primitive root; to *become sapless* through drought; used only as denominative from H7179; to *forage* for straw, stubble or wood; figuratively to *assemble:*— gather, gather together, gather selves together.

H7198 קֶשֶׁת *qešet* from H7185 in the original sense (of H6983) of *bending;* a *bow,* for *shooting* (hence figuratively *strength*) or the *iris:*— archer, arrow, bow, bowman, bowshot.

H7199 קַשָּׁת *qaššāt* intensive (as denominative) from H7198; a *bowman:*— archer.

ר

H7200 רָאָה *rā᾽â* a primitive root; to *see,* literally or figuratively (in numerous applications, direct and implied, transitively, intransitively and causatively) :— advise self, appear, approve, behold, certainly, consider, discern, enjoy, make to enjoy, have experience, gaze, take heed, indeed, joyfully, lo, look, look on, look one another, look one on another, look one upon another, look out, look up, look upon, mark, meet, be near, perceive, present, provide, regard, respect, have respect, see, forsee, cause to see, let see, seer, seem, see one another, shew, shew self, sight of others, spy, espy, stare, surely, think, view, visions.

H7201 רָאָה *rā᾽â* from H7200; a *bird* of prey (probably the *vulture,* from its sharp *sight*):— glede. Compare H1676

H7202 רָאֶה *rā᾽eh* from H7200; *seeing,* i.e. experiencing:— see.

H7203 רֹאֶה *rō᾽eh* active participle of H7200; a *seer* (as often rendered); but also (abstractly) a *vision:*— vision.

H7204 רֹאֵה *rō᾽ēh* for H7203; *prophet; Roëh,* an Israelite:— Haroeh *[including the article].*

H7205 רְאוּבֵן *rĕ᾽ûbēn* from the imperative of H7200 and H1121; *see* ye a *son; Reüben,* a son of Jacob:— Reuben.

H7206 רְאוּבֵנִי *rĕ᾽ûbēnî* patronymic from H7205; a *Reübenite* or descendant of Reüben:— children of Reuben, Reubenites.

H7207 רַאֲוָה *ra᾽ăwâ* from H7200; *sight,* i.e. satisfaction:— behold.

H7208 רְאוּמָה *rĕ᾽ûmâ* feminine passive participle of H7213; *raised; Reümah,* a Syrian woman:— Reumah.

H7209 רְאִי *rĕ᾽î* from H7200; a *mirror* (as *seen*):— looking glass.

H7210 רֳאִי *rŏ᾽î* from H7200; *sight,* whether abstract *(vision)* or concrete (a *spectacle*):— gazingstock, look to, see, that seeth.

H7211 רְאָיָה *rĕ᾽āyâ* from H7200 and H3050; *Jah has seen; Reäjah,* the name of three Israelites:— Reaia, Reaiah.

H7212 רְאִית *rĕ᾽ît* from H7200; *sight:*— beholding.

H7213 רָאַם *rā᾽am* a primitive root; to *rise:*— be lifted up.

H7214 רְאֵם *rĕ᾽ēm* or

רְאֵים *rĕ᾽êm* or

רֵים *rêm* or

רֵם *rēm* from H7213; a wild *bull* (from its *conspicuousness*):— unicorn.

H7215 רָאמָה *rā᾽mâ* from H7213; something *high* in value, i.e. perhaps *coral:*— coral.

H7216 רָאמוֹת *rā᾽môt* or

רָאמֹת *rā᾽mōt* plural of H7215; *heights; Ramoth,* the name of two places in Palestine:— Ramoth.

H7217 רֵאשׁ *rē᾽š* (Aramaic) corresponding to H7218; the *head;* figuratively the *sum:*— chief, head, sum.

H7218 רֹאשׁ *rō᾽š* from an unused root apparently meaning to *shake;* the *head* (as most easily *shaken*), whether literally or figuratively (in many applications, of place, time, rank, etc.):— band, beginning, captain, chapiter, chief, chiefest place, chief man, chief things, company, end, every man, excellent, first, forefront, head, behead, height, high, on high, highest part, high priest, lead, poor, principal, ruler, sum, top.

H7219 רֹאשׁ *rō᾽š* or

רוֹשׁ *rôš* (Deut. 32:32), apparently the same as H7218; a poisonous *plant,* probably the *poppy* (from its conspicuous *head*); generally *poison* (even of serpents):— gall, hemlock, poison, venom.

H7220 רֹאשׁ *rō᾽š* probably the same as H7218; *Rosh,* the name of an Israelite and of a foreign nation:— Rosh.

H7221 רִאשָׁה *ri᾽šâ* from the same as H7218; a *beginning:*— beginning.

H7222 רֹאשָׁה *rō᾽šâ* feminine of H7218; the *head* :— headstone.

H7223 רִאשׁוֹן *ri᾽šôn* or

רִאשֹׁן *ri᾽šōn* from H7221; *first,* in place, time or rank (as adjective or noun):— ancestor, before, that were before, beforetime, beginning, eldest, first, forefather, foremost, former, former thing, of old time, past.

H7224 רִאשֹׁנִי *ri᾽šōnî* from H7223; *first:*— first.

H7225 רֵאשִׁית *rē᾽šît* from the same as H7218; the *first,* in place, time, order or rank (specifically a *firstfruit*):— beginning, chief, chiefest, first, firstfruits, first part, first time, principal thing.

H7226 רַאֲשֹׁת *ra᾽ăšōt* from H7218; a *pillow* (being for the *head*):— bolster.

H7227 רַב *rab* by contraction from H7231; *abundant* (in quantity, size, age, number, rank, quality) :— abound, in abundance, abundant, abundantly, captain, elder, enough, exceedingly, full, great, greatly, great man, great one, increase, long, long enough, long time, many, do many, have many, manifold, many things, many a time, master, shipmaster, mighty, more, much, too much, very much, multiply, multitude, officer, oftentimes, plenteous, populous, prince, process of time, suffice, sufficient.

H7228 רַב *rab* by contraction from H7232; an *archer* [or perhaps the same as H7227]:— archer.

H7229 רַב *rab* (Aramaic) corresponding to H7227 :— captain, chief, great, lord, master, stout.

H7230 רֹב *rōb* from H7231; *abundance* (in any respect):— abundance, abundantly, all, common sort, excellent, great, greatly, greatness, great number, huge, be increased, long, many, more in number, most, much, multitude, plenty, plentifully, very age.

H7231 רָבַב *rābab* a primitive root; properly to *cast* together [compare H7241], i.e. *increase,* especially in number; also (as denominative from H7233) to *multiply by the myriad:*— increase, be many, be manifold, be more, multiply, ten thousands.

H7232 רָבַב *rābab* a primitive root [rather identical with H7231 through the idea of *projection]; to shoot* an arrow:— shoot.

H7233 רְבָבָה *rĕbābâ* from H7231; *abundance* (in number), i.e. (specifically) a *myriad* (whether definite or indefinite):— many, million, multiply, ten thousand.

H7234 רָבַד *rābad* a primitive root; to *spread:*— deck.

H7235 רָבָה *rābâ* a primitive root; to *increase* (in whatever respect):— abundance, bring in abundance, abundantly, archer *[by mistake for H7232],* be in authority, bring up, continue, enlarge, excel, exceeding, exceedingly, be full of, great, be greater, make great, greatly, greatness, grow up, heap, increase, be long, many, be many, give many, have many, make many, use many, many a time, more, any more, be more, give more, give the more, have more, more in number, much, ask much, be much greater, be so much, gather much, over much, take much, yield much, much more, multiply, make to multiply, nourish, plenty, plenteous, process of time, sore, store, thoroughly, very.

H7236 רְבָה *rĕbâ* (Aramaic) corresponding to H7235 :— make a great man, grow.

H7237 רַבָּה *rabbâ* feminine of H7227; *great; Rabbah,* the name of two places in Palestine, east and west:— Rabbah, Rabbath.

H7238 רְבוּ *rĕbû* (Aramaic) from a root corresponding to H7235; *increase* (of dignity):— greatness, majesty.

H7239 רִבּוֹ *ribbô* or

רִבּוֹא *ribbô᾽* from H7231; a *myriad,* i.e. indefinitely *large number:*— great things, ten thousand, eighteen thousand, forty thousand, sixscore thousand, threescore thousand, twenty thousand, twenty thousand.

HEB

H7240 רִבּוֹ *ribbô* (Aramaic) corresponding to H7239 :— ten thousand times ten thousand.

H7241 רָבִיב *rābîb* from H7231; a *rain* (as an *accumulation* of drops):— shower.

H7242 רָבִיד *rābîd* from H7234; a *collar* (as *spread* around the neck):— chain.

H7243 רְבִיעִי *rĕbîʿî* or

רְבִעִי *rĕbīʿî* from H7251; *fourth;* also (fractionally) a *fourth:*— foursquare, fourth, fourth part.

H7244 רְבִיעַי *rĕbîʿay* (Aramaic) corresponding to H7243:— fourth.

H7245 רַבִּית *rabbît* from H7231; *multitude; Rabbiyth,* a place in Palestine:— Rabbith.

H7246 רָבַךְ *rābak* a primitive root; to *soak* (bread in oil):— baken, fried, that which is fried.

H7247 רִבְלָה *riblâ* from an unused root meaning to *be fruitful; fertile; Riblah,* a place in Syria:— Riblah.

H7248 רַב־מָג *rab-māg* from H7227 and a foreign word for a Magian; *chief Magian; Rab-Mag,* a Babylonian official:— Rab-mag.

H7249 רַב־סָרִיס *rab-sārîs* from H7227 and a foreign word for a eunuch; *chief chamberlain; Rab-Saris,* a Babylonian official:— Rab-saris.

H7250 רָבַע *rābaʿ* a primitive root; to *squat* or *lie* out flat, i.e. (specifically) in copulation:— let gender, lie down.

H7251 רָבַע *rābaʿ* a primitive root [rather identical with H7250 through the idea of *sprawling* "at all fours" (or possibly the reverse is the order, of derivation); compare H702]; properly to *be four* (sided); used only as denominative of H7253; to *be quadrate:*— square, foursquare, squared.

H7252 רֶבַע *rebaʿ* from H7250; *prostration* (for sleep) :— lying down.

H7253 רֶבַע *rebaʿ* from H7251; a *fourth* (part or side):— fourth part, side, square.

H7254 רֶבַע *rebaʿ* the same as H7253; *Reba,* a Midianite:— Reba.

H7255 רֹבַע *rōbaʿ* from H7251; a *quarter:*— fourth part.

H7256 רִבֵּעַ *ribbēaʿ* from H7251; a descendant of the *fourth* generation, i.e. *great great grandchild:*— fourth.

H7257 רָבַץ *rābaṣ* a primitive root; to *crouch* (on all four legs folded, like a recumbent animal); by implication to *recline, repose, brood, lurk, imbed:*— crouch, crouch down, fall down, make a fold, lay, lie, cause to lie down, make to lie down, lie down, make to rest, sit.

H7258 רֵבֶץ *rēbeṣ* from H7257; a *couch* or place of repose:— where each lay, lie down in, resting place.

H7259 רִבְקָה *ribqâ* from an unused root probably meaning to *clog* by tying up the fetlock; *fettering* (by beauty); *Birkah,* the wife of Isaac:— Rebekah.

H7260 רַבְרַב *rabrab* (Aramaic) from H7229; *huge* (in size); *domineering* (in character):— great, very great things, great things.

H7261 רַבְרְבָן *rabrĕbān* (Aramaic) from H7260; a *magnate:*— lord, prince.

H7262 רַבְשָׁקֵה *rabšāqēh* from H7227 and H8248; *chief butler; Rabshakeh,* a Babylonian official:— Rabshakeh.

H7263 רֶגֶב *regeb* from an unused root meaning to *pile* together; a *lump* of clay:— clod.

H7264 רָגַז *rāgaz* a primitive root; to *quiver* (with any violent emotion, especially anger or fear):— be afraid, stand in awe, disquiet, fall out, fret, move, provoke, quake, rage, shake, tremble, trouble, be wroth.

H7265 רְגַז *rĕgaz* (Aramaic) corresponding to H7264 :— provoke unto wrath.

H7266 רְגַז *rĕgaz* (Aramaic) from H7265; violent *anger:*— rage.

H7267 רֹגֶז *rōgez* from H7264; *commotion, restlessness* (of a horse), *crash* (of thunder), *disquiet, anger:*— fear, noise, rage, trouble, troubling, wrath.

H7268 רַגָּז *raggāz* intensive from H7264; *timid:*— trembling.

H7269 רָגְזָה *rogzâ* feminine of H7267; *trepidation* :— trembling.

H7270 רָגַל *rāgal* a primitive root; to *walk* along; but only in specific applications, to *reconnoitre,* to *be a tale-bearer* (i.e. slander); also (as denominative from H7272) to *lead about:*— backbite, search, slander, spy, espy out, spy out, teach to go, view.

H7271 רְגַל *rĕgal* (Aramaic) corresponding to H7272 :— foot.

H7272 רֶגֶל *regel* from H7270; a *foot* (as used in *walking*); by implication a *step;* by euphemism the *pudenda:*— be able to endure, according as, after, coming, follow, foot, brokenfooted, footstool, great toe, haunt, journey, leg, piss, possession, time.

H7273 רַגְלִי *raglî* from H7272; a *footman* (soldier) :— on foot, footman.

H7274 רֹגְלִים *rōgĕlîm* plural or active participle of H7270; *fullers* (as *tramping* the cloth in washing); *Rogelim,* a place east of the Jordan:— Rogelim.

H7275 רָגַם *rāgam* a primitive root [compare H7263, H7321, H7551]; to *cast* together (stones), i.e. to *lapidate:*— certainly, stone.

H7276 רֶגֶם *regem* from H7275; stone-*heap; Regem,* an Israelite:— Regem.

H7277 רִגְמָה *rigmâ* feminine of the same as H7276; a *pile* (of stones), i.e. (figuratively) a *throng:*— council.

H7278 רֶגֶם מֶלֶךְ *regem melek* from H7276 and H4428; *king's heap; Regem-Melek,* an Israelite:— Regem-melech.

H7279 רָגַן *rāgan* a primitive root; to *grumble,* i.e. *rebel:*— murmur.

H7280 רָגַע *rāgaʿ* a primitive root; properly to *toss* violently and suddenly (the sea with waves, the skin with boils); figuratively (in a favorable manner) to *settle,* i.e. quiet; specifically to *wink* (from the motion of the eye-lids):— break, divide, find ease, be a moment, rest, cause rest, give rest, make to rest, make suddenly.

H7281 רֶגַע *regaʿ* from H7280; a *wink* (of the eyes), i.e. a very *short space* of time:— instant, moment, space, suddenly.

H7282 רָגֵעַ *rāgēaʿ* from H7280; *restful,* i.e. peaceable:— that are quiet.

H7283 רָגַשׁ *rāgaš* a primitive root; to *be tumultuous:*— rage.

H7284 רְגַשׁ *rĕgaš* (Aramaic) corresponding to H7283; to *gather* tumultuously:— assemble, assemble together.

H7285 רֶגֶשׁ *regeš* or (feminine)

רִגְשָׁה *rigšâ* from H7283; a tumultuous *crowd* :— company, insurrection.

H7286 רָדַד *rādad* a primitive root; to *tread* in pieces, i.e. (figuratively) to *conquer,* or (specifically) to *overlay:*— spend, spread, subdue.

H7287 רָדָה *rādâ* a primitive root; to *tread* down, i.e. *subjugate;* specifically to *crumble* off:— have dominion, come to have dominion, make to have dominion, prevail against, reign, rule, bear rule, make to rule, ruler, rule over, take.

H7288 רַדַּי *radday* intensive from H7287; *domineering; Raddai,* an Israelite:— Raddai.

H7289 רָדִיד *rādîd* from H7286 in the sense of *spreading;* a *veil* (as expanded):— vail, veil.

H7290 רָדַם *rādam* a primitive root; to *stun,* i.e. *stupefy* (with sleep or death):— be fast asleep, be in a deep sleep, cast into a dead sleep, that sleepeth, sleeper.

H7291 רָדַף *rādap* a primitive root; to *run after* (usually with hostile intent; figuratively [of time] *gone by*):— chase, put to flight, follow, follow after, follow on, hunt, persecute, be under persecution, persecutor, pursue, pursuer.

H7292 רָהַב *rāhab* a primitive root; to *urge* severely, i.f. (figuratively) *importune, embolden, capture, act insolently:*— overcome, behave self proudly, make sure, strengthen.

H7293 רַהַב *rahab* from H7292; *bluster (-er):*— proud, strength.

H7294 רַהַב *rahab* the same as H7293; *Rahab* (i.e. *boaster*), an epithet of Egypt:— Rahab.

H7295 רָהָב *rāhāb* from H7292; *insolent:*— proud.

H7296 רֹהַב *rōhāb* from H7292; *pride:*— strength.

H7297 רָהָה *rāhâ* a primitive root; to *fear:*— be afraid.

H7298 רַהַט *rahaṭ* from an unused root apparently meaning to *hollow out;* a *channel* or watering-box; by resemblance a *ringlet* of hair (as forming parallel lines):— gallery, gutter, trough.

H7299 רֵו *rēw* (Aramaic) from a root corresponding to H7200; *aspect:*— form.

H7300 רוּד *rûd* a primitive root; to *tramp* about, i.e. *ramble* (free or disconsolate):— have the dominion, be lord, mourn, rule.

H7301 רָוָה *rāwâ* a primitive root; to *slake* the thirst (occasionally of other appetites):— bathe, make drunk, fill, take the fill, satiate, satisfy, abundantly satisfy, soak, water, water abundantly.

H7302 רָוֶה *rāweh* from H7301; *sated* (with drink) :— drunkenness, watered.

H7303 רוֹהֲגָה *rôhăgâ* from an unused root probably meaning to *cry* out; *outcry; Rohagah,* an Israelite:— Rohgah.

H7304 רָוַח *rāwaḥ* a primitive root; [rather identical with H7306]; properly to *breathe* freely, i.e. *revive;* by implication to *have ample room:*— be refreshed, large.

H7305 רֶוַח *rewaḥ* from H7304; *room,* literally (an *interval*) or figuratively *(deliverance)*:— enlargement, space.

H7306 רוּחַ *rûaḥ* a primitive root; properly to *blow,* i.e. *breathe;* only (literally) to *smell* or (by implication) *perceive* (figuratively to *anticipate, enjoy*):— accept, smell, touch, make of quick understanding.

H7307 רוּחַ *rûaḥ* from H7306; *wind;* by resemblance *breath,* i.e. a sensible (or even violent) exhalation; figuratively *life, anger, unsubstantiality;*

by extension a *region* of the sky; by resemblance *spirit,* but only of a rational being (including its expression and functions):— air, anger, blast, breath, cool, courage, mind, quarter, side, spiritual, tempest, vain, wind, whirlwind, windy.

H7308 רוּחַ *rûaḥ* (Aramaic) corresponding to H7307 :— mind, spirit, wind.

H7309 רְוָחָה *rĕwāḥâ* feminine of H7305; *relief:—* breathing, respite.

H7310 רְוָיָה *rĕwāyâ* from H7301; *satisfaction:—* runneth over, wealthy.

H7311 רוּם *rûm* a primitive root; to *be high,* active to *rise* or *raise* (in various applications, literal or figurative):— bring up, exalt, exalt self, extol, give, go up, haughty; heave, heave up, high, be high, lift up on high, make on high, set up on high, too high, be higher, high one, hold up, levy, lift up, lifter up, lofty, be lofty, loud, aloud, mount up, offer, offer up, presumptuously, promote, promotion, be promotion, proud, set up, tall, taller, take, take away, take off, take up, breed worms.

H7312 רוּם *rûm* or

רֻם *rūm* from H7311; (literally) *elevation* or (figuratively) *elation:—* haughtiness, height, high.

H7313 רוּם *rûm* (Aramaic) corresponding to H7311; figuratively only:— extol, lift up, lift up self, set up.

H7314 רוּם *rûm* (Aramaic) from H7313; (literally) *altitude:—* height.

H7315 רוֹם *rôm* from H7311; *elevation,* i.e. (adverbially) *aloft:—* on high.

H7316 רוּמָה *rûmâ* from H7311; *height; Rumah,* a place in Palestine:— Rumah.

H7317 רוֹמָה *rômâ* feminine of H7315; *elation,* i.e. (adverbially) *proudly:—* haughtily.

H7318 רוֹמָם *rômām* from H7426; *exaltation,* i.e. (figuratively and specifically) *praise:—* be extolled.

H7319 רוֹמְמָה *rômĕmâ* feminine active participle of H7426; *exaltation,* i.e. *praise:—* high.

H7320 רוֹמַמְתִּי עֶזֶר *rômamtî ʿezer* or

רֹמַמְתִּי *rōmamtî* from H7311 and H5828; *I have raised* up a *help; Romamti-Ezer,* an Israelite:— Romamti-ezer.

H7321 רוּעַ *rûaʿ* a primitive root; to *mar* (especially by breaking); figuratively to *split* the ears (with sound), i.e. *shout* (for alarm or joy):— blow an alarm, cry, cry alarm, cry aloud, cry out, destroy, make a joyful noise, smart, shout, shout for joy, sound an alarm, triumph.

H7322 רוּף *rûp* a primitive root; properly to *triturate* (in a mortar), i.e. (figuratively) to *agitate* (by concussion):— tremble.

H7323 רוּץ *rûṣ* a primitive root; to *run* (for whatever reason, especially to *rush*):— break down, divide speedily, footman, guard, bring hastily, run, make run away, run through, post.

H7324 רוּק *rûq* a primitive root; to *pour* out (literally or figuratively), i.e. *empty:—* arm, cast out, draw, draw out, empty, make empty, pour forth, pour out.

H7325 רוּר *rûr* a primitive root; to *slaver* (with spittle), i.e. (by analogy) to *emit* a fluid (ulcerous or natural):— run.

H7326 רוּשׁ *rûš* a primitive root; to *be destitute:—* lack, needy, poor, make self poor, poor man.

H7327 רוּת *rût* probably for H7468; *friend; Ruth,* a Moabitess:— Ruth.

H7328 רָז *rāz* (Aramaic) from an unused root probably meaning to *attenuate,* i.e. (figuratively) *hide;* a *mystery:—* secret.

H7329 רָזָה *rāzâ* a primitive root; to *emaciate,* i.e. *make (become) thin* (literally or figuratively):— famish, wax lean.

H7330 רָזֶה *rāzeh* from H7329; *thin:—* lean.

H7331 רְזוֹן *rĕzôn* from H7336; *prince; Rezon,* a Syrian:— Rezon.

H7332 רָזוֹן *rāzôn* from H7329; *thinness:—* leanness, scant.

H7333 רָזוֹן *rāzôn* from H7336; a *dignitary:—* prince.

H7334 רָזִי *rāzî* from H7329; *thinness:—* leanness.

H7335 רָזַם *rāzam* a primitive root; to *twinkle* the eye (in mockery):— wink.

H7336 רָזַן *rāzan* a primitive root; probably to be *heavy,* i.e. (figuratively) *honorable:—* prince, ruler.

H7337 רָחַב *rāḥab* a primitive root; to *broaden* (intransitively or transitively, literally or figuratively) :— be an enlarging, enlarge, make large, make room, make wide, open wide.

H7338 רַחַב *raḥab* from H7337; a *width:—* breadth, broad place.

H7339 רְחֹב *rĕḥōb* or

רְחוֹב *rĕḥôb* from H7337; a *width,* i.e. (concretely) *avenue* or *area:—* broad place, broad way, street. See also H1050

H7340 רְחֹב *rĕḥōb* or

רְחוֹב *rĕḥôb* the same as H7339; *Rechob,* the name of a place in Syria, also of a Syrian and an Israelite:— Rehob.

H7341 רֹחַב *rōḥab* from H7337; *width* (literal or figurative):— breadth, broad, largeness, thickness, wideness.

H7342 רָחָב *rāḥāb* from H7337; *roomy,* in any (or every) direction, literally or figuratively:— broad, large, at liberty, proud, wide.

H7343 רָחָב *rāḥāb* the same as H7342; *proud; Rachab,* a Canaanitess:— Rahab.

H7344 רְחֹבוֹת *rĕḥōbôt* or

רְחֹבֹת *rĕḥōbōt* plural of H7339; *streets; Rechoboth,* a place in Assyria and one in Palestine:— Rehoboth.

H7345 רְחַבְיָה *rĕḥabyâ* or

רְחַבְיָהוּ *rĕḥabyāhû* from H7337 and H3050; *Jah has enlarged; Rechabjah,* an Israelite:— Rehabiah.

H7346 רְחַבְעָם *rĕḥabʿām* from H7337 and H5971; a *people has enlarged; Rechabam,* an Israelite king:— Rehoboam.

H7347 רֵחֶה *rēḥeh* from an unused root meaning to *pulverize;* a *mill*-stone:— mill, mill stone.

H7348 רְחוּם *rĕḥûm* a form of H7349; *Rechum,* the name of a Persian and of three Israelites:— Rehum.

H7349 רַחוּם *raḥûm* from H7355; *compassionate:—* full of compassion, merciful.

H7350 רָחוֹק *rāḥôq* or

רָחֹק *rāḥōq* from H7368; *remote,* literally or figuratively, of place or time; specifically *precious;* often used adverbially (with preposition):— afar off, far, far abroad, far off, long ago, of old, space, great while to come.

H7351 רְהִיט *rĕhîṭ* from the same as H7298; a *panel* (as resembling a *trough*):— rafter.

H7352 רַחִיק *raḥîq* (Aramaic) corresponding to H7350 :— far.

H7353 רָחֵל *rāḥēl* from an unused root meaning to *journey;* a *ewe* [the *females* being the predominant element of a flock] (as a good *traveller*):— ewe, sheep.

H7354 רָחֵל *rāḥēl* the same as H7353; *Rachel,* a wife of Jacob:— Rachel.

H7355 רָחַם *rāḥam* a primitive root; to *fondle;* by implication to *love,* especially to *compassionate:—* have compassion, have compassion on, have compassion upon, love, mercy, find mercy, have mercy, obtain mercy, shew mercy, merciful, have mercy on, have mercy upon, pity, have pity, Ruhamah, surely.

H7356 רַחַם *raḥam* from H7355; *compassion* (in the plural); by extension the *womb* (as *cherishing* the foetus); by implication a *maiden:—* bowels, compassion, damsel, tender love, mercy, great mercy, tender mercy, pity, womb.

H7357 רַחַם *raḥam* the same as H7356; *pity; Racham,* an Israelite:— Raham.

H7358 רֶחֶם *reḥem* from H7355; the *womb* [compare H7356]:— matrix, womb.

H7359 רְחֵם *rĕḥēm* (Aramaic) corresponding to H7356; (plural) *pity:—* mercy.

H7360 רָחָם *rāḥām* or (feminine)

רָחָמָה *rāḥāmâ* from H7355; a kind of *vulture* (supposed to be *tender* towards its young):— gier-eagle.

H7361 רַחֲמָה *raḥămâ* feminine of H7356; a *maiden* :— damsel.

H7362 רַחְמָנִי *raḥmānî* from H7355; *compassionate* :— pitiful.

H7363 רָחַף *rāḥap* a primitive root; to *brook;* by implication to *be relaxed:—* flutter, move, shake.

H7364 רָחַץ *rāḥaṣ* a primitive root; to *lave* (the whole or a part of a thing):— bathe, bathe self, wash, wash self.

H7365 רְחַץ *rĕḥaṣ* (Aramaic) corresponding to H7364 [probably through the accessory idea of *ministering* as a servant at the bath]; to *attend* upon:— trust.

H7366 רַחַץ *raḥaṣ* from H7364; a *bath:—* washpot.

H7367 רַחְצָה *raḥṣâ* feminine of H7366; a *bathing* place:— washing.

H7368 רָחַק *rāḥaq* a primitive root; to *widen* (in any direction), i.e. (intransitively) *recede* or (transitively) *remove* (literally or figuratively, of place or relation):— far, afar off, be far, be far away, be far off, be too far, cast far off, drive far, get far, go far, go far away, keep self far, put far, put far away, remove far, remove far away, be too far, wander far off, withdraw far, far off, loose, refrain, very, a good way off, be a good way off.

H7369 רָחֵק *rāḥēq* from H7368; *remote:—* that are far.

H7370 רָחַשׁ *rāḥaš* a primitive root; to *gush:—* indite.

H7371 רַחַת *raḥat* from H7306; a *winnowing*-fork (as *blowing* the chaff away):— shovel.

H7372 רָטַב *rāṭab* a primitive root; to *be moist:—* be wet.

H7373 רָטֹב *rāṭōb* from H7372; *moist* (with sap):— green.

H7374 רֶטֶט *reṭeṭ* from an unused root meaning to *tremble; terror:*— fear.

H7375 רֻטֲפַשׁ *ruṭăpaš* a root compounded from H7373 and H2954; to *be rejuvenated:*— be fresh.

H7376 רָטַשׁ *rāṭāš* a primitive root; to *dash* down :— dash, dash in pieces.

H7377 רִי *rî* from H7301; *irrigation,* i.e. a shower :— watering.

H7378 רִיב *rîb* or

רוּב *rûb* a primitive root; properly to *toss,* i.e. *grapple;* mostly figuratively to *wrangle,* i.e. *hold a controversy;* (by implication) to *defend:*— adversary, chide, complain, contend, debate, ever, lay wait, plead, rebuke, strive, thoroughly.

H7379 רִיב *rîb* or

רִב *rīb* from H7378; a *contest* (personal or legal):— adversary, cause, chiding, contend, contention, controversy, multitude *[from the margin],* pleading, strife, strive, striving, suit.

H7380 רִיבַי *rîbay* from H7378; *contentious; Ribai,* an Israelite:— Ribai.

H7381 רֵיחַ *rêaḥ* from H7306; *odor* (as if *blown*):— savour, scent, smell.

H7382 רֵיחַ *rêaḥ* (Aramaic) corresponding to H7381 :— smell.

H7383 רִיפָה *rîpâ* or

רִפָה *rīpâ* from H7322; (only plural), *grits* (as *pounded*):— ground corn, wheat.

H7384 רִיפַת *rîpat* or (probably by orthographical error)

דִּיפַת *dîpat* of foreign origin; *Riphath,* a grandson of Japheth and his descendants:— Riphath.

H7385 רִיק *rîq* from H7324; *emptiness;* figuratively a *worthless* thing; adverbially *in vain:*— empty, to no purpose, in vain, vain thing, vanity.

H7386 רֵיק *rêq* or (shorter)

רֵק *rēq* from H7324; *empty;* figuratively *worthless:*— emptied, empty, vain, vain fellow, vain man.

H7387 רֵיקָם *reyqām* from H7386; *emptily;* figuratively (objectively) *ineffectually,* (subjectively) *undeservedly:*— without cause, empty, in vain, void.

H7388 רִיר *rîr* from H7325; *saliva;* by resemblance *broth:*— spittle, white of an egg.

H7389 רֵישׁ *rêš* or

רֵאשׁ *rēʾš* or

רִישׁ *rîš* from H7326; *poverty:*— poverty.

H7390 רַךְ *rak* from H7401; *tender* (literally or figuratively); by implication *weak:*— fainthearted, soft, tender, tenderhearted, tender one, weak.

H7391 רֹךְ *rōk* from H7401; *softness* (figurative):— tenderness.

H7392 רָכַב *rākab* a primitive root; to *ride* (on an animal or in a vehicle); causatively to *place upon* (for riding or generally), to *despatch:*— bring, bring on horseback, carry, get oneself up, on horseback, put, ride, cause to ride, make to ride, ride in a chariot, ride on, rider, set.

H7393 רֶכֶב *rekeb* from H7392; a *vehicle;* by implication a *team;* by extension *cavalry;* by analogy a *rider,* i.e. the upper millstone:— chariot, millstone, upper millstone, multitude *[from the margin],* wagon.

H7394 רֵכָב *rēkāb* from H7392; *rider; Rekab,* the name of two Arabs and of two Israelites:— Rechab.

H7395 רַכָּב *rakkāb* from H7392; a *charioteer:*— chariot man, driver of a chariot, horseman.

H7396 רִכְבָּה *rikbâ* feminine of H7393; a *chariot* (collectively):— chariots.

H7397 רֵכָה *rēkâ* probably feminine from H7401; *softness; Rekah,* a place in Palestine:— Rechah.

H7398 רְכוּב *rĕkûb* from passive participle of H7392; a *vehicle* (as *ridden* on):— chariot.

H7399 רְכוּשׁ *rĕkûš* or

רְכֻשׁ *rĕkūš* from passive participle of H7408; *property* (as *gathered*):— good, riches, substance.

H7400 רָכִיל *rākîl* from H7402; a *scandal-monger* (as *travelling* about):— slander, carry tales, talebearer.

H7401 רָכַךְ *rākak* a primitive root; to *soften* (intransitively or transitively), used figuratively:— faint, be fainthearted, mollify, be softer, make soft, be tender.

H7402 רָכַל *rākal* a primitive root; to *travel* for trading:— merchant, spice merchant.

H7403 רָכָל *rākāl* from H7402; *merchant; Rakal,* a place in Palestine:— Rachal.

H7404 רְכֻלָּה *rĕkullâ* feminine passive participle of H7402; *trade* (as *peddled*):— merchandise, traffic.

H7405 רָכַס *rākas* a primitive root; to *tie:*— bind.

H7406 רֶכֶס *rekes* from H7405; a mountain *ridge* (as if *tied* summits):— rough place.

H7407 רֹכֶס *rōkes* from H7405; a *snare* (as of *tied* meshes):— pride.

H7408 רָכַשׁ *rākaš* a primitive root; to *lay up,* i.e. collect:— gather, get.

H7409 רֶכֶשׁ *rekeš* from H7408; a *relay* of animals on a post-route (as *stored* up for that purpose); by implication a *courser:*— dromedary, mule, swift beast.

H7410 רָם *rām* active participle of H7311; *high; Ram,* the name of an Arabian and of an Israelite:— Ram. See also H1027

H7411 רָמָה *rāmâ* a primitive root; to *hurl;* specifically to *shoot;* figuratively to *delude* or *betray* (as if causing to fall):— beguile, betray, bowman, carry, deceive, throw.

H7412 רְמָה *rĕmâ* (Aramaic) corresponding to H7411; to *throw, set,* (figuratively) *assess:*— cast, cast down, impose.

H7413 רָמָה *rāmâ* feminine active participle of H7311; a *height* (as a seat of idolatry):— high place.

H7414 רָמָה *rāmâ* the same as H7413; *Ramah,* the name of four places in Palestine:— Ramah.

H7415 רִמָּה *rimmâ* from H7426 in the sense of *breeding* [compare H7311]; a *maggot* (as rapidly *bred*), literally or figuratively:— worm.

H7416 רִמּוֹן *rimmôn* or

רִמֹּן *rimmōn* from H7426; a *pomegranate,* the tree (from its *upright* growth) or the fruit (also an artificial ornament):— pomegranate.

H7417 רִמּוֹן *rimmôn* or (shorter)

רִמֹּן *rimmōn* or

רִמּוֹנוֹ *rimmônô* (1 Chron. 6:62 [47]), the same as H7416. The addition "-methoar" (Josh 19:13) is

הַמְּתֹאָר *hammĕtōʾār* , passive participle of H8388 with the article, *the* (one) *marked off,* i.e. *which pertains,* mistaken for part of the name.; *Rimmon,* the name of a Syrian deity, also of five places in Palestine:— Remmon, Rimmon.

H7418 רָמוֹת־נֶגֶב *rāmôt-negeb* or

רָמַת נֶגֶב *rāmat negeb* from the plural or construct of H7413 and H5045; *heights* (or *height*) *of* the *South; Ramoth-Negeb* or *Ramath-Negeb,* a place in Palestine:— south Ramoth, Ramath of the south.

H7419 רָמוּת *rāmût* from H7311; a *heap* (of carcases):— height.

H7420 רֹמַח *rōmaḥ* from an unused root meaning to *hurl;* a *lance* (as *thrown*); especially the iron *point:*— buckler, javelin, lancet, spear.

H7421 רַמִּי *rammî* for H761; a *Ramite,* i.e. Aramaean:— Syrian.

H7422 רַמְיָה *ramyâ* from H7311 and H3050; *Jah has raised; Ramjah,* an Israelite:— Ramiah.

H7423 רְמִיָּה *rĕmîyâ* from H7411; *remissness, treachery:*— deceit, deceitful, deceitfully, false, guile, idle, slack, slothful.

H7424 רַמָּךְ *rammāk* of foreign origin; a brood *mare* :— dromedary.

H7425 רְמַלְיָהוּ *rĕmalyāhû* from an unused root and H3050 (perhaps meaning to *deck*); *Jah has bedecked; Remaljah,* an Israelite:— Remaliah.

H7426 רָמַם *rāmam* a primitive root; to *rise* (literally or figuratively):— exalt, get [oneself] up, lift up (self), mount up.

H7427 רֹמֵמֻת *rōmēmūt* from the active participle of H7426; *exaltation:*— lifting up of self.

H7428 רִמֹּן פֶּרֶץ *rimmōn pereṣ* from H7416 and H6556; *pomegranate of* the *breach; Rimmon-Perets,* a place in the Desert:— Rimmon-parez.

H7429 רָמַס *rāmas* a primitive root; to *tread* upon (as a potter, in walking or abusively):— oppressor, stamp upon, trample, trample under feet, tread, tread down, tread upon.

H7430 רָמַשׂ *rāmaś* a primitive root; properly to *glide* swiftly, i.e. to *crawl* or *move* with short steps; by analogy to *swarm:*— creep, move.

H7431 רֶמֶשׂ *remeś* from H7430; a *reptile* or any other rapidly moving animal:— that creepeth, creeping thing, moving thing.

H7432 רֶמֶת *remet* from H7411; *height; Remeth,* a place in Palestine:— Remeth.

H7433 רָמֹת גִּלְעָד *rāmōt gilʿād* or

רָמוֹת גִּלְעָד *rāmôt gilʿād* (2 Chron. 22:5), from the plural of H7413 and H1568; *heights of Gilad; Ramoth-Gilad,* a place east of the Jordan:— Ramoth-gilead, Ramoth in Gilead. See also H7216

H7434 רָמַת הַמִּצְפֶּה *rāmat hammiṣpeh* from H7413 and H4707 with the article interp; *height of the watch-*tower; *Ramoth-ham-Mitspeh,* a place in Palestine:— Ramath-mizpeh.

H7435 רָמָתִי *rāmātî* patronymic of H7414; a *Ramathite* or inhabitant of Ramah:— Ramathite.

H7436 רָמָתַיִם צוֹפִים *rāmātayim ṣôpîm* from the dual of H7413 and the plural of the active participle of H6822; *double height of watchers; Ramathajim-Tsophim,* a place in Palestine:— Ramathaim-zophim.

H7437 רָמַת לֶחִי *rāmat leḥî* from H7413 and H3895; *height of a jaw-bone; Ramath-Lechi,* a place in Palestine:— Ramath-lehi.

H7438 רֹן *rōn* from H7442; a *shout* (of deliverance):— song.

H7439 רָנָה *rānâ* a primitive root; to *whiz:*— rattle.

H7440 רִנָּה *rinnâ* from H7442; properly a *creaking* (or shrill sound), i.e. *shout* (of joy or grief):— cry, gladness, joy, proclamation, rejoicing, shouting, sing, singing, triumph.

H7441 רִנָּה *rinnâ* the same as H7440; *Rinnah,* an Israelite:— Rinnah.

H7442 רָנַן *rānan* a primitive root; properly to *creak* (or emit a stidulous sound), i.e. to *shout* (usually for joy):— aloud for joy, cry out, be joyful, rejoice, greatly rejoice, make to rejoice, shout, cause to shout, shout for joy, sing, cause to sing for joy, sing aloud, sing out, triumph.

H7443 רֶנֶן *renen* from H7442; an *ostrich* (from its *wail*):— goodly.

H7444 רַנֵּן *rannēn* intensive from H7442; *shouting* (for joy):— singing.

H7445 רְנָנָה *rĕnānâ* from H7442; a *shout* (for joy) :— joyful, joyful voice, singing, triumphing.

H7446 רִסָּה *rissâ* from H7450; a *ruin* (as *dripping* to pieces); *Rissah,* a place in the Desert:— Rissah.

H7447 רָסִיס *rāsîs* from H7450; properly *dripping* to pieces, i.e. a *ruin;* also a dew-*drop:*— breach, drop.

H7448 רֶסֶן *resen* from an unused root meaning to *curb;* a *halter* (as *restraining*); by implication the *jaw:*— bridle.

H7449 רֶסֶן *resen* the same as H7448; *Resen,* a place in Assyria:— Resen.

H7450 רָסַס *rāsas* a primitive root; to *comminute;* used only as denominatively from H7447, to *moisten* (with drops):— temper.

H7451 רַע *ra*ᶜ from H7489; *bad* or (as noun) *evil* (natural or moral):— adversity, affliction, bad, calamity, displease, displeasure, distress, evil, evil-favouredness, evil man, evil thing, exceedingly, great, grief, grievous, harm, heavy, hurt, hurtful, ill, ill favoured, mark, mischief, mischievous, misery, naught, naughty, noisome, not please, sad, sadly, sore, sorrow, trouble, vex, wicked, wickedly, wickedness, wicked one, worse, worst, wretchedness, wrong. [Including feminine

רָעָה *rāᶜā* as adjective or noun.].

H7452 רֵעַ *rēa*ᶜ from H7321; a *crash* (of thunder), *noise* (of war), *shout* (of joy):— aloud, noise, shouted.

H7453 רֵעַ *rēa*ᶜ or

רֵיעַ *rêa*ᶜ from H7462; an *associate* (more or less close):— brother, companion, fellow, friend, husband, lover, neighbour, other, another.

H7454 רֵעַ *rēa*ᶜ from H7462; a *thought* (as *association* of ideas):— thought.

H7455 רֹעַ *rōa*ᶜ from H7489; *badness* (as *marring*), physically or morally:— be so bad, badness, evil, be so evil, naughtiness, sadness, sorrow, wickedness.

H7456 רָעֵב *rāᶜēb* a primitive root; to *hunger:*— famsh, suffer to famish, hunger, be hungry, have hunger, suffer hunger, suffer to hunger.

H7457 רָעֵב *rāᶜēb* from H7456; *hungry* (more or less intensely):— hunger bitten, hungry.

H7458 רָעָב *rāᶜāb* from H7456; *hunger* (more or less extensive):— dearth, famine, famished, hunger.

H7459 רְעָבוֹן *rĕᶜābôn* from H7456; *famine:*— famine.

H7460 רָעַד *rāᶜad* a primitive root; to *shudder* (more or less violently):— tremble.

H7461 רַעַד *raᶜad* or (feminine)

רְעָדָה *rĕᶜādâ* from H7460; a *shudder:*— trembling.

H7462 רָעָה *rāᶜâ* a primitive root; to *tend* a flock, i.e. *pasture* it; intransitively to *graze* (literally or figuratively); generally to *rule;* by extension to *associate* with (as a friend):— break, companion, keep company with, devour, eat up, evil entreat, feed, use as a friend, make friendship with, herdman, keeper, keep sheep, pastor, shearing house, shepherd, wander, waste.

H7463 רֵעֶה *rēᶜeh* from H7462; a (male) *companion:*— friend.

H7464 רֵעָה *rēᶜâ* feminine of H7453; a female *associate:*— companion, fellow.

H7465 רֹעָה *rōᶜâ* for H7455; *breakage:*— broken, utterly.

H7466 רְעוּ *rĕᶜû* for H7471 in the sense of H7453; *friend; Reü,* a postdiluvian patriarch:— Reu.

H7467 רְעוּאֵל *rĕᶜûᵓēl* from the same as H7466 and H410; *friend of God; Reüel,* the name of Moses' father-in-law, also of an Edomite and an Israelite:— Raguel, Reuel.

H7468 רְעוּת *rĕᶜût* from H7462 in the sense of H7453; a female *associate;* generally an *additional* one:— another, mate, neighbour.

H7469 רְעוּת *rĕᶜût* probably from H7462; a *feeding* upon, i.e. grasping after:— vexation.

H7470 רְעוּת *rĕᶜût* (Aramaic) corresponding to H7469; *desire:*— pleasure, will.

H7471 רְעִי *rĕᶜî* from H7462; *pasture:*— pasture.

H7472 רֵעִי *rēᶜî* from H7453; *social; Reï,* an Israelite:— Rei.

H7473 רֹעִי *rōᶜî* from active participle of H7462; *pastoral;* as noun, a *shepherd:*— shepherd.

H7474 רַעְיָה *raᶜyâ* feminine of H7453; a female *associate:*— fellow, love.

H7475 רַעְיוֹן *raᶜyôn* from H7462 in the sense of H7469; *desire:*— vexation.

H7476 רַעְיוֹן *raᶜyôn* (Aramaic) corresponding to H7475; a *grasp,* i.e. (figuratively) mental *conception:*— cogitation, thought.

H7477 רָעַל *rāᶜal* a primitive root; to *reel,* i.e. (figuratively) to *brandish:*— terribly shake.

H7478 רַעַל *raᶜal* from H7477; a *reeling* (from intoxication):— trembling.

H7479 רַעֲלָה *raᶜălâ* feminine of H7478; a long *veil* (as *fluttering*):— muffler.

H7480 רְעֵלָיָה *rĕᶜēlāyâ* from H7477 and H3050; *made to tremble* (i.e. *fearful*) *of Jah; Reëlajah,* an Israelite:— Reeliah.

H7481 רָעַם *rāᶜam* a primitive root; to *tumble,* i.e. *be* violently *agitated;* specifically to *crash* (of thunder); figuratively to *irritate* (with anger):— make to fret, roar, thunder, trouble.

H7482 רַעַם *raᶜam* from H7481; a *peal* of thunder:— thunder.

H7483 רַעְמָה *raᶜmâ* feminine of H7482; the *mane* of a horse (as *quivering* in the wind):— thunder.

H7484 רַעְמָה *raᶜmâ* the same as H7483; *Ramah,* the name of a grandson of Ham, and of a place (perhaps founded by him):— Raamah.

H7485 רַעַמְיָה *raᶜamyâ* from H7481 and H3050; *Jah has shaken; Raamjah,* an Israelite:— Raamiah.

H7486 רַעְמְסֵס *raᶜmĕsēs* or

רַעַמְסֵס *raᶜamsēs* of Egyptian origin; *Rameses* or *Raamses,* a place in Egypt:— Raamses, Rameses.

H7487 רַעֲנַן *raᶜănan* (Aramaic) corresponding to H7488; *green,* i.e. (figuratively) *prosperous:*— flourishing.

H7488 רַעֲנָן *raᶜănān* from an unused root meaning to *be green; verdant;* by analogy *new;* figuratively *prosperous:*— green, flourishing.

H7489 רָעַע *rāᶜaᶜ* a primitive root; properly to *spoil* (literally by *breaking* to pieces); figuratively to *make* (or *be*) *good for nothing,* i.e. *bad* (physically, socially or morally):— afflict, associate selves *[by mistake for H7462],* break, break down, break in pieces, displease, evil, be evil, bring evil, do evil, evil doer, evil entreat, evil man, show self friendly *[by mistake for H7462],* do harm, hurt, do hurt, ill, behave self ill, deal ill, indeed, do mischief, punish, still, vex, wicked, do wickedly, wicked doer, be worse, deal worse, do worse.

H7490 רְעַע *rĕᶜaᶜ* (Aramaic) corresponding to H7489 :— break, bruise.

H7491 רָעַף *rāᶜap* a primitive root; to *drip:*— distil, drop, drop down.

H7492 רָעַץ *rāᶜaṣ* a primitive root; to *break* in pieces; figuratively *harass:*— dash in pieces, vex.

H7493 רָעַשׁ *rāᶜaš* a primitive root; to *undulate* (as the earth, the sky, etc.; also a field of grain), particularly through fear; specifically to *spring* (as a locust):— make afraid, move, remove, quake, shake, make to shake, tremble, make to tremble.

H7494 רַעַשׁ *raᶜaš* from H7493; *vibration, bounding, uproar:*— commotion, confused noise, earthquake, fierceness, quaking, rattling, rushing, shaking.

H7495 רָפָא *rāpāᵓ* or

רָפָה *rāpâ* a primitive root; properly to *mend* (by stitching), i.e. (figuratively) to *cure:*— cure, heal, cause to heal, physician, repair, thoroughly, make whole. See H7503

H7496 רָפָא *rāpāᵓ* from H7495 in the sense of H7503; properly *lax,* i.e. (figuratively) a *ghost* (as *dead;* in plural only):— dead, deceased.

H7497 רָפָא *rāpāᵓ* or

רָפָה *rāpâ* from H7495 in the sense of *invigorating;* a *giant:*— giant, Rapha, Rephaim, Rephaims. See also H1051

H7498 רָפָא *rāpāᵓ* or

רָפָה *rāpâ* probably the same as H7497; *giant; Rapha* or *Raphah,* the name of two Israelites:— Rapha.

H7499 רְפֻאָה *rĕpūᵓâ* feminine passive participle of H7495; a *medicament:*— healed, medicine.

H7500 רִפְאוּת *ripᵓût* from H7495; a *cure:*— health.

H7501 רְפָאֵל *rĕpāᵓēl* from H7495 and H410; *God has cured; Rephaël,* an Israelite:— Rephael.

H7502 רָפַד *rāpad* a primitive root; to *spread* (a bed); by implication to *refresh:*— comfort, make a bed, spread.

H7503 רָפָה *rāpâ* a primitive root; to *slacken* (in many applications, literally or figuratively):— abate, cease, consume, draw toward evening, fail, faint, be faint, be feeble, wax feeble, forsake, idle, leave, let alone, let go, let down, slack, be slack, stay, be still, be slothful, weaken, be weak. See H7495

H7504 רָפֶה *rāpeh* from H7503; *slack* (in body or mind):— weak.

H7505 רָפוּא *rāpû'* passive participle of H7495; *cured; Raphu,* an Israelite:— Raphu.

H7506 רֶפַח *repaḥ* from an unused root apparently meaning to *sustain; support; Rephach,* an Israelite:— Rephah.

H7507 רְפִידָה *rĕpîdâ* from H7502; a *railing* (as *spread* along):— bottom.

H7508 רְפִידִים *rĕpîdîm* plural of the masculine of the same as H7507; *ballusters; Rephidim,* a place in the Desert:— Rephidim.

H7509 רְפָיָה *rĕpāyâ* from H7495 and H3050; *Jah has cured; Rephajah,* the name of five Israelites:— Rephaiah.

H7510 רִפְיוֹן *ripyôn* from H7503; *slackness:*— feebleness.

H7511 רָפַס *rāpas* a primitive root; to *trample,* i.e. *prostrate:*— humble self, submit self.

H7512 רְפַס *rĕpas* (Aramaic) corresponding to H7511 :— stamp.

H7513 רַפְסֹדָה *rapsōdâ* from H7511; a *raft* (as *flat* on the water):— flote.

H7514 רָפַק *rāpaq* a primitive root; to *recline:*— lean.

H7515 רָפַשׂ *rāpaś* a primitive root; to *trample,* i.e. *roil* water:— foul, trouble.

H7516 רֶפֶשׁ *repeš* from H7515; *mud* (as *roiled*):— mire.

H7517 רֶפֶת *repet* probably from H7503; a *stall* for cattle (from their *resting* there):— stall.

H7518 רַץ *raṣ* contracted from H7533; a *fragment* :— piece.

H7519 רָצָא *rāṣā'* a primitive root; to *run;* also to *delight* in:— accept, run.

H7520 רָצַד *rāṣad* a primitive root; probably to *look askant,* i.e. (figuratively) *be jealous:*— leap.

H7521 רָצָה *rāṣâ* a primitive root; to *be pleased with;* specifically to *satisfy* a debt:— accept, be acceptable, accomplish, set affection, approve, consent with, delight, delight self, enjoy, be favourable, have a favour, like, observe, pardon, please, be pleased with, have pleasure, take pleaseure, reconcile self.

H7522 רָצוֹן *rāṣôn* or

רָצֹן *rāṣōn* from H7521; *delight* (especially as shown):— acceptable, be acceptable, be accepted, acceptance, delight, desire, favour, pleasure, good pleasure, will, own will, self will, voluntary will, as . . . would, what would.

H7523 רָצַח *rāṣaḥ* a primitive root; properly to *dash* in pieces, i.e. *kill* (a human being), especially to *murder:*— put to death, kill, slay, slayer, manslayer, murder, murderer.

H7524 רֶצַח *reṣaḥ* from H7523; a *crushing;* specifically a *murder*-cry:— slaughter, sword.

H7525 רִצְיָא *riṣyā'* from H7521; *delight; Ritsjah,* an Israelite:— Rezia.

H7526 רְצִין *rĕṣîn* probably for H7522; *Retsin,* the name of a Syrian and of an Israelite:— Rezin.

H7527 רָצַע *rāṣa^c* a primitive root; to *pierce:*— bore.

H7528 רָצַף *rāṣap* a denominative from H7529; to *tessellate,* i.e. embroider (as if with bright stones):— pave.

H7529 רֶצֶף *reṣep* for H7565; a red-hot *stone* (for baking):— coal.

H7530 רֶצֶף *reṣep* the same as H7529; *Retseph,* a place in Assyrian:— Rezeph.

H7531 רִצְפָּה *riṣpâ* feminine of H7529; a hot *stone;* also a tessellated *pavement:*— live coal, pavement.

H7532 רִצְפָּה *riṣpâ* the same as H7531; *Ritspah,* an Israelitess:— Rizpah.

H7533 רָצַץ *rāṣaṣ* a primitive root; to *crack* in pieces, literally or figuratively:— break, bruise, crush, discourage, oppress, struggle together.

H7534 רַק *raq* from H7556 in its original sense; *emaciated* (as if *flattened* out):— lean, leanfleshed, thin.

H7535 רַק *raq* the same as H7534 as a noun; properly *leanness,* i.e. (figuratively) limitation; only adverbially *merely,* or conjunctionally *although:*— but, even, except, howbeit, howsoever, at the least, nevertheless, nothing but, notwithstanding, only, save, so that, surely, yet, yet so, in any wise.

H7536 רֹק *rōq* from H7556; *spittle:*— spit, spitting, spittle.

H7537 רָקַב *rāqab* a primitive root; to *decay* (as by worm-eating):— rot.

H7538 רָקָב *rāqāb* from H7537; *decay* (by *caries*) :— rottenness, rotten thing.

H7539 רִקָּבוֹן *riqqābôn* from H7538; *decay* (by *caries*):— rotten.

H7540 רָקַד *rāqad* a primitive root; properly to *stamp,* i.e. to *spring* about (wildly or for joy):— dance, jump, leap, skip.

H7541 רַקָּה *raqqâ* feminine of H7534; properly *thinness,* i.e. the *side* of the head:— temple.

H7542 רַקּוֹן *raqqôn* from H7534; *thinness; Rakkon,* a place in Palestine:— Rakkon.

H7543 רָקַח *rāqaḥ* a primitive root; to *perfume:*— apothecary, compound, make ointment, prepare, spice.

H7544 רֶקַח *reqaḥ* from H7543; properly *perfumery,* i.e. (by implication) *spicery* (for flavor):— spiced.

H7545 רֹקַח *rōqaḥ* from H7542; an *aromatic:*— confection, ointment.

H7546 רַקָּח *raqqāḥ* from H7543; a male *perfumer* :— apothecary.

H7547 רַקּוּחַ *raqqûaḥ* from H7543; a *scented* substance:— perfume.

H7548 רַקָּחָה *raqqāḥâ* feminine of H7547; a female *perfumer:*— confectioner.

H7549 רָקִיעַ *rāqîa^c* from H7554; properly an *expanse,* i.e. the *firmament* or (apparently) visible arch of the sky:— firmament.

H7550 רָקִיק *rāqîq* from H7556 in its original sense; a thin *cake:*— cake, wafer.

H7551 רָקַם *rāqam* a primitive root; to *variegate* color, i.e. *embroider;* by implication to *fabricate:*— embroiderer, needlework, curiously work.

H7552 רֶקֶם *reqem* from H7551; *versicolor; Rekem,* the name of a place in Palestine, also of a Midianite and an Israelite:— Rekem.

H7553 רִקְמָה *riqmâ* from H7551; *variegation* of color; specifically *embroidery:*— broidered, embroidered work, divers colours, needlework, raiment of needlework, needlework on both sides.

H7554 רָקַע *rāqa^c* a primitive root; to *pound* the earth (as a sign of passion); by analogy to *expand* (by hammering); by implication to *overlay* (with thin sheets of metal):— beat, make broad, spread abroad, spread forth, spread over, spread out, spread into plates, stamp, stretch.

H7555 רִקֻּעַ *riqqūa^c* from H7554; *beaten* out, i.e. a (metallic) *plate:*— broad.

H7556 רָקַק *rāqaq* a primitive root; to *spit:*— spit.

H7557 רַקַּת *raqqat* from H7556 in its original sense of *diffusing;* a *beach* (as *expanded* single); *Rakkath,* a place in Palestine:— Rakkath.

H7558 רִשְׁיוֹן *rišyôn* from an unused root meaning to *have leave;* a *permit:*— grant.

H7559 רָשַׁם *rāšam* a primitive root; to *record:*— note.

H7560 רְשַׁם *rĕšam* (Aramaic) corresponding to H7559:— sign, write.

H7561 רָשַׁע *rāša^c* a primitive root; to *be* (causatively *do* or *declare*) *wrong;* by implication to *disturb, violate:*— condemn, make trouble, vex, be wicked, commit wickedness, deal wickedly, depart wickedly, do wickedly.

H7562 רֶשַׁע *reša^c* from H7561; a *wrong* (especially moral):— iniquity, wicked, wickedness.

H7563 רָשָׁע *rāšā^c* from H7561; morally *wrong;* concretely an (actively) *bad* person:— condemned, guilty, ungodly, wicked, wicked man, that did wrong.

H7564 רִשְׁעָה *riš^câ* feminine of H7562; *wrong* (especially moral):— fault, wickedly, wickedness.

H7565 רֶשֶׁף *rešep* from H8313; a live *coal;* by analogy *lightning;* figuratively an *arrow* (as *flashing* through the air); specifically *fever:*— arrow, coal, burning coal, burning heat, spark, hot thunderbolt.

H7566 רֶשֶׁף *rešep* the same as H7565; *Resheph,* an Israelite:— Resheph.

H7567 רָשַׁשׁ *rāšaš* a primitive root; to *demolish:*— impoverish.

H7568 רֶשֶׁת *rešet* from H3423; a *net* (as *catching* animals):— net, network.

H7569 רַתּוֹק *rattôq* from H7576; a *chain:*— chain.

H7570 רָתַח *rātaḥ* a primitive root; to *boil:*— boil.

H7571 רֶתַח *retaḥ* from H7570; a *boiling:*— boil well.

H7572 רַתִּיקָה *rattîqâ* from H7576; a *chain:*— chain.

H7573 רָתַם *rātam* a primitive root; to *yoke* up (to the pole of a vehicle):— bind.

H7574 רֶתֶם *retem* or

רֹתֶם *rōtem* from H7573; the Spanish *broom* (from its pole-like stems):— juniper, juniper tree.

H7575 רִתְמָה *ritmâ* feminine of H7574; *Rithmah,* a place in the Desert:— Rithmah.

H7576 רָתַק *rātaq* a primitive root; to *fasten:*— bind.

H7577 רְתֻקָה *rĕtūqâ* feminine passive participle of H7576; something *fastened,* i.e. a *chain:*— chain.

H7578 רְתֵת *rĕtēt* for H7374; *terror:*— trembling.

שׁ

H7579 שָׁאַב *šā'ab* a primitive root; to *bale* up water :— woman to draw, drawer, draw water.

H7580 שָׁאַג *šāʾag* a primitive root; to *rumble* or *moan:*— mightily, roar.

H7581 שְׁאָגָה *šĕʾāgâ* from H7580; a *rumbling* or *moan:*— roaring.

H7582 שָׁאָה *šāʾâ* a primitive root; to *rush;* by implication to *desolate:*— be desolate, rush, make a rushing, waste, lay waste.

H7583 שָׁאָה *šāʾâ* a primitive root; [rather identical with H7582 through the idea of *whirling* to giddiness]; to *stun,* i.e. (intransitively) *be astonished:*— wonder.

H7584 שַׁאֲוָה *šaʾăwâ* from H7582; a *tempest* (as *rushing*):— desolation.

H7585 שְׁאוֹל *šĕʾôl* or

שְׁאֹל *šĕʾōl* from H7592; *hades* or the world of the dead (as if a subterranean *retreat*), including its accessories and inmates:— grave, hell, pit.

H7586 שָׁאוּל *šāʾûl* passive participle of H7592; *asked; Shaül,* the name of an Edomite and two Israelites:— Saul, Shaul.

H7587 שָׁאוּלִי *šāʾûlî* patronymic from H7856; a *Shaülite* or descendant of Shaul:— Shaulites.

H7588 שָׁאוֹן *šāʾôn* from H7582; *uproar* (as of *rushing*); by implication *destruction:*— horrible, noise, pomp, rushing, tumult, tumultuous.

H7589 שְׁאָט *šĕʾāṭ* from an unused root meaning to *push* aside; *contempt:*— despite, despiteful.

H7590 שָׁאט *šāʾṭ* for active participle of H7750 [compare H7589]; one *contemning:*— that despise, that despised, which despise.

H7591 שְׁאִיָּה *šĕʾiyâ* from H7582; *desolation:*— destruction.

H7592 שָׁאַל *šāʾal* or

שָׁאֵל *šāʾēl* a primitive root; to *inquire;* by implication to *request;* by extension to *demand:*— ask, ask counsel, ask on, beg, borrow, lay to charge, consult, demand, desire, earnestly, enquire, greet, obtain leave, lend, pray, request, require, salute, straitly, surely, wish.

H7593 שְׁאֵל *šĕʾēl* (Aramaic) corresponding to H7592 :— ask, demand, require.

H7594 שְׁאָל *šĕʾāl* from H7592; *request; Sheäl,* an Israelite:— Sheal.

H7595 שְׁאֵלָא *šĕʾēlāʾ* (Aramaic) from H7593; properly a *question* (at law), i.e. judicial *decision* or mandate:— demand.

H7596 שְׁאֵלָה *šĕʾēlâ* or

שֵׁלָה *šēlâ* (1 Sam. 1:17), from H7592; a *petition;* by implication a *loan:*— loan, petition, request.

H7597 שְׁאַלְתִּיאֵל *šĕʾaltîʾēl* or

שַׁלְתִּיאֵל *šaltîʾēl* from H7592 and H410; *I have asked God; Sheältiël,* an Israelite:— Shalthiel, Shealtiel.

H7598 שְׁאַלְתִּיאֵל *šĕʾaltîʾēl* (Aramaic) corresponding to H7597:— Shealtiel.

H7599 שָׁאַן *šāʾan* a primitive root; to *loll,* i.e. *be peaceful:*— be at ease, be quiet, rest. See also H1052

H7600 שַׁאֲנָן *šaʾănān* from H7599; *secure;* in a bad sense, *haughty:*— that is at ease, quiet, tumult. Compare H7946

H7601 שָׁאַס *šāʾas* a primitive root; to *plunder:*— spoil.

H7602 שָׁאַף *šāʾap* a primitive root; to *inhale* eagerly; figuratively to *covet;* by implication to *be angry;* also to *hasten:*— desire, desire earnestly, devour, haste, pant, snuff up, swallow up.

H7603 שְׂאֹר *śĕʾōr* from H7604; *barm* or yeast-cake (as *swelling* by fermentation):— leaven.

H7604 שָׁאַר *šāʾar* a primitive root; properly to *swell* up, i.e. *be* (causatively *make*) *redundant:*— leave, left, be left, let, remain, remnant, reserve, the rest.

H7605 שְׁאָר *šĕʾār* from H7604; a *remainder:*— other, remnant, residue, rest.

H7606 שְׁאָר *šĕʾār* (Aramaic) corresponding to H7605:— whatsoever more, residue, rest.

H7607 שְׁאֵר *šĕʾēr* from H7604; *flesh* (as *swelling* out), as living or for food; generally *food* of any kind; figuratively *kindred* by blood:— body, flesh, food, kin, near kin, kinsman, near kinsman, kinswoman, near of kin, nigh of kin.

H7608 שַׁאֲרָה *šaʾărâ* feminine of H7607; female *kindred* by blood:— near kinswomen.

H7609 שֶׁאֱרָה *šeʾĕrâ* the same as H7608; *Sheërah,* an Israelitess:— Sherah.

H7610 שְׁאָר יָשׁוּב *šĕʾār yāšûb* from H7605 and H7725; a *remnant will return; Sheär-Jashub,* the symbolic name of one of Isaiah's sons:— Shear-jashub.

H7611 שְׁאֵרִית *šĕʾērît* from H7604; a *remainder* or residual (surviving, final) portion:— that had escaped, be left, posterity, remain, remainder, remnant, residue, rest.

H7612 שֵׁאת *šēʾt* from H7582; *devastation:*— desolation.

H7613 שְׂאֵת *śĕʾēt* from H5375; an *elevation* or leprous scab; figuratively *elation* or cheerfulness; *exaltation* in rank or character:— be accepted, dignity, excellency, highness, raise up self, rising.

H7614 שְׁבָא *šĕbāʾ* of foreign origin; *Sheba,* the name of three early progenitors of tribes and of an Ethiopian district:— Sheba, Sabeans.

H7615 שְׁבָאִי *šĕbāʾî* patronymic from H7614; a *Shebaïte* or descendant of Sheba:— Sabean.

H7616 שָׁבָב *šābāb* from an unused root meaning to *break* up; a *fragment,* i.e. *ruin:*— broken in pieces.

H7617 שָׁבָה *šābâ* a primitive root; to *transport* into captivity:— captive, bring away captive, carry captives, carry away captive, lead captive, lead away captive, take captive, drive away, take away.

H7618 שְׁבוּ *šĕbû* from an unused root (probably identical with that of H7617 through the idea of *subdivision* into flashes or streamers [compare H7632]) meaning to *flame;* a *gem* (from its sparkle), probably the *agate:*— agate.

H7619 שְׁבוּאֵל *šĕbûʾēl* or

שׁוּבָאֵל *šûbāʾēl* from H7617 (abbreviated) or H7725 and H410; *captive* (or *returned*) *of God; Shebuël* or *Shebaël,* the name of two Israelites:— Shebuel, Shubael.

H7620 שָׁבוּעַ *šābûaʿ* or

שָׁבֻעַ *šābūaʿ* also (feminine)

שְׁבֻעָה *šĕbūʿâ* properly passive participle of H7650 as a denominative of H7651; literally *sevened,* i.e. a *week* (specifically of years):— seven, week.

H7621 שְׁבוּעָה *šĕbûʿâ* feminine passive participle of H7650; properly something *sworn,* i.e. an *oath:*— curse, oath, sworn.

H7622 שְׁבוּת *šĕbût* or

שְׁבִית *šĕbît* from H7617; *exile;* concretely *prisoners;* figuratively a *former state* of prosperity:— *captive, captivity.*

H7623 שָׁבַח *šābaḥ* a primitive root; properly to address in a loud tone, i.e. (specifically) *loud;* figuratively to *pacify* (as if by words):— commend, glory, keep in, praise, still, triumph.

H7624 שְׁבַח *šĕbaḥ* (Aramaic) corresponding to H7623; to *adulate,* i.e. *adore:*— praise.

H7625 שְׁבַט *šĕbaṭ* (Aramaic) corresponding to H7626; a *clan:*— tribe.

H7626 שֵׁבֶט *šēbeṭ* from an unused root probably meaning to *branch* off; a *scion,* i.e. (literally) a *stick* (for punishing, writing, fighting, ruling, walking, etc.) or (figuratively) a *clan:*— correction, dart, rod, sceptre, staff, tribe.

H7627 שְׁבָט *šĕbāṭ* of foreign origin; *Shebat,* a Jewish month:— Sebat.

H7628 שְׁבִי *šĕbî* from H7618; *exiled; captured;* as noun, *exile* (abstractly or concretely and collectively); by extension *booty:*— captive, captivity, prisoners, take away, that was taken.

H7629 שֹׁבִי *šōbî* from H7617; *captor; Shobi,* an Ammonite:— Shobi.

H7630 שֹׁבַי *šōbay* for H7629; *Shobai,* an Israelite:— Shobai.

H7631 שְׁבִיב *šĕbîb* (Aramaic) corresponding to H7632 :— flame.

H7632 שָׁבִיב *šābîb* from the same as H7616; *flame* (as *split* into tongues):— spark.

H7633 שִׁבְיָה *šibyâ* feminine of H7628; *exile* (abstractly or concretely and collectively):— captives, captivity.

H7634 שָׁבְיָה *šobyâ* feminine of the same as H7629; *captivation; Shobjah,* and Israelite:— Shachia *[from the margin].*

H7635 שָׁבִיל *šābîl* from the same as H7640; a *track* or passage-way (as if *flowing* along):— path.

H7636 שָׁבִיס *šābîs* from an unused root meaning to *interweave;* a *netting* for the hair:— caul.

H7637 שְׁבִיעִי *šĕbîʿî* or

שְׁבִעִי *šĕbīʿî* ordinal from H7657; *seventh:*— seventh, seventh time.

H7638 שָׂבָךְ *śābāk* from an unused root meaning to *intwine;* a *netting* (ornament to the capital of a column):— net.

H7639 שְׂבָכָה *śĕbākâ* feminine of H7638; a *network,* i.e. (in hunting) a *snare,* (in architecture) a *ballustrade;* also a *reticulated* ornament to a pillar:— checker, lattice, network, snare, wreath, wreathenwork.

H7640 שֹׁבֶל *šebel* from an unused root meaning to *flow;* a lady's *train* (as *trailing* after her):— leg.

H7641 שִׁבֹּל *šibbōl* or (feminine)

שִׁבֹּלֶת *šibbōlet* from the same as H7640; a *stream* (as *flowing*); also an *ear* of grain (as *growing* out); by analogy a *branch:*— branch, channel, ear, ear of corn, flood, waterflood, Shibboleth. Compare H5451

H7642 שַׁבְלוּל *šablûl* from the same as H7640; a *snail* (as if *floating* in its own slime):— snail.

H7643 שְׂבָם *śĕbām* or (feminine)

שִׂבְמָה *śibmâ* probably from H1313; *spice; Sebam* or *Sibmah*, a place in Moab:— Shebam, Shibmah, Sibmah.

H7644 שֶׁבְנָא *šebnāʾ* or

שֶׁבְנָה *šebnâ* from an unused root meaning to *grow; growth; Shebna* or *Shebnah*, an Israelite:— Shebna, Shebnah.

H7645 שְׁבַנְיָה *šĕbanyâ* or

שְׁבַנְיָהוּ *šĕbanyāhû* from the same as H7644 and H3050; *Jah has grown* (i.e. *prospered*); *Shebanjah*, the name of three or four Israelites:— Shebaniah.

H7646 שָׂבַע *śābaᶜ* or

שָׂבֵעַ *śābēaᶜ* a primitive root; to *sate*, i.e. *fill* to satisfaction (literally or figuratively):— have enough, fill, fill full, fill self, fill with, be full, be full of, to the full, have plenty of, be satiate, satisfy, satisfy with, suffice, be weary of.

H7647 שָׂבָע *śābāᶜ* from H7646; *copiousness:*— abundance, plenteous, plenteousness, plenteously.

H7648 שֹׂבַע *śōbaᶜ* from H7646; *satisfaction* (of food or [figuratively] joy):— fill, full, fullness, satisfying, be satisfied.

H7649 שָׂבֵעַ *śābēaᶜ* from H7646; *satiated* (in a pleasant or disagreeable sense):— full, full of, satisfied, satisfied with.

H7650 שָׁבַע *šābaᶜ* a primitive root; properly to *be complete*, but used only as a denominative from H7651; to *seven* oneself, i.e. *swear* (as if by repeating a declaration seven times):— adjure, charge, charge by an oath, charge with an oath, feed to the full *[by mistake for H7646]*, take an oath, straitly, swear, cause to swear, make to swear.

H7651 שֶׁבַע *šebaᶜ* or (masculine)

שִׁבְעָה *šibᶜâ* from H7650; a primitive cardinal number; *seven* (as the sacred *full* one); also (adverbially) *seven times*; by implication a *week*; by extension an *indefinite* number:— seven, by sevens, sevenfold, +seventeen, seventeenth, seventh, seven times. Compare H7658

H7652 שֶׁבַע *šebaᶜ* the same as H7651; *seven; Sheba*, the name of a place in Palestine, and of two Israelites:— Sheba.

H7653 שִׂבְעָה *śibᶜâ* feminine of H7647; *satiety:*— fulness.

H7654 שָׂבְעָה *śobᶜâ* feminine of H7648; *satiety:*— enough, to have enough, till . . . be full, unsatiable, satisfy, sufficiently.

H7655 שִׁבְעָה *šibᶜâ* (Aramaic) corresponding to H7651:— seven, seven times.

H7656 שִׁבְעָה *šibᶜâ* masculine of H7651; *seven (-th); Shebah*, a well in Palestine:— Shebah.

H7657 שִׁבְעִים *šibᶜîm* multiple of H7651; *seventy* :— seventy, threescore and ten, threescore and fifteen, threescore and fourteen, threescore and seventeen, threescore and sixteen, threescore and thirteen, threescore and twelve.

H7658 שִׁבְעָנָה *šibᶜānâ* prolonged for the masculine of H7651; *seven:*— seven.

H7659 שִׁבְעָתַיִם *šibᶜātayim* dual (adverbial) of H7651; *seventimes:*— seven, sevenfold, seven times.

H7660 שָׁבַץ *šābaṣ* a primitive root; to *interweave* (colored) threads in squares; by implication *(of reticulation)* to *inchase* gems in gold:— embroider, set.

H7661 שָׁבָץ *šābāṣ* from H7660; *intanglement*, i.e. (figuratively) *perplexity:*— anguish.

H7662 שְׁבַק *šĕbaq* (Aramaic) corresponding to the root of H7733; to *quit*, i.e. allow to remain:— leave, let alone.

H7663 שָׂבַר *śābar* erroneously

שָׂבַר *śābar* (Neh. 2:13, 15), a primitive root; to *scrutinize;* by implication (of *watching*) to *expect* (with hope and patience):— hope, tarry, view, wait.

H7664 שֵׂבֶר *śēber* from H7663; *expectation:*— hope.

H7665 שָׁבַר *šābar* a primitive root; to *burst* (literally or figuratively):— break, break down, break off, break in pieces, break up, broken, brokenhearted, bring to the birth, crush, destroy, hurt, quench, quite, tear, view *[by mistake for H7663]*.

H7666 שָׁבַר *šābar* denominative from H7668; to *deal* in grain:— buy, sell.

H7667 שֶׁבֶר *šeber* or

שֵׁבֶר *šēber* from H7665; a *fracture*, figuratively *ruin;* specifically a *solution* (of a dream):— affliction, breach, breaking, brokenfooted, brokenhanded, bruise, crashing, destruction, hurt, interpretation, vexation.

H7668 שֶׁבֶר *šeber* the same as H7667; *grain* (as if *broken* into kernels):— corn, victuals.

H7669 שֶׁבֶר *šeber* the same as H7667; *Sheber*, an Israelite:— Sheber.

H7670 שִׁבְרוֹן *šibrôn* from H7665; *rupture*, i.e. a *pang;* figuratively *ruin:*— breaking, destruction.

H7671 שְׁבָרִים *šĕbārîm* plural of H7667; *ruins; Shebarim*, a place in Palestine:— Shebarim.

H7672 שְׁבַשׁ *šĕbaš* (Aramaic) corresponding to H7660; to *intangle*, i.e. *perplex:*— be astonished.

H7673 שָׁבַת *šābat* a primitive root; to *repose*, i.e. *desist* from exertion; used in many implied relations (causatively, figuratively or specifically):— cease, cause to cease, let cease, make to cease, celebrate, cause to fail, make to fail, keep, keep sabbath, suffer to be lacking, leave, put away, put down, rest, make to rest, rid, still, take away.

H7674 שֶׁבֶת *šebet* from H7673; *rest, interruption, cessation:*— cease, sit still, loss of time.

H7675 שֶׁבֶת *šebet* infinitive of H3427; properly *session;* but used also concretely an *abode* or *locality:*— place, seat. Compare H3429

H7676 שַׁבָּת *šabbāt* intensive from H7673; *intermission*, i.e. (specifically) the *Sabbath:*— sabbath, every sabbath.

H7677 שַׁבָּתוֹן *šabbātôn* from H7676; a *sabbatism* or special holiday:— rest, sabbath.

H7678 שַׁבְּתַי *šabbĕtay* from H7676; *restful; Shabbethai*, the name of three Israelites:— Shabbethai.

H7679 שָׂגָא *śāgāʾ* a primitive root; to *grow*, i.e. (causatively) to *enlarge*, (figuratively) *laud:*— increase, magnify.

H7680 שְׂגָא *śĕgāʾ* (Aramaic) corresponding to H7679; to *increase:*— grow, be multiplied.

H7681 שָׁגֶא *šāgeʾ* probably from H7686; *erring; Shagè*, an Israelite:— Shage.

H7682 שָׂגַב *śāgab* a primitive root; to *be* (causatively *make*) *lofty*, especially *inaccessible;* by implication *safe, strong;* used literally and figuratively:— defend, exalt, be excellent, high, be high, set on high, lofty, be safe, set up, set up on high, be too strong.

H7683 שָׁגַג *šāgag* a primitive root; to *stray*, i.e. (figuratively) *sin* (with more or less apology):— also for that, deceived, err, go astray, sin ignorantly.

H7684 שְׁגָגָה *šĕgāgâ* from H7683; a *mistake* or inadvertent *transgression:*— error, ignorance, at unawares, unwittingly.

H7685 שָׂגָה *śāgâ* a primitive root; to *enlarge* (especially upward, also figuratively):— grow, grow up, increase.

H7686 שָׁגָה *šāgâ* a primitive root; to *stray* (causatively *mislead*), usually (figuratively) to *mistake*, especially (morally) to *transgress;* by extension (through the idea of intoxication) to *reel*, (figuratively) *be enraptured:*— go astray, cause to go astray, deceive, err, be ravished, sin through ignorance, wander, let wander, make to wander.

H7687 שְׂגוּב *śĕgûb* from H7682; *aloft; Segub*, the name of two Israelites:— Segub.

H7688 שָׁגַח *šāgaḥ* a primitive root; to *peep*, i.e. *glance* sharply at:— look, look narrowly.

H7689 שַׂגִּיא *śaggîʾ* from H7679; (superlatively) *mighty:*— excellent, great.

H7690 שַׂגִּיא *śaggîʾ* (Aramaic) corresponding to H7689; *large* (in size, quantity or number, also adverbially):— exceeding, great, greatly, many, much, sore, very.

H7691 שְׁגִיאָה *šĕgîʾâ* from H7686; a moral *mistake* :— error.

H7692 שִׁגָּיוֹן *šiggāyôn* or

שִׁגָּיֹנָה *šiggāyōnâ* from H7686; properly *aberration*, i.e. (technically) a *dithyramb* or rambling poem:— Shiggaion, Shigionoth.

H7693 שָׁגַל *šāgal* a primitive root; to *copulate* with :— lie with, ravish.

H7694 שֵׁגָל *šēgāl* from H7693; a *queen* (from cohabitation):— queen.

H7695 שֵׁגָל *šēgāl* (Aramaic) corresponding to H7694; a (legitimate) *queen:*— wife.

H7696 שָׁגַע *šāgaᶜ* a primitive root; to *rave* through insanity:— mad, mad man, be mad, play the mad man.

H7697 שִׁגָּעוֹן *šiggāᶜôn* from H7696; *craziness:*— furiously, madness.

H7698 שֶׁגֶר *šeger* from an unused root probably meaning to *eject;* the *foetus* (as finally *expelled*):— that cometh of, increase.

H7699 שַׁד *šad* or

שֹׁד *šōd* probably from H7736 (in its original sense) contracted; the *breast* of a woman or animal (as *bulging*):— breast, pap, teat.

H7700 שֵׁד *šēd* from H7736; a *daemon* (as *malignant*):— devil.

H7701 שֹׁד *šōd* or

שׁוֹד *šôd* (Job 5:21), from H7736; *violence, ravage:*— desolation, destruction, oppression, robbery, spoil, spoiled, spoiler, spoiling, wasting.

H7702 שָׂדַד *śādad* a primitive root; to *abrade*, i.e. *harrow* a field:— break clods, harrow.

H7703 שָׁדַד *šādad* a primitive root; properly to *be burly*, i.e. (figuratively) *powerful* (passive *impregnable*); by implication to *ravage:*— dead, destroy, destroyer, oppress, robber, spoil, spoiler, utterly, waste, lay waste.

H7704 שָׂדֶה *śādeh* or

שָׂדַי *śāday* from an unused root meaning to *spread* out; a *field* (as *flat*):— country, field, ground, land, soil, wild.

H7705 שִׁדָּה *šiddâ* from H7703; a *wife* (as *mistress* of the house):— all sorts, musical instrument.

H7706 שַׁדַּי *šadday* from H7703; the *Almighty:*— Almighty.

H7707 שְׁדֵיאוּר *šĕdêʾûr* from the same as H7704 and H217; *spreader of light; Shedejur,* an Israelite:— Shedeur.

H7708 שִׂדִּים *śiddîm* plural from the same as H7704; *flats; Siddim,* a valley in Palestine:— Siddim.

H7709 שְׁדֵמָה *šĕdēmâ* apparently from H7704; a cultivated *field:*— blasted, field.

H7710 שָׁדַף *šādap* a primitive root; to *scorch:*— blast.

H7711 שְׁדֵפָה *šĕdēpâ* or

שִׁדָּפוֹן *šiddāpôn* from H7710; *blight:*— blasted, blasting.

H7712 שְׁדַר *šĕdar* (Aramaic) a primitive root; to *endeavor:*— labour.

H7713 שְׂדֵרָה *śĕdērâ* from an unused root meaning to *regulate;* a *row,* i.e. *rank* (of soldiers), *story* (of rooms):— board, range.

H7714 שַׁדְרַךְ *šadrak* probably of foreign origin; *Shadrak,* the Babylonian name of one of Daniel's companions:— Shadrach.

H7715 שַׁדְרַךְ *šadrak* (Aramaic) the same as H7714 :— Shadrach.

H7716 שֶׂה *śeh* or

שֵׂי *śê* probably from H7582 through the idea of *pushing* out to graze; a member of a flock, i.e. a *sheep* or *goat:*— cattle, lesser cattle, small cattle, ewe, goat, lamb, sheep. Compare H2089

H7717 שָׂהֵד *śāhēd* from an unused root meaning to *testify;* a *witness:*— record.

H7718 שֹׁהַם *šōham* from an unused root probably meaning to *blanch;* a gem, probably the *beryl* (from its *pale* green color):— onyx.

H7719 שֹׁהַם *šōham* the same as H7718; *Shoham,* an Israelite:— Shoham.

H7720 שַׂהֲרֹן *śahărōn* from the same as H5469; a round *pendant* for the neck:— ornament, round tire like the moon.

H7721 שׂוֹא *śôʾ* from an unused root (akin to H5375 and H7722) meaning to *rise;* a *rising:*— arise.

H7722 שׁוֹא *šôʾ* or (feminine)

שׁוֹאָה *šōʾâ* or

שֹׁאָה *šōʾâ* from an unused root meaning to *rush* over; a *tempest;* by implication *devastation:*— desolate, desolation, destroy, destruction, storm, wasteness.

H7723 שָׁוְא *šowʾ* or

שַׁו *šaw* from the same as H7722 in the sense of *desolating; evil* (as *destructive*), literally *(ruin)* or morally (especially *guile*); figuratively *idolatry* (as false, subjectively), *uselessness* (as deceptive, objectively; also adverbially in *vain*):— false, falsely, lie, lying, vain, vanity.

H7724 שְׁוָא *šĕwāʾ* from the same as H7723; *false; Sheva,* an Israelite:— Sheva.

H7725 שׁוּב *šûb* a primitive root; to *turn* back (hence, away) transitively or intransitively, literally or figuratively (not necessarily with the idea of *return* to the starting point); generally to *retreat;* often adverbially *again:*— again, break again, build again, circumcise again, dig again, do anything again, do evil again, feed again, lay down again, lie down again, lodge again, make again, rejoice again, send again, take again, weep again, answer, answer, cause to answer, answer again, in any case, in any wise, at all, averse, bring, bring again, bring back, bring home again, call to mind, carry again, carry back, cease, certainly, come again, come back, consider, continually, convert, deliver, deliver again, deny, draw back, fetch home again, fro, get oneself again, get oneself back again, give, give again, go again, go back, go home, go out, hinder, let, see more, needs, be past, pay, pervert, pull in again, put, put again, put up again, recall, recompense, recover, refresh, relieve, render, render again, requite, rescue, restore, retrieve, return, cause to return, make to return, reverse, reward, say nay, send back, set again, slide back, still, surely, take back, take off, turn, cause to turn, make to turn, turn again, turn self again, turn away, turn back, turn back again, turn backward, turn from, turn off, withdraw.

H7726 שׁוֹבָב *šôbāb* from H7725; *apostate,* i.e. idolatrous:— backsliding, frowardly, turn away *[from margin].*

H7727 שׁוֹבָב *šôbāb* the same as H7726; *rebellious; Shobab,* the name of two Israelites:— Shobabh.

H7728 שׁוֹבֵב *šôbēb* from H7725; *apostate,* i.e. heathenish or (actually) heathen:— backsliding.

H7729 שׁוּבָה *šûbâ* from H7725; a *return:*— returning.

H7730 שׂוֹבֶךְ *śôbek* for H5441; a *thicket,* i.e. interlaced branches:— thick boughs.

H7731 שׁוֹבָךְ *šôbāk* perhaps for H7730; *Shobak,* a Syrian:— Shobach.

H7732 שׁוֹבָל *šôbāl* from the same as H7640; *overflowing; Shobal,* the name of an Edomite and two Israelites:— Shobal.

H7733 שׁוֹבֵק *šôbēq* active participle from a primitive root meaning to *leave* (compare H7662); *forsaking; Shobek,* an Israelite:— Shobek.

H7734 שׂוּג *śûg* a primitive root; to *retreat:*— turn back.

H7735 שׂוּג *śûg* a primitive root; to *hedge* in:— make to grow.

H7736 שׁוּד *šûd* a primitive root; properly to *swell* up, i.e. figuratively (by implication of *insolence*) to *devastate:*— waste.

H7737 שָׁוָה *šāwâ* a primitive root; properly to *level,* i.e. *equalize;* figuratively to *resemble;* by implication to *adjust* (i.e. counterbalance, be suitable, compose, place, yield, etc.):— avail, behave, bring forth, compare, countervail, equal, be equal, make equal, lay, be like, make like, be alike, make plain, profit, reckon.

H7738 שָׁוָה *šāwâ* a primitive root; to *destroy:*— substance *[from the margin].*

H7739 שְׁוָה *šĕwâ* (Aramaic) corresponding to H7737; to *resemble:*— make like.

H7740 שָׁוֵה *šāwēh* from H7737; *plain; Shaveh,* a place in Palestine:— Shaveh.

H7741 שָׁוֵה קִרְיָתַיִם *šāwēh qiryātayim* from the same as H7740 and the dual of H7151; *plain of a double city; Shaveh-Kirjathajim,* a place east of the Jordan:— Shaveh Kiriathaim.

H7742 שׂוּחַ *śûaḥ* a primitive root; to *muse* pensively:— meditate.

H7743 שׁוּחַ *šûaḥ* a primitive root; to *sink,* literally or figuratively:— bow down, incline, humble.

H7744 שׁוּחַ *šûaḥ* from H7743; *dell; Shuăch,* a son of Abraham:— Shuah.

H7745 שׁוּחָה *šûḥâ* from H7743; a *chasm:*— ditch, pit.

H7746 שׁוּחָה *šûḥâ* the same as H7745; *Shuchah,* an Israelite:— Shuah.

H7747 שׁוּחִי *šûḥî* patronymic from H7744; a *Shuchite* or descendant of Shuach:— Shuhite.

H7748 שׁוּחָם *šûḥām* from H7743; *humbly; Shucham,* an Israelite:— Shuham.

H7749 שׁוּחָמִי *šûḥāmî* patronymic from H7748; a *Shuchamite* (collectively):— Shuhamites.

H7750 שׂוּט *śûṭ* or (by permutation)

סוּט *sûṭ* a primitive root; to *detrude,* i.e. (intransitively and figuratively) *become derelict* (wrongly practise; namely, idolatry):— turn aside to.

H7751 שׁוּט *šûṭ* a primitive root; properly to *push* forth; (but used only figuratively) to *lash,* i.e. (the sea with oars) to *row;* by implication to *travel:*— go, go about, go through, go to and fro, mariner, rower, run to and fro.

H7752 שׁוֹט *šôṭ* from H7751; a *lash* (literally or figuratively):— scourge, whip.

H7753 שׂוּךְ *śûk* a primitive root; to *entwine,* i.e. *shut* in (for formation, protection or restraint):— fence, make an hedge, hedge up.

H7754 שׂוֹךְ *śôk* or (feminine)

שׂוֹכָה *śôkâ* from H7753; a *branch* (as *interleaved*):— bough.

H7755 שׂוֹכֹה *śôkōh* or

שֹׂכֹה *śōkōh* or

שׂוֹכוֹ *śôkô* from H7753; *Sokoh* or *Soko,* the name of two places in Palestine:— Shocho, Shochoh, Sochoh, Soco, Socoh.

H7756 שׂוּכָתִי *śûkātî* probably patronymic from a name corresponding to H7754 (feminine); a *Sukathite* or descendant of an unknown Israelite named Sukah:— Suchathite.

H7757 שׁוּל *šûl* from an unused root meaning to *hang* down; a *skirt;* by implication a bottom *edge:*— hem, skirt, train.

H7758 שׁוֹלָל *šôlāl* or

שֵׁילָל *šēlāl* (Mic. 1:8), from H7997; *nude* (especially bare-foot); by implication *captive:*— spoiled, stripped.

H7759 שׁוּלַמִּית *šûlammît* from H7999; *peaceful* (with the article always prefixed, making it a pet name); the *Shulammith,* an epithet of Solomon's queen:— Shulamite.

H7760 שׂוּם *śûm* or

שִׂים *śîm* a primitive root; to *put* (used in a great variety of applications, literal, figurative, inferential and elliptical):— any wise, appoint, bring, call a name, care, cast in, change, charge, commit, consider, convey, determine, disguise, dispose, do, get, give, heap up, hold, impute, lay, lay down, lay up, leave, look, make, make out, mark, name, on, ordain, order, paint, place, preserve, purpose, put, put on, regard, rehearse, reward, set, cause to set, set on, set up, shew, stedfastly, take, tell, tread down, turn, overturn, wholly, work.

H7761 שׂוּם *śûm* (Aramaic) corresponding to H7760 :— command, give, lay, make, name, regard, set.

H7762 שׁוּם *šûm* from an unused root meaning to *exhale; garlic* (from its rank *odor*):— garlic.

H7763 שׁוֹמֵר *šômēr* or

שֹׁמֵר *šōmēr* active participle of H8104; *keeper; Shomer,* the name of two Israelites:— Shomer.

H7764 שׁוּנִי *šûnî* from an unused root meaning to *rest; quiet, Shuni,* an Israelite:— Shuni.

H7765 שׁוּנִי *šûnî* patronymic from H7764; a *Shunite* (collectively) or descendant of Shuni:— Shunites.

H7766 שׁוּנֵם *šûnēm* probably from the same as H7764; *quietly; Shunem,* a place in Palestine:— Shunem.

H7767 שׁוּנַמִּית *šûnammît* patrial from H7766; a *Shunammitess,* or female inhabitant of Shunem :— Shunamite.

H7768 שָׁוַע *šāwaᶜ* a primitive root; properly to *be free;* but used only causatively and reflexively to *halloo* (for help, i.e. *freedom* from some trouble):— cry, cry aloud, cry out, shout.

H7769 שׁוַע *šûaᶜ* from H7768; a *halloo:*— cry, riches.

H7770 שׁוּעַ *šûaᶜ* the same as H7769; *Shuä,* a Canaanite:— Shua, Shuah.

H7771 שׁוֹעַ *šôaᶜ* from H7768 in the original sense of *freedom;* a *noble,* i.e. *liberal, opulent;* also (as noun in the derived sense) a *halloo:*— bountiful, crying, rich.

H7772 שׁוֹעַ *šôaᶜ* the same as H7771; *rich; Shoä,* an Oriental people:— Shoa.

H7773 שֶׁוַע *šewaᶜ* from H7768; a *halloo:*— cry.

H7774 שׁוּעָא *šûᶜāᵓ* from H7768; *wealth; Shuä,* an Israelitess:— Shua.

H7775 שַׁוְעָה *šawᶜâ* feminine of H7773; a *hallooing:*— crying.

H7776 שׁוּעָל *šûᶜāl* or

שֻׁעָל *šūᶜāl* from the same as H8168; a *jackal* (as *burrower*):— fox.

H7777 שׁוּעָל *šûᶜāl* the same as H7776; *Shuäl,* the name of an Israelite and of a place in Palestine:— Shual.

H7778 שׁוֹעֵר *šôᶜēr* or

שֹׁעֵר *šōᶜēr* active participle of H8176 (as denominative from H8179); a *janitor:*— doorkeeper, porter.

H7779 שׁוּף *šûp* a primitive root; properly to *gape,* i.e. *snap* at; figuratively to *overwhelm:*— break, bruise, cover.

H7780 שׁוֹפָךְ *šôpāk* from H8210; *poured; Shophak,* a Syrian:— Shophach.

H7781 שׁוּפָמִי *šûpāmî* patronymic from H8197; a *Shuphamite* (collectively) or descendant of Shephupham:— Shuphamite.

H7782 שׁוֹפָר *šôpār* or

שֹׁפָר *šōpār* from H8231 in the original sense of *incising;* a *cornet* (as giving a *clear* sound) or curved horn:— cornet, trumpet.

H7783 שׁוּק *šûq* a primitive root; to *run* after or over, i.e. *overflow:*— overflow, water.

H7784 שׁוּק *šûq* from H7783; a *street* (as *run* over) :— street.

H7785 שׁוֹק *šôq* from H7783; the (lower) *leg* (as a *runner*):— hip, let, shoulder, thigh.

H7786 שׂוּר *śûr* a primitive root; properly to *vanquish;* by implication to *rule* (causatively *crown*):— make princes, have power, reign. See H5493

H7787 שׂוּר *śûr* a primitive root [rather identical with H7786 through the idea of *reducing* to pieces; compare H4883]; to *saw:*— cut.

H7788 שׁוּר *šûr* a primitive root; properly to *turn,* i.e. *travel* about (as a harlot or a merchant):— go, sing. See also H7891

H7789 שׁוּר *šûr* a primitive root [rather identical with H7788 through the idea of *going round* for inspection]; to *spy* out, i.e. (generally) *survey,* (for evil) *lurk for,* (for good) *care for:*— behold, lay wait, look, observe, perceive, regard, see.

H7790 שׁוּר *šûr* from H7889; a *foe* (as *lying in wait*) :— enemy.

H7791 שׁוּר *šûr* from H7788; a *wall* (as *going about*) :— wall.

H7792 שׁוּר *šûr* (Aramaic) corresponding to H7791 :— wall.

H7793 שׁוּר *šûr* the same as H7791; *Shur,* a region of the Desert:— Shur.

H7794 שׁוֹר *šôr* from H7788; a *bullock* (as a *traveller*):— bull, bullock, cow, ox, wall *[by mistake for H7791].*

H7795 שׂוֹרָה *śôrâ* from H7786 in the primitive sense of H5493; properly a *ring,* i.e. (by analogy) a *row* (adverbially):— principal.

H7796 שׂוֹרֵק *śôrēq* the same as H8321; a *vine; Sorek,* a valley in Palestine:— Sorek.

H7797 שׂוּשׂ *śûś* or

שִׂישׂ *śîś* a primitive root; to *be bright,* i.e. *cheerful:*— be glad, greatly, joy, make mirth, rejoice.

H7798 שַׁוְשָׁא *šawšāᵓ* from H7797; *joyful; Shavsha,* an Israelite:— Shavsha.

H7799 שׁוּשַׁן *šûšan* or

שׁוֹשָׁן *šôšān* or

שֹׁשָׁן *šōšān* and (feminine)

שׁוֹשַׁנָּה *šôšannâ* from H7797; a *lily* (from its *whiteness*), as a flower or architectural ornament; also a (straight) *trumpet* (from the *tubular* shape) :— lily, Shoshannim.

H7800 שׁוּשַׁן *šûšan* the same as H7799; *Shushan,* a place in Persia:— Shushan.

H7801 שׁוּשַׁנְכִי *šûšankî* (Aramaic) of foreign origin; a *Shushankite* (collectively) or inhabitant of some unknown place in Assyria:— Susanchites.

H7802 שׁוּשַׁן עֵדוּת *šûšan ᶜēdût* or (plural of former)

שׁוֹשַׁנִּים עֵדוּת *šôšannîm ᶜēdût* from H7799 and H5715; *lily* (or *trumpet*) *of assemblage; Shushan-Eduth* or *Shoshannim-Eduth,* the title of a popular song:— Shoshannim-Eduth, Shushan-eduth.

H7803 שׁוּתֶלַח *šûtelaḥ* probably from H7682 and the same as H8520; *crash of breakage; Shuthelach,* the name of two Israelites:— Shuthelah.

H7804 שְׁזַב *šězab* (Aramaic) corresponding to H5800; to *leave,* i.e. (causatively) *free:*— deliver.

H7805 שָׁזַף *šāzap* a primitive root; to *tan* (by sunburning); figuratively (as if by a piercing ray) to *scan:*— look up, see.

H7806 שָׁזַר *šāzar* a primitive root; to *twist* (a thread of straw):— twine.

H7807 שַׁח *šaḥ* from H7817; *sunk,* i.e. *downcast:*— humble.

H7808 שֵׂחַ *śēaḥ* for H7879; *communion,* i.e. (reflexively) *meditation:*— thought.

H7809 שָׁחַד *šāḥad* a primitive root; to *donate,* i.e. *bribe:*— hire, give a reward.

H7810 שַׁחַד *šaḥad* from H7809; a *donation* (venal or redemptive):— bribe, bribery, gift, present, reward.

H7811 שָׂחָה *śāḥâ* a primitive root; to *swim;* causatively to *inundate:*— swim, make to swim.

H7812 שָׁחָה *šāḥâ* a primitive root; to *depress,* i.e. *prostrate* (especially reflexively in homage to royalty or God):— bow, bow self, bow self down, bow down, crouch, fall down, fall flat, humbly beseech, do obeisance, make obeisance, do reverence, make to stoop, worship.

H7813 שָׂחוּ *śāḥû* from H7811; a *pond* (for *swimming*):— to swim in.

H7814 שְׂחוֹק *śěḥôq* or

שְׂחֹק *śěḥōq* from H7832; *laughter* (in merriment or defiance):— derision, laughter, laughed to scorn, laughing, mocked, sport.

H7815 שְׁחוֹר *šěḥôr* from H7835; *dinginess,* i.e. perhaps *soot:*— coal.

H7816 שְׁחוּת *šěḥût* from H7812; *pit:*— pit.

H7817 שָׁחַח *šāḥaḥ* a primitive root; to *sink* or *depress* (reflexively or causatively):— bend, bow, bow down, bring down, cast down, couch, humble self, be low, bring low, stoop.

H7818 שָׂחַט *śāḥaṭ* a primitive root; to *tread* out, i.e. *squeeze* (grapes):— press.

H7819 שָׁחַט *šāḥaṭ* a primitive root; to *slaughter* (in sacrifice or massacre):— kill, offer, shoot out, slay, slaughter.

H7820 שָׁחַט *šāḥaṭ* a primitive root [rather identical with H7819 through the idea of *striking];* to *hammer* out:— beat.

H7821 שְׁחִיטָה *šěḥîṭâ* from H7819; *slaughter:*— killing.

H7822 שְׁחִין *šěḥîn* from an unused root probably meaning to *burn; inflammation,* i.e. an *ulcer:*— boil, botch.

H7823 שָׁחִיס *šāḥîs* or

סָחִישׁ *sāḥîš* from an unused root apparently meaning to *sprout; after-growth:*— that which springeth of the same, which springeth of the same.

H7824 שָׁחִיף *šāḥîp* from the same as H7828; a *board* (as *chipped* thin):— cieled with.

H7825 שְׁחִית *šěḥît* from H7812; a *pit*-fall (literal or figurative):— destruction, pit.

H7826 שַׁחַל *šaḥal* from an unused root probably meaning to *roar;* a *lion* (from his characteristic *roar*):— lion, fierce lion.

H7827 שְׁחֵלֶת *šěḥelet* apparently from the same as H7826 through some obscure idea, perhaps that of *peeling* off by concussion of sound; a *scale* or shell, i.e. the aromatic *mussel:*— onycha.

H7828 שַׁחַף *šaḥap* from an unused root meaning to *peel,* i.e. *emaciate;* the *gull* (as *thin*):— cuckoo.

H7829 שַׁחֶפֶת *šaḥepet* from the same as H7828; *emaciation:*— consumption.

H7830 שַׁחַץ *šaḥaṣ* from an unused root apparently meaning to *strut; haughtiness* (as evinced by the attitude):— lion, pride.

H7831 שַׁחֲצוֹם *šaḥăṣôm* from the same as H7830; *proudly; Shachatsom,* a place in Palestine:— Shahazimah *[from the margin]*.

H7832 שָׂחַק *śāḥaq* a primitive root; to *laugh* (in pleasure or detraction); by implication to *play:*— deride, have in derision, laugh, make merry, mock, mocker, play, rejoice, scorn, laugh to scorn, be in sport, make sport.

H7833 שָׁחַק *šāḥaq* a primitive root; to *comminate* (by trituration or attrition):— beat, wear.

H7834 שַׁחַק *šaḥaq* from H7833; a *powder* (as *beaten* small); by analogy a thin *vapor;* by extension the *firmament:*— cloud, small dust, heaven, sky.

H7835 שָׁחַר *šāḥar* a primitive root [rather identical with H7836 through the idea of the *duskiness* of early dawn]; to be *dim* or dark (in color):— be black.

H7836 שָׁחַר *šāḥar* a primitive root; properly to *dawn,* i.e. (figuratively) *be* (up) *early* at any task (with the implication of earnestness); by extension to *search* for (with painstaking):— do something betimes, enquire early, rise betimes, seek betimes, seek early, seek, diligently, seek in the morning.

H7837 שַׁחַר *šaḥar* from H7836; *dawn* (literally, figuratively or adverbially):— day, dayspring, early, light, morning, whence riseth.

H7838 שָׁחֹר *šāḥōr* or

שָׁחוֹר *šāḥôr* from H7835; properly *dusky,* but also (absolutely) *jetty:*— black.

H7839 שַׁחֲרוּת *šaḥărût* from H7836; a *dawning,* i.e. (figuratively) *juvenescence:*— youth.

H7840 שְׁחַרְחֹרֶת *šĕḥarḥōret* from H7835; *swarthy* :— black.

H7841 שְׁחַרְיָה *šĕḥaryâ* from H7836 and H3050; *Jah has sought; Shecharjah,* an Israelite:— Sheariah.

H7842 שַׁחֲרַיִם *šaḥărayim* dual of H7837; *double dawn; Shacharajim,* an Israelite:— Shaharaim.

H7843 שָׁחַת *šāḥat* a primitive root; to *decay,* i.e. (causatively) *ruin* (literally or figuratively):— batter, cast off, corrupt, corrupter, corrupt thing, destroy, destroyer, destruction, lose, mar, perish, spill, spoiler, utterly, waste, waster.

H7844 שְׁחַת *šĕḥat* (Aramaic) corresponding to H7843 :— corrupt, fault.

H7845 שַׁחַת *šaḥat* from H7743; a *pit* (especially as a trap); figuratively *destruction:*— corruption, destruction, ditch, grave, pit.

H7846 שֵׂט *śēṭ* or

סֵט *sēṭ* from H7750; a *departure* from right, i.e. *sin:*— revolter, that turn aside.

H7847 שָׂטָה *śāṭâ* a primitive root; to *deviate* from duty:— decline, go aside, turn.

H7848 שִׁטָּה *šiṭṭâ* feminine of a derivative [only in the plural

שִׁטִּים *šiṭṭîm* meaning the *sticks* of wood] a derivative from the same as H7850; the *acacia* (from its *scourging* thorns):— shittah, shittim. See also H1029

H7849 שָׁטַח *šāṭaḥ* a primitive root; to *expand:*— all abroad, enlarge, spread, stretch out.

H7850 שֹׁטֵט *šōṭēṭ* active participle of an otherwise unused root meaning (properly) to *pierce;* but only as a denominative from H7752) to *flog;* a *goad:*— scourge.

H7851 שִׁטִּים *šiṭṭîm* the same as the plural of H7848; *acacia* trees; *Shittim,* a place east of the Jordan:— Shittim.

H7852 שָׂטַם *śāṭam* a primitive root; properly to *lurk* for, i.e. *persecute:*— hate, oppose self against.

H7853 שָׂטַן *śāṭan* a primitive root; to *attack,* (figuratively) *accuse:*— (be an) adversary, resist.

H7854 שָׂטָן *śāṭān* from H7853; an *opponent;* especially (with the article prefixed) *Satan,* the arch-enemy of good:— adversary, Satan, withstand.

H7855 שִׂטְנָה *śiṭṭĕnâ* from H7853; *opposition* (by letter):— accusation.

H7856 שִׂטְנָה *śiṭnâ* the same as H7855; *Sitnah,* the name of a well in Palestine:— Sitnah.

H7857 שָׁטַף *šāṭap* a primitive root; to *gush;* by implication to *inundate, cleanse;* by analogy to *gallop, conquer:*— drown, flow, overflow, overwhelm, rinse, run, rush, wash, wash away, throughly wash away.

H7858 שֶׁטֶף *šeṭep* or

שֵׁטֶף *šēṭep* from H7857; a *deluge* (literally or figuratively):— flood, outrageous, overflowing.

H7859 שְׁטַר *šĕṭar* (Aramaic) of uncertain derivation; a *side:*— side.

H7860 שֹׁטֵר *šōṭēr* active participle of an otherwise unused root probably meaning to *write;* properly a *scribe,* i.e. (by analogy or implication) an official *superintendent* or *magistrate:*— officer, overseer, ruler.

H7861 שִׁטְרַי *šiṭray* from the same as H7860; *magisterial; Shitrai,* an Israelite:— Shitrai.

H7862 שַׁי *šay* probably from H7737; a *gift* (as *available*):— present.

H7863 שִׂיא *śî᾽* from the same as H7721 by permutation; *elevation:*— excellency.

H7864 שְׁיָא *šĕyā᾽* for H7724; *Sheja,* an Israelite:— Sheva *[from the margin]*.

H7865 שִׂיאֹן *śî᾽ōn* from H7863; *peak; Sion,* the summit of Mount Hermon:— Sion.

H7866 שִׁיאוֹן *šî᾽ôn* from the same as H7722; *ruin; Shijon,* a place in Palestine:— Shihon.

H7867 שִׂיב *śîb* a primitive root; properly to *become aged,* i.e. (by implication) to *grow gray:*— grayheaded, be grayheaded.

H7868 שִׂיב *śîb* (Aramaic) corresponding to H7867 :— elder.

H7869 שֵׂיב *śîb* from H7867; old *age:*— age.

H7870 שִׁיבָה *šîbâ* by permutation from H7725; a *return* (of property):— captivity.

H7871 שִׁיבָה *šîbâ* from H3427; *residence:*— while . . . lay.

H7872 שֵׂיבָה *śêbâ* feminine of H7869; old *age:*— gray hairs, gray headed, gray head, hoar hairs, hoar head, be hoary, hoary head, old age.

H7873 שִׂיג *śîg* from H7734; a *withdrawal* (into a private place):— pursuing.

H7874 שִׂיד *śîd* a primitive root probably meaning to *boil* up (compare H7736); used only as denominative from H7875; to *plaster:*— plaister.

H7875 שִׂיד *śîd* from H7874; *lime* (as *boiling* when slacked):— lime, plaister.

H7876 שָׁיָה *šāyâ* a primitive root; to *keep* in memory:— be unmindful. [Render Deut 21:18, "A Rock bore thee, *thou must recollect;* and (yet) thou hast forgotten," etc.].

H7877 שִׁיזָא *šîzā᾽* of unknown derivation; *Shiza,* an Israelite:— Shiza.

H7878 שִׂיחַ *śîaḥ* a primitive root; to *ponder,* i.e. (by implication) *converse* (with oneself, and hence aloud) or (transitively) *utter:*— commune, complain, declare, meditate, muse, pray, speak, talk, talk with.

H7879 שִׂיחַ *śîaḥ* from H7878; a *contemplation;* by implication an *utterance:*— babbling, communication, complaint, meditation, prayer, talk.

H7880 שִׂיחַ *śîaḥ* from H7878; a *shoot* (as if *uttered* or put forth), i.e. (generally) *shrubbery:*— bush, plant, shrub.

H7881 שִׂיחָה *śîḥâ* feminine of H7879; *reflection;* by extension *devotion:*— meditation, prayer.

H7882 שִׁיחָה *šîḥâ* for H7745; a *pit-fall:*— pit.

H7883 שִׁיחוֹר *šîḥôr* or

שִׁחוֹר *šiḥôr* or

שִׁחֹר *šiḥōr* probably from H7835; *dark,* i.e. *turbid: Shichor,* a stream of Egypt:— Shihor, Sihor.

H7884 שִׁיחוֹר לִבְנָת *šîḥôr libnāt* from the same as H7883 and H3835; *darkish whiteness; Shichor-Libnath,* a stream of Palestine:— Shihor-libnath.

H7885 שַׁיִט *šayiṭ* from H7751; an *oar;* also (compare H7752) a *scourge* (figuratively):— oar, scourge.

H7886 שִׁילֹה *šîlōh* from H7951; *tranquil; Shiloh,* an epithet of the Messiah:— Shiloh.

H7887 שִׁילֹה *šîlōh* or

שִׁלֹה *šilōh* or

שִׁילוֹ *šîlô* or

שִׁלוֹ *šilô* from the same as H7886; *Shiloh,* a place in Palestine:— Shiloh.

H7888 שִׁילוֹנִי *šîlônî* or

שִׁילֹנִי *šîlōnî* or

שִׁלֹנִי *šilōnî* from H7887; a *Shilonite* or inhabitant of Shiloh:— Shilonite.

H7889 שִׁימוֹן *šîmôn* apparently for H3452; *desert; Shimon,* an Israelite:— Shimon.

H7890 שַׁיִן *šayin* from an unused root meaning to *urinate; urine:*— piss.

H7891 שִׁיר *šîr* or the original form

שׁוּר *šûr* (1 Sam. 18:6), a primitive root [rather identical with H7788 through the idea of *strolling* minstrelsy]; to *sing:*— behold *[by mistake for H7789]*, sing, singer, singing man, singing woman.

H7892 שִׁיר *šîr* or feminine

שִׁירָה *šîrâ* from H7891; a *song;* abstractly *singing:*— musical, musick, singer, singing, song.

H7893 שַׁיִשׁ *šayiš* from an unused root meaning to *bleach,* i.e. *whiten; white,* i.e. *marble:*— marble. See H8336

H7894 שִׁישָׁא *šîšā᾽* from the same as H7893; *whiteness; Shisha,* an Israelite:— Shisha.

H7895 שִׁישַׁק *šîšaq* or

שׁוּשַׁק *šûšaq* of Egyptian derivation; *Shishak,* an Egyptian king:— Shishak.

H7896 שִׁית *šît* to *place* (in a very wide application):— apply, appoint, array, bring, consider, lay, lay up, let alone, look, make, mark, put, put on, regard, set, shew, be stayed, take.

H7897 שִׁית *šît* from H7896; a *dress* (as *put* on):— attire.

H7898 שַׁיִת *šayit* from H7896; *scrub* or *trash,* i.e. wild *growth* of weeds or briers (as if *put* on the field):— thorns.

H7899 שֵׂךְ *śēk* from H5526 in the sense of H7753; a *brier* (as of a hedge):— prick.

H7900 שֹׂךְ *śōk* from H5526 in the sense of H7753; a *booth* (as *interlaced*):— tabernacle.

H7901 שָׁכַב *šākab* a primitive root; to *lie* down (for rest, sexual connection, decease or any other purpose):— at all, cast down, lay, overlay, lay down, lay self down, lie, make to lie down, lie down, lie down to sleep, lie still, lie with, lodge, ravish, take rest, sleep, stay.

H7902 שְׁכָבָה *šĕkābâ* from H7901; a *lying* down (of dew, or for the sexual act):— carnally, copulation, lay, seed.

H7903 שְׁכֹבֶת *šekōbet* from H7901; a (sexual) *lying* with:— lie.

H7904 שָׁכָה *šākâ* a primitive root; to *roam* (through lust):— in the morning *[by mistake for H7925].*

H7905 שֻׂכָּה *śukkâ* feminine of H7900 in the sense of H7899; a *dart* (as pointed like a *thorn*):— barbed iron.

H7906 שֵׂכוּ *śēkû* from an unused root apparently meaning to *surmount;* an *observatory* (with the article); *Seku,* a place in Palestine:— Sechu.

H7907 שֶׂכְוִי *śekwî* from the same as H7906; *observant,* i.e. (concretely) the *mind:*— heart.

H7908 שְׁכוֹל *šĕkôl* infinitive of H7921; *bereavement* :— loss of children, spoiling.

H7909 שַׁכּוּל *šakkûl* or

שַׁכֻּל *šakkūl* from H7921; *bereaved:*— barren, bereaved of children, bereaved of whelps, robbed of whelps.

H7910 שִׁכּוֹר *šikkôr* or

שִׁכֹּר *šikkōr* from H7937; *intoxicated,* as a state or a habit:— drunk, drunkard, drunken, drunken man.

H7911 שָׁכַח *šākaḥ* or

שָׁכֵחַ *šākēaḥ* a primitive root; to *mislay,* i.e. to *be oblivious* of, from want of memory or attention:— at all, forget, cause to forget.

H7912 שְׁכַח *šĕkaḥ* (Aramaic) corresponding to H7911 through the idea of disclosure of a *covered* or *forgotten* thing; to *discover* (literally or figuratively):— find.

H7913 שָׁכֵחַ *šākēaḥ* from H7911; *oblivious:*— forget.

H7914 שְׂכִיָּה *śĕkîyâ* feminine from the same as H7906; a *conspicuous* object:— picture.

H7915 שַׂכִּין *śakkîn* intensive perhaps from the same as H7906 in the sense of H7753; a *knife* (as *pointed* or edged):— knife.

H7916 שָׂכִיר *śākîr* from H7936; a man *at wages* by the day or year:— hired, hired man, hired servant, hireling.

H7917 שְׂכִירָה *śĕkîrâ* feminine of H7916; a *hiring* :— that is hired.

H7918 שָׁכַךְ *šākak* a primitive root; to *weave* (i.e. *lay*) a trap; figuratively (through the idea of *secreting*) to *allay* (passions; physically *abate* a flood):— appease, assuage, make to cease, pacify, set.

H7919 שָׂכַל *śākal* a primitive root; to *be* (causatively *make* or *act*) *circumspect* and hence *intelligent:*— consider, expert, instruct, prosper, prudent, deal prudently, skill, give skill, skillful, have good success, teach, understand, have understanding, make to understand, understanding, wisdom, wise, be wise, behave self wisely, consider wisely, make wise, wisely, guide wittingly.

H7920 שְׂכַל *śĕkal* (Aramaic) corresponding to H7919 :— consider.

H7921 שָׁכֹל *šākōl* a primitive root; properly to *miscarry,* i.e. *suffer abortion;* by analogy to *bereave* (literally or figuratively):— bereave, bereave of children, barren, cast calf, cast fruit, cast young, be childless, make childless, deprive, destroy, expect, lose children, miscarry, rob of children, spoil.

H7922 שֶׂכֶל *śekel* or

שֵׂכֶל *śēkel* from H7919; *intelligence;* by implication *success:*— discretion, knowledge, policy, prudence, sense, understanding, wisdom, wise.

H7923 שִׁכֻּלִים *šikkūlîm* plural from H7921; *childlessness* (by continued bereavements):— to have after loss of others.

H7924 שׇׂכְלְתָנוּ *śoklĕtānû* (Aramaic) from H7920; *intelligence:*— understanding.

H7925 שָׁכַם *šākam* a primitive root; properly to *incline* (the shoulder to a burden); but used only as denominative from H7926; literally to *load up* (on the back of man or beast), i.e. to *start early* in the morning:— early, arise early, be up early, get up early, get oneself up early, rise up early, rise up betimes, morning.

H7926 שְׁכֶם *šĕkem* from H7925; the *neck* (between the shoulders) as the place of burdens; figuratively the *spur* of a hill:— back, consent, portion, shoulder.

H7927 שְׁכֶם *šĕkem* the same as H7926; *ridge; Shekem,* a place in Palestine:— Shechem.

H7928 שֶׁכֶם *šekem* for H7926; *Shekem,* the name of a Hivite and two Israelites:— Shechem.

H7929 שִׁכְמָה *šikmâ* feminine of H7926; the *shoulder*-bone:— shoulder blade.

H7930 שִׁכְמִי *šikmî* patronymic from H7928; a *Shikmite* (Collectively), or descendant of Shekem:— Shichemites.

H7931 שָׁכַן *šākan* a primitive root [apparently akin (by transmutation) to H7901 through the idea of *lodging;* compare H5531, H7925]; to *reside* or permanently stay (literally or figuratively):— abide, continue, dwell, cause to dwell, make to dwell, dweller, have habitation, inhabit, lay, place, remain, cause to remain, rest, set, set up.

H7932 שְׁכַן *šĕkan* (Aramaic) corresponding to H7931:— cause to dwell, have habitation.

H7933 שֶׁכֶן *šeken* from H7931; a *residence:*— habitation.

H7934 שָׁכֵן *šākēn* from H7931; a *resident;* by extension a fellow-*citizen:*— inhabitant, neighbour, nigh.

H7935 שְׁכַנְיָה *šĕkanyâ* or (prolonged)

שְׁכַנְיָהוּ *šĕkanyāhû* from H7931 and H3050; *Jah has dwelt; Shekanjah,* the name of nine Israelites:— Shecaniah, Shechaniah.

H7936 שָׂכַר *śākar* or (by permutation)

סָכַר *sākar* (Ezra 4:5), a primitive root [apparently akin (by prosthesis) to H3739 through the idea of temporary *purchase;* compare H7937]; to *hire:*— earn wages, hire, hire out self, reward, surely.

H7937 שָׁכַר *šākar* a primitive root. [Superlative of H8248.]; to *become tipsy;* in a qualified sense, to *satiate* with a stimulating drink or (figuratively) influence:— be filled with drink, drink abundantly, drunk, be drunken, make drunk, make drunken, be merry.

H7938 שֶׂכֶר *śeker* from H7936; *wages:*— reward, sluices.

H7939 שָׂכָר *śākār* from H7936; *payment* of contract; concretely *salary, fare, maintenance;* by implication *compensation, benefit:*— hire, price, reward, rewarded, wages, worth.

H7940 שָׂכָר *śākār* the same as H7939; *recompense; Sakar,* the name of two Israelites:— Sacar.

H7941 שֵׁכָר *šēkār* from H7937; an *intoxicant,* i.e. intensely alcoholic *liquor:*— strong drink, drunkard, strong wine.

H7942 שִׁכְּרוֹן *šikkĕrôn* for H7943; *drunkenness; Shikkeron,* a place in Palestine:— Shicron.

H7943 שִׁכָּרוֹן *šikkārôn* from H7937; *intoxication* :— be drunken, drunkenness.

H7944 שַׁל *šal* from H7952 abbreviated; a *fault:*— error.

H7945 שֶׁל *šel* for the relative H834; used with preposition prefixed, and often followed by some pronoun affixed; on *account* of, *what*soever, *which*soever:— cause, sake.

H7946 שַׁלְאֲנָן *šalʾănān* for H7600; *tranquil:*— being at east.

H7947 שָׁלַב *šālab* a primitive root; to *space* off; intensively *(evenly)* to *make equidistant:*— equally distant, set in order.

H7948 שָׁלָב *šālāb* from H7947; a *spacer* or raised *interval,* i.e. the *stile* in a frame or panel:— ledge.

H7949 שָׁלַג *šālag* a primitive root; properly meaning to be *white;* used only as denominative from H7950; to be *snow-white* (with the linen clothing of the slain):— be as snow.

H7950 שֶׁלֶג *šeleg* from H7949; *snow* (probably from its *whiteness*):— snow, snowy.

H7951 שָׁלָה *šālâ* or

שָׁלַו *šālaw* (Job 3:26), a primitive root; to be *tranquil,* i.e. *secure* or *successful:*— be happy, prosper, be in safety.

H7952 שָׁלָה *šālâ* a primitive root [probably rather identical with H7953 through the idea of *educing];* to *mislead:*— deceive, be negligent.

H7953 שָׁלָה *šālâ* a primitive root [rather cognate (by contraction) to the base of H5394, H7997 and their congeners through the idea of *extracting];* to *draw* out or off, i.e. *remove* (the soul by death):— take away.

H7954 שְׁלָה *šĕlâ* (Aramaic) corresponding to H7951; to *be secure:*— at rest.

H7955 שָׁלָה *šālâ* (Aramaic) from a root corresponding to H7952; a *wrong:*— thing amiss.

H7956 שֵׁלָה *šēlâ* the same as H7596 (shortened); *request; Shelah,* the name of a postdiluvian patriarch and of an Israelite:— Shelah.

H7957 שַׁלְהֶבֶת *šalhebet* from the same as H3851 with sibilant prefixed; a *flare* of fire:— flame, flaming flame.

H7958 שְׂלָו *śĕlāw* or

שְׂלָיו *śĕlāyw* by orthographical variation from H7951 through the idea of *sluggishness;* the *quail* collectively (as *slow* in flight from its weight):— quails.

H7959 שֶׁלֶו *šelew* from H7951; *security:*— prosperity.

H7960 שָׁלוּ *šālû* or

שָׁלוּת *šālût* (Aramaic) from the same as H7955; a *fault:*— error, fail, thing amiss.

H7961 שָׁלֵו *šālēw* or

שָׁלֵיו *šālêw* feminine

שְׁלֵוָה *šĕlēwâ* from H7951; *tranquil;* (in a bad sense) *careless;* abstractly *security:*— at ease, being at ease, peaceable, prosper, in prosperity, quiet, quietness, wealthy.

H7962 שַׁלְוָה *šalwâ* from H7951; *security* (genuine or false):— abundance, peace, peacably, prosperity, quietness.

H7963 שְׁלֵוָה *šĕlēwâ* (Aramaic) correspondingly to H7962; *safety:*— tranquillity. See also H7961

H7964 שִׁלּוּחַ *šillûaḥ* or

שִׁלֻּחַ *šillūaḥ* from H7971; (only in plural) a *dismissal,* i.e. (of a wife) *divorce* (especially the document); also (of a daughter) *dower:*— presents, have sent back.

H7965 שָׁלוֹם *šālôm* or

שָׁלֹם *šālōm* from H7999; *safe;* i.e. (figuratively) *well, happy, friendly;* also (abstractly) *welfare,* i.e. health, prosperity, peace:— do, familiar, fare, favour, friend, great, health, good health, peace, perfect peace, such as be at peace, peaceable, peaceably, prosper, prosperity, prosperous, rest, safe, safety, salute, welfare, well, all is well, be well, wholly.

H7966 שִׁלּוּם *šillûm* or

שִׁלֻּם *šillūm* from H7999; a *requital,* i.e. (secure) *retribution,* (venal) a *fee:*— recompense, reward.

H7967 שַׁלּוּם *šallûm* or (shorter)

שַׁלֻּם *šallūm* the same as H7966; *Shallum,* the name of fourteen Israelites:— Shallum.

H7968 שַׁלּוּן *šallûn* probably for H7967; *Shallun,* an Israelite:— Shallum.

H7969 שָׁלוֹשׁ *šālôš* or

שָׁלֹשׁ *šālōš* masculine

שְׁלוֹשָׁה *šĕlôšâ* or

שְׁלֹשָׁה *šĕlōšâ* a primitive number; *three;* occasionally (ordinal) *third,* or (multiplied) *thrice:*— fork, oftentimes, third, thirteen, thirteenth, three, thrice. Compare H7991

H7970 שְׁלוֹשִׁים *šĕlôšîm* or

שְׁלֹשִׁים *šĕlōšîm* multiple of H7969; *thirty;* or (ordinal) *thirtieth:*— thirty, thirtieth. Compare H7991

H7971 שָׁלַח *šālaḥ* a primitive root; to *send* away, for, or out (in a great variety of applications):— any wise, appoint, bring, bring on the way, cast, cast away, cast out, conduct, earnestly, forsake, give, give up, grow long, lay, leave, let depart, let down, let go, let loose, push away, put, put away, put forth, put in, put out, reach forth, send, send away, send forth, send out, set, shoot, shoot forth, shoot out, sow, spread, stretch forth, stretch out.

H7972 שְׁלַח *šĕlaḥ* (Aramaic) corresponding to H7971 :— put, send.

H7973 שֶׁלַח *šelaḥ* from H7971; a *missile* of attack, i.e. *spear;* also (figuratively) a *shoot* of growth, i.e. *branch:*— dart, plant, put off, sword, weapon.

H7974 שֶׁלַח *šelaḥ* the same as H7973; *Shelach,* a postdiluvian patriarch:— Salah, Shelah. Compare H7975

H7975 שִׁלֹּחַ *šillōaḥ* or in imitation of H7974

שֶׁלַח *šelaḥ* (Neh. 3:15), from H7971; *rill; Shiloäch,* a fountain of Jerusalem:— Shiloah, Siloah.

H7976 שִׁלֻּחָה *šillūḥâ* feminine of H7964; a *shoot* :— branch.

H7977 שִׁלְחִי *šilḥî* from H7973; *missive,* i.e. *armed; Shilchi,* an Israelite:— Shilhi.

H7978 שִׁלְחִים *šilḥîm* plural of H7973; *javelins* or *sprouts; Shilchim,* a place in Palestine:— Shilhim.

H7979 שֻׁלְחָן *šulḥān* from H7971; a *table* (as *spread* out); by implication a *meal:*— table.

H7980 שָׁלַט *šālaṭ* a primitive root; to *dominate,* i.e. *govern;* by implication to *permit:*— rule, bear rule, have rule, have dominion, give power, have power.

H7981 שְׁלֵט *šĕlēṭ* (Aramaic) corresponding to H7980 :— have the mastery, have power, bear rule, be ruler, make ruler.

H7982 שֶׁלֶט *šeleṭ* from H7980; probably a *shield* (as *controlling,* i.e. protecting the person):— shield.

H7983 שִׁלְטוֹן *šilṭôn* from H7980; a *potentate:*— power.

H7984 שִׁלְטוֹן *šilṭôn* (Aramaic) or

שִׁלְטֹן *šilṭōn* corresponding to H7983:— ruler.

H7985 שָׁלְטָן *šolṭān* (Aramaic) from H7981; *empire* (abstractly or concretely):— dominion.

H7986 שַׁלֶּטֶת *šalleṭet* feminine from H7980; a *vixen* :— imperious.

H7987 שְׁלִי *šĕlî* from H7951; *privacy:*— quietly.

H7988 שִׁלְיָה *šilyâ* feminine from H7953; a *foetus* or *babe* (as *extruded* in birth):— young one.

H7989 שַׁלִּיט *šallîṭ* from H7980; *potent;* concretely a *prince* or *warrior:*— governor, mighty, that hath power, ruler.

H7990 שַׁלִּיט *šallîṭ* (Aramaic) corresponding to H7989; *mighty;* abstractly *permission;* concretely a *premier:*— captain, be lawful, rule, ruler.

H7991 שָׁלִישׁ *šālîš* or

שָׁלוֹשׁ *šālôš* (1 Chron. 11:11; 12:18),

שָׁלשׁ *šālōš* (2 Sam. 23:13), from H7969; a *triple,* i.e. (as a musical instrument) a *triangle* (or perhaps rather *three*-stringed lute); also (as an indefinitely great quantity) a *three*-fold measure (perhaps a *treble* ephah); also (as an officer) a general of the *third* rank (upward, i.e. the highest):— captain, instrument of musick, lord, great lord, measure, great measure, prince, three *[from the margin].*

H7992 שְׁלִישִׁי *šĕlîšî* ordinal from H7969; *third;* feminine a *third* (part); by extension a *third* (day, year or time); specifically a *third*-story cell):— third, third part, third rank, third time, three, three years old.

H7993 שָׁלַךְ *šālak* a primitive root; to *throw* out, down or away (literally or figuratively):— adventure, cast, cast away, cast down, cast forth, cast off, cast out, hurl, pluck, throw.

H7994 שָׁלָךְ *šālāk* from H7993; *bird of prey,* usually thought to be the *pelican* (from *casting* itself into the sea):— cormorant.

H7995 שַׁלֶּכֶת *šalleket* from H7993; a *felling* (of trees) :— when cast.

H7996 שַׁלֶּכֶת *šalleket* the same as H7995; *Shalleketh,* a gate in Jerusalem:— Shalleketh.

H7997 שָׁלַל *šālal* a primitive root; to *drop* or *strip;* by implication to *plunder:*— let fall, make self a prey, of purpose, spoil, make a spoil, take spoil.

H7998 שָׁלָל *šālāl* from H7997; *booty:*— prey, spoil.

H7999 שָׁלַם *šālam* a primitive root; to *be safe* (in mind, body or estate); figuratively to *be* (causatively *make*) *completed;* by implication to *be friendly;* by extension to *reciprocate* (in various applications):— make amends, end, make an end, finish, full, give again, make good, pay, repay, pay again, make peace, make to be at peace, be at peace, peaceable, that is perfect, perform, prosper, make prosperous, recompense, render, requite, make restitution, restore, reward, surely.

H8000 שְׁלַם *šĕlam* (Aramaic) corresponding to H7999; to *complete,* to *restore:*— deliver, finish.

H8001 שְׁלָם *šĕlām* (Aramaic) corresponding to H7965; *prosperity:*— peace.

H8002 שֶׁלֶם *šelem* from H7999; properly *requital,* i.e. a (voluntary) sacrifice in *thanks:*— peace offering.

H8003 שָׁלֵם *šālēm* from H7999; *complete* (literally or figuratively); especially *friendly:*— full, just, made ready, peaceable, perfect, perfected, quiet, Shalem *[by mistake for a name],* whole.

H8004 שָׁלֵם *šālēm* the same as H8003; *peaceful; Shalem,* an early name of Jerusalem:— Salem.

H8005 שִׁלֵּם *šillēm* from H7999; *requital:*— recompense.

H8006 שִׁלֵּם *šillēm* the same as H8005; *Shillem,* an Israelite:— Shillem.

H8007 שַׂלְמָא *śalmāʾ* probably for H8008; *clothing; Salma,* the name of two Israelites:— Salma.

H8008 שַׂלְמָה *śalmâ* transposed for H8071; a *dress* :— clothes, garment, raiment.

H8009 שַׂלְמָה *śalmâ* the same as H8008; *clothing; Salmah,* an Israelite:— Salmon. Compare H8012

H8010 שְׁלֹמֹה *šĕlōmōh* from H7965; *peaceful; Shelomoh,* David's successor:— Solomon.

H8011 שִׁלֻּמָה *šillūmâ* feminine of H7966; *retribution:*— recompense.

H8012 שַׂלְמוֹן *śalmôn* from H8008; *investitute; Salmon,* an Israelite:— Salmon. Compare H8009

H8013 שְׁלֹמוֹת *šĕlōmôt* feminine plural of H7965; *pacifications; Shelomoth,* the name of two Israelites:— Shelomith *[from the margin],* Shelomoth. Compare H8019

H8014 שַׂלְמַי *śalmay* from H8008; *clothed; Salmai,* an Israelite:— Shalmai.

H8015 שְׁלֹמִי *šĕlōmî* from H7965; *peaceable; Shelomi,* an Israelite:— Shelomi.

H8016 שִׁלֵּמִי *šillēmî* patronymic from H8006; a *Shilemite* (collectively) or descendant of Shillem:— Shillemites.

H8017 שְׁלֻמִיאֵל *šělumîʾēl* from H7965 and H410; *peace of God; Shelumiël,* an Israelite:— Shelumiel.

H8018 שֶׁלֶמְיָה *šelemyâ* or

שֶׁלֶמְיָהוּ *šelemyāhû* from H8002 and H3050; *thank-offering of Jah; Shelemjah,* the name of nine Israelites:— Shelemiah.

H8019 שְׁלֹמִית *šělōmît* or

שְׁלוֹמִית *šělōmît* (Ezra 8:10), from H7965; *peaceableness; Shelomith,* the name of five Israelites and three Israelitesses:— Shelomith.

H8020 שַׁלְמַן *šalman* of foreign derivation; *Shalman,* a king apparently of Assyria:— Shalman. Compare H8022

H8021 שַׁלְמֹן *šalmōn* from H7999; a *bribe:*— reward.

H8022 שַׁלְמַנְאֶסֶר *šalmanʾeser* of foreign derivation; *Shalmaneser,* an Assyrian king:— Shalmaneser. Compare H8020

H8023 שִׁלֹנִי *šilōnî* the same as H7888; *Shiloni,* an Israelite:— Shiloni.

H8024 שֵׁלָנִי *šēlānî* from H7956; a *Shelanite* (collectively), or descendant of Shelah:— Shelanites.

H8025 שָׁלַף *šālap* a primitive root; to *pull* out, up or off:— draw, draw off, grow up, pluck off.

H8026 שֶׁלֶף *šelep* from H8025; *extract; Sheleph,* a son of Jokthan:— Sheleph.

H8027 שָׁלַשׁ *šālaš* a primitive root perhaps originally to *intensify,* i.e. *treble;* but apparently used only as denominative from H7969, to *be* (causatively *make*) *triplicate* (by restoration, in portions, strands, days or years):— do the third time, three, divide into three parts, stay three days, threefold, three years old.

H8028 שֶׁלֶשׁ *šeleš* from H8027; *triplet; Shelesh,* an Israelite:— Shelesh.

H8029 שִׁלֵּשׁ *šillēš* from H8027; a descendant of the *third* degree, i.e. *great grandchild:*— third generation.

H8030 שִׁלְשָׁה *šilšâ* feminine from the same as H8028; *triplication; Shilshah,* an Israelite:— Shilshah.

H8031 שָׁלִשָׁה *šālīšâ* feminine from H8027; *trebled* land; *Shalishah,* a place in Palestine:— Shalisha.

H8032 שִׁלְשׁוֹם *šilšôm* or

שִׁלְשֹׁם *šilšōm* from the same as H8028; *trebly,* i.e. (in time) *day before yesterday:*— before, before that time, beforetime, excellent things *[from the margin],* heretofore, three days, time past.

H8033 שָׁם *šām* a primitive particle [rather from the relative H834]; *there* (transferred to time) *then;* often *thither,* or *thence:*— in it, thence, there, therein, thereof, thereout, thither, whither.

H8034 שֵׁם *šēm* a primitive word [perhaps rather from H7760 through the idea of definite and conspicuous *position;* compare H8064]; an *appellation,* as a mark or memorial of individuality; by implication *honor, authority, character:*— base, fame, infamous, +famous, name, named, renown, report.

H8035 שֵׁם *šēm* the same as H8034; *name; Shem,* a son of Noah (often including his posterity):— Sem, Shem.

H8036 שֻׁם *šūm* (Aramaic) corresponding to H8034 :— name.

H8037 שַׁמָּא *šammāʾ* from H8074; *desolation; Shamma,* an Israelite:— Shamma.

H8038 שֶׁמְאֵבֶר *šemʾēber* apparently from H8034 and H83; *name of pinion,* i.e. *illustrious; Shemeber,* a king of Zeboim:— Shemeber.

H8039 שִׁמְאָה *šimʾâ* perhaps for H8093; *Shimah,* an Israelite:— Shimah. Compare H8043

H8040 שְׂמֹאול *śěmōʾwl* or

שְׂמֹאל *śěmōʾl* a primitive word [rather perhaps from the same as H8071 (by insertion of [HEB]a) through the idea of *wrapping* up]; properly *dark* (as *enveloped*), i.e. the *north;* hence (by orientation) the *left* hand:— left, left hand, left side.

H8041 שָׂמַאל *śāmaʾl* a primitive root [rather denominative from H8040]; to use the *left* hand or pass in that direction:— left, go to the left, turn to the left, on the left, to the left.

H8042 שְׂמָאלִי *śěmāʾlî* from H8040; situated on the *left* side:— left.

H8043 שִׁמְאָם *šimʾām* for H8039 [compare H38]; *Shimam,* an Israelite:— Shimeam.

H8044 שַׁמְגַּר *šamgar* of uncertain derivation; *Shamgar,* an Israelite judge:— Shamgar.

H8045 שָׁמַד *šāmad* a primitive root; to *desolate:*— destroy, destruction, bring to nought, overthrow, perish, pluck down, utterly.

H8046 שְׁמַד *šěmad* (Aramaic) corresponding to H8045:— consume.

H8047 שַׁמָּה *šammâ* from H8074; *ruin;* by implication *consternation:*— astonishment, desolate, desolation, waste, wonderful thing.

H8048 שַׁמָּה *šammâ* the same as H8047; *Shammah,* the name of an Edomite and four Israelites:— Shammah.

H8049 שַׁמְהוּת *šamhût* for H8048; *desolation; Shamhuth,* an Israelite:— Shamhuth.

H8050 שְׁמוּאֵל *šěmûʾēl* from the passive participle of H8085 and H410; *heard of God; Shemuël,* the name of three Israelites:— Samuel, Shemuel.

H8051 שַׁמּוּעַ *šammûaʿ* from H8074; *renowned; Shammua,* the name of four Israelites:— Shammua, Shammuah.

H8052 שְׁמוּעָה *šěmûʿâ* feminine passive participle of H8074; something *heard,* i.e. an *announcement* :— bruit, doctrine, fame, mentioned, news, report, rumor, tidings.

H8053 שָׁמוּר *šāmûr* passive participle of H8103; *observed; Shamur,* an Israelite:— Shamir *[from the margin].*

H8054 שַׁמּוֹת *šammôt* plural of H8047; *ruins; Shammoth,* an Israelite:— Shamoth.

H8055 שָׂמַח *śāmaḥ* a primitive root; probably to *brighten* up, i.e. (figuratively) *be* (causatively make) *blithe* or *gleesome:*— cheer up, be glad, make glad, joy, have joy, make joyful, be merry, make merry, rejoice, cause to rejoice, make to rejoice, very.

H8056 שָׂמֵחַ *śāmēaḥ* from H8055; *blithe* or *gleeful:*— glad, be glad, joyful, merry, making merry, merryhearted, merrily, rejoice, rejoicing.

H8057 שִׂמְחָה *śimḥâ* from H8056; *blithesomeness* or *glee,* (religious or festival):— exceeding, exceedingly, gladness, joy, joyfulness, mirth, pleasure, rejoice, rejoicing.

H8058 שָׁמַט *šāmaṭ* a primitive root; to *fling* down; incipiently to *jostle;* figuratively to *let alone, desist, remit:*— discontinue, overthrow, release, let rest, shake, stumble, throw down.

H8059 שְׁמִטָּה *šěmiṭṭâ* from H8058; *remission* (of debt) or *suspension* of labor):— release.

H8060 שַׁמַּי *šammay* from H8073; *destructive; Shammai,* the name of three Israelites:— Shammai.

H8061 שְׁמִידָע *šěmîdāʿ* apparently from H8034 and H3045; *name of knowing; Shemida,* an Israelite:— Shemida, Shemidah.

H8062 שְׁמִידָעִי *šěmîdāʿî* patronymic from H8061; a *Shemidaïte* (collectively) or descendant of Shemida:— Shemidaites.

H8063 שְׂמִיכָה *śěmîkâ* from H5564; a *rug* (as *sustaining* the Oriental sitter):— mantle.

H8064 שָׁמַיִם *šāmayim* dual of an unused singular

שָׁמֶה *šāmeh* from an unused root meaning to *be lofty;* the *sky* (as *aloft;* the dual perhaps alluding to the visible arch in which the clouds move, as well as to the higher ether where the celestial bodies revolve):— air, astrologer, heaven, heavens.

H8065 שָׁמַיִן *šāmayin* (Aramaic) corresponding to H8064:— heaven.

H8066 שְׁמִינִי *šěmînî* from H8083; *eight:*— eight.

H8067 שְׁמִינִית *šěmînît* feminine of H8066; probably an *eight*-stringed lyre:— Sheminith.

H8068 שָׁמִיר *šāmîr* from H8104 in the original sense of *pricking;* a *thorn;* also (from its *keenness* for scratching) a gem, probably the *diamond:*— adamant, adamant stone, brier, diamond.

H8069 שָׁמִיר *šāmîr* the same as H8068; *Shamir,* the name of two places in Palestine:— Shamir. Compare H8053

H8070 שְׁמִירָמוֹת *šěmîrāmôt* or

שְׁמָרִימוֹת *šěmārîmôt* probably from H8034 and plural of H7413; *name of heights; Shemiramoth,* the name of two Israelites:— Shemiramoth.

H8071 שִׂמְלָה *śimlâ* perhaps by permutation for the feminine of H5566 (through the idea of a *cover* assuming the shape of the object beneath); a *dress,* especially a *mantle:*— apparel, cloth, clothes, clothing, garment, raiment. Compare H8008

H8072 שַׂמְלָה *śamlâ* probably for the same as H8071; *Samlah,* an Edomite:— Samlah.

H8073 שַׁמְלַי *šamlay* for H8014; *Shamlai,* one of the Nethinim:— Shalmai *[from the margin].*

H8074 שָׁמֵם *šāmēm* a primitive root; to *stun* (or intransitively *grow numb*), i.e. *devastate* or (figuratively) *stupefy* (both usually in a passive sense):— make amazed, be astonied, be astonished, astonish, be an astonishment, desolate, be desolate, bring into desolation, bring unto desolation, lay desolate, lie desolate, make desolate, desolate places, be destitute, destroy, destroy self, waste, lay waste, lie waste, make waste, wonder.

H8075 שְׁמַם *šěmam* (Aramaic) corresponding to H8074:— be astonied.

H8076 שָׁמֵם *šāmēm* from H8074; *ruined:*— desolate.

H8077 שְׁמָמָה *šěmāmâ* or

שִׁמָמָה *šimāmâ* feminine of H8076; *devastation;* figuratively *astonishment:*— desolate, laid desolate, most desolate, desolation, waste.

H8078 שִׁמָּמוֹן *šimmāmôn* from H8074; *stupefaction* :— astonishment.

H8079 שְׂמָמִית *śĕmāmît* probably from H8074 (in the sense of *poisoning*); a *lizard* (from the superstition of its *noxiousness*):— spider.

H8080 שָׁמַן *šāman* a primitive root; to *shine*, i.e. (by analogy) *be* (causatively *make*) *oily* or *gross:*— become fat, make fat, wax fat.

H8081 שֶׁמֶן *šemen* from H8080; *grease*, especially liquid (as from the olive, often perfumed); figuratively *richness:*— anointing, fat, fat things, fruitful, oil, oiled, ointment, olive, pine.

H8082 שָׁמֵן *šāmēn* from H8080; *greasy*, i.e. *gross;* figuratively *rich:*— fat, lusty, plenteous.

H8083 שְׁמֹנֶה *šĕmōneh* or

שְׁמוֹנֶה *šĕmôneh* feminine

שְׁמֹנָה *šĕmūnâ* or

שְׁמוֹנָה *šĕmônâ* apparently from H8082 through the idea of *plumpness;* a cardinal number, *eight* (as if a *surplus* above the "perfect" seven); also (as ordinal) *eighth:*— eight, eighteen, eighteenth, eighth.

H8084 שְׁמֹנִים *šĕmōnîm* or

שְׁמוֹנִים *šĕmônîm* multiplied from H8083; *eighty;* also *eightieth:*— eighty, eightieth, fourscore.

H8085 שָׁמַע *šāmaᶜ* a primitive root; to *hear* intelligently (often with implication of attention, obedience, etc.; causatively to *tell*, etc.):— attentively, call together, gather together, carefully, certainly, consent, consider, be content, declare, diligently, discern, give ear, cause to hear, let hear, make to hear, hearken, hear tell, indeed, listen, make noise, make a noise, obient, be obedient, obey, perceive, proclaim, make a proclation, publish, regard, report, shew, shew forth, sound, make a sound, surely, tell, understand, whosoever heareth, witness.

H8086 שְׁמַע *šĕmaᶜ* (Aramaic) corresponding to H8085:— hear, obey.

H8087 שֶׁמַע *šemaᶜ* for the same as H8088; *Shema*, the name of a place in Palestine and of four Israelites:— Shema.

H8088 שֵׁמַע *šēmaᶜ* from H8085; something *heard*, i.e. a *sound, rumor, announcement;* abstractly *audience:*— bruit, fame, hear, hearing, loud, report, speech, tidings.

H8089 שֹׁמַע *šōmaᶜ* from H8085; a *report:*— fame.

H8090 שְׁמָע *šĕmāᶜ* for H8087; *Shema*, a place in Palestine:— Shema.

H8091 שָׁמָע *šāmāᶜ* from H8085; *obedient; Shama*, an Israelite:— Shama.

H8092 שִׁמְעָא *šimᶜāʾ* for H8093; *Shima*, the name of four Israelites:— Shimea, Shimei, Shamma.

H8093 שִׁמְעָה *šimᶜâ* feminine of H8088; *annunciation; Shimah*, an Israelite:— Shimeah.

H8094 שְׁמָעָה *šĕmāᶜâ* for H8093; *Shemaah*, an Israelite:— Shemaah.

H8095 שִׁמְעוֹן *šimᶜôn* from H8085; *hearing; Shimon*, one of Jacob's sons, also the tribe descendant from him:— Simeon.

H8096 שִׁמְעִי *šimᶜî* from H8088; *famous; Shimi*, the name of twenty Israelites:— Shimeah *[from the margin]*, Shimei, Shimhi, Shimi.

H8097 שִׁמְעִי *šimᶜî* patronymic from H8096; a *Shimite* (collectively) or descendant of Shimi:— of Shimi, Shimites.

H8098 שְׁמַעְיָה *šĕmaᶜyâ* or

שְׁמַעְיָהוּ *šĕmaᶜyāhû* from H8085 and H3050; *Jah has heard; Shemajah*, the name of twenty-five Israelites:— Shemaiah.

H8099 שִׁמְעֹנִי *šimᶜōnî* patronymic from H8095; a *Shimonite* (collectively) or descendant of Shimon:— tribe of Simeon, Simeonites.

H8100 שִׁמְעָת *šimᶜat* feminine of H8088; *annunciation; Shimath*, an Ammonitess:— Shimath.

H8101 שִׁמְעָתִי *šimᶜātî* patronymic from H8093; a *Shimathite* (collectively) or descendant of Shimah :— Shimeathites.

H8102 שֶׁמֶץ *šemeṣ* from an unused root meaning to *emit* a sound; an *inkling:*— a little.

H8103 שִׁמְצָה *šimṣâ* feminine of H8102; scornful *whispering* (of hostile spectators):— shame.

H8104 שָׁמַר *šāmar* a primitive root; properly to *hedge* about (as with thorns), i.e. *guard;* generally to *protect, attend to*, etc:— beware, be circumspect, take heed, take heed to self, keep, keeper, keep self, mark, look narrowly, observe, preserve, regard, reserve, save, save self, sure, wait, wait for, that lay wait, watch, watchman.

H8105 שֶׁמֶר *šemer* from H8104; something *preserved*, i.e. the *settlings* (plural only) of wine:— dregs, lees, wines on the lees.

H8106 שֶׁמֶר *šemer* the same as H8105; *Shemer*, the name of three Israelites:— Shamer, Shemer.

H8107 שִׁמֻּר *šimmūr* from H8104; an *observance:*— be observed, be much observed.

H8108 שָׁמְרָה *šomrâ* feminine of an unused noun from H8104 meaning a *guard; watchfulness:*— watch.

H8109 שְׁמֻרָה *šĕmūrâ* feminine of passive participle of H8104; something *guarded*, i.e. an *eye-lid:*— waking.

H8110 שִׁמְרוֹן *šimrôn* from H8105 in its original sense; *guardianship; Shimron*, the name of an Israelite and of a place in Palestine:— Shimron.

H8111 שֹׁמְרוֹן *šōmĕrôn* from the active participle of H8104; *watch-station; Shomeron*, a place in Palestine:— Samaria.

H8112 שִׁמְרוֹן מְראוֹן *šimrôn mĕrʾôn* from H8110 and a derivation of H4754; *guard of lashing; Shimron-Meron*, a place in Palestine:— Shimon-meron.

H8113 שִׁמְרִי *šimrî* from H8105 in its original sense; *watchful; Shimri*, the name of four Israelites:— Shimri.

H8114 שְׁמַרְיָה *šĕmaryâ* or

שְׁמַרְיָהוּ *šĕmaryāhû* from H8104 and H3050; *Jah has guarded; Shemarjah*, the name of four Israelites:— Shamariah, Shemariah.

H8115 שָׁמְרַיִן *šomrayin* (Aramaic) corresponding to H8111; *Shomraïn*, a place in Palestine:— Samaria.

H8116 שִׁמְרִית *šimrît* feminine of H8113; *female guard; Shimrith*, a Moabitess:— Shimrith.

H8117 שִׁמְרֹנִי *šimrōnî* patronymic from H8110; a *Shimronite* (collectively) or descendant or Shimron:— Shimronites.

H8118 שֹׁמְרֹנִי *šōmĕrōnî* patrial from H8111; a *Shomeronite* (collectively) or inhabitant of Shomeron:— Samaritans.

H8119 שִׁמְרָת *šimrāt* from H8104; *guardianship; Shimrath*, an Israelite:— Shimrath.

H8120 שְׁמַשׁ *šĕmaš* (Aramaic) corresponding to the root of H8121 through the idea of *activity* implied in day-light; to *serve:*— minister.

H8121 שֶׁמֶשׁ *šemeš* from an unused root meaning to be *brilliant;* the *sun;* by implication the *east;* figuratively a *ray*, i.e. (architecturally) a notched *battlement:*— east side, eastward, sun, sun rising, west, westward, window. See also H1053

H8122 שֶׁמֶשׁ *šemeš* (Aramaic) corresponding to H8121; the *sun:*— sun.

H8123 שִׁמְשׁוֹן *šimšôn* from H8121; *sunlight; Shimshon*, an Israelite:— Samson.

H8124 שִׁמְשַׁי *šimšay* (Aramaic) from H8122; *sunny; Shimshai*, a Samaritan:— Shimshai.

H8125 שַׁמְשְׁרַי *šamšĕray* apparently for H8121; *sunlike; Shamsherai*, an Israelite:— Shamsherai.

H8126 שֻׁמָתִי *šumātî* patronymic from an unused name from H7762 probably meaning *garlic*-smell; a *Shumathite* (collectively) or descendant of Shumah:— Shumathites.

H8127 שֵׁן *šēn* from H8150; a *tooth* (as *sharp*); specifically (for H8143) *ivory;* figuratively a *cliff:*— crag, forefront, ivory, sharp, tooth.

H8128 שֵׁן *šēn* (Aramaic) corresponding to H8127; a *tooth:*— tooth.

H8129 שֵׁן *šēn* the same as H8127; *crag; Shen*, a place in Palestine:— Shen.

H8130 שָׂנֵא *śānēʾ* a primitive root; to *hate* (personally):— enemy, foe, hate, be hateful, hater, odious, utterly.

H8131 שְׂנֵא *śĕnēʾ* (Aramaic) corresponding to H8130 :— hate.

H8132 שָׁנָא *šānāʾ* a primitive root; to *alter:*— change.

H8133 שְׁנָא *šĕnāʾ* (Aramaic) corresponding to H8132 :— alter, change, diverse, be diverse.

H8134 שִׁנְאָב *šinʾāb* probably from H8132 and H1; a *father has turned; Shinab*, a Canaanite:— Shinab.

H8135 שִׂנְאָה *śinʾâ* from H8130; *hate:*— exceedingly, hate, hateful, hatred.

H8136 שִׁנְאָן *šinʾān* from H8132; *change*, i.e. *repetition:*— angels.

H8137 שֶׁנְאַצַּר *šenʾaṣṣar* apparently of Babylonian origin; *Shenatstsar*, an Israelite:— Senazar.

H8138 שָׁנָה *šānâ* a primitive root; to *fold*, i.e. *duplicate* (literally or figuratively); by implication to *transmute* (transitively or intransitively):— do again, speak again, strike again, alter, double, change, be given to change, disguise, diverse, be diverse, pervert, prefer, repeat, return, do the second time.

H8139 שְׁנָה *šĕnâ* (Aramaic) corresponding to H8142 :— sleep.

H8140 שְׁנָה *šĕnâ* (Aramaic) corresponding to H8141 :— year.

H8141 שָׁנֶה *šāneh* (in plural only), or (feminine)

שָׁנָה *šānâ* from H8138; a *year* (as a *revolution* of time):— whole age, long, old, year, yearly.

H8142 שֵׁנָה *šēnâ* or

שֵׁנָא *šēnāʾ* (Ps. 127:2), from H3462; *sleep:*— sleep.

HEB

H8143 שֶׁנְהַבִּים *šenhabbîm* from H8127 and the plural apparently of a foreign word; probably *tooth of elephants,* i.e. *ivory tusk:*— ivory.

H8144 שָׁנִי *šānî* of uncertain derivation; *crimson,* properly the insect or its color, also stuff dyed with it:— crimson, scarlet, scarlet thread.

H8145 שֵׁנִי *šēnî* from H8138; properly *double,* i.e. *second;* also adverbially *again:*— again, either of them, other, another, second, second time.

H8146 שָׂנִיא *śānîʾ* from H8130; *hated:*— hated.

H8147 שְׁנַיִם *šĕnayim* or (feminine)

שְׁתַּיִם *šĕtayim* dual of H8145; also (as ordinal) *twofold:*— both, couple, double, second, twain, twelfth, twelve, twenty thousand, sixscore thousand, twice, two.

H8148 שְׁנִינָה *šĕnînâ* from H8150; something *pointed,* i.e. a *gibe:*— byword, taunt.

H8149 שְׁנִיר *šĕnîr* or

שְׂנִיר *śĕnîr* from an unused root meaning to *be pointed; peak; Shenir* or *Senir,* a summit of Lebanon:— Senir, Shenir.

H8150 שָׁנַן *šānan* a primitive root; to *point* (transitively or intransitively); intensively to *pierce;* figuratively to *inculcate:*— prick, sharp, sharpen, teach diligently, whet.

H8151 שָׁנַס *šānas* a primitive root; to *compress* (with a belt):— gird up.

H8152 שִׁנְעָר *šinʿār* probably of foreign derivation; *Shinar,* a plain in Babylonia:— Shinar.

H8153 שְׁנָת *šĕnāt* from H3462; *sleep:*— sleep.

H8154 שָׁסָה *šāsâ* or

שָׁשָׂה *šāśâ* (Isa. 10:13), a primitive root; to *plunder:*— destroyer, rob, spoil, spoiler.

H8155 שָׁסַס *šāsas* a primitive root; to *plunder:*— rifle, spoil.

H8156 שָׁסַע *šāsaʿ* a primitive root; to *split* or *tear;* figuratively to *upbraid:*— cleave, cloven, be clovenfooted, rend, stay.

H8157 שֶׁסַע *šesaʿ* from H8156; a *fissure:*— cleft, clovenfooted.

H8158 שָׁסַף *šāsap* a primitive root; to *cut* in pieces, i.e. slaughter:— hew in pieces.

H8159 שָׁעָה *šāʿâ* a primitive root; to *gaze* at or about (properly for help); by implication to *inspect, consider, compassionate, be non-plussed* (as looking around in amazement) or *bewildered:*— depart, be dim, be dismayed, look, look away, regard, have respect, spare, turn.

H8160 שָׁעָה *šāʿâ* (Aramaic) from a root corresponding to H8159; properly a *look,* i.e. a *moment:*— hour.

H8161 שַׁעֲטָה *šaʿăṭâ* feminine from an unused root meaning to *stamp;* a *clatter* (of hoofs):— stamping.

H8162 שַׁעַטְנֵז *šaʿaṭnēz* probably of foreign derivation; *linsey-woolsey,* i.e. cloth of linen and wool carded and spun together:— garment of divers sorts, linen and woollen.

H8163 שָׂעִיר *śāʿîr* or

שָׂעִר *śāʿir* from H8175; *shaggy;* as noun, a *he-goat;* by analogy a *faun:*— devil, goat, hairy, kid, rough, satyr.

H8164 שָׂעִיר *śāʿîr* formed the same as H8163; a *shower* (as *tempestuous*):— small rain.

H8165 שֵׂעִיר *śēʿîr* formed like H8163; *rough; Seïr,* a mountain of Idumaea and its aboriginal occupants, also one in Palestine:— Seir.

H8166 שְׂעִירָה *śĕʿîrâ* feminine of H8163; a *she-goat* :— kid.

H8167 שְׂעִירָה *śĕʿîrâ* formed as H8166; *roughness; Seïrah,* a place in Palestine:— Seirath.

H8168 שֹׁעַל *šōʿal* from an unused root meaning to *hollow* out; the *palm;* by extension a *handful:*— handful, hollow of the hand.

H8169 שַׁעַלְבִים *šaʿalbîm* or

שַׁעֲלַבִּין *šaʿălabbîn* plural from H7776; *foxholes; Shaalbim* or *Shaalabbin,* a place in Palestine:— Shaalabbin, Shaalbim.

H8170 שַׁעַלְבֹנִי *šaʿalbōnî* patrial from H8169; a *Shaalbonite* or inhabitant of Shaalbin:— Shaalbonite.

H8171 שַׁעֲלִים *šaʿălîm* plural of H7776; *foxes; Shaalim,* a place in Palestine:— Shalim.

H8172 שָׁעַן *šāʿan* a primitive root; to *support* one's self:— lean, lie, rely, rest, rest on, rest self, stay.

H8173 שָׁעַע *šāʿaʿ* a primitive root; (in a good acceptation) to *look* upon (with complacency), i.e. *fondle, please* or *amuse* (self); (in a bad one) to *look* about (in dismay), i.e. *stare:*— cry, cry out *[by confusion with H7768],* dandle, delight, delight self, play, shut.

H8174 שַׁעַף *šaʿap* from H5586; *fluctuation; Shaaph,* the name of two Israelites:— Shaaph.

H8175 שָׂעַר *śāʿar* a primitive root; to *storm;* by implication to *shiver,* i.e. *fear:*— be afraid, be horribly afraid, fear, hurl as a storm, be tempestuous, come like a whirlwind, take away as with a whirlwind.

H8176 שָׁעַר *šāʿar* a primitive root; to *split* or *open,* i.e. (literally, but only as denominative from H8179) to *act as gate-keeper* (see H7778); (figuratively) to *estimate:*— think.

H8177 שְׂעַר *śĕʿar* (Aramaic) corresponding to H8181; *hair:*— hair.

H8178 שַׂעַר *śaʿar* from H8175; a *tempest;* also a *terror:*— affrighted, horribly, sore, storm. See H8181

H8179 שַׁעַר *šaʿar* from H8176 in its original sense; an *opening,* i.e. *door* or *gate:*— city, door, gate, port, porter.

H8180 שַׁעַר *šaʿar* from H8176; a *measure* (as a *section*):— hundredfold.

H8181 שֵׂעָר *śēʿār* or

שַׂעַר *śaʿar* (Isa. 7:20), from H8175 in the sense of *dishevelling; hair* (as if *tossed* or *bristling*):— hair, hairy, rough.

H8182 שֹׁעָר *šōʿār* from H8176; *harsh* or *horrid,* i.e. *offensive:*— vile.

H8183 שְׂעָרָה *śĕʿārâ* feminine of H8178; a *hurricane:*— storm, tempest.

H8184 שְׂעֹרָה *śĕʿōrâ* or

שְׂעוֹרָה *śĕʿôrâ* (feminine, meaning the *plant*); and (masculine, meaning the *grain*); also

שְׂעֹר *śĕʿōr* or

שְׂעוֹר *śĕʿôr* from H8175 in the sense of *roughness; barley* (as *villose*):— barley.

H8185 שַׂעֲרָה *śaʿărâ* feminine of H8181; *hairiness* :— hair.

H8186 שַׁעֲרוּרָה *šaʿărûrâ* or

שַׁעֲרִירִיָּה *šaʿărîrîyâ* or

שַׁעֲרֻרִת *šaʿărūrīt* feminine from H8176 in the sense of H8175; something *fearful:*— horrible thing.

H8187 שְׁעַרְיָה *šĕʿaryâ* from H8176 and H3050; *Jah has stormed; Sheärjah,* an Israelite:— Sheariah.

H8188 שְׂעֹרִים *śĕʿōrîm* masculine plural of H8184; *barley* grains; *Seörim,* an Israelite:— Seorim.

H8189 שַׁעֲרַיִם *šaʿărayim* dual of H8179; *double gates; Shaarajim,* a place in Palestine:— Shaaraim.

H8190 שַׁעַשְׁגַז *šaʿašgaz* of Persian derivation; *Shaashgaz,* a eunuch of Xerxes:— Shaashgaz.

H8191 שַׁעְשֻׁעַ *šaʿšūaʿ* from H8173; *enjoyment:*— delight, pleasure.

H8192 שָׁפָה *šāpâ* a primitive root; to *abrade,* i.e. *bare:*— high, stick out.

H8193 שָׂפָה *śāpâ* or (in dual and plural)

שֶׂפֶת *śepet* probably from H5595 or H8192 through the idea of *termination* (compare H5490); the *lip* (as a natural boundary); by implication *language;* by analogy a *margin* (of a vessel, water, cloth, etc.):— band, bank, binding, border, brim, brink, edge, language, lip, prating, shore, seashore, side, speech, talk, vain words.

H8194 שָׁפָה *šāpâ* from H8192 in the sense of *clarifying;* a *cheese* (as *strained* from the whey):— cheese.

H8195 שְׁפוֹ *šĕpô* or

שְׁפִי *šĕpî* from H8192; *baldness* [compare H8205]; *Shepho* or *Shephi,* an Idumaean:— Shephi, Shepho.

H8196 שְׁפוֹט *šĕpôṭ* or

שְׁפוּט *šĕpûṭ* from H8199; a judicial *sentence,* i.e. *punishment:*— judgment.

H8197 שְׁפוּפָם *šĕpûpām* or

שְׁפוּפָן *šĕpûpān* from the same as H8207; *serpent-like; Shephupham* or *Shephuphan,* an Israelite:— Shephuphan, Shupham.

H8198 שִׁפְחָה *šiphâ* feminine from an unused root meaning to *spread* out (as a *family;* see H4940); a *female slave* (as a member of the *household*):— maid, bondmaid, handmaid, maiden, maidservant, wench, bondwoman, womanservant.

H8199 שָׁפַט *šāpaṭ* a primitive root; to *judge,* i.e. pronounce *sentence* (for or against); by implication to *vindicate* or *punish;* by extension to *govern;* passive to *litigate* (literally or figuratively):— avenge, that condemn, contend, defend, execute, execute judgment, judge, be a judge, judgement, needs, plead, reason, rule.

H8200 שְׁפַט *šĕpaṭ* (Aramaic) corresponding to H8199; to *judge:*— magistrate.

H8201 שֶׁפֶט *šepeṭ* from H8199; a *sentence,* i.e. *infliction:*— judgment.

H8202 שָׁפָט *šāpāṭ* from H8199; *judge; Shaphat,* the name of four Israelites:— Shaphat.

H8203 שְׁפַטְיָה *šĕpaṭyâ* or

שְׁפַטְיָהוּ *šĕpaṭyāhû* from H8199 and H3050; *Jah has judged; Shephatjah,* the name of ten Israelites:— Shephatiah.

H8204 שִׁפְטָן *šipṭān* from H8199; *judge-like; Shiphtan,* an Israelite:— Shiphtan.

H8205 שְׁפִי *šĕpî* from H8192; *bareness;* concretely a *bare* hill or plain:— high place, stick out.

H8206 שֻׁפִּים *šuppîm* plural of an unused noun from the same as H8207 and meaning the same; *serpents; Shuppim,* an Israelite:— Shuppim.

H8207 שְׁפִיפֹן *šĕpîpōn* from an unused root meaning the same as H7779; a kind of *serpent* (as *snapping*), probably the *cerastes* or horned adder:— adder.

H8208 שָׁפִיר *šāpîr* from H8231; *beautiful; Shaphir,* a place in Palestine:— Saphir.

H8209 שַׁפִּיר *šappîr* (Aramaic) intensive of a form corresponding to H8208; *beautiful:*— fair.

H8210 שָׁפַךְ *šāpak* a primitive root; to *spill* forth (blood, a libation, liquid metal; or even a solid, i.e. to *mound* up); also (figuratively) to *expend* (life, soul, complaint, money, etc.); intensively to *sprawl* out:— cast, cast up, gush out, pour, pour out, shed, shedder, shed out, slip.

H8211 שֶׁפֶךְ *šepek* from H8210; an *emptying* place, e.g. an ash-*heap:*— are poured out.

H8212 שָׁפְכָה *šopkâ* feminine of a derivative from H8210; a *pipe* (for *pouring* forth, e.g. wine), i.e. the *penis:*— privy member.

H8213 שָׁפֵל *šāpēl* a primitive root; to *depress* or *sink* (especially figuratively to *humiliate,* intransitively or transitively):— abase, bring down, cast down, put down, debase, humble, humble self, be low, bring low, lay low, make low, put lower.

H8214 שְׁפַל *šĕpal* (Aramaic) corresponding to H8213 :— abase, humble, put down, subdue.

H8215 שְׁפַל *šĕpal* (Aramaic) from H8214; *low:*— basest.

H8216 שֵׁפֶל *šēpel* from H8213; an *humble* rank:— low estate, low place.

H8217 שָׁפָל *šāpāl* from H8213; *depressed,* literally or figuratively:— base, basest, humble, low, lower, lowly.

H8218 שִׁפְלָה *šiplâ* feminine of H8216; *depression* :— low place.

H8219 שְׁפֵלָה *šĕpēlâ* from H8213; *Lowland,* i.e. (with the article) the maritime slope of Palestine:— low country, plain, low plain, vale, valley.

H8220 שִׁפְלוּת *šiplût* from H8213; *remissness:*— idleness.

H8221 שְׁפָם *šĕpām* probably from H8192; *bare* spot; *Shepham,* a place in or near Palestine:— Shepham.

H8222 שָׂפָם *śāpām* from H8193; the *beard* (as a *lip-piece*):— beard, lip, upper lip.

H8223 שָׁפָם *šāpām* formed like H8221; *baldly; Shapham,* an Israelite:— Shapham.

H8224 שִׂפְמוֹת *śipmôt* feminine plural of H8221; *Siphmoth,* a place in Palestine:— Siphmoth.

H8225 שִׁפְמִי *šipmî* patrial from H8221; a *Shiphmite* or inhabitant of Shepham:— Shiphmite.

H8226 שָׂפַן *śāpan* a primitive root; to *conceal* (as a valuable):— treasure.

H8227 שָׁפָן *šāpān* from H8226; a species of *rock-rabbit* (from its *hiding*), i.e. probably the *hyrax:*— coney.

H8228 שֶׁפַע *šepaᶜ* from an unused root meaning to *abound; resources:*— abundance.

H8229 שִׁפְעָה *šipᶜâ* feminine of H8228; *copiousness* :— abundance, company, multitude.

H8230 שִׁפְעִי *šipᶜî* from H8228; *copious; Shiphi,* an Israelite:— Shiphi.

H8231 שָׁפַר *šāpar* a primitive root; to *glisten,* i.e. (figuratively) *be* (causatively *make*) *fair:*— goodly.

H8232 שְׁפַר *šĕpar* (Aramaic) corresponding to H8231; to *be beautiful:*— be acceptable, please, think good.

H8233 שֶׁפֶר *šeper* from H8231; *beauty:*— goodly.

H8234 שֶׁפֶר *šeper* the same as H8233; *Shepher,* a place in the Desert:— Shapper.

H8235 שִׁפְרָה *šiprâ* from H8231; *brightness:*— garnish.

H8236 שִׁפְרָה *šiprâ* the same as H8235; *Shiphrah,* an Israelitess:— Shiphrah.

H8237 שַׁפְרוּר *šaprûr* from H8231; *splendid,* i.e. a *tapestry* or *canopy:*— royal pavilion.

H8238 שְׁפַרְפַּר *šĕparpar* (Aramaic) from H8231; the *dawn* (as *brilliant* with aurora):— very early in the morning.

H8239 שָׁפַת *šāpat* a primitive root; to *locate,* i.e. (generally) *hang* on or (figuratively) *establish, reduce:*— bring, ordain, set on.

H8240 שְׁפָת *šāpāt* from H8239; a (double) *stall* (for cattle); also a (two-pronged) *hook* (for flaying animals on):— hook, pot.

H8241 שֶׁצֶף *šeṣep* from H7857 (for alliteration with H7110); an *outburst* (of anger):— little.

H8242 שַׂק *śaq* from H8264; properly a *mesh* (as allowing a liquid to *run* through), i.e. coarse loose cloth or *sacking* (used in mourning and for bagging); hence a *bag* (for grain, etc.):— sack, sackcloth, sackclothes.

H8243 שָׁק *šāq* (Aramaic) corresponding to H7785; the *leg:*— leg.

H8244 שָׂקַד *śāqad* a primitive root; to *fasten:*— bind.

H8245 שָׁקַד *šāqad* a primitive root; to *be alert,* i.e. *sleepless;* hence to *be on the lookout* (whether for good or ill):— hasten, remain, wake, watch, watch for.

H8246 שָׁקַד *šāqad* a denominative from H8247; to *be* (intensively *make*) *almond-shaped:*— make like almonds, make like unto almonds, make after the fashion of almonds.

H8247 שָׁקֵד *šāqēd* from H8245; the *almond* (tree or nut; as being the *earliest* in bloom):— almond, almond tree.

H8248 שָׁקָה *šāqâ* a primitive root; to *quaff,* i.e. (causatively) to *irrigate* or *furnish a potion* to:— cause to drink, give drink, give to drink, let drink, make to drink, drown, moisten, water. See H7937, H8354

H8249 שִׁקֻּו *šiqqūw* from H8248; (plural collective) a *draught:*— drink.

H8250 שִׁקּוּי *šiqqûy* from H8248; a *beverage; moisture,* i.e. (figuratively) *refreshment:*— drink, marrow.

H8251 שִׁקּוּץ *šiqqûṣ* or

שִׁקֻּץ *šiqqūṣ* from H8262; *disgusting,* i.e. *filthy;* especially *idolatrous* or (concretely) an *idol:*— abominable filth, abominable idol, abomination, detestable, detestable thing.

H8252 שָׁקַט *šāqaṭ* a primitive root; to *repose* (usually figuratively):— appease, idleness, quiet, at quiet, be at quiet, be in quietness, give quiet, rest, be at rest, be in rest, give rest, have rest, take rest, settle, be still.

H8253 שֶׁקֶט *šeqeṭ* from H8252; *tranquillity:*— quietness.

H8254 שָׁקַל *šāqal* a primitive root; to *suspend* or *poise* (especially in trade):— pay, receive, receiver, spend, throughly, weigh.

H8255 שֶׁקֶל *šeqel* from H8254; probably a *weight;* used as a commercial standard:— shekel.

H8256 שָׁקָם *šāqām* or (feminine)

שִׁקְמָה *šiqmâ* of uncertain derivation; a *sycamore* (usually the tree):— sycamore, sycamore fruit, sycamore tree.

H8257 שָׁקַע *šāqaᶜ* (abbreviated, Amos 8:8), a primitive root; to *subside;* by implication to *be overflowed, cease;* causatively to *abate, subdue:*— make deep, let down, drown, quench, sink.

H8258 שְׁקַעֲרוּרָה *šĕqaᶜrûrâ* from H8257; a *depression:*— hollow strake.

H8259 שָׁקַף *šāqap* a primitive root; properly to *lean out* (of a window), i.e. (by implication) *peep* or *gaze* (passive *be a spectacle*):— appear, look, look down, look forth, look out.

H8260 שֶׁקֶף *šeqep* from H8259; a *loophole* (for *looking out*), to admit light and air:— window.

H8261 שָׁקֻף *šāqūp* passive participle of H8259; an *embrasure* or opening [compare H8260] with bevelled jam:— light, window.

H8262 שָׁקַץ *šāqaṣ* a primitive root; to *be filthy,* i.e. (intensively) to *loathe, pollute:*— abhor, make abominable, have in abominations, detest, utterly.

H8263 שֶׁקֶץ *šeqeṣ* from H8262; *filth,* i.e. (figuratively and specifically) an *idolatrous* object:— abominable, abomination.

H8264 שָׁקַק *šāqaq* a primitive root; to *course* (like a beast of prey); by implication to *seek* greedily:— have appetite, justle one against another, long, range, run, run to and fro.

H8265 שָׂקַר *śāqar* a primitive root; to *ogle,* i.e. *blink* coquettishly:— wanton.

H8266 שָׁקַר *šāqar* a primitive root; to *cheat,* i.e. *be untrue* (usually in words):— fail, deal falsely, lie.

H8267 שֶׁקֶר *šeqer* from H8266; an *untruth;* by implication a *sham* (often adverbially):— without a cause, deceit, deceitful, false, falsehood, falsely, feignedly, liar, lie, lying, vain, vain thing, wrongfully.

H8268 שֹׁקֶת *šōqet* from H8248; a *trough* (for *watering*):— trough.

H8269 שַׂר *śar* from H8323; a *head* person (of any rank or class):— captain, captain that had rule, chief, chief captain, general, governor, keeper, lord, master, taskmaster, prince, principal, ruler, steward.

H8270 שֹׁר *šōr* from H8324; a *string* (as *twisted* [compare H8306]), i.e. (specifically) the umbilical cord (also figuratively as the centre of strength):— navel.

H8271 שְׁרֵא *šĕrēʾ* (Aramaic) a root corresponding to that of H8293; to *free, separate;* figuratively to *unravel, commence;* by implication (of unloading beasts) to *reside:*— begin, dissolve, dwell, loose.

H8272 שַׁרְאֶצֶר *šarʾeṣer* of foreign derivation; *Sharetser,* the name of an Assyrian and an Israelite:— Sharezer.

H8273 שָׁרָב *šārāb* from an unused root meaning to *glare;* quivering *glow* (of the air), especially the *mirage:*— heat, parched ground.

H8274 שֵׁרֵבְיָה *šērēbĕyâ* from H8273 and H3050; *Jah has brought heat; Sherebjah,* the name of two Israelites:— Sherebiah.

H8275 שַׁרְבִּיט *šarbîṭ* for H7626; a *rod* of empire:— sceptre.

H8276 שָׂרַג *śārag* a primitive root; to *intwine:—* wrap together, wreath.

H8277 שָׂרַד *śārad* a primitive root; properly to *puncture* [compare H8279], i.e. (figuratively through the idea of *slipping* out) to *escape* or survive:— remain.

H8278 שְׂרָד *śĕrād* from H8277; *stitching* (as *pierced* with a needle):— service.

H8279 שֶׂרֶד *śered* from H8277; a (carpenter's) *scribing-awl* (for *pricking* or scratching measurements):— line.

H8280 שָׂרָה *śārâ* a primitive root; to *prevail:—* have power, have power as a prince.

H8281 שָׁרָה *šārâ* a primitive root; to *free:—* direct.

H8282 שָׂרָה *śārâ* feminine of H8269; a *mistress,* i.e. female noble:— lady, princess, queen.

H8283 שָׂרָה *śārâ* the same as H8282; *Sarah,* Abraham's wife:— Sarah.

H8284 שָׁרָה *šārâ* probably feminine of H7791; a *fortification* (literal or figurative):— sing *[by mistake for H7891]*, wall.

H8285 שֵׁרָה *šērâ* from H8324 in its original sense of *pressing;* a wrist-*band* (as *compact* or *clasping*):— bracelet.

H8286 שְׂרוּג *śĕrûg* from H8276; *tendril; Serug,* a postdiluvian patriarch:— Serug.

H8287 שָׁרוּחֶן *šārûḥen* probably from H8281 (in the sense of *dwelling* [compare H8271]) and H2580; *abode of pleasure; Sharuchen,* a place in Palestine:— Sharuhen.

H8288 שְׂרוֹךְ *śĕrôk* from H8308; a *thong* (as *laced* or *tied*):— latched, shoelatchet.

H8289 שָׁרוֹן *šārôn* probably abridged from H3474; *plain; Sharon,* the name of a place in Palestine:— Lasharon, Sharon.

H8290 שָׁרוֹנִי *šārônî* patrial from H8289; a *Sharonite* or inhabitant of Sharon:— Sharonite.

H8291 שָׂרוּק *śārûq* passive participle from the same as H8231; a *grapevine:—* principal plant. See H8320, H8321

H8292 שְׁרוּקָה *šĕrûqâ* or (by permutation)

שְׁרִיקָה *šĕrîqâ* feminine passive participle of H8319; a *whistling* (in scorn); by analogy a *piping:—* bleating, hissing.

H8293 שֵׁרוּת *šērût* from H8281 abbreviated; *freedom:—* remnant.

H8294 שֶׂרַח *śeraḥ* by permutation for H5629; *superfluity; Serach,* an Israelitess:— Sarah, Serah.

H8295 שָׂרַט *śāraṭ* a primitive root; to *gash:—* cut in pieces, make cuttings, pieces.

H8296 שֶׂרֶט *śereṭ* and

שָׂרֶטֶת *śāreṭet* from H8295; an *incision:—* cutting.

H8297 שָׂרַי *śāray* from H8269; *dominative; Sarai,* the wife of Abraham:— Sarai.

H8298 שָׁרַי *šāray* probably from H8324; *hostile; Sharay,* an Israelite:— Sharai.

H8299 שָׂרִיג *śārîg* from H8276; a *tendril* (as *intwining*):— branch.

H8300 שָׂרִיד *śārîd* from H8277; a *survivor:—* alive, left, remain, remaining, remnant, rest.

H8301 שָׂרִיד *śārîd* the same as H8300; *Sarid,* a place in Palestine:— Sarid.

H8302 שִׁרְיוֹן *širyôn* or

שִׁרְיֹן *širyōn* and

שִׁרְיָן *širyān* also (feminine)

שִׁרְיָה *širyâ* and

שִׁרְיֹנָה *širyōnâ* from H8281 in the original sense of *turning;* a *corslet* (as if *twisted*):— breastplate, coat of mail, habergeon, harness. See H5630

H8303 שִׂרְיוֹן *śiryôn* and

שִׂרְיֹן *śiryōn* the same as H8304 (i.e. *sheeted* with snow); *Shirjon* or *Sirjon,* a peak of the Lebanon:— Sirion.

H8304 שְׂרָיָה *śĕrāyâ* or

שְׂרָיָהוּ *śĕrāyāhû* from H8280 and H3050; *Jah has prevailed; Serajah,* the name of nine Israelites:— Seraiah.

H8305 שְׂרִיקָה *śĕrîqâ* from the same as H8321 in the original sense of *piercing; hetchelling* (or combing flax), i.e. (concretely) *tow* (by extension *linen* cloth):— fine.

H8306 שָׁרִיר *šārîr* from H8324 in the original sense as in H8270 (compare H8326); a *cord,* i.e. (by analogy) *sinew:—* navel.

H8307 שְׁרִירוּת *šĕrîrût* from H8324 in the sense of *twisted,* i.e. *firm; obstinacy:—* imagination, lust.

H8308 שָׂרַךְ *śārak* a primitive root; to *interlace:—* traverse.

H8309 שְׁרֵמָה *šĕrēmâ* probably by orthographical error for H7709; a *common:—* field.

H8310 שַׂרְסְכִים *śarsĕkîm* of foreign derivation; *Sarsekim,* a Babylonian general:— Sarsechim.

H8311 שָׂרַע *śāraᶜ* a primitive root; to *prolong,* i.e. (reflexively) *be deformed* by excess of members:— stretch out self, superfluous thing, have any superfluous thing.

H8312 שַׂרְעַף *śarᶜap* for H5587; *cogitation:—* thought.

H8313 שָׂרַף *śārap* a primitive root; to *be* (causatively *set*) *on fire:—* burn, cause to burn, make a burning, burn up, kindle, utterly.

H8314 שָׂרָף *śārāp* from H8313; *burning,* i.e. (figuratively) *poisonous* (serpent); specifically a *saraph* or symbolic creature (from their copper color):— fiery, fiery serpent, seraph.

H8315 שָׂרָף *śārāp* the same as H8314; *Saraph,* an Israelite:— Saraph.

H8316 שְׂרֵפָה *śĕrēpâ* from H8313; *cremation:—* burning.

H8317 שָׁרַץ *šāraṣ* a primitive root; to *wriggle,* i.e. (by implication) *swarm* or *abound:—* breed abundantly, bring forth abundantly, increase abundantly, bring forth in abundance, creep, move.

H8318 שֶׁרֶץ *šereṣ* from H8317; a *swarm,* i.e. active mass of minute animals:— creep, creeping thing, move, moving creature.

H8319 שָׁרַק *šāraq* a primitive root; properly to *be shrill,* i.e. to whistle or *hiss* (as a call or in scorn):— hiss.

H8320 שָׂרֻק *śārūq* from H8319; *bright red* (as *piercing* to the sight), i.e. *bay:—* speckled. See H8291

H8321 שֹׂרֵק *śōrēq* or

שׂוֹרֵק *śôrēq* and (feminine)

שֹׂרֵקָה *śōrēqâ* from H8319 in the sense of *redness* (compare H8320); a *vine* stock (properly one yielding *purple* grapes, the richest variety):— choice vine, choicest vine, noble wine. Compare H8291

H8322 שְׁרֵקָה *šĕrēqâ* from H8319; a *derision:—* hissing.

H8323 שָׂרַר *śārar* a primitive root; to *have* (transitively *exercise;* reflexively *get*) *dominion:—* altogether, make self a prince, rule, bear rule.

H8324 שָׁרַר *šārar* a primitive root; to *be hostile* (only active participle an *opponent*):— enemy.

H8325 שָׁרַר *šārar* from H8324; *hostile; Sharar,* an Israelite:— Sharar.

H8326 שֹׁרֶר *šōrer* from H8324 in the sense of *twisting* (compare H8270); the umbilical *cord,* i.e. (by extension) a *bodice:—* navel.

H8327 שָׁרַשׁ *šāraš* a primitive root; to *root,* i.e. strike into the soil, or (by implication) to pluck from it:— take root, cause to take root, root out.

H8328 שֶׁרֶשׁ *šereš* from H8327; a *root* (literal or figurative):— bottom, deep, heel, root.

H8329 שֶׁרֶשׁ *šereš* the same as H8328; *Sheresh,* an Israelite:— Sharesh.

H8330 שֹׁרֶשׁ *šōreš* (Aramaic) corresponding to H8328 :— root.

H8331 שַׁרְשָׁה *šaršâ* from H8327; a *chain* (as *rooted,* i.e. *linked*):— chain. Compare H8333

H8332 שְׁרֹשׁוּ *šĕrōšû* (Aramaic) from a root corresponding to H8327; *eradication,* i.e. (figuratively) *exile:—* banishment.

H8333 שַׁרְשְׁרָה *šaršĕrâ* from H8327 [compare H8331]; a *chain;* (architecturally) probably a *garland:—* chain.

H8334 שָׁרַת *šārat* a primitive root; to *attend* as a menial or worshipper; figuratively to *contribute* to:— minister, minister unto, serve, do service, servant, servitor, wait on.

H8335 שָׁרֵת *šārēt* infinitive of H8334; *service* (in the Temple):— minister, ministry.

H8336 שֵׁשׁ *šēš* or (for alliteration with H4897)

שְׁשִׁי *šĕšî* for H7893; *bleached* stuff, i.e. *white* linen or (by analogy) marble:— blue, fine linen, fine twined linen, marble, silk.

H8337 שֵׁשׁ *šēš* masculine

שִׁשָּׁה *šiššâ* a primitive number; *six* (as an overplus [see H7797] beyond five or the fingers of the hand); as ordinal *sixth:—* six, sixteen, sixteenth, sixth.

H8338 שָׁשָׁא *šāšāʾ* a primitive root; apparently to *annihilate:—* leave but the sixth part *[by confusion with H8341]*.

H8339 שֵׁשְׁבַּצַּר *šēšĕbaṣṣar* of foreign derivation; *Sheshbatstsar,* Zerubbabel's Persian name:— Sheshbazzar.

H8340 שֵׁשְׁבַּצַּר *šēšĕbaṣṣar* (Aramaic) corresponding to H8339:— Sheshbazzar.

H8341 שָׁשָׁה *šāšâ* a denominative from H8337; to *sixth* or divide into sixths:— give the sixth part.

H8342 שָׂשׂוֹן *śāśôn* or

שָׂשֹׂן *śāśōn* from H7797; *cheerfulness;* specifically *welcome:—* gladness, joy, mirth, rejoicing.

H8343 שָׁשַׁי *šāšay* perhaps from H8336; *whitish; Shashai,* an Israelite:— Shashai.

H8344 שֵׁשַׁי *šēšay* probably for H8343; *Sheshai,* a Canaanite:— Sheshai.

H8345 שִׁשִּׁי *šiššî* from H8337; *sixth,* ordinal or (feminine) fractional:— sixth, sixth part.

H8346 שִׁשִּׁים *šiššîm* multiple of H8337; *sixty:*— sixty, three score.

H8347 שֵׁשַׁךְ *šēšak* of foreign derivation; *Sheshak,* a symbolic name of Babylon:— Sheshach.

H8348 שֵׁשָׁן *šēšān* perhaps for H7799; *lily, Sheshan,* an Israelite:— Sheshan.

H8349 שָׁשַׁק *šāšaq* probably from the base of H7785; *pedestrian; Shashak,* an Israelite:— Shashak.

H8350 שָׁשַׁר *šāšar* perhaps from the base of H8324 in the sense of that of H8320; *red* ochre (from its *piercing* color):— vermillion.

H8351 שֵׁת *šēt* (Num 24:17) from H7582; *tumult* :— Sheth.

H8352 שֵׁת *šēt* from H7896; *put,* i.e. *substituted; Sheth,* third son of Adam:— Seth, Sheth.

H8353 שֵׁת *šēt* or

שֹׁת *šōt* (Aramaic) corresponding to H8337 :— six, sixth.

H8354 שָׁתָה *šātâ* a primitive root. [Properly intensive of H8248.]; to *imbibe* (literally or figuratively):— assuredly, banquet, certainly, drink, drinker, drinking, drunk, drunkard, surely.

H8355 שְׁתָה *šĕtâ* (Aramaic) corresponding to H8354 :— drink.

H8356 שָׁתָה *šātâ* from H7896; a *basis,* i.e. (figuratively) political or moral *support:*— foundation, purpose.

H8357 שֵׁתָה *šētâ* from H7896; the *seat* (of the person):— buttock.

H8358 שְׁתִי *šĕtî* from H8354; *intoxication:*— drunkenness.

H8359 שְׁתִי *šĕtî* from H7896; a *fixture,* i.e. the *warp* in weaving:— warp.

H8360 שְׁתִיָּה *šĕtîyâ* feminine of H8358; *potation:*— drinking.

H8361 שִׁתִּין *šittîn* (Aramaic) corresponding to H8346 [compare H8353]; *sixty:*— threescore.

H8362 שָׁתַל *šātal* a primitive root; to *transplant:*— plant.

H8363 שְׁתִל *šĕtil* from H8362; a *sprig* (as if *transplanted*), i.e. *sucker:*— plant.

H8364 שֻׁתַלְחִי *šutalḥî* patronymic from H7803; a *Shuthalchite* (collectively) or descendant of Shuthelach:— Shuthalhites.

H8365 שָׁתַם *šātam* a primitive root; to *unveil* (figuratively):— be open.

H8366 שָׁתַן *šātan* a primitive root; (causatively) to *make water,* i.e. *urinate:*— piss.

H8367 שָׁתַק *šātaq* a primitive root; to *subside:*— be calm, cease, be quiet.

H8368 שָׂתַר *śātar* a primitive root; to *break* out (as an eruption):— have in one's secret parts.

H8369 שֵׁתָר *šētār* of foreign derivation; *Shethar,* a Persian satrap:— Shethar.

H8370 שְׁתַר בּוֹזְנַי *šĕtar bôzĕnay* of foreign derivation; *Shethar-Bozenai,* a Persian officer:— Shethar-boznai.

H8371 שָׁתַת *šātat* a primitive root; to *place,* i.e. *array;* reflexively to *lie:*— be laid, set.

ת

H8372 תָּא *tāʾ* and (feminine)

תָּאָה *tāʾâ* (Ezek. 40:12), from (the base of) H8376); a *room* (as *circumscribed*):— chamber, little chamber.

H8373 תָּאַב *tāʾab* a primitive root; to *desire:*— long.

H8374 תָּאַב *tāʾab* a primitive root [probably rather identical with H8373 through the idea of *puffing* disdainfully at; compare H340]; to *loathe* (morally):— abhor.

H8375 תַּאֲבָה *taʾăbâ* from H8374 [compare H15]; *desire:*— longing.

H8376 תָּאָה *tāʾâ* a primitive root; to *mark* off, i.e. (intensively) *designate:*— point out.

H8377 תְּאוֹ *tĕʾô* and

תּוֹא *tôʾ* (the original form) from H8376; a *species of antelope* (probably from the white *stripe* on the cheek):— wild bull, wild ox.

H8378 תַּאֲוָה *taʾăwâ* from H183 (abbreviated); a *longing;* by implication a *delight* (subjectively *satisfaction,* objectively a *charm*):— dainty, desire, exceedingly, greedily, lust, lusting, pleasant. See also H6914

H8379 תַּאֲוָה *taʾăwâ* from H8376; a *limit,* i.e. full extent:— utmost bound.

H8380 תָּאוֹם *tāʾôm* or

תָּאֹם *tāʾōm* from H8382; a *twin* (in plural only), literally or figuratively:— twins.

H8381 תַּאֲלָה *taʾălâ* from H422; an *imprecation:*— curse.

H8382 תָּאַם *tāʾam* a primitive root; to *be complete;* but used only as denominative from H8380, to *be* (causatively *make*) *twinned,* i.e. (figuratively) *duplicate* or (architecturally) *jointed:*— coupled, coupled together, bear twins.

H8383 תְּאֻן *tĕʾūn* from H205; *naughtiness,* i.e. *toil* :— lie.

H8384 תְּאֵן *tĕʾēn* or (in the singular, feminine)

תְּאֵנָה *tĕʾēnâ* perhaps of foreign derivation; the *fig* (tree or fruit):— fig, fig tree.

H8385 תַּאֲנָה *taʾănâ* or

תֹּאֲנָה *tōʾănâ* from H579; an *opportunity* or (subjectively) *purpose:*— occasion.

H8386 תַּאֲנִיָּה *taʾănîyâ* from H578; *lamentation:*— heaviness, mourning.

H8387 תַּאֲנַת שִׁלֹה *taʾănat šilōh* from H8385 and H7887; *approach of Shiloh; Taanath-Shiloh,* a place in Palestine:— Taanath-shiloh.

H8388 תָּאַר *tāʾar* a primitive root; to *delineate;* reflexively to *extend:*— be drawn, mark out, Rimmon-methoar *[by union with H7417].*

H8389 תֹּאַר *tōʾar* from H8388; *outline,* i.e. *figure* or *appearance:*— beautiful, comely, countenance, fair, favoured, form, goodly, resemble, visage.

H8390 תַּאֲרֵעַ *taʾărēaʿ* perhaps from H772; *Taareä,* an Israelite:— Tarea. See H8475

H8391 תְּאַשּׁוּר *tĕʾaššûr* from H833; a species of *cedar* (from its *erectness*):— box, box tree.

H8392 תֵּבָה *tēbâ* perhaps of foreign derivation; a *box:*— ark.

H8393 תְּבוּאָה *tĕbûʾâ* from H935; *income,* i.e. *produce* (literal or figurative):— fruit, gain, increase, revenue.

H8394 תָּבוּן *tābûn* and (feminine)

תְּבוּנָה *tĕbûnâ* or

תּוֹבֻנָה *tôbūnâ* from H995; *intelligence;* by implication an *argument;* by extension *caprice:*— discretion, reason, skilfulness, understanding, wisdom.

H8395 תְּבוּסָה *tĕbûsâ* from H947; a *treading down,* i.e. *ruin:*— destruction.

H8396 תָּבוֹר *tābôr* from a root corresponding to H8406; *broken* region; *Tabor,* a mountain in Palestine, also a city adjacent:— Tabor.

H8397 תֶּבֶל *tebel* apparently from H1101; *mixture,* i.e. *unnatural* bestiality:— confusion.

H8398 תֵּבֵל *tēbēl* from H2986; the *earth* (as *moist* and therefore inhabited); by extension the *globe;* by implication its *inhabitants;* specifically a particular *land,* as Babylonia, Palestine:— habitable part, world.

H8399 תַּבְלִית *tablît* from H1086; *consumption:*— destruction.

H8400 תְּבַלֻּל *tĕballūl* from H1101 in the original sense of *flowing;* a *cataract* (in the eye):— blemish.

H8401 תֶּבֶן *teben* probably from H1129; properly *material,* i.e. (specifically) refuse *haum* or stalks of grain (as *chopped* in threshing and used for fodder):— chaff, straw, stubble.

H8402 תִּבְנִי *tibnî* from H8401; *strawy; Tibni,* an Israelite:— Tibni.

H8403 תַּבְנִית *tabnît* from H1129; *structure;* by implication a *model, resemblance:*— figure, form, likeness, pattern, similitude.

H8404 תַּבְעֵרָה *tabʿērâ* from H1197; *burning; Taberah,* a place in the Desert:— Taberah.

H8405 תֵּבֵץ *tēbēṣ* from the same as H948; *whiteness; Tebets,* a place in Palestine:— Thebez.

H8406 תְּבַר *tĕbar* (Aramaic) corresponding to H7665; to *be fragile* (figuratively):— broken.

H8407 תִּגְלַת פִּלְאֶסֶר *tiglat pilʾeser* or

תִּגְלַת פְּלֶסֶר *tiglat pĕleser* or

תִּלְגַת פִּלְנְאֶסֶר *tilgat pilnĕʾeser* or

תִּלְגַת פִּלְנֶסֶר *tilgat pilneser* of foreign derivation; *Tiglath-Pileser* or *Tilgath-pilneser,* an Assyrian king:— Tiglath-pileser, Tilgath-pilneser.

H8408 תַּגְמוּל *tagmûl* from H1580; a *bestowment* :— benefit.

H8409 תִּגְרָה *tigrâ* from H1624; *strife,* i.e. *infliction* :— blow.

H8410 תִּדְהָר *tidhār* apparently from H1725; *enduring;* a species of hard-wood or *lasting* tree (perhaps *oak*):— pine, pine tree.

H8411 תְּדִירָא *tĕdîrāʾ* (Aramaic) from H1753 in the original sense of *enduring; permanence,* i.e. (adverbially) *constantly:*— continually.

H8412 תַּדְמֹר *tadmōr* or

תַּמֹּר *tammōr* (1 Kings 9:18), apparently from H8558; *palm*-city; *Tadmor,* a place near Palestine:— Tadmor.

H8413 תִּדְעָל *tidʿāl* perhaps from H1763; *fearfulness; Tidal,* a Canaanite:— Tidal.

H8414 תֹּהוּ *tōhû* from an unused root meaning to lie *waste;* a *desolation* (of surface), i.e. *desert;* figuratively a *worthless* thing; adverbially in *vain:*— confusion, empty place, without form, nothing, nought, thing of nought, vain, vanity, waste, wilderness.

H8415 תְּהוֹם *tĕhôm* or

תְּהֹם *tĕhōm* (usually feminine) from H1949; an *abyss* (as a *surging* mass of water), especially the *deep* (the *main* sea or the subterranean *water-supply*):— deep, deep place, depth.

H8416 תְּהִלָּה *tĕhillâ* from H1984; *laudation;* specifically (concretely) a *hymn:*— praise.

H8417 תָּהֳלָה *tohŏlâ* feminine of an unused noun (apparently from H1984) meaning *bluster; braggadocio,* i.e. (by implication) *fatuity:*— folly.

H8418 תַּהֲלֻכָה *tahălūkâ* from H1980; a *procession* :— went.

H8419 תַּהְפֻּכָה *tahpūkâ* from H2015; a *perversity* or *fraud:*— froward, very froward, frowardness, froward thing, perverse thing.

H8420 תָּו *tāw* from H8427; a *mark;* by implication a *signature:*— desire, mark.

H8421 תּוּב *tûb* (Aramaic) corresponding to H7725; to *come back;* specifically (transitively and elliptically) to *reply*):— answer, restore, return, return an answer.

H8422 תּוּבַל *tûbal* or

תֻּבַל *tūbal* probably of foreign derivation; *Tubal,* a postdiluvian patriarch and his posterity:— Tubal.

H8423 תּוּבַל קַיִן *tûbal qayin* apparently from H2986 (compare H2981) and H7014; *offspring of Cain; Tubal-Kajin,* an antediluvian patriarch:— Tubal-cain.

H8424 תּוּגָה *tûgâ* from H3013; *depression* (of spirits); concretely a *grief:*— heaviness, sorrow.

H8425 תּוֹגַרְמָה *tôgarmâ* or

תֹּגַרְמָה *tōgarmâ* probably of foreign derivation; *Togarmah,* a son of Gomer and his posterity:— Togarmah.

H8426 תּוֹדָה *tôdâ* from H3034; properly an *extension* of the hand, i.e. (by implication) *avowal,* or (usually) *adoration;* specifically a *choir* of worshippers:— confession, praise, sacrifice of praise, thanks, thanksgiving, thank offering.

H8427 תָּוָה *tāwâ* a primitive root; to *mark* out, i.e. (primitively) *scratch* or (definitely) *imprint:*— scrabble, set a mark.

H8428 תָּוָה *tāwâ* a primitive root [or perhaps identical with H8427 through a similar idea from *scraping* to pieces]; to *grieve:*— limit *[by confusion with H8427].*

H8429 תְּוַהּ *tĕwah* (Aramaic) corresponding to H8539 or perhaps to H7582 through the idea of *sweeping* to ruin [compare H8428]; to *amaze,* i.e. (reflexively by implication) *take alarm:*— be astonied.

H8430 תּוֹחַ *tôaḥ* from an unused root meaning to *depress; humble; Toäch,* an Israelite:— Toah.

H8431 תּוֹחֶלֶת *tôḥelet* from H3176; *expectation:*— hope.

H8432 תָּוֶךְ *tāwek* from an unused root meaning to *sever;* a *bisection,* i.e. (by implication) the *centre:*— among, amongst, between, half, in, therein, wherein, whereinto, middle, midnight, midst, midst among, out, out of, through, with, within.

H8433 תּוֹכֵחָה *tôkēḥâ* and

תּוֹכַחַת *tôkaḥat* from H3198; *chastisement;* figuratively (by words) *correction, refutation, proof* (even in defence):— argument, chastened, correction, reasoning, rebuke, reproof, be reproved, often reproved.

H8434 תּוֹלָד *tôlād* from H3205; *posterity; Tolad,* a place in Palestine:— Tolad. Compare H513

H8435 תּוֹלְדָה *tôlĕdâ* or

תֹּלְדָה *tōlĕdâ* from H3205; (plural only) *descent,* i.e. *family;* (figuratively) *history:*— birth, generations.

H8436 תּוּלֹן *tûlôn* from H8524; *suspension; Tulon,* an Israelite:— Tilon *[from the margin].*

H8437 תּוֹלָל *tôlāl* from H3213; *causing to howl,* i.e. an *oppressor:*— that wasted.

H8438 תּוֹלָע *tôlāᶜ* and (feminine)

תּוֹלֵעָה *tôlēᶜâ* or

תּוֹלַעַת *tôlaᶜat* or

תֹּלַעַת *tōlaᶜat* from H3216; a *maggot* (as *voracious*); specifically (often with ellipsis of H8144) the crimson-*grub,* but used only (in this connection) of the color from it, and cloths dyed therewith:— crimson, scarlet, worm.

H8439 תּוֹלָע *tôlāᶜ* the same as H8438; *worm; Tola,* the name of two Israelites:— Tola.

H8440 תּוֹלָעִי *tôlāᶜî* patronymic from H8439; a *Tolaïte* (collectively) or descendant of Tola:— Tolaites.

H8441 תּוֹעֵבָה *tôᶜēbah* or

תֹּעֵבָה *tōᶜēbah* feminine active participle of H8581; properly something *disgusting* (morally), i.e. (as noun) an *abhorrence;* especially *idolatry* or (concretely) an *idol:*— abominable, abominable custom, abominable thing, abomination.

H8442 תּוֹעָה *tôᶜâ* feminine active participle of H8582; *mistake,* i.e. (moral) *impiety,* or (political) *injury:*— error, hinder.

H8443 תּוֹעָפָה *tôᶜāpâ* from H3286; (only in plural collective) *weariness,* i.e. (by implication) *toil (treasure* so obtained) or *speed:*— plenty, strength.

H8444 תּוֹצָאָה *tôṣāʾâ* or

תֹּצָאָה *tōṣāʾâ* from H3318; (only in plural collective) *exit,* i.e. (geographical) *boundary,* or (figuratively) *deliverance,* (actively) *source:*— border, borders, going forth, going out, goings forth, going out, issues, outgoings.

H8445 תּוֹקַהַת *tôqahat* from the same as H3349; *obedience; Tokahath,* an Israelite:— Tikvath *[by correction for H8616].*

H8446 תּוּר *tûr* a primitive root; to *meander* (causatively *guide*) about, especially for trade of reconnoitring:— chapman, sent to descry, be excellent, merchantman, search, search out, seek, espy, spy out.

H8447 תּוֹר *tôr* or

תֹּר *tōr* from H8446; a *succession,* i.e. a *string* or (abstractly) *order:*— border, row, turn.

H8448 תּוֹר *tôr* probably the same as H8447; a *manner* (as a sort of *turn*):— estate.

H8449 תּוֹר *tôr* or

תֹּר *tōr* probably the same as H8447; a *ring-dove,* often (figuratively) as a term of endearment :— turtle, turtledove.

H8450 תּוֹר *tôr* (Aramaic) corresponding (by permutation) to H7794; a *bull:*— bullock, ox.

H8451 תּוֹרָה *tôrâ* or

תֹּרָה *tōrâ* from H3384; a *precept* or *statute,* especially the *Decalogue* or *Pentateuch:*— law.

H8452 תּוֹרָה *tôrâ* probably feminine of H8448; a *custom:*— manner.

H8453 תּוֹשָׁב *tôšāb* or

תֹּשָׁב *tōšāb* (1 Kings 17:1), from H3427; a *dweller* (but not outlandish [H5237]); especially (as distinguished from a native citizen [active participle of H3427] and a temporary inmate [H1616] or mere lodger [H3885]) resident *alien:*— foreigner, inhabitant, sojourner, stranger.

H8454 תּוּשִׁיָּה *tûšîyâ* or

תֻּשִׁיָּה *tušîyâ* from an unused root probably meaning to *substantiate; support* or (by implication) *ability,* i.e. (direct) *help,* (in purpose) an *undertaking,* (intellectual) *understanding:*— enterprise, that which is, thing as it is, substance, wisdom, sound wisdom, working.

H8455 תּוֹתָח *tôtāḥ* from an unused root meaning to *smite;* a *club:*— darts.

H8456 תָּזַז *tāzaz* a primitive root; to *lop* off:— cut down.

H8457 תַּזְנוּת *taznût* or

תַּזְנֻת *taznūt* from H2181; *harlotry,* i.e. (figuratively) *idolatry:*— fornication, whoredom.

H8458 תַּחְבֻּלָה *taḥbūlâ* or

תַּחְבּוּלָה *taḥbûlâ* from H2254 as denominative from H2256; (only in plural) properly *steerage* (as a management of *ropes*), i.e. (figuratively) *guidance* or (by implication) a *plan:*— good advice, counsels, wise counsels.

H8459 תֹּחוּ *tōḥû* from an unused root meaning to *depress; abasement; Tochu,* an Israelite:— Tohu.

H8460 תְּחוֹת *tĕḥôt* or

תְּחֹת *tĕḥōt* (Aramaic) corresponding to H8478; *beneath:*— under.

H8461 תַּחְכְּמֹנִי *taḥkĕmōnî* probably fro H2453; *sagacious; Tachkemoni,* an Israelite:— Tachmonite.

H8462 תְּחִלָּה *tĕḥillâ* from H2490 in the sense of *opening;* a *commencement;* relatively *original* (adverbially *-ly*):— begin, beginning, first, first time.

H8463 תַּחֲלוּא *taḥălûʾ* or

תַּחֲלֻא *taḥălūʾ* from H2456; a *malady:*— disease, grievous, that are sick, sickness.

H8464 תַּחְמָס *taḥmās* from H2554; a species of unclean bird (from its *violence*), perhaps an *owl:*— night hawk.

H8465 תַּחַן *taḥan* probably from H2583; *station; Tachan,* the name of two Israelites:— Tahan.

H8466 תַּחֲנָה *taḥănâ* from H2583; (only plural collectively) an *encampment:*— camp.

H8467 תְּחִנָּה *tĕḥinnâ* from H2603; *graciousness;* causatively *entreaty:*— favour, grace, supplication.

H8468 תְּחִנָּה *tĕḥinnâ* the same as H8467; *Techinnah,* an Israelite:— Tehinnah.

H8469 תַּחֲנוּן *taḥănûn* or (feminine)

תַּחֲנוּנָה *taḥănûnâ* from H2603; earnest *prayer* :— intreaty, supplication.

H8470 תַּחֲנִי *taḥănî* patronymic from H8465; a *Tachanite* (collectively) or descendant of Tachan:— Tahanites.

H8471 תַּחְפַּנְחֵס *taḥpanḥēs* or

תְּחַפְנְחֵס *tĕhapnĕhēs* (Ezek. 30:18), or

תַּחְפְּנֵס *taḥpĕnēs* (Jer. 2:16), of Egyptian derivation; *Tachpanches, Techaphneches* or *Tachpenes,* a place in Egypt:— Tahapanes, Tahpanhes, Tehaphnehes.

H8472 תַּחְפְּנֵיס *taḥpĕnês* of Egyptian derivation; *Tachpenes,* an Egyptian woman:— Tahpenes.

H8473 תַּחֲרָא *taḥărāʾ* from H2734 in the original sense of H2352 or H2353; a linen *corslet* (as *white* or *hollow*):— habergeon.

H8474 תַּחֲרָה *taḥărâ* a factitious root from H2734 through the idea of the *heat* of jealousy; to *vie* with a rival:— close, contend.

H8475 תַּחְרֵעַ *taḥrēaᶜ* for H8390; *Tachreä*, an Israelite:— Tahrea.

H8476 תַּחַשׁ *taḥaš* probably of foreign derivation; a (clean) animal with fur, probably a species of *antelope:*— badger.

H8477 תַּחַשׁ *taḥaš* the same as H8476; *Tachash*, a relative of Abraham:— Thahash.

H8478 תַּחַת *taḥat* from the same as H8430; the *bottom* (as *depressed*); only adverbially *below* (often with preposition prefixed *underneath*), in *lieu of*, etc:— as, beneath, flat, in, instead, place, same place, place where . . . is, room, for . . . sake, stead of, under, unto, when . . . was mine, whereas, wherefore, with.

H8479 תַּחַת *taḥat* (Aramaic) corresponding to H8478 :— under.

H8480 תַּחַת *taḥat* the same as H8478; *Tachath*, the name of a place in the Desert, also of three Israelites:— Tahath.

H8481 תַּחְתּוֹן *taḥtôn* or

תַּחְתֹּן *taḥtōn* from H8478; *bottommost:*— lower, lowest, nether, nethermost.

H8482 תַּחְתִּי *taḥtî* from H8478; *lowermost;* as noun (feminine plural) the *depths* (figuratively a *pit*, the *womb*):— low, low parts, lower, lower parts, lowest, nether, nether part.

H8483 תַּחְתִּים חָדְשִׁי *taḥtîm ḥodšî* apparently from the plural masculine of H8482 or H8478 and H2320; *lower* (ones) *monthly; Tachtim-Chodshi*, a place in Palestine:— Tahtim-hodshi.

H8484 תִּיכוֹן *tîkôn* or

תִּיכֹן *tîkōn* from H8432; *central:*— middle, middlemost, midst.

H8485 תֵּימָא *têmāʾ* or

תֵּמָא *têmāʾ* probably of foreign derivation; *Tema*, a son of Ishmael, and the region settled by him:— Tema.

H8486 תֵּימָן *têmān* or

תֵּמָן *têmān* denominative from H3225; the *south* (as being on the *right* hand of a person facing the east):— south, south side, southward, south wind.

H8487 תֵּימָן *têmān* or

תֵּמָן *têmān* the same as H8486; *Teman*, the name of two Edomites, and of the region and descendants of one of them:— south, Teman.

H8488 תֵּימְנִי *têmĕnî* probably for H8489; *Temeni*, an Israelite:— Temeni.

H8489 תֵּימָנִי *têmānî* patronymic from H8487; a *Temanite* or descendant of Teman:— Temani, Temanite.

H8490 תִּימָרָה *tîmārâ* or

תִּמָרָה *timārâ* from the same as H8558; a *column*, i.e. cloud:— pillar.

H8491 תִּיצִי *tîṣî* patrial or patronymic from an unused noun of uncertain meaning; a *Titsite* or descendant or inhabitant of an unknown Tits:— Tizite.

H8492 תִּירוֹשׁ *tîrôš* or

תִּירֹשׁ *tîrōš* from H3423 in the sense of *expulsion; must* or fresh grape-juice (as just *squeezed* out); by implication (rarely) fermented *wine:*— wine, new wine, sweet wine.

H8493 תִּירְיָא *tîrĕyāʾ* probably from H3372; *fearful; Tirja*, an Israelite:— Tiria.

H8494 תִּירָס *tîrās* probably of foreign derivation; *Tiras*, a son of Japheth:— Tiras.

H8495 תַּיִשׁ *tayiš* from an unused root meaning to *butt;* a *buck* or he-goat (as given to *butting*):— he goat.

H8496 תֹּךְ *tōk* or

תּוֹךְ *tôk* (Ps. 72:14), from the same base as H8432 (in the sense of *cutting* to pieces); *oppression:*— deceit, fraud.

H8497 תָּכָה *tākâ* a primitive root; to *strew*, i.e. *encamp:*— sit down.

H8498 תְּכוּנָה *tĕkûnâ* feminine passive participle of H8505; *adjustment*, i.e. *structure;* by implication *equipage:*— fashion, store.

H8499 תְּכוּנָה *tĕkûnâ* from H3559; or probably identical with H8498; something *arranged* or *fixed*, i.e. a *place:*— seat.

H8500 תֻּכִּי *tukkî* or

תּוּכִּי *tûkkî* probably of foreign derivation; some imported creature, probably a *peacock:*— peacock.

H8501 תָּכָךְ *tākāk* from an unused root meaning to *dissever*, i.e. *crush:*— deceitful.

H8502 תִּכְלָה *tiklâ* from H3615; *completeness:*— perfection.

H8503 תַּכְלִית *taklît* from H3615; *completion;* by implication an *extremity:*— end, perfect, perfection.

H8504 תְּכֵלֶת *tĕkēlet* probably for H7827; the cerulean *mussel*, i.e. the color (*violet*) obtained therefrom or stuff dyed therewith:— blue.

H8505 תָּכַן *tākan* a primitive root; to *balance*, i.e. *measure* out (by weight or dimension); figuratively to *arrange, equalize*, through the idea of *levelling* (mentally *estimate, test*):— bear up, direct, be equal, be unequal, mete, ponder, tell, weigh.

H8506 תֹּכֶן *tōken* from H8505; a fixed *quantity:*— measure, tale.

H8507 תֹּכֶן *tōken* the same as H8506; *Token*, a place in Palestine:— Tochen.

H8508 תָּכְנִית *toknît* from H8506; *admeasurement*, i.e. *consummation:*— pattern, sum.

H8509 תַּכְרִיךְ *takrîk* apparently from an unused root meaning to *encompass;* a *wrapper* or robe:— garment.

H8510 תֵּל *tēl* by contraction from H8524; a *mound* :— heap, strength.

H8511 תָּלָא *tālāʾ* a primitive root; to *suspend;* figuratively (through *hesitation*) to *be uncertain;* by implication (of mental *dependence*) to *habituate:*— be bent, hang, hang in doubt.

H8512 תֵּל אָבִיב *tēl ʾābîb* from H8510 and H24; *mound* of *green* growth; *Tel-Abib*, a place in Chaldaea:— Tel-abib.

H8513 תְּלָאָה *tĕlāʾâ* from H3811; *distress:*— travail, travel, trouble.

H8514 תַּלְאוּבָה *talʾûbâ* from H3851; *desiccation:*— great drought.

H8515 תְּלַאשָּׂר *tĕlaʾśśar* or

תְּלַשָּׂר *tĕlaśśar* of foreign derivation; *Telassar*, a region of Assyria:— Tel-assar.

H8516 תַּלְבֹּשֶׁת *talbōšet* from H3847; a *garment:*— clothing.

H8517 תְּלַג *tĕlag* (Aramaic) corresponding to H7950; *snow:*— snow.

H8518 תָּלָה *tālâ* a primitive root; to *suspend* (especially to *gibbet*):— hang, hang up.

H8519 תְּלוּנָה *tĕlûnâ* or

תְּלֻנָּה *tĕlunnâ* from H3885 in the sense of *obstinacy;* a *grumbling:*— murmuring.

H8520 תֶּלַח *telaḥ* probably from an unused root meaning to *dissever; breach; Telach*, an Israelite :— Telah.

H8521 תֵּל חַרְשָׁא *tēl ḥaršāʾ* from H8510 and the feminine of H2798; *mound of workmanship; Tel-Charsha*, a place in Babylonia:— Tel-haresha, Tel-harsa.

H8522 תְּלִי *tĕlî* probably from H8518; a *quiver* (as *slung*):— quiver.

H8523 תְּלִיתַי *tĕlîtay* or

תַּלְתִּי *taltî* (Aramaic) ordinal from H8532; *third:*— third.

H8524 תָּלַל *tālal* a primitive root; to *pile up*, i.e. *elevate:*— eminent. Compare H2048

H8525 תֶּלֶם *telem* from an unused root meaning to *accumulate;* a *bank* or *terrace:*— furrow, ridge.

H8526 תַּלְמַי *talmay* from H8525; *ridged; Talmai*, the name of a Canaanite and a Syrian:— Talmai.

H8527 תַּלְמִיד *talmîd* from H3925; a *pupil:*— scholar.

H8528 תֵּל מֶלַח *tēl melaḥ* from H8510 and H4417; *mound of salt; Tel-Melach*, a place in Babylonia:— Tel-melah.

H8529 תָּלַע *tālaᶜ* a denominative from H8438; to *crimson*, i.e. dye that color:— scarlet.

H8530 תַּלְפִּיָּה *talpîyâ* feminine from an unused root meaning to *tower;* something *tall*, i.e. (plural collectively) *slenderness:*— armoury.

H8531 תְּלַת *tĕlat* (Aramaic) from H8532; a *tertiary* rank:— third.

H8532 תְּלָת *tĕlāt* masculine

תְּלָתָה *tĕlātâ* or

תְּלָתָא *tĕlātāʾ* (Aramaic) corresponding to H7969; *three* or *third:*— third, three.

H8533 תְּלָתִין *tĕlātîn* (Aramaic) multiple of H8532; *ten times three:*— thirty.

H8534 תַּלְתַּל *taltal* by reduplication from H8524 through the idea of *vibration;* a trailing *bough* (as *pendulous*):— bushy.

H8535 תָּם *tām* from H8552; *complete;* usually (morally) *pious;* specifically *gentle, dear:*— coupled together, perfect, plain, undefiled, upright.

H8536 תָּם *tām* (Aramaic) corresponding to H8033; *there:*— thence, there, where.

H8537 תֹּם *tōm* from H8552; *completeness;* figuratively *prosperity;* usually (morally) *innocence:*— fully, integrity, perfect, perfection, simplicity, upright, uprightly, uprightness, at a venture. See H8550

H8538 תֻּמָּה *tummâ* feminine of H8537; *innocence* :— integrity.

H8539 תָּמַהּ *tāmah* a primitive root; to *be in consternation:*— be amazed, be astonished, marvel, marvellously, wonder.

H8540 תְּמַהּ *tĕmah* (Aramaic) from a root corresponding to H8539; a *miracle:*— wonder.

H8541 תִּמָּהוֹן *timmāhôn* from H8539; *consternation* :— astonishment.

H8542 תַּמּוּז *tammûz* of uncertain derivation; *Tammuz*, a Phoenician deity:— Tammuz.

H8543 תְּמוֹל *tĕmôl* or

תְּמֹל *tĕmōl* probably for H865; properly *ago,* i.e. a (short or long) *time since;* especially *yesterday,* or (with H8032) *day before* yesterday:— before, beforetime, these three days, heretofore, time past, yesterday.

H8544 תְּמוּנָה *tĕmûnâ* or

תְּמֻנָה *tĕmūnâ* from H4327; *something portioned* (i.e. *fashioned*) out, as a *shape,* i.e. (indefinitely) *phantom,* or (specifically) *embodiment,* or (figuratively) *manifestation* (of favor):— image, likeness, similitude.

H8545 תְּמוּרָה *tĕmûrâ* from H4171; *barter, compensation:*— change, exchange, changing, recompense, restitution.

H8546 תְּמוּתָה *tĕmûtâ* from H4191; *execution* (as a doom):— death, die.

H8547 תֶּמַח *temaḥ* of uncertain derivation; *Temach,* one of the Nethinim:— Tamah, Thamah.

H8548 תָּמִיד *tāmîd* from an unused root meaning to *stretch;* properly *continuance* (as indefinite *extension*); but used only attributively (as adjective *constant*) or adverbially (*constantly*); elliptically the *regular* (daily) sacrifice:— alway, always, continual, continual employment, continually, daily, ever, never, evermore, perpetual.

H8549 תָּמִים *tāmîm* from H8552; *entire* (literally, figuratively or morally); also (as noun) *integrity, truth:*— without blemish, complete, full, perfect, sincerely, sincerity, sound, without spot, undefiled, upright, uprightly, whole.

H8550 תֻּמִּים *tūmîm* plural of H8537; *perfections,* i.e. (technically) one of the epithets of the objects in the high-priest's breastplate as an emblem of *complete* Truth:— Thummim.

H8551 תָּמַךְ *tāmak* a primitive root; to *sustain;* by implication to *obtain, keep fast;* figuratively to *help, follow close:*— hold, take hold, uphold, hold up, maintain, retain, stay, stay up.

H8552 תָּמַם *tāmam* a primitive root; to *complete,* in a good or a bad sense, literally or figuratively, transitively or intransitively (as follows):— accomplish, cease, be clean passed, consume, have done, end, come to an end, have an end, make an end, fail, come to the full, be all gone, be all here, be perfect, make perfect, be spent, sum, be upright, shew self upright, be wasted, whole.

H8553 תִּמְנָה *timnâ* from H4487; a *portion* assigned; *Timnah,* the name of two places in Palestine:— Timnah, Timnath, Thimnathah.

H8554 תִּמְנִי *timnî* patrial from H8553; a *Timnite* or inhabitant of Timnah:— Timnite.

H8555 תִּמְנָע *timnā*ᶜ from H4513; *restraint; Timna,* the name of two Edomites:— Timna, Timnah.

H8556 תִּמְנַת חֶרֶס *timnat ḥeres* or

תִּמְנַת סֶרַח *timnat serah* from H8553 and H2775; *portion of* (the) *sun; Timnath-Cheres,* a place in Palestine:— Timnath-heres, Timnath-serah.

H8557 תֶּמֶס *temes* from H4529; *liquefaction,* i.e. *disappearance:*— melt.

H8558 תָּמָר *tāmār* from an unused root meaning to *be erect;* a *palm* tree:— palm, palm tree.

H8559 תָּמָר *tāmār* the same as H8558; *Tamar,* the name of three women and a place:— Tamar.

H8560 תֹּמֶר *tōmer* from the same root as H8558; a *palm* trunk:— palm tree.

H8561 תִּמֹּר *timmōr* (plural only); or (feminine)

תִּמֹּרָה *timmōrâ* (singular and plural) from the same root as H8558; (architecturally) a *palm*-like pilaster (i.e. umbellate):— palm tree.

H8562 תַּמְרוּק *tamrûq* or

תַּמְרֻק *tamrūq* or

תַּמְרִיק *tamrîq* from H4838; properly a *scouring,* i.e. *soap* or *perfumery* for the bath; figuratively a *detergent:*— cleanse, thing for purification, purifying.

H8563 תַּמְרוּר *tamrûr* from H4843; *bitterness* (plural as collective):— most bitter, most bitterly.

H8564 תַּמְרוּר *tamrûr* from the same root as H8558; an *erection,* i.e. *pillar* (probably for a guide-board):— high heap.

H8565 תַּן *tan* from an unused root probably meaning to *elongate;* a *monster* (as preternaturally formed), i.e. a *sea-serpent* (or other huge marine animal); also a *jackal* (or other hideous land animal):— dragon, whale. Compare H8577

H8566 תָּנָה *tānâ* a primitive root; to *present* (a mercenary inducement), i.e. *bargain* with (a harlot):— hire.

H8567 תָּנָה *tānâ* a primitive root [rather identical with H8566 through the idea of *attributing* honor]; to *ascribe* (praise), i.e. *celebrate, commemorate:*— lament, rehearse.

H8568 תַּנָּה *tannâ* probably feminine of H8565; a female *jackal:*— dragon.

H8569 תְּנוּאָה *tĕnûʾâ* from H5106; *alienation;* by implication *enmity:*— breach of promise, occasion.

H8570 תְּנוּבָה *tĕnûbâ* from H5107; *produce:*— fruit, increase.

H8571 תְּנוּךְ *tĕnûk* perhaps from the same as H594 through the idea of *protraction;* a *pinnacle,* i.e. *extremity:*— tip.

H8572 תְּנוּמָה *tĕnûmâ* from H5123; *drowsiness,* i.e. *sleep:*— slumber, slumbering.

H8573 תְּנוּפָה *tĕnûpâ* from H5130; a *brandishing* (in threat); by implication *tumult;* specifically the official *undulation* of sacrificial offerings:— offering, shaking, wave, wave offering.

H8574 תַּנּוּר *tannûr* from H5216; a *fire-pot:*— furnace, oven.

H8575 תַּנְחוּם *tanḥûm* or

תַּנְחֻם *tanḥūm* and (feminine)

תַּנְחוּמָה *tanḥûmâ* from H5162; *compassion, solace:*— comfort, consolation.

H8576 תַּנְחֻמֶת *tanḥumet* for H8575 (feminine); *Tanchumeth,* an Israelite:— Tanhumeth.

H8577 תַּנִּין *tannîn* or

תַּנִּים *tannîm* (Ezek. 29:3), intensive from the same as H8565; a marine or land *monster,* i.e. *sea-serpent* or *jackal:*— dragon, sea-monster, serpent, whale.

H8578 תִּנְיָן *tinyān* (Aramaic) corresponding to H8147; *second:*— second.

H8579 תִּנְיָנוּת *tinyānût* (Aramaic) from H8578; a *second time:*— again.

H8580 תַּנְשֶׁמֶת *tanšemet* from H5395; properly a hard *breather,* i.e. the name of two unclean creatures, a lizard and a bird (both perhaps from changing color through their *irascibility*), both the *tree-toad* and the *water-hen:*— mole, swan.

H8581 תָּעַב *tāᶜab* a primitive root; to *loathe,* i.e. (morally) *detest:*— abhor, make to be abhorred, abominable, be abominable, commit more abominable, do abominable, do abominably, utterly.

H8582 תָּעָה *tāᶜâ* a primitive root; to *vacillate,* i.e. *reel* or *stray* (literally or figuratively); also causative of both :— go astray, cause to go astray, deceive, dissemble, err, cause to err, make to err, pant, seduce, stagger, make to stagger, wander, cause to wander, be out of the way.

H8583 תֹּעוּ *tōᶜû* or

תֹּעִי *tōᶜî* from H8582; *error; Toü* or *Toï,* a Syrian king:— Toi, Tou.

H8584 תְּעוּדָה *tĕᶜûdâ* from H5749; *attestation,* i.e. a *precept, usage:*— testimony.

H8585 תְּעָלָה *tĕᶜālâ* from H5927; a *channel* (into which water is *raised* for irrigation); also a *bandage* or *plaster* (as placed *upon* a wound):— conduit, cured, healing, little river, trench, watercourse.

H8586 תַּעֲלוּל *taᶜălûl* from H5953; *caprice* (as a fit *coming on*), i.e. *vexation;* concretely a *tyrant:*— babe, delusion.

H8587 תַּעֲלֻמָּה *taᶜălummâ* from H5956; a *secret:*— thing that is hid, secret.

H8588 תַּעֲנוּג *taᶜănûg* or

תַּעֲנֻג *taᶜănūg* and (feminine)

תַּעֲנֻגָה *taᶜănūgâ* from H6026; *luxury:*— delicate, delight, pleasant.

H8589 תַּעֲנִית *taᶜănît* from H6031; *affliction* (of self), i.e. *fasting:*— heaviness.

H8590 תַּעֲנָךְ *taᶜănāk* or

תַּעְנָךְ *taᶜnāk* of uncertain derivation; *Taanak* or *Tanak,* a place in Palestine:— Taanach, Tanach.

H8591 תָּעַע *tāᶜaᶜ* a primitive root; to *cheat;* by analogy to *maltreat:*— deceive, misuse.

H8592 תַּעֲצֻמָה *taᶜăṣūmâ* from H6105; *might* (plural collective):— power.

H8593 תַּעַר *taᶜar* from H6168; a *knife* or *razor* (as *making* bare); also a *scabbard* (as *being bare,* i.e. empty):— penknife, rasor, scabbard, shave, sheath.

H8594 תַּעֲרֻבָה *taᶜărūbâ* from H6148; *suretyship,* i.e. (concretely) a *pledge:*— hostage.

H8595 תַּעְתֻּעַ *taᶜtūaᶜ* from H8591; a *fraud:*— error.

H8596 תֹּף *tōp* from H8608 contracted; a *tambourine:*— tabret, timbrel.

H8597 תִּפְאָרָה *tipʾārâ* or

תִּפְאֶרֶת *tipʾeret* from H6286; *ornament* (abstractly or concretely, literally or figuratively):— beauty, beautiful, bravery, comely, fair, glory, glorious, honour, majesty.

H8598 תַּפּוּחַ *tappûaḥ* from H5301; an *apple* (from its *fragrance*), i.e. the fruit or the tree (probably including others of the *pome* order, as the quince, the orange, etc.):— apple, apple tree. See also H1054

H8599 תַּפּוּחַ *tappûaḥ* the same as H8598; *Tappuäch,* the name of two places in Palestine, also of an Israelite:— Tappuah.

H8600 תְּפוֹצָה *tĕpôṣâ* from H6327; a *dispersal:*— dispersion.

H8601 תֻּפִין *tūpîn* from H644; *cookery,* i.e. (concretely) a *cake:*— baked piece.

H8602 תָּפֵל *tāpēl* from an unused root meaning to *smear; plaster* (as *gummy*) or *slime;* (figuratively) *frivolity:*— foolish things, unsavoury, untempered.

H8603 תֹּפֶל *tōpel* from the same as H8602; *quagmire; Tophel,* a place near the Desert:— Tophel.

H8604 תִּפְלָה *tiplâ* from the same as H8602; *frivolity:*— folly, foolishly.

H8605 תְּפִלָּה *tĕpillâ* from H6419; *intercession, supplication;* by implication a *hymn:*— prayer.

H8606 תִּפְלֶצֶת *tipleṣet* from H6426; *fearfulness:*— terrible.

H8607 תִּפְסַח *tipsaḥ* from H6452; *ford; Tiphsach,* a place in Mesopotamia:— Tipsah.

H8608 תָּפַף *tāpap* a primitive root; to *drum,* i.e. play (as) on the tambourine:— taber, play with timbrels.

H8609 תָּפַר *tāpar* a primitive root; to *dew:*— sew, women that sew, sew together.

H8610 תָּפַשׂ *tāpaś* a primitive root; to *manipulate,* i.e. *seize;* chiefly to *capture, wield;* specifically to *overlay;* figuratively to *use* unwarrantably:— catch, handle, hold, lay hold on, take hold, lay over, stop, surely, surprise, take.

H8611 תֹּפֶת *tōpet* from the base of H8608; a *smiting,* i.e. (figuratively) *contempt:*— tabret.

H8612 תֹּפֶת *tōpet* the same as H8611; *Topheth,* a place near Jerus:— Tophet, Topheth.

H8613 תָּפְתֶּה *topteh* probably a form of H8612; *Tophteh,* a place of cremation:— Tophet.

H8614 תִּפְתָּי *tiptay* (Aramaic) perhaps from H8199; *judicial,* i.e. a *lawyer:*— sheriff.

H8615 תִּקְוָה *tiqwâ* from H6960; literally a *cord* (as an *attachment* [compare H6961]); figuratively *expectancy:*— expectation, expected, hope, live, thing that I long for.

H8616 תִּקְוָה *tiqwâ* the same as H8615; *Tikvah,* the name of two Israelites:— Tikvah.

H8617 תְּקוּמָה *tĕqûmâ* from H6965; *resistfulness:*— power to stand.

H8618 תְּקוֹמֵם *tĕqômēm* from H6965; an *opponent* :— rise up against.

H8619 תָּקוֹעַ *tāqôa*ᶜ from H8628 (in the musical sense); a *trumpet:*— trumpet.

H8620 תְּקוֹעַ *tĕqôa*ᶜ a form of H8619; *Tekoä,* a place in Palestine:— Tekoa, Tekoah.

H8621 תְּקוֹעִי *tĕqôᶜî* or

תְּקֹעִי *tĕqōᶜî* patronymic from H8620; a *Tekoïte* or inhabitant of Tekoah:— Tekoite.

H8622 תְּקוּפָה *tĕqûpâ* or

תְּקֻפָה *tĕqūpâ* from H5362; a *revolution,* i.e. (of the sun) *course,* (of time) *lapse:*— circuit, come about, end.

H8623 תַּקִּיף *taqqîp* from H8630; *powerful:*— mightier.

H8624 תַּקִּיף *taqqîp* (Aramaic) corresponding to H8623:— mighty, strong.

H8625 תְּקַל *tĕqal* (Aramaic) corresponding to H8254; to *balance:*— Tekel, be weighed.

H8626 תָּקַן *tāqan* a primitive root; to *equalize,* i.e. *straighten* (intransitively or transitively); figuratively to *compose:*— set in order, make straight.

H8627 תְּקַן *tĕqan* (Aramaic) corresponding to H8626; to *straighten* up, i.e. *confirm:*— establish.

H8628 תָּקַע *tāqa*ᶜ a primitive root; to *clatter,* i.e. *slap* (the hands together), *clang* (an instrument); by analogy to *drive* (a nail or tent-pin, a dart, etc.); by implication to *become bondsman* (by handclasping):— blow, blow a trumpet, cast, clap, fasten, pitch tent, smite, sound, strike, suretiship, thrust.

H8629 תֵּקַע *tēqa*ᶜ from H8628; a *blast* of a trumpet:— sound.

H8630 תָּקַף *tāqap* a primitive root; to *overpower* :— prevail, prevail against.

H8631 תְּקֵף *tĕqēp* (Aramaic) corresponding to H8630; to *become* (causatively *make*) *mighty* or (figuratively) *obstinate:*— make firm, harden, be strong, become strong.

H8632 תְּקֹף *tĕqōp* (Aramaic) corresponding to H8633; *power:*— might, strength.

H8633 תֹּקֶף *tōqep* from H8630; *might* or (figuratively) *positiveness:*— authority, power, strength.

H8634 תַּרְאֲלָה *tarʾălâ* probably for H8653; a *reeling; Taralah,* a place in Palestine:— Taralah.

H8635 תַּרְבּוּת *tarbût* from H7235; *multiplication,* i.e. *progeny:*— increase.

H8636 תַּרְבִּית *tarbît* from H7235; *multiplication,* i.e. *percentage* or *bonus* in addition to principal:— increase, unjust gain.

H8637 תִּרְגַּל *tirgal* a denominative from H7270; to *cause to walk:*— teach to go.

H8638 תִּרְגַּם *tirgam* a denominative from H7275 in the sense of *throwing* over; to *transfer,* i.e. *translate:*— interpret.

H8639 תַּרְדֵּמָה *tardēmâ* from H7290; a *lethargy* or (by implication) *trance:*— deep sleep.

H8640 תִּרְהָקָה *tirhāqâ* of foreign derivation; *Tirhakah,* a king of Kush:— Tirhakah.

H8641 תְּרוּמָה *tĕrûmâ* or

תְּרֻמָה *tĕrūmâ* (Deut. 12:11), from H7311; a *present* (as offered *up*), especially in *sacrifice* or as *tribute:*— gift, heave offering, heave shoulder, oblation, offered, offering.

H8642 תְּרוּמִיָּה *tĕrûmîyâ* formed as H8641; a sacrificial *offering:*— oblation.

H8643 תְּרוּעָה *tĕrûᶜâ* from H7321; *clamor,* i.e. *acclamation* of joy or a *battle-cry;* especially *clangor* of trumpets, as an *alarum:*— alarm, blow, blowing the trumptets, blowing of trumpets, joy, jubile, loud noise, rejoicing, shout, shouting, high sound, joyful sound, sounding.

H8644 תְּרוּפָה *tĕrûpâ* from H7322 in the sense of its congener H7495; a *remedy:*— medicine.

H8645 תִּרְזָה *tirzâ* probably from H7329; a species of tree (apparently from its *slenderness*), perhaps the *cypress:*— cypress.

H8646 תֶּרַח *teraḥ* of uncertain derivation; *Terach,* the father of Abraham; also a place in the Desert:— Tarah, Terah.

H8647 תִּרְחֲנָה *tirḥănâ* of uncertain derivation; *Tirchanah,* an Israelite:— Tirhanah.

H8648 תְּרֵין *tĕrên* (Aramaic), feminine

תַּרְתֵּין *tartên* corresponding to H8147; *two* :— second, twelve, two.

H8649 תָּרְמָה *tormâ* and

תַּרְמוּת *tarmût* or

תַּרְמִית *tarmît* from H7411; *fraud:*— deceit, deceitful, privily.

H8650 תֹּרֶן *tōren* probably for H766; a *pole* (as a mast or flag-staff):— beacon, mast.

H8651 תְּרַע *tĕra*ᶜ (Aramaic) corresponding to H8179; a *door;* by implication a *palace:*— gate mouth.

H8652 תָּרָע *tārā*ᶜ (Aramaic) from H8651; a *doorkeeper:*— porter.

H8653 תַּרְעֵלָה *tarᶜēlâ* from H7477; *reeling:*— astonishment, trembling.

H8654 תִּרְעָתִי *tirᶜātî* patrial from an unused name meaning *gate;* a *Tirathite* or inhabitant of an unknown Tirah:— Tirathite.

H8655 תְּרָפִים *tĕrāpîm* plural perhaps from H7495; a *healer; Teraphim* (singular or plural) a family idol:— idols, idolatry, images, teraphim.

H8656 תִּרְצָה *tirṣâ* from H7521; *delightsomeness; Tirtsah,* a place in Palestine; also an Israelitess:— Tirzah.

H8657 תֶּרֶשׁ *tereš* of foreign derivation; *Teresh,* a eunuch of Xerxes:— Teresh.

H8658 תַּרְשִׁישׁ *taršîš* probably of foreign derivation [compare H8659]; a gem, perhaps the *topaz:*— beryl.

H8659 תַּרְשִׁישׁ *taršîš* probably the same as H8658 (as the region of the stone, or the reverse); *Tarshish,* a place on the Mediterranean, hence the epithet of a *merchant* vessel (as if for or from that port); also the name of a Persian and of an Israelite:— Tarshish, Tharshish.

H8660 תִּרְשָׁתָא *tiršātāʾ* of foreign derivation; the title of a Persian deputy or *governor:*— Tirshatha.

H8661 תַּרְתָּן *tartān* of foreign derivation; *Tartan,* an Assyrian:— Tartan.

H8662 תַּרְתָּק *tartāq* of foreign derivation; *Tartak,* a deity of the Avvites:— Tartak.

H8663 תְּשֻׁאָה *tĕšuʾâ* from H7722; a *crashing* or loud *clamor:*— crying, noise, shouting, stir.

H8664 תִּשְׁבִּי *tišbî* patrial from an unused name meaning *recourse;* a *Tishbite* or inhabitant of Tishbeh (in Gilead):— Tishbite.

H8665 תַּשְׁבֵּץ *tašbēṣ* from H7660; *checkered* stuff (as *reticulated*):— broidered.

H8666 תְּשׁוּבָה *tĕšûbâ* or

תְּשֻׁבָה *tĕšūbâ* from H7725; a *recurrence* (of time or place); a *reply* (as *returned*):— answer, be expired, return.

H8667 תְּשׂוּמֶת *tĕśûmet* from H7760; a *deposit,* i.e. *pledging:*— fellowship.

H8668 תְּשׁוּעָה *tĕšûᶜâ* or

תְּשֻׁעָה *tĕšūᶜâ* from H7768 in the sense of H3467; *rescue* (literal or figurative, personal, national or spiritual):— deliverance, help, safety, salvation, victory.

H8669 תְּשׁוּקָה *tĕšûqâ* from H7783 in the original sense of *stretching* out after; a *longing:*— desire.

H8670 תְּשׁוּרָה *tĕšûrâ* from H7788 in the sense of *arrival;* a *gift:*— present.

H8671 תְּשִׁיעִי *tĕšîᶜî* ordinal from H8672; *ninth:*— ninth.

H8672 תֵּשַׁע *tēša*ᶜ or (masculine)

תִּשְׁעָה *tišᶜâ* perhaps from H8159 through the idea of a *turn* to the next or full number ten; *nine* or (ordinal) *ninth:*— nine, nineteen, nineteenth, ninth.

H8673 תִּשְׁעִים *tišᶜîm* multiple from H8672; *ninety* :— ninety.

H8674 תַּתְּנַי *tattĕnay* of foreign derivation; *Tattenai,* a Persian:— Tatnai.

Dictionary of Greek Words

Dictionary Features

Strong's Number
Each Greek word has a unique number, prefixed by "G" and italicized. This simple reference system allows anyone, whether or not they read Greek, to easily find the root word behind the English translation.

Lexical Form
Gives the root form of the Greek word in Greek type.

Transliteration
The English transliteration of the Greek word. (See Transliteration Table below.)

Definition
Gives a general sense of the derivation and meaning of the word and how it is used.

KJV Use
Preceded by ":—"
Gives the English words used to translate this word in the KJV.

Alternate or Related forms
The same Greek word may have more than one spelling or lexical form. When this is the case, multiple spellings will be listed. Th common elements of related forms can often be seen when they are placed side by side.

Related words
Related Greek, Hebrew, or Aramaic words are referenced by Strong's number.

G1823 **ἐξαστράπτω** *exastraptō* from *G1537* and *G797*; to *lighten forth,* i.e. (figuratively) to *be radiant* (of very white garments):— glistening.

G1824 **ἐξαυτῆς** *exautēs* from *G1537* and the generic singular feminine of *G846* (*G5610* being understood); *from that* hour, i.e. *instantly*:— by and by, immediately, presently, straightway.

G1825 **ἐξεγείρω** *exegeirō* from *G1537* and *G1453*; to *rouse fully,* i.e. (figuratively) to *resuscitate* (from death), *release* (from infliction):— raise up.

G1826 **ἔξειμι** *exeimi* from *G1537* and **εἶμι** *eimi* (to *go*); to *issue,* i.e. *leave* (a place), *escape* (to the shore):— depart, get [*to land*], go out.

Greek Transliteration Table

Character		Transliteration	Character		Transliteration
Α, α	*alpha*	*A, a*	Π, π	*pi*	*P, p*
Β, β	*bēta*	*B, b*	Ρ, ρ	*rho*	*R, r*
Γ, γ	*gamma*	*G, g*	ῥ	initial *rho* (or in medial double *rho:* e.g., *Pyrrhos)*	*rh*
γ	*gamma* nasal	*n* (before γ, κ, ξ, χ)	Σ, σ	*sigma*	*S, s*
Δ, δ	*delta*	*D, d*	Τ, τ	*tau*	*T, t*
Ε, ε	*epsilon*	*E, e*	Υ, υ	*upsilon*	*Y, y* (not in diphthong)
Ζ, ζ	*zēta*	*Z, z*	υ	*upsilon*	*u* (in diphthongs: *au, eu, ēu, ou, ui*)
Η, η	*ēta*	*¼, ē*	Φ, φ	*phi*	*Ph, ph*
Θ, θ	*thēta*	*Th, th*	Χ, χ	*chi*	*Ch, ch*
Ι, ι	*iōta*	*I, i*	Ψ, ψ	*psi*	*Ps, ps*
Κ, κ	*kappa*	*K, k*	Ω, ω	*ōmega*	*½, ō*
Λ, λ	*lambda*	*L, l*	῾	rough breathing	*H, h* (preceding initial vowel or diphthong)
Μ, μ	*mu*	*M, m*			
Ν, ν	*nu*	*N, n*			
Ξ, ξ	*xi*	*X, x*			
Ο, ο	*omicron*	*O, o*			

Dictionary of Greek Words

The over 5,500 entries in this dictionary provide the user with a listing of the Greek words translated into the English of the King James Version. See the diagram of features on the facing page for an explanation of the entries. See the section "Exploring the original languages" in the Introduction (beginning on page x) for ideas on how to use this in Bible study.

The reader should note that when the original edition of this dictionary was compiled and published, there were 101 numbers that were not used. The original edition included the following explanation: "Owing to changes in the enumeration while in progress, there were no words left for Nos. *[G]2717* and *[G]3203-3302,* which were therefore silently dropped out of the vocabulary and references as redundant. This will occasion no practical mistake or inconvenience."

A

G1 **Α α** *A a* of Semitic origin; the first letter of the alphabet; figuratively only (from its use as a numeral) the *first.*

ἀν *an* (usually before a vowel) also used in compounds (as a contraction from *G427*) in the sense of *privation;* so in many words beginning with this letter; occasionally in the sense of *union* (as a contraction of *G260*):— Alpha.

G2 **Ἀαρών** *Aarōn* of Hebrew origin [H175]; *Aaron,* the brother of Moses:— Aaron.

G3 **Ἀβαδδών** *Abaddōn* of Hebrew origin [H11]; a destroying *angel:*— Abaddon.

G4 **ἀβαρής** *abarēs* from *G1* (as a negative particle) and *G922*; *weightless,* i.e. (figuratively) *not burdensome:*— not burdensome.

G5 **Ἀββᾶ** *Abba* of Aramaic origin [H2]; *father* (as a vocative):— Abba.

G6 **Ἄβελ** *Abel* of Hebrew origin [H1893]; *Abel,* the son of Adam:— Abel.

G7 **Ἀβιά** *Abia* of Hebrew origin [H29]; *Abijah,* the name of two Israelites:— Abia.

G8 **Ἀβιάθαρ** *Abiathar* of Hebrew origin [H54]; *Abiathar,* an Israelite:— Abiathar.

G9 **Ἀβιληνή** *Abilēnē* of foreign origin [compare H58]; *Abilene,* a region of Syria:— Abilene.

G10 **Ἀβιούδ** *Abioud* of Hebrew origin [H31]; *Abihud,* an Israelite:— Abiud.

G11 **Ἀβραάμ** *Abraam* of Hebrew origin [H85]; *Abraham,* the Hebrew patriarch:— Abraham.

G12 **ἄβυσσος** *abyssos* from *G1* (as a negative particle) and a variation of *G1037*; *depthless,* i.e. (specifically infernal) *"abyss":*— deep, (bottomless) pit.

G13 **Ἄγαβος** *Agabos* of Hebrew origin [compare H2285]; *Agabus,* an Israelite:— Agabus.

G14 **ἀγαθοεργέω** *agathoergeō* from *G18* and *G2041*; to *work good:*— do good.

G15 **ἀγαθοποιέω** *agathopoieō* from *G17*; to *be a well-doer* (as a favor or a duty):— (when) do good (well).

G16 **ἀγαθοποιΐα** *agathopoiia* from *G17*; *well-doing,* i.e. *virtue:*— well-doing.

G17 **ἀγαθοποιός** *agathopoios* from *G18* and *G4160*; a *well-doer,* i.e. *virtuous:*— them that do well.

G18 **ἀγαθός** *agathos* a primary word; *"good"* (in any sense, often as noun):— benefit, good, goods, good things, well. Compare *G2570*.

G19 **ἀγαθωσύνη** *agathōsynē* from *G18*; *goodness,* i.e. *virtue* or *beneficence:*— goodness.

G20 **ἀγαλλίασις** *agalliasis* from *G21*; *exultation;* specifically *welcome:*— gladness, (exceeding) joy.

G21 **ἀγαλλιάω** *agalliaō* from

ἄγαν *agan* (*much*) and *G242*; properly to *jump for joy,* i.e. *exult:*— be (exceeding) glad, with exceeding joy, rejoice (greatly).

G22 **ἄγαμος** *agamos* from *G1* (as a negative particle) and *G1062*; *unmarried:*— unmarried.

G23 **ἀγανακτέω** *aganakteō* from

ἄγαν *agan* (*much*) and

ἄχθος *achthos* (*grief;* akin to the base of *G43*); to *be greatly afflicted,* i.e. (figuratively) *indignant:*— be much (sore) displeased, have (be moved with, with) indignation.

G24 **ἀγανάκτησις** *aganaktēsis* from *G23*; *indignation:*— indignation.

G25 **ἀγαπάω** *agapaō* perhaps from

ἄγαν *agan* (*much*) [or compare H5689]; to *love* (in a social or moral sense):— love, beloved. Compare *G5368*.

G26 **ἀγάπη** *agapē* from *G25*; *love,* i.e. *affection* or *benevolence;* specifically (plural) a *love-feast:*— charity, feast of charity, charitably, dear, love.

G27 **ἀγαπητός** *agapētos* from *G25*; *beloved:*— (dearly, well) beloved, dear.

G28 **Ἄγαρ** *Agar* of Hebrew origin [H1904]; *Hagar,* the concubine of Abraham:— Hagar.

G29 **ἀγγαρεύω** *angareuō* of foreign origin [compare H104]; properly to *be a courier,* i.e., (by implication) to *press* into public service:— compel (to go).

G30 **ἀγγεῖον** *angeion* from

ἄγγος *angos* (a *pail,* perhaps as *bent;* compare the base of *G43*); a *receptacle:*— vessel.

G31 **ἀγγελία** *angelia* from *G32*; an *announcement,* i.e. (by implication) *precept:*— message.

G32 **ἄγγελος** *angelos* from

ἀγγέλλω *angellō* [probably derived from *G71*; compare *G34*] (to *bring tidings*); a *messenger;* especially an *"angel";* by implication a *pastor:*— angel, messenger.

G33 **ἄγε** *age* imperative of *G71*; properly *lead,* i.e. *come on:*— go to.

G34 **ἀγέλη** *agelē* from *G71* [compare *G32*]; a *drove* :— herd.

G35 **ἀγενεαλόγητος** *agenealogētos* from *G1* (as negative particle) and *G1075*; *unregistered* as to birth:— without descent.

G36 **ἀγενής** *agenēs* from *G1* (as negative particle) and *G1085*; properly *without kin,* i.e. (of unknown descent, and by implication) *ignoble:*— base things.

G37 **ἁγιάζω** *hagiazō* from *G40*; to *make holy,* i.e. (ceremonially) *purify* or *consecrate;* (mentally) to *venerate:*— hallow, be holy, sanctify.

G38 **ἁγιασμός** *hagiasmos* from *G37*; properly *purification,* i.e. (the state) *purity;* concretely (by Hebrew) a *purifier:*— holiness, sanctification.

G39 **ἅγιον** *hagion* neuter of *G40*; a *sacred* thing (i.e. spot):— holiest (of all), holy place, sanctuary.

G40 **ἅγιος** *hagios* from

ἅγος *hagos* (an *awful* thing) [compare *G53*, H2282]; *sacred* (physically *pure,* morally *blameless* or *religious,* ceremonially *consecrated*):— (most) holy (one, thing), saint.

G41 **ἁγιότης** *hagiotēs* from *G40*; *sanctity* (i.e. properly the state):— holiness.

G42 **ἁγιωσύνη** *hagiōsynē* from *G40*; *sacredness* (i.e. properly the quality):— holiness.

G43 **ἀγκάλη** *ankalē* from

ἄγκος *ankos* (a *bend,* "ache"); an *arm* (as *curved*):— arm.

G44 **ἄγκιστρον** *ankistron* from the same as *G43*; a *hook* (as *bent*):— hook.

G45 **ἄγκυρα** *ankyra* from the same as *G43*; an *"anchor"* (as *crooked*):— anchor.

G46 **ἄγναφος** *agnaphos* from *G1* (as a negative particle) and the same as *G1102*; properly *unshrunk,* i.e. (by implication) *new* (cloth):— new.

G47 **ἁγνεία** *hagneia* from *G53*; *cleanliness* (the quality), i.e. (specifically) *chastity:*— purity.

G48 **ἁγνίζω** *hagnizō* from *G53*; to *make clean,* i.e. (figuratively) *sanctify* (ceremonially or morally):— purify (self).

G49 **ἁγνισμός** *hagnismos* from *G48*; a *cleansing* (the act), i.e. (ceremonial) *lustration:*— purification.

G50 **ἀγνοέω** *agnoeō* from *G1* (as a negative particle) and *G3539*; *not to know* (through lack of information or intelligence); by implication to *ignore* (through disinclination):— (be) ignorant, ignorantly, not know, not understand, unknown.

G51 **ἀγνόημα** *agnoēma* from *G50*; a thing *ignored,* i.e. *shortcoming:*— error.

G52 **ἄγνοια** *agnoia* from *G50*; *ignorance* (properly the quality):— ignorance.

G53 **ἁγνός** *hagnos* from the same as *G40*; properly *clean,* i.e. (figuratively) *innocent, modest, perfect:*— chaste, clean, pure.

G54 **ἁγνότης** *hagnotēs* from *G53*; *cleanness* (the state), i.e. (figuratively) *blamelessness:*— pureness.

G55 **ἁγνῶς** *hagnōs* adverb from *G53*; *purely,* i.e. *honestly:*— sincerely.

G56 **ἀγνωσία** *agnōsia* from *G1* (as negative particle) and *G1108*; *ignorance* (properly the state):— ignorance, not the knowledge.

G57 **ἄγνωστος** *agnōstos* from *G1* (as negative particle) and *G1110*; *unknown:*— unknown.

G58 **ἀγορά** *agora* from

ἀγείρω *ageirō* (to *gather;* probably akin to *G1453*); properly the *town-square* (as a place of public resort); by implication a *market* or *thoroughfare:*— market, marketplace, street.

G59 **ἀγοράζω** *agorazō* from *G58*; properly to *go to market,* i.e. (by implication) to *purchase;* specifically to *redeem:*— buy, redeem.

G60 **ἀγοραῖος** *agoraios* from *G58*; *relating to the market-place,* i.e. *forensic* (times); by implication *vulgar:*— baser sort, low.

G61 **ἄγρα** *agra* from *G71*; (abstractly) a *catching* (of fish); also (concretely) a *haul* (of fish):— draught.

G62 **ἀγράμματος** *agrammatos* from *G1* (as negative particle) and *G1121*; *unlettered,* i.e. *illiterate:*— unlearned.

G63 **ἀγραυλέω** *agrauleō* from *G68* and *G832* (in the sense of *G833*); to *camp out:*— abide in the field.

G64 **ἀγρεύω** *agreuō* from *G61*; to *hunt,* i.e. (figuratively) to *entrap:*— catch.

G65 **ἀγριέλαιος** *agrielaios* from *G66* and *G1636*; an *oleaster:*— olive tree (which is) wild.

G66 **ἄγριος** *agrios* from *G68*; *wild* (as pertaining to the *country*), literally (*natural*) or figuratively (*fierce*):— wild, raging.

G67 **Ἀγρίππας** *Agrippas* apparently from *G66* and *G2462*; *wild-horse* tamer; *Agrippas,* one of the Herods:— Agrippa.

G68 **ἀγρός** *agros* from *G71*; a *field* (as a *drive* for cattle); generically the *country;* specially a *farm,* i.e. *hamlet:*— country, farm, piece of ground, land.

G69 ἀγρυπνέω *agrypneō* ultimately from *G1* (as negative particle) and *G5258*; to *be sleepless,* i.e. *keep awake:*— watch.

G70 ἀγρυπνία *agrypnia* from *G69*; *sleeplessness,* i.e. a *keeping awake:*— watch.

G71 ἄγω *agō* a primary verb; properly to *lead;* by implication to *bring, drive,* (reflexive) *go,* (specifically) *pass* (time), or (figuratively) *induce:*— be, bring (forth), carry, (let) go, keep, lead away, be open.

G72 ἀγωγή *agōgē* reduplication from *G71*; a *bringing* up, i.e. *mode of living:*— manner of life.

G73 ἀγών *agōn* from *G71*; properly a place of *assembly* (as if *led*), i.e. (by implication) a *contest* (held there); figuratively an *effort* or *anxiety:*— conflict, contention, fight, race.

G74 ἀγωνία *agōnia* from *G73*; *struggle* (properly the state), i.e. (figuratively) *anguish:*— agony.

G75 ἀγωνίζομαι *agōnizomai* from *G73*; to *struggle,* literally (to *compete* for a prize), figuratively (to *contend* with an adversary), or generally (to *endeavor* to accomplish something):— fight, labor fervently, strive.

G76 Ἀδάμ *Adam* of Hebrew origin [H121]; *Adam,* the first man; typical (of Jesus) *man* (as his representative):— Adam.

G77 ἀδάπανος *adapanos* from *G1* (as negative particle) and *G1160*; *costless,* i.e. *gratuitous:*— without expense.

G78 Ἀδδί *Addi* probably of Hebrew origin [compare H5716]; *Addi,* an Israelite:— Addi.

G79 ἀδελφή *adelphē* feminine of *G80*; a *sister* (natural or ecclesiastical):— sister.

G80 ἀδελφός *adelphos* from *G1* (as a connective particle) and

δελφύς *delphys* (the *womb*); a *brother* (literally or figuratively) near or remote [much like H1]:— brother.

G81 ἀδελφότης *adelphotēs* from *G80*; *brotherhood* (properly the feeling of *brotherliness*), i.e. the (Christian) *fraternity:*— brethren, brotherhood.

G82 ἄδηλος *adēlos* from *G1* (as a negative particle) and *G1212*; *hidden,* figuratively *indistinct:*— appear not, uncertain.

G83 ἀδηλότης *adēlotēs* from *G82*; *uncertainty:*— uncertainty.

G84 ἀδήλως *adēlōs* adverb from *G82*; *uncertainly* :— uncertainly.

G85 ἀδημονέω *adēmoneō* from a derivative of

ἀδέω *adeō* (to be *sated* to loathing); to *be in distress* (of mind):— be full of heaviness, be very heavy.

G86 ᾅδης *hadēs* from *G1* (as a negative particle) and *G1492*; properly *unseen,* i.e. *"Hades"* or the place (state) of departed souls:— grave, hell.

G87 ἀδιάκριτος *adiakritos* from *G1* (as a negative particle) and a derivative of *G1252*; properly *undistinguished,* i.e. (active) *impartial:*— without partiality.

G88 ἀδιάλειπτος *adialeiptos* from *G1* (as a negative particle) and a derivative of a compound of *G1223* and *G3007*; *without intermission,* i.e. *permanent:*— without ceasing, continual.

G89 ἀδιαλείπτως *adialeiptōs* adverb from *G88*; *uninterruptedly,* i.e. *without omission* (on an appropriate occasion):— without ceasing.

G90 ἀδιαφθορία *adiaphthoria* from a derivative of a compound of *G1* (as a negative particle) and a derivative of *G1311*; *not corruption,* i.e. (figuratively) *purity* (of doctrine):— integrity.

G91 ἀδικέω *adikeō* from *G94*; to *be unjust,* i.e. (active) *do wrong* (morally, socially or physically):— hurt, injure, be an offender, be unjust, (do, suffer, take) wrong.

G92 ἀδίκημα *adikēma* from *G91*; a *wrong* done :— evil doing, iniquity, matter of wrong.

G93 ἀδικία *adikia* from *G94*; (legal) *injustice* (properly the quality, by implication the act); moral *wrongfulness* (of character, life or act):— iniquity, unjust, unrighteousness, wrong.

G94 ἄδικος *adikos* from *G1* (as a negative particle) and *G1349*; *unjust;* by extension *wicked;* by implication *treacherous;* specifically *heathen:*— unjust, unrighteous.

G95 ἀδίκως *adikōs* adverb from *G94*; *unjustly:*— wrongfully.

G96 ἀδόκιμος *adokimos* from *G1* (as a negative particle) and *G1384*; *unapproved,* i.e. *rejected;* by implication *worthless* (literally or morally):— castaway, rejected, reprobate.

G97 ἄδολος *adolos* from *G1* (as a negative particle) and *G1388*; *not deceitful,* i.e. (figuratively) *unadulterated:*— sincere.

G98 Ἀδραμυττηνός *Adramyttēnos* from

Ἀδραμύττειον *Adramytteion* (a place in Asia Minor); *Adramyttene* or belonging to Adramyttium:— of Adramyttium.

G99 Ἀδρίας *Adrias* from

Ἀδρία *Adria* (a place near its shore); the *Adriatic* sea (including the Ionian):— Adria.

G100 ἁδρότης *hadrotēs* from

ἁδρός *hadros* (*stout*); *plumpness,* i.e. (figuratively) *liberality:*— abundance.

G101 ἀδυνατέω *adynateō* from *G102*; to *be unable,* i.e. (passive) *impossible:*— be impossible.

G102 ἀδύνατος *adynatos* from *G1* (as a negative particle) and *G1415*; *unable,* i.e. *weak* (literally or figuratively); passive *impossible:*— could not do, impossible, impotent, not possible, weak.

G103 ᾄδω *adō* a primary verb; to *sing:*— sing.

G104 ἀεί *aei* from an obsolete primary noun (apparently meaning continued *duration*); *"ever;"* by qualification *regularly;* by implication *earnestly:*— always, ever.

G105 ἀετός *aetos* from the same as *G109*; an *eagle* (from its *wind*-like flight):— eagle.

G106 ἄζυμος *azymos* from *G1* (as a negative particle) and *G2219*; *unleavened,* i.e. (figuratively) *uncorrupted;* (in the neuter plural) specifically (by implication) the *Passover* week:— unleavened (bread).

G107 Ἀζώρ *Azōr* of Hebrew origin [compare H5809]; *Azor,* an Israelite:— Azor.

G108 Ἄζωτος *Azōtos* of Hebrew origin [H795]; *Azotus* (i.e. Ashdod), a place in Palestine:— Azotus.

G109 ἀήρ *aēr* from

ἄημι *aēmi* (to *breathe* unconsciously, i.e. *respire;* by analogy to *blow*); *"air"* (as naturally *circumambient*):— air. Compare *G5594*.

G110 ἀθανασία *athanasia* from a compound of *G1* (as a negative particle) and *G2288*; *deathlessness:*— immortality.

G111 ἀθέμιτος *athemitos* from *G1* (as a negative particle) and a derivative of

θέμις *themis* (*statute;* from the base of *G5087*); *illegal;* by implication *flagitious:*— abominable, unlawful thing.

G112 ἄθεος *atheos* from *G1* (as a negative particle) and *G2316*; *godless:*— without God.

G113 ἄθεσμος *athesmos* from *G1* (as a negative particle) and a derivative of *G5087* (in the sense of *enacting*); *lawless,* i.e. (by implication) *criminal:*— wicked.

G114 ἀθετέω *atheteō* from a compound of *G1* (as a negative particle) and a derivative of *G5087*; to *set aside,* i.e. (by implication) to *disesteem, neutralize* or *violate:*— cast off, despise, disannul, frustrate, bring to nought, reject.

G115 ἀθέτησις *athetēsis* from *G114*; *cancellation* (literal or figurative):— disannulling, put away.

G116 Ἀθῆναι *Athēnai* plural of

Ἀθήνη *Athēnē* (the goddess of wisdom, who was reputed to have founded the city); *Athenae,* the capital of Greece:— Athens.

G117 Ἀθηναῖος *Athēnaios* from *G116*; an *Athenaean* or inhabitant of Athenae:— Athenian.

G118 ἀθλέω *athleō* from

ἆθλος *athlos* (a *contest* in the public lists); to *contend* in the competitive games:— strive.

G119 ἄθλησις *athlēsis* from *G118*; a *struggle* (figurative):— fight.

G120 ἀθυμέω *athymeō* from a compound of *G1* (as a negative particle) and *G2372*; to *be spiritless,* i.e. *disheartened:*— be dismayed.

G121 ἄθωος *athōos* from *G1* (as a negative particle) and a probable derivative of *G5087* (meaning a *penalty*); *not guilty:*— innocent.

G122 αἴγειος *aigeios* from

αἴξ *aix* (a *goat*); belonging to a *goat:*— goat.

G123 αἰγιαλός *aigialos* from

ἀΐσσω *aissō* (to *rush*) and *G251* (in the sense of the *sea*); a *beach* (on which the *waves dash*):— shore.

G124 Αἰγύπτιος *Aigyptios* from *G125*; an *Aegyptian* or inhabitant of Aegyptus:— Egyptian.

G125 Αἴγυπτος *Aigyptos* of uncertain derivation; *Aegyptus,* the land of the Nile:— Egypt.

G126 ἀΐδιος *aidios* from *G104*; *ever enduring* (forward and backward, or forward only):— eternal, everlasting.

G127 αἰδώς *aidōs* perhaps from *G1* (as a negative particle) and *G1492* (through the idea of *downcast* eyes); *bashfulness,* i.e. (towards men), *modesty* or (towards God) *awe:*— reverence, shamefacedness.

G128 Αἰθίοψ *Aithiops* from

αἴθω *aithō* (to *scorch*) and

ὤψ *ōps* (the *face,* from *G3700*); an *Aethiopian:*— Ethiopian.

G129 αἷμα *haima* of uncertain derivation; *blood,* literal (of men or animals), figurative (the *juice* of grapes) or specifically (the atoning *blood* of Christ); by implication *bloodshed,* also *kindred:*— blood.

G130 **αἱματεκχυσία** *haimatekchysia* from Greek *G129* and a derivative of Greek *G1632*; an *effusion of blood:*— shedding of blood.

G131 **αἱμορροέω** *haimorroeo* from *G129* and *G4482*; to *flow blood,* i.e. *have a hemorrhage:*— diseased with an issue of blood.

G132 **Αἰνέας** *Aineas* of uncertain derivation; *Aeneas,* an Israelite:— Aeneas.

G133 **αἴνεσις** *ainesis* from *G134*; a *praising* (the act), i.e. (specificallly) a *thanking* (thank offering):— praise.

G134 **αἰνέω** *aineō* from *G136*; to *praise* (God):— praise.

G135 **αἴνιγμα** *ainigma* from a derivative of Greek *G136* (in its primary sense); an *obscure* saying ("enigma"), i.e. (abstract) *obscureness:*— darkly.

G136 **αἶνος** *ainos* apparently a primary word; properly a *story,* but used in the sense of *G1868*; *praise* (of God):— praise.

G137 **Αἰνών** *Ainōn* of Hebrew origin [a derivative of H5869, *place of springs*]; *Aenon,* a place in Palestine:— Aenon.

G138 **αἱρέομαι** *haireomai* probably akin to *G142*; to *take for oneself,* i.e. to *prefer:*— choose. Some of the forms are borrowed from a cognate **ἕλλομαι** *hellomai* which is otherwise obsolete.

G139 **αἵρεσις** *hairesis* from *G138*; properly a *choice,* i.e. (specifically) a *party* or (abstractly) *disunion:*— heresy [*which is the Greek word itself*], sect.

G140 **αἱρετίζω** *hairetizō* from a derivative of *G138*; to *make a choice:*— choose.

G141 **αἱρετικός** *hairetikos* from the same as *G140*; a *schismatic:*— heretic [*the Greek word itself*].

G142 **αἴρω** *airō* a primary verb; to *lift;* by implication to *take up* or *away;* figuratively to *raise* (the voice), *keep in suspense* (the mind); specifically to *sail* away (i.e. *weigh anchor*); by Hebrew [compare H5375] to *expiate* sin:— away with, bear (up), carry, lift up, loose, make to doubt, put away, remove, take (away, up).

G143 **αἰσθάνομαι** *aisthanomai* of uncertain derivation; to *apprehend* (properly by the senses):— perceive.

G144 **αἴσθησις** *aisthēsis* from *G143*; *perception,* i.e. (figuratively) *discernment:*— judgment.

G145 **αἰσθητήριον** *aisthētērion* from a derivative of *G143*; properly an *organ of perception,* i.e. (figuratively) *judgment:*— senses.

G146 **αἰσχροκερδής** *aischrokerdēs* from *G150* and **κέρδος** *kerdos* (*gain*); *sordid:*— given to (greedy of) filthy lucre.

G147 **αἰσχροκερδῶς** *aischrokerdōs* adverb from *G146*; *sordidly:*— for filthy lucre's sake.

G148 **αἰσχρολογία** *aischrologia* from *G150* and *G3056*; *vile conversation:*— filthy communication.

G149 **αἰσχρόν** *aischron* neuter of *G150*; a *shameful* thing, i.e. *indecorum:*— shame.

G150 **αἰσχρός** *aischros* from the same as *G153*; *shameful,* i.e. *base* (specifically *venal*):— filthy.

G151 **αἰσχρότης** *aischrotēs* from *G150*; *shamefulness,* i.e. *obscenity:*— filthiness.

G152 **αἰσχύνη** *aischynē* from *G153*; *shame* or *disgrace* (abstract or concrete):— dishonesty, shame.

G153 **αἰσχύνομαι** *aischynomai* from **αἶσχος** *aischos* (*disfigurement,* i.e. *disgrace*); to *feel shame* (for oneself):— be ashamed.

G154 **αἰτέω** *aiteō* of uncertain derivation; to *ask* (in general):— ask, beg, call for, crave, desire, require. Compare *G4441*.

G155 **αἴτημα** *aitēma* from *G154*; a *thing asked* or (abstractly) an *asking:*— petition, request, required.

G156 **αἰτία** *aitia* from the same as *G154*; a *cause* (as if *asked* for), i.e. (logical) *reason* (motive, matter), (legal) *crime* (alleged or proved):— accusation, case, cause, crime, fault.

G157 **αἰτίαμα** *aitiama* from a derivative of *G156*; a *thing charged:*— complaint.

G158 **αἴτιον** *aition* neuter of *G159*; a *reason* or *crime* [like *G156*]:— cause, fault.

G159 **αἴτιος** *aitios* from the same as *G154*; *causative,* i.e. (concretely) that which *causes:*— author.

G160 **αἰφνίδιος** *aiphnidios* from a compound of *G1* (as a negative particle) and *G5316* [compare *G1810*] (meaning *non-apparent*); *unexpected,* i.e. (adverbially) *suddenly:*— sudden, unawares.

G161 **αἰχμαλωσία** *aichmalōsia* from *G164*; *captivity:*— captivity.

G162 **αἰχμαλωτεύω** *aichmalōteuō* from **αἰχμαλωτός** *aichmalōtos*; to *capture* [like *G163*]:— lead captive.

G163 **αἰχμαλωτίζω** *aichmalōtizō* from *G164*; to *make captive:*— lead away captive, bring into captivity.

G164 **αἰχμαλωτός** *aichmalōtos* from **αἰχμή** *aichmē* (a *spear*) and a derivative of the same as *G259*; properly a *prisoner of war,* i.e. (generally) a *captive:*— captive.

G165 **αἰών** *aiōn* from the same as *G104*; properly an *age;* by extension *perpetuity* (also past); by implication the *world;* specifically (Jewish) a Messianic period (present or future):— age, course, eternal, (for) ever, (for) evermore, never, ever, (beginning of the, while the) world (began, without end). Compare *G5550*.

G166 **αἰώνιος** *aiōnios* from *G165*; *perpetual* (also used of past time, or past and future as well):— eternal, for ever, everlasting, world (began).

G167 **ἀκαθαρσία** *akatharsia* from *G169*; *impurity* (the quality), physical or moral:— uncleanness.

G168 **ἀκαθάρτης** *akathartēs* from *G169*; *impurity* (the state), morally:— filthiness.

G169 **ἀκάθαρτος** *akathartos* from *G1* (as a negative particle) and a presumed derivative of **καθαίρω** *kathairō* (meaning *cleansed*); *impure* (ceremonially, morally [*lewd*] or specifically [*daemonic*]):— foul, unclean.

G170 **ἀκαιρέομαι** *akaireomai* from a compound of *G1* (as a negative particle) and *G2540* (meaning *unseasonable*); to *be inopportune* (for oneself), i.e. to *fail of a proper occasion:*— lack opportunity.

G171 **ἀκαίρως** *akairōs* adverb from the same as *G170*; *inopportunely:*— out of season.

G172 **ἄκακος** *akakos* from *G1* (as a negative particle) and *G2556*; *not bad,* i.e. (objectively) *innocent* or (subjectively) *unsuspecting:*— harmless, simple.

G173 **ἄκανθα** *akantha* probably from the same as *G188*; a *thorn:*— thorn.

G174 **ἀκάνθινος** *akanthinos* from *G173*; *thorny* :— *of thorns.*

G175 **ἄκαρπος** *akarpos* from *G1* (as a negative particle) and *G2590*; *barren* (literally or figuratively):— without fruit, unfruitful.

G176 **ἀκατάγνωστος** *akatagnōstos* from *G1* (as a negative particle) and a derivative of *G2607*; *not blamable:*— that cannot be condemned.

G177 **ἀκατακάλυπτος** *akatakalyptos* from *G1* (as a negative particle) and a derivative of a compound of *G2596* and *G2572*; *unveiled:*— uncovered.

G178 **ἀκατάκριτος** *akatakritos* from *G1* (as a negative particle) and a derivative of *G2632*; *without* (legal) *trial:*— not condemned.

G179 **ἀκατάλυτος** *akatalytos* from *G1* (as a negative particle) and a derivative of *G2647*; *indissoluble,* i.e. (figuratively) *permanent:*— endless.

G180 **ἀκατάπαυστος** *akatapaustos* from *G1* (as a negative particle) and a derivative of *G2664*; *not refraining:*— that cannot cease.

G181 **ἀκαταστασία** *akatastasia* from *G182*; *instability,* i.e. *disorder:*— commotion, confusion, tumult.

G182 **ἀκατάστατος** *akatastatos* from *G1* (as a negative particle) and a derivative of *G2525*; *inconstant:*— unstable.

G183 **ἀκατάσχετος** *akataschetos* from *G1* (as a negative particle) and a derivative of *G2722*; *not restrainable:*— unruly.

G184 **Ἀκελδαμά** *Akeldama* of Aramaic origin [meaning *field of blood;* corresponding to H2506 and H1818]; *Akeldama,* a place near Jerusalem:— Aceldama.

G185 **ἀκέραιος** *akeraios* from *G1* (as a negative particle) and a presumed derivative of *G2767*; *unmixed,* i.e. (figuratively) *innocent:*— harmless, simple.

G186 **ἀκλινής** *aklinēs* from *G1* (as a negative particle) and *G2827*; *not leaning,* i.e. (figuratively) *firm:*— without wavering.

G187 **ἀκμάζω** *akmazō* from the same as *G188*; to *make a point,* i.e. (figuratively) *mature:*— be fully ripe.

G188 **ἀκμήν** *akmēn* accusative of a noun ("*acme*") akin to **ἀκή** *akē* (a *point*) and meaning the same; adverbially *just* now, i.e. *still:*— yet.

G189 **ἀκοή** *akoē* from *G191*; *hearing* (the act, the sense or the thing heard):— audience, ear, fame, which ye heard, hearing, preached, report, rumor.

G190 **ἀκολουθέω** *akoloutheō* from *G1* (as a particle of union) and **κέλευθος** *keleuthos* (a *road*); properly to *be in the same way with,* i.e. to *accompany* (specifically as a disciple):— follow, reach.

G191 **ἀκούω** *akouō* a primary verb; to *hear* (in various senses):— give (in the) audience (of), come (to the ears), (shall) hear, hearer, hearken, be noised, be reported, understand.

G192 **ἀκρασία** *akrasia* from *G193*; *want of self-restraint:*— excess, incontinence.

G193 **ἀκράτης** *akratēs* from *G1* (as a negative particle) and *G2904*; *powerless,* i.e. *without self-control:*— incontinent.

G194 **ἄκρατος** *akratos* from *G1* (as a negative particle) and a presumed derivative of *G2767*; *undiluted:*— without mixture.

G195 ἀκρίβεια *akribeia* from the same as *G196*; *exactness:*— perfect manner.

G196 ἀκριβέστατος *akribestatos* superlative of **ἀκριβής** *akribēs* (a derivative of the same as Greek *G206*); *most exact:*— most exact.

G197 ἀκριβέστερον *akribesteron* neuter of the comparative of the same as *G196*; (adverbially) *more exactly:*— more perfect, more perfectly.

G198 ἀκριβόω *akriboō* from the same as *G196*; to *be exact,* i.e. *ascertain:*— inquire diligently.

G199 ἀκριβῶς *akribōs* adverb from the same as *G196*; *exactly:*— circumspectly, diligently, perfect, perfectly.

G200 ἀκρίς *akris* apparently from the same as *G206*; a *locust* (as *pointed,* or as *lighting* on the *top* of vegetation):— locust.

G201 ἀκροατήριον *akroatērion* from *G202*; an *audience-room:*— place of hearing.

G202 ἀκροατής *akroatēs* from **ἀκροάομαι** *akroaomai* (to *listen;* apparently an intensive of *G191*); a *hearer* (merely):— hearer.

G203 ἀκροβυστία *akrobystia* from *G206* and probably a modified form of **πόσθη** *posthē* (the *penis* or male sexual organ); the *prepuce;* by implication an *uncircumcised* (i.e. *gentile,* figuratively *unregenerate*) state or person:— not circumcised, uncircumcised [*with G2192*], uncircumcision.

G204 ἀκρογωνιαῖος *akrogōniaios* from *G206* and *G1137*; belonging to the extreme *corner:*— chief corner.

G205 ἀκροθίνιον *akrothinion* from *G206* and **θίς** *this* (a *heap*); properly (in the plural) the *top of the heap,* i.e. (by implication) *best of the booty:*— spoils.

G206 ἄκρον *akron* neuter of an adjective probably akin to the base of *G188*; the *extremity:*— one end . . . other, tip, top, uttermost part.

G207 Ἀκύλας *Akylas* probably for Latin *aquila* (an *eagle*); *Akulas,* an Israelite:— Aquila.

G208 ἀκυρόω *akyroō* from *G1* (as a negative particle) and *G2964*; to *invalidate:*— disannul, make of none effect.

G209 ἀκωλύτως *akōlytōs* adverb from a compound of *G1* (as a negative particle) and a derivative of *G2967*; in *an unhindered manner,* i.e. *freely:*— no man forbidding him.

G210 ἄκων *akōn* from *G1* (as a negative particle) and *G1635*; *unwilling:*— against the will.

G211 ἀλάβαστρον *alabastron* neuter of **ἀλάβαστρος** *alabastros* (of uncertain derivation), the name of a stone; properly an *"alabaster"* box, i.e. (by extension) a perfume *vase* (of any material):— (alabaster) box.

G212 ἀλαζονεία *alazoneia* from *G213*; *braggadocio,* i.e. (by implication) *self-confidence:*— boasting, pride.

G213 ἀλαζών *alazōn* from **ἄλη** *alē* (*vagrancy*); *braggart:*— boaster.

G214 ἀλαλάζω *alalazō* from **ἀλαλή** *alalē* (a *shout, "halloo"*); to *vociferate,* i.e. (by implication) to *wail;* figuratively to *clang:*— tinkle, wail.

G215 ἀλάλητος *alalētos* from *G1* (as a negative particle) and a derivative of *G2980*; *unspeakable:*— unutterable, which cannot be uttered.

G216 ἄλαλος *alalos* from *G1* (as a negative particle) and *G2980*; *mute:*— dumb.

G217 ἅλας *halas* from *G251*; *salt;* figuratively *prudence:*— salt.

G218 ἀλείφω *aleiphō* from *G1* (as particle of union) and the base of *G3045*; to *oil* (with perfume):— anoint.

G219 ἀλεκτοροφωνία *alektorophōnia* from *G220* and *G5456*; *cock-crow,* i.e. the third night-watch:— cockcrowing.

G220 ἀλέκτωρ *alektōr* from **ἀλέκω** *alekō* (to *ward* off); a *cock* or male fowl:— cock.

G221 Ἀλεξανδρεύς *Alexandreus* from **Ἀλεξάνδρεια** *Alexandreia* (the city so called); an *Alexandreian* or inhabitant of Alexandria:— of Alexandria, Alexandrian.

G222 Ἀλεξανδρῖνος *Alexandrinos* from the same as *G221*; *Alexandrine,* or belonging to Alexandria:— of Alexandria.

G223 Ἀλέξανδρος *Alexandros* from the same as (the first part of) *G220* and *G435*; *mandefender; Alexander,* the name of three Israelites and one other man:— Alexander.

G224 ἄλευρον *aleuron* from **ἀλέω** *aleō* (to *grind*); *flour:*— meal.

G225 ἀλήθεια *alētheia* from *G227*; *truth:*— true, truly, truth, verity.

G226 ἀληθεύω *alētheuō* from *G227*; to *be true* (in doctrine and profession):— speak (tell) the truth.

G227 ἀληθής *alēthēs* from *G1* (as a negative particle) and *G2990*; *true* (as *not concealing*):— true, truly, truth.

G228 ἀληθινός *alēthinos* from *G227*; *truthful:*— true.

G229 ἀλήθω *alēthō* from the same as *G224*; to *grind:*— grind.

G230 ἀληθῶς *alēthōs* adverb from *G227*; *truly:*— indeed, surely, of a surety, truly, of a (in) truth, verily, very.

G231 ἁλιεύς *halieus* from *G251*; a *sailor* (as engaged on the *salt* water), i.e. (by implication) a *fisher:*— fisher, fisherman.

G232 ἁλιεύω *halieuō* from *G231*; to *be a fisher,* i.e. (by implication) to *fish:*— go a-fishing.

G233 ἁλίζω *halizō* from *G251*; to *salt:*— salt.

G234 ἀλίσγημα *alisgēma* from **ἀλισγέω** *alisgeō* (to *soil*); (ceremonial) *defilement:*— pollution.

G235 ἀλλά *alla* neuter plural of *G243*; properly *other* things, i.e. (adverbially) *contrariwise* (in many relations):— and, but (even), howbeit, indeed, nay, nevertheless, no, notwithstanding, save, therefore, yea, yet.

G236 ἀλλάσσω *allassō* from *G243*; to *make different:*— change.

G237 ἀλλαχόθεν *allachothen* from *G243*; *from elsewhere:*— some other way.

G238 ἀλληγορέω *allēgoreō* from *G243* and **ἀγορέω** *agoreō* (to *harangue* [compare *G58*]); to *allegorize:*— be an allegory [*the Greek word itself*].

G239 ἀλληλουϊά *allēlouia* of Hebrew origin [imperative of H1984 and H3050]; *praise ye Jah!,* an adoring exclamation:— alleluiah.

G240 ἀλλήλων *allēlōn* genitive plural from *G243* reduplication; *one another:*— each other, mutual, one another, (the other), themselves, yourselves, selves, (selves) together [*sometimes with G3326 or G4314*].

G241 ἀλλογενής *allogenēs* from *G243* and *G1085*; *foreign,* i.e. not a Jew:— stranger.

G242 ἅλλομαι *hallomai* middle of apparently a primary verb; to *jump;* figuratively to *gush:*— leap, spring up.

G243 ἄλλος *allos* a primary word; *"else,"* i.e. *different* (in many applications):— more, one (another), another, some another, other, others, otherwise.

G244 ἀλλοτριεπίσκοπος *allotriepiskopos* from *G245* and *G1985*; *overseeing others'* affairs, i.e. a *meddler* (specifically in Gentile customs):— busybody in other men's matters.

G245 ἀλλότριος *allotrios* from *G243*; *another's,* i.e. not one's own; by extension *foreign, not akin, hostile:*— alien, other (man's, men's), another (man's, men's), strange, stranger.

G246 ἀλλόφυλος *allophylos* from *G243* and *G5443*; *foreign,* i.e. (specifically) *Gentile:*— one of another nation.

G247 ἄλλως *allōs* adverb from *G243*; *differently* :— otherwise.

G248 ἀλοάω *aloaō* from the same as *G257*; to *tread* out grain:— thresh, tread out the corn.

G249 ἄλογος *alogos* from *G1* (as a negative particle) and *G3056*; *irrational:*— brute, unreasonable.

G250 ἀλοή *aloē* of foreign origin [compare H174]; *aloes* (the gum):— aloes.

G251 ἅλς *hals* a primary word; *"salt":*— salt.

G252 ἁλυκός *halykos* from *G251*; *briny:*— salt.

G253 ἀλυπότερος *alypoteros* comparative of a compound of *G1* (as a negative particle) and *G3077*; *more without grief:*— less sorrowful.

G254 ἅλυσις *halysis* of uncertain derivation; a *fetter* or *manacle:*— bonds, chain.

G255 ἀλυσιτελής *alysitelēs* from *G1* (as a negative particle) and the base of *G3081*; *without gain,* i.e. (by implication) *pernicious:*— unprofitable.

G256 Ἀλφαῖος *Alphaios* of Hebrew origin [compare H2501]; *Alphaeus,* an Israelite:— Alpheus.

G257 ἅλων *halōn* probably from the base of *G1507*; a threshing-*floor* (as *rolled* hard), i.e. (figuratively) the *grain* (and chaff, as just threshed):— floor.

G258 ἀλώπηξ *alōpēx* of uncertain derivation; a *fox,* i.e. (figuratively) a *cunning* person:— fox.

G259 ἅλωσις *halōsis* from a collateral form of *G138*; *capture:*— be taken.

G260 ἅμα *hama* a primary particle; properly *at the "same" time,* but freely used as a preposition or adverb denoting close association:— also, and, together, with, withal.

G261 ἀμαθής *amathēs* from *G1* (as a negative particle) and *G3129*; *ignorant:*— unlearned.

G262 ἀμαράντινος *amarantinos* from *G263*; *"amaranthine"*, i.e. (by implication) *fadeless:*— that fadeth not away.

G263 ἀμάραντος *amarantos* from *G1* (as a negative particle) and a presumed derivative of *G3133*; *unfading,* i.e. (by implication) *perpetual:*— that fadeth not away.

G264 ἁμαρτάνω *hamartanō* perhaps from *G1* (as a negative particle) and the base of *G3313*; properly to *miss* the mark (and so *not share* in the prize), i.e. (figuratively) to *err,* especially (morally) to *sin:*— for your faults, offend, sin, trespass.

G265 ἁμάρτημα *hamartēma* from *G264*; a *sin* (properly concrete):— sin.

G266 ἁμαρτία *hamartia* from *G264*; *sin* (properly abstract):— offence, sin, sinful.

G267 ἀμάρτυρος *amartyros* from *G1* (as a negative particle) and a form of *G3144*; *unattested:*— without witness.

G268 ἁμαρτωλός *hamartōlos* from *G264*; *sinful,* i.e. a *sinner:*— sinful, sinner.

G269 ἄμαχος *amachos* from *G1* (as a negative particle) and *G3163*; *peaceable:*— not a brawler.

G270 ἀμάω *amaō* from *G260*; properly to *collect,* i.e. (by implication) *reap:*— reap down.

G271 ἀμέθυστος *amethystos* from *G1* (as a negative particle) and a derivative of *G3184*; the *"amethyst"* (supposed to *prevent intoxication*):— amethyst.

G272 ἀμελέω *ameleō* from *G1* (as a negative particle) and *G3199*; to *be careless* of:— make light of, neglect, be negligent, not regard.

G273 ἄμεμπτος *amemptos* from *G1* (as a negative particle) and a derivative of *G3201*; *irreproachable:*— blameless, faultless, unblamable.

G274 ἀμέμπτως *amemptōs* adverb from *G273*; *faultlessly:*— blameless, unblamably.

G275 ἀμέριμνος *amerimnos* from *G1* (as a negative particle) and *G3308*; *not anxious:*— without care, without carefulness, secure.

G276 ἀμετάθετος *ametathetos* from *G1* (as a negative particle) and a derivative of *G3346*; *unchangeable,* or (neuter as abstract) *inability to be changed:*— immutable, immutability.

G277 ἀμετακίνητος *ametakinētos* from *G1* (as a negative particle) and a derivative of *G3334*; *immovable:*— unmovable.

G278 ἀμεταμέλητος *ametamelētos* from *G1* (as a negative particle) and a presumed derivative of *G3338*; *irrevocable:*— without repentance, not to be repented of.

G279 ἀμετανόητος *ametanoētos* from *G1* (as a negative particle) and a presumed derivative of *G3340*; *unrepentant:*— impenitent.

G280 ἄμετρος *ametros* from *G1* (as a negative particle) and *G3358*; *immoderate:*— without measure, thing without measure.

G281 ἀμήν *amēn* of Hebrew origin [H543]; properly *firm,* i.e. (figuratively) *trustworthy;* adverb *surely* (often as interjection *so be it*):— amen, verily.

G282 ἀμήτωρ *amētōr* from *G1* (as a negative particle) and *G3384*; *motherless,* i.e. *of unknown maternity:*— without mother.

G283 ἀμίαντος *amiantos* from *G1* (as a negative particle) and a derivative of *G3392*; *unsoiled,* i.e. (figuratively) *pure:*— undefiled.

G284 Ἀμιναδάβ *Aminadab* of Hebrew origin [H5992]; *Aminadab,* an Israelite:— Aminadab.

G285 ἄμμος *ammos* perhaps from *G260*; *sand* (as *heaped* on the beach):— sand.

G286 ἀμνός *amnos* apparently a primary word; a *lamb:*— lamb.

G287 ἀμοιβή *amoibē* from

ἀμείβω *ameibō* (to *exchange*); *requital:*— requite.

G288 ἄμπελος *ampelos* probably from the base of *G297* and that of *G257*; a *vine* (as *coiling about* a support):— vine.

G289 ἀμπελουργός *ampelourgos* from *G288* and *G2041*; a *vine-worker,* i.e. *pruner:*— vine-dresser.

G290 ἀμπελών *ampelōn* from *G288*; a *vineyard* :— vineyard.

G291 Ἀμπλίας *Amplias* contracted for Latin *ampliatus* [*enlarged*]; *Amplias,* a Roman Christian:— Amplias.

G292 ἀμύνομαι *amynomai* middle of a primary verb; to *ward off* (for oneself), i.e. *protect:*— defend.

G293 ἀμφίβληστρον *amphiblēstron* from a compound of the base of *G297* and *G906*; a (fishing) *net* (as *thrown about* the fish):— net.

G294 ἀμφιέννυμι *amphiennymi* from the base of *G297* and

ἕννυμι *hennymi* (to *invest*); to *enrobe:*— clothe.

G295 Ἀμφίπολις *Amphipolis* from the base of *G297* and *G4172*; a *city surrounded* by a river; *Amphipolis,* a place in Macedonia:— Amphipolis.

G296 ἄμφοδον *amphodon* from the base of *G297* and *G3598*; a *fork* in the road:— where two ways meet.

G297 ἀμφότερος *amphoteros* comparative of

ἀμφί *amphi* (*around*); (in plural) *both:*— both.

G298 ἀμώμητος *amōmētos* from *G1* (as a negative particle) and a derivative of *G3469*; *not blamable:*— blameless.

G299 ἄμωμος *amōmos* from *G1* (as a negative particle) and *G3470*; *unblemished* (literally or figuratively):— without blame (blemish, fault, spot), faultless, unblamable.

G300 Ἀμών *Amōn* of Hebrew origin [H526]; *Amon,* an Israelite:— Amon.

G301 Ἀμώς *Amōs* of Hebrew origin [H531]; *Amos,* an Israelite:— Amos.

G302 ἄν *an* a primary particle, denoting a *supposition, wish, possibility* or *uncertainty;* Usually unexpressed except by the subjunctive or potential mood. Also contracted for *G1437*:— whatsoever, whereso-ever, whithersoever, whosoever.

G303 ἀνά *ana* a primary preposition and adverb; properly *up;* but (by extension) used (distributively) *severally,* or (locally) *at* (etc.). In compounds (as a prefix) it often means (by implication) *repetition, intensity, reversal,* etc.:— and, apiece, by, each, every, every (man), in, through.

G304 ἀναβαθμός *anabathmos* from *G305* [compare *G898*]; a *stairway:*— stairs.

G305 ἀναβαίνω *anabainō* from *G303* and the base of Greek *G939*; to *go up* (literally or figuratively):— arise, ascend (up), climb (go, grow, rise, spring) up, come (up).

G306 ἀναβάλλομαι *anaballomai* middle from *G303* and *G906*; to *put off* (for oneself):— defer.

G307 ἀναβιβάζω *anabibazō* from *G303* and a derivative of the base of *G939*; to *cause to go up,* i.e. *haul* (a net):— draw.

G308 ἀναβλέπω *anablepō* from *G303* and *G991*; to *look up;* by implication to *recover sight:*— look (up), see, receive sight.

G309 ἀνάβλεψις *anablepsis* from *G308*; *restoration of sight:*— recovering of sight.

G310 ἀναβοάω *anaboaō* from *G303* and *G994*; to *halloo:*— cry (aloud, out).

G311 ἀναβολή *anabolē* from *G306*; a *putting off* :— delay.

G312 ἀναγγέλλω *anangellō* from *G303* and the base of *G32*; to *announce* (in detail):— declare, rehearse, report, show, speak, tell.

G313 ἀναγεννάω *anagennaō* from *G303* and *G1080*; to *beget* or (by extension) *bear* (again):— beget, (bear) again.

G314 ἀναγινώσκω *anaginōskō* from *G303* and *G1097*; to *know again,* i.e. (by extension) to *read:*— read.

G315 ἀναγκάζω *anankazō* from *G318*; to *necessitate;:*— compel, constrain.

G316 ἀναγκαῖος *anankaios* from *G318*; *necessary;* by implication *close* (of kin):— near, necessary, necessity, needful.

G317 ἀναγκαστῶς *anankastōs* adverb from a derivative of *G315*; *compulsorily:*— by constraint.

G318 ἀνάγκη *anankē* from *G303* and the base of *G43*; *constraint* (literal or figurative); by implication *distress:*— distress, must needs, (of) necessity, necessary, needeth, needful.

G319 ἀναγνωρίζομαι *anagnōrizomai* middle from *G303* and *G1107*; to *make* (oneself) *known:*— be made known.

G320 ἀνάγνωσις *anagnōsis* from *G314*; (the act of) *reading:*— reading.

G321 ἀνάγω *anagō* from *G303* and *G71*; to *lead up;* by extension to *bring out;* specifically to *sail* away:— bring (again, forth, up again), depart, launch (forth), lead (up), loose, offer, sail, set forth, take up.

G322 ἀναδείκνυμι *anadeiknymi* from *G303* and *G1166*; to *exhibit,* i.e. (by implication) to *indicate, appoint:*— appoint, shew.

G323 ἀνάδειξις *anadeixis* from *G322*; (the act of) *exhibition:*— shewing.

G324 ἀναδέχομαι *anadechomai* from *G303* and *G1209*; to *entertain* (as a guest):— receive.

G325 ἀναδίδωμι *anadidōmi* from *G303* and *G1325*; to *hand over:*— deliver.

G326 ἀναζάω *anazaō* from *G303* and *G2198*; to *recover life* (literally or figuratively):— be alive again, live again, revive.

G327 ἀναζητέω *anazēteō* from *G303* and *G2212*; to *search* out:— seek.

G328 ἀναζώννυμι *anazōnnymi* from *G303* and *G2224*; to *gird afresh:*— gird up.

G329 ἀναζωπυρέω *anazōpyreō* from *G303* and a compound of the base of *G2226* and *G4442*; to *re-enkindle:*— stir up.

G330 ἀναθάλλω *anathallō* from *G303* and

θάλλω *thallō* (to *flourish*); to *revive:*— flourish again.

G331 **ἀνάθεμα** *anathema* from *G394*; a (religious) *ban* or (concretely) *excommunicated* (thing or person):— accused, anathema, curse, great.

G332 **ἀναθεματίζω** *anathematizō* from *G331*; to *declare* or *vow* under penalty of execration:— (bind under a) curse, bind with an oath.

G333 **ἀναθεωρέω** *anatheōreō* from *G303* and *G2334*; to *look again* (i.e. *attentively*) at (literally or figuratively):— behold, consider.

G334 **ἀνάθημα** *anathēma* from *G394* [like *G331*, but in a good sense]; a *votive* offering:— gift.

G335 **ἀναίδεια** *anaideia* from a compound of *G1* (as a negative particle [compare *G427*]) and *G127*; *impudence*, i.e. (by implication) *importunity*:— importunity.

G336 **ἀναίρεσις** *anairesis* from *G337*; (the act of) *killing*:— death.

G337 **ἀναιρέω** *anaireō* from *G303* and (the active of) *G138*; to *take up*, i.e. *adopt*; by implication to *take away* (violently), i.e. *abolish, murder*:— put to death, kill, slay, take away, take up.

G338 **ἀναίτιος** *anaitios* from *G1* (as a negative particle) and *G159* (in the sense of *G156*); *innocent*:— blameless, guiltless.

G339 **ἀνακαθίζω** *anakathizō* from *G303* and *G2523*; properly to *set up*, i.e. (reflexive) to *sit up*:— sit up.

G340 **ἀνακαινίζω** *anakainizō* from *G303* and a derivative of *G2537*; to *restore*:— renew.

G341 **ἀνακαινόω** *anakainoō* from *G303* and a derivative of *G2537*; to *renovate*:— renew.

G342 **ἀνακαίνωσις** *anakainōsis* from *G341*; *renovation*:— renewing.

G343 **ἀνακαλύπτω** *anakalyptō* from *G303* (in the sense of *reversal*) and *G2572*; to *unveil*:— open, ([un-]) taken away.

G344 **ἀνακάμπτω** *anakamptō* from *G303* and *G2578*; to *turn back*:— return, turn.

G345 **ἀνακεῖμαι** *anakeimai* from *G303* and *G2749*; to *recline* (as a corpse or at a meal):— guest, lean, lie, sit (down, at meat), at the table.

G346 **ἀνακεφαλαιόομαι** *anakephalaioomai* from *G303* and *G2775* (in its original sense); to *sum up*:— briefly comprehend, gather together in one.

G347 **ἀνακλίνω** *anaklinō* from *G303* and *G2827*; to *lean back*:— lay, (make) sit down.

G348 **ἀνακόπτω** *anakoptō* from *G303* and *G2875*; to *beat back*, i.e. *check*:— hinder.

G349 **ἀνακράζω** *anakrazō* from *G303* and *G2896*; to *scream up* (aloud):— cry out.

G350 **ἀνακρίνω** *anakrinō* from *G303* and *G2919*; properly to *scrutinize*, i.e. (by implication) *investigate, interrogate, determine*:— ask, question, discern, examine, judge, search.

G351 **ἀνάκρισις** *anakrisis* from *G350*; a (judicial) *investigation*:— examination.

G352 **ἀνακύπτω** *anakyptō* from *G303* (in the sense of *reversal*) and *G2955*; to *unbend*, i.e. *rise*; figuratively *be elated*:— lift up, look up.

G353 **ἀναλαμβάνω** *analambanō* from *G303* and *G2983*; to *take up*:— receive up, take (in, unto, up).

G354 **ἀνάληψις** *analēpsis* from Greek *G353*; *ascension*:— taking up.

G355 **ἀναλίσκω** *analiskō* from *G303* and a form of the alternate of *G138*; properly to *use up*, i.e. *destroy*:— consume.

G356 **ἀναλογία** *analogia* from a compound of *G303* and *G3056*; *proportion*:— proportion.

G357 **ἀναλογίζομαι** *analogizomai* middle from *G356*; to *estimate*, i.e. (figuratively) *contemplate* :— consider.

G358 **ἄναλος** *analos* from *G1* (as a negative particle) and *G251*; *without salt*, i.e. *insipid*:— lose saltness.

G359 **ἀνάλυσις** *analysis* from *G360*; *departure*:— departure.

G360 **ἀναλύω** *analyō* from *G303* and *G3089*; to *break up*, i.e. *depart* (literally or figuratively):— depart, return.

G361 **ἀναμάρτητος** *anamartētos* from *G1* (as a negative particle) and a presumed derivative of *G264*; *sinless*:— that is without sin.

G362 **ἀναμένω** *anamenō* from *G303* and *G3306*; to *await*:— wait for.

G363 **ἀναμιμνήσκω** *anamimnēskō* from *G303* and *G3403*; to *remind*; reflexive to *recollect*:— call to mind, remember, (bring to, call to, put in), remembrance.

G364 **ἀνάμνησις** *anamnēsis* from *G363*; *recollection*:— *remembrance* (again).

G365 **ἀνανεόω** *ananeoō* from *G303* and a derivative of *G3501*; to *renovate*, i.e. *reform*:— renew.

G366 **ἀνανήφω** *ananēphō* from *G303* and *G3525*; to become *sober again*, i.e. (figuratively) *regain* (one's) *senses*:— recover self.

G367 **Ἀνανίας** *Ananias* of Hebrew origin [H2608]; *Ananias*, the name of three Israelites:— Ananias.

G368 **ἀναντίρρητος** *anantirrhētos* from *G1* (as a negative particle) and a presumed derivative of a compound of *G473* and *G4483*; *indisputable*:— cannot be spoken against.

G369 **ἀναντιρρήτως** *anantirrhētōs* adverb from *G368*; *promptly*:— without gainsaying.

G370 **ἀνάξιος** *anaxios* from *G1* (as a negative particle) and *G514*; *unfit*:— unworthy.

G371 **ἀναξίως** *anaxiōs* adverb from *G370*; *irreverently*:— unworthily.

G372 **ἀνάπαυσις** *anapausis* from *G373*; *intermission*; by implication *recreation*:— rest.

G373 **ἀναπαύω** *anapauō* from *G303* and *G3973*; (reflexive) to *repose* (literally or figuratively [*be exempt*], *remain*); by implication to *refresh*:— take ease, refresh, (give, take) rest.

G374 **ἀναπείθω** *anapeithō* from *G303* and *G3982*; to *incite*:— persuade.

G375 **ἀναπέμπω** *anapempō* from *G303* and *G3992*; to *send up* or *back*:— send (again).

G376 **ἀνάπηρος** *anapēros* from *G303* (in the sense of *intensity*) and
πῆρος *pēros* (*maimed*); *crippled*:— maimed.

G377 **ἀναπίπτω** *anapiptō* from *G303* and *G4098*; to *fall back*, i.e. *lie down, lean back*:— lean, sit down (to meat).

G378 **ἀναπληρόω** *anaplēroō* from *G303* and *G4137*; to *complete*; by implication to *occupy, supply*; figurative to *accomplish* (by coincidence or obedience):— fill up, fulfil, occupy, supply.

G379 **ἀναπολόγητος** *anapologētos* from *G1* (as a negative particle) and a presumed derivative of *G626*; *indefensible*:— without excuse, inexcusable.

G380 **ἀναπτύσσω** *anaptyssō* from *G303* (in the sense of *reversal*) and *G4428*; to *unroll* (a scroll or volume):— open.

G381 **ἀνάπτω** *anaptō* from *G303* and *G681*; to *enkindle*:— kindle, light.

G382 **ἀναρίθμητος** *anarithmētos* from *G1* (as a negative particle) and a derivative of *G705*; *unnumbered*, i.e. *without number*:— innumerable.

G383 **ἀνασείω** *anaseiō* from *G303* and *G4579*; figuratively to *excite*:— move, stir up.

G384 **ἀνασκευάζω** *anaskeuazō* from *G303* (in the sense of *reversal*) and a derivative of *G4632*; properly to *pack up* (baggage), i.e. (by implication and figuratively) to *upset*:— subvert.

G385 **ἀνασπάω** *anaspaō* from *G303* and *G4685*; to *take up* or *extricate*:— draw up, pull out.

G386 **ἀνάστασις** *anastasis* from *G450*; a *standing up* again, i.e. (literally) a *resurrection* from death (individual, general or by implication [its author]), or (figuratively) a (moral) *recovery* (of spiritual truth) :— raised to life again, resurrection, rise from the dead, that should rise, rising again.

G387 **ἀναστατόω** *anastatoō* from a derivative of *G450* (in the sense of *removal*); properly to *drive out* of home, i.e. (by implication) to *disturb* (literally or figuratively):— trouble, turn upside down, make an uproar.

G388 **ἀνασταυρόω** *anastauroō* from *G303* and *G4717*; to *crucify again* (figuratively):— crucify afresh.

G389 **ἀναστενάζω** *anastenazō* from *G303* and *G4727*; to *sigh deeply*:— sigh deeply.

G390 **ἀναστρέφω** *anastrephō* from *G303* and *G4762*; to *overturn*; also to *return*; by implication to *busy* oneself, i.e. *remain, live*:— abide, behave self, have conversation, live, overthrow, pass, return, be used.

G391 **ἀναστροφή** *anastrophē* from *G390*; *behavior*:— conversation.

G392 **ἀνατάσσομαι** *anatassomai* from *G303* and the middle of *G5021*; to *arrange*:— set in order.

G393 **ἀνατέλλω** *anatellō* from *G303* and the base of *G5056*; to (*cause* to) *arise*:— arise, make to rise, at the rising of, spring (up), be up.

G394 **ἀνατίθεμαι** *anatithemai* from *G303* and the middle of *G5087*; to *set forth* (for oneself), i.e. *propound*:— communicate, declare.

G395 **ἀνατολή** *anatolē* from *G393*; a *rising* of light, i.e. *dawn* (figuratively); by implication the *east* (also in plural):— dayspring, east, rising.

G396 **ἀνατρέπω** *anatrepō* from *G303* and the base of *G5157*; to *overturn* (figuratively):— overthrow, subvert.

G397 **ἀνατρέφω** *anatrephō* from *G303* and *G5142*; to *rear* (physically or mentally):— bring up, nourish (up).

G398 **ἀναφαίνω** *anaphainō* from *G303* and *G5316*; to *show*, i.e. (reflexive) *appear*, or (passive) *have pointed* out:— (should) appear, discover.

G399 **ἀναφέρω** *anapherō* from *G303* and *G5342*; to *take up* (literally or figuratively):— bear, bring (carry, lead) up, offer (up).

G400 **ἀναφωνέω** *anaphōneō* from *G303* and *G5455*; to *exclaim:*— speak out.

G401 **ἀνάχυσις** *anachysis* from a compound of *G303* and
χέω *cheō* (to *pour*); properly *effusion,* i.e. (figuratively) *license:*— excess.

G402 **ἀναχωρέω** *anachōreō* from *G303* and *G5562*; to *retire:*— depart, give place, go (turn) aside, withdraw self.

G403 **ἀνάψυξις** *anapsyxis* from *G404*; properly a *recovery of breath,* i.e. (figuratively) *revival:*— revival.

G404 **ἀναψύχω** *anapsychō* from *G303* and *G5594*; properly to *cool off,* i.e. (figuratively) *relieve:*— refresh.

G405 **ἀνδραποδιστής** *andrapodistēs* from a derivative of a compound of *G435* and *G4228*; an *enslaver* (as bringing *men* to his *feet*):— men-stealer.

G406 **Ἀνδρέας** *Andreas* from *G435*; *manly; Andreas,* an Israelite:— Andrew.

G407 **ἀνδρίζομαι** *andrizomai* middle from *G435*; to *act manly:*— quit like men.

G408 **Ἀνδρόνικος** *Andronikos* from *G435* and *G3534*; *man of victory; Andronicos,* an Israelite:— Andronicus.

G409 **ἀνδροφόνος** *androphonos* from *G435* and *G5408*; a *murderer:*— manslayer.

G410 **ἀνέγκλητος** *anenklētos* from *G1* (as a negative particle) and a derivative of *G1458*; *not accused,* i.e. (by implication) *irreproachable:*— blameless.

G411 **ἀνεκδιήγητος** *anekdiēgētos* from *G1* (as a negative particle) and a presumed derivative of *G1555*; *not expounded* in full, i.e. *indescribable:*— unspeakable.

G412 **ἀνεκλάλητος** *aneklalētos* from *G1* (as a negative particle) and a presumed derivative of *G1583*; *not spoken out,* i.e. (by implication) *unutterable:*— unspeakable.

G413 **ἀνέκλειπτος** *anekleiptos* from *G1* (as a negative particle) and a presumed derivative of *G1587*; *not left out,* i.e. (by implication) *inexhaustible:*— that faileth not.

G414 **ἀνεκτότερος** *anektoteros* comparative of a derivative of *G430*; *more endurable:*— more tolerable.

G415 **ἀνελεήμων** *aneleēmōn* from *G1* (as a negative particle) and *G1655*; *merciless:*— unmerciful.

G416 **ἀνεμίζω** *anemizō* from *G417*; to *toss with the wind:*— drive with the wind.

G417 **ἄνεμος** *anemos* from the base of *G109*; *wind;* (plural) by implication (the four) *quarters* (of the earth):— wind.

G418 **ἀνένδεκτος** *anendektos* from *G1* (as a negative particle) and a derivative of the same as *G1735*; *not admitted,* i.e. (by implication) *not supposable:*— impossible.

G419 **ἀνεξερεύνητος** *anexereunētos* from *G1* (as a negative particle) and a presumed derivative of *G1830*; *not searched out,* i.e. (by implication) *inscrutable:*— unsearchable.

G420 **ἀνεξίκακος** *anexikakos* from *G430* and *G2556*; *enduring of ill,* i.e. *forbearing:*— patient.

G421 **ἀνεξιχνίαστος** *anexichniastos* from *G1* (as a negative particle) and a presumed derivative of a compound of *G1537* and a derivative of *G2487*; *not tracked out,* i.e. (by implication) *untraceable:*— past finding out, unsearchable.

G422 **ἀνεπαίσχυντος** *anepaischyntos* from *G1* (as a negative particle) and a presumed derivative of a compound of *G1909* and *G153*; *not ashamed,* i.e. (by implication) *not reprehensible:*— that needeth not to be ashamed.

G423 **ἀνεπίληπτος** *anepilēptos* from *G1* (as a negative particle) and a derivative of *G1949*; *not arrested,* i.e. (by implication) *inculpable:*— blameless, unrebukeable.

G424 **ἀνέρχομαι** *anerchomai* from *G303* and *G2064*; to *ascend:*— go up.

G425 **ἄνεσις** *anesis* from *G447*; *relaxation* or (figuratively) *relief:*— eased, liberty, rest.

G426 **ἀνετάζω** *anetazō* from *G303* and
ἐτάζω *etazō* (to *test*); to *investigate* (judicially):— examine, should have examined.

G427 **ἄνευ** *aneu* a primary particle; *without:*— without. Compare *G1*.

G428 **ἀνεύθετος** *aneuthetos* from *G1* (as a negative particle) and *G2111*; *not well set,* i.e. *inconvenient:*— not commodious.

G429 **ἀνευρίσκω** *aneuriskō* from *G303* and *G2147*; to *find out:*— find.

G430 **ἀνέχομαι** *anechomai* middle from *G303* and
ἔχω *echō*; to *hold oneself up* against, i.e. (figuratively) *put up* with:— bear with, endure, forbear, suffer.

G431 **ἀνέψιος** *anepsios* from *G1* (as a particle of union) and an obsolete
νέπος *nepos* (a *brood*); properly *akin,* i.e. (specifically) a *cousin:*— sister's son.

G432 **ἄνηθον** *anēthon* probably of foreign origin; *dill:*— anise.

G433 **ἀνήκω** *anēkō* from *G303* and *G2240*; to *attain to,* i.e. (figuratively) *be proper:*— convenient, be fit.

G434 **ἀνήμερος** *anēmeros* from *G1* (as a negative particle) and
ἥμερος *hēmeros* (*lame*); *savage:*— fierce.

G435 **ἀνήρ** *anēr* a primary word [compare *G444*]; a *man* (properly as an individual male):— fellow, husband, man, sir.

G436 **ἀνθίστημι** *anthistēmi* from *G473* and *G2476*; to *stand against,* i.e. *oppose:*— resist, withstand.

G437 **ἀνθομολογέομαι** *anthomologeomai* from *G473* and the middle of *G3670*; to *confess in turn,* i.e. *respond* in praise:— give thanks.

G438 **ἄνθος** *anthos* a primary word; a *blossom:*— flower.

G439 **ἀνθρακιά** *anthrakia* from *G440*; a bed of burning *coals:*— fire of coals.

G440 **ἄνθραξ** *anthrax* of uncertain derivation; a live *coal:*— coal of fire.

G441 **ἀνθρωπάρεσκος** *anthrōpareskos* from *G444* and *G700*; *man-courting,* i.e. *fawning:*— men-pleaser.

G442 **ἀνθρώπινος** *anthrōpinos* from *G444*; *human* :— common to man, man, man's, mankind, men's, after the manner of men.

G443 **ἀνθρωποκτόνος** *anthrōpoktonos* from *G444* and
κτείνω *kteinō* (to *kill*); a *manslayer:*— murderer. Compare *G5406*.

G444 **ἄνθρωπος** *anthrōpos* from *G435* and
ὤψ *ōps* (the *countenance;* from *G3700*); *man-faced,* i.e. a *human* being:— certain, man.

G445 **ἀνθυπατεύω** *anthypateuō* from *G446*; to *act as proconsul:*— be the deputy.

G446 **ἀνθύπατος** *anthypatos* from *G473* and a superlative of *G5228*; *instead* of the *highest* officer, i.e. (specifically) a Roman *proconsul:*— deputy.

G447 **ἀνίημι** *aniēmi* from *G303* and
ἵημι *hiēmi* (to *send*); to *let up,* i.e. (literally) *slacken,* or (figuratively) *desert, desist* from:— forbear, leave, loose.

G448 **ἀνίλεως** *anileōs* from *G1* (as a negative particle) and *G2436*; *inexorable:*— without mercy.

G449 **ἄνιπτος** *aniptos* from *G1* (as a negative particle) and a presumed derivative of *G3538*; *without ablution:*— unwashen.

G450 **ἀνίστημι** *anistēmi* from *G303* and *G2476*; to *stand up* (literally or figuratively, transitive or intransitive):— arise, lift up, raise up (again), rise (again), stand up, stand upright.

G451 **Ἄννα** *Anna* of Hebrew origin [H2584]; *Anna,* an Israelitess:— Anna.

G452 **Ἄννας** *Annas* of Hebrew origin [H2608]; *Annas* (i.e. *G367*), an Israelite:— Annas.

G453 **ἀνόητος** *anoētos* from *G1* (as a negative particle) and a derivative of *G3539*; *unintelligent;* by implication *sensual:*— fool, foolish, unwise.

G454 **ἄνοια** *anoia* from a compound of *G1* (as a negative particle) and *G3563*; *stupidity;* by implication *rage:*— folly, madness.

G455 **ἀνοίγω** *anoigō* from *G303* and
οἴγω *oigō* (to *open*); to *open up* (literally or figuratively, in various applications):— open.

G456 **ἀνοικοδομέω** *anoikodomeō* from *G303* and *G3618*; to *rebuild:*— build again.

G457 **ἄνοιξις** *anoixis* from *G455*; *opening* (throat) :— open.

G458 **ἀνομία** *anomia* from *G459*; *illegality,* i.e. *violation of law* or (generally) *wickedness:*— iniquity, transgress, transgression of the law, unrighteousness.

G459 **ἄνομος** *anomos* from *G1* (as a negative particle) and *G3551*; *lawless,* i.e. (negatively) *not subject to* (the Jewish) *law;* (by implication a *Gentile*), or (positively) *wicked:*— without law, lawless, transgressor, unlawful, wicked.

G460 **ἀνόμως** *anomōs* adverb from *G459*; *lawlessly,* i.e. (specifically) *not amenable to* (the Jewish) *law:*— without law.

G461 **ἀνορθόω** *anorthoō* from *G303* and a derivative of the base of *G3717*; to *straighten up:*— lift (set) up, make straight.

G462 **ἀνόσιος** *anosios* from *G1* (as a negative particle) and *G3741*; *wicked:*— unholy.

G463 **ἀνοχή** *anochē* from *G430*; *self-restraint,* i.e. *tolerance:*— forbearance.

G464 **ἀνταγωνίζομαι** *antagōnizomai* from *G473* and *G75*; to *struggle against* (figuratively) ["antagonize"]:— strive against.

G465 **ἀντάλλαγμα** *antallagma* from a compound of *G473* and *G236*; an *equivalent* or *ransom:*— in exchange.

G466 **ἀνταναπληρόω** *antanaplēroō* from *G473* and *G378*; to *supplement:*— fill up.

G467 ἀνταποδίδωμι *antapodidōmi* from *G473* and *G591*; to *requite* (good or evil):— recompense, render, repay.

G468 ἀνταπόδομα *antapodoma* from *G467*; a *requital* (properly the thing):— recompense.

G469 ἀνταπόδοσις *antapodosis* from *G467*; *requital* (properly the act):— reward.

G470 ἀνταποκρίνομαι *antapokrinomai* from *G473* and *G611*; to *contradict* or *dispute:*— answer again, reply against.

G471 ἀντέπω *antepō* from *G473* and *G2036*; to *refute* or *deny:*— gainsay, say against.

G472 ἀντέχομαι *antechomai* from *G473* and the middle of *G2192*; to *hold* oneself *opposite* to, i.e. (by implication) *adhere to;* by extension to *care for:*— hold fast, hold to, support.

G473 ἀντί *anti* a primary particle; *opposite,* i.e. *instead* or *because* of (rarely *in addition* to). Often used in compounds to denote *contrast, requital, substitution, correspondence,* etc.:— for, in the room of.

G474 ἀντιβάλλω *antiballō* from *G473* and *G906*; to *bandy:*— have.

G475 ἀντιδιατίθεμαι *antidiatithemai* from *G473* and *G1303*; to *set oneself opposite,* i.e. *be disputatious:*— that oppose themselves.

G476 ἀντίδικος *antidikos* from *G473* and *G1349*; an *opponent* (in a lawsuit); specifically *Satan* (as the arch-enemy):— adversary.

G477 ἀντίθεσις *antithesis* from a compound of *G473* and *G5087*; *opposition,* i.e. a *conflict* (of theories):— opposition.

G478 ἀντικαθίστημι *antikathistēmi* from *G473* and *G2525*; to *set down* (troops) *against,* i.e. *withstand:*— resist.

G479 ἀντικαλέω *antikaleō* from *G473* and *G2564*; to *invite in return:*— bid again.

G480 ἀντίκειμαι *antikeimai* from *G473* and *G2749*; to *lie opposite,* i.e. *be adverse* (figuratively *repugnant*) to:— adversary, be contrary, oppose.

G481 ἀντικρύ *antikry* prolonged from *G473*; *opposite:*— over against.

G482 ἀντιλαμβάνομαι *antilambanomai* from *G473* and the middle of *G2983*; to *take* hold of *in turn,* i.e. *succor;* also to *participate:*— help, partaker, support.

G483 ἀντίλεγω *antilegō* from *G473* and *G3004*; to *dispute, refuse:*— answer again, contradict, deny, gainsay, gainsayer, speak against.

G484 ἀντίληψις *antilēpsis* from *G482*; *relief:*— help.

G485 ἀντιλογία *antilogia* from a derivative of *G483*; *dispute, disobedience:*— contradiction, gainsaying, strife.

G486 ἀντιλοιδορέω *antiloidoreō* from *G473* and *G3058*; to *rail in reply:*— revile again.

G487 ἀντίλυτρον *antilytron* from *G473* and *G3083*; a *redemption-price:*— ransom.

G488 ἀντιμετρέω *antimetreō* from *G473* and *G3354*; to *mete in return:*— measure again.

G489 ἀντιμισθία *antimisthia* from a compound of *G473* and *G3408*; *requital, correspondence:*— recompense.

G490 Ἀντιόχεια *Antiocheia* from
Ἀντίοχος *Antiochos* (a Syrian king); *Antiochia,* a place in Syria:— Antioch.

G491 Ἀντιοχεύς *Antiocheus* from *G490*; an *Antiochian* or inhabitant of Antiochia:— of Antioch.

G492 ἀντιπαρέρχομαι *antiparerchomai* from *G473* and *G3928*; to *go along opposite:*— pass by on the other side.

G493 Ἀντίπας *Antipas* contracted for a compound of *G473* and a derivative of *G3962*; *Antipas,* a Christian:— Antipas.

G494 Ἀντιπατρίς *Antipatris* from the same as *G493*; *Antipatris,* a place in Palestine:— Antipatris.

G495 ἀντιπέραν *antiperan* from *G473* and *G4008*; *on the opposite side:*— over against.

G496 ἀντιπίπτω *antipiptō* from *G473* and *G4098* (including its alternate); to *oppose:*— resist.

G497 ἀντιστρατεύομαι *antistrateuomai* from *G473* and *G4754*; (figuratively) to *attack,* i.e. (by implication) *destroy:*— war against.

G498 ἀντιτάσσομαι *antitassomai* from *G473* and the middle of *G5021*; to *range oneself against,* i.e. *oppose:*— oppose themselves, resist.

G499 ἀντίτυπον *antitypon* neuter of a compound of *G473* and *G5179*; *corresponding* ["antitype"], i.e. a *representative, counterpart:*— (like) figure (whereunto).

G500 ἀντίχριστος *antichristos* from *G473* and *G5547*; an *opponent of the Messiah:*— antichrist.

G501 ἀντλέω *antleō* from
ἄντλος *antlos* (the *hold* of a ship); to *bale* up (properly bilge water), i.e. *dip* water (with a bucket, pitcher, etc.):— draw (out).

G502 ἄντλημα *antlēma* from *G501*; a *baling-vessel:*— thing to draw with.

G503 ἀντοφθαλμέω *antophthalmeō* from a compound of *G473* and *G3788*; to *face:*— bear up into.

G504 ἄνυδρος *anydros* from *G1* (as a negative particle) and *G5204*; *waterless,* i.e. *dry:*— dry, without water.

G505 ἀνυπόκριτος *anypokritos* from *G1* (as a negative particle) and a presumed derivative of *G5271*; *not dissembled,* i.e. *sincere:*— without dissimulation (hypocrisy), unfeigned.

G506 ἀνυπότακτος *anypotaktos* from *G1* (as a negative particle) and a presumed derivative of *G5293*; *not subdued,* i.e. *insubordinate* (in fact or temper):— disobedient, that is not put under, unruly.

G507 ἄνω *anō* adverb from *G473*; *upward* or *on the top:*— above, brim, high, up.

G508 ἀνώγεον *anōgeon* from *G507* and *G1093*; *above* the *ground,* i.e. (properly) the *second floor* of a building; used for a *dome* or a *balcony* on the upper story:— upper room.

G509 ἄνωθεν *anōthen* from *G507*; *from above;* by analogy *from the first;* by implication *anew:*— from above, again, from the beginning (very first), the top.

G510 ἀνωτερικός *anōterikos* from *G511*; *superior,* i.e. (locally) *more remote:*— upper.

G511 ἀνώτερος *anōteros* comparative degree of *G507*; *upper,* i.e. (neuter as adverb) to a *more conspicuous* place, in a *former* part of the book:— above, higher.

G512 ἀνωφέλες *anōpheles* from *G1* (as a negative particle) and the base of *G5624*; *useless* or (neuter) *inutility:*— unprofitable, unprofitableness.

G513 ἀξίνη *axinē* probably from
ἄγνυμι *agnymi* (to *break;* compare *G4486*); an *axe:*— axe.

G514 ἄξιος *axios* probably from *G71*; *deserving, comparable* or *suitable* (as if *drawing* praise):— due reward, meet, worthy, unworthy.

G515 ἀξιόω *axioō* from *G514*; to *deem entitled* or *fit:*— desire, think good, count (think) worthy.

G516 ἀξίως *axiōs* adverb from *G514*; *appropriately:*— as becometh, after a godly sort, worthily, worthy.

G517 ἀόρατος *aoratos* from *G1* (as a negative particle) and *G3707*; *invisible:*— invisible (thing).

G518 ἀπαγγέλλω *apangellō* from *G575* and the base of *G32*; to *announce:*— bring word (again), declare, report, shew (again), tell.

G519 ἀπάγχομαι *apanchomai* from *G575* and
ἄγχω *anchō* (to *choke;* akin to the base of *G43*); to *strangle oneself off* (i.e. to death):— hang himself.

G520 ἀπάγω *apagō* from *G575* and *G71*; to *take off* (in various senses):— bring, carry away, lead (away), put to death, take away.

G521 ἀπαίδευτος *apaideutos* from *G1* (as a negative particle) and a derivative of *G3811*; *uninstructed,* i.e. (figuratively) *stupid:*— unlearned.

G522 ἀπαίρω *apairō* from *G575* and *G142*; to *lift off,* i.e. *remove:*— take (away).

G523 ἀπαιτέω *apaiteō* from *G575* and *G154*; to *demand back:*— ask again, require.

G524 ἀπαλγέω *apalgeō* from *G575* and
ἀλγέω *algeō* (to *smart*); to *grieve out,* i.e. *become apathetic:*— be past feeling.

G525 ἀπαλλάσσω *apallassō* from *G575* and *G236*; to *change away,* i.e. *release,* (reflexive) *remove:*— deliver, depart.

G526 ἀπαλλοτριόω *apallotrioō* from *G575* and a derivative of *G245*; to *estrange away,* i.e. (passive and figuratively) to *be non-participant:*— alienate, be alien.

G527 ἁπαλός *apalos* of uncertain derivation; *soft* :— tender.

G528 ἀπαντάω *apantaō* from *G575* and a derivative of *G473*; to *meet away,* i.e. *encounter:*— meet.

G529 ἀπάντησις *apantēsis* from *G528*; a (friendly) *encounter:*— meet.

G530 ἅπαξ *hapax* probably from *G537*; *one* (or a *single*) *time* (numerically or conclusively):— once.

G531 ἀπαράβατος *aparabatos* from *G1* (as a negative particle) and a derivative of *G3845*; *not passing away,* i.e. *not transferable* (perpetual):— unchangeable.

G532 ἀπαρασκεύαστος *aparaskeuastos* from *G1* (as a negative particle) and a derivative of *G3903*; *unready:*— unprepared.

G533 ἀπαρνέομαι *aparneomai* from *G575* and *G720*; to *deny utterly,* i.e. *disown, abstain:*— deny.

G534 ἀπάρτι *aparti* from *G575* and *G737*; *from now,* i.e. *henceforth* (*already*):— from henceforth.

G535 ἀπαρτισμός *apartismos* from a derivative of *G534*; *completion:*— finishing.

G536 ἀπαρχή *aparchē* from a compound of *G575* and *G756*; a *beginning* of sacrifice, i.e. the (Jewish) *first-fruit* (figuratively):— first-fruits.

G537 **ἅπας** *hapas* from *G1* (as a particle of union) and *G3956*; absolutely *all* or (singular) *every* one:— all (things), every (one), whole.

G538 **ἀπατάω** *apataō* of uncertain derivation; to *cheat,* i.e. *delude:*— deceive.

G539 **ἀπάτη** *apatē* from *G538*; *delusion:*— deceit, deceitful, deceitfulness, deceivableness, deceiving.

G540 **ἀπάτωρ** *apatōr* from *G1* (as a negative particle) and *G3962*; *fatherless,* i.e. *of unrecorded paternity:*— without father.

G541 **ἀπαύγασμα** *apaugasma* from a compound of *G575* and *G826*; an *off-flash,* i.e. *effulgence:*— brightness.

G542 **ἀπείδω** *apeidō* from *G575* and the same as *G1492*; to *see* fully:— see.

G543 **ἀπείθεια** *apeitheia* from *G545*; *disbelief* (obstinate and rebellious):— disobedience, unbelief.

G544 **ἀπειθέω** *apeitheō* from *G545*; to *disbelieve* (willfully and perversely):— not believe, disobedient, obey not, unbelieving.

G545 **ἀπειθής** *apeithēs* from *G1* (as a negative particle) and *G3982*; *not persuadable,* i.e. *contumacious:*— disobedient.

G546 **ἀπειλέω** *apeileō* of uncertain derivation; to *menace;* by implication to *forbid:*— threaten.

G547 **ἀπειλή** *apeilē* from *G546*; a *menace:*— straitly, threatening.

G548 **ἄπειμι** *apeimi* from *G575* and *G1510*; to *be away:*— be absent. Compare *G549*.

G549 **ἄπειμι** *apeimi* from *G575* and
εἶμι *eimi* (to *go*); to *go away:*— go. Compare *G548*.

G550 **ἀπειπόμην** *apeipomēn* reflexive past of a compound of *G575* and *G2036*; to *say off* for oneself, i.e. *disown:*— renounce.

G551 **ἀπείραστος** *apeirastos* from *G1* (as a negative particle) and a presumed derivative of *G3987*; *untried,* i.e. *unable to be tempted:*— not to be tempted.

G552 **ἄπειρος** *apeiros* from *G1* (as a negative particle) and *G3984*; *inexperienced,* i.e. *ignorant:*— unskillful.

G553 **ἀπεκδέχομαι** *apekdechomai* from *G575* and *G1551*; to *expect fully:*— look (wait) for.

G554 **ἀπεκδύομαι** *apekdyomai* middle from *G575* and *G1562*; to *divest wholly* oneself, or (for oneself) *despoil:*— put off, spoil.

G555 **ἀπέκδυσις** *apekdysis* from *G554*; *divestment* :— putting off.

G556 **ἀπελαύνω** *apelaunō* from *G575* and *G1643*; to *dismiss:*— drive.

G557 **ἀπελεγμός** *apelegmos* from a compound of *G575* and *G1651*; *refutation,* i.e. (by implication) *contempt:*— nought.

G558 **ἀπελεύθερος** *apeleutheros* from *G575* and *G1658*; one *freed away,* i.e. a *freedman:*— freeman.

G559 **Ἀπελλῆς** *Apellēs* of Latin origin; *Apelles,* a Christian:— Apelles.

G560 **ἀπελπίζω** *apelpizō* from *G575* and *G1679*; to *hope out,* i.e. *fully expect:*— hope for again.

G561 **ἀπέναντι** *apenanti* from *G575* and *G1725*; *from in front,* i.e. *opposite, before* or *against:*— before, contrary, over against, in the presence of.

G562 **ἀπέραντος** *aperantos* from *G1* (as a negative particle) and a secondary derivative of *G4008*; *unfinished,* i.e. (by implication) *interminable:*— endless.

G563 **ἀπερισπάστως** *aperispastōs* adverb from a compound of *G1* (as a negative particle) and a presumed derivative of *G4049*; *not distractedly,* i.e. *free from* (domestic) *solicitude:*— without distraction.

G564 **ἀπερίτμητος** *aperitmētos* from *G1* (as a negative particle) and a presumed derivative of *G4059*; *uncircumcised* (figuratively):— uncircumcised.

G565 **ἀπέρχομαι** *aperchomai* from *G575* and *G2064*; to *go off* (i.e. *depart*), *aside* (i.e. *apart*) or *behind* (i.e. *follow*), literally or figuratively:— come, depart, go (aside, away, back, out, . . . ways), pass away, be past.

G566 **ἀπέχει** *apechei* 3rd person singular present indicative active of *G568* used impersonally; *it is sufficient:*— it is enough.

G567 **ἀπέχομαι** *apechomai* middle (reflexive) of *G568*; to *hold oneself off,* i.e. *refrain:*— abstain.

G568 **ἀπέχω** *apechō* from *G575* and *G2192*; (active) to *have out,* i.e. *receive in full;* (intransitive) to *keep* (oneself) *away,* i.e. *be distant* (literally or figuratively):— be, have, receive.

G569 **ἀπιστέω** *apisteō* from *G571*; to *be unbelieving,* i.e. (transitive) *disbelieve,* or (by implication) *disobey:*— believe not.

G570 **ἀπιστία** *apistia* from *G571*; *faithlessness,* i.e. (negatively) *disbelief* (*want of* Christian *faith*), or (positively) *unfaithfulness* (*disobedience*):— unbelief.

G571 **ἄπιστος** *apistos* from *G1* (as a negative particle) and *G4103*; (active) *disbelieving,* i.e. *without* Christian *faith* (specifically a *heathen*); (passive) *untrustworthy* (person), or *incredible* (thing):— that believeth not, faithless, incredible thing, infidel, unbeliever, unbelieving.

G572 **ἁπλότης** *haplotēs* from *G573*; *singleness,* i.e. (subjectively) *sincerity* (*without dissimulation* or *self-seeking*), or (objectively) *generosity* (*copious bestowal*):— bountifulness, liberal, liberality, simplicity, singleness.

G573 **ἁπλοῦς** *haplous* probably from *G1* (as a particle of union) and the base of *G4120*; properly *folded together,* i.e. *single* (figuratively *clear*):— single.

G574 **ἁπλῶς** *haplōs* adverb from *G573* (in the objective sense of *G572*); *bountifully:*— liberally.

G575 **ἀπό** *apo* a primary particle; *"off,"* i.e. *away* (from something near), in various senses (of place, time, or relation; literal or figurative). In compounds (as a prefix) it usually denotes *separation, departure, cessation, completion, reversal,* etc.:— after, hereafter, ago, at, because of, before, by (the space of), for, forth, from, in, (out) of, off, on, upon, once, since, with.

G576 **ἀποβαίνω** *apobainō* from *G575* and the base of *G939*; literally to *disembark;* figuratively to *eventuate:*— become, go out, turn.

G577 **ἀποβάλλω** *apoballō* from *G575* and *G906*; to *throw off;* figuratively to *lose:*— cast away.

G578 **ἀποβλέπω** *apoblepō* from *G575* and *G991*; to *look away* from everything else, i.e. (figuratively) intently *regard:*— have respect.

G579 **ἀπόβλητος** *apoblētos* from *G577*; *cast off,* i.e. (figuratively) such as to *be rejected:*— be refused.

G580 **ἀποβολή** *apobolē* from *G577*; *rejection;* figuratively *loss:*— casting away, loss.

G581 **ἀπογενόμενος** *apogenomenos* past participle of a compound of *G575* and *G1096*; *absent,* i.e. *deceased* (figuratively *renounced*):— being dead.

G582 **ἀπογραφή** *apographē* from *G583*; an *enrollment;* by implication an *assessment:*— taxing.

G583 **ἀπογράφω** *apographō* from *G575* and *G1125*; to *write off* (a copy or list), i.e. *enroll:*— tax, write.

G584 **ἀποδείκνυμι** *apodeiknymi* from *G575* and *G1166*; to *show off,* i.e. *exhibit;* figuratively to *demonstrate,* i.e. *accredit:*— prove, approve, set forth, shew.

G585 **ἀπόδειξις** *apodeixis* from *G584*; *manifestation:*— demonstration.

G586 **ἀποδεκατόω** *apodekatoō* from *G575* and *G1183*; to *tithe* (as debtor or creditor):— (give, pay, take) tithe.

G587 **ἀπόδεκτος** *apodektos* from *G588*; *accepted,* i.e. *agreeable:*— acceptable.

G588 **ἀποδέχομαι** *apodechomai* from *G575* and *G1209*; to *take fully,* i.e. *welcome* (persons), *approve* (things):— accept, receive (gladly).

G589 **ἀποδημέω** *apodēmeō* from *G590*; to *go abroad,* i.e. *visit a foreign land:*— go (travel) into a far country, journey.

G590 **ἀπόδημος** *apodēmos* from *G575* and *G1218*; *absent from* one's own *people,* i.e. a *foreign traveler:*— taking a far journey.

G591 **ἀποδίδωμι** *apodidōmi* from *G575* and *G1325*; to *give away,* i.e. *up, over, back,* etc. (in various applications):— deliver (again), give (again), pay, repay, payment be made, perform, recompense, render, requite, restore, reward, sell, yield.

G592 **ἀποδιορίζω** *apodiorizō* from *G575* and a compound of *G1223* and *G3724*; to *disjoin* (by a boundary, figuratively a party):— separate.

G593 **ἀποδοκιμάζω** *apodokimazō* from *G575* and *G1381*; to *disapprove,* i.e. (by implication) to *repudiate:*— disallow, reject.

G594 **ἀποδοχή** *apodochē* from *G588*; *acceptance* :— acceptation.

G595 **ἀπόθεσις** *apothesis* from *G659*; a *laying aside* (literal or figurative):— putting away (off).

G596 **ἀποθήκη** *apothēkē* from *G659*; a *repository,* i.e. *granary:*— barn, garner.

G597 **ἀποθησαυρίζω** *apothēsaurizō* from *G575* and *G2343*; to *treasure away:*— lay up in store.

G598 **ἀποθλίβω** *apothlibō* from *G575* and *G2346*; to *crowd* from (every side):— press.

G599 **ἀποθνήσκω** *apothnēskō* from *G575* and *G2348*; to *die* off (literally or figuratively):— be dead, death, die, lie-a-dying, be slain (with).

G600 **ἀποκαθίστημι** *apokathistēmi* from *G575* and *G2525*; to *reconstitute* (in health, home or organization):— restore (again).

G601 **ἀποκαλύπτω** *apokalyptō* from *G575* and *G2572*; to take *off the cover,* i.e. *disclose:*— reveal.

G602 **ἀποκάλυψις** *apokalypsis* from *G601*; *disclosure:*— appearing, coming, lighten, manifestation, be revealed, revelation.

G603 **ἀποκαραδοκία** *apokaradokia* from a compound of *G575* and a compound of
κάρα *kara* (the *head*) and *G1380* (in the sense of *watching*); *intense anticipation:*— earnest expectation.

G604 **ἀποκαταλλάσσω** *apokatallassō* from *G575* and *G2644*; to *reconcile fully:*— reconcile.

G605 **ἀποκατάστασις** *apokatastasis* from *G600*; *reconstitution:*— restitution.

G606 **ἀπόκειμαι** *apokeimai* from *G575* and *G2749*; to *be reserved;* figuratively to *await:*— be appointed, (be) laid up.

G607 **ἀποκεφαλίζω** *apokephalizō* from *G575* and *G2776*; to *decapitate:*— behead.

G608 **ἀποκλείω** *apokleiō* from *G575* and *G2808*; to *close fully:*— shut up.

G609 **ἀποκόπτω** *apokoptō* from *G575* and *G2875*; to *amputate;* reflexive (by irony) to *mutilate* (the privy parts):— cut off. Compare *G2699*.

G610 **ἀπόκριμα** *apokrima* from *G611* (in its original sense of *judging*); a judicial *decision:*— sentence.

G611 **ἀποκρίνομαι** *apokrinomai* from *G575* and
κρίνω *krinō*; to *conclude for oneself,* i.e. (by implication) to *respond;* by Hebrew [compare H6030] to *begin to speak* (where an address is expected):— answer.

G612 **ἀπόκρισις** *apokrisis* from *G611*; a *response* :— answer.

G613 **ἀποκρύπτω** *apokryptō* from *G575* and *G2928*; to *conceal away* (i.e. *fully*); figuratively to *keep secret:*— hide.

G614 **ἀπόκρυφος** *apokryphos* from *G613*; *secret;* by implication *treasured:*— hid, kept secret.

G615 **ἀποκτείνω** *apokteinō* from *G575* and
κτείνω *kteinō* (to *slay*); to *kill* outright; figuratively to *destroy:*— put to death, kill, slay.

G616 **ἀποκυέω** *apokyeō* from *G575* and the base of *G2949*; to *breed forth,* i.e. (by transfer) to *generate* (figuratively):— beget, produce.

G617 **ἀποκυλίω** *apokyliō* from *G575* and *G2947*; to *roll away:*— roll away (back).

G618 **ἀπολαμβάνω** *apolambanō* from *G575* and *G2983*; to *receive* (specifically in *full,* or as a host); also to *take aside:*— receive, take.

G619 **ἀπόλαυσις** *apolausis* from a compound of *G575* and
λαύω *lauō* (to *enjoy*); full *enjoyment:*— enjoy, enjoyment.

G620 **ἀπολείπω** *apoleipō* from *G575* and *G3007*; to *leave* behind (passive *remain*); by implication to *forsake:*— leave, remain.

G621 **ἀπολείχω** *apoleichō* from *G575* and
λείχω *leichō* (to *"lick"*); to *lick* clean:— lick.

G622 **ἀπόλλυμι** *apollymi* from *G575* and the base of *G3639*; to *destroy* fully (reflexive to *perish,* or *lose*), literally or figuratively:— destroy, die, lose, mar, perish.

G623 **Ἀπολλύων** *Apollyōn* active participle of *G622*; a *destroyer* (i.e. *Satan*):— Appollyon.

G624 **Ἀπολλωνία** *Apollōnia* from the pagan deity
Ἀπόλλων *Apollōn* (i.e. the *sun;* from *G622*); *Apollonia,* a place in Macedonia:— Apollonia.

G625 **Ἀπολλώς** *Apollōs* probably from the same as Greek *G624*; *Apollos,* an Israelite:— Apollos.

G626 **ἀπολογέομαι** *apologeomai* middle from a compound of *G575* and *G3056*; to give an *account* (legal *plea*) of oneself, i.e. *exculpate* (self):— answer (for self), make defence, excuse (self), speak for self.

G627 **ἀπολογία** *apologia* from the same as *G626*; a *plea* ("apology"):— answer (for self), clearing of self, defence.

G628 **ἀπολούω** *apolouō* from *G575* and *G3068*; to *wash* fully, i.e. (figuratively) *have remitted* (reflexive):— wash (away).

G629 **ἀπολύτρωσις** *apolytrōsis* from a compound of *G575* and *G3083*; (the act) *ransom* in full, i.e. (figuratively) *riddance,* or (specifically) Christian *salvation:*— deliverance, redemption.

G630 **ἀπολύω** *apolyō* from *G575* and *G3089*; to *free* fully, i.e. (literally) *relieve, release, dismiss* (reflexive *depart*), or (figuratively) *let die, pardon,* or (specifically) *divorce:*— (let) depart, dismiss, divorce, forgive, let go, loose, put (send) away, release, set at liberty.

G631 **ἀπομάσσομαι** *apomassomai* middle from *G575* and
μάσσω *massō* (to *squeeze, knead, smear*); to *scrape away:*— wipe off.

G632 **ἀπονέμω** *aponemō* from *G575* and the base of *G3551*; to *apportion,* i.e. *bestow:*— give.

G633 **ἀπονίπτω** *aponiptō* from *G575* and *G3538*; to *wash off* (reflexive one's own hands, symbolically):— wash.

G634 **ἀποπίπτω** *apopiptō* from *G575* and *G4098*; to *fall off:*— fall.

G635 **ἀποπλανάω** *apoplanaō* from *G575* and *G4105*; to *lead astray* (figuratively), passive to *stray* (from truth):— err, seduce.

G636 **ἀποπλέω** *apopleō* from *G575* and *G4126*; to *set sail:*— sail away.

G637 **ἀποπλύνω** *apoplynō* from *G575* and *G4150*; to *rinse off:*— wash.

G638 **ἀποπνίγω** *apopnigō* from *G575* and *G4155*; to *stifle* (by drowning or overgrowth):— choke.

G639 **ἀπορέω** *aporeō* from a compound of *G1* (as a negative particle) and the base of *G4198*; to *have no way* out, i.e. *be at a loss* (mentally):— (stand in) doubt, be perplexed.

G640 **ἀπορία** *aporia* from the same as *G639*; a (state of) *quandary:*— perplexity.

G641 **ἀπορρίπτω** *aporrhiptō* from *G575* and *G4496*; to *hurl off,* i.e. *precipitate* (oneself):— cast.

G642 **ἀπορφανίζω** *aporphanizō* from *G575* and a derivative of *G3737*; to *bereave wholly,* i.e. (figuratively) *separate* (from intercourse):— take.

G643 **ἀποσκευάζω** *aposkeuazō* from *G575* and a derivative of *G4632*; to *pack up* (one's) *baggage:*— take up . . . carriages.

G644 **ἀποσκίασμα** *aposkiasma* from a compound of *G575* and a derivative of *G4639*; a *shading off,* i.e. *obscuration:*— shadow.

G645 **ἀποσπάω** *apospaō* from *G575* and *G4685*; to *drag forth,* i.e. (literally) *unsheathe* (a sword), or relatively (with a degree of force implied) *retire* (personally or factiously):— draw (away), withdraw, after we were gotten from.

G646 **ἀποστασία** *apostasia* feminine of the same as *G647*; *defection* from truth (properly the state) ["apostasy"]:— falling away, forsake.

G647 **ἀποστάσιον** *apostasion* neuter of a (presumed) adjective from a derivative of *G868*; properly something *separative,* i.e. (specifically) *divorce:*— (writing of) divorcement.

G648 **ἀποστεγάζω** *apostegazō* from *G575* and a derivative of *G4721*; to *unroof:*— uncover.

G649 **ἀποστέλλω** *apostellō* from *G575* and *G4724*; *set apart,* i.e. (by implication) to *send out* (properly on a mission) literally or figuratively:— put in, send (away, forth, out), set [at liberty].

G650 **ἀποστερέω** *apostereō* from *G575* and
στερέω *stereō* (to *deprive*); to *despoil:*— defraud, destitute, kept back by fraud.

G651 **ἀποστολή** *apostolē* from *G649*; *commission,* i.e. (specifically) *apostolate:*— apostleship.

G652 **ἀπόστολος** *apostolos* from *G649*; a *delegate;* specifically an *ambassador* of the Gospel; officially a *commissioner* of Christ [*"apostle"*] (with miraculous powers):— apostle, messenger, he that is sent.

G653 **ἀποστοματίζω** *apostomatizō* from *G575* and a (presumed) derivative of *G4750*; to *speak off-hand* (properly *dictate*), i.e. to *catechize* (in an invidious manner):— provoke to speak.

G654 **ἀποστρέφω** *apostrephō* from *G575* and *G4762*; to *turn away* or *back* (literally or figuratively):— bring again, pervert, turn away (from).

G655 **ἀποστυγέω** *apostygeō* from *G575* and the base of *G4767*; to *detest* utterly:— abhor.

G656 **ἀποσυνάγωγος** *aposynagōgos* from *G575* and *G4864*; *excommunicated:*— (put) out of the synagogue, (put) out of the synagogues.

G657 **ἀποτάσσομαι** *apotassomai* middle from *G575* and *G5021*; literally to *say adieu* (by departing or dismissing); figuratively to *renounce:*— bid farewell, forsake, take leave, send away.

G658 **ἀποτελέω** *apoteleō* from *G575* and *G5055*; to *complete entirely,* i.e. *consummate:*— finish.

G659 **ἀποτίθημι** *apotithēmi* from *G575* and *G5087*; to *put away* (literally or figuratively):— cast off, lay apart (aside, down), put away (off).

G660 **ἀποτινάσσω** *apotinassō* from *G575* and
τινάσσω *tinassō* (to *jostle*); to *brush off:*— shake off.

G661 **ἀποτίνω** *apotinō* from *G575* and *G5099*; to *pay* in full:— repay.

G662 **ἀποτολμάω** *apotolmaō* from *G575* and *G5111*; to *venture* plainly:— be very bold.

G663 **ἀποτομία** *apotomia* from the base of *G664*; (figuratively) *decisiveness,* i.e. *rigor:*— severity.

G664 **ἀποτόμως** *apotomōs* adverb from a derivative of a compound of *G575* and
τέμνω *temnō* (to *cut*); *abruptly,* i.e. *peremptorily:*— sharply, sharpness.

G665 **ἀποτρέπω** *apotrepō* from *G575* and the base of *G5157*; to *deflect,* i.e. (reflexive) *avoid:*— turn away.

G666 **ἀπουσία** *apousia* from the participle of *G548*; a *being away:*— absence.

G667 **ἀποφέρω** *apopherō* from *G575* and *G5342*; to *bear off* (literally or relatively):— bring, carry (away).

G668 ἀποφεύγω *apopheugō* from *G575* and *G5343*; (figuratively) to *escape:*— escape.

G669 ἀποφθέγγομαι *apophthengomai* from *G575* and *G5350*; to *enunciate* plainly, i.e. *declare:*— say, speak forth, utterance.

G670 ἀποφορτίζομαι *apophortizomai* from *G575* and the middle of *G5412*; to *unload:*— unlade.

G671 ἀπόχρησις *apochrēsis* from a compound of *G575* and *G5530*; the act of *using up,* i.e. *consumption:*— using.

G672 ἀποχωρέω *apochōreō* from *G575* and *G5562*; to *go away:*— depart.

G673 ἀποχωρίζω *apochōrizō* from *G575* and *G5563*; to *rend apart;* reflexive to *separate:*— depart (asunder).

G674 ἀποψύχω *apopsychō* from *G575* and *G5594*; to *breathe out,* i.e. *faint:*— hearts failing.

G675 Ἄππιος *Appios* of Latin origin; (in the genitive, i.e. possessive case) *of Appius,* the name of a Roman:— Appii.

G676 ἀπρόσιτος *aprositos* from *G1* (as a negative particle) and a derivative of a compound of *G4314* and

εἶμι *eimi* (to *go*); *inaccessible:*— which no man can approach.

G677 ἀπρόσκοπος *aproskopos* from *G1* (as a negative particle) and a presumed derivative of *G4350*; active *inoffensive,* i.e. *not leading into sin;* passive *faultless,* i.e. *not led into sin:*— none (void of, without) offence.

G678 ἀπροσωπολήπτως *aprosōpolēptōs* adverb from a compound of *G1* (as a negative particle) and a presumed derivative of a presumed compound of *G4383* and *G2983* [compare *G4381*]; in a way *not accepting* the *person,* i.e. *impartially:*— without respect of persons.

G679 ἄπταιστος *aptaistos* from *G1* (as a negative particle) and a derivative of *G4417*; *not stumbling,* i.e. (figuratively) *without sin:*— from falling.

G680 ἅπτομαι *haptomai* reflexive of *G681*; properly to *attach* oneself to, i.e. to *touch* (in many implied relations):— touch.

G681 ἅπτω *haptō* a primary verb; properly to *fasten* to, i.e. (specifically) to *set* on fire:— kindle, light.

G682 Ἀπφία *Apphia* probably of foreign origin; *Apphia,* a woman of Colossae:— Apphia.

G683 ἀπωθέομαι *apōtheomai* or

ἀπώθομαι *apōthomai* from *G575* and the middle of

ὠθέω *ōtheō* or

ὤθω *ōthō* (to *shove*); to *push off,* figuratively to *reject:*— cast away, put away (from), thrust away (from).

G684 ἀπώλεια *apōleia* from a presumed derivative of *G622*; *ruin* or *loss* (physical, spiritual or eternal):— damnable, damnation, destruction, die, perdition, perish, pernicious ways, waste.

G685 ἀρά *ara* probably from *G142*; properly *prayer* (as *lifted* to Heaven), i.e. (by implication) *imprecation:*— curse.

G686 ἄρα *ara* probably from *G142* (through the idea of *drawing* a conclusion); a particle denoting an *inference* more or less decisive (as follows). Often used in connection with other particles, especially *G1065* or *G3767* (after) or *G1487* (before). Compare also *G687*:— haply, (what) manner (of man), no doubt, perhaps, so be, then, therefore, truly, wherefore.

G687 ἆρα *ara* a form of *G686*; denoting an *interrogation* to which a negative answer is presumed:— therefore.

G688 Ἀραβία *Arabia* of Hebrew origin [H6152]; *Arabia,* a region of Asia:— Arabia.

G689 Ἀράμ *Aram* of Hebrew origin [H7410]; *Aram* (i.e. *Ram*), an Israelite:— Aram.

G690 Ἄραψ *Araps* from *G688*; an *Arab* or native of Arabia:— Arabian.

G691 ἀργέω *argeō* from *G692*; to *be idle,* i.e. (figuratively) to *delay:*— linger.

G692 ἀργός *argos* from *G1* (as a negative particle) and *G2041*; *inactive,* i.e. *unemployed;* (by implication) *lazy, useless:*— barren, idle, slow.

G693 ἀργύρεος *argyreos* from *G696*; made *of silver:*— (of) silver.

G694 ἀργύριον *argyrion* neuter of a presumed derivative of *G696*; *silvery,* i.e. (by implication) *cash;* specifically a *silverling* (i.e. *drachma* or *shekel*):— money, (piece of) silver (piece).

G695 ἀργυροκόπος *argyrokopos* from *G696* and *G2875*; a *beater* (i.e. *worker*) *of silver:*— silversmith.

G696 ἄργυρος *argyros* from

ἀργός *argos* (*shining*); *silver* (the metal, in the articles or coin):— silver.

G697 Ἄρειος Πάγος *Areios Pagos* from

Ἄρης *Arēs* (the name of the Greek deity of war) and a derivative of *G4078*; *rock of Ares,* a place in Athens:— Areopagus, Mars' Hill.

G698 Ἀρεοπαγίτης *Areopagitēs* from *G697*; an *Areopagite* or member of the court held on Mars' Hill:— Areopagite.

G699 ἀρέσκεια *areskeia* from a derivative of *G700*; *complaisance:*— pleasing.

G700 ἀρέσκω *areskō* probably from *G142* (through the idea of *exciting* emotion); to *be agreeable* (or by implication to seek to be so):— please.

G701 ἀρεστός *arestos* from *G700*; *agreeable;* by implication *fit:*— (things that) please, pleasing, reason.

G702 Ἀρέτας *Aretas* of foreign origin; *Aretas,* an Arabian:— Aretas.

G703 ἀρετή *aretē* from the same as *G730*; properly *manliness* (valor), i.e. *excellence* (intrinsic or attributed):— praise, virtue.

G704 ἀρήν *arēn* perhaps the same as *G730*; a *lamb* (as a *male*):— lamb.

G705 ἀριθμέω *arithmeō* from *G706*; to *enumerate* or *count:*— number.

G706 ἀριθμός *arithmos* from *G142*; a *number* (as reckoned *up*):— number.

G707 Ἀριμαθαία *Arimathaia* of Hebrew origin [H7414]; *Arimathaea* (or *Ramah*), a place in Palestine:— Arimathaea.

G708 Ἀρίσταρχος *Aristarchos* from the same as *G712* and *G757*; *best ruling; Aristarchus,* a Macedonian:— Aristarchus.

G709 ἀριστάω *aristaō* from *G712*; to *take the principal meal:*— dine.

G710 ἀριστερός *aristeros* apparently a compound of the same as *G712*; the *left* hand (as *second-best*):— left [hand].

G711 Ἀριστόβουλος *Aristoboulos* from the same as *G712* and *G1012*; *best counseling; Aristobulus,* a Christian:— Aristobulus.

G712 ἄριστον *ariston* apparently neuter of a superlative from the same as *G730*; the *best* meal [or *breakfast;* perhaps from

ἦρι *ēri* (*"early"*)], i.e. *luncheon:*— dinner.

G713 ἀρκετός *arketos* from *G714*; *satisfactory:*— enough, suffice, sufficient.

G714 ἀρκέω *arkeō* apparently a primary verb [but probably akin to *G142* through the idea of *raising* a barrier]; properly to *ward off,* i.e. (by implication) to *avail* (figuratively *be satisfactory*):— be content, be enough, suffice, be sufficient.

G715 ἄρκτος *arktos* probably from *G714*; a *bear* (as *obstructing* by ferocity):— bear.

G716 ἅρμα *harma* probably from *G142* [perhaps with *G1* (as a particle of union) prefixed]; a *chariot* (as *raised* or fitted *together* [compare *G719*]):— chariot.

G717 Ἀρμαγεδδών *Armageddōn* of Hebrew origin [H2022 and H4023]; *Armageddon* (or *Har-Megiddon*), a symbolic name:— Armageddon.

G718 ἁρμόζω *harmozō* from *G719*; to *joint,* i.e. (figuratively) to *woo* (reflexive to *betroth*):— espouse.

G719 ἁρμός *harmos* from the same as *G716*; an *articulation* (of the body):— joint.

G720 ἀρνέομαι *arneomai* perhaps from *G1* (as a negative particle) and the middle of *G4483*; to *contradict,* i.e. *disavow, reject, abnegate:*— deny, refuse.

G721 ἀρνίον *arnion* diminutive from *G704*; a *lambkin:*— lamb.

G722 ἀροτριάω *arotriaō* from *G723*; to *plough:*— plow.

G723 ἄροτρον *arotron* from

ἀρόω *aroō* (to *till*); a *plough:*— plow.

G724 ἁρπαγή *harpagē* from *G726*; *pillage* (properly abstract):— extortion, ravening, spoiling.

G725 ἁρπαγμός *harpagmos* from *G726*; *plunder* (properly concrete):— robbery.

G726 ἁρπάζω *harpazō* from a derivative of *G138*; to *seize* (in various applications):— catch (away, up), pluck, pull, take (by force).

G727 ἅρπαξ *harpax* from *G726*; *rapacious:*— extortion, ravening.

G728 ἀρραβών *arrhabōn* of Hebrew origin [H6162]; a *pledge,* i.e. part of the purchase-money or property given in advance as *security* for the rest:— earnest.

G729 ἄρραφος *arrhaphos* from *G1* (as a negative particle) and a presumed derivative of the same as *G4476*; *not sewn,* i.e. of a single piece:— without seam.

G730 ἄρρην *arrhēn* or

ἄρσην *arsēn* probably from *G142*; *male* (as stronger for *lifting*):— male, man.

G731 ἄρρητος *arrhētos* from *G1* (as a negative particle) and the same as *G4490*; *unsaid,* i.e. (by implication) *inexpressible:*— unspeakable.

G732 ἄρρωστος *arrhōstos* from *G1* (as a negative particle) and a presumed derivative of *G4517*; *infirm:*— sick (folk), sickly.

G733 ἀρσενοκοίτης *arsenokoitēs* from *G730* and *G2845*; a *sodomite:—* abuser of (that defile) self with mankind.

G734 Ἀρτεμᾶς *Artemas* contracted from a compound of *G735* and *G1435*; *gift of Artemis; Artemas* (or *Artemidorus*), a Christian:— Artemas.

G735 Ἄρτεμις *Artemis* probably from the same as *G736*; *prompt; Artemis*, the name of a Grecian goddess borrowed by the Asiatics for one of their deities:— Diana.

G736 ἀρτέμων *artemōn* from a derivative of *G737*; properly something *ready* [or else more remotely from *G142* (compare *G740*); something *hung* up], i.e. (specifically) the *topsail* (rather *foresail* or *jib*) of a vessel:— mainsail.

G737 ἄρτι *arti* adverb from a derivative of *G142* (compare *G740*) through the idea of *suspension; just now:—* this day (hour), hence, henceforth, here, hereafter, hither, hitherto, (even) now, (this) present.

G738 ἀρτιγέννητος *artigennētos* from *G737* and *G1084*; *just born*, i.e. (figuratively) a *young convert:—* new born.

G739 ἄρτιος *artios* from *G737*; *fresh*, i.e. (by implication) *complete:—* perfect.

G740 ἄρτος *artos* from *G142*; *bread* (as *raised*) or a *loaf:—* bread, shewbread, loaf.

G741 ἀρτύω *artyō* from a presumed derivative of *G142*; to *prepare*, i.e. *spice* (with *stimulating* condiments):— season.

G742 Ἀρφαξάδ *Arphaxad* of Hebrew origin [*H775*]; *Arphaxad*, a post-diluvian patriarch:— Arphaxad.

G743 ἀρχάγγελος *archangelos* from *G757* and *G32*; a *chief angel:—* archangel.

G744 ἀρχαῖος *archaios* from *G746*; *original* or *primeval:—* (them of) old (time).

G745 Ἀρχέλαος *Archelaos* from *G757* and *G2994*; *people-ruling; Archelaus*, a Jewish king:— Archelaus.

G746 ἀρχή *archē* from *G756*; (properly abstract) a *commencement*, or (concrete) *chief* (in various applications of order, time, place or rank):— beginning, corner, (at the, the) first (estate), magistrate, power, principality, principle, rule.

G747 ἀρχηγός *archēgos* from *G746* and *G71*; a *chief leader:—* author, captain, prince.

G748 ἀρχιερατικός *archieratikos* from *G746* and a derivative of *G2413*; *high-priestly:—* of the high-priest.

G749 ἀρχιερεύς *archiereus* from *G746* and *G2409*; the *high-priest* (literally of the Jews, typically Christ); by extension a *chief priest:—* chief (high) priest, chief of the priests.

G750 ἀρχιποίμην *archipoimēn* from *G746* and *G4166*; a *head shepherd:—* chief shepherd.

G751 Ἄρχιππος *Archippos* from *G746* and *G2462*; *horse-ruler; Archippus*, a Christian:— Archippus.

G752 ἀρχισυνάγωγος *archisynagōgos* from *G746* and *G4864*; *director of* the *synagogue* services:— (chief) ruler of the synagogue.

G753 ἀρχιτέκτων *architektōn* from *G746* and *G5045*; a *chief constructor*, i.e. *"architect":—* masterbuilder.

G754 ἀρχιτελώνης *architelōnēs* from *G746* and *G5057*; a *principal tax-gatherer:—* chief among the publicans.

G755 ἀρχιτρίκλινος *architriklinos* from *G746* and a compound of *G5140* and *G2827* (a *dinner-bed*, because composed of three couches); *director of* the *entertainment:—* governor (ruler) of the feast.

G756 ἄρχομαι *archomai* middle of *G757* (through the by implication of *precedence*); to *commence* (in order of time):— begin, (rehearse from the) beginning.

G757 ἄρχω *archō* a primary verb; to be *first* (in political rank or power):— reign (rule) over.

G758 ἄρχων *archōn* present participle of *G757*; a *first* (in rank or power):— chief (ruler), magistrate, prince, ruler.

G759 ἄρωμα *arōma* from *G142* (in the sense of *sending* off scent); an *aromatic:—* (sweet) spice.

G760 Ἀσά *Asa* of Hebrew origin [*H609*]; *Asa*, an Israelite:— Asa.

G761 ἀσάλευτος *asaleutos* from *G1* (as a negative particle) and a derivative of *G4531*; *unshaken*, i.e. (by implication) *immovable* (figuratively):— which cannot be moved, unmovable.

G762 ἄσβεστος *asbestos* from *G1* (as a negative particle) and a derivative of *G4570*; *not extinguished*, i.e. (by implication) *perpetual:—* not to be quenched, unquenchable.

G763 ἀσέβεια *asebeia* from *G765*; *impiety*, i.e. (by implication) *wickedness:—* ungodly, ungodliness.

G764 ἀσεβέω *asebeō* from *G765*; to *be* (by implication *act*) *impious* or *wicked:—* commit (live, that after should live) ungodly.

G765 ἀσεβής *asebēs* from *G1* (as a negative particle) and a presumed derivative of *G4576*; *irreverent*, i.e. (by extension) *impious* or *wicked:—* ungodly (man).

G766 ἀσέλγεια *aselgeia* from a compound of *G1* (as a negative particle) and a presumed

σελγής *selgēs* (of uncertain derivation, but apparently meaning *continent*); *licentiousness* (sometimes including other vices):— filthy, lasciviousness, wantonness.

G767 ἄσημος *asēmos* from *G1* (as a negative particle) and the base of *G4591*; *unmarked*, i.e. (figuratively) *ignoble:—* mean.

G768 Ἀσήρ *Asēr* of Hebrew origin [*H836*]; *Aser* (i.e. *Asher*), an Israelite tribe:— Aser.

G769 ἀσθένεια *astheneia* from *G772*; *feebleness* (of body or mind); by implication *malady*; moral *frailty:—* disease, infirmity, sickness, weakness.

G770 ἀσθενέω *astheneō* from *G772*; to *be feeble* (in any sense):— be diseased, impotent folk (man), (be) sick, (be, be made) weak.

G771 ἀσθένημα *asthenēma* from *G770*; a *scruple* of conscience:— infirmity.

G772 ἀσθενής *asthenēs* from *G1* (as a negative particle) and the base of *G4599*; *without strength* (in various applications, literally, figuratively and morally):— more feeble, impotent, sick, without strength, weak, weaker, weakness, weak thing.

G773 Ἀσία *Asia* of uncertain derivation; *Asia*, i.e. *Asia Minor*, or (usually) only its western shore:— Asia.

G774 Ἀσιανός *Asianos* from *G773*; an *Asian* (i.e. *Asiatic*) or inhabitant of Asia:— of Asia.

G775 Ἀσιάρχης *Asiarchēs* from *G773* and *G746*; an *Asiarch* or president of the public festivities in a city of Asia Minor:— chief of Asia.

G776 ἀσιτία *asitia* from *G777*; *fasting* (the state) :— abstinence.

G777 ἄσιτος *asitos* from *G1* (as a negative particle) and *G4621*; *without* (taking) *food:—* fasting.

G778 ἀσκέω *askeō* probably from the same as *G4632*; to *elaborate*, i.e. (figuratively) *train* (by implication *strive*):— exercise.

G779 ἀσκός *askos* from the same as *G778*; a leathern (or skin) *bag* used as a bottle:— bottle.

G780 ἀσμένως *asmenōs* adverb from a derivative of the base of *G2237*; *with pleasure:—* gladly.

G781 ἄσοφος *asophos* from *G1* (as a negative particle) and *G4680*; *unwise:—* fool.

G782 ἀσπάζομαι *aspazomai* from *G1* (as a particle of union) and a presumed form of *G4685*; to *enfold* in the arms, i.e. (by implication) to *salute*, (figuratively) to *welcome:—* embrace, greet, salute, take leave.

G783 ἀσπασμός *aspasmos* from *G782*; a *greeting* (in person or by letter):— greeting, salutation.

G784 ἄσπιλος *aspilos* from *G1* (as a negative particle) and *G4695*; *unblemished* (physically or morally):— without spot, unspotted.

G785 ἀσπίς *aspis* of uncertain derivation; a *buckler* (or *round* shield); used of a serpent (as *coiling* itself), probably the *"asp":—* asp.

G786 ἄσπονδος *aspondos* from *G1* (as a negative particle) and a derivative of *G4689*; literally *without libation* (which usually accompanied a treaty), i.e. (by implication) *without truce:—* implacable, truce-breaker.

G787 ἀσσάριον *assarion* of Latin origin; an *assarius* or *as*, a Roman coin:— farthing.

G788 ἆσσον *asson* neuter comparative of the base of *G1451*; *more nearly*, i.e. *very near:—* close.

G789 Ἄσσος *Assos* probably of foreign origin; *Assus*, a city of Asia Minor:— Assos.

G790 ἀστατέω *astateō* from *G1* (as a negative particle) and a derivative of *G2476*; to *be non-stationary*, i.e. (figuratively) *homeless:—* have no certain dwelling-place.

G791 ἀστεῖος *asteios* from

ἄστυ *asty* (a *city*); *urbane*, i.e. (by implication) *handsome:—* fair.

G792 ἀστήρ *astēr* probably from the base of *G4766*; a *star* (as *strewn* over the sky), literally or figuratively:— star.

G793 ἀστήρικτος *astēriktos* from *G1* (as a negative particle) and a presumed derivative of *G4741*; *unfixed*, i.e. (figuratively) *vacillating:—* unstable.

G794 ἄστοργος *astorgos* from *G1* (as a negative particle) and a presumed derivative of

στέργω *stergō* (to *cherish* affectionately); *hard-hearted* towards kindred:— without natural affection.

G795 ἀστοχέω *astocheō* from a compound of *G1* (as a negative particle) and

στοίχος *stoichos* (an *aim*); to *miss* the mark, i.e. (figuratively) *deviate* from truth:— err, swerve.

G796 ἀστραπή *astrapē* from *G797*; *lightning*; by analogy *glare:—* lightning, bright shining.

G797 ἀστράπτω *astraptō* probably from *G792*; to *flash* as lightning:— lighten, shine.

G798 **ἄστρον** *astron* neuter from *G792*; properly a *constellation;* put for a single *star* (natural or artificial):— star.

G799 **Ἀσύγκριτος** *Asynkritos* from *G1* (as a negative particle) and a derivative of *G4793*; *incomparable; Asyncritus,* a Christian:— Asyncritus.

G800 **ἀσύμφωνος** *asymphōnos* from *G1* (as a negative particle) and *G4859*; *inharmonious* (figuratively):— agree not.

G801 **ἀσύνετος** *asynetos* from *G1* (as a negative particle) and *G4908*; *unintelligent;* by implication *wicked:*— foolish, without understanding.

G802 **ἀσύνθετος** *asynthetos* from *G1* (as a negative particle) and a derivative of *G4934*; properly *not agreed,* i.e. *treacherous* to compacts:— covenant-breaker.

G803 **ἀσφάλεια** *asphaleia* from *G804*; *security* (literal or figurative):— certainty, safety.

G804 **ἀσφαλής** *asphalēs* from *G1* (as a negative particle) and

σφάλλω *sphallō* (to *"fail"*); *secure* (literally or figuratively):— certain, certainty, safe, sure.

G805 **ἀσφαλίζω** *asphalizō* from *G804*; to *render secure:*— make fast (sure).

G806 **ἀσφαλῶς** *asphalōs* adverb from *G804*; *securely* (literally or figuratively):— assuredly, safely.

G807 **ἀσχημονέω** *aschēmoneō* from *G809*; to *be* (i.e. *act*) *unbecoming:*— behave self uncomely (unseemly).

G808 **ἀσχημοσύνη** *aschēmosynē* from *G809*; an *indecency;* by implication the *pudenda:*— shame, that which is unseemly.

G809 **ἀσχήμων** *aschēmōn* from *G1* (as a negative particle) and a presumed derivative of *G2192* (in the sense of its congener *G4976*); properly *shapeless,* i.e. (figuratively) *inelegant:*— uncomely.

G810 **ἀσωτία** *asōtia* from a compound of *G1* (as a negative particle) and a presumed derivative of *G4982*; properly *not being saved,* i.e. (by implication) *profligacy:*— excess, riot.

G811 **ἀσώτως** *asōtōs* adverb from the same as *G810*; *dissolutely:*— riotous.

G812 **ἀτακτέω** *atakteō* from *G813*; to *be* (i.e. *act*) *irregular:*— behave self disorderly.

G813 **ἄτακτος** *ataktos* from *G1* (as a negative particle) and a derivative of *G5021*; *not arranged,* i.e. (by implication) *insubordinate* (religiously):— unruly.

G814 **ἀτάκτως** *ataktōs* adverb from *G813*; *irregularly* (morally):— disorderly.

G815 **ἄτεκνος** *ateknos* from *G1* (as a negative particle) and *G5043*; *childless:*— childless, without children.

G816 **ἀτενίζω** *atenizō* from a compound of *G1* (as a particle of union) and

τείνω *teinō* (to *stretch*); to *gaze* intently:— behold earnestly (steadfastly), fasten (eyes), look (earnestly, steadfastly, up steadfastly), set eyes.

G817 **ἄτερ** *ater* a particle probably akin to *G427*; *aloof,* i.e. *apart* from (literally or figuratively):— in the absence of, without.

G818 **ἀτιμάζω** *atimazō* from *G820*; to *render infamous,* i.e. (by implication) *contemn* or *maltreat:*— despise, dishonour, suffer shame, entreat shamefully.

G819 **ἀτιμία** *atimia* from *G820*; *infamy,* i.e. (subjectively) comparative *indignity,* (objectively) *disgrace:*— dishonour, reproach, shame, vile.

G820 **ἄτιμος** *atimos* from *G1* (as a negative particle) and *G5092*; (negatively) *not honoured* or (positively) *dishonoured:*— despised, without honour, less honourable [*comparative degree*].

G821 **ἀτιμόω** *atimoō* from *G820*; used like *G818*; to *maltreat:*— handle shamefully.

G822 **ἀτμίς** *atmis* from the same as *G109*; *mist:*— vapour.

G823 **ἄτομος** *atomos* from *G1* (as a negative particle) and the base of *G5114*; *uncut,* i.e. (by implication) *indivisible* [an *"atom"* of time]:— moment.

G824 **ἄτοπος** *atopos* from *G1* (as a negative particle) and *G5117*; *out of place,* i.e. (figuratively) *improper, injurious, wicked:*— amiss, harm, unreasonable.

G825 **Ἀττάλεια** *Attaleia* from

Ἄτταλος *Attalos* (a king of Pergamus); *Attaleia,* a place in Pamphylia:— Attalia.

G826 **αὐγάζω** *augazō* from *G827*; to *beam* forth (figuratively):— shine.

G827 **αὐγή** *augē* of uncertain derivation; a *ray* of light, i.e. (by implication) *radiance, dawn:*— break of day.

G828 **Αὔγουστος** *Augoustos* from Latin ["august"]; *Augustus,* a title of the Roman emperor:— Augustus.

G829 **αὐθάδης** *authadēs* from *G846* and the base of *G2237*; *self-pleasing,* i.e. *arrogant:*— self-willed.

G830 **αὐθαίρετος** *authairetos* from *G846* and the same as *G140*; *self-chosen,* i.e. (by implication) *voluntary:*— of own accord, willing of self.

G831 **αὐθεντέω** *authenteō* from a compound of *G846* and an obsolete

ἕντης *hentēs* (a *worker*); to *act of oneself,* i.e. (figuratively) *dominate:*— usurp authority over.

G832 **αὐλέω** *auleō* from *G836*; to play the *flute:*— pipe.

G833 **αὐλή** *aulē* from the same as *G109*; a *yard* (as open to the *wind*); by implication a *mansion:*— court, fold, sheepfold, hall, palace.

G834 **αὐλητής** *aulētēs* from *G832*; a *flute-player* :— minstrel, piper.

G835 **αὐλίζομαι** *aulizomai* middle from *G833*; to *pass the night* (properly in the open air):— abide, lodge.

G836 **αὐλός** *aulos* from the same as *G109*; a *flute* (as *blown*):— pipe.

G837 **αὐξάνω** *auxanō* a prolonged form of a primary verb; to *grow* (*"wax"*), i.e. *enlarge* (literally or figuratively, active or passive):— grow (up), (give the) increase.

G838 **αὔξησις** *auxēsis* from *G837*; *growth:*— increase.

G839 **αὔριον** *aurion* from a derivative of the same as *G109* (meaning a *breeze,* i.e. the morning *air*); properly *fresh,* i.e. (adverbially with ellipsis of *G2250*) *tomorrow:*— morrow, tomorrow, next day.

G840 **αὐστηρός** *austēros* from a (presumed) derivative of the same as *G109* (meaning *blown*); *rough* (properly as a *gale*), i.e. (figuratively) *severe:*— austere.

G841 **αὐτάρκεια** *autarkeia* from *G842*; *self-satisfaction,* i.e. (abstractly) *contentedness,* or (concretely) a *competence:*— contentment, sufficiency.

G842 **αὐτάρκης** *autarkēs* from *G846* and *G714*; *self-complacent,* i.e. *contented:*— content.

G843 **αὐτοκατάκριτος** *autokatakritos* from *G846* and a derivative of *G2632*; *self-condemned:*— condemned of self.

G844 **αὐτόματος** *automatos* from *G846* and the same as *G3155*; *self-moved* ["automatic"], i.e. *spontaneous:*— of own accord, of self.

G845 **αὐτόπτης** *autoptēs* from *G846* and *G3700*; *self-seeing,* i.e. an *eye-witness:*— eye-witness.

G846 **αὐτός** *autos* from the particle

αὖ *au* [perhaps akin to the base of *G109* through the idea of a *baffling* wind] (*backward*); the reflexive pronoun *self,* used (alone or in the compound *G1438*) of the third person, and (with the properly personal pronoun) of the other persons:— her, it, itself, one, the other, (mine) own, said, same, selfsame, the same, self, himself, myself, thyself, selves, yourselves, she, that, their, theirs, them, themselves, there, thereat, thereby, therein, thereinto, thereof, thereon, therewith, they, (these) things, this (man), those, together, very, which. Compare *G848*.

G847 **αὐτοῦ** *autou* genitive (i.e. possessive) of *G846*, used as an adverb of location; properly belonging to the *same* spot, i.e. *in this* (or *that*) *place:*— here, there.

G848 **αὑτοῦ** *hautou* contracted for *G1438*; *self* (in some oblique case or reflexive relation):— her (own), (of) him, (of) himself, his (own), of it, thee, their (own), them, themselves, they.

G849 **αὐτόχειρ** *autocheir* from *G846* and *G5495*; *self-handed,* i.e. doing *personally:*— with . . . own hands.

G850 **αὐχμηρός** *auchmēros* from

αὐχμός *auchmos* [probably from a base akin to that of *G109*] (*dust,* as *dried* by wind); properly *dirty,* i.e. (by implication) *obscure:*— dark.

G851 **ἀφαιρέω** *aphaireō* from *G575* and *G138*; to *remove* (literally or figuratively):— cut (smite) off, take away.

G852 **ἀφανής** *aphanēs* from *G1* (as a negative particle) and *G5316*; *non-apparent:*— that is not manifest.

G853 **ἀφανίζω** *aphanizō* from *G852*; to *render not apparent,* i.e. (active) *consume* (*becloud*), or (passive) *disappear* (*be destroyed*):— corrupt, disfigure, perish, vanish away.

G854 **ἀφανισμός** *aphanismos* from *G853*; *disappearance,* i.e. (figuratively) *abrogation:*— vanish away.

G855 **ἄφαντος** *aphantos* from *G1* (as a negative particle) and a derivative of *G5316*; *non-manifested,* i.e. *invisible:*— vanished out of sight.

G856 **ἀφεδρών** *aphedrōn* from a compound of *G575* and the base of *G1476*; a place of *sitting apart,* i.e. a *privy:*— draught.

G857 **ἀφειδία** *apheidia* from a compound of *G1* (as a negative particle) and *G5339*; *being unsparing,* i.e. *austerity* (*asceticism*):— neglecting.

G858 **ἀφελότης** *aphelotēs* from a compound of *G1* (as a negative particle) and

φέλλος *phellos* (in the sense of a *stone* as *stubbing* the foot); *smoothness,* i.e. (figuratively) *simplicity:*— singleness.

***G859* ἄφεσις** *aphesis* from *G863*; *freedom;* (figuratively) *pardon:*— deliverance, forgiveness, liberty, remission.

***G860* ἁφή** *haphē* from *G680*; probably a *ligament* (as *fastening*):— joint.

***G861* ἀφθαρσία** *aphtharsia* from *G862*; *incorruptibility;* generally *unending existence;* (figuratively) *genuineness:*— immortality, incorruption, sincerity.

***G862* ἄφθαρτος** *aphthartos* from *G1* (as a negative particle) and a derivative of Greek *G5351*; *not decaying* (in essence or continuance):— not corruptible, incorruptible, uncorruptible, immortal.

***G863* ἀφίημι** *aphiēmi* from *G575* and
ἵημι *hiēmi* (to *send;* an intensive form of
εἶμι *eimi* to *go*); to *send forth,* in various applications (as follow):— cry, forgive, forsake, lay aside, leave, let (alone, be, go, have), omit, put (send) away, remit, suffer, yield up.

***G864* ἀφικνέομαι** *aphikneomai* from *G575* and the base of *G2425*; to *go* (i.e. *spread*) *forth* (by rumor):— come abroad.

***G865* ἀφιλάγαθος** *aphilagathos* from *G1* (as a negative particle) and *G5358*; *hostile to virtue:*— despiser of those that are good.

***G866* ἀφιλάργυρος** *aphilargyros* from *G1* (as a negative particle) and *G5366*; *not avaricious:*— without covetousness, not greedy of filthy lucre.

***G867* ἄφιξις** *aphixis* from *G864*; properly *arrival,* i.e. (by implication) *departure:*— departing.

***G868* ἀφίστημι** *aphistēmi* from *G575* and *G2476*; to *remove,* i.e. (active) *instigate* to revolt; usually (reflexive) to *desist, desert,* etc.:— depart, draw (fall) away, refrain, withdraw self.

***G869* ἄφνω** *aphnō* adverb from *G852* (contraction); *unawares,* i.e. *unexpectedly:*— suddenly.

***G870* ἀφόβως** *aphobōs* adverb from a compound of *G1* (as a negative particle) and *G5401*; *fearlessly:*— without fear.

***G871* ἀφομοιόω** *aphomoioō* from *G575* and *G3666*; to *assimilate* closely:— make like.

***G872* ἀφοράω** *aphoraō* from *G575* and *G3708*; to *consider* attentively:— look.

***G873* ἀφορίζω** *aphorizō* from *G575* and *G3724*; to *set off* by boundary, i.e. (figuratively) *limit, exclude, appoint,* etc.:— divide, separate, sever.

***G874* ἀφορμή** *aphormē* from a compound of *G575* and *G3729*; a *starting*-point, i.e. (figuratively) an *opportunity:*— occasion.

***G875* ἀφρίζω** *aphrizō* from *G876*; to *froth* at the mouth (in epilepsy):— foam.

***G876* ἀφρός** *aphros* apparently a primary word; *froth,* i.e. *slaver:*— foaming.

***G877* ἀφροσύνη** *aphrosynē* from *G878*; *senselessness,* i.e. (euphemistic) *egotism;* (moral) *recklessness:*— folly, foolishly, foolishness.

***G878* ἄφρων** *aphrōn* from *G1* (as a negative particle) and *G5424*; properly *mindless,* i.e. *stupid,* (by implication) *ignorant,* (specifically) *egotistic,* (practically) *rash,* or (morally) *unbelieving:*— fool, foolish, unwise.

***G879* ἀφυπνόω** *aphypnoō* from a compound of *G575* and *G5258*; properly to *become awake,* i.e. (by implication) to *drop* (off) in slumber:— fall asleep.

***G880* ἄφωνος** *aphōnos* from *G1* (as a negative particle) and *G5456*; *voiceless,* i.e. *mute* (by nature or choice); figuratively *unmeaning:*— dumb, without signification.

***G881* Ἀχάζ** *Achaz* of Hebrew origin [H271]; *Achaz,* an Israelite:— Achaz.

***G882* Ἀχαΐα** *Achaia* of uncertain derivation; *Achaïa* (i.e. *Greece*), a country of Europe:— Achaia.

***G883* Ἀχαϊκός** *Achaikos* from *G882*; an *Achaïan; Achaïus,* a Christian:— Achaicus.

***G884* ἀχάριστος** *acharistos* from *G1* (as a negative particle) and a presumed derivative of *G5483*; *thankless,* i.e. *ungrateful:*— unthankful.

***G885* Ἀχείμ** *Acheim* probably of Hebrew origin [compare H3137]; *Achim,* an Israelite:— Achim.

***G886* ἀχειροποίητος** *acheiropoiētos* from *G1* (as a negative particle) and *G5499*; *not manufactured,* i.e. *not artificial:*— made without (not made with) hands.

***G887* ἀχλύς** *achlys* of uncertain derivation; *dimness* of sight, i.e. (probably) a *cataract:*— mist.

***G888* ἀχρεῖος** *achreios* from *G1* (as a negative particle) and a derivative of *G5534* [compare *G5532*]; *useless,* i.e. (euphemistically) *unmeritorious:*— unprofitable.

***G889* ἀχρειόω** *achreioō* from *G888*; to *render useless,* i.e. *spoil:*— become unprofitable.

***G890* ἄχρηστος** *achrēstos* from *G1* (as a negative particle) and *G5543*; *inefficient,* i.e. (by implication) *detrimental:*— unprofitable.

***G891* ἄχρι** *achri* or
ἄχρις *achris* akin to *G206* (through the idea of a *terminus*); (of time) *until* or (of place) *up to:*— as far as, for, in, into, till, to, (even) unto, until, while. Compare *G3360*.

***G892* ἄχυρον** *achyron* perhaps remotely from
χέω *cheō* (to *shed* forth); *chaff* (as *diffusive*):— chaff.

***G893* ἀψευδής** *apseudēs* from *G1* (as a negative particle) and *G5579*; *veracious:*— that cannot lie.

***G894* ἄψινθος** *apsinthos* of uncertain derivation; *wormwood* (as a type of *bitterness,* i.e. [figuratively] *calamity*):— wormwood.

***G895* ἄψυχος** *apsychos* from *G1* (as a negative particle) and *G5590*; *lifeless,* i.e. *inanimate* (mechanical):— without life.

B

***G896* Βάαλ** *Baal* of Hebrew origin [H1168]; *Baal,* a Phoenician deity (used as a symbol of idolatry):— Baal.

***G897* Βαβυλών** *Babylōn* of Hebrew origin [H894]; *Babylon,* the capital of Chaldaea (literally or figuratively [as a type of tyranny]):— Babylon.

***G898* βαθμός** *bathmos* from the same as *G899*; a *step,* i.e. (figuratively) *grade* (of dignity):— degree.

***G899* βάθος** *bathos* from the same as *G901*; *profundity,* i.e. (by implication) *extent;* (figuratively) *mystery:*— deep (things), deepness, depth.

***G900* βαθύνω** *bathynō* from *G901*; to *deepen:*— deep.

***G901* βαθύς** *bathys* from the base of *G939*; *profound* (as *going* down), literally or figuratively:— deep, very early.

***G902* βαΐον** *baion* a diminutive of a derivative probably of the base of *G939*; a palm *twig* (as *going* out far):— branch.

***G903* Βαλαάμ** *Balaam* of Hebrew origin [H1109]; *Balaam,* a Mesopotamian (symbolic of a false teacher) :— Balaam.

***G904* Βαλάκ** *Balak* of Hebrew origin [H1111]; *Balak,* a Moabite:— Balac.

***G905* βαλάντιον** *balantion* probably remotely from *G906* (as a *depository*); a *pouch* (for money):— bag, purse.

***G906* βάλλω** *ballō* a primary verb; to *throw* (in various applications, more or less violent or intense):— arise, cast (out), dung, lay, lie, pour, put (up), send, strike, throw (down), thrust. Compare *G4496*.

***G907* βαπτίζω** *baptizō* from a derivative of *G911*; to *make whelmed* (i.e. *fully wet*); used only (in the N.T.) of ceremonial *ablution,* especially (technically) of the ordinance of Christian *baptism:*— baptist, baptize, wash.

***G908* βάπτισμα** *baptisma* from *G907*; *baptism* (technical or figurative):— baptism.

***G909* βαπτισμός** *baptismos* from *G907*; *ablution* (ceremonially or Christian):— baptism, washing.

***G910* Βαπτιστής** *Baptistēs* from *G907*; a *baptizer,* as an epithet of Christ's forerunner:— Baptist.

***G911* βάπτω** *baptō* a primary verb; to *whelm,* i.e. cover wholly with a fluid; in the N.T. only in a qualified or specific sense, i.e. (literally) to *moisten* (a part of one's person), or (by implication) to *stain* (as with dye):— dip.

***G912* Βαραββᾶς** *Barabbas* of Aramaic origin [H1347 and *G5*]; *son of Abba; Bar-abbas,* an Israelite:— Barabbas.

***G913* Βαράκ** *Barak* of Hebrew origin [H1301]; *Barak,* an Israelite:— Barak.

***G914* Βαραχίας** *Barachias* of Hebrew origin [H1296]; *Barachias* (i.e. *Berechijah*), an Israelite:— Barachias.

***G915* βάρβαρος** *barbaros* of uncertain derivation; a *foreigner* (i.e. *non-Greek*):— barbarian, barbarous.

***G916* βαρέω** *bareō* from *G926*; to *weigh* down (figuratively):— burden, charge, heavy, press.

***G917* βαρέως** *bareōs* adverb from *G926*; *heavily* (figuratively):— dull.

***G918* Βαρθολομαῖος** *Bartholomaios* of Aramaic origin [H1247 and H8526]; *son of Tolmai; Bartholomaeus,* a Christian apostle:— Bartholomeus.

***G919* Βαριησοῦς** *Bariēsous* of Aramaic origin [H1247 and H3091]; *son of Jesus* (or *Joshua*); *Barjesus,* an Israelite:— Barjesus.

***G920* Βαριωνᾶς** *Bariōnas* of Aramaic origin [H1247 and H3124]; *son of Jonas* (or *Jonah*); *Bar-jonas,* an Israelite:— Bar-jona.

***G921* Βαρνάβας** *Barnabas* of Aramaic origin [H1247 and H5029]; *son of Nabas* (i.e. *prophecy*); *Barnabas,* an Israelite:— Barnabas.

***G922* βάρος** *baros* probably from the same as *G939* (through the notion of *going* down; compare *G899*); *weight;* in the N.T. only figuratively a *load, abundance, authority:*— burden, burdensome, weight.

***G923* Βαρσαβᾶς** *Barsabas* of Aramaic origin [H1247 and probably H6634]; *son of Sabas* (or

Tsaba); *Bar-sabas,* the name of two Israelites:— Barsabas.

G924 **Βαρτιμαῖος** *Bartimaios* of Aramaic origin [H1247 and H2931]; *son of Timaeus* (or the *unclean*); *Bar-timaeus,* an Israelite:— Bartimaeus.

G925 **βαρύνω** *barynō* from *G926*; to *burden* (figuratively):— overcharge.

G926 **βαρύς** *barys* from the same as *G922*; *weighty,* i.e. (figuratively) *burdensome, grave:*— grievous, heavy, weightier.

G927 **βαρύτιμος** *barytimos* from *G926* and *G5092*; highly *valuable:*— very precious.

G928 **βασανίζω** *basanizō* from *G931*; to *torture* :— pain, toil, torment, toss, vex.

G929 **βασανισμός** *basanismos* from *G928*; *torture* :— torment.

G930 **βασανιστής** *basanistēs* from *G928*; a *torturer:*— tormentor.

G931 **βάσανος** *basanos* perhaps remotely from the same as *G939* (through the notion of *going* to the bottom); a *touch-stone,* i.e. (by analogy) *torture:*— torment.

G932 **βασιλεία** *basileia* from *G935*; properly *royalty,* i.e. (abstractly) *rule,* or (concretely) a *realm* (literal or figurative):— kingdom, reign.

G933 **βασίλειον** *basileion* neuter of *G934*; a *palace:*— king's court.

G934 **βασίλειος** *basileios* from *G935*; *kingly* (in nature):— royal.

G935 **βασιλεύς** *basileus* probably from *G939* (through the notion of a *foundation* of power); a *sovereign* (abstract, relative or figurative):— king.

G936 **βασιλεύω** *basileuō* from *G935*; to *rule* (literally or figuratively):— king, reign.

G937 **βασιλικός** *basilikos* from *G935*; *regal* (in relation), i.e. (literally) belonging to (or befitting) the sovereign (as land, dress, or a *courtier*), or (figuratively) *preeminent:*— king's, nobleman, royal.

G938 **βασίλισσα** *basilissa* feminine from *G936*; a *queen:*— queen.

G939 **βάσις** *basis* from
βαίνω *bainō* (to *walk*); a *pace* ("base"), i.e. (by implication) the *foot:*— foot.

G940 **βασκαίνω** *baskainō* akin to *G5335*; to *malign,* i.e. (by extension) to *fascinate* (by false representations):— bewitch.

G941 **βαστάζω** *bastazō* perhaps remotely derived from the base of *G939* (through the idea of *removal*); to *lift,* literally or figuratively (*endure, declare, sustain, receive,* etc.):— bear, carry, take up.

G942 **βάτος** *batos* of uncertain derivation; a *brier* shrub:— bramble, bush.

G943 **βάτος** *batos* of Hebrew origin [H1324]; a *bath,* or measure for liquids:— measure.

G944 **βάτραχος** *batrachos* of uncertain derivation; a *frog:*— frog.

G945 **βαττολογέω** *battologeō* from
Βάττος *Battos* (a proverbial stammerer) and *G3056*; to *stutter,* i.e. (by implication) to *prate* tediously:— use vain repetitions.

G946 **βδέλυγμα** *bdelygma* from *G948*; a *detestation,* i.e. (specifically) *idolatry:*— abomination.

G947 **βδελυκτός** *bdelyktos* from *G948*; *detestable,* i.e. (specifically) *idolatrous:*— abominable.

G948 **βδελύσσω** *bdelyssō* from a (presumed) derivative of
βδέω *bdeō* (to *stink*); to *be disgusted,* i.e. (by implication) *detest* (especially of idolatry):— abhor, abominable.

G949 **βέβαιος** *bebaios* from the base of *G939* (through the idea of *basality*); *stable* (literally or figuratively):— firm, of force, steadfast, sure.

G950 **βεβαιόω** *bebaioō* from *G949*; to *stabilize* (figuratively):— confirm, stablish, establish.

G951 **βεβαίωσις** *bebaiōsis* from *G950*; *stabilization* :— confirmation.

G952 **βέβηλος** *bebēlos* from the base of *G939* and
βηλός *bēlos* (a *threshold*); *accessible* (as by *crossing the door-way*), i.e. (by implication of Jewish notions) *heathenish, wicked:*— profane (person).

G953 **βεβηλόω** *bebēloō* from *G952*; to *desecrate:*— profane.

G954 **Βεελζεβούλ** *Beelzeboul* of Aramaic origin [by parody upon H1176]; *dung-god; Beelzebul,* a name of Satan:— Beelzebub.

G955 **Βελίαλ** *Belial* of Hebrew origin [H1100], *worthlessness; Belial,* as an epithet of Satan:— Belial.

G956 **βέλος** *belos* from *G906*; a *missile,* i.e. *spear* or *arrow:*— dart.

G957 **βελτίον** *beltion* neuter of a compound of a derivative of *G906* (used for the comparative of *G18*); *better:*— very well.

G958 **Βενιαμίν** *Beniamin* of Hebrew origin [H1144]; *Benjamin,* an Israelite:— Benjamin.

G959 **Βερνίκη** *Bernikē* from a provincial form of *G5342* and *G3529*; *victorious; Bernicè,* a member of the Herodian family:— Bernice.

G960 **Βέροια** *Beroia* perhaps a provincial from a derivative of *G4008* [*Peraea,* i.e. the region *beyond* the coast-line]; *Beroea,* a place in Macedonia:— Berea.

G961 **Βεροιαῖος** *Beroiaios* from *G960*; a *Beroean* or native of Beroea:— of Berea.

G962 **Βηθαβαρά** *Bēthabara* of Hebrew origin [H1004 and H5679]; *ferry-house; Bethabara* (i.e. *Bethabarah*), a place on the Jordan:— Bethabara.

G963 **Βηθανία** *Bēthania* of Aramaic origin; *date-house; Beth-any,* a place in Palestine:— Bethany.

G964 **Βηθεσδά** *Bēthesda* of Aramaic origin [compare H1004 and H2617]; *house of kindness; Beth-esda,* a pool in Jerusalem:— Bethesda.

G965 **Βηθλεέμ** *Bēthleem* of Hebrew origin [H1036]; *Bethleem* (i.e. *Beth-lechem*), a place in Palestine:— Bethlehem.

G966 **Βηθσαϊδά** *Bēthsaida* of Aramaic origin [compare H1004 and H6719]; *fishing-house; Bethsaïda,* a place in Palestine:— Bethsaida.

G967 **Βηθφαγή** *Bēthphagē* of Aramaic origin [compare H1004 and H6291]; *fig-house; Bethphagè,* a place in Palestine:— Bethphage.

G968 **βῆμα** *bēma* from the base of *G939*; a *step,* i.e. *foot-breath;* by implication a *rostrum,* i.e. *tribunal:*— judgment-seat, set [foot] on, throne.

G969 **βήρυλλος** *bēryllos* of uncertain derivation; a *"beryl":*— beryl.

G970 **βία** *bia* probably akin to *G979* (through the idea of *vital* activity); *force:*— violence.

G971 **βιάζω** *biazō* from *G970*; to *force,* i.e. (reflexive) to *crowd oneself* (into), or (passive) to *be seized:*— press, suffer violence.

G972 **βίαιος** *biaios* from *G970*; *violent:*— mighty.

G973 **βιαστής** *biastēs* from *G971*; a *forcer,* i.e. (figuratively) *energetic:*— violent.

G974 **βιβλαρίδιον** *biblaridion* a diminutive of *G975*; a *booklet:*— little book.

G975 **βιβλίον** *biblion* a diminutive of *G976*; a *roll:*— bill, book, scroll, writing.

G976 **βίβλος** *biblos*; properly the inner *bark* of the papyrus plant, i.e. (by implication) a *sheet* or *scroll* of writing:— book.

G977 **βιβρώσκω** *bibrōskō* a reduplicated and prolonged form of an obsolete primary verb [perhaps causative of *G1006*]; to *eat:*— eat.

G978 **Βιθυνία** *Bithynia* of uncertain derivation; *Bithynia,* a region of Asia:— Bithynia.

G979 **βίος** *bios* a primary word; *life,* i.e. (literally) the present state of existence; by implication the means of *livelihood:*— good, life, living.

G980 **βιόω** *bioō* from *G979*; to *spend* existence:— live.

G981 **βίωσις** *biōsis* from *G980*; *living* (properly the act, by implication the mode):— manner of life.

G982 **βιωτικός** *biōtikos* from a derivative of *G980*; *relating to* the present *existence:*— of (pertaining to, things that pertain to) this life.

G983 **βλαβερός** *blaberos* from *G984*; *injurious:*— hurtful.

G984 **βλάπτω** *blaptō* a primary verb; properly to *hinder,* i.e. (by implication) to *injure:*— hurt.

G985 **βλαστάνω** *blastanō* from
βλαστός *blastos* (a *sprout*); to *germinate;* by implication to *yield* fruit:— bring forth, bud, spring (up).

G986 **Βλάστος** *Blastos* perhaps the same as the base of *G985*; *Blastus,* an officer of Herod Agrippa :— Blastus.

G987 **βλασφημέω** *blasphēmeō* from *G989*; to *vilify;* specifically to *speak impiously:*— blaspheme, blasphemer, speak blasphemously, speak blasphemy, defame, rail on, revile, speak evil.

G988 **βλασφημία** *blasphēmia* from *G989*; *vilification* (especially against God):— blasphemy, evil speaking, railing.

G989 **βλάσφημος** *blasphēmos* from a derivative of *G984* and *G5345*; *scurrilous,* i.e. *calumnious* (against man), or (specifically) *impious* (against God):— blasphemer, blasphemous, railing.

G990 **βλέμμα** *blemma* from *G991*; *vision* (properly concrete; by implication abstract):— seeing.

G991 **βλέπω** *blepō* a primary verb; to *look* at (literally or figuratively):— behold, beware, lie, look (on, to), perceive, regard, see, sight, take heed. Compare *G3700*.

G992 **βλητέος** *blēteos* from *G906*; fit *to be cast* (i.e. *applied*):— must be put.

G993 **Βοανεργές** *Boanerges* of Aramaic origin [H1123 and H7266]; *sons of commotion; Boa'nerges,* an epithet of two of the Apostles:— Boanerges.

G994 **βοάω** *boaō* apparently a prolonged form of a primary verb; to *halloo,* i.e. *shout* (for help or in a tumultuous way):— cry.

G995 **βοή** *boē* from *G994*; a *halloo,* i.e. *call* (for aid, etc.):— cry.

G996 **βοήθεια** *boētheia* from *G998*; *aid;* specifically a rope or chain for *securing* a vessel:— help.

G997 **βοηθέω** *boētheō* from *G998*; to *aid* or *relieve:*— help, succour.

G998 **βοηθός** *boēthos* from Greek *G995* and
θέω *theō* (to *run*); a *rescuer:*— helper.

G999 **βόθυνος** *bothynos* akin to *G900*; a *hole* (in the ground); specifically a *cistern:*— ditch, pit.

G1000 **βολή** *bolē* from *G906*; a *throw* (as a measure of distance):— cast.

G1001 **βολίζω** *bolizō* from *G1002*; to *heave* the lead:— sound.

G1002 **βολίς** *bolis* from *G906*; a *missile,* i.e. *javelin:*— dart.

G1003 **Βοόζ** *Booz* of Hebrew origin [H1162]; *Bo'oz,* (i.e. *Bo'az*), an Israelite:— Booz.

G1004 **βόρβορος** *borboros* of uncertain derivation; *mud:*— mire.

G1005 **βορρᾶς** *borrhas* of uncertain derivation; the *north* (properly wind):— north.

G1006 **βόσκω** *boskō* a prolonged form of a primary verb [compare *G977*, *G1016*]; to *pasture;* by extension to *fodder;* reflexive to *graze:*— feed, keep.

G1007 **Βοσόρ** *Bosor* of Hebrew origin [H1160]; *Bosor* (i.e. *Beo'r*), a Moabite:— Bosor.

G1008 **βοτάνη** *botanē* from *G1006*; *herbage* (as if for *grazing*):— herb.

G1009 **βότρυς** *botrys* of uncertain derivation; a *bunch* (of grapes):— (vine) cluster (of the vine).

G1010 **βουλευτής** *bouleutēs* from *G1011*; an *adviser,* i.e. (specifically) a *councilor* or member of the Jewish Sanhedrin:— counsellor.

G1011 **βουλεύω** *bouleuō* from *G1012*; to *advise,* i.e. (reflexive) *deliberate,* or (by implication) *resolve:*— consult, take counsel, determine, be minded, purpose.

G1012 **βουλή** *boulē* from *G1014*; *volition,* i.e. (objectively) *advice,* or (by implication) *purpose:*— advise, counsel, will.

G1013 **βούλημα** *boulēma* from *G1014*; a *resolve* :— purpose, will.

G1014 **βούλομαι** *boulomai* middle of a primary verb; to *"will,"* i.e. (reflexive) *be willing:*— be disposed, minded, intend, list, be willing, of own will. Compare *G2309*.

G1015 **βουνός** *bounos* probably of foreign origin; a *hillock:*— hill.

G1016 **βοῦς** *bous* probably from the base of *G1006*; an *ox* (as *grazing*), i.e. an animal of that species ("beef"):— ox.

G1017 **βραβεῖον** *brabeion* from
βραβεύς *brabeus* (an *umpire;* of uncertain derivation); an *award* (of arbitration), i.e. (specifically) a *prize* in the public games:— prize.

G1018 **βραβεύω** *brabeuō* from the same as *G1017*; to *arbitrate,* i.e. (generally) to *govern* (figuratively *prevail*):— rule.

G1019 **βραδύνω** *bradynō* from *G1021*; to *delay:*— be slack, tarry.

G1020 **βραδυπλοέω** *bradyploeō* from *G1021* and a prolonged form of Greek *G4126*; to *sail slowly:*— sail slowly.

G1021 **βραδύς** *bradys* of uncertain affinity; *slow;* figuratively *dull:*— slow.

G1022 **βραδύτης** *bradytēs* from *G1021*; *tardiness* :— slackness.

G1023 **βραχίων** *brachiōn* properly, comparitive of *G1024*, but apparently in the sense of
βράσσω *brassō* (to *wield*); the *arm,* i.e. (figuratively) *strength:*— arm.

G1024 **βραχύς** *brachys* of uncertain affinity; *short* (of time, place, quantity, or number):— few words, little (space, while).

G1025 **βρέφος** *brephos* of uncertain affinity; an *infant* (properly unborn) literal or figurative:— babe, (young) child, infant.

G1026 **βρέχω** *brechō* a primary verb; to *moisten* (especially by a shower):— (send) rain, wash.

G1027 **βροντή** *brontē* akin to
βρέμω *bremō* (to *roar*); *thunder:*— thunder, thundering.

G1028 **βροχή** *brochē* from H1026; *rain:*— rain.

G1029 **βρόχος** *brochos* of uncertain derivation; a *noose:*— snare.

G1030 **βρυγμός** *brygmos* from *G1031*; a *grating* (of the teeth):— gnashing.

G1031 **βρύχω** *brychō* a primary verb; to *grate* the teeth (in pain or rage):— gnash.

G1032 **βρύω** *bryō* a primary verb; to *swell* out, i.e. (by implication) to *gush:*— send forth.

G1033 **βρῶμα** *brōma* from the base of *G977*; *food* (literal or figurative), especially (ceremonial) articles allowed or forbidden by the Jewish law:— meat, victuals.

G1034 **βρώσιμος** *brōsimos* from *G1035*; *eatable:*— *meat.*

G1035 **βρῶσις** *brōsis* from the base of *G977*; (abstractly) *eating* (literal or figurative); by extension (concretely) *food* (literal or figurative):— eating, food, meat.

G1036 **βυθίζω** *bythizō* from *G1037*; to *sink;* by implication to *drown:*— begin to sink, drown.

G1037 **βυθός** *bythos* a variation of *G899*; *depth,* i.e. (by implication) the *sea:*— deep.

G1038 **βυρσεύς** *byrseus* from
βύρσα *byrsa* (a *hide*); a *tanner:*— tanner.

G1039 **βύσσινος** *byssinos* from *G1040*; made of *linen* (neuter a linen *cloth*):— fine linen.

G1040 **βύσσος** *byssos* of Hebrew origin [H948]; white *linen:*— fine linen.

G1041 **βῶμος** *bōmos* from the base of *G939*; properly a *stand,* i.e. (specifically) an *altar:*— altar.

Γ

G1042 **γαββαθά** *gabbatha* of Aramaic origin [compare H1355]; *the knoll; gabbatha,* a vernacular term for the Roman tribunal in Jerusalem:— Gabbatha.

G1043 **Γαβριήλ** *Gabriēl* of Hebrew origin [H1403]; *Gabriel,* an archangel:— Gabriel.

G1044 **γάγγραινα** *gangraina* from
γραίνω *grainō* (to *gnaw*); an *ulcer* ("gangrene"):— canker.

G1045 **Γάδ** *Gad* of Hebrew origin [H1410]; *Gad,* a tribe of Israel:— Gad.

G1046 **Γαδαρηνός** *Gadarēnos* from
Γαδαρά *Gadara* (a town East of the Jordan); a *Gadarene* or inhabitant of Gadara:— Gadarene.

G1047 **γάζα** *gaza* of foreign origin; a *treasure:*— treasure.

G1048 **Γάζα** *Gaza* of Hebrew origin [H5804]; *Gazah* (i.e. *Azzah*), a place in Palestine:— Gaza.

G1049 **γαζοφυλάκιον** *gazophylakion* from *G1047* and *G5438*; a *treasure-house,* i.e. a court in the temple for the collection-boxes:— treasury.

G1050 **Γάϊος** *Gaios* of Latin origin; *Gaïus* (i.e. *Caius*), a Christian:— Gaius.

G1051 **γάλα** *gala* of uncertain affinity; *milk* (figurative):— milk.

G1052 **Γαλάτης** *Galatēs* from *G1053*; a *Galatian* or inhabitant of Galatia:— Galatian.

G1053 **Γαλατία** *Galatia* of foreign origin; *Galatia,* a region of Asia:— Galatia.

G1054 **Γαλατικός** *Galatikos* from *G1053*; *Galatic* or relating to Galatia:— of Galatia.

G1055 **γαλήνη** *galēnē* of uncertain derivation; *tranquillity:*— calm.

G1056 **Γαλιλαία** *Galilaia* of Hebrew origin [H1551]; *Galilaea* (i.e. the heathen *circle*), a region of Palestine:— Galilee.

G1057 **Γαλιλαῖος** *Galilaios* from *G1056*; *Galilaean* or belonging to Galilaea:— Galilaean, of Galilee.

G1058 **Γαλλίων** *Galliōn* of Latin origin; *Gallion* (i.e. *Gallio*), a Roman officer:— Gallio.

G1059 **Γαμαλιήλ** *Gamaliēl* of Hebrew origin [H1583]; *Gamaliel* (i.e. *Gamliel*), an Israelite:— Gamaliel.

G1060 **γαμέω** *gameō* from *G1062*; to *wed* (of either sex):— marry (a wife).

G1061 **γαμίσκω** *gamiskō* from *G1062*; to *espouse* (a daughter to a husband):— give in marriage.

G1062 **γάμος** *gamos* of uncertain affinity; *nuptials* :— marriage, wedding.

G1063 **γάρ** *gar* a primary particle; properly assigning a *reason* (used in argument, explanation or intensification; often with other particles):— and, as, because (that), but, even, for, indeed, no doubt, seeing, then, therefore, verily, what, why, yet.

G1064 **γαστήρ** *gastēr* of uncertain derivation; the *stomach;* by analogy the *matrix;* figuratively a *gourmand:*— belly, with child, womb.

G1065 **γέ** *ge* a primary particle of *emphasis* or *qualification;* often used with other particles prefixed:— and besides, doubtless, at least, yet.

G1066 **Γεδεών** *Gedeōn* of Hebrew origin [H1439]; *Gedeon* (i.e. *Gid[e]on*), an Israelite:— Gedeon.

G1067 **γέεννα** *geenna* of Hebrew origin [H1516 and H2011]; *valley of* (the son of) *Hinnom; gehenna* (or *Ge-Hinnom*), a valley of Jerusalem, used (figuratively) as a name for the place (or state) of everlasting punishment:— hell.

G1068 **Γεθσημανῆ** *Gethsēmanē* of Aramaic origin [compare H1660 and H8081]; *oil-press; Gethsemane,* a garden near Jerusalem:— Gethsemane.

G1069 **γείτων** *geitōn* from *G1093*; a *neighbor* (as adjoining one's *ground*); by implication a *friend:*— neighbour.

G1070 **γελάω** *gelaō* of uncertain affinity; to *laugh* (as a sign of joy or satisfaction):— laugh.

G1071 **γέλως** *gelōs* from *G1070*; *laughter* (as a mark of gratification):— laughter.

G1072 **γεμίζω** *gemizō* transitive from *G1073*; to *fill* entirely:— fill, (be) full.

G1073 **γέμω** *gemō* a primary verb; to *swell* out, i.e. *be full:*— be full.

G1074 **γενεά** *genea* from (a presumed derivative of) *G1085*; a *generation;* by implication an *age* (the period or the persons):— age, generation, nation, time.

G1075 **γενεαλογέω** *genealogeō* from *G1074* and *G3056*; to *reckon by generations,* i.e. *trace in genealogy:*— count by descent.

G1076 **γενεαλογία** *genealogia* from the same as *G1075*; *tracing by generations,* i.e. *"genealogy":*— genealogy.

G1077 **γενέσια** *genesia* neuter plural of a derivative of *G1078*; *birthday* ceremonies:— birthday.

G1078 **γένεσις** *genesis* from the same as Greek *G1074*; *nativity;* figuratively *nature:*— generation, nature, natural.

G1079 **γενετή** *genetē* feminine of a presumed derivative of the base of *G1074*; *birth:*— birth.

G1080 **γεννάω** *gennaō* from a variation of *G1085*; to *procreate* (properly of the father, but by extension of the mother); figuratively to *regenerate:*— bear, beget, be born, bring forth, conceive, be delivered of, gender, make, spring.

G1081 **γέννημα** *gennēma* from *G1080*; *offspring;* by analogy *produce* (literal or figurative):— fruit, generation.

G1082 **Γεννησαρέτ** *Gennēsaret* of Hebrew origin [compare H3672]; *Gennesaret* (i.e. *Kinnereth*), a lake and plain in Palestine:— Gennesaret.

G1083 **γέννησις** *gennēsis* from *G1080*; *nativity:*— birth.

G1084 **γεννητός** *gennētos* from *G1080*; *born:*— they that are born.

G1085 **γένος** *genos* from *G1096*; *"kin"* (abstract or concrete, literal or figurative, individual or collective):— born, country, countryman, diversity, generation, kind, kindred, nation, offspring, stock.

G1086 **Γεργεσηνός** *Gergesēnos* of Hebrew origin [H1622]; a *Gergesene* (i.e. *Girgashite*) or one of the aborigines of Palestine:— Gergesene.

G1087 **γερουσία** *gerousia* from *G1088*; the *eldership,* i.e. (collectively) the Jewish *Sanhedrin:*— senate.

G1088 **γέρων** *gerōn* of uncertain affinity [compare *G1094*]; *aged:*— old.

G1089 **γεύομαι** *geuomai* a primary verb; to *taste;* by implication to *eat;* figuratively to *experience* (good or ill):— eat, taste.

G1090 **γεωργέω** *geōrgeō* from Greek *G1092*; to *till* (the soil):— dress.

G1091 **γεώργιον** *geōrgion* neuter of a (presumed) derivative of *G1092*; *cultivable,* i.e. a *farm:*— husbandry.

G1092 **γεωργός** *geōrgos* from *G1093* and the base of *G2041*; a *land-worker,* i.e. *farmer:*— husbandman.

G1093 **γῆ** *gē* contracted from a primary word; *soil;* by extension a *region,* or the solid part or the whole of the *terrene* globe (including the occupants in each application):— country, earth, earthly, ground, land, world.

G1094 **γῆρας** *gēras* akin to *G1088*; *senility:*— old age.

G1095 **γηράσκω** *gēraskō* from *G1094*; to *be senescent:*— be (wax) old.

G1096 **γίνομαι** *ginomai* a prolonged and middle form of a primary verb; to *cause to be* (*"gen"-erate*), i.e. (reflexive) to *become* (*come into being*), used with great latitude (literally, figuratively, intensively, etc.) :— arise, be assembled, be, become, befall, behave self, be brought (to pass), (be) come (to pass), continue, be divided, draw, be ended, fall, be finished, follow, be found, be fulfilled, God forbid, grow, happen, have, be kept, be made, be married, be ordained to be, partake, pass, be performed, be published, require, seem, be showed, soon as it was, sound, be taken, be turned, use, wax, will, would, be wrought.

G1097 **γινώσκω** *ginōskō* a prolonged form of a primary verb; to *"know"* (absolutely), in a great variety of applications and with many by implications (as follow, with others not thus clearly expressed):— allow, be aware (of), feel, know, have knowledge, perceive, be resolved, can speak, be sure, understand.

G1098 **γλεῦκος** *gleukos* akin to *G1099*; *sweet* wine, i.e. (properly) *must* (fresh juice), but used of the more saccharine (and therefore highly inebriating) fermented *wine:*— new wine.

G1099 **γλυκύς** *glykys* of uncertain affinity; *sweet* (i.e. not bitter nor salt):— sweet, fresh.

G1100 **γλῶσσα** *glōssa* of uncertain affinity; the *tongue;* by implication a *language* (specifically one not acquired naturally):— tongue.

G1101 **γλωσσόκομον** *glōssokomon* from *G1100* and the base of *G2889*; properly a *case* (to keep mouthpieces of wind-instruments in), i.e. (by extension) a *casket* or (special) *purse:*— bag.

G1102 **γναφεύς** *gnapheus* by variation for a derived from

κνάπτω *knaptō* (to *tease* cloth); a cloth *dresser:*— fuller.

G1103 **γνήσιος** *gnēsios* from the same as *G1077*; *legitimate* (of birth), i.e. *genuine:*— own, sincerity, true.

G1104 **γνησίως** *gnēsiōs* adverb from *G1103*; *genuinely,* i.e. *really:*— naturally.

G1105 **γνόφος** *gnophos* akin to *G3509*; *gloom* (as of a storm):— blackness.

G1106 **γνώμη** *gnōmē* from *G1097*; *cognition,* i.e. (subjectively) *opinion,* or (objectively) *resolve* (*counsel, consent,* etc.):— advice, agree, judgment, mind, purpose, will.

G1107 **γνωρίζω** *gnōrizō* from a derivative of *G1097*; to *make known;* subject to *know:*— certify, declare, make known, give to understand, do to wit, wot.

G1108 **γνῶσις** *gnōsis* from *G1097*; *knowing* (the act), i.e. (by implication) *knowledge:*— knowledge, science.

G1109 **γνώστης** *gnōstēs* from *G1097*; one who *knows:*— expert.

G1110 **γνωστός** *gnōstos* from *G1097*; well *known* :— acquaintance, (which may be) known, notable.

G1111 **γογγύζω** *gongyzō* of uncertain derivation; to *grumble:*— murmur.

G1112 **γογγυσμός** *gongysmos* from *G1111*; a *grumbling:*— grudging, murmuring.

G1113 **γογγυστής** *gongystēs* from *G1111*; a *grumbler:*— murmurer.

G1114 **γόης** *goēs* from

γοάω *goaō* (to *wail*); properly a *wizard* (as *muttering* spells), i.e. (by implication) an *imposter:*— seducer.

G1115 **Γολγοθᾶ** *Golgotha* of Aramaic origin [compare H1538]; *the skull; Golgotha,* a knoll near Jerusalem:— Golgotha.

G1116 **Γόμορρα** *Gomorrha* of Hebrew origin [H6017]; *Gomorrha* (i.e. *Amorah*), a place near the Dead Sea:— Gomorrha.

G1117 **γόμος** *gomos* from *G1073*; a *load* (as *filling*), i.e. (specifically) a *cargo,* or (by extension) *wares:*— burden, merchandise.

G1118 **γονεύς** *goneus* from the base of *G1096*; a *parent:*— parent.

G1119 **γονύ** *gony* of uncertain affinity; the *"knee"* :— knee, kneel.

G1120 **γονυπετέω** *gonypeteō* from a compound of *G1119* and the alternative of *G4098*; to *fall* on the *knee:*— bow the knee, kneel down.

G1121 **γράμμα** *gramma* from *G1125*; a *writing,* i.e. a *letter, note, epistle, book,* etc.; plural *learning:*— bill, learning, letter, scripture, writing, written.

G1122 **γραμματεύς** *grammateus* from *G1121*; a *writer,* i.e. (professional) *scribe* or *secretary:*— scribe, town-clerk.

G1123 **γραπτός** *graptos* from *G1125*; *inscribed* (figuratively):— written.

G1124 **γραφή** *graphē* from *G1125*; a *document,* i.e. holy *Writ* (or its contents or a statement in it):— scripture.

G1125 **γράφω** *graphō* a primary verb; to *"grave"*, especially to *write;* figuratively to *describe:*— describe, write, writing, written.

G1126 **γραώδης** *graōdēs* from

γραῦς *graus* (an *old woman*) and *G1491*; *crone-like,* i.e. *silly:*— old wives'.

G1127 **γρηγορέω** *grēgoreō* from *G1453*; to *keep awake,* i.e. *watch* (literally or figuratively):— be vigilant, wake, watch, be watchful.

G1128 **γυμνάζω** *gymnazō* from *G1131*; to *practice naked* (in the games), i.e. *train* (figuratively):— exercise.

G1129 **γυμνασία** *gymnasia* from *G1128*; *training,* i.e. (figuratively) *asceticism:*— exercise.

G1130 **γυμνητεύω** *gymnēteuō* from a derivative of *G1131*; to *strip,* i.e. (reflexive) *go poorly clad:*— be naked.

G1131 **γυμνός** *gymnos* of uncertain affinity; *nude* (absolutely or relatively, literally or figuratively):— naked.

G1132 **γυμνότης** *gymnotēs* from *G1131*; *nudity* (absolute or comparative):— nakedness.

G1133 **γυναικάριον** *gynaikarion* a diminutive from *G1135*; a *little* (i.e. *foolish*) *woman:*— silly woman.

G1134 **γυναικεῖος** *gynaikeios* from *G1135*; *feminine:*— wife.

G1135 **γυνή** *gynē* probably from the base of *G1096*; a *woman;* specifically a *wife:*— wife, woman.

G1136 **Γώγ** *Gōg* of Hebrew origin [H1463]; *Gog,* a symbolic name for some future Antichrist:— Gog.

G1137 **γωνία** *gōnia* probably akin to *G1119*; an *angle:*— corner, quarter.

Δ

G1138 **Δαβίδ** *Dabid* of Hebrew origin [H1732]; *Dabid* (i.e. *David*), the Israelite king:— David.

G1139 **δαιμονίζομαι** *daimonizomai* middle from *G1142*; to *be exercised by a daemon:*— have a (be vexed with, be possessed with) devil, have (be vexed with, be possessed with) devils.

G1140 **δαιμόνιον** *daimonion* neuter of a derivative of *G1142*; a *daemonic being;* by extension a *deity:*— devil, god.

G1141 **δαιμονιώδης** *daimoniōdēs* from *G1140* and *G1142*; *daemon-like:*— devilish.

G1142 **δαίμων** *daimōn* from
δαίω *daiō* (to *distribute* fortunes); a *daemon* or supernatural spirit (of a bad nature):— devil.

G1143 **δάκνω** *daknō* a prolonged form of a primary root; to *bite,* i.e. (figuratively) *thwart:*— bite.

G1144 **δάκρυ** *dakry* or
δάκρυον *dakryon* of uncertain affinity; a *tear:*— tear.

G1145 **δακρύω** *dakryō* from *G1144*; to *shed tears* :— weep. Compare *G2799*.

G1146 **δακτύλιος** *daktylios* from *G1147*; a *finger-*ring:— ring.

G1147 **δάκτυλος** *daktylos* probably from *G1176*; a *finger:*— finger.

G1148 **Δαλμανουθά** *Dalmanoutha* probably of Aramaic origin; *Dalmanutha,* a place in Palestine:— Dalmanutha.

G1149 **Δαλματία** *Dalmatia* probably of foreign derivation; *Dalmatia,* a region of Europe:— Dalmatia.

G1150 **δαμάζω** *damazō* a variation of an obsolete primary of the same meaning; to *tame:*— tame.

G1151 **δάμαλις** *damalis* probably from the base of *G1150*; a *heifer* (as *tame*):— heifer.

G1152 **Δάμαρις** *Damaris* probably from the base of *G1150*; perhaps *gentle; Damaris,* an Athenian woman:— Damaris.

G1153 **Δαμασκηνός** *Damaskēnos* from *G1154*; a *Damascene* or inhabitant of Damascus:— Damascene.

G1154 **Δαμασκός** *Damaskos* of Hebrew origin [H1834]; *Damascus,* a city of Syria:— Damascus.

G1155 **δανείζω** *daneizō* from *G1156*; to *loan* on interest; reflexive to *borrow:*— borrow, lend.

G1156 **δάνειον** *daneion* from
δάνος *danos* (a *gift*); probably akin to the base of *G1325*; a *loan:*— debt.

G1157 **δανειστής** *daneistēs* from *G1155*; a *lender* :— creditor.

G1158 **Δανιήλ** *Daniēl* of Hebrew origin [H1840]; *Daniel,* an Israelite:— Daniel.

G1159 **δαπανάω** *dapanaō* from *G1160*; to *expend,* i.e. (in a good sense) to *incur cost,* or (in a bad one) to *waste:*— be at charges, consume, spend.

G1160 **δαπάνη** *dapanē* from
δάπτω *daptō* (to *devour*); *expense* (as *consuming*):— cost.

G1161 **δέ** *de* a primary particle (adversative or continuative); *but, and,* etc.:— also, and, but, moreover, now [*often unexpressed in English*].

G1162 **δέησις** *deēsis* from *G1189*; a *petition:*— prayer, request, supplication.

G1163 **δεῖ** *dei* third person singular active present of *G1210*; also
δεόν *deon* neuter active participle of *G1210*; both used impersonally; *it is* (*was,* etc.) *necessary* (as *binding*):— behoved, be meet, must (needs), need, be needful, ought, should.

G1164 **δεῖγμα** *deigma* from the base of *G1166*; a *specimen* (as *shown*):— example.

G1165 **δειγματίζω** *deigmatizō* from *G1164*; to *exhibit:*— make a shew.

G1166 **δεικνύω** *deiknyō* a prolonged form of an obsolete primary of the same meaning; to *show* (literally or figuratively):— shew.

G1167 **δειλία** *deilia* from *G1169*; *timidity:*— fear.

G1168 **δειλιάω** *deiliaō* from *G1167*; to *be timid:*— be afraid.

G1169 **δειλός** *deilos* from
δέος *deos* (*dread*); *timid,* i.e. (by implication) *faithless:*— fearful.

G1170 **δεῖνα** *deina* probably from the same as *G1171* (through the idea of forgetting the name as *fearful,* i.e. *strange*); *so and so* (when the person is not specified):— such a man.

G1171 **δεινῶς** *deinōs* adverb from a derivative of the same as *G1169*; *terribly,* i.e. *excessively:*— grievously, vehemently.

G1172 **δειπνέω** *deipneō* from *G1173*; to *dine,* i.e. take the principal (or evening) meal:— sup, supper.

G1173 **δεῖπνον** *deipnon* from the same as *G1160*; *dinner,* i.e. the chief meal (usually in the evening):— feast, supper.

G1174 **δεισιδαιμονέστερος** *deisidaimonesteros* the compound of a derivative of the base of *G1169* and *G1142*; *more religious* than others:— too superstitious.

G1175 **δεισιδαιμονία** *deisidaimonia* from the same as *G1174*; *religion:*— superstition.

G1176 **δέκα** *deka* a primary number; *ten:*— ten, -teen (e.g., eighteen).

G1177 **δεκαδύο** *dekadyo* from *G1176* and *G1417*; *two* and *ten,* i.e. *twelve:*— twelve.

G1178 **δεκαπέντε** *dekapente* from *G1176* and *G4002*; *ten* and *five,* i.e. *fifteen:*— fifteen.

G1179 **Δεκάπολις** *Dekapolis* from *G1176* and *G4172*; the *ten-city* region; the *Decapolis,* a district in Syria:— Decapolis.

G1180 **δεκατέσσαρες** *dekatessares* from *G1176* and *G5064*; *ten* and *four,* i.e. *fourteen:*— fourteen.

G1181 **δεκάτη** *dekatē* feminine of *G1182*; a *tenth,* i.e. as a percentage or (technical) *tithe:*— tenth (part), tithe.

G1182 **δέκατος** *dekatos* ordinal from *G1176*; *tenth* :— tenth.

G1183 **δεκατόω** *dekatoō* from *G1181*; to *tithe,* i.e. to *give* or *take a tenth:*— pay (receive) tithes.

G1184 **δεκτός** *dektos* from *G1209*; *approved;* (figuratively) *propitious:*— accepted, acceptable.

G1185 **δελεάζω** *deleazō* from the base of *G1388*; to *entrap,* i.e. (figuratively) *delude:*— allure, beguile, entice.

G1186 **δένδρον** *dendron* probably from
δρύς *drys* (an *oak*); a *tree:*— tree.

G1187 **δεξιολάβος** *dexiolabos* from *G1188* and *G2983*; a *guardsman* (as if *taking the right*) or light-armed soldier:— spearman.

G1188 **δεξιός** *dexios* from *G1209*; the *right* side or (feminine) hand (as that which usually *takes*):— right (hand, side).

G1189 **δέομαι** *deomai* middle of *G1210*; to *beg* (as *binding oneself*), i.e. *petition:*— beseech, pray (to), make request. Compare *G4441*.

G1190 **Δερβαῖος** *Derbaios* from *G1191*; a *Derbaean* or inhabitant of Derbe:— of Derbe.

G1191 **Δέρβη** *Derbē* of foreign origin; *Derbè,* a place in Asia Minor:— Derbe.

G1192 **δέρμα** *derma* from *G1194*; a *hide:*— skin.

G1193 **δερμάτινος** *dermatinos* from *G1192*; made of *hide:*— leathern, of a skin.

G1194 **δέρω** *derō* a primary verb; properly to *flay,* i.e. (by implication) to *scourge,* or (by analogy) to *thrash:*— beat, smite.

G1195 **δεσμεύω** *desmeuō* from a (presumed) derivative of *G1196*; to *be a binder* (*captor*), i.e. to *enchain* (a prisoner), to *tie on* (a load):— bind.

G1196 **δεσμέω** *desmeō* from *G1199*; to *tie,* i.e. *shackle:*— bind.

G1197 **δεσμή** *desmē* from *G1196*; a *bundle:*— bundle.

G1198 **δέσμιος** *desmios* from *G1199*; a *captive* (as *bound*):— in bonds, prisoner.

G1199 **δεσμόν** *desmon* neuter or masculine
δεσμός *desmos* from *G1210*; a *band,* i.e. *ligament* (of the body) or *shackle* (of a prisoner); figuratively an *impediment* or *disability:*— band, bond, chain, string.

G1200 **δεσμοφύλαξ** *desmophylax* from *G1199* and *G5441*; a *jailer* (as *guarding* the *prisoners*):— jailor, keeper of the prison.

G1201 **δεσμωτήριον** *desmōtērion* from a derivative of *G1199* (equivalent to *G1196*); a *place of bondage,* i.e. a *dungeon:*— prison.

G1202 **δεσμώτης** *desmōtēs* from the same as *G1201*; (passive) a *captive:*— prisoner.

G1203 **δεσπότης** *despotēs* perhaps from *G1210* and
πόσις *posis* (a *husband*); an absolute *ruler* ("despot"):— Lord, master.

G1204 **δεῦρο** *deuro* of uncertain affinity; *here;* used also imperatively *hither!;* and of time, *hitherto:*— come (hither), hither, hitherto.

G1205 **δεῦτε** *deute* from *G1204* and an imperative form of
εἶμι *eimi* (to *go*); *come hither!:*— come, follow.

G1206 **δευτεραῖος** *deuteraios* from *G1208*; *secondary,* i.e. (specifically) on the *second* day:— next day.

G1207 **δευτερόπρωτος** *deuteroprōtos* from *G1208* and *G4413*; *second-first,* i.e. (specifically) a designation of the Sabbath immediately after the Paschal week (being the *second* after Passover day, and the *first* of the seven Sabbaths intervening before Pentecost):— second . . . after the first.

G1208 δεύτερος *deuteros* as the comparative of *G1417*; (ordinal) *second* (in time, place or rank; also adverbially):— afterward, again, second, secondarily, second time.

G1209 δέχομαι *dechomai* middle of a primary verb; to *receive* (in various applications, literally or figuratively):— accept, receive, take. Compare *G2983*.

G1210 δέω *deō* a primary verb; to *bind* (in various applications, literally or figuratively):— bind, be in bonds, knit, tie, wind. See also *G1163*, *G1189*.

G1211 δή *dē* probably akin to *G1161*; a particle of emphasis or explicitness; *now, then,* etc.:— also, and, doubtless, now, therefore.

G1212 δῆλος *dēlos* of uncertain derivation; *clear* :— bewray, certain, evident, manifest.

G1213 δηλόω *dēloō* from *G1212*; to *make plain* (by words):— declare, shew, signify.

G1214 Δημᾶς *Dēmas* probably for *G1216*; *Demas,* a Christian:— Demas.

G1215 δημηγορέω *dēmēgoreō* from a compound of *G1218* and *G58*; to *be a people-gatherer,* i.e. to *address* a public assembly:— make an oration.

G1216 Δημήτριος *Dēmētrios* from **Δημήτηρ** *Dēmētēr* (*Ceres*); *Demetrius,* the name of an Ephesian and of a Christian:— Demetrius.

G1217 δημιουργός *dēmiourgos* from *G1218* and *G2041*; a *worker* for the *people,* i.e. *mechanic* (spoken of the *Creator*):— maker.

G1218 δῆμος *dēmos* from *G1210*; the *public* (as *bound* together socially):— people.

G1219 δημόσιος *dēmosios* from *G1218*; *public;* (feminine singular dative as adverb) *in public:*— common, openly, publickly.

G1220 δηνάριον *dēnarion* of Latin origin; a *denarius* (or *ten asses*):— pence, penny, pennyworth.

G1221 δήποτε *dēpote* from *G1211* and *G4218*; a particle of generalization; *indeed, at any time:*— -soever (e.g., whatsoever).

G1222 δήπου *dēpou* from *G1211* and *G4225*; a particle of asseveration; *indeed doubtless:*— verily.

G1223 διά *dia* a primary preposition denoting the *channel* of an act; *through* (in very wide applications, local, causal or occasional). In compounds it retains the same general import:— after, always, among, at, to avoid, because of (that), briefly, by, for (cause) . . . fore, from, in, by occasion of, of, by reason of, forsake, that, thereby, therefore, though, through, throughout, to, wherefore, with, within.

G1224 διαβαίνω *diabainō* from *G1223* and the base of *G939*; to *cross:*— come over, pass (through).

G1225 διαβάλλω *diaballō* from *G1223* and *G906*; (figuratively) to *traduce:*— accuse.

G1226 διαβεβαιόομαι *diabebaioomai* middle of a compound of *G1223* and *G950*; to *confirm thoroughly* (by words), i.e. *asseverate:*— affirm constantly.

G1227 διαβλέπω *diablepō* from *G1223* and *G991*; to *look through,* i.e. *recover* full *vision:*— see clearly.

G1228 διάβολος *diabolos* from *G1225*; a *traducer;* specifically *Satan* [compare H7854]:— false accuser, devil, slanderer.

G1229 διαγγέλλω *diangellō* from *G1223* and the base of *G32*; to *herald thoroughly:*— declare, preach, signify.

G1230 διαγίνομαι *diaginomai* from *G1223* and *G1096*; to *elapse meanwhile:*— after, be past, be spent.

G1231 διαγινώσκω *diaginōskō* from *G1223* and *G1097*; to *know thoroughly,* i.e. *ascertain exactly:*— (would) inquire, know the uttermost.

G1232 διαγνωρίζω *diagnōrizō* from *G1123* and *G1107*; to *tell abroad:*— make known.

G1233 διάγνωσις *diagnōsis* from *G1231*; (magisterial) *examination* ("diagnosis"):— hearing.

G1234 διαγογγύζω *diagongyzō* from *G1223* and *G1111*; to *complain throughout* a crowd:— murmur.

G1235 διαγρηγορέω *diagrēgoreō* from *G1223* and *G1127*; to *waken thoroughly:*— be awake.

G1236 διάγω *diagō* from *G1223* and *G71*; to *pass* time or life:— lead life, living.

G1237 διαδέχομαι *diadechomai* from *G1223* and *G1209*; to *receive in turn,* i.e. (figuratively) *succeed to:*— come after.

G1238 διάδημα *diadēma* from a compound of *G1223* and *G1210*; a *"diadem"* (as *bound about* the head):— crown. Compare *G4735*.

G1239 διαδίδωμι *diadidōmi* from *G1223* and *G1325*; to *give throughout* a crowd, i.e. *deal out;* also to *deliver* over (as to a successor):— distribute, make distribution, divide, give.

G1240 διάδοχος *diadochos* from *G1237*; a *successor* in office:— room.

G1241 διαζώννυμι *diazōnnymi* from *G1223* and *G2224*; to *gird tightly:*— gird.

G1242 διαθήκη *diathēkē* from *G1303*; properly a *disposition,* i.e. (specifically) a *contract* (especially a devisory *will*):— covenant, testament.

G1243 διαίρεσις *diairesis* from *G1244*; a *distinction* or (concrete) *variety:*— difference, diversity.

G1244 διαιρέω *diaireō* from *G1223* and *G138*; to *separate,* i.e. *distribute:*— divide.

G1245 διακαθαρίζω *diakatharizō* from *G1223* and *G2511*; to *cleanse perfectly,* i.e. (specifically) *winnow:*— throughly purge.

G1246 διακατελέγχομαι *diakatelenchomai* middle from *G1223* and a compound of *G2596* and *G1651*; to *prove downright,* i.e. *confute:*— convince.

G1247 διακονέω *diakoneō* from *G1249*; to *be an attendant,* i.e. *wait upon* (menially or as a host, friend or [figuratively] teacher); technically to *act as a* Christian *deacon:*— minister (unto), administer, serve, use the office of a deacon.

G1248 διακονία *diakonia* from *G1249*; *attendance* (as a servant, etc.); figuratively (eleemosynary) *aid,* (official) *service* (especially of the Christian teacher, or technically of the *diaconate*):— minister, administer, ministering, ministration, administration, ministry, office, relief, service, servicing.

G1249 διάκονος *diakonos* probably from an obsolete **διάκω** *diakō* (to *run* on errands; compare *G1377*); an *attendant,* i.e. (generally) a *waiter* (at table or in other menial duties); specifically a Christian *teacher* and *pastor* (technically a *deacon* or *deaconess*):— deacon, minister, servant.

G1250 διακόσιοι *diakosioi* from *G1364* and *G1540*; *two hundred:*— two hundred.

G1251 διακούομαι *diakouomai* middle from *G1223* and *G191*; to *hear throughout,* i.e. *patiently listen* (to a prisoner's plea):— hear.

G1252 διακρίνω *diakrinō* from *G1223* and *G2919*; to *separate thoroughly* i.e. (literally and reflexive) to *withdraw* from, or (by implication) *oppose;* figuratively to *discriminate* (by implication *decide*), or (reflexive) *hesitate:*— contend, make (to) differ, difference, discern, doubt, judge, be partial, stagger, waver.

G1253 διάκρισις *diakrisis* from *G1252*; judicial *estimation:*— discern, discerning, disputation.

G1254 διακωλύω *diakōlyō* from *G1223* and *G2967*; to *hinder altogether,* i.e. *utterly prohibit:*— forbid.

G1255 διαλαλέω *dialaleō* from *G1223* and *G2980*; to *talk throughout* a company, i.e. *converse* or (generally) *publish:*— commune, noise abroad.

G1256 διαλέγομαι *dialegomai* middle from *G1223* and *G3004*; to *say thoroughly,* i.e. *discuss* (in argument or exhortation):— dispute, preach (unto), reason (with), speak.

G1257 διαλείπω *dialeipō* from *G1223* and *G3007*; to *leave off in the middle,* i.e. *intermit:*— cease.

G1258 διάλεκτος *dialektos* from *G1256*; a (mode of) *discourse,* i.e. *"dialect":*— language, tongue.

G1259 διαλλάσσω *diallassō* from *G1223* and *G236*; to *change thoroughly,* i.e. (mentally) to *conciliate:*— reconcile.

G1260 διαλογίζομαι *dialogizomai* from *G1223* and *G3049*; to *reckon thoroughly,* i.e. (generally) to *deliberate* (by reflection or discussion):— cast in mind, consider, dispute, muse, reason, think.

G1261 διαλογισμός *dialogismos* from *G1260*; *discussion,* i.e. (internal) *consideration* (by implication *purpose*), or (external) *debate:*— dispute, doubtful, doubting, imagination, reasoning, thought.

G1262 διαλύω *dialyō* from *G1223* and *G3089*; to *dissolve utterly:*— scatter.

G1263 διαμαρτύρομαι *diamartyromai* from *G1223* and *G3140*; to *attest* or *protest earnestly,* or (by implication) *hortatively:*— charge, testify (unto), witness.

G1264 διαμάχομαι *diamachomai* from *G1223* and *G3164*; to *fight fiercely* (in altercation):— strive.

G1265 διαμένω *diamenō* from *G1223* and *G3306*; to *stay constantly* (in being or relation):— continue, remain.

G1266 διαμερίζω *diamerizō* from *G1223* and *G3307*; to *partition thoroughly* (literally in distribution, figuratively in dissension):— cloven, divide, part.

G1267 διαμερισμός *diamerismos* from *G1266*; *disunion* (of opinion and conduct):— division.

G1268 διανέμω *dianemō* from *G1223* and the base of *G3551*; to *distribute,* i.e. (of information) to *disseminate:*— spread.

G1269 διανεύω *dianeuō* from *G1223* and *G3506*; to *nod* (or *express* by signs) *across* an intervening space:— beckon.

G1270 διανόημα *dianoēma* from a compound of *G1223* and *G3539*; something *thought through* i.e. a *sentiment:*— thought.

G1271 διάνοια *dianoia* from *G1223* and *G3563*; *deep thought,* properly the faculty (*mind* or its *disposition*), by implication its exercise:— imagination, mind, understanding.

G1272 διανοίγω *dianoigō* from *G1223* and *G455*; to *open thoroughly*, literally (as a first-born) or figuratively (to *expound*):— open.

G1273 διανυκτερεύω *dianyktereuō* from *G1223* and a derivative of *G3571*; to *sit up the whole night*:— continue all night.

G1274 διανύω *dianyō* from *G1223* and
ἀνύω *anyō* (to *effect*); to *accomplish thoroughly*:— finish.

G1275 διαπαντός *diapantos* from *G1223* and the genitive of *G3956*; *through all* time, i.e. (adverbially) *constantly*:— alway, always, continually.

G1276 διαπεράω *diaperaō* from *G1223* and a derivative of the base of *G4008*; to *cross entirely*:— go over, pass (over), sail over.

G1277 διαπλέω *diapleō* from *G1223* and *G4126*; to *sail through*:— sail over.

G1278 διαπονέω *diaponeō* from *G1223* and a derivative of *G4192*; to *toil through*, i.e. (passive) *be worried*:— be grieved.

G1279 διαπορεύομαι *diaporeuomai* from *G1223* and *G4198*; to *travel through*:— go through, journey in, pass by.

G1280 διαπορέω *diaporeō* from *G1223* and *G639*; to *be thoroughly nonplussed*:— (be in) doubt, be (much) perplexed.

G1281 διαπραγματεύομαι *diapragmateuomai* from *G1223* and *G4231*; to *thoroughly occupy oneself*, i.e. (transitive and by implication) to *earn* in business:— gain by trading.

G1282 διαπρίω *diapriō* from *G1223* and the base of *G4249*; to *saw asunder*, i.e. (figuratively) to *exasperate*:— cut (to the heart).

G1283 διαρπάζω *diarpazō* from *G1223* and *G726*; to *seize asunder*, i.e. *plunder*:— spoil.

G1284 διαρρήσσω *diarrhēssō* from *G1223* and *G4486*; to *tear asunder*:— break, rend.

G1285 διασαφέω *diasapheō* from *G1223* and
σαφής *saphēs* (*clear*); to *clear thoroughly*, i.e. (figuratively) *declare*:— tell unto.

G1286 διασείω *diaseiō* from *G1223* and *G4579*; to *shake thoroughly*, i.e. (figuratively) to *intimidate*:— do violence to.

G1287 διασκορπίζω *diaskorpizō* from *G1223* and *G4650*; to *dissipate*, i.e. (generally) to *rout* or *separate*; specifically to *winnow*; figuratively to *squander*:— disperse, scatter (abroad), strew, waste.

G1288 διασπάω *diaspaō* from *G1223* and *G4685*; to *draw apart*, i.e. *sever* or *dismember*:— pluck asunder, pull in pieces.

G1289 διασπείρω *diaspeirō* from *G1223* and *G4687*; to *sow throughout*, i.e. (figuratively) *distribute* in foreign lands:— scatter abroad.

G1290 διασπορά *diaspora* from *G1289*; *dispersion*, i.e. (specifically and concretely) the (converted) Israelite *resident* in Gentile countries:— (which are) scattered (abroad).

G1291 διαστέλλομαι *diastellomai* middle from *G1223* and *G4724*; to *set* (oneself) *apart* (figuratively *distinguish*), i.e. (by implication) to *enjoin*:— charge, that which was commanded, give commandment.

G1292 διάστημα *diastēma* from *G1339*; an *interval*:— space.

G1293 διαστολή *diastolē* from *G1291*; a *variation* :— difference, distinction.

G1294 διαστρέφω *diastrephō* from *G1223* and *G4762*; to *distort*, i.e. (figuratively) *misinterpret*, or (morally) *corrupt*:— perverse, pervert, turn away.

G1295 διασώζω *diasōzō* from *G1223* and *G4982*; to *save thoroughly*, i.e. (by implication or analogy) to *cure, preserve, rescue*, etc.:— bring safe, escape (safe), heal, make perfectly whole, save.

G1296 διαταγή *diatagē* from *G1299*; *arrangement*, i.e. *institution*:— instrumentality.

G1297 διάταγμα *diatagma* from *G1299*; an *arrangement*, i.e. (authoritative) *edict*:— commandment.

G1298 διαταράσσω *diatarassō* from *G1223* and *G5015*; to *disturb wholly*, i.e. *agitate* (with alarm) :— trouble.

G1299 διατάσσω *diatassō* from *G1223* and *G5021*; to *arrange thoroughly*, i.e. (specifically) *institute, prescribe*, etc.:— appoint, command, give, (set in) order, ordain.

G1300 διατελέω *diateleō* from *G1223* and *G5055*; to *accomplish thoroughly*, i.e. (subjectively) to *persist*:— continue.

G1301 διατηρέω *diatēreō* from *G1223* and *G5083*; to *watch thoroughly*, i.e. (positive and transitive) to *observe* strictly, or (negatively and reflexive) to *avoid* wholly:— keep.

G1302 διατί *diati* from *G1223* and *G5101*; *through what* cause?, i.e. *why?*:— wherefore, why.

G1303 διατίθεμαι *diatithemai* middle from *G1223* and *G5087*; to *put apart*, i.e. (figuratively) *dispose* (by assignment, compact or bequest):— appoint, make, testator.

G1304 διατρίβω *diatribō* from *G1223* and the base of *G5147*; to *wear through* (time), i.e. *remain*:— abide, be, continue, tarry.

G1305 διατροφή *diatrophē* from a compound of *G1223* and *G5142*; *nourishment*:— food.

G1306 διαυγάζω *diaugazō* from *G1223* and *G826*; to *glimmer through*, i.e. *break* (as day):— dawn.

G1307 διαφανής *diaphanēs* from *G1223* and *G5316*; *appearing through*, i.e. *"diaphanous"*:— transparent.

G1308 διαφέρω *diapherō* from *G1223* and *G5342*; to *bear through*, i.e. (literally) *transport*; usually to *bear apart*, i.e. (objectively) to *toss about* (figuratively *report*); subjectively to *"differ,"* or (by implication) *surpass*:— be better, carry, differ from, drive up and down, be (more) excellent, make matter, publish, be of more value.

G1309 διαφεύγω *diapheugō* from *G1223* and *G5343*; to *flee through*, i.e. *escape*:— escape.

G1310 διαφημίζω *diaphēmizō* from *G1223* and a derivative of *G5345*; to *report thoroughly*, i.e. *divulge*:— blaze abroad, commonly report, spread abroad, fame.

G1311 διαφθείρω *diaphtheirō* from *G1225* and *G5351*; to *rot thoroughly*, i.e. (by implication) to *ruin* (passive *decay* utterly, figuratively *pervert*):— corrupt, destroy, perish.

G1312 διαφθορά *diaphthora* from *G1311*; *decay* :— corruption.

G1313 διάφορος *diaphoros* from *G1308*; *varying*; also *surpassing*:— differing, divers, more excellent.

G1314 διαφυλάσσω *diaphylassō* from *G1223* and *G5442*; to *guard thoroughly*, i.e. *protect*:— keep.

G1315 διαχειρίζομαι *diacheirizomai* from *G1223* and a derivative of *G5495*; to *handle thoroughly*, i.e. *lay* violent *hands* upon:— kill, slay.

G1316 διαχωρίζομαι *diachōrizomai* from *G1223* and the middle of *G5563*; to *remove* (oneself) *wholly*, i.e. *retire*:— depart.

G1317 διδακτικός *didaktikos* from *G1318*; *instructive* ("didactic"):— apt to teach.

G1318 διδακτός *didaktos* from *G1321*; (subjectively) *instructed* or (objectively) *communicated* by teaching:— taught, which . . . teacheth.

G1319 διδασκαλία *didaskalia* from *G1320*; *instruction* (the function or the information):— doctrine, learning, teaching.

G1320 διδάσκαλος *didaskalos* from *G1321*; an *instructor* (generally or specifically):— doctor, master, teacher.

G1321 διδάσκω *didaskō* a prolonged (causative) form of a primary verb
δάω *daō* (to *learn*); to *teach* (in the same broad application):— teach.

G1322 διδαχή *didachē* from *G1321*; *instruction* (the act or the matter):— doctrine, hath been taught.

G1323 δίδραχμον *didrachmon* from *G1364* and *G1406*; a *double drachma* (*didrachm*):— tribute.

G1324 Δίδυμος *Didymos* prolonged from *G1364*; *double*, i.e. *twin*; *Didymus*, a Christian:— Didymus.

G1325 δίδωμι *didōmi* a prolonged form of a primary verb (which is used as an alternative in most of the tenses); to *give* (used in a very wide application, properly or by implication, literally or figuratively; greatly modified by the connection):— adventure, bestow, bring forth, commit, deliver (up), give, grant, hinder, make, minister, number, offer, have power, put, receive, set, shew, smite (+ with the hand), strike (+ with the palm of the hand), suffer, take, utter, yield.

G1326 διεγείρω *diegeirō* from *G1223* and *G1453*; to *wake fully*, i.e. *arouse* (literally or figuratively):— arise, awake, raise, stir up.

G1327 διέξοδος *diexodos* from *G1223* and *G1841*; an *outlet through*, i.e. probably an open *square* (from which roads diverge):— highway.

G1328 διερμηνευτής *diermēneutēs* from *G1329*; an *explainer*:— interpreter.

G1329 διερμηνεύω *diermēneuō* from *G1223* and *G2059*; to *explain thoroughly*; by implication to *translate*:— expound, interpret, interpretation.

G1330 διέρχομαι *dierchomai* from *G1223* and *G2064*; to *traverse* (literally):— come, depart, go (about, abroad, every where, over, through, throughout), pass (by, over, through, throughout), pierce through, travel, walk through.

G1331 διερωτάω *dierōtaō* from *G1223* and *G2065*; to *question throughout*, i.e. *ascertain* by interrogation:— make inquiry for.

G1332 διετής *dietēs* from *G1364* and *G2094*; *of two years* (in age):— two years old.

G1333 διετία *dietia* from *G1332*; a space of *two years* (*biennium*):— two years.

G1334 διηγέομαι *diēgeomai* from *G1223* and *G2233*; to *relate fully*:— declare, shew, tell.

G1335 διήγησις *diēgēsis* from *G1334*; a *recital:*— declaration.

G1336 διηνεκές *diēnekes* neuter of a compound of *G1223* and a derivative of an alternate of *G5342*; *carried through,* i.e. (adverbially with *G1519* and *G3588* prefix) *perpetually:*— continually, for ever.

G1337 διθάλασσος *dithalassos* from *G1364* and *G2281*; *having two seas,* i.e. a *sound* with a double outlet:— where two seas met.

G1338 διϊκνέομαι *diikneomai* from *G1223* and the base of *G2425*; to *reach through,* i.e. *penetrate:*— pierce.

G1339 διΐστημι *diistēmi* from *G1223* and *G2476*; to *stand apart,* i.e. (reflexive) to *remove, intervene:*— go further, be parted, after the space of.

G1340 διϊσχυρίζομαι *diischyrizomai* from *G1223* and a derivative of *G2478*; to *stout* it *through,* i.e. *asseverate:*— confidently (constantly) affirm.

G1341 δικαιοκρισία *dikaiokrisia* from *G1342* and Greek *G2920*; a *just sentence:*— righteous judgment.

G1342 δίκαιος *dikaios* from *G1349*; *equitable* (in character or act); by implication *innocent, holy* (absolutely or relatively):— just, meet, right, righteous.

G1343 δικαιοσύνη *dikaiosynē* from *G1342*; *equity* (of character or act); specifically (Christian) *justification:*— righteousness.

G1344 δικαιόω *dikaioō* from *G1342*; to *render* (i.e. *show* or *regard* as) *just* or *innocent:*— free, justify, justifier, be righteous.

G1345 δικαίωμα *dikaiōma* from *G1344*; an *equitable deed;* by implication a *statute* or *decision:*— judgment, justification, ordinance, righteousness.

G1346 δικαίως *dikaiōs* adverb from *G1342*; *equitably:*— justly, righteously, to righteousness.

G1347 δικαίωσις *dikaiōsis* from *G1344*; *acquittal* (for Christ's sake):— justification.

G1348 δικαστής *dikastēs* from a derivative of *G1349*; a *judger:*— judge.

G1349 δίκη *dikē* probably from *G1166*; *right* (as self-*evident*), i.e. *justice* (the principle, a decision, or its execution):— judgment, punish, vengeance.

G1350 δίκτυον *diktyon* probably from a primary verb

δίκω *dikō* (to *cast*); a *seine* (for fishing):— net.

G1351 δίλογος *dilogos* from *G1364* and *G3056*; *equivocal,* i.e. telling a different story:— double-tongued.

G1352 διό *dio* from *G1223* and *G3739*; *through which* thing, i.e. *consequently:*— for which cause, therefore, wherefore.

G1353 διοδεύω *diodeuō* from *G1223* and *G3593*; to *travel through:*— go throughout, pass through.

G1354 Διονύσιος *Dionysios* from

Διόνυσος *Dionysos* (*Bacchus*); *reveller; Dionysius,* an Athenian:— Dionysius.

G1355 διόπερ *dioper* from *G1352* and *G4007*; *on which very account:*— wherefore.

G1356 διοπετής *diopetēs* from the alternate of *G2203* and the alternate of *G4098*; *sky-fallen* (i.e. an *aerolite*):— which fell down from Jupiter.

G1357 διόρθωσις *diorthōsis* from a compound of *G1223* and a derivative of *G3717*, meaning to *straighten thoroughly; rectification,* i.e. (specifically) the Messianic *restoration:*— reformation.

G1358 διορύσσω *dioryssō* from *G1223* and *G3736*; to *penetrate* like a burglar:— break through (up).

G1359 Διόσκουροι *Dioskouroi* from the alternate of *G2203* and a form of the base of *G2877*; *sons of Jupiter,* i.e. the twins *Dioscuri:*— Castor and Pollux.

G1360 διότι *dioti* from *G1223* and *G3754*; *on the very account that,* or *inasmuch as:*— because (that), for, therefore.

G1361 Διοτρεφής *Diotrephēs* from the alternate of *G2203* and *G5142*; *Jove-nourished; Diotrephes,* an opponent of Christianity:— Diotrephes.

G1362 διπλοῦς *diplous* from *G1364* and (probably) the base of *G4119*; *two-fold:*— double, two-fold more.

G1363 διπλόω *diploō* from *G1362*; to *render two-fold:*— double.

G1364 δίς *dis* adverb from *G1417*; *twice:*— again, twice.

G1365 διστάζω *distazō* from *G1364*; properly to *duplicate,* i.e. (mentally) to *waver* (in opinion):— doubt.

G1366 δίστομος *distomos* from *G1364* and *G4750*; *double-edged:*— with two edges, two-edged.

G1367 δισχίλιοι *dischilioi* from *G1364* and *G5507*; *two thousand:*— two thousand.

G1368 διϋλίζω *diylizō* from *G1223* and

ὑλίζω *hylizō* (to *filter*); to *strain out:*— strain at [*probably by misprint*].

G1369 διχάζω *dichazō* from a derivative of *G1364*; to *make apart,* i.e. *sunder* (figuratively *alienate*):— set at variance.

G1370 διχοστασία *dichostasia* from a derivative of *G1364* and *G4714*; *disunion,* i.e. (figuratively) *dissension:*— division, sedition.

G1371 διχοτομέω *dichotomeō* from a compound of a derivative of *G1364* and a derivative of

τέμνω *temnō* (to *cut*); to *bisect,* i.e. (by extension) to *flog* severely:— cut asunder (in sunder).

G1372 διψάω *dipsaō* from a variation of *G1373*; to *thirst* for (literally or figuratively):— be thirsty, be athirst.

G1373 δίψος *dipsos* of uncertain affinity; *thirst:*— thirst.

G1374 δίψυχος *dipsychos* from *G1364* and *G5590*; *two-spirited,* i.e. *vacillating* (in opinion or purpose):— double minded.

G1375 διωγμός *diōgmos* from *G1377*; *persecution* :— persecution.

G1376 διώκτης *diōktēs* from *G1377*; a *persecutor* :— persecutor.

G1377 διώκω *diōkō* a prolonged (and causative) form of a primary verb

δίω *diō* (to *flee;* compare the base of *G1169* and *G1249*); to *pursue* (literally or figuratively); by implication to *persecute:*— ensue, follow (after), given to, (suffer) persecute, persecution, press forward.

G1378 δόγμα *dogma* from the base of *G1380*; a *law* (civil, ceremonial or ecclesiastical):— decree, ordinance.

G1379 δογματίζω *dogmatizō* from *G1378*; to *prescribe* by statute, i.e. (reflexive) to *submit to* ceremonial *rule:*— be subject to ordinances.

G1380 δοκέω *dokeō* a prolonged form of a primary verb

δόκω *dokō* (used only as an alternate in certain tenses; compare the base of *G1166*) of the same meaning; to *think;* by implication to *seem* (truthfully or uncertainly):— be accounted, please, of own pleasure, be of reputation, seem (good), suppose, think, trow.

G1381 δοκιμάζω *dokimazō* from *G1384*; to *test* (literally or figuratively); by implication to *approve:*— allow, discern, examine, like, approve, prove, try.

G1382 δοκιμή *dokimē* from the same as *G1384*; *test* (abstractly or concretely); by implication *trustiness:*— experience, experiment, proof, trial.

G1383 δοκίμιον *dokimion* neuter of a presumed derivative of *G1382*; a *testing;* by implication *trustworthiness:*— trial, trying.

G
R
K

G1384 δόκιμος *dokimos* from *G1380*; properly *acceptable* (*current* after assayal), i.e. *approved:*— approved, tried.

G1385 δοκός *dokos* from *G1209* (through the idea of *holding* up); a *stick* of timber:— beam.

G1386 δόλιος *dolios* from *G1388*; *guileful:*— deceitful.

G1387 δολιόω *dolioō* from *G1386*; to *be guileful* :— use deceit.

G1388 δόλος *dolos* from an obsolete primary

δέλλω *dellō* (probably meaning to *decoy;* compare *G1185*); a *trick* (*bait*), i.e. (figuratively) *wile:*— craft, deceit, guile, subtilty.

G1389 δολόω *doloō* from *G1388*; to *ensnare,* i.e. (figuratively) *adulterate:*— handle deceitfully.

G1390 δόμα *doma* from the base of *G1325*; a *present:*— gift.

G1391 δόξα *doxa* from the base of Greek

δοκέω *dokeō*; *glory* (as very *apparent*), in a wide application (literally or figuratively, objectively or subjectively):— dignity, glory, glorious, honour, praise, worship.

G1392 δοξάζω *doxazō* from *G1391*; to *render* (or *esteem*) *glorious* (in a wide application):— glorify, make glorious, full of (have) glory, honour, magnify.

G1393 Δορκάς *Dorkas*; *gazelle; Dorcas,* a Christian woman:— Dorcas.

G1394 δόσις *dosis* from the base of *G1325*; a *giving;* by implication (concretely) a *gift:*— gift, giving.

G1395 δότης *dotēs* from the base of *G1325*; a *giver* :— giver.

G1396 δουλαγωγέω *doulagōgeō* from a presumed compound of *G1401* and *G71*; to *be a slave-driver,* i.e. to *enslave* (figuratively *subdue*):— bring into subjection.

G1397 δουλεία *douleia* from *G1398*; *slavery* (ceremonial or figurative):— bondage.

G1398 δουλεύω *douleuō* from *G1401*; to *be a slave* to (literally or figuratively, involuntarily or voluntarily):— be in bondage, serve, do service.

G1399 δούλη *doulē* feminine of *G1401*; a *female slave* (involuntary or voluntary):— handmaid, handmaiden.

G1400 δοῦλον *doulon* neuter of *G1401*; *subservient:*— servant.

G1401 δοῦλος *doulos* from *G1210*; a *slave* (literal or figurative, involuntary or voluntary; frequently therefore in a qualified sense of *subjection* or *subservience*):— bond, bondman, servant.

G1402 **δουλόω** *douloō* from *G1401*; to *enslave* (literally or figuratively):— bring into (be under) bondage, given, become (make) servant.

G1403 **δοχή** *dochē* from *G1209*; a *reception*, i.e. convivial *entertainment*:— feast.

G1404 **δράκων** *drakōn* probably from an alternate form of

δέρκομαι *derkomai* (to *look*); a fabulous kind of *serpent* (perhaps as supposed to *fascinate*):— dragon.

G1405 **δράσσομαι** *drassomai* perhaps akin to the base of *G1404* (through the idea of *capturing*); to *grasp*, i.e. (figuratively) *entrap*:— take.

G1406 **δραχμή** *drachmē* from *G1405*; a *drachma* or (silver) coin (as *handled*):— piece (of silver).

G1407 **δρέπανον** *drepanon* from

δρέπω *drepō* (to *pluck*); a gathering *hook* (especially for harvesting):— sickle.

G1408 **δρόμος** *dromos* from the alternate of *G5143*; a *race*, i.e. (figuratively) *career*:— course.

G1409 **Δρούσιλλα** *Drousilla* a feminine diminutive of *Drusus* (a Roman name); *Drusilla*, a member of the Herodian family:— Drusilla.

G1410 **δύναμαι** *dynamai* of uncertain affinity; to *be able* or *possible*:— be able, can (do), +cannot, could, may, might, be possible, be of power.

G1411 **δύναμις** *dynamis* from *G1410*; *force* (literal or figurative); specifically miraculous *power* (usually by implication a *miracle* itself):— ability, abundance, meaning, might, mightily, mighty, mighty deed, (worker of) miracle, worker of miracles, power, strength, violence, might (wonderful) work.

G1412 **δυναμόω** *dynamoō* from *G1411*; to *enable* :— strengthen.

G1413 **δυνάστης** *dynastēs* from *G1410*; a *ruler* or *officer*:— of great authority, mighty, potentate.

G1414 **δυνατέω** *dynateō* from *G1415*; to *be efficient* (figuratively):— be mighty.

G1415 **δυνατός** *dynatos* from *G1410*; *powerful* or *capable* (literally or figuratively); neuter *possible*:— able, could, (that is) mighty (man), possible, power, strong.

G1416 **δύνω** *dynō* or

δῦμι *dymi* prolonged forms of an obsolete primary

δύω *dyō* (to *sink*); to go *"down"*:— set.

G1417 **δύο** *dyo* a primary numeral; *"two"*:— both, twain, two.

G1418 **δυς-** *dys-* a primary inseparable particle of uncertain derivation; used only in compounds as a prefix; *hard*, i.e. *with difficulty*:— hard, grievous, *etc.*

G1419 **δυσβάστακτος** *dysbastaktos* from *G1418* and a derivative of *G941*; *oppressive*:— grievous to be borne.

G1420 **δυσεντερία** *dysenteria* from *G1418* and a compound of *G1787* (meaning a *bowel*); a *"dysentery"*:— bloody flux.

G1421 **δυσερμήνευτος** *dysermēneutos* from *G1418* and a presumed derivative of *G2059*; *difficult of explanation*:— hard to be uttered.

G1422 **δύσκολος** *dyskolos* from *G1418* and

κόλον *kolon* (*food*); properly *fastidious about eating* (*peevish*), i.e. (generally) *impracticable*:— hard.

G1423 **δυσκόλως** *dyskolōs* adverb from *G1422*; *impracticably*:— hardly.

G1424 **δυσμή** *dysmē* from *G1416*; the sun-*set*, i.e. (by implication) the *western* region:— west.

G1425 **δυσνόητος** *dysnoētos* from *G1418* and a derivative of *G3539*; *difficult of perception*:— hard to be understood.

G1426 **δυσφημία** *dysphēmia* from a compound of *G1418* and *G5345*; *defamation*:— evil report.

G1427 **δώδεκα** *dōdeka* from *G1417* and *G1176*; *two* and *ten*, i.e. a *dozen*:— twelve.

G1428 **δωδέκατος** *dōdekatos* from *G1427*; *twelfth* :— twelfth.

G1429 **δωδεκάφυλον** *dōdekaphylon* from *G1427* and *G5443*; the *commonwealth* of Israel:— twelve tribes.

G1430 **δῶμα** *dōma* from

δέμω *demō* (to *build*); properly an *edifice*, i.e. (specifically) a *roof*:— housetop.

G1431 **δωρεά** *dōrea* from *G1435*; a *gratuity*:— gift.

G1432 **δωρεάν** *dōrean* accusative of *G1431* as adverb; *gratuitously* (literally or figuratively):— without a cause, freely, for naught, in vain.

G1433 **δωρέομαι** *dōreomai* middle from *G1435*; to *bestow* gratuitously:— give.

G1434 **δώρημα** *dōrēma* from *G1433*; a *bestowal* :— gift.

G1435 **δῶρον** *dōron*; a *present*; specifically a *sacrifice*:— gift, offering.

E

G1436 **ἔα** *ea* apparently imperative of *G1439*; properly *let it be*, i.e. (as interjection) *aha!*:— let alone.

G1437 **ἐάν** *ean* from *G1487* and *G302*; a *conditional* particle; *in case* that, *provided*, etc.; often used in connection with other particles to denote *indefiniteness* or *uncertainty*:— before, but, except, (and) if, (if) so, whatsoever, whithersoever, though, when, whensoever, whether (or), to whom, whoso, whosoever). See *G3361*.

G1438 **ἑαυτοῦ** *heautou* (including all the other cases); from a reflexive pronoun otherwise obsolete and the genitive (dative or accusative) of *G846*; *himself, herself, itself, themselves*, also [in conjunction with the personal pronoun of the other persons] *myself, thyself, ourselves, yourself, yourselves*, etc.:— alone, her (own), herself, (he) himself, his (own), itself, one (to) another, our (thine) own, ourselves), that she had, their (own, own selves), (of) them, themselves, they, thyself, you, your (own, own conceits, own selves, yourselves).

G1439 **ἐάω** *eaō* of uncertain affinity; to *let be*, i.e. *permit* or *leave* alone:— commit, leave, let (alone), suffer. See also *G1436*.

G1440 **ἑβδομήκοντα** *hebdomēkonta* from *G1442* and a modified form of *G1176*; *seventy*:— seventy, three score and ten.

G1441 **ἑβδομηκοντάκις** *hebdomēkontakis* multiple adverb from *G1440*; *seventy times*:— seventy times.

G1442 **ἕβδομος** *hebdomos* ordinal from *G2033*; *seventh*:— seventh.

G1443 **Ἐβέρ** *Eber* of Hebrew origin [H5677]; *Eber*, a patriarch:— Eber.

G1444 **Ἑβραϊκός** *Hebraikos* from *G1443*; *Hebraïc* or the *Jewish* language:— Hebrew.

G1445 **Ἑβραῖος** *Hebraios* from *G1443*; a *Hebraean* (i.e. Hebrew) or *Jew*:— Hebrew.

G1446 **Ἑβραΐς** *Hebrais* from *G1443*; the *Hebraistic* (i.e. *Hebrew*) or *Jewish* (*Aramaic*) language:— Hebrew.

G1447 **Ἑβραϊστί** *Hebraisti* adverb from *G1446*; *Hebraistically* or in the Jewish (Aramaic) language:— in (the) Hebrew (tongue).

G1448 **ἐγγίζω** *engizō* from *G1451*; to make *near*, i.e. (reflexive) *approach*:— approach, be at hand, come (draw) near, be (come, draw) nigh.

G1449 **ἐγγράφω** *engraphō* from *G1722* and *G1125*; to *"engrave"*, i.e. *inscribe*:— write (in).

G1450 **ἔγγυος** *engyos* from *G1722* and

γυῖον *guion* (a *limb*); *pledged* (as if *articulated* by a member), i.e. a *bondsman*:— surety.

G1451 **ἐγγύς** *engys* from a primary verb

ἄγχω *anchō* (to *squeeze* or *throttle*; akin to the base of *G43*); *near* (literally or figuratively, of place or time):— from, at hand, near, nigh (at hand, unto), ready.

G1452 **ἐγγύτερον** *engyteron* neuter of the comparative of *G1451*; *nearer*:— nearer.

G1453 **ἐγείρω** *egeirō* probably akin to the base of *G58* (through the idea of *collecting* one's faculties); to *waken* (transitive or intransitive), i.e. *rouse* (literally from sleep, from sitting or lying, from disease, from death; or figuratively from obscurity, inactivity, ruins, nonexistence):— awake, lift (up), raise (again, up), rear up, arise, rise (again, up), stand, take up.

G1454 **ἔγερσις** *egersis* from *G1453*; a *resurgence* (from death):— resurrection.

G1455 **ἐγκάθετος** *enkathetos* from *G1722* and a derivative of *G2524*; *subinduced*, i.e. surreptitiously *suborned* as one who lies in wait:— spy.

G1456 **ἐγκαίνια** *enkainia* neuter plural of a presumed compound from *G1722* and *G2537*; *innovations*, i.e. (specifically) *renewal* (of religious services after the Antiochian interruption):— dedication.

G1457 **ἐγκαινίζω** *enkainizō* from *G1456*; to *renew*, i.e. *inaugurate*:— consecrate, dedicate.

G1458 **ἐγκαλέω** *enkaleō* from *G1722* and *G2564*; to *call in* (as a debt or demand), i.e. *bring to account* (*charge, criminate, etc.*):— accuse, call in question, implead, lay to the charge.

G1459 **ἐγκαταλείπω** *enkataleipō* from *G1722* and *G2641*; to *leave behind in* some place, i.e. (in a good sense) *let remain over*, or (in a bad one) to *desert*:— forsake, leave.

G1460 **ἐγκατοικέω** *enkatoikeō* from *G1722* and *G2730*; to *settle down in* a place, i.e. *reside*:— dwell among.

G1461 **ἐγκεντρίζω** *enkentrizō* from *G1722* and a derivative of *G2759*; to *prick in*, i.e. *ingraft*:— graff in, graff into.

G1462 **ἔγκλημα** *enklēma* from *G1458*; an *accusation*, i.e. *offence* alleged:— crime laid against, laid to charge.

G1463 **ἐγκομβόομαι** *enkomboomai* middle from *G1722* and

κομβόω *komboō* (to *gird*); to *gird* oneself (for labor), i.e. figuratively (the apron being a badge of servitude) to *wear* (in token of mutual deference):— be clothed with.

G1464 ἐγκοπή *enkopē* from *G1465*; a *hindrance* :— hinder.

G1465 ἐγκόπτω *enkoptō* from *G1722* and *G2875*; to *cut into,* i.e. (figuratively) *impede, detain:*— hinder, be tedious unto.

G1466 ἐγκράτεια *enkrateia* from *G1468*; *self-control* (especially *continence*):— temperance.

G1467 ἐγκρατεύομαι *enkrateuomai* middle from *G1468*; to *exercise self-restraint* (in diet and chastity):— can ([-not]) contain, be temperate.

G1468 ἐγκρατής *enkratēs* from *G1722* and *G2904*; *strong in* a thing (*masterful*), i.e. (figuratively and reflexive) *self-controlled* (in appetite, etc.):— temperate.

G1469 ἐγκρίνω *enkrinō* from *G1722* and *G2919*; to *judge in,* i.e. *count* among:— make of the number.

G1470 ἐγκρύπτω *enkryptō* from *G1722* and *G2928*; to *conceal in,* i.e. *incorporate with:*— hid in.

G1471 ἔγκυος *enkyos* from *G1722* and the base of *G2949*; *swelling inside,* i.e. *pregnant:*— great with child.

G1472 ἐγχρίω *enchriō* from *G1722* and *G5548*; to *rub in* (oil), i.e. *besmear:*— anoint.

G1473 ἐγώ *egō* a primary pronoun of the first person; only expressed when emphatic:— I, me. For the other cases and the plural see *G1691, G1698, G1700, G2248, G2249, G2254, G2257*, etc.

G1474 ἐδαφίζω *edaphizō* from Greek *G1475*; to *raze:*— lay even with the ground.

G1475 ἔδαφος *edaphos* from the base of *G1476*; a *basis* (*bottom*), i.e. the *soil:*— ground.

G1476 ἑδραῖος *hedraios* from a derivative of **ἕζομαι** *hezomai* (to *sit*); *sedentary,* i.e. (by implication) *immovable:*— settled, stedfast.

G1477 ἑδραίωμα *hedraiōma* from a derivative of *G1476*; a *support,* i.e. (figuratively) *basis:*— ground.

G1478 Ἐζεκίας *Ezekias* of Hebrew origin [H2396]; *Ezekias* (i.e. *Hezekiah*), an Israelite:— Ezekias.

G1479 ἐθελοθρησκεία *ethelothrēskeia* from *G2309* and *G2356*; *voluntary* (*arbitrary* and *unwarranted*) *piety,* i.e. *sanctimony:*— will worship.

G1480 ἐθίζω *ethizō* from *G1485*; to *accustom,* i.e. (neuter passive participle) *customary:*— custom.

G1481 ἐθνάρχης *ethnarchēs* from *G1484* and *G746*; the *governor* [not king] *of a district:*— ethnarch.

G1482 ἐθνικός *ethnikos* from *G1484*; *national* ("*ethnic*"), i.e. (specifically) a *Gentile:*— heathen (man).

G1483 ἐθνικῶς *ethnikōs* adverb from *G1482*; *as a Gentile:*— after the manner of Gentiles.

G1484 ἔθνος *ethnos* probably from *G1486*; a *race* (as of the same *habit*), i.e. a *tribe;* specifically a *foreign* (*non-Jewish*) one (usually by implication *pagan*):— Gentile, heathen, nation, people.

G1485 ἔθος *ethos* from *G1486*; a *usage* (prescribed by habit or law):— custom, manner, be wont.

G1486 ἔθω *ethō* a primary verb; to *be used* (by habit or conventionality); neuter perfect participle *usage:*— be custom (manner, wont).

G1487 εἰ *ei* a primary particle of conditionality; *if, whether, that,* etc. Often used in connection or compounds with other particles, especially as in *G1489, G1490*), *G1499, G1508, G1509, G1512, G1513, G1536, G1537*:— forasmuch as, if, that, although, though, whether. See also *G1437*.

G1488 εἶ *ei* second personal singular present of *G1510*; thou *art:*— art, be.

G1489 εἴγε *eige* from *G1487* and *G1065*; *if indeed, seeing that, unless,* (with negative) *otherwise:*— if (so be that, yet).

G1490 εἰ δὲ μή(γε) *ei de mē(ge)* from *G1487, G1161* and *G3361* (sometimes with *G1065* added); *but if not:*— (or) else, if (not, otherwise), otherwise.

G1491 εἶδος *eidos* from *G1492*; a *view,* i.e. *form* (literal or figurative):— appearance, fashion, shape, sight.

G1492 εἴδω *eidō* a primary verb; used only in certain past tenses, the others being borrowed from the equivalent *G3700* and *G3708*; properly to *see* (literally or figuratively); by implication (in the perfect only) to *know:*— be aware, behold, can (+ not tell), consider, know, have knowledge, look (on), perceive, see, be sure, tell, understand, wish, wot. Compare *G3700*.

G1493 εἰδωλεῖον *eidōleion* neuter of a presumed derivative of *G1497*; an *image-temple:*— idol's temple.

G1494 εἰδωλόθυτον *eidōlothyton* neuter of a compound of *G1497* and a presumed derivative of *G2380*; an *image-sacrifice,* i.e. part of an *idolatrous offering:*— (meat, thing that is) offered (in sacrifice, sacrificed) to (unto) idols.

G1495 εἰδωλολατρεία *eidōlolatreia* from *G1497* and *G2999*; *image-worship* (literal or figurative) :— idolatry.

G1496 εἰδωλολάτρης *eidōlolatrēs* from *G1497* and the base of *G3000*; an *image-* (*servant* or) *worshipper* (literal or figurative):— idolater.

G1497 εἴδωλον *eidōlon* from *G1491*; an *image* (i.e. for worship); by implication a heathen *god,* or (plural) the *worship* of such:— idol.

G1498 εἴην *eiēn* optative (i.e. English subjunctive) present of *G1510* (including the other persons); *might* (*could, would* or *should*) *be:*— mean, perish, should be, was, were.

G1499 εἰ καί *ei kai* from *G1487* and *G2532*; *if also* (or *even*):— if (that), though.

G1500 εἰκῆ *eikē* probably from *G1502* (through the idea of *failure*); *idly,* i.e. *without reason* (or *effect*):— without a cause, (in) vain, vainly.

G1501 εἴκοσι *eikosi* of uncertain affinity; a *score* :— twenty.

G1502 εἴκω *eikō* apparently a primary verb; properly to *be weak,* i.e. *yield:*— give place.

G1503 εἴκω *eikō* apparently a primary verb [perhaps akin to *G1502* through the idea of *faintness* as a copy]; to *resemble:*— be like.

G1504 εἰκών *eikōn* from *G1503*; a *likeness,* i.e. (literally) *statue, profile,* or (figuratively) *representation, resemblance:*— image.

G1505 εἰλικρίνεια *eilikrineia* from *G1506*; *clearness,* i.e. (by implication) *purity* (figuratively):— sincerity.

G1506 εἰλικρινής *eilikrinēs* from **εἵλη** *heilē* (the sun's *ray*) and *G2919*; *judged by sunlight,* i.e. tested as *genuine* (figuratively):— pure, sincere.

G1507 εἱλίσσω *heilissō* a prolonged form of a primary but defective verb **εἵλω** *heilō* (of the same meaning); to *coil* or *wrap:*— roll together. See also *G1667*.

G1508 εἰ μή *ei mē* from *G1487* and *G3361*; *if not* :— but, except (that), if not, more than, save (only) that, saving, till.

G1509 εἰ μή τι *ei mē ti* from *G1508* and the neuter of *G5100*; *if not somewhat:*— except.

G1510 εἰμί *eimi* first person singular present indicative; a prolonged form of a primary and defective verb; *I exist* (used only when emphatic):— am, have been, it is I, was. See also *G1488, G1498, G1511, G1527, G2070, G2071, G2075, G2076, G2258, G2468, G2771, G5600*.

G1511 εἶναι *einai* present infinitive from *G1510*; *to exist:*— am, are, come, is, lust after, please well, there is, to be, was.

G1512 εἴ περ *ei per* from *G1487* and *G4007*; *if perhaps:*— if so be (that), seeing, though.

G1513 εἴ πως *ei pōs* from *G1487* and *G4458*; *if somehow:*— if by any means.

G1514 εἰρηνεύω *eirēneuō* from *G1515*; to *be* (*act*) *peaceful:*— be at (have, live in) peace, live peaceably.

G1515 εἰρήνη *eirēnē* probably from a primary verb **εἴρω** *eirō* (to *join*); *peace* (literal or figurative); by implication *prosperity:*— one, peace, quietness, rest, set at one again.

G1516 εἰρηνικός *eirēnikos* from *G1515*; *pacific;* by implication *salutary:*— peaceable.

G1517 εἰρηνοποιέω *eirēnopoieō* from *G1518*; to *be a peace-maker,* i.e. (figuratively) to *harmonize:*— make peace.

G1518 εἰρηνοποιός *eirēnopoios* from *G1518* and *G4160*; *pacificatory,* i.e. (subjectively) *peaceable:*— peacemaker.

G1519 εἰς *eis* a primary prepostition; *to* or *into* (indicating the point reached or entered), of place, time, or (figuratively) purpose (result, etc.); also in adverbial phrases:— abundant, abundantly, against, among, as, at, back, backward, before, by, concerning, continual, far more exceeding, for [intent, purpose], fore, forth, in (among, at, unto), inso much that, into, to the intent that, of one mind, never, of, on, upon, perish, set at one again, (so) that, therefore, thereunto, throughout, till, to (be, the end), toward), heretoward, until to . . . ward, fore, wherefore, with. Often used in compounds with the same general import, but only with verbs (etc.) expressing motion (literal or figurative).

G1520 εἷς *heis* Including the neuter [etc.] **ἕν** *hen* a primary numeral; *one:*— a, an, any, a certain, abundantly, man, one (another), only, other, some. See also *G1527, G3367, G3391, G3762*.

G1521 εἰσάγω *eisagō* from *G1519* and *G71*; to *introduce* (literally or figuratively):— bring in, bring into, (+ was to) lead into.

G1522 εἰσακούω *eisakouō* from *G1519* and *G191*; to *listen* to:— hear.

G1523 εἰσδέχομαι *eisdechomai* from *G1519* and *G1209*; to *take into* one's favor:— receive.

G1524 εἴσειμι *eiseimi* from *G1519* and **εἶμι** *eimi* (to *go*); to *enter:*— enter (go) into.

G1525 εἰσέρχομαι *eiserchomai* from *G1519* and *G2064*; to *enter* (literally or figuratively):— arise, come (in, into), enter in, enter into, go in (through).

G1526 εἰσί *eisi* 3rd person plural present indicative of *G1510*; they *are:*— agree, are, be, dure, is, were.

G1527 εἷς καθ' εἷς *heis kath' heis* from *G1520* repeated with *G2596* inserted; *severally:*— one by one.

G1528 εἰσκαλέω *eiskaleō* from *G1519* and *G2564*; to *invite* in:— call in.

G1529 εἴσοδος *eisodos* from *G1519* and *G3598*; an *entrance* (literal or figurative):— coming, enter in (to), entering in (to).

G1530 εἰσπηδάω *eispēdaō* from *G1519* and **πηδάω** *pēdaō* (to *leap*); to *rush in:*— run (spring) in.

G1531 εἰσπορεύομαι *eisporeuomai* from *G1519* and *G4198*; to *enter* (literally or figuratively):— come (enter) in, go into.

G1532 εἰστρέχω *eistrechō* from *G1519* and *G5143*; to *hasten inward:*— run in.

G1533 εἰσφέρω *eispherō* from *G1519* and *G5342*; to *carry inward* (literally or figuratively):— bring (in), lead into.

G1534 εἶτα *eita* of uncertain affinity; a particle of *succession* (in time or logical enumeration), *then, moreover:*— after that, afterward, furthermore, then. See also *G1899*.

G1535 εἴτε *eite* from *G1487* and *G5037*; *if too:*— if, or, whether.

G1536 εἴ τις *ei tis* from *G1487* and *G5100*; *if any* :— he that, if a/any man/man's, thing, from any, ought, whether any, whosoever.

G1537 ἐκ *ek* or **ἐξ** *ex* a primary preposition denoting *origin* (the point *whence* motion or action proceeds); *from, out* (of place, time or cause; literally or figuratively; direct or remote). Often used in compounds, with the same general import; often of *completion:*— after, among, are, at, betwixt, beyond, by (the means of), exceedingly, (abundantly above), for, forth, from (among, forth, up), grudgingly, heartily, heavenly, hereby, very highly, (because, by reason) of, off (from), on, out among (from, of), over, since, thenceforth, through, unto, vehemently, with, without.

G1538 ἕκαστος *hekastos* as if a superlative of **ἕκας** *hekas* (*afar*); *each* or *every:*— any, both, each (one), every (man, one, woman), particularly.

G1539 ἑκάστοτε *hekastote* as if from *G1538* and *G5119*; at *every time:*— always.

G1540 ἑκατόν *hekaton* of uncertain affinity; a *hundred:*— hundred.

G1541 ἑκατονταέτης *hekatontaetēs* from *G1540* and *G2094*; *centenarian:*— hundred years old.

G1542 ἑκατονταπλασίων *hekatontaplasiōn* from *G1540* and a presumed derivative of *G4111*; a *hundred times:*— hundredfold.

G1543 ἑκατοντάρχης *hekatontarchēs* or **ἑκατόνταρχος** *hekatontarchos* from *G1540* and *G757*; the *captain of one hundred men:*— centurion.

G1544 ἐκβάλλω *ekballō* from *G1537* and *G906*; to *eject* (literally or figuratively):— bring forth, cast (forth, out), drive (out), expel, leave, pluck (pull, take, thrust) out, put forth (out), send away (forth, out).

G1545 ἔκβασις *ekbasis* from a compound of *G1537* and the base of *G939* (meaning to *go out*); an *exit* (literal or figurative):— end, way to escape.

G1546 ἐκβολή *ekbolē* from *G1544*; *ejection,* i.e. (specifically) a *throwing overboard* of the cargo :— lighten the ship.

G1547 ἐκγαμίζω *ekgamizō* from *G1537* and a form of *G1061* [compare *G1548*]; to *marry off* a daughter:— give in marriage.

G1548 ἐκγαμίσκω *ekgamiskō* from *G1537* and *G1061*; the same as *G1547:*— give in marriage.

G1549 ἔκγονον *ekgonon* neuter of a derivative of a compound of *G1537* and *G1096*; a *descendant,* i.e. (specifically) *grandchild:*— nephew.

G1550 ἐκδαπανάω *ekdapanaō* from *G1537* and *G1159*; to *expend* (wholly), i.e. (figuratively) *exhaust:*— spend.

G1551 ἐκδέχομαι *ekdechomai* from *G1537* and *G1209*; to *accept from* some source, i.e. (by implication) to *await:*— expect, look (tarry) for, wait (for).

G1552 ἔκδηλος *ekdēlos* from *G1537* and *G1212*; *wholly evident:*— manifest.

G1553 ἐκδημέω *ekdēmeō* from a compound of *G1537* and *G1218*; to *emigrate,* i.e. (figuratively) *vacate* or *quit:*— be absent.

G1554 ἐκδίδωμι *ekdidōmi* from *G1537* and *G1325*; to *give forth,* i.e. (specifically) to *lease:*— let forth (out).

G1555 ἐκδιηγέομαι *ekdiēgeomai* from *G1537* and a compound of *G1223* and *G2233*; to *narrate* through wholly:— declare.

G1556 ἐκδικέω *ekdikeō* from *G1558*; to *vindicate, retaliate, punish:*— avenge, revenge.

G1557 ἐκδίκησις *ekdikēsis* from *G1556*; *vindication, retribution:*— avenge, revenge, vengeance, punishment.

G1558 ἔκδικος *ekdikos* from *G1537* and *G1349*; carrying *justice out,* i.e. a *punisher:*— avenger, revenger.

G1559 ἐκδιώκω *ekdiōkō* from *G1537* and *G1377*; to *pursue out,* i.e. *expel* or *persecute* implacably:— persecute.

G1560 ἔκδοτος *ekdotos* from *G1537* and a derivative of *G1325*; *given out* or *over,* i.e. *surrendered:*— delivered.

G1561 ἐκδοχή *ekdochē* from *G1551*; *expectation* :— looking for.

G1562 ἐκδύω *ekdyō* from *G1537* and the base of *G1416*; to cause to *sink out* of, i.e. (specifically as of clothing) to *divest:*— strip, take off from, unclothe.

G1563 ἐκεῖ *ekei* of uncertain affinity; *there;* by extension *thither:*— there, thither, thitherward, (to) yonder (place).

G1564 ἐκεῖθεν *ekeithen* from *G1563*; *thence:*— from that place, (from) thence, there.

G1565 ἐκεῖνος *ekeinos* from *G1563*; *that* one (or [neuter] thing); often intensified by the article prefixed:— he, it, the other (same), selfsame, that (same, very), their, them, they, this, those. See also *G3778*.

G1566 ἐκεῖσε *ekeise* from *G1563*; *thither:*— there.

G1567 ἐκζητέω *ekzēteō* from *G1537* and *G2212*; to *search out,* i.e. (figuratively) *investigate, crave, demand,* (by Hebrew) *worship:*— inquire, require, seek after (carefully, diligently).

G1568 ἐκθαμβέω *ekthambeō* from *G1569*; to *astonish* utterly:— affright, greatly (sore) amaze.

G1569 ἔκθαμβος *ekthambos* from *G1537* and *G2285*; *utterly astounded:*— greatly wondering.

G1570 ἔκθετος *ekthetos* from *G1537* and a derivative of *G5087*; *put out,* i.e. *exposed* to perish:— cast out.

G1571 ἐκκαθαίρω *ekkathairō* from *G1537* and *G2508*; to *cleanse thoroughly:*— purge (out).

G1572 ἐκκαίω *ekkaiō* from *G1537* and *G2545*; to *inflame* deeply:— burn.

G1573 ἐκκακέω *ekkakeō* from *G1537* and *G2556*; to *be* (*bad* or) *weak,* i.e. (by implication) to *fail* (in heart):— faint, be weary.

G1574 ἐκκεντέω *ekkenteō* from *G1537* and the base of *G2759*; to *transfix:*— pierce.

G1575 ἐκκλάω *ekklaō* from *G1537* and *G2806*; to *exscind:*— break off.

G1576 ἐκκλείω *ekkleiō* from *G1537* and *G2808*; to *shut out* (literally or figuratively):— exclude.

G1577 ἐκκλησία *ekklēsia* from a compound of *G1537* and a derivative of *G2564*; a *calling out,* i.e. (concretely) a popular *meeting,* especially a religious *congregation* (Jewish *synagogue,* or Christian community of members on earth or saints in heaven or both):— assembly, church.

G1578 ἐκκλίνω *ekklinō* from *G1537* and *G2827*; to *deviate,* i.e. (absolutely) to *shun* (literally or figuratively), or (relatively) to *decline* (from piety):— avoid, eschew, go out of the way.

G1579 ἐκκολυμβάω *ekkolymbaō* from *G1537* and *G2860*; to *escape* by *swimming:*— swim out.

G1580 ἐκκομίζω *ekkomizō* from *G1537* and *G2865*; to *bear forth* (to burial):— carry out.

G1581 ἐκκόπτω *ekkoptō* from *G1537* and *G2875*; to *excise;* figuratively to *frustrate:*— cut down (off, out), hew down, hinder.

G1582 ἐκκρέμαμαι *ekkremamai* middle from *G1537* and *G2910*; to *hang upon* the lips of a speaker, i.e. *listen closely:*— be very attentive.

G1583 ἐκλαλέω *eklaleō* from *G1537* and *G2980*; to *divulge:*— tell.

G1584 ἐκλάμπω *eklampō* from *G1537* and *G2989*; to *be resplendent:*— shine forth.

G1585 ἐκλανθάνομαι *eklanthanomai* middle from *G1537* and *G2990*; to *be* utterly *oblivious* of:— forget.

G1586 ἐκλέγομαι *eklegomai* middle from *G1537* and *G3004* (in its primary sense); to *select:*— make choice, choose (out), chosen.

G1587 ἐκλείπω *ekleipō* from *G1537* and *G3007*; to *omit,* i.e. (by implication) *cease* (*die*):— fail.

G1588 ἐκλεκτός *eklektos* from *G1586*; *select;* by implication *favorite:*— chosen, elect.

G1589 ἐκλογή *eklogē* from *G1586*; (divine) *selection* (abstract or concrete):— chosen, election.

G1590 ἐκλύω *eklyō* from *G1537* and *G3089*; to *relax* (literally or figuratively):— faint.

G1591 ἐκμάσσω *ekmassō* from *G1537* and the base of *G3145*; to *knead out,* i.e. (by analogy) to *wipe dry:*— wipe.

G1592 ἐκμυκτερίζω *ekmykterizō* from *G1537* and *G3456*; to *sneer* outright at:— deride.

G1593 ἐκνεύω *ekneuō* from *G1537* and *G3506*; (by analogy) to *slip off*, i.e. quietly *withdraw:*— convey self away.

G1594 ἐκνήφω *eknēphō* from *G1537* and *G3525*; (figuratively) to *rouse* (oneself) *out* of stupor:— awake.

G1595 ἑκούσιον *hekousion* neuter of a derived from *G1635*; *voluntariness:*— willingly.

G1596 ἑκουσίως *hekousiōs* adverb from the same as *G1595*; *voluntarily:*— wilfully, willingly.

G1597 ἔκπαλαι *ekpalai* from *G1537* and *G3819*; *long ago, for a long while:*— of a long time, of old.

G1598 ἐκπειράζω *ekpeirazō* from *G1537* and *G3985*; to *test thoroughly:*— tempt.

G1599 ἐκπέμπω *ekpempō* from *G1537* and *G3992*; to *dispatch:*— send away (forth).

G1600 ἐκπετάννυμι *ekpetannymi* from *G1537* and a form of *G4072*; to *fly out*, i.e. (by analogy) *extend:*— stretch forth.

G1601 ἐκπίπτω *ekpiptō* from *G1537* and *G4098*; to *drop away;* specifically *be driven out* of one's course; figuratively to *lose, become inefficient:*— be cast, fail, fall (away, off), take none effect.

G1602 ἐκπλέω *ekpleō* from *G1537* and *G4126*; to *depart* by ship:— sail (away, thence).

G1603 ἐκπληρόω *ekplēroō* from *G1537* and *G4137*; to *accomplish* entirely:— fulfill.

G1604 ἐκπλήρωσις *ekplērōsis* from *G1603*; *completion:*— accomplishment.

G1605 ἐκπλήσσω *ekplēssō* from *G1537* and *G4141*; to *strike* with astonishment:— amaze, astonish.

G1606 ἐκπνέω *ekpneō* from *G1537* and *G4154*; to *expire:*— give up the ghost.

G1607 ἐκπορεύομαι *ekporeuomai* from *G1537* and *G4198*; to *depart, be discharged, proceed, project:*— come (forth, out of), depart, go (forth, out), issue, proceed (out of).

G1608 ἐκπορνεύω *ekporneuō* from *G1537* and *G4203*; to *be utterly unchaste:*— give self over to fornication.

G1609 ἐκπτύω *ekptyō* from *G1537* and *G4429*; to *spit out*, i.e. (figuratively) *spurn:*— reject.

G1610 ἐκριζόω *ekrizoō* from *G1537* and *G4492*; to *uproot:*— pluck up by the root, root up.

G1611 ἔκστασις *ekstasis* from *G1839*; a *displacement* of the mind, i.e. *bewilderment, "ecstasy":*— be amazed, amazement, astonishment, trance.

G1612 ἐκστρέφω *ekstrephō* from *G1537* and *G4762*; to *pervert* (figuratively):— subvert.

G1613 ἐκταράσσω *ektarassō* from *G1537* and *G5015*; to *disturb wholly:*— exceedingly trouble.

G1614 ἐκτείνω *ekteinō* from *G1537* and
τείνω *teinō* (to *stretch*); to *extend:*— cast, put forth, stretch forth (out).

G1615 ἐκτελέω *ekteleō* from *G1537* and *G5055*; to *complete* fully:— finish.

G1616 ἐκτένεια *ekteneia* from *G1618*; *intentness* :— instantly.

G1617 ἐκτενέστερον *ektenesteron* neuter of the comparative of *G1618*; *more intently:*— more earnestly.

G1618 ἐκτενής *ektenēs* from *G1614*; *intent:*— without ceasing, fervent.

G1619 ἐκτενῶς *ektenōs* adverb from *G1618*; *intently:*— fervently.

G1620 ἐκτίθημι *ektithēmi* from *G1537* and *G5087*; to *expose;* figuratively to *declare:*— cast out, expound.

G1621 ἐκτινάσσω *ektinassō* from *G1537* and
τινάσσω *tinassō* (to *swing*); to *shake* violently:— shake (off).

G1622 ἐκτός *ektos* from *G1537*; the *exterior;* figuratively (as a preposition) *aside from, besides:*— but, except, excepted, other than, out of, outside, unless, without.

G1623 ἕκτος *hektos* ordinal from *G1803*; *sixth:*— sixth.

G1624 ἐκτρέπω *ektrepō* from *G1537* and the base of *G5157*; to *deflect*, i.e. *turn away* (literally or figuratively):— avoid, turn (aside, out of the way).

G1625 ἐκτρέφω *ektrephō* from *G1537* and *G5142*; to *rear up* to maturity, i.e. (generally) to *cherish* or *train:*— bring up, nourish.

G1626 ἔκτρωμα *ektrōma* from a compound of *G1537* and
τιτρώσκω *titrōskō* (to *wound*); a *miscarriage* (*abortion*), i.e. (by analogy) *untimely birth:*— born out of due time.

G1627 ἐκφέρω *ekpherō* from *G1537* and *G5342*; to *bear out* (literally or figuratively):— bear, bring forth, carry forth (out).

G1628 ἐκφεύγω *ekpheugō* from *G1537* and *G5343*; to *flee out:*— escape, flee.

G1629 ἐκφοβέω *ekphobeō* from *G1537* and *G5399*; to *frighten utterly:*— terrify.

G1630 ἔκφοβος *ekphobos* from *G1537* and *G5401*; *frightened out* of one's wits:— sore afraid, exceedingly fear.

G1631 ἐκφύω *ekphyō* from *G1537* and *G5453*; to *sprout up:*— put forth.

G1632 ἐκχέω *ekcheō* or by variation
ἐκχύνω *ekchynō* from *G1537* and
χέω *cheō* (to *pour*); to *pour forth;* figuratively to *bestow:*— gush (pour) out, run greedily (out), shed (abroad, forth), spill.

G1633 ἐκχωρέω *ekchōreō* from *G1537* and *G5562*; to *depart:*— depart out.

G1634 ἐκψύχω *ekpsychō* from *G1537* and *G5594*; to *expire:*— give (yield) up the ghost.

G1635 ἑκών *hekōn* of uncertain affinity; *voluntary:*— willingly.

G1636 ἐλαία *elaia* feminine of a presumed derived from an obsolete primary; an *olive* (the tree or the fruit):— olive (berry, tree).

G1637 ἔλαιον *elaion* neuter of the same as *G1636*; olive *oil:*— oil.

G1638 ἐλαιών *elaiōn* from *G1636*; an *olive-orchard*, i.e. (specifically) the *Mt. of Olives:*— Olivet.

G1639 Ἐλαμίτης *Elamitēs* of Hebrew origin [H5867]; an *Elamite* or Persian:— Elamite.

G1640 ἐλάσσων *elassōn* or
ἐλάττων *elattōn* comparative of the same as *G1646*; *smaller* (in size, quantity, age or quality):— less, under, worse, younger.

G1641 ἐλαττονέω *elattoneō* from *G1640*; to *diminish*, i.e. *fall short:*— have lack.

G1642 ἐλαττόω *elattoō* from *G1640*; to *lessen* (in rank or influence):— decrease, make lower.

G1643 ἐλαύνω *elaunō* a prolonged form of a primary verb (obsolete except in certain tenses as an alternative of this) of uncertain affinity; to *push* (as wind, oars or daemoniacal power):— carry, drive, row.

G1644 ἐλαφρία *elaphria* from *G1645*; *levity* (figurative), i.e. *fickleness:*— lightness.

G1645 ἐλαφρός *elaphros* probably akin to *G1643* and the base of *G1640*; *light*, i.e. *easy:*— light.

G1646 ἐλάχιστος *elachistos* superlative of
ἔλαχυς *elachys* (*short*); used as equivalent to *G3398*; *least* (in size, amount, dignity, etc.):— least, very little (small), smallest.

G1647 ἐλαχιστότερος *elachistoteros* comparative of *G1646*; *far less:*— less than the least.

G1648 Ἐλεάζαρ *Eleazar* of Hebrew origin [H499]; *Eleazar*, an Israelite:— Eleazar.

G1649 ἔλεγξις *elenxis* from *G1651*; *refutation*, i.e. *reproof:*— rebuke.

G1650 ἔλεγχος *elenchos* from *G1651*; *proof, conviction:*— evidence, reproof.

G1651 ἐλέγχω *elenchō* of uncertain affinity; to *confute, admonish:*— convict, convince, tell a fault, rebuke, reprove.

G1652 ἐλεεινός *eleeinos* from *G1656*; *pitiable:*— miserable.

G1653 ἐλεέω *eleeō* from *G1656*; to *compassionate* (by word or deed, specifically by divine grace):— have compassion (pity on), have (obtain, receive, shew) mercy (on).

G1654 ἐλεημοσύνη *eleēmosynē* from *G1656*; *compassion*, i.e. (as exercised towards the poor) *beneficence*, or (concretely) a *benefaction:*— alms, almsdeeds.

G1655 ἐλεήμων *eleēmōn* from *G1653*; ; *compassionate* (active):— merciful.

G1656 ἔλεος *eleos* of uncertain affinity; *compassion* (human or divine, especially active):— (+ tender) mercy.

G1657 ἐλευθερία *eleutheria* from *G1658*; *freedom* (legitimate or licentious, chiefly moral or ceremonial):— liberty.

G1658 ἐλεύθερος *eleutheros* probably from the alternative of *G2064*; *unrestrained* (to *go* at pleasure), i.e. (as a citizen) *not a slave* (whether *freeborn* or *manumitted*), or (generally) *exempt* (from obligation or liability):— free (man, woman), at liberty.

G1659 ἐλευθερόω *eleutheroō* from *G1658*; to *liberate*, i.e. (figuratively) to *exempt* (from moral, ceremonial or mortal liability):— deliver, make free.

G1660 ἔλευσις *eleusis* from the alternative of *G2064*; an *advent:*— coming.

G1661 ἐλεφάντινος *elephantinos* from
ἔλεφας *elephas* (an *"elephant"*); *elephantine*, i.e. (by implication) composed of *ivory:*— of ivory.

G1662 Ἐλιακείμ *Eliakeim* of Hebrew origin [H471]; *Eliakim*, an Israelite:— Eliakim.

G1663 Ἐλιέζερ *Eliezer* of Hebrew origin [H461]; *Eliezer*, an Israelite:— Eliezer.

G1664 Ἐλιούδ *Elioud* of Hebrew origin [H410 and H1935]; *God of majesty; Eliud*, an Israelite:— Eliud.

G1665 Ἐλισάβετ *Elisabet* of Hebrew origin [H472]; *Elisabet,* an Israelitess:— Elisabeth.

G1666 Ἐλισσαῖος *Elissaios* of Hebrew origin [H477]; *Elissaeus,* an Israelite:— Elissaeus.

G1667 ἑλίσσω *helissō* a form of G1507; to *coil* or *wrap:*— fold up.

G1668 ἕλκος *helkos* probably from G1670; an *ulcer* (as if drawn together):— sore.

G1669 ἑλκόω *helkoō* from G1668; to *cause to ulcerate,* i.e. (passive) *be ulcerous:*— full of sores.

G1670 ἑλκύω *helkyō* or
ἕλκω *helkō* probably akin to G138; to *drag* (literally or figuratively):— draw. Compare G1667.

G1671 Ἑλλάς *Hellas* of uncertain affinity; *Hellas* (or *Greece*), a country of Europe:— Greece.

G1672 Ἕλλην *Hellēn* from G1671; a *Hellen* (*Grecian*) or inhabitant of Hellas; by extension a *Greek-speaking* person, especially a *non-Jew:*— Gentile, Greek.

G1673 Ἑλληνικός *Hellēnikos* from G1672; *Hellenic,* i.e. *Grecian* (in language):— Greek.

G1674 Ἑλληνίς *Hellēnis* feminine of G1672; a *Grecian* (i.e. *non-Jewish*) woman:— Greek.

G1675 Ἑλληνιστής *Hellēnistēs* from a derivative of G1672; a *Hellenist* or Greek-speaking Jew:— Grecian.

G1676 Ἑλληνιστί *Hellēnisti* adverb from the same as G1675; *Hellenistically,* i.e. in the Grecian language:— Greek.

G1677 ἐλλογέω *ellogeō* from G1722 and G3056 (in the sense of *account*); to *reckon in,* i.e. *attribute:*— impute, put on account.

G1678 Ἐλμωδάμ *Elmōdam* of Hebrew origin [perhaps for H486]; *Elmodam,* an Israelite:— Elmodam.

G1679 ἐλπίζω *elpizō* from G1680; to *expect* or *confide:*— (have) hope (for), (have) hoped (for), thing hoped for, trust.

G1680 ἐλπίς *elpis* from a primary
ἔλπω *elpō* (to *anticipate,* usually with pleasure); *expectation* (abstract or concrete) or *confidence:*— faith, hope.

G1681 Ἐλύμας *Elymas* of foreign origin; *Elymas,* a wizard:— Elymas.

G1682 ἐλωΐ *elōi* of Aramaic origin [H426 with pronominal suffix]; *my God:*— Eloi.

G1683 ἐμαυτοῦ *emautou* general compound of G1700 and G846; *of myself* (so likewise the dative)
ἐμαυτῷ *emautō* and accusative
ἐμαυτόν *emauton* :— me, mine own (self), myself.

G1684 ἐμβαίνω *embainō* from G1722 and the base of G939; to *walk on,* i.e. *embark* (aboard a vessel), *reach* (a pool):— come (get) into, enter (into), go (up) into, step in, take ship.

G1685 ἐμβάλλω *emballō* from G1722 and G906; to *throw on,* i.e. (figuratively) *subject to* (eternal punishment):— cast into.

G1686 ἐμβάπτω *embaptō* from G1722 and G911; to *whelm on,* i.e. *wet* (a part of the person, etc.) by contact with a fluid:— dip.

G1687 ἐμβατεύω *embateuō* from G1722 and a presumed derivative of the base of G939; equivalent to G1684; to *intrude on* (figuratively):— intrude into.

G1688 ἐμβιβάζω *embibazō* from G1722 and
βιβάζω *bibazō* (to *mount;* causative of G1684); to *place on,* i.e. *transfer* (aboard a vessel):— put in.

G1689 ἐμβλέπω *emblepō* from G1722 and G991; to *look on,* i.e. (relatively) to *observe* fixedly, or (absolutely) to *discern* clearly:— behold, gaze up, look upon, (could) see.

G1690 ἐμβριμάομαι *embrimaomai* from G1722 and
βριμάομαι *brimaomai* (to *snort* with anger); to have *indignation on,* i.e. (transitive) to *blame,* (intransitive) to *sigh* with chagrin, (specifically) to sternly *enjoin:*— straitly charge, groan, murmur against.

G1691 ἐμέ *eme* a prolonged form of G3165; *me:*— I, me, my, myself.

G1692 ἐμέω *emeō* of uncertain affinity; to *vomit* :— (will) spue.

G1693 ἐμμαίνομαι *emmainomai* from G1722 and G3105; to *rave on,* i.e. *rage at:*— be mad against.

G1694 Ἐμμανουήλ *Emmanouēl* of Hebrew origin [H6005]; *God with us; Emmanuel,* a name of Christ :— Emmanuel.

G1695 Ἐμμαούς *Emmaous* probably of Hebrew origin [compare H3222]; *Emmaus,* a place in Palestine:— Emmaus.

G1696 ἐμμένω *emmenō* from G1722 and G3306; to *stay in* the same place, i.e. (figuratively) to *persevere:*— continue.

G1697 Ἐμμόρ *Emmor* of Hebrew origin [H2544]; *Emmor* (i.e. *Chamor*), a Canaanite:— Emmoral.

G1698 ἐμοί *emoi* a prolonged form of G3427; *to me:*— I, me, mine, my.

G1699 ἐμός *emos* from the oblique cases of G1473 (G1698, G1700, G1691); *my:*— of me, mine (own), my.

G1700 ἐμοῦ *emou* a prolonged form of G3449; *of me:*— me, mine, my.

G1701 ἐμπαιγμός *empaigmos* from G1702; *derision* :— mocking.

G1702 ἐμπαίζω *empaizō* from G1722 and G3815; to *jeer at,* i.e. *deride:*— mock.

G1703 ἐμπαίκτης *empaiktēs* from G1702; one who *derides,* i.e. (by implication) a *false teacher:*— mocker, scoffer.

G1704 ἐμπεριπατέω *emperipateō* from G1722 and G4043; to *perambulate on* a place, i.e. (figuratively) to *be occupied among* persons:— walk in.

G1705 ἐμπίπλημι *empiplēmi* or
ἐμπλήθω *emplēthō* from G1722 and the base of G4118; to *fill in* (*up*), i.e. (by implication) to *satisfy* (literally or figuratively):— fill.

G1706 ἐμπίπτω *empiptō* from G1722 and G4098; to *fall on,* i.e. (literally) *be entrapped by,* or (figuratively) *be overwhelmed with:*— fall among (into).

G1707 ἐμπλέκω *emplekō* from G1722 and G4120; to *entwine,* i.e. (figuratively) *involve* with:— entangle (in, self with).

G1708 ἐμπλοκή *emplokē* from G1707; elaborate *braiding* of the hair:— plaiting.

G1709 ἐμπνέω *empneō* from G1722 and G4154; to *inhale,* i.e. (figuratively) to *be animated by* (*bent upon*):— breathe.

G1710 ἐμπορεύομαι *emporeuomai* from G1722 and G4198; to *travel in* (a country as a peddler), i.e. (by implication) to *trade:*— buy and sell, make merchandise.

G1711 ἐμπορία *emporia* feminine from G1713; *traffic:*— merchandise.

G1712 ἐμπόριον *emporion* neuter from G1713; a *mart* (*"emporium"*):— merchandise.

G1713 ἔμπορος *emporos* from G1722 and the base of G4198; a (wholesale) *tradesman:*— merchant.

G1714 ἐμπρήθω *emprēthō* from G1722 and
πρήθω *prēthō* (to *blow* a flame); to *enkindle,* i.e. *set on fire:*— burn up.

G1715 ἔμπροσθεν *emprosthen* from G1722 and G4314; *in front of* (in place [literal or figurative] or time):— against, at, before, (in presence, sight) of.

G1716 ἐμπτύω *emptyō* from G1722 and G4429; to *spit at* or *on:*— spit (upon).

G1717 ἐμφανής *emphanēs* from a compound of G1722 and G5316; *apparent in* self:— manifest, openly.

G1718 ἐμφανίζω *emphanizō* from G1717; to *exhibit* (in person) or *disclose* (by words):— appear, declare (plainly), inform, (will) manifest, shew, signify.

G1719 ἔμφοβος *emphobos* from G1722 and G5401; *in fear,* i.e. *alarmed:*— affrighted, afraid, tremble.

G1720 ἐμφυσάω *emphysaō* from G1722 and
φυσαω *physaō* (to *puff*) [compare G5453]; to *blow at* or *on:*— breathe on.

G1721 ἔμφυτος *emphytos* from G1722 and a derivative of G5453; *implanted* (figuratively):— engrafted.

G1722 ἐν *en* a primary preposition denoting (fixed) *position* (in place, time or state), and (by implication) *instrumentality* (medially or constructively), i.e. a relation of *rest* (intermediate between G1519 and G1537); *"in," at, on, upon, by,* etc. Often used in compounds, with substantially the same import; rarely with verbs of motion, and then not to indicate direction, except (elliptically) by a separate (and different) preposition:— about, after, against, almost, altogether, among, as, at, before, between, by, here by (+ all means), for (. . . sake of), give self wholly to, in, herein, into, inwardly, mightily, (because) of, on, upon, -ly (e.g., openly, speedily), outwardly, one, quickly, shortly, that, there, therein, thereon, through, throughout, to, unto, toward, under, when, where, wherewith, while, with, within.

G1723 ἐναγκαλίζομαι *enankalizomai* from G1722 and a derivative of G43; to *take in* one's *arms,* i.e. *embrace:*— take up in arms.

G1724 ἐνάλιος *enalios* from G1722 and G251; *in* the *sea,* i.e. *marine:*— thing in the sea.

G1725 ἔναντι *enanti* from G1722 and G473; *in front* (i.e. figuratively *presence*) *of:*— before.

G1726 ἐναντίον *enantion* neuter of G1727; (adverbially) *in* the *presence* (*view*) *of:*— before, in the presence of.

G1727 ἐναντίος *enantios* from G1725; *opposite;* figuratively *antagonistic:*— (over) against, contrary.

G1728 ἐνάρχομαι *enarchomai* from G1722 and G756; to *commence on:*— rule [*by mistake* for G757].

G1729 ἐνδεής *endeēs* from a compound of G1722 and G1210 (in the sense of *lacking*); *deficient in:*— lacking.

G1730 ἔνδειγμα *endeigma* from G1731; an *indication* (concrete):— manifest token.

G1731 ἐνδείκνυμι *endeiknymi* from *G1722* and *G1166*; to *indicate* (by word or act):— do, show (forth).

G1732 ἔνδειξις *endeixis* from *G1731*; *indication* (abstract):— declare, evident token, proof.

G1733 ἕνδεκα *hendeka* from (the neuter of) *G1520* and *G1176*; *one* and *ten*, i.e. *eleven:*— eleven.

G1734 ἑνδέκατος *hendekatos* ordinal from *G1733*; *eleventh:*— eleventh.

G1735 ἐνδέχεται *endechetai* third person singular present of a compound of *G1722* and *G1209*; (impersonally) *it is accepted in*, i.e. *admitted* (*possible*):— can (+ not) be.

G1736 ἐνδημέω *endēmeō* from a compound of *G1722* and *G1218*; to *be in* one's own *country*, i.e. *home* (figuratively):— be at home (present).

G1737 ἐνδιδύσκω *endidyskō* a prolonged form of *G1746*; to *invest* (with a garment):— clothe in, wear.

G1738 ἔνδικος *endikos* from *G1722* and *G1349*; *in* the *right*, i.e. *equitable:*— just.

G1739 ἐνδόμησις *endomēsis* from a compound of *G1722* and a derivative of the base of *G1218*; a *housing in* (*residence*), i.e. *structure:*— building.

G1740 ἐνδοξάζω *endoxazō* from *G1741*; to *glorify:*— glorify.

G1741 ἔνδοξος *endoxos* from *G1722* and *G1391*; *in glory*, i.e. *splendid*, (figuratively) *noble:*— glorious, gorgeous, gorgeously, honourable.

G1742 ἔνδυμα *endyma* from *G1746*; *apparel* (especially the outer *robe*):— clothing, garment, raiment.

G1743 ἐνδυναμόω *endynamoō* from *G1722* and *G1412*; to *empower:*— enable, (increase in) strength, strengthen, be (make) strong.

G1744 ἐνδύνω *endynō* from *G1772* and *G1416*; to *sink* (by implication *wrap* [compare *G1746*]) *on*, i.e. (figuratively) *sneak:*— creep.

G1745 ἔνδυσις *endysis* from *G1746*; *investment* with clothing:— putting on.

G1746 ἐνδύω *endyō* from *G1722* and *G1416* (in the sense of *sinking* into a garment); to *invest* with clothing (literally or figuratively):— array, clothe (with), endue, have (put) on.

G1747 ἐνέδρα *enedra* feminine from *G1722* and the base of *G1476*; an *ambuscade*, i.e. (figuratively) murderous *purpose:*— lay wait. See also Greek *G1749*.

G1748 ἐνεδρεύω *enedreuō* from *G1747*; to *lurk*, i.e. (figuratively) *plot* assassination:— lay wait for.

G1749 ἔνεδρον *enedron* neuter of the same as *G1747*; an *ambush*, i.e. (figuratively) murderous *design:*— lying in wait.

G1750 ἐνειλέω *eneileō* from *G1772* and the base of *G1507*; to *enwrap:*— wrap in.

G1751 ἔνειμι *eneimi* from *G1772* and *G1510*; to *be within* (neuter participle plural):— such things as . . . have. See also *G1762*.

G1752 ἕνεκα *heneka* or
ἕνεκεν *heneken* or
εἵνεκεν *heineken* of uncertain affinity; *on account of:*— because, for (cause, sake), fore, wherefore, by reason of, that.

G1753 ἐνέργεια *energeia* from *G1756*; *efficiency* ("energy"):— operation, strong, (effectual) working.

G1754 ἐνεργέω *energeō* from *G1756*; to *be active, efficient:*— do, (be) effectual (fervent), be mighty in, shew forth self, work (effectually in).

G1755 ἐνέργημα *energēma* from *G1754*; an *effect* :— operation, working.

G1756 ἐνεργής *energēs* from *G1722* and *G2041*; *active, operative:*— effectual, powerful.

G1757 ἐνευλογέω *eneulogeō* from *G1722* and *G2127*; to *confer a benefit on:*— bless.

G1758 ἐνέχω *enechō* from *G1722* and *G2192*; to *hold in* or *upon*, i.e. *ensnare;* by implication to *keep a grudge:*— entangle with, have a quarrel against, urge.

G1759 ἐνθάδε *enthade* from a prolonged form of *G1722*; properly *within*, i.e. (of place) *here, hither:*— here, there, hither.

G1760 ἐνθυμέομαι *enthymeomai* from a compound of *G1722* and *G2372*; to *be inspirited*, i.e. *ponder:*— think.

G1761 ἐνθύμησις *enthymēsis* from *G1760*; *deliberation:*— device, thought.

G1762 ἔνι *eni* contracted for third person singular present indicative of *G1751*; impersonal *there is* in or among:— be, (there) is.

G1763 ἐνιαυτός *eniautos* prolonged from a primary
ἔνος *enos* (a *year*); a *year:*— year.

G1764 ἐνίστημι *enistēmi* from *G1722* and *G2476*; to *place on* hand, i.e. (reflexive) *impend*, (participle) be *instant:*— come, be at hand, present.

G1765 ἐνισχύω *enischyō* from *G1722* and *G2480*; to *invigorate* (transitive or reflexive):— strengthen.

G1766 ἔννατος *ennatos* ordinal from *G1767*; *ninth* :— ninth.

G1767 ἐννέα *ennea* a primary number; *nine:*— nine.

G1768 ἐννενηκονταεννέα *ennenēkontaennea* from a (tenth) multiple of *G1767* and *G1767* itself; *ninety-nine:*— ninety and nine.

G1769 ἐννεός *enneos* from *G1770*; *dumb* (as *making signs*), i.e. *silent* from astonishment:— speechless.

G1770 ἐννεύω *enneuō* from *G1722* and *G3506*; to *nod at*, i.e. *beckon* or *communicate by gesture:*— make signs.

G1771 ἔννοια *ennoia* from a compound of *G1722* and *G3563*; *thoughtfulness*, i.e. moral *understanding:*— intent, mind.

G1772 ἔννομος *ennomos* from *G1722* and *G3551*; (subjectively) *legal*, or (objectively) *subject* to:— lawful, under law.

G1773 ἔννυχον *ennychon* neuter of a compound of *G1722* and *G3571*; (adverbially) *by night:*— before day.

G1774 ἐνοικέω *enoikeō* from *G1722* and *G3611*; to *inhabit* (figuratively):— dwell in.

G1775 ἑνότης *henotēs* from *G1520*; *oneness*, i.e. (figuratively) *unanimity:*— unity.

G1776 ἐνοχλέω *enochleō* from *G1722* and *G3791*; to *crowd in*, i.e. (figuratively) to *annoy:*— trouble.

G1777 ἔνοχος *enochos* from *G1758*; *liable* to (a condition, penalty or imputation):— in danger of, guilty of, subject to.

G1778 ἔνταλμα *entalma* from *G1781*; an *injunction*, i.e. religious *precept:*— commandment.

G1779 ἐνταφιάζω *entaphiazō* from a compound of *G1722* and *G5028*; to *swathe* with cerements for interment:— bury.

G1780 ἐνταφιασμός *entaphiasmos* from *G1779*; *preparation* for interment:— burying.

G1781 ἐντέλλομαι *entellomai* from *G1722* and the base of *G5056*; to *enjoin:*— (give) charge, command, give commandments, injoin.

G1782 ἐντεῦθεν *enteuthen* from the same as *G1759*; *hence* (literally or figuratively); (repeated) *on both sides:*— (from) hence, on either side.

G1783 ἔντευξις *enteuxis* from *G1793*; an *interview*, i.e. (specifically) *supplication:*— intercession, prayer.

G1784 ἔντιμος *entimos* from *G1722* and *G5092*; *valued* (figuratively):— dear, more honourable, precious, in reputation.

G1785 ἐντολή *entolē* from *G1781*; *injunction*, i.e. an authoritative *prescription:*— commandment, precept.

G1786 ἐντόπιος *entopios* from *G1722* and *G5117*; a *resident:*— of that place.

G1787 ἐντός *entos* from *G1722*; *inside* (adverb or noun):— within.

G1788 ἐντρέπω *entrepō* from *G1722* and the base of *G5157*; to *invert*, i.e. (figuratively and reflexive) in a good sense, to *respect;* or in a bad one, to *confound:*— regard, (give) reverence, shame.

G1789 ἐντρέφω *entrephō* from *G1722* and *G5142*; (figuratively) to *educate:*— nourish up in.

G1790 ἔντρομος *entromos* from *G1722* and *G5156*; *terrified:*— quake, trembled.

G1791 ἐντροπή *entropē* from *G1788*; *confusion:*— shame.

G1792 ἐντρυφάω *entryphaō* from *G1722* and *G5171*; to *revel in:*— sporting selves.

G1793 ἐντυγχάνω *entynchanō* from *G1722* and *G5177*; to *chance upon*, i.e. (by implication) *confer with;* by extension to *entreat* (in favor or against):— deal with, make intercession.

G1794 ἐντυλίσσω *entylissō* from *G1722* and
τυλίσσω *tylissō* (to *twist;* probably akin to *G1507*); to *entwine*, i.e. *wind up* in:— wrap in (together).

G1795 ἐντυπόω *entypoō* from *G1722* and a derivative of *G5179*; to *enstamp*, i.e. *engrave:*— engrave.

G1796 ἐνυβρίζω *enybrizō* from *G1722* and *G5195*; to *insult:*— do despite unto.

G1797 ἐνυπνιάζομαι *enypniazomai* middle from *G1798*; to *dream:*— dream, dreamer.

G1798 ἐνύπνιον *enypnion* from *G1722* and *G5258*; something seen *in sleep*, i.e. a *dream* (*vision* in a dream):— dream.

G1799 ἐνώπιον *enōpion* neuter of a compound of *G1722* and a derivative of *G3700*; *in the face* of (literally or figuratively):— before, in the presence (sight) of, to.

G1800 Ἐνώς *Enōs* of Hebrew origin [H583]; *Enos* (i.e. *Enosh*), a patriarch:— Enos.

G1801 ἐνωτίζομαι *enōtizomai* middle from a compound of *G1722* and *G3775*; to take *in one's ear*, i.e. to *listen:*— hearken.

G1802 Ἐνώχ *Enōch* of Hebrew origin [H2585]; *Enoch* (i.e. *Chanok*), an antediluvian:— Enoch.

G1803 ἕξ *hex* a primary numeral; *six:*— six.

G1804 **ἐξαγγέλλω** *exangellō* from *G1537* and the base of *G32*; to *publish* i.e. *celebrate:*— shew forth.

G1805 **ἐξαγοράζω** *exagorazō* from *G1537* and *G59*; to *buy up,* i.e. *ransom;* figuratively to *rescue* from loss (*improve* opportunity):— redeem.

G1806 **ἐξάγω** *exagō* from *G1537* and *G71*; to *lead forth:*— bring forth (out), fetch (lead) out.

G1807 **ἐξαιρέω** *exaireō* from *G1537* and *G138*; active, to *tear out;* middle, to *select;* figuratively, to *release:*— deliver, pluck out, rescue.

G1808 **ἐξαίρω** *exairō* from *G1537* and *G142*; to *remove:*— put (take) away.

G1809 **ἐξαιτέομαι** *exaiteomai* middle from *G1537* and *G154*; to *demand* (for trial):— desire.

G1810 **ἐξαίφνης** *exaiphnēs* from *G1537* and the base of *G160*; *of a sudden* (*unexpectedly*):— suddenly. Compare *G1819*.

G1811 **ἐξακολουθέω** *exakoloutheō* from *G1537* and *G190*; to *follow out,* i.e. (figuratively) to *imitate, obey,* yield to:— follow.

G1812 **ἑξακόσιοι** *hexakosioi* plural ordinal from *G1803* and *G1540*; *six hundred:*— six hundred.

G1813 **ἐξαλείφω** *exaleiphō* from *G1537* and *G218*; to *smear out,* i.e. *obliterate* (*erase* tears, figuratively *pardon* sin):— blot out, wipe away.

G1814 **ἐξάλλομαι** *exallomai* from *G1537* and *G242*; to *spring forth:*— leap up.

G1815 **ἐξανάστασις** *exanastasis* from *G1817*; a *rising from* death:— resurrection.

G1816 **ἐξανατέλλω** *exanatellō* from *G1537* and *G393*; to *start up out* of the ground, i.e. *germinate:*— spring up.

G1817 **ἐξανίστημι** *exanistēmi* from *G1537* and *G450*; objectively to *produce,* i.e. (figuratively) *beget;* subjectively to *arise,* i.e. (figuratively) *object:*— raise (rise) up.

G1818 **ἐξαπατάω** *exapataō* from *G1537* and *G538*; to *seduce wholly:*— beguile, deceive.

G1819 **ἐξάπινα** *exapina* from *G1537* and a derivative of the same as *G160*; *of a sudden,* i.e. *unexpectedly:*— suddenly. Compare *G1810*.

G1820 **ἐξαπορέομαι** *exaporeomai* middle from *G1537* and *G639*; to *be utterly at a loss,* i.e. *despond:*— (in) despair.

G1821 **ἐξαποστέλλω** *exapostellō* from *G1537* and *G649*; to *send away forth,* i.e. (on a mission) to *despatch,* or (peremptorily) to *dismiss:*— send (away, forth, out).

G1822 **ἐξαρτίζω** *exartizō* from *G1537* and a derivative of *G739*; to *finish out* (time); figuratively to *equip fully* (a teacher):— accomplish, thoroughly furnish.

G1823 **ἐξαστράπτω** *exastraptō* from *G1537* and *G797*; to *lighten forth,* i.e. (figuratively) to *be radiant* (of very white garments):— glistening.

G1824 **ἐξαυτῆς** *exautēs* from *G1537* and the genetic singular feminine of *G846* (*G5610* being understood); *from that* hour, i.e. *instantly:*— by and by, immediately, presently, straightway.

G1825 **ἐξεγείρω** *exegeirō* from *G1537* and *G1453*; to *rouse fully,* i.e. (figuratively) to *resuscitate* (from death), *release* (from infliction):— raise up.

G1826 **ἔξειμι** *exeimi* from *G1537* and
εἶμι *eimi* (to *go*); to *issue,* i.e. *leave* (a place), *escape* (to the shore):— depart, get [*to land*], go out.

G1827 **ἐξελέγχω** *exelenchō* from *G1537* and *G1651*; to *convict fully,* i.e. (by implication) to *punish:*— convince.

G1828 **ἐξέλκω** *exelkō* from *G1537* and *G1670*; to *drag forth,* i.e. (figuratively) to *entice* (to sin):— draw away.

G1829 **ἐξέραμα** *exerama* from a compound of *G1537* and a presumed
ἐράω *eraō* (to *spew*); *vomit,* i.e. *food disgorged:*— vomit.

G1830 **ἐξερευνάω** *exereunaō* from *G1537* and *G2045*; to *explore* (figuratively):— search diligently.

G1831 **ἐξέρχομαι** *exerchomai* from *G1537* and *G2064*; to *issue* (literally or figuratively):— come (forth, out), depart (out of), escape, get out, go (abroad, away, forth, out, thence), proceed (forth), spread abroad.

G1832 **ἔξεστι** *exesti* third person singular present indicative of a compound of *G1537*and *G1510*; so also
ἐξόν *exon* neuter present participle (with or without some form of *G1510* expressed); impersonal *it is right* (through the figurative idea of *being out* in public):— be lawful, let, may, mayest.

G1833 **ἐξετάζω** *exetazō* from *G1537* and
ἐτάζω *etazō* (to *examine*); to *test thoroughly* (by questions), i.e. *ascertain* or *interrogate:*— ask, inquire, search.

G1834 **ἐξηγέομαι** *exēgeomai* from *G1537* and *G2233*; to *consider out* (aloud), i.e. *rehearse, unfold:*— declare, tell.

G1835 **ἑξήκοντα** *hexēkonta* the tenth multiple of *G1803*; *sixty:*— sixty, sixtyfold, threescore.

G1836 **ἑξῆς** *hexēs* from *G2192* (in the sense of *taking hold* of, i.e. *adjoining*); *successive:*— after, following, morrow, next.

G1837 **ἐξηχέομαι** *exēcheomai* middle from *G1537* and *G2278*; to *"echo" forth,* i.e. *resound* (*be* generally *reported*):— sound forth.

G1838 **ἕξις** *hexis* from *G2192*; *habit,* i.e. (by implication) *practice:*— use.

G1839 **ἐξίστημι** *existēmi* from *G1537* and *G2476*; to *put* (*stand*) out of wits, i.e. *astound,* or (reflexive) *become astounded, insane:*— amaze, be (make) astonished, be beside self (selves), bewitch, wonder.

G1840 **ἐξισχύω** *exischyō* from *G1537* and *G2480*; to *have full strength,* i.e. *be entirely competent:*— be able.

G1841 **ἔξοδος** *exodos* from *G1537* and *G3598*; an *exit,* i.e. (figuratively) *death:*— decease, departing.

G1842 **ἐξολοθρεύω** *exolothreuō* from *G1537* and *G3645*; to *extirpate:*— destroy.

G1843 **ἐξομολογέω** *exomologeō* from *G1537* and *G3670*; to *acknowledge* or (by implication of *assent*) *agree fully:*— confess, profess, promise.

G1844 **ἐξορκίζω** *exorkizō* from *G1537* and *G3726*; to *exact an oath,* i.e. *conjure:*— adjure.

G1845 **ἐξορκιστής** *exorkistēs* from *G1844*; *one that binds by an oath* (or *spell*), i.e. (by implication) an *"exorcist"* (*conjurer*):— exorcist.

G1846 **ἐξορύσσω** *exoryssō* from *G1537* and *G3736*; to *dig out,* i.e. (by extension) to *extract* (an eye), *remove* (a roofing):— break up, pluck out.

G1847 **ἐξουδενόω** *exoudenoō* from *G1537* and a derivative of the neuter of *G3762*; to *make utterly nothing of,* i.e. *despise:*— set at nought. See also *G1848*.

G1848 **ἐξουθενέω** *exoutheneō* a variation of *G1847*; meaning the same as *G1847:*— contemptible, despise, least esteemed, set at nought.

G1849 **ἐξουσία** *exousia* from *G1832* (in the sense of *ability*); *privilege,* i.e. (subjectively) *force, capacity, competency, freedom,* or (objectively) *mastery* (concretely *magistrate, superhuman, potentate, token of control*), delegated *influence:*— authority, jurisdiction, liberty, power, right, strength.

G1850 **ἐξουσιάζω** *exousiazō* from *G1849*; to *control:*— exercise authority upon, bring under the (have) power of.

G1851 **ἐξοχή** *exochē* from a compound of *G1537* and *G2192* (meaning to *stand out*); *prominence* (figurative):— principal.

G1852 **ἐξυπνίζω** *exypnizō* from *G1853*; to *waken* :— awake out of sleep.

G1853 **ἔξυπνος** *exypnos* from *G1537* and *G5258*; *awake:*— out of sleep.

G1854 **ἔξω** *exō* adverb from *G1537*; *out, outside, out of doors,* literally or figuratively:— away, forth, out, without, out of, outward, strange.

G1855 **ἔξωθεν** *exōthen* from *G1854*; *external, externally:*— out, outside, outward, outwardly, (from) without.

G1856 **ἐξωθέω** *exōtheō* or
ἐξώθω *exōthō* from *G1537* and
ὠθέω *ōtheō* (to *push*); to *expel;* by implication to *propel:*— drive out, thrust in.

G1857 **ἐξώτερος** *exōteros* comparative of *G1854*; *exterior:*— outer.

G1858 **ἑορτάζω** *heortazō* from *G1859*; to *observe a festival:*— keep the feast.

G1859 **ἑορτή** *heortē* of uncertain affinity; a *festival:*— feast, holyday.

G1860 **ἐπαγγελία** *epangelia* from *G1861*; an *announcement* (for information, assent or pledge; especially a divine *assurance* of good):— message, promise.

G1861 **ἐπαγγέλλω** *epangellō* from *G1909* and the base of *G32*; to *announce upon* (reflexive), i.e. (by implication) to *engage* to do something, to *assert* something respecting oneself:— profess, (make) promise.

G1862 **ἐπάγγελμα** *epangelma* from *G1861*; a *self-committal* (by *assurance* of conferring some good) :— promise.

G1863 **ἐπάγω** *epagō* from *G1909* and *G71*; to *superinduce,* i.e. *inflict* (an evil), *charge* (a crime):— bring upon.

G1864 **ἐπαγωνίζομαι** *epagōnizomai* from *G1909* and *G75*; to *struggle for:*— earnestly contend for.

G1865 **ἐπαθροίζω** *epathroizō* from *G1909* and
ἀθροίζω *athroizō* (to *assemble*); to *accumulate:*— gather thick together.

G1866 **Ἐπαίνετος** *Epainetos* from *G1867*; *praised; Epaenetus,* a Christian:— Epenetus.

G1867 **ἐπαινέω** *epaineō* from *G1909* and *G134*; to *applaud:*— commend, laud, praise.

G1868 **ἔπαινος** *epainos* from *G1909* and the base of *G134*; *laudation;* concretely a *commendable* thing :— praise.

G1869 ἐπαίρω *epairō* from G1909 and G142; to *raise up* (literally or figuratively):— exalt self, poise (lift, take) up.

G1870 ἐπαισχύνομαι *epaischynomai* from G1909 and G153; to *feel shame for* something:— be ashamed.

G1871 ἐπαιτέω *epaiteō* from G1909 and G154; to *ask for:*— beg.

G1872 ἐπακολουθέω *epakoloutheō* from G1909 and G190; to *accompany:*— follow (after).

G1873 ἐπακούω *epakouō* from G1909 and G191; to *hearken* (favorably) *to:*— hear.

G1874 ἐπακροάομαι *epakroaomai* from G1909 and the base of G202; to *listen* (intently) *to:*— hear.

G1875 ἐπάν *epan* from G1909 and G302; a particle of indefinite contemporaneousness; *whenever, as soon as:*— when.

G1876 ἐπάναγκες *epanankes* neuter of a presumed compound of G1909 and G318; (adverbly) *on necessity,* i.e. *necessarily:*— necessary.

G1877 ἐπανάγω *epanagō* from G1909 and G321; to *lead up on,* i.e. (technically) to *put out* (to sea); (intransitive) to *return:*— launch (thrust) out, return.

G1878 ἐπαναμιμνήσκω *epanamimnēskō* from G1909 and G363; to *remind of:*— put in mind.

G1879 ἐπαναπαύομαι *epanapauomai* middle from G1909 and G373; to *settle on;* literally (*remain*) or figuratively (*rely*):— rest in (upon).

G1880 ἐπανέρχομαι *epanerchomai* from G1909 and G424; to *come up on,* i.e. *return:*— come again, return.

G1881 ἐπανίσταμαι *epanistamai* middle from G1909 and G450; to *stand up on,* i.e. (figuratively) to *attack:*— rise up against.

G1882 ἐπανόρθωσις *epanorthōsis* from a compound of G1909 and G461; a *straightening up again,* i.e. (figuratively) *rectification* (*reformation*):— correction.

G1883 ἐπάνω *epanō* from G1909 and G507; *up above,* i.e. *over* or *on* (of place, amount, rank, etc.):— above, more than, on, upon, over.

G1884 ἐπαρκέω *eparkeō* from G1909 and G714; to *avail for,* i.e. *help:*— relieve.

G1885 ἐπαρχία *eparchia* from a compound of G1909 and G757 (meaning a *governor* of a district, "eparch"); a special *region* of government, i.e. a Roman *praefecture:*— province.

G1886 ἔπαυλις *epaulis* from G1909 and an equivalent of G833; a *hut over* the head, i.e. a *dwelling:*— habitation.

G1887 ἐπαύριον *epaurion* from G1909 and G839; occurring *on* the *succeeding* day, i.e. (G2250 being implied) *to-morrow:*— day following, morrow, next day (after).

G1888 ἐπαυτοφώρῳ *epautophōrō* from G1909 and G846 and (the dative singular of) a derivative of

φώρ *phōr* (a *thief*); *in theft itself,* i.e. (by analogy) *in actual crime:*— in the very act.

G1889 Ἐπαφρᾶς *Epaphras* contraction from G1891; *Epaphras,* a Christian:— Epaphras.

G1890 ἐπαφρίζω *epaphrizō* from G1909 and G875; to *foam upon,* i.e. (figuratively) to *exhibit* (a vile passion):— foam out.

G1891 Ἐπαφρόδιτος *Epaphroditos* from G1909 (in the sense of *devoted* to) and

Ἀφροδίτη *Aphroditē* (*Venus*); *Epaphroditus,* a Christian:— Epaphroditus. Compare G1889.

G1892 ἐπεγείρω *epegeirō* from G1909 and G1453; to *rouse upon,* i.e. (figuratively) to *excite* against:— raise, stir up.

G1893 ἐπεί *epei* from G1909 and G1487; *thereupon,* i.e. *since* (of time or cause):— because, else, for that (then), forasmuch as, otherwise, seeing that, since, when.

G1894 ἐπειδή *epeidē* from G1893 and G1211; *since now,* i.e. (of time) *when* or (of cause) *whereas:*— after that, because, for (that), forasmuch as, seeing, since.

G1895 ἐπειδήπερ *epeidēper* from G1894 and G4007; *since indeed* (of cause):— forasmuch.

G1896 ἐπεῖδον *epeidon* and other moods and persons of the same tense; from G1909 and G1492; to *regard* (favorably or otherwise):— behold, look upon.

G1897 ἐπείπερ *epeiper* from G1893 and G4007; *since* indeed (of cause):— seeing.

G1898 ἐπεισαγωγή *epeisagōgē* from a compound of G1909 and G1521; an *introduction in addition:*— bringing in.

G1899 ἔπειτα *epeita* from G1909 and G1534; *thereafter:*— after that, afterward, then.

G1900 ἐπέκεινα *epekeina* from G1909 and (the accusative plural neuter of) G1565; *upon those* parts of, i.e. *on the further side of:*— beyond.

G1901 ἐπεκτείνομαι *epekteinomai* middle from G1909 and G1614; to *stretch* (oneself) forward *upon:*— reach forth.

G1902 ἐπενδύομαι *ependyomai* middle from G1909 and G1746; to *invest upon* oneself:— be clothed upon.

G1903 ἐπενδύτης *ependytēs* from G1902; a *wrapper,* i.e. outer garment:— fisher's coat.

G1904 ἐπέρχομαι *eperchomai* from G1909 and G2064; to *supervene,* i.e. *arrive, occur, impend, attack,* (figuratively) *influence:*— come (in, upon).

G1905 ἐπερωτάω *eperōtaō* from G1909 and G2065; to *ask for,* i.e. *inquire, seek:*— ask (after, questions), demand, desire, question.

G1906 ἐπερώτημα *eperōtēma* from G1905; an *inquiry:*— answer.

G1907 ἐπέχω *epechō* from G1909 and G2192; to *hold upon,* i.e. (by implication) to *retain;* (by extension) to *detain;* (with by implication of G3563) to *pay attention to:*— give (take) heed unto, hold forth, mark, stay.

G1908 ἐπηρεάζω *epēreazō* from a compound of G1909 and (probably)

ἀρειά *areia* (*threats*); to *insult, slander:*— use despitefully, falsely accuse.

G1909 ἐπί *epi* a primary preposition properly meaning *superimposition* (of time, place, order, etc.); as a relation of *distribution* [with the genitive], i.e. *over, upon,* etc.; of *rest* (with the dative) *at, on,* etc.; of *direction* (with the accusative) *towards, upon,* etc. In compounds it retains essentially the same import, *at, upon,* etc. (literally or figuratively):— about (the times), above, after, against, among, as long as (touching), at, beside, have charge of, fore, before, wherefore, in (a place, as much as, the time of), into, (because) of, on (behalf of), upon, over, (by, for) the space of, through, throughout, to, unto, toward, with.

G1910 ἐπιβαίνω *epibainō* from G1909 and the base of G939; to *walk upon,* i.e. *mount, ascend, embark, arrive:*— come (into), enter into, go abroad, sit upon, take ship.

G1911 ἐπιβάλλω *epiballō* from G1909 and G906; to *throw upon* (literally or figuratively, transitive or reflexive; usually with more or less force); specifically (with G1438 implied) to *reflect;* impersonally to *belong to:*— beat into, cast on, cast upon, fall, lay (on), put (unto), stretch forth, think on.

G1912 ἐπιβαρέω *epibareō* from G1909 and G916; to *be heavy upon,* i.e. (in a pecuniary sense) to *be expensive to;* figuratively to *be severe towards:*— be chargeable to, overcharge.

G1913 ἐπιβιβάζω *epibibazō* from G1909 and a reduplicated derivative of the base of G939 [compare G307]; to *cause to mount* (an animal):— set on.

G1914 ἐπιβλέπω *epiblepō* from G1909 and G991; to *gaze at* (with favor, pity or partiality):— look upon, regard, have respect to.

G1915 ἐπίβλημα *epiblēma* from G1911; a *patch* :— piece.

G1916 ἐπιβοάω *epiboaō* from G1909 and G994; to *exclaim against:*— cry.

G1917 ἐπιβουλή *epiboulē* from a presumed compound of G1909 and G1014; a *plan against* someone, i.e. a *plot:*— laying (lying) in wait.

G1918 ἐπιγαμβρεύω *epigambreuō* from G1909 and a derivative of G1062; to *form affinity with,* i.e. (specifically) in a levirate way:— marry.

G1919 ἐπίγειος *epigeios* from G1909 and G1093; *worldly* (physically or morally):— earthly, in earth, terrestrial.

G1920 ἐπιγίνομαι *epiginomai* from G1909 and G1096; to *arrive upon,* i.e. *spring up* (as a wind) :— blow.

G1921 ἐπιγινώσκω *epiginōskō* from G1909 and G1097; to *know upon* some mark, i.e. *recognize;* by implication to *become fully acquainted with,* to *acknowledge:*— know (well), acknowledge, (have, take) knowledge, perceive.

G1922 ἐπίγνωσις *epignōsis* from G1921; *recognition,* i.e. (by implication) full *discernment, acknowledgment:*— knowledge, acknowledge, acknowledging, acknowledgement.

G1923 ἐπιγραφή *epigraphē* from G1924; an *inscription:*— superscription.

G1924 ἐπιγράφω *epigraphō* from G1909 and G1125; to *inscribe* (physically or mentally):— inscription, write in (over, thereon).

G1925 ἐπιδείκνυμι *epideiknymi* from G1909 and G1166; to *exhibit* (physically or mentally):— shew.

G1926 ἐπιδέχομαι *epidechomai* from G1909 and G1209; to *admit* (as a guest or [figuratively] teacher):— receive.

G1927 ἐπιδημέω *epidēmeō* from a compound of G1909 and G1218; to *make oneself at home,* i.e. (by extension) to *reside* (in a foreign country):— [be] dwelling (which were) there, stranger.

G1928 ἐπιδιατάσσομαι *epidiatassomai* middle from G1909 and G1299; to *appoint besides,* i.e. *supplement* (as a codicil):— add to.

G1929 ἐπιδίδωμι *epididōmi* from G1909 and G1325; to *give over* (by hand or surrender):— deliver unto, give, let (+ [her drive]), offer.

G1930 **ἐπιδιορθόω** *epidiorthoō* from *G1909* and a derivative of *G3717*; to *straighten further,* i.e. (figuratively) *arrange additionally:—* set in order.

G1931 **ἐπιδύω** *epidyō* from *G1909* and *G1416*; to *set* fully (as the sun):— go down.

G1932 **ἐπιείκεια** *epieikeia* from *G1933*; *suitableness,* i.e. (by implication) *equity, mildness:—* clemency, gentleness.

G1933 **ἐπιεικής** *epieikēs* from *G1909* and *G1503*; *appropriate,* i.e. (by implication) *mild:—* gentle, moderation, patient.

G1934 **ἐπιζητέω** *epizēteō* from *G1909* and *G2212*; to *search* (*inquire*) *for;* intensively to *demand,* to *crave:—* desire, inquire, seek (after, for).

G1935 **ἐπιθανάτιος** *epithanatios* from *G1909* and *G2288*; doomed *to death:—* appointed to death.

G1936 **ἐπίθεσις** *epithesis* from *G2007*; an *imposition* (of hands officially):— laying (putting) on.

G1937 **ἐπιθυμέω** *epithymeō* from *G1909* and *G2372*; to set the *heart upon,* i.e. *long* for (rightfully or otherwise):— covet, desire, would fain, lust (after).

G1938 **ἐπιθυμητής** *epithymētēs* from *G1937*; a *craver:—* lust after.

G1939 **ἐπιθυμία** *epithymia* from *G1937*; a *longing* (especially for what is forbidden):— concupiscence, desire, lust (after).

G1940 **ἐπικαθίζω** *epikathizō* from *G1909* and *G2523*; to *seat upon:—* set upon.

G1941 **ἐπικαλέομαι** *epikaleomai* middle from *G1909* and *G2564*; to *entitle;* by implication to *invoke* (for aid, worship, testimony, decision, etc.):— appeal (unto), call (on, upon), surname.

G1942 **ἐπικάλυμμα** *epikalymma* from *G1943*; a *covering,* i.e. (figuratively) *pretext:—* cloke.

G1943 **ἐπικαλύπτω** *epikalyptō* from *G1909* and *G2572*; to *conceal,* i.e. (figuratively) *forgive:—* cover.

G1944 **ἐπικατάρατος** *epikataratos* from *G1909* and a derivative of *G2672*; *imprecated,* i.e. *execrable:—* accursed.

G1945 **ἐπίκειμαι** *epikeimai* from *G1909* and *G2749*; to *rest upon* (literally or figuratively):— impose, be instant, (be) laid (on, thereon, upon), (when) lay (on), lie (on), press upon.

G1946 **Ἐπικούρειος** *Epikoureios* from **Ἐπίκουρος** *Epikouros* [compare *G1947*] (a noted philosopher); an *Epicurean* or follower of Epicurus:— Epicurean.

G1947 **ἐπικουρία** *epikouria* from a compound of *G1909* and a (prolonged) form of the base of *G2877* (in the sense of *servant*); *assistance:—* help.

G1948 **ἐπικρίνω** *epikrinō* from *G1909* and *G2919*; to *adjudge:—* give sentence.

G1949 **ἐπιλαμβάνομαι** *epilambanomai* middle from *G1909* and *G2983*; to *seize* (for help, injury, attainment or any other purpose; literally or figuratively):— catch, lay hold (on upon), take (by, hold of, on).

G1950 **ἐπιλανθάνομαι** *epilanthanomai* middle from *G1909* and *G2990*; to *lose out* of mind; by implication to *neglect:—* forget, be forgetful (of).

G1951 **ἐπιλέγομαι** *epilegomai* middle from *G1909* and *G3004*; to *surname, select:—* call, choose.

G1952 **ἐπιλείπω** *epileipō* from *G1909* and *G3007*; to *leave upon,* i.e. (figuratively) to *be insufficient for:—* fail.

G1953 **ἐπιλησμονή** *epilēsmonē* from a derivative of *G1950*; *negligence:—* forgetful.

G1954 **ἐπίλοιπος** *epiloipos* from *G1909* and *G3062*; *left over,* i.e. *remaining:—* rest.

G1955 **ἐπίλυσις** *epilysis* from *G1956*; *explanation,* i.e. *application:—* interpretation.

G1956 **ἐπιλύω** *epilyō* from *G1909* and *G3089*; to *solve further,* i.e. (figuratively) to *explain, decide:—* determine, expound.

G1957 **ἐπιμαρτυρέω** *epimartyreō* from *G1909* and *G3140*; to *attest further,* i.e. *corroborate:—* testify.

G1958 **ἐπιμέλεια** *epimeleia* from *G1959*; *carefulness,* i.e. kind *attention* (*hospitality*):— refresh self.

G1959 **ἐπιμελέομαι** *epimeleomai* middle from *G1909* and the same as *G3199*; to *care for* (physically or otherwise):— take care of.

G1960 **ἐπιμελῶς** *epimelōs* adverb from a derivative of *G1959*; *carefully:—* diligently.

G1961 **ἐπιμένω** *epimenō* from *G1909* and *G3306*; to *stay over,* i.e. *remain* (figuratively *persevere*):— abide (in), continue (in), tarry.

G1962 **ἐπινεύω** *epineuō* from *G1909* and *G3506*; to *nod at,* i.e. (by implication) to *assent:—* consent.

G1963 **ἐπίνοια** *epinoia* from *G1909* and *G3563*; *attention* of the mind, i.e. (by implication) *purpose:—* thought.

G1964 **ἐπιορκέω** *epiorkeō* from *G1965*; to *commit perjury:—* forswear self.

G1965 **ἐπίορκος** *epiorkos* from *G1909* and *G3727*; *on oath,* i.e. (falsely) a *forswearer:—* perjured person.

G1966 **ἐπιοῦσα** *epiousa* feminine singular participle of a compound of *G1909* and **εἶμι** *heimi* (to *go*); *supervening,* i.e. (*G2250* or *G3571* being expressed or implied) the *ensuing* day or night:— following, next.

G1967 **ἐπιούσιος** *epiousios* perhaps from the same as *G1966*; *to-morrow's;* but more probably from *G1909* and a derivative of the present participle feminine of *G1510*; *for subsistence,* i.e. *needful:—* daily.

G1968 **ἐπιπίπτω** *epipiptō* from *G1909* and *G4098*; to *embrace* (with affection) or *seize* (with more or less violence; literal or figurative):— fall into (on, upon), lie on, press upon.

G1969 **ἐπιπλήσσω** *epiplēssō* from *G1909* and *G4141*; to *chastise,* i.e. (with words) to *upbraid:—* rebuke.

G1970 **ἐπιπνίγω** *epipnigō* from *G1909* and *G4155*; to *throttle upon,* i.e. (figuratively) *overgrow:—* choke.

G1971 **ἐπιποθέω** *epipotheō* from *G1909* and **ποθέω** *potheō* (to *yearn*); to *dote upon,* i.e. *intensely crave* possession (lawfully or wrongfully):— (earnestly) desire (greatly), (greatly) long (after), lust.

G1972 **ἐπιπόθησις** *epipothēsis* from *G1971*; a *longing for:—* earnest (vehement) desire.

G1973 **ἐπιπόθητος** *epipothētos* from *G1909* and a derivative of the latter part of *G1971*; *yearned upon,* i.e. *greatly loved:—* longed for.

G1974 **ἐπιποθία** *epipothia* from *G1971*; *intense longing:—* great desire.

G1975 **ἐπιπορεύομαι** *epiporeuomai* from *G1909* and *G4198*; to *journey further,* i.e. *travel on* (*reach*):— come.

G1976 **ἐπιρράπτω** *epirrhaptō* from *G1909* and the base of *G4476*; to *stitch upon,* i.e. *fasten* with the needle:— sew on.

G1977 **ἐπιρρίπτω** *epirrhiptō* from *G1909* and *G4496*; to *throw upon* (literally or figuratively):— cast upon.

G1978 **ἐπίσημος** *episēmos* from *G1909* and some form of the base of *G4591*; *remarkable,* i.e. (figuratively) *eminent:—* notable, of note.

G1979 **ἐπισιτισμός** *episitismos* from a compound of *G1909* and a derivative of *G4621*; a *provisioning,* i.e. (concretely) *food:—* victuals.

G1980 **ἐπισκέπτομαι** *episkeptomai* middle from *G1909* and the base of *G4649*; to *inspect,* i.e. (by implication) to *select;* by extension to *go to see, relieve:—* look out, visit.

G1981 **ἐπισκηνόω** *episkēnoō* from *G1909* and *G4637*; to *tent upon,* i.e. (figuratively) *abide with* :— rest upon.

G1982 **ἐπισκιάζω** *episkiazō* from *G1909* and a derivative of *G4639*; to *cast a shade upon,* i.e. (by analogy) to *envelop* in a haze of brilliancy; figuratively to *invest* with preternatural influence:— overshadow.

G1983 **ἐπισκοπέω** *episkopeō* from *G1909* and *G4648*; to *oversee;* by implication to *beware:—* look diligently, take the oversight.

G1984 **ἐπισκοπή** *episkopē* from *G1980*; *inspection* (for relief); by implication *superintendence;* specifically the Christian *"episcopate":—* the office of a "bishop", bishoprick, visitation.

G1985 **ἐπίσκοπος** *episkopos* from *G1909* and *G4649* (in the sense of *G1983*); a *superintendent,* i.e. Christian officer in general charge of a (or the) church (literally or figuratively):— bishop, overseer.

G1986 **ἐπισπάομαι** *epispaomai* from *G1909* and *G4685*; to *draw over,* i.e. (with *G203* implied) *efface* the mark of *circumcision* (by recovering with the foreskin):— become uncircumcised.

G1987 **ἐπίσταμαι** *epistamai* apparently a middle of *G2186* (with *G3563* implied); to *put* the mind *upon,* i.e. *comprehend,* or *be acquainted with:—* know, understand.

G1988 **ἐπιστάτης** *epistatēs* from *G1909* and a presumed derivative of *G2476*; an *appointee over,* i.e. *commander* (*teacher*):— master.

G1989 **ἐπιστέλλω** *epistellō* from *G1909* and *G4724*; to *enjoin* (by writing), i.e. (generally) to *communicate by letter* (for any purpose):— write (a letter, unto).

G1990 **ἐπιστήμων** *epistēmōn* from *G1987*; *intelligent:—* endued with knowledge.

G1991 **ἐπιστηρίζω** *epistērizō* from *G1909* and *G4741*; to *support further,* i.e. *reestablish:—* confirm, strengthen.

G1992 **ἐπιστολή** *epistolē* from *G1989*; a *written message:—* "epistle", letter.

G1993 **ἐπιστομίζω** *epistomizō* from *G1909* and *G4750*; to put something *over* the *mouth,* i.e. (figuratively) to *silence:—* stop mouths.

G1994 **ἐπιστρέφω** *epistrephō* from *G1909* and *G4762*; to *revert* (literally, figuratively or morally):— come (go) again, convert, turn (about, again), return.

G1995 **ἐπιστροφή** *epistrophē* from *G1994*; *reversion,* i.e. moral *revolution:*— conversion.

G1996 **ἐπισυνάγω** *episynagō* from *G1909* and *G4863*; to *collect upon* the same place:— gather (together).

G1997 **ἐπισυναγωγή** *episynagōgē* from *G1996*; a complete *collection;* specifically a Christian *meeting* (for worship):— assembling (gathering) together.

G1998 **ἐπισυντρέχω** *episyntrechō* from *G1909* and *G4936*; to *hasten together upon* one place (or a particular occasion):— come running together.

G1999 **ἐπισύστασις** *episystasis* from the middle of a compound of *G1909* and *G4921*; a *conspiracy,* i.e. *concourse* (riotous or friendly):— that which cometh upon, raising up.

G2000 **ἐπισφαλής** *episphalēs* from a compound of *G1909* and

σφάλλω *sphallō* (to *trip*); figuratively *insecure:*— dangerous.

G2001 **ἐπισχύω** *epischyō* from *G1909* and *G2480*; to *avail further,* i.e. (figuratively) *insist stoutly:*— be the more fierce.

G2002 **ἐπισωρεύω** *episōreuō* from *G1909* and *G4987*; to *accumulate further,* i.e. (figuratively) *seek* additionally:— heap.

G2003 **ἐπιταγή** *epitagē* from *G2004*; an *injunction* or *decree;* by implication *authority:*— authority, commandment.

G2004 **ἐπιτάσσω** *epitassō* from *G1909* and *G5021*; to *arrange upon,* i.e. *order:*— charge, command, injoin.

G2005 **ἐπιτελέω** *epiteleō* from *G1909* and *G5055*; to *fulfill further* (or *completely*), i.e. *execute;* by implication to *terminate, undergo:*— accomplish, do, finish, (make) (perfect), perform, performance.

G2006 **ἐπιτήδειος** *epitēdeios* from

ἐπιτηδές *epitēdes* (*enough*); *serviceable,* i.e. (by implication) *requisite:*— things which are needful.

G2007 **ἐπιτίθημι** *epitithēmi* from *G1909* and *G5087*; to *impose* (in a friendly or hostile sense) :— add unto, lade, lay upon, put (up) on, set on (up), surname, wound.

G2008 **ἐπιτιμάω** *epitimaō* from *G1909* and *G5091*; to *tax upon,* i.e. *censure* or *admonish;* by implication *forbid:*— (straitly) charge, rebuke.

G2009 **ἐπιτιμία** *epitimia* from a compound of *G1909* and *G5092*; properly *esteem,* i.e. *citizenship;* used (in the sense of *G2008*) of a *penalty:*— punishment.

G2010 **ἐπιτρέπω** *epitrepō* from *G1909* and the base of *G5157*; to *turn over* (*transfer*), i.e. *allow:*— give leave (liberty, license), let, permit, suffer.

G2011 **ἐπιτροπή** *epitropē* from *G2010*; *permission,* i.e. (by implication) full *power:*— commission.

G2012 **ἐπίτροπος** *epitropos* from *G1909* and *G5158* (in the sense of *G2011*); a *commissioner,* i.e. domestic *manager, guardian:*— steward, tutor.

G2013 **ἐπιτυγχάνω** *epitynchanō* from *G1909* and *G5177*; to *chance upon,* i.e. (by implication) *attain:*— obtain.

G2014 **ἐπιφαίνω** *epiphainō* from *G1909* and *G5316*; to *shine upon,* i.e. *become* (literally) *visible* or (figuratively) *known:*— appear, give light.

G2015 **ἐπιφάνεια** *epiphaneia* from *G2016*; a *manifestation,* i.e. (specifically) the *advent* of Christ (past or future):— appearing, brightness.

G2016 **ἐπιφανής** *epiphanēs* from *G2014*; *conspicuous,* i.e. (figuratively) *memorable:*— notable.

G2017 **ἐπιφαύω** *epiphauō* a form of *G2014*; to *illuminate* (figuratively):— give light.

G2018 **ἐπιφέρω** *epipherō* from *G1909* and *G5342*; to *bear upon* (or *further*), i.e. *adduce* (personally or judicially [*accuse, inflict*]), *induce additionally:*— add, bring (against), take.

G2019 **ἐπιφωνέω** *epiphōneō* from *G1909* and *G5455*; to *call at* something, i.e. *exclaim:*— cry (against), give a shout.

G2020 **ἐπιφώσκω** *epiphōskō* a form of *G2017*; to begin to *grow light:*— begin to dawn, draw on.

G2021 **ἐπιχειρέω** *epicheireō* from *G1909* and *G5495*; to put the *hand upon,* i.e. *undertake:*— go about, take in hand (upon).

G2022 **ἐπιχέω** *epicheō* from *G1909* and

χέω *cheō* (to *pour*); to *pour upon:*— pour in.

G2023 **ἐπιχορηγέω** *epichorēgeō* from *G1909* and *G5524*; to *furnish besides,* i.e. fully *supply,* (figuratively) *aid* or *contribute:*— add, minister (nourishment, unto).

G2024 **ἐπιχορηγία** *epichorēgia* from *G2023*; *contribution:*— supply.

G2025 **ἐπιχρίω** *epichriō* from *G1909* and *G5548*; to *smear over:*— anoint.

G2026 **ἐποικοδομέω** *epoikodomeō* from *G1909* and *G3618*; to *build upon,* i.e. (figuratively) to *rear up:*— build thereon (thereupon, on, upon).

G2027 **ἐποκέλλω** *epokellō* from *G1909* and

ὀκέλλω *okellō* (to *urge*); to *drive upon* the shore, i.e. to *beach* a vessel:— run aground.

G2028 **ἐπονομάζω** *eponomazō* from *G1909* and *G3687*; to *name further,* i.e. *denominate:*— call.

G2029 **ἐποπτεύω** *epopteuō* from *G1909* and a derivative of *G3700*; to *inspect,* i.e. *watch:*— behold.

G2030 **ἐπόπτης** *epoptēs* from *G1909* and a presumed derivative of *G3700*; a *looker- on:*— eye-witness.

G2031 **ἔπος** *epos* from *G2036*; a *word:*— say.

G2032 **ἐπουράνιος** *epouranios* from *G1909* and *G3772*; *above* the *sky:*— celestial, (in) heaven, heavenly, high.

G2033 **ἑπτά** *hepta* a primary number; *seven:*— seven.

G2034 **ἑπτάκις** *heptakis* adverb from *G2033*; *seven times:*— seven times.

G2035 **ἑπτακισχίλιοι** *heptakischilioi* from *G2034* and *G5507*; *seven times a thousand:*— seven thousand.

G2036 **ἔπω** *epō* a primary verb (used only in the definite past tense, the others being borrowed from *G2046*, *G4483* and *G5346*); to *speak* or *say* (by word or writing):— answer, bid, bring word, call, command, grant, say (on), speak, tell. Compare *G3004*.

G2037 **Ἔραστος** *Erastos* from

ἐράω *eraō* (to *love*); *beloved; Erastus,* a Christian:— Erastus.

G2038 **ἐργάζομαι** *ergazomai* middle from *G2041*; to *toil* (as a task, occupation, etc.), (by implication) *effect, be engaged in* or *with,* etc.:— commit, do, labor for, minister about, trade (by), work.

G2039 **ἐργασία** *ergasia* from *G2040*; *occupation;* by implication *profit, pains:*— craft, diligence, gain, work.

G2040 **ἐργάτης** *ergatēs* from *G2041*; a *toiler;* figuratively a *teacher:*— labourer, worker, workmen.

G2041 **ἔργον** *ergon* from a primary (but obsolete)

ἔργον *ergon* (to *work*); *toil* (as an effort or occupation); by implication an *act:*— deed, doing, labour, work.

G2042 **ἐρεθίζω** *erethizō* from a presumed prolonged form of *G2054*; to *stimulate* (especially to anger):— provoke.

G2043 **ἐρείδω** *ereidō* of obscure affinity; to *prop,* i.e. (reflexive) *get fast:*— stick fast.

G2044 **ἐρεύγομαι** *ereugomai* of uncertain affinity; to *belch,* i.e. (figuratively) to *speak out:*— utter.

G2045 **ἐρευνάω** *ereunaō* apparently from *G2046* (through the idea of *inquiry*); to *seek,* i.e. (figuratively) to *investigate:*— search.

G2046 **ἐρέω** *ereō* probably a fuller form of *G4483*; an alternate for *G2036* in certain tenses; to *utter,* i.e. *speak* or *say:*— call, say, speak (of), tell.

G2047 **ἐρημία** *erēmia* from *G2048*; *solitude* (concrete):— desert, wilderness.

G2048 **ἔρημος** *erēmos* of uncertain affinity; *lonesome,* i.e. (by implication) *waste* (usually as a noun, *G5561* being implied):— desert, desolate, solitary, wilderness.

G2049 **ἐρημόω** *erēmoō* from *G2048*; to *lay waste* (literally or figuratively):— (bring to, make) desolate, desolation, come to nought.

G2050 **ἐρήμωσις** *erēmōsis* from *G2049*; *despoliation:*— desolation.

G2051 **ἐρίζω** *erizō* from *G2054*; to *wrangle:*— strive.

G2052 **ἐριθεία** *eritheia* perhaps from the same as *G2042*; properly *intrigue,* i.e. (by implication) *faction:*— contention, contentious, strife.

G2053 **ἔριον** *erion* of obscure affinity; *wool:*— wool.

G2054 **ἔρις** *eris* of uncertain affinity; a *quarrel,* i.e. (by implication) *wrangling:*— contention, debate, strife, variance.

G2055 **ἐρίφιον** *eriphion* from *G2056*; a *small kid,* i.e. (generally) *goat* (symbolically *wicked* person):— goat.

G2056 **ἔριφος** *eriphos* perhaps from the same as *G2053* (through the idea of *hairiness*); a *kid* or (generally) *goat:*— goat, kid.

G2057 **Ἑρμᾶς** *Hermas* probably from *G2060*; *Hermas,* a Christian:— Hermas.

G2058 **ἑρμηνεία** *hermēneia* from the same as *G2059*; *translation:*— interpretation.

G2059 **ἑρμηνεύω** *hermēneuō* from a presumed derivative of *G2060* (as the god of language); to *translate:*— interpret.

G2060 **Ἑρμῆς** *Hermēs* perhaps from *G2046*; *Hermes,* the name of the messenger of the Greek deities; also of a Christian:— Hermes, Mercury.

G2061 **Ἑρμογένης** *Hermogenēs* from *G2060* and *G1096*; *born of Hermes; Hermogenes,* an apostate Christian:— Hermogenes.

G2062 ἑρπετόν *herpeton* neuter of a derivative of **ἕρπω** *herpō* (to *creep*); a *reptile,* i.e. (by Hebrew [compare H7431]) a small *animal:*— creeping thing, serpent.

G2063 ἐρυθρός *erythros* of uncertain affinity; *red,* i.e. (with G2281) the *Red* Sea:— red.

G2064 ἔρχομαι *erchomai* middle of a primary verb (used only in the presonal and imperfect tenses, the others being supplied by a kindred [middle] **ἐλεύθομαι** *eleuthomai* or [active] **ἔλθω** *elthō* which do not otherwise occur); to *come* or *go* (in a great variety of applications, literally and figuratively):— accompany, appear, bring, come, enter, fall out, go, grow, light, next, pass, resort, be set.

G2065 ἐρωτάω *erōtaō* apparently from G2046 [compare G2045]; to *interrogate;* by implication to *request:*— ask, beseech, desire, intreat, pray. Compare G4441.

G2066 ἐσθής *esthēs* from **ἕννυμι** *hennymi* (to *clothe*); *dress:*— apparel, clothing, raiment, robe.

G2067 ἔσθησις *esthēsis* from a derivative of G2066; *clothing* (concrete):— government.

G2068 ἐσθίω *esthiō* strengthened for a primary **ἔδω** *edō* (to *eat*); used only in certain tenses, the rest being supplied by G5315; to *eat* (usually literally):— devour, eat, live.

G2069 Ἐσλί *Esli* of Hebrew origin [probably for H454]; *Esli,* an Israelite:— Esli.

G2070 ἐσμέν *esmen* first person plural indicative of G1510; we *are:*— are, be, have our being, have hope, [the gospel] was [preached unto] us.

G2071 ἔσομαι *esomai* future of G1510; *will be:*— shall (should) be (have), (shall) come (to pass), may have, fall, what would follow, live long, sojourn.

G2072 ἔσοπτρον *esoptron* from G1519 and a presumed derivative of G3700; a *mirror* (for *looking into*):— glass. Compare G2734.

G2073 ἑσπέρα *hespera* feminine of an adjective **ἑσπερος** *hesperos* (*evening*); the *eve* (G5610 being implied):— evening, eventide.

G2074 Ἐσρώμ *Esrōm* of Hebrew origin [H2696]; *Esrom* (i.e. *Chetsron*), an Israelite:— Esrom.

G2075 ἐστέ *este* second person plural present indicative of G1510; ye *are:*— be, have been, belong.

G2076 ἐστί *esti* third person singular present indicative of G1510; he (she or it) *is;* also (with neuter plural) they *are:*— are, be, belong, call, can, cannot, come, consisteth, dure for awhile, follow, have, (that) is (to say), make, meaneth, must needs, profit, remaineth, wrestle.

G2077 ἔστω *estō* second person singular present imperative of G1510; *be* thou; also **ἔστωσαν** *estōsan* third person plural; *let* them *be:*— be.

G2078 ἔσχατος *eschatos* a superlative probably from G2192 (in the sense of *contiguity*); *farthest, final* (of place or time):— ends of, last, latter end, lowest, uttermost.

G2079 ἐσχάτως *eschatōs* adverb from G2078; *finally,* i.e. (with G2192) *at the extremity* of life:— point of death.

G2080 ἔσω *esō* from G1519; *inside* (as preposition or adjective):— in, within, inner, into, inward.

G2081 ἔσωθεν *esōthen* from G2080; *from inside;* also used as equivalent to G2080 (*inside*):— inward, inwardly, (from) within, without.

G2082 ἐσώτερος *esōteros* comparative of G2080; *interior:*— inner, within.

G2083 ἑταῖρος *hetairos* from **ἔτης** *etēs* (a *clansman*); a *comrade:*— fellow, friend.

G2084 ἑτερόγλωσσος *heteroglōssos* from G2087 and G1100; *other-tongued,* i.e. a *foreigner:*— man of other tongue.

G2085 ἑτεροδιδασκαλέω *heterodidaskaleō* from G2087 and G1320; to *instruct differently:*— teach other doctrine, teach otherwise.

G2086 ἑτεροζυγέω *heterozygeō* from a compound of G2087 and G2218; to *yoke* up *differently,* i.e. (figuratively) to *associate discordantly:*— unequally yoke together with.

G2087 ἕτερος *heteros* of uncertain affinity; *another,* (the) *other* or *different:*— altered, else, next (day), one, other, another, some, strange.

G2088 ἑτέρως *heterōs* adverb from G2087; *differently:*— otherwise.

G2089 ἔτι *eti* perhaps akin to G2094; *"yet," still* (of time or degree):— after that, also, ever, (any) further, henceforth (more), thenceforth (more), hereafter, (any) longer, (any, anyone) more, now, still, yet.

G2090 ἑτοιμάζω *hetoimazō* from G2092; to *prepare:*— prepare, provide, make ready. Compare G2680.

G2091 ἑτοιμασία *hetoimasia* from G2090; *preparation:*— preparation.

G2092 ἕτοιμος *hetoimos* from an old noun **ἔτεος** *heteos* (*fitness*); *adjusted,* i.e. *ready:*— prepared, (made) ready (to our hand), readiness.

G2093 ἑτοίμως *hetoimōs* adverb from G2092; *in readiness:*— ready.

G2094 ἔτος *etos* apparently a primary word; a *year* :— year.

G2095 εὖ *eu* neuter of a primary **εὖς** *eus* (*good*); (adverb) *well:*— good, well (done).

G2096 Εὕα *Eua* of Hebrew origin [H2332]; *Eua* (or *Eva,* i.e. *Chavvah*), the first woman:— Eve.

G2097 εὐαγγελίζω *euangelizō* from G2095 and G32; to *announce good* news ("evangelize") especially the gospel:— declare, bring (declare, show) glad (good) tidings, preach (the gospel).

G2098 εὐαγγέλιον *euangelion* from the same as G2097; a *good message,* i.e. the *gospel:*— gospel.

G2099 εὐαγγελιστής *euangelistēs* from G2097; a *preacher* of the gospel:— evangelist.

G2100 εὐαρεστέω *euaresteō* from G2101; to *gratify entirely:*— please (well).

G2101 εὐάρεστος *euarestos* from G2095 and G701; *fully agreeable:*— acceptable, accepted, wellpleasing.

G2102 εὐαρέστως *euarestōs* adverb from G2101; *quite agreeably:*— acceptably, please well.

G2103 Εὔβουλος *Euboulos* from G2095 and G1014; *good-willer; Eubulus,* a Christian:— Eubulus.

G2104 εὐγενής *eugenēs* from G2095 and G1096; *well born,* i.e. (literally) *high* in rank, or (figuratively) *generous:*— more noble, nobleman.

G2105 εὐδία *eudia* feminine from G2095 and the alternate of G2203 (as the god of the weather); a *clear sky,* i.e. *fine weather:*— fair weather.

G2106 εὐδοκέω *eudokeō* from G2095 and G1380; to *think well* of, i.e. *approve* (an act); specifically to *approbate* (a person or thing):— think good, please, pleased, be well pleased, be the good (have, take) pleasure, be willing.

G2107 εὐδοκία *eudokia* from a presumed compound of G2095 and the base of G1380; *satisfaction,* i.e. (subjectively) *delight,* or (objectively) *kindness, wish, purpose:*— desire, good pleasure (will), seem good.

G2108 εὐεργεσία *euergesia* from G2110; *beneficence* (generally or specifically):— benefit, good deed done.

G2109 εὐεργετέω *euergeteō* from G2110; to *be philanthropic:*— do good.

G2110 εὐεργέτης *euergetēs* from G2095 and the base of G2041; a *worker of good,* i.e. (specifically) a *philanthropist:*— benefactor.

G2111 εὔθετος *euthetos* from G2095 and a derivative of G5087; *well placed,* i.e. (figuratively) *appropriate:*— fit, meet.

G2112 εὐθέως *eutheōs* adverb from G2117; *directly,* i.e. *at once* or *soon:*— anon, as soon as, forthwith, immediately, shortly, straightway.

G2113 εὐθυδρομέω *euthydromeō* from G2117 and G1408; to *lay a straight course,* i.e. *sail direct:*— (come) with a straight course.

G2114 εὐθυμέω *euthymeō* from G2115; to *cheer up,* i.e. (intransitive) *be cheerful;* neuter comparative (adverbially) *more cheerfully:*— be of good cheer (merry).

G2115 εὔθυμος *euthymos* from G2095 and G2372; in *fine spirits,* i.e. *cheerful:*— of good cheer, the more cheerfully.

G2116 εὐθύνω *euthynō* from G2117; to *straighten* (*level*); technically to *steer:*— governor, make straight.

G2117 εὐθύς *euthys* perhaps from G2095 and G5087; *straight,* i.e. (literally) *level,* or (figuratively) *true;* adverbially (of time) *at once:*— anon, by and by, forthwith, immediately, straightway.

G2118 εὐθύτης *euthytēs* from G2117; *rectitude:*— righteousness.

G2119 εὐκαιρέω *eukaireō* from G2121; to *have good time,* i.e. *opportunity* or *leisure:*— have leisure (convenient time), spend time.

G2120 εὐκαιρία *eukairia* from G2121; a favorable *occasion:*— opportunity.

G2121 εὔκαιρος *eukairos* from G2095 and G2540; *well-timed,* i.e. *opportune:*— convenient, in time of need.

G2122 εὐκαίρως *eukairōs* adverb from G2121; *opportunely:*— conveniently, in season.

G2123 εὐκοπώτερος *eukopōteros* comparative of a compound of G2095 and G2873; *better for toil,* i.e. *more facile:*— easier.

G2124 εὐλάβεια *eulabeia* from G2126; properly *caution,* i.e. (religiously) *reverence* (*piety*); by implication *dread* (concrete):— fear, feared.

G2125 εὐλαβέομαι *eulabeomai* middle from G2126; to *be circumspect,* i.e. (by implication) to *be apprehensive;* religiously, to *reverence:*— (moved with) fear.

G2126 εὐλαβής *eulabēs* from *G2095* and *G2983*; *taking well* (*carefully*), i.e. *circumspect* (religiously, *pious*):— devout.

G2127 εὐλογέω *eulogeō* from a compound of *G2095* and *G3056*; to *speak well of,* i.e. (religiously) to *bless* (*thank* or *invoke a benediction upon, prosper*):— bless, praise.

G2128 εὐλογητός *eulogētos* from *G2127*; *adorable* :— blessed.

G2129 εὐλογία *eulogia* from the same as *G2127*; *fine speaking,* i.e. *elegance of language; commendation* (*"eulogy"*), i.e. (reverentially) *adoration;* religiously, *benediction;* by implication *consecration;* by extension *benefit* or *largess:*— blessing (a matter of) bounty, bountifully, fair speech.

G2130 εὐμετάδοτος *eumetadotos* from *G2095* and a presumed derivative of *G3330*; *good at imparting,* i.e. *liberal:*— ready to distribute.

G2131 Εὐνίκη *Eunikē* from *G2095* and *G3529*; *victorious; Eunice,* a Jewess:— Eunice.

G2132 εὐνοέω *eunoeō* from a compound of *G2095* and *G3563*; to *be well-minded,* i.e. *reconcile:*— agree.

G2133 εὔνοια *eunoia* from the same as *G2132*; *kindness;* euphemistically *conjugal duty:*— benevolence, good will.

G2134 εὐνουχίζω *eunouchizō* from *G2135*; to *castrate* (figuratively *live unmarried*):— make . . . eunuch.

G2135 εὐνοῦχος *eunouchos* from

εὐνή *eunē* (a *bed*) and *G2192*; a *castrated* person (such being employed in Oriental bed-chambers); by extension an *impotent* or *unmarried* man; by implication a *chamberlain* (*state-officer*):— eunuch.

G2136 Εὐοδία *Euodia* from the same as *G2137*; *fine travelling; Euodia,* a Christian woman:— Euodias.

G2137 εὐοδόω *euodoō* from a compound of *G2095* and *G3598*; to *help* on the *road,* i.e. (passive) *succeed in reaching;* figuratively to *succeed* in business affairs:— prosper, have a prosperous journey.

G2138 εὐπειθής *eupeithēs* from *G2095* and *G3982*; *good* for *persuasion,* i.e. (intransitive) *compliant:*— easy to be intreated.

G2139 εὐπερίστατος *euperistatos* from *G2095* and a derivative of a presumed compound of *G4012* and *G2476*; *well standing around,* i.e. (*a competitor*) *thwarting* (a racer) in every direction (figuratively of sin in general):— which doth so easily beset.

G2140 εὐποιΐα *eupoiia* from a compound of *G2095* and *G4160*; *well doing,* i.e. *beneficence:*— to do good.

G2141 εὐπορέω *euporeō* from a compound of *G2090* and the base of *G4197*; (intransitive) to *be good* for *passing* through, i.e. (figuratively) *have* pecuniary *means:*— ability.

G2142 εὐπορία *euporia* from the same as *G2141*; pecuniary *resources:*— wealth.

G2143 εὐπρέπεια *euprepeia* from a compound of *G2095* and *G4241*; *good suitableness,* i.e. *gracefulness:*— grace.

G2144 εὐπρόσδεκτος *euprosdektos* from *G2095* and a derivative of *G4327*; *well-received,* i.e. *approved, favorable:*— acceptable, accepted.

G2145 εὐπρόσεδρος *euprosedros* from *G2095* and the same as *G4332*; *sitting well towards,* i.e. (figuratively) *assiduous* (neuter *diligent service*):— attend upon.

G2146 εὐπροσωπέω *euprosōpeō* from a compound of *G2095* and *G4383*; to *be of good countenance,* i.e. (figuratively) to *make a display:*— make a fair show.

G2147 εὑρίσκω *heuriskō* a prolonged form of a primary

εὕρω, *heurō,* which (together with another cognate form

εὑρέω *heureō*) is used for it in all the tenses except the present and imperfect; to *find* (literally or figuratively):— find, get, obtain, perceive, see.

G2148 Εὐροκλύδων *Euroklydōn* from

Εὖρος *Euros* (the *east* wind) and *G2830*; a *storm from the East* (or Southeast), i.e. (in modern phrase) a *Levanter:*— Euroklydon.

G2149 εὐρύχωρος *eurychōros* from

εὐρύς *eurys* (*wide*) and *G5561*; *spacious:*— broad.

G2150 εὐσέβεια *eusebeia* from *G2152*; *piety;* specifically the *gospel* scheme:— godliness, holiness.

G2151 εὐσεβέω *eusebeō* from *G2152*; to *be pious,* i.e. (towards God) to *worship,* or (towards parents) to *respect* (*support*):— show piety, worship.

G2152 εὐσεβής *eusebēs* from *G2095* and *G4576*; *well-reverent,* i.e. *pious:*— devout, godly.

G2153 εὐσεβῶς *eusebōs* adverb from *G2152*; *piously:*— godly.

G2154 εὔσημος *eusēmos* from *G2095* and the base of *G4591*; *well indicated,* i.e. (figuratively) *significant:*— easy to be understood.

G2155 εὔσπλαγχνος *eusplanchnos* from *G2095* and *G4698*; *well compassionate,* i.e. *sympathetic* :— pitiful, tender-hearted.

G2156 εὐσχημόνως *euschēmonōs* adverb from *G2158*; *decorously:*— decently, honestly.

G2157 εὐσχημοσύνη *euschēmosynē* from *G2158*; *decorousness:*— comeliness.

G2158 εὐσχήμων *euschēmōn* from *G2095* and *G4976*; *well-formed,* i.e. (figuratively) *decorous, noble* (in rank):— comely, honourable.

G2159 εὐτόνως *eutonōs* adverb from a compound of *G2095* and a derivative of

τείνω *teinō* (to *stretch*); *in a well-strung manner,* i.e. (figuratively) *intensely* (in a good sense, *cogently;* in a bad one, *fiercely*):— mightily, vehemently.

G2160 εὐτραπελία *eutrapelia* from a compound of *G2095* and a derivative of the base of *G5157* (meaning *well-turned,* i.e. *ready at repartee, jocose*); *witticism,* i.e. (in a vulgar sense) *ribaldry:*— jesting.

G2161 Εὔτυχος *Eutychos* from *G2095* and a derivative of *G5177*; *well-fated,* i.e. *fortunate; Eutychus,* a young man:— Eutychus.

G2162 εὐφημία *euphēmia* from *G2163*; *good language* (*"euphemy"*), i.e. *praise* (*repute*):— good report.

G2163 εὔφημος *euphēmos* from *G2095* and *G5345*; *well spoken of,* i.e. *reputable:*— of good report.

G2164 εὐφορέω *euphoreō* from *G2095* and *G5409*; to *bear well,* i.e. *be fertile:*— bring forth abundantly.

G2165 εὐφραίνω *euphrainō* from *G2095* and *G5424*; to *put* (middle or passive *be*) *in a good* frame of *mind,* i.e. *rejoice:*— fare, make glad, be (make) merry, rejoice.

G2166 Εὐφράτης *Euphratēs* of foreign origin [compare H6578]; *Euphrates,* a river of Asia:— Euphrates.

G2167 εὐφροσύνη *euphrosynē* from the same as *G2165*; *joyfulness:*— gladness, joy.

G2168 εὐχαριστέω *eucharisteō* from *G2170*; to *be grateful,* i.e. (active) to *express gratitude* (towards); specifically to *say grace* at a meal:— thank, give thanks, thankful.

G2169 εὐχαριστία *eucharistia* from *G2170*; *gratitude;* active *grateful language* (to God, as an act of worship):— thankfulness, (giving of) thanks, thanksgiving.

G2170 εὐχάριστος *eucharistos* from *G2095* and a derivative of *G5483*; *well favored,* i.e. (by implication) *grateful:*— thankful.

G2171 εὐχή *euchē* from *G2172*; properly a *wish,* expressed as a *petition* to God, or in *votive* obligation:— prayer, vow.

GRK

G2172 εὔχομαι *euchomai* middle of a primary verb; to *wish;* by implication to *pray* to God:— pray, will, wish.

G2173 εὔχρηστος *euchrēstos* from *G2095* and *G5543*; *easily used,* i.e. *useful:*— profitable, meet for use.

G2174 εὐψυχέω *eupsycheō* from a compound of *G2095* and *G5590*; to *be in good spirits,* i.e. *feel encouraged:*— be of good comfort.

G2175 εὐωδία *euōdia* from a compound of *G2095* and a derivative of *G3605*; *good-scent,* i.e. *fragrance:*— sweet savour (smell), sweetsmelling.

G2176 εὐώνυμος *euōnymos* from *G2095* and *G3686*; properly *well-named* (*good-omened*), i.e. the *left* (which was the *lucky* side among the pagan Greeks); neuter as adverb *at the left* hand:— (on the) left.

G2177 ἐφάλλομαι *ephallomai* from *G1909* and *G242*; to *spring upon:*— leap on.

G2178 ἐφάπαξ *ephapax* from *G1909* and *G530*; *upon one occasion* (only):— (at) once (for all).

G2179 Ἐφεσῖνος *Ephesinos* from *G2181*; *Ephesine,* or situated at Ephesus:— of Ephesus.

G2180 Ἐφέσιος *Ephesios* from *G2181*; an *Ephesian* or inhabitant of Ephesus:— Ephesian, of Ephesus.

G2181 Ἔφεσος *Ephesos* probably of foreign origin; *Ephesus,* a city of Asia Minor:— Ephesus.

G2182 ἐφευρετής *epheuretēs* from a compound of *G1909* and *G2147*; a *discoverer,* i.e. *contriver:*— inventor.

G2183 ἐφημερία *ephēmeria* from *G2184*; *diurnal arrangement,* i.e. (specifically) the quotidian *rotation* or *class* of the Jewish priests' service at the Temple, as distributed by families:— course.

G2184 ἐφήμερος *ephēmeros* from *G1909* and *G2250*; *for a day* ("ephemeral"), i.e. *diurnal:*— daily.

G2185 ἐφικνέομαι *ephikneomai* from *G1909* and a cognate of *G2240*; to *arrive upon,* i.e. *extend to:*— reach.

G2186 ἐφίστημι *ephistēmi* from *G1909* and *G2476*; to *stand upon,* i.e. *be present* (in various applications, friendly or otherwise, usually literal):— assault, come (in, to, unto, upon), be at hand (instant), present, stand (before, by, over).

G2187 Ἐφραΐμ *Ephraim* of Hebrew origin [H669 or better H6085]; *Ephraïm,* a place in Palestine:— Ephraim.

G2188 ἐφφαθά *ephphatha* of Aramaic origin [H6606]; *be opened!*:— Ephphatha.

G2189 ἔχθρα *echthra* feminine of G2190 ; *hostility;* by implication a reason for *opposition:*— enmity, hatred.

G2190 ἐχθρός *echthros* from a primary **ἔχθω** *echthō* (to *hate*); *hateful* (passive *odious,* or active *hostile*); usually as a noun, an *adversary* (especially *Satan*):— enemy, foe.

G2191 ἔχιδνα *echidna* of uncertain origin; an *adder* or other poisonous snake (literal or figurative):— viper.

G2192 ἔχω *echō* including an alternate form **σχέω** *scheō* (used in certain tenses only); a primary verb; to *hold* (used in very various applications, literal or figurative, direct or remote; such as *possession, ability, contiguity, relation* or *condition*) :— be (able, hold, possessed with), accompany, begin to amend, can, cannot, conceive, count, diseased, do, eat, enjoy, fear, following, have, hold, keep, lack, go to law, lie, must needs, of necessity, need, next, recover, reign, rest, return, sick, take for, tremble, uncircumcised, use.

G2193 ἕως *heōs* of uncertain affinity; a conjunction, preposition and adverb of continuance, *until* (of time and place):— even (until, unto), (as) far (as), how long, till, until, (up) to, hitherto, unto, while, whiles.

Z

G2194 Ζαβουλών *Zaboulōn* of Hebrew origin [H2074]; *Zabulon* (i.e. *Zebulon*), a region of Palestine:— Zabulon.

G2195 Ζακχαῖος *Zakchaios* of Hebrew origin [compare H2140]; *Zacchaeus,* an Israelite:— Zacchaeus.

G2196 Ζαρά *Zara* of Hebrew origin [H2226]; *Zara* (i.e. *Zerach*), an Israelite:— Zara.

G2197 Ζαχαρίας *Zacharias* of Hebrew origin [H2148]; *Zacharias* (i.e. *Zechariah*), the name of two Israelites:— Zacharias.

G2198 ζάω *zaō* a primary verb; to *live* (literally or figuratively):— life, lifetime, live, alive, lively, quick.

G2199 Ζεβεδαῖος *Zebedaios* of Hebrew origin [compare H2067]; *Zebedaeus,* an Israelite:— Zebedee.

G2200 ζεστός *zestos* from G2204; *boiled,* i.e. (by implication) *hot* (figuratively *fervent*):— hot.

G2201 ζεῦγος *zeugos* from the same as G2218; a *couple,* i.e. a *team* (of oxen yoked together) or *brace* (of birds tied together):— yoke, pair.

G2202 ζευκτηρία *zeuktēria* feminine of a derivative (at the second stage) from the same as G2218; a *fastening* (*tiller-rope*):— band.

G2203 Ζεύς *Zeus* of uncertain affinity; in the oblique cases there is used instead of it a (probably cognate) name **Δίς** *Dis* which is otherwise obsolete; *Zeus* or *Dis* (among the Latins *Jupiter* or *Jove*), the supreme deity of the Greeks:— Jupiter.

G2204 ζέω *zeō* a primary verb; to *be hot* (*boil,* of liquids; or *glow,* of solids), i.e. (figuratively) *be fervid* (*earnest*):— be fervent.

G2205 ζῆλος *zēlos* from G2204; properly *heat,* i.e. (figuratively) *"zeal"* (in a favorable sense, *ardor;* in an unfavorable one, *jealousy,* as of a husband [figuratively of God], or an enemy, *malice*):— emulation, envy, envying, fervent mind, indignation, jealousy, zeal.

G2206 ζηλόω *zēloō* from G2205; to *have warmth* of feeling for or against:— affect, covet (earnestly), (have) desire, (move with) envy, be jealous over, (be) zealous, zealously affect.

G2207 ζηλωτής *zēlōtēs* from G2206; a *"zealot"*:— zealous.

G2208 Ζηλωτής *Zēlōtēs* the same as G2208; a *Zealot,* i.e. (specifically) *partisan* for Jewish political independence:— Zelotes.

G2209 ζημία *zēmia* probably akin to the base of G1150 (through the idea of *violence*); *detriment:*— damage, loss.

G2210 ζημιόω *zēmioō* from G2209; to *injure,* i.e. (reflexive or passive) to *experience detriment:*— be cast away, receive damage, lose, suffer loss.

G2211 Ζηνᾶς *Zēnas* probably contracted from a poetic form of G2203 and G1435; *Jove-given; Zenas,* a Christian:— Zenas.

G2212 ζητέω *zēteō* of uncertain affinity; to *seek* (literally or figuratively); specifically (by Hebrew) to *worship* (God), or (in a bad sense) to *plot* (against life):— be (go) about, desire, endeavour, inquire (for), require, (will) seek (after, for, means). Compare G4441.

G2213 ζήτημα *zētēma* from G2212; a *search* (properly concrete), i.e. (in words) a *debate:*— question.

G2214 ζήτησις *zētēsis* from G2212; a *searching* (properly the act), i.e. a *dispute* or its *theme:*— question.

G2215 ζιζάνιον *zizanion* of uncertain origin; *darnel* or false grain:— tares.

G2216 Ζοροβάβελ *Zorobabel* of Hebrew origin [H2216]; *Zorobabel* (i.e. *Zerubbabel*), an Israelite:— Zorobabel.

G2217 ζόφος *zophos* akin to the base of G3509; *gloom* (as shrouding like a *cloud*):— blackness, darkness, mist.

G2218 ζυγός *zygos* from the root of **ζεύγνυμι** *zeugnymi* (to *join,* especially by a "yoke"); a *coupling,* i.e. (figuratively) *servitude* (a *law* or *obligation*); also (literally) the *beam* of the balance (as *connecting* the scales):— pair of balances, yoke.

G2219 ζύμη *zymē* probably from G2204; *ferment* (as if *boiling* up):— leaven.

G2220 ζυμόω *zymoō* from G2219; to *cause to ferment:*— leaven.

G2221 ζωγρέω *zōgreō* from the same as G2226 and G64; to *take alive* (*make a prisoner of war*), i.e. (figuratively) to *capture* or *ensnare:*— take captive, catch.

G2222 ζωή *zōē* from G2198; *life* (literal or figurative):— life, lifetime. Compare G5590.

G2223 ζώνη *zōnē* probably akin to the base of G2218; a *belt;* by implication a *pocket:*— girdle, purse.

G2224 ζώννυμι *zōnnymi* from G2223; to *bind about* (especially with a belt):— gird.

G2225 ζωογονέω *zōogoneō* from the same as G2226 and a derivative of G1096; to *engender alive,* i.e. (by analogy) to *rescue* (passive *be saved*) from death:— live, preserve.

G2226 ζῷον *zōon* neuter of a derivative of G2198; a *live* thing, i.e. an *animal:*— beast.

G2227 ζωοποιέω *zōopoieō* from the same as G2226 and G4160; to *vitalize, revitalize* (literally or figuratively):— make alive, give life, quicken.

H

G2228 ἤ *ē* a primary particle of distinction between two connected terms; disjunctive, *or;* comparative, *than.* Often used in connection with other particles:— and, but (either), either, neither, except it be, or (else), nor, rather, save, than, that, what, yea. Compare especially G2235, G2260, G2273.

G2229 ἦ *ē* an adverb of *confirmation;* perhaps intensive of G2228; used only (in the N.T.) before G3303; *assuredly:*— surely.

G2230 ἡγεμονεύω *hēgemoneuō* from G2232; to *act as ruler:*— be governor.

G2231 ἡγεμονία *hēgemonia* from G2232; *government,* i.e. (in time) official *term:*— reign.

G2232 ἡγεμών *hēgemōn* from G2233; a *leader,* i.e. *chief* person (or figuratively place) of a province:— governor, prince, ruler.

G2233 ἡγέομαι *hēgeomai* middle of a (presumed) strengthened form of G71; to *lead,* i.e. *command* (with official authority); figuratively to *deem,* i.e. *consider:*— account, (be) chief, count, esteem, governor, judge, have the rule over, suppose, think.

G2234 ἡδέως *hēdeōs* adverb from a derivative of the base of G2237; *sweetly,* i.e. (figuratively) *with pleasure:*— gladly.

G2235 ἤδη *ēdē* apparently from G2228 (or possibly G2229) and G1211; *even now:*— already, (even) now (already), by this time.

G2236 ἥδιστα *hēdista* neuter plural of the superlative of the same as G2234; *with great pleasure:*— most (very) gladly.

G2237 ἡδονή *hēdonē* from **ἁνδάνω** *handanō* (to *please*); sensual *delight;* by implication *desire:*— lust, pleasure.

G2238 ἡδύοσμον *hēdyosmon* neuter of a compound of the same as G2234 and G3744; a *sweet-scented* plant, i.e. *mint:*— mint.

G2239 ἦθος *ēthos* a strengthened form of G1485; *usage,* i.e. (plural) moral *habits:*— manners.

G2240 ἥκω *hēkō* a primary verb; to *arrive,* i.e. *be present* (literally or figuratively):— come.

G2241 ἠλί *ēli* of Hebrew origin [H410 with pronoun suffix]; *my God:*— Eli.

G2242 Ἡλί *hēli* of Hebrew origin [H5941]; *Heli* (i.e. *Eli*), an Israelite:— Heli.

G2243 Ἡλίας *Hēlias* of Hebrew origin [H452]; *Helias* (i.e. *Elijah*), an Israelite:— Elias.

G2244 ἡλικία *hēlikia* from the same as G2245; *maturity* (in years or size):— age, stature.

G2245 ἡλίκος *hēlikos* from **ἧλιξ** *hēlix* (a *comrade,* i.e. one of the same age); *as big as,* i.e. (as an interjection) *how much:*— how (what) great.

G2246 ἥλιος *hēlios* from
ἕλη *helē* (*a ray;* perhaps akin to the alternate of *G138*); the *sun;* by implication *light:*— east, sun.

G2247 ἧλος *hēlos* of uncertain affinity; a *stud,* i.e. *spike:*— nail.

G2248 ἡμᾶς *hēmas* accusative plural of *G1473*; *us* :— our, us, we.

G2249 ἡμεῖς *hēmeis* nominative plural of *G1473*; *we* (only used when emphatic):— us, we (ourselves).

G2250 ἡμέρα *hēmera* feminine (with *G5610* implied) of a derivative of
ἧμαι *hēmai* (to *sit;* akin to the base of *G1476*) meaning *tame,* i.e. *gentle; day,* i.e. (literally) the time space between dawn and dark, or the whole twenty-four hours (but several days were usually reckoned by the Jews as inclusive of the parts of both extremes); figuratively a *period* (always defined more or less clearly by the context):— age, alway, day (by day), daily, midday, for ever, judgment, (day) time, while, years.

G2251 ἡμέτερος *hēmeteros* from *G2349*; *our:*— our, your [*by a different reading*].

G2252 ἤμην *ēmēn* a prolonged form of *G2358*; I *was* [*Sometimes unexpressed*]:— be, was.

G2253 ἡμιθανής *hēmithanēs* from a presumed compound of the base of *G2255* and *G2348*; *half dead,* i.e. *entirely exhausted:*— half dead.

G2254 ἡμῖν *hēmin* dative plural of *G1473*; *to* (or *for, with, by*) *us:*— our, (for) us, we.

G2255 ἥμισυ *hēmisy* neuter of a derived from an inseparable prefix akin to *G260* (through the idea of *partition* involved in *connection*) and meaning *semi-*; (as noun) *half:*— half.

G2256 ἡμιώριον *hēmiōrion* from the base of *G2255* and *G5610*; a *half-hour:*— half an hour.

G2257 ἡμῶν *hēmōn* genetive plural of *G1473*; *of* (or *from*) *us:*— our (company), us, we.

G2258 ἦν *ēn* imperfect of *G1510*; *I* (*thou,* etc.) *was* (*wast* or *were*):— agree, be, have (+ charge of), hold, use, was, wast, were.

G2259 ἡνίκα *hēnika* of uncertain affinity; *at which time:*— when.

G2260 ἤπερ *ēper* from *G2228* and *G4007*; *than at all* (or *than perhaps, than indeed*):— than.

G2261 ἤπιος *ēpios* probably from *G2031*; properly *affable,* i.e. *mild* or *kind:*— gentle.

G2262 Ἤρ *Ēr* of Hebrew origin [H6147]; *Er,* an Israelite:— Er.

G2263 ἤρεμος *ēremos* perhaps by transposition from *G2048* (through the idea of *stillness*); *tranquil:*— quiet.

G2264 Ἡρώδης *Hērōdēs* compound of
ἥρως *hērōs* (a *"hero"*) and *G1491*; *heroic; Herodes,* the name of four Jewish kings:— Herod.

G2265 Ἡρῳδιανοί *Hērōdianoi* plural of a derivative of *G2264*; *Herodians,* i.e. partisans of Herodes:— Herodians.

G2266 ἡρωδιάς *hērōdias* from *G2264*; *Herodias,* a woman of the Herodian family:— Herodias.

G2267 ἡρῳδίων *hērōdiōn* from *G2264*; *Herodion,* a Christian:— Herodion.

G2268 Ἡσαΐας *Hēsaias* of Hebrew origin [H3470]; *Hesaias* (i.e. *Jeshajah*), an Israelite:— Esaias.

G2269 Ἠσαῦ *Ēsau* of Hebrew origin [H6215]; *Esau,* an Edomite:— Esau.

G2270 ἡσυχάζω *hēsychazō* from the same as *G2272*; to *keep still* (intransitive), i.e. *refrain* from labor, meddling, or speech:— cease, hold peace, be quiet, rest.

G2271 ἡσυχία *hēsychia* feminine of *G2272*; (as noun) *stillness,* i.e. desisting from bustle or language:— quietness, silence.

G2272 ἡσύχιος *hēsychios* a prolonged form of a compound probably of a derivative of the base of *G1476* and perhaps *G2192*; properly *keeping* one's *seat* (*sedentary*), i.e. (by implication) *still* (*undisturbed, not disturbing*):— peaceable, quiet.

G2273 ἤτοι *ētoi* from *G2228* and *G5104*; *either indeed:*— whether.

G2274 ἡττάω *hēttaō* from the same as *G2276*; to *make worse,* i.e. *vanquish* (literally or figuratively); by implication to *rate lower:*— be inferior, overcome.

G2275 ἥττημα *hēttēma* from *G2274*; a *deterioration,* i.e. (objectively) *failure* or (subjectively) *loss:*— diminishing, fault.

G2276 ἥττον *hētton* neuter of comparative of
ἧκα *hēka* (*slightly*) used for that of *G2556*; *worse* (as noun); by implication *less* (as adverb):— less, worse.

G2277 ἤτω *ētō* third person singular imperative of *G1510*; *let him* (or *it*) *be:*— let . . . be.

G2278 ἠχέω *ēcheō* from *G2279*; to *make a* loud *noise,* i.e. *reverberate:*— roar, sound.

G2279 ἦχος *ēchos* of uncertain affinity; a loud or confused *noise* (*"echo"*), i.e. *roar;* figuratively a *rumor:*— fame, sound.

Θ

G2280 Θαδδαῖος *Thaddaios* of uncertain origin; *Thaddaeus,* one of the Apostles:— Thaddaeus.

G2281 θάλασσα *thalassa* probably prolonged from *G251*; the *sea* (generally or specifically):— sea.

G2282 θάλπω *thalpō* probably akin to
θάλλω *thallō* (to *warm*); to *brood,* i.e. (figuratively) to *foster:*— cherish.

G2283 Θάμαρ *Thamar* of Hebrew origin [H8559]; *Thamar* (i.e. *Tamar*), an Israelitess:— Thamar.

G2284 θαμβέω *thambeō* from *G2285*; to *stupefy* (with surprise), i.e. *astound:*— amaze, astonish.

G2285 θάμβος *thambos* akin to an obsolete
τάφω *taphō* (to *dumbfound*); *stupefaction* (by surprise), i.e. *astonishment:*— amazed, astonished, wonder.

G2286 θανάσιμος *thanasimos* from *G2288*; *fatal,* i.e. *poisonous:*— deadly.

G2287 θανατηφόρος *thanatēphoros* from (the feminine form of) *G2288* and *G5342*; *death-bearing,* i.e. *fatal:*— deadly.

G2288 θάνατος *thanatos* from *G2348*; (properly an adjective used as a noun) *death* (literally or figuratively):— deadly, (be . . .) death.

G2289 θανατόω *thanatoō* from *G2288*; to *kill* (literally or figuratively):— become dead, (cause to be) put to death, kill, mortify.

G2290 θάπτω *thaptō* a primary verb; to *celebrate funeral rites,* i.e. *inter:*— bury.

G2291 Θάρα *Thara* of Hebrew origin [H8646]; *Thara* (i.e. *Terach*), the father of Abraham:— Thara.

G2292 θαρρέω *tharrheō* another form for *G2293*; to *exercise courage:*— be bold, boldly, have confidence, be confident. Compare *G5111*.

G2293 θαρσέω *tharseō* from *G2294*; to *have courage:*— be of good cheer (comfort). Compare *G2292*.

G2294 θάρσος *tharsos* akin (by transposition) to
θράσος *thrasos* (*daring*); *boldness* (subjective):— courage.

G2295 θαῦμα *thauma* apparently from a form of *G2300*; *wonder* (properly concrete; but by implication abstract):— admiration.

G2296 θαυμάζω *thaumazō* from *G2295*; to *wonder;* by implication to *admire:*— admire, have in admiration, marvel, wonder.

G2297 θαυμάσιος *thaumasios* from *G2295*; *wondrous,* i.e. (neuter as noun) a *miracle:*— wonderful thing.

G2298 θαυμαστός *thaumastos* from *G2296*; *wondered* at, i.e. (by implication) *wonderful:*— marvel, marvelous.

G2299 θεά *thea* feminine of *G2316*; a female *deity* :— goddess.

G2300 θεάομαι *theaomai* a prolonged form of a primary verb; to *look* closely at, i.e. (by implication) to *perceive* (literally or figuratively); by extension to *visit:*— behold, look (upon), see. Compare *G3700*.

G2301 θεατρίζω *theatrizō* from *G2302*; to *expose as a spectacle:*— make a gazing stock.

G2302 θέατρον *theatron* from *G2300*; *a place for public show* (*"theatre"*), i.e. general *audience-room;* by implication a *show* itself (figuratively):— spectacle, theatre.

G2303 θεῖον *theion* probably neuter of *G2304* (in its origin sense of *flashing*); *sulphur:*— brimstone.

G2304 θεῖος *theios* from *G2316*; *godlike* (neuter as noun, *divinity*):— divine, godhead.

G2305 θειότης *theiotēs* from *G2304*; *divinity* (abstract):— godhead.

G2306 θειώδης *theiōdēs* from *G2303* and *G1491*; *sulphur-like,* i.e. *sulphurous:*— brimstone.

G2307 θέλημα *thelēma* from the prolonged form of *G2309*; a *determination* (properly the thing), i.e. (active) *choice* (specifically *purpose, decree;* abstractly *volition*) or (passive) *inclination:*— desire, pleasure, will.

G2308 θέλησις *thelēsis* from *G2309*; *determination* (properly the act), i.e. *option:*— will.

G2309 θέλω *thelō* or
ἐθέλω *ethelō* in certain tenses
θελέω *theleō* and
ἐθελέω *etheleō* which are otherwise obsolete; apparently strengthened from the alternate form of *G138*; to *determine* (as an active *option* from subjective impulse; whereas *G1014* properly denotes rather a passive *acquiescence* in objective considerations), i.e., *choose* or *prefer* (literally or figuratively); by implication to *wish,* i.e. *be inclined* to (sometimes adverbially *gladly*); impersonally for the future tense, to *be about to;* by Hebrew to *delight in:*— desire, be disposed (forward), intend, list, love, mean, please, have rather, will (have), (be) willing, willingly.

G2310 θεμέλιος *themelios* from a derivative of *G5087*; something *put* down, i.e. a *substructure* (of a building, etc.), (literally or figuratively):— foundation.

G2311 θεμελιόω *themelioō* from *G2310*; to *lay a basis* for, i.e. (literally) *erect*, or (figuratively) *consolidate:*— found, lay the foundation, ground, settle.

G2312 θεοδίδακτος *theodidaktos* from *G2316* and *G1321*; *divinely instructed:*— taught of God.

G2312¢θεολόγος *theologos* from *G2316* and *G3004*; a "theologian":— divine.

G2313 θεομαχέω *theomacheō* from *G2314*; to *resist deity:*— fight against God.

G2314 θεόμαχος *theomachos* from *G2316* and *G3164*; an *opponent of deity:*— to fight against God.

G2315 θεόπνευστος *theopneustos* from *G2316* and a presumed derivative of *G4154*; *divinely breathed* in:— given by inspiration of God.

G2316 θεός *theos* of uncertain affinity; a *deity*, especially (with *G3588*) *the* supreme *Divinity;* figuratively a *magistrate;* by Hebrew *very:*— exceeding, God, god, godly, godward.

G2317 θεοσέβεια *theosebeia* from *G2318*; *devoutness*, i.e. *piety:*— godliness.

G2318 θεοσεβής *theosebēs* from *G2316* and *G4576*; *reverent of God*, i.e. *pious:*— worshipper of God.

G2319 θεοστυγής *theostygēs* from *G2316* and the base of *G4767*; *hateful to God*, i.e. *impious:*— hater of God.

G2320 θεότης *theotēs* from *G2316*; *divinity* (abstract):— godhead.

G2321 Θεόφιλος *Theophilos* from *G2316* and *G5384*; *friend of God; Theophilus*, a Christian:— Theophilus.

G2322 θεραπεία *therapeia* from *G2323*; *attendance* (specifically medical, i.e. *cure*); figuratively and collectively *domestics:*— healing, household.

G2323 θεραπεύω *therapeuō* from the same as *G2324*; to *wait upon* menially, i.e. (figuratively) to *adore* (God), or (specifically) to *relieve* (of disease):— cure, heal, worship.

G2324 θεράπων *therapōn* apparently a participle from an otherwise obsolete derivative of the base of *G2330*; a menial *attendant* (as if *cherishing*):— servant.

G2325 θερίζω *therizō* from *G2330* (in the sense of the *crop*); to *harvest:*— reap.

G2326 θερισμός *therismos* from *G2325*; *reaping*, i.e. the *crop:*— harvest.

G2327 θεριστής *theristēs* from *G2325*; a *harvester* :— reaper.

G2328 θερμαίνω *thermainō* from *G2329*; to *heat* (oneself):— (be) warm, be warmed, warm self.

G2329 θέρμη *thermē* from the base of *G2330*; *warmth:*— heat.

G2330 θέρος *theros* from a primary

θέρω *therō* (to *heat*); properly *heat*, i.e. *summer:*— summer.

G2331 Θεσσαλονικεύς *Thessalonikeus* from *G2332*; a *Thessalonican*, i.e. inhabitant of Thessalonice:— Thessalonian.

G2332 Θεσσαλονίκη *Thessalonikē* from

Θεσσαλός *Thessalos* (a *Thessalian*) and *G3529*; *Thessalonice*, a place in Asia Minor:— Thessalonica.

G2333 Θευδᾶς *Theudas* of uncertain origin; *Theudas*, an Israelite:— Theudas.

G2334 θεωρέω *theōreō* from a derivative of *G2300* (perhaps by addition of *G3708*); to *be a spectator* of, i.e. *discern*, (literally, figuratively [*experience*] or intensively [*acknowledge*]):— behold, consider, look on, perceive, see. Compare *G3700*.

G2335 θεωρία *theōria* from the same as *G2334*; *spectatorship*, i.e. (concretely) a *spectacle:*— sight.

G2336 θήκη *thēkē* from *G5087*; a *receptacle*, i.e. *scabbard:*— sheath.

G2337 θηλάζω *thēlazō* from

θηλή *thēlē* (the *nipple*); to *suckle;* by implication to *suck:*— (give) suck, suckling.

G2338 θῆλυς *thēlys* from the same as *G2337*; *female:*— female, woman.

G2339 θήρα *thēra* from

θήρ *thēr* (a wild *animal*, as *game*); *hunting*, i.e. (figuratively) *destruction:*— trap.

G2340 θηρεύω *thēreuō* from *G2339*; to *hunt* (an animal), i.e. (figuratively) to *carp at:*— catch.

G2341 θηριομαχέω *thēriomacheō* from a compound of *G2342* and *G3164*; to *be a beast-fighter* (in the gladiatorial show), i.e. (figuratively) to *encounter* (furious men):— fight with wild beasts.

G2342 θηρίον *thērion* diminutive from the same as *G2339*; a *dangerous animal:*— (venomous, wild) beast.

G2343 θησαυρίζω *thēsaurizō* from *G2344*; to *amass* or *reserve* (literally or figuratively):— lay up (treasure), (keep) in store, (heap) treasure (together, up).

G2344 θησαυρός *thēsauros* from *G5087*; a *deposit*, i.e. *wealth* (literal or figurative):— treasure.

G2345 θιγγάνω *thinganō* a prolonged form of an obsolete primary

θίγω *thigō* (to *finger*); to *manipulate*, i.e. *have to do with;* by implication to *injure:*— handle, touch.

G2346 θλίβω *thlibō* akin to the base of *G5147*; to *crowd* (literally or figuratively):— afflict, narrow, throng, suffer tribulation, trouble.

G2347 θλῖψις *thlipsis* from *G2346*; *pressure* (literal or figurative):— afflicted, affliction, anguish, burdened, persecution, tribulation, trouble.

G2348 θνήσκω *thnēskō* a strengthened form of a simpler primary

θάνω *thanō* (which is used for it only in certain tenses); to *die* (literally or figuratively):— be dead, die.

G2349 θνητός *thnētos* from *G2348*; *liable to die:*— mortal, mortality.

G2350 θορυβέω *thorybeō* from *G2351*; to *be in tumult*, i.e. *disturb, clamor:*— make ado (a noise), trouble self, set on an uproar.

G2351 θόρυβος *thorybos* from the base of *G2360*; a *disturbance:*— tumult, uproar.

G2352 θραύω *thrauō* a primary verb; to *crush:*— bruise. Compare *G4486*.

G2353 θρέμμα *thremma* from *G5142*; *stock* (as *raised* on a farm):— cattle.

G2354 θρηνέω *thrēneō* from *G2355*; to *bewail:*— lament, mourn.

G2355 θρῆνος *thrēnos* from the base of *G2360*; *wailing:*— lamentation.

G2356 θρησκεία *thrēskeia* from a derivative of *G2357*; ceremonial *observance:*— religion, worshipping.

G2357 θρῆσκος *thrēskos* probably from the base of *G2360*; *ceremonious* in worship (as *demonstrative*), i.e. *pious:*— religious.

G2358 θριαμβεύω *thriambeuō* from a prolonged compound of the base of *G2360* and a derivative of *G680* (meaning a *noisy iambus*, sung in honor of Bacchus); to *make an acclamatory procession*, i.e. (figuratively) to *conquer* or (by Hebrew) to *give victory:*— (cause) to triumph (over).

G2359 θρίξ *thrix* genetive

τριχός *trichos* etc.; of uncertain derivation; *hair:*— hair. Compare *G2864*.

G2360 θροέω *throeō* from

θρέομαι *threomai* (to *wail*); to *clamor*, i.e. (by implication) to *frighten:*— trouble.

G2361 θρόμβος *thrombos* perhaps from *G5142* (in the sense of *thickening*); a *clot:*— great drop.

G2362 θρόνος *thronos* from

θράω *thraō* (to *sit*); a stately *seat* ("*throne*"); by implication *power* or (concretely) a *potentate:*— seat, throne.

G2363 Θυάτειρα *Thyateira* of uncertain derivation; *Thyatira*, a place in Asia Minor:— Thyatira.

G2364 θυγάτηρ *thygatēr* apparently a primary word [compare "daughter"]; a *female child*, or (by Hebrew) *descendant* (or *inhabitant*):— daughter.

G2365 θυγάτριον *thygatrion* from *G2364*; a *little daughter:*— little (young) daughter.

G2366 θύελλα *thyella* from *G2380* (in the sense of *blowing*); a storm:— tempest.

G2367 θύϊνος *thyinos* from a derivative of *G2380* (in the sense of *blowing;* denoting a certain *fragrant* tree); made of *citron*-wood:— thyine.

G2368 θυμίαμα *thymiama* from *G2370*; an *aroma*, i.e. fragrant *powder* burnt in religious service; by implication the *burning* itself:— incense, odour.

G2369 θυμιατήριον *thymiatērion* from a derivative of *G2370*; a *place of fumigation*, i.e. the *altar of incense* (in the Temple):— censer.

G2370 θυμιάω *thymiaō* from a derivative of *G2380* (in the sense of *smoking*); to *fumigate*, i.e. *offer* aromatic *fumes:*— burn incense.

G2371 θυμομαχέω *thymomacheō* from a presumed compound of *G2372* and *G3164*; to *be in a furious fight*, i.e. (figuratively) to *be exasperated:*— be highly displeased.

G2372 θυμός *thymos* from *G2380*; *passion* (as if *breathing* hard):— fierceness, indignation, wrath. Compare *G5590*.

G2373 θυμόω *thymoō* from *G2372*; to *put in a passion*, i.e. *enrage:*— be wroth.

G2374 θύρα *thyra* apparently a primary word [compare "door"]; a *portal* or entrance (the opening or the closure, literally or figuratively):— door, gate.

G2375 θυρεός *thyreos* from *G2374*; a large *shield* (as *door*-shaped):— shield.

G2376 θυρίς *thyris* from *G2374*; an *aperture*, i.e. *window:*— window.

G2377 θυρωρός *thyrōros* from *G2374* and
οὖρος *ouros* (a *watcher*); a *gate-warden:*— that kept the door, porter.

G2378 θυσία *thysia* from *G2380*; *sacrifice* (the act or the victim, literally or figuratively):— sacrifice.

G2379 θυσιαστήριον *thysiastērion* from a derivative of *G2378*; a *place of sacrifice,* i.e. an *altar* (specifically or generally, literally or figuratively):— altar.

G2380 θύω *thyō* a primary verb; properly to *rush* (*breathe* hard, *blow, smoke*), i.e. (by implication) to *sacrifice* (properly by fire, but generally); by extension to *immolate* (*slaughter* for any purpose):— kill, (do) sacrifice, slay.

G2381 Θωμᾶς *Thōmas* of Aramaic origin [compare H8380]; *the twin; Thomas,* a Christian:— Thomas.

G2382 θώραξ *thōrax* of uncertain affinity; the *chest* (*"thorax"*), i.e. (by implication) a *corselet:*— breastplate.

I

G2383 Ἰάειρος *Iaeiros* of Hebrew origin [H2971]; *Ja'ïrus* (i.e. *Jair*), an Israelite:— Jairus.

G2384 Ἰακώβ *Iakōb* of Hebrew origin [H3290]; *Jacob* (i.e. *Jaaeakob*), the progenitor of the Israelite; also an Israelite:— Jacob.

G2385 Ἰάκωβος *Iakōbos* the same as *G2384* Graecized; *Jacobus,* the name of three Israelites:— James.

G2386 ἴαμα *iama* from *G2390*; a *cure* (the effect):— healing.

G2387 Ἰαμβρῆς *Iambrēs* of Egyptian origin; *Jambres,* an Egyptian:— Jambres.

G2388 Ἰαννά *Ianna* probably of Hebrew origin [compare H3238]; *Janna,* an Israelite:— Janna.

G2389 Ἰαννῆς *Iannēs* of Egyptian origin; *Jannes,* an Egyptian:— Jannes.

G2390 ἰάομαι *iaomai* middle of apparently a primary verb; to *cure* (literally or figuratively):— heal, make whole.

G2391 Ἰάρεδ *Iared* of Hebrew origin [H3382]; *Jared* (i.e. *Jered*), an antediluvian:— Jared.

G2392 ἴασις *iasis* from *G2390*; *curing* (the act):— cure, heal, healing.

G2393 ἴασπις *iaspis* probably of foreign origin [see H3471]; *"jasper",* a gem:— jasper.

G2394 Ἰάσων *Iasōn* future active participle masculine of *G2390*; *about to cure; Jason,* a Christian:— Jason.

G2395 ἰατρός *iatros* from *G2390*; a *physician:*— physician.

G2396 ἴδε *ide* second person singular imperfect active of *G1492*; used as interjection to denote *surprise; lo!:*— behold, lo, see.

G2397 ἰδέα *idea* from *G1492*; a *sight* [compare figuratively "idea"], i.e. *aspect:*— countenance.

G2398 ἴδιος *idios* of uncertain affinity; *pertaining to self,* i.e. one's *own;* by implication *private* or *separate:*— his acquaintance, when they were alone, apart, aside, due, his (own, proper, several), home, (her, our, thine, your) own (business), private, privately, proper, severally, their (own).

G2399 ἰδιώτης *idiōtēs* from *G2398*; a *private* person, i.e. (by implication) an *ignoramus* (compare "idiot"):— ignorant, rude, unlearned.

G2400 ἰδού *idou* second person singular imperfect middle of *G1492*; used as imperative *lo!:*— behold, lo, see.

G2401 Ἰδουμαία *Idoumaia* of Hebrew origin [H123]; *Idumaea* (i.e. *Edom*), a region East (and South) of Palestine:— Idumaea.

G2402 ἱδρώς *hidrōs* a strengthened form of a primary
ἴδος *idos* (*sweat*); *perspiration:*— sweat.

G2403 Ἰεζαβήλ *Iezabēl* of Hebrew origin [H348]; *Jezabel* (i.e. *Jezebel*), a Tyrian woman (used as a synonym of a termagant or false teacher):— Jezabel.

G2404 Ἱεράπολις *Hierapolis* from *G2413* and *G4172*; *holy city; Hierapolis,* a place in Asia Minor:— Hierapolis.

G2405 ἱερατεία *hierateia* from *G2407*; *that which is priestly,* i.e. the *sacerdotal function:*— office of the priesthood, priest's office.

G2406 ἱεράτευμα *hierateuma* from *G2407*; the *priestly fraternity,* i.e. a *sacerdotal order* (figuratively):— priesthood.

G2407 ἱερατεύω *hierateuō* prolonged from *G2409*; to *be a priest,* i.e. *perform his functions:*— execute the priest's office.

G2408 Ἱερεμίας *Hieremias* of Hebrew origin [H3414]; *Hieremias* (i.e. *Jermijah*), an Israelite:— Jeremiah.

G2409 ἱερεύς *hiereus* from *G2413*; a *priest* (literally or figuratively):— (high) priest.

G2410 Ἱεριχώ *Hierichō* of Hebrew origin [H3405]; *Jericho,* a place in Palestine:— Jericho.

G2411 ἱερόν *hieron* neuter of *G2413*; a *sacred* place, i.e. the entire precincts (whereas *G3485* denotes the central *sanctuary* itself) of the *Temple* (at Jerusalem or elsewhere):— temple.

G2412 ἱεροπρεπής *hieroprepēs* from *G2413* and the same as *G4241*; *reverent:*— as becometh holiness.

G2413 ἱερός *hieros* of uncertain affinity; *sacred:*— holy.

G2414 Ἱεροσόλυμα *Hierosolyma* of Hebrew origin [H3389]; *Hierosolyma* (i.e. *Jerushalaïm*), the capital of Palestine:— Jerusalem. Compare *G2419*.

G2415 Ἱεροσολυμίτης *Hierosolymitēs* from *G2414*; a *Hierosolymite,* i.e. inhabitant of Hierosolyma:— of Jerusalem.

G2416 ἱεροσυλεω *hierosyleō* from Greek *G2417*; to *be a temple-robber* (figuratively):— commit sacrilege.

G2417 ἱερόσυλος *hierosylos* from *G2411* and *G4813*; a *temple-despoiler:*— robber of churches.

G2418 ἱερουργέω *hierourgeō* from a compound of *G2411* and the base of *G2041*; to *be a temple-worker,* i.e. *officiate as a priest* (figuratively):— minister.

G2419 Ἱερουσαλήμ *Hierousalēm* of Hebrew origin [H3389]; *Hierusalem* (i.e. *Jerushalem*), the capital of Palestine:— Jerusalem. Compare *G2414*.

G2420 ἱερωσύνη *hierōsynē* from *G2413*; *sacredness,* i.e. (by implication) the *priestly office:*— priesthood.

G2421 Ἰεσσαί *Iessai* of Hebrew origin [H3448]; *Jessae* (i.e. *Jishai*), an Israelite:— Jesse.

G2422 Ἰεφθάε *Iephthae* of Hebrew origin [H3316]; *Jephthae'* (i.e. *Jiphtach*), an Israelite:— Jephthah.

G2423 Ἰεχονίας *Iechonias* of Hebrew origin [H3204]; *Jechonias* (i.e. *Jekonjah*), an Israelite:— Jechonias.

G2424 Ἰησοῦς *Iēsous* of Hebrew origin [H3091]; *Jesus* (i.e. *Jehoshua*), the name of our Lord and two (three) other Israelites:— Jesus.

G2425 ἱκανός *hikanos* from
ἵκω *hikō* or
ἱκάνω *hikanō* or
ἱκνέομαι *hikneomai* akin to *G2240* (to *arrive*); *competent* (as if *coming* in season), i.e. *ample* (in amount) or *fit* (in character):— able, content, enough, good, great, large, long (while), many, meet, much, security, sore, sufficient, worthy.

G2426 ἱκανότης *hikanotēs* from *G2425*; *ability* :— sufficiency.

G2427 ἱκανόω *hikanoō* from *G2425*; to *enable,* i.e. *qualify:*— make able (meet).

G2428 ἱκετηρία *hiketēria* from a derivative of the base of *G2425* (through the idea of *approaching* for a favor); *entreaty:*— supplication.

G2429 ἰκμάς *ikmas* of uncertain affinity; *dampness:*— moisture.

G2430 Ἰκόνιον *Ikonion* perhaps from *G1504*; *image-like; Iconium,* a place in Asia Minor:— Iconium.

G2431 ἱλαρός *hilaros* from the same as *G2436*; *propitious* or *merry* (*"hilarious"*), i.e. *prompt* or *willing:*— cheerful.

G2432 ἱλαρότης *hilarotēs* from *G2431*; *alacrity* :— cheerfulness.

G2433 ἱλάσκομαι *hilaskomai* middle from the same as *G2436*; to *conciliate,* i.e. (transitive) to *atone* for (sin), or (intransitive) *be propitious:*— be merciful, make reconciliation for.

G2434 ἱλασμός *hilasmos*; *atonement,* i.e. (concretely) an *expiator:*— propitiation.

G2435 ἱλαστήριον *hilastērion* neuter of a derivative of *G2433*; an *expiatory* (place or thing), i.e. (concretely) an atoning *victim,* or (specifically) the *lid* of the Ark (in the Temple):— mercyseat, propitiation.

G2436 ἵλεως *hileōs* perhaps from the alternate form of *G138*; *cheerful* (as *attractive*), i.e. *propitious;* adverbially (by Hebrew) God be *gracious!,* i.e. (in averting some calamity) *far* be it:— be it far, merciful.

G2437 Ἰλλυρικόν *Illyrikon* neuter of an adjective from a name of uncertain derivation; (the) *Illyrican* (shore), i.e. (as a name itself) *Illyricum,* a region of Europe:— Illyricum.

G2438 ἱμάς *himas* perhaps from the same as *G260*; a *strap,* i.e. (specifically) the *tie* (of a sandal) or the *lash* (of a scourge):— latchet, thong.

G2439 ἱματίζω *himatizō* from *G2440*; to *dress:*— clothe.

G2440 ἱμάτιον *himation* neuter of a presumed derivative of
ἕννυμι *hennymi* (to *put on*); a *dress* (inner or outer):— apparel, cloke, clothes, garment, raiment, robe, vesture.

G2441 ἱματισμός *himatismos* from *G2439*; *clothing:*— apparel (appareled), array, raiment, vesture.

GRK

G2442 **ἱμείρομαι** *himeiromai* middle from
ἵμερος *himeros* (a *yearning;* of uncertain affinity); to *long for:*— be affectionately desirous.

G2443 **ἵνα** *hina* probably from the same as the former part of *G1438* (through the *demonstrative* idea; compare *G3588*); in order *that* (denoting the *purpose* or the *result*):— albeit, because, to the intent (that), lest, so as, (so) that, (for) to. Compare *G3363*.

G2444 **ἱνατί** *hinati* from *G2443* and *G5101*; *for what* reason?, i.e. *why?:*— wherefore, why.

G2445 **Ἰόππη** *Ioppē* of Hebrew origin [H3305]; *Joppe* (i.e. *Japho*), a place in Palestine:— Joppa.

G2446 **Ἰορδάνης** *Iordanēs* of Hebrew origin [H3383]; the *Jordanes* (i.e. *Jarden*), a river of Palestine:— Jordan.

G2447 **ἰός** *ios* perhaps from
εἶμι *eimi* (to *go*) or
ἵημι *hiēmi* (to *send*); *rust* (as if *emitted* by metals); also *venom* (as *emitted* by serpents):— poison, rust.

G2448 **Ἰουδά** *Iouda* of Hebrew origin [H3063 or perhaps H3194]; *Judah* (i.e. *Jehudah* or *Juttah*), a part of (or place in) Palestine:— Judah.

G2449 **Ἰουδαία** *Ioudaia* feminine of *G2453* (with *G1093* implied); the *Judaean* land (i.e. *Judaea*), a region of Palestine:— Judaea.

G2450 **Ἰουδαΐζω** *Ioudaizō* from *G2453*; to *become a Judaean,* i.e. *"Judaize":*— live as the Jews.

G2451 **Ἰουδαϊκός** *Ioudaikos* from *G2453*; *Judaïc,* i.e. *resembling a Judaean:*— Jewish.

G2452 **Ἰουδαϊκῶς** *Ioudaikōs* adverb from *G2451*; *Judaïcally* or *in a manner resembling a Judaean:*— as do the Jews.

G2453 **Ἰουδαῖος** *Ioudaios* from *G2448* (in the sense of *G2455* as a country); *Judaean,* i.e. belonging to *Jehudah:*— Jew, Jewess, of Judaea.

G2454 **Ἰουδαϊσμός** *Ioudaismos* from *G2450*; *"Judaïsm",* i.e. the *Jewish faith* and usages:— Jewsae religion.

G2455 **Ἰουδάς** *Ioudas* of Hebrew origin [H3063]; *Judas* (i.e. *Jehudah*), the name of ten Israelites; also of the posterity of one of them and its region:— Juda, Judah, Judas, Jude.

G2456 **Ἰουλία** *Ioulia* feminine of the same as *G2457*; *Julia,* a Christian woman:— Julia.

G2457 **Ἰούλιος** *Ioulios* of Latin origin; *Julius,* a centurion:— Julius.

G2458 **Ἰουνίας** *Iounias* of Latin origin; *Junias,* a Christian:— Junias.

G2459 **Ἰοῦστος** *Ioustos* of Latin origin (*"just"*); *Justus,* the name of three Christians:— Justus.

G2460 **ἱππεύς** *hippeus* from *G2462*; an *equestrian,* i.e. member of a *cavalry* corps:— horseman.

G2461 **ἱππικόν** *hippikon* neuter of a derivative of *G2462*; the *cavalry* force:— horse, horsemen.

G2462 **ἵππος** *hippos* of uncertain affinity; a *horse* :— horse.

G2463 **ἶρις** *iris* perhaps from *G2046* (as a symbolical of the female *messenger* of the pagan deities); a *rainbow* (*"iris"*):— rainbow.

G2464 **Ισαάκ** *Isaak* of Hebrew origin [H3327]; *Isaac* (i.e. *Jitschak*), the son of Abraham:— Isaac.

G2465 **ἰσάγγελος** *isangelos* from *G2470* and *G32*; *like an angel,* i.e. *angelic:*— equal unto the angels.

G2466 **Ἰσαχάρ** *Isachar* of Hebrew origin [H3485]; *Isachar* (i.e. *Jissaskar*), a son of Jacob (figuratively his descendants):— Issachar.

G2467 **ἴσημι** *isēmi* assumed by some as the base of certain irregular forms of *G1942*; to *know:*— know.

G2468 **ἴσθι** *isthi* second person imperative present of *G1510*; *be* thou:— agree, be, give thyself wholly to.

G2469 **Ἰσκαριώτης** *Iskariōtēs* of Hebrew origin [probably H377 and H7149]; *inhabitant of Kerioth; Iscariotes* (i.e. *Keriothite*), an epithet of Judas the traitor:— Iscariot.

G2470 **ἴσος** *isos* probably from *G1492* (through the idea of *seeming*); *similar* (in amount or kind):— agree, as much, equal, like.

G2471 **ἰσότης** *isotēs*; *likeness* (in condition or proportion); by implication *equity:*— equal, equality.

G2472 **ἰσότιμος** *isotimos* from *G2470* and *G5092*; *of equal value* or *honor:*— like precious.

G2473 **ἰσόψυχος** *isopsychos* from *G2470* and *G5590*; *of similar spirit:*— likeminded.

G2474 **Ἰσραήλ** *Israēl* of Hebrew origin [H3478]; *Israel* (i.e. *Jisrael*), the adopted name of Jacob, including his descendants (literal or figurative):— Israel.

G2475 **Ἰσραηλίτης** *Israēlitēs* from *G2474*; an *"Israelite",* i.e. descendant of Israel (literally or figuratively):— Israelite.

G2476 **ἵστημι** *histēmi* a prolonged form of a primary
στάω *staō* (of the same meaning, and used for it in certain tenses); to *stand* (transitive or intransitive), used in various applications (literally or figuratively):— abide, appoint, bring, continue, covenant, establish, hold up, lay, present, set (up), stanch, stand (by, forth, still, up). Compare *G5087*.

G2477 **ἱστορέω** *historeō* from a derivative of *G1492*; to *be knowing* (*learned*), i.e. (by implication) to *visit* for information (*interview*):— see.

G2478 **ἰσχυρός** *ischyros* from *G2479*; *forcible* (literally or figuratively):— boisterous, mighty, mightier, powerful, strong (man), stronger, valiant.

G2479 **ἰσχύς** *ischys* from a derivative of
ἱς *his* (*force;* compare
ἔσχον *eschon* a form of *G2192*); *forcefulness* (literal or figurative):— ability, might, mightily, power, strength.

G2480 **ἰσχύω** *ischyō* from *G2479*; to *have* (or *exercise*) *force* (literally or figuratively):— be able, avail, can do, cannot do, could, be good, might, prevail, be of strength, be whole, much work.

G2481 **ἴσως** *isōs* adverb from *G2470*; *likely,* i.e. *perhaps:*— it may be.

G2482 **Ἰταλία** *Italia* probably of foreign origin; *Italia,* a region of Europe:— Italy.

G2483 **Ἰταλικός** *Italikos* from *G2482*; *Italic,* i.e. belonging to Italia:— Italian.

G2484 **Ἰτουραΐα** *Itouraia* of Hebrew origin [H3195]; *Ituraea* (i.e. *Jetur*), a region of Palestine:— Ituraea.

G2485 **ἰχθύδιον** *ichthydion* diminutive from *G2486*; a *petty fish:*— little (small) fish.

G2486 **ἰχθύς** *ichthys* of uncertain affinity; a *fish:*— fish.

G2487 **ἴχνος** *ichnos* from
ἰκνέομαι *ikneomai* (to *arrive;* compare *G2240*); a *track* (figurative):— step.

G2488 **Ἰωάθαμ** *Iōatham* of Hebrew origin [H3147]; *Joatham* (i.e. *Jotham*), an Israelite:— Joatham.

G2489 **Ἰωάννα** *Iōanna* feminine of the same as *G2491*; *Joanna,* a Christian:— Joanna.

G2490 **Ἰωαννᾶς** *Iōannas* a form of *G2491*; *Joannas,* an Israelite:— Joannas.

G2491 **Ἰωάννης** *Iōannēs* of Hebrew origin [H3110]; *Joannes* (i.e. *Jochanan*), the name of four Israelites:— John.

G2492 **Ἰώβ** *Iōb* of Hebrew origin [H347]; *Job* (i.e. *Ijob*), a patriarch:— Job.

G2493 **Ἰωήλ** *Iōēl* of Hebrew origin [H3100]; *Joel,* an Israelite:— Joel.

G2494 **Ἰωνάν** *Iōnan* probably for *G2491* or *G2495*; *Jonan,* an Israelite:— Jonan.

G2495 **Ἰωνᾶς** *Iōnas* of Hebrew origin [H3124]; *Jonas* (i.e. *Jonah*), the name of two Israelites:— Jonas.

G2496 **Ἰωράμ** *Iōram* of Hebrew origin [H3141]; *Joram,* an Israelite:— Joram.

G2497 **Ἰωρείμ** *Iōreim* perhaps for *G2496*; *Jorim,* an Israelite:— Jorim.

G2498 **Ἰωσαφάτ** *Iōsaphat* of Hebrew origin [H3092]; *Josaphat* (i.e. *Jehoshaphat*), an Israelite:— Josaphat.

G2499 **Ἰωσή** *Iōsē* genitive of *G2500*; *Jose,* an Israelite:— Jose.

G2500 **Ἰωσῆς** *Iōsēs* perhaps for *G2501*; *Joses,* the name of two Israelites:— Joses. Compare Greek *G2499*.

G2501 **Ἰωσήφ** *Iōsēph* of Hebrew origin [H3130]; *Joseph,* the name of seven Israelites:— Joseph.

G2502 **Ἰωσίας** *Iōsias* of Hebrew origin [H2977]; *Josias* (i.e. *Joshiah*), an Israelite:— Josias.

G2503 **ἰῶτα** *iōta* of Hebrew origin [the tenth letter of the Hebrew alphabet]; *"iota",* the name of the eighth letter of the Greek alphabet, put (figuratively) for a very small part of anything:— jot.

K

G2504 **κἀγώ** *kagō* from *G2532* and *G1473*; so also the dataive
κἀμοί *kamoi* and accusative
κἀμέ *kame*; *and* (or *also, even,* etc.) *I,* (*to*) *me:*— (and, even, even so, so) I (also, in like wise), both me, me also.

G2505 **καθά** *katha* from *G2596* and the neuter plural of *G3739*; *according to which* things, i.e. *just as:*— as.

G2506 **καθαίρεσις** *kathairesis* from *G2507*; *demolition;* figuratively *extinction:*— destruction, pulling down.

G2507 **καθαιρέω** *kathaireō* from *G2596* and *G138* (including its alternate); to *lower* (or with violence) *demolish* (literally or figuratively):— cast (pull, put, take) down, destroy.

G2508 **καθαίρω** *kathairō* from *G2513*; to *cleanse,* i.e. (specifically) to *prune;* figuratively to *expiate:*— purge.

G2509 **καθάπερ** *kathaper* from *G2505* and *G4007*; *exactly as:*— (even, as well) as.

G2510 **καθάπτω** *kathaptō* from *G2596* and *G680*; to *seize upon:*— fasten on.

G2511 **καθαρίζω** *katharizō* from *G2513*; to *cleanse* (literally or figuratively):— (make) clean, cleanse, purge, purify.

G2512 **καθαρισμός** *katharismos* from *G2511*; a *washing* off, i.e. (ceremonial) *ablution,* (moral) *expiation:*— cleansing, purge, purification, purifying.

G2513 **καθαρός** *katharos* of uncertain affinity; *clean* (literally or figuratively):— clean, clear, pure.

G2514 **καθαρότης** *katharotēs* from *G2513*; *cleanness* (ceremonial):— purification.

G2515 **καθέδρα** *kathedra* from *G2596* and the same as *G1476*; a *bench* (literal or figurative):— seat.

G2516 **καθέζομαι** *kathezomai* from *G2596* and the base of *G1476*; to *sit down:*— sit.

G2517 **καθεξῆς** *kathexēs* from *G2596* and *G1836*; *thereafter,* i.e. *consecutively;* as a noun (by ellipsis of noun) a *subsequent* person or time:— after, afterward, by (in) order.

G2518 **καθεύδω** *katheudō* from *G2596* and **εὕδω** *heudō* (to *sleep*); to lie *down* to *rest,* i.e. (by implication) to *fall asleep* (literally or figuratively):— sleep, be asleep.

G2519 **καθηγητής** *kathēgētēs* from a compound of *G2596* and *G2233*; a *guide,* i.e. (figuratively) a *teacher:*— master.

G2520 **καθήκω** *kathēkō* from *G2596* and *G2240*; to *reach to,* i.e. (neuter of present active participle, figuratively as adjective) *becoming:*— convenient, fit.

G2521 **κάθημαι** *kathēmai* from *G2596* and hemai (to *sit;* akin to the base of *G1476*); to *sit down;* figuratively to *remain, reside:*— dwell, sit (by, down).

G2522 **καθημερινός** *kathēmerinos* from *G2596* and *G2250*; *quotidian:*— daily.

G2523 **καθίζω** *kathizō* another (active) form for *G2516*; to *seat down,* i.e. *set* (figuratively *appoint*); intransitive to *sit* (down); figuratively to *settle* (*hover, dwell*):— continue, set, sit (down), tarry.

G2524 **καθίημι** *kathiēmi* from *G2596* and **ἵημι** *hiēmi* (to *send*); to *lower:*— let down.

G2525 **καθίστημι** *kathistēmi* from *G2596* and *G2476*; to *place down* (permanently), i.e. (figuratively) to *designate, constitute, convoy:*— appoint, be, conduct, make, ordain, set.

G2526 **καθό** *katho* from *G2596* and *G3739*; *according to which* thing, i.e. *precisely as, in proportion as:*— according to that, (inasmuch) as.

G2526¢ **καθόλικος** *katholikos* from *G2527*; *universal:*— general.

G2527 **καθόλου** *katholou* from *G2596* and *G3650*; *on the whole,* i.e. *entirely:*— at all.

G2528 **καθοπλίζω** *kathoplizō* from *G2596* and *G3695*; to *equip fully* with armor:— arm.

G2529 **καθοράω** *kathoraō* from *G2596* and *G3708*; to *behold fully,* i.e. (figuratively) *distinctly apprehend:*— clearly see.

G2530 **καθότι** *kathoti* from *G2596* and *G3739* and *G5100*; *according to which certain* thing, i.e. *as far* (or *inasmuch*) *as:*— (according, forasmuch) as, because (that).

G2531 **καθώς** *kathōs* from *G2596* and *G5613*; *just* (or *inasmuch*) *as, that:*— according to, (according, even) as, how, when.

G2532 **καί** *kai* apparently a primary particle, having a *copulative* and sometimes also a *cumulative* force; *and, also, even, so, then, too,* etc.; often used in connection (or compounds) with other particles or small words:— and, also, both, but, even, for, if, or, so, that, then, therefore, when, yet.

G2533 **Καϊάφας** *Kaiaphas* of Aramaic origin; *the dell; Caïaphas* (i.e. *Cajepha*), an Israelite:— Caiaphas.

G2534 **καίγε** *kaige* from *G2532* and *G1065*; *and at least* (or *even, indeed*):— and, at least.

G2535 **Κάϊν** *Kain* of Hebrew origin [H7014]; *Caïn* (i.e. *Cajin*), the son of Adam:— Cain.

G2536 **Καϊνάν** *Kainan* of Hebrew origin [H7018]; *Caïnan* (i.e. *Kenan*), the name of two patriarchs:— Cainan.

G2537 **καινός** *kainos* of uncertain affinity; *new* (especially in *freshness;* while *G3501* is properly so with respect to *age*):— new.

G2538 **καινότης** *kainotēs* from *G2537*; *renewal* (figurative):— newness.

G2539 **καίπερ** *kaiper* from *G2532* and *G4007*; *and indeed,* i.e. *nevertheless* or *notwithstanding:*— and yet, although.

G2540 **καιρός** *kairos* of uncertain affinity; an *occasion,* i.e. *set* or *proper* time:— always, opportunity, (convenient, due) season, (due, short, while) time, a while. Compare *G5550*.

G2541 **Καῖσαρ** *Kaisar* of Latin origin; *Caesar,* a title of the Roman emperor:— Caesar.

G2542 **Καισάρεια** *Kaisareia* from *G2541*; *Caesaria,* the name of two places in Palestine:— Caesarea.

G2543 **καίτοι** *kaitoi* from *G2532* and *G5104*; *and yet,* i.e. *nevertheless:*— although.

G2544 **καίτοιγε** *kaitoige* from *G2543* and *G1065*; *and yet indeed,* i.e. *although really:*— nevertheless, though.

G2545 **καίω** *kaiō* apparently a primary verb; to *set on fire,* i.e. *kindle* or (by implication) *consume:*— burn, light.

G2546 **κἀκεῖ** *kakei* from *G2532* and *G1563*; *likewise in that place:*— and there, there (thither) also.

G2547 **κἀκεῖθεν** *kakeithen* from *G2532* and *G1564*; *likewise from that place* (or *time*):— and afterward (from) (thence), thence also.

G2548 **κἀκεῖνος** *kakeinos* from *G2532* and *G1565*; *likewise that* (or *those*):— and him (other, them), even he, him also, them (also), (and) they.

G2549 **κακία** *kakia* from *G2556*; *badness,* i.e. (subjectively) *depravity,* or (active) *malignity,* or (passive) *trouble:*— evil, malice, maliciousness, naughtiness, wickedness.

G2550 **κακοήθεια** *kakoētheia* from a compound of *G2556* and *G2239*; *bad character,* i.e. (specifically) *mischievousness:*— malignity.

G2551 **κακολογέω** *kakologeō* from a compound of *G2556* and *G3056*; to *revile:*— curse, speak evil of.

G2552 **κακοπάθεια** *kakopatheia* from a compound of *G2556* and *G3806*; *hardship:*— suffering affliction.

G2553 **κακοπαθέω** *kakopatheō* from the same as *G2552*; to *undergo hardship:*— be afflicted, endure afflictions (hardness), suffer trouble.

G2554 **κακοποιέω** *kakopoieō* from *G2555*; to *be a bad-doer,* i.e. (object) to *injure,* or (generally) to *sin:*— do evil, doing evil.

G2555 **κακοποιός** *kakopoios* from *G2556* and *G4160*; a *bad-doer;* (specificaly) a *criminal:*— evil-doer, malefactor.

G2556 **κακός** *kakos* apparently a primary word; *worthless* (*intrinsically* such; whereas *G4190* properly refers to *effects*), i.e. (subjectively) *depraved,* or (objectively) *injurious:*— bad, evil, harm, ill, noisome, wicked.

G2557 **κακοῦργος** *kakourgos* from *G2556* and the base of *G2041*; a *wrong-doer,* i.e. *criminal:*— evil-doer, malefactor.

G2558 **κακουχέω** *kakoucheō* from a presumed compound of *G2556* and *G2192*; to *maltreat:*— which suffer adversity, torment.

G2559 **κακόω** *kakoō* from *G2556*; to *injure;* figuratively to *exasperate:*— make evil affected, entreat evil, harm, hurt, vex.

G2560 **κακῶς** *kakōs* adverb from *G2556*; *badly* (physically or morally):— amiss, diseased, evil, grievously, miserably, sick, sore.

G2561 **κάκωσις** *kakōsis* from *G2559*; *maltreatment* :— affliction.

G2562 **καλάμη** *kalamē* feminine of *G2563*; a *stalk* of grain, i.e. (collectively) *stubble:*— stubble.

G2563 **κάλαμος** *kalamos* of uncertain affinity; a *reed* (the plant or its stem, or that of a similar plant); by implication a *pen:*— pen, reed.

G2564 **καλέω** *kaleō* akin to the base of *G2753*; to *"call"* (properly aloud, but used in a variety of applications, directly or otherwise):— bid, call (forth), (whose) name (was [called]), (whose) surname (was [called]).

G2565 **καλλιέλαιος** *kallielaios* from the base of *G2566* and *G1636*; a *cultivated olive* tree, i.e. a *domesticated* or *improved* one:— good olive tree.

G2566 **κάλλιον** *kallion* neuter of the (irregular) comparative of *G2570*; (adverbially) *better* than many:— very well.

G2567 **καλοδιδάσκαλος** *kalodidaskalos* from *G2570* and *G1320*; a *teacher of* the *right:*— teacher of good things.

G2568 **Καλοὶ Λιμένες** *Kaloi Limenes* plural of *G2570* and *G3040*; *Good Harbors,* i.e. *Fairhaven,* a bay of Crete:— fair havens.

G2569 **καλοποιέω** *kalopoieō* from *G2570* and *G4160*; to *do well,* i.e. live virtuously:— well doing.

G2570 **καλός** *kalos* of uncertain affinity; properly *beautiful,* but chiefly (figuratively) *good* (literally or morally), i.e. *valuable* or *virtuous* (for *appearance* or *use,* and thus distinguished from *G18*, which is properly *intrinsic*):— better, fair, good, goodly, honest, meet, well, worthy.

G2571 **κάλυμμα** *kalymma* from *G2572*; a *cover,* i.e. *veil:*— vail.

G2572 **καλύπτω** *kalyptō* akin to *G2813* and *G2928*; to *cover* up (literally or figuratively):— cover, hide.

G2573 **καλῶς** *kalōs* adverb from *G2570*; *well* (usually morally):— (in a) good (place), honestly, recover, (full) well.

G2574 **κάμηλος** *kamēlos* of Hebrew origin [H1581]; a *"camel"*:— camel.

G2575 κάμινος *kaminos* probably from G2545; a *furnace:*— furnace.

G2576 καμμύω *kammyō* for a compound of G2596 and the base of G3466; to *shut down,* i.e. *close* the eyes:— close.

G2577 κάμνω *kamnō* apparently a primary verb; properly to *toil,* i.e. (by implication) to *tire* (figuratively *faint, sicken*):— faint, sick, be wearied.

G2578 κάμπτω *kamptō* apparently a primary verb; to *bend:*— bow.

G2579 κἄν *kan* from G2532 and G1437; *and* (or *even*) *if:*— and (also) if (so much as), if but, at the least, though, yet.

G2580 Κανᾶ *Kana* of Hebrew origin [compare H7071]; *Cana,* a place in Palestine:— Cana.

G2581 Κανανίτης *Kananitēs* of Aramaic origin [compare H7067]; *zealous; Cananitès,* an epithet:— Canaanite [*by mistake for a derived from G5477*].

G2582 Κανδάκη *Kandakē* of foreign origin; *Candacè,* an Egyptian queen:— Candace.

G2583 κανών *kanōn* from
κάνη *kanē* (a straight *reed,* i.e. *rod*); a *rule* (*"canon"*), i.e. (figuratively) a *standard* (of faith and practice); by implication a *boundary,* i.e. (figuratively) a *sphere* (of activity):— line, rule.

G2584 Καπερναούμ *Kapernaoum* of Hebrew origin [probably H3723 and H5151]; *Capernaum* i.e. *Caphanachum*), a place in Palestine:— Capernaum.

G2585 καπηλεύω *kapēleuō* from
κάπηλος *kapēlos* (a *huckster*); to *retail,* i.e. (by implication) to *adulterate* (figuratively):— corrupt.

G2586 καπνός *kapnos* of uncertain affinity; *smoke* :— smoke.

G2587 Καππαδοκία *Kappadokia* of foreign origin; *Cappadocia,* a region of Asia Minor:— Cappadocia.

G2588 καρδία *kardia* prolonged from a primary
κάρ *kar* (Latin *cor,* "*heart*"); the *heart,* i.e. (figuratively) the *thoughts* or *feelings* (*mind*); also (by analogy) the *middle:*— heart, broken hearted.

G2589 καρδιογνώστης *kardiognōstēs* from G2588 and G1097; *one who knows the heart:*— which knowest the hearts.

G2590 καρπός *karpos* probably from the base of G726; *fruit* (as *plucked*), literally or figuratively:— fruit.

G2591 Κάρπος *Karpos* perhaps for G2590; *Carpus,* probably a Christian:— Carpus.

G2592 καρποφορέω *karpophoreō* from G2593; to *be fertile* (literally or figuratively):— (bear, bring forth) fruit, be fruitful.

G2593 καρποφόρος *karpophoros* from G2590 and G5342; *fruitbearing* (figuratively):— fruitful.

G2594 καρτερέω *kartereō* from a derivative of G2904 (transposed); to *be strong,* i.e. (figuratively) *steadfast* (*patient*):— endure.

G2595 κάρφος *karphos* from
κάρφω *karphō* (to *wither*); a dry *twig* or *straw:*— mote.

G2596 κατά *kata* a primary particle; (preposition) *down* (in place or time), in varied relations (according to the case [genitive, dative or accusative] with which it is joined). In compounds it retains many of these applications, and frequently denotes *opposition, distribution* or *intensity:*— about, according as (to), after, against, (when they were) alone, among, and, apart, (even, like) as (concerning, pertaining to, touching), aside, at, before, beyond, by, to the charge of, [charita-]bly, concerning, covered, [dai-]ly, down, every, (+ far more) exceeding, more excellent, for, from . . . to, godly, in (divers, every, respect of), inasmuch, into, . . . by, after the manner of, by any means, beyond (out of) measure, mightily, more, natural, of, on (part), upon, out (of every), over against, (+ your) own, particularly, so, through, throughout (every), thus, to, unto, together, toward, uttermost, where, whereby, with.

G2597 καταβαίνω *katabainō* from G2596 and the base of G939; to *descend* (literally or figuratively):— come (get, go, step) down, fall (down).

G2598 καταβάλλω *kataballō* from G2596 and G906; to *throw down:*— cast down, lay.

G2599 καταβαρέω *katabareō* from G2596 and G916; to *impose upon:*— burden.

G2600 κατάβασις *katabasis* from G2597; a *declivity:*— descent.

G2601 καταβιβάζω *katabibazō* from G2596 and a derivative of the base of G939; to *cause to go down,* i.e. *precipitate:*— bring (thrust) down.

G2602 καταβολή *katabolē* from G2598; a *deposition,* i.e. *founding;* figuratively *conception:*— conceive, foundation.

G2603 καταβραβεύω *katabrabeuō* from G2596 and G1018 (in its original sense); to *award* the price *against,* i.e. (figuratively) to *defraud* (of salvation):— beguile of reward.

G2604 καταγγελεύς *katangeleus* from G2605; a *proclaimer:*— setter forth.

G2605 καταγγέλλω *katangellō* from G2596 and the base of G32; to *proclaim, promulgate:*— declare, preach, shew, speak of, teach.

G2606 καταγελάω *katagelaō*; to *laugh down,* i.e. *deride:*— laugh to scorn.

G2607 καταγινώσκω *kataginōskō* from G2596 and G1097; to *note against,* i.e. *find fault with:*— blame, condemn.

G2608 κατάγνυμι *katagnymi* from G2596 and the base of G4486; to *rend in pieces,* i.e. *crack apart:*— break.

G2609 κατάγω *katagō* from G2596 and G71; to *lead down;* specifically to *moor* a vessel:— bring (down, forth), (bring to) land, touch.

G2610 καταγωνίζομαι *katagōnizomai* from G2596 and G75; to *struggle against,* i.e. (by implication) to *overcome:*— subdue.

G2611 καταδέω *katadeō* from G2596 and G1210; to *tie down,* i.e. *bandage* (a wound):— bind up.

G2612 κατάδηλος *katadēlos* from G2596 intensive and G1212; *manifest:*— far more evident.

G2613 καταδικάζω *katadikazō* from G2596 and a derivative of G1349; to *adjudge against,* i.e. *pronounce guilty:*— condemn.

G2614 καταδιώκω *katadiōkō* from G2596 and G1377; to *hunt down,* i.e. *search for:*— follow after.

G2615 καταδουλόω *katadouloō* from G2596 and G1402; to *enslave utterly:*— bring into bondage.

G2616 καταδυναστεύω *katadynasteuō* from Greek G2596 and a derivative of G1413; to *exercise dominion against,* i.e. *oppress:*— oppress.

G2617 καταισχύνω *kataischynō* from G2596 and G153; to *shame down,* i.e. *disgrace* or (by implication) *put to the blush:*— confound, dishonour, shame, be ashamed, make ashamed.

G2618 κατακαίω *katakaiō* from G2596 and G2545; to *burn down* (to the ground), i.e. *consume wholly:*— burn (up, utterly).

G2619 κατακαλύπτω *katakalyptō* from G2596 and G2572; to *cover wholly,* i.e. *veil:*— cover, hide.

G2620 κατακαυχάομαι *katakauchaomai* from G2596 and G2744; to *exult against* (i.e. *over*):— boast (against), glory, rejoice against.

G2621 κατάκειμαι *katakeimai* from G2596 and G2749; to *lie down,* i.e. (by implication) *be sick;* specifically to *recline* at a meal:— keep, lie, sit at meat (down).

G2622 κατακλάω *kataklaō* from G2596 and G2806; to *break down,* i.e. *divide:*— break.

G2623 κατακλείω *katakleiō* from G2596 and G2808; to *shut down* (in a dungeon), i.e. *incarcerate:*— shut up.

G2624 κατακληροδοτέω *kataklērodoteō* from G2596 and a derivative of a compound of G2819 and G1325; to *be a giver of lots to each,* i.e. (by implication) to *apportion an estate:*— divide by lot.

G2625 κατακλίνω *kataklinō* from G2596 and G2827; to *recline down,* i.e. (specifically) to *take a place* at table:— (make) sit down (at meat).

G2626 κατακλύζω *kataklyzō* from G2596 and the base of G2830; to *dash* (*wash*) *down,* i.e. (by implication) to *deluge:*— overflow.

G2627 κατακλυσμός *kataklysmos* from G2626; an *inundation:*— flood.

G2628 κατακολουθέω *katakoloutheō* from G2596 and G190; to *accompany closely:*— follow (after).

G2629 κατακόπτω *katakoptō* from G2596 and G2875; to *chop down,* i.e. *mangle:*— cut.

G2630 κατακρημνίζω *katakrēmnizō* from G2596 and a derivative of G2911; to *precipitate down:*— cast down headlong.

G2631 κατάκριμα *katakrima* from G2632; an *adverse sentence* (the verdict):— condemnation.

G2632 κατακρίνω *katakrinō* from G2596 and G2919; to *judge against,* i.e. *sentence:*— condemn, damn.

G2633 κατάκρισις *katakrisis* from G2632; *sentencing adversely* (the act):— condemn, condemnation.

G2634 κατακυριεύω *katakyrieuō* from G2596 and G2961; to *lord against,* i.e. *control, subjugate:*— exercise dominion over (lordship), be lord over, overcome.

G2635 καταλαλέω *katalaleō* from G2637; to *be a traducer,* i.e. to *slander:*— speak against (evil of).

G2636 καταλαλιά *katalalia* from G2637; *defamation:*— backbiting, evil speaking.

G2637 κατάλαλος *katalalos* from G2596 and the base of G2980; *talkative against,* i.e. a *slanderer:*— backbiter.

G2638 καταλαμβάνω *katalambanō* from G2596 and G2983; to *take eagerly,* i.e. *seize, possess,* etc. (literally or figuratively):— apprehend, attain, come upon, comprehend, find, obtain, perceive, take, overtake.

G2639 καταλέγω *katalegō* from *G2596* and *G3004* (in its original meaning); to *lay down,* i.e. (figuratively) to *enroll:*— take into the number.

G2640 κατάλειμμα *kataleimma* from *G2641*; a *remainder,* i.e. (by implication) a *few:*— remnant.

G2641 καταλείπω *kataleipō* from *G2596* and *G3007*; to *leave down,* i.e. *behind;* by implication to *abandon, have remaining:*— forsake, leave, reserve.

G2642 καταλιθάζω *katalithazō* from *G2596* and *G3034*; to *stone down,* i.e. *to death:*— stone.

G2643 καταλλαγή *katallagē* from *G2644*; *exchange* (figuratively *adjustment*), i.e. *restoration* to (the divine) favor:— atonement, reconciling, reconciliation.

G2644 καταλλάσσω *katallassō* from *G2596* and *G236*; to *change mutually,* i.e. (figuratively) to *compound* a difference:— reconcile.

G2645 κατάλοιπος *kataloipos* from *G2596* and *G3062*; *left down* (*behind*) i.e. *remaining* (plural the *rest*):— residue.

G2646 κατάλυμα *katalyma* from *G2647*; properly a *dissolution* (breaking up of a journey), i.e. (by implication) a *lodging-place:*— guestchamber, inn.

G2647 καταλύω *katalyō* from *G2596* and *G3089*; to *loosen down* (*disintegrate*), i.e. (by implication) to *demolish* (literally or figuratively); specifically [compare *G2646*] to *halt* for the night:— destroy, dissolve, be guest, lodge, come to nought, overthrow, throw down.

G2648 καταμανθάνω *katamanthanō* from *G2596* and *G3129*; to *learn thoroughly,* i.e. (by implication) to *note carefully:*— consider.

G2649 καταμαρτυρέω *katamartyreō* from *G2596* and *G3140*; to *testify against:*— witness against.

G2650 καταμένω *katamenō* from *G2596* and *G3306*; to *stay fully,* i.e. *reside:*— abide.

G2651 καταμόνας *katamonas* from *G2596* and accusative plural feminine of *G3441* (with *G5561* implied); *according to sole* places, i.e. (adverbially) *separately:*— alone.

G2652 κατανάθεμα *katanathema* from *G2596* (intensive) and *G331*; an *imprecation:*— curse.

G2653 καταναθεματίζω *katanathematizō* from *G2596* (intensive) and *G332*; to *imprecate:*— curse.

G2654 καταναλίσκω *katanaliskō* from *G2596* and *G355*; to *consume utterly:*— consume.

G2655 καταναρκάω *katanarkaō* from *G2596* and **ναρκάω** *narkaō* (to *be numb*); to *grow utterly torpid,* i.e. (by implication) *slothful* (figuratively *expensive*):— be burdensome (chargeable).

G2656 κατανεύω *kataneuō* from *G2596* and *G3506*; to *nod down* (*towards*), i.e. (by analogy) to *make signs* to:— beckon.

G2657 κατανοέω *katanoeō* from *G2596* and *G3539*; to *observe fully:*— behold, consider, discover, perceive.

G2658 καταντάω *katantaō* from *G2596* and a derivative of *G473*; to *meet against,* i.e. *arrive* at (literally or figuratively):— attain, come.

G2659 κατάνυξις *katanyxis* from *G2660*; a *prickling* (sensation, as of the limbs *asleep*), i.e. (by implication [perhaps by some confusion with *G3506* or even with *G3571*]) *stupor* (*lethargy*):— slumber.

G2660 κατανύσσω *katanyssō* from *G2596* and *G3572*; to *pierce thoroughly,* i.e. (figuratively) to *agitate* violently ("sting to the quick"):— prick.

G2661 καταξιόω *kataxioō* from *G2596* and *G515*; to *deem entirely deserving:*— account worthy, count worthy.

G2662 καταπατέω *katapateō* from *G2596* and *G3961*; to *trample down;* figuratively to *reject* with disdain:— trample, tread (down, underfoot).

G2663 κατάπαυσις *katapausis* from *G2664*; *reposing down,* i.e. (by Hebrew) *abode:*— rest.

G2664 καταπαύω *katapauō* from *G2596* and *G3973*; to *settle down,* i.e. (literally) to *colonize,* or (figuratively) to (*cause to*) *desist:*— cease, (give) rest, restrain.

G2665 καταπέτασμα *katapetasma* from a compound of *G2596* and a congener of *G4072*; something *spread thoroughly,* i.e. (specifically) the door *screen* (to the Most Holy Place) in the Jewish Temple:— vail.

G2666 καταπίνω *katapinō* from *G2596* and *G4095*; to *drink down,* i.e. *gulp entire* (literally or figuratively):— devour, drown, swallow (up).

G2667 καταπίπτω *katapiptō* from *G2596* and *G4098*; to *fall down:*— fall (down).

G2668 καταπλέω *katapleō* from *G2596* and *G4126*; to *sail down* upon a place, i.e. to *land* at:— arrive.

G2669 καταπονέω *kataponeō* from *G2596* and a derivative of *G4192*; to *labor down* i.e. *wear with toil* (figuratively *harass*):— oppress, vex.

G2670 καταποντίζω *katapontizō* from *G2596* and a derivative of the same as *G4195*; to *plunge down,* i.e. *submerge:*— drown, sink.

G2671 κατάρα *katara* from *G2596* (intensive) and *G685*; *imprecation, execration:*— curse, cursed, cursing.

G2672 καταράομαι *kataraomai* middle from *G2671*; to *execrate;* by analogy to *doom:*— curse.

G2673 καταργέω *katargeō* from *G2596* and *G691*; to *be* (*render*) *entirely idle* (*useless*), literally or figuratively:— abolish, cease, cumber, deliver, destroy, do away, become (make) of no (none, without) effect, fail, loose, bring (come) to nought, put away (down), vanish away, make void.

G2674 καταριθμέω *katarithmeō* from *G2596* and *G705*; to *reckon among:*— number with.

G2675 καταρτίζω *katartizō* from *G2596* and a derivative of *G739*; to *complete thoroughly,* i.e. *repair* (literally or figuratively) or *adjust:*— fit, frame, mend, (make) perfect, perfectly join together, prepare, restore.

G2676 κατάρτισις *katartisis* from *G2675*; *thorough equipment* (subjectively):— perfection.

G2677 καταρτισμός *katartismos* from *G2675*; *complete furnishing* (objectively):— perfecting.

G2678 κατασείω *kataseiō* from *G2596* and *G4579*; to *sway downward,* i.e. *make a signal:*— beckon.

G2679 κατασκάπτω *kataskaptō* from *G2596* and *G4626*; to *undermine,* i.e. (by implication) *destroy* :— dig down, ruin.

G2680 κατασκευάζω *kataskeuazō* from *G2596* and a derivative of *G4632*; to *prepare thoroughly* (properly by external *equipment;* whereas *G2090* refers rather to internal *fitness*); by implication to *construct, create:*— build, make, ordain, prepare.

G2681 κατασκηνόω *kataskēnoō* from *G2596* and *G4637*; to *camp down,* i.e. *haunt;* figuratively to *remain:*— lodge, rest.

G2682 κατασκήνωσις *kataskēnōsis* from *G2681*; an *encamping,* i.e. (figuratively) a *perch:*— nest.

G2683 κατασκιάζω *kataskiazō* from *G2596* and a derivative of *G4639*; to *overshade,* i.e. *cover:*— shadow.

G2684 κατασκοπέω *kataskopeō* from *G2685*; to *be a sentinel,* i.e. to *inspect* insidiously:— spy out.

G2685 κατάσκοπος *kataskopos* from *G2596* (intensive) and *G4649* (in the sense of a *watcher*); a *reconnoiterer:*— spy.

G2686 κατασοφίζομαι *katasophizomai* middle from *G2596* and *G4679*; to *be crafty against,* i.e. *circumvent:*— deal subtilly with.

G2687 καταστέλλω *katastellō* from *G2596* and *G4724*; to *put down,* i.e. *quell:*— appease, quiet.

G2688 κατάστημα *katastēma* from *G2525*; properly a *position* or *condition,* i.e. (subjectively) *demeanor:*— behaviour.

GRK

G2689 καταστολή *katastolē* from *G2687*; a *deposit,* i.e. (specifically) *costume:*— apparel.

G2690 καταστρέφω *katastrephō* from *G2596* and *G4762*; to *turn* upside *down,* i.e. *upset:*— overthrow.

G2691 καταστρηνιάω *katastrēniaō* from *G2596* and *G4763*; to *become voluptuous against:*— begin to wax wanton against.

G2692 καταστροφή *katastrophē* from *G2690*; an *overturn* ("*catastrophe*"), i.e. *demolition;* figuratively *apostasy:*— overthrow, subverting.

G2693 καταστρώννυμι *katastrōnnymi* from *G2596* and *G4766*; to *strew down,* i.e. (by implication) to *prostrate* (*slay*):— overthrow.

G2694 κατασύρω *katasyrō* from *G2596* and *G4951*; to *drag down,* i.e. *arrest* judicially:— hale.

G2695 κατασφάττω *katasphattō* from *G2596* and *G4969*; to *kill down,* i.e. *slaughter:*— slay.

G2696 κατασφραγίζω *katasphragizō* from *G2596* and *G4972*; to *seal closely:*— seal.

G2697 κατάσχεσις *kataschesis* from *G2722*; a *holding down,* i.e. *occupancy:*— possession.

G2698 κατατίθημι *katatithēmi* from *G2596* and *G5087*; to *place down,* i.e. *deposit* (literally or figuratively):— do, lay, shew.

G2699 κατατομή *katatomē* from a compound of *G2596* and **τέμνω** *temnō* (to *cut*); a *cutting down* (*off*), i.e. *mutilation* (ironically):— concision. Compare *G609*.

G2700 κατατοξεύω *katatoxeuō* from *G2596* and a derivative of *G5115*; to *shoot down* with an arrow or other missile:— thrust through.

G2701 κατατρέχω *katatrechō* from *G2596* and *G5143*; to *run down,* i.e. *hasten* from a tower:— run down.

G2702 καταφέρω *katapherō* from *G2596* and *G5342* (including its alternate); to *bear down,* i.e. (figuratively) *overcome* (with drowsiness); specifically to *cast* a vote:— fall, give, sink down.

G2703 καταφεύγω *katapheugō* from *G2596* and *G5343*; to *flee down* (*away*):— flee.

G2704 καταφθείρω *kataphtheirō* from *G2596* and *G5351*; to *spoil entirely,* i.e. (literally) to *destroy;* or (figuratively) to *deprave:*— corrupt, utterly perish.

G2705 καταφιλέω *kataphileō* from *G2596* and *G5368*; to *kiss earnestly:*— kiss.

G2706 καταφρονέω *kataphroneō* from G2596 and G5426; to *think against*, i.e. *disesteem:*— despise.

G2707 καταφρονητής *kataphronētēs* from G2706; *one who feels contempt:*— despiser.

G2708 καταχέω *katacheō* from G2596 and **χέω** *cheō* (to *pour*); to *pour down* (*out*):— pour.

G2709 καταχθόνιος *katachthonios* from G2596 and **χθών** *chthōn* (the *ground*); *subterranean*, i.e. *infernal* (belonging to the world of departed spirits):— under the earth.

G2710 καταχράομαι *katachraomai* from G2596 and G5530; to *overuse* i.e. *misuse:*— abuse.

G2711 καταψύχω *katapsychō* from G2596 and G5594; to *cool down* (*off*), i.e. *refresh:*— cool.

G2712 κατείδωλος *kateidōlos* from G2596 (intensive) and G1497; *utterly idolatrous:*— wholly given to idolatry.

G2713 κατέναντι *katenanti* from G2596 and G1725; *directly opposite:*— before, over against.

G2714 κατενώπιον *katenōpion* from G2596 and G1799; *directly in front of:*— before (the presence of), in the sight of.

G2715 κατεξουσιάζω *katexousiazō* from G2596 and G1850; to *have* (*wield*) *full privilege over:*— exercise authority.

G2716 κατεργάζομαι *katergazomai* from G2596 and G2038; to *work fully*, i.e. *accomplish;* by implication to *finish, fashion:*— cause, do (deed), perform, work (out).

G2718 κατέρχομαι *katerchomai* from G2596 and G2064 (including its alternate); to *come* (or *go*) *down* (literally or figuratively):— come (down), depart, descend, go down, land.

G2719 κατεσθίω *katesthiō* from G2596 and G2068 (including its alternate); to *eat down*, i.e. *devour* (literally or figuratively):— devour.

G2720 κατευθύνω *kateuthynō* from G2596 and G2116; to *straighten fully*, i.e. (figuratively) *direct:*— guide, direct.

G2721 κατεφίστημι *katephistēmi* from G2596 and G2186; to *stand over against*, i.e. *rush upon* (*assault*):— make insurrection against.

G2722 κατέχω *katechō* from G2596 and G2192; to *hold down* (*fast*), in various applications (literally or figuratively):— have, hold (fast), keep (in memory), let, make toward, possess, retain, seize on, stay, take, withhold.

G2723 κατηγορέω *katēgoreō* from G2725; to *be a plaintiff*, i.e. to *charge* with some offence:— accuse, object.

G2724 κατηγορία *katēgoria* from G2725; a *complaint* ("category"), i.e. criminal *charge:*— accusation (accused).

G2725 κατήγορος *katēgoros* from G2596 and G58; *against* one in the *assembly*, i.e. a *complainant* at law; specifically *Satan:*— accuser.

G2726 κατήφεια *katēpheia* from a compound of G2596 and perhaps a derivative of the base of G5316 (meaning *downcast* in look); *demureness*, i.e. (by implication) *sadness:*— heaviness.

G2727 κατηχέω *katēcheō* from G2596 and G2279; to *sound down* into the ears, i.e. (by implication) to *indoctrinate* ("catechize") or (generally) to *apprise* of:— inform, instruct, teach.

G2728 κατιόω *katioō* from G2596 and a derivative of G2447; to *rust down*, i.e. *corrode:*— canker.

G2729 κατισχύω *katischyō* from G2596 and G2480; to *overpower:*— prevail (against).

G2730 κατοικέω *katoikeō* from G2596 and G3611; to *house permanently*, i.e. *reside* (literally or figuratively):— dwell, dweller, inhabitant, inhabiter.

G2731 κατοίκησις *katoikēsis* from G2730; *residence* (properly the act; but by implication concretely the mansion):— dwelling.

G2732 κατοικητήριον *katoikētērion* from a derivative of G2730; a *dwelling-place:*— habitation.

G2733 κατοικία *katoikia*; *residence* (properly the condition; but by implication the abode itself):— habitation.

G2734 κατοπτρίζομαι *katoptrizomai* middle from a compound of G2596 and a derivative of G3700 [compare G2072]; to *mirror oneself*, i.e. to *see reflected* (figuratively):— behold as in a glass.

G2735 κατόρθωμα *katorthōma* from a compound of G2596 and a derivative of G3717 [compare G1357]; something *made fully upright*, i.e. (figuratively) *rectification* (specifically *good* public *administration*):— very worthy deed.

G2736 κάτω *katō* also comparative **κατωτέρω** *katōterō* [compare G2737]; adverb from G2596; *downwards:*— beneath, bottom, down, under.

G2737 κατώτερος *katōteros* comparative from G2736; *inferior* (locally, of Hades):— lower.

G2738 καῦμα *kauma* from G2545; properly a *burn* (concrete), but used (abstractly) of a *glow:*— heat.

G2739 καυματίζω *kaumatizō* from G2738; to *burn* :— scorch.

G2740 καῦσις *kausis* from G2545; *burning* (the act):— be burned.

G2741 καυσόω *kausoō* from G2740; to *set on fire* :— with fervent heat.

G2742 καύσων *kausōn* from G2741; a *glare:*— (burning) heat.

G2743 καυτηριάζω *kautēriazō* from a derivative of G2545; to *brand* ("*cauterize*"), i.e. (by implication) to *render insensitive* (figuratively):— sear with a hot iron.

G2744 καυχάομαι *kauchaomai* from some (obsolete) base akin to that of **αὐχέω** *aucheō* (to *boast*) and G2172; to *vaunt* (in a good or a bad sense):— (make) boast, glory, joy, rejoice.

G2745 καύχημα *kauchēma* from G2744; a *boast* (properly the object; by implication the act) in a good or a bad sense:— boasting, (whereof) to glory (of), glorying, rejoice, rejoicing.

G2746 καύχησις *kauchēsis* from G2744; *boasting* (properly the act; by implication the object), in a good or a bad sense:— boasting, whereof I may glory, glorying, rejoicing.

G2747 Κεγχρεαί *Kenchreai* probably from **κέγχρος** *kenchros* (*millet*); *Cenchreae*, a port of Corinth:— Cenchrea.

G2748 Κεδρών *Kedrōn* of Hebrew origin [H6939]; *Cedron* (i.e. *Kidron*), a brook near Jerusalem:— Cedron.

G2749 κεῖμαι *keimai* middle of a primary verb; to *lie* outstretched (literally or figuratively):— be (appointed, laid up, made, set), lay, lie. Compare G5087.

G2750 κειρία *keiria* of uncertain affinity; a *swathe*, i.e. *winding-sheet:*— graveclothes.

G2751 κείρω *keirō* a primary verb; to *shear:*— shear, shearer.

G2752 κέλευσμα *keleusma* from G2753; a *cry* of incitement:— shout.

G2753 κελεύω *keleuō* from a primary **κέλλω** *kellō* (to *urge* on); "hail"; to *incite* by word, i.e. *order:*— bid, (at, give) command, commandment.

G2754 κενοδοξία *kenodoxia* from G2755; *empty glorying*, i.e. *self-conceit:*— vain-glory.

G2755 κενόδοξος *kenodoxos* from G2756 and G1391; *vainly glorifying*, i.e. *self-conceited:*— desirous of vain-glory.

G2756 κενός *kenos* apparently a primary word; *empty* (literally or figuratively):— empty, (in) vain.

G2757 κενοφωνία *kenophōnia* from a presumed compound of G2756 and G5456; *empty sounding*, i.e. *fruitless discussion:*— vain.

G2758 κενόω *kenoō* from G2756; to *make empty*, i.e. (figuratively) to *abase, neutralize, falsify:*— make (of none effect, of no reputation, void), be in vain.

G2759 κέντρον *kentron* from **κεντέω** *kenteō* (to *prick*); a *point* ("centre"), i.e. a *sting* (figuratively *poison*) or *goad* (figuratively divine *impulse*):— prick, sting.

G2760 κεντυρίων *kentyriōn* of Latin origin; a *centurion*, i.e. *captain* of one hundred soldiers:— centurion.

G2761 κενῶς *kenōs* adverb from G2756; *vainly*, i.e. *to no purpose:*— in vain.

G2762 κεραία *keraia* feminine of a presumed derivative of the base of G2768; something *horn-like*, i.e. (specifically) the *apex* of a Hebrew letter (figuratively the least *particle*):— tittle.

G2763 κεραμεύς *kerameus* from G2766; a *potter* :— potter.

G2764 κεραμικός *keramikos* from G2766; *made of clay*, i.e. *earthen:*— of a potter.

G2765 κεράμιον *keramion* neuter of a presumed derivative of G2766; an *earthenware* vessel, i.e. *jar:*— pitcher.

G2766 κέραμος *keramos* probably from the base of G2767 (through the idea of *mixing* clay and water); *earthenware*, i.e. a *tile* (by analogy a thin *roof* or *awning*):— tiling.

G2767 κεράννυμι *kerannymi* a prolonged form of a more primary **κεράω** *keraō* (which is used in certain tenses); to *mingle*, i.e. (by implication) to *pour* out (for drinking):— fill, pour out. Compare G3396.

G2768 κέρας *keras* from a primary **κάρ** *kar* (the *hair* of the head); a *horn* (literal or figurative):— horn.

G2769 κεράτιον *keration* neuter of a presumed derivative of G2768; something *horned*, i.e. (specifically) the *pod* of the carob-tree:— husk.

G2770 κερδαίνω *kerdainō* from G2771; to *gain* (literally or figuratively):— (get) gain, win.

G2771 κέρδος *kerdos* of uncertain affinity; *gain* (pecuniary or general):— gain, lucre.

G2772 κέρμα *kerma* from G2751; a *clipping* (*bit*), i.e. (specifically) a *coin*:— money.

G2773 κερματιστής *kermatistēs* from a derivative of G2772; a *handler of coins,* i.e. *money-broker*:— changer of money.

G2774 κεφάλαιον *kephalaion* neuter of a derivative of G2776; a *principal* thing, i.e. *main point;* specifically an *amount* (of money):— sum.

G2775 κεφαλαιόω *kephalaioō* from the same as G2774; (specifically) to *strike on the head*:— wound in the head.

G2776 κεφαλή *kephalē* probably from the primary **κάπτω** *kaptō* (in the sense of *seizing*); the *head* (as the part most readily *taken* hold of), literally or figuratively:— head.

G2777 κεφαλίς *kephalis* from G2776; properly a *knob,* i.e. (by implication) a *roll* (by extension from the *end* of a stick on which the manuscript was rolled):— volume.

G2778 κῆνσος *kēnsos* of Latin origin; properly an *enrolment* (*"census"*), i.e. (by implication) a *tax*:— tribute.

G2779 κῆπος *kēpos* of uncertain affinity; a *garden*:— garden.

G2780 κηπουρός *kēpouros* from G2779 and **οὖρος** *ouros* (a *warden*); a *garden-keeper,* i.e. *gardener*:— gardener.

G2781 κηρίον *kērion* diminutive from **κηός** *kēos*; (*wax*); a *cell* for honey, i.e. (collectively) the *comb*:— comb, honeycomb.

G2782 κήρυγμα *kērygma* from G2784; a *proclamation* (especially of the gospel; by implication the *gospel* itself):— preaching.

G2783 κήρυξ *kēryx* from G2784; a *herald,* i.e. of divine truth (especially of the gospel):— preacher.

G2784 κηρύσσω *kēryssō* of uncertain affinity; to *herald* (as a public *crier*), especially divine truth (the gospel):— preach, preacher, proclaim, publish.

G2785 κῆτος *kētos* probably from the base of G5490; a huge *fish* (as *gaping* for prey):— whale.

G2786 Κηφᾶς *Kēphas* of Aramaic origin [compare H3710]; *the Rock; Cephas* (i.e. *Kepha*), a surname of Peter:— Cephas.

G2787 κιβωτός *kibōtos* of uncertain derivation; a *box,* i.e. the sacred *ark* and that of Noah:— ark.

G2788 κιθάρα *kithara* of uncertain affinity; a *lyre*:— harp.

G2789 κιθαρίζω *kitharizō* from G2788; to *play on a lyre*:— harp.

G2790 κιθαρῳδός *kitharōdos* from G2788 and a derivative of the same as G5603; a *lyre-singer* (*lyre-player*), i.e. *harpist*:— harper.

G2791 Κιλικία *Kilikia* probably of foreign origin; *Cilicia,* a region of Asia Minor:— Cilicia.

G2792 κινάμωμον *kinamōmon* of foreign origin [compare H7076]; *cinnamon*:— cinnamon.

G2793 κινδυνεύω *kindyneyō* from G2794; to *undergo peril*:— be in danger, be (stand) in jeopardy.

G2794 κίνδυνος *kindynos* of uncertain derivation; *danger*:— peril.

G2795 κινέω *kineō* from **κιω** *kio* (poetic for **εἶμι** *eimi to go*); to *stir* (transitive), literally or figuratively:— move, remove, mover, way.

G2796 κίνησις *kinēsis* from G2795; a *stirring*:— moving.

G2797 Κίς *Kis* of Hebrew origin [H7027]; *Cis* (i.e. *Kish*), an Israelite:— Cis.

G2798 κλάδος *klados* from G2806; a *twig* or *bough* (as if broken off):— branch.

G2799 κλαίω *klaiō* of uncertain affinity; to *sob,* i.e. *wail* aloud (whereas G1145 is rather to *cry* silently):— bewail, weep.

G2800 κλάσις *klasis* from G2806; *fracture* (the act):— breaking.

G2801 κλάσμα *klasma* from G2806; a *piece* (*bit*):— broken, fragment.

G2802 Κλαύδη *Klaudē* of uncertain derivation; *Claude,* an island near Crete:— Clauda.

G2803 Κλαυδία *Klaudia* feminine of G2804; *Claudia,* a Christian woman:— Claudia.

G2804 Κλαύδιος *Klaudios* of Latin origin; *Claudius,* the name of two Romans:— Claudius.

G2805 κλαυθμός *klauthmos* from G2799; *lamentation*:— wailing, weeping, wept.

G2806 κλάω *klaō* a primary verb; to *break* (specifically of bread):— break.

G2807 κλείς *kleis* from G2808; a *key* (as *shutting* a lock), literal or figurative:— key.

G2808 κλείω *kleiō* a primary verb; to *close* (literally or figuratively):— shut (up).

G2809 κλέμμα *klemma* from G2813; *stealing* (properly the thing stolen, but used of the act):— theft.

G2810 Κλεόπας *Kleopas* probably contracted from **Κλεόπατρος** *Kleopatros* (compound of G2811 and G3962); *Cleopas,* a Christian:— Cleopas.

G2811 κλέος *kleos* from a shorter form of G2564; *renown* (as if *being called*):— glory.

G2812 κλέπτης *kleptēs* from G2813; a *stealer* (literal or figurative):— thief. Compare G3027.

G2813 κλέπτω *kleptō* a primary verb; to *filch*:— steal.

G2814 κλῆμα *klēma* from G2806; a *limb* or *shoot* (as if *broken* off):— branch.

G2815 Κλήμης *Klēmēs* of Latin origin; *merciful; Clemes* (i.e. *Clemens*), a Christian:— Clement.

G2816 κληρονομέω *klēronomeō* from G2818; to *be an heir* to (literally or figuratively):— be heir, (obtain by) inherit, inheritance.

G2817 κληρονομία *klēronomia* from G2818; *heirship,* i.e. (concretely) a *patrimony* or (generally) a *possession*:— inheritance.

G2818 κληρονόμος *klēronomos* from G2819 and the base of G3551 (in its original sense of *partitioning,* i.e. [reflexive] *getting* by apportionment); a *sharer by lot,* i.e. an *inheritor* (literal or figurative); by implication a *possessor*:— heir.

G2819 κλῆρος *klēros* probably from G2806 (through the idea of using *bits* of wood, etc., for the purpose); a *die* (for drawing chances); by implication a *portion* (as if so secured); by extension an *acquisition* (especially a *patrimony,* figuratively):— heritage, inheritance, lot, participle.

G2820 κληρόω *klēroō* from G2819; to *allot,* i.e. (figuratively) to *assign* (a privilege):— obtain an inheritance.

G2821 κλῆσις *klēsis* from a shorter form of G2564; an *invitation* (figurative):— calling.

G2822 κλητός *klētos* from the same as G2821; *invited,* i.e. *appointed,* or (specifically) a *saint*:— called.

G2823 κλίβανος *klibanos* of uncertain derivation; an earthen *pot* used for baking in:— oven.

G2824 κλίμα *klima* from G2827; a *slope,* i.e. (specifically) a *"clime"* or *tract* of country:— part, region.

G2825 κλίνη *klinē* from G2827; a *couch* (for sleep, sickness, sitting or eating):— bed, table.

G2826 κλινίδιον *klinidion* neuter of a presumed derivative of G2825; a *pallet* or *little couch*:— bed.

G2827 κλίνω *klinō* a primary verb; to *slant* or *slope,* i.e. *incline* or *recline* (literally or figuratively):— bow (down), be far spent, lay, turn to flight, wear away.

G2828 κλισία *klisia* from a derivative of G2827; properly a *reclining,* i.e. (concretely and specifically) a *party* at a meal:— company.

G2829 κλοπή *klopē* from G2813; *stealing*:— theft.

G2830 κλύδων *klydōn* from **κλύζω** *klyzō* (to *billow* or *dash* over); a *surge* of the sea (literal or figurative):— raging, wave.

G2831 κλυδωνίζομαι *klydōnizomai* middle from G2830; to *surge,* i.e. (figuratively) to *fluctuate*:— toss to and fro.

G2832 Κλωπᾶς *Klōpas* of Aramaic origin (corresponding to G256); *Clopas,* an Israelite:— Clopas.

G2833 κνήθω *knēthō* from a primary **κνάω** *knaō* (to *scrape*); to *scratch,* i.e. (by implication) to *tickle*:— itching.

G2834 Κνίδος *Knidos* probably of foreign origin; *Cnidus,* a place in Asia Minor:— Cnidus.

G2835 κοδράντης *kodrantēs* of Latin origin; a *quadrans,* i.e. the fourth part of an as:— farthing.

G2836 κοιλία *koilia* from **κοῖλος** *koilos* (*"hollow"*); a *cavity,* i.e. (specifically) the *abdomen;* by implication the *matrix;* figuratively the *heart*:— belly, womb.

G2837 κοιμάω *koimaō* from G2749; to *put to sleep,* i.e. (passive or reflexive) to *slumber;* figuratively to *decease*:— sleep, be asleep, fall asleep, fall on sleep, be dead.

G2838 κοίμησις *koimēsis* from G2837; *sleeping,* i.e. (by implication) *repose*:— taking of rest.

G2839 κοινός *koinos* probably from G4862; *common,* i.e. (literally) shared by all or several, or (ceremonially) *profane*:— common, defiled, unclean, unholy.

G2840 κοινόω *koinoō* from G2839; to *make* (or *consider*) *profane* (ceremonially):— call common, defile, pollute, unclean.

G2841 κοινωνέω *koinōneō* from G2844; to *share* with others (objectively or subjectively):— communicate, distribute, be partaker.

G2842 κοινωνία *koinōnia* from G2844; *partnership,* i.e. (literal) *participation,* or (social) *intercourse,* or (pecuniary) *benefaction*:— (to) communicate, communication, communion, distribution, contribution, fellowship.

G2843 κοινωνικός *koinōnikos* from *G2844*; *communicative,* i.e. (in a pecuniary sense) *liberal:*— willing to communicate.

G2844 κοινωνός *koinōnos* from *G2839*; a *sharer,* i.e. *associate:*— companion, fellowship, partaker, partner.

G2845 κοίτη *koitē* from *G2749*; a *couch;* by extension *cohabitation;* by implication the male *sperm:*— bed, chambering, conceive.

G2846 κοιτών *koitōn* from *G2845*; a *bedroom:*— chamberlain.

G2847 κόκκινος *kokkinos* from *G2848* (from the *kernel*-shape of the insect); *crimson*-colored:— scarlet (colour, coloured).

G2848 κόκκος *kokkos* apparently a primary word; a *kernel* of seed:— corn, grain.

G2849 κολάζω *kolazō* from

κόλος *kolos* (*dwarf*); properly to *curtail,* i.e. (figuratively) to *chastise* (or *reserve* for infliction):— punish.

G2850 κολακεία *kolakeia* from a derivative of

κόλαξ *kolax* (a *fawner*); *flattery:*— flattering.

G2851 κόλασις *kolasis* from *G2849*; penal *infliction:*— punishment, torment.

G2852 κολαφίζω *kolaphizō* from a derivative of the base of *G2849*; to *rap* with the fist:— buffet.

G2853 κολλάω *kollaō* from

κόλλα *kolla* (*"glue"*); to *glue,* i.e. (passive or reflexive) to *stick* (figuratively):— cleave, join (self), keep company.

G2854 κολλούριον *kollourion* neuter of a presumed derivative of

κολλύρα *kollyra* (a *cake;* probably akin to the base of *G2853*); properly a *poultice* (as made of or in the form of *crackers*), i.e. (by analogy) a *plaster:*— eyesalve.

G2855 κολλυβιστής *kollybistēs* from a presumed derivative of

κόλλυβος *kollybos* (a small *coin;* probably akin to *G2854*); a *coin-dealer:*— changer, money-changer.

G2856 κολοβόω *koloboō* from a derivative of the base of *G2849*; to *dock,* i.e. (figuratively) *abridge:*— shorten.

G2857 Κολοσσαί *Kolossai* apparently feminine plural of

κολοσσός *kolossos* (*"colossal"*); *Colossae,* a place in Asia Minor:— Colosse.

G2858 Κολοσσαεύς *Kolossaeus* from *G2857*; a *Colossaean,* i.e. inhabitant of Colossae:— Colossian.

G2859 κόλπος *kolpos* apparently a primary word; the *bosom;* by analogy a *bay:*— bosom, creek.

G2860 κολυμβάω *kolymbaō* from

κόλυμβος *kolymbos* (a *diver*); to *plunge* into water:— swim.

G2861 κολυμβήθρα *kolymbēthra* from *G2860*; a *diving-place,* i.e. *pond* for bathing (or swimming):— pool.

G2862 κολωνία *kolōnia* of Latin origin; a Roman *"colony"* for veterans:— colony.

G2863 κομάω *komaō* from *G2864*; to *wear tresses* of hair:— have long hair.

G2864 κόμη *komē* apparently from the same as *G2865*; the *hair* of the head (*locks,* as *ornamental,* and thus differing from *G2359*, which properly denotes merely the *scalp*):— hair.

G2865 κομίζω *komizō* from a primary

κομέω *komeō* (to *tend,* i.e. take care of); properly to *provide* for, i.e. (by implication) to *carry* off (as if from harm; generally *obtain*):— bring, receive.

G2866 κομψότερον *kompsoteron* neuter comparative of a derivative of the base of *G2865* (meaning properly *well dressed,* i.e. *nice*); figuratively *convalescent:*— began to amend.

G2867 κονιάω *koniaō* from

κονία *konia* (*dust;* by analogy *lime*); to *whitewash:*— whiten.

G2868 κονιορτός *koniortos* from the base of *G2867* and

ὄρνυμι *ornymi* (to *"rouse"*); *pulverulence* (as *blown* about):— dust.

G2869 κοπάζω *kopazō* from *G2873*; to *tire,* i.e. (figuratively) to *relax:*— cease.

G2870 κοπετός *kopetos* from *G2875*; *mourning* (properly by *beating* the breast):— lamentation.

G2871 κοπή *kopē* from *G2875*; *cutting,* i.e. *carnage:*— slaughter.

G2872 κοπιάω *kopiaō* from a derivative of *G2873*; to *feel fatigue;* by implication to *work hard:*— (bestow) labour, toil, be wearied.

G2873 κόπος *kopos* from *G2875*; a *cut,* i.e. (by analogy) *toil* (as *reducing* the strength), literally or figuratively; by implication *pains:*— labour, trouble, weariness.

G2874 κοπρία *kopria* from

κόπρος *kopros* (*ordure;* perhaps akin to *G2875*); *manure:*— dung, dunghill.

G2875 κόπτω *koptō* a primary verb; to *"chop"*; specifically to *beat* the breast in grief:— cut down, lament, mourn, wail, bewail. Compare the base of *G5114*.

G2876 κόραξ *korax* perhaps from *G2880*; a *crow* (from its *voracity*):— raven.

G2877 κοράσιον *korasion* neuter of a presumed derivative of

κόρη *korē* (a *maiden*); a (little) *girl:*— damsel, maid.

G2878 κορβᾶν *korban* and

κορβανᾶς *korbanas* of Hebrew and Aramaic origin respectively [H7133]; a votive *offering* and *the offering;* a *consecrated present* (to the Temple fund); by extension (the latter term) the *Treasury* itself, i.e. the room where the contribution boxes stood:— Corban, treasury.

G2879 Κορέ *Kore* of Hebrew origin [H7141]; *Corè* (i.e. *Korach*), an Israelite:— Core.

G2880 κορέννυμι *korennymi* a primary verb; to *cram,* i.e. *glut* or *sate:*— eat enough, full.

G2881 Κορίνθιος *Korinthios* from *G2882*; a *Corinthian,* i.e. inhabitant of Corinth:— Corinthian.

G2882 Κόρινθος *Korinthos* of uncertain derivation; *Corinthus,* a city of Greece:— Corinth.

G2883 Κορνήλιος *Kornēlios* of Latin origin; *Cornelius,* a Roman:— Cornelius.

G2884 κόρος *koros* of Hebrew origin [H3734]; a *cor,* i.e. a specific measure:— measure.

G2885 κοσμέω *kosmeō* from *G2889*; to *put in* proper *order,* i.e. *decorate* (literally or figuratively); specifically to *snuff* (a wick):— adorn, garnish, trim.

G2886 κοσμικός *kosmikos* from *G2889* (in its secondary sense); *terrene* (*"cosmic"*), literally (*mundane*) or figuratively (*corrupt*):— worldly.

G2887 κόσμιος *kosmios* from *G2889* (in its primary sense); *orderly,* i.e. *decorous:*— of good behaviour, modest.

G2888 κοσμοκράτωρ *kosmokratōr* from *G2889* and *G2902*; a *world-ruler,* an epithet of Satan:— ruler.

G2889 κόσμος *kosmos* probably from the base of *G2865*; orderly *arrangement,* i.e. *decoration;* by implication the *world* (in a wide or narrow sense, including its inhabitants, literally or figuratively [morally]):— adorning, world.

G2890 Κούαρτος *Kouartos* of Latin origin (*fourth*); *Quartus,* a Christian:— Quartus.

G2891 κοῦμι *koumi* of Aramaic origin [H6966]; *cumi* (i.e. *rise!*):— cumi.

G2892 κουστωδία *koustōdia* of Latin origin; *"custody",* i.e. a Roman *sentry:*— watch.

G2893 κουφίζω *kouphizō* from

κοῦφος *kouphos* (*light* in weight); to *unload:*— lighten.

G2894 κόφινος *kophinos* of uncertain derivation; a (small) *basket:*— basket.

G2895 κράββατος *krabbatos* probably of foreign origin; a *mattress:*— bed.

G2896 κράζω *krazō* a primary verb; properly to *"croak"* (as a raven) or *scream,* i.e. (generally) to *call* aloud (*shriek, exclaim, intreat*):— cry (out).

G2897 κραιπάλη *kraipalē* probably from the same as *G726*; properly a *headache* (as a *seizure* of pain) from drunkenness, i.e. (by implication) a *debauch* (by analogy a *glut*):— surfeiting.

G2898 κρανίον *kranion* diminutive of a derivative of the base of *G2768*; a *skull* (*"cranium"*):— Calvary, skull.

G2899 κράσπεδον *kraspedon* of uncertain derivation; a *margin,* i.e. (specifically) a *fringe* or *tassel:*— border, hem.

G2900 κραταιός *krataios* from *G2904*; *powerful* :— mighty.

G2901 κραταιόω *krataioō* from *G2900*; to *empower,* i.e. (passive) *increase in vigor:*— be strengthened, be (wax) strong.

G2902 κρατέω *krateō* from *G2904*; to *use strength,* i.e. *seize* or *retain* (literally or figuratively):— hold (by, fast), keep, lay hand (hold) on, obtain, retain, take (by).

G2903 κράτιστος *kratistos* superlative of a derivative of *G2904*; *strongest,* i.e. (in dignity) *very honorable:*— most excellent (noble).

G2904 κράτος *kratos* perhaps a primary word; *vigor* ["great"] (literal or figurative):— dominion, might, mightily, power, strength.

G2905 κραυγάζω *kraugazō* from *G2906*; to *clamor* :— cry out.

G2906 κραυγή *kraugē* from *G2896*; an *outcry* (in notification, tumult or grief):— clamour, cry, crying.

G2907 κρέας *kreas* perhaps a primary word; (butcher's) *meat:*— flesh.

G2908 κρεῖσσον *kreisson* neuter of an alternate form of G2909; (as noun) *better,* i.e. *greater advantage:*— better.

G2909 κρείττων *kreittōn* comparative of a derivative of G2904; *stronger,* i.e. (figuratively) *better,* i.e. *nobler:*— best, better.

G2910 κρεμάννυμι *kremannymi* a prolonged form of a primary verb; to *hang:*— hang.

G2911 κρημνός *krēmnos* from G2910; *overhanging,* i.e. a *precipice:*— steep place.

G2912 Κρής *Krēs* from G2914; a *Cretan,* i.e. inhabitant of Crete:— Crete, Cretian.

G2913 Κρήσκης *Krēskēs* of Latin origin; *growing; Cresces* (i.e. *Crescens*), a Christian:— Crescens.

G2914 Κρήτη *Krētē* of uncertain derivation; *Crete,* an island in the Mediterranean:— Crete.

G2915 κριθή *krithē* of uncertain derivation; *barley:*— barley.

G2916 κρίθινος *krithinos* from G2915; consisting *of barley:*— barley.

G2917 κρίμα *krima* from G2919; a *decision* (the function or the effect, for or against ["crime"]):— avenge, condemned, condemnation, damnation, go to law, judgment.

G2918 κρίνον *krinon* perhaps a primary word; a *lily:*— lily.

G2919 κρίνω *krinō*; properly to *distinguish,* i.e. *decide* (mentally or judicially); by implication to *try, condemn, punish:*— avenge, conclude, condemn, damn, decree, determine, esteem, judge, go to (sue at the) law, ordain, call in question, sentence to, think.

G2920 κρίσις *krisis*; *decision* (subjective or objective, for or against); by extension a *tribunal;* by implication *justice* (specifically divine *law*):— accusation, condemnation, damnation, judgment.

G2921 Κρίσπος *Krispos* of Latin origin; *"crisp"; Crispus,* a Corinthian:— Crispus.

G2922 κριτήριον *kritērion* neuter of a presumed derivative of G2923; a *rule* of judging (*"criterion"*), i.e. (by implication) a *tribunal:*— to judge, judgment (seat).

G2923 κριτής *kritēs* from G2919; a *judge* (general or specific):— judge.

G2924 κριτικός *kritikos* from G2923; *decisive* (*"critical"*), i.e. *discriminative:*— discerner.

G2925 κρούω *krouō* apparently a primary verb; to *rap:*— knock.

G2926 κρυπτή *kryptē* feminine of G2927; a *hidden* place, i.e. *cellar* (*"crypt"*):— secret.

G2927 κρυπτός *kryptos* from G2928; *concealed,* i.e. *private:*— hid, hidden, inward, inwardly, secret.

G2928 κρύπτω *kryptō* a primary verb; to *conceal* (properly by *covering*):— hide (self), keep secret, secret, secretly.

G2929 κρυσταλλίζω *krystallizō* from G2930; to *make* (i.e. intransitive *resemble*) *ice* ("crystallize") :— be clear as crystal.

G2930 κρύσταλλος *krystallos* from a derivative of
κρύος *kryos* (*frost*); *ice,* i.e. (by analogy) rock *"crystal"*:— crystal.

G2931 κρυφῆ *kryphē* adverb from G2928; *privately* :— in secret.

G2932 κτάομαι *ktaomai* a primary verb; to *get,* i.e. *acquire* (by any means; *own*):— obtain, possess, provide, purchase.

G2933 κτῆμα *ktēma* from G2932; an *acquirement,* i.e. *estate:*— possession.

G2934 κτῆνος *ktēnos* from G2932; *property,* i.e. (specifically) a domestic *animal:*— beast.

G2935 κτήτωρ *ktētōr* from G2932; an *owner:*— possessor.

G2936 κτίζω *ktizō* probably akin to G2932 (through the idea of the *proprietorship* of the *manufacturer*); to *fabricate,* i.e. *found* (*form* originally):— create, Creator, make.

G2937 κτίσις *ktisis* from G2936; original *formation* (properly the act; by implication the thing, literal or figurative):— building, creation, creature, ordinance.

G2938 κτίσμα *ktisma* from G2936; an original *formation* (concrete), i.e. *product* (created thing) :— creature.

G2939 κτίστης *ktistēs* from G2936; a *founder,* i.e. *God* (as author of all things):— Creator.

G2940 κυβεία *kybeia* from
κύβος *kybos* (a *"cube",* i.e. *die* for playing); *gambling,* i.e. (figuratively) *artifice* or *fraud:*— sleight.

G2941 κυβέρνησις *kybernēsis* from
κυβερνάω *kybernaō* (of Latin origin, to *steer*); *piloting,* i.e. (figuratively) *directorship* (in the church):— government.

G2942 κυβερνήτης *kybernētēs* from the same as G2941; *helmsman,* i.e. (by implication) *captain:*— (ship) master.

G2943 κυκλόθεν *kyklothen* adverb from the same as G2945; *from* the *circle,* i.e. *all around:*— (round) about.

G2944 κυκλόω *kykloō* from the same as G2945; to *encircle,* i.e. *surround:*— compass (about), come (stand) round about.

G2945 κύκλῳ *kyklō* as if dative of
κύκλος *kyklos* (a *ring, "cycle";* akin to G2947); i.e. *in a circle* (by implication of G1722), i.e. (adverbially) *all around:*— round about.

G2946 κύλισμα *kylisma* from G2947; a *wallow* (the effect of *rolling*), i.e. *filth:*— wallowing.

G2947 κυλιόω *kyliō* from the base of G2949 (through the idea of *circularity;* compare G2945, G1507); to *roll* about:— wallow.

G2948 κυλλός *kyllos* from the same as G2947; *rocking* about, i.e. *crippled* (*maimed,* in feet or hands):— maimed.

G2949 κῦμα *kyma* from
κύω *kyō* (to *swell* [with young], i.e. *bend, curve*); a *billow* (as *bursting* or *toppling*):— wave.

G2950 κύμβαλον *kymbalon* from a derivative of the base of G2949; a *"cymbal"* (as *hollow*):— cymbal.

G2951 κύμινον *kyminon* of foreign origin [compare H3646]; *dill* or *fennel* ("cummin"):— cummin.

G2952 κυνάριον *kynarion* neuter of a presumed derivative of G2965; a *puppy:*— dog.

G2953 Κύπριος *Kyprios* from G2954; a *Cyprian* (*Cypriot*), i.e. inhabitant of Cyprus:— of Cyprus.

G2954 Κύπρος *Kypros* of uncertain origin; *Cyprus,* an island in the Mediterranean:— Cyprus.

G2955 κύπτω *kyptō* probably from the base of G2949; to *bend* forward:— stoop (down).

G2956 Κυρηναῖος *Kyrēnaios* from G2957; a *Cyrenaean,* i.e. inhabitant of Cyrene:— of Cyrene, Cyrenian.

G2957 Κυρήνη *Kyrēnē* of uncertain derivation; *Cyrenè,* a region of Africa:— Cyrene.

G2958 Κυρήνιος *Kyrēnios* of Latin origin; *Cyrenius* (i.e. *Quirinus*), a Roman:— Cyrenius.

G2959 Κυρία *Kyria* feminine of G2962; *Cyria,* a Christian woman:— lady.

G2960 κυριακός *kyriakos* from G2962; *belonging to* the *Lord* (Jehovah or Jesus):— Lord's.

G2961 κυριεύω *kyrieuō* from G2962; to *rule:*— have dominion over, lord, be lord of, exercise lordship over.

G2962 κύριος *kyrios* from
κῦρος *kyros* (*supremacy*); *supreme* in authority, i.e. (as noun) *controller;* by implication *Mister* (as a respectful title):— God, Lord, master, Sir.

G2963 κυριότης *kyriotēs* from G2962; *mastery,* i.e. (concrete and collective) *rulers:*— dominion, government.

G2964 κυρόω *kyroō* from the same as G2962; to *make authoritative,* i.e. *ratify:*— confirm.

G2965 κύων *kyōn* a primary word; a *dog* [*"hound"*] (literal or figurative):— dog.

G2966 κῶλον *kōlon* from the base of G2849; a *limb* of the body (as if *lopped*):— carcase.

G2967 κωλύω *kōlyō* from the base of G2849; to *hinder,* i.e. *prevent* (by word or act):— forbid, hinder, keep from, let, not suffer, withstand.

G2968 κώμη *kōmē* from G2749; a *hamlet* (as if *laid* down):— town, village.

G2969 κωμόπολις *kōmopolis* from G2968 and G4172; an unwalled *city:*— town.

G2970 κῶμος *kōmos* from G2749; a *carousal* (as if a *letting loose*):— revelling, rioting.

G2971 κώνωψ *kōnōps* apparently from a derivative of the base of G2759 and a derivative of G3700; a *mosquito* (from its *stinging proboscis*):— gnat.

G2972 Κῶς *Kōs* of uncertain origin; *Cos,* an island in the Mediterranean:— Cos.

G2973 Κωσάμ *Kōsam* of Hebrew origin [compare H7081]; *Cosam* (i.e. *Kosam*), an Israelite:— Cosam.

G2974 κωφός *kōphos* from G2875; *blunted,* i.e. (figuratively) of hearing (*deaf*) or speech (*dumb*):— deaf, dumb, speechless.

Λ

G2975 λαγχάνω *lanchanō* a prolonged form of a primary verb, which is only used as an alternate in certain tenses; to *lot,* i.e. *determine* (by implication *receive*) especially by lot:— his lot be, cast lots, obtain.

G2976 Λάζαρος *Lazaros* probably of Hebrew origin [H499]; *Lazarus* (i.e. *Elazar*), the name of two Israelites (one imaginary):— Lazarus.

G2977 λάθρα *lathra* adverb from G2990; *privately* :— privily, secretly.

G2978 λαῖλαψ *lailaps* of uncertain derivation; a *whirlwind* (*squall*):— storm, tempest.

G2979 λακτίζω *laktizō* from adverb
λάξ *lax* (*with the foot*); to *be recalcitrant:*— kick.

G2980 λαλέω *laleō* a prolonged form of an otherwise obsolete verb; to *talk,* i.e. *utter* words:— preach, say, speak (after), talk, tell, utter. Compare *G3004*.

G2981 λαλιά *lalia* from *G2980*; *talk:*— saying, speech.

G2982 λαμά *lama* or
λαμμᾶ *lamma* of Hebrew origin [H4100 with prepositional prefix]; *lama* (i.e. *why*):— lama.

G2983 λαμβάνω *lambanō* a prolonged form of a primary verb, which is used only as an alternate in certain tenses; to *take* (in very many applications, literally and figuratively [properly objective or active, to *get hold* of; whereas *G1209* is rather subjective or passive, to *have offered* to one; while *G138* is more violent, to *seize* or *remove*]):— accept, be amazed, assay, attain, bring, when I call, catch, come on (unto), forget, have, hold, obtain, receive (after), take (away, up).

G2984 Λάμεχ *Lamech* of Hebrew origin [H3929]; *Lamech* (i.e. *Lemek*), a patriarch:— Lamech.

G2985 λαμπάς *lampas* from *G2989*; a *"lamp"* or *flambeau:*— lamp, light, torch.

G2986 λαμπρός *lampros* from the same as *G2985*; *radiant;* by analogy *limpid;* figuratively *magnificent* or *sumptuous* (in appearance):— bright, clear, gay, goodly, gorgeous, white.

G2987 λαμπρότης *lamprotēs* from *G2896*; *brilliancy* :— brightness.

G2988 λαμπρῶς *lamprōs* adverb from *G2986*; *brilliantly,* i.e. (figuratively) *luxuriously:*— sumptuously.

G2989 λάμπω *lampō* a primary verb; to *beam,* i.e. *radiate* brilliancy (literally or figuratively):— give light, shine.

G2990 λανθάνω *lanthanō* a prolonged form of a primary verb, which is used only as an alternate in certain tenses; to *lie hid* (literally or figuratively); often used adverbially *unwittingly:*— be hid, be ignorant of, unawares.

G2991 λαξευτός *laxeutos* from a compound of
λᾶς *las* (*a stone*) and the base of *G3584* (in its origin sense of *scraping*); *rock-quarried:*— hewn in stone.

G2992 λαός *laos* apparently a primary word; a *people* (in general; thus differing from *G1218*, which denotes one's *own* populace):— people.

G2993 Λαοδίκεια *Laodikeia* from a compound of *G2992* and *G1349*; *Laodicia,* a place in Asia Minor :— Laodicea.

G2994 Λαοδικεύς *Laodikeus* from *G2993*; a *Laodicean,* i.e. inhabitant of Laodicia:— Laodicean.

G2995 λάρυγξ *larynx* of uncertain derivation; the *throat* (*"larynx"*):— throat.

G2996 Λασαία *Lasaia* of uncertain origin; *Lasaea,* a place in Crete:— Lasea.

G2997 λάσκω *laskō* a strengthened form of a primary verb, which only occurs in this and another prolonged form as alternate in certain tenses; to *crack* open (from a fall):— burst asunder.

G2998 λατομέω *latomeō* from the same as the first part of *G2991* and the base of *G5114*; to *quarry:*— hew.

G2999 λατρεία *latreia* from *G3000*; *ministration* of God, i.e. *worship:*— (divine) service.

G3000 λατρεύω *latreuō* from
λάτρις *latris* (a hired *menial*); to *minister* (to God), i.e. *render* religious *homage:*— serve, do the service, worship, worshiper.

G3001 λάχανον *lachanon* from
λαχαίνω *lachainō* (to *dig*); a *vegetable:*— herb.

G3002 Λεββαῖος *Lebbaios* of uncertain origin; *Lebbaeus,* a Christian:— Lebbaeus.

G3003 λεγεών *legeōn* of Latin origin; a *"legion",* i.e. Roman *regiment* (figuratively):— legion.

G3004 λέγω *legō* a primary verb; properly to *"lay"* forth, i.e. (figuratively) *relate* (in words [usually of systematic or set *discourse;* whereas *G2036* and *G5346* generally refer to an *individual* expression or speech respectively; while *G4483* is properly to *break silence* merely, and *G2980* means an *extended* or random harangue]); by implication to *mean:*— ask, bid, boast, call, describe, give out, name, put forth, say (on), saying, shew, speak, tell, utter.

G3005 λεῖμμα *leimma* from *G3007*; a *remainder* :— remnant.

G3006 λεῖος *leios* apparently a primary word; *smooth,* i.e. *"level":*— smooth.

G3007 λείπω *leipō* a primary verb; to *leave,* i.e. (intransitive or passive) to *fail* or *be absent:*— be destitute (wanting), lack.

G3008 λειτουργέω *leitourgeō* from *G3011*; to be a *public servant,* i.e. (by analogy) to *perform* religious or charitable *functions* (*worship, obey, relieve*):— minister.

G3009 λειτουργία *leitourgia* from *G3008*; *public function* (as priest ["liturgy"] or almsgiver):— ministration, ministry, service.

G3010 λειτουργικός *leitourgikos* from the same as *G3008*; *functional publicly* ("liturgic"), i.e. *beneficent:*— ministering.

G3011 λειτουργός *leitourgos* from a derivative of *G2992* and *G2041*; a *public servant,* i.e. a *functionary* in the Temple or Gospel, or (generally) a *worshipper* (of God) or *benefactor* (of man):— minister, ministered.

G3012 λέντιον *lention* of Latin origin; a *"linen"* cloth, i.e. *apron:*— towel.

G3013 λεπίς *lepis* from
λέπω *lepō* (to *peel*); a *flake:*— scale.

G3014 λέπρα *lepra* from the same as *G3013*; *scaliness,* i.e. *"leprosy":*— leprosy.

G3015 λεπρός *lepros* from the same as *G3014*; *scaly,* i.e. *leprous* (a *leper*):— leper.

G3016 λεπτόν *lepton* neuter of a derivative of the same as *G3013*; something *scaled* (*light*), i.e. a small *coin:*— mite.

G3017 Λευΐ *Leui* of Hebrew origin [H3878]; *Levi,* the name of three Israelites:— Levi. Compare *G3018*.

G3018 Λευΐς *Leuis* a form of *G3017*; *Lewis* (i.e. *Levi*), a Christian:— Levi.

G3019 Λευΐτης *Leuitēs* from *G3017*; a *Levite,* i.e. descendant of Levi:— Levite.

G3020 Λευϊτικός *Leuitikos* from *G3019*; *Levitic,* i.e. relating to the Levites:— Levitical.

G3021 λευκαίνω *leukainō* from *G3022*; to *whiten* :— make white, whiten.

G3022 λευκός *leukos* from
λύκη *lykē* (*"light"*); *white:*— white.

G3023 λέων *leōn* a primary word; a *"lion":*— lion.

G3024 λήθη *lēthē* from *G2990*; *forgetfulness:*— forget.

G3025 ληνός *lēnos* apparently a primary word; a *trough,* i.e. wine-*vat:*— winepress.

G3026 λῆρος *lēros* apparently a primary word; *twaddle,* i.e. an *incredible* story:— idle tale.

G3027 λῃστής *lēstēs* from
ληΐζομαι *lēizomai* (to *plunder*); a *brigand* :— robber, thief.

G3028 λῆψις *lēpsis* from *G2983*; *receipt* (the act) :— receiving.

G3029 λίαν *lian* of uncertain affinity; *much* (adverbially):— exceeding, great, greatly, sore, very (+ chiefest).

G3030 λίβανος *libanos* of foreign origin [H3828]; the *incense*-tree, i.e. (by implication) *incense* itself:— frankincense.

G3031 λιβανωτός *libanōtos* from *G3030*; *frankincense,* i.e. (by extension) a *censer* for burning it:— censer.

G3032 Λιβερτῖνος *Libertinos* of Latin origin; a Roman *freedman:*— Libertine.

G3033 Λιβύη *Libyē* probably from *G3047*; *Libye,* a region of Africa:— Libya.

G3034 λιθάζω *lithazō* from *G3037*; to *pelt with stones:*— stone.

G3035 λίθινος *lithinos* from *G3037*; *stony,* i.e. made of *stone:*— of stone.

G3036 λιθοβολέω *lithoboleō* from a compound of *G3037* and *G906*; to *throw stones,* i.e. *pelt with stones:*— stone, cast stones.

G3037 λίθος *lithos* apparently a primary word; a *stone* (literal or figurative):— stone, mill-stone, stumbling-stone.

G3038 λιθόστρωτος *lithostrōtos* from *G3037* and a derivative of *G4766*; *strewn with stones,* i.e. a tessellated *mosaic* on which the Roman tribunal was placed:— Pavement.

G3039 λικμάω *likmaō* from
λικμός *likmos* the equivalent of
λίκνον *liknon* (a winnowing *fan* or basket); to *winnow,* i.e. (by analogy) to *pulverize:*— grind to powder.

G3040 λιμήν *limēn* apparently a primary word; a *harbor:*— haven. Compare *G2568*.

G3041 λίμνη *limnē* probably from *G3040* (through the idea of the nearness of shore); a *pond* (large or small):— lake.

G3042 λιμός *limos* probably from *G3007* (through the idea of *destitution*); a *scarcity* of food:— dearth, famine, hunger.

G3043 λίνον *linon* probably a primary word; *flax,* i.e. (by implication) *"linen":*— linen.

G3044 Λῖνος *Linos* perhaps from *G3043*; *Linus,* a Christian:— Linus.

G3045 λιπαρός *liparos* from
λίπος *lipos* (*grease*); *fat,* i.e. (figuratively) *sumptuous:*— dainty.

G3046 λίτρα *litra* of Latin origin [*libra*]; a *pound* in weight:— pound.

G3047 λίψ *lips* probably from

λείβω *leibō* (to *pour* a "libation"); the *south* (southwest) wind (as bringing rain), i.e. (by extension) the *south* quarter:— southwest.

G3048 λογία *logia* from *G3056* (in the commercial sense); a *contribution:*— collection, gathering.

G3049 λογίζομαι *logizomai* middle from *G3056*; to *take an inventory,* i.e. *estimate* (literally or figuratively):— conclude, count, account (of), despise, esteem, impute, lay, number, reason, reckon, suppose, think (on).

G3050 λογικός *logikos* from *G3056*; *rational* (*"logical"*):— reasonable, of the word.

G3051 λόγιον *logion* neuter of *G3052*; an *utterance* (of God):— oracle.

G3052 λόγιος *logios* from *G3056*; *fluent,* i.e. an *orator:*— eloquent.

G3053 λογισμός *logismos* from *G3049*; *computation,* i.e. (figuratively) *reasoning* (*conscience, conceit*):— imagination, thought.

G3054 λογομαχέω *logomacheō* from a compound of *G3056* and *G3164*; to *be disputatious* (on trifles):— strive about words.

G3055 λογομαχία *logomachia* from the same as *G3054*; *disputation* about trifles (*"logomachy"*):— strife of words.

G3056 λόγος *logos* from *G3004*; something *said* (including the *thought*); by implication a *topic* (subject of discourse), also *reasoning* (the mental faculty) or *motive;* by extension a *computation;* specifically (with the art. in John) the Divine *Expression* (i.e. *Christ*):— account, cause, communication, concerning, doctrine, fame, have to do, intent, matter, mouth, preaching, question, reason, reckon, remove, say, saying, shew, speaker, speech, talk, thing, none of these things move me, tidings, treatise, utterance, word, work.

G3057 λόγχη *lonchē* perhaps a primary word; a *"lance"*:— spear.

G3058 λοιδορέω *loidoreō* from *G3060*; to *reproach,* i.e. *vilify:*— revile.

G3059 λοιδορία *loidoria* from *G3060*; *slander* or *vituperation:*— railing, reproach, reproachfully.

G3060 λοίδορος *loidoros* from

λοιδός *loidos* (*mischief*); *abusive,* i.e. a *blackguard:*— railer, reviler.

G3061 λοιμός *loimos* of uncertain affinity; a *plague* (literally the *disease,* or figuratively a *pest*):— pestilence, pestilent.

G3062 λοιποί *loipoi* masculine plural of a derivative of *G3007*; *remaining* ones:— other, which remain, remnant, residue, rest.

G3063 λοιπόν *loipon* neuter singular of the same as *G3062*; something *remaining* (adverb):— besides, finally, furthermore, (from) henceforth, moreover, now, it remaineth, then.

G3064 λοιποῦ *loipou* genetive singular of the same as *G3062*; *remaining* time:— from henceforth.

G3065 Λουκᾶς *Loukas* contracted from Latin *Lucanus; Lucas,* a Christian:— Lucas, Luke.

G3066 Λούκιος *Loukios* of Latin origin; *illuminative; Lucius,* a Christian:— Lucius.

G3067 λουτρόν *loutron* from *G3068*; a *bath,* i.e. (figuratively) *baptism:*— washing.

G3068 λούω *louō* a primary verb; to *bathe* (the *whole* person; whereas *G3538* means to wet a *part* only, and *G4150* to wash, cleanse *garments* exclusively):— wash.

G3069 Λύδδα *Lydda* of Hebrew origin [H3850]; *Lydda* (i.e. *Lod*), a place in Palestine:— Lydda.

G3070 Λυδία *Lydia* properly femine of

Λύδιος *Lydios* [of foreign origin] (a *Lydian,* in Asia Minor); *Lydia,* a Christian woman:— Lydia.

G3071 Λυκαονία *Lykaonia* perhaps remotely from *G3074*; *Lycaonia,* a region of Asia Minor:— Lycaonia.

G3072 Λυκαονιστί *Lykaonisti* adverb from a derivative of *G3071*; *Lycaonistically,* i.e. in the language of the Lycaonians:— in the speech of Lycaonia.

G3073 Λυκία *Lykia* probably remotely from *G3074*; *Lycia,* a province of Asia Minor:— Lycia.

G3074 λύκος *lykos* perhaps akin to the base of Greek *G3022* (from the *whitish* hair); a *wolf:*— wolf.

G3075 λυμαίνομαι *lymainomai* middle from a probable derivative of *G3089* (meaning *filth*); properly to *soil,* i.e. (figuratively) *insult* (*maltreat*):— make havock of.

G3076 λυπέω *lypeō* from *G3077*; to *distress;* reflexive or passive to *be sad:*— cause grief, grieve, be in heaviness, (be) sorrow, sorrowful, be (make) sorry.

G3077 λύπη *lypē* apparently a primaive word; *sadness:*— grief, grievous, grudgingly, heaviness, sorrow.

G3078 Λυσανίας *Lysanias* from *G3080* and

ἀνία *ania* (*trouble*); *grief-dispelling; Lysanias,* a governor of Abilene:— Lysanias.

G3079 Λυσίας *Lysias* of uncertain affinity; *Lysias,* a Roman:— Lysias.

G3080 λύσις *lysis* from *G3089*; a *loosening,* i.e. (specifically) *divorce:*— to be loosed.

G3081 λυσιτελεῖ *lysitelei* third person singular present indicative active of a derivative of a compound of *G3080* and *G5056*; impersonally, it *answers* the *purpose,* i.e. *is advantageous:*— it is better.

G3082 Λύστρα *Lystra* of uncertain origin; *Lystra,* a place in Asia Minor:— Lystra.

G3083 λύτρον *lytron* from *G3089*; something to *loosen* with, i.e. a redemption *price* (figuratively *atonement*):— ransom.

G3084 λυτρόω *lytroō* from *G3083*; to *ransom* (literally or figuratively):— redeem.

G3085 λύτρωσις *lytrōsis* from *G3084*; a *ransoming* (figurative):— redeemed, redemption.

G3086 λυτρωτής *lytrōtēs* from *G3084*; a *redeemer* (figurative):— deliverer.

G3087 λυχνία *lychnia* from *G3088*; a *lamp-stand* (literal or figurative):— candlestick.

G3088 λύχνος *lychnos* from the base of *G3022*; a portable *lamp* or other *illuminator* (literal or figurative):— candle, light.

G3089 λύω *lyō* a primary verb; to *"loosen"* (literally or figuratively):— break (up), destroy, dissolve, loose, unloose, melt, put off. Compare *G4486*.

G3090 Λωΐς *Lōis* of uncertain origin; *Loïs,* a Christian woman:— Lois.

G3091 Λώτ *Lōt* of Hebrew origin [H3876]; *Lot,* a patriarch:— Lot.

M

G3092 Μαάθ *Maath* probably of Hebrew origin; *Maath,* an Israelite:— Maath.

G3093 Μαγδαλά *Magdala* of Aramaic origin [compare H4026]; *the tower; Magdala* (i.e., *Migdala*), a place in Palestine:— Magdala.

G3094 Μαγδαληνή *Magdalēnē* femine of a derivative of *G3093*; a female *Magdalene,* i.e. inhabitant of Magdala:— Magdalene.

G3095 μαγεία *mageia* from *G3096*; *"magic"*:— sorcery.

G3096 μαγεύω *mageuō* from *G3097*; to *practice magic:*— use sorcery.

G3097 μάγος *magos* of foreign origin [H7248]; a *Magian,* i.e. Oriental *scientist;* by implication a *magician:*— sorcerer, wise man.

G3098 Μαγώγ *Magōg* of Hebrew origin [H4031]; *Magog,* a foreign nation, i.e. (figuratively) an Antichristian party:— Magog.

G3099 Μαδιάν *Madian* of Hebrew origin [H4080]; *Madian* (i.e. *Midian*), a region of Arabia:— Madian.

G3100 μαθητεύω *mathēteuō* from *G3101*; intransitive to *become a pupil;* transitive to *disciple,* i.e. enroll as scholar:— be disciple, instruct, teach.

G3101 μαθητής *mathētēs* from *G3129*; a *learner,* i.e. *pupil:*— disciple.

G3102 μαθήτρια *mathētria* feminine from *G3101*; a female *pupil:*— disciple.

G3103 Μαθουσάλα *Mathousala* of Hebrew origin [H4968]; *Mathusala* (i.e. *Methushelach*), an antediluvian:— Mathusala.

G3104 Μαϊνάν *Mainan* probably of Hebrew origin; *Maïnan,* an Israelite:— Mainan.

G3105 μαίνομαι *mainomai* middle from a primary

μάω *maō* (to *long* for; through the idea of insensate *craving*); to *rave* as a "maniac":— be beside self (mad).

G3106 μακαρίζω *makarizō* from *G3107*; to *beatify,* i.e. *pronounce* (or *esteem*) *fortunate:*— call blessed, count happy.

G3107 μακάριος *makarios* a prolonged form of the poetical

μάκαρ *makar* (meaning the same); supremely *blest;* by extension *fortunate, well off:*— blessed, happy (happier).

G3108 μακαρισμός *makarismos* from *G3106*; *beatification,* i.e. *attribution of good fortune:*— blessedness.

G3109 Μακεδονία *Makedonia* from *G3110*; *Macedonia,* a region of Greece:— Macedonia.

G3110 Μακεδών *Makedōn* of uncertain derivation; a *Macedon* (*Macedonian*), i.e. inhabitant of Macedonia:— of Macedonia, Macedonian.

G3111 μάκελλον *makellon* of Latin origin [*macellum*]; a *butcher's stall, meat market* or *provision-shop:*— shambles.

G3112 μακράν *makran* feminine accusative singular of *G3117* (*G3598* being implied); *at a distance* (literally or figuratively):— far (off), afar (off), good (great) way off.

G3113 μακρόθεν *makrothen* adverb from *G3117*; *from a distance* or *afar:*— afar off, from far.

G3114 μακροθυμέω *makrothymeō* from the same as G3116; to *be long-spirited,* i.e. (objectively) *forbearing* or (subjectively) *patient:*— bear (suffer) long, be longsuffering, have (long) patience, be patient, patiently endure.

G3115 μακροθυμία *makrothymia* from the same as G3116; *longsuffering,* i.e. (objective) *forbearance* or (subjective) *fortitude:*— longsuffering, patience.

G3116 μακροθύμως *makrothymōs* adverb of a compound of G3117 and G2372; *with long (enduring) temper,* i.e. *leniently:*— patiently.

G3117 μακρός *makros* from G3372; *long* (in place [*distant*] or time [neuter plural]):— far, long.

G3118 μακροχρόνιος *makrochronios* from G3117 and G5550; *long-timed,* i.e. *long-lived:*— live long.

G3119 μαλακία *malakia* from G3120; *softness,* i.e. *enervation (debility):*— disease.

G3120 μαλακός *malakos* of uncertain affinity; *soft,* i.e. *fine* (clothing); figuratively a *catamite:*— effeminate, soft.

G3121 Μαλελεήλ *Maleleēl* of Hebrew origin [H4111]; *Malelee'l* (i.e. *Mahalalel*), an antediluvian:— Maleleel.

G3122 μάλιστα *malista* neuter plural of the superlative of an apparently primary adverb

μάλα *mala* (*very*); (adverbially) *most* (*in the greatest degree*) or *particularly:*— chiefly, most of all, specially, especially.

G3123 μᾶλλον *mallon* neuter of the comparative of the same as G3122; (adverbially) *more* (*in a greater degree*) or *rather:*— better, far, (the) more (and more), (so) much (the more), rather.

G3124 Μάλχος *Malchos* of Hebrew origin [H4429]; *Malchus,* an Israelite:— Malchus.

G3125 μάμμη *mammē* of native origin ["mammy"]; a *grandmother:*— grandmother.

G3126 μαμμωνᾶς *mammōnas* of Aramaic origin (*confidence,* i.e. figuratively *wealth,* personified); *mammonas,* i.e. *avarice* (deified):— mammon.

G3127 Μαναήν *Manaēn* of uncertain origin; *Manae'n,* a Christian:— Manaen.

G3128 Μανασσῆς *Manassēs* of Hebrew origin [H4519]; *Manasses* (i.e. *Menashsheh*), an Israelite:— Manasses.

G3129 μανθάνω *manthanō* prolonged from a primary verb, another form of which,

μαθέω *matheō* is used as an alternate in certain tenses; to *learn* (in any way):— learn, understand.

G3130 μανία *mania* from G3105; *craziness:*— [+ make] mad.

G3131 μάννα *manna* of Hebrew origin [H4478]; *manna* (i.e. *man*), an edible gum:— manna.

G3132 μαντεύομαι *manteuomai* from a derivative of G3105 (meaning a *prophet,* as supposed to *rave* through *inspiration*); to *divine,* i.e. *utter spells* (under pretence of foretelling):— by soothsaying.

G3133 μαραίνω *marainō* of uncertain affinity; to *extinguish* (as fire), i.e. (figuratively and passive) to *pass away:*— fade away.

G3134 μαρὰν ἀθά *maran atha* of Aramaic origin (meaning *our Lord has come*); *maranatha,* i.e. an exclamation of the approaching *divine judgment:*— Maran-atha.

G3135 μαργαρίτης *margaritēs* from

μάργαρος *margaros* (a pearl-*oyster*); a *pearl* :— pearl.

G3136 Μάρθα *Martha* probably of Aramaic origin (meaning *mistress*); *Martha,* a Christian woman :— Martha.

G3137 Μαρία *Maria* or

Μαριάμ *Mariam* of Hebrew origin [H4813]; *Maria* or *Mariam* (i.e. *Mirjam*), the name of six Christian females:— Mary.

G3138 Μάρκος *Markos* of Latin origin; *Marcus,* a Christian:— Marcus, Mark.

G3139 μάρμαρος *marmaros* from

μαρμαίρω *marmairō* (to *glisten*); *marble* (as sparkling *white*):— marble.

G3140 μαρτυρέω *martyreō* from G3144; to *be a witness,* i.e. *testify* (literally or figuratively):— charge, give [*evidence*], bear record, have (obtain, of) good (honest) report, be well reported of, testify, give (have) testimony, (be, bear, give, obtain) witness.

G3141 μαρτυρία *martyria* from G3144; *evidence* given (judicially or generally):— record, report, testimony, witness.

G3142 μαρτύριον *martyrion* neuter of a presumed derivative of G3144; something *evidential,* i.e. (generally) *evidence* given or (specifically) the *Decalogue* (in the sacred Tabernacle):— to be testified, testimony, witness.

G3143 μαρτύρομαι *martyromai* middle from G3144; to *be adduced* as *a witness,* i.e. (figuratively) to *testify* (in affirmation or exhortation):— take to record, testify.

G3144 μάρτυς *martys* of uncertain affinity; a *witness* (literal [judicially] or figurative [generally]); by analogy a *"martyr":*— martyr, record, witness.

G3145 μασσάομαι *massaomai* from a primary

μάσσω *massō* (to *handle* or *squeeze*); to *chew:*— gnaw.

G3146 μαστιγόω *mastigoō* from G3148; to *flog* (literally or figuratively):— scourge.

G3147 μαστίζω *mastizō* from G3149; to *whip* (literally):— scourge.

G3148 μάστιξ *mastix* probably from the base of G3145 (through the idea of *contact*); a *whip* (literally the Roman *flagellum* for criminals; figuratively a *disease*):— plague, scourging.

G3149 μαστός *mastos* from the base of G3145; a (properly female) *breast* (as if *kneaded* up):— pap.

G3150 ματαιολογία *mataiologia* from G3151; *random talk,* i.e. *babble:*— vain jangling.

G3151 ματαιολόγος *mataiologos* from G3152 and G3004; an *idle* (i.e. *senseless* or *mischievous*) *talker,* i.e. a *wrangler:*— vain talker.

G3152 μάταιος *mataios* from the base of G3155; *empty,* i.e. (literally) *profitless,* or (specifically) an *idol:*— vain, vanity.

G3153 ματαιότης *mataiotēs* from G3152; *inutility;* figuratively *transience;* moral *depravity:*— vanity.

G3154 ματαιόω *mataioō* from G3152; to *render* (passive *become*) *foolish,* i.e. (morally) *wicked* or (specifically) *idolatrous:*— become vain.

G3155 μάτην *matēn* accusative of a derivative of the base of G3145 (through the idea of tentative *manipulation,* i.e. unsuccessful *search,* or else of *punishment*); *folly,* i.e. (adverbially) *to no purpose:*— in vain.

G3156 Ματθαῖος *Matthaios* a shorter form of G3161; *Matthoeus* (i.e. *Matthitjah*), an Israelite and Christian:— Matthew.

G3157 Ματθάν *Matthan* of Hebrew origin [H4977]; *Matthan* (i.e. *Mattan*), an Israelite:— Matthan.

G3158 Ματθάτ *Matthat* probably a shortened form of G3161; *Matthat* (i.e. *Mattithjah*), the name of two Israelites:— Mathat.

G3159 Ματθίας *Matthias* apparently a shortened form of G3161; *Matthias* (i.e. *Mattithjah*), an Israelite:— Matthias.

G3160 Ματταθά *Mattatha* probably a shortened form of G3161 [compare H4992]; *Mattatha* (i.e. *Mattithjah*), an Israelite:— Mattatha.

G3161 Ματταθίας *Mattathias* of Hebrew origin [H4993]; *Mattathias* (i.e. *Mattithjah*), an Israelite and Christian:— Mattathias.

G3162 μάχαιρα *machaira* probably feminine of a presumed derivative of G3163; a *knife,* i.e. *dirk;* figuratively *war,* judicially *punishment:*— sword.

G3163 μάχη *machē* from G3164; a *battle,* i.e. (figuratively) *controversy:*— fighting, strive, striving.

G3164 μάχομαι *machomai* middle of an apparently primary verb; to *war,* i.e. (figuratively) to *quarrel, dispute:*— fight, strive.

G3165 μέ *me* a shorter (and probably original) form of G1691; *me:*— I, me, my.

G3166 μεγαλαυχέω *megalaucheō* from a compound of G3173 and

αὐχέω *aucheō* (to *boast;* akin to G837 and G2744); to *talk big,* i.e. *be grandiloquent* (*arrogant, egotistic*):— boast great things.

G3167 μεγαλεῖος *megaleios* from G3173; *magnificent,* i.e. (neuter plural as noun) a conspicuous *favor,* or (subjectively) *perfection:*— great things, wonderful works.

G3168 μεγαλειότης *megaleiotēs* from G3167; *grandeur,* i.e. *glory* or *splendor:*— magnificence, majesty, mighty power.

G3169 μεγαλοπρεπής *megaloprepēs* from G3173 and G4241; *befitting greatness* or *magnificence* (*majestic*):— excellent.

G3170 μεγαλύνω *megalynō* from G3173; to *make* (or *declare*) *great,* i.e. *increase* or (figuratively) *extol:*— enlarge, magnify, shew great.

G3171 μεγάλως *megalōs* adverb from G3173; *much* :— greatly.

G3172 μεγαλωσύνη *megalōsynē* from G3173; *greatness,* i.e. (figuratively) *divinity* (often *God* himself):— majesty.

G3173 μέγας *megas* including the prolonged forms, feminine

μεγάλη *megalē* plural

μεγάλοι *megaloi* etc.; compare also G3176, G3187; *big* (literally or figuratively, in a very wide application):— (+ fear) exceedingly, great, greatest, high, large, loud, mighty, (be) sore (afraid), strong, to years.

G3174 μέγεθος *megethos* from G3173; *magnitude* (figurative):— greatness.

G3175 μεγιστᾶνες *megistanes* plural from G3176; *grandees:*— great men, lords.

G3176 μέγιστος *megistos* superlative of G3173; *greatest* or *very great:*— exceeding great.

G3177 μεθερμηνεύω *methermēneuō* from *G3326* and *G2059*; to *explain over,* i.e. *translate:*— interpret, by interpretation.

G3178 μέθη *methē* apparently a primary word; an *intoxicant,* i.e. (by implication) *intoxication:*— drunkenness.

G3179 μεθίστημι *methistēmi* or 1 Cor. 13:2
μεθιστάνω *methistanō* from *G3326* and *G2476*; to *transfer,* i.e. *carry away, depose* or (figuratively) *exchange, seduce:*— put out, remove, translate, turn away.

G3180 μεθοδεία *methodeia* from a compound of *G3326* and *G3593* [compare "method"]; *travelling over,* i.e. *travesty* (*trickery*):— wile, lie in wait.

G3181 μεθόριος *methorios* from *G3326* and *G3725*; *bounded alongside,* i.e. *contiguous* (neuter plural as noun, *frontier*):— border.

G3182 μεθύσκω *methyskō* a prolonged (transitive) form of *G3184*; to *intoxicate:*— be drunk, drunken.

G3183 μέθυσος *methysos* from *G3184*; *tipsy,* i.e. (as noun) a *sot:*— drunkard.

G3184 μεθύω *methyō* from another form of *G3178*; to *drink* to *intoxication,* i.e. *get drunk:*— drink well, make (be) drunk, make (be) drunken.

G3185 μεῖζον *meizon* neuter of *G3187*; (adverbially) in a *greater* degree:— the more.

G3186 μειζότερος *meizoteros* continued comparative of *G3187*; *still larger* (figuratively):— greater.

G3187 μείζων *meizōn* irregular comparative of *G3173*; *larger* (literally or figuratively, specifically in age):— elder, greater, greatest, more.

G3188 μέλαν *melan* neuter of *G3189* as noun; *ink:*— ink.

G3189 μέλας *melas* apparently a primary word; *black:*— black.

G3190 Μελεᾶς *Meleas* of uncertain origin; *Meleas,* an Israelite:— Meleas.

G3191 μελετάω *meletaō* from a presumed derivative of *G3199*; to *take care of,* i.e. (by implication) *revolve* in the mind:— imagine, meditate, premeditate.

G3192 μέλι *meli* apparently a primary word; *honey* :— honey.

G3193 μελίσσιος *melissios* from *G3192*; *relating to honey,* i.e. *bee* (comb):— honeycomb.

G3194 Μελίτη *Melitē* of uncertain origin; *Melita,* an island in the Mediterranean:— Melita.

G3195 μέλλω *mellō* a strengthened form of *G3199* (through the idea of *expectation*); to *intend,* i.e. *be about* to be, do, or suffer something (of persons or things, especially events; in the sense of *purpose, duty, necessity, probability, possibility,* or *hesitation*) :— about, after that, be (almost), (that which is, things, which was for) to come, intend, was to (be), mean, mind, be at the point, (be) ready, return, shall (begin), (which, that) should (after, afterwards, hereafter) tarry, which was for, will, would, be yet.

G3196 μέλος *melos* of uncertain affinity; a *limb* or *part* of the body:— member.

G3197 Μελχί *Melchi* of Hebrew origin [H4428 with pronoun suffix, *my king*]; *Melchi* (i.e. *Malki*), the name of two Israelites:— Melchi.

G3198 Μελχισεδέκ *Melchisedek* of Hebrew origin [H4442]; *Melchisedek* (i.e. *Malkitsedek*), a patriarch:— Melchisedec.

G3199 μέλω *melō* a primary verb; to *be of interest* to, i.e. to *concern* (only third person singular present indicative used impersonally *it matters*):— (take) care.

G3200 μεμβράνα *membrana* of Latin origin ("*membrane*"); a (written) sheep-*skin:*— parchment.

G3201 μέμφομαι *memphomai* middle of an apparently primary verb; to *blame:*— find fault.

G3202 μεμψίμοιρος *mempsimoiros* from a presumed derivative of *G3201* and
μοῖρα *moira* (*fate;* akin to the base of *G3313*); *blaming fate,* i.e. *querulous* (*discontented*) :— complainer.

G3303 μέν *men* a primary particle; properly indicative of *affirmation* or *concession* (*in fact*); usually followed by a *contrasted* clause with *G1161* (*this* one, the *former,* etc.). Often compounded with other particles in an *intensive* or *asseverative* sense:— even, indeed, so, some, truly, verily.

G3304 μενοῦνγε *menounge* from *G3303* and *G3767* and *G1065*; *so then at least:*— nay but, yea doubtless (rather, verily).

G3305 μέντοι *mentoi* from *G3303* and *G5104*; *indeed though,* i.e. *however:*— also, but, howbeit, nevertheless, yet.

G3306 μένω *menō* a primary verb; to *stay* (in a given place, state, relation or expectancy):— abide, continue, dwell, endure, be present, remain, stand, tarry (for), thine own.

G3307 μερίζω *merizō* from *G3313*; to *part,* i.e. (literally) to *apportion, bestow, share,* or (figuratively) to *disunite, differ:*— deal, be difference between, distribute, divide, give part.

G3308 μέριμνα *merimna* from *G3307* (through the idea of *distraction*); *solicitude:*— care.

G3309 μεριμνάω *merimnaō* from *G3308*; to *be anxious* about:— (have) care, (be) careful, take thought.

G3310 μερίς *meris* feminine of *G3313*; a *portion,* i.e. *province, share* or (abstractly) *participation:*— part, partakers.

G3311 μερισμός *merismos* from *G3307*; a *separation* or *distribution:*— dividing asunder, gift.

G3312 μεριστής *meristēs* from *G3307*; an *apportioner* (*administrator*):— divider.

G3313 μέρος *meros* from an obsolete but more primary form of
μείρομαι *meiromai* (to *get* as a *section* or *allotment*); a *division* or *share* (literal or figurative, in a wide application):— behalf, coast, course, craft, particular, particularly, part, partly, piece, portion, respect, side, some sort, somewhat.

G3314 μεσημβρία *mesēmbria* from *G3319* and *G2250*; *midday;* by implication the *south:*— noon, south.

G3315 μεσιτεύω *mesiteuō* from *G3316*; to *interpose* (as arbiter), i.e. (by implication) to *ratify* (as surety):— confirm.

G3316 μεσίτης *mesitēs* from *G3319*; a *go-between,* i.e. (simply) an *intermediary,* or (by implication) a *reconciler* (*intercessor*):— mediator.

G3317 μεσονύκτιον *mesonyktion* neuter of a compound of *G3319* and *G3571*; *midnight* (especially as a watch):— midnight.

G3318 Μεσοποταμία *Mesopotamia* from *G3319* and *G4215*; *Mesopotamia* (as lying between the Euphrates and the Tigris; compare H763), a region of Asia:— Mesopotamia.

G3319 μέσος *mesos* from *G3326*; *middle* (as adjective or [neuter] noun):— among, before them, between, forth, midday, midnight, midst, way.

G3320 μεσότοιχον *mesotoichon* from *G3319* and *G5109*; a *partition* (figurative):— middle wall.

G3321 μεσουράνημα *mesouranēma* from a presumed compound of *G3319* and *G3772*; *mid-sky:*— midst of heaven.

G3322 μεσόω *mesoō* from *G3319*; to *form* the *middle,* i.e. (in point of time), to *be half-way* over:— be about the midst.

G3323 Μεσσίας *Messias* of Hebrew origin [H4899]; the *Messias* (i.e. *Mashiach*), or Christ:— Messias.

G3324 μεστός *mestos* of uncertain derivation; *replete* (literally or figuratively):— full.

G3325 μεστόω *mestoō* from *G3324*; to *replenish,* i.e. (by implication) to *intoxicate:*— fill.

G3326 μετά *meta* a primary preposition (often used adverbially); properly denoting *accompaniment; "amid"* (locally or causally); modified variously according to the case (genitive *association,* or accusative *succession*) with which it is joined; occupying an intermediate position between *G575* or *G1537* and *G1519* or *G4314*; less intimate than *G1722,* and less close than *G4862*). Often used in compounds, in substantially the same relations of *participation* or *proximity,* and *transfer* or *sequence:*— after, afterward, that be again, against, among, and, follow, hence, hereafter, in, of, on, upon, our, and setting, since, to, unto, together, when, with, without.

G3327 μεταβαίνω *metabainō* from *G3326* and the base of *G939*; to *change place:*— depart, go, pass, remove.

G3328 μεταβάλλω *metaballō* from *G3326* and *G906*; to *throw over,* i.e. (middle figuratively) to *turn about* in opinion:— change mind.

G3329 μετάγω *metagō* from *G3326* and *G71*; to *lead over,* i.e. *transfer* (*direct*):— turn about.

G3330 μεταδίδωμι *metadidōmi* from *G3326* and *G1325*; to *give over,* i.e. *share:*— give, impart.

G3331 μετάθεσις *metathesis* from *G3346*; *transposition,* i.e. *transferral* (to heaven), *disestablishment* (of a law):— change, removing, translation.

G3332 μεταίρω *metairō* from *G3326* and *G142*; to *betake* oneself, i.e. *remove* (locally):— depart.

G3333 μετακαλέω *metakaleō* from *G3326* and *G2564*; to *call elsewhere,* i.e. *summon:*— call (for, hither).

G3334 μετακινέω *metakineō* from *G3326* and *G2795*; to *stir* to a place *elsewhere,* i.e. *remove* (figuratively):— move away.

G3335 μεταλαμβάνω *metalambanō* from *G3326* and *G2983*; to *participate;* generally to *accept* (and use):— eat, have, be partaker, receive, take.

G3336 μετάληψις *metalēpsis* from *G3335*; *participation:*— taking.

G3337 μεταλλάσσω *metallassō* from *G3326* and *G236*; to *exchange:*— change.

G3338 μεταμέλομαι *metamelomai* from *G3326* and the middle of *G3199*; to *care afterwards,* i.e. *regret:*— repent (self).

G3339 μεταμορφόω *metamorphoō* from G3326 and G3445; to *transform* (literally or figuratively "metamorphose"):— change, transfigure, transform.

G3340 μετανοέω *metanoeō* from G3326 and G3539; to *think differently* or *afterwards,* i.e. *reconsider* (morally *feel compunction*):— repent.

G3341 μετάνοια *metanoia* from G3340; (subjectively) *compunction* (for guilt, including *reformation*); by implication *reversal* (of [another's] decision):— repentance.

G3342 μεταξύ *metaxy* from G3326 and a form of G4862; *betwixt* (of place or person); (of time) as adjective *intervening,* or (by implication) *adjoining:*— between, meanwhile, next.

G3343 μεταπέμπω *metapempō* from G3326 and G3992; to *send* from *elsewhere,* i.e. (middle) to *summon* or *invite:*— call (send) for.

G3344 μεταστρέφω *metastrephō* from G3326 and G4762; to *turn across,* i.e. *transmute* or (figuratively) *corrupt:*— pervert, turn.

G3345 μετασχηματίζω *metaschēmatizō* from G3326 and a derivative of G4976; to *transfigure* or *disguise;* figuratively to *apply* (by accommodation):— transfer, transform (self).

G3346 μετατίθημι *metatithēmi* from G3326 and G5087; to *transfer,* i.e. (literally) *transport,* (by implication) *exchange,* (reflexive) *change sides,* or (figuratively) *pervert:*— carry over, change, remove, translate, turn.

G3347 μετέπειτα *metepeita* from G3326 and G1899; *thereafter:*— afterward.

G3348 μετέχω *metechō* from G3326 and G2192; to *share* or *participate;* by implication *belong* to, *eat* (or *drink*):— be partaker, pertain, take part, use.

G3349 μετεωρίζω *meteōrizō* from a compound of G3326 and a collateral form of G142 or perhaps rather of G109 (compare "meteor"); to *raise in midair,* i.e. (figuratively) *suspend* (passive *fluctuate* or *be anxious*):— be of doubtful mind.

G3350 μετοικεσία *metoikesia* from a derivative of a compound of G3326 and G3624; a *change of abode,* i.e. (specifically) *expatriation:*— brought, carried away to, carried away into, carrying away to, carrying away into.

G3351 μετοικίζω *metoikizō* from the same as G3350; to *transfer* as a *settler* or *captive,* i.e. *colonize* or *exile:*— carry away, remove into.

G3352 μετοχή *metochē* from G3348; *participation,* i.e. *intercourse:*— fellowship.

G3353 μέτοχος *metochos* from G3348; *participant,* i.e. (as noun) a *sharer;* by implication an *associate:*— fellow, partaker, partner.

G3354 μετρέω *metreō* from G3358; to *measure* (i.e. ascertain in size by a fixed standard); by implication to *admeasure* (i.e. allot by rule); figuratively to *estimate:*— measure, mete.

G3355 μετρητής *metrētēs* from G3354; a *measurer,* i.e. (specifically) a certain standard *measure* of capacity for liquids:— firkin.

G3356 μετριοπαθέω *metriopatheō* from a compound of the base of G3357 and G3806; to *be moderate in passion,* i.e. *gentle* (to *treat indulgently*):— have compassion.

G3357 μετρίως *metriōs* adverb from a derivative of G3358; *moderately,* i.e. *slightly:*— a little.

G3358 μέτρον *metron* an apparently primary word; a *measure* ("meter"), literal or figurative; by implication a limited *portion* (*degree*):— measure.

G3359 μέτωπον *metōpon* from G3326 and
ὤψ *ōps* (the *face*); the *forehead* (as *opposite* the *countenance*):— forehead.

G3360 μέχρι *mechri* or
μεχρίς *mechris* from G3372; *as far as,* i.e. *up to* a certain point (as preposition of extent [denoting the *terminus,* whereas G891 refers especially to the *space* of time or place intervening] or conjecture):— till, to, unto, until.

G3361 μή *mē* a primary particle of qualified *negation* (whereas G3756 expresses an absolute denial); (adverb) *not,* (conjunction) *lest;* also (as interrogative implying a *negative* answer [whereas G3756 expects an *affirmative* one]) *whether.* Often used in compounds in substantially the same relations:— any, but (that), forbear, God forbid, lack, lest, neither, never, no (wise in), none, nor, not, cannot, nothing, that not, un- (e.g., untaken), without. See also G3362, G3363, G3364, G3372, G3373, G3375, G3378.

G3362 ἐὰν μή *ean mē* i.e. G1437 and G3361; *if not,* i.e. *unless:*— before, but, except, if no, (if, whosoever) not.

G3363 ἵνα μή *hina mē* i.e. G2443 and G3361; *in order* (or *so*) *that not:*— albeit not, lest, that no, that not, that nothing.

G3364 οὐ μή *ou mē* i.e. G3756 and G3361; a double negative strengthening the denial; *not at all:*— any more, at all, by any (no) means, neither, never, no (at all), in no case (wise), nor ever, not (at all, in any wise). Compare G3378.

G3365 μηδαμῶς *mēdamōs* adverb from a compound of G3361 and
ἀμός *amos* (*somebody*); *by no means:*— not so.

G3366 μηδέ *mēde* from G3361 and G1161; *but not, not even;* in a continued negation, *nor:*— neither, nor (yet), (no) not (once, so much as).

G3367 μηδείς *mēdeis* including the irregular feminine
μηδεμία *mēdemia* and the neuter
μηδέν *mēden* from G3361 and G1520; *not even one* (man, woman, thing):— any (man, thing), no (man), none, not (at all, any man, a whit), nothing, without delay.

G3368 μηδέποτε *mēdepote* from G3366 and G4218; *not even ever:*— never.

G3369 μηδέπω *mēdepō* from G3366 and G4452; *not even yet:*— not yet.

G3370 Μῆδος *Mēdos* of foreign origin [compare H4074]; a *Median,* or inhabitant of Media:— Mede.

G3371 μηκέτι *mēketi* from G3361 and G2089; *no further:*— any longer, (not) henceforth, hereafter, no henceforward (longer, more, soon), not any more.

G3372 μῆκος *mēkos* probably akin to G3173; *length* (literal or figurative):— length.

G3373 μηκύνω *mēkynō* from G3372; to *lengthen,* i.e. (middle) to *enlarge:*— grow up.

G3374 μηλωτή *mēlōtē* from
μελον *melon* (a *sheep*); a *sheep-skin:*— sheepskin.

G3375 μήν *mēn* a stronger form of G3303; a particle of affirmation (only with G2229); *assuredly:*— surely.

G3376 μήν *mēn* a primary word; a *month:*— month.

G3377 μηνύω *mēnyō* probably from the same base as G3145 and G3415 (i.e.
μάω *maō* to *strive*); to *disclose* (through the idea of mental *effort* and thus calling to *mind*), i.e. *report, declare, intimate:*— shew, tell.

G3378 μὴ οὐκ *mē ouk* i.e. G3361 and G3756; as interrogative and negative *is it not that?:*— neither (followed by *no*), never, not. Compare G3364.

G3379 μήποτε *mēpote* or
μή ποτε *mē pote* from G3361 and G4218; *not ever;* also *if* (or *lest*) *ever* (or *perhaps*):— if peradventure, lest (at any time, haply), not at all, whether or not.

G3380 μήπω *mēpō* from G3361 and G4452; *not yet:*— not yet.

G3381 μήπως *mēpōs* or
μή πως *mē pōs* from G3361 and G4458; *lest somehow:*— lest (by any means, by some means, haply, perhaps).

G3382 μηρός *mēros* perhaps a primary word; a *thigh:*— thigh.

G3383 μήτε *mēte* from G3361 and G5037; *not too,* i.e. (in continued negation) *neither* or *nor;* also, *not even:*— neither, or, nor, so much as.

G3384 μήτηρ *mētēr* apparently a primary word; a *"mother"* (literal or figurative, immediate or remote):— mother.

G3385 μήτι *mēti* from G3361 and the neuter of G5100; *whether at all:*— not [*the particle usually not expressed, except by the form of the question*].

G3386 μήτιγε *mētige* from G3385 and G1065; *not at all then,* i.e. *not to say* (*the rather still*):— how much more.

G3387 μήτις *mētis* or
μή τις *mē tis* from G3361 and G5100; *whether any:*— any [*sometimes unexpressed except by the simple interrogative form of the sentence*].

G3388 μήτρα *mētra* from G3384; the *matrix:*— womb.

G3389 μητρολῴας *mētrolōas* from G3384 and the base of G257; a *mother-thresher,* i.e. *matricide:*— murderer of mothers.

G3390 μητρόπολις *mētropolis* from G3384 and G4172; a *mother city,* i.e. *"metropolis":*— chiefest city.

G3391 μία *mia* irregular feminine of G1520; *one* or *first:*— a (certain), agree, first, one, other.

G3392 μιαίνω *miainō* perhaps a primary verb; to *sully* or *taint,* i.e. *contaminate* (ceremonially or morally):— defile.

G3393 μίασμα *miasma* from G3392 (*"miasma"*); (moral) *foulness* (properly the effect):— pollution.

G3394 μιασμός *miasmos* from G3392; (morally) *contamination* (properly the act):— uncleanness.

G3395 μίγμα *migma* from G3396; a *compound:*— mixture.

G3396 μίγνυμι *mignymi* a primary verb; to *mix* :— mingle.

G3397 μικρόν *mikron* masculine or neuter singular of G3398 (as noun); a *small* space of *time* or *degree:*— a (little) (while).

G3398 μικρός *mikros* including the comparative **μικρότερος** *mikroteros* apparently a primary word; *small* (in size, quantity, number) or (figuratively) dignity):— least, less, little, small.

G3399 Μίλητος *Milētos* of uncertain origin; *Miletus*, a city of Asia Minor:— Miletus.

G3400 μίλιον *milion* of Latin origin; a *thousand* paces, i.e. a *"mile"*:— mile.

G3401 μιμέομαι *mimeomai* middle from **μῖμος** *mimos* (a *"mimic"*); to *imitate:*— follow.

G3402 μιμητής *mimētēs* from G3401; an *imitator:*— follower.

G3403 μιμνήσκω *mimnēskō* a prolonged form of G3415 (from which some of the tenses are borrowed); to *remind*, i.e. (middle) to *recall to mind:*— be mindful, remember.

G3404 μισέω *miseō* from a primary **μῖσος** *misos* (*hatred*); to *detest* (especially to *persecute*); by extension to *love less:*— hate, hateful.

G3405 μισθαποδοσία *misthapodosia* from G3406; *requital* (good or bad):— recompence of reward.

G3406 μισθαποδότης *misthapodotēs* from G3409 and G591; a *remunerator:*— rewarder.

G3407 μίσθιος *misthios* from G3408; a *wage-earner* :— hired servant.

G3408 μισθός *misthos* apparently a primary word; *pay* for service (literal or figurative), good or bad:— hire, reward, wages.

G3409 μισθόω *misthoō* from G3408; to *let* out for wages, i.e. (middle) to *hire:*— hire.

G3410 μίσθωμα *misthōma* from G3409; a *rented* building:— hired house.

G3411 μισθωτός *misthōtos* from G3409; a *wage-worker* (good or bad):— hired servant, hireling.

G3412 Μιτυλήνη *Mitylēnē* for **μυτιλήνη** *mytilēnē* (*abounding in shell-fish*); *Mitylene* (or *Mytilene*), a town in the island Lesbos:— Mitylene.

G3413 Μιχαήλ *Michaēl* of Hebrew origin [H4317]; *Michae'l*, an archangel:— Michael.

G3414 μνᾶ *mna* of Latin origin; a *mna* (i.e. *mina*), a certain *weight:*— pound.

G3415 μνάομαι *mnaomai* middle of a derivative of G3306 or perhaps of the base of G3145 (through the idea of *fixture* in the mind or of mental *grasp*); to *bear in mind*, i.e. *recollect;* by implication to *reward* or *punish:*— be mindful, remember, come (have) in remembrance. Compare G3403.

G3416 Μνάσων *Mnasōn* of uncertain origin; *Mnason*, a Christian:— Mnason.

G3417 μνεία *mneia* from G3415 or G3403; *recollection;* by implication *recital:*— mention, remembrance.

G3418 μνῆμα *mnēma* from G3415; a *memorial*, i.e. sepulchral *monument* (*burial-place*):— grave, sepulchre, tomb.

G3419 μνημεῖον *mnēmeion* from G3420; a *remembrance*, i.e. *cenotaph* (*place of interment*):— grave, sepulchre, tomb.

G3420 μνήμη *mnēmē* from G3403; *memory:*— remembrance.

G3421 μνημονεύω *mnēmoneuō* from a derivative of G3420; to *exercise memory*, i.e. *recollect;* by implication to *punish;* also to *rehearse:*— make mention, be mindful, remember.

G3422 μνημόσυνον *mnēmosynon* from G3421; a *reminder* (*memorandum*), i.e. *record:*— memorial.

G3423 μνηστεύω *mnēsteuō* from a derivative of G3415; to *give a souvenir* (engagement present), i.e. *betroth:*— espouse.

G3424 μογιλάλος *mogilalos* from G3425 and G2980; *hardly talking*, i.e. *dumb* (*tongue-tied*):— having an impediment in his speech.

G3425 μόγις *mogis* adverb from a primary **μόγος** *mogos* (*toil*); *with difficulty:*— hardly.

G3426 μόδιος *modios* of Latin origin; a *modius*, i.e. certain measure for things dry (the quantity or the utensil):— bushel.

G3427 μοί *moi* the simpler form of G1698; *to me* :— I, me, mine, my.

G3428 μοιχαλίς *moichalis* a prolonged form of the feminine of G3432; an *adulteress* (literal or figurative):— adulteress, adulterous, adulterously.

G3429 μοιχάω *moichaō* from G3432; (middle) to *commit adultery:*— commit adultery.

G3430 μοιχεία *moicheia* from G3431; *adultery:*— adultery.

G3431 μοιχεύω *moicheuō* from G3432; to *commit adultery:*— commit adultery.

G3432 μοιχός *moichos* perhaps a primary word; a (male) *paramour;* figuratively *apostate:*— adulterer.

G3433 μόλις *molis* probably by variation for G3425; *with difficulty:*— hardly, scarce, scarcely, with much work.

G3434 Μολόχ *Moloch* of Hebrew origin [H4432]; *Moloch* (i.e. *Molek*), an idol:— Moloch.

G3435 μολύνω *molynō* probably from G3189; to *soil* (figuratively):— defile.

G3436 μολυσμός *molysmos* from G3435; a *stain*, i.e. (figuratively) *immorality:*— filthiness.

G3437 μομφή *momphē* from G3201; *blame*, i.e. (by implication) a *fault:*— quarrel.

G3438 μονή *monē* from G3306; a *staying*, i.e. *residence* (the act or the place):— abode, mansion.

G3439 μονογενής *monogenēs* from G3441 and G1096; *only-born*, i.e. *sole:*— only (begotten, child).

G3440 μόνον *monon* neuter of G3441 as adverb; *merely:*— alone, but, only.

G3441 μόνος *monos* probably from G3306; *remaining*, i.e. *sole* or *single;* by implication *mere:*— alone, only, by themselves.

G3442 μονόφθαλμος *monophthalmos* from G3441 and G3788; *one-eyed:*— with one eye.

G3443 μονόω *monoō* from G3441; to *isolate*, i.e. *bereave:*— be desolate.

G3444 μορφή *morphē* perhaps from the base of G3313 (through the idea of *adjustment* of parts); *shape;* figuratively *nature:*— form.

G3445 μορφόω *morphoō* from the same as G3444; to *fashion* (figuratively):— form.

G3446 μόρφωσις *morphōsis* from G3445; *formation*, i.e. (by implication) *appearance* (*semblance* or [concrete] *formula*):— form.

G3447 μοσχοποιέω *moschopoieō* from G3448 and G4160; to *fabricate* the image of a *bullock:*— make a calf.

G3448 μόσχος *moschos* probably strengthened for **ὄσχος** *oschos* (a *shoot*); a young *bullock:*— calf.

G3449 μόχθος *mochthos* from the base of G3425; *toil*, i.e. (by implication) *sadness:*— painfulness, travail.

G3450 μοῦ *mou* the simpler form of G1700; *of me:*— I, me, mine (own), my.

G3451 μουσικός *mousikos* from **Μοῦσα** *Mousa* (a *Muse*); *"musical"*, i.e. (as noun) a *minstrel:*— musician.

G3452 μυελός *myelos* perhaps a primary word; the *marrow:*— marrow.

G3453 μυέω *myeō* from the base of G3466; to *initiate*, i.e. (by implication) to *teach:*— instruct.

G3454 μῦθος *mythos* perhaps from the same as G3453 (through the idea of *tuition*); a *tale*, i.e. *fiction* (*"myth"*):— fable.

G3455 μυκάομαι *mykaomai* from a presumed derivative of **μύζω** *myzō* (to *"moo"*); to *bellow* (*roar*):— roar.

G3456 μυκτηρίζω *myktērizō* from a derivative of the base of G3455 (meaning *snout*, as that whence *lowing* proceeds); to *make mouths* at, i.e. *ridicule:*— mock.

G3457 μυλικός *mylikos* from G3458; *belonging to a mill:*— mill, millstone.

G3458 μύλος *mylos* probably ultimately from the base of G3433 (through the idea of *hardship*); a *"mill"*, i.e. (by implication) a *grinder* (*millstone*):— millstone.

G3459 μύλων *mylōn* from G3458; a *mill-house:*— mill.

G3460 Μύρα *Myra* of uncertain derivation; *Myra*, a place in Asia Minor:— Myra.

G3461 μυρίας *myrias* from G3463; a *ten-thousand;* by extension a *"myriad"* or indefinite number:— ten thousand.

G3462 μυρίζω *myrizō* from G3464; to *apply* (perfumed) *unguent* to:— anoint.

G3463 μύριοι *myrioi* plural of an apparently primary word (properly meaning *very many*); *ten thousand;* by extension *innumerably* many:— ten thousand.

G3464 μύρον *myron* probably of foreign origin [compare H4753, G4666]; *"myrrh"*, i.e. (by implication) *perfumed oil:*— ointment.

G3465 Μυσία *Mysia* of uncertain origin; *Mysia*, a region of Asia Minor:— Mysia.

G3466 μυστήριον *mystērion* from a derivative of **μύω** *myō* (to *shut* the mouth); a *secret* or *"mystery"* (through the idea of *silence* imposed by *initiation* into religious rites):— mystery.

G3467 μυωπάζω *myōpazō* from a compound of the base of G3466 and **ὤψ** *ōps* (the *face;* from G3700); to *shut* the *eyes*, i.e. *blink* (*see indistinctly*):— cannot see afar off.

G3468 μώλωψ *mōlōps* from **μῶλος** *mōlos* (*"moil"*; probably akin to the base of G3433) and probably **ὤψ** *ōps* (the *face;* from G3700); a *mole* ("black eye") or *blow-mark:*— stripe.

G3469 **μωμάομαι** *mōmaomai* from *G3470*; to *carp* at, i.e. *censure* (*discredit*):— blame.

G3470 **μῶμος** *mōmos* perhaps from *G3201*; a *flaw* or *blot*, i.e. (figuratively) *disgraceful* person:— blemish.

G3471 **μωραίνω** *mōrainō* from *G3474*; to *become insipid;* figuratively to *make* (passive *act*) as a *simpleton:*— become fool, make foolish, lose savour.

G3472 **μωρία** *mōria* from *G3474*; *silliness,* i.e. *absurdity:*— foolishness.

G3473 **μωρολογία** *mōrologia* from a compound of *G3474* and *G3004*; *silly talk,* i.e. *buffoonery:*— foolish talking.

G3474 **μωρός** *mōros* probably from the base of *G3466*; *dull* or *stupid* (as if *shut* up), i.e. *heedless,* (moral) *blockhead,* (apparently) *absurd:*— fool, foolish, foolishness.

G3475 **Μωσεύς** *Mōseus* or
Μωσῆς *Mōsēs* or
Μωϋσῆς *Mōysēs* of Hebrew origin; [H4872]; *Moseus, Moses* or *Mou'ses* (i.e. *Mosheh*), the Hebrew lawgiver:— Moses.

N

G3476 **Ναασσών** *Naassōn* of Hebrew origin [H5177]; *Naasson* (i.e. *Nachshon*), an Israelite:— Naasson.

G3477 **Ναγγαί** *Nangai* probably of Hebrew origin [compare H5052]; *Nangae* (i.e. perhaps *Nogach*), an Israelite:— Nagge.

G3478 **Ναζαρέθ** *Nazareth* or
Ναζαρέτ *Nazaret* of uncertain derivation; *Nazareth* or *Nazaret,* a place in Palestine:— Nazareth.

G3479 **Ναζαρηνός** *Nazarēnos* from *G3478*; a *Nazarene,* i.e. inhabitant of Nazareth:— of Nazareth.

G3480 **Ναζωραῖος** *Nazōraios* from *G3478*; a *Nazoraean,* i.e. inhabitant of Nazareth; by extension a *Christian:*— Nazarene, of Nazareth.

G3481 **Ναθάν** *Nathan* of Hebrew origin [H5416]; *Nathan,* an Israelite:— Nathan.

G3482 **Ναθαναήλ** *Nathanaēl* of Hebrew origin [H5417]; *Nathanae'l* (i.e. *Nathanel*), an Israelite and Christian:— Nathanael.

G3483 **ναί** *nai* a primary particle of strong affirmation; *yes:*— even so, surely, truth, verily, yea, yes.

G3484 **Ναΐν** *Nain* probably of Hebrew origin [compare H4999]; *Naïn,* a place in Palestine:— Nain.

G3485 **ναός** *naos* from a primary
ναίω *naiō* (to *dwell*); a *fane, shrine, temple* :— shrine, temple. Compare *G2411*.

G3486 **Ναούμ** *Naoum* of Hebrew origin [H5151]; *Nau'm* (i.e. *Nachum*), an Israelite:— Naum.

G3487 **νάρδος** *nardos* of foreign origin [compare H5373]; *"nard":*— nard, spikenard.

G3488 **Νάρκισσος** *Narkissos* a flower of the same name, from
ναρκη *narkē* (*stupefaction,* as a "narcotic"); *Narcissus,* a Roman:— Narcissus.

G3489 **ναυαγέω** *nauageō* from a compound of *G3491* and *G71*; to *be shipwrecked* (*stranded,* "navigate"), literally or figuratively:— make (suffer) shipwreck.

G3490 **ναύκληρος** *nauklēros* from *G3491* and *G2819* ("clerk"); a *captain:*— owner of a ship.

G3491 **ναῦς** *naus* from
νάω *naō* or
νέω *neō* (to *float*); a *boat* (of any size):— ship.

G3492 **ναύτης** *nautēs* from *G3491*; a *boatman,* i.e. *seaman:*— sailor, shipman.

G3493 **Ναχώρ** *Nachōr* of Hebrew origin [H5152]; *Nachor,* the grandfather of Abraham:— Nachor.

G3494 **νεανίας** *neanias* from a derivative of *G3501*; a *youth* (up to about forty years):— young man.

G3495 **νεανίσκος** *neaniskos* from the same as *G3494*; a *youth* (under forty):— young man.

G3496 **Νεάπολις** *Neapolis* from *G3501* and *G4172*; *new town; Nea'polis,* a place in Macedonia:— Neapolis.

G3497 **Νεεμάν** *Neeman* of Hebrew origin [H5283]; *Nee'man* (i.e. *Naaman*), a Syrian:— Naaman.

G3498 **νεκρός** *nekros* from an apparently primary
νέκυς *nekys* (a *corpse*); *dead* (literally or figuratively; also as noun):— dead.

G3499 **νεκρόω** *nekroō* from *G3498*; to *deaden,* i.e. (figuratively) to *subdue:*— be dead, mortify.

G3500 **νέκρωσις** *nekrōsis* from *G3499*; *decease;* figuratively *impotency:*— deadness, dying.

G3501 **νέος** *neos* including the comparative
νεώτερος *neōteros* a primary word; *"new",* i.e. (of persons) *youthful,* or (of things) *fresh;* figuratively *regenerate:*— new, young.

G3502 **νεοσσός** *neossos* from *G3501*; a *youngling* (*nestling*):— young.

G3503 **νεότης** *neotēs* from *G3501*; *newness,* i.e. *youthfulness:*— youth.

G3504 **νεόφυτος** *neophytos* from *G3501* and a derivative of *G5453*; *newly planted,* i.e. (figuratively) a *young convert* (*"neophyte"*):— novice.

G3505 **Νέρων** *Nerōn* of Latin origin; *Neron* (i.e. *Nero*), a Roman emperor:— Nero.

G3506 **νεύω** *neuō* apparently a primary verb; to *"nod",* i.e. (by analogy) to *signal:*— beckon.

G3507 **νεφέλη** *nephelē* from *G3509*; properly *cloudiness,* i.e. (concrete) a *cloud:*— cloud.

G3508 **Νεφθαλείμ** *Nephthaleim* of Hebrew origin [H5321]; *Nephthaleim* (i.e. *Naphthali*), a tribe in Palestine:— Nephthalim.

G3509 **νέφος** *nephos* apparently a primary word; a *cloud:*— cloud.

G3510 **νεφρός** *nephros* of uncertain affinity; a *kidney* (plural), i.e. (figuratively) the inmost *mind:*— reins.

G3511 **νεωκόρος** *neōkoros* from a form of *G3485* and
κορέω *koreō* (to *sweep*); a *temple-servant,* i.e. (by implication) a *votary:*— worshipper.

G3512 **νεωτερικός** *neōterikos* from the comparative of *G3501*; *appertaining to younger* persons, i.e. *juvenile:*— youthful.

G3513 **νή** *nē* probably an intensive form of *G3483*; a particle of attestation (accompanied by the object invoked or appealed to in confirmation); *as sure as:*— I protest by.

G3514 **νήθω** *nēthō* from
νέω *neō* (of like meaning); to *spin:*— spin.

G3515 **νηπιάζω** *nēpiazō* from *G3516*; to *act* as a *babe,* i.e. (figuratively) *innocently:*— be a child.

G3516 **νήπιος** *nēpios* from an obsolete particle
νη *nē* (implying *negation*) and *G2031*; *not speaking,* i.e. an *infant* (*minor*); figuratively a *simple-minded* person, an *immature* Christian:— babe, child, childish.

G3517 **Νηρεύς** *Nēreus* apparently from a derivative of the base of *G3491* (meaning *wet*); *Nereus,* a Christian:— Nereus.

G3518 **Νηρί** *Nēri* of Hebrew origin [H5374]; *Neri* (i.e. *Nerijah*), an Israelite:— Neri.

G3519 **νησίον** *nēsion* diminutive of *G3520*; an *islet* :— island.

G3520 **νῆσος** *nēsos* probably from the base of *G3491*; an *island:*— island, isle.

G3521 **νηστεία** *nēsteia* from *G3522*; *abstinence* (from lack of food, or voluntary and religious); specifically the *fast* of the Day of Atonement:— fast, fasting.

G3522 **νηστεύω** *nēsteuō* from *G3523*; to *abstain* from food (religiously):— fast.

G3523 **νῆστις** *nēstis* from the inseparable negative particle
νη *nē* (*not*) and *G2068*; *not eating,* i.e. *abstinent* from food (religiously):— fasting.

G3524 **νηφάλεος** *nēphaleos* or
νηφάλιος *nēphalios* from *G3525*; *sober,* i.e. (figuratively) *circumspect:*— sober.

G3525 **νήφω** *nēphō* of uncertain affinity; to *abstain* from wine (*keep sober*), i.e. (figuratively) *be discreet:*— be sober, watch.

G3526 **Νίγερ** *Niger* of Latin origin; *black; Niger,* a Christian:— Niger.

G3527 **Νικάνωρ** *Nikanōr* probably from *G3528*; *victorious; Nicanor,* a Christian:— Nicanor.

G3528 **νικάω** *nikaō* from *G3529*; to *subdue* (literally or figuratively):— conquer, overcome, prevail, get the victory.

G3529 **νίκη** *nikē* apparently a primary word; *conquest* (abstract), i.e. (figuratively) the *means of success:*— victory.

G3530 **Νικόδημος** *Nikodēmos* from *G3534* and *G1218*; *victorious* among his *people; Nicodemus,* an Israelite:— Nicodemus.

G3531 **Νικολαΐτης** *Nikolaitēs* from *G3532*; a *Nicolaïte,* i.e. adherent of *Nicolau's:*— *Nicolaitane.*

G3532 **Νικόλαος** *Nikolaos* from *G3534* and *G2994*; *victorious* over the *people; Nicolau's,* a heretic:— Nicolaus.

G3533 **Νικόπολις** *Nikopolis* from *G3534* and *G4172*; *victorious city; Nicopolis,* a place in Macedonia:— Nicopolis.

G3534 **νῖκος** *nikos* from *G3529*; a *conquest* (concrete), i.e. (by implication) *triumph:*— victory.

G3535 **Νινευΐ** *Nineui* of Hebrew origin [H5210]; *Ninevi* (i.e. *Nineveh*), the capital of Assyria:— Nineve.

G3536 **Νινευΐτης** *Nineuitēs* from *G3535*; a *Ninevite,* i.e. inhabitant of Nineveh:— of Nineve, Ninevite.

G3537 **νιπτήρ** *niptēr* from *G3538*; a *ewer:*— bason.

G3538 **νίπτω** *niptō*; to *cleanse* (especially the hands or the feet or the face); ceremonially to *perform ablution:*— wash. Compare *G3068*.

G3539 νοέω *noeō* from *G3563*; to *exercise* the *mind* (*observe*), i.e. (figuratively) to *comprehend, heed:*— consider, perceive, think, understand.

G3540 νόημα *noēma* from *G3539*; a *perception,* i.e. *purpose,* or (by implication) the *intellect, disposition,* itself:— device, mind, thought.

G3541 νόθος *nothos* of uncertain affinity; a *spurious* or *illegitimate* son:— bastard.

G3542 νομή *nomē* feminine from the same as *G3551*; *pasture,* i.e. (the act) *feeding* (figuratively *spreading* of a gangrene), or (the food) *pasturage:*— eat, pasture.

G3543 νομίζω *nomizō* from *G3551*; properly to *do* by *law* (*usage*), i.e. to *accustom* (passive *be usual*); by extension to *deem* or *regard:*— suppose, think, be wont.

G3544 νομικός *nomikos* from *G3551*; *according* (or *pertaining*) *to law,* i.e. *legal* (ceremonially); as noun, an *expert in* the (Mosaic) *law:*— about the law, lawyer.

G3545 νομίμως *nomimōs* adverb from a derivative of *G3551*; *legitimately* (specifically agreeably to the rules of the lists):— lawfully.

G3546 νόμισμα *nomisma* from *G3543*; *what is reckoned* as of value (after the Latin *numisma*), i.e. current *coin:*— money.

G3547 νομοδιδάσκαλος *nomodidaskalos* from *G3551* and *G1320*; an *expounder of* the (Jewish) *law,* i.e. a *Rabbi:*— doctor (teacher) of the law.

G3548 νομοθεσία *nomothesia* from *G3550*; *legislation* (specifically the *institution of* the Mosaic *code*):— giving of the law.

G3549 νομοθετέω *nomotheteō* from *G3550*; to *legislate,* i.e. (passive) to *have* (the Mosaic) *enactments* enjoined, *be sanctioned* (by them):— establish, receive the law.

G3550 νομοθέτης *nomothetēs* from *G3551* and a derivative of *G5087*; a *legislator:*— lawgiver.

G3551 νόμος *nomos* from a primary

νέμω *nemō* (to *parcel* out, especially *food* or *grazing* to animals); *law* (through the idea of prescriptive *usage*), general (*regulation*), specific (of Moses [including the volume]; also of the Gospel), or figurative (a *principle*):— law.

G3552 νοσέω *noseō* from *G3554*; to *be sick,* i.e. (by implication of a diseased appetite) to *hanker* after (figuratively to *harp* upon):— dote.

G3553 νόσημα *nosēma* from *G3552*; an *ailment* :— disease.

G3554 νόσος *nosos* of uncertain affinity; a *malady* (rarely figurative of moral *disability*):— disease, infirmity, sickness.

G3555 νοσσιά *nossia* from *G3502*; a *brood* (of chickens):— brood.

G3556 νοσσίον *nossion* diminutive of *G3502*; a *little bird:*— chicken.

G3557 νοσφίζομαι *nosphizomai* middle from

νοσφί *nosphi* (*apart* or *clandestinely*); to *sequestrate* for oneself, i.e. *embezzle:*— keep back, purloin.

G3558 νότος *notos* of uncertain affinity; the *south* (*southwest*) *wind;* by extension the *southern quarter* itself:— south (wind).

G3559 νουθεσία *nouthesia* from *G3563* and a derivative of *G5087*; calling *attention* to, i.e. (by implication) mild *rebuke* or *warning:*— admonition.

G3560 νουθετέω *noutheteō* from the same as *G3559*; to *put in mind,* i.e. (by implication) to *caution* or *reprove* gently:— admonish, warn.

G3561 νουμηνία *noumēnia* feminine of a compound of *G3501* and *G3376* (as noun by implication of *G2250*); the festival of *new moon:*— new moon.

G3562 νουνεχῶς *nounechōs* adverb from a compound of the accusative of *G3563* and *G2192*; in a *mind-having* way, i.e. *prudently:*— discreetly.

G3563 νοῦς *nous* probably from the base of *G1097*; the *intellect,* i.e. *mind* (divine or human; in thought, feeling, or will); by implication *meaning:*— mind, understanding. Compare *G5590*

G3564 Νυμφᾶς *Nymphas* probably contracted for a compound of *G3565* and *G1435*; *nymph-given* (i.e. *nymph-born*); *Nymphas,* a Christian:— Nymphas.

G3565 νύμφη *nymphē* from a primary but obsolete verb.

νύπτω *nyptō* (to *veil* as a bride; compare Latin *"nupto,"* to *marry*); a young *married* woman (as *veiled*), including a *betrothed* girl; by implication a *son's wife:*— bride, daughter-in-law.

G3566 νυμφίος *nymphios* from *G3565*; a *bridegroom* (literal or figurative):— bridegroom.

G3567 νυμφών *nymphōn* from *G3565*; the *bridal* room:— bridechamber.

G3568 νῦν *nyn* a primary particle of present time; *"now"* (as adverb of date, a transition, or emphasis); also as noun or adjective *present* or *immediate:*— henceforth, hereafter, of late, soon, present, this (time). See also *G3569, G3570.*

G3569 τανῦν *tanyn* or

τᾶ νῦν *ta nyn* from neuter plural of *G3588* and *G3568*; *the* things *now,* i.e. (adverbially) *at present:*— (but) now.

G3570 νυνί *nyni* a prolonged form of *G3568* for emphasis; *just now:*— now.

G3571 νύξ *nyx* a primary word; *"night"* (literal or figurative):— night, midnight.

G3572 νύσσω *nyssō* apparently a primary word; to *prick* ("nudge"):— pierce.

G3573 νυστάζω *nystazō* from a presumed derivative of *G3506*; to *nod,* i.e. (by implication) to *fall asleep;* figuratively to *delay:*— slumber.

G3574 νυχθήμερον *nychthēmeron* from *G3571* and *G2250*; a *day-and-night,* i.e. full *day* of twenty-four hours:— night and day.

G3575 Νῶε *Nōe* of Hebrew origin [H5146]; *Noe',* (i.e. *Noa'ch*), a patriarch:— Noe.

G3576 νωθρός *nōthros* from a derivative of *G3541*; *sluggish,* i.e. (literally) *lazy,* or (figuratively) *stupid:*— dull, slothful.

G3577 νῶτος *nōtos* of uncertain affinity; the *back* :— back.

Ξ

G3578 ξενία *xenia* from *G3581*; *hospitality,* i.e. (by implication) a *place of entertainment:*— lodging.

G3579 ξενίζω *xenizō* from *G3581*; to *be a host* (passive a *guest*); by implication *be* (*make, appear*) *strange:*— entertain, lodge, (think it) strange.

G3580 ξενοδοχέω *xenodocheō* from a compound of *G3581* and *G1209*; to *be hospitable:*— lodge strangers.

G3581 ξένος *xenos* apparently a primary word; *foreign* (literally *alien,* or figuratively *novel*); by implication a *guest* or (vice-versa) *entertainer:*— host, strange, stranger.

G3582 ξέστης *xestēs* as if from

ξέω *xeō* (properly to *smooth;* by implication [of *friction*] to *boil* or *heat*); a *vessel* (as *fashioned* or for *cooking*) [or perhaps by corruption from the Latin *sextarius,* the *sixth* of a modius, i.e. about a *pint*], i.e. (specifically) a *measure* for liquids or solids, (by analogy a *pitcher*):— pot.

G3583 ξηραίνω *xērainō* from *G3584*; to *desiccate;* by implication to *shrivel,* to *mature:*— dry up, pine away, be ripe, wither (away).

G3584 ξηρός *xēros* from the base of *G3582* (through the idea of *scorching*); *arid;* by implication *shrunken, earth* (as opposed to water):— dry, land, withered.

G3585 ξύλινος *xylinos* from *G3586*; *wooden:*— of wood.

G3586 ξύλον *xylon* from another form of the base of Greek *G3582*; *timber* (as fuel or material); by implication a *stick, club* or *tree* or other wooden article or substance:— staff, stocks, tree, wood.

G3587 ξυράω *xyraō* from a derivative of the same as *G3586* (meaning a *razor*); to *shave* or *"shear"* the hair:— shave.

O

G3588 ὁ *ho* including the feminine

ἡ *hē* and the neuter

τό *to* in all their inflections; the definite article; *the* (sometimes to be supplied, at others omitted, in English idiom):— the, this, that, one, he, she, it, etc.

G3589 ὀγδοήκοντα *ogdoēkonta* from *G3590*; *ten times eight:*— fourscore.

G3590 ὄγδοος *ogdoos* from *G3638*; the *eighth:*— eighth.

G3591 ὄγκος *onkos* probably from the same as *G43*; a *mass* (as *bending* or *bulging* by its load), i.e. *burden* (*hindrance*):— weight.

G3592 ὅδε *hode* including the feminine form

ἥδε *hēde* and the neuter

τόδε *tode* from *G3588* and *G1161*; the *same,* i.e. *this* or *that* one (plural *these* or *those*); often used as personal pronoun:— he, she, such, these, thus.

G3593 ὁδεύω *hodeuō* from *G3598*; to *travel:*— journey.

G3594 ὁδηγέω *hodēgeō* from *G3595*; to *show* the *way* (literally or figuratively [*teach*]):— guide, lead.

G3595 ὁδηγός *hodēgos* from *G3598* and *G2233*; a *conductor* (literal or figurative [*teacher*]):— guide, leader.

G3596 ὁδοιπορέω *hodoiporeō* from a compound of *G3598* and *G4198*; to *be a wayfarer,* i.e. *travel:*— go on a journey.

G3597 ὁδοιπορία *hodoiporia* from the same as *G3596*; *travel:*— journey, journeying.

G3598 ὁδός *hodos* apparently a primary word; a *road;* by implication a *progress* (the route, act, or distance); figuratively a *mode* or *means:*— journey, way, highway.

G3599 ὀδούς *odous* perhaps from the base of *G2068*; a *"tooth"*:— tooth.

GRK

G3600 ὀδυνάω *odynaō* from *G3601*; to *grieve*:— sorrow, torment.

G3601 ὀδύνη *odynē* from *G1416*; *grief* (as *dejecting*):— sorrow.

G3602 ὀδυρμός *odyrmos* from a derivative of the base of *G1416*; *moaning*, i.e. *lamentation*:— mourning.

G3603 ὅ εστι *ho esti* from the neuter of *G3739* and the third person singular present indicative of *G1510*; *which is*:— called, which is (make), that is (to say).

G3604 Ὀζίας *Ozias* of Hebrew origin [H5818]; *Ozias* (i.e. *Uzzijah*), an Israelite:— Ozias.

G3605 ὄζω *ozō* a primary verb (in a strengthened form); to *scent* (usually an ill "odor"):— stink.

G3606 ὅθεν *hothen* from *G3739* with the directive enclitic of source; *from which* place or source or cause (adverb or conjunction):— from thence, (from) whence, where, whereby, wherefore, whereupon.

G3607 ὀθόνη *othonē* of uncertain affinity; a *linen* cloth, i.e. (especially) a *sail*:— sheet.

G3608 ὀθόνιον *othonion* neuter of a presumed derivative of *G3607*; a linen *bandage*:— linen clothes.

G3609 οἰκεῖος *oikeios* from *G3624*; *domestic*, i.e. (as noun), a *relative, adherent*:— (those) of the (his own) house, (those) of the (his own) household.

G3610 οἰκέτης *oiketēs* from *G3611*; a fellow *resident*, i.e. menial *domestic*:— (household) servant.

G3611 οἰκέω *oikeō* from *G3624*; to *occupy a house*, i.e. *reside* (figuratively *inhabit, remain, inhere*); by implication to *cohabit*:— dwell. See also *G3625*.

G3612 οἴκημα *oikēma* from *G3611*; a *tenement*, i.e. (specifically) a *jail*:— prison.

G3613 οἰκητήριον *oikētērion* neuter of a presumed derivative of *G3611* (equivalent to *G3612*); a *residence* (literal or figurative):— habitation, house.

G3614 οἰκία *oikia* from *G3624*; properly *residence* (abstract), but usually (concrete) an *abode* (literal or figurative); by implication a *family* (especially *domestics*):— home, house, household.

G3615 οἰκιακός *oikiakos* from *G3614*; *familiar*, i.e. (as noun) *relatives*:— they (them) of (his own) household.

G3616 οἰκοδεσποτέω *oikodespoteō* from *G3617*; to *be the head of* (i.e. *rule*) *a family*:— guide the house.

G3617 οἰκοδεσπότης *oikodespotēs* from *G3624* and *G1203*; *the head of a family*:— goodman (of the house), householder, master of the house.

G3618 οἰκοδομέω *oikodomeō* from the same as *G3619*; to *be a house-builder*, i.e. *construct* or (figuratively) *confirm*:— build (up), builder (up), (be in) building (up), edify, embolden.

G3619 οἰκοδομή *oikodomē* feminine (abstract) of a compound of *G3624* and the base of *G1430*; *architecture*, i.e. (concretely) a *structure*; figuratively *confirmation*:— building, edify, edification, edifying.

G3620 οἰκοδομία *oikodomia* from the same as *G3619*; *confirmation*:— edifying.

G3621 οἰκονομέω *oikonomeō* from *G3623*; to *manage* (a house, i.e. an estate):— be steward.

G3622 οἰκονομία *oikonomia* from *G3623*; *administration* (of a household or estate); specifically a (religious) *"economy"*:— dispensation, stewardship.

G3623 οἰκονόμος *oikonomos* from *G3624* and the base of *G3551*; a *house-distributor* (i.e. *manager*), or *overseer*, i.e. an employee in that capacity; by extension a fiscal *agent* (*treasurer*); figuratively a *preacher* (of the Gospel):— chamberlain, governor, steward.

G3624 οἶκος *oikos* of uncertain affinity; a *dwelling* (more or less extensive, literal or figurative); by implication a *family* (more or less related, literal or figurative):— home, house, household, temple.

G3625 οἰκουμένη *oikoumenē* feminine participle present passive of *G3611* (as noun, by implication of *G1093*); *land*, i.e. the (terrene part of the) *globe*; specifically the Roman *empire*:— earth, world.

G3626 οἰκουρός *oikouros* from *G3624* and

οὖρος *ouros* (a *guard*; be "ware"); one who *stays at home*, i.e. *domestically inclined* (a "good housekeeper"):— keeper at home.

G3627 οἰκτείρω *oikteirō* also (in certain tenses) prolonged

οἰκτερέω *oiktereō* from

οἶκτος *oiktos* (*pity*); to *exercise pity*:— have compassion on.

G3628 οἰκτιρμός *oiktirmos* from *G3627*; *pity*:— mercy.

G3629 οἰκτίρμων *oiktirmōn* from *G3627*; *compassionate*:— merciful, of tender mercy.

G3630 οἰνοπότης *oinopotēs* from *G3631* and a derivative of the alternate of *G4095*; a *tippler*:— winebibber.

G3631 οἶνος *oinos* a primary word (or perhaps of Hebrew origin [H3196]); *"wine"* (literal or figurative):— wine.

G3632 οἰνοφλυγία *oinophlygia* from *G3631* and a form of the base of *G5397*; an *overflow* (or surplus) of *wine*, i.e. *wine-drunkenness* (*drunkenness*):— excess of wine.

G3633 οἴομαι *oiomai* or (shorter)

οἶμαι *oimai* middle apparently from Greek *G3634*; to *make like* (oneself), i.e. *imagine* (*be of* the *opinion*):— suppose, think.

G3634 οἷος *hoios* probably akin to *G3588*, *G3739*, and *G3745*; *such* or *what sort* of (as a correlation or exclamation); especially the neuter (adverbially) with negative not *so*:— so (as), such as, what (manner of), which.

G3635 ὀκνέω *okneō* from

ὄκνος *oknos* (*hesitation*); to *be slow* (figuratively *loath*):— delay.

G3636 ὀκνηρός *oknēros* from *G3635*; *tardy*, i.e. *indolent*; (figuratively) *irksome*:— grievous, slothful.

G3637 ὀκταήμερος *oktaēmeros* from *G3638* and *G2250*; an *eight-day* old person or act:— the eighth day.

G3638 ὀκτώ *oktō* a primary numeral; *"eight"*:— eight.

G3639 ὄλεθρος *olethros* from a primary

ὄλλυμι *ollymi* (to *destroy*; a prolonged form); *ruin*, i.e. *death, punishment*:— destruction.

G3640 ὀλιγόπιστος *oligopistos* from *G3641* and *G4102*; *incredulous*, i.e. *lacking confidence* (in Christ):— of little faith.

G3641 ὀλίγος *oligos* of uncertain affinity; *puny* (in extent, degree, number, duration or value); especially neuter (adverbially) *somewhat*:— almost, brief, briefly, few, (a) little, long, a season, short, small, a while.

G3642 ὀλιγόψυχος *oligopsychos* from *G3641* and *G5590*; *little-spirited*, i.e. *faint-hearted*:— feebleminded.

G3643 ὀλιγωρέω *oligōreō* from a compound of *G3641* and

ὥρα *ōra* (*"care"*); to *have little regard* for, i.e. to *disesteem*:— despise.

G3644 ὀλοθρευτής *olothreutēs* from *G3645*; a *ruiner*, i.e. (specifically) a venomous *serpent*:— destroyer.

G3645 ὀλοθρεύω *olothreuō* from *G3639*; to *spoil*, i.e. *slay*:— destroy.

G3646 ὁλοκαύτωμα *holokautōma* from a derivative of a compound of *G3650* and a derivative of *G2545*; a *wholly-consumed* sacrifice ("holocaust") :— (whole) burnt offering.

G3647 ὁλοκληρία *holoklēria* from *G3648*; *integrity*, i.e. physical *wholeness*:— perfect soundness.

G3648 ὁλόκληρος *holoklēros* from *G3650* and *G2819*; *complete* in every *part*, i.e. perfectly *sound* (in body):— entire, whole.

G3649 ὀλολύζω *ololyzō* a reduplicated primary verb; to *"howl"* or *"halloo"*, i.e. *shriek*:— howl.

G3650 ὅλος *holos* a primary word; *"whole"* or *"all"*, i.e. *complete* (in extent, amount, time or degree), especially (neuter) as noun or adverb:— all, altogether, every whit, throughout, whole.

G3651 ὁλοτελής *holotelēs* from *G3650* and *G5056*; *complete* to the *end*, i.e. *absolutely perfect*:— wholly.

G3652 Ὀλυμπᾶς *Olympas* probably a contracted from

Ὀλυμπιόδωρος *Olympiodōros* (*Olympian-bestowed*, i.e. *heaven-descended*); *Olympas*, a Christian:— Olympas.

G3653 ὄλυνθος *olynthos* of uncertain derivation; an *unripe* (because out of season) *fig*:— untimely fig.

G3654 ὅλως *holōs* adverb from *G3650*; *completely*, i.e. *altogether*; (by analogy) *everywhere*; (negative) not *by any means*:— at all, commonly, utterly.

G3655 ὄμβρος *ombros* of uncertain affinity; a thunder *storm*:— shower.

G3656 ὁμιλέω *homileō* from *G3658*; to *be in company* with, i.e. (by implication) to *converse*:— commune, talk.

G3657 ὁμιλία *homilia* from *G3658*; *companionship* ("homily"), i.e. (by implication) *intercourse* :— communication.

G3658 ὅμιλος *homilos* from the base of *G3674* and a derivative of the alternate of *G138* (meaning a *crowd*); *association together*, i.e. a *multitude*:— company.

G3659 ὄμμα *omma* from *G3700*; a *sight*, i.e. (by implication) the *eye*:— eye.

G3660 ὀμνύω *omnyō* a prolonged form of a primary but obsolete

ὄμω *omō* for which another prolonged form

ὀμόω *omoō* is used in certain tenses; to *swear*, i.e. *take* (or *declare on*) *oath*:— swear.

G3661 ὁμοθυμαδόν *homothymadon* adverb from a compound of the base of *G3674* and *G2372*; *unanimously*:— with one accord (mind).

G3662 ὁμοιάζω *homoiazō* from *G3664*; to *resemble* :— agree.

G3663 ὁμοιοπαθής *homoiopathēs* from *G3664* and the alternate of *G3958*; *similarly affected:*— of (subject to) like passions.

G3664 ὅμοιος *homoios* from the base of *G3674*; *similar* (in appearance or character):— like, manner.

G3665 ὁμοιότης *homoiotēs* from *G3664*; *resemblance:*— like as, similitude.

G3666 ὁμοιόω *homoioō* from *G3664*; to *assimilate*, i.e. *compare;* passive to *become similar:*— be (make) like, liken, in the likeness, resemble.

G3667 ὁμοίωμα *homoiōma* from *G3666*; a *form;* abstractly *resemblance:*— made like to, likeness, shape, similitude.

G3668 ὁμοίως *homoiōs* adverb from *G3664*; *similarly:*— likewise, so.

G3669 ὁμοίωσις *homoiōsis* from *G3666*; *assimilation,* i.e. *resemblance:*— similitude.

G3670 ὁμολογέω *homologeō* from a compound of the base of *G3674* and *G3056*; to *assent,* i.e. *covenant, acknowledge:*— confess, profess, confession is made, give thanks, promise.

G3671 ὁμολογία *homologia* from the same as *G3670*; *acknowledgment:*— confession, profession, professed.

G3672 ὁμολογουμένος *homologoumenos* adverb of present passive participle of *G3670*; *by confession:*— without controversy.

G3673 ὁμότεχνος *homotechnos* from the base of *G3674* and *G5078*; a *fellow-artificer:*— of the same craft.

G3674 ὁμοῦ *homou* genetive of

ὁμός *homos* (the *same;* akin to *G260*) as adverb; *at* the *same* place or time:— together.

G3675 ὁμόφρων *homophrōn* from the base of *G3674* and *G5424*; *like-minded,* i.e. *harmonious:*— of one mind.

G3676 ὅμως *homōs* adverb from the base of *G3674*; *at* the *same* time, i.e. (conjunction) *notwithstanding, yet still:*— and even, nevertheless, though, but.

G3677 ὄναρ *onar* of uncertain derivation; a *dream* :— dream.

G3678 ὀνάριον *onarion* neuter of a presumed derivative of *G3688*; a *little ass:*— young ass.

G3679 ὀνειδίζω *oneidizō* from *G3681*; to *defame,* i.e. *rail at, chide, taunt:*— cast in teeth, (suffer) reproach, revile, upbraid.

G3680 ὀνειδισμός *oneidismos* from *G3679*; *contumely:*— reproach.

G3681 ὄνειδος *oneidos* probably akin to the base of *G3686*; *notoriety,* i.e. a *taunt* (*disgrace*):— reproach.

G3682 Ὀνήσιμος *Onēsimos* from *G3685*; *profitable; Onesimus,* a Christian:— Onesimus.

G3683 Ὀνησίφορος *Onēsiphoros* from a derivative of *G3685* and *G5411*; *profit-bearer; Onesiphorus,* a Christian:— Onesiphorus.

G3684 ὀνικός *onikos* from *G3688*; *belonging to* an *ass,* i.e. *large* (so as to be turned by an ass):— millstone.

G3685 ὀνίνημι *oninēmi* a prolonged form of an apparent primary verb

(**ὄνομαι** *onomai* to *slur*); for which another prolonged form

ὀνάω *onaō* is used as an alternate in some tenses [unless indeed it be identical with the base of *G3686* through the idea of *notoriety*]; to *gratify,* i.e. (middle) to *derive pleasure* or *advantage* from:— have joy.

G3686 ὄνομα *onoma* from a presumed derivative of the base of *G1097* (compare *G3685*); a *"name"* (literal or figurative) [*authority, character*]:— called, name, named, surnamed.

G3687 ὀνομάζω *onomazō* from *G3686*; to *name,* i.e. *assign an appellation;* by extension to *utter, mention, profess:*— call, name.

G3688 ὄνος *onos* apparently a primary word; a *donkey:*— ass.

G3689 ὄντως *ontōs* adverb of the oblique cases of *G5607*; *really:*— certainly, clean, indeed, of a truth, verily.

G3690 ὄξος *oxos* from *G3691*; *vinegar,* i.e. *sour* wine:— vinegar.

G3691 ὀξύς *oxys* probably akin to the base of *G188* [*"acid"*]; *keen;* by analogy *rapid:*— sharp, swift.

G3692 ὀπή *opē* probably from *G3700*; a *hole* (as if for light), i.e. *cavern;* by analogy a *spring* (of water):— cave, place.

G3693 ὄπισθεν *opisthen* from

ὄπις *opis* (*regard;* from *G3700*) with enclitic of source; *from the rear* (as a secure *aspect*), i.e. *at* the *back* (adverb and preposition of place or time):— after, backside, behind.

G3694 ὀπίσω *opisō* from the same as *G3693* with enclitic of direction; *to the back,* i.e. *aback* (as adverb or preposition of time or place; or as noun):— after, back, backward, (+ get) behind, follow.

G3695 ὁπλίζω *hoplizō* from *G3696*; to *equip* (with weapons [middle and figuratively]):— arm self.

G3696 ὅπλον *hoplon* probably from a primary

ἕπω *hepō* (to be *busy* about); an *implement* or *utensil* or *tool* (literal or figurative, especially offensive for war):— armour, instrument, weapon.

G3697 ὁποῖος *hopoios* from *G3739* and *G4169*; of *what* kind *that,* i.e. *how* (*as*) *great* (*excellent*) (specifically as indefinite correlation to antecedent definite *G5108* of quality):— what manner (sort) of, such as, whatsoever.

G3698 ὁπότε *hopote* from *G3739* and *G4218*; *what then, whatever then,* i.e. (of time) *as soon as:*— when.

G3699 ὅπου *hopou* from *G3739* and *G4225*; *what where, whatever where,* i.e. *at whichever* spot:— in what place, where, whereas, wheresoever), whither, whithersoever.

G3700 ὀπτάνομαι *optanomai* a (middle) prolonged form of the primary (middle)

ὄπτομαι *optomai* which is used for it in certain tenses; and both as an alternate of *G3708*; to *gaze* (i.e. with wide-open eyes, as at something remarkable; and thus differing from *G991*, which denotes simply *voluntary* observation; and from *G1492*, which expresses merely mechanical, passive or casual vision; while *G2300*, and still more emphatically its intensive *G2334*, signifies an earnest but more continued *inspection;* and *G4648* a watching *from a distance*):— appear, look, see, shew self.

G3701 ὀπτασία *optasia* from a presumed derivative of *G3700*; *vision,* i.e. (concretely) an *apparition:*— vision.

G3702 ὀπτός *optos* from an obsolete verb akin to

ἕψω *hepsō* (to *"steep"*); *cooked,* i.e. *roasted:*— broiled.

G3703 ὀπώρα *opōra* apparently from the base of *G3796* and *G5610*; properly *even-tide* of the (summer) season (*dog-days*), i.e. (by implication) *ripe* fruit:— fruit.

G3704 ὅπως *hopōs* from *G3739* and *G4459*; *what, whatever, how,* i.e. *in* the *manner that* (as adverb or conjecture of coincidence, intentional or actual):— because, how, (so) that, to, when.

G3705 ὅραμα *horama* from *G3708*; *something gazed at,* i.e. a *spectacle* (especially supernatural):— sight, vision.

GRK

G3706 ὅρασις *horasis* from *G3708*; the act of *gazing,* i.e. (externally) an *aspect* or (internally) an inspired *appearance:*— sight, vision.

G3707 ὁρατός *horatos* from *G3708*; *gazed at,* i.e. (by implication) *capable of being seen:*— visible.

G3708 ὁράω *horaō*; properly to *stare* at [compare *G3700*], i.e. (by implication) to *discern* clearly (physically or mentally); by extension to *attend* to; by Hebrew to *experience;* passive to *appear:*— behold, perceive, see, take heed.

G3709 ὀργή *orgē* from *G3713*; properly *desire* (as a *reaching* forth or *excitement* of the mind), i.e. (by analogy) violent *passion* (*ire,* or [justifiable] *abhorrence*); by implication *punishment:*— anger, indignation, vengeance, wrath.

G3710 ὀργίζω *orgizō* from *G3709*; to *provoke* or *enrage,* i.e. (passive) *become exasperated:*— be angry (wroth).

G3711 ὀργίλος *orgilos* from *G3709*; *irascible:*— soon angry.

G3712 ὀργυιά *orguia* from *G3713*; a *stretch* of the arms, i.e. a *fathom:*— fathom.

G3713 ὀρέγομαι *oregomai* middle of apparently a prolonged form of an obsolete primary [compare *G3735*]; to *stretch* oneself, i.e. *reach* out after (*long* for):— covet after, desire.

G3714 ὀρεινός *oreinos* from *G3735*; *mountainous,* i.e. (feminine by implication of *G5561*) the *Highlands* (of Judaea):— hill country.

G3715 ὄρεξις *orexis* from *G3713*; *excitement* of the mind, i.e. *longing* after:— lust.

G3716 ὀρθοποδέω *orthopodeō* from a compound of *G3717* and *G4228*; to *be straight-footed,* i.e. (figuratively) to *go directly* forward:— walk uprightly.

G3717 ὀρθός *orthos* probably from the base of *G3735*; *right* (as *rising*), i.e. (perpendicularly) *erect* (figuratively *honest*), or (horizontally) *level* or *direct:*— straight, upright.

G3718 ὀρθοτομέω *orthotomeō* from a compound of *G3717* and the base of *G5114*; to *make a straight cut,* i.e. (figuratively) to *dissect* (*expound*) *correctly* (the divine message):— rightly divide.

G3719 ὀρθρίζω *orthrizō* from *G3722*; to *use* the *dawn,* i.e. (by implication) to *repair betimes:*— come early in the morning.

G3720 ὀρθρινός *orthrinos* from *G3722*; *relating to* the *dawn,* i.e. *matutinal* (as an epithet of Venus, especially brilliant in the early day):— morning.

G3721 ὄρθριος *orthrios* from *G3722*; *in the dawn,* i.e. up *at day-break:*— early.

G3722 ὄρθρος *orthros* from the same as *G3735*; *dawn* (as *sun-rise, rising* of light); by extension *morn:*— early in the morning.

G3723 ὀρθῶς *orthōs* adverb from *G3717*; *in a straight* manner, i.e. (figuratively) *correctly* (also morally):— plain, right, rightly.

G3724 ὁρίζω *horizō* from *G3725*; to *mark* out or *bound* ("horizon"), i.e. (figuratively) to *appoint, decree, specify:*— declare, determine, limit, ordain.

G3725 ὅριον *horion* neuter of a derivative of an apparently primary

ὅρος *horos* (a *bound* or *limit*); a *boundary-*line, i.e. (by implication) a *frontier* (*region*):— border, coast.

G3726 ὁρκίζω *horkizō* from *G3727*; to *put on oath,* i.e. *make swear;* by analogy to solemnly *enjoin:*— adjure, charge.

G3727 ὅρκος *horkos* from

ἕρκος *herkos* (a *fence;* perhaps akin to *G3725*); a *limit,* i.e. (sacred) *restraint* (specifically *oath*):— oath.

G3728 ὁρκωμοσία *horkōmosia* from a compound of *G3727* and a derivative of *G3660*; *asseveration on oath:*— oath.

G3729 ὁρμάω *hormaō* from *G3730*; to *start, spur* or *urge* on, i.e. (reflexive) to *dash* or *plunge:*— run (violently), rush.

G3730 ὁρμή *hormē* of uncertain affinity; a violent *impulse,* i.e. *onset:*— assault.

G3731 ὅρμημα *hormēma* from *G3730*; an *attack,* i.e. (abstractly) *precipitancy:*— violence.

G3732 ὄρνεον *orneon* neuter of a presumed derivative of *G3733*; a *little bird:*— bird, fowl.

G3733 ὄρνις *ornis* probably from a prolonged form of the base of *G3735*; a *bird* (as *rising* in the air), i.e. (specifically) a *hen* (or female domestic fowl):— hen.

G3734 ὁροθεσία *horothesia* from a compound of the base of *G3725* and a derivative of *G5087*; a *limit-placing,* i.e. (concrete) *boundary-line:*— bound.

G3735 ὄρος *oros* probably from an obsolete

ὄρω *orō* (to *rise* or *"rear";* perhaps akin to *G142*; compare *G3733*); a *mountain* (as *lifting* itself above the plain):— hill, mount, mountain.

G3736 ὀρύσσω *orussō* apparently a primary verb; to *"burrow"* in the ground, i.e. *dig:*— dig.

G3737 ὀρφανός *orphanos* of uncertain affinity; *bereaved* ("*orphan*"), i.e. *parentless:*— comfortless, fatherless.

G3738 ὀρχέομαι *orcheomai* middle from

ὄρχος *orchos* (a *row* or *ring*); to *dance* (from the *rank-like* or *regular* motion):— dance.

G3739 ὅς *hos* including feminine

ἥ *hē* and neuter

ὅ *ho* probably a primary word (or perhaps a form of the article *G3588*); the relative (sometimes demonstrative) pronoun, *who, which, what, that:*— one, other, another, the other, some, that, what, which, who, whom, whose, etc. See also *G3757*.

G3740 ὁσάκις *hosakis* multiple adverb from *G3739*; *how* (i.e. with *G302, so*) *many times* as:— as oft as, as often as.

G3741 ὅσιος *hosios* of uncertain affinity; properly *right* (by intrinsic or divine character; thus distinguished from *G1342*, which refers rather to *human* statutes and relations; from *G2413*, which denotes formal *consecration;* and from *G40*, which relates to *purity* from defilement), i.e. *hallowed* (*pious, sacred, sure*):— holy, mercy, shalt be.

G3742 ὁσιότης *hosiotēs* from *G3741*; *piety:*— holiness.

G3743 ὁσίως *hosiōs* adverb from *G3741*; *piously* :— holily.

G3744 ὀσμή *osmē* from *G3605*; *fragrance* (literal or figurative):— odour, savour.

G3745 ὅσος *hosos* by reduplicated from *G3739*; *as* (*much, great, long,* etc.) *as:*— all (that), as (long, many, much) (as), how great (many, much), asmuch as, inasmuch as, so many as, that (ever), the more, those things, what (great), whatsoever, wheresoever, wherewithsoever, which, while, who, whosoever.

G3746 ὅσπερ *hosper* from *G3739* and *G4007*; *who especially:*— whomsoever.

G3747 ὀστέον *osteon* or contracted

ὀστοῦν *ostoun* of uncertain affinity; a *bone* :— bone.

G3748 ὅστις *hostis* including the feminine

ἥτις *hētis* and the neuter

ὅ τι *ho ti* from *G3739* and *G5100*; *which some,* i.e. *any that;* also (definite) *which same:*— and (they), (such) as, (they) that, in that they, what, whatsoever, whereas ye, (they) which, who, whosoever. Compare *G3754*.

G3749 ὀστράκινος *ostrakinos* from

ὄστρακον *ostrakon* ["oyster"] (a *tile,* i.e. *terra cotta*); *earthen-*ware, i.e. *clayey;* by implication *frail:*— of earth, earthen.

G3750 ὄσφρησις *osphrēsis* from a derivative of *G3605*; *smell* (the sense):— smelling.

G3751 ὀσφύς *osphys* of uncertain affinity; the *loin* (external), i.e. the *hip;* internal (by extension) *procreative power:*— loin.

G3752 ὅταν *hotan* from *G3753* and *G302*; *whenever* (implying *hypothesis* or more or less *uncertainty*); also causative (conjunction) *inasmuch as:*— as long (soon) as, that, till, when, whensoever, while.

G3753 ὅτε *hote* from *G3739* and *G5037*; at *which* (thing) *too,* i.e. *when:*— after (that), as soon as, that, when, while.

ὅ τε *ho, te* also feminine

ἥ τε *hē, te* and neuter

τό τε *to, te* simply the article *G3588* followed by *G5037*; so written (in some editions) to distinguish them from *G3752* and *G5119*.

G3754 ὅτι *hoti* neuter of *G3748* as conjecture; demonstrative *that* (sometimes redundant); causative *because:*— as concerning that, as though, because (that), for (that), how (that), (in) that, though, why.

G3755 ὅτου *hotou* for the genetive of *G3748* (as adverb); during *which same* time, i.e. *whilst:*— whiles.

G3756 οὐ *ou* Also (before a vowel)

οὐκ *ouk* and (before an aspirate)

οὐχ *ouch* a primary word; the absolute negative [compare *G3361*] adverb; *no* or *not:*— long, nay, neither, never, no (man), none, not, cannot, nothing, special, un- (e.g., unworthy), when, without, yet but. See also *G3364*, *G3372*.

G3757 οὗ *hou* genetive of *G3739* as adverb; at *which* place, i.e. *where:*— where, wherein whither, whithersoever.

G3758 οὐά *oua* a primary exclamation of surprise; *"ah":*— ah.

G3759 οὐαί *ouai* a primary exclamation of grief; *"woe":*— alas, woe.

G3760 οὐδαμῶς *oudamōs* adverb from (the feminine) of *G3762*; *by no means:*— not.

G3761 οὐδέ *oude* from *G3756* and *G1161*; *not however,* i.e. *neither, nor, not even:*— neither (indeed), never, no (more, nor, not), nor (yet), (also, even, then) not (even, so much as), nothing, so much as.

G3762 οὐδείς *oudeis* including the feminine

οὐδεμία *oudemia* neuter

οὐδέν *ouden* from *G3761* and *G1520*; *not even one* (man, woman or thing), i.e. *none, nobody, nothing:*— any (man), aught, man, neither any (thing), never (man), no (man), none (+ of these things), not (any, at all), nothing, nought.

G3763 οὐδέποτε *oudepote* from *G3761* and *G4218*; *not even at any time,* i.e. *never at all:*— neither at any time, never, nothing at any time.

G3764 οὐδέπω *oudepō* from *G3761* and *G4452*; *not even yet:*— as yet not, never before (yet), (not) yet.

G3765 οὐκέτι *ouketi* also (separately)

οὐκ ἔτι *ouk eti* from *G3756* and *G2089*; *not yet, no longer:*— after that (not), (not) any more, henceforth (hereafter) not, no longer (more), not as yet (now), now no more (not), yet (not).

G3766 οὐκοῦν *oukoun* from *G3756* and *G3767*; is it *not therefore* that, i.e. (affirmative) *hence* or *so:*— then.

G3767 οὖν *oun* apparently a primary word; (adverb) *certainly,* or (conjunction) *accordingly:*— and (so, truly), but, now (then), so (likewise then), then, therefore, verily, wherefore.

G3768 οὔπω *oupō* from *G3756* and *G4452*; *not yet:*— hitherto not, (no . . .) as yet, not yet.

G3769 οὐρά *oura* apparently a primary word; a *tail:*— tail.

G3770 οὐράνιος *ouranios* from *G3772*; *celestial,* i.e. *belonging to* or *coming from* the *sky:*— heavenly.

G3771 οὐρανόθεν *ouranothen* from *G3772* and the enclitic of source; *from* the *sky:*— from heaven.

G3772 οὐρανός *ouranos* perhaps from the same as *G3735* (through the idea of *elevation*); the *sky;* by extension *heaven* (as the abode of God); by implication *happiness, power, eternity;* specifically the *Gospel* (*Christianity*):— air, heaven, heavenly, sky.

G3773 Οὐρβανός *Ourbanos* of Latin origin; *Urbanus* (*of the city, "urbane"*), a Christian:— Urbanus.

G3774 Οὐρίας *Ourias* of Hebrew origin [H223]; *Urias* (i.e. *Urijah*), a Hittite:— Urias.

G3775 οὖς *ous* apparently a primary word; the *ear* (physical or mental):— ear.

G3776 οὐσία *ousia* from the feminine of *G5607*; *substance,* i.e. *property* (*possessions*):— goods, substance.

G3777 οὔτε *oute* from *G3756* and *G5037*; *not too,* i.e. *neither* or *nor;* by analogy *not even:*— neither, none, nor (yet), (no, yet) not, nothing.

G3778 οὗτος *houtos* including nominative masculine plural
οὗτοι *houtoi* nominative feminine singular
αὕτη *hautē* and nominative feminine plural
αὗται *hautai* from the article *G3588* and *G846*; *the he* (*she* or *it*), i.e. *this* or *that* (often with article repeated):— he (it was that), hereof, it, she, such as, the same, these, they, this (man, same, woman), which, who.

G3779 οὕτω *houtō* or (before a vowel)
οὕτως *houtōs* adverb from *G3778*; *in this way* (referring to what precedes or follows):— after that, after (in) this manner, as, even (so), for all that, like, likewise, no more, on this fashion, on this wise, so (in like manner), thus, what.

G3780 οὐχί *ouchi* intensive of *G3756*; *not indeed* :— nay, not.

G3781 ὀφειλέτης *opheiletēs* from *G3784*; *one who owes*, i.e. a person *indebted*; figuratively a *delinquent*; morally a *transgressor* (against God):— debtor, which owed, sinner.

G3782 ὀφειλή *opheilē* from *G3784*; *indebtedness*, i.e. (concretely) a *sum* owed; figuratively *obligation*, i.e. (conjugal) *duty*:— debt, due.

G3783 ὀφείλημα *opheilēma* from (the alternate of) *G3784*; *something owed*, i.e. (figuratively) a *due*; morally a *fault*:— debt.

G3784 ὀφείλω *opheilō* or (in certain tenses) prolonged form
ὀφειλέω *opheileō* probably from the base of *G3786* (through the idea of *accruing*); to *owe* (monetarily); figuratively to *be under obligation* (*ought, must, should*); morally to *fail* in duty:— behove, be bound, debt, be debtor, (be) due, duty, be guilty (indebted), (must) need, must needs, ought, owe, should. See also *G3785*.

G3785 ὄφελον *ophelon* first person singular of a past tense of *G3784*; *I ought* (*wish*), i.e. (interjection) *oh that!*:— would (to God).

G3786 ὄφελος *ophelos* from
ὀφέλλω *ophellō* (to *heap* up, i.e. *accumulate* or *benefit*); *gain*:— advantageth, profit.

G3787 ὀφθαλμοδουλεία *ophthalmodouleia* from *G3788* and *G1397*; *sight-labor*, i.e. that needs watching (*remissness*):— eye-service.

G3788 ὀφθαλμός *ophthalmos* from *G3700*; the *eye* (literal or figurative); by implication *vision*; figuratively *envy* (from the jealous side-glance):— eye, sight.

G3789 ὄφις *ophis* probably from *G3700* (through the idea of *sharpness* of vision); a *snake*, figuratively (as a type of sly cunning) an artful *malicious* person, especially *Satan*:— serpent.

G3790 ὀφρύς *ophrys* perhaps from *G3700* (through the idea of the shading or proximity to the organ of *vision*); the eye-*"brow"* or *forehead*, i.e. (figuratively) the *brink* of a precipice:— brow.

G3791 ὀχλέω *ochleō* from *G3793*; to *mob*, i.e. (by implication) to *harass*:— vex.

G3792 ὀχλοποιέω *ochlopoieō* from *G3793* and *G4160*; to *make a crowd*, i.e. *raise a* public *disturbance*:— gather a company.

G3793 ὄχλος *ochlos* from a derivative of *G2192* (meaning a *vehicle*); a *throng* (as *borne* along); by implication the *rabble*; by extension a *class* of people; figuratively a *riot*:— company, multitude, number (of people), people, press.

G3794 ὀχύρωμα *ochyrōma* from a remote derivative of *G2192* (meaning to *fortify*, through the idea of *holding* safely); a *castle* (figuratively *argument*):— stronghold.

G3795 ὀψάριον *opsarion* neuter of a presumed derivative of the base of *G3702*; a *relish* to other food (as if cooked *sauce*), i.e. (specifically) *fish* (presumably salted and dried as a condiment):— fish.

G3796 ὀψέ *opse* from the same as *G3694* (through the idea of *backwardness*); (adverb) *late* in the day; by extension *after the close* of the day:— (at) even, in the end.

G3797 ὄψιμος *opsimos* from *G3796*; *later*, i.e. *vernal* (showering):— latter.

G3798 ὄψιος *opsios* from *G3796*; *late*; feminine (as noun) *afternoon* (early eve) or *nightfall* (later eve) :— even, evening, eventide.

G3799 ὄψις *opsis* from *G3700*; properly *sight* (the act), i.e. (by implication) the *visage*, an external *show* :— appearance, countenance, face.

G3800 ὀψώνιον *opsōnion* neuter of a presumed derivative of the same as *G3795*; *rations* for a soldier, i.e. (by extension) his *stipend* or *pay*:— wages.

G3801 ὁ ὢν καὶ ὁ ἦν καὶ ὁ ἐρχόμενος *ho ōn kai ho ēn kai ho erchomenos* a phrase combining *G3588* with the present participle and imperfect of *G1510* and the present participle of *G2064* by means of *G2532*; *the* one *being and the* one that *was and the* one *coming*, i.e. *the Eternal*, as a divine epithet of Christ:— which art (is, was), and (which) wast (is, was), and art (is) to come (shalt be).

Π

G3802 παγιδεύω *pagideuō* from *G3803*; to *ensnare* (figuratively):— entangle.

G3803 παγίς *pagis* from *G4078*; a *trap* (as *fastened* by a noose or notch); figuratively a *trick* or *strategem* (*temptation*):— snare.

G3804 πάθημα *pathēma* from a presumed derivative of *G3806*; something *undergone*, i.e. *hardship* or *pain*; subjectively an *emotion* or *influence*:— affection, affliction, motion, suffering.

G3805 παθητός *pathētos* from the same as *G3804*; *liable* (i.e. *doomed*) *to* experience *pain*:— suffer.

G3806 πάθος *pathos* from the alternate of *G3958*; properly *suffering* (*"pathos"*), i.e. (subjectively) a *passion* (especially *concupiscence*):— (inordinate) affection, lust.

G3807 παιδαγωγός *paidagōgos* from *G3816* and a reduplicated form of *G71*; a *boy-leader*, i.e. a servant whose office it was to take the children to school; (by implication [figuratively] a *tutor* [*"paedagogue"*]) :— instructor, schoolmaster.

G3808 παιδάριον *paidarion* neuter of a presumed derivative of *G3816*; a *little boy*:— child, lad.

G3809 παιδεία *paideia* from *G3811*; *tutorage*, i.e. *education* or *training*; by implication disciplinary *correction*:— chastening, chastisement, instruction, nurture.

G3810 παιδευτής *paideutēs* from *G3811*; a *trainer*, i.e. *teacher* or (by implication) *discipliner*:— which corrected, instructor.

G3811 παιδεύω *paideuō* from *G3816*; to *train* up a child, i.e. *educate*, or (by implication) *discipline* (by punishment):— chasten, chastise, instruct, learn, teach.

G3812 παιδιόθεν *paidiothen* adverb (of *source*) from *G3813*; *from infancy*:— of a child.

G3813 παιδίον *paidion* neuter diminutive of *G3816*; a *little child* (of either sex), i.e. (properly) an infant, or (by extension) a half-grown *boy* or *girl*; figuratively an *immature* Christian:— (little, young) child, damsel.

G3814 παιδίσκη *paidiskē* feminine diminutive of *G3816*; a *girl*, i.e. (specifically) a *female slave* or *servant*:— bondmaid, bondwoman, damsel, maid, maiden.

GRK

G3815 παίζω *paizō* from *G3816*; to *sport* (as a boy):— play.

G3816 παῖς *pais* perhaps from *G3817*; a *boy* (as often *beaten* with impunity), or (by analogy) a *girl*, and (generally) a *child*; specifically a *slave* or *servant* (especially a *minister* to a king; and by eminence to God):— child, maid, maiden, (man) servant, son, young man.

G3817 παίω *paiō* a primary verb; to *hit* (as if by a single blow and less violently than *G5180*); specifically to *sting* (as a scorpion):— smite, strike.

G3818 Πακατιανή *Pakatianē* feminine of an adjective of uncertain derivation; *Pacatianian*, a section of Phrygia:— Pacatiana.

G3819 πάλαι *palai* probably another form for *G3825* (through the idea of *retrocession*); (adverbially) *formerly*, or (by relationship) *sometime since*; (elliptically as adjective) *ancient*:— any while, a great while ago, (of) old, in time past.

G3820 παλαιός *palaios* from *G3819*; *antique*, i.e. *not recent, worn out*:— old.

G3821 παλαιότης *palaiotēs* from *G3820*; *antiquatedness*:— oldness.

G3822 παλαιόω *palaioō* from *G3820*; to *make* (passive *become*) *worn out*, or *declare obsolete*:— decay, make (wax) old.

G3823 πάλη *palē* from
πάλλω *pallō* (to *vibrate*; another form for *G906*); *wrestling*:— wrestle.

G3824 παλιγγενεσία *palingenesia* from *G3825* and *G1078*; (spiritual) *rebirth* (the state or the act), i.e. (figuratively) spiritual *renovation*; specifically Messianic *restoration*:— regeneration.

G3825 πάλιν *palin* probably from the same as *G3823* (through the idea of *oscillatory* repetition); (adverb) *anew*, i.e. (of place) *back*, (of time) *once more*, or (conjunction) *furthermore* or *on the other hand*:— again.

G3826 παμπληθεί *pamplēthei* dative (adverbial) of a compound of *G3956* and *G4128*; *in full multitude*, i.e. *concertedly* or *simultaneously*:— all at once.

G3827 πάμπολυς *pampolys* from *G3956* and *G4183*; *full many*, i.e. *immense*:— very great.

G3828 Παμφυλία *Pamphylia* from a compound of *G3956* and *G5443*; *every-tribal*, i.e. *heterogeneous* (*G5561* being implied); *Pamphylia*, a region of Asia Minor:— Pamphylia.

G3829 πανδοχεῖον *pandocheion* neuter of a presumed compound of *G3956* and a derivative of *G1209*; *all-receptive*, i.e. a public *lodging*-place (*caravanserai* or *khan*):— inn.

G3830 πανδοχεύς *pandocheus* from the same as *G3829*; an *innkeeper* (*warden of a caravanserai*):— host.

G3831 πανήγυρις *panēgyris* from *G3956* and a derivative of *G58*; a *mass-meeting*, i.e. (figuratively) *universal companionship*:— general assembly.

G3832 πανοικί *panoiki* adverb from *G3956* and *G3624*; *with* the *whole family*:— with all his house.

G3833 πανοπλία *panoplia* from a compound of *G3956* and *G3696*; *full armor* (*"panoply"*):— all (whole) armour.

G3834 πανουργία *panourgia* from *G3835*; *adroitness*, i.e. (in a bad sense) *trickery* or *sophistry*:— (cunning) craftiness, subtlety.

G3835 πανοῦργος *panourgos* from *G3956* and *G2041*; *all-working*, i.e. *adroit* (*shrewd*):— crafty.

G3836 πανταχόθεν *pantachothen* adverb (of *source*) from *G3837*; *from all* directions:— from every quarter.

G3837 πανταχοῦ *pantachou* genetive (as adverb of *place*) of a presumed derivative of *G3956*; *universally*:— in all places, everywhere.

G3838 παντελής *pantelēs* from *G3956* and *G5056*; *full-ended*, i.e. *entire* (neuter as noun, *completion*) :— in [no] wise, uttermost.

G3839 πάντη *pantē* adverb (of *manner*) from *G3956*; *wholly*:— always.

G3840 πάντοθεν *pantothen* adverb (of *source*) from *G3956*; *from* (i.e. *on*) *all* sides:— on every side, round about.

G3841 παντοκράτωρ *pantokratōr* from *G3956* and *G2904*; the *all-ruling*, i.e. *God* (as absolute and universal *sovereign*):— Almighty, Omnipotent.

G3842 πάντοτε *pantote* from *G3956* and *G3753*; *every when*, i.e. *at all* times:— alway, always, ever, evermore.

G3843 πάντως *pantōs* adverb from *G3956*; *entirely*; specifically *at all events*, (with negative following) *in* no *event*:— by all means, altogether, at all, needs, no doubt, in [no] wise, surely.

G3844 παρά *para* a primary preposition; properly *near*, i.e. (with genetive) *from beside* (literally or figuratively), (with dative) *at* (or *in*) the *vicinity* of (objectively or subjectively), (with accusative) to the *proximity* with (local [especially *beyond* or *opposed* to] or causal [*on account* of]). In compounds it retains the same variety of application:— above, against, among, at, before, by, contrary to, friend, from, give [such things as they], that [she] had, his, in, more than, nigh unto, (out) of, past, save, side . . . by, in the sight of, than, fore, therefore, with.

G3845 παραβαίνω *parabainō* from *G3844* and the base of *G939*; to *go contrary to*, i.e. *violate* a command:— transgress, by transgression.

G3846 παραβάλλω *paraballō* from *G3844* and *G906*; to *throw alongside*, i.e. (reflexive) to *reach* a place, or (figuratively) to *liken*:— arrive, compare.

G3847 παράβασις *parabasis* from *G3845*; *violation*:— breaking, transgression.

G3848 παραβάτης *parabatēs* from *G3845*; a *violator*:— breaker, transgress, transgressor.

G3849 παραβιάζομαι *parabiazomai* from *G3844* and the middle of *G971*; to *force contrary* to (nature), i.e. *compel* (by entreaty):— constrain.

G3850 παραβολή *parabolē* from *G3846*; a *similitude* (*"parable"*), i.e. (symbolic) *fictitious narrative* (of common life conveying a moral), *apothegm* or *adage*:— comparison, figure, parable, proverb.

G3851 παραβουλεύομαι *parabouleuomai* from *G3844* and the middle of *G1011*; to *misconsult*, i.e. *disregard*:— not (to) regard, not regarding.

G3852 παραγγελία *parangelia* from *G3853*; a *mandate*:— charge, command.

G3853 παραγγέλλω *parangellō* from *G3844* and the base of *G32*; to *transmit a message*, i.e. (by implication) to *enjoin*:— (give in) charge, (give) command, commandment, declare.

G3854 παραγίνομαι *paraginomai* from *G3844* and *G1096*; to *become near*, i.e. *approach* (*have arrived*); by implication to *appear* publicly:— come, go, be present.

G3855 παράγω *paragō* from *G3844* and *G71*; to *lead near*, i.e. (reflexive or intransitive) to *go along* or *away*:— depart, pass (away, by, forth).

G3856 παραδειγματίζω *paradeigmatizō* from *G3844* and *G1165*; to *show alongside* (the public), i.e. *expose to infamy*:— make a public example, put to an open shame.

G3857 παράδεισος *paradeisos* of Oriental origin [compare H6508]; a *park*, i.e. (specifically) an *Eden* (place of future happiness, *"paradise"*):— paradise.

G3858 παραδέχομαι *paradechomai* from *G3844* and *G1209*; to *accept near*, i.e. *admit* or (by implication) *delight* in:— receive.

G3859 παραδιατριβή *paradiatribē* from a compound of *G3844* and *G1304*; *misemployment*, i.e. *meddlesomeness*:— perverse disputing.

G3860 παραδίδωμι *paradidōmi* from *G3844* and *G1325*; to *surrender*, i.e. *yield up*, *entrust*, *transmit*:— betray, bring forth, cast, commit, deliver (up), give (over, up), hazard, put in prison, recommend.

G3861 παράδοξος *paradoxos* from *G3844* and *G1391* (in the sense of *seeming*); *contrary to expectation*, i.e. *extraordinary* (*"paradox"*):— strange.

G3862 παράδοσις *paradosis* from *G3860*; *transmission*, i.e. (concretely) a *precept*; specifically the Jewish *traditional law*:— ordinance, tradition.

G3863 παραζηλόω *parazēloō* from *G3844* and *G2206*; to *stimulate alongside*, i.e. *excite to rivalry*:— provoke to emulation (jealousy).

G3864 παραθαλάσσιος *parathalassios* from *G3844* and *G2281*; *along the sea*, i.e. *maritime* (*lacustrine*):— upon the sea coast.

G3865 παραθεωρέω *paratheōreō* from *G3844* and *G2334*; to *overlook* or *disregard*:— neglect.

G3866 παραθήκη *parathēkē* from *G3908*; a *deposit*, i.e. (figuratively) *trust*:— committed unto.

G3867 παραινέω *paraineō* from *G3844* and *G134*; to *mispraise*, i.e. *recommend* or *advise* (a different course):— admonish, exhort.

G3868 παραιτέομαι *paraiteomai* from *G3844* and the middle of *G154*; to *beg off*, i.e. *deprecate*, *decline*, *shun*:— avoid, (make) excuse, entreat, refuse, reject.

G3869 παρακαθίζω *parakathizō* from *G3844* and *G2523*; to *sit down near*:— sit.

G3870 παρακαλέω *parakaleō* from *G3844* and *G2564*; to *call near*, i.e. *invite*, *invoke* (by *imploration*, *exhortation* or *consolation*):— beseech, call for, (be of good) comfort, desire, exhort, (give) exhortation, entreat, pray.

G3871 παρακαλύπτω *parakalyptō* from *G3844* and *G2572*; to *cover alongside*, i.e. *veil* (figuratively):— hide.

G3872 παρακαταθήκη *parakatathēkē* from a compound of *G3844* and *G2698*; something *put down alongside*, i.e. a *deposit* (sacred *trust*):— that (thing) which is committed to/unto (trust).

G3873 παράκειμαι *parakeimai* from *G3844* and *G2749*; to *lie near*, i.e. *be at hand* (figuratively *be prompt* or *easy*):— be present.

G3874 παράκλησις *paraklēsis* from *G3870*; *imploration*, *exhortation*, *solace*:— comfort, consolation, exhortation, entreaty.

G3875 παράκλητος *paraklētos*; an *intercessor*, *consoler*:— advocate, comforter.

G3876 παρακοή *parakoē* from *G3878*; *inattention*, i.e. (by implication) *disobedience*:— disobedience.

G3877 παρακολουθέω *parakoloutheō* from *G3844* and *G190*; to *follow near*, i.e. (figuratively) *attend* (as a result), *trace out*, *conform* to:— attain, follow, fully know, have understanding.

G3878 παρακούω *parakouō* from *G3844* and *G191*; to *mishear*, i.e. (by implication) to *disobey*:— neglect to hear.

G3879 παρακύπτω *parakyptō* from *G3844* and *G2955*; to *bend beside*, i.e. *lean over* (so as to *peer within*):— look (into), stoop down.

G3880 παραλαμβάνω *paralambanō* from *G3844* and *G2983*; to *receive near*, i.e. *associate with* oneself (in any familiar or intimate act or relation); by analogy to *assume* an office; figuratively to *learn*:— receive, take (unto, with).

G3881 παραλέγομαι *paralegomai* from *G3844* and the middle of *G3004* (in its original sense); (specifically) to *lay* one's course *near*, i.e. *sail past*:— pass, sail by.

G3882 παράλιος *paralios* from *G3844* and *G251*; *beside* the *salt* (*sea*), i.e. *maritime*:— sea coast.

G3883 παραλλαγή *parallagē* from a compound of *G3844* and *G236*; *transmutation* (of phase or orbit), i.e. (figuratively) *fickleness*:— variableness.

G3884 παραλογίζομαι *paralogizomai* from *G3844* and *G3049*; to *misreckon*, i.e. *delude*:— beguile, deceive.

G3885 παραλυτικός *paralytikos* from a derivative of *G3886*; as if *dissolved*, i.e. *"paralytic"*:— that had (sick of) the palsy.

G3886 παραλύω *paralyō* from *G3844* and *G3089*; to *loosen beside*, i.e. *relax* (perfect passive participle *paralyzed* or *enfeebled*):— feeble, sick of the (taken with) palsy.

G3887 παραμένω *paramenō* from *G3844* and *G3306*; to *stay near*, i.e. *remain* (literally *tarry*; or figuratively *be permanent*, *persevere*):— abide, continue.

G3888 παραμυθέομαι *paramytheomai* from *G3844* and the middle of a derivative of *G3454*; to *relate near*, i.e. (by implication) *encourage*, *console*:— comfort.

G3889 παραμυθία *paramythia* from *G3888*; *consolation* (properly abstract):— comfort.

G3890 **παραμύθιον** *paramythion* neuter of *G3889*; *consolation* (properly concrete):— comfort.

G3891 **παρανομέω** *paranomeō* from a compound of *G3844* and *G3551*; to *be opposed to law,* i.e. to *transgress:*— contrary to law.

G3892 **παρανομία** *paranomia* from the same as *G3891*; *transgression:*— iniquity.

G3893 **παραπικραίνω** *parapikrainō* from *G3844* and *G4087*; to *embitter alongside,* i.e. (figuratively) to *exasperate:*— provoke.

G3894 **παραπικρασμός** *parapikrasmos* from *G3893*; *irritation:*— provocation.

G3895 **παραπίπτω** *parapiptō* from *G3844* and *G4098*; to *fall aside,* i.e. (figuratively) to *apostatize:*— fall away.

G3896 **παραπλέω** *parapleō* from *G3844* and *G4126*; to *sail near:*— sail by.

G3897 **παραπλήσιον** *paraplēsion* neuter of a compound of *G3844* and the base of *G4139* (as adverb); *close by,* i.e. (figuratively) *almost:*— nigh unto.

G3898 **παραπλησίως** *paraplēsiōs* adverb from the same as *G3897*; *in a manner near by,* i.e. (figuratively) *similarly:*— likewise.

G3899 **παραπορεύομαι** *paraporeuomai* from *G3844* and *G4198*; to *travel near:*— go, pass (by).

G3900 **παράπτωμα** *paraptōma* from *G3895*; a *side-slip* (*lapse* or *deviation*), i.e. (unintentional) *error* or (willful) *transgression:*— fall, fault, offence, sin, trespass.

G3901 **παραρρυέω** *pararrhyeō* from *G3844* and the alternate of *G4482*; to *flow by,* i.e. (figuratively) carelessly *pass* (*miss*):— let slip.

G3902 **παράσημος** *parasēmos* from *G3844* and the base of *G4591*; *side-marked,* i.e. *labeled* (with a *badge* [*figure-head*] of a ship):— sign.

G3903 **παρασκευάζω** *paraskeuazō* from *G3844* and a derivative of *G4632*; to *furnish aside,* i.e. *get ready:*— prepare self, be (make) ready.

G3904 **παρασκευή** *paraskeuē* as if from *G3903*; *readiness:*— preparation.

G3905 **παρατείνω** *parateinō* from *G3844* and
τείνω *teinō* (to *stretch*); to *extend along,* i.e. *prolong* (in point of time):— continue.

G3906 **παρατηρέω** *paratēreō* from *G3844* and *G5083*; to *inspect alongside,* i.e. *note insidiously* or *scrupulously:*— observe, watch.

G3907 **παρατήρησις** *paratērēsis* from *G3906*; *inspection,* i.e. *ocular evidence:*— observation.

G3908 **παρατίθημι** *paratithēmi* from *G3844* and *G5087*; to *place alongside,* i.e. *present* (food, truth); by implication to *deposit* (as a trust or for protection):— allege, commend, commit (the keeping of), put forth, set before.

G3909 **παρατυγχάνω** *paratynchanō* from *G3844* and *G5177*; to *chance near,* i.e. *fall in with:*— meet with.

G3910 **παραυτίκα** *parautika* from *G3844* and a derivative of *G846*; *at the very* instant, i.e. *momentary:*— but for a moment.

G3911 **παραφέρω** *parapherō* from *G3844* and *G5342* (including its alternate forms); to *bear along* or *aside,* i.e. *carry off* (literally or figuratively); by implication to *avert:*— remove, take away.

G3912 **παραφρονέω** *paraphroneō* from *G3844* and *G5426*; to *misthink,* i.e. *be insane* (*silly*):— as a fool.

G3913 **παραφρονία** *paraphronia* from *G3912*; *insanity,* i.e. *foolhardiness:*— madness.

G3914 **παραχειμάζω** *paracheimazō* from *G3844* and *G5492*; to *winter near,* i.e. *stay* with over the *rainy* season:— winter.

G3915 **παραχειμασία** *paracheimasia* from *G3914*; a *wintering* over:— winter in.

G3916 **παραχρῆμα** *parachrēma* from *G3844* and *G5536* (in its original sense); *at the thing* itself, i.e. *instantly:*— forthwith, immediately, presently, straightway, soon.

G3917 **πάρδαλις** *pardalis* feminine of
πάρδος *pardos* (a *panther*); a *leopard:*— leopard.

G3918 **πάρειμι** *pareimi* from *G3844* and *G1510* (including its various forms); to *be near,* i.e. *at hand;* neuter present participle (singular) *time being,* or (plural) *property:*— come, have, be here, lack, (be here) present.

G3919 **παρεισάγω** *pareisagō* from *G3844* and *G1521*; to *lead in aside,* i.e. *introduce surreptitiously:*— privily bring in.

G3920 **παρείσακτος** *pareisaktos* from *G3919*; *smuggled in:*— unawares brought in.

G3921 **παρεισδύνω** *pareisdynō* from *G3844* and a compound of *G1519* and *G1416*; to *settle in alongside,* i.e. *lodge stealthily:*— creep in unawares.

G3922 **παρεισέρχομαι** *pareiserchomai* from *G3844* and *G1525*; to *come in alongside,* i.e. *supervene additionally* or *stealthily:*— come in privily, enter.

G3923 **παρεισφέρω** *pareispherō* from *G3844* and *G1533*; to *bear in alongside,* i.e. *introduce simultaneously:*— give.

G3924 **παρεκτός** *parektos* from *G3844* and *G1622*; *near outside,* i.e. *besides:*— except, saving, without.

G3925 **παρεμβολή** *parembolē* from a compound of *G3844* and *G1685*; a *throwing in beside (juxtaposition);* i.e. (specifically) *battle-array, encampment* or *barracks* (tower Antonia):— army, camp, castle.

G3926 **παρενοχλέω** *parenochleō* from *G3844* and *G1776*; to *harass further,* i.e. *annoy:*— trouble.

G3927 **παρεπίδημος** *parepidēmos* from *G3844* and the base of *G1927*; an *alien alongside,* i.e. a *resident foreigner:*— pilgrim, stranger.

G3928 **παρέρχομαι** *parerchomai* from *G3844* and *G2064*; to *come near* or *aside,* i.e. to *approach* (*arrive*), *go by* (or *away*), (figuratively) *perish* or *neglect,* (causative) *avert:*— come (forth), go, pass (away, by, over), past, transgress.

G3929 **πάρεσις** *paresis* from *G2935*; *pretermission,* i.e. *toleration:*— remission.

G3930 **παρέχω** *parechō* from *G3844* and *G2192*; to *hold near,* i.e. *present, afford, exhibit, furnish occasion:*— bring, do, give, keep, minister, offer, shew, trouble.

G3931 **παρηγορία** *parēgoria* from a compound of *G3844* and a derivative of *G58* (meaning to *harangue* an assembly); an *address alongside,* i.e. (specifically) *consolation:*— comfort.

G3932 **παρθενία** *parthenia* from *G3933*; *maidenhood:*— virginity.

G3933 **παρθένος** *parthenos* of unknown origin; a *maiden;* by implication an unmarried *daughter:*— virgin.

G3934 **Πάρθος** *Parthos* probably of foreign origin; a *Parthian,* i.e. inhabitant of Parthia:— Parthian.

G3935 **παρίημι** *pariēmi* from *G3844* and
ἵημι *hiēmi* (to *send*); to *let by,* i.e. *relax:*— hang down.

G3936 **παρίστημι** *paristēmi* or prolonged
παριστάνω *paristanō* from *G3844* and *G2476*; to *stand beside,* i.e. (transitive) to *exhibit, proffer,* (specifically) *recommend,* (figuratively) *substantiate;* or (intransitive) to *be at hand* (or *ready*), *aid:*— assist, bring before, command, commend, give presently, present, prove, provide, shew, stand (before, by, here, up, with), yield.

GRK

G3937 **Παρμενᾶς** *Parmenas* probably by contraction for
Παρμενίδης *Parmenidēs* (a derivative of a compound of *G3844* and *G3306*); *constant; Parmenas,* a Christian:— Parmenas.

G3938 **πάροδος** *parodos* from *G3844* and *G3598*; a *by-road,* i.e. (active) a *route:*— way.

G3939 **παροικέω** *paroikeō* from *G3844* and *G3611*; to *dwell near,* i.e. *reside* as a *foreigner:*— sojourn in, be a stranger.

G3940 **παροικία** *paroikia* from *G3941*; *foreign residence:*— sojourning, as strangers.

G3941 **πάροικος** *paroikos* from *G3844* and *G3624*; having a *home near,* i.e. (as noun) a *by-dweller* (*alien resident*):— foreigner, sojourn, stranger.

G3942 **παροιμία** *paroimia* from a compound of *G3844* and perhaps a derivative of *G3633*; apparently a state *alongside of supposition,* i.e. (concretely) an *adage;* specifically an enigmatical or fictitious *illustration:*— parable, proverb.

G3943 **πάροινος** *paroinos* from *G3844* and *G3631*; staying *near wine,* i.e. *tippling* (a *toper*):— given to wine.

G3944 **παροίχομαι** *paroichomai* from *G3844* and
οἴχομαι *oichomai* (to *depart*); to *escape along,* i.e. *be gone:*— past.

G3945 **παρομοιάζω** *paromoiazō* from *G3946*; to *resemble:*— be like unto.

G3946 **παρόμοιος** *paromoios* from *G3844* and *G3664*; *alike nearly,* i.e. *similar:*— like.

G3947 **παροξύνω** *paroxynō* from *G3844* and a derivative of *G3691*; to *sharpen alongside,* i.e. (figuratively) to *exasperate:*— easily provoke, stir.

G3948 **παροξυσμός** *paroxysmos* from *G3947* (*"paroxysm"*); *incitement* (to good), or *dispute* (in anger):— contention, provoke unto.

G3949 **παροργίζω** *parorgizō* from *G3844* and *G3710*; to *anger alongside,* i.e. *enrage:*— anger, provoke to wrath.

G3950 **παροργισμός** *parorgismos* from *G3949*; *rage* :— wrath.

G3951 **παροτρύνω** *parotrynō* from *G3844* and
ὀτρύνω *otrynō* (to *spur*); to *urge along,* i.e. *stimulate* (to hostility):— stir up.

G3952 **παρουσία** *parousia* from the present participle of *G3918*; a *being near,* i.e. *advent* (often, *return;* specifically of Christ to punish Jerusalem, or finally the wicked); (by implication) physical *aspect:*— coming, presence.

G3953 παροψίς *paropsis* from G3844 and the base of G3795; a *side-dish* (the receptacle):— platter.

G3954 παρρησία *parrhēsia* from G3956 and a derivative of G4483; *all* out-*spokenness,* i.e. *frankness, bluntness, publicity;* by implication *assurance:*— bold, -boldly, boldness, boldness of speech, confidence, freely, openly, plainly, plainness.

G3955 παρρησιάζομαι *parrhēsiazomai* middle from G3954; to *be frank* in utterance, or *confident* in spirit and demeanor:— be (wax) bold, (preach, speak) boldly.

G3956 πᾶς *pas* including all the forms of declension; apparently a primary word; *all, any, every,* the *whole:*— all (manner of, means), always, always, any (one), daily, ever, every (one, way), as many as, no, nothing, thoroughly, whatsoever, whole, whosoever.

G3957 πάσχα *pascha* of Aramaic origin [compare H6453]; the *Passover* (the meal, the day, the festival or the special sacrifices connected with it):— Easter, Passover.

G3958 πάσχω *paschō* including the forms
πάθω *pathō* and
πένθω *penthō* used only in certain tenses for it; apparently a primary verb; to *experience* a sensation or impression (usually painful):— feel, passion, suffer, vex.

G3959 Πάταρα *Patara* probably of foreign origin; *Patara,* a place in Asia Minor:— Patara.

G3960 πατάσσω *patassō* probably prolonged from G3817; to *knock* (gently or with a weapon or fatally):— smite, strike. Compare G5180.

G3961 πατέω *pateō* from a derivative probably of G3817 (meaning a *"path"*); to *trample* (literally or figuratively):— tread (down, under foot).

G3962 πατήρ *patēr* apparently a primary word; a *"father"* (literal or figurative, near or more remote):— father, parent.

G3963 Πάτμος *Patmos* of uncertain derivation; *Patmus,* an islet in the Mediterranean:— Patmos.

G3964 πατραλῴας *patralōias* from G3962 and the same as the latter part of G3389; a *parricide:*— murderer of fathers.

G3965 πατριά *patria* as if feminine of a derivative of G3962; paternal *descent,* i.e. (concretely) a *group* of families or a whole *race* (*nation*):— family, kindred, lineage.

G3966 πατριάρχης *patriarchēs* from G3965 and G757; a *progenitor* ("patriarch"):— patriarch.

G3967 πατρικός *patrikos* from G3962; *paternal,* i.e. *ancestral:*— of fathers.

G3968 πατρίς *patris* from G3962; a *father-land,* i.e. *native town;* (figuratively) heavenly *home:*— (own) country.

G3969 Πατρόβας *Patrobas* perhaps contracted for
Πατρόβιος *Patrobios* (a compound of G3962 and G979); *father's life; Patrobas,* a Christian:— Patrobas.

G3970 πατροπαράδοτος *patroparadotos* from G3962 and a derivative of G3860 (in the sense of *handing over* or *down*); *traditional:*— received by tradition from fathers.

G3971 πατρῷος *patrōos* from G3962; *paternal,* i.e. *hereditary:*— of fathers.

G3972 Παῦλος *Paulos* of Latin origin; (*little;* but remotely from a derivative of G3973, meaning the same); *Paulus,* the name of a Roman and of an apostle:— Paul, Paulus.

G3973 παύω *pauō* a primary verb (*"pause"*); to *stop* (transitive or intransitive), i.e. *restrain, quit, desist, come to an end:*— cease, leave, refrain.

G3974 Πάφος *Paphos* of uncertain derivation; *Paphus,* a place in Cyprus:— Paphos.

G3975 παχύνω *pachynō* from a derivative of G4078 (meaning *thick*); to *thicken,* i.e. (by implication) to *fatten* (figuratively *stupefy* or *render callous*):— wax gross.

G3976 πέδη *pedē* ultimately from G4228; a *shackle* for the feet:— fetter.

G3977 πεδινός *pedinos* from a derivative of G4228 (meaning the *ground*); *level* (as easy for the *feet*):— plain.

G3978 πεζεύω *pezeuō* from the same as G3979; to *foot* a journey, i.e. *travel* by land:— go afoot.

G3979 πεζῇ *pezē* dative feminine of a derivative of G4228 (as adverb); *foot-wise,* i.e. by *walking:*— (on) foot, afoot.

G3980 πειθαρχέω *peitharcheō* from a compound of G3982 and G757; to *be persuaded* by a *ruler,* i.e. (generally) to *submit* to authority; by analogy to *conform* to advice:— hearken, obey (magistrates).

G3981 πειθός *peithos* from G3982; *persuasive:*— enticing.

G3982 πείθω *peithō* a primary verb; to *convince* (by argument, true or false); by analogy to *pacify* or *conciliate* (by other fair means); reflexive or passive to *assent* (to evidence or authority), to *rely* (by inward certainty):— agree, assure, believe, have confidence, be (wax) confident, make friend, obey, persuade, trust, yield.

G3983 πεινάω *peinaō* from the same as G3993 (through the idea of pinching *toil; "pine"*); to *famish* (absolutely or comparatively); figuratively to *crave* :— be an hungered.

G3984 πεῖρα *peira* from the base of G4008 (through the idea of *piercing*); a *test,* i.e. *attempt, experience:*— assaying, trial.

G3985 πειράζω *peirazō* from G3984; to *test* (objectively), i.e. *endeavor, scrutinize, entice, discipline* :— assay, examine, go about, prove, tempt, tempter, try.

G3986 πειρασμός *peirasmos* from G3985; a putting to *proof* (by experiment [of good], *experience* [of evil], solicitation, discipline or provocation); by implication *adversity:*— temptation, try.

G3987 πειράω *peiraō* from G3984; to *test* (subjectively), i.e. (reflexive) to *attempt:*— assay.

G3988 πεισμονή *peismonē* from a presumed derivative of G3982; *ease of persuasion,* i.e. *credulity:*— persuasion.

G3989 πέλαγος *pelagos* of uncertain affinity; deep or open *sea,* i.e. the *main:*— depth, sea.

G3990 πελεκίζω *pelekizō* from a derivative of G4141 (meaning an *axe*); to *chop* off (the head), i.e. *truncate:*— behead.

G3991 πέμπτος *pemptos* from G4002; *fifth:*— fifth.

G3992 πέμπω *pempō* apparently a primary verb; to *dispatch* (from the subjective view or point of *departure,* whereas
ἵημι *hiēmi* [as a stronger form of
εἶμι *eimi* refers rather to the objective point or *terminus ad quem,* and G4724 denotes properly the *orderly* motion involved), especially on a temporary errand; also to *transmit, bestow,* or *wield:*— send, thrust in.

G3993 πένης *penēs* from a primary
πένω *penō* (to *toil* for daily subsistence); *starving,* i.e. *indigent:*— poor. Compare G4434.

G3994 πενθερά *penthera* feminine of G3995; a *wife's mother:*— mother-in-law, wife's mother.

G3995 πενθερός *pentheros* of uncertain affinity; a *wife's father:*— father-in-law.

G3996 πενθέω *pentheō* from G3997; to *grieve* (the feeling or the act):— mourn, wail, bewail.

G3997 πένθος *penthos* strengthened from the alternate of G3958; *grief:*— mourning, sorrow.

G3998 πενιχρός *penichros* prolonged from the base of G3993; *necessitous:*— poor.

G3999 πεντακίς *pentakis* multiple adverb from G4002; *five times:*— five times.

G4000 πεντακισχίλιοι *pentakischilioi* from G3999 and G5507; *five times a thousand:*— five thousand.

G4001 πεντακόσιοι *pentakosioi* from G4002 and G1540; *five hundred:*— five hundred.

G4002 πέντε *pente* a primary number; *"five":*— five.

G4003 πεντεκαιδέκατος *pentekaidekatos* from G4002 and G2532 and G1182; *five and tenth:*— fifteenth.

G4004 πεντήκοντα *pentēkonta* multiple of G4002; *fifty:*— fifty.

G4005 πεντηκοστή *pentēkostē* feminine of the order of G4004; *fiftieth* (G2250 being implied) from Passover, i.e. the festival of *"Pentecost":*— Pentecost.

G4006 πεποίθησις *pepoithēsis* from the perfect of the alternate of G3958; *reliance:*— confidence, trust.

G4007 περ *per* from the base of G4008; an enclitic particle significant of *abundance* (*thoroughness*), i.e. *emphasis; much, very* or *ever:*— -soever (e.g., whomsoever).

G4008 πέραν *peran* apparently accusative of an obsolete derivative of
πείρω *peirō* (to *"pierce"*); *through* (as adverb or prep.), i.e. *across:*— beyond, farther (other) side, over.

G4009 πέρας *peras* from the same as G4008; an *extremity:*— end, most, utmost, uttermost part.

G4010 Πέργαμος *Pergamos* from G4444; *fortified; Pergamus,* a place in Asia Minor:— Pergamos.

G4011 Πέργη *Pergē* probably from the same as G4010; a *tower; Perga,* a place in Asia Minor:— Perga.

G4012 περί *peri* from the base of G4008; properly *through* (all over), i.e. *around;* figuratively *with respect* to; used in various applications, of place, cause or time (with the genitive denoting the *subject* or *occasion* or *superlative* point; with the accusative the *locality, circuit, matter, circumstance* or general *period*). In compounds it retains substantially the same meaning of circuit (*around*), excess (*beyond*), or completeness (*through*) :— about, thereabout, above, against, at, on behalf of, and his company, which concern, (as) concerning, for, how it will go with, of, thereof, whereof, on, over, pertaining (to), for sake, state, estate, (as) touching, by, whereby (in), with.

G4013 περιάγω *periagō* from G4012 and G71; to *take around* (as a companion); reflexive to *walk around:*— compass, go (round) about, lead about.

G4014 **περιαιρέω** *periaireō* from *G4012* and *G138* (including its alternate); to *remove* all *around,* i.e. *unveil, cast off* (anchor); figuratively to *expiate:*— take away (up).

G4015 **περιαστράπτω** *periastraptō* from *G4012* and *G797*; to *flash* all *around,* i.e. *envelop in light:*— shine round (about).

G4016 **περιβάλλω** *periballō* from *G4012* and *G906*; to *throw* all *around,* i.e. *invest* (with a palisade or with clothing):— array, cast about, clothe, clothed me, put on.

G4017 **περιβλέπω** *periblepō* from *G4012* and *G991*; to *look* all *around:*— look (round) about (on).

G4018 **περιβόλαιον** *peribolaion* neuter of a presumed derivative of *G4016*; something *thrown around* one, i.e. a *mantle, veil:*— covering, vesture.

G4019 **περιδέω** *perideō* from *G4012* and *G1210*; to *bind around* one, i.e. *enwrap:*— bind about.

G4020 **περιεργάζομαι** *periergazomai* from *G4012* and *G2038*; to *work* all *around,* i.e. *bustle about (meddle):*— be a busybody.

G4021 **περίεργος** *periergos* from *G4012* and *G2041*; *working* all *around,* i.e. *officious* (*meddlesome,* neuter plural *magic*):— busybody, curious arts.

G4022 **περιέρχομαι** *perierchomai* from *G4012* and *G2064* (including its alternate); to *come* all *around,* i.e. *stroll, vacillate, veer:*— fetch a compass, vagabond, wandering about.

G4023 **περιέχω** *periechō* from *G4012* and *G2192*; to *hold* all *around,* i.e. *include, clasp* (figuratively):— astonished, contain, after [this manner].

G4024 **περιζώννυμι** *perizōnnymi* from *G4012* and *G2224*; to *gird* all *around,* i.e. (middle or passive) to *fasten on one's belt* (literally or figuratively):— gird (about, self).

G4025 **περίθεσις** *perithesis* from *G4060*; a *putting* all *around,* i.e. *decorating* oneself with:— wearing.

G4026 **περιΐστημι** *periistēmi* from *G4012* and *G2476*; to *stand* all *around,* i.e. (near) to *be a bystander,* or (aloof) to *keep away* from:— avoid, shun, stand by (round about).

G4027 **περικάθαρμα** *perikatharma* from a compound of *G4012* and *G2508*; something *cleaned* off all *around,* i.e. *refuse* (figurative):— filth.

G4028 **περικαλύπτω** *perikalyptō* from *G4012* and *G2572*; to *cover* all *around,* i.e. *entirely* (the face, a surface):— blindfold, cover, overlay.

G4029 **περίκειμαι** *perikeimai* from *G4012* and *G2749*; to *lie* all *around,* i.e. *enclose, encircle, hamper* (literally or figuratively):— be bound (compassed) with, hang about.

G4030 **περικεφαλαία** *perikephalaia* feminine of a compound of *G4012* and *G2776*; *encirclement of* the *head,* i.e. a *helmet:*— helmet.

G4031 **περικρατής** *perikratēs* from *G4012* and *G2904*; *strong* all *around,* i.e. a *master* (*manager*):— come by.

G4032 **περικρύβω** *perikrybō* from *G4012* and *G2928*; to *conceal* all *around,* i.e. *entirely:*— hide.

G4033 **περικυκλόω** *perikykloō* from *G4012* and *G2944*; to *encircle* all *around,* i.e. *blockade completely:*— compass round.

G4034 **περιλάμπω** *perilampō* from *G4012* and *G2989*; to *illuminate* all *around,* i.e. *invest with a halo:*— shine round about.

G4035 **περιλείπω** *perileipō* from *G4012* and *G3007*; to *leave* all *around,* i.e. (passive) *survive:*— remain.

G4036 **περίλυπος** *perilypos* from *G4012* and *G3077*; *grieved* all *around,* i.e. *intensely sad:*— exceeding (very) sorry, exceeding (very) sorrowful.

G4037 **περιμένω** *perimenō* from *G4012* and *G3306*; to *stay around,* i.e. *await:*— wait for.

G4038 **πέριξ** *perix* adverb from *G4012*; all *around,* i.e. (as adjective) *surrounding:*— round about.

G4039 **περιοικέω** *perioikeō* from *G4012* and *G3611*; to *reside around,* i.e. *be a neighbor:*— dwell round about.

G4040 **περίοικος** *perioikos* from *G4012* and *G3611*; *housed around,* i.e. *neighboring* (elliptically as noun):— neighbour.

G4041 **περιούσιος** *periousios* from the present participle feminine of a compound of *G4012* and *G1510*; *being beyond* usual, i.e. *special* (one's *own*):— peculiar.

G4042 **περιοχή** *periochē* from *G4023*; a *being held around,* i.e. (concretely) a *passage* (of Scripture, as *circumscribed*):— place.

G4043 **περιπατέω** *peripateō* from *G4012* and *G3961*; to *tread* all *around,* i.e. *walk* at large (especially as proof of ability); figuratively to *live, deport oneself, follow* (as a companion or votary):— go, be occupied with, walk (about).

G4044 **περιπείρω** *peripeirō* from *G4012* and the base of *G4008*; to *penetrate entirely,* i.e. *transfix* (figuratively):— pierce through.

G4045 **περιπίπτω** *peripiptō* from *G4012* and *G4098*; to *fall* into something that is all *around,* i.e. *light among* or *upon, be surrounded with:*— fall among (into).

G4046 **περιποιέομαι** *peripoieomai* middle from *G4012* and *G4160*; to *make around oneself,* i.e. *acquire* (*buy*):— purchase.

G4047 **περιποίησις** *peripoiēsis* from *G4046*; *acquisition* (the act or the thing); by extension *preservation:*— obtain, obtaining, peculiar, purchased, possession, saving.

G4048 **περιρρήγνυμι** *perirrhēgnymi* from *G4012* and *G4486*; to *tear* all *around,* i.e. *completely away* :— rend off.

G4049 **περισπάω** *perispaō* from *G4012* and *G4685*; to *drag* all *around,* i.e. (figuratively) to *distract* (with care):— cumber.

G4050 **περισσεία** *perisseia* from *G4052*; *surplus,* i.e. *superabundance:*— abundance, abundant, abundantly, superfluity.

G4051 **περίσσευμα** *perisseuma* from *G4052*; a *surplus,* or *superabundance:*— abundance, that was left, over and above.

G4052 **περισσεύω** *perisseuō* from *G4053*; to *superabound* (in quantity or quality), *be in excess, be superfluous;* also (transposed) to *cause to superabound* or *excel:*— (make, more) abound, (have, have more) abundance, (be more) abundant, be the better, enough and to spare, exceed, excel, increase, be left, redound, remain (over and above).

G4053 **περισσός** *perissos* from *G4012* (in the sense of *beyond*); *superabundant* (in quantity) or *superior* (in quality); by implication *excessive;* adverbially (with *G1537*) *violently;* neuter (as noun) *preeminence:*— exceeding abundantly above, more abundantly, advantage, exceedingly, very highly, beyond measure, more, superfluous, vehement, vehemently.

G4054 **περισσότερον** *perissoteron* neuter of *G4055* (as adverb); in a *more superabundant* way:— more abundantly, a great deal, far more.

G4055 **περισσότερος** *perissoteros* comparative of *G4053*; *more superabundant* (in number, degree or character):— more abundant, greater (much) more, overmuch.

G4056 **περισσοτέρως** *perissoterōs* adverb from *G4055*; *more superabundantly:*— more abundant, more abundantly, the more earnest, (more) exceedingly, more frequent, much more, the rather.

G4057 **περισσῶς** *perissōs* adverb from *G4053*; *superabundantly:*— exceedingly, out of measure, the more.

G4058 **περιστερά** *peristera* of uncertain derivation; a *pigeon:*— dove, pigeon.

G4059 **περιτέμνω** *peritemnō* from *G4012* and the base of *G5114*; to *cut around,* i.e. (specifically) to *circumcise:*— circumcise.

G4060 **περιτίθημι** *peritithēmi* from *G4012* and *G5087*; to *place around;* by implication to *present:*— bestow upon, hedge round about, put about (on, upon), set about.

G4061 **περιτομή** *peritomē* from *G4059*; *circumcision* (the rite, the condition or the people, literal or figurative):— circumcised, circumcision.

G4062 **περιτρέπω** *peritrepō* from *G4012* and the base of *G5157*; to *turn around,* i.e. (mentally) to *craze:*— make mad.

G4063 **περιτρέχω** *peritrechō* from *G4012* and *G5143* (including its alternate); to *run around,* i.e. *traverse:*— run through.

G4064 **περιφέρω** *peripherō* from *G4012* and *G5342*; to *convey around,* i.e. *transport hither and thither:*— bear (carry) about.

G4065 **περιφρονέω** *periphroneō* from *G4012* and *G5426*; to *think beyond,* i.e. *depreciate* (*condemn*):— despise.

G4066 **περίχωρος** *perichōros* from *G4012* and *G5561*; *around* the *region,* i.e. *surrounding* (as noun, with *G1093* implied *vicinity*):— country (round) about, region (that lieth) round about.

G4067 **περίψημα** *peripsēma* from a compound of *G4012* and

ψάω *psaō* (to *rub*); something *brushed* all *around,* i.e. *off-scrapings* (figuratively *scum*):— offscouring.

G4068 **περπερεύομαι** *perpereuomai* middle from

πέρπερος *perperos* (*braggart;* perhaps by reduplication of the base of *G4008*); to *boast:*— vaunt itself.

G4069 **Περσίς** *Persis*; a *Persian* woman; *Persis,* a Christian female:— Persis.

G4070 **πέρυσι** *perysi* adverb from *G4009*; the *bygone,* i.e. (as noun) *last year:*— a year ago.

G4071 **πετεινόν** *peteinon* neuter of a derivative of *G4072*; a *flying* animal, i.e. *bird:*— bird, fowl.

G4072 **πέτομαι** *petomai* or prolonged

πετάομαι *petaomai* or contracted

πτάομαι *ptaomai* middle of a primary verb; to *fly:*— fly, flying.

G4073 **πέτρα** *petra* feminine of the same as *G4074*; a (mass of) *rock* (literal or figurative):— rock.

G4074 **Πέτρος** *Petros* apparently a primary word; a (piece of) *rock* (larger than *G3037*); as a name, *Petrus,* an apostle:— Peter, rock. Compare *G2786.*

G4075 **πετρώδης** *petrōdēs* from *G4073* and *G1491*; *rock-like,* i.e. *rocky:*— stony.

G4076 **πήγανον** *pēganon* from *G4078*; *rue* (from its *thick* or *fleshy* leaves):— rue.

G4077 **πηγή** *pēgē* probably from *G4078* (through the idea of *gushing* plumply); a *fount* (literal or figurative), i.e. *source* or *supply* (of water, blood, enjoyment) (not necessarily the original spring):— fountain, well.

G4078 **πήγνυμι** *pēgnymi* a prolonged form of a primary verb (which in its simpler form occurs only as an alternate in certain tenses); to *fix* (*"peg"*), i.e. (specifically) to *set up* (a tent):— pitch.

G4079 **πηδάλιον** *pēdalion* neuter of a (presumed) derivative of

πηδόν *pēdon* (the *blade* of an oar; from the same as *G3976*); a *"pedal"*, i.e. *helm:*— rudder.

G4080 **πηλίκος** *pēlikos* a quantitative form (the feminine) of the base of *G4225*; *how much* (as indefinite), i.e. in size or (figuratively) dignity:— how great (large).

G4081 **πηλός** *pēlos* perhaps a primary word; *clay:*— clay.

G4082 **πήρα** *pēra* of uncertain affinity; a *wallet* or leather *pouch* for food:— scrip.

G4083 **πῆχυς** *pēchys* of uncertain affinity; the *forearm,* i.e. (as a measure) a *cubit:*— cubit.

G4084 **πιάζω** *piazō* probably another form of *G971*; to *squeeze,* i.e. *seize* (gently by the hand [*press*], or officially [*arrest*], or in hunting [*capture*]):— apprehend, catch, lay hand on, take. Compare *G4085.*

G4085 **πιέζω** *piezō* another form for *G4084*; to *pack:*— press down.

G4086 **πιθανολογία** *pithanologia* from a compound of a derivative of *G3982* and *G3056*; *persuasive language:*— enticing words.

G4087 **πικραίνω** *pikrainō* from *G4089*; to *embitter* (literally or figuratively):— be (make) bitter.

G4088 **πικρία** *pikria* from *G4089*; *acridity* (especially *poison*), literal or figurative:— bitterness.

G4089 **πικρός** *pikros* perhaps from *G4078* (through the idea of *piercing*); *sharp* (*pungent*), i.e. *acrid* (literally or figuratively):— bitter.

G4090 **πικρῶς** *pikrōs* adverb from *G4089*; *bitterly,* i.e. (figuratively) *violently:*— bitterly.

G4091 **Πιλάτος** *Pilatos* of Latin origin; *close-pressed,* i.e. *firm; Pilatus,* a Roman:— Pilate.

G4092 **πίμπρημι** *pimprēmi* a reduplicated and prolonged form of a primary

πρέω *preō* (which occurs only as an alternate in certain tenses); to *fire,* i.e. *burn* (figuratively and passive *become inflamed* with fever):— be (should have) swollen.

G4093 **πινακίδιον** *pinakidion* diminutive of *G4094*; a *tablet* (for writing on):— writing table.

G4094 **πίναξ** *pinax* apparently a form of *G4109*; a *plate:*— charger, platter.

G4095 **πίνω** *pinō* a prolonged form of

πίω *piō* which (together with another form

πόω *poō*) occurs only as an alternate in certain tenses; to *imbibe* (literally or figuratively):— drink.

G4096 **πιότης** *piotēs* from

πίων *piōn* (*fat;* perhaps akin to the alternate of *G4095* through the idea of *repletion*); *plumpness,* i.e. (by implication) *richness* (*oiliness*):— fatness.

G4097 **πιπράσκω** *pipraskō* a reduplicated and prolonged form of

πράω *praō* (which occurs only as an alternate in certain tenses); contracted from

περάω *peraō* (to *traverse;* from the base of *G4008*); to *traffic* (by *travelling*), i.e. *dispose* of as merchandise or into slavery (literally or figuratively):— sell.

G4098 **πίπτω** *piptō* a reduplicated and contracted form of

πέτω *petō* (which occurs only as an alternate in certain tenses); probably akin to *G4072* through the idea of *alighting;* to *fall* (literally or figuratively):— fail, fall (down), light on.

G4099 **Πισιδία** *Pisidia* probably of foreign origin; *Pisidia,* a region of Asia Minor:— Pisidia.

G4100 **πιστεύω** *pisteuō* from *G4102*; to *have faith* (in, upon, or with respect to, a person or thing), i.e. *credit;* by implication to *entrust* (especially one's spiritual well-being to Christ):— believe, believer, commit (to trust), put in trust with.

G4101 **πιστικός** *pistikos* from *G4102*; *trustworthy,* i.e. *genuine* (*unadulterated*):— spike, spikenard.

G4102 **πίστις** *pistis* from *G3982*; *persuasion,* i.e. *credence;* moral *conviction* (of *religious* truth, or the truthfulness of God or a religious teacher), especially *reliance* upon Christ for salvation; abstractly *constancy* in such profession; by extension the system of religious (Gospel) *truth* itself:— assurance, belief, believe, faith, fidelity.

G4103 **πιστός** *pistos* from *G3982*; objectively *trustworthy;* subjectively *trustful:*— believe, believing, believer, faithful, faithfully, sure, true.

G4104 **πιστόω** *pistoō* from *G4103*; to *assure:*— assure of.

G4105 **πλανάω** *planaō* from *G4106*; to (properly *cause* to) *roam* (from safety, truth, or virtue):— go astray, deceive, err, seduce, wander, be out of the way.

G4106 **πλάνη** *planē* feminine of *G4108* (as abstract); objective *fraudulence;* subjectively a *straying* from orthodoxy or piety:— deceit, to deceive, delusion, error.

G4107 **πλανήτης** *planētēs* from *G4108*; a *rover* ("planet"), i.e. (figuratively) an *erratic* teacher:— wandering.

G4108 **πλάνος** *planos* of uncertain affinity; *roving* (as a *tramp*), i.e. (by implication) an *impostor* or *misleader:*— deceiver, seducing.

G4109 **πλάξ** *plax* from *G4111*; a *molding-board,* i.e. *flat* surface (*"plate"*, or *tablet,* literal or figurative):— table.

G4110 **πλάσμα** *plasma* from *G4111*; something *molded:*— thing formed.

G4111 **πλάσσω** *plassō* a primary verb; to *mold,* i.e. *shape* or *fabricate:*— form.

G4112 **πλαστός** *plastos* from *G4111*; *molded,* i.e. (by implication) *artificial* or (figuratively) *fictitious* (*false*):— feigned.

G4113 **πλατεῖα** *plateia* feminine of *G4116*; a *wide "plat"* or *"place"*, i.e. open *square:*— street.

G4114 **πλάτος** *platos* from *G4116*; *width:*— breadth.

G4115 **πλατύνω** *platynō* from *G4116*; to *widen* (literally or figuratively):— make broad, enlarge.

G4116 **πλατύς** *platys* from *G4111*; spread out *"flat"* ("plot"), i.e. *broad:*— wide.

G4117 **πλέγμα** *plegma* from *G4120*; a *plait* (of hair) :— broidered hair.

G4118 **πλεῖστος** *pleistos* irregular superlative of *G4183*; the *largest number* or *very large:*— very great, most.

G4119 **πλείων** *pleiōn* neuter

πλεῖον *pleion* or

πλέον *pleon* comparative of *G4183*; *more* in quantity, number, or quality; also (in plural) the *major portion:*— above, exceed, more excellent, further, (very) great, greater, long, longer, (very) many, greater (more) part, yet but.

G4120 **πλέκω** *plekō* a primary word; to *twine* or *braid:*— plait.

G4121 **πλεονάζω** *pleonazō* from *G4119*; to *do, make* or *be more,* i.e. *increase* (transitive or intransitive); by extension to *superabound:*— abound, abundant, make to increase, have over.

G4122 **πλεονεκτέω** *pleonekteō* from *G4123*; to *be covetous,* i.e. (by implication) to *overreach:*— get an advantage, defraud, make a gain.

G4123 **πλεονέκτης** *pleonektēs* from *G4119* and *G2192*; *holding* (*desiring*) *more,* i.e. *eager for gain* (*avaricious,* hence a *defrauder*):— covetous.

G4124 **πλεονεξία** *pleonexia* from *G4123*; *avarice,* i.e. (by implication) *fraudulence, extortion:*— covetous practices, covetousness, greediness.

G4125 **πλευρά** *pleura* of uncertain affinity; a *rib,* i.e. (by extension) *side:*— side.

G4126 **πλέω** *pleō* another form for

πλεύω *pleuō* which is used as an alternate in certain tenses; probably a form of *G4150* (through the idea of *plunging* through the water); to *pass* in a vessel:— sail. See also *G4130.*

G4127 **πληγή** *plēgē* from *G4141*; a *stroke;* by implication a *wound;* figuratively a *calamity:*— plague, stripe, wound, wounded.

G4128 **πλῆθος** *plēthos* from *G4130*; a *fullness,* i.e. a *large number, throng, populace:*— bundle, company, multitude.

G4129 **πληθύνω** *plēthynō* from another form of *G4128*; to *increase* (transitive or intransitive):— abound, multiply.

G4130 **πλήθω** *plēthō* a prolonged form of a primary

πλέω *pleō* (which appears only as an alternate in certain tenses and in the reduplication form

πίμπλημι *pimplēmi*); to *"fill"* (literally or figuratively [*imbue, influence, supply*]); specifically to *fulfil* (time):— accomplish, full (. . . come), furnish.

G4131 **πλήκτης** *plēktēs* from *G4141*; a *smiter,* i.e. *pugnacious* (*quarrelsome*):— striker.

G4132 **πλημμύρα** *plēmmyra* prolonged from *G4130*; *flood-tide,* i.e. (by analogy) a *freshet:*— flood.

G4133 **πλήν** *plēn* from *G4119*; *moreover* (*besides*), i.e. *albeit, save that, rather, yet:*— but (rather), except, nevertheless, notwithstanding, save, than.

G4134 **πλήρης** *plērēs* from *G4130*; *replete,* or *covered* over; by analogy *complete:*— full.

G4135 **πληροφορέω** *plērophoreō* from *G4134* and *G5409*; to *carry out fully* (in evidence), i.e. *completely assure* (or *convince*), *entirely accomplish:*—

most surely believe, fully know (persuade), make full proof of.

***G4136* πληροφορία** *plērophoria* from *G4135*; *entire confidence:*— (full) assurance.

***G4137* πληρόω** *plēroō* from *G4134*; to *make replete,* i.e. (literally) to *cram* (a net), *level* up (a hollow), or (figuratively) to *furnish* (or *imbue, diffuse, influence*), *satisfy, execute* (an office), *finish* (a period or task), *verify* (or *coincide* with a prediction), etc.:— accomplish, after, (be) complete, end, expire, fill (up), fulfil, (be, make) full (come), fully preach, perfect, supply.

***G4138* πλήρωμα** *plērōma* from *G4137*; *repletion* or *completion,* i.e. (subjectively) what *fills* (as contents, supplement, copiousness, multitude), or (objectively) what is *filled* (as container, performance, period):— which is put in to fill up, piece that filled up, fulfilling, full, fulness.

***G4139* πλησίον** *plēsion* neuter of a derivative of
πέλας *pelas* (*near*); (adverbially) *close* by; as noun, a *neighbor,* i.e. *fellow* (as man, countryman, Christian or friend):— near, neighbour.

***G4140* πλησμονή** *plēsmonē* from a presumed derivative of *G4130*; a *filling* up, i.e. (figuratively) *gratification:*— satisfying.

***G4141* πλήσσω** *plēssō* apparently another form of *G4111* (through the idea of *flattening* out); to *pound,* i.e. (figuratively) to *inflict* with (calamity):— smite. Compare *G5180*.

***G4142* πλοιάριον** *ploiarion* neuter of a presumed derivative of *G4143*; a *boat:*— boat, little (small) ship.

***G4143* πλοῖον** *ploion* from *G4126*; a *sailer,* i.e. *vessel:*— ship, shipping.

***G4144* πλόος** *ploos* from *G4126*; a *sail,* i.e. *navigation:*— course, sailing, voyage.

***G4145* πλούσιος** *plousios* from *G4149*; *wealthy;* figuratively *abounding* with:— rich.

***G4146* πλουσίως** *plousiōs* adverb from *G4145*; *copiously:*— abundantly, richly.

***G4147* πλουτέω** *plouteō* from *G4148*; to *be* (or *become*) *wealthy* (literally or figuratively):— be increased with goods, (be made, wax) rich.

***G4148* πλουτίζω** *ploutizō* from *G4149*; to *make wealthy* (figuratively):— enrich, (make) rich.

***G4149* πλοῦτος** *ploutos* from the base of *G4130*; *wealth* (as *fullness*), i.e. (literally) *money, possessions,* or (figuratively) *abundance, richness,* (specifically) valuable *bestowment:*— riches.

***G4150* πλύνω** *plynō* a prolonged form of an obsolete
πλύω *plyō* (to *"flow"*); to *"plunge"*, i.e. *launder* clothing:— wash. Compare *G3068*, *G3538*.

***G4151* πνεῦμα** *pneuma* from *G4154*; a *current* of air, i.e. *breath* (*blast*) or a *breeze;* by analogy or figuratively a *spirit,* i.e. (human) the rational *soul,* (by implication) *vital principle,* mental *disposition,* etc., or (superhuman) an *angel, daemon,* or (divine) *God,* Christ's *spirit,* the Holy *Spirit:*— ghost, life, spirit, spiritual, spiritually, mind. Compare *G5590*.

***G4152* πνευματικός** *pneumatikos* from *G4151*; *non-carnal,* i.e. (humanly) *ethereal* (as opposed to gross), or (daemoniacally) a *spirit* (concretely), or (divinely) *supernatural, regenerate, religious:*— spiritual. Compare *G5591*.

***G4153* πνευματικῶς** *pneumatikōs* adverb from *G4152*; *non-physically,* i.e. *divinely, figuratively:*— spiritually.

***G4154* πνέω** *pneō* a primary word; to *breathe* hard, i.e. *breeze:*— blow. Compare *G5594*.

***G4155* πνίγω** *pnigō* strengthened from *G4154*; to *wheeze,* i.e. (causatively, by implication) to *throttle* or *strangle* (*drown*):— choke, take by the throat.

***G4156* πνικτός** *pniktos* from *G4155*; *throttled,* i.e. (neuter concretely) an animal *choked* to death (*not bled*):— strangled.

***G4157* πνοή** *pnoē* from *G4154*; *respiration,* a *breeze* :— breath, wind.

***G4158* ποδήρης** *podērēs* from *G4228* and another element of uncertain affinity; a *dress* (*G2066* implied) *reaching* the *ankles:*— garment down to the foot.

***G4159* πόθεν** *pothen* from the base of *G4213* with enclitic adverb of origin; *from which* (as interrogative) or *what* (as relative) place, state, source or cause:— whence.

***G4160* ποιέω** *poieō* apparently a prolonged form of an obsolete primary; to *make* or *do* (in a very wide application, more or less direct):— abide, agree, appoint, avenge, band together, be, bear, bewray, bring (forth), cast out, cause, commit, content, continue, deal, without any delay, (would) do, doing, execute, exercise, fulfil, gain, give, have, hold, journeying, keep, lay wait, lighten the ship, make, mean, none of these things move me, observe, ordain, perform, provide, have purged, purpose, put, raising up, secure, shew, shoot out, spend, take, tarry, transgress the law, work, yield. Compare *G4238*.

***G4161* ποίημα** *poiēma* from *G4160*; a *product,* i.e. *fabric* (literal or figurative):— thing that is made, workmanship.

***G4162* ποίησις** *poiēsis* from *G4160*; *action,* i.e. *performance* (of the law):— deed.

***G4163* ποιητής** *poiētēs* from *G4160*; a *performer;* specifically a *"poet"*:— doer, poet.

***G4164* ποικίλος** *poikilos* of uncertain derivation; *motley,* i.e. *various* in character:— divers, manifold.

***G4165* ποιμαίνω** *poimainō* from *G4166*; to *tend* as a shepherd (or figuratively *supervisor*):— feed (cattle), rule.

***G4166* ποιμήν** *poimēn* of uncertain affinity; a *shepherd* (literal or figurative):— shepherd, pastor.

***G4167* ποίμνη** *poimnē* contracted from *G4165*; a *flock* (literal or figurative):— flock, fold.

***G4168* ποίμνιον** *poimnion* neuter of a presumed derivative of *G4167*; a *flock,* i.e. (figuratively) *group* (of believers):— flock.

***G4169* ποῖος** *poios* from the base of *G4226* and *G3634*; individualizing interrogative (of character) *what* sort of, or (of number) *which* one:— what (manner of), which.

***G4170* πολεμέω** *polemeō* from *G4171*; to *be* (engaged) in *warfare,* i.e. to *battle* (literally or figuratively):— fight, (make) war.

***G4171* πόλεμος** *polemos* from
πέλομαι *pelomai* (to *bustle*); *warfare* (literal or figurative; a single encounter or a series):— battle, fight, war.

***G4172* πόλις** *polis* probably from the same as *G4171*, or perhaps from *G4183*; a *town* (properly with walls, of greater or less size):— city.

***G4173* πολιτάρχης** *politarchēs* from *G4172* and Greek *G757*; a *town-officer,* i.e. *magistrate:*— ruler of the city.

***G4174* πολιτεία** *politeia* from *G4177* (*"polity"*); *citizenship;* concretely a *community:*— commonwealth, freedom.

***G4175* πολίτευμα** *politeuma* from *G4176*; a *community,* i.e. (abstractly) *citizenship* (figuratively):— conversation.

***G4176* πολιτεύομαι** *politeuomai* middle of a derivative of *G4177*; to *behave* as a citizen (figuratively):— let conversation be, live.

***G4177* πολίτης** *politēs* from *G4172*; a *townsman* :— citizen.

***G4178* πολλάκις** *pollakis* multiple adverb from *G4183*; *many times,* i.e. *frequently:*— oft, often, oftentimes, ofttimes.

***G4179* πολλαπλασίων** *pollaplasiōn* from *G4183* and probably a derivative of *G4120*; *manifold,* i.e. (neuter as noun) *very much more:*— manifold more.

***G4180* πολυλογία** *polylogia* from a compound of *G4183* and *G3056*; *loquacity,* i.e. *prolixity:*— much speaking.

***G4181* πολυμέρως** *polymerōs* adverb from a compound of *G4183* and *G3313*; *in many portions,* i.e. *variously* as to time and agency (*piecemeal*):— at sundry times.

***G4182* πολυποίκιλος** *polypoikilos* from *G4183* and *G4164*; *much variegated,* i.e. *multifarious:*— manifold.

***G4183* πολύς** *polys* including the forms from the alternate
πολλός *pollos*; (singular) *much* (in any respect) or (plural) *many;* neuter (singular) as adverb *largely;* neuter (plural) as adverb or noun *often, mostly, largely:*— abundant, altogether, common, far (passed, spent), (+ be of a) great (age, deal, while), greatly, long, many, much, oft, often, ofttimes, plenteous, sore, straitly. Compare *G4118*, *G4119*.

***G4184* πολύσπλαγχνος** *polysplanchnos* from *G4183* and *G4698* (figuratively); *extremely compassionate:*— very pitiful.

***G4185* πολυτελής** *polytelēs* from *G4183* and *G5056*; *extremely expensive:*— costly, very precious, of great price.

***G4186* πολύτιμος** *polytimos* from *G4183* and *G5092*; *extremely valuable:*— very costly, of great price.

***G4187* πολυτρόπως** *polytropōs* adverb from a compound of *G4183* and *G5158*; *in many ways,* i.e. *variously* as to method or form:— in divers manners.

***G4188* πόμα** *poma* from the alternate of *G4095*; a *beverage:*— drink.

***G4189* πονηρία** *ponēria* from *G4190*; *depravity,* i.e. (specifically) *malice;* plural (concretely) *plots, sins:*— iniquity, wickedness.

***G4190* πονηρός** *ponēros* from a derivative of *G4192*; *hurtful,* i.e. *evil* (properly in effect or influence, and thus differing from *G2556*, which refers rather to *essential* character, as well as from *G4550*, which indicates *degeneracy* from original virtue); figuratively *calamitous;* also (passive) *ill,* i.e. *diseased;* but especially (morally) *culpable,* i.e. *derelict, vicious,* *wicked;* neuter (singular) *mischief, malice,* or (plural) *guilt;* masculine (singular) the *devil,* or (plural) *sinners:*— bad, evil, grievous, harm, lewd, malicious, wicked, wickedness. See also G4191.

***G4191* πονηρότερος** *ponēroteros* comparative of G4190; *more evil:*— more wicked.

***G4192* πόνος** *ponos* from the base of G3993; *toil,* i.e. (by implication) *anguish:*— pain.

***G4193* Ποντικός** *Pontikos* from G4195; a *Pontican,* i.e. native of Pontus:— born in Pontus.

***G4194* Πόντιος** *Pontios* of Latin origin; apparently *bridged; Pontius,* a Roman:— Pontius.

***G4195* Πόντος** *Pontos;* a *sea; Pontus,* a region of Asia Minor:— Pontus.

***G4196* Πόπλιος** *Poplios* of Latin origin; apparently *"popular"; Poplius* (i.e. *Publius*), a Roman:— Publius.

***G4197* πορεία** *poreia* from G4198; *travel* (by land); figuratively (plural) *proceedings,* i.e. *career:*— journey, journeying, ways.

***G4198* πορεύομαι** *poreuomai* middle from a derivative of the same as G3984; to *traverse,* i.e. *travel* (literally or figuratively; especially to *remove* [figuratively *die*], *live,* etc.):— depart, go (away, forth, one's way, up), (make a, take a) journey, walk.

***G4199* πορθέω** *portheō* prolonged from
πέρθω *perthō* (to *sack*); to *ravage* (figurative):— destroy, waste.

***G4200* πορισμός** *porismos* from a derivative of
πόρος *poros* (a *way,* i.e. *means*); *furnishing* (*procuring*), i.e. (by implication) *money-getting* (*acquisition*):— gain.

***G4201* Πόρκιος** *Porkios* of Latin origin; apparently *swinish; Porcius,* a Roman:— Porcius.

***G4202* πορνεία** *porneia* from G4203; *harlotry* (including *adultery* and *incest*); figurative *idolatry:*— fornication.

***G4203* πορνεύω** *porneuō* from G4204; to *act* the *harlot,* i.e. (literally) *indulge* unlawful *lust* (of either sex), or (figuratively) *practice idolatry:*— commit (fornication).

***G4204* πόρνη** *pornē* feminine of G4205; a *strumpet;* figuratively an *idolater:*— harlot, whore.

***G4205* πόρνος** *pornos* from
πέρνημι *pernēmi* (to *sell;* akin to the base of G4097); a (male) *prostitute* (as *venal*), i.e. (by analogy) a *debauchee* (*libertine*):— fornicator, whoremonger.

***G4206* πόρρω** *porrhō* adverb from G4253; *forwards,* i.e. *at a distance:*— far, a great way off. See also G4207.

***G4207* πόρρωθεν** *porrhōthen* from G4206 with adverbial enclitic of source; *from far,* or (by implication) *at a distance,* i.e. *distantly:*— afar off.

***G4208* πορρωτέρω** *porrhōterō* adverbial comparative of G4206; *farther,* i.e. *a greater distance:*— further.

***G4209* πορφύρα** *porphyra* of Latin origin; the *"purple"* mussel, i.e. (by implication) the *red-blue* color itself, and finally a garment dyed with it:— purple.

***G4210* πορφυροῦς** *porphyrous* from G4209; *purplish,* i.e. *bluish red:*— purple.

***G4211* πορφυρόπωλις** *porphyropōlis* feminine of a compound of G4209 and G4453; a *female trader in purple* cloth:— seller of purple.

***G4212* ποσάκις** *posakis* multiple from G4214; *how many times:*— how oft, how often.

***G4213* πόσις** *posis* from the alternate of G4095; a *drinking* (the act), i.e. (concretely) a *draught:*— drink.

***G4214* πόσος** *posos* from an obsolete
πός *pos* (*who, what*) and G3739; interrogative pronoun (of amount) *how much* (*large, long* or [plural] *many*):— how great (long, many), what.

***G4215* ποταμός** *potamos* probably from a derivative of the alternate of G4095 (compare G4224); a *current, brook* or *freshet* (as *drinkable*), i.e. *running water:*— flood, river, stream, water.

***G4216* ποταμοφόρητος** *potamophorētos* from G4215 and a derivative of G5409; *river-borne,* i.e. *overwhelmed by a stream:*— carried away of the flood.

***G4217* ποταπός** *potapos* apparently from G4219 and the base of G4226; interrogative *whatever,* i.e. of *what possible* sort:— what (manner of).

***G4218* ποτέ** *pote* from the base of G4225 and G5037; indefinite adverb, at *sometime, ever:*— (any) time(s), aforetime(s), time(s), at length (the last), ever, never, in the old time, in time past, once, when.

***G4219* πότε** *pote* from the base of G4225 and G5037; interrogative adverb, at *what time:*— how long, when.

***G4220* πότερον** *poteron* neuter of a comparative of the base of G4226; interrogative as adverb, *which* (of two), i.e. *is it* this or that:— whether.

***G4221* ποτήριον** *potērion* neuter of a derivative of the alternate of G4095; a *drinking-vessel;* by extension the contents thereof, i.e. a *cupful* (*draught*); figuratively a *lot* or *fate:*— cup.

***G4222* ποτίζω** *potizō* from a derivative of the alternate of G4095; to *furnish drink, irrigate:*— give (make) to drink, feed, water.

***G4223* Ποτίολοι** *Potioloi* of Latin origin; *little wells,* i.e. *mineral springs; Potioli* (i.e. *Puteoli*), a place in Italy:— Puteoli.

***G4224* πότος** *potos* from the alternate of G4095; a *drinking-bout* or *carousal:*— banqueting.

***G4225* πού** *pou* genitive of an indefinite pronoun
πός *pos* (*some*) otherwise obsolete (compare G4214); as adverb of place, *somewhere,* i.e. *nearly:*— about, a certain place.

***G4226* ποῦ** *pou* genitive of an interrogative pronoun
πός *pos* (*what*) otherwise obsolete (perhaps the same as G4225 used with the rising slide of inquiry); as adverb of place; *at* (by implication *to*) *what* locality:— where, whither.

***G4227* Πούδης** *Poudēs* of Latin origin; *modest; Pudes* (i.e. *Pudens*), a Christian:— Pudens.

***G4228* πούς** *pous* a primary word; a *"foot"* (figurative or literal):— foot, footstool.

***G4229* πρᾶγμα** *pragma* from G4238; a *deed;* by implication an *affair;* by extension an *object* (material):— business, matter, thing, work.

***G4230* πραγματεία** *pragmateia* from G4231; a *transaction,* i.e. *negotiation:*— affair.

***G4231* πραγματεύομαι** *pragmateuomai* from G4229; to *busy oneself* with, i.e. to *trade:*— occupy.

***G4232* πραιτώριον** *praitōrion* of Latin origin; the *praetorium* or governor's *courtroom* (sometimes including the whole *edifice* and *camp*):— (common, judgment) hall (of judgment), palace, praetorium.

***G4233* πράκτωρ** *praktōr* from a derivative of G4238; a *practitioner,* i.e. (specifically) an official *collector:*— officer.

***G4234* πρᾶξις** *praxis* from G4238; *practice,* i.e. (concretely) an *act;* by extension a *function:*— deed, office, work.

***G4235* πρᾷος** *praos* a form of G4239, used in certain parts; *gentle,* i.e. *humble:*— meek.

***G4236* πρᾳότης** *praotēs* from G4235; *gentleness;* by implication *humility:*— meekness.

***G4237* πρασιά** *prasia* perhaps from
πράσον *prason* (a *leek,* and so an *onion-patch*); a garden-*plot,* i.e. (by implication of regular *beds*) a *row* (repeated in plural by Hebrew to indicate an arrangement):— in ranks.

***G4238* πράσσω** *prassō* a primary verb; to *"practice"*, i.e. *perform repeatedly* or *habitually* (thus differing from G4160, which properly refers to a *single* act); by implication to *execute, accomplish,* etc.; specifically to *collect* (dues), *fare* (personally):— commit, deeds, do, exact, keep, require, use arts.

***G4239* πραΰς** *praus* apparently a primary word; *mild,* i.e. (by implication) *humble:*— meek. See also G4235.

***G4240* πραΰτης** *prautēs* from G4239; *mildness,* i.e. (by implication) *humility:*— meekness.

***G4241* πρέπω** *prepō* apparently a primary verb; to *tower* up (*be conspicuous*), i.e. (by implication) to *be suitable* or *proper* (third person singular present indicative, often used impersonally, it is *fit* or *right*):— become, comely.

***G4242* πρεσβεία** *presbeia* from G4243; *seniority* (*status of elder*), i.e. (by implication) an *embassy* (concrete *ambassadors*):— ambassage, message.

***G4243* πρεσβεύω** *presbeuō* from the base of Greek G4245; to be a *senior,* i.e. (by implication) *act as a representative* (figuratively *preacher*):— be an ambassador.

***G4244* πρεσβυτέριον** *presbyterion* neuter of a presumed derivative of G4245; the *order of elders,* i.e. (specifically) Israelite *Sanhedrin* or Christian *"presbytery"*:— (estate of) elder(s), presbytery.

***G4245* πρεσβύτερος** *presbyteros* comparative of
πρέσβυς *presbys* (*elderly*); *older;* as noun, a *senior;* specially an Israelite member of the *Sanhedrin* (also figuratively member of the celestial council) or Christian *"presbyter"*:— elder, eldest, old.

***G4246* πρεσβύτης** *presbytēs* from the same as G4245; an *old man:*— aged (man), old man.

***G4247* πρεσβῦτις** *presbytis* feminine of G4246; an *old woman:*— aged woman.

***G4248* πρηνής** *prēnēs* from G4253; *leaning* (*falling*) *forward* (*"prone"*), i.e. *head foremost:*— headlong.

***G4249* πρίζω** *prizō* a strengthened form of a primary
πρίω *priō* (to *saw*); to *saw* in two:— saw asunder.

***G4250* πρίν** *prin* adverb from G4253; *prior, sooner* :— before (that), ere.

***G4251* Πρίσκα** *Priska* of Latin origin; feminine of *Priscus, ancient; Priska,* a Christian woman:— Prisca. See also G4252.

***G4252* Πρίσκιλλα** *Priskilla* diminative of G4251; *Priscilla* (i.e. *little Prisca*), a Christian woman:— Priscilla.

G4253 πρό *pro* a primary preposition; *"fore"*, i.e. *in front of, prior* (figuratively *superior*) *to*. In compounds it retains the same meanings:— above, ago, before, or ever.

G4254 προάγω *proagō* from *G4253* and *G71*; to *lead forward* (magisterially); intransitive to *precede* (in place or time [participle *previous*]):— bring (forth, out), go before.

G4255 προαιρέομαι *proaireomai* from *G4253* and *G138*; to *choose* for oneself *before* another thing (*prefer*), i.e. (by implication) to *propose* (*intend*):— purpose.

G4256 προαιτιάομαι *proaitiaomai* from *G4253* and a derivative of *G156*; to *accuse already*, i.e. *previously charge*:— prove before.

G4257 προακούω *proakouō* from *G4253* and *G191*; to *hear already*, i.e. *anticipate*:— hear before.

G4258 προαμαρτάνω *proamartanō* from *G4253* and *G264*; to *sin previously* (to conversion):— sin already, heretofore sin.

G4259 προαύλιον *proaulion* neuter of a presumed compound of *G4253* and *G833*; a *forecourt*, i.e. *vestibule* (*alley-way*):— porch.

G4260 προβαίνω *probainō* from *G4253* and the base of *G939*; to *walk forward*, i.e. *advance* (literally or in years):— be of a great age, go farther (on), be well stricken.

G4261 προβάλλω *proballō* from *G4253* and *G906*; to *throw forward*, i.e. *push to the front, germinate*:— put forward, shoot forth.

G4262 προβατικός *probatikos* from *G4263*; *relating to sheep*, i.e. (a *gate*) through which they were led into Jerusalem:— sheep (market).

G4263 πρόβατον *probaton* properly neuter of a presumed derivative of *G4260*; *something that walks forward* (a *quadruped*), i.e. (specifically) a *sheep* (literal or figurative):— sheep, sheepfold.

G4264 προβιβάζω *probibazō* from *G4253* and a reduplicated form of *G971*; to *force forward*, i.e. *bring to the front, instigate*:— draw, before instruct.

G4265 προβλέπω *problepō* from *G4253* and *G991*; to *look out beforehand*, i.e. *furnish in advance*:— provide.

G4266 προγίνομαι *proginomai* from *G4253* and *G1096*; to *be already*, i.e. *have previously transpired*:— be past.

G4267 προγινώσκω *proginōskō* from *G4253* and *G1097*; to *know beforehand*, i.e. *foresee*:— foreknow (ordain), know (before).

G4268 πρόγνωσις *prognōsis* from *G4267*; *forethought*:— foreknowledge.

G4269 πρόγονος *progonos* from *G4266*; an *ancestor, parent, grandparent*:— forefather, parent.

G4270 προγράφω *prographō* from *G4253* and *G1125*; to *write previously*; figuratively to *announce, prescribe*:— before ordain, evidently set forth, write (afore, aforetime).

G4271 πρόδηλος *prodēlos* from *G4253* and *G1212*; *plain before* all men, i.e. *obvious*:— evident, manifest (open) beforehand.

G4272 προδίδωμι *prodidōmi* from *G4253* and *G1325*; to *give before* the other party has given:— first give.

G4273 προδότης *prodotēs* from *G4272* (in the sense of *giving forward* into another's [the enemy's] hands); a *surrender*:— betrayer, traitor.

G4274 πρόδρομος *prodromos* from the alternate of *G4390*; a *runner ahead*, i.e. *scout* (figuratively *precursor*):— forerunner.

G4275 προείδω *proeidō* from *G4253* and *G1492*; *foresee*:— foresee, saw before.

G4276 προελπίζω *proelpizō* from *G4253* and *G1679*; to *hope in advance* of other confirmation:— first trust.

G4277 προέπω *proepō* from *G4253* and *G2036*; to *say already*, to *predict*:— forewarn, say (speak, tell) before. Compare *G4280*.

G4278 προενάρχομαι *proenarchomai* from *G4253* and *G1728*; to *commence already*:— begin (before).

G4279 προεπαγγέλλομαι *proepangellomai* middle from *G4253* and *G1861*; to *promise of old*:— promise before.

G4280 προερέω *proereō* from *G4253* and *G2046*; used as alternate of *G4277*; to *say already, predict*:— foretell, say (speak, tell) before.

G4281 προέρχομαι *proerchomai* from *G4253* and *G2064* (including its alternate); to *go onward, precede* (in place or time):— go before (farther, forward), outgo, pass on.

G4282 προετοιμάζω *proetoimazō* from *G4253* and *G2090*; to *fit up in advance* (literally or figuratively):— ordain before, prepare afore.

G4283 προευαγγελίζομαι *proeuangelizomai* middle from *G4253* and *G2097*; to *announce* glad news *in advance*:— preach before the gospel.

G4284 προέχομαι *proechomai* middle from *G4253* and *G2192*; to *hold* oneself *before* others, i.e. (figuratively) to *excel*:— be better.

G4285 προηγέομαι *proēgeomai* from *G4253* and *G2233*; to *lead the way* for others, i.e. *show deference*:— prefer.

G4286 πρόθεσις *prothesis* from *G4388*; a *setting forth*, i.e. (figuratively) *proposal* (*intention*); specifically the *show*-bread (in the Temple) as *exposed* before God:— purpose, shew, shewbread.

G4287 προθέσμιος *prothesmios* from *G4253* and a derivative of *G5087*; *fixed beforehand*, i.e. (feminine with *G2250* implied) a *designated* day:— time appointed.

G4288 προθυμία *prothymia* from *G4289*; *predisposition*, i.e. *alacrity*:— forwardness of mind, readiness (of mind), ready (willing) mind.

G4289 πρόθυμος *prothymos* from *G4253* and *G2372*; *forward* in *spirit*, i.e. *predisposed*; neuter (as noun) *alacrity*:— ready, willing.

G4290 προθύμως *prothymōs* adverb from *G4289*; *with alacrity*:— willingly.

G4291 προΐστημι *proistēmi* from *G4253* and *G2476*; to *stand before*, i.e. (in rank) to *preside*, or (by implication) to *practice*:— maintain, be over, rule.

G4292 προκαλέομαι *prokaleomai* middle from *G4253* and *G2564*; to *call forth to oneself* (*challenge*), i.e. (by implication) to *irritate*:— provoke.

G4293 προκαταγγέλλω *prokatangellō* from *G4253* and *G2605*; to *announce beforehand*, i.e. *predict, promise*:— foretell, have notice, (shew) before.

G4294 προκαταρτίζω *prokatartizō* from *G4253* and *G2675*; to *prepare in advance*:— make up beforehand.

G4295 πρόκειμαι *prokeimai* from *G4253* and *G2749*; to *lie before* the view, i.e. (figuratively) to *be present* (to the mind), to *stand forth* (as an example or reward):— be first, set before (forth).

G4296 προκηρύσσω *prokēryssō* from *G4253* and *G2784*; to *herald* (i.e. *proclaim*) *in advance*:— before (first) preach.

G4297 προκοπή *prokopē* from *G4298*; *progress*, i.e. *advancement* (subjective or objective):— furtherance, profit.

G4298 προκόπτω *prokoptō* from *G4253* and *G2875*; to *drive forward* (as if by beating), i.e. (figuratively and intransitive) to *advance* (in amount, to *grow*; in time, to *be well along*):— increase, proceed, profit, be far spent, wax.

GRK

G4299 πρόκριμα *prokrima* from a compound of *G4253* and *G2919*; a *prejudgment* (*prejudice*), i.e. *prepossession*:— prefer one before another.

G4300 προκυρόω *prokyroō* from *G4253* and *G2964*; to *ratify previously*:— confirm before.

G4301 προλαμβάνω *prolambanō* from *G4253* and *G2983*; to *take in advance*, i.e. (literally) *eat before* others have an opportunity; (figuratively) to *anticipate, surprise*:— come aforehand, overtake, take before.

G4302 προλέγω *prolegō* from *G4253* and *G3004*; to *say beforehand*, i.e. *predict, forewarn*:— foretell, tell before.

G4303 προμαρτύρομαι *promartyromai* from *G4253* and *G3143*; to *be a witness in advance*, i.e. *predict*:— testify beforehand.

G4304 προμελετάω *promeletaō* from *G4253* and *G3191*; to *premeditate*:— meditate before.

G4305 προμεριμνάω *promerimnaō* from *G4253* and *G3309*; to *care* (anxiously) *in advance*:— take thought beforehand.

G4306 προνοέω *pronoeō* from *G4253* and *G3539*; to *consider in advance*, i.e. *look* out for *beforehand* (active by way of *maintenance* for others; middle by way of *circumspection* for oneself):— provide (for).

G4307 πρόνοια *pronoia* from *G4306*; *forethought*, i.e. provident *care* or *supply*:— providence, provision.

G4308 προοράω *prooraō* from *G4253* and *G3708*; to *behold in advance*, i.e. (active) to *notice* (another) *previously*, or (middle) to *keep in* (one's own) *view*:— foresee, see before.

G4309 προορίζω *proorizō* from *G4253* and *G3724*; to *limit in advance*, i.e. (figuratively) *predetermine*:— determine before, ordain, predestinate.

G4310 προπάσχω *propaschō* from *G4253* and *G3958*; to *undergo* hardship *previously*:— suffer before.

G4311 προπέμπω *propempō* from *G4253* and *G3992*; to *send forward*, i.e. *escort* or *aid* in travel:— accompany, bring (forward) on journey (way), conduct forth.

G4312 προπετής *propetēs* from a compound of *G4253* and *G4098*; *falling forward*, i.e. *headlong* (figuratively *precipitate*):— heady, rash, rashly.

G4313 προπορεύομαι *proporeuomai* from *G4253* and *G4198*; to *precede* (as guide or herald):— go before.

G4314 πρός *pros* a strengthened form of G4253; a preposition of direction; *forward to,* i.e. *toward* (with the genitive *the side* of, i.e. *pertaining to;* with the dative *by the side of,* i.e. *near to;* usually with the accusative, the place, time, occasion, or respect, which is the *destination* of the relation, i.e. *whither* or *for* which it is predicated). In compounds it denotes essentially the same applications, namely, motion *towards,* accession *to,* or nearness *at:*— about, according to, against, among, at, because of, before, between, by, whereby, for, at thy house, in, for intent, nigh unto, of, which pertain to, that, to (the end that), together, to, toward, to youward, unto, with (-in).

G4315 προσάββατον *prosabbaton* from G4253 and G4521; a *fore-sabbath,* i.e. the *Sabbath-eve:*— day before the sabbath. Compare G3904.

G4316 προσαγορεύω *prosagoreuō* from G4314 and a derivative of G58 (meaning to *harangue*); to *address,* i.e. salute by *name:*— call.

G4317 προσάγω *prosagō* from G4314 and G71; to *lead towards,* i.e. (transitive) to *conduct near* (*summon, present*), or (intransitive) to *approach:*— bring, draw near.

G4318 προσαγωγή *prosagōgē* from G4317 (compare G72); *admission:*— access.

G4319 προσαιτέω *prosaiteō* from G4314 and G154; to *ask repeatedly* (*importune*), i.e. *solicit:*— beg.

G4320 προσαναβαίνω *prosanabainō* from G4314 and G305; to *ascend farther,* i.e. *be promoted* (*take an upper* [*more honorable*] *seat*):— go up.

G4321 προσαναλίσκω *prosanaliskō* from G4314 and G355; to *expend further:*— spend.

G4322 προσαναπληρόω *prosanaplēroō* from G4314 and G378; to *fill up further,* i.e. *furnish fully:*— supply.

G4323 προσανατίθημι *prosanatithēmi* from G4314 and G394; to *lay up in addition,* i.e. (middle and figuratively) to *impart* or (by implication) to *consult:*— in conference add, confer.

G4324 προσαπειλέω *prosapeileō* from G4314 and G546; to *menace additionally:*— threaten further.

G4325 προσδαπανάω *prosdapanaō* from G4314 and G1159; to *expend additionally:*— spend more.

G4326 προσδέομαι *prosdeomai* from G4314 and G1189; to *require additionally,* i.e. *want further:*— need.

G4327 προσδέχομαι *prosdechomai* from G4314 and G1209; to *admit* (to intercourse, hospitality, credence or [figuratively] endurance); by implication to *await* (with confidence or patience):— accept, allow, look (wait) for, take.

G4328 προσδοκάω *prosdokaō* from G4314 and **δοκεύω** *dokeuō* (to *watch*); to *anticipate* (in thought, hope or fear); by implication to *await:*— expect, (be in) expectation, look (for), when looked, tarry, wait for.

G4329 προσδοκία *prosdokia* from G4328; *apprehension* (of evil); by implication *infliction* anticipated:— expectation, looking after.

G4330 προσεάω *proseaō* from G4314 and G1439; to *permit further* progress:— suffer.

G4331 προσεγγίζω *prosengizō* from G4314 and G1448; to *approach near:*— come nigh.

G4332 προσεδρεύω *prosedreuō* from a compound of G4314 and the base of G1476; to *sit near,* i.e. *attend* as a servant:— wait at.

G4333 προσεργάζομαι *prosergazomai* from G4314 and G2038; to *work additionally,* i.e. (by implication) *acquire besides:*— gain.

G4334 προσέρχομαι *proserchomai* from G4314 and G2064 (including its alternate); to *approach,* i.e. (literally) *come near, visit,* or (figuratively) *worship, assent to:*— (as soon as he) come (unto), come thereunto, consent, draw near, go (near, to, unto).

G4335 προσευχή *proseuchē* from G4336; *prayer* (*worship*); by implication an *oratory* (*chapel*):— pray earnestly, prayer.

G4336 προσεύχομαι *proseuchomai* from G4314 and G2172; to *pray to* God, i.e. *supplicate, worship:*— pray (earnestly, for), make prayer.

G4337 προσέχω *prosechō* from G4314 and G2192; (figuratively) to *hold* the mind (G3563 implied) *towards,* i.e. *pay attention to, be cautious about, apply oneself* to, *adhere to:*— attend, (give) attendance (at, to, unto), beware, be given to, give (take) heed (to, unto) have regard.

G4338 προσηλόω *prosēloō* from G4314 and a derivative of G2247; to *peg to,* i.e. *spike* fast:— nail to.

G4339 προσήλυτος *prosēlytos* from the alternate of G4334; an *arriver* from a foreign region, i.e. (specifically) *one who accedes* (a *convert*) to Judaism (*"proselyte"*):— proselyte.

G4340 πρόσκαιρος *proskairos* from G4314 and G2540; *for the occasion* only, i.e. *temporary:*— dur for awhile, dureth for awhile, endure for a time, for a season, temporal.

G4341 προσκαλέομαι *proskaleomai* middle from G4314 and G2564; to *call toward oneself,* i.e. *summon, invite:*— call (for, to, unto).

G4342 προσκαρτερέω *proskartereō* from G4314 and G2594; to *be earnest towards,* i.e. (to a thing) to *persevere, be constantly* diligent, or (in a place) to *attend* assiduously all the exercises, or (to a person) to *adhere* closely *to* (as a servitor):— attend (give self) continually (upon), continue (in, instant in, with), wait on (continually).

G4343 προσκαρτέρησις *proskarterēsis* from G4342; *persistency:*— perseverance.

G4344 προσκεφάλαιον *proskephalaion* neuter of a presumed compound of G4314 and G2776; something *for the head,* i.e. a *cushion:*— pillow.

G4345 προσκληρόω *prosklēroō* from G4314 and G2820; to *give* a common *lot to,* i.e. (figuratively) to *associate with:*— consort with.

G4346 πρόσκλισις *prosklisis* from a compound of G4314 and G2827; a *leaning towards,* i.e. (figuratively) *proclivity* (*favoritism*):— partiality.

G4347 προσκολλάω *proskollaō* from G4314 and G2853; to *glue to,* i.e. (figuratively) to *adhere:*— cleave, join (self).

G4348 πρόσκομμα *proskomma* from G4350; a *stub,* i.e. (figuratively) *occasion of apostasy:*— offence, stumbling, stumbling-block, stumbling-stone.

G4349 προσκοπή *proskopē* from G4350; a *stumbling,* i.e. (figuratively and concretely) *occasion of sin:*— offence.

G4350 προσκόπτω *proskoptō* from G4314 and G2875; to *strike at,* i.e. *surge against* (as water); specifically to *stub on,* i.e. *trip up* (literally or figuratively):— beat upon, dash, stumble (at).

G4351 προσκυλίω *proskyliō* from G4314 and G2947; to *roll towards,* i.e. *block against:*— roll (to).

G4352 προσκυνέω *proskyneō* from G4314 and a probably derivative of G2965 (meaning to *kiss,* like a dog *licking* his master's hand); to *fawn* or *crouch to,* i.e. (literally or figuratively) *prostrate* oneself in homage (*do reverence* to, *adore*):— worship.

G4353 προσκυνητής *proskynētēs* from G4352; an *adorer:*— worshipper.

G4354 προσλαλέω *proslaleō* from G4314 and G2980; to *talk to,* i.e. *converse with:*— speak to (with).

G4355 προσλαμβάνω *proslambanō* from G4314 and G2983; to *take to* oneself, i.e. *use* (food), *lead* (aside), *admit* (to friendship or hospitality):— receive, take (unto).

G4356 πρόσληψις *proslēpsis* from G4355; *admission:*— receiving.

G4357 προσμένω *prosmenō* from G4314 and G3306; to *stay further,* i.e. *remain* in a place, with a person: figuratively to *adhere* to, *persevere* in:— abide still, be with, cleave unto, continue in (with).

G4358 προσορμίζω *prosormizō* from G4314 and a derivative of the same as G3730 (meaning to *tie* [*anchor*] or *lull*); to *moor to,* i.e. (by implication) *land at:*— draw to the shore.

G4359 προσοφείλω *prosopheilō* from G4314 and G3784; to *be indebted additionally:*— over besides.

G4360 προσοχθίζω *prosochthizō* from G4314 and a form of **ὀχθέω** *ochtheō* (to *be vexed* with something irksome); to *feel indignant at:*— be grieved with.

G4361 πρόσπεινος *prospeinos* from G4314 and the same as G3983; *hungering further,* i.e. *intensely hungry:*— very hungry.

G4362 προσπήγνυμι *prospēgnymi* from G4314 and G4078; to *fasten to,* i.e. (specifically) to *impale* (on a cross):— crucify.

G4363 προσπίπτω *prospiptō* from G4314 and G4098; to *fall towards,* i.e. (gently) *prostrate* oneself (in supplication or homage), or (violently) to *rush* upon (in storm):— beat upon, fall (down) at (before).

G4364 προσποιέομαι *prospoieomai* middle from G4314 and G4160; to *do forward for oneself,* i.e. *pretend* (as if about to do a thing):— make as though.

G4365 προσπορεύομαι *prosporeuomai* from G4314 and G4198; to *journey towards,* i.e. *approach* [not the same as G4313]:— go before.

G4366 προσρήγνυμι *prosrēgnymi* from G4314 and G4486; to *tear towards,* i.e. *burst upon* (as a tempest or flood):— beat vehemently against (upon).

G4367 προστάσσω *prostassō* from G4314 and G5021; to *arrange towards,* i.e. (figuratively) *enjoin:*— bid, command.

G4368 προστάτις *prostatis* feminine of a derivative of G4291; a *patroness,* i.e. *assistant:*— succourer.

G4369 προστίθημι *prostithēmi* from G4314 and G5087; to *place additionally,* i.e. *lay beside, annex, repeat:*— add, again, give more, increase, lay unto, proceed further, speak to any more.

G4370 προστρέχω *prostrechō* from G4314 and G5143 (including its alternate); to *run towards,* i.e. *hasten* to meet or join:— run (thither to, to).

G4371 προσφάγιον *prosphagion* neuter of a presumed derivative of a compound of G4314 and

G5315; something *eaten in addition* to bread, i.e. a *relish* (specifically *fish;* compare *G3795*):— meat.

G4372 **πρόσφατος** *prosphatos* from *G4253* and a derivative of *G4969*; *previously* (*recently*) *slain* (*fresh*), i.e. (figuratively) *lately made:*— new.

G4373 **προσφάτως** *prosphatōs* adverb from *G4372*; *recently:*— lately.

G4374 **προσφέρω** *prospherō* from *G4314* and *G5342* (including its alternate); to *bear towards,* i.e. *lead to, tender* (especially to God), *treat:*— bring (to, unto) deal with, do, offer (unto, up), present unto, put to.

G4375 **προσφιλής** *prosphilēs* from a presumed compound of *G4314* and *G5368*; *friendly towards,* i.e. *acceptable:*— lovely.

G4376 **προσφορά** *prosphora* from *G4374*; *presentation;* concretely an *oblation* (bloodless) or *sacrifice:*— offering (up).

G4377 **προσφωνέω** *prosphōneō* from *G4314* and *G5455*; to *sound towards,* i.e. *address, exclaim, summon:*— call unto, speak to, speak unto.

G4378 **πρόσχυσις** *proschysis* from a compound of *G4314* and
χέω *cheō* (to *pour*); a *shedding forth,* i.e. a *pouring on:*— sprinkling.

G4379 **προσψαύω** *prospsauō* from *G4314* and
ψαύω *psauō* (to *touch*); to *impinge,* i.e. *lay a finger on* (in order to relieve):— touch.

G4380 **προσωποληπτέω** *prosōpolēpteō* from *G4381*; to *favor an individual,* i.e. *show partiality:*— have respect to persons.

G4381 **προσωπολήπτης** *prosōpolēptēs* from *G4383* and *G2983*; an *acceptor* of *a face* (*individual*), i.e. (specifically) one *exhibiting partiality:*— respecter of persons.

G4382 **προσωποληψία** *prosōpolēpsia* from *G4381*; *partiality,* i.e. *favoritism:*— respect of persons.

G4383 **πρόσωπον** *prosōpon* from *G4314* and
ὤψ *ōps* (the *visage;* from *G3700*); the *front* (as being *towards view*), i.e. the *countenance, aspect, appearance, surface;* by implication *presence, person:*— (outward) appearance, before, countenance, face, fashion, (men's) person, presence.

G4384 **προτάσσω** *protassō* from *G4253* and *G5021*; to *pre-arrange,* i.e. *prescribe:*— before appoint.

G4385 **προτείνω** *proteinō* from *G4253* and
τείνω *teinō* (to *stretch*); to *stretch forth,* i.e. *tie prostrate* (for scourging):— bind.

G4386 **πρότερον** *proteron* neuter of *G4387* as adverb (with or without the article); *previously:*— before, (at the) first, former.

G4387 **πρότερος** *proteros* comparative of *G4253*; *prior* or *previous:*— former.

G4388 **προτίθεμαι** *protithemai* middle from *G4253* and *G5087*; to *place before,* i.e. (for oneself) to *exhibit;* (to oneself) to *propose* (*determine*):— purpose, set forth.

G4389 **προτρέπομαι** *protrepomai* middle from *G4253* and the base of *G5157*; to *turn forward* for oneself, i.e. *encourage:*— exhort.

G4390 **προτρέχω** *protrechō* from *G4253* and *G5143* (including its alternate); to *run forward,* i.e. *outstrip, precede:*— outrun, run before.

G4391 **προϋπάρχω** *proyparchō* from *G4253* and *G5225*; to *exist before,* i.e. (adverbially) to *be* or *do* something *previously:*— be before, be before-time.

G4392 **πρόφασις** *prophasis* from a compound of *G4253* and *G5316*; an *outward showing,* i.e. *pretext:*— cloke, colour, pretence, show.

G4393 **προφέρω** *propherō* from *G4253* and *G5342*; to *bear forward,* i.e. *produce:*— bring forth.

G4394 **προφητεία** *prophēteia* from *G4396* (*"prophecy"*); *prediction* (scriptural or other):— prophecy, prophesying.

G4395 **προφητεύω** *prophēteuō* from *G4396*; to *foretell* events, *divine, speak* under *inspiration, exercise* the prophetic *office:*— prophesy.

G4396 **προφήτης** *prophētēs* from a compound of *G4253* and *G5346*; a *foreteller* (*"prophet"*); by analogy an *inspired speaker;* by extension a *poet:*— prophet.

G4397 **προφητικός** *prophētikos* from *G4396*; *pertaining to a foreteller* (*"prophetic"*):— of prophecy, of the prophets.

G4398 **προφῆτις** *prophētis* feminine of *G4396*; a *female foreteller* or an *inspired woman:*— prophetess.

G4399 **προφθάνω** *prophthanō* from *G4253* and *G5348*; to *get an earlier start of,* i.e. *anticipate:*— prevent.

G4400 **προχειρίζομαι** *procheirizomai* middle from *G4253* and a derivative of *G5495*; to *handle* for oneself *in advance,* i.e. (figuratively) to *purpose:*— choose, make.

G4401 **προχειροτονέω** *procheirotoneō* from *G4253* and *G5500*; to *elect in advance:*— choose before.

G4402 **Πρόχορος** *Prochoros* from *G4253* and *G5525*; *before* the *dance; Prochorus,* a Christian:— Prochorus.

G4403 **πρύμνα** *prymna* feminine of
πρυμνύς *prymnys* (*hindmost*); the *stern* of a ship:— hinder part, stern.

G4404 **πρωΐ** *prōi* adverb from *G4253*; at *dawn;* by implication the *day-break* watch:— early (in the morning), (in the) morning.

G4405 **πρωΐα** *prōia* feminine of a derivative of *G4404* as noun; *day-dawn:*— early, morning.

G4406 **πρώϊμος** *prōimos* from *G4404*; *dawning,* i.e. (by analogy) *autumnal* (showering, the first of the rainy season):— early.

G4407 **πρωϊνός** *prōinos* from *G4404*; pertaining to the *dawn,* i.e. *matutinal:*— morning.

G4408 **πρῴρα** *prōra* feminine of a presumed derivative of *G4253* as noun; the *prow,* i.e. forward part of a vessel:— forepart, foreship.

G4409 **πρωτεύω** *prōteuō* from *G4413*; to *be first* (in rank or influence):— have the preeminence.

G4410 **πρωτοκαθεδρία** *prōtokathedria* from *G4413* and *G2515*; a *sitting first* (in the front row), i.e. *preeminence* in council:— chief (highest, uppermost) seat.

G4411 **πρωτοκλισία** *prōtoklisia* from *G4413* and *G2828*; a *reclining first* (in the place of honor) at the dinner-bed, i.e. *preeminence* at meals:— chief (highest, uppermost) room.

G4412 **πρῶτον** *prōton* neuter of *G4413* as adverb (with or without *G3588*); *firstly* (in time, place, order, or importance):— before, at the beginning, chiefly, (at, at the) first (of all).

G4413 **πρῶτος** *prōtos* contracted superlative of *G4253*; *foremost* (in time, place, order or importance):— before, beginning, best, chief, chiefest, first (of all), former.

G4414 **πρωτοστάτης** *prōtostatēs* from *G4413* and *G2476*; one *standing first* in the ranks, i.e. a *captain* (*champion*):— ringleader.

G4415 **πρωτοτόκια** *prōtotokia* from *G4416*; *primogeniture* (as a privilege):— birthright.

G4416 **πρωτότοκος** *prōtotokos* from *G4413* and the alternate of *G5088*; *first-born* (usually as noun, literal or figurative):— firstbegotten, firstborn.

G4417 **πταίω** *ptaiō* a form of *G4098*; to *trip,* i.e. (figuratively) to *err, sin, fail* (of salvation):— fall, offend, stumble.

G4418 **πτέρνα** *pterna* of uncertain derivation; the *heel* (figuratively):— heel.

G4419 **πτερύγιον** *pterygion* neuter of a presumed derivative of *G4420*; a *little wing,* i.e. (figuratively) *extremity* (top corner):— pinnacle.

G4420 **πτέρυξ** *pteryx* from a derivative of *G4072* (meaning a *feather*); a *wing:*— wing.

G4421 **πτηνόν** *ptēnon* contracted for *G4071*; a *bird* :— bird.

G4422 **πτοέω** *ptoeō* probably akin to the alternate of *G4098* (through the idea of causing to *fall*) or to *G4072* (through that of causing to *fly* away); to *scare:*— frighten.

G4423 **πτόησις** *ptoēsis* from *G4422*; *alarm:*— amazement.

G4424 **Πτολεμαΐς** *Ptolemais* from
Πτολεμαῖς *Ptolemais* (*Ptolemy,* after whom it was named); *Ptolemaïs,* a place in Palestine:— Ptolemais.

G4425 **πτύον** *ptyon* from *G4429*; a *winnowing-fork* (as *scattering* like spittle):— fan.

G4426 **πτύρω** *ptyrō* from a presumed derivative of *G4429* (and thus akin to *G4422*); to *frighten:*— terrify.

G4427 **πτύσμα** *ptysma* from *G4429*; *saliva:*— spittle.

G4428 **πτύσσω** *ptyssō* probably akin to
πετάννυμι *petannymi* (to *spread;* and thus apparently allied to *G4072* through the idea of *expansion,* and to *G4429* through that of *flattening;* compare *G3961*); to *fold,* i.e. *furl* a scroll:— close.

G4429 **πτύω** *ptyō* a primary verb (compare *G4428*); to *spit:*— spit.

G4430 **πτῶμα** *ptōma* from the alternate of *G4098*; a *ruin,* i.e. (specifically) lifeless *body* (*corpse, carrion*):— dead body, carcase, corpse.

G4431 **πτῶσις** *ptōsis* from the alternate of *G4098*; a *crash,* i.e. *downfall* (literal or figurative):— fall.

G4432 **πτωχεία** *ptōcheia* from *G4433*; *beggary,* i.e. *indigence* (literal or figurative):— poverty.

G4433 **πτωχεύω** *ptōcheuō* from *G4434*; to *be a beggar,* i.e. (by implication) to *become indigent* (figuratively):— become poor.

G4434 **πτωχός** *ptōchos* from
πτώσσω *ptōssō* (to *crouch;* akin to *G4422* and the alternate of *G4098*); a *beggar* (as *cringing*), i.e. *pauper* (strictly denoting absolute or public *mendicancy,* although also used in a qualified or relative sense; whereas *G3993* properly means only *straitened* circumstances in private), literal (often as noun) or figurative (*distressed*):— beggar, beggarly, poor.

G4435 πυγμή *pygmē* from a primary

πύξ *pyx* (the *fist* as a weapon); the clenched *hand,* i.e. (only in dative as adverb) *with* the *fist* (hard *scrubbing*):— oft.

G4436 Πύθων *Pythōn* from

Πυθώ *Pythō* (the name of the region where Delphi, the seat of the famous *oracle,* was located); a *Python,* i.e. (by analogy with the supposed *diviner* there) *inspiration* (*soothsaying*):— divination.

G4437 πυκνός *pyknos* from the same as *G4635*; *clasped* (*thick*), i.e. (figuratively) *frequent;* neuter plural (as adverb) *frequently:*— often, oftener.

G4438 πυκτέυω *pykteuō* from a derivative of the same as *G4435*; to *box* (with the fist), i.e. *contend* (as a boxer) at the games (figuratively):— fight.

G4439 πύλη *pylē* apparently a primary word; a *gate,* i.e. the leaf or wing of a folding *entrance* (literal or figurative):— gate.

G4440 πυλών *pylōn* from *G4439*; a *gateway, doorway* of a building or city; by implication a *portal* or *vestibule:*— gate, porch.

G4441 πυνθάνομαι *pynthanomai* middle prolonged from a primary

πύθω *pythō* (which occurs only as an alternate in certain tenses); to *question,* i.e. *ascertain* by inquiry (as a matter of *information* merely; and thus differing from *G2065*, which properly means a *request* as a favor; and from *G154*, which is strictly a *demand* of something due; as well as from *G2212*, which implies a *search* for something hidden; and from *G1189*, which involves the idea of urgent *need*); by implication to *learn* (by casual intelligence):— ask, demand, inquire, understand.

G4442 πῦρ *pyr* a primary word; *"fire"* (literal or figurative, specifically *lightning*):— fiery, fire.

G4443 πυρά *pyra* from *G4442*; a *fire* (concrete):— fire.

G4444 πύργος *pyrgos* apparently a primary word (*"burgh"*); a *tower* or *castle:*— tower.

G4445 πυρέσσω *pyressō* from *G4443*; to *be on fire,* i.e. (specifically) to *have a fever:*— be sick of a fever.

G4446 πυρετός *pyretos* from *G4445*; *inflamed,* i.e. (by implication) *feverish* (as noun, *fever*):— fever.

G4447 πύρινος *pyrinos* from *G4443*; *fiery,* i.e. (by implication) *flaming:*— of fire.

G4448 πυρόω *pyroō* from *G4442*; to *kindle,* i.e. (passive) to *be ignited, glow* (literally), *be refined* (by implication), or (figuratively) to *be inflamed* (with anger, grief, lust):— burn, fiery, be on fire, try.

G4449 πυρράζω *pyrrhazō* from *G4450*; to *redden* (intransitive):— be red.

G4450 πυρρός *pyrrhos* from *G4442*; *fire-like,* i.e. (specifically) *flame-colored:*— red.

G4451 πύρωσις *pyrōsis* from *G4448*; *ignition,* i.e. (specifically) *smelting* (figuratively *conflagration, calamity* as a *test*):— burning, trial.

G4452 -πω *-pō* another form of the base of *G4458*; an enclitic particle of indefiniteness; *yet, even;* used only in compounds:— See *G3369*, *G3380*, *G3764*, *G3768*, *G4455*.

G4453 πωλέω *pōleō* probably ultimately from

πέλομαι *pelomai* (to *be busy,* to *trade*); to *barter* (as a *peddler*), i.e. to *sell:*— sell, whatever is sold.

G4454 πῶλος *pōlos* apparently a primary word; a *"foal"* or *"filly"*, i.e. (specifically) a *young ass:*— colt.

G4455 πώποτε *pōpote* from *G4452* and *G4218*; *at any time,* i.e. (with negative particle) *at no time:*— at any time, never (. . . to any man), yet never man.

G4456 πωρόω *pōroō* apparently from

πῶρος *pōros* (a kind of *stone*); to *petrify,* i.e. (figuratively) to *indurate* (*render stupid* or *callous*):— blind, harden.

G4457 πώρωσις *pōrōsis* from *G4456*; *stupidity* or *callousness:*— blindness, hardness.

G4458 πώς *pōs* adverb from the base of *G4225*; an enclitic particle of indefiniteness of manner; *somehow* or *anyhow;* used only in compounds:— haply, by any (some) means, perhaps. See *G1513*, *G3381*. Compare *G4459*.

G4459 πῶς *pōs* adverb from the base of *G4226*; an interrogative particle of manner; *in what way?* (sometimes the question is indirect, *how?*); also as exclamation, *how much!* [*Occasionally unexpressed in English*]:— how, after (by) what manner (means), that.

Ρ

G4460 Ῥαάβ *Rhaab* of Hebrew origin [H7343]; *Raab* (i.e. *Rachab*), a Canaanitess:— Rahab. See also Greek *G4477*.

G4461 ῥαββί *rhabbi* of Hebrew origin [H7227 with pronominal suffix]; *my master,* i.e. *Rabbi,* as an official title of honor:— Master, Rabbi.

G4462 ῥαββονί *rhabboni* or

ῥαββουνί *rhabbouni* of Aramaic origin; corresponding to *G4461*:— Lord, Rabboni.

G4463 ῥαβδίζω *rhabdizō* from *G4464*; to *strike with a stick,* i.e. *bastinado:*— beat (with rods).

G4464 ῥάβδος *rhabdos* from the base of *G4474*; a *stick* or *wand* (as a *cudgel,* a *cane* or a *baton* of royalty):— rod, sceptre, staff.

G4465 ῥαβδοῦχος *rhabdouchos* from *G4464* and *G2192*; a *rod-* (the Latin *fasces*) *holder,* i.e. a Roman *lictor* (*constable* or *executioner*):— sergeant.

G4466 Ῥαγαῦ *Rhagau* of Hebrew origin [H7466]; *Ragau* (i.e. *Reu'*), a patriarch:— Ragau.

G4467 ῥᾳδιούργημα *rhadiourgēma* from a compound of

ῥᾴδιος *rhadios* (*easy,* i.e. *reckless*) and *G2041*; *easy-going behavior,* i.e. (by extension) a *crime:*— lewdness.

G4468 ῥᾳδιουργία *rhadiourgia* from the same as *G4467*; *recklessness,* i.e. (by extension) *malignity:*— mischief.

G4469 ῥακά *rhaka* of Aramaic origin [compare H7386]; O *empty* one, i.e. thou *worthless* (as a term of utter vilification):— Raca.

G4470 ῥάκος *rhakos* from *G4486*; a *"rag,"* i.e. *piece* of cloth:— cloth.

G4471 Ῥαμᾶ *Rhama* of Hebrew origin [H7414]; *Rama* (i.e. *Ramah*), a place in Palestine:— Rama.

G4472 ῥαντίζω *rhantizō* from a derivative of

ῥαίνω *rhainō* (to *sprinkle*); to *render besprinkled,* i.e. *asperse* (ceremonially or figuratively) :— sprinkle.

G4473 ῥαντισμός *rhantismos* from *G4472*; *aspersion* (ceremonial or figurative):— sprinkling.

G4474 ῥαπίζω *rhapizō* from a derivative of a primary

ῥέπω *rhepō* (to *let fall, "rap"*); to *slap:*— smite (with the palm of the hand). Compare *G5180*.

G4475 ῥάπισμα *rhapisma* from *G4474*; a *slap:*— (+ strike with the) palm of the hand, smite with the hand.

G4476 ῥαφίς *rhaphis* from a primary

ῥάπτω *rhaptō* (to *sew;* perhaps rather akin to the base of *G4474* through the idea of *puncturing*); a *needle:*— needle.

G4477 Ῥαχάβ *Rhachab* from the same as *G4460*; *Rachab,* a Canaanitess:— Rachab.

G4478 Ῥαχήλ *Rhachēl* of Hebrew origin [H7354]; *Rachel,* the wife of Jacob:— Rachel.

G4479 Ῥεβέκκα *Rhebekka* of Hebrew origin [H7259]; *Rebecca* (i.e. *Ribkah*), the wife of Isaac:— Rebecca.

G4480 ῥέδα *rheda* of Latin origin; a *rheda,* i.e. four-wheeled *carriage* (*wagon* for riding):— chariot.

G4481 Ῥεμφάν *Rhemphan* by incorrect transliteration for a word of Hebrew origin [H3594]; *Remphan* (i.e. *Kijun*), an Egyptian idol:— Remphan.

G4482 ῥέω *rheō* a primary verb; for some tenses of which a prolonged form

ῥεύω *rheuō* is used; to *flow* (*"run"*, as water) :— flow.

G4483 ῥέω *rheō* for certain tenses of which a prolonged form

ἐρέω *ereō* is used; and both as alternate for *G2036*; perhaps akin (or identical) with *G4482* (through the idea of *pouring* forth); to *utter,* i.e. *speak* or *say:*— command, make, say, speak (of). Compare *G3004*.

G4484 Ῥήγιον *Rhēgion* of Latin origin; *Rhegium,* a place in Italy:— Rhegium.

G4485 ῥῆγμα *rhēgma* from *G4486*; something *torn,* i.e. a *fragment* (by implication and abstractly a *fall*):— ruin.

G4486 ῥήγνυμι *rhēgnymi* or

ῥήσσω *rhēssō* both prolonged forms of

ῥήκω *rhēkō* (which appears only in certain forms, and is itself probably a strengthened form of

ἄγνυμι *agnymi* [see in *G2608*]); to *"break"*, *"wreck"* or *"crack"*, i.e. (especially) to *sunder* (by *separation* of the parts; *G2608* being its intensive [with the preposition in compound], and *G2352* a *shattering* to minute fragments; but not a *reduction* to the constituent particles, like *G3089*) or *disrupt, lacerate;* by implication to *convulse* (with *spasms*); figuratively to *give vent* to joyful emotions:— break (forth), burst, rend, tear.

G4487 ῥῆμα *rhēma* from *G4483*; an *utterance* (individual, collective or specific); by implication a *matter* or *topic* (especially of narration, command or dispute); with a negative *naught* whatever:— evil, nothing, saying, word.

G4488 Ῥησά *Rhēsa* probably of Hebrew origin [apparently for H7509]; *Resa* (i.e. *Rephajah*), an Israelite:— Rhesa.

G4489 ῥήτωρ *rhētōr* from *G4483*; a *speaker,* i.e. (by implication) a forensic *advocate:*— orator.

G4490 ῥητῶς *rhētōs* adverb from a derivative of *G4483*; out-*spokenly,* i.e. *distinctly:*— expressly.

G4491 ῥίζα *rhiza* apparently a primary word; a *"root"* (literal or figurative):— root.

G4492 ῥιζόω *rhizoō* from *G4491*; to *root* (figuratively *become stable*):— root.

G4493 ῥιπή *rhipē* from *G4496*; a *jerk* (of the eye, i.e. [by analogy] an *instant*):— twinkling.

G4494 ῥιπίζω *rhipizō* from a derivative of *G4496* (meaning a *fan* or *bellows*); to *breeze up*, i.e. (by analogy) to *agitate* (into waves):— toss.

G4495 ῥιπτέω *rhipteō* from a derivative of *G4496*; to *toss* up:— cast off.

G4496 ῥίπτω *rhiptō* a primary verb (perhaps rather akin to the base of *G4474*, through the idea of sudden *motion*); to *fling* (properly with a quick *toss*, thus differing from *G906*, which denotes a *deliberate* hurl; and from

τείνω *teinō* [see in *G1614*], which indicates an *extended* projection); by qualification, to *deposit* (as if a load); by extension to *disperse:*— cast (down, out), scatter abroad, throw.

G4497 Ῥοβοάμ *Rhoboam* of Hebrew origin [H7346]; *Roboa'm* (i.e. *Rechabam*), an Israelite:— Roboam.

G4498 Ῥόδη *Rhodē* probably for

ῥοδή *rhodē* (a *rose*); *Rode*, a servant girl:— Rhoda.

G4499 Ῥόδος *Rhodos* probably from

ῥόδον *rhodon* (a *rose*); *Rhodus*, an island of the Mediterranean:— Rhodes.

G4500 ῥοιζηδόν *rhoizēdon* adverb from a derivative of

ῥοῖζος *rhoizos* (a *whir*); *whizzingly*, i.e. *with a crash:*— with a great noise.

G4501 ῥομφαία *rhomphaia* probably of foreign origin; a *saber*, i.e. a long and broad *cutlass* (any *weapon* of the kind, literal or figurative):— sword.

G4502 Ῥουβήν *Rhoubēn* of Hebrew origin [H7205]; *Ruben* (i.e. *Reuben*), an Israelite:— Reuben.

G4503 Ῥούθ *Rhouth* of Hebrew origin [H7827]; *Ruth*, a Moabitess:— Ruth.

G4504 Ῥοῦφος *Rhouphos* of Latin origin; *red; Rufus*, a Christian:— Rufus.

G4505 ῥύμη *rhymē* prolonged from *G4506* in its original sense; an *alley* or *avenue* (as crowded):— lane, street.

G4506 ῥύομαι *rhyomai* middle of an obsolete verb, akin to *G4482* (through the idea of a *current;* compare *G4511*); to *rush* or *draw* (for oneself), i.e. *rescue:*— deliver, deliverer.

G4507 ῥυπαρία *rhyparia* from *G4508*; *dirtiness* (moral):— turpitude.

G4508 ῥυπαρός *rhyparos* from *G4509*; *dirty*, i.e. (relatively) *cheap* or *shabby;* morally *wicked:*— vile.

G4509 ῥύπος *rhypos* of uncertain affinity; *dirt*, i.e. (moral) *depravity:*— filth.

G4510 ῥύπῳ *rhypō* from *G4509*; to *soil*, i.e. (intransitive) to *become dirty* (morally):— be filthy.

G4511 ῥύσις *rhysis* from *G4506* in the sense of its congener *G4482*; a *flux* (of blood):— issue.

G4512 ῥυτίς *rhytis* from *G4506*; a *fold* (as *drawing* together), i.e. a *wrinkle* (especially on the face):— wrinkle.

G4513 Ῥωμαϊκός *Rhōmaikos* from *G4514*; *Roman*, i.e. *Latin:*— Latin.

G4514 Ῥωμαῖος *Rhōmaios* from *G4516*; *Romaean*, i.e. *Roman* (as noun):— Roman, of Rome.

G4515 Ῥωμαϊστί *Rhōmaisti* adverb from a presumed derivative of *G4516*; *Romaïstically*, i.e. *in* the *Latin* language:— Latin.

G4516 Ῥώμη *Rhōmē* from the base of *G4517*; *strength; Roma*, the capital of Italy:— Rome.

G4517 ῥώννυμι *rhōnnymi* prolonged from

ῥώομαι *rhōomai* (to *dart;* probably akin to *G4506*); to *strengthen*, i.e. (impersonal passive) *have health* (as a parting exclamation, *goodbye*):— farewell.

Σ

G4518 σαβαχθανί *sabachthani* of Aramaic origin [H7662 with pronoun suffix]; *thou hast left me; sabachthani* (i.e. *shebakthani*), a cry of distress:— sabachthani.

G4519 σαβαώθ *sabaōth* of Hebrew origin [H6635 in feminine plural]; *armies; sabaoth* (i.e. *tsebaoth*), a military epithet of God:— sabaoth.

G4520 σαββατισμός *sabbatismos* from a derivative of *G4521*; a *"sabbatism"*, i.e. (figuratively) the *repose* of Christianity (as a type of heaven):— rest.

G4521 σάββατον *sabbaton* of Hebrew origin [H7676]; the *Sabbath* (i.e. *Shabbath*), or day of weekly *repose* from secular avocations (also the observance or institution itself); by extension a *week*, i.e. the interval between two Sabbaths; likewise the plural in all the above applications:— sabbath (day), week.

G4522 σαγήνη *sagēnē* from a derivative of

σάττω *sattō* (to *equip*) meaning *furniture*, especially a *pack-saddle* (which in the East is merely a bag of *netted* rope); a *"seine"* for fishing:— net.

G4523 Σαδδουκαῖος *Saddoukaios* probably from *G4524*; a *Sadducaean* (i.e. *Tsadokian*), or follower of a certain heretical Israelite:— Sadducee.

G4524 Σαδώκ *Sadōk* of Hebrew origin [H6659]; *Sadoc* (i.e. *Tsadok*), an Israelite:— Sadoc.

G4525 σαίνω *sainō* akin to *G4579*; to *wag* (as a dog its tail fawningly), i.e. (generally) to *shake* (figuratively *disturb*):— move.

G4526 σάκκος *sakkos* of Hebrew origin [H8242]; *"sack"*-cloth, i.e. *mohair* (the material or garments made of it, worn as a sign of grief):— sackcloth.

G4527 Σαλά *Sala* of Hebrew origin [H7974]; *Sala* (i.e. *Shelach*), a patriarch:— Sala.

G4528 Σαλαθιήλ *Salathiēl* of Hebrew origin [H7597]; *Salathie'l* (i.e. *Shea'ltie'l*), an Israelite:— Salathiel.

G4529 Σαλαμίς *Salamis* probably from *G4535* (from the *surge* on the shore); *Salamis*, a place in Cyprus:— Salamis.

G4530 Σαλείμ *Saleim* probably from the same as *G4531*; *Salim*, a place in Palestine:— Salim.

G4531 σαλεύω *saleuō* from *G4535*; to *waver*, i.e. *agitate, rock, topple* or (by implication) *destroy;* figuratively to *disturb, incite:*— move, shake (together), which can be shaken, which cannot be shaken, stir up.

G4532 Σαλήμ *Salēm* of Hebrew origin [H8004]; *Salem* (i.e. *Shalem*), a place in Palestine:— Salem.

G4533 Σαλμών *Salmōn* of Hebrew origin [H8012]; *Salmon*, an Israelite:— Salmon.

G4534 Σαλμώνη *Salmōnē* perhaps of similar origin to *G4529*; *Salmone*, a place in Crete:— Salmone.

G4535 σάλος *salos* probably from the base of *G4525*; a *vibration*, i.e. (specifically) *billow:*— wave.

G4536 σάλπιγξ *salpinx* perhaps from *G4535* (through the idea of *quavering* or *reverberation*); a *trumpet:*— trump, trumpet.

G4537 σαλπίζω *salpizō* from *G4536*; to *trumpet*, i.e. *sound a blast* (literally or figuratively):— (which are yet to) sound (a trumpet).

G4538 σαλπιστής *salpistēs* from *G4537*; a *trumpeter:*— trumpeter.

G4539 Σαλώμη *Salōmē* probably of Hebrew origin [feminine from H7965]; *Salomè* (i.e. *Shelomah*), an Israelitess:— Salome.

G4540 Σαμάρεια *Samareia* of Hebrew origin [H8111]; *Samaria* (i.e. *Shomeron*), a city and region of Palestine:— Samaria.

G4541 Σαμαρείτης *Samareitēs* from *G4540*; a *Samarite*, i.e. inhabitant of Samaria:— Samaritan.

G4542 Σαμαρεῖτις *Samareitis* feminine of *G4541*; a *Samaritess*, i.e. woman of Samaria:— of Samaria.

G4543 Σαμοθρᾴκη *Samothrakē* from *G4544* and

Θρᾴκη *Thrakē* (*Thrace*); *Samo-thracè* (*Samos of Thrace*), an island in the Mediterranean:— Samothracia.

G4544 Σάμος *Samos* of uncertain affinity; *Samus*, an island of the Mediterranean:— Samos.

G4545 Σαμουήλ *Samouēl* of Hebrew origin [H8050]; *Samuel* (i.e. *Shemuel*), an Israelite:— Samuel.

G4546 Σαμψών *Sampsōn* of Hebrew origin [H8123]; *Sampson* (i.e. *Shimshon*), an Israelite:— Samson.

G4547 σανδάλιον *sandalion* neuter of a derivative of

σάνδαλον *sandalon* (a *"sandal";* of uncertain origin); a *slipper* or *sole-pad:*— sandal.

G4548 σανίς *sanis* of uncertain affinity; a *plank* :— *board.*

G4549 Σαούλ *Saoul* of Hebrew origin [H7586]; *Sau'l* (i.e. *Shau'l*), the Jewish name of *Paul:*— Saul. Compare *G4569*.

G4550 σαπρός *sapros* from *G4595*; *rotten*, i.e. *worthless* (literally or morally):— bad, corrupt. Compare *G4190*.

G4551 Σαπφείρη *Sappheirē* feminine of *G4552*; *Sapphirè*, an Israelitess:— Sapphira.

G4552 σάπφειρος *sappheiros* of Hebrew origin [H5601]; a *"sapphire"* or *lapis-lazuli* gem:— sapphire.

G4553 σαργάνη *sarganē* apparently of Hebrew origin [H8276]; a *basket* (as *interwoven* or *wicker*-work):— basket.

G4554 Σάρδεις *Sardeis* plural of uncertain derivation; *Sardis*, a place in Asia Minor:— Sardis.

G4555 σάρδινος *sardinos* from the same as *G4556*; *sardine* (*G3037* being implied), i.e. a gem, so called:— sardine.

G4556 σάρδιος *sardios* proper adjective from an uncertain base; *sardian* (*G3037* being implied), i.e. (as noun) the gem so called:— sardius.

G4557 σαρδόνυξ *sardonyx* from the base of *G4556* and

ὄνυξ *onyx* (the *nail* of a finger; hence the *"onyx"* stone); a *"sardonyx"*, i.e. the gem so called:— sardonyx.

GRK

G4558 **Σάρεπτα** *Sarepta* of Hebrew origin [H6886]; *Sarepta* (i.e. *Tsarephath*), a place in Palestine:— Sarepta.

G4559 **σαρκικός** *sarkikos* from *G4561*; *pertaining to flesh,* i.e. (by extension) *bodily, temporal,* or (by implication) *animal, unregenerate:*— carnal, fleshly.

G4560 **σάρκινος** *sarkinos* from *G4561*; *similar to flesh,* i.e. (by analogy) *soft:*— fleshly.

G4561 **σάρξ** *sarx* probably from the base of *G4563*; *flesh* (as *stripped* of the skin), i.e. (strictly) the *meat* of an animal (as food), or (by extension) the *body* (as opposed to the soul [or spirit], or as the symbol of what is external, or as the means of kindred), or (by implication) *human nature* (with its frailties [physical or moral] and passions), or (specifically) a *human being* (as such):— carnal, carnally, carnally minded, flesh, fleshly.

G4562 **Σαρούχ** *Sarouch* of Hebrew origin [H8286]; *Saruch* (i.e. *Serug*), a patriarch:— Saruch.

G4563 **σαρόω** *saroō* from a derivative of

σαίρω *sairō* (to *brush* off; akin to *G4951*) meaning a *broom;* to *sweep:*— sweep.

G4564 **Σάρρα** *Sarrha* of Hebrew origin [H8283]; *Sarra* (i.e. *Sarah*), the wife of Abraham:— Sara, Sarah.

G4565 **Σάρων** *Sarōn* of Hebrew origin [H8289]; *Saron* (i.e. *Sharon*), a district of Palestine:— Saron.

G4566 **Σατᾶν** *Satan* of Hebrew origin [H7854]; *Satan,* i.e. the *devil:*— Satan. Compare *G4567*.

G4567 **Σατανᾶς** *Satanas* of Aramaic origin corresponding to *G4566* (with the definite affix); *the accuser,* i.e. the *devil:*— Satan.

G4568 **σάτον** *saton* of Hebrew origin [H5429]; a certain *measure* for things dry:— measure.

G4569 **Σαῦλος** *Saulos* of Hebrew origin, the same as *G4549*; *Saulus* (i.e. *Shau'l*), the Jewish name of *Paul:*— Saul.

G4570 **σβέννυμι** *sbennymi* a prolonged form of an apparently primary verb; to *extinguish* (literally or figuratively):— go out, quench.

G4571 **σέ** *se* accusative singular of *G4771*; *thee:*— thee, thou, thy house.

G4572 **σεαυτοῦ** *seautou* genitive from *G4571* and *G846*; also dative of the same

σεαυτῷ *seautō* and accusative

σεαυτόν *seauton* likewise contracted genitive

σαυτοῦ *sautou* contracted dative

σαυτῷ *sautō* and contracted accusative

σαυτόν *sauton* ; *of* (*with, to*) *thyself:*— thee, thine own self, thy, thou thyself.

G4573 **σεβάζομαι** *sebazomai* middle from a derivative of *G4576*; to *venerate,* i.e. *adore:*— worship.

G4574 **σέβασμα** *sebasma* from *G4573*; something *adored,* i.e. an *object of worship* (god, altar, etc.):— devotion, that is worshipped.

G4575 **σεβαστός** *sebastos* from *G4573*; *venerable* (*august*), i.e. (as noun) a title of the Roman *Emperor,* or (as adjective) *imperial:*— Augustus, Augustusae.

G4576 **σέβομαι** *sebomai* middle of an apparently primary verb; to *revere,* i.e. *adore:*— devout, religious, worship.

G4577 **σειρά** *seira* probably from *G4951* through its congener

εἴρω *eirō* (to *fasten;* akin to *G138*); a *chain* (as *binding* or *drawing*):— chain.

G4578 **σεισμός** *seismos* from *G4579*; a *commotion,* i.e. (of the air) a *gale,* (of the ground) an *earthquake:*— earthquake, tempest.

G4579 **σείω** *seiō* apparently a primary verb; to *rock* (*vibrate,* properly sideways or to and fro), i.e. (generally) to *agitate* (in any direction; cause to *tremble*); figuratively to throw into a *tremor* (of fear or concern):— move, quake, shake.

G4580 **Σεκοῦνδος** *Sekoundos* of Latin origin; *"second"; Secundus,* a Christian:— Secundus.

G4581 **Σελεύκεια** *Seleukeia* from

Σέλευκος *Seleukos* (*Seleucus,* a Syrian king); *Seleuceia,* a place in Syria:— Seleucia.

G4582 **σελήνη** *selēnē* from

σέλας *selas* (*brilliancy;* probably akin to the alternate of *G138*, through the idea of *attractiveness*); the *moon:*— moon.

G4583 **σεληνιάζομαι** *selēniazomai* middle or passive from a presumed derivative of *G4582*; to *be moonstruck,* i.e. *crazy:*— be lunatic.

G4584 **Σεμεΐ** *Semei* of Hebrew origin [H8096]; *Semeï* (i.e. *Shimi*), an Israelite:— Semei.

G4585 **σεμίδαλις** *semidalis* probably of foreign origin; fine wheaten *flour:*— fine flour.

G4586 **σεμνός** *semnos* from *G4576*; *venerable,* i.e. *honorable:*— grave, honest.

G4587 **σεμνότης** *semnotēs* from *G4586*; *venerability,* i.e. *probity:*— gravity, honesty.

G4588 **Σέργιος** *Sergios* of Latin origin; *Sergius,* a Roman:— Sergius.

G4589 **Σήθ** *Sēth* of Hebrew origin [H8352]; *Seth* (i.e. *Sheth*), a patriarch:— Seth.

G4590 **Σήμ** *Sēm* of Hebrew origin [H8035]; *Sem* (i.e. *Shem*), a patriarch:— Sem.

G4591 **σημαίνω** *sēmainō* from

σῆμα *sēma* (a *mark;* of uncertain derivation); to *indicate:*— signify.

G4592 **σημεῖον** *sēmeion* neuter of a presumed derivative of the base of *G4591*; an *indication,* especially ceremonial or supernatural:— miracle, sign, token, wonder.

G4593 **σημειόω** *sēmeioō* from *G4592*; to *distinguish,* i.e. *mark* (for avoidance):— note.

G4594 **σήμερον** *sēmeron* neuter (as adverb) of a presumed compound of the article *G3588* (**τ** changed to **σ**) and *G2250*; on *the* (i.e. *this*) *day* (or *night* current or just passed); generally *now* (i.e. at *present, hitherto*):— this day, today.

G4595 **σήπω** *sēpō* apparently a primary verb; to *putrefy,* i.e. (figuratively) *perish:*— be corrupted.

G4596 **σηρικός** *sērikos* from

Σήρ *Sēr* (an Indian tribe from whom *silk* was procured; hence the name of the *silk-worm*); *Seric,* i.e. *silken* (neuter as noun, a *silky* fabric):— silk.

G4597 **σής** *sēs* apparently of Hebrew origin [H5580]; a *moth:*— moth.

G4598 **σητόβρωτος** *sētobrōtos* from *G4597* and a derivative of *G977*; *moth-eaten:*— motheaten.

G4599 **σθενόω** *sthenoō* from

σθενόω *sthenoō* (bodily *vigor;* probably akin to the base of *G2476*); to *strengthen,* i.e. (figuratively) *confirm* (in spiritual knowledge and power):— strengthen.

G4600 **σιαγών** *siagōn* of uncertain derivation; the *jaw*-bone, i.e. (by implication) the *cheek* or side of the face:— cheek.

G4601 **σιγάω** *sigaō* from *G4602*; to *keep silent* (transitive or intransitive):— keep close (secret, silence), hold peace.

G4602 **σιγή** *sigē* apparently from

σίζω *sizō* (to *hiss,* i.e. *hist* or *hush*); *silence:*— silence. Compare *G4623*.

G4603 **σιδήρεος** *sidēreos* from *G4604*; made *of iron:*— (of) iron.

G4604 **σίδηρος** *sidēros* of uncertain derivation; *iron:*— iron.

G4605 **Σιδών** *Sidōn* of Hebrew origin [H6721]; *Sidon* (i.e. *Tsidon*), a place in Palestine:— Sidon.

G4606 **Σιδώνιος** *Sidōnios* from *G4605*; a *Sidonian,* i.e. inhabitant of Sidon:— of Sidon.

G4607 **σικάριος** *sikarios* of Latin origin; a *daggerman* or *assassin;* a *freebooter* (Jewish *fanatic* outlawed by the Romans):— murderer. Compare *G5406*.

G4608 **σίκερα** *sikera* of Hebrew origin [H7941]; an *intoxicant,* i.e. intensely fermented *liquor:*— strong drink.

G4609 **Σίλας** *Silas* contracted for *G4610*; *Silas,* a Christian:— Silas.

G4610 **Σιλουανός** *Silouanos* of Latin origin; *"silvan"; Silvanus,* a Christian:— Silvanus. Compare *G4609*.

G4611 **Σιλωάμ** *Silōam* of Hebrew origin [H7975]; *Siloa'm* (i.e. *Shiloa'ch*), a pool of Jerusalem:— Siloam.

G4612 **σιμικίνθιον** *simikinthion* of Latin origin; a *semicinctium* or *half-girding,* i.e. narrow covering (*apron*):— apron.

G4613 **Σίμων** *Simōn* of Hebrew origin [H8095]; *Simon* (i.e. *Shimon*), the name of nine Israelites:— Simon. Compare *G4826*.

G4614 **Σινᾶ** *Sina* of Hebrew origin [H5514]; *Sina* (i.e. *Sinai*), a mountain in Arabia:— Sina.

G4615 **σίναπι** *sinapi* perhaps from

σίνομαι *sinomai* (to *hurt,* i.e. *sting*); *mustard* (the plant):— mustard.

G4616 **σινδών** *sindōn* of uncertain (perhaps foreign) origin; *byssos,* i.e. bleached *linen* (the cloth or a garment of it):— (fine) linen (cloth).

G4617 **σινιάζω** *siniazō* from

σινίον *sinion* (a *sieve*); to *riddle* (figuratively):— sift.

G4618 **σιτευτός** *siteutos* from a derivative of *G4621*; *grain-fed,* i.e. *fattened:*— fatted.

G4619 **σιτιστός** *sitistos* from a derivative of *G4621*; *grained,* i.e. *fatted:*— fatling.

G4620 **σιτομέτριον** *sitometrion* from *G4621* and *G3358*; a *grain-measure,* i.e. (by implication) *ration* (*allowance* of food):— portion of meat.

G4621 **σῖτος** *sitos* plural irregular neuter

σῖτα *sita* of uncertain derivation; *grain,* especially *wheat:*— corn, wheat.

G4622 **Σιών** *Siōn* of Hebrew origin [H6726]; *Sion* (i.e. *Tsijon*), a hill of Jerusalem; figuratively the *Church* (militant or triumphant):— Sion.

G4623 **σιωπάω** *siōpaō* from

σιωπή *siōpē* (*silence,* i.e. a *hush;* properly *muteness,* i.e. *involuntary* stillness, or *inability* to speak; and thus differing from *G4602*, which is rather a voluntary *refusal* or *indisposition* to speak, although the terms are often used synonymously); to *be dumb* (but not *deaf* also, like *G2974* properly); figuratively to *be calm* (as *quiet* water):— dumb, (hold) peace.

G4624 σκανδαλίζω *skandalizō* ("scandalize"); from *G4625*; to *entrap*, i.e. *trip* up (figuratively *stumble* [transitive] or *entice* to sin, apostasy or displeasure):— (make to) offend.

G4625 σκάνδαλον *skandalon* ("scandal"); probably from a derivative of *G2578*; a *trap-stick* (*bent* sapling), i.e. *snare* (figuratively *cause* of displeasure or sin):— occasion to fall (of stumbling), offence, thing that offends, stumblingblock.

G4626 σκάπτω *skaptō* apparently a primary verb; to *dig*:— dig.

G4627 σκάφη *skaphē*; a *"skiff"* (as if *dug* out), or *yawl* (carried aboard a large vessel for landing):— boat.

G4628 σκέλος *skelos* apparently from
 σκέλλω *skellō* (to *parch*; through the idea of *leanness*); the *leg* (as *lank*):— leg.

G4629 σκέπασμα *skepasma* from a derivative of
 σκέπας *skepas* (a *covering*; perhaps akin to the base of *G4649* through the idea of *being noticeable*); *clothing*:— raiment.

G4630 Σκευᾶς *Skeuas* apparently of Latin origin; *left-handed*; *Scevas* (i.e. *Scaevus*), an Israelite:— Sceva.

G4631 σκευή *skeuē* from *G4632*; *furniture*, i.e. spare *tackle*:— tackling.

G4632 σκεῦος *skeuos* of uncertain affinity; a *vessel*, *implement*, *equipment* or *apparatus* (literal or figurative [specifically a *wife* as contributing to the usefulness of the husband]):— goods, sail, stuff, vessel.

G4633 σκηνή *skēnē* apparently akin to *G4632* and *G4639*; a *tent* or cloth hut (literal or figurative):— habitation, tabernacle.

G4634 σκηνοπηγία *skēnopēgia* from *G4636* and *G4078*; the *Festival of Tabernacles* (so called from the custom of erecting booths for temporary homes):— tabernacles.

G4635 σκηνοποιός *skēnopoios* from *G4633* and *G4160*; a *manufacturer of tents*:— tentmaker.

G4636 σκῆνος *skēnos* from *G4633*; a *hut* or temporary residence, i.e. (figuratively) the human *body* (as the abode of the spirit):— tabernacle.

G4637 σκηνόω *skēnoō* from *G4636*; to *tent* or *encamp*, i.e. (figuratively) to *occupy* (as a mansion) or (specifically) to *reside* (as God did in the Tabernacle of old, a symbol of protection and communion):— dwell.

G4638 σκήνωμα *skēnōma* from *G4637*; an *encampment*, i.e. (figuratively) the *Temple* (as God's residence), the *body* (as a tenement for the soul) :— tabernacle.

G4639 σκιά *skia* apparently a primary word; *"shade"* or a shadow (literal or figurative [darkness of *error* or an *adumbration*]):— shadow.

G4640 σκιρτάω *skirtaō* akin to
 σκαίρω *skairō* (to *skip*); to *jump*, i.e. sympathetically *move* (as the *quickening* of a fetus):— leap (for joy).

G4641 σκληροκαρδία *sklērokardia* feminine of a compound of *G4642* and *G2588*; *hard-heartedness*, i.e. (specifically) *destitution of* (spiritual) *perception*:— hardness of heart.

G4642 σκληρός *sklēros* from the base of *G4628*; *dry*, i.e. *hard* or *tough* (figuratively *harsh*, *severe*):— fierce, hard.

G4643 σκληρότης *sklērotēs* from *G4642*; *callousness*, i.e. (figuratively) *stubbornness*:— hardness.

G4644 σκληροτράχηλος *sklērotrachēlos* from *G4642* and *G5137*; having a *hard nape*, i.e. (figuratively) *obstinate*:— stiffnecked.

G4645 σκληρύνω *sklērynō* from *G4642*; to *indurate*, i.e. (figuratively) *render stubborn*:— harden.

G4646 σκολιός *skolios* from the base of *G4628*; *warped*, i.e. *winding*; figuratively *perverse*:— crooked, froward, untoward.

G4647 σκόλοψ *skolops* perhaps from the base of *G4628* and *G3700*; *withered* at the *front*, i.e. a *point* or *prickle* (figuratively a bodily *annoyance* or *disability*):— thorn.

G4648 σκοπέω *skopeō* from *G4649*; to take *aim* at (*spy*), i.e. (figuratively) *regard*:— consider, take heed, look at (on), mark. Compare *G3700*.

G4649 σκοπός *skopos* ("scope"); from
 σκέπτομαι *skeptomai* (to *peer* about ["skeptic"]; perhaps akin to *G4626* through the idea of *concealment*; compare *G4629*); a *watch* (*sentry* or *scout*), i.e. (by implication) a *goal*:— mark.

G4650 σκορπίζω *skorpizō* apparently from the same as *G4651* (through the idea of *penetrating*); to *dissipate*, i.e. (figuratively) *put to flight*, *waste*, *be liberal*:— disperse abroad, scatter (abroad).

G4651 σκορπίος *skorpios* probably from an obsolete
 σκέρπω *skerpō* (perhaps strengthened from the base of *G4649* and meaning to *pierce*); a *"scorpion"* (from its *sting*):— scorpion.

G4652 σκοτεινός *skoteinos* from *G4655*; *opaque*, i.e. (figuratively) *benighted*:— dark, full of darkness.

G4653 σκοτία *skotia* from *G4655*; *dimness*, *obscurity* (literal or figurative):— dark, darkness.

G4654 σκοτίζω *skotizō* from *G4655*; to *obscure* (literally or figuratively):— darken.

G4655 σκότος *skotos* from the base of *G4639*; *shadiness*, i.e. *obscurity* (literal or figurative):— darkness.

G4656 σκοτόω *skotoō* from *G4655*; to *obscure* or *blind* (literally or figuratively):— be full of darkness.

G4657 σκύβαλον *skybalon* neuter of a presumed derivative of *G1519* and *G2965* and *G906*; what is *thrown to* the *dogs*, i.e. *refuse* (*ordure*):— dung.

G4658 Σκύθης *Skythēs* probably of foreign origin; a *Scythene* or *Scythian*, i.e. (by implication) a *savage*:— Scythian.

G4659 σκυθρωπός *skythrōpos* from
 σκυθρός *skythros* (*sullen*) and a derivative of *G3700*; *angry of visage*, i.e. *gloomy* or affecting a *mournful* appearance:— of a sad countenance.

G4660 σκύλλω *skyllō* apparently a primary verb; to *flay*, i.e. (figuratively) to *harass*:— trouble (self).

G4661 σκῦλον *skylon* neuter from *G4660*; something *stripped* (as a *hide*), i.e. *booty*:— spoil.

G4662 σκωληκόβρωτος *skōlēkobrōtos* from *G4663* and a derivative of *G977*; *worm-eaten*, i.e. *diseased with maggots*:— eaten of worms.

G4663 σκώληξ *skōlēx* of uncertain derivation; a *grub*, *maggot* or *earth-worm*:— worm.

G4664 σμαράγδινος *smaragdinos* from *G4665*; consisting *of emerald*:— emerald.

G4665 σμάραγδος *smaragdos* of uncertain derivation; the *emerald* or green gem so called:— emerald.

G4666 σμύρνα *smyrna* apparently strengthened for *G3464*; *myrrh*:— myrrh.

G4667 Σμύρνα *Smyrna* the same as *G4666*; *Smyrna*, a place in Asia Minor:— Smyrna.

G4668 Σμυρναῖος *Smyrnaios* from *G4667*; a *Smyrnaean*:— in Smyrna.

G4669 σμυρνίζω *smyrnizō* from *G4667*; to *tincture with myrrh*, i.e. *embitter* (as a narcotic):— mingle with myrrh.

G4670 Σόδομα *Sodoma* plural of Hebrew origin [H5467]; *Sodoma* (i.e. *Sedom*), a place in Palestine:— Sodom.

G4671 σοί *soi* dative of *G4771*; *to thee*:— thee, thine own, thou, thy.

G4672 Σολομών *Solomōn* of Hebrew origin [H8010]; *Solomon* (i.e. *Shelomoh*), the son of David:— Solomon.

G4673 σορός *soros* probably akin to the base of *G4987*; a *funereal receptacle* (*urn*, *coffin*), i.e. (by analogy) a *bier*:— bier.

G4674 σός *sos* from *G4771*; *thine*:— thine (own), thy (friend).

G4675 σοῦ *sou* genitive of *G4771*; *of thee*, *thy*:— home, thee, thine (own), thou, thy.

G4676 σουδάριον *soudarion* of Latin origin; a *sudarium* (*sweat-cloth*), i.e. *towel* (for wiping the perspiration from the face, or binding the face of a corpse):— handkerchief, napkin.

G4677 Σουσάννα *Sousanna* of Hebrew origin [H7799 feminine]; *lily*; *Susannah* (i.e. *Shoshannah*), an Israelitess:— Susanna.

G4678 σοφία *sophia* from *G4680*; *wisdom* (higher or lower, worldly or spiritual):— wisdom.

G4679 σοφίζω *sophizō* from *G4680*; to *render wise*; in a sinister acceptation, to *form "sophisms"*, i.e. *continue plausible error*:— cunningly devised, make wise.

G4680 σοφός *sophos* akin to
 σαφής *saphēs* (*clear*); *wise* (in a most general application):— wise. Compare *G5429*.

G4681 Σπανία *Spania* probably of foreign origin; *Spania*, a region of Europe:— Spain.

G4682 σπαράσσω *sparassō* prolonged from
 σπαίρω *spairō* (to *gasp*; apparently strengthened from *G4685* through the idea of *spasmodic* contraction); to *mangle*, i.e. *convulse* with epilepsy:— rend, tear.

G4683 σπαργανόω *sparganoō* from
 σπάργανον *sparganon* (a *strip*; from a derivative of the base of *G4682* meaning to *strap* or *wrap* with strips); to *swathe* (an infant after the Oriental custom):— wrap in swaddling clothes.

G4684 σπαταλάω *spatalaō* from
 σπατάλη *spatalē* (*luxury*); to *be voluptuous* :— live in pleasure, be wanton.

G4685 σπάω *spaō* a primary verb; to *draw*:— draw (out).

G4686 σπεῖρα *speira* of immediate Latin origin, but ultimately a derivative of *G138* in the sense of its cognate *G1507*; a *coil* (*spira*, "spire"), i.e. (figuratively) a *mass* of men (a Roman military *cohort*; also [by analogy] a *squad* of Levites):— band.

G4687 **σπείρω** *speirō* probably strengthened from *G4685* (through the idea of *extending*); to *scatter,* i.e. *sow* (literally or figuratively):— sow, sower, receive seed.

G4688 **σπεκουλάτωρ** *spekoulatōr* of Latin origin; a *speculator,* i.e. military *scout* (*spy* or [by extension] *life-guardsman*):— executioner.

G4689 **σπένδω** *spendō* apparently a primary verb; to *pour* out as a libation, i.e. (figuratively) to *devote* (one's life or blood, as a sacrifice) (*"spend"*):— (be ready to) be offered.

G4690 **σπέρμα** *sperma* from *G4687*; something *sown,* i.e. *seed* (including the male *"sperm"*); by implication *offspring;* specifically a *remnant* (figuratively as if kept over for planting):— issue, seed.

G4691 **σπερμολόγος** *spermologos* from *G4690* and *G3004*; a *seed-picker* (as the crow), i.e. (figuratively) a *sponger, loafer* (specifically a *gossip* or *trifler* in talk):— babbler.

G4692 **σπεύδω** *speudō* probably strengthened from *G4228*; to *"speed"* ("study"), i.e. *urge* on (diligently or earnestly); by implication to *await* eagerly:— (make, with) haste unto.

G4693 **σπήλαιον** *spēlaion* neuter of a presumed derivative of

σπέος *speos* (a *grotto*); a *cavern;* by implication a *hiding-place* or *resort:*— cave, den.

G4694 **σπιλάς** *spilas* of uncertain derivation; a *ledge* or *reef* of rock in the sea:— spot [*by confusion with G4696*].

G4695 **σπιλόω** *spiloō* from *G4696*; to *stain* or *soil* (literal or figurative):— defile, spot.

G4696 **σπίλος** *spilos* of uncertain derivation; a *stain* or *blemish,* i.e. (figuratively) *defect, disgrace:*— spot.

G4697 **σπλαγχνίζομαι** *splanchnizomai* middle from *G4698*; to have the *bowels* yearn, i.e. (figuratively) *feel sympathy,* to *pity:*— have (be moved with) compassion.

G4698 **σπλάγχνον** *splanchnon* probably strengthened from

σπλήν *splēn* (the *"spleen"*); an *intestine* (plural); figuratively *pity* or *sympathy:*— bowels, inward affection, tender mercy.

G4699 **σπόγγος** *spongos* perhaps of foreign origin; a *"sponge"*:— spunge.

G4700 **σποδός** *spodos* of uncertain derivation; *ashes* :— ashes.

G4701 **σπορά** *spora* from *G4687*; a *sowing,* i.e. (by implication) *parentage:*— seed.

G4702 **σπόριμος** *sporimos* from *G4703*; *sown,* i.e. (neuter plural) a planted *field:*— corn, cornfield.

G4703 **σπόρος** *sporos* from *G4687*; a *scattering* (of seed), i.e. (concretely) *seed* (as sown):— seed (sown).

G4704 **σπουδάζω** *spoudazō* from *G4710*; to *use speed,* i.e. to *make effort, be prompt* or *earnest:*— do (give) diligence, be diligent (forward), endeavour, labour, study.

G4705 **σπουδαῖος** *spoudaios* from *G4710*; *prompt, energetic, earnest:*— diligent.

G4706 **σπουδαιότερον** *spoudaioteron* neuter of *G4707* as adverb; *more earnestly* than others), i.e. very *promptly:*— very diligently.

G4707 **σπουδαιότερος** *spoudaioteros* comparative of *G4705*; *more prompt, more earnest:*— more diligent (forward).

G4708 **σπουδαιοτέρως** *spoudaioterōs* adverb from *G4707*; *more speedily,* i.e. *sooner* than otherwise:— more carefully.

G4709 **σπουδαίως** *spoudaiōs* adverb from *G4705*; *earnestly, promptly:*— diligently, instantly.

G4710 **σπουδή** *spoudē* from *G4692*; *"speed"*, i.e. (by implication) *dispatch, eagerness, earnestness* :— business, (earnest) care, carefulness, diligence, forwardness, haste.

G4711 **σπυρίς** *spyris* from *G4687* (as *woven*); a *hamper* or *lunch-receptacle:*— basket.

G4712 **στάδιον** *stadion* or masculine (in plural)

στάδιος *stadios* from the base of *G2476* (as *fixed*); a *stade* or certain measure of distance; by implication a *stadium* or *race-course:*— furlong, race.

G4713 **στάμνος** *stamnos* from the base of *G2476* (as *stationary*); a *jar* or earthen *tank:*— pot.

G4714 **στάσις** *stasis* from the base of *G2476*; a *standing* (properly the act), i.e. (by analogy) *position* (*existence*); by implication a popular *uprising;* figuratively *controversy:*— dissension, insurrection, standing, uproar.

G4715 **στατήρ** *statēr* from the base of *G2746*; a *stander* (*standard* of value), i.e. (specifically) a *stater* or certain coin:— piece of money.

G4716 **σταυρός** *stauros* from the base of *G2476*; a *stake* or *post* (as *set* upright), i.e. (specifically) a *pole* or *cross* (as an instrument of capital punishment); figuratively *exposure to death,* i.e. *self-denial;* by implication the *atonement* of Christ:— cross.

G4717 **σταυρόω** *stauroō* from *G4716*; to *impale* on the cross; figuratively to *extinguish* (*subdue*) passion or selfishness:— crucify.

G4718 **σταφυλή** *staphylē* probably from the base of *G4735*; a *cluster* of grapes (as if *intertwined*):— grapes.

G4719 **στάχυς** *stachys* from the base of *G2476*; a *head* of grain (as *standing* out from the stalk):— ear (of corn).

G4720 **Στάχυς** *Stachys* the same as *G4719*; *Stachys,* a Christian:— Stachys.

G4721 **στέγη** *stegē* strengthened from a primary

τέγος *tegos* (a *"thatch"* or *"deck"* of a building); a *roof:*— roof.

G4722 **στέγω** *stegō* from *G4721*; to *roof* over, i.e. (figuratively) to *cover* with silence (*endure* patiently):— bear, forbear, suffer.

G4723 **στεῖρος** *steiros* a contracted from *G4731* (as *stiff* and *unnatural*); *"sterile"*:— barren.

G4724 **στέλλω** *stellō* probably strengthened from the base of *G2476*; properly to *set* fast (*"stall"*), i.e. (figuratively) to *repress* (reflexive *abstain* from associating with):— avoid, withdraw self.

G4725 **στέμμα** *stemma* from the base of *G4735*; a *wreath* for show:— garland.

G4726 **στεναγμός** *stenagmos* from *G4727*; a *sigh* :— groaning.

G4727 **στενάζω** *stenazō* from *G4728*; to *make* (intransitive *be*) *in straits,* i.e. (by implication) to *sigh, murmur, pray* inaudibly:— with grief, groan, grudge, sigh.

G4728 **στενός** *stenos* probably from the base of *G2476*; *narrow* (from obstacles *standing* close about) :— strait.

G4729 **στενοχωρέω** *stenochōreō* from the same as *G4730*; to *hem* in closely, i.e. (figuratively) *cramp:*— distress, straiten.

G4730 **στενοχωρία** *stenochōria* from a compound of *G4728* and *G5561*; *narrowness of room,* i.e. (figuratively) *calamity:*— anguish, distress.

G4731 **στερεός** *stereos* from *G2476*; *stiff,* i.e. *solid, stable* (literally or figuratively):— stedfast, strong, sure.

G4732 **στερεόω** *stereoō* from *G4731*; to *solidify,* i.e. *confirm* (literally or figuratively):— establish, receive strength, make strong.

G4733 **στερέωμα** *stereōma* from *G4732*; something *established,* i.e. (abstract) *confirmation* (*stability*):— stedfastness.

G4734 **Στεφανᾶς** *Stephanas* probably contraction for

στεφανωτός *stephanōtos* (*crowned;* from *G4737*); *Stephanas,* a Christian:— Stephanas.

G4735 **στέφανος** *stephanos* from an apparently primary

στέφω *stephō* (to *twine* or *wreathe*); a *chaplet* (as a badge of royalty, a prize in the public games or a symbol of honor generally; but more conspicuous and elaborate than the simple *fillet, G1238*), literally or figuratively:— crown.

G4736 **Στέφανος** *Stephanos* the same as *G4735*; *Stephanus,* a Christian:— Stephen.

G4737 **στεφανόω** *stephanoō* from *G4735*; to *adorn with* an honorary *wreath* (literally or figuratively) :— crown.

G4738 **στῆθος** *stēthos* from *G2476* (as *standing* prominently); the (entire external) *bosom,* i.e. *chest:*— breast.

G4739 **στήκω** *stēkō* from the perfect tense of *G2476*; to *be stationary,* i.e. (figuratively) to *persevere:*— stand (fast).

G4740 **στηριγμός** *stērigmos* from *G4741*; *stability* (figurative):— stedfastness.

G4741 **στηρίζω** *stērizō* from a presumed derivative of *G2476* (like *G4731*); to *set fast,* i.e. (literally) to *turn resolutely* in a certain direction, or (figuratively) to *confirm:*— fix, stablish, establish, stedfastly set, strengthen.

G4742 **στίγμα** *stigma* from a primary

στίζω *stizō* (to *"stick"*, i.e. *prick*); a *mark* incised or punched (for recognition of ownership), i.e. (figuratively) *scar* of service:— mark.

G4743 **στιγμή** *stigmē* feminine of *G4742*; a *point* of time, i.e. an *instant:*— moment.

G4744 **στίλβω** *stilbō* apparently a primary verb; to *gleam,* i.e. *flash* intensely:— shining.

G4745 **στοά** *stoa* probably from *G2476*; a *colonnade* or interior *piazza:*— porch.

G4746 **στοιβάς** *stoibas* from a primary

στείβω *steibō* (to *"step"* or *"stamp"*); a *spread* (as if *tramped* flat) of loose materials for a couch, i.e. (by implication) a *bough* of a tree so employed:— branch.

G4747 **στοιχεῖον** *stoicheion* neuter of a presumed derivative of the base of *G4748*; something *orderly* in arrangement, i.e. (by implication) a *serial* (*basal,* *fundamental, initial*) constituent (literal), proposition (figurative):— element, principle, rudiment.

G4748 στοιχέω *stoicheō* from a derivative of
στείχω *steichō* (to *range* in regular line); to *march* in (military) rank (*keep step*), i.e. (figuratively) to *conform* to virtue and piety:— walk (orderly).

G4749 στολή *stolē* from *G4724*; *equipment*, i.e. (specifically) a *"stole"* or long-fitting *gown* (as a mark of dignity):— long clothing (garment), (long) robe.

G4750 στόμα *stoma* probably strengthened from a presumed derivative of the base of *G5114*; the *mouth* (as if a *gash* in the face); by implication *language* (and its relations); figuratively an *opening* (in the earth); specifically the *front* or *edge* (of a weapon):— edge, face, mouth.

G4751 στόμαχος *stomachos* from *G4750*; an *orifice* (the *gullet*), i.e. (specifically) the *"stomach"*:— stomach.

G4752 στρατεία *strateia* from *G4754*; military *service*, i.e. (figuratively) the apostolic *career* (as one of hardship and danger):— warfare.

G4753 στράτευμα *strateuma* from *G4754*; an *armament*, i.e. (by implication) a body of *troops* (more or less extensive or systematic):— army, soldier, man of war.

G4754 στρατεύομαι *strateuomai* middle from the base of *G4756*; to *serve* in a military campaign; figuratively to *execute the apostolate* (with its arduous duties and functions), to *contend* with carnal inclinations:— soldier, (go to) war, warfare.

G4755 στρατηγός *stratēgos* from the base of *G4756* and *G71* or *G2233*; a *general*, i.e. (by implication or analogy) a (military) *governor* (*praetor*), the *chief* (*prefect*) of the (Levitical) temple-wardens:— captain, magistrate.

G4756 στρατιά *stratia* feminine of a derivative of
στρατός *stratos* (an *army*; from the base of *G4766*, as *encamped*); *camp-likeness*, i.e. an *army*, i.e. (figuratively) the *angels*, the celestial *luminaries*:— host.

G4757 στρατιώτης *stratiōtēs* from a presumed derivative of the same as *G4756*; a *camper out*, i.e. a (common) *warrior* (literal or figurative):— soldier.

G4758 στρατολογέω *stratologeō* from a compound of the base of *G4756* and *G3004* (in its original sense); to *gather* (or *select*) as a *warrior*, i.e. *enlist* in the army:— choose to be a soldier.

G4759 στρατοπεδάρχης *stratopedarchēs* from *G4760* and *G757*; a *ruler of an army*, i.e. (specifically) a Praetorian *prefect*:— captain of the guard.

G4760 στρατόπεδον *stratopedon* from the base of *G4756* and the same as *G3977*; a *camping-ground*, i.e. (by implication) a body of *troops*:— army.

G4761 στρεβλόω *strebloō* from a derivative of *G4762*; to *wrench*, i.e. (specifically) to *torture* (by the rack), but only figuratively to *pervert*:— wrest.

G4762 στρέφω *strephō* strengthened from the base of *G5157*; to *twist*, i.e. *turn* quite around or *reverse* (literally or figuratively):— convert, turn (again, back again, self, self about).

G4763 στρηνιάω *strēniaō* from a presumed derivative of *G4764*; to *be luxurious*:— live deliciously.

G4764 στρῆνος *strēnos* akin to *G4731*; a *"straining"*, *"strenuousness"* or "strength", i.e. (figuratively) *luxury* (*voluptuousness*):— delicacy.

G4765 στρουθίον *strouthion* diminutive of
στρουθός *strouthos* (a *sparrow*); a *little sparrow*:— sparrow.

G4766 στρώννυμι *strōnnymi* or simpler
στρωννύω *strōnnyō* prolonged from a still simpler
στρόω *stroō* (used only as an alternate in certain tenses; probably akin to *G4731* through the idea of *positing*); to *"strew"*, i.e. *spread* (as a carpet or couch):— make bed, furnish, spread, strew.

G4767 στυγητός *stygētos* from a derivative of an obsolete apparently primary
στύγω *stygō* (to *hate*); *hated*, i.e. *odious*:— hateful.

G4768 στυγνάζω *stygnazō* from the same as *G4767*; to *render gloomy*, i.e. (by implication) *glower* (*be overcast* with clouds, or *somberness* of speech):— lower, be sad.

G4769 στῦλος *stylos* from
στύω *styō* (to *stiffen*; properly akin to the base of *G2476*); a *post* (*"style"*), i.e. (figuratively) *support*:— pillar.

G4770 Στωϊκός *Stōikos* from *G4745*; a *"Stoïc"* (as occupying a particular porch in Athens), i.e. adherent of a certain philosophy:— Stoick.

G4771 σύ *sy* the personal pronoun of the second person singular; *thou*:— thou. See also *G4571*, *G4671*, *G4675*; and for the plural *G5209*, *G5210*, *G5213*, *G5216*.

G4772 συγγένεια *syngeneia* from *G4773*; *relationship*, i.e. (concretely) *relatives*:— kindred.

G4773 συγγενής *syngenēs* from *G4862* and *G1085*; a *relative* (by blood); by extension a fellow *countryman*:— cousin, kin, kinsfolk, kinsman.

G4774 συγγνώμη *syngnōmē* from a compound of *G4862* and *G1097*; *fellow knowledge*, i.e. *concession*:— permission.

G4775 συγκάθημαι *synkathēmai* from *G4862* and *G2521*; to *seat oneself* in company *with*:— sit with.

G4776 συγκαθίζω *synkathizō* from *G4862* and *G2523*; to *give* (or *take*) *a seat* in company *with*:— (make) sit (down) together.

G4777 συγκακοπαθέω *synkakopatheō* from *G4862* and *G2553*; to *suffer hardship* in company *with*:— be partaker of afflictions.

G4778 συγκακουχέω *synkakoucheō* from *G4862* and *G2558*; to *maltreat* in company *with*, i.e. (passive) *endure persecution together*:— suffer affliction with.

G4779 συγκαλέω *synkaleō* from *G4862* and *G2564*; to *convoke*:— call together.

G4780 συγκαλύπτω *synkalyptō* from *G4862* and *G2572*; to *conceal altogether*:— cover.

G4781 συγκάμπτω *synkamptō* from *G4862* and *G2578*; to *bend together*, i.e. (figuratively) to *afflict*:— bow down.

G4782 συγκαταβαίνω *synkatabainō* from *G4862* and *G2597*; to *descend* in company *with*:— go down with.

G4783 συγκατάθεσις *synkatathesis* from *G4784*; a *deposition* (of sentiment) in company *with*, i.e. (figuratively) *accord* with:— agreement.

G4784 συγκατατίθεμαι *synkatatithemai* middle from *G4862* and *G2698*; to *deposit* (one's vote or opinion) in company *with*, i.e. (figuratively) to *accord* with:— consent.

G4785 συγκαταψηφίζω *synkatapsēphizō* from *G4862* and a compound of *G2596* and *G5585*; to *count down* in company *with*, i.e. *enroll among*:— number with.

G4786 συγκεράννυμι *synkerannymi* from *G4862* and *G2767*; to *commingle*, i.e. (figuratively) to *combine* or *assimilate*:— mix with, temper together.

G4787 συγκινέω *synkineō* from *G4682* and *G2795*; to *move together*, i.e. (specifically) to *excite* as a mass (to sedition):— stir up.

G4788 συγκλείω *synkleiō* from *G4862* and *G2808*; to *shut together*, i.e. *include* or (figuratively) *embrace* in a common subjection to:— conclude, inclose, shut up.

G4789 συγκληρονόμος *synklēronomos* from *G4862* and *G2818*; a *co-heir*, i.e. (by analogy) *participant in common*:— fellow heir, joint-heir, heir together, heir with.

G4790 συγκοινωνέω *synkoinōneō* from *G4862* and *G2841*; to *share* in company *with*, i.e. *co-participate* in :— communicate (have fellowship) with, be partaker of.

G4791 συγκοινωνός *synkoinōnos* from *G4862* and *G2844*; a *co-participant*:— companion, partake, partaker (with).

G4792 συγκομίζω *synkomizō* from *G4862* and *G2865*; to *convey together*, i.e. *collect* or *bear* away in company *with* others:— carry.

G4793 συγκρίνω *synkrinō* from *G4862* and *G2919*; to *judge* of one thing in connection *with* another, i.e. *combine* (spiritual ideas with appropriate expressions) or *collate* (one person with another by way of contrast or resemblance):— compare among (with).

G4794 συγκύπτω *synkyptō* from *G4862* and *G2955*; to *stoop altogether*, i.e. *be completely overcome* by:— bow together.

G4795 συγκυρία *synkyria* from a compound of *G4862* and
κυρέω *kyreō* (to *light* or *happen*; from the base of *G2962*); *concurrence*, i.e. *accident*:— chance.

G4796 συγχαίρω *synchairō* from *G4862* and *G5463*; to *sympathize in gladness, congratulate*:— rejoice in (with).

G4797 συγχέω *syncheō* or
συγχύνω *synchynō* from *G4862* and
χέω *cheō* (to *pour*) or its alternate; to *commingle* promiscuously, i.e. (figuratively) to *throw* (an assembly) *into disorder*, to *perplex* (the mind):— confound, confuse, stir up, be in an uproar.

G4798 συγχράομαι *synchraomai* from *G4862* and *G5530*; to *use jointly*, i.e. (by implication) to *hold intercourse in common*:— have dealings with.

G4799 σύγχυσις *synchysis* from *G4797*; *commixture*, i.e. (figuratively) riotous *disturbance*:— confusion.

G4800 συζάω *syzaō* from *G4862* and *G2198*; to continue to *live* in common *with*, i.e. *co-survive* (literally or figuratively):— live with.

G4801 συζεύγνυμι *syzeugnymi* from *G4862* and the base of *G2201*; to *yoke together*, i.e. (figuratively) *conjoin* (in marriage):— join together.

G4802 συζητέω *syzēteō* from *G4862* and *G2212*; to investigate *jointly*, i.e. *discuss, controvert, cavil*:— dispute (with), inquire, question (with), reason (together).

G4803 **συζήτησις** *syzētēsis* from *G4802*; *mutual questioning,* i.e. *discussion:*— disputation, disputing, reasoning.

G4804 **συζητητής** *syzētētēs* from *G4802*; a *disputant,* i.e. *sophist:*— disputer.

G4805 **σύζυγος** *syzygos* from *G4801*; *co-yoked,* i.e. (figuratively) as noun, a *colleague;* probably rather as proper name; *Syzygus,* a Christian:— yokefellow.

G4806 **συζωοποιέω** *syzōopoieō* from *G4862* and *G2227*; to *reanimate conjointly* with (figuratively) :— quicken together with.

G4807 **συκάμινος** *sykaminos* of Hebrew origin [H8256] in imitation of *G4809*; a *sycamore*-fig tree:— sycamine tree.

G4808 **συκῆ** *sykē* from *G4810*; a *fig-tree:*— fig tree.

G4809 **συκομωραία** *sykomōraia* from *G4810* and **μόρον** *moron* (the *mulberry*); the *"sycamore"*-fig tree:— sycamore tree. Compare *G4807*.

G4810 **σῦκον** *sykon* apparently a primary word; a *fig:*— figurative.

G4811 **συκοφαντέω** *sykophanteō* from a compound of *G4810* and a derivative of *G5316*; to *be a fig-informer* (reporter of the law forbidding the exportation of figs from Greece), *"sycophant"*, i.e. (generally and by extension) to *defraud* (*exact* unlawfully, *extort*):— accuse falsely, take by false accusation.

G4812 **συλαγωγέω** *sylagōgeō* from the base of *G4813* and (the reduplicated form of) *G71*; to *lead* away as *booty,* i.e. (figuratively) *seduce:*— spoil.

G4813 **συλάω** *sylaō* from a derivative of **σύλλω** *syllō* (to *strip;* probably akin to *G138*; compare *G4661*); to *despoil:*— rob.

G4814 **συλλαλέω** *syllaleō* from *G4862* and *G2980*; to *talk together,* i.e. *converse:*— commune (confer, talk) with, speak among.

G4815 **συλλαμβάνω** *syllambanō* from *G4862* and *G2983*; to *clasp,* i.e. *seize* (*arrest, capture*); specifically to *conceive* (literally or figuratively); by implication to *aid:*— catch, conceive, help, take.

G4816 **συλλέγω** *syllegō* from *G4862* and *G3004* in its original sense; to *collect:*— gather (together, up).

G4817 **συλλογίζομαι** *syllogizomai* from *G4862* and *G3049*; to *reckon together* (with oneself), i.e. *deliberate:*— reason with.

G4818 **συλλυπέω** *syllypeō* from *G4862* and *G3076*; to *afflict jointly,* i.e. (passive) *sorrow at* (on account of) some one:— be grieved.

G4819 **συμβαίνω** *symbainō* from *G4862* and the base of *G939*; to *walk* (figuratively *transpire*) *together,* i.e. *concur* (*take place*):— be, befall, happen (unto).

G4820 **συμβάλλω** *symballō* from *G4862* and *G906*; to *combine,* i.e. (in speaking) to *converse, consult, dispute,* (mentally) to *consider,* (by implication) to *aid,* (personally) to *join, attack:*— confer, encounter, help, make, meet with, ponder.

G4821 **συμβασιλεύω** *symbasileuō* from *G4862* and *G936*; to *be co-regent* (figuratively):— reign with.

G4822 **συμβιβάζω** *symbibazō* from *G4862* and **βιβάζω** *bibazō* (to *force;* causative [by reduplication] of the base of *G939*); to *drive together,* i.e. *unite* (in association or affection), (mentally) to *infer, show, teach:*— compact, assuredly gather, intrust, knit together, prove.

G4823 **συμβουλεύω** *symbouleuō* from *G4862* and *G1011*; to *give* (or *take*) *advice jointly,* i.e. *recommend, deliberate* or *determine:*— consult, (give, take) counsel (together).

G4824 **συμβούλιον** *symboulion* neuter of a presumed derivative of *G4825*; *advisement;* specifically a *deliberative* body, i.e. the provincial *assessors* or lay-court:— consultation, counsel, council.

G4825 **σύμβουλος** *symboulos* from *G4862* and *G1012*; *one who consults,* i.e. an *adviser:*— counsellor.

G4826 **Συμεών** *Symeōn* from the same as Greek *G4613*; *Symeon* (i.e. *Shimon*), the name of five Israelites:— Simeon, Simon.

G4827 **συμμαθητής** *symmathētēs* from a compound of *G4862* and *G3129*; a *co-learner* (of Christianity):— fellowdisciple.

G4828 **συμμαρτυρέω** *symmartyreō* from *G4862* and *G3140*; to *testify jointly,* i.e. *corroborate* by (concurrent) evidence:— testify unto, (also) bear witness (with).

G4829 **συμμερίζομαι** *symmerizomai* middle from *G4862* and *G3307*; to *share jointly,* i.e. *participate* in:— be partaker with.

G4830 **συμμέτοχος** *symmetochos* from *G4862* and *G3353*; a *co-participant:*— partaker.

G4831 **συμμιμητής** *symmimētēs* from a presumed compound of *G4862* and *G3401*; a *co-imitator,* i.e. *fellow votary:*— follower together.

G4832 **σύμμορφος** *symmorphos* from *G4862* and *G3444*; *jointly formed,* i.e. (figuratively) *similar:*— conformed to, fashioned like unto.

G4833 **συμμορφόω** *symmorphoō* from *G4832*; to *render like,* i.e. (figuratively) to *assimilate:*— make conformable unto.

G4834 **συμπαθέω** *sympatheō* from *G4835*; to *feel "sympathy"* with, i.e. (by implication) to *commiserate:*— have compassion, be touched with a feeling of.

G4835 **συμπαθής** *sympathēs* from *G4841*; *having a fellow-feeling* (*"sympathetic"*), i.e. (by implication) *mutually commiserative:*— having compassion one of another.

G4836 **συμπαραγίνομαι** *symparaginomai* from *G4862* and *G3854*; to *be present together,* i.e. to *convene;* by implication to *appear in aid:*— come together, stand with.

G4837 **συμπαρακαλέω** *symparakaleō* from *G4862* and *G3870*; to *console jointly:*— comfort together.

G4838 **συμπαραλαμβάνω** *symparalambanō* from *G4862* and *G3880*; to *take along in company:*— take with.

G4839 **συμπαραμένω** *symparamenō* from *G4862* and *G3887*; to *remain in company,* i.e. *still live:*— continue with.

G4840 **συμπάρειμι** *sympareimi* from *G4862* and *G3918*; to *be at hand together,* i.e. *now present:*— be here present with.

G4841 **συμπάσχω** *sympaschō* from *G4862* and *G3958* (including its alternate); to *experience pain jointly* or of the *same kind* (specifically *persecution;* to *"sympathize"*):— suffer with.

G4842 **συμπέμπω** *sympempō* from *G4862* and *G3992*; to *dispatch in company:*— send with.

G4843 **συμπεριλαμβάνω** *symperilambanō* from *G4862* and a compound of *G4012* and *G2983*; to *take by inclosing altogether,* i.e. *earnestly throw the arms about one:*— embrace.

G4844 **συμπίνω** *sympinō* from *G4862* and *G4095*; to *partake a beverage in company:*— drink with.

G4845 **συμπληρόω** *symplēroō* from *G4862* and *G4137*; to *fill completely,* i.e. (of space) to *swamp* (a boat), or (of time) to *accomplish* (passive be *complete*):— (fully) come, fill up.

G4846 **συμπνίγω** *sympnigō* from *G4862* and *G4155*; to *strangle completely,* i.e. (literally) to *drown,* or (figuratively) to *crowd:*— choke, throng.

G4847 **συμπολίτης** *sympolitēs* from *G4862* and *G4177*; a *native of the same town,* i.e. (figuratively) *co-religionist* (*fellow-Christian*):— fellowcitizen.

G4848 **συμπορεύομαι** *symporeuomai* from *G4862* and *G4198*; to *journey together;* by implication to *assemble:*— go with, resort.

G4849 **συμπόσιον** *symposion* neuter of a derivative of the alternate of *G4844*; a *drinking*-party (*"symposium"*), i.e. (by extension) a *room* of guests :— company.

G4850 **συμπρεσβύτερος** *sympresbyteros* from *G4862* and *G4245*; a *co-presbyter:*— presbyter, also an elder.

G4851 **συμφέρω** *sympherō* from *G4862* and *G5342* (including its alternate); to *bear together* (*contribute*), i.e. (literally) to *collect,* or (figuratively) to *conduce;* especially (neuter participle as noun) *advantage:*— be better for, bring together, be expedient (for), be good, profit, be profitable for.

G4852 **σύμφημι** *symphēmi* from *G4862* and *G5346*; to *say jointly,* i.e. *assent to:*— consent unto.

G4853 **συμφυλέτης** *symphyletēs* from *G4862* and a derivative of *G5443*; a *co-tribesman,* i.e. *native of the same country:*— countryman.

G4854 **σύμφυτος** *symphytos* from *G4862* and a derivative of *G5453*; *grown* along *with* (*connate*), i.e. (figuratively) closely *united* to:— planted together.

G4855 **συμφύω** *symphyō* from *G4862* and *G5453*; passive to *grow jointly:*— spring up with.

G4856 **συμφωνέω** *symphōneō* from *G4859*; to be *harmonious,* i.e. (figuratively) to *accord* (*be suitable, concur*) or *stipulate* (by compact):— agree (together, with).

G4857 **συμφώνησις** *symphōnēsis* from *G4856*; *accordance:*— concord.

G4858 **συμφωνία** *symphōnia* from *G4859*; *unison* of sound (*"symphony"*), i.e. a *concert* of instruments (harmonious *note*):— music.

G4859 **σύμφωνος** *symphōnos* from *G4862* and *G5456*; *sounding together* (*alike*), i.e. (figuratively) *accordant* (neuter as noun, *agreement*):— consent.

G4860 **συμψηφίζω** *sympsēphizō* from *G4862* and *G5585*; to *compute jointly:*— reckon.

G4861 **σύμψυχος** *sympsychos* from *G4862* and *G5590*; *co-spirited,* i.e. *similar in sentiment:*— like-minded.

G4862 **σύν** *syn* a primary preposition denoting *union; with* or *together* (but much closer than *G3326* or *G3844*), i.e. by association, companionship, process, resemblance, possession, instrumentality, addition, etc. In compounds it has similar applications, including *completeness:*— beside, with.

G4863 **συνάγω** *synagō* from *G4862* and *G71*; to *lead together,* i.e. *collect* or *convene;* specifically to *entertain* (hospitably):— accompany, assemble (selves, together), bestow, come together, gather (selves together, up, together), lead into, resort, take in.

G4864 **συναγωγή** *synagōgē* from (the reduplicated form of) *G4863*; an *assemblage* of persons; specifically a Jewish *"synagogue"* (the meeting or the place); by analogy a Christian *church:*— assembly, congregation, synagogue.

G4865 **συναγωνίζομαι** *synagōnizomai* from *G4862* and *G75*; to *struggle* in company *with,* i.e. (figuratively) to *be a partner* (*assistant*):— strive together with.

G4866 **συναθλέω** *synathleō* from *G4862* and *G118*; to *wrestle* in company *with,* i.e. (figuratively) to *seek jointly:*— labour with, strive together for.

G4867 **συναθροίζω** *synathroizō* from *G4862* and **ἀθροίζω** *athroizō* (to *hoard*); to *convene:*— call (gather) together.

G4868 **συναίρω** *synairō* from *G4862* and *G142*; to *make up together,* i.e. (figuratively) to *compute* (an account):— reckon, take.

G4869 **συναιχμάλωτος** *synaichmalōtos* from *G4862* and *G164*; a *co-captive:*— fellowprisoner.

G4870 **συνακολουθέω** *synakoloutheō* from *G4862* and *G190*; to *accompany:*— follow.

G4871 **συναλίζω** *synalizō* from *G4862* and **ἁλίζω** *halizō* (to *throng*); to *accumulate,* i.e. *convene:*— assemble together.

G4872 **συναναβαίνω** *synanabainō* from *G4862* and *G305*; to *ascend* in company *with:*— come up with.

G4873 **συνανάκειμαι** *synanakeimai* from *G4862* and *G345*; to *recline* in company *with* (at a meal):— sit (down, at the table, together) with (at meat).

G4874 **συναναμίγνυμι** *synanamignymi* from *G4862* and a compound of *G303* and *G3396*; to *mix up together,* i.e. (figuratively) *associate with:*— (have, keep) company (with).

G4875 **συναναπαύομαι** *synanapauomai* middle from *G4862* and *G373*; to *recruit oneself* in company *with:*— refresh with.

G4876 **συναντάω** *synantaō* from *G4862* and a derivative of *G473*; to *meet with;* figuratively to *occur* :— befall, meet.

G4877 **συνάντησις** *synantēsis* from *G4876*; a *meeting with:*— meet.

G4878 **συναντιλαμβάνομαι** *synantilambanomai* from *G4862* and *G482*; to *take* hold of *opposite together,* i.e. *co-operate* (*assist*):— help.

G4879 **συναπάγω** *synapagō* from *G4862* and *G520*; to *take off together,* i.e. *transport with* (*seduce,* passive *yield*):— carry (lead) away with, condescend.

G4880 **συναποθνήσκω** *synapothnēskō* from *G4862* and *G599*; to *decease* (literally) in company *with,* or (figuratively) similarly *to:*— be dead (die) with.

G4881 **συναπόλλυμι** *synapollymi* from *G4862* and *G622*; to *destroy* (middle or passive *be slain*) in company *with:*— perish with.

G4882 **συναποστέλλω** *synapostellō* from *G4862* and *G649*; to *dispatch* (on an errand) in company *with:*— send with.

G4883 **συναρμολογέω** *synarmologeō* from *G4862* and a derivative of a compound of *G719* and *G3004* (in its original sense of *laying*); to *render close-jointed together,* i.e. *organize compactly:*— be fitly framed (joined) together.

G4884 **συναρπάζω** *synarpazō* from *G4862* and *G726*; to *snatch together,* i.e. *seize:*— catch.

G4885 **συναυξάνω** *synauxanō* from *G4862* and *G837*; to *increase* (*grow up*) *together:*— grow together.

G4886 **σύνδεσμος** *syndesmos* from *G4862* and *G1199*; a *joint tie,* i.e. *ligament,* (figuratively) *uniting principle, control:*— band, bond.

G4887 **συνδέω** *syndeō* from *G4862* and *G1210*; to *bind with,* i.e. (passive) *be a fellow-prisoner* (figuratively):— be bound with.

G4888 **συνδοξάζω** *syndoxazō* from *G4862* and *G1392*; to *exalt* to dignity in company (i.e. *similarly*) *with:*— glorify together.

G4889 **σύνδουλος** *syndoulos* from *G4862* and *G1401*; a *co-slave,* i.e. *servitor* or *ministrant of the same master* (human or divine):— fellowservant.

G4890 **συνδρομή** *syndromē* from (the alternate of) *G4936*; a *running together,* i.e. (riotous) *concourse:*— run together.

G4891 **συνεγείρω** *synegeirō* from *G4862* and *G1453*; to *rouse* (from death) in company *with,* i.e. (figuratively) to *revivify* (spiritually) in resemblance to:— raise up together, rise with.

G4892 **συνέδριον** *synedrion* neuter of a presumed derivative of a compound of *G4862* and the base of *G1476*; a *joint session,* i.e. (specifically) the Jewish *Sanhedrin;* by analogy a subordinate *tribunal:*— council.

G4893 **συνείδησις** *syneidēsis* from a prolonged form of *G4894*; *co-perception,* i.e. moral *consciousness:*— conscience.

G4894 **συνείδω** *syneidō* from *G4862* and *G1492*; to *see completely;* used (like its primary) only in two past tenses, respectively meaning to *understand* or *become aware,* and to *be conscious* or (clandestinely) *informed of:*— consider, know, be privy, be ware of.

G4895 **σύνειμι** *syneimi* from *G4862* and *G1510* (including its various inflections); to *be* in company *with,* i.e. *present* at the time:— be with.

G4896 **σύνειμι** *syneimi* from *G4862* and **εἶμι** *eimi* (to *go*); to *assemble:*— gather together.

G4897 **συνεισέρχομαι** *syneiserchomai* from *G4862* and *G1525*; to *enter* in company *with:*— go in with, go with into.

G4898 **συνέκδημος** *synekdēmos* from *G4862* and the base of *G1553*; a *co-absentee* from home, i.e. *fellow-traveler:*— companion in travel, travel with.

G4899 **συνεκλεκτός** *syneklektos* from a compound of *G4862* and *G1586*; *chosen* in company *with,* i.e. *co-elect* (*fellow Christian*):— elected together with.

G4900 **συνελαύνω** *synelaunō* from *G4862* and *G1643*; to *drive together,* i.e. (figuratively) *exhort* (to reconciliation):— set at one again.

G4901 **συνεπιμαρτυρέω** *synepimartyreō* from *G4862* and *G1957*; to *testify further jointly,* i.e. *unite in adding evidence:*— also bear witness.

G4902 **συνέπομαι** *synepomai* middle from *G4862* and a primary **ἕπω** *hepō* (to *follow*); to *attend* (*travel*) in company *with:*— accompany.

G4903 **συνεργέω** *synergeō* from *G4904*; to *be a fellow-worker,* i.e. *co-operate:*— help (work) with, work together, worker together.

G4904 **συνεργός** *synergos* from a presumed compound of *G4862* and the base of *G2041*; a *co-laborer,* i.e. *coadjutor:*— companion in labour, helper, fellow-helper, fellow-labourer, fellow-worker, labourer together with, workfellow.

G4905 **συνέρχομαι** *synerchomai* from *G4862* and *G2064*; to *convene, depart* in company *with, associate* with, or (specifically) *cohabit* (conjugally):— accompany, assemble (with), come (together), come (company, go) with, resort.

G4906 **συνεσθίω** *synesthiō* from *G4862* and *G2068* (including its alternate); to *take food* in company *with:*— eat with.

G4907 **σύνεσις** *synesis* from *G4920*; a mental *putting together,* i.e. *intelligence* or (concretely) the *intellect:*— knowledge, understanding.

G4908 **συνετός** *synetos* from *G4920*; mentally *put* (or *putting*) *together,* i.e. *sagacious:*— prudent. Compare *G5429*.

G4909 **συνευδοκέω** *syneudokeō* from *G4862* and *G2106*; to *think well of in common,* i.e. *assent* to, *feel gratified with:*— allow, assent, be pleased, have pleasure.

G4910 **συνευωχέω** *syneuōcheō* from *G4862* and a derivative of a presumed compound of *G2095* and a derivative of *G2192* (meaning to *be in good condition,* i.e. [by implication] to *fare well,* or *feast*); to *entertain* sumptuously in company *with,* i.e. (middle or passive) to *revel together:*— feast with.

G4911 **συνεφίστημι** *synephistēmi* from *G4862* and *G2186*; to *stand up together,* i.e. to *resist* (or *assault*) *jointly:*— rise up together.

G4912 **συνέχω** *synechō* from *G4862* and *G2192*; to *hold together,* i.e. to *compress* (the ears, with a crowd or siege) or *arrest* (a prisoner); figuratively to *compel, perplex, afflict, preoccupy:*— constrain, hold, keep in, press, lie sick of, stop, be in a strait, straiten, be taken with, throng.

G4913 **συνήδομαι** *synēdomai* middle from *G4862* and the base of *G2237*; to *rejoice in with* oneself, i.e. *feel satisfaction* concerning:— delight.

G4914 **συνήθεια** *synētheia* from a compound of *G4862* and *G2239*; *mutual habituation,* i.e. *usage:*— custom.

G4915 **συνηλικιώτης** *synēlikiōtēs* from *G4862* and a derivative of *G2244*; a *co-aged* person, i.e. *alike* in years:— equal.

G4916 **συνθάπτω** *synthaptō* from *G4862* and *G2290*; to *inter* in company *with,* i.e. (figuratively) to *assimilate* spiritually (to Christ by a sepulture as to sin):— bury with.

G4917 **συνθλάω** *synthlaō* from *G4862* and **θλάω** *thlaō* (to *crush*); to *dash together,* i.e. *shatter:*— break.

G4918 **συνθλίβω** *synthlibō* from *G4862* and *G2346*; to *compress,* i.e. *crowd* on all sides:— throng.

G4919 **συνθρύπτω** *synthryptō* from *G4862* and **θρύπτω** *thryptō* (to *crumble*); to *crush together,* i.e. (figuratively) to *dispirit:*— break.

G4920 **συνίημι** *syniēmi* from *G4862* and **ἵημι** *hiēmi* (to *send*); to *put together,* i.e. (mentally) to *comprehend;* by implication to *act piously:*— consider, understand, be wise.

G4921 **συνιστάω** *synistaō* or strengthened
συνιστάνω *synistanō* or
συνίστημι *synistēmi* from *G4862* and *G2476* (including its collective forms); to *set together,* i.e. (by implication) to *introduce* (favorably), or (figuratively) to *exhibit;* intransitive to *stand near,* or (figuratively) to *constitute:*— approve, commend, consist, make, stand (with).

G4922 **συνοδεύω** *synodeuō* from *G4862* and *G3593*; to *travel* in company *with:*— journey with.

G4923 **συνοδία** *synodia* from a compound of *G4862* and *G3598* (*"synod"*); *companionship* on a journey, i.e. (by implication) a *caravan:*— company.

G4924 **συνοικέω** *synoikeō* from *G4862* and *G3611*; to *reside together* (as a family):— dwell together.

G4925 **συνοικοδομέω** *synoikodomeō* from *G4862* and *G3618*; to *construct,* i.e. (passive) to *compose* (in company with other Christians, figuratively):— build together.

G4926 **συνομιλέω** *synomileō* from *G4862* and *G3656*; to *converse* mutually:— talk with.

G4927 **συνομορέω** *synomoreō* from *G4862* and a derivative of a compound of the base of *G3674* and the base of *G3725*; to *border together,* i.e. *adjoin:*— join hard.

G4928 **συνόχη** *synochē* from *G4912*; *restraint,* i.e. (figuratively) *anxiety:*— anguish, distress.

G4929 **συντάσσω** *syntassō* from *G4862* and *G5021*; to *arrange jointly,* i.e. (figuratively) to *direct:*— appoint.

G4930 **συντέλεια** *synteleia* from *G4931*; *entire completion,* i.e. *consummation* (of a dispensation):— end.

G4931 **συντελέω** *synteleō* from *G4862* and *G5055*; to *complete entirely;* generally to *execute* (literally or figuratively):— end, finish, fulfill, make.

G4932 **συντέμνω** *syntemnō* from *G4862* and the base of *G5114*; to *contract* by cutting, i.e. (figuratively) *do concisely* (*speedily*):— (cut) short.

G4933 **συντηρέω** *syntēreō* from *G4862* and *G5083*; to *keep* closely *together,* i.e. (by implication) to *conserve* (from ruin); mentally to *remember* (and *obey*):— keep, observe, preserve.

G4934 **συντίθεμαι** *syntithemai* middle from *G4862* and *G5087*; to *place jointly,* i.e. (figuratively) to *consent* (*bargain, stipulate*), *concur:*— agree, assent, covenant.

G4935 **συντόμως** *syntomōs* adverb from a derivative of *G4932*; *concisely* (*briefly*):— a few words.

G4936 **συντρέχω** *syntrechō* from *G4862* and *G5143* (including its alternate); to *rush together* (hastily *assemble*) or *headlong* (figuratively):— run (together, with).

G4937 **συντρίβω** *syntribō* from *G4862* and the base of *G5147*; to *crush completely,* i.e. to *shatter* (literally or figuratively):— break (in pieces), broken to shivers, broken-hearted, bruise.

G4938 **σύντριμμα** *syntrimma* from *G4937*; *concussion* or utter *fracture* (properly concrete), i.e. complete *ruin:*— destruction.

G4939 **σύντροφος** *syntrophos* from *G4862* and *G5162* (in a passive sense); a *fellow-nursling,* i.e. *comrade:*— brought up with.

G4940 **συντυγχάνω** *syntynchanō* from *G4862* and *G5177*; to *chance together,* i.e. *meet* with (*reach*):— come at.

G4941 **Συντύχη** *Syntychē* from *G4940*; an *accident; Syntyche,* a Christian female:— Syntyche.

G4942 **συνυποκρίνομαι** *synypokrinomai* from *G4862* and *G5271*; to *act hypocritically* in concert *with:*— dissemble with.

G4943 **συνυπουργέω** *synypourgeō* from *G4862* and a derivative of a compound of *G5259* and the base of *G2041*; to *be a co-auxiliary,* i.e. *assist:*— help together.

G4944 **συνωδίνω** *synōdinō* from *G4862* and *G5605*; to *have* (parturition) *pangs* in company (concert, simultaneously) *with,* i.e. (figuratively) to *sympathize* (in expectation of relief from suffering):— travail in pain together.

G4945 **συνωμοσία** *synōmosia* from a compound of *G4862* and *G3660*; a *swearing together,* i.e. (by implication) a *plot:*— conspiracy.

G4946 **Συράκουσαι** *Syrakousai* plural of uncertain derivation; *Syracusae,* the capital of Sicily:— Syracuse.

G4947 **Συρία** *Syria* probably of Hebrew origin [H6865]; *Syria* (i.e. *Tsyria* or *Tyre*), a region of Asia:— Syria.

G4948 **Σύρος** *Syros* from the same as *G4947*; a *Syran* (i.e. probably *Tyrian*), a native of Syria:— Syrian.

G4949 **Συροφοίνισσα** *Syrophoinissa* feminine of a compound of *G4948* and the same as *G5403*; a *Syrophoenician* woman, i.e. a female native of Phoenicia in Syria:— Syrophenician.

G4950 **σύρτις** *syrtis* from *G4951*; a *shoal* (from the sand *drawn* thither by the waves), i.e. the *Syrtis* Major or great bay on the North coast of Africa:— quicksands.

G4951 **σύρω** *syrō* probably akin to *G138*; to *trail* :— drag, draw, hale.

G4952 **συσπαράσσω** *sysparassō* from *G4862* and *G4682*; to *rend completely,* i.e. (by analogy) to *convulse* violently:— throw down.

G4953 **σύσσημον** *syssēmon* neuter of a compound of *G4862* and the base of *G4591*; a *sign in common,* i.e. prearranged *signal:*— token.

G4954 **σύσσωμος** *syssōmos* from *G4862* and *G4983*; *of a joint body,* i.e. (figuratively) a *fellow-member* of the Christian community:— of the same body.

G4955 **συστασιαστής** *systasiastēs* from a compound of *G4862* and a derivative of *G4714*; a *fellow-insurgent:*— make insurrection with.

G4956 **συστατικός** *systatikos* from a derivative of *G4921*; *introductory,* i.e. *recommendatory:*— of commendation.

G4957 **συσταυρόω** *systauroō* from *G4862* and *G4717*; to *impale* in company *with* (literally or figuratively):— crucify with.

G4958 **συστέλλω** *systellō* from *G4862* and *G4724*; to *send* (*draw*) *together,* i.e. *enwrap* (*enshroud* a corpse for burial), *contract* (an interval):— short, wind up.

G4959 **συστενάζω** *systenazō* from *G4862* and *G4727*; to *moan jointly,* i.e. (figuratively) *experience a common calamity:*— groan together.

G4960 **συστοιχέω** *systoicheō* from *G4862* and *G4748*; to *file together* (as soldiers in ranks), i.e. (figuratively) to *correspond* to:— answer to.

G4961 **συστρατιώτης** *systratiōtēs* from *G4862* and *G4757*; a *co-campaigner,* i.e. (figuratively) an *associate* in Christian toil:— fellowsoldier.

G4962 **συστρέφω** *systrephō* from *G4862* and *G4762*; to *twist together,* i.e. *collect* (a bundle, a crowd):— gather.

G4963 **συστροφή** *systrophē* from *G4962*; a *twisting together,* i.e. (figuratively) a secret *coalition,* riotous *crowd:*— band together, concourse.

G4964 **συσχηματίζω** *syschēmatizō* from *G4862* and a derivative of *G4976*; to *fashion alike,* i.e. *conform* to the same pattern (figuratively):— conform to, fashion self according to.

G4965 **Συχάρ** *Sychar* of Hebrew origin [H7941]; *Sychar* (i.e. *Sheḳar*), a place in Palestine:— Sychar.

G4966 **Συχέμ** *Sychem* of Hebrew origin [H7927]; *Sychem* (i.e. *Shekem*), the name of a Canaanite and of a place in Palestine:— Sychem.

G4967 **σφαγή** *sphagē* from *G4969*; *butchery* (of animals for food or sacrifice, or [figuratively] of men [*destruction*]):— slaughter.

G4968 **σφάγιον** *sphagion* neuter of a derivative of *G4967*; a *victim* (in sacrifice):— slain beast.

G4969 **σφάζω** *sphazō* a primary verb; to *butcher* (especially an animal for food or in sacrifice) or (generally) to *slaughter,* or (specifically) to *maim* (violently):— kill, slay, wound.

G4970 **σφόδρα** *sphodra* neuter plural of
σφοδρός *sphodros* (*violent;* of uncertain derivation) as adverb; *vehemently,* i.e. in *a high degree, much:*— exceeding, exceedingly, greatly, sore, very.

G4971 **σφοδρῶς** *sphodrōs* adverb from the same as *G4970*; *very much:*— exceedingly.

G4972 **σφραγίζω** *sphragizō* from *G4973*; to *stamp* (with a signet or private mark) for security or preservation (literally or figuratively); by implication to *keep secret,* to *attest:*— (set a, set to) seal up, stop.

G4973 **σφραγίς** *sphragis* probably strengthened from *G5420*; a *signet* (as *fencing* in or protecting from misappropriation); by implication the *stamp* impressed (as a mark of privacy, or genuineness), literal or figurative:— seal.

G4974 **σφυρόν** *sphyron* neuter of a presumed derivative probably of the same as
σφαῖρα *sphaira* (a *ball, "sphere";* compare the feminine
σφῦρα *sphyra* a *hammer*); the *ankle* (as *globular*):— ankle bone.

G4975 **σχεδόν** *schedon* neuter of a presumed derivative of the alternate of *G2192* as adverb; *nigh,* i.e. *nearly:*— almost.

G4976 **σχῆμα** *schēma* from the alternate of *G2192*; a *figure* (as a *mode* or *circumstance*), i.e. (by implication) external *condition:*— fashion.

G4977 **σχίζω** *schizō* apparently a primary verb; to *split* or *sever* (literally or figuratively):— break, divide, open, rend, make a rent.

G4978 **σχίσμα** *schisma* from *G4977*; a *split* or *gap* (*"schism"*), literal or figurative:— division, rent, schism.

G4979 **σχοινίον** *schoinion* diminutive of
σχοῖνος *schoinos* (a *rush* or *flag*-plant; of uncertain derivation); a *small rush,* i.e. *grass-withe* or *tie* (generally):— small cord, rope.

G4980 **σχολάζω** *scholazō* from *G4981*; to *take a holiday,* i.e. *be at leisure* for (by implication *devote oneself* wholly to); figuratively to *be vacant* (of a house):— empty, give self.

G4981 **σχολή** *scholē* probable feminine of a presumed derivative of the alternate of *G2192*; properly *loitering* (as a *withholding* of oneself from work) or *leisure,* i.e. (by implication) a *"school"* (as *vacation* from physical employment):— school.

G4982 **σώζω** *sōzō* from a primary
σῶς *sōs* (contracted for obsolete
σάος *saos "safe"*); to *save,* i.e. *deliver* or *protect* (literally or figuratively):— heal, preserve, save (self), do well, be (make) whole.

G4983 **σῶμα** *sōma* from *G4982*; the *body* (as a *sound* whole), used in a very wide application, literal or figurative:— bodily, body, slave.

G4984 **σωματικός** *sōmatikos* from *G4983*; *corporeal* or *physical:*— bodily.

G4985 **σωματικῶς** *sōmatikōs* adverb from *G4984*; *corporeally* or *physically:*— bodily.

G4986 **Σώπατρος** *Sōpatros* from the base of *G4982* and *G3962*; *of a safe father; Sopatrus,* a Christian:— Sopater. Compare *G4989*.

G4987 **σωρεύω** *sōreuō* from another form of *G4673*; to *pile* up (literally or figuratively):— heap, load.

G4988 **Σωσθένης** *Sōsthenēs* from the base of *G4982* and that of *G4599*; *of safe strength; Sosthenes,* a Christian:— Sosthenes.

G4989 **Σωσίπατρος** *Sōsipatros* prolonged for *G4986*; *Sosipatrus,* a Christian:— Sosipater.

G4990 **σωτήρ** *sōtēr* from *G4982*; a *deliverer,* i.e. God or Christ:— saviour.

G4991 **σωτηρία** *sōtēria* feminine of a derivative of *G4990* as (properly abstract) noun; *rescue* or *safety* (physical or moral):— deliver, health, salvation, save, saving.

G4992 **σωτήριον** *sōtērion* neuter of the same as *G4991* as (properly concrete) noun; *defender* or (by implication) *defence:*— salvation.

G4993 **σωφρονέω** *sōphroneō* from *G4998*; to *be of sound mind,* i.e. *sane,* (figuratively) *moderate:*— be in right mind, be sober (minded), soberly.

G4994 **σωφρονίζω** *sōphronizō* from *G4998*; to *make of sound mind,* i.e. (figuratively) to *discipline* or *correct:*— teach to be sober.

G4995 **σωφρονισμός** *sōphronismos* from *G4994*; *discipline,* i.e. *self-control:*— sound mind.

G4996 **σωφρόνως** *sōphronōs* adverb from *G4998*; *with sound mind,* i.e. *moderately:*— soberly.

G4997 **σωφροσύνη** *sōphrosynē* from *G4998*; *soundness of mind,* i.e. (literally) *sanity* or (figuratively) *self-control:*— soberness, sobriety.

G4998 **σώφρων** *sōphrōn* from the base of *G4982* and that of *G5424*; *safe* (*sound*) in *mind,* i.e. *self-controlled* (*moderate* as to opinion or passion):— discreet, sober, temperate.

T

G4999 **Ταβέρναι** *Tabernai* plural of Latin origin; *huts* or *wooden-walled* buildings; *Tabernae:*— taverns.

G5000 **Ταβιθά** *Tabitha* of Aramaic origin [compare H6646]; *the gazelle; Tabitha* (i.e. *Tabjetha*), a Christian female:— Tabitha.

G5001 **τάγμα** *tagma* from *G5021*; something orderly in *arrangement* (a *troop*), i.e. (figuratively) a *series* or *succession:*— order.

G5002 **τακτός** *taktos* from *G5021*; *arranged,* i.e. *appointed* or *stated:*— set.

G5003 **ταλαιπωρέω** *talaipōreō* from *G5005*; to *be wretched,* i.e. *realize* one's own *misery:*— be afflicted.

G5004 **ταλαιπωρία** *talaipōria* from *G5005*; *wretchedness,* i.e. *calamity:*— misery.

G5005 **ταλαίπωρος** *talaipōros* from the base of *G5007* and a derivative of the base of *G3984*; *enduring trial,* i.e. *miserable:*— wretched.

G5006 **ταλαντιαῖος** *talantiaios* from *G5007*; *talent-like* in weight:— weight of a talent.

G5007 **τάλαντον** *talanton* neuter of a presumed derivative of the original form of
τλάω *tlaō* (to *bear;* equivalent to *G5342*); a *balance* (as *supporting* weights), i.e. (by implication) a certain *weight* (and thence a *coin* or rather *sum* of money) or *"talent":*— talent.

G5008 **ταλιθά** *talitha* of Aramaic origin [compare H2924]; *the fresh,* i.e. young *girl; talitha* (*O maiden*):— talitha.

G5009 **ταμεῖον** *tameion* neuter contraction of a presumed derivative of
ταμίας *tamias* (a *dispenser* or *distributor;* akin to
τέμνω *temnō* to *cut*); a *dispensary* or *magazine,* i.e. a chamber on the ground-floor or interior of an Oriental house (generally used for *storage* or *privacy,* a spot for retirement):— secret chamber, closet, storehouse.

G5010 **τάξις** *taxis* from *G5021*; regular *arrangement,* i.e. (in time) fixed *succession* (of rank or character), official *dignity:*— order.

G5011 **ταπεινός** *tapeinos* of uncertain derivation; *depressed,* i.e. (figuratively) *humiliated* (in circumstances or disposition):— base, cast down, humble, of low degree (estate), lowly.

G5012 **ταπεινοφροσύνη** *tapeinophrosynē* from a compound of *G5011* and the base of *G5424*; *humiliation of mind,* i.e. *modesty:*— humbleness of mind, humility (of mind), lowliness (of mind).

G5013 **ταπεινόω** *tapeinoō* from *G5011*; to *depress;* figuratively to *humiliate* (in condition or heart):— abase, bring low, humble (self).

G5014 **ταπείνωσις** *tapeinōsis* from *G5013*; *depression* (in rank or feeling):— humiliation, be made low, low estate, vile.

G5015 **ταράσσω** *tarassō* of uncertain affinity; to *stir* or *agitate* (*roil* water):— trouble.

G5016 **ταραχή** *tarachē* feminine from *G5015*; *disturbance,* i.e. (of water) *roiling,* or (of a mob) *sedition:*— trouble, troubling.

G5017 **τάραχος** *tarachos* masculine from *G5015*; a *disturbance,* i.e. (popular) *tumult:*— stir.

G5018 **Ταρσεύς** *Tarseus* from *G5019*; a *Tarsean,* i.e. native of Tarsus:— of Tarsus.

G5019 **Ταρσός** *Tarsos* perhaps the same as
ταρσός *tarsos* (a *flat* basket); *Tarsus,* a place in Asia Minor:— Tarsus.

G5020 **ταρταρόω** *tartaroō* from
Τάρταρος *Tartaros* (the deepest *abyss* of Hades); to *incarcerate* in eternal torment:— cast down to hell.

G5021 **τάσσω** *tassō* a prolonged form of a primary verb (which latter appears only in certain tenses); to *arrange* in an orderly manner, i.e. *assign* or *dispose* (to a certain position or lot):— addict, appoint, determine, ordain, set.

G5022 **ταῦρος** *tauros* apparently a primary word [compare H8450, *"steer"*]; a *bullock:*— bull, ox.

G5023 **ταῦτα** *tauta* nominative or accusative neuter plural of *G3778*; *these* things:— afterward, follow, hereafter, him, the same, so, such, that, then, these, they, this, those, thus.

G5024 **ταὐτά** *tauta* neuter plural of *G3588* and *G846* as adverb; in *the same* way:— even thus, (manner) like, so.

G5025 **ταύταις** *tautais* dative feminine plural and
ταύτας *tautas* accusative feminine plural forms of *G3778*; (*to* or *with* or *by,* etc.) *these:*— hence, that, then, these, those.

G5026 **ταύτῃ** *tautē* dative feminine singular and
ταύτην *tautēn* accusative feminine singular and
ταύτης *tautēs* genitive feminine singular forms of *G3778*; (*towards* or *of*) *this:*— her, hereof, it, that, thereby, the (same), this (same).

G5027 **ταφή** *taphē* feminine from *G2290*; *burial* (the act):— bury.

G5028 **τάφος** *taphos* masculine from *G2290*; a *grave* (the place of interment):— sepulchre, tomb.

G5029 **τάχα** *tacha* as if neuter plural of *G5036* (adverb); *shortly,* i.e. (figuratively) *possibly:*— peradventure (-haps).

G5030 **ταχέως** *tacheōs* adverb from *G5036*; *briefly,* i.e. (in time) *speedily,* or (in manner) *rapidly:*— hastily, quickly, shortly, soon, suddenly.

G5031 **ταχινός** *tachinos* from *G5034*; *curt,* i.e. *impending:*— shortly, swift.

G5032 **τάχιον** *tachion* neuter singular of the comparative of *G5036* (as adverb); *more swiftly,* i.e. (in manner) *more rapidly,* or (in time) *more speedily:*— out [run], quickly, shortly, sooner.

G5033 **τάχιστα** *tachista* neuter plural of the superlative of *G5036* (as adverb); *most quickly,* i.e. (with *G5613* prefixed) *as soon* as possible:— with all speed.

G5034 **τάχος** *tachos* from the same as *G5036*; a *brief* space (of time), i.e. *with G1722* prefixed) in *haste:*— quickly, shortly, speedily.

G5035 **ταχύ** *tachy* neuter singular of *G5036* (as adverb); *shortly,* i.e. *without delay, soon,* or (by surprise) *suddenly,* or (by implication of ease) *readily:*— lightly, quickly.

G5036 **ταχύς** *tachys* of uncertain affinity; *fleet,* i.e. (figuratively) *prompt* or *ready:*— swift.

G5037 **τε** *te* a primary particle (enclitic) of connection or addition; *both* or *also* (properly as correlation of *G2532*). Often used in compounds, usually as the latter part:— also, and, both, even, then, whether.

G5038 **τεῖχος** *teichos* akin to the base of *G5088*; a *wall* (as *formative* of a house):— wall.

GRK

G5039 τεκμήριον *tekmērion* neuter of a presumed derivative of
τεκμάρ *tekmar* (a *goal* or fixed *limit*); a *token* (as *defining* a fact), i.e. *criterion* of certainty:— infallible proof.

G5040 τεκνίον *teknion* diminutive of *G5043*; an *infant,* i.e. (plural figurative) *darlings* (Christian *converts*):— little children.

G5041 τεκνογονέω *teknogoneō* from a compound of *G5043* and the base of *G1096*; to *be a child-bearer,* i.e. *parent* (*mother*):— bear children.

G5042 τεκνογονία *teknogonia* from the same as *G5041*; *childbirth* (*parentage*), i.e. (by implication) *maternity* (the performance of *maternal duties*):— childbearing.

G5043 τέκνον *teknon* from the base of *G5098*; a *child* (as *produced*):— child, daughter, son.

G5044 τεκνοτροφέω *teknotropheō* from a compound of *G5043* and *G5142*; to *rear a child,* i.e. *fulfill* the duties of *a female parent:*— bring up children.

G5045 τέκτων *tektōn* from the base of *G5098*; an *artificer* (as *producer* of fabrics), i.e. (specifically) a *craftsman* in wood:— carpenter.

G5046 τέλειος *teleios* from *G5056*; *complete* (in various applications of labor, growth, mental and moral character, etc.); neuter (as noun, with *G3588*) *completeness:*— of full age, man, perfect.

G5047 τελειότης *teleiotēs* from *G5046*; (the state) *completeness* (mental or moral):— perfection, perfectness.

G5048 τελειόω *teleioō* from *G5046*; to *complete,* i.e. (literally) *accomplish,* or (figuratively) *consummate* (in character):— consecrate, finish, fulfill, make) perfect.

G5049 τελείως *teleiōs* adverb from *G5046*; *completely,* i.e. (of hope) *without wavering:*— to the end.

G5050 τελείωσις *teleiōsis* from *G5448*; (the act) *completion,* i.e. (of prophecy) *verification,* or (of expiation) *absolution:*— perfection, performance.

G5051 τελειωτής *teleiōtēs* from *G5048*; *one who completes,* i.e. *one who consummates:*— finisher.

G5052 τελεσφορέω *telesphoreō* from a compound of *G5056* and *G5342*; to *be a bearer to completion* (maturity), i.e. to *ripen* fruit (figuratively):— bring fruit to perfection.

G5053 τελευτάω *teleutaō* from a presumed derivative of *G5055*; to *finish* life (by implication of *G979*), i.e. *expire* (*demise*):— be dead, decease, die.

G5054 τελευτή *teleutē* from *G5053*; *decease:*— death.

G5055 τελέω *teleō* from *G5056*; to *end,* i.e. *complete, execute, conclude, discharge* (a debt):— accomplish, make an end, expire, fill up, finish, go over, pay, perform.

G5056 τέλος *telos* from a primary
τέλλω *tellō* (to *set out* for a definite point or *goal*); properly the point aimed at as a *limit,* i.e. (by implication) the *conclusion* of an act or state (*termination* [literal, figurative or indefinite], *result* [immediate, ultimate or prophetic], *purpose*); specifically an *impost* or *levy* (as *paid*):— continual, custom, end, ending, finally, uttermost. Compare *G5411*.

G5057 τελώνης *telōnēs* from *G5056* and *G5608*; a *tax-farmer,* i.e. *collector of* public *revenue:*— publican.

G5058 τελώνιον *telōnion* neuter of a presumed derivative of *G5057*; a *tax-gatherer's* place of business:— receipt of custom.

G5059 τέρας *teras* of uncertain affinity; a *prodigy* or *omen:*— wonder.

G5060 Τέρτιος *Tertios* of Latin origin; *third; Tertius,* a Christian:— Tertius.

G5061 Τέρτυλλος *Tertyllos* of uncertain derivation; *Tertullus,* a Roman:— Tertullus.

G5062 τεσσαράκοντα *tessarakonta* the decade of *G5064*; *forty:*— forty.

G5063 τεσσαρακονταετής *tessarakontaetēs* from *G5062* and *G2094*; *of forty years* of age:— (+ full, of) forty years (old).

G5064 τέσσαρες *tessares* neuter
τέσσαρα *tessara*; a plural number; *four:*— four.

G5065 τεσσαρεσκαιδέκατος *tessareskaidekatos* from *G5064* and *G2532* and *G1182*; *fourteenth:*— fourteenth.

G5066 τεταρταῖος *tetartaios* from *G5064*; pertaining to the *fourth* day:— four days.

G5067 τέταρτος *tetartos* ordinal from *G5064*; *fourth:*— four, fourth.

G5068 τετράγωνος *tetragōnos* from *G5064* and *G1137*; *four-cornered,* i.e. *square:*— foursquare.

G5069 τετράδιον *tetradion* neuter of a presumed derivative of
τέτρας *tetras* (a *tetrad;* from *G5064*); a *quaternion* or squad (picket) of four Roman soldiers:— quaternion.

G5070 τετρακισχίλιοι *tetrakischilioi* from the multiple adverb of *G5064* and *G5507*; *four times a thousand:*— four thousand.

G5071 τετρακόσιοι *tetrakosioi* neuter
τετρακόσια *tetrakosia* plural from *G5064* and *G1540*; *four hundred:*— four hundred.

G5072 τετράμηνον *tetramēnon* neuter of a compound of *G5064* and *G3376*; a *four monthsae* space:— four months.

G5073 τετραπλόος *tetraploos* from *G5064* and a derivative of the base of *G4118*; *quadruple:*— fourfold.

G5074 τετράπους *tetrapous* from *G5064* and *G4228*; a *quadruped:*— fourfooted beast.

G5075 τετραρχέω *tetrarcheō* from *G5076*; to *be a tetrarch:*— (be) tetrarch.

G5076 τετράρχης *tetrarchēs* from *G5064* and *G757*; the *ruler of a fourth* part of a country ("*tetrarch*"):— tetrarch.

G5077 τεφρόω *tephroō* from
τέφρα *tephra* (*ashes*); to *incinerate,* i.e. *consume:*— turn to ashes.

G5078 τέχνη *technē* from the base of *G5088*; *art* (as *productive*), i.e. (specifically) a *trade,* or (generally) *skill:*— art, craft, occupation.

G5079 τεχνίτης *technitēs* from *G5078*; an *artisan;* figuratively a *founder* (*Creator*):— builder, craftsman.

G5080 τήκω *tēkō* apparently a primary verb; to *liquefy:*— melt.

G5081 τηλαυγῶς *tēlaugōs* adverb from a compound of a derivative of *G5056* and *G827*; in a *far-shining* manner, i.e. *plainly:*— clearly.

G5082 τηλικοῦτος *tēlikoutos* feminine
τηλικαύτη *tēlikautē* from a compound of *G3588* with *G2245* and *G3778*; *such as this,* i.e. (in [figurative] magnitude) *so vast:*— so great, so mighty.

G5083 τηρέω *tēreō* from
τηρός *tēros* (a *watch;* perhaps akin to *G2334*); to *guard* (from *loss* or *injury,* properly by keeping *the eye* upon; and thus differing from *G5442*, which is properly to *prevent* escaping; and from *G2892*, which implies a *fortress* or full military lines of apparatus), i.e. to *note* (a prophecy; figuratively to *fulfill* a command); by implication to *detain* (in custody; figuratively to *maintain*); by extension to *withhold* (for personal ends; figuratively to *keep unmarried*):— hold fast, keep, keeper, serve, preserve, reserve, watch.

G5084 τήρησις *tērēsis* from *G5083*; a *watching,* i.e. (figuratively) *observance,* or (concretely) a *prison:*— hold.

G5085 Τιβεριάς *Tiberias* from *G5086*; *Tiberias,* the name of a town and a lake in Palestine:— Tiberias.

G5086 Τιβέριος *Tiberios* of Latin origin; probably *pertaining to the* river *Tiberis* or *Tiber; Tiberius,* a Roman emperor:— Tiberius.

G5087 τίθημι *tithēmi* a prolonged form of a primary
θέω *theō* (which is used only as alternate in certain tenses); to *place* (in the widest application, literally and figuratively; properly in a passive or horizontal posture, and thus different from *G2476*, which properly denotes an upright and active position, while *G2749* is properly reflexive and utterly prostrate):— advise, appoint, bow, commit, conceive, give, kneel down, lay (aside, down, up), make, ordain, purpose, put, set (forth), settle, sink down.

G5088 τίκτω *tiktō* a strengthened form of a primary
τέκω *tekō* (which is used only as alternate in certain tenses); to *produce* (from seed, as a mother, a plant, the earth, etc.), literally or figuratively:— bear, be born, bring forth, be delivered, be in travail.

G5089 τίλλω *tillō* perhaps akin to the alternate of *G138*, and thus to *G4951*; to *pull* off:— pluck.

G5090 Τίμαιος *Timaios* probably of Aramaic origin [compare H2931]; *Timaeus* (i.e. *Timay*), an Israelite:— Timaeus.

G5091 τιμάω *timaō* from *G5093*; to *prize,* i.e. *fix* a *valuation* upon; by implication to *revere:*— honour, value.

G5092 τιμή *timē* from *G5099*; a *value,* i.e. *money* paid, or (concretely and collectively) *valuables;* by analogy *esteem* (especially of the highest degree), or the *dignity* itself:— honour, precious, price, some.

G5093 τίμιος *timios* including the comparative
τιμιώτερος *timiōteros* and the superlative
τιμιώτατος *timiōtatos* from *G5092*; *valuable,* i.e. (objectively) *costly,* or (subjectively) *honored, esteemed,* or (figuratively) *beloved:*— dear, honourable, (more, most) precious, had in reputation.

G5094 τιμιότης *timiotēs* from *G5093*; *expensiveness,* i.e. (by implication) *magnificence:*— costliness.

G5095 Τιμόθεος *Timotheos* from *G5092* and *G2316*; *dear to God; Timotheus,* a Christian:— Timotheus, Timothy.

G5096 Τίμων *Timōn* from *G5092*; *valuable; Timon,* a Christian:— Timon.

G5097 **τιμωρέω** *timōreō* from a compound of *G5092* and
οὖρος *ouros* (a *guard*); properly to *protect* one's *honor*, i.e. to *avenge* (*inflict a penalty*):— punish.

G5098 **τιμωρία** *timōria* from *G5097*; *vindication*, i.e. (by implication) a *penalty*:— punishment.

G5099 **τίνω** *tinō* strengthened for a primary
τίω *tiō* (which is only used as an alternate in certain tenses); to *pay* a price, i.e. as a *penalty*:— be punished with.

G5100 **τὶς** *tis* an enclitic indefinite pronoun; *some* or *any* person or object:— a (kind of), any (man, thing, thing at all), certain (thing), divers, he (every) man, one (thing), ought, partly, some (man), somebody, something, somewhat, thing, that nothing, what, whatsoever, wherewith, whom, whomsoever, whose, whosoever.

G5101 **τίς** *tis* probably emphatic of *G5100*; an interrogative pronoun, *who, which* or *what* (in direct or indirect questions):— every man, how (much), no, none, nothing, what (manner, thing), where, whereby, wherefore, whereof, whereunto, wherewith, wherewithal, whether, which, who, whom, whose, why.

G5102 **τίτλος** *titlos* of Latin origin; a *titulus* or *"title"* (*placard*):— title.

G5103 **Τίτος** *Titos* of Latin origin but uncertain significance; *Titus*, a Christian:— Titus.

G5104 **τοί** *toi* probably for the dative of *G3588*; an enclitic particle of *asseveration* by way of contrast; *in sooth*:— [*used only with other particles in compounds, as G2544, G3305, G5105, G5106, etc.*].

G5105 **τοιγαροῦν** *toigaroun* from *G5104* and *G1063* and *G3767*; *truly for then*, i.e. *consequently*:— therefore, wherefore.

G5106 **τοίνυν** *toinyn* from *G5104* and *G3568*; *truly now*, i.e. *accordingly*:— then, therefore.

G5107 **τοιόσδε** *toiosde* (including the other inflections); from a derivative of *G5104* and *G1161*; *such-like then*, i.e. *so great*:— such.

G5108 **τοιοῦτος** *toioutos* (including the other inflections); from *G5104* and *G3778*; *truly this*, i.e. *of this sort* (to denote character or individuality):— like, such (an one).

G5109 **τοῖχος** *toichos* another form of *G5038*; a *wall*:— wall.

G5110 **τόκος** *tokos* from the base of *G5088*; *interest* on money loaned (as a *produce*):— usury.

G5111 **τολμάω** *tolmaō* from
τόλμα *tolma* (*boldness*; probably itself from the base of *G5056* through the idea of *extreme* conduct); to *venture* (objectively or in *act*; while *G2292* is rather subjective or in *feeling*); by implication to be *courageous*:— be bold, boldly, dare, durst.

G5112 **τολμηρότερον** *tolmēroteron* neuter of the comparative of a derivative of the base of *G5111* (as adverb); *more daringly*, i.e. *with greater confidence* than otherwise:— the more boldly.

G5113 **τολμητής** *tolmētēs* from *G5111*; a *daring* (*audacious*) man:— presumptuous.

G5114 **τομώτερος** *tomōteros* comparative of a derivative of the primary
τέμνω *temnō* (to *cut*, more comprehensive or decisive than *G2875*, as if by a *single* stroke; whereas that implies repeated blows, like *hacking*); *more keen*:— sharper.

G5115 **τόξον** *toxon* from the base of *G5088*; a *bow* (apparently as the simplest fabric):— bow.

G5116 **τοπάζιον** *topazion* neuter of a presumed derivative (alternate) of
τόπαζος *topazos* (a *"topaz"*; of uncertain origin); a gem, probably the *chrysolite*:— topaz.

G5117 **τόπος** *topos* apparently a primary word; a *spot* (generally in *space*, but limited by occupancy; whereas *G5561* is a larger but particular *locality*), i.e. *location* (as a position, home, tract, etc.); figuratively *condition, opportunity*; specifically a *scabbard*:— coast, licence, place, plain, quarter, rock, room, where.

G5118 **τοσοῦτος** *tosoutos* from
τόσος *tosos* (*so much*; apparently from *G3588* and *G3739*) and *G3778* (including its variations); so *vast as this*, i.e. *such* (in quantity, amount, number or space):— as large, so great (long, many, much), these many.

G5119 **τότε** *tote* from (the neuter of) *G3588* and *G3753*; *the when*, i.e. *at the time* that (of the past or future, also in consecution):— that time, then.

G5120 **τοῦ** *tou* properly the genitive of *G3588*; sometimes used for *G5127*; *of this person*:— his.

G5121 **τοὐναντίον** *tounantion* contracted for the neuter of *G3588* and *G1726*; *on the contrary*:— contrariwise.

G5122 **τοὔνομα** *tounoma* contracted for the neuter of *G3588* and *G3686*; *the name* (is):— named.

G5123 **τουτέστι** *toutesti* contracted for *G5124* and *G2076*; *that is*:— that is (to say).

G5124 **τοῦτο** *touto* neuter singular nominative or accusative of *G3778*; *that* thing:— here, hereunto, it, partly, self, selfsame, so, that (intent), the same, there, therefore, thereunto, this, thus, where, wherefore.

G5125 **τούτοις** *toutois* dative plural masculine or neuter of *G3778*; *to* (*for, in, with* or *by*) *these* (persons or things):— such, them, there, therein, therewith, these, this, those.

G5126 **τοῦτον** *touton* accusative singular masculine of *G3778*; *this* (person, as object of verb or preposition):— him, the same, that, this.

G5127 **τούτου** *toutou* genitive singular masculine or neuter of *G3778*; *of* (*from* or *concerning*) *this* (person or thing):— here, hereby, him, it, such manner of, that, thence, thenceforth, thereabout, this, thus.

G5128 **τούτους** *toutous* accusative plural masculine of *G3778*; *these* (persons, as object of verb or preposition):— such, them, these, this.

G5129 **τούτῳ** *toutō* dative singular masculine or neuter of *G3778*; *to* (*in, with or by*) *this* (person or thing):— here, hereby, herein, him, one, the same, there, therein, this.

G5130 **τούτων** *toutōn* genitive plural masculine or neuter of *G3778*; *of* (*from* or *concerning*) *these* (persons or things):— such, their, these (things), they, this sort, those.

G5131 **τράγος** *tragos* from the base of *G5176*; a *he-goat* (as a *gnawing one*):— goat.

G5132 **τράπεζα** *trapeza* probably contracted from *G5064* and *G3979*; a *table* or *stool* (as being *four-legged*), usually for food (figuratively a *meal*); also a *counter* for money (figuratively a broker's *office* for loans at interest):— bank, meat, table.

G5133 **τραπεζίτης** *trapezitēs* from *G5132*; a money-*broker* or *banker*:— exchanger.

G5134 **τραῦμα** *trauma* from the base of
τιτρώσκω *titrōskō* (to *wound*; akin to the base of *G2352*, *G5147*, *G5149*, etc.); a *wound*:— wound.

G5135 **τραυματίζω** *traumatizō* from *G5134*; to *inflict a wound*:— wound.

G5136 **τραχηλίζω** *trachēlizō* from *G5137*; to *seize* by *the throat* or *neck*, i.e. to *expose* the *gullet* of a victim for killing (generally to *lay bare*):— opened.

G5137 **τράχηλος** *trachēlos* probably from *G5143* (through the idea of *mobility*); the *throat* (*neck*), i.e. (figuratively) *life*:— neck.

G5138 **τραχύς** *trachys* perhaps strengthened from the base of *G4486* (as if *jagged* by rents); *uneven, rocky* (*reef-like*):— rock, rough.

G5139 **Τραχωνῖτις** *Trachōnitis* from a derivative of *G5138*; *rough* district; *Trachonitis*, a region of Syria:— Trachonitis.

G5140 **τρεῖς** *treis* neuter
τρία *tria* a primary (plural) number; *three* :— three.

G5141 **τρέμω** *tremō* strengthened from a primary
τρέω *treō* (to *"dread"*, *"terrify"*); to *"tremble"* or *fear*:— be afraid, trembling.

G5142 **τρέφω** *trephō* a primary verb (properly
θρέφω *threphō* but perhaps strengthened from the base of *G5157* through the idea of *convolution*); properly to *stiffen*, i.e. *fatten* (by implication to *cherish* [with food, etc.], *pamper, rear*):— bring up, feed, nourish.

G5143 **τρέχω** *trechō* apparently a primary verb (properly
θρέχω *threchō* compare *G2359*); which uses
δρέμω *dremō* (the base of *G1408*) as alternate in certain tenses; to *run* or *walk hastily* (literally or figuratively):— have course, run.

G5144 **τριάκοντα** *triakonta* the decade of *G5140*; *thirty*:— thirty.

G5145 **τριακόσιοι** *triakosioi* plural from *G5140* and *G1540*; *three hundred*:— three hundred.

G5146 **τρίβολος** *tribolos* from *G5140* and *G956*; properly a *crow-foot* (*three-pronged* obstruction in war), i.e. (by analogy) a *thorny* plant (*caltrop*):— brier, thistle.

G5147 **τρίβος** *tribos* from
τρίβω *tribō* (to *"rub"*; akin to
τείρω *teirō* or
τρύω *tryō* and the base of *G5131*, *G5134*); a *rut* or worn *track*:— path.

G5148 **τριετία** *trietia* from a compound of *G5140* and *G2094*; a *three yearsae period* (*triennium*):— space of three years.

G5149 **τρίζω** *trizō* apparently a primary verb; to *creak* (*squeak*), i.e. (by analogy) to *grate* the teeth (in frenzy):— gnash.

G5150 **τρίμηνον** *trimēnon* neuter of a compound of *G5140* and *G3376* as noun; a *three monthsae* space:— three months.

G5151 **τρίς** *tris* adverb from *G5140*; *three times*:— three times, thrice.

G5152 **τρίστεγον** *tristegon* neuter of a compound of *G5140* and *G4721* as noun; a *third roof* (*story*):— third loft.

G5153 **τρισχίλιοι** *trischilioi* from *G5151* and *G5507*; *three times a thousand*:— three thousand.

GRK

G5154 **τρίτος** *tritos* ordinal from *G5140*; *third;* neuter (as noun) a *third part,* or (as adverb) a (or the) *third* time, *thirdly:*— third, thirdly.

G5155 **τρίχινος** *trichinos* from *G2359*; *hairy,* i.e. made *of hair* (*mohair*):— of hair.

G5156 **τρόμος** *tromos* from *G5141*; a *"trembling"*, i.e. quaking with *fear:*— tremble, trembling.

G5157 **τροπή** *tropē* from an apparently primary
τρέπω *trepō* (to *turn*); a *turn* ("trope"), i.e. *revolution* (figuratively *variation*):— turning.

G5158 **τρόπος** *tropos* from the same as *G5157*; a *turn,* i.e. (by implication) *mode* or *style* (especially with preposition or relative prefixed as adverb *like*); figuratively *deportment* or *character:*— (even) as, conversation, [+ like] manner, (+ by any) means, way.

G5159 **τροποφορέω** *tropophoreō* from *G5158* and *G5409*; to *endure* one's *habits:*— suffer the manners.

G5160 **τροφή** *trophē* from *G5142*; *nourishment* (literal or figurative); by implication *rations* (*wages*):— food, meat.

G5161 **Τρόφιμος** *Trophimos* from *G5160*; *nutritive; Trophimus,* a Christian:— Trophimus.

G5162 **τροφός** *trophos* from *G5142*; one who *nourishes,* i.e. *nurse:*— nurse.

G5163 **τροχιά** *trochia* from *G5164*; a *track* (as a wheel-*rut*), i.e. (figuratively) a *course* of conduct:— path.

G5164 **τροχός** *trochos* from *G5143*; a *wheel* (as a *runner*), i.e. (figuratively) a *circuit* of physical effects:— course.

G5165 **τρύβλιον** *tryblion* neuter of a presumed derivative of uncertain affinity; a *bowl:*— dish.

G5166 **τρυγάω** *trygaō* from a derivative of
τρύγω *trygō* (to *dry*) meaning ripe *fruit* (as if *dry*); to *collect* the vintage:— gather.

G5167 **τρυγών** *trygōn* from
τρύζω *tryzō* (to *murmur;* akin to *G5149*; but denoting a *duller* sound); a *turtle-dove* (as *cooing*):— turtle-dove.

G5168 **τρυμαλιά** *trymalia* from a derivative of
τρύω *tryō* (to *wear* away; akin to the base of *G5134*, *G5147* and *G5176*); an *orifice,* i.e. a needle's *eye:*— eye. Compare *G5169*.

G5169 **τρύπημα** *trypēma* from a derivative of the base of *G5168*; an *aperture,* i.e. a needle's *eye:*— eye.

G5170 **Τρύφαινα** *Tryphaina* from *G5172*; *luxurious; Tryphaena,* a Christian woman:— Tryphena.

G5171 **τρυφάω** *tryphaō* from *G5172*; to *indulge in luxury:*— live in pleasure.

G5172 **τρυφή** *tryphē* from
θρύπτω *thryptō* (to *break* up or [figuratively] *enfeeble,* especially the mind and body by indulgence); *effeminacy,* i.e. *luxury* or *debauchery:*— delicately, riot.

G5173 **Τρυφῶσα** *Tryphōsa* from *G5172*; *luxuriating; Tryphosa,* a Christian female:— Tryphosa.

G5174 **Τρῳάς** *Trōas* from
Τρός *Tros* (a *Trojan*); the *Troad* (or plain of Troy), i.e. *Troas,* a place in Asia Minor:— Troas.

G5175 **Τρωγύλλιον** *Trōgyllion* of uncertain derivation; *Trogyllium,* a place in Asia Minor:— Trogyllium.

G5176 **τρώγω** *trōgō* probably strengthened from a collateral form of the base of *G5134* and *G5147* through the idea of *corrosion* or *wear;* or perhaps rather of a base of *G5167* and *G5149* through the idea of a *crunching* sound; to *gnaw* or *chew,* i.e. (generally) to *eat:*— eat.

G5177 **τυγχάνω** *tynchanō* probably for an obsolete
τύχω *tychō* (for which the middle of another alternate
τεύχω *teuchō* [to *make ready* or *bring to pass*] is used in certain tenses); akin to the base of *G5088* through the idea of *effecting;* properly to *affect;* or (specifically) to *hit* or *light upon* (as a mark to be reached), i.e. (transitive) to *attain* or *secure* an object or end, or (intransitive) to *happen* (as if *meeting* with); but in the latter application only impersonal (with *G1487*), i.e. *perchance;* or (present participle) as adjective *usual* (as if commonly *met with,* with *G3756*, *extraordinary*), neuter (as adverb) *perhaps;* or (with another verb) as adverb by *accident* (*as it were*):— be, chance, enjoy, little, obtain, refresh . . . self, special. Compare *G5180*.

G5178 **τυμπανίζω** *tympanizō* from a derivative of *G5180* (meaning a *drum, "tympanum"*); to stretch on an instrument of *torture* resembling a drum, and thus *beat* to death:— torture.

G5179 **τύπος** *typos* from *G5180*; a *die* (as *struck*), i.e. (by implication) a *stamp* or *scar;* by analogy a *shape,* i.e. a *statue,* (figuratively) *style* or *resemblance;* specifically a *sampler* (*"type"*), i.e. a *model* (for imitation) or *instance* (for warning):— example, fashion, figure, form, manner, pattern, print.

G5180 **τύπτω** *typtō* a primary verb (in a strengthened form); to *"thump"*, i.e. *cudgel* or *pummel* (properly with a stick or *bastinado*), but in any case by *repeated* blows; thus differing from *G3817* and *G3960*, which denote a [usually single] blow with the hand or any instrument, or *G4141* with the *fist* [or a *hammer*], or *G4474* with the *palm;* as well as from *G5177*, an *accidental* collision); by implication to *punish;* figuratively to *offend* (the conscience):— beat, smite, strike, wound.

G5181 **Τύραννος** *Tyrannos* a provincial form of the derivative of the base of *G2962*; a *"tyrant"*; *Tyrannus,* an Ephesian:— Tyrannus.

G5182 **τυρβάζω** *tyrbazō* from
τύρβη *tyrbē* (Latin *turba,* a *crowd;* akin to *G2351*); to *make "turbid"*, i.e. *disturb:*— trouble.

G5183 **Τύριος** *Tyrios* from *G5184*; a *Tyrian,* i.e. inhabitant of Tyrus:— of Tyre.

G5184 **Τύρος** *Tyros* of Hebrew origin [*H6865*]; *Tyrus* (i.e. *Tsor*), a place in Palestine:— Tyre.

G5185 **τυφλός** *typhlos* from *G5187*; *opaque* (as if *smoky*), i.e. (by analogy) *blind* (physically or mentally):— blind.

G5186 **τυφλόω** *typhloō* from *G5185*; to *make blind,* i.e. (figuratively) to *obscure:*— blind.

G5187 **τυφόω** *typhoō* from a derivative of *G5188*; to envelop with *smoke,* i.e. (figuratively) to *inflate* with self-conceit:— high-minded, be lifted up with pride, be proud.

G5188 **τύφω** *typhō* apparently a primary verb; to make a *smoke,* i.e. slowly *consume* without flame:— smoke.

G5189 **τυφωνικός** *typhōnikos* from a derivative of *G5188*; *stormy* (as if *smoky*):— tempestuous.

G5190 **Τυχικός** *Tychikos* from a derivative of *G5177*; *fortuitous,* i.e. *fortunate; Tychicus,* a Christian:— Tychicus.

Υ

G5191 **ὑακίνθινος** *hyakinthinos* from *G5192*; *"hyacinthine"* or *"jacinthine"*, i.e. deep *blue:*— jacinth.

G5192 **ὑάκινθος** *hyakinthos* of uncertain derivation; the *"hyacinth"* or *"jacinth"*, i.e. some gem of a deep *blue* color, probably the *zirkon:*— jacinth.

G5193 **ὑάλινος** *hyalinos* from *G5194*; *glassy,* i.e. *transparent:*— of glass.

G5194 **ὕαλος** *hyalos* perhaps from the same as *G5205* (as being transparent like *rain); glass:*— glass.

G5195 **ὑβρίζω** *hybrizō* from *G5196*; to *exercise violence,* i.e. *abuse:*— use despitefully, reproach, entreat shamefully (spitefully).

G5196 **ὕβρις** *hybris* from *G5228*; *insolence* (as *overbearing*), i.e. *insult, injury:*— harm, hurt, reproach.

G5197 **ὑβριστής** *hybristēs* from *G5195*; one who *insults,* i.e. one who *maltreats:*— despiteful, injurious.

G5198 **ὑγιαίνω** *hygiainō* from *G5199*; to *have* sound *health,* i.e. *be well* (in body); figuratively to be *uncorrupt* (*true* in doctrine):— be in health, (be safe and) sound, (be) whole, (be) wholesome.

G5199 **ὑγιής** *hygiēs* from the base of *G837*; *healthy,* i.e. *well* (in body); figuratively *true* (in doctrine):— sound, whole.

G5200 **ὑγρός** *hygros* from the base of *G5205*; *wet* (as if with *rain*), i.e. (by implication) *sappy* (*fresh*) :— green.

G5201 **ὑδρία** *hydria* from *G5204*; a *water-jar,* i.e. *receptacle* for family supply:— waterpot.

G5202 **ὑδροποτέω** *hydropoteō* from a compound of *G5204* and a derivative of *G4095*; to *be a water-drinker,* i.e. to *abstain from vinous beverages:*— drink water.

G5203 **ὑδρωπικός** *hydrōpikos* from a compound of *G5204* and a derivative of *G3700* (as if *looking watery*); to be *"dropsical"*:— have the dropsy.

G5204 **ὕδωρ** *hydōr* genitive
ὕδατος *hydatos* etc.; from the base of *G5205*; *water* (as if *rainy*) literal or figurative:— water.

G5205 **ὑετός** *hyetos* from a primary
ὕω *hyō* (to *rain*); *rain,* especially a *shower:*— rain.

G5206 **υἱοθεσία** *huiothesia* from a presumed compound of *G5207* and a derivative of *G5087*; the *placing* as a *son,* i.e. *adoption* (figuratively Christian *sonship* in respect to God):— adoption (of children, of sons).

G5207 **υἱός** *huios* apparently a primary word; a *"son"* (sometimes of animals), used very widely of immediate, remote or figurative kinship:— child, foal, son.

G5208 **ὕλη** *hylē* perhaps akin to *G3586*; a *forest,* i.e. (by implication) *fuel:*— matter.

G5209 **ὑμᾶς** *hymas* accusative of *G5210*; *you* (as the object of a verb or preposition):— ye, you, youward, your, your own.

G5210 **ὑμεῖς** *hymeis* irregular plural of *G4771*; *you* (as subject of verb):— ye (yourselves), you.

G5211 **Ὑμεναῖος** *Hymenaios* from
Ὑμήν *Hymēn* (the god of *weddings*); *"hymenaeal"*; *Hymenaeus,* an opponent of Christianity :— Hymenaeus.

G5212 **ὑμέτερος** *hymeteros* from *G5210*; *yours,* i.e. *pertaining to you:*— your (own).

G5213 ὑμῖν *hymin* irregular dative of *G5210*; *to* (*with* or *by*) *you:*— ye, you, your, yourselves.

G5214 ὑμνέω *hymneō* from *G5215*; to *hymn,* i.e. sing a religious ode; by implication to *celebrate* (God) in song:— sing an hymn (praise unto).

G5215 ὕμνος *hymnos* apparently from a simpler (obsolete) form of

ὑδέω *hydeō* (to *celebrate;* probably akin to *G103*; compare *G5567*); a *"hymn"* or religious ode, (one of the Psalms):— hymn.

G5216 ὑμῶν *hymōn* genetive of *G5210*; *of* (*from* or *concerning*) *you:*— ye, you, your (own), yourselves.

G5217 ὑπάγω *hypagō* from *G5259* and *G71*; to *lead* (oneself) *under,* i.e. *withdraw* or *retire* (as if *sinking* out of sight), literally or figuratively:— depart, get hence, go way, go away.

G5218 ὑπακοή *hypakoē* from *G5219*; *attentive hearkening,* i.e. (by implication) *compliance* or *submission:*— obedience, (make) obedient, obey, obeying.

G5219 ὑπακούω *hypakouō* from *G5259* and *G191*; to *hear under* (as a *subordinate*), i.e. to *listen attentively;* by implication to *heed* or *conform* to a command or authority:— hearken, be obedient to, obey.

G5220 ὕπανδρος *hypandros* from *G5259* and *G435*; in subjection *under a man,* i.e. a *married* woman:— which hath an husband.

G5221 ὑπαντάω *hypantaō* from *G5259* and a derivative of *G473*; to *go opposite* (*meet*) *under* (*quietly*), i.e. to *encounter, fall in with:*— (go to) meet.

G5222 ὑπάντησις *hypantēsis* from *G5221*; an *encounter* or *concurrence* (with *G1519* for infinitive, in order to *fall in with*):— meeting.

G5223 ὕπαρξις *hyparxis* from *G5225*; *existence* or *proprietorship,* i.e. (concretely) *property, wealth:*— goods, substance.

G5224 ὑπάρχοντα *hyparchonta* neuter plural of present participle active of *G5225* as noun; things *extant* or *in hand,* i.e. *property* or *possessions:*— goods, that which one has, things which (one) possesseth, substance, that hast.

G5225 ὑπάρχω *hyparchō* from *G5259* and *G756*; to *begin under* (*quietly*), i.e. *come into existence* (*be present* or *at hand*); expletively, to *exist* (as copula or subordinate to an adjective, participle, adverb or preposition, or as auxiliary to principal verb):— after, behave, live.

G5226 ὑπείκω *hypeikō* from *G5259* and

εἴκω *eikō* (to *yield,* be *"weak"*); to *surrender:*— submit self.

G5227 ὑπεναντίος *hypenantios* from *G5259* and *G1727*; *under* (*covertly*), *contrary* to, i.e. *opposed* or (as noun) an *opponent:*— adversary, against.

G5228 ὑπέρ *hyper* a primary preposition; *"over"*, i.e. (with the genetive) of place, *above, beyond, across,* or causal, *for* the sake of, *instead, regarding;* with the accusative *superior to,* more *than.* In compounds it retains many of the above applications:— (exceeding abundantly) above, in (on) behalf of, beyond, by, very chiefest, concerning, exceeding (above), exceedingly, for, very highly, more (than), of, over, on the part of, for sake of, in stead, than, to, toward, very.

G5229 ὑπεραίρομαι *hyperairomai* middle from *G5228* and *G142*; to *raise* oneself *over,* i.e. (figuratively) to *become haughty:*— exalt self, be exalted above measure.

G5230 ὑπέρακμος *hyperakmos* from *G5228* and the base of *G188*; *beyond* the *"acme"*, i.e. figuratively (of a daughter) *past* the *bloom* (*prime*) of youth:— pass the flower of (her) age.

G5231 ὑπεράνω *hyperanō* from *G5228* and *G507*; *above upward,* i.e. *greatly higher* (in place or rank) :— far above, over.

G5232 ὑπεραυξάνω *hyperauxanō* from *G5228* and *G837*; to *increase above* ordinary degree:— grow exceedingly.

G5233 ὑπερβαίνω *hyperbainō* from *G5228* and the base of *G939*; to *transcend,* i.e. (figuratively) to *overreach:*— go beyond.

G5234 ὑπερβαλλόντως *hyperballontōs* adverb from present participle active of *G5235*; *excessively:*— beyond measure.

G5235 ὑπερβάλλω *hyperballō* from *G5228* and *G906*; to *throw beyond* the usual mark, i.e. (figuratively) to *surpass* (only active participle *supereminent*):— exceeding, excel, pass.

G5236 ὑπερβολή *hyperbolē* from *G5235*; a *throwing beyond* others, i.e. (figuratively) *supereminence;* adverb (with *G1519* or *G2596*) *pre-eminently:*— abundance, (far more) exceeding, excellency, more excellent, beyond (out of) measure.

G5237 ὑπερείδω *hypereidō* from *G5228* and *G1492*; to *overlook,* i.e. *not punish:*— wink at.

G5238 ὑπερέκεινα *hyperekeina* from *G5228* and the neuter plural of *G1565*; *above those* parts, i.e. *still farther:*— beyond.

G5239 ὑπερεκτείνω *hyperekteinō* from *G5228* and *G1614*; to *extend inordinately:*— stretch beyond.

G5240 ὑπερεκχύνω *hyperekchynō* from *G5228* and the alternate form of *G1632*; to *pour out over,* i.e. (passive) to *overflow:*— run over.

G5241 ὑπερεντυγχάνω *hyperentynchanō* from *G5228* and *G1793*; to *intercede in behalf of:*— make intercession for.

G5242 ὑπερέχω *hyperechō* from *G5228* and *G2192*; to *hold* oneself *above,* i.e. (figuratively) to *excel;* participle (as adjective, or neuter as noun) *superior, superiority:*— better, excellency, higher, pass, supreme.

G5243 ὑπερηφανία *hyperēphania* from *G5244*; *haughtiness:*— pride.

G5244 ὑπερήφανος *hyperēphanos* from *G5228* and *G5316*; *appearing above* others (*conspicuous*), i.e. (figuratively) *haughty:*— proud.

G5245 ὑπερνικάω *hypernikaō* from *G5228* and *G3528*; to *vanquish beyond,* i.e. *gain* a decisive *victory:*— more than conquer.

G5246 ὑπέρογκος *hyperonkos* from *G5228* and *G3591*; *bulging over,* i.e. (figuratively) *insolent:*— great swelling.

G5247 ὑπεροχή *hyperochē* from *G5242*; *prominence,* i.e. (figuratively) *superiority* (in rank or character):— authority, excellency.

G5248 ὑπερπερισσεύω *hyperperisseuō* from *G5228* and *G4052*; to *super-abound:*— abound much more, exceeding.

G5249 ὑπερπερισσῶς *hyperperissōs* from *G5228* and *G4057*; *superabundantly,* i.e. *exceedingly:*— beyond measure.

G5250 ὑπερπλεονάζω *hyperpleonazō* from *G5228* and *G4121*; to *super-abound:*— be exceeding abundant.

G5251 ὑπερυψόω *hyperypsoō* from *G5228* and *G5312*; to *elevate above* others, i.e. *raise* to the *highest* position:— highly exalt.

G5252 ὑπερφρονέω *hyperphroneō* from *G5228* and *G5426*; to *esteem* oneself *overmuch,* i.e. *be vain* or *arrogant:*— think more highly.

G5253 ὑπερῷον *hyperōon* neuter of a derivative of *G5228*; a *higher* part of the house, i.e. apartment in the *third story:*— upper chamber (room).

G5254 ὑπέχω *hypechō* from *G5259* and *G2192*; to *hold* oneself *under,* i.e. *endure* with patience:— suffer.

G5255 ὑπήκοος *hypēkoos* from *G5219*; *attentively listening,* i.e. (by implication) *submissive:*— obedient.

G5256 ὑπηρετέω *hypēreteō* from *G5257*; to *be a subordinate,* i.e. (by implication) *serve as a subordinate:*— minister (unto), serve.

G5257 ὑπηρέτης *hypēretēs* from *G5259* and a derivative of

ἐρέσσω *eressō* (to *row*); an *under-oarsman,* i.e. (generally) *subordinate* (*assistant, sexton, constable*):— minister, officer, servant.

G5258 ὕπνος *hypnos* from an obsolete primary (perhaps akin to *G5259* through the idea of *subsilience*); *sleep,* i.e. (figuratively) spiritual *torpor:*— sleep.

G5259 ὑπό *hypo* a primary preposition; *under,* i.e. (with the genitive) of place (*beneath*), or with verbs (the agency or means, *through*); (with the accusative) of place (whither [*underneath*] or where [*below*]) or time (when [*at*]). In compounds it retains the same general applications, especially of *inferior* position or condition, and specifically *covertly* or *moderately:*— among, by, from, in, of, under, with.

G5260 ὑποβάλλω *hypoballō* from *G5259* and *G906*; to *throw* in *stealthily,* i.e. *introduce* by collusion:— suborn.

G5261 ὑπογραμμός *hypogrammos* from a compound of *G5259* and *G1125*; an *underwriting,* i.e. *copy* for imitation (figuratively):— example.

G5262 ὑπόδειγμα *hypodeigma* from *G5263*; an *exhibit* for imitation or warning (figuratively *specimen, adumbration*):— example, pattern.

G5263 ὑποδείκνυμι *hypodeiknymi* from *G5259* and *G1166*; to *exhibit under* the eyes, i.e. (figuratively) to *exemplify* (*instruct, admonish*):— show, warn, forewarn.

G5264 ὑποδέχομαι *hypodechomai* from *G5259* and *G1209*; to *admit under* one's roof, i.e. *entertain* hospitably:— receive.

G5265 ὑποδέω *hypodeō* from *G5259* and *G1210*; to *bind under* one's feet, i.e. *put on* shoes or sandals:— bind on, (be) shod.

G5266 ὑπόδημα *hypodēma* from *G5265*; something *bound under* the feet, i.e. a *shoe* or *sandal:*— shoe.

G5267 ὑπόδικος *hypodikos* from *G5259* and *G1349*; *under sentence,* i.e. (by implication) *condemned:*— guilty.

G5268 ὑποζύγιον *hypozygion* neuter of a compound of *G5259* and *G2218*; an animal *under* the *yoke* (*draught-beast*), i.e. (specifically) a *donkey*:— ass.

G5269 **ὑποζώννυμι** *hypozōnnymi* from *G5259* and *G2224*; to *gird under,* i.e. *bind* (a vessel with cables across the keel, sides and deck):— undergirt.

G5270 **ὑποκάτω** *hypokatō* from *G5259* and *G2736*; *down under,* i.e. *beneath*:— under.

G5271 **ὑποκρίνομαι** *hypokrinomai* middle from *G5259* and *G2919*; to *decide* (*speak* or *act*) *under* a false part, i.e. (figuratively) *dissemble* (*pretend*) :— feign.

G5272 **ὑπόκρισις** *hypokrisis* from *G5271*; *acting under* a feigned part, i.e. (figuratively) *deceit* ("*hypocrisy*"):— condemnation, dissimulation, hypocrisy.

G5273 **ὑποκριτής** *hypokritēs* from *G5271*; an *actor under* an assumed character (*stage-player*), i.e. (figuratively) a *dissembler* ("*hypocrite*"):— hypocrite.

G5274 **ὑπολαμβάνω** *hypolambanō* from *G5259* and *G2983*; to *take* from *below,* i.e. *carry upward;* figuratively to *take up,* i.e. *continue* a discourse or topic; mentally to *assume* (*presume*):— answer, receive, suppose.

G5275 **ὑπολείπω** *hypoleipō* from *G5295* and Greek *G3007*; to *leave under* (*behind*), i.e. (passive) to *remain* (*survive*):— be left.

G5276 **ὑπολήνιον** *hypolēnion* neuter of a presumed compound of *G5259* and *G3025*; vessel or receptacle *under* the *press,* i.e. lower *wine vat*:— winefat.

G5277 **ὑπολιμπάνω** *hypolimpanō* a prolonged form for *G5275*; to *leave behind,* i.e. *bequeath*:— leave.

G5278 **ὑπομένω** *hypomenō* from *G5259* and *G3306*; to *stay under* (*behind*), i.e. *remain;* figuratively to *undergo,* i.e. *bear* (trials), *have fortitude, persevere*:— abide, endure, patient, take patiently, suffer, tarry behind.

G5279 **ὑπομιμνήσκω** *hypomimnēskō* from *G5259* and *G3403*; to *remind quietly,* i.e. *suggest* to the (middle, one's own) memory:— put in mind, remember, bring to (put in) remembrance.

G5280 **ὑπόμνησις** *hypomnēsis* from *G5279*; a *reminding* or (reflexive) *recollection*:— remembrance.

G5281 **ὑπομονή** *hypomonē* from *G5278*; cheerful (or hopeful) *endurance, constancy*:— enduring, patience, patient continuance (waiting).

G5282 **ὑπονοέω** *hyponoeō* from *G5259* and *G3539*; to *think under* (*privately*), i.e. to *surmise* or *conjecture*:— think, suppose, deem.

G5283 **ὑπόνοια** *hyponoia* from *G5282*; *suspicion* :— surmising.

G5284 **ὑποπλέω** *hypopleō* from *G5259* and *G4126*; to *sail under* the lee of:— sail under.

G5285 **ὑποπνέω** *hypopneō* from *G5259* and *G4154*; to *breathe gently,* i.e. *breeze*:— blow softly.

G5286 **ὑποπόδιον** *hypopodion* neuter of a compound of *G5259* and *G4228*; something *under* the *feet,* i.e. a *foot-rest* (figurative):— footstool.

G5287 **ὑπόστασις** *hypostasis* from a compound of *G5259* and *G2476*; a *setting under* (*support*), i.e. (figuratively) concrete *essence,* or abstract *assurance* (objective or subjective):— confidence, confident, person, substance.

G5288 **ὑποστέλλω** *hypostellō* from *G5259* and *G4724*; to *withhold under* (*out of sight*), i.e. (reflexive) to *cower* or *shrink,* (figuratively) to *conceal* (*reserve*):— draw (keep) back, shun, withdraw.

G5289 **ὑποστολή** *hypostolē* from *G5288*; *shrinkage* (*timidity*), i.e. (by implication) *apostasy*:— draw back.

G5290 **ὑποστρέφω** *hypostrephō* from *G5259* and *G4762*; to *turn under* (*behind*), i.e. to *return* (literally or figuratively):— come again, return (again, back again), turn back (again).

G5291 **ὑποστρώννυμι** *hypostrōnnymi* from *G5259* and *G4766*; to *strew underneath* (the feet as a carpet):— spread.

G5292 **ὑποταγή** *hypotagē* from *G5293*; *subordination*:— subjection.

G5293 **ὑποτάσσω** *hypotassō* from *G5259* and *G5021*; to *subordinate;* reflexive to *obey*:— be under obedience (obedient), put under, subdue unto, (be, make) subject (to, unto), be (put) in subjection (to, under), submit self unto.

G5294 **ὑποτίθημι** *hypotithēmi* from *G5259* and *G5087*; to *place underneath,* i.e. (figuratively) to *hazard,* (reflexive) to *suggest*:— lay down, put in remembrance.

G5295 **ὑποτρέχω** *hypotrechō* from *G5259* and *G5143* (including its alternate); to *run under,* i.e. (specifically) to *sail past*:— run under.

G5296 **ὑποτύπωσις** *hypotypōsis* from a compound of *G5259* and a derivative of *G5179*; *typification under* (*after*), i.e. (concretely) a *sketch* (figuratively) for imitation:— form, pattern.

G5297 **ὑποφέρω** *hypopherō* from *G5259* and *G5342*; to *bear* from *underneath,* i.e. (figuratively) to *undergo* hardship:— bear, endure.

G5298 **ὑποχωρέω** *hypochōreō* from *G5259* and *G5562*; to *vacate down,* i.e. *retire* quietly:— go aside, withdraw self.

G5299 **ὑπωπιάζω** *hypōpiazō* from a compound of *G5259* and a derivative of *G3700*; to hit *under* the *eye* (*buffet* or *disable* an antagonist as a pugilist), i.e. (figuratively) to *tease* or *annoy* (into compliance), *subdue* (one's passions):— keep under, weary.

G5300 **ὗς** *hys* apparently a primary word; a *hog* ("*swine*"):— sow.

G5301 **ὕσσωπος** *hyssōpos* of foreign origin [H231]; "*hyssop*":— hyssop.

G5302 **ὑστερέω** *hystereō* from *G5306*; to *be later,* i.e. (by implication) to *be inferior;* generally to *fall short (be deficient)*:— come behind (short), be destitute, fail, lack, suffer need, (be in) want, be the worse.

G5303 **ὑστέρημα** *hysterēma* from *G5302*; a *deficit;* specifically *poverty*:— that which is behind, lack, that which was lacking, penury, want.

G5304 **ὑστέρησις** *hysterēsis* from *G5302*; a *falling short,* i.e. (specifically) *penury*:— want.

G5305 **ὕστερον** *hysteron* neuter of *G5306* as adverb; *more lately,* i.e. *eventually*:— afterward, (at the) last (of all).

G5306 **ὕστερος** *hysteros* comparative from *G5259* (in the sense of *behind*); *later*:— latter.

G5307 **ὑφαντός** *hyphantos* from **ὑφαίνω** *hyphainō* (to *weave*); *woven,* i.e. (perhaps) *knitted*:— woven.

G5308 **ὑψηλός** *hypsēlos* from *G5311*; *lofty* (in place or character):— high, higher, highly (esteemed).

G5309 **ὑψηλοφρονέω** *hypsēlophroneō* from a compound of *G5308* and *G5424*; to *be lofty in mind,* i.e. *arrogant*:— be highminded.

G5310 **ὕψιστος** *hypsistos* superlative from the base of *G5311*; *highest,* i.e. (masculine singular) the *Supreme* (God), or (neuter plural) the *heavens*:— most high, highest.

G5311 **ὕψος** *hypsos* from a derivative of *G5228*; *elevation,* i.e. (abstract) *altitude,* (specifically) the *sky,* or (figuratively) *dignity*:— be exalted, height, (on) high.

G5312 **ὑψόω** *hypsoō* from *G5311*; to *elevate* (literally or figuratively):— exalt, lift up.

G5313 **ὕψωμα** *hypsōma* from *G5312*; an *elevated* place or thing, i.e. (abstract) *altitude,* or (by implication) a *barrier* (figurative):— height, high thing.

Φ

G5314 **φάγος** *phagos* from *G5315*; a *glutton*:— gluttonous.

G5315 **φάγω** *phagō* a primary verb (used as an alternate of *G2068* in certain tenses); to *eat* (literally or figuratively):— eat, meat.

G5316 **φαίνω** *phainō* prolonged for the base of *G5457*; to *lighten* (*shine*), i.e. *show* (transitive or intransitive, literally or figuratively):— appear, seem, be seen, shine, think.

G5317 **Φάλεκ** *Phalek* of Hebrew origin [H6389]; *Phalek* (i.e. *Peleg*), a patriarch:— Phalec.

G5318 **φανερός** *phaneros* from *G5316*; *shining,* i.e. *apparent* (literally or figuratively); neuter (as adverb) *publicly, externally*:— abroad, appear, known, manifest, open, openly, outward, outwardly.

G5319 **φανερόω** *phaneroō* from *G5318*; to *render apparent* (literally or figuratively):— appear, manifestly declare, (make) manifest (forth), shew (self).

G5320 **φανερῶς** *phanerōs* adverb from *G5318*; *plainly,* i.e. *clearly* or *publicly*:— evidently, openly.

G5321 **φανέρωσις** *phanerōsis* from *G5319*; *exhibition,* i.e. (figuratively) *expression,* (by extension) a *bestowment*:— manifestation.

G5322 **φανός** *phanos* from *G5316*; that which *lightens,* i.e. *light; lantern*:— lantern.

G5323 **Φανουήλ** *Phanouēl* of Hebrew origin [H6439]; *Phanue'l* (i.e. *Penue'l*), an Israelite:— Phanuel.

G5324 **φαντάζω** *phantazō* from a derivative of *G5316*; to *make apparent,* i.e. (passive) to *appear* (neuter participle as noun, a *spectacle*):— sight.

G5325 **φαντασία** *phantasia* from a derivative of *G5324*; (properly abstract) a (vain) *show* ("fantasy"):— pomp.

G5326 **φάντασμα** *phantasma* from *G5324*; (properly concrete) a (mere) *show* ("phantasm"), i.e. *specter*:— spirit.

G5327 **φάραγξ** *pharanx* properly strengthened from the base of *G4008* or rather of *G4486*; a *gap* or *chasm,* i.e. *ravine* (*winter-torrent*):— valley.

G5328 **Φαραώ** *Pharaō* of foreign origin [H6547]; *Pharao'* (i.e. *Pharoh*), an Egyptian king:— Pharaoh.

G5329 **Φαρές** *Phares* of Hebrew origin [H6557]; *Phares* (i.e. *Perets*), an Israelite:— Phares.

G5330 **Φαρισαῖος** *Pharisaios* of Hebrew origin [compare H6567]; a *separatist,* i.e. exclusively *religious;* a *Pharisaean,* i.e. Jewish sectary:— Pharisee.

***G5331* φαρμακεία** *pharmakeia* from *G5332*; *medication* ("pharmacy"), i.e. (by extension) *magic* (literal or figurative):— sorcery, witchcraft.

***G5332* φαρμακεύς** *pharmakeus* from
φάρμακον *pharmakon* (a *drug,* i.e. spell-giving *potion*); a *druggist* ("pharmacist") or *poisoner,* i.e. (by extension) a *magician:*— sorcerer.

***G5333* φαρμακός** *pharmakos* the same as *G5332*; the same as *G5332*:— sorcerer.

***G5334* φάσις** *phasis* from *G5346* (not the same as "phase", which is from *G5316*); a *saying,* i.e. *report:*— tidings.

***G5335* φάσκω** *phaskō* prolonged from the same as *G5346*; to *assert:*— affirm, profess, say.

***G5336* φάτνη** *phatnē* from
πατέομαι *pateomai* (to *eat*); a *crib* (for fodder):— manger, stall.

***G5337* φαῦλος** *phaulos* apparently a primary word; *"foul"* or *"flawed"*, i.e. (figuratively) *wicked:*— evil.

***G5338* φέγγος** *phengos* probably akin to the base of *G5457* [compare *G5350*]; *brilliancy:*— light.

***G5339* φείδομαι** *pheidomai* of uncertain affinity; to *be chary* of, i.e. (subjectively) to *abstain* or (objectively) to *treat leniently:*— forbear, spare.

***G5340* φειδομένως** *pheidomenōs* adverb from participle of *G5339*; *abstemiously,* i.e. *stingily:*— sparingly.

***G5341* φελόνης** *phelonēs* by transposition for a derivative probably of *G5316* (as *showing* outside the other garments); a *mantle* (*overcoat*):— cloke.

***G5342* φέρω** *pherō* a primary verb (for which other and apparently not cognate ones are used in certain tenses only; namely,
οἴω *oiō* and
ἐνέγκω *enenkō*); to *"bear"* or *carry* (in a very wide application, literally and figuratively, as follows):— be, bear, bring (forth), carry, come, let her drive, be driven, endure, go on, lay, lead, move, reach, rushing, uphold.

***G5343* φεύγω** *pheugō* apparently a primary verb; to *run away* (literally or figuratively); by implication to *shun;* by analogy to *vanish:*— escape, flee (away).

***G5344* Φῆλιξ** *Phēlix* of Latin origin; *happy; Phelix* (i.e. *Felix*), a Roman:— Felix.

***G5345* φήμη** *phēmē* from *G5346*; a *saying,* i.e. *rumor* ("fame"):— fame.

***G5346* φημί** *phēmi* properly the same as the base of *G5457* and *G5316*; to *show* or *make known* one's thoughts, i.e. *speak* or *say:*— affirm, say. Compare *G3004*.

***G5347* Φῆστος** *Phēstos* of Latin derivation; *festal; Phestus* (i.e. *Festus*), a Roman:— Festus.

***G5348* φθάνω** *phthanō* apparently a primary verb; to *be beforehand,* i.e. *anticipate* or *precede;* by extension to *have arrived* at:— (already) attain, come, prevent.

***G5349* φθαρτός** *phthartos* from *G5351*; *decayed,* i.e. (by implication) *perishable:*— corruptible.

***G5350* φθέγγομαι** *phthengomai* probably akin to *G5338* and thus to *G5346*; to *utter* a clear sound, i.e. (generally) to *proclaim:*— speak.

***G5351* φθείρω** *phtheirō* probably strengthened from
φθίω *phthiō* (to *pine* or *waste*); properly to *shrivel* or *wither,* i.e. to *spoil* (by any process) or (generally) to *ruin* (especially figuratively by moral influences, to *deprave*):— corrupt (self), defile, destroy.

***G5352* φθινοπωρινός** *phthinopōrinos* from a derivative of
φθίνω *phthinō* (to *wane;* akin to the base of *G5351*) and *G3703* (meaning *late autumn*); *autumnal* (as *stripped* of leaves):— whose fruit withereth.

***G5353* φθόγγος** *phthongos* from *G5350*; *utterance,* i.e. a *musical* note (vocal or instrumental):— sound.

***G5354* φθονέω** *phthoneō* from *G5355*; to *be jealous* of:— envy.

***G5355* φθόνος** *phthonos* probably akin to the base of *G5351*; *ill-will* (as *detraction*), i.e. *jealousy* (*spite*) :— envy.

***G5356* φθορά** *phthora* from *G5351*; *decay,* i.e. *ruin* (spontaneous or inflicted, literal or figurative):— corruption, destroy, perish.

***G5357* φιάλη** *phialē* of uncertain affinity; a broad shallow *cup* ("phial"):— vial.

***G5358* φιλάγαθος** *philagathos* from *G5384* and *G18*; *fond to good,* i.e. a *promoter of virtue:*— love of good men.

***G5359* Φ*λαδέλφεια** *Philadelpheia* from
Φ*λάδελφος *Philadelphos* (the same as *G5361*), a king of Pergamos; *Philadelphia,* a place in Asia Minor:— Philadelphia.

***G5360* φιλαδελφία** *philadelphia* from *G5361*; *fraternal affection:*— brotherly love (kindness), love of the brethren.

***G5361* φιλάδελφος** *philadelphos* from *G5384* and *G80*; *fond of brethren,* i.e. *fraternal:*— love as brethren.

***G5362* φίλανδρος** *philandros* from *G5384* and *G435*; *fond of man,* i.e. *affectionate* as a wife:— love their husbands.

***G5363* φιλανθρωπία** *philanthrōpia* from the same as *G5364* and *G444*; *fondly to man* ("philanthropically"), i.e. *humanely:*— courteously.

***G5364* φιλανθρώπως** *philanthrōpōs* adverb from a compound of *G5384* and *G444*; *fondly to man* ("philanthropically"), i.e. *humanely:*— courteously.

***G5365* φιλαργυρία** *philargyria* from *G5366*; *avarice:*— love of money.

***G5366* φιλάργυρος** *philargyros* from *G5384* and *G696*; *fond of silver* (*money*), i.e. *avaricious:*— covetous.

***G5367* φίλαυτος** *philautos* from *G5384* and *G846*; *fond of self,* i.e. *selfish:*— lover of own self.

***G5368* φιλέω** *phileō* from *G5384*; to *be a friend to* (*fond of* [an individual or an object]), i.e. *have affection* for (denoting *personal* attachment, as a matter of sentiment or feeling; while *G25* is wider, embracing especially the judgment and the *deliberate* assent of the will as a matter of principle, duty and propriety: the two thus stand related very much as *G2309* and *G1014*, or as *G2372* and *G3563* respectively; the former being chiefly of the *heart* and the latter of the *head*); specifically to *kiss* (as a mark of tenderness):— kiss, love.

***G5369* φιλήδονος** *philēdonos* from *G5384* and *G2237*; *fond of pleasure,* i.e. *voluptuous:*— lover of pleasure.

***G5370* φίλημα** *philēma* from *G5368*; a *kiss:*— kiss.

***G5371* Φ*λήμων** *Philēmōn* from *G5368*; *friendly; Philemon,* a Christian:— Philemon.

***G5372* Φ*λητός** *Philētos* from *G5368*; *amiable; Philetus,* an opponent of Christianity:— Philetus.

***G5373* φιλία** *philia* from *G5384*; *fondness:*— friendship.

***G5374* Φ*λιππήσιος** *Philippēsios* from *G5375*; a *Philippesian* (*Philippian*), i.e. native of Philippi:— Philippian.

***G5375* Φίλιπποι** *Philippoi* plural of *G5376*; *Philippi,* a place in Macedonia:— Philippi.

***G5376* Φίλιππος** *Philippos* from *G5384* and *G2462*; *fond of horses; Philippus,* the name of four Israelites:— Philip.

***G5377* φιλόθεος** *philotheos* from *G5384* and *G2316*; *fond of God,* i.e. *pious:*— lover of God.

GRK

***G5378* Φ*λόλογος** *Philologos* from *G5384* and *G3056*; *fond of words,* i.e. *talkative* (*argumentative, learned, "philological"*); *Philologus,* a Christian:— Philologus.

***G5379* φιλονεικία** *philoneikia* from *G5380*; *quarrelsomeness,* i.e. a *dispute:*— strife.

***G5380* φιλόνεικος** *philoneikos* from *G5384* and
νεῖκος *neikos* (a *quarrel;* probably akin to *G3534*); *fond of strife,* i.e. *disputatious:*— contentious.

***G5381* φιλονεξία** *philonexia* from *G5382*; *hospitality:*— entertain strangers, hospitality.

***G5382* φιλόξενος** *philoxenos* from *G5384* and *G3581*; *fond of guests,* i.e. *hospitable:*— given to (lover of, use) hospitality.

***G5383* φιλοπρωτεύω** *philoprōteuō* from a compound of *G5384* and *G4413*; to *be fond of being first,* i.e. *ambitious* of distinction:— love to have the preeminence.

***G5384* φίλος** *philos*; properly *dear,* i.e. a *friend;* active *fond,* i.e. *friendly* (still as a noun, an *associate, neighbor,* etc.):— friend.

***G5385* φιλοσοφία** *philosophia* from *G5386*; *"philosophy"*, i.e. (specifically) Jewish *sophistry:*— philosophy.

***G5386* φιλόσοφος** *philosophos* from *G5384* and *G4680*; *fond of wise* things, i.e. a *"philosopher"*:— philosopher.

***G5387* φιλόστοργος** *philostorgos* from *G5384* and
στοργή *storgē* (*cherishing* one's kindred, especially parents or children); *fond of* natural *relatives,* i.e. *fraternal* towards fellow Christians:— kindly affectioned.

***G5388* φιλότεκνος** *philoteknos* from *G5384* and *G5043*; *fond of* one's *children,* i.e. *maternal:*— love their children.

***G5389* φιλοτιμέομαι** *philotimeomai* middle from a compound of *G5384* and *G5092*; to be *fond of honor,* i.e. *emulous* (*eager* or *earnest* to do something):— labour, strive, study.

***G5390* φιλοφρόνως** *philophronōs* adverb from *G5391*; *with friendliness of mind,* i.e. *kindly:*— courteously.

***G5391* φιλόφρων** *philophrōn* from *G5384* and *G5424*; *friendly of mind,* i.e. *kind:*— courteous.

***G5392* φιμόω** *phimoō* from
φιμός *phimos* (a *muzzle*); to *muzzle:*— muzzle.

G5393 Φλέγων *Phlegōn* active participle of the base of *G5395*; *blazing; Phlegon,* a Christian:— Phlegon.

G5394 φλογίζω *phlogizō* from *G5395*; to *cause a blaze,* i.e. *ignite* (figuratively to *inflame* with passion):— set on fire.

G5395 φλόξ *phlox* from a primary
φλέγω *phlegō* (to *"flash"* or *"flame"*); a *blaze* :— flame, flaming.

G5396 φλυαρέω *phlyareō* from *G5397*; to *be a babbler* or *trifler,* i.e. (by implication) to *berate* idly or mischievously:— prate against.

G5397 φλύαρος *phlyaros* from
φλύω *phlyō* (to *bubble*); a *garrulous* person, i.e. *prater:*— tattler.

G5398 φοβερός *phoberos* from *G5401*; *frightful,* i.e. (objectively) *formidable:*— fearful, terrible.

G5399 φοβέω *phobeō* from *G5401*; to *frighten,* i.e. (passive) to *be alarmed;* by analogy to *be in awe* of, i.e. *revere:*— be (+ sore) afraid, fear (exceedingly), reverence.

G5400 φόβητρον *phobētron* neuter of a derivative of *G5399*; a *frightening* thing, i.e. *terrific* portent:— fearful sight.

G5401 φόβος *phobos* from a primary
φήβομαι *phēbomai* (to *be* put in *fear*); *alarm* or *fright:*— be afraid, exceedingly, fear, terror.

G5402 Φοίβη *Phoibē* feminine of
φοῖβος *phoibos* (*bright;* probably akin to the base of *G5457*); *Phoebe,* a Christian woman:— Phebe.

G5403 Φοινίκη *Phoinikē* from *G5404*; *palm-*country; *Phoenice* (or *Phoenicia*), a region of Palestine:— Phenice, Phenicia.

G5404 φοῖνιξ *phoinix* of uncertain derivation; a *palm-*tree:— palm (tree).

G5405 Φοῖνιξ *Phoinix* probably the same as *G5404*; *Phoenix,* a place in Crete:— Phenice.

G5406 φονεύς *phoneus* from *G5408*; a *murderer* (always of *criminal* [or at least *intentional*] homicide; which *G443* does not necessarily imply; while *G4607* is a special term for a *public* bandit):— murderer.

G5407 φονεύω *phoneuō* from *G5406*; to *be a murderer* (of):— kill, do murder, slay.

G5408 φόνος *phonos* from an obsolete primary
φένω *phenō* (to *slay*); *murder:*— murder, be slain with, slaughter.

G5409 φορέω *phoreō* from *G5411*; to *have a burden,* i.e. (by analogy) to *wear* as clothing or a constant accompaniment:— bear, wear.

G5410 Φόρον *Phoron* of Latin origin; a *forum* or market-place; only in compound with *G675*; a *station* on the Appian road:— forum.

G5411 φόρος *phoros* from *G5342*; a *load* (as *borne*), i.e. (figuratively) a *tax* (properly an individual *assessment* on persons or property; whereas *G5056* is usually a generic *toll* on goods or travel):— tribute.

G5412 φορτίζω *phortizō* from *G5414*; to *load* up (properly as a vessel or animal), i.e. (figuratively) to *overburden* with ceremony (or spiritual anxiety):— lade, be heavy laden.

G5413 φορτίον *phortion* diminutive of *G5414*; an *invoice* (as part of *freight*), i.e. (figuratively) a *task* or *service:*— burden.

G5414 φόρτος *phortos* from *G5342*; something *carried,* i.e. the *cargo* of a ship:— lading.

G5415 Φορτουνάτος *Phortounatos* of Latin origin; *"fortunate"; Fortunatus,* a Christian:— Fortunatus.

G5416 φραγέλλιον *phragellion* neuter of a derived from the base of *G5417*; a *whip,* i.e. Roman *lash* as a public punishment:— scourge.

G5417 φραγελλόω *phragelloō* from a presumed equivalent of the Latin *flagellum;* to *whip,* i.e. *lash* as a public punishment:— scourge.

G5418 φραγμός *phragmos* from *G5420*; a *fence,* or inclosing *barrier* (literal or figurative):— hedge (+ round about), partition.

G5419 φράζω *phrazō* probably akin to *G5420* through the idea of *defining;* to *indicate* (by word or act), i.e. (specifically) to *expound:*— declare.

G5420 φράσσω *phrassō* apparently a strengthened form of the base of *G5424*; to *fence* or enclose, i.e. (specifically) to *block* up (figuratively to *silence*):— stop.

G5421 φρέαρ *phrear* of uncertain derivation; a *hole* in the ground (dug for obtaining or holding water or other purposes), i.e. a *cistern* or *well;* figuratively an *abyss* (as a *prison*):— well, pit.

G5422 φρεναπατάω *phrenapataō* from *G5423*; to *be a mind-misleader,* i.e. *delude:*— deceive.

G5423 φρεναπάτης *phrenapatēs* from *G5424* and *G539*; a *mind-misleader,* i.e. *seducer:*— deceiver.

G5424 φρήν *phrēn* probably from an obsolete
φράω *phraō* (to *rein* in or *curb;* compare *G5420*); the *midriff* (as a *partition* of the body), i.e. (figuratively and by implication of sympathy) the *feelings* (or sensitive nature; by extension [also in the plural] the *mind* or cognitive faculties):— understanding.

G5425 φρίσσω *phrissō* apparently a primary verb; to *"bristle"* or *chill,* i.e. *shudder* (*fear*):— tremble.

G5426 φρονέω *phroneō* from *G5424*; to *exercise* the *mind,* i.e. *entertain* or *have a sentiment* or *opinion;* by implication to *be* (mentally) *disposed* (more or less earnestly in a certain direction); intensively to *interest oneself* in (with concern or obedience):— set the affection on, care, be careful, (+ be of one, be of the same, let this) mind, (be like) minded, regard, savour, think.

G5427 φρόνημα *phronēma* from *G5426*; (mental) *inclination* or *purpose:*— mind, (be, be carnally, be spiritually) minded.

G5428 φρόνησις *phronēsis* from *G5426*; mental *action* or *activity,* i.e. intellectual or moral *insight:*— prudence, wisdom.

G5429 φρόνιμος *phronimos* from *G5424*; *thoughtful,* i.e. *sagacious* or *discreet* (implying a *cautious* character; while *G4680* denotes *practical* skill or acumen; and *G4908* indicates rather *intelligence* or mental acquirement); in a bad sense *conceited* (also in the comparative):— wise, wiser.

G5430 φρονίμως *phronimōs* adverb from *G5429*; *prudently:*— wisely.

G5431 φροντίζω *phrontizō* from a derivative of *G5424*; to *exercise thought,* i.e. *be anxious:*— be careful.

G5432 φρουρέω *phroureō* from a compound of *G4253* and *G3708*; to *be a watcher in advance,* i.e. to *mount guard* as a sentinel (*post spies* at gates); figuratively to *hem in, protect:*— keep (with a garrison). Compare *G5083*.

G5433 φρυάσσω *phryassō* akin to *G1032*, *G1031*; to *snort* (as a spirited horse), i.e. (figuratively) to *make a tumult:*— rage.

G5434 φρύγανον *phryganon* neuter of a presumed derivative of
φρύγω *phrygō* (to *roast* or *parch;* akin to the base of *G5395*); something *desiccated,* i.e. a dry *twig:*— stick.

G5435 Φρυγία *Phrygia* probably of foreign origin; *Phrygia,* a region of Asia Minor:— Phrygia.

G5436 Φύγελλος *PHygellos* probably from *G5343*; *fugitive; Phygellus,* an apostate Christian:— Phygellus.

G5437 φυγή *phygē* from *G5343*; a *fleeing,* i.e. *escape:*— flight.

G5438 φυλακή *phylakē* from *G5442*; a *guarding* (or concretely *guard*), the act, the person; figuratively the place, the condition, or (specifically) the time (as a division of day or night), literally or figuratively:— cage, hold, prison, imprisonment, ward, watch.

G5439 φυλακίζω *phylakizō* from *G5441*; to *incarcerate:*— imprison.

G5440 φυλακτήριον *phylaktērion* neuter of a derivative of *G5442*; a *guard-case,* i.e. *"phylactery"* for wearing slips of Scripture texts:— phylactery.

G5441 φύλαξ *phylax* from *G5442*; a *watcher* or *sentry:*— keeper.

G5442 φυλάσσω *phylassō* probably from *G5443* through the idea of *isolation;* to *watch,* i.e. *be on guard* (literally or figuratively); by implication to *preserve, obey, avoid:*— beware, keep (self), observe, save. Compare *G5083*.

G5443 φυλή *phylē* from *G5453* (compare *G5444*); an *offshoot,* i.e. *race* or *clan:*— kindred, tribe.

G5444 φύλλον *phyllon* from the same as *G5443*; a *sprout,* i.e. *leaf:*— leaf.

G5445 φύραμα *phyrama* from a prolonged form of
φύρω *phyrō* (to *mix* a liquid with a solid; perhaps akin to *G5453* through the idea of *swelling* in bulk), mean to *knead;* a *mass* of dough:— lump.

G5446 φυσικός *physikos* from *G5449*; *"physical"*, i.e. (by implication) *instinctive:*— natural. Compare *G5591*.

G5447 φυσικῶς *physikōs* adverb from *G5446*; *"physically"*, i.e. (by implication) *instinctively:*— naturally.

G5448 φυσιόω *physioō* from *G5449* in the primary sense of *blowing;* to *inflate,* i.e. (figuratively) *make proud* (*haughty*):— puff up.

G5449 φύσις *physis* from *G5453*; *growth* (by *germination* or *expansion*), i.e. (by implication) natural *production* (lineal *descent*); by extension a *genus* or *sort;* figuratively native *disposition, constitution* or *usage:*— kind, mankind, nature, natural.

G5450 φυσίωσις *physiōsis* from *G5448*; *inflation,* i.e. (figuratively) *haughtiness:*— swelling.

G5451 φυτεία *phyteia* from *G5452*; *planting* or *transplanting,* i.e. (concretely) a *shrub* or *vegetable:*— plant.

G5452 φυτεύω *phyteuō* from a derivative of *G5453*; to *set out* in the earth, i.e. *implant;* figuratively to *instill* doctrine:— plant.

G5453 φύω *phyō* a primary verb; probably originally to *"puff"* or *blow,* i.e. to *swell* up; but only used in the implied sense, to *germinate* or *grow* (*sprout, produce*), literally or figuratively:— spring (up).

G5454 φωλεός *phōleos* of uncertain derivation; a *burrow* or *lurking-place:*— hole.

G5455 φωνέω *phōneō* from G5456; to emit a *sound* (animal, human or instrumental); by implication to *address* in words or by name, also in imitation:— call (for), crow, cry.

G5456 φωνή *phōnē* probably akin to G5316 through the idea of *disclosure;* a *tone* (articulate, bestial or artificial); by implication an *address* (for any purpose), *saying* or *language:*— noise, sound, voice.

G5457 φῶς *phōs* from an obsolete

φάω *phaō* (to *shine* or make *manifest,* especially by *rays;* compare G5316, G5346); *luminosity* (in the widest application, natural or artificial, abstract or concrete, literal or figurative):— fire light.

G5458 φωστήρ *phōstēr* from G5457; an *illuminator,* i.e. (concretely) a *luminary,* or (abstractly) *brilliancy:*— light.

G5459 φωσφόρος *phōsphoros* from G5457 and G5342; *light-bearing* ("phosphorus"), i.e. (specifically) the *morning-star* (figuratively):— day star.

G5460 φωτεινός *phōteinos* from G5457; *lustrous,* i.e. *transparent* or *well-illuminated* (figuratively):— bright, full of light.

G5461 φωτίζω *phōtizō* from G5457; to *shed rays,* i.e. to *shine* or (transitive) to *brighten* up (literally or figuratively):— enlighten, illuminate, (bring to, give) light, make to see.

G5462 φωτισμός *phōtismos* from G5461; *illumination* (figurative):— light.

X

G5463 χαίρω *chairō* a primary verb; to *be cheerful,* i.e. calmly *happy* or well-off; impersonally especially as salutation (on meeting or parting), *be well:*— farewell, be glad, God speed, greeting, hail, joy, joyfully, rejoice.

G5464 χάλαζα *chalaza* probably from G5465; *hail* :— hail.

G5465 χαλάω *chalaō* from the base of G5490; to *lower* (as into a *void*):— let down, strike.

G5466 Χαλδαῖος *Chaldaios* probably of Hebrew origin [H3778]; a *Chaldaean* (i.e. *Kasdi*), or native of the region of the lower Euphrates:— Chaldaean.

G5467 χαλεπός *chalepos* perhaps from G5465 through the idea of *reducing* the strength; *difficult,* i.e. *dangerous,* or (by implication) *furious:*— fierce, perilous.

G5468 χαλιναγωγέω *chalinagōgeō* from a compound of G5469 and the reduplicated form of G71; to *be* a *bit-leader,* i.e. to *curb* (figuratively):— bridle.

G5469 χαλινός *chalinos* from G5465; a *curb* or *head-stall* (as *curbing* the spirit):— bit, bridle.

G5470 χάλκεος *chalkeos* from G5475; *coppery:*— brass.

G5471 χαλκεύς *chalkeus* from G5475; a *copper-worker* or *brazier:*— coppersmith.

G5472 χαλκηδών *chalkēdōn* from G5475 and perhaps G1491; *copper-like,* i.e. *"chalcedony":*— chalcedony.

G5473 χαλκίον *chalkion* diminutive from G5475; a *copper dish:*— brazen vessel.

G5474 χαλκολίβανον *chalkolibanon* neuter of a compound of G5475 and G3030 (in the implied meaning of *whiteness* or *brilliancy*); *burnished copper,* an alloy of copper (or gold) and silver having a brilliant luster:— fine brass.

G5475 χαλκός *chalkos* perhaps from Greek G5465 through the idea of *hollowing* out as a vessel (this metal being chiefly used for that purpose); *copper* (the substance, or some implement or coin made of it):— brass, money.

G5476 χαμαί *chamai* adverb perhaps from the base of G5490 through the idea of a *fissure* in the soil; *earthward,* i.e. *prostrate:*— on (to) the ground.

G5477 Χανάαν *Chanaan* of Hebrew origin [H3667]; *Chanaan* (i.e. *Kenaan*), the early name of Palestine:— Chanaan.

G5478 Χαναναῖος *Chananaios* from G5477; a *Chananaean* (i.e. *Kenaanite*), or native of gentile Palestine:— of Canaan.

G5479 χαρά *chara* from G5463; *cheerfulness,* i.e. calm *delight:*— gladness, greatly, joy, (be exceeding) joyful, joyfully, joyfulness, joyous.

G5480 χάραγμα *charagma* from the same as G5482; a *scratch* or *etching,* i.e. *stamp* (as a *badge* of servitude), or *sculptured* figure (*statue*):— graven, mark.

G5481 χαρακτήρ *charaktēr* from the same as G5482; a *graver* (the tool or the person), i.e. (by implication) *engraving* ([*"character"*], the *figure* stamped, i.e. an exact *copy* or [figurative] *representation*):— express image.

G5482 χάραξ *charax* from

χαράσσω *charassō* (to *sharpen* to a point; akin to G1125 through the idea of *scratching*); a *stake,* i.e. (by implication) a *palisade* or *rampart* (military *mound* or surrounding rampart in a siege) :— trench.

G5483 χαρίζομαι *charizomai* middle from G5485; to grant as a *favor,* i.e. gratuitously, in kindness, pardon or rescue:— deliver, (frankly) forgive, (freely) give, grant.

G5484 χάριν *charin* accusative of G5485 as preposition; through *favor* of, i.e. *on account* of:— be (for) cause of, for sake of, + . . . fore, reproachfully.

G5485 χάρις *charis* from G5463; *graciousness* (as *gratifying*), of manner or act (abstract or concrete; literal, figurative or spiritual; especially the divine influence upon the heart, and its reflection in the life; including *gratitude*):— acceptable, benefit, favour, gift, grace, gracious, joy, liberality, pleasure, thank, thanks, thankworthy.

G5486 χάρισμα *charisma* from G5483; a (divine) *gratuity,* i.e. *deliverance* (from danger or passion); (specifically) a (spiritual) *endowment,* i.e. (subjectively) religious *qualification,* or (objectively) miraculous *faculty:*— (free) gift.

G5487 χαριτόω *charitoō* from G5485; to *grace,* i.e. impart special *honor:*— make accepted, be highly favoured.

G5488 Χαρράν *Charrhan* of Hebrew origin [H2771]; *Charrhan* (i.e. *Charan*), a place in Mesopotamia:— Charran.

G5489 χάρτης *chartēs* from the same as G5482; a *sheet* ("chart") of writing-material (as to be *scribbled* over):— paper.

G5490 χάσμα *chasma* from a form of an obsolete primary

χηαο *chēao* (to *"gape"* or *"yawn"*); a *"chasm"* or *vacancy* (impassable *interval*):— gulf.

G5491 χεῖλος *cheilos* from a form of the same as G5490; a *lip* (as a *pouring* place); figuratively a *margin* (of water):— lip, shore.

G5492 χειμάζω *cheimazō* from the same as G5494; to *storm,* i.e. (passive) to *labor under a gale:*— be tossed with tempest.

G5493 χείμαρρος *cheimarrhos* from the base of G5494 and G4482; a *storm-runlet,* i.e. *winter-torrent:*— brook.

G5494 χειμών *cheimōn* from a derivative of

χέω *cheō* (to *pour;* akin to the base of G5490 through the idea of a *channel*), meaning a *storm* (as *pouring* rain); by implication the *rainy* season, i.e. *winter:*— tempest, foul weather, winter.

G5495 χείρ *cheir* perhaps from the base of G5494 in the sense of its congener the base of G5490 (through the idea of *hollowness* for grasping); the *hand* (literal or figurative [*power*]; especially [by Hebrew] a *means* or *instrument*):— hand.

G5496 χειραγωγέω *cheiragōgeō* from G5497; to be a *hand-leader,* i.e. to *guide* (a blind person):— lead by the hand.

G5497 χειραγωγός *cheiragōgos* from G5495 and a reduplicated form of G71; a *hand-leader,* i.e. personal *conductor* (of a blind person):— some to lead by the hand.

G5498 χειρόγραφον *cheirographon* neuter of a compound of G5495 and G1125; something *handwritten* (*"chirograph"*), i.e. a *manuscript* (specifically a legal *document* or *bond* [figurative]):— handwriting.

G5499 χειροποίητος *cheiropoiētos* from G5495 and a derivative of G4160; *manufactured,* i.e. *of human construction:*— made by (make with) hands.

G5500 χειροτονέω *cheirotoneō* from a compound of G5495 and

τείνω *teinō* (to *stretch*); to *reach with the hand* or *vote* (by raising the hand), i.e. (generally) to *select* or *appoint:*— choose, ordain.

G5501 χείρων *cheirōn* irregular comparative of G2556; from an obsolete equivalent

χέρης *cherēs* (of uncertain derivation); *more evil* or *aggravated* (physically, mentally or morally):— sorer, worse.

G5502 χερουβίμ *cheroubim* plural of Hebrew origin [H3742]; *"cherubim"* (i.e. *cherubs* or *kerubim*):— cherubims.

G5503 χήρα *chēra* feminine of a presumed derivative apparently from the base of G5490 through the idea of *deficiency;* a *widow* (as *lacking* a husband), literal or figurative:— widow.

G5504 χθές *chthes* of uncertain derivation; *"yesterday";* by extension *in time past* or *hitherto:*— yesterday.

G5505 χιλιάς *chilias* from G5507; one *thousand* (*"chiliad"*):— thousand.

G5506 χιλίαρχος *chiliarchos* from G5507 and G757; the *commander of a thousand* soldiers (*"chiliarch"*), i.e. *colonel:*— (chief, high) captain.

G5507 **χίλιοι** *chilioi* plural of uncertain affinity; a *thousand:*— thousand.

G5508 **Χίος** *Chios* of uncertain derivation; *Chios,* an island in the Mediterranean:— Chios.

G5509 **χιτών** *chitōn* of foreign origin [H3801]; a *tunic* or *shirt:*— clothes, coat, garment.

G5510 **χιών** *chiōn* perhaps akin to the base of *G5490* (*G5465*) or *G5494* (as *descending* or *empty*); *snow:*— snow.

G5511 **χλαμύς** *chlamys* of uncertain derivation; a military *cloak:*— robe.

G5512 **χλευάζω** *chleuazō* from a derivative probably of Greek *G5491*; to *throw out* the *lip,* i.e. *jeer* at:— mock.

G5513 **χλιαρός** *chliaros* from
χλίω *chliō* (to *warm*); *tepid:*— lukewarm.

G5514 **Χλόη** *Chloē* feminine of apparently a primary word; *"green"; Chloe',* a Christian female:— Chloe.

G5515 **χλωρός** *chlōros* from the same as *G5514*; *greenish,* i.e. *verdant, dun-colored:*— green, pale.

G5516 **χξα†&&&** *chxs* the twenty-second, fourteenth and an obsolete letter (*G4742* as a *cross*) of the Greek alphabet (intermediate between the fifth and sixth), used as numbers; denoting respectively six hundred, sixty and six; six hundred sixty-six as a numeral:— six hundred threescore and six.

G5517 **χοϊκός** *choikos* from *G5522*; *dusty* or *dirty* (*soil*-like), i.e. (by implication) *terrene:*— earthy.

G5518 **χοῖνιξ** *choinix* of uncertain derivation; a *choenix* or certain dry measure:— measure.

G5519 **χοῖρος** *choiros* of uncertain derivation; a *hog:*— swine.

G5520 **χολάω** *cholaō* from *G5521*; to *be bilious,* i.e. (by implication) *irritable* (*enraged,* "choleric"):— be angry.

G5521 **χολή** *cholē* feminine of an equivalent perhaps akin to the same as *G5514* (from the *greenish* hue); *"gall"* or *bile,* i.e. (by analogy) *poison* or an *anodyne* (wormwood, poppy, etc.):— gall.

G5522 **χόος** *choos* from the base of *G5494*; a *heap* (as *poured* out), i.e. *rubbish; loose dirt:*— dust.

G5523 **Χοραζίν** *Chorazin* of uncertain derivation; *Chorazin,* a place in Palestine:— Chorazin.

G5524 **χορηγέω** *chorēgeō* from a compound of *G5525* and *G71*; to be a *dance-leader,* i.e. (generally) to *furnish:*— give, minister.

G5525 **χορός** *choros* of uncertain derivation; a *ring,* i.e. round *dance* ("choir"):— dancing.

G5526 **χορτάζω** *chortazō* from *G5528*; to *fodder,* i.e. (generally) to *gorge* (*supply food* in abundance):— feed, fill, satisfy.

G5527 **χόρτασμα** *chortasma* from *G5526*; *forage,* i.e. *food:*— sustenance.

G5528 **χόρτος** *chortos* apparently a primary word; a *"court"* or *"garden",* i.e. (by implication of *pasture*) *herbage* or *vegetation:*— blade, grass, hay.

G5529 **Χουζᾶς** *Chouzas* of uncertain origin; *Chuzas,* an officer of Herod:— Chuza.

G5530 **χράομαι** *chraomai* middle of a primary verb (perhaps rather from *G5495*, to *handle*); to *furnish* what is needed; (give an *oracle, "graze"* [touch slightly], *light* upon, etc.), i.e. (by implication) to *employ* or (by extension) to *act towards* one in a given manner:— entreat, use. Compare *G5531, G5534*.

G5531 **χράω** *chraō* probably the same as the base of *G5530*; to *loan:*— lend.

G5532 **χρεία** *chreia* from the base of *G5530* or *G5534*; *employment,* i.e. an *affair;* also (by implication) *occasion, demand, requirement* or *destitution:*— business, lack, necessary, necessity, need, needful, use, want.

G5533 **χρεωφειλέτης** *chreōpheiletēs* from a derivative of *G5531* and *G3781*; one who *owes a loan,* i.e. *indebted* person:— debtor.

G5534 **χρή** *chrē* third person singular of the same as *G5530* or *G5531* used impersonally; it *needs* (*must* or *should*) be:— ought.

G5535 **χρῄζω** *chrēzō* from *G5532*; to *make* (i.e. *have*) *necessity,* i.e. *be in want* of:— (have) need.

G5536 **χρῆμα** *chrēma*; something *useful* or *needed,* i.e. *wealth, price:*— money, riches.

G5537 **χρηματίζω** *chrēmatizō* from *G5536*; to *utter an oracle* (compare the original sense of *G5530*), i.e. divinely *intimate;* by implication (compare the secular sense of *G5532*) to constitute a *firm* for business, i.e. (generally) *bear* as a *title:*— be called, be admonished (warned) of God, reveal, speak.

G5538 **χρηματισμός** *chrēmatismos* from *G5537*; a divine *response* or *revelation:*— answer of God.

G5539 **χρήσιμος** *chrēsimos* from *G5540*; *serviceable:*— profit.

G5540 **χρῆσις** *chrēsis* from *G5530*; *employment,* i.e. (specifically) sexual *intercourse* (as an *occupation* of the body):— use.

G5541 **χρηστεύομαι** *chrēsteuomai* middle from *G5543*; to *show oneself useful,* i.e. *act benevolently:*— be kind.

G5542 **χρηστολογία** *chrēstologia* from a compound of *G5543* and *G3004*; *fair speech,* i.e. *plausibility:*— good words.

G5543 **χρηστός** *chrēstos* from *G5530*; *employed,* i.e. (by implication) *useful* (in manner or morals):— better, easy, good, goodness, gracious, kind.

G5544 **χρηστότης** *chrēstotēs* from *G5543*; *usefulness,* i.e. moral *excellence* (in character or demeanor):— gentleness, good, goodness, kindness.

G5545 **χρίσμα** *chrisma* from *G5548*; an *unguent* or *smearing,* i.e. (figuratively) the special *endowment* ("chrism") of the Holy Spirit:— anointing, unction.

G5546 **Χριστιανός** *Christianos* from *G5547*; a *Christian,* i.e. follower of Christ:— Christian.

G5547 **Χριστός** *Christos* from *G5548*; *anointed,* i.e. the *Messiah,* an epithet of Jesus:— Christ.

G5548 **χρίω** *chriō* probably akin to *G5530* through the idea of *contact;* to *smear* or *rub* with oil, i.e. (by implication) to *consecrate* to an office or religious service:— anoint.

G5549 **χρονίζω** *chronizō* from *G5550*; to *take time,* i.e. *linger:*— delay, tarry.

G5550 **χρόνος** *chronos* of uncertain derivation; a space of *time* (in general, and thus properly distinguished from *G2540*, which designates a *fixed* or special occasion; and from *G165*, which denotes a particular *period*) or *interval;* by extension an individual *opportunity;* by implication *delay:*— years old, season, space, time, times, oftentimes, while, awhile.

G5551 **χρονοτριβέω** *chronotribeō* from a presumed compound of *G5550* and the base of *G5147*; to be a *time-wearer,* i.e. to *procrastinate* (*linger*):— spend time.

G5552 **χρύσεος** *chryseos* from *G5557*; made *of gold:*— of gold, golden.

G5553 **χρυσίον** *chrysion* diminutive of *G5557*; a *golden* article, i.e. gold plating, ornament, or coin:— gold.

G5554 **χρυσοδακτύλιος** *chrysodaktylios* from *G5557* and *G1146*; *gold-ringed,* i.e. *wearing* a golden finger-ring or similar *jewelry:*— with a gold ring.

G5555 **χρυσόλιθος** *chrysolithos* from *G5557* and Greek *G3037*; *gold-stone,* i.e. a *yellow gem* (*"chrysolite"*):— chrysolite.

G5556 **χρυσόπρασος** *chrysoprasos* from *G5557* and
πράσον *prason* (a *leek*); a *greenish-yellow* gem (*"chrysoprase"*):— chrysoprase.

G5557 **χρυσός** *chrysos* perhaps from the base of *G5530* (through the idea of the *utility* of the metal); *gold;* by extension a *golden* article, as an ornament or coin:— gold.

G5558 **χρυσόω** *chrysoō* from *G5557*; to *gild,* i.e. *bespangle* with golden ornaments:— deck.

G5559 **χρώς** *chrōs* probably akin to the base of *G5530* through the idea of *handling;* the *body* (properly its *surface* or *skin*):— body.

G5560 **χωλός** *chōlos* apparently a primary word; *"halt",* i.e. *limping:*— cripple, halt, lame.

G5561 **χώρα** *chōra* feminine of a derivative of the base of *G5490* through the idea of *empty* expanse; *room,* i.e. a space of *territory* (more or less extensive; often including its inhabitants):— coast, county, fields, ground, land, region. Compare *G5117*.

G5562 **χωρέω** *chōreō* from *G5561*; to *be* in (*give*) *space,* i.e. (intransitive) to *pass, enter,* or (transitive) to *hold, admit* (literally or figuratively):— come, contain, go, have place, (can, be room to) receive.

G5563 **χωρίζω** *chōrizō* from *G5561*; to *place room* between, i.e. *part;* reflexive to *go away:*— depart, put asunder, separate.

G5564 **χωρίον** *chōrion* diminutive of *G5561*; a *spot* or *plot* of ground:— field, land, parcel of ground, place, possession.

G5565 **χωρίς** *chōris* adverb from *G5561*; *at a space,* i.e. *separately* or *apart* from (often as preposition):— beside, by itself, without.

G5566 **χῶρος** *chōros* of Latin origin; the *northwest* wind:— north west.

Ψ

G5567 **ψάλλω** *psallō* probably strengthened from
ψάω *psaō* (to *rub* or *touch* the surface; compare *G5597*); to *twitch* or *twang,* i.e. to *play* on a stringed instrument (*celebrate* the divine worship *with music* and accompanying odes):— make melody, sing (psalms).

G5568 **ψαλμός** *psalmos* from *G5567*; a set piece of *music,* i.e. a sacred *ode* (accompanied with the voice, harp or other instrument; a *"psalm"*); collectively the book of the *Psalms:*— psalm. Compare *G5603*.

G5569 **ψευδάδελφος** *pseudadelphos* from *G5571* and *G80*; a *spurious brother,* i.e. *pretended associate:*— false brethren.

G5570 ψευδαπόστολος *pseudapostolos* from *G5571* and *G652*; a *spurious apostle,* i.e. *pretended preacher:*— false teacher.

G5571 ψευδής *pseudēs* from *G5574*; *untrue,* i.e. *erroneous, deceitful; wicked:*— false, liar.

G5572 ψευδοδιδάσκαλος *pseudodidaskalos* from *G5571* and *G1320*; a *spurious teacher,* i.e. *propagator* of *erroneous* Christian *doctrine:*— false teacher.

G5573 ψευδολόγος *pseudologos* from Greek *G5571* and *G3004*; *mendacious,* i.e. *promulgating erroneous* Christian *doctrine:*— speaking lies.

G5574 ψεύδομαι *pseudomai* middle of an apparently primary verb; to *utter an untruth* or attempt to *deceive* by falsehood:— falsely, lie.

G5575 ψευδομάρτυς *pseudomartys* from *G5571* and a kindred form of *G3144*; a *spurious witness,* i.e. *bearer of untrue testimony:*— false witness.

G5576 ψευδομαρτυρέω *pseudomartyreō* from *G5575*; to *be an untrue testifier,* i.e. offer *falsehood in evidence:*— be a false witness.

G5577 ψευδομαρτυρία *pseudomartyria* from *G5575*; *untrue testimony:*— false witness.

G5578 ψευδοπροφήτης *pseudoprophētēs* from *G5571* and *G4396*; a *spurious prophet,* i.e. *pretended foreteller* or religious *impostor:*— false prophet.

G5579 ψεῦδος *pseudos* from *G5574*; a *falsehood* :— lie, lying.

G5580 ψευδόχριστος *pseudochristos* from *G5571* and *G5547*; a *spurious Messiah:*— false Christ.

G5581 ψευδώνυμος *pseudōnymos* from *G5571* and *G3686*; *untruly named:*— falsely so called.

G5582 ψεῦσμα *pseusma* from *G5574*; a *fabrication,* i.e. *falsehood:*— lie.

G5583 ψεύστης *pseustēs* from *G5574*; a *falsifier* :— liar.

G5584 ψηλαφάω *psēlaphaō* from the base of *G5567* (compare *G5586*); to *manipulate,* i.e. *verify* by contact; figuratively to *search* for:— feel after, handle, touch.

G5585 ψηφίζω *psēphizō* from *G5586*; to *use pebbles* in enumeration, i.e. (generally) to *compute:*— count.

G5586 ψῆφος *psēphos* from the same as *G5584*; a *pebble* (as worn smooth by *handling*), i.e. (by implication of use as a *counter* or *ballot*) a *verdict* (of acquittal) or *ticket* (of admission); a *vote:*— stone, voice.

G5587 ψιθυρισμός *psithyrismos* from a derivative of

ψίθος *psithos* (a *whisper;* by implication a *slander;* probably akin to *G5574*); *whispering,* i.e. secret *detraction:*— whispering.

G5588 ψιθυριστής *psithyristēs* from the same as *G5587*; a secret *calumniator:*— whisperer.

G5589 ψιχίον *psichion* diminutive from a derivative of the base of *G5567* (meaning a *crumb*); a *little bit* or *morsel:*— crumb.

G5590 ψυχή *psychē* from *G5594*; *breath,* i.e. (by implication) *spirit,* abstract or concrete (the *animal* sentient principle only; thus distinguished on the one hand from *G4151*, which is the rational and immortal *soul;* and on the other from *G2222*, which is mere *vitality,* even of plants: these terms thus exactly correspond respectively to the Hebrew H5315, H7307 and H2416):— heart, heartily, life, mind, soul, us, you.

G5591 ψυχικός *psychikos* from *G5590*; *sensitive,* i.e. *animate* (in distinction on the one hand from *G4152*, which is the higher or *renovated* nature; and on the other from *G5446*, which is the lower or *bestial* nature):— natural, sensual.

G5592 ψύχος *psychos* from *G5594*; *coolness:*— cold.

G5593 ψυχρός *psychros* from *G5592*; *chilly* (literally or figuratively):— cold.

G5594 ψύχω *psychō* a primary verb; to *breathe* (*voluntarily* but *gently;* thus differing on the one hand from *G4154*, which denotes properly a *forcible* respiration; and on the other from the base of *G109*, which refers properly to an inanimate *breeze*), i.e. (by implication of reduction of temperature by evaporation) to *chill* (figuratively):— wax cold.

G5595 ψωμίζω *psōmizō* from the base of *G5596*; to *supply* with *bits,* i.e. (generally) to *nourish:*— (bestow to) feed.

G5596 ψωμίον *psōmion* diminutive from a derivative of the base of *G5597*; a *crumb* or *morsel* (as if *rubbed* off), i.e. a *mouthful:*— sop.

G5597 ψώχω *psōchō* prolonged from the same base as Greek *G5567*; to *triturate,* i.e. (by analogy) to *rub* out (kernels from husks with the fingers or hand):— rub.

Ω

G5598 Ω *Ō* i.e.

ὦμεγα *ōmega*; the last letter of the Greek alphabet, i.e. (figuratively) the *finality:*— Omega.

G5599 ὦ *ō* a primary interjection; as a sign of the vocative *O;* as a note of exclamation, *oh:*— O.

G5600 ὦ *ō* including the oblique forms, as well as

ᾖς *ēs* and

ᾖ *ē* etc.; the subjunctive of *G1510*; (*may, might, can, could, would, should, must,* etc.; also with *G1487* and its comparative, as well as with other particles) *be:*— appear, are, (may, might, should) be, have, is, pass the flower of her age, should stand, were.

G5601 Ὠβήδ *Ōbēd* of Hebrew origin [H5744]; *Obed,* an Israelite:— Obed.

G5602 ὧδε *hōde* from an adverbial form of *G3592*; *in this* same spot, i.e. *here* or *hither:*— here, hither, (in) this place, there.

G5603 ᾠδή *ōdē* from *G103*; a *chant* or *"ode"* (the general term for any words sung; while *G5215* denotes especially a *religious* metrical composition, and *G5568* still more specifically a *Hebrew* metrical composition):— song.

G5604 ὠδίν *ōdin* akin to *G3601*; a *pang* or *throe,* especially of childbirth:— pain, sorrow, travail.

G5605 ὠδίνω *ōdinō* from *G5604*; to *experience* the *pains* of parturition (literally or figuratively):— travail in (birth).

G5606 ὦμος *ōmos* perhaps from the alternate of *G5342*; the *shoulder* (as that on which burdens are *borne*):— shoulder.

G5607 ὤν *ōn* including the feminine

οὖσα *ousa* and the neuter

ὄν *on* present participle of *G1510*; *being:*— be, come, have.

G5608 ὠνέομαι *ōneomai* middle from an apparently primary

ὦνος *ōnos* (a *sum* or *price*); to *purchase* (synonymous with the earlier *G4092*):— buy.

G5609 ᾠόν *ōon* apparently a primary word; an *"egg":*— egg.

G5610 ὥρα *hōra* apparently a primary word; an *"hour"* (literal or figurative):— day, hour, instant, season, short, -tide (e.g., eventide), (high) time.

G5611 ὡραῖος *hōraios* from *G5610*; *belonging* to the right *hour* or *season* (*timely*), i.e. (by implication) *flourishing* (*beauteous* [figuratively]):— beautiful.

G5612 ὠρύομαι *ōryomai* middle of an apparently primary verb; to *"roar":*— roar.

G5613 ὡς *hōs* probably adverb of comparison from *G3739*; *which how,* i.e. *in that manner* (very variously used, as follows):— about, after (that), (according) as (it had been, it were), as soon (as), even as (like), for, how (greatly), like (as, unto), since, so (that), that, to wit, unto, when, whensoever, while, with all speed.

G5614 ὡσαννά *hōsanna* of Hebrew origin [H3467 and H4994]; *oh save!; hosanna* (i.e. *hoshia-na*), an exclamation of adoration:— hosanna.

G5615 ὡσαύτως *hōsautōs* from *G5613* and an adverb from *G846*; *as thus,* i.e. *in the same way:*— even so, likewise, after the same (in like) manner.

G5616 ὡσεί *hōsei* from *G5613* and *G1487*; *as if:*— about, as (it had been, it were), like (as).

G5617 Ὡσηέ *Hōsēe* of Hebrew origin [H1954]; *Hosee'* (i.e. *Hoshea'*), an Israelite:— Osee.

G5618 ὥσπερ *hōsper* from *G5613* and *G4007*; *just as,* i.e. *exactly like:*— (even, like) as.

G5619 ὡσπερεί *hōsperei* from *G5618* and *G1487*; *just as if,* i.e. *as it were:*— as.

G5620 ὥστε *hōste* from *G5613* and *G5037*; *so too,* i.e. *thus therefore* (in various relations of *consecution,* as follow):— (insomuch) as, so that (then), (insomuch) that, therefore, to, wherefore.

G5621 ὠτίον *ōtion* diminutive of *G3775*; a *little ear,* i.e. *one* of the ears, or perhaps the *lobe* of the ear:— ear.

G5622 ὠφέλεια *ōpheleia* from a derivative of the base of *G5624*; *usefulness,* i.e. *benefit:*— advantage, profit.

G5623 ὠφελέω *ōpheleō* from the same as *G5622*; to *be useful,* i.e. to *benefit:*— advantage, better, prevail, profit.

G5624 ὠφέλιμος *ōphelimos* from a form of *G3786*; *helpful* or *serviceable,* i.e. *advantageous:*— profit, profitable.

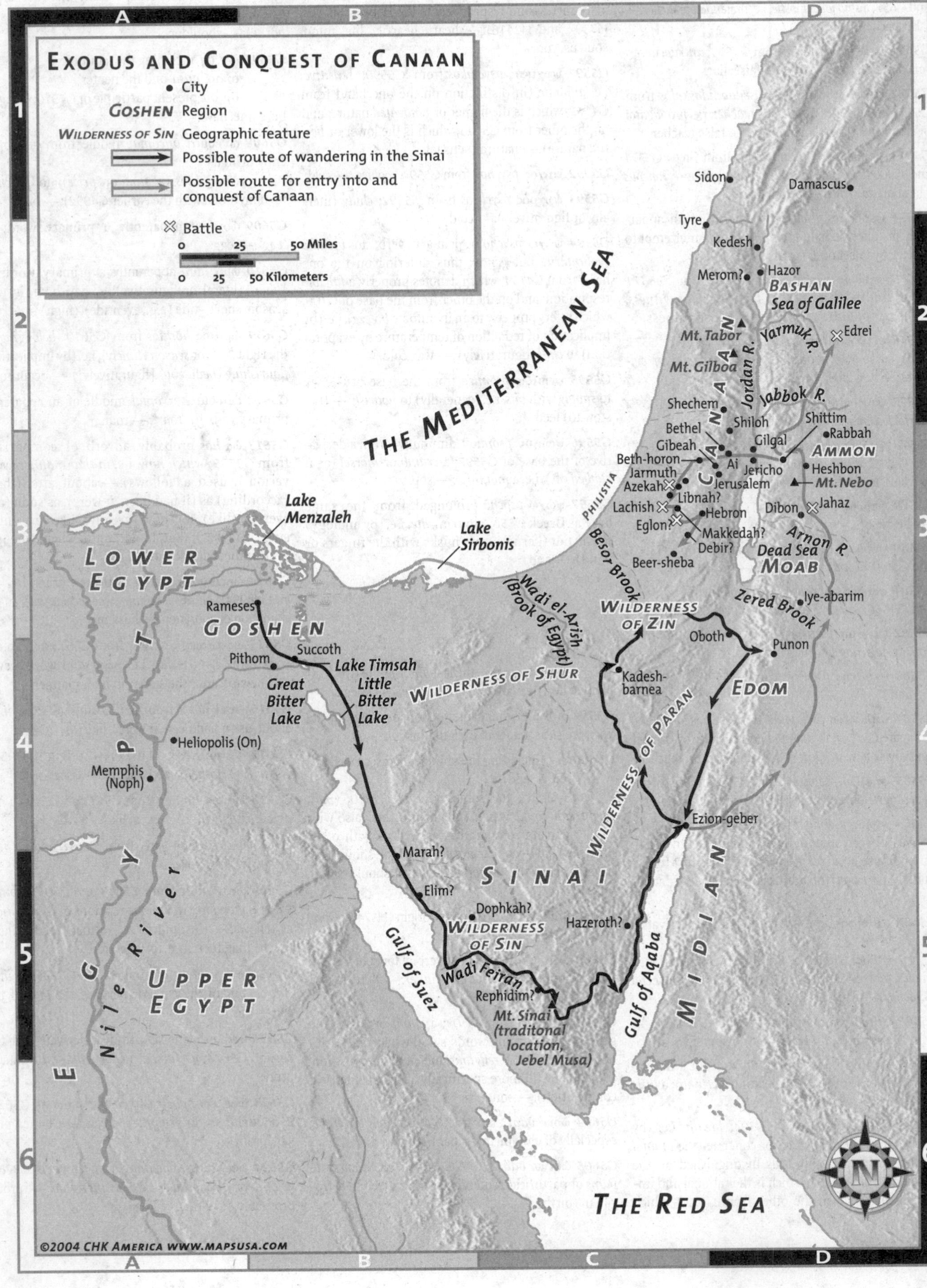
EXODUS AND CONQUEST OF CANAAN
City
GOSHEN Region
WILDERNESS OF SIN Geographic feature
Possible route of wandering in the Sinai
Possible route for entry into and conquest of Canaan
Battle
0 25 50 Miles
0 25 50 Kilometers
THE MEDITERRANEAN SEA
Sidon
Damascus
Tyre
Kedesh
Merom?
Hazor
BASHAN
Sea of Galilee
Mt. Tabor
Yarmuk R.
Edrei
Mt. Gilboa
Jordan R.
CANAAN
Jabbok R.
Shechem
Bethel
Shiloh
Shittim
Gibeah
Gilgal
Rabbah
Beth-horon
Ai
AMMON
Jarmuth
Jericho
Heshbon
Azekah
Jerusalem
Mt. Nebo
Libnah?
Lachish
Hebron
Dibon
Jahaz
Eglon?
Makkedah?
Debir?
Arnon R.
Dead Sea
Beer-sheba
MOAB
PHILISTIA
Besor Brook
Lake Menzaleh
Lake Sirbonis
LOWER EGYPT
Wadi el-Arish (Brook of Egypt)
WILDERNESS OF ZIN
Zered Brook
Iye-abarim
Rameses
GOSHEN
Oboth
Punon
Succoth
Pithom
Lake Timsah
Kadesh-barnea
Great Bitter Lake
Little Bitter Lake
WILDERNESS OF SHUR
EDOM
WILDERNESS OF PARAN
Heliopolis (On)
Memphis (Noph)
Ezion-geber
Marah?
SINAI
Elim?
Dophkah?
WILDERNESS OF SIN
Hazeroth?
Gulf of Suez
Wadi Feiran
Rephidim?
Mt. Sinai (traditonal location, Jebel Musa)
Gulf of Aqaba
MIDIAN
Nile River
UPPER EGYPT
EGYPT
THE RED SEA
N
A B C D
1 2 3 4 5 6
©2004 CHK AMERICA WWW.MAPSUSA.COM

The Land of Israel/ Palestine in the First Century of the Common Era
City
Mt. Nebo Geographic feature
GALILEE Region
NABATEAN Kingdom/province
Boundary of Herod's kingdom – greatest extent
Province boundaries
0 10 20 Miles
0 10 20 Kilometers
Sidon
Sarepta
Tyre
Damascus
Abana R.
Pharpar R.
Mt. Hermon
Leontes R.
Iturea
Abilene
Province of Syria
Phoenicia
Panias
Dan(Caesarea Philippi)
Kedesh
Lake Huleh
Gaulanitis
Batanea
Trachonitis
Gischala
Merom?
Ptolemais (Akko)
Chorazin
Capernaum
Beth-saida
Gennesaret
Magdala/ Taricheae
Sea of Galilee
Raphana
Gamala
Hippos
Dion?
Yarmuk R.
Abila
Mt. Carmel
Sepphoris
Nazareth
Mt. Tabor
Galilee
Geba/Hippeum
Gedor(Gadara)
Auranitis
Dor
Caesarea (Strato's Tower)
The Mediterranean Sea
Plain of Sharon
Scythopolis (Beth-shan)
Mt. Gilboa
Pella
Decapolis
Kingdom of Herod
Sebaste (Samaria)
Jordan River
Gerasa (Jerash)
Amathus
Mt. Ebal
Neapolis (Nablus)
Mt. Gerazim
Apollonia
Yarkon R.
Jabbok R.
Antipatris(Aphek)
Joppa
Samaria
Alexandrium
Phasaelis
Gadara
Thamna
Lydda(Lod)
Gophna
Archelais
Gazara(Gezer)
Modein
Philadelphia (Amman)
Jamnia (Jabneh)
Emmaus
Jericho
Cyprus
Perea
Betharamphtha
Azotus (Ashdod)
Jerusalem
Bethany
Esbus(Heshbon)
Judea
Mt. Nebo
Bethlehem
Hyrcania
Qumran
Medeba
Ascalon (Ashkelon) (free city)
Herodium
Betogabri (Beth-guvrin)
Callirrhoe
Anthedon
Marisa (Maresha)
Machaerus
Adora
Hebron
Gaza
En-gedi
The Dead Sea
Arnon R.
Besor Brook
Idumea
Raphia
Masada
Bersabe (Beer-sheba)
Malatha
Mampsis
The Negeb
Nabatean Kingdom
Khirbet Tannur
Zered Brook
Nessana
N
©2003 CHK America www.mapsusa.com

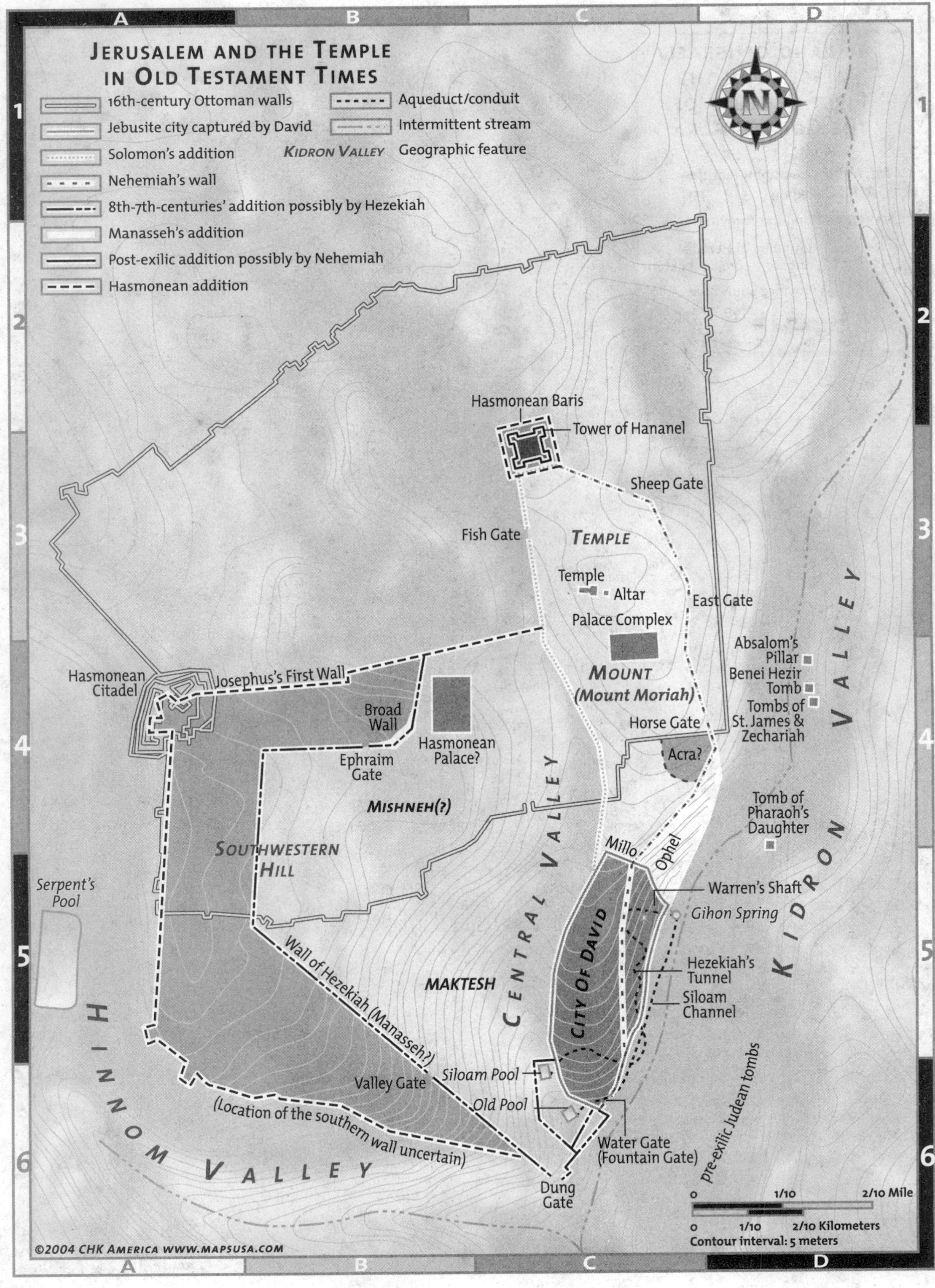

Jerusalem and the Temple in Old Testament Times
16th-century Ottoman walls
Jebusite city captured by David
Solomon's addition
Nehemiah's wall
8th-7th-centuries' addition possibly by Hezekiah
Manasseh's addition
Post-exilic addition possibly by Nehemiah
Hasmonean addition
Aqueduct/conduit
Intermittent stream
Kidron Valley
Geographic feature
N
Hasmonean Baris
Tower of Hananel
Sheep Gate
Fish Gate
Temple
Temple
Altar
East Gate
Palace Complex
Mount
(Mount Moriah)
Horse Gate
Acra?
Absalom's Pillar
Benei Hezir Tomb
Tombs of St. James & Zechariah
Kidron Valley
Hasmonean Citadel
Josephus's First Wall
Broad Wall
Hasmonean Palace?
Ephraim Gate
Mishneh(?)
Southwestern Hill
Central Valley
Tomb of Pharaoh's Daughter
Millo
Ophel
Warren's Shaft
Gihon Spring
City of David
Hezekiah's Tunnel
Siloam Channel
Serpent's Pool
Wall of Hezekiah (Manasseh?)
Maktesh
Siloam Pool
Valley Gate
Old Pool
(Location of the southern wall uncertain)
Hinnom Valley
Water Gate (Fountain Gate)
pre-exilic Judean tombs
Dung Gate
0 1/10 2/10 Mile
0 1/10 2/10 Kilometers
Contour interval: 5 meters
©2004 CHK America www.mapsusa.com
A B C D
1 2 3 4 5 6

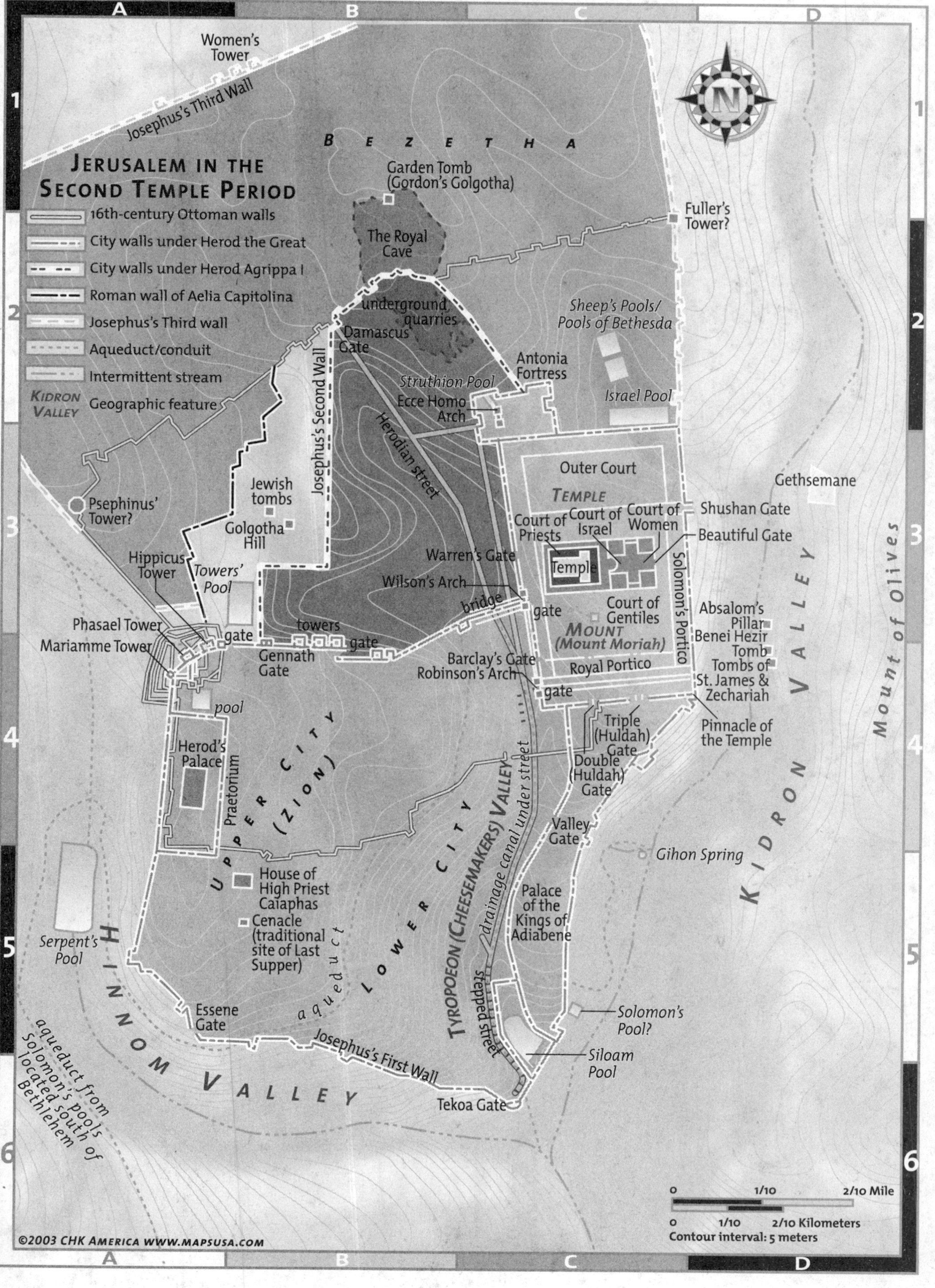

Jerusalem in the Second Temple Period
16th-century Ottoman walls
City walls under Herod the Great
City walls under Herod Agrippa I
Roman wall of Aelia Capitolina
Josephus's Third wall
Aqueduct/conduit
Intermittent stream
Kidron Valley Geographic feature
Women's Tower
Josephus's Third Wall
Bezetha
Garden Tomb (Gordon's Golgotha)
The Royal Cave
Fuller's Tower?
underground quarries
Damascus Gate
Sheep's Pools/ Pools of Bethesda
Antonia Fortress
Struthion Pool
Ecce Homo Arch
Israel Pool
Herodian street
Josephus's Second Wall
Outer Court
Temple
Court of Priests
Court of Israel
Court of Women
Shushan Gate
Beautiful Gate
Gethsemane
Jewish tombs
Psephinus' Tower?
Golgotha Hill
Temple
Warren's Gate
Wilson's Arch
Hippicus Tower
Towers' Pool
bridge
gate
Court of Gentiles
Solomon's Portico
Absalom's Pillar
Benei Hezir Tomb
Tombs of St. James & Zechariah
Mount (Mount Moriah)
Phasael Tower
Mariamme Tower
gate
towers
gate
Gennath Gate
Barclay's Gate
Robinson's Arch
Royal Portico
gate
pool
Triple (Huldah) Gate
Pinnacle of the Temple
Herod's Palace
Praetorium
Upper City (Zion)
Double (Huldah) Gate
Kidron Valley
Mount of Olives
Tyropoeon (Cheesemakers) Valley
drainage canal under street
Valley Gate
Gihon Spring
House of High Priest Caiaphas
Lower City
Palace of the Kings of Adiabene
Cenacle (traditional site of Last Supper)
Serpent's Pool
aqueduct
stepped street
Solomon's Pool?
Essene Gate
Siloam Pool
Hinnom Valley
Josephus's First Wall
Tekoa Gate
aqueduct from Solomon's pools located south of Bethlehem
0 1/10 2/10 Mile
0 1/10 2/10 Kilometers
Contour interval: 5 meters
©2003 CHK America www.mapsusa.com

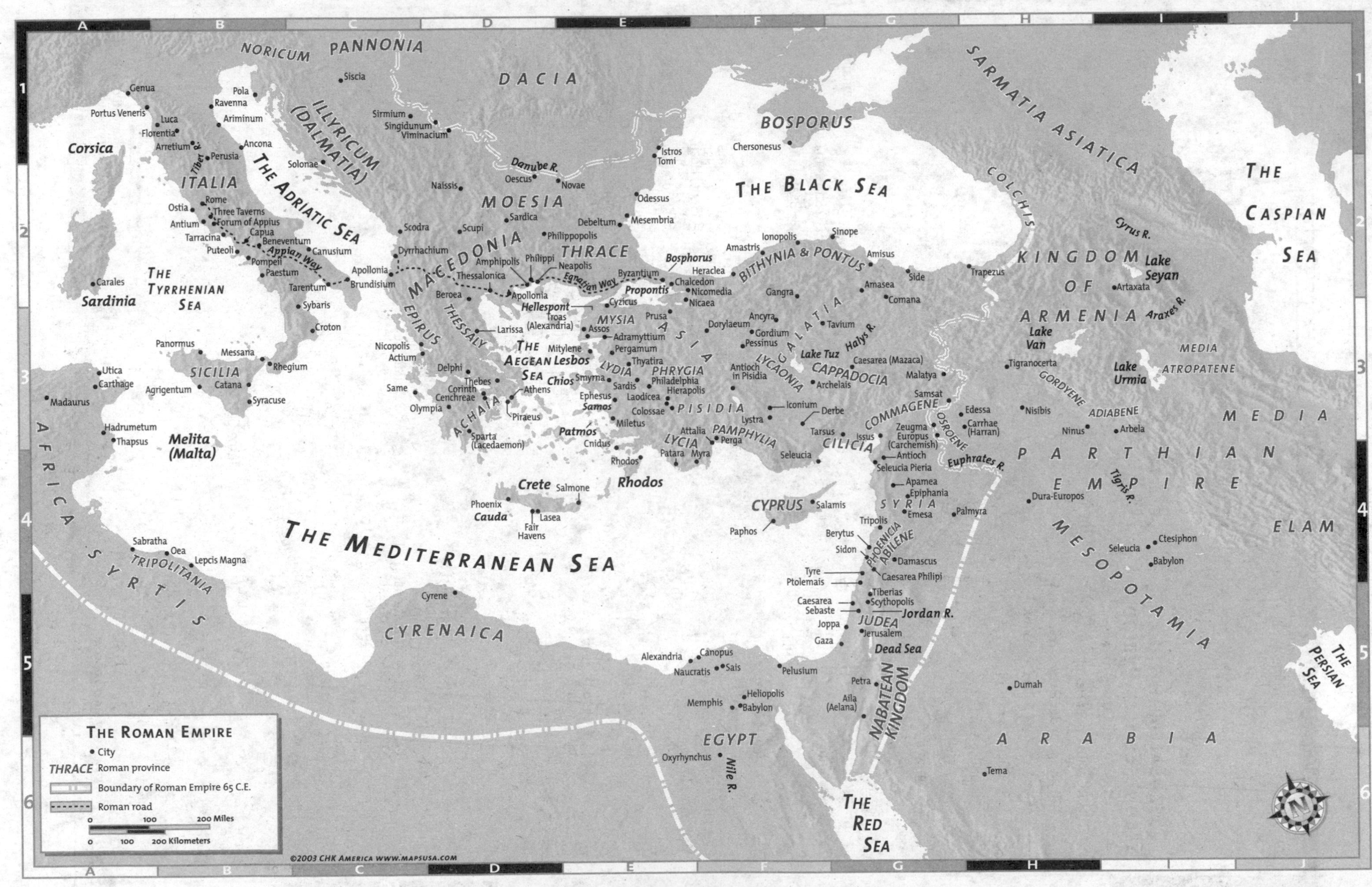

The Roman Empire
City
THRACE Roman province
Boundary of Roman Empire 65 C.E.
Roman road
0 100 200 Miles
0 100 200 Kilometers
©2003 CHK America www.mapsusa.com
The Mediterranean Sea
The Black Sea
The Caspian Sea
The Adriatic Sea
The Tyrrhenian Sea
The Aegean Sea
The Red Sea
The Persian Sea
Noricum
Pannonia
Dacia
Illyricum (Dalmatia)
Moesia
Macedonia
Thrace
Epirus
Thessaly
Achaia
Italia
Sicilia
Sardinia
Corsica
Melita (Malta)
Crete
Cauda
Rhodos
Cyprus
Bosporus
Sarmatia Asiatica
Colchis
Kingdom of Armenia
Bithynia & Pontus
Galatia
Asia
Mysia
Lydia
Phrygia
Pisidia
Lycia
Pamphylia
Lycaonia
Cappadocia
Cilicia
Commagene
Osroene
Syria
Phoenicia
Abilene
Judea
Nabatean Kingdom
Egypt
Cyrenaica
Tripolitania
Syrtis
Africa
Parthian Empire
Mesopotamia
Media
Atropatene
Gordyene
Adiabene
Elam
Arabia
Danube R.
Tiber R.
Nile R.
Jordan R.
Euphrates R.
Tigris R.
Halys R.
Araxes R.
Cyrus R.
Lake Van
Lake Urmia
Lake Seyan
Lake Tuz
Dead Sea
Appian Way
Egnatian Way
Hellespont
Proponits
Bosphorus
Chios
Samos
Patmos
Lesbos
Genua
Portus Veneris
Luca
Florentia
Arretium
Perusia
Pola
Ravenna
Ariminum
Ancona
Rome
Ostia
Antium
Three Taverns
Forum of Appius
Capua
Tarracina
Beneventum
Puteoli
Pompeii
Paestum
Canusium
Tarentum
Brundisium
Sybaris
Croton
Rhegium
Messana
Panormus
Agrigentum
Catana
Syracuse
Carales
Utica
Carthage
Madaurus
Hadrumetum
Thapsus
Sabratha
Oea
Lepcis Magna
Cyrene
Siscia
Solonae
Sirmium
Singidunum
Viminacium
Naissis
Oescus
Novae
Istros
Tomi
Odessus
Mesembria
Debeltum
Scodra
Scupi
Sardica
Philippopolis
Dyrrhachium
Apollonia
Amphipolis
Philippi
Neapolis
Thessalonica
Beroea
Larissa
Nicopolis
Actium
Delphi
Thebes
Corinth
Cenchreae
Athens
Piraeus
Same
Olympia
Sparta (Lacedaemon)
Phoenix
Lasea
Fair Havens
Salmone
Byzantium
Chalcedon
Nicomedia
Nicaea
Heraclea
Cyzicus
Troas (Alexandria)
Assos
Adramyttium
Pergamum
Mitylene
Thyatira
Smyrna
Sardis
Philadelphia
Hierapolis
Ephesus
Laodicea
Colossae
Miletus
Cnidus
Rhodos
Patara
Myra
Attalia
Perga
Prusa
Dorylaeum
Ancyra
Gordium
Pessinus
Antioch in Pisidia
Iconium
Lystra
Derbe
Tarsus
Seleucia
Amastris
Ionopolis
Sinope
Amisus
Side
Gangra
Amasea
Comana
Tavium
Caesarea (Mazaca)
Archelais
Trapezus
Malatya
Samsat
Zeugma
Europus (Carchemish)
Issus
Antioch
Seleucia Pieria
Apamea
Epiphania
Emesa
Palmyra
Edessa
Carrhae (Harran)
Chersonesus
Artaxata
Tigranocerta
Nisibis
Ninus
Arbela
Dura-Europos
Seleucia
Ctesiphon
Babylon
Salamis
Paphos
Tripolis
Berytus
Sidon
Damascus
Tyre
Ptolemais
Caesarea Philipi
Tiberias
Scythopolis
Caesarea
Sebaste
Joppa
Jerusalem
Gaza
Alexandria
Canopus
Naucratis
Sais
Pelusium
Heliopolis
Memphis
Babylon
Oxyrhynchus
Petra
Aila (Aelana)
Dumah
Tema